Racehorse Record

JUMPS 2001-2002

Sponsored by:

Editor Ashley Rumney
Comments by David Bellingham, Nicki Bowen, Mark Brown, Steffan Edwards, Keith Hewitt, Walter Glynn, Richard Lowther, Ashley Rumney, Ronald Wood,
Development Phillip Lamphee, Dan Di Pol

Typeset and Published by Raceform Ltd,
Compton, Newbury, Berkshire, RG20 6NL
Tel: 01635 578080
Fax: 01635 578101
Web http://www.raceform.co.uk
EMail: raceform@raceform.co.uk
Printed by Polestar Wheatons Ltd, Exeter

ISBN 1 901100 59 6

£23.00

CONTENTS

Full details of all Raceform services and publications are available from
Raceform, Compton, Newbury, Berkshire RG20 6NL.
Tel: 01635 578080 Fax: 01635 578101.
Web http://www.raceform.co.uk
Email: raceform@raceform.co.uk

Cover Photo: Shooting Light (A. P. McCoy)
on his way to winning the Tote Silver Cup at Ascot in December 2001

INTRODUCTION

Raceform's *Racehorse Record* has been designed not only as an historical reference, but also as a guide to the future, with the aim being to provide factual information about individual horses that ran under Jump racing Rules in Britain during the 2001-2002 season, and also to pinpoint conditions that are likely to prove conducive to future success.

For full season's results and ratings, refer to the *Chaseform 2001-2002 Jumps Annual*.

The horses are listed in alphabetical order.

KEY TO HORSE RECORDS

Best Mate (IRE)

121 (111h) (155h) 186

7-y-o b g Un Desperado (FR)-Katday (FR) (Miller's Mate)
Miss H C Knight Jim Lewis

Placings: *11221*/**1112-1221** **(4252)**
2001/02: 17^{1}GF, 19^{2}G, 24^{2}G, 26^{1}G

	Starts	1st	2nd	3rd	Win & Pl
Chases	4	2	2	0	239500
Career Total	**13**	**8**	**5**	**0**	**364629**

186	3/02	Chel	3m2f110y	A Ch	GD	£174000
182	11/01	Extr	2m1f110y	A HCh	G-F	£21000
177	2/01	Sand	2m4f110y	A Ch	HVY	£24000
166	11/00	Chel	2m	A Ch	G-S	£15000
161	10/00	Extr	2m1f110y	D Ch	GD	£3926
146	4/00	Aint	2m4f	A Hdl	GD	£21000
137	12/99	Sand	2m110y	D Hdl	G-S	£3680
133	11/99	Chel	2m110y	B NHF	GD	£7197

Total win prize-money £269804

Going: Sf: 0-0 GS: 0-0 Gd: 1-3 GF: - Fm: 1-1
Distance: 2m/2m3: 1-1 2m4-2m7: 0-1 3m+: 1-2
Track: LH: 1-1 RH: 1-3 Tight: 0-0 **Gall: 1-1**
Aids: Bl: 0-0 Vi: 0-0 Tstrap: 0-0
Best Rating: 186 3/02 Chel 3m2f110y good Ch

The leading novice chaser in 2000/01, unbeaten in three starts over fences and especially impressive in the Scilly Isles at Sandown. He was regarded as an Arkle banker, but foot and mouth put paid to that target and, rerouted to Aintree, found only Barton too good in the Martell Aintree Hurdle. He made a winning reappearance in 2001/02 in the Haldon Gold Cup at Exeter, but was held at the weights at Ascot. Passed his biggest test when runner-up in the King George, before running out an impressive winner of the Gold Cup. He jumps well, has a fine turn of foot, and stays three and a quarter miles and being only seven years old seems to have several good seasons ahead of him.

Name of horse, plus country of origin suffix in brackets

Master Split Second speed rating on left, Raceform rating on right (hurdles ratings in brackets)

Age, colour, sex and pedigree. The sire's name is followed by the dam's name, then the dam's sire's name in brackets

Trainer's name in bold (plus date of transfer and previous trainer's name if the horse changed stables during the season), followed by the owner's name

Complete list of the horse's placings, starting with its first recorded race. Bumper outings are in italic, hurdles outings in roman type and chase or hunter chase outings in bold type. A slash '/' or dash '-' indicates a change of season. This is followed in brackets by the Raceform number of the last race in the Form Book in which the horse competed

2001-2002 season's record, broken down into race types followed by career record

Career wins, showing (left to right) winning Raceform rating, date of win (month/year), course, distance, race conditions and type, going, win prize money

Going record for the season (wins-runs)

Distance record for the season

Track type record for the season *

Aids record for the season (blinkers, visor, tongue strap)

Best Raceform rating achieved during the season, followed by the relevant date, course, distance, going and race type

Raceform master comment on selected horses only. (These comments may refer in some instances to races which have already taken place during the 2002-2003 season).

Scale of Weight for Age for Steeple Chases and Hurdle Races

HURDLE RACES

The allowances, assessed in lbs, which three-year-olds and four-year-olds will receive from five-year-olds and upwards

Distance		JAN		FEB		MAR		APR		MAY		JUNE		JULY		AUG		SEPT		OCT		NOV		DEC	
Miles	**Age**	**1/15**	16/31	**1/14**	15/29	**1/15**	16/31	**1/15**	16/30	**1/15**	16/31	**1/15**	16/30	**1/15**	16/31	**1/15**	16/31	**1/15**	16/30	**1/15**	16/31	**1/15**	16/30	**1/15**	16/31
2	3	-	-	-	-	-	-	-	-	-	-	-	-	20	20	19	19	18	18	17	17	16	15	14	13
	4	12	11	10	9	8	7	6	5	4	4	3	3	2	2	1	1	-	-	-	-	-	-	-	-
2½	3	-	-	-	-	-	-	-	-	-	-	-	-	21	21	20	20	19	19	18	18	17	16	15	14
	4	13	12	11	10	9	8	7	6	5	5	4	4	3	3	2	2	1	1	-	-	-	-	-	-
3	3	-	-	-	-	-	-	-	-	-	-	-	-	22	22	21	21	20	20	19	19	18	17	16	15
	4	14	13	12	11	10	9	8	7	6	6	5	5	4	4	3	3	2	2	1	1	-	-	-	-

Scale of Weight for Age for Steeple Chases and Hurdle Races

STEEPLE CHASES

The allowances, assessed in lbs, which four-year-olds and five-year-olds will receive from five-year-olds and upwards

Distance		JAN		FEB		MAR		APR		MAY		JUNE		JULY		AUG		SEPT		OCT		NOV		DEC	
Miles	**Age**	**1/15**	16/31	**1/14**	15/29	**1/15**	16/31	**1/15**	16/30	**1/15**	16/31	**1/15**	16/30	**1/15**	16/31	**1/15**	16/31	**1/15**	16/30	**1/15**	16/31	**1/15**	16/30	**1/15**	16/31
2	4	-	-	-	-	-	-	-	-	-	-	-	-	-	-	15	15	14	14	13	13	12	12	11	10
	5	9	8	7	6	5	4	3	3	2	2	1	1	-	-	-	-	-	-	-	-	-	-	-	-
2½	4	-	-	-	-	-	-	-	-	-	-	-	-	-	-	16	16	15	15	14	14	13	13	12	11
	5	10	9	8	7	6	5	4	4	3	3	2	2	1	1	-	-	-	-	-	-	-	-	-	-
3	4	-	-	-	-	-	-	-	-	-	-	-	-	-	-	17	17	16	16	15	15	14	14	13	13
	5	12	12	11	11	10	10	9	8	7	7	6	6	5	5	4	4	3	3	2	2	1	1	-	-

RACEFORM RATINGS

Raceform Ratings for each horse are listed after the Starting Price and indicate the actual level of performance attained in that race. The figure in the back index represents the BEST public form that Raceform's Handicappers still believe the horse capable of reproducing.

To use the ratings constructively in determining those horses best-in in future events, the following procedures should be followed:

(i) In races where all runners are set to carry the same weight, no calculations are necessary. The horse with the highest rating is best in.

(ii) In races where all runners are set to carry different weights, add one point to the Raceform Rating for every pound less than 12 st to be carried; deduct one point for every pound more than 12 st.

For example,

Horse	Age & Weight	Adjustment from 12st	RR base rating	Adjusted rating
Flagship Uberalles	8-12-00	0	172	172
Edredon Bleu	10-11-12	+2	168	170
Fadalko	9-11-10	+4	168	172
Cenkos	8-11-06	+8	166	174

Therefore Cenkos is top-rated (best-in)

NB No adjustments are made for weight for age in Chaseform ratings. The official weight for age scale is displayed for information purposes while any live weight for age conditions are displayed underneath each individual result.

The following symbols are used in conjunction with the ratings:

++ almost certain to prove better
+ likely to prove better
d disappointing (has run well below best recently)
? form hard to evaluate, may prove unreliable
t tentative rating based on race-time

REVIEW OF THE SEASON

by Richard Lowther

The 2001/2002 season was one in which jump racing acclaimed yet more feats by its greatest champion, while saying goodbye to its most famous patron.

The magnificent Tony McCoy landed his seventh consecutive jockeys' championship, with Richard Johnson runner-up for the fifth year in a row. As early as September 17th, McCoy broke his own record for the fastest century in a season when partnering Present Bleu to victory at Plumpton. The fastest 200 came on Native Man at Huntingdon on January 11th, and by this stage not only did his own seasonal record seem there for the taking, but Sir Gordon Richards' all-time record of 269, set on the Flat in 1947, looked within reach. McCoy duly set a new jumps total of 254 when successful on Firetree at Huntingdon on March 2nd, and a month later he topped Sir Gordon's tally when driving Valfonic to victory at Warwick. At one stage 300 winners for the season seemed within reach, but he eventually had to settle for 289.

On Easter Saturday, March 30th, Queen Elizabeth the Queen Mother passed away at the age of 101. She had been in declining health for some months. Racing was cancelled on the day of her funeral, April 9th, as a mark of respect. The Queen Mother's first winner, owned jointly with her daughter the future Queen, was Monaveen at Fontwell in 1949, and the last of 461 winners under Rules had been First Love at Sandown on March 8th. Her blue and buff colours will always be associated especially with Devon Loch, who collapsed with victory in sight in the 1956 Grand National, and Special Cargo, winner of a memorable Whitbread Gold Cup in 1984. She was a great enthusiast, and the sport will miss her patronage.

The previous season had been blighted by the Foot and Mouth outbreak, and in the early weeks of the new campaign a number of fixtures were still being lost. By the autumn things were back in full swing, however. Cheltenham's 'Open' fixture was held on November 16th-18th, something of a misnomer as the season it opened had begun more than six months earlier. The feature race on the Saturday, the Thomas Pink Gold Cup, fell to the Martin Pipe-trained, Tony McCoy-ridden favourite Shooting Light. Carrying the colours of John Brown, Executive Chairman of William Hill, the blinkered gelding beat Foly Pleasant by an easy three lengths to land an ante-post gamble. McCoy was back for more next day, booting home a treble on Tarxien, Seebald and Westender, all for Pipe.

There was some excellent sport the following weekend. On Saturday November 24th, owner Jim Lewis and trainer Henrietta Knight had the enviable choice of attending either Ascot, where their brilliant prospect Best Mate was running in the First National Gold Cup, or Huntingdon, to watch Edredon Bleu bid to win the Peterborough Chase for a fourth year running. Lewis and Knight chose the latter option, and were proved right as Edredon Bleu made all to land the odds. Over at Ascot Best Mate, who had been so impressive on his seasonal reappearance at Exeter, ran well but was unable to concede 20lb to Wahiba Sands, another big-race winner for Pipe and McCoy. The years were rolled back at Aintree the next day when Amberleigh House, trained by Ginger McCain, was a big-priced winner of the Tote Becher Chase. Given a fine ride by Warren Marston, Amberleigh House was McCain's first winner over the famous Aintree fences since Red Rum in the 1977 Grand National.

Newbury's Hennessy Cognac Gold Cup on December 1st gave trainer Philip Hobbs the most valuable win of his career so far. The grey, partnered by former champion amateur Paul Flynn, rallied to beat Behrajan a neck after a rousing finish. This was one of the closest winning margins in the race's long history.

On December 8th Flagship Uberalles landed the big two-miler at Sandown, the Mitsubishi Shogun Tingle Creek Trophy, for the third year running, each for a different trainer. The gelding had been trained by Paul Nicholls when successful in 1999, by Noel Chance the next season (the race was run at Cheltenham, as Sandown had been waterlogged), and had already had a brief spell in Henrietta Knight's care before moving on again to the yard of Philip Hobbs. Ridden by Robert Widger, whose career in the saddle was later put in doubt due to weight problems, Flagship Uberalles beat Edredon Bleu by four lengths.

Cheltenham's meeting on December 15th was lost to the weather, but the Bula Hurdle was transferred to Newbury's card the following Wednesday. With doubts already surrounding the future of reigning Champion hurdler Istabraq, Martin Pipe's Valiramix took the opportunity to lay down his Champion Hurdle credentials with a smooth victory.

There were two excellent days' racing at Ascot on December 21st and 22nd. The Cantor Sport Long Walk Hurdle, put back to the Friday, was won in brilliant style by the Francois Doumen-trained Baracouda, who had already made a successful raid on Ascot earlier in the season. Saturday's card only received the green light after four inspections owing to a heavy frost. There were a number of withdrawals, but Tony McCoy was not complaining as he compiled a brilliant near 127/1 five-timer, spearheaded by Shooting Light in the Tote Silver Cup Chase. The day also saw the first running at Ascot of the Ladbroke, the richly endowed handicap hurdle previously held at Leopardstown. Victory went to Marble Arch, the biggest winner so far for trainer Hughie Morrison. Despite the quality on show at Ascot throughout the season, runners were in relatively short supply, and it was disconcerting to hear the management express doubts about the long-term future of jump racing at the Berkshire track.

The big freeze had now set in, and only two of the nine meetings scheduled for Boxing Day beat the weather. Happily, one of these was Kempton, where racegoers were treated to an excellent renewal of the Pertemps King George VI Chase. It had a popular winner in Florida Pearl, so often the nearly horse in the top chasing events, who beat Best Mate by half a length. Trainer Willie Mullins had booked J. P. McNamara to ride Florida Pearl, but when Wetherby was abandoned he was able to secure the services of Adrian Maguire instead. The previous month Maguire had ridden his 1,000th career winner, achieving the landmark aboard Fiori at Carlisle, but in March he was sidelined for the rest of the season after suffering a serious neck injury in a fall from Luzcadou at Warwick.

The Coral Eurobet Welsh National at Chepstow on December 27th went to 10/1 shot Supreme Glory, who beat the previous year's winner Jocks Cross by two lengths. Bindaree plugged on well for third, with What's Up Boys fading into fourth. Supreme Glory was the biggest career success to date for both trainer Pat Murphy and rider Leighton Aspell, each of whom has suffered more than their fair share of tribulations, but was ruled out of a crack at the Aintree National when he damaged a tendon in March.

Istabraq made his eagerly anticipated return to action at Leopardstown shortly after Christmas, but he made heavy weather of beating the greatly inferior Bust Out, the margin only a head. Trainer Aidan O'Brien suggested that the Champion would go to Cheltenham without another prep race.

Tony McCoy's most bizarre success of the season occurred at Southwell on January 23rd. Unseated from the odds-on favourite Family Business before halfway in a novice chase, he threw his crash helmet to the ground in disgust, but one by one each of the other six runners also fell by the wayside. Seizing his chance, McCoy remounted and completed more than a circuit of the course alone to claim the prize. His action did not meet with universal acclaim, however; one layer made the costly mistake of offering 1000/1 in running about Family Business on a betting exchange.

The feature attraction at Ascot on January 12th, the Victor Chandler Chase, saw a progressive winner in Turgeonev who was landing a four-timer. The grey, trained by Tim Easterby, was a first Ascot ride for jockey Richard McGrath. Easterby was also on the mark at Newcastle, where his exciting prospect Barton completed a hat-trick over fences in the Dipper Novices' Chase.

Looks Like Trouble, whose career had appeared in serious doubt, made an impressive return to the racecourse at Wincanton on January 19th, winning the John Bull Chase very easily. Off the track since injuring a tendon in November 2000, Noel chance's ten-year-old was now on track to defend his Gold Cup crown.

Conditions were appalling for participant and punter alike at Cheltenham on Saturday January 26th, as heavy rain in the morning and early afternoon turned the ground into a quagmire. The racing was still of a high quality, however. The featured Pillar Property Chase was won by Irish raider Rince Ri, trained by Ted Walsh and ridden by his son Ruby. The chestnut went off at 9/2, but had been available at 20/1 in the morning before the heavens opened. The bottomless ground and the slow pace, coupled with the withdrawal of the fancied Marlborough, rendered the Pillar of limited value as a Gold Cup trial.

With Istabraq an absentee, the way was clear for favourite Ned Kelly to win the AIG Europe Champion Hurdle at Leopardstown on January 27th. The chestnut scored comfortably in the hands of Norman Williamson and had his price for Cheltenham reduced from 16/1 to just 5/1.

Bacchanal was cut to 5/1 second favourite for the Gold Cup after his decisive win in Newbury's Aon Chase on February 9th. Nicky Henderson's gelding, third in the King George on his previous start, again displayed a tendency to jump out to his right but still beat Shotgun Willy and Marlborough by twelve lengths and a neck. Feature race of Newbury's card, the Tote Gold Trophy Hurdle, went to Copeland and Tony McCoy. The weights for this valuable handicap had been raised 16lb at the overnight stage following the defection of Valiramix, like Copeland trained by Martin Pipe.

The Grade One Hennessy Cognac Gold Cup at Leopardstown the next day was run in gruelling conditions, Alexander Banquet battled on dourly to hold off Behrajan with Rince Ri back in third. The winner's stablemate Florida Pearl, bidding for his fourth win in this event, was well beaten in fourth.

The last significant trials for the Cheltenham showcases took place at Wincanton on February 21st. 1999 Gold Cup winner See More Business confirmed himself on course for another crack at the big race with a thirty-length victory in the Country Gentlemen's Association Jim Ford Chase. Earlier in the season, Paul Nicholls' veteran had lain winded after a fall at Chepstow, and many observers feared the worst. The Axminster Carpets Kingwell Hurdle saw a return to form for former Champion Hurdle runner-up Hors La Loi III, who had no problem in disposing of Copeland.

The valuable Racing Post Chase, run at Kempton on February 22nd, was won in dashing style by former point-to-pointer Gunther McBride. The winner, who is missing most of his tail, was the third consecutive winner of the Kempton feature for Ricahrd Johnson, successful on Gloria Victis and Young Spartacus in the previous two runnings. Johnson had spent three months of the season on the sidelines after breaking his right leg in a fall from novice chaser Ilico II at Exeter on October 23rd.

The first Cheltenham Festival for two years opened on March 12th. After weeks of speculation about his well-being Istabraq made the line-up for the Smurfit Champion Hurdle, and was sent off the 2/1 favourite to win the title for the fourth time. Valiramix, who had disputed favouritism, was next best at 3/1. The line-up lost some of its lustre when Ned Kelly was withdrawn three days beforehand, apparently after an unsatisfactory tracheal scope. It was a sensational race. Istabraq, who had moved poorly to post, dropped back to last place after the second flight of hurdles and, on the bend going away from the stands, was pulled up by Charlie Swan. The huge crowd burst into spontaneous applause, knowing they had witnessed the swansong of a great hurdler. There was further drama to come. Valiramix, cruising behind the leaders with two flights to jump, suddenly crashed to the ground on the flat. He had broken his shoulder and had to be destroyed. His departure left the way clear for Hors La Loi II to beat outsider Marble Arch by three lengths. Trained by James Fanshawe, who had been responsible for most of the training of Royal Gait, Champion Hurdler of 1992, Hors La Loi II was ridden by Dean Gallagher who had made a comeback to the saddle after overcoming a drugs problem which threatened his career. As for Istabraq, it transpired that he had damaged a tendon, and his retirement was soon announced.

The opening day began in traditional fashion with the victory of an Irish-trained favourite, Like-A-Butterfly, in the Gerrard Supreme Novices' Hurdle. The eight-year-old mare, carrying the colours of J. P. McManus, had been many people's idea of the week's banker.

The Irish made it two out of two when Moscow Flyer was an impressive winner over Seebald and Armaturk in the Irish Independent Arkle Challenge Trophy. Jessica Harrington's charge went on to score at the Punchestown Festival, confirming himself the pick of the season's two-mile novices.

Hughie Morrison, whose first ever Festival runner Marble Arch had done him proud earlier in the afternoon, went one better when Frenchman's Creek landed the William Hill National Hunt Handicap Chase. Given a superbly cool ride by Paul Carberry, the 8/1 shot was still on the bridle when leading on the run-in.

Wednesday's highlight, the Queen Mother Champion Chase, saw Flagship Uberalles land a hefty gamble under a strong ride by Richard Johnson. The favourite was on and off the bridle at various stages, but responded to Johnson's urgings to collar Cenkos on the run-in. Cenkos, who held a clear lead at the final fence, was pipped by the rallying Native Upmanship for second spot. For winning trainer Philip Hobbs it was another highlight in a memorable season.

Galileo won day two's opener, the Royal and SunAlliance Novices' Hurdle, but this was not the dual Derby hero of 2001. This Galileo, who provided trainer Tom

George and jockey Jason Maguire with their first Festival victories, was still a 'Classic' winner, having won the St Leger in his native Poland.

The Royal and SunAlliance Novices' Chase went to outsider Hussard Collonges, in the hands of Russ Garritty. Sent off a 33/1 chance, the winner is from the Yorkshire stable of Peter Beaumont, who has enjoyed great success with chasers Jodami and Young Kenny.

A field of eighteen went to post for what promised to be a vintage Tote Gold Cup, and it certainly did not disappoint. One of the brightest jumping prospects for years, Best Mate, proved he had what it takes with an impressive victory, with Irish raider Commanche Court second and See More Business an honourable third. Best Mate's win justified the high hopes that trainer Henrietta Knight had always held for him, and was a personal triumph for Jim Culloty who had regained the mount on the gelding after breaking his arm earlier in the season. Naturally, there were disappointments. Florida Pearl, who seems destined never to win a Gold Cup, faded to finish tenth while Bacchanal finished two places behind, having been outpaced on the good ground. Sent off favourite, Looks Like Trouble made much of the running, but dropped away to walk over the line in last place. His tendon injury had recurred, and he was immediately retired.

Earlier in the afternoon Baracouda stamped himself an outstanding performer with a cheeky victory in the Bonusprint Stayers' Hurdle. Thierry Doumen gave the favourite a very confident ride, holding him up off the pace before cruising through to beat Irish hope Bannow Bay by a neck. Charlie Swan, criticised in some quarters for his ride on Bannow Bay, had begun the day with victory in the JCB Triumph Hurdle aboard Scolardy. Five of the first six home in the Triumph were Irish-trained.

It was a Festival to forget for Tony McCoy, who was inconsolable after the death of Valiramix. He had to wait until the penultimate race of the whole meeting, the Cathcart Challenge Cup, before riding a winner, 2/1 favourite Royal Auclair.

The Bunny Boiler, trained by Noel Meade, completed a National double in the period between Cheltenham and Aintree. The eight-year-old landed the Marstons Pedigree Midlands Grand National at Uttoxeter on March 16th in the hands of Norman Williamson, and added the Powers Gold Label Irish Grand National at Fairyhouse on Easter Monday under claimer Ross Geraghty. This was technically the second Irish National to be run during the latest season, the 2001 version, won by Davids Lad and Timmy Murphy, having been deferred until May due to Foot and Mouth.

Three weeks on from the Gold Cup, and the Aintree Grand National meeting got under way on April 4th. Florida Pearl, who was found to have had a lung infection at Cheltenham, returned to form with an impressive victory in the Martell Cup Chase, slamming Cyfor Malta by eleven lengths. Florida Pearl was to complete his campaign by taking the Punchestown Heineken Gold Cup, and was officially rated the season's best chaser.

Polly Gundry became only the third woman to ride a winner over the Grand National fences when her mount Torduff Express beat 29 rivals in the Martell Fox Hunters' Chase. Officially trained by Paul Nicholls, Torduff Express's daily routine had been supervised by point-to-point handler Richard Barber.

Aintree's second day feature, the Martell Melling Chase, went to Native

Upmanship, who appreciated the intermediate trip of two and a half miles and thoroughly deserved his big-race victory, while Barton, found to have a sore back after disappointing in the Arkle, returned to form when upped in trip in the Martell Mildmay Novices' Chase.

Ilnamar, a surprise winner of the Coral Cup at Cheltenham, maintained his improvement by taking the Martell Aintree Hurdle on Grand National day. The French import was partnered by Ruby Walsh, Tony McCoy having opted to ride another Martin Pipe runner, third-placed It Takes Time.

A typically dramatic Martell Grand National was won by 20/1 shot Bindaree, who rallied to beat What's Up Boys by a length and three-quarters with the favourite Blowing Wind and Tony McCoy well adrift in third. Bindaree's trainer Nigel Twiston-Davies, who had won the race with Earth Summit four years earlier, had endured a nightmare season, and revealed after the race that he was giving serious thought to handing in his trainer's licence. A few weeks later Twiston-Davies parted company with his assistant, former champion jockey Peter Scudamore. Bindaree was ridden by Jim Culloty, who only came in for the ride after intended jockey Jamie Goldstein had broken his leg at Ludlow three days before the race. Culloty thus became the first rider since John Burke in 1976 to complete the Gold Cup/Grand National double in the same year. No fewer than nine horses came to grief at the first fence, among then the fancied Paris Pike and Marlborough, the most casualties at the first since 1951. Another pivotal moment in the race came at the fourth from home with the departures of Ad Hoc and Davids Lad, both of whom had been travelling well. Sadly there were two fatailities, The Last Fling and Manx Magic.

Ruby Walsh was the man in form at Ayr's big meeting on April 20th. The stylish Irish rider notched a brilliant 5,716/1 four-timer, notably a memorable win on Take Control in the Gala Casinos Daily Record Scottish National. The 20/1 shot, rejected by Tony McCoy, almost ran off the track while switching around the dolled-off final fence, before being driven to catch Shotgun Willy close home, with Gunther McBride third. Walsh, also successful on Kadarann, Saint Par and Maybe The Business, all for Paul Nicholls, came within a whisker of landing the Scottish Champion Hurdle too, but his mount Vol Solitaire was pipped by Milligan and Norman Williamson.

Cenkos, who had run so well in the Queen Mother Champion Chase at the Festival, gained compensation with a defeat of Flagship Uberalles in the two-miler at Sandown on April 27th. First run the previous year, this well-endowed event was retitled the Queen Elizabeth the Queen Mother Celebration Chase.

There was also a change of identity for the season's last big race. Whitbread had pulled out of their sponsorship after forty-five years, to be replaced by the new satellite television channel Attheraces. The inaugural Attheraces Gold Cup went, appropriately, to Martin Pipe and Tony McCoy courtesy of the novice Bounce Back. Pipe was crowned champion trainer for the twelfth time, with 235 winners from nearly a thousand runners, and accrued record prizemoney of £2.6 million. His principal patron, David Johnson, was champion owner.

A less palatable aspect of the season was the persistent rumour that drug abuse was rife in jump racing. In December Lambourn trainer Charlie Mann urged the Jockey Club to act over the use of Erythropoietin (EPO), a performance-enhancing drug that stimulates the production of red blood cells. In February, a team of Jockey Club officials and vets carried out dawn raids on five randomly selected trainers, among them Martin Pipe, and tested each member of their strings for EPO. It was subsequently announced that every test proved negative.

Later in the season, however, a winner tested positive for Acetylpromazine (ACP), a 'stopping' drug which was at the centre of the long-running race-fixing saga which rocked the sport a couple of years earlier. The horse in question was Ashgar, a novice hurdler trained by Philip Hobbs, who failed the dope test after a race at Plumpton over Easter.

There were a number of notable retirements from the ranks of the jockeys. Peter Niven, who had reached the career landmark of 1000 winners at the end of the previous season, called it a day in September to begin a training career. Chris Maude, who had a fine record over the Grand National fences, hung up his boots in December to concentrate on his other role of jockeys' valet. Jimmy Frost, who in a long career won the Grand National on Little Polveir and the Champion Hurdle on Beech Road, retired from the saddle in March after partnering Bohill Lad to victory at Newton Abbot, which was also his first victory as a trainer.

The Queen Mother apart, the sport mourned a number of others during the season. These included owner Robert Hitchins, 86, who owned good jumpers with Jenny Pitman such as Toby Tobias and Princeful, and who was noted for his donations to charity; Terry Casey, 56, trainer of 1996 Grand National winner Rough Quest; Evan Williams, 89, who won the 1936 Gold Cup on Golden Miller and the folowing year's National on Royal Mail; and Dick Saunders, 68, who won the 1982 Grand National on Grittar at the age of 48, the oldest jockey to win the Aintree race.

RACEFORM TOP RATED CHASERS

Horse	Rating
First Gold	177
Best Mate	174
Florida Pearl	174
Flagship Uberalles	172
Commanche Court	171
Alexander Banquet	169
Bacchanal	169
Behrajan	168
Edredon Bleu	168
Lord Noelie	168
Native Upmanship	167
Cenkos	166
Latalomne	166
See More Business	166
Rince Ri	165
Foxchapel King	164
Fadalko	168
Legal Right	163
Marlborough	163
Sleeping Night	166
Wahiba Sands	163
Cyfor Malta	161
Shooting Light	161

RACEFORM TOP RATED HURDLERS

Horse	Rating
Istabraq	174
Baracouda	170
Limestone Lad	170
Hors La Loi III	167
Landing Light	165
Marble Arch	165
Geos	164
Valiramix	162
Bannow Bay	161
Bilboa	159
Ned Kelly	159
Rodock	157
Copeland	156

***NB: the above figures are as at 27th April 2002. A ratings revision will take place in May 2002 for the 2002-03 season.**

A Chef Too Far

101

9-y-o b g Be My Chief (USA)-Epithet (Mill Reef (USA))
R G Frost Merlin Pippa Partnership

Placings:203/221/2-P (0924)
2001/02: 17^{P}GF

	Starts	1st	2nd	3rd	Win & Pl
Hurdles	1	0	0	0	
Career Total	8	1	4	1	5768

99	1/00	Ludl	2m	E(0-105)HHdl	G-S	£2562

Total win prize-money £2562

Going: Sf: 0-0 GS: 0-0 Gd: 0-0 GF: - Fm: 0-1
Distance: 2m/2m3: 0-1 2m4-2m7: 0-0 3m+: 0-0
Track: LH: 0-1 RH: 0-0 Tight: 0-1 Gall: 0-0
Aids: Bl: 0-0 Vi: 0-0 Tstrap: 0-0
Best Rating: 105 3/01 Font 2m2f110y soft Hdl

A Day On The Dub

59

9-y-o b g Presidium-Border Mouse (Border Chief)
D Eddy Revblayd

Placings:0/0P5562/P0/5**F1PP6**/1500-P (1501)
2001/02: 17^{P}G

	Starts	1st	2nd	3rd	Win & Pl
Hurdles	1	0	0	0	
Career Total	20	2	1	0	4991

111	9/00	Sedg	2m1f	E Hdl	GD	£1862
112	1/00	Catt	2m	F(0-100)HCh	GD	£2453

Total win prize-money £4316

Going: Sf: 0-0 GS: 0-0 Gd: 0-1 GF: - Fm: 0-0
Distance: 2m/2m3: 0-1 2m4-2m7: 0-0 3m+: 0-0
Track: LH: 0-1 RH: 0-0 Tight: 0-1 Gall: 0-0
Aids: Bl: 0-0 Vi: 0-0 Tstrap: 0-0
Best Rating: 112 1/00 Catt 2m good Ch

A Few Bob Back (IRE)

105 108

6-y-o b g Bob Back (USA)-Kottna (USA) (Lyphard (USA))
D Eddy (J L Hassett 11/11) Brian Chicken

Placings:000-55P41F0012P (3790)
2001/02: 16^{5}HY, 16^{5}HY, 24^{P}G, 20^{4}YS, 20^{1}SH, 20^{F}SH, 18^{0}YS, 24^{0}Y, 24^{1}S, 25^{2}S, 20^{P}S

	Starts	1st	2nd	3rd	Win & Pl
NH Flat	2	0	0	0	0
Hurdles	9	2	1	0	9689
Career Total	14	2	1	0	9689

108	1/02	Newc	3m	D(0-125)HHdl	SFT	£3542
99	8/01	Slig	2m4f	(0-95)HHdl	SH	£4312

Total win prize-money £7855

Going: Sf: 1-5 GS: 0-0 Gd: 0-1 GF: - Fm: 0-0
Distance: 2m/2m3: 0-3 2m4-2m7: 1-4 3m+: 1-4
Track: **LH: 1-3** RH: 0-0 Tight: 0-1 **Gall: 1-2**
Aids: **Bl: 1-5** Vi: 0-0 Tstrap: 0-0
Best Rating: 108 1/02 Catt 3m1f110y soft Hdl

Handicap hurdler, he acts on a soft surface and stays three miles. Has worn sheepskin cheekpieces and blinkers.

A Piece Of Cake (IRE)

109(53h) 144

9-y-o gr g Roselier (FR)-Boreen Bro (Boreen (FR))
Mrs M Reveley Lightbody Celebration Cakes Ltd

Placings:0/15**F2123131**-6F1450 (4897)
2001/02: 20^{6}G, 20^{F}G, 20^{1}S, 19^{4}GS, 24^{5}GS, 24^{0}G

	Starts	1st	2nd	3rd	Win & Pl
Chases	6	1	0	0	10299
Career Total	17	5	2	2	40476

144	2/02	Newc	2m4f	B(0-140)HCh	SFT	£8853
144	4/01	Asct	2m3f110y	C(0-130)HCh	SFT	£14040
132	1/01	Newc	2m4f	E Ch	HVY	£3120
120	11/00	Kels	2m6f110y	E Ch	SFT	£3315
89	5/00	Weth	2m4f110y	D Hdl	G-F	£3432

Total win prize-money £32761

Going: Sf: 1-1 GS: 0-2 Gd: 0-3 GF: - Fm: 0-0
Distance: 2m/2m3: 0-0 **2m4-2m7: 1-4** 3m+: 0-2
Track: **LH: 1-5** RH: 0-1 Tight: 0-0 **Gall: 1-3**
Aids: Bl: 0-0 Vi: 0-0 Tstrap: 0-0
Best Rating: 144 2/02 Newc 2m4f soft Ch

A sound jumper, he was most consistent in novice chases in the 2000/2001 season, putting up his best effort when winning a valuable novices' handicap at Ascot in April 2001, and landed a Newcastle handicap on his third run of 2001/02. Suited by soft ground, he is normally ridden patiently and promises to stay three miles.

A Proper Charlie

78 52

6-y-o b g Cashwyn-Kate's Girl (Lighter)
R J Price R J Lewis

Placings:0/0-0U0 (0495)
2001/02: 16^{0}GF, 19^{U}G, 19^{0}G

	Starts	1st	2nd	3rd	Win & Pl
Hurdles	3	0	0	0	
Career Total	5	0	0	0	

Going: Sf: 0-0 GS: 0-0 Gd: 0-2 GF: - Fm: 0-1
Distance: 2m/2m3: 0-1 2m4-2m7: 0-2 3m+: 0-0
Track: LH: 0-0 RH: 0-3 Tight: 0-0 Gall: 0-1
Aids: Bl: 0-0 Vi: 0-0 Tstrap: 0-0
Best Rating: 52 5/01 Hntg 2m110y gd-fm Hdl

A Right Set Two

94 109

10-y-o ch g Island Set (USA)-Super Sol (Rolfe (USA))
J S King Jim Short

Placings:PF34/12/40-2 (0208)
2001/02: 24^{2}F

	Starts	1st	2nd	3rd	Win & Pl
Chases	1	0	1	0	1171
Career Total	9	1	2	1	6296

114	5/99	Hntg	3m	F(0-100)HCh	G-F	£3406

Total win prize-money £3407

Going: Sf: 0-0 GS: 0-0 Gd: 0-0 GF: - Fm: 0-1
Distance: 2m/2m3: 0-0 2m4-2m7: 0-0 3m+: 0-1
Track: LH: 0-1 RH: 0-0 Tight: 0-1 Gall: 0-0
Aids: Bl: 0-0 Vi: 0-0 Tstrap: 0-0
Best Rating: 114 5/99 Hntg 3m gd-fm Ch

A Romp Too Far (IRE)

80 84

6-y-o b g Eurobus-Saxa Princess (IRE) (Lancastrian)
C J Mann Roger Maggs

Placings:06 (2392)
2001/02: 16^{0}G, 20^{6}S

	Starts	1st	2nd	3rd	Win & Pl
NH Flat	1	0	0	0	0
Hurdles	1	0	0	0	0
Career Total	2	0	0	0	0

Going: Sf: 0-1 GS: 0-0 Gd: 0-1 GF: - Fm: 0-0
Distance: 2m/2m3: 0-1 2m4-2m7: 0-1 3m+: 0-0
Track: LH: 0-2 RH: 0-0 Tight: 0-0 Gall: 0-0
Aids: Bl: 0-0 Vi: 0-0 Tstrap: 0-0
Best Rating: 98 10/01 Chel 2m110y good NHF

A S Jim

99 87

11-y-o b g Welsh Captain-Cawston's Arms (Cawston's Clown)
O O'Neill James A Atkin

Placings:020321/4513611F212/5F/054-0001 (0846)
2001/02: 16^{0}GF, 20^{0}GF, 19^{0}GF, 22^{1}GF

	Starts	1st	2nd	3rd	Win & Pl
Hurdles	4	1	0	0	1680
Career Total	26	6	4	2	15936

87	7/01	Strf	2m6f110y	G(0-95)HHdl	G-F	£1680
101	2/98	Hrfd	2m1f	F(0-105)HHdl	GD	£2766
88	11/97	Tntn	2m3f110y	G(0-110)HHdl	GD	£1917
88	11/97	Wwck	2m	F(0-100)HHdl	GD	£2092
87	9/97	Hrfd	2m3f110y	F(0-100)HHdl	GD	£2374
87	4/97	Worc	2m	G Hdl	GD	£2048

Total win prize-money £12879

Going: Sf: 0-0 GS: 0-0 Gd: 0-0 GF: - Fm: 1-4
Distance: 2m/2m3: 0-1 **2m4-2m7: 1-3** 3m+: 0-0
Track: **LH: 1-3** RH: 0-1 **Tight: 1-3** Gall: 0-0
Aids: Bl: 0-0 Vi: 0-0 Tstrap: 0-0
Best Rating: 113 3/98 Ludl 2m5f110y good Hdl

Plating-class hurdler, has deteriorated in last couple of seasons. Best on good ground or faster.

A Second Sloe

7-y-o gr g Scallywag-Cherry Morello (Bargello)
R H Alner Dr S G F Cave

Placings:S (0436)
2001/02: 17^{S}GF

	Starts	1st	2nd	3rd	Win & Pl
NH Flat	1	0	0	0	
Career Total	1	0	0	0	

Going: Sf: 0-0 GS: 0-0 Gd: 0-0 GF: - Fm: 0-1
Distance: 2m/2m3: 0-1 2m4-2m7: 0-0 3m+: 0-0
Track: LH: 0-0 RH: 0-0 Tight: 0-1 Gall: 0-0
Aids: Bl: 0-0 Vi: 0-0 Tstrap: 0-0
Best Rating: mfy

A Thousand Dreams (IRE)

97(94h) (70h)75

12-y-o b g Aristocracy-Ardellis Lady (Pollerton)
L Waring Mrs J Waring

Placings:0/34460/000/0144/0015P/00P-000500000065 (4734)
2001/02: 17^{0}G, 17^{0}G, 16^{0}G, 17^{6}G, 16^{5}GF, 17^{0}GF, 16^{0}GF, 17^{0}GF, 16^{0}GF, 16^{0}GF, 17^{0}G, 17^{6}G, 19^{5}F

	Starts	1st	2nd	3rd	Win & Pl
Hurdles	12	0	0	0	0
Chases	1	0	0	0	0
Career Total	34	2	0	1	5935

105	1/00	Ludl	2m	E Ch	GD	£3209
80	7/98	Wolv	2m	E(0-105)HHdl	G-F	£2144

Total win prize-money £5354

Going: Sf: 0-0 GS: 0-0 Gd: 0-6 GF: - Fm: 0-7
Distance: 2m/2m3: 0-12 2m4-2m7: 0-1 3m+: 0-0
Track: LH: 0-8 RH: 0-5 Tight: 0-6 Gall: 0-0
Aids: Bl: 0-0 Vi: 0-0 Tstrap: 0-0
Best Rating: **105** 1/00 Ludl 2m good Ch

Plating class hurdler who races at around two miles. Has won over fences at two miles. Acts on a sound surface.

A Venture To Phar (IRE)

8-y-o br g Phardante (FR)-Loughaderra (IRE) (Strong Gale)
N G Richards Ashleybank Investments Limited

Placings: *0U/0-F* (1459)
2001/02: 24^{F}G

	Starts	1st	2nd	3rd	Win & Pl
Hurdles	1	0	0	0	
Career Total	4	0	0	0	

Going: Sf: 0-0 GS: 0-0 Gd: 0-1 GF: - Fm: 0-0
Distance: 2m/2m3: 0-0 2m4-2m7: 0-0 3m+: 0-1
Track: LH: 0-0 RH: 0-1 Tight: 0-0 Gall: 0-0
Aids: Bl: 0-0 Vi: 0-0 Tstrap: 0-0
Best Rating: **93** 1/00 Donc 2m110y gd-fm NHF

A Verse To Order

11-y-o b g Rymer-Born Bossy (Eborneezer)
Mrs P Ford K R Ford

Placings: *006050*P5/PP (1801)
2001/02: 20^{P}GF, 20^{P}GF

	Starts	1st	2nd	3rd	Win & Pl
Hurdles	1	0	0	0	0
Chases	1	0	0	0	0
Career Total	10	0	0	0	0

Going: Sf: 0-0 GS: 0-0 Gd: 0-0 GF: - Fm: 0-2
Distance: 2m/2m3: 0-0 2m4-2m7: 0-2 3m+: 0-0
Track: LH: 0-1 RH: 0-1 Tight: 0-1 Gall: 0-0
Aids: Bl: 0-0 Vi: 0-0 Tstrap: 0-2
Best Rating: **80** 10/97 Tntn 2m1f gd-fm NHF

A-Time Of Peace (IRE)

9-y-o b m Royal Fountain-Sparkle For Me (Baragoi)
R Lee Mr C R Elliott & Mr R Brereton

Placings: *00*/PPC (4682)
2001/02: 16^{P}S, 24^{P}GS, 17^{C}GF

	Starts	1st	2nd	3rd	Win & Pl
Hurdles	2	0	0	0	0
Chases	1	0	0	0	0
Career Total	5	0	0	0	

Going: Sf: 0-1 GS: 0-1 Gd: 0-0 GF: - Fm: 0-1
Distance: 2m/2m3: 0-2 2m4-2m7: 0-0 3m+: 0-1
Track: LH: 0-1 RH: 0-2 Tight: 0-2 Gall: 0-0
Aids: Bl: 0-0 Vi: 0-0 Tstrap: 0-0
Best Rating: **82** 10/99 Tntn 2m1f gd-fm NHF

Abacus (IRE)

93 116

8-y-o ch g Be My Native (USA)-Millers Run (Deep Run)
F Flood (M C Pipe 19/11) Kildare Racing Club

Placings: *1*/P31/U430PP (4461a)
2001/02: 25^{U}GF, 24^{4}GS, 20^{3}GF, 20^{0}HY, 24^{P}SH, 24^{P}S

	Starts	1st	2nd	3rd	Win & Pl
Chases	6	0	0	1	447
Career Total	10	2	0	2	6588

107	1/00	Sthl	2m	E Ch	G-S	£2596
111	2/99	Punc	2m	NHF	HVY	£2915

Total win prize-money £5512

Going: Sf: 0-2 GS: 0-1 Gd: 0-0 GF: - Fm: 0-2
Distance: 2m/2m3: 0-0 2m4-2m7: 0-2 3m+: 0-4
Track: LH: 0-1 RH: 0-3 Tight: 0-0 Gall: 0-0
Aids: Bl: 0-0 Vi: 0-0 Tstrap: 0-0
Best Rating: **123** 1/00 Extr 2m7f110y heavy Ch

Abajany

101 93

8-y-o b g Akarad (FR)-Miss Ivory Coast (USA) (Sir Ivor)
M R Channon M Channon

Placings: P45/260/3/4-03000 (4185)
2001/02: 16^{0}G, 16^{3}GF, 16^{0}GS, 17^{0}G, 17^{0}S

	Starts	1st	2nd	3rd	Win & Pl
Hurdles	5	0	0	1	361
Career Total	13	0	1	2	3467

Going: Sf: 0-1 GS: 0-1 Gd: 0-2 GF: - Fm: 0-1
Distance: 2m/2m3: 0-5 2m4-2m7: 0-0 3m+: 0-0
Track: LH: 0-1 RH: 0-4 Tight: 0-1 Gall: 0-1
Aids: Bl: 0-0 Vi: 0-2 Tstrap: 0-0
Best Rating: **106** 10/98 Plum 2m1f good Hdl

A Flat winner, he has shown bits and pieces of form over timber and looks to need a sound surface.

Abalvino (FR)

112 140

8-y-o ch g Sillery (USA)-Abalvina (FR) (Abdos)
P R Webber I M S Racing & Noel Caronin

Placings: *3130/45*/**F3124321-15132U0** (4649)
2001/02: 16^{1}G, 17^{5}GS, 17^{1}S, 16^{3}HY, 16^{2}GS, 17^{U}S, 16^{0}G

	Starts	1st	2nd	3rd	Win & Pl
Chases	7	2	1	1	16512
Career Total	21	5	3	5	31463

140	12/01	Strf	2m1f110y	D(0-120)HCh	SFT	£8580
140	5/01	Hntg	2m110y	E Ch	GD	£3752
140	4/01	MRas	2m1f110y	D Ch	G-S	£4849
127	12/00	Leic	2m	E(0-105)HCh	G-S	£3133
114	1/99	Towc	2m	H NHF	HVY	£1420

Total win prize-money £21734

Going: Sf: 1-3 GS: 0-2 Gd: 1-2 GF: - Fm: 0-0
Distance: **2m/2m3: 2-7** 2m4-2m7: 0-0 3m+: 0-0
Track: LH: 1-4 RH: 1-3 Tight: 1-3 Gall: 1-2
Aids: Bl: 0-0 Vi: 0-0 Tstrap: 0-0
Best Rating: **140** 2/02 Sand 2m gd-sft Ch

Fair handicap chaser, effective at around two miles and acts on good and soft ground.

Abandon Hope

69f 21f

6-y-o ch m Jupiter Island-Band Of Hope (USA) (Dixieland Band (USA))
W Clay P Riley & N Brown

Placings: *0* (1263)
2001/02: 16^{0}GF

	Starts	1st	2nd	3rd	Win & Pl
NH Flat	1	0	0	0	
Career Total	1	0	0	0	

Going: Sf: 0-0 GS: 0-0 Gd: 0-0 GF: - Fm: 0-1
Distance: 2m/2m3: 0-1 2m4-2m7: 0-0 3m+: 0-0
Track: LH: 0-0 RH: 0-1 Tight: 0-0 Gall: 0-1
Aids: Bl: 0-0 Vi: 0-0 Tstrap: 0-0
Best Rating: **15** 8/01 Hntg 2m110y gd-fm NHF

Abbey Flyer

10-y-o b g Minster Son-Miss Felham (Malinowski (USA))
Mrs P Sly Mrs J Woollatt

Placings: P/P (1909)
2001/02: 20^{P}S

	Starts	1st	2nd	3rd	Win & Pl
Chases	1	0	0	0	
Career Total	2	0	0	0	

Going: Sf: 0-1 GS: 0-0 Gd: 0-0 GF: - Fm: 0-0
Distance: 2m/2m3: 0-0 2m4-2m7: 0-1 3m+: 0-0
Track: LH: 0-1 RH: 0-0 Tight: 0-1 Gall: 0-0
Aids: Bl: 0-0 Vi: 0-0 Tstrap: 0-0
Best Rating:

Abbey Hill

5-y-o b m Then Again-Galley Bay (Welsh Saint)
W S Kittow J A Aldworth

Placings: *0* (3345)
2001/02: 17^{0}S

	Starts	1st	2nd	3rd	Win & Pl
NH Flat	1	0	0	0	
Career Total	1	0	0	0	

Going: Sf: 0-1 GS: 0-0 Gd: 0-0 GF: - Fm: 0-0
Distance: 2m/2m3: 0-1 2m4-2m7: 0-0 3m+: 0-0
Track: LH: 0-0 RH: 0-0 Tight: 0-0 Gall: 0-0
Aids: Bl: 0-0 Vi: 0-0 Tstrap: 0-0
Best Rating:

Abbeyknock Boy (IRE)

94 75

5-y-o b/br g Alphabatim (USA)-Haha Dash (IRE) (Lord Ha Ha)
Ian Williams Westbourne Leisure Ltd

Placings: *4*-04U (4850)
2001/02: 16^{0}GF, 22^{4}S, 22^{U}G

	Starts	1st	2nd	3rd	Win & Pl
NH Flat	1	0	0	0	0
Hurdles	2	0	0	0	0
Career Total	**4**	**0**	**0**	**0**	**326**

Going: Sf: 0-1 GS: 0-0 Gd: 0-1 GF: - Fm: 0-1
Distance: 2m/2m3: 0-1 2m4-2m7: 0-2 3m+: 0-0
Track: LH: 0-2 RH: 0-1 Tight: 0-2 Gall: 0-1
Aids: Bl: 0-0 Vi: 0-0 Tstrap: 0 0
Best Rating: **71** 2/01 Wwck 2m soft NHF

Ran by far his best race over hurdles when third in three mile novices' handicap at Worcester June 2002.

Abbiejo (IRE)

5-y-o b m Blues Traveller (IRE)-Chesham Lady (IRE) (Fayruz)
G Fierro G Fierro

Placings:*0* **(0684)**
2001/02: 17^{0}G

	Starts	1st	2nd	3rd	Win & Pl
NH Flat	1	0	0	0	
Career Total	**1**	**0**	**0**	**0**	

Going: Sf: 0-0 GS: 0-0 Gd: 0-1 GF: - Fm: 0-0
Distance: 2m/2m3: 0-1 2m4-2m7: 0-0 3m+: 0-0
Track: LH: 0-1 RH: 0-0 Tight: 0-1 Gall: 0-0
Aids: Bl: 0-0 Vi: 0-0 Tstrap: 0-0
Best Rating:

Abbot

118 **130**
4-y-o b g Bishop Of Cashel-Gifted (Shareef Dancer (USA))
C J Mann (B J Meehan 16/7) Abbott Racing Limited

Placings:1642 **(4651)**
2001/02: 16^{1}G, 16^{6}G, 16^{4}G, 16^{2}G

	Starts	1st	2nd	3rd	Win & Pl
Hurdles	4	1	1	0	26740
Career Total	**4**	**1**	**1**	**0**	**26740**

124	11/01	Newb	2m110y	D Hdl	GD	£3640

Total win prize-money £3640

Going: Sf: 0-0 GS: 0-0 Gd: 1-4 GF: - Fm: 0-0
Distance: **2m/2m3: 1-4** 2m4-2m7: 0-0 3m+: 0-0
Track: **LH: 1-2** RH: 0-2 Tight: 0-1 **Gall: 1-1**
Aids: Bl: 0-0 Vi: 0-0 Tstrap: 0-0
Best Rating: **130** 4/02 Aint 2m110y good Hdl

A huge sort for his age, he won on his debut over hurdles in fine style at Newbury in November 2001. Flopped next time but went on to prove himself a leading juvenile. Chasing will be his game in time.

Abbots Court (IRE)

79 **73**
7-y-o b g Hallowed Turf (USA)-Coronea Sea Queen (IRE) (Bassompierre)
R H Alner H Wellstead

Placings:*0-PP* **(2113)**
2001/02: 25^{P}S, 25^{P}G

	Starts	1st	2nd	3rd	Win & Pl
Chases	2	0	0	0	
Career Total	**3**	**0**	**0**	**0**	

Going: Sf: 0-1 GS: 0-0 Gd: 0-1 GF: - Fm: 0-0
Distance: 2m/2m3: 0-0 2m4-2m7: 0-0 3m+: 0-2
Track: LH: 0-0 RH: 0-2 Tight: 0-1 Gall: 0-0
Aids: Bl: 0-0 Vi: 0-0 Tstrap: 0-0
Best Rating: **95** 3/01 Hntg 2m110y soft NHF

A winner of point-to-points in 2000. Lightly-raced since.

Abinitio Lady (IRE)

109 **103**
7-y-o br m Be My Native (USA)-Chake-Chake (Goldhill)
Mrs M Reveley Michael Ahern

Placings:*30432/12*-32FU **(4237)**
2001/02: 16^{3}GS, 16^{2}S, 16^{F}GS, 16^{U}GF

	Starts	1st	2nd	3rd	Win & Pl
Hurdles	4	0	1	1	1162
Career Total	**11**	**1**	**3**	**3**	**6587**

93	7/00	Tipp	2m	NHF	G-F	£3312

Total win prize-money £3312

Going: Sf: 0-1 GS: 0-2 Gd: 0-0 GF: - Fm: 0-1
Distance: 2m/2m3: 0-4 2m4-2m7: 0-0 3m+: 0-0
Track: LH: 0-2 RH: 0-2 Tight: 0-1 Gall: 0-2
Aids: Bl: 0-0 Vi: 0-0 Tstrap: 0-0
Best Rating: **103** 2/02 Hntg 2m110y soft Hdl

A fast-ground bumper winner in Ireland, she won a weak novices' hurdle at Hexham in June 2002. Effective at two miles on good ground.

Able Native (IRE)

101(105h) (113h)**86**
5-y-o b m Thatching-Native Joy (IRE) (Be My Native (USA))
N B Mason (G M Moore 21/6) N B Mason

Placings:204-0051342122055133 **(4869)**
2001/02: 20^{0}G, 16^{0}G, 20^{5}GS, 16^{1}S, 21^{3}S, 20^{4}GS, 20^{2}S, 16^{1}S, 16^{2}GS, 16^{2}S, 20^{0}S, 16^{5}S, 16^{5}G, 20^{1}HY, 20^{3}G, 20^{3}GF

	Starts	1st	2nd	3rd	Win & Pl
Hurdles	16	3	3	3	15310
Career Total	**19**	**3**	**4**	**3**	**16201**

113	3/02	Newc	2m4f	E(0-110)HHdl	HVY	£3493
104	1/02	Fknm	2m	E(0-110)HHdl	SFT	£2408
100	10/01	Fknm	2m	F(0-105)HHdl	SFT	£3342

Total win prize-money £9245

Going: Sf: 3-8 GS: 0-3 Gd: 0-4 GF: - Fm: 0-1
Distance: **2m/2m3: 2-7** 2m4-2m7: 1-9 3m+: 0-0
Track: **LH: 3-11** RH: 0-3 **Tight: 2-8** Gall: 1-2
Aids: Bl: 0-0 Vi: 0-0 **Tstrap: 3-14**
Best Rating: **113** 3/02 Newc 2m4f heavy Hdl

Fair hurdler, seems to have improved for the fitting of a tongue tie towards the end of 2001. Goes well with cut and likes a sharp track. Best over two miles, stays two and a half. Goes well at Fakenham.

Able Pete

70 **27**
6-y-o b g Formidable (USA)-An Empress (USA) (Affirmed (USA))
A G Newcombe A G Newcombe

Placings:0 **(1567)**
2001/02: 20^{0}GS

	Starts	1st	2nd	3rd	Win & Pl
Hurdles	1	0	0	0	
Career Total	**1**	**0**	**0**	**0**	

Going: Sf: 0-0 GS: 0-1 Gd: 0-0 GF: - Fm: 0-0
Distance: 2m/2m3: 0-0 2m4-2m7: 0-1 3m+: 0-0
Track: LH: 0-0 RH: 0-0 Tight: 0-1 Gall: 0-0
Aids: Bl: 0-0 Vi: 0-0 Tstrap: 0-0
Best Rating: **27** 10/01 Font 2m4f gd-sft Hdl

Above The Cut (USA)

108(73c) **99**
10-y-o ch g Topsider (USA)-Placer Queen (Habitat)
C P Morlock J P M & J W Cook

Placings:25662152/216/64/253606645/22244-000520142105 **(4877)**
2001/02: 19^{0}F, 19^{0}GF, 17^{0}G, 20^{5}S, 22^{2}GS, 17^{0}GF, 24^{1}GF, 24^{4}G, 24^{2}GF, 24^{1}GS, 24^{0}G, 24^{5}G

	Starts	1st	2nd	3rd	Win & Pl
Hurdles	12	2	2	0	8935
Career Total	**39**	**4**	**10**	**1**	**22826**

99	12/01	Tntn	3m110y	D(0-120)HHdl	G-S	£3510
94	10/01	Ludl	3m	F(0-95)HHdl	G-F	£3209
108	5/97	Towc	2m	D(0-125)HHdl	GD	£2840
104	3/97	Ludl	2m	E(0-115)HHdl	G-F	£2584

Total win prize-money £12144

Going: Sf: 0-1 GS: 1-2 Gd: 0-4 GF: - Fm: 1-5
Distance: 2m/2m3: 0-3 2m4-2m7: 0-3 **3m+: 2-6**
Track: LH: 0-4 **RH: 2-8 Tight: 1-5** Gall: 0-0
Aids: Bl: 0-0 Vi: 0-0 Tstrap: 0-0
Best Rating: **110** 7/00 NAbb 2m110y gd-fm Ch

Fair three-mile handicap hurdler. Does not want the ground too soft. Acts on a sound surface.

Absolutely Hopeful

103(98c) **89**
9-y-o ch g Nearly A Hand-Owena Deep (Deep Run)
C P Morlock Michael Padfield

Placings:*304/0/022PP/2FP5556P*-P4536410P **(4316)**
2001/02: 25^{P}S, 23^{4}G, 22^{5}GS, 22^{3}HY, 21^{6}GS, 24^{4}G, 22^{1}S, 24^{0}G, 24^{P}HY

	Starts	1st	2nd	3rd	Win & Pl
Hurdles	9	1	0	1	3141
Career Total	**26**	**1**	**3**	**2**	**6063**

89	2/02	Folk	2m6f110y	E(0-110)HHdl	SFT	£2555

Total win prize-money £2555

Going: Sf: 1-4 GS: 0-2 Gd: 0-3 GF: - Fm: 0-0
Distance: 2m/2m3: 0-0 **2m4-2m7: 1-5** 3m+: 0-4
Track: LH: 0-2 **RH: 1-6 Tight: 1-3** Gall: 0-1
Aids: Bl: 1-4 Vi: 0-0 Tstrap: 1-5
Best Rating: **90** 5/00 Towc 3m1f soft Ch

Inconsistent staying hurdler, he broke his duck in fine style at the 25th attempt.

Abu Dancer (IRE)

74 **53**
6-y-o b m Vestris Abu-Oonagh's Teddy (Quayside)
Miss H C Knight David & Elaine Long

Placings:*0*PU00 **(4881)**
2001/02: 17^{0}G, 16^{P}S, 19^{U}GS, 16^{0}G, 18^{0}GF

	Starts	1st	2nd	3rd	Win & Pl
NH Flat	1	0	0	0	0
Hurdles	4	0	0	0	0
Career Total	**5**	**0**	**0**	**0**	

Going: Sf: 0-1 GS: 0-1 Gd: 0-2 GF: - Fm: 0-1
Distance: 2m/2m3: 0-4 2m4-2m7: 0-1 3m+: 0-0
Track: LH: 0-1 RH: 0-4 Tight: 0-2 Gall: 0-0

Aids: Bl: 0-0 Vi: 0-0 Tstrap: 0-0
Best Rating: 70 10/01 Hrfd 2m1f good NHF

Abzuson

95f **102f**

5-y-o b g Abzu-Mellouise (Handsome Sailor)
J R Norton Abzuson Syndicate

Placings:*24* **(4771)**
2001/02: 17^{2}S, 16^{4}GF

	Starts	1st	2nd	3rd	Win & Pl
NH Flat	2	0	1	0	494
Career Total	**2**	**0**	**1**	**0**	**494**

Going: Sf: 0-1 GS: 0-0 Gd: 0-0 GF: - Fm: 0-1
Distance: 2m/2m3: 0-2 2m4-2m7: 0-0 3m+: 0-0
Track: LH: 0-1 RH: 0-0 Tight: 0-1 Gall: 0-0
Aids: Bl: 0-0 Vi: 0-0 Tstrap: 0-0
Best Rating: 93 4/02 Hexm 2m110y gd-fm NHF

Posted a solid effort on his racecourse debut, finishing runner-up in a soft ground bumper at Bangor.

Academic Accuracy

4-y-o b f Environment Friend-Branitska (Mummy's Pet)
P S McEntee (M J Gingell 25/11) M J Gingell

Placings:PPP **(2324)**
2001/02: 16^{P}G, 16^{P}G, 16^{P}S

	Starts	1st	2nd	3rd	Win & Pl
Hurdles	3	0	0	0	
Career Total	**3**	**0**	**0**	**0**	

Going: Sf: 0-1 GS: 0-0 Gd: 0-2 GF: - Fm: 0-0
Distance: 2m/2m3: 0-3 2m4-2m7: 0-0 3m+: 0-0
Track: LH: 0-1 RH: 0-2 Tight: 0-1 Gall: 0-2
Aids: Bl: 0-0 Vi: 0-0 Tstrap: 0-0
Best Rating:

Academic Record

89 **62**

4-y-o b g Royal Academy (USA)-Bala Monaafis (IRE) (In The Wings)
N M Babbage (Gerard Cully 24/9) B Babbage

Placings:F03600 **(2204)**
2001/02: 16^{F}G, 16^{0}GF, 16^{3}GF, 17^{6}GS, 17^{0}G, 16^{0}GS

	Starts	1st	2nd	3rd	Win & Pl
Hurdles	6	0	0	1	423
Career Total	**6**	**0**	**0**	**1**	**423**

Going: Sf: 0-0 GS: 0-2 Gd: 0-2 GF: - Fm: 0-2
Distance: 2m/2m3: 0-6 2m4-2m7: 0-0 3m+: 0-0
Track: LH: 0-2 RH: 0-3 Tight: 0-1 Gall: 0-0
Aids: Bl: 0-5 Vi: 0-0 Tstrap: 0-0
Best Rating: 62 10/01 Ludl 2m gd-fm Hdl

Academy (IRE)

91 **81**

7-y-o ch g Archway (IRE)-Dream Academy (Town And Country)
Andrew Turnell Mrs M R Taylor

Placings:01/3/50P0 **(4160)**
2001/02: 16^{5}G, 16^{0}G, 16^{P}S, 16^{0}GS

	Starts	1st	2nd	3rd	Win & Pl
Hurdles	4	0	0	0	0
Career Total	**7**	**1**	**0**	**1**	**2451**

98 4/99 Sedg 2m1f E Hdl FRM £2022
Total win prize-money £2023

Going: Sf: 0-1 GS: 0-1 Gd: 0-2 GF: - Fm: 0-0
Distance: 2m/2m3: 0-4 2m4-2m7: 0-0 3m+: 0-0
Track: LH: 0-1 RH: 0-3 Tight: 0-0 Gall: 0-1
Aids: Bl: 0-0 Vi: 0-0 Tstrap: 0-0
Best Rating: 98 11/99 Wwck 2m good Hdl

Lightly-raced hurdler, he won a weak event on firm ground back in 1999, but has been held in handicap company since.

Accademia (IRE)

82 **65**

9-y-o b g Top Of The World-Lady Gondola (Tug Of War)
M J Wilkinson Accademia Partners

Placings:*60643P/F420/50-0* **(0374)**
2001/02: 26^{0}GF

	Starts	1st	2nd	3rd	Win & Pl
Hurdles	1	0	0	0	
Career Total	**13**	**0**	**1**	**1**	**1079**

Going: Sf: 0-0 GS: 0-0 Gd: 0-0 GF: - Fm: 0-1
Distance: 2m/2m3: 0-0 2m4-2m7: 0-0 3m+: 0-1
Track: LH: 0-0 RH: 0-1 Tight: 0-0 Gall: 0-1
Aids: Bl: 0-0 Vi: 0-0 Tstrap: 0-0
Best Rating: 87 4/99 Strf 2m6f110y gd-sft Hdl

Access Overseas

100 **91**

5-y-o b m Access Ski-Access Advantage (Infantry)
J D Frost (R G Frost 20/12) Miss Elaine D Williams

Placings:45-1U4040 **(4866)**
2001/02: 17^{1}G, 17^{U}G, 16^{4}GF, 16^{0}G, 17^{4}G, 17^{0}F

	Starts	1st	2nd	3rd	Win & Pl
Hurdles	6	1	0	0	2275
Career Total	**8**	**1**	**0**	**0**	**2275**

91 6/01 NAbb 2m1f G Hdl GD £2275
Total win prize-money £2275

Going: Sf: 0-0 GS: 0-0 Gd: 1-4 GF: - Fm: 0-2
Distance: **2m/2m3: 1-6** 2m4-2m7: 0-0 3m+: 0-0
Track: **LH: 1-3** RH: 0-3 **Tight: 1-3** Gall: 0-0
Aids: Bl: 0-0 Vi: 0-0 Tstrap: 0-0
Best Rating: 91 6/01 NAbb 2m1f good Hdl

Plating-class hurdler at around two miles. Acts on good ground.

Accystan

91 **77**

7-y-o ch g Efisio-Amia (CAN) (Nijinsky (CAN))
A Crook G Heap

Placings:241204/0/05-000PP **(4670)**
2001/02: 16^{0}S, 16^{0}GS, 16^{0}GS, 19^{P}S, 21^{P}GF

	Starts	1st	2nd	3rd	Win & Pl
Hurdles	5	0	0	0	
Career Total	**14**	**1**	**2**	**0**	**3007**

89 11/98 Catt 2m G Hdl GD £1509
Total win prize-money £1509

Going: Sf: 0-2 GS: 0-2 Gd: 0-0 GF: - Fm: 0-1
Distance: 2m/2m3: 0-4 2m4-2m7: 0-1 3m+: 0-0
Track: LH: 0-5 RH: 0-0 Tight: 0-5 Gall: 0-0
Aids: Bl: 0-2 Vi: 0-0 Tstrap: 0-0
Best Rating: 94 2/99 Muss 2m firm Hdl

Ace Of Spades (IRE)

95 **81**

6-y-o b g Treasure Hunter-Jamie's Lady (Ashmore (FR))
I A Duncan Good Time Managers Syndicate

Placings:*020* **(4067a)**
2001/02: 16^{0}S, 24^{2}HY, 22^{0}HY

	Starts	1st	2nd	3rd	Win & Pl
NH Flat	1	0	0	0	0
Hurdles	2	0	1	0	880
Career Total	**3**	**0**	**1**	**0**	**880**

Going: Sf: 0-3 GS: 0-0 Gd: 0-0 GF: - Fm: 0-0
Distance: 2m/2m3: 0-1 2m4-2m7: 0-1 3m+: 0-1
Track: LH: 0-1 RH: 0-1 Tight: 0-0 Gall: 0-0
Aids: Bl: 0-0 Vi: 0-0 Tstrap: 0-3
Best Rating: 81 2/02 Ayr 3m110y heavy Hdl

Runner-up in a novices' hurdle at Ayr in February, he stays well.

Achill Rambler

71 **42**

9-y-o b m Rakaposhi King-One More Try (Kemal (FR))
D M Lloyd D M Lloyd

Placings:*566*/0230/0514P/243-P0 **(3334)**
2001/02: 16^{P}S, 16^{0}G

	Starts	1st	2nd	3rd	Win & Pl
Hurdles	2	0	0	0	
Career Total	**17**	**1**	**2**	**2**	**3906**

85 6/99 Worc 2m F Hdl G-F £2269
Total win prize-money £2269

Going: Sf: 0-1 GS: 0-0 Gd: 0-1 GF: - Fm: 0-0
Distance: 2m/2m3: 0-2 2m4-2m7: 0-0 3m+: 0-0
Track: LH: 0-1 RH: 0-1 Tight: 0-1 Gall: 0-0
Aids: Bl: 0-0 Vi: 0-0 Tstrap: 0-0
Best Rating: 86 7/00 Wolv 2m gd-sft Hdl

Achilles Sun

81 **68**

4-y-o b g Deploy-Tsungani (Cure The Blues (USA))
T D McCarthy (Jamie Poulton 30/11) Achilles International

Placings:6P **(2427)**
2001/02: 16^{6}GS, 16^{P}G

	Starts	1st	2nd	3rd	Win & Pl
Hurdles	2	0	0	0	0
Career Total	**2**	**0**	**0**	**0**	**0**

Going: Sf: 0-0 GS: 0-1 Gd: 0-1 GF: - Fm: 0-0
Distance: 2m/2m3: 0-2 2m4-2m7: 0-0 3m+: 0-0
Track: LH: 0-1 RH: 0-1 Tight: 0-0 Gall: 0-1
Aids: Bl: 0-0 Vi: 0-0 Tstrap: 0-0
Best Rating: 68 10/01 Kemp 2m gd-sft Hdl

Achilles Wings (USA)

113 **127**

6-y-o b g Irish River (FR)-Shirley Valentine (Shirley Heights)

Miss K M George Exterior Profiles Ltd

Placings:20-43P41U1153 (4531)

2001/02: 17^{4}F, 17^{3}GF, 20^{P}G, 16^{4}S, 19^{1}G, 17^{U}G, 16^{1}GS, 16^{1}S, 16^{5}GS, 16^{3}GS

	Starts	1st	2nd	3rd	Win & Pl
Hurdles	10	3	0	2	14967
Career Total	**12**	**3**	**1**	**2**	**15727**

127	2/02	Winc	2m	D(0-125)HHdl	SFT	£3514
118	1/02	Winc	2m	D(0-125)HHdl	G-S	£6890
114	11/01	Hrfd	2m3f110y	F(0-100)HHdl	GD	£2639

Total win prize-money £13043

Going: Sf: 1-2 GS: 1-3 Gd: 1-3 GF: - Fm: 0-2
Distance: **2m/2m3: 2-8** 2m4-2m7: 1-2 3m+: 0-0
Track: LH: 0-3 **RH: 3-7** Tight: 0-2 Gall: 0-0
Aids: Bl: 0-0 Vi: 0-0 Tstrap: 0-0
Best Rating: **127** 4/02 Chep 2m110y gd-sft Hdl

He has progressed well in 2001/02, unfortunate not to complete a four-timer before being outclassed in the Kingwell Hurdle. Suited by two miles on soft ground and a flat, right-handed track.

Ackzo

104 **149**

9-y-o b g Ardross-Trimar Gold (Goldhill)

Ferdy Murphy Mrs N L Spence

Placings:3222112/52121P/6P-363PP (4677)

2001/02: 26^{3}G, 24^{6}S, 33^{3}S, 24^{P}GS, 36^{P}G

	Starts	1st	2nd	3rd	Win & Pl
Chases	5	0	0	2	8880
Career Total	**20**	**4**	**6**	**3**	**78927**

149	3/00	Uttx	4m2f	A HCh	GD	£43500
130	1/00	Hntg	3m	E Ch	G-S	£3562
125	4/99	Carl	2m4f110y	E Hdl	GD	£2654
125	2/99	Newc	2m4f	E Hdl	G-S	£2536

Total win prize-money £52253

Going: Sf: 0-2 GS: 0-1 Gd: 0-2 GF: - Fm: 0-0
Distance: 2m/2m3: 0-0 2m4-2m7: 0-0 3m+: 0-5
Track: LH: 0-5 RH: 0-0 Tight: 0-1 Gall: 0-4
Aids: Bl: 0-5 Vi: 0-0 Tstrap: 0-0
Best Rating: **149** 2/02 Newc 4m1f soft Ch

A smart staying novice chaser during 1999/2000, he was lightly raced the following season as the ground turned unsuitably soft. Good run in the Eider on his third start of 2001/2002. At his best on a quick surface, he stays all day.

Acoustic (IRE)

87(79h) (88h)**103**

8-y-o br g Orchestra-Rambling Ivy (Mandalus)

O Brennan Lady Anne Bentinck

Placings:3/0054 (4592)

2001/02: 20^{0}S, 20^{0}S, 23^{5}GS, 26^{4}G

	Starts	1st	2nd	3rd	Win & Pl
Hurdles	2	0	0	0	0
Chases	2	0	0	0	265
Career Total	**5**	**0**	**0**	**1**	**829**

Going: Sf: 0-2 GS: 0-1 Gd: 0-1 GF: - Fm: 0-0
Distance: 2m/2m3: 0-0 2m4-2m7: 0-2 3m+: 0-2
Track: LH: 0-3 RH: 0-0 Tight: 0-0 Gall: 0-0
Aids: Bl: 0-0 Vi: 0-0 Tstrap: 0-0

Best Rating: 103 1/02 Weth 2m7f110y gd-sft Ch

Act In Time (IRE)

111 **128**

10-y-o b g Actinium (FR)-Anvil Chorus (Levanter)

T R George Mrs G C McFerran

Placings:0P/424/1P2251/515200/4U4415-1P501532 (4503)

2001/02: 28^{1}G, 26^{P}GS, 25^{5}G, 30^{0}GS, 27^{1}G, 25^{5}G, 24^{3}G, 26^{2}G

	Starts	1st	2nd	3rd	Win & Pl
Chases	8	2	1	1	21929
Career Total	**31**	**6**	**5**	**1**	**51805**

128	12/01	Ludl	3m3f110y	D(0-120)HCh	GD	£7956
128	5/01	Sedg	3m4f	D(0-125)HCh	GD	£11163
128	2/01	Fknm	3m110y	F(0-100)HCh	SFT	£4046
131	12/99	Winc	3m1f110y	C(0-130)HCh	SFT	£8976
131	4/99	Chel	2m5f	D(0-115)HCh	GD	£5836
112	12/98	Chel	2m5f	E(0-125)HCh	GD	£3452

Total win prize-money £41431

Going: Sf: 0-0 GS: 0-2 Gd: 2-6 GF: - Fm: 0-0
Distance: 2m/2m3: 0-0 2m4-2m7: 0-0 **3m+: 2-8**
Track: LH: 1-3 RH: 1-5 **Tight: 2-3** Gall: 0-1
Aids: Bl: 0-0 Vi: 0-0 Tstrap: 0-0
Best Rating: **131** 2/00 Leic 2m7f110y gd-sft Ch

He is able on his day at up to three and a half miles, but is a little in and out. Although he has won on soft, he looks better on genuinely good ground. Successful at Ludlow in December 2001.

Action Jackson

10-y-o ch g Hadeer-Water Woo (USA) (Tom Rolfe)

A W Carroll D Morgan

Placings:P (1567)

2001/02: 20^{P}GS

	Starts	1st	2nd	3rd	Win & Pl
Hurdles	1	0	0	0	
Career Total	**1**	**0**	**0**	**0**	

Going: Sf: 0-0 GS: 0-1 Gd: 0-0 GF: - Fm: 0-0
Distance: 2m/2m3: 0-0 2m4-2m7: 0-1 3m+: 0-0
Track: LH: 0-0 RH: 0-0 Tight: 0-1 Gall: 0-0
Aids: Bl: 0-1 Vi: 0-0 Tstrap: 0-1
Best Rating:

Active Account (USA)

5-y-o b/br g Unaccounted For (USA)-Ameritop (USA) (Topsider (USA))

Mrs H Dalton Mrs Heather Dalton

Placings:6P (4275)

2001/02: 16^{6}G, 16^{P}G

	Starts	1st	2nd	3rd	Win & Pl
NH Flat	1	0	0	0	0
Hurdles	1	0	0	0	0
Career Total	**2**	**0**	**0**	**0**	**0**

Going: Sf: 0-0 GS: 0-0 Gd: 0-2 GF: - Fm: 0-0
Distance: 2m/2m3: 0-2 2m4-2m7: 0-0 3m+: 0-0
Track: LH: 0-1 RH: 0-1 Tight: 0-2 Gall: 0-0
Aids: Bl: 0-0 Vi: 0-0 Tstrap: 0-0
Best Rating: **73** 12/01 Muss 2m good NHF

Activist

106 **106**

4-y-o ch g Diesis-Shicklah (USA) (The Minstrel (CAN))

G M Moore (M L W Bell 30/8) John Robson

Placings:043326 (4840)

2001/02: 16^{0}G, 16^{4}G, 16^{3}S, 16^{3}GS, 16^{2}G, 16^{6}G

	Starts	1st	2nd	3rd	Win & Pl
Hurdles	6	0	1	2	3350
Career Total	**6**	**0**	**1**	**2**	**3350**

Going: Sf: 0-1 GS: 0-1 Gd: 0-4 GF: - Fm: 0-0
Distance: 2m/2m3: 0-6 2m4-2m7: 0-0 3m+: 0-0
Track: LH: 0-6 RH: 0-0 Tight: 0-0 Gall: 0-1
Aids: Bl: 0-0 Vi: 0-0 Tstrap: 0-0
Best Rating: **106** 11/01 Weth 2m good Hdl

In the frame in decent novice hurdles, but has fluffed easier opportunities and does not look one to trust.

Acton Bank

90 **105**

8-y-o b g Teenoso (USA)-Lavenham Blue (Streetfighter)

P R Webber Geoffrey Reeve

Placings:P5P22 (4405)

2001/02: 21^{P}G, 20^{5}S, 24^{P}S, 17^{2}GS, 17^{2}S

	Starts	1st	2nd	3rd	Win & Pl
Chases	5	0	2	0	2936
Career Total	**5**	**0**	**2**	**0**	**2936**

Going: Sf: 0-3 GS: 0-1 Gd: 0-1 GF: - Fm: 0-0
Distance: 2m/2m3: 0-2 2m4-2m7: 0-2 3m+: 0-1
Track: LH: 0-2 RH: 0-3 Tight: 0-3 Gall: 0-1
Aids: Bl: 0-0 Vi: 0-0 Tstrap: 0-0
Best Rating: **105** 3/02 MRas 2m1f110y gd-sft Ch

Point winner who is finding it difficult to adapt to regulation fences.

Acuteangle (IRE)

62 **12**

6-y-o b/br m Cataldi-Sharp Mama Vii (Damsire Unregistered)

Mrs S Wall J P C Wall

Placings:0 (0230)

2001/02: 16^{0}GF

	Starts	1st	2nd	3rd	Win & Pl
Hurdles	1	0	0	0	
Career Total	**1**	**0**	**0**	**0**	

Going: Sf: 0-0 GS: 0-0 Gd: 0-0 GF: - Fm: 0-1
Distance: 2m/2m3: 0-1 2m4-2m7: 0-0 3m+: 0-0
Track: LH: 0-0 RH: 0-1 Tight: 0-0 Gall: 0-1
Aids: Bl: 0-0 Vi: 0-0 Tstrap: 0-0
Best Rating: **12** 5/01 Hntg 2m110y gd-fm Hdl

Ad Hoc (IRE)

111 **172**

8-y-o b g Strong Gale-Knockarctic (Quayside)

P F Nicholls Sir Robert Ogden

Placings:3111/FFP521-053B4 (4913)

2001/02: 26^{0}S, 24^{5}G, 24^{3}GS, 36^{B}G, 29^{4}G

	Starts	1st	2nd	3rd	Win & Pl

	Starts	1st	2nd	3rd	Win & Pl
Chases	5	0	0	1	13250
Career Total	**15**	**4**	**1**	**2**	**140903**

172	4/01	Sand	3m5f110y	A HCh	SFT	£72500
159	4/00	Ayr	3m1f	C HCh	GD	£21970
123	1/00	Ayr	2m5f110y	D Ch	SFT	£3945
116	12/99	Leic	2m7f110y	E Ch	G-F	£3613

Total win prize-money £102029

Going: Sf: 0-1 GS: 0-1 Gd: 0-3 GF: - Fm: 0-0
Distance: 2m/2m3: 0-0 2m4-2m7: 0-0 3m+: 0-5
Track: LH: 0-3 RH: 0-2 Tight: 0-1 Gall: 0-2
Aids: Bl: 0-0 Vi: 0-0 Tstrap: 0-0
Best Rating: **172** 4/01 Sand 3m5f110y soft Ch

A high-class novice chaser in 1999-2000, he had jumping problems which have blighted his progress. Got his act together in the spring of 2001, chasing home Gingembre in the Scottish National, before gaining compensation with an easy win in the Whitbread. He was well beaten on his return in the Hennessy in December 2001, before disappointing behind Shooting Light at Ascot. However he was a good third at Cheltenham in March 2002 and looked full of running when knocked out of the Grand National four out. Ran another fair race in the Atheraces Gold Cup. He handles the soft ground, although gives the impression he is best suited by faster.

Adalie

103 **98**

8-y-o b m Absalom-Allied Newcastle (Crooner)
P J Hobbs Jack Joseph

Placings:001/0F32 **(4504)**
2001/02: 20^{0}S, 19^{F}G, 19^{3}S, 17^{2}G

	Starts	1st	2nd	3rd	Win & Pl
Hurdles	4	0	1	1	1393
Career Total	**7**	**1**	**1**	**1**	**3164**

105	4/00	NAbb	2m1f	H NHF	HVY	£1771

Total win prize-money £1771

Going: Sf: 0-2 GS: 0-0 Gd: 0-2 GF: - Fm: 0-0
Distance: 2m/2m3: 0-2 2m4-2m7: 0-2 3m+: 0-0
Track: LH: 0-1 RH: 0-2 Tight: 0-3 Gall: 0-0
Aids: Bl: 0-0 Vi: 0-0 Tstrap: 0-0
Best Rating: **106** 2/00 Kemp 2m soft NHF

Bumper winner, modest maiden over hurdles, acts in soft ground. Best trip around two and a quarter miles.

Adamant Approach (IRE)

121 **152**

8-y-o b g Mandalus-Crash Approach (Crash Course)
W P Mullins Greenstar Syndicate

Placings: *1*/P2422-152413F35 **(4959a)**
2001/02: 16^{1}G, 16^{5}S, 16^{2}Y, 16^{4}G, 16^{1}YS, 18^{3}HY, 16^{F}GS, 16^{3}Y, 16^{5}GY

	Starts	1st	2nd	3rd	Win & Pl
Hurdles	9	2	1	2	73137
Career Total	**15**	**3**	**4**	**2**	**82719**

139	1/02	Leop	2m	(0-140)HHdl	Y-S	£48251
107	10/01	Fair	2m	Hdl	GD	£5564
136	2/00	Leop	2m	NHF	YLD	£4140

Total win prize-money £57957

Going: Sf: 0-2 GS: 0-1 Gd: 1-2 GF: - Fm: 0-0
Distance: **2m/2m3: 2-9** 2m4-2m7: 0-0 3m+: 0-0
Track: LH: 1-3 RH: 1-5 Tight: 0-0 Gall: 0-0
Aids: Bl: 0-0 Vi: 0-0 Tstrap: 0-0
Best Rating: **152** 3/02 Chel 2m110y gd-sft Hdl

A useful Irish hurdler, took the valuable Pierce Hurdle in January 2002. Probably at his best over two miles on good ground. Would have gone close but for falling at the last when bang in contention in the Supreme Novices' at the Cheltenham Festival and ran well in top company subsequently.

Adamatic (IRE)

11-y-o b g Henbit (USA)-Arpal Magic (Master Owen)
Neil King (R Allan 17/2) Mrs R N Jarvis

Placings:*241323*/12213600/3**F12U/P202F3/314132110/401 UP66PP-25U40** **(4650)**
2001/02: 16^{2}GF, 16^{5}GS, 24^{U}GF, 20^{4}S, 21^{0}G

	Starts	1st	2nd	3rd	Win & Pl
Chases	5	0	1	0	1445
Career Total	**48**	**9**	**9**	**7**	**46452**

135	6/00	Hexm	2m110y	D(0-125)HCh	G-F	£5915
127	10/99	Kels	2m1f	E(0-115)HCh	GD	£3127
119	10/99	Carl	2m	D(0-125)HCh	GD	£4535
117	7/99	Sedg	2m110y	E(0-115)HCh	G-F	£3488
119	6/99	Hexm	2m110y	D(0-125)HCh	SFT	£5572
106	1/98	Muss	2m	E Ch	GD	£2786
100	11/96	Kels	2m2f	D(0-125)HHdl	GD	£2736
71	5/96	Prth	2m110y	D Hdl	FRM	£2905
97	12/95	Muss	2m	H NHF	G-F	£1446

Total win prize-money £32512

Going: Sf: 0-1 GS: 0-1 Gd: 0-1 GF: - Fm: 0-2
Distance: 2m/2m3: 0-2 2m4-2m7: 0-2 3m+: 0-1
Track: LH: 0-3 RH: 0-2 Tight: 0-1 Gall: 0-1
Aids: Bl: 0-0 Vi: 0-0 Tstrap: 0-0
Best Rating: **135** 6/00 Hexm 2m110y gd-fm Ch

Added Dimension (IRE)

107 **96**

11-y-o b g Top Ville-Lassalia (Sallust)
N A Dunger N A Dunger

Placings:P/P42636/031112/0/00/303-425014 **(3229)**
2001/02: 17^{4}HY, 16^{2}S, 17^{5}S, 16^{0}G, 16^{1}HY, 21^{4}GS

	Starts	1st	2nd	3rd	Win & Pl
Hurdles	6	1	1	0	3015
Career Total	**25**	**4**	**3**	**4**	**12034**

96	12/01	Towc	2m	G(0-95)HHdl	HVY	£1659
109	2/97	Tntn	2m1f	F(0-105)HHdl	GD	£1962
102	2/97	Hrfd	2m1f	F(0-105)HHdl	G-S	£2318
96	1/97	Folk	2m1f110y	F(0-105)HHdl	SFT	£2180

Total win prize-money £8120

Going: Sf: 1-4 GS: 0-1 Gd: 0-1 GF: - Fm: 0-0
Distance: **2m/2m3: 1-5** 2m4-2m7: 0-1 3m+: 0-0
Track: LH: 0-1 **RH: 1-5** Tight: 0-3 Gall: 0-1
Aids: Bl: 0-0 Vi: 0-0 Tstrap: 0-4
Best Rating: **109** 3/97 Hrfd 2m1f good Hdl

Has had a patchy career, with relatively few runs and few wins, bar a purple patch in 1997. Has worn a tongue-tie of late. Appears to like Towcester.

Addington Boy (IRE)

96 **114**

14-y-o br g Callernish-Ballaroe Bar (Bargello)
Ferdy Murphy W J Gott

Placings:*4/45*/1311502/**1121U111/312/50P/PF354/U035/26 UP-6** **(0675)**
2001/02: 23^{6}GF

	Starts	1st	2nd	3rd	Win & Pl
Chases	1	0	0	0	0
Career Total	**38**	**10**	**4**	**4**	**194235**

158	12/96	Chel	2m5f	A HCh	G-F	£37690
157	4/96	Ayr	2m4f	A Ch	SFT	£13470
151	3/96	Aint	3m1f	A Ch	GD	£23656
133	3/96	Donc	3m2f	B(0-145)HCh	GD	£21397
134	11/95	Kels	3m1f	D Ch	GD	£3881
120	10/95	Bang	2m4f110y	D Ch	G-S	£3533
105	9/95	Sedg	2m5f	E Ch	G-F	£2838
106	11/94	Aint	2m110y	Hdl	GD	£3038
104	11/94	Hayd	2m	HHdl	GD	£2900
86	8/94	Prth	2m110y	Hdl	G-F	£2190

Total win prize-money £114595

Going: Sf: 0-0 GS: 0-0 Gd: 0-0 GF: - Fm: 0-1
Distance: 2m/2m3: 0-0 2m4-2m7: 0-0 3m+: 0-1
Track: LH: 0-1 RH: 0-0 Tight: 0-0 Gall: 0-0
Aids: Bl: 0-0 Vi: 0-0 Tstrap: 0-0
Best Rating: **161** 11/96 Chel 2m4f110y gd-fm Ch

Twice brought out of retirement, he shaped with promise on his return to action over an inadequate trip at Huntingdon in March 2001 and clearly retains ability. He needs a sound surface to run to his best and has an admirable record in the National, finishing fourth in 1999 and fifth in 2000, but only got to the second in 2001. Believed to have been retired.

Adelphi Theatre (USA)

104 **128**

5-y-o b g Sadler's Wells (USA)-Truly Bound (USA) (In Reality)
R Rowe The Encore Partnership

Placings:312100 **(4155)**
2001/02: 17^{3}G, 20^{1}GS, 20^{2}G, 18^{1}G, 20^{0}S, 16^{0}GS

	Starts	1st	2nd	3rd	Win & Pl
Hurdles	6	2	1	1	11483
Career Total	**6**	**2**	**1**	**1**	**11483**

127	12/01	Font	2m2f110y	C(0-130)HHdl	GD	£6916
128	11/01	Font	2m4f	E Hdl	G-S	£2387

Total win prize-money £9303

Going: Sf: 0-1 GS: 1-2 Gd: 1-3 GF: - Fm: 0-0
Distance: 2m/2m3: 1-3 2m4-2m7: 1-3 3m+: 0-0
Track: **LH: 1-1** RH: 0-4 **Tight: 2-2** Gall: 0-1
Aids: Bl: 0-0 Vi: 0-0 Tstrap: 0-0
Best Rating: **128** 11/01 Font 2m4f gd-sft Hdl

A decent handicapper on the level, he has shown useful form over hurdles, winning twice at Fontwell. Best suited by two and a half miles. Well held this year.

Adeney Moss

9-y-o b m Le Moss-Adeney Lass (Space King)
W M Brisbourne Michael F Blackham

Placings:P **(0054)**
2001/02: 24^{P}G

	Starts	1st	2nd	3rd	Win & Pl
Hurdles	1	0	0	0	
Career Total	**1**	**0**	**0**	**0**	

Going: Sf: 0-0 GS: 0-0 Gd: 0-1 GF: - Fm: 0-0
Distance: 2m/2m3: 0-0 2m4-2m7: 0-0 3m+: 0-1
Track: LH: 0-1 RH: 0-0 Tight: 0-1 Gall: 0-0
Aids: Bl: 0-0 Vi: 0-0 Tstrap: 0-0
Best Rating:

Adjiram (IRE)

97 **79**

6-y-o b g Be My Guest (USA)-Adjriyna (Top Ville)
D C O'Brien K Marshall

Placings:2P/0-0406 **(4535)**
2001/02: 16^{0}S, 20^{4}S, 17^{0}S, 20^{6}G

	Starts	1st	2nd	3rd	Win & Pl
Hurdles	4	0	0	0	0
Career Total	**7**	**0**	**1**	**0**	**744**

Going: Sf: 0-3 GS: 0-0 Gd: 0-1 GF: - Fm: 0-0
Distance: 2m/2m3: 0-2 2m4-2m7: 0-2 3m+: 0-0
Track: LH: 0-2 RH: 0-1 Tight: 0-4 Gall: 0-0
Aids: Bl: 0-0 Vi: 0-0 Tstrap: 0-0
Best Rating: **66** 3/02 Font 2m4f soft Hdl

Admiral Peary (IRE)

6-y-o b/br g Lord Americo-Arctic Brief (Buckskin (FR))
C R Egerton M Haynes

Placings:*33* **(4329)**
2001/02: 18^{3}S, 17^{3}S

	Starts	1st	2nd	3rd	Win & Pl
NH Flat	2	0	0	2	477
Career Total	**2**	**0**	**0**	**2**	**477**

Going: Sf: 0-2 GS: 0-0 Gd: 0-0 GF: - Fm: 0-0
Distance: 2m/2m3: 0-2 2m4-2m7: 0-0 3m+: 0-0
Track: LH: 0-1 RH: 0-1 Tight: 0-1 Gall: 0-0
Aids: Bl: 0-0 Vi: 0-0 Tstrap: 0-0
Best Rating: **115** 2/02 Font 2m2f110y soft NHF

Promising efforts in bumpers. Races a bit keenly at present.

Admiral's Guest (IRE)

73 **39**

10-y-o ch g Be My Guest (USA)-Watership (USA) (Foolish Pleasure (USA))
W Clay Mrs M Robertson

Placings:0P560600/406236343/3**F**0320P0042/650P0/BP0 **(1387)**
2001/02: 16^{B}GF, 24^{P}GF, 16^{0}G

	Starts	1st	2nd	3rd	Win & Pl
Hurdles	3	0	0	0	
Career Total	**36**	**0**	**3**	**5**	**3065**

Going: Sf: 0-0 GS: 0-0 Gd: 0-1 GF: - Fm: 0-2
Distance: 2m/2m3: 0-2 2m4-2m7: 0-0 3m+: 0-1
Track: LH: 0-2 RH: 0-1 Tight: 0-1 Gall: 0-1
Aids: Bl: 0-0 Vi: 0-2 Tstrap: 0-2
Best Rating: **82** 6/99 Uttx 3m110y good Hdl

Adoran

64 **13**

7-y-o ch g Gildoran-Millie Duffer (Furry Glen)
Mrs H Dalton The Haydock Club

Placings:*00* **(4025)**
2001/02: 17^{0}GS, 16^{0}S

	Starts	1st	2nd	3rd	Win & Pl
NH Flat	1	0	0	0	0

	Starts	1st	2nd	3rd	Win & Pl
Hurdles	1	0	0	0	0
Career Total	**2**	**0**	**0**	**0**	

Going: Sf: 0-1 GS: 0-1 Gd: 0-0 GF: - Fm: 0-0
Distance: 2m/2m3: 0-2 2m4-2m7: 0-0 3m+: 0-0
Track: LH: 0-0 RH: 0-1 Tight: 0-0 Gall: 0-1
Aids: Bl: 0-0 Vi: 0-0 Tstrap: 0-0
Best Rating: **33** 11/01 Aint 2m1f gd-sft NHF

Adronikus (IRE)

104 **83+**

5-y-o ch g Monsun (GER)-Arionette (Lombard (GER))
D J Wintle (P Schiergen 22/9) Mrs B Grainger

Placings:0P **(4820)**
2001/02: 16^{0}GS, 17^{P}G

	Starts	1st	2nd	3rd	Win & Pl
Hurdles	2	0	0	0	
Career Total	**2**	**0**	**0**	**0**	

Going: Sf: 0-0 GS: 0-1 Gd: 0-1 GF: - Fm: 0-0
Distance: 2m/2m3: 0-2 2m4-2m7: 0-0 3m+: 0-0
Track: LH: 0-1 RH: 0-1 Tight: 0-0 Gall: 0-2
Aids: Bl: 0-0 Vi: 0-0 Tstrap: 0-0
Best Rating:

Got off the mark in a moderate novices' handicap hurdle in the summer of 2002. Suited by fast ground.

Ads-Sixty-Five

65f **45f**

5-y-o b g Casteddu-Come On Lucy (Reesh)
D J Wintle A D Bennett

Placings:*0* **(0032)**
2001/02: 16^{0}G

	Starts	1st	2nd	3rd	Win & Pl
NH Flat	1	0	0	0	
Career Total	**1**	**0**	**0**	**0**	

Going: Sf: 0-0 GS: 0-0 Gd: 0-1 GF: - Fm: 0-0
Distance: 2m/2m3: 0-1 2m4-2m7: 0-0 3m+: 0-0
Track: LH: 0-0 RH: 0-1 Tight: 0-0 Gall: 0-1
Aids: Bl: 0-0 Vi: 0-0 Tstrap: 0-0
Best Rating: **45** 5/01 Hntg 2m110y good NHF

Aduka (IRE)

6-y-o b g Pursuit Of Love-Nsx (Roi Danzig (USA))
D W Whillans D W Whillans

Placings:*0-P* **(2188)**
2001/02: 16^{P}GS

	Starts	1st	2nd	3rd	Win & Pl
NH Flat	1	0	0	0	
Career Total	**2**	**0**	**0**	**0**	

Going: Sf: 0-0 GS: 0-1 Gd: 0-0 GF: - Fm: 0-0
Distance: 2m/2m3: 0-1 2m4-2m7: 0-0 3m+: 0-0
Track: LH: 0-1 RH: 0-0 Tight: 0-0 Gall: 0-0
Aids: Bl: 0-0 Vi: 0-0 Tstrap: 0-0
Best Rating:

Adulation (USA)

80 **32**

8-y-o ch g Sheikh Albadou-Pedestal (High Line)
Mrs D A Butler Mrs D Butler

Placings:0/60F0/2-000 **(1240)**
2001/02: 16^{0}GF, 20^{0}GF, 24^{0}GF

	Starts	1st	2nd	3rd	Win & Pl
Hurdles	3	0	0	0	
Career Total	**9**	**0**	**1**	**0**	**548**

Going: Sf: 0-0 GS: 0-0 Gd: 0-0 GF: - Fm: 0-3
Distance: 2m/2m3: 0-1 2m4-2m7: 0-1 3m+: 0-1
Track: LH: 0-2 RH: 0-1 Tight: 0-1 Gall: 0-1
Aids: Bl: 0-0 Vi: 0-0 Tstrap: 0-0
Best Rating: **91** 11/99 Carl 2m1f gd-sft Hdl

Advance East

103 **114**

10-y-o b g Polish Precedent (USA)-Startino (Bustino)
M J M Evans Mrs J Z Munday

Placings:150/23**B4U**0356/24**6**0133200/**23355**6**54123**/**F-1** **(4596)**
2001/02: 20^{1}G

	Starts	1st	2nd	3rd	Win & Pl
Chases	1	1	0	0	3838
Career Total	**35**	**4**	**5**	**7**	**22740**

114	4/02	Uttx	2m4f	E(0-110)HCh	GD	£3838
100	2/00	Leic	2m	E(0-115)HCh	SFT	£3103
92	2/99	Plum	2m4f	G Hdl	SFT	£2215
110	11/96	Hayd	2m	D Hdl	GD	£3011

Total win prize-money £12168

Going: Sf: 0-0 GS: 0-0 Gd: 1-1 GF: - Fm: 0-0
Distance: 2m/2m3: 0-0 **2m4-2m7: 1-1** 3m+: 0-0
Track: **LH: 1-1** RH: 0-0 Tight: 0-0 Gall: 0-0
Aids: Bl: 0-0 Vi: 0-0 Tstrap: 0-0
Best Rating: **114** 4/02 Uttx 2m4f good Ch

Fair chaser. Suited by soft ground and between two/ two and a half miles. Lightly raced in the last couple of years.

Advanta Pride (IRE)

93f **75f**

6-y-o ch g Pips Pride-Mia Gigi (Hard Fought)
J R Best H J Jarvis

Placings:*64* **(1650)**
2001/02: 16^{6}GF, 16^{4}G

	Starts	1st	2nd	3rd	Win & Pl
NH Flat	2	0	0	0	0
Career Total	**2**	**0**	**0**	**0**	**0**

Going: Sf: 0-0 GS: 0-0 Gd: 0-1 GF: - Fm: 0-1
Distance: 2m/2m3: 0-2 2m4-2m7: 0-0 3m+: 0-0
Track: LH: 0-0 RH: 0-2 Tight: 0-0 Gall: 0-2
Aids: Bl: 0-0 Vi: 0-0 Tstrap: 0-0
Best Rating: **75** 10/01 Hntg 2m110y good NHF

Adventino

88f **92f**

7-y-o gr g Neltino-My Miss Adventure (New Member)
N A Twiston-Davies Nick Seal

Placings:*06-3* **(0239)**
2001/02: 16^{3}GF

	Starts	1st	2nd	3rd	Win & Pl
NH Flat	1	0	0	1	224
Career Total	**3**	**0**	**0**	**1**	**224**

Going: Sf: 0-0 GS: 0-0 Gd: 0-0 GF: - Fm: 0-1
Distance: 2m/2m3: 0-1 2m4-2m7: 0-0 3m+: 0-0
Track: LH: 0-1 RH: 0-0 Tight: 0-1 Gall: 0-0
Aids: Bl: 0-0 Vi: 0-0 Tstrap: 0-0
Best Rating: **92** 5/01 Sthl 2m gd-fm NHF

Aegean

114 **122**

8-y-o b g Rock Hopper-Sayulita (Habitat)
Mrs S J Smith Mrs Alicia Skene & W S Skene

Placings:43030/3**251112-0332444** **(1134)**
2001/02: 27^{0}G, 25^{3}G, 25^{3}F, 24^{2}GF, 32^{4}GF, 24^{4}G, 23^{4}GF

	Starts	1st	2nd	3rd	Win & Pl
Chases	7	0	1	2	7324
Career Total	**19**	**3**	**3**	**5**	**21609**

126	8/00	Worc	2m7f110y	E(0-105)HCh	G-F	£3454
120	7/00	Worc	2m7f110y	E Ch	G-F	£3376
106	6/00	Hexm	3m1f	E(0-105)HCh	G-F	£3120

Total win prize-money £9952

Going: Sf: 0-0 GS: 0-0 Gd: 0-3 GF: - Fm: 0-4
Distance: 2m/2m3: 0-0 2m4-2m7: 0-0 3m+: 0-7
Track: LH: 0-5 RH: 0-1 Tight: 0-3 Gall: 0-0
Aids: Bl: 0-0 Vi: 0-0 Tstrap: 0-0
Best Rating: **126** 10/00 Aint 3m1f good Ch

Handicap chaser, effective over three miles and on a sound surface.

Aegean Glory

6-y-o b m Shareef Dancer (USA)-Sayulita (Habitat)
J G M O'Shea Gary Roberts

Placings:P0/64022-PP0PP **(2719)**
2001/02: 16^{P}GF, 17^{P}G, 16^{0}S, 17^{P}S, 17^{P}G

	Starts	1st	2nd	3rd	Win & Pl
Hurdles	5	0	0	0	
Career Total	**12**	**0**	**2**	**0**	**960**

Going: Sf: 0-2 GS: 0-0 Gd: 0-2 GF: - Fm: 0-1
Distance: 2m/2m3: 0-5 2m4-2m7: 0-0 3m+: 0-0
Track: LH: 0-2 RH: 0-3 Tight: 0-1 Gall: 0-0
Aids: Bl: 0-1 Vi: 0-1 Tstrap: 0-0
Best Rating: **69** 8/00 Worc 2m gd-fm Hdl

Aegean Sunrise

94 **96**

4-y-o ch g Deploy-Dizzydaisy (Sharpo)
R M Flower K Panos

Placings:2 **(1444)**
2001/02: 18^{2}GF

	Starts	1st	2nd	3rd	Win & Pl
Hurdles	1	0	1	0	688
Career Total	**1**	**0**	**1**	**0**	**688**

Going: Sf: 0-0 GS: 0-0 Gd: 0-0 GF: - Fm: 0-1
Distance: 2m/2m3: 0-1 2m4-2m7: 0-0 3m+: 0-0
Track: LH: 0-1 RH: 0-0 Tight: 0-1 Gall: 0-0
Aids: Bl: 0-0 Vi: 0-0 Tstrap: 0-0
Best Rating: **96** 9/01 Font 2m2f110y gd-fm Hdl

Aelred

109(99h) (83h)**125**

9-y-o b g Ovac (ITY)-Sponsorship (Sparkler)
R Johnson J L Gledson

Placings:000/**556043463642/1212320125-P23216050** **(4876)**
2001/02: 16^{3}S, 22^{P}GF, 16^{2}GS, 16^{3}G, 20^{2}GS, 16^{1}S, 17^{6}S, 19^{0}GS, 16^{5}HY, 20^{0}G

	Starts	1st	2nd	3rd	Win & Pl
Chases	10	1	2	2	7830
Career Total	**35**	**4**	**7**	**5**	**25457**

125	1/02	Newc	2m110y	E(0-110)HCh	SFT	£3370
115	1/01	Newc	2m110y	F(0-110)HCh	SFT	£2912
108	5/00	Ctml	2m1f110y	F(0-100)HCh	GD	£2990
109	5/00	Kels	2m1f	E Ch	G-S	£3445

Total win prize-money £12718

Going: Sf: 1-4 GS: 0-3 Gd: 0-2 GF: - Fm: 0-1
Distance: **2m/2m3: 1-6** 2m4-2m7: 0-4 3m+: 0-0
Track: **LH: 1-8** RH: 0-2 Tight: 0-1 **Gall: 1-6**
Aids: Bl: 0-0 Vi: 0-0 Tstrap: 0-0
Best Rating: **125** 1/02 Newc 2m110y soft Ch

Fair two-mile handicap chaser who wins in his turn. Best with some cut in the ground.

Afadan (IRE)

85 **110**

4-y-o br g Royal Academy (USA)-Afasara (IRE) (Shardari)
J R Jenkins (John M Oxx 4/10) St Albans Chasers

Placings:P1PP **(3860)**
2001/02: 16^{P}G, 16^{1}S, 16^{P}G, 20^{P}S

	Starts	1st	2nd	3rd	Win & Pl
Hurdles	4	1	0	0	3526
Career Total	**4**	**1**	**0**	**0**	**3526**

110	12/01	Sand	2m110y	D Hdl	SFT	£3526

Total win prize-money £3526

Going: Sf: 1-2 GS: 0-0 Gd: 0-2 GF: - Fm: 0-0
Distance: **2m/2m3: 1-3** 2m4-2m7: 0-1 3m+: 0-0
Track: LH: 0-2 **RH: 1-2** Tight: 0-0 Gall: 0-2
Aids: Bl: 0-0 Vi: 0-0 Tstrap: 0-1
Best Rating: **110** 12/01 Sand 2m110y soft Hdl

Ex-Irish, showed a useful turn of foot to land a novice hurdle at Sandown in December. Has won on soft ground.

Aficionado (IRE)

8-y-o b g Marju (IRE)-Haneena (Habitat)
R Williams R Williams

Placings:3B5560/00060/06064/000-6 **(4544)**
2001/02: 26^{6}G

	Starts	1st	2nd	3rd	Win & Pl
Hurdles	1	0	0	0	0
Career Total	**20**	**0**	**0**	**1**	**261**

Going: Sf: 0-0 GS: 0-0 Gd: 0-1 GF: - Fm: 0-0
Distance: 2m/2m3: 0-0 2m4-2m7: 0-0 3m+: 0-1
Track: LH: 0-0 RH: 0-1 Tight: 0-0 Gall: 0-0
Aids: Bl: 0-0 Vi: 0-0 Tstrap: 0-0
Best Rating: **73** 11/98 Hrfd 2m1f good Hdl

Africa (IRE)

87 **82**

5-y-o b m Namaqualand (USA)-Tannerrun (IRE) (Runnett)
A Streeter Malt 'N' Hops

Placings:0-03FF **(4904)**
2001/02: 16^{0}GF, 16^{3}GF, 16^{F}GF, 17^{F}G

	Starts	1st	2nd	3rd	Win & Pl
Hurdles	4	0	0	1	486
Career Total	**5**	**0**	**0**	**1**	**486**

Going: Sf: 0-0 GS: 0-0 Gd: 0-1 GF: - Fm: 0-3
Distance: 2m/2m3: 0-4 2m4-2m7: 0-0 3m+: 0-0
Track: LH: 0-3 RH: 0-1 Tight: 0-2 Gall: 0-0
Aids: Bl: 0-0 Vi: 0-0 Tstrap: 0-0
Best Rating: **82** 7/01 Uttx 2m gd-fm Hdl

After Galway (IRE)

88f **107f**

6-y-o b g Camden Town-Money For Honey (New Brig)
A Scott A Butler

Placings:3-0 **(0181)**
2001/02: 16^{0}GF

	Starts	1st	2nd	3rd	Win & Pl
NH Flat	1	0	0	0	
Career Total	**2**	**0**	**0**	**1**	**241**

Going: Sf: 0-0 GS: 0-0 Gd: 0-0 GF: - Fm: 0-1
Distance: 2m/2m3: 0-1 2m4-2m7: 0-0 3m+: 0-0
Track: LH: 0-1 RH: 0-0 Tight: 0-0 Gall: 0-0
Aids: Bl: 0-0 Vi: 0-0 Tstrap: 0-0
Best Rating: **107** 4/01 Muss 2m1f gd-fm NHF

After Me Boys

101 **114**

8-y-o b g Arzanni-Realm Wood (Precipice Wood)
Mrs S J Smith Keith Nicholson

Placings:21421-212P **(1751)**
2001/02: 20^{2}F, 20^{1}GF, 24^{2}S, 21^{P}G

	Starts	1st	2nd	3rd	Win & Pl
Hurdles	4	1	2	0	6218
Career Total	**9**	**3**	**4**	**0**	**13655**

112	8/01	Sthl	2m4f110y	E(0-115)HHdl	G-F	£2380
110	4/01	MRas	2m3f110y	D Hdl	HVY	£4403
109	6/00	Hexm	2m	H NHF	G-F	£1641

Total win prize-money £8426

Going: Sf: 0-1 GS: 0-0 Gd: 0-1 GF: - Fm: 1-2
Distance: 2m/2m3: 0-0 **2m4-2m7: 1-3** 3m+: 0-1
Track: **LH: 1-2** RH: 0-2 **Tight: 1-4** Gall: 0-0
Aids: Bl: 0-0 Vi: 0-0 Tstrap: 0-0
Best Rating: **114** 9/01 MRas 3m soft Hdl

Fair hurdler, acts on any ground.

After The Blue (IRE)

104 **100+**

5-y-o b g Last Tycoon-Sudden Interest (FR) (Highest Honor (FR))
C J Mann John & Doreen Tubb

Placings:544442P **(4739)**
2001/02: 17^{5}G, 18^{4}S, 17^{4}F, 16^{4}G, 21^{4}GF, 21^{2}G, 21^{P}GF

	Starts	1st	2nd	3rd	Win & Pl
Hurdles	7	0	1	0	1342
Career Total	**7**	**0**	**1**	**0**	**1342**

Going: Sf: 0-1 GS: 0-0 Gd: 0-3 GF: - Fm: 0-3

Distance: 2m/2m3: 0-4 2m4-2m7: 0-3 3m+: 0-0
Track: LH: 0-4 RH: 0-3 Tight: 0-4 Gall: 0-0
Aids: Bl: 0-0 Vi: 0-0 Tstrap: 0-7
Best Rating: 94 10/01 Chel 2m110y good Hdl

Modest form in novice hurdles over around two and a half miles.

Afterjacko (IRE)

95 **101**

6-y-o ch g Seattle Dancer (USA)-Shilka (Soviet Star (USA))
D R C Elsworth Mcdowell Racing

Placings:5 (2300)
2001/02: 16^{5}G

	Starts	1st	2nd	3rd	Win & Pl
Hurdles	1	0	0	0	0
Career Total	**1**	**0**	**0**	**0**	**0**

Going: Sf: 0-0 GS: 0-0 Gd: 0-1 GF: - Fm: 0-0
Distance: 2m/2m3: 0-1 2m4-2m7: 0-0 3m+: 0-0
Track: LH: 0-0 RH: 0-1 Tight: 0-0 Gall: 0-0
Aids: Bl: 0-0 Vi: 0-0 Tstrap: 0-0
Best Rating: 101 11/01 Asct 2m110y good Hdl

Agassi's Ace

84(89h) (48h)**37**

9-y-o b g Vital Season-Welsh Flower (Welsh Saint)
N A Twiston-Davies Mio Blagojevic

Placings:053PF0-0P5P0 (1241)
2001/02: 20^{0}G, 21^{P}G, 27^{5}G, 21^{P}G, 20^{0}CF

	Starts	1st	2nd	3rd	Win & Pl
Hurdles	3	0	0	0	0
Chases	2	0	0	0	0
Career Total	**11**	**0**	**0**	**1**	**454**

Going: Sf: 0-0 GS: 0-0 Gd: 0-4 GF: - Fm: 0-1
Distance: 2m/2m3: 0-0 2m4-2m7: 0-2 3m+: 0-3
Track: LH: 0-5 RH: 0-0 Tight: 0-2 Gall: 0-0
Aids: Bl: 0-0 Vi: 0-0 Tstrap: 0-2
Best Rating: 81 9/00 Worc 2m4f gd-fm Hdl

Agent Provocateur (NZ)

79 **66**

6-y-o b g Racing Is Fun (USA)-Silver Crest (NZ) (Silver Dream)
S B Clark S B Clark

Placings:*3-0*F03 (4434)
2001/02: 16^{0}G, 23^{F}GS, 16^{0}GS, 20^{3}HY

	Starts	1st	2nd	3rd	Win & Pl
NH Flat	1	0	0	0	0
Hurdles	3	0	0	1	386
Career Total	**5**	**0**	**0**	**2**	**609**

Going: Sf: 0-1 GS: 0-2 Gd: 0-1 GF: - Fm: 0-0
Distance: 2m/2m3: 0-2 2m4-2m7: 0-2 3m+: 0-0
Track: LH: 0-4 RH: 0-0 Tight: 0-1 Gall: 0-2
Aids: Bl: 0-0 Vi: 0-0 Tstrap: 0-0
Best Rating: 93 10/00 Hntg 2m110y gd-fm NHF

Agift

67 **42**

8-y-o b m Cadeaux Genereux-Aspark (Sparkler)

Mrs P Robeson Mrs P Robeson

Placings:F06/0/0F (4867)
2001/02: 20^{0}G, 16^{F}GF

	Starts	1st	2nd	3rd	Win & Pl
Hurdles	2	0	0	0	
Career Total	**6**	**0**	**0**	**0**	**0**

Going: Sf: 0-0 GS: 0-0 Gd: 0-1 GF: - Fm: 0-1
Distance: 2m/2m3: 0-1 2m4-2m7: 0-1 3m+: 0-0
Track: LH: 0-1 RH: 0-1 Tight: 0-0 Gall: 0-1
Aids: Bl: 0-0 Vi: 0-0 Tstrap: 0-0
Best Rating: 68 3/99 Winc 2m good Hdl

Agile King

80

11-y-o b g Rakaposhi King-My Aisling (John De Coombe)
A J Tizzard A J Tizzard

Placings:6/5 (0228)
2001/02: 20^{5}GF

	Starts	1st	2nd	3rd	Win & Pl
Chases	1	0	0	0	0
Career Total	**2**	**0**	**0**	**0**	**0**

Going: Sf: 0-0 GS: 0-0 Gd: 0-0 GF: - Fm: 0-1
Distance: 2m/2m3: 0-0 2m4-2m7: 0-1 3m+: 0-0
Track: LH: 0-0 RH: 0-1 Tight: 0-0 Gall: 0-1
Aids: Bl: 0-0 Vi: 0-0 Tstrap: 0-0
Best Rating: 80 5/01 Hntg 2m4f110y gd-fm Ch

Agincourt (IRE)

79 **79**

6-y-o b g Alphabatim (USA)-Miss Brantridge (Riboboy (USA))
John R Upson Middleham Park Racing Xxi

Placings:*000*-065100P (4577)
2001/02: 20^{0}G, 16^{6}S, 20^{5}HY, 25^{1}GS, 27^{0}HY, 21^{0}S, 24^{P}G

	Starts	1st	2nd	3rd	Win & Pl
Hurdles	7	1	0	0	2688
Career Total	**10**	**1**	**0**	**0**	**2688**

79 12/01 Weth 3m1f F(0-95)HHdl G-S £2688
Total win prize-money £2688

Going: Sf: 0-4 GS: 1-1 Gd: 0-2 GF: - Fm: 0-0
Distance: 2m/2m3: 0-1 2m4-2m7: 0-3 **3m+: 1-3**
Track: **LH: 1-5** RH: 0-1 Tight: 0-1 Gall: 0-1
Aids: Bl: 0-1 Vi: 0-0 Tstrap: 0-0
Best Rating: 80 10/00 Sedg 2m1f gd-sft NHF

A real stayer, his stamina won him the day when scoring at Wetherby in December 2001.

Aginor

102 **94**

8-y-o b g Slip Anchor-Fairy Feet (Sadler's Wells (USA))
Mrs V C Ward The Late Mrs R F Key & Mrs V C Ward

Placings:P030/0015/0020 (0909)
2001/02: 19^{0}G, 19^{0}G, 17^{2}F, 16^{0}G

	Starts	1st	2nd	3rd	Win & Pl
Hurdles	4	0	1	0	1090
Career Total	**12**	**1**	**1**	**1**	**3666**

109 9/99 Hrfd 2m1f F(0-100)HHdl GD £2304
Total win prize-money £2304

Going: Sf: 0-0 GS: 0-0 Gd: 0-3 GF: - Fm: 0-1

Distance: 2m/2m3: 0-2 2m4-2m7: 0-2 3m+: 0-0
Track: LH: 0-1 RH: 0-3 Tight: 0-0 Gall: 0-0
Aids: Bl: 0-0 Vi: 0-0 Tstrap: 0-4
Best Rating: 109 9/99 Hrfd 2m1f good Hdl

Agitando (IRE)

106 **120**

6-y-o b g Tenby-Crown Rose (Dara Monarch)
B De Haan (R Charlton 25/10) The Inspirations Partnership

Placings:511 (4774)
2001/02: 16^{5}S, 16^{1}G, 17^{1}G

	Starts	1st	2nd	3rd	Win & Pl
Hurdles	3	2	0	0	6538
Career Total	**3**	**2**	**0**	**0**	**6538**

118 4/02 MRas 2m1f110y D Hdl GD £3836
111 4/02 Uttx 2m E Hdl GD £2702
Total win prize-money £6538

Going: Sf: 0-1 GS: 0-0 Gd: 2-2 GF: - Fm: 0-0
Distance: **2m/2m3: 2-3** 2m4-2m7: 0-0 3m+: 0-0
Track: LH: 1-1 RH: 1-2 **Tight: 1-1** Gall: 0-0
Aids: Bl: 0-0 Vi: 0-0 Tstrap: 0-0
Best Rating: 118 4/02 MRas 2m1f110y good Hdl

Formerly a fair sort on the Flat, he won two novice hurdles in April 2002. Effective at two miles.

Ahouod

65 **40**

6-y-o b m Merdon Melody-Balidilemma (Balidar)
P S McEntee (T Keddy 10/10) Miss Debbie Mountain

Placings:0P (1618)
2001/02: 16^{0}GF, 21^{P}G

	Starts	1st	2nd	3rd	Win & Pl
Hurdles	2	0	0	0	
Career Total	**2**	**0**	**0**	**0**	

Going: Sf: 0-0 GS: 0-0 Gd: 0-1 GF: - Fm: 0-1
Distance: 2m/2m3: 0-1 2m4-2m7: 0-1 3m+: 0-0
Track: LH: 0-1 RH: 0-1 Tight: 0-1 Gall: 0-0
Aids: Bl: 0-0 Vi: 0-0 Tstrap: 0-0
Best Rating: 40 9/01 Plum 2m gd-fm Hdl

Ahraydoubleyou

103 **123**

9-y-o b/br g Teenoso (USA)-Minigale (Strong Gale)
Mrs S J Smith Mrs Alicia Skene & W S Skene

Placings:*2451/512P30/035/5F343F53P*-1F (0849)
2001/02: 20^{1}GF, 21^{F}GF

	Starts	1st	2nd	3rd	Win & Pl
Chases	2	1	0	0	6971
Career Total	**24**	**3**	**2**	**5**	**15541**

123 6/01 Prth 2m4f110y E(0-105)HCh G-F £6971
101 11/98 MRas 2m1f110y D Hdl G-S £3018
109 4/98 Carl 2m1f H NHF GD £1423
Total win prize-money £11414

Going: Sf: 0-0 GS: 0-0 Gd: 0-0 GF: - Fm: 1-2
Distance: 2m/2m3: 0-0 **2m4-2m7: 1-2** 3m+: 0-0
Track: LH: 0-1 **RH: 1-1** Tight: 0-1 Gall: 0-0
Aids: Bl: 0-0 Vi: 0-0 Tstrap: 0-0
Best Rating: 123 6/01 Prth 2m4f110y gd-fm Ch

Aiden (IRE)

104 **98**

8-y-o b g Supreme Leader-Chevaux-Vapeur (Le Moss)
Mrs L Richards The Aiden Partnership

Placings: 0463-233044P **(4039)**
2001/02: 25^{2}G, 24^{3}GS, 24^{3}G, 24^{0}GS, 25^{4}HY, 24^{4}S, 27^{P}S

	Starts	1st	2nd	3rd	Win & Pl
Hurdles	7	0	1	2	2282
Career Total	**11**	**0**	**1**	**3**	**2786**

Going: Sf: 0-3 GS: 0-2 Gd: 0-2 GF: - Fm: 0-0
Distance: 2m/2m3: 0-0 2m4-2m7: 0-0 3m+: 0-7
Track: LH: 0-3 RH: 0-1 Tight: 0-1 Gall: 0-2
Aids: Bl: 0-0 Vi: 0-4 Tstrap: 0-0
Best Rating: **98** 2/02 Kemp 3m110y soft Hdl

Moderate novice hurdler who acts well with cut in the ground. Stays three miles one.

Ailsa Craig

10-y-o b g Torus-Mashin Time (Palm Track)
R H Goldie Robert H Goldie

Placings: 0P0/0/6-4 **(4525)**
2001/02: 26^{4}GS

	Starts	1st	2nd	3rd	Win & Pl
Chases	1	0	0	0	110
Career Total	**6**	**0**	**0**	**0**	**110**

Going: Sf: 0-0 GS: 0-1 Gd: 0-0 GF: - Fm: 0-0
Distance: 2m/2m3: 0-0 2m4-2m7: 0-0 3m+: 0-1
Track: LH: 0-0 RH: 0-1 Tight: 0-0 Gall: 0-0
Aids: Bl: 0-0 Vi: 0-0 Tstrap: 0-0
Best Rating: **91** 11/98 Ayr 2m gd-sft NHF

Aintgottime (IRE)

10-y-o ch g Decent Fellow-Spoonbender (Mr Bigmore)
Mrs F Kehoe (J Cullinan 31/5) Mrs F Kehoe

Placings: 6/342 **(0556)**
2001/02: 24^{3}GF, 21^{4}G, 24^{2}GF

	Starts	1st	2nd	3rd	Win & Pl
Chases	3	0	1	1	1037
Career Total	**4**	**0**	**1**	**1**	**1037**

Going: Sf: 0-0 GS: 0-0 Gd: 0-1 GF: - Fm: 0-2
Distance: 2m/2m3: 0-0 2m4-2m7: 0-1 3m+: 0-2
Track: LH: 0-1 RH: 0-1 Tight: 0-1 Gall: 0-1
Aids: Bl: 0-1 Vi: 0-0 Tstrap: 0-0
Best Rating: **97** 5/01 Chel 2m5f good Ch

Air Control (IRE)

68 34

7-y-o b g Executive Perk-Sandy Jayne (IRE) (Royal Fountain)
L Lungo Mrs Barbara Lungo

Placings: 4/5-006 **(4431)**
2001/02: 16^{0}GS, 16^{0}S, 16^{6}HY

	Starts	1st	2nd	3rd	Win & Pl
Hurdles	3	0	0	0	0
Career Total	**5**	**0**	**0**	**0**	**0**

Going: Sf: 0-2 GS: 0-1 Gd: 0-0 GF: - Fm: 0-0
Distance: 2m/2m3: 0-3 2m4-2m7: 0-0 3m+: 0-0
Track: LH: 0-3 RH: 0-0 Tight: 0-1 Gall: 0-1
Aids: Bl: 0-0 Vi: 0-0 Tstrap: 0-0
Best Rating: **100** 5/00 Uttx 2m good NHF

Air Shot

88(104h) (71h)83

12-y-o b g Gunner B-Dans Le Vent (Pollerton)
Mrs P Robeson Mrs P Prowting & Mrs P Bates

Placings: 112/51124220/U12322/113/34/PP54F/2-0P56 **(3276)**
2001/02: 21^{0}S, 24^{P}S, 21^{5}S, 20^{6}S

	Starts	1st	2nd	3rd	Win & Pl
Hurdles	2	0	0	0	0
Chases	2	0	0	0	0
Career Total	**32**	**7**	**8**	**3**	**51103**

144	2/97	Chep	2m3f110y	B Ch	SFT	£6775
128	5/96	NAbb	2m5f110y	D Ch	SFT	£3827
118	1/96	Ling	2m	E Ch	SFT	£3290
110	12/94	Ling	2m110y	Hdl	HVY	£2559
95	12/94	Uttx	2m	Hdl	GD	£2113
105	3/94	Bang	2m1f	NHF	G-S	£1924
112	3/94	Chep	2m1f	NHF	SFT	£1276

Total win prize-money £21767

Going: Sf: 0-4 GS: 0-0 Gd: 0-0 GF: - Fm: 0-0
Distance: 2m/2m3: 0-0 2m4-2m7: 0-3 3m+: 0-1
Track: LH: 0-2 RH: 0-2 Tight: 0-2 Gall: 0-0
Aids: Bl: 0-0 Vi: 0-0 Tstrap: 0-0
Best Rating: **144** 5/97 Strf 2m5f110y good Ch

Aircon (IRE)

104(70h) (44h)119

7-y-o ch g Moscow Society (USA)-Corrielek (Menelek)
R Dickin G Hutsby

Placings: 5/56613-FUF5P300P22 **(4740)**
2001/02: 25^{F}G, 26^{U}GF, 28^{F}GF, 24^{5}G, 21^{P}GS, 24^{3}S, 24^{0}G, 16^{0}G, 20^{P}HY, 20^{2}GF, 20^{2}GF

	Starts	1st	2nd	3rd	Win & Pl
Hurdles	2	0	0	0	0
Chases	9	0	2	1	3024
Career Total	**17**	**1**	**2**	**2**	**8676**

119	2/01	Wwck	2m4f110y	D Ch	SFT	£5008

Total win prize-money £5008

Going: Sf: 0-2 GS: 0-1 Gd: 0-4 GF: - Fm: 0-4
Distance: 2m/2m3: 0-1 2m4-2m7: 0-4 3m+: 0-6
Track: LH: 0-6 RH: 0-5 Tight: 0-5 Gall: 0-1
Aids: Bl: 0-0 Vi: 0-7 Tstrap: 0-0
Best Rating: **119** 5/01 NAbb 3m2f110y gd-fm Ch

Moderate handicap chaser who does not have the best completion record. Stays three miles. Regularly visored.

Airoski

75f

6-y-o b g Petoski-Thames Air (Crash Course)
Mrs C J Robinson Jeremy Beasley

Placings: 00PP **(4373)**
2001/02: 16^{0}S, 16^{0}GS, 21^{P}HY, 21^{P}S

	Starts	1st	2nd	3rd	Win & Pl
NH Flat	2	0	0	0	0
Hurdles	2	0	0	0	0
Career Total	**4**	**0**	**0**	**0**	

Going: Sf: 0-3 GS: 0-1 Gd: 0-0 GF: - Fm: 0-0
Distance: 2m/2m3: 0-2 2m4-2m7: 0-2 3m+: 0-0
Track: LH: 0-1 RH: 0-2 Tight: 0-0 Gall: 0-1
Aids: Bl: 0-0 Vi: 0-0 Tstrap: 0-0
Best Rating: **75** 12/01 Wwck 2m soft NHF

Airs'N'Laces

5-y-o b m Neltino-Dime And Lace (Spare A Dime)
J L Harris R Andrew

Placings: 0 **(0506)**
2001/02: 16^{0}GF

	Starts	1st	2nd	3rd	Win & Pl
NH Flat	1	0	0	0	
Career Total	**1**	**0**	**0**	**0**	

Going: Sf: 0-0 GS: 0-0 Gd: 0-0 GF: - Fm: 0-1
Distance: 2m/2m3: 0-1 2m4-2m7: 0-0 3m+: 0-0
Track: LH: 0-0 RH: 0-1 Tight: 0-0 Gall: 0-1
Aids: Bl: 0-0 Vi: 0-0 Tstrap: 0-0
Best Rating:

Ajar (IRE)

104 114

12-y-o b g Avocat-Door Belle (Fidel)
J W Mullins Col R I Webb-Bowen

Placings: 60/32FU/60110215F2/F6103335/0406U0222-U42111 **(4416)**
2001/02: 21^{U}GF, 21^{4}GF, 21^{2}G, 20^{1}S, 20^{1}G, 20^{1}S

	Starts	1st	2nd	3rd	Win & Pl
Chases	6	3	1	0	9744
Career Total	**39**	**7**	**7**	**4**	**34403**

114	3/02	Font	2m4f	H Ch	SFT	£2226
114	3/02	Sand	2m4f110y	H Ch	GD	£3354
108	2/02	Sand	2m4f110y	H Ch	SFT	£2324
123	12/99	Thur	2m	Hdl	SFT	£6160
121	3/99	Limk	2m	Ch	SFT	£3989
116	1/99	Gowr	2m2f	Hdl	SFT	£3437
112	1/99	Tram	2m	Hdl	SH	£2608

Total win prize-money £24102

Going: Sf: 2-2 GS: 0-0 Gd: 1-2 GF: - Fm: 0-2
Distance: 2m/2m3: 0-0 **2m4-2m7: 3-6** 3m+: 0-0
Track: LH: 0-2 **RH: 2-3 Tight: 1-4** Gall: 0-0
Aids: Bl: 0-0 Vi: 0-0 Tstrap: 0-0
Best Rating: **132** 4/00 Fair 2m soft Hdl

Ex-Irish chaser. A fair hunter chaser, he scored twice over two and a half miles at Sandown and once at Fontwell early in 2002 and likes the ground good or softer. Jumps right-handed.

Akina (NZ)

98 92d

11-y-o b g Ivory Hunter (USA)-Wairoa Belle (NZ) (Bold Venture (NZ))
J Neville N Brookes

Placings: 1F4F0/F0UP/0FP-FU0F2U2PP **(4505)**
2001/02: 24^{F}GF, 20^{U}GF, 21^{0}GF, 20^{F}S, 23^{2}G, 24^{U}G, 26^{2}HY, 26^{P}S, 21^{P}G

	Starts	1st	2nd	3rd	Win & Pl
Chases	9	0	2	0	1867
Career Total	**21**	**1**	**2**	**0**	**3927**

8/98	Awap	1m5f	Hdl	HVY	£2060

Total win prize-money £2060

Going: Sf: 0-3 GS: 0-0 Gd: 0-3 GF: - Fm: 0-3
Distance: 2m/2m3: 0-0 2m4-2m7: 0-4 3m+: 0-5
Track: LH: 0-6 RH: 0-2 Tight: 0-4 Gall: 0-1
Aids: Bl: 0-0 Vi: 0-0 Tstrap: 0-0
Best Rating: **96** 7/01 Worc 2m7f110y good Ch

He is a winner over hurdles in New Zealand, but took a long time before he showed anything over here. Not the best jumper, he is an extremely inconsistent sort.

Al Mabrook (IRE)

101 **88**

7-y-o b g Rainbows For Life (CAN)-Sky Lover (Ela-Mana-Mou)
K A Ryan (Ferdy Murphy 24/6) The Gloria Darley Racing Partnership

Placings:2P26332 **(4917)**
2001/02: 16^{2}F, 20^{P}GF, 17^{2}S, 20^{6}G, 17^{3}S, 17^{3}S, 21^{2}GF

	Starts	1st	2nd	3rd	Win & Pl
Hurdles	7	0	3	2	4919
Career Total	**7**	**0**	**3**	**2**	**4919**

Going: Sf: 0-3 GS: 0-0 Gd: 0-1 GF: - Fm: 0-3
Distance: 2m/2m3: 0-4 2m4-2m7: 0-3 3m+: 0-0
Track: LH: 0-6 RH: 0-1 Tight: 0-4 Gall: 0-0
Aids: Bl: 0-0 Vi: 0-0 Tstrap: 0-0
Best Rating: **88** 4/02 Sedg 2m5f110y gd-fm Hdl

A winner on the Flat, he has yet to get off the mark over hurdles.

Al Towd (USA)

101 **110**

5-y-o b g Kingmambo (USA)-Toujours Elle (USA) (Lyphard (USA))
M Halford (S Dow 25/8) Paul Rooney

Placings:2 0251200 **(4790a)**
2001/02: 18^{6}GF, 22^{2}GF, 20^{5}GF, 16^{1}S, 19^{2}HY, 16^{0}Y, 20^{0}Y

	Starts	1st	2nd	3rd	Win & Pl
Hurdles	7	1	2	0	7919
Career Total	**8**	**1**	**3**	**0**	**8581**

99 3/02 Thur 2m Hdl SFT £3809
Total win prize-money £3810

Going: Sf: 1-2 GS: 0-0 Gd: 0-0 GF: - Fm: 0-3
Distance: **2m/2m3: 1-4** 2m4-2m7: 0-3 3m+: 0-0
Track: LH: 0-4 **RH: 1-2** Tight: 0-2 Gall: 0-0
Aids: Bl: 0-0 Vi: 0-0 Tstrap: 0-0
Best Rating: **110** 3/02 Naas 2m3f heavy Hdl

Al's Fella (IRE)

66 **53**

7-y-o br g Alzao (USA)-Crystal Cross (USA) (Roberto (USA))
D J S Ffrench Davis (Miss K M George 16/7) Mrs S Liddiard

Placings:5243/06 **(0929)**
2001/02: 17^{0}G, 20^{6}GF

	Starts	1st	2nd	3rd	Win & Pl
Hurdles	2	0	0	0	0
Career Total	**6**	**0**	**1**	**1**	**978**

Going: Sf: 0-0 GS: 0-0 Gd: 0-1 GF: - Fm: 0-1
Distance: 2m/2m3: 0-1 2m4-2m7: 0-1 3m+: 0-0
Track: LH: 0-2 RH: 0-0 Tight: 0-2 Gall: 0-0
Aids: Bl: 0-1 Vi: 0-0 Tstrap: 0-2
Best Rating: **91** 9/99 Sedg 2m1f gd-fm Hdl

Alabaster

7-y-o gr m Gran Alba (USA)-Last Ditch (Ben Novus)
N J Hawke Mrs D R Whigham

Placings:PP **(3655)**
2001/02: 19^{P}S, 22^{P}S

	Starts	1st	2nd	3rd	Win & Pl
Hurdles	2	0	0	0	
Career Total	**2**	**0**	**0**	**0**	

Going: Sf: 0-2 GS: 0-0 Gd: 0-0 GF: - Fm: 0-0
Distance: 2m/2m3: 0-0 2m4-2m7: 0-2 3m+: 0-0
Track: LH: 0-0 RH: 0-2 Tight: 0-1 Gall: 0-0
Aids: Bl: 0-0 Vi: 0-0 Tstrap: 0-0
Best Rating:

Alackaday (GER)

104 **109**

6-y-o b g Nebos (GER)-Aminata (GER) (Local Suitor (USA))
G Macaire (Mme E Mader 2/12) Mlle Y Shen

Placings:126-B0430
2001/02: 17^{B}HY, 18^{0}HY, 19^{4}HY, 17^{3}GS, 18^{0}VS

	Starts	1st	2nd	3rd	Win & Pl
Hurdles	4	0	0	1	2791
Chases	1	0	0	0	0
Career Total	**8**	**1**	**1**	**1**	**5694**

9/00 Brem 2m1f Ch SFT £1613
Total win prize-money £1613

Going: Sf: 0-3 GS: 0-1 Gd: 0-0 GF: - Fm: 0-0
Distance: 2m/2m3: 0-4 2m4-2m7: 0-1 3m+: 0-0
Track: LH: 0-1 RH: 0-1 Tight: 0-1 Gall: 0-0
Aids: Bl: 0-0 Vi: 0-0 Tstrap: 0-0
Best Rating: **109** 12/01 Tntn 2m1f gd-sft Hdl

Alagazam

77 **44**

4-y-o ch g Alhijaz-Maziere (Mazilier (USA))
B I Case Paul Rackham

Placings:0 **(4737)**
2001/02: 16^{0}GF

	Starts	1st	2nd	3rd	Win & Pl
Hurdles	1	0	0	0	
Career Total	**1**	**0**	**0**	**0**	

Going: Sf: 0-0 GS: 0-0 Gd: 0-0 GF: - Fm: 0-1
Distance: 2m/2m3: 0-1 2m4-2m7: 0-0 3m+: 0-0
Track: LH: 0-0 RH: 0-1 Tight: 0-0 Gall: 0-0
Aids: Bl: 0-0 Vi: 0-0 Tstrap: 0-0
Best Rating: **44** 4/02 Ludl 2m gd-fm Hdl

Alakdar (CAN)

109(62h) **98**

8-y-o ch g Green Dancer (USA)-Population (General Assembly (USA))
Jane Southcombe Online Racing Club

Placings:00/30/0464235/25300-010602F443P **(2940)**
2001/02: 21^{0}GF, 21^{1}GS, 21^{0}G, 23^{6}G, 26^{0}GF, 21^{2}GF, 20^{F}GF, 24^{4}S, 21^{4}S, 21^{3}HY, 22^{P}G

	Starts	1st	2nd	3rd	Win & Pl
Chases	11	1	1	1	6329
Career Total	**27**	**1**	**3**	**4**	**8307**

98 6/01 NAbb 2m5f110y D Ch G-S £4202
Total win prize-money £4202

Going: Sf: 0-3 **GS: 1-1** Gd: 0-3 GF: - Fm: 0-4
Distance: 2m/2m3: 0-0 **2m4-2m7: 1-8** 3m+: 0-3
Track: **LH: 1-10** RH: 0-0 **Tight: 1-8** Gall: 0-1
Aids: Bl: 0-0 Vi: 0-0 Tstrap: 0-0
Best Rating: **98** 6/01 NAbb 2m5f110y gd-sft Ch

Alanna's Gold (IRE)

71 **33**

9-y-o ch g Ajraas (USA)-Val Gardena (Ahonoora)
J W Mullins Mrs Sally Mullins

Placings:5260/40/52/0-0 **(0060)**
2001/02: 17^{0}GS

	Starts	1st	2nd	3rd	Win & Pl
Hurdles	1	0	0	0	
Career Total	**10**	**0**	**2**	**0**	**1065**

Going: Sf: 0-0 GS: 0-1 Gd: 0-0 GF: - Fm: 0-0
Distance: 2m/2m3: 0-1 2m4-2m7: 0-0 3m+: 0-0
Track: LH: 0-0 RH: 0-1 Tight: 0-1 Gall: 0-0
Aids: Bl: 0-0 Vi: 0-0 Tstrap: 0-0
Best Rating: **86** 9/99 NAbb 2m6f gd-fm Hdl

Alaskan Heir

11-y-o b g Northern State (USA)-Royal Meeting (Dara Monarch)
Miss W M Bayliss Miss W M Bayliss

Placings:32U2113P0/04300/F0055632/25224P0632/24463 00/P **(3707)**
2001/02: 25^{P}HY

	Starts	1st	2nd	3rd	Win & Pl
Chases	1	0	0	0	
Career Total	**40**	**2**	**8**	**6**	**14762**

76 1/95 Muss 2m4f F(0-100)HHdl GD £2780
75 12/94 Leic 2m Hdl HVY £1960
Total win prize-money £4740

Going: Sf: 0-1 GS: 0-0 Gd: 0-0 GF: - Fm: 0-0
Distance: 2m/2m3: 0-0 2m4-2m7: 0-0 3m+: 0-1
Track: LH: 0-0 RH: 0-1 Tight: 0-0 Gall: 0-0
Aids: Bl: 0-0 Vi: 0-1 Tstrap: 0-1
Best Rating: **83** 12/98 Hayd 3m soft Ch

Alba Street

7-y-o gr m Gran Alba (USA)-Kerry Street (Dairialatan)
C Tizzard Mr & Mrs E Vickery

Placings:00-4 **(0920)**
2001/02: 27^{4}GF

	Starts	1st	2nd	3rd	Win & Pl
Hurdles	1	0	0	0	0
Career Total	**3**	**0**	**0**	**0**	**0**

Going: Sf: 0-0 GS: 0-0 Gd: 0-0 GF: - Fm: 0-1
Distance: 2m/2m3: 0-0 2m4-2m7: 0-0 3m+: 0-1
Track: LH: 0-1 RH: 0-0 Tight: 0-1 Gall: 0-0
Aids: Bl: 0-0 Vi: 0-0 Tstrap: 0-0
Best Rating: **58** 12/00 Ludl 2m soft NHF

Albahi (IRE)

86 **74**

5-y-o ch g Indian Ridge-Ghanimah (Caerleon (USA))
M G Quinlan Twincroft Partnerships

Placings: *345* (2131)
2001/02: 16^{3}GF, 16^{4}G, 16^{5}GF

	Starts	1st	2nd	3rd	Win & Pl
NH Flat	2	0	0	1	217
Hurdles	1	0	0	0	0
Career Total	**3**	**0**	**0**	**1**	**217**

Going: Sf: 0-0 GS: 0-0 Gd: 0-1 GF: - Fm: 0-2
Distance: 2m/2m3: 0-3 2m4-2m7: 0-0 3m+: 0-0
Track: LH: 0-1 RH: 0-2 Tight: 0-0 Gall: 0-1
Aids: Bl: 0-0 Vi: 0-0 Tstrap: 0-0
Best Rating: **91** 9/01 Worc 2m gd-fm NHF

Albermarle (IRE)

100 90

11-y-o ch g Phardante (FR)-Clarahill (Menelek)
J S King Terry Bailey

Placings: 0/1F31/**13450/P2PUF/**0-04 (0419)
2001/02: 21^{0}GF, 20^{4}G

	Starts	1st	2nd	3rd	Win & Pl
Hurdles	2	0	0	0	0
Career Total	**18**	**3**	**1**	**2**	**11585**
103 5/98	MRas	2m4f	D Ch	G-F	£4261
116 4/98	Extr	2m3f110y	E Hdl	SFT	£2444
107 5/97	Wwck	2m4f110y	E Hdl	GD	£2761

Total win prize-money £9466

Going: Sf: 0-0 GS: 0-0 Gd: 0-1 GF: - Fm: 0-1
Distance: 2m/2m3: 0-0 2m4-2m7: 0-2 3m+: 0-0
Track: LH: 0-1 RH: 0-0 Tight: 0-1 Gall: 0-0
Aids: Bl: 0-0 Vi: 0-0 Tstrap: 0-0
Best Rating: **116** 4/98 Extr 2m3f110y soft Hdl

Albert The Lion (IRE)

10-y-o gr g Celio Rufo-Esker Lady (Gala Performance (USA))
Mrs Beverley Moore-Williams 1st Regiment Royal Horse Artillery

Placings: *00/P/P040O60/P* (3753)
2001/02: 24^{P}S

	Starts	1st	2nd	3rd	Win & Pl
Chases	1	0	0	0	
Career Total	**11**	**0**	**0**	**0**	**0**

Going: Sf: 0-1 GS: 0-0 Gd: 0-0 GF: - Fm: 0-0
Distance: 2m/2m3: 0-0 2m4-2m7: 0-0 3m+: 0-1
Track: LH: 0-0 RH: 0-1 Tight: 0-0 Gall: 0-0
Aids: Bl: 0-0 Vi: 0-0 Tstrap: 0-0
Best Rating: **57** 12/97 Ludl 2m good Hdl

Albertino Lad

90f 102f

5-y-o ch g Mystiko (USA)-Siokra (Kris)
L Lungo A Saccomando

Placings: *5* (4841)
2001/02: 16^{5}G

	Starts	1st	2nd	3rd	Win & Pl
NH Flat	1	0	0	0	0
Career Total	**1**	**0**	**0**	**0**	**0**

Going: Sf: 0-0 GS: 0-0 Gd: 0-1 GF: - Fm: 0-0
Distance: 2m/2m3: 0-1 2m4-2m7: 0-0 3m+: 0-0
Track: LH: 0-1 RH: 0-0 Tight: 0-0 Gall: 0-0
Aids: Bl: 0-0 Vi: 0-0 Tstrap: 0-0
Best Rating: **102** 4/02 Ayr 2m good NHF

Albertridge (IRE)

62

9-y-o gr g Moscow Society (USA)-Abigail's Dream (Kalaglow)
V R A Dartnall Bertie's Allsorts

Placings: 0/6F/52605/**F-00** (0600)
2001/02: 22^{0}F, 27^{0}G

	Starts	1st	2nd	3rd	Win & Pl
Hurdles	2	0	0	0	
Career Total	**11**	**0**	**1**	**0**	**703**

Going: Sf: 0-0 GS: 0-0 Gd: 0-1 GF: - Fm: 0-1
Distance: 2m/2m3: 0-0 2m4-2m7: 0-1 3m+: 0-1
Track: LH: 0-1 RH: 0-0 Tight: 0-1 Gall: 0-0
Aids: Bl: 0-1 Vi: 0-0 Tstrap: 0-0
Best Rating: **89** 5/99 DRoy 3m soft Hdl

Albright

6-y-o b m Teenoso (USA)-Bright-One (Electric)
C W Thornton Peter Rawson

Placings: *0-P* (1025)
2001/02: 17^{P}GF

	Starts	1st	2nd	3rd	Win & Pl
NH Flat	1	0	0	0	
Career Total	**2**	**0**	**0**	**0**	

Going: Sf: 0-0 GS: 0-0 Gd: 0-0 GF: - Fm: 0-1
Distance: 2m/2m3: 0-1 2m4-2m7: 0-0 3m+: 0-0
Track: LH: 0-1 RH: 0-0 Tight: 0-1 Gall: 0-0
Aids: Bl: 0-0 Vi: 0-0 Tstrap: 0-0
Best Rating: **79** 5/00 Bang 2m1f good NHF

Alcapone (IRE)

109 (113h)153

8-y-o b g Roselier (FR)-Ann's Cap (IRE) (Cardinal Flower)
M F Morris Mrs A M Daly

Placings: 0F263121436/**F55U21F031-34523FPP** (4938a)
2001/02: 20^{3}G, 16^{4}Y, 18^{5}YS, 17^{2}Y, 16^{3}YS, 20^{F}SH, 20^{P}G, 16^{P}YS

	Starts	1st	2nd	3rd	Win & Pl
Chases	8	0	1	2	11234
Career Total	**31**	**4**	**4**	**5**	**60854**
153 4/01	Fair	2m	Ch	Y-S	£32500
140 12/00	Fair	2m100y	Ch	SFT	£3864
112 2/00	Clon	2m	(0-95)Hdl	SFT	£2760
103 1/00	Tram	2m	Hdl	Y-S	£3588

Total win prize-money £42712

Going: Sf: 0-0 GS: 0-0 Gd: 0-2 GF: - Fm: 0-0
Distance: 2m/2m3: 0-5 2m4-2m7: 0-3 3m+: 0-0
Track: LH: 0-3 RH: 0-2 Tight: 0-1 Gall: 0-0
Aids: Bl: 0-0 Vi: 0-0 Tstrap: 0-1
Best Rating: **153** 1/02 Fair 2m100y yld-sft Ch

A useful Irish chaser, he stays two and a half miles but is probably better over slightly shorter trips, having won a Grade One novice chase at Fairyhouse in April 2001. Normally a sound jumper, he ran well in good company in 2001/2002 and is capable of winning a decent two-mile handicap. Suited by cut in the ground.

Alcayde

94 90

7-y-o ch g Alhijaz-Lucky Flinders (Free State)
J Akehurst A D Spence

Placings: 6/30-5456 (2567)
2001/02: 21^{5}GS, 22^{4}GS, 21^{5}GS, 16^{6}S

	Starts	1st	2nd	3rd	Win & Pl
Hurdles	4	0	0	0	281
Career Total	**7**	**0**	**0**	**1**	**1029**

Going: Sf: 0-1 GS: 0-3 Gd: 0-0 GF: - Fm: 0-0
Distance: 2m/2m3: 0-1 2m4-2m7: 0-3 3m+: 0-0
Track: LH: 0-1 RH: 0-3 Tight: 0-0 Gall: 0-1
Aids: Bl: 0-0 Vi: 0-0 Tstrap: 0-0
Best Rating: **109** 11/00 Asct 2m4f soft Hdl

Aldenham (IRE)

80 37

5-y-o b m Namaqualand (USA)-Lamp Of Phoebus (USA) (Sunshine Forever (USA))
Andrew Reid A S Reid

Placings: *0-0PP* (2642)
2001/02: 16^{0}GS, 16^{P}S, 21^{P}GS

	Starts	1st	2nd	3rd	Win & Pl
Hurdles	3	0	0	0	
Career Total	**4**	**0**	**0**	**0**	

Going: Sf: 0-1 GS: 0-2 Gd: 0-0 GF: - Fm: 0-0
Distance: 2m/2m3: 0-2 2m4-2m7: 0-1 3m+: 0-0
Track: LH: 0-1 RH: 0-2 Tight: 0-1 Gall: 0-1
Aids: Bl: 0-0 Vi: 0-0 Tstrap: 0-0
Best Rating: **37** 11/01 Plum 2m gd-sft Hdl

Aldington Annie

8-y-o gr m Baron Blakeney-Aldington Princess (Cavo Doro)
N Waggott Mrs J Waggott

Placings: P (0659)
2001/02: 20^{P}F

	Starts	1st	2nd	3rd	Win & Pl
Hurdles	1	0	0	0	
Career Total	**1**	**0**	**0**	**0**	

Going: Sf: 0-0 GS: 0-0 Gd: 0-0 GF: - Fm: 0-1
Distance: 2m/2m3: 0-0 2m4-2m7: 0-1 3m+: 0-0
Track: LH: 0-0 RH: 0-1 Tight: 0-0 Gall: 0-0
Aids: Bl: 0-0 Vi: 0-0 Tstrap: 0-0
Best Rating:

Aldwych Arrow (IRE)

78 51

7-y-o ch g Rainbows For Life (CAN)-Shygate (Shy Groom (USA))
M A Buckley M A Buckley

Placings: 0 (2399)
2001/02: 16^{0}G

	Starts	1st	2nd	3rd	Win & Pl
Hurdles	1	0	0	0	
Career Total	**1**	**0**	**0**	**0**	

Going: Sf: 0-0 GS: 0-0 Gd: 0-1 GF: - Fm: 0-0

Distance: 2m/2m3: 0-1 2m4-2m7: 0-0 3m+: 0-0
Track: LH: 0-1 RH: 0-0 Tight: 0-0 Gall: 0-0
Aids: Bl: 0-0 Vi: 0-0 Tstrap: 0-0
Best Rating: 51 11/01 Weth 2m good Hdl

Alena H Banks

80

8-y-o b g Milieu-Widow Trellerne (Cool Guy (USA))
N B Mason N B Mason

Placings:50**PPP-P0U5P** (1622)
2001/02: 20^{P}GF, 17^{0}GS, 21^{U}GF, 24^{5}GF, 25^{P}G

	Starts	1st	2nd	3rd	Win & Pl
Chases	5	0	0	0	0
Career Total	**10**	**0**	**0**	**0**	**0**

Going: Sf: 0-0 GS: 0-1 Gd: 0-1 GF: - Fm: 0-3
Distance: 2m/2m3: 0-1 2m4-2m7: 0-2 3m+: 0-2
Track: LH: 0-3 RH: 0-2 Tight: 0-2 Gall: 0-1
Aids: Bl: 0-0 Vi: 0-0 Tstrap: 0-3
Best Rating: 80 9/01 Sedg 2m5f gd-fm Ch

Alex Thuscombe

14-y-o ch g Takachiho-Portate (Articulate)
Mrs Peter Shaw Mrs Peter Shaw

Placings:00/05000/**P2/U/400** (4763)
2001/02: 21^{4}GF, 24^{0}GF, 24^{0}GF

	Starts	1st	2nd	3rd	Win & Pl
Chases	3	0	0	0	0
Career Total	**13**	**0**	**1**	**0**	**836**

Going: Sf: 0-0 GS: 0-0 Gd: 0-0 GF: - Fm: 0-3
Distance: 2m/2m3: 0-0 2m4-2m7: 0-1 3m+: 0-2
Track: LH: 0-1 RH: 0-2 Tight: 0-1 Gall: 0-0
Aids: Bl: 0-3 Vi: 0-0 Tstrap: 0-0
Best Rating: 111 4/99 Asct 3m110y gd-fm Ch

Alexander Banquet (IRE)

124 178

9-y-o b g Glacial Storm (USA)-Black Nancy (Monksfield)
W P Mullins Mrs N O'Callaghan

Placings:*11*/11110/**1144512/32-316U3** (4945a)
2001/02: 24^{3}Y, 24^{1}HY, 26^{6}G, 36^{U}G, 25^{3}G

	Starts	1st	2nd	3rd	Win & Pl
Chases	5	1	0	2	83092
Career Total	**21**	**10**	**2**	**3**	**241195**

178	2/02	Leop	3m	Ch	HVY	£61411
160	2/00	Naas	2m4f	Ch	SFT	£10400
157	11/99	Fair	2m4f	Ch	SFT	£26116
150	11/99	Naas	2m3f	Ch	Y-S	£4620
146	2/99	Leop	2m2f	Hdl	SH	£17343
148	11/98	Fair	2m	Hdl	Y-S	£16956
116	11/98	Punc	2m	Hdl	HVY	£4483
120	11/98	Fair	2m4f	Hdl	Y-S	£2690
142	3/98	Chel	2m110y	A NHF	GD	£18448
115	2/98	Gowr	2m1f	NHF	YLD	£2978

Total win prize-money £165449

Going: Sf: 1-1 GS: 0-0 Gd: 0-3 GF: - Fm: 0-0
Distance: 2m/2m3: 0-0 2m4-2m7: 0-0 **3m+: 1-5**
Track: **LH: 1-4** RH: 0-1 Tight: 0-1 Gall: 0-1
Aids: Bl: 0-0 Vi: 0-0 Tstrap: 0-0
Best Rating: 178 2/02 Leop 3m heavy Ch

A very useful performer, he was restricted to just two runs, in the English and Irish versions of the Hennessy Gold Cup, in 2000/01. Third, albeit well beaten at Newbury, he ran better when two lengths runner-up to Florida Pearl at Leopardstown. Reportedly strained a tendon in the latter race and was sidelined for the rest of the campaign, but came back in 2001/02 to run well in the Ericcson prior to winning the Hennessy at Leopardstown. He ran a good trial for the Grand National when staying on well in the Gold Cup, but unseated early at Aintree and found the ground too quick behind Florida Peal at Punchestown. Granted a test of stamina and soft ground, this game individual will win plenty more races.

Alexander Boyzone (IRE)

8-y-o gr g Mandalus-Fane Bridge (Random Shot)
Miss M E Rowland Paul Mayo

Placings:*30000/3-6* (1597)
2001/02: 16^{6}G

	Starts	1st	2nd	3rd	Win & Pl
Hurdles	1	0	0	0	0
Career Total	**7**	**0**	**0**	**2**	**727**

Going: Sf: 0-0 GS: 0-0 Gd: 0-1 GF: - Fm: 0-0
Distance: 2m/2m3: 0-1 2m4-2m7: 0-0 3m+: 0-0
Track: LH: 0-1 RH: 0-0 Tight: 0-1 Gall: 0-0
Aids: Bl: 0-0 Vi: 0-0 Tstrap: 0-0
Best Rating: 85 5/00 Punc 2m good NHF

Alexander Milenium (IRE)

112f 136f

6-y-o b g Be My Native (USA)-Kissowen (Pitpan)
W P Mullins Mrs N O'Callaghan

Placings:*1P2* (4948a)
2001/02: 16^{1}Y, 16^{P}GS, 16^{2}G

	Starts	1st	2nd	3rd	Win & Pl
NH Flat	3	1	1	0	9061
Career Total	**3**	**1**	**1**	**0**	**9061**

136 12/01 Leop 2m NHF YLD £5564
Total win prize-money £5565

Going: Sf: 0-0 GS: 0-1 Gd: 0-1 GF: - Fm: 0-0
Distance: **2m/2m3: 1-3** 2m4-2m7: 0-0 3m+: 0-0
Track: LH: 0-1 RH: 0-1 Tight: 0-0 Gall: 0-0
Aids: Bl: 0-0 Vi: 0-0 Tstrap: 0-0
Best Rating: 136 12/01 Leop 2m yield NHF

A high-class irish bumper performer, winning at leopardstown and, after pulling up at Cheltenham, was narrowly beaten at Punchestown. Looks to have a bright future over hurdles.

Alexander Nevsky

95 86

6-y-o b g Be My Native (USA)-Tsarella (Mummy's Pet)
N J Henderson Mrs Hugh Maitland-Jones

Placings:*15-3*P0 (4007)
2001/02: 17^{3}G, 20^{P}G, 19^{0}S

	Starts	1st	2nd	3rd	Win & Pl
NH Flat	1	0	0	1	280
Hurdles	2	0	0	0	0
Career Total	**5**	**1**	**0**	**1**	**1757**

101 5/00 Worc 2m H NHF GD £1477
Total win prize-money £1477

Going: Sf: 0-1 GS: 0-0 Gd: 0-2 GF: - Fm: 0-0
Distance: 2m/2m3: 0-2 2m4-2m7: 0-1 3m+: 0-0
Track: LH: 0-2 RH: 0-1 Tight: 0-0 Gall: 0-2
Aids: Bl: 0-0 Vi: 0-0 Tstrap: 0-0
Best Rating: 101 5/01 Hrfd 2m1f good NHF

Decent bumper performer. Apparently has had breathing problems. Well beaten over hurdles so far. Has won on good ground.

Alexandra Parade (IRE)

97f 109f

5-y-o b m Mister Lord (USA)-Ballyanihan (Le Moss)
B De Haan Campbell Ross

Placings:*515* (4823)
2001/02: 16^{5}G, 16^{1}GS, 17^{5}G

	Starts	1st	2nd	3rd	Win & Pl
NH Flat	3	1	0	0	1548
Career Total	**3**	**1**	**0**	**0**	**1548**

96 2/02 Fknm 2m H NHF G-S £1548
Total win prize-money £1548

Going: Sf: 0-0 GS: 1-1 Gd: 0-2 GF: - Fm: 0-0
Distance: **2m/2m3: 1-3** 2m4-2m7: 0-0 3m+: 0-0
Track: **LH: 1-3** RH: 0-0 **Tight: 1-2** Gall: 0-1
Aids: Bl: 0-0 Vi: 0-0 Tstrap: 0-0
Best Rating: 109 4/02 Chel 2m1f good NHF

Half-sister to winning stayer Cottstown Boy, won her second bumper at Fakenham.

Alfa Sunrise

94f 89f

5-y-o b g Alflora (IRE)-Gipsy Dawn (Lighter)
C R Barwell Robin Barwell

Placings:*5* (2048)
2001/02: 16^{5}G

	Starts	1st	2nd	3rd	Win & Pl
NH Flat	1	0	0	0	0
Career Total	**1**	**0**	**0**	**0**	**0**

Going: Sf: 0-0 GS: 0-0 Gd: 0-1 GF: - Fm: 0-0
Distance: 2m/2m3: 0-1 2m4-2m7: 0-0 3m+: 0-0
Track: LH: 0-0 RH: 0-1 Tight: 0-0 Gall: 0-0
Aids: Bl: 0-0 Vi: 0-0 Tstrap: 0-0
Best Rating: 89 11/01 Winc 2m good NHF

Alfalfa

76 58

4-y-o b g Rudimentary (USA)-Zalfa (Luthier)
G B Balding Mrs P Gulliver Mrs K Perrin G Balding

Placings:00OP (2594)
2001/02: 16^{0}GS, 17^{0}G, 16^{0}G, 17^{P}S

	Starts	1st	2nd	3rd	Win & Pl
Hurdles	4	0	0	0	
Career Total	**4**	**0**	**0**	**0**	

Going: Sf: 0-1 GS: 0-1 Gd: 0-2 GF: - Fm: 0-0
Distance: 2m/2m3: 0-4 2m4-2m7: 0-0 3m+: 0-0
Track: LH: 0-0 RH: 0-4 Tight: 0-1 Gall: 0-0
Aids: Bl: 0-0 Vi: 0-0 Tstrap: 0-0
Best Rating: 58 12/01 Winc 2m good Hdl

Alfies Dream (IRE)

53f 46f

7-y-o b g Hollow Hand-Tower Alum (Niels)

Jane Southcombe A G Varney

Placings: *00* (1245)

2001/02: 16^{0}GF, 16^{0}GF

	Starts	1st	2nd	3rd	Win & Pl
NH Flat	2	0	0	0	
Career Total	**2**	**0**	**0**	**0**	

Going: Sf: 0-0 GS: 0-0 Gd: 0-0 GF: - Fm: 0-2
Distance: 2m/2m3: 0-2 2m4-2m7: 0-0 3m+: 0-0
Track: LH: 0-2 RH: 0-0 Tight: 0-0 Gall: 0-0
Aids: Bl: 0-0 Vi: 0-0 Tstrap: 0-1
Best Rating: 46 8/01 Worc 2m gd-fm NHF

Alfies Rocket

68f 19f

5-y-o ch g Hatim (USA)-Run Pet Run (Deep Run)

D M Grissell Chartwell Racing

Placings: *0* (3811)

2001/02: 18^{0}S

	Starts	1st	2nd	3rd	Win & Pl
NH Flat	1	0	0	0	
Career Total	**1**	**0**	**0**	**0**	

Going: Sf: 0-1 GS: 0-0 Gd: 0-0 GF: - Fm: 0-0
Distance: 2m/2m3: 0-1 2m4-2m7: 0-0 3m+: 0-0
Track: LH: 0-1 RH: 0-0 Tight: 0-1 Gall: 0-0
Aids: Bl: 0-0 Vi: 0-0 Tstrap: 0-0
Best Rating: 19 2/02 Font 2m2f110y soft NHF

Alfred The Grey

86(90h) (85h)88

5-y-o gr g Environment Friend-Ranyah (USA) (Our Native (USA))

R Hollinshead Saloop

Placings: *60-066P6* (4905)

2001/02: 16^{0}GF, 20^{6}HY, 20^{6}HY, 20^{P}GS, 17^{6}GF

	Starts	1st	2nd	3rd	Win & Pl
Hurdles	4	0	0	0	
Chases	1	0	0	0	
Career Total	**7**	**0**	**0**	**0**	**0**

Going: Sf: 0-2 GS: 0-1 Gd: 0-0 GF: - Fm: 0-2
Distance: 2m/2m3: 0-2 2m4-2m7: 0-3 3m+: 0-0
Track: LH: 0-3 RH: 0-2 Tight: 0-3 Gall: 0-0
Aids: Bl: 0-0 Vi: 0-0 Tstrap: 0-0
Best Rating: 85 12/01 Hayd 2m4f heavy Hdl

Sprang a 33/1 shock when winning a poor three and a quarter mile maiden chase on first outing for new trainer at Southwell July 2002.

Alfy Rich

75 41

6-y-o b g Alflora (IRE)-Weareagrandmother (Prince Tenderfoot (USA))

P M Rich P M Rich

Placings: *006* (2388)

2001/02: 17^{0}GS, 22^{0}G, 20^{6}S

	Starts	1st	2nd	3rd	Win & Pl
NH Flat	1	0	0	0	0
Hurdles	2	0	0	0	0

Career Total	**3**	**0**	**0**	**0**	**0**

Going: Sf: 0-1 GS: 0-1 Gd: 0-1 GF: - Fm: 0-0
Distance: 2m/2m3: 0-1 2m4-2m7: 0-2 3m+: 0-0
Track: LH: 0-1 RH: 0-2 Tight: 0-1 Gall: 0-0
Aids: Bl: 0-0 Vi: 0-0 Tstrap: 0-0
Best Rating: 53 10/01 MRas 2m1f110y gd-sft NHF

Alheri

99 (76c)75

11-y-o gr g Puget (USA)-Miss Haddon (Free Boy)

J A T De Giles J A T De Giles

Placings: 0P6P/3U20/03P (2308)

2001/02: 24^{0}GF, 22^{3}GF, 26^{P}G

	Starts	1st	2nd	3rd	Win & Pl
Hurdles	3	0	0	1	360
Career Total	**11**	**0**	**1**	**2**	**1560**

Going: Sf: 0-0 GS: 0-0 Gd: 0-1 GF: - Fm: 0-2
Distance: 2m/2m3: 0-0 2m4-2m7: 0-1 3m+: 0-2
Track: LH: 0-0 RH: 0-2 Tight: 0-0 Gall: 0-1
Aids: Bl: 0-0 Vi: 0-0 Tstrap: 0-0
Best Rating: 80 7/99 Worc 2m4f110y gd-fm Ch

Ali Oop

43

5-y-o b g Shareef Dancer (USA)-Happydrome (Ahonoora)

P Beaumont (J D Bethell 21/5) Mrs J M Plummer

Placings: 0 (1251)

2001/02: 17^{0}G

	Starts	1st	2nd	3rd	Win & Pl
Hurdles	1	0	0	0	
Career Total	**1**	**0**	**0**	**0**	

Going: Sf: 0-0 GS: 0-0 Gd: 0-1 GF: - Fm: 0-0
Distance: 2m/2m3: 0-1 2m4-2m7: 0-0 3m+: 0-0
Track: LH: 0-1 RH: 0-0 Tight: 0-1 Gall: 0-0
Aids: Bl: 0-0 Vi: 0-0 Tstrap: 0-1
Best Rating: mfy

Aliabad (IRE)

73 33

7-y-o b/br g Doyoun-Alannya (FR) (Relko)

J G M O'Shea (D Haydn Jones 8/6) N G H Ayliffe

Placings: 600534/2032300503P/0-0 (0907)

2001/02: 24^{0}G

	Starts	1st	2nd	3rd	Win & Pl
Hurdles	1	0	0	0	
Career Total	**19**	**0**	**2**	**4**	**3022**

Going: Sf: 0-0 GS: 0-0 Gd: 0-1 GF: - Fm: 0-0
Distance: 2m/2m3: 0-0 2m4-2m7: 0-0 3m+: 0-1
Track: LH: 0-1 RH: 0-0 Tight: 0-0 Gall: 0-0
Aids: Bl: 0-0 Vi: 0-0 Tstrap: 0-0
Best Rating: 87 4/00 Ludl 2m5f good Hdl

Alice

102 68

5-y-o b m Rambo Dancer (CAN)-Cold Line (Exdirectory)

J Hetherton N Hetherton

Placings: *6504P0* (4867)

2001/02: 16^{6}GS, 16^{5}G, 16^{0}S, 16^{4}GS, 20^{P}S, 16^{0}GF

	Starts	1st	2nd	3rd	Win & Pl
NH Flat	4	0	0	0	0
Hurdles	2	0	0	0	0

Career Total	**6**	**0**	**0**	**0**	**0**

Going: Sf: 0-2 GS: 0-2 Gd: 0-1 GF: - Fm: 0-1
Distance: 2m/2m3: 0-5 2m4-2m7: 0-1 3m+: 0-0
Track: LH: 0-5 RH: 0-0 Tight: 0-2 Gall: 0-1
Aids: Bl: 0-0 Vi: 0-0 Tstrap: 0-1
Best Rating: 81 2/02 Fknm 2m gd-sft NHF

Moderate form in bumpers so far.

Alice Baring

5-y-o gr m Roselier (FR)-Forty Watts (Sparkler)

H D Daly M Ward-Thomas

Placings: 4 (4087)

2001/02: 17^{4}S

	Starts	1st	2nd	3rd	Win & Pl
Hurdles	1	0	0	0	0
Career Total	**1**	**0**	**0**	**0**	**0**

Going: Sf: 0-1 GS: 0-0 Gd: 0-0 GF: - Fm: 0-0
Distance: 2m/2m3: 0-1 2m4-2m7: 0-0 3m+: 0-0
Track: LH: 0-1 RH: 0-0 Tight: 0-1 Gall: 0-0
Aids: Bl: 0-0 Vi: 0-0 Tstrap: 0-0
Best Rating:

Alice Reigns

49f 95f

5-y-o b m Sir Harry Lewis (USA)-Richards Kate (Fidel)

Mrs A J Perrett S P Tindall

Placings: *1* (3290)

2001/02: 17^{1}S

	Starts	1st	2nd	3rd	Win & Pl
NH Flat	1	1	0	0	1610
Career Total	**1**	**1**	**0**	**0**	**1610**

95 1/02 Folk 2m1f110y H NHF SFT £1610

Total win prize-money £1610

Going: Sf: 1-1 GS: 0-0 Gd: 0-0 GF: - Fm: 0-0
Distance: **2m/2m3: 1-1** 2m4-2m7: 0-0 3m+: 0-0
Track: LH: 0-0 RH: 0-0 **Tight: 1-1** Gall: 0-0
Aids: Bl: 0-0 Vi: 0-0 Tstrap: 0-0
Best Rating: 95 1/02 Folk 2m1f110y soft NHF

A half-sister to Jane Lechat, a bumper winner who became disappointing. Won a Folkestone bumper on her debut on soft ground. Has the build of a chaser.

Alice Rose

68f

6-y-o b m Afzal-Rose Orchard (Rouser)

Mrs S M Johnson Mrs M Marfell

Placings: *0P* (0366)

2001/02: 18^{0}GF, 25^{P}G

	Starts	1st	2nd	3rd	Win & Pl
NH Flat	1	0	0	0	0
Hurdles	1	0	0	0	0
Career Total	**2**	**0**	**0**	**0**	

Going: Sf: 0-0 GS: 0-0 Gd: 0-1 GF: - Fm: 0-1
Distance: 2m/2m3: 0-1 2m4-2m7: 0-0 3m+: 0-1
Track: LH: 0-1 RH: 0-0 Tight: 0-1 Gall: 0-0
Aids: Bl: 0-0 Vi: 0-0 Tstrap: 0-0
Best Rating: 68 5/01 Font 2m2f110y gd-fm NHF

Alka International

105 121

10-y-o b g Northern State (USA)-Cachucha (Gay Fandango (USA))

Mrs P Townsley Paul Townsley

Placings:3240/242P/3212532/262360/11240/0-5246615 (4413)

2001/02: 16^{5}G, 18^{2}G, 21^{4}G, 21^{6}GS, 16^{6}S, 16^{1}HY, 18^{5}S

	Starts	1st	2nd	3rd	Win & Pl
Hurdles	7	1	1	0	6128
Career Total	**34**	**4**	**10**	**4**	**28660**

121	2/02	Plum	2m	D(0-115)HHdl	HVY	£3430
133	12/99	Ling	2m110y	D(0-125)HHdl	SFT	£2851
133	12/99	Font	2m2f110y	C(0-130)HHdl	GD	£7002
103	12/97	Hayd	2m	E(0-120)HHdl	SFT	£2221

Total win prize-money £15506

Going: Sf: 1-3 GS: 0-1 Gd: 0-3 GF: - Fm: 0-0
Distance: 2m/2m3: 1-5 2m4-2m7: 0-2 3m+: 0-0
Track: LH: 1-4 RH: 0-3 Tight: 1-4 Gall: 0-0
Aids: Bl: 1-2 Vi: 0-0 Tstrap: 0-0
Best Rating: 133 12/99 Kemp 2m soft Hdl

Decent, if fragile, handicap hurdler, stays two miles plus, suited by cut in the ground. Best on a sharp track. Winner of a fair two-mile handicap in the mud in Febraury.

Alkateb

102 90

10-y-o ch g Rock City-Corley Moor (Habitat)

A E Jones Mrs J Whitburn

Placings:6PP/3 (1034)

2001/02: 17^{3}G

	Starts	1st	2nd	3rd	Win & Pl
Hurdles	1	0	0	1	520
Career Total	**4**	**0**	**0**	**1**	**520**

Going: Sf: 0-0 GS: 0-0 Gd: 0-1 GF: - Fm: 0-0
Distance: 2m/2m3: 0-1 2m4-2m7: 0-0 3m+: 0-0
Track: LH: 0-1 RH: 0-0 Tight: 0-1 Gall: 0-0
Aids: Bl: 0-0 Vi: 0-0 Tstrap: 0-0
Best Rating: 91 11/98 Extr 2m1f soft Hdl

All Bleevable

101 72

5-y-o b g Presidium-Eve's Treasure (Bustino)

Mrs S Lamyman Mike & Tony Blee And Roy Allerston

Placings:6P005-PP20 (4904)

2001/02: 19^{P}GF, 21^{P}GS, 16^{2}G, 17^{0}G

	Starts	1st	2nd	3rd	Win & Pl
Hurdles	4	0	1	0	539
Career Total	**9**	**0**	**1**	**0**	**539**

Going: Sf: 0-0 GS: 0-1 Gd: 0-2 GF: - Fm: 0-1
Distance: 2m/2m3: 0-2 2m4-2m7: 0-2 3m+: 0-0
Track: LH: 0-1 RH: 0-3 Tight: 0-4 Gall: 0-0
Aids: Bl: 0-0 Vi: 0-0 Tstrap: 0-0
Best Rating: 72 4/02 Fknm 2m good Hdl

Plating-class hurdler.

All But (IRE)

103f 82f

10-y-o b g Roselier (FR)-Cloncunny (Teofane)

J Clements (P J Rothwell 16/1) J Clements

Placings:0/4/F0064523B24P/46S0064-PFU040500F0 (4951a)

2001/02: 25^{P}G, 24^{F}GF, 24^{U}GY, 22^{0}Y, 24^{4}S, 16^{0}S, 28^{5}S, 16^{0}S, 25^{0}GY, 33^{F}G, 31^{0}G

	Starts	1st	2nd	3rd	Win & Pl
NH Flat	2	0	0	0	0
Chases	9	0	0	0	282
Career Total	**32**	**0**	**2**	**1**	**5449**

Going: Sf: 0-4 GS: 0-0 Gd: 0-3 GF: - Fm: 0-1
Distance: 2m/2m3: 0-2 2m4-2m7: 0-1 3m+: 0-8
Track: LH: 0-1 RH: 0-4 Tight: 0-0 Gall: 0-0
Aids: Bl: 0-3 Vi: 0-0 Tstrap: 0-0
Best Rating: 89 4/97 Fair 2m2f gd-fm NHF

Moderate Irish handicap chaser, stays three miles.

All Guns Blazing (IRE)

104 108

6-y-o b g Un Desperado (FR)-Malone Ranger (Noble Philip (USA))

K C Bailey The All Guns Blazing Partnership

Placings:00P4364 (4513)

2001/02: 16^{0}GS, 18^{0}G, 24^{P}HY, 24^{4}S, 22^{3}S, 26^{6}S, 24^{4}GS

	Starts	1st	2nd	3rd	Win & Pl
NH Flat	2	0	0	0	0
Hurdles	5	0	0	1	794
Career Total	**7**	**0**	**0**	**1**	**794**

Going: Sf: 0-4 GS: 0-2 Gd: 0-1 GF: - Fm: 0-0
Distance: 2m/2m3: 0-2 2m4-2m7: 0-1 3m+: 0-4
Track: LH: 0 3 RH: 0 4 Tight: 0 3 Gall: 0 2
Aids: Bl: 0-0 Vi: 0-0 Tstrap: 0-0
Best Rating: 108 2/02 Font 2m6f110y soft Hdl

In the frame in staying novice hurdles.

All Honey (IRE)

99 84

5-y-o ch m Fourstars Allstar (USA)-A Bit Of Honey (The Parson)

Miss K Marks Nick Shutts

Placings:61-433540 (4420)

2001/02: 17^{4}HY, 17^{3}S, 19^{3}S, 19^{5}HY, 21^{4}S, 21^{0}GS

	Starts	1st	2nd	3rd	Win & Pl
NH Flat	2	0	0	1	302
Hurdles	4	0	0	1	483
Career Total	**8**	**1**	**0**	**2**	**4680**

105	4/01	List	2m	NHF	HVY	£3895

Total win prize-money £3895

Going: Sf: 0-5 GS: 0-1 Gd: 0-0 GF: - Fm: 0-0
Distance: 2m/2m3: 0-3 2m4-2m7: 0-3 3m+: 0-0
Track: LH: 0-2 RH: 0-2 Tight: 0-2 Gall: 0-1
Aids: Bl: 0-1 Vi: 0-0 Tstrap: 0-0
Best Rating: 105 4/01 List 2m heavy NHF

A bumper winner in Ireland, she acts on heavy ground. Fair form since switching to race in England at trips around two and a half miles. Has given the impression that she will stay further.

All On My Own (USA)

81(101h) (76h)85

7-y-o ch g Unbridled (USA)-Someforall (USA) (One For All (USA))

I W McInnes Ian McInnes

Placings:450/000P00-0006 (2305)

2001/02: 16^{0}GF, 16^{0}G, 17^{0}G, 16^{6}GF

	Starts	1st	2nd	3rd	Win & Pl
Hurdles	3	0	0	0	0
Chases	1	0	0	0	0
Career Total	**13**	**0**	**0**	**0**	**0**

Going: Sf: 0-0 GS: 0-0 Gd: 0-2 GF: - Fm: 0-2
Distance: 2m/2m3: 0-4 2m4-2m7: 0-0 3m+: 0-0
Track: LH: 0-4 RH: 0-0 Tight: 0-4 Gall: 0-0
Aids: Bl: 0-3 Vi: 0-0 Tstrap: 0-0
Best Rating: 90 10/99 Hexm 2m good NHF

All Sewn Up

10-y-o ch g Jazetas-Rose Of Bradford (Levanter)

R J Baker Trefusis Farm

Placings:6/0630P/6 (1726)

2001/02: 19^{6}F

	Starts	1st	2nd	3rd	Win & Pl
Chases	1	0	0	0	0
Career Total	**7**	**0**	**0**	**1**	**381**

Going: Sf: 0-0 GS: 0-0 Gd: 0-0 GF: - Fm: 0-1
Distance: 2m/2m3: 0-1 2m4-2m7: 0-0 3m+: 0-0
Track: LH: 0-0 RH: 0-1 Tight: 0-1 Gall: 0-0
Aids: Bl: 0-0 Vi: 0-0 Tstrap: 0-0
Best Rating: 64 10/96 Chel 2m110y firm Hdl

All Sonsilver (FR)

86 102

5-y-o b g Son Of Silver-All Licette (FR) (Native Guile (USA))

M Todhunter Sir Robert Ogden

Placings:01 (4438)

2001/02: 16^{0}S, 16^{1}S

	Starts	1st	2nd	3rd	Win & Pl
Hurdles	2	1	0	0	3063
Career Total	**2**	**1**	**0**	**0**	**3063**

93	3/02	Kels	2m110y	E Hdl	SFT	£3062

Total win prize-money £3063

Going: Sf: 1-2 GS: 0-0 Gd: 0-0 GF: - Fm: 0-0
Distance: 2m/2m3: 1-2 2m4-2m7: 0-0 3m+: 0-0
Track: LH: 1-2 RH: 0-0 Tight: 1-1 Gall: 0-0
Aids: Bl: 0-0 Vi: 0-0 Tstrap: 0-0
Best Rating: 93 3/02 Kels 2m110y soft Hdl

A brother to a winning chaser in France, he has a pronounced knee action. He did not show much on this racecourse debut but stayed on well to win at Kelso on his second start. Followed up at Hexham early in the new season.

All Things Nice

11-y-o ch m Sweet Monday-Penny's Affair (Chingnu)

M R Daniell Mrs M R Daniell

Placings:P53 (4685)

2001/02: 19^{P}S, 16^{5}S, 16^{3}GF

	Starts	1st	2nd	3rd	Win & Pl
Chases	3	0	0	1	273
Career Total	**3**	**0**	**0**	**1**	**273**

Going: Sf: 0-2 GS: 0-0 Gd: 0-0 GF: - Fm: 0-1
Distance: 2m/2m3: 0-2 2m4-2m7: 0-1 3m+: 0-0
Track: LH: 0-1 RH: 0-2 Tight: 0-0 Gall: 0-1

Aids: Bl: 0-0 Vi: 0-0 Tstrap: 0-0
Best Rating: 70 4/02 Hrfd 2m gd-fm Ch

All Trix (IRE)

96 **93**

9-y-o br g Buckskin (FR)-Night Trix (IRE) (Spin Of A Coin)
Miss Lucinda V Russell (A Crook 15/5) A D Stewart

Placings:P0F2305/P24F/PPF513P-0P45P (2586)
2001/02: 26^{0}GF, 27^{P}G, 20^{4}S, 24^{5}GS, 29^{P}S

	Starts	1st	2nd	3rd	Win & Pl
Chases	5	0	0	0	535
Career Total	**23**	**1**	**2**	**2**	**6380**

86 1/01 Sthl 3m110y F(0-90)HCh HVY £2548
Total win prize-money £2548

Going: Sf: 0-2 GS: 0-1 Gd: 0-1 GF: - Fm: 0-1
Distance: 2m/2m3: 0-0 2m4-2m7: 0-1 3m+: 0-4
Track: LH: 0-3 RH: 0-1 Tight: 0-1 Gall: 0-1
Aids: Bl: 0-1 Vi: 0-0 Tstrap: 0-0
Best Rating: 112 1/99 Punc 2m4f heavy Ch

All-Allone

9-y-o ch g Adbass (USA)-Lady Alone (Mr Fluorocarbon)
D Mullarkey Dune Racing

Placings:FP-5 (0593)
2001/02: 20^{5}GF

	Starts	1st	2nd	3rd	Win & Pl
Hurdles	1	0	0	0	0
Career Total	**3**	**0**	**0**	**0**	**0**

Going: Sf: 0-0 GS: 0-0 Gd: 0-0 GF: - Fm: 0-1
Distance: 2m/2m3: 0-0 2m4-2m7: 0-1 3m+: 0-0
Track: LH: 0-1 RH: 0-0 Tight: 0-1 Gall: 0-0
Aids: Bl: 0-0 Vi: 0-0 Tstrap: 0-0
Best Rating: 80 10/00 Bang 2m1f soft Hdl

Allanton Brig

6-y-o b g Milieu-Lurdenlaw Rose (New Brig)
C W Fairhurst I Anderson

Placings:0 (4436)
2001/02: 16^{0}HY

	Starts	1st	2nd	3rd	Win & Pl
NH Flat	1	0	0	0	
Career Total	**1**	**0**	**0**	**0**	

Going: Sf: 0-1 GS: 0-0 Gd: 0-0 GF: - Fm: 0-0
Distance: 2m/2m3: 0-1 2m4-2m7: 0-0 3m+: 0-0
Track: LH: 0-0 RH: 0-0 Tight: 0-0 Gall: 0-0
Aids: Bl: 0-0 Vi: 0-0 Tstrap: 0-0
Best Rating:

Allegation

91 **88**

12-y-o b g Dominion-Pageantry (Welsh Pageant)
M C Pipe Martin Pipe Racing Club

Placings:32211103/2121112P110/00P0/6125/56500026/04440/36002/040P45P5-0 (0073)
2001/02: 19^{0}G

	Starts	1st	2nd	3rd	Win & Pl
Hurdles	1	0	0	0	
Career Total	**54**	**10**	**8**	**3**	**65426**

143 2/97 Hayd 2m4f B(0-145)HHdl G-S £4815
137 3/95 Chel 2m4f110y B Hdl SFT £10601
142 2/95 Wwck 2m4f110y A Hdl SFT £9920
145 12/94 Wwck 2m4f110y (0-135)HHdl GD £3756
137 11/94 Worc 2m4f (0-125)HHdl SFT £2075
131 11/94 Chep 2m110y (0-135)HHdl SFT £3600
116 10/94 Chep 2m110y (0-115)HHdl GD £2202
109 2/94 Sthl 2m2f Hdl STD £1484
90 1/94 Sthl 2m6f Hdl STD £1698
96 12/93 Donc 2m110y HHdl GD £2110
Total win prize-money £42261

Going: Sf: 0-0 GS: 0-0 Gd: 0-1 GF: - Fm: 0-0
Distance: 2m/2m3: 0-1 2m4-2m7: 0-0 3m+: 0-0
Track: LH: 0-0 RH: 0-1 Tight: 0-0 Gall: 0-0
Aids: Bl: 0-0 Vi: 0-1 Tstrap: 0-0
Best Rating: 146 4/98 Chel 2m5f110y heavy Hdl

Allegiance

85 **60**

7-y-o b g Rock Hopper-So Precise (FR) (Balidar)
P Wegmann P Wegmann

Placings:P15000532040/004/11626430P-0 (1653)
2001/02: 17^{0}G

	Starts	1st	2nd	3rd	Win & Pl
Hurdles	1	0	0	0	
Career Total	**25**	**3**	**2**	**2**	**10600**

100 11/00 Wwck 2m F(0-100)HHdl HVY £1940
100 11/00 NAbb 2m1f F(0-110)HHdl HVY £2678
79 9/98 MRas 2m1f110y G Hdl GD £1562
Total win prize-money £6180

Going: Sf: 0-0 GS: 0-0 Gd: 0-1 GF: - Fm: 0-0
Distance: 2m/2m3: 0-1 2m4-2m7: 0-0 3m+: 0-0
Track: LH: 0-1 RH: 0-0 Tight: 0-1 Gall: 0-0
Aids: Bl: 0-0 Vi: 0-0 Tstrap: 0-0
Best Rating: 100 12/00 Chep 2m110y soft Hdl

Allied Imperial

95 **75**

6-y-o b m Morpeth-Super Sarena (IRE) (Taufan (USA))
R G Frost Mrs J McCormack

Placings:54063/02505-606 (1629)
2001/02: 17^{6}GS, 16^{0}GF, 21^{6}GF

	Starts	1st	2nd	3rd	Win & Pl
Hurdles	3	0	0	0	0
Career Total	**13**	**0**	**1**	**1**	**682**

Going: Sf: 0-0 GS: 0-1 Gd: 0-0 GF: - Fm: 0-2
Distance: 2m/2m3: 0-2 2m4-2m7: 0-1 3m+: 0-0
Track: LH: 0-1 RH: 0-1 Tight: 0-0 Gall: 0-0
Aids: Bl: 0-0 Vi: 0-0 Tstrap: 0-2
Best Rating: 81 7/00 Worc 2m4f gd-fm Hdl

Allimac (IRE)

109(102h) (104h)**123**

5-y-o b g Alphabatim (USA)-Firewood (IRE) (Brush Aside (USA))
Miss H C Knight Mrs T P Radford

Placings:20-2204 (4540)
2001/02: 19^{2}GS, 16^{2}G, 20^{0}G, 19^{4}G

	Starts	1st	2nd	3rd	Win & Pl
Hurdles	4	0	2	0	1722
Career Total	**6**	**0**	**3**	**0**	**2218**

Going: Sf: 0-0 GS: 0-1 Gd: 0-3 GF: - Fm: 0-0
Distance: 2m/2m3: 0-1 2m4-2m7: 0-3 3m+: 0-0
Track: LH: 0-1 RH: 0-3 Tight: 0-1 Gall: 0-1
Aids: Bl: 0-0 Vi: 0-0 Tstrap: 0-0
Best Rating: 104 11/01 Winc 2m good Hdl

Novice hurder. Acts on fast ground and is effective at around two miles.

Allotrope (IRE)

102 **86**

7-y-o b g Nashwan (USA)-Graphite (USA) (Mr Prospector (USA))
Mrs M Reveley Mrs M Reveley

Placings:525/3P05430-10 (1744)
2001/02: 22^{1}G, 22^{0}GS

	Starts	1st	2nd	3rd	Win & Pl
Hurdles	2	1	0	0	2856
Career Total	**12**	**1**	**1**	**2**	**4099**

86 10/01 Kels 2m6f110y F(0-105)HHdl GD £2856
Total win prize-money £2856

Going: Sf: 0-0 GS: 0-1 Gd: 1-1 GF: - Fm: 0-0
Distance: 2m/2m3: 0-0 **2m4-2m7: 1-2** 3m+: 0-0
Track: **LH: 1-2** RH: 0-0 **Tight: 1-2** Gall: 0-0
Aids: Bl: 0-0 Vi: 0-0 Tstrap: 0-0
Best Rating: 98 10/99 Kels 2m6f110y good Hdl

Allow (IRE)

11-y-o b g Glow (USA)-All Found (USA) (Alleged (USA))
Ms Nicky Hugo (B Llewellyn 17/2) K Rowlands

Placings:03500340/51414254/P222/P41/4564440/320P5P-P (4091)
2001/02: 24^{P}S

	Starts	1st	2nd	3rd	Win & Pl
Chases	1	0	0	0	
Career Total	**37**	**3**	**5**	**3**	**18301**

117 11/98 Extr 2m6f110y D(0-125)HCh SFT £4182
94 11/96 Newb 2m5f E(0-110)HHdl G-S £2880
91 11/96 Extr 2m3f E(0-100)HHdl G-S £2547
Total win prize-money £9609

Going: Sf: 0-1 GS: 0-0 Gd: 0-0 GF: - Fm: 0-0
Distance: 2m/2m3: 0-0 2m4-2m7: 0-0 3m+: 0-1
Track: LH: 0-0 RH: 0-0 Tight: 0-0 Gall: 0-0
Aids: Bl: 0-0 Vi: 0-0 Tstrap: 0-0
Best Rating: 117 11/98 Extr 2m6f110y soft Ch

Allten Grazed

66 **40**

6-y-o b m Sea Raven (IRE)-Ellerton Song (Cree Song)
C Grant J B Farnaby Turf Growers

Placings:00-0P (1346)
2001/02: 17^{0}G, 17^{P}GF

	Starts	1st	2nd	3rd	Win & Pl
Hurdles	2	0	0	0	
Career Total	**4**	**0**	**0**	**0**	

Going: Sf: 0-0 GS: 0-0 Gd: 0-1 GF: - Fm: 0-1
Distance: 2m/2m3: 0-2 2m4-2m7: 0-0 3m+: 0-0
Track: LH: 0-2 RH: 0-0 Tight: 0-2 Gall: 0-0
Aids: Bl: 0-0 Vi: 0-0 Tstrap: 0-0
Best Rating: 45 12/00 Newc 2m soft NHF

Allthewayfromtuam (IRE)

(88h) (62h)

8-y-o b/br m Mandalus-Chancery Vision (Pauper)

Mrs A M Naughton Andrew Nicholls

Placings:PP-064603P (2634)

2001/02: 19^{P}GF, 17^{6}G, 24^{4}GS, 20^{6}G, 20^{0}G, 20^{3}GS, 25^{P}S

	Starts	1st	2nd	3rd	Win & Pl
Hurdles	5	0	0	0	0
Chases	2	0	0	1	600
Career Total	**9**	**0**	**0**	**1**	**600**

Going: Sf: 0-1 GS: 0-2 Gd: 0-3 GF: - Fm: 0-1
Distance: 2m/2m3: 0-1 2m4-2m7: 0-4 3m+: 0-2
Track: LH: 0-4 RH: 0-3 Tight: 0-5 Gall: 0-0
Aids: Bl: 0-0 Vi: 0-0 Tstrap: 0-0
Best Rating: **62** 9/01 Sedg 2m1f good Hdl

Alltime Dancer (IRE)

10-y-o b g Waajib-Dance On Lady (Grundy)

Mrs C F Lambert (Dr J R J Naylor 11/6) Major Charles Lambert

Placings:1213141144/5450003651/6-4540 (4135)

2001/02: 20^{4}GF, 21^{5}GF, 26^{4}G, 24^{0}G

	Starts	1st	2nd	3rd	Win & Pl
Chases	4	0	0	0	407
Career Total	**25**	**6**	**1**	**2**	**21185**

116	4/97	Plum	2m4f	E(0-115)HHdl	G-F	£2241
110	3/96	Newb	2m110y	D Hdl	G-S	£2941
122	12/95	Sand	2m110y	C Hdl	GD	£3525
122	11/95	Sand	2m110y	C Hdl	G-F	£3355
110	10/95	Extr	2m1f110y	E Hdl	GD	£2122
83	7/95	MRas	2m1f110y	D Hdl	G-F	£2630

Total win prize-money £16816

Going: Sf: 0-0 GS: 0-0 Gd: 0-2 GF: - Fm: 0-2
Distance: 2m/2m3: 0-0 2m4-2m7: 0-2 3m+: 0-2
Track: LH: 0-2 RH: 0-2 Tight: 0-2 Gall: 0-1
Aids: Bl: 0-0 Vi: 0-0 Tstrap: 0-0
Best Rating: **125** 10/96 Chep 2m110y good Hdl

Almanoso

99 78

6-y-o b m Teenoso (USA)-Almanot (Remainder Man)

R Curtis Guildings Racing Club

Placings:*6/40*550-6230U (4108)

2001/02: 22^{6}GS, 26^{2}G, 24^{3}S, 24^{0}S, 24^{U}S

	Starts	1st	2nd	3rd	Win & Pl
Hurdles	5	0	1	1	855
Career Total	**11**	**0**	**1**	**1**	**855**

Going: Sf: 0-3 GS: 0-1 Gd: 0-1 GF: - Fm: 0-0
Distance: 2m/2m3: 0-0 2m4-2m7: 0-1 3m+: 0-4
Track: LH: 0-1 RH: 0-4 Tight: 0-3 Gall: 0-1
Aids: Bl: 0-0 Vi: 0-0 Tstrap: 0-0
Best Rating: **99** 4/00 Asct 2m110y soft NHF

Plating-class staying hurdler, best efforts when ridden from the front.

Almapa

105(59c) 86

10-y-o ch g Absalom-More Fun (Malicious)

R J Baker P Slade

Placings:23341330226333/U4P112334U6/F34213446U4/4332/343512-4063 (0841)

2001/02: 19^{4}F, 16^{0}GF, 17^{6}G, 16^{3}G

	Starts	1st	2nd	3rd	Win & Pl
Hurdles	4	0	0	1	276
Career Total	**50**	**5**	**7**	**16**	**21258**

96	8/00	NAbb	2m1f	F(0-100)HHdl	GD	£2604
96	10/98	Tntn	2m1f	G(0-90)HHdl	FRM	£1836
94	10/97	Tntn	2m1f	E(0-115)HHdl	FRM	£3737
82	9/97	Strf	2m110y	F Hdl	GD	£1931
79	10/96	Tntn	2m1f	G Hdl	HRD	£2005

Total win prize-money £12115

Going: Sf: 0-0 GS: 0-0 Gd: 0-2 GF: - Fm: 0-2
Distance: 2m/2m3: 0-3 2m4-2m7: 0-1 3m+: 0-0
Track: LH: 0-2 RH: 0-2 Tight: 0-2 Gall: 0-1
Aids: Bl: 0-0 Vi: 0-0 Tstrap: 0-0
Best Rating: **97** 9/00 NAbb 2m110y gd-fm Ch

Pays his way in lowly company on fast ground.

Almikino (IRE)

(80c) (55c)39

9-y-o b g Altountash-Lucky Penny Lass (Kampala)

Miss S E Forster (R A Ross 26/5) A S Nelson

Placings:646 (1238)

2001/02: 20^{6}GF, 20^{4}GF, 22^{6}GS

	Starts	1st	2nd	3rd	Win & Pl
Hurdles	1	0	0	0	0
Chases	2	0	0	0	0
Career Total	**3**	**0**	**0**	**0**	**0**

Going: Sf: 0-0 GS: 0-1 Gd: 0-0 GF: - Fm: 0-2
Distance: 2m/2m3: 0-0 2m4-2m7: 0-3 3m+: 0-0
Track: LH: 0-3 RH: 0-0 Tight: 0-2 Gall: 0-0
Aids: Bl: 0-0 Vi: 0-0 Tstrap: 0-0
Best Rating: **55** 5/01 Strf 2m4f gd-fm Ch

Alminstar

87 69

6-y-o br m Minshaanshu Amad (USA)-Joytime (John De Coombe)

Mrs L Richards Mrs G M Gooderham

Placings:F4 (1222)

2001/02: 16^{F}S, 18^{4}GF

	Starts	1st	2nd	3rd	Win & Pl
Hurdles	2	0	0	0	0
Career Total	**2**	**0**	**0**	**0**	**0**

Going: Sf: 0-1 GS: 0-0 Gd: 0-0 GF: - Fm: 0-1
Distance: 2m/2m3: 0-2 2m4-2m7: 0-0 3m+: 0-0
Track: LH: 0-2 RH: 0-0 Tight: 0-2 Gall: 0-0
Aids: Bl: 0-0 Vi: 0-0 Tstrap: 0-0
Best Rating: **69** 8/01 Font 2m2f110y gd-fm Hdl

Almost An Angel (IRE)

74 29

12-y-o ch g Lancastrian-Ballykytton (Signa Infesta)

Simon T Lewis Simon T Lewis

Placings:0P00/PPPP0 (3815)

2001/02: 19^{P}GF, 22^{P}HY, 20^{P}G, 19^{P}S, 16^{0}S

	Starts	1st	2nd	3rd	Win & Pl
Chases	5	0	0	0	
Career Total	**9**	**0**	**0**	**0**	

Going: Sf: 0-3 GS: 0-0 Gd: 0-1 GF: - Fm: 0-1
Distance: 2m/2m3: 0-2 2m4-2m7: 0-3 3m+: 0-0
Track: LH: 0-0 RH: 0-5 Tight: 0-2 Gall: 0-0
Aids: Bl: 0-0 Vi: 0-0 Tstrap: 0-0
Best Rating: **70** 7/98 Limk 2m2f yield Hdl

Almost Broke

90f 104f

5-y-o ch g Nearly A Hand-Teletex (Pollerton)

Ferdy Murphy A Howland Jackson

Placings:2 (4377)

2001/02: 16^{2}S

	Starts	1st	2nd	3rd	Win & Pl
NH Flat	1	0	1	0	584
Career Total	**1**	**0**	**1**	**0**	**584**

Going: Sf: 0-1 GS: 0-0 Gd: 0-0 GF: - Fm: 0-0
Distance: 2m/2m3: 0-1 2m4-2m7: 0-0 3m+: 0-0
Track: LH: 0-0 RH: 0-1 Tight: 0-0 Gall: 0-0
Aids: Bl: 0-0 Vi: 0-0 Tstrap: 0-0
Best Rating: **104** 3/02 Ludl 2m soft NHF

Just caught on his bumper debut.

Alpenstock (FR)

6-y-o b g Mister Mat (FR)-Altaraza (FR) (Jolie Mars (FR))

A Hollingsworth D Wellon

Placings:34000/P (0421)

2001/02: 24^{P}G

	Starts	1st	2nd	3rd	Win & Pl
Hurdles	1	0	0	0	
Career Total	**6**	**0**	**0**	**1**	**372**

Going: Sf: 0-0 GS: 0-0 Gd: 0-1 GF: - Fm: 0-0
Distance: 2m/2m3: 0-0 2m4-2m7: 0-0 3m+: 0-1
Track: LH: 0-1 RH: 0-0 Tight: 0-1 Gall: 0-0
Aids: Bl: 0-0 Vi: 0-0 Tstrap: 0-0
Best Rating: **93** 11/99 Uttx 2m gd-sft Hdl

Alpha Gold (IRE)

102(88h) (71h)97

7-y-o ch g Alphabatim (USA)-Show M How (Ashmore (FR))

H D Daly Alpha Gold Partnership

Placings:60P21U2FU (4889)

2001/02: 21^{6}GF, 20^{0}S, 22^{P}S, 23^{2}S, 24^{1}S, 25^{U}S, 24^{2}GF, 25^{F}GF, 26^{U}G

	Starts	1st	2nd	3rd	Win & Pl
Hurdles	3	0	0	0	0
Chases	6	1	2	0	4905
Career Total	**9**	**1**	**2**	**0**	**4905**

91	3/02	Hntg	3m	F(0-90)HCh	SFT	£2646

Total win prize-money £2646

Going: Sf: 1-5 GS: 0-0 Gd: 0-1 GF: - Fm: 0-3
Distance: 2m/2m3: 0-0 2m4-2m7: 0-3 **3m+: 1-6**
Track: LH: 0-2 **RH: 1-5** Tight: 0-1 **Gall: 1-1**

Aids: Bl: 0-0 Vi: 0-0 Tstrap: 0-0
Best Rating: 97 4/02 Wwck 3m110y gd-fm Ch

Ex-pointer, confirmed promise he showed on chasing debut with a win over three miles in a weak event in March 2002. Acts on soft ground, but has handled faster.

Alpha Leather

87(86h) (62h)46
11-y-o b g Zambrano-Harvey's Choice (Whistlefield)
L P Grassick Postlip Racing

Placings:6400000/B605555/2632P400/306S**5064545U0**/P6000 (4131)
2001/02: 24^{P}G, 22^{6}G, 22^{0}G, 24^{0}GF, 26^{0}G

	Starts	1st	2nd	3rd	Win & Pl
Hurdles	5	0	0	0	0
Career Total	**40**	**0**	**2**	**2**	**2608**

Going: Sf: 0-0 GS: 0-0 Gd: 0-4 GF: - Fm: 0-1
Distance: 2m/2m3: 0-0 2m4-2m7: 0-2 3m+: 0-3
Track: LH: 0-3 RH: 0-2 Tight: 0-2 Gall: 0-0
Aids: Bl: 0-0 Vi: 0-0 Tstrap: 0-0
Best Rating: 85 11/95 Uttx 2m gd-fm NHF

Alpha Romana (IRE)

116+
8-y-o b g Alphabatim (USA)-Stella Romana (Roman Warrior)
Mrs Susan E Busby Miss Susan E Busby

Placings:06056/0030/**P21** (4534)
2001/02: 20^{P}S, 21^{2}G, 21^{1}G

	Starts	1st	2nd	3rd	Win & Pl
Chases	3	1	1	0	2834
Career Total	**12**	**1**	**1**	**1**	**3097**

99 4/02 Fknm 2m5f110y H Ch GD £2212
Total win prize-money £2212

Going: Sf: 0-1 GS: 0-0 Gd: 1-2 GF: - Fm: 0-0
Distance: 2m/2m3: 0-0 **2m4-2m7: 1-3** 3m+: 0-0
Track: **LH: 1-2** RH: 0-1 **Tight: 1-2** Gall: 0-0
Aids: Bl: 0-0 Vi: 0-0 Tstrap: 0-0
Best Rating: 99 4/02 Fknm 2m5f110y good Ch

Hunter chaser, effective at below three miles and suited by good/fast ground. Progressive.

Alpha Two (IRE)

72 65
8-y-o ch g Alphabatim (USA)-Marys Bard (Le Bavard (FR))
R T Phillips Gerald Myers

Placings:PP/216P-60 (1395)
2001/02: 22^{6}G, 24^{0}GF

	Starts	1st	2nd	3rd	Win & Pl
Hurdles	2	0	0	0	0
Career Total	**8**	**1**	**1**	**0**	**3351**

95 8/00 Uttx 3m110y E Hdl G-F £2687
Total win prize-money £2688

Going: Sf: 0-0 GS: 0-0 Gd: 0-1 GF: - Fm: 0-1
Distance: 2m/2m3: 0-0 2m4-2m7: 0-1 3m+: 0-1
Track: LH: 0-2 RH: 0-0 Tight: 0-1 Gall: 0-0
Aids: Bl: 0-0 Vi: 0-0 Tstrap: 0-0
Best Rating: 95 8/00 Uttx 3m110y gd-fm Hdl

Alphacall

94 78
4-y-o b f Forzando-Second Call (Kind Of Hush)
T D Walford (T D Easterby 6/8) J W Nellis

Placings:14600 (4765)
2001/02: 16^{1}GF, 16^{4}GF, 17^{6}G, 16^{0}G, 16^{0}GF

	Starts	1st	2nd	3rd	Win & Pl
Hurdles	5	1	0	0	2933
Career Total	**5**	**1**	**0**	**0**	**2933**

78 8/01 Uttx 2m E Hdl G-F £2933
Total win prize-money £2933

Going: Sf: 0-0 GS: 0-0 Gd: 0-2 GF: - Fm: 1-3
Distance: **2m/2m3: 1-5** 2m4-2m7: 0-0 3m+: 0-0
Track: **LH: 1-4** RH: 0-0 Tight: 0-2 Gall: 0-1
Aids: Bl: 0-0 Vi: 0-0 Tstrap: 0-0
Best Rating: 78 9/01 Sedg 2m1f good Hdl

Regressive hurdle form since winning over the minimum trip in summer 2001.

Alpheus (IRE)

101 103
7-y-o b/br g Alphabatim (USA)-Cold Evening (IRE) (Strong Gale)
O Sherwood Miss Liz Clark

Placings:40B5-1P (0502)
2001/02: 21^{1}G, 21^{P}GF

	Starts	1st	2nd	3rd	Win & Pl
Hurdles	2	1	0	0	3024
Career Total	**6**	**1**	**0**	**0**	**3024**

103 5/01 Sedg 2m5f110y F(0-100)HHdl GD £3024
Total win prize-money £3024

Going: Sf: 0-0 GS: 0-0 Gd: 1-1 GF: - Fm: 0-1
Distance: 2m/2m3: 0-0 **2m4-2m7: 1-2** 3m+: 0-0
Track: **LH: 1-1** RH: 0-1 **Tight: 1-1** Gall: 0-1
Aids: Bl: 0-0 Vi: 0-0 Tstrap: 0-0
Best Rating: 103 5/01 Sedg 2m5f110y good Hdl

Alpine Hideaway (IRE)

96 81
9-y-o b g Tirol-Arbour (USA) (Graustark)
J S Wainwright Peter Easterby

Placings:534341/1135**PP**6050/34/0-554000 (2903)
2001/02: 17^{5}GF, 17^{5}GS, 17^{4}G, 20^{0}G, 16^{0}S, 16^{0}GS

	Starts	1st	2nd	3rd	Win & Pl
Hurdles	6	0	0	0	0
Career Total	**25**	**3**	**0**	**4**	**8832**

113 6/98 MRas 2m1f110y E(0-110)HHdl GD £2903
112 5/98 Weth 2m D Hdl G-F £2897
102 3/98 Newc 2m F Hdl G-F £1896
Total win prize-money £7697

Going: Sf: 0-1 GS: 0-2 Gd: 0-2 GF: - Fm: 0-1
Distance: 2m/2m3: 0-5 2m4-2m7: 0-1 3m+: 0-0
Track: LH: 0-3 RH: 0-3 Tight: 0-4 Gall: 0-1
Aids: Bl: 0-0 Vi: 0-2 Tstrap: 0-0
Best Rating: 113 9/98 Sedg 2m1f good Hdl

A winner of two handicap hurdles in the summer of 1998. Lightly-raced and dropped to selling company since.

Alpine Message

99 79
5-y-o b m Tirol-Jupiter's Message (Jupiter Island)
J R Jenkins The Wayward Lads

Placings:5-600P (4315)
2001/02: 16^{6}G, 16^{0}G, 16^{0}S, 16^{P}HY

	Starts	1st	2nd	3rd	Win & Pl
NH Flat	2	0	0	0	0
Hurdles	2	0	0	0	0
Career Total	**5**	**0**	**0**	**0**	**0**

Going: Sf: 0-2 GS: 0-0 Gd: 0-2 GF: - Fm: 0-0
Distance: 2m/2m3: 0-4 2m4-2m7: 0-0 3m+: 0-0
Track: LH: 0-3 RH: 0-1 Tight: 0-1 Gall: 0-1
Aids: Bl: 0-0 Vi: 0-0 Tstrap: 0-0
Best Rating: 83 11/01 Chel 2m110y good NHF

Alpine Star

90f 106f
5-y-o ch g Alflora (IRE)-Northwood Star (IRE) (Henbit (USA))
J T Gifford S N J Embiricos

Placings:30 (4639)
2001/02: 16^{3}GS, 16^{0}GF

	Starts	1st	2nd	3rd	Win & Pl
NH Flat	2	0	0	1	365
Career Total	**2**	**0**	**0**	**1**	**365**

Going: Sf: 0-0 GS: 0-1 Gd: 0-0 GF: - Fm: 0-1
Distance: 2m/2m3: 0-2 2m4-2m7: 0-0 3m+: 0-0
Track: LH: 0-0 RH: 0-2 Tight: 0-0 Gall: 0-0
Aids: Bl: 0-0 Vi: 0-0 Tstrap: 0-0
Best Rating: 106 3/02 Sand 2m110y gd-sft NHF

Ran a promising debut in a Sandown bumper and looks to have a future.

Alscot Foxy Lady (IRE)

74 36
5-y-o b m Foxhound (USA)-Arena (Sallust)
R Dickin Warwick Members Two

Placings:0F00 (4654)
2001/02: 17^{0}G, 16^{F}S, 16^{0}GS, 17^{0}GS

	Starts	1st	2nd	3rd	Win & Pl
NH Flat	1	0	0	0	0
Hurdles	3	0	0	0	0
Career Total	**4**	**0**	**0**	**0**	

Going: Sf: 0-1 GS: 0-2 Gd: 0-1 GF: - Fm: 0-0
Distance: 2m/2m3: 0-4 2m4-2m7: 0-0 3m+: 0-0
Track: LH: 0-2 RH: 0-2 Tight: 0-3 Gall: 0-0
Aids: Bl: 0-0 Vi: 0-0 Tstrap: 0-0
Best Rating: 37 10/01 Bang 2m1f good NHF

Alsina

11-y-o b g Alias Smith (USA)-Tersina (Lighter)
Peter Innes Peter Innes

Placings:P (4335)
2001/02: 27^{P}S

	Starts	1st	2nd	3rd	Win & Pl
Chases	1	0	0	0	
Career Total	**1**	**0**	**0**	**0**	

Going: Sf: 0-1 GS: 0-0 Gd: 0-0 GF: - Fm: 0-0

Distance: 2m/2m3: 0-0 2m4-2m7: 0-0 3m+: 0-1
Track: LH: 0-1 RH: 0-0 Tight: 0-1 Gall: 0-0
Aids: Bl: 0-0 Vi: 0-0 Tstrap: 0-0
Best Rating:

Multiple point winner but flopped under Rules on his debut at an advanced age.

Alska (FR)

9-y-o b/br m Leading Counsel (USA)-Kolkwitzia (FR) (The Wonder (FR))
P L Southcombe P L Southcombe

Placings:P00UUP00/332/U05P6P-3U02U (4638)
2001/02: 21[3]GF, 24[U]GF, 24[0]S, 25[2]G, 19[U]GF

	Starts	1st	2nd	3rd	Win & Pl
Chases	5	0	1	1	739
Career Total	**22**	**0**	**2**	**3**	**2529**

Going: Sf: 0-1 GS: 0-0 Gd: 0-1 GF: - Fm: 0-3
Distance: 2m/2m3: 0-0 2m4-2m7: 0-2 3m+: 0-3
Track: LH: 0-1 RH: 0-4 Tight: 0-1 Gall: 0-0
Aids: Bl: 0-0 Vi: 0-0 Tstrap: 0-0
Best Rating: **85** 3/02 Winc 3m1f110y good Ch

Alstack (IRE)

81 **44**
11-y-o ch g Mister Lord (USA)-Laura Nore (Laurence O)
R Curtis Cohen Glazer Green Harriers

Placings:430-00P (1443)
2001/02: 24[0]F, 24[0]GF, 26[P]GF

	Starts	1st	2nd	3rd	Win & Pl
Chases	3	0	0	0	
Career Total	**6**	**0**	**0**	**1**	**740**

Going: Sf: 0-0 GS: 0-0 Gd: 0-0 GF: - Fm: 0-3
Distance: 2m/2m3: 0-0 2m4-2m7: 0-0 3m+: 0-3
Track: LH: 0-0 RH: 0-2 Tight: 0-2 Gall: 0-1
Aids: Bl: 0-3 Vi: 0-0 Tstrap: 0-0
Best Rating: **84** 8/00 NAbb 3m2f110y gd-sft Ch

Alta

97(82h) **124**
9-y-o b m Arctic Lord-Thames Air (Crash Course)
N A Twiston-Davies The Alchemists

Placings:2/211103522/1F5F5003/04053223-5 (0074)
2001/02: 19[5]G

	Starts	1st	2nd	3rd	Win & Pl
Chases	1	0	0	0	0
Career Total	**27**	**4**	**6**	**4**	**20195**

110	5/99	Extr	2m1f110y	E Hdl	G-F	£2705
111	10/98	Extr	2m1f	E Hdl	GD	£2389
116	10/98	Bang	2m1f	H NHF	GD	£1350
101	5/98	Bang	2m1f	H NHF	GD	£1318

Total win prize-money £7764

Going: Sf: 0-0 GS: 0-0 Gd: 0-1 GF: - Fm: 0-0
Distance: 2m/2m3: 0-0 2m4-2m7: 0-1 3m+: 0-0
Track: LH: 0-0 RH: 0-1 Tight: 0-0 Gall: 0-0
Aids: Bl: 0-0 Vi: 0-0 Tstrap: 0-1
Best Rating: **130** 2/01 Ludl 3m gd-sft Ch

A bumpes and hurdle winner, she finished lame in May 2001 and has been absent since. Looks to need a sound surface.

Altapeter

105(108h) (112h)**125**
7-y-o b g Mandalus-Always Shining (Tug Of War)
P Beaumont Miss J Hey

Placings:566014/421500201-3**P16P** (3857)
2001/02: 21[3]S, 20[P]GS, 25[1]GS, 24[6]S, 24[P]S

	Starts	1st	2nd	3rd	Win & Pl
Hurdles	1	0	0	1	1298
Chases	4	1	0	0	4362
Career Total	**20**	**4**	**2**	**1**	**16020**

125	1/02	Weth	3m1f	D Ch	G-S	£4361
112	4/01	MRas	2m5f110y	F(0-100)HHdl	HVY	£2992
110	10/00	Sedg	2m5f110y	F(0-105)HHdl	G-S	£2688
105	4/00	Kels	2m110y	D Hdl	SFT	£2744

Total win prize-money £12787

Going: Sf: 0-3 GS: 1-2 Gd: 0-0 GF: - Fm: 0-0
Distance: 2m/2m3: 0-0 2m4-2m7: 0-2 **3m+: 1-3**
Track: **LH: 1-3** RH: 0-2 Tight: 0-2 Gall: 0-2
Aids: Bl: 0-0 Vi: 0-0 Tstrap: 0-0
Best Rating: **125** 1/02 Weth 3m1f gd-sft Ch

A fair hurdler, he likes testing ground. Pulled up on chasing debut, but scored in good style at Wetherby in January 2002, proving he gets three miles plus.

Altareek (USA)

101f **110f**
5-y-o b g Alleged (USA)-Black Tulip (FR) (Fabulous Dancer (USA))
J M Jefferson Dean Bostock And Raymond Bostock

Placings:100 (1873)
2001/02: 17[1]GS, 16[0]S, 16[0]GF

	Starts	1st	2nd	3rd	Win & Pl
NH Flat	3	1	0	0	1743
Career Total	**3**	**1**	**0**	**0**	**1743**

110	3/02	MRas	2m1f110y	H NHF	G-S	£1743

Total win prize-money £1743

Going: Sf: 0-1 GS: 1-1 Gd: 0-0 GF: - Fm: 0-1
Distance: **2m/2m3: 1-3** 2m4-2m7: 0-0 3m+: 0-0
Track: LH: 0-2 **RH: 1-1 Tight: 1-1** Gall: 0-0
Aids: Bl: 0-0 Vi: 0-0 Tstrap: 0-0
Best Rating: **110** 3/02 MRas 2m1f110y gd-sft NHF

Bumper winner who will need a stamina test over hurdles.

Althrey Dandy (IRE)

84f **89f**
7-y-o ch g Good Thyne (USA)-Hawthorn Dandy (Deep Run)
F Lloyd F Lloyd

Placings:3 (0377)
2001/02: 16[3]GF

	Starts	1st	2nd	3rd	Win & Pl
NH Flat	1	0	0	1	247
Career Total	**1**	**0**	**0**	**1**	**247**

Going: Sf: 0-0 GS: 0-0 Gd: 0-0 GF: - Fm: 0-1
Distance: 2m/2m3: 0-1 2m4-2m7: 0-0 3m+: 0-0
Track: LH: 0-0 RH: 0-1 Tight: 0-0 Gall: 0-1
Aids: Bl: 0-0 Vi: 0-0 Tstrap: 0-0
Best Rating: **89** 5/01 Hntg 2m110y gd-fm NHF

Althrey Riverside (IRE)

76 **32**
6-y-o b g Grand Plaisir (IRE)-Miss Riversfield (IRE) (Sandalay)
F Lloyd F Lloyd

Placings:0-00P5 (1227)
2001/02: 17[0]G, 16[0]G, 16[P]GF, 20[5]GF

	Starts	1st	2nd	3rd	Win & Pl
NH Flat	2	0	0	0	0
Hurdles	2	0	0	0	0
Career Total	**5**	**0**	**0**	**0**	**0**

Going: Sf: 0-0 GS: 0-0 Gd: 0-2 GF: - Fm: 0-2
Distance: 2m/2m3: 0-3 2m4-2m7: 0-1 3m+: 0-0
Track: LH: 0-4 RH: 0-0 Tight: 0-2 Gall: 0-0
Aids: Bl: 0-0 Vi: 0-0 Tstrap: 0-0
Best Rating: **65** 5/01 Bang 2m1f good NHF

Althrey Ruler (IRE)

102 **84**
9-y-o b g Phardante (FR)-Keego's Aunt (Tyrant (USA))
F Lloyd F Lloyd

Placings:0062F/020P1/660-F5P55P440026P (3704)
2001/02: 17[F]G, 16[5]GF, 19[P]GF, 16[5]G, 20[5]G, 16[P]GF, 16[4]GF, 16[4]GS, 20[0]S, 16[0]GF, 17[2]GS, 16[6]G, 17[P]HY

	Starts	1st	2nd	3rd	Win & Pl
Hurdles	13	0	1	0	1095
Career Total	**26**	**1**	**3**	**0**	**5321**

97	3/00	Uttx	2m	F(0-100)HHdl	GD	£2789

Total win prize-money £2790

Going: Sf: 0-2 GS: 0-2 Gd: 0-4 GF: - Fm: 0-5
Distance: 2m/2m3: 0-10 2m4-2m7: 0-3 3m+: 0-0
Track: LH: 0-9 RH: 0-4 Tight: 0-6 Gall: 0-0
Aids: Bl: 0-4 Vi: 0-0 Tstrap: 0-0
Best Rating: **97** 3/00 Uttx 2m good Hdl

Last and only win came back in 2000, although he has run with credit since then. Acts on good ground and is effective over two miles.

Althrey Torch (IRE)

104 **95**
10-y-o b g Torus-Keep The Cut (Tarqogan)
W Clay (F Lloyd 6/3) F Lloyd

Placings:6054/2003460/6-P3U260P46 (4842)
2001/02: 20[P]F, 17[3]GS, 17[U]GS, 17[2]HY, 20[6]S, 20[0]S, 20[P]S, 16[4]G, 20[6]G

	Starts	1st	2nd	3rd	Win & Pl
Hurdles	9	0	1	1	1176
Career Total	**21**	**0**	**2**	**2**	**2673**

Going: Sf: 0-4 GS: 0-2 Gd: 0-2 GF: - Fm: 0-1
Distance: 2m/2m3: 0-4 2m4-2m7: 0-5 3m+: 0-0
Track: LH: 0-7 RH: 0-2 Tight: 0-5 Gall: 0-2
Aids: Bl: 0-0 Vi: 0-0 Tstrap: 0-0
Best Rating: **95** 2/02 Hntg 2m4f110y soft Hdl

Modest hurdler, effective in heavy ground. Best form shown around two miles.

Altregan Boy (IRE)

92 **58**
10-y-o b g Lancastrian-Please Oblige (Le Levanstell)
C N Kellett A M Egan

Placings:60000/11B0/F0U020/FP06F-**PPP0PP** (4908)
2001/02: 21[P]HY, 24[P]S, 20[P]HY, 21[0]GS, 20[P]GF, 21[P]G

	Starts	1st	2nd	3rd	Win & Pl
Hurdles	2	0	0	0	0

	Starts	1st	2nd	3rd	Win & Pl
Chases	4	0	0	0	0
Career Total	**26**	**2**	**1**	**0**	**8305**

106 5/98 Dund 2m4f153y (0-123)HHdl G-Y £5026
104 5/98 Limk 3m (0-102)HHdl Y-S £2382
Total win prize-money £7409

Going: Sf: 0-3 GS: 0-1 Gd: 0-1 GF: - Fm: 0-1
Distance: 2m/2m3: 0-0 2m4-2m7: 0-5 3m+: 0-1
Track: LH: 0-4 RH: 0-1 Tight: 0-3 Gall: 0-0
Aids: Bl: 0-3 Vi: 0-0 Tstrap: 0-3
Best Rating: **111** 4/00 Fair 2m6f yld-sft Hdl

Bad novice chaser.

Alva (IRE)

8-y-o b m Good Thyne (USA)-Tiffany Downs (Green Shoon)
G M McCourt Graham McCourt

Placings:P (0774)
2001/02: 23^{P}GF

	Starts	1st	2nd	3rd	Win & Pl
Chases	1	0	0	0	
Career Total	**1**	**0**	**0**	**0**	

Going: Sf: 0-0 GS: 0-0 Gd: 0-0 GF: - Fm: 0-1
Distance: 2m/2m3: 0-0 2m4-2m7: 0-0 3m+: 0-1
Track: LH: 0-1 RH: 0-0 Tight: 0-0 Gall: 0-0
Aids: Bl: 0-0 Vi: 0-0 Tstrap: 0-0
Best Rating:

Alvarez

87f 89f
5-y-o b g Gran Alba (USA)-Glorious Jane (Hittite Glory)
C W Thornton Mrs C Wilson

Placings:_4053_ (4860)
2001/02: 16^{4}G, 16^{0}S, 16^{5}GF, 16^{3}G

	Starts	1st	2nd	3rd	Win & Pl
NH Flat	4	0	0	1	243
Career Total	**4**	**0**	**0**	**1**	**243**

Going: Sf: 0-1 GS: 0-0 Gd: 0-2 GF: - Fm: 0-1
Distance: 2m/2m3: 0-4 2m4-2m7: 0-0 3m+: 0-0
Track: LH: 0-0 RH: 0-1 Tight: 0-1 Gall: 0-0
Aids: Bl: 0-0 Vi: 0-0 Tstrap: 0-0
Best Rating: **89** 4/02 Hexm 2m110y good NHF

Alvaro (IRE)

99 83
5-y-o ch g Priolo (USA)-Gezalle (Shareef Dancer (USA))
M C Chapman Sir Clement Freud

Placings:60R0-60 (1146)
2001/02: 17^{6}GF, 16^{0}GF

	Starts	1st	2nd	3rd	Win & Pl
Hurdles	2	0	0	0	0
Career Total	**6**	**0**	**0**	**0**	**0**

Going: Sf: 0-0 GS: 0-0 Gd: 0-0 GF: - Fm: 0-2
Distance: 2m/2m3: 0-2 2m4-2m7: 0-0 3m+: 0-0
Track: LH: 0-1 RH: 0-1 Tight: 0-2 Gall: 0-0
Aids: Bl: 0-1 Vi: 0-0 Tstrap: 0-0
Best Rating: **81** 11/00 Catt 2m gd-sft Hdl

Alvino

103f 130f
5-y-o b g Alflora (IRE)-Rose Ravine (Deep Run)
Miss H C Knight Martin Broughton

Placings:_110_ (4235)
2001/02: 16^{1}GF, 16^{1}G, 16^{0}GS

	Starts	1st	2nd	3rd	Win & Pl
NH Flat	3	2	0	0	11945
Career Total	**3**	**2**	**0**	**0**	**11945**

130 12/01 Asct 2m110y B NHF GD £10426
114 11/01 Ludl 2m H NHF G-F £1519
Total win prize-money £11945

Going: Sf: 0-0 GS: 0-1 Gd: 1-1 GF: - Fm: 1-1
Distance: **2m/2m3: 2-3** 2m4-2m7: 0-0 3m+: 0-0
Track: LH: 0-1 **RH: 2-2** Tight: 0-0 Gall: 0-0
Aids: Bl: 0-0 Vi: 0-0 Tstrap: 0-0
Best Rating: **130** 12/01 Asct 2m110y good NHF

Out of top staying hurdler Rose Ravine, he won a Ludlow bumper on his racecourse debut in November 2001and followed up at Ascot. Limitations exposed in the Festival bumper.

Always Avon

80f 69f
5-y-o b m Afzal-Always Alex (Final Straw)
John Allen Avon Estates Ltd

Placings:_00-0_ (1959)
2001/02: 16^{0}G

	Starts	1st	2nd	3rd	Win & Pl
NH Flat	1	0	0	0	
Career Total	**3**	**0**	**0**	**0**	

Going: Sf: 0-0 GS: 0-0 Gd: 0-1 GF: - Fm: 0-0
Distance: 2m/2m3: 0-1 2m4-2m7: 0-0 3m+: 0-0
Track: LH: 0-1 RH: 0-0 Tight: 0-0 Gall: 0-0
Aids: Bl: 0-0 Vi: 0-0 Tstrap: 0-0
Best Rating: **70** 2/01 Donc 2m110y good NHF

Always Trying

7-y-o b g Always Fair (USA)-Bassita (Bustino)
Mrs Sarah Horner-Harker P A Horner-Harker

Placings:0P0/**PP0** (4692)
2001/02: 25^{P}G, 21^{P}G, 25^{0}GF

	Starts	1st	2nd	3rd	Win & Pl
Chases	3	0	0	0	
Career Total	**6**	**0**	**0**	**0**	

Going: Sf: 0-0 GS: 0-0 Gd: 0-2 GF: - Fm: 0-1
Distance: 2m/2m3: 0-0 2m4-2m7: 0-1 3m+: 0-2
Track: LH: 0-3 RH: 0-0 Tight: 0-3 Gall: 0-0
Aids: Bl: 0-0 Vi: 0-0 Tstrap: 0-0
Best Rating: **69** 3/99 Muss 2m good Hdl

Alzaro (IRE)

83 58
8-y-o b g Alzao (USA)-Merriment (USA) (Go Marching (USA))
P R Chamings P R Chamings

Placings:33/0 (2719)
2001/02: 17^{0}G

	Starts	1st	2nd	3rd	Win & Pl
Hurdles	1	0	0	0	
Career Total	**3**	**0**	**0**	**2**	**714**

Going: Sf: 0-0 GS: 0-0 Gd: 0-1 GF: - Fm: 0-0
Distance: 2m/2m3: 0-1 2m4-2m7: 0-0 3m+: 0-0
Track: LH: 0-0 RH: 0-1 Tight: 0-0 Gall: 0-0
Aids: Bl: 0-0 Vi: 0-0 Tstrap: 0-0
Best Rating: **111** 5/98 Uttx 2m gd-fm Hdl

Amadeus (AUS)

75 21
5-y-o ch g Brief Truce (USA)-Amazaan (NZ) (Zamazaan (FR))
J M Bradley Miss S Howell

Placings:F0P (3357)
2001/02: 19^{F}G, 20^{0}GS, 24^{P}HY

	Starts	1st	2nd	3rd	Win & Pl
Hurdles	3	0	0	0	
Career Total	**3**	**0**	**0**	**0**	

Going: Sf: 0-1 GS: 0-1 Gd: 0-1 GF: - Fm: 0-0
Distance: 2m/2m3: 0-1 2m4-2m7: 0-1 3m+: 0-1
Track: LH: 0-2 RH: 0-1 Tight: 0-0 Gall: 0-0
Aids: Bl: 0-0 Vi: 0-0 Tstrap: 0-0
Best Rating: **21** 12/01 Chep 2m4f gd-sft Hdl

Amarach (IRE)

102 94
8-y-o ch g Ballinvella Boy-Bold Sea Reef (Main Reef)
Noel T Chance (A J Martin 10/6) M Worcester

Placings:5-F002 (1379)
2001/02: 24^{F}G, 25^{0}G, 24^{0}F, 25^{2}GF

	Starts	1st	2nd	3rd	Win & Pl
Chases	4	0	1	0	1087
Career Total	**5**	**0**	**1**	**0**	**1087**

Going: Sf: 0-0 GS: 0-0 Gd: 0-2 GF: - Fm: 0-2
Distance: 2m/2m3: 0-0 2m4-2m7: 0-0 3m+: 0-4
Track: LH: 0-0 RH: 0-1 Tight: 0-0 Gall: 0-0
Aids: Bl: 0-0 Vi: 0-0 Tstrap: 0-0
Best Rating: **94** 9/01 Hrfd 3m1f110y gd-fm Ch

Amarettoforanna (IRE)

101 119
9-y-o b g Satco (FR)-Candy Slam (Candy Cane)
Ferdy Murphy R J V Partnership

Placings:_035/_**32052R0/124-14463500** (4749)
2001/02: 16^{1}GF, 17^{4}GF, 16^{4}S, 22^{6}G, 19^{3}G, 25^{5}GS, 16^{0}G, 20^{0}GF

	Starts	1st	2nd	3rd	Win & Pl
Chases	8	1	0	1	5408
Career Total	**21**	**2**	**3**	**3**	**15925**

119 5/01 Ayr 2m E Ch G-F £3471
112 10/00 MRas 2m6f110y E(0-105)HCh GD £3900
Total win prize-money £7371

Going: Sf: 0-1 GS: 0-1 Gd: 0-3 GF: - Fm: 1-3
Distance: **2m/2m3: 1-4** 2m4-2m7: 0-3 3m+: 0-1
Track: **LH: 1-6** RH: 0-1 Tight: 0-2 Gall: 0-1
Aids: Bl: 0-0 Vi: 0-0 Tstrap: 0-0
Best Rating: **119** 5/01 Ayr 2m gd-fm Ch

Moderate front-running chaser. Suited by two miles to two miles six, and a sound surface.

Amari (IRE)

98(88h) 105
7-y-o ch g Grand Plaisir (IRE)-Teazle (Quayside)
H D Daly M Ward-Thomas

Placings:5543/P6-**5660** (1076)
2001/02: 17^{5}GS, 20^{6}G, 23^{6}G, 24^{0}GF

	Starts	1st	2nd	3rd	Win & Pl
Chases	4	0	0	0	0
Career Total	**10**	**0**	**0**	**1**	**523**

Going: Sf: 0-0 GS: 0-1 Gd: 0-2 GF: - Fm: 0-1
Distance: 2m/2m3: 0-1 2m4-2m7: 0-1 3m+: 0-2
Track: LH: 0-4 RH: 0-0 Tight: 0-2 Gall: 0-0
Aids: Bl: 0-0 Vi: 0-0 Tstrap: 0-0
Best Rating: **105** 6/01 Worc 2m4f110y good Ch

Amarone

98 **85**
4-y-o b g Young Ern-Tendresse (IRE) (Tender King)
M J Ryan M J Ryan

Placings:2P100 (4601)
2001/02: 16^{2}G, 16^{P}G, 16^{1}S, 16^{0}GS, 16^{0}GF

	Starts	1st	2nd	3rd	Win & Pl
Hurdles	5	1	1	0	3256
Career Total	**5**	**1**	**1**	**0**	**3256**
85 2/02 Donc 2m110y G Hdl				SFT	£2404

Total win prize-money £2405

Going: Sf: 1-1 GS: 0-1 Gd: 0-2 GF: - Fm: 0-1
Distance: **2m/2m3: 1-5** 2m4-2m7: 0-0 3m+: 0-0
Track: **LH: 1-4** RH: 0-1 Tight: 0-1 **Gall: 1-3**
Aids: **Bl: 1-3** Vi: 0-0 Tstrap: 0-0
Best Rating: **85** 2/02 Donc 2m110y soft Hdl

Amateur Dramatics

94 **50**
6-y-o b g Theatrical Charmer-Chaconia Girl (Bay Express)
Mrs P A Tetley Mrs P A Tetley

Placings:0-0P0P4 (4779)
2001/02: 17^{0}GS, 22^{P}GF, 22^{0}S, 20^{P}S, 21^{4}GF

	Starts	1st	2nd	3rd	Win & Pl
Hurdles	5	0	0	0	0
Career Total	**6**	**0**	**0**	**0**	**0**

Going: Sf: 0-2 GS: 0-1 Gd: 0-0 GF: - Fm: 0-2
Distance: 2m/2m3: 0-1 2m4-2m7: 0-4 3m+: 0-0
Track: LH: 0-4 RH: 0-0 Tight: 0-5 Gall: 0-0
Aids: Bl: 0-0 Vi: 0-0 Tstrap: 0-0
Best Rating: **50** 4/02 Plum 2m5f gd-fm Hdl

Amazing Fact (USA)

94 **66**
7-y-o b g Known Fact (USA)-Itsamazing (USA) (The Minstrel (CAN))
D Burchell (M Salaman 20/6) Mrs Ruth Burchell

Placings:0P/25P-0U0P (2476)
2001/02: 17^{0}GF, 16^{U}GF, 16^{0}GF, 17^{P}S

	Starts	1st	2nd	3rd	Win & Pl
Hurdles	4	0	0	0	0
Career Total	**9**	**0**	**1**	**0**	**570**

Going: Sf: 0-1 GS: 0-0 Gd: 0-0 GF: - Fm: 0-3
Distance: 2m/2m3: 0-4 2m4-2m7: 0-0 3m+: 0-0
Track: LH: 0-3 RH: 0-1 Tight: 0-2 Gall: 0-0
Aids: Bl: 0-0 Vi: 0-0 Tstrap: 0-0
Best Rating: **75** 6/00 Worc 2m gd-fm Hdl

Amber Castle

7-y-o ch g Carlingford Castle-Hardwick Amber (Tanfirion)
C Tizzard R E Dimond

Placings:00-P (0214)
2001/02: 22^{P}GF

	Starts	1st	2nd	3rd	Win & Pl
Hurdles	1	0	0	0	
Career Total	**3**	**0**	**0**	**0**	

Going: Sf: 0-0 GS: 0-0 Gd: 0-0 GF: - Fm: 0-1
Distance: 2m/2m3: 0-0 2m4-2m7: 0-1 3m+: 0-0
Track: LH: 0-0 RH: 0-1 Tight: 0-0 Gall: 0-0
Aids: Bl: 0-0 Vi: 0-0 Tstrap: 0-0
Best Rating: **89** 2/01 Winc 2m good NHF

Amber Go Go

86 **71+**
5-y-o ch m Rudimentary (USA)-Plaything (High Top)
K W Hogg K W Hogg

Placings:O-00PP (1747)
2001/02: 21^{0}G, 22^{0}G, 17^{P}G, 17^{P}G

	Starts	1st	2nd	3rd	Win & Pl
Hurdles	4	0	0	0	
Career Total	**5**	**0**	**0**	**0**	

Going: Sf: 0-0 GS: 0-0 Gd: 0-4 GF: - Fm: 0-0
Distance: 2m/2m3: 0-2 2m4-2m7: 0-2 3m+: 0-0
Track: LH: 0-3 RH: 0-1 Tight: 0-4 Gall: 0-0
Aids: Bl: 0-0 Vi: 0-0 Tstrap: 0-0
Best Rating: **22** 10/01 Kels 2m6f110y good Hdl

Amber Life

84f **98f**
6-y-o b h Lyphento (USA)-Amber Marsh (Arctic Kanda)
R H York R H York

Placings:0 (0064)
2001/02: 17^{0}GS

	Starts	1st	2nd	3rd	Win & Pl
NH Flat	1	0	0	0	
Career Total	**1**	**0**	**0**	**0**	

Going: Sf: 0-0 GS: 0-1 Gd: 0-0 GF: - Fm: 0-0
Distance: 2m/2m3: 0-1 2m4-2m7: 0-0 3m+: 0-0
Track: LH: 0-0 RH: 0-0 Tight: 0-1 Gall: 0-0
Aids: Bl: 0-0 Vi: 0-0 Tstrap: 0-0
Best Rating: **98** 5/01 Folk 2m1f110y gd-sft NHF

Amber Lily

85 **58**
10-y-o ch m Librate-Just Bluffing (Green Shoon)
Mrs S M Johnson S J Merrick

Placings:00/0P1P030P000/F263050-P (4869)
2001/02: 20^{P}GF

	Starts	1st	2nd	3rd	Win & Pl
Hurdles	1	0	0	0	
Career Total	**21**	**1**	**1**	**2**	**2989**
96 9/99 Hrfd 2m1f E Hdl				GD	£1954

Total win prize-money £1954

Going: Sf: 0-0 GS: 0-0 Gd: 0-0 GF: - Fm: 0-1
Distance: 2m/2m3: 0-0 2m4-2m7: 0-1 3m+: 0-0
Track: LH: 0-1 RH: 0-0 Tight: 0-0 Gall: 0-0
Aids: Bl: 0-0 Vi: 0-0 Tstrap: 0-0
Best Rating: **96** 9/99 Hrfd 2m1f good Hdl

Amber Moss

100 **103**
7-y-o ch g Phardante (FR)-Queen's Darling (Le Moss)
Mrs S C Bradburne Mrs C J Kerr

Placings:0052311/**F33U0PF-242P26332P** (4895)
2001/02: 24^{2}GS, 17^{4}G, 25^{2}GS, 25^{P}GS, 25^{2}S, 23^{6}GS, 21^{3}S, 17^{3}S, 25^{2}GF, 20^{P}G

	Starts	1st	2nd	3rd	Win & Pl
Chases	10	0	4	2	6783
Career Total	**24**	**2**	**5**	**5**	**20288**
116 4/00 Ayr 2m6f C HHdl				GD	£7488
113 3/00 Uttx 2m4f110y D Hdl				GD	£3802

Total win prize-money £11291

Going: Sf: 0-3 GS: 0-4 Gd: 0-2 GF: - Fm: 0-1
Distance: 2m/2m3: 0-2 2m4-2m7: 0-2 3m+: 0-6
Track: LH: 0-7 RH: 0-2 Tight: 0-5 Gall: 0-0
Aids: Bl: 0-0 Vi: 0-0 Tstrap: 0-0
Best Rating: **121** 10/00 Kels 2m1f soft Ch

Some ability in novice chases and looks a real stayer. Suited by good or slightly softer. Usually in the frame.

Amber Spark (IRE)

13-y-o ch g The Parson-La Dragonlere (Hot Spark)
G Harris N J Hamer

Placings:6340666/05500526/32F33U1/3640024/P0/P (0227)
2001/02: 24^{P}GF

	Starts	1st	2nd	3rd	Win & Pl
Chases	1	0	0	0	
Career Total	**32**	**1**	**3**	**5**	**7833**
106 3/97 Ling 2m4f110y E Ch				G-S	£2946

Total win prize-money £2947

Going: Sf: 0-0 GS: 0-0 Gd: 0-0 GF: - Fm: 0-1
Distance: 2m/2m3: 0-0 2m4-2m7: 0-0 3m+: 0-1
Track: LH: 0-0 RH: 0-1 Tight: 0-0 Gall: 0-1
Aids: Bl: 0-0 Vi: 0-0 Tstrap: 0-0
Best Rating: **106** 3/97 Ling 2m4f110y gd-sft Ch

Amberleigh House (IRE)

113(89h) (91h)**151**
10-y-o br g Buckskin (FR)-Chancy Gal (Al Sirat (USA))
D McCain Halewood International Ltd

Placings:00/3613213144024/**2145345B/622F43210/1550PB-5216501** (4845)
2001/02: 20^{5}S, 16^{2}S, 27^{1}S, 20^{6}HY, 17^{5}S, 21^{0}G, 24^{1}G

	Starts	1st	2nd	3rd	Win & Pl
Hurdles	1	0	0	0	0
Chases	6	2	1	0	37821
Career Total	**45**	**8**	**7**	**5**	**100164**
151 4/02 Bang 3m110y C(0-135)HCh				GD	£7572
142 11/01 Aint 3m3f B HCh				SFT	£29000
155 5/00 Punc 2m4f HCh				GD	£11440
153 2/00 Thur 2m4f Ch				HVY	£13000
124 10/98 Gowr 2m1f Ch				Y-S	£2989
129 2/98 Leop 2m HHdl				Y-S	£5956
120 1/98 Navn 2m Hdl				HVY	£2680
111 11/97 Naas 2m NHF				SH	£3051

Total win prize-money £75691

Going: Sf: 1-5 GS: 0-0 Gd: 1-2 GF: - Fm: 0-0

Distance: 2m/2m3: 0-2 2m4-2m7: 0-3 **3m+: 2-2**
Track: **LH: 2-7** RH: 0-0 **Tight: 2-4** Gall: 0-1
Aids: Bl: 0-0 Vi: 0-0 Tstrap: 0-0
Best Rating: 155 5/00 Punc 2m4f good Ch

Useful ex-Irish staying handicap chaser. Best in decent races getting weight rather than giving weight away. Has won on good and soft ground. Winner of the Becher Chase in November 2001, he failed to make the cut in the Grand National and was well held in the Topham but bounced back to score at Bangor two weeks later.. He is not very big but jumps well. Stays three and a half miles.

Ambersam

103 **93**

7-y-o b g Gildoran-Golden Valley (Hotfoot)
T D Walford Jim Burns

Placings:000-3 (0203)
2001/02: 20^{3}G

	Starts	1st	2nd	3rd	Win & Pl
Hurdles	1	0	0	1	573
Career Total	**4**	**0**	**0**	**1**	**573**

Going: Sf: 0-0 GS: 0-0 Gd: 0-1 GF: - Fm: 0-0
Distance: 2m/2m3: 0-0 2m4-2m7: 0-1 3m+: 0-0
Track: LH: 0-1 RH: 0-0 Tight: 0-0 Gall: 0-0
Aids: Bl: 0-0 Vi: 0-0 Tstrap: 0-0
Best Rating: 93 5/01 Weth 2m4f110y good Hdl

Ambience

73f **58f**

5-y-o ch g Wolfhound (USA)-Amber Fizz (USA) (Effervescing (USA))
G A Swinbank Miss Sally R Haynes

Placings:0 (0239)
2001/02: 16^{0}GF

	Starts	1st	2nd	3rd	Win & Pl
NH Flat	1	0	0	0	
Career Total	**1**	**0**	**0**	**0**	

Going: Sf: 0-0 GS: 0-0 Gd: 0-0 GF: - Fm: 0-1
Distance: 2m/2m3: 0-1 2m4-2m7: 0-0 3m+: 0-0
Track: LH: 0-1 RH: 0-0 Tight: 0-1 Gall: 0-0
Aids: Bl: 0-0 Vi: 0-0 Tstrap: 0-0
Best Rating: 58 5/01 Sthl 2m gd-fm NHF

Ambleside (IRE)

114 **137**

11-y-o b g Kambalda-Noellespir (Bargello)
Mrs S D Williams B M Yin

Placings:62140/312403/**2U44112**/**U354122U23**/**31213125**/ 34442-0302146 (4661)
2001/02: 23^{0}GS, 19^{3}S, 26^{0}S, 25^{2}GS, 24^{1}S, 34^{4}HY, 25^{6}G

	Starts	1st	2nd	3rd	Win & Pl
Chases	7	1	1	1	18373
Career Total	**48**	**9**	**11**	**8**	**89193**

137	2/02	Sand	3m110y	B(0-140)HCh	SFT	£10695
140	2/00	Chep	3m2f110y	C(0-135)HCh	SFT	£6890
141	12/99	Chep	2m3f110y	C(0-130)HCh	HVY	£7197
133	12/99	Winc	2m5f	E(0-115)HCh	GD	£3464
131	2/99	Winc	2m5f	D(0-125)HCh	G-S	£7392
117	4/98	Bang	2m1f110y	D Ch	SFT	£4221
111	4/98	Tntn	2m110y	D Ch	GD	£3856
117	12/96	Ling	2m110y	C(0-130)HHdl	G-S	£3403
96	2/96	Chep	2m110y	E Hdl	SFT	£2542

Total win prize-money £49664

Going: Sf: 1-4 GS: 0-2 Gd: 0-1 GF: - Fm: 0-0
Distance: 2m/2m3: 0-0 2m4-2m7: 0-1 **3m+: 1-6**
Track: LH: 0-4 **RH: 1-3** Tight: 0-1 Gall: 0-0
Aids: Bl: 0-1 Vi: 0-0 Tstrap: 0-0
Best Rating: 141 3/00 Chep 3m2f110y gd-sft Ch

A consistent staying chaser, he goes well at Chepstow and won his first race in two years at Sandown in February 2002. However, he was well beaten in a better race at Uttoxeter next time. Suited by soft ground.

Ambry

112 **124**

5-y-o br g Machiavellian (USA)-Alkaffeyeh (IRE) (Sadler's Wells (USA))
G L Moore Raymond Gross, Ms Adrienne Gross

Placings:2124-0230210 (4418)
2001/02: 16^{0}G, 20^{2}G, 21^{3}S, 20^{0}S, 16^{2}HY, 18^{1}S, 16^{0}GS

	Starts	1st	2nd	3rd	Win & Pl
Hurdles	7	1	2	1	6378
Career Total	**11**	**2**	**4**	**1**	**11880**

111	3/02	Font	2m2f110y	E(0-110)HHdl	SFT	£2646
94	3/01	Plum	2m	E Hdl	HVY	£3304

Total win prize-money £5950

Going: Sf: 1-4 GS: 0-1 Gd: 0-2 GF: - Fm: 0-0
Distance: **2m/2m3: 1-4** 2m4-2m7: 0-3 3m+: 0-0
Track: **LH: 1-4** RH: 0-2 **Tight: 1-4** Gall: 0-2
Aids: **Bl: 1-6** Vi: 0-0 Tstrap: 0-0
Best Rating: 114 1/02 Font 2m4f good Hdl

Handicap hurdler, suited by soft ground and trips up to two and a half miles. Often blinkered.

Ambushed (IRE)

105 **101**

6-y-o b g Indian Ridge-Surprise Move (IRE) (Simply Great (FR))
P Monteith Allan W Melville

Placings:343-230 (3504)
2001/02: 16^{2}GF, 16^{3}G, 16^{0}S

	Starts	1st	2nd	3rd	Win & Pl
Hurdles	3	0	1	1	1465
Career Total	**6**	**0**	**1**	**3**	**2044**

Going: Sf: 0-1 GS: 0-0 Gd: 0-1 GF: - Fm: 0-1
Distance: 2m/2m3: 0-3 2m4-2m7: 0-0 3m+: 0-0
Track: LH: 0-0 RH: 0-3 Tight: 0-2 Gall: 0-0
Aids: Bl: 0-0 Vi: 0-0 Tstrap: 0-0
Best Rating: 101 1/02 Muss 2m good Hdl

Amercius

(85h) (69h)

10-y-o ch g Old Vic-Elarrih (USA) (Sharpen Up)
A W Carroll R Clarke

Placings:22235/64/**2125P**/**0U15**/2-3 (0553)
2001/02: 26^{3}GF

	Starts	1st	2nd	3rd	Win & Pl
Hurdles	1	0	0	1	367
Career Total	**18**	**2**	**6**	**2**	**12468**

111	7/99	Worc	2m7f110y	F(0-100)HCh	G-F	£3050
85	6/98	MRas	2m6f110y	E(0-100)HCh	G-F	£3808

Total win prize-money £6858

Going: Sf: 0-0 GS: 0-0 Gd: 0-0 GF: - Fm: 0-1
Distance: 2m/2m3: 0-0 2m4-2m7: 0-0 3m+: 0-1
Track: LH: 0-0 RH: 0-1 Tight: 0-0 Gall: 0-1
Aids: Bl: 0-1 Vi: 0-0 Tstrap: 0-0
Best Rating: 111 7/99 Worc 2m7f110y gd-fm Ch

American President (IRE)

93 **72**

6-y-o br g Lord Americo-Deceptive Response (Furry Glen)
O Brennan Lady Anne Bentinck

Placings:0050 (4873)
2001/02: 16^{0}G, 16^{0}GS, 16^{5}G, 16^{0}GF

	Starts	1st	2nd	3rd	Win & Pl
NH Flat	4	0	0	0	0
Career Total	**4**	**0**	**0**	**0**	**0**

Going: Sf: 0-0 GS: 0-1 Gd: 0-2 GF: - Fm: 0-1
Distance: 2m/2m3: 0-4 2m4-2m7: 0-0 3m+: 0-0
Track: LH: 0-3 RH: 0-1 Tight: 0-1 Gall: 0-1
Aids: Bl: 0-0 Vi: 0-0 Tstrap: 0-0
Best Rating: 93 4/02 Towc 2m good NHF

Amica Bella

5-y-o b m Environment Friend-Pontevecchio Bella (Main Reef)
Mrs L C Jewell Helen Clark & Frank Brawn

Placings:P0 (4881)
2001/02: 17^{P}GF, 18^{0}GF

	Starts	1st	2nd	3rd	Win & Pl
Hurdles	2	0	0	0	
Career Total	**2**	**0**	**0**	**0**	

Going: Sf: 0-0 GS: 0-0 Gd: 0-0 GF: - Fm: 0-2
Distance: 2m/2m3: 0-2 2m4-2m7: 0-0 3m+: 0-0
Track: LH: 0-1 RH: 0-1 Tight: 0-1 Gall: 0-0
Aids: Bl: 0-0 Vi: 0-0 Tstrap: 0-0
Best Rating:

Amigo (IRE)

93 **85**

4-y-o b c Spectrum (IRE)-Eleanor Antoinette (IRE) (Double Schwartz)
P Mitchell Sir Peter O'Sullevan

Placings:6 (2891)
2001/02: 16^{6}G

	Starts	1st	2nd	3rd	Win & Pl
Hurdles	1	0	0	0	
Career Total	**1**	**0**	**0**	**0**	

Going: Sf: 0-0 GS: 0-0 Gd: 0-1 GF: - Fm: 0-0
Distance: 2m/2m3: 0-1 2m4-2m7: 0-0 3m+: 0-0
Track: LH: 0-0 RH: 0-1 Tight: 0-0 Gall: 0-0
Aids: Bl: 0-0 Vi: 0-0 Tstrap: 0-0
Best Rating: 85 12/01 Kemp 2m good Hdl

Amitge (FR)

88(100h) **86**

8-y-o ch m Vaguely Pleasant (FR)-Ribbon In Her Hair (USA) (Sauce Boat (USA))
Miss Venetia Williams The Winning Line

Placings:111225P/3536405U/0**1F1F6**/**F21111P-4** (4740)
2001/02: 20^{4}GF

	Starts	1st	2nd	3rd	Win & Pl
Chases	1	0	0	0	386
Career Total	**29**	**9**	**3**	**2**	**39576**

113	12/00	Font	2m2f110y	G Hdl	SFT	£2795
110	10/00	Hrfd	2m3f110y	G Hdl	GD	£1883
106	8/00	Font	2m2f110y	G Hdl	G-F	£2268
105	6/00	Folk	2m1f110y	G Hdl	GD	£1554
128	2/00	Wwck	2m4f	D Ch	GD	£4628
122	11/99	Plum	2m4f	D Ch	G-F	£4135
106	10/97	Hrfd	2m1f	E Hdl	G-F	£2220
106	8/97	Worc	2m	E Hdl	GD	£2232
87	8/97	Bang	2m1f	E Hdl	G-F	£2710

Total win prize-money £24426

Going: Sf: 0-0 GS: 0-0 Gd: 0-0 GF: - Fm: 0-1
Distance: 2m/2m3: 0-0 2m4-2m7: 0-1 3m+: 0-0
Track: LH: 0-0 RH: 0-1 Tight: 0-1 Gall: 0-0
Aids: Bl: 0-0 Vi: 0-0 Tstrap: 0-0
Best Rating: **139** 2/99 Newb 2m110y good Hdl

Completed a hat-trick over hurdles in 2000 for Martin Pipe but was off the track after pulling up the following January.

Amjad

102 **102**

5-y-o ch g Cadeaux Genereux-Babita (Habitat)
Miss Kate Milligan (P C Haslam 7/2) Miss Kate Milligan

Placings:F3410 **(4858)**
2001/02: 16^{F}GS, 16^{3}GF, 17^{4}G, 16^{1}G, 16^{0}G

	Starts	1st	2nd	3rd	Win & Pl
Hurdles	5	1	0	1	2753
Career Total	**5**	**1**	**0**	**1**	**2753**

102	12/01	Donc	2m110y	G Hdl	GD	£2331

Total win prize-money £2331

Going: Sf: 0-0 GS: 0-1 Gd: 1-3 GF: - Fm: 0-1
Distance: **2m/2m3: 1-5** 2m4-2m7: 0-0 3m+: 0-0
Track: **LH: 1-4** RH: 0-0 Tight: 0-2 **Gall: 1-1**
Aids: Bl: 0-0 Vi: 0-0 Tstrap: 0-0
Best Rating: **102** 12/01 Donc 2m110y good Hdl

Moderate hurdler, suited by a sound surface.

Amlwch

85(90c) **76**

9-y-o b g Weld-Connaughts' Trump (Connaught)
C Tizzard The Butterwick Syndicate

Placings:4/342U024/6120312/R132F126/4323UR-U0RR **(3987)**
2001/02: 19^{U}GS, 17^{0}GS, 18^{R}HY, 19^{R}S

	Starts	1st	2nd	3rd	Win & Pl
Hurdles	3	0	0	0	0
Chases	1	0	0	0	0
Career Total	**33**	**4**	**7**	**5**	**23008**

128	2/00	Sedg	2m110y	F(0-110)HCh	G-S	£3139
96	9/99	Sedg	2m1f	E Hdl	GD	£2285
120	4/99	Sedg	2m110y	D Ch	FRM	£3925
125	12/98	Donc	2m110y	D Ch	GD	£3574

Total win prize-money £12924

Going: Sf: 0-2 GS: 0-2 Gd: 0-0 GF: - Fm: 0-0
Distance: 2m/2m3: 0-2 2m4-2m7: 0-2 3m+: 0-0
Track: LH: 0-0 RH: 0-3 Tight: 0-4 Gall: 0-0
Aids: Bl: 0-0 Vi: 0-1 Tstrap: 0-3
Best Rating: **131** 7/00 Wolv 2m gd-sft Ch

Ammieanne (IRE)

100 **96**

7-y-o b m Zaffaran (USA)-Joyful Rosanna (Kemal (FR))
B R Hamilton R W Donaldson

Placings:0443300 **(4894)**
2001/02: 16^{0}YS, 20^{4}S, 20^{4}S, 20^{3}S, 17^{3}S, 20^{0}S, 16^{0}G

	Starts	1st	2nd	3rd	Win & Pl
NH Flat	1	0	0	0	0
Hurdles	6	0	0	2	1521
Career Total	**7**	**0**	**0**	**2**	**1521**

Going: Sf: 0-5 GS: 0-0 Gd: 0-1 GF: - Fm: 0-0
Distance: 2m/2m3: 0-3 2m4-2m7: 0-4 3m+: 0-0
Track: LH: 0-0 RH: 0-3 Tight: 0-0 Gall: 0-0
Aids: Bl: 0-0 Vi: 0-0 Tstrap: 0-0
Best Rating: **96** 1/02 DRoy 2m4f soft Hdl

Amoebic (IRE)

100 **83**

9-y-o b g Prince Rupert (FR)-Redington Belle (Ahonoora)
T H Caldwell Mrs Rita Butler

Placings:2400/3404P/P-63 **(0724)**
2001/02: 17^{6}G, 17^{3}F

	Starts	1st	2nd	3rd	Win & Pl
Hurdles	2	0	0	1	389
Career Total	**12**	**0**	**1**	**2**	**1545**

Going: Sf: 0-0 GS: 0-0 Gd: 0-1 GF: - Fm: 0-1
Distance: 2m/2m3: 0-2 2m4-2m7: 0-0 3m+: 0-0
Track: LH: 0-0 RH: 0-2 Tight: 0-0 Gall: 0-0
Aids: Bl: 0-0 Vi: 0-0 Tstrap: 0-0
Best Rating: **100** 10/97 Hexm 2m gd-fm NHF

Amos

39f

6-y-o ch g Then Again-Amethystine (USA) (Barachois (CAN))
R J Hodges R J Hodges

Placings:0 **(1731)**
2001/02: 17^{0}F

	Starts	1st	2nd	3rd	Win & Pl
NH Flat	1	0	0	0	
Career Total	**1**	**0**	**0**	**0**	

Going: Sf: 0-0 GS: 0-0 Gd: 0-0 GF: - Fm: 0-1
Distance: 2m/2m3: 0-1 2m4-2m7: 0-0 3m+: 0-0
Track: LH: 0-0 RH: 0-0 Tight: 0-0 Gall: 0-0
Aids: Bl: 0-0 Vi: 0-0 Tstrap: 0-0
Best Rating: **39** 10/01 Tntn 2m1f firm NHF

Amtrak Express

15-y-o ch g Black Minstrel-Four In A Row (Cracksman)
P E Froud (Mrs J Pitman 27/1) Mr & Mrs P E Froud

Placings:1513110/1FF3/1113B0/25U1U53/3/5P4F/P **(3861)**
2001/02: 19^{P}S

	Starts	1st	2nd	3rd	Win & Pl
Chases	1	0	0	0	
Career Total	**30**	**9**	**1**	**5**	**87165**

145	2/96	Sand	3m110y	A HCh	G-F	£18990
147	12/94	Kemp	2m4f110y	HCh	SFT	£14810
142	12/94	Uttx	2m5f	(0-130)HCh	GD	£4143
138	11/94	Winc	2m5f	(0-125)HCh	GD	£3548
120	10/93	Newb	2m1f	Ch	GD	£3626
113	3/93	Winc	2m	Hdl	G-F	£2162
119	2/93	Winc	2m	Hdl	GD	£11200
92	12/92	Tntn	2m1f	Hdl	SFT	£1502
	10/92	Chel	2m110y	NHF	GD	£1553

Total win prize-money £61536

Going: Sf: 0-1 GS: 0-0 Gd: 0-0 GF: - Fm: 0-0
Distance: 2m/2m3: 0-0 2m4-2m7: 0-1 3m+: 0-0
Track: LH: 0-1 RH: 0-0 Tight: 0-0 Gall: 0-1
Aids: Bl: 0-0 Vi: 0-0 Tstrap: 0-0
Best Rating: **148** 4/97 Asct 2m3f110y gd-fm Ch

Amusement

86 **64**

6-y-o ch g Mystiko (USA)-Jolies Eaux (Shirley Heights)
D G Bridgwater Daltagh Construction Ltd

Placings:00-200 **(2208)**
2001/02: 16^{2}GF, 16^{0}G, 16^{0}GS

	Starts	1st	2nd	3rd	Win & Pl
NH Flat	1	0	1	0	419
Hurdles	2	0	0	0	0
Career Total	**5**	**0**	**1**	**0**	**419**

Going: Sf: 0-0 GS: 0-1 Gd: 0-1 GF: - Fm: 0-1
Distance: 2m/2m3: 0-3 2m4-2m7: 0-0 3m+: 0-0
Track: LH: 0-0 RH: 0-3 Tight: 0-0 Gall: 0-2
Aids: Bl: 0-0 Vi: 0-0 Tstrap: 0-0
Best Rating: **89** 8/01 Hntg 2m110y gd-fm NHF

Amwell Star (USA)

82 **87**

4-y-o gr f Silver Buck (USA)-Markham Fair (CAN) (Woodman (USA))
J R Jenkins Amwell Racing

Placings:F40 **(3460)**
2001/02: 16^{F}G, 16^{4}HY, 16^{0}HY

	Starts	1st	2nd	3rd	Win & Pl
Hurdles	3	0	0	0	0
Career Total	**3**	**0**	**0**	**0**	**0**

Going: Sf: 0-2 GS: 0-0 Gd: 0-1 GF: - Fm: 0-0
Distance: 2m/2m3: 0-3 2m4-2m7: 0-0 3m+: 0-0
Track: LH: 0-1 RH: 0-2 Tight: 0-0 Gall: 0-1
Aids: Bl: 0-0 Vi: 0-0 Tstrap: 0-0
Best Rating: **87** 11/01 Hntg 2m110y good Hdl

An Jolien

5-y-o b m Aragon-Joli's Girl (Mansingh (USA))
M J Ryan Mr & Mrs W J Foley

Placings:P **(1074)**
2001/02: 16^{P}GF

	Starts	1st	2nd	3rd	Win & Pl
Hurdles	1	0	0	0	
Career Total	**1**	**0**	**0**	**0**	

Going: Sf: 0-0 GS: 0-0 Gd: 0-0 GF: - Fm: 0-1
Distance: 2m/2m3: 0-1 2m4-2m7: 0-0 3m+: 0-0
Track: LH: 0-1 RH: 0-0 Tight: 0-1 Gall: 0-0
Aids: Bl: 0-0 Vi: 0-0 Tstrap: 0-0
Best Rating:

Anador

7-y-o b m Gildoran-Ancella (Tycoon Ii)

Mrs P Ford K R Ford

Placings:U-0 (0720)
2001/02: 26^{0}F

	Starts	1st	2nd	3rd	Win & Pl
Hurdles	1	0	0	0	
Career Total	**2**	**0**	**0**	**0**	

Going: Sf: 0-0 GS: 0-0 Gd: 0-0 GF: - Fm: 0-1
Distance: 2m/2m3: 0-0 2m4-2m7: 0-0 3m+: 0-1
Track: LH: 0-0 RH: 0-1 Tight: 0-0 Gall: 0-0
Aids: Bl: 0-0 Vi: 0-0 Tstrap: 0-0
Best Rating:

Anatar (IRE)

87 86

4-y-o b g Caerleon (USA)-Anaza (Darshaan)
M C Pipe Eminence Grise Partnership

Placings:050 (4724)
2001/02: 17^{0}GS, 17^{5}GS, 16^{0}GF

	Starts	1st	2nd	3rd	Win & Pl
Hurdles	3	0	0	0	0
Career Total	**3**	**0**	**0**	**0**	**0**

Going: Sf: 0-0 GS: 0-2 Gd: 0-0 GF: - Fm: 0-1
Distance: 2m/2m3: 0-3 2m4-2m7: 0-0 3m+: 0-0
Track: LH: 0-1 RH: 0-2 Tight: 0-2 Gall: 0-0
Aids: Bl: 0-0 Vi: 0-0 Tstrap: 0-0
Best Rating: **86** 3/02 MRas 2m1f110y gd-sft Hdl

An Aga Khan-bred gelding, he finished runner-up twice from three starts in the French Provinces. A leggy type, he disappointed when sent off favourite on his hurdling debut.

Andaleer (IRE)

98(97c) (92c)83

7-y-o b m Phardante (FR)-Dunleer Duchess (Our Mirage)
Mrs H Dalton M Richards And G Stone

Placings:4-2333 (1013)
2001/02: 17^{2}GS, 20^{3}G, 19^{3}GF, 20^{3}G

	Starts	1st	2nd	3rd	Win & Pl
NH Flat	1	0	1	0	511
Hurdles	3	0	0	3	1050
Career Total	**5**	**0**	**1**	**3**	**1561**

Going: Sf: 0-0 GS: 0-1 Gd: 0-2 GF: - Fm: 0-1
Distance: 2m/2m3: 0-2 2m4-2m7: 0-2 3m+: 0-0
Track: LH: 0-4 RH: 0-0 Tight: 0-2 Gall: 0-0
Aids: Bl: 0-0 Vi: 0-0 Tstrap: 0-0
Best Rating: **93** 5/01 Bang 2m1f gd-sft NHF

Regularly placed over hurdles and on her chasing debut.

Andoli

79 33

6-y-o b g Out Of Hand-Sulamar (Sulaafah (USA))
L G Cottrell Mrs G O Green

Placings:3U0 (2217)
2001/02: 17^{3}F, 16^{U}G, 17^{0}G

	Starts	1st	2nd	3rd	Win & Pl
NH Flat	1	0	0	1	329
Hurdles	2	0	0	0	0
Career Total	**3**	**0**	**0**	**1**	**329**

Going: Sf: 0-0 GS: 0-0 Gd: 0-2 GF: - Fm: 0-1
Distance: 2m/2m3: 0-3 2m4-2m7: 0-0 3m+: 0-0
Track: LH: 0-1 RH: 0-1 Tight: 0-1 Gall: 0-0
Aids: Bl: 0-0 Vi: 0-0 Tstrap: 0-0
Best Rating: **78** 10/01 Tntn 2m1f firm NHF

Andre Laval (IRE)

92

13-y-o ch g Over The River (FR)-French Academy (Le Bavard (FR))
M J M Evans M J M Evans

Placings:11/16/U22342/4426630/5536234553-P (0378)
2001/02: 24^{P}GF

	Starts	1st	2nd	3rd	Win & Pl
Chases	1	0	0	0	
Career Total	**28**	**3**	**5**	**5**	**27793**

115	11/96	Winc	3m1f110y	C(0-130)HCh	GD	£6775
108	3/96	Wind	3m	E Ch	G-S	£3241
108	2/96	Nott	2m5f110y	E Ch	GD	£3600

Total win prize-money £13616

Going: Sf: 0-0 GS: 0-0 Gd: 0-0 GF: - Fm: 0-1
Distance: 2m/2m3: 0-0 2m4-2m7: 0-0 3m+: 0-1
Track: LH: 0-0 RH: 0-1 Tight: 0-0 Gall: 0-1
Aids: Bl: 0-0 Vi: 0-0 Tstrap: 0-0
Best Rating: **122** 2/98 Wwck 3m5f good Ch

Andrelot

15-y-o b g Caerleon (USA)-Seminar (Don (ITY))
D M Grissell Mrs D M Grissell

Placings:6523146/45323052/133003240/3P/444U1/113124 30240FP/322414132P360/22341P23U434P/00/5R-U0 (0556)
2001/02: 31^{U}G, 24^{0}GF

	Starts	1st	2nd	3rd	Win & Pl
Chases	2	0	0	0	
Career Total	**76**	**9**	**12**	**15**	**48770**

112	8/97	Worc	2m4f110y	E(0-115)HCh	GD	£3087
126	9/96	MRas	2m4f	D(0-120)HCh	G-F	£4497
120	8/96	Sthl	3m110y	C(0-130)HCh	GD	£5287
126	7/95	MRas	2m4f	D(0-120)HCh	G-F	£3910
115	5/95	Wwck	2m4f110y	H Ch	GD	£2018
115	5/95	Hrfd	2m3f	H Ch	G-F	£1725
112	4/95	Hrfd	2m3f	H Ch	FRM	£2164
95	5/92	Ludl	2m	Hdl	G-F	£1518
	2/91	Winc	2m	Hdl	GD	£2110

Total win prize-money £26318

Going: Sf: 0-0 GS: 0-0 Gd: 0-1 GF: - Fm: 0-1
Distance: 2m/2m3: 0-0 2m4-2m7: 0-0 3m+: 0-2
Track: LH: 0-0 RH: 0-2 Tight: 0-1 Gall: 0-1
Aids: Bl: 0-2 Vi: 0-0 Tstrap: 0-0
Best Rating: **127** 8/95 Gway 2m6f gd-fm Ch

Andsuephi (IRE)

95(96h) (85h)108

10-y-o b g Montelimar (USA)-Butler's Daughter (Rhett Butler)
A M Hales Mrs J A Cohen

Placings:111140P/13U23/11F40/1P-00P (2892)
2001/02: 23^{0}GF, 20^{0}G, 24^{P}G

	Starts	1st	2nd	3rd	Win & Pl
Hurdles	1	0	0	0	0
Chases	2	0	0	0	0
Career Total	**22**	**8**	**1**	**2**	**37643**

146	5/00	Strf	3m	C(0-135)HCh	G-F	£6337
146	12/99	Leic	2m7f110y	D(0-125)HCh	G-F	£4272
140	11/99	Worc	2m7f110y	C(0-135)HCh	G-S	£5889
137	1/99	Winc	2m5f	D Ch	SFT	£3831
105	12/97	Leic	2m	E Hdl	SFT	£3239
118	10/97	Strf	2m110y	E Hdl	GD	£2670
107	5/97	Worc	2m	H NHF	SFT	£1255
106	5/97	Wwck	2m	H NHF	GD	£1028

Total win prize-money £28525

Going: Sf: 0-0 GS: 0-0 Gd: 0-2 GF: - Fm: 0-1
Distance: 2m/2m3: 0-0 2m4-2m7: 0-1 3m+: 0-2
Track: LH: 0-2 RH: 0-1 Tight: 0-1 Gall: 0-0
Aids: Bl: 0-0 Vi: 0-0 Tstrap: 0-0
Best Rating: **146** 5/00 Strf 3m gd-fm Ch

One-time useful chaser, well beaten in three starts last term.

Andy Clyde

93 60

9-y-o b g Rambo Dancer (CAN)-Leprechaun Lady (Royal Blend)
A Bailey Sandybrow Stables Ltd

Placings:5/000450/F20405/0506/060P-P066 (2269)
2001/02: 17^{P}G, 16^{0}GF, 20^{6}G, 19^{6}G

	Starts	1st	2nd	3rd	Win & Pl
Hurdles	4	0	0	0	0
Career Total	**25**	**0**	**1**	**0**	**1025**

Going: Sf: 0-0 GS: 0-0 Gd: 0-3 GF: - Fm: 0-1
Distance: 2m/2m3: 0-3 2m4-2m7: 0-1 3m+: 0-0
Track: LH: 0-3 RH: 0-1 Tight: 0-1 Gall: 0-0
Aids: Bl: 0-1 Vi: 0-0 Tstrap: 0-0
Best Rating: **93** 8/98 Bang 2m4f good Hdl

Andy's Birthday (IRE)

105(82h) (79h)113

11-y-o ch g King Luthier-Clonroche Abendego (Pauper)
Miss S J Wilton John Pointon And Sons

Placings:0P0/1F254P1/P23P6-PP42131 (4428)
2001/02: 28^{P}S, 26^{P}HY, 20^{4}S, 23^{2}G, 24^{1}S, 29^{3}HY, 23^{1}HY

	Starts	1st	2nd	3rd	Win & Pl
Hurdles	1	0	0	0	0
Chases	6	2	1	1	10570
Career Total	**22**	**4**	**3**	**2**	**22995**

113	3/02	Uttx	2m7f	D(0-115)HCh	HVY	£5068
112	2/02	Kemp	3m	D(0-115)HCh	SFT	£3640
119	4/00	Uttx	3m	D(0-125)HCh	SFT	£4567
117	12/99	Uttx	3m	E(0-105)HCh	SFT	£3288

Total win prize-money £16565

Going: Sf: 2-6 GS: 0-0 Gd: 0-1 GF: - Fm: 0-0
Distance: 2m/2m3: 0-0 2m4-2m7: 1-2 3m+: 1-5
Track: LH: 1-4 RH: 1-3 Tight: 0-1 Gall: 0-0
Aids: Bl: 0-0 Vi: 0-1 **Tstrap: 2-5**
Best Rating: **119** 4/00 Uttx 3m soft Ch

Fair staying chaser when on song. Goes well in soft ground and has benefited from the fitting of a tongue-strap this year.

Andy's Lad (IRE)

102(95h) 105

10-y-o br g Versailles Road (USA)-Ah Ye Know (Wolverlife)
D Burchell (Ferdy Murphy 27/9) Primeshade Contracts Ltd

Placings:00P0*2031*0620/63200124/311/00-554F6P (4529)
2001/02: 16^{5}G, 20^{5}GS, 19^{4}GS, 20^{F}G, 20^{6}S, 19^{P}GS

	Starts	1st	2nd	3rd	Win & Pl
Chases	6	0	0	0	790
Career Total	**31**	**4**	**4**	**3**	**18900**

120	1/00	Catt	2m3f	D Ch	GD	£3965
124	1/00	Catt	2m3f	E Ch	GD	£3888
108	12/98	Wwck	2m3f	E(0-100)HHdl	G-S	£2582
103	12/97	Cork	2m	NHF	HVY	£3391

Total win prize-money £13827

Going: Sf: 0-1 GS: 0-3 Gd: 0-2 GF: - Fm: 0-0
Distance: 2m/2m3: 0-1 2m4-2m7: 0-5 3m+: 0-0
Track: LH: 0-3 RH: 0-3 Tight: 0-3 Gall: 0-0
Aids: Bl: 0-0 Vi: 0-0 Tstrap: 0-0
Best Rating: 124 1/00 Catt 2m3f good Ch

He made a promising start to his chasing career with two victories over 2m 3f at Catterick in January, but has not built on that.

Andys Joy (IRE)

50

8-y-o ch g Phardante (FR)-Meandering (Le Moss)
O Brennan O Brennan

Placings:5 (0451)
2001/02: 23^{5}F

	Starts	1st	2nd	3rd	Win & Pl
Hurdles	1	0	0	0	0
Career Total	**1**	**0**	**0**	**0**	**0**

Going: Sf: 0-0 GS: 0-0 Gd: 0-0 GF: - Fm: 0-1
Distance: 2m/2m3: 0-0 2m4-2m7: 0-1 3m+: 0-0
Track: LH: 0-1 RH: 0-0 Tight: 0-0 Gall: 0-0
Aids: Bl: 0-0 Vi: 0-0 Tstrap: 0-0
Best Rating: 50 5/01 Weth 2m7f firm Hdl

Anemos (IRE)

92 81

7-y-o ch g Be My Guest (USA)-Frendly Persuasion (General Assembly (USA))
T D McCarthy (Ian Williams 6/7) Andreas Michael

Placings:60 (0827)
2001/02: 16^{6}GF, 16^{0}GF

	Starts	1st	2nd	3rd	Win & Pl
Hurdles	2	0	0	0	0
Career Total	**2**	**0**	**0**	**0**	**0**

Going: Sf: 0-0 GS: 0-0 Gd: 0-0 GF: - Fm: 0-2
Distance: 2m/2m3: 0-2 2m4-2m7: 0-0 3m+: 0-0
Track: LH: 0-1 RH: 0-1 Tight: 0-1 Gall: 0-1
Aids: Bl: 0-0 Vi: 0-0 Tstrap: 0-0
Best Rating: 81 5/01 Hntg 2m110y gd-fm Hdl

Angel Delight

96 68

6-y-o gr m Seymour Hicks (FR)-Bird's Custard (Birdbrook)
Miss Venetia Williams Croome Cavaliers

Placings:6-560 (4850)
2001/02: 16^{5}G, 16^{6}GS, 22^{0}G

	Starts	1st	2nd	3rd	Win & Pl
NH Flat	2	0	0	0	0
Hurdles	1	0	0	0	0
Career Total	**4**	**0**	**0**	**0**	**0**

Going: Sf: 0-0 GS: 0-1 Gd: 0-2 GF: - Fm: 0-0
Distance: 2m/2m3: 0-2 2m4-2m7: 0-1 3m+: 0-0
Track: LH: 0-1 RH: 0-1 Tight: 0-1 Gall: 0-0
Aids: Bl: 0-0 Vi: 0-0 Tstrap: 0-0
Best Rating: 91 3/01 Hayd 2m heavy NHF

Angel Dust (FR)

102(103h) (67h)94

6-y-o b m Cadoudal (FR)-Silicity (FR) (Son Of Silver)
C Grant Akv Cladding Fabrications Ltd

Placings:0/001R41500-**0323PP** (4144)
2001/02: 17^{0}G, 16^{3}S, 16^{2}HY, 16^{3}S, 16^{P}S, 16^{P}HY

	Starts	1st	2nd	3rd	Win & Pl
Chases	6	0	1	2	2390
Career Total	**16**	**2**	**1**	**2**	**8245**

100	12/00	Sthl	2m	E Hdl	SFT	£2331
86	6/00	Prth	2m110y	F(0-100)HHdl	HVY	£3298

Total win prize-money £5630

Going: Sf: 0-5 GS: 0-0 Gd: 0-1 GF: - Fm: 0-0
Distance: 2m/2m3: 0-6 2m4-2m7: 0-0 3m+: 0-0
Track: LH: 0-5 RH: 0-1 Tight: 0-2 Gall: 0-1
Aids: Bl: 0-0 Vi: 0-0 Tstrap: 0-0
Best Rating: 100 12/00 Sthl 2m soft Hdl

A modest hurdler, she is only small and appears to struggle with the larger obstacles.

Angel In Disguise

10-y-o b m Kind Of Hush-Kasu (Try My Best (USA))
N B Mason Mrs D B Mason

Placings:6/46P-00 (4859)
2001/02: 21^{0}S, 25^{0}G

	Starts	1st	2nd	3rd	Win & Pl
Chases	2	0	0	0	
Career Total	**6**	**0**	**0**	**0**	**0**

Going: Sf: 0-1 GS: 0-0 Gd: 0-1 GF: - Fm: 0-0
Distance: 2m/2m3: 0-0 2m4-2m7: 0-1 3m+: 0-1
Track: LH: 0-2 RH: 0-0 Tight: 0-1 Gall: 0-0
Aids: Bl: 0-0 Vi: 0-0 Tstrap: 0-0
Best Rating: 60 9/00 Sedg 2m110y good Ch

Modest dual-purpose novice.

Angel Lane

79 44

5-y-o b m Merdon Melody-Young Whip (Bold Owl)
A W Carroll Aramis Racing Syndicate

Placings:00 (2204)
2001/02: 16^{0}GS, 16^{0}GS

	Starts	1st	2nd	3rd	Win & Pl
Hurdles	2	0	0	0	
Career Total	**2**	**0**	**0**	**0**	

Going: Sf: 0-0 GS: 0-2 Gd: 0-0 GF: - Fm: 0-0
Distance: 2m/2m3: 0-2 2m4-2m7: 0-0 3m+: 0-0
Track: LH: 0-1 RH: 0-1 Tight: 0-1 Gall: 0-0
Aids: Bl: 0-0 Vi: 0-0 Tstrap: 0-0
Best Rating: 44 11/01 Plum 2m gd-sft Hdl

Angels Venture

107 117

6-y-o ch g Unfuwain (USA)-City Of Angels (Woodman (USA))
J R Jenkins J Buffenbarger

Placings:1033/5P5-634 (4758)
2001/02: 16^{6}GF, 16^{3}GF, 16^{4}GF

	Starts	1st	2nd	3rd	Win & Pl
Hurdles	3	0	0	1	1093
Career Total	**10**	**1**	**0**	**3**	**4879**

100	11/99	Uttx	2m	E Hdl	G-S	£2347

Total win prize-money £2348

Going: Sf: 0-0 GS: 0-0 Gd: 0-0 GF: - Fm: 0-3
Distance: 2m/2m3: 0-3 2m4-2m7: 0-0 3m+: 0-0
Track: LH: 0-1 RH: 0-2 Tight: 0-1 Gall: 0-0
Aids: Bl: 0-0 Vi: 0-0 Tstrap: 0-2
Best Rating: 117 4/02 Asct 2m110y gd-fm Hdl

He made a winning debut over hurdles in a modest event at Uttoxeter in 1999, but finished tailed off in Lingfield's Summit Junior Hurdle. Well held in decent company, until third when dropped right down in class at the end of 2001. Has run his better races with give in the ground.

Angharad's Angel (IRE)

(98h) (77h)92

8-y-o b m Macmillion-West Along Lucy (IRE) (Dromod Hill)
Mrs A M Thorpe Mrs A M Thorpe

Placings:*520/0*P06**P**-060**UP** (1033)
2001/02: 22^{0}GF, 16^{6}G, 17^{0}G, 20^{U}GF, 16^{P}G

	Starts	1st	2nd	3rd	Win & Pl
Hurdles	3	0	0	0	0
Chases	2	0	0	0	0
Career Total	**13**	**0**	**1**	**0**	**427**

Going: Sf: 0-0 GS: 0-0 Gd: 0-3 GF: - Fm: 0-2
Distance: 2m/2m3: 0-3 2m4-2m7: 0-2 3m+: 0-0
Track: LH: 0-5 RH: 0-0 Tight: 0-4 Gall: 0-0
Aids: Bl: 0-0 Vi: 0-0 Tstrap: 0-0
Best Rating: 98 11/99 Hrfd 2m1f good NHF

Angie Gold

88f 61f

5-y-o b m Mesleh-Gold Duchess (Sonnen Gold)
Miss V Halgh Town Moor Golf Racing Syndicate

Placings:0 (4873)
2001/02: 16^{0}GF

	Starts	1st	2nd	3rd	Win & Pl
NH Flat	1	0	0	0	
Career Total	**1**	**0**	**0**	**0**	

Going: Sf: 0-0 GS: 0-0 Gd: 0-0 GF: - Fm: 0-1
Distance: 2m/2m3: 0-1 2m4-2m7: 0-0 3m+: 0-0
Track: LH: 0-1 RH: 0-0 Tight: 0-0 Gall: 0-0
Aids: Bl: 0-0 Vi: 0-0 Tstrap: 0-0
Best Rating: 61 4/02 Weth 2m gd-fm NHF

Angies Quest

5-y-o b m Inchinor-Chanson D'Avril (Chief Singer)
P W D'Arcy Mrs A Lovat

Placings:0 (3319)
2001/02: 16^{0}GS

	Starts	1st	2nd	3rd	Win & Pl
Hurdles	1	0	0	0	
Career Total	**1**	**0**	**0**	**0**	

Going: Sf: 0-0 GS: 0-1 Gd: 0-0 GF: - Fm: 0-0
Distance: 2m/2m3: 0-1 2m4-2m7: 0-0 3m+: 0-0
Track: LH: 0-0 RH: 0-1 Tight: 0-0 Gall: 0-1
Aids: Bl: 0-0 Vi: 0-0 Tstrap: 0-0
Best Rating:

Anglesey Dream

8-y-o b m Scottish Reel-Lexham View (Abwah)
J Mackie (T R George 19/5) Mrs P Hewitt

Placings:PP (3705)
2001/02: 17^{P}GS, 19^{P}HY

	Starts	1st	2nd	3rd	Win & Pl
Hurdles	2	0	0	0	
Career Total	**2**	**0**	**0**	**0**	

Going: Sf: 0-1 GS: 0-1 Gd: 0-0 GF: - Fm: 0-0
Distance: 2m/2m3: 0-1 2m4-2m7: 0-1 3m+: 0-0
Track: LH: 0-1 RH: 0-1 Tight: 0-1 Gall: 0-0
Aids: Bl: 0-0 Vi: 0-0 Tstrap: 0-0
Best Rating:

Anglesey Roseview

88 68

9-y-o b m Roscoe Blake-Lexham View (Abwah)
J Mackie Mrs P Hewitt

Placings:0P-000400 (1623)
2001/02: 24^{0}G, 20^{0}GS, 16^{0}GF, 20^{4}GS, 16^{0}G, 21^{0}G

	Starts	1st	2nd	3rd	Win & Pl
Hurdles	6	0	0	0	0
Career Total	**8**	**0**	**0**	**0**	**0**

Going: Sf: 0-0 GS: 0-2 Gd: 0-3 GF: - Fm: 0-1
Distance: 2m/2m3: 0-2 2m4-2m7: 0-3 3m+: 0-1
Track: LH: 0-5 RH: 0-1 Tight: 0-2 Gall: 0-0
Aids: Bl: 0-0 Vi: 0-0 Tstrap: 0-5
Best Rating: **68** 7/01 Uttx 2m gd-fm Hdl

Angry Native (IRE)

97 100

10-y-o b g Be My Native (USA)-An Grianan (Ballymore)
J Wade John Wade

Placings:0/5F66/600P0/031540006/53-450 (1904)
2001/02: 21^{4}G, 21^{5}G, 27^{0}G

	Starts	1st	2nd	3rd	Win & Pl
Chases	3	0	0	0	236
Career Total	**24**	**1**	**0**	**2**	**3076**

98 10/99 Hexm 2m4f110y F Hdl GD £2102
Total win prize-money £2102

Going: Sf: 0-0 GS: 0-0 Gd: 0-3 GF: - Fm: 0-0
Distance: 2m/2m3: 0-0 2m4-2m7: 0-2 3m+: 0-1
Track: LH: 0-3 RH: 0-0 Tight: 0-3 Gall: 0-0
Aids: Bl: 0-0 Vi: 0-0 Tstrap: 0-0
Best Rating: **100** 10/01 Sedg 2m5f good Ch

Anguilla

94 68

7-y-o b g Rudimentary (USA)-More Wise (Ballymore)
P T Dalton Mrs Lucia Farmer

Placings:4/0 (3368)
2001/02: 16^{0}GS

	Starts	1st	2nd	3rd	Win & Pl
NH Flat	1	0	0	0	
Career Total	**2**	**0**	**0**	**0**	**0**

Going: Sf: 0-0 GS: 0-1 Gd: 0-0 GF: - Fm: 0-0
Distance: 2m/2m3: 0-1 2m4-2m7: 0-0 3m+: 0-0
Track: LH: 0-1 RH: 0-0 Tight: 0-1 Gall: 0-0
Aids: Bl: 0-0 Vi: 0-0 Tstrap: 0-0
Best Rating: **75** 5/99 Hntg 2m110y gd-fm NHF

Angus-G

10-y-o br g Chief Singer-Horton Line (High Line)
Mrs M Reveley W Ginzel

Placings:P (3319)
2001/02: 16^{P}GS

	Starts	1st	2nd	3rd	Win & Pl
Hurdles	1	0	0	0	
Career Total	**1**	**0**	**0**	**0**	

Going: Sf: 0-0 GS: 0-1 Gd: 0-0 GF: - Fm: 0-0
Distance: 2m/2m3: 0-1 2m4-2m7: 0-0 3m+: 0-0
Track: LH: 0-0 RH: 0-1 Tight: 0-0 Gall: 0-1
Aids: Bl: 0-0 Vi: 0-0 Tstrap: 0-0
Best Rating:

Anna Almost

80 68+

4-y-o b f Tragic Role (USA)-Princess Hotpot (IRE) (King's Ride)
S Gollings Mrs Shirley Brasher

Placings:006 (4539)
2001/02: 16^{0}GS, 16^{0}S, 16^{6}G

	Starts	1st	2nd	3rd	Win & Pl
NH Flat	3	0	0	0	0
Career Total	**3**	**0**	**0**	**0**	**0**

Going: Sf: 0-1 GS: 0-1 Gd: 0-1 GF: - Fm: 0-0
Distance: 2m/2m3: 0-3 2m4-2m7: 0-0 3m+: 0-0
Track: LH: 0-2 RH: 0-1 Tight: 0-2 Gall: 0-0
Aids: Bl: 0-0 Vi: 0-0 Tstrap: 0-0
Best Rating: **74** 4/02 Fknm 2m good NHF

Annabee

5-y-o gr m Norton Challenger-Annaway (New Brig)
J C McConnochie P P Hall

Placings:0P (4315)
2001/02: 16^{0}S, 16^{P}HY

	Starts	1st	2nd	3rd	Win & Pl
NH Flat	1	0	0	0	0
Hurdles	1	0	0	0	0
Career Total	**2**	**0**	**0**	**0**	

Going: Sf: 0-2 GS: 0-0 Gd: 0-0 GF: - Fm: 0-0
Distance: 2m/2m3: 0-2 2m4-2m7: 0-0 3m+: 0-0
Track: LH: 0-2 RH: 0-0 Tight: 0-1 Gall: 0-1
Aids: Bl: 0-0 Vi: 0-0 Tstrap: 0-0
Best Rating:

Annadawi

99 78

7-y-o b g Sadler's Wells (USA)-Prayers'n Promises (USA) (Foolish Pleasure (USA))
M E Sowersby (C N Kellett 5/11) Paul Clifton

Placings:34/50/00-466 (4013)
2001/02: 16^{4}S, 16^{6}S, 16^{6}GS

	Starts	1st	2nd	3rd	Win & Pl
Hurdles	3	0	0	0	0
Career Total	**9**	**0**	**0**	**1**	**424**

Going: Sf: 0-2 GS: 0-1 Gd: 0-0 GF: - Fm: 0-0
Distance: 2m/2m3: 0-3 2m4-2m7: 0-0 3m+: 0-0
Track: LH: 0-2 RH: 0-1 Tight: 0-1 Gall: 0-2

Aids: Bl: 0-0 Vi: 0-0 Tstrap: 0-0
Best Rating: **99** 2/99 Thur 2m heavy NHF

A winner on the flat, he is a maiden over hurdles. Acts on good to soft ground.

Annapurna Boufrey (IRE)

57f 60f

6-y-o b m Roselier (FR)-Vulcash (IRE) (Callernish)
Mrs S A Bramall Mrs S A Bramall

Placings:00 (3999)
2001/02: 16^{0}Y, 16^{0}S

	Starts	1st	2nd	3rd	Win & Pl
NH Flat	2	0	0	0	
Career Total	**2**	**0**	**0**	**0**	

Going: Sf: 0-1 GS: 0-0 Gd: 0-0 GF: - Fm: 0-0
Distance: 2m/2m3: 0-2 2m4-2m7: 0-0 3m+: 0-0
Track: LH: 0-1 RH: 0-0 Tight: 0-0 Gall: 0-1
Aids: Bl: 0-0 Vi: 0-0 Tstrap: 0-0
Best Rating: **60** 12/01 Navn 2m yield NHF

Annespride

98 75

5-y-o b m Komaite (USA)-Lindrake's Pride (Mandrake Major)
Mrs M Reveley Mrs Muriel Ward

Placings:F40F-005 (1068)
2001/02: 17^{0}G, 16^{0}GF, 17^{5}GF

	Starts	1st	2nd	3rd	Win & Pl
Hurdles	3	0	0	0	0
Career Total	**7**	**0**	**0**	**0**	**222**

Going: Sf: 0-0 GS: 0-0 Gd: 0-1 GF: - Fm: 0-2
Distance: 2m/2m3: 0-3 2m4-2m7: 0-0 3m+: 0-0
Track: LH: 0-2 RH: 0-1 Tight: 0-2 Gall: 0-0
Aids: Bl: 0-2 Vi: 0-0 Tstrap: 0-0
Best Rating: **77** 8/00 Bang 2m1f good Hdl

Annie's Alfie

8-y-o b g Afzal-Annie's Daughter (Majestic Maharaj)
H W Lavis Mrs S M Farr

Placings:PP (0957)
2001/02: 16^{P}G, 16^{P}S

	Starts	1st	2nd	3rd	Win & Pl
Hurdles	2	0	0	0	
Career Total	**2**	**0**	**0**	**0**	

Going: Sf: 0-1 GS: 0-0 Gd: 0-1 GF: - Fm: 0-0
Distance: 2m/2m3: 0-2 2m4-2m7: 0-0 3m+: 0-0
Track: LH: 0-2 RH: 0-0 Tight: 0-0 Gall: 0-0
Aids: Bl: 0-0 Vi: 0-0 Tstrap: 0-0
Best Rating:

Annies Lad (IRE)

9-y-o ch g Un Desperado (FR)-Conductress (Orchestra)
Simon T Lewis Simon T Lewis

Placings:00/00/P (2929)

2001/02: 24^{P}GS

	Starts	1st	2nd	3rd	Win & Pl
Chases	1	0	0	0	
Career Total	**5**	**0**	**0**	**0**	

Going: Sf: 0-0 GS: 0-1 Gd: 0-0 GF: - Fm: 0-0
Distance: 2m/2m3: 0-0 2m4-2m7: 0-0 3m+: 0-1
Track: LH: 0-0 RH: 0-1 Tight: 0-1 Gall: 0-0
Aids: Bl: 0-0 Vi: 0-0 Tstrap: 0-0
Best Rating: **65** 7/99 Khgn 2m6f gd-fm Hdl

Annodyce

97 **71**

4-y-o b f Faustus (USA)-Coleford (USA) (Secreto (USA))
C A Dwyer S B Components (international) Ltd

Placings:4 **(1486)**
2001/02: 16^{4}GF

	Starts	1st	2nd	3rd	Win & Pl
Hurdles	1	0	0	0	0
Career Total	**1**	**0**	**0**	**0**	**0**

Going: Sf: 0-0 GS: 0-0 Gd: 0-0 GF: - Fm: 0-1
Distance: 2m/2m3: 0-1 2m4-2m7: 0-0 3m+: 0-0
Track: LH: 0-0 RH: 0-1 Tight: 0-0 Gall: 0-1
Aids: Bl: 0-0 Vi: 0-0 Tstrap: 0-0
Best Rating: **73** 9/01 Hntg 2m110y gd-fm Hdl

Made a promising enough debut at Huntingdon over two miles on good to firm.

Anns Girl

100(67c) **106**

9-y-o br m Newski (USA)-Nearly Married (Nearly A Hand)
J C Fox Mrs J A Cleary

Placings:061022413/6563F3P000/2454432111F460-P000 **(4853)**
2001/02: 19^{P}GS, 16^{0}GF, 16^{0}GF, 16^{0}G

	Starts	1st	2nd	3rd	Win & Pl
Hurdles	3	0	0	0	0
Chases	1	0	0	0	0
Career Total	**37**	**5**	**4**	**4**	**18671**

111	10/00	Extr	2m1f	D(0-125)HHdl	GD	£3419
105	9/00	Extr	2m1f	D(0-120)HHdl	GD	£3159
98	9/00	Worc	2m	E(0-115)HHdl	G-F	£2765
104	4/99	NAbb	2m1f	E Hdl	GD	£2421
83	6/98	Worc	2m	H NHF	GD	£1213

Total win prize-money £12979

Going: Sf: 0-0 GS: 0-1 Gd: 0-1 GF: - Fm: 0-2
Distance: 2m/2m3: 0-3 2m4-2m7: 0-1 3m+: 0-0
Track: LH: 0-3 RH: 0-1 Tight: 0-2 Gall: 0-0
Aids: Bl: 0-3 Vi: 0-0 Tstrap: 0-0
Best Rating: **111** 11/00 Newb 2m3f soft Hdl

Fair handicap hurdler on fast ground.

Anorak (USA)

96 **78**

12-y-o b g Storm Bird (CAN)-Someway Somehow (USA) (What Luck (USA))
N J Pomfret W J Turcan

Placings:54/1224B432/P4426/3054620062/P-6 **(0588)**
2001/02: 16^{6}GF

	Starts	1st	2nd	3rd	Win & Pl
Hurdles	1	0	0	0	0
Career Total	**27**	**1**	**6**	**2**	**6019**

87	9/94	Sedg	2m1f110y	Hdl	FRM	£1940

Total win prize-money £1940

Going: Sf: 0-0 GS: 0-0 Gd: 0-0 GF: - Fm: 0-1
Distance: 2m/2m3: 0-1 2m4-2m7: 0-0 3m+: 0-0
Track: LH: 0-1 RH: 0-0 Tight: 0-1 Gall: 0-0
Aids: Bl: 0-0 Vi: 0-0 Tstrap: 0-0
Best Rating: **93** 12/94 Muss 2m good Hdl

Another Alice

6-y-o b/br m Primitive Rising (USA)-Dragons Daughter (Mandrake Major)
C R Wilson W R Wilson

Placings:0 **(2401)**
2001/02: 16^{0}G

	Starts	1st	2nd	3rd	Win & Pl
NH Flat	1	0	0	0	
Career Total	**1**	**0**	**0**	**0**	

Going: Sf: 0-0 GS: 0-0 Gd: 0-1 GF: - Fm: 0-0
Distance: 2m/2m3: 0-1 2m4-2m7: 0-0 3m+: 0-0
Track: LH: 0-1 RH: 0-0 Tight: 0-0 Gall: 0-0
Aids: Bl: 0-0 Vi: 0-0 Tstrap: 0-0
Best Rating:

Another Chance

109 **132**

7-y-o b g Golden Heights-Lapopie (Deep Run)
J M Jefferson North South Partnership

Placings:33/326F-22F2122140 **(4667)**
2001/02: 16^{2}S, 17^{2}G, 17^{F}GS, 16^{2}G, 20^{1}S, 20^{2}G, 22^{2}S, 20^{1}S, 20^{4}G, 20^{0}G

	Starts	1st	2nd	3rd	Win & Pl
Hurdles	10	2	5	0	20597
Career Total	**16**	**2**	**6**	**3**	**22044**

132	2/02	Hntg	2m4f110y	B Hdl	SFT	£10504
125	10/01	Bang	2m4f	F(0-110)HHdl	SFT	£3510

Total win prize-money £14014

Going: Sf: 2-5 GS: 0-1 Gd: 0-4 GF: - Fm: 0-0
Distance: 2m/2m3: 0-4 **2m4-2m7: 2-6** 3m+: 0-0
Track: LH: 1-7 RH: 1-3 Tight: 1-4 Gall: 1-2
Aids: Bl: 0-0 Vi: 0-0 Tstrap: 0-0
Best Rating: **132** 2/02 Hntg 2m4f110y soft Hdl

Front-running hurdler, he was an easy winner of a Bangor handicap when stepped up in trip in October 2001. Came back from a break to win a decent Huntingdon novice. Stays two and a half miles plus, and suited by cut in the ground.

Another Chancer

85 **77**

11-y-o ch g Scallywag-Acuity (Sharp Edge)
D R Gandolfo Peter Melotti & Andy Chalmers

Placings:33533UR215/35320P-00 **(2926)**
2001/02: 24^{0}S, 24^{0}GS

	Starts	1st	2nd	3rd	Win & Pl
Hurdles	2	0	0	0	
Career Total	**18**	**1**	**2**	**6**	**5411**

91	3/99	Ling	2m7f	F(0-100)HHdl	G-S	£2277

Total win prize-money £2278

Going: Sf: 0-1 GS: 0-1 Gd: 0-0 GF: - Fm: 0-0
Distance: 2m/2m3: 0-0 2m4-2m7: 0-0 3m+: 0-2
Track: LH: 0-0 RH: 0-2 Tight: 0-1 Gall: 0-0
Aids: Bl: 0-1 Vi: 0-1 Tstrap: 0-0
Best Rating: **91** 3/99 Ling 2m7f gd-sft Hdl

Another Copper

82 (77h)**87**

6-y-o ch g Bandmaster (USA)-Letitica (Deep Run)
Mrs S D Williams Mrs E J Taplin

Placings:301 **(4732)**
2001/02: 22^{3}GF, 22^{0}G, 23^{1}F

	Starts	1st	2nd	3rd	Win & Pl
Hurdles	2	0	0	1	350
Chases	1	1	0	0	3640
Career Total	**3**	**1**	**0**	**1**	**3990**

87	4/02	Extr	2m7f110y	E Ch	FRM	£3640

Total win prize-money £3640

Going: Sf: 0-0 GS: 0-0 Gd: 0-1 GF: - Fm: 1-2
Distance: 2m/2m3: 0-0 2m4-2m7: 0-2 **3m+: 1-1**
Track: LH: 0-0 **RH: 1-1** Tight: 0-0 Gall: 0-0
Aids: Bl: 0-0 Vi: 0-0 Tstrap: 0-0
Best Rating: **87** 4/02 Extr 2m7f110y firm Ch

Lightly-raced, he ran well on his hurdling debut at Exeter in October 2001. Got off the mark on his chasing debut in April 2002. Appreciates fast ground.

Another Dude (IRE)

102 **100**

5-y-o br g Shardari-Gemma's Fridge (Frigid Aire)
J Howard Johnson Maurice Hutchinson

Placings:0442P **(4857)**
2001/02: 19^{0}G, 16^{4}G, 19^{4}S, 17^{2}S, 20^{P}G

	Starts	1st	2nd	3rd	Win & Pl
Hurdles	5	0	1	0	726
Career Total	**5**	**0**	**1**	**0**	**726**

Going: Sf: 0-2 GS: 0-0 Gd: 0-3 GF: - Fm: 0-0
Distance: 2m/2m3: 0-4 2m4-2m7: 0-1 3m+: 0-0
Track: LH: 0-4 RH: 0-1 Tight: 0-4 Gall: 0-0
Aids: Bl: 0-0 Vi: 0-0 Tstrap: 0-0
Best Rating: **100** 3/02 Sedg 2m1f soft Hdl

Showed much improved form when narrowly held under top-weight in a novices' handicap hurdle at Sedgefield.

Another Fine Mess (IRE)

82 **74**

6-y-o b/br g Supreme Leader-Galamear (Strong Gale)
T R George Mrs Sharon C Nelson

Placings:0PF **(4584)**
2001/02: 16^{0}HY, 21^{P}HY, 16^{F}G

	Starts	1st	2nd	3rd	Win & Pl
Hurdles	3	0	0	0	
Career Total	**3**	**0**	**0**	**0**	

Going: Sf: 0-2 GS: 0-0 Gd: 0-1 GF: - Fm: 0-0
Distance: 2m/2m3: 0-2 2m4-2m7: 0-1 3m+: 0-0
Track: LH: 0-1 RH: 0-1 Tight: 0-0 Gall: 0-0
Aids: Bl: 0-0 Vi: 0-0 Tstrap: 0-0
Best Rating: **74** 2/02 Hayd 2m heavy Hdl

Another Fly

8-y-o b m Buckley-March Fly (Sousa)
A H Mactaggart A H Mactaggart

Placings:0/0 **(4859)**
2001/02: 25^{0}G

	Starts	1st	2nd	3rd	Win & Pl
Chases	1	0	0	0	
Career Total	**2**	**0**	**0**	**0**	

Going: Sf: 0-0 GS: 0-0 Gd: 0-1 GF: - Fm: 0-0
Distance: 2m/2m3: 0-0 2m4-2m7: 0-0 3m+: 0-1
Track: LH: 0-1 RH: 0-0 Tight: 0-0 Gall: 0-0
Aids: Bl: 0-0 Vi: 0-0 Tstrap: 0-0
Best Rating: **39** 5/99 Prth 2m110y heavy NHF

Another General (IRE)

107 **134**

7-y-o ch g Glacial Storm (USA)-What's In A Name (IRE) (Le Moss)
R T Phillips Paul Duffy, Alan Beard, Brian Beard

Placings: *14*-1111P (4229)
2001/02: 20^{1}HY, 22^{1}HY, 22^{1}S, 24^{1}GS, 21^{P}GS

	Starts	1st	2nd	3rd	Win & Pl
Hurdles	5	4	0	0	20178
Career Total	**7**	**5**	**0**	**0**	**21830**

133	3/02	Newb	3m110y	D Hdl	G-S	£4641
134	2/02	Winc	2m6f	B Hdl	SFT	£9282
113	1/02	Folk	2m6f110y	E Hdl	HVY	£2667
105	12/01	Leic	2m4f110y	D Hdl	HVY	£3588
116	12/00	Towc	2m	H NHF	HVY	£1652

Total win prize-money £21830

Going: Sf: 3-3 GS: 1-2 Gd: 0-0 GF: - Fm: 0-0
Distance: 2m/2m3: 0-0 **2m4-2m7: 3-4** 3m+: 1-1
Track: LH: 1-2 **RH: 3-3** Tight: 1-1 Gall: 1-2
Aids: Bl: 0-0 Vi: 0-0 Tstrap: 0-0
Best Rating: **134** 2/02 Winc 2m6f soft Hdl

A bumper winner and four times a winner over hurdles, he acts on testing ground and firmer. Stays very well. Likely to have a big future as a chaser.

Another Helping (FR)

4-y-o gr g Turgeon (USA)-Tabelbala (FR) (Nashamaa)
J R Best Second Helping Associated Group

Placings: *0* (3503)
2001/02: 16^{0}S

	Starts	1st	2nd	3rd	Win & Pl
NH Flat	1	0	0	0	
Career Total	**1**	**0**	**0**	**0**	

Going: Sf: 0-1 GS: 0-0 Gd: 0-0 GF: - Fm: 0-0
Distance: 2m/2m3: 0-1 2m4-2m7: 0-0 3m+: 0-0
Track: LH: 0-0 RH: 0-1 Tight: 0-0 Gall: 0-0
Aids: Bl: 0-0 Vi: 0-0 Tstrap: 0-0
Best Rating:

Another Islay

98 **84**

11-y-o b g Tobin Lad (USA)-Coincidence Girl (Manacle)
R Johnson A Cowen

Placings: *0/00/*P5/0/P-P0P343PPP4 (1071)
2001/02: 25^{P}S, 20^{0}G, 20^{P}F, 16^{3}F, 16^{4}GF, 25^{3}G, 17^{P}G, 24^{P}GF, 27^{P}GF, 16^{4}GF

	Starts	1st	2nd	3rd	Win & Pl
Chases	10	0	0	2	1552
Career Total	**17**	**0**	**0**	**2**	**1552**

Going: Sf: 0-1 GS: 0-0 Gd: 0-3 GF: - Fm: 0-6
Distance: 2m/2m3: 0-4 2m4-2m7: 0-2 3m+: 0-4
Track: LH: 0-8 RH: 0-2 Tight: 0-4 Gall: 0-0
Aids: Bl: 0-5 Vi: 0-0 Tstrap: 0-1
Best Rating: **84** 5/01 Hexm 2m110y firm Ch

Another Joker

107 **97**

7-y-o b g Commanche Run-Just For A Laugh (Idiots Delight)
J L Needham Miss Joanna Needham

Placings: *0-2*0U02 (4540)
2001/02: 16^{2}GF, 20^{0}G, 17^{U}S, 16^{0}G, 19^{2}G

	Starts	1st	2nd	3rd	Win & Pl
NH Flat	1	0	1	0	446
Hurdles	4	0	1	0	980
Career Total	**6**	**0**	**2**	**0**	**1426**

Going: Sf: 0-1 GS: 0-0 Gd: 0-3 GF: - Fm: 0-1
Distance: 2m/2m3: 0-3 2m4-2m7: 0-2 3m+: 0-0
Track: LH: 0-2 RH: 0-3 Tight: 0-1 Gall: 0-0
Aids: Bl: 0-0 Vi: 0-0 Tstrap: 0-0
Best Rating: **102** 4/02 Hrfd 2m3f110y good Hdl

Modest novice hurdler, stays two and a half miles.

Another King

67

7-y-o ch g Primitive Rising (USA)-Knocksharry (Palm Track)
K W Hogg K W Hogg

Placings: *60/6*-P0 (1576)
2001/02: 17^{P}G, 22^{0}G

	Starts	1st	2nd	3rd	Win & Pl
Hurdles	2	0	0	0	
Career Total	**5**	**0**	**0**	**0**	**0**

Going: Sf: 0-0 GS: 0-0 Gd: 0-2 GF: - Fm: 0-0
Distance: 2m/2m3: 0-1 2m4-2m7: 0-1 3m+: 0-0
Track: LH: 0-2 RH: 0-0 Tight: 0-2 Gall: 0-0
Aids: Bl: 0-0 Vi: 0-0 Tstrap: 0-0
Best Rating: **79** 10/99 MRas 1m5f110y good NHF

Another Laura

87 (87h) (62h) **72**

7-y-o gr m Puissance-Traumatic Laura (Pragmatic)
J W F Aynsley Miss Susan J Blain

Placings: 0P-064**0640P** (4856)
2001/02: 24^{0}S, 20^{6}GF, 16^{4}GF, 19^{0}G, 19^{6}GS, 16^{4}S, 25^{0}GF, 25^{P}G

	Starts	1st	2nd	3rd	Win & Pl
Hurdles	3	0	0	0	0
Chases	5	0	0	0	233
Career Total	**10**	**0**	**0**	**0**	**233**

Going: Sf: 0-2 GS: 0-1 Gd: 0-2 GF: - Fm: 0-3
Distance: 2m/2m3: 0-4 2m4-2m7: 0-1 3m+: 0-3
Track: LH: 0-8 RH: 0-0 Tight: 0-3 Gall: 0-2
Aids: Bl: 0-0 Vi: 0-0 Tstrap: 0-1
Best Rating: **72** 4/02 Kels 3m1f gd-fm Ch

She is not a natural jumper and has achieved little over fences so far.

Another Man (IRE)

(93h) (68h)

7-y-o gr g Cataldi-Steal On (General Ironside)
N G Richards (Mrs H Dalton 31/5) J Hales

Placings: *0P*-06P (4671)
2001/02: 20^{0}G, 20^{6}F, 21^{P}GF

	Starts	1st	2nd	3rd	Win & Pl
Hurdles	2	0	0	0	0
Chases	1	0	0	0	0
Career Total	**5**	**0**	**0**	**0**	**0**

Going: Sf: 0-0 GS: 0-0 Gd: 0-1 GF: - Fm: 0-2
Distance: 2m/2m3: 0-0 2m4-2m7: 0-3 3m+: 0-0
Track: LH: 0-3 RH: 0-0 Tight: 0-1 Gall: 0-0
Aids: Bl: 0-1 Vi: 0-0 Tstrap: 0-0
Best Rating: **73** 1/01 Donc 2m110y good NHF

Another Question (USA)

(90h) **85**

6-y-o b g Quest For Fame-Another Notch (USA) (Cox's Ridge (USA))
A Dickman Mike Smallman

Placings: 3P3/033P43**200-0FF** (2530)
2001/02: 16^{0}G, 16^{F}F, 17^{F}S

	Starts	1st	2nd	3rd	Win & Pl
Chases	3	0	0	0	
Career Total	**15**	**0**	**1**	**5**	**4132**

Going: Sf: 0-1 GS: 0-0 Gd: 0-1 GF: - Fm: 0-1
Distance: 2m/2m3: 0-3 2m4-2m7: 0-0 3m+: 0-0
Track: LH: 0-1 RH: 0-2 Tight: 0-1 Gall: 0-0
Aids: Bl: 0-0 Vi: 0-0 Tstrap: 0-0
Best Rating: **100** 11/99 Newc 2m good Hdl

Another Raleagh (IRE)

106 (110h) (123h) **133**

8-y-o b g Be My Native (USA)-Caffra Mills (Pitpan)
A Ennis A T A Wates

Placings: *3/5*141-4222 (4386)
2001/02: 16^{4}GS, 16^{2}G, 16^{2}G, 16^{2}S

	Starts	1st	2nd	3rd	Win & Pl
Hurdles	1	0	0	0	651
Chases	3	0	3	0	5472
Career Total	**9**	**2**	**3**	**1**	**12600**

123	4/01	Winc	2m	E Hdl	SFT	£3066
109	2/01	Towc	2m	E Hdl	HVY	£2506

Total win prize-money £5572

Going: Sf: 0-1 GS: 0-1 Gd: 0-2 GF: - Fm: 0-0
Distance: 2m/2m3: 0-4 2m4-2m7: 0-0 3m+: 0-0
Track: LH: 0-0 RH: 0-4 Tight: 0-0 Gall: 0-0
Aids: Bl: 0-0 Vi: 0-0 Tstrap: 0-0
Best Rating: **133** 3/02 Sand 2m good Ch

Showed progressive form over hurdles and has offered encouragement in his attempts over fences. Handles a sound surface though his wins have come on soft.

Another Wagon (IRE)

98 **80**

9-y-o b g Yashgan-Dawn Even (Laurence O)
A M Crow The Ancrum Pointer

Placings: *0*003P/0/**P-UPP3PP** (4523)
2001/02: 24^{U}GF, 24^{P}S, 27^{P}S, 32^{3}HY, 32^{P}HY, 26^{P}GS

	Starts	1st	2nd	3rd	Win & Pl

	Starts	1st	2nd	3rd	Win & Pl
Hurdles	1	0	0	0	0
Chases	5	0	0	1	603
Career Total	**13**	**0**	**0**	**2**	**844**

Going: Sf: 0-4 GS: 0-1 Gd: 0-0 GF: - Fm: 0-1
Distance: 2m/2m3: 0-0 2m4-2m7: 0-0 3m+: 0-6
Track: LH: 0-3 RH: 0-3 Tight: 0-3 Gall: 0-0
Aids: Bl: 0-0 Vi: 0-0 Tstrap: 0-0
Best Rating: **80** 3/02 Hexm 4m heavy Ch

Very moderate staying chase with poor completion record. Suited by long distances and soft ground.

Anotherhandyman

95 **100**

8-y-o ch g Jupiter Island-Handbelle (Nearly A Hand)
R Johnson J L Gledson

Placings:*000*/**P44**P **(4890)**
2001/02: 27^{P}HY, 21^{4}S, 20^{4}S, 24^{P}G

	Starts	1st	2nd	3rd	Win & Pl
Hurdles	1	0	0	0	0
Chases	3	0	0	0	507
Career Total	**7**	**0**	**0**	**0**	**507**

Going: Sf: 0-3 GS: 0-0 Gd: 0-1 GF: - Fm: 0-0
Distance: 2m/2m3: 0-0 2m4-2m7: 0-2 3m+: 0-2
Track: LH: 0-2 RH: 0-2 Tight: 0-3 Gall: 0-0
Aids: Bl: 0-0 Vi: 0-0 Tstrap: 0-0
Best Rating: **100** 2/02 Sedg 2m5f soft Ch

Winning pointer, lightly raced under Rules so far.

Ansar (IRE)

(120li) (154h) **132+**

6-y-o b g Kahyasi-Anaza (Darshaan)
D K Weld Mrs K Devlin

Placings:52/1-11156604 **(4959a)**
2001/02: 16^{1}Y, 16^{1}GY, 16^{1}S, 20^{5}Y, 16^{6}S, 16^{6}GS, 16^{0}Y, 16^{4}GY

	Starts	1st	2nd	3rd	Win & Pl
Hurdles	8	3	0	0	102402
Career Total	**11**	**4**	**1**	**0**	**107714**

154	10/01	Tipp	2m	Hdl	SFT	£34072
145	8/01	Gway	2m	HHdl	G-Y	£53931
137	7/01	Gway	2m	(0-123)HHdl	YLD	£7062
118	8/00	Gway	2m	Hdl	G-Y	£4416

Total win prize-money £100283

Going: Sf: 1-2 GS: 0-1 Gd: 0-0 GF: - Fm: 0-0
Distance: **2m/2m3: 3-7** 2m4-2m7: 0-1 3m+: 0-0
Track: LH: 0-1 RH: 0-3 Tight: 0-0 Gall: 0-0
Aids: Bl: 0-0 Vi: 0-0 Tstrap: 0-0
Best Rating: **154** 3/02 Chel 2m110y gd-sft Hdl

Winner of the Galway Hurdle in August, he likes soft ground and improved to beat Grimes and Liss A Paoraigh at Tipperary in October. Below par at Gowran Park in February,he was a respectable sixth in the Champion Hurdle but was held in good races in ireland subsequently.

Ansari (IRE)

113 **123**

5-y-o b g Selkirk (USA)-Anaza (Darshaan)
Patrick O Brady Miss Rita Shah

Placings:0000-0230421135110100 **(4256)**
2001/02: 16^{0}G, 16^{2}G, 17^{3}GF, 16^{0}GF, 18^{4}F, 18^{2}GY, 16^{1}S, 16^{1}G, 16^{3}GY, 16^{5}GF, 16^{1}F, 16^{1}G, 16^{0}S, 16^{1}HY, 16^{0}GS, 17^{0}G

	Starts	1st	2nd	3rd	Win & Pl
Hurdles	16	5	2	2	42330
Career Total	**20**	**5**	**2**	**2**	**42330**

123	2/02	Naas	2m	HHdl	HVY	£11963
116	10/01	Gowr	2m	(0-135)HHdl	GD	£13104
112	9/01	DRoy	2m	(0-116)HHdl	FRM	£3895
105	8/01	Baln	2m	(0-95)HHdl	GD	£5008
99	8/01	Rosc	2m	(0-116)HHdl	SFT	£5008

Total win prize-money £38979

Going: Sf: 2-3 GS: 0-1 Gd: 2-5 GF: - Fm: 1-5
Distance: **2m/2m3: 5-16** 2m4-2m7: 0-0 3m+: 0-0
Track: **LH: 1-3** RH: 0-1 Tight: 0-0 Gall: 0-1
Aids: Bl: 0-0 Vi: 0-0 Tstrap: 0-0
Best Rating: **123** 2/02 Naas 2m heavy Hdl

Fair Irish hurdler, acts on any ground.

Anse (IRE)

77f **70f**

5-y-o b g Mujadil (USA)-Mevlana (IRE) (Red Sunset)
J R Norton Jaffa Racing Syndicate

Placings:*0P* **(2007)**
2001/02: 17^{0}GF, 16^{P}S

	Starts	1st	2nd	3rd	Win & Pl
NH Flat	2	0	0	0	
Career Total	**2**	**0**	**0**	**0**	

Going: Sf: 0-1 GS: 0-0 Gd: 0-0 GF: - Fm: 0-1
Distance: 2m/2m3: 0-2 2m4-2m7: 0-0 3m+: 0-0
Track: LH: 0-1 RH: 0-1 Tight: 0-1 Gall: 0-0
Aids: Bl: 0-0 Vi: 0-0 Tstrap: 0-0
Best Rating: **70** 6/01 MRas 2m1f110y gd-fm NHF

Ansias (USA)

97 **102**

9-y-o b g Diesis-Alia (Sun Prince)
N P McCormack (Mrs D McCormack 1/6) Mrs D McCormack

Placings:030F/P/**41FP** **(4487)**
2001/02: 21^{4}G, 24^{1}GF, 28^{F}GF, 26^{P}GS

	Starts	1st	2nd	3rd	Win & Pl
Chases	4	1	0	0	3021
Career Total	**9**	**1**	**0**	**1**	**3275**

102	5/01	Prth	3m	H Ch	G-F	£3020

Total win prize-money £3021

Going: Sf: 0-0 GS: 0-1 Gd: 0-1 GF: - Fm: 1-2
Distance: 2m/2m3: 0-0 2m4-2m7: 0-1 **3m+: 1-3**
Track: LH: 0-2 **RH: 1-2** Tight: 0-2 Gall: 0-0
Aids: Bl: 0-0 Vi: 0-0 Tstrap: 0-0
Best Rating: **109** 4/99 Carl 2m4f110y good Hdl

Antenne (IRE)

72 **61**

5-y-o b m Roakarad-Secrete Envie (USA) (Secreto (USA))
A Crook (J Ortet 22/7) Hope Springs Eternal

Placings:05**056**-23453 **(4315)**
2001/02: 17^{2}GS, 19^{3}G, 17^{4}G, 16^{5}GS, 16^{3}HY

	Starts	1st	2nd	3rd	Win & Pl
Hurdles	3	0	1	1	2312
Chases	2	0	0	1	1057
Career Total	**10**	**0**	**1**	**2**	**4484**

Going: Sf: 0-1 GS: 0-2 Gd: 0-2 GF: - Fm: 0-0
Distance: 2m/2m3: 0-4 2m4-2m7: 0-1 3m+: 0-0
Track: LH: 0-2 RH: 0-0 Tight: 0-2 Gall: 0-0
Aids: Bl: 0-3 Vi: 0-0 Tstrap: 0-0
Best Rating: **61** 1/02 Sthl 2m gd-sft Hdl

Modest hurdler.

Anthemion (IRE)

76

5-y-o ch g Night Shift (USA)-New Sensitive (Wattlefield)
Mrs D Thomson The Coutts McGregor Clan

Placings:0P-FPF **(4888)**
2001/02: 17^{F}GS, 16^{P}G, 16^{F}G

	Starts	1st	2nd	3rd	Win & Pl
Hurdles	3	0	0	0	
Career Total	**5**	**0**	**0**	**0**	

Going: Sf: 0-0 GS: 0-1 Gd: 0-2 GF: - Fm: 0-0
Distance: 2m/2m3: 0-3 2m4-2m7: 0-0 3m+: 0-0
Track: LH: 0-1 RH: 0-2 Tight: 0-0 Gall: 0-0
Aids: Bl: 0-0 Vi: 0-0 Tstrap: 0-0
Best Rating: **76** 4/02 Prth 2m110y good Hdl

Antiguan Flyer

77 **32**

13-y-o b g Shirley Heights-Fleet Girl (Habitat)
G Prodromou George Prodromou

Placings:21562240/3/24400121/1P26451/54210050/11PP/6 **(1221)**
2001/02: 18^{6}GF

	Starts	1st	2nd	3rd	Win & Pl
Hurdles	1	0	0	0	0
Caroor Total	**37**	**8**	**7**	**1**	**25243**

106	5/99	Towc	2m	D(0-125)HHdl	G-F	£2802
106	5/99	MRas	2m1f110y	F(0-105)HHdl	G-F	£2080
104	11/98	Wind	2m	E(0-120)HHdl	GD	£2921
104	3/98	Fknm	2m	E(0-115)HHdl	GD	£3625
95	5/97	Hntg	2m110y	D(0-120)HHdl	G-F	£2756
94	4/97	Towc	2m	F(0-105)HHdl	G-F	£2034
83	3/97	Fknm	2m	G(0-90)HHdl	GD	£2785
86	1/93	Sthl	2m	Hdl	STD	£1484

Total win prize-money £20568

Going: Sf: 0-0 GS: 0-0 Gd: 0-0 GF: - Fm: 0-1
Distance: 2m/2m3: 0-1 2m4-2m7: 0-0 3m+: 0-0
Track: LH: 0-1 RH: 0-0 Tight: 0-1 Gall: 0-0
Aids: Bl: 0-0 Vi: 0-1 Tstrap: 0-0
Best Rating: **106** 5/99 Towc 2m gd-fm Hdl

Antique Gold

78 **59**

8-y-o b g Gildoran-Chanelle (The Parson)
R Allan Mrs L A Ogilvie

Placings:*52/22/6* **(4120)**
2001/02: 16^{6}HY

	Starts	1st	2nd	3rd	Win & Pl
Hurdles	1	0	0	0	0
Career Total	**5**	**0**	**3**	**0**	**3158**

Going: Sf: 0-1 GS: 0-0 Gd: 0-0 GF: - Fm: 0-0
Distance: 2m/2m3: 0-1 2m4-2m7: 0-0 3m+: 0-0
Track: LH: 0-1 RH: 0-0 Tight: 0-0 Gall: 0-0
Aids: Bl: 0-0 Vi: 0-0 Tstrap: 0-0
Best Rating: **125** 11/99 Asct 3m good Hdl

He has shown enough promise to suggest that he can win staying events over hurdles.

Antonio Mariano (SWE)

111 123

11-y-o b g Mango Express-Mango Sampaquita (SWE) (Colombian Friend (USA))

Mrs L C Taylor (Lady Herries 12/6) Mrs Mette Campbell

Placings:1/006/**11**/**1**F32F52/3-21 **(4886)**

2001/02: 16^{2}G, 18^{1}GF

	Starts	1st	2nd	3rd	Win & Pl
Chases	2	1	1	0	5050
Career Total	**16**	**5**	**3**	**2**	**21931**

123	4/02	Font	2m2f	D(0-110)HCh	G-F	£3657
118	11/99	Winc	2m	D(0-120)HCh	GD	£5095
111	12/97	Folk	2m	E(0-100)HCh	GD	£3517
111	11/97	Plum	2m	F(0-105)HCh	SFT	£2707
105	4/96	Font	2m2f	E Hdl	G-F	£2098

Total win prize-money £17077

Going: Sf: 0-0 GS: 0-0 Gd: 0-1 GF: - Fm: 1-1
Distance: **2m/2m3: 1-2** 2m4-2m7: 0-0 3m+: 0-0
Track: LH: 0-0 RH: 0-1 **Tight: 1-1** Gall: 0-0
Aids: Bl: 0-0 Vi: 0-0 Tstrap: 0-0
Best Rating: **123** 4/02 Font 2m2f gd-fm Ch

Lightly-raced handicap chaser, suited by two miles plus, good ground and a sharp track.

Anubis Quercus (FR)

9-y-o b g Kadrou (FR)-Polish Maid (FR) (Bolkonski)

G C Evans (B Ellison 5/5) C E Sherry

Placings:02/004231/20-PUPPF **(4650)**

2001/02: 20^{P}S, 19^{U}S, 20^{P}S, 20^{P}S, 21^{F}G

	Starts	1st	2nd	3rd	Win & Pl
Hurdles	1	0	0	0	0
Chases	4	0	0	0	0
Career Total	**15**	**1**	**3**	**1**	**10381**

104	3/00	Sedg	2m110y	C Ch	G-F	£5817

Total win prize-money £5818

Going: Sf: 0-4 GS: 0-0 Gd: 0-1 GF: - Fm: 0-0
Distance: 2m/2m3: 0-0 2m4-2m7: 0-5 3m+: 0-0
Track: LH: 0-3 RH: 0-2 Tight: 0-2 Gall: 0-1
Aids: Bl: 0-0 Vi: 0-0 Tstrap: 0-0
Best Rating: **107** 1/00 Uttx 2m soft Ch

Anugraha (IRE)

9-y-o gr g Supreme Leader-Nanny Kehoe (IRE) (Sexton Blake)

H H G Owen (A W Carroll 31/5) J P Owen

Placings:*00*P3P/PF024/50-PP **(4724)**

2001/02: 21^{P}GF, 16^{P}GF

	Starts	1st	2nd	3rd	Win & Pl
Hurdles	2	0	0	0	
Career Total	**14**	**0**	**1**	**1**	**1595**

Going: Sf: 0-0 GS: 0-0 Gd: 0-0 GF: - Fm: 0-2
Distance: 2m/2m3: 0-1 2m4-2m7: 0-1 3m+: 0-0
Track: LH: 0-1 RH: 0-1 Tight: 0-0 Gall: 0-1
Aids: Bl: 0-1 Vi: 0-0 Tstrap: 0-0
Best Rating: **94** 4/00 Hntg 2m5f110y good Hdl

Anxious Moments (IRE)

116 129

7-y-o b g Supreme Leader-Ms Brooks (IRE) (Lord Ha Ha)

C F Swan J P McManus

Placings:0*1*-016151 **(4712a)**

2001/02: 16^{0}S, 16^{1}Y, 16^{6}G, 16^{1}Y, 16^{5}YS, 16^{1}Y

	Starts	1st	2nd	3rd	Win & Pl
NH Flat	1	0	0	0	0
Hurdles	5	3	0	0	61407
Career Total	**8**	**4**	**0**	**0**	**64719**

129	4/02	Fair	2m	HHdl	YLD	£39877
126	12/01	Navn	2m	HHdl	YLD	£12580
114	11/01	Cork	2m	Hdl	YLD	£6955
112	10/00	Fair	2m	NHF	Y-S	£3312

Total win prize-money £62726

Going: Sf: 0-1 GS: 0-0 Gd: 0-1 GF: - Fm: 0-0
Distance: **2m/2m3: 3-6** 2m4-2m7: 0-0 3m+: 0-0
Track: LH: 1-3 RH: 1-1 Tight: 0-0 Gall: 0-0
Aids: Bl: 0-0 Vi: 0-0 Tstrap: 0-0
Best Rating: **129** 4/02 Fair 2m yield Hdl

An Irish-trained novice, he was off the track for a year after winning a bumper at Fairyhouse in October 2000, but got off the mark over hurdles at Cork in November 2001 and won his handicap debut a month later. Impressive at fairyhouse over Easter. Suited by soft ground and two miles.

Anzal (IRE)

4-y-o b g Kahyasi-Anazara (USA) (Trempolino (USA))

D R Gandolfo Peter Melotti

Placings:0 **(3502)**

2001/02: 16^{0}S

	Starts	1st	2nd	3rd	Win & Pl
NH Flat	1	0	0	0	
Career Total	**1**	**0**	**0**	**0**	

Going: Sf: 0-1 GS: 0-0 Gd: 0-0 GF: - Fm: 0-0
Distance: 2m/2m3: 0-1 2m4-2m7: 0-0 3m+: 0-0
Track: LH: 0-0 RH: 0-1 Tight: 0-0 Gall: 0-0
Aids: Bl: 0-0 Vi: 0-0 Tstrap: 0-0
Best Rating:

Apache Park (USA)

95 101

9-y-o b g Alleged (USA)-Fairly Magic (USA) (Raise A Native)

J Mackie Mrs Sue Adams

Placings:06P145/62F5124500P/20344514PP/F3500/012 **(2901)**

2001/02: 20^{0}HY, 20^{1}GS, 20^{2}S

	Starts	1st	2nd	3rd	Win & Pl
Hurdles	3	1	1	0	4611
Career Total	**35**	**4**	**4**	**2**	**14824**

99	12/01	Leic	2m4f110y	D(0-120)HHdl	G-S	£3471
99	12/98	Leic	2m4f110y	G(0-90)HHdl	G-S	£2220
87	6/97	Uttx	2m4f110y	F Hdl	GD	£2316
96	2/97	Leic	2m	F Hdl	G-S	£2595

Total win prize-money £10602

Going: Sf: 0-2 GS: 1-1 Gd: 0-0 GF: - Fm: 0-0
Distance: 2m/2m3: 0-0 **2m4-2m7: 1-3** 3m+: 0-0
Track: LH: 0-0 **RH: 1-3** Tight: 0-0 Gall: 0-0
Aids: Bl: 0-0 Vi: 0-0 **Tstrap: 1-3**
Best Rating: **106** 2/00 Leic 2m4f110y gd-sft Hdl

Modest hurdler, acts on good and soft ground.

Apachee Flower

94 56

12-y-o ch m Formidable (USA)-Molucella (Connaught)

H S Howe John Bull

Placings:432536606/404/241043/502546/21P13P/F00/215 02520454P4/100-00 **(0979)**

2001/02: 27^{0}G, 27^{0}G

	Starts	1st	2nd	3rd	Win & Pl
Hurdles	2	0	0	0	
Career Total	**51**	**5**	**7**	**4**	**19395**

95	9/00	NAbb	3m3f	D(0-125)HHdl	G-F	£2871
98	5/99	Strf	3m3f	D(0-125)HHdl	GD	£2960
89	7/97	Sthl	3m110y	E(0-110)HHdl	G-F	£2310
88	5/97	NAbb	3m3f	F(0-105)HHdl	GD	£1944
88	11/95	Uttx	3m110y	E Hdl	GD	£2165

Total win prize-money £12253

Going: Sf: 0-0 GS: 0-0 Gd: 0-2 GF: - Fm: 0-0
Distance: 2m/2m3: 0-0 2m4-2m7: 0-0 3m+: 0-2
Track: LH: 0-2 RH: 0-0 Tight: 0-2 Gall: 0-0
Aids: Bl: 0-0 Vi: 0-0 Tstrap: 0-0
Best Rating: **98** 10/99 Ludl 3m gd-fm Hdl

Apachevere (IRE)

(85h)

7-y-o b g Commanche Run-Vent Vert (IRE) (Green Shoon)

Mrs H Dalton Norton Natives

Placings:400-PP4 **(3767)**

2001/02: 25^{P}G, 25^{P}GS, 24^{4}GS

	Starts	1st	2nd	3rd	Win & Pl
Hurdles	1	0	0	0	0
Chases	2	0	0	0	319
Career Total	**6**	**0**	**0**	**0**	**589**

Going: Sf: 0-0 GS: 0-2 Gd: 0-1 GF: - Fm: 0-0
Distance: 2m/2m3: 0-0 2m4-2m7: 0-0 3m+: 0-3
Track: LH: 0-2 RH: 0-1 Tight: 0-1 Gall: 0-0
Aids: Bl: 0-0 Vi: 0-0 Tstrap: 0-0
Best Rating: **72** 1/01 Donc 3m110y good Hdl

Moderate ability shown over both hurdles and fences so far.

Apadi (USA)

108 106

6-y-o ch g Diesis-Ixtapa (USA) (Chief's Crown (USA))

M C Chapman (K Bell 22/7) Barry Brown & Kenny Blanch

Placings:6403-521511620F6000F0 **(4848)**

2001/02: 16^{5}GF, 16^{2}GF, 16^{1}GF, 17^{5}GS, 17^{1}G, 16^{1}GF, 24^{6}S, 17^{2}GS, 16^{0}GF, 16^{F}G, 16^{6}GS, 16^{0}G, 16^{0}G, 16^{0}GS, 17^{F}G, 16^{0}G

	Starts	1st	2nd	3rd	Win & Pl
Hurdles	16	3	2	0	10607
Career Total	**20**	**3**	**2**	**1**	**10982**

102	9/01	Worc	2m	E(0-115)HHdl	G-F	£3083
95	8/01	Ctml	2m1f110y	G(0-90)HHdl	GD	£3657
86	7/01	Sthl	2m	G Hdl	G-F	£1596

Total win prize-money £8338

Going: Sf: 0-1 GS: 0-4 Gd: 1-6 GF: - Fm: 2-5
Distance: **2m/2m3: 3-15** 2m4-2m7: 0-0 3m+: 0-1
Track: **LH: 3-10** RH: 0-6 **Tight: 2-10** Gall: 0-1
Aids: Bl: 0-0 Vi: 0-0 Tstrap: 0-0
Best Rating: **106** 10/01 MRas 2m1f110y gd-sft Hdl

Fair handicap hurdler. Best at two miles on a sound surface. Suited by a strong pace.

Apatura King

106 110

12-y-o ch g Button Bright (USA)-Apatura Iris (Space King)
R H Alner C E Gibbs

Placings:0/6/3/12/30-60 (0422)
2001/02: 25^{6}GF, 30^{0}G

	Starts	1st	2nd	3rd	Win & Pl
Chases	2	0	0	0	0
Career Total	9	1	1	2	4392

109 5/99 Folk 3m7f H Ch G-F £2682
Total win prize-money £2682

Going: Sf: 0-0 GS: 0-0 Gd: 0-1 GF: - Fm: 0-1
Distance: 2m/2m3: 0-0 2m4-2m7: 0-0 3m+: 0-2
Track: LH: 0-1 RH: 0-1 Tight: 0-1 Gall: 0-0
Aids: Bl: 0-0 Vi: 0-0 Tstrap: 0-0
Best Rating: 119 10/00 Chel 3m110y good Ch

Apple Joe

85(77h) (41h)73

6-y-o b g Sula Bula-Hazelwain (Hard Fact)
Dr P Pritchard A J Whiting

Placings:FP304 (4182)
2001/02: 18^{F}GS, 24^{P}G, 21^{3}HY, 16^{0}S, 19^{4}S

	Starts	1st	2nd	3rd	Win & Pl
Hurdles	4	0	0	1	372
Chases	1	0	0	0	368
Career Total	5	0	0	1	740

Going: Sf: 0-3 GS: 0-1 Gd: 0-1 GF: - Fm: 0-0
Distance: 2m/2m3: 0-3 2m4-2m7: 0-1 3m+: 0-1
Track: LH: 0-3 RH: 0-2 Tight: 0-4 Gall: 0-1
Aids: Bl: 0-0 Vi: 0-0 Tstrap: 0-0
Best Rating: 73 3/02 Tntn 2m3f soft Ch

Apple John

102 101

13-y-o b g Sula Bula-Hazelwain (Hard Fact)
Dr P Pritchard A J Whiting

Placings:3F/1PUPP/P/050-4P04402142UPU (4664)
2001/02: 24^{4}GF, 20^{P}G, 31^{0}GS, 22^{4}G, 20^{4}GS, 23^{0}G, 24^{2}S, 22^{1}HY, 24^{4}S, 24^{2}S, 20^{U}S, 24^{P}S, 21^{U}G

	Starts	1st	2nd	3rd	Win & Pl
Chases	13	1	2	0	5351
Career Total	24	2	2	1	8810

101 2/02 Font 2m6f F(0-90)HCh HVY £3108
89 3/99 Tntn 3m H Ch SFT £2931
Total win prize-money £6039

Going: Sf: 1-6 GS: 0-2 Gd: 0-4 GF: - Fm: 0-1
Distance: 2m/2m3: 0-0 **2m4-2m7: 1-6** 3m+: 0-7
Track: LH: 0-3 RH: 0-8 **Tight: 1-7** Gall: 0-3
Aids: Bl: 0-1 Vi: 0-0 Tstrap: 0-0
Best Rating: 109 11/96 Kemp 3m gd-sft Ch

A winner over fences, he acts on good and soft ground and is effective at around three miles.

Apple Saft (IRE)

11-y-o b g Arapahos (FR)-Why Cry (Pry)
M S Wilesmith M S Wilesmith

Placings:P-P (0267)
2001/02: 17^{P}G

	Starts	1st	2nd	3rd	Win & Pl
Hurdles	1	0	0	0	
Career Total	2	0	0	0	

Going: Sf: 0-0 GS: 0-0 Gd: 0-1 GF: - Fm: 0-0
Distance: 2m/2m3: 0-1 2m4-2m7: 0-0 3m+: 0-0
Track: LH: 0-0 RH: 0-1 Tight: 0-0 Gall: 0-0
Aids: Bl: 0-0 Vi: 0-1 Tstrap: 0-0
Best Rating:

Applemir George

71 41

7-y-o b g Almushmmir-Lady Sweetapples (Super Song)
Jane Southcombe Mrs J C Duffy

Placings:5-000FP (4883)
2001/02: 17^{0}GS, 17^{0}GS, 22^{0}G, 22^{F}G, 22^{P}GF

	Starts	1st	2nd	3rd	Win & Pl
NH Flat	1	0	0	0	0
Hurdles	4	0	0	0	0
Career Total	6	0	0	0	0

Going: Sf: 0-0 GS: 0-2 Gd: 0-2 GF: - Fm: 0-1
Distance: 2m/2m3: 0-2 2m4-2m7: 0-3 3m+: 0-0
Track: LH: 0-1 RH: 0-4 Tight: 0-2 Gall: 0-0
Aids: Bl: 0-0 Vi: 0-2 Tstrap: 0-0
Best Rating: 97 4/01 Tntn 2m1f gd-fm NHF

Applepie Lady (IRE)

101f 96f

5-y-o b m Lord Americo-Lady Bow (Deep Run)
A J Liddordale A Franklin

Placings:25 (4269)
2001/02: 16^{2}HY, 16^{5}S

	Starts	1st	2nd	3rd	Win & Pl
NH Flat	2	0	1	0	542
Career Total	2	0	1	0	542

Going: Sf: 0-2 GS: 0-0 Gd: 0-0 GF: - Fm: 0-0
Distance: 2m/2m3: 0-2 2m4-2m7: 0-0 3m+: 0-0
Track: LH: 0-2 RH: 0-0 Tight: 0-0 Gall: 0-0
Aids: Bl: 0-0 Vi: 0-0 Tstrap: 0-0
Best Rating: 94 2/02 Wwck 2m heavy NHF

Runner-up in a bumper on her debut.

April Ace

74 46

6-y-o ch g First Trump-Champ D'Avril (Northfields (USA))
R J Baker Graham Brown

Placings:0 (2719)
2001/02: 17^{0}G

	Starts	1st	2nd	3rd	Win & Pl
Hurdles	1	0	0	0	
Career Total	1	0	0	0	

Going: Sf: 0-0 GS: 0-0 Gd: 0-1 GF: - Fm: 0-0
Distance: 2m/2m3: 0-1 2m4-2m7: 0-0 3m+: 0-0
Track: LH: 0-0 RH: 0-1 Tight: 0-0 Gall: 0-0
Aids: Bl: 0-0 Vi: 0-0 Tstrap: 0-0
Best Rating: 33 12/01 Hrfd 2m1f good Hdl

April Call

6-y-o b m Gildoran-Cloud Cuckoo (Idiots Delight)
P F Nicholls Richard Barber

Placings:0-6P (4655)
2001/02: 17^{6}G, 17^{P}GS

	Starts	1st	2nd	3rd	Win & Pl
NH Flat	1	0	0	0	0
Hurdles	1	0	0	0	0
Career Total	3	0	0	0	0

Going: Sf: 0-0 GS: 0-1 Gd: 0-1 GF: - Fm: 0-0
Distance: 2m/2m3: 0-2 2m4-2m7: 0-0 3m+: 0-0
Track: LH: 0-0 RH: 0-1 Tight: 0-1 Gall: 0-0
Aids: Bl: 0-0 Vi: 0-0 Tstrap: 0-0
Best Rating: 78 11/01 Tntn 2m1f good NHF

April Louise

112 117

6-y-o b m Meqdaam (USA)-California Dreamin (Slip Anchor)
T Wall Harton Manor Racing Club

Placings:0000630-34205051023 (4662)
2001/02: 19^{3}GF, 20^{4}G, 16^{2}G, 16^{0}G, 20^{5}GS, 21^{0}G, 16^{5}GS, 16^{1}S, 16^{0}G, 16^{2}S, 16^{3}G

	Starts	1st	2nd	3rd	Win & Pl
Hurdles	11	1	2	2	12439
Career Total	18	1	2	3	12758

109 2/02 Ludl 2m D(0-115)HHdl SFT £4056
Total win prize-money £4056

Going: Sf: 1-2 GS: 0-2 Gd: 0-6 GF: - Fm: 0-1
Distance: **2m/2m3: 1-7** 2m4-2m7: 0-4 3m+: 0-0
Track: LH: 0-4 **RH: 1-7** Tight: 0-3 Gall: 0-1
Aids: Bl: 0-0 Vi: 0-0 Tstrap: 0-0
Best Rating: 117 4/02 Aint 2m110y good Hdl

Seemingly exposed before winning a mares' handicap hurdle at Ludlow in February 2002. Possibly flattered when third in smart company at Aintree. Goes well in soft ground.

April Spirit

105(102h) (80h)101

7-y-o b m Nomination-Seraphim (FR) (Lashkari)
Mrs S J Smith Mrs B Ramsden

Placings:06/24533230/03-4051F546 (1752)
2001/02: 19^{4}GF, 22^{0}GF, 21^{5}GS, 20^{1}GF, 20^{F}G, 24^{5}G, 20^{4}G, 22^{6}G

	Starts	1st	2nd	3rd	Win & Pl
Hurdles	3	0	0	0	0
Chases	5	1	0	0	3720
Career Total	20	1	2	4	5560

101 8/01 Worc 2m4f110y E(0-105)HCh G-F £3484
Total win prize-money £3484

Going: Sf: 0-0 GS: 0-1 Gd: 0-4 GF: - Fm: 1-3
Distance: 2m/2m3: 0-0 **2m4-2m7: 1-7** 3m+: 0-1
Track: **LH: 1-5** RH: 0-2 Tight: 0-6 Gall: 0-0
Aids: Bl: 0-0 Vi: 0-0 Tstrap: 0-0
Best Rating: 101 10/01 Sthl 2m4f110y good Ch

April Treasure

96 73

7-y-o b m Stani (USA)-Eleri (Rolfe (USA))
Mrs P Ford W E Donohue

Placings:PP0/P0F25P050P-65005 (1733)
2001/02: 16^{6}GF, 16^{5}GF, 16^{0}GF, 16^{0}GS, 19^{5}GS

	Starts	1st	2nd	3rd	Win & Pl
Hurdles	5	0	0	0	0
Career Total	18	0	1	0	576

Going: Sf: 0-0 GS: 0-2 Gd: 0-0 GF: - Fm: 0-3
Distance: 2m/2m3: 0-4 2m4-2m7: 0-1 3m+: 0-0
Track: LH: 0-4 RH: 0-1 Tight: 0-0 Gall: 0-0
Aids: Bl: 0-0 Vi: 0-0 Tstrap: 0-0
Best Rating: 77 10/00 Strf 2m110y soft Hdl

She has become very modest.

Aqribaa (IRE)

79 66

4-y-o b g Pennekamp (USA)-Karayb (IRE) (Last Tycoon)
K A Morgan (D Hanley 18/7) Mrs P A L Butler

Placings:3P (1486)
2001/02: 17^{3}G, 16^{P}GF

	Starts	1st	2nd	3rd	Win & Pl
Hurdles	2	0	0	1	486
Career Total	**2**	**0**	**0**	**1**	**486**

Going: Sf: 0-0 GS: 0-0 Gd: 0-1 GF: - Fm: 0-1
Distance: 2m/2m3: 0-2 2m4-2m7: 0-0 3m+: 0-0
Track: LH: 0-1 RH: 0-1 Tight: 0-1 Gall: 0-1
Aids: Bl: 0-0 Vi: 0-0 Tstrap: 0-0
Best Rating: 66 9/01 Bang 2m1f good Hdl

Raced on the flat in Ireland, before being well beaten on his hurdling debut, and has since been pulled up in a weak event at Huntingdon.

Aquiline

92 100

4-y-o ch g Sanglamore (USA)-Fantasy Flyer (USA) (Lear Fan (USA))
John A Harris Risley Hall Partnership

Placings:206 (4044)
2001/02: 16^{2}S, 16^{0}S, 17^{6}GS

	Starts	1st	2nd	3rd	Win & Pl
Hurdles	3	0	1	0	1998
Career Total	3	0	1	0	1998

Going: Sf: 0-2 GS: 0-1 Gd: 0-0 GF: - Fm: 0-0
Distance: 2m/2m3: 0-3 2m4-2m7: 0-0 3m+: 0-0
Track: LH: 0-1 RH: 0-2 Tight: 0-1 Gall: 0-2
Aids: Bl: 0-0 Vi: 0-0 Tstrap: 0-0
Best Rating: 100 1/02 Donc 2m110y soft Hdl

Runner-up on his hurdles debut on soft ground but saddle slipped on second start and that can be forgiven.

Arab Gold

7-y-o b g Presidium-Parklands Belle (Stanford)
J S Moore The Country Life Partnership

Placings:P (4127)
2001/02: 17^{P}G

	Starts	1st	2nd	3rd	Win & Pl
Hurdles	1	0	0	0	
Career Total	**1**	**0**	**0**	**0**	

Going: Sf: 0-0 GS: 0-0 Gd: 0-1 GF: - Fm: 0-0
Distance: 2m/2m3: 0-1 2m4-2m7: 0-0 3m+: 0-0
Track: LH: 0-0 RH: 0-1 Tight: 0-0 Gall: 0-0
Aids: Bl: 0-0 Vi: 0-0 Tstrap: 0-0
Best Rating:

Arabian Moon (IRE)

105 121

6-y-o ch h Barathea (IRE)-Excellent Alibi (USA) (Exceller (USA))
S Dow Byerley Bloodstock

Placings:46-111023 (4633)
2001/02: 23^{1}GF, 22^{1}G, 20^{1}GF, 21^{0}GS, 24^{2}G, 20^{3}GF

	Starts	1st	2nd	3rd	Win & Pl
Hurdles	6	3	1	1	11613
Career Total	**8**	**3**	**1**	**1**	**11909**

110	8/01	Uttx	2m4f110y	D Hdl	G-F	£3360
110	8/01	Strf	2m6f110y	D Hdl	GD	£3523
115	5/01	Fknm	2m7f110y	E Hdl	G-F	£2374

Total win prize-money £9257

Going: Sf: 0-0 GS: 0-1 Gd: 1-2 GF: - Fm: 2-3
Distance: 2m/2m3: 0-0 **2m4-2m7: 2-4** 3m+: 1-2
Track: **LH: 3-3** RH: 0-3 **Tight: 2-2** Gall: 0-0
Aids: Bl: 0-0 Vi: 0-0 Tstrap: 0-0
Best Rating: 121 4/02 Asct 2m4f gd-fm Hdl

Useful hurdler, stays three miles, but better over a shorter trip. Goes well when ridden close to the pace and best suited by fast ground.

Aragant (FR)

53 10

6-y-o b/br g Aragon-Soolaimon (IRE) (Shareef Dancer (USA))
R J Hodges Joli Racing

Placings:0/0 (0841)
2001/02: 16^{0}G

	Starts	1st	2nd	3rd	Win & Pl
Hurdles	1	0	0	0	
Career Total	2	0	0	0	

Going: Sf: 0-0 GS: 0-0 Gd: 0-1 GF: - Fm: 0-0
Distance: 2m/2m3: 0-1 2m4-2m7: 0-0 3m+: 0-0
Track: LH: 0-1 RH: 0-0 Tight: 0-0 Gall: 0-0
Aids: Bl: 0-0 Vi: 0-0 Tstrap: 0-0
Best Rating: 61 10/99 Tntn 2m1f gd-fm Hdl

Araminta

101 87

8-y-o ch m Carlingford Castle-Abinovian (Ra Nova)
N J Pomfret Mrs A J Higgins

Placings:000/UB-16634405 (4646)
2001/02: 20^{1}GF, 20^{6}G, 20^{6}GF, 24^{3}S, 20^{4}S, 20^{4}S, 20^{0}S, 21^{5}G

	Starts	1st	2nd	3rd	Win & Pl
Hurdles	8	1	0	1	3530
Career Total	13	1	0	1	3530

87	6/01	Fknm	2m4f	E Hdl	G-F	£2898

Total win prize-money £2898

Going: Sf: 0-4 GS: 0-0 Gd: 0-2 GF: - Fm: 1-2
Distance: 2m/2m3: 0-0 **2m4-2m7: 1-7** 3m+: 0-1
Track: **LH: 1-3** RH: 0-5 **Tight: 1-2** Gall: 0-2
Aids: Bl: 0-0 Vi: 0-0 Tstrap: 0-0
Best Rating: 87 6/01 Fknm 2m4f gd-fm Hdl

Her only win to date came on fast ground when she was held up, but she has not been getting home when ridden positively in soft ground.

Arawak Prince (IRE)

105 106

6-y-o ch g College Chapel-Alpine Symphony (Northern Dancer)
G Prodromou (D G Bridgwater 5/5) C Karavias

Placings:P1045/140P60 (3449)
2001/02: 17^{1}G, 17^{4}GS, 16^{0}S, 20^{P}S, 19^{6}S, 16^{0}GS

	Starts	1st	2nd	3rd	Win & Pl
Hurdles	6	1	0	0	2527
Career Total	**11**	**2**	**0**	**0**	**4865**

106	5/01	Hrfd	2m1f	G(0-95)HHdl	GD	£2100
107	3/00	Plum	2m	E Hdl	GD	£2338

Total win prize-money £4438

Going: Sf: 0-3 GS: 0-2 Gd: 1-1 GF: - Fm: 0-0
Distance: **2m/2m3: 1-4** 2m4-2m7: 0-2 3m+: 0-0
Track: LH: 0-3 **RH: 1-3** Tight: 0-5 Gall: 0-0
Aids: Bl: 0-0 **Vi: 1-4** Tstrap: 0-0
Best Rating: 107 3/00 Plum 2m good Hdl

Arbenig (IRE)

7-y-o b m Anita's Prince-Out On Her Own (Superlative)
B Palling Andrew Smallwood

Placings:0 (3408)
2001/02: 16^{0}S

	Starts	1st	2nd	3rd	Win & Pl
Hurdles	1	0	0	0	
Career Total	1	0	0	0	

Going: Sf: 0-1 GS: 0-0 Gd: 0-0 GF: - Fm: 0-0
Distance: 2m/2m3: 0-1 2m4-2m7: 0-0 3m+: 0-0
Track: LH: 0-0 RH: 0-1 Tight: 0-0 Gall: 0-0
Aids: Bl: 0-0 Vi: 0-0 Tstrap: 0-0
Best Rating:

Arc (IRE)

86(98h) 101

8-y-o b g Archway (IRE)-Columbian Sand (IRE) (Salmon Leap (USA))
G M Moore Mrs A Roddis

Placings:4P0/4/005-5P (2425)
2001/02: 17^{5}G, 17^{P}S

	Starts	1st	2nd	3rd	Win & Pl
Chases	2	0	0	0	0
Career Total	9	0	0	0	0

Going: Sf: 0-1 GS: 0-0 Gd: 0-1 GF: - Fm: 0-0
Distance: 2m/2m3: 0-2 2m4-2m7: 0-0 3m+: 0-0
Track: LH: 0-2 RH: 0-0 Tight: 0-2 Gall: 0-0
Aids: Bl: 0-0 Vi: 0-0 Tstrap: 0-0
Best Rating: 101 11/01 Kels 2m1f good Ch

Archbishop

73 21

5-y-o ch g Minster Son-Elitist (Keren)
T D Walford G E Dempsey

Placings:0000 (4583)
2001/02: 17^{0}G, 16^{0}S, 16^{0}G, 20^{0}G

	Starts	1st	2nd	3rd	Win & Pl
NH Flat	2	0	0	0	0
Hurdles	2	0	0	0	0
Career Total	4	0	0	0	

Going: Sf: 0-1 GS: 0-0 Gd: 0-3 GF: - Fm: 0-0
Distance: 2m/2m3: 0-3 2m4-2m7: 0-1 3m+: 0-0
Track: LH: 0-3 RH: 0-1 Tight: 0-1 Gall: 0-1
Aids: Bl: 0-0 Vi: 0-0 Tstrap: 0-0

Best Rating: 67 11/01 Hayd 2m soft NHF

Archies Oats

13-y-o ch g Oats-Archetype (Over The River (FR))
Jon Trice-Rolph Jon Trice-Rolph

Placings:15/4246/446/P6/0P (4055)
2001/02: 24^{0}S, 23^{P}S

	Starts	1st	2nd	3rd	Win & Pl
Chases	2	0	0	0	
Career Total	13	1	1	0	4011

97	3/97	Sand	2m4f110y	H Ch	GD	£2684

Total win prize-money £2684

Going: Sf: 0-2 GS: 0-0 Gd: 0-0 GF: - Fm: 0-0
Distance: 2m/2m3: 0-0 2m4-2m7: 0-0 3m+: 0-2
Track: LH: 0-0 RH: 0-2 Tight: 0-0 Gall: 0-0
Aids: Bl: 0-0 Vi: 0-0 Tstrap: 0-0
Best Rating: 97 3/98 Sand 3m110y good Ch

Archon (IRE)

87 **92**
5-y-o ch g Archway (IRE)-Lindas Delight (Batshoof)
Mrs P N Dutfield Simon Dutfield

Placings:20 (0843)
2001/02: 17^{2}G, 16^{0}G

	Starts	1st	2nd	3rd	Win & Pl
NH Flat	2	0	1	0	652
Career Total	2	0	1	0	652

Going: Sf: 0-0 GS: 0-0 Gd: 0-2 GF: - Fm: 0-0
Distance: 2m/2m3: 0-2 2m4-2m7: 0-0 3m+: 0-0
Track: LH: 0-2 RH: 0-0 Tight: 0-1 Gall: 0-0
Aids: Bl: 0-0 Vi: 0-0 Tstrap: 0-0
Best Rating: 101 6/01 NAbb 2m1f good NHF

Runner-up in Newton Abbot bumper June 2001. Won over seven furlongs on the Polytrack at Lingfield May 2002. May find stamina a problem over hurdles.

Arctic Affair (IRE)

9-y-o b m Glacial Storm (USA)-Moonlight Romance (Teenoso (USA))
K A Morgan Mrs S J Storer

Placings:00555P3P/563/0654F-P (0591)
2001/02: 23^{P}GF

	Starts	1st	2nd	3rd	Win & Pl
Hurdles	1	0	0	0	
Career Total	17	0	0	2	629

Going: Sf: 0-0 GS: 0-0 Gd: 0-0 GF: - Fm: 0-1
Distance: 2m/2m3: 0-0 2m4-2m7: 0-0 3m+: 0-1
Track: LH: 0-1 RH: 0-0 Tight: 0-1 Gall: 0-0
Aids: Bl: 0-0 Vi: 0-0 Tstrap: 0-0
Best Rating: 92 6/99 Strf 2m6f110y gd-fm Hdl

Arctic Burner (IRE)

102(62c) **84**
8-y-o b g Glacial Storm (USA)-Lucky Appeal (Star Appeal)
M Pitman (P F Nicholls 28/7) The Fountains Partnership

Placings:00/06006/4240241U-PR515500 (1611)
2001/02: 20^{P}GF, 16^{R}GS, 22^{5}GF, 19^{1}G, 18^{5}GF, 16^{5}GF, 21^{0}GS, 19^{0}GF

	Starts	1st	2nd	3rd	Win & Pl
Hurdles	6	1	0	0	3010
Chases	2	0	0	0	0
Career Total	23	2	2	0	7367

81	7/01	Strf	2m3f	E(0-105)HHdl	GD	£3010
100	9/00	NAbb	2m110y	F(0-100)HCh	G-F	£2527

Total win prize-money £5537

Going: Sf: 0-0 GS: 0-2 Gd: 1-1 GF: - Fm: 0-5
Distance: **2m/2m3: 1-5** 2m4-2m7: 0-3 3m+: 0-0
Track: **LH: 1-6** RH: 0-2 **Tight: 1-6** Gall: 0-1
Aids: Bl: 0-1 Vi: 0-0 Tstrap: 0-0
Best Rating: 100 9/00 NAbb 2m110y gd-fm Ch

Arctic Camper

111 **163**
10-y-o b g Arctic Lord-Mayotte (Little Buskins)
Miss Venetia Williams Lady Harris

Placings:1221/2P/116/21/PR-14 (2801)
2001/02: 24^{1}S, 24^{4}G

	Starts	1st	2nd	3rd	Win & Pl
Chases	2	1	0	0	25940
Career Total	15	6	4	0	78526

163	12/01	Chep	3m	A HCh	SFT	£23440
152	1/00	Weth	3m1f	A Ch	SFT	£17190
129	2/99	Font	2m6f110y	E Hdl	GD	£2810
124	11/98	Chel	2m5f	B Hdl	G-S	£7100
129	4/97	Punc	2m	NHF	GD	£12772
103	1/97	Fair	2m	NHF	GD	£3051

Total win prize-money £66364

Going: Sf: 1-1 GS: 0-0 Gd: 0-1 GF: - Fm: 0-0
Distance: 2m/2m3: 0-0 2m4-2m7: 0-0 **3m+: 1-2**
Track: **LH: 1-1** RH: 0-1 Tight: 0-0 Gall: 0-0
Aids: Bl: 0-0 Vi: 0-0 Tstrap: 0-0
Best Rating: 163 12/01 Chep 3m soft Ch

Very useful but lightly-raced due to injury, he looked a useful prospect when landing an uncompetitive Grade Two novice chase at Wetherby in January 2000. Restricted to two outings in 2000/2001, he failed to complete on both starts. He showed his true form on his seasonal debut, winning the Rehearsal Chase, but was subsequently held in Listed company at Ascot. Best on soft ground. Stays three miles and suited by left-handed tracks.

Arctic Challenge (IRE)

105(108h) **136**
8-y-o b g Glacial Storm (USA)-Ruckinge Girl (Eborneezer)
K R Burke Mr I & Mrs A Russell

Placings:4/33/3336-2013P01P2 (4907)
2001/02: 21^{2}G, 20^{0}G, 20^{1}G, 19^{3}G, 20^{P}G, 23^{0}GS, 20^{1}GF, 20^{P}GF, 20^{2}GF

	Starts	1st	2nd	3rd	Win & Pl
Chases	9	2	2	1	11933
Career Total	16	2	2	6	14057

121	4/02	Hntg	2m4f110y	E Ch	G-F	£3078
130	11/01	Kemp	2m4f110y	D Ch	GD	£4936

Total win prize-money £8015

Going: Sf: 0-0 GS: 0-1 Gd: 1-5 GF: - Fm: 1-3
Distance: 2m/2m3: 0-0 **2m4-2m7: 2-8** 3m+: 0-1
Track: LH: 0-2 **RH: 2-6** Tight: 0-2 **Gall: 1-1**
Aids: Bl: 0-0 Vi: 0-0 Tstrap: 0-0
Best Rating: 136 11/01 Asct 2m3f110y good Ch

A fair maiden hurdler. Jumped soundly on his chasing debut, his first run since March and won a novice chase at Kempton in October over two and a half miles. Held in better company next time. Acts on a sound surface.

Arctic Cirrus

9-y-o b m Arctic Lord-Silver Cirrus (General Ironside)
J C McConnochie Major R G Wilson

Placings:P000P6/6F-5 (0212)
2001/02: 20^{5}F

	Starts	1st	2nd	3rd	Win & Pl
Hurdles	1	0	0	0	0
Career Total	9	0	0	0	0

Going: Sf: 0-0 GS: 0-0 Gd: 0-0 GF: - Fm: 0-1
Distance: 2m/2m3: 0-0 2m4-2m7: 0-1 3m+: 0-0
Track: LH: 0-1 RH: 0-0 Tight: 0-1 Gall: 0-0
Aids: Bl: 0-1 Vi: 0-0 Tstrap: 0-0
Best Rating: 76 1/00 Hntg 3m good Ch

Arctic Copper (IRE)

112 **153**
8-y-o b g Montelimar (USA)-Miss Penguin (General Assembly (USA))
Noel Meade Grand Alliance Racing Club

Placings:02133142/411232122-642F513U45 (4938a)
2001/02: 20^{6}G, 24^{4}Y, 18^{2}YS, 24^{F}YS, 17^{5}Y, 16^{1}YS, 16^{3}HY, 21^{U}G, 29^{4}GY, 16^{5}YS

	Starts	1st	2nd	3rd	Win & Pl
Chases	10	1	1	1	25793
Career Total	27	6	7	4	82924

153	1/02	Fair	2m100y	Ch	Y-S	£10368
140	2/01	Navn	3m	Ch	SFT	£7790
147	10/00	Gowr	2m6f	Ch	SFT	£5520
122	5/00	Gowr	2m4f	Hdl	Y-S	£3864
109	2/00	Navn	2m2f	Hdl	SH	£3588
100	12/99	Navn	2m	NHF	HVY	£3080

Total win prize-money £34210

Going: Sf: 0-1 GS: 0-0 Gd: 0-2 GF: - Fm: 0-0
Distance: **2m/2m3: 1-5** 2m4-2m7: 0-2 3m+: 0-3
Track: LH: 0-4 RH: 0-3 Tight: 0-0 Gall: 0-1
Aids: **Bl: 1-8** Vi: 0-0 Tstrap: 0-0
Best Rating: 153 2/02 Naas 2m heavy Ch

He spent most of the 2000/2001 season being beaten by Sackville in valuable novice chases, but is a useful performer in his own right. Some decent efforts in 2001/02, but an early casualty at Cheltenham. Probably best at distances short of three miles, he goes well on easy ground.

Arctic Double (IRE)

93f **102f**
5-y-o b g Insan (USA)-Icy Queen (IRE) (Callernish)
Miss H C Knight T M Curtis

Placings:30 (4158)
2001/02: 16^{3}G, 16^{0}GS

	Starts	1st	2nd	3rd	Win & Pl
NH Flat	2	0	0	1	229
Career Total	2	0	0	1	229

Going: Sf: 0-0 GS: 0-1 Gd: 0-1 GF: - Fm: 0-0
Distance: 2m/2m3: 0-2 2m4-2m7: 0-0 3m+: 0-0
Track: LH: 0-0 RH: 0-2 Tight: 0-0 Gall: 0-0
Aids: Bl: 0-0 Vi: 0-0 Tstrap: 0-0
Best Rating: 102 3/02 Sand 2m110y gd-sft NHF

Arctic Earl

(90h) (55h)

8-y-o br g Arctic Lord-Moy Ran Lady (Black Minstrel)

A Streeter Malt 'N' Hops

Placings:_05/P/P5_**PPPFF** (4020)

2001/02: 20^{P}G, 20^{5}G, 20^{P}GS, 24^{P}GS, 23^{P}S, 19^{F}S, 24^{F}S

	Starts	1st	2nd	3rd	Win & Pl
Hurdles	3	0	0	0	0
Chases	4	0	0	0	0
Career Total	**10**	**0**	**0**	**0**	**0**

Going: Sf: 0-3 GS: 0-2 Gd: 0-2 GF: - Fm: 0-0
Distance: 2m/2m3: 0-0 2m4-2m7: 0-4 3m+: 0-3
Track: LH: 0-4 RH: 0-3 Tight: 0-3 Gall: 0-3
Aids: Bl: 0-0 Vi: 0-0 Tstrap: 0-4
Best Rating: **80** 3/99 Newb 2m110y gd-fm NHF

Arctic Fancy (USA)

106 136

9-y-o ch g Arctic Tern (USA)-Fit And Fancy (USA) (Vaguely Noble)

Miss H C Knight (J G Smyth-Osbourne 9/6) Another Chance Partnership

Placings:21135/**12151/63550-4402224** (4635)

2001/02: 24^{4}GF, 20^{4}G, 19^{0}GS, 20^{2}S, 24^{2}S, 18^{2}GS, 19^{4}GF

	Starts	1st	2nd	3rd	Win & Pl
Chases	7	0	3	0	8839
Career Total	**22**	**5**	**5**	**2**	**36599**

145	4/00	Chep	2m110y	E Ch	SFT	£3575
147	1/00	Donc	2m110y	D Ch	G-F	£3789
137	11/99	Chep	2m110y	E Ch	GD	£2989
125	2/99	Folk	2m1f110y	E Hdl	SFT	£2853
119	1/99	Plum	2m1f	E Hdl	HVY	£2407

Total win prize-money £15617

Going: Sf: 0-2 GS: 0-2 Gd: 0-1 GF: - Fm: 0-2
Distance: 2m/2m3: 0-1 2m4-2m7: 0-4 3m+: 0-2
Track: LH: 0-5 RH: 0-2 Tight: 0-1 Gall: 0-1
Aids: Bl: 0-0 Vi: 0-0 Tstrap: 0-0
Best Rating: **149** 5/00 Punc 2m good Ch

Showed useful form as a novice hurdler in 1998/1999 and won three times over fences in 1999/2000. He has changed stables and has run well in 2002. Stays two and a half miles, but does not quite get three miles and acts on a soft surface.

Arctic Flame

(71h) (35h)

11-y-o b m Arctic Lord-Rekindle (Relkino)

A W Carroll Stable Tavern

Placings:_5/000_**PP** (1244)

2001/02: 16^{0}G, 22^{0}GF, 20^{0}GF, 16^{P}S, 23^{P}GF

	Starts	1st	2nd	3rd	Win & Pl
Hurdles	3	0	0	0	0
Chases	2	0	0	0	0
Career Total	**6**	**0**	**0**	**0**	**0**

Going: Sf: 0-1 GS: 0-0 Gd: 0-1 GF: - Fm: 0-3
Distance: 2m/2m3: 0-2 2m4-2m7: 0-2 3m+: 0-1
Track: LH: 0-5 RH: 0-0 Tight: 0-1 Gall: 0-0
Aids: Bl: 0-0 Vi: 0-0 Tstrap: 0-3
Best Rating: **80** 10/96 Hntg 2m110y gd-fm NHF

Arctic Fusilier

96(79h) (39h)96

11-y-o gr g Gunner B-Arctic Advert (Birdbrook)

R Williams R Williams

Placings:_0/20/354P/_**2333124/U-04U235** (0913)

2001/02: 19^{0}G, 16^{4}G, 25^{U}F, 21^{2}GF, 20^{3}G, 24^{5}G

	Starts	1st	2nd	3rd	Win & Pl
Hurdles	1	0	0	0	0
Chases	5	0	1	1	2280
Career Total	**21**	**1**	**4**	**5**	**8451**

92	8/99	Bang	2m4f	E Hdl	GD	£1882

Total win prize-money £1882

Going: Sf: 0-0 GS: 0-0 Gd: 0-4 GF: - Fm: 0-2
Distance: 2m/2m3: 0-1 2m4-2m7: 0-3 3m+: 0-2
Track: LH: 0-3 RH: 0-3 Tight: 0-4 Gall: 0-0
Aids: Bl: 0-1 Vi: 0-0 Tstrap: 0-0
Best Rating: **114** 5/99 Strf 2m5f110y good Ch

Arctic Gamble

102 100

10-y-o b g Arctic Lord-Honey Gamble (Gambling Debt)

L G Cottrell Miss S Lock

Placings:42F (4482)

2001/02: 23^{4}GS, 23^{2}GF, 25^{F}G

	Starts	1st	2nd	3rd	Win & Pl
Chases	3	0	1	0	2071
Career Total	**3**	**0**	**1**	**0**	**2071**

Going: Sf: 0-0 GS: 0-1 Gd: 0-1 GF: - Fm: 0-1
Distance: 2m/2m3: 0-0 2m4-2m7: 0-0 3m+: 0-3
Track: LH: 0-0 RH: 0-2 Tight: 0-0 Gall: 0-0
Aids: Bl: 0-0 Vi: 0-0 Tstrap: 0-0
Best Rating: **100** 11/01 Extr 2m7f110y gd-fm Ch

Lightly-raced chaser, stays three miles and appreciates a sound surface.

Arctic King

100 84

9-y-o b g Arctic Lord-Dunsilly Bell (London Bells (CAN))

M Tate D H Cowgill

Placings:_06/4636U/02P3F5P_**-P5P** (0829)

2001/02: 24^{P}G, 21^{5}GF, 24^{P}GF

	Starts	1st	2nd	3rd	Win & Pl
Chases	3	0	0	0	0
Career Total	**17**	**0**	**1**	**2**	**2660**

Going: Sf: 0-0 GS: 0-0 Gd: 0-1 GF: - Fm: 0-2
Distance: 2m/2m3: 0-0 2m4-2m7: 0-1 3m+: 0-2
Track: LH: 0-2 RH: 0-0 Tight: 0-2 Gall: 0-0
Aids: Bl: 0-1 Vi: 0-0 Tstrap: 0-0
Best Rating: **97** 11/00 Hrfd 2m3f gd-sft Ch

Arctic Melody (IRE)

(85h)

9-y-o b g Orchestra-Arctic Brief (Buckskin (FR))

B De Haan The Longhedge Partnership

Placings:_30/P/000_**-BP** (1030)

2001/02: 16^{B}GF, 17^{P}G

	Starts	1st	2nd	3rd	Win & Pl
Chases	2	0	0	0	
Career Total	**8**	**0**	**0**	**1**	**158**

Going: Sf: 0-0 GS: 0-0 Gd: 0-1 GF: - Fm: 0-1
Distance: 2m/2m3: 0-2 2m4-2m7: 0-0 3m+: 0-0
Track: LH: 0-1 RH: 0-0 Tight: 0-1 Gall: 0-0
Aids: Bl: 0-0 Vi: 0-0 Tstrap: 0-0
Best Rating: **83** 5/98 Fknm 2m good NHF

Arctic Owl

88 95

8-y-o b g Most Welcome-Short Rations (Lorenzaccio)

J R Fanshawe The Owl Society

Placings:4 (3469)

2001/02: 16^{4}S

	Starts	1st	2nd	3rd	Win & Pl
Hurdles	1	0	0	0	0
Career Total	**1**	**0**	**0**	**0**	**0**

Going: Sf: 0-1 GS: 0-0 Gd: 0-0 GF: - Fm: 0-0
Distance: 2m/2m3: 0-1 2m4-2m7: 0-0 3m+: 0-0
Track: LH: 0-1 RH: 0-0 Tight: 0-0 Gall: 0-1
Aids: Bl: 0-0 Vi: 0-0 Tstrap: 0-0
Best Rating: **95** 1/02 Donc 2m110y soft Hdl

A top-class stayer on the Flat, including winning an Irish St Leger. He was a disappointing fourth on his hurdles debut at Doncaster in January 2002.

Arctic Penguin

5-y-o gr g Absalom-Sedge Warbler (Scallywag)

Mrs P Robeson Mrs P Robeson

Placings:_0006_**P** (3600)

2001/02: 16^{0}G, 17^{0}S, 16^{0}GS, 20^{6}S, 18^{P}HY

	Starts	1st	2nd	3rd	Win & Pl
NH Flat	3	0	0	0	0
Hurdles	2	0	0	0	0
Career Total	**5**	**0**	**0**	**0**	**0**

Going: Sf: 0-3 GS: 0-1 Gd: 0-1 GF: - Fm: 0-0
Distance: 2m/2m3: 0-4 2m4-2m7: 0-1 3m+: 0-0
Track: LH: 0-2 RH: 0-3 Tight: 0-2 Gall: 0-2
Aids: Bl: 0-0 Vi: 0-0 Tstrap: 0-0
Best Rating: **74** 5/01 Hntg 2m110y good NHF

Arctic Playboy

91f 83f

6-y-o b g Petoski-Arctic Oats (Oats)

M Wellings R P Dineen

Placings:_0-O3_ (1019)

2001/02: 16^{0}G, 16^{3}G

	Starts	1st	2nd	3rd	Win & Pl
NH Flat	2	0	0	1	211
Career Total	**3**	**0**	**0**	**1**	**211**

Going: Sf: 0-0 GS: 0-0 Gd: 0-2 GF: - Fm: 0-0
Distance: 2m/2m3: 0-2 2m4-2m7: 0-0 3m+: 0-0
Track: LH: 0-2 RH: 0-0 Tight: 0-0 Gall: 0-0
Aids: Bl: 0-0 Vi: 0-0 Tstrap: 0-0
Best Rating: **83** 7/01 Worc 2m good NHF

Arctic Puffin

7-y-o b g Petoski-Arctic Warbler (Deep Run)

Mrs P Robeson Mrs P Robeson

Placings:P (2798)

2001/02: 20^{P}S

	Starts	1st	2nd	3rd	Win & Pl
Hurdles	1	0	0	0	
Career Total	**1**	**0**	**0**	**0**	

Going: Sf: 0-1 GS: 0-0 Gd: 0-0 GF: - Fm: 0-0
Distance: 2m/2m3: 0-0 2m4-2m7: 0-1 3m+: 0-0
Track: LH: 0-1 RH: 0-0 Tight: 0-0 Gall: 0-0
Aids: Bl: 0-0 Vi: 0-0 Tstrap: 0-0
Best Rating:

Arctic Sandy (IRE)

105(91h) (83h)85

12-y-o ch g Sandalay-Reach Here (Hereford)
Mrs J K M Oliver Mr & Mrs Raymond Anderson Green

Placings: *112/4330/12F1/P6642521/246505460-4P6* (1576)
2001/02: 17^{4}GF, 24^{P}G, 22^{6}G

	Starts	1st	2nd	3rd	Win & Pl
Hurdles	2	0	0	0	0
Chases	1	0	0	0	0
Career Total	**31**	**5**	**5**	**2**	**22238**

106	4/00	Kels	2m1f	F(0-110)HCh	SFT	£3945
109	3/98	Newc	2m4f	E Ch	GD	£2814
112	1/98	Muss	2m	D(0-125)HCh	G-S	£3355
112	4/96	Carl	2m1f	H NHF	FRM	£1528
106	10/95	Tipp	2m	NHF	FRM	£3391

Total win prize-money £15035

Going: Sf: 0-0 GS: 0-0 Gd: 0-2 GF: - Fm: 0-1
Distance: 2m/2m3: 0-1 2m4-2m7: 0-1 3m+: 0-1
Track: LH: 0-2 RH: 0-1 Tight: 0-2 Gall: 0-0
Aids: Bl: 0-0 Vi: 0-1 Tstrap: 0-0
Best Rating: 112 1/98 Muss 2m gd-sft Ch

Arctic Sky (IRE)

99f 100+f

5-y-o b g Arctic Lord-Lake Garden Park (Comedy Star (USA))
N J Henderson Mrs Christopher Pugh

Placings: *0* (4158)
2001/02: 16^{0}GS

	Starts	1st	2nd	3rd	Win & Pl
NH Flat	1	0	0	0	
Career Total	**1**	**0**	**0**	**0**	

Going: Sf: 0-0 GS: 0-1 Gd: 0-0 GF: - Fm: 0-0
Distance: 2m/2m3: 0-1 2m4-2m7: 0-0 3m+: 0-0
Track: LH: 0-0 RH: 0-1 Tight: 0-0 Gall: 0-0
Aids: Bl: 0-0 Vi: 0-0 Tstrap: 0-0
Best Rating: 94 3/02 Sand 2m110y gd-sft NHF

Arctic Spirit

103(104h) (65h)106

7-y-o b g Arctic Lord-Dickies Girl (Saxon Farm)
R Dickin The Lordy Racing Partnership

Placings: *0P005/60246532-0001U1F561* (4566)
2001/02: 16^{0}F, 16^{0}G, 16^{0}S, 16^{1}G, 17^{U}S, 16^{1}GF, 16^{F}G, 18^{5}HY, 20^{6}G, 16^{1}G

	Starts	1st	2nd	3rd	Win & Pl
Hurdles	2	0	0	0	0
Chases	8	3	0	0	9910
Career Total	**23**	**3**	**2**	**1**	**11983**

106	4/02	Towc	2m110y	E(0-105)HCh	GD	£4202
106	12/01	Leic	2m	E(0-105)HCh	G-F	£3146
92	11/01	Wwck	2m110y	F(0-100)HCh	GD	£2562

Total win prize-money £9910

Going: Sf: 0-3 GS: 0-0 Gd: 2-5 GF: - Fm: 1-2
Distance: **2m/2m3: 3-9** 2m4-2m7: 0-1 3m+: 0-0
Track: LH: 0-4 **RH: 2-4** Tight: 0-4 Gall: 0-0
Aids: Bl: 0-0 Vi: 0-0 Tstrap: 0-0
Best Rating: 106 4/02 Towc 2m110y good Ch

He was winning his first ever race when landing a handicap on only his second ever start over fences at Warwick in November, and has added wins at Leicester and Towcester since. A Game sort, he enjoys fast ground and is best at around two miles.

Arctic Splash

98 71

7-y-o ch m St Ninian-Arctic Oats (Oats)
G A Swinbank (M Wellings 31/7) R P Dineen

Placings: *2343454/5-0P040* (4061)
2001/02: 20^{0}GF, 24^{P}GF, 22^{0}GF, 16^{4}S, 17^{0}S

	Starts	1st	2nd	3rd	Win & Pl
Hurdles	5	0	0	0	0
Career Total	**13**	**0**	**1**	**2**	**806**

Going: Sf: 0-2 GS: 0-0 Gd: 0-0 GF: - Fm: 0-3
Distance: 2m/2m3: 0-2 2m4-2m7: 0-2 3m+: 0-1
Track: LH: 0-5 RH: 0-0 Tight: 0-3 Gall: 0-1
Aids: Bl: 0-0 Vi: 0-0 Tstrap: 0-0
Best Rating: 90 11/99 Hexm 2m good NHF

Arctic Times (IRE)

103 94

6-y-o ch g Montelimar (USA)-Miss Penguin (General Assembly (USA))
Miss H C Knight Trevor Hemmings

Placings: *40*-0F40 (3222)
2001/02: 16^{0}G, 16^{F}GF, 20^{4}G, 22^{0}G

	Starts	1st	2nd	3rd	Win & Pl
Hurdles	4	0	0	0	0
Career Total	**6**	**0**	**0**	**0**	**0**

Going: Sf: 0-0 GS: 0-0 Gd: 0-3 GF: - Fm: 0-1
Distance: 2m/2m3: 0-2 2m4-2m7: 0-2 3m+: 0-0
Track: LH: 0-2 RH: 0-2 Tight: 0-1 Gall: 0-1
Aids: Bl: 0-0 Vi: 0-0 Tstrap: 0-0
Best Rating: 100 1/01 Kemp 2m soft NHF

Arctictaldi (IRE)

107(93h) (88h)116

12-y-o br g Cataldi-Arctic Sue (Arctic Slave)
B Ellison Bridgecastle Properties Ltd

Placings: *00/P40/F/6P5U3/2F15322214412-2312234PPP3* (4778)
2001/02: 16^{2}S, 20^{3}GF, 17^{1}G, 16^{2}GF, 21^{2}G, 16^{3}G, 16^{4}S, 20^{P}S, 20^{P}GS, 17^{P}G, 17^{3}G

	Starts	1st	2nd	3rd	Win & Pl
Hurdles	2	0	0	1	340
Chases	9	1	3	2	8780
Career Total	**35**	**4**	**8**	**5**	**24848**

116	8/01	Ctml	2m1f110y	D(0-120)HCh	GD	£5292
110	3/01	MRas	2m1f110y	F(0-105)HCh	HVY	£3360
114	12/00	Sedg	2m110y	F(0-105)HCh	SFT	£3591
115	10/00	Sthl	2m	F(0-100)HCh	G-S	£2164

Total win prize-money £14408

Going: Sf: 0-3 GS: 0-1 Gd: 1-5 GF: - Fm: 0-2
Distance: **2m/2m3: 1-7** 2m4-2m7: 0-4 3m+: 0-0
Track: **LH: 1-9** RH: 0-2 **Tight: 1-9** Gall: 0-0
Aids: Bl: 0-1 Vi: 0-0 Tstrap: 0-0
Best Rating: 116 11/01 Sedg 2m110y soft Ch

Moderate if consistent chaser. Goes well on a sharp track but prone to jumping errors.

Ard Drum (IRE)

10-y-o b g Febrino-Miss Maraise (Grange Melody)
C E N Smith Mrs J Smith

Placings: 3/060/P (4769)
2001/02: 25^{P}GF

	Starts	1st	2nd	3rd	Win & Pl
Chases	1	0	0	0	
Career Total	**5**	**0**	**0**	**1**	**147**

Going: Sf: 0-0 GS: 0-0 Gd: 0-0 GF: - Fm: 0-1
Distance: 2m/2m3: 0-0 2m4-2m7: 0-0 3m+: 0-1
Track: LH: 0-1 RH: 0-0 Tight: 0-0 Gall: 0-0
Aids: Bl: 0-0 Vi: 0-0 Tstrap: 0-0
Best Rating: 71 9/99 Sedg 2m110y gd-fm Ch

Ard Na Carrig (IRE)

9-y-o ch g Mister Lord (USA)-Coxtown Lass (IRE) (Selko)
M Sheppard Simon Gegg

Placings: 0/0/P/4-PP (0429)
2001/02: 19^{P}G, 25^{P}G

	Starts	1st	2nd	3rd	Win & Pl
Chases	2	0	0	0	
Career Total	**6**	**0**	**0**	**0**	**285**

Going: Sf: 0-0 GS: 0-0 Gd: 0-2 GF: - Fm: 0-0
Distance: 2m/2m3: 0-1 2m4-2m7: 0-0 3m+: 0-1
Track: LH: 0-0 RH: 0-1 Tight: 0-0 Gall: 0-0
Aids: Bl: 0-0 Vi: 0-0 Tstrap: 0-0
Best Rating: 8 12/98 Wxfd 2m sft-hvy Ch

Ardeal

99 86

10-y-o ch m Ardross-Rare Deal (Pitpan)
C C Bealby Mrs S M V Bealby

Placings: 5/PP-PUP3P32P (4916)
2001/02: 25^{P}S, 24^{U}S, 26^{P}S, 16^{3}S, 24^{P}S, 24^{3}HY, 25^{2}G, 27^{P}GF

	Starts	1st	2nd	3rd	Win & Pl
Chases	8	0	1	2	2414
Career Total	**11**	**0**	**1**	**2**	**2414**

Going: Sf: 0-6 GS: 0-0 Gd: 0-1 GF: - Fm: 0-1
Distance: 2m/2m3: 0-1 2m4-2m7: 0-0 3m+: 0-7
Track: LH: 0-5 RH: 0-3 Tight: 0-3 Gall: 0-1
Aids: Bl: 0-0 Vi: 0-0 Tstrap: 0-0
Best Rating: 86 4/02 MRas 3m1f good Ch

A winner of point-to-points, but she has yet to show the same level of form under Rules and has bled.

Ardent Oliver

9-y-o b g Ardross-Olnistar (FR) (Balsamo (FR))
N M Babbage Mrs Joan Nelson

Placings: *0614/F5F2/P* (3983)
2001/02: 24^{P}G

	Starts	1st	2nd	3rd	Win & Pl
Hurdles	1	0	0	0	
Career Total	**9**	**1**	**1**	**0**	**3392**

94	1/99	Ling	2m7f	E Hdl	HVY	£2256

Total win prize-money £2257

Going: Sf: 0-0 GS: 0-0 Gd: 0-1 GF: - Fm: 0-0
Distance: 2m/2m3: 0-0 2m4-2m7: 0-0 3m+: 0-1
Track: LH: 0-0 RH: 0-1 Tight: 0-0 Gall: 0-0
Aids: Bl: 0-0 Vi: 0-0 Tstrap: 0-0
Best Rating: **97** 12/99 Towc 2m6f good Ch

Ardent Scout

109(110h) **133**

10-y-o b g Ardross-Vidette (Billion (USA))
Mrs S J Smith Mrs Alicia Skene & W S Skene

Placings: *53F013104B/***1U31P32PP/32134/123PP-3403P50** (4845)
2001/02: 24^{3}G, 27^{4}S, 26^{0}G, 24^{3}HY, 28^{P}S, 33^{5}S, 24^{0}G

	Starts	1st	2nd	3rd	Win & Pl
Chases	7	0	0	2	5747
Career Total	**36**	**6**	**3**	**9**	**52705**

139	11/00	Ayr	3m1f	C(0-135)HCh	G-S	£6942
124	11/99	Bang	3m110y	C(0-130)HCh	HVY	£6087
139	12/98	Weth	3m1f	D Ch	SFT	£3756
121	11/98	Carl	2m4f110y	D Ch	SFT	£3501
114	12/97	Weth	2m4f110y	D(0-110)HHdl	SFT	£3304
96	11/97	Carl	2m4f110y	E Hdl	GD	£2500

Total win prize-money £26091

Going: Sf: 0-4 GS: 0-0 Gd: 0-3 GF: - Fm: 0-0
Distance: 2m/2m3: 0-0 2m4-2m7: 0-0 3m+: 0-7
Track: LH: 0-6 RH: 0-0 Tight: 0-2 Gall: 0-3
Aids: Bl: 0-0 Vi: 0-0 Tstrap: 0-0
Best Rating: **144** 11/00 Aint 3m3f soft Ch

He stays and goes well under testing condition.

Ardfinnan (IRE)

96(90c) (101c)**97**

9-y-o b g Torus-O Tuk Deep (Deep Run)
Ian Williams Willsford Racing Incorporated

Placings: *220/52U41/235032/***632F-3P0P00** (4847)
2001/02: 20^{3}G, 24^{P}G, 16^{0}GF, 20^{P}G, 19^{0}G, 20^{0}G

	Starts	1st	2nd	3rd	Win & Pl
Hurdles	2	0	0	0	0
Chases	4	0	0	1	620
Career Total	**24**	**1**	**6**	**4**	**11609**

111	4/99	Hntg	2m5f110y	E Hdl	G-F	£2962

Total win prize-money £2962

Going: Sf: 0-0 GS: 0-0 Gd: 0-5 GF: - Fm: 0-1
Distance: 2m/2m3: 0-1 2m4-2m7: 0-4 3m+: 0-1
Track: LH: 0-3 RH: 0-2 Tight: 0-2 Gall: 0-0
Aids: Bl: 0-0 Vi: 0-2 Tstrap: 0-0
Best Rating: **127** 11/99 Wwck 2m good Ch

He has made the frame over fences, but does not seem to be progressing.

Ardmayle (IRE)

8-y-o b g Be My Native (USA)-Serena Bay (Furry Glen)
Mrs Richard Arthur Mrs Richard Arthur

Placings: PP (4525)
2001/02: 27^{P}S, 26^{P}GS

	Starts	1st	2nd	3rd	Win & Pl
Chases	2	0	0	0	
Career Total	**2**	**0**	**0**	**0**	

Going: Sf: 0-1 GS: 0-1 Gd: 0-0 GF: - Fm: 0-0
Distance: 2m/2m3: 0-0 2m4-2m7: 0-0 3m+: 0-2
Track: LH: 0-1 RH: 0-1 Tight: 0-1 Gall: 0-0
Aids: Bl: 0-0 Vi: 0-0 Tstrap: 0-0
Best Rating:

Ardrich

100 **110**

8-y-o b g Ardross-Randama (Akarad (FR))
S A Brookshaw (P M Rich 2/2) T G K Construction Ltd

Placings: *0/4/***623P** (3821)
2001/02: 19^{6}S, 16^{2}HY, 16^{3}HY, 17^{P}S

	Starts	1st	2nd	3rd	Win & Pl
Hurdles	4	0	1	1	1130
Career Total	**6**	**0**	**1**	**1**	**1130**

Going: Sf: 0-4 GS: 0-0 Gd: 0-0 GF: - Fm: 0-0
Distance: 2m/2m3: 0-3 2m4-2m7: 0-1 3m+: 0-0
Track: LH: 0-3 RH: 0-1 Tight: 0-1 Gall: 0-0
Aids: Bl: 0-0 Vi: 0-0 Tstrap: 0-0
Best Rating: **110** 2/02 Hayd 2m heavy Hdl

A lightly-raced individual. Has shown modest form to date at around two miles on soft ground.

Ardross Gem (IRE)

85 **50**

8-y-o b m Ardross-Forty Watts (Sparkler)
Jane Southcombe P L Southcombe

Placings: *60/***060** (0734)
2001/02: 22^{0}GF, 25^{6}G, 22^{0}G

	Starts	1st	2nd	3rd	Win & Pl
Hurdles	3	0	0	0	0
Career Total	**5**	**0**	**0**	**0**	**0**

Going: Sf: 0-0 GS: 0-0 Gd: 0-2 GF: - Fm: 0-1
Distance: 2m/2m3: 0-0 2m4-2m7: 0-2 3m+: 0-1
Track: LH: 0-1 RH: 0-1 Tight: 0-1 Gall: 0-0
Aids: Bl: 0-0 Vi: 0-0 Tstrap: 0-0
Best Rating: **62** 12/99 Hrfd 2m1f good NHF

Ardstown

99 **115**

11-y-o b m Ardross-Booterstown (Master Owen)
R F Knipe Mrs R F Knipe

Placings: 232/113122/21-04P (4419)
2001/02: 26^{0}S, 28^{4}HY, 24^{P}GS

	Starts	1st	2nd	3rd	Win & Pl
Chases	3	0	0	0	3500
Career Total	**14**	**4**	**5**	**2**	**28723**

141	3/01	Newb	3m	B(0-140)HCh	HVY	£10152
116	3/00	Leic	2m7f110y	H Ch	G-S	£5018
121	2/00	Chep	3m	H Ch	SFT	£1785
100	5/99	Strf	3m	H Ch	GD	£2784

Total win prize-money £19741

Going: Sf: 0-2 GS: 0-1 Gd: 0-0 GF: - Fm: 0-0
Distance: 2m/2m3: 0-0 2m4-2m7: 0-0 3m+: 0-3
Track: LH: 0-3 RH: 0-0 Tight: 0-0 Gall: 0-1
Aids: Bl: 0-0 Vi: 0-0 Tstrap: 0-0
Best Rating: **141** 3/01 Newb 3m heavy Ch

A smart hunter chaser, she made a successful debut for Venetia Williams when winning a Class B handicap chase on heavy ground at Newbury in March 2001. Held in handicaps for her owner/trainer last season, she has been retired.

Are You With Me

90 **81**

5-y-o ch g Rudimentary (USA)-Evening Star (Red Sunset)
A Dickman (J A Glover 25/7) Parklea Partnership

Placings: *45605* (3349)
2001/02: 16^{4}GF, 17^{5}GF, 16^{6}G, 17^{0}S, 16^{5}G

	Starts	1st	2nd	3rd	Win & Pl
NH Flat	3	0	0	0	0
Hurdles	2	0	0	0	0
Career Total	**5**	**0**	**0**	**0**	**0**

Going: Sf: 0-1 GS: 0-0 Gd: 0-2 GF: - Fm: 0-2
Distance: 2m/2m3: 0-5 2m4-2m7: 0-0 3m+: 0-0
Track: LH: 0-2 RH: 0-3 Tight: 0-4 Gall: 0-0
Aids: Bl: 0-0 Vi: 0-0 Tstrap: 0-0
Best Rating: **87** 6/01 MRas 2m1f110y gd-fm NHF

Arellano (IRE)

98 **112**

4-y-o ch g Erin's Isle-Volnost (USA) (Lyphard (USA))
C F Swan (J S Bolger 27/5) J P McManus

Placings: 2330 (3316a)
2001/02: 16^{2}HY, 16^{3}G, 16^{3}SH, 16^{0}YS

	Starts	1st	2nd	3rd	Win & Pl
Hurdles	4	0	1	2	3068
Career Total	**4**	**0**	**1**	**2**	**3068**

Going: Sf: 0-1 GS: 0-0 Gd: 0-1 GF: - Fm: 0-0
Distance: 2m/2m3: 0-4 2m4-2m7: 0-0 3m+: 0-0
Track: LH: 0-2 RH: 0-0 Tight: 0-0 Gall: 0-0
Aids: Bl: 0-0 Vi: 0-0 Tstrap: 0-0
Best Rating: **112** 10/01 Tipp 2m heavy Hdl

Placed in his first three starts over hurdles, his jumping was a bit awkward at Cheltenham, but the ground was not ideal as he prefers to get his toe in.

Argamia (GER)

91 **96**

6-y-o b m Orfano (GER)-Arkona (GER) (Aspros (GER))
M G Quinlan P J McBride

Placings: 30 (3696)
2001/02: 21^{3}GS, 16^{0}S

	Starts	1st	2nd	3rd	Win & Pl
Hurdles	2	0	0	1	781
Career Total	**2**	**0**	**0**	**1**	**781**

Going: Sf: 0-1 GS: 0-1 Gd: 0-0 GF: - Fm: 0-0
Distance: 2m/2m3: 0-1 2m4-2m7: 0-1 3m+: 0-0
Track: LH: 0-1 RH: 0-1 Tight: 0-0 Gall: 0-1
Aids: Bl: 0-0 Vi: 0-0 Tstrap: 0-0
Best Rating: **96** 1/02 Kemp 2m5f gd-sft Hdl

A winning stayer on the Flat, she showed promise on her hurdling bow in January 2002.

Argento

98 **86+**

5-y-o b g Weldnaas (USA)-Four M'S (Majestic Maharaj)
G M Moore Mrs Susan Moore

Placings: *654* (4860)
2001/02: 16^{6}G, 16^{5}S, 16^{4}G

	Starts	1st	2nd	3rd	Win & Pl
NH Flat	3	0	0	0	0
Career Total	**3**	**0**	**0**	**0**	**0**

Going: Sf: 0-1 GS: 0-0 Gd: 0-2 GF: - Fm: 0-0

Distance: 2m/2m3: 0-3 2m4-2m7: 0-0 3m+: 0-0
Track: LH: 0-1 RH: 0-0 Tight: 0-1 Gall: 0-0
Aids: Bl: 0-0 Vi: 0-0 Tstrap: 0-0
Best Rating: **86** 4/02 Hexm 2m110y good NHF

Some ability in bumpers and novice hurdles, but looks to need at least two and a half miles.

Ariala

92 **77**

5-y-o b m Arazi (USA)-Kashtala (Lord Gayle (USA))
G L Moore (K R Burke 3/5) Leydens Farm Stud

Placings:300 **(2204)**
2001/02: 18^{3}S, 16^{0}GS, 16^{0}GS

	Starts	1st	2nd	3rd	Win & Pl
Hurdles	3	0	0	1	352
Career Total	**3**	**0**	**0**	**1**	**352**

Going: Sf: 0-1 GS: 0-2 Gd: 0-0 GF: - Fm: 0-0
Distance: 2m/2m3: 0-3 2m4-2m7: 0-0 3m+: 0-0
Track: LH: 0-2 RH: 0-1 Tight: 0-2 Gall: 0-0
Aids: Bl: 0-0 Vi: 0-0 Tstrap: 0-0
Best Rating: **77** 10/01 Font 2m2f110y soft Hdl

Arijaz

85f **74f**

5-y-o b g Teenoso (USA)-Zajira (IRE) (Ela-Mana-Mou)
P R Hedger Zajira Racing

Placings:6 **(0253)**
2001/02: 17^{6}GF

	Starts	1st	2nd	3rd	Win & Pl
NH Flat	1	0	0	0	0
Career Total	**1**	**0**	**0**	**0**	**0**

Going: Sf: 0-0 GS: 0-0 Gd: 0-0 GF: - Fm: 0-1
Distance: 2m/2m3: 0-1 2m4-2m7: 0-0 3m+: 0-0
Track: LH: 0-1 RH: 0-0 Tight: 0-1 Gall: 0-0
Aids: Bl: 0-0 Vi: 0-0 Tstrap: 0-0
Best Rating: **74** 5/01 NAbb 2m1f gd-fm NHF

Arizona Bold

76(91h) (48h)**63**

9-y-o b g Skyliner-Bold Event (Persian Bold)
N B Mason N B Mason

Placings:330P0F/6PP32PP6500PP3-3P0650 **(1623)**
2001/02: 26^{3}G, 22^{P}GF, 21^{0}GF, 20^{6}GF, 25^{5}G, 21^{0}G

	Starts	1st	2nd	3rd	Win & Pl
Hurdles	1	0	0	0	0
Chases	5	0	0	1	528
Career Total	**26**	**0**	**1**	**5**	**3247**

Going: Sf: 0-0 GS: 0-0 Gd: 0-3 GF: - Fm: 0-3
Distance: 2m/2m3: 0-0 2m4-2m7: 0-4 3m+: 0-2
Track: LH: 0-4 RH: 0-2 Tight: 0-5 Gall: 0-0
Aids: Bl: 0-0 Vi: 0-0 Tstrap: 0-0
Best Rating: **80** 10/00 Towc 3m1f gd-fm Ch

Arkley Royal

11-y-o b g Ardross-Lady Geneva (Royalty)
J A B Old Arkley Royal Partnership

Placings:113/221/41/445/3-FP **(3700)**
2001/02: 24^{F}HY, 24^{P}S

	Starts	1st	2nd	3rd	Win & Pl
Hurdles	1	0	0	0	0
Chases	1	0	0	0	0
Career Total	**14**	**4**	**2**	**2**	**16154**

137 3/99 Wwck 2m4f110y C(0-135)HHdl SFT £5060
127 2/98 Wwck 2m4f110y D Hdl GD £3790
115 1/97 Ling 2m110y H NHF SFT £1306
98 12/96 Ling 2m110y H NHF G-S £1311
Total win prize-money £11469

Going: Sf: 0-2 GS: 0-0 Gd: 0-0 GF: - Fm: 0-0
Distance: 2m/2m3: 0-0 2m4-2m7: 0-0 3m+: 0-2
Track: LH: 0-2 RH: 0-0 Tight: 0-0 Gall: 0-1
Aids: Bl: 0-0 Vi: 0-0 Tstrap: 0-0
Best Rating: **141** 4/00 Chel 2m5f110y soft Hdl

A fair hurdler, he has yet to show much over fences and appears to lack confidence. Suited by two and a half miles. Has won on good and heavy ground.

Arlas (FR)

114(111h) (142h)**157**

7-y-o b g Northern Fashion (USA)-Ribbon In Her Hair (USA) (Sauce Boat (USA))
M C Pipe (P F Nicholls 15/5) Matt Archer & Miss Jean Broadhurst

Placings:2P3164**62/51F12424/P**1**U**0**P**-12**1112**4 **(2029)**
2001/02: 19^{1}G, 20^{2}G, 26^{1}GF, 23^{1}GF, 23^{1}GF, 24^{2}G, 24^{4}GS

	Starts	1st	2nd	3rd	Win & Pl
Hurdles	3	1	1	0	4268
Chases	4	3	1	0	22514
Career Total	**28**	**8**	**6**	**1**	**121922**

157 0/01 Worc 2m7f110y C(0-135)HCh G-F £6864
153 8/01 Worc 2m7f110y C(0-130)HCh G-F £6745
152 7/01 NAbb 3m2f110y C(0-135)HCh G-F £5846
123 5/01 Hrfd 2m3f110y G Hdl GD £2044
127 11/00 NAbb 2m6f C(0-130)HHdl HVY £6743
129 1/00 Font 2m6f D Ch GD £3906
5/99 Autl 2m5f110y Ch HLD £53821
12/98 Cagn 2m1f110y Hdl GD £6061
Total win prize-money £92034

Going: Sf: 0-0 GS: 0-1 Gd: 1-3 GF: - Fm: 3-3
Distance: 2m/2m3: 0-0 2m4-2m7: 1-2 **3m+: 3-5**
Track: **LH: 3-6** RH: 1-1 **Tight: 1-1** Gall: 0-0
Aids: Bl: 0-2 Vi: 0-0 Tstrap: 0-0
Best Rating: **157** 10/01 Chep 3m good Ch

He was in fine form during the summer completing a hat trick over fences and had previously won over hurdles. Suited by trips of around three miles, he has won on heavy ground over hurdles, but is especially well suited by faster conditions.

Arleneseoin (IRE)

(93h) (86h)

10-y-o b g Aristocracy-Lady Flair (Flair Path)
J T Gifford Mrs Sarah Dunsdon

Placings:000UF0*56*/1F/06/1142F-3 **(1672)**
2001/02: 22^{3}HY

	Starts	1st	2nd	3rd	Win & Pl
Hurdles	1	0	0	1	335
Career Total	**18**	**3**	**1**	**1**	**10461**

120 7/00 Worc 2m4f110y F(0-100)HCh G-F £2756
120 6/00 Strf 2m4f E(0-115)HCh G-S £3159
90 8/98 Tram 2m Ch G-F £2540
Total win prize-money £8456

Going: Sf: 0-1 GS: 0-0 Gd: 0-0 GF: - Fm: 0-0
Distance: 2m/2m3: 0-0 2m4-2m7: 0-1 3m+: 0-0
Track: LH: 0-0 RH: 0-1 Tight: 0-1 Gall: 0-0
Aids: Bl: 0-0 Vi: 0-0 Tstrap: 0-0
Best Rating: **120** 9/00 Strf 2m4f good Ch

Arlequin De Sou (FR)

103(88h) (89h)**131**

8-y-o b g Sir Brink (FR)-Colombine (USA) (Empery (USA))
P J Hobbs Mrs Karola Vann

Placings:1141356/2112P5/1321433F-002 **(4497)**
2001/02: 20^{0}HY, 20^{0}GS, 24^{2}G

	Starts	1st	2nd	3rd	Win & Pl
Hurdles	1	0	0	0	0
Chases	2	0	1	0	2180
Career Total	**24**	**7**	**4**	**4**	**53272**

147 12/00 Chel 2m5f E(0-125)HCh SFT £7247
121 11/00 Winc 2m6f E(0-115)HHdl G-S £4426
116 2/00 Font 2m6f110y D(0-125)HHdl G-S £5499
105 2/00 Chep 2m4f D(0-125)HHdl SFT £3087
12/98 Autl 2m1f110y Ch HVY £6566
11/98 Engh 2m2f Ch VS £6566
10/98 Autl 2m4f110y Ch HLD £6566
Total win prize-money £39960

Going: Sf: 0-1 GS: 0-1 Gd: 0-1 GF: - Fm: 0-0
Distance: 2m/2m3: 0-0 2m4-2m7: 0-2 3m+: 0-1
Track: LH: 0-3 RH: 0-0 Tight: 0-0 Gall: 0-1
Aids: Bl: 0-3 Vi: 0-0 Tstrap: 0-0
Best Rating: **147** 12/00 Chel 2m5f soft Ch

He is best when bullying the opposition and made all to win a couple of weakly contested handicaps at the end of 2000. Disappointing afterwards, he jumped badly left on one occasion and fell in the John Hughes Trophy at Aintree in 2001. Reappeared after nearly a year off in spring of 2002. He wears blinkers and is suited by trips around two and a half miles on easy ground.

Armageddon

94 **76**

5-y-o b g Deploy-Arusha (IRE) (Dance Of Life (USA))
N J Henderson Raymond Tooth

Placings:12-P6 **(4518)**
2001/02: 21^{P}HY, 21^{6}GS

	Starts	1st	2nd	3rd	Win & Pl
Hurdles	2	0	0	0	0
Career Total	**4**	**1**	**1**	**0**	**4004**

108 1/01 Chep 2m110y H NHF G-S £1484
Total win prize-money £1484

Going: Sf: 0-1 GS: 0-1 Gd: 0-0 GF: - Fm: 0-0
Distance: 2m/2m3: 0-0 2m4-2m7: 0-2 3m+: 0-0
Track: LH: 0-0 RH: 0-1 Tight: 0-0 Gall: 0-0
Aids: Bl: 0-0 Vi: 0-0 Tstrap: 0-0
Best Rating: **110** 2/01 Newb 2m110y soft NHF

A useful bumper winner early in 2001, he was pulled up on his hurdling debut after a year's absence. Has won on good to soft ground.

Armaguedon (FR)

101f **119f**

4-y-o b g Garde Royale-Miss Dundee (FR) (Esprit Du Nord (USA))
L Lungo Ashleybank Investments Limited

Placings:3 **(4841)**
2001/02: 16^{3}G

	Starts	1st	2nd	3rd	Win & Pl

	Starts	1st	2nd	3rd	Win & Pl
NH Flat	1	0	0	1	478
Career Total	**1**	**0**	**0**	**1**	**478**

Going: Sf: 0-0 GS: 0-0 Gd: 0-1 GF: - Fm: 0-0
Distance: 2m/2m3: 0-1 2m4-2m7: 0-0 3m+: 0-0
Track: LH: 0-1 RH: 0-0 Tight: 0-0 Gall: 0-0
Aids: Bl: 0-0 Vi: 0-0 Tstrap: 0-0
Best Rating: **119** 4/02 Ayr 2m good NHF

Armaturk (FR)

120(123h) (151h)**161**
5-y-o ch g Baby Turk-Armalita (FR) (Goodland (FR))
P F Nicholls B C Marshall

Placings:332111-3121131 **(4675)**
2001/02: 16^{3}G, 16^{1}GS, 16^{2}G, 18^{1}G, 16^{1}S, 16^{3}GS, 16^{1}G

	Starts	1st	2nd	3rd	Win & Pl
Hurdles	2	1	0	1	8403
Chases	5	3	1	1	91055
Career Total	**13**	**7**	**2**	**4**	**116289**

161	4/02	Aint	2m	A Ch	GD	£46500
152	2/02	Wwck	2m110y	A Ch	SFT	£18000
146	12/01	Newb	2m2f110y	D Ch	GD	£5905
151	10/01	Kemp	2m	B Hdl	G-S	£6890
130	4/01	Kemp	2m	D Hdl	GD	£3939
128	4/01	Plum	2m	E Hdl	HVY	£2513
	1/01	Pau	2m110y	Hdl	SFT	£6305

Total win prize-money £90052

Going: Sf: 1-1 GS: 1-2 Gd: 2-4 GF: - Fm: 0-0
Distance: **2m/2m3: 4-7** 2m4-2m7: 0-0 3m+: 0-0
Track: **LH: 2-5** RH: 1-1 Tight: 1-1 Gall: 1-3
Aids: Bl: 0-0 Vi: 0-0 Tstrap: 0-0
Best Rating: **161** 4/02 Aint 2m good Ch

A French import, he shaped with promise on his chasing debut before getting off the mark over the larger obstacles at Newbury in December. He followed up at Warwick the following month before a fair third in the Arkle and went on to reverse that form with Seebald at Aintree. Best at around two miles and versatile regarding ground, he might find life a little tougher against experienced chasers in 2002/03.

Aroseforclare

71 **30**
6-y-o b m Royal Vulcan-Lovelyroseofclare (Torus)
Miss K M George Michael Mingay

Placings:*06*-000 **(0720)**
2001/02: 17^{0}F, 17^{0}G, 26^{0}F

	Starts	1st	2nd	3rd	Win & Pl
NH Flat	1	0	0	0	0
Hurdles	2	0	0	0	0
Career Total	**5**	**0**	**0**	**0**	**0**

Going: Sf: 0-0 GS: 0-0 Gd: 0-1 GF: - Fm: 0-2
Distance: 2m/2m3: 0-2 2m4-2m7: 0-0 3m+: 0-1
Track: LH: 0-0 RH: 0-3 Tight: 0-0 Gall: 0-0
Aids: Bl: 0-0 Vi: 0-0 Tstrap: 0-0
Best Rating: **62** 5/01 Extr 2m1f firm NHF

Around The Gale (IRE)

11-y-o b g Strong Gale-Ring Road (Giolla Mear)
D R Gandolfo Starlight Racing

Placings:*21*/562151/**12123**/05544/**PP1**/**3P3356**/**231434**-PPP **(4177)**
2001/02: 25^{P}G, 23^{P}GF, 24^{P}GS

	Starts	1st	2nd	3rd	Win & Pl
Chases	3	0	0	0	0
Career Total	**36**	**7**	**5**	**6**	**50207**

126	11/00	Kemp	3m	D(0-120)HCh	SFT	£7722
124	2/99	Sand	2m4f110y	C(0-130)HCh	GD	£5654
134	12/96	Bang	2m4f110y	D Ch	GD	£4357
124	11/96	Bang	2m1f110y	D Ch	G-S	£4032
126	4/96	Bang	2m4f	E Hdl	SFT	£3284
117	3/96	NAbb	2m1f	Hdl	HVY	£2358
91	4/95	NAbb	2m1f	H NHF	G-S	£1628

Total win prize-money £29037

Going: Sf: 0-0 GS: 0-1 Gd: 0-1 GF: - Fm: 0-1
Distance: 2m/2m3: 0-0 2m4-2m7: 0-0 3m+: 0-3
Track: LH: 0-1 RH: 0-2 Tight: 0-2 Gall: 0-0
Aids: Bl: 0-1 Vi: 0-2 Tstrap: 0-0
Best Rating: **137** 2/97 Kemp 2m4f110y good Ch

A fair staying handicapper. Has won at up to three miles. Acts on soft ground. Normally runs blinkered or visored. Pulled up on all three of his starts this term.

Arribilo (GER)

98 **91**
8-y-o b g Top Ville-Arborea (GER) (Priamos (GER))
P R Johnson (G M McCourt 12/1) Mrs L V Durnall

Placings:0-P62P045 **(4531)**
2001/02: 16^{P}S, 16^{6}GS, 16^{2}G, 16^{P}G, 20^{0}S, 17^{4}S, 16^{5}GS

	Starts	1st	2nd	3rd	Win & Pl
Hurdles	7	0	1	0	681
Career Total	**8**	**0**	**1**	**0**	**681**

Going: Sf: 0-3 GS: 0-2 Gd: 0-2 GF: - Fm: 0-0
Distance: 2m/2m3: 0-6 2m4-2m7: 0-1 3m+: 0-0
Track: LH: 0-3 RH: 0-4 Tight: 0-1 Gall: 0-1
Aids: Bl: 0-0 Vi: 0-2 Tstrap: 0-0
Best Rating: **91** 4/02 Chep 2m110y gd-sft Hdl

Modest form over hurdles, including claimers.

Arrogant Lord

10-y-o b g Arctic Lord-Warham Fantasy (Barolo)
D M Grissell Cockerell Cowing Racing

Placings:*0*/PP **(0325)**
2001/02: 18^{P}GF, 21^{P}G

	Starts	1st	2nd	3rd	Win & Pl
Chases	2	0	0	0	0
Career Total	**3**	**0**	**0**	**0**	**0**

Going: Sf: 0-0 GS: 0-0 Gd: 0-1 GF: - Fm: 0-1
Distance: 2m/2m3: 0-1 2m4-2m7: 0-1 3m+: 0-0
Track: LH: 0-0 RH: 0-1 Tight: 0-2 Gall: 0-0
Aids: Bl: 0-0 Vi: 0-0 Tstrap: 0-0
Best Rating:

Art Nouveau

78f **53f**
4-y-o b f Cyrano De Bergerac-Norska (Northfields (USA))
J A Moore Mrs J M Moore

Placings:*0* **(4771)**
2001/02: 16^{0}GF

	Starts	1st	2nd	3rd	Win & Pl
NH Flat	1	0	0	0	
Career Total	**1**	**0**	**0**	**0**	

Going: Sf: 0-0 GS: 0-0 Gd: 0-0 GF: - Fm: 0-1
Distance: 2m/2m3: 0-1 2m4-2m7: 0-0 3m+: 0-0
Track: LH: 0-0 RH: 0-1 Tight: 0-0 Gall: 0-0
Aids: Bl: 0-0 Vi: 0-0 Tstrap: 0-0
Best Rating: **43** 4/02 Hexm 2m110y gd-fm NHF

Art Prince (IRE)

(83h)**92**
12-y-o b g Aristocracy-Come Now (Prince Hansel)
M C Pipe Terry Neill

Placings:*032***F11**/**3F3P33F4**/**1U1220134P3**/**P123221213F**/**513PPF-P0P** **(0927)**
2001/02: 21^{P}GF, 24^{0}GF, 25^{P}GF

	Starts	1st	2nd	3rd	Win & Pl
Hurdles	1	0	0	0	0
Chases	2	0	0	0	0
Career Total	**45**	**9**	**7**	**10**	**58438**

143	6/00	NAbb	3m2f110y	D(0-120)HCh	G-F	£4036
141	11/99	Sand	3m110y	B HCh	GD	£10987
141	10/99	Tntn	3m	D(0-120)HCh	G-F	£5108
130	8/99	Worc	2m7f110y	C(0-130)HCh	G-F	£5743
107	8/98	Strf	2m6f110y	D Hdl	G-F	£2973
114	6/98	Hrfd	3m2f	E Hdl	G-F	£2305
133	5/98	Winc	3m1f110y	D(0-120)HCh	GD	£3707
123	12/96	Uttx	2m5f	E(0-100)HCh	G-S	£3087
123	12/96	Donc	2m3f110y	D Ch	G-F	£3626

Total win prize-money £41576

Going: Sf: 0-0 GS: 0-0 Gd: 0-0 GF: - Fm: 0-3
Distance: 2m/2m3: 0-0 2m4-2m7: 0-1 3m+: 0-2
Track: LH: 0-3 RH: 0-0 Tight: 0-3 Gall: 0-0
Aids: Bl: 0-0 Vi: 0-0 Tstrap: 0-3
Best Rating: **143** 8/00 Uttx 2m5f gd-fm Ch

A fast ground specialist who front runs and races in a tongue tie, he lost his way last season and looks on the downgrade.

Art Stones (FR)

104 **122**
7-y-o b g Dark Stone (FR)-Aktia (FR) (Lyphard's Special (USA))
Mrs S A Bramall Mrs S A Bramall

Placings:035201/15366 **(4447a)**
2001/02: 20^{1}S, 24^{5}YS, 16^{3}YS, 20^{6}HY, 20^{6}S

	Starts	1st	2nd	3rd	Win & Pl
Chases	5	1	0	1	5229
Career Total	**11**	**2**	**1**	**2**	**23610**

122	10/01	Carl	2m4f	D Ch	SFT	£4563
91	3/00	Gowr	2m4f	Hdl	YLD	£3312

Total win prize-money £7875

Going: Sf: 1-3 GS: 0-0 Gd: 0-0 GF: - Fm: 0-0
Distance: 2m/2m3: 0-1 **2m4-2m7: 1-3** 3m+: 0-1
Track: LH: 0-1 **RH: 1-3** Tight: 0-0 Gall: 0-0
Aids: Bl: 0-1 Vi: 0-0 Tstrap: 0-0
Best Rating: **122** 10/01 Carl 2m4f soft Ch

Artadoin Lad (IRE)

100 **110**
9-y-o b g King's Ride-Nun Merrier (The Parson)
M Pitman J Shaw

Placings:*0*/*1*F1312/56P/U3 **(3642)**
2001/02: 20^{U}G, 24^{3}GS

	Starts	1st	2nd	3rd	Win & Pl
Chases	2	0	0	1	636
Career Total	**12**	**3**	**1**	**2**	**27760**

131	3/99	Newb	2m110y	D Hdl	SFT	£3610
105	11/98	Wwck	2m	E Hdl	GD	£2731
112	5/98	Uttx	2m	H NHF	G-S	£1826

Total win prize-money £8168

Going: Sf: 0-0 GS: 0-1 Gd: 0-1 GF: - Fm: 0-0
Distance: 2m/2m3: 0-0 2m4-2m7: 0-1 3m+: 0-1
Track: LH: 0-0 RH: 0-2 Tight: 0-1 Gall: 0-0
Aids: Bl: 0-0 Vi: 0-0 Tstrap: 0-0
Best Rating: **146** 3/99 Chel 2m5f gd-sft Hdl

A former very useful hurdler, he is now novice chasing. Stays three miles, acts on good and soft ground.

Artemesia

99 86

7-y-o b m Teenoso (USA)-Annicombe Run (Deep Run)
Ferdy Murphy Beautifully Bred Partnership

Placings: *3/024*-03U6R4 (4919)
2001/02: 16^{0}G, 16^{3}S, 19^{U}GF, 19^{6}S, 20^{R}G, 21^{4}GF

	Starts	1st	2nd	3rd	Win & Pl
Hurdles	6	0	0	1	374
Career Total	**10**	**0**	**1**	**2**	**1289**

Going: Sf: 0-2 GS: 0-0 Gd: 0-2 GF: - Fm: 0-2
Distance: 2m/2m3: 0-4 2m4-2m7: 0-2 3m+: 0-0
Track: LH: 0-5 RH: 0-1 Tight: 0-3 Gall: 0-0
Aids: Bl: 0-0 Vi: 0-0 Tstrap: 0-0
Best Rating: **102** 1/01 Fknm 2m soft NHF

Handicap hurdler. Stays three miles and acts on a soft surface.

Arterxerxes

95 96

9-y-o b g Anshan-Hanglands (Bustino)
C G Cox S P Tindall

Placings: 0-3 (0209)
2001/02: 16^{3}F

	Starts	1st	2nd	3rd	Win & Pl
Hurdles	1	0	0	1	523
Career Total	**2**	**0**	**0**	**1**	**523**

Going: Sf: 0-0 GS: 0-0 Gd: 0-0 GF: - Fm: 0-1
Distance: 2m/2m3: 0-1 2m4-2m7: 0-0 3m+: 0-0
Track: LH: 0-1 RH: 0-0 Tight: 0-1 Gall: 0-0
Aids: Bl: 0-0 Vi: 0-0 Tstrap: 0-0
Best Rating: **96** 5/01 Sthl 2m firm Hdl

Arthur Porter

9-y-o ch g Crawter-Chetsford Water (Sir Lark)
P R Hedger Ms L Angell

Placings: 6P (4036)
2001/02: 20^{6}S, 20^{P}S

	Starts	1st	2nd	3rd	Win & Pl
Chases	2	0	0	0	0
Career Total	**2**	**0**	**0**	**0**	**0**

Going: Sf: 0-2 GS: 0-0 Gd: 0-0 GF: - Fm: 0-0
Distance: 2m/2m3: 0-0 2m4-2m7: 0-2 3m+: 0-0
Track: LH: 0-0 RH: 0-1 Tight: 0-1 Gall: 0-0
Aids: Bl: 0-0 Vi: 0-0 Tstrap: 0-0
Best Rating:

Arthur-K

74 43

5-y-o ch g Greensmith-Classy Miss (Homeboy)
R H Alner Kavanagh Roofing Southern Limited

Placings: 0PP (4518)
2001/02: 17^{0}S, 24^{P}S, 21^{P}GS

	Starts	1st	2nd	3rd	Win & Pl
Hurdles	3	0	0	0	
Career Total	**3**	**0**	**0**	**0**	

Going: Sf: 0-2 GS: 0-1 Gd: 0-0 GF: - Fm: 0-0
Distance: 2m/2m3: 0-1 2m4-2m7: 0-1 3m+: 0-1
Track: LH: 0-0 RH: 0-3 Tight: 0-2 Gall: 0-0
Aids: Bl: 0-0 Vi: 0-0 Tstrap: 0-0
Best Rating: **43** 1/02 Tntn 2m1f soft Hdl

Arthurs Kingdom (IRE)

98 79

6-y-o b g Roi Danzig (USA)-Merrie Moment (IRE) (Taufan (USA))
Miss Kate Milligan Dr Roy Palmer

Placings: 603450-05325105P (4766)
2001/02: 21^{0}G, 19^{5}GF, 20^{3}G, 24^{2}GF, 24^{5}G, 22^{1}GS, 21^{0}GF, 25^{5}G, 20^{P}GF

	Starts	1st	2nd	3rd	Win & Pl
Hurdles	9	1	1	1	3728
Career Total	**15**	**1**	**1**	**2**	**4124**

79	8/01	Ctml	2m6f	G(0-90)HHdl	G-S	£2772

Total win prize-money £2772

Going: Sf: 0-0 GS: 1-1 Gd: 0-4 GF: - Fm: 0-4
Distance: 2m/2m3: 0-0 **2m4-2m7: 1-6** 3m+: 0-3
Track: **LH: 1-7** RH: 0-2 **Tight: 1-5** Gall: 0 0
Aids: Bl: 0-0 Vi: 0-1 Tstrap: 0-0
Best Rating: **90** 9/00 Sedg 2m1f soft Hdl

Moderate staying hurdler, got off the mark at the 31st attempt at Cartmel in August 2001. Seems to handle any ground.

Artic Jack (FR)

111(109h) 150

6-y-o b g Cadoudal (FR)-Si Jamais (FR) (Arctic Tern (USA))
N J Henderson Trevor Hemmings

Placings: 2/616-2F114PU3 (4835)
2001/02: 19^{2}G, 22^{F}G, 21^{1}G, 24^{1}G, 24^{4}GS, 24^{P}GS, 25^{U}G, 25^{3}G

	Starts	1st	2nd	3rd	Win & Pl
Chases	8	2	1	1	19888
Career Total	**12**	**3**	**2**	**1**	**31035**

150	1/02	Asct	3m110y	B Ch	GD	£9035
121	12/01	Folk	2m5f	D Ch	GD	£4459
126	1/01	Hayd	2m	D Hdl	SFT	£3612

Total win prize-money £17106

Going: Sf: 0-0 GS: 0-2 Gd: 2-6 GF: - Fm: 0-0
Distance: 2m/2m3: 0-0 2m4-2m7: 1-3 3m+: 1-5
Track: LH: 0-3 **RH: 2-4 Tight: 1-2** Gall: 0-1
Aids: Bl: 0-0 Vi: 0-0 Tstrap: 0-0
Best Rating: **150** 1/02 Asct 3m110y good Ch

Handicap chaser. Has won on soft and good ground. Stays three miles.

Artist's Model

(89h) (47h)

7-y-o b m Petoski-Henry's True Love (Random Shot)
H D Daly Mrs Philip Humphries-Cuff

Placings: 446/3360-F60F (3980)
2001/02: 20^{F}GS, 17^{6}S, 16^{0}S, 20^{F}GS

	Starts	1st	2nd	3rd	Win & Pl
Hurdles	3	0	0	0	0
Chases	1	0	0	0	0
Career Total	**11**	**0**	**0**	**2**	**818**

Going: Sf: 0-2 GS: 0-2 Gd: 0-0 GF: - Fm: 0-0
Distance: 2m/2m3: 0-2 2m4-2m7: 0-2 3m+: 0-0
Track: LH: 0-1 RH: 0-3 Tight: 0-1 Gall: 0-0
Aids: Bl: 0-0 Vi: 0-0 Tstrap: 0-0
Best Rating: **98** 11/00 Hayd 2m soft Hdl

Arvi's Way

72f 95f

5-y-o b g Alflora (IRE)-Gentle Madam (Camden Town)
Mrs S J Smith Mrs Alicia Skene & W S Skene

Placings: *6* (4526)
2001/02: 17^{6}G

	Starts	1st	2nd	3rd	Win & Pl
NH Flat	1	0	0	0	0
Career Total	**1**	**0**	**0**	**0**	**0**

Going: Sf: 0-0 GS: 0-0 Gd: 0-1 GF: - Fm: 0-0
Distance: 2m/2m3: 0-1 2m4-2m7: 0-0 3m+: 0-0
Track: LH: 0-0 RH: 0-1 Tight: 0-0 Gall: 0-0
Aids: Bl: 0-0 Vi: 0-0 Tstrap: 0-0
Best Rating: **95** 4/02 Carl 2m1f good NHF

As Time Goes By

4-y-o ch g Timeless Times (USA)-Parfait Amour (Clantime)
B S Rothwell Brian Rothwell

Placings: P (3460)
2001/02: 16^{P}HY

	Starts	1st	2nd	3rd	Win & Pl
Hurdles	1	0	0	0	
Career Total	**1**	**0**	**0**	**0**	

Going: Sf: 0-1 GS: 0-0 Gd: 0-0 GF: - Fm: 0-0
Distance: 2m/2m3: 0-1 2m4-2m7: 0-0 3m+: 0-0
Track: LH: 0-1 RH: 0-0 Tight: 0-0 Gall: 0-0
Aids: Bl: 0-0 Vi: 0-0 Tstrap: 0-0
Best Rating:

Asador (FR)

105 140

6-y-o ch g Kadounor (FR)-Apos (FR) (Baillamont (USA))
P F Nicholls Darren C Mercer

Placings: 1110/1F1P (4254)
2001/02: 16^{1}HY, 16^{F}S, 17^{1}HY, 16^{P}G

	Starts	1st	2nd	3rd	Win & Pl
Chases	4	2	0	0	7100
Career Total	**8**	**5**	**0**	**0**	**31661**

140	2/02	Plum	2m1f	E Ch	HVY	£3360
140	12/01	NAbb	2m110y	D Ch	HVY	£3740
	2/00	Ange	2m1f110y	Hdl	VS	£10567
	1/00	Pau	2m2f	Hdl	VS	£7535
	12/99	Pau	2m110y	Hdl	HVY	£6459

Total win prize-money £31661

Going: Sf: 2-3 GS: 0-0 Gd: 0-1 GF: - Fm: 0-0
Distance: **2m/2m3: 2-4** 2m4-2m7: 0-0 3m+: 0-0
Track: **LH: 2-3** RH: 0-1 **Tight: 2-3** Gall: 0-1
Aids: Bl: 0-0 Vi: 0-0 Tstrap: 0-0
Best Rating: **140** 2/02 Plum 2m1f heavy Ch

A mud-lover, he won his first three races over hurdles in the

French Provinces and showed plenty of ability before breaking down in the Triumph at Cheltenham. Suited by left-handed tracks and heavy ground around two miles. Won his chasing bow after an absence of 21 months. Won an easy race at Plumpton after falling the time before.

Ascari

6-y-o br g Presidium-Ping Pong (Petong)
W Jarvis (M C Banks 29/9) M C Banks

Placings:0P4/6-F (1483)
2001/02: 17^{F}GS

	Starts	1st	2nd	3rd	Win & Pl
Chases	1	0	0	0	
Career Total	**5**	**0**	**0**	**0**	**0**

Going: Sf: 0-0 GS: 0-1 Gd: 0-0 GF: - Fm: 0-0
Distance: 2m/2m3: 0-1 2m4-2m7: 0-0 3m+: 0-0
Track: LH: 0-1 RH: 0-0 Tight: 0-1 Gall: 0-0
Aids: Bl: 0-0 Vi: 0-0 Tstrap: 0-0
Best Rating: **80** 3/00 Fknm 2m good Hdl

Ascot Boy

90 68
7-y-o b g Puissance-Our Aisling (Blakeney)
Graeme Roe Roe Racing Ltd

Placings:*0/60-6*6P (1392)
2001/02: 16^{6}GF, 16^{6}GF, 20^{P}GF

	Starts	1st	2nd	3rd	Win & Pl
NH Flat	1	0	0	0	0
Hurdles	2	0	0	0	0
Career Total	**6**	**0**	**0**	**0**	**0**

Going: Sf: 0-0 GS: 0-0 Gd: 0-0 GF: - Fm: 0-3
Distance: 2m/2m3: 0-2 2m4-2m7: 0-1 3m+: 0-0
Track: LH: 0-3 RH: 0-0 Tight: 0-0 Gall: 0-0
Aids: Bl: 0-0 Vi: 0-0 Tstrap: 0-0
Best Rating: **68** 8/01 Worc 2m gd-fm Hdl

Ash Branch (IRE)

87 81
8-y-o ch g Shardari-Etnas Princess (The Parson)
Sir John Barlow Bt Sir John & Lady Barlow

Placings:*0*-500P (4757)
2001/02: 16^{5}GF, 16^{0}G, 16^{0}S, 16^{P}GF

	Starts	1st	2nd	3rd	Win & Pl
Hurdles	4	0	0	0	0
Career Total	**5**	**0**	**0**	**0**	**0**

Going: Sf: 0-1 GS: 0-0 Gd: 0-1 GF: - Fm: 0-2
Distance: 2m/2m3: 0-4 2m4-2m7: 0-0 3m+: 0-0
Track: LH: 0-4 RH: 0-0 Tight: 0-1 Gall: 0-0
Aids: Bl: 0-0 Vi: 0-0 Tstrap: 0-0
Best Rating: **81** 9/01 Worc 2m gd-fm Hdl

Poor hurdler.

Ashbury Star (NZ)

104(101h) (105h)111
7-y-o ch g Sumayr-Piaf's Star (NZ) (Famous Star)
Mrs N Smith Tony Hayward

Placings:P1-3040234222 (4508)
2001/02: 17^{3}G, 17^{0}GF, 22^{4}S, 16^{0}G, 17^{2}S, 17^{3}G, 16^{4}HY, 17^{2}HY, 17^{2}HY, 17^{2}G

	Starts	1st	2nd	3rd	Win & Pl
Hurdles	6	0	1	1	1320
Chases	4	0	3	1	3484
Career Total	**12**	**1**	**4**	**2**	**7527**

103	4/01	Plum	2m	E Hdl	HVY	£2723

Total win prize-money £2723

Going: Sf: 0-5 GS: 0-0 Gd: 0-4 GF: - Fm: 0-1
Distance: 2m/2m3: 0-9 2m4-2m7: 0-1 3m+: 0-0
Track: LH: 0-7 RH: 0-3 Tight: 0-9 Gall: 0-0
Aids: Bl: 0-1 Vi: 0-0 Tstrap: 0-0
Best Rating: **111** 3/02 Plum 2m1f good Ch

Modest hurdler, who has done enough over fences to suggest that he can add to his tally. Acts in soft ground. Suited by two miles.

Ashfield Jake (IRE)

62(61c) (19c)37
10-y-o br g Jolly Jake (NZ)-Ashfield Rose (Mon Capitaine)
Simon T Lewis Simon T Lewis

Placings:0U00P (1664)
2001/02: 20^{0}G, 22^{U}GF, 22^{0}G, 19^{0}G, 24^{P}G

	Starts	1st	2nd	3rd	Win & Pl
Hurdles	3	0	0	0	0
Chases	2	0	0	0	0
Career Total	**5**	**0**	**0**	**0**	

Going: Sf: 0-0 GS: 0-0 Gd: 0-4 GF: - Fm: 0-1
Distance: 2m/2m3: 0-1 2m4-2m7: 0-3 3m+: 0-1
Track: LH: 0-3 RH: 0-2 Tight: 0-3 Gall: 0-1
Aids: Bl: 0-0 Vi: 0-0 Tstrap: 0-0
Best Rating: **37** 5/01 Hntg 2m4f110y good Hdl

Ashgan (IRE)

102(107h) (120h)119+
9-y-o br g Yashgan-Nicky's Dilemma (Kambalda)
Mrs H Dalton Mr A J & Mrs L Brazier

Placings:2FP215P/4**P5P**115/P11**3-41** (0505)
2001/02: 25^{4}G, 20^{1}GF

	Starts	1st	2nd	3rd	Win & Pl
Chases	2	1	0	0	3562
Career Total	**20**	**6**	**2**	**1**	**20162**

118	5/01	Hntg	2m4f110y	E Ch	G-F	£3262
128	8/00	Bang	2m4f110y	F(0-100)HCh	GD	£4251
123	7/00	Sedg	2m5f110y	D(0-125)HHdl	G-F	£3139
114	3/00	Folk	2m6f110y	F(0-110)HHdl	GD	£2416
118	2/00	MRas	2m5f110y	F(0-110)HHdl	G-S	£1921
98	3/99	Hntg	2m5f110y	E Hdl	G-S	£2740

Total win prize-money £17731

Going: Sf: 0-0 GS: 0-0 Gd: 0-1 GF: - Fm: 1-1
Distance: 2m/2m3: 0-0 **2m4-2m7: 1-1** 3m+: 0-1
Track: LH: 0-0 **RH: 1-2** Tight: 0-0 **Gall: 1-1**
Aids: Bl: 0-0 Vi: 0-0 Tstrap: 0-0
Best Rating: **128** 8/00 Bang 2m4f110y good Ch

Useful handicap hurdler and chaser at distances short of three miles. Acts on fast ground but was successful on good to soft in his younger days.

Ashgar (USA)

103(108h) (122h)131
6-y-o ch g Bien Bien (USA)-Ardisia (USA) (Affirmed (USA))
P J Hobbs Jay Dee Bloodstock Limited

Placings:2-1124323 (4817)
2001/02: 21^{1}GF, 21^{1}GF, 24^{2}GS, 24^{4}G, 21^{3}G, 24^{2}GF, 24^{3}GF

	Starts	1st	2nd	3rd	Win & Pl
Hurdles	7	2	2	2	9707
Career Total	**8**	**2**	**3**	**2**	**10452**

109	11/01	Ludl	2m5f	E Hdl	G-F	£2803
109	11/01	Ludl	2m5f	E Hdl	G-F	£2712

Total win prize-money £5517

Going: Sf: 0-0 GS: 0-1 Gd: 0-2 GF: - Fm: 2-4
Distance: 2m/2m3: 0-0 **2m4-2m7: 2-3** 3m+: 0-4
Track: LH: 0-1 **RH: 2-5** Tight: 0-2 Gall: 0-0
Aids: Bl: 0-0 Vi: 0-0 Tstrap: 0-0
Best Rating: **122** 4/02 Chel 3m gd-fm Hdl

A one-time useful stayer on the Flat, he went on to score twice at Ludlow in under two weeks in the autumn of 2001, but was found out subsequently in handicaps. Quirky sort, acts on fast ground.

Ashgreen

87 68
5-y-o b g Afzal-Space Kate (Space King)
M Sheppard C J Green

Placings:FP50P (4131)
2001/02: 16^{F}S, 16^{P}S, 19^{5}S, 19^{0}S, 26^{P}G

	Starts	1st	2nd	3rd	Win & Pl
Hurdles	5	0	0	0	0
Career Total	**5**	**0**	**0**	**0**	**0**

Going: Sf: 0-4 GS: 0-0 Gd: 0-1 GF: - Fm: 0-0
Distance: 2m/2m3: 0-2 2m4-2m7: 0-2 3m+: 0-1
Track: LH: 0-1 RH: 0-4 Tight: 0-0 Gall: 0-0
Aids: Bl: 0-0 Vi: 0-0 Tstrap: 0-0
Best Rating: **68** 12/01 Hrfd 2m3f110y soft Hdl

Ashley Muck

113(101h) (126h)146
9-y-o b g Gunner B-Miss Muck (Balinger)
M C Pipe Matt Archer & Miss Jean Broadhurst

Placings:*U5/32*F12/3/50P13-2**1111123** (1889)
2001/02: 19^{2}G, 21^{1}GF, 21^{1}GF, 21^{1}G, 21^{1}GF, 21^{1}G, 19^{2}G, 24^{3}G

	Starts	1st	2nd	3rd	Win & Pl
Hurdles	1	0	1	0	1093
Chases	7	5	1	1	25101
Career Total	**21**	**7**	**4**	**4**	**43038**

146	9/01	Uttx	2m5f	D(0-125)HCh	GD	£4920
146	8/01	Uttx	2m5f	C(0-135)HCh	G-F	£5872
144	8/01	NAbb	2m5f110y	D Ch	GD	£3721
141	7/01	NAbb	2m5f110y	E Ch	G-F	£3376
122	6/01	NAbb	2m5f110y	D Ch	G-F	£3840
123	3/01	Strf	2m110y	D(0-125)HHdl	SFT	£7436
126	11/98	Extr	2m1f	E Hdl	SFT	£2805

Total win prize-money £31973

Going: Sf: 0-0 GS: 0-0 Gd: 2-5 GF: - Fm: 3-3
Distance: 2m/2m3: 0-0 **2m4-2m7: 5-7** 3m+: 0-1
Track: **LH: 5-7** RH: 0-1 **Tight: 3-3** Gall: 0-1
Aids: Bl: 0-0 Vi: 0-0 Tstrap: 0-0
Best Rating: **146** 9/01 Uttx 2m5f good Ch

Certainly has plenty of ability, but has temperament problems too and has had a tendency to lose ground at the start. Not much wrong with his attitude in 2001 however, rattling off a five timer on fast ground in the summer. Had a tough task at the weights at Chepstow and did not stay three miles at Cheltenham. Suited by trips of around two and a half miles.

Ashman (IRE)

86(95c) 73

9-y-o b g Ashmolean (USA)-Rhein Maiden (Rheingold)
H D Daly The Hon Mr Simon Sainsbury

Placings:5/0**F**01216/0**4**-**F**0PP (2220)
2001/02: 16^{F}GF, 16^{0}GF, 16^{P}GF, 17^{P}G

	Starts	1st	2nd	3rd	Win & Pl
Hurdles	3	0	0	0	0
Chases	1	0	0	0	0
Career Total	**14**	**2**	**1**	**0**	**7361**

123	3/00	Bang	2m1f	E Hdl	GD	£3038
113	2/00	Hrfd	2m1f	F(0-100)HHdl	GD	£2884

Total win prize-money £5922

Going: Sf: 0-0 GS: 0-0 Gd: 0-1 GF: - Fm: 0-3
Distance: 2m/2m3: 0-4 2m4-2m7: 0-0 3m+: 0-0
Track: LH: 0-3 RH: 0-0 Tight: 0-1 Gall: 0-0
Aids: Bl: 0-0 Vi: 0-0 Tstrap: 0-0
Best Rating: **123** 3/00 Bang 2m1f good Hdl

A former successful point to pointer, is a keen sort and a top of the ground performer. Successful twice at two miles one, he is prone to the odd mistake. Capable of adding to his tally when the ground dries out.

Ashnaya (FR)

76 **57**

4-y-o b f Ashkalani (IRE)-Upend (Main Reef)
W Storey (J L Dunlop 22/10) Tony Stafford

Placings:06 (4198)
2001/02: 16^{0}GS, 21^{6}S

	Starts	1st	2nd	3rd	Win & Pl
Hurdles	2	0	0	0	0
Career Total	**2**	**0**	**0**	**0**	**0**

Going: Sf: 0-1 GS: 0-1 Gd: 0-0 GF: - Fm: 0-0
Distance: 2m/2m3: 0-1 2m4-2m7: 0-1 3m+: 0-0
Track: LH: 0-2 RH: 0-0 Tight: 0-2 Gall: 0-0
Aids: Bl: 0-0 Vi: 0-0 Tstrap: 0-0
Best Rating: **60** 3/02 Catt 2m gd-sft Hdl

Has cut little ice to date.

Ashwell Boy (IRE)

108 **144**

11-y-o b g Strong Gale-Billys Pet (Le Moss)
M C Pipe A B S Racing

Placings:*125/0*F1052F/14PF261/P**11F334223/11142313/5 22F2/F00-23125** (4960a)
2001/02: 16^{2}GF, 17^{3}GF, 16^{1}GS, 16^{2}GF, 16^{5}GY

	Starts	1st	2nd	3rd	Win & Pl
Chases	5	1	2	1	17500
Career Total	**48**	**11**	**11**	**6**	**109902**

143	10/01	Kemp	2m	B(0-140)HCh	G-S	£8957
144	3/99	Newb	2m4f	C(0-135)HCh	SFT	£7035
137	10/98	Chep	2m3f110y	C(0-130)HCh	GD	£5085
144	5/98	Strf	2m5f110y	D Ch	GD	£3730
116	5/98	Strf	2m5f110y	D Ch	FRM	£4068
133	10/97	NAbb	2m110y	E Ch	G-F	£2859
133	9/97	Strf	2m4f	D Ch	GD	£3890
125	4/97	Chep	2m110y	B HHdl	G-F	£4674
121	5/96	Winc	2m	E Hdl	FRM	£2442
123	1/96	Asct	2m110y	D Hdl	SFT	£3988
98	3/95	Newb	2m110y	H NHF	GD	£2248

Total win prize-money £48981

Going: Sf: 0-0 GS: 1-1 Gd: 0-0 GF: - Fm: 0-3
Distance: **2m/2m3: 1-5** 2m4-2m7: 0-0 3m+: 0-0
Track: LH: 0-1 **RH: 1-3** Tight: 0-1 Gall: 0-0
Aids: Bl: 0-1 **Vi: 1-4** Tstrap: 0-0
Best Rating: **144** 11/01 Asct 2m gd-fm Ch

A useful chaser, he is not easy to train or a straightforward ride. Broke a lengthy losing run at Kempton in October 2001. Suited by fast ground, he has been fitted with a visor of late.

Ask June (IRE)

108 **119**

7-y-o b m Shernazar-Slim-N-Lite (Furry Glen)
Miss Venetia Williams Mrs Toni S Tipper

Placings:0P50*210*/3-2115PP (4500)
2001/02: 16^{2}S, 16^{1}S, 16^{1}HY, 20^{5}S, 19^{P}HY, 17^{P}G

	Starts	1st	2nd	3rd	Win & Pl
Hurdles	6	2	1	0	7501
Career Total	**14**	**3**	**2**	**1**	**11489**

119	12/01	Hayd	2m	D Hdl	HVY	£3675
110	12/01	Sthl	2m	E Hdl	SFT	£2506
90	4/00	Clon	2m4f	NHF	GD	£2760

Total win prize-money £8941

Going: Sf: 2-5 GS: 0-0 Gd: 0-1 GF: - Fm: 0-0
Distance: **2m/2m3: 2-4** 2m4-2m7: 0-2 3m+: 0-0
Track: **LH: 2-4** RH: 0-2 **Tight: 1-3** Gall: 0-0
Aids: Bl: 0-0 Vi: 0-0 Tstrap: 0-0
Best Rating: **119** 12/01 Hayd 2m heavy Hdl

Won two weak novice hurdles in testing ground in December 2001, but was then disappointing under big weights. Suited by two miles and soft ground.

Ask The Natives (IRE)

(113h) (124h)

8-y-o br g Be My Native (USA)-Ask The Lady (Over The River (FR))
P F Nicholls Paul K Barber

Placings:*21*/11/**FF4**B3-P**5** (1749)
2001/02: 16^{P}G, 17^{5}G

	Starts	1st	2nd	3rd	Win & Pl
Hurdles	1	0	0	0	0
Chases	1	0	0	0	0
Career Total	**11**	**3**	**1**	**1**	**15845**

126	12/99	Chel	2m1f	C Hdl	GD	£5459
126	11/99	Extr	2m3f	D Hdl	G-S	£3522
109	3/99	Winc	2m	H NHF	GD	£1682

Total win prize-money £10664

Going: Sf: 0-0 GS: 0-0 Gd: 0-2 GF: - Fm: 0-0
Distance: 2m/2m3: 0-2 2m4-2m7: 0-0 3m+: 0-0
Track: LH: 0-1 RH: 0-1 Tight: 0-1 Gall: 0-0
Aids: Bl: 0-0 Vi: 0-0 Tstrap: 0-0
Best Rating: **136** 11/00 Chep 2m3f110y soft Ch

He looked an outstanding prospect over hurdles in the 1999-2000 season but made an unfortunate start to his chasing career, taking two heavy falls in November 2000. Third in a valuable handicap hurdle at Aintree in April 2001, he broke a blood-vessel on his return to fences in October that year.

Askadari (IRE)

82f **55f**

5-y-o ch g Shardari-Maevepatricia (Artaius (USA))
Mrs H Dalton J & G Sporting Partners

Placings:*0* (4873)
2001/02: 16^{0}GF

	Starts	1st	2nd	3rd	Win & Pl
NH Flat	1	0	0	0	
Career Total	**1**	**0**	**0**	**0**	

Going: Sf: 0-0 GS: 0-0 Gd: 0-0 GF: - Fm: 0-1
Distance: 2m/2m3: 0-1 2m4-2m7: 0-0 3m+: 0-0
Track: LH: 0-1 RH: 0-0 Tight: 0-0 Gall: 0-0
Aids: Bl: 0-0 Vi: 0-0 Tstrap: 0-0
Best Rating: **55** 4/02 Weth 2m gd-fm NHF

Asking

106 **95**

10-y-o b g Skyliner-Ma Famille (Welsh Saint)
M Bradstock Miss J C Blackwell

Placings:34613/02/520/5P/243**F**0/3240-20164 (3404)
2001/02: 17^{2}G, 16^{0}G, 19^{1}S, 19^{6}G, 16^{4}S

	Starts	1st	2nd	3rd	Win & Pl
Hurdles	5	1	1	0	2175
Career Total	**26**	**2**	**5**	**4**	**10363**

95	12/01	MRas	2m3f110y	G(0-95)HHdl	SFT	£1575
86	11/95	MRas	2m1f110y	D Hdl	G-F	£3134

Total win prize-money £4709

Going: Sf: 1-2 GS: 0-0 Gd: 0-3 GF: - Fm: 0-0
Distance: 2m/2m3: 0-4 **2m4-2m7: 1-1** 3m+: 0-0
Track: LH: 0-1 **RH: 1-4** **Tight: 1-1** Gall: 0-1
Aids: Bl: 0-0 **Vi: 1-4** Tstrap: 0-0
Best Rating: **99** 2/00 Folk 2m good Ch

Plating-class hurdler. Stays two miles-three, handles any ground. Sometimes wears a visor.

Askrigg Venture (IRE)

98(49c) **80**

9-y-o br m Jurado (USA)-Brave Polly (Brave Invader (USA))
A Crook Keith Johnson

Placings:*0*/0305/**62**/**3PP**-1PF5**P**6P (4919)
2001/02: 16^{1}GS, 20^{P}GS, 20^{F}G, 16^{5}S, 19^{P}GS, 21^{6}HY, 21^{P}GF

	Starts	1st	2nd	3rd	Win & Pl
Hurdles	6	1	0	0	2979
Chases	1	0	0	0	0
Career Total	**17**	**1**	**1**	**2**	**5334**

80	5/01	Prth	2m110y	E Hdl	G-S	£2078

Total win prize-money £2979

Going: Sf: 0-2 GS: 1-3 Gd: 0-1 GF: - Fm: 0-1
Distance: **2m/2m3: 1-3** 2m4-2m7: 0-4 3m+: 0-0
Track: LH: 0-6 **RH: 1-1** Tight: 0-4 Gall: 0-1
Aids: **Bl: 1-4** Vi: 0-1 Tstrap: 0-0
Best Rating: **98** 2/00 Newc 2m4f heavy Ch

Asparagus (IRE)

117(114h) (115h)**125**

8-y-o b g Roselier (FR)-Arctic Bead (IRE) (Le Moss)
M Sheppard Simon Gegg

Placings:23FF-F1434**211** (4430)
2001/02: 20^{F}S, 16^{1}HY, 16^{4}S, 20^{3}S, 20^{4}HY, 19^{2}HY, 16^{1}S, 16^{1}HY

	Starts	1st	2nd	3rd	Win & Pl
Hurdles	5	1	0	1	4330
Chases	3	2	1	0	7430
Career Total	**12**	**3**	**2**	**2**	**14426**

125	3/02	Uttx	2m	F(0-100)HCh	HVY	£3445
120	3/02	Chep	2m110y	F(0-95)HCh	SFT	£2989
115	11/01	Uttx	2m	E Hdl	HVY	£2730

Total win prize-money £9164

Going: Sf: 3-8 GS: 0-0 Gd: 0-0 GF: - Fm: 0-0
Distance: **2m/2m3: 3-5** 2m4-2m7: 0-3 3m+: 0-0
Track: **LH: 3-6** RH: 0-2 Tight: 0-0 Gall: 0-0

Aids: Bl: 0-0 Vi: 0-0 **Tstrap: 3-7**
Best Rating: 125 3/02 Uttx 2m heavy Ch

Fell on his last two starts over fences before switching to hurdles. Fell on his hurdles debut but scored next time with a tongue tie. Decent effort back over fences and proved very game when winning under top-weight at Uttoxeter in March. Stays two and a half miles, but best over two miles on heavy.

Aspirant Dancer

114 **150**

7-y-o b g Marju (IRE)-Fairy Ballerina (Fairy King (USA))
Mrs L Wadham (M L W Bell 20/10) Peter Coe

Placings:221/1FP266-11361006 **(4667)**
2001/02: 20^{1}G, 21^{1}GS, 20^{3}S, 20^{6}G, 20^{1}S, 20^{0}S, 25^{0}GS, 20^{6}G

	Starts	1st	2nd	3rd	Win & Pl
Hurdles	8	3	0	1	30098
Career Total	**17**	**5**	**3**	**1**	**44166**

150	1/02	Hayd	2m4f	B HHdl	SFT	£9262
143	11/01	MRas	2m5f110y	B HHdl	G-S	£8157
132	11/01	Hayd	2m4f	B(0-140)HHdl	GD	£10244
131	11/00	MRas	2m5f110y	B HHdl	G-S	£8235
111	12/99	MRas	2m3f110y	F Hdl	GD	£2388

Total win prize-money £38289

Going: Sf: 1-3 GS: 1-2 Gd: 1-3 GF: - Fm: 0-0
Distance: 2m/2m3: 0-0 **2m4-2m7: 3-7** 3m+: 0-1
Track: **LH: 2-5** RH: 1-2 **Tight: 1-3** Gall: 0-1
Aids: Bl: 0-0 Vi: 0-0 Tstrap: 0-1
Best Rating: 150 1/02 Hayd 2m4f soft Hdl

Genuine, front-running hurdler, he stays two and a half miles plus, suited by good or easy ground.

Assessed (IRE)

117 (130h) **150**

8-y-o b g Montelimar (USA)-Tax Code (Workboy)
W P Mullins Festival Syndicate

Placings:*132*-1112U311563 **(4953a)**
2001/02: 20^{1}G, 24^{1}G, 16^{1}YS, 24^{2}HY, 16^{U}YS, 24^{3}Y, 16^{1}YS, 17^{1}HY, 21^{5}HY, 16^{6}GS, 16^{3}G

	Starts	1st	2nd	3rd	Win & Pl
Hurdles	2	2	0	0	10294
Chases	9	3	1	2	56292
Career Total	**14**	**6**	**2**	**3**	**71950**

149	1/02	Leop	2m1f	Ch	HVY	£31901
130	1/02	Punc	2m	Ch	Y-S	£7975
132	11/01	Thur	2m	Ch	Y-S	£6120
122	5/01	Navn	3m	(0-116)HHdl	GD	£5564
130	5/01	Gowr	2m4f	Hdl	GD	£4729
114	1/01	Thur	2m	NHF	HVY	£3895

Total win prize-money £60188

Going: Sf: 1-3 GS: 0-1 Gd: 2-3 GF: - Fm: 0-0
Distance: **2m/2m3: 3-6** 2m4-2m7: 1-2 3m+: 1-3
Track: LH: 1-4 RH: 1-3 Tight: 0-0 Gall: 0-1
Aids: Bl: 0-0 Vi: 0-0 Tstrap: 0-0
Best Rating: 150 4/02 Punc 2m good Ch

Useful bumper horse. Decent hurdler over two and a half/ three miles. Has done well since switching to fences and was a fair sixth in the Arkle at Cheltenham. Suited by two miles on soft ground over fences.

Assured Movements (USA)

107 **95**

6-y-o b g Northern Flagship (USA)-Love At Dawn (USA) (Grey Dawn Ii)
Mrs D A Hamer Twelly Davies

Placings:623F02/4035-031 **(4724)**
2001/02: 19^{0}S, 17^{3}G, 16^{1}GF

	Starts	1st	2nd	3rd	Win & Pl
Hurdles	3	1	0	1	3268
Career Total	**13**	**1**	**2**	**3**	**5942**

91	4/02	Chep	2m110y	E Hdl	G-F	£2856

Total win prize-money £2856

Going: Sf: 0-1 GS: 0-0 Gd: 0-1 GF: - Fm: 1-1
Distance: **2m/2m3: 1-2** 2m4-2m7: 0-1 3m+: 0-0
Track: **LH: 1-1** RH: 0-2 Tight: 0-0 Gall: 0-0
Aids: Bl: 0-0 Vi: 0-0 **Tstrap: 1-3**
Best Rating: 91 4/02 Chep 2m110y gd-fm Hdl

Modest hurdler, suited by two miles and acts on fast and soft ground.

Assured Physique

95 **81**

5-y-o b g Salse (USA)-Metaphysique (FR) (Law Society (USA))
R J Baker Graham Brown

Placings:0045 **(4866)**
2001/02: 17^{0}GF, 16^{0}G, 17^{4}F, 17^{5}F

	Starts	1st	2nd	3rd	Win & Pl
Hurdles	4	0	0	0	0
Career Total	**4**	**0**	**0**	**0**	**0**

Going: Sf: 0-0 GS: 0-0 Gd: 0-1 GF: - Fm: 0-3
Distance: 2m/2m3: 0-4 2m4-2m7: 0-0 3m+: 0-0
Track: LH: 0-0 RH: 0-4 Tight: 0-0 Gall: 0-0
Aids: Bl: 0-0 Vi: 0-0 Tstrap: 0-0
Best Rating: 81 4/02 Extr 2m1f firm Hdl

Modest performer on Flat and over hurdles.

Astley Gold (IRE)

97 **83**

8-y-o ch g Big Sink Hope (USA)-Ascot Princess (Prince Hansel)
R H Buckler Mrs Liz Jones

Placings:2000U4/20P00 **(4757)**
2001/02: 17^{2}GF, 21^{0}G, 21^{P}GS, 20^{0}G, 16^{0}GF

	Starts	1st	2nd	3rd	Win & Pl
Hurdles	5	0	1	0	790
Career Total	**11**	**0**	**2**	**0**	**1617**

Going: Sf: 0-0 GS: 0-1 Gd: 0-2 GF: - Fm: 0-2
Distance: 2m/2m3: 0-2 2m4-2m7: 0-3 3m+: 0-0
Track: LH: 0-4 RH: 0-1 Tight: 0-1 Gall: 0-2
Aids: Bl: 0-0 Vi: 0-0 Tstrap: 0-0
Best Rating: 102 11/99 Wwck 2m good NHF

Modest hurdler/chaser.

Aston Mara

103 **101**

5-y-o b g Bering-Coigach (Niniski (USA))
Mrs M Reveley Mrs D J Buckley

Placings:42003-0144230624 **(4670)**
2001/02: 16^{0}G, 20^{1}F, 21^{4}GF, 24^{4}GF, 19^{2}S, 24^{3}GF, 24^{0}GF, 21^{6}GS, 19^{2}GS, 21^{4}GF

	Starts	1st	2nd	3rd	Win & Pl
Hurdles	10	1	2	1	5707
Career Total	**15**	**1**	**3**	**2**	**6950**

101	6/01	Prth	2m4f110y	E Hdl	FRM	£2961

Total win prize-money £2961

Going: Sf: 0-1 GS: 0-2 Gd: 0-1 GF: - Fm: 1-6
Distance: 2m/2m3: 0-2 **2m4-2m7: 1-5** 3m+: 0-3
Track: LH: 0-4 **RH: 1-5** Tight: 0-7 Gall: 0-0
Aids: Bl: 0-0 Vi: 0-0 Tstrap: 0-0
Best Rating: 101 9/01 MRas 2m3f110y soft Hdl

A modest performer, he is best at two and a half miles, but stays three and is suited by fast ground.

Astral Prince

77 **67**

4-y-o ch g Efisio-Val D'Erica (Ashmore (FR))
A Crook (B J Meehan 19/12) Matham Investments

Placings:006 **(4915)**
2001/02: 16^{0}GS, 17^{0}G, 17^{6}GF

	Starts	1st	2nd	3rd	Win & Pl
Hurdles	3	0	0	0	0
Career Total	**3**	**0**	**0**	**0**	**0**

Going: Sf: 0-0 GS: 0-1 Gd: 0-1 GF: - Fm: 0-1
Distance: 2m/2m3: 0-3 2m4-2m7: 0-0 3m+: 0-0
Track: LH: 0-2 RH: 0-1 Tight: 0-3 Gall: 0-0
Aids: Bl: 0-0 Vi: 0-0 Tstrap: 0-0
Best Rating: 67 4/02 Sedg 2m1f gd-fm Hdl

Astro Lines (IRE)

101(96h) (63+h)**106**

8-y-o ch g Classic Secret (USA)-Fado's Delight (Orchestra)
Ferdy Murphy K Lee And Mr I Davies

Placings:F134431/33/**14F-46P505** **(4920)**
2001/02: 17^{4}GS, 19^{6}G, 17^{P}S, 16^{5}S, 17^{0}G, 21^{5}GF

	Starts	1st	2nd	3rd	Win & Pl
Chases	6	0	0	0	346
Career Total	**18**	**3**	**0**	**4**	**11299**

105	11/00	Newc	2m4f	E Ch	SFT	£3279
121	3/98	Kels	2m2f	E Hdl	GD	£2318
106	9/97	Fair	2m	Hdl	G-Y	£3051

Total win prize-money £8650

Going: Sf: 0-2 GS: 0-1 Gd: 0-2 GF: - Fm: 0-1
Distance: 2m/2m3: 0-4 2m4-2m7: 0-2 3m+: 0-0
Track: LH: 0-4 RH: 0-2 Tight: 0-4 Gall: 0-2
Aids: Bl: 0-0 Vi: 0-0 Tstrap: 0-0
Best Rating: 124 11/00 Carl 2m soft Ch

Winner of two hurdle races and a chase but has been out of sorts.

Astronaut

81 **103**

5-y-o b g Sri Pekan (USA)-Wild Abandon (USA) (Graustark)
Mrs L A Murphy (T Casey 7/5) Mrs Louise Murphy

Placings:4R6-40 **(1088)**
2001/02: 18^{4}GF, 16^{0}GF

	Starts	1st	2nd	3rd	Win & Pl
Hurdles	2	0	0	0	0
Career Total	**5**	**0**	**0**	**0**	**0**

Going: Sf: 0-0 GS: 0-0 Gd: 0-0 GF: - Fm: 0-2
Distance: 2m/2m3: 0-2 2m4-2m7: 0-0 3m+: 0-0
Track: LH: 0-2 RH: 0-0 Tight: 0-1 Gall: 0-0
Aids: Bl: 0-0 Vi: 0-0 Tstrap: 0-0
Best Rating: 103 5/01 Font 2m2f110y gd-fm Hdl

At The Double

100 76

6-y-o b g Sure Blade (USA)-Moheli (Ardross)
P Winkworth The Main Group Limited

Placings:0-40065 (4568)
2001/02: 17^{4}HY, 21^{0}S, 22^{0}S, 25^{6}GS, 24^{5}G

	Starts	1st	2nd	3rd	Win & Pl
Hurdles	5	0	0	0	0
Career Total	**6**	**0**	**0**	**0**	**0**

Going: Sf: 0-3 GS: 0-1 Gd: 0-1 GF: - Fm: 0-0
Distance: 2m/2m3: 0-1 2m4-2m7: 0-2 3m+: 0-2
Track: LH: 0-2 RH: 0-2 Tight: 0-3 Gall: 0-0
Aids: Bl: 0-0 Vi: 0-1 Tstrap: 0-0
Best Rating: **76** 4/02 Towc 3m good Hdl

Atalya

95 102

5-y-o ch g Afzal-Sandy Looks (Music Boy)
G A Ham W E Catstrey

Placings:0024313-23P (1653)
2001/02: 17^{2}G, 16^{3}GF, 17^{P}G

	Starts	1st	2nd	3rd	Win & Pl
Hurdles	3	0	1	1	1763
Career Total	**10**	**1**	**2**	**3**	**5596**

88	1/01	Winc	2m	F Hdl	SFT	£2513

Total win prize-money £2513

Going: Sf: 0-0 GS: 0-0 Gd: 0-2 GF: - Fm: 0-1
Distance: 2m/2m3: 0-3 2m4-2m7: 0-0 3m+: 0-0
Track: LH: 0-2 RH: 0-1 Tight: 0-2 Gall: 0-1
Aids: Bl: 0-0 Vi: 0-0 Tstrap: 0-0
Best Rating: **102** 5/01 Hntg 2m110y gd-fm Hdl

Atavistic (IRE)

114(85h) 146

10-y-o b g Architect (USA)-Saceili (Saher)
P J Hobbs Mrs Jill Emery, Mr A Staple, Mr E Morris

Placings:0210/3P13F/12111P/1PF1/35B12PP-22223P0 (4913)
2001/02: 26^{2}GS, 28^{2}S, 29^{2}G, 25^{2}G, 27^{3}S, 34^{P}HY, 29^{0}G

	Starts	1st	2nd	3rd	Win & Pl
Chases	7	0	4	1	10758
Career Total	**33**	**9**	**7**	**4**	**65989**

146	1/01	Tntn	3m3f	C(0-130)HCh	SFT	£7150
149	1/00	Tntn	3m3f	C(0-130)HCh	G-S	£6955
135	11/99	NAbb	3m2f110y	D(0-120)HCh	SFT	£3838
132	2/99	Tntn	3m	D Ch	G-S	£4572
133	2/99	NAbb	3m2f110y	E Ch	HVY	£2892
110	1/99	Kemp	3m110y	D(0-120)HHdl	SFT	£5503
106	10/98	Font	2m6f110y	E(0-115)HHdl	GD	£2302
95	1/97	Tntn	2m3f110y	E Hdl	GD	£1945
107	3/96	Ayr	2m	H NHF	GD	£1250

Total win prize-money £36409

Going: Sf: 0-3 GS: 0-1 Gd: 0-3 GF: - Fm: 0-0
Distance: 2m/2m3: 0-0 2m4-2m7: 0-0 3m+: 0-7
Track: LH: 0-2 RH: 0-2 Tight: 0-2 Gall: 0-0
Aids: Bl: 0-0 Vi: 0-0 Tstrap: 0-0
Best Rating: **149** 1/00 Tntn 3m3f gd-sft Ch

He ran his best race when chasing Flaked Oats home in the Singer & Friedlander National Trial at Uttoxeter in February 2001. Ran well in 2001/2002, if proving the bridesmaid more often than ideal. He goes well on sharp tracks, but can make mistakes. Goes well fresh, stays three and a half miles plus and acts on soft ground.

Athena's Profile

6-y-o b m Sir Harry Lewis (USA)-Caoimhe (Pollerton)
Miss K M George Exterior Profiles Ltd

Placings:000 (3759)
2001/02: 16^{0}G, 16^{0}G, 17^{0}S

	Starts	1st	2nd	3rd	Win & Pl
NH Flat	2	0	0	0	0
Hurdles	1	0	0	0	0
Career Total	**3**	**0**	**0**	**0**	

Going: Sf: 0-1 GS: 0-0 Gd: 0-2 GF: - Fm: 0-0
Distance: 2m/2m3: 0-3 2m4-2m7: 0-0 3m+: 0-0
Track: LH: 0-1 RH: 0-2 Tight: 0-1 Gall: 0-0
Aids: Bl: 0-0 Vi: 0-0 Tstrap: 0-0
Best Rating: **58** 11/01 Wwck 2m good NHF

Athenian Law

103 95

5-y-o br g Darshaan-Titania's Way (Fairy King (USA))
P J Hobbs Richard Green (fine Paintings)

Placings:11 (2353)
2001/02: 17^{1}G, 17^{1}GS

	Starts	1st	2nd	3rd	Win & Pl
NH Flat	1	1	0	0	1596
Hurdles	1	1	0	0	2996
Career Total	**2**	**2**	**0**	**0**	**4592**

95	11/01	MRas	2m1f110y	E Hdl	G-S	£2996
99	10/01	Hrfd	2m1f	H NHF	GD	£1596

Total win prize-money £4592

Going: Sf: 0-0 GS: 1-1 Gd: 1-1 GF: - Fm: 0-0
Distance: **2m/2m3: 2-2** 2m4-2m7: 0-0 3m+: 0-0
Track: LH: 0-0 **RH: 2-2 Tight: 1-1** Gall: 0-0
Aids: Bl: 0-0 Vi: 0-0 Tstrap: 0-0
Best Rating: **99** 10/01 Hrfd 2m1f good NHF

He won his only start in bumpers at Hereford and got off the mark over hurdles with a workmanlike win at Market Rasen.

Athens Abercadabra

5-y-o gr h Abergwiffy-Athensmidnitemagic (Athens Treasure)
Miss Lucinda V Russell Girls On Tour

Placings:20P (0801)
2001/02: 16^{2}S, 16^{0}GS, 20^{P}GF

	Starts	1st	2nd	3rd	Win & Pl
NH Flat	2	0	1	0	654
Hurdles	1	0	0	0	0
Career Total	**3**	**0**	**1**	**0**	**654**

Going: Sf: 0-1 GS: 0-1 Gd: 0-0 GF: - Fm: 0-1
Distance: 2m/2m3: 0-2 2m4-2m7: 0-1 3m+: 0-0
Track: LH: 0-1 RH: 0-2 Tight: 0-0 Gall: 0-0
Aids: Bl: 0-0 Vi: 0-0 Tstrap: 0-0
Best Rating:

Athirty (IRE)

71f 66f

5-y-o ch g Denel (FR)-Terrific Temp (Kemal (FR))
C Tizzard Mrs P Tizzard

Placings:0 (4391)
2001/02: 16^{0}S

	Starts	1st	2nd	3rd	Win & Pl
NH Flat	1	0	0	0	
Career Total	**1**	**0**	**0**	**0**	

Going: Sf: 0-1 GS: 0-0 Gd: 0-0 GF: - Fm: 0-0
Distance: 2m/2m3: 0-1 2m4-2m7: 0-0 3m+: 0-0
Track: LH: 0-0 RH: 0-1 Tight: 0-0 Gall: 0-0
Aids: Bl: 0-0 Vi: 0-0 Tstrap: 0-0
Best Rating: **66** 3/02 Winc 2m soft NHF

Athleague Guest (IRE)

100(109h) (107h)111

9-y-o b g Be My Guest (USA)-Santella Bell (Ballad Rock)
A Sadik A Sadik

Placings:4/3162P/060/16FP6332 (4433)
2001/02: 20^{1}GS, 20^{6}G, 20^{F}GS, 22^{P}HY, 19^{6}S, 19^{3}GS, 21^{3}HY, 20^{2}HY

	Starts	1st	2nd	3rd	Win & Pl
Hurdles	4	1	0	0	6500
Chases	4	0	1	2	2709
Career Total	**17**	**2**	**2**	**3**	**13307**

107	10/01	Uttx	2m4f110y	C(0-130)HHdl	G-S	£6500
107	2/98	Naas	2m	Hdl	SFT	£2680

Total win prize-money £9180

Going: Sf: 0-4 GS: 1-3 Gd: 0-1 GF: - Fm: 0-0
Distance: 2m/2m3: 0-0 **2m4-2m7: 1-8** 3m+: 0-0
Track: **LH: 1-8** RH: 0-0 Tight: 0-0 Gall: 0-3
Aids: Bl: 0-1 Vi: 0-0 Tstrap: 0-0
Best Rating: **113** 2/98 Naas 2m4f yield Hdl

Formerly Irish-trained, he was off the track for nearly three years before causing a 66/1 upset in a handicap hurdle at Uttoxeter in October 2001. Has not shown a great deal since, including over fences. He is suited by cut in the ground. Stays two and a half miles.

Athnowen (IRE)

99 100

10-y-o b g Lord Americo-Lady Bluebird (Arapaho)
J R Payne (C L Popham 8/1) R J Payne

Placings:PF6510U2344/05365FU-P0P1 (4505)
2001/02: 16^{P}S, 19^{0}GS, 25^{P}S, 21^{1}G

	Starts	1st	2nd	3rd	Win & Pl
Hurdles	1	0	0	0	0
Chases	3	1	0	0	2282
Career Total	**22**	**2**	**1**	**2**	**8486**

94	3/02	NAbb	2m5f110y	G(0-95)HCh	GD	£2282
105	1/00	Hrfd	2m	E(0-105)HCh	G-S	£3103

Total win prize-money £5386

Going: Sf: 0-2 GS: 0-1 Gd: 1-1 GF: - Fm: 0-0
Distance: 2m/2m3: 0-2 **2m4-2m7: 1-1** 3m+: 0-1
Track: **LH: 1-1** RH: 0-3 **Tight: 1-2** Gall: 0-0
Aids: Bl: 0-0 Vi: 0-0 Tstrap: 0-0
Best Rating: **111** 3/00 Tntn 2m3f good Ch

Won a 21 furlong selling chase at Newton Abbot in March 2002 on first outing for his present trainer.

Atlantic Charter (USA)

102 105

6-y-o b g Gone West (USA)-Silk Slippers (USA) (Nureyev (USA))

J J O'Neill Strathayr Publishing Ltd

Placings:300-2P1 **(1195)**
2001/02: 16^{2}G, 17^{P}G, 20^{1}G

	Starts	1st	2nd	3rd	Win & Pl
Hurdles	3	1	1	0	3850
Career Total	**6**	**1**	**1**	**1**	**4208**

105 8/01 Prth 2m4f110y E Hdl GD £2905
Total win prize-money £2905

Going: Sf: 0-0 GS: 0-0 Gd: 1-3 GF: - Fm: 0-0
Distance: 2m/2m3: 0-2 **2m4-2m7: 1-1** 3m+: 0-0
Track: LH: 0-2 **RH: 1-1** Tight: 0-1 Gall: 0-0
Aids: Bl: 0-0 Vi: 0-0 Tstrap: 0-0
Best Rating: **105** 8/01 Prth 2m4f110y good Hdl

Atlantic Crossing (IRE)

86f 85f
5-y-o b g Roselier (FR)-Ocean Mist (IRE) (Crash Course)
P Beaumont N W A Bannister

Placings:*000* **(4750)**
2001/02: 17^{0}GS, 16^{0}G, 17^{0}G

	Starts	1st	2nd	3rd	Win & Pl
NH Flat	3	0	0	0	
Career Total	**3**	**0**	**0**	**0**	

Going: Sf: 0-0 GS: 0-1 Gd: 0-2 GF: - Fm: 0-0
Distance: 2m/2m3: 0-3 2m4-2m7: 0-0 3m+: 0-0
Track: LH: 0-1 RH: 0-2 Tight: 0-1 Gall: 0-0
Aids: Bl: 0-0 Vi: 0-0 Tstrap: 0-0
Best Rating: **85** 4/02 Carl 2m1f good NHF

Atlantic Drift (IRE)

89 67
8-y-o b g Commanche Run-Cantafleur (Cantab)
J A Moore J A Moore

Placings:*53*/6430-U060R0 **(4871)**
2001/02: 26^{U}G, 22^{0}G, 23^{6}G, 21^{0}GS, 25^{R}GF, 25^{0}GF

	Starts	1st	2nd	3rd	Win & Pl
Hurdles	5	0	0	0	0
Chases	1	0	0	0	0
Career Total	**12**	**0**	**0**	**2**	**822**

Going: Sf: 0-0 GS: 0-1 Gd: 0-3 GF: - Fm: 0-2
Distance: 2m/2m3: 0-0 2m4-2m7: 0-3 3m+: 0-3
Track: LH: 0-4 RH: 0-2 Tight: 0-2 Gall: 0-1
Aids: Bl: 0-0 Vi: 0-0 Tstrap: 0-0
Best Rating: **100** 11/99 Chep 2m110y gd-sft NHF

Atlantic Power

101(88h) (37h)88
9-y-o gr g Golden Lahab (USA)-She Say She Will (Roselier (FR))
W Storey Thistle And Rose Racing

Placings:*0300655*/531352/210-0PF0 **(4877)**
2001/02: 20^{0}GS, 25^{P}G, 24^{F}HY, 24^{0}G

	Starts	1st	2nd	3rd	Win & Pl
Hurdles	4	0	0	0	
Career Total	**20**	**2**	**2**	**3**	**7735**

101 6/00 Prth 3m110y F(0-110)HHdl HVY £2691
95 2/00 Ayr 2m4f F(0-95)HHdl HVY £2730
Total win prize-money £5421

Going: Sf: 0-1 GS: 0-1 Gd: 0-2 GF: - Fm: 0-0
Distance: 2m/2m3: 0-0 2m4-2m7: 0-1 3m+: 0-3
Track: LH: 0-3 RH: 0-1 Tight: 0-1 Gall: 0-1
Aids: Bl: 0-0 Vi: 0-0 Tstrap: 0-0
Best Rating: **101** 6/00 Prth 3m110y heavy Hdl

Won twice over hurdles in bad ground. Stayed on to finish runner-up on his chasing bow and will be suited by three miles.

Atlantic Prince (IRE)

77 55
6-y-o b g Fairy King (USA)-Idle Chat (USA) (Assert)
Mrs K M Lamb Mrs K M Lamb

Placings:00/P0-06006P00U **(4673)**
2001/02: 16^{0}F, 17^{6}GF, 21^{0}GF, 17^{0}GF, 17^{6}G, 17^{P}GS, 22^{0}GS, 16^{0}GS, 17^{U}GF

	Starts	1st	2nd	3rd	Win & Pl
Hurdles	9	0	0	0	0
Career Total	**13**	**0**	**0**	**0**	**0**

Going: Sf: 0-0 GS: 0-3 Gd: 0-1 GF: - Fm: 0-5
Distance: 2m/2m3: 0-7 2m4-2m7: 0-2 3m+: 0-0
Track: LH: 0-8 RH: 0-1 Tight: 0-7 Gall: 0-1
Aids: Bl: 0-0 Vi: 0-0 Tstrap: 0-8
Best Rating: **55** 9/01 Sedg 2m1f gd-fm Hdl

Atomic Breeze (IRE)

95 98
8-y-o b/br g Strong Gale-Atomic Lady (Over The River (FR))
D M Forster D M Forster

Placings:0P/0P-0P3 **(4671)**
2001/02: 21^{0}G, 25^{P}G, 21^{3}GF

	Starts	1st	2nd	3rd	Win & Pl
Chases	3	0	0	1	598
Career Total	**7**	**0**	**0**	**1**	**598**

Going: Sf: 0-0 GS: 0-0 Gd: 0-2 GF: - Fm: 0-1
Distance: 2m/2m3: 0-0 2m4-2m7: 0-2 3m+: 0-1
Track: LH: 0-3 RH: 0-0 Tight: 0-2 Gall: 0-0
Aids: Bl: 0-0 Vi: 0-0 Tstrap: 0-0
Best Rating: **98** 4/02 Sedg 2m5f gd-fm Ch

Moderate, lightly-raced chaser, seems to need a sound surface.

Attacker (USA)

53 44
5-y-o b g Defensive Play (USA)-Bold Ballerina (Sadler's Wells (USA))
Miss L C Siddall Mrs Ann Morgan

Placings:03P **(4583)**
2001/02: 17^{0}GS, 20^{3}HY, 20^{P}G

	Starts	1st	2nd	3rd	Win & Pl
Hurdles	3	0	0	1	536
Career Total	**3**	**0**	**0**	**1**	**536**

Going: Sf: 0-1 GS: 0-1 Gd: 0-1 GF: - Fm: 0-0
Distance: 2m/2m3: 0-1 2m4-2m7: 0-2 3m+: 0-0
Track: LH: 0-2 RH: 0-1 Tight: 0-1 Gall: 0-0
Aids: Bl: 0-0 Vi: 0-0 Tstrap: 0-0
Best Rating: **44** 3/02 Uttx 2m4f110y heavy Hdl

Poor on the Flat and over hurdles.

Atto (IRE)

(85h) (63h)
8-y-o b g Mandalus-Deep Cristina (Deep Run)
P R Webber (J S King 19/7) S Clough

Placings:0PPP/0/0445-FP0 **(2137)**
2001/02: 21^{F}GF, 16^{P}S, 17^{0}G

	Starts	1st	2nd	3rd	Win & Pl
Hurdles	2	0	0	0	0
Chases	1	0	0	0	0
Career Total	**12**	**0**	**0**	**0**	**794**

Going: Sf: 0-1 GS: 0-0 Gd: 0-1 GF: - Fm: 0-1
Distance: 2m/2m3: 0-2 2m4-2m7: 0-1 3m+: 0-0
Track: LH: 0-1 RH: 0-2 Tight: 0-1 Gall: 0-0
Aids: Bl: 0-1 Vi: 0-0 Tstrap: 0-0
Best Rating: **97** 11/00 Tntn 2m3f gd-sft Ch

Atum Re (IRE)

97f 108f
5-y-o br g Be My Native (USA)-Collopy's Cross (Pragmatic)
P R Webber Paul Green

Placings:*10* **(3701)**
2001/02: 16^{1}G, 16^{0}S

	Starts	1st	2nd	3rd	Win & Pl
NH Flat	2	1	0	0	1603
Career Total	**2**	**1**	**0**	**0**	**1603**

108 12/01 Ludl 2m H NHF GD £1603
Total win prize-money £1603

Going: Sf: 0-1 GS: 0-0 Gd: 1-1 GF: - Fm: 0-0
Distance: **2m/2m3: 1-2** 2m4-2m7: 0-0 3m+: 0-0
Track: LH: 0-1 **RH: 1-1** Tight: 0-0 Gall: 0-1
Aids: Bl: 0-0 Vi: 0-0 Tstrap: 0-0
Best Rating: **108** 12/01 Ludl 2m good NHF

Au Lac

99 94
8-y-o b g North Col-Janlarmar (Habat)
J W Mullins Don Hazzard

Placings:*26220*/F223310F2/0P-2360 **(4119)**
2001/02: 22^{2}GS, 19^{3}S, 22^{6}S, 22^{0}G

	Starts	1st	2nd	3rd	Win & Pl
Hurdles	4	0	1	1	1500
Career Total	**20**	**1**	**7**	**3**	**9358**

112 2/00 Folk 2m4f110y E Hdl SFT £2539
Total win prize-money £2540

Going: Sf: 0-2 GS: 0-1 Gd: 0-1 GF: - Fm: 0-0
Distance: 2m/2m3: 0-0 2m4-2m7: 0-4 3m+: 0-0
Track: LH: 0-0 RH: 0-4 Tight: 0-2 Gall: 0-0
Aids: Bl: 0-0 Vi: 0-0 Tstrap: 0-0
Best Rating: **112** 2/00 Folk 2m4f110y soft Hdl

Auburn Spirit

97(101h) (69h)94
7-y-o ch g Teamster-Spirit Of Youth (Kind Of Hush)
M D I Usher G A Summers

Placings:*04*/5000/514306-**6031463** **(4312)**
2001/02: 19^{6}GS, 23^{0}G, 20^{3}HY, 19^{1}HY, 21^{4}S, 25^{6}S, 20^{3}HY

	Starts	1st	2nd	3rd	Win & Pl
Chases	7	1	0	2	4121
Career Total	**19**	**2**	**0**	**3**	**7131**

94 2/02 Hrfd 2m3f E(0-105)HCh HVY £3237
68 11/00 Winc 2m6f F(0-100)HHdl SFT £2639

Total win prize-money £5876

Going:	Sf: 1-5 GS: 0-1 Gd: 0-1 GF: - Fm: 0-0
Distance:	**2m/2m3: 1-2** 2m4-2m7: 0-3 3m+: 0-2
Track:	LH: 0-2 **RH: 1-5** Tight: 0-4 Gall: 0-0
Aids:	Bl: 0-0 Vi: 0-0 Tstrap: 0-0
Best Rating:	**94** 2/02 Hrfd 2m3f heavy Ch

Very moderate chaser at around two and a half miles, acts on heavy ground.

Audacter (IRE)

105(112h) **120**

9-y-o b g Strong Gale-Sue's A Lady (Le Moss)
L Wells Mrs Carrie Zetter-Wells

Placings:20/430/1223/1543-321 **(1770)**
2001/02: 22^{3}S, 23^{2}GF, 23^{1}GS

	Starts	1st	2nd	3rd	Win & Pl
Chases	3	1	1	1	6560
Career Total	**16**	**3**	**4**	**4**	**37995**

120	10/01	Extr	2m7f110y	D Ch	G-S	£4192
150	5/00	Hayd	2m7f110y	B Hdl	GD	£7085
117	1/00	Kemp	2m5f	C(0-130)HHdl	GD	£7052

Total win prize-money £18331

Going:	Sf: 0-1 GS: 1-1 Gd: 0-0 GF: - Fm: 0-1
Distance:	2m/2m3: 0-0 2m4-2m7: 0-1 **3m+: 1-2**
Track:	LH: 0-0 **RH: 1-3** Tight: 0-1 Gall: 0-0
Aids:	Bl: 0-0 Vi: 0-0 Tstrap: 0-0
Best Rating:	**150** 5/00 Hayd 2m7f110y good Hdl

He started 2000/01 in the best possible way by winning a conditions hurdle at Haydock, but then found himself outclassed by the likes of Baracouda, Deano's Beeno and Merry Masquerade in Class A staying events at Ascot, Doncaster and Kempton. Switched to fences, he did better on faster ground at Exeter than he had on his debut, and won next time again at Exeter. Most effective when able to dictate from the front against lesser opposition and needs a sound surface. Poor run on his return to action in August 2002.

Audiostreetdotcom

95 **94**

5-y-o ch g Risk Me (FR)-Ballagarrow Girl (North Stoke)
G B Balding Audiostreetdotcom Partnership

Placings:426-0U34236441 **(4502)**
2001/02: 16^{0}S, 16^{U}G, 21^{3}GS, 19^{4}G, 21^{2}HY, 18^{3}HY, 22^{6}S, 21^{4}GS, 19^{4}S, 22^{1}G

	Starts	1st	2nd	3rd	Win & Pl
Hurdles	10	1	1	2	5120
Career Total	**13**	**1**	**2**	**2**	**6881**

94	3/02	NAbb	2m6f	E(0-105)HHdl	GD	£3136

Total win prize-money £3136

Going:	Sf: 0-5 GS: 0-2 Gd: 1-3 GF: - Fm: 0-0
Distance:	2m/2m3: 0-5 **2m4-2m7: 1-5** 3m+: 0-0
Track:	**LH: 1-7** RH: 0-1 **Tight: 1-3** Gall: 0-3
Aids:	Bl: 0-0 Vi: 0-0 Tstrap: 0-0
Best Rating:	**105** 1/01 Wwck 2m soft Hdl

Quirky sort, suited by soft ground, appreciated returning to a longer trip when winning 22 furlong novices' handicap at Newton Abbot in March 2002.

Auditty (IRE)

131

9-y-o b g Montelimar (USA)-Tax Code (Workboy)
A L T Moore Peter M Law

Placings:060/0605F/F410150/P1521565-2310121U0P **(4960a)**
2001/02: 18^{2}F, 20^{3}GF, 16^{1}F, 18^{0}G, 16^{1}G, 17^{2}GF, 16^{1}GF, 16^{U}G, 16^{0}GY, 16^{P}GY

	Starts	1st	2nd	3rd	Win & Pl
Hurdles	1	0	0	0	0
Chases	9	3	2	1	25048
Career Total	**33**	**7**	**3**	**1**	**41744**

131	9/01	List	2m	(0-130)HCh	G-F	£7790
131	8/01	Tram	2m	(0-109)HCh	GD	£7233
118	6/01	Tram	2m	(0-123)HCh	FRM	£6399
119	8/00	Tram	2m4f	(0-109)HCh	G-F	£5520
95	6/00	Dund	2m1f	(0-102)HCh	G-Y	£4140
102	10/99	Navn	2m1f	(0-102)HCh	GD	£3388
92	9/99	Dund	2m3f	(0-102)HCh	FRM	£2464

Total win prize-money £36935

Going:	Sf: 0-0 GS: 0-0 Gd: 1-3 GF: - Fm: 2-5
Distance:	**2m/2m3: 3-9** 2m4-2m7: 0-1 3m+: 0-0
Track:	**LH: 1-1** RH: 0-2 Tight: 0-0 Gall: 0-0
Aids:	Bl: 0-0 Vi: 0-0 Tstrap: 0-0
Best Rating:	**131** 9/01 List 2m gd-fm Ch

In fine form in Ireland in the summer and autumn of 2001, he loves fast ground and is effective at up to two and a half miles.

Auetaler (GER)

121(105c) (124c)**150**

8-y-o gr g Niniski (USA)-Astica (GER) (Surumu (GER))
M C Pipe The Macca & Growler Partnership

Placings:1023/1110341242/06-**1F14**34P0 **(4256)**
2001/02: 21^{1}GF, 21^{F}GS, 16^{1}GF, 16^{4}GF, 16^{3}GS, 22^{4}G, 16^{P}S, 17^{U}G

	Starts	1st	2nd	3rd	Win & Pl
Hurdles	4	0	0	1	1709
Chases	4	2	0	0	7915
Career Total	**24**	**7**	**3**	**3**	**58637**

111	8/01	NAbb	2m110y	E Ch	G-F	£3342
124	5/01	NAbb	2m5f110y	D Ch	G-F	£4270
151	2/00	Sand	2m110y	B Hdl	G-S	£8112
114	5/99	Uttx	2m	E Hdl	GD	£2472
122	5/99	Strf	2m6f110y	D Hdl	GD	£3428
115	5/99	Aint	2m4f	D Hdl	G-S	£2983
128	2/99	Tntn	2m1f	E Hdl	G-S	£2472

Total win prize-money £27082

Going:	Sf: 0-1 GS: 0-2 Gd: 0-2 GF: - Fm: 2-3
Distance:	2m/2m3: 1-5 2m4-2m7: 1-3 3m+: 0-0
Track:	**LH: 2-6** RH: 0-2 **Tight: 2-3** Gall: 0-2
Aids:	Bl: 0-0 Vi: 0-1 Tstrap: 0-0
Best Rating:	**158** 4/00 Aint 2m4f good Hdl

He fell just below top class over hurdles, but was not convincing over fences despite winning two of his first four starts in the summer of 2001. Fair return to hurdles at Kempton, but has not built on that. Suited by quick ground.

August Twelfth

59 **14**

14-y-o b g Full Of Hope-Espanita (Riboboy (USA))
D C O'Brien D C O'Brien

Placings:50345/0/31120/01220/050/F3442245/1325**P2P**/03 3225/500/5PP **(4507)**
2001/02: 16^{5}G, 22^{P}S, 21^{P}G

	Starts	1st	2nd	3rd	Win & Pl
Hurdles	3	0	0	0	0
Career Total	**46**	**4**	**9**	**6**	**15311**

89	12/97	Wind	2m4f	F(0-105)HHdl	GD	£2188
88	12/94	Folk	2m1f110y	(0-115)HHdl	SFT	£1917
82	3/94	Plum	2m4f	(0-105)HHdl	HVY	£2045
72	2/94	Folk	2m1f110y	(0-100)HHdl	HVY	£1553

Total win prize-money £7706

Going:	Sf: 0-1 GS: 0-0 Gd: 0-2 GF: - Fm: 0-0
Distance:	2m/2m3: 0-1 2m4-2m7: 0-2 3m+: 0-0
Track:	LH: 0-2 RH: 0-1 Tight: 0-3 Gall: 0-0
Aids:	Bl: 0-0 Vi: 0-0 Tstrap: 0-0
Best Rating:	**999** 2/92 Ling 2m4f stand

Augusta Brook (IRE)

100 **97**

9-y-o b m Over The River (FR)-Augusta Victoria (Callernish)
Dr P Pritchard Mrs T Pritchard

Placings:0/45U3U43005/4220036-P204465226565 **(3797)**
2001/02: 21^{P}G, 16^{2}GF, 16^{0}GF, 19^{4}G, 16^{4}S, 16^{6}G, 20^{5}G, 20^{2}G, 21^{2}S, 19^{6}S, 27^{5}HY, 16^{6}S, 26^{5}S

	Starts	1st	2nd	3rd	Win & Pl
Chases	13	0	3	0	3970
Career Total	**31**	**0**	**5**	**3**	**10023**

Going:	Sf: 0-6 GS: 0-0 Gd: 0-5 GF: - Fm: 0-2
Distance:	2m/2m3: 0-6 2m4-2m7: 0-5 3m+: 0-2
Track:	LH: 0-7 RH: 0-5 Tight: 0-8 Gall: 0-0
Aids:	Bl: 0-0 Vi: 0-0 Tstrap: 0-0
Best Rating:	**100** 2/01 Newb 2m1f soft Ch

Moderate staying chaser, who is thoroughly exposed.

Auk

103 **72**

7-y-o ch g Absalom-Lady Stock (Crofter (USA))
Mrs P Robeson Mrs P Robeson

Placings:0P-0P0613F0 **(4110)**
2001/02: 16^{0}G, 17^{P}S, 16^{0}G, 21^{6}GS, 16^{1}S, 16^{3}HY, 16^{F}HY, 16^{0}S

	Starts	1st	2nd	3rd	Win & Pl
Hurdles	8	1	0	1	2365
Career Total	**10**	**1**	**0**	**1**	**2365**

72	1/02	Leic	2m	G(0-90)HHdl	SFT	£1939

Total win prize-money £1939

Going:	Sf: 1-5 GS: 0-1 Gd: 0-2 GF: - Fm: 0-0
Distance:	**2m/2m3: 1-7** 2m4-2m7: 0-1 3m+: 0-0
Track:	LH: 0-2 **RH: 1-6** Tight: 0-2 Gall: 0-2
Aids:	Bl: 0-0 Vi: 0-0 Tstrap: 0-0
Best Rating:	**72** 1/02 Towc 2m heavy Hdl

Free-running, plating-class hurdler, he handles testing ground and is effective over two miles.

Auntie Bob

57f

4-y-o b f Overbury (IRE)-Kadari (Commanche Run)
W Clay G A Greaves

Placings:5 **(4429)**
2001/02: 16^{5}HY

	Starts	1st	2nd	3rd	Win & Pl
NH Flat	1	0	0	0	0
Career Total	**1**	**0**	**0**	**0**	**0**

Going:	Sf: 0-1 GS: 0-0 Gd: 0-0 GF: - Fm: 0-0
Distance:	2m/2m3: 0-1 2m4-2m7: 0-0 3m+: 0-0
Track:	LH: 0-1 RH: 0-0 Tight: 0-0 Gall: 0-0
Aids:	Bl: 0-0 Vi: 0-0 Tstrap: 0-0
Best Rating:	mfy

Autcaesar Autnihil (IRE)

93(82h) (82h)77+

7-y-o b g Supreme Leader-Monagey (Pimpernel's Tune)
Noel T Chance Whistlejacket Partnership

Placings:000 (4906)
2001/02: 21^{0}G, 21^{0}S, 19^{0}G

	Starts	1st	2nd	3rd	Win & Pl
Hurdles	3	0	0	0	
Career Total	**3**	**0**	**0**	**0**	

Going: Sf: 0-1 GS: 0-0 Gd: 0-2 GF: - Fm: 0-0
Distance: 2m/2m3: 0-0 2m4-2m7: 0-3 3m+: 0-0
Track: LH: 0-1 RH: 0-2 Tight: 0-1 Gall: 0-1
Aids: Bl: 0-0 Vi: 0-0 Tstrap: 0-0
Best Rating: **82** 3/02 Newb 2m5f soft Hdl

Avalanche (FR)

99 97

5-y-o gr g Highest Honor (FR)-Fairy Gold (Golden Fleece (USA))
J R Best The Downhill Partnership

Placings:200-U3P (1646)
2001/02: 18^{U}GF, 19^{3}GF, 20^{P}G

	Starts	1st	2nd	3rd	Win & Pl
Hurdles	3	0	0	1	406
Career Total	**6**	**0**	**1**	**1**	**2676**

Going: Sf: 0-0 GS: 0-0 Gd: 0-1 GF: - Fm: 0-2
Distance: 2m/2m3: 0-1 2m4-2m7: 0-2 3m+: 0-0
Track: LH: 0-2 RH: 0-1 Tight: 0-2 Gall: 0-1
Aids: Bl: 0-0 Vi: 0-0 Tstrap: 0-0
Best Rating: **103** 12/00 Kemp 2m gd-sft Hdl

Avalon Buck (IRE)

103(108h) (118h)133

9-y-o b g Buckskin (FR)-Lilly's Way (Golden Love)
Miss Venetia Williams B C Dice

Placings:1/2211134-1PP (3867)
2001/02: 24^{1}S, 24^{P}S, 24^{P}G

	Starts	1st	2nd	3rd	Win & Pl
Chases	3	1	0	0	3476
Career Total	**11**	**5**	**2**	**1**	**16299**

133	12/01	Sthl	3m110y	E Ch	SFT	£3475
116	2/01	Uttx	2m4f110y	D Hdl	SFT	£3475
111	1/01	Chep	2m4f	E Hdl	G-S	£2439
124	1/01	Extr	2m1f	E Hdl	HVY	£2136
110	12/99	Wwck	2m	H NHF	SFT	£1912

Total win prize-money £13440

Going: Sf: 1-2 GS: 0-0 Gd: 0-1 GF: - Fm: 0-0
Distance: 2m/2m3: 0-0 2m4-2m7: 0-0 **3m+: 1-3**
Track: **LH: 1-2** RH: 0-1 **Tight: 1-3** Gall: 0-0
Aids: Bl: 0-0 Vi: 0-0 Tstrap: 0-0
Best Rating: **133** 12/01 Sthl 3m110y soft Ch

A winner of a bumper and three hurdles, he made an impressive start to his chasing career when winning easily at Southwell but flopped next time. Suited by soft ground.

Avanti

88 91

6-y-o gr h Reprimand-Dolly Bevan (Another Realm)
Dr J R J Naylor A R M Galbraith

Placings:0-3 (0216)
2001/02: 16^{3}GF

	Starts	1st	2nd	3rd	Win & Pl
Hurdles	1	0	0	1	439
Career Total	**2**	**0**	**0**	**1**	**439**

Going: Sf: 0-0 GS: 0-0 Gd: 0-0 GF: - Fm: 0-1
Distance: 2m/2m3: 0-1 2m4-2m7: 0-0 3m+: 0-0
Track: LH: 0-0 RH: 0-1 Tight: 0-0 Gall: 0-0
Aids: Bl: 0-0 Vi: 0-0 Tstrap: 0-0
Best Rating: **91** 5/01 Winc 2m gd-fm Hdl

Avanti Blue

90 81

8-y-o b g Emarati (USA)-Dominion Blue (Dominion)
C C Bealby Mrs Jennifer C Skelton

Placings:P06 (4553)
2001/02: 23^{P}S, 17^{0}GS, 17^{6}GF

	Starts	1st	2nd	3rd	Win & Pl
Hurdles	3	0	0	0	0
Career Total	**3**	**0**	**0**	**0**	**0**

Going: Sf: 0-1 GS: 0-1 Gd: 0-0 GF: - Fm: 0-1
Distance: 2m/2m3: 0-2 2m4-2m7: 0-0 3m+: 0-1
Track: LH: 0-1 RH: 0-2 Tight: 0-3 Gall: 0-0
Aids: Bl: 0-0 Vi: 0-0 Tstrap: 0-1
Best Rating: **81** 4/02 MRas 2m1f110y gd-fm Hdl

Avanti Express (IRE)

114 120

12-y-o b g Supreme Leader-Muckride Lady (Deep Run)
Miss E C Lavelle Mrs Sarah Stevens

Placings:2/2210/2421311/1/2243250/6-36 (4635)
2001/02: 24^{3}G, 19^{6}GF

	Starts	1st	2nd	3rd	Win & Pl
Chases	2	0	0	1	1075
Career Total	**23**	**5**	**8**	**3**	**31998**

131	4/99	MRas	2m1f110y	D(0-120)HCh	GD	£3925
114	4/98	Worc	2m	E Ch	G-S	£3206
131	4/98	MRas	2m1f110y	D Ch	SFT	£4027
128	3/98	Tntn	2m3f	D Ch	G-S	£4369
111	2/97	Hrfd	2m1f	E Hdl	SFT	£2347

Total win prize-money £17875

Going: Sf: 0-0 GS: 0-0 Gd: 0-1 GF: - Fm: 0-1
Distance: 2m/2m3: 0-0 2m4-2m7: 0-1 3m+: 0-1
Track: LH: 0-0 RH: 0-2 Tight: 0-0 Gall: 0-0
Aids: Bl: 0-0 Vi: 0-0 Tstrap: 0-0
Best Rating: **138** 3/00 Chel 3m110y good Ch

Fair handicap chaser a few seasons ago, but was off the track for 22 months until reappearing at Sandown in March 2002. Effective at two and a half/three miles, he acts on good and soft ground.

Away Game (IRE)

96f 104f

5-y-o b m Bob's Return (IRE)-Balancing Act (Balinger)
Miss H C Knight W Shand Kydd

Placings:2 (2294)
2001/02: 17^{2}GF

	Starts	1st	2nd	3rd	Win & Pl
NH Flat	1	0	1	0	505
Career Total	**1**	**0**	**1**	**0**	**505**

Going: Sf: 0-0 GS: 0-0 Gd: 0-0 GF: - Fm: 0-1
Distance: 2m/2m3: 0-1 2m4-2m7: 0-0 3m+: 0-0
Track: LH: 0-0 RH: 0-1 Tight: 0-0 Gall: 0-0
Aids: Bl: 0-0 Vi: 0-0 Tstrap: 0-0
Best Rating: **104** 11/01 Extr 2m1f gd-fm NHF

Awesome Aunt (IRE)

103(97h) (85h)120

6-y-o br m Vestris Abu-Rose-Anore (Roselier (FR))
Miss H C Knight Mrs Gwen Meacham & Alan Briscoe

Placings:1/045-5552113 (2130)
2001/02: 17^{5}GS, 17^{5}G, 20^{5}G, 16^{2}GF, 16^{1}GF, 19^{1}S, 20^{3}GF

	Starts	1st	2nd	3rd	Win & Pl
Hurdles	5	1	1	0	3940
Chases	2	1	0	1	4084
Career Total	**11**	**3**	**1**	**1**	**9669**

120	10/01	Hrfd	2m3f	E(0-105)HCh	SFT	£3503
81	9/01	Strf	2m110y	E Hdl	G-F	£2968
95	3/00	Donc	2m110y	H NHF	G-S	£1645

Total win prize-money £8117

Going: Sf: 1-1 GS: 0-1 Gd: 0-2 GF: - Fm: 1-3
Distance: **2m/2m3: 2-5** 2m4-2m7: 0-2 3m+: 0-0
Track: LH: 1-3 RH: 1-4 **Tight: 1-2** Gall: 0-0
Aids: Bl: 0-0 Vi: 0-0 Tstrap: 0-2
Best Rating: **120** 10/01 Hrfd 2m3f soft Ch

Jumped well when winning on her chasing debut but broke a blood-vessel next time.

Awesome Wells (IRE)

84 76

8-y-o b g Sadler's Wells (USA)-Shadywood (Habitat)
D J Wintle M Tuerks

Placings:P-P (4850)
2001/02: 22^{P}G

	Starts	1st	2nd	3rd	Win & Pl
Hurdles	1	0	0	0	
Career Total	**2**	**0**	**0**	**0**	

Going: Sf: 0-0 GS: 0-0 Gd: 0-1 GF: - Fm: 0-0
Distance: 2m/2m3: 0-0 2m4-2m7: 0-1 3m+: 0-0
Track: LH: 0-1 RH: 0-0 Tight: 0-1 Gall: 0-0
Aids: Bl: 0-0 Vi: 0-0 Tstrap: 0-0
Best Rating:

Ayem (IRE)

101 103

7-y-o ch g Sharp Victor (USA)-Morning Crown (USA) (Chief's Crown (USA))
C Weedon Mrs M A Peet

Placings:0254422/U11/602-541 (1142)
2001/02: 19^{5}GF, 20^{4}G, 16^{1}G

	Starts	1st	2nd	3rd	Win & Pl
Hurdles	3	1	0	0	2819
Career Total	**16**	**3**	**4**	**0**	**10849**

103	8/01	Strf	2m110y	F(0-105)HHdl	GD	£2394
113	9/99	Plum	2m5f	E Hdl	GD	£2337
105	5/99	Fknm	2m4f	D Hdl	G-F	£2344

Total win prize-money £7077

Going: Sf: 0-0 GS: 0-0 Gd: 1-2 GF: - Fm: 0-1
Distance: **2m/2m3: 1-1** 2m4-2m7: 0-2 3m+: 0-0
Track: **LH: 1-3** RH: 0-0 **Tight: 1-2** Gall: 0-0

Aids: Bl: 0-0 Vi: 0-0 Tstrap: 1-3
Best Rating: 113 9/99 Plum 2m5f good Hdl

Azertyuiop (FR)

113 162

5-y-o b g Baby Turk-Temara (FR) (Rex Magna (FR))
P F Nicholls J Hales

Placings:112-1545 (4676)
2001/02: 16^{1}G, 16^{5}G, 16^{4}GS, 20^{5}G

	Starts	1st	2nd	3rd	Win & Pl
Hurdles	4	1	0	0	21175
Career Total	**7**	**3**	**1**	**0**	**77624**

162	11/01	Winc	2m	A HHdl	GD	£15000
155	2/01	Winc	2m	A Hdl	GD	£21000
	10/00	Autl	1m7f	Hdl	VS	£13449

Total win prize-money £49449

Going: Sf: 0-0 GS: 0-1 Gd: 1-3 GF: - Fm: 0-0
Distance: **2m/2m3: 1-3** 2m4-2m7: 0-1 3m+: 0-0
Track: LH: 0-1 **RH: 1-3** Tight: 0-1 Gall: 0-0
Aids: Bl: 0-0 Vi: 0-0 Tstrap: 0-0
Best Rating: **162** 11/01 Winc 2m good Hdl

A decent performer in France, he made a fine debut in this country when beating Hors La Loi III in the Axminster Hurdle at Wincanton in February 2001, but probably found the desperate ground against him behind Bilboa at Aintree. He made a good reappearance when winning back at Wincanton in November 2001, but disappointed in high-class hurdles subsequently. Suited by good ground and two miles.

Aztec Rule (IRE)

86 87

9-y-o b g Strong Gale-Monksville (Monksfield)
R Curtis Eddie Gloyne

Placings:503P/022-F5 (4726)
2001/02: 21^{F}GF, 20^{5}GF

	Starts	1st	2nd	3rd	Win & Pl
Hurdles	1	0	0	0	0
Chases	1	0	0	0	0
Career Total	**9**	**0**	**2**	**1**	**1932**

Going: Sf: 0-0 GS: 0-0 Gd: 0-0 GF: - Fm: 0-2
Distance: 2m/2m3: 0-0 2m4-2m7: 0-2 3m+: 0-0
Track: LH: 0-1 RH: 0-1 Tight: 0-0 Gall: 0-0
Aids: Bl: 0-0 Vi: 0-0 Tstrap: 0-0
Best Rating: **94** 12/99 Donc 2m4f gd-fm Hdl

Azzan (USA)

6-y-o b/br g Gulch (USA)-Dixieland Dream (USA) (Dixieland Band (USA))
T Keddy Brensway Partnership

Placings:PP/P0-PP (1618)
2001/02: 20^{P}G, 21^{P}G

	Starts	1st	2nd	3rd	Win & Pl
Hurdles	2	0	0	0	
Career Total	**6**	**0**	**0**	**0**	

Going: Sf: 0-0 GS: 0-0 Gd: 0-2 GF: - Fm: 0-0
Distance: 2m/2m3: 0-0 2m4-2m7: 0-2 3m+: 0-0
Track: LH: 0-1 RH: 0-1 Tight: 0-0 Gall: 0-0
Aids: Bl: 0-0 Vi: 0-0 Tstrap: 0-0
Best Rating: 15 6/00 Uttx 2m good Hdl

B B Boy

86f 82f

6-y-o br g Arctic Lord-Belle Muguet (Bargello)
K C Bailey T Benfield And Mr W Brown

Placings:*00* (4423)
2001/02: 16^{0}GS, 16^{0}GS

	Starts	1st	2nd	3rd	Win & Pl
NH Flat	2	0	0	0	
Career Total	**2**	**0**	**0**	**0**	

Going: Sf: 0-0 GS: 0-2 Gd: 0-0 GF: - Fm: 0-0
Distance: 2m/2m3: 0-2 2m4-2m7: 0-0 3m+: 0-0
Track: LH: 0-1 RH: 0-1 Tight: 0-0 Gall: 0-1
Aids: Bl: 0-0 Vi: 0-0 Tstrap: 0-0
Best Rating: **82** 2/02 Winc 2m gd-sft NHF

B J Zusjack (IRE)

7-y-o ch g Broken Hearted-Tuney Blade (Fine Blade (USA))
B G Powell The Heartbeakers

Placings:*00*/0-P (0981)
2001/02: 22^{P}G

	Starts	1st	2nd	3rd	Win & Pl
Hurdles	1	0	0	0	
Career Total	**4**	**0**	**0**	**0**	

Going: Sf: 0-0 GS: 0-0 Gd: 0-1 GF: - Fm: 0-0
Distance: 2m/2m3: 0-0 2m4-2m7: 0-1 3m+: 0-0
Track: LH: 0-1 RH: 0-0 Tight: 0-1 Gall: 0-0
Aids: Bl: 0-0 Vi: 0-0 Tstrap: 0-0
Best Rating: **72** 11/00 Kemp 2m soft Hdl

B The One

111 147

11-y-o b g Gunner B-Half Asleep (Quiet Fling (USA))
J J Quinn Andrew Page And Mr John Pollard

Placings:1/P12/U3303/1PP6/P113342-13214 (3494)
2001/02: 16^{1}S, 17^{3}S, 16^{2}S, 16^{1}HY, 16^{4}S

	Starts	1st	2nd	3rd	Win & Pl
Chases	5	2	1	1	16207
Career Total	**25**	**7**	**3**	**6**	**35734**

147	1/02	Uttx	2m	C(0-135)HCh	HVY	£6812
147	11/01	Hayd	2m	D(0-125)HCh	SFT	£4056
138	12/00	Sthl	2m	F(0-110)HCh	SFT	£2345
126	11/00	Sedg	2m110y	F(0-100)HCh	SFT	£2782
120	12/99	Sthl	2m4f110y	E(0-105)HCh	SFT	£3086
94	11/96	Newc	2m	E Hdl	GD	£2295
94	4/96	Hexm	2m	H NHF	G-F	£1301

Total win prize-money £22677

Going: Sf: 2-5 GS: 0-0 Gd: 0-0 GF: - Fm: 0-0
Distance: **2m/2m3: 2-5** 2m4-2m7: 0-0 3m+: 0-0
Track: **LH: 2-5** RH: 0-0 Tight: 0-0 Gall: 0-2
Aids: Bl: 0-0 Vi: 0-0 Tstrap: 0-0
Best Rating: **147** 1/02 Uttx 2m heavy Ch

He had a cracking season in 2000/1 and has scored twice in decent handicap company since then. Should continue to pay his way in two-mile handicaps. Best in the mud.

Baba Au Rhum (IRE)

106(99h) (100h)130

10-y-o b g Baba Karam-Spring About (Hard Fought)
Ian Williams Horses For Courses Partnership

Placings:P6/124/P411/133-41334 (1542)
2001/02: 16^{4}GS, 16^{1}GF, 16^{3}GF, 17^{3}GF, 16^{4}G

	Starts	1st	2nd	3rd	Win & Pl
Chases	5	1	0	2	6168
Career Total	**17**	**5**	**1**	**4**	**24728**

130	7/01	Sthl	2m	F(0-105)HCh	G-F	£4134
120	10/00	MRas	2m1f110y	D(0-120)HHdl	GD	£7020
111	3/99	Ludl	2m	E(0-115)HHdl	GD	£2866
105	10/98	Ludl	2m	E Hdl	G-F	£2402
112	9/97	Worc	2m	D Ch	GD	£3728

Total win prize-money £20151

Going: Sf: 0-0 GS: 0-1 Gd: 0-1 GF: - Fm: 1-3
Distance: **2m/2m3: 1-5** 2m4-2m7: 0-0 3m+: 0-0
Track: **LH: 1-4** RH: 0-1 **Tight: 1-4** Gall: 0-0
Aids: Bl: 0-0 Vi: 0-0 Tstrap: 0-0
Best Rating: **130** 7/01 Sthl 2m gd-fm Ch

Babs Wheal

6-y-o b m Petoski-Releta (Relkino)
D J Wintle Mrs Helen Hogben

Placings:*00* (2757)
2001/02: 16^{0}G, 17^{0}GS

	Starts	1st	2nd	3rd	Win & Pl
NH Flat	2	0	0	0	
Career Total	**2**	**0**	**0**	**0**	

Going: Sf: 0-0 GS: 0-1 Gd: 0-1 GF: - Fm: 0-0
Distance: 2m/2m3: 0-2 2m4-2m7: 0-0 3m+: 0-0
Track: LH: 0-2 RH: 0-0 Tight: 0-1 Gall: 0-0
Aids: Bl: 0-0 Vi: 0-0 Tstrap: 0-0
Best Rating:

Baby Carrot (IRE)

105 88

7-y-o ch g Good Thyne (USA)-Partners In Crime (Crofthall)
P Winkworth Giles Dixon, John Winkworth

Placings:0/6243PO-03 (4724)
2001/02: 16^{0}GS, 16^{3}GF

	Starts	1st	2nd	3rd	Win & Pl
Hurdles	2	0	0	1	408
Career Total	**9**	**0**	**1**	**2**	**1507**

Going: Sf: 0-0 GS: 0-1 Gd: 0-0 GF: - Fm: 0-1
Distance: 2m/2m3: 0-2 2m4-2m7: 0-0 3m+: 0-0
Track: LH: 0-1 RH: 0-1 Tight: 0-0 Gall: 0-1
Aids: Bl: 0-0 Vi: 0-0 Tstrap: 0-0
Best Rating: **88** 4/02 Chep 2m110y gd-fm Hdl

Novice hurdler, exposed as moderate.

Baby Gee

112 80

8-y-o ch m King Among Kings-Market Blues (Porto Bello)
D W Whillans Chas N Whillans

Placings:004/011123 (4440)
2001/02: 20^{0}G, 16^{1}G, 16^{1}S, 16^{1}GS, 16^{2}HY, 16^{3}S

	Starts	1st	2nd	3rd	Win & Pl
Hurdles	6	3	1	1	8516
Career Total	**9**	**3**	**1**	**1**	**8725**

79	2/02	Muss	2m	E(0-105)HHdl	G-S	£2996
80	1/02	Newc	2m	E(0-100)HHdl	SFT	£2534
73	1/02	Catt	2m	G(0-90)HHdl	G-S	£1764

Total win prize-money £7294

Going: Sf: 1-3 GS: 2-2 Gd: 0-1 GF: - Fm: 0-0
Distance: **2m/2m3: 3-5** 2m4-2m7: 0-1 3m+: 0-0
Track: **LH: 2-5** RH: 1-1 **Tight: 2-3** Gall: 1-1

Aids: Bl: 0-0 Vi: 0-0 Tstrap: 0-0
Best Rating: **80** 3/02 Kels 2m110y soft Hdl

Modest hurdler, and not the biggest, she cracked a bone in her foot and was absent for seven months, but came back to land a treble at the start of 2002. Suited by cut in the ground.

Baby John (IRE)

100(99c) (73c)98

9-y-o b g Celio Rufo-Kings Princess (King's Ride)
Miss H C Knight The Father John Partnership

Placings:0/33**PF**/3245**1**3-34350 **(4550)**
2001/02: 22^{3}GF, 24^{4}GF, 22^{3}GF, 22^{5}G, 21^{0}GF

	Starts	1st	2nd	3rd	Win & Pl
Hurdles	4	0	0	2	885
Chases	1	0	0	0	271
Career Total	16	1	1	6	8782

119	11/00	Tntn	2m3f	D(0-105)HCh	GD	£4793

Total win prize-money £4794

Going: Sf: 0-0 GS: 0-0 Gd: 0-1 GF: - Fm: 0-4
Distance: 2m/2m3: 0-0 2m4-2m7: 0-4 3m+: 0-1
Track: LH: 0-1 RH: 0-4 Tight: 0-1 Gall: 0-2
Aids: Bl: 0-0 Vi: 0-0 Tstrap: 0-0
Best Rating: **119** 11/00 Tntn 2m3f gd-sft Ch

Bacardi Boy (IRE)

109 122

6-y-o b g Lord Americo-Little Welly (Little Buskins)
T R George Allan Stennett & Terry Warner

Placings:*13332* **(3805)**
2001/02: 17^{1}S, 16^{3}HY, 16^{3}GS, 20^{3}HY, 22^{2}S

	Starts	1st	2nd	3rd	Win & Pl
NH Flat	3	1	0	2	3658
Hurdles	2	0	1	1	3252
Career Total	5	1	1	3	6910

118	11/01	Carl	2m1f	H NHF	SFT	£1610

Total win prize-money £1610

Going: Sf: 1-4 GS: 0-1 Gd: 0-0 GF: - Fm: 0-0
Distance: **2m/2m3: 1-3** 2m4-2m7: 0-2 3m+: 0-0
Track: LH: 0-3 **RH: 1-2** Tight: 0-1 Gall: 0-0
Aids: Bl: 0-0 Vi: 0-0 Tstrap: 0-0
Best Rating: **126** 12/01 Chep 2m110y gd-sft NHF

Bred to stay. He fell when in the lead in an Irish point-to-point last season. Stayed on well to land a Carlisle bumper in November on soft ground and has continued to run well in bumpers since then. Placed in novice hurdles.

Baccarat (IRE)

100 128

8-y-o b g Bob Back (USA)-Sarahlee (Sayyaf)
J G Fitzgerald Lady Lloyd Webber

Placings:*1230/4*/F33-3 **(0066)**
2001/02: 21^{3}G

	Starts	1st	2nd	3rd	Win & Pl
Chases	1	0	0	1	543
Career Total	9	1	1	4	4299

115	12/98	Donc	2m110y	H NHF	GD	£1413

Total win prize-money £1413

Going: Sf: 0-0 GS: 0-0 Gd: 0-1 GF: - Fm: 0-0
Distance: 2m/2m3: 0-0 2m4-2m7: 0-1 3m+: 0-0
Track: LH: 0-1 RH: 0-0 Tight: 0-1 Gall: 0-0
Aids: Bl: 0-0 Vi: 0-0 Tstrap: 0-0
Best Rating: **128** 5/01 Sedg 2m5f good Ch

Bacchanal (IRE)

115 (124h)180

8-y-o ch g Bob Back (USA)-Justitia (Dunbeath (USA))
N J Henderson Lady Lloyd Webber

Placings:2115/121/4111F0-1310 **(4252)**
2001/02: 24^{1}GS, 24^{3}G, 24^{1}S, 26^{0}G

	Starts	1st	2nd	3rd	Win & Pl
Chases	4	2	0	1	62116
Career Total	17	9	2	1	228898

180	2/02	Newb	3m	A Ch	SFT	£34800
172	12/01	Sand	3m110y	B Ch	G-S	£10816
172	2/01	Asct	3m110y	A Ch	SFT	£22925
172	12/00	Kemp	3m	A Ch	G-S	£26200
165	11/00	Newb	2m4f	C Ch	G-S	£7772
168	3/00	Chel	3m	A Hdl	G-F	£66700
163	11/99	Newb	2m110y	A(0-145)Hdl	G-S	£13090
159	3/99	Chep	2m110y	B Hdl	SFT	£13550
134	2/99	Sand	2m110y	D Hdl	G-S	£3009

Total win prize-money £198862

Going: Sf: 1-1 GS: 1-1 Gd: 0-2 GF: - Fm: 0-0
Distance: 2m/2m3: 0-0 2m4-2m7: 0-0 **3m+: 2-4**
Track: LH: 1-2 RH: 1-2 Tight: 0-0 **Gall: 1-2**
Aids: Bl: 0-0 Vi: 0-0 Tstrap: 0-0
Best Rating: **180** 2/02 Newb 3m soft Ch

A decisive winner of the 2000 Stayers' Hurdle at Cheltenham, he took well to fences in 2000/01, landing the Grade One Feltham Novices' Chase at the Kempton Christmas meeting impressively and following up in a weakly-contested Reynoldstown at Ascot, but got no further than the first fence at Aintree. He made an encouraging return at Sandown in December 2001 before running a good third in the King George. Decisive winner of the Aon Chase at Newbury, he disappointed in the Gold Cup. He stays three miles plus and acts on most ground. Has shown a tendency to jump to the right.

Bacchus Du Berlais (FR)

95 121

5-y-o b h Saint Preuil (FR)-Cindy Cad (FR) (Cadoudal (FR))
G Macaire J-M Vergnaud

Placings:1111-222021030
2001/02: 17^{2}, 17^{2}S, 17^{2}GS, 17^{0}VS, 17^{2}VS, 36^{1}HY, 20^{0}HO, 19^{3}GS, 18^{0}HY

	Starts	1st	2nd	3rd	Win & Pl
Hurdles	1	0	0	0	0
Chases	8	1	4	1	29399
Career Total	13	5	4	1	44288

11/01	Autl	4m4f110y	Ch	HVY	£21339
8/00	Vich	2m110y	Hdl	VS	£5764
7/00	Vich	2m110y	Hdl	G-S	£3842
6/00	Diep	1m7f	Hdl	GD	£3074
6/00	Jall	1m7f	Hdl	GD	£2209

Total win prize-money £36228

Going: Sf: 1-3 GS: 0-2 Gd: 0-0 GF: - Fm: 0-0
Distance: 2m/2m3: 0-6 2m4-2m7: 0-2 **3m+: 1-1**
Track: LH: 0-1 RH: 0-0 Tight: 0-0 Gall: 0-0
Aids: Bl: 0-1 Vi: 0-0 Tstrap: 0-0
Best Rating: **121** 12/01 Chep 2m3f110y gd-sft Ch

Bachelor's Tonic (IRE)

82f 81f

4-y-o b g Fayruz-Dance Alone (USA) (Monteverdi)
C J Mann Stamford Bridge Partnership

Placings:*0* **(3910)**
2001/02: 16^{0}G

	Starts	1st	2nd	3rd	Win & Pl
NH Flat	1	0	0	0	
Career Total	1	0	0	0	

Going: Sf: 0-0 GS: 0-0 Gd: 0-1 GF: - Fm: 0-0
Distance: 2m/2m3: 0-1 2m4-2m7: 0-0 3m+: 0-0
Track: LH: 0-0 RH: 0-1 Tight: 0-0 Gall: 0-0
Aids: Bl: 0-0 Vi: 0-0 Tstrap: 0-0
Best Rating: **81** 2/02 Kemp 2m good NHF

Bachelors Pad

105 86

8-y-o b g Pursuit Of Love-Note Book (Mummy's Pet)
Miss S J Wilton John Pointon And Sons

Placings:05-00155361030 **(3765)**
2001/02: 17^{0}GS, 20^{0}G, 16^{1}S, 16^{5}S, 17^{5}G, 16^{3}HY, 17^{6}G, 16^{1}S, 16^{0}GS, 16^{3}S, 16^{0}GS

	Starts	1st	2nd	3rd	Win & Pl
Hurdles	11	2	0	2	4529
Career Total	13	2	0	2	4529

86	12/01	Strf	2m110y	G(0-95)HHdl	SFT	£2002
86	10/01	Fknm	2m	G(0-90)HHdl	SFT	£1862

Total win prize-money £3865

Going: Sf: 2-5 GS: 0-3 Gd: 0-3 GF: - Fm: 0-0
Distance: **2m/2m3: 2-10** 2m4-2m7: 0-1 3m+: 0-0
Track: **LH: 2-9** RH: 0-2 **Tight: 2-8** Gall: 0-1
Aids: Bl: 0-0 Vi: 0-0 Tstrap: 0-0
Best Rating: **86** 12/01 Strf 2m110y soft Hdl

Moderate hurdler, he acts on soft ground and is effective over two miles.

Bachiana (FR)

97 87

5-y-o ch m Exit To Nowhere (USA)-Etoile D'Ocean (USA) (Northern Dancer)
M C Pipe (D G Bridgwater 29/9) Ray Ransom

Placings:P-0450P **(3449)**
2001/02: 16^{0}GS, 17^{4}HY, 17^{5}GS, 16^{0}G, 16^{P}GS

	Starts	1st	2nd	3rd	Win & Pl
Hurdles	5	0	0	0	0
Career Total	6	0	0	0	0

Going: Sf: 0-1 GS: 0-3 Gd: 0-1 GF: - Fm: 0-0
Distance: 2m/2m3: 0-5 2m4-2m7: 0-0 3m+: 0-0
Track: LH: 0-4 RH: 0-1 Tight: 0-4 Gall: 0-0
Aids: Bl: 0-0 Vi: 0-1 Tstrap: 0-0
Best Rating: **87** 12/01 NAbb 2m1f heavy Hdl

Back In Front (IRE)

116f 149f

5-y-o br g Bob Back (USA)-Storm Front (IRE) (Strong Gale)
E J O'Grady Nelius Hayes

Placings:*1130* **(4948a)**
2001/02: 16^{1}G, 16^{1}G, 16^{3}GS, 16^{0}G

	Starts	1st	2nd	3rd	Win & Pl
NH Flat	4	2	0	1	16159
Career Total	4	2	0	1	16159

131	11/01	Chel	2m110y	A NHF	GD	£8814
111	7/01	Naas	2m	NHF	GD	£3895

Total win prize-money £12709

Going: Sf: 0-0 GS: 0-1 Gd: 2-3 GF: - Fm: 0-0
Distance: **2m/2m3: 2-4** 2m4-2m7: 0-0 3m+: 0-0
Track: **LH: 1-2** RH: 0-1 Tight: 0-0 Gall: 0-0
Aids: Bl: 0-0 Vi: 0-0 Tstrap: 0-0
Best Rating: **149** 3/02 Chel 2m110y gd-sft NHF

Useful bumper horse, winner at Naas in July and Cheltenham in November before running third in the Festival bumper.

Back In Thyne (IRE)

(44h) **103**

7-y-o b g Good Thyne (USA)-Black Again (Strong Gale)
E Bolger (C F Swan 5/9) E Kavanagh

Placings:*6030000*0510U460-B360P4PU30F2FP1244211P (4802a)
2001/02: 25^{B}GY, 25^{3}G, 24^{6}G, 24^{0}GF, 22^{P}YS, 25^{4}G, 22^{P}G, 24^{U}GF, 21^{3}HY, 24^{0}Y, 31^{F}G, 24^{2}YS, 26^{F}S, 22^{P}S, 22^{1}Y, 28^{2}YS, 20^{4}SH, 20^{4}HY, 24^{2}HY, 28^{1}S, 24^{1}S, 20^{P}GF

	Starts	1st	2nd	3rd	Win & Pl
Hurdles	1	0	0	0	0
Chases	21	3	3	2	33568
Career Total	**37**	**4**	**3**	**3**	**36442**

103	3/02	Limk	3m	HCh	SFT	£13159
102	3/02	Dpat	3m4f	(0-116)HCh	SFT	£7975
102	1/02	Tram	2m6f	(0-102)HCh	YLD	£5926
98	8/00	Dpat	3m	Ch	G-F	£2345

Total win prize-money £29407

Going: Sf: 2-7 GS: 0-0 Gd: 0-5 GF: - Fm: 0-3
Distance: 2m/2m3: 0-0 2m4-2m7: 1-8 **3m+: 2-14**
Track: LH: 0-3 **RH: 2-5** Tight: 0-0 Gall: 0-0
Aids: **Bl: 3-17** Vi: 0-0 Tstrap: 0-8
Best Rating: **103** 3/02 Limk 3m soft Ch

Back To Business (IRE)

9-y-o br m Creative Plan (USA)-Dark Foam (Bustineto)
P F Nicholls A G Fear

Placings:306/P (3655)
2001/02: 22^{P}S

	Starts	1st	2nd	3rd	Win & Pl
Hurdles	1	0	0	0	
Career Total	**4**	**0**	**0**	**1**	**221**

Going: Sf: 0-1 GS: 0-0 Gd: 0-0 GF: - Fm: 0-0
Distance: 2m/2m3: 0-0 2m4-2m7: 0-1 3m+: 0-0
Track: LH: 0-0 RH: 0-1 Tight: 0-0 Gall: 0-0
Aids: Bl: 0-0 Vi: 0-0 Tstrap: 0-0
Best Rating: **86** 12/99 Tntn 2m1f soft NHF

Back To Nature (IRE)

79 **76**

5-y-o b g Zaffaran (USA)-Late Night Caller (IRE) (Waajib)
M Pitman H J Jarvis

Placings:*5-0*56 (3383)
2001/02: 17^{0}GS, 17^{5}S, 16^{6}GS

	Starts	1st	2nd	3rd	Win & Pl
NH Flat	2	0	0	0	0
Hurdles	1	0	0	0	0
Career Total	**4**	**0**	**0**	**0**	**0**

Going: Sf: 0-1 GS: 0-2 Gd: 0-0 GF: - Fm: 0-0

Distance: 2m/2m3: 0-3 2m4-2m7: 0-0 3m+: 0-0
Track: LH: 0-0 RH: 0-1 Tight: 0-1 Gall: 0-0
Aids: Bl: 0-0 Vi: 0-0 Tstrap: 0-0
Best Rating: **84** 12/01 Folk 2m1f110y soft NHF

He is well regarded but has shown little so far.

Backbeat (IRE)

87 **93**

5-y-o ch g Bob Back (USA)-Pinata (Deep Run)
D R C Elsworth W V M W & Mrs E S Robins

Placings:240 (4138)
2001/02: 16^{2}G, 16^{4}GS, 16^{0}GS

	Starts	1st	2nd	3rd	Win & Pl
NH Flat	1	0	1	0	0
Hurdles	2	0	0	0	0
Career Total	**3**	**0**	**1**	**0**	**0**

Going: Sf: 0-0 GS: 0-2 Gd: 0-1 GF: - Fm: 0-0
Distance: 2m/2m3: 0-3 2m4-2m7: 0-0 3m+: 0-0
Track: LH: 0-0 RH: 0-3 Tight: 0-0 Gall: 0-0
Aids: Bl: 0-0 Vi: 0-0 Tstrap: 0-0
Best Rating: **121** 12/01 Asct 2m110y good NHF

Out of a winning hurdler, made an encouraging debut in a decent Ascot bumper.

Backcraft (IRE)

105 **120**

4-y-o b g Bob Back (USA)-Bawnanell (Viking (USA))
L Lungo (D K Weld 24/9) M Magowan

Placings:313 (4840)
2001/02: 16^{3}GF, 18^{1}HY, 16^{3}G

	Starts	1st	2nd	3rd	Win & Pl
Hurdles	3	1	0	2	4373
Career Total	**3**	**1**	**0**	**2**	**4373**

102	3/02	Kels	2m2f	E Hdl	HVY	£2786

Total win prize-money £2786

Going: Sf: 1-1 GS: 0-0 Gd: 0-1 GF: - Fm: 0-1
Distance: **2m/2m3: 1-3** 2m4-2m7: 0-0 3m+: 0-0
Track: **LH: 1-3** RH: 0-0 **Tight: 1-1** Gall: 0-0
Aids: Bl: 0-0 Vi: 0-0 Tstrap: 0-0
Best Rating: **111** 4/02 Ayr 2m good Hdl

Backend Charlie

8-y-o b g Sylvan Express-Red Eska (Smackover)
B W Murray G Bulmer

Placings:*0050*/P (3993)
2001/02: 20^{P}S

	Starts	1st	2nd	3rd	Win & Pl
Hurdles	1	0	0	0	
Career Total	**5**	**0**	**0**	**0**	**0**

Going: Sf: 0-1 GS: 0-0 Gd: 0-0 GF: - Fm: 0-0
Distance: 2m/2m3: 0-0 2m4-2m7: 0-1 3m+: 0-0
Track: LH: 0-1 RH: 0-0 Tight: 0-0 Gall: 0-1
Aids: Bl: 0-0 Vi: 0-0 Tstrap: 0-0
Best Rating: **83** 12/98 Catt 2m good NHF

Backitbob (IRE)

95f **111f**

6-y-o br g Bob Back (USA)-Winter Fox (Martinmas)
A J Martin (George Stewart 16/1) Seamus Ross

Placings:*205* (4716a)
2001/02: 16^{2}GY, 16^{0}GS, 16^{5}Y

	Starts	1st	2nd	3rd	Win & Pl
NH Flat	3	0	1	0	1031
Career Total	**3**	**0**	**1**	**0**	**1031**

Going: Sf: 0-0 GS: 0-1 Gd: 0-0 GF: - Fm: 0-0
Distance: 2m/2m3: 0-3 2m4-2m7: 0-0 3m+: 0-0
Track: LH: 0-1 RH: 0-2 Tight: 0-0 Gall: 0-0
Aids: Bl: 0-0 Vi: 0-0 Tstrap: 0-0
Best Rating: **111** 3/02 Chel 2m110y gd-sft NHF

Backpacker (IRE)

67 **70**

5-y-o b g Petoski-Yellow Iris (Le Bavard (FR))
T P McGovern (John Joseph Murphy 22/11) C R H Racing

Placings:*355* (4883)
2001/02: 16^{3}YS, 20^{5}S, 22^{5}GF

	Starts	1st	2nd	3rd	Win & Pl
NH Flat	1	0	0	1	508
Hurdles	2	0	0	0	0
Career Total	**3**	**0**	**0**	**1**	**508**

Going: Sf: 0-1 GS: 0-0 Gd: 0-0 GF: - Fm: 0-1
Distance: 2m/2m3: 0-1 2m4-2m7: 0-2 3m+: 0-0
Track: LH: 0-1 RH: 0-0 Tight: 0-2 Gall: 0-0
Aids: Bl: 0-0 Vi: 0-0 Tstrap: 0-0
Best Rating: **90** 11/01 Cork 2m yld-sft NHF

Backsheesh (IRE)

7-y-o b g Bob Back (USA)-Kottna (USA) (Lyphard (USA))
G Tuer (E W Tuer 17/10) G Tuer

Placings:*00/040614/062406*-0341 (4288)
2001/02: 17^{0}F, 21^{3}G, 25^{4}G, 25^{1}GS

	Starts	1st	2nd	3rd	Win & Pl
Chases	4	1	0	1	2177
Career Total	**18**	**2**	**1**	**1**	**6510**

116	3/02	MRas	3m1f	H Ch	G-S	£1528
99	4/00	DRoy	2m	NHF	G-F	£2760

Total win prize-money £4288

Going: Sf: 0-0 GS: 1-1 Gd: 0-2 GF: - Fm: 0-1
Distance: 2m/2m3: 0-1 2m4-2m7: 0-1 **3m+: 1-2**
Track: LH: 0-2 **RH: 1-1 Tight: 1-2** Gall: 0-0
Aids: Bl: 0-0 Vi: 0-0 **Tstrap: 1-4**
Best Rating: **116** 3/02 MRas 3m1f gd-sft Ch

Ex-Irish novice chaser, he has shown some fair form in points and hunter chases and jumped well when making all at Market Rasen in March 2002.

Backview

105 **82**

10-y-o ch g Backchat (USA)-Book Review (Balidar)
M Salaman Graham Hunt

Placings:0/56/14/0/0/000-031643P0 (4917)
2001/02: 16^{0}S, 24^{3}GS, 21^{1}HY, 20^{6}S, 19^{4}S, 22^{3}S, 20^{P}G, 21^{0}GF

	Starts	1st	2nd	3rd	Win & Pl
Hurdles	8	1	0	2	2232
Career Total	**18**	**2**	**0**	**2**	**3930**

82	1/02	Sedg	2m5f110y	G(0-90)HHdl	HVY	£1701
91	4/98	Hrfd	2m1f	G Hdl	SFT	£1698

Total win prize-money £3399

Going: Sf: 1-5 GS: 0-1 Gd: 0-1 GF: - Fm: 0-1

Distance: 2m/2m3: 0-1 **2m4-2m7: 1-6** 3m+: 0-1
Track: **LH: 1-5** RH: 0-3 **Tight: 1-5** Gall: 0-1
Aids: Bl: 0-0 Vi: 0-0 **Tstrap: 1-6**
Best Rating: 91 4/98 Hrfd 2m1f soft Hdl

Ran out a ready winner at Sedgefield in January 2002. Stays two miles five. Acts on heavy ground.

Baclama (FR)

105(101c) (113c)107

6-y-o b m Siam (USA)-Santa Ana Wind (USA) (Empery (USA))
M C Pipe Glenmore Investments Ltd

Placings:50121206/PP0P-2100351**2014PF**34 (4371)
2001/02: 19^{2}F, 19^{1}G, 20^{0}GF, 17^{0}GF, 20^{3}GS, 17^{5}G, 18^{1}GF, 17^{2}GF, 16^{0}GS, 18^{1}GS, 24^{4}GF, 21^{P}HY, 17^{F}G, 16^{3}S, 16^{4}GS

	Starts	1st	2nd	3rd	Win & Pl
Hurdles	10	2	2	1	6610
Chases	5	1	0	1	4218
Career Total	**27**	**5**	**4**	**2**	**33356**

113	11/01	Font	2m2f	F(0-110)HCh	G-S	£3290
93	8/01	Font	2m2f110y	G Hdl	G-F	£2341
89	5/01	Hrfd	2m3f110y	G Hdl	GD	£2380
	11/99	Autl	2m2f	Hdl	HLD	£6997
	10/99	Autl	2m2f	Hdl	HVY	£6997

Total win prize-money £22006

Going: Sf: 0-2 GS: 1-4 Gd: 1-3 GF: - Fm: 1-6
Distance: **2m/2m3: 2-9** 2m4-2m7: 1-5 3m+: 0-1
Track: LH: 1-9 RH: 1-5 **Tight: 2-9** Gall: 0-1
Aids: Bl: 0-0 Vi: 0-0 Tstrap: 0-0
Best Rating: 113 11/01 Font 2m2f gd-sft Ch

Modest hurdler/chaser, stays two miles three furlongs and acts on most types of ground.

Bad Bertrich (IRE)

87 49

11-y-o b g Waajib-Sweet Unison (USA) (One For All (USA))
Graeme Roe Roe Racing Ltd

Placings:000/02223055U/01041550P/0/**PP0P036** (1487)
2001/02: 24^{P}G, 22^{P}GF, 20^{0}S, 21^{P}G, 20^{0}GF, 23^{3}GF, 24^{6}GF

	Starts	1st	2nd	3rd	Win & Pl
Hurdles	2	0	0	0	0
Chases	5	0	0	1	600
Career Total	**29**	**2**	**3**	**2**	**9993**

87	7/98	Strf	2m6f110y	D Hdl	G-F	£2960
97	5/98	Chep	2m4f110y	E Hdl	GD	£1996

Total win prize-money £4956

Going: Sf: 0-1 GS: 0-0 Gd: 0-2 GF: - Fm: 0-4
Distance: 2m/2m3: 0-0 2m4-2m7: 0-4 3m+: 0-3
Track: LH: 0-5 RH: 0-1 Tight: 0-2 Gall: 0-1
Aids: Bl: 0-0 Vi: 0-4 Tstrap: 0-0
Best Rating: 100 9/97 List 2m gd-yld Hdl

Baden Vugie (IRE)

90 47

5-y-o bl g Hamas (IRE)-Bag Lady (Be My Guest (USA))
H D Daly Mrs D N Carr-Smith

Placings:*00*-000 (4518)
2001/02: 16^{0}G, 17^{0}GS, 21^{0}GS

	Starts	1st	2nd	3rd	Win & Pl
Hurdles	3	0	0	0	
Career Total	**5**	**0**	**0**	**0**	

Going: Sf: 0-0 GS: 0-2 Gd: 0-1 GF: - Fm: 0-0
Distance: 2m/2m3: 0-2 2m4-2m7: 0-1 3m+: 0-0
Track: LH: 0-1 RH: 0-2 Tight: 0-1 Gall: 0-0
Aids: Bl: 0-0 Vi: 0-0 Tstrap: 0-0
Best Rating: 58 2/01 Wwck 2m soft NHF

Badge Of Fame (IRE)

100

8-y-o gr g Caerleon (USA)-Infamy (Shirley Heights)
J L Eyre (M Pitman 9/6) John Law

Placings:3111/134/**P4-PP** (1502)
2001/02: 23^{P}G, 21^{P}G

	Starts	1st	2nd	3rd	Win & Pl
Chases	2	0	0	0	
Career Total	**11**	**4**	**0**	**2**	**14869**

134	11/98	Worc	2m4f	C(0-135)HHdl	HVY	£3767
124	4/98	Ludl	2m5f110y	E(0-100)HHdl	GD	£3074
102	3/98	Ling	2m3f110y	D Hdl	GD	£3209
107	3/98	Ling	2m110y	E Hdl	G-S	£2549

Total win prize-money £12601

Going: Sf: 0-0 GS: 0-0 Gd: 0-2 GF: - Fm: 0-0
Distance: 2m/2m3: 0-0 2m4-2m7: 0-1 3m+: 0-1
Track: LH: 0-2 RH: 0-0 Tight: 0-1 Gall: 0-0
Aids: Bl: 0-0 Vi: 0-0 Tstrap: 0-1
Best Rating: 134 12/98 Hayd 2m4f soft Hdl

Badger Beer

10-y-o b g Town And Country-Panda Pops (Cornuto)
J W Dufosee Mrs R H Woodhouse

Placings:4/43P/20P-**014P0B4** (4865)
2001/02: 23^{0}G, 21^{1}GF, 16^{4}G, 21^{P}GF, 19^{0}G, 19^{B}GF, 23^{4}F

	Starts	1st	2nd	3rd	Win & Pl
Chases	7	1	0	0	2223
Career Total	**14**	**1**	**1**	**1**	**3020**

105	5/01	Winc	2m5f	H Ch	G-F	£2222

Total win prize-money £2223

Going: Sf: 0-0 GS: 0-0 Gd: 0-3 GF: - Fm: 1-4
Distance: 2m/2m3: 0-1 **2m4-2m7: 1-4** 3m+: 0-2
Track: LH: 0-1 **RH: 1-5** Tight: 0-1 Gall: 0-0
Aids: Bl: 0-0 Vi: 0-0 **Tstrap: 1-7**
Best Rating: 108 4/02 Extr 2m7f110y firm Ch

Hunter chaser, likes fast ground. Best at around two and a half miles.

Badgers Glory

84 72

6-y-o gr/ro g Neltino-Shedid (St Columbus)
G P Enright Frederick Gray

Placings:*00*PP4 (4780)
2001/02: 17^{0}GS, 17^{0}GF, 21^{P}G, 18^{P}G, 17^{4}GF

	Starts	1st	2nd	3rd	Win & Pl
NH Flat	2	0	0	0	0
Hurdles	2	0	0	0	0
Chases	1	0	0	0	263
Career Total	**5**	**0**	**0**	**0**	**263**

Going: Sf: 0-0 GS: 0-1 Gd: 0-2 GF: - Fm: 0-2
Distance: 2m/2m3: 0-4 2m4-2m7: 0-1 3m+: 0-0
Track: LH: 0-3 RH: 0-0 Tight: 0-5 Gall: 0-0
Aids: Bl: 0-0 Vi: 0-0 Tstrap: 0-0
Best Rating: 71 5/01 Folk 2m1f110y gd-sft NHF

Bahamas (IRE)

105 91

5-y-o b g Barathea (IRE)-Rum Cay (USA) (Our Native (USA))
M A Barnes (J A B Old 10/12) Thirdtimelucky

Placings:P-**056001FU** (4867)
2001/02: 17^{0}G, 16^{5}G, 17^{6}G, 16^{0}S, 17^{0}HY, 16^{1}HY, 16^{F}S, 16^{U}GF

	Starts	1st	2nd	3rd	Win & Pl
Hurdles	8	1	0	0	3472
Career Total	**9**	**1**	**0**	**0**	**3472**

90	3/02	Ayr	2m	D(0-110)HHdl	HVY	£3472

Total win prize-money £3472

Going: Sf: 1-4 GS: 0-0 Gd: 0-3 GF: - Fm: 0-1
Distance: **2m/2m3: 1-8** 2m4-2m7: 0-0 3m+: 0-0
Track: **LH: 1-6** RH: 0-2 Tight: 0-3 Gall: 0-0
Aids: Bl: 0-2 Vi: 0-0 Tstrap: 0-0
Best Rating: 91 3/02 Kels 2m110y soft Hdl

Half-brother to Persian Punch and formerly a fair Flat handicapper, showed his best form over hurdles on his second run for Maurice Barnes when landing a fair handicap in heavy ground.

Baie Des Singes

71

8-y-o b g Royal Vulcan-Mikey's Monkey (Monksfield)
H D Daly S Preston

Placings:2/0343F5/**24P4FP-5** (0367)
2001/02: 24^{5}G

	Starts	1st	2nd	3rd	Win & Pl
Chases	1	0	0	0	0
Career Total	**14**	**0**	**2**	**2**	**4556**

Going: Sf: 0-0 GS: 0-0 Gd: 0-1 GF: - Fm: 0-0
Distance: 2m/2m3: 0-0 2m4-2m7: 0-0 3m+: 0-1
Track: LH: 0-0 RH: 0-0 Tight: 0-0 Gall: 0-0
Aids: Bl: 0-0 Vi: 0-0 Tstrap: 0-0
Best Rating: 117 10/00 Strf 2m4f gd-sft Ch

Bailieborough Boy (IRE)

8-y-o ch g Shalford (IRE)-Salique (Sallust)
D C O'Brien D C O'Brien

Placings:0/6/P (0230)
2001/02: 16^{P}GF

	Starts	1st	2nd	3rd	Win & Pl
Hurdles	1	0	0	0	
Career Total	**3**	**0**	**0**	**0**	**0**

Going: Sf: 0-0 GS: 0-0 Gd: 0-0 GF: - Fm: 0-1
Distance: 2m/2m3: 0-1 2m4-2m7: 0-0 3m+: 0-0
Track: LH: 0-0 RH: 0-1 Tight: 0-0 Gall: 0-1
Aids: Bl: 0-0 Vi: 0-0 Tstrap: 0-0
Best Rating: 70 4/99 Font 2m2f110y good Hdl

Baisse D'Argent (IRE)

97 94

6-y-o b g Common Grounds-Fabulous Pet (Somethingfabulous (USA))
D J S Cosgrove Winning Circle Racing Club Ltd

Placings:1152/30 (3378)

2001/02: 16³S, 21⁰GS

	Starts	1st	2nd	3rd	Win & Pl
Hurdles	2	0	0	1	344
Career Total	**6**	**2**	**1**	**1**	**6084**

94	11/99	Hntg	2m110y	E Hdl	GD	£2232
83	9/99	Hntg	2m110y	E Hdl	GD	£2481

Total win prize-money £4715

Going: Sf: 0-1 GS: 0-1 Gd: 0-0 GF: - Fm: 0-0
Distance: 2m/2m3: 0-1 2m4-2m7: 0-1 3m+: 0-0
Track: LH: 0-1 RH: 0-1 Tight: 0-1 Gall: 0-0
Aids: Bl: 0-0 Vi: 0-0 Tstrap: 0-0
Best Rating: **101** 3/00 MRas 2m1f110y gd-fm Hdl

Made an encouraging return to action over hurdles in January 2002 after a lengthy absence. He acts on well on good ground and is effective at around two miles.

Bajan Sunset (IRE)

86 71

5-y-o ch g Mujtahid (USA)-Dubai Lady (Kris)
D R Gandolfo (J D Bethell 22/6) Mrs John Lee

Placings:0 **(2289)**
2001/02: 17⁰GF

	Starts	1st	2nd	3rd	Win & Pl
Hurdles	1	0	0	0	
Career Total	**1**	**0**	**0**	**0**	

Going: Sf: 0-0 GS: 0-0 Gd: 0-0 GF: - Fm: 0-1
Distance: 2m/2m3: 0-1 2m4-2m7: 0-0 3m+: 0-0
Track: LH: 0-0 RH: 0-1 Tight: 0-0 Gall: 0-0
Aids: Bl: 0-0 Vi: 0-0 Tstrap: 0-0
Best Rating: **71** 11/01 Extr 2m1f gd-fm Hdl

Bak On Board

78 70

6-y-o b g Sula Bula-Kirstins Pride (Silly Prices)
Mrs S Gardner D V Gardner

Placings:*000*-05P35 **(4861)**
2001/02: 17⁰GS, 19⁵S, 22ᴾS, 17³GS, 22ᶠF

	Starts	1st	2nd	3rd	Win & Pl
Hurdles	5	0	0	1	400
Career Total	**8**	**0**	**0**	**1**	**400**

Going: Sf: 0-2 GS: 0-2 Gd: 0-0 GF: - Fm: 0-1
Distance: 2m/2m3: 0-2 2m4-2m7: 0-3 3m+: 0-0
Track: LH: 0-0 RH: 0-4 Tight: 0-1 Gall: 0-0
Aids: Bl: 0-0 Vi: 0-0 Tstrap: 0-0
Best Rating: **74** 1/01 Kemp 2m soft NHF

Lacks stamina over hurdles, despite being tried at various trips.

Bak To Bill

104 107

7-y-o b g Nicholas Bill-Kirstins Pride (Silly Prices)
Mrs S Gardner Thurlestone Hotel Racing Club

Placings:4/63ROP2PP-2062P3065425412 **(4502)**
2001/02: 19²G, 22⁰F, 19⁶GF, 20²GF, 20ᴾG, 22³G, 19⁰G, 22⁶G, 19⁵G, 22⁴GF, 22²G, 26⁵S, 19⁴S, 22¹G, 22²G

	Starts	1st	2nd	3rd	Win & Pl
Hurdles	15	1	4	1	6988
Career Total	**24**	**1**	**5**	**2**	**8121**

105	3/02	Winc	2m6f	F(0-100)HHdl	GD	£3402

Total win prize-money £3402

Going: Sf: 0-2 GS: 0-0 Gd: 1-9 GF: - Fm: 0-4
Distance: 2m/2m3: 0-3 **2m4-2m7: 1-11** 3m+: 0-1
Track: LH: 0-7 **RH: 1-6** Tight: 0-8 Gall: 0-0
Aids: Bl: 0-0 Vi: 0-0 Tstrap: 0-0
Best Rating: **107** 3/02 NAbb 2m6f good Hdl

A maiden until getting off the mark in a handicap at Wincanton in March 2002. Stays well and looks best on a sound surface.

Balanak (USA)

106 96

11-y-o b g Shahrastani (USA)-Banque Privee (USA) (Private Account (USA))
D R Gandolfo M A Dore

Placings:11104/400000/351F/5354404/042214203/34/0612 262-22455P **(4572)**
2001/02: 22²HY, 21²GS, 20⁴S, 22⁵S, 21⁵HY, 20ᴾG

	Starts	1st	2nd	3rd	Win & Pl
Hurdles	6	0	2	0	1493
Career Total	**46**	**6**	**8**	**4**	**36323**

96	12/00	Folk	2m6f110y	F(0-105)HHdl	HVY	£1890
111	8/98	Ctml	2m6f	D(0-120)HHdl	G-S	£2878
122	11/96	Wwck	2m3f	B(0-145)HHdl	GD	£5052
127	2/95	Kemp	2m	A Hdl	HVY	£8438
125	1/95	Wind	2m	D Hdl	SFT	£3113
106	1/95	Towc	2m	E Hdl	HVY	£2267

Total win prize-money £23640

Going: Sf: 0-4 GS: 0-1 Gd: 0-1 GF: - Fm: 0-0
Distance: 2m/2m3: 0-0 2m4-2m7: 0-6 3m+: 0-0
Track: LH: 0-2 RH: 0-4 Tight: 0-3 Gall: 0-1
Aids: Bl: 0-0 Vi: 0-0 Tstrap: 0-0
Best Rating: **127** 2/95 Kemp 2m heavy Hdl

Balapour (IRE)

107 135

4-y-o b g Kahyasi-Balaniya (USA) (Diesis)
Patrick O Brady (John M Oxx 16/6) Miss Rita Shah

Placings:51031000423 **(4952a)**
2001/02: 16⁵G, 16¹F, 16⁰YS, 16³S, 16¹Y, 16⁰Y, 16⁰SH, 16⁰HY, 17⁴G, 16²GY, 16³G

	Starts	1st	2nd	3rd	Win & Pl
Hurdles	11	2	1	2	36742
Career Total	**11**	**2**	**1**	**2**	**36742**

119	12/01	Fair	2m	Hdl	YLD	£13104
111	9/01	Fair	2m	Hdl	FRM	£5564

Total win prize-money £18670

Going: Sf: 0-2 GS: 0-0 Gd: 0-3 GF: - Fm: 1-1
Distance: **2m/2m3: 2-11** 2m4-2m7: 0-0 3m+: 0-0
Track: LH: 0-3 **RH: 2-6** Tight: 0-0 Gall: 0-1
Aids: Bl: 0-0 Vi: 0-0 **Tstrap: 2-11**
Best Rating: **135** 4/02 Punc 2m good Hdl

Fair stayer on the Flat. Twice successful over hurdles at two miles, he is tough but hardly an outstanding performer. Finished well into fourth in the Triumph Hurdle. Has won on a sound surface and good to soft.

Balcony Boy

10-y-o b g Palm Track-Energia (Alias Smith (USA))
S R Bolton Mrs Cheryl L Owen

Placings:P/UPP/P/P **(0556)**
2001/02: 24ᴾGF

	Starts	1st	2nd	3rd	Win & Pl
Chases	1	0	0	0	
Career Total	**6**	**0**	**0**	**0**	

Going: Sf: 0-0 GS: 0-0 Gd: 0-0 GF: - Fm: 0-1
Distance: 2m/2m3: 0-0 2m4-2m7: 0-0 3m+: 0-1
Track: LH: 0-0 RH: 0-1 Tight: 0-0 Gall: 0-1
Aids: Bl: 0-0 Vi: 0-0 Tstrap: 0-0
Best Rating:

Baldhu Chance

14-y-o ch g Chaparly (FR)-Galla Currency (Galeopsis)
S P Long Terry Long

Placings:P00/P/P/4/P0P-P **(0563)**
2001/02: 26ᴾGF

	Starts	1st	2nd	3rd	Win & Pl
Chases	1	0	0	0	
Career Total	**10**	**0**	**0**	**0**	**114**

Going: Sf: 0-0 GS: 0-0 Gd: 0-0 GF: - Fm: 0-1
Distance: 2m/2m3: 0-0 2m4-2m7: 0-0 3m+: 0-1
Track: LH: 0-1 RH: 0-0 Tight: 0-1 Gall: 0-0
Aids: Bl: 0-0 Vi: 0-0 Tstrap: 0-0
Best Rating: **100** 3/00 NAbb 2m5f110y good Ch

Bali Strong (IRE)

102 101

8-y-o b g Strong Gale-Greavesfind (The Parson)
Ferdy Murphy Exors Of The Late Mr G A Hubbard

Placings:243662U1/32110646/6-024 **(4747)**
2001/02: 20⁰GS, 24²G, 20⁴G

	Starts	1st	2nd	3rd	Win & Pl
Hurdles	3	0	1	0	766
Career Total	**20**	**3**	**4**	**2**	**13861**

114	11/99	Kemp	3m110y	D(0-120)HHdl	GD	£3485
111	10/99	Plum	3m1f110y	D(0-125)HHdl	G-F	£3187
108	4/99	Hntg	2m5f110y	E(0-115)HHdl	GD	£2722

Total win prize-money £9396

Going: Sf: 0-0 GS: 0-1 Gd: 0-2 GF: - Fm: 0-0
Distance: 2m/2m3: 0-0 2m4-2m7: 0-2 3m+: 0-1
Track: LH: 0-1 RH: 0-1 Tight: 0-0 Gall: 0-0
Aids: Bl: 0-0 Vi: 0-0 Tstrap: 0-3
Best Rating: **114** 11/99 Kemp 3m110y good Hdl

Formerly a fairly useful staying handicap hurdler. Best on a sound surface.

Balisteros (FR)

13-y-o b g Bad Conduct (USA)-Oldburry (FR) (Fin Bon)
Mrs B K Thomson Mrs B K Thomson

Placings:*00*/005FU50/2/35/112/124F4P-2353 **(3916)**
2001/02: 24²GS, 26³G, 28⁵GF, 24³GS

	Starts	1st	2nd	3rd	Win & Pl
Chases	4	0	1	2	2755
Career Total	**25**	**3**	**4**	**3**	**14466**

127	5/00	Uttx	3m2f	H Ch	G-F	£3393
113	3/00	Kels	3m1f	H Ch	G-S	£1960
115	2/00	Sedg	2m5f	H Ch	G-S	£1582

Total win prize-money £6936

Going: Sf: 0-0 GS: 0-2 Gd: 0-1 GF: - Fm: 0-1
Distance: 2m/2m3: 0-0 2m4-2m7: 0-0 3m+: 0-4

Track: LH: 0-2 RH: 0-1 Tight: 0-3 Gall: 0-0
Aids: Bl: 0-0 Vi: 0-0 Tstrap: 0-0
Best Rating: 128 6/00 Strf 3m4f good Ch

He registered 13 wins in point-to-points and hunter chases during 2000, but struggled in 2001. Prone to mistakes (including when tried in a visor), he has looked more like his old self in 2002.

Balkirk

5-y-o ch g Selkirk (USA)-Balenare (Pharly (FR))
Mrs Mary Hambro (R T Phillips 28/1) Richard Hambro

Placings:*006* (4637)
2001/02: 16^{0}GF, 16^{0}S, 20^{6}GF

	Starts	1st	2nd	3rd	Win & Pl
NH Flat	2	0	0	0	0
Hurdles	1	0	0	0	0
Career Total	**3**	**0**	**0**	**0**	**0**

Going: Sf: 0-1 GS: 0-0 Gd: 0-0 GF: - Fm: 0-2
Distance: 2m/2m3: 0-2 2m4-2m7: 0-1 3m+: 0-0
Track: LH: 0-1 RH: 0-2 Tight: 0-0 Gall: 0-0
Aids: Bl: 0-0 Vi: 0-0 Tstrap: 0-0
Best Rating: 48 1/02 Kemp 2m soft NHF

Ball Games

91 72
4-y-o b g Mind Games-Deb's Ball (Glenstal (USA))
D Moffatt Cartmel Bloodstock

Placings:00 (2907)
2001/02: 16^{0}S, 16^{0}GS

	Starts	1st	2nd	3rd	Win & Pl
Hurdles	2	0	0	0	
Career Total	**2**	**0**	**0**	**0**	

Going: Sf: 0-1 GS: 0-1 Gd: 0-0 GF: - Fm: 0-0
Distance: 2m/2m3: 0-2 2m4-2m7: 0-0 3m+: 0-0
Track: LH: 0-2 RH: 0-0 Tight: 0-1 Gall: 0-0
Aids: Bl: 0-0 Vi: 0-0 Tstrap: 0-0
Best Rating: 67 12/01 Weth 2m gd-sft Hdl

Ball In The Net

9-y-o b g Arctic Lord-Courtlands Girl (Crimson Beau)
D Rees (B G Powell 31/5) D A Rees

Placings:*0/04P* (4865)
2001/02: 22^{0}GS, 24^{4}GF, 23^{P}F

	Starts	1st	2nd	3rd	Win & Pl
Hurdles	1	0	0	0	0
Chases	2	0	0	0	0
Career Total	**4**	**0**	**0**	**0**	**0**

Going: Sf: 0-0 GS: 0-1 Gd: 0-0 GF: - Fm: 0-2
Distance: 2m/2m3: 0-0 2m4-2m7: 0-1 3m+: 0-2
Track: LH: 0-0 RH: 0-2 Tight: 0-0 Gall: 0-1
Aids: Bl: 0-0 Vi: 0-0 Tstrap: 0-0
Best Rating: 92 5/01 Hntg 3m gd-fm Ch

Balla D'Aire (IRE)

90 67
7-y-o b/br g Balla Cove-Silius (Junius (USA))
C N Kellett Ms L Whitehorn

Placings:324/P0044/00545P-5 (0192)
2001/02: 24^{5}GF

	Starts	1st	2nd	3rd	Win & Pl
Chases	1	0	0	0	0
Career Total	**15**	**0**	**1**	**1**	**1385**

Going: Sf: 0-0 GS: 0-0 Gd: 0-0 GF: - Fm: 0-1
Distance: 2m/2m3: 0-0 2m4-2m7: 0-0 3m+: 0-1
Track: LH: 0-1 RH: 0-0 Tight: 0-1 Gall: 0-0
Aids: Bl: 0-0 Vi: 0-0 Tstrap: 0-0
Best Rating: 91 2/99 Plum 2m1f gd-sft Hdl

Ballet G

79f 57f
6-y-o ch m Gunner B-Nicolene (Nice Music)
J Neville Gallagher Enterprises Ltd

Placings:*00* (4823)
2001/02: 16^{0}G, 17^{0}G

	Starts	1st	2nd	3rd	Win & Pl
NH Flat	2	0	0	0	
Career Total	**2**	**0**	**0**	**0**	

Going: Sf: 0-0 GS: 0-0 Gd: 0-2 GF: - Fm: 0-0
Distance: 2m/2m3: 0-2 2m4-2m7: 0-0 3m+: 0-0
Track: LH: 0-2 RH: 0-0 Tight: 0-0 Gall: 0-1
Aids: Bl: 0-0 Vi: 0-1 Tstrap: 0-0
Best Rating: 57 4/02 Uttx 2m good NHF

Half-sister to Ballet-K, well held on bumper debut.

Ballet High (IRE)

87 49
9-y-o b g Sadler's Wells (USA)-Marie D'Argonne (FR) (Jefferson)
R Dickin Wholebuild Ltd

Placings:430/P13/0/60-0 (0918)
2001/02: 22^{0}GF

	Starts	1st	2nd	3rd	Win & Pl
Hurdles	1	0	0	0	
Career Total	**10**	**1**	**0**	**2**	**3876**

106	3/99	Chep	2m110y	D Hdl	G-S	£2931

Total win prize-money £2931

Going: Sf: 0-0 GS: 0-0 Gd: 0-0 GF: - Fm: 0-1
Distance: 2m/2m3: 0-0 2m4-2m7: 0-1 3m+: 0-0
Track: LH: 0-1 RH: 0-0 Tight: 0-1 Gall: 0-0
Aids: Bl: 0-1 Vi: 0-0 Tstrap: 0-0
Best Rating: 121 11/97 Newb 2m110y soft Hdl

Ballet Red

85 57
5-y-o b m Sea Raven (IRE)-Cailin Rua (IRE) (Montelimar (USA))
R D Wylie Dennis Patrick Flynn

Placings:*000-024* (1424)
2001/02: 17^{0}GF, 22^{2}GS, 21^{4}G

	Starts	1st	2nd	3rd	Win & Pl
Hurdles	3	0	1	0	1147
Career Total	**6**	**0**	**1**	**0**	**1147**

Going: Sf: 0-0 GS: 0-1 Gd: 0-1 GF: - Fm: 0-1
Distance: 2m/2m3: 0-1 2m4-2m7: 0-2 3m+: 0-0
Track: LH: 0-3 RH: 0-0 Tight: 0-3 Gall: 0-0
Aids: Bl: 0-0 Vi: 0-0 Tstrap: 0-0
Best Rating: 57 9/01 Sedg 2m5f110y good Hdl

Ballet-K

116 147
8-y-o ch m Gunner B-Nicolene (Nice Music)
J Neville Gallagher Enterprises Ltd

Placings:*1115/F*120212/6320-46200P (4193)
2001/02: 23^{4}G, 21^{6}GS, 25^{2}G, 25^{0}S, 22^{0}S, 25^{P}GS

	Starts	1st	2nd	3rd	Win & Pl
Hurdles	6	0	1	0	13438
Career Total	**21**	**5**	**5**	**1**	**42790**

130	4/00	Chep	2m4f	E Hdl	SFT	£2170
129	2/00	Uttx	2m	D Hdl	SFT	£3672
114	2/99	Donc	2m110y	H NHF	G-F	£1514
95	2/99	Ayr	2m	H NHF	SFT	£1464
96	6/98	MRas	1m5f110y	H NHF	G-F	£1308

Total win prize-money £10130

Going: Sf: 0-2 GS: 0-2 Gd: 0-2 GF: - Fm: 0-0
Distance: 2m/2m3: 0-0 2m4-2m7: 0-2 3m+: 0-4
Track: LH: 0-2 RH: 0-3 Tight: 0-1 Gall: 0-1
Aids: Bl: 0-0 Vi: 0-0 Tstrap: 0-0
Best Rating: 150 2/01 Sand 2m6f heavy Hdl

A useful staying handicap hurdler. Stays three miles plus and suited by soft ground. Appeared to run above herself when second in the Long Walk Hurdle in December 2001 but has not run up to that form since.

Ballinclay King (IRE)

97 162
8-y-o b g Asir-Clonroche Artic (Pauper)
Ferdy Murphy I Guise, B Leatherday & N L Spence

Placings:*14/*115102/1314214-04PP (3697)
2001/02: 20^{0}G, 16^{4}G, 16^{P}GS, 17^{P}S

	Starts	1st	2nd	3rd	Win & Pl
Chases	4	0	0	0	684
Career Total	**19**	**7**	**2**	**1**	**77592**

162	4/01	Aint	2m	A Ch	HVY	£46500
154	12/00	Ayr	2m	D Ch	SFT	£3705
155	10/00	Weth	2m	E Ch	G-S	£3206
131	2/00	Ayr	2m4f	E Hdl	HVY	£2747
116	12/99	Hayd	2m	D Hdl	HVY	£3322
122	11/99	Ayr	2m	E Hdl	GD	£2670
130	4/99	Ayr	2m	H NHF	SFT	£3548

Total win prize-money £65700

Going: Sf: 0-1 GS: 0-1 Gd: 0-2 GF: - Fm: 0-0
Distance: 2m/2m3: 0-3 2m4-2m7: 0-1 3m+: 0-0
Track: LH: 0-4 RH: 0-0 Tight: 0-0 Gall: 0-1
Aids: Bl: 0-0 Vi: 0-0 Tstrap: 0-0
Best Rating: 162 4/01 Aint 2m heavy Ch

A decent novice hurdler in 1999/2000 winning three of his six races and running second in the Scottish Champion Hurdle, he switched to fences the following season and added another three victories. His best win was in the Maghull Novices Chase at Aintree, although he has disappointed since then. He is well suited by two miles and soft ground, although he stays further. All his wins have been on flat, left-handed tracks, including four at Ayr. He has given problems at the start on occasions, but is talented nonetheless.

Ballinliss Lad (IRE)

94(79h) 103
9-y-o ch g Bustomi-Sea Shrub (Ballymore)
R Dickin The Classic Chance Partnership

Placings:0/00-34P1PP3 (2205)
2001/02: 19^{3}G, 16^{4}G, 16^{P}S, 20^{1}GF, 20^{P}G, 16^{P}GF, 16^{3}GF

	Starts	1st	2nd	3rd	Win & Pl
Chases	7	1	0	2	5892
Career Total	**10**	**1**	**0**	**2**	**5892**

103	8/01	MRas	2m4f	D Ch	G-F	£4959

Total win prize-money £4960

Going: Sf: 0-1 GS: 0-0 Gd: 0-3 GF: - Fm: 1-3
Distance: 2m/2m3: 0-5 **2m4-2m7: 1-2** 3m+: 0-0
Track: LH: 0-2 **RH: 1-5 Tight: 1-3** Gall: 0-0
Aids: Bl: 0-0 Vi: 0-0 Tstrap: 0-0
Best Rating: **103** 8/01 MRas 2m4f gd-fm Ch

Ballistic Boy

106 **100**

5-y-o ch g First Trump-Be Discreet (Junius (USA))
J J O'Neill A & G Oliver

Placings:2-525211 **(1240)**
2001/02: 16^{5}GF, 16^{2}GS, 16^{5}GF, 19^{2}G, 20^{1}G, 24^{1}GF

	Starts	1st	2nd	3rd	Win & Pl
Hurdles	6	2	2	0	7097
Career Total	**7**	**2**	**3**	**0**	**8167**

100	8/01	Worc	3m	F(0-95)HHdl	G-F	£1946
92	8/01	Bang	2m4f	F(0-105)HHdl	GD	£3688

Total win prize-money £5635

Going: Sf: 0-0 GS: 0-1 **Gd: 1-2** GF: - Fm: 1-3
Distance: 2m/2m3: 0-4 2m4-2m7: 1-1 3m+: 1-1
Track: **LH: 2-6** RH: 0-0 **Tight: 1-5** Gall: 0-0
Aids: Bl: 0-0 Vi: 0-0 Tstrap: 0-0
Best Rating: **100** 8/01 Worc 3m gd-fm Hdl

Ballochan Linn

10-y-o ch g Denel (FR)-Kawarau Queen (Taufan (USA))
A P James The Festival Racing Partnership

Placings:P/2/00P-0 **(0082)**
2001/02: 19^{0}G

	Starts	1st	2nd	3rd	Win & Pl
Chases	1	0	0	0	
Career Total	**6**	**0**	**1**	**0**	**337**

Going: Sf: 0-0 GS: 0-0 Gd: 0-1 GF: - Fm: 0-0
Distance: 2m/2m3: 0-1 2m4-2m7: 0-0 3m+: 0-0
Track: LH: 0-0 RH: 0-1 Tight: 0-0 Gall: 0-0
Aids: Bl: 0-0 Vi: 0-0 Tstrap: 0-1
Best Rating: **70** 5/00 Bang 2m1f good Hdl

Ballon Point (IRE)

12-y-o b g Bulldozer-Trigonella (Balliol)
R H Buckler R H Buckler

Placings:*22223/23/34*PF/6-P0P **(3149)**
2001/02: 25^{P}G, 20^{0}G, 22^{P}G

	Starts	1st	2nd	3rd	Win & Pl
Chases	3	0	0	0	
Career Total	**15**	**0**	**5**	**3**	**5244**

Going: Sf: 0-0 GS: 0-0 Gd: 0-3 GF: - Fm: 0-0
Distance: 2m/2m3: 0-0 2m4-2m7: 0-2 3m+: 0-1
Track: LH: 0-0 RH: 0-1 Tight: 0-2 Gall: 0-0
Aids: Bl: 0-0 Vi: 0-0 Tstrap: 0-0
Best Rating: **107** 7/97 Gway 2m good NHF

Showed good form in bumpers in 1997, but is still a maiden and has shown little over fences.

Bally Lir Lady

100 **76**

8-y-o b m Lir-Ballyorney Girl (New Member)
P R Rodford P R Rodford

Placings:*0540*/P-F363056 **(1846)**
2001/02: 21^{F}GF, 16^{3}S, 16^{6}GF, 20^{3}GF, 18^{0}GF, 22^{5}GF, 22^{6}G

	Starts	1st	2nd	3rd	Win & Pl
Hurdles	6	0	0	2	642
Chases	1	0	0	0	0
Career Total	**12**	**0**	**0**	**2**	**642**

Going: Sf: 0-1 GS: 0-0 Gd: 0-1 GF: - Fm: 0-5
Distance: 2m/2m3: 0-3 2m4-2m7: 0-4 3m+: 0-0
Track: LH: 0-5 RH: 0-1 Tight: 0-2 Gall: 0-0
Aids: Bl: 0-0 Vi: 0-0 Tstrap: 0-0
Best Rating: **76** 8/01 Worc 2m4f gd-fm Hdl

Bally Lira

99 **119**

10-y-o b m Lir-Ballyorney Girl (New Member)
P R Rodford Victor Thorne

Placings:*633045521*/**24P36541U33/6343P242/322635101-65U0356** **(4049)**
2001/02: 25^{6}F, 24^{5}GS, 32^{U}GS, 29^{0}GS, 25^{3}GS, 25^{5}HY, 30^{6}G

	Starts	1st	2nd	3rd	Win & Pl
Chases	7	0	0	1	1320
Career Total	**44**	**4**	**6**	**10**	**32689**

119	4/01	Extr	3m1f110y	E(0-115)HCh	SFT	£4355
119	3/01	Wwck	3m2f	F(0-100)HCh	HVY	£2786
103	3/99	Chep	3m	D Ch	HVY	£3870
89	3/98	Extr	3m2f	D(0-125)HHdl	G-S	£3353

Total win prize-money £14364

Going: Sf: 0-1 GS: 0-4 Gd: 0-1 GF: - Fm: 0-1
Distance: 2m/2m3: 0-0 2m4-2m7: 0-0 3m+: 0-7
Track: LH: 0-2 RH: 0-2 Tight: 0-0 Gall: 0-0
Aids: Bl: 0-0 Vi: 0-0 Tstrap: 0-0
Best Rating: **119** 4/01 Extr 3m1f110y soft Ch

She stays forever, but is painfully slow and would ideally like five miles in treacle. She managed a couple of wins early in 2001 when she was able to take advantage of the leaders falling in a heap, although she has been held since then.

Bally's Heart

60 **23**

6-y-o b g Ballacashtal (CAN)-Wilhemina Crusty (Jester)
Dr P Pritchard Three Of A Kind Racing

Placings:P-00PP **(3863)**
2001/02: 16^{0}G, 21^{0}G, 20^{P}HY, 21^{P}GS

	Starts	1st	2nd	3rd	Win & Pl
Hurdles	4	0	0	0	
Career Total	**5**	**0**	**0**	**0**	

Going: Sf: 0-1 GS: 0-1 Gd: 0-2 GF: - Fm: 0-0
Distance: 2m/2m3: 0-1 2m4-2m7: 0-3 3m+: 0-0
Track: LH: 0-2 RH: 0-2 Tight: 0-0 Gall: 0-1
Aids: Bl: 0-0 Vi: 0-0 Tstrap: 0-0
Best Rating: **23** 10/01 Winc 2m good Hdl

Ballyamber (IRE)

104 (134c)**136**

7-y-o b g Glacial Storm (USA)-El Scarsdale (Furry Glen)
W P Mullins David Doane

Placings:*410/16*-42311500 **(4944a)**
2001/02: 22^{4}Y, 22^{2}Y, 16^{3}Y, 24^{1}YS, 24^{1}S, 21^{5}GS, 24^{0}G, 20^{0}G

	Starts	1st	2nd	3rd	Win & Pl
Hurdles	5	2	0	0	23765
Chases	3	0	1	1	3911
Career Total	**13**	**4**	**1**	**1**	**36777**

136	2/02	Fair	3m	HHdl	SFT	£15950
127	12/01	Punc	3m	Hdl	Y-S	£5564
115	5/00	Punc	2m	NHF	GD	£5520
118	1/00	Naas	2m3f	NHF	SH	£3312

Total win prize-money £30348

Going: Sf: 1-1 GS: 0-1 Gd: 0-2 GF: - Fm: 0-0
Distance: 2m/2m3: 0-1 2m4-2m7: 0-4 **3m+: 2-3**
Track: LH: 0-2 **RH: 2-4** Tight: 0-1 Gall: 0-1
Aids: Bl: 0-0 Vi: 0-0 Tstrap: 0-0
Best Rating: **136** 3/02 Chel 2m5f gd-sft Hdl

Useful Irish novice hurdler, stays three miles and is suited by soft ground.

Ballybentragh (IRE)

107 **104**

8-y-o b g Over The River (FR)-Ballymas (Martinmas)
S Dow (O Sherwood 28/5) The Ballybentragh Partnership

Placings:0P0P/314P-PP622PPP **(4783)**
2001/02: 24^{P}F, 24^{P}GF, 20^{6}GF, 25^{2}G, 25^{2}G, 24^{P}G, 25^{P}GS, 29^{P}GF

	Starts	1st	2nd	3rd	Win & Pl
Chases	8	0	2	0	2706
Career Total	**16**	**1**	**2**	**1**	**6580**

100	10/00	Font	2m6f	F(0-95)HCh	GD	£2821

Total win prize-money £2821

Going: Sf: 0-0 GS: 0-1 Gd: 0-3 GF: - Fm: 0-4
Distance: 2m/2m3: 0-0 2m4-2m7: 0-1 3m+: 0-7
Track: LH: 0-1 RH: 0-5 Tight: 0-4 Gall: 0-1
Aids: Bl: 0-1 Vi: 0-0 Tstrap: 0-0
Best Rating: **104** 10/01 Aint 3m1f good Ch

Modest staying chaser, runner-up at Towcester and Aintree in October. Suited by good ground.

Ballybough Rasher (IRE)

111(102h) (108h)**135**

7-y-o b g Broken Hearted-Chat Her Up (Proverb)
J Howard Johnson Comtake-Welding Engineering Specialists

Placings:0001-1F121PP **(4835)**
2001/02: 24^{1}GF, 25^{F}G, 25^{1}G, 25^{2}GS, 24^{1}G, 25^{P}G, 25^{P}G

	Starts	1st	2nd	3rd	Win & Pl
Hurdles	1	1	0	0	2232
Chases	6	2	1	0	14796
Career Total	**11**	**4**	**1**	**0**	**19029**

135	1/02	Donc	3m	D Ch	GD	£4273
132	10/01	Aint	3m1f	C Ch	GD	£7252
108	5/01	Hexm	3m	F(0-100)HHdl	G-F	£2231
100	2/01	Catt	3m1f110y	F(0-100)HHdl	SFT	£2002

Total win prize-money £15760

Going: Sf: 0-0 GS: 0-1 **Gd: 2-5** GF: - Fm: 1-1
Distance: 2m/2m3: 0-0 2m4-2m7: 0-0 **3m+: 3-7**
Track: **LH: 3-7** RH: 0-0 Tight: 1-4 Gall: 1-1
Aids: Bl: 0-0 Vi: 0-0 Tstrap: 0-0
Best Rating: **135** 1/02 Donc 3m good Ch

Progressing well over fences, he stays three miles and is effective on good ground. Usually held up.

Ballycassidy (IRE)

109 131

6-y-o br g Insan (USA)-Bitofabreeze (IRE) (Callernish)

A King C G Clarke,G C Mordaunt,Hon D Whitfield

Placings:2233-111F2310 **(4665)**

2001/02: 26^{1}G, 22^{1}G, 27^{1}GF, 24^{F}G, 24^{2}G, 24^{3}G, 26^{1}GS, 24^{0}G

	Starts	1st	2nd	3rd	Win & Pl
Hurdles	8	4	1	1	26632
Career Total	**12**	**4**	**3**	**3**	**29589**

131	1/02	Hntg	3m2f	A Hdl	G-S	£12127
129	6/01	Strf	3m3f	D(0-125)HHdl	G-F	£3666
122	5/01	Strf	2m6f110y	D Hdl	GD	£3900
108	5/01	Hrfd	3m2f	E Hdl	GD	£2800

Total win prize-money £22494

Going: Sf: 0-0 GS: 1-1 Gd: 2-6 GF: - Fm: 1-1
Distance: 2m/2m3: 0-0 2m4-2m7: 1-1 **3m+: 3-7**
Track: LH: 2-4 RH: 2-4 **Tight: 2-4** Gall: 1-1
Aids: Bl: 0-0 Vi: 0-0 Tstrap: 0-0
Best Rating: 131 1/02 Hntg 3m2f gd-sft Hdl

A winning point-to-pointer in Ireland, he went from strength to strength to score a hat-trick in the summer of 2001 and has run well since, including when successful at Huntingdon in January 2002. He handles fast ground but acts on soft. Stays three and a half miles.

Ballydavid (IRE)

72 48

10-y-o br g Lord Americo-Arctic Bavard (Le Bavard (FR))

G M Moore Mrs Alurie O'Sullivan

Placings:300/405PP/5 **(4668)**

2001/02: 17^{5}GF

	Starts	1st	2nd	3rd	Win & Pl
Hurdles	1	0	0	0	0
Career Total	**9**	**0**	**0**	**1**	**350**

Going: Sf: 0-0 GS: 0-0 Gd: 0-0 GF: - Fm: 0-1
Distance: 2m/2m3: 0-1 2m4-2m7: 0-0 3m+: 0-0
Track: LH: 0-1 RH: 0-0 Tight: 0-1 Gall: 0-0
Aids: Bl: 0-0 Vi: 0-0 Tstrap: 0-0
Best Rating: 88 2/98 Sedg 2m5f110y good Hdl

Moderate hurdler, returned from three year absence in April 2002.

Ballydonnelly (IRE)

102 (61h)100

10-y-o br g Be My Native (USA)-Madam Milan (Milan)

David M O'Brien G Thomson

Placings:*1F/20/03F300401* **(1628)**

2001/02: 17^{0}GF, 18^{3}G, 20^{F}G, 17^{3}F, 20^{0}G, 16^{0}GF, 16^{4}G, 19^{0}GF, 20^{1}GF

	Starts	1st	2nd	3rd	Win & Pl
Hurdles	1	0	0	0	0
Chases	8	1	0	2	4744
Career Total	**13**	**2**	**1**	**2**	**8141**

100	10/01	Ludl	2m4f	E Ch	G-F	£3376
97	12/97	Clon	2m	NHF	HVY	£2712

Total win prize-money £6090

Going: Sf: 0-0 GS: 0-0 Gd: 0-4 GF: - Fm: 1-5
Distance: 2m/2m3: 0-6 **2m4-2m7: 1-3** 3m+: 0-0
Track: LH: 0-0 **RH: 1-1 Tight: 1-1** Gall: 0-0
Aids: Bl: 0-0 Vi: 0-0 Tstrap: 0-1
Best Rating: 103 7/98 Kiny 2m1f gd-fm NHF

Ballyduff Bay (IRE)

74 43

7-y-o b g Jolly Jake (NZ)-Loughrealt (Carlingford Castle)

M Sheppard Simon Gegg

Placings:000P-0 **(0666)**

2001/02: 20^{0}G

	Starts	1st	2nd	3rd	Win & Pl
Hurdles	1	0	0	0	
Career Total	**5**	**0**	**0**	**0**	

Going: Sf: 0-0 GS: 0-0 Gd: 0-1 GF: - Fm: 0-0
Distance: 2m/2m3: 0-0 2m4-2m7: 0-1 3m+: 0-0
Track: LH: 0-1 RH: 0-0 Tight: 0-0 Gall: 0-0
Aids: Bl: 0-0 Vi: 0-0 Tstrap: 0-0
Best Rating: 69 9/00 Chep 2m110y good Hdl

Ballyea Boy (IRE)

12-y-o gr g Sandalay-Nesford (Walshford)

J W Mullins Miss Suzannah Cotterill

Placings:*224345/223204/***116502/52FP/U4P/RR-5F** **(0256)**

2001/02: 26^{5}G, 28^{F}GF

	Starts	1st	2nd	3rd	Win & Pl
Chases	2	0	0	0	0
Career Total	**29**	**2**	**7**	**2**	**15116**

122	12/96	Extr	2m7f110y	D(0-120)HCh	GD	£4192
109	11/96	Towc	3m1f	D(0-125)HCh	GD	£3738

Total win prize-money £7930

Going: Sf: 0-0 GS: 0-0 Gd: 0-1 GF: - Fm: 0-1
Distance: 2m/2m3: 0-0 2m4-2m7: 0-0 3m+: 0-2
Track: LH: 0-1 RH: 0-1 Tight: 0-2 Gall: 0-0
Aids: Bl: 0-0 Vi: 0-2 Tstrap: 0-0
Best Rating: 126 10/98 Winc 3m1f110y gd-sft Ch

Ballygarvan (IRE)

101(105h) (93h)142

7-y-o gr g King Luthier-Lackengarra Wood (Prince Regent (FR))

Ferdy Murphy Jobs Racing

Placings:*550520/242-31* **(1722)**

2001/02: 20^{3}G, 25^{1}G

	Starts	1st	2nd	3rd	Win & Pl
Hurdles	1	0	0	1	556
Chases	1	1	0	0	2288
Career Total	**11**	**1**	**3**	**1**	**5095**

142	10/01	Weth	3m1f	F Ch	GD	£2288

Total win prize-money £2288

Going: Sf: 0-0 GS: 0-0 Gd: 1-2 GF: - Fm: 0-0
Distance: 2m/2m3: 0-0 2m4-2m7: 0-1 **3m+: 1-1**
Track: **LH: 1-1** RH: 0-1 Tight: 0-0 Gall: 0-1
Aids: Bl: 0-0 Vi: 0-0 Tstrap: 0-0
Best Rating: 142 10/01 Weth 3m1f good Ch

Ballygobackwards (IRE)

99 75

10-y-o b g Lord Americo-Bargy Fancy (Crash Course)

C T Pogson C T Pogson

Placings:34432043/PU3P4PP40-PP0P0P20 **(4917)**

2001/02: 21^{P}G, 24^{P}GF, 20^{0}F, 23^{P}GS, 17^{0}S, 24^{P}HY, 16^{2}GF, 21^{0}GF

	Starts	1st	2nd	3rd	Win & Pl
Hurdles	7	0	1	0	762
Chases	1	0	0	0	0
Career Total	**25**	**0**	**2**	**4**	**4989**

Going: Sf: 0-2 GS: 0-1 Gd: 0-1 GF: - Fm: 0-4
Distance: 2m/2m3: 0-2 2m4-2m7: 0-4 3m+: 0-2
Track: LH: 0-8 RH: 0-0 Tight: 0-5 Gall: 0-0
Aids: Bl: 0-2 Vi: 0-0 Tstrap: 0-0
Best Rating: 98 1/00 Sthl 2m gd-sft Ch

Still a maiden. Suited by fast ground.

Ballygriffin Lad (IRE)

101(81h) (90h)103

13-y-o ch g Carlingford Castle-Calfstown Night (Bargello)

T P McGovern Anthony O'Gorman

Placings:0PP405/**PP5611F/1F33U1/P0-053R21** **(3813)**

2001/02: 24^{0}GF, 28^{5}GF, 25^{3}S, 26^{R}S, 22^{2}HY, 21^{1}S

	Starts	1st	2nd	3rd	Win & Pl
Chases	6	1	1	1	4899
Career Total	**27**	**5**	**1**	**3**	**17299**

103	2/02	Folk	2m5f	F(0-90)HCh	SFT	£3423
107	4/00	Towc	3m1f	F(0-100)HCh	GD	£3911
107	12/99	Plum	2m5f	E Hdl	HVY	£2040
95	3/98	Plum	3m1f110y	F(0-100)HCh	SFT	£2467
107	3/98	Hntg	3m	F(0-100)HCh	SFT	£3001

Total win prize-money £14843

Going: Sf: 1-4 GS: 0-0 Gd: 0-0 GF: - Fm: 0-2
Distance: 2m/2m3: 0-0 **2m4-2m7: 1-2** 3m+: 0-4
Track: LH: 0-2 **RH: 1-2 Tight: 1-4** Gall: 0-0
Aids: Bl: 0-0 Vi: 0-0 Tstrap: 0-0
Best Rating: 107 4/00 Towc 3m1f good Ch

Lightly-raced consistent handicap chaser, he is a real fighter who is suited by testing ground. Stays three miles.

Ballyhackamore (IRE)

8-y-o b g Insan (USA)-Augustaeliza (IRE) (Callernish)

Miss E J Baker Mrs M J Arnold

Placings:P-P **(0090)**

2001/02: 25^{P}S

	Starts	1st	2nd	3rd	Win & Pl
Chases	1	0	0	0	
Career Total	**2**	**0**	**0**	**0**	

Going: Sf: 0-1 GS: 0-0 Gd: 0-0 GF: - Fm: 0-0
Distance: 2m/2m3: 0-0 2m4-2m7: 0-0 3m+: 0-1
Track: LH: 0-1 RH: 0-0 Tight: 0-0 Gall: 0-0
Aids: Bl: 0-0 Vi: 0-0 Tstrap: 0-0
Best Rating:

Ballyhampshire Boy (IRE)

120 152

6-y-o b g Husyan (USA)-Dante's Ville (IRE) (Phardante (FR))

Sean Aherne Kilmeadan Racing Syndicate

Placings:*311114B2* **(4940a)**

2001/02: 18^{3}G, 16^{1}G, 16^{1}SH, 16^{1}Y, 16^{1}S, 16^{4}Y, 21^{B}GS, 16^{2}Y

	Starts	1st	2nd	3rd	Win & Pl
NH Flat	3	2	0	1	10750
Hurdles	5	2	1	0	25352
Career Total	**8**	**4**	**1**	**1**	**36102**

142 12/01 Punc 2m Hdl SFT £8911
132 12/01 Fair 2m Hdl YLD £5564
125 10/01 Gway 2m NHF SH £5564
113 10/01 Gowr 2m NHF GD £4451
Total win prize-money £24493

Going: Sf: 1-1 GS: 0-1 Gd: 1-2 GF: - Fm: 0-0
Distance: **2m/2m3: 4-7** 2m4-2m7: 0-1 3m+: 0-0
Track: LH: 0-2 **RH: 2-3** Tight: 0-0 Gall: 0-1
Aids: Bl: 0-0 Vi: 0-0 Tstrap: 0-0
Best Rating: **152** 4/02 Punc 2m yield Hdl

Dual bumper winner, he scored on his first two starts over hurdles before his limitations were exposed in better company. He is suited by cut.

Ballyhand

61f **63f**

5-y-o b g Nearly A Hand-Ballynora (Ballacashtal (CAN))
R H Alner Sir Richard Sutton

Placings:*0* **(1093)**
2001/02: 16^{0}GF

	Starts	1st	2nd	3rd	Win & Pl
NH Flat	1	0	0	0	
Career Total	**1**	**0**	**0**	**0**	

Going: Sf: 0-0 GS: 0-0 Gd: 0-0 GF: - Fm: 0-1
Distance: 2m/2m3: 0-1 2m4-2m7: 0-0 3m+: 0-0
Track: LH: 0-1 RH: 0-0 Tight: 0 0 Gall: 0-0
Aids: Bl: 0-0 Vi: 0-0 Tstrap: 0-0
Best Rating: **63** 8/01 Worc 2m gd-fm NHF

Ballyhannon (IRE)

13-y-o b g Strong Gale-Chestnut Fire (Deep Run)
R Hollinshead (E W Froggatt 1/6) E W Froggatt

Placings:*52005*/**U/P5-UUPPP** **(0972)**
2001/02: 24^{U}GF, 24^{U}GF, 23^{P}GF, 25^{P}GF, 24^{P}GF

	Starts	1st	2nd	3rd	Win & Pl
Hurdles	1	0	0	0	0
Chases	4	0	0	0	0
Career Total	**13**	**0**	**1**	**0**	**482**

Going: Sf: 0-0 GS: 0-0 Gd: 0-0 GF: - Fm: 0-5
Distance: 2m/2m3: 0-0 2m4-2m7: 0-0 3m+: 0-5
Track: LH: 0-5 RH: 0-0 Tight: 0-4 Gall: 0-0
Aids: Bl: 0-0 Vi: 0-0 Tstrap: 0-0
Best Rating: **78** 10/94 Tipp 2m soft NHF

Ballyharry (IRE)

12-y-o b g Phardante (FR)-Oakville Lady (Menelek)
P Grindey Manton Hire Ltd

Placings:5P2603/PP3/**FP-P** **(0358)**
2001/02: 24^{P}GS

	Starts	1st	2nd	3rd	Win & Pl
Chases	1	0	0	0	
Career Total	**12**	**0**	**1**	**2**	**1243**

Going: Sf: 0-0 GS: 0-1 Gd: 0-0 GF: - Fm: 0-0
Distance: 2m/2m3: 0-0 2m4-2m7: 0-0 3m+: 0-1
Track: LH: 0-1 RH: 0-0 Tight: 0-1 Gall: 0-0
Aids: Bl: 0-0 Vi: 0-0 Tstrap: 0-0
Best Rating: **80** 1/98 Ling 2m7f gd-sft Hdl

Ballykissann

99 **67**

7-y-o ch g Ballacashtal (CAN)-Mybella Ann (Anfield)
J C Tuck Paul De Weck

Placings:P02P0P/604640P/0-00000300 **(3334)**
2001/02: 17^{0}G, 17^{0}GF, 17^{0}GF, 16^{0}GF, 19^{0}GF, 19^{3}F, 20^{0}GS, 16^{0}G

	Starts	1st	2nd	3rd	Win & Pl
Hurdles	8	0	0	1	242
Career Total	**22**	**0**	**1**	**1**	**675**

Going: Sf: 0-0 GS: 0-1 Gd: 0-2 GF: - Fm: 0-5
Distance: 2m/2m3: 0-6 2m4-2m7: 0-2 3m+: 0-0
Track: LH: 0-4 RH: 0-3 Tight: 0-5 Gall: 0-0
Aids: Bl: 0-0 Vi: 0-0 Tstrap: 0-0
Best Rating: **75** 11/98 Tntn 2m1f good Hdl

Ballyline (IRE)

110 **102**

11-y-o b g Electric-Miss Dikler (Tepukei)
B G Powell The 49 Partnership

Placings:F20122F23PP24/F1234612B/F321025P330/P062 P0/35245 **(4497)**
2001/02: 25^{3}G, 24^{5}G, 25^{2}GS, 24^{4}GS, 24^{5}G

	Starts	1st	2nd	3rd	Win & Pl
Chases	5	0	1	1	2458
Career Total	**44**	**4**	**11**	**6**	**40146**

126 10/98 Worc 2m7f110y C(0-135)HCh GD £4796
119 3/98 Uttx 2m5f C(0-135)HCh GD £7132
113 11/97 Kels 2m6f110y C(0-135)HCh GD £5158
88 10/96 Weth 2m D(0-105)HCh GD £3561
Total win prize-money £20648

Going: Sf: 0-0 GS: 0-2 Gd: 0-3 GF: - Fm: 0-0
Distance: 2m/2m3: 0-0 2m4-2m7: 0-0 3m+: 0-5
Track: LH: 0-5 RH: 0-0 Tight: 0-1 Gall: 0-1
Aids: Bl: 0-0 Vi: 0-0 Tstrap: 0-0
Best Rating: **126** 10/98 Worc 2m7f110y good Ch

A front-running chaser. Having his first run for a year and a half when third at Wetherby in November 2001 and has run fairly well since, but has not won since October 1998. Best on good ground. Stays three miles.

Ballymaloe Boy (IRE)

9-y-o b g Cataldi-Tartan Sash (Crofter (USA))
Graham Richards Graham Richards

Placings:543/16065/50 **(0428)**
2001/02: 20^{5}GF, 21^{0}G

	Starts	1st	2nd	3rd	Win & Pl
Chases	2	0	0	0	0
Career Total	**10**	**1**	**0**	**1**	**3477**

92 5/99 Uttx 2m7f E Ch GD £2840
Total win prize-money £2840

Going: Sf: 0-0 GS: 0-0 Gd: 0-1 GF: - Fm: 0-1
Distance: 2m/2m3: 0-0 2m4-2m7: 0-2 3m+: 0-0
Track: LH: 0-1 RH: 0-0 Tight: 0-0 Gall: 0-0
Aids: Bl: 0-0 Vi: 0-0 Tstrap: 0-0
Best Rating: **92** 5/99 Uttx 2m7f good Ch

Ballymenagh (IRE)

10-y-o br g Buckskin (FR)-Breeze Dancer (Torus)
K Robson (J Barclay 27/10) Mrs M Armstrong

Placings:*02001*PF00/60**54P**0/003 **(4859)**
2001/02: 20^{0}GS, 20^{0}S, 25^{3}G

	Starts	1st	2nd	3rd	Win & Pl
Hurdles	2	0	0	0	0
Chases	1	0	0	1	241
Career Total	**18**	**1**	**1**	**1**	**2078**

92 8/98 Dpat 2m1f172y NHF G-F £1494
Total win prize-money £1495

Going: Sf: 0-1 GS: 0-1 Gd: 0-1 GF: - Fm: 0-0
Distance: 2m/2m3: 0-0 2m4-2m7: 0-2 3m+: 0-1
Track: LH: 0-1 RH: 0-0 Tight: 0-0 Gall: 0-0
Aids: Bl: 0-0 Vi: 0-0 Tstrap: 0-0
Best Rating: **92** 8/98 Dpat 2m1f172y gd-fm NHF

Modest pointer/hunter chaser. Stays well but not the best of jumpers.

Ballymore Rover (IRE)

(83h) (59h)

8-y-o b g Euphemism-Tots Paradise (Roi Guillaume (FR))
O Brennan O Brennan

Placings:*45606*-0U0 **(3993)**
2001/02: 16^{0}GF, 23^{U}G, 20^{0}S

	Starts	1st	2nd	3rd	Win & Pl
Hurdles	3	0	0	0	
Career Total	**8**	**0**	**0**	**0**	**0**

Going: Sf: 0-1 GS: 0-0 Gd: 0-1 GF: - Fm: 0-1
Distance: 2m/2m3: 0-1 2m4-2m7: 0-2 3m+: 0-0
Track: LH: 0-3 RH: 0-0 Tight: 0-0 Gall: 0-1
Aids: Bl: 0-0 Vi: 0-0 Tstrap: 0-0
Best Rating: **97** 5/00 Worc 2m good NHF

Ballynabragget (IRE)

103

9-y-o ch g Zaffaran (USA)-Dalaray (Dalesa)
N A Twiston-Davies The Double Octagon Partnership

Placings:*20443320*/2110116/**F2216P15-P** **(0041)**
2001/02: 23^{P}GS

	Starts	1st	2nd	3rd	Win & Pl
Chases	1	0	0	0	
Career Total	**24**	**6**	**5**	**2**	**25970**

136 3/01 Ling 3m D Ch HVY £4017
136 11/00 Newb 2m6f110y D Ch SFT £5264
129 4/00 Towc 3m E Hdl GD £3007
126 3/00 Newb 3m110y D Hdl SFT £3932
112 10/99 Extr 2m6f E Hdl GD £2542
119 10/99 Extr 2m6f F(0-100)HHdl GD £2430
Total win prize-money £21193

Going: Sf: 0-0 GS: 0-1 Gd: 0-0 GF: - Fm: 0-0
Distance: 2m/2m3: 0-0 2m4-2m7: 0-0 3m+: 0-1
Track: LH: 0-0 RH: 0-1 Tight: 0-0 Gall: 0-0
Aids: Bl: 0-0 Vi: 0-0 Tstrap: 0-1
Best Rating: **136** 3/01 Ling 3m heavy Ch

A progressive staying hurdler in 1999/2000, he did not fulfil expectations in novice chases (won two weak events), often ruining his chance with sloppy jumping. Absent since pulling up in May 2001, he is best on left handed tracks, he is capable of better and can win a decent long distance handicap from his current mark.

Ballynattin Blue (IRE)

99 **116**

9-y-o ch g Good Thyne (USA)-Ballynattin Moss (Le Moss)
J N R Billinge Sceptre House Golf Society

Placings:505412/410P4-14P6 **(4834)**
2001/02: 24^{1}G, 22^{4}S, 24^{P}S, 22^{6}G

	Starts	1st	2nd	3rd	Win & Pl
Hurdles	4	1	0	0	7504
Career Total	**15**	**3**	**1**	**0**	**15074**

116	10/01	Aint	3m110y	C(0-135)HHdl	GD	£6870
111	1/01	Ayr	3m110y	F(0-100)HHdl	SFT	£3094
102	3/00	Kels	2m6f110y	E Hdl	G-S	£2044

Total win prize-money £12009

Going: Sf: 0-2 GS: 0-0 Gd: 1-2 GF: - Fm: 0-0
Distance: 2m/2m3: 0-0 2m4-2m7: 0-2 **3m+: 1-2**
Track: **LH: 1-4** RH: 0-0 **Tight: 1-1** Gall: 0-1
Aids: Bl: 0-0 Vi: 0-0 Tstrap: 0-0
Best Rating: **116** 10/01 Aint 3m110y good Hdl

He stays three miles over hurdles and acts on good and soft ground. Suited by racing prominently and a left-handed galloping track.

Ballyquintet (IRE)

11-y-o ch m Orchestra-Ollie's Pet (Tiepolo Ii)
H B Hodge A H B Hodge

Placings:0/00P/P4U **(0592)**
2001/02: 26^{P}G, 25^{4}GF, 21^{U}GF

	Starts	1st	2nd	3rd	Win & Pl
Chases	3	0	0	0	244
Career Total	**7**	**0**	**0**	**0**	**244**

Going: Sf: 0-0 GS: 0-0 Gd: 0-1 GF: - Fm: 0-2
Distance: 2m/2m3: 0-0 2m4-2m7: 0-1 3m+: 0-2
Track: LH: 0-1 RH: 0-2 Tight: 0-3 Gall: 0-0
Aids: Bl: 0-0 Vi: 0-0 Tstrap: 0-0
Best Rating:

Ballysicyos (FR)

105(97c) (130c)**142**

7-y-o b g Nikos-Bally Duke (FR) (Iron Duke (FR))
M C Pipe Mrs P A Deal

Placings:FFF304152/240/11F0U6-1P665163 **(4821)**
2001/02: 25^{1}F, 22^{P}S, 24^{6}GS, 22^{6}G, 25^{5}HY, 25^{1}S, 25^{6}GS, 24^{3}G

	Starts	1st	2nd	3rd	Win & Pl
Hurdles	7	1	0	1	6873
Chases	1	1	0	0	4680
Career Total	**26**	**5**	**2**	**2**	**37857**

142	2/02	Wwck	3m1f	D(0-125)HHdl	SFT	£5200
130	5/01	Extr	3m1f110y	E(0-115)HCh	FRM	£4680
136	11/00	Plum	2m4f	D Ch	SFT	£3948
142	10/00	Strf	2m3f	C(0-135)HHdl	SFT	£5118
114	2/99	Ludl	2m	E Hdl	GD	£2038

Total win prize-money £20986

Going: Sf: 1-3 GS: 0-2 Gd: 0-2 GF: - Fm: 1-1
Distance: 2m/2m3: 0-0 2m4-2m7: 0-2 **3m+: 2-6**
Track: LH: 0-3 RH: 0-1 Tight: 0-1 Gall: 0-1
Aids: Bl: 0-0 Vi: 0-0 Tstrap: 0-0
Best Rating: **142** 2/02 Wwck 3m1f soft Hdl

A smart staying hurdler. Made a winning debut over fences at Plumpton in November 2000, but struggled in novice chases on bad ground afterwards. Won back on fast ground at the beginning of 2001 season, but reverted to hurdles subsequently and was on his best behaviour when winning at Warwick in February 2002 and ran a fair race at Cheltenham in March, but was just outclassed. Stays three miles plus and has won on fast ground and soft.

Ballystone (IRE)

106 **133**

9-y-o ch g Roselier (FR)-Gusserane Princess (Paddy's Stream)
L Lungo A W Duncan And S E Constable

Placings:266F2/1121P-2U10 **(4831)**
2001/02: 26^{2}S, 29^{U}S, 25^{1}G, 20^{0}G

	Starts	1st	2nd	3rd	Win & Pl
Chases	4	1	1	0	7112
Career Total	**14**	**4**	**4**	**0**	**22456**

133	12/01	Catt	3m1f110y	D(0-120)HCh	GD	£4982
132	2/01	Carl	3m2f	D(0-125)HCh	SFT	£4270
132	11/00	Newc	3m	D Ch	SFT	£4580
127	11/00	Ayr	2m5f110y	D(0-110)HCh	SFT	£3861

Total win prize-money £17694

Going: Sf: 0-2 GS: 0-0 Gd: 1-2 GF: - Fm: 0-0
Distance: 2m/2m3: 0-0 2m4-2m7: 0-1 **3m+: 1-3**
Track: **LH: 1-3** RH: 0-1 **Tight: 1-1** Gall: 0-0
Aids: Bl: 0-0 Vi: 0-0 Tstrap: 0-0
Best Rating: **133** 12/01 Catt 3m1f110y good Ch

Much improved over fences, he does nothing but jump and stay. Stays three and a quarter miles. Has won on soft ground and good.

Ballyvaddy (IRE)

99(76c) (102c)**100**

6-y-o gr g Roselier (FR)-Bodalmore Kit (Bargello)
G B Balding Lady Wates (london)

Placings:0-4UP312 **(4817)**
2001/02: 20^{4}GS, 22^{U}GS, 22^{P}G, 20^{3}GS, 22^{1}G, 24^{2}GF

	Starts	1st	2nd	3rd	Win & Pl
Hurdles	3	1	1	1	6591
Chases	3	0	0	0	237
Career Total	**7**	**1**	**1**	**1**	**6828**

96	4/02	Winc	2m6f	E(0-105)HHdl	GD	£3458

Total win prize-money £3458

Going: Sf: 0-0 GS: 0-3 Gd: 1-2 GF: - Fm: 0-1
Distance: 2m/2m3: 0-0 **2m4-2m7: 1-5** 3m+: 0-1
Track: LH: 0-1 **RH: 1-2** Tight: 0-2 Gall: 0-2
Aids: Bl: 0-0 **Vi: 1-2** Tstrap: 0-0
Best Rating: **102** 10/01 Font 2m4f gd-sft Ch

Lightly-raced, well held over fences in 2001/2, but broke his duck over jumps in a modest hurdle in April. Good effort next time.

Ballyvaughan (IRE)

(80h)

12-y-o ch g Carlingford Castle-Fahy Quay (Quayside)
E A Elliott Mrs Anne E Elliott

Placings:56/2/30/423/S331/51F-P **(2448)**
2001/02: 30^{P}GS

	Starts	1st	2nd	3rd	Win & Pl
Chases	1	0	0	0	
Career Total	**16**	**2**	**2**	**4**	**12828**

117	2/01	Kels	2m6f110y	E(0-115)HCh	SFT	£3575
117	12/99	Sthl	3m110y	E Ch	SFT	£4650

Total win prize-money £8225

Going: Sf: 0-0 GS: 0-1 Gd: 0-0 GF: - Fm: 0-0
Distance: 2m/2m3: 0-0 2m4-2m7: 0-0 3m+: 0-1
Track: LH: 0-1 RH: 0-0 Tight: 0-0 Gall: 0-1
Aids: Bl: 0-0 Vi: 0-0 Tstrap: 0-0
Best Rating: **117** 2/01 Kels 2m6f110y soft Ch

Best on good ground or softer.

Balmoral Spring (IRE)

101 **67**

9-y-o b g Royal Fountain-The Best I Can (Derring Rose)
C R Millington C R Millington

Placings:006/30/400P **(4590)**
2001/02: 19^{4}G, 22^{0}S, 24^{0}GS, 24^{P}G

	Starts	1st	2nd	3rd	Win & Pl
Chases	4	0	0	0	336
Career Total	**9**	**0**	**0**	**1**	**537**

Going: Sf: 0-1 GS: 0-1 Gd: 0-2 GF: - Fm: 0-0
Distance: 2m/2m3: 0-0 2m4-2m7: 0-2 3m+: 0-2
Track: LH: 0-1 RH: 0-3 Tight: 0-0 Gall: 0-1
Aids: Bl: 0-0 Vi: 0-0 Tstrap: 0-0
Best Rating: **85** 5/99 Font 2m2f110y firm NHF

Balnagreine (IRE)

108 **104**

9-y-o b g Strong Gale-Regent Miss (Prince Regent (FR))
J Mackie (J J Lambe 22/6) Peter McMahon

Placings:0460/0000/50F000-32U **(4909)**
2001/02: 24^{3}F, 24^{2}F, 20^{U}GF

	Starts	1st	2nd	3rd	Win & Pl
Chases	3	0	1	1	1200
Career Total	**18**	**0**	**1**	**1**	**1330**

Going: Sf: 0-0 GS: 0-0 Gd: 0-0 GF: - Fm: 0-3
Distance: 2m/2m3: 0-0 2m4-2m7: 0-1 3m+: 0-2
Track: LH: 0-0 RH: 0-1 Tight: 0-1 Gall: 0-0
Aids: Bl: 0-0 Vi: 0-0 Tstrap: 0-0
Best Rating: **100** 6/01 Clon 3m firm Ch

Moderate ex-Irish chaser. Stays three miles and suited by fast ground.

Baloo

103 **100+**

6-y-o b g Morpeth-Moorland Nell (Neltino)
J D Frost (R G Frost 28/11) Cloud Nine-Premier Cru

Placings:3540550-3364104 **(4502)**
2001/02: 22^{3}GF, 22^{3}GF, 22^{6}GF, 19^{4}GF, 22^{1}GF, 16^{0}S, 22^{4}G

	Starts	1st	2nd	3rd	Win & Pl
Hurdles	7	1	0	2	3406
Career Total	**14**	**1**	**0**	**3**	**3619**

87	11/01	Extr	2m6f110y	E(0-105)HHdl	G-F	£2520

Total win prize-money £2520

Going: Sf: 0-1 GS: 0-0 Gd: 0-1 GF: - Fm: 1-5
Distance: 2m/2m3: 0-2 **2m4-2m7: 1-5** 3m+: 0-0
Track: LH: 0-5 RH: 0-1 Tight: 0-4 Gall: 0-0
Aids: Bl: 0-0 Vi: 0-0 **Tstrap: 1-3**
Best Rating: **92** 10/00 Tntn 2m1f good NHF

Won a novices' handicap over 22 furlongs at Exeter in November 2001. Returned after a three month break to win 27 furlong handicap at Newton Abbot July 2002. Stays well and likes the top of the ground.

Baltic Fleet

101 **85**

7-y-o b/br m Arzanni-Misty Sunset (Le Bavard (FR))
J J O'Neill A & G Oliver

Placings:656300-5 **(1395)**
2001/02: 24^{5}GF

	Starts	1st	2nd	3rd	Win & Pl
Hurdles	1	0	0	0	0
Career Total	**7**	**0**	**0**	**1**	**453**

Going: Sf: 0-0 GS: 0-0 Gd: 0-0 GF: - Fm: 0-1
Distance: 2m/2m3: 0-0 2m4-2m7: 0-0 3m+: 0-1
Track: LH: 0-1 RH: 0-0 Tight: 0-0 Gall: 0-0
Aids: Bl: 0-0 Vi: 0-0 Tstrap: 0-0
Best Rating: **92** 12/00 Leic 2m heavy Hdl

Baltic Magic (IRE)

102 **102**

8-y-o b g Yashgan-Woolly (Giolla Mear)
J L Spearing The Square Milers

Placings:5P0P431PF-02P134P **(4168)**
2001/02: 22^{0}GS, 21^{2}G, 26^{P}S, 19^{1}S, 21^{3}HY, 19^{4}S, 20^{P}GS

	Starts	1st	2nd	3rd	Win & Pl
Hurdles	5	1	1	1	4723
Chases	2	0	0	0	0
Career Total	**16**	**2**	**1**	**2**	**12284**

93 1/02 Hrfd 2m3f110y E Hdl SFT £2849
117 1/01 Tram 2m4f Ch SH £6677
Total win prize-money £9526

Going: Sf: 1-4 GS: 0-2 Gd: 0-1 GF: - Fm: 0-0
Distance: 2m/2m3: 0-0 **2m4-2m7: 1-6** 3m+: 0-1
Track: LH: 0-4 **RH: 1-3** Tight: 0-4 Gall: 0-0
Aids: **Bl: 1-4** Vi: 0-2 Tstrap: 0-0
Best Rating: **119** 1/01 Thur 3m heavy Ch

Baltic Oak (IRE)

7-y-o ch g Cardinal Flower-Bustomi Lass (Bustomi)
T P Tate T P Tate

Placings:0-P **(0449)**
2001/02: 20^{P}F

	Starts	1st	2nd	3rd	Win & Pl
Hurdles	1	0	0	0	
Career Total	**2**	**0**	**0**	**0**	

Going: Sf: 0-0 GS: 0-0 Gd: 0-0 GF: - Fm: 0-1
Distance: 2m/2m3: 0-0 2m4-2m7: 0-1 3m+: 0-0
Track: LH: 0-1 RH: 0-0 Tight: 0-0 Gall: 0-0
Aids: Bl: 0-0 Vi: 0-0 Tstrap: 0-0
Best Rating:

Bandit Brown (IRE)

92 **91**

6-y-o b g Supreme Leader-Parkroe Lady (IRE) (Deep Run)
P Winkworth R D Barber & R J B Blake

Placings:4043 **(4171)**
2001/02: 17^{4}S, 18^{0}G, 16^{4}HY, 16^{3}GS

	Starts	1st	2nd	3rd	Win & Pl
NH Flat	1	0	0	0	0
Hurdles	3	0	0	1	351
Career Total	**4**	**0**	**0**	**1**	**351**

Going: Sf: 0-2 GS: 0-1 Gd: 0-1 GF: - Fm: 0-0
Distance: 2m/2m3: 0-4 2m4-2m7: 0-0 3m+: 0-0
Track: LH: 0-3 RH: 0-0 Tight: 0-4 Gall: 0-0
Aids: Bl: 0-0 Vi: 0-0 Tstrap: 0-0
Best Rating: **91** 3/02 Plum 2m gd-sft Hdl

Shaped as if further would suit when finishing one-paced in a two-mile hurdle in March.

Bangabunny

97 **120**

12-y-o ch g Gunner B-Olympian Princess (Master Owen)
Mrs S A Bramall Winning Post Racing Syndicate

Placings:02/43/100354F5/U6330/252224F0/052411530/30F-6412100 **(4664)**
2001/02: 20^{6}S, 20^{4}S, 22^{1}GS, 28^{2}S, 28^{1}YS, 20^{0}SH, 21^{0}G

	Starts	1st	2nd	3rd	Win & Pl
Hurdles	1	0	0	0	0
Chases	6	2	1	0	13066
Career Total	**44**	**5**	**7**	**6**	**33998**

110 1/02 Punc 3m4f Ch Y-S £6984
10/01 Saum 2m6f110y Ch G-S £3104
125 2/00 Carl 2m D(0-120)Ch HVY £4075
125 1/00 Kels 2m1f D(0-120)HCh GD £3789
99 10/96 Punc 2m4f Hdl G-Y £3177
Total win prize-money £21133

Going: Sf: 0-3 GS: 1-1 Gd: 0-1 GF: - Fm: 0-0
Distance: 2m/2m3: 0-0 2m4-2m7: 1-5 3m+: 1-2
Track: LH: 0-1 RH: 0-1 Tight: 0-1 Gall: 0-0
Aids: Bl: 0-0 Vi: 0-0 Tstrap: 0-0
Best Rating: **125** 2/00 Carl 2m heavy Ch

Handicap chaser. A winner at two miles, he stays beyond three miles and acts on good ground and soft ground.

Bangor Erris (IRE)

100(98h) (50h)**91**

9-y-o ch g Executive Perk-Dawn Infidel (IRE) (Fidel)
A J Chamberlain (P Bowen 8/1) Mike Ledbury

Placings:4FPP/43/236-004F36P51F5P4 **(4886)**
2001/02: 20^{0}GF, 22^{0}GF, 24^{4}G, 19^{F}G, 19^{3}S, 27^{6}G, 26^{P}S, 19^{5}GS, 22^{1}G, 25^{F}S, 20^{5}S, 24^{P}GF, 18^{4}GF

	Starts	1st	2nd	3rd	Win & Pl
Hurdles	2	0	0	0	0
Chases	11	1	0	1	3912
Career Total	**22**	**1**	**1**	**3**	**5270**

91 1/02 Font 2m6f F(0-90)HCh GD £3220
Total win prize-money £3220

Going: Sf: 0-4 GS: 0-1 Gd: 1-4 GF: - Fm: 0-4
Distance: 2m/2m3: 0-3 **2m4-2m7: 1-5** 3m+: 0-5
Track: LH: 0-5 RH: 0-6 **Tight: 1-8** Gall: 0-1
Aids: Bl: 0-0 Vi: 0-1 Tstrap: 0-0
Best Rating: **91** 1/02 Font 2m6f good Ch

Fair handicap chaser. Got off the mark over fences at Fontwell early in 2002. Best over two miles-six. Acts on a sound surface.

Banjo Hill

98 **100**

8-y-o b g Arctic Lord-Just Hannah (Macmillion)
Mrs L Richards John B Hobbs

Placings:454000016/12200/1-P **(2259)**
2001/02: 24^{P}G

	Starts	1st	2nd	3rd	Win & Pl
Hurdles	1	0	0	0	
Career Total	**16**	**3**	**2**	**0**	**10467**

105 5/00 Extr 2m6f D(0-120)HHdl FRM £3692
99 9/99 Font 2m6f110y E(0-115)HHdl GD £2267
89 4/99 Winc 2m6f F(0-105)HHdl GD £2570
Total win prize-money £8530

Going: Sf: 0-0 GS: 0-0 Gd: 0-1 GF: - Fm: 0-0
Distance: 2m/2m3: 0-0 2m4-2m7: 0-0 3m+: 0-1
Track: LH: 0-0 RH: 0-1 Tight: 0-0 Gall: 0-0
Aids: Bl: 0-0 Vi: 0-0 Tstrap: 0-0
Best Rating: **105** 5/00 Extr 2m6f firm Hdl

Bank Avenue

104 **135**

11-y-o b g Buckley-Woodram Delight (Idiots Delight)
M Pitman S D Hemstock

Placings:30/60U/435PFP526/1313344/21/F305-3520PP **(3493)**
2001/02: 24^{3}G, 24^{5}G, 25^{2}G, 24^{0}G, 25^{P}GS, 24^{P}S

	Starts	1st	2nd	3rd	Win & Pl
Chases	6	0	1	1	2711
Career Total	**33**	**3**	**3**	**7**	**46305**

137 10/99 Kemp 3m B HCh G-F £14096
135 10/98 Kemp 3m B(0-150)HCh GD £10435
117 9/98 Worc 2m7f110y E(0-110)HCh G-F £2906
Total win prize-money £27438

Going: Sf: 0-1 GS: 0-1 Gd: 0-4 GF: - Fm: 0-0
Distance: 2m/2m3: 0-0 2m4-2m7: 0-0 3m+: 0-6
Track: LH: 0-3 RH: 0-3 Tight: 0-0 Gall: 0-3
Aids: Bl: 0-1 Vi: 0-0 Tstrap: 0-0
Best Rating: **137** 10/00 Kemp 3m gd-fm Ch

A dual winner of Kempton's Charisma Gold Cup, he has lost his way in recent seasons. Suited by fast ground.

Banker Count

118 **167**

10-y-o b g Lord Bud-Gilzie Bank (New Brig)
Miss Venetia Williams (M W Easterby 8/12) Mrs H Brown

Placings:6632/1/P221F/13/FB2121-12132U0 **(4827a)**
2001/02: 20^{1}G, 24^{2}G, 20^{1}S, 24^{3}S, 19^{2}GS, 24^{U}GS, 21^{0}GF

	Starts	1st	2nd	3rd	Win & Pl
Chases	7	2	2	1	50693
Career Total	**25**	**7**	**7**	**3**	**85708**

167 12/01 Weth 2m4f110y B(0-145)HCh SFT £10436
152 11/01 Weth 2m4f110y B(0-150)HCh GD £10656
144 4/01 Weth 3m1f B(0-150)HCh G-S £7215
135 2/01 Kels 2m6f110y C(0-130)HCh SFT £7020
129 12/99 Donc 2m110y C(0-130)HCh G-F £5743
106 3/99 Catt 2m3f E Ch SFT £2979
113 11/97 Weth 2m C Hdl G-F £3652
Total win prize-money £47703

Going: Sf: 1-2 GS: 0-2 Gd: 1-2 GF: - Fm: 0-1
Distance: 2m/2m3: 0-0 **2m4-2m7: 2-4** 3m+: 0-3
Track: **LH: 2-5** RH: 0-1 Tight: 0-0 Gall: 0-1
Aids: Bl: 0-0 Vi: 0-0 Tstrap: 0-0
Best Rating: **167** 12/01 Weth 2m4f110y soft Ch

He used to be prone to jumping errors but is useful when putting in a clear round. He is effective at up to three miles and a furlong but is better over shorter. He has improved and scored twice last season over two and a half. Handles most types of ground, but does not want it too soft. Has a useful turn of foot.

Bankersdraft

81 **37**

7-y-o ch g Mazaad-Overdraft (Bustino)
N B Mason (D McCain 26/5) N B Mason

Placings: *0*PP6-PP0 **(1403)**
2001/02: 19^{PG}, 20^{PGF}, 24^{G}

	Starts	1st	2nd	3rd	Win & Pl
Chases	3	0	0	0	
Career Total	**7**	**0**	**0**	**0**	**0**

Going: Sf: 0-0 GS: 0-0 Gd: 0-2 GF: - Fm: 0-1
Distance: 2m/2m3: 0-1 2m4-2m7: 0-1 3m+: 0-1
Track: LH: 0-2 RH: 0-1 Tight: 0-1 Gall: 0-0
Aids: Bl: 0-0 Vi: 0-0 Tstrap: 0-0
Best Rating: **37** 9/01 Bang 3m110y good Ch

Bankhead (IRE)

80 **90**

13-y-o gr g Roselier (FR)-Coolcanute (Hardicanute)
J L Spearing Mrs Melanie Williams

Placings: P216312/**11PP**11424/2446/P0-0 **(0347)**
2001/02: 27^{0}G

	Starts	1st	2nd	3rd	Win & Pl
Hurdles	1	0	0	0	
Career Total	**23**	**6**	**4**	**1**	**25485**

133	2/97	Chep	3m	C(0-135)HHdl	SFT	£3715
130	2/97	Newb	3m110y	C(0-130)HHdl	GD	£3727
116	11/96	Bang	3m110y	D Ch	SFT	£3745
117	11/96	Towc	3m1f	D Ch	GD	£3942
113	2/95	Nott	3m110y	E Hdl	SFT	£2598
96	12/94	Hrfd	3m2f	Hdl	GD	£1919

Total win prize-money £19648

Going: Sf: 0-0 GS: 0-0 Gd: 0-1 GF: - Fm: 0-0
Distance: 2m/2m3: 0-0 2m4-2m7: 0-0 3m+: 0-1
Track: LH: 0-1 RH: 0-0 Tight: 0-1 Gall: 0-0
Aids: Bl: 0-0 Vi: 0-0 Tstrap: 0-0
Best Rating: **133** 11/98 Chep 3m gd-sft Hdl

Bannagh Lord (IRE)

92 **67**

7-y-o ch g Montelimar (USA)-Lady Karola (Lord Gayle (USA))
Michael McNeilly Michael McNeilly

Placings: *5506/0000*-0FPP00 **(4877)**
2001/02: 16^{0}G, 22^{F}GY, 20^{P}S, 22^{P}S, 20^{0}GY, 24^{0}G

	Starts	1st	2nd	3rd	Win & Pl
NH Flat	1	0	0	0	0
Hurdles	5	0	0	0	0
Career Total	**14**	**0**	**0**	**0**	

Going: Sf: 0-2 GS: 0-0 Gd: 0-2 GF: - Fm: 0-0
Distance: 2m/2m3: 0-1 2m4-2m7: 0-4 3m+: 0-1
Track: LH: 0-0 RH: 0-2 Tight: 0-0 Gall: 0-0
Aids: Bl: 0-0 Vi: 0-0 Tstrap: 0-0
Best Rating: **87** 2/01 Fair 2m heavy Hdl

Bannagh Mor (IRE)

11-y-o b g Detroit Sam (FR)-Castle Ita (Midland Gayle)
L G Cottrell J H Burbidge

Placings: *00*6/P/FU **(1848)**
2001/02: 23^{F}GS, 25^{U}G

	Starts	1st	2nd	3rd	Win & Pl

	Starts	1st	2nd	3rd	Win & Pl
Chases	2	0	0	0	
Career Total	**6**	**0**	**0**	**0**	

Going: Sf: 0-0 GS: 0-1 Gd: 0-1 GF: - Fm: 0-0
Distance: 2m/2m3: 0-0 2m4-2m7: 0-0 3m+: 0-2
Track: LH: 0-0 RH: 0-2 Tight: 0-0 Gall: 0-0
Aids: Bl: 0-0 Vi: 0-0 Tstrap: 0-0
Best Rating: **60** 10/96 Fair 2m gd-fm NHF

A multiple winning pointer in 1998, but lightly raced in recent seasons.

Banneret (USA)

77 **44**

9-y-o b g Imperial Falcon (CAN)-Dashing Partner (Formidable (USA))
F L Matthews (A G Juckes 10/3) F L Matthews

Placings: 334/0-FR **(4741)**
2001/02: 19^{F}GF, 24^{R}GF

	Starts	1st	2nd	3rd	Win & Pl
Chases	2	0	0	0	
Career Total	**6**	**0**	**0**	**2**	**450**

Going: Sf: 0-0 GS: 0-0 Gd: 0-0 GF: - Fm: 0-2
Distance: 2m/2m3: 0-0 2m4-2m7: 0-1 3m+: 0-1
Track: LH: 0-0 RH: 0-2 Tight: 0-1 Gall: 0-0
Aids: Bl: 0-1 Vi: 0-1 Tstrap: 0-0
Best Rating: **83** 1/00 Ludl 2m gd-sft Hdl

Bannow Bay (IRE)

113 **171**

7-y-o b g Good Thyne (USA)-Derry Girl (Rarity)
C Roche Mrs Paul Shanahan & Mrs John Magnier

Placings: 401/201111211-44112 **(4251)**
2001/02: 16^{4}S, 20^{4}Y, 24^{1}Y, 24^{1}S, 24^{2}G

	Starts	1st	2nd	3rd	Win & Pl
Hurdles	5	2	1	0	71431
Career Total	**17**	**9**	**3**	**0**	**153203**

157	2/02	Navn	3m	Hdl	SFT	£19938
171	12/01	Leop	3m	Hdl	YLD	£20967
144	4/01	Fair	3m	Hdl	Y-S	£32500
152	12/00	Leop	3m	Hdl	HVY	£13000
150	10/00	Cork	2m4f	Hdl	SFT	£4968
162	8/00	Tral	2m6f	(0-123)HHdl	SFT	£4692
143	8/00	Gway	2m5f190y	HHdl	GD	£10400
123	8/00	Gway	3m	(0-130)HHdl	GD	£7176
87	2/00	Clon	2m4f	Hdl	SFT	£2760

Total win prize-money £116403

Going: Sf: 1-2 GS: 0-0 Gd: 0-1 GF: - Fm: 0-0
Distance: 2m/2m3: 0-1 2m4-2m7: 0-1 **3m+: 2-3**
Track: **LH: 2-2** RH: 0-1 Tight: 0-0 Gall: 0-0
Aids: Bl: 0-0 Vi: 0-0 Tstrap: 0-0
Best Rating: **171** 12/01 Leop 3m yield Hdl

One of Ireland's top staying hurdlers, he needs three miles and goes on good ground and soft. He won the Boyne Hurdle in February and found only Baracouda too good in the Stayers' at Cheltenham. He looks a high-class chasing prospect.

Banny Hill Lad

12-y-o gr g Pragmatic-Four M'S (Majestic Maharaj)
Mrs J Fitzgerald Pan Of Scouse Partnership

Placings: *3*/6432/52202**P22**/5P6P/P **(0063)**
2001/02: 26^{P}G

	Starts	1st	2nd	3rd	Win & Pl

	Starts	1st	2nd	3rd	Win & Pl
Chases	1	0	0	0	
Career Total	**18**	**0**	**6**	**2**	**5932**

Going: Sf: 0-0 GS: 0-0 Gd: 0-1 GF: - Fm: 0-0
Distance: 2m/2m3: 0-0 2m4-2m7: 0-0 3m+: 0-1
Track: LH: 0-0 RH: 0-1 Tight: 0-1 Gall: 0-0
Aids: Bl: 0-0 Vi: 0-0 Tstrap: 0-0
Best Rating: **103** 12/97 Hntg 3m2f gd-sft Hdl

Banteer Bet (IRE)

104

10-y-o ch m Black Minstrel-Deirdre Elizabeth (Salluceva)
R Lee C H Gittins

Placings: 3/P/1-0P **(0576)**
2001/02: 24^{0}G, 28^{P}GF

	Starts	1st	2nd	3rd	Win & Pl
Chases	2	0	0	0	
Career Total	**5**	**1**	**0**	**1**	**3685**

104	4/01	Hrfd	3m1f110y	E Ch	GD	£3474

Total win prize-money £3474

Going: Sf: 0-0 GS: 0-0 Gd: 0-1 GF: - Fm: 0-1
Distance: 2m/2m3: 0-0 2m4-2m7: 0-0 3m+: 0-2
Track: LH: 0-1 RH: 0-0 Tight: 0-1 Gall: 0-0
Aids: Bl: 0-0 Vi: 0-0 Tstrap: 0-2
Best Rating: **104** 4/01 Hrfd 3m1f110y good Ch

Baracouda (FR)

124 **176**

7-y-o b g Alesso (USA)-Peche Aubar (FR) (Zino)
F Doumen J P McManus

Placings: 52/112211111-1111 **(4251)**
2001/02: 20^{1}G, 25^{1}G, 24^{1}GS, 24^{1}G

	Starts	1st	2nd	3rd	Win & Pl
Hurdles	4	4	0	0	136100
Career Total	**15**	**11**	**3**	**0**	**395528**

171	3/02	Chel	3m	A Hdl	GD	£72500
156	2/02	Kemp	3m110y	A Hdl	G-S	£15000
176	12/01	Asct	3m1f110y	A Hdl	GD	£33000
171	11/01	Asct	2m4f	A Hdl	GD	£15600
155	4/01	Sand	3m	A Hdl	G-S	£37700
	3/01	Autl	2m3f110y	Hdl	HVY	£31038
161	2/01	Font	2m4f	B Hdl	G-S	£14365
175	12/00	Asct	3m1f110y	A Hdl	HVY	£33000
	11/00	Autl	2m4f110y	Hdl	HVY	£48031
	7/00	Autl	2m2f	Hdl	HLD	£14409
	5/00	Autl	2m3f110y	HHdl	VS	£25937

Total win prize-money £340580

Going: Sf: 0-0 GS: 1-1 Gd: 3-3 GF: - Fm: 0-0
Distance: 2m/2m3: 0-0 2m4-2m7: 1-1 **3m+: 3-3**
Track: LH: 0-0 **RH: 3-3** Tight: 0-0 Gall: 0-0
Aids: Bl: 0-0 Vi: 0-0 Tstrap: 0-0
Best Rating: **176** 12/01 Asct 3m1f110y good Hdl

A top-class staying hurdler, he showed that he had retained all his ability when scoring on his seasonal debut at Ascot in November 2001 and when going on to win his second Long Walk Hurdle at the same track. Followed up at Kempton before confirming himself the top stayer with a cheeky win at the Festival. Usually held up and has a fine turn of foot, it will be interesting to see if he is .

Barakana (IRE)

88 **77**

4-y-o b g Barathea (IRE)-Safkana (IRE) (Doyoun)
N B Mason (P Haley 21/7) N B Mason

Placings:0600 **(4757)**
2001/02: 16^{0}GF, 16^{6}G, 16^{0}GF, 16^{0}GF

	Starts	1st	2nd	3rd	Win & Pl
Hurdles	4	0	0	0	0
Career Total	**4**	**0**	**0**	**0**	**0**

Going: Sf: 0-0 GS: 0-0 Gd: 0-1 GF: - Fm: 0-3
Distance: 2m/2m3: 0-4 2m4-2m7: 0-0 3m+: 0-0
Track: LH: 0-2 RH: 0-2 Tight: 0-1 Gall. 0-1
Aids: Bl: 0-0 Vi: 0-0 Tstrap: 0-0
Best Rating: **77** 9/01 Plum 2m gd-fm Hdl

Modest hurdling form.

Barashan

8-y-o ch g Anshan-Gohar (USA) (Barachois (CAN))
M Salaman M Salaman

Placings:00/6P0/P **(0060)**
2001/02: 17^{P}GS

	Starts	1st	2nd	3rd	Win & Pl
Hurdles	1	0	0	0	
Career Total	**6**	**0**	**0**	**0**	**0**

Going: Sf: 0-0 GS: 0-1 Gd: 0-0 GF: - Fm: 0-0
Distance: 2m/2m3: 0-1 2m4-2m7: 0-0 3m+: 0-0
Track: LH: 0-0 RH: 0-1 Tight: 0-1 Gall: 0-0
Aids: Bl: 0-0 Vi: 0-0 Tstrap: 0-1
Best Rating: **64** 3/99 Chep 2m110y gd-sft NHF

Barba Papa (IRE)

90 **134**
8-y-o b h Mujadil (USA)-Baby's Smile (Shirley Heights)
A J Martin Glen Devlin

Placings:601525/55/13300-1130P **(4193)**
2001/02: 20^{1}GF, 16^{1}G, 20^{3}SH, 23^{0}HY, 25^{P}GS

	Starts	1st	2nd	3rd	Win & Pl
Hurdles	5	2	0	1	14973
Career Total	**18**	**4**	**1**	**3**	**35234**

130	9/01	Punc	2m	Hdl	GD	£7790
134	6/01	Tral	2m4f	Hdl	G-F	£5967
108	5/00	Rosc	2m	Hdl	G-F	£4002
113	2/99	Punc	2m	Hdl	HVY	£3069

Total win prize-money £20829

Going: Sf: 0-1 GS: 0-1 Gd: 1-1 GF: - Fm: 1-1
Distance: 2m/2m3: 1-1 2m4-2m7: 1-2 3m+: 0-2
Track: LH: 0-2 **RH: 1-1** Tight: 0-0 Gall: 0-1
Aids: Bl: 0-0 Vi: 0-0 **Tstrap: 2-3**
Best Rating: **134** 6/01 Tral 2m4f gd-fm Hdl

High-class stayer on the Flat, he has won over hurdles on fast ground, although he acts on softer. Has run in decent hurdle company in Britain. Has won over two and two and a half miles over hurdles. Broke down at Cheltenham.

Barbizon (NZ)

95 **87**
8-y-o b g Oregon (USA)-Fleece Tum (NZ) (Umteen (NZ))
B De Haan Plough Racing

Placings:0660/3F01/1PF-60P **(4908)**
2001/02: 22^{6}HY, 21^{0}GS, 21^{P}G

	Starts	1st	2nd	3rd	Win & Pl
Hurdles	3	0	0	0	0
Career Total	**14**	**2**	**0**	**1**	**4997**

96	5/00	Ludl	2m5f	E(0-105)HHdl	GD	£2600
96	4/00	Towc	2m5f	F Hdl	GD	£1909

Total win prize-money £4510

Going: Sf: 0-1 GS: 0-1 Gd: 0-1 GF: - Fm: 0-0
Distance: 2m/2m3: 0-0 2m4-2m7: 0-3 3m+: 0-0
Track: LH: 0-1 RH: 0-2 Tight: 0-1 Gall: 0-1
Aids: Bl: 0-0 Vi: 0-0 Tstrap: 0-2
Best Rating: **96** 5/00 Ludl 2m5f good Hdl

Barbury Hill (IRE)

80 **49**
6-y-o b g Rashar (USA)-Supreme Rehearsal (IRE) (Supreme Leader)
A King Mrs A Shutes,Mrs L Field & J E Brown

Placings:656 **(4303)**
2001/02: 17^{6}G, 19^{5}G, 16^{6}HY

	Starts	1st	2nd	3rd	Win & Pl
NH Flat	1	0	0	0	0
Hurdles	2	0	0	0	0
Career Total	**3**	**0**	**0**	**0**	**0**

Going: Sf: 0-1 GS: 0-0 Gd: 0-2 GF: - Fm: 0-0
Distance: 2m/2m3: 0-2 2m4-2m7: 0-1 3m+: 0-0
Track: LH: 0-2 RH: 0-1 Tight: 0-1 Gall: 0-0
Aids: Bl: 0-0 Vi: 0-0 Tstrap: 0-0
Best Rating: **87** 11/01 NAbb 2m1f good NHF

Modest form in three races to date.

Barcelona

110 **117**
5-y-o b g Barathea (IRE)-Pipitina (Bustino)
G L Moore George Smith Ltd

Placings:1406541 **(4762)**
2001/02: 18^{1}GS, 16^{4}G, 19^{0}G, 19^{6}S, 16^{5}S, 18^{4}S, 20^{1}GF

	Starts	1st	2nd	3rd	Win & Pl
Hurdles	7	2	0	0	20242
Career Total	**7**	**2**	**0**	**0**	**20242**

110	4/02	Asct	2m4f	B Hdl	G-F	£17400
117	10/01	Font	2m2f110y	E Hdl	G-S	£2460

Total win prize-money £19861

Going: Sf: 0-3 GS: 1-1 Gd: 0-2 GF: - Fm: 1-1
Distance: 2m/2m3: 1-6 2m4-2m7: 1-1 3m+: 0-0
Track: LH: 1-4 RH: 1-3 **Tight: 1-2** Gall: 0-1
Aids: Bl: 0-1 Vi: 0-0 **Tstrap: 2-7**
Best Rating: **117** 10/01 Font 2m2f110y gd-sft Hdl

A fair stayer on the level, he made a winning debut over hurdles at Fontwell but was been slightly disappointing until winning at Ascot. Stays at least two and a quarter miles. Acts on an easy surface.

Barden Lady

91 **64**
5-y-o b m Presidium-Pugilistic (Hard Fought)
H D Daly D G Blagden

Placings:P05 **(4682)**
2001/02: 16^{P}GS, 16^{0}S, 17^{5}GF

	Starts	1st	2nd	3rd	Win & Pl
Hurdles	3	0	0	0	0
Career Total	**3**	**0**	**0**	**0**	**0**

Going: Sf: 0-1 GS: 0-1 Gd: 0-0 GF: - Fm: 0-1
Distance: 2m/2m3: 0-3 2m4-2m7: 0-0 3m+: 0-0
Track: LH: 0-0 RH: 0-3 Tight: 0-0 Gall: 0-0
Aids: Bl: 0-0 Vi: 0-0 Tstrap: 0-0
Best Rating: **64** 4/02 Hrfd 2m1f gd-fm Hdl

Barito (GER)

101 **126**
5-y-o b g Winged Love (IRE)-Blumme (CHI) (Jadar (CHI))
F Doumen (C Von Der Recke 24/8) Mrs Michaela Faust

Placings:311213015 **(3795)**
2001/02: 16^{3}, 17^{1}S, 17^{1}S, 20^{2}G, 16^{1}G, 16^{3}HY, 18^{0}HY, 16^{1}G, 21^{5}S

	Starts	1st	2nd	3rd	Win & Pl
Hurdles	9	4	1	2	24240
Career Total	**9**	**4**	**1**	**2**	**24240**

126	12/01	Kemp	2m	B Hdl	GD	£7085
	9/01	Maia	2m110y	Hdl	GD	£6212
	7/01	Aabe	2m1f	HHdl	SFT	£1607
	7/01	Aabe	2m1f	Hdl	SFT	£1607

Total win prize-money £16511

Going: Sf: 2-5 GS: 0-0 Gd: 2-3 GF: - Fm: 0-0
Distance: **2m/2m3: 4-7** 2m4-2m7: 0-2 3m+: 0-0
Track: LH: 0-0 **RH: 1-1** Tight: 0-0 Gall: 0-0
Aids: Bl: 0-0 Vi: 0-0 Tstrap: 0-0
Best Rating: **126** 12/01 Kemp 2m good Hdl

Winning ex-German hurdler. Now with Francois Doumen. His wins have come at around two miles on good and soft ground.

Barkingatthemoon

86 **89**
8-y-o b g Seymour Hicks (FR)-China's Way (USA) (Native Uproar (USA))
J Mackie Fools Who Dream

Placings:4/050044/22/3 **(0777)**
2001/02: 16^{3}GF

	Starts	1st	2nd	3rd	Win & Pl
Hurdles	1	0	0	1	290
Career Total	**10**	**0**	**2**	**1**	**1719**

Going: Sf: 0-0 GS: 0-0 Gd: 0-0 GF: - Fm: 0-1
Distance: 2m/2m3: 0-1 2m4-2m7: 0-0 3m+: 0-0
Track: LH: 0-1 RH: 0-0 Tight: 0-0 Gall: 0-0
Aids: Bl: 0-0 Vi: 0-0 Tstrap: 0-1
Best Rating: **101** 12/98 Donc 2m110y good NHF

Barley Meadow (IRE)

104(78c) (61c)**70**
10-y-o ch g Phardante (FR)-Foredefine (Bonne Noel)
R Ford R Burgess

Placings:650000/000UP002065/30U35002141612433/452 51464/4325562P6005-1530220P0P60 **(4786)**
2001/02: 21^{1}GS, 22^{5}GS, 17^{3}G, 22^{0}GF, 16^{2}GF, 20^{2}G, 16^{0}GS, 16^{P}S, 20^{0}S, 16^{P}GS, 17^{6}GS, 20^{0}F

	Starts	1st	2nd	3rd	Win & Pl
Hurdles	11	1	2	1	3696
Chases	1	0	0	0	0
Career Total	**66**	**5**	**8**	**6**	**16713**

79	7/01	MRas	2m5f110y	G(0-90)HHdl	G-S	£1624
98	7/99	Worc	2m	G Hdl	G-F	£1730
92	11/98	Ludl	2m	G(0-95)HHdl	GD	£1660
91	10/98	Hexm	2m	G Hdl	GD	£2158
82	9/98	Worc	2m	G(0-90)HHdl	G-F	£2460

Total win prize-money £9632

Going: Sf: 0-2 GS: 1-5 Gd: 0-2 GF: - Fm: 0-3
Distance: 2m/2m3: 0-6 **2m4-2m7: 1-6** 3m+: 0-0
Track: LH: 0-8 RH: 0-3 Tight: 0-7 Gall: 0-1
Aids: Bl: 0-0 Vi: 1-9 Tstrap: 1-12
Best Rating: **98** 7/99 Worc 2m gd-fm Hdl

Barn Dancer (IRE)

7-y-o b m Cataldi-Dancing Gale (Strong Gale)
G P Kelly G P Kelly

Placings: 00P0-F (4673)
2001/02: 17^{F}GF

	Starts	1st	2nd	3rd	Win & Pl
Hurdles	1	0	0	0	
Career Total	**5**	**0**	**0**	**0**	

Going: Sf: 0-0 GS: 0-0 Gd: 0-0 GF: - Fm: 0-1
Distance: 2m/2m3: 0-1 2m4-2m7: 0-0 3m+: 0-0
Track: LH: 0-1 RH: 0-0 Tight: 0-1 Gall: 0-0
Aids: Bl: 0-0 Vi: 0-0 Tstrap: 0-0
Best Rating: **59** 7/00 Rosc 2m gd-fm NHF

Barnaby

5-y-o b g Theatrical Charmer-Fruitful Affair (IRE) (Taufan (USA))
M R Bosley The Ann & Daisy George Partnership

Placings: PP-0 (3510)
2001/02: 17^{0}S

	Starts	1st	2nd	3rd	Win & Pl
Hurdles	1	0	0	0	
Career Total	**3**	**0**	**0**	**0**	

Going: Sf: 0-1 GS: 0-0 Gd: 0-0 GF: - Fm: 0-0
Distance: 2m/2m3: 0-1 2m4-2m7: 0-0 3m+: 0-0
Track: LH: 0-0 RH: 0-1 Tight: 0-1 Gall: 0-0
Aids: Bl: 0-0 Vi: 0-0 Tstrap: 0-0
Best Rating: mfy

Barnane Walk (IRE)

103(84h) (85h)**91**

10-y-o b g Supreme Leader-Little Pride (Tepukei)
J C Tuck J C Tuck

Placings: 00P004/F1100P/3-04U045 (2214)
2001/02: 22^{0}GF, 21^{4}GF, 26^{U}GF, 24^{0}G, 25^{4}G, 25^{5}G

	Starts	1st	2nd	3rd	Win & Pl
Hurdles	1	0	0	0	0
Chases	5	0	0	0	548
Career Total	**19**	**2**	**0**	**1**	**6670**
88	12/99	Extr	2m7f	F(0-100)HHdl	G-S £2547
83	11/99	Extr	2m6f	F(0-100)HHdl	G-S £2924

Total win prize-money £5472

Going: Sf: 0-0 GS: 0-0 Gd: 0-3 GF: - Fm: 0-3
Distance: 2m/2m3: 0-0 2m4-2m7: 0-2 3m+: 0-4
Track: LH: 0-3 RH: 0-3 Tight: 0-3 Gall: 0-0
Aids: Bl: 0-0 Vi: 0-0 Tstrap: 0-0
Best Rating: **91** 8/01 NAbb 3m2f110y gd-fm Ch

Barnburgh Boy

105(105h) (117h)**134**

8-y-o ch g Shalford (IRE)-Tuxford Hideaway (Cawston's Clown)
Miss Venetia Williams Mrs H Spencer

Placings: 513P4222/422111212/205/2134216-360F (4838)
2001/02: 16^{3}G, 16^{6}HY, 16^{0}G, 16^{F}G

	Starts	1st	2nd	3rd	Win & Pl
Chases	4	0	0	1	3436
Career Total	**31**	**7**	**10**	**3**	**45411**
134	2/01	Hntg	2m110y	D(0-120)HCh	G-S £4231
126	11/00	MRas	2m1f110y	D(0-120)HCh	G-S £5379
125	3/99	Newc	2m110y	E Ch	SFT £3420
113	2/99	Catt	2m	D Ch	GD £4302
118	2/99	Muss	2m	E Ch	GD £2788
110	1/99	Catt	2m	D Ch	SFT £3684
100	12/97	Weth	2m	D Hdl	SFT £3127

Total win prize-money £26933

Going: Sf: 0-1 GS: 0-0 Gd: 0-3 GF: - Fm: 0-0
Distance: 2m/2m3: 0-4 2m4-2m7: 0-0 3m+: 0-0
Track: LH: 0-3 RH: 0-1 Tight: 0-0 Gall: 0-1
Aids: Bl: 0-0 Vi: 0-0 Tstrap: 0-0
Best Rating: **134** 11/01 Asct 2m good Ch

Rejoined Tim Easterby after a spell in Ireland and showed fair form in handicap chases around two miles, but did not always look totally in love with the game. Now with Venetia Williams, he was third in a Listed race at Ascot in November 2001, but well held in similar company in the spring. Finished alone at Market Rasen in July 2002. Acts on good/good to soft ground.

Barney Knows (IRE)

101 **119**

7-y-o b g In The Wings-Afeefa (Lyphard (USA))
Ian Williams C N Barnes

Placings: 2101/F22104/0005 (4636)
2001/02: 25^{0}S, 22^{0}GS, 25^{0}GS, 24^{5}GF

	Starts	1st	2nd	3rd	Win & Pl
Hurdles	4	0	0	0	0
Career Total	**14**	**3**	**3**	**0**	**26038**
142	1/00	Donc	2m4f	A Hdl	GD £9600
109	3/99	Asct	2m110y	H NHF	G-F £2505
102	1/99	Donc	2m110y	H NHF	GD £1767

Total win prize-money £13872

Going: Sf: 0-1 GS: 0-2 Gd: 0-0 GF: - Fm: 0-1
Distance: 2m/2m3: 0-0 2m4-2m7: 0-1 3m+: 0-3
Track: LH: 0-1 RH: 0-2 Tight: 0-0 Gall: 0-1
Aids: Bl: 0-0 Vi: 0-0 Tstrap: 0-0
Best Rating: **142** 1/00 Donc 2m4f good Hdl

A useful hurdler in 1999/2000, he has been well held since returning from a break of 16 months in January 2002. Handles any ground, although may not want it too soft. Stays two miles-six.

Barneysian

89 **74**

6-y-o b g Petoski-Rosemoss (Le Moss)
A Streeter Mrs Margaret James

Placings: 0-05 (3626)
2001/02: 20^{0}S, 19^{5}GS

	Starts	1st	2nd	3rd	Win & Pl
Hurdles	2	0	0	0	0
Career Total	**3**	**0**	**0**	**0**	**0**

Going: Sf: 0-1 GS: 0-1 Gd: 0-0 GF: - Fm: 0-0
Distance: 2m/2m3: 0-0 2m4-2m7: 0-2 3m+: 0-0
Track: LH: 0-1 RH: 0-1 Tight: 0-1 Gall: 0-1
Aids: Bl: 0-0 Vi: 0-0 Tstrap: 0-0
Best Rating: **74** 2/02 MRas 2m3f110y gd-sft Hdl

Baron Allfours

97 **88**

10-y-o gr g Baron Blakeney-Georgian Quickstep (Dubassoff (USA))
Miss Z C Davison (P J Millington 1/6) The Secret Circle (1)

Placings: O/0P/2U25F3PP-PPPPPP34454P2F (4563)
2001/02: 24^{P}GS, 21^{P}G, 28^{P}GF, 24^{P}GF, 26^{P}GF, 24^{P}GF, 26^{3}GF, 22^{4}S, 21^{4}G, 21^{5}S, 26^{4}GS, 25^{P}G, 26^{2}G, 26^{F}GF

	Starts	1st	2nd	3rd	Win & Pl
Hurdles	1	0	0	0	0
Chases	13	0	1	1	2038
Career Total	**25**	**0**	**3**	**2**	**4412**

Going: Sf: 0-2 GS: 0-2 Gd: 0-4 GF: - Fm: 0-6
Distance: 2m/2m3: 0-0 2m4-2m7: 0-4 3m+: 0-10
Track: LH: 0-5 RH: 0-3 Tight: 0-9 Gall: 0-0
Aids: Bl: 0-0 Vi: 0-0 Tstrap: 0-0
Best Rating: **96** 7/00 MRas 2m6f110y good Ch

Modest maiden chaser, stays three miles plus.

Baron Bernard

95 **84**

5-y-o b g Baron Blakeney-Rosie Vii (Damsire Unregistered)
C A Dwyer Larkwood Stud

Placings: 05600 (3672)
2001/02: 16^{0}GF, 16^{5}G, 16^{6}G, 20^{0}G, 24^{0}S

	Starts	1st	2nd	3rd	Win & Pl
NH Flat	2	0	0	0	0
Hurdles	3	0	0	0	0
Career Total	**5**	**0**	**0**	**0**	**0**

Going: Sf: 0-1 GS: 0-0 Gd: 0-3 GF: - Fm: 0-1
Distance: 2m/2m3: 0-3 2m4-2m7: 0-1 3m+: 0-1
Track: LH: 0-1 RH: 0-4 Tight: 0-0 Gall: 0-4
Aids: Bl: 0-0 Vi: 0-0 Tstrap: 0-0
Best Rating: **84** 2/02 Kemp 3m110y soft Hdl

Baron De Pichon (IRE)

103 **116**

6-y-o b g Perugino (USA)-Ariadne (Bustino)
Miss S J Wilton John Pointon And Sons

Placings: 4541U (4662)
2001/02: 17^{4}GS, 20^{5}G, 16^{4}S, 16^{1}G, 16^{U}G

	Starts	1st	2nd	3rd	Win & Pl
Hurdles	5	1	0	0	3336
Career Total	**5**	**1**	**0**	**0**	**3336**
116	2/02	Ludl	2m	E Hdl	GD £3335

Total win prize-money £3336

Going: Sf: 0-1 GS: 0-1 Gd: 1-3 GF: - Fm: 0-0
Distance: **2m/2m3: 1-4** 2m4-2m7: 0-1 3m+: 0-0
Track: LH: 0-3 **RH: 1-2** Tight: 0-2 Gall: 0-1
Aids: Bl: 0-0 Vi: 0-0 Tstrap: 0-0
Best Rating: **116** 2/02 Ludl 2m good Hdl

A prolific winner on the sand, he is suited by two miles on good ground over hurdles. Won at Ludlow in February 2002 wearing sheepskin cheekpieces, but unseated rider in the valuable Novices' Hurdle at Aintree.

Baron's Pharaoh (IRE)

106 **106**

7-y-o b g Phardante (FR)-Katomi (Monksfield)
A W Carroll R H Harris & Barry Veasey

Placings: *000*/11 **(0880)**
2001/02: 16^{1}G, 19^{1}G

	Starts	1st	2nd	3rd	Win & Pl
Hurdles	2	2	0	0	6019
Career Total	**5**	**2**	**0**	**0**	**6019**

106	7/01	MRas	2m3f110y	D Hdl	GD	£3558
96	5/01	Wwck	2m	F Hdl	GD	£2460

Total win prize-money £6020

Going: Sf: 0-0 GS: 0-0 Gd: 2-2 GF: - Fm: 0-0
Distance: 2m/2m3: 1-1 2m4-2m7: 1-1 3m+: 0-0
Track: LH: 1-1 RH: 1-1 **Tight: 1-1** Gall: 0-0
Aids: Bl: 0-0 Vi: 0-0 Tstrap: 0-0
Best Rating: **106** 7/01 MRas 2m3f110y good Hdl

Fair hurdler, winner of novice events in the summer of 2001. Handles good ground.

Baroncelli

12-y-o ch g Baron Blakeney-Toumanova (High Line)
M J Wilkinson The Gardians

Placings: 0200/35/6U3412/2132124/2P/33-PUPP **(3893)**
2001/02: 25^{P}G, 26^{U}G, 26^{P}G, 29^{P}HY

	Starts	1st	2nd	3rd	Win & Pl
Chases	4	0	0	0	
Career Total	**27**	**3**	**6**	**5**	**21613**

106	4/99	Plum	3m1f110y	F(0-95)HCh	GD	£3020
106	12/98	NAbb	3m2f110y	E(0-110)HCh	SFT	£6775
98	4/98	Plum	3m1f110y	F(0-95)HCh	SFT	£3046

Total win prize-money £12841

Going: Sf: 0-1 GS: 0-0 Gd: 0-3 GF: - Fm: 0-0
Distance: 2m/2m3: 0-0 2m4-2m7: 0-0 3m+: 0-4
Track: LH: 0-1 RH: 0-1 Tight: 0-1 Gall: 0-0
Aids: Bl: 0-0 Vi: 0-0 Tstrap: 0-0
Best Rating: **106** 4/99 Chep 3m heavy Ch

Fair handicap chaser. Stays three miles plus. Acts on a sound surface. Does not appear the easiest horse to train.

Barons Court (IRE)

8-y-o b g Mandalus-Princess Rapunzel (Ete Indien (USA))
T R George Timothy N Chick

Placings: *0*/400/**PP** **(0424)**
2001/02: 19^{P}G, 20^{P}G

	Starts	1st	2nd	3rd	Win & Pl
Chases	2	0	0	0	
Career Total	**6**	**0**	**0**	**0**	**0**

Going: Sf: 0-0 GS: 0-0 Gd: 0-2 GF: - Fm: 0-0
Distance: 2m/2m3: 0-1 2m4-2m7: 0-1 3m+: 0-0
Track: LH: 0-1 RH: 0-1 Tight: 0-1 Gall: 0-0
Aids: Bl: 0-0 Vi: 0-0 Tstrap: 0-0
Best Rating: **83** 10/99 Worc 2m2f gd-fm Hdl

Barrelbio (IRE)

110(94c) (99c)**123**
7-y-o b g Elbio-Esther (Persian Bold)
F P Murtagh (J J O'Neill 26/1) W Four Times

Placings: 30P/6442040/222111551004-421333U61134220PP5 **(4834)**
2001/02: 24^{4}GS, 20^{2}F, 20^{1}GF, 20^{3}GF, 24^{3}GF, 16^{3}G, 22^{U}GF, 20^{6}GF, 21^{1}G, 21^{1}G, 21^{3}G, 21^{4}G, 21^{2}GS, 20^{2}S, 20^{0}S, 20^{P}HY, 18^{P}HY, 22^{5}G

	Starts	1st	2nd	3rd	Win & Pl
Hurdles	16	3	3	3	19707
Chases	2	0	0	1	624
Career Total	**40**	**7**	**7**	**5**	**37532**

123	10/01	Sedg	2m5f110y	D(0-125)HHdl	GD	£3171
115	9/01	Sedg	2m5f110y	D(0-120)HHdl	GD	£3337
115	6/01	Prth	2m4f110y	D(0-125)HHdl	G-F	£3406
116	12/00	Weth	2m	C(0-135)HHdl	SFT	£4940
117	7/00	Worc	2m4f	E Hdl	G-F	£2387
106	7/00	Wolv	2m	E Hdl	G-S	£2298
100	6/00	Prth	2m4f110y	D Hdl	GD	£3435

Total win prize-money £22976

Going: Sf: 0-4 GS: 0-2 Gd: 2-6 GF: - Fm: 1-6
Distance: 2m/2m3: 0-2 **2m4-2m7: 3-14** 3m+: 0-2
Track: **LH: 2-12** RH: 1-6 **Tight: 2-7** Gall: 0-3
Aids: Bl: 0-1 Vi: 0-0 Tstrap: 0-0
Best Rating: **123** 11/01 MRas 2m5f110y gd-sft Hdl

Suited by decent ground and hold-up tactics, he has shown consistent form in modest handicap hurdles in the last couple of years. Acts on most types of ground and is most effective over trips of around two and a half miles.

Barren Lands

85(114h) (120h)**90**
7-y-o b g Green Desert (USA)-Current Raiser (Filiberto (USA))
K Bishop Mrs E K Ellis

Placings: 62314102/031P106-2004342F22 **(4593)**
2001/02: 16^{2}G, 16^{0}GF, 17^{0}S, 16^{4}GS, 19^{3}GS, 19^{4}GS, 17^{2}GS, 16^{F}G, 16^{2}GS, 16^{2}G

	Starts	1st	2nd	3rd	Win & Pl
Hurdles	10	0	4	1	8380
Career Total	**25**	**4**	**6**	**3**	**24211**

116	1/01	Tntn	2m1f	D(0-120)HHdl	SFT	£3575
116	10/00	Winc	2m	E(0-110)HHdl	G-S	£3250
104	1/00	Tntn	2m1f	D(0-120)HHdl	G-S	£3526
109	12/99	Winc	2m	F(0-100)HHdl	SFT	£2402

Total win prize-money £12753

Going: Sf: 0-1 GS: 0-5 Gd: 0-3 GF: - Fm: 0-1
Distance: 2m/2m3: 0-8 2m4-2m7: 0-2 3m+: 0-0
Track: LH: 0-3 RH: 0-7 Tight: 0-4 Gall: 0-0
Aids: Bl: 0-0 Vi: 0-0 Tstrap: 0-0
Best Rating: **116** 4/02 Uttx 2m good Hdl

Moderate hurdler, he is best on a right-handed track over two miles with give in the ground.

Barresbo

108 **110**
8-y-o b g Barrys Gamble-Bo' Babbity (Strong Gale)
A C Whillans E Waugh

Placings: 0/2023044/1-22302142 **(4877)**
2001/02: 16^{2}GF, 17^{2}S, 20^{3}HY, 19^{0}G, 17^{2}S, 20^{1}HY, 16^{4}S, 24^{2}G

	Starts	1st	2nd	3rd	Win & Pl
Hurdles	8	1	4	1	8250
Career Total	**17**	**2**	**6**	**2**	**13886**

110	2/02	Ayr	2m4f	F(0-95)HHdl	HVY	£3150
104	4/01	Prth	2m110y	G Hdl	HVY	£3614

Total win prize-money £6764

Going: Sf: 1-5 GS: 0-0 Gd: 0-2 GF: - Fm: 0-1
Distance: 2m/2m3: 0-5 **2m4-2m7: 1-2** 3m+: 0-1
Track: **LH: 1-2** RH: 0-5 Tight: 0-2 Gall: 0-0
Aids: Bl: 0-0 Vi: 0-0 Tstrap: 0-0
Best Rating: **110** 4/02 Prth 3m110y good Hdl

Handicap hurdler, effective at up to three miles, likes soft ground but handles faster.

Barrigan's Hill (IRE)

92(101h) (103h)**100**
12-y-o b g Lafontaine (USA)-Limerick Lady (The Parson)
D L Williams N F Dawe

Placings: *00/0F/00363330*060/0520/41F21026/036640P1106-43023 **(1354)**
2001/02: 16^{4}G, 17^{3}GF, 20^{0}G, 22^{2}GF, 21^{3}GF

	Starts	1st	2nd	3rd	Win & Pl
Hurdles	4	0	1	1	921
Chases	1	0	0	1	648
Career Total	**43**	**4**	**4**	**7**	**17143**

113	2/01	Hntg	2m4f110y	F(0-95)HHdl	G-S	£2265
101	2/01	Ludl	2m	G Hdl	G-S	£2128
98	1/00	Punc	2m4f	(0-109)HHdl	SFT	£3588
88	10/99	Thur	2m	(0-95)HHdl	G-Y	£2587

Total win prize-money £10570

Going: Sf: 0-0 GS: 0-0 Gd: 0-2 GF: - Fm: 0-3
Distance: 2m/2m3: 0-2 2m4-2m7: 0-3 3m+: 0-0
Track: LH: 0-4 RH: 0-1 Tight: 0-5 Gall: 0-0
Aids: Bl: 0-0 Vi: 0-0 Tstrap: 0-0
Best Rating: **113** 2/01 Hntg 2m4f110y gd-sft Hdl

Barron Bay (USA)

10-y-o br g Track Barron (USA)-In Bay (ARG) (Halpern Bay (USA))
Mrs P A Tetley Brian Tetley

Placings: *0*/P/P **(0913)**
2001/02: 24^{P}G

	Starts	1st	2nd	3rd	Win & Pl
Chases	1	0	0	0	
Career Total	**3**	**0**	**0**	**0**	

Going: Sf: 0-0 GS: 0-0 Gd: 0-1 GF: - Fm: 0-0
Distance: 2m/2m3: 0-0 2m4-2m7: 0-0 3m+: 0-1
Track: LH: 0-1 RH: 0-0 Tight: 0-1 Gall: 0-0
Aids: Bl: 0-0 Vi: 0-0 Tstrap: 0-0
Best Rating: **74** 5/96 Extr 2m2f gd-fm NHF

Barrow (SWI)

100 **113**
5-y-o br h Caerleon (USA)-Bestow (Shirley Heights)
Ferdy Murphy Janet & Myrtle

Placings: 4324-2 **(0178)**
2001/02: 22^{2}GF

Starts	1st	2nd	3rd	Win & Pl
Hurdles	1	0	1	0	848
Career Total	**5**	**0**	**2**	**1**	**3498**

Going: Sf: 0-0 GS: 0-0 Gd: 0-0 GF: - Fm: 0-1
Distance: 2m/2m3: 0-0 2m4-2m7: 0-1 3m+: 0-0
Track: LH: 0-1 RH: 0-0 Tight: 0-0 Gall: 0-0
Aids: Bl: 0-0 Vi: 0-0 Tstrap: 0-0
Best Rating: **113** 5/01 Ayr 2m6f gd-fm Hdl

Barrow Boy Lad

5-y-o b g Lyphento (USA)-Miss Sula Bula (Sula Bula)
J M Bradley John Brookman

Placings: U **(0083)**
2001/02: 19^{U}G

	Starts	1st	2nd	3rd	Win & Pl

	Starts	1st	2nd	3rd	Win & Pl
Hurdles	1	0	0	0	
Career Total	**1**	**0**	**0**	**0**	

Going: Sf: 0-0 GS: 0-0 Gd: 0-1 GF: - Fm: 0-0
Distance: 2m/2m3: 0-0 2m4-2m7: 0-1 3m+: 0-0
Track: LH: 0-0 RH: 0-1 Tight: 0-0 Gall: 0-0
Aids: Bl: 0-0 Vi: 0-0 Tstrap: 0-0
Best Rating:

Barryscourt Lad (IRE)

8-y-o b g Glacial Storm (USA)-Clonana (Le Bavard (FR))
D Pipe Miss Joanna Holmes

Placings:2252 (4678)
2001/02: 24^{2}S, 26^{2}HY, 24^{5}G, 25^{2}G

	Starts	1st	2nd	3rd	Win & Pl
Chases	4	0	3	0	5422
Career Total	**4**	**0**	**3**	**0**	**5422**

Going: Sf: 0-2 GS: 0-0 Gd: 0-2 GF: - Fm: 0-0
Distance: 2m/2m3: 0-0 2m4-2m7: 0-0 3m+: 0-4
Track: LH: 0-2 RH: 0-2 Tight: 0-1 Gall: 0-0
Aids: Bl: 0-0 Vi: 0-0 Tstrap: 0-0
Best Rating: **117** 4/02 Aint 3m1f good Ch

Promising hunter chaser, stays four miles but might benefit from stronger handling.

Barton

110(117h) (170h)**165**
9-y-o ch g Port Etienne (FR)-Peanuts (FR) (Mistigri)
T D Easterby Stanley W Clarke

Placings:*O2*/1111111/12514-**2111101** (4666)
2001/02: 16^{2}G, 20^{1}G, 24^{1}GS, 16^{1}GS, 20^{1}S, 16^{0}GS, 25^{1}G

	Starts	1st	2nd	3rd	Win & Pl
Chases	7	5	1	0	78675
Career Total	**21**	**14**	**3**	**0**	**286357**

165	4/02	Aint	3m1f	A Ch	GD	£46500
149	1/02	Newc	2m4f	A Ch	SFT	£14875
147	12/01	Weth	2m	C Ch	G-S	£6376
151	12/01	Newc	3m	C Ch	G-S	£6711
139	11/01	Newc	2m4f	E Ch	GD	£3110
170	4/01	Aint	2m4f	A Hdl	HVY	£71400
163	11/00	Newc	2m	A Hdl	SFT	£22200
163	4/99	Aint	2m4f	A Hdl	GD	£17850
160	3/99	Chel	2m5f	A Hdl	G-S	£45960
158	1/99	Donc	2m4f	A Hdl	GD	£10087
149	12/98	Sand	2m6f	A Hdl	GD	£9689
148	11/98	Uttx	2m4f110y	A Hdl	GD	£9419
119	10/98	Weth	2m7f	C Hdl	SFT	£4185
113	10/98	Weth	2m4f110y	D Hdl	GD	£3037

Total win prize-money £271404

Going: Sf: 1-1 GS: 2-3 Gd: 2-3 GF: - Fm: 0-0
Distance: 2m/2m3: 1-3 2m4-2m7: 2-2 3m+: 2-2
Track: **LH: 5-7** RH: 0-0 Tight: 1-1 **Gall: 3-4**
Aids: Bl: 0-0 Vi: 0-0 Tstrap: 0-0
Best Rating: **170** 4/01 Aint 2m4f heavy Hdl

A top-class hurdler, he has switched his attentions to chasing and, after a minor hiccup when beaten on his chasing debut at Wetherby in November 2001, managed to win two uncompetitive events at Newcastle, but his jumping was much improved when winning at Wetherby after Christmas. He then returned to Newcastle to gain his fourth straight success over fences in emphatic fashion, but he was very disappointing in the Arkle at Cheltenham in March 2002. Bounced back better than ever at Aintree (his third success at the meeting). Acts on good and soft ground. Stays three miles but has won over two miles.

Barton Account (NZ)

103 **98**
7-y-o b g Accountant (NZ)-Wheels (NZ) (Redolent Ii (AUS))
T H Caldwell (H D Daly 19/5) M J Caldwell

Placings:61-554 (1280)
2001/02: 25^{5}G, 20^{5}G, 24^{4}GF

	Starts	1st	2nd	3rd	Win & Pl
Hurdles	3	0	0	0	0
Career Total	**5**	**1**	**0**	**0**	**2296**

98	4/01	Hrfd	3m2f	E Hdl	GD	£2296

Total win prize-money £2296

Going: Sf: 0-0 GS: 0-0 Gd: 0-2 GF: - Fm: 0-1
Distance: 2m/2m3: 0-0 2m4-2m7: 0-1 3m+: 0-2
Track: LH: 0-2 RH: 0-0 Tight: 0-1 Gall: 0-0
Aids: Bl: 0-0 Vi: 0-0 Tstrap: 0-0
Best Rating: **98** 8/01 Bang 2m4f good Hdl

Barton Bandit

97(83h) (78h)**100**
6-y-o ch g Sula Bula-Yamrah (Milford)
D McCain (H D Daly 23/5) D McCain

Placings:4-0P4PF4 (4843)
2001/02: 20^{0}G, 17^{P}S, 16^{4}S, 16^{P}S, 17^{F}S, 17^{4}G

	Starts	1st	2nd	3rd	Win & Pl
Hurdles	2	0	0	0	0
Chases	4	0	0	0	607
Career Total	**7**	**0**	**0**	**0**	**607**

Going: Sf: 0-4 GS: 0-0 Gd: 0-2 GF: - Fm: 0-0
Distance: 2m/2m3: 0-5 2m4-2m7: 0-1 3m+: 0-0
Track: LH: 0-3 RH: 0-3 Tight: 0-4 Gall: 0-0
Aids: Bl: 0-0 Vi: 0-0 Tstrap: 0-3
Best Rating: **100** 4/02 Bang 2m1f110y good Ch

Modest novice chaser and a rather clumsy jumper.

Barton Bog (IRE)

99(99h) (89h)**96**
8-y-o gr g Roselier (FR)-Al's Niece (Al Sirat (USA))
J R Cornwall (N A Twiston-Davies 23/10) J R Cornwall

Placings:630232-**23523P0** (4634)
2001/02: 24^{2}GF, 24^{3}G, 25^{5}G, 25^{2}GS, 24^{3}S, 23^{P}S, 24^{0}GF

	Starts	1st	2nd	3rd	Win & Pl
Hurdles	1	0	1	0	1028
Chases	6	0	1	2	2155
Career Total	**13**	**0**	**4**	**4**	**5398**

Going: Sf: 0-2 GS: 0-1 Gd: 0-2 GF: - Fm: 0-2
Distance: 2m/2m3: 0-0 2m4-2m7: 0-0 3m+: 0-7
Track: LH: 0-2 RH: 0-4 Tight: 0-1 Gall: 0-0
Aids: Bl: 0-3 Vi: 0-0 Tstrap: 0-0
Best Rating: **96** 10/01 Extr 3m1f110y gd-sft Ch

A winning point to pointer, he made the frame over hurdles but does not have much in the way of toe and needs staying distances over fences. Suited by soft ground but acts on a sound surface as well. Stays three miles.

Barton Buster

66f **35f**
7-y-o b g Bustino-Chicory (Vaigly Great)
T R George C N Walker

Placings:*0*/0 (1019)
2001/02: 16^{0}G

	Starts	1st	2nd	3rd	Win & Pl
NH Flat	1	0	0	0	
Career Total	**2**	**0**	**0**	**0**	

Going: Sf: 0-0 GS: 0-0 Gd: 0-1 GF: - Fm: 0-0
Distance: 2m/2m3: 0-1 2m4-2m7: 0-0 3m+: 0-0
Track: LH: 0-1 RH: 0-0 Tight: 0-0 Gall: 0-0
Aids: Bl: 0-0 Vi: 0-0 Tstrap: 0-0
Best Rating: **71** 11/99 Chep 2m110y gd-sft NHF

Barton Dante

104 **107**
5-y-o b m Phardante (FR)-Cindie Girl (Orchestra)
M W Easterby Stanley W Clarke

Placings:*22-21*31210 (4420)
2001/02: 16^{2}G, 17^{1}G, 17^{3}G, 19^{1}GF, 19^{2}G, 21^{1}HY, 21^{0}GS

	Starts	1st	2nd	3rd	Win & Pl
NH Flat	2	1	1	0	2420
Hurdles	5	2	1	1	5566
Career Total	**9**	**3**	**4**	**1**	**9121**

107	1/02	Sedg	2m5f110y	E Hdl	HVY	£2450
105	11/01	Catt	2m3f	F Hdl	G-F	£1907
97	10/01	Bang	2m1f	H NHF	GD	£1767

Total win prize-money £6126

Going: Sf: 1-1 GS: 0-1 Gd: 1-4 GF: - Fm: 1-1
Distance: **2m/2m3: 2-5** 2m4-2m7: 1-2 3m+: 0-0
Track: **LH: 3-6** RH: 0-1 **Tight: 3-5** Gall: 0-1
Aids: Bl: 0-0 Vi: 0-0 **Tstrap: 1-3**
Best Rating: **107** 1/02 Sedg 2m5f110y heavy Hdl

A half-sister to the chaser Dorans Gold, she was runner-up in three bumpers before scoring at Bangor in October 2001 and has continued in good form over hurdles in modest company, gaining further victories at Catterick and Sedgefield. She carries her head high and wears a sheepskin noseband and a tongue strap. Stays two miles five furlongs and acts on any ground.

Barton Dream (IRE)

97 **76?**
6-y-o b g Le Bavard (FR)-Tax Dream (IRE) (Electric)
John Allen (D McCain 18/5) Nic Allen

Placings:*0*000 (2514)
2001/02: 17^{0}G, 16^{0}S, 16^{0}S, 19^{0}S

	Starts	1st	2nd	3rd	Win & Pl
NH Flat	2	0	0	0	0
Hurdles	2	0	0	0	0
Career Total	**4**	**0**	**0**	**0**	

Going: Sf: 0-3 GS: 0-0 Gd: 0-1 GF: - Fm: 0-0
Distance: 2m/2m3: 0-4 2m4-2m7: 0-0 3m+: 0-0
Track: LH: 0-3 RH: 0-1 Tight: 0-2 Gall: 0-0
Aids: Bl: 0-0 Vi: 0-0 Tstrap: 0-0
Best Rating: **72** 5/01 Extr 2m1f good NHF

Barton Heights

97 **78**
10-y-o b g Primitive Rising (USA)-Changatre (Malinowski (USA))
Miss M Bragg W H Whitley

Placings:000211/305431/224/**44P3F**/45-0P4P25F (1269)
2001/02: 19^{0}G, 22^{P}G, 17^{4}G, 22^{P}GF, 17^{2}G, 22^{5}G, 17^{F}GF

	Starts	1st	2nd	3rd	Win & Pl
Hurdles	7	0	1	0	662
Career Total	**29**	**3**	**4**	**3**	**13388**

88	3/97	Weth	2m7f	G(0-100)HHdl	GD	£2250
85	4/96	Carl	2m4f110y	D(0-105)HHdl	FRM	£3123
82	3/96	Catt	2m3f	F(0-100)HHdl	GD	£2101

Total win prize-money £7474

Going: Sf: 0-0 GS: 0-0 Gd: 0-5 GF: - Fm: 0-2
Distance: 2m/2m3: 0-4 2m4-2m7: 0-3 3m+: 0-0
Track: LH: 0-6 RH: 0-1 Tight: 0-6 Gall: 0-0
Aids: Bl: 0-6 Vi: 0-1 Tstrap: 0-0
Best Rating: **105** 11/99 NAbb 2m5f110y gd-sft Ch

Barton Lass

8-y-o gr m Jester-Deauville Duchess (Ballad Rock)
M R Ewer-Hoad (D M Grissell 1/6) Mrs S M Becvar

Placings:*0/00*B/0P **(0872)**
2001/02: 16^{0}GF, 16^{P}GS

	Starts	1st	2nd	3rd	Win & Pl
Hurdles	2	0	0	0	
Career Total	6	0	0	0	

Going: Sf: 0-0 GS: 0-1 Gd: 0-0 GF: - Fm: 0-1
Distance: 2m/2m3: 0-2 2m4-2m7: 0-0 3m+: 0-0
Track: LH: 0-2 RH: 0-0 Tight: 0-2 Gall: 0-0
Aids: Bl: 0-0 Vi: 0-0 Tstrap: 0-0
Best Rating: **80** 10/98 Chel 2m110y gd-sft NHF

Barton Nlc

9-y-o b g Nicholas Bill-Dutch Majesty (Homing)
Paul Keane (A Streeter 20/1) Mrs Liz Harrington

Placings:*4625/0/0*P-2F **(4172)**
2001/02: 26^{2}HY, 26^{F}GS

	Starts	1st	2nd	3rd	Win & Pl
Chases	2	0	1	0	328
Career Total	**9**	**0**	**2**	**0**	**750**

Going: Sf: 0-1 GS: 0-1 Gd: 0-0 GF: - Fm: 0-0
Distance: 2m/2m3: 0-0 2m4-2m7: 0-0 3m+: 0-2
Track: LH: 0-0 RH: 0-0 Tight: 0-0 Gall: 0-0
Aids: Bl: 0-1 Vi: 0-0 Tstrap: 0-0
Best Rating: **102** 2/99 Sedg 2m1f good NHF

Moderate ex-pointer, distant runner-up on his hunter chase debut.

Barton Rose

11-y-o b g Derring Rose-Barton Sauce (Saucy Kit)
Mrs S J Evans Mrs S J Evans

Placings:F-0P **(0579)**
2001/02: 19^{0}F, 24^{P}GF

	Starts	1st	2nd	3rd	Win & Pl
Chases	2	0	0	0	
Career Total	**3**	**0**	**0**	**0**	

Going: Sf: 0-0 GS: 0-0 Gd: 0-0 GF: - Fm: 0-2
Distance: 2m/2m3: 0-0 2m4-2m7: 0-1 3m+: 0-1
Track: LH: 0-1 RH: 0-1 Tight: 0-1 Gall: 0-0
Aids: Bl: 0-0 Vi: 0-0 Tstrap: 0-0
Best Rating: **65** 5/01 Extr 2m3f110y firm Ch

Barton Saint (NZ)

90(94h) (65h)76
7-y-o ch g St Hilarion (USA)-Aquatramp (NZ) (Pevero)
T D Easterby Mrs E Harrington

Placings:P00-0 **(0071)**
2001/02: 21^{0}G

	Starts	1st	2nd	3rd	Win & Pl
Hurdles	1	0	0	0	
Career Total	**4**	**0**	**0**	**0**	

Going: Sf: 0-0 GS: 0-0 Gd: 0-1 GF: - Fm: 0-0
Distance: 2m/2m3: 0-0 2m4-2m7: 0-1 3m+: 0-0
Track: LH: 0-1 RH: 0-0 Tight: 0-1 Gall: 0-0
Aids: Bl: 0-0 Vi: 0-0 Tstrap: 0-0
Best Rating: **85** 12/00 Donc 2m110y gd-sft Hdl

Barton Scamp

83 64
10-y-o ch g Sadeem (USA)-Hachimitsu (Vaigly Great)
D L Williams Miss B W Palmer

Placings:*0/046604/*UPF06/P0P055113440/5F5U00/500-00P **(0953)**
2001/02: 16^{0}GF, 22^{0}GF, 20^{P}S

	Starts	1st	2nd	3rd	Win & Pl
Hurdles	3	0	0	0	
Career Total	**36**	**2**	**0**	**1**	**4267**

92	12/98	Strf	2m110y	G(0-95)HHdl	SFT	£1772
77	11/98	Uttx	2m	G(0-90)HHdl	SFT	£1647

Total win prize-money £3420

Going: Sf: 0-1 GS: 0-0 Gd: 0-0 GF: - Fm: 0-2
Distance: 2m/2m3: 0-1 2m4-2m7: 0-2 3m+: 0-0
Track: LH: 0-3 RH: 0-0 Tight: 0-1 Gall: 0-0
Aids: Bl: 0-0 Vi: 0-0 Tstrap: 0-1
Best Rating: **101** 2/97 Newc 2m good Hdl

Basil

97(79h) 76
9-y-o br g Lighter-Thrupence (Royal Highway)
S G Knight Mrs C J Dunn

Placings:PU00-RU3P5 **(0919)**
2001/02: 26^{R}GF, 25^{U}G, 21^{3}GS, 26^{P}GF, 21^{5}GF

	Starts	1st	2nd	3rd	Win & Pl
Chases	5	0	0	1	647
Career Total	**9**	**0**	**0**	**1**	**647**

Going: Sf: 0-0 GS: 0-1 Gd: 0-1 GF: - Fm: 0-3
Distance: 2m/2m3: 0-0 2m4-2m7: 0-2 3m+: 0-3
Track: LH: 0-4 RH: 0-1 Tight: 0-4 Gall: 0-0
Aids: Bl: 0-0 Vi: 0-0 Tstrap: 0-0
Best Rating: **76** 7/01 NAbb 2m5f110y gd-fm Ch

Basil Grainger (IRE)

5-y-o ch g Good Thyne (USA)-Lynn Grange (Northern Guest (USA))
J T Gifford Martin & Valerie Slade

Placings:*000* **(4138)**
2001/02: 16^{0}G, 16^{0}S, 16^{0}GS

	Starts	1st	2nd	3rd	Win & Pl
NH Flat	2	0	0	0	0
Hurdles	1	0	0	0	0
Career Total	**3**	**0**	**0**	**0**	

Going: Sf: 0-1 GS: 0-1 Gd: 0-1 GF: - Fm: 0-0
Distance: 2m/2m3: 0-3 2m4-2m7: 0-0 3m+: 0-0
Track: LH: 0-0 RH: 0-3 Tight: 0-0 Gall: 0-0
Aids: Bl: 0-0 Vi: 0-0 Tstrap: 0-0
Best Rating: **81** 12/01 Asct 2m110y good NHF

Basil Street (IRE)

10-y-o b g Glenstal (USA)-Pockatello (Commanche Run)
Mrs P D Innes (S Flook 10/3) Peter Innes

Placings:422F00/24/**30**/P **(4690)**
2001/02: 25^{P}GF

	Starts	1st	2nd	3rd	Win & Pl
Chases	1	0	0	0	
Career Total	**11**	**0**	**3**	**1**	**2872**

Going: Sf: 0-0 GS: 0-0 Gd: 0-0 GF: - Fm: 0-1
Distance: 2m/2m3: 0-0 2m4-2m7: 0-0 3m+: 0-1
Track: LH: 0-1 RH: 0-0 Tight: 0-1 Gall: 0-0
Aids: Bl: 0-0 Vi: 0-0 Tstrap: 0-0
Best Rating: **99** 10/95 Asct 2m110y gd-fm Hdl

Basincroft

12-y-o b g Celtic Cone-Somay (Tarkhun)
Miss C F Elliott R Cook

Placings:*000/*03BP/6323/600/**U**/2P3-04 **(0322)**
2001/02: 24^{0}GS, 21^{4}G

	Starts	1st	2nd	3rd	Win & Pl
Chases	2	0	0	0	168
Career Total	**20**	**0**	**2**	**4**	**2227**

Going: Sf: 0-0 GS: 0-1 Gd: 0-1 GF: - Fm: 0-0
Distance: 2m/2m3: 0-0 2m4-2m7: 0-1 3m+: 0-1
Track: LH: 0-1 RH: 0-1 Tight: 0-2 Gall: 0-0
Aids: Bl: 0-0 Vi: 0-0 Tstrap: 0-0
Best Rating: **92** 2/01 Folk 2m5f soft Ch

Bassenhally

101 113
12-y-o ch g Celtic Cone-Milly Kelly (Murrayfield)
Mrs P Sly Thorney Racing Club

Placings:00/4F2263/**10UP**306/**F11441U**/6**12**/**11PP6P**/P-12P **(4537)**
2001/02: 24^{1}S, 24^{2}S, 21^{P}G

	Starts	1st	2nd	3rd	Win & Pl
Chases	3	1	1	0	6095
Career Total	**35**	**8**	**4**	**2**	**37909**

113	10/01	Fknm	3m110y	F(0-110)HCh	SFT	£4760
130	12/99	Fknm	3m110y	D(0-120)HCh	GD	£4905
130	10/99	Fknm	3m110y	F(0-110)HCh	GD	£4606
123	10/98	Fknm	3m110y	E(0-110)HCh	GD	£4597
110	3/98	Fknm	2m5f110y	D(0-120)HCh	GD	£4265
110	12/97	MRas	3m1f	E(0-105)HCh	HVY	£3434
112	11/97	MRas	3m1f	E(0-105)HCh	G-S	£3678
85	11/96	Uttx	2m	E(0-100)HHdl	GD	£2347

Total win prize-money £32598

Going: Sf: 1-2 GS: 0-0 Gd: 0-1 GF: - Fm: 0-0
Distance: 2m/2m3: 0-0 2m4-2m7: 0-1 **3m+: 1-2**
Track: **LH: 1-3** RH: 0-0 **Tight: 1-3** Gall: 0-0

Aids: Bl: 0-0 Vi: 0-0 Tstrap: 0-0
Best Rating: **130** 12/99 Fknm 3m110y good Ch

Veteran handicap chaser. He goes well at Fakenham and seems to run his best races when fresh. Handles good ground or softer and often front runs.

Bath House Boy (IRE)

104 **89**

9-y-o b g Don't Forget Me-Domiciliate (King's Lake (USA))
Mrs Pippa Bickerton David Bickerton

Placings:3010P4/**4F2P4540**/0-030020 **(1492)**
2001/02: 20^{0}GF, 22^{3}GF, 22^{0}GF, 20^{0}G, 24^{2}GF, 26^{0}G

	Starts	1st	2nd	3rd	Win & Pl
Hurdles	6	0	1	1	762
Career Total	**21**	**1**	**2**	**2**	**5531**

109 12/98 Uttx 2m4f110y E Hdl G-S £1955
Total win prize-money £1956

Going: Sf: 0-0 GS: 0-0 Gd: 0-2 GF: - Fm: 0-4
Distance: 2m/2m3: 0-0 2m4-2m7: 0-4 3m+: 0-2
Track: LH: 0-5 RH: 0-1 Tight: 0-4 Gall: 0-1
Aids: Bl: 0-0 Vi: 0-0 Tstrap: 0-0
Best Rating: **120** 12/99 Towc 2m6f good Ch

Batoutoftheblue

101 **120**

9-y-o br g Batshoof-Action Belle (Auction Ring (USA))
G A Swinbank Mrs I Gibson

Placings:333220/2B3-1 **(0178)**
2001/02: 22^{1}GF

	Starts	1st	2nd	3rd	Win & Pl
Hurdles	1	1	0	0	2968
Career Total	**10**	**1**	**3**	**4**	**7265**

120 5/01 Ayr 2m6f E Hdl G-F £2968
Total win prize-money £2968

Going: Sf: 0-0 GS: 0-0 Gd: 0-0 GF: - Fm: 1-1
Distance: 2m/2m3: 0-0 **2m4-2m7: 1-1** 3m+: 0-0
Track: **LH: 1-1** RH: 0-0 Tight: 0-0 Gall: 0-0
Aids: Bl: 0-0 Vi: 0-0 Tstrap: 0-0
Best Rating: **120** 5/01 Ayr 2m6f gd-fm Hdl

Batswing

113(110h) (130h)**142**

7-y-o b g Batshoof-Magic Milly (Simply Great (FR))
B Ellison Ashley Carr

Placings:13/4/21B3-300**112041** **(4960a)**
2001/02: 16^{3}G, 16^{0}GS, 16^{0}G, 16^{1}G, 16^{1}S, 21^{2}S, 16^{0}G, 16^{4}G, 16^{1}GY

	Starts	1st	2nd	3rd	Win & Pl
Hurdles	3	0	0	1	5000
Chases	6	3	1	0	21244
Career Total	**16**	**5**	**2**	**3**	**40972**

142 4/02 Punc 2m (0-127)HCh G-Y £9969
124 1/02 Muss 2m E Ch SFT £3107
117 1/02 Muss 2m D Ch GD £4192
122 2/01 Donc 2m110y C(0-130)HHdl GD £5534
113 3/99 Tntn 2m3f110y E Hdl SFT £2452
Total win prize-money £25257

Going: Sf: 1-2 GS: 0-1 Gd: 1-5 GF: - Fm: 0-0
Distance: **2m/2m3: 3-8** 2m4-2m7: 0-1 3m+: 0-0
Track: LH: 0-5 **RH: 3-4 Tight: 2-4** Gall: 0-2
Aids: Bl: 0-0 Vi: 0-0 Tstrap: 0-0
Best Rating: **142** 4/02 Punc 2m gd-yld Ch

Decent on the Flat, he failed to build on the promise he showed over hurdles at Cheltenham in November, but made up for it when switched to fences, wining his first two races in fine style over two miles. Was not disgraced in Listed company this spring before winning at Punchestown. Acts well with cut in the ground.

Battle Cruiser (USA)

88 **64**

4-y-o b g Sea Hero (USA)-Wholey Ghost (USA) (Rare Performer (USA))
Miss S J Wilton (Charles O'Brien 9/10) John Pointon And Sons

Placings:3 **(2421)**
2001/02: 17^{3}GS

	Starts	1st	2nd	3rd	Win & Pl
Hurdles	1	0	0	1	385
Career Total	**1**	**0**	**0**	**1**	**385**

Going: Sf: 0-0 GS: 0-1 Gd: 0-0 GF: - Fm: 0-0
Distance: 2m/2m3: 0-1 2m4-2m7: 0-0 3m+: 0-0
Track: LH: 0-1 RH: 0-0 Tight: 0-1 Gall: 0-0
Aids: Bl: 0-0 Vi: 0-0 Tstrap: 0-0
Best Rating: **64** 11/01 Bang 2m1f gd-sft Hdl

Battle Royal (IRE)

99 **124**

8-y-o b g Phardante (FR)-Bargara (Bargello)
P F Nicholls Sir Robert Ogden

Placings:FU/13 **(2028)**
2001/02: 19^{1}G, 20^{3}GS

	Starts	1st	2nd	3rd	Win & Pl
Hurdles	2	1	0	1	5247
Career Total	**4**	**1**	**0**	**1**	**5247**

123 10/01 MRas 2m3f110y E Hdl GD £3234
Total win prize-money £3234

Going: Sf: 0-0 GS: 0-1 Gd: 1-1 GF: - Fm: 0-0
Distance: 2m/2m3: 0-0 **2m4-2m7: 1-2** 3m+: 0-0
Track: LH: 0-1 **RH: 1-1 Tight: 1-1** Gall: 0-0
Aids: Bl: 0-0 Vi: 0-0 Tstrap: 0-0
Best Rating: **124** 11/01 Chep 2m4f gd-sft Hdl

A half-brother to Cahervillahow, returned from almost two years off to score on his hurdling debut at Market Rasen and ran a good race when making a huge step up in grade at Chepstow in November. Likely to return to fences in due course.

Battling Buster (IRE)

5-y-o b g Glacial Storm (USA)-Flutter (IRE) (Floriferous)
P R Webber G Regan

Placings:*0* **(4158)**
2001/02: 16^{0}GS

	Starts	1st	2nd	3rd	Win & Pl
NH Flat	1	0	0	0	
Career Total	**1**	**0**	**0**	**0**	

Going: Sf: 0-0 GS: 0-1 Gd: 0-0 GF: - Fm: 0-0
Distance: 2m/2m3: 0-1 2m4-2m7: 0-0 3m+: 0-0
Track: LH: 0-0 RH: 0-1 Tight: 0-0 Gall: 0-0
Aids: Bl: 0-0 Vi: 0-0 Tstrap: 0-0
Best Rating:

Bauble

(86h) **68**

7-y-o ch g Sanglamore (USA)-Princess Borghese (USA) (Nijinsky (CAN))
G L Moore Paul Chapman

Placings:55500/120/P6P-4 **(0061)**
2001/02: 26^{4}G

	Starts	1st	2nd	3rd	Win & Pl
Chases	1	0	0	0	282
Career Total	**12**	**1**	**1**	**0**	**3369**

96 11/99 Folk 2m6f110y F(0-110)HHdl G-S £2162
Total win prize-money £2163

Going: Sf: 0-0 GS: 0-0 Gd: 0-1 GF: - Fm: 0-0
Distance: 2m/2m3: 0-0 2m4-2m7: 0-0 3m+: 0-1
Track: LH: 0-0 RH: 0-1 Tight: 0-1 Gall: 0-0
Aids: Bl: 0-0 Vi: 0-0 Tstrap: 0-0
Best Rating: **96** 12/99 Font 2m2f110y gd-sft Hdl

Bay Island (IRE)

81 **66**

6-y-o b/br g Treasure Hunter-Wild Deer (Royal Buck)
Mrs H Dalton B Perkins

Placings:PP5 **(4241)**
2001/02: 24^{P}HY, 24^{P}G, 20^{5}GF

	Starts	1st	2nd	3rd	Win & Pl
Hurdles	1	0	0	0	0
Chases	2	0	0	0	0
Career Total	**3**	**0**	**0**	**0**	**0**

Going: Sf: 0-1 GS: 0-0 Gd: 0-1 GF: - Fm: 0-1
Distance: 2m/2m3: 0-0 2m4-2m7: 0-1 3m+: 0-2
Track: LH: 0-1 RH: 0-2 Tight: 0-1 Gall: 0-1
Aids: Bl: 0-0 Vi: 0-0 Tstrap: 0-1
Best Rating: **66** 3/02 Hntg 2m4f110y gd-fm Ch

Irish point winner but has achieved little over fences here so far.

Bay Lightning (IRE)

97 **101**

5-y-o b g Un Desperado (FR)-Glendale Charmer (Down The Hatch)
Miss H C Knight David & Elaine Long

Placings:*0-62* **(1539)**
2001/02: 17^{6}G, 19^{2}G

	Starts	1st	2nd	3rd	Win & Pl
NH Flat	1	0	0	0	0
Hurdles	1	0	1	0	784
Career Total	**3**	**0**	**1**	**0**	**784**

Going: Sf: 0-0 GS: 0-0 Gd: 0-2 GF: - Fm: 0-0
Distance: 2m/2m3: 0-1 2m4-2m7: 0-1 3m+: 0-0
Track: LH: 0-1 RH: 0-1 Tight: 0-1 Gall: 0-0
Aids: Bl: 0-0 Vi: 0-0 Tstrap: 0-0
Best Rating: **101** 10/01 Hrfd 2m3f110y good Hdl

Bay Magic (IRE)

100 **97**

9-y-o b g Ela-Mana-Mou-Come In (Be My Guest (USA))
J Howard Johnson J Howard Johnson

Placings:*61/45*02245000/32/2P4344-2545 **(4432)**

2001/02: 20^{2}GF, 21^{5}GF, 20^{4}HY, 20^{5}HY

	Starts	1st	2nd	3rd	Win & Pl
Hurdles	4	0	1	0	663
Career Total	**24**	**1**	**5**	**2**	**9853**

112 9/97 List 2m NHF SFT £3730
Total win prize-money £3730

Going: Sf: 0-2 GS: 0-0 Gd: 0-0 GF: - Fm: 0-2
Distance: 2m/2m3: 0-0 2m4-2m7: 0-4 3m+: 0-0
Track: LH: 0-4 RH: 0-0 Tight: 0-1 Gall: 0-1
Aids: Bl: 0-1 Vi: 0-0 Tstrap: 0-0
Best Rating: **112** 5/98 Leop 2m gd-fm NHF

Mainly consistent, he proved he goes on heavy ground, but the fact that he has yet to win over hurdles is a bit of a concern.

Bay Maid

77f **68f**

4-y-o b f Karinga Bay-Maid To Match (Matching Pair)
P R Webber Mrs Helen Mobley

Placings:*00* **(4539)**
2001/02: 16^{0}G, 16^{0}G

	Starts	1st	2nd	3rd	Win & Pl
NH Flat	2	0	0	0	
Career Total	**2**	**0**	**0**	**0**	

Going: Sf: 0-0 GS: 0-0 Gd: 0-2 GF: - Fm: 0-0
Distance: 2m/2m3: 0-2 2m4-2m7: 0-0 3m+: 0-0
Track: LH: 0-1 RH: 0-1 Tight: 0-1 Gall: 0-0
Aids: Bl: 0-0 Vi: 0-0 Tstrap: 0-0
Best Rating: **68** 2/02 Ludl 2m good NHF

Bayar (IRE)

74 **49**

5-y-o b g Thatching-Bayrika (IRE) (Kahyasi)
H D Daly Ludlow Racing Partnership

Placings:00-0 **(0495)**
2001/02: 19^{0}G

	Starts	1st	2nd	3rd	Win & Pl
Hurdles	1	0	0	0	
Career Total	**3**	**0**	**0**	**0**	

Going: Sf: 0-0 GS: 0-0 Gd: 0-1 GF: - Fm: 0-0
Distance: 2m/2m3: 0-0 2m4-2m7: 0-1 3m+: 0-0
Track: LH: 0-0 RH: 0-1 Tight: 0-0 Gall: 0-0
Aids: Bl: 0-0 Vi: 0-0 Tstrap: 0-0
Best Rating: **49** 4/01 Hrfd 2m1f good Hdl

Be Fair

103f **104f**

4-y-o br c Blushing Flame (USA)-Tokyo (Mtoto)
D E Cantillon Mrs Edward Cantillon

Placings:*1* **(4552)**
2001/02: 16^{1}GF

	Starts	1st	2nd	3rd	Win & Pl
NH Flat	1	1	0	0	1792
Career Total	**1**	**1**	**0**	**0**	**1792**

104 4/02 Hntg 2m110y H NHF G-F £1792
Total win prize-money £1792

Going: Sf: 0-0 GS: 0-0 Gd: 0-0 GF: - Fm: 1-1
Distance: **2m/2m3: 1-1** 2m4-2m7: 0-0 3m+: 0-0
Track: LH: 0-0 **RH: 1-1** Tight: 0-0 **Gall: 1-1**
Aids: Bl: 0-0 Vi: 0-0 Tstrap: 0-0
Best Rating: **104** 4/02 Hntg 2m110y gd-fm NHF

Be Gone

81 **87**

7-y-o ch g Be My Chief (USA)-Hence (USA) (Mr Prospector (USA))
C A Dwyer K Kyriacou

Placings:510/3-0 **(0104)**
2001/02: 18^{0}GF

	Starts	1st	2nd	3rd	Win & Pl
Hurdles	1	0	0	0	
Career Total	**5**	**1**	**0**	**1**	**2869**

104 3/00 Folk 2m4f110y E Hdl G-F £2528
Total win prize-money £2528

Going: Sf: 0-0 GS: 0-0 Gd: 0-0 GF: - Fm: 0-1
Distance: 2m/2m3: 0-1 2m4-2m7: 0-0 3m+: 0-0
Track: LH: 0-1 RH: 0-0 Tight: 0-1 Gall: 0-0
Aids: Bl: 0-0 Vi: 0-0 Tstrap: 0-0
Best Rating: **104** 6/00 Folk 2m6f110y good Hdl

Be My Destiny (IRE)

98f **96f**

5-y-o b g Be My Native (USA)-Miss Cali (Young Man (FR))
M Pitman Mrs Elizabeth Pearce

Placings:*206* **(3701)**
2001/02: 17^{2}S, 16^{0}G, 16^{6}S

	Starts	1st	2nd	3rd	Win & Pl
NH Flat	3	0	1	0	448
Career Total	**3**	**0**	**1**	**0**	**448**

Going: Sf: 0-2 GS: 0-0 Gd: 0-1 GF: - Fm: 0-0
Distance: 2m/2m3: 0-3 2m4-2m7: 0-0 3m+: 0-0
Track: LH: 0-2 RH: 0-0 Tight: 0-1 Gall: 0-2
Aids: Bl: 0-0 Vi: 0-0 Tstrap: 0-0
Best Rating: **96** 2/02 Newb 2m110y soft NHF

Be My Dream (IRE)

109(102h) (111h)**121**

7-y-o b g Be My Native (USA)-Dream Toi (Carlburg)
J J O'Neill Darren C Mercer

Placings:06-311**32** **(3591)**
2001/02: 20^{3}G, 24^{1}GS, 25^{1}G, 22^{3}S, 26^{2}HY

	Starts	1st	2nd	3rd	Win & Pl
Hurdles	3	2	0	1	5529
Chases	2	0	1	1	4591
Career Total	**7**	**2**	**1**	**2**	**10120**

111 10/01 Weth 3m1f F(0-90)HHdl GD £2492
111 10/01 MRas 3m F(0-100)HHdl G-S £2712
Total win prize-money £5205

Going: Sf: 0-2 GS: 1-1 Gd: 1-2 GF: - Fm: 0-0
Distance: 2m/2m3: 0-0 2m4-2m7: 0-2 **3m+: 2-3**
Track: LH: 1-3 RH: 1-1 **Tight: 1-2** Gall: 0-0
Aids: Bl: 0-0 Vi: 0-0 Tstrap: 0-0
Best Rating: **111** 1/02 Hayd 2m6f soft Ch

Staying novice hurdler, improved for the step up to three miles when taking novice events at Market Rasen and Wetherby in the autumn of 2001. Has shown ability over fences and should find success at a modest level

Be My Manager (IRE)

105 **136**

7-y-o b g Be My Native (USA)-Fahy Quay (Quayside)
Miss H C Knight The Earl Cadogan

Placings:2143/**11-P4F** **(2548)**
2001/02: 20^{P}G, 20^{4}G, 24^{F}GS

	Starts	1st	2nd	3rd	Win & Pl
Chases	3	0	0	0	692
Career Total	**9**	**3**	**1**	**1**	**25740**

156 1/01 Chel 2m5f C HCh SFT £11212
130 10/00 Tntn 2m3f D Ch GD £5642
117 1/00 Leic 2m4f110y D Hdl SFT £3705
Total win prize-money £20560

Going: Sf: 0-0 GS: 0-1 Gd: 0-2 GF: - Fm: 0-0
Distance: 2m/2m3: 0-0 2m4-2m7: 0-2 3m+: 0-1
Track: LH: 0-1 RH: 0-2 Tight: 0-0 Gall: 0-1
Aids: Bl: 0-0 Vi: 0-0 Tstrap: 0-0
Best Rating: **156** 1/01 Chel 2m5f soft Ch

A winning Irish pointer, he was successful on both his starts over fences as a novice, landing a valuable ' handicap at Cheltenham in late January 2001. He is reported to prefer good ground and will stay three miles.

Be My Mot (IRE)

87 **75**

10-y-o b m Be My Native (USA)-Madam Butterfly (Deep Run)
D M Grissell R Winchester & Son

Placings:*50/45*P2122200/**U**122530/33**1PUP**00/351300-F0 **(2895)**
2001/02: 20^{F}S, 24^{0}G

	Starts	1st	2nd	3rd	Win & Pl
Hurdles	2	0	0	0	
Career Total	**35**	**4**	**6**	**5**	**32666**

115 11/00 Folk 2m6f110y F(0-105)HHdl HVY £1839
130 12/99 Ling 3m A Ch G-S £14300
109 11/98 Kemp 3m110y C(0-130)HHdl SFT £3720
86 12/97 Folk 2m6f110y E Hdl GD £2490
Total win prize-money £22351

Going: Sf: 0-1 GS: 0-0 Gd: 0-1 GF: - Fm: 0-0
Distance: 2m/2m3: 0-0 2m4-2m7: 0-1 3m+: 0-1
Track: LH: 0-0 RH: 0-2 Tight: 0-1 Gall: 0-0
Aids: Bl: 0-2 Vi: 0-0 Tstrap: 0-2
Best Rating: **130** 12/99 Ling 3m gd-sft Ch

Be My Own (IRE)

95 **71**

6-y-o b g Lord Americo-No Slow (King's Ride)
R H Buckler The Desirables

Placings:*40*P00B0 **(4731)**
2001/02: 17^{4}G, 16^{0}G, 20^{P}S, 19^{0}G, 16^{0}GS, 17^{B}G, 17^{0}F

	Starts	1st	2nd	3rd	Win & Pl
NH Flat	2	0	0	0	0
Hurdles	5	0	0	0	0
Career Total	**7**	**0**	**0**	**0**	**0**

Going: Sf: 0-1 GS: 0-1 Gd: 0-4 GF: - Fm: 0-1
Distance: 2m/2m3: 0-6 2m4-2m7: 0-1 3m+: 0-0
Track: LH: 0-2 RH: 0-5 Tight: 0-0 Gall: 0-0
Aids: Bl: 0-0 Vi: 0-0 Tstrap: 0-0
Best Rating: **82** 10/01 Hrfd 2m1f good NHF

Be My Raleagh (IRE)

102(99h) (46h)101

9-y-o b g Be My Native (USA)-Mrs Hooters (Glint Of Gold)
D J Wintle Mrs Joan L Egan

Placings:0040P4/0P0P-06P5353 (2599)
2001/02: 16^{0}GF, 20^{6}GF, 16^{P}GF, 19^{5}S, 16^{3}S, 16^{5}S, 20^{3}G

	Starts	1st	2nd	3rd	Win & Pl
Hurdles	2	0	0	0	0
Chases	5	0	0	2	1413
Career Total	**17**	**0**	**0**	**2**	**1413**

Going: Sf: 0-3 GS: 0-0 Gd: 0-1 GF: - Fm: 0-3
Distance: 2m/2m3: 0-5 2m4-2m7: 0-2 3m+: 0-0
Track: LH: 0-3 RH: 0-2 Tight: 0-3 Gall: 0-0
Aids: Bl: 0-1 Vi: 0-0 Tstrap: 0-0
Best Rating: **101** 12/01 Wwck 2m110y soft Ch

Be My Romany (IRE)

10-y-o ch m Be My Native (USA)-Romany Fortune (Sunyboy)
J L Needham Miss Joanna Needham

Placings:30/0/0P65/304-F (2640)
2001/02: 16^{F}GF

	Starts	1st	2nd	3rd	Win & Pl
Chases	1	0	0	0	
Career Total	**11**	**0**	**0**	**2**	**711**

Going: Sf: 0-0 GS: 0-0 Gd: 0-0 GF: - Fm: 0-1
Distance: 2m/2m3: 0-1 2m4-2m7: 0-0 3m+: 0-0
Track: LH: 0-0 RH: 0-1 Tight: 0-0 Gall: 0-0
Aids: Bl: 0-0 Vi: 0-0 Tstrap: 0-0
Best Rating: **87** 12/97 Ludl 2m good NHF

Be My Tinker

4-y-o ch f Be My Chief (USA)-Tinkerbird (Music Boy)
G Brown J Cleeve

Placings:6U (1486)
2001/02: 17^{6}GF, 16^{U}GF

	Starts	1st	2nd	3rd	Win & Pl
Hurdles	2	0	0	0	0
Career Total	**2**	**0**	**0**	**0**	**0**

Going: Sf: 0-0 GS: 0-0 Gd: 0-0 GF: - Fm: 0-2
Distance: 2m/2m3: 0-2 2m4-2m7: 0-0 3m+: 0-0
Track: LH: 0-1 RH: 0-1 Tight: 0-1 Gall: 0-1
Aids: Bl: 0-0 Vi: 0-0 Tstrap: 0-0
Best Rating:

Be Thankfull (IRE)

88 97

6-y-o gr m Linamix (FR)-Thank One's Stars (Alzao (USA))
Miss H C Knight Mrs G C Maxwell

Placings:42 (0504)
2001/02: 17^{4}G, 20^{2}GF

	Starts	1st	2nd	3rd	Win & Pl
Hurdles	2	0	1	0	765
Career Total	**2**	**0**	**1**	**0**	**765**

Going: Sf: 0-0 GS: 0-0 Gd: 0-1 GF: - Fm: 0-1
Distance: 2m/2m3: 0-1 2m4-2m7: 0-1 3m+: 0-0
Track: LH: 0-0 RH: 0-2 Tight: 0-0 Gall: 0-1
Aids: Bl: 0-0 Vi: 0-0 Tstrap: 0-0
Best Rating: **102** 5/01 Hrfd 2m1f good Hdl

Be Upstanding

104 106

7-y-o ch g Hubbly Bubbly (USA)-Two Travellers (Deep Run)
Ferdy Murphy (R Wilman 10/5) M Holmes

Placings:UF-01345 (4857)
2001/02: 20^{0}G, 20^{1}GS, 21^{3}S, 26^{4}G, 20^{5}G

	Starts	1st	2nd	3rd	Win & Pl
Hurdles	5	1	0	1	3790
Career Total	**7**	**1**	**0**	**1**	**3790**

86 2/02 Fknm 2m4f D Hdl G-S £3343
Total win prize-money £3343

Going: Sf: 0-1 GS: 1-1 Gd: 0-3 GF: - Fm: 0-0
Distance: 2m/2m3: 0-0 **2m4-2m7: 1-4** 3m+: 0-1
Track: **LH: 1-3** RH: 0-2 **Tight: 1-1** Gall: 0-1
Aids: Bl: 0-0 Vi: 0-0 Tstrap: 0-0
Best Rating: **106** 3/02 Ludl 2m5f soft Hdl

Modest novice hurdler, stays two and a half miles.

Beachtime

83 71

6-y-o b g Lugana Beach-Time Warp (Town And Country)
N R Mitchell Mrs Sarah Faulks

Placings:0-20P (1847)
2001/02: 17^{2}GF, 16^{0}GS, 16^{P}G

	Starts	1st	2nd	3rd	Win & Pl
NH Flat	1	0	1	0	449
Hurdles	2	0	0	0	0
Career Total	**4**	**0**	**1**	**0**	**449**

Going: Sf: 0-0 GS: 0-1 Gd: 0-1 GF: - Fm: 0-1
Distance: 2m/2m3: 0-3 2m4-2m7: 0-0 3m+: 0-0
Track: LH: 0-1 RH: 0-1 Tight: 0-2 Gall: 0-0
Aids: Bl: 0-0 Vi: 0-0 Tstrap: 0-0
Best Rating: **83** 5/01 Folk 2m1f110y gd-fm NHF

Still a maiden, and has been well beaten on all starts to date, tried only at around two miles.

Beacon Boy

77 17

7-y-o ch g Barrish-Lirella (Lir)
P R Rodford B R Brereton

Placings:00PP-0F0 (0836)
2001/02: 22^{0}GF, 22^{F}GF, 22^{0}GF

	Starts	1st	2nd	3rd	Win & Pl
Hurdles	3	0	0	0	
Career Total	**7**	**0**	**0**	**0**	

Going: Sf: 0-0 GS: 0-0 Gd: 0-0 GF: - Fm: 0-3
Distance: 2m/2m3: 0-0 2m4-2m7: 0-3 3m+: 0-0
Track: LH: 0-3 RH: 0-0 Tight: 0-3 Gall: 0-0
Aids: Bl: 0-0 Vi: 0-0 Tstrap: 0-0
Best Rating: **87** 5/00 Chep 2m110y firm NHF

Beamish (IRE)

8-y-o ch g Caesar Imperator (FR)-Super Slaney (Brave Invader (USA))
Dr J R J Naylor Mrs K A Davis

Placings:3404-PP (2519)
2001/02: 24^{P}G, 25^{P}S

	Starts	1st	2nd	3rd	Win & Pl
Hurdles	2	0	0	0	
Career Total	**6**	**0**	**0**	**1**	**575**

Going: Sf: 0-1 GS: 0-0 Gd: 0-1 GF: - Fm: 0-0
Distance: 2m/2m3: 0-0 2m4-2m7: 0-0 3m+: 0-2
Track: LH: 0-0 RH: 0-1 Tight: 0-1 Gall: 0-0
Aids: Bl: 0-0 Vi: 0-1 Tstrap: 0-0
Best Rating: **108** 7/00 Worc 2m good NHF

Bearys Cross (IRE)

(88h) (28h)

10-y-o gr g Runnett-Etnas Princess (The Parson)
R J Hodges Miss L Crossman

Placings:366P6/5202B34U1B21/00FP-0P0 (3287)
2001/02: 19^{0}S, 26^{P}HY, 22^{0}S

	Starts	1st	2nd	3rd	Win & Pl
Hurdles	1	0	0	0	0
Chases	2	0	0	0	0
Career Total	**24**	**2**	**3**	**2**	**9725**

93 4/00 NAbb 2m5f110y G(0-95)HCh HVY £2373
93 3/00 Tntn 2m110y F(0-100)HCh SFT £3071
Total win prize-money £5444

Going: Sf: 0-3 GS: 0-0 Gd: 0-0 GF: - Fm: 0-0
Distance: 2m/2m3: 0-0 2m4-2m7: 0-2 3m+: 0-1
Track: LH: 0-2 RH: 0-1 Tight: 0-2 Gall: 0-0
Aids: Bl: 0-2 Vi: 0-0 Tstrap: 0-0
Best Rating: **96** 11/98 NAbb 3m3f soft Hdl

Beat The Retreat

93 107

7-y-o b g Terimon-Carpet Slippers (Daring March)
A King Mrs Peter Mason

Placings:43/33 (3766)
2001/02: 16^{3}GS, 20^{3}GS

	Starts	1st	2nd	3rd	Win & Pl
Hurdles	2	0	0	2	845
Career Total	**4**	**0**	**0**	**3**	**1601**

Going: Sf: 0-0 GS: 0-2 Gd: 0-0 GF: - Fm: 0-0
Distance: 2m/2m3: 0-1 2m4-2m7: 0-1 3m+: 0-0
Track: LH: 0-1 RH: 0-1 Tight: 0-1 Gall: 0-1
Aids: Bl: 0-0 Vi: 0-0 Tstrap: 0-0
Best Rating: **107** 1/02 Hntg 2m110y gd-sft Hdl

Returned from a two-year absence to finish third in a novice hurdle in January 2002.

Beat The Ring (IRE)

92 92+

4-y-o br g Tagula (IRE)-Pursue (Auction Ring (USA))
C A Dwyer (G Brown 8/8) Mrs K W Sneath

Placings:644 (4854)
2001/02: 16^{6}GF, 16^{4}G, 22^{4}G

	Starts	1st	2nd	3rd	Win & Pl
Hurdles	3	0	0	0	0
Career Total	**3**	**0**	**0**	**0**	**0**

Going: Sf: 0-0 GS: 0-0 Gd: 0-2 GF: - Fm: 0-1
Distance: 2m/2m3: 0-2 2m4-2m7: 0-1 3m+: 0-0
Track: LH: 0-2 RH: 0-1 Tight: 0-1 Gall: 0-1
Aids: Bl: 0-0 Vi: 0-0 Tstrap: 0-0

Best Rating: 86 4/02 Uttx 2m good Hdl

May struggle to stay two miles over hurdles but could do better in novice handicaps.

Beatson (IRE)

101 **91**

13-y-o gr g Roselier (FR)-Toevarro (Raga Navarro (ITY))
R H Buckler Mrs E B Gardiner

Placings: *12000/212306/11425213*/**F111423/565541/32154/43P4313/4432P1-PP4P** (3813)
2001/02: 20^{P}GS, 16^{P}HY, 18^{4}HY, 21^{P}S

	Starts	1st	2nd	3rd	Win & Pl
Chases	4	0	0	0	0
Career Total	54	12	8	8	57983

111	2/01	Towc	2m110y	D(0-120)HCh	HVY	£4672
120	12/99	Towc	2m110y	D(0-125)HCh	SFT	£3767
127	1/99	Towc	2m110y	D(0-125)HCh	HVY	£3580
111	12/97	Plum	2m5f	D(0-120)HCh	SFT	£3557
118	12/96	Towc	2m110y	D(0-125)HCh	G-S	£4565
108	12/96	Chel	2m5f	E(0-125)HCh	G-F	£3160
105	12/96	Plum	2m5f	D(0-120)HCh	G-S	£4077
89	11/95	Chel	3m110y	E Ch	G-F	£4182
98	5/95	Wwck	2m4f110y	E(0-115)HHdl	G-F	£2382
97	5/95	Uttx	2m4f110y	D(0-125)HHdl	G-F	£2801
95	10/94	Bang	2m4f	HHdl	G-S	£2410
104	12/93	Wwck	2m	NHF	HVY	£2087

Total win prize-money £41246

Going: Sf: 0-3 GS: 0-1 Gd: 0-0 GF: - Fm: 0-0
Distance: 2m/2m3: 0-2 2m4-2m7: 0-2 3m+: 0-0
Track: LH: 0-1 RH: 0-2 Tight: 0-3 Gall: 0-0
Aids: Bl: 0-3 Vi: 0-0 Tstrap: 0-0
Best Rating: 127 1/99 Towc 2m110y heavy Ch

Beau (IRE)

117 **168**

9-y-o b g Zaffaran (USA)-Sand Martin (Menelek)
N A Twiston-Davies Trevor Hemmings

Placings: *1212254*/**24121121/3P42U5-6200U0** (4913)
2001/02: 25^{6}G, 27^{2}G, 25^{0}G, 26^{0}S, 36^{U}G, 29^{0}G

	Starts	1st	2nd	3rd	Win & Pl
Chases	6	0	1	0	10750
Career Total	27	6	8	1	199785

183	4/00	Sand	3m5f110y	A HCh	SFT	£66700
160	2/00	Asct	3m110y	A Ch	G-S	£22925
157	1/00	Donc	3m	B(0-145)HCh	GD	£30914
156	12/99	Hayd	2m4f	C Ch	SFT	£6071
125	12/98	NAbb	2m1f	E Hdl	SFT	£2232
108	5/98	Towc	2m	H NHF	GD	£1285

Total win prize-money £130128

Going: Sf: 0-1 GS: 0-0 Gd: 0-5 GF: - Fm: 0-0
Distance: 2m/2m3: 0-0 2m4-2m7: 0-0 3m+: 0-6
Track: LH: 0-5 RH: 0-1 Tight: 0-1 Gall: 0-2
Aids: Bl: 0-0 Vi: 0-0 Tstrap: 0-0
Best Rating: 183 4/00 Sand 3m5f110y soft Ch

Runaway winner of the Whitbread in 2000, he took time to find his form last term but ran well when fourth in the King George. Beaten a distance into second by See More Business at Cheltenham, he was going well when unshipping Carl Llewellyn in the 2001 Grand National. Best effort since when runner-up at Cheltenham on his second start of last season when a mistake at the last arguably cost him victory. Up with the pace and going well when unluckily departing with over a circuit to go in the 2002 National. Usually jumps well and is most effective when making the running. Stays at least three and a half miles.

Beau Brun (FR)

6-y-o b/br g Cadoudal (FR)-Atakaia (FR) (Ataxerxes (GER))
Graeme Roe Roe Racing Ltd

Placings: P53/P (2060)
2001/02: 20^{P}GS

	Starts	1st	2nd	3rd	Win & Pl
Hurdles	1	0	0	0	
Career Total	4	0	0	1	675

Going: Sf: 0-0 GS: 0-1 Gd: 0-0 GF: - Fm: 0-0
Distance: 2m/2m3: 0-0 2m4-2m7: 0-1 3m+: 0-0
Track: LH: 0-0 RH: 0-0 Tight: 0-1 Gall: 0-0
Aids: Bl: 0-0 Vi: 0-0 Tstrap: 0-0
Best Rating: 55 11/99 Hntg 2m110y good Hdl

Beau Coup

100 **100**

5-y-o b g Toulon-Energance (IRE) (Salmon Leap (USA))
John R Upson Mrs Ann Key

Placings: 635 (4874)
2001/02: 19^{6}S, 18^{3}S, 20^{5}G

	Starts	1st	2nd	3rd	Win & Pl
Hurdles	3	0	0	1	504
Career Total	3	0	0	1	504

Going: Sf: 0-2 GS: 0-0 Gd: 0-1 GF: - Fm: 0-0
Distance: 2m/2m3: 0-1 2m4-2m7: 0-2 3m+: 0-0
Track: LH: 0-1 RH: 0-2 Tight: 0-2 Gall: 0-0
Aids: Bl: 0-0 Vi: 0-0 Tstrap: 0-0
Best Rating: 100 3/02 Font 2m2f110y soft Hdl

Has shown ability over hurdles.

Beau George

10-y-o ch g Lir-Thing O'Beauty (Sir Lark)
Miss S Young B R J.Young

Placings: P (1494)
2001/02: 22^{P}GF

	Starts	1st	2nd	3rd	Win & Pl
Hurdles	1	0	0	0	
Career Total	1	0	0	0	

Going: Sf: 0-0 GS: 0-0 Gd: 0-0 GF: - Fm: 0-1
Distance: 2m/2m3: 0-0 2m4-2m7: 0-1 3m+: 0-0
Track: LH: 0-0 RH: 0-0 Tight: 0-0 Gall: 0-0
Aids: Bl: 0-0 Vi: 0-0 Tstrap: 0-0
Best Rating:

Beau Jake (IRE)

93 **64**

7-y-o b g Jolly Jake (NZ)-Cool Mary (Beau Charmeur (FR))
N M Babbage John Cantrill

Placings: *44*003000 (4110)
2001/02: 16^{4}GF, 17^{4}GF, 16^{0}G, 20^{0}G, 21^{3}GF, 17^{0}GS, 22^{0}S, 16^{0}S

	Starts	1st	2nd	3rd	Win & Pl
NH Flat	3	0	0	0	0
Hurdles	5	0	0	1	401
Career Total	8	0	0	1	401

Going: Sf: 0-2 GS: 0-1 Gd: 0-2 GF: - Fm: 0-3
Distance: 2m/2m3: 0-5 2m4-2m7: 0-3 3m+: 0-0
Track: LH: 0-3 RH: 0-5 Tight: 0-4 Gall: 0-1
Aids: Bl: 0-0 Vi: 0-0 Tstrap: 0-0
Best Rating: 104 5/01 Hntg 2m110y gd-fm NHF

Beau Joueur (FR)

9-y-o ch g Tagel (USA)-Bille En Tete (FR) (Green Dancer (USA))
P L Gilligan D Heath

Placings: PPP (3153)
2001/02: 16^{P}HY, 20^{P}S, 20^{P}G

	Starts	1st	2nd	3rd	Win & Pl
Hurdles	2	0	0	0	0
Chases	1	0	0	0	0
Career Total	3	0	0	0	

Going: Sf: 0-2 GS: 0-0 Gd: 0-1 GF: - Fm: 0-0
Distance: 2m/2m3: 0-1 2m4-2m7: 0-2 3m+: 0-0
Track: LH: 0-0 RH: 0-2 Tight: 0-1 Gall: 0-0
Aids: Bl: 0-1 Vi: 0-0 Tstrap: 0-2
Best Rating:

Beauanarrow (IRE)

93(77h) (80h)**105**

7-y-o b g Beau Sher-Ardnasagh Rose (Crash Course)
N M Babbage John Cantrill

Placings: *21*-31642 (4598)
2001/02: 16^{3}GF, 16^{1}G, 16^{6}HY, 16^{4}S, 16^{2}GF

	Starts	1st	2nd	3rd	Win & Pl
NH Flat	2	1	0	1	2198
Hurdles	1	0	0	0	0
Chases	2	0	1	0	1382
Career Total	7	2	2	1	5844

104	12/01	Ludl	2m	H NHF	GD	£1981
102	4/01	MRas	2m1f110y	H NHF	HVY	£1764

Total win prize-money £3745

Going: Sf: 0-2 GS: 0-0 Gd: 1-1 GF: - Fm: 0-2
Distance: **2m/2m3: 1-5** 2m4-2m7: 0-0 3m+: 0-0
Track: LH: 0-0 **RH: 1-4** Tight: 0-0 Gall: 0-0
Aids: Bl: 0-0 Vi: 0-0 Tstrap: 0-0
Best Rating: 107 11/01 Ludl 2m gd-fm NHF

Effective at around two miles, he acts on good and heavy ground.

Beauty Star (IRE)

74 **32**

5-y-o b m Shalford (IRE)-Dream Academy (Town And Country)
N M Babbage B Babbage

Placings: *500* (4597)
2001/02: 16^{5}HY, 16^{0}GS, 19^{0}GF

	Starts	1st	2nd	3rd	Win & Pl
NH Flat	2	0	0	0	0
Hurdles	1	0	0	0	0
Career Total	3	0	0	0	0

Going: Sf: 0-1 GS: 0-1 Gd: 0-0 GF: - Fm: 0-1
Distance: 2m/2m3: 0-3 2m4-2m7: 0-0 3m+: 0-0
Track: LH: 0-3 RH: 0-0 Tight: 0-0 Gall: 0-0
Aids: Bl: 0-0 Vi: 0-0 Tstrap: 0-0
Best Rating: 80 2/02 Wwck 2m heavy NHF

Modest bumper form.

Beaver Lodge (IRE)

105 **112**

5-y-o gr g Grand Lodge (USA)-Thistlewood (Kalamoun)
C J Mann (Kevin Prendergast 1/11) Granville J Harper

Placings:0234-445011 (4842)
2001/02: 16^{4}Y, 16^{4}G, 16^{5}HY, 16^{0}GS, 19^{1}GF, 20^{1}G

	Starts	1st	2nd	3rd	Win & Pl
Hurdles	6	2	0	0	8010
Career Total	**10**	**2**	**1**	**1**	**9629**

112 4/02 Bang 2m4f E Hdl GD £3962
112 4/02 MRas 2m3f110y D(0-120)HHdl G-F £3500
Total win prize-money £7462

Going: Sf: 0-1 GS: 0-1 Gd: 1-2 GF: - Fm: 1-1
Distance: 2m/2m3: 0-4 **2m4-2m7: 2-2** 3m+: 0-0
Track: LH: 1-3 RH: 1-2 **Tight: 2-2** Gall: 0-1
Aids: Bl: 0-0 Vi: 0-0 Tstrap: 0-0
Best Rating: 112 4/02 Bang 2m4f good Hdl

Some ability in maiden hurdles in Ireland, and won a handicap at Market Rasen in April 2002. Followed up easing right down in novice company next time at Bangor and needs fast ground.

Bebe Bleu (IRE)

100f

6-y-o b m Terimon-Fu's Lady (Netherkelly)
M C Pipe Mrs Angie Malde

Placings:*20*F (3150)
2001/02: 16^{2}G, 17^{0}GF, 18^{F}G

	Starts	1st	2nd	3rd	Win & Pl
NH Flat	2	0	1	0	446
Hurdles	1	0	0	0	0
Career Total	**3**	**0**	**1**	**0**	**446**

Going: Sf: 0-0 GS: 0-0 Gd: 0-2 GF: - Fm: 0-1
Distance: 2m/2m3: 0-3 2m4-2m7: 0-0 3m+: 0-0
Track: LH: 0-2 RH: 0-1 Tight: 0-1 Gall: 0-0
Aids: Bl: 0-0 Vi: 0-0 Tstrap: 0-0
Best Rating: 100 11/01 Wwck 2m good NHF

Probably ran into a decent sort when runner-up on her debut in a Warwick bumper.

Because I Am

4-y-o b f Tragic Role (USA)-Ketti (Hotfoot)
G Brown Mrs Amanda Killick

Placings:0P (1481)
2001/02: 16^{0}GF, 16^{P}GS

	Starts	1st	2nd	3rd	Win & Pl
Hurdles	2	0	0	0	
Career Total	**2**	**0**	**0**	**0**	

Going: Sf: 0-0 GS: 0-1 Gd: 0-0 GF: - Fm: 0-1
Distance: 2m/2m3: 0-2 2m4-2m7: 0-0 3m+: 0-0
Track: LH: 0-2 RH: 0-0 Tight: 0-1 Gall: 0-0
Aids: Bl: 0-0 Vi: 0-0 Tstrap: 0-0
Best Rating:

Because I Do

66 **24**

5-y-o b m Tragic Role (USA)-Ketti (Hotfoot)
D L Williams Mrs Amanda Killick

Placings:*005-00* (0912)
2001/02: 17^{0}F, 16^{0}GF

	Starts	1st	2nd	3rd	Win & Pl
NH Flat	1	0	0	0	0
Hurdles	1	0	0	0	0
Career Total	**5**	**0**	**0**	**0**	**0**

Going: Sf: 0-0 GS: 0-0 Gd: 0-0 GF: - Fm: 0-2
Distance: 2m/2m3: 0-2 2m4-2m7: 0-0 3m+: 0-0
Track: LH: 0-1 RH: 0-1 Tight: 0-1 Gall: 0-0
Aids: Bl: 0-0 Vi: 0-0 Tstrap: 0-0
Best Rating: 57 5/01 Extr 2m1f firm NHF

Beckdale

103 **89**

6-y-o b g Perpendicular-Knocksharry (Palm Track)
Andrew Turnell Dr John Hollowood

Placings:*3224000*-**F**P6P10 (4579)
2001/02: 20^{F}GF, 24^{P}S, 21^{6}GS, 24^{P}G, 17^{1}S, 16^{0}G

	Starts	1st	2nd	3rd	Win & Pl
Hurdles	5	1	0	0	2541
Chases	1	0	0	0	0
Career Total	**13**	**1**	**2**	**1**	**3982**

82 3/02 Sedg 2m1f E(0-105)HHdl SFT £2541
Total win prize-money £2541

Going: Sf: 1-2 GS: 0-1 Gd: 0-2 GF: - Fm: 0-1
Distance: **2m/2m3: 1-2** 2m4-2m7: 0-2 3m+: 0-2
Track: **LH: 1-3** RH: 0-3 **Tight: 1-2** Gall: 0-1
Aids: Bl: 0-1 Vi: 0-0 Tstrap: 0-0
Best Rating: 110 12/00 Donc 2m110y heavy NHF

Took advantage of a lenient mark to take a two mile novices' handicap at Sedgefield in March narrowly.

Beckley (IRE)

88 **82**

6-y-o b g Phardante (FR)-Baybush (Boreen (FR))
C Grant J Henderson (co Durham)

Placings:*2306* (4828)
2001/02: 17^{2}G, 17^{3}GF, 16^{0}G, 16^{6}G

	Starts	1st	2nd	3rd	Win & Pl
NH Flat	3	0	1	1	676
Hurdles	1	0	0	0	0
Career Total	**4**	**0**	**1**	**1**	**676**

Going: Sf: 0-0 GS: 0-0 Gd: 0-3 GF: - Fm: 0-1
Distance: 2m/2m3: 0-4 2m4-2m7: 0-0 3m+: 0-0
Track: LH: 0-3 RH: 0-0 Tight: 0-1 Gall: 0-0
Aids: Bl: 0-0 Vi: 0-0 Tstrap: 0-0
Best Rating: 100 10/01 Sedg 2m1f good NHF

A half-brother to Sparky Gayle, he has shown ability in bumpers.

Beckwith Magic (IRE)

8-y-o b g Ilium-Miss Fortsir (Al Sirat (USA))
S Magnier White Rose Racing Syndicate

Placings:0/P (4053)
2001/02: 20^{P}S

	Starts	1st	2nd	3rd	Win & Pl
Chases	1	0	0	0	
Career Total	**2**	**0**	**0**	**0**	

Going: Sf: 0-1 GS: 0-0 Gd: 0-0 GF: - Fm: 0-0
Distance: 2m/2m3: 0-0 2m4-2m7: 0-1 3m+: 0-0
Track: LH: 0-0 RH: 0-1 Tight: 0-0 Gall: 0-0
Aids: Bl: 0-0 Vi: 0-0 Tstrap: 0-0
Best Rating:

Bede (IRE)

89(98h) (92h)**87**

6-y-o b g Spanish Place (USA)-Midnight Oil (Menelek)
P J Hobbs M G St Quinton

Placings:*6650* (4138)
2001/02: 17^{6}G, 17^{6}GS, 16^{5}GS, 16^{0}GS

	Starts	1st	2nd	3rd	Win & Pl
NH Flat	1	0	0	0	0
Hurdles	3	0	0	0	0
Career Total	**4**	**0**	**0**	**0**	**0**

Going: Sf: 0-0 GS: 0-3 Gd: 0-1 GF: - Fm: 0-0
Distance: 2m/2m3: 0-4 2m4-2m7: 0-0 3m+: 0-0
Track: LH: 0-0 RH: 0-4 Tight: 0-0 Gall: 0-0
Aids: Bl: 0-0 Vi: 0-0 Tstrap: 0-0
Best Rating: 95 5/01 Extr 2m1f good NHF

Bedtime Boogie

7-y-o b g Carlton (GER)-Saruk (IRE) (Tate Gallery (USA))
Mrs P Townsley Alan Walder

Placings:PP/0 (0058)
2001/02: 17^{0}GS

	Starts	1st	2nd	3rd	Win & Pl
Hurdles	1	0	0	0	
Career Total	**3**	**0**	**0**	**0**	

Going: Sf: 0-0 GS: 0-1 Gd: 0-0 GF: - Fm: 0-0
Distance: 2m/2m3: 0-1 2m4-2m7: 0-0 3m+: 0-0
Track: LH: 0-0 RH: 0-1 Tight: 0-1 Gall: 0-0
Aids: Bl: 0-0 Vi: 0-0 Tstrap: 0-0
Best Rating:

Bee

86 **54**

8-y-o b g Scorpio (FR)-Course Weed (Crash Course)
Mrs S J Smith Mrs S Smith

Placings:56F-000 (2909)
2001/02: 20^{0}G, 16^{0}GF, 25^{0}GS

	Starts	1st	2nd	3rd	Win & Pl
Hurdles	3	0	0	0	
Career Total	**6**	**0**	**0**	**0**	**0**

Going: Sf: 0-0 GS: 0-1 Gd: 0-1 GF: - Fm: 0-1
Distance: 2m/2m3: 0-1 2m4-2m7: 0-1 3m+: 0-1
Track: LH: 0-3 RH: 0-0 Tight: 0-1 Gall: 0-1
Aids: Bl: 0-0 Vi: 0-0 Tstrap: 0-0
Best Rating: 94 2/01 Towc 2m heavy NHF

Bee An Bee (IRE)

107f **105f**

5-y-o b g Phardante (FR)-Portia's Delight (IRE) (The Parson)
P Winkworth Stan Moore

Placings:*2200* (3811)
2001/02: 18^{2}GS, 16^{2}S, 16^{0}S, 18^{0}S

	Starts	1st	2nd	3rd	Win & Pl
NH Flat	4	0	2	0	940
Career Total	**4**	**0**	**2**	**0**	**940**

Going: Sf: 0-3 GS: 0-1 Gd: 0-0 GF: - Fm: 0-0

Distance: 2m/2m3: 0-4 2m4-2m7: 0-0 3m+: 0-0
Track: LH: 0-3 RH: 0-0 Tight: 0-1 Gall: 0-1
Aids: Bl: 0-0 Vi: 0-0 Tstrap: 0-0
Best Rating: 105 11/01 Chep 2m110y soft NHF

By Phardante, he made an encouraging debut in a bumper at Plumpton in November on easy ground. Runner-up again next time.

Bee Foxed

8-y-o gr m Bold Fox-Annie Bee (Rusticaro (FR))
Jane Southcombe The Broadway Bells

Placings: *06/P* (4152)
2001/02: 20^{P}GS

	Starts	1st	2nd	3rd	Win & Pl
Hurdles	1	0	0	0	
Career Total	**3**	**0**	**0**	**0**	**0**

Going: Sf: 0-0 GS: 0-1 Gd: 0-0 GF: - Fm: 0-0
Distance: 2m/2m3: 0-0 2m4-2m7: 0-1 3m+: 0-0
Track: LH: 0-1 RH: 0-0 Tight: 0-0 Gall: 0-0
Aids: Bl: 0-0 Vi: 0-0 Tstrap: 0-1
Best Rating: 69 6/99 Worc 2m gd-fm NHF

Beechbrook Gale (IRE)

89 93
6-y-o b g Toulon-Swan Upping (Lord Gayle (USA))
John R Upson Jim Bath & Martin Tucker

Placings: 5FP3 (4516)
2001/02: 16^{5}G, 20^{F}S, 24^{P}GS, 16^{3}GS

	Starts	1st	2nd	3rd	Win & Pl
Chases	4	0	0	1	943
Career Total	**4**	**0**	**0**	**1**	**943**

Going: Sf: 0-1 GS: 0-2 Gd: 0-1 GF: - Fm: 0-0
Distance: 2m/2m3: 0-2 2m4-2m7: 0-1 3m+: 0-1
Track: LH: 0-2 RH: 0-2 Tight: 0-2 Gall: 0-1
Aids: Bl: 0-0 Vi: 0-0 Tstrap: 0-0
Best Rating: 93 3/02 Towc 2m110y gd-sft Ch

Beechcourt

109f 131f
5-y-o b g Son Pardo-Calametta (Oats)
M J P O'Brien Pierse Contracting Limited

Placings: *1-140* (4235)
2001/02: 16^{1}Y, 16^{4}Y, 16^{0}GS

	Starts	1st	2nd	3rd	Win & Pl
NH Flat	3	1	0	0	5411
Career Total	**4**	**2**	**0**	**0**	**10976**

131 12/01 Fair 2m NHF YLD £5008
135 1/01 Leop 2m NHF SFT £5564
Total win prize-money £10573

Going: Sf: 0-0 GS: 0-1 Gd: 0-0 GF: - Fm: 0-0
Distance: **2m/2m3: 1-3** 2m4-2m7: 0-0 3m+: 0-0
Track: LH: 0-1 **RH: 1-1** Tight: 0-0 Gall: 0-0
Aids: Bl: 0-0 Vi: 0-0 Tstrap: 0-0
Best Rating: 135 1/01 Leop 2m soft NHF

Beeches Boy (IRE)

101 113
7-y-o b/br g Doubletour (USA)-Tutti Frutti (Tarboosh (USA))
R Dickin E R C Beech & B Wilkinson

Placings: PUP0/132 (1190)
2001/02: 16^{1}GF, 17^{3}G, 20^{2}G

	Starts	1st	2nd	3rd	Win & Pl
Chases	3	1	1	1	5789
Career Total	**7**	**1**	**1**	**1**	**5789**

113 5/01 Wwck 2m110y E Ch G-F £3159
Total win prize-money £3159

Going: Sf: 0-0 GS: 0-0 Gd: 0-2 GF: - Fm: 1-1
Distance: **2m/2m3: 1-2** 2m4-2m7: 0-1 3m+: 0-0
Track: LH: 0-2 RH: 0-0 Tight: 0-2 Gall: 0-0
Aids: Bl: 0-0 Vi: 0-0 Tstrap: 0-0
Best Rating: 113 7/01 Strf 2m1f110y good Ch

Beeches Girl

(98h) (76h)
7-y-o b m Lord Americo-Phyll-Tarquin (Tarqogan)
R Dickin E R C Beech & B Wilkinson

Placings: *060P-50PF65* (3623)
2001/02: 16^{5}G, 16^{0}S, 19^{P}GS, 19^{F}GS, 16^{6}S, 20^{5}S

	Starts	1st	2nd	3rd	Win & Pl
Hurdles	4	0	0	0	0
Chases	2	0	0	0	0
Career Total	**10**	**0**	**0**	**0**	**0**

Going: Sf: 0-3 GS: 0-2 Gd: 0-1 GF: - Fm: 0-0
Distance: 2m/2m3: 0-5 2m4-2m7: 0-1 3m+: 0-0
Track: LH: 0-3 RH: 0-3 Tight: 0-4 Gall: 0-0
Aids: Bl: 0-0 Vi: 0-0 Tstrap: 0-0
Best Rating: 82 11/00 Towc 2m soft NHF

Beechfield Flyer

(101h) (68h)
11-y-o ch g Northern State (USA)-Djimbaran Bay (Le Levanstell)
W Clay Mrs M Robertson

Placings: 05/354504/5213262/2411150/00/P24P00206-0U (0723)
2001/02: 20^{0}G, 25^{U}F

	Starts	1st	2nd	3rd	Win & Pl
Hurdles	1	0	0	0	0
Chases	1	0	0	0	0
Career Total	**35**	**4**	**6**	**2**	**16537**

113 1/98 Leic 2m4f110y D(0-120)HHdl SFT £2846
114 12/97 Leic 2m4f110y D(0-120)HHdl SFT £3292
104 11/97 Leic 2m4f110y D(0-120)HHdl G-S £2950
95 1/97 Leic 2m (0-90)HHdl G-S £1952
Total win prize-money £11041

Going: Sf: 0-0 GS: 0-0 Gd: 0-1 GF: - Fm: 0-1
Distance: 2m/2m3: 0-0 2m4-2m7: 0-1 3m+: 0-1
Track: LH: 0-1 RH: 0-1 Tight: 0-1 Gall: 0-0
Aids: Bl: 0-0 Vi: 0-0 Tstrap: 0-0
Best Rating: 114 2/98 Hayd 2m4f good Hdl

Beehive Lad

(100h) (87h)
8-y-o b g Then Again-Steel Typhoon (General Ironside)
R Ford Dave Teasdale

Placings: *00/034-24F* (4556)
2001/02: 16^{2}GF, 17^{4}S, 17^{F}G

	Starts	1st	2nd	3rd	Win & Pl
Hurdles	2	0	1	0	776
Chases	1	0	0	0	0
Career Total	**8**	**0**	**1**	**1**	**1322**

Going: Sf: 0-1 GS: 0-0 Gd: 0-1 GF: - Fm: 0-1
Distance: 2m/2m3: 0-3 2m4-2m7: 0-0 3m+: 0-0
Track: LH: 0-2 RH: 0-1 Tight: 0-2 Gall: 0-0
Aids: Bl: 0-0 Vi: 0-0 Tstrap: 0-0
Best Rating: 98 3/01 MRas 2m1f110y gd-sft Hdl

Best effort when runner-up in a novices' hurdle at Hexham in May 2001.

Beethoven (IRE)

100 119
6-y-o b/br g Yashgan-Adare Princess (Paico)
Noel T Chance T Collins

Placings: *12-31P* (3586)
2001/02: 16^{3}S, 20^{1}G, 20^{P}HY

	Starts	1st	2nd	3rd	Win & Pl
NH Flat	1	0	0	1	244
Hurdles	2	1	0	0	10348
Career Total	**5**	**2**	**1**	**1**	**13878**

119 12/01 Asct 2m4f B Hdl GD £10348
126 2/01 Asct 2m110y H NHF HVY £2485
Total win prize-money £12833

Going: Sf: 0-2 GS: 0-0 Gd: 1-1 GF: - Fm: 0-0
Distance: 2m/2m3: 0-1 **2m4-2m7: 1-2** 3m+: 0-0
Track: LH: 0-2 **RH: 1-1** Tight: 0-0 Gall: 0-0
Aids: Bl: 0-0 Vi: 0-0 Tstrap: 0-0
Best Rating: 126 3/01 Sand 2m110y heavy NHF

Useful bumper performer who won well at Ascot on his hurdling debut in December 2001. Acts on good ground or easier.

Before The Mast (IRE)

96f 117f
5-y-o br g Broken Hearted-Kings Reserve (King's Ride)
Noel T Chance A D Weller

Placings: *2* (3777)
2001/02: 16^{2}S

	Starts	1st	2nd	3rd	Win & Pl
NH Flat	1	0	1	0	650
Career Total	**1**	**0**	**1**	**0**	**650**

Going: Sf: 0-1 GS: 0-0 Gd: 0-0 GF: - Fm: 0-0
Distance: 2m/2m3: 0-1 2m4-2m7: 0-0 3m+: 0-0
Track: LH: 0-0 RH: 0-1 Tight: 0-0 Gall: 0-0
Aids: Bl: 0-0 Vi: 0-0 Tstrap: 0-0
Best Rating: 117 2/02 Sand 2m110y soft NHF

Beggars Balm

97f 98f
6-y-o b m North Col-Beggars Lane (Capitano)
P R Webber B E Merriman

Placings: *16P* (3345)
2001/02: 17^{1}GS, 17^{6}HY, 17^{P}S

	Starts	1st	2nd	3rd	Win & Pl
NH Flat	3	1	0	0	1789
Career Total	**3**	**1**	**0**	**0**	**1789**

98 5/01 Bang 2m1f H NHF G-S £1788
Total win prize-money £1789

Going: Sf: 0-2 GS: 1-1 Gd: 0-0 GF: - Fm: 0-0
Distance: **2m/2m3: 1-3** 2m4-2m7: 0-0 3m+: 0-0
Track: **LH: 1-1** RH: 0-0 **Tight: 1-2** Gall: 0-0
Aids: Bl: 0-0 Vi: 0-0 Tstrap: 0-0

Best Rating: 98 5/01 Bang 2m1f gd-sft NHF

Beggars Hollow

8-y-o b m Teenoso (USA)-Dutch Princess (Royalty)
J R Jenkins Miss J G Collins

Placings:*060*P-6 (0504)
2001/02: 20^{6}GF

	Starts	1st	2nd	3rd	Win & Pl
Hurdles	1	0	0	0	0
Career Total	**5**	**0**	**0**	**0**	**0**

Going: Sf: 0-0 GS: 0-0 Gd: 0-0 GF: - Fm: 0-1
Distance: 2m/2m3: 0-0 2m4-2m7: 0-1 3m+: 0-0
Track: LH: 0-0 RH: 0-1 Tight: 0-0 Gall: 0-1
Aids: Bl: 0-0 Vi: 0-0 Tstrap: 0-0
Best Rating: 47 12/00 Folk 2m1f110y heavy Hdl

Begin Again

98 114

8-y-o b g Neltino-The Beginning (Goldhill)
P R Webber Mrs Anne Seyfriend

Placings:*036*/42/10 (2939)
2001/02: 23^{1}G, 24^{0}G

	Starts	1st	2nd	3rd	Win & Pl
Chases	2	1	0	0	3146
Career Total	**7**	**1**	**1**	**1**	**4098**

114 12/01 Leic 2m7f110y E Ch GD £3146
Total win prize-money £3146

Going: Sf: 0-0 GS: 0-0 Gd: 1-2 GF: - Fm: 0-0
Distance: 2m/2m3: 0-0 2m4-2m7: 0-0 **3m+: 1-2**
Track: LH: 0-1 **RH: 1-1** Tight: 0-0 Gall: 0-1
Aids: Bl: 0-0 Vi: 0-0 Tstrap: 0-0
Best Rating: 114 12/01 Leic 2m7f110y good Ch

Lightly raced. Acts on good ground and is suited by around three miles.

Behamore (IRE)

9-y-o b g Brush Aside (USA)-Dilkusha Girl (Prince Tenderfoot (USA))
R Rowe Mrs Jean R Bishop

Placings:*160*/513652/**15-F** (2126)
2001/02: 20^{F}G

	Starts	1st	2nd	3rd	Win & Pl
Chases	1	0	0	0	
Career Total	**12**	**3**	**1**	**1**	**16080**

127 5/00 Extr 2m1f E Ch GD £3006
98 11/99 Kemp 2m D Hdl G-F £3100
99 10/98 Cork 2m NHF YLD £2989
Total win prize-money £9095

Going: Sf: 0-0 GS: 0-0 Gd: 0-1 GF: 0-0 Fm: 0-0
Distance: 2m/2m3: 0-0 2m4-2m7: 0-1 3m+: 0-0
Track: LH: 0-1 RH: 0-0 Tight: 0-0 Gall: 0-1
Aids: Bl: 0-0 Vi: 0-0 Tstrap: 0-0
Best Rating: 127 5/00 Extr 2m1f good Ch

Behari (IRE)

86 60

8-y-o b g Kahyasi-Berhala (IRE) (Doyoun)
F M Barton (R Hollinshead 15/11) F M Barton

Placings:000/04222F550/33F423345-000P005 (4742)
2001/02: 16^{0}S, 16^{0}GF, 20^{0}GS, 21^{P}G, 17^{0}GS, 20^{0}G, 24^{5}GF

	Starts	1st	2nd	3rd	Win & Pl
Hurdles	7	0	0	0	0
Career Total	**28**	**0**	**4**	**4**	**4561**

Going: Sf: 0-1 GS: 0-2 Gd: 0-2 GF: - Fm: 0-2
Distance: 2m/2m3: 0-3 2m4-2m7: 0-3 3m+: 0-1
Track: LH: 0-3 RH: 0-4 Tight: 0-1 Gall: 0-0
Aids: Bl: 0-0 Vi: 0-0 Tstrap: 0-3
Best Rating: 88 8/00 Bang 2m4f good Hdl

Behavingbadly (IRE)

106 125

7-y-o b g Lord Americo-Audrey's Turn (Strong Gale)
A Parker (I R Ferguson 21/11) R A Bartlett

Placings:*521122* (4890)
2001/02: 16^{5}S, 17^{2}S, 24^{1}S, 25^{1}GS, 20^{2}GS, 24^{2}G

	Starts	1st	2nd	3rd	Win & Pl
NH Flat	2	0	1	0	677
Hurdles	4	2	2	0	9752
Career Total	**6**	**2**	**3**	**0**	**10430**

112 1/02 Catt 3m1f110y E Hdl G-S £2807
95 12/01 Hexm 3m E Hdl SFT £2439
Total win prize-money £5247

Going: Sf: 1-3 GS: 1-2 Gd: 0-1 GF: - Fm: 0-0
Distance: 2m/2m3: 0-2 2m4-2m7: 0-1 **3m+: 2-3**
Track: **LH: 2-2** RH: 0-1 **Tight: 1-1** Gall: 0-0
Aids: Bl: 0-0 Vi: 0-0 Tstrap: 0-0
Best Rating: 125 4/02 Prth 3m110y good Hdl

Modest ex-Irish staying novice hurdler, he scored a double on his first two starts in Britain. Suited by soft ground.

Behrajan (IRE)

123(105h) (152h)177

7-y-o b g Arazi (USA)-Behera (Mill Reef (USA))
H D Daly The Behrajan Partnership

Placings:11215/52113/**112213-33212P** (4252)
2001/02: 23^{3}G, 24^{3}G, 26^{2}S, 25^{1}GS, 24^{2}HY, 26^{P}G

	Starts	1st	2nd	3rd	Win & Pl
Hurdles	1	0	0	1	1575
Chases	5	1	2	1	64940
Career Total	**22**	**9**	**6**	**4**	**161424**

177 12/01 Weth 3m1f A HCh G-S £19053
154 3/01 Hntg 3m E Ch SFT £3562
132 11/00 Extr 2m7f110y D Ch G-S £5330
150 10/00 Weth 3m1f D Ch G-S £4186
164 1/00 Hayd 2m7f110y A Hdl SFT £15000
164 12/99 Chel 3m B Hdl SFT £8286
138 2/99 Wwck 2m4f110y B Hdl G-S £7385
138 1/99 Sand 2m110y A Hdl SFT £15699
125 12/98 Wwck 2m E Hdl G-S £2792
Total win prize-money £81296

Going: Sf: 0-2 GS: 1-1 Gd: 0-3 GF: - Fm: 0-0
Distance: 2m/2m3: 0-0 2m4-2m7: 0-0 **3m+: 1-6**
Track: **LH: 1-6** RH: 0-0 Tight: 0-0 Gall: 0-2
Aids: Bl: 0-0 Vi: 0-0 Tstrap: 0-0
Best Rating: 177 2/02 Leop 3m heavy Ch

A very useful hurdler at staying trips, he won three times in his first season over fences, but also suffered two defeats on soft ground after finding little on the run-in. Reverted to hurdles at the end of the 2000/2001 campaign. A real chasing type, he ran well on his Haydock reappearance and was just touched off in the Hennessy. Stamped himself a Gold Cup candidate with an impressive victory in the Rowland Meyrick and a good second in the Hennessy at Leopardstown, but disappointed in the Gold Cup itself.

Suited by three miles plus and easy ground, but does not find a great deal when in front.

Behrani (IRE)

67

6-y-o gr g Linamix (FR)-Behera (Mill Reef (USA))
Ian Williams Hardwood Timber Products Ltd

Placings:*0*/*00*P-66 (0641)
2001/02: 21^{6}GF, 24^{6}GF

	Starts	1st	2nd	3rd	Win & Pl
Hurdles	2	0	0	0	0
Career Total	**6**	**0**	**0**	**0**	**0**

Going: Sf: 0-0 GS: 0-0 Gd: 0-0 GF: - Fm: 0-2
Distance: 2m/2m3: 0-0 2m4-2m7: 0-1 3m+: 0-1
Track: LH: 0-0 RH: 0-1 Tight: 0-1 Gall: 0-0
Aids: Bl: 0-2 Vi: 0-0 Tstrap: 0-0
Best Rating: 84 4/00 Hntg 2m110y good NHF

Bekstar

100 101

7-y-o br m Nicholas Bill-Murex (Royalty)
J C Tuck J C Tuck

Placings:*400*/0064-0031F46 (3389)
2001/02: 17^{0}G, 22^{0}GF, 17^{3}GF, 19^{1}GF, 19^{F}GS, 19^{4}GS, 22^{6}GS

	Starts	1st	2nd	3rd	Win & Pl
Hurdles	7	1	0	1	2051
Career Total	**14**	**1**	**0**	**1**	**2368**

91 10/01 Extr 2m3f G(0-95)HHdl G-F £1792
Total win prize-money £1792

Going: Sf: 0-0 GS: 0-3 Gd: 0-1 GF: - Fm: 1-3
Distance: **2m/2m3: 1-5** 2m4-2m7: 0-2 3m+: 0-0
Track: LH: 0-1 **RH: 1-6** Tight: 0-1 Gall: 0-0
Aids: Bl: 0-0 Vi: 0-0 Tstrap: 0-0
Best Rating: 91 10/01 Extr 2m3f gd-sft Hdl

First sign of form when dropped into selling grade at Exeter, and scored at the same track next time. Stays two miles three, acts on fast ground.

Belisario (IRE)

103(80h) 133

8-y-o b/br g Distinctly North (USA)-Bold Kate (Bold Lad (IRE))
M W Easterby Paul G Jacobs

Placings:*413*/562/1F-3131 (3996)
2001/02: 20^{3}GS, 23^{1}GS, 22^{3}HY, 24^{1}S

	Starts	1st	2nd	3rd	Win & Pl
Chases	4	2	0	2	8059
Career Total	**12**	**4**	**1**	**3**	**12603**

125 3/02 Donc 3m E Ch SFT £3302
129 1/02 Weth 2m7f110y E Ch G-S £3363
112 10/00 Weth 2m7f F(0-100)HHdl G-S £1970
106 3/98 MRas 1m5f110y H NHF G-S £1287
Total win prize-money £9924

Going: Sf: 1-2 GS: 1-2 Gd: 0-1 GF: - Fm: 0-0
Distance: 2m/2m3: 0-0 2m4-2m7: 0-2 **3m+: 2-2**
Track: **LH: 1-2** RH: 0-0 Tight: 0-0 **Gall: 1-1**
Aids: Bl: 0-0 Vi: 0-0 Tstrap: 0-0
Best Rating: 133 2/02 Hayd 2m6f heavy Ch

A winner of a bumper back in 1998, he won a novice hurdle at Wetherby in 2000. Has taken well to fences this season, but does not stand much racing. Acts on good to soft ground.

Belitlir

82(76h) (37h)80

10-y-o b m Lir-Kimberley Ann (St Columbus)

Miss S Young B R J Young

Placings:0/00-P5542 (4482)

2001/02: 33^{P}G, 16^{5}S, 24^{5}S, 24^{4}S, 25^{2}G

	Starts	1st	2nd	3rd	Win & Pl
Hurdles	1	0	0	0	0
Chases	4	0	1	0	1607
Career Total	**8**	**0**	**1**	**0**	**1607**

Going: Sf: 0-3 GS: 0-0 Gd: 0-2 GF: - Fm: 0-0
Distance: 2m/2m3: 0-1 2m4-2m7: 0-0 3m+: 0-4
Track: LH: 0-1 RH: 0-2 Tight: 0-2 Gall: 0-0
Aids: Bl: 0-0 Vi: 0-0 Tstrap: 0-0
Best Rating: **80** 2/02 Tntn 3m soft Ch

Modest, lightly-raced chaser, ran above herself at Exeter in March 2002.

Bell Lane Lad (IRE)

76f 77f

5-y-o b g Wakashan-Busti Lass (IRE) (Bustineto)

Ferdy Murphy Jack McGrath

Placings:0 (3375)

2001/02: 16^{0}S

	Starts	1st	2nd	3rd	Win & Pl
NH Flat	1	0	0	0	
Career Total	**1**	**0**	**0**	**0**	

Going: Sf: 0-1 GS: 0 0 Gd: 0-0 GF: - Fm: 0-0
Distance: 2m/2m3: 0-1 2m4-2m7: 0-0 3m+: 0-0
Track: LH: 0-1 RH: 0-0 Tight: 0-0 Gall: 0-0
Aids: Bl: 0-0 Vi: 0-0 Tstrap: 0-0
Best Rating: **77** 1/02 Hayd 2m soft NHF

Bell Rock

82 79

4-y-o ch g Charmer-Sule Skerry (Scottish Rifle)

Miss E C Lavelle A J Struthers

Placings:40 (1800)

2001/02: 16^{4}GF, 16^{0}GF

	Starts	1st	2nd	3rd	Win & Pl
Hurdles	2	0	0	0	0
Career Total	**2**	**0**	**0**	**0**	**0**

Going: Sf: 0-0 GS: 0-0 Gd: 0-0 GF: - Fm: 0-2
Distance: 2m/2m3: 0-2 2m4-2m7: 0-0 3m+: 0-0
Track: LH: 0-0 RH: 0-2 Tight: 0-0 Gall: 0-0
Aids: Bl: 0-0 Vi: 0-0 Tstrap: 0-0
Best Rating: **79** 10/01 Winc 2m gd-fm Hdl

Bell Tex (IRE)

76 85

10-y-o br g Orchestra-Lyngard (Balliol)

J C Fox Shirley M & Peter G Palmer

Placings:P/P040-2 (0432)

2001/02: 20^{2}GF

	Starts	1st	2nd	3rd	Win & Pl
Hurdles	1	0	1	0	582
Career Total	**6**	**0**	**1**	**0**	**582**

Going: Sf: 0-0 GS: 0-0 Gd: 0-0 GF: - Fm: 0-1
Distance: 2m/2m3: 0-0 2m4-2m7: 0-1 3m+: 0-0
Track: LH: 0-0 RH: 0-1 Tight: 0-1 Gall: 0-0
Aids: Bl: 0-0 Vi: 0-0 Tstrap: 0-0
Best Rating: **85** 5/01 Folk 2m4f110y gd-fm Hdl

Bell Tor (IRE)

91f 88f

5-y-o b m King's Ride-Shannon Juliette (Julio Mariner)

D R Gandolfo T J Whitley

Placings:*6* (0843)

2001/02: 16^{6}G

	Starts	1st	2nd	3rd	Win & Pl
NH Flat	1	0	0	0	0
Career Total	**1**	**0**	**0**	**0**	**0**

Going: Sf: 0-0 GS: 0-0 Gd: 0-1 GF: - Fm: 0-0
Distance: 2m/2m3: 0-1 2m4-2m7: 0-0 3m+: 0-0
Track: LH: 0-1 RH: 0-0 Tight: 0-0 Gall: 0-0
Aids: Bl: 0-0 Vi: 0-0 Tstrap: 0-0
Best Rating: **88** 6/01 Worc 2m good NHF

Bella Macrae

99 113

7-y-o b m Bustino-Highland Lyric (Rymer)

N J Henderson Queen Elizabeth

Placings:*31025*/21421UF-2 (0372)

2001/02: 16^{2}GF

	Starts	1st	2nd	3rd	Win & Pl
Hurdles	1	0	1	0	896
Career Total	**13**	**3**	**4**	**1**	**12329**

129	3/01	Sand	2m110y	E(0-115)HHdl	HVY	£4368
121	12/00	Winc	2m	E Hdl	G-S	£2653
105	2/00	Fknm	2m	H NHF	GD	£1445

Total win prize-money £8467

Going: Sf: 0-0 GS: 0-0 Gd: 0-0 GF: - Fm: 0-1
Distance: 2m/2m3: 0-1 2m4-2m7: 0-0 3m+: 0-0
Track: LH: 0-0 RH: 0-1 Tight: 0-0 Gall: 0-1
Aids: Bl: 0-0 Vi: 0-0 Tstrap: 0-0
Best Rating: **129** 3/01 Sand 2m110y heavy Hdl

Bella Pupa

55

6-y-o ch m Theatrical Charmer-Louisa Anne (Mummy's Pet)

N M Babbage Colin Rashbrook

Placings:00-PP (0976)

2001/02: 19^{P}G, 16^{P}GF

	Starts	1st	2nd	3rd	Win & Pl
Hurdles	2	0	0	0	
Career Total	**4**	**0**	**0**	**0**	

Going: Sf: 0-0 GS: 0-0 Gd: 0-1 GF: - Fm: 0-1
Distance: 2m/2m3: 0-1 2m4-2m7: 0-1 3m+: 0-0
Track: LH: 0-1 RH: 0-1 Tight: 0-1 Gall: 0-0
Aids: Bl: 0-0 Vi: 0-1 Tstrap: 0-0
Best Rating: **55** 4/01 Hrfd 2m1f good Hdl

Bellabaloo

96 83

7-y-o b m Seymour Hicks (FR)-Supreme Issue (Bustiki)

J A Glover R W Metcalfe

Placings:*3*/55551P (1853)

2001/02: 17^{5}GF, 17^{5}GS, 16^{5}GF, 19^{5}GF, 17^{1}S, 17^{P}S

	Starts	1st	2nd	3rd	Win & Pl
Hurdles	6	1	0	0	2765
Career Total	**7**	**1**	**0**	**1**	**2980**

83	9/01	MRas	2m1f110y	F(0-100)HHdl	SFT	£2765

Total win prize-money £2765

Going: Sf: 1-2 GS: 0-1 Gd: 0-0 GF: - Fm: 0-3
Distance: **2m/2m3: 1-5** 2m4-2m7: 0-1 3m+: 0-0
Track: LH: 0-2 **RH: 1-3 Tight: 1-4** Gall: 0-0
Aids: Bl: 0-0 Vi: 0-0 Tstrap: 0-0
Best Rating: **83** 9/01 MRas 2m1f110y soft Hdl

Bellacaccia (IRE)

94f 99f

6-y-o ch m Beau Sher-Game Gambler (IRE) (Long Pond)

C W Thornton D B Dennison

Placings:*4*-324 (2055)

2001/02: 17^{3}GS, 17^{2}GS, 17^{4}S

	Starts	1st	2nd	3rd	Win & Pl
NH Flat	3	0	1	1	738
Career Total	**4**	**0**	**1**	**1**	**738**

Going: Sf: 0-1 GS: 0-2 Gd: 0-0 GF: - Fm: 0-0
Distance: 2m/2m3: 0-3 2m4-2m7: 0-0 3m+: 0-0
Track: LH: 0-1 RH: 0-2 Tight: 0-1 Gall: 0-0
Aids: Bl: 0-0 Vi: 0-0 Tstrap: 0-0
Best Rating: **99** 10/01 Carl 2m1f gd-sft NHF

Bellaney King (IRE)

10-y-o b g King's Ride-Girseach (Furry Glen)

Mrs A Price Mrs A Price

Placings:00P/P6 (4684)

2001/02: 20^{P}G, 19^{6}GF

	Starts	1st	2nd	3rd	Win & Pl
Hurdles	1	0	0	0	0
Chases	1	0	0	0	0
Career Total	**5**	**0**	**0**	**0**	**0**

Going: Sf: 0-0 GS: 0-0 Gd: 0-1 GF: - Fm: 0-1
Distance: 2m/2m3: 0-0 2m4-2m7: 0-2 3m+: 0-0
Track: LH: 0-0 RH: 0-2 Tight: 0-1 Gall: 0-0
Aids: Bl: 0-0 Vi: 0-0 Tstrap: 0-0
Best Rating: **51** 3/00 DRoy 3m1f gd-yld Ch

Bellator

106 169

9-y-o b g Simply Great (FR)-Jupiter's Message (Jupiter Island)

Miss Venetia Williams Peter Richardson

Placings:11/0604U1/02554044/**11154P/12331R44-35RR** (3385)

2001/02: 21^{3}G, 24^{5}G, 24^{R}G, 21^{R}GS

	Starts	1st	2nd	3rd	Win & Pl
Chases	4	0	0	1	4025
Career Total	**34**	**8**	**2**	**3**	**156025**

162	1/01	Winc	2m5f	B Ch	G-S	£12635
170	10/00	Extr	2m1f110y	A HCh	SFT	£21000
164	1/00	Asct	2m	A Ch	GD	£15600
160	1/00	Hayd	2m	C Ch	SFT	£6272
141	11/99	NAbb	2m110y	E Ch	SFT	£2954
158	4/98	Aint	2m110y	B HHdl	SFT	£18635
125	11/96	Aint	2m110y	B Hdl	GD	£5151
119	11/96	Weth	2m	A Hdl	GD	£9690

Total win prize-money £91940

Going: Sf: 0-0 GS: 0-1 Gd: 0-3 GF: - Fm: 0-0
Distance: 2m/2m3: 0-0 2m4-2m7: 0-2 3m+: 0-2
Track: LH: 0-1 RH: 0-3 Tight: 0-0 Gall: 0-0
Aids: Bl: 0-0 Vi: 0-0 Tstrap: 0-0
Best Rating: 170 11/00 Asct 2m3f110y soft Ch

A high-class performer in his time over both hurdles and fences, he has now been retired.

Bell Bird

107 **93**

6-y-o gr m Bob's Return (IRE)-Tangara (Town Crier)
Mrs P Robeson Mrs P Robeson

Placings:30P-P3312P (4535)
2001/02: 20^{P}G, 17^{3}G, 17^{3}G, 19^{1}GS, 19^{2}S, 20^{P}G

	Starts	1st	2nd	3rd	Win & Pl
Hurdles	6	1	1	2	4340
Career Total	**9**	**1**	**1**	**3**	**4545**

81 12/01 Tntn 2m3f110y F(0-95)HHdl G-S £2856
Total win prize-money £2856

Going: Sf: 0-1 GS: 1-1 Gd: 0-4 GF: - Fm: 0-0
Distance: 2m/2m3: 0-2 **2m4-2m7: 1-4** 3m+: 0-0
Track: LH: 0-1 **RH: 1-5 Tight: 1-5** Gall: 0-1
Aids: Bl: 0-0 Vi: 0-0 Tstrap: 0-0
Best Rating: 93 4/02 Fknm 2m4f good Hdl

Landed a weak novices' handicap hurdle at Taunton in December, runner-up over course and distance next time. Broke down when looking sure to win at Fakenham in April.

Belle Amour

63 **56**

5-y-o b m Inchinor-Mossy Rose (King Of Spain)
Miss H M Irving Miss H M Irving

Placings:00-0 (0102)
2001/02: 18^{0}GF

	Starts	1st	2nd	3rd	Win & Pl
Hurdles	1	0	0	0	
Career Total	**3**	**0**	**0**	**0**	

Going: Sf: 0-0 GS: 0-0 Gd: 0-0 GF: - Fm: 0-1
Distance: 2m/2m3: 0-1 2m4-2m7: 0-0 3m+: 0-0
Track: LH: 0-1 RH: 0-0 Tight: 0-1 Gall: 0-0
Aids: Bl: 0-0 Vi: 0-0 Tstrap: 0-0
Best Rating: 56 5/01 Font 2m2f110y gd-fm Hdl

Belle D'Anjou (FR)

(111h) (135h)

5-y-o b m Saint Cyrien (FR)-Epsibelle (IRE) (Darshaan)
M C Pipe Network Training

Placings:4/211111530-1101B3 (4822)
2001/02: 16^{1}G, 19^{1}GS, 16^{0}S, 16^{1}GS, 16^{B}S, 21^{3}G

	Starts	1st	2nd	3rd	Win & Pl
Hurdles	6	3	0	1	23734
Career Total	**16**	**8**	**1**	**2**	**48116**

131 12/01 Newb 2m110y B Hdl G-S £7250
135 11/01 Tntn 2m3f110y D(0-120)HHdl G-S £3633
120 10/01 Chep 2m110y B HHdl GD £9834
109 9/00 Plum 2m C Hdl GD £4845
112 9/00 Strf 2m110y E Hdl GD £2795
109 8/00 NAbb 2m1f E Hdl G-F £2506
104 8/00 Bang 2m1f E Hdl GD £2886
6/00 Autl 1m7f Hdl VS £6244
Total win prize-money £39995

Going: Sf: 0-2 GS: 2-2 Gd: 1-2 GF: - Fm: 0-0
Distance: **2m/2m3: 2-4** 2m4-2m7: 1-2 3m+: 0-0
Track: **LH: 2-4** RH: 1-2 Tight: 1-1 Gall: 1-3
Aids: Bl: 0-0 Vi: 0-0 Tstrap: 0-0
Best Rating: 135 11/01 Tntn 2m3f110y gd-sft Hdl

Ex-French, she scored four facile victories in late summer 2000, sent off at odds-on each time, but was held afterwards on softer ground. Successful twice on the Flat in the summer of 2001 before scoring three times in decent company over hurdles before Christmas. Useful when the ground is in her favour.

Belle D'Orsini (FR)

77 **41**

7-y-o ch m Le Nain Jaune (FR)-Ma Belle (FR) (Lightning (FR))
J J O'Neill V N Stroud

Placings:3F/41P30F/22311-0 (1668)
2001/02: 20^{0}G

	Starts	1st	2nd	3rd	Win & Pl
Hurdles	1	0	0	0	
Career Total	**14**	**3**	**2**	**3**	**13755**

132 1/01 Donc 2m4f C(0-135)HHdl GD £5430
120 1/01 Donc 2m4f E(0-115)HHdl GD £2733
109 5/99 Ctml 2m1f110y G Hdl G-F £2556
Total win prize-money £10721

Going: Sf: 0-0 GS: 0-0 Gd: 0-1 GF: - Fm: 0-0
Distance: 2m/2m3: 0-0 2m4-2m7: 0-1 3m+: 0-0
Track: LH: 0-1 RH: 0-0 Tight: 0-1 Gall: 0-0
Aids: Bl: 0-0 Vi: 0-0 Tstrap: 0-0
Best Rating: 132 1/01 Donc 2m4f good Hdl

Belle Dancer

8-y-o b m Rambo Dancer (CAN)-Warning Bell (Bustino)
T Wall Harton Manor Racing Club

Placings:P/00/P0000/00000-00 (1405)
2001/02: 17^{0}GS, 16^{0}GF

	Starts	1st	2nd	3rd	Win & Pl
Hurdles	2	0	0	0	
Career Total	**16**	**0**	**0**	**0**	

Going: Sf: 0-0 GS: 0-1 Gd: 0-0 GF: - Fm: 0-1
Distance: 2m/2m3: 0-2 2m4-2m7: 0-0 3m+: 0-0
Track: LH: 0-2 RH: 0-0 Tight: 0-1 Gall: 0-0
Aids: Bl: 0-0 Vi: 0-0 Tstrap: 0-0
Best Rating: 58 11/99 Ludl 2m good Hdl

Belle Derriere

85 **85**

7-y-o b m Kylian (USA)-Metannee (The Brianstan)
S E H Sherwood R J Bassett

Placings:2141/60PP (4853)
2001/02: 17^{6}G, 16^{0}G, 16^{P}S, 16^{P}G

	Starts	1st	2nd	3rd	Win & Pl
Hurdles	4	0	0	0	0
Career Total	**8**	**2**	**1**	**0**	**5794**

121 12/99 Leic 2m E Hdl GD £3340
100 10/99 Ludl 2m H NHF G-F £1721
Total win prize-money £5061

Going: Sf: 0-1 GS: 0-0 Gd: 0-3 GF: - Fm: 0-0
Distance: 2m/2m3: 0-4 2m4-2m7: 0-0 3m+: 0-0
Track: LH: 0-1 RH: 0-3 Tight: 0-1 Gall: 0-0
Aids: Bl: 0-1 Vi: 0-0 Tstrap: 0-0
Best Rating: 121 12/99 Leic 2m good Hdl

Belle Des Poires

7-y-o ch m Alnasr Alwasheek-Plum Tree (Dominion)
G E Jones G Elwyn Jones

Placings:0-00 (2215)
2001/02: 17^{0}GF, 17^{0}G

	Starts	1st	2nd	3rd	Win & Pl
NH Flat	2	0	0	0	
Career Total	**3**	**0**	**0**	**0**	

Going: Sf: 0-0 GS: 0-0 Gd: 0-1 GF: - Fm: 0-1
Distance: 2m/2m3: 0-2 2m4-2m7: 0-0 3m+: 0-0
Track: LH: 0-0 RH: 0-2 Tight: 0-0 Gall: 0-0
Aids: Bl: 0-0 Vi: 0-0 Tstrap: 0-0
Best Rating: 50 5/00 Bang 2m1f good NHF

Belle's Boy

9-y-o b g Nalchik (USA)-Ty-With-Belle (Pamroy)
P Williams Mrs D J Hughes

Placings:P/0 (0226)
2001/02: 20^{0}GF

	Starts	1st	2nd	3rd	Win & Pl
Chases	1	0	0	0	
Career Total	**2**	**0**	**0**	**0**	

Going: Sf: 0-0 GS: 0-0 Gd: 0-0 GF: - Fm: 0-1
Distance: 2m/2m3: 0-0 2m4-2m7: 0-1 3m+: 0-0
Track: LH: 0-0 RH: 0-1 Tight: 0-0 Gall: 0-1
Aids: Bl: 0-0 Vi: 0-0 Tstrap: 0-0
Best Rating:

Belleave It Or Not

77 **46**

9-y-o b g Long Leave-Bellerica (Spirit Of St Louis)
Miss D Cole J F R Chapple

Placings:P0 (1849)
2001/02: 19^{P}G, 22^{0}G

	Starts	1st	2nd	3rd	Win & Pl
Hurdles	2	0	0	0	
Career Total	**2**	**0**	**0**	**0**	

Going: Sf: 0-0 GS: 0-0 Gd: 0-2 GF: - Fm: 0-0
Distance: 2m/2m3: 0-0 2m4-2m7: 0-2 3m+: 0-0
Track: LH: 0-0 RH: 0-2 Tight: 0-0 Gall: 0-0
Aids: Bl: 0-0 Vi: 0-0 Tstrap: 0-0
Best Rating: 46 10/01 Winc 2m6f good Hdl

Bellefleur

88f **81f**

5-y-o b m Alflora (IRE)-Isabeau (Law Society (USA))
J M Jefferson Pryke Hygeine Group,J Wilkinson,B Wade

Placings:055 (4289)
2001/02: 16^{0}S, 16^{5}S, 17^{5}GS

	Starts	1st	2nd	3rd	Win & Pl
NH Flat	3	0	0	0	0
Career Total	**3**	**0**	**0**	**0**	**0**

Going: Sf: 0-2 GS: 0-1 Gd: 0-0 GF: - Fm: 0-0
Distance: 2m/2m3: 0-3 2m4-2m7: 0-0 3m+: 0-0
Track: LH: 0-1 RH: 0-1 Tight: 0-1 Gall: 0-1
Aids: Bl: 0-0 Vi: 0-0 Tstrap: 0-0

Best Rating: 81 2/02 Donc 2m110y soft NHF

Has shown some ability in bumpers.

Bellino Spirit (IRE)

93 **74**

6-y-o b m Robellino (USA)-Working Model (Ile De Bourbon (USA))

M Todhunter Tim Kilroe

Placings:00/F4P3 **(4431)**

2001/02: 16^{F}GS, 16^{4}HY, 16^{P}S, 16^{3}HY

	Starts	1st	2nd	3rd	Win & Pl
Hurdles	4	0	0	1	380
Career Total	**6**	**0**	**0**	**1**	**380**

Going: Sf: 0-3 GS: 0-1 Gd: 0-0 GF: - Fm: 0-0
Distance: 2m/2m3: 0-4 2m4-2m7: 0-0 3m+: 0-0
Track: LH: 0-4 RH: 0-0 Tight: 0-1 Gall: 0-1
Aids: Bl: 0-0 Vi: 0-0 Tstrap: 0-0
Best Rating: 74 3/02 Ayr 2m heavy Hdl

Showed a little ability over hurdles in heavy ground in March. Benefits from being held up.

Belloc

97 **75**

7-y-o gr g Arzanni-Princess Story (Prince De Galles)

Mrs D Haine Mrs Solna Thomson Jones

Placings:0/2200P-4P **(2112)**

2001/02: 20^{4}G, 20^{P}S

	Starts	1st	2nd	3rd	Win & Pl
Hurdles	2	0	0	0	0
Career Total	**8**	**0**	**2**	**0**	**868**

Going: Sf: 0-1 GS: 0-0 Gd: 0-1 GF: - Fm: 0-0
Distance: 2m/2m3: 0-0 2m4-2m7: 0-2 3m+: 0-0
Track: LH: 0-1 RH: 0-1 Tight: 0-2 Gall: 0-0
Aids: Bl: 0-0 Vi: 0-0 Tstrap: 0-2
Best Rating: 95 11/00 Wwck 2m heavy NHF

Belovodsk (SU)

107 **129**

10-y-o b g Eten (SU)-Bavariya (SU) (Avat (SU))

Zdena Havlickova Stall Pegas-Znojmo

Placings:3/3/U2-341U5 **(2146)**

2001/02: 22^{3}GF, 29^{4}G, 25^{1}GF, 34^{U}GF, 31^{5}G

	Starts	1st	2nd	3rd	Win & Pl
Chases	5	1	0	1	1604
Career Total	**9**	**1**	**1**	**3**	**26967**

8/01 Pard 3m1f Ch G-F £903
Total win prize-money £903

Going: Sf: 0-0 GS: 0-0 Gd: 0-2 GF: - Fm: 1-3
Distance: 2m/2m3: 0-0 2m4-2m7: 0-1 **3m+: 1-4**
Track: **LH: 1-3** RH: 0-0 Tight: 0-0 Gall: 0-0
Aids: Bl: 0-0 Vi: 0-0 Tstrap: 0-0
Best Rating: 129 11/01 Chel 3m7f good Ch

Chaser trained in the Czech Republic. Acts over staying trips.

Ben Cohan (IRE)

104(103h) (109h)**119**

9-y-o b g Brush Aside (USA)-Lornaaron (Tanfirion)

K C Bailey A Heyes & M Barlow

Placings:U40022/41350/3F402-6165412 **(1804)**

2001/02: 17^{6}G, 21^{1}GF, 19^{6}GF, 22^{5}GF, 20^{4}GF, 20^{1}GF, 24^{2}GF

	Starts	1st	2nd	3rd	Win & Pl
Hurdles	5	1	0	0	3962
Chases	2	1	1	0	3937
Career Total	**23**	**3**	**4**	**2**	**14107**

115 8/01 Hntg 2m4f110y E Ch G-F £3061
109 5/01 Hntg 2m5f110y D(0-125)HHdl G-F £3444
109 5/99 DRoy 2m Hdl SFT £2455
Total win prize-money £8961

Going: Sf: 0-0 GS: 0-0 Gd: 0-1 GF: - Fm: 2-6
Distance: 2m/2m3: 0-1 **2m4-2m7: 2-5** 3m+: 0-1
Track: LH: 0-3 **RH: 2-4** Tight: 0-5 **Gall: 2-2**
Aids: Bl: 0-0 Vi: 0-0 **Tstrap: 2-7**
Best Rating: 119 10/01 Ludl 3m gd-fm Ch

Won a novice chase in August and ran well in handicap company next time. Effective on fast ground.

Ben Ewar

116 **139**

8-y-o b g Old Vic-Sunset Reef (Mill Reef (USA))

K O Cunningham-Brown (F Doumen 11/10) A J Richards

Placings:16501-035 **(4758)**

2001/02: 18^{0}GS, 17^{3}G, 16^{5}GF

	Starts	1st	2nd	3rd	Win & Pl
Hurdles	3	0	0	1	6325
Career Total	**8**	**2**	**0**	**1**	**35324**

4/01 Engh 2m1f110y Hdl HVY £19399
128 12/00 Asct 2m110y A Hdl HVY £9600
Total win prize-money £28999

Going: Sf: 0-0 GS: 0-1 Gd: 0-1 GF: - Fm: 0-1
Distance: 2m/2m3: 0-3 2m4-2m7: 0-0 3m+: 0-0
Track: LH: 0-1 RH: 0-1 Tight: 0-0 Gall: 0-1
Aids: Bl: 0-0 Vi: 0-0 Tstrap: 0-0
Best Rating: 139 3/02 Chel 2m1f good Hdl

Useful on the Flat in France. Having his first run over hurdles for more than a year when third in the County Hurdle at Cheltenham in 2002. Probably needs to be held up off a decent pace over two miles. Has won on heavy, handles good ground.

Ben From Ketton

7-y-o b g Cruise Missile-Saucy Girl (Saucy Kit)

S J Robinson S J Robinson

Placings:P **(0473)**

2001/02: 20^{P}GF

	Starts	1st	2nd	3rd	Win & Pl
Chases	1	0	0	0	
Career Total	**1**	**0**	**0**	**0**	

Going: Sf: 0-0 GS: 0-0 Gd: 0-0 GF: - Fm: 0-1
Distance: 2m/2m3: 0-0 2m4-2m7: 0-1 3m+: 0-0
Track: LH: 0-1 RH: 0-0 Tight: 0-0 Gall: 0-0
Aids: Bl: 0-0 Vi: 0-0 Tstrap: 0-0
Best Rating:

Benbecula (IRE)

101f **113f**

5-y-o b g Glacial Storm (USA)-Lough View (Radical)

P R Webber J Dougall

Placings:20 **(4158)**

2001/02: 16^{2}G, 16^{0}GS

	Starts	1st	2nd	3rd	Win & Pl
NH Flat	2	0	1	0	765
Career Total	**2**	**0**	**1**	**0**	**765**

Going: Sf: 0-0 GS: 0-1 Gd: 0-1 GF: - Fm: 0-0
Distance: 2m/2m3: 0-2 2m4-2m7: 0-0 3m+: 0-0
Track: LH: 0-1 RH: 0-1 Tight: 0-0 Gall: 0-1
Aids: Bl: 0-0 Vi: 0-0 Tstrap: 0-0
Best Rating: 113 12/01 Newb 2m110y good NHF

Acts on good ground and is effective at two miles.

Benbradagh (IRE)

8-y-o b g Mister Lord (USA)-Meenia (Black Minstrel)

Brendan W Duke Cotswold Coppington Connection

Placings:P/35P-PP00 **(4577)**

2001/02: 22^{P}GS, 20^{P}S, 26^{0}G, 24^{0}G

	Starts	1st	2nd	3rd	Win & Pl
Hurdles	4	0	0	0	
Career Total	**8**	**0**	**0**	**1**	**366**

Going: Sf: 0-1 GS: 0-1 Gd: 0-2 GF: - Fm: 0-0
Distance: 2m/2m3: 0-0 2m4-2m7: 0-2 3m+: 0-2
Track: LH: 0-1 RH: 0-3 Tight: 0-0 Gall: 0-1
Aids: Bl: 0-0 Vi: 0-1 Tstrap: 0-4
Best Rating: 95 12/00 MRas 2m3f110y gd-sft Hdl

Benbyas

112 **134**

5-y-o b g Rambo Dancer (CAN)-Light The Way (Nicholas Bill)

J L Eyre C H Stephenson & Partners

Placings:223-21113340 **(4674)**

2001/02: 19^{2}G, 16^{1}G, 16^{1}G, 17^{1}G, 16^{3}GS, 16^{3}S, 17^{4}G, 16^{0}G

	Starts	1st	2nd	3rd	Win & Pl
Hurdles	8	3	1	2	45074
Career Total	**11**	**3**	**3**	**3**	**47140**

134 12/01 Chel 2m1f C(0-135)HHdl GD £17875
113 11/01 Weth 2m D Hdl GD £3948
117 11/01 Weth 2m C Hdl GD £5635
Total win prize-money £27459

Going: Sf: 0-1 GS: 0-1 Gd: 3-6 GF: - Fm: 0-0
Distance: **2m/2m3: 3-7** 2m4-2m7: 0-1 3m+: 0-0
Track: **LH: 3-6** RH: 0-2 Tight: 0-2 **Gall: 1-3**
Aids: Bl: 0-0 Vi: 0-0 Tstrap: 0-0
Best Rating: 134 12/01 Chel 2m1f good Hdl

A front-running hurdler, he won two novice events at Wetherby in November 2001 before taking a handicap hurdle at Cheltenham in December in battling fashion. Consistent efforts since. A brave sort, suited by the minimum trip and good ground.

Bendor Mark

(79h) (34h)

13-y-o b g Lighter-Montana (Puissance)

D C Turner Mrs Mandy Hand

Placings:0P03/0533U10/P12/3PF4/PP/0P0 **(1150)**

2001/02: 16^{0}GF, 21^{P}G, 22^{0}GF

	Starts	1st	2nd	3rd	Win & Pl
Hurdles	1	0	0	0	0
Chases	2	0	0	0	0
Career Total	**23**	**2**	**1**	**4**	**10894**

108 1/97 Leic 3m F(0-105)HCh G-F £3566
97 3/96 Ling 2m4f110y E Ch SFT £3234
Total win prize-money £6801

Going: Sf: 0-0 GS: 0-0 Gd: 0-1 GF: - Fm: 0-2
Distance: 2m/2m3: 0-1 2m4-2m7: 0-2 3m+: 0-0
Track: LH: 0-3 RH: 0-0 Tight: 0-3 Gall: 0-0
Aids: Bl: 0-0 Vi: 0-0 Tstrap: 0-0
Best Rating: **109** 1/98 Hntg 3m gd-sft Ch

Benefit

(104h) (91h)**88**
8-y-o b g Primitive Rising (USA)-Sobriquet (Roan Rocket)
Miss L C Siddall Mrs D Ibbotson

Placings:34/213040206-13534P5 **(4572)**
2001/02: 21^{1}G, 20^{3}S, 23^{5}G, 21^{3}GS, 21^{4}GS, 24^{P}HY, 20^{5}G

	Starts	1st	2nd	3rd	Win & Pl
Hurdles	7	1	0	2	3662
Career Total	**18**	**2**	**2**	**4**	**9363**

89 5/01 Wwck 2m5f F(0-90)HHdl GD £2597
103 6/00 Uttx 2m4f110y D Hdl GD £2947
Total win prize-money £5545

Going: Sf: 0-2 GS: 0-2 Gd: 1-3 GF: - Fm: 0-0
Distance: 2m/2m3: 0-0 **2m4-2m7: 1-5** 3m+: 0-2
Track: LH: 0-4 RH: 0-2 Tight: 0-3 Gall: 0-0
Aids: Bl: 0-0 Vi: 0-0 Tstrap: 0-0
Best Rating: **103** 6/00 Uttx 2m4f110y good Hdl

He tends to run in snatches, his last victory being at Warwick over two and a half miles in May 2001 on good ground.

Bengal Boy

101(100h) (95h)**107**
6-y-o b g Gildoran-Bengal Lady (Celtic Cone)
P Beaumont Brandsby Racing

Placings:0004P-PP46**P2U5315** **(4746)**
2001/02: 21^{P}G, 24^{P}G, 17^{4}GF, 16^{8}GS, 17^{P}S, 16^{2}G, 19^{U}S, 20^{5}S, 16^{3}GS, 17^{1}S, 20^{5}GF

	Starts	1st	2nd	3rd	Win & Pl
Hurdles	5	0	0	0	0
Chases	6	1	1	1	6293
Career Total	**16**	**1**	**1**	**1**	**6293**

107 3/02 Bang 2m1f110y D Ch SFT £4340
Total win prize-money £4340

Going: Sf: 1-4 GS: 0-2 Gd: 0-3 GF: - Fm: 0-2
Distance: **2m/2m3: 1-6** 2m4-2m7: 0-4 3m+: 0-1
Track: **LH: 1-9** RH: 0-2 **Tight: 1-6** Gall: 0-3
Aids: Bl: 0-0 Vi: 0-0 Tstrap: 0-1
Best Rating: **107** 3/02 Bang 2m1f110y soft Ch

Modest hurdler/novice chaser prone to jumping errors and made mistakes before winning a terrible Bangor novice chase by a wide margin in March 2002. Handles soft ground and should stay two and a half miles.

Benick (IRE)

9-y-o b g Yashgan-Sounds Symphonic (Orchestra)
N A Twiston-Davies (R J Smith 15/1) M P Wareing & D J Owen

Placings:PF/0F112P53P-0P05 **(4150)**
2001/02: 22^{0}GS, 24^{P}S, 26^{0}HY, 24^{5}GS

	Starts	1st	2nd	3rd	Win & Pl
Hurdles	2	0	0	0	0
Chases	2	0	0	0	0
Career Total	**15**	**2**	**1**	**1**	**5701**

107 11/00 Sedg 3m3f110y E Hdl SFT £2348
107 11/00 Chep 3m F Hdl SFT £1883
Total win prize-money £4232

Going: Sf: 0-2 GS: 0-2 Gd: 0-0 GF: - Fm: 0-0
Distance: 2m/2m3: 0-0 2m4-2m7: 0-1 3m+: 0-3
Track: LH: 0-2 RH: 0-2 Tight: 0-0 Gall: 0-0
Aids: Bl: 0-1 Vi: 0-0 Tstrap: 0-0
Best Rating: **107** 11/00 Plum 3m1f110y heavy Hdl

He won twice in November 2000, but then rather lost his form afterwards. Suited by a test of stamina and is suited by soft ground.

Benova Boy

10-y-o ch g Ra Nova-Alithorne (Kinglet)
Mrs K J Gilmore (S J Gilmore 31/5) Brian Gurney

Placings:6-F0630 **(4179)**
2001/02: 21^{F}GF, 16^{0}G, 24^{6}GF, 20^{3}S, 24^{0}GS

	Starts	1st	2nd	3rd	Win & Pl
Chases	5	0	0	1	332
Career Total	**6**	**0**	**0**	**1**	**332**

Going: Sf: 0-1 GS: 0-1 Gd: 0-1 GF: - Fm: 0-2
Distance: 2m/2m3: 0-1 2m4-2m7: 0-2 3m+: 0-2
Track: LH: 0-2 RH: 0-2 Tight: 0-2 Gall: 0-1
Aids: Bl: 0-1 Vi: 0-4 Tstrap: 0-0
Best Rating: **81** 5/01 Hntg 3m gd-fm Ch

Benrajah (IRE)

94f **108f**
5-y-o b g Lord Americo-Andy's Fancy (IRE) (Andretti)
H D Daly The Behrajan Partnership

Placings:2 **(4329)**
2001/02: 17^{2}S

	Starts	1st	2nd	3rd	Win & Pl
NH Flat	1	0	1	0	486
Career Total	**1**	**0**	**1**	**0**	**486**

Going: Sf: 0-1 GS: 0-0 Gd: 0-0 GF: - Fm: 0-0
Distance: 2m/2m3: 0-1 2m4-2m7: 0-0 3m+: 0-0
Track: LH: 0-0 RH: 0-1 Tight: 0-0 Gall: 0-0
Aids: Bl: 0-0 Vi: 0-0 Tstrap: 0-0
Best Rating: **108** 3/02 Hrfd 2m1f soft NHF

Runner-up in a bumper on his debut.

Benson (IRE)

75 **82**
7-y-o b/br g Hawkstone (IRE)-Erin St Helen (IRE) (Seclude (USA))
H D Daly Midavon Partnership

Placings:4P5-6 **(0054)**
2001/02: 24^{6}G

	Starts	1st	2nd	3rd	Win & Pl
Hurdles	1	0	0	0	0
Career Total	**4**	**0**	**0**	**0**	**0**

Going: Sf: 0-0 GS: 0-0 Gd: 0-1 GF: - Fm: 0-0
Distance: 2m/2m3: 0-0 2m4-2m7: 0-0 3m+: 0-1
Track: LH: 0-1 RH: 0-0 Tight: 0-1 Gall: 0-0
Aids: Bl: 0-0 Vi: 0-0 Tstrap: 0-0
Best Rating: **82** 4/01 Winc 2m soft Hdl

Bentyheath Lane

92 **73**
5-y-o b g Puissance-Eye Sight (Roscoe Blake)
M Mullineaux The Hon Mrs S Pakenham

Placings:500P **(4642)**
2001/02: 16^{5}GF, 16^{0}GS, 16^{0}GF, 16^{P}G

	Starts	1st	2nd	3rd	Win & Pl
Hurdles	4	0	0	0	0
Career Total	**4**	**0**	**0**	**0**	**0**

Going: Sf: 0-0 GS: 0-1 Gd: 0-1 GF: - Fm: 0-2
Distance: 2m/2m3: 0-4 2m4-2m7: 0-0 3m+: 0-0
Track: LH: 0-3 RH: 0-1 Tight: 0-2 Gall: 0-0
Aids: Bl: 0-0 Vi: 0-0 Tstrap: 0-0
Best Rating: **73** 6/01 Worc 2m gd-fm Hdl

Little signs of ability.

Benvolio

91(91h) (69h)**75**
5-y-o br g Cidrax (FR)-Miss Capulet (Commanche Run)
C N Kellett 7 A.D. Racing

Placings:0P000000-00000**PP** **(4405)**
2001/02: 20^{0}G, 19^{0}G, 24^{0}GS, 25^{0}G, 26^{0}G, 23^{P}S, 17^{P}S

	Starts	1st	2nd	3rd	Win & Pl
Hurdles	5	0	0	0	0
Chases	2	0	0	0	0
Career Total	**15**	**0**	**0**	**0**	

Going: Sf: 0-2 GS: 0-1 Gd: 0-4 GF: - Fm: 0-0
Distance: 2m/2m3: 0-1 2m4-2m7: 0-2 3m+: 0-4
Track: LH: 0-2 RH: 0-5 Tight: 0-2 Gall: 0-2
Aids: Bl: 0-0 Vi: 0-0 Tstrap: 0-0
Best Rating: **69** 5/01 Hrfd 2m3f110y good Hdl

Berewolf (IRE)

97(91h) (93h)**54**
8-y-o b g Commanche Run-Iron Star (General Ironside)
J T Gifford The Arkle Bar Partnership

Placings:5/4/06000B0F **(4563)**
2001/02: 16^{0}G, 20^{6}G, 22^{0}G, 22^{0}G, 23^{0}S, 24^{B}S, 24^{0}GF, 26^{F}GF

	Starts	1st	2nd	3rd	Win & Pl
Hurdles	4	0	0	0	0
Chases	4	0	0	0	0
Career Total	**10**	**0**	**0**	**0**	**218**

Going: Sf: 0-2 GS: 0-0 Gd: 0-4 GF: - Fm: 0-2
Distance: 2m/2m3: 0-1 2m4-2m7: 0-3 3m+: 0-4
Track: LH: 0-2 RH: 0-5 Tight: 0-1 Gall: 0-2
Aids: Bl: 0-0 Vi: 0-0 Tstrap: 0-0
Best Rating: **102** 3/99 Asct 2m110y gd-fm NHF

Bergamo

104 **109**
6-y-o b g Robellino (USA)-Pretty Thing (Star Appeal)
B Ellison Ashley Young

Placings:0324P-21423124 **(4776)**
2001/02: 16^{2}GF, 20^{1}G, 20^{4}G, 16^{2}S, 16^{3}S, 16^{1}G, 17^{2}GF, 17^{4}G

	Starts	1st	2nd	3rd	Win & Pl
Hurdles	8	2	3	1	12721
Career Total	**13**	**2**	**4**	**2**	**14343**

109 3/02 Fknm 2m D(0-120)HHdl GD £5408
98 12/01 Muss 2m4f E Hdl GD £3052
Total win prize-money £8460

Going: Sf: 0-2 GS: 0-0 Gd: 2-4 GF: - Fm: 0-2
Distance: 2m/2m3: 1-6 2m4-2m7: 1-2 3m+: 0-0
Track: LH: 1-3 RH: 1-5 **Tight: 2-7** Gall: 0-1
Aids: **Bl: 2-8** Vi: 0-0 Tstrap: 0-0
Best Rating: **109** 4/02 Sedg 2m1f gd-fm Hdl

Fair hurdler, suited by a sound surface and a sharp track, goes well at Musselburgh. Wears blinkers and usually held up.

Bering Gifts (IRE)

107 **118**

7-y-o b g Bering-Bobbysoxer (Valiyar)
C J Mann J E Brown

Placings:6/3601F0-10512140 **(1498)**
2001/02: 16^{1}GF, 16^{0}GF, 16^{5}GF, 17^{1}GF, 16^{2}G, 16^{1}GF, 16^{4}GF, 17^{0}GF

	Starts	1st	2nd	3rd	Win & Pl
Hurdles	8	3	1	0	9325
Career Total	**15**	**4**	**1**	**1**	**11590**

118	8/01	Hntg	2m110y	F(0-110)HHdl	G-F	£1946
107	7/01	NAbb	2m1f	D(0-120)HHdl	G-F	£3114
113	5/01	Hntg	2m110y	E Hdl	G-F	£3136
100	8/00	Worc	2m	F Hdl	G-F	£1897

Total win prize-money £10093

Going: Sf: 0-0 GS: 0-0 Gd: 0-1 GF: - Fm: 3-7
Distance: **2m/2m3: 3-8** 2m4-2m7: 0-0 3m+: 0-0
Track: LH: 1-5 **RH: 2-3** Tight: 1-4 **Gall: 2-2**
Aids: Bl: 0-0 Vi: 0-0 Tstrap: 0-0
Best Rating: **118** 8/01 Hntg 2m110y gd-fm Hdl

Decent handicap hurdler, likes fast ground, needs to be produced late.

Berkeley Frontier (IRE)

106(81c) (73c)**99**

9-y-o ch g Imperial Frontier (USA)-Harristown Rose (Miami Springs)
M R Bosley (N A Gaselee 28/5) Miss N Henton

Placings:200/**6P**F135/U252461/0**5U53-06**PP0201 **(4568)**
2001/02: 16^{0}GF, 16^{6}GF, 19^{P}G, 19^{P}G, 16^{0}G, 16^{2}HY, 20^{0}S, 24^{1}G

	Starts	1st	2nd	3rd	Win & Pl
Hurdles	6	1	1	0	3532
Chases	2	0	0	0	0
Career Total	**29**	**3**	**4**	**2**	**12900**

99	4/02	Towc	3m	E(0-105)HHdl	GD	£2681
110	3/00	Winc	2m	D(0-125)HHdl	G-S	£2977
94	3/99	Towc	2m	E(0-105)HHdl	GD	£2617

Total win prize-money £8276

Going: Sf: 0-2 GS: 0-0 Gd: 1-4 GF: - Fm: 0-2
Distance: 2m/2m3: 0-5 2m4-2m7: 0-2 **3m+: 1-1**
Track: LH: 0-2 **RH: 1-5** Tight: 0-1 Gall: 0-1
Aids: Bl: 0-0 Vi: 0-2 Tstrap: 0-0
Best Rating: **118** 5/00 Towc 2m gd-fm Hdl

Handicap hurdler, he acts on good and good to soft ground and is effective between two and three miles. Goes well at Towcester.

Berlin Blue

(92h) (118h)**114**

9-y-o b g Belmez (USA)-Blue Brocade (Reform)
R M Stronge Peter J Douglas Engineering

Placings:444F0/52116/642322/4111-54 **(3878)**
2001/02: 24^{5}G, 25^{4}GS

	Starts	1st	2nd	3rd	Win & Pl
Hurdles	1	0	0	0	0
Chases	1	0	0	0	1290
Career Total	**22**	**5**	**4**	**1**	**47545**

148	7/00	Uttx	4m110y	B(0-140)HCh	G-F	£26000
125	6/00	Uttx	3m	D Ch	G-F	£3718
120	5/00	Uttx	3m2f	E Ch	G-F	£3159
119	3/99	Newb	3m110y	D Hdl	G-F	£2997
113	2/99	Hntg	2m4f110y	E(0-105)HHdl	G-S	£2808

Total win prize-money £38683

Going: Sf: 0-0 GS: 0-1 Gd: 0-1 GF: - Fm: 0-0
Distance: 2m/2m3: 0-0 2m4-2m7: 0-0 3m+: 0-2
Track: LH: 0-0 RH: 0-1 Tight: 0-0 Gall: 0-0
Aids: Bl: 0-0 Vi: 0-0 Tstrap: 0-0
Best Rating: **148** 7/00 Uttx 4m110y gd-fm Ch

He thrived when returned to fences in the spring of 2000, scoring a hat-trick at Uttoxeter. Absent from July 2000, he returned in December 2001 over hurdles, but was well held behind some good rivals. Best on good ground or faster and stays marathon distances. A sound jumper.

Bernard Seven (IRE)

104 **96**

10-y-o b g Taufan (USA)-Madame Nureyev (USA) (Nureyev (USA))
Miss Lucinda V Russell The Heavy Going Partnership

Placings:3132/54464/3325-10P4 **(2158)**
2001/02: 20^{1}S, 24^{0}G, 22^{P}G, 24^{4}GS

	Starts	1st	2nd	3rd	Win & Pl
Hurdles	4	1	0	0	3820
Career Total	**17**	**2**	**2**	**4**	**10026**

96	5/01	Prth	2m4f110y	F(0-110)HHdl	SFT	£3552
97	8/97	Ctml	2m1f110y	E Hdl	G-F	£2215

Total win prize-money £5767

Going: Sf: 1-1 GS: 0-1 Gd: 0-2 GF: - Fm: 0-0
Distance: 2m/2m3: 0-0 **2m4-2m7: 1-2** 3m+: 0-2
Track: LH: 0-2 **RH: 1-2** Tight: 0-1 Gall: 0-0
Aids: Bl: 0-0 Vi: 0-0 Tstrap: 0-0
Best Rating: **105** 9/97 Sedg 2m1f gd-fm Hdl

A fair handicap hurdler, he is best suited by testing conditions. He stays three miles but he has never won beyond two and a half miles.

Bernardon (GER)

110 **133**

6-y-o b g Suave Dancer (USA)-Bejaria (GER) (Konigsstuhl (GER))
M C Pipe (P Schiergen 22/9) The Macca & Growler Partnership

Placings:1F0 **(4724)**
2001/02: 17^{1}S, 16^{F}GS, 16^{0}GF

	Starts	1st	2nd	3rd	Win & Pl
Hurdles	3	1	0	0	3815
Career Total	**3**	**1**	**0**	**0**	**3815**

114	2/02	Tntn	2m1f	D Hdl	SFT	£3815

Total win prize-money £3815

Going: Sf: 1-1 GS: 0-1 Gd: 0-0 GF: - Fm: 0-1
Distance: **2m/2m3: 1-3** 2m4-2m7: 0-0 3m+: 0-0
Track: LH: 0-2 **RH: 1-1 Tight: 1-1** Gall: 0-0
Aids: Bl: 0-0 Vi: 0-0 Tstrap: 0-0
Best Rating: **126** 3/02 Chel 2m110y gd-sft Hdl

Ex-German trained, he hacked up on his hurdles debut in this country in impressive style, but limitations exposed at the Festival. Acts on soft ground.

Bernini's Quest (IRE)

91 **58**

7-y-o b m Royal Fountain-Our Quest (Private Walk)
T J Etherington London Racing Club Owners Group

Placings:0000-0P **(1913)**
2001/02: 20^{0}G, 23^{P}G

	Starts	1st	2nd	3rd	Win & Pl
Hurdles	2	0	0	0	
Career Total	**6**	**0**	**0**	**0**	

Going: Sf: 0-0 GS: 0-0 Gd: 0-2 GF: - Fm: 0-0
Distance: 2m/2m3: 0-0 2m4-2m7: 0-2 3m+: 0-0
Track: LH: 0-2 RH: 0-0 Tight: 0-0 Gall: 0-0
Aids: Bl: 0-0 Vi: 0-0 Tstrap: 0-0
Best Rating: **72** 6/00 MRas 2m1f110y gd-fm NHF

Berrington (NZ)

70f **50f**

5-y-o b g Fort Prospect (USA)-Calamity (NZ) (Bally Royal)
B P J Baugh M W & A N Harris

Placings:00 **(3338)**
2001/02: 16^{0}G, 16^{0}G

	Starts	1st	2nd	3rd	Win & Pl
NH Flat	2	0	0	0	
Career Total	**2**	**0**	**0**	**0**	

Going: Sf: 0-0 GS: 0-0 Gd: 0-2 GF: - Fm: 0-0
Distance: 2m/2m3: 0-2 2m4-2m7: 0-0 3m+: 0-0
Track: LH: 0-0 RH: 0-2 Tight: 0-0 Gall: 0-0
Aids: Bl: 0-0 Vi: 0-0 Tstrap: 0-0
Best Rating: **50** 12/01 Ludl 2m good NHF

Bersaglio

81 **74**

7-y-o ch h Rainbow Quest (USA)-Escrime (USA) (Sharpen Up)
K A Morgan J A Outwin

Placings:P/P0-06P **(2349)**
2001/02: 23^{0}GF, 21^{6}G, 19^{P}GS

	Starts	1st	2nd	3rd	Win & Pl
Hurdles	3	0	0	0	0
Career Total	**6**	**0**	**0**	**0**	**0**

Going: Sf: 0-0 GS: 0-1 Gd: 0-1 GF: - Fm: 0-1
Distance: 2m/2m3: 0-0 2m4-2m7: 0-2 3m+: 0-1
Track: LH: 0-2 RH: 0-1 Tight: 0-3 Gall: 0-0
Aids: Bl: 0-0 Vi: 0-3 Tstrap: 0-3
Best Rating: **74** 4/01 MRas 2m1f110y gd-sft Hdl

Berude Not To (IRE)

13-y-o b g Roselier (FR)-Decent Debbie (Decent Fellow)
Mrs A L Tory J & B Cullen, P Moore & Ms M Malgarin

Placings:11/111120/**22/11414/P0/4-0UP** **(0426)**
2001/02: 26^{0}G, 28^{U}GF, 26^{P}G

	Starts	1st	2nd	3rd	Win & Pl
Chases	3	0	0	0	
Career Total	**21**	**9**	**3**	**0**	**74285**

136	2/97	Kemp	3m	D Ch	GD	£3485
113	12/96	Donc	3m	D Ch	G-F	£3756
127	12/94	Newb	2m5f	Hdl	HVY	£18020
130	12/94	Asct	2m110y	Hdl	GD	£6280
130	11/94	Chel	2m110y	Hdl	SFT	£6520

107	10/94	Asct	2m110y	Hdl	G-F	£4533
116	4/94	Uttx	2m	NHF	G-F	£2060
102	3/94	Winc	2m	NHF	G-S	£2230

Total win prize-money £46886

Going: Sf: 0-0 GS: 0-0 Gd: 0-2 GF: - Fm: 0-1
Distance: 2m/2m3: 0-0 2m4-2m7: 0-0 3m+: 0-3
Track: LH: 0-1 RH: 0-1 Tight: 0-2 Gall: 0-0
Aids: Bl: 0-3 Vi: 0-0 Tstrap: 0-0
Best Rating: **146** 3/97 Chel 3m110y gd-fm Ch

Berzoud

72 **42**

5-y-o b m Ezzoud (IRE)-Bertie's Girl (Another Realm)
J R Jenkins Miss I Leitendorfa

Placings:0 **(2208)**
2001/02: 16^{0}GS

	Starts	1st	2nd	3rd	Win & Pl
Hurdles	1	0	0	0	
Career Total	**1**	**0**	**0**	**0**	

Going: Sf: 0-0 GS: 0-1 Gd: 0-0 GF: - Fm: 0-0
Distance: 2m/2m3: 0-1 2m4-2m7: 0-0 3m+: 0-0
Track: LH: 0-0 RH: 0-1 Tight: 0-0 Gall: 0-0
Aids: Bl: 0-0 Vi: 0-0 Tstrap: 0-0
Best Rating: **42** 11/01 Leic 2m gd-sft Hdl

Beseiged (USA)

103 **102+**

5-y-o ch g Cadeaux Genereux-Munnaya (USA) (Nijinsky (CAN))
R A Fahey Mike Caulfield

Placings:*525* **(3354)**
2001/02: 16^{5}GS, 16^{2}G, 16^{5}G

	Starts	1st	2nd	3rd	Win & Pl
NH Flat	3	0	1	0	466
Career Total	**3**	**0**	**1**	**0**	**466**

Going: Sf: 0-0 GS: 0-1 Gd: 0-2 GF: - Fm: 0-0
Distance: 2m/2m3: 0-3 2m4-2m7: 0-0 3m+: 0-0
Track: LH: 0-2 RH: 0-1 Tight: 0-2 Gall: 0-0
Aids: Bl: 0-0 Vi: 0-0 Tstrap: 0-0
Best Rating: **95** 1/02 Muss 2m good NHF

Fair form in bumpers, winning at Perth in May 2002. Suited by a sound surface.

Bessie Bunter

88 **59**

6-y-o b m Rakaposhi King-Black H'Penny (Town And Country)
J A B Old Bessie Bunter Partnership

Placings:*500* **(4181)**
2001/02: 17^{5}S, 16^{0}HY, 19^{0}S

	Starts	1st	2nd	3rd	Win & Pl
NH Flat	2	0	0	0	0
Hurdles	1	0	0	0	0
Career Total	**3**	**0**	**0**	**0**	**0**

Going: Sf: 0-3 GS: 0-0 Gd: 0-0 GF: - Fm: 0-0
Distance: 2m/2m3: 0-2 2m4-2m7: 0-1 3m+: 0-0
Track: LH: 0-1 RH: 0-1 Tight: 0-1 Gall: 0-0
Aids: Bl: 0-0 Vi: 0-0 Tstrap: 0-0
Best Rating: **82** 1/02 Tntn 2m1f soft NHF

Best Available (IRE)

104(105h) (102h)**105**

7-y-o b g Accordion-Grangeshoon (Green Shoon)
P J Hobbs Aiden Murphy

Placings:*30*/P3150 **(4540)**
2001/02: 20^{P}GS, 24^{3}S, 19^{1}S, 19^{5}S, 19^{0}G

	Starts	1st	2nd	3rd	Win & Pl
Hurdles	5	1	0	1	5193
Career Total	**7**	**1**	**0**	**2**	**5585**

102	2/02	Tntn	2m3f110y	D Hdl	SFT	£4556

Total win prize-money £4557

Going: Sf: 1-3 GS: 0-1 Gd: 0-1 GF: - Fm: 0-0
Distance: 2m/2m3: 0-0 **2m4-2m7: 1-4** 3m+: 0-1
Track: LH: 0-0 **RH: 1-5 Tight: 1-3** Gall: 0-0
Aids: Bl: 0-0 Vi: 0-0 Tstrap: 0-0
Best Rating: **102** 3/02 Tntn 2m3f110y soft Hdl

Fair novice hurdler who got off the mark at Taunton in February 2002. Runner-up on his chasing debut. Stays two and a half miles and is suited by soft ground. Not entirely straightforward.

Best Mate (IRE)

121(111h) (155h)**186**

7-y-o b g Un Desperado (FR)-Katday (FR) (Miller's Mate)
Miss H C Knight Jim Lewis

Placings:*11221*/**1112-1221** **(4252)**
2001/02: 17^{1}GF, 19^{2}G, 24^{2}G, 26^{1}G

	Starts	1st	2nd	3rd	Win & Pl
Chases	4	2	2	0	239500
Career Total	**13**	**8**	**5**	**0**	**364629**

186	3/02	Chel	3m2f110y	A Ch	GD	£174000
182	11/01	Extr	2m1f110y	A HCh	G-F	£21000
177	2/01	Sand	2m4f110y	A Ch	HVY	£24000
166	11/00	Chel	2m	A Ch	G-S	£15000
161	10/00	Extr	2m1f110y	D Ch	GD	£3926
146	4/00	Aint	2m4f	A Hdl	GD	£21000
137	12/99	Sand	2m110y	D Hdl	G-S	£3680
133	11/99	Chel	2m110y	B NHF	GD	£7197

Total win prize-money £269804

Going: Sf: 0-0 GS: 0-0 Gd: 1-3 GF: - Fm: 1-1
Distance: 2m/2m3: 1-1 2m4-2m7: 0-1 3m+: 1-2
Track: LH: 1-1 RH: 1-3 Tight: 0-0 **Gall: 1-1**
Aids: Bl: 0-0 Vi: 0-0 Tstrap: 0-0
Best Rating: **186** 3/02 Chel 3m2f110y good Ch

The leading novice chaser in 2000/01, unbeaten in three starts over fences and especially impressive in the Scilly Isles at Sandown. He was regarded as an Arkle banker, but foot and mouth put paid to that target and, rerouted to Aintree, found only Barton too good in the Martell Aintree Hurdle. He made a winning reappearance in 2001/02 in the Haldon Gold Cup at Exeter, but was held at the weights at Ascot. Passed his biggest test when runner-up in the King George, before running out an impressive winner of the Gold Cup. He jumps well, has a fine turn of foot, and stays three and a quarter miles and being only seven years old seems to have several good seasons ahead of him.

Best Of The Girls (IRE)

76 **58**

7-y-o b m Supreme Leader-Belinda Vard (Le Bavard (FR))
S E H Sherwood Aiden Murphy

Placings:*12140*-4P **(3655)**
2001/02: 19^{4}S, 22^{P}S

	Starts	1st	2nd	3rd	Win & Pl
Hurdles	2	0	0	0	0
Career Total	**7**	**2**	**1**	**0**	**7831**

108	2/01	Wwck	2m	H NHF	SFT	£4241
117	11/00	Hrfd	2m1f	H NHF	SFT	£1512

Total win prize-money £5753

Going: Sf: 0-2 GS: 0-0 Gd: 0-0 GF: - Fm: 0-0
Distance: 2m/2m3: 0-0 2m4-2m7: 0-2 3m+: 0-0
Track: LH: 0-0 RH: 0-2 Tight: 0-0 Gall: 0-0
Aids: Bl: 0-0 Vi: 0-0 Tstrap: 0-0
Best Rating: **117** 1/01 Folk 2m1f110y heavy NHF

Best On Show (IRE)

6-y-o br g King's Ride-Tawney Lass (Over The River (FR))
J J O'Neill Mr Richard Seed & Mrs Maralyn Seed

Placings:*0/5*-P **(2527)**
2001/02: 20^{P}HY

	Starts	1st	2nd	3rd	Win & Pl
Hurdles	1	0	0	0	
Career Total	**3**	**0**	**0**	**0**	**0**

Going: Sf: 0-1 GS: 0-0 Gd: 0-0 GF: - Fm: 0-0
Distance: 2m/2m3: 0-0 2m4-2m7: 0-1 3m+: 0-0
Track: LH: 0-0 RH: 0-1 Tight: 0-0 Gall: 0-0
Aids: Bl: 0-0 Vi: 0-0 Tstrap: 0-0
Best Rating: **89** 11/00 Ayr 2m soft NHF

Best Wait (IRE)

114 **125**

5-y-o b m Insan (USA)-Greek Melody (IRE) (Trojan Fort)
T Hogan (Donal Hassett 7/7) J M Ryan

Placings:61241530305F0 **(4803a)**
2001/02: 16^{6}GF, 16^{1}F, 16^{2}SH, 17^{4}G, 16^{1}Y, 16^{5}S, 16^{3}Y, 16^{0}Y, 16^{3}S, 16^{0}YS, 16^{5}HY, 16^{F}GS, 16^{0}GF

	Starts	1st	2nd	3rd	Win & Pl
NH Flat	3	1	0	0	6073
Hurdles	10	1	1	2	14371
Career Total	**13**	**2**	**1**	**2**	**20444**

105	10/01	Limk	2m	Hdl	YLD	£8387
101	7/01	Cork	2m	NHF	FRM	£5564

Total win prize-money £13952

Going: Sf: 0-3 GS: 0-1 Gd: 0-1 GF: - Fm: 1-3
Distance: **2m/2m3: 2-13** 2m4-2m7: 0-0 3m+: 0-0
Track: LH: 0-4 RH: 0-3 Tight: 0-0 Gall: 0-0
Aids: Bl: 0-0 Vi: 0-0 **Tstrap: 2-13**
Best Rating: **125** 12/01 Fair 2m yield Hdl

An Irish-trained novice, she won two small events in the autumn. Seems to handle any ground, wears a tongue tie.

Betabatim (IRE)

100 **94**

7-y-o b g Alphabatim (USA)-Lucy Platter (FR) (Record Token)
J E Brockbank J E Brockbank

Placings:*5/P*-P0FP54 **(4857)**
2001/02: 17^{P}GS, 16^{0}G, 20^{F}S, 22^{P}HY, 16^{5}GF, 20^{4}G

	Starts	1st	2nd	3rd	Win & Pl
Hurdles	6	0	0	0	0
Career Total	**8**	**0**	**0**	**0**	**0**

Going: Sf: 0-2 GS: 0-1 Gd: 0-2 GF: - Fm: 0-1
Distance: 2m/2m3: 0-3 2m4-2m7: 0-3 3m+: 0-0
Track: LH: 0-3 RH: 0-1 Tight: 0-2 Gall: 0-0
Aids: Bl: 0-0 Vi: 0-0 Tstrap: 0-0

Best Rating: **95** 4/00 Carl 2m1f gd-sft NHF

A tall, angular sort, has shown modest ability over hurdles.

Better Days (IRE)

105 **122**

6-y-o b g Supreme Leader-Kilkilrun (Deep Run)
N J Henderson Trevor Hemmings

Placings:2-160 **(4653)**
2001/02: 16^{1}GS, 20^{6}S, 20^{0}G

	Starts	1st	2nd	3rd	Win & Pl
Hurdles	3	1	0	0	4212
Career Total	**4**	**1**	**1**	**0**	**5157**

122 11/01 Aint 2m110y D Hdl G-S £4212
Total win prize-money £4212

Going: Sf: 0-1 GS: 1-1 Gd: 0-1 GF: - Fm: 0-0
Distance: **2m/2m3: 1-1** 2m4-2m7: 0-2 3m+: 0-0
Track: **LH: 1-3** RH: 0-0 **Tight: 1-2** Gall: 0-0
Aids: Bl: 0-0 Vi: 0-0 Tstrap: 0-0
Best Rating: **122** 11/01 Aint 2m110y gd-sft Hdl

Showed promise on his sole bumper start in 2000/2001 season when with Nicky Richards. Won his hurdles debut in good style but could not repeat that effort when a disappointing sixth next time out . A chaser in the making.

Better Moment (IRE)

106 **96**

5-y-o b g Turtle Island (IRE)-Snoozeandyoulose (IRE) (Scenic)
M C Pipe (John Berry 28/7) P M Harley

Placings:0105434-3U2 **(4640)**
2001/02: 16^{3}S, 19^{U}S, 16^{2}G

	Starts	1st	2nd	3rd	Win & Pl
Hurdles	3	0	1	1	1271
Career Total	**10**	**1**	**1**	**2**	**3090**

86 1/01 Catt 2m G Hdl G-S £1596
Total win prize-money £1596

Going: Sf: 0-2 GS: 0-0 Gd: 0-1 GF: - Fm: 0-0
Distance: 2m/2m3: 0-2 2m4-2m7: 0-1 3m+: 0-0
Track: LH: 0-1 RH: 0-2 Tight: 0-1 Gall: 0-0
Aids: Bl: 0-1 Vi: 0-2 Tstrap: 0-1
Best Rating: **86** 1/01 Catt 2m gd-sft Hdl

Modest winning hurdler who just about stays two miles four. Has proved too keen for his own good so far for Martin Pipe. Acts on fast ground but has scored on good to soft.

Better Offer (IRE)

96(106h) (136h)**131**

10-y-o b g Waajib-Camdens Gift (Camden Town)
M C Pipe (P F Nicholls 6/8) Stuart M Mercer

Placings:122201F/5P520F/21F421/1F02F-03U11 **(1281)**
2001/02: 23^{0}GS, 21^{3}G, 24^{U}GF, 22^{1}G, 20^{1}GF

	Starts	1st	2nd	3rd	Win & Pl
Hurdles	2	2	0	0	5555
Chases	3	0	0	1	629
Career Total	**29**	**7**	**7**	**1**	**36060**

136	8/01	Uttx	2m4f110y	D(0-125)HHdl	G-F	£3307
125	8/01	NAbb	2m6f	F Hdl	GD	£2247
146	11/00	Extr	2m3f110y	D(0-125)HCh	G-S	£4173
127	3/00	Tntn	2m3f	D Ch	GD	£4845
120	10/99	Tntn	2m3f	D Ch	G-F	£3783
135	4/98	Asct	2m4f	D Hdl	G-S	£3533
119	11/97	Hntg	2m110y	E Hdl	G-F	£2722

Total win prize-money £24615

Going: Sf: 0-0 GS: 0-1 Gd: 1-2 GF: - Fm: 1-2
Distance: 2m/2m3: 0-0 **2m4-2m7: 2-3** 3m+: 0-2
Track: **LH: 2-4** RH: 0-1 **Tight: 1-3** Gall: 0-0
Aids: Bl: 0-1 **Vi: 1-1** Tstrap: 0-0
Best Rating: **146** 11/00 Extr 2m3f110y gd-sft Ch

Better Think Again (IRE)

106(103h) (127h)**134**

8-y-o b g Brush Aside (USA)-Ride The Rapids (Bulldozer)
D P Kelly (M C Pipe 11/6) John J Burns

Placings:1/13P/63P0-2F300 **(2627a)**
2001/02: 26^{2}GF, 23^{F}F, 26^{3}G, 16^{0}Y, 20^{0}S

	Starts	1st	2nd	3rd	Win & Pl
Hurdles	2	0	0	0	0
Chases	3	0	1	1	1620
Career Total	**13**	**2**	**1**	**3**	**16228**

127 11/99 Chep 2m4f C Hdl G-S £5356
121 4/99 Punc 2m NHF YLD £6138
Total win prize-money £11495

Going: Sf: 0-1 GS: 0-0 Gd: 0-1 GF: - Fm: 0-2
Distance: 2m/2m3: 0-1 2m4-2m7: 0-1 3m+: 0-3
Track: LH: 0-2 RH: 0-2 Tight: 0-2 Gall: 0-0
Aids: Bl: 0-0 Vi: 0-1 Tstrap: 0-0
Best Rating: **134** 6/01 NAbb 3m2f110y good Ch

Better Thyne (IRE)

101 **102**

6-y-o ch g Good Thyne (USA)-Cailin Cainnteach (Le Bavard (FR))
V R A Dartnall R F Woodward

Placings:P3310 **(3672)**
2001/02: 24^{P}GF, 17^{3}HY, 22^{3}S, 24^{1}HY, 24^{0}S

	Starts	1st	2nd	3rd	Win & Pl
Hurdles	5	1	0	2	2923
Career Total	**5**	**1**	**0**	**2**	**2923**

102 1/02 Uttx 3m110y F Hdl HVY £1974
Total win prize-money £1974

Going: Sf: 1-4 GS: 0-0 Gd: 0-0 GF: - Fm: 0-1
Distance: 2m/2m3: 0-1 2m4-2m7: 0-1 **3m+: 1-3**
Track: **LH: 1-4** RH: 0-1 Tight: 0-2 Gall: 0-0
Aids: Bl: 0-0 Vi: 0-0 Tstrap: 0-0
Best Rating: **102** 1/02 Uttx 3m110y heavy Hdl

He does not do anything quickly but stays particularly well. He loves the mud.

Better Times Ahead

109 **119**

16-y-o ro g Scallywag-City's Sister (Maystreak)
N G Richards E Briggs

Placings:2UU2/11251/365402P/34112PP/111P/11116/505 6PP0/2061053/P12111122P/1123140/2260-11 **(0661)**
2001/02: 24^{1}GS, 24^{1}F

	Starts	1st	2nd	3rd	Win & Pl
Hurdles	2	2	0	0	6389
Career Total	**69**	**23**	**12**	**4**	**118926**

119	6/01	Prth	3m110y	F(0-110)HHdl	FRM	£2954
122	5/01	Prth	3m110y	D(0-120)HHdl	G-S	£3435
122	3/00	Newc	3m	C(0-130)HHdl	GD	£5284
145	8/99	Ctml	3m2f	D(0-125)HCh	GD	£3847
134	5/99	Ctml	2m5f110y	E(0-125)HCh	GD	£3245
138	11/98	Carl	3m2f	C(0-130)HCh	SFT	£4719
144	10/98	Carl	3m2f	D(0-125)HCh	HVY	£3550
130	10/98	Carl	3m2f	C(0-130)HCh	GD	£5845
131	8/98	Ctml	3m2f	D(0-120)HCh	GD	£3587
120	5/98	Ctml	2m5f110y	E(0-125)HCh	G-F	£3117
137	3/98	Kels	3m4f	E(0-125)HCh	GD	£3203
147	1/96	Hayd	2m7f110y	A Hdl	SFT	£12740
142	12/95	Chel	3m	B HHdl	GD	£5639
138	11/95	Bang	2m4f110y	C(0-130)HCh	GD	£4585
142	11/95	Ayr	3m110y	C(0-130)HHdl	GD	£3452
134	11/93	Weth	2m4f110y	(0-145)HCh	G-S	£3340
128	10/93	Bang	2m4f110y	(0-140)HCh	GD	£4546
106	5/93	Ctml	3m2f	Ch	GD	£2398
112	12/92	Bang	2m4f110y	Ch	SFT	£2554
96	11/92	Bang	3m110y	Ch	SFT	£2697
	2/91	Wwck	2m5f	Hdl	G-S	£7717
	11/90	Ayr	2m	Hdl	G-S	£2278
	11/90	Weth	2m	Hdl	GD	£1949

Total win prize-money £96688

Going: Sf: 0-0 GS: 1-1 Gd: 0-0 GF: - Fm: 1-1
Distance: 2m/2m3: 0-0 2m4-2m7: 0-0 **3m+: 2-2**
Track: LH: 0-0 **RH: 2-2** Tight: 0-0 Gall: 0-0
Aids: Bl: 0-0 Vi: 0-0 Tstrap: 0-0
Best Rating: **159** 2/92 Hayd 2m gd-sft Hdl

He became a legend in the north west and Cumbria winning 23 races, but has now been retired.

Bewleys Hotels (IRE)

92f

6-y-o ch g Muharib (USA)-Alchymya (Cosmo)
Mrs M Reveley Bewley's Hotels, Glasgow (bsh Ltd)

Placings:3 **(4438)**
2001/02: 16^{3}HY

	Starts	1st	2nd	3rd	Win & Pl
NH Flat	1	0	0	1	260
Career Total	**1**	**0**	**0**	**1**	**260**

Going: Sf: 0-1 GS: 0-0 Gd: 0-0 GF: - Fm: 0-0
Distance: 2m/2m3: 0-1 2m4-2m7: 0-0 3m+: 0-0
Track: LH: 0-0 RH: 0-0 Tight: 0-0 Gall: 0-0
Aids: Bl: 0-0 Vi: 0-0 Tstrap: 0-0
Best Rating: **92** 3/02 Newc 2m heavy NHF

Beyond Control (IRE)

104(103c) (119c)**109**

7-y-o b g Supreme Leader-Bucktina (Buckskin (FR))
P F Nicholls Paul K Barber

Placings:F31P **(4150)**
2001/02: 21^{F}GS, 26^{3}HY, 24^{1}S, 24^{P}GS

	Starts	1st	2nd	3rd	Win & Pl
Hurdles	2	1	0	0	3087
Chases	2	0	0	1	610
Career Total	**4**	**1**	**0**	**1**	**3697**

109 2/02 Tntn 3m110y E Hdl SFT £3087
Total win prize-money £3087

Going: Sf: 1-2 GS: 0-2 Gd: 0-0 GF: - Fm: 0-0
Distance: 2m/2m3: 0-0 2m4-2m7: 0-1 **3m+: 1-3**
Track: LH: 0-1 **RH: 1-2 Tight: 1-2** Gall: 0-0
Aids: Bl: 0-0 Vi: 0-0 Tstrap: 0-0
Best Rating: **119** 2/02 Font 3m2f110y heavy Ch

Staying chaser, not always the most fluent jumper. Won his hurdles debut over three miles in February.

Beyond Our Reach

70(88h) (56h)**42**

14-y-o br g Reach-Over Beyond (Bold Lad (IRE))
R J Hodges Miss L Crossman

Placings:3543/3U/14205/P6132P6/0/14225/5636**511P/125 343P5P/4256-FU**06 **(0737)**
2001/02: 20^{F}GF, 18^{U}GF, 19^{0}GF, 16^{6}GS

	Starts	1st	2nd	3rd	Win & Pl
Hurdles	1	0	0	0	0
Chases	3	0	0	0	0
Career Total	**49**	**6**	**6**	**7**	**24373**

114	5/98	Towc	2m110y	E(0-115)HCh	GD	£2883
114	3/98	Font	2m2f	E(0-100)HCh	G-F	£3808
103	3/98	Tntn	2m110y	F(0-105)HCh	G-S	£2542
91	5/96	Ludl	2m	G Hdl	G-F	£2102
102	1/95	Ludl	2m5f110y	E(0-115)HHdl	SFT	£2500
100	11/93	Wind	2m6f110y	Hdl	GD	£1480

Total win prize-money £15317

Going: Sf: 0-0 GS: 0-1 Gd: 0-0 GF: - Fm: 0-3
Distance: 2m/2m3: 0-2 2m4-2m7: 0-2 3m+: 0-0
Track: LH: 0-2 RH: 0-1 Tight: 0-4 Gall: 0-0
Aids: Bl: 0-0 Vi: 0-0 Tstrap: 0-0
Best Rating: **129** 2/92 Sand 2m good Hdl

Beyond The Pale (IRE)

93f **101f**

4-y-o b g Be My Native (USA)-Cyrano Imperial (IRE) (Cyrano De Bergerac)
Noel T Chance A D Weller

Placings:*40* **(4713a)**
2001/02: 16^{4}GS, 16^{0}Y

	Starts	1st	2nd	3rd	Win & Pl
NH Flat	2	0	0	0	0
Career Total	**2**	**0**	**0**	**0**	**0**

Going: Sf: 0-0 GS: 0-1 Gd: 0-0 GF: - Fm: 0-0
Distance: 2m/2m3: 0-2 2m4-2m7: 0-0 3m+: 0-0
Track: LH: 0-1 RH: 0-1 Tight: 0-0 Gall: 0-1
Aids: Bl: 0-0 Vi: 0-0 Tstrap: 0-0
Best Rating: **101** 3/02 Newb 2m110y gd-sft NHF

Beytadj (FR)

(100h) (77h)

6-y-o b g Beyssac (FR)-Centadj (FR) (Tadj (FR))
Jack Barbe (R H Buckler 9/5) Ecurie Gebeka

Placings:P5P50652/1013F-5400
2001/02: 16^{5}S, 16^{4}GF, 17^{0}VS, 17^{0}VS

	Starts	1st	2nd	3rd	Win & Pl
Hurdles	2	0	0	0	0
Chases	2	0	0	0	0
Career Total	**17**	**2**	**1**	**1**	**8221**

	7/00	Leto	2m1f	Ch	HVY	£2786
	5/00	Mans	2m2f	Ch	HVY	£2690

Total win prize-money £5476

Going: Sf: 0-1 GS: 0-0 Gd: 0-0 GF: - Fm: 0-1
Distance: 2m/2m3: 0-4 2m4-2m7: 0-0 3m+: 0-0
Track: LH: 0-2 RH: 0-0 Tight: 0-2 Gall: 0-0
Aids: Bl: 0-0 Vi: 0-0 Tstrap: 0-0
Best Rating: **90** 1/01 Folk 2m1f110y heavy Hdl

Bhutan (IRE)

112 **130**

7-y-o b g Polish Patriot (USA)-Bustinetta (Bustino)
Mrs M Reveley P D Savill

Placings:3P624/21113/1000-4141556 **(2893)**
2001/02: 16^{4}G, 16^{1}S, 16^{4}G, 18^{1}GS, 20^{5}GS, 16^{5}GS, 16^{6}G

	Starts	1st	2nd	3rd	Win & Pl
Hurdles	7	2	0	0	5743
Career Total	**21**	**6**	**2**	**2**	**26184**

130	11/01	Font	2m2f110y	F Hdl	G-S	£2352
129	10/01	Plum	2m	F Hdl	SFT	£2310
130	10/00	Kels	2m110y	D(0-120)HHdl	GD	£7117
127	12/99	Weth	2m	C(0-135)HHdl	G-S	£4760
116	11/99	Newc	2m	E(0-115)HHdl	G-S	£2232
87	6/99	MRas	2m1f110y	E Hdl	GD	£2652

Total win prize-money £21425

Going: Sf: 1-1 GS: 1-3 Gd: 0-3 GF: - Fm: 0-0
Distance: **2m/2m3: 2-6** 2m4-2m7: 0-1 3m+: 0-0
Track: **LH: 2-4** RH: 0-3 **Tight: 2-4** Gall: 0-1
Aids: Bl: 0-0 Vi: 0-0 Tstrap: 0-0
Best Rating: **130** 11/01 Font 2m2f110y gd-sft Hdl

Suited by a strong pace, he is a fair sort at a modest level although he has his quirks. Effective on varying ground and likes to be held up.

Bibury Court (IRE)

92 **68**

10-y-o b g Henbit (USA)-Hard Lady (Hard Boy)
Mrs S D Williams H Davies/a Johnston Partnership

Placings:*50/65*/P6P **(3158)**
2001/02: 22^{P}G, 23^{6}G, 25^{P}S

	Starts	1st	2nd	3rd	Win & Pl
Chases	3	0	0	0	0
Career Total	**7**	**0**	**0**	**0**	**0**

Going: Sf: 0-1 GS: 0-0 Gd: 0-2 GF: - Fm: 0-0
Distance: 2m/2m3: 0-0 2m4-2m7: 0-1 3m+: 0-2
Track: LH: 0-1 RH: 0-2 Tight: 0-0 Gall: 0-1
Aids: Bl: 0-0 Vi: 0-0 Tstrap: 0-0
Best Rating: **91** 10/97 Bang 2m1f good NHF

Bicycle Thief (IRE)

103 **116**

9-y-o ch g Archway (IRE)-Push Bike (Ballad Rock)
Miss Venetia Williams B Moore & E C Stephens

Placings:52/13110/0014-0046 **(3908)**
2001/02: 21^{0}G, 20^{0}S, 22^{4}HY, 21^{6}G

	Starts	1st	2nd	3rd	Win & Pl
Hurdles	4	0	0	0	808
Career Total	**15**	**4**	**1**	**1**	**25625**

138	3/01	Ling	2m3f110y	B(0-140)HHdl	HVY	£14040
127	1/00	Kemp	2m5f	D Hdl	GD	£3835
125	12/99	Hrfd	2m3f110y	E Hdl	HVY	£2850
129	12/99	Hrfd	2m3f110y	E Hdl	GD	£2682

Total win prize-money £23407

Going: Sf: 0-2 GS: 0-0 Gd: 0-2 GF: - Fm: 0-0
Distance: 2m/2m3: 0-0 2m4-2m7: 0-4 3m+: 0-0
Track: LH: 0-3 RH: 0-1 Tight: 0-0 Gall: 0-1
Aids: Bl: 0-2 Vi: 0-0 Tstrap: 0-0
Best Rating: **138** 3/01 Ling 2m3f110y heavy Hdl

Decent handicap hurdler, effective at trips of around two and a half miles. Acts on most types of ground.

Big Boy Sid (IRE)

8-y-o b g Denel (FR)-There There (Mummy's Pet)
Mrs L B Normile The Heatheryfour

Placings:*0*-**PPF**PPPP **(4877)**
2001/02: 20^{P}GS, 25^{P}G, 25^{F}GS, 22^{P}GS, 21^{P}S, 24^{P}S, 24^{P}G

	Starts	1st	2nd	3rd	Win & Pl
Hurdles	3	0	0	0	0
Chases	4	0	0	0	0
Career Total	**8**	**0**	**0**	**0**	

Going: Sf: 0-2 GS: 0-3 Gd: 0-2 GF: - Fm: 0-0
Distance: 2m/2m3: 0-0 2m4-2m7: 0-3 3m+: 0-4
Track: LH: 0-5 RH: 0-1 Tight: 0-3 Gall: 0-0
Aids: Bl: 0-0 Vi: 0-0 Tstrap: 0-0
Best Rating: **28** 10/00 Leop 2m4f heavy NHF

Big Brazil (IRE)

41f

6-y-o ch g Executive Perk-Lady Denys (Saint Denys)
Miss K Marks Nick Shutts

Placings:*0* **(0032)**
2001/02: 16^{0}G

	Starts	1st	2nd	3rd	Win & Pl
NH Flat	1	0	0	0	
Career Total	**1**	**0**	**0**	**0**	

Going: Sf: 0-0 GS: 0-0 Gd: 0-1 GF: - Fm: 0-0
Distance: 2m/2m3: 0-1 2m4-2m7: 0-0 3m+: 0-0
Track: LH: 0-0 RH: 0-1 Tight: 0-0 Gall: 0-1
Aids: Bl: 0-0 Vi: 0-0 Tstrap: 0-0
Best Rating:

Big For Money (IRE)

6-y-o b/br m Glacial Storm (USA)-Cailin Dubh (IRE) (Le Bavard (FR))
Cecil Mahon Coleman Rooney

Placings:P0 **(4621a)**
2001/02: 22^{P}GS, 16^{0}GY

	Starts	1st	2nd	3rd	Win & Pl
NH Flat	1	0	0	0	0
Hurdles	1	0	0	0	0
Career Total	**2**	**0**	**0**	**0**	

Going: Sf: 0-0 GS: 0-1 Gd: 0-0 GF: - Fm: 0-0
Distance: 2m/2m3: 0-1 2m4-2m7: 0-1 3m+: 0-0
Track: LH: 0-1 RH: 0-0 Tight: 0-1 Gall: 0-0
Aids: Bl: 0-0 Vi: 0-0 Tstrap: 0-0
Best Rating:

Big Horn (IRE)

73 **40**

8-y-o b g Little Bighorn-Fast Girl (IRE) (Tumble Gold)
C W Thornton P Sadler

Placings:5P **(0644)**
2001/02: 16^{5}GF, 17^{P}GF

	Starts	1st	2nd	3rd	Win & Pl
Hurdles	2	0	0	0	0
Career Total	**2**	**0**	**0**	**0**	**0**

Going: Sf: 0-0 GS: 0-0 Gd: 0-0 GF: - Fm: 0-2
Distance: 2m/2m3: 0-2 2m4-2m7: 0-0 3m+: 0-0

Track: LH: 0-1 RH: 0-1 Tight: 0-1 Gall: 0-1
Aids: Bl: 0-0 Vi: 0-0 Tstrap: 0-0
Best Rating: 40 5/01 Newc 2m gd-fm Hdl

Big Lil (IRE)

8-y-o ch m Montelimar (USA)-Romany Fortune (Sunyboy)
J L Needham Miss Joanna Needham

Placings:P (1912)
2001/02: 22^{P}S

	Starts	1st	2nd	3rd	Win & Pl
Hurdles	1	0	0	0	
Career Total	**1**	**0**	**0**	**0**	

Going: Sf: 0-1 GS: 0-0 Gd: 0-0 GF: - Fm: 0-0
Distance: 2m/2m3: 0-0 2m4-2m7: 0-1 3m+: 0-0
Track: LH: 0-1 RH: 0-0 Tight: 0-1 Gall: 0-0
Aids: Bl: 0-0 Vi: 0-0 Tstrap: 0-0
Best Rating:

Big Lugs

62f 66f
6-y-o ch g Rakaposhi King-Winnowing (IRE) (Strong Gale)
J S Haldane J S Haldane

Placings:00 (4098)
2001/02: 16^{0}S, 16^{0}GS

	Starts	1st	2nd	3rd	Win & Pl
NH Flat	2	0	0	0	
Career Total	**2**	**0**	**0**	**0**	

Going: Sf: 0-1 GS: 0-1 Gd: 0-0 GF: - Fm: 0-0
Distance: 2m/2m3: 0-2 2m4-2m7: 0-0 3m+: 0-0
Track: LH: 0-1 RH: 0-0 Tight: 0-1 Gall: 0-0
Aids: Bl: 0-0 Vi: 0-0 Tstrap: 0-0
Best Rating: 66 1/02 Newc 2m soft NHF

Big Max

85(108h) (113h)110
7-y-o b g Rakaposhi King-Edwina's Dawn (Space King)
J Howard Johnson Peter Gormley

Placings:0P414/1231-364P013 (4558)
2001/02: 21^{3}G, 16^{6}GS, 24^{4}GF, 24^{P}G, 20^{0}S, 21^{1}GS, 19^{3}GF

	Starts	1st	2nd	3rd	Win & Pl
Hurdles	7	1	0	2	5412
Career Total	**16**	**4**	**1**	**3**	**17360**

100	3/02	MRas	2m5f110y	D(0-120)HHdl	G-S	£4069
113	4/01	Muss	3m	F(0-100)HHdl	G-F	£3251
104	10/00	MRas	3m	F(0-100)HHdl	GD	£2646
85	1/00	Muss	2m4f	F(0-100)HHdl	GD	£3493

Total win prize-money £13461

Going: Sf: 0-1 GS: 1-2 Gd: 0-2 GF: - Fm: 0-2
Distance: 2m/2m3: 0-1 **2m4-2m7: 1-4** 3m+: 0-2
Track: LH: 0-2 **RH: 1-5 Tight: 1-6** Gall: 0-1
Aids: Bl: 0-0 Vi: 0-0 Tstrap: 0-0
Best Rating: 113 4/01 Muss 3m gd-fm Hdl

A free-runner, he seems to appreciate a sharp right-handed track and good or fast ground. Runner-up on his chasing debut.

Big Perks (IRE)

98 119
10-y-o ch g Executive Perk-Secret Ocean (Most Secret)
P T Dalton R A H Perkins

Placings:21/0333/4/22262-02 (1666)
2001/02: 19^{0}G, 16^{2}G

	Starts	1st	2nd	3rd	Win & Pl
Chases	2	0	1	0	1033
Career Total	**14**	**1**	**6**	**3**	**9244**

100	1/97	Wwck	2m	H NHF	G-F	£1476

Total win prize-money £1476

Going: Sf: 0-0 GS: 0-0 Gd: 0-2 GF: - Fm: 0-0
Distance: 2m/2m3: 0-2 2m4-2m7: 0-0 3m+: 0-0
Track: LH: 0-1 RH: 0-1 Tight: 0-1 Gall: 0-0
Aids: Bl: 0-0 Vi: 0-0 Tstrap: 0-0
Best Rating: 126 1/01 Donc 2m110y good Ch

Big Quick (IRE)

94 98
7-y-o ch g Glacial Storm (USA)-Furryvale (Furry Glen)
L Wells R A Gadd

Placings:32 (4167)
2001/02: 17^{3}GF, 21^{2}GS

	Starts	1st	2nd	3rd	Win & Pl
NH Flat	1	0	0	1	242
Hurdles	1	0	1	0	711
Career Total	**2**	**0**	**1**	**1**	**953**

Going: Sf: 0-0 GS: 0-1 Gd: 0-0 GF: - Fm: 0-1
Distance: 2m/2m3: 0-1 2m4-2m7: 0-1 3m+: 0-0
Track: LH: 0-2 RH: 0-0 Tight: 0-2 Gall: 0-0
Aids: Bl: 0-0 Vi: 0-0 Tstrap: 0-0
Best Rating: 102 5/01 NAbb 2m1f gd-fm NHF

A maiden over hurdles, but has shown bits of form. Acts on acts on a sound surface, but also effective with cut in the ground.

Big Red

41 82
9-y-o ch g Left To Me-Backherorbust (Casino Boy)
Miss K M George Miss K George

Placings:P-F00 (1352)
2001/02: 16^{F}GF, 16^{0}GF, 17^{0}GF

	Starts	1st	2nd	3rd	Win & Pl
Hurdles	3	0	0	0	
Career Total	**4**	**0**	**0**	**0**	

Going: Sf: 0-0 GS: 0-0 Gd: 0-0 GF: - Fm: 0-3
Distance: 2m/2m3: 0-3 2m4-2m7: 0-0 3m+: 0-0
Track: LH: 0-2 RH: 0-1 Tight: 0-1 Gall: 0-0
Aids: Bl: 0-0 Vi: 0-0 Tstrap: 0-0
Best Rating: 82 5/01 Winc 2m gd-fm Hdl

Big Thyne

77 33
7-y-o b g Good Thyne (USA)-Cala Conta (Deep Run)
T J Etherington Mrs J E Todd

Placings:0PFP52/0-5 (1827)
2001/02: 24^{5}G

	Starts	1st	2nd	3rd	Win & Pl
Chases	1	0	0	0	0
Career Total	**8**	**0**	**1**	**0**	**546**

Going: Sf: 0-0 GS: 0-0 Gd: 0-1 GF: - Fm: 0-0
Distance: 2m/2m3: 0-0 2m4-2m7: 0-0 3m+: 0-1
Track: LH: 0-1 RH: 0-0 Tight: 0-1 Gall: 0-0
Aids: Bl: 0-0 Vi: 0-0 Tstrap: 0-0
Best Rating: 98 11/99 Weth 2m good NHF

Big Trouble

88 74
7-y-o b g Gildoran-Bengal Lady (Celtic Cone)
N A Twiston-Davies H B Shouler

Placings:0/5-0F00 (1923)
2001/02: 17^{0}G, 16^{F}G, 17^{0}G, 20^{0}G

	Starts	1st	2nd	3rd	Win & Pl
Hurdles	4	0	0	0	
Career Total	**6**	**0**	**0**	**0**	**0**

Going: Sf: 0-0 GS: 0-0 Gd: 0-4 GF: - Fm: 0-0
Distance: 2m/2m3: 0-3 2m4-2m7: 0-1 3m+: 0-0
Track: LH: 0-2 RH: 0-2 Tight: 0-2 Gall: 0-0
Aids: Bl: 0-0 Vi: 0-0 Tstrap: 0-1
Best Rating: 80 11/99 Chel 2m110y good NHF

He has faced some stiff tasks in his brief career and has yet to show much.

Big-And-Bold (IRE)

110 146
6-y-o b g Legal Circles (USA)-Kodak Lady (IRE) (Entre Nous)
G M Lyons Mrs Alix Stevenson

Placings:6/1210-34113 (4836)
2001/02: 18^{3}Y, 24^{4}Y, 20^{1}S, 20^{1}Y, 20^{3}G

	Starts	1st	2nd	3rd	Win & Pl
Chases	5	2	0	2	43429
Career Total	**10**	**4**	**1**	**2**	**56905**

145	4/02	Fair	2m4f	Ch	YLD	£34168
126	2/02	DRoy	2m4f	Ch	SFT	£4868
126	1/01	Leop	2m4f	Hdl	SFT	£9435
109	11/00	Thur	2m2f	NHF	HVY	£2760

Total win prize-money £51231

Going: Sf: 1-1 GS: 0-0 Gd: 0-1 GF: - Fm: 0-0
Distance: 2m/2m3: 0-1 **2m4-2m7: 2-3** 3m+: 0-1
Track: LH: 0-2 **RH: 1-2** Tight: 0-0 Gall: 0-0
Aids: Bl: 0-0 Vi: 0-0 **Tstrap: 2-5**
Best Rating: 146 4/02 Ayr 2m4f good Ch

Fair novice hurdler. Suited by two and a half miles and soft ground.

Bignoyse (IRE)

9-y-o b g Little Bighorn-Black River Lady (River Beauty)
C R Wilson (Mrs A Duffield 3/11) Bill Martin

Placings:P/PPP (3996)
2001/02: 20^{P}S, 22^{P}G, 24^{P}S

	Starts	1st	2nd	3rd	Win & Pl
Hurdles	1	0	0	0	0
Chases	2	0	0	0	0
Career Total	**4**	**0**	**0**	**0**	

Going: Sf: 0-2 GS: 0-0 Gd: 0-1 GF: - Fm: 0-0
Distance: 2m/2m3: 0-0 2m4-2m7: 0-2 3m+: 0-1
Track: LH: 0-2 RH: 0-1 Tight: 0-1 Gall: 0-1
Aids: Bl: 0-0 Vi: 0-0 Tstrap: 0-0
Best Rating:

Bigwig (IRE)

102 **104**

9-y-o ch g Thatching-Sabaah (USA) (Nureyev (USA))
G L Moore Mrs Elizabeth Kiernan

Placings:6504/405P0034/511562026/62O250411/06F3301-204406011 **(4561)**
2001/02: 21^{2}S, 21^{0}GF, 20^{4}G, 21^{4}GS, 24^{0}G, 21^{6}S, 20^{0}S, 21^{1}GS, 21^{1}GF

	Starts	1st	2nd	3rd	Win & Pl
Hurdles	9	2	1	0	5982
Career Total	**46**	**7**	**5**	**3**	**22918**

99	4/02	Plum	2m5f	E(0-105)HHdl	G-F	£2975
95	3/02	Plum	2m5f	F(0-90)Hdl	G-S	£1928
104	4/01	Plum	2m5f	F(0-105)HHdl	HVY	£2901
110	4/00	Plum	2m5f	F(0-105)HHdl	G-S	£2800
110	4/00	Plum	2m5f	F Hdl	G-S	£2758
97	8/98	Worc	2m2f	E(0-115)HHdl	GD	£2442
78	5/98	Hntg	2m110y	G(0-95)HHdl	G-F	£1716

Total win prize-money £17523

Going: Sf: 0-3 GS: 1-2 Gd: 0-2 GF: - Fm: 1-2
Distance: 2m/2m3: 0-0 **2m4-2m7: 2-8** 3m+: 0-1
Track: **LH: 2-5** RH: 0-4 **Tight: 2-5** Gall: 0-2
Aids: **Bl: 2-9** Vi: 0-0 Tstrap: 0-0
Best Rating: **110** 4/00 Plum 2m5f gd-sft Hdl

Moderate handicap hurdler, suited by cut but acts on faster. A course specialist at Plumpton, he usually wears blinkers. He is best in the spring.

Bija

80 **69**

7-y-o b g Librate-Guilty Sparkle (Roc Imp)
F P Murtagh F P Murtagh

Placings:0/00P-06 **(1931)**
2001/02: 16^{0}GS, 16^{6}G

	Starts	1st	2nd	3rd	Win & Pl
Hurdles	2	0	0	0	0
Career Total	**6**	**0**	**0**	**0**	**0**

Going: Sf: 0-0 GS: 0-1 Gd: 0-1 GF: - Fm: 0-0
Distance: 2m/2m3: 0-2 2m4-2m7: 0-0 3m+: 0-0
Track: LH: 0-2 RH: 0-0 Tight: 0-2 Gall: 0-0
Aids: Bl: 0-0 Vi: 0-0 Tstrap: 0-0
Best Rating: **76** 9/00 Worc 2m gd-fm Hdl

Bilboa (FR)

116 **157**

5-y-o b m Phantom Breeze-Maisonnaise (FR) (Labus (FR))
F Doumen Jorg Vasicek

Placings:1212115-2222213P **(4676)**
2001/02: 19^{2}S, 19^{2}VS, 19^{2}VS, 19^{2}HY, 16^{2}G, 16^{1}S, 16^{3}GS, 20^{P}G

	Starts	1st	2nd	3rd	Win & Pl
Hurdles	8	1	5	1	121645
Career Total	**15**	**5**	**7**	**1**	**247920**

129	2/02	Sand	2m110y	B Hdl	SFT	£10140
157	4/01	Aint	2m110y	A Hdl	SFT	£58000
146	2/01	Kemp	2m	A Hdl	G-S	£12000
	11/00	Engh	2m1f110y	Hdl	HVY	£28818
	9/00	Autl	2m2f	Hdl	VS	£13449

Total win prize-money £122407

Going: Sf: 1-3 GS: 0-1 Gd: 0-2 GF: - Fm: 0-0
Distance: **2m/2m3: 1-4** 2m4-2m7: 0-4 3m+: 0-0
Track: LH: 0-3 **RH: 1-2** Tight: 0-1 Gall: 0-0
Aids: Bl: 0-0 Vi: 0-0 Tstrap: 0-0
Best Rating: **157** 3/02 Chel 2m110y gd-sft Hdl

A winning hurdler in France, she ran well in defeat at Chepstow on her debut in this country in December 2000, especially as her rider appeared to set her a bit too much to do, and confirmed herself to be one of the best of her generation with clear wins at Kempton and Aintree over two miles. Finished runner-up on five consecutive occasions last season before running out a convincing winner of the Agfa Hurdle in 2002 then finishing third in the Champion Hurdle. Her trainer believes she is at her best on a sound surface, although all her wins have come with plenty of give in the ground. Suited by two miles.

Biliverdin (IRE)

110(55h) **150**

8-y-o b g Bob Back (USA)-Straw Beret (USA) (Chief's Crown (USA))
G B Balding Theo Waddington And Bernard Keay

Placings:*21/100*/00/1P**25-FF3234** **(4914)**
2001/02: 19^{F}G, 19^{F}G, 20^{3}S, 20^{2}G, 20^{3}Y, 20^{4}G

	Starts	1st	2nd	3rd	Win & Pl
Chases	6	0	1	2	12759
Career Total	**17**	**3**	**3**	**2**	**50258**

105	5/00	Hntg	2m110y	E Hdl	GD	£2564
124	2/99	Punc	2m	NHF	HVY	£3683
116	4/98	Fair	2m	NHF	G-Y	£25652

Total win prize-money £31900

Going: Sf: 0-1 GS: 0-0 Gd: 0-4 GF: - Fm: 0-0
Distance: 2m/2m3: 0-0 2m4-2m7: 0-6 3m+: 0-0
Track: LH: 0-0 RH: 0-6 Tight: 0-0 Gall: 0-0
Aids: Bl: 0-0 Vi: 0-0 Tstrap: 0-0
Best Rating: **150** 4/02 Sand 2m4f110y good Ch

Very lightly raced since arriving from Ireland, he ran a cracker behind Crocadee in a Grade 2 novice chase at Kempton in February 2001. Failed to get off the mark in 2001/02 despite being placed in good races. He has plenty of ability but is not the best of jumpers. Stays two and a half miles. Acts on a good or softer.

Bill And Win

11-y-o b g Faustus (USA)-Water Folly (Sharpo)
T Wall Harton Manor Racing Club

Placings:46154/4/P0P00/**F**00 **(2901)**
2001/02: 16^{F}GF, 19^{0}G, 20^{0}S

	Starts	1st	2nd	3rd	Win & Pl
Hurdles	2	0	0	0	0
Chases	1	0	0	0	0
Career Total	**14**	**1**	**0**	**0**	**2057**

78	11/94	Nott	2m	Hdl	SFT	£2056

Total win prize-money £2057

Going: Sf: 0-1 GS: 0-0 Gd: 0-1 GF: - Fm: 0-1
Distance: 2m/2m3: 0-2 2m4-2m7: 0-1 3m+: 0-0
Track: LH: 0-2 RH: 0-1 Tight: 0-0 Gall: 0-0
Aids: Bl: 0-1 Vi: 0-0 Tstrap: 0-0
Best Rating: **80** 5/95 Uttx 2m gd-fm Hdl

Bill Joyce (IRE)

68

11-y-o b g Lord Americo-French Academy (Le Bavard (FR))
R Williams R Williams

Placings:*03*/0*00*/*0*6-0 **(0914)**
2001/02: 22^{0}GF

	Starts	1st	2nd	3rd	Win & Pl
Hurdles	1	0	0	0	
Career Total	**8**	**0**	**0**	**1**	**283**

Going: Sf: 0-0 GS: 0-0 Gd: 0-0 GF: - Fm: 0-1
Distance: 2m/2m3: 0-0 2m4-2m7: 0-1 3m+: 0-0
Track: LH: 0-1 RH: 0-0 Tight: 0-1 Gall: 0-0
Aids: Bl: 0-0 Vi: 0-0 Tstrap: 0-0
Best Rating: **88** 6/98 Cork 2m4f good NHF

Bill's Integrity

69f **44f**

7-y-o b m Bold Fox-Emlyn Princess (Julio Mariner)
Miss Venetia Williams W E Prichard

Placings:*0* **(0678)**
2001/02: 16^{0}GF

	Starts	1st	2nd	3rd	Win & Pl
NH Flat	1	0	0	0	
Career Total	**1**	**0**	**0**	**0**	

Going: Sf: 0-0 GS: 0-0 Gd: 0-0 GF: - Fm: 0-1
Distance: 2m/2m3: 0-1 2m4-2m7: 0-0 3m+: 0-0
Track: LH: 0-1 RH: 0-0 Tight: 0-0 Gall: 0-0
Aids: Bl: 0-0 Vi: 0-0 Tstrap: 0-0
Best Rating: **44** 6/01 Worc 2m gd-fm NHF

Billie John (IRE)

106 **96**

7-y-o ch g Boyne Valley-Lovestream (Sandy Creek)
Mrs K Walton Mrs Patricia M Wilson

Placings:*0-60*620 **(4894)**
2001/02: 17^{6}GS, 16^{0}G, 19^{6}G, 16^{2}GF, 16^{0}G

	Starts	1st	2nd	3rd	Win & Pl
NH Flat	2	0	0	0	0
Hurdles	3	0	1	0	860
Career Total	**6**	**0**	**1**	**0**	**860**

Going: Sf: 0-0 GS: 0-1 Gd: 0-3 GF: - Fm: 0-1
Distance: 2m/2m3: 0-5 2m4-2m7: 0-0 3m+: 0-0
Track: LH: 0-3 RH: 0-2 Tight: 0-2 Gall: 0-0
Aids: Bl: 0-0 Vi: 0-0 Tstrap: 0-0
Best Rating: **103** 4/02 Kels 2m110y gd-fm Hdl

Improved a great deal during the spring of 2002. Suited by fast ground and probably best over two miles.

Billingsgate

109(107h) (105h)**140**

10-y-o ch g Nicholas Bill-Polly Washdish (Oats)
P J Hobbs Dr D Chesney & Mrs B Chesney

Placings:*124*/05/21**333**/11**P** **(4148)**
2001/02: 24^{1}G, 24^{1}GS, 26^{P}GS

	Starts	1st	2nd	3rd	Win & Pl
Hurdles	1	1	0	0	5473
Chases	2	1	0	0	23200
Career Total	**13**	**4**	**2**	**3**	**54636**

140	2/02	Sand	3m110y	B(0-145)HCh	G-S	£23200
105	11/01	Newb	3m110y	C Hdl	GD	£5473
136	11/98	Asct	2m	B Ch	GD	£7650
101	12/96	Worc	2m	H NHF	G-S	£1448

Total win prize-money £37771

Going: Sf: 0-0 GS: 1-2 Gd: 1-1 GF: - Fm: 0-0
Distance: 2m/2m3: 0-0 2m4-2m7: 0-0 **3m+: 2-3**
Track: LH: 1-2 RH: 1-1 Tight: 0-0 **Gall: 1-1**
Aids: Bl: 0-0 Vi: 0-0 Tstrap: 0-0
Best Rating: **147** 12/98 Sand 2m good Ch

A decent novice chaser in the 1998/1999 season, he was off the track for two and a half years before landing a double over both types of obstacle in the 2001/2002 season.

Staying is his game and he acts on good to soft ground, but he is a fragile sort.

Billy Ballbreaker (IRE)

104f 106f

6-y-o b g Good Thyne (USA)-Droichead Dhamhile (IRE) (The Parson)

P F Nicholls C G Roach

Placings:*50* (2942)

2001/02: 16^{5}S, 16^{0}G

	Starts	1st	2nd	3rd	Win & Pl
NH Flat	2	0	0	0	0
Career Total	**2**	**0**	**0**	**0**	**0**

Going: Sf: 0-1 GS: 0-0 Gd: 0-1 GF: - Fm: 0-0
Distance: 2m/2m3: 0-2 2m4-2m7: 0-0 3m+: 0-0
Track: LH: 0-2 RH: 0-0 Tight: 0-0 Gall: 0-1
Aids: Bl: 0-0 Vi: 0-0 Tstrap: 0-0
Best Rating: **106** 12/01 Newb 2m110y good NHF

Billy Nomaite

107 129+

8-y-o ch g Komaite (USA)-Lucky Monashka (Lucky Wednesday)

Mrs S J Smith R Preston

Placings:66020U4600P/2211351/162-63F (4749)

2001/02: 18^{6}HY, 20^{3}GS, 20^{F}GF

	Starts	1st	2nd	3rd	Win & Pl
Hurdles	1	0	0	0	0
Chases	2	0	0	1	568
Career Total	**24**	**4**	**4**	**2**	**17981**

123	10/00	Kels	2m1f	E Ch	SFT	£3510
113	12/99	Uttx	2m	C(0-130)HHdl	SFT	£5135
110	9/99	Worc	2m	E(0-115)HHdl	G-F	£2250
100	8/99	Strf	2m110y	F(0-105)HHdl	GD	£1976

Total win prize-money £12873

Going: Sf: 0-1 GS: 0-1 Gd: 0-0 GF: - Fm: 0-1
Distance: 2m/2m3: 0-1 2m4-2m7: 0-2 3m+: 0-0
Track: LH: 0-1 RH: 0-2 Tight: 0-1 Gall: 0-0
Aids: Bl: 0-0 Vi: 0-0 Tstrap: 0-0
Best Rating: **123** 3/02 Carl 2m4f gd-sft Ch

A keen sort, he has been successful over hurdles and fences. Acts on most types of ground and stays two and a half miles.

Billy The Snake (IRE)

(109h) (119h)110

9-y-o b g Yashgan-Kathy's Trix (Callernish)

P Hughes Ouncle Syndicate

Placings:*002310*4-332F11**1F** (4233)

2001/02: 20^{3}G, 20^{3}YS, 18^{2}Y, 22^{F}YS, 24^{1}SH, 18^{1}S, 32^{F}GS

	Starts	1st	2nd	3rd	Win & Pl
Hurdles	5	1	1	2	9154
Chases	2	1	0	0	6773
Career Total	**14**	**3**	**2**	**3**	**20751**

110	2/02	Gowr	2m2f	Ch	SFT	£6773
106	1/02	Punc	3m	Hdl	SH	£6561
120	2/01	Clon	2m2f	NHF	HVY	£3338

Total win prize-money £16673

Going: Sf: 1-1 GS: 0-1 Gd: 0-1 GF: - Fm: 0-0
Distance: 2m/2m3: 1-2 2m4-2m7: 0-3 3m+: 1-2
Track: LH: 0-2 **RH: 2-3** Tight: 0-0 Gall: 0-1
Aids: Bl: 0-0 Vi: 0-0 Tstrap: 0-0
Best Rating: **120** 2/01 Clon 2m2f heavy NHF

Irish staying novice chaser, ran well for a long way before falling in the Cheltenham National Hunt Chase.

Billyjo (IRE)

4-y-o b g Idris (IRE)-Village Countess (IRE) (Reasonable (FR))

Miss A Stokell Ms Caron Stokell

Placings:P (4424)

2001/02: 16^{P}HY

	Starts	1st	2nd	3rd	Win & Pl
Hurdles	1	0	0	0	
Career Total	**1**	**0**	**0**	**0**	

Going: Sf: 0-1 GS: 0-0 Gd: 0-0 GF: - Fm: 0-0
Distance: 2m/2m3: 0-1 2m4-2m7: 0-0 3m+: 0-0
Track: LH: 0-1 RH: 0-0 Tight: 0-0 Gall: 0-0
Aids: Bl: 0-0 Vi: 0-0 Tstrap: 0-0
Best Rating:

Bin It (IRE)

109 119

6-y-o b m Supreme Leader-Castle Stream (Paddy's Stream)

C J Mann John Seth-Smith

Placings:3235-F2121220 (4149)

2001/02: 22^{F}S, 20^{2}S, 21^{1}S, 21^{2}HY, 19^{1}S, 20^{2}S, 21^{2}S, 20^{0}GS

	Starts	1st	2nd	3rd	Win & Pl
Hurdles	8	2	4	0	12293
Career Total	**12**	**2**	**5**	**2**	**14909**

119	1/02	Hrfd	2m3f110y	E(0-110)HHdl	SFT	£3475
108	11/01	Towc	2m5f	D Hdl	SFT	£3913

Total win prize-money £7389

Going: Sf: 2-7 GS: 0-1 Gd: 0-0 GF: - Fm: 0-0
Distance: 2m/2m3: 0-0 **2m4-2m7: 2-8** 3m+: 0-0
Track: LH: 0-2 **RH: 2-5** Tight: 0-3 Gall: 0-0
Aids: Bl: 0-0 Vi: 0-0 Tstrap: 0-0
Best Rating: **119** 2/02 Kemp 2m5f soft Hdl

A half-sister to winning jumpers Native Shore and Native Recruit, she has proven admirably consistent in novice hurdles, showing progressive form in the process. Stays two miles five and likes soft ground.

Bindaree (IRE)

113 158

8-y-o ch g Roselier (FR)-Flowing Tide (Main Reef)

N A Twiston-Davies H R Mould

Placings:*3*1111240/**1213U124U-0533601** (4677)

2001/02: 20^{0}G, 26^{5}S, 24^{3}S, 29^{3}GS, 24^{6}S, 24^{0}GS, 36^{1}G

	Starts	1st	2nd	3rd	Win & Pl
Chases	7	1	0	2	306375
Career Total	**24**	**8**	**3**	**4**	**398516**

158	4/02	Aint	4m4f	A HCh	GD	£290000
154	1/01	Asct	3m110y	B Ch	G-S	£8807
143	11/00	Chep	2m3f110y	A Ch	SFT	£18000
146	9/00	Prth	2m4f110y	D Ch	HVY	£4771
153	12/99	Chel	2m5f110y	A Hdl	SFT	£16375
153	12/99	Chel	3m	A Hdl	G-S	£9525
141	11/99	Chep	3m	B Hdl	SFT	£7132
135	10/99	Carl	3m110y	E Hdl	GD	£2346

Total win prize-money £356958

Going: Sf: 0-3 GS: 0-2 Gd: 1-2 GF: - Fm: 0-0
Distance: 2m/2m3: 0-0 2m4-2m7: 0-1 **3m+: 1-6**
Track: **LH: 1-7** RH: 0-0 **Tight: 1-1** Gall: 0-3
Aids: Bl: 0-0 Vi: 0-0 Tstrap: 0-0
Best Rating: **158** 4/02 Aint 4m4f good Ch

Winner of the Grade One Challow Hurdle in 1999/2000, he made up into a good novice and handicap chaser. Stays particularly well, and was third in the 2001 Welsh National before gaining his biggest success in the 2002 Grand National. Acts on anything from good to heavy and is suited by going left-handed.

Binny Bay

99 85

6-y-o b m Karinga Bay-Binny Grove (Sunyboy)

D McCain D McCain

Placings:*00*0030034612 (4919)

2001/02: 17^{0}GS, 16^{0}GS, 17^{0}G, 17^{0}G, 19^{3}GS, 16^{0}G, 21^{0}HY, 16^{3}HY, 21^{4}GS, 27^{6}S, 16^{1}GF, 21^{2}GF

	Starts	1st	2nd	3rd	Win & Pl
NH Flat	2	0	0	0	0
Hurdles	10	1	1	2	3470
Career Total	**12**	**1**	**1**	**2**	**3470**

84	4/02	Uttx	2m	G Hdl	G-F	£1946

Total win prize-money £1946

Going: Sf: 0-3 GS: 0-4 Gd: 0-3 GF: - Fm: 1-2
Distance: **2m/2m3: 1-7** 2m4-2m7: 0-4 3m+: 0-1
Track: **LH: 1-10** RH: 0-2 Tight: 0-8 Gall: 0-0
Aids: Bl: 0-0 Vi: 0-0 **Tstrap: 1-3**
Best Rating: **85** 2/02 Uttx 2m heavy Hdl

Got up in final stride to land two mile seller at Uttoxeter in April 2002 when appearing to settle better with the aid of a tongue-tie and a new bit.

Bint Aljood

5-y-o b m Bin Ajwaad (IRE)-Shareehan (Dancing Brave (USA))

A J Chamberlain A C Ledbury

Placings:0PP (2274)

2001/02: 17^{0}G, 20^{P}S, 16^{P}G

	Starts	1st	2nd	3rd	Win & Pl
Hurdles	3	0	0	0	
Career Total	**3**	**0**	**0**	**0**	

Going: Sf: 0-1 GS: 0-0 Gd: 0-2 GF: - Fm: 0-0
Distance: 2m/2m3: 0-2 2m4-2m7: 0-1 3m+: 0-0
Track: LH: 0-2 RH: 0-1 Tight: 0-0 Gall: 0-0
Aids: Bl: 0-0 Vi: 0-0 Tstrap: 0-0
Best Rating:

Bint St James

96 82

7-y-o b m Shareef Dancer (USA)-St James's Antigua (IRE) (Law Society (USA))

W Clay Mrs Janet Dutton

Placings:550/P4U3F0P01P/402FPP0 (4573)

2001/02: 22^{4}GS, 22^{0}GF, 16^{2}GS, 16^{F}GS, 20^{P}HY, 17^{P}S, 20^{0}G

	Starts	1st	2nd	3rd	Win & Pl
Hurdles	7	0	1	0	500
Career Total	**20**	**1**	**1**	**1**	**2443**

85	11/99	MRas	2m3f110y	G(0-90)HHdl	G-S	£1490

Total win prize-money £1490

Going: Sf: 0-2 GS: 0-3 Gd: 0-1 GF: - Fm: 0-1
Distance: 2m/2m3: 0-3 2m4-2m7: 0-4 3m+: 0-0
Track: LH: 0-6 RH: 0-1 Tight: 0-4 Gall: 0-0
Aids: Bl: 0-0 Vi: 0-1 Tstrap: 0-0
Best Rating: 85 11/99 MRas 2m3f110y gd-sft Hdl

Bird King

5-y-o b g Rakaposhi King-Miss Wrensborough (Buckskin (FR))
D R Gandolfo G C Hartigan

Placings: *0* (3375)
2001/02: 16^{0}S

	Starts	1st	2nd	3rd	Win & Pl
NH Flat	1	0	0	0	
Career Total	**1**	**0**	**0**	**0**	

Going: Sf: 0-1 GS: 0-0 Gd: 0-0 GF: - Fm: 0-0
Distance: 2m/2m3: 0-1 2m4-2m7: 0-0 3m+: 0-0
Track: LH: 0-1 RH: 0-0 Tight: 0-0 Gall: 0-0
Aids: Bl: 0-0 Vi: 0-0 Tstrap: 0-0
Best Rating:

Birkdale (IRE)

110(95h) (128h)153
11-y-o gr g Roselier (FR)-Clonroche Lady (Charlottesvilles Flyer)
Ferdy Murphy Duncan Norbury

Placings: 02/221111P/**215211134**/4511101P/50-**232P0** (4677)
2001/02: 25^{2}S, 25^{3}GS, 24^{2}HY, 28^{P}HY, 36^{0}G

	Starts	1st	2nd	3rd	Win & Pl
Chases	5	0	2	1	15681
Career Total	**33**	**12**	**7**	**2**	**65722**

144	3/00	Ayr	3m1f	D(0-125)HCh	HVY	£5215
144	1/00	Kels	3m1f	D(0-125)HCh	GD	£3867
139	12/99	Ayr	3m1f	D(0-125)HCh	HVY	£4198
155	12/99	Hayd	2m4f	B HHdl	HVY	£6781
148	2/99	Weth	2m7f	C(0-135)HHdl	GD	£4435
152	1/99	Weth	3m1f	D(0-125)HHdl	SFT	£2786
145	1/99	Newc	3m	D(0-125)HHdl	SFT	£2775
131	11/98	Kels	2m6f110y	E Ch	HVY	£3290
127	3/98	Ayr	3m110y	D(0-125)HHdl	SFT	£2747
120	1/98	Catt	3m1f110y	E Hdl	SFT	£2598
118	12/97	Sedg	3m3f110y	E Hdl	SFT	£2355
103	12/97	Hexm	3m	E Hdl	SFT	£2511

Total win prize-money £43560

Going: Sf: 0-3 GS: 0-1 Gd: 0-1 GF: - Fm: 0-0
Distance: 2m/2m3: 0-0 2m4-2m7: 0-0 3m+: 0-5
Track: LH: 0-4 RH: 0-1 Tight: 0-1 Gall: 0-0
Aids: Bl: 0-0 Vi: 0-0 Tstrap: 0-0
Best Rating: 155 12/99 Hayd 2m4f heavy Hdl

Genuine front-running stayer who is better over hurdles than he is over fences. Best suited by a soft surface. Stays three miles plus.

Birotex Boy (IRE)

99 102
9-y-o b g Meneval (USA)-Ballymorris Belle (Laurence O)
C Grant Birotex

Placings: *00063/2/50/0P*2P-R5333P (4310)
2001/02: 20^{R}G, 17^{5}S, 16^{3}S, 16^{3}S, 16^{3}S, 16^{P}S

	Starts	1st	2nd	3rd	Win & Pl
Chases	6	0	0	3	1592
Career Total	**18**	**0**	**2**	**4**	**3172**

Going: Sf: 0-5 GS: 0-0 Gd: 0-1 GF: - Fm: 0-0
Distance: 2m/2m3: 0-5 2m4-2m7: 0-1 3m+: 0-0
Track: LH: 0-5 RH: 0-1 Tight: 0-1 Gall: 0-4
Aids: Bl: 0-2 Vi: 0-0 Tstrap: 0-0
Best Rating: 102 2/02 Newc 2m110y soft Ch

Moderate maiden over hurdles and fences, he acts on good and soft ground.

Bishop's Secret

75 58
4-y-o b g Bishop Of Cashel-Secret Rapture (USA) (Woodman (USA))
P T Dalton (Mrs N Macauley 17/8) Thringstone Racing Club

Placings: 000P (2794)
2001/02: 16^{0}G, 17^{0}G, 16^{0}HY, 16^{P}S

	Starts	1st	2nd	3rd	Win & Pl
Hurdles	4	0	0	0	
Career Total	**4**	**0**	**0**	**0**	

Going: Sf: 0-2 GS: 0-0 Gd: 0-2 GF: - Fm: 0-0
Distance: 2m/2m3: 0-4 2m4-2m7: 0-0 3m+: 0-0
Track: LH: 0-2 RH: 0-2 Tight: 0-0 Gall: 0-0
Aids: Bl: 0-0 Vi: 0-0 Tstrap: 0-0
Best Rating: 59 12/01 Leic 2m heavy Hdl

Bishopstone Belle

5-y-o b m Formidable (USA)-Relatively Easy (Relkino)
J A Moore J A Moore

Placings: P-PP (0929)
2001/02: 20^{P}GF, 20^{P}GF

	Starts	1st	2nd	3rd	Win & Pl
Hurdles	2	0	0	0	
Career Total	**3**	**0**	**0**	**0**	

Going: Sf: 0-0 GS: 0-0 Gd: 0-0 GF: - Fm: 0-2
Distance: 2m/2m3: 0-0 2m4-2m7: 0-2 3m+: 0-0
Track: LH: 0-1 RH: 0-1 Tight: 0-1 Gall: 0-0
Aids: Bl: 0-0 Vi: 0-0 Tstrap: 0-0
Best Rating:

Bisquet-De-Bouche

81 97
8-y-o ch m Most Welcome-Larive (Blakeney)
A W Carroll Martin Brook

Placings: 0/0202B12P/63641-35 (0347)
2001/02: 22^{3}GS, 27^{5}G

	Starts	1st	2nd	3rd	Win & Pl
Hurdles	2	0	0	1	478
Career Total	**16**	**2**	**3**	**2**	**9190**

97	4/01	Winc	2m6f	F(0-105)HHdl	SFT	£3724
87	2/00	Catt	3m1f110y	F(0-100)HHdl	GD	£2012

Total win prize-money £5737

Going: Sf: 0-0 GS: 0-1 Gd: 0-1 GF: - Fm: 0-0
Distance: 2m/2m3: 0-0 2m4-2m7: 0-1 3m+: 0-1
Track: LH: 0-1 RH: 0-0 Tight: 0-1 Gall: 0-0
Aids: Bl: 0-0 Vi: 0-0 Tstrap: 0-0
Best Rating: 97 4/01 Winc 2m6f soft Hdl

Bit O Magic (IRE)

100(54h) 111
10-y-o ch g Henbit (USA)-Arpal Magic (Master Owen)
Ferdy Murphy Geoff Adam

Placings: *1/20/*4F15344/650/31-**U2P41** (4551)
2001/02: 20^{U}GS, 22^{2}GS, 19^{P}GS, 16^{4}S, 16^{1}GF

	Starts	1st	2nd	3rd	Win & Pl
Chases	5	1	1	0	5547
Career Total	**20**	**4**	**2**	**2**	**13138**

111	4/02	Hntg	2m110y	D(0-115)HCh	G-F	£4059
101	10/00	Kels	2m2f	F(0-110)HHdl	SFT	£1879
88	12/98	Muss	2m4f	E Hdl	GD	£2262
95	5/96	Prth	2m110y	H NHF	FRM	£1966

Total win prize-money £10167

Going: Sf: 0-1 GS: 0-3 Gd: 0-0 GF: - Fm: 1-1
Distance: **2m/2m3: 1-3** 2m4-2m7: 0-2 3m+: 0-0
Track: LH: 0-3 **RH: 1-2** Tight: 0-4 **Gall: 1-1**
Aids: Bl: 0-0 Vi: 0-0 Tstrap: 0-0
Best Rating: 111 4/02 Hntg 2m110y gd-fm Ch

Winning hurdler who has shown promise over fences. Probably best at two and a half miles.

Bit Of A Snob

99(59h) (19h)108
11-y-o b g St Columbus-Classey (Dubassoff (USA))
J S King Miss S Douglas-Pennant

Placings: PP02043/1P1313P-P01 (1259)
2001/02: 21^{P}GF, 17^{0}GF, 16^{1}GF

	Starts	1st	2nd	3rd	Win & Pl
Chases	3	1	0	0	2660
Career Total	**17**	**4**	**1**	**3**	**14662**

108	8/01	Hntg	2m110y	F(0-100)HCh	G-F	£2660
114	8/00	NAbb	2m110y	F(0-110)HCh	GD	£4065
108	6/00	Hrfd	2m	E Ch	G-F	£3110
100	5/00	Winc	2m	E Hdl	FRM	£2751

Total win prize-money £12587

Going: Sf: 0-0 GS: 0-0 Gd: 0-0 GF: - Fm: 1-3
Distance: **2m/2m3: 1-2** 2m4-2m7: 0-1 3m+: 0-0
Track: LH: 0-2 **RH: 1-1** Tight: 0-2 **Gall: 1-1**
Aids: Bl: 0-1 Vi: 0-0 Tstrap: 0-0
Best Rating: 114 8/00 NAbb 2m110y good Ch

Bit Of Minster

105(96h) (60h)102
6-y-o b g Minster Son-Bit On Edge (Henbit (USA))
P Monteith Burns Partnership

Placings: 0P-0043442 (4856)
2001/02: 20^{0}GF, 20^{0}G, 20^{4}S, 24^{3}S, 24^{4}HY, 21^{4}S, 25^{2}G

Starts		1st	2nd	3rd	Win & Pl
Hurdles	5	0	0	1	601
Chases	2	0	1	0	1447
Career Total	**9**	**0**	**1**	**1**	**2048**

Going: Sf: 0-4 GS: 0-0 Gd: 0-2 GF: - Fm: 0-1
Distance: 2m/2m3: 0-0 2m4-2m7: 0-4 3m+: 0-3
Track: LH: 0-3 RH: 0-4 Tight: 0-4 Gall: 0-0
Aids: Bl: 0-0 Vi: 0-0 Tstrap: 0-0
Best Rating: 102 4/02 Hexm 3m1f good Ch

Modest hurdler, yet to prove he truly gets three miles.

	Starts	1st	2nd	3rd	Win & Pl
Hurdles	1	0	0	0	0
Chases	1	0	0	0	0
Career Total	**19**	**3**	**4**	**3**	**19141**

116	2/00	Leic	2m	E Ch	SFT	£4750
119	2/00	Newc	2m110y	E Ch	SFT	£2983
102	12/98	MRas	2m1f110y	D Hdl	SFT	£3029

Total win prize-money £10763

Going: Sf: 0-2 GS: 0-0 Gd: 0-0 GF: - Fm: 0-0
Distance: 2m/2m3: 0-0 2m4-2m7: 0-2 3m+: 0-0
Track: LH: 0-2 RH: 0-0 Tight: 0-0 Gall: 0-1
Aids: Bl: 0-0 Vi: 0-0 Tstrap: 0-0
Best Rating: **119** 3/00 Newb 2m2f110y gd-fm Ch

Handicap chaser, best at around two miles. A mudlark.

Bitofamixup (IRE)

94 **89**

11-y-o br g Strong Gale-Geeaway (Gala Performance (USA))
M J Roberts Mike Roberts

Placings:011/**12122/164U/P2PP/63P3** (4783)
2001/02: 24^{6}G, 25^{3}GF, 26^{P}GF, 29^{3}GF

	Starts	1st	2nd	3rd	Win & Pl
Chases	4	0	0	2	1825
Career Total	**20**	**5**	**4**	**2**	**34611**

142	5/98	Worc	2m7f110y	E Ch	GD	£3566
133	2/98	Font	3m2f110y	D Ch	GD	£3975
124	5/97	Bang	3m110y	H Ch	GD	£1548
135	4/97	Aint	3m1f	B Ch	GD	£7107
106	2/97	Hntg	3m	H Ch	G-S	£1262

Total win prize-money £17459

Going: Sf: 0-0 GS: 0-0 Gd: 0-1 GF: - Fm: 0-3
Distance: 2m/2m3: 0-0 2m4-2m7: 0-0 3m+: 0-4
Track: LH: 0-1 RH: 0-2 Tight: 0-0 Gall: 0-0
Aids: Bl: 0-0 Vi: 0-0 Tstrap: 0-2
Best Rating: **148** 4/98 Ayr 3m1f good Ch

Former highly-regarded hunter chaser, he has not shown much form in handicap chases in recent years.

Bitter Sweet

100 **90**

6-y-o gr m Deploy-Julia Flyte (Drone (USA))
J L Spearing Masonaires

Placings:000/132403 (2408)
2001/02. 16^{1}GF, 16^{3}GF, 17^{2}S, 10^{4}G, 10^{0}G, 17^{3}GS

	Starts	1st	2nd	3rd	Win & Pl
Hurdles	6	1	1	2	4804
Career Total	**9**	**1**	**1**	**2**	**4804**

83	9/01	Worc	2m	E Hdl	G-F	£2443

Total win prize-money £2443

Going: Sf: 0-1 GS: 0-1 Gd: 0-2 GF: - Fm: 1-2
Distance: **2m/2m3: 1-6** 2m4-2m7: 0-0 3m+: 0-0
Track: **LH: 1-3** RH: 0-3 Tight: 0-3 Gall: 0-1
Aids: Bl: 0-0 Vi: 0-0 Tstrap: 0-0
Best Rating: **90** 11/01 NAbb 2m1f soft Hdl

She has won three races, two of which on the flat at around ten furlongs and the other over two miles over hurdles, and she is holding her hurdling form well, including a good second at Newton Abbot in November. Acts on a sound surface.

Bittern

61

9-y-o b m Henbit (USA)-Anamasi (Idiots Delight)
A J Chamberlain A J Chamberlain

Placings:*0*PU/0-P00P (1886)
2001/02: 19^{P}GF, 22^{0}GF, 22^{0}G, 21^{P}G

	Starts	1st	2nd	3rd	Win & Pl
Hurdles	4	0	0	0	
Career Total	**8**	**0**	**0**	**0**	

Going: Sf: 0-0 GS: 0-0 Gd: 0-2 GF: - Fm: 0-2
Distance: 2m/2m3: 0-0 2m4-2m7: 0-4 3m+: 0-0
Track: LH: 0-1 RH: 0-2 Tight: 0-0 Gall: 0-1
Aids: Bl: 0-0 Vi: 0-0 Tstrap: 0-0
Best Rating: **57** 11/99 Wwck 2m good NHF

Bivowag

9-y-o gr g Scallywag-Bivadell (Bivouac)
J R Weymes S A Blyth

Placings:PP-F (0233)
2001/02: 24^{F}GF

	Starts	1st	2nd	3rd	Win & Pl
Chases	1	0	0	0	
Career Total	**3**	**0**	**0**	**0**	

Going: Sf: 0-0 GS: 0-0 Gd: 0-0 GF: - Fm: 0-1
Distance: 2m/2m3: 0-0 2m4-2m7: 0-0 3m+: 0-1
Track: LH: 0-1 RH: 0-0 Tight: 0-1 Gall: 0-0
Aids: Bl: 0-0 Vi: 0-0 Tstrap: 0-0
Best Rating:

Biya (IRE)

98 **78**

10-y-o ch g Shadeed (USA)-Rosie Potts (Shareef Dancer (USA))
D McCain Champ Chicken Co Ltd

Placings:6/0600054/55**F30/P**0510U235/24154/00-040 (0741)
2001/02: 16^{0}GF, 20^{4}F, 16^{0}GS

	Starts	1st	2nd	3rd	Win & Pl
Hurdles	1	0	0	0	0
Chases	2	0	0	0	0
Career Total	**32**	**2**	**2**	**2**	**9868**

95	12/99	Sedg	2m110y	F(0-105)HCh	G-S	£3533
88	10/98	Bang	2m1f110y	E(0-110)HCh	GD	£3371

Total win prize money £6005

Going: Sf: 0-0 GS: 0-1 Gd: 0-0 GF: - Fm: 0-2
Distance: 2m/2m3: 0-2 2m4-2m7: 0-1 3m+: 0-0
Track: LH: 0-3 RH: 0-0 Tight: 0-0 Gall: 0-0
Aids: Bl: 0-3 Vi: 0-0 Tstrap: 0-0
Best Rating: **95** 12/99 Sedg 2m110y gd-sft Ch

Black Abbey (IRE)

76 **69**

11-y-o b g Black Minstrel-Abbey Belle (Kambalda)
B Scriven B Scriven

Placings:*0/00***PP/FP/34PPP** (1848)
2001/02: 16^{3}G, 16^{4}GF, 26^{P}GF, 16^{P}GF, 25^{P}G

	Starts	1st	2nd	3rd	Win & Pl
Chases	5	0	0	1	837
Career Total	**12**	**0**	**0**	**1**	**837**

Going: Sf: 0-0 GS: 0-0 Gd: 0-2 GF: - Fm: 0-3
Distance: 2m/2m3: 0-3 2m4-2m7: 0-0 3m+: 0-2
Track: LH: 0-4 RH: 0-1 Tight: 0-4 Gall: 0-0
Aids: Bl: 0-0 Vi: 0-0 Tstrap: 0-0
Best Rating: **72** 8/01 NAbb 2m110y gd-fm Ch

Black Bullet (NZ)

105 **105**

9-y-o br g Silver Pistol (AUS)-Monte D'Oro (NZ) (Cache Of Gold (USA))
A Streeter Martin Jump

Placings:*0/0*34162/**3F2113/2U02**-P**P** (3998)
2001/02: 20^{P}HY, 19^{P}S

Black Fashion (IRE)

101 **100**

10-y-o br m Boreen (FR)-Thethingtodo (Kambalda)
P J Hobbs C De P Berry

Placings:400F0**P/4001/P021322-63105334** (3289)
2001/02: 24^{6}G, 21^{3}GF, 19^{1}S, 19^{0}GF, 21^{5}G, 20^{3}G, 22^{3}G, 21^{4}S

	Starts	1st	2nd	3rd	Win & Pl
Chases	8	1	0	3	3713
Career Total	**25**	**3**	**3**	**4**	**13961**

100	10/01	Chep	2m3f110y	G(0-90)HCh	SFT	£2023
99	10/00	Winc	3m1f110y	F(0-95)HCh	G-S	£3315
81	4/00	DRoy	3m	Ch	G-F	£2960

Total win prize-money £8298

Going: Sf: 1-2 GS: 0-0 Gd: 0-4 GF: - Fm: 0-2
Distance: 2m/2m3: 0-0 **2m4-2m7: 1-7** 3m+: 0-1
Track: **LH: 1-2** RH: 0-5 Tight: 0-3 Gall: 0-0
Aids: Bl: 0-0 Vi: 0-1 Tstrap: 0-0
Best Rating: **100** 1/02 Font 2m6f good Ch

Modest chaser who landed a seller at Chepstow in October. Genuine and jumps well enough.

Black Frost (IRE)

6-y-o ch g Glacial Storm (USA)-Black Tulip (Pals Passage)
H D Daly Trevor Hemmings

Placings:*23*-50 (3909)
2001/02: 16^{5}HY, 21^{0}G

	Starts	1st	2nd	3rd	Win & Pl
Hurdles	2	0	0	0	0
Career Total	**4**	**0**	**1**	**1**	**730**

Going: Sf: 0-1 GS: 0-0 Gd: 0-1 GF: - Fm: 0-0
Distance: 2m/2m3: 0-1 2m4-2m7: 0-1 3m+: 0-0
Track: LH: 0-1 RH: 0-1 Tight: 0-0 Gall: 0-0
Aids: Bl: 0-0 Vi: 0-0 Tstrap: 0-0
Best Rating: **111** 3/01 Hayd 2m heavy NHF

Black Ice Boy (IRE)

92 **80**

11-y-o b g Law Society (USA)-Hogan's Sister (USA) (Speak John)
R Bastiman Mrs Judith Marshall

Placings:6/P/0560/200/5/02-0400 (4196)
2001/02: 20^{0}G, 25^{4}GS, 24^{0}S, 27^{0}S

	Starts	1st	2nd	3rd	Win & Pl
Hurdles	4	0	0	0	
Career Total	**16**	**0**	**2**	**0**	**1212**

Going: Sf: 0-2 GS: 0-1 Gd: 0-1 GF: - Fm: 0-0
Distance: 2m/2m3: 0-0 2m4-2m7: 0-1 3m+: 0-3
Track: LH: 0-4 RH: 0-0 Tight: 0-1 Gall: 0-1
Aids: Bl: 0-3 Vi: 0-0 Tstrap: 0-0
Best Rating: **91** 11/98 Kels 2m6f110y soft Hdl

Black Is Beautiful (IRE)

99 **105**

10-y-o b/br g Black Minstrel-Sueyenka (Malinowski (USA))
Mrs M Reveley Frank Nolan

Placings:0U00/5404/104/6530-165 **(0961)**
2001/02: 16^{1}GF, 16^{6}GF, 16^{5}GF

	Starts	1st	2nd	3rd	Win & Pl
Chases	3	1	0	0	3290
Career Total	**18**	**2**	**0**	**1**	**6575**

97 5/01 Hntg 2m110y E Ch G-F £3290
84 6/99 Dund 2m135y Hdl G-F £2455
Total win prize-money £5745

Going: Sf: 0-0 GS: 0-0 Gd: 0-0 GF: - Fm: 1-3
Distance: **2m/2m3: 1-3** 2m4-2m7: 0-0 3m+: 0-0
Track: LH: 0-1 **RH: 1-2** Tight: 0-1 **Gall: 1-1**
Aids: Bl: 0-0 Vi: 0-0 Tstrap: 0-0
Best Rating: **105** 7/01 Sedg 2m110y gd-fm Ch

Black Jolly (IRE)

71f **74f**

7-y-o br g Jolly Jake (NZ)-Black Betty (Furry Glen)
M J Gingell B M Gray

Placings:*S0* **(2648)**
2001/02: 16^{S}S, 16^{0}GS

	Starts	1st	2nd	3rd	Win & Pl
NH Flat	2	0	0	0	
Career Total	**2**	**0**	**0**	**0**	

Going: Sf: 0-1 GS: 0-1 Gd: 0-0 GF: - Fm: 0-0
Distance: 2m/2m3: 0-2 2m4-2m7: 0-0 3m+: 0-0
Track: LH: 0-1 RH: 0-1 Tight: 0-1 Gall: 0-1
Aids: Bl: 0-0 Vi: 0-0 Tstrap: 0-0
Best Rating: **74** 12/01 Hntg 2m110y gd-sft NHF

Black Optimist (IRE)

104 **122**

8-y-o br g Roselier (FR)-Borys Glen (Furry Glen)
M Bradstock Ever The Optimists

Placings:2R **(4233)**
2001/02: 26^{2}HY, 32^{R}GS

	Starts	1st	2nd	3rd	Win & Pl
Chases	2	0	1	0	1220
Career Total	**2**	**0**	**1**	**0**	**1220**

Going: Sf: 0-1 GS: 0-1 Gd: 0-0 GF: - Fm: 0-0
Distance: 2m/2m3: 0-0 2m4-2m7: 0-0 3m+: 0-2
Track: LH: 0-1 RH: 0-0 Tight: 0-1 Gall: 0-1
Aids: Bl: 0-0 Vi: 0-0 Tstrap: 0-0
Best Rating: **122** 2/02 Font 3m2f110y heavy Ch

Black Rainbow (IRE)

91f **88f**

4-y-o br f Definite Article-Inonder (Belfort (FR))
A Dickman Mike Smallman

Placings:*43* **(3999)**
2001/02: 16^{4}S, 16^{3}S

	Starts	1st	2nd	3rd	Win & Pl
NH Flat	2	0	0	1	238
Career Total	**2**	**0**	**0**	**1**	**238**

Going: Sf: 0-2 GS: 0-0 Gd: 0-0 GF: - Fm: 0-0
Distance: 2m/2m3: 0-2 2m4-2m7: 0-0 3m+: 0-0
Track: LH: 0-2 RH: 0-0 Tight: 0-0 Gall: 0-2
Aids: Bl: 0-0 Vi: 0-0 Tstrap: 0-0
Best Rating: **84** 3/02 Donc 2m110y soft NHF

Has looked devoid of pace in mares' only bumpers.

Black Saint

94 **73**

5-y-o br g Perpendicular-Fool's Errand (Milford)
P Wegmann (B A McMahon 2/8) R Koniger

Placings:300P **(2716)**
2001/02: 16^{3}GS, 16^{0}GF, 16^{0}S, 19^{P}G

	Starts	1st	2nd	3rd	Win & Pl
Hurdles	4	0	0	1	339
Career Total	**4**	**0**	**0**	**1**	**339**

Going: Sf: 0-1 GS: 0-1 Gd: 0-1 GF: - Fm: 0-1
Distance: 2m/2m3: 0-3 2m4-2m7: 0-1 3m+: 0-0
Track: LH: 0-3 RH: 0-1 Tight: 0-2 Gall: 0-0
Aids: Bl: 0-0 Vi: 0-0 Tstrap: 0-1
Best Rating: **73** 7/01 Wolv 2m gd-sft Hdl

Black Secret

88 **76**

9-y-o br m Gildoran-Polypodium (Politico (USA))
R J Baker T Hubbard

Placings:1/2/P0-50 **(0799)**
2001/02: 17^{5}G, 17^{0}GF

	Starts	1st	2nd	3rd	Win & Pl
Hurdles	2	0	0	0	0
Career Total	**6**	**1**	**1**	**0**	**1665**

104 3/98 Folk 2m1f110y H NHF GD £1308
Total win prize-money £1308

Going: Sf: 0-0 GS: 0-0 Gd: 0-1 GF: - Fm: 0-1
Distance: 2m/2m3: 0-2 2m4-2m7: 0-0 3m+: 0-0
Track: LH: 0-2 RH: 0-0 Tight: 0-2 Gall: 0-0
Aids: Bl: 0-0 Vi: 0-0 Tstrap: 0-0
Best Rating: **104** 11/98 Extr 2m1f soft NHF

Black Weasel (IRE)

7-y-o br g Lahib (USA)-Glowlamp (IRE) (Glow (USA))
A Bailey S A Pritchard

Placings:05/120-4 **(0738)**
2001/02: 22^{4}GS

	Starts	1st	2nd	3rd	Win & Pl
Hurdles	1	0	0	0	0
Career Total	**6**	**1**	**1**	**0**	**3810**

92 8/00 Ctml 2m6f E Hdl GD £2852
Total win prize-money £2853

Going: Sf: 0-0 GS: 0-1 Gd: 0-0 GF: - Fm: 0-0
Distance: 2m/2m3: 0-0 2m4-2m7: 0-1 3m+: 0-0
Track: LH: 0-1 RH: 0-0 Tight: 0-1 Gall: 0-0
Aids: Bl: 0-0 Vi: 0-0 Tstrap: 0-0
Best Rating: **92** 8/00 Ctml 2m6f good Hdl

Black Zena (IRE)

72f **91f**

6-y-o b/br m Supreme Leader-Black Gayle (IRE) (Strong Gale)
G M Lyons Mrs Alix Stevenson

Placings:*400* **(4841)**
2001/02: 16^{4}Y, 16^{0}Y, 16^{0}G

	Starts	1st	2nd	3rd	Win & Pl
NH Flat	3	0	0	0	323
Career Total	**3**	**0**	**0**	**0**	**323**

Going: Sf: 0-0 GS: 0-0 Gd: 0-1 GF: - Fm: 0-0
Distance: 2m/2m3: 0-3 2m4-2m7: 0-0 3m+: 0-0
Track: LH: 0-1 RH: 0-0 Tight: 0-0 Gall: 0-0
Aids: Bl: 0-0 Vi: 0-0 Tstrap: 0-3
Best Rating: **91** 12/01 Navn 2m yield NHF

Blackberry Way

8-y-o ch m Almoojid-Prickly Path (Royal Match)
Dr J R J Naylor Mrs Stella Watson

Placings:P-5 **(0191)**
2001/02: 23^{5}GF

	Starts	1st	2nd	3rd	Win & Pl
Hurdles	1	0	0	0	0
Career Total	**2**	**0**	**0**	**0**	**0**

Going: Sf: 0-0 GS: 0-0 Gd: 0-0 GF: - Fm: 0-1
Distance: 2m/2m3: 0-0 2m4-2m7: 0-0 3m+: 0-1
Track: LH: 0-1 RH: 0-0 Tight: 0-1 Gall: 0-0
Aids: Bl: 0-0 Vi: 0-0 Tstrap: 0-0
Best Rating: **83** 5/01 Fknm 2m7f110y gd-fm Hdl

Lightly-raced ex-pointer, appreciates fast ground. Won over two and a half miles at Huntingdon in May 2002.

Blackchesters

9-y-o bl g Genuine Gift (CAN)-Newgrove (Cantab)
Mrs Antonia Bealby (Tim Brown 10/3) Irvin S Naylor

Placings:4530 **(4678)**
2001/02: 24^{4}GS, 21^{5}G, 25^{3}G, 25^{0}G

	Starts	1st	2nd	3rd	Win & Pl
Chases	4	0	0	1	393
Career Total	**4**	**0**	**0**	**1**	**393**

Going: Sf: 0-0 GS: 0-1 Gd: 0-3 GF: - Fm: 0-0
Distance: 2m/2m3: 0-0 2m4-2m7: 0-1 3m+: 0-3
Track: LH: 0-2 RH: 0-1 Tight: 0-2 Gall: 0-0
Aids: Bl: 0-0 Vi: 0-0 Tstrap: 0-0
Best Rating: **94** 5/01 Chel 2m5f good Ch

Blackchurch Lass (IRE)

4-y-o b f Taum Go Leor (IRE)-Melons Lady (IRE) (The

Noble Player (USA))
Brendan W Duke Brendan W Duke Racing

Placings:03P (4575)
2001/02: 16^{0}S, 17^{3}S, 20^{P}G

	Starts	1st	2nd	3rd	Win & Pl
NH Flat	1	0	0	0	0
Hurdles	2	0	0	1	446
Career Total	**3**	**0**	**0**	**1**	**446**

Going: Sf: 0-2 GS: 0-0 Gd: 0-1 GF: - Fm: 0-0
Distance: 2m/2m3: 0-2 2m4-2m7: 0-1 3m+: 0-0
Track: LH: 0-2 RH: 0-1 Tight: 0-1 Gall: 0-0
Aids: Bl: 0-0 Vi: 0-0 Tstrap: 0-1
Best Rating: **47** 2/02 Asct 2m110y soft NHF

Blackjack Lir

8-y-o b g Lir-Miss Black Glama (Derrylin)
P R Rodford P R Rodford

Placings:0 (0559)
2001/02: 22^{0}GF

	Starts	1st	2nd	3rd	Win & Pl
Hurdles	1	0	0	0	
Career Total	**1**	**0**	**0**	**0**	

Going: Sf: 0-0 GS: 0-0 Gd: 0-0 GF: - Fm: 0-1
Distance: 2m/2m3: 0-0 2m4-2m7: 0-1 3m+: 0-0
Track: LH: 0-1 RH: 0-0 Tight: 0-1 Gall: 0-0
Aids: Bl: 0-0 Vi: 0-0 Tstrap: 0-0
Best Rating:

Blackwater Bay (IRE)

83 93
8-y-o br m Supreme Leader-Maypole Gayle (Strong Gale)
J Neville M Andrews

Placings:26/251320/0P0004-F0 (0775)
2001/02: 21^{F}G, 20^{0}GF

	Starts	1st	2nd	3rd	Win & Pl
Hurdles	2	0	0	0	
Career Total	**16**	**1**	**3**	**1**	**4606**

102	2/00	Newc	2m	E Hdl	SFT	£2537

Total win prize-money £2538

Going: Sf: 0-0 GS: 0-0 Gd: 0-1 GF: - Fm: 0-1
Distance: 2m/2m3: 0-0 2m4-2m7: 0-2 3m+: 0-0
Track: LH: 0-1 RH: 0-0 Tight: 0-0 Gall: 0-0
Aids: Bl: 0-0 Vi: 0-0 Tstrap: 0-0
Best Rating: **105** 4/00 Tntn 2m1f gd-sft Hdl

Blackwater Brave (IRE)

112 128
9-y-o b g Commanche Run-Ardmore Lady (Quayside)
P F Nicholls Mrs Bunty Millard

Placings:4/24P23/0/1123P-15PUP (3388)
2001/02: 25^{1}G, 26^{5}G, 32^{P}GS, 25^{U}G, 25^{P}GS

	Starts	1st	2nd	3rd	Win & Pl
Chases	5	1	0	0	5421
Career Total	**17**	**3**	**3**	**2**	**19710**

128	10/01	Winc	3m1f110y	F(0-110)HCh	GD	£5421
118	11/00	Winc	2m5f	F(0-105)Ch	SFT	£3536
112	11/00	Winc	3m1f110y	E(0-105)HCh	G-S	£6987

Total win prize-money £15945

Going: Sf: 0-0 GS: 0-2 Gd: 1-3 GF: - Fm: 0-0
Distance: 2m/2m3: 0-0 2m4-2m7: 0-0 **3m+: 1-5**
Track: LH: 0-1 **RH: 1-3** Tight: 0-1 Gall: 0-0
Aids: Bl: 0-1 Vi: 0-0 Tstrap: 0-0
Best Rating: **128** 10/01 Winc 3m1f110y good Ch

Fair handicap chaser, stays three miles plus, suited by right-handed tracks. Goes well fresh and likes Wincanton.

Blade Of Fortune

14-y-o b g Beldale Flutter (USA)-Foil 'Em (USA) (Blade (USA))
V G Greenway V G Greenway

Placings:460102/5110400140/616405/0636502P/0P44-P (4483)
2001/02: 19^{P}G

	Starts	1st	2nd	3rd	Win & Pl
Chases	1	0	0	0	
Career Total	**35**	**5**	**2**	**1**	**14564**

105	11/98	NAbb	2m110y	E(0-105)HCh	SFT	£4492
90	3/98	Tntn	2m1f	G(0-95)HHdl	G-S	£1551
95	5/97	NAbb	2m1f	F(0-105)HHdl	G-S	£1971
90	5/97	Chep	2m110y	F Hdl	G-S	£2108
95	2/97	Tntn	2m1f	G(0-95)HHdl	G-S	£1931

Total win prize-money £12054

Going: Sf: 0-0 GS: 0-0 Gd: 0-1 GF: - Fm: 0-0
Distance: 2m/2m3: 0-0 2m4-2m7: 0-1 3m+: 0-0
Track: LH: 0-0 RH: 0-1 Tight: 0-0 Gall: 0-0
Aids: Bl: 0-0 Vi: 0-0 Tstrap: 0-0
Best Rating: **105** 12/98 NAbb 2m110y soft Ch

Blagdon Hill (IRE)

105
6-y-o b g Spanish Place (USA)-Fairogan (Tarqogan)
P J Hobbs R H Dunn

Placings:60545-F (1497)
2001/02: 19^{F}GF

	Starts	1st	2nd	3rd	Win & Pl
Hurdles	1	0	0	0	
Career Total	**6**	**0**	**0**	**0**	**0**

Going: Sf: 0-0 GS: 0-0 Gd: 0-0 GF: - Fm: 0-1
Distance: 2m/2m3: 0-1 2m4-2m7: 0-0 3m+: 0-0
Track: LH: 0-0 RH: 0-1 Tight: 0-0 Gall: 0-0
Aids: Bl: 0-0 Vi: 0-0 Tstrap: 0-0
Best Rating: **107** 10/00 Extr 2m1f good NHF

Blakeney Coast (IRE)

86f 91f
5-y-o b g Satco (FR)-Up To More Trix (IRE) (Torus)
Mrs M Reveley Cristiana's Crew

Placings:660 (4019)
2001/02: 16^{6}GS, 16^{6}HY, 16^{0}GS

	Starts	1st	2nd	3rd	Win & Pl
NH Flat	3	0	0	0	0
Career Total	**3**	**0**	**0**	**0**	**0**

Going: Sf: 0-1 GS: 0-2 Gd: 0-0 GF: - Fm: 0-0
Distance: 2m/2m3: 0-3 2m4-2m7: 0-0 3m+: 0-0
Track: LH: 0-2 RH: 0-1 Tight: 0-0 Gall: 0-2
Aids: Bl: 0-0 Vi: 0-0 Tstrap: 0-0
Best Rating: **91** 12/01 Hntg 2m110y gd-sft NHF

Blakeney Hill

7-y-o ch m Baron Blakeney-Hillgate Lady (Rustingo)
Mrs N S Sharpe Miss M J Ward

Placings:00P (4385)
2001/02: 17^{0}G, 17^{0}S, 22^{P}S

	Starts	1st	2nd	3rd	Win & Pl
NH Flat	2	0	0	0	0
Hurdles	1	0	0	0	0
Career Total	**3**	**0**	**0**	**0**	

Going: Sf: 0-2 GS: 0-0 Gd: 0-1 GF: - Fm: 0-0
Distance: 2m/2m3: 0-2 2m4-2m7: 0-1 3m+: 0-0
Track: LH: 0-0 RH: 0-3 Tight: 0-0 Gall: 0-0
Aids: Bl: 0-0 Vi: 0-0 Tstrap: 0-0
Best Rating: **17** 12/01 Hrfd 2m1f soft NHF

Blakeneys Ghost

8-y-o gr m Baron Blakeney-Night Pry (Pry)
S J Gilmore R A Jeffery

Placings:00/PP/P6P (3159)
2001/02: 16^{P}S, 21^{6}G, 19^{P}S

	Starts	1st	2nd	3rd	Win & Pl
Hurdles	3	0	0	0	0
Career Total	**7**	**0**	**0**	**0**	**0**

Going: Sf: 0-2 GS: 0-0 Gd: 0-1 GF: - Fm: 0-0
Distance: 2m/2m3: 0-1 2m4-2m7: 0-2 3m+: 0-0
Track: LH: 0-0 RH: 0-2 Tight: 0-0 Gall: 0-0
Aids: Bl: 0-0 Vi: 0-1 Tstrap: 0-0
Best Rating:

Blank Cheque

12-y-o b g Idiots Delight-Quickapenny (Espresso)
J J Coates J J Coates

Placings:503P/3/3/4-0 (0090)
2001/02: 25^{0}S

	Starts	1st	2nd	3rd	Win & Pl
Chases	1	0	0	0	
Career Total	**8**	**0**	**0**	**3**	**1131**

Going: Sf: 0-1 GS: 0-0 Gd: 0-0 GF: - Fm: 0-0
Distance: 2m/2m3: 0-0 2m4-2m7: 0-0 3m+: 0-1
Track: LH: 0-1 RH: 0-0 Tight: 0-0 Gall: 0-0
Aids: Bl: 0-0 Vi: 0-0 Tstrap: 0-0
Best Rating: **106** 4/98 Chel 3m1f110y good Ch

Blanville (FR)

13-y-o b g Pot D'Or (FR)-Nordica Iii (FR) (Orvilliers)
M C Pipe P A D Scouller

Placings:2/2/11-1P (0584)
2001/02: 26^{1}G, 28^{P}GF

	Starts	1st	2nd	3rd	Win & Pl
Chases	2	1	0	0	8775
Career Total	**6**	**3**	**2**	**0**	**29121**

139	5/01	Chel	3m2f110y	H Ch	GD	£8775
148	4/01	Newb	3m2f110y	H Ch	SFT	£2926
115	5/00	Strf	3m	H Ch	GD	£2268

Total win prize-money £13969

Going: Sf: 0-0 GS: 0-0 Gd: 1-1 GF: - Fm: 0-1
Distance: 2m/2m3: 0-0 2m4-2m7: 0-0 **3m+: 1-2**
Track: LH: 0-1 RH: 0-0 Tight: 0-1 Gall: 0-0
Aids: Bl: 0-0 Vi: 0-0 Tstrap: 0-0
Best Rating: **148** 4/01 Newb 3m2f110y soft Ch

Twice placed in the French Grand National, he was unbeaten in completed point to points and quickly developed into a top-class hunter chaser. He pulled up in June 2001 at Stratford and has not been seen since. Best on soft ground and a thorough stayer.

Blarney Stone (IRE)

97 **67**

8-y-o ch g Commanche Run-Lils Girl (Dunphy)
Miss Kate Milligan Miss A M Smith

Placings: *20*/200-0PP6 **(3350)**
2001/02: 22^{0}GS, 27^{P}S, 16^{P}GF, 20^{6}G

	Starts	1st	2nd	3rd	Win & Pl
Hurdles	4	0	0	0	0
Career Total	**9**	**0**	**2**	**0**	**914**

Going: Sf: 0-1 GS: 0-1 Gd: 0-1 GF: - Fm: 0-1
Distance: 2m/2m3: 0-1 2m4-2m7: 0-2 3m+: 0-1
Track: LH: 0-3 RH: 0-1 Tight: 0-4 Gall: 0-0
Aids: Bl: 0-0 Vi: 0-0 Tstrap: 0-0
Best Rating: **96** 10/00 MRas 2m1f110y good NHF

Blasket Sound (IRE)

105(42c) **110**

10-y-o b g Lancastrian-June's Friend (Laurence O)
D J Wintle R H L Barnes

Placings: 541235**331/464UP643201****45FU**/45**PU3F1143/2**64
221P0-20P0P216 **(4059)**
2001/02: 27^{2}G, 20^{0}GF, 22^{P}GF, 20^{0}S, 24^{P}G, 26^{2}S, 26^{1}S, 27^{6}S

	Starts	1st	2nd	3rd	Win & Pl
Hurdles	8	1	2	0	4268
Career Total	**50**	**7**	**7**	**6**	**31423**

100	2/02	Hntg	3m2f	E(0-110)HHdl	SFT	£2576
113	3/01	Hntg	3m2f	F(0-110)HHdl	SFT	£2051
115	3/00	Towc	3m1f	D(0-120)HCh	SFT	£3848
110	3/00	Chep	3m2f110y	E(0-115)HCh	HVY	£2879
110	1/99	Naas	3m	(0-116)HCh	HVY	£3989
103	4/98	Clon	3m	Ch	HVY	£1935
104	11/97	Limk	2m4f	Hdl	HVY	£2712

Total win prize-money £19994

Going: Sf: 1-4 GS: 0-0 Gd: 0-2 GF: - Fm: 0-2
Distance: 2m/2m3: 0-0 2m4-2m7: 0-3 **3m+: 1-5**
Track: LH: 0-5 **RH: 1-3** Tight: 0-4 **Gall: 1-1**
Aids: Bl: 0-0 Vi: 0-0 Tstrap: 0-0
Best Rating: **115** 3/00 Towc 3m1f soft Ch

Modest staying hurdler, he acts on an easy surface and is best around three miles two.

Blayney Dancer

75 **32**

5-y-o b g Contract Law (USA)-Lady Poly (Dunbeath (USA))
J J O'Neill (Jamie Poulton 25/10) Mrs M Liston

Placings: 2015-0 **(3229)**
2001/02: 21^{0}GS

	Starts	1st	2nd	3rd	Win & Pl
Hurdles	1	0	0	0	
Career Total	**5**	**1**	**1**	**0**	**4273**
96 10/00 Kemp 2m	D Hdl			G-S	£3412

Total win prize-money £3413

Going: Sf: 0-0 GS: 0-1 Gd: 0-0 GF: - Fm: 0-0
Distance: 2m/2m3: 0-0 2m4-2m7: 0-1 3m+: 0-0
Track: LH: 0-0 RH: 0-1 Tight: 0-0 Gall: 0-1
Aids: Bl: 0-0 Vi: 0-0 Tstrap: 0-0
Best Rating: **96** 10/00 Kemp 2m gd-sft Hdl

Blaze Of Oak (USA)

79 **82**

11-y-o ch g Green Forest (USA)-Magic Robe (USA) (Grey Dawn Ii)
M R Bosley Mrs Hilary Putt

Placings: 530/260P/066/511201/4466P/4243-0 **(0052)**
2001/02: 20^{0}G

	Starts	1st	2nd	3rd	Win & Pl
Hurdles	1	0	0	0	
Career Total	**26**	**3**	**3**	**2**	**8257**

96	4/99	Tntn	2m3f110y	G(0-100)HHdl	G-S	£1720
96	3/99	Plum	2m4f	F(0-100)HHdl	SFT	£2232
98	3/99	Tntn	2m1f	G(0-95)HHdl	SFT	£1621

Total win prize-money £5575

Going: Sf: 0-0 GS: 0-0 Gd: 0-1 GF: - Fm: 0-0
Distance: 2m/2m3: 0-0 2m4-2m7: 0-1 3m+: 0-0
Track: LH: 0-1 RH: 0-0 Tight: 0-1 Gall: 0-0
Aids: Bl: 0-0 Vi: 0-0 Tstrap: 0-0
Best Rating: **103** 12/95 Hrfd 2m1f good Hdl

Blaze Of Song

10-y-o ch g Jester-Intellect (Frimley Park)
William Hayes Mrs L P Vaughan

Placings: 6406/45334U300P/52/PPPP5P5/24P6-P **(4376)**
2001/02: 20^{P}S

	Starts	1st	2nd	3rd	Win & Pl
Chases	1	0	0	0	
Career Total	**28**	**0**	**2**	**3**	**2666**

Going: Sf: 0-1 GS: 0-0 Gd: 0-0 GF: - Fm: 0-0
Distance: 2m/2m3: 0-0 2m4-2m7: 0-1 3m+: 0-0
Track: LH: 0-0 RH: 0-1 Tight: 0-1 Gall: 0-0
Aids: Bl: 0-0 Vi: 0-0 Tstrap: 0-0
Best Rating: **96** 5/98 Hrfd 2m3f110y good Hdl

Blazing Batman

102 **107**

9-y-o ch g Shaab-Cottage Blaze (Sunyboy)
Dr P Pritchard Docs'R'Us

Placings: *50*/**42/F/FP04-PU415P41542PP0** **(4814)**
2001/02: 24^{P}GF, 23^{U}GF, 24^{4}G, 24^{1}GF, 23^{5}GF, 22^{P}S, 25^{4}G, 29^{1}S, 24^{5}G, 21^{4}HY, 16^{2}S, 26^{P}HY, 26^{P}GS, 21^{0}GF

	Starts	1st	2nd	3rd	Win & Pl
Chases	14	2	1	0	10236
Career Total	**23**	**2**	**2**	**0**	**12194**

103	11/01	Fknm	3m5f110y	F(0-100)HCh	SFT	£4123
103	7/01	Sthl	3m110y	E Ch	G-F	£3406

Total win prize-money £7530

Going: Sf: 1-5 GS: 0-1 Gd: 0-3 GF: - Fm: 1-5
Distance: 2m/2m3: 0-1 2m4-2m7: 0-3 **3m+: 2-10**
Track: **LH: 1-9** RH: 0-4 **Tight: 1-5** Gall: 0-2
Aids: Bl: 0-0 Vi: 0-0 Tstrap: 0-0
Best Rating: **111** 1/01 Weth 2m4f110y heavy Ch

Moderate staying chaser who won at Southwell and Fakenham in the second half of 2001. Suited by a sharp track and acts on any ground.

Blazing Hills

108(93h) (77h)**110**

6-y-o ch g Shaab-Cottage Blaze (Sunyboy)
K C Bailey Mrs Julie Martin

Placings: *0*-5623B**115** **(1771)**
2001/02: 26^{5}G, 24^{6}G, 26^{2}F, 26^{3}GF, 24^{B}GF, 26^{1}GF, 25^{1}G, 25^{5}GS

	Starts	1st	2nd	3rd	Win & Pl
Hurdles	4	0	1	0	908
Chases	4	2	0	1	7005
Career Total	**9**	**2**	**1**	**1**	**7913**

110	10/01	Towc	3m1f	F(0-90)HCh	GD	£3562
101	9/01	Uttx	3m2f	E Ch	G-F	£3012

Total win prize-money £6575

Going: Sf: 0-0 GS: 0-1 Gd: 1-3 GF: - Fm: 1-4
Distance: 2m/2m3: 0-0 2m4-2m7: 0-0 **3m+: 2-8**
Track: LH: 1-4 RH: 1-3 Tight: 0-2 Gall: 0-0
Aids: **Bl: 1-2** Vi: 0-0 Tstrap: 0-0
Best Rating: **110** 10/01 Towc 3m1f good Ch

A promising young staying chaser, he won at Uttoxeter before defying 12 stone in first-time blinkers at Towcester.

Blazing Storm (IRE)

40

10-y-o ch g Keen-Raging Storm (Horage)
Mrs P Ford K R Ford

Placings: *015064/232***F5/PU36114**/446*0*-**06P5P** **(4020)**
2001/02: 24^{0}GF, 16^{6}G, 25^{P}G, 16^{5}S, 24^{P}S

	Starts	1st	2nd	3rd	Win & Pl
Chases	5	0	0	0	0
Career Total	**27**	**3**	**2**	**2**	**14536**

112	11/99	Chep	2m110y	E(0-115)HCh	SFT	£2821
112	10/99	Chel	2m	D Ch	GD	£5199
99	5/96	Tipp	2m4f	NHF	GD	£2824

Total win prize-money £10845

Going: Sf: 0-2 GS: 0-0 Gd: 0-2 GF: - Fm: 0-1
Distance: 2m/2m3: 0-2 2m4-2m7: 0-0 3m+: 0-3
Track: LH: 0-1 RH: 0-3 Tight: 0-2 Gall: 0-1
Aids: Bl: 0-0 Vi: 0-0 Tstrap: 0-0
Best Rating: **112** 11/99 Chel 2m good Ch

Bless Yourself (IRE)

35f

6-y-o b g Shardari-Wee Madge (Apollo Eight)
D McCain John Singleton

Placings: *0* **(2321)**
2001/02: 17^{0}GS

	Starts	1st	2nd	3rd	Win & Pl
NH Flat	1	0	0	0	
Career Total	**1**	**0**	**0**	**0**	

Going: Sf: 0-0 GS: 0-1 Gd: 0-0 GF: - Fm: 0-0
Distance: 2m/2m3: 0-1 2m4-2m7: 0-0 3m+: 0-0
Track: LH: 0-0 RH: 0-0 Tight: 0-0 Gall: 0-0
Aids: Bl: 0-0 Vi: 0-0 Tstrap: 0-0
Best Rating: **35** 11/01 Aint 2m1f gd-sft NHF

Blessed Oliver

12-y-o ch g Relkino-Oca (O'Grady)
N A Twiston-Davies O D Plunkett

Placings:14P435/**3F/P** (0429)
2001/02: 25^{P}G

	Starts	1st	2nd	3rd	Win & Pl
Chases	1	0	0	0	
Career Total	**9**	**1**	**0**	**2**	**3197**

80	10/95	Ludl	2m5f110y	E Hdl	FRM	£2094

Total win prize-money £2094

Going: Sf: 0-0 GS: 0-0 Gd: 0-1 GF: - Fm: 0-0
Distance: 2m/2m3: 0-0 2m4-2m7: 0-0 3m+: 0-1
Track: LH: 0-0 RH: 0-0 Tight: 0-0 Gall: 0-0
Aids: Bl: 0-0 Vi: 0-0 Tstrap: 0-0
Best Rating: **97** 4/96 Extr 2m3f110y good Hdl

Bleu Superbe (FR)

110 **145**

7-y-o b g Epervier Bleu-Brett's Dream (FR) (Pharly (FR))
Miss Venetia Williams P A Deal

Placings:111113/F603P122/**5PPP13P-F3P** (4876)
2001/02: 16^{F}G, 16^{3}G, 20^{P}G

	Starts	1st	2nd	3rd	Win & Pl
Chases	3	0	0	1	1085
Career Total	**24**	**7**	**2**	**4**	**108184**

145	3/01	Hayd	2m	D(0-120)HCh	HVY	£7117
	1/00	Cagn	2m7f	Ch	SFT	£21133
	3/99	Pau	2m2f110y	Ch	VS	£7535
	1/99	Pau	2m2f	Hdl	VS	£15070
	1/99	Pau	2m2f	Hdl	HVY	£7535
	12/98	Bord	2m2f	Hdl	VS	£5051
	11/98	Bord	2m2f	Hdl	VS	£3030

Total win prize-money £66472

Going: Sf: 0-0 GS: 0-0 Gd: 0-3 GF: - Fm: 0-0
Distance: 2m/2m3: 0-2 2m4-2m7: 0-1 3m+: 0-0
Track: LH: 0-2 RH: 0-1 Tight: 0-1 Gall: 0-0
Aids: Bl: 0-0 Vi: 0-0 Tstrap: 0-0
Best Rating: **145** 4/01 Kemp 2m good Ch

Successful over three miles in France, he was very disappointing until winning over the minimum trip at Haydock in March 2001. Off the track for ten months until finishing third in the same race in 2002. Easy winner at Aintree and Towcester in May and his jumping is improving.

Blin (CZE)

92 **71**

7-y-o ch g Lincoln (CZE)-Brenda (CZE) (Coulstry)
Josef Piruch West Country Racing

Placings:54650 (2146)
2001/02: 23^{5}G, 21^{4}G, 29^{6}G, 26^{5}GF, 31^{0}G

	Starts	1st	2nd	3rd	Win & Pl
Chases	5	0	0	0	
Career Total	**5**	**0**	**0**	**0**	

Going: Sf: 0-0 GS: 0-0 Gd: 0-4 GF: - Fm: 0-1
Distance: 2m/2m3: 0-0 2m4-2m7: 0-2 3m+: 0-3
Track: LH: 0-1 RH: 0-0 Tight: 0-0 Gall: 0-0
Aids: Bl: 0-0 Vi: 0-0 Tstrap: 0-0
Best Rating: **71** 11/01 Chel 3m7f good Ch

Bloomfield Storm (IRE)

92 **122**

9-y-o b g Glacial Storm (USA)-Mylie's Response (Moyrath Response)
K C Bailey W H Ponsonby

Placings:11464/**4P-353** (4549)
2001/02: 20^{3}G, 27^{5}G, 24^{3}GF

	Starts	1st	2nd	3rd	Win & Pl
Chases	3	0	0	2	1247
Career Total	**10**	**2**	**0**	**2**	**10396**

148	1/00	Leic	2m4f110y	D Ch	GD	£4615
117	12/99	Hrfd	2m	F Ch	SFT	£2567

Total win prize-money £7182

Going: Sf: 0-0 GS: 0-0 Gd: 0-2 GF: - Fm: 0-1
Distance: 2m/2m3: 0-0 2m4-2m7: 0-1 3m+: 0-2
Track: LH: 0-1 RH: 0-2 Tight: 0-1 Gall: 0-1
Aids: Bl: 0-0 Vi: 0-0 Tstrap: 0-0
Best Rating: **148** 1/00 Leic 2m4f110y good Ch

Winner of his first two starts over fences in fine style in 1999/2000 season, he beat quite a decent field on the second occasion, but has lost his way since. Best form around two and a half miles. Acts on good to soft/soft ground.

Blotoft

91(93h) (73h)**68**

10-y-o b g High Kicker (USA)-Foothold (Hotfoot)
S Gollings R N Forman

Placings:002P/0614/130/4443024/0R146**2203661/0232534 4500-0P** (0882)
2001/02: 21^{0}GF, 17^{P}G

	Starts	1st	2nd	3rd	Win & Pl
Chases	2	0	0	0	
Career Total	**43**	**4**	**6**	**5**	**18141**

97	4/00	MRas	2m1f110y	F(0-105)HCh	G-F	£3029
87	10/99	Fknm	2m	G(0-95)HHdl	GD	£1811
81	5/97	Uttx	2m	G(0-95)HHdl	G-S	£1878
78	3/97	Fknm	2m	G(0-90)HHdl	GD	£3071

Total win prize-money £9791

Going: Sf: 0-0 GS: 0-0 Gd: 0-1 GF: - Fm: 0-1
Distance: 2m/2m3: 0-1 2m4-2m7: 0-1 3m+: 0-0
Track: LH: 0-1 RH: 0-1 Tight: 0-2 Gall: 0-0
Aids: Bl: 0-0 Vi: 0-0 Tstrap: 0-0
Best Rating: **97** 6/00 Uttx 2m good Ch

Blowing Away (IRE)

83(87h) (66h)**70**

8-y-o b/br m Last Tycoon-Taken By Force (Persian Bold)
J E Long (Julian Poulton 11/2) Mrs Elizabeth Reed

Placings:301/6365F (4780)
2001/02: 18^{6}G, 16^{3}G, 16^{6}S, 16^{5}HY, 17^{F}GF

	Starts	1st	2nd	3rd	Win & Pl
Hurdles	4	0	0	1	545
Chases	1	0	0	0	0
Career Total	**8**	**1**	**0**	**2**	**2456**

71	3/98	Uttx	2m	G Hdl	GD	£1595

Total win prize-money £1595

Going: Sf: 0-2 GS: 0-0 Gd: 0-2 GF: - Fm: 0-1
Distance: 2m/2m3: 0-5 2m4-2m7: 0-0 3m+: 0-0
Track: LH: 0-4 RH: 0-1 Tight: 0-4 Gall: 0-0
Aids: Bl: 0-0 Vi: 0-0 Tstrap: 0-0
Best Rating: **80** 2/98 Catt 2m good Hdl

Blowing Rock (IRE)

111 **136**

10-y-o b g Strong Gale-Poor Elsie (Crash Course)
Miss H C Knight Mrs Peter Andrews

Placings:562/P21404/**S1F0423/2U24212/1U340-2122501** (4549)
2001/02: 25^{2}GF, 25^{1}G, 23^{2}GF, 20^{2}G, 24^{5}GS, 25^{0}G, 24^{1}GF

	Starts	1st	2nd	3rd	Win & Pl
Chases	7	2	3	0	14736
Career Total	**35**	**6**	**10**	**2**	**40106**

136	4/02	Hntg	3m	D(0-120)HCh	G-F	£3952
131	5/01	Hrfd	3m1f110y	E(0-115)HCh	GD	£4338
116	5/00	MRas	3m1f	E(0-115)HCh	G-F	£4290
112	11/99	Leic	2m7f110y	E(0-115)HCh	G-F	£3525
104	5/98	Towc	2m6f	E(0-100)HCh	G-F	£3315
104	10/97	Chel	2m110y	D Hdl	G-F	£2918

Total win prize-money £22340

Going: Sf: 0-0 GS: 0-1 Gd: 1-3 GF: - Fm: 1-3
Distance: 2m/2m3: 0-0 2m4-2m7: 0-1 **3m+: 2-6**
Track: LH: 0-1 **RH: 2-6** Tight: 0-0 **Gall: 1-2**
Aids: Bl: 0-0 Vi: 0-0 Tstrap: 0-0
Best Rating: **136** 4/02 Hntg 3m gd-fm Ch

Useful handicap chaser. Inclined to run in snatches though. He is best in small fields and needs a decent surface. Usually kept to right-handed tracks. Stays three miles.

Blowing Wind (FR)

115 **160**

9-y-o b/br g Fabulous Dancer (USA)-Bassita (Bustino)
M C Pipe P A Deal

Placings:02403111/4F2B0/**4112106/303113-P513** (4677)
2001/02: 20^{P}G, 16^{5}GS, 20^{1}GS, 36^{3}G

	Starts	1st	2nd	3rd	Win & Pl
Chases	4	1	0	1	100500
Career Total	**30**	**9**	**3**	**5**	**278289**

160	3/02	Chel	2m4f110y	A HCh	G-S	£45500
144	2/01	Sand	2m	B HCh	HVY	£10071
157	1/01	Donc	2m3f110y	C(0-130)HCh	GD	£6545
150	2/00	Asct	2m3f110y	B Ch	G-S	£10114
148	1/00	Leic	2m	E Ch	GD	£3315
128	12/99	Ludl	2m	E Ch	G-S	£3048
155	4/98	Ayr	2m	A HHdl	GD	£15669
156	3/98	Chel	2m1f	A HHdl	GD	£26974
147	3/98	Sand	2m110y	B(0-150)HHdl	SFT	£21495

Total win prize-money £142735

Going: Sf: 0-0 GS: 1-2 Gd: 0-2 GF: - Fm: 0-0
Distance: 2m/2m3: 0-1 **2m4-2m7: 1-2** 3m+: 0-1
Track: **LH: 1-2** RH: 0-2 Tight: 0-1 **Gall: 1-1**
Aids: Bl: 0-0 Vi: 0-0 Tstrap: 0-0
Best Rating: **160** 3/02 Chel 2m4f110y gd-sft Ch

Previously a useful hurdler and decent novice in 1999/2000, he was carried out by a loose horse at the 19th in the 2001 Grand National, but eventually carried on to finish a very remote third. He returned from a break at Kempton in January of 2002, but was below his best until running out a surprise winner of the Mildmay of Flete at the Festival. Seemed not to fully see out the trip when a remote third in this year's National. Acts on good, soft and heavy ground.

Blue (IRE)

109 **118**

6-y-o b h Bluebird (USA)-Watership (USA) (Foolish Pleasure (USA))
Noel Meade The High Street Racing Synd

Placings:0-33121000 (4712a)
2001/02: 16^{3}F, 16^{3}GY, 16^{1}G, 16^{2}GF, 16^{1}GF, 16^{0}G, 16^{0}YS, 16^{0}Y

	Starts	1st	2nd	3rd	Win & Pl
Hurdles	8	2	1	2	25919
Career Total	**9**	**2**	**1**	**2**	**25919**

118	9/01	List	2m	HHdl	G-F	£18830

110	8/01	Kbgn	2m	Hdl	GD	£4451

Total win prize-money £23283

Going: Sf: 0-0 GS: 0-0 Gd: 1-2 GF: - Fm: 1-3
Distance: **2m/2m3: 2-8** 2m4-2m7: 0-0 3m+: 0-0
Track: **LH: 1-3** RH: 0-2 Tight: 0-0 Gall: 0-0
Aids: Bl: 0-2 Vi: 0-0 Tstrap: 0-0
Best Rating: **118** 9/01 List 2m gd-fm Hdl

Won a maiden hurdle in August of 2001, he was then a good second, before gaining another victory at the end of September in a handicap hurdle. Beaten in decent handicaps since, he acts on most types of ground, and is suited by two miles.

Blue Anchor

7-y-o b g Robellino (USA)-Fair Seas (General Assembly (USA))
D R Wellicome D R Wellicome

Placings:0/P (1087)
2001/02: 16^{P}GF

	Starts	1st	2nd	3rd	Win & Pl
Hurdles	1	0	0	0	
Career Total	**2**	**0**	**0**	**0**	

Going: Sf: 0-0 GS: 0-0 Gd: 0-0 GF: - Fm: 0-1
Distance: 2m/2m3: 0-1 2m4-2m7: 0-0 3m+: 0-0
Track: LH: 0-1 RH: 0-0 Tight: 0-0 Gall: 0-0
Aids: Bl: 0-0 Vi: 0-0 Tstrap: 0-0
Best Rating: **53** 12/98 Leic 2m gd-sft Hdl

Blue Bud

29

8-y-o b g Lord Bud-Hodsock Venture (Major Portion)
Mrs M Reveley R & H Burridge, M Matheson, A S Wing

Placings:045/620P/032040-00 (0225)
2001/02: 21^{0}G, 24^{0}GF

	Starts	1st	2nd	3rd	Win & Pl
Hurdles	1	0	0	0	0
Chases	1	0	0	0	0
Career Total	**15**	**0**	**2**	**1**	**2016**

Going: Sf: 0-0 GS: 0-0 Gd: 0-1 GF: - Fm: 0-1
Distance: 2m/2m3: 0-0 2m4-2m7: 0-1 3m+: 0-1
Track: LH: 0-2 RH: 0-0 Tight: 0-1 Gall: 0-0
Aids: Bl: 0-1 Vi: 0-0 Tstrap: 0-0
Best Rating: **106** 2/99 Hayd 2m soft NHF

Blue Chieftain

8-y-o gr g Zambrano-Lady Crusty (Golden Dipper)
L P Grassick Baskerville Racing Club

Placings:000/0005P/P0P00 (4850)
2001/02: 24^{P}S, 20^{0}S, 21^{P}S, 20^{0}S, 22^{0}G

	Starts	1st	2nd	3rd	Win & Pl
Hurdles	5	0	0	0	
Career Total	**13**	**0**	**0**	**0**	**0**

Going: Sf: 0-4 GS: 0-0 Gd: 0-1 GF: - Fm: 0-0
Distance: 2m/2m3: 0-0 2m4-2m7: 0-4 3m+: 0-1
Track: LH: 0-3 RH: 0-1 Tight: 0-1 Gall: 0-0
Aids: Bl: 0-1 Vi: 0-0 Tstrap: 0-0
Best Rating: **69** 6/99 MRas 1m5f110y gd-fm NHF

Blue Dante (IRE)

102f 139f

5-y-o b m Phardante (FR)-Weather Line (IRE) (Strong Gale)
P F Nicholls Mrs Angela Tincknell

Placings:*11* (4823)
2001/02: 16^{1}G, 17^{1}G

	Starts	1st	2nd	3rd	Win & Pl
NH Flat	2	2	0	0	18119
Career Total	**2**	**2**	**0**	**0**	**18119**

139	4/02	Chel	2m1f	A NHF	GD	£18118

Total win prize-money £18119

Going: Sf: 0-0 GS: 0-0 Gd: 2-2 GF: - Fm: 0-0
Distance: **2m/2m3: 2-2** 2m4-2m7: 0-0 3m+: 0-0
Track: **LH: 2-2** RH: 0-0 Tight: 0-0 **Gall: 1-1**
Aids: Bl: 0-0 Vi: 0-0 Tstrap: 0-0
Best Rating: **139** 4/02 Chel 2m1f good NHF

From the family of Marlborough, she dead-heated in a bumper on her debut. Followed up in better company when winning a Class A mares only bumper at Cheltenham next time.

Blue Falcon (IRE)

57 10

4-y-o b g Eagle Eyed (USA)-Indian Sand (Indian King (USA))
I W McInnes I W McInnes

Placings:0 (0965)
2001/02: 17^{0}GS

	Starts	1st	2nd	3rd	Win & Pl
Hurdles	1	0	0	0	
Career Total	**1**	**0**	**0**	**0**	

Going: Sf: 0-0 GS: 0-1 Gd: 0-0 GF: - Fm: 0-0
Distance: 2m/2m3: 0-1 2m4-2m7: 0-0 3m+: 0-0
Track: LH: 0-0 RH: 0-0 Tight: 0-0 Gall: 0-0
Aids: Bl: 0-0 Vi: 0-0 Tstrap: 0-0
Best Rating: **10** 7/01 MRas 2m1f110y gd-sft Hdl

Blue Haze

71f 58f

6-y-o ch g Ardkinglass-Cold Line (Exdirectory)
J Hetherton N Hetherton

Placings:*0/0* (4750)
2001/02: 17^{0}G

	Starts	1st	2nd	3rd	Win & Pl
NH Flat	1	0	0	0	
Career Total	**2**	**0**	**0**	**0**	

Going: Sf: 0-0 GS: 0-0 Gd: 0-1 GF: - Fm: 0-0
Distance: 2m/2m3: 0-1 2m4-2m7: 0-0 3m+: 0-0
Track: LH: 0-0 RH: 0-1 Tight: 0-0 Gall: 0-0
Aids: Bl: 0-0 Vi: 0-0 Tstrap: 0-0
Best Rating: **58** 4/02 Carl 2m1f good NHF

Blue Irish (IRE)

11-y-o gr g Roselier (FR)-Grannie No (Brave Invader (USA))
Mrs S A Bramall Winning Post Racing

Placings:2066353/141/41/4FPP3UP/U-F (4650)
2001/02: 21^{F}G

	Starts	1st	2nd	3rd	Win & Pl
Chases	1	0	0	0	
Career Total	**21**	**3**	**1**	**3**	**19902**

126	11/98	Carl	3m2f	C(0-130)HCh	HVY	£4856
127	2/98	Naas	3m	Ch	Y-S	£5956
120	11/97	Navn	2m4f	Ch	HVY	£4069

Total win prize-money £14882

Going: Sf: 0-0 GS: 0-0 Gd: 0-1 GF: - Fm: 0-0
Distance: 2m/2m3: 0-0 2m4-2m7: 0-1 3m+: 0-0
Track: LH: 0-1 RH: 0-0 Tight: 0-1 Gall: 0-0
Aids: Bl: 0-0 Vi: 0-0 Tstrap: 0-0
Best Rating: **138** 11/99 DRoy 3m1f soft Ch

Good form in 97/98 and by no means disgraced behind Florida Pearl at Down Royal the following year, but has been most disappointing since then, failing to complete six times from his last seven runs. His jumping let him down that year (2000) and he has been lightly-raced since then.

Blue Is The Colour (IRE)

13-y-o ch g The Parson-Avocan (Avocat)
A J Walker Miss E M Hewitt

Placings:0006/3/2/0P (0427)
2001/02: 25^{0}G, 33^{P}G

	Starts	1st	2nd	3rd	Win & Pl
Chases	2	0	0	0	
Career Total	**8**	**0**	**1**	**1**	**794**

Going: Sf: 0-0 GS: 0-0 Gd: 0-2 GF: - Fm: 0-0
Distance: 2m/2m3: 0-0 2m4-2m7: 0-0 3m+: 0-2
Track: LH: 0-1 RH: 0-0 Tight: 0-0 Gall: 0-0
Aids: Bl: 0-0 Vi: 0-0 Tstrap: 0-0
Best Rating: **105** 5/99 Aint 3m1f gd-sft Ch

Blue Jar

71f 65f

4-y-o b g Royal Abjar (USA)-Artist's Glory (Rarity)
M Mullineaux T Clarke

Placings:*00* (4377)
2001/02: 16^{0}GF, 16^{0}S

	Starts	1st	2nd	3rd	Win & Pl
NH Flat	2	0	0	0	
Career Total	**2**	**0**	**0**	**0**	

Going: Sf: 0-1 GS: 0-0 Gd: 0-0 GF: - Fm: 0-1
Distance: 2m/2m3: 0-2 2m4-2m7: 0-0 3m+: 0-0
Track: LH: 0-0 RH: 0-2 Tight: 0-0 Gall: 0-1
Aids: Bl: 0-0 Vi: 0-0 Tstrap: 0-0
Best Rating: **65** 3/02 Hntg 2m110y gd-fm NHF

Blue Label

6-y-o b g Tragic Role (USA)-Grecian Belle (Ilium)
D C Gibbs D C Gibbs

Placings:*06*-P (0231)
2001/02: 24^{P}GF

	Starts	1st	2nd	3rd	Win & Pl
Chases	1	0	0	0	
Career Total	**3**	**0**	**0**	**0**	**0**

Going: Sf: 0-0 GS: 0-0 Gd: 0-0 GF: - Fm: 0-1
Distance: 2m/2m3: 0-0 2m4-2m7: 0-0 3m+: 0-1
Track: LH: 0-0 RH: 0-1 Tight: 0-0 Gall: 0-1

Aids: Bl: 0-0 Vi: 0-0 Tstrap: 0-0
Best Rating: 72 6/00 NAbb 2m1f gd-fm NHF

Blue Moon (IRE)

98(105h) (99h)99
7-y-o b g Scenic-Debach Delight (Great Nephew)
N Wilson (Ferdy Murphy 8/7) Alderclad Roofing Ltd

Placings:33/21035/420F66-003502P (1904)
2001/02: 16^{0}G, 21^{0}G, 27^{3}GF, 25^{5}GF, 17^{0}G, 27^{2}G, 27^{P}G

	Starts	1st	2nd	3rd	Win & Pl
Hurdles	3	0	0	1	402
Chases	4	0	1	0	830
Career Total	**20**	**1**	**3**	**4**	**6698**

105 11/99 Hexm 2m E Hdl GD £2280
Total win prize-money £2280

Going: Sf: 0-0 GS: 0-0 Gd: 0-5 GF: - Fm: 0-2
Distance: 2m/2m3: 0-2 2m4-2m7: 0-1 3m+: 0-4
Track: LH: 0-5 RH: 0-2 Tight: 0-6 Gall: 0-0
Aids: Bl: 0-1 Vi: 0-0 Tstrap: 0-0
Best Rating: 105 2/00 Newc 2m4f heavy Hdl

Won an awful four-runner novice hurdle at Hexham in November 1999, but looks pretty moderate.

Blue Music (IRE)

110 122
7-y-o ch g Keen-Coast Wind (USA) (Chief's Crown (USA))
R G Frost Jack Joseph

Placings:P04/6201113O/00-53111F (2287)
2001/02: 17^{5}GF, 16^{3}GF, 16^{1}GF, 16^{1}GF, 17^{1}G, 16^{F}G

	Starts	1st	2nd	3rd	Win & Pl
Hurdles	6	3	0	1	14099
Career Total	**19**	**6**	**1**	**2**	**23402**

122	9/01	Bang	2m1f	C(0-135)HHdl	GD	£6857
112	8/01	Uttx	2m	D(0-125)HHdl	G-F	£3339
121	8/01	Strf	2m110y	D(0-125)HHdl	G-F	£3380
125	8/99	Prth	2m110y	D(0-120)HHdl	G-F	£3420
115	7/99	Strf	2m110y	E(0-115)HHdl	GD	£2804
104	7/99	Strf	2m110y	G Hdl	GD	£1593

Total win prize-money £21394

Going: Sf: 0-0 GS: 0-0 Gd: 1-2 GF: - Fm: 2-4
Distance: **2m/2m3: 3-6** 2m4-2m7: 0-0 3m+: 0-0
Track: **LH: 3-5** RH: 0-1 **Tight: 2-4** Gall: 0-0
Aids: Bl: 0-0 Vi: 0-0 Tstrap: 0-0
Best Rating: 125 9/99 Strf 2m110y gd-fm Hdl

An habitual front-runner, he was in fine form during the summer winning three in a row at around two miles. Acted on fast ground. (DEAD)

Blue Orleans

72 72
4-y-o b g Dancing Spree (USA)-Blues Player (Jaazeiro (USA))
A G Newcombe Advanced Marketing Services Ltd

Placings:1P (2162)
2001/02: 16^{1}G, 16^{P}G

	Starts	1st	2nd	3rd	Win & Pl
Hurdles	2	1	0	0	2979
Career Total	**2**	**1**	**0**	**0**	**2979**

72 7/01 Strf 2m110y E Hdl GD £2978
Total win prize-money £2979

Going: Sf: 0-0 GS: 0-0 Gd: 1-2 GF: - Fm: 0-0
Distance: **2m/2m3: 1-2** 2m4-2m7: 0-0 3m+: 0-0
Track: **LH: 1-2** RH: 0-0 **Tight: 1-1** Gall: 0-0
Aids: Bl: 0-0 Vi: 0-0 Tstrap: 0-0
Best Rating: 72 7/01 Strf 2m110y good Hdl

Blue Planet (IRE)

71 80
4-y-o b g Bluebird (USA)-Millie Musique (Miller's Mate)
P G Murphy (Sir Mark Prescott 27/9) Miss J Collison

Placings:30 (2758)
2001/02: 16^{3}S, 16^{0}GS

	Starts	1st	2nd	3rd	Win & Pl
Hurdles	2	0	0	1	543
Career Total	**2**	**0**	**0**	**1**	**543**

Going: Sf: 0-1 GS: 0-1 Gd: 0-0 GF: - Fm: 0-0
Distance: 2m/2m3: 0-2 2m4-2m7: 0-0 3m+: 0-0
Track: LH: 0-1 RH: 0-1 Tight: 0-0 Gall: 0-1
Aids: Bl: 0-0 Vi: 0-0 Tstrap: 0-0
Best Rating: 80 12/01 Sand 2m110y soft Hdl

Blue Rain

75f 60f
7-y-o b g Salse (USA)-Collage (Ela-Mana-Mou)
C N Kellett Sean A Taylor

Placings:3/0-0P (1019)
2001/02: 16^{0}G, 16^{P}G

	Starts	1st	2nd	3rd	Win & Pl
NH Flat	2	0	0	0	
Career Total	**4**	**0**	**0**	**1**	**224**

Going: Sf: 0-0 GS: 0-0 Gd: 0-2 GF: - Fm: 0-0
Distance: 2m/2m3: 0-2 2m4-2m7: 0-0 3m+: 0-0
Track: LH: 0-2 RH: 0-0 Tight: 0-0 Gall: 0-0
Aids: Bl: 0-0 Vi: 0-0 Tstrap: 0-0
Best Rating: 100 11/99 Sand 2m110y good NHF

Blue Ribbon (IRE)

6-y-o b g Bluebird (USA)-Sweet Justice (Law Society (USA))
G M Moore J R F (management Consultants) Ltd

Placings:60/450P-0P (3469)
2001/02: 16^{0}G, 16^{P}S

	Starts	1st	2nd	3rd	Win & Pl
Hurdles	2	0	0	0	
Career Total	**8**	**0**	**0**	**0**	**0**

Going: Sf: 0-1 GS: 0-0 Gd: 0-1 GF: - Fm: 0-0
Distance: 2m/2m3: 0-2 2m4-2m7: 0-0 3m+: 0-0
Track: LH: 0-2 RH: 0-0 Tight: 0-0 Gall: 0-2
Aids: Bl: 0-0 Vi: 0-0 Tstrap: 0-0
Best Rating: 92 10/00 MRas 2m1f110y good NHF

Blue Ride (IRE)

103f 96f
5-y-o b m King's Ride-Charmere's Beauty (IRE) (Phardante (FR))
P F Nicholls Mrs Angela Tincknell

Placings:1 (4743)
2001/02: 16^{1}GF

	Starts	1st	2nd	3rd	Win & Pl
NH Flat	1	1	0	0	2223
Career Total	**1**	**1**	**0**	**0**	**2223**

96 4/02 Ludl 2m H NHF G-F £2222
Total win prize-money £2223

Going: Sf: 0-0 GS: 0-0 Gd: 0-0 GF: - Fm: 1-1
Distance: **2m/2m3: 1-1** 2m4-2m7: 0-0 3m+: 0-0
Track: LH: 0-0 **RH: 1-1** Tight: 0-0 Gall: 0-0
Aids: Bl: 0-0 Vi: 0-0 Tstrap: 0-0
Best Rating: 96 4/02 Ludl 2m gd-fm NHF

Made a winning debut in an ordinary Ludlow bumper.

Blue Royal (FR)

7-y-o b g Dauphin Du Bourg (FR)-Before The Flag (IRE) (Lomond (USA))
N J Henderson Lynn Wilson

Placings:2211/103/0-P (4676)
2001/02: 20^{P}G

	Starts	1st	2nd	3rd	Win & Pl
Hurdles	1	0	0	0	
Career Total	**9**	**3**	**2**	**1**	**49625**

157	12/99	Asct	2m110y	B Hdl	SFT	£8208
130	4/99	Punc	2m	Hdl	GD	£6138
122	4/99	Towc	2m	F Hdl	GD	£1653

Total win prize-money £15999

Going: Sf: 0-0 GS: 0-0 Gd: 0-1 GF: - Fm: 0-0
Distance: 2m/2m3: 0-0 2m4-2m7: 0-1 3m+: 0-0
Track: LH: 0-1 RH: 0-0 Tight: 0-1 Gall: 0-0
Aids: Bl: 0-0 Vi: 0-0 Tstrap: 0-0
Best Rating: 164 3/00 Chel 2m110y good Hdl

Ex-French, he created a big impression when winning at Punchestown in the spring of 1999. Took the notable scalp of Sir Talbot on his seasonal return at Ascot and faced a stiff task off top weight in the Tote Gold Trophy, before showing his true colours with a fine third in the 2000 Champion Hurdle. Best at around two miles. Acts on good, handles heavy. Lightly-raced of late and should now be ready to tackle fences.

Blue Toski

61f 72f
4-y-o b f Petoski-Trecauldah (Treboro (USA))
W S Kittow Mrs Angela Tincknell

Placings:6 (4603)
2001/02: 16^{6}GF

	Starts	1st	2nd	3rd	Win & Pl
NH Flat	1	0	0	0	0
Career Total	**1**	**0**	**0**	**0**	**0**

Going: Sf: 0-0 GS: 0-0 Gd: 0-0 GF: - Fm: 0-1
Distance: 2m/2m3: 0-1 2m4-2m7: 0-0 3m+: 0-0
Track: LH: 0-1 RH: 0-0 Tight: 0-0 Gall: 0-0
Aids: Bl: 0-0 Vi: 0-0 Tstrap: 0-0
Best Rating: 72 4/02 Wwck 2m gd-fm NHF

Blue Wave (IRE)

10-y-o b g Project Manager-Over The Seas (North Summit)
G W Briscoe G W Briscoe

Placings:600/0411/PP/P (3694)
2001/02: 22^{P}HY

	Starts	1st	2nd	3rd	Win & Pl
Chases	1	0	0	0	
Career Total	**10**	**2**	**0**	**0**	**6320**

112	1/97	Punc	2m4f	Hdl	YLD	£3051
104	1/97	Navn	2m	NHF	G-Y	£3051

Total win prize-money £6104

Going: Sf: 0-1 GS: 0-0 Gd: 0-0 GF: - Fm: 0-0

Distance: 2m/2m3: 0-0 2m4-2m7: 0-1 3m+: 0-0
Track: LH: 0-0 RH: 0-0 Tight: 0-0 Gall: 0-0
Aids: Bl: 0-0 Vi: 0-0 Tstrap: 0-1
Best Rating: 112 1/97 Punc 2m4f yield Hdl

Blues Story (FR)

79f 73f

4-y-o b g Pistolet Bleu (IRE)-Herbe Sucree (FR) (Tiffauges)
P R Webber D Heath

Placings:00 (4506)
2001/02: 16^{0}S, 17^{0}G

	Starts	1st	2nd	3rd	Win & Pl
NH Flat	2	0	0	0	
Career Total	**2**	**0**	**0**	**0**	

Going: Sf: 0-1 GS: 0-0 Gd: 0-1 GF: - Fm: 0-0
Distance: 2m/2m3: 0-2 2m4-2m7: 0-0 3m+: 0-0
Track: LH: 0-2 RH: 0-0 Tight: 0-1 Gall: 0-0
Aids: Bl: 0-0 Vi: 0-0 Tstrap: 0-0
Best Rating: 73 1/02 Hayd 2m soft NHF

Blues Whisperer (IRE)

62 41

5-y-o b g Blues Traveller (IRE)-Princess Roxanne (Prince Tenderfoot (USA))
B R Millman R C D Martin

Placings:0P (2204)
2001/02: 17^{0}S, 16^{P}GS

	Starts	1st	2nd	3rd	Win & Pl
Hurdles	2	0	0	0	
Career Total	**2**	**0**	**0**	**0**	

Going: Sf: 0-1 GS: 0-1 Gd: 0-0 GF: - Fm: 0-0
Distance: 2m/2m3: 0-2 2m4-2m7: 0-0 3m+: 0-0
Track: LH: 0-1 RH: 0-1 Tight: 0-1 Gall: 0-0
Aids: Bl: 0-0 Vi: 0-0 Tstrap: 0-2
Best Rating: 41 11/01 NAbb 2m1f soft Hdl

Blueshaan (IRE)

107 85

9-y-o b g Darshaan-Pale Blue (Kris)
Dr P Pritchard Not Going To Cheltenham Partnership

Placings:03/1U2P35/P6P-PP00006 (4573)
2001/02: 19^{P}G, 19^{P}S, 24^{0}S, 20^{0}S, 17^{0}G, 22^{0}S, 20^{6}G

	Starts	1st	2nd	3rd	Win & Pl
Hurdles	7	0	0	0	0
Career Total	**18**	**1**	**1**	**2**	**4334**

120 10/98 Chep 2m4f110y E Hdl G-S £1982
Total win prize-money £1982

Going: Sf: 0-4 GS: 0-0 Gd: 0-3 GF: - Fm: 0-0
Distance: 2m/2m3: 0-2 2m4-2m7: 0-4 3m+: 0-1
Track: LH: 0-4 RH: 0-3 Tight: 0-2 Gall: 0-3
Aids: Bl: 0-0 Vi: 0-0 Tstrap: 0-0
Best Rating: 120 10/98 Chep 2m4f110y gd-sft Hdl

Blurred Image (IRE)

11-y-o ch g Exactly Sharp (USA)-Bear's Affair (Gay Fandango (USA))
Mrs A Price Mrs A Price

Placings:U36/00/P3426/530/3/000**U/PP** (1543)

2001/02: 20^{P}G, 19^{P}G

	Starts	1st	2nd	3rd	Win & Pl
Chases	2	0	0	0	
Career Total	**20**	**0**	**1**	**4**	**1694**

Going: Sf: 0-0 GS: 0-0 Gd: 0-2 GF: - Fm: 0-0
Distance: 2m/2m3: 0-1 2m4-2m7: 0-1 3m+: 0-0
Track: LH: 0-1 RH: 0-1 Tight: 0-1 Gall: 0-0
Aids: Bl: 0-0 Vi: 0-0 Tstrap: 0-0
Best Rating: 87 2/95 Winc 2m soft Hdl

Blyth Brook

97 115

10-y-o b g Meadowbrook-The Bean-Goose (King Sitric)
C Storey Mrs S A Sutton

Placings:000/25P2-65 (4678)
2001/02: 25^{6}GS, 25^{5}G

	Starts	1st	2nd	3rd	Win & Pl
Chases	2	0	0	0	0
Career Total	**9**	**0**	**2**	**0**	**1834**

Going: Sf: 0-0 GS: 0-1 Gd: 0-1 GF: - Fm: 0-0
Distance: 2m/2m3: 0-0 2m4-2m7: 0-0 3m+: 0-2
Track: LH: 0-1 RH: 0-0 Tight: 0-1 Gall: 0-0
Aids: Bl: 0-0 Vi: 0-0 Tstrap: 0-0
Best Rating: 115 4/01 Ayr 3m3f110y good Ch

Headstrong hunter who prefers fast ground.

Blythe Lady

95 87

8-y-o b m Warrshan (USA)-Aldwick Colonnade (Kind Of Hush)
T Wall John Reynolds & Derek Dean

Placings:264302P/P302/3F43400FP-223000 (0977)
2001/02: 20^{2}GF, 17^{2}G, 17^{3}F, 20^{0}G, 16^{0}G, 24^{0}GF

	Starts	1st	2nd	3rd	Win & Pl
Hurdles	6	0	2	1	1710
Career Total	**26**	**0**	**5**	**5**	**5680**

Going: Sf: 0-0 GS: 0-0 Gd: 0-3 GF: - Fm: 0-3
Distance: 2m/2m3: 0-3 2m4-2m7: 0-2 3m+: 0-1
Track: LH: 0-4 RH: 0-2 Tight: 0-2 Gall: 0-0
Aids: Bl: 0-0 Vi: 0-0 Tstrap: 0-0
Best Rating: 93 3/00 Uttx 2m4f110y good Hdl

Bo Dancer (IRE)

102 94

8-y-o ch g Magical Wonder (USA)-Pitty Pal (USA) (Caracolero (USA))
Mrs E Slack A Slack

Placings:00/10/211/060-06 (4747)
2001/02: 17^{0}G, 20^{6}G

	Starts	1st	2nd	3rd	Win & Pl
Hurdles	2	0	0	0	0
Career Total	**12**	**3**	**1**	**0**	**7532**

101 12/99 Catt 2m3f F(0-110)HHdl G-F £1924
97 11/99 Carl 2m4f110y F(0-105)HHdl G-S £2430
83 11/98 Hexm 2m4f110y E Hdl HVY £2553
Total win prize-money £6907

Going: Sf: 0-0 GS: 0-0 Gd: 0-2 GF: - Fm: 0-0
Distance: 2m/2m3: 0-1 2m4-2m7: 0-1 3m+: 0-0
Track: LH: 0-0 RH: 0-1 Tight: 0-0 Gall: 0-0
Aids: Bl: 0-0 Vi: 0-0 Tstrap: 0-0
Best Rating: 101 12/99 Catt 2m3f gd-fm Hdl

Board Walk (IRE)

103 107

7-y-o b g Commanche Run-Swift Tide (Hard Boy)
Mrs M Reveley Mrs M Hoey

Placings:0P0-P3F1U (3625)
2001/02: 25^{P}G, 27^{3}G, 24^{F}GS, 24^{1}S, 22^{U}S

	Starts	1st	2nd	3rd	Win & Pl
Chases	5	1	0	1	3918
Career Total	**8**	**1**	**0**	**1**	**3918**

107 1/02 Newc 3m F(0-100)HCh SFT £3496
Total win prize-money £3497

Going: Sf: 1-2 GS: 0-1 Gd: 0-2 GF: - Fm: 0-0
Distance: 2m/2m3: 0-0 2m4-2m7: 0-1 **3m+: 1-4**
Track: **LH: 1-4** RH: 0-1 Tight: 0-2 **Gall: 1-2**
Aids: Bl: 0-0 Vi: 0-0 Tstrap: 0-0
Best Rating: 107 1/02 Newc 3m soft Ch

An enormous, lightly-raced gelding. Looked on the upgrade in 2001/02, winning at Newcastle. Suited by a test of stamina, handles soft ground.

Boater

107 111

8-y-o b g Batshoof-Velvet Beret (IRE) (Dominion)
R J Baker Christine And Aubrey Loze

Placings:23/42P61/02211402/3F5-032252426 (2850)
2001/02: 16^{0}GF, 17^{3}GF, 17^{2}GF, 16^{2}GF, 17^{5}GF, 19^{2}GF, 19^{4}GS, 19^{2}GS, 21^{6}G

	Starts	1st	2nd	3rd	Win & Pl
Hurdles	9	0	4	1	4293
Career Total	**27**	**3**	**9**	**3**	**19925**

118 8/99 NAbb 2m1f C(0-130)HHdl GD £4662
112 7/99 NAbb 2m1f F(0-100)HHdl G-F £2640
99 4/99 Tntn 2m1f F(0-100)HHdl G-S £1966
Total win prize-money £9268

Going: Sf: 0-0 GS: 0-2 Gd: 0-1 GF: - Fm: 0-6
Distance: 2m/2m3: 0-6 2m4-2m7: 0-3 3m+: 0-0
Track: LH: 0-4 RH: 0-5 Tight: 0-5 Gall: 0-0
Aids: Bl: 0-3 Vi: 0-0 Tstrap: 0-0
Best Rating: 122 7/00 NAbb 2m1f gd-fm Hdl

Fair handicap hurdler, suited by fast ground but acts on easier. Returned after a five month absence to narrowly win a handicap at Newton Abbot May 2002.

Boatswain

79f 42f

7-y-o b g Pursuit Of Love-Bay Bay (Bay Express)
I A Wood Neardown Stables

Placings:0/00 (1411)
2001/02: 16^{0}GF, 16^{0}GF

	Starts	1st	2nd	3rd	Win & Pl
NH Flat	2	0	0	0	
Career Total	**3**	**0**	**0**	**0**	

Going: Sf: 0-0 GS: 0-0 Gd: 0-0 GF: - Fm: 0-2
Distance: 2m/2m3: 0-2 2m4-2m7: 0-0 3m+: 0-0
Track: LH: 0-1 RH: 0-1 Tight: 0-0 Gall: 0-1
Aids: Bl: 0-0 Vi: 0-0 Tstrap: 0-0
Best Rating: 47 3/99 Ludl 2m good NHF

Bob Ar Aghaidh (IRE)

94f 105f

6-y-o b g Bob Back (USA)-Shuil Ar Aghaidh (The Parson)
A J Lidderdale (E Stanners 10/11) George Ward

Placings: *260* (4032)
2001/02: 16^{2}GS, 16^{6}S, 16^{0}GS

	Starts	1st	2nd	3rd	Win & Pl
NH Flat	3	0	1	0	693
Career Total	**3**	**0**	**1**	**0**	**693**

Going: Sf: 0-1 GS: 0-2 Gd: 0-0 GF: - Fm: 0-0
Distance: 2m/2m3: 0-3 2m4-2m7: 0-0 3m+: 0-0
Track: LH: 0-1 RH: 0-2 Tight: 0-0 Gall: 0-1
Aids: Bl: 0-0 Vi: 0-0 Tstrap: 0-0
Best Rating: **105** 3/02 Newb 2m110y gd-sft NHF

Out of the 1993 Stayers' Hurdle winner, showed ability in a Sandown bumper on his debut and will relish a test of stamina.

Bob Justice (IRE)

117(108c) (118+c)147

6-y-o b g Bob Back (USA)-Bramdean (Niniski (USA))
T M Walsh Ms Breda Brady

Placings: *22/44*012251-03433022 (4954a)
2001/02: 16^{0}G, 16^{3}Y, 16^{4}YS, 16^{3}S, 16^{3}HY, 21^{0}GS, 18^{2}GY, 24^{2}G

	Starts	1st	2nd	3rd	Win & Pl
Hurdles	8	0	2	3	21058
Career Total	**18**	**2**	**6**	**3**	**51046**
136 4/01 Fair	2m	Hdl		SFT	£7862
135 12/00 Leop	2m	Hdl		SH	£5520

Total win prize-money £13383

Going: Sf: 0-2 GS: 0-1 Gd: 0-2 GF: - Fm: 0-0
Distance: 2m/2m3: 0-6 2m4-2m7: 0-1 3m+: 0-1
Track: LH: 0-4 RH: 0-2 Tight: 0-0 Gall: 0-1
Aids: Bl: 0-0 Vi: 0-0 Tstrap: 0-0
Best Rating: **147** 4/02 Punc 3m good Hdl

Irish handicap hurdler. Suited by soft ground. Stepped up in trip, he ran his best race when runner-up to Limestone Lad at the Punchestown Festival.

Bob Knows

8-y-o br g Robellino (USA)-Snowline (Bay Express)
Mrs Rosemary Gasson Mrs Rosemary Gasson

Placings: F50004/3 (0226)
2001/02: 20^{3}GF

	Starts	1st	2nd	3rd	Win & Pl
Chases	1	0	0	1	169
Career Total	**7**	**0**	**0**	**1**	**169**

Going: Sf: 0-0 GS: 0-0 Gd: 0-0 GF: - Fm: 0-1
Distance: 2m/2m3: 0-0 2m4-2m7: 0-1 3m+: 0-0
Track: LH: 0-0 RH: 0-1 Tight: 0-0 Gall: 0-1
Aids: Bl: 0-0 Vi: 0-0 Tstrap: 0-0
Best Rating: **102** 5/01 Hntg 2m4f110y gd-fm Ch

Bob Le Gaoth (IRE)

83

6-y-o br g Bob Back (USA)-Shuil Le Gaoth (IRE) (Strong Gale)
E Stanners Bonusprint

Placings: *31*-U (1941)
2001/02: 21^{U}GS

	Starts	1st	2nd	3rd	Win & Pl
Hurdles	1	0	0	0	
Career Total	**3**	**1**	**0**	**1**	**2830**
110 4/01 NAbb	2m1f	H NHF		SFT	£2450

Total win prize-money £2450

Going: Sf: 0-0 GS: 0-1 Gd: 0-0 GF: - Fm: 0-0
Distance: 2m/2m3: 0-0 2m4-2m7: 0-1 3m+: 0-0
Track: LH: 0-1 RH: 0-0 Tight: 0-1 Gall: 0-0
Aids: Bl: 0-0 Vi: 0-0 Tstrap: 0-0
Best Rating: **110** 4/01 NAbb 2m1f soft NHF

Bob's Buster

92(105c) (102c)92

6-y-o b g Bob's Return (IRE)-Saltina (Bustino)
R Johnson Mrs Geraldine Jones

Placings: FP0/02053444-252F4331 (4858)
2001/02: 16^{2}GF, 16^{5}S, 16^{2}G, 16^{F}S, 16^{4}S, 16^{3}S, 16^{3}S, 16^{1}G

	Starts	1st	2nd	3rd	Win & Pl
Hurdles	2	1	0	1	3490
Chases	6	0	2	1	3060
Career Total	**19**	**1**	**3**	**3**	**8724**
90 4/02 Hexm	2m110y	E(0-110)HHdl		GD	£3052

Total win prize-money £3052

Going: Sf: 0-5 GS: 0-0 Gd: 1-2 GF: - Fm: 0-1
Distance: **2m/2m3: 1-8** 2m4-2m7: 0-0 3m+: 0-0
Track: LH: 0-7 RH: 0-0 Tight: 0-2 Gall: 0-3
Aids: Bl: 0-0 Vi: 0-0 Tstrap: 0-0
Best Rating: **102** 3/02 Sedg 2m110y soft Ch

He has shown ability in ordinary company in novice chases, but won over hurdles at Hexham in April.

Bob's Gray

8-y-o gr g Scallywag-Summer Path (Warpath)
Mrs D McCormack Mrs D McCormack

Placings: *60*/PP0P-F (0473)
2001/02: 20^{F}GF

	Starts	1st	2nd	3rd	Win & Pl
Chases	1	0	0	0	
Career Total	**7**	**0**	**0**	**0**	

Going: Sf: 0-0 GS: 0-0 Gd: 0-0 GF: - Fm: 0-1
Distance: 2m/2m3: 0-0 2m4-2m7: 0-1 3m+: 0-0
Track: LH: 0-1 RH: 0-0 Tight: 0-0 Gall: 0-0
Aids: Bl: 0-0 Vi: 0-0 Tstrap: 0-0
Best Rating: **72** 10/99 Sedg 2m1f gd-fm NHF

Bobanvi

95 72

4-y-o b f Timeless Times (USA)-Bobanlyn (IRE) (Dance Of Life (USA))
J S Wainwright S Pedersen

Placings: 0002044P (4752)
2001/02: 16^{0}G, 16^{0}G, 16^{0}G, 16^{2}G, 16^{0}GS, 16^{4}GS, 16^{4}S, 16^{P}GF

	Starts	1st	2nd	3rd	Win & Pl
Hurdles	8	0	1	0	666
Career Total	**8**	**0**	**1**	**0**	**666**

Going: Sf: 0-1 GS: 0-2 Gd: 0-4 GF: - Fm: 0-1
Distance: 2m/2m3: 0-8 2m4-2m7: 0-0 3m+: 0-0
Track: LH: 0-8 RH: 0-0 Tight: 0-1 Gall: 0-3
Aids: Bl: 0-0 Vi: 0-0 Tstrap: 0-0
Best Rating: **72** 11/01 Weth 2m good Hdl

Moderate hurdler, whose best effort was a second when dropped to selling class at the end of 2001.

Bobaway (IRE)

78f 76f

5-y-o br g Bob Back (USA)-Baybush (Boreen (FR))
A J Lidderdale Tripleprint

Placings: *0* (4032)
2001/02: 16^{0}GS

	Starts	1st	2nd	3rd	Win & Pl
NH Flat	1	0	0	0	
Career Total	**1**	**0**	**0**	**0**	

Going: Sf: 0-0 GS: 0-1 Gd: 0-0 GF: - Fm: 0-0
Distance: 2m/2m3: 0-1 2m4-2m7: 0-0 3m+: 0-0
Track: LH: 0-1 RH: 0-0 Tight: 0-0 Gall: 0-1
Aids: Bl: 0-0 Vi: 0-0 Tstrap: 0-0
Best Rating: **76** 3/02 Newb 2m110y gd-sft NHF

Bobayaro (IRE)

105 108

6-y-o b g Bob Back (USA)-Instanter (Morston (FR))
N G Richards (P F McEnery 11/9) It's A Bargain Syndicate

Placings: *2-641*3321 (4880)
2001/02: 16^{6}GY, 16^{4}GY, 16^{1}GF, 20^{3}G, 20^{3}S, 22^{2}S, 20^{1}G

	Starts	1st	2nd	3rd	Win & Pl
NH Flat	3	1	0	0	5226
Hurdles	4	1	1	2	5236
Career Total	**8**	**2**	**2**	**2**	**11166**
108 4/02 Prth	2m4f110y	D Hdl		GD	£3718
99 9/01 Gway	2m	NHF		GF	£5008

Total win prize-money £8726

Going: Sf: 0-2 GS: 0-0 Gd: 1-2 GF: - Fm: 1-1
Distance: 2m/2m3: 1-3 2m4-2m7: 1-4 3m+: 0-0
Track: LH: 0-3 **RH: 1-1** Tight: 0-1 Gall: 0-2
Aids: Bl: 0-1 Vi: 0-0 Tstrap: 0-0
Best Rating: **108** 4/02 Prth 2m4f110y good Hdl

Ex-Irish bumper winner, successful over hurdles at Perth in April.

Bobbi Rose Red

85f 83f

5-y-o ch m Bob Back (USA)-Lady Rosanna (Kind Of Hush)
P T Dalton Mrs Julie Martin

Placings: *53* (4429)
2001/02: 16^{5}S, 16^{3}HY

	Starts	1st	2nd	3rd	Win & Pl
NH Flat	2	0	0	1	223
Career Total	**2**	**0**	**0**	**1**	**223**

Going: Sf: 0-2 GS: 0-0 Gd: 0-0 GF: - Fm: 0-0
Distance: 2m/2m3: 0-2 2m4-2m7: 0-0 3m+: 0-0
Track: LH: 0-1 RH: 0-1 Tight: 0-0 Gall: 0-0
Aids: Bl: 0-0 Vi: 0-0 Tstrap: 0-0
Best Rating: **83** 3/02 Towc 2m soft NHF

Has shown little in bumpers.

Bobby Grant

106 142

11-y-o ch g Gunner B-Goldaw (Gala Performance (USA))
P Beaumont John J Thompson

Placings:*31115/2/2F2310/121124/251*-6 **(2694)**
2001/02: 24^{6}S

	Starts	1st	2nd	3rd	Win & Pl
Chases	1	0	0	0	675
Career Total	**22**	**8**	**6**	**2**	**111352**

173	12/00	Hayd	3m	A Ch	HVY	£25200
163	1/00	Hayd	3m	B(0-140)HCh	SFT	£8827
170	12/99	Hayd	3m	A Ch	HVY	£25000
147	11/99	Newc	3m	D(0-125)HCh	GD	£3810
148	1/99	Newc	2m4f	A Ch	SFT	£12834
110	2/97	Newc	2m4f	E Hdl	GD	£2473
99	1/97	Weth	2m4f110y	E Hdl	GD	£2587
98	12/96	Hexm	2m	H NHF	G-S	£1406

Total win prize-money £82139

Going: Sf: 0-1 GS: 0-0 Gd: 0-0 GF: - Fm: 0-0
Distance: 2m/2m3: 0-0 2m4-2m7: 0-0 3m+: 0-1
Track: LH: 0-1 RH: 0-0 Tight: 0-0 Gall: 0-0
Aids: Bl: 0-0 Vi: 0-0 Tstrap: 0-0
Best Rating: **173** 12/00 Hayd 3m heavy Ch

He enjoyed a fine season in 1999/2000 after switching to Beaumont's yard, going up 38lb in the official ratings through the campaign. Needed his first two runs in 2000/2001, but put up a good performance to beat the Hennessy winner King's Road in the Tommy Whittle at Haydock in December. A sound jumper who stays well, he missed the remainder of the season with a hairline fracture. Ran well on his sole start of 2001/02.

Bobby Wonder

9-y-o ch g Highlands-Friendly Wonder (Be Friendly)
Mrs Lynne Ward (R E Barr 10/2) A Jackson

Placings:*00/*63-4P6PP **(4672)**
2001/02: 25^{4}S, 20^{P}F, 20^{6}GS, 20^{P}G, 27^{P}GF

	Starts	1st	2nd	3rd	Win & Pl
Chases	5	0	0	0	262
Career Total	**9**	**0**	**0**	**1**	**1158**

Going: Sf: 0-1 GS: 0-1 Gd: 0-1 GF: - Fm: 0-2
Distance: 2m/2m3: 0-0 2m4-2m7: 0-3 3m+: 0-2
Track: LH: 0-5 RH: 0-0 Tight: 0-1 Gall: 0-0
Aids: Bl: 0-0 Vi: 0-0 Tstrap: 0-0
Best Rating: **82** 4/01 MRas 2m4f heavy Ch

Bobona

76 **40**

6-y-o b g Interrex (CAN)-Puella Bona (Handsome Sailor)
B J Llewellyn Miss Emily Jane Jones

Placings:04 **(1733)**
2001/02: 20^{0}GS, 19^{4}GS

	Starts	1st	2nd	3rd	Win & Pl
Hurdles	2	0	0	0	0
Career Total	**2**	**0**	**0**	**0**	**0**

Going: Sf: 0-0 GS: 0-2 Gd: 0-0 GF: - Fm: 0-0
Distance: 2m/2m3: 0-0 2m4-2m7: 0-2 3m+: 0-0
Track: LH: 0-0 RH: 0-1 Tight: 0-1 Gall: 0-0
Aids: Bl: 0-0 Vi: 0-0 Tstrap: 0-0
Best Rating: **40** 10/01 Font 2m4f gd-sft Hdl

Bobosh

105 **101**

6-y-o b g Devil's Jump-Jane Craig (Rapid Pass)
R Dickin Mrs Steffi Vine

Placings:*00/0*-025025523404021 **(4739)**
2001/02: 26^{0}G, 17^{2}GS, 20^{5}GF, 20^{0}G, 16^{2}S, 16^{5}GF, 17^{5}GS, 16^{2}G, 16^{3}G, 16^{4}G, 16^{0}S, 16^{4}S, 17^{0}HY, 21^{2}G, 21^{1}GF

	Starts	1st	2nd	3rd	Win & Pl
Hurdles	15	1	4	1	11028
Career Total	**18**	**1**	**4**	**1**	**11028**

92	4/02	Ludl	2m5f	D(0-120)HHdl	G-F	£4336

Total win prize-money £4337

Going: Sf: 0-4 GS: 0-2 Gd: 0-6 GF: - Fm: 1-3
Distance: 2m/2m3: 0-10 **2m4-2m7: 1-4** 3m+: 0-1
Track: LH: 0-11 **RH: 1-4** Tight: 0-2 Gall: 0-1
Aids: Bl: 0-0 Vi: 0-1 Tstrap: 0-0
Best Rating: **101** 11/01 Chel 2m110y good Hdl

Modest hurdler, seems to act on any surface but lacks a change of gear.

Bobsbest (IRE)

105 **81**

6-y-o b g Lashkari-Bobs (Warpath)
R Dickin R H Harris And R A Jefferies

Placings:*04*00-06634040 **(4646)**
2001/02: 17^{0}G, 20^{6}GS, 20^{6}G, 22^{3}GF, 16^{4}GS, 16^{0}GS, 19^{4}S, 21^{0}G

	Starts	1st	2nd	3rd	Win & Pl
Hurdles	8	0	0	1	630
Career Total	**12**	**0**	**0**	**1**	**630**

Going: Sf: 0-1 GS: 0-3 Gd: 0-3 GF: - Fm: 0-1
Distance: 2m/2m3: 0-3 2m4-2m7: 0-5 3m+: 0-0
Track: LH: 0-4 RH: 0-4 Tight: 0-2 Gall: 0-1
Aids: Bl: 0-0 Vi: 0-0 Tstrap: 0-0
Best Rating: **88** 10/00 Chel 2m110y good NHF

Respectable hurdles efforts without getting his head in front.

Bobstown (IRE)

5-y-o b h Bob's Return (IRE)-Minerstown (IRE) (Miners Lamp)
Ferdy Murphy Exors Of The Late Mr G A Hubbard

Placings:*P* **(3338)**
2001/02: 16^{P}G

	Starts	1st	2nd	3rd	Win & Pl
NH Flat	1	0	0	0	
Career Total	**1**	**0**	**0**	**0**	

Going: Sf: 0-0 GS: 0-0 Gd: 0-1 GF: - Fm: 0-0
Distance: 2m/2m3: 0-1 2m4-2m7: 0-0 3m+: 0-0
Track: LH: 0-0 RH: 0-1 Tight: 0-0 Gall: 0-0
Aids: Bl: 0-0 Vi: 0-0 Tstrap: 0-0
Best Rating:

Bodfari Cream

103 **133**

7-y-o b g Rudimentary (USA)-Final Attraction (Jalmood (USA))
Andrew Turnell Dr John Hollowood

Placings:*1122P0/0*2 **(1933)**
2001/02: 20^{2}G

	Starts	1st	2nd	3rd	Win & Pl
Chases	1	0	1	0	1653
Career Total	**7**	**2**	**3**	**0**	**6834**

117	12/99	Donc	2m110y	H NHF	G-F	£1628
117	11/99	Weth	2m	H NHF	GD	£1604

Total win prize-money £3232

Going: Sf: 0-0 GS: 0-0 Gd: 0-1 GF: - Fm: 0-0
Distance: 2m/2m3: 0-0 2m4-2m7: 0-1 3m+: 0-0
Track: LH: 0-1 RH: 0-0 Tight: 0-0 Gall: 0-0
Aids: Bl: 0-0 Vi: 0-0 Tstrap: 0-0
Best Rating: **133** 11/01 Weth 2m4f110y good Ch

Won a brace of bumpers in good style for Mick Easterby, and made a promising hurdles debut in January 2000. Failed to cope with softer ground on his next two runs, before being well beaten at Newbury in March of 2000, he nearly made a successful return after over a year off the track at Wetherby in November of 2001 over fences, when second.

Bodfari Creek

99 **98+**

5-y-o ch g In The Wings-Cormorant Creek (Gorytus (USA))
P R Webber Bodfari Stud Ltd

Placings:*1* **(4499)**
2001/02: 16^{1}G

	Starts	1st	2nd	3rd	Win & Pl
NH Flat	1	1	0	0	1932
Career Total	**1**	**1**	**0**	**0**	**1932**

98	3/02	Hayd	2m	H NHF	GD	£1932

Total win prize-money £1932

Going: Sf: 0-0 GS: 0-0 Gd: 1-1 GF: - Fm: 0-0
Distance: **2m/2m3: 1-1** 2m4-2m7: 0-0 3m+: 0-0
Track: **LH: 1-1** RH: 0-0 Tight: 0-0 Gall: 0-0
Aids: Bl: 0-0 Vi: 0-0 Tstrap: 0-0
Best Rating: **98** 3/02 Hayd 2m good NHF

Grand-type, successfull on his bow in a bumper at Haydock in March. Could prove useful.

Bodfari Millennium

66 **28**

4-y-o b g Tragic Role (USA)-Petomania (Petong)
M W Easterby Bodfari Stud Ltd

Placings:0 **(1418)**
2001/02: 17^{0}G

	Starts	1st	2nd	3rd	Win & Pl
Hurdles	1	0	0	0	
Career Total	**1**	**0**	**0**	**0**	

Going: Sf: 0-0 GS: 0-0 Gd: 0-1 GF: - Fm: 0-0
Distance: 2m/2m3: 0-1 2m4-2m7: 0-0 3m+: 0-0
Track: LH: 0-1 RH: 0-0 Tight: 0-1 Gall: 0-0
Aids: Bl: 0-0 Vi: 0-0 Tstrap: 0-0
Best Rating: **28** 9/01 Sedg 2m1f good Hdl

Bodfari Signet

112 **109**

6-y-o ch g King's Signet (USA)-Darakah (Doulab (USA))
Mrs S C Bradburne Strath Pack Partnership

Placings:4130P/00F316-4F541422246 **(4879)**
2001/02: 16^{4}GF, 16^{F}F, 16^{5}G, 16^{4}G, 17^{1}GF, 16^{4}S, 16^{2}S, 20^{2}GS, 16^{2}S, 16^{4}G, 16^{6}G

	Starts	1st	2nd	3rd	Win & Pl
Hurdles	11	1	3	0	7584
Career Total	**22**	**3**	**3**	**2**	**15281**

103	12/01	Muss	2m1f	G(0-95)HHdl	G-F	£2341
92	4/01	Muss	2m1f	F(0-100)HHdl	G-F	£3230
91	9/99	Strf	2m110y	E Hdl	G-F	£3096

Total win prize-money £8670

Going: Sf: 0-3 GS: 0-1 Gd: 0-4 GF: - Fm: 1-3

Distance: **2m/2m3: 1-10** 2m4-2m7: 0-1 3m+: 0-0
Track: LH: 0-4 RH: 0-6 Tight: 0-6 Gall: 0-0
Aids: Bl: 0-0 Vi: 0-0 Tstrap: 0-0
Best Rating: **109** 2/02 Muss 2m4f gd-sft Hdl

Fair hurdler at up to two and a half miles, acts on any ground, likes Musselburgh.

Bohill Lad (IRE)

105(108h) (118h)130

8-y-o b g Contract Law (USA)-La Sass (Sassafras (FR))
J D Frost (R G Frost 7/11) Mrs J McCormack

Placings:*000/444*00000/U343P3015/1534422UP-121226312 **(4863)**
2001/02: 17^{1}GF, 16^{2}GS, 16^{1}G, 16^{2}GF, 16^{2}GF, 19^{6}GF, 16^{3}S, 19^{1}G, 19^{2}F

	Starts	1st	2nd	3rd	Win & Pl
Hurdles	5	2	2	0	9159
Chases	4	1	2	1	8262
Career Total	**38**	**5**	**6**	**5**	**27115**

118	3/02	Extr	2m3f	D(0-115)HHdl	GD	£3542
130	7/01	NAbb	2m110y	D Ch	GD	£4057
105	6/01	NAbb	2m1f	F(0-105)HHdl	G-F	£3073
103	5/00	Extr	2m1f	E(0-115)HHdl	G-F	£3201
97	3/00	Tntn	2m1f	G Hdl	GD	£1526

Total win prize-money £15399

Going: Sf: 0-1 GS: 0-1 Gd: 2-2 GF: - Fm: 1-5
Distance: **2m/2m3: 3-8** 2m4-2m7: 0-1 3m+: 0-0
Track: **LH: 2-6** RH: 1-3 **Tight: 2-6** Gall: 0-0
Aids: Bl: 0-0 Vi: 0-0 Tstrap: 0-0
Best Rating: **130** 7/01 NAbb 2m110y good Ch

He mixes hurdling and chasing these days and is a fair tool under both codes around the minor tracks. Suited by two to two and a half miles and though he has run well on soft ground, is better on faster.

Bold Action (IRE)

106 105

11-y-o b g Denel (FR)-Loughan-Na-Curry (No Argument)
J R Turner Yarm Racing Partnership

Placings:223/306/1/4214UP224P/64P23/011460-2PPR3P1P **(4889)**
2001/02: 24^{2}S, 26^{P}S, 25^{P}HY, 25^{R}HY, 20^{3}S, 32^{P}HY, 26^{1}GS, 26^{P}G

	Starts	1st	2nd	3rd	Win & Pl
Chases	8	1	1	1	6450
Career Total	**36**	**5**	**7**	**4**	**27744**

103	4/02	Carl	3m2f	F(0-95)HCh	G-S	£3997
111	1/01	Weth	3m1f	E(0-115)HCh	HVY	£3360
104	12/00	Towc	3m1f	F(0-110)HCh	HVY	£5018
111	11/98	Hexm	3m1f	E(0-105)HCh	HVY	£3425
92	11/97	Hexm	2m4f110y	E Hdl	G-F	£2532

Total win prize-money £18333

Going: Sf: 0-6 GS: 1-1 Gd: 0-1 GF: - Fm: 0-0
Distance: 2m/2m3: 0-0 2m4-2m7: 0-1 **3m+: 1-7**
Track: LH: 0-2 **RH: 1-5** Tight: 0-0 Gall: 0-0
Aids: Bl: 0-2 Vi: 0-0 Tstrap: 0-0
Best Rating: **111** 1/01 Weth 3m1f heavy Ch

Marathon handicap chaser, he loves the mud and sometimes wears blinkers. Suited by a stiff track.

Bold Baby

74f 31f

6-y-o b m El Conquistador-Sizzling Sun (Sunyboy)
B G Powell R B Felmingham

Placings:*00* **(1384)**
2001/02: 16^{0}GF, 17^{0}GF

	Starts	1st	2nd	3rd	Win & Pl
NH Flat	2	0	0	0	
Career Total	**2**	**0**	**0**	**0**	

Going: Sf: 0-0 GS: 0-0 Gd: 0-0 GF: - Fm: 0-2
Distance: 2m/2m3: 0-2 2m4-2m7: 0-0 3m+: 0-0
Track: LH: 0-0 RH: 0-2 Tight: 0-0 Gall: 0-1
Aids: Bl: 0-0 Vi: 0-0 Tstrap: 0-0
Best Rating: **31** 9/01 Hrfd 2m1f gd-fm NHF

Bold Bird

95 78

5-y-o b g Puissance-Plum Bold (Be My Guest (USA))
D J Coakley David F Wilson

Placings:5560 **(1624)**
2001/02: 16^{5}GF, 16^{5}GF, 16^{6}GF, 16^{0}GF

	Starts	1st	2nd	3rd	Win & Pl
Hurdles	4	0	0	0	0
Career Total	**4**	**0**	**0**	**0**	**0**

Going: Sf: 0-0 GS: 0-0 Gd: 0-0 GF: - Fm: 0-4
Distance: 2m/2m3: 0-4 2m4-2m7: 0-0 3m+: 0-0
Track: LH: 0-2 RH: 0-2 Tight: 0-0 Gall: 0-1
Aids: Bl: 0-0 Vi: 0-4 Tstrap: 0-0
Best Rating: **78** 8/01 Worc 2m gd-fm Hdl

Bold Bishop (IRE)

109f 111f

5-y-o b g Religiously (USA)-Ladybojangles (IRE) (Buckskin (FR))
J I A Charlton J I A Charlton

Placings: / **(4873)**
2001/02: 16^{1}GF

	Starts	1st	2nd	3rd	Win & Pl
NH Flat	1	1	0	0	1939
Career Total	**1**	**1**	**0**	**0**	**1939**

111	4/02	Weth	2m	H NHF	G-F	£1939

Total win prize-money £1939

Going: Sf: 0-0 GS: 0-0 Gd: 0-0 GF: - Fm: 1-1
Distance: **2m/2m3: 1-1** 2m4-2m7: 0-0 3m+: 0-0
Track: **LH: 1-1** RH: 0-0 Tight: 0-0 Gall: 0-0
Aids: Bl: 0-0 Vi: 0-0 Tstrap: 0-0
Best Rating: **111** 4/02 Weth 2m gd-fm NHF

Started favourite first time when a ready winner of a bumper at Wetherby in April. Looks a useful prospect.

Bold Buccaneer (IRE)

98f

8-y-o br g Trigon-Maggies Turn (Garda's Revenge (USA))
M C Pipe A P Brady

Placings:PP/*00*F-0 **(0314)**
2001/02: 17^{0}F

	Starts	1st	2nd	3rd	Win & Pl
Hurdles	1	0	0	0	
Career Total	**6**	**0**	**0**	**0**	

Going: Sf: 0-0 GS: 0-0 Gd: 0-0 GF: - Fm: 0-1
Distance: 2m/2m3: 0-1 2m4-2m7: 0-0 3m+: 0-0
Track: LH: 0-0 RH: 0-1 Tight: 0-0 Gall: 0-0
Aids: Bl: 0-0 Vi: 0-0 Tstrap: 0-0
Best Rating: **98** 3/01 Extr 2m3f heavy Hdl

Bold Cardowan (IRE)

(108h) (93h)

6-y-o b g Persian Bold-Moving Trend (IRE) (Be My Guest (USA))
John Berry J McCarthy

Placings:340-03620 **(4599)**
2001/02: 20^{0}GS, 16^{3}HY, 17^{6}S, 21^{2}GS, 25^{0}GF

	Starts	1st	2nd	3rd	Win & Pl
Hurdles	5	0	1	1	1023
Career Total	**8**	**0**	**1**	**2**	**1389**

Going: Sf: 0-2 GS: 0-2 Gd: 0-0 GF: - Fm: 0-1
Distance: 2m/2m3: 0-2 2m4-2m7: 0-2 3m+: 0-1
Track: LH: 0-3 RH: 0-1 Tight: 0-3 Gall: 0-0
Aids: Bl: 0-0 Vi: 0-0 Tstrap: 0-0
Best Rating: **93** 3/02 Plum 2m5f gd-sft Hdl

Fair hurdler, stays three miles and effective on good ground. Jumped badly and was pulled up on chasing bow.

Bold Classic (IRE)

9-y-o b g Persian Bold-Bay Street (Grundy)
C Grant (J R Adam 23/6) Chris Grant

Placings:5023/11164/2PP5/300-P001420 **(4650)**
2001/02: 24^{P}GF, 21^{0}GF, 22^{0}GF, 26^{1}G, 22^{4}HY, 21^{2}HY, 21^{0}G

	Starts	1st	2nd	3rd	Win & Pl
Hurdles	1	0	0	0	0
Chases	0	1	1	0	4413
Career Total	**23**	**4**	**3**	**2**	**18354**

110	8/01	Ctml	3m2f	E Ch	GD	£3428
127	3/98	Uttx	3m110y	B(0-140)HHdl	GD	£5103
112	1/98	Sand	2m6f	D(0-110)HHdl	SFT	£3095
107	11/97	Carl	2m4f110y	F(0-105)HHdl	GD	£2052

Total win prize-money £13680

Going: Sf: 0-2 GS: 0-0 Gd: 1-2 GF: - Fm: 0-3
Distance: 2m/2m3: 0-0 2m4-2m7: 0-5 **3m+: 1-2**
Track: **LH: 1-5** RH: 0-1 **Tight: 1-5** Gall: 0-0
Aids: Bl: 0-0 Vi: 0-0 Tstrap: 0-0
Best Rating: **127** 3/98 Uttx 3m110y good Hdl

Lightly-raced over recent years, he does not look the same horse over fences as he was over hurdles. He is often reverted to the level for a sharpener between jump races. Goes on most ground.

Bold Conqueror

6-y-o br m Anshan-Freudenau (Wassl)
P D Evans A Shields

Placings:P/P **(2134)**
2001/02: 21^{P}GF

	Starts	1st	2nd	3rd	Win & Pl
Hurdles		1	0	0	0
Career Total		**2**	**0**	**0**	**0**

Going: Sf: 0-0 GS: 0-0 Gd: 0-0 GF: - Fm: 0-1
Distance: 2m/2m3: 0-0 2m4-2m7: 0-1 3m+: 0-0
Track: LH: 0-0 RH: 0-1 Tight: 0-0 Gall: 0-0
Aids: Bl: 0-0 Vi: 0-0 Tstrap: 0-0
Best Rating:

Bold Hunter

100(94h) (58h)96

8-y-o b g Polish Precedent (USA)-Pumpona (USA) (Sharpen Up)

M J M Evans M J M Evans

Placings:0U/2126453/06404P53-00P035 **(4843)**

2001/02: 16^{0}S, 17^{0}HY, 19^{P}S, 19^{0}S, 19^{3}GF, 17^{5}G

	Starts	1st	2nd	3rd	Win & Pl
Hurdles	4	0	0	0	0
Chases	2	0	0	1	639
Career Total	**23**	**1**	**2**	**3**	**5310**

96	8/99	Strf	2m110y	E Hdl	GD	£2537

Total win prize-money £2538

Going: Sf: 0-4 GS: 0-0 Gd: 0-1 GF: - Fm: 0-1
Distance: 2m/2m3: 0-4 2m4-2m7: 0-2 3m+: 0-0
Track: LH: 0-1 RH: 0-5 Tight: 0-2 Gall: 0-0
Aids: Bl: 0-0 Vi: 0-0 Tstrap: 0-0
Best Rating: 97 8/99 NAbb 2m1f good Hdl

Bold Investor

107 129

5-y-o b g Anshan-Shirlstar Investor (Some Hand)

J J O'Neill Mrs A R Thompson

Placings:F412306-31416 **(4821)**

2001/02: 17^{3}S, 20^{1}G, 22^{4}GS, 22^{1}GS, 24^{6}G

	Starts	1st	2nd	3rd	Win & Pl
Hurdles	5	2	0	1	11460
Career Total	**12**	**3**	**1**	**2**	**16339**

129	3/02	Sand	2m6f	D(0-120)HHdl	G-S	£7280
120	1/02	Donc	2m4f	E(0-110)HHdl	GD	£3104
105	11/00	Newc	2m	E Hdl	SFT	£2415

Total win prize-money £12800

Going: Sf: 0-1 GS: 1-2 Gd: 1-2 GF: - Fm: 0-0
Distance: 2m/2m3: 0-1 **2m4-2m7: 2-3** 3m+: 0-1
Track: LH: 1-1 RH: 1-3 Tight: 0-0 **Gall: 1-1**
Aids: Bl: 0-0 Vi: 0-0 Tstrap: 0-0
Best Rating: 129 3/02 Sand 2m6f gd-sft Hdl

Fair handicap hurdler at up to two miles-six. Suited by good and soft ground and will eventually make a chaser.

Bold King (FR)

104(100c) (113c)114

7-y-o gr g Turgeon (USA)-Vanila Fudge (USA) (Bold Bidder)

Ian Williams (N A Callaghan 15/5) Favourites Racing Ltd

Placings:1050000/46112/11235-5413212035 **(4821)**

2001/02: 19^{5}G, 20^{4}G, 19^{1}GF, 24^{3}GS, 24^{2}G, 24^{1}G, 26^{2}GS, 24^{0}GS, 24^{3}G, 24^{5}G

	Starts	1st	2nd	3rd	Win & Pl
Hurdles	8	2	2	1	11877
Chases	2	0	0	1	1090
Career Total	**27**	**7**	**4**	**3**	**40722**

114	1/02	Ludl	3m	D(0-115)HHdl	GD	£3415
109	11/01	Extr	2m3f	D(0-125)HHdl	G-F	£3510
137	11/00	Leic	2m	E Ch	G-S	£3022
117	10/00	Towc	2m110y	D Ch	GD	£3835
101	3/00	Ludl	2m	F(0-105)HHdl	GD	£4111
101	3/00	Hntg	2m110y	F(0-110)HHdl	G-F	£1806
	6/98	Autl	1m7f	Hdl	VS	£10101

Total win prize-money £29802

Going: Sf: 0-0 GS: 0-3 Gd: 1-6 GF: - Fm: 1-1
Distance: 2m/2m3: 1-1 2m4-2m7: 0-2 3m+: 1-7
Track: LH: 0-4 **RH: 2-5** Tight: 0-1 Gall: 0-1
Aids: Bl: 0-0 Vi: 0-1 Tstrap: 0-0
Best Rating: 137 11/00 Newb 2m1f heavy Ch

Fair hurdler, useful chaser. He took well to fences in 2000/1, winning twice. He has been mixing hurdling and chasing since and has managed to win twice over the smaller obstacles. Stays three miles plus and appreciates decent ground. Best on a right-handed track, he does not want to hit the front too soon.

Bold McLaughlan

4-y-o b g Mind Games-Stoneydale (Tickled Pink)

Miss M Bragg (J S Goldie 16/7) W H Whitley

Placings:PP **(4724)**

2001/02: 20^{P}GS, 16^{P}GF

	Starts	1st	2nd	3rd	Win & Pl
Hurdles	2	0	0	0	
Career Total	**2**	**0**	**0**	**0**	

Going: Sf: 0-0 GS: 0-1 Gd: 0-0 GF: - Fm: 0-1
Distance: 2m/2m3: 0-1 2m4-2m7: 0-1 3m+: 0-0
Track: LH: 0-2 RH: 0-0 Tight: 0-0 Gall: 0-0
Aids: Bl: 0-0 Vi: 0-0 Tstrap: 0-0
Best Rating:

Bold Navigator

97 99

12-y-o b g Lighter-Drummond Lass (Peacock (FR))

A M Crow A M Crow

Placings:P/0-5 **(3996)**

2001/02: 24^{5}S

	Starts	1st	2nd	3rd	Win & Pl
Chases	1	0	0	0	0
Career Total	**3**	**0**	**0**	**0**	**0**

Going: Sf: 0-1 GS: 0-0 Gd: 0-0 GF: - Fm: 0-0
Distance: 2m/2m3: 0-0 2m4-2m7: 0-0 3m+: 0-1
Track: LH: 0-1 RH: 0-0 Tight: 0-0 Gall: 0-1
Aids: Bl: 0-0 Vi: 0-0 Tstrap: 0-0
Best Rating: 99 3/02 Donc 3m soft Ch

Bolder Alexander (IRE)

96 63

5-y-o b g Persian Bold-Be Yourself (USA) (Noalcoholic (FR))

F Jordan M W Doyle

Placings:600000 **(2510)**

2001/02: 20^{6}G, 18^{0}GF, 16^{5}S, 17^{0}G, 20^{0}GS, 16^{0}S

	Starts	1st	2nd	3rd	Win & Pl
Hurdles	6	0	0	0	0
Career Total	**6**	**0**	**0**	**0**	**0**

Going: Sf: 0-2 GS: 0-1 Gd: 0-2 GF: - Fm: 0-1
Distance: 2m/2m3: 0-4 2m4-2m7: 0-2 3m+: 0-0
Track: LH: 0-5 RH: 0-1 Tight: 0-6 Gall: 0-0
Aids: Bl: 0-0 Vi: 0-0 Tstrap: 0-0
Best Rating: 63 11/01 Strf 2m110y soft Hdl

Bolshie Baron

13-y-o b g Baron Blakeney-Contrary Lady (Conwyn)

H W Wheeler (M F Harris 16/5) E O Steward

Placings:6620422/P0P50P/4/P2PP-43P3 **(4741)**

2001/02: 31^{4}G, 24^{3}G, 25^{P}G, 24^{3}GF

	Starts	1st	2nd	3rd	Win & Pl
Chases	4	0	0	2	1066
Career Total	**22**	**0**	**4**	**2**	**5405**

Going: Sf: 0-0 GS: 0-0 Gd: 0-3 GF: - Fm: 0-1
Distance: 2m/2m3: 0-0 2m4-2m7: 0-0 3m+: 0-4
Track: LH: 0-1 RH: 0-3 Tight: 0-3 Gall: 0-0
Aids: Bl: 0-0 Vi: 0-0 Tstrap: 0-4
Best Rating: 92 5/00 Folk 3m7f good Ch

A modest pointer and poor hunter.

Bolton Forest (IRE)

9-y-o b g Be My Native (USA)-Tickenor Wood (Le Bavard (FR))

C Storey Mrs C Strang Steel

Placings:0/12200/04413055P/51/16204-6 **(4833)**

2001/02: 27^{6}G

	Starts	1st	2nd	3rd	Win & Pl
Chases	1	0	0	0	0
Career Total	**23**	**4**	**3**	**1**	**17093**

125	5/00	MRas	2m6f110y	E Ch	G-F	£3526
107	4/00	Font	2m4f	F(0-100)HHdl	GD	£2744
93	7/98	Limk	2m2f	Hdl	YLD	£2989
100	9/97	List	2m	NHF	G-Y	£4069

Total win prize-money £13328

Going: Sf: 0-0 GS: 0-0 Gd: 0-1 GF: - Fm: 0-0
Distance: 2m/2m3: 0-0 2m4-2m7: 0-0 3m+: 0-1
Track: LH: 0-1 RH: 0-0 Tight: 0-0 Gall: 0-0
Aids: Bl: 0-0 Vi: 0-0 Tstrap: 0-0
Best Rating: 125 5/00 MRas 2m6f110y gd-fm Ch

Bomb Alaska

71 57

7-y-o br g Polar Falcon (USA)-So True (So Blessed)

G B Balding Miss B Swire

Placings:60 **(2936)**

2001/02: 16^{6}GS, 16^{0}G

	Starts	1st	2nd	3rd	Win & Pl
Hurdles	2	0	0	0	188
Career Total	**2**	**0**	**0**	**0**	**188**

Going: Sf: 0-0 GS: 0-1 Gd: 0-1 GF: - Fm: 0-0
Distance: 2m/2m3: 0-2 2m4-2m7: 0-0 3m+: 0-0
Track: LH: 0-2 RH: 0-0 Tight: 0-0 Gall: 0-2
Aids: Bl: 0-0 Vi: 0-0 Tstrap: 0-1
Best Rating: 57 12/01 Newb 2m110y good Hdl

Smart handicapper on the Flat at around a mile. Has yet to show much over hurdles.

Bondosan

6-y-o b g Barathea (IRE)-Fern (Shirley Heights)

J F Coupland J F Coupland

Placings:U00/PP **(2175)**

2001/02: 16^{P}G, 16^{P}G

	Starts	1st	2nd	3rd	Win & Pl
Hurdles	2	0	0	0	
Career Total	**5**	**0**	**0**	**0**	

Going: Sf: 0-0 GS: 0-0 Gd: 0-2 GF: - Fm: 0-0
Distance: 2m/2m3: 0-2 2m4-2m7: 0-0 3m+: 0-0
Track: LH: 0-2 RH: 0-0 Tight: 0-1 Gall: 0-0
Aids: Bl: 0-0 Vi: 0-0 Tstrap: 0-0
Best Rating: 33 2/00 Catt 2m good Hdl

Boneyarrow (IRE)

117 **144**

6-y-o ch g Over The River (FR)-Apicat (Buckskin (FR))
W P Mullins J Comerford

Placings:1262312134 **(4944a)**
2001/02: 17^{1}G, 16^{2}S, 24^{6}YS, 24^{2}S, 16^{3}Y, 18^{1}YS, 18^{2}HY, 20^{1}S, 20^{3}G, 20^{4}G

	Starts	1st	2nd	3rd	Win & Pl
NH Flat	2	1	1	0	5702
Hurdles	8	2	2	2	23140
Career Total	**10**	**3**	**3**	**2**	**28842**

144	3/02	Punc	2m4f	Hdl	SFT	£7975
108	1/02	Thur	2m2f	Hdl	Y-S	£3809
120	9/01	Tral	2m1f	NHF	GD	£3895

Total win prize-money £15680

Going: Sf: 1-4 GS: 0-0 Gd: 1-3 GF: - Fm: 0-0
Distance: **2m/2m3: 2-5** 2m4-2m7: 1-3 3m+: 0-2
Track: LH: 0-2 **RH: 1-3** Tight: 0-1 Gall: 0-0
Aids: Bl: 0-0 Vi: 0-0 Tstrap: 0-0
Best Rating: 144 4/02 Punc 2m4f good Hdl

Decent Irish hurdler, stays two and a quarter miles, handles soft ground.

Bonny Rigg (IRE)

70 **31**

10-y-o b m Phardante (FR)-Open Your Eyes (Beau Charmeur (FR))
B J Llewellyn N B Jones

Placings:00/P0000/00U/0456055/3422/0P **(0643)**
2001/02: 21^{0}G, 22^{P}GF

	Starts	1st	2nd	3rd	Win & Pl
Chases	2	0	0	0	
Career Total	**23**	**0**	**2**	**1**	**2282**

Going: Sf: 0-0 GS: 0-0 Gd: 0-1 GF: - Fm: 0-1
Distance: 2m/2m3: 0-0 2m4-2m7: 0-2 3m+: 0-0
Track: LH: 0-0 RH: 0-1 Tight: 0-1 Gall: 0-0
Aids: Bl: 0-0 Vi: 0-0 Tstrap: 0-0
Best Rating: 88 6/99 MRas 2m6f110y good Ch

Bonus Bridge (IRE)

100 **108**

7-y-o b g Executive Perk-Corivia (Over The River (FR))
H D Daly Lady Knutsford

Placings:34-123P4 **(4597)**
2001/02: 17^{1}S, 16^{2}GF, 17^{3}GS, 20^{P}GS, 19^{4}GF

	Starts	1st	2nd	3rd	Win & Pl
Hurdles	5	1	1	1	4879
Career Total	**7**	**1**	**1**	**2**	**5174**

103	10/01	Hrfd	2m1f	E Hdl	SFT	£3328

Total win prize-money £3329

Going: Sf: 1-1 GS: 0-2 Gd: 0-0 GF: - Fm: 0-2
Distance: **2m/2m3: 1-4** 2m4-2m7: 0-1 3m+: 0-0
Track: LH: 0-1 **RH: 1-4** Tight: 0-0 Gall: 0-0
Aids: Bl: 0-0 Vi: 0-0 Tstrap: 0-0
Best Rating: 117 1/01 Ludl 2m soft NHF

A chaser in the making. Has won over hurdles. Acts on soft ground, but handles a sounder surface and is likely to stay two and a half miles.

Bonus Trix (IRE)

103f **95f**

6-y-o b g Executive Perk-Black Trix (Peacock (FR))
A J Lidderdale (E Stanners 23/5) Team George I

Placings:P-10 **(4423)**
2001/02: 17^{1}G, 16^{0}GS

	Starts	1st	2nd	3rd	Win & Pl
NH Flat	2	1	0	0	1666
Career Total	**3**	**1**	**0**	**0**	**1666**

95	5/01	Bang	2m1f	H NHF	GD	£1666

Total win prize-money £1666

Going: Sf: 0-0 GS: 0-1 Gd: 1-1 GF: - Fm: 0-0
Distance: **2m/2m3: 1-2** 2m4-2m7: 0-0 3m+: 0-0
Track: **LH: 1-2** RH: 0-0 **Tight: 1-1** Gall: 0-1
Aids: Bl: 0-0 Vi: 0-0 Tstrap: 0-0
Best Rating: 95 3/02 Newb 2m110y gd-sft NHF

Boogy Woogy

98(99h) (116h)**103**

6-y-o ch g Rock Hopper-Primulette (Mummy's Pet)
T D Easterby Mrs P D Croft

Placings:312/13P00643-450 **(2579)**
2001/02: 21^{4}G, 21^{5}G, 20^{0}S

	Starts	1st	2nd	3rd	Win & Pl
Chases	3	0	0	0	232
Career Total	**14**	**2**	**1**	**3**	**13191**

125	10/00	Weth	2m	D(0-125)HHdl	G-S	£2957
90	11/99	MRas	2m1f110y	D Hdl	G-S	£3504

Total win prize-money £6462

Going: Sf: 0-1 GS: 0-0 Gd: 0-2 GF: - Fm: 0-0
Distance: 2m/2m3: 0-0 2m4-2m7: 0-3 3m+: 0-0
Track: LH: 0-3 RH: 0-0 Tight: 0-2 Gall: 0-0
Aids: Bl: 0-2 Vi: 0-0 Tstrap: 0-0
Best Rating: 125 10/00 Weth 2m gd-sft Hdl

Books Whirl

72f **44f**

5-y-o b m Henbit (USA)-In A Whirl (USA) (Island Whirl (USA))
Mrs D A Hamer Gwynne Phillips

Placings:00 **(1799)**
2001/02: 17^{0}GF, 16^{0}S

	Starts	1st	2nd	3rd	Win & Pl
NH Flat	2	0	0	0	
Career Total	**2**	**0**	**0**	**0**	

Going: Sf: 0-1 GS: 0-0 Gd: 0-0 GF: - Fm: 0-1
Distance: 2m/2m3: 0-2 2m4-2m7: 0-0 3m+: 0-0
Track: LH: 0-1 RH: 0-1 Tight: 0-0 Gall: 0-0
Aids: Bl: 0-0 Vi: 0-0 Tstrap: 0-0
Best Rating: 44 9/01 Hrfd 2m1f gd-fm NHF

Booming Business (IRE)

95 **91**

7-y-o b/br g Good Thyne (USA)-Hurricane Girl (IRE) (Strong Gale)
R Rowe Mrs Jean R Bishop

Placings:P00/3-34 **(1897)**

2001/02: 25^{3}G, 26^{4}GS

	Starts	1st	2nd	3rd	Win & Pl
Chases	2	0	0	1	755
Career Total	**6**	**0**	**0**	**2**	**1085**

Going: Sf: 0-0 GS: 0-1 Gd: 0-1 GF: - Fm: 0-0
Distance: 2m/2m3: 0-0 2m4-2m7: 0-0 3m+: 0-2
Track: LH: 0-0 RH: 0-1 Tight: 0-2 Gall: 0-0
Aids: Bl: 0-0 Vi: 0-0 Tstrap: 0-0
Best Rating: 91 10/01 Font 3m2f110y gd-sft Ch

An improving sort, this lightly-raced novice chaser will stay three miles in time.

Boozeandyoulose (IRE)

7-y-o b g Noble Patriarch-Kates Fling (USA) (Quiet Fling (USA))
John Moore (J Neville 10/3) Barrie Allen

Placings:30/50 **(0430)**
2001/02: 20^{5}GF, 16^{0}G

	Starts	1st	2nd	3rd	Win & Pl
Chases	2	0	0	0	0
Career Total	**4**	**0**	**0**	**1**	**224**

Going: Sf: 0-0 GS: 0-0 Gd: 0-1 GF: - Fm: 0-1
Distance: 2m/2m3: 0-1 2m4-2m7: 0-1 3m+: 0-0
Track: LH: 0-1 RH: 0-0 Tight: 0-1 Gall: 0-0
Aids: Bl: 0-0 Vi: 0-0 Tstrap: 0-0
Best Rating: 99 7/99 Worc 2m gd-fm NHF

Boozi Birthday

8-y-o b m Crested Lark-Pollygloss (Doctor Pangloss)
B I Case Morning After The Night Before P/ship

Placings:PUP3F **(3444)**
2001/02: 24^{P}S, 24^{U}S, 22^{P}S, 24^{3}G, 24^{F}GS

	Starts	1st	2nd	3rd	Win & Pl
Hurdles	1	0	0	0	0
Chases	4	0	0	1	550
Career Total	**5**	**0**	**0**	**1**	**550**

Going: Sf: 0-3 GS: 0-1 Gd: 0-1 GF: - Fm: 0-0
Distance: 2m/2m3: 0-0 2m4-2m7: 0-1 3m+: 0-4
Track: LH: 0-3 RH: 0-2 Tight: 0-2 Gall: 0-0
Aids: Bl: 0-0 Vi: 0-0 Tstrap: 0-0
Best Rating:

Borani

109 **118**

7-y-o b g Shirley Heights-Ower (IRE) (Lomond (USA))
J J O'Neill G McManus

Placings:0/00-B1F361 **(4848)**
2001/02: 17^{B}S, 16^{1}S, 21^{F}HY, 16^{3}G, 16^{6}G, 16^{1}G

	Starts	1st	2nd	3rd	Win & Pl
Hurdles	6	2	0	1	8265
Career Total	**9**	**2**	**0**	**1**	**8265**

122	4/02	Strf	2m110y	D(0-110)HHdl	GD	£3783
105	2/02	Sand	2m110y	D(0-115)HHdl	SFT	£3672

Total win prize-money £7456

Going: Sf: 1-3 GS: 0-0 Gd: 1-3 GF: - Fm: 0-0
Distance: **2m/2m3: 2-5** 2m4-2m7: 0-1 3m+: 0-0

Track: LH: 1-2 RH: 1-3 **Tight: 1-3** Gall: 0-0
Aids: Bl: 0-0 Vi: 0-0 Tstrap: 0-0
Best Rating: **122** 4/02 Strf 2m110y good Hdl

He left his previous hurdling form behind when winning comfortably at Sandown in February 2002 and just got up to win at Stratford in April, but he is a very difficult ride who needs to be produced right on the line. Acts on any ground.

Border Burn

90 **91**

8-y-o ch g Safawan-Burning Ryme (Rymer)
N M L Ewart N M L Ewart

Placings:6P-450 **(4859)**
2001/02: 21^{4}HY, 26^{5}GS, 25^{0}G

	Starts	1st	2nd	3rd	Win & Pl
Chases	3	0	0	0	0
Career Total	**5**	**0**	**0**	**0**	**0**

Going: Sf: 0-1 GS: 0-1 Gd: 0-1 GF: - Fm: 0-0
Distance: 2m/2m3: 0-0 2m4-2m7: 0-1 3m+: 0-2
Track: LH: 0-2 RH: 0-1 Tight: 0-0 Gall: 0-0
Aids: Bl: 0-0 Vi: 0-0 Tstrap: 0-0
Best Rating: **91** 3/02 Ayr 2m5f110y heavy Ch

Former smart pointer, he has been lightly raced.

Border Edge

4-y-o b g Beveled (USA)-Seymour Ann (Krayyan)
K McAuliffe Allsorts

Placings:6 **(2162)**
2001/02: 16^{6}G

	Starts	1st	2nd	3rd	Win & Pl
Hurdles	1	0	0	0	0
Career Total	**1**	**0**	**0**	**0**	**0**

Going: Sf: 0-0 GS: 0-0 Gd: 0-1 GF: - Fm: 0-0
Distance: 2m/2m3: 0-1 2m4-2m7: 0-0 3m+: 0-0
Track: LH: 0-1 RH: 0-0 Tight: 0-0 Gall: 0-0
Aids: Bl: 0-0 Vi: 0-0 Tstrap: 0-0
Best Rating:

Border Farmer (IRE)

9-y-o b g Riverhead (USA)-Double Figures (FR) (Double Form)
Mrs S Richardson James Richardson

Placings:006/04P/06-U26 **(0429)**
2001/02: 24^{U}G, 24^{2}GF, 25^{6}G

	Starts	1st	2nd	3rd	Win & Pl
Chases	3	0	1	0	530
Career Total	**11**	**0**	**1**	**0**	**530**

Going: Sf: 0-0 GS: 0-0 Gd: 0-2 GF: - Fm: 0-1
Distance: 2m/2m3: 0-0 2m4-2m7: 0-0 3m+: 0-3
Track: LH: 0-1 RH: 0-1 Tight: 0-1 Gall: 0-1
Aids: Bl: 0-0 Vi: 0-0 Tstrap: 0-0
Best Rating: **89** 5/01 Strf 3m gd-fm Ch

Border Glory

11-y-o ch g Derrylin-Boreen's Glory (Boreen (FR))
C Storey The Hon Gerald Maitland-Carew

Placings:U/P4UU/6PP6P/52/00PPU-PP **(0338)**
2001/02: 25^{P}S, 20^{P}S

	Starts	1st	2nd	3rd	Win & Pl
Chases	2	0	0	0	
Career Total	**19**	**0**	**1**	**0**	**666**

Going: Sf: 0-2 GS: 0-0 Gd: 0-0 GF: - Fm: 0-0
Distance: 2m/2m3: 0-0 2m4-2m7: 0-1 3m+: 0-1
Track: LH: 0-1 RH: 0-1 Tight: 0-0 Gall: 0-0
Aids: Bl: 0-2 Vi: 0-0 Tstrap: 0-0
Best Rating: **92** 4/00 Kels 3m1f soft Ch

Border Light

91 **91**

9-y-o ch g Lighter-Border Cherry (Deep Run)
H J Manners H J Manners

Placings:0/0/45P-03PP **(1897)**
2001/02: 17^{0}GS, 25^{3}G, 24^{P}S, 26^{P}GS

	Starts	1st	2nd	3rd	Win & Pl
Chases	4	0	0	1	568
Career Total	**9**	**0**	**0**	**1**	**809**

Going: Sf: 0-1 GS: 0-2 Gd: 0-1 GF: - Fm: 0-0
Distance: 2m/2m3: 0-1 2m4-2m7: 0-0 3m+: 0-3
Track: LH: 0-1 RH: 0-1 Tight: 0-1 Gall: 0-0
Aids: Bl: 0-0 Vi: 0-0 Tstrap: 0-0
Best Rating: **91** 5/01 Chel 3m1f110y good Ch

Border Run

(94h)

5-y-o b g Missed Flight-Edraianthus (Windjammer (USA))
M Mullineaux P T Hollins

Placings:0031306-PPPF5P **(4751)**
2001/02: 16^{P}GF, 17^{P}GS, 16^{P}GS, 16^{F}S, 16^{5}S, 20^{P}GF

	Starts	1st	2nd	3rd	Win & Pl
Hurdles	3	0	0	0	0
Chases	3	0	0	0	0
Career Total	**13**	**1**	**0**	**2**	**3574**

78 12/00 Ludl 2m G Hdl SFT £2853
Total win prize-money £2854

Going: Sf: 0-2 GS: 0-2 Gd: 0-0 GF: - Fm: 0-2
Distance: 2m/2m3: 0-5 2m4-2m7: 0-1 3m+: 0-0
Track: LH: 0-3 RH: 0-3 Tight: 0-3 Gall: 0-0
Aids: Bl: 0-0 Vi: 0-0 Tstrap: 0-0
Best Rating: **84** 1/01 Tntn 2m1f heavy Hdl

Poor dual-purpose handicapper, has more letters by his name than numbers.

Border Star (IRE)

92 **94**

5-y-o b g Parthian Springs-Tengello (Bargello)
J M Jefferson Mrs Kathleen Campey

Placings:0655005 **(4867)**
2001/02: 16^{0}S, 17^{6}GS, 16^{5}S, 17^{5}HY, 16^{0}HY, 20^{0}HY, 16^{5}GF

	Starts	1st	2nd	3rd	Win & Pl
NH Flat	2	0	0	0	0
Hurdles	5	0	0	0	0
Career Total	**7**	**0**	**0**	**0**	**0**

Going: Sf: 0-5 GS: 0-1 Gd: 0-0 GF: - Fm: 0-1
Distance: 2m/2m3: 0-6 2m4-2m7: 0-1 3m+: 0-0
Track: LH: 0-6 RH: 0-1 Tight: 0-2 Gall: 0-1
Aids: Bl: 0-0 Vi: 0-0 Tstrap: 0-0
Best Rating: **94** 2/02 Hayd 2m heavy Hdl

Limited ability in novice hurdles around two miles. Should do better over further and looks more of a chaser.

Borderline Case

94f **97f**

6-y-o b g Homo Sapien-Our Chrisy (Carlburg)
O Sherwood Dougal Duff Watt Partners

Placings:20-4 **(0078)**
2001/02: 17^{4}G

	Starts	1st	2nd	3rd	Win & Pl
NH Flat	1	0	0	0	0
Career Total	**3**	**0**	**1**	**0**	**494**

Going: Sf: 0-0 GS: 0-0 Gd: 0-1 GF: - Fm: 0-0
Distance: 2m/2m3: 0-1 2m4-2m7: 0-0 3m+: 0-0
Track: LH: 0-0 RH: 0-1 Tight: 0-0 Gall: 0-0
Aids: Bl: 0-0 Vi: 0-0 Tstrap: 0-0
Best Rating: **101** 2/01 Winc 2m good NHF

Borehill Joker

108(93c) (107c)**104**

6-y-o ch g Pure Melody (USA)-Queen Matilda (Castle Keep)
E Haddock (W G M Turner 6/2) Miss H M Newell

Placings:3/0021P3062115-415452452236 **(4589)**
2001/02: 16^{4}S, 16^{1}G, 17^{5}GS, 18^{4}GS, 18^{5}G, 20^{2}G, 20^{4}G, 16^{5}S, 16^{2}S, 16^{2}GS, 16^{3}S, 16^{6}G

	Starts	1st	2nd	3rd	Win & Pl
Hurdles	11	1	3	1	5207
Chases	1	0	0	0	0
Career Total	**25**	**4**	**5**	**3**	**13209**

104	10/01	Sthl	2m	F(0-105)HHdl	GD	£2240
102	1/01	Leic	2m	F Hdl	HVY	£2646
101	1/01	Leic	2m	G(0-90)HHdl	HVY	£1967
89	10/00	Towc	2m	G Hdl	G-S	£1575

Total win prize-money £8428

Going: Sf: 0-4 GS: 0-3 Gd: 1-5 GF: - Fm: 0-0
Distance: **2m/2m3: 1-10** 2m4-2m7: 0-2 3m+: 0-0
Track: **LH: 1-6** RH: 0-6 **Tight: 1-7** Gall: 0-1
Aids: Bl: 0-0 Vi: 0-0 **Tstrap: 1-12**
Best Rating: **107** 11/01 Plum 2m1f gd-sft Ch

Plating-class hurdler, suited by a right-handed track and soft ground.

Boring Goring (IRE)

(107h) (90h)

8-y-o b g Aristocracy-Coolrusk (IRE) (Millfontaine)
Miss A M Newton-Smith Goring Hotel

Placings:40/0P2P54/44FF-PUF2161 **(4512)**
2001/02: 26^{P}G, 22^{U}GF, 22^{F}G, 21^{2}GS, 22^{1}GF, 22^{6}G, 21^{1}G

	Starts	1st	2nd	3rd	Win & Pl
Hurdles	6	2	1	0	6129
Chases	1	0	0	0	0
Career Total	**19**	**2**	**2**	**0**	**7517**

90	3/02	Plum	2m5f	E Hdl	GD	£2719
90	11/01	Extr	2m6f110y	F(0-100)HHdl	G-F	£2727

Total win prize-money £5447

Going: Sf: 0-0 GS: 0-1 Gd: 1-4 GF: - Fm: 1-2
Distance: 2m/2m3: 0-0 **2m4-2m7: 2-6** 3m+: 0-1
Track: **LH: 1-3** RH: 0-1 **Tight: 1-4** Gall: 0-0
Aids: Bl: 0-0 Vi: 0-0 **Tstrap: 2-7**
Best Rating: **95** 2/99 Folk 2m1f110y soft NHF

A controversial winner at Exeter in November, he scored on

his own merits at Plumpton over Easter. Stays two miles five furlongs, likes good ground.

Borleagh Pilot (IRE)

11-y-o ch g Torus-Pilots Row (Tanavar)
Miss Tina Jackson H L Thompson

Placings:0040/500630/FF/P00P (4856)
2001/02: 25^{P}S, 16^{0}G, 19^{0}GS, 25^{P}G

	Starts	1st	2nd	3rd	Win & Pl
Chases	4	0	0	0	
Career Total	**16**	**0**	**0**	**1**	**350**

Going: Sf: 0-1 GS: 0-1 Gd: 0-2 GF: - Fm: 0-0
Distance: 2m/2m3: 0-2 2m4-2m7: 0-0 3m+: 0-2
Track: LH: 0-4 RH: 0-0 Tight: 0-2 Gall: 0-1
Aids: Bl: 0-0 Vi: 0-0 Tstrap: 0-0
Best Rating: **92** 1/98 Gowr 2m yield Hdl

Ex-Irish, modest form over hurdles and fences.

Born Of Fubar

90 **88**
8-y-o gr g North Col-Scallykath (Scallywag)
B J M Ryall B J M Ryall

Placings:06/3F/5000F (4484)
2001/02: 17^{5}HY, 17^{0}S, 21^{0}S, 19^{0}S, 17^{F}G

	Starts	1st	2nd	3rd	Win & Pl
Hurdles	5	0	0	0	0
Career Total	**9**	**0**	**0**	**1**	**391**

Going: Sf: 0-4 GS: 0-0 Gd: 0-1 GF: - Fm: 0-0
Distance: 2m/2m3: 0-3 2m4-2m7: 0-2 3m+: 0-0
Track: LH: 0-1 RH: 0-4 Tight: 0-3 Gall: 0-0
Aids: Bl: 0-0 Vi: 0-0 Tstrap: 0-0
Best Rating: **93** 11/99 Tntn 2m1f good Hdl

Born To Please (IRE)

(63h)
10-y-o ch g Waajib-Gratify (Grundy)
R T Phillips A B S Racing

Placings:3021322161154/503/53P121/022421U23125/P24 1206P-6 (0433)
2001/02: 25^{6}GF

	Starts	1st	2nd	3rd	Win & Pl
Chases	1	0	0	0	0
Career Total	**43**	**9**	**11**	**5**	**32740**

111	9/00	Font	2m6f110y	F(0-110)HHdl	G-S	£2646
110	10/99	Sedg	3m3f110y	F(0-100)HHdl	GD	£2302
100	9/99	NAbb	2m6f	G Hdl	G-F	£1846
95	10/98	Hrfd	2m3f110y	G Hdl	G-F	£1679
95	9/98	NAbb	2m6f	G Hdl	G-F	£1665
101	10/96	Hrfd	2m3f110y	D(0-120)HHdl	G-F	£2717
90	10/96	Hntg	2m5f110y	E(0-110)HHdl	G-F	£2215
100	8/96	Prth	2m4f110y	E(0-110)HHdl	G-F	£2710
82	7/96	Worc	2m4f	D Hdl	G-F	£2973

Total win prize-money £20754

Going: Sf: 0-0 GS: 0-0 Gd: 0-0 GF: - Fm: 0-1
Distance: 2m/2m3: 0-0 2m4-2m7: 0-0 3m+: 0-1
Track: LH: 0-0 RH: 0-1 Tight: 0-1 Gall: 0-0
Aids: Bl: 0-0 Vi: 0-1 Tstrap: 0-0
Best Rating: **112** 10/00 Tntn 3m110y good Hdl

Born Winner

77 **37**
7-y-o b g Rainbow Quest (USA)-Tinaca (USA) (Manila (USA))
Miss L Bower Christopher J Halpin

Placings:00/0-P0 (3765)
2001/02: 16^{P}S, 16^{0}GS

	Starts	1st	2nd	3rd	Win & Pl
Hurdles	2	0	0	0	
Career Total	**5**	**0**	**0**	**0**	

Going: Sf: 0-1 GS: 0-1 Gd: 0-0 GF: - Fm: 0-0
Distance: 2m/2m3: 0-2 2m4-2m7: 0-0 3m+: 0-0
Track: LH: 0-1 RH: 0-1 Tight: 0-1 Gall: 0-0
Aids: Bl: 0-0 Vi: 0-0 Tstrap: 0-0
Best Rating: **73** 2/00 Sand 2m110y soft Hdl

Boro Sovereign (IRE)

111(105c) (125c)**129**
9-y-o b g King's Ride-Boro Penny (Normandy)
Miss Venetia Williams (N J Henderson 11/7) Mrs P De W Johnson

Placings: 1/122/13/402-21PPU230F0 (4149)
2001/02: 16^{2}G, 20^{1}G, 20^{P}G, 24^{P}G, 22^{U}G, 24^{2}S, 22^{3}HY, 22^{0}S, 20^{F}S, 20^{0}GS

	Starts	1st	2nd	3rd	Win & Pl
Hurdles	6	0	1	1	2500
Chases	4	1	1	0	5233
Career Total	**19**	**4**	**5**	**2**	**18445**

125	9/01	Bang	2m4f110y	D Ch	GD	£4309
106	12/99	Towc	2m	E Hdl	SFT	£2740
109	12/98	Hntg	2m110y	H NHF	SFT	£1392
103	4/97	Tipp	2m	NHF	GD	£2712

Total win prize-money £11155

Going: Sf: 0-4 GS: 0-1 Gd: 1-5 GF: - Fm: 0-0
Distance: 2m/2m3: 0-1 **2m4-2m7: 1-7** 3m+: 0-2
Track: **LH: 1-7** RH: 0-3 **Tight: 1-4** Gall: 0-0
Aids: Bl: 0-0 Vi: 0-0 Tstrap: 0-0
Best Rating: **129** 11/01 Chep 3m soft Hdl

Useful in bumpers and over hurdles for Nicky Henderson, he got off the mark over fences for Venetia Williams at Bangor in September 2001, but then appeared to lose his confidence and appreciated a return to hurdles.

Boro Vacation (IRE)

67(57h) (29h)**23**
13-y-o b g Ovac (ITY)-Boro Quarter (Normandy)
L Waring Mrs J Waring

Placings:050142060030/F203301/111S0U6/P4455/0P0344 60/066P064P0-P006FP0 (1994)
2001/02: 16^{P}GF, 16^{0}GF, 16^{0}GF, 21^{6}G, 16^{F}G, 16^{P}GF, 17^{0}S

	Starts	1st	2nd	3rd	Win & Pl
Hurdles	2	0	0	0	0
Chases	5	0	0	0	0
Career Total	**55**	**5**	**2**	**4**	**19122**

129	5/96	Wxfd	2m4f	(0-135)HCh	GD	£4237
129	5/96	Rosc	2m4f	Ch	G-F	£3530
118	5/96	Tram	2m	Ch	GD	£2295
105	4/96	Thur	2m2f	Ch	G-Y	£3177
	10/94	Thur	2m2f	NHF	GD	£2120

Total win prize-money £15361

Going: Sf: 0-1 GS: 0-0 Gd: 0-2 GF: - Fm: 0-4
Distance: 2m/2m3: 0-6 2m4-2m7: 0-1 3m+: 0-0
Track: LH: 0-6 RH: 0-1 Tight: 0-6 Gall: 0-0
Aids: Bl: 0-0 Vi: 0-0 Tstrap: 0-6
Best Rating: **129** 5/96 Wxfd 2m4f good Ch

Borrisheen Bay

106 **83**
7-y-o b g Arctic Lord-Soraway (Choral Society)
Mrs Richard Arthur Mrs Richard Arthur

Placings:FF6P6F20P6 (4766)
2001/02: 20^{F}GF, 19^{F}GF, 17^{6}GF, 24^{P}G, 22^{6}G, 20^{F}G, 25^{2}GF, 19^{0}G, 25^{P}GS, 20^{6}GF

	Starts	1st	2nd	3rd	Win & Pl
Hurdles	10	0	1	0	780
Career Total	**10**	**0**	**1**	**0**	**780**

Going: Sf: 0-0 GS: 0-1 Gd: 0-4 GF: - Fm: 0-5
Distance: 2m/2m3: 0-2 2m4-2m7: 0-5 3m+: 0-3
Track: LH: 0-7 RH: 0-3 Tight: 0-5 Gall: 0-0
Aids: Bl: 0-0 Vi: 0-0 Tstrap: 0-5
Best Rating: **83** 11/01 Catt 3m1f110y gd-fm Hdl

Maiden hurdler.

Boss Doyle (IRE)

113 **158**
10-y-o b g Lapierre-Prolific Scot (Northern Guest (USA))
M F Morris Mrs A M Daly

Placings:4221201/1111211F/242P0/14215/P153225-1320 (4251)
2001/02: 25^{1}G, 24^{3}Y, 24^{2}HY, 24^{0}G

	Starts	1st	2nd	3rd	Win & Pl
Hurdles	4	1	1	1	17772
Career Total	**36**	**12**	**10**	**2**	**155762**

158	11/01	Weth	3m1f	A Hdl	GD	£13200
153	10/00	Weth	3m1f	A Hdl	SFT	£13200
140	1/00	Leop	2m6f	(0-140)HHdl	YLD	£4692
152	11/99	Navn	3m	HHdl	Y-S	£7392
168	4/98	Aint	3m1f	A Ch	SFT	£26344
146	3/98	Fair	3m1f	HCh	YLD	£8739
158	12/97	Leop	3m	Ch	HVY	£6782
132	10/97	Gowr	2m2f	Ch	G-F	£3051
114	10/97	Thur	2m6f	Ch	YLD	£2543
112	9/97	List	2m6f	Ch	G-Y	£4069
114	3/97	Thur	3m	Hdl	GD	£2712
116	1/97	Thur	2m	Hdl	GD	£2204

Total win prize-money £94931

Going: Sf: 0-1 GS: 0-0 Gd: 1-2 GF: - Fm: 0-0
Distance: 2m/2m3: 0-0 2m4-2m7: 0-0 **3m+: 1-4**
Track: **LH: 1-2** RH: 0-0 Tight: 0-0 Gall: 0-0
Aids: **Bl: 1-4** Vi: 0-0 Tstrap: 0-0
Best Rating: **168** 4/98 Aint 3m1f soft Ch

On his return in November of 2001 he won the West Yorkshire Hurdle for a second time, but he has been held since, including in the Stayers' Hurdle at Cheltenham in March 2002. Best when fresh and with cut in the ground. Stays three miles.

Boss Morton (IRE)

98 **70+**
11-y-o b g Tremblant-Sandy Kelly (Ovac (ITY))
S G Chadwick S Chadwick

Placings:0051F000/4/U0U0P/FU0P2316F33402P/6UU/003 F-00600P (3553)
2001/02: 17^{0}G, 22^{0}G, 17^{6}S, 17^{0}S, 17^{0}GF, 19^{P}S

	Starts	1st	2nd	3rd	Win & Pl
Hurdles	6	0	0	0	0
Career Total	**42**	**2**	**2**	**4**	**10144**

95	7/98	Klny	2m1f	(0-102)HCh	G-F	£3288
103	9/95	Gway	2m	Hdl	G-F	£3391

Total win prize-money £6679

Going: Sf: 0-3 GS: 0-0 Gd: 0-2 GF: - Fm: 0-1
Distance: 2m/2m3: 0-5 2m4-2m7: 0-1 3m+: 0-0
Track: LH: 0-4 RH: 0-1 Tight: 0-4 Gall: 0-0
Aids: Bl: 0-0 Vi: 0-0 Tstrap: 0-0
Best Rating: **105** 10/98 Cork 2m5f yield Ch

Elderly selling hurdler.

Boss Royal

103 **90**

5-y-o ch g Afzal-Born Bossy (Eborneezer)
G A Ham W E Catstrey

Placings:P-0003P341 **(4847)**
2001/02: 17^{0}G, 21^{0}G, 16^{0}GF, 17^{3}HY, 16^{P}GS, 16^{3}S, 16^{4}G, 20^{1}G

	Starts	1st	2nd	3rd	Win & Pl
Hurdles	8	1	0	2	6022
Career Total	**9**	**1**	**0**	**2**	**6022**

90	4/02	Bang	2m4f	F(0-100)HHdl	GD	£5245

Total win prize-money £5246

Going: Sf: 0-2 GS: 0-1 Gd: 1-4 GF: - Fm: 0-1
Distance: 2m/2m3: 0-6 **2m4-2m7: 1-2** 3m+: 0-0
Track: **LH: 1-4** RH: 0-4 **Tight: 1-2** Gall: 0-1
Aids: Bl: 0-0 Vi: 0-0 **Tstrap: 1-3**
Best Rating: **90** 4/02 Bang 2m4f good Hdl

Very modest hurdler, likes to front run. Appreciated the step up to two and a half miles when getting off the mark in a handicap at Bangor in April and will make a chaser in time.

Boss Tweed (IRE)

87 **103+**

5-y-o b g Persian Bold-Betty Kenwood (Dominion)
B Mactaggart (Ronald Thompson 19/7) Graeme Renton

Placings:02 **(4888)**
2001/02: 16^{0}S, 16^{2}G

	Starts	1st	2nd	3rd	Win & Pl
Hurdles	2	0	1	0	1192
Career Total	**2**	**0**	**1**	**0**	**1192**

Going: Sf: 0-1 GS: 0-0 Gd: 0-1 GF: - Fm: 0-0
Distance: 2m/2m3: 0-2 2m4-2m7: 0-0 3m+: 0-0
Track: LH: 0-1 RH: 0-1 Tight: 0-1 Gall: 0-0
Aids: Bl: 0-0 Vi: 0-0 Tstrap: 0-1
Best Rating: **100** 4/02 Prth 2m110y good Hdl

Bosscat

5-y-o b g Presidium-Belltina (Belfort (FR))
R G Frost (K McAuliffe 18/7) Mrs Carol Pope

Placings:PP **(3340)**
2001/02: 17^{P}HY, 17^{P}S

	Starts	1st	2nd	3rd	Win & Pl
Hurdles	2	0	0	0	
Career Total	**2**	**0**	**0**	**0**	

Going: Sf: 0-2 GS: 0-0 Gd: 0-0 GF: - Fm: 0-0
Distance: 2m/2m3: 0-2 2m4-2m7: 0-0 3m+: 0-0
Track: LH: 0-1 RH: 0-1 Tight: 0-2 Gall: 0-0
Aids: Bl: 0-0 Vi: 0-0 Tstrap: 0-0
Best Rating:

Bossy Spice

79 **54**

5-y-o br m Emperor Jones (USA)-Million Heiress (Auction Ring (USA))
N M Babbage B & M Babbage & Co Ltd

Placings:6F005-3 **(0122)**
2001/02: 19^{3}F

	Starts	1st	2nd	3rd	Win & Pl
Hurdles	1	0	0	1	232
Career Total	**6**	**0**	**0**	**1**	**232**

Going: Sf: 0-0 GS: 0-0 Gd: 0-0 GF: - Fm: 0-1
Distance: 2m/2m3: 0-0 2m4-2m7: 0-1 3m+: 0-0
Track: LH: 0-0 RH: 0-1 Tight: 0-1 Gall: 0-0
Aids: Bl: 0-0 Vi: 0-0 Tstrap: 0-0
Best Rating: **54** 5/01 Tntn 2m3f110y firm Hdl

Boston Lass

99 **93**

5-y-o br m Terimon-Larksmore (Royal Fountain)
R D E Woodhouse M K Oldham

Placings:*4004P063* **(4871)**
2001/02: 17^{4}GS, 16^{0}G, 16^{0}G, 16^{4}S, 21^{P}S, 22^{0}HY, 20^{6}G, 25^{3}GF

	Starts	1st	2nd	3rd	Win & Pl
NH Flat	3	0	0	0	0
Hurdles	5	0	0	1	349
Career Total	**8**	**0**	**0**	**1**	**349**

Going: Sf: 0-3 GS: 0-1 Gd: 0-3 GF: - Fm: 0-1
Distance: 2m/2m3: 0-4 2m4-2m7: 0-3 3m+: 0-1
Track: LH: 0-6 RH: 0-2 Tight: 0-2 Gall: 0-1
Aids: Bl: 0-0 Vi: 0-0 Tstrap: 0-0
Best Rating: **93** 1/02 Newc 2m soft Hdl

Has shown some ability in novices' hurdles.

Bosuns Mate

106 **136**

9-y-o ch g Yachtsman (USA)-Langton Lass (Nearly A Hand)
N A Twiston-Davies Howard Parker

Placings:41/1211200/0U361231/FPPF032-P1656 **(2776)**
2001/02: 25^{P}G, 25^{1}GF, 23^{6}GF, 26^{5}HY, 25^{6}G

	Starts	1st	2nd	3rd	Win & Pl
Chases	5	1	0	0	5440
Career Total	**29**	**7**	**4**	**3**	**68033**

136	10/01	Extr	3m1f110y	D(0-120)HCh	G-F	£5440
155	4/00	Sand	3m110y	B Ch	SFT	£16883
155	3/00	Bang	3m110y	D Ch	GD	£4719
137	1/99	Newb	3m110y	C Hdl	HVY	£4781
137	12/98	Chel	3m	A Hdl	GD	£9375
113	5/98	Worc	2m	H NHF	G-F	£1560
101	3/98	Ludl	2m	H NHF	GD	£1203

Total win prize-money £43963

Going: Sf: 0-1 GS: 0-0 Gd: 0-2 GF: - Fm: 1-2
Distance: 2m/2m3: 0-0 2m4-2m7: 0-0 **3m+: 1-5**
Track: LH: 0-1 RH: 0-2 Tight: 0-1 Gall: 0-0
Aids: **Bl: 1-2** Vi: 0-2 Tstrap: 0-0
Best Rating: **155** 4/00 Sand 3m110y soft Ch

Possibly best in the spring, he stays well and won a farce of a race at Exeter in October after five-month break.

Bosworth Boy

100f **87f**

4-y-o b g Deploy-Krill (Kris)
Ian Williams John L Marriott

Placings:*630* **(4873)**
2001/02: 16^{6}GS, 16^{3}GF, 16^{0}GF

	Starts	1st	2nd	3rd	Win & Pl
NH Flat	3	0	0	1	387
Career Total	**3**	**0**	**0**	**1**	**387**

Going: Sf: 0-0 GS: 0-1 Gd: 0-0 GF: - Fm: 0-2
Distance: 2m/2m3: 0-3 2m4-2m7: 0-0 3m+: 0-0
Track: LH: 0-2 RH: 0-1 Tight: 0-0 Gall: 0-0
Aids: Bl: 0-0 Vi: 0-0 Tstrap: 0-0
Best Rating: **87** 4/02 Asct 2m110y gd-fm NHF

Bouchasson (FR)

115 **139**

9-y-o b g Big John (FR)-Kizil Ayak (FR) (Stratege (USA))
P J Hobbs R M E Wright

Placings:051P/0311/42234U4/5P03-00312000 **(4913)**
2001/02: 23^{0}GS, 24^{0}GF, 24^{3}G, 20^{1}G, 22^{2}G, 24^{0}G, 19^{0}GF, 29^{0}G

	Starts	1st	2nd	3rd	Win & Pl
Chases	8	1	1	1	12187
Career Total	**27**	**4**	**3**	**4**	**74689**

139	11/01	Kemp	2m4f110y	B(0-140)HCh	GD	£8999
150	4/99	Punc	2m4f	HCh	YLD	£12718
150	4/99	Ayr	2m4f	A Ch	SFT	£15840
	1/98	Cagn	2m110y	HHdl	GD	£6566

Total win prize-money £44124

Going: Sf: 0-0 GS: 0-1 Gd: 1-5 GF: - Fm: 0-2
Distance: 2m/2m3: 0-0 **2m4-2m7: 1-3** 3m+: 0-5
Track: LH: 0-2 **RH: 1-6** Tight: 0-1 Gall: 0-1
Aids: Bl: 0-1 Vi: 0-0 Tstrap: 0-0
Best Rating: **150** 3/00 Chel 3m110y good Ch

A fair handicapper, he benefited from a drop in the handicap when winning at Kempton in November 2001, but rising back up the weights again seems to have found him out. Effective at up to three miles, he is suited by right-handed tracks and after an abject effort at Uttoxeter was just denied at Perth.

Boulevard Bay (IRE)

99 **94**

11-y-o b g Royal Fountain-Cairita (Pitcairn)
Mrs P Robeson Mrs P Robeson

Placings:0/F0FP3P1316/41/3623-55500613 **(4268)**
2001/02: 16^{5}S, 16^{5}GS, 16^{5}S, 20^{0}G, 20^{0}GS, 20^{6}S, 16^{1}S, 16^{3}S

	Starts	1st	2nd	3rd	Win & Pl
Chases	8	1	0	1	3437
Career Total	**25**	**4**	**1**	**5**	**17476**

90	2/02	Leic	2m	F(0-90)HCh	SFT	£3010
116	11/99	Towc	2m110y	D(0-120)HCh	GD	£3722
113	3/99	Ling	2m	F(0-110)HCh	G-S	£3501
113	2/99	Leic	2m1f	E Ch	G-S	£3080

Total win prize-money £13313

Going: Sf: 1-5 GS: 0-2 Gd: 0-1 GF: - Fm: 0-0
Distance: **2m/2m3: 1-5** 2m4-2m7: 0-3 3m+: 0-0
Track: LH: 0-3 **RH: 1-5** Tight: 0-0 Gall: 0-1
Aids: **Bl: 1-3** Vi: 0-0 Tstrap: 0-1
Best Rating: **116** 11/99 Towc 2m110y good Ch

Fair chaser, he acts on ground with some ease, but cannot cope with very soft ground and is most effective over two miles.

Boulta (IRE)

86 **101**

8-y-o ch g Commanche Run-Boulta View (Beau Chapeau)
Mrs Clare Moore (Trainer Unknown 10/2) Mrs Clare Moore

Placings:0 **(4690)**
2001/02: 25^{0}GF

	Starts	1st	2nd	3rd	Win & Pl
Chases	1	0	0	0	
Career Total	**1**	**0**	**0**	**0**	

Going: Sf: 0-0 GS: 0-0 Gd: 0-0 GF: - Fm: 0-1
Distance: 2m/2m3: 0-0 2m4-2m7: 0-0 3m+: 0-1
Track: LH: 0-1 RH: 0-0 Tight: 0-1 Gall: 0-0
Aids: Bl: 0-0 Vi: 0-0 Tstrap: 0-1
Best Rating: **54** 4/02 Kels 3m1f gd-fm Ch

Modest pointer, handles any ground. Has worn a tongue tie.

Bounce Back (USA)

111(115h) (153h)**167**

6-y-o ch g Trempolino (USA)-Lattaquie (FR) (Fast Topaze (USA))
M C Pipe (F Doumen 16/6) Mrs Belinda Harvey

Placings:21F/1332224-23**21433561** **(4913)**
2001/02: 21^{2}S, 25^{3}VS, 19^{2}G, 19^{1}S, 25^{4}G, 21^{3}G, 20^{3}GS, 24^{5}G, 20^{6}G, 29^{1}G

	Starts	1st	2nd	3rd	Win & Pl
Hurdles	5	0	1	1	50627
Chases	5	2	1	2	84844
Career Total	**20**	**4**	**6**	**5**	**255507**

167	4/02	Sand	3m5f110y	A HCh	GD	£72500
148	12/01	Chep	2m3f110y	D Ch	SFT	£4124
	5/00	Autl	2m3f110y	Hdl	VS	£28818
	3/00	Engh	2m2f	Hdl	HLD	£11527

Total win prize-money £116969

Going: Sf: 1-2 GS: 0-1 Gd: 1-6 GF: - Fm: 0-0
Distance: 2m/2m3: 0-0 2m4-2m7: 1-6 3m+: 1-4
Track: LH: 1-2 RH: 1-5 Tight: 0-1 Gall: 0-0
Aids: Bl: 0-0 **Vi: 1-3** Tstrap: 0-0
Best Rating: **167** 4/02 Sand 3m5f110y good Ch

Formerly a high-class hurdler in France, he won a novice chase at Chepstow in December 2001, but did not look a natural over fences. Proved a revelation when stepped up to three miles-five in the Attheraces Gold Cup at Sandown in April. Acts on good and soft ground. Has worn a visor.

Bouncinoffthewalls (IRE)

6-y-o b g Cataldi-River Craig (IRE) (Over The River (FR))
K C Bailey Graham And Alison Jelley

Placings:*0-PPP* **(3162)**
2001/02: 17^{P}S, 16^{P}G, 16^{P}S

	Starts	1st	2nd	3rd	Win & Pl
Hurdles	3	0	0	0	
Career Total	**4**	**0**	**0**	**0**	

Going: Sf: 0-2 GS: 0-0 Gd: 0-1 GF: - Fm: 0-0
Distance: 2m/2m3: 0-3 2m4-2m7: 0-0 3m+: 0-0
Track: LH: 0-0 RH: 0-3 Tight: 0-0 Gall: 0-1
Aids: Bl: 0-0 Vi: 0-0 Tstrap: 0-0
Best Rating: **77** 4/01 Ayr 2m gd-fm NHF

Bound

105 **114**

4-y-o b g Kris-Tender Moment (IRE) (Caerleon (USA))
Mrs L Wadham (R Curtis 27/12) Dingley Dell Racing Ltd

Placings:3P203112 **(4774)**
2001/02: 16^{3}S, 16^{P}G, 17^{2}GS, 16^{0}HY, 17^{3}GS, 17^{1}GS, 16^{1}GF, 17^{2}G

	Starts	1st	2nd	3rd	Win & Pl
Hurdles	8	2	2	2	9357
Career Total	**8**	**2**	**2**	**2**	**9357**

110	4/02	Plum	2m	E Hdl	G-F	£2698
109	3/02	MRas	2m1f110y	D Hdl	G-S	£3672

Total win prize-money £6372

Going: Sf: 0-2 GS: 1-3 Gd: 0-2 GF: - Fm: 1-1
Distance: **2m/2m3: 2-8** 2m4-2m7: 0-0 3m+: 0-0
Track: LH: 1-3 RH: 1-5 **Tight: 2-6** Gall: 0-0
Aids: Bl: 0-0 Vi: 0-0 **Tstrap: 2-3**
Best Rating: **116** 4/02 MRas 2m1f110y good Hdl

Some ability over hurdles before winning at Market Rasen and Plumpton in spring 2002. Suited by forcing tactics, has worn a tongue tie.

Boundtohonour (IRE)

73(93h) **89**

10-y-o b g Rashar (USA)-Densidal (Tanfirion)
Ian Williams Newhaven Racing Club

Placings:*3006/40P/F5P0P/F2166154/33PP51P450-6PP* **(3876)**
2001/02: 25^{6}S, 25^{P}S, 20^{P}S

	Starts	1st	2nd	3rd	Win & Pl
Hurdles	1	0	0	0	0
Chases	2	0	0	0	0
Career Total	**33**	**3**	**1**	**3**	**11180**

104	12/00	Hntg	3m	F(0-110)HCh	HVY	£2925
100	3/00	Sedg	2m5f	F(0-110)HCh	G-F	£3500
94	12/99	Folk	2m6f110y	F(0-105)HHdl	SFT	£1960

Total win prize-money £8385

Going: Sf: 0-3 GS: 0-0 Gd: 0-0 GF: - Fm: 0-0
Distance: 2m/2m3: 0-0 2m4-2m7: 0-1 3m+: 0-2
Track: LH: 0-0 RH: 0-3 Tight: 0-0 Gall: 0-1
Aids: Bl: 0-1 Vi: 0-0 Tstrap: 0-0
Best Rating: **104** 12/00 Hntg 3m heavy Ch

Bourbon County (IRE)

12-y-o ch g The Parson-Money Spinner (Even Money)
Miss S J Wilton John Pointon And Sons

Placings:UPP5P/PP-R0P **(1443)**
2001/02: 16^{R}GF, 16^{0}GF, 26^{P}GF

	Starts	1st	2nd	3rd	Win & Pl
Hurdles	2	0	0	0	0
Chases	1	0	0	0	0
Career Total	**10**	**0**	**0**	**0**	**0**

Going: Sf: 0-0 GS: 0-0 Gd: 0-0 GF: - Fm: 0-3
Distance: 2m/2m3: 0-2 2m4-2m7: 0-0 3m+: 0-1
Track: LH: 0-2 RH: 0-0 Tight: 0-1 Gall: 0-0
Aids: Bl: 0-0 Vi: 0-0 Tstrap: 0-0
Best Rating: **75** 2/98 Leic 2m4f110y good Ch

Bourdonner

10-y-o b g Pharly (FR)-Buzzbomb (Bustino)
A Crook Cornelius Lysaght

Placings:UF000/14121521/222343/4533/P **(1258)**
2001/02: 20^{P}GF

	Starts	1st	2nd	3rd	Win & Pl
Hurdles	1	0	0	0	
Career Total	**24**	**4**	**5**	**4**	**17203**

110	4/97	Prth	2m4f110y	D(0-125)HHdl	GD	£3647
94	8/96	Prth	3m110y	E(0-110)HHdl	G-F	£3048
83	8/96	Worc	2m4f	E(0-100)HHdl	G-S	£2320
95	6/96	Prth	2m110y	E(0-100)HHdl	G-F	£2388

Total win prize-money £11404

Going: Sf: 0-0 GS: 0-0 Gd: 0-0 GF: - Fm: 0-1
Distance: 2m/2m3: 0-0 2m4-2m7: 0-1 3m+: 0-0
Track: LH: 0-0 RH: 0-1 Tight: 0-0 Gall: 0-1
Aids: Bl: 0-0 Vi: 0-0 Tstrap: 0-0
Best Rating: **110** 6/97 Worc 2m4f gd-fm Hdl

Bow Bells

90 **32**

7-y-o b m Absalom-Dancing Chimes (London Bells (CAN))
J Joseph Jack Joseph

Placings:5264545/06/00 **(1353)**
2001/02: 24^{0}G, 22^{0}GF

	Starts	1st	2nd	3rd	Win & Pl
Hurdles	2	0	0	0	
Career Total	**11**	**0**	**1**	**0**	**635**

Going: Sf: 0-0 GS: 0-0 Gd: 0-1 GF: - Fm: 0-1
Distance: 2m/2m3: 0-0 2m4-2m7: 0-1 3m+: 0-1
Track: LH: 0-2 RH: 0-0 Tight: 0-1 Gall: 0-0
Aids: Bl: 0-0 Vi: 0-0 Tstrap: 0-0
Best Rating: **82** 2/99 Plum 2m4f gd-sft Hdl

Bow Strada

114 **132**

5-y-o ch g Rainbow Quest (USA)-La Strada (Niniski (USA))
P J Hobbs (P W Harris 10/11) M J Tuckey

Placings:23-11F01 **(4862)**
2001/02: 16^{1}G, 17^{1}GS, 19^{F}GS, 16^{0}G, 19^{1}F

	Starts	1st	2nd	3rd	Win & Pl
Hurdles	5	3	0	0	12393
Career Total	**7**	**3**	**1**	**1**	**15552**

132	4/02	Extr	2m3f	D(0-125)HHdl	FRM	£3575
121	12/01	Tntn	2m1f	D Hdl	G-S	£5528
123	12/01	Donc	2m110y	E Hdl	GD	£3290

Total win prize-money £12393

Going: Sf: 0-0 GS: 1-2 Gd: 1-2 GF: - Fm: 1-1
Distance: **2m/2m3: 3-5** 2m4-2m7: 0-0 3m+: 0-0
Track: LH: 1-3 **RH: 2-2** Tight: 1-2 Gall: 1-2
Aids: Bl: 0-0 Vi: 0-0 Tstrap: 0-0
Best Rating: **132** 4/02 Extr 2m3f firm Hdl

A decent Flat handicapper, he made a good start over hurdles with wins at Doncaster and Taunton in December 2001, but was beaten when falling at Newbury in January 2002. Handled fast ground when winning 19 furlong handicap at Exeter in April 2002. Thought likely to prove best at around two and a half miles.

Bowcliffe

11-y-o b g Petoski-Gwiffina (Welsh Saint)
W Storey J P Hames

Placings:00P34/P/43305P/3/P (1501)
2001/02: 17^{P}G

	Starts	1st	2nd	3rd	Win & Pl
Hurdles	1	0	0	0	
Career Total	**14**	**0**	**0**	**4**	**1728**

Going: Sf: 0-0 GS: 0-0 Gd: 0-1 GF: - Fm: 0-0
Distance: 2m/2m3: 0-1 2m4-2m7: 0-0 3m+: 0-0
Track: LH: 0-1 RH: 0-0 Tight: 0-1 Gall: 0-0
Aids: Bl: 0-0 Vi: 0-0 Tstrap: 0-0
Best Rating: **89** 1/00 Hntg 2m110y good Hdl

Bowcliffe Court (IRE)

98 64
10-y-o b g Slip Anchor-Res Nova (USA) (Blushing Groom (FR))
G H Jones John Priday Construction Ltd

Placings:P130/6443/511/P600 (4680)
2001/02: 20^{P}S, 17^{6}G, 17^{0}GS, 17^{0}GF

	Starts	1st	2nd	3rd	Win & Pl
Hurdles	4	0	0	0	0
Career Total	**15**	**3**	**0**	**2**	**10295**

113	12/98	Leic	2m	E(0-110)HHdl	SFT	£3028
104	12/98	Leic	2m	E(0-110)HHdl	G-S	£2206
96	12/96	Chep	2m110y	D Hdl	SFT	£2693

Total win prize-money £7928

Going: Sf: 0-1 GS: 0-1 Gd: 0-1 GF: - Fm: 0-1
Distance: 2m/2m3: 0-3 2m4-2m7: 0-1 3m+: 0-0
Track: LH: 0-2 RH: 0-2 Tight: 0-2 Gall: 0-0
Aids: Bl: 0-0 Vi: 0-0 Tstrap: 0-0
Best Rating: **113** 12/98 Leic 2m soft Hdl

Bowden Surprise

101 91
12-y-o ch g Morgans Choice-Bankers Surprise (Golden Surprise)
R J Baker R J Baker

Placings:U5/P15/3426/245P/5122-605 (1635)
2001/02: 21^{6}G, 23^{0}GF, 25^{5}GF

	Starts	1st	2nd	3rd	Win & Pl
Chases	3	0	0	0	0
Career Total	**20**	**2**	**4**	**1**	**10782**

91	8/00	NAbb	3m2f110y	F(0-100)HCh	GD	£3386
65	3/97	NAbb	2m6f	G(0-95)HHdl	G-F	£1932

Total win prize-money £5320

Going: Sf: 0-0 GS: 0-0 Gd: 0-1 GF: - Fm: 0-2
Distance: 2m/2m3: 0-0 2m4-2m7: 0-1 3m+: 0-2
Track: LH: 0-1 RH: 0-2 Tight: 0-1 Gall: 0-0
Aids: Bl: 0-2 Vi: 0-0 Tstrap: 0-0
Best Rating: **91** 10/01 Extr 2m7f110y gd-fm Ch

Bowfell

75 41
4-y-o b f Alflora (IRE)-April City (Lidhame)
C Smith Mr & Mrs T I Gourley

Placings:0FUU (4284)
2001/02: 17^{0}GS, 16^{F}HY, 17^{U}GS, 17^{U}GS

	Starts	1st	2nd	3rd	Win & Pl
Hurdles	4	0	0	0	
Career Total	**4**	**0**	**0**	**0**	

Going: Sf: 0-1 GS: 0-3 Gd: 0-0 GF: - Fm: 0-0
Distance: 2m/2m3: 0-4 2m4-2m7: 0-0 3m+: 0-0
Track: LH: 0-1 RH: 0-3 Tight: 0-3 Gall: 0-0
Aids: Bl: 0-0 Vi: 0-0 Tstrap: 0-0
Best Rating: **41** 2/02 MRas 2m1f110y gd-sft Hdl

Bowl Of Gold

11
9-y-o ch m Gildoran-Bishop's Bow (Crozier)
A G Hobbs David Urquhart

Placings:2/224/56106/P-P0 (0371)
2001/02: 22^{P}GS, 21^{0}G

	Starts	1st	2nd	3rd	Win & Pl
Hurdles	2	0	0	0	
Career Total	**12**	**1**	**3**	**0**	**2880**

102	1/00	Folk	2m1f110y	F(0-100)HHdl	HVY	£1785

Total win prize-money £1785

Going: Sf: 0-0 GS: 0-1 Gd: 0-1 GF: - Fm: 0-0
Distance: 2m/2m3: 0-0 2m4-2m7: 0-2 3m+: 0-0
Track: LH: 0-0 RH: 0-0 Tight: 0-0 Gall: 0-0
Aids: Bl: 0-0 Vi: 0-0 Tstrap: 0-0
Best Rating: **102** 1/00 Folk 2m1f110y heavy Hdl

Bowles Patrol (IRE)

106(104h) (75h)113
10-y-o gr g Roselier (FR)-Another Dud (Le Bavard (FR))
John R Upson Bill Ellis

Placings:00F3/00**22/3/UP**12134414/**12235FP3**1/1U36523 5-**0P611**03 (3982)
2001/02: 24^{0}F, 25^{P}F, 20^{6}G, 27^{1}S, 24^{1}GS, 25^{0}S, 24^{3}GS

	Starts	1st	2nd	3rd	Win & Pl
Hurdles	1	0	0	0	0
Chases	6	2	0	1	8234
Career Total	**44**	**8**	**6**	**8**	**37629**

113	12/01	Tntn	3m	F(0-105)HCh	G-S	£3802
108	11/01	Sedg	3m3f	F(0-105)HCh	SFT	£2863
111	5/00	Hntg	2m5f110y	F(0-110)HHdl	GD	£2710
112	4/00	MRas	2m5f110y	F(0-100)HHdl	SFT	£1542
111	11/99	NAbb	2m5f110y	F(0-100)HCh	SFT	£3120
107	3/99	Newb	2m5f	E(0-115)HHdl	SFT	£3057
91	12/98	Plum	3m110y	E(0-105)HHdl	G-S	£2775
86	11/98	Carl	2m4f110y	E(0-100)HHdl	SFT	£2402

Total win prize-money £22274

Going: Sf: 1-2 GS: 1-2 Gd: 0-1 GF: - Fm: 0-2
Distance: 2m/2m3: 0-0 2m4-2m7: 0-1 **3m+: 2-6**
Track: LH: 1-4 RH: 1-2 **Tight: 2-6** Gall: 0-0
Aids: Bl: 0-0 Vi: 0-0 Tstrap: 0-0
Best Rating: **113** 2/02 Ludl 3m gd-sft Ch

Staying chaser, genuine if a little one-paced.

Bowling On

8-y-o b m Gildoran-Bishop's Bow (Crozier)
Mrs S D Williams Alan Hewings

Placings:0/54P/005PP/FF (0681)
2001/02: 23^{F}F, 26^{F}G

	Starts	1st	2nd	3rd	Win & Pl
Chases	2	0	0	0	
Career Total	**11**	**0**	**0**	**0**	0

Going: Sf: 0-0 GS: 0-0 Gd: 0-1 GF: - Fm: 0-1
Distance: 2m/2m3: 0-0 2m4-2m7: 0-0 3m+: 0-2
Track: LH: 0-1 RH: 0-1 Tight: 0-1 Gall: 0-0
Aids: Bl: 0-0 Vi: 0-0 Tstrap: 0-0
Best Rating: **85** 11/99 Towc 2m good Hdl

Box Builder

(104h) (110h)82
5-y-o ch g Fraam-Ena Olley (Le Moss)
B G Powell M Hutchinson

Placings:4025 (2429)
2001/02: 21^{4}S, 22^{0}S, 21^{2}GF, 24^{5}G

	Starts	1st	2nd	3rd	Win & Pl
Hurdles	4	0	1	0	775
Career Total	**4**	**0**	**1**	**0**	**775**

Going: Sf: 0-2 GS: 0-0 Gd: 0-1 GF: - Fm: 0-1
Distance: 2m/2m3: 0-0 2m4-2m7: 0-3 3m+: 0-1
Track: LH: 0-3 RH: 0-1 Tight: 0-1 Gall: 0-1
Aids: Bl: 0-0 Vi: 0-0 Tstrap: 0-2
Best Rating: **104** 11/01 Ludl 2m5f gd-fm Hdl

Box Car (IRE)

98 75
5-y-o b g Blues Traveller (IRE)-Racey Naskra (USA) (Star De Naskra (USA))
R Wilman (G L Moore 23/5) Mrs Joanna Hughes

Placings:540-4360 (4904)
2001/02: 16^{4}G, 17^{3}GF, 16^{6}GF, 17^{0}G

	Starts	1st	2nd	3rd	Win & Pl
Hurdles	4	0	0	1	301
Career Total	**7**	**0**	**0**	**1**	**301**

Going: Sf: 0-0 GS: 0-0 Gd: 0-2 GF: - Fm: 0-2
Distance: 2m/2m3: 0-4 2m4-2m7: 0-0 3m+: 0-0
Track: LH: 0-2 RH: 0-2 Tight: 0-1 Gall: 0-1
Aids: Bl: 0-0 Vi: 0-0 Tstrap: 0-0
Best Rating: **75** 4/02 Hrfd 2m1f gd-fm Hdl

Selling plater class over hurdles.

Boxer's Double

87 75
5-y-o b g Petoski-Grayrose Double (Celtic Cone)
G A Ham K C White

Placings:*600*0PP (3657)
2001/02: 17^{6}G, 16^{0}G, 17^{0}G, 16^{0}G, 24^{P}S, 22^{P}S

	Starts	1st	2nd	3rd	Win & Pl
NH Flat	3	0	0	0	0
Hurdles	3	0	0	0	0
Career Total	**6**	**0**	**0**	**0**	**0**

Going: Sf: 0-2 GS: 0-0 Gd: 0-4 GF: - Fm: 0-0
Distance: 2m/2m3: 0-4 2m4-2m7: 0-1 3m+: 0-1
Track: LH: 0-1 RH: 0-4 Tight: 0-1 Gall: 0-0
Aids: Bl: 0-0 Vi: 0-0 Tstrap: 0-0
Best Rating: **76** 10/01 Hrfd 2m1f good NHF

Boy Band (IRE)

75 39
4-y-o b g Desert Style (IRE)-Arab Scimetar (IRE) (Sure Blade (USA))
J W Mullins (M R Channon 17/5) Seamus Mullins

Placings:U0P0P (4657)

2001/02: 16^{U}G, 18^{0}G, 16^{P}G, 17^{0}S, 24^{P}G

	Starts	1st	2nd	3rd	Win & Pl
Hurdles	5	0	0	0	
Career Total	**5**	**0**	**0**	**0**	

Going: Sf: 0-1 GS: 0-0 Gd: 0-4 GF: - Fm: 0-0
Distance: 2m/2m3: 0-4 2m4-2m7: 0-0 3m+: 0-1
Track: LH: 0-2 RH: 0-3 Tight: 0-3 Gall: 0-0
Aids: Bl: 0-0 Vi: 0-0 Tstrap: 0-0
Best Rating: **39** 12/01 Font 2m2f110y good Hdl

Boyne Banks (IRE)

7-y-o ch g Boyne Valley-Pallatess (Pall Mall)
N A Twiston-Davies James Cheetham

Placings:P (1865)
2001/02: 25^{P}G

	Starts	1st	2nd	3rd	Win & Pl
Hurdles	1	0	0	0	
Career Total	**1**	**0**	**0**	**0**	

Going: Sf: 0-0 GS: 0-0 Gd: 0-1 GF: - Fm: 0-0
Distance: 2m/2m3: 0-0 2m4-2m7: 0-0 3m+: 0-1
Track: LH: 0-1 RH: 0-0 Tight: 0-0 Gall: 0-1
Aids: Bl: 0-0 Vi: 0-0 Tstrap: 0-0
Best Rating:

Boyzontoowa (IRE)

110 **113**
10-y-o b g Beau Sher-Lindabell (Over The River (FR))
W Storey John J Maguire

Placings:06000/12332P4/6F160012/PF01232/4133UP-4P2 (4489)
2001/02: 20^{4}GS, 25^{P}G, 26^{2}GS

	Starts	1st	2nd	3rd	Win & Pl
Chases	3	0	1	0	2018
Career Total	**36**	**5**	**6**	**5**	**26802**

120	6/00	Prth	3m	E(0-115)HCh	HVY	£4810
120	1/00	Catt	3m1f110y	F(0-105)HCh	GD	£2730
105	4/99	Hexm	2m4f110y	F(0-105)HCh	GD	£3160
94	12/98	Catt	2m3f	E(0-100)HCh	GD	£3571
84	11/97	Hexm	2m4f110y	G(0-90)HHdl	G-F	£1725

Total win prize-money £15996

Going: Sf: 0-0 GS: 0-2 Gd: 0-1 GF: - Fm: 0-0
Distance: 2m/2m3: 0-0 2m4-2m7: 0-1 3m+: 0-2
Track: LH: 0-2 RH: 0-1 Tight: 0-1 Gall: 0-1
Aids: Bl: 0-0 Vi: 0-0 Tstrap: 0-0
Best Rating: **120** 11/00 Newc 2m4f soft Ch

Consistent staying chaser who wins in his turn. Best with some cut in the ground.

Bozo (IRE)

101(80h) (37h)**115**
11-y-o b g Kefaah (USA)-Hossvend (Malinowski (USA))
B J M Ryall B J M Ryall

Placings:30/30022F20P/33PP30/321U415/02P3P0-24PP33P06 (4543)
2001/02: 21^{2}G, 20^{4}GF, 23^{P}G, 21^{P}G, 19^{3}GF, 20^{3}G, 24^{P}S, 24^{0}S, 19^{6}G

	Starts	1st	2nd	3rd	Win & Pl
Chases	9	0	1	2	2799
Career Total	**39**	**2**	**6**	**9**	**21868**

114	4/00	Ludl	2m4f	D(0-120)HCh	GD	£5476
118	11/99	Tntn	2m3f	C Ch	GD	£6045

Total win prize-money £11522

Going: Sf: 0-2 GS: 0-0 Gd: 0-5 GF: - Fm: 0-2
Distance: 2m/2m3: 0-1 2m4-2m7: 0-5 3m+: 0-3
Track: LH: 0-3 RH: 0-6 Tight: 0-3 Gall: 0-0
Aids: Bl: 0-0 Vi: 0-0 Tstrap: 0-0
Best Rating: **119** 3/97 Chel 2m110y gd-fm NHF

Modest handicapper, his best form has come on good ground round right-handed tracks.

Bracey Run (IRE)

103 **114**
12-y-o b g The Parson-Outdoor Ivy (Deep Run)
A J Lidderdale (E Stanners 28/11) Bonusprint

Placings:2/31334P/FF/33203/311U-40004 (4561)
2001/02: 18^{4}GS, 19^{0}G, 24^{0}S, 21^{0}GS, 21^{4}GF

	Starts	1st	2nd	3rd	Win & Pl
Hurdles	5	0	0	0	0
Career Total	**23**	**3**	**2**	**7**	**20859**

126	5/00	Uttx	2m4f110y	B(0-140)HHdl	G-F	£6227
119	5/00	Hrfd	2m3f110y	D(0-120)HHdl	GD	£3269
110	12/97	Towc	2m	E Hdl	SFT	£2705

Total win prize-money £12203

Going: Sf: 0-1 GS: 0-2 Gd: 0-1 GF: - Fm: 0-1
Distance: 2m/2m3: 0-2 2m4-2m7: 0-2 3m+: 0-1
Track: LH: 0-4 RH: 0-1 Tight: 0-3 Gall: 0-1
Aids: Bl: 0-0 Vi: 0-0 Tstrap: 0-0
Best Rating: **130** 2/98 Chep 2m4f110y gd-sft Hdl

Veteran hurdler, on the downgrade. Had slipped to a useful mark when winning moderate handicap at Southwell in May 2002. Acts on all types of ground.

Braceys Girl (IRE)

96 **71**
5-y-o b/br m Be My Native (USA)-Minigirls Niece (IRE) (Strong Gale)
D Brace (P J Hobbs 20/2) David Brace

Placings:360053 (4646)
2001/02: 16^{3}GF, 16^{6}S, 20^{0}S, 22^{0}S, 16^{5}GS, 21^{3}G

	Starts	1st	2nd	3rd	Win & Pl
NH Flat	2	0	0	1	210
Hurdles	4	0	0	1	600
Career Total	**6**	**0**	**0**	**2**	**810**

Going: Sf: 0-3 GS: 0-1 Gd: 0-1 GF: - Fm: 0-1
Distance: 2m/2m3: 0-3 2m4-2m7: 0-3 3m+: 0-0
Track: LH: 0-2 RH: 0-3 Tight: 0-1 Gall: 0-0
Aids: Bl: 0-0 Vi: 0-0 Tstrap: 0-0
Best Rating: **77** 10/01 Chep 2m110y soft NHF

Has shown modest form on all starts to date.

Brachvogel (GER)

90 **109**
8-y-o gr g Val Des Pres (FR)-Bastei (GER) (Authi)
Ronald O'Leary D S T Syndicate

Placings:600-2433200500 (4340a)
2001/02: 17^{2}G, 16^{4}YS, 16^{3}S, 17^{3}GY, 16^{2}GF, 16^{0}Y, 16^{0}G, 16^{5}S, 17^{0}HY, 16^{0}S

	Starts	1st	2nd	3rd	Win & Pl
Hurdles	10	0	2	2	3669
Career Total	**13**	**0**	**2**	**2**	**3669**

Going: Sf: 0-4 GS: 0-0 Gd: 0-2 GF: - Fm: 0-1
Distance: 2m/2m3: 0-10 2m4-2m7: 0-0 3m+: 0-0
Track: LH: 0-2 RH: 0-0 Tight: 0-0 Gall: 0-0
Aids: Bl: 0-0 Vi: 0-0 Tstrap: 0-10
Best Rating: **109** 7/01 Klny 2m1f good Hdl

An Irish-trained hurdler, he has made the frame a few times but has yet to get off the mark. Acts on any ground.

Brackenheath (IRE)

11-y-o b g Le Moss-Stable Lass (Golden Love)
Mrs D M Grissell (D M Grissell 3/2) John Grist

Placings:0220/F142120/P022F240/3F5/PP-1R (3714)
2001/02: 26^{1}G, 26^{R}HY

	Starts	1st	2nd	3rd	Win & Pl
Chases	2	1	0	0	1463
Career Total	**26**	**3**	**7**	**1**	**24568**

110	5/01	Folk	3m2f	H Ch	GD	£1462
118	2/98	Folk	2m6f110y	E Hdl	G-F	£2731
109	11/97	Asct	3m	C Hdl	SFT	£3582

Total win prize-money £7778

Going: Sf: 0-1 GS: 0-0 Gd: 1-1 GF: - Fm: 0-0
Distance: 2m/2m3: 0-0 2m4-2m7: 0-0 **3m+: 1-2**
Track: LH: 0-0 **RH: 1-1 Tight: 1-1** Gall: 0-0
Aids: Bl: 0-0 Vi: 0-0 Tstrap: 0-0
Best Rating: **139** 4/98 Aint 3m110y soft Hdl

Formerly useful hurdler.chaser, now hunter chasing. Best on a sound surface although handles softer, likes Folkestone.

Brad

101f **97f**
4-y-o b g Deploy-Celia Brady (Last Tycoon)
P R Webber Mrs David Blackburn

Placings:20 (4019)
2001/02: 10^{2}HY, 16^{0}GS

	Starts	1st	2nd	3rd	Win & Pl
NH Flat	2	0	1	0	662
Career Total	**2**	**0**	**1**	**0**	**662**

Going: Sf: 0-1 GS: 0-1 Gd: 0-0 GF: - Fm: 0-0
Distance: 2m/2m3: 0-2 2m4-2m7: 0-0 3m+: 0-0
Track: LH: 0-1 RH: 0-1 Tight: 0-0 Gall: 0-1
Aids: Bl: 0-0 Vi: 0-0 Tstrap: 0-0
Best Rating: **97** 1/02 Towc 2m heavy NHF

Showed promise in bumper on heavy ground.

Bradley My Boy (IRE)

93 **102**
6-y-o ch g Treasure Hunter-Clonaslee Baby (Konigssee)
V Bowens (J C Harley 26/12) A P Brady

Placings:45-10050 (3035a)
2001/02: 17^{1}GF, 20^{0}G, 16^{0}S, 16^{5}Y, 20^{0}S

	Starts	1st	2nd	3rd	Win & Pl
NH Flat	1	1	0	0	1694
Hurdles	4	0	0	0	0
Career Total	**7**	**1**	**0**	**0**	**1886**

103	5/01	NAbb	2m1f	H NHF	G-F	£1694

Total win prize-money £1694

Going: Sf: 0-2 GS: 0-0 Gd: 0-1 GF: - Fm: 1-1
Distance: **2m/2m3: 1-3** 2m4-2m7: 0-2 3m+: 0-0
Track: **LH: 1-2** RH: 0-3 **Tight: 1-1** Gall: 0-0
Aids: Bl: 0-0 Vi: 0-0 Tstrap: 0-0
Best Rating: **103** 5/01 NAbb 2m1f gd-fm NHF

Brady Boys (USA)

98 **87**

5-y-o b g Cozzene (USA)-Elvia (USA) (Roberto (USA))
J G M O'Shea K W Bell & Son Ltd

Placings:5P **(2474)**
2001/02: 16^{5}S, 19^{P}S

	Starts	1st	2nd	3rd	Win & Pl
Hurdles	2	0	0	0	0
Career Total	**2**	**0**	**0**	**0**	**0**

Going: Sf: 0-2 GS: 0-0 Gd: 0-0 GF: - Fm: 0-0
Distance: 2m/2m3: 0-1 2m4-2m7: 0-1 3m+: 0-0
Track: LH: 0-1 RH: 0-1 Tight: 0-0 Gall: 0-0
Aids: Bl: 0-0 Vi: 0-0 Tstrap: 0-0
Best Rating: **79** 11/01 Uttx 2m soft Hdl

Braeburn

108 **105**

7-y-o b g Petoski-Great Granny Smith (Fine Blue)
N J Henderson Mrs T Stopford-Sackville

Placings:2P **(4825)**
2001/02: 24^{2}GS, 25^{P}G

	Starts	1st	2nd	3rd	Win & Pl
Chases	2	0	1	0	1242
Career Total	**2**	**0**	**1**	**0**	**1242**

Going: Sf: 0-0 GS: 0-1 Gd: 0-1 GF: - Fm: 0-0
Distance: 2m/2m3: 0-0 2m4-2m7: 0-0 3m+: 0-2
Track: LH: 0-1 RH: 0-1 Tight: 0-1 Gall: 0-1
Aids: Bl: 0-0 Vi: 0-0 Tstrap: 0-0
Best Rating: **105** 3/02 Ludl 3m gd-sft Ch

Runner-up in a Ludlow three-mile novice chase on his racecourse debut.

Braidwater (IRE)

44

6-y-o b g Glacial Storm (USA)-Felicity Lot (Malacate (USA))
J Howard Johnson Mrs T McIlhagga

Placings:00P-P **(1465)**
2001/02: 20^{P}G

	Starts	1st	2nd	3rd	Win & Pl
Hurdles	1	0	0	0	
Career Total	**4**	**0**	**0**	**0**	

Going: Sf: 0-0 GS: 0-0 Gd: 0-1 GF: - Fm: 0-0
Distance: 2m/2m3: 0-0 2m4-2m7: 0-1 3m+: 0-0
Track: LH: 0-0 RH: 0-1 Tight: 0-0 Gall: 0-0
Aids: Bl: 0-0 Vi: 0-0 Tstrap: 0-0
Best Rating: **53** 3/01 MRas 2m1f110y good NHF

Bramble Fair (IRE)

103(109h) **116**

8-y-o ch m Montelimar (USA)-Gold Label (Deep Run)
Mrs M Reveley Mrs K Quinn

Placings:3063/04511130P-**24P34UP5** **(4748)**
2001/02: 25^{2}G, 25^{4}G, 25^{P}GS, 25^{3}GS, 23^{4}GS, 20^{U}S, 21^{P}HY, 26^{5}GF

	Starts	1st	2nd	3rd	Win & Pl
Chases	8	0	1	1	2605
Career Total	**21**	**3**	**1**	**4**	**11428**

111	1/01	Newc	3m	F(0-100)HHdl	HVY	£2296
106	1/01	Weth	2m4f110y	F(0-105)HHdl	G-S	£2075
97	11/00	Kels	2m6f110y	E(0-105)HHdl	SFT	£2899

Total win prize-money £7271

Going: Sf: 0-2 GS: 0-3 Gd: 0-2 GF: - Fm: 0-1
Distance: 2m/2m3: 0-0 2m4-2m7: 0-2 3m+: 0-6
Track: LH: 0-5 RH: 0-2 Tight: 0-2 Gall: 0-0
Aids: Bl: 0-1 Vi: 0-1 Tstrap: 0-0
Best Rating: **116** 11/01 Weth 3m1f good Ch

Completed a hat-trick over hurdles in the 2000/01 season before her form tailed off. Made a highly satisfactory reappearance in November 2001 when second on her chasing debut at Wetherby and has continued to run well over fences since then. Stays three miles and likes to get her toe in. Has worn blinkers to winning effect over hurdles.

Bramblehill Duke (IRE)

107 **142**

10-y-o b g Kambalda-Scat-Cat (Furry Glen)
Miss Venetia Williams South Wales Shower Supplies T/a Faucets

Placings:143P/11331/**F2R21/5P1165-03P20** **(4191)**
2001/02: 20^{0}G, 24^{3}G, 24^{P}GS, 19^{2}GS, 24^{0}GS

	Starts	1st	2nd	3rd	Win & Pl
Chases	5	0	1	1	4460
Career Total	**25**	**7**	**3**	**4**	**45504**

145	1/01	Wwck	2m4f110y	C(0-135)HCh	SFT	£8424
145	1/01	Uttx	2m4f	B(0-140)HCh	HVY	£10426
135	2/00	Hayd	2m6f	C Ch	HVY	£7315
119	11/98	Newb	2m5f	E(0-110)HHdl	GD	£3566
109	5/98	Towc	2m	E Hdl	G-F	£2460
109	5/98	Chep	2m110y	E(0-100)HHdl	GD	£2416
107	11/97	Hayd	2m	H NHF	GD	£1278

Total win prize-money £35885

Going: Sf: 0-0 GS: 0-3 Gd: 0-2 GF: - Fm: 0-0
Distance: 2m/2m3: 0-0 2m4-2m7: 0-2 3m+: 0-3
Track: LH: 0-4 RH: 0-1 Tight: 0-1 Gall: 0-2
Aids: Bl: 0-0 Vi: 0-0 Tstrap: 0-0
Best Rating: **145** 1/01 Wwck 2m4f110y soft Ch

Handicap chaser, stays three miles although effective at shorter. Acts on most types of ground.

Brambling

5-y-o b m Rambo Dancer (CAN)-By Line (High Line)
N J Henderson Tom Wilson

Placings:00P **(3148)**
2001/02: 17^{0}G, 17^{0}S, 22^{P}G

	Starts	1st	2nd	3rd	Win & Pl
NH Flat	2	0	0	0	0
Hurdles	1	0	0	0	0
Career Total	**3**	**0**	**0**	**0**	

Going: Sf: 0-1 GS: 0-0 Gd: 0-2 GF: - Fm: 0-0
Distance: 2m/2m3: 0-2 2m4-2m7: 0-1 3m+: 0-0
Track: LH: 0-1 RH: 0-2 Tight: 0-1 Gall: 0-0
Aids: Bl: 0-1 Vi: 0-0 Tstrap: 0-0
Best Rating: **66** 12/01 Hrfd 2m1f soft NHF

Bramblings Boy (IRE)

74 **39**

8-y-o b g Cataldi-Ballybeg Rose (IRE) (Roselier (FR))
G H Yardley (N A Twiston-Davies 11/5) Mrs S Tainton

Placings:0/00/0-06PP **(4265)**
2001/02: 22^{0}GF, 17^{6}GS, 24^{P}S, 20^{P}S

	Starts	1st	2nd	3rd	Win & Pl
Hurdles	4	0	0	0	0
Career Total	**8**	**0**	**0**	**0**	**0**

Going: Sf: 0-2 GS: 0-1 Gd: 0-0 GF: - Fm: 0-1
Distance: 2m/2m3: 0-1 2m4-2m7: 0-2 3m+: 0-1
Track: LH: 0-2 RH: 0-2 Tight: 0-2 Gall: 0-0
Aids: Bl: 0-1 Vi: 0-0 Tstrap: 0-0
Best Rating: **78** 3/00 Carl 2m1f gd-sft NHF

Brambly Hedge

102(102h) (110h)**114**

8-y-o b m Teenoso (USA)-True Clown (True Song)
N A Twiston-Davies Mr & Mrs Peter Orton

Placings:12112/2445221-**02P1213** **(4107)**
2001/02: 24^{0}G, 25^{2}S, 24^{P}G, 25^{1}S, 25^{2}HY, 22^{1}HY, 22^{3}S

	Starts	1st	2nd	3rd	Win & Pl
Chases	7	2	2	1	12275
Career Total	**19**	**6**	**7**	**1**	**29476**

114	1/02	Towc	2m6f	D Ch	HVY	£5427
114	11/01	Towc	3m1f	F(0-100)HCh	SFT	£3822
110	4/01	Prth	3m110y	C Hdl	HVY	£5850
108	12/99	Tntn	2m1f	H NHF	SFT	£1637
108	12/99	Towc	2m	H NHF	SFT	£1688
108	11/99	Hrfd	2m1f	H NHF	GD	£1532

Total win prize-money £19957

Going: Sf: 2-5 GS: 0-0 Gd: 0-2 GF: - Fm: 0-0
Distance: 2m/2m3: 0-0 2m4-2m7: 1-2 3m+: 1-5
Track: LH: 0-1 **RH: 2-5** Tight: 0-0 Gall: 0-1
Aids: Bl: 0-0 Vi: 0-0 Tstrap: 0-0
Best Rating: **114** 1/02 Towc 2m6f heavy Ch

Novice chaser. Stays well and is suited by plenty of give in the ground.

Brand New Dance

8-y-o b g Gildoran-Starawak (Star Appeal)
D J Wintle J P Dickinson

Placings:23-P **(4682)**
2001/02: 17^{P}GF

	Starts	1st	2nd	3rd	Win & Pl
Hurdles	1	0	0	0	
Career Total	**3**	**0**	**1**	**1**	**976**

Going: Sf: 0-0 GS: 0-0 Gd: 0-0 GF: - Fm: 0-1
Distance: 2m/2m3: 0-1 2m4-2m7: 0-0 3m+: 0-0
Track: LH: 0-0 RH: 0-1 Tight: 0-0 Gall: 0-0
Aids: Bl: 0-0 Vi: 0-0 Tstrap: 0-0
Best Rating: **115** 9/00 Rosc 2m good Hdl

Branksome (IRE)

8-y-o b g Commanche Run-Heather Point (Pollerton)
P J Millington P J Millington

Placings:PPPP **(0474)**
2001/02: 25^{P}S, 24^{P}GF, 21^{P}G, 22^{P}G

	Starts	1st	2nd	3rd	Win & Pl
Chases	4	0	0	0	
Career Total	**4**	**0**	**0**	**0**	

Going: Sf: 0-1 GS: 0-0 Gd: 0-2 GF: - Fm: 0-1

Distance: 2m/2m3: 0-0 2m4-2m7: 0-2 3m+: 0-2
Track: LH: 0-2 RH: 0-2 Tight: 0-3 Gall: 0-0
Aids: Bl: 0-2 Vi: 0-2 Tstrap: 0-0
Best Rating:

Brassis Hill (IRE)

98 87

11-y-o b g Marktingo-Mystery Woman (Tula Rocket)
Miss A M Newton-Smith (R Rowe 18/7) The Sleeping Partnership

Placings: *0/40400*/1655/6020P/2/3234-5300P3 **(4560)**
2001/02: 18^{5}GF, 16^{3}G, 20^{0}S, 16^{0}S, 20^{P}S, 17^{3}GF

	Starts	1st	2nd	3rd	Win & Pl
Chases	6	0	0	2	752
Career Total	**26**	**1**	**3**	**4**	**6868**

93	5/97	Clon	2m	NHF	GD	£2204

Total win prize-money £2204

Going: Sf: 0-3 GS: 0-0 Gd: 0-1 GF: - Fm: 0-2
Distance: 2m/2m3: 0-4 2m4-2m7: 0-2 3m+: 0-0
Track: LH: 0-3 RH: 0-1 Tight: 0-4 Gall: 0-0
Aids: Bl: 0-0 Vi: 0-0 Tstrap: 0-6
Best Rating: **93** 5/97 Clon 2m good NHF

Moderate chaser, seems tho handle any ground, usually tongue tied.

Bravanti

72f 46f

4-y-o b g Ashkalani (IRE)-Javandra (USA) (Lyphard (USA))
M C Chapman Paul Stead

Placings: *000* **(4910)**
2001/02: 16^{0}S, 17^{0}GS, 17^{0}G

	Starts	1st	2nd	3rd	Win & Pl
NH Flat	3	0	0	0	
Career Total	**3**	**0**	**0**	**0**	

Going: Sf: 0-1 GS: 0-1 Gd: 0-1 GF: - Fm: 0-0
Distance: 2m/2m3: 0-3 2m4-2m7: 0-0 3m+: 0-0
Track: LH: 0-1 RH: 0-2 Tight: 0-2 Gall: 0-0
Aids: Bl: 0-0 Vi: 0-0 Tstrap: 0-0
Best Rating: **46** 4/02 MRas 2m1f110y good NHF

Brave Dane (IRE)

95 72

4-y-o b g Danehill (USA)-Nuriva (USA) (Woodman (USA))
G M McCourt (Mme C Head-Maarek 13/9) Graham McCourt

Placings: 0PF05 **(4904)**
2001/02: 16^{0}GS, 16^{P}S, 18^{F}S, 16^{0}GS, 17^{5}G

	Starts	1st	2nd	3rd	Win & Pl
Hurdles	5	0	0	0	0
Career Total	**5**	**0**	**0**	**0**	**0**

Going: Sf: 0-2 GS: 0-2 Gd: 0-1 GF: - Fm: 0-0
Distance: 2m/2m3: 0-5 2m4-2m7: 0-0 3m+: 0-0
Track: LH: 0-3 RH: 0-2 Tight: 0-2 Gall: 0-1
Aids: Bl: 0-0 Vi: 0-0 Tstrap: 0-0
Best Rating: **72** 4/02 MRas 2m1f110y good Hdl

Failed to complete two of his first four starts, otherwise well held. Has yet to show he stays further than the minimum trip.

Brave Dream (IRE)

96(89h) (80h)101

8-y-o b g Commanche Run-Sleepy Bye Byes (IRE) (Supreme Leader)
J A B Old R P Fry

Placings: *45/*13161/PFP-P664 **(2545)**
2001/02: 17^{P}HY, 21^{6}GS, 21^{6}G, 23^{4}GS

	Starts	1st	2nd	3rd	Win & Pl
Hurdles	2	0	0	0	0
Chases	2	0	0	0	292
Career Total	**14**	**3**	**0**	**1**	**7561**

112	4/00	NAbb	2m1f	D(0-125)HHdl	HVY	£2934
106	11/99	NAbb	2m1f	E Hdl	SFT	£2326
115	10/99	Tntn	2m1f	H NHF	G-F	£1700

Total win prize-money £6961

Going: Sf: 0-1 GS: 0-2 Gd: 0-1 GF: - Fm: 0-0
Distance: 2m/2m3: 0-1 2m4-2m7: 0-2 3m+: 0-1
Track: LH: 0-1 RH: 0-3 Tight: 0-2 Gall: 0-0
Aids: Bl: 0-0 Vi: 0-0 Tstrap: 0-0
Best Rating: **127** 2/01 Towc 2m110y heavy Ch

Ran in a couple of fairly hot bumpers last season, but had a rather easier task when winning a fast-ground bumper at Taunton on his reappearance. Got off the mark at Newton Abbot on his second start over hurdles when encountering soft ground for the first time. He will be suited by two and a half miles plus.

Brave Effect (IRE)

107 97

6-y-o br g Bravefoot-Crupney Lass (Ardoon)
M Todhunter P E Sowerby, K A Sowerby, R E Bell

Placings: 2 **(4522)**
2001/02: 17^{2}G

	Starts	1st	2nd	3rd	Win & Pl
Hurdles	1	0	1	0	850
Career Total	**1**	**0**	**1**	**0**	**850**

Going: Sf: 0-0 GS: 0-0 Gd: 0-1 GF: - Fm: 0-0
Distance: 2m/2m3: 0-1 2m4-2m7: 0-0 3m+: 0-0
Track: LH: 0-0 RH: 0-1 Tight: 0-0 Gall: 0-0
Aids: Bl: 0-0 Vi: 0-0 Tstrap: 0-0
Best Rating: **100** 4/02 Carl 2m1f good Hdl

Promising debut in a novices hurdle at Carlisle in April 2002.

Brave King (IRE)

74 74

9-y-o b g King's Ride-Arumah (Arapaho)
M J Wilkinson M Batchelor & D Batchelor

Placings: *1/*6P5/5 **(3754)**
2001/02: 16^{5}HY

	Starts	1st	2nd	3rd	Win & Pl
Hurdles	1	0	0	0	0
Career Total	**5**	**1**	**0**	**0**	**1371**

107	4/98	Towc	2m	H NHF	SFT	£1371

Total win prize-money £1371

Going: Sf: 0-1 GS: 0-0 Gd: 0-0 GF: - Fm: 0-0
Distance: 2m/2m3: 0-1 2m4-2m7: 0-0 3m+: 0-0
Track: LH: 0-0 RH: 0-1 Tight: 0-0 Gall: 0-0
Aids: Bl: 0-0 Vi: 0-0 Tstrap: 0-0
Best Rating: **107** 4/98 Towc 2m soft NHF

Brave Knight

5-y-o b g Presidium-Agnes Jane (Sweet Monday)
N Bycroft P Casimir-Mrowczynsk

Placings: 5 **(1590)**
2001/02: 17^{5}GS

	Starts	1st	2nd	3rd	Win & Pl
Hurdles	1	0	0	0	0
Career Total	**1**	**0**	**0**	**0**	**0**

Going: Sf: 0-0 GS: 0-1 Gd: 0-0 GF: - Fm: 0-0
Distance: 2m/2m3: 0-1 2m4-2m7: 0-0 3m+: 0-0
Track: LH: 0-1 RH: 0-0 Tight: 0-1 Gall: 0-0
Aids: Bl: 0-0 Vi: 0-0 Tstrap: 0-0
Best Rating:

Brave Run (IRE)

67 55

6-y-o b g Commanche Run-Evergreen Lady (Smartset)
G A Swinbank Leading Star Racing

Placings: *0*-0 **(2514)**
2001/02: 19^{0}S

	Starts	1st	2nd	3rd	Win & Pl
Hurdles	1	0	0	0	
Career Total	**2**	**0**	**0**	**0**	

Going: Sf: 0-1 GS: 0-0 Gd: 0-0 GF: - Fm: 0-0
Distance: 2m/2m3: 0-1 2m4-2m7: 0-0 3m+: 0-0
Track: LH: 0-1 RH: 0-0 Tight: 0-1 Gall: 0-0
Aids: Bl: 0-0 Vi: 0-0 Tstrap: 0-0
Best Rating: **60** 3/01 Hayd 2m heavy NHF

Brave The Waves (IRE)

10-y-o b g Black Minstrel-Edna Cottage (The Parson)
J R Jenkins P J Jarvis

Placings: 0 **(0230)**
2001/02: 16^{0}GF

	Starts	1st	2nd	3rd	Win & Pl
Hurdles	1	0	0	0	
Career Total	**1**	**0**	**0**	**0**	

Going: Sf: 0-0 GS: 0-0 Gd: 0-0 GF: - Fm: 0-1
Distance: 2m/2m3: 0-1 2m4-2m7: 0-0 3m+: 0-0
Track: LH: 0-0 RH: 0-1 Tight: 0-0 Gall: 0-1
Aids: Bl: 0-0 Vi: 0-0 Tstrap: 0-0
Best Rating:

Brave Vision

113 100+

6-y-o b g Clantime-Kinlet Vision (IRE) (Vision (USA))
A C Whillans Mrs S Harrow

Placings: F/534622-54U556221 **(4440)**
2001/02: 17^{5}G, 16^{4}S, 16^{U}GF, 18^{5}GS, 16^{5}GS, 20^{6}G, 16^{2}S, 16^{2}HY, 16^{1}S

	Starts	1st	2nd	3rd	Win & Pl
Hurdles	9	1	2	0	5379
Career Total	**16**	**1**	**4**	**1**	**7650**

89	3/02	Kels	2m110y	E(0-110)HHdl	SFT	£3435

Total win prize-money £3435

Going: Sf: 1-4 GS: 0-2 Gd: 0-2 GF: - Fm: 0-1

Distance: **2m/2m3: 1-8** 2m4-2m7: 0-1 3m+: 0-0
Track: **LH: 1-6** RH: 0-3 **Tight: 1-4** Gall: 0-1
Aids: Bl: 0-0 Vi: 0-0 Tstrap: 0-0
Best Rating: **92** 4/01 Weth 2m gd-sft Hdl

Consistent, if somewhat fustrating before scoring at Kelso in March 2002. Appears best at the minimum trip. Effective on most ground but best with some cut.

Bravo

79 **71**

4-y-o b/br g Efisio-Apache Squaw (Be My Guest (USA))
J Mackie (C W Thornton 19/9) Paul D Leech

Placings:4 **(3495)**
2001/02: 16^{4}S

	Starts	1st	2nd	3rd	Win & Pl
Hurdles	1	0	0	0	500
Career Total	**1**	**0**	**0**	**0**	**500**

Going: Sf: 0-1 GS: 0-0 Gd: 0-0 GF: - Fm: 0-0
Distance: 2m/2m3: 0-1 2m4-2m7: 0-0 3m+: 0-0
Track: LH: 0-1 RH: 0-0 Tight: 0-0 Gall: 0-1
Aids: Bl: 0-0 Vi: 0-0 Tstrap: 0-0
Best Rating: **71** 1/02 Donc 2m110y soft Hdl

Well held on hurdles debut.

Braw Lass

72 **35**

5-y-o b m Alflora (IRE)-Mirthful (Will Somers)
J Howard Johnson The Braw Partnership

Placings:*000* **(3326)**
2001/02: 17^{0}G, 16^{0}G, 16^{0}S

	Starts	1st	2nd	3rd	Win & Pl
NH Flat	2	0	0	0	0
Hurdles	1	0	0	0	0
Career Total	**3**	**0**	**0**	**0**	

Going: Sf: 0-1 GS: 0-0 Gd: 0-2 GF: - Fm: 0-0
Distance: 2m/2m3: 0-3 2m4-2m7: 0-0 3m+: 0-0
Track: LH: 0-3 RH: 0-0 Tight: 0-1 Gall: 0-1
Aids: Bl: 0-0 Vi: 0-0 Tstrap: 0-0
Best Rating: **82** 11/01 Weth 2m good NHF

Bray Hill (IRE)

101 **88**

9-y-o b g King Luthier-Pixies Glen (Furry Glen)
N A Twiston-Davies Fairfield Millennium Ltd

Placings:*23P000/36-*200F **(1240)**
2001/02: 20^{2}G, 20^{0}GF, 19^{0}G, 24^{F}GF

	Starts	1st	2nd	3rd	Win & Pl
Hurdles	4	0	1	0	723
Career Total	**12**	**0**	**2**	**2**	**1730**

Going: Sf: 0-0 GS: 0-0 Gd: 0-2 GF: - Fm: 0-2
Distance: 2m/2m3: 0-1 2m4-2m7: 0-2 3m+: 0-1
Track: LH: 0-4 RH: 0-0 Tight: 0-2 Gall: 0-0
Aids: Bl: 0-0 Vi: 0-0 Tstrap: 0-1
Best Rating: **93** 7/99 Worc 2m gd-fm NHF

Brea Hill

105 **88**

9-y-o b g Brotherly (USA)-Top Feather (High Top)
Ferdy Murphy A W K Merriam

Placings:*650/635F3UP/P-*P42U6F26 **(4856)**
2001/02: 27^{P}G, 27^{4}S, 27^{2}S, 27^{U}HY, 27^{6}S, 24^{F}S, 25^{2}GF, 25^{6}G

	Starts	1st	2nd	3rd	Win & Pl
Chases	8	0	2	0	1808
Career Total	**19**	**0**	**2**	**2**	**2826**

Going: Sf: 0-5 GS: 0-0 Gd: 0-2 GF: - Fm: 0-1
Distance: 2m/2m3: 0-0 2m4-2m7: 0-0 3m+: 0-8
Track: LH: 0-7 RH: 0-1 Tight: 0-5 Gall: 0-1
Aids: Bl: 0-0 Vi: 0-0 Tstrap: 0-3
Best Rating: **99** 12/98 Newc 2m soft NHF

Modest staying maiden chaser, who has done much of his racing at Sedgefield. Not the best jumper and often pulls up.

Break The Glass (USA)

67 **34**

5-y-o b/br g Dynaformer (USA)-Greek Wedding (USA) (Blushing Groom (FR))
R Ford Nick Shutts

Placings:*0P-*0 **(1931)**
2001/02: 16^{0}G

	Starts	1st	2nd	3rd	Win & Pl
Hurdles	1	0	0	0	
Career Total	**3**	**0**	**0**	**0**	

Going: Sf: 0-0 GS: 0-0 Gd: 0-1 GF: - Fm: 0-0
Distance: 2m/2m3: 0-1 2m4-2m7: 0-0 3m+: 0-0
Track: LH: 0-1 RH: 0-0 Tight: 0-1 Gall: 0-0
Aids: Bl: 0-0 Vi: 0-0 Tstrap: 0-0
Best Rating: **39** 11/00 Chel 2m110y gd-sft Hdl

Break The Rules

97 **77**

10-y-o b g Dominion-Surf Bird (Shareef Dancer (USA))
A G Juckes Whistlejacket Partnership

Placings:*0421132/00/PP/02222650/505-*305P **(1147)**
2001/02: 16^{3}GF, 17^{0}G, 22^{5}GF, 24^{P}GF

	Starts	1st	2nd	3rd	Win & Pl
Hurdles	4	0	0	1	286
Career Total	**26**	**2**	**6**	**2**	**10673**

113	2/97	Hayd	2m	D Hdl	GD	£3039
104	2/97	Tntn	2m1f	F Hdl	GD	£1707

Total win prize-money £4746

Going: Sf: 0-0 GS: 0-0 Gd: 0-1 GF: - Fm: 0-3
Distance: 2m/2m3: 0-2 2m4-2m7: 0-1 3m+: 0-1
Track: LH: 0-4 RH: 0-0 Tight: 0-4 Gall: 0-0
Aids: Bl: 0-0 Vi: 0-0 Tstrap: 0-0
Best Rating: **113** 4/97 Chep 2m110y firm Hdl

Breakin Glass

80 **60**

5-y-o b m Ardkinglass-Bee Dee Dancer (Ballacashtal (CAN))
A Bailey Mrs J Bailey

Placings:*53-*0 **(0348)**
2001/02: 16^{0}G

	Starts	1st	2nd	3rd	Win & Pl
Hurdles	1	0	0	0	
Career Total	**3**	**0**	**0**	**1**	**401**

Going: Sf: 0-0 GS: 0-0 Gd: 0-1 GF: - Fm: 0-0
Distance: 2m/2m3: 0-1 2m4-2m7: 0-0 3m+: 0-0
Track: LH: 0-1 RH: 0-0 Tight: 0-1 Gall: 0-0
Aids: Bl: 0-0 Vi: 0-0 Tstrap: 0-0
Best Rating: **85** 10/00 Ludl 2m gd-fm Hdl

Breaking Breeze (IRE)

105(105h) (105h)**115**

7-y-o b g Mandalus-Knockacool Breeze (Buckskin (FR))
J S King H Porter, N Rich, V Askew

Placings:*1040-*321400 **(4848)**
2001/02: 20^{3}F, 16^{2}GF, 16^{1}G, 17^{4}GS, 22^{0}GS, 16^{0}G

	Starts	1st	2nd	3rd	Win & Pl
Hurdles	6	1	1	1	5513
Career Total	**10**	**2**	**1**	**1**	**9101**

103	12/01	Ludl	2m	E(0-115)HHdl	GD	£4046
111	8/00	Cork	2m	NHF	Y-S	£3588

Total win prize-money £7634

Going: Sf: 0-0 GS: 0-2 Gd: 1-2 GF: - Fm: 0-2
Distance: **2m/2m3: 1-4** 2m4-2m7: 0-2 3m+: 0-0
Track: LH: 0-2 **RH: 1-4** Tight: 0-3 Gall: 0-0
Aids: Bl: 0-0 Vi: 0-0 Tstrap: 0-0
Best Rating: **111** 8/00 Cork 2m yld-sft NHF

Improved over hurdles to win a two-mile handicap on good ground in December 2001. Acts on good ground.

Breath Of Scandal (IRE)

11-y-o br g Strong Gale-Her Name Was Lola (Pitskelly)
D R Stoddart (C Grant 10/2) Mrs D R Stoddart

Placings:*60/P1/15P6F3/*P **(3875)**
2001/02: 24^{P}GS

	Starts	1st	2nd	3rd	Win & Pl
Chases	1	0	0	0	
Career Total	**11**	**2**	**0**	**1**	**7768**

123	5/99	Hexm	3m1f	E Ch	SFT	£3310
113	4/99	Hexm	3m1f	E Ch	GD	£3284

Total win prize-money £6596

Going: Sf: 0-0 GS: 0-1 Gd: 0-0 GF: - Fm: 0-0
Distance: 2m/2m3: 0-0 2m4-2m7: 0-0 3m+: 0-1
Track: LH: 0-0 RH: 0-1 Tight: 0-0 Gall: 0-1
Aids: Bl: 0-0 Vi: 0-0 Tstrap: 0-0
Best Rating: **123** 5/99 Hexm 3m1f soft Ch

Breathless Dreams (IRE)

75 **58**

5-y-o ch g College Chapel-Foston Bridge (Relkino)
M Wigham (G Brown 29/9) Cable Media Consultancy Ltd

Placings:0P **(1484)**
2001/02: 16^{0}GF, 16^{P}GS

	Starts	1st	2nd	3rd	Win & Pl
Hurdles	2	0	0	0	
Career Total	**2**	**0**	**0**	**0**	

Going: Sf: 0-0 GS: 0-1 Gd: 0-0 GF: - Fm: 0-1
Distance: 2m/2m3: 0-2 2m4-2m7: 0-0 3m+: 0-0
Track: LH: 0-2 RH: 0-0 Tight: 0-1 Gall: 0-0
Aids: Bl: 0-0 Vi: 0-0 Tstrap: 0-0
Best Rating: **58** 9/01 Worc 2m gd-fm Hdl

Breeze Home

6-y-o b g Homo Sapien-Poppy's Pride (Uncle Pokey)
Ian Williams Mrs M Mann

Placings:P0 (1619)
2001/02: 16^{P}GF, 16^{0}G

	Starts	1st	2nd	3rd	Win & Pl
Hurdles	2	0	0	0	
Career Total	**2**	**0**	**0**	**0**	

Going: Sf: 0-0 GS: 0-0 Gd: 0-1 GF: - Fm: 0-1
Distance: 2m/2m3: 0-2 2m4-2m7: 0-0 3m+: 0-0
Track: LH: 0-0 RH: 0-2 Tight: 0-0 Gall: 0-1
Aids: Bl: 0-0 Vi: 0-0 Tstrap: 0-0
Best Rating:

Breezy Betsy (IRE)

6-y-o br m Phardante (FR)-Aughclogeen Run (Deep Run)
Lady Earle (Mrs S D Williams 10/3) Lady Earle

Placings:3PPP (4735)
2001/02: 23^{3}GF, 24^{P}S, 25^{P}G, 23^{P}F

	Starts	1st	2nd	3rd	Win & Pl
Chases	4	0	0	1	636
Career Total	**4**	**0**	**0**	**1**	**636**

Going: Sf: 0-1 GS: 0-0 Gd: 0-1 GF: - Fm: 0-2
Distance: 2m/2m3: 0-0 2m4-2m7: 0-0 3m+: 0-4
Track: LH: 0-1 RH: 0-3 Tight: 0-0 Gall: 0-0
Aids: Bl: 0-1 Vi: 0-0 Tstrap: 0-0
Best Rating:

Breithorn Piper

9-y-o b g Scottish Reel-Miss Wrensborough (Buckskin (FR))
D R Gandolfo A W F Clapperton

Placings:0/00/056/P-F (0375)
2001/02: 16^{P}GF

	Starts	1st	2nd	3rd	Win & Pl
Hurdles	1	0	0	0	
Career Total	**8**	**0**	**0**	**0**	**0**

Going: Sf: 0-0 GS: 0-0 Gd: 0-0 GF: - Fm: 0-1
Distance: 2m/2m3: 0-1 2m4-2m7: 0-0 3m+: 0-0
Track: LH: 0-0 RH: 0-1 Tight: 0-0 Gall: 0-1
Aids: Bl: 0-0 Vi: 0-0 Tstrap: 0-0
Best Rating: **82** 12/99 Towc 2m soft Hdl

Bremridge (IRE)

5-y-o ch g Ridgewood Ben-Eimkar (Junius (USA))
G Brown Gary Brown

Placings:6-0P (0875)
2001/02: 18^{0}GF, 16^{P}GS

	Starts	1st	2nd	3rd	Win & Pl
Hurdles	2	0	0	0	
Career Total	**3**	**0**	**0**	**0**	**0**

Going: Sf: 0-0 GS: 0-1 Gd: 0-0 GF: - Fm: 0-1
Distance: 2m/2m3: 0-2 2m4-2m7: 0-0 3m+: 0-0
Track: LH: 0-2 RH: 0-0 Tight: 0-2 Gall: 0-0
Aids: Bl: 0-0 Vi: 0-0 Tstrap: 0-0
Best Rating:

Brenda's Delight (IRE)

87 **36**
4-y-o b f Blues Traveller (IRE)-Tara's Delight (Dunbeath (USA))
P Butler E H Whatmough

Placings:P (3396)
2001/02: 18^{P}S

	Starts	1st	2nd	3rd	Win & Pl
Hurdles	1	0	0	0	
Career Total	**1**	**0**	**0**	**0**	

Going: Sf: 0-1 GS: 0-0 Gd: 0-0 GF: - Fm: 0-0
Distance: 2m/2m3: 0-1 2m4-2m7: 0-0 3m+: 0-0
Track: LH: 0-1 RH: 0-0 Tight: 0-1 Gall: 0-0
Aids: Bl: 0-0 Vi: 0-0 Tstrap: 0-0
Best Rating:

Brereton (IRE)

96 **94**
6-y-o b g Be My Native (USA)-Society News (Law Society (USA))
N J Henderson Paul Sandy

Placings:205 (3647)
2001/02: 16^{2}S, 16^{0}G, 21^{5}S

	Starts	1st	2nd	3rd	Win & Pl
NH Flat	2	0	1	0	488
Hurdles	1	0	0	0	0
Career Total	**3**	**0**	**1**	**0**	**488**

Going: Sf: 0-2 GS: 0-0 Gd: 0-1 GF: - Fm: 0-0
Distance: 2m/2m3: 0-2 2m4-2m7: 0-1 3m+: 0-0
Track: LH: 0-2 RH: 0-1 Tight: 0-0 Gall: 0-1
Aids: Bl: 0-0 Vi: 0-0 Tstrap: 0-0
Best Rating: **120** 12/01 Wwck 2m soft NHF

Encouraging debut in a Warwick bumper. Looked to need further when fifth on his hurdles bow over two miles five. Acts on soft ground.

Breteche (FR)

7-y-o b m Fijar Tango (FR)-Foinery (Reference Point)
N J Hawke Roland John Hair Studio

Placings:2F064120452/30130/061P6PP6P346U636-004 (0682)
2001/02: 19^{0}G, 18^{0}GF, 22^{4}G

	Starts	1st	2nd	3rd	Win & Pl
Hurdles	2	0	0	0	0
Chases	1	0	0	0	0
Career Total	**35**	**3**	**3**	**4**	**11528**

96	5/00	NAbb	2m110y	D Ch	G-F	£3750
86	5/99	Ctml	2m1f110y	G(0-100)HHdl	GD	£3503
74	1/99	Folk	2m1f110y	G Hdl	HVY	£1618

Total win prize-money £8873

Going: Sf: 0-0 GS: 0-0 Gd: 0-2 GF: - Fm: 0-1
Distance: 2m/2m3: 0-1 2m4-2m7: 0-2 3m+: 0-0
Track: LH: 0-1 RH: 0-1 Tight: 0-2 Gall: 0-0
Aids: Bl: 0-0 Vi: 0-3 Tstrap: 0-0
Best Rating: **96** 5/00 NAbb 2m110y gd-fm Ch

Brexent (FR)

99 **76**

7-y-o ch g Funambule (USA)-Vertevoie (FR) (Tip Moss (FR))
A Scott Mrs D M Stevenson

Placings:40/5004002/45-660 (2471)
2001/02: 17^{6}G, 24^{6}S, 18^{0}GS

	Starts	1st	2nd	3rd	Win & Pl
Hurdles	3	0	0	0	0
Career Total	**14**	**0**	**1**	**0**	**890**

Going: Sf: 0-1 GS: 0-1 Gd: 0-1 GF: - Fm: 0-0
Distance: 2m/2m3: 0-2 2m4-2m7: 0-0 3m+: 0-1
Track: LH: 0-2 RH: 0-1 Tight: 0-2 Gall: 0-0
Aids: Bl: 0-0 Vi: 0-0 Tstrap: 0-0
Best Rating: **89** 11/98 Wwck 2m soft Hdl

Brian James

105(46c) **102**
8-y-o ch g River God (USA)-Rose Orchard (Rouser)
F P Murtagh Brian Callaghan

Placings:04PPP/45216FP3-23332 (3437)
2001/02: 27^{2}G, 24^{3}GS, 24^{3}S, 24^{3}S, 27^{2}HY

	Starts	1st	2nd	3rd	Win & Pl
Hurdles	5	0	2	3	2714
Career Total	**18**	**1**	**3**	**4**	**6485**

102	12/00	Sedg	3m3f110y	E Hdl	SFT	£2380

Total win prize-money £2380

Going: Sf: 0-3 GS: 0-1 Gd: 0-1 GF: - Fm: 0-0
Distance: 2m/2m3: 0-0 2m4-2m7: 0-0 3m+: 0-5
Track: LH: 0-5 RH: 0-0 Tight: 0-2 Gall: 0-1
Aids: Bl: 0-1 Vi: 0-0 Tstrap: 0-0
Best Rating: **102** 1/02 Sedg 3m3f110y heavy Hdl

A big, strongly-made chasing type, his only victory has come on the sharp left-handed Sedgefield track over an extended three miles three furlongs on easy ground.

Briano (FR)

102(57h) **106**
7-y-o br g Tropular-Heracleia (FR) (Kenmare (FR))
A Parker Mr & Mrs Raymond Anderson Green

Placings:42/423214/22402653F12/543362-0442 (2160)
2001/02: 16^{0}G, 16^{4}GS, 16^{4}GS, 20^{2}GS

	Starts	1st	2nd	3rd	Win & Pl
Chases	4	0	1	0	1830
Career Total	**29**	**2**	**9**	**4**	**30335**

107	3/00	Ayr	2m	D(0-125)HCh	HVY	£4452
103	3/99	Kels	2m2f	E Hdl	GD	£2318

Total win prize-money £6770

Going: Sf: 0-0 GS: 0-3 Gd: 0-1 GF: - Fm: 0-0
Distance: 2m/2m3: 0-3 2m4-2m7: 0-1 3m+: 0-0
Track: LH: 0-2 RH: 0-2 Tight: 0-1 Gall: 0-0
Aids: Bl: 0-1 Vi: 0-3 Tstrap: 0-0
Best Rating: **113** 3/00 Carl 2m4f110y gd-sft Ch

Consistently in the frame at up to two and a half miles in fair hurdling company, he took well to fences with a win in the mud at Ayr in March 2000. He has regularly been in the shake up, but has proved hard to win with since then.

Briar's Delight

80 **67**
14-y-o b g Idiots Delight-Briar Park (Timolin (FR))
R Allan A Clark

Placings:0006U/0P32/423114026324/13243433131/U12/333P21432/2P13242P35/5415P43/5130324-0P0 (4691)
2001/02: 16^{0}GF, 20^{P}G, 17^{0}GF

	Starts	1st	2nd	3rd	Win & Pl

	Starts	1st	2nd	3rd	Win & Pl
Chases	3	0	0	0	
Career Total	**71**	**10**	**12**	**17**	**57004**

112	5/00	MRas	2m1f110y	F(0-110)HCh	G-S	£3110
112	6/99	Prth	2m4f110y	E(0-115)HCh	SFT	£4201
113	10/98	Carl	2m	D(0-95)HCh	GD	£3371
111	2/98	Kels	2m1f	C(0-135)HCh	G-S	£4719
98	11/96	Kels	2m1f	D(0-120)HCh	G-F	£4006
98	5/96	Kels	2m1f	C Ch	SFT	£4817
83	3/96	Kels	2m1f	D Ch	GD	£3820
88	10/95	Kels	2m110y	E(0-115)HHdl	G-F	£2318
83	11/94	Newc	2m110y	Hdl	GD	£1955
81	9/94	Sedg	2m1f110y	(0-100)HHdl	GD	£1548

Total win prize-money £33870

Going: Sf: 0-0 GS: 0-0 Gd: 0-1 GF: - Fm: 0-2
Distance: 2m/2m3: 0-2 2m4-2m7: 0-1 3m+: 0-0
Track: LH: 0-1 RH: 0-2 Tight: 0-3 Gall: 0-0
Aids: Bl: 0-0 Vi: 0-3 Tstrap: 0-0
Best Rating: **113** 4/99 Kels 2m1f gd-fm Ch

Briar's Mist (IRE)

90 **103**

5-y-o gr g Roselier (FR)-Claycastle (IRE) (Carlingford Castle)
Miss H C Knight Southern Brick & Tile Co Ltd

Placings:*0035* (4400)
2001/02: 17^{0}G, 16^{0}S, 21^{3}HY, 21^{5}S

	Starts	1st	2nd	3rd	Win & Pl
NH Flat	2	0	0	0	0
Hurdles	2	0	0	1	583
Career Total	**4**	**0**	**0**	**1**	**583**

Going: Sf: 0-3 GS: 0-0 Gd: 0-1 GF: - Fm: 0-0
Distance: 2m/2m3: 0-2 2m4-2m7: 0-2 3m+: 0-0
Track: LH: 0-2 RH: 0-1 Tight: 0-1 Gall: 0-1
Aids: Bl: 0-0 Vi: 0-0 Tstrap: 0-0
Best Rating: **103** 3/02 Newb 2m5f soft Hdl

Promising effort on novice hurdle debut over two miles and five furlongs, looks well up to winning races. Acts on soft/heavy ground.

Briary Boy (IRE)

10-y-o ch g Mister Lord (USA)-Aprolon Princess (IRE) (Duky)
L J Williams L J Williams

Placings:000/**FP** (3398)
2001/02: 19^{F}S, 22^{P}S

	Starts	1st	2nd	3rd	Win & Pl
Chases	2	0	0	0	
Career Total	**5**	**0**	**0**	**0**	

Going: Sf: 0-2 GS: 0-0 Gd: 0-0 GF: - Fm: 0-0
Distance: 2m/2m3: 0-1 2m4-2m7: 0-1 3m+: 0-0
Track: LH: 0-0 RH: 0-1 Tight: 0-1 Gall: 0-0
Aids: Bl: 0-0 Vi: 0-0 Tstrap: 0-0
Best Rating: **51** 12/97 Cork 2m yld-sft Hdl

Bric A Brac

5-y-o ch m Minster Son-Greenhill's Girl (Radetzky)
W G Young W G Young

Placings:*000* (3613)
2001/02: 16^{0}G, 17^{0}GS, 16^{0}S

	Starts	1st	2nd	3rd	Win & Pl
NH Flat	3	0	0	0	
Career Total	**3**	**0**	**0**	**0**	

Going: Sf: 0-1 GS: 0-1 Gd: 0-1 GF: - Fm: 0-0
Distance: 2m/2m3: 0-3 2m4-2m7: 0-0 3m+: 0-0
Track: LH: 0-0 RH: 0-3 Tight: 0-1 Gall: 0-0
Aids: Bl: 0-0 Vi: 0-0 Tstrap: 0-0
Best Rating:

Bridal White

51 **61**

6-y-o b m Robellino (USA)-Alwatar (USA) (Caerleon (USA))
M J Ryan Peter P Scott

Placings:60/**5P** (4175)
2001/02: 16^{5}S, 20^{P}GS

	Starts	1st	2nd	3rd	Win & Pl
Chases	2	0	0	0	0
Career Total	**4**	**0**	**0**	**0**	**0**

Going: Sf: 0-1 GS: 0-1 Gd: 0-0 GF: - Fm: 0-0
Distance: 2m/2m3: 0-1 2m4-2m7: 0-1 3m+: 0-0
Track: LH: 0-1 RH: 0-1 Tight: 0-1 Gall: 0-1
Aids: Bl: 0-0 Vi: 0-0 Tstrap: 0-0
Best Rating: **65** 11/99 Hntg 2m110y gd-fm Hdl

Bridgend Blue (IRE)

92 **57**

6-y-o b g Up And At 'Em-Sperrin Mist (Camden Town)
J S Hubbuck J S Hubbuck

Placings:53P/P60P00P06P05 (4858)
2001/02: 24^{P}S, 16^{6}GF, 16^{0}F, 16^{P}GS, 16^{0}G, 17^{0}GF, 22^{P}G, 20^{0}G, 18^{6}GS, 16^{P}GF, 16^{0}GF, 16^{5}G

	Starts	1st	2nd	3rd	Win & Pl
Hurdles	12	0	0	0	0
Career Total	**15**	**0**	**0**	**1**	**341**

Going: Sf: 0-1 GS: 0-2 Gd: 0-4 GF: - Fm: 0-5
Distance: 2m/2m3: 0-9 2m4-2m7: 0-2 3m+: 0-1
Track: LH: 0-9 RH: 0-1 Tight: 0-4 Gall: 0-1
Aids: Bl: 0-1 Vi: 0-0 Tstrap: 0-3
Best Rating: **71** 9/99 Hntg 2m110y good Hdl

Modest hurdler.

Brief Contact (IRE)

94 **76**

4-y-o b g Brief Truce (USA)-Incommunicado (IRE) (Sadler's Wells (USA))
Jamie Poulton George H Gibson

Placings:*025* (1558)
2001/02: 16^{0}GF, 16^{2}GS, 16^{5}G

	Starts	1st	2nd	3rd	Win & Pl
Hurdles	3	0	1	0	975
Career Total	**3**	**0**	**1**	**0**	**975**

Going: Sf: 0-0 GS: 0-1 Gd: 0-1 GF: - Fm: 0-1
Distance: 2m/2m3: 0-3 2m4-2m7: 0-0 3m+: 0-0
Track: LH: 0-3 RH: 0-0 Tight: 0-2 Gall: 0-0
Aids: Bl: 0-2 Vi: 0-0 Tstrap: 0-0
Best Rating: **76** 10/01 Chep 2m110y good Hdl

Improved on his debut when runner-up in a moderate Plumpton juvenile event in September.

Briery Ann

100(102h) **103**

8-y-o b m Anshan-Fall About (Comedy Star (USA))
H D Daly Mrs Helen Plumbly

Placings:*343*/60411/**F43P-42P** (3321)
2001/02: 21^{4}G, 19^{2}G, 24^{P}GS

	Starts	1st	2nd	3rd	Win & Pl
Chases	3	0	1	0	1660
Career Total	**15**	**2**	**1**	**3**	**10475**

120	3/00	Towc	2m5f	D Hdl	SFT	£3591
118	2/00	Carl	2m4f110y	D Hdl	HVY	£3575

Total win prize-money £7166

Going: Sf: 0-0 GS: 0-1 Gd: 0-2 GF: - Fm: 0-0
Distance: 2m/2m3: 0-0 2m4-2m7: 0-2 3m+: 0-1
Track: LH: 0-1 RH: 0-2 Tight: 0-1 Gall: 0-1
Aids: Bl: 0-0 Vi: 0-0 Tstrap: 0-0
Best Rating: **120** 3/00 Towc 2m5f soft Hdl

A mud lover whose best form over hurdles was over two and a half miles in the early part of 2000.

Briery Ella

63 **57**

6-y-o ch m Good Thyne (USA)-Oranella (Orange Bay)
H D Daly Mrs Helen Plumbly

Placings:*00-0* (0346)
2001/02: 20^{0}G

	Starts	1st	2nd	3rd	Win & Pl
Hurdles	1	0	0	0	
Career Total	**3**	**0**	**0**	**0**	

Going: Sf: 0-0 GS: 0-0 Gd: 0-1 GF: - Fm: 0-0
Distance: 2m/2m3: 0-1 2m4-2m7: 0-1 3m+: 0-0
Track: LH: 0-1 RH: 0-0 Tight: 0-1 Gall: 0-0
Aids: Bl: 0-0 Vi: 0-0 Tstrap: 0-0
Best Rating: **73** 2/01 Donc 2m110y good NHF

Brig A Deer

58f **78f**

6-y-o b g Presidium-Brig's Gazelle (Lord Nelson (FR))
I Park Mrs C Park

Placings:*000* (4860)
2001/02: 16^{0}GS, 16^{0}HY, 16^{0}G

	Starts	1st	2nd	3rd	Win & Pl
NH Flat	3	0	0	0	
Career Total	**3**	**0**	**0**	**0**	

Going: Sf: 0-1 GS: 0-1 Gd: 0-1 GF: - Fm: 0-0
Distance: 2m/2m3: 0-3 2m4-2m7: 0-0 3m+: 0-0
Track: LH: 0-1 RH: 0-0 Tight: 0-0 Gall: 0-1
Aids: Bl: 0-0 Vi: 0-0 Tstrap: 0-0
Best Rating: **78** 3/02 Newc 2m heavy NHF

Brig O'Turk

68 **72**

5-y-o ch g Inchinor-Sharmood (USA) (Sharpen Up)
J S Moore (C J Mann 23/7) David & Stewart Yates

Placings:*0P* (4176)
2001/02: 18^{0}GF, 19^{P}GS

	Starts	1st	2nd	3rd	Win & Pl
Hurdles	2	0	0	0	
Career Total	**2**	**0**	**0**	**0**	

Going: Sf: 0-0 GS: 0-1 Gd: 0-0 GF: - Fm: 0-1
Distance: 2m/2m3: 0-2 2m4-2m7: 0-0 3m+: 0-0
Track: LH: 0-2 RH: 0-0 Tight: 0-2 Gall: 0-0
Aids: Bl: 0-1 Vi: 0-0 Tstrap: 0-0

Best Rating: 72 5/01 Font 2m2f110y gd-fm Hdl

Briggs Turn

101 **107**

8-y-o b g Rudimentary (USA)-Turnabout (Tyrnavos)
B Llewellyn Mrs M Llewellyn

Placings:P/562221220/300-031 (3334)
2001/02: 17^{0}G, 16^{3}S, 16^{1}G

	Starts	1st	2nd	3rd	Win & Pl
Hurdles	3	1	0	1	2393
Career Total	**16**	**2**	**5**	**2**	**9054**

107	1/02	Ludl	2m	G(0-95)HHdl	GD	£2107
96	12/98	Ludl	2m	E(0-110)HHdl	G-S	£2722

Total win prize-money £4830

Going: Sf: 0-1 GS: 0-0 Gd: 1-2 GF: - Fm: 0-0
Distance: **2m/2m3: 1-3** 2m4-2m7: 0-0 3m+: 0-0
Track: LH: 0-1 **RH: 1-2** Tight: 0-1 Gall: 0-0
Aids: Bl: 0-0 Vi: 0-0 Tstrap: 0-0
Best Rating: **107** 1/02 Ludl 2m good Hdl

Plating-class hurdler, he is a better horse on good ground. Best at two miles.

Bright Approach (IRE)

9-y-o gr g Roselier (FR)-Dysart Lady (King's Ride)
Mrs O Bush (L G Cottrell 2/10) J H Burbidge

Placings:5/141P66 (4826)
2001/02: 23^{1}G, 24^{4}GS, 33^{1}G, 28^{P}GF, 23^{6}GF, 26^{6}G

	Starts	1st	2nd	3rd	Win & Pl
Chases	6	2	0	0	7514
Career Total	**7**	**2**	**0**	**0**	**7514**

113	5/01	Chel	4m1f	H Ch	GD	£5528
108	5/01	Extr	2m7f110y	H Ch	GD	£1715

Total win prize-money £7243

Going: Sf: 0-0 GS: 0-1 Gd: 2-3 GF: - Fm: 0-2
Distance: 2m/2m3: 0-0 2m4-2m7: 0-0 **3m+: 2-6**
Track: LH: 0-3 **RH: 1-2** Tight: 0-2 Gall: 0-1
Aids: Bl: 0-0 Vi: 0-0 Tstrap: 0-0
Best Rating: **113** 5/01 Chel 4m1f good Ch

Decent hunter chaser, stays four miles, does not want the ground too soft.

Bright Buck (IRE)

90(50h) **74**

9-y-o b g Glacial Storm (USA)-Bright News (Buckskin (FR))
F Lloyd F Lloyd

Placings:*60/604420000O0/63004*/02212415-**0P05U33U** (1403)
2001/02: 17^{0}GS, 24^{P}GF, 22^{0}GF, 23^{5}G, 20^{U}G, 24^{3}GF, 24^{3}GF, 24^{U}G

	Starts	1st	2nd	3rd	Win & Pl
Hurdles	1	0	0	0	0
Chases	7	0	0	2	968
Career Total	**34**	**2**	**4**	**3**	**10088**

93	10/00	Ludl	2m5f	F(0-90)Hdl	G-F	£2576
89	8/00	Bang	2m4f	F Hdl	GD	£2320

Total win prize-money £4897

Going: Sf: 0-0 GS: 0-1 Gd: 0-3 GF: - Fm: 0-4
Distance: 2m/2m3: 0-1 2m4-2m7: 0-2 3m+: 0-5
Track: LH: 0-7 RH: 0-1 Tight: 0-6 Gall: 0-0
Aids: Bl: 0-1 Vi: 0-0 Tstrap: 0-0
Best Rating: **93** 10/00 Ludl 2m5f gd-fm Hdl

Bright Destiny

95(69h) **104**

11-y-o br g Destroyer-Bright Suggestion (Magnate)
J S Goldie Strathayr Publishing Ltd

Placings:*000P*/**0446P05P031F6/646/35225132134O/36P1P246/3PPP4P04P04-46515346P** (4523)
2001/02: 29^{4}S, 24^{6}S, 24^{5}S, 25^{1}HY, 24^{5}S, 20^{3}HY, 25^{4}HY, 32^{6}HY, 26^{P}GS

	Starts	1st	2nd	3rd	Win & Pl
Chases	9	1	0	1	9152
Career Total	**60**	**5**	**4**	**7**	**45714**

104	2/02	Ayr	3m1f	D(0-120)HCh	HVY	£7560
113	2/00	Ayr	3m1f	D(0-120)HCh	HVY	£10980
113	3/99	Ayr	3m1f	D(0-125)HCh	SFT	£6020
111	2/99	Ayr	3m1f	E(0-115)HCh	SFT	£3548
86	3/97	Hexm	3m1f	G(0-90)HCh	SFT	£2357

Total win prize-money £30465

Going: Sf: 1-8 GS: 0-1 Gd: 0-0 GF: - Fm: 0-0
Distance: 2m/2m3: 0-0 2m4-2m7: 0-1 **3m+: 1-8**
Track: **LH: 1-6** RH: 0-3 Tight: 0-3 Gall: 0-1
Aids: Bl: 0-0 Vi: 0-3 Tstrap: 0-0
Best Rating: **113** 5/00 Sedg 3m4f gd-fm Ch

A one-time decent handicap chaser, he had lost his way before winning at Ayr in February 2002. Stays well and is effective in soft ground.

Bright November

101 **140**

11-y-o b g Niniski (USA)-Brigata (Brigadier Gerard)
D R Gandolfo Mrs C Skipworth

Placings:05522216/110/3F/2P/11115-24P (3671)
2001/02: 17^{2}S, 20^{4}G, 20^{P}S

	Starts	1st	2nd	3rd	Win & Pl
Chases	3	0	1	0	2892
Career Total	**23**	**7**	**5**	**1**	**41539**

144	2/01	Asct	2m3f110y	B Ch	SFT	£10166
140	11/00	Kemp	2m	D Ch	SFT	£4251
144	11/00	Kemp	2m4f110y	D Ch	SFT	£5096
134	10/00	Hrfd	2m	F(0-110)HCh	GD	£3711
118	4/98	Uttx	2m	B(0-140)HHdl	G-S	£5003
107	4/98	Hrfd	2m1f	F(0-105)HHdl	SFT	£3048
87	4/96	Hrfd	2m3f110y	F(0-95)HHdl	G-F	£2906

Total win prize-money £34183

Going: Sf: 0-2 GS: 0-0 Gd: 0-1 GF: - Fm: 0-0
Distance: 2m/2m3: 0-1 2m4-2m7: 0-2 3m+: 0-0
Track: LH: 0-1 RH: 0-2 Tight: 0-1 Gall: 0-0
Aids: Bl: 0-0 Vi: 0-0 Tstrap: 0-0
Best Rating: **144** 2/01 Asct 2m3f110y soft Ch

A smart front runner, he had a good season in novice chases in 2000/2001, winning four times over distances ranging from two to two and a half miles. Second of two finishers on his reappearance, he is best going right-handed and races enthusiastically. Acts on an easy surface.

Bright Question

90 **64**

5-y-o ch g Nashwan (USA)-Ozone Friendly (USA) (Green Forest (USA))
Mrs Merrita Jones R K McCafferty

Placings:00P0 (4601)
2001/02: 16^{0}G, 21^{0}S, 16^{P}HY, 16^{0}GF

	Starts	1st	2nd	3rd	Win & Pl
Hurdles	4	0	0	0	
Career Total	**4**	**0**	**0**	**0**	

Going: Sf: 0-2 GS: 0-0 Gd: 0-1 GF: - Fm: 0-1
Distance: 2m/2m3: 0-3 2m4-2m7: 0-1 3m+: 0-0
Track: LH: 0-3 RH: 0-1 Tight: 0-1 Gall: 0-1
Aids: Bl: 0-0 Vi: 0-0 Tstrap: 0-0
Best Rating: **64** 4/02 Wwck 2m gd-fm Hdl

Bright Steel (IRE)

76f **58f**

5-y-o gr g Roselier (FR)-Ikeathy (Be Friendly)
A Parker Mr & Mrs Raymond Anderson Green

Placings:*0* (2923)
2001/02: 16^{0}G

	Starts	1st	2nd	3rd	Win & Pl
NH Flat	1	0	0	0	
Career Total	**1**	**0**	**0**	**0**	

Going: Sf: 0-0 GS: 0-0 Gd: 0-1 GF: - Fm: 0-0
Distance: 2m/2m3: 0-1 2m4-2m7: 0-0 3m+: 0-0
Track: LH: 0-0 RH: 0-1 Tight: 0-1 Gall: 0-0
Aids: Bl: 0-0 Vi: 0-0 Tstrap: 0-0
Best Rating: **58** 12/01 Muss 2m good NHF

Brilliancy (USA)

89 **60**

7-y-o b g Alleged (USA)-Crystal Gazing (USA) (El Gran Senor (USA))
M Pitman Mrs M A Hoffman

Placings:*45/0* (1087)
2001/02: 16^{0}GF

	Starts	1st	2nd	3rd	Win & Pl
Hurdles	1	0	0	0	
Career Total	**3**	**0**	**0**	**0**	**0**

Going: Sf: 0-0 GS: 0-0 Gd: 0-0 GF: - Fm: 0-1
Distance: 2m/2m3: 0-1 2m4-2m7: 0-0 3m+: 0-0
Track: LH: 0-1 RH: 0-0 Tight: 0-0 Gall: 0-0
Aids: Bl: 0-0 Vi: 0-0 Tstrap: 0-0
Best Rating: **94** 4/99 MRas 1m5f110y soft NHF

Brilliant Star (NZ)

105 **125**

10-y-o b g Star Way-Karman Gal (Persian Bold)
S A Brookshaw T G K Construction Ltd

Placings:B1410/0035**143F/FP**044121-03P021 (4740)
2001/02: 20^{0}GS, 16^{3}GF, 20^{P}G, 17^{0}G, 20^{2}G, 20^{1}GF

	Starts	1st	2nd	3rd	Win & Pl
Chases	6	1	1	1	8044
Career Total	**27**	**6**	**2**	**3**	**27784**

125	4/02	Ludl	2m4f	D(0-120)HCh	G-F	£5018
126	9/00	Hrfd	2m	E(0-115)HCh	G-S	£3415
126	9/00	Hrfd	2m3f	F(0-110)HCh	G-F	£4075
122	10/99	Ludl	2m4f	E Ch	G-F	£3403
117	3/99	Ludl	2m	E Hdl	SFT	£2626
110	1/99	Ludl	2m	F Hdl	SFT	£2053

Total win prize-money £20594

Going: Sf: 0-0 GS: 0-1 Gd: 0-3 GF: - Fm: 1-2
Distance: 2m/2m3: 0-2 **2m4-2m7: 1-4** 3m+: 0-0
Track: LH: 0-2 **RH: 1-4 Tight: 1-4** Gall: 0-1
Aids: Bl: 0-0 Vi: 0-0 Tstrap: 0-0
Best Rating: **126** 9/00 Hrfd 2m gd-sft Ch

Decent handicap chaser, suited by fast ground over two and a half miles.

Bring Sweets

151

6-y-o b g Sabrehill (USA)-Che Gambe (USA) (Lyphard (USA))
B Ellison Spring Cottage Syndicate

Placings:11110/6300612-F **(0080)**
2001/02: 16^{F}G

	Starts	1st	2nd	3rd	Win & Pl
Hurdles	1	0	0	0	
Career Total	**13**	**5**	**1**	**1**	**45357**

149	2/01	Hayd	2m	B Hdl	SFT	£16900
126	2/00	Newb	2m110y	C Hdl	G-S	£4966
120	11/99	Newb	2m110y	D Hdl	G-F	£3496
123	10/99	Chel	2m110y	C Hdl	GD	£5121
128	10/99	Kemp	2m	D Hdl	G-F	£3139

Total win prize-money £33622

Going: Sf: 0-0 GS: 0-0 Gd: 0-1 GF: - Fm: 0-0
Distance: 2m/2m3: 0-1 2m4-2m7: 0-0 3m+: 0-0
Track: LH: 0-1 RH: 0-0 Tight: 0-0 Gall: 0-0
Aids: Bl: 0-0 Vi: 0-0 Tstrap: 0-0
Best Rating: **151** 5/01 Hayd 2m good Hdl

A very smart hurdle,r he tragically took a fatal fall in the Swinton Hurdle at Haydock when still just holding the lead. (DEAD)

Brinton

76 90

7-y-o b g Minster Son-River Chimes (Forlorn River)
J N R Billinge Hilton Racing Partnership

Placings:00-00 **(1746)**
2001/02: 20^{0}G, 16^{0}GS

	Starts	1st	2nd	3rd	Win & Pl
Hurdles	2	0	0	0	
Career Total	**4**	**0**	**0**	**0**	

Going: Sf: 0-0 GS: 0-1 Gd: 0-1 GF: - Fm: 0-0
Distance: 2m/2m3: 0-1 2m4-2m7: 0-1 3m+: 0-0
Track: LH: 0-1 RH: 0-1 Tight: 0-1 Gall: 0-0
Aids: Bl: 0-0 Vi: 0-0 Tstrap: 0-0
Best Rating: **90** 4/01 Ayr 2m good Hdl

Brioney (IRE)

77 62

5-y-o ch m Barathea (IRE)-La Vigie (King Of Clubs)
J A Glover David Jenkins

Placings:0 **(1042)**
2001/02: 16^{0}GF

	Starts	1st	2nd	3rd	Win & Pl
Hurdles	1	0	0	0	
Career Total	**1**	**0**	**0**	**0**	

Going: Sf: 0-0 GS: 0-0 Gd: 0-0 GF: - Fm: 0-1
Distance: 2m/2m3: 0-1 2m4-2m7: 0-0 3m+: 0-0
Track: LH: 0-1 RH: 0-0 Tight: 0-0 Gall: 0-0
Aids: Bl: 0-0 Vi: 0-0 Tstrap: 0-1
Best Rating: **62** 7/01 Uttx 2m gd-fm Hdl

Britannia Mills

78 24

11-y-o gr m Nordico (USA)-May Fox (Healaugh Fox)
R J Price Don Gould

Placings:F2/01633023P03060P0/P56/23/1F6160000PF2/0012S6000/20065300-000000 **(2308)**
2001/02: 17^{0}G, 22^{0}G, 22^{0}GS, 17^{0}G, 24^{0}GF, 26^{0}G

	Starts	1st	2nd	3rd	Win & Pl
Hurdles	6	0	0	0	
Career Total	**58**	**4**	**6**	**6**	**15532**

78	8/99	Ctml	2m6f	G(0-90)HHdl	GD	£2864
80	8/98	Ctml	2m6f	G(0-90)HHdl	GD	£2262
86	6/98	Uttx	2m4f110y	G(0-90)HHdl	GD	£1752
80	8/95	Ctml	2m1f110y	G(0-90)HHdl	FRM	£2324

Total win prize-money £9203

Going: Sf: 0-0 GS: 0-1 Gd: 0-4 GF: - Fm: 0-1
Distance: 2m/2m3: 0-2 2m4-2m7: 0-2 3m+: 0-2
Track: LH: 0-4 RH: 0-2 Tight: 0-4 Gall: 0-1
Aids: Bl: 0-4 Vi: 0-0 Tstrap: 0-0
Best Rating: **86** 6/98 Uttx 2m4f110y good Hdl

British Volunteer (IRE)

88 96

6-y-o br g Executive Perk-Dante Light (IRE) (Phardante (FR))
C J Mann Roy Wright And The Volunteers

Placings:0-33P **(2765)**
2001/02: 20^{3}GS, 21^{3}S, 19^{P}GS

	Starts	1st	2nd	3rd	Win & Pl
Hurdles	3	0	0	2	747
Career Total	**4**	**0**	**0**	**2**	**747**

Going: Sf: 0-1 GS: 0-2 Gd: 0-0 GF: - Fm: 0-0
Distance: 2m/2m3: 0-1 2m4-2m7: 0-2 3m+: 0-0
Track: LH: 0-1 RH: 0-0 Tight: 0-1 Gall: 0-1
Aids: Bl: 0-0 Vi: 0-0 Tstrap: 0-0
Best Rating: **96** 11/01 Font 2m4f gd-sft Hdl

Showed promise on hurdling debut.

Broad Statement

9-y-o br g Broadsword (USA)-Spartiquick (Spartan General)
J M Castle J M Castle

Placings:P-P **(0194)**
2001/02: 24^{P}GF

	Starts	1st	2nd	3rd	Win & Pl
Chases	1	0	0	0	
Career Total	**2**	**0**	**0**	**0**	

Going: Sf: 0-0 GS: 0-0 Gd: 0-0 GF: - Fm: 0-1
Distance: 2m/2m3: 0-0 2m4-2m7: 0-0 3m+: 0-1
Track: LH: 0-1 RH: 0-0 Tight: 0-1 Gall: 0-0
Aids: Bl: 0-0 Vi: 0-0 Tstrap: 0-0
Best Rating:

Broadgate Flyer (IRE)

99 90

8-y-o b g Silver Kite (USA)-Fabulous Pet (Somethingfabulous (USA))
D A Lamb D G Pryde

Placings:343165/R05P00UF/4005P450616/P6026-P546260P **(4855)**
2001/02: 16^{P}GS, 16^{5}G, 17^{4}G, 16^{6}S, 16^{2}GF, 20^{6}S, 17^{0}GF, 20^{P}G

	Starts	1st	2nd	3rd	Win & Pl
Chases	8	0	1	0	1162
Career Total	**38**	**2**	**2**	**2**	**9365**

90	3/00	Sedg	2m110y	D Ch	G-F	£4119
72	10/97	Kels	2m110y	E Hdl	FRM	£2192

Total win prize-money £6312

Going: Sf: 0-2 GS: 0-1 Gd: 0-3 GF: - Fm: 0-2
Distance: 2m/2m3: 0-6 2m4-2m7: 0-2 3m+: 0-0
Track: LH: 0-6 RH: 0-2 Tight: 0-7 Gall: 0-0
Aids: Bl: 0-0 Vi: 0-0 Tstrap: 0-8
Best Rating: **90** 12/01 Muss 2m gd-fm Ch

Broadway Boy

48

6-y-o b g Regal Embers (IRE)-Masters Magic (Current Magic)
John Allen Forever Optimistic

Placings:U00 **(0778)**
2001/02: 16^{U}GF, 16^{0}GF, 20^{0}GF

	Starts	1st	2nd	3rd	Win & Pl
NH Flat	2	0	0	0	0
Hurdles	1	0	0	0	0
Career Total	**3**	**0**	**0**	**0**	

Going: Sf: 0-0 GS: 0-0 Gd: 0-0 GF: - Fm: 0-3
Distance: 2m/2m3: 0-2 2m4-2m7: 0-1 3m+: 0-0
Track: LH: 0-2 RH: 0-1 Tight: 0-1 Gall: 0-1
Aids: Bl: 0-0 Vi: 0-0 Tstrap: 0-0
Best Rating: **57** 5/01 Hntg 2m110y gd-fm NHF

Brockbuster

100 106

7-y-o b g Syrtos-Ruby's Vision (Balinger)
N A Twiston-Davies Michael J Arnold

Placings:2062-P45P4 **(4514)**
2001/02: 24^{P}G, 21^{4}S, 24^{5}GS, 32^{P}GS, 25^{4}GS

	Starts	1st	2nd	3rd	Win & Pl
Hurdles	1	0	0	0	0
Chases	4	0	0	0	316
Career Total	**9**	**0**	**2**	**0**	**1275**

Going: Sf: 0-1 GS: 0-3 Gd: 0-1 GF: - Fm: 0-0
Distance: 2m/2m3: 0-0 2m4-2m7: 0-1 3m+: 0-4
Track: LH: 0-3 RH: 0-2 Tight: 0-0 Gall: 0-3
Aids: Bl: 0-0 Vi: 0-0 Tstrap: 0-0
Best Rating: **106** 12/01 Uttx 2m5f soft Ch

Likes to force the pace and put in some good efforts in bumpers, but flopped on his hurdling debut. He is named after the Japanese version of the 1973 number one hit by The Sweet.

Brockhall Boy

79f 85f

6-y-o b g Royal Fountain-Ribo Melody (Riboboy (USA))
D Eddy Brockhall Village Ltd

Placings:00 **(3368)**
2001/02: 16^{0}S, 16^{0}GS

	Starts	1st	2nd	3rd	Win & Pl
NH Flat	2	0	0	0	
Career Total	**2**	**0**	**0**	**0**	

Going: Sf: 0-1 GS: 0-1 Gd: 0-0 GF: - Fm: 0-0
Distance: 2m/2m3: 0-2 2m4-2m7: 0-0 3m+: 0-0
Track: LH: 0-2 RH: 0-0 Tight: 0-1 Gall: 0-0
Aids: Bl: 0-0 Vi: 0-0 Tstrap: 0-0
Best Rating: **85** 12/01 Wwck 2m soft NHF

Brockhall Lad

4-y-o b g Primo Dominie-Cremets (Mummy's Pet)
D Eddy Brockhall Village Ltd

Placings:0 **(3744)**
2001/02: 16^{0}S

	Starts	1st	2nd	3rd	Win & Pl
Hurdles	1	0	0	0	
Career Total	**1**	**0**	**0**	**0**	

Going: Sf: 0-1 GS: 0-0 Gd: 0-0 GF: - Fm: 0-0
Distance: 2m/2m3: 0-1 2m4-2m7: 0-0 3m+: 0-0
Track: LH: 0-0 RH: 0-1 Tight: 0-1 Gall: 0-0
Aids: Bl: 0-0 Vi: 0-0 Tstrap: 0-0
Best Rating:

Brockton Mist (IRE)

105 **109+**

7-y-o ch g Mister Lord (USA)-Glens Princess (Prince Hansel)
R H Buckler Mrs D A La Trobe

Placings:*2-050* **(2942)**
2001/02: 16^{0}G, 16^{5}HY, 16^{0}G

	Starts	1st	2nd	3rd	Win & Pl
NH Flat	3	0	0	0	0
Career Total	**4**	**0**	**1**	**0**	**500**

Going: Sf: 0-1 GS: 0-0 Gd: 0-2 GF: - Fm: 0-0
Distance: 2m/2m3: 0-3 2m4-2m7: 0-0 3m+: 0-0
Track: LH: 0-2 RH: 0-1 Tight: 0-0 Gall: 0-1
Aids: Bl: 0-0 Vi: 0-0 Tstrap: 0-0
Best Rating: **96** 12/01 Towc 2m heavy NHF

A half-brother to Grand National winner Papillon, he will make a chaser in time.

Broctune Line

82 **44**

8-y-o ch g Safawan-Ra Ra (Lord Gayle (USA))
Mrs P Ford M Sweeney

Placings:2006/P/04000P3/0-00P **(4405)**
2001/02: 16^{0}S, 21^{0}GF, 17^{P}S

	Starts	1st	2nd	3rd	Win & Pl
Hurdles	2	0	0	0	0
Chases	1	0	0	0	0
Career Total	**16**	**0**	**1**	**1**	**1177**

Going: Sf: 0-2 GS: 0-0 Gd: 0-0 GF: - Fm: 0-1
Distance: 2m/2m3: 0-2 2m4-2m7: 0-1 3m+: 0-0
Track: LH: 0-1 RH: 0-2 Tight: 0-1 Gall: 0-2
Aids: Bl: 0-0 Vi: 0-0 Tstrap: 0-0
Best Rating: **87** 11/97 Weth 2m gd-sft Hdl

Brodante King (IRE)

103 **97**

8-y-o b g Phardante (FR)-Pedigree Corner (Pollerton)
C Tizzard R G Tizzard

Placings:*3-P4262* **(3400)**
2001/02: 25^{P}S, 21^{4}GF, 26^{2}G, 22^{6}G, 26^{2}S

	Starts	1st	2nd	3rd	Win & Pl
Chases	5	0	2	0	2216
Career Total	**6**	**0**	**2**	**1**	**2427**

Going: Sf: 0-2 GS: 0-0 Gd: 0-2 GF: - Fm: 0-1
Distance: 2m/2m3: 0-0 2m4-2m7: 0-2 3m+: 0-3
Track: LH: 0-0 RH: 0-2 Tight: 0-3 Gall: 0-0
Aids: Bl: 0-0 Vi: 0-0 Tstrap: 0-0
Best Rating: **97** 12/01 Font 3m2f110y good Ch

Winner of a point to point, is effective on a sound surface but has only shown moderate form over regulation fences.

Broguestown Breeze (IRE)

(90h) (92h)

9-y-o b g Montelimar (USA)-Spin A Coin (Torus)
L A Dace Danny O'Sullivan

Placings:*0321/P00P25/34PP-3* **(0374)**
2001/02: 26^{3}GF

	Starts	1st	2nd	3rd	Win & Pl
Hurdles	1	0	0	1	360
Career Total	**15**	**1**	**2**	**3**	**6399**

111	1/99	DRoy	2m4f	Ch	HVY	£3376

Total win prize-money £3376

Going: Sf: 0-0 GS: 0-0 Gd: 0-0 GF: - Fm: 0-1
Distance: 2m/2m3: 0-0 2m4-2m7: 0-0 3m+: 0-1
Track: LH: 0-0 RH: 0-1 Tight: 0-0 Gall: 0-1
Aids: Bl: 0-0 Vi: 0-0 Tstrap: 0-0
Best Rating: **112** 3/00 Carl 2m4f110y gd-sft Ch

Broke Road (IRE)

109(106h) (110h)**117+**

8-y-o b g Deploy-Shamaka (Kris)
Mrs V C Ward Broke Road Partnerhsip

Placings:44315/06403P1-0522P6110 **(4273)**
2001/02: 17^{0}G, 17^{5}GS, 16^{2}S, 16^{2}G, 16^{P}S, 16^{6}GS, 16^{1}GS, 16^{1}GS, 16^{0}G

	Starts	1st	2nd	3rd	Win & Pl
Hurdles	9	2	2	0	12597
Career Total	**21**	**4**	**2**	**2**	**18883**

110	2/02	Fknm	2m	D(0-115)HHdl	G-S	£3334
104	1/02	Catt	2m	E(0-110)HHdl	G-S	£7280
97	2/01	Fknm	2m	E(0-115)HHdl	SFT	£3292
98	3/00	Fknm	2m	E Hdl	GD	£2320

Total win prize-money £16229

Going: Sf: 0-2 GS: 2-4 Gd: 0-3 GF: - Fm: 0-0
Distance: **2m/2m3: 2-9** 2m4-2m7: 0-0 3m+: 0-0
Track: **LH: 2-9** RH: 0-0 **Tight: 2-6** Gall: 0-0
Aids: Bl: 0-0 Vi: 0-0 Tstrap: 0-0
Best Rating: **110** 2/02 Fknm 2m gd-sft Hdl

A winner twice over hurdles at the start of 2002, he made a successful debut over fences at Fakenham in May and won again over fences at Worcester in July. Suited by a sharp left-handed track.

Broken Arrow (IRE)

97 **99**

5-y-o b g Sri Pekan (USA)-Domniga (IRE) (Be My Guest (USA))
A J Lidderdale (E Stanners 15/11) Bernard Gover Bloodstock Trading Ltd

Placings:*1-004* **(4564)**
2001/02: 17^{0}GS, 17^{0}G, 16^{4}GF

	Starts	1st	2nd	3rd	Win & Pl
NH Flat	2	0	0	0	0
Hurdles	1	0	0	0	0
Career Total	**4**	**1**	**0**	**0**	**1568**

105	4/01	Tntn	2m1f	H NHF	G-F	£1568

Total win prize-money £1568

Going: Sf: 0-0 GS: 0-1 Gd: 0-1 GF: - Fm: 0-1
Distance: 2m/2m3: 0-3 2m4-2m7: 0-0 3m+: 0-0
Track: LH: 0-1 RH: 0-1 Tight: 0-1 Gall: 0-0
Aids: Bl: 0-0 Vi: 0-0 Tstrap: 0-1
Best Rating: **105** 4/01 Tntn 2m1f gd-fm NHF

Fast-ground bumper winner, given too much to do on his hurdling debut. Wears a tongue tie.

Broken Dream (IRE)

104 **97**

5-y-o b g Broken Hearted-A Little Further (Mandalus)
Miss H C Knight Ms Linda Agran

Placings:204 **(4485)**
2001/02: 17^{2}G, 19^{0}S, 19^{4}G

	Starts	1st	2nd	3rd	Win & Pl
Hurdles	3	0	1	0	931
Career Total	**3**	**0**	**1**	**0**	**931**

Going: Sf: 0-1 GS: 0-0 Gd: 0-2 GF: - Fm: 0-0
Distance: 2m/2m3: 0-3 2m4-2m7: 0-0 3m+: 0-0
Track: LH: 0-2 RH: 0-1 Tight: 0-1 Gall: 0-1
Aids: Bl: 0-0 Vi: 0-0 Tstrap: 0-0
Best Rating: **97** 3/02 Newb 2m3f soft Hdl

Made a creditable hurdling debut over two miles and a furlong but looks to need further and has not built on that since. Acts on good ground.

Brokenborough

5-y-o ch g Beveled (USA)-Swilly Express (Ballacashtal (CAN))
C R Egerton P J Doherty

Placings:0-P **(1147)**
2001/02: 24^{P}GF

	Starts	1st	2nd	3rd	Win & Pl
Hurdles	1	0	0	0	
Career Total	**2**	**0**	**0**	**0**	

Going: Sf: 0-0 GS: 0-0 Gd: 0-0 GF: - Fm: 0-1
Distance: 2m/2m3: 0-0 2m4-2m7: 0-0 3m+: 0-1
Track: LH: 0-1 RH: 0-0 Tight: 0-1 Gall: 0-0
Aids: Bl: 0-0 Vi: 0-0 Tstrap: 0-0
Best Rating: **47** 3/01 Hntg 2m110y soft Hdl

Bronzesmith

99 **104**

6-y-o b g Greensmith-Bronze Age (Celtic Cone)
B J M Ryall Mrs M E Ash

Placings:*062-13* **(1947)**
2001/02: 17^{1}GF, 19^{3}GF

	Starts	1st	2nd	3rd	Win & Pl
Hurdles	2	1	0	1	3392
Career Total	**5**	**1**	**1**	**1**	**4092**

89	10/01	Extr	2m1f	E Hdl	G-F	£2765

Total win prize-money £2765

Going: Sf: 0-0 GS: 0-0 Gd: 0-0 GF: - Fm: 1-2
Distance: **2m/2m3: 1-2** 2m4-2m7: 0-0 3m+: 0-0
Track: LH: 0-0 **RH: 1-2** Tight: 0-0 Gall: 0-0
Aids: Bl: 0-0 Vi: 0-0 Tstrap: 0-0

Best Rating: 107 4/01 NAbb 2m1f soft NHF

Modest novice, placed on soft ground in the spring of 2001 before getting off the mark on his reappearance on fast ground in the autumn.

Brook Street

83f 89f

5-y-o b g Cruise Missile-Sweet Spice (Native Bazaar)
C Tizzard C L Tizzard

Placings:4 (4391)
2001/02: 16^{4}S

	Starts	1st	2nd	3rd	Win & Pl
NH Flat	1	0	0	0	0
Career Total	**1**	**0**	**0**	**0**	**0**

Going: Sf: 0-1 GS: 0-0 Gd: 0-0 GF: - Fm: 0-0
Distance: 2m/2m3: 0-1 2m4-2m7: 0-0 3m+: 0-0
Track: LH: 0-0 RH: 0-1 Tight: 0-0 Gall: 0-0
Aids: Bl: 0-0 Vi: 0-0 Tstrap: 0-0
Best Rating: 89 3/02 Winc 2m soft NHF

Brooklyn Breeze (IRE)

66f 95f

5-y-o b/br g Be My Native (USA)-Moss Gale (Strong Gale)
L Lungo Ashleybank Investments Limited

Placings:4 (4499)
2001/02: 16^{4}G

	Starts	1st	2nd	3rd	Win & Pl
NH Flat	1	0	0	0	0
Career Total	**1**	**0**	**0**	**0**	**0**

Going: Sf: 0-0 GS: 0-0 Gd: 0-1 GF: - Fm: 0-0
Distance: 2m/2m3: 0-1 2m4-2m7: 0-0 3m+: 0-0
Track: LH: 0-1 RH: 0-0 Tight: 0-0 Gall: 0-0
Aids: Bl: 0-0 Vi: 0-0 Tstrap: 0-0
Best Rating: 95 3/02 Hayd 2m good NHF

Chasing-type who made a satisfactory bumper debut.

Brooklyn's Gold (USA)

108 107

7-y-o b g Seeking The Gold (USA)-Brooklyn's Dance (FR) (Shirley Heights)
Ian Williams Terry Warner

Placings:0-60F1254222 (4915)
2001/02: 16^{6}G, 16^{0}GS, 16^{F}G, 16^{1}S, 17^{2}S, 16^{5}S, 16^{4}G, 17^{2}G, 16^{2}G, 17^{2}GF

	Starts	1st	2nd	3rd	Win & Pl
Hurdles	10	1	4	0	10771
Career Total	**11**	**1**	**4**	**0**	**10771**

107	1/02	Wwck	2m	D(0-110)HHdl	SFT £5174

Total win prize-money £5174

Going: Sf: 1-3 GS: 0-1 Gd: 0-5 GF: - Fm: 0-1
Distance: **2m/2m3: 1-10** 2m4-2m7: 0-0 3m+: 0-0
Track: **LH: 1-6** RH: 0-4 Tight: 0-5 Gall: 0-1
Aids: Bl: 0-0 Vi: 0-0 Tstrap: 0-0
Best Rating: 107 1/02 Wwck 2m soft Hdl

Useful on the Flat when younger, he easily won a weak novices' handicap hurdle at Warwick in January 2002.

Brooksby Whorlton (IRE)

95 84

8-y-o b g Commanche Run-Superlee (IRE) (Le Moss)
R Bastiman G L Mason

Placings:4/11/0PP00-P3PP0F (4670)
2001/02: 21^{P}G, 19^{3}GS, 20^{P}S, 19^{P}S, 17^{0}S, 21^{F}GF

	Starts	1st	2nd	3rd	Win & Pl
Hurdles	6	0	0	1	233
Career Total	**14**	**2**	**0**	**1**	**4589**

107	12/99	Sedg	2m5f110y	E Hdl	SFT	£1940
95	11/99	Kels	2m2f	E Hdl	GD	£2416

Total win prize-money £4356

Going: Sf: 0-3 GS: 0-1 Gd: 0-1 GF: - Fm: 0-1
Distance: 2m/2m3: 0-2 2m4-2m7: 0-4 3m+: 0-0
Track: LH: 0-4 RH: 0-1 Tight: 0-4 Gall: 0-1
Aids: Bl: 0-3 Vi: 0-0 Tstrap: 0-0
Best Rating: 107 12/99 Sedg 2m5f110y soft Hdl

Selling-class hurdler, he is not the most reliable.

Brooksie

105 102

7-y-o b g Efisio-Elkie Brooks (Relkino)
Miss K M George Stableline

Placings:00030330/64366P0/313663262-00023463P31 (4660)
2001/02: 19^{0}G, 19^{0}GS, 17^{0}GS, 16^{2}HY, 19^{3}S, 19^{4}S, 16^{6}HY, 17^{3}S, 19^{P}S, 17^{3}G, 17^{1}G

	Starts	1st	2nd	3rd	Win & Pl
Hurdles	11	1	1	3	4895
Career Total	**35**	**2**	**3**	**10**	**11984**

102	4/02	Tntn	2m1f	E(0-110)HHdl	GD	£2674
91	1/01	Tntn	2m3f110y	G Hdl	HVY	£1596

Total win prize-money £4270

Going: Sf: 0-6 GS: 0-2 Gd: 1-3 GF: - Fm: 0-0
Distance: **2m/2m3: 1-7** 2m4-2m7: 0-4 3m+: 0-0
Track: LH: 0-3 **RH: 1-8 Tight: 1-9** Gall: 0-0
Aids: Bl: 0-1 **Vi: 1-10** Tstrap: 0-0
Best Rating: 102 4/02 Tntn 2m1f good Hdl

Modest hurdler between two and two and a half miles and appears to like Taunton. Seems to handle most types of ground.

Brooksy's Castle

8-y-o ch g Carlingford Castle-Hovian (Hotfoot)
T Wall T Wall

Placings:0P (1842)
2001/02: 19^{0}G, 24^{P}S

	Starts	1st	2nd	3rd	Win & Pl
Hurdles	2	0	0	0	
Career Total	**2**	**0**	**0**	**0**	

Going: Sf: 0-1 GS: 0-0 Gd: 0-1 GF: - Fm: 0-0
Distance: 2m/2m3: 0-0 2m4-2m7: 0-1 3m+: 0-1
Track: LH: 0-0 RH: 0-2 Tight: 0-1 Gall: 0-0
Aids: Bl: 0-0 Vi: 0-0 Tstrap: 0-0
Best Rating:

Broom Close (IRE)

8-y-o b g Yashgan-Pick Nine (Tumble Wind (USA))
R Johnson (J R Turner 20/1) Robert Johnson

Placings:4P-0 (4525)
2001/02: 26^{0}GS

	Starts	1st	2nd	3rd	Win & Pl
Chases	1	0	0	0	
Career Total	**3**	**0**	**0**	**0**	**0**

Going: Sf: 0-0 GS: 0-1 Gd: 0-0 GF: - Fm: 0-0
Distance: 2m/2m3: 0-0 2m4-2m7: 0-0 3m+: 0-1
Track: LH: 0-0 RH: 0-1 Tight: 0-0 Gall: 0-0
Aids: Bl: 0-0 Vi: 0-0 Tstrap: 0-0
Best Rating: 74 5/00 Towc 2m soft Hdl

Brostaig Ort (IRE)

94(91h) (50h)72

11-y-o br g Radical-Logical View (Mandalus)
R Curtis Hurryup Partners

Placings:650/0132/113P-PP0P3 (2572)
2001/02: 28^{P}G, 26^{P}GF, 26^{0}G, 25^{P}S, 25^{3}HY

	Starts	1st	2nd	3rd	Win & Pl
Hurdles	1	0	0	0	0
Chases	4	0	0	1	634
Career Total	**16**	**3**	**1**	**3**	**14346**

114	6/00	Strf	3m4f	D(0-120)HCh	GD	£4231
102	5/00	Towc	3m1f	F(0-105)HCh	SFT	£3262
93	12/99	Font	3m2f110y	F(0-100)HCh	G-S	£3192

Total win prize-money £10687

Going: Sf: 0-2 GS: 0-0 Gd: 0-2 GF: - Fm: 0-1
Distance: 2m/2m3: 0-0 2m4-2m7: 0-0 3m+: 0-5
Track: LH: 0-2 RH: 0-3 Tight: 0-2 Gall: 0-1
Aids: Bl: 0-0 Vi: 0-0 Tstrap: 0-0
Best Rating: 114 6/00 Strf 3m4f good Ch

Formerly useful staying chaser who has become disappointing. Better effort at Towcester in December where he at least completed the course. Seems to act on most ground.

Brother Beacon

99 81

11-y-o ch g High Line-Flaming Peace (Queens Hussar)
P R Chamings Mrs J E L Wright

Placings:0U320/522 (1221)
2001/02: 17^{5}G, 16^{2}GF, 18^{2}GF

	Starts	1st	2nd	3rd	Win & Pl
Hurdles	3	0	2	0	1165
Career Total	**8**	**0**	**3**	**1**	**2109**

Going: Sf: 0-0 GS: 0-0 Gd: 0-1 GF: - Fm: 0-2
Distance: 2m/2m3: 0-3 2m4-2m7: 0-0 3m+: 0-0
Track: LH: 0-1 RH: 0-2 Tight: 0-1 Gall: 0-1
Aids: Bl: 0-0 Vi: 0-0 Tstrap: 0-0
Best Rating: 88 11/98 Ludl 2m good Hdl

Brother Ernest

93 73

7-y-o b/br g Phardante (FR)-Minerstown (IRE) (Miners Lamp)
Ferdy Murphy Exors Of The Late Mr G A Hubbard

Placings:0000/PUP-506 (3551)
2001/02: 20^{5}G, 26^{0}S, 19^{6}S

	Starts	1st	2nd	3rd	Win & Pl
Hurdles	3	0	0	0	0
Career Total	**10**	**0**	**0**	**0**	**0**

Going: Sf: 0-2 GS: 0-0 Gd: 0-1 GF: - Fm: 0-0
Distance: 2m/2m3: 0-1 2m4-2m7: 0-1 3m+: 0-1

Track: LH: 0-2 RH: 0-1 Tight: 0-2 Gall: 0-0
Aids: Bl: 0-0 Vi: 0-0 Tstrap: 0-1
Best Rating: 84 1/00 Hntg 2m110y good NHF

Brother Joe (NZ)

118 155

8-y-o ch g Hula Town (NZ)-Olivia Rose (NZ) (Travolta (FR))
P J Hobbs Sir Robert Ogden

Placings:2111/F55F1-123U023 (4911)
2001/02: 21^{1}G, 25^{2}G, 16^{3}GS, 24^{U}G, 20^{0}G, 24^{2}GF, 24^{3}G

	Starts	1st	2nd	3rd	Win & Pl
Hurdles	7	1	2	2	33935
Career Total	**16**	**5**	**3**	**2**	**57128**

155	10/01	Chel	2m5f	B(0-145)HHdl	GD	£9282
142	4/01	Ayr	2m6f	B(0-150)HHdl	GD	£7124
140	4/00	Ayr	2m6f	B HHdl	GD	£6988
140	3/00	Chep	2m4f	B(0-140)HHdl	G-S	£6825
110	11/99	Folk	2m4f110y	F Hdl	G-S	£1499

Total win prize-money £31719

Going: Sf: 0-0 GS: 0-1 Gd: 1-5 GF: - Fm: 0-1
Distance: 2m/2m3: 0-1 **2m4-2m7: 1-2** 3m+: 0-4
Track: **LH: 1-3** RH: 0-2 Tight: 0-1 **Gall: 1-2**
Aids: Bl: 0-0 Vi: 0-0 Tstrap: 0-0
Best Rating: **155** 2/02 Winc 2m gd-sft Hdl

An ex-New Zealand gelding, he won three hurdle races at the start of his career in this country during the 1999/2000 season. Described by his trainer as quirky, he won a decent two miles-five handicap at Cheltenham in October 2001, but was subsequently beaten over longer and shorter trips, including when unseating in the Stayers Hurdle at Cheltenham in March 2002. He gets three miles on a sound surface as when runner-up at Ascot the following month, but does not want it too soft.

Brother Of Iris (IRE)

9-y-o b g Decent Fellow-Granita Cafe (FR) (Arctic Tern (USA))
Mrs M Reveley W J Smith And M D Dudley

Placings:1/4P14/2111F/11P/F4PP-P (0969)
2001/02: 20^{P}GS

	Starts	1st	2nd	3rd	Win & Pl
Chases	1	0	0	0	
Career Total	**18**	**7**	**1**	**0**	**37034**

164	12/99	Weth	3m1f	B(0-140)HCh	G-S	£9085
157	11/99	Ayr	3m1f	B(0-140)HCh	GD	£8401
147	1/99	Donc	3m	D(0-115)HCh	GD	£4846
130	12/98	Donc	3m	D Ch	GD	£3652
125	11/98	Hntg	2m4f110y	D Ch	G-S	£3692
103	2/98	Carl	2m4f110y	E Hdl	SFT	£2528
103	3/97	Carl	2m1f	H NHF	GD	£1035

Total win prize-money £33240

Going: Sf: 0-0 GS: 0-1 Gd: 0-0 GF: - Fm: 0-0
Distance: 2m/2m3: 0-0 2m4-2m7: 0-1 3m+: 0-0
Track: LH: 0-0 RH: 0-0 Tight: 0-0 Gall: 0-0
Aids: Bl: 0-0 Vi: 0-0 Tstrap: 0-0
Best Rating: **164** 12/99 Weth 3m1f gd-sft Ch

A high-class but injury-prone chaser, he has been retired.

Brother William (IRE)

10-y-o ch g Phardante (FR)-Cloughoola Lady (Black Minstrel)
J R Jenkins The West's Awake Racing Partnership

Placings:PUUP (1015)
2001/02: 25^{P}GF, 23^{U}GF, 24^{U}GF, 23^{P}G

	Starts	1st	2nd	3rd	Win & Pl
Chases	4	0	0	0	
Career Total	**4**	**0**	**0**	**0**	

Going: Sf: 0-0 GS: 0-0 Gd: 0-1 GF: - Fm: 0-3
Distance: 2m/2m3: 0-0 2m4-2m7: 0-0 3m+: 0-4
Track: LH: 0-3 RH: 0-1 Tight: 0-2 Gall: 0-0
Aids: Bl: 0-0 Vi: 0-0 Tstrap: 0-0
Best Rating:

Broughty Castle (IRE)

4-y-o b g Inzar (USA)-Heavenly Note (Chief Singer)
Mrs Sarah Horner-Harker (B J Meehan 30/9) Mrs Sarah Horner-Harker

Placings:P40 (3251)
2001/02: 16^{P}GS, 16^{4}S, 16^{0}S

	Starts	1st	2nd	3rd	Win & Pl
Hurdles	3	0	0	0	0
Career Total	**3**	**0**	**0**	**0**	**0**

Going: Sf: 0-2 GS: 0-1 Gd: 0-0 GF: - Fm: 0-0
Distance: 2m/2m3: 0-3 2m4-2m7: 0-0 3m+: 0-0
Track: LH: 0-3 RH: 0-0 Tight: 0-0 Gall: 0-2
Aids: Bl: 0-0 Vi: 0-0 Tstrap: 0-0
Best Rating:

Browjoshy (IRE)

105(112c) (117c)112

9-y-o b g Zaffaran (USA)-Keeping Company (Kings Company)
M Pitman B D L Racing

Placings:5/3F00/410353/321135P/3P1P0-60P653 (4951a)
2001/02: 31^{6}GS, 26^{0}S, 24^{P}S, 25^{6}S, 26^{5}GF, 31^{3}G

	Starts	1st	2nd	3rd	Win & Pl
Hurdles	3	0	0	0	0
Chases	3	0	0	1	1325
Career Total	**29**	**4**	**1**	**7**	**63889**

154	1/01	Wwck	3m2f	B(0-150)HCh	SFT	£27391
140	2/00	Uttx	3m2f	C HCh	SFT	£15570
142	1/00	Folk	2m5f	D(0-110)HCh	G-S	£3993
107	11/98	Towc	2m5f	F Hdl	SFT	£2092

Total win prize-money £49048

Going: Sf: 0-3 GS: 0-1 Gd: 0-1 GF: - Fm: 0-1
Distance: 2m/2m3: 0-0 2m4-2m7: 0-0 3m+: 0-6
Track: LH: 0-2 RH: 0-3 Tight: 0-0 Gall: 0-1
Aids: Bl: 0-1 Vi: 0-1 Tstrap: 0-0
Best Rating: **154** 1/01 Wwck 3m2f soft Ch

He developed into a useful handicap chaser and won well at Warwick in 2001, but struggled when tried against the better staying chasers. Three and a quarter miles on soft ground looks as far as he wants. Wears blinkers or a visor, but his resolution is not in doubt.

Brown Esquire

11-y-o b g Broadleaf-Ana Brown (Souvran)
Miss G Dewhurst Miss G Dewhurst

Placings:0PP/PP-2 (4741)
2001/02: 24^{2}GF

	Starts	1st	2nd	3rd	Win & Pl
Chases	1	0	1	0	751
Career Total	**6**	**0**	**1**	**0**	**751**

Going: Sf: 0-0 GS: 0-0 Gd: 0-0 GF: - Fm: 0-1
Distance: 2m/2m3: 0-0 2m4-2m7: 0-0 3m+: 0-1
Track: LH: 0-0 RH: 0-1 Tight: 0-1 Gall: 0-0
Aids: Bl: 0-0 Vi: 0-0 Tstrap: 0-0
Best Rating: **99** 4/02 Ludl 3m gd-fm Ch

Brown Seal

10-y-o b m Arctic Lord-Brown Veil (Don't Look)
Mrs Merrita Jones Mrs P Corbett

Placings:50/5P34P3/U/0P (3333)
2001/02: 20^{0}S, 24^{P}G

	Starts	1st	2nd	3rd	Win & Pl
Hurdles	1	0	0	0	0
Chases	1	0	0	0	0
Career Total	**11**	**0**	**0**	**2**	**734**

Going: Sf: 0-1 GS: 0-0 Gd: 0-1 GF: - Fm: 0-0
Distance: 2m/2m3: 0-0 2m4-2m7: 0-1 3m+: 0-1
Track: LH: 0-1 RH: 0-1 Tight: 0-1 Gall: 0-0
Aids: Bl: 0-0 Vi: 0-0 Tstrap: 0-0
Best Rating: **85** 3/99 Ludl 2m5f110y soft Hdl

Brown Teddy

105f 101f

5-y-o b g Afzal-Quadrapol (Pollerton)
R Ford G B Barlow

Placings:4 (4873)
2001/02: 16^{4}GF

	Starts	1st	2nd	3rd	Win & Pl
NH Flat	1	0	0	0	0
Career Total	**1**	**0**	**0**	**0**	**0**

Going: Sf: 0-0 GS: 0-0 Gd: 0-0 GF: - Fm: 0-1
Distance: 2m/2m3: 0-1 2m4-2m7: 0-0 3m+: 0-0
Track: LH: 0-1 RH: 0-0 Tight: 0-0 Gall: 0-0
Aids: Bl: 0-0 Vi: 0-0 Tstrap: 0-0
Best Rating: **101** 4/02 Weth 2m gd-fm NHF

Chasing bred, showed ability on his bumper debut.

Brown's Flight

71 24

6-y-o b m Jupiter Island-Fearless Princess (Tyrnavos)
W G M Turner Mrs Tracy Turner

Placings:2-0 (1624)
2001/02: 16^{0}GF

	Starts	1st	2nd	3rd	Win & Pl
Hurdles	1	0	0	0	
Career Total	**2**	**0**	**1**	**0**	**818**

Going: Sf: 0-0 GS: 0-0 Gd: 0-0 GF: - Fm: 0-1
Distance: 2m/2m3: 0-1 2m4-2m7: 0-0 3m+: 0-0
Track: LH: 0-0 RH: 0-1 Tight: 0-0 Gall: 0-0
Aids: Bl: 0-0 Vi: 0-0 Tstrap: 0-1
Best Rating: **80** 6/00 Fknm 2m4f good Hdl

Brownes Hill Lad (IRE)

83(105h) (97h)93

10-y-o ch g King Of Clubs-Record Finish (Record Token)

R J O'Sullivan Mrs R J Doorgachurn

Placings:31120/11P3024/**206P**/**50F2**/**4F**4-00043105 **(2592)**

2001/02: 17^{0}GS, 18^{0}GF, 17^{0}GF, 22^{4}GF, 22^{3}GF, 22^{1}GF, 24^{0}GF, 25^{5}G

	Starts	1st	2nd	3rd	Win & Pl
Hurdles	7	1	0	1	2675
Chases	1	0	0	0	0
Career Total	**31**	**5**	**4**	**3**	**16049**

97	8/01	Font	2m6f110y	F(0-100)HHdl	G-F	£2289
113	10/97	Hrfd	2m1f	E Hdl	GD	£2360
116	9/97	Worc	2m	E Hdl	G-F	£2302
101	8/96	Tral	2m1f	NHF	G-Y	£3530

Total win prize-money £10483

Going: Sf: 0-0 GS: 0-1 Gd: 0-1 GF: - Fm: 1-6
Distance: 2m/2m3: 0-3 **2m4-2m7: 1-3** 3m+: 0-2
Track: **LH: 1-6** RH: 0-2 **Tight: 1-6** Gall: 0-0
Aids: Bl: 0-1 Vi: 0-0 Tstrap: 0-0
Best Rating: **125** 3/98 Sand 2m110y soft Hdl

Browns Delight

73 32

5-y-o b m Runnett-Fearless Princess (Tyrnavos)

Mrs A C Tate (M Tate 15/11) B Staight

Placings:PPP0PP0 **(4752)**

2001/02: 19^{P}G, 16^{P}GF, 21^{P}GF, 16^{0}GS, 16^{P}GF, 17^{P}G, 16^{0}GF

	Starts	1st	2nd	3rd	Win & Pl
Hurdles	7	0	0	0	
Career Total	**7**	**0**	**0**	**0**	

Going: Sf: 0-0 GS: 0-1 Gd: 0-2 GF: - Fm: 0-4
Distance: 2m/2m3: 0-5 2m4-2m7: 0-2 3m+: 0-0
Track: LH: 0-3 RH: 0-4 Tight: 0-1 Gall: 0-1
Aids: Bl: 0-4 Vi: 0-0 Tstrap: 0-0
Best Rating: **32** 4/02 Uttx 2m gd-fm Hdl

Bruan (IRE)

(88h) (28h)

6-y-o b g Be My Native (USA)-Celtic Cygnet (Celtic Cone)

A Crook Trevor Hemmings

Placings:00-0P **(0670)**

2001/02: 20^{0}G, 23^{P}G

	Starts	1st	2nd	3rd	Win & Pl
Hurdles	1	0	0	0	0
Chases	1	0	0	0	0
Career Total	**4**	**0**	**0**	**0**	

Going: Sf: 0-0 GS: 0-0 Gd: 0-2 GF: - Fm: 0-0
Distance: 2m/2m3: 0-0 2m4-2m7: 0-1 3m+: 0-1
Track: LH: 0-2 RH: 0-0 Tight: 0-1 Gall: 0-0
Aids: Bl: 0-0 Vi: 0-0 Tstrap: 0-0
Best Rating: **72** 11/00 Aint 2m1f gd-sft NHF

Brumalis (NZ)

10-y-o b g High Ice (USA)-Kerry Sue (NZ) (Knighthood (NZ))

Miss Laura Cottam (B D Leavy 1/6) K J Condliffe

Placings:4503P6/6PP6FP53P602/UF3PP-00 **(4525)**

2001/02: 27^{0}GF, 26^{0}GS

	Starts	1st	2nd	3rd	Win & Pl
Hurdles	1	0	0	0	0
Chases	1	0	0	0	0
Career Total	**25**	**0**	**1**	**3**	**3031**

Going: Sf: 0-0 GS: 0-1 Gd: 0-0 GF: - Fm: 0-1
Distance: 2m/2m3: 0-0 2m4-2m7: 0-0 3m+: 0-2
Track: LH: 0-1 RH: 0-1 Tight: 0-1 Gall: 0-0
Aids: Bl: 0-1 Vi: 0-0 Tstrap: 0-0
Best Rating: **87** 4/99 Bang 3m gd-sft Hdl

Brush A King

103 85+

7-y-o b g Derrylin-Colonial Princess (Roscoe Blake)

C T Pogson C T Pogson

Placings:560/03-0PP **(4915)**

2001/02: 20^{0}G, 20^{P}HY, 17^{P}GF

	Starts	1st	2nd	3rd	Win & Pl
Hurdles	3	0	0	0	
Career Total	**8**	**0**	**0**	**1**	**267**

Going: Sf: 0-1 GS: 0-0 Gd: 0-1 GF: - Fm: 0-1
Distance: 2m/2m3: 0-1 2m4-2m7: 0-2 3m+: 0-0
Track: LH: 0-3 RH: 0-0 Tight: 0-2 Gall: 0-0
Aids: Bl: 0-0 Vi: 0-0 Tstrap: 0-0
Best Rating: **96** 11/00 Weth 2m heavy NHF

Placed a couple of times in novices' hurdles but is only very moderate.

Brush And Go (IRE)

8-y-o b g Brush Aside (USA)-Knockacool Breeze (Buckskin (FR))

Mrs S Shirley-Beavan Mrs S H Shirley-Beavan

Placings:4 **(4335)**

2001/02: 27^{4}S

	Starts	1st	2nd	3rd	Win & Pl
Chases	1	0	0	0	0
Career Total	**1**	**0**	**0**	**0**	**0**

Going: Sf: 0-1 GS: 0-0 Gd: 0-0 GF: - Fm: 0-0
Distance: 2m/2m3: 0-0 2m4-2m7: 0-0 3m+: 0-1
Track: LH: 0-1 RH: 0-0 Tight: 0-1 Gall: 0-0
Aids: Bl: 0-1 Vi: 0-0 Tstrap: 0-0
Best Rating:

Placed in points but will struggle to make an impact under Rules.

Brush The Ark

101 90

8-y-o b m Brush Aside (USA)-Expensive Lark (Sir Lark)

J S Smith Donald Smith

Placings:125-362PP04 **(4875)**

2001/02: 17^{3}GS, 19^{6}G, 16^{2}S, 20^{P}S, 19^{P}HY, 21^{0}GS, 24^{4}G

	Starts	1st	2nd	3rd	Win & Pl
Hurdles	7	0	1	1	1531
Career Total	**10**	**1**	**2**	**1**	**3746**

100	10/00	Bang	2m1f	H NHF	SFT	£1704

Total win prize-money £1705

Going: Sf: 0-3 GS: 0-2 Gd: 0-2 GF: - Fm: 0-0
Distance: 2m/2m3: 0-2 2m4-2m7: 0-4 3m+: 0-1
Track: LH: 0-2 RH: 0-5 Tight: 0-2 Gall: 0-1
Aids: Bl: 0-0 Vi: 0-0 Tstrap: 0-0
Best Rating: **100** 10/00 Bang 2m1f soft NHF

Bumper winner. Acts on soft ground, but is still a maiden over hurdles.

Brush With Fame (IRE)

88(91c) (64c)23

10-y-o b g Brush Aside (USA)-Cheeney's Gift (Quayside)

S H Shirley-Beavan S H Shirley-Beavan

Placings:3/0U0536/111F2P6/151361P/52235-0P **(0324)**

2001/02: 24^{0}GF, 31^{P}G

	Starts	1st	2nd	3rd	Win & Pl
Chases	2	0	0	0	
Career Total	**28**	**6**	**3**	**4**	**21212**

95	11/99	Wwck	3m1f110y	E(0-115)HCh	GD	£3080
107	9/99	NAbb	3m2f110y	E Ch	G-F	£3036
95	7/99	Worc	3m	D(0-125)HHdl	G-F	£2968
97	9/98	Worc	3m	E(0-100)HHdl	G-F	£2460
97	8/98	Worc	3m	F(0-95)HHdl	GD	£1954
94	7/98	NAbb	2m6f	E(0-100)HHdl	G-F	£2670

Total win prize-money £16169

Going: Sf: 0-0 GS: 0-0 Gd: 0-1 GF: - Fm: 0-1
Distance: 2m/2m3: 0-0 2m4-2m7: 0-0 3m+: 0-2
Track: LH: 0-1 RH: 0-1 Tight: 0-2 Gall: 0-0
Aids: Bl: 0-1 Vi: 0-0 Tstrap: 0-0
Best Rating: **107** 6/00 NAbb 3m2f110y gd-fm Ch

Bruthuinne (IRE)

103 119

7-y-o ch g Vaquillo (USA)-Portane Miss (Salluceva)

Miss H C Knight Martin Broughton

Placings:63/34-4PU3223P **(4634)**

2001/02: 20^{4}G, 20^{P}S, 23^{U}G, 19^{3}S, 24^{2}GS, 24^{2}G, 21^{3}G, 24^{P}GF

	Starts	1st	2nd	3rd	Win & Pl
Chases	8	0	2	2	4166
Career Total	**12**	**0**	**2**	**4**	**5919**

Going: Sf: 0-2 GS: 0-1 Gd: 0-4 GF: - Fm: 0-1
Distance: 2m/2m3: 0-1 2m4-2m7: 0-3 3m+: 0-4
Track: LH: 0-2 RH: 0-6 Tight: 0-2 Gall: 0-2
Aids: Bl: 0-0 Vi: 0-0 Tstrap: 0-0
Best Rating: **121** 11/00 Kemp 2m soft Ch

A half-brother to Aghawadda Gold, he has shown potential in novice chases. Acts on the soft. Two and a half miles looks more suitable than three miles at present.

Brutus McGregor (IRE)

85 84

6-y-o ch g Be My Native (USA)-Pisa (IRE) (Carlingford Castle)

C J Mann (E J O'Grady 14/6) Martin Myers

Placings:120 **(2128)**

2001/02: 16^{1}GF, 17^{2}G, 19^{0}G

	Starts	1st	2nd	3rd	Win & Pl
NH Flat	2	1	1	0	5827
Hurdles	1	0	0	0	0
Career Total	**3**	**1**	**1**	**0**	**5827**

110	5/01	Tipp	2m	NHF	G-F	£4729

Total win prize-money £4730

Going: Sf: 0-0 GS: 0-0 Gd: 0-2 GF: - Fm: 1-1

Distance: 2m/2m3: 1-3 2m4-2m7: 0-0 3m+: 0-0
Track: LH: 0-1 RH: 0-0 Tight: 0-0 Gall: 0-1
Aids: Bl: 0-0 Vi: 0-0 Tstrap: 0-0
Best Rating: 112 6/01 Tipp 2m1f good NHF

Brydferth Ddu (IRE)

86f 53f

7-y-o b m Supreme Leader-Mantas Melody (IRE) (Orchestra)
D Brace David Brace

Placings: *5* (1154)
2001/02: 17^{5}GF

	Starts	1st	2nd	3rd	Win & Pl
NH Flat	1	0	0	0	0
Career Total	**1**	**0**	**0**	**0**	**0**

Going: Sf: 0-0 GS: 0-0 Gd: 0-0 GF: - Fm: 0-1
Distance: 2m/2m3: 0-1 2m4-2m7: 0-0 3m+: 0-0
Track: LH: 0-1 RH: 0-0 Tight: 0-1 Gall: 0-0
Aids: Bl: 0-0 Vi: 0-0 Tstrap: 0-0
Best Rating: 53 8/01 NAbb 2m1f gd-fm NHF

Buadhach (IRE)

93 86

6-y-o b g Petoski-Viking Rocket (Viking (USA))
A Parker Mr & Mrs Raymond Anderson Green

Placings: *P20-0*P0210P0 (4786)
2001/02: 16^{0}G, 17^{P}GS, 18^{0}G, 16^{2}G, 20^{1}GS, 20^{0}S, 24^{P}S, 20^{P}F

	Starts	1st	2nd	3rd	Win & Pl
NH Flat	1	0	0	0	0
Hurdles	7	1	1	0	4174
Career Total	**11**	**1**	**2**	**0**	**4640**

84	11/01	Ayr	2m4f	D(0-110)HHdl	G-S	£3402

Total win prize-money £3402

Going: Sf: 0-2 GS: 1-2 Gd: 0-3 GF: - Fm: 0-1
Distance: 2m/2m3: 0-4 **2m4-2m7: 1-3** 3m+: 0-1
Track: **LH: 1-6** RH: 0-2 Tight: 0-4 Gall: 0-1
Aids: Bl: 0-0 Vi: 0-0 Tstrap: 0-0
Best Rating: 103 6/00 Hexm 2m gd-fm NHF

He improved to win an ordinary seller at Ayr over two and a half miles in November with cut in the ground.

Buck Lad (IRE)

10-y-o b g Buckskin (FR)-Left Hand Woman (Energist)
Miss L C Siddall Miss Sue Vinden

Placings: P/PP53P/32PUUP-PPF (2344)
2001/02: 20^{P}G, 20^{P}G, 24^{F}GS

	Starts	1st	2nd	3rd	Win & Pl
Chases	3	0	0	0	
Career Total	**15**	**0**	**1**	**2**	**2365**

Going: Sf: 0-0 GS: 0-1 Gd: 0-2 GF: - Fm: 0-0
Distance: 2m/2m3: 0-0 2m4-2m7: 0-2 3m+: 0-1
Track: LH: 0-3 RH: 0-0 Tight: 0-0 Gall: 0-2
Aids: Bl: 0-0 Vi: 0-0 Tstrap: 0-0
Best Rating: 91 3/00 Newc 2m4f good Ch

Buck's Palace

9-y-o ch g Buckley-Lady Geneva (Royalty)
B Mactaggart (P F Nicholls 14/5) The Potassium Partnership

Placings: *1*216144/223P3/1312-33 (2470)
2001/02: 26^{3}GF, 25^{3}GS

	Starts	1st	2nd	3rd	Win & Pl
Chases	2	0	0	2	2078
Career Total	**18**	**5**	**4**	**5**	**31403**

136	10/00	Ludl	3m	E Ch	G-F	£3328
115	5/00	Ludl	2m4f	D Ch	GD	£4257
116	2/99	Uttx	3m110y	C Hdl	HVY	£5295
121	11/98	Winc	2m6f	C Hdl	GD	£4279
109	5/98	Hrfd	2m1f	H NHF	GD	£1229

Total win prize-money £18390

Going: Sf: 0-0 GS: 0-1 Gd: 0-0 GF: - Fm: 0-1
Distance: 2m/2m3: 0-0 2m4-2m7: 0-0 3m+: 0-2
Track: LH: 0-2 RH: 0-0 Tight: 0-2 Gall: 0-0
Aids: Bl: 0-0 Vi: 0-0 Tstrap: 0-0
Best Rating: 136 11/00 Ludl 3m good Ch

Something of a quirky character, he was given the full Tony McCoy treatment when winning a three miles novice chase at Ludlow in October 2000. Lightly-raced of late.

Buckby Lane

95 82

6-y-o b g Nomadic Way (USA)-Buckby Folly (Netherkelly)
P R Webber Mrs P Starkey

Placings: 4P (3355)
2001/02: 20^{4}S, 24^{P}HY

	Starts	1st	2nd	3rd	Win & Pl
Hurdles	2	0	0	0	0
Career Total	**2**	**0**	**0**	**0**	**0**

Going: Sf: 0-2 GS: 0-0 Gd: 0-0 GF: - Fm: 0-0
Distance: 2m/2m3: 0-0 2m4-2m7: 0-1 3m+: 0-1
Track: LH: 0-2 RH: 0-0 Tight: 0-0 Gall: 0-0
Aids: Bl: 0-0 Vi: 0-0 Tstrap: 0-0
Best Rating: 82 12/01 Uttx 2m4f110y soft Hdl

Buckland Knight (IRE)

103 115

6-y-o b/br g Commanche Run-Myra Gaye (Buckskin (FR))
D M Grissell Mrs R M Hepburn

Placings: *400*-U1P (3754)
2001/02: 22^{U}HY, 17^{1}HY, 16^{P}HY

	Starts	1st	2nd	3rd	Win & Pl
Hurdles	3	1	0	0	2744
Career Total	**6**	**1**	**0**	**0**	**2744**

115	1/02	Folk	2m1f110y	E Hdl	HVY	£2744

Total win prize-money £2744

Going: Sf: 1-3 GS: 0-0 Gd: 0-0 GF: - Fm: 0-0
Distance: **2m/2m3: 1-2** 2m4-2m7: 0-1 3m+: 0-0
Track: LH: 0-0 **RH: 1-3 Tight: 1-2** Gall: 0-0
Aids: Bl: 0-0 Vi: 0-0 Tstrap: 0-0
Best Rating: 115 1/02 Folk 2m1f110y heavy Hdl

Caused a 100/1 surprise when winning at Folkestone in January 2002, but there was no fluke about it. Very much suited by heavy ground.

Buckland Lad (IRE)

11-y-o ch g Phardante (FR)-Belcraig (Foggy Bell)
D M Grissell Mrs R M Hepburn

Placings: *0*/054312/3121/21/1214112/3F12/25RP-P (3500)
2001/02: 24^{P}S

	Starts	1st	2nd	3rd	Win & Pl
Chases	1	0	0	0	
Career Total	**29**	**9**	**7**	**3**	**56689**

130	12/99	Kemp	2m4f110y	D(0-120)HCh	SFT	£11040
123	3/99	Folk	2m	D(0-125)HCh	GD	£3622
133	3/99	Newb	2m1f	C(0-135)HCh	SFT	£5970
123	1/99	Kemp	2m	C(0-135)HCh	SFT	£5420
113	12/98	Wind	2m	D(0-125)HCh	G-S	£3418
116	12/97	Font	2m3f	D(0-120)HCh	SFT	£3557
93	3/97	Ling	2m	F(0-95)HCh	G-F	£2467
89	2/97	Folk	2m	F(0-100)HCh	SFT	£2612
89	4/96	Folk	2m1f110y	E(0-100)HHdl	G-F	£2678

Total win prize-money £40788

Going: Sf: 0-1 GS: 0-0 Gd: 0-0 GF: - Fm: 0-0
Distance: 2m/2m3: 0-0 2m4-2m7: 0-0 3m+: 0-1
Track: LH: 0-0 RH: 0-1 Tight: 0-0 Gall: 0-0
Aids: Bl: 0-0 Vi: 0-0 Tstrap: 0-0
Best Rating: 135 1/01 Kemp 3m soft Ch

Formerly genuine and reliable, he goes well at Kempton.

Buckley House

10-y-o b g Buckley-Reperage (USA) (Key To Content (USA))
J M Bradley W M Kathrens

Placings: *4/04*P2/P/UF (0842)
2001/02: 20^{U}G, 16^{F}G

	Starts	1st	2nd	3rd	Win & Pl
Chases	2	0	0	0	
Career Total	**8**	**0**	**1**	**0**	**676**

Going: Sf: 0-0 GS: 0-0 Gd: 0-2 GF: - Fm: 0-0
Distance: 2m/2m3: 0-1 2m4-2m7: 0-1 3m+: 0-0
Track: LH: 0-2 RH: 0-0 Tight: 0-0 Gall: 0-0
Aids: Bl: 0-0 Vi: 0-0 Tstrap: 0-0
Best Rating: 82 10/97 Kels 2m110y gd-fm Hdl

Buckley Star

6-y-o b g Buckley-Kiki Star (Some Hand)
R J Hodges The Gardens Entertainments Ltd

Placings: *40*OU (4501)
2001/02: 17^{4}F, 16^{0}G, 20°S, 27^{U}G

	Starts	1st	2nd	3rd	Win & Pl
NH Flat	2	0	0	0	0
Hurdles	2	0	0	0	0
Career Total	**4**	**0**	**0**	**0**	**0**

Going: Sf: 0-1 GS: 0-0 Gd: 0-2 GF: - Fm: 0-1
Distance: 2m/2m3: 0-2 2m4-2m7: 0-1 3m+: 0-1
Track: LH: 0-2 RH: 0-1 Tight: 0-1 Gall: 0-0
Aids: Bl: 0-0 Vi: 0-0 Tstrap: 0-0
Best Rating: 74 11/01 Winc 2m good NHF

Bucks Gala (IRE)

10-y-o b g Buckskin (FR)-Queen's Gala (Gala Performance (USA))
D A Lamb D A Lamb

Placings: *0*/P0PP/0UP04P/PUP-P0 (4766)
2001/02: 24^{P}G, 20^{0}GF

	Starts	1st	2nd	3rd	Win & Pl
Hurdles	1	0	0	0	0

	Starts	1st	2nd	3rd	Win & Pl
Chases	1	0	0	0	0
Career Total	**16**	**0**	**0**	**0**	**206**

Going: Sf: 0-0 GS: 0-0 Gd: 0-1 GF: - Fm: 0-1
Distance: 2m/2m3: 0-0 2m4-2m7: 0-1 3m+: 0-1
Track: LH: 0-1 RH: 0-1 Tight: 0-1 Gall: 0-0
Aids: Bl: 0-0 Vi: 0-0 Tstrap: 0-0
Best Rating: 53 10/98 Sedg 2m1f gd-sft Hdl

Dismal form over both types of obstacle.

Bucks View (IRE)

12-y-o b g Buckskin (FR)-Our View (Our Mirage)
G D Hanmer H R Hocknell

Placings:4 (0358)
2001/02: 24^{4}GS

	Starts	1st	2nd	3rd	Win & Pl
Chases	1	0	0	0	0
Career Total	**1**	**0**	**0**	**0**	**0**

Going: Sf: 0-0 GS: 0-1 Gd: 0-0 GF: - Fm: 0-0
Distance: 2m/2m3: 0-0 2m4-2m7: 0-0 3m+: 0-1
Track: LH: 0-1 RH: 0-0 Tight: 0-1 Gall: 0-0
Aids: Bl: 0-0 Vi: 0-0 Tstrap: 0-0
Best Rating:

Buckshee (IRE)

99 102

11-y-o ch g Buckskin (FR)-Georgina Victoria (Laser Light)
H J Collingridge Mrs T M Gibson

Placings:1/F5P43P/0650P (0848)
2001/02: 24^{0}G, 28^{6}GF, 33^{5}G, 24^{0}GF, 32^{P}GF

	Starts	1st	2nd	3rd	Win & Pl
Chases	5	0	0	0	0
Career Total	**12**	**1**	**0**	**1**	**3382**

103	3/99	Newc	3m	H Ch	SFT	£2666

Total win prize-money £2666

Going: Sf: 0-0 GS: 0-0 Gd: 0-2 GF: - Fm: 0-3
Distance: 2m/2m3: 0-0 2m4-2m7: 0-0 3m+: 0-5
Track: LH: 0-2 RH: 0-1 Tight: 0-2 Gall: 0-1
Aids: Bl: 0-0 Vi: 0-2 Tstrap: 0-0
Best Rating: 103 3/99 Newc 3m soft Ch

Buddy Diver

83 52

9-y-o br g Revlow-Rely-On-Pearl (Deep Diver)
C J Gray (C L Popham 3/2) A J Hutchings

Placings:0PP/6 (4682)
2001/02: 17^{6}GF

	Starts	1st	2nd	3rd	Win & Pl
Hurdles	1	0	0	0	0
Career Total	**4**	**0**	**0**	**0**	**0**

Going: Sf: 0-0 GS: 0-0 Gd: 0-0 GF: - Fm: 0-1
Distance: 2m/2m3: 0-1 2m4-2m7: 0-0 3m+: 0-0
Track: LH: 0-0 RH: 0-1 Tight: 0-0 Gall: 0-0
Aids: Bl: 0-0 Vi: 0-0 Tstrap: 0-0
Best Rating: 52 4/02 Hrfd 2m1f gd-fm Hdl

Buddy Marvel (IRE)

105(108c) (131c)126

8-y-o b g Law Society (USA)-Rosa Van Fleet (Sallust)
Mrs M Reveley Sir Robert Ogden

Placings:111P110P/45006/011U23122/F46-515P00615P (4834)
2001/02: 17^{5}G, 20^{1}G, 16^{5}G, 20^{P}GS, 16^{0}S, 21^{0}GS, 22^{6}HY, 20^{1}HY, 21^{5}GS, 22^{P}G

	Starts	1st	2nd	3rd	Win & Pl
Hurdles	6	1	0	0	3798
Chases	4	1	0	0	13367
Career Total	**35**	**10**	**3**	**1**	**69883**

126	2/02	Hayd	2m4f	D(0-120)HHdl	HVY	£3797
131	10/01	Aint	2m4f	D(0-125)HCh	GD	£12586
127	3/00	Kels	2m1f	D Ch	G-S	£5746
147	12/99	MRas	2m1f110y	D Ch	G-S	£4305
136	11/99	Catt	2m	D Ch	G-F	£5004
135	2/98	Kemp	2m	A Hdl	G-F	£9375
129	1/98	Donc	2m110y	C Hdl	GD	£4744
118	12/97	Ling	2m110y	A Hdl	SFT	£9176
125	11/97	Cork	2m	Hdl	Y-S	£3391
116	11/97	Fair	2m	Hdl	YLD	£3051

Total win prize-money £61177

Going: Sf: 1-3 GS: 0-3 Gd: 1-4 GF: - Fm: 0-0
Distance: 2m/2m3: 0-3 **2m4-2m7: 2-7** 3m+: 0-0
Track: **LH: 2-7** RH: 0-3 **Tight: 1-3** Gall: 0-2
Aids: Bl: 0-0 **Vi: 2-8** Tstrap: 0-0
Best Rating: 147 12/99 MRas 2m1f110y gd-sft Ch

He mixed hurdling and chasing in recent seasons. Stayed two and a half miles, aced on most ground but probably best on good, suited by a sharp track.Broke a leg at Ayr in April 2002. (DEAD)

Buddy's Toy (IRE)

107 107

8-y-o b/br m Be My Native (USA)-Righthand Lady (Buckskin (FR))
R J Smith (James Joseph Mangan 19/7) Ankor Express Syndicate

Placings:0PP/00-00012636130 (4420)
2001/02: 20^{0}GF, 16^{0}F, 17^{0}G, 16^{1}S, 21^{2}S, 17^{6}S, 17^{3}S, 24^{6}S, 19^{1}HY, 21^{3}S, 21^{0}GS

	Starts	1st	2nd	3rd	Win & Pl
Hurdles	11	2	1	2	8353
Career Total	**16**	**2**	**1**	**2**	**8353**

107	2/02	Hrfd	2m3f110y	D Hdl	HVY	£3542
107	11/01	Towc	2m	E Hdl	SFT	£2618

Total win prize-money £6161

Going: Sf: 2-7 GS: 0-1 Gd: 0-1 GF: - Fm: 0-2
Distance: 2m/2m3: 1-5 2m4-2m7: 1-5 3m+: 0-1
Track: LH: 0-1 **RH: 2-7** Tight: 0-2 Gall: 0-1
Aids: Bl: 0-0 Vi: 0-0 Tstrap: 0-1
Best Rating: 107 2/02 Hrfd 2m3f110y heavy Hdl

A poor performer over hurdles in Ireland, perhaps due to a virus, she caused a major surprise when winning on her return to hurdles in this country at Towcester in November 2001. Fair efforts under a penalty, winning at Hereford in February 2001.

Bukehorn

102 94

11-y-o b g Bold Owl-Milly Kelly (Murrayfield)
Mrs P Sly Mrs P M Sly

Placings:400/06000/6/U445P-002F0 (2647)
2001/02: 16^{0}GF, 16^{0}G, 16^{2}G, 16^{F}G, 16^{0}GS

	Starts	1st	2nd	3rd	Win & Pl
Chases	5	0	1	0	848
Career Total	**19**	**0**	**1**	**0**	**1313**

Going: Sf: 0-0 GS: 0-1 Gd: 0-3 GF: - Fm: 0-1
Distance: 2m/2m3: 0-5 2m4-2m7: 0-0 3m+: 0-0
Track: LH: 0-3 RH: 0-2 Tight: 0-2 Gall: 0-1
Aids: Bl: 0-0 Vi: 0-0 Tstrap: 0-0
Best Rating: 103 7/00 Worc 2m good Ch

A half-brother to Singlesole and Bassenhally. Showed ability over hurdles without winning. Has been let down by his jumping so far over fences. Two and a half miles is probably his trip at present over fences. Best efforts on a sound surface.

Bula Rose (IRE)

104 113

4-y-o ch f Alphabatim (USA)-Titled Dancer (IRE) (Where To Dance (USA))
E W Tuer E Tuer

Placings:3111221 (3495)
2001/02: 17^{3}GS, 17^{1}G, 17^{1}G, 16^{1}G, 16^{2}G, 16^{2}G, 16^{1}S

	Starts	1st	2nd	3rd	Win & Pl
Hurdles	7	4	2	1	20825
Career Total	**7**	**4**	**2**	**1**	**20825**

103	1/02	Donc	2m110y	C Hdl	SFT	£6493
96	9/01	Prth	2m110y	E Hdl	GD	£2915
102	9/01	Sedg	2m1f	E Hdl	GD	£2387
99	8/01	Ctml	2m1f110y	E Hdl	GD	£2642

Total win prize-money £14440

Going: Sf: 1-1 GS: 0-1 Gd: 3-5 GF: - Fm: 0-0
Distance: **2m/2m3: 4-7** 2m4-2m7: 0-0 3m+: 0-0
Track: **LH: 3-4** RH: 1-2 **Tight: 2-2** Gall: 1-1
Aids: Bl: 0-0 Vi: 0-0 Tstrap: 0-0
Best Rating: 113 11/01 Asct 2m110y good Hdl

She has taken well to hurdles completing a hat-trick in the late summer, and ran very well when second to Quazar, at Wetherby in November. No match for Live The Dream at Ascot, but made up for that next time. Jumps well and suited by good ground.

Bullens Bay (IRE)

109(102c) 101

13-y-o b g Hallodri (ATA)-Coolgreen Lolly (Blue Chariot)
B J Llewellyn B W Parren

Placings:6/3323P/52103215P511354/044/24P4/R41641UCP40-53356 (2008)
2001/02: 24^{5}F, 27^{3}G, 27^{3}GF, 25^{6}GF, 24^{6}S

	Starts	1st	2nd	3rd	Win & Pl
Hurdles	5	0	0	2	1183
Career Total	**44**	**6**	**4**	**7**	**32806**

101	1/01	Uttx	2m4f110y	G Hdl	HVY	£1918
105	5/00	NAbb	2m5f110y	B HCh	G-F	£8739
117	3/98	NAbb	3m3f	D(0-125)HHdl	SFT	£3254
120	2/98	Chep	3m	C(0-135)HHdl	G-S	£4474
114	7/97	Sthl	3m110y	F(0-100)HHdl	GD	£2088
92	5/97	Strf	2m6f110y	D Hdl	GD	£3183

Total win prize-money £23657

Going: Sf: 0-1 GS: 0-0 Gd: 0-1 GF: - Fm: 0-3
Distance: 2m/2m3: 0-0 2m4-2m7: 0-0 3m+: 0-5
Track: LH: 0-4 RH: 0-1 Tight: 0-4 Gall: 0-0
Aids: Bl: 0-0 Vi: 0-0 Tstrap: 0-0
Best Rating: 120 2/98 Chep 3m gd-sft Hdl

A doughty staying hurdler, he has shown some fair form in point to points and hunter chases without setting the world alight.

Bullfinch

108 122

9-y-o ch g Anshan-Lambay (Lorenzaccio)

R T Phillips Paul Duffy, Alan Beard, Brian Beard

Placings:5526/1316/**UP03P**014/1120P0-64144P005 **(4844)**

2001/02: 27^{6}G, 27^{4}GF, 22^{1}GS, 27^{4}GF, 22^{4}S, 22^{P}HY, 24^{0}S, 22^{0}G, 24^{5}G

	Starts	1st	2nd	3rd	Win & Pl
Hurdles	9	1	0	0	4396
Career Total	**31**	**6**	**2**	**2**	**21030**

122	6/01	NAbb	2m6f	D(0-120)HHdl	G-S	£3368
118	8/00	Uttx	3m110y	D(0-120)HHdl	G-F	£3059
112	5/00	Chep	3m	E(0-115)HHdl	FRM	£2726
112	4/00	Tntn	3m110y	G(0-95)HHdl	G-S	£1722
100	7/98	Worc	2m	E Hdl	G-F	£2512
104	5/98	MRas	2m1f110y	E Hdl	G-F	£2862

Total win prize-money £16252

Going: Sf: 0-3 GS: 1-1 Gd: 0-3 GF: - Fm: 0-2
Distance: 2m/2m3: 0-0 **2m4-2m7: 1-4** 3m+: 0-5
Track: **LH: 1-7** RH: 0-2 **Tight: 1-6** Gall: 0-0
Aids: Bl: 0-0 Vi: 0-0 Tstrap: 0-0
Best Rating: **122** 6/01 NAbb 3m3f gd-fm Hdl

Fair staying hurdler who has won on fast ground and good to soft.

Bumpse A Daisy

93 79

8-y-o b m Lord Bud-Zarnina (The Brianstan)

D C O'Brien D C O'Brien

Placings:0/400FF/06331-56 **(2709)**

2001/02: 17^{5}GS, 16^{0}G

	Starts	1st	2nd	3rd	Win & Pl
Hurdles	2	0	0	0	0
Career Total	**13**	**1**	**0**	**2**	**2897**

80	2/01	Folk	2m1f110y	F(0-90)HHdl	HVY	£2394

Total win prize-money £2394

Going: Sf: 0-0 GS: 0-1 Gd: 0-1 GF: - Fm: 0-0
Distance: 2m/2m3: 0-2 2m4-2m7: 0-0 3m+: 0-0
Track: LH: 0-1 RH: 0-1 Tight: 0-2 Gall: 0-0
Aids: Bl: 0-0 Vi: 0-0 Tstrap: 0-0
Best Rating: **84** 12/99 Plum 2m good Hdl

Bungee Jumper

12-y-o b g Idiots Delight-Catherine Bridge (Pitpan)

J K Cresswell J K S Cresswell

Placings:20/002/2113/00/P40/42P26P0/2F431/3-P **(1140)**

2001/02: 17^{P}G

	Starts	1st	2nd	3rd	Win & Pl
Chases	1	0	0	0	
Career Total	**28**	**3**	**6**	**3**	**14991**

115	7/99	Strf	2m1f110y	D Ch	GD	£4318
100	10/95	Ludl	2m	E Hdl	FRM	£2332
93	9/95	Hntg	2m110y	E Hdl	G-F	£2442

Total win prize-money £9094

Going: Sf: 0-0 GS: 0-0 Gd: 0-1 GF: - Fm: 0-0
Distance: 2m/2m3: 0-1 2m4-2m7: 0-0 3m+: 0-0
Track: LH: 0-1 RH: 0-0 Tight: 0-1 Gall: 0-0
Aids: Bl: 0-0 Vi: 0-0 Tstrap: 0-0
Best Rating: **119** 5/00 Worc 2m gd-fm Ch

Bunker Buster

5-y-o b g Neltino-Bright Bomb (Cruise Missile)

P Winkworth P Winkworth

Placings:0 **(1947)**

2001/02: 19^{0}GF

	Starts	1st	2nd	3rd	Win & Pl
Hurdles	1	0	0	0	
Career Total	**1**	**0**	**0**	**0**	

Going: Sf: 0-0 GS: 0-0 Gd: 0-0 GF: - Fm: 0-1
Distance: 2m/2m3: 0-1 2m4-2m7: 0-0 3m+: 0-0
Track: LH: 0-0 RH: 0-1 Tight: 0-0 Gall: 0-0
Aids: Bl: 0-0 Vi: 0-0 Tstrap: 0-0
Best Rating:

Bunkum

104 106

4-y-o b g Robellino (USA)-Spinning Mouse (Bustino)

R Lee (M L W Bell 5/7) John Jackson And Maggie Pope

Placings:441 **(4263)**

2001/02: 16^{4}HY, 16^{4}HY, 16^{1}S

	Starts	1st	2nd	3rd	Win & Pl
Hurdles	3	1	0	0	2667
Career Total	**3**	**1**	**0**	**0**	**2667**

107	3/02	Chep	2m110y	E Hdl	SFT	£2667

Total win prize-money £2667

Going: Sf: 1-3 GS: 0-0 Gd: 0-0 GF: - Fm: 0-0
Distance: **2m/2m3: 1-3** 2m4-2m7: 0-0 3m+: 0-0
Track: **LH: 1-3** RH: 0-0 Tight: 0-0 Gall: 0-0
Aids: Bl: 0-0 Vi: 0-0 Tstrap: 0-0
Best Rating: **107** 3/02 Chep 2m110y soft Hdl

Fair novice hurdler at the minimum trip. A ready winner on his third start over hurdles at Chepstow. Acts on soft/heavy ground.

Bunratty Castle (IRE)

107 (114h) 137

7-y-o b g Supreme Leader-Shannon Foam (Le Bavard (FR))

P F Nicholls (Anthony Mullins 4/7) T J Hawkins, D J Nichols, A J White

Placings:212-4P42323 **(4634)**

2001/02: 20^{4}HY, 20^{P}G, 20^{4}GF, 19^{2}S, 16^{3}HY, 21^{2}G, 24^{3}GF

	Starts	1st	2nd	3rd	Win & Pl
Hurdles	3	0	0	0	661
Chases	4	0	2	2	5073
Career Total	**10**	**1**	**4**	**2**	**13723**

115	1/01	Cork	2m	Hdl	SFT	£4729

Total win prize-money £4730

Going: Sf: 0-3 GS: 0-0 Gd: 0-2 GF: - Fm: 0-2
Distance: 2m/2m3: 0-1 2m4-2m7: 0-5 3m+: 0-1
Track: LH: 0-2 RH: 0-2 Tight: 0-0 Gall: 0-0
Aids: Bl: 0-0 Vi: 0-0 Tstrap: 0-0
Best Rating: **137** 12/01 Chep 2m3f110y soft Ch

A useful novice hurdler when with Tony Mullins in Ireland. Bought for 27,000gns and now with Paul Nicholls. Has shown ability with a couple of placed efforts over fences and is suited by soft ground.

Bunty

86 60

6-y-o b m Presidium-Shirlstar Investor (Some Hand)

R C Spicer G D J Linder

Placings:6-0003 **(1807)**

2001/02: 16^{0}F, 16^{0}G, 16^{0}G, 16^{3}S

	Starts	1st	2nd	3rd	Win & Pl
Hurdles	4	0	0	1	266
Career Total	**5**	**0**	**0**	**1**	**266**

Going: Sf: 0-1 GS: 0-0 Gd: 0-2 GF: - Fm: 0-1
Distance: 2m/2m3: 0-4 2m4-2m7: 0-0 3m+: 0-0
Track: LH: 0-4 RH: 0-0 Tight: 0-3 Gall: 0-0
Aids: Bl: 0-0 Vi: 0-0 Tstrap: 0-0
Best Rating: **76** 2/01 Hntg 2m110y gd-sft Hdl

Burcot Girl (IRE)

5-y-o b m Petardia-Phoenix Forli (USA) (Forli (ARG))

Mrs A C Tate M Tate

Placings:P0 **(4594)**

2001/02: 19^{P}G, 16^{0}G

	Starts	1st	2nd	3rd	Win & Pl
Hurdles	2	0	0	0	
Career Total	**2**	**0**	**0**	**0**	

Going: Sf: 0-0 GS: 0-0 Gd: 0-2 GF: - Fm: 0-0
Distance: 2m/2m3: 0-1 2m4-2m7: 0-1 3m+: 0-0
Track: LH: 0-1 RH: 0-1 Tight: 0-0 Gall: 0-0
Aids: Bl: 0-0 Vi: 0-0 Tstrap: 0-0
Best Rating:

Burdens Boy

79 107

6-y-o b g Alflora (IRE)-Dalbeattie (Phardante (FR))

H D Daly Furrows Ltd

Placings:36-1F **(2458)**

2001/02: 16^{1}S, 19^{F}S

	Starts	1st	2nd	3rd	Win & Pl
Hurdles	2	1	0	0	4290
Career Total	**4**	**1**	**0**	**1**	**4543**

107	10/01	Towc	2m	D Hdl	SFT	£4290

Total win prize-money £4290

Going: Sf: 1-2 GS: 0-0 Gd: 0-0 GF: - Fm: 0-0
Distance: **2m/2m3: 1-2** 2m4-2m7: 0-0 3m+: 0-0
Track: LH: 0-1 **RH: 1-1** Tight: 0-0 Gall: 0-0
Aids: Bl: 0-0 Vi: 0-0 Tstrap: 0-0
Best Rating: **107** 10/01 Towc 2m soft Hdl

Made a good start to his jumping career with a comfortable win in an uncompetitive event at Towcester.

Burdens Girl

83f 89f

5-y-o ch m Alflora (IRE)-Dalbeattie (Phardante (FR))

H D Daly Furrows Ltd

Placings:4 **(3985)**

2001/02: 16^{4}G

	Starts	1st	2nd	3rd	Win & Pl
NH Flat	1	0	0	0	0
Career Total	**1**	**0**	**0**	**0**	**0**

Going: Sf: 0-0 GS: 0-0 Gd: 0-1 GF: - Fm: 0-0
Distance: 2m/2m3: 0-1 2m4-2m7: 0-0 3m+: 0-0

Track: LH: 0-0 RH: 0-1 Tight: 0-0 Gall: 0-0
Aids: Bl: 0-0 Vi: 0-0 Tstrap: 0-0
Best Rating: 89 2/02 Ludl 2m good NHF

Burgundy Bob (IRE)

110 125

8-y-o gr g Roselier (FR)-Katebeaujolais (Politico (USA))
Mrs Susan Nock Gerard Nock

Placings: *00*/P45-2PPPP (4399)
2001/02: 24^{2}G, 20^{P}G, 25^{P}G, 24^{P}GS, 22^{P}GS

	Starts	1st	2nd	3rd	Win & Pl
Chases	5	0	1	0	1332
Career Total	**10**	**0**	**1**	**0**	**2542**

Going: Sf: 0-0 GS: 0-2 Gd: 0-3 GF: - Fm: 0-0
Distance: 2m/2m3: 0-0 2m4-2m7: 0-2 3m+: 0-3
Track: LH: 0-2 RH: 0-3 Tight: 0-0 Gall: 0-3
Aids: Bl: 0-0 Vi: 0-0 Tstrap: 0-0
Best Rating: 125 5/01 Hntg 3m good Ch

A winning point to pointer. Looking to be getting the hang of things with some useful placed efforts in the spring/summer of 2001 but has been pulled up on his last few starts. Best at three miles on a sound surface.

Burning Cost

90 56

12-y-o br m Lochnager-Sophie Avenue (Guillaume Tell (USA))
R E Peacock R E Peacock

Placings: 5/00P-6 (0872)
2001/02: 16^{6}GS

	Starts	1st	2nd	3rd	Win & Pl
Hurdles	1	0	0	0	0
Career Total	**5**	**0**	**0**	**0**	**0**

Going: Sf: 0-0 GS: 0-1 Gd: 0-0 GF: - Fm: 0-0
Distance: 2m/2m3: 0-1 2m4-2m7: 0-0 3m+: 0-0
Track: LH: 0-1 RH: 0-0 Tight: 0-1 Gall: 0-0
Aids: Bl: 0-0 Vi: 0-0 Tstrap: 0-0
Best Rating: 83 5/98 Strf 2m110y gd-fm Hdl

Burning Impulse

111 125

4-y-o b c Cadeaux Genereux-Isle Of Flame (Shirley Heights)
Thomas Foley (P R Webber 4/4) P E Delaney

Placings: 15000 (4952a)
2001/02: 16^{1}GS, 16^{5}S, 17^{0}G, 16^{0}G, 16^{0}G

	Starts	1st	2nd	3rd	Win & Pl
Hurdles	5	1	0	0	4310
Career Total	**5**	**1**	**0**	**0**	**4310**
125 1/02 Kemp 2m	D Hdl			G-S	£4309

Total win prize-money £4310

Going: Sf: 0-1 GS: 1-1 Gd: 0-3 GF: - Fm: 0-0
Distance: **2m/2m3: 1-5** 2m4-2m7: 0-0 3m+: 0-0
Track: LH: 0-2 **RH: 1-3** Tight: 0-1 Gall: 0-1
Aids: Bl: 0-0 Vi: 0-0 Tstrap: 0-0
Best Rating: 125 4/02 Punc 2m good Hdl

An expensive buy off the Flat, he made a successful hurdling debut at Kempton in January, but was then held when tried on softer ground and in better company.

Burning Scally

105 (88h) (95h) 110

10-y-o gr m Scallywag-Burning Mirage (Pamroy)
N M L Ewart N M L Ewart

Placings: 540F3/20U555-505F3214 (3791)
2001/02: 26^{5}GS, 20^{0}S, 25^{5}GS, 24^{F}GS, 25^{3}S, 24^{2}S, 24^{1}S, 24^{4}S

	Starts	1st	2nd	3rd	Win & Pl
Hurdles	1	0	0	0	0
Chases	7	1	1	1	5598
Career Total	**19**	**1**	**2**	**2**	**6980**
110 1/02 Newc 3m	D(0-115)HCh			SFT	£4046

Total win prize-money £4046

Going: Sf: 1-5 GS: 0-3 Gd: 0-0 GF: - Fm: 0-0
Distance: 2m/2m3: 0-0 2m4-2m7: 0-1 **3m+: 1-7**
Track: **LH: 1-6** RH: 0-2 Tight: 0-1 **Gall: 1-4**
Aids: Bl: 0-1 Vi: 0-0 Tstrap: 0-0
Best Rating: 110 1/02 Newc 3m soft Ch

Modest staying chaser, handles soft ground and looks suited by racing prominently.

Burnt Imp (USA)

101 108

12-y-o ch g Imp Society (USA)-Flaming Reason (USA) (Limit To Reason (USA))
N B Mason N B Mason

Placings: 111423245/F5211400/000405/11205/**3112F444/1 3333253250/341055312552462430 3/35402233434-02243** (1812)
2001/02: 27^{0}G, 21^{2}G, 25^{2}GF, 24^{4}G, 21^{3}S

	Starts	1st	2nd	3rd	Win & Pl		
Chases	5	0	2	1	3520		
Career Total	**82**	**12**	**14**	**16**	**85261**		
120	11/99	Hexm	2m4f110y	F(0-105)HCh		GD	£3184
115	6/99	Hexm	2m4f110y	E(0-115)HCh		SFT	£3234
120	10/98	Kels	2m6f110y	D(0-120)HCh		SFT	£4318
117	12/97	Bang	2m4f110y	D Ch		G-S	£3550
120	11/97	Newc	2m4f	C Ch		GD	£4355
122	11/96	Ayr	2m4f	D(0-120)HHdl		GD	£3629
119	11/96	Weth	2m4f110y	C(0-135)HHdl		GD	£2792
125	1/95	Chel	2m5f110y	C(0-130)HHdl		G-S	£7392
118	12/94	Weth	2m4f110y	HHdl		SFT	£2860
103	10/93	Weth	2m	Hdl		GD	£6340
103	10/93	Weth	2m	Hdl		SFT	£2110
96	8/93	Ctml	2m1f110y	Hdl		FRM	£2005

Total win prize-money £45775

Going: Sf: 0-1 GS: 0-0 Gd: 0-3 GF: - Fm: 0-1
Distance: 2m/2m3: 0-0 2m4-2m7: 0-2 3m+: 0-3
Track: LH: 0-3 RH: 0-2 Tight: 0-4 Gall: 0-0
Aids: Bl: 0-0 Vi: 0-0 Tstrap: 0-5
Best Rating: 128 11/96 Hayd 2m6f good Hdl

He was a useful sort once, but is merely a journeyman northern handicapper these days. He looks best suited by trips short of three miles though he has run pretty well over further. He seems to go well at Hexham.

Burra Sahib

(74h) (50h)

6-y-o b g First Trump-Old Flower (Persian Bold)
P C Ritchens (J Akehurst 5/9) Fraser Miller Racing

Placings: P0 (4854)
2001/02: 24^{P}G, 22^{0}G

	Starts	1st	2nd	3rd	Win & Pl
Hurdles	2	0	0	0	
Career Total	**2**	**0**	**0**	**0**	

Going: Sf: 0-0 GS: 0-0 Gd: 0-2 GF: - Fm: 0-0
Distance: 2m/2m3: 0-0 2m4-2m7: 0-1 3m+: 0-1
Track: LH: 0-1 RH: 0-1 Tight: 0-1 Gall: 0-0
Aids: Bl: 0-0 Vi: 0-0 Tstrap: 0-0
Best Rating: 50 4/02 Strf 2m6f110y good Hdl

Burundi (IRE)

111 120

8-y-o b g Danehill (USA)-Sofala (Home Guard (USA))
A W Carroll K Marshall, M Lennon

Placings: 1162/P40-223P436 (4593)
2001/02: 17^{2}GS, 16^{2}GS, 16^{3}G, 17^{P}HY, 20^{4}GS, 16^{3}GS, 16^{6}G

	Starts	1st	2nd	3rd	Win & Pl
Hurdles	7	0	2	2	6393
Career Total	**14**	**2**	**3**	**2**	**12998**
120 12/98 Leic 2m	E Hdl			G-S	£2882
109 11/98 Leic 2m	E Hdl			SFT	£2903

Total win prize-money £5785

Going: Sf: 0-1 GS: 0-4 Gd: 0-2 GF: - Fm: 0-0
Distance: 2m/2m3: 0-6 2m4-2m7: 0-1 3m+: 0-0
Track: LH: 0-4 RH: 0-3 Tight: 0-1 Gall: 0-2
Aids: Bl: 0-0 Vi: 0-0 Tstrap: 0-0
Best Rating: 120 3/02 Newb 2m110y gd-sft Hdl

Won his first two starts over hurdles towards the end of 1998, but then lost his way and was lightly raced, missing the whole of 2000. Fair efforts since returning and has often made the frame, but has yet to recapture his very best.

Burwood Breeze (IRE)

98 100

6-y-o b g Fresh Breeze (USA)-Shuil Le Cheile (Quayside)
T R George David & Lesley Byrne

Placings: *544420* (4502)
2001/02: 16^{5}S, 17^{4}HY, 16^{4}S, 17^{4}S, 19^{2}S, 22^{0}G

	Starts	1st	2nd	3rd	Win & Pl
NH Flat	2	0	0	0	0
Hurdles	4	0	1	0	1402
Career Total	**6**	**0**	**1**	**0**	**1402**

Going: Sf: 0-5 GS: 0-0 Gd: 0-1 GF: - Fm: 0-0
Distance: 2m/2m3: 0-4 2m4-2m7: 0-2 3m+: 0-0
Track: LH: 0-4 RH: 0-2 Tight: 0-5 Gall: 0-0
Aids: Bl: 0-0 Vi: 0-0 Tstrap: 0-0
Best Rating: 100 2/02 Tntn 2m1f soft Hdl

Fair novice. Suited by two and a half miles. Acts on soft/heavy ground.

Busela Lady

5-y-o ch m Alflora (IRE)-Burling Moss (Le Moss)
B D Leavy R W Russell

Placings: *0* (3999)
2001/02: 16^{0}S

	Starts	1st	2nd	3rd	Win & Pl
NH Flat	1	0	0	0	
Career Total	**1**	**0**	**0**	**0**	

Going: Sf: 0-1 GS: 0-0 Gd: 0-0 GF: - Fm: 0-0
Distance: 2m/2m3: 0-1 2m4-2m7: 0-0 3m+: 0-0
Track: LH: 0-1 RH: 0-0 Tight: 0-0 Gall: 0-1
Aids: Bl: 0-0 Vi: 0-0 Tstrap: 0-0

Bush Hill Bandit (IRE)

7-y-o b/br g Executive Perk-Baby Isle (Menelek)
P R Webber The Large G & T Partnership

Placings: *06*/006-P (0191)
2001/02: 23^{P}GF

	Starts	1st	2nd	3rd	Win & Pl
Hurdles	1	0	0	0	
Career Total	**6**	**0**	**0**	**0**	**0**

Going: Sf: 0-0 GS: 0-0 Gd: 0-0 GF: - Fm: 0-1
Distance: 2m/2m3: 0-0 2m4-2m7: 0-0 3m+: 0-1
Track: LH: 0-1 RH: 0-0 Tight: 0-1 Gall: 0-0
Aids: Bl: 0-0 Vi: 0-0 Tstrap: 0-0
Best Rating: **84** 2/00 Sand 2m110y soft NHF

Bush Park (IRE)

109(104h) (102h)**122**
7-y-o b g Be My Native (USA)-By All Means (Pitpan)
R H Alner Mrs U Wainwright

Placings: *325*/3503-00**12312**3**1**0 (4814)
2001/02: 22^{0}GF, 16^{0}GF, 16^{1}G, 19^{2}S, 20^{3}G, 19^{1}G, 20^{2}GS, 20^{3}G, 16^{1}S, 21^{0}GF

	Starts	1st	2nd	3rd	Win & Pl
Hurdles	3	1	0	0	2730
Chases	7	2	2	2	12609
Career Total	**17**	**3**	**3**	**5**	**16895**

102	3/02	Winc	2m	E(0-105)HHdl	SFT	£2730
122	11/01	Hnfd	2m3f	E(0-115)HCh	GD	£3435
111	10/01	Strf	2m	F(0-100)HCh	GD	£2756

Total win prize-money £8921

Going: Sf: 1-2 GS: 0-1 Gd: 2-4 GF: - Fm: 0-3
Distance: **2m/2m3: 3-5** 2m4-2m7: 0-5 3m+: 0-0
Track: LH: 1-4 **RH: 2-6 Tight: 1-2** Gall: 0-2
Aids: Bl: 0-0 Vi: 0-0 Tstrap: 0-0
Best Rating: **122** 12/01 Kemp 2m4f110y good Ch

A winner over both hurdles and fences. Stays two and a half miles. A sound jumper who handles good ground or softer.

Bushehr (IRE)

96 **90**
10-y-o b g Persian Bold-Shejrah (USA) (Northjet)
Mrs A M Thorpe Mrs A M Thorpe

Placings: 30500245/4-40 (0842)
2001/02: 18^{4}GF, 16^{0}G

	Starts	1st	2nd	3rd	Win & Pl
Chases	2	0	0	0	206
Career Total	**11**	**0**	**1**	**1**	**1414**

Going: Sf: 0-0 GS: 0-0 Gd: 0-1 GF: - Fm: 0-1
Distance: 2m/2m3: 0-2 2m4-2m7: 0-0 3m+: 0-0
Track: LH: 0-1 RH: 0-0 Tight: 0-1 Gall: 0-0
Aids: Bl: 0-0 Vi: 0-0 Tstrap: 0-0
Best Rating: **90** 5/01 Font 2m2f gd-fm Ch

Bushie Bill

99 **97**
4-y-o ch g Captain Webster-Mistress Royal (Royalty)
P R Hedger Bill Broomfield

Placings: 43 (2597)

2001/02: 16^{4}G, 18^{3}G

	Starts	1st	2nd	3rd	Win & Pl
Hurdles	2	0	0	1	638
Career Total	**2**	**0**	**0**	**1**	**638**

Going: Sf: 0-0 GS: 0-0 Gd: 0-2 GF: - Fm: 0-0
Distance: 2m/2m3: 0-2 2m4-2m7: 0-0 3m+: 0-0
Track: LH: 0-2 RH: 0-0 Tight: 0-1 Gall: 0-1
Aids: Bl: 0-0 Vi: 0-0 Tstrap: 0-0
Best Rating: **97** 12/01 Font 2m2f110y good Hdl

Business Class (NZ)

102 **119**
10-y-o b g Accountant (NZ)-Fury's Princess (NZ) (Our Kungfu (NZ))
Mrs M Reveley Ernie Fenwick

Placings: 5531104 (4920)
2001/02: 16^{5}G, 25^{5}G, 16^{3}GF, 16^{1}GS, 21^{1}GF, 21^{0}GF, 21^{4}GF

	Starts	1st	2nd	3rd	Win & Pl
Chases	7	2	0	1	9029
Career Total	**7**	**2**	**0**	**1**	**9029**

115	4/02	Sedg	2m5f	D Ch	G-F	£3883
104	3/02	Catt	2m	D Ch	G-S	£4192

Total win prize-money £8077

Going: Sf: 0-0 GS: 1-1 Gd: 0-2 GF: - Fm: 1-4
Distance: 2m/2m3: 1-3 2m4-2m7: 1-3 3m+: 0-1
Track: **LH: 2-6** RH: 0-1 **Tight: 2-4** Gall: 0-1
Aids: Bl: 0-0 Vi: 0-0 Tstrap: 0-0
Best Rating: **115** 4/02 Sedg 2m5f gd-fm Ch

Former three-day eventer. Moderate pointer. Jumps soundly and took two modest novice chases in the spring of 2002. Stays two miles-five, handles any ground.

Busky Gorse

59
6-y-o gr m Scallywag-Miss Anax (Anax)
P Beaumont Josttigo Racing

Placings: *0-R0* (2321)
2001/02: 16^{R}G, 17^{0}GS

	Starts	1st	2nd	3rd	Win & Pl
NH Flat	2	0	0	0	
Career Total	**3**	**0**	**0**	**0**	

Going: Sf: 0-0 GS: 0-1 Gd: 0-1 GF: - Fm: 0-0
Distance: 2m/2m3: 0-2 2m4-2m7: 0-0 3m+: 0-0
Track: LH: 0-1 RH: 0-0 Tight: 0-0 Gall: 0-0
Aids: Bl: 0-0 Vi: 0-0 Tstrap: 0-0
Best Rating: **32** 1/01 Catt 2m gd-sft NHF

Bustamante

6-y-o ch g Sir Harry Lewis (USA)-Carribean Sound (Good Times (ITY))
P Monteith Hamilton House Limited

Placings: 0 (2473)
2001/02: 16^{0}GS

	Starts	1st	2nd	3rd	Win & Pl
Hurdles	1	0	0	0	
Career Total	**1**	**0**	**0**	**0**	

Going: Sf: 0-0 GS: 0-1 Gd: 0-0 GF: - Fm: 0-0
Distance: 2m/2m3: 0-1 2m4-2m7: 0-0 3m+: 0-0
Track: LH: 0-1 RH: 0-0 Tight: 0-1 Gall: 0-0
Aids: Bl: 0-0 Vi: 0-0 Tstrap: 0-0
Best Rating:

Busted Flat (IRE)

(85h)
9-y-o br g Bustino-Trailing Rose (Undulate (USA))
Mrs M Reveley R Burridge

Placings: 000V/4131F/50-6 (3776)
2001/02: 24^{6}S

	Starts	1st	2nd	3rd	Win & Pl
Chases	1	0	0	0	0
Career Total	**12**	**2**	**0**	**1**	**5145**

106	1/00	Weth	2m4f110y	F(0-105)HHdl	SFT	£2170
85	11/99	Weth	2m4f110y	F(0-110)HHdl	GD	£2304

Total win prize-money £4474

Going: Sf: 0-1 GS: 0-0 Gd: 0-0 GF: - Fm: 0-0
Distance: 2m/2m3: 0-0 2m4-2m7: 0-0 3m+: 0-1
Track: LH: 0-0 RH: 0-1 Tight: 0-0 Gall: 0-0
Aids: Bl: 0-0 Vi: 0-0 Tstrap: 0-0
Best Rating: **106** 2/00 Weth 2m7f soft Hdl

Bustling Rio (IRE)

96(106h) (123h)**109**
6-y-o b g Up And At 'Em-Une Venitienne (FR) (Green Dancer (USA))
P C Haslam Rio Stainless Engineering Limited

Placings: 111-**141**20 (4633)
2001/02: 20^{1}GS, 20^{4}S, 20^{1}GF, 24^{2}S, 20^{0}GF

	Starts	1st	2nd	3rd	Win & Pl
Hurdles	2	0	1	0	1605
Chases	3	2	0	0	7454
Career Total	**8**	**5**	**1**	**0**	**17751**

93	3/02	Hntg	2m4f110y	E Ch	G-F	£3035
109	11/01	Newc	2m4f	E Ch	G-S	£3168
124	1/01	Weth	2m7f	E Hdl	HVY	£2660
120	10/00	Aint	2m4f	E Hdl	GD	£3120
113	10/00	MRas	2m3f110y	E Hdl	GD	£2912

Total win prize-money £14897

Going: Sf: 0-2 GS: 1-1 Gd: 0-0 GF: - Fm: 1-2
Distance: 2m/2m3: 0-0 **2m4-2m7: 2-4** 3m+: 0-1
Track: LH: 1-3 RH: 1-2 Tight: 0-1 **Gall: 2-3**
Aids: Bl: 0-0 Vi: 0-0 Tstrap: 0-0
Best Rating: **124** 1/01 Weth 2m7f heavy Hdl

A winner on the Flat on both turf and sand, he has been winning over hurdles and fences in 2001/2002 and is very versatile. Probably best over trips of around two and a half miles though he does stay further and acts on any ground.

Busty Girl

7-y-o br m Be My Native (USA)-Busy Girl (Bustiki)
C N Kellett I P Crane

Placings: *0*/R-0 (0593)
2001/02: 20^{0}GF

	Starts	1st	2nd	3rd	Win & Pl
Hurdles	1	0	0	0	
Career Total	**3**	**0**	**0**	**0**	

Going: Sf: 0-0 GS: 0-0 Gd: 0-0 GF: - Fm: 0-1
Distance: 2m/2m3: 0-0 2m4-2m7: 0-1 3m+: 0-0
Track: LH: 0-1 RH: 0-0 Tight: 0-1 Gall: 0-0
Aids: Bl: 0-0 Vi: 0-0 Tstrap: 0-0
Best Rating:

Busy Busy Bee

84 **54**

5-y-o gr m Batshoof-Rectitude (Runnymede)
M E Sowersby (N P Littmoden 15/2) Neville Saunders

Placings:F5P0 **(4904)**
2001/02: 16^{F}G, 16^{5}S, 17^{P}G, 17^{0}G

	Starts	1st	2nd	3rd	Win & Pl
Hurdles	4	0	0	0	0
Career Total	**4**	**0**	**0**	**0**	**0**

Going: Sf: 0-1 GS: 0-0 Gd: 0-3 GF: - Fm: 0-0
Distance: 2m/2m3: 0-4 2m4-2m7: 0-0 3m+: 0-0
Track: LH: 0-0 RH: 0-4 Tight: 0-2 Gall: 0-0
Aids: Bl: 0-0 Vi: 0-0 Tstrap: 0-0
Best Rating: **54** 4/02 MRas 2m1f110y good Hdl

Busy Gunner

5-y-o ch m Gunner B-Bustle'Em (IRE) (Burslem)
D McCain D McCain

Placings:P **(1042)**
2001/02: 16^{P}GF

	Starts	1st	2nd	3rd	Win & Pl
Hurdles	1	0	0	0	
Career Total	**1**	**0**	**0**	**0**	

Going: Sf: 0-0 GS: 0-0 Gd: 0-0 GF: - Fm: 0-1
Distance: 2m/2m3: 0-1 2m4-2m7: 0-0 3m+: 0-0
Track: LH: 0-1 RH: 0-0 Tight: 0-0 Gall: 0-0
Aids: Bl: 0-0 Vi: 0-0 Tstrap: 0-0
Best Rating:

Butch Cassidy

6-y-o b g Rambo Dancer (CAN)-Sioux Be It (Warpath)
T H Caldwell Hogarth Racing

Placings:1/0 **(2173)**
2001/02: 16^{0}S

	Starts	1st	2nd	3rd	Win & Pl
NH Flat	1	0	0	0	
Career Total	**2**	**1**	**0**	**0**	**1663**

95 2/00 Sedg 2m1f H NHF G-S £1662
Total win prize-money £1663

Going: Sf: 0-1 GS: 0-0 Gd: 0-0 GF: - Fm: 0-0
Distance: 2m/2m3: 0-1 2m4-2m7: 0-0 3m+: 0-0
Track: LH: 0-1 RH: 0-0 Tight: 0-0 Gall: 0-0
Aids: Bl: 0-0 Vi: 0-0 Tstrap: 0-0
Best Rating: **95** 2/00 Sedg 2m1f gd-sft NHF

Butchers Minstrel

10-y-o ch g Brotherly (USA)-Flash Bunny (Flashback)
Mrs N S Sharpe J R B Williams

Placings:P/P/P **(3642)**
2001/02: 24^{P}GS

	Starts	1st	2nd	3rd	Win & Pl
Chases	1	0	0	0	
Career Total	**3**	**0**	**0**	**0**	

Going: Sf: 0-0 GS: 0-1 Gd: 0-0 GF: - Fm: 0-0
Distance: 2m/2m3: 0-0 2m4-2m7: 0-0 3m+: 0-1
Track: LH: 0-0 RH: 0-1 Tight: 0-1 Gall: 0-0
Aids: Bl: 0-0 Vi: 0-0 Tstrap: 0-0

Buteland Boy

10-y-o b g Buckskin (FR)-Dark Trix (Peacock (FR))
R Johnson J L Gledson

Placings:00660/0U **(0467)**
2001/02: 21^{0}G, 20^{U}GF

	Starts	1st	2nd	3rd	Win & Pl
Chases	2	0	0	0	
Career Total	**7**	**0**	**0**	**0**	**0**

Going: Sf: 0-0 GS: 0-0 Gd: 0-1 GF: - Fm: 0-1
Distance: 2m/2m3: 0-0 2m4-2m7: 0-2 3m+: 0-0
Track: LH: 0-2 RH: 0-0 Tight: 0-1 Gall: 0-0
Aids: Bl: 0-0 Vi: 0-0 Tstrap: 0-0
Best Rating: **80** 12/98 Muss 2m good NHF

Butler John (IRE)

108 **96**

13-y-o b g The Parson-Corrielek (Menelek)
V R A Dartnall Nick Viney

Placings:00/016U044/1F42/35243P **(1344)**
2001/02: 25^{3}G, 22^{5}GF, 26^{2}G, 26^{4}GF, 26^{3}GF, 26^{P}GF

	Starts	1st	2nd	3rd	Win & Pl
Chases	6	0	1	2	1879
Career Total	**19**	**2**	**2**	**2**	**8857**

97 5/95 Aint 2m4f E Ch FRM £2964
77 9/94 Kbgn 2m3f Hdl GD £2609
Total win prize-money £5575

Going: Sf: 0-0 GS: 0-0 Gd: 0-2 GF: 0-4
Distance: 2m/2m3: 0-0 2m4-2m7: 0-1 3m+: 0-5
Track: LH: 0-3 RH: 0-1 Tight: 0-5 Gall: 0-0
Aids: Bl: 0-0 Vi: 0-0 Tstrap: 0-0
Best Rating: **99** 9/94 List 2m gd-yld Hdl

Butlers Hall

68 **18**

6-y-o b m Saddlers' Hall (IRE)-Debate (High Line)
Ferdy Murphy The Ferdy Murphy Racing Club

Placings:000/000-0 **(1588)**
2001/02: 17^{0}GS

	Starts	1st	2nd	3rd	Win & Pl
Hurdles	1	0	0	0	
Career Total	**7**	**0**	**0**	**0**	

Going: Sf: 0-0 GS: 0-1 Gd: 0-0 GF: - Fm: 0-0
Distance: 2m/2m3: 0-1 2m4-2m7: 0-0 3m+: 0-0
Track: LH: 0-1 RH: 0-0 Tight: 0-1 Gall: 0-0
Aids: Bl: 0-0 Vi: 0-0 Tstrap: 0-0
Best Rating: **48** 4/00 Wxfd 2m good Hdl

Butterwick Chief

92 **66**

5-y-o b g Be My Chief (USA)-Swift Return (Double Form)
R A Fahey P S Cresswell

Placings:000 **(3463)**
2001/02: 16^{0}G, 20^{0}G, 16^{0}S

	Starts	1st	2nd	3rd	Win & Pl
Hurdles	3	0	0	0	
Career Total	**3**	**0**	**0**	**0**	

Going: Sf: 0-1 GS: 0-0 Gd: 0-2 GF: - Fm: 0-0
Distance: 2m/2m3: 0-2 2m4-2m7: 0-1 3m+: 0-0
Track: LH: 0-3 RH: 0-0 Tight: 0-0 Gall: 0-3

Aids: Bl: 0-0 Vi: 0-0 Tstrap: 0-0
Best Rating: **66** 1/02 Donc 2m4f good Hdl

Buxted's First

75 **54**

5-y-o gr m Mystiko (USA)-Sea Fairy (Wollow)
G L Moore Buxted Partnership

Placings:600 **(2204)**
2001/02: 16^{6}GS, 16^{0}S, 16^{0}GS

	Starts	1st	2nd	3rd	Win & Pl
Hurdles	3	0	0	0	0
Career Total	**3**	**0**	**0**	**0**	**0**

Going: Sf: 0-1 GS: 0-2 Gd: 0-0 GF: - Fm: 0-0
Distance: 2m/2m3: 0-3 2m4-2m7: 0-0 3m+: 0-0
Track: LH: 0-2 RH: 0-1 Tight: 0-1 Gall: 0-0
Aids: Bl: 0-0 Vi: 0-0 Tstrap: 0-0
Best Rating: **54** 9/01 Plum 2m gd-sft Hdl

Buying A Dream (IRE)

80 **72**

5-y-o ch g Prince Of Birds (USA)-Cartagena Lady (IRE) (Prince Rupert (FR))
Andrew Turnell Robinson Webster (holdings) Ltd

Placings:00P **(2896)**
2001/02: 16^{0}S, 16^{0}G, 20^{P}S

	Starts	1st	2nd	3rd	Win & Pl
Hurdles	3	0	0	0	
Career Total	**3**	**0**	**0**	**0**	

Going: Sf: 0-2 GS: 0-0 Gd: 0-1 GF: - Fm: 0-0
Distance: 2m/2m3: 0-2 2m4-2m7: 0-1 3m+: 0-0
Track: LH: 0-2 RH: 0-1 Tight: 0-0 Gall: 0-1
Aids: Bl: 0-1 Vi: 0-0 Tstrap: 0-0
Best Rating: **72** 11/01 Uttx 2m soft Hdl

Buzz O'The Crowd

15-y-o br g Sousa-Dotted Swiss (Super Slip)
Jane Southcombe P J Quinn

Placings:P6/P6353/4/113125/512/P/BP **(0494)**
2001/02: 28^{B}GF, 25^{P}G

	Starts	1st	2nd	3rd	Win & Pl
Chases	2	0	0	0	
Career Total	**20**	**4**	**2**	**3**	**8640**

112 4/99 Tntn 3m H Ch FRM £2337
114 3/98 Hrfd 3m1f110y H Ch G-F £1590
110 2/98 Hrfd 3m1f110y H Ch GD £1255
114 5/97 NAbb 3m2f110y H Ch G-S £1152
Total win prize-money £6335

Going: Sf: 0-0 GS: 0-0 Gd: 0-1 GF: - Fm: 0-1
Distance: 2m/2m3: 0-0 2m4-2m7: 0-0 3m+: 0-2
Track: LH: 0-1 RH: 0-1 Tight: 0-1 Gall: 0-0
Aids: Bl: 0-0 Vi: 0-0 Tstrap: 0-0
Best Rating: **114** 4/99 Hntg 3m good Ch

Buzzsword

74(84h) **43**

8-y-o ch m Broadsword (USA)-Heron Valley (Remezzo)
R H Buckler Mrs Jean Clemoes

Placings: *00/06*P/05P/06**55-6U6P** (4563)
2001/02: 22^{6}HY, 24^{U}S, 25^{6}G, 26^{P}GF

	Starts	1st	2nd	3rd	Win & Pl
Chases	4	0	0	0	0
Career Total	**16**	**0**	**0**	**0**	**0**

Going: Sf: 0-2 GS: 0-0 Gd: 0-1 GF: - Fm: 0-1
Distance: 2m/2m3: 0-0 2m4-2m7: 0-1 3m+: 0-3
Track: LH: 0-0 RH: 0-2 Tight: 0-1 Gall: 0-1
Aids: Bl: 0-0 Vi: 0-0 Tstrap: 0-0
Best Rating: 69 11/00 Intn 2m3f110y gd-sft Hdl

By Jove

84f 90f
7-y-o ch g Jupiter Island-Joscilla (Joshua)
Miss H C Knight D C G Gyle-Thompson

Placings: *3* (0032)
2001/02: 16^{3}G

	Starts	1st	2nd	3rd	Win & Pl
NH Flat	1	0	0	1	257
Career Total	**1**	**0**	**0**	**1**	**257**

Going: Sf: 0-0 GS: 0-0 Gd: 0-1 GF: - Fm: 0-0
Distance: 2m/2m3: 0-1 2m4-2m7: 0-0 3m+: 0-0
Track: LH: 0-0 RH: 0-1 Tight: 0-0 Gall: 0-1
Aids: Bl: 0-0 Vi: 0-0 Tstrap: 0-0
Best Rating: 90 5/01 Hntg 2m110y good NHF

By My Side (IRE)

102 87
8-y-o b/br g Brush Aside (USA)-Stay As You Are (Buckskin (FR))
Miss Jacqueline S Doyle A W Regan

Placings: P-6603P0 (1268)
2001/02: 22^{6}GS, 22^{6}GF, 24^{0}G, 17^{3}G, 16^{P}G, 17^{0}GF

	Starts	1st	2nd	3rd	Win & Pl
Hurdles	6	0	0	1	420
Career Total	**7**	**0**	**0**	**1**	**420**

Going: Sf: 0-0 GS: 0-1 Gd: 0-3 GF: - Fm: 0-2
Distance: 2m/2m3: 0-3 2m4-2m7: 0-2 3m+: 0-1
Track: LH: 0-5 RH: 0-0 Tight: 0-4 Gall: 0-0
Aids: Bl: 0-3 Vi: 0-0 Tstrap: 0-0
Best Rating: 87 5/01 Extr 2m6f110y gd-sft Hdl

By N By (IRE)

88f 93f
6-y-o b g Un Desperado (FR)-Andonova (Prince Tenderfoot (USA))
Miss Venetia Williams The Down South Syndicate

Placings: *0* (3503)
2001/02: 16^{0}S

	Starts	1st	2nd	3rd	Win & Pl
NH Flat	1	0	0	0	
Career Total	**1**	**0**	**0**	**0**	

Going: Sf: 0-1 GS: 0-0 Gd: 0-0 GF: - Fm: 0-0
Distance: 2m/2m3: 0-1 2m4-2m7: 0-0 3m+: 0-0
Track: LH: 0-0 RH: 0-1 Tight: 0-0 Gall: 0-0
Aids: Bl: 0-0 Vi: 0-0 Tstrap: 0-0
Best Rating: 93 1/02 Kemp 2m soft NHF

Bydemill Brook

77 45
8-y-o b m Baron Blakeney-Amazon Gold (Whistlefield)
J A T De Giles J A T De Giles

Placings: *0566*P-P0P (0929)
2001/02: 25^{P}G, 20^{0}G, 20^{P}GF

	Starts	1st	2nd	3rd	Win & Pl
Hurdles	3	0	0	0	
Career Total	**8**	**0**	**0**	**0**	**0**

Going: Sf: 0-0 GS: 0-0 Gd: 0-2 GF: - Fm: 0-1
Distance: 2m/2m3: 0-0 2m4-2m7: 0-2 3m+: 0-1
Track: LH: 0-2 RH: 0-0 Tight: 0-1 Gall: 0-0
Aids: Bl: 0-0 Vi: 0-0 Tstrap: 0-0
Best Rating: 81 7/00 Worc 2m gd-fm NHF

Byron Lamb

108 122
5-y-o b g Rambo Dancer (CAN)-Caroline Lamb (Hotfoot)
N G Richards Edward Melville

Placings: *1*3111 (4486)
2001/02: 16^{1}GS, 16^{3}G, 16^{1}HY, 16^{1}S, 17^{1}GS

	Starts	1st	2nd	3rd	Win & Pl
NH Flat	1	1	0	0	1789
Hurdles	4	3	0	1	9507
Career Total	**5**	**4**	**0**	**1**	**11296**

113	3/02	Carl	2m1f	E Hdl	G-S	£3094
122	3/02	Ayr	2m	D Hdl	SFT	£3465
112	3/02	Ayr	2m	F Hdl	HVY	£2478
112	11/01	Ayr	2m	H NHF	G-S	£1788

Total win prize-money £10826

Going: Sf: 2-2 GS: 2-2 Gd: 0-1 GF: - Fm: 0-0
Distance: **2m/2m3: 4-5** 2m4-2m7: 0-0 3m+: 0-0
Track: **LH: 3-4** RH: 1-1 Tight: 0-0 Gall: 0-1
Aids: Bl: 0-0 Vi: 0-0 Tstrap: 0-0
Best Rating: 122 3/02 Ayr 2m soft Hdl

From a good family, he won a bumper first time and confirmed the promise he showed on his hurdles debut when winning in the mud next time at Ayr. Went on to complete a hat-trick and looks a nice prospect for novice chases.

Byzantium

98 100
8-y-o b g Shirley Heights-Dulceata (IRE) (Rousillon (USA))
H D Daly R Van Gelder

Placings: 02-33 (0778)
2001/02: 16^{3}GF, 20^{3}GF

	Starts	1st	2nd	3rd	Win & Pl
Hurdles	2	0	0	2	819
Career Total	**4**	**0**	**1**	**2**	**1568**

Going: Sf: 0-0 GS: 0-0 Gd: 0-0 GF: - Fm: 0-2
Distance: 2m/2m3: 0-1 2m4-2m7: 0-1 3m+: 0-0
Track: LH: 0-1 RH: 0-1 Tight: 0-0 Gall: 0-1
Aids: Bl: 0-0 Vi: 0-0 Tstrap: 0-0
Best Rating: 100 5/01 Hntg 2m110y gd-fm Hdl

C J's Will

(88h) (77h)
8-y-o b/br g Teenoso (USA)-Grayrose Double (Celtic Cone)
Mrs S Lamyman Miss J Robinson

Placings: *05/005*P-0 (0207)
2001/02: 16^{0}F

	Starts	1st	2nd	3rd	Win & Pl
Chases	1	0	0	0	
Career Total	**7**	**0**	**0**	**0**	**0**

Going: Sf: 0-0 GS: 0-0 Gd: 0-0 GF: - Fm: 0-1
Distance: 2m/2m3: 0-1 2m4-2m7: 0-0 3m+: 0-0
Track: LH: 0-1 RH: 0-0 Tight: 0-1 Gall: 0-0
Aids: Bl: 0-0 Vi: 0-1 Tstrap: 0-0
Best Rating: 93 2/00 Towc 2m heavy NHF

C'Est Deja Vu (IRE)

94 83
6-y-o b g Phardante (FR)-Quayside Romance (Quayside)
P F Nicholls C R Barnett

Placings: *05*F660 (4646)
2001/02: 17^{0}G, 18^{5}GS, 24^{F}S, 22^{6}S, 20^{6}S, 21^{0}G

	Starts	1st	2nd	3rd	Win & Pl
NH Flat	2	0	0	0	0
Hurdles	4	0	0	0	0
Career Total	**6**	**0**	**0**	**0**	**0**

Going: Sf: 0-3 GS: 0-1 Gd: 0-2 GF: - Fm: 0-0
Distance: 2m/2m3: 0-2 2m4-2m7: 0-3 3m+: 0-1
Track: LH: 0-1 RH: 0-3 Tight: 0-3 Gall: 0-0
Aids: Bl: 0-0 Vi: 0-0 Tstrap: 0-0
Best Rating: 93 11/01 Plum 2m2f gd-sft NHF

Ca Ne Fait Rien (IRE)

93f 85f
6-y-o gr g Denel (FR)-Fairytale-Ending (Sweet Story)
N M Babbage Ford Associated Racing Team Ii

Placings: *04* (4910)
2001/02: 16^{0}GF, 17^{4}G

	Starts	1st	2nd	3rd	Win & Pl
NH Flat	2	0	0	0	0
Career Total	**2**	**0**	**0**	**0**	**0**

Going: Sf: 0-0 GS: 0-0 Gd: 0-1 GF: - Fm: 0-1
Distance: 2m/2m3: 0-2 2m4-2m7: 0-0 3m+: 0-0
Track: LH: 0-0 RH: 0-2 Tight: 0-1 Gall: 0-0
Aids: Bl: 0-0 Vi: 0-0 Tstrap: 0-0
Best Rating: 80 4/02 MRas 2m1f110y good NHF

Caballe (USA)

102 121
5-y-o ch m Opening Verse (USA)-Attirance (FR) (Crowned Prince (USA))
N J Henderson (S P C Woods 3/9) The Caballeros

Placings: 133350 (4842)
2001/02: 16^{1}S, 17^{3}GS, 16^{3}G, 17^{3}HY, 16^{5}GF, 20^{0}G

	Starts	1st	2nd	3rd	Win & Pl
Hurdles	6	1	0	3	3705
Career Total	**6**	**1**	**0**	**3**	**3705**

121	12/01	Plum	2m	E Hdl	SFT	£2492

Total win prize-money £2492

Going: Sf: 1-2 GS: 0-1 Gd: 0-2 GF: - Fm: 0-1
Distance: **2m/2m3: 1-5** 2m4-2m7: 0-1 3m+: 0-0
Track: **LH: 1-4** RH: 0-2 **Tight: 1-5** Gall: 0-0
Aids: Bl: 0-0 Vi: 0-0 Tstrap: 0-0
Best Rating: 121 12/01 Plum 2m soft Hdl

Made a winning hurdles debut in testing ground at Plumpton, but failed to get home on several occasions subsequently and probably needs a sharp track and decent ground.

Cabaret Quest

(88h) (68h)

6-y-o ch g Pursuit Of Love-Cabaret Artiste (Shareef Dancer (USA))

J M Bradley Miss S Howell

Placings:0P40F **(1544)**

2001/02: 16^{0}GF, 19^{P}GF, 16^{4}GF, 17^{0}S, 17^{F}G

	Starts	1st	2nd	3rd	Win & Pl
Hurdles	5	0	0	0	0
Career Total	**5**	**0**	**0**	**0**	**0**

Going: Sf: 0-1 GS: 0-0 Gd: 0-1 GF: - Fm: 0-3
Distance: 2m/2m3: 0-4 2m4-2m7: 0-1 3m+: 0-0
Track: LH: 0-2 RH: 0-3 Tight: 0-1 Gall: 0-0
Aids: Bl: 0-0 Vi: 0-0 Tstrap: 0-2
Best Rating: 68 9/01 Worc 2m gd-fm Hdl

Caddy's First

94 **87**

10-y-o b g Petong-Love Scene (Carwhite)

P R Rodford P R Rodford

Placings:4406P45/P203525/40B106F60/6525511060/50/64-664 **(0956)**

2001/02: 20^{6}GF, 26^{6}GF, 20^{4}S

	Starts	1st	2nd	3rd	Win & Pl
Chases	3	0	0	0	0
Career Total	**40**	**3**	**3**	**1**	**12818**

87	10/98	Ludl	2m	G(0-95)HCh	G-F	£2864
87	10/98	MRas	2m4f	D Ch	SFT	£4760
83	7/97	Sthl	2m	G(0-95)HHdl	G-F	£2085

Total win prize-money £9709

Going: Sf: 0-1 GS: 0-0 Gd: 0-0 GF: - Fm: 0-2
Distance: 2m/2m3: 0-0 2m4-2m7: 0-2 3m+: 0-1
Track: LH: 0-2 RH: 0-0 Tight: 0-2 Gall: 0-0
Aids: Bl: 0-1 Vi: 0-0 Tstrap: 0-0
Best Rating: 100 11/95 Newb 2m110y good Hdl

Cades Bay

11-y-o b g Unfuwain (USA)-Antilla (Averof)

Miss L Gardner (Mrs S Gardner 2/8) Miss L Gardner

Placings:03/00F3/5P/0F-P0U55500 **(4483)**

2001/02: 19^{P}F, 24^{0}GF, 21^{U}GF, 16^{5}G, 21^{5}G, 21^{5}G, 24^{0}GF, 19^{0}G

	Starts	1st	2nd	3rd	Win & Pl
Chases	8	0	0	0	0
Career Total	**18**	**0**	**0**	**2**	**695**

Going: Sf: 0-0 GS: 0-0 Gd: 0-4 GF: - Fm: 0-4
Distance: 2m/2m3: 0-1 2m4-2m7: 0-5 3m+: 0-2
Track: LH: 0-6 RH: 0-2 Tight: 0-5 Gall: 0-0
Aids: Bl: 0-2 Vi: 0-0 Tstrap: 0-0
Best Rating: 94 3/00 Uttx 2m4f good Ch

Cadmax (IRE)

106 **92**

7-y-o b g Second Set (IRE)-Stella Ann (Ahonoora)

P J Hobbs A J Allright

Placings:34030/35 **(0587)**

2001/02: 16^{3}G, 16^{5}GF

	Starts	1st	2nd	3rd	Win & Pl
Hurdles	2	0	0	1	418
Career Total	**7**	**0**	**0**	**3**	**1111**

Going: Sf: 0-0 GS: 0-0 Gd: 0-1 GF: - Fm: 0-1
Distance: 2m/2m3: 0-2 2m4-2m7: 0-0 3m+: 0-0
Track: LH: 0-1 RH: 0-1 Tight: 0-1 Gall: 0-1
Aids: Bl: 0-0 Vi: 0-0 Tstrap: 0-0
Best Rating: 92 5/01 Hntg 2m110y good Hdl

Cadougold (FR)

115 **144**

11-y-o b g Cadoudal (FR)-Fontaine Aux Faons (FR) (Nadjar (FR))

M C Pipe D A Johnson

Placings:F316511/00253/34141/22022/2/1P1F13-1434P342 **(4845)**

2001/02: 21^{1}GF, 20^{4}G, 24^{3}G, 20^{4}S, 24^{P}G, 24^{3}GS, 25^{4}G, 24^{2}G

	Starts	1st	2nd	3rd	Win & Pl
Chases	8	1	1	2	23007
Career Total	**37**	**9**	**7**	**6**	**132923**

147	5/01	NAbb	2m5f110y	E Ch	G-F	£3614
124	4/01	Hayd	2m	C Ch	SFT	£6776
134	3/01	Wwck	2m4f110y	E Ch	HVY	£3133
140	11/00	Tntn	2m3f	C Ch	G-S	£6080
146	4/97	Aint	2m4f	B HHdl	GD	£12653
137	12/96	Chep	2m4f110y	B(0-140)HHdl	SFT	£4935
95	4/95	Chep	2m110y	E Hdl	GD	£2500
108	4/95	Chep	2m110y	E Hdl	FRM	£2794
120	3/95	Wind	2m4f	E Hdl	HVY	£2267

Total win prize-money £44755

Going: Sf: 0-1 GS: 0-1 Gd: 0-5 GF: - Fm: 1-1
Distance: 2m/2m3: 0-0 **2m4-2m7: 1-3** 3m+: 0-5
Track: **LH: 1-6** RH: 0-2 **Tight: 1-3** Gall: 0-2
Aids: Bl: 0-0 Vi: 0-0 Tstrap: 0-0
Best Rating: 153 4/98 Chep 2m110y heavy Hdl

Handicap hurdler/ chaser. Seemingly effective on a variety of ground, he has a high cruising speed and is effective at around two and a half miles but has shown he stays three.

Cadrillon (FR)

12-y-o br g Le Pontet (FR)-Jenvraie (FR) (Night And Day)

Miss J E Foster (A J Lockwood 7/4) Miss J E Foster

Placings:4000F4/0/13P45326P0/54P4545443P/6464P2550P0P-PP **(4892)**

2001/02: 25^{P}GF, 31^{P}G

	Starts	1st	2nd	3rd	Win & Pl
Chases	2	0	0	0	
Career Total	**42**	**1**	**2**	**3**	**8365**

95	5/98	Hexm	3m1f	H Ch	G-S	£2583

Total win prize-money £2583

Going: Sf: 0-0 GS: 0-0 Gd: 0-1 GF: - Fm: 0-1
Distance: 2m/2m3: 0-0 2m4-2m7: 0-0 3m+: 0-2
Track: LH: 0-1 RH: 0-0 Tight: 0-0 Gall: 0-0
Aids: Bl: 0-0 Vi: 0-0 Tstrap: 0-0
Best Rating: 95 3/99 Hexm 4m soft Ch

Cadw (IRE)

71 **27**

7-y-o b g Cadeaux Genereux-Night Jar (Night Shift (USA))

John Allen Nicholson Jones

Placings:0-0 **(0058)**

2001/02: 17^{0}GS

	Starts	1st	2nd	3rd	Win & Pl
Hurdles	1	0	0	0	
Career Total	**2**	**0**	**0**	**0**	

Going: Sf: 0-0 GS: 0-1 Gd: 0-0 GF: - Fm: 0-0
Distance: 2m/2m3: 0-1 2m4-2m7: 0-0 3m+: 0-0
Track: LH: 0-0 RH: 0-1 Tight: 0-1 Gall: 0-0
Aids: Bl: 0-0 Vi: 0-0 Tstrap: 0-0
Best Rating: 47 3/01 MRas 2m1f110y gd-sft Hdl

Caen Dancer

7-y-o gr g Thethingaboutitis (USA)-Interview (Interrex (CAN))

F Jordan Trevor Price

Placings:00 **(1799)**

2001/02: 16^{0}GF, 16^{0}S

	Starts	1st	2nd	3rd	Win & Pl
NH Flat	2	0	0	0	
Career Total	**2**	**0**	**0**	**0**	

Going: Sf: 0-1 GS: 0-0 Gd: 0-0 GF: - Fm: 0-1
Distance: 2m/2m3: 0-2 2m4-2m7: 0-0 3m+: 0-0
Track: LH: 0-2 RH: 0-0 Tight: 0-1 Gall: 0-0
Aids: Bl: 0-0 Vi: 0-0 Tstrap: 0-0
Best Rating:

Caernarfon Bay (IRE)

7-y-o ch g Royal Academy (USA)-Bay Shade (USA) (Sharpen Up)

R J Hodges A Barrow

Placings:00/06064-P **(1340)**

2001/02: 22^{P}GF

	Starts	1st	2nd	3rd	Win & Pl
Hurdles	1	0	0	0	
Career Total	**8**	**0**	**0**	**0**	**0**

Going: Sf: 0-0 GS: 0-0 Gd: 0-0 GF: - Fm: 0-1
Distance: 2m/2m3: 0-0 2m4-2m7: 0-1 3m+: 0-0
Track: LH: 0-1 RH: 0-0 Tight: 0-1 Gall: 0-0
Aids: Bl: 0-0 Vi: 0-0 Tstrap: 0-0
Best Rating: 85 3/00 Winc 2m gd-sft Hdl

Caesar's Palace (GER)

106 **127**

5-y-o ch g Lomitas-Caraveine (FR) (Nikos)

M C Pipe Pipe Monkees

Placings:111156-25000P4410 **(4939a)**

2001/02: 18^{2}GF, 19^{5}GS, 19^{0}GS, 17^{0}GS, 19^{0}S, 16^{P}HY, 17^{4}S, 22^{4}G, 24^{1}F, 20^{0}Y

	Starts	1st	2nd	3rd	Win & Pl
Hurdles	10	1	1	0	6137
Career Total	**16**	**5**	**1**	**0**	**22530**

125	4/02	Extr	3m110y	D(0-120)HHdl	FRM	£5401
124	12/00	Chel	2m1f	B Hdl	SFT	£7150
119	11/00	Newb	2m110y	D Hdl	SFT	£3887
119	9/00	Plum	2m	E Hdl	G-F	£2352
105	8/00	Font	2m2f110y	E Hdl	G-F	£2254

Total win prize-money £21045

Going: Sf: 0-3 GS: 0-3 Gd: 0-1 GF: - Fm: 1-2
Distance: 2m/2m3: 0-4 2m4-2m7: 0-5 **3m+: 1-1**
Track: LH: 0-2 **RH: 1-8** Tight: 0-7 Gall: 0-0
Aids: Bl: 0-1 **Vi: 1-7** Tstrap: 0-0
Best Rating: 125 4/02 Extr 3m110y firm Hdl

A prolific winning novice hurdler in 2000. Showed the benefit of a return to fast ground when stepped up to three miles at Exeter in April 2002 and looked most progressive when winning at Chepstow the following month. At his best when making the running.

Cage Aux Folles (IRE)

94 **120**
7-y-o b g Kenmare (FR)-Ivory Thread (USA) (Sir Ivor)
R Lee The Cage Aux Folles Partnership

Placings:403/P3032534451/4511P31443021-0P **(1583)**
2001/02: 17°GS, 17^{P}GS

	Starts	1st	2nd	3rd	Win & Pl
Hurdles	2	0	0	0	
Career Total	**29**	**5**	**2**	**6**	**22402**

120 4/01 NAbb 2m1f E(0-115)HHdl SFT £5590
117 10/00 Bang 2m1f F(0-110)HHdl SFT £4309
107 7/00 Worc 2m E(0-115)HHdl G-F £3464
108 6/00 NAbb 2m1f F(0-105)HHdl G-F £2597
96 4/00 Winc 2m F(0-110)HHdl G-S £2247
Total win prize-money £18209

Going: Sf: 0-0 GS: 0-2 Gd: 0-0 GF: - Fm: 0-0
Distance: 2m/2m3: 0-2 2m4-2m7: 0-0 3m+: 0-0
Track: LH: 0-1 RH: 0-1 Tight: 0-2 Gall: 0-0
Aids: Bl: 0-0 Vi: 0-0 Tstrap: 0-2
Best Rating: 120 4/01 NAbb 2m1f soft Hdl

Caher Society (IRE)

10-y-o ch g Moscow Society (USA)-Dame's Delight (Ballymoss)
Paul Morris R D J Swinburne

Placings:0/05/P33P0P/35F-261P **(4678)**
2001/02: 24^{2}GS, 23^{6}S, 20^{1}S, 25^{P}G

	Starts	1st	2nd	3rd	Win & Pl
Chases	4	1	1	0	3537
Career Total	**16**	**1**	**1**	**3**	**5322**

116 3/02 Ludl 2m4f H Ch SFT £2786
Total win prize-money £2786

Going: Sf: 1-2 GS: 0-1 Gd: 0-1 GF: - Fm: 0-0
Distance: 2m/2m3: 0-0 **2m4-2m7: 1-1** 3m+: 0-3
Track: LH: 0-1 **RH: 1-3 Tight: 1-3** Gall: 0-0
Aids: Bl: 0-0 Vi: 0-0 Tstrap: 0-0
Best Rating: 116 3/02 Ludl 2m4f soft Ch

Modest pointer/hunter chaser.

Cake O' The North (IRE)

81(97h) (85h)**45**
6-y-o ch g Eve's Error-Butlers Pier (Good Thyne (USA))
L Lungo Lightbody Celebration Cakes Ltd

Placings:0/5-00350 **(4769)**
2001/02: 17°HY, 20°S, 24^{3}HY, 27^{5}S, 25°GF

	Starts	1st	2nd	3rd	Win & Pl
Hurdles	4	0	0	1	292
Chases	1	0	0	0	0
Career Total	**7**	**0**	**0**	**1**	**292**

Going: Sf: 0-4 GS: 0-0 Gd: 0-0 GF: - Fm: 0-1
Distance: 2m/2m3: 0-1 2m4-2m7: 0-1 3m+: 0-3
Track: LH: 0-4 RH: 0-1 Tight: 0-1 Gall: 0-1
Aids: Bl: 0-0 Vi: 0-0 Tstrap: 0-0
Best Rating: 85 4/01 Weth 2m4f110y gd-sft Hdl

Lightly-raced staying hurdler, stays three miles and needs soft ground.

Caldamus

10-y-o gr g Scallywag-Portodamus (Porto Bello)
Miss S Waugh J W Elliott

Placings:465/3514/**B46**/**P2** **(4416)**
2001/02: 20^{P}GF, 20^{2}S

	Starts	1st	2nd	3rd	Win & Pl
Chases	2	0	1	0	636
Career Total	**12**	**1**	**1**	**1**	**4153**

110 2/99 Sedg 2m5f110y E Hdl GD £2582
Total win prize-money £2583

Going: Sf: 0-1 GS: 0-0 Gd: 0-0 GF: - Fm: 0-1
Distance: 2m/2m3: 0-0 2m4-2m7: 0-2 3m+: 0-0
Track: LH: 0-1 RH: 0-0 Tight: 0-1 Gall: 0-0
Aids: Bl: 0-0 Vi: 0-0 Tstrap: 0-0
Best Rating: 110 2/99 Sedg 2m5f110y good Hdl

Caledonian Express

98 **76**
7-y-o b m Northern Park (USA)-New Edition (Great Nephew)
J R Best Inside Track Racing Club

Placings:0044/24016/512230P-00F424F **(1479)**
2001/02: 20°GF, 19°G, 17^{F}G, 16^{4}GF, 22^{2}GF, 22^{4}GF, 21^{F}GS

	Starts	1st	2nd	3rd	Win & Pl
Hurdles	7	0	1	0	654
Career Total	**23**	**2**	**4**	**1**	**6103**

82 5/00 Fknm 2m G Hdl FRM £1466
76 2/00 Fknm 2m G(0-90)HHdl GD £1830
Total win prize-money £3298

Going: Sf: 0-0 GS: 0-1 Gd: 0-2 GF: - Fm: 0-4
Distance: 2m/2m3: 0-3 2m4-2m7: 0-4 3m+: 0-0
Track: LH: 0-7 RH: 0-0 Tight: 0-6 Gall: 0-0
Aids: Bl: 0-0 Vi: 0-0 Tstrap: 0-0
Best Rating: 94 10/00 Folk 2m1f110y gd-fm Hdl

Caley Gold (IRE)

99
6-y-o ch g Houmayoun (FR)-Flashy Gold (Le Bavard (FR))
B Ellison B J Tennant

Placings:430/550-P **(1500)**
2001/02: 21^{P}G

	Starts	1st	2nd	3rd	Win & Pl
Hurdles	1	0	0	0	
Career Total	**7**	**0**	**0**	**1**	**300**

Going: Sf: 0-0 GS: 0-0 Gd: 0-1 GF: - Fm: 0-0
Distance: 2m/2m3: 0-0 2m4-2m7: 0-1 3m+: 0-0
Track: LH: 0-1 RH: 0-0 Tight: 0-1 Gall: 0-0
Aids: Bl: 0-0 Vi: 0-0 Tstrap: 0-0
Best Rating: 99 4/01 Ayr 2m4f good Hdl

Calfstown Lord

95 **87**
10-y-o b g Arctic Lord-Calfstown Maid (Master Buck)
C J Gray (B G Powell 1/5) P Popham, F D Popham, T Bartlett

Placings:005/02220P/P-04FU604023 **(4864)**
2001/02: 24°G, 21^{4}HY, 24^{F}GS, 25^{U}S, 26^{6}S, 24°GS, 24^{4}S, 21°G, 23^{2}F, 25^{3}F

	Starts	1st	2nd	3rd	Win & Pl
Chases	10	0	1	1	2589
Career Total	**20**	**0**	**4**	**1**	**5889**

Going: Sf: 0-4 GS: 0-2 Gd: 0-2 GF: - Fm: 0-2
Distance: 2m/2m3: 0-0 2m4-2m7: 0-2 3m+: 0-8
Track: LH: 0-2 RH: 0-6 Tight: 0-6 Gall: 0-1
Aids: Bl: 0-2 Vi: 0-1 Tstrap: 0-4
Best Rating: 109 2/00 Tntn 3m soft Ch

Moderate chaser, stays three miles and handles any ground. Has worn headgear.

Calhoun (FR)

97(104h) (121h)**104**
7-y-o b g Sheyrann-Blanche Dame (FR) (Saint Cyrien (FR))
P J Hobbs Mrs R J Skan

Placings:32/12501/F6P-6434060 **(2640)**
2001/02: 16^{6}GF, 18^{4}GF, 16^{3}GF, 16^{4}GS, 19^{0}F, 16^{6}GF, 16^{0}GF

	Starts	1st	2nd	3rd	Win & Pl
Hurdles	2	0	0	0	0
Chases	5	0	0	1	893
Career Total	**17**	**2**	**2**	**2**	**7594**

124 3/00 Winc 2m E(0-105)HHdl G-S £2611
113 11/99 Winc 2m E Hdl GD £2276
Total win prize-money £4887

Going: Sf: 0-0 GS: 0-1 Gd: 0-0 GF: - Fm: 0-6
Distance: 2m/2m3: 0-7 2m4-2m7: 0-0 3m+: 0-0
Track: LH: 0-4 RH: 0-3 Tight: 0-5 Gall: 0-0
Aids: Bl: 0-0 Vi: 0-0 Tstrap: 0-0
Best Rating: 126 5/00 Strf 2m110y good Hdl

Caliban (IRE)

107 **95**
4-y-o ch g Rainbows For Life (CAN)-Amour Toujours (IRE) (Law Society (USA))
Ian Williams Jim Edmunds

Placings:522224323445 **(4813)**
2001/02: 17^{5}G, 17^{2}G, 16^{2}GF, 17^{2}G, 16^{2}GF, 18^{4}GF, 17^{3}GS, 16^{2}S, 17^{3}G, 20^{4}S, 17^{4}S, 17^{5}GF

	Starts	1st	2nd	3rd	Win & Pl
Hurdles	12	0	5	2	5170
Career Total	**12**	**0**	**5**	**2**	**5170**

Going: Sf: 0-3 GS: 0-1 Gd: 0-4 GF: - Fm: 0-4
Distance: 2m/2m3: 0-11 2m4-2m7: 0-1 3m+: 0-0
Track: LH: 0-9 RH: 0-3 Tight: 0-5 Gall: 0-2
Aids: Bl: 0-0 Vi: 0-1 Tstrap: 0-0
Best Rating: 95 3/02 Hrfd 2m1f soft Hdl

Regularly in the frame in juvenile hurdles, but does not seem to want to win. Looks best suited by soft ground and trips around two miles.

Calidar (IRE)

104 **95**
5-y-o b g Shernazar-Caladira (IRE) (Darshaan)
Ian Williams Andrew & Philipa Wyer

Placings:_0-200_ **(2683)**
2001/02: 17^{2}G, 16^{0}S, 16^{0}G

	Starts	1st	2nd	3rd	Win & Pl
NH Flat	2	0	1	0	476
Hurdles	1	0	0	0	0
Career Total	**4**	**0**	**1**	**0**	**476**

Going: Sf: 0-1 GS: 0-0 Gd: 0-2 GF: - Fm: 0-0
Distance: 2m/2m3: 0-3 2m4-2m7: 0-0 3m+: 0-0
Track: LH: 0-3 RH: 0-0 Tight: 0-1 Gall: 0-1
Aids: Bl: 0-0 Vi: 0-0 Tstrap: 0-0
Best Rating: 95 12/01 Donc 2m110y good Hdl

Caliwag (IRE)

85 **74**

6-y-o b g Lahib (USA)-Mitsubishi Style (Try My Best (USA))
Jamie Poulton Lottie Collins Partnership

Placings:006 **(2515)**
2001/02: 16^{0}GS, 16^{0}G, 16^{6}S

	Starts	1st	2nd	3rd	Win & Pl
Hurdles	3	0	0	0	0
Career Total	**3**	**0**	**0**	**0**	**0**

Going: Sf: 0-1 GS: 0-1 Gd: 0-1 GF: - Fm: 0-0
Distance: 2m/2m3: 0-3 2m4-2m7: 0-0 3m+: 0-0
Track: LH: 0-2 RH: 0-1 Tight: 0-2 Gall: 0-0
Aids: Bl: 0-0 Vi: 0-0 Tstrap: 0-0
Best Rating: 74 11/01 Plum 2m good Hdl

Call Bob (IRE)

12-y-o ch g Lancastrian-Call Bird (Le Johnstan)
Mrs Edward Crow R J French

Placings:_0/0/500/_**P6510PP/4P3044202413104P04/40 4013F0016/40650-F2P** **(4376)**
2001/02: 24^{F}GF, 21^{2}GF, 20^{P}S

	Starts	1st	2nd	3rd	Win & Pl
Chases	3	0	1	0	911
Career Total	**49**	**5**	**3**	**3**	**31325**

114	10/99	Punc	2m2f	(0-116)HCh	YLD	£4928
103	7/99	Klny	2m1f	(0-95)HCh	GD	£3683
119	10/98	Gowr	2m	(0-116)HCh	Y-S	£8445
101	9/98	List	2m4f	Ch	SH	£3586
100	10/97	Tipp	2m	Ch	GD	£3730

Total win prize-money £24375

Going: Sf: 0-1 GS: 0-0 Gd: 0-0 GF: - Fm: 0-2
Distance: 2m/2m3: 0-0 2m4-2m7: 0-2 3m+: 0-1
Track: LH: 0-1 RH: 0-2 Tight: 0-2 Gall: 0-1
Aids: Bl: 0-0 Vi: 0-0 Tstrap: 0-0
Best Rating: 119 10/98 Gowr 2m yld-sft Ch

Call For Gold (USA)

82f **88f**

5-y-o ch g Caerleon (USA)-Norfolk Lily (Blakeney)
J R Norton J Norton

Placings:_0500_ **(4873)**
2001/02: 17^{0}GF, 17^{5}G, 17^{0}GS, 16^{0}GF

	Starts	1st	2nd	3rd	Win & Pl
NH Flat	4	0	0	0	0
Career Total	**4**	**0**	**0**	**0**	**0**

Going: Sf: 0-0 GS: 0-1 Gd: 0-1 GF: - Fm: 0-2
Distance: 2m/2m3: 0-4 2m4-2m7: 0-0 3m+: 0-0
Track: LH: 0-2 RH: 0-1 Tight: 0-2 Gall: 0-0
Aids: Bl: 0-0 Vi: 0-1 Tstrap: 0-0
Best Rating: 88 10/01 Sedg 2m1f good NHF

Call It A Day (IRE)

12-y-o b g Callernish-Arctic Bavard (Le Bavard (FR))
Michael Appleby Mrs Jane Lane

Placings:01135/**122122/131454/3224F31/2P44323/3 FP56/06-30** **(4826)**
2001/02: 26^{3}S, 26^{0}G

	Starts	1st	2nd	3rd	Win & Pl
Chases	2	0	0	1	1065
Career Total	**40**	**7**	**8**	**8**	**221614**

155	4/98	Sand	3m5f110y	A HCh	G-S	£63490
147	2/97	Newb	3m2f110y	B(0-145)HCh	GD	£7196
139	11/96	Uttx	2m5f	B(0-145)HCh	G-F	£6827
118	2/96	Uttx	2m5f	E Ch	GD	£3022
126	12/95	Chep	2m3f110y	D Ch	G-S	£3488
101	1/95	Nott	2m5f110y	F(0-100)HHdl	SFT	£2390
95	12/94	Hrfd	2m3f110y	Hdl	G-S	£2108

Total win prize-money £88523

Going: Sf: 0-1 GS: 0-0 Gd: 0-1 GF: - Fm: 0-0
Distance: 2m/2m3: 0-0 2m4-2m7: 0-0 3m+: 0-2
Track: LH: 0-1 RH: 0-0 Tight: 0-1 Gall: 0-1
Aids: Bl: 0-0 Vi: 0-0 Tstrap: 0-0
Best Rating: 155 3/99 Uttx 4m2f gd-sft Ch

A one-time high-class staying handicapper (Whitbread winner) he now plies his trade in hunter chases.

Call Me Ash (IRE)

53 **82**

7-y-o b g Religiously (USA)-Arctic Laura (Le Bavard (FR))
Miss Venetia Williams Favourites Racing Ltd

Placings:1P5 **(4544)**
2001/02: 23^{1}S, 22^{P}S, 26^{5}G

	Starts	1st	2nd	3rd	Win & Pl
Hurdles	3	1	0	0	2422
Career Total	**3**	**1**	**0**	**0**	**2422**

82	1/02	Fknm	2m7f110y	E Hdl	SFT	£2422

Total win prize-money £2422

Going: Sf: 1-2 GS: 0-0 Gd: 0-1 GF: - Fm: 0-0
Distance: 2m/2m3: 0-0 2m4-2m7: 0-1 **3m+: 1-2**
Track: **LH: 1-1** RH: 0-2 **Tight: 1-2** Gall: 0-0
Aids: Bl: 0-0 Vi: 0-0 Tstrap: 0-0
Best Rating: 82 1/02 Fknm 2m7f110y soft Hdl

Made a winning debut in a Fakenham novice hurdle in January 2002. Stays well.

Call Me Jack (IRE)

(107h) (102h)**107**

6-y-o b g Lord Americo-Tawney Rose (Tarqogan)
B Ellison R G Fell

Placings:_6/_026521-431F **(2530)**
2001/02: 17^{4}S, 17^{3}S, 17^{1}S, 17^{F}S

	Starts	1st	2nd	3rd	Win & Pl
Hurdles	3	1	0	1	2719
Chases	1	0	0	0	0
Career Total	**11**	**2**	**2**	**1**	**8135**

102	11/01	Sedg	2m1f	E(0-115)HHdl	SFT	£2338
97	4/01	Prth	2m110y	D Hdl	HVY	£3332

Total win prize-money £5670

Going: Sf: 1-4 GS: 0-0 Gd: 0-0 GF: - Fm: 0-0
Distance: **2m/2m3: 1-4** 2m4-2m7: 0-0 3m+: 0-0
Track: **LH: 1-1** RH: 0-3 **Tight: 1-2** Gall: 0-0
Aids: Bl: 0-0 Vi: 0-0 **Tstrap: 1-4**
Best Rating: 108 12/01 MRas 2m1f110y soft Ch

Call Me Sonic

88 **92**

6-y-o b g Henbit (USA)-Call-Me-Dinky (Mart Lane)
R H Alner (B J Llewellyn 29/12) C A Fuller

Placings:_0_P45 **(4850)**
2001/02: 16^{0}G, 16^{P}S, 16^{4}G, 22^{5}G

	Starts	1st	2nd	3rd	Win & Pl
NH Flat	1	0	0	0	0
Hurdles	3	0	0	0	0
Career Total	**4**	**0**	**0**	**0**	**0**

Going: Sf: 0-1 GS: 0-0 Gd: 0-3 GF: - Fm: 0-0
Distance: 2m/2m3: 0-3 2m4-2m7: 0-1 3m+: 0-0
Track: LH: 0-2 RH: 0-2 Tight: 0-2 Gall: 0-0
Aids: Bl: 0-0 Vi: 0-0 Tstrap: 0-0
Best Rating: 92 4/02 Winc 2m good Hdl

Shaped with promise on his second run over hurdles, but has yet to prove his stamina.

Call My Guest (IRE)

102 **102**

12-y-o b g Be My Guest (USA)-Overcall (Bustino)
R E Peacock Mr Derek D & Mrs Jean P Clee

Placings:2232322P/2211310212/54F0/5220005F4/23 /U41P13F053/66U046231/34F404-5503 **(4149)**
2001/02: 17^{5}G, 20^{5}G, 20^{0}GS, 20^{3}GS

	Starts	1st	2nd	3rd	Win & Pl
Hurdles	4	0	0	1	772
Career Total	**62**	**7**	**13**	**9**	**55283**

110	4/00	Ludl	2m5f	D(0-120)HHdl	G-S	£4160
121	7/98	MRas	2m1f110y	C(0-135)HHdl	G-F	£10317
121	6/98	Worc	2m4f	D(0-120)HHdl	GD	£2979
130	4/95	Weth	2m4f110y	C(0-135)HHdl	GD	£4207
128	3/95	Weth	2m4f110y	D(0-125)HHdl	SFT	£2924
121	11/94	Weth	2m4f110y	HHdl	G-S	£2807
109	11/94	Carl	2m4f110y	Hdl	GD	£2233

Total win prize-money £29631

Going: Sf: 0-0 GS: 0-2 Gd: 0-2 GF: - Fm: 0-0
Distance: 2m/2m3: 0-1 2m4-2m7: 0-3 3m+: 0-0
Track: LH: 0-4 RH: 0-0 Tight: 0-2 Gall: 0-0
Aids: Bl: 0-0 Vi: 0-0 Tstrap: 0-0
Best Rating: 130 5/95 Asct 2m4f gd-fm Hdl

A useful handicap hurdler in his younger days, he retains ability. Effective at two and a half miles, does not want the ground too soft.

Call The Shots (IRE)

103 **107**

13-y-o br g Callernish-Golden Strings (Perspex)
J Wade John Wade

Placings:0U0000/**0033/412U/421/P/PPPPP/6531/61** **(1348)**
2001/02: 25^{6}GF, 27^{1}GF

	Starts	1st	2nd	3rd	Win & Pl
Chases	2	1	0	0	3543
Career Total	**29**	**4**	**2**	**3**	**21011**

107	9/01	Sedg	3m3f	E(0-115)HCh	G-F	£3542
101	10/99	Sedg	3m3f	F(0-100)HCh	G-F	£3022
108	3/97	Kels	3m4f	C(0-130)HCh	GD	£6775
104	1/96	Sedg	3m3f	E Ch	G-F	£3647

Total win prize-money £16987

Going: Sf: 0-0 GS: 0-0 Gd: 0-0 GF: - Fm: 1-2
Distance: 2m/2m3: 0-0 2m4-2m7: 0-0 **3m+: 1-2**
Track: **LH: 1-1** RH: 0-1 **Tight: 1-2** Gall: 0-0
Aids: Bl: 0-0 Vi: 0-0 Tstrap: 0-0
Best Rating: 108 3/97 Kels 3m4f good Ch

Call The Tune

10-y-o b m Lancastrian-Wand Of Youth (Mandamus)
P J Lutman P J Lutman

Placings: *06/0/5*-P (0321)
2001/02: 26^{P}G

	Starts	1st	2nd	3rd	Win & Pl
Chases	1	0	0	0	
Career Total	**5**	**0**	**0**	**0**	**0**

Going: Sf: 0-0 GS: 0-0 Gd: 0-1 GF: - Fm: 0-0
Distance: 2m/2m3: 0-0 2m4-2m7: 0-0 3m+: 0-1
Track: LH: 0-0 RH: 0-1 Tight: 0-1 Gall: 0-0
Aids: Bl: 0-0 Vi: 0-0 Tstrap: 0-0
Best Rating: 88 3/98 Ayr 2m gd-sft NHF

Calladine (IRE)

109 **142**

6-y-o b g Erin's Isle-Motus (Anfield)
C Roche S J Murphy

Placings: 1F6000/031613-50 (4193)
2001/02: 24^{5}YS, 25^{0}GS

	Starts	1st	2nd	3rd	Win & Pl
Hurdles	2	0	0	0	
Career Total	**14**	**3**	**0**	**2**	**33985**

145	12/00	Leop	3m	HHdl	SH	£7176
131	11/00	Naas	2m4f	HHdl	Y-S	£10400
127	12/99	Leop	2m	Hdl	SH	£14508

Total win prize-money £32085

Going: Sf: 0-0 GS: 0-1 Gd: 0-0 GF: - Fm: 0-0
Distance: 2m/2m3: 0-0 2m4-2m7: 0-0 3m+: 0-2
Track: LH: 0-2 RH: 0-0 Tight: 0-0 Gall: 0-1
Aids: Bl: 0-0 Vi: 0-0 Tstrap: 0-0
Best Rating: 145 12/00 Leop 3m sft-hvy Hdl

He developed into a decent staying hurdler in 2000/1. He has a decent turn of foot and is often held up.

Calldat Seventeen

106 **114**

6-y-o b g Komaite (USA)-Westminster Waltz (Dance In Time (CAN))
P W D'Arcy Keith Harrison & Terry Miller

Placings: P-1R (3872)
2001/02: 16^{1}GS, 20^{R}S

	Starts	1st	2nd	3rd	Win & Pl
Hurdles	2	1	0	0	2562
Career Total	**3**	**1**	**0**	**0**	**2562**

114	1/02	Hntg	2m110y	E Hdl	G-S	£2562

Total win prize-money £2562

Going: Sf: 0-1 GS: 1-1 Gd: 0-0 GF: - Fm: 0-0
Distance: **2m/2m3: 1-1** 2m4-2m7: 0-1 3m+: 0-0
Track: LH: 0-0 **RH: 1-2** Tight: 0-0 **Gall: 1-2**
Aids: Bl: 0-0 Vi: 0-0 Tstrap: 0-0
Best Rating: 114 1/02 Hntg 2m110y gd-sft Hdl

A decent Flat handicapper, he made all in a novice hurdle at Huntingdon in January.

Calleva Star (IRE)

11-y-o b g Over The River (FR)-Ask The Madam (Strong Gale)
Mrs F E Needham Michael D Abrahams

Placings: 6P/**442342/332413/P3F431FP/4U3-PB0U02** (4833)
2001/02: 25^{P}G, 28^{B}GF, 33^{0}G, 25^{U}GS, 21^{0}G, 27^{2}G

	Starts	1st	2nd	3rd	Win & Pl
Chases	6	0	1	0	868
Career Total	**31**	**2**	**4**	**7**	**16140**

108	3/99	Plum	3m1f110y	E(0-125)HCh	HVY	£3420
104	3/98	Plum	3m1f110y	E Ch	GD	£3130

Total win prize-money £6550

Going: Sf: 0-1 GS: 0-1 Gd: 0-3 GF: - Fm: 0-1
Distance: 2m/2m3: 0-0 2m4-2m7: 0-1 3m+: 0-5
Track: LH: 0-4 RH: 0-1 Tight: 0-3 Gall: 0-0
Aids: Bl: 0-0 Vi: 0-0 Tstrap: 0-0
Best Rating: 108 3/99 Plum 3m1f110y heavy Ch

Fair pointer who generally struggles in hunter chases.

Callfourseasons (IRE)

10-y-o b g Euphemism-Home And Dry (Crash Course)
L Lungo R Hewitt And C & J Stockton

Placings: *66/5*6041160/**14P16/51PPP-P** (2770)
2001/02: 25^{P}G

	Starts	1st	2nd	3rd	Win & Pl
Hurdles	1	0	0	0	
Career Total	**21**	**5**	**0**	**0**	**16185**

135	12/00	Sthl	3m110y	E(0-115)HCh	SFT	£2798
135	3/00	Bang	3m110y	D(0-125)HCh	SFT	£4777
121	11/99	Hayd	2m6f	D(0-115)HCh	GD	£3922
110	11/98	Kels	2m6f110y	E(0-100)HHdl	SFT	£2290
97	10/98	Weth	3m1f	F(0-105)HHdl	GD	£1917

Total win prize-money £15706

Going: Sf: 0-0 GS: 0-0 Gd: 0-1 GF: - Fm: 0-0
Distance: 2m/2m3: 0-0 2m4-2m7: 0-0 3m+: 0-1
Track: LH: 0-1 RH: 0-0 Tight: 0-1 Gall: 0-0
Aids: Bl: 0-0 Vi: 0-0 Tstrap: 0-0
Best Rating: 135 12/00 Sthl 3m110y soft Ch

Formerly a fair sort in modest handicap chases at around three miles, but has a job to complete these days.

Callindoe (IRE)

12-y-o b m Callernish-Winsome Doe (Buckskin (FR))
J L Needham Miss Joanna Needham

Placings: *425/600*/6-**PPUP** (4541)
2001/02: 22^{P}G, 25^{P}G, 24^{U}S, 25^{P}G

	Starts	1st	2nd	3rd	Win & Pl
Hurdles	1	0	0	0	0
Chases	3	0	0	0	0
Career Total	**11**	**0**	**1**	**0**	**463**

Going: Sf: 0-1 GS: 0-0 Gd: 0-3 GF: - Fm: 0-0
Distance: 2m/2m3: 0-0 2m4-2m7: 0-1 3m+: 0-3
Track: LH: 0-1 RH: 0-3 Tight: 0-1 Gall: 0-0
Aids: Bl: 0-0 Vi: 0-0 Tstrap: 0-0
Best Rating: 85 12/96 Bang 2m1f good NHF

Calling Brave (IRE)

101f **132f**

6-y-o ch g Bob Back (USA)-Queenie Kelly (The Parson)
N J Henderson Sir Robert Ogden

Placings: *1420* (4235)
2001/02: 17^{1}GS, 16^{4}GS, 16^{2}S, 16^{0}GS

	Starts	1st	2nd	3rd	Win & Pl
NH Flat	4	1	1	0	3674
Career Total	**4**	**1**	**1**	**0**	**3674**

132	11/01	Aint	2m1f	H NHF	G-S	£2149

Total win prize-money £2149

Going: Sf: 0-1 GS: 1-3 Gd: 0-0 GF: - Fm: 0-0
Distance: **2m/2m3: 1-4** 2m4-2m7: 0-0 3m+: 0-0
Track: LH: 0-2 RH: 0-1 Tight: 0-0 Gall: 0-0
Aids: Bl: 0-0 Vi: 0-0 Tstrap: 0-0
Best Rating: 132 11/01 Aint 2m1f gd-sft NHF

A half-brother to Queens Harbour and Ottowa. He made an impressive debut in an Aintree bumper, but struggled in good races subsequently. Needs soft ground.

Callisoe Bay (IRE)

13-y-o b/br g Callernish-Granagh Bay (Cade's County)
O Sherwood O M C Sherwood

Placings: *14/11250/***F132115/122U0025/11F1P33/523 P0/21PP0/6-5** (3875)
2001/02: 24^{5}GS

	Starts	1st	2nd	3rd	Win & Pl
Chases	1	0	0	0	0
Career Total	**41**	**11**	**7**	**4**	**94268**

150	11/99	Hayd	3m4f110y	C(0-135)HCh	G-S	£9987
152	1/98	Winc	2m5f	B Ch	G-S	£8772
152	11/97	Newb	2m4f	B HCh	G-S	£7451
152	11/97	Uttx	2m5f	B(0-145)HCh	SFT	£6976
141	10/96	Strf	2m1f110y	C(0-135)HCh	GD	£4815
124	3/96	Sand	2m	C Ch	G-S	£4735
119	3/96	Donc	2m110y	D Ch	G-F	£3822
104	11/95	Uttx	2m	D Ch	GD	£3452
125	11/94	Newb	2m110y	Hdl	G-S	£4012
114	10/94	Weth	2m	Hdl	GD	£2805
	10/93	Mall	2m	NHF	G-Y	£2411

Total win prize-money £59244

Going: Sf: 0-0 GS: 0-1 Gd: 0-0 GF: - Fm: 0-0
Distance: 2m/2m3: 0-0 2m4-2m7: 0-0 3m+: 0-1
Track: LH: 0-0 RH: 0-1 Tight: 0-0 Gall: 0-1
Aids: Bl: 0-0 Vi: 0-0 Tstrap: 0-0
Best Rating: 152 1/98 Winc 2m5f gd-sft Ch

Calon Lan (IRE)

103 **102**

11-y-o b g Bustineto-Cherish (Bargello)
R Williams R Williams

Placings: *3*/F/4P13/**233P12/41545/1-0P004P** (4740)
2001/02: 16^{0}GS, 19^{P}G, 16^{0}G, 16^{0}S, 19^{4}G, 20^{P}GF

	Starts	1st	2nd	3rd	Win & Pl
Chases	6	0	0	0	326
Career Total	**24**	**4**	**2**	**4**	**27630**

115	3/01	Hntg	2m110y	D(0-125)HCh	SFT	£4108
126	10/99	Strf	2m1f110y	D(0-120)HCh	G-F	£3821
115	4/99	Ayr	2m	C Ch	HVY	£5865
112	3/98	Newb	2m110y	C Hdl	SFT	£4237

Total win prize-money £18031

Going: Sf: 0-1 GS: 0-1 Gd: 0-3 GF: - Fm: 0-1
Distance: 2m/2m3: 0-5 2m4-2m7: 0-1 3m+: 0-0

Track: LH: 0-2 RH: 0-4 Tight: 0-1 Gall: 0-0
Aids: Bl: 0-2 Vi: 0-0 Tstrap: 0-0
Best Rating: 131 11/98 Chep 2m3f110y gd-sft Ch

Camair Commander (IRE)

52f

4-y-o b g Beau Sher-Miss Josephine (IRE) (Kemal (FR))
W McKeown Colin W German

Placings:*0* **(4860)**
2001/02: 16^{0}G

	Starts	1st	2nd	3rd	Win & Pl
NH Flat	1	0	0	0	
Career Total	**1**	**0**	**0**	**0**	

Going: Sf: 0-0 GS: 0-0 Gd: 0-1 GF: - Fm: 0-0
Distance: 2m/2m3: 0-1 2m4-2m7: 0-0 3m+: 0-0
Track: LH: 0-0 RH: 0-0 Tight: 0-0 Gall: 0-0
Aids: Bl: 0-0 Vi: 0-0 Tstrap: 0-0
Best Rating: 52 4/02 Hexm 2m110y good NHF

Camair Crusader (IRE)

100(72c) (82c)91

8-y-o br g Jolly Jake (NZ)-Sigrid's Dream (USA) (Triple Bend (USA))
F P Murtagh (W McKeown 16/5) Colin W German

Placings:*00*/00P6F0245/33232S414-P6FF044 **(4765)**
2001/02: 16^{P}GS, 16^{6}S, 16^{F}GF, 16^{F}GF, 16^{0}GS, 16^{4}G, 16^{4}GF

	Starts	1st	2nd	3rd	Win & Pl
Hurdles	4	0	0	0	0
Chases	3	0	0	0	0
Career Total	**27**	**1**	**3**	**3**	**4746**

91	4/01	MRas	2m1f110y	G Hdl	G-S	£1890

Total win prize-money £1890

Going: Sf: 0-1 GS: 0-2 Gd: 0-1 GF: - Fm: 0-3
Distance: 2m/2m3: 0-7 2m4-2m7: 0-0 3m+: 0-0
Track: LH: 0-3 RH: 0-3 Tight: 0-3 Gall: 0-0
Aids: Bl: 0-0 Vi: 0-0 Tstrap: 0-0
Best Rating: 93 9/00 Sedg 2m1f soft Hdl

Camaraderie

90

6-y-o b g Most Welcome-Secret Valentine (Wollow)
Mrs M Reveley The Mary Reveley Racing Club

Placings:010-6 **(1578)**
2001/02: 16^{6}G

	Starts	1st	2nd	3rd	Win & Pl
Hurdles	1	0	0	0	0
Career Total	**4**	**1**	**0**	**0**	**2373**

104	10/00	Kels	2m110y	G Hdl	SFT	£2373

Total win prize-money £2373

Going: Sf: 0-0 GS: 0-0 Gd: 0-1 GF: - Fm: 0-0
Distance: 2m/2m3: 0-1 2m4-2m7: 0-0 3m+: 0-0
Track: LH: 0-1 RH: 0-0 Tight: 0-1 Gall: 0-0
Aids: Bl: 0-1 Vi: 0-0 Tstrap: 0-0
Best Rating: 104 10/00 Kels 2m110y soft Hdl

Cambio (IRE)

103 91+

4-y-o b g Turtle Island (IRE)-Motley (Rainbow Quest (USA))
B R Johnson (T D Easterby 29/5) Mrs Beryl Williams

Placings:64 **(4781)**
2001/02: 16^{6}HY, 16^{4}GF

	Starts	1st	2nd	3rd	Win & Pl
Hurdles	2	0	0	0	0
Career Total	**2**	**0**	**0**	**0**	**0**

Going: Sf: 0-1 GS: 0-0 Gd: 0-0 GF: - Fm: 0-1
Distance: 2m/2m3: 0-2 2m4-2m7: 0-0 3m+: 0-0
Track: LH: 0-2 RH: 0-0 Tight: 0-2 Gall: 0-0
Aids: Bl: 0-0 Vi: 0-0 Tstrap: 0-0
Best Rating: 79 4/02 Plum 2m gd-fm Hdl

Did not jump fluently on first two hurdles starts.

Cambrian Dawn

113 122

8-y-o b g Danehill (USA)-Welsh Daylight (Welsh Pageant)
J J O'Neill Out The Box Racing

Placings:*41*/*41*123/1 **(4893)**
2001/02: 20^{1}G

	Starts	1st	2nd	3rd	Win & Pl
Hurdles	1	1	0	0	5931
Career Total	**8**	**4**	**1**	**1**	**13462**

122	4/02	Prth	2m4f110y	C(0-130)HHdl	GD	£5931
108	1/00	Catt	3m1f110y	E Hdl	GD	£2817
113	11/99	Hexm	2m	H NHF	GD	£1595
113	4/99	Hexm	2m	H NHF	GD	£1640

Total win prize-money £11985

Going: Sf: 0-0 GS: 0-0 Gd: 1-1 GF: - Fm: 0-0
Distance: 2m/2m3: 0-0 **2m4-2m7: 1-1** 3m+: 0-0
Track: LH: 0-0 **RH: 1-1** Tight: 0-0 Gall: 0-0
Aids: Bl: 0-0 Vi: 0-0 Tstrap: 0-0
Best Rating: 122 4/02 Prth 2m4f110y good Hdl

Camden Dolphin (IRE)

76f 39f

5-y-o gr m Camden Town-Ackle Backle (Furry Glen)
C J Hemsley Mark Hoaren

Placings:*0* **(4166)**
2001/02: 16^{0}GS

	Starts	1st	2nd	3rd	Win & Pl
NH Flat	1	0	0	0	
Career Total	**1**	**0**	**0**	**0**	

Going: Sf: 0-0 GS: 0-1 Gd: 0-0 GF: - Fm: 0-0
Distance: 2m/2m3: 0-1 2m4-2m7: 0-0 3m+: 0-0
Track: LH: 0-1 RH: 0-0 Tight: 0-0 Gall: 0-0
Aids: Bl: 0-0 Vi: 0-0 Tstrap: 0-0
Best Rating: 39 3/02 Wwck 2m gd-sft NHF

Camden King (IRE)

(99h) (61h)

7-y-o b/br g Camden Town-Valerie Owens (IRE) (Lancastrian)
T P McGovern Wellpool Ltd And Mark Holman

Placings:*00*/3455-60 **(4772)**
2001/02: 21^{6}GF, 21^{0}G

	Starts	1st	2nd	3rd	Win & Pl
Hurdles	2	0	0	0	0
Career Total	**8**	**0**	**0**	**1**	**250**

Going: Sf: 0-0 GS: 0-0 Gd: 0-1 GF: - Fm: 0-1
Distance: 2m/2m3: 0-0 2m4-2m7: 0-2 3m+: 0-0
Track: LH: 0-1 RH: 0-1 Tight: 0-2 Gall: 0-0
Aids: Bl: 0-0 Vi: 0-0 Tstrap: 0-0
Best Rating: 94 5/00 Folk 2m1f110y good NHF

Camden Road (IRE)

107(99h) 107

9-y-o b g Camden Town-Kinnagh Pet (Roselier (FR))
Miss S Edwards Coldharbour Racing Ltd

Placings:400P/026112/UF04-2 **(3871)**
2001/02: 16^{2}GS

	Starts	1st	2nd	3rd	Win & Pl
Chases	1	0	1	0	1189
Career Total	**15**	**2**	**3**	**0**	**10341**

113	2/00	Hrfd	2m3f	F(0-100)HCh	GD	£3493
103	1/00	Folk	2m	E(0-105)HCh	G-S	£2934

Total win prize-money £6429

Going: Sf: 0-0 GS: 0-1 Gd: 0-0 GF: - Fm: 0-0
Distance: 2m/2m3: 0-1 2m4-2m7: 0-0 3m+: 0-0
Track: LH: 0-0 RH: 0-1 Tight: 0-0 Gall: 0-1
Aids: Bl: 0-0 Vi: 0-0 Tstrap: 0-0
Best Rating: 113 2/00 Hrfd 2m3f good Ch

Suited by a sound surface and trips around two to two and a half miles. Seems suited by a right-handed track.

Camdenation (IRE)

98f 100f

6-y-o b g Camden Town-Out The Nav (IRE) (Over The River (FR))
J T Gifford Unstable Companions

Placings:50 **(0377)**
2001/02: 18^{5}GF, 16^{0}GF

	Starts	1st	2nd	3rd	Win & Pl
NH Flat	2	0	0	0	0
Career Total	**2**	**0**	**0**	**0**	**0**

Going: Sf: 0-0 GS: 0-0 Gd: 0-0 GF: - Fm: 0-2
Distance: 2m/2m3: 0-2 2m4-2m7: 0-0 3m+: 0-0
Track: LH: 0-1 RH: 0-1 Tight: 0-1 Gall: 0-1
Aids: Bl: 0-0 Vi: 0-0 Tstrap: 0-0
Best Rating: 100 5/01 Font 2m2f110y gd-fm NHF

Cameron Bridge (IRE)

104 105

6-y-o b g Camden Town-Arctic Raheen (Over The River (FR))
P J Hobbs The Country Side

Placings:*F5*-55532112 **(4660)**
2001/02: 17^{5}S, 16^{5}G, 17^{5}GF, 16^{3}G, 16^{2}G, 16^{1}G, 16^{1}GS, 17^{2}G

	Starts	1st	2nd	3rd	Win & Pl
Hurdles	8	2	2	1	8198
Career Total	**10**	**2**	**2**	**1**	**8198**

101	1/02	Winc	2m	E Hdl	G-S	£3136
105	1/02	Winc	2m	E(0-110)HHdl	GD	£2989

Total win prize-money £6125

Going: Sf: 0-1 GS: 1-1 Gd: 1-5 GF: - Fm: 0-1
Distance: **2m/2m3: 2-8** 2m4-2m7: 0-0 3m+: 0-0

Track: LH: 0-0 **RH: 2-8** Tight: 0-1 Gall: 0-0
Aids: Bl: 0-0 Vi: 0-0 Tstrap: 0-0
Best Rating: 108 4/02 Tntn 2m1f good Hdl

Fair hurdler. Suited by two miles and a sound surface. Won twice at Wincanton in January 2002.

Camitrov (FR)

12-y-o b g Sharken (FR)-Emitrovna (FR) (Buisson D'Or)
G R Kerr G R Kerr

Placings:11341/42/55/3/243F/1/2UP (4852)
2001/02: 24^{2}G, 23^{U}GF, 24^{P}G

	Starts	1st	2nd	3rd	Win & Pl
Chases	3	0	1	0	832
Career Total	**18**	**4**	**3**	**3**	**48501**

128 3/00 Sand 3m110y E Ch GD £6380
123 4/95 Punc 2m4f Ch YLD £12871
95 12/94 MRas 2m1f110y Ch SFT £4056
110 11/94 Wwck 2m Ch G-S £3600
Total win prize-money £26908

Going: Sf: 0-0 GS: 0-0 Gd: 0-2 GF: - Fm: 0-1
Distance: 2m/2m3: 0-0 2m4-2m7: 0-1 3m+: 0-2
Track: LH: 0-2 RH: 0-1 Tight: 0-1 Gall: 0-0
Aids: Bl: 0-0 Vi: 0-0 Tstrap: 0-0
Best Rating: 142 11/97 Hntg 2m4f110y good Ch

Formerly a useful chaser, but is now just an ordinary pointer/hunter.

Camp Hill

103(104h) (94h)91
8-y-o gr g Ra Nova-Baytino (Neltino)
J S Haldane Mrs Hugh Fraser

Placings:00/6P00/P5542-50436U42F (4433)
2001/02: 16^{5}GS, 20^{0}S, 20^{4}G, 20^{3}S, 16^{6}S, 20^{U}S, 16^{4}S, 21^{2}S, 20^{F}HY

	Starts	1st	2nd	3rd	Win & Pl
Hurdles	4	0	0	1	857
Chases	5	0	1	0	1503
Career Total	**20**	**0**	**2**	**1**	**3312**

Going: Sf: 0-7 GS: 0-1 Gd: 0-1 GF: - Fm: 0-0
Distance: 2m/2m3: 0-3 2m4-2m7: 0-6 3m+: 0-0
Track: LH: 0-8 RH: 0-0 Tight: 0-1 Gall: 0-4
Aids: Bl: 0-0 Vi: 0-0 Tstrap: 0-0
Best Rating: 94 12/01 Hayd 2m4f soft Hdl

Modest maiden hurdler, suited by soft ground.

Camp Nou (IRE)

91 92
5-y-o b g Sadler's Wells (USA)-Campestral (USA) (Alleged (USA))
J J O'Neill M Tabor

Placings:3-0405 (4138)
2001/02: 16^{0}S, 16^{4}S, 17^{0}GS, 16^{5}GS

	Starts	1st	2nd	3rd	Win & Pl
NH Flat	1	0	0	0	0
Hurdles	3	0	0	0	350
Career Total	**5**	**0**	**0**	**1**	**630**

Going: Sf: 0-2 GS: 0-2 Gd: 0-0 GF: - Fm: 0-0
Distance: 2m/2m3: 0-4 2m4-2m7: 0-0 3m+: 0-0
Track: LH: 0-1 RH: 0-3 Tight: 0-1 Gall: 0-0
Aids: Bl: 0-0 Vi: 0-0 Tstrap: 0-0
Best Rating: 96 3/01 Hntg 2m110y soft NHF

Campaign Trail (IRE)

96 94
4-y-o b g Sadler's Wells (USA)-Campestral (USA) (Alleged (USA))
J J O'Neill (J E Hammond 23/9) M Tabor

Placings:5660 (3890)
2001/02: 16^{5}GS, 16^{6}HY, 17^{6}GS, 16^{0}HY

	Starts	1st	2nd	3rd	Win & Pl
Hurdles	4	0	0	0	0
Career Total	**4**	**0**	**0**	**0**	**0**

Going: Sf: 0-2 GS: 0-2 Gd: 0-0 GF: - Fm: 0-0
Distance: 2m/2m3: 0-4 2m4-2m7: 0-0 3m+: 0-0
Track: LH: 0-3 RH: 0-1 Tight: 0-1 Gall: 0-1
Aids: Bl: 0-0 Vi: 0-0 Tstrap: 0-0
Best Rating: 94 2/02 MRas 2m1f110y gd-sft Hdl

Lightly raced on the Flat in France over staying trips. Now with Jonjo O'Neill.

Campden Kitty

99 51
8-y-o b m Henbit (USA)-Catherine Tudor (Tudor Wood)
D J Wintle J C Collett

Placings:0/P0506 (1492)
2001/02: 22^{P}G, 17^{0}G, 24^{5}GF, 22^{0}GF, 26^{6}G

	Starts	1st	2nd	3rd	Win & Pl
Hurdles	5	0	0	0	0
Career Total	**6**	**0**	**0**	**0**	**0**

Going: Sf: 0-0 GS: 0-0 Gd: 0-3 GF: - Fm: 0-2
Distance: 2m/2m3: 0-1 2m4-2m7: 0-2 3m+: 0-2
Track: LH: 0-3 RH: 0-2 Tight: 0-4 Gall: 0-1
Aids: Bl: 0-0 Vi: 0-0 Tstrap: 0-0
Best Rating: 62 5/99 Worc 2m gd-fm NHF

Camross

89 81
6-y-o b g Teenoso (USA)-Arizona Belle (Arab Chieftain)
J C Fox Shannon Racing Partnership

Placings:0003R0 (4398)
2001/02: 19^{0}G, 20^{0}S, 19^{0}GS, 24^{3}HY, 24^{R}G, 24^{0}S

	Starts	1st	2nd	3rd	Win & Pl
Hurdles	6	0	0	1	282
Career Total	**6**	**0**	**0**	**1**	**282**

Going: Sf: 0-3 GS: 0-1 Gd: 0-2 GF: - Fm: 0-0
Distance: 2m/2m3: 0-2 2m4-2m7: 0-1 3m+: 0-3
Track: LH: 0-5 RH: 0-1 Tight: 0-0 Gall: 0-3
Aids: Bl: 0-0 Vi: 0-0 Tstrap: 0-0
Best Rating: 81 1/02 Uttx 3m110y heavy Hdl

Camtex Capers (IRE)

95(96h) (76h)94
10-y-o b g Boreen (FR)-Night Number (Crash Course)
Mrs S J Smith David Campbell

Placings:00F4100/F/210-64 (3217)
2001/02: 20^{6}HY, 25^{4}GS

	Starts	1st	2nd	3rd	Win & Pl
Hurdles	1	0	0	0	0
Chases	1	0	0	0	336
Career Total	**13**	**2**	**1**	**0**	**7386**

98 10/00 Sthl 2m4f110y D(0-120)HHdl SFT £3406
96 3/99 Newc 2m E Hdl SFT £2990
Total win prize-money £6396

Going: Sf: 0-1 GS: 0-1 Gd: 0-0 GF: - Fm: 0-0
Distance: 2m/2m3: 0-0 2m4-2m7: 0-1 3m+: 0-1
Track: LH: 0-2 RH: 0-0 Tight: 0-0 Gall: 0-0
Aids: Bl: 0-0 Vi: 0-0 Tstrap: 0-0
Best Rating: 98 10/00 Sthl 2m4f110y soft Hdl

A winner on soft ground over hurdles, has shown ability over fences. Stays two and a half miles.

Camus Des Mottes (FR)

66
6-y-o b g Africanus (FR)-Camille Des Mottes (FR) (Abdonski (FR))
Dr P Pritchard The Retreat Racing Club

Placings:46/056PF6-PP (4814)
2001/02: 16^{P}G, 21^{P}GF

	Starts	1st	2nd	3rd	Win & Pl
Chases	2	0	0	0	
Career Total	**10**	**0**	**0**	**0**	**753**

Going: Sf: 0-0 GS: 0-0 Gd: 0-1 GF: - Fm: 0-1
Distance: 2m/2m3: 0-1 2m4-2m7: 0-1 3m+: 0-0
Track: LH: 0-1 RH: 0-1 Tight: 0-0 Gall: 0-1
Aids: Bl: 0-0 Vi: 0-0 Tstrap: 0-0
Best Rating: 100 2/01 Ludl 2m4f good Ch

Lightly-raced chaser, has shown moderate form in chases so far.

Can Cortana (IRE)

97 83
6-y-o b g Supreme Leader-Glen Boosh (Furry Glen)
T D Easterby David & Steven Dudley

Placings:0430 (2916)
2001/02: 16^{0}G, 17^{4}GS, 17^{3}S, 20^{0}HY

	Starts	1st	2nd	3rd	Win & Pl
NH Flat	1	0	0	0	0
Hurdles	3	0	0	1	492
Career Total	**4**	**0**	**0**	**1**	**492**

Going: Sf: 0-2 GS: 0-1 Gd: 0-1 GF: - Fm: 0-0
Distance: 2m/2m3: 0-3 2m4-2m7: 0-1 3m+: 0-0
Track: LH: 0-2 RH: 0-2 Tight: 0-2 Gall: 0-0
Aids: Bl: 0-0 Vi: 0-0 Tstrap: 0-0
Best Rating: 83 11/01 MRas 2m1f110y gd-sft Hdl

Canada

109 117
4-y-o b g Ezzoud (IRE)-Chancel (USA) (Al Nasr (FR))
M C Pipe (B W Hills 5/10) W J Gredley

Placings:1P (4250)
2001/02: 16^{1}HY, 17^{P}G

	Starts	1st	2nd	3rd	Win & Pl
Hurdles	2	1	0	0	3903
Career Total	**2**	**1**	**0**	**0**	**3903**

117 2/02 Hayd 2m D Hdl HVY £3902
Total win prize-money £3903

Going: Sf: 1-1 GS: 0-0 Gd: 0-1 GF: - Fm: 0-0

Distance: 2m/2m3: 1-2 2m4-2m7: 0-0 3m+: 0-0
Track: LH: 1-2 RH: 0-0 Tight: 0-0 Gall: 0-1
Aids: Bl: 0-0 Vi: 0-0 Tstrap: 0-0
Best Rating: 117 2/02 Hayd 2m heavy Hdl

Smart handicapper on the Flat at around ten furlongs. Made a satisfactory winning debut over hurdles. Seems to handle any ground.

Canadiane (FR)

108(102h) (120h)130
7-y-o ch m Nikos-Carmonera (FR) (Carmont (FR))
M C Pipe M C Pipe

Placings:664F/454562125/06503242P4 (4500)
2001/02: 20^{0}G, 19^{6}GS, 16^{5}G, 19^{0}GS, 17^{3}GS, 16^{2}S, 17^{4}S, 16^{2}S, 24^{P}S, 17^{4}G

	Starts	1st	2nd	3rd	Win & Pl
Hurdles	10	0	2	1	3233
Career Total	23	1	4	1	26548

120 12/99 Chep 2m110y D Hdl G-S £3347
Total win prize-money £3347

Going: Sf: 0-4 GS: 0-3 Gd: 0-3 GF: - Fm: 0-0
Distance: 2m/2m3: 0-6 2m4-2m7: 0-3 3m+: 0-1
Track: LH: 0-3 RH: 0-7 Tight: 0-5 Gall: 0-0
Aids: Bl: 0-0 Vi: 0-0 Tstrap: 0-0
Best Rating: 120 2/02 Sand 2m110y soft Hdl

A winning hurdler, shewas switched successfully to fences in the early summer of 2002. Stays two and a half miles, acts on most types of ground.

Candarli (IRE)

100 106
6-y-o ch g Polish Precedent (USA)-Calounia (IRE) (Pharly (FR))
D R Gandolfo A E Frost

Placings:5-301 (4116)
2001/02: 16^{3}G, 16^{0}S, 16^{1}G

	Starts	1st	2nd	3rd	Win & Pl
Hurdles	3	1	0	1	6392
Career Total	4	1	0	1	6392

106 3/02 Winc 2m D(0-125)HHdl GD £5261
Total win prize-money £5262

Going: Sf: 0-1 GS: 0-0 Gd: 1-2 GF: - Fm: 0-0
Distance: 2m/2m3: 1-3 2m4-2m7: 0-0 3m+: 0-0
Track: LH: 0-2 RH: 1-1 Tight: 0-0 Gall: 0-1
Aids: Bl: 0-0 Vi: 0-0 Tstrap: 0-0
Best Rating: 106 3/02 Winc 2m good Hdl

Ex-Irish, he made a successful handicap debut in a decent event at Wincanton in March 2002 and should win more races. Suited by good ground.

Candy Copper

90 68
9-y-o b m Nicholas Bill-Chocolate Drop (Goldhill)
Mrs P Ford K R Ford

Placings:50000P3/P042/612600-000U0 (2140)
2001/02: 17^{0}GF, 20^{0}G, 16^{0}GF, 16^{U}GS, 19^{0}G

	Starts	1st	2nd	3rd	Win & Pl
Hurdles	5	0	0	0	
Career Total	22	1	2	1	4393

89 5/00 Hrfd 2m1f E Hdl G-S £2775
Total win prize-money £2776

Going: Sf: 0-0 GS: 0-1 Gd: 0-2 GF: - Fm: 0-2
Distance: 2m/2m3: 0-3 2m4-2m7: 0-2 3m+: 0-0
Track: LH: 0-3 RH: 0-2 Tight: 0-4 Gall: 0-1
Aids: Bl: 0-0 Vi: 0-0 Tstrap: 0-4
Best Rating: 89 5/00 Hrfd 2m1f gd-sft Hdl

Cannon Bridge (IRE)

94 70
4-y-o ch g Definite Article-Hit For Six (Tap On Wood)
D Shaw J C Fretwell

Placings:6 (3368)
2001/02: 16^{6}GS

	Starts	1st	2nd	3rd	Win & Pl
NH Flat	1	0	0	0	0
Career Total	1	0	0	0	0

Going: Sf: 0-0 GS: 0-1 Gd: 0-0 GF: - Fm: 0-0
Distance: 2m/2m3: 0-1 2m4-2m7: 0-0 3m+: 0-0
Track: LH: 0-1 RH: 0-0 Tight: 0-1 Gall: 0-0
Aids: Bl: 0-0 Vi: 0-0 Tstrap: 0-0
Best Rating: 64 1/02 Catt 2m gd-sft NHF

Canny Chiftane

107 86
6-y-o b g Be My Chief (USA)-Prudence (Grundy)
Miss C J E Caroe Miss C J E Caroe

Placings:04461/30PP5-0P0PP16400P (4283)
2001/02: 17^{0}GS, 26^{P}G, 24^{0}GS, 16^{P}S, 24^{P}S, 20^{1}S, 22^{6}HY, 16^{4}HY, 21^{0}HY, 20^{0}S, 17^{P}GS

	Starts	1st	2nd	3rd	Win & Pl
Hurdles	11	1	0	0	1868
Career Total	21	2	0	1	4135

86 11/01 Fknm 2m4f G(0-95)HHdl SFT £1867
77 4/00 Newc 2m F Hdl G-S £1897
Total win prize-money £3765

Going: Sf: 1-7 GS: 0-3 Gd: 0-1 GF: - Fm: 0-0
Distance: 2m/2m3: 0-4 2m4-2m7: 1-4 3m+: 0-3
Track: LH: 1-1 RH: 0-9 Tight: 1-5 Gall: 0-2
Aids: Bl: 0-4 Vi: 1-6 Tstrap: 0-0
Best Rating: 86 11/01 Fknm 2m4f soft Hdl

Plating-class hurdler, suited by cut in the ground. Stays two and a half miles, often wears a visor.

Canon McCarthy (IRE)

105(94h) 97
6-y-o ch g Be My Native (USA)-Archetype (Over The River (FR))
A W Carroll Gary J Roberts

Placings:34563-0332 (3776)
2001/02: 22^{0}G, 24^{3}G, 24^{3}S, 24^{2}S

	Starts	1st	2nd	3rd	Win & Pl
Chases	4	0	1	2	2751
Career Total	9	0	1	4	3685

Going: Sf: 0-2 GS: 0-0 Gd: 0-2 GF: - Fm: 0-0
Distance: 2m/2m3: 0-0 2m4-2m7: 0-1 3m+: 0-3
Track: LH: 0-2 RH: 0-2 Tight: 0-1 Gall: 0-2
Aids: Bl: 0-0 Vi: 0-0 Tstrap: 0-0
Best Rating: 97 2/02 Sand 3m110y soft Ch

Moderate form in novice and handicaps chases. Stays three miles.

Canterbury (IRE)

85 75
9-y-o b g King's Ride-Private Dancer (Deep Run)
R J Baker Churchgoers Anonymous

Placings:0P/02-6 (0121)
2001/02: 19^{6}F

	Starts	1st	2nd	3rd	Win & Pl
Hurdles	1	0	0	0	0
Career Total	5	0	1	0	552

Going: Sf: 0-0 GS: 0-0 Gd: 0-0 GF: - Fm: 0-1
Distance: 2m/2m3: 0-0 2m4-2m7: 0-1 3m+: 0-0
Track: LH: 0-0 RH: 0-1 Tight: 0-1 Gall: 0-0
Aids: Bl: 0-0 Vi: 0-0 Tstrap: 0-0
Best Rating: 75 4/01 Extr 2m1f gd-sft Hdl

Canton Venture

10-y-o ch g Arctic Tern (USA)-Ski Michaela (USA) (Devil's Bag (USA))
A W Carroll Miss E J Marley

Placings:231F0/11214/4F34221300/0460P3/P (1618)
2001/02: 21^{P}G

	Starts	1st	2nd	3rd	Win & Pl
Hurdles	1	0	0	0	
Career Total	27	5	4	4	18824

116 9/98 Font 2m6f110y E(0-110)HHdl G-F £2337
113 10/97 Font 2m2f110y D(0-120)HHdl GD £2863
115 9/97 Plum 2m4f D(0-120)HHdl G-F £2771
105 8/97 Font 2m2f110y E(0-110)HHdl GD £2238
98 10/96 Chel 2m5f D Hdl FRM £2906
Total win prize-money £13117

Going: Sf: 0-0 GS: 0-0 Gd: 0-1 GF: - Fm: 0-0
Distance: 2m/2m3: 0-0 2m4-2m7: 0-1 3m+: 0-0
Track: LH: 0-0 RH: 0-1 Tight: 0-0 Gall: 0-0
Aids: Bl: 0-0 Vi: 0-0 Tstrap: 0-0
Best Rating: 120 10/98 Font 2m6f110y good Hdl

Canyoubatim (IRE)

97 83
8-y-o b g Alphabatim (USA)-Boat Whistle (Amoristic (USA))
H D Daly Strachan,Griffith,Park'Son,Grieve,Barlow

Placings:6-F04P (4686)
2001/02: 22^{F}HY, 24^{0}GS, 24^{4}S, 26^{P}GF

	Starts	1st	2nd	3rd	Win & Pl
Hurdles	2	0	0	0	0
Chases	2	0	0	0	0
Career Total	5	0	0	0	0

Going: Sf: 0-2 GS: 0-1 Gd: 0-0 GF: - Fm: 0-1
Distance: 2m/2m3: 0-0 2m4-2m7: 0-1 3m+: 0-3
Track: LH: 0-0 RH: 0-4 Tight: 0-0 Gall: 0-1
Aids: Bl: 0-1 Vi: 0-0 Tstrap: 0-0
Best Rating: 107 10/00 Chel 3m1f110y good Hdl

Cap It If You Can (IRE)

102 100
9-y-o b m Capitano-Lady Of Tara (Deep Run)
T H Caldwell Mrs C J Cadwallader

Placings:00502001210/62U3364/03PP3621P25/P504 2P-01306PU643053540 (4908)
2001/02: 17^{0}G, 21^{1}GF, 17^{3}GS, 20^{0}G, 20^{6}S, 21^{P}S, 20^{U}HY, 19^{6}G, 23^{4}HY, 20^{3}G, 21^{0}HY, 19^{5}G, 21^{3}GS, 21^{5}GF, 24^{4}G, 21^{0}G

	Starts	1st	2nd	3rd	Win & Pl
Hurdles	16	1	0	3	4405

	Starts	1st	2nd	3rd	Win & Pl
Career Total	**51**	**4**	**6**	**7**	**19877**

96	5/01	Hntg	2m5f110y	F(0-110)HHdl	G-F	£2018
100	2/00	Carl	2m1f	D(0-120)HHdl	HVY	£3074
109	3/98	Wxfd	2m4f	(0-116)HHdl	SH	£2382
99	2/98	Gowr	2m	Hdl	YLD	£2680

Total win prize-money £10157

Going: Sf: 0-5 GS: 0-2 Gd: 0-7 GF: - Fm: 1-2
Distance: 2m/2m3: 0-3 **2m4-2m7: 1-11** 3m+: 0-2
Track: LH: 0-9 **RH: 1-5** Tight: 0-9 **Gall: 1-3**
Aids: Bl: 0-0 Vi: 0-0 Tstrap: 0-0
Best Rating: 109 3/98 Wxfd 2m4f sft-hvy Hdl

Handicap hurdler, suited by around two and a half miles.

Cape Stormer (IRE)

105 **101**

7-y-o b g Be My Native (USA)-My Sunny South (Strong Gale)
Miss H C Knight (Mrs A J Perrett 4/5) Mrs Anne Miller

Placings:*0*P225 **(4584)**
2001/02: 17^{0}GS, 16^{P}S, 16^{2}GS, 19^{2}G, 16^{5}G

	Starts	1st	2nd	3rd	Win & Pl
NH Flat	1	0	0	0	0
Hurdles	4	0	2	0	1567
Career Total	**5**	**0**	**2**	**0**	**1567**

Going: Sf: 0-1 GS: 0-2 Gd: 0-2 GF: - Fm: 0-0
Distance: 2m/2m3: 0-4 2m4-2m7: 0-1 3m+: 0-0
Track: LH: 0-1 RH: 0-3 Tight: 0-2 Gall: 0-0
Aids: Bl: 0-0 Vi: 0-0 Tstrap: 0-0
Best Rating: 101 3/02 Hrfd 2m3f110y good Hdl

Runner-up in novice hurdles, stays two and a half miles.

Capitaine Leau (FR)

7-y-o b g Ganges (USA)-Disco Dancer (FR) (Green Dancer (USA))
N J Henderson Lynn Wilson

Placings:0150/200604/1PP-P **(1891)**
2001/02: 20^{P}G

	Starts	1st	2nd	3rd	Win & Pl
Chases	1	0	0	0	
Career Total	**14**	**2**	**1**	**0**	**29062**

137	11/00	Chel	2m4f110y	B Ch	G-S	£10627
	10/98	Autl	2m2f	Hdl	SFT	£10101

Total win prize-money £20729

Going: Sf: 0-0 GS: 0-0 Gd: 0-1 GF: - Fm: 0-0
Distance: 2m/2m3: 0-0 2m4-2m7: 0-1 3m+: 0-0
Track: LH: 0-1 RH: 0-0 Tight: 0-0 Gall: 0-1
Aids: Bl: 0-0 Vi: 0-0 Tstrap: 0-0
Best Rating: 137 11/00 Chel 2m4f110y gd-sft Ch

Capital Breeze (IRE)

4-y-o b c Shareef Dancer (USA)-Crystal Land (Kris)
G L Moore (D R C Elsworth 19/5) Rdm Racing

Placings:P **(1481)**
2001/02: 16^{P}GS

	Starts	1st	2nd	3rd	Win & Pl
Hurdles	1	0	0	0	
Career Total	**1**	**0**	**0**	**0**	

Going: Sf: 0-0 GS: 0-1 Gd: 0-0 GF: - Fm: 0-0
Distance: 2m/2m3: 0-1 2m4-2m7: 0-0 3m+: 0-0
Track: LH: 0-1 RH: 0-0 Tight: 0-1 Gall: 0-0
Aids: Bl: 0-0 Vi: 0-0 Tstrap: 0-0
Best Rating:

Cappadrummin (IRE)

93f **112f**

5-y-o ch g Bob Back (USA)-Out And About (Orchestra)
N J Henderson Lady Lloyd Webber

Placings:*1* **(3910)**
2001/02: 16^{1}G

	Starts	1st	2nd	3rd	Win & Pl
NH Flat	1	1	0	0	2562
Career Total	**1**	**1**	**0**	**0**	**2562**

112	2/02	Kemp	2m	H NHF	GD	£2562

Total win prize-money £2562

Going: Sf: 0-0 GS: 0-0 Gd: 1-1 GF: - Fm: 0-0
Distance: **2m/2m3: 1-1** 2m4-2m7: 0-0 3m+: 0-0
Track: LH: 0-0 **RH: 1-1** Tight: 0-0 Gall: 0-0
Aids: Bl: 0-0 Vi: 0-0 Tstrap: 0-0
Best Rating: 112 2/02 Kemp 2m good NHF

Capriccio (IRE)

98 **100**

5-y-o gr g Robellino (USA)-Yamamah (Siberian Express (USA))
C G Cox The C. O. G. S.

Placings:11-0660 **(4267)**
2001/02: 21^{0}GS, 17^{6}HY, 19^{6}G, 24^{0}S

	Starts	1st	2nd	3rd	Win & Pl
Hurdles	4	0	0	0	0
Career Total	**6**	**2**	**0**	**0**	**5457**

117	2/01	Wwck	2m	E Hdl	SFT	£2870
115	1/01	Folk	2m1f110y	E Hdl	HVY	£2586

Total win prize-money £5457

Going: Sf: 0-2 GS: 0-1 Gd: 0-1 GF: - Fm: 0-0
Distance: 2m/2m3: 0-2 2m4-2m7: 0-1 3m+: 0-1
Track: LH: 0-1 RH: 0-3 Tight: 0-0 Gall: 0-0
Aids: Bl: 0-1 Vi: 0-0 Tstrap: 0-0
Best Rating: 117 2/01 Wwck 2m soft Hdl

Twice a winner over hurdles in the mud at the beginning of 2001, hewas out of form in 2001/02. Effective at around two miles.

Capricorn

80f **89f**

4-y-o b g Minster Son-Loch Scavaig (IRE) (The Parson)
W McKeown Ian Ives

Placings:*40* **(4750)**
2001/02: 16^{4}S, 17^{0}G

	Starts	1st	2nd	3rd	Win & Pl
NH Flat	2	0	0	0	0
Career Total	**2**	**0**	**0**	**0**	**0**

Going: Sf: 0-1 GS: 0-0 Gd: 0-1 GF: - Fm: 0-0
Distance: 2m/2m3: 0-2 2m4-2m7: 0-0 3m+: 0-0
Track: LH: 0-0 RH: 0-1 Tight: 0-0 Gall: 0-0
Aids: Bl: 0-0 Vi: 0-0 Tstrap: 0-0
Best Rating: 89 1/02 Newc 2m soft NHF

Made a fair racecourse debut in a bumper at Newcastle.

Capricorn Princess

106 **102**

8-y-o b m Nicholas Bill-Yamrah (Milford)
A Streeter Capricorn Hospitality

Placings:*00*P635/424112-0230P5 **(1401)**
2001/02: 17^{0}G, 16^{2}GF, 17^{3}G, 16^{0}GF, 20^{P}GF, 20^{5}G

	Starts	1st	2nd	3rd	Win & Pl
Hurdles	6	0	1	1	1056
Career Total	**18**	**2**	**3**	**2**	**12363**

95	8/00	Bang	2m1f	D Hdl	GD	£3477
93	7/00	Uttx	2m	E(0-105)I Hdl	G-F	£3552

Total win prize-money £7030

Going: Sf: 0-0 GS: 0-0 Gd: 0-3 GF: - Fm: 0-3
Distance: 2m/2m3: 0-4 2m4-2m7: 0-2 3m+: 0-0
Track: LH: 0-5 RH: 0-1 Tight: 0-4 Gall: 0-0
Aids: Bl: 0-0 Vi: 0-0 Tstrap: 0-0
Best Rating: 102 6/01 Worc 2m gd-fm Hdl

Capriolo (IRE)

93 **83**

6-y-o ch g Priolo (USA)-Carroll's Canyon (IRE) (Hatim (USA))
J C Fox (R Hannon 25/10) S J Kingshott

Placings:040P **(3361)**
2001/02: 16^{0}S, 16^{4}GS, 16^{0}G, 16^{P}HY

	Starts	1st	2nd	3rd	Win & Pl
Hurdles	4	0	0	0	625
Career Total	**4**	**0**	**0**	**0**	**625**

Going: Sf: 0-2 GS: 0-1 Gd: 0-1 GF: - Fm: 0-0
Distance: 2m/2m3: 0-4 2m4-2m7: 0-0 3m+: 0-0
Track: LH: 0-4 RH: 0-0 Tight: 0-0 Gall: 0-3
Aids: Bl: 0-0 Vi: 0-0 Tstrap: 0-0
Best Rating: 83 12/01 Newb 2m110y good Hdl

A middle-distance performer on the Flat, has shown little over hurdles so far.

Captain Biggles

90 **74**

10-y-o br g My Richard-Kiltipper (Menelek)
Miss A Stokell Ms Caron Stokell

Placings:*0/066*0022/4/0P00-6 **(0220)**
2001/02: 16^{6}GF

	Starts	1st	2nd	3rd	Win & Pl
Hurdles	1	0	0	0	0
Career Total	**14**	**0**	**2**	**0**	**1391**

Going: Sf: 0-0 GS: 0-0 Gd: 0-0 GF: - Fm: 0-1
Distance: 2m/2m3: 0-1 2m4-2m7: 0-0 3m+: 0-0
Track: LH: 0-1 RH: 0-0 Tight: 0-0 Gall: 0-0
Aids: Bl: 0-0 Vi: 0-0 Tstrap: 0-0
Best Rating: 100 3/99 Hntg 2m110y gd-sft Hdl

Captain Brady (IRE)

76

7-y-o ch g Soviet Lad (USA)-Eight Mile Rock (Dominion)
J S Goldie Frank Brady

Placings:204/12/P-0P **(3329)**
2001/02: 17^{0}GF, 16^{P}S

	Starts	1st	2nd	3rd	Win & Pl
Hurdles	2	0	0	0	
Career Total	**8**	**1**	**2**	**0**	**4168**

95	5/99	Prth	2m110y	E Hdl	SFT	£2724

Total win prize-money £2724

Going: Sf: 0-1 GS: 0-0 Gd: 0-0 GF: - Fm: 0-1

Distance: 2m/2m3: 0-2 2m4-2m7: 0-0 3m+: 0-0
Track: LH: 0-1 RH: 0-0 Tight: 0-0 Gall: 0-1
Aids: Bl: 0-0 Vi: 0-0 Tstrap: 0-0
Best Rating: 98 6/99 Prth 2m110y gd-sft Hdl

Captain Bravado (IRE)

78 53

8-y-o b g Torus-Miss Bavard (Le Bavard (FR))
D J Caro J A S Hardcastle

Placings:P (4051)
2001/02: 24^{P}G

	Starts	1st	2nd	3rd	Win & Pl
Hurdles	1	0	0	0	
Career Total	**1**	**0**	**0**	**0**	

Going: Sf: 0-0 GS: 0-0 Gd: 0-1 GF: - Fm: 0-0
Distance: 2m/2m3: 0-0 2m4-2m7: 0-0 3m+: 0-1
Track: LH: 0-0 RH: 0-1 Tight: 0-0 Gall: 0-0
Aids: Bl: 0-0 Vi: 0-0 Tstrap: 0-0
Best Rating:

Captain Clooney (IRE)

36

9-y-o b g Supreme Leader-Capincur Lady (Over The River (FR))
N R Mitchell (John Brassil 5/8) Michael Green

Placings:42551000/40/5P-0PU (4388)
2001/02: 24^{0}G, 22^{P}GY, 25^{U}S

	Starts	1st	2nd	3rd	Win & Pl
Chases	3	0	0	0	
Career Total	**15**	**1**	**1**	**0**	**5207**

116 1/99 Punc 3m Hdl HVY £3989
Total win prize-money £3990

Going: Sf: 0-1 GS: 0-0 Gd: 0-1 GF: - Fm: 0-0
Distance: 2m/2m3: 0-0 2m4-2m7: 0-1 3m+: 0-2
Track: LH: 0-0 RH: 0-1 Tight: 0-0 Gall: 0-0
Aids: Bl: 0-0 Vi: 0-0 Tstrap: 0-0
Best Rating: 116 1/99 Punc 3m heavy Hdl

Captain Corelli

96f 104f

5-y-o b g Weld-Deaconess (The Parson)
M Pitman Patrick Bancroft

Placings:30 (4679)
2001/02: 16^{3}GS, 17^{0}G

	Starts	1st	2nd	3rd	Win & Pl
NH Flat	2	0	0	1	244
Career Total	**2**	**0**	**0**	**1**	**244**

Going: Sf: 0-0 GS: 0-1 Gd: 0-1 GF: - Fm: 0-0
Distance: 2m/2m3: 0-2 2m4-2m7: 0-0 3m+: 0-0
Track: LH: 0-0 RH: 0-1 Tight: 0-0 Gall: 0-0
Aids: Bl: 0-0 Vi: 0-0 Tstrap: 0-0
Best Rating: 104 2/02 Winc 2m gd-sft NHF

Just failed to get up on his hurdles debut.

Captain George

85 68

9-y-o br g Arctic Lord-Bonne Fille (Bonne Noel)
D G Bridgwater J M I Evetts

Placings:0P (3230)
2001/02: 23^{0}G, 24^{P}GS

	Starts	1st	2nd	3rd	Win & Pl
Chases	2	0	0	0	
Career Total	**2**	**0**	**0**	**0**	

Going: Sf: 0-0 GS: 0-1 Gd: 0-1 GF: - Fm: 0-0
Distance: 2m/2m3: 0-0 2m4-2m7: 0-0 3m+: 0-2
Track: LH: 0-0 RH: 0-2 Tight: 0-0 Gall: 0-1
Aids: Bl: 0-0 Vi: 0-1 Tstrap: 0-2
Best Rating: 68 12/01 Leic 2m7f110y good Ch

Captain Gibson

95 98

4-y-o b g Beveled (USA)-Little Egret (Carwhite)
D J S Ffrench Davis M Duthie

Placings:05043F (4757)
2001/02: 16^{0}GS, 16^{5}S, 16^{0}G, 17^{4}S, 16^{3}GS, 16^{F}GF

	Starts	1st	2nd	3rd	Win & Pl
Hurdles	6	0	0	1	636
Career Total	**6**	**0**	**0**	**1**	**636**

Going: Sf: 0-2 GS: 0-2 Gd: 0-1 GF: - Fm: 0-1
Distance: 2m/2m3: 0-6 2m4-2m7: 0-0 3m+: 0-0
Track: LH: 0-3 RH: 0-3 Tight: 0-1 Gall: 0-3
Aids: Bl: 0-1 Vi: 0-0 Tstrap: 0-0
Best Rating: 98 2/02 Kemp 2m good Hdl

Fair two-mile novice hurdler. Acts with cut. Not an easy ride.

Captain Kozando

4-y-o b g Komaite (USA)-Times Zando (Forzando)
P C Haslam Mrs B Hawkins

Placings:P (2301)
2001/02: 16^{P}GF

	Starts	1st	2nd	3rd	Win & Pl
Hurdles	1	0	0	0	
Career Total	**1**	**0**	**0**	**0**	

Going: Sf: 0-0 GS: 0-0 Gd: 0-0 GF: - Fm: 0-1
Distance: 2m/2m3: 0-1 2m4-2m7: 0-0 3m+: 0-0
Track: LH: 0-1 RH: 0-0 Tight: 0-1 Gall: 0-0
Aids: Bl: 0-0 Vi: 0-0 Tstrap: 0-0
Best Rating:

Captain O'Neill

99(101h) (90h)101

8-y-o b g Welsh Captain-The Last Tune (Gunner B)
J G M O'Shea Gary Roberts

Placings:600P303P/36-001PP0P (4847)
2001/02: 17^{0}G, 16^{0}S, 20^{1}S, 25^{P}HY, 17^{P}HY, 21^{0}S, 20^{P}G

	Starts	1st	2nd	3rd	Win & Pl
Hurdles	7	1	0	0	1946
Career Total	**17**	**1**	**0**	**3**	**2924**

90 12/01 Chep 2m4f G Hdl SFT £1946
Total win prize-money £1946

Going: Sf: 1-5 GS: 0-0 Gd: 0-2 GF: - Fm: 0-0
Distance: 2m/2m3: 0-3 **2m4-2m7: 1-3** 3m+: 0-1
Track: **LH: 1-4** RH: 0-2 Tight: 0-1 Gall: 0-1
Aids: Bl: 0-0 Vi: 0-0 Tstrap: 0-0
Best Rating: 90 12/01 Chep 2m4f soft Hdl

Plating-class hurdler, best at around two and a half miles. Struggles to stay three miles over fences.

Captain Oates

9-y-o b g Arctic Lord-Captain's Cottage (Relkino)
W A Bethell W A Bethell

Placings:0/0-P (4057)
2001/02: 23^{P}S

	Starts	1st	2nd	3rd	Win & Pl
Chases	1	0	0	0	
Career Total	**3**	**0**	**0**	**0**	

Going: Sf: 0-1 GS: 0-0 Gd: 0-0 GF: - Fm: 0-0
Distance: 2m/2m3: 0-0 2m4-2m7: 0-0 3m+: 0-1
Track: LH: 0-0 RH: 0-1 Tight: 0-0 Gall: 0-0
Aids: Bl: 0-0 Vi: 0-0 Tstrap: 0-0
Best Rating: 61 11/97 Worc 2m good NHF

Captain Ron (IRE)

86 47

6-y-o b g Marju (IRE)-Callas Star (Chief Singer)
P D Evans N E Powell

Placings:0 (0914)
2001/02: 22^{0}GF

	Starts	1st	2nd	3rd	Win & Pl
Hurdles	1	0	0	0	
Career Total	**1**	**0**	**0**	**0**	

Going: Sf: 0-0 GS: 0-0 Gd: 0-0 GF: - Fm: 0-1
Distance: 2m/2m3: 0-0 2m4-2m7: 0-1 3m+: 0-0
Track: LH: 0-1 RH: 0-0 Tight: 0-1 Gall: 0-0
Aids: Bl: 0-0 Vi: 0-0 Tstrap: 0-0
Best Rating: 47 7/01 Strf 2m6f110y gd-fm Hdl

Captain Rose

10-y-o b g Soldier Rose-Miss Oxstall'S (The Brianstan)
R Evans Mrs Richard Evans

Placings:P/P-P (4545)
2001/02: 19^{P}G

	Starts	1st	2nd	3rd	Win & Pl
Chases	1	0	0	0	
Career Total	**3**	**0**	**0**	**0**	

Going: Sf: 0-0 GS: 0-0 Gd: 0-1 GF: - Fm: 0-0
Distance: 2m/2m3: 0-1 2m4-2m7: 0-0 3m+: 0-0
Track: LH: 0-0 RH: 0-1 Tight: 0-0 Gall: 0-0
Aids: Bl: 0-0 Vi: 0-0 Tstrap: 0-0
Best Rating:

Captain Zinzan (NZ)

(98h) 111

7-y-o b g Zabeel (NZ)-Lady Springfield (NZ) (Sharivari (USA))
Mrs A J Perrett Michael H Watt

Placings:44/121-2 (0243)
2001/02: 16^{2}GF

	Starts	1st	2nd	3rd	Win & Pl
Chases	1	0	1	0	972
Career Total	**6**	**2**	**2**	**0**	**6811**

119 1/01 Donc 2m110y E Hdl GD £3080
108 8/00 Hntg 2m110y H NHF G-F £1477

Total win prize-money £4557

Going: Sf: 0-0 GS: 0-0 Gd: 0-0 GF: - Fm: 0-1
Distance: 2m/2m3: 0-1 2m4-2m7: 0-0 3m+: 0-0
Track: LH: 0-0 RH: 0-0 Tight: 0-0 Gall: 0-0
Aids: Bl: 0-0 Vi: 0-0 Tstrap: 0-0
Best Rating: 119 1/01 Donc 2m110y good Hdl

Captain's Leap (IRE)

97f **102f**
6-y-o ch g Grand Plaisir (IRE)-Ballingowan Star (Le Moss)
L Lungo J Regan

Placings:216 **(4309)**
2001/02: 17^{2}G, 16^{1}G, 16^{6}S

	Starts	1st	2nd	3rd	Win & Pl
NH Flat	3	1	1	0	2002
Career Total	**3**	**1**	**1**	**0**	**2002**

99	12/01	Muss	2m	H NHF	GD	£1554

Total win prize-money £1554

Going: Sf: 0-1 GS: 0-0 Gd: 1-2 GF: - Fm: 0-0
Distance: **2m/2m3: 1-3** 2m4-2m7: 0-0 3m+: 0-0
Track: LH: 0-2 **RH: 1-1 Tight: 1-2** Gall: 0-0
Aids: Bl: 0-0 Vi: 0-0 Tstrap: 0-0
Best Rating: 102 3/02 Ayr 2m soft NHF

A well regarded individual. He was runner-up on his bumper debut at Sedgefield in November 2001 on good ground, and got off the mark at Musselburgh the following month.

Captain's Walk

6-y-o b g Seymour Hicks (FR)-Mayina (Idiots Delight)
P Bowen John O'Sullivan

Placings:60-40P **(1397)**
2001/02: 17^{4}F, 16^{0}GF, 24^{P}GF

	Starts	1st	2nd	3rd	Win & Pl
NH Flat	2	0	0	0	0
Hurdles	1	0	0	0	0
Career Total	**5**	**0**	**0**	**0**	**0**

Going: Sf: 0-0 GS: 0-0 Gd: 0-0 GF: - Fm: 0-3
Distance: 2m/2m3: 0-2 2m4-2m7: 0-0 3m+: 0-1
Track: LH: 0-1 RH: 0-2 Tight: 0-0 Gall: 0-1
Aids: Bl: 0-0 Vi: 0-0 Tstrap: 0-0
Best Rating: 95 5/01 Hntg 2m110y gd-fm NHF

Captains Table

94 **108**
9-y-o b g Welsh Captain-Wensum Girl (Ballymoss)
R Dickin Les Pike

Placings:6 **(0677)**
2001/02: 16^{6}GF

	Starts	1st	2nd	3rd	Win & Pl
Chases	1	0	0	0	0
Career Total	**1**	**0**	**0**	**0**	**0**

Going: Sf: 0-0 GS: 0-0 Gd: 0-0 GF: - Fm: 0-1
Distance: 2m/2m3: 0-1 2m4-2m7: 0-0 3m+: 0-0
Track: LH: 0-1 RH: 0-0 Tight: 0-0 Gall: 0-0
Aids: Bl: 0-0 Vi: 0-0 Tstrap: 0-0
Best Rating: 108 6/01 Worc 2m gd-fm Ch

Captaintwothousand

107 **92**
7-y-o b g Milieu-Royal Scarlet (Royal Fountain)
C W Fairhurst Mrs A M Leggett

Placings:*0/2P*6U50-0P22123 **(4668)**
2001/02: 16^{0}S, 20^{P}G, 17^{2}S, 16^{2}GS, 19^{1}GS, 16^{2}HY, 17^{3}GF

	Starts	1st	2nd	3rd	Win & Pl
Hurdles	7	1	3	1	5417
Career Total	**14**	**1**	**4**	**1**	**5892**

92	3/02	Catt	2m3f	F(0-100)HHdl	G-S	£2096

Total win prize-money £2097

Going: Sf: 0-3 GS: 1-2 Gd: 0-1 GF: - Fm: 0-1
Distance: **2m/2m3: 1-6** 2m4-2m7: 0-1 3m+: 0-0
Track: **LH: 1-7** RH: 0-0 **Tight: 1-4** Gall: 0-2
Aids: Bl: 0-0 Vi: 0-0 Tstrap: 0-1
Best Rating: 106 10/00 Sedg 2m1f gd-sft NHF

Modest hurdler. Proved suited by two and a half miles when opening his account in handicap company at Catterick in March 2002. Appreciates cut in the ground.

Captivated (IRE)

93f **69f**
5-y-o b g King's Ride-Ivy Green (Green Shoon)
S E H Sherwood The Hon Mrs S Sherwood

Placings:6 **(1630)**
2001/02: 16^{6}GF

	Starts	1st	2nd	3rd	Win & Pl
NH Flat	1	0	0	0	0
Career Total	**1**	**0**	**0**	**0**	**0**

Going: Sf: 0-0 GS: 0-0 Gd: 0-0 GF: 0-0 Fm: 0-1
Distance: 2m/2m3: 0-1 2m4-2m7: 0-0 3m+: 0-0
Track: LH: 0-0 RH: 0-1 Tight: 0-0 Gall: 0-0
Aids: Bl: 0-0 Vi: 0-0 Tstrap: 0-0
Best Rating: 69 10/01 Ludl 2m gd-fm NHF

Captive (IRE)

96(98h) (90h)**94**
6-y-o br g Be My Native (USA)-La Capitana (Mon Capitaine)
A Crook (N G Richards 9/5) Trevor Hemmings

Placings:*04*5-3065**04P** **(4521)**
2001/02: 16^{3}GS, 17^{0}G, 16^{6}S, 16^{5}G, 16^{0}S, 16^{4}GS, 20^{P}GS

	Starts	1st	2nd	3rd	Win & Pl
Hurdles	4	0	0	1	349
Chases	3	0	0	0	323
Career Total	**10**	**0**	**0**	**1**	**671**

Going: Sf: 0-2 GS: 0-3 Gd: 0-2 GF: - Fm: 0-0
Distance: 2m/2m3: 0-6 2m4-2m7: 0-1 3m+: 0-0
Track: LH: 0-5 RH: 0-2 Tight: 0-4 Gall: 0-1
Aids: Bl: 0-0 Vi: 0-0 Tstrap: 0-5
Best Rating: 94 3/02 Catt 2m gd-sft Ch

Maiden hurdler-chaser. Has worn a tongue tie.

Caracciola (NZ)

6-y-o ch g Fiesta Star (AUS)-Striking Princess (NZ) (Straight Strike (USA))
G M McCourt N H Oliver

Placings:0PP **(3702)**
2001/02: 16^{0}S, 22^{P}S, 19^{P}HY

	Starts	1st	2nd	3rd	Win & Pl
Hurdles	3	0	0	0	
Career Total	3	0	0	0	

Going: Sf: 0-3 GS: 0-0 Gd: 0-0 GF: - Fm: 0-0
Distance: 2m/2m3: 0-1 2m4-2m7: 0-2 3m+: 0-0
Track: LH: 0-2 RH: 0-1 Tight: 0-1 Gall: 0-0
Aids: Bl: 0-0 Vi: 0-0 Tstrap: 0-0
Best Rating:

Caradoc

(65h)
7-y-o ch g Bustino-Hathaway (Connaught)
Mrs L C Jewell John D Hurd

Placings:0/P042PP-0 **(0103)**
2001/02: 26^{0}GF

	Starts	1st	2nd	3rd	Win & Pl
Chases	1	0	0	0	
Career Total	**8**	**0**	**1**	**0**	**896**

Going: Sf: 0-0 GS: 0-0 Gd: 0-0 GF: - Fm: 0-1
Distance: 2m/2m3: 0-0 2m4-2m7: 0-0 3m+: 0-1
Track: LH: 0-0 RH: 0-0 Tight: 0-1 Gall: 0-0
Aids: Bl: 0-0 Vi: 0-0 Tstrap: 0-0
Best Rating: 81 1/01 Plum 2m4f heavy Ch

Caramore

7-y-o b g Puget (USA)-Security Pacific (Sonnen Gold)
C J Drewe Trip Syndicate

Placings:PP **(4405)**
2001/02: 20^{P}GS, 17^{P}S

	Starts	1st	2nd	3rd	Win & Pl
Hurdles	1	0	0	0	0
Chases	1	0	0	0	0
Career Total	**2**	**0**	**0**	**0**	

Going: Sf: 0-1 GS: 0-1 Gd: 0-0 GF: - Fm: 0-0
Distance: 2m/2m3: 0-1 2m4-2m7: 0-1 3m+: 0-0
Track: LH: 0-2 RH: 0-0 Tight: 0-1 Gall: 0-0
Aids: Bl: 0-0 Vi: 0-0 Tstrap: 0-0
Best Rating:

Carandrew (FR)

107(63c) **136**
9-y-o b g Saint Andrews (FR)-Cara Maria (FR) (Cadoudal (FR))
M C Pipe D A Johnson

Placings:0/0166541/00**F4121FU2/235**4050P-111145000511 **(4728)**
2001/02: 17^{1}F, 16^{1}GF, 17^{1}F, 17^{1}GF, 16^{4}GF, 16^{5}GF, 16^{0}GS, 19^{0}GS, 25^{0}S, 16^{5}G, 16^{1}GS, 16^{1}GF

	Starts	1st	2nd	3rd	Win & Pl
Hurdles	12	6	0	0	18796
Career Total	**38**	**10**	**3**	**1**	**54662**

136	4/02	Chep	2m110y	C(0-130)HHdl	G-F	£5509
127	4/02	Chep	2m110y	F Hdl	G-S	£1897
136	5/01	Folk	2m1f110y	F(0-110)HHdl	G-F	£2982
110	5/01	Extr	2m1f	E(0-115)HHdl	FRM	£3108
120	5/01	Sthl	2m	F(0-105)HHdl	G-F	£2086
106	5/01	Tntn	2m1f	F(0-100)HHdl	FRM	£2107
146	2/00	Plum	2m1f	E Ch	HVY	£3585
130	1/00	Extr	2m7f110y	D Ch	HVY	£5040
	5/99	Autl	2m1f110y	HHdl	VS	£10764
	9/98	Nior	2m3f	Hdl	SFT	£3030

Total win prize-money £40108

Going: Sf: 0-1 GS: 1-3 Gd: 0-1 GF: - Fm: 5-7

Distance: 2m/2m3: 6-11 2m4-2m7: 0-0 3m+: 0-1
Track: LH: 3-7 RH: 3-4 Tight: 3-4 Gall: 0-2
Aids: Bl: 0-0 Vi: 0-0 Tstrap: 0-0
Best Rating: 146 6/00 Strf 2m1f110y good Ch

A winner over hurdles in France and England, he has also won over fences. He completed a four-timer over hurdles in the spring of 2001, but shot up the handicap as a result and his two victories at Chepstow in April 2002 were in weak events. Suited by two miles and fast ground.

Carbonado

8-y-o b g Anshan-Virevoite (Shareef Dancer (USA))
H R Tuck Mrs M J Tuck

Placings: *546*F0/42 (4645)
2001/02: 24^{4}S, 24^{2}G

	Starts	1st	2nd	3rd	Win & Pl
Chases	2	0	1	0	800
Career Total	**7**	**0**	**1**	**0**	**800**

Going: Sf: 0-1 GS: 0-0 Gd: 0-1 GF: - Fm: 0-0
Distance: 2m/2m3: 0-0 2m4-2m7: 0-0 3m+: 0-2
Track: LH: 0-0 RH: 0-2 Tight: 0-2 Gall: 0-0
Aids: Bl: 0-0 Vi: 0-0 Tstrap: 0-0
Best Rating: 105 4/02 Ludl 3m good Ch

Hunter chaser, effective over three miles on a sound surface.

Carbury Cross (IRE)

119(87h) (105h)163

8-y-o b g Mandalus-Brickey Gazette (Fine Blade (USA))
J J O'Neill Anne Duchess Of Westminster

Placings: 41306/211/111-62021U6 (4913)
2001/02: 24^{6}G, 25^{2}G, 24^{0}G, 24^{2}GS, 25^{1}G, 33^{U}G, 29^{6}G

	Starts	1st	2nd	3rd	Win & Pl
Hurdles	1	0	0	0	0
Chases	6	1	2	0	49875
Career Total	**18**	**7**	**3**	**1**	**87783**

163	4/02	Aint	3m1f	B HCh	GD	£26000
144	4/01	Ayr	3m1f	B HCh	G-F	£21385
140	2/01	Donc	3m	E Ch	GD	£3225
134	1/01	Muss	3m	E Ch	G-S	£3575
122	11/99	Hayd	2m7f110y	D(0-120)HHdl	GD	£3078
126	10/99	Carl	3m110y	E(0-115)HHdl	GD	£2402
108	1/99	Weth	2m4f110y	D Hdl	SFT	£3116

Total win prize-money £62782

Going: Sf: 0-0 GS: 0-1 Gd: 1-6 GF: - Fm: 0-0
Distance: 2m/2m3: 0-0 2m4-2m7: 0-0 3m+: 1-7
Track: LH: 1-5 RH: 0-2 Tight: 1-2 Gall: 0-2
Aids: Bl: 1-4 Vi: 0-0 Tstrap: 0-0
Best Rating: 163 4/02 Aint 3m1f good Ch

He won all three of his starts over fences in 2000/2001, including a valuable novices' handicap at Ayr. He was disappointing on his reappearance over hurdles at Aintree and did not hit top form over fences until running a good second in the Ritz Club at the Festival when blinkered for the first time. Scored in fine style at Aintree and was still going well behind the leaders when unseating in the Scottish National. Looked to be feeling the effects of those races in the Attheraces Gold Cup. Normally a sound jumper, he stays well.

Cardiff Arms (NZ)

85 94

8-y-o b g Lowell (USA)-Shuzohra (NZ) (Tom's Shu (USA))
Ian Williams The Winning Line & J M Kinnear

Placings: 151-0 (1955)
2001/02: 16^{0}G

	Starts	1st	2nd	3rd	Win & Pl
Hurdles	1	0	0	0	0
Career Total	**4**	**2**	**0**	**0**	**4234**

129	12/00	Fknm	2m	E Hdl	G-S	£1764
131	10/00	Aint	2m110y	E Hdl	GD	£2470

Total win prize-money £4234

Going: Sf: 0-0 GS: 0-0 Gd: 0-1 GF: - Fm: 0-0
Distance: 2m/2m3: 0-1 2m4-2m7: 0-0 3m+: 0-0
Track: LH: 0-1 RH: 0-0 Tight: 0-0 Gall: 0-0
Aids: Bl: 0-0 Vi: 0-0 Tstrap: 0-1
Best Rating: 131 10/00 Aint 2m110y good Hdl

Useful Flat performer, won hurdling debut at Aintree but subsequently beaten favourite at Cheltenham. Better suited to sharp Fakenham track when winning there in December 2000. Blew up on his sole start in 2001/02.

Cardinal Fair (IRE)

5-y-o b m Namaqualand (USA)-Irish Affaire (IRE) (Fairy King (USA))
B P J Baugh Mrs Joan M Chrimes

Placings: PP0P-FP (0875)
2001/02: 16^{F}GF, 16^{P}GS

	Starts	1st	2nd	3rd	Win & Pl
Hurdles	2	0	0	0	
Career Total	**6**	**0**	**0**	**0**	

Going: Sf: 0-0 GS: 0-1 Gd: 0-0 GF: - Fm: 0-1
Distance: 2m/2m3: 0-2 2m4-2m7: 0-0 3m+: 0-0
Track: LH: 0-2 RH: 0-0 Tight: 0-1 Gall: 0-0
Aids: Bl: 0-0 Vi: 0-0 Tstrap: 0-0
Best Rating:

Cardinal Gayle (IRE)

73 104

12-y-o b g Cardinal Flower-Bettica (Lord Gayle (USA))
R H Alner The Wedding Party

Placings: 03PPF0/302023/3/5/1-0 (0084)
2001/02: 25^{0}G

	Starts	1st	2nd	3rd	Win & Pl
Chases	1	0	0	0	
Career Total	**16**	**1**	**2**	**4**	**6435**

104	4/01	Plum	3m2f	F(0-95)HCh	SFT	£3246

Total win prize-money £3247

Going: Sf: 0-0 GS: 0-0 Gd: 0-1 GF: - Fm: 0-0
Distance: 2m/2m3: 0-0 2m4-2m7: 0-0 3m+: 0-1
Track: LH: 0-0 RH: 0-1 Tight: 0-0 Gall: 0-0
Aids: Bl: 0-0 Vi: 0-0 Tstrap: 0-0
Best Rating: 104 4/01 Plum 3m2f soft Ch

Cardinal Rule (IRE)

13-y-o ch g Carlingford Castle-Lady Of Rathleek (Furry Glen)
R Ford D E Harrison

Placings: *65556*/PUP331115P2/131/UP1132/4433063/U-P (0043)
2001/02: 19^{P}GS

	Starts	1st	2nd	3rd	Win & Pl
Chases	1	0	0	0	
Career Total	**34**	**7**	**2**	**7**	**32743**

136	1/99	Weth	2m4f110y	D(0-125)HCh	SFT	£3710
128	12/98	Wwck	2m4f110y	D(0-120)HCh	G-S	£3947
106	10/97	Uttx	2m4f	D(0-125)HCh	GD	£4338
113	5/97	Towc	2m6f	E(0-100)HCh	GD	£3182
108	2/97	Hrfd	2m3f	E(0-105)HCh	SFT	£2875
106	2/97	Hrfd	2m3f	E(0-100)HCh	G-S	£3100
80	1/97	Plum	2m5f	E(0-100)HCh	GD	£3503

Total win prize-money £24659

Going: Sf: 0-0 GS: 0-1 Gd: 0-0 GF: - Fm: 0-0
Distance: 2m/2m3: 0-0 2m4-2m7: 0-1 3m+: 0-0
Track: LH: 0-0 RH: 0-1 Tight: 0-0 Gall: 0-0
Aids: Bl: 0-0 Vi: 0-0 Tstrap: 0-0
Best Rating: 136 2/99 Sand 2m4f110y good Ch

Cardinal Way (IRE)

9-y-o b/br g Cardinal Flower-Loving Way (Golden Love)
Mrs Julie Read (L Wells 10/3) A F J J Moss

Placings: 66/4/P (4777)
2001/02: 25^{P}G

	Starts	1st	2nd	3rd	Win & Pl
Chases	1	0	0	0	
Career Total	**4**	**0**	**0**	**0**	**0**

Going: Sf: 0-0 GS: 0-0 Gd: 0-1 GF: - Fm: 0-0
Distance: 2m/2m3: 0-0 2m4-2m7: 0-0 3m+: 0-1
Track: LH: 0-0 RH: 0-1 Tight: 0-1 Gall: 0-0
Aids: Bl: 0-0 Vi: 0-0 Tstrap: 0-0
Best Rating: 89 3/98 Font 2m2f110y gd-fm Hdl

Carew

72 27

6-y-o b g Minster Son-The White Lion (Flying Tyke)
C Grant D Vic Roper

Placings: *52B-40* (4679)
2001/02: 16^{4}HY, 17^{0}G

	Starts	1st	2nd	3rd	Win & Pl
NH Flat	2	0	0	0	0
Career Total	**5**	**0**	**1**	**0**	**450**

Going: Sf: 0-1 GS: 0-0 Gd: 0-1 GF: - Fm: 0-0
Distance: 2m/2m3: 0-2 2m4-2m7: 0-0 3m+: 0-0
Track: LH: 0-0 RH: 0-0 Tight: 0-0 Gall: 0-0
Aids: Bl: 0-0 Vi: 0-0 Tstrap: 0-0
Best Rating: 102 12/00 Muss 2m good NHF

Careysville (IRE)

102 122

11-y-o b g Carmelite House (USA)-Kavali (Blakeney)
Miss Venetia Williams R T Sturgis

Placings: *6500*P/06/5F11PF5/2101/F424/3-02 (4135)
2001/02: 24^{0}S, 24^{2}G

	Starts	1st	2nd	3rd	Win & Pl
Chases	2	0	1	0	2210
Career Total	**25**	**4**	**3**	**1**	**27605**

135	3/99	Newb	3m	C(0-135)HCh	SFT	£5524
135	1/99	Folk	3m2f	D(0-125)HCh	SFT	£7335
120	1/98	Ludl	3m	E(0-115)HCh	G-S	£3048
124	12/97	Font	3m2f110y	E(0-100)HCh	SFT	£3603

Total win prize-money £19511

Going: Sf: 0-1 GS: 0-0 Gd: 0-1 GF: - Fm: 0-0
Distance: 2m/2m3: 0-0 2m4-2m7: 0-0 3m+: 0-2

Track: LH: 0-0 RH: 0-2 Tight: 0-0 Gall: 0-0
Aids: Bl: 0-0 Vi: 0-0 Tstrap: 0-0
Best Rating: 135 3/99 Newb 3m soft Ch

He is a fair chaser at a modest level, but is pretty slow and needs an extreme test of stamina to show his best. He was off the track for a long time before the start of 2002, but ran well on his second start back in the Grand Military Gold Cup.

Cargo Flight

7-y-o br g Seymour Hicks (FR)-Lilac Wood (Precipice Wood)
G B Balding Bernard Keay

Placings:0/0P **(3657)**
2001/02: 21^{0}S, 22^{P}S

	Starts	1st	2nd	3rd	Win & Pl
Hurdles	2	0	0	0	
Career Total	**3**	**0**	**0**	**0**	

Going: Sf: 0-2 GS: 0-0 Gd: 0-0 GF: - Fm: 0-0
Distance: 2m/2m3: 0-0 2m4-2m7: 0-2 3m+: 0-0
Track: LH: 0-1 RH: 0-1 Tight: 0-1 Gall: 0-0
Aids: Bl: 0-0 Vi: 0-0 Tstrap: 0-0
Best Rating: 94 4/00 Font 2m2f110y good NHF

Caribbean Lad (IRE)

91 **77**
6-y-o ch g Denel (FR)-Daisy Star (Star Appeal)
J R Turner Mrs Sylvia Blakeley

Placings:00-0F **(1842)**
2001/02: 17^{0}GS, 24^{F}S

	Starts	1st	2nd	3rd	Win & Pl
Hurdles	2	0	0	0	
Career Total	**4**	**0**	**0**	**0**	

Going: Sf: 0-1 GS: 0-1 Gd: 0-0 GF: - Fm: 0-0
Distance: 2m/2m3: 0-1 2m4-2m7: 0-0 3m+: 0-1
Track: LH: 0-0 RH: 0-2 Tight: 0-0 Gall: 0-0
Aids: Bl: 0-0 Vi: 0-0 Tstrap: 0-0
Best Rating: 77 10/01 Carl 2m1f gd-sft Hdl

Caribbean Twist (IRE)

8-y-o b g Montelimar (USA)-Ye Little Daisy (Prince Tenderfoot (USA))
Mrs L Williamson Halewood International Ltd

Placings:00/0 **(1833)**
2001/02: 20^{0}G

	Starts	1st	2nd	3rd	Win & Pl
Hurdles	1	0	0	0	
Career Total	**3**	**0**	**0**	**0**	

Going: Sf: 0-0 GS: 0-0 Gd: 0-1 GF: - Fm: 0-0
Distance: 2m/2m3: 0-0 2m4-2m7: 0-1 3m+: 0-0
Track: LH: 0-1 RH: 0-0 Tight: 0-1 Gall: 0-0
Aids: Bl: 0-0 Vi: 0-0 Tstrap: 0-0
Best Rating: 83 1/00 Donc 2m110y gd-fm NHF

Carins Hill

51 **10**
8-y-o b g High Kicker (USA)-Ishaarah (IRE) (Top Ville)
Ronald Thompson Ronald Thompson

Placings:00P/P-0 **(0646)**
2001/02: 17^{0}GF

	Starts	1st	2nd	3rd	Win & Pl
Hurdles	1	0	0	0	
Career Total	**5**	**0**	**0**	**0**	

Going: Sf: 0-0 GS: 0-0 Gd: 0-0 GF: - Fm: 0-1
Distance: 2m/2m3: 0-1 2m4-2m7: 0-0 3m+: 0-0
Track: LH: 0-0 RH: 0-1 Tight: 0-1 Gall: 0-0
Aids: Bl: 0-0 Vi: 0-0 Tstrap: 0-0
Best Rating: 93 11/99 Carl 2m1f soft NHF

Carley Lad (IRE)

14-y-o br g Crash Course-Leveret (Le Bavard (FR))
N B Mason N B Mason

Placings:00P/2121/**PP/61F405110/26531/**40**P40-P5** **(2153)**
2001/02: 25^{P}G, 24^{5}G

	Starts	1st	2nd	3rd	Win & Pl
Chases	2	0	0	0	0
Career Total	**30**	**6**	**3**	**1**	**34980**

127	4/00	Weth	3m1f	B(0-150)HCh	SFT	£10062
122	4/99	Towc	2m6f	D(0-125)HCh	GD	£5563
116	3/99	Newc	3m	E(0-115)HCh	SFT	£3550
114	12/98	Weth	2m4f110y	D(0-110)HCh	SFT	£4004
98	3/96	Newc	3m	C(0-130)HHdl	SFT	£3436
100	2/96	Newc	3m	F(0-105)HHdl	SFT	£2344

Total win prize-money £28959

Going: Sf: 0-0 GS: 0-0 Gd: 0-2 GF: - Fm: 0-0
Distance: 2m/2m3: 0-0 2m4-2m7: 0-0 3m+: 0-2
Track: LH: 0-2 RH: 0-0 Tight: 0-1 Gall: 0-1
Aids: Bl: 0-0 Vi: 0-0 Tstrap: 0-2
Best Rating: 127 4/00 Weth 3m1f soft Ch

Carlinare

12-y-o b g Sousa-Demetria (GER) (Basalt (GER))
Mrs L B Normile Mrs L Normile

Placings:55P2-4 **(4892)**
2001/02: 31^{4}G

	Starts	1st	2nd	3rd	Win & Pl
Chases	1	0	0	0	322
Career Total	**5**	**0**	**1**	**0**	**1130**

Going: Sf: 0-0 GS: 0-0 Gd: 0-1 GF: - Fm: 0-0
Distance: 2m/2m3: 0-0 2m4-2m7: 0-0 3m+: 0-1
Track: LH: 0-0 RH: 0-0 Tight: 0-0 Gall: 0-0
Aids: Bl: 0-0 Vi: 0-0 Tstrap: 0-0
Best Rating: 81 4/01 Prth 2m4f110y heavy Hdl

Carling Elect

90(78c) (50c)**67**
6-y-o ch m Carlingford Castle-Electress (Baron Blakeney)
J Neville J S Payne

Placings:00054P **(4173)**
2001/02: 22^{0}G, 21^{0}G, 21^{0}G, 21^{5}G, 22^{4}HY, 25^{P}GS

	Starts	1st	2nd	3rd	Win & Pl
Hurdles	5	0	0	0	0
Chases	1	0	0	0	0
Career Total	**6**	**0**	**0**	**0**	**0**

Going: Sf: 0-1 GS: 0-1 Gd: 0-4 GF: - Fm: 0-0
Distance: 2m/2m3: 0-0 2m4-2m7: 0-5 3m+: 0-1
Track: LH: 0-2 RH: 0-2 Tight: 0-3 Gall: 0-0
Aids: Bl: 0-0 Vi: 0-0 Tstrap: 0-3
Best Rating: 67 1/02 Ludl 2m5f good Hdl

Carlingbrook

69
8-y-o ch g Carlingford Castle-Siliferous (Sandy Creek)
T R George Mrs Sharon C Nelson

Placings:54/P4 **(4303)**
2001/02: 16^{P}HY, 16^{4}HY

	Starts	1st	2nd	3rd	Win & Pl
Hurdles	2	0	0	0	273
Career Total	**4**	**0**	**0**	**0**	**491**

Going: Sf: 0-2 GS: 0-0 Gd: 0-0 GF: - Fm: 0-0
Distance: 2m/2m3: 0-2 2m4-2m7: 0-0 3m+: 0-0
Track: LH: 0-2 RH: 0-0 Tight: 0-0 Gall: 0-0
Aids: Bl: 0-0 Vi: 0-0 Tstrap: 0-0
Best Rating: 100 2/00 Asct 2m110y soft NHF

Carlovent (FR)

116(126c) **150**
7-y-o b g Cadoudal (FR)-Carlaya (FR) (Carmarthen (FR))
M C Pipe C M , B J & R F Batterham

Placings:11F113/1111FF11160/**514PU**612-543535034 **(4911)**
2001/02: 20^{5}GS, 24^{4}S, 25^{3}G, 23^{5}S, 22^{3}S, 24^{5}GS, 24^{0}G, 24^{3}GF, 24^{4}G

	Starts	1st	2nd	3rd	Win & Pl
Hurdles	9	0	0	3	19525
Career Total	**34**	**13**	**1**	**4**	**142945**

149	4/01	Aint	3m110y	B HHdl	SFT	£26000
154	11/00	Asct	2m	B HCh	G-S	£13312
136	11/99	Chep	2m110y	B Hdl	G-S	£6710
147	11/99	Chep	2m4f	B HHdl	SFT	£22073
142	10/99	Chep	2m110y	B HHdl	SFT	£6710
134	7/99	Wolv	2m4f110y	C(0-130)HHdl	G-F	£6563
	6/99	Autl	2m1f110y	Ch	SFT	£6997
	6/99	Toul	2m1f110y	Hdl	GD	£3767
	5/99	Dax	2m3f	Ch	SFT	£3767
	10/98	Mesl	2m1f110y	Ch	HVY	£3535
	9/98	Jarn	2m	Hdl	GD	£1515
	7/98	Pomp	1m5f110y	Hdl	GD	£2828
	6/98	Pomp	1m5f110y	Hdl	GD	£2525

Total win prize-money £106303

Going: Sf: 0-3 GS: 0-2 Gd: 0-3 GF: - Fm: 0-1
Distance: 2m/2m3: 0-0 2m4-2m7: 0-2 3m+: 0-7
Track: LH: 0-3 RH: 0-4 Tight: 0-0 Gall: 0-1
Aids: Bl: 0-0 Vi: 0-0 Tstrap: 0-0
Best Rating: 154 11/00 Asct 2m gd-sft Ch

A winner over hurdles and fences in both France and England, he just misses out at the top level. Best these days at around three miles, but held in hot company since winning at Aintree in April 2001. Suited by testing ground, he is reportedly blind in one eye.

Carlton Cracker

112(82h) **107**
10-y-o b g Primitive Rising (USA)-Miss Cracker Jack (Ancient Monro)
J G Given J E Titley

Placings:3F-PUP5321 **(4557)**
2001/02: 20^{P}GS, 20^{U}S, 19^{P}G, 16^{5}GS, 20^{3}S, 20^{2}GS, 25^{1}G

	Starts	1st	2nd	3rd	Win & Pl

	Starts	1st	2nd	3rd	Win & Pl
Chases	7	1	1	1	5050
Career Total	**9**	**1**	**1**	**2**	**5878**

107 4/02 MRas 3m1f F(0-95)Ch GD £3556
Total win prize-money £3556

Going: Sf: 0-2 GS: 0-3 Gd: 1-2 GF: - Fm: 0-0
Distance: 2m/2m3: 0-1 2m4-2m7: 0-5 **3m+: 1-1**
Track: LH: 0-2 **RH: 1-5 Tight: 1-4** Gall: 0-2
Aids: Bl: 0-0 Vi: 0-0 Tstrap: 0-0
Best Rating: 110 3/02 MRas 2m4f gd-sft Ch

Winning pointer but is headstrong and has taken time to get his act together under Rules.

Carlyta

6-y-o ch m Carlingford Castle-Baryta (Nishapour (FR))
M J Gingell (G L Moore 4/5) Lime Street Racing Syndicate

Placings: 0P4PP (3449)
2001/02: 17^{0}GS, 21^{P}S, 16^{4}S, 16^{P}S, 16^{P}GS

	Starts	1st	2nd	3rd	Win & Pl
NH Flat	1	0	0	0	0
Hurdles	4	0	0	0	0
Career Total	**5**	**0**	**0**	**0**	**0**

Going: Sf: 0-3 GS: 0-2 Gd: 0-0 GF: - Fm: 0-0
Distance: 2m/2m3: 0-4 2m4-2m7: 0-1 3m+: 0-0
Track: LH: 0-3 RH: 0-1 Tight: 0-4 Gall: 0-0
Aids: Bl: 0-0 Vi: 0-0 Tstrap: 0-0
Best Rating: 46 5/01 Folk 2m1f110y gd-sft NHF

Carmichael (NZ)

82 66

7-y-o b g Lord Ballina (AUS)-Zamyntor (NZ) (Amyntor (FR))
Lady Connell Lady Connell

Placings: 0004 (4640)
2001/02: 17^{0}S, 16^{0}G, 16^{0}G, 16^{4}G

	Starts	1st	2nd	3rd	Win & Pl
NH Flat	1	0	0	0	0
Hurdles	3	0	0	0	250
Career Total	**4**	**0**	**0**	**0**	**250**

Going: Sf: 0-1 GS: 0-0 Gd: 0-3 GF: - Fm: 0-0
Distance: 2m/2m3: 0-4 2m4-2m7: 0-0 3m+: 0-0
Track: LH: 0-0 RH: 0-4 Tight: 0-1 Gall: 0-1
Aids: Bl: 0-0 Vi: 0-0 Tstrap: 0-0
Best Rating: 66 10/01 Winc 2m good Hdl

Carna Too

48f 18f

5-y-o br m Afzal-H And K Punter (Mandalus)
C J Drewe Rw2

Placings: 00 (4571)
2001/02: 16^{0}HY, 16^{0}G

	Starts	1st	2nd	3rd	Win & Pl
NH Flat	2	0	0	0	
Career Total	**2**	**0**	**0**	**0**	

Going: Sf: 0-1 GS: 0-0 Gd: 0-1 GF: - Fm: 0-0
Distance: 2m/2m3: 0-2 2m4-2m7: 0-0 3m+: 0-0
Track: LH: 0-1 RH: 0-1 Tight: 0-0 Gall: 0-0
Aids: Bl: 0-0 Vi: 0-0 Tstrap: 0-0
Best Rating: 18 2/02 Wwck 2m heavy NHF

Carnaven

94 80

10-y-o b g Le Coq D'Or-Carney (New Brig)
R Allan Mrs L A Ogilvie

Placings: 00P/P0PP/4P/PP-P523602 (1022)
2001/02: 25^{P}S, 20^{5}GF, 20^{2}GF, 24^{3}F, 20^{6}GF, 21^{0}GF, 27^{2}GF

	Starts	1st	2nd	3rd	Win & Pl
Chases	7	0	2	1	2587
Career Total	**18**	**0**	**2**	**1**	**2587**

Going: Sf: 0-1 GS: 0-0 Gd: 0-0 GF: - Fm: 0-6
Distance: 2m/2m3: 0-0 2m4-2m7: 0-4 3m+: 0-3
Track: LH: 0-5 RH: 0-2 Tight: 0-2 Gall: 0-0
Aids: Bl: 0-1 Vi: 0-5 Tstrap: 0-0
Best Rating: 80 7/01 Sedg 3m3f gd-fm Ch

Carnoustie (USA)

99 104

4-y-o gr f Ezzoud (IRE)-Sarba (USA) (Persepolis (FR))
R T Phillips (M A Jarvis 21/9) Dozen Dreamers Partnership

Placings: 3 (4504)
2001/02: 17^{3}G

	Starts	1st	2nd	3rd	Win & Pl
Hurdles	1	0	0	1	436
Career Total	**1**	**0**	**0**	**1**	**436**

Going: Sf: 0-0 GS: 0-0 Gd: 0-1 GF: - Fm: 0-0
Distance: 2m/2m3: 0-1 2m4-2m7: 0-0 3m+: 0-0
Track: LH: 0-1 RH: 0-0 Tight: 0-1 Gall: 0-0
Aids: Bl: 0-0 Vi: 0-0 Tstrap: 0-0
Best Rating: 92 3/02 NAbb 2m1f good Hdl

Showed plenty of promise on hurdling debut.

Carole's Dove

94 71

6-y-o b m Manhal-Nimble Dove (Starch Reduced)
C J Price Mrs C A Crawford

Placings: 605P365 (4408)
2001/02: 16^{6}S, 16^{0}GS, 16^{5}S, 19^{P}GS, 19^{3}S, 19^{6}S, 17^{5}S

	Starts	1st	2nd	3rd	Win & Pl
Hurdles	7	0	0	1	497
Career Total	**7**	**0**	**0**	**1**	**497**

Going: Sf: 0-5 GS: 0-2 Gd: 0-0 GF: - Fm: 0-0
Distance: 2m/2m3: 0-4 2m4-2m7: 0-3 3m+: 0-0
Track: LH: 0-3 RH: 0-4 Tight: 0-3 Gall: 0-0
Aids: Bl: 0-0 Vi: 0-0 Tstrap: 0-0
Best Rating: 71 12/01 Chep 2m110y soft Hdl

Carousing

99 106

5-y-o b g Selkirk (USA)-Moon Carnival (Be My Guest (USA))
A Bailey Willie McKay

Placings: 54522-440 (2435)
2001/02: 20^{4}G, 20^{4}G, 16^{0}S

	Starts	1st	2nd	3rd	Win & Pl
Hurdles	3	0	0	0	0
Career Total	**8**	**0**	**2**	**0**	**1194**

Going: Sf: 0-1 GS: 0-0 Gd: 0-2 GF: - Fm: 0-0
Distance: 2m/2m3: 0-1 2m4-2m7: 0-2 3m+: 0-0
Track: LH: 0-3 RH: 0-0 Tight: 0-2 Gall: 0-0
Aids: Bl: 0-0 Vi: 0-0 Tstrap: 0-0

Best Rating: 106 10/01 Aint 2m4f good Hdl

Carradium

98 77

6-y-o b g Presidium-Carrapateira (Gunner B)
R Shiels R Shiels

Placings: 0-P00004 (4788)
2001/02: 16^{P}G, 17^{0}G, 22^{0}G, 16^{0}G, 22^{0}GS, 20^{4}F

	Starts	1st	2nd	3rd	Win & Pl
Hurdles	6	0	0	0	0
Career Total	**7**	**0**	**0**	**0**	**0**

Going: Sf: 0-0 GS: 0-1 Gd: 0-4 GF: - Fm: 0-1
Distance: 2m/2m3: 0-3 2m4-2m7: 0-3 3m+: 0-0
Track: LH: 0-5 RH: 0-1 Tight: 0-4 Gall: 0-1
Aids: Bl: 0-0 Vi: 0-0 Tstrap: 0-1
Best Rating: 70 4/02 Newc 2m4f firm Hdl

Carrick Troop (IRE)

107 134

9-y-o gr g Roselier (FR)-Over The Pond (IRE) (Over The River (FR))
Mrs M Reveley Major J C K Young

Placings: P4/6B112/322PPU3P-P13B114 (4831)
2001/02: 22^{P}G, 16^{1}S, 17^{3}G, 17^{B}S, 17^{1}S, 18^{1}GS, 20^{4}G

	Starts	1st	2nd	3rd	Win & Pl
Chases	7	3	0	1	26162
Career Total	**22**	**5**	**3**	**3**	**40815**

134	3/02	Newb	2m2f110y	D(0-125)HCh	G-S	£7182
128	3/02	Newb	2m1f	C(0-135)HCh	SFT	£8268
124	12/01	Hayd	2m	D(0-125)HCh	SFT	£9051
126	1/00	Sedg	3m3f	F(0-105)HCh	SFT	£2873
120	12/99	MRas	3m1f	E(0-105)HCh	G-S	£3481

Total win prize-money £30857

Going: Sf: 2-3 GS: 1-1 Gd: 0-3 GF: - Fm: 0-0
Distance: **2m/2m3: 3-5** 2m4-2m7: 0-2 3m+: 0-0
Track: **LH: 3-5** RH: 0-1 Tight: 0-1 **Gall: 2-3**
Aids: Bl: 0-0 Vi: 0-0 Tstrap: 0-0
Best Rating: 134 3/02 Newb 2m2f110y gd-sft Ch

Handicap chaser who used to race over three miles plus but now seems perfectly capable at trips around two miles. Suited by soft ground. Needs a strong pace in order to show his best.

Carried Interest (IRE)

109 127

8-y-o br g Celio Rufo-Laurie Belle (Boreen (FR))
N A Gaselee Michael Stoddart

Placings: 33/5333/106462-24P344 (4390)
2001/02: 21^{2}GF, 23^{4}GF, 22^{P}G, 21^{3}S, 24^{4}S, 21^{4}S

	Starts	1st	2nd	3rd	Win & Pl
Chases	6	0	1	1	2826
Career Total	**18**	**1**	**2**	**6**	**10508**

127 12/00 Hntg 3m E(0-105)HCh SFT £3289
Total win prize-money £3290

Going: Sf: 0-3 GS: 0-0 Gd: 0-1 GF: - Fm: 0-2
Distance: 2m/2m3: 0-0 2m4-2m7: 0-4 3m+: 0-2
Track: LH: 0-2 RH: 0-4 Tight: 0-1 Gall: 0-1
Aids: Bl: 0-2 Vi: 0-0 Tstrap: 0-0
Best Rating: 127 4/01 Font 2m6f good Ch

Fair chaser who stays well and is versatile with regard to ground conditions. Has lost his way somewhat this year.

Carrig Boy (IRE)

2-y-o ch g Long Pond-Shining Brightly (Giolla Mear)
Anderson Ian Anderson

Placings:*00/PB* (4846)
2001/02: 25^{P}S, 24^{B}G

	Starts	1st	2nd	3rd	Win & Pl
Chases	2	0	0	0	
Career Total	4	0	0	0	

Going: Sf: 0-1 GS: 0-0 Gd: 0-1 GF: - Fm: 0-0
Distance: 2m/2m3: 0-0 2m4-2m7: 0-0 3m+: 0-2
Track: LH: 0-2 RH: 0-0 Tight: 0-1 Gall: 0-0
Aids: Bl: 0-0 Vi: 0-0 Tstrap: 0-0
Best Rating: 82 12/96 Clon 2m yield NHF

Carrigafoyle

85 65
-y-o b g Young Senor (USA)-Miss Skindles (Taufan (USA))
O Brennan O Brennan

Placings:*40-06* (4774)
2001/02: 16^{0}GF, 17^{6}G

	Starts	1st	2nd	3rd	Win & Pl
NH Flat	1	0	0	0	0
Hurdles	1	0	0	0	0
Career Total	4	0	0	0	0

Going: Sf: 0-0 GS: 0-0 Gd: 0-1 GF: - Fm: 0-1
Distance: 2m/2m3: 0-2 2m4-2m7: 0-0 3m+: 0-0
Track: LH: 0-1 RH: 0-1 Tight: 0-1 Gall: 0-0
Aids: Bl: 0-0 Vi: 0-0 Tstrap: 0-0
Best Rating: 93 5/00 Chep 2m110y firm NHF

Carrington House

98(93c) (43c)81
9-y-o b g Teenoso (USA)-Erica Superba (Langton Heath)
K C Bailey I F W Buchan

Placings:*U/06/6P4P/434F4U4-P502650* (4110)
2001/02: 20^{P}S, 20^{5}GF, 24^{0}GF, 20^{2}GS, 16^{6}HY, 20^{5}S, 16^{0}S

	Starts	1st	2nd	3rd	Win & Pl
Hurdles	5	0	1	0	578
Chases	2	0	0	0	0
Career Total	21	0	1	1	2282

Going: Sf: 0-4 GS: 0-1 Gd: 0-0 GF: - Fm: 0-2
Distance: 2m/2m3: 0-2 2m4-2m7: 0-4 3m+: 0-1
Track: LH: 0-1 RH: 0-6 Tight: 0-0 Gall: 0-2
Aids: Bl: 0-1 Vi: 0-0 Tstrap: 0-0
Best Rating: 110 5/00 Towc 2m6f gd-fm Ch

Modest form over both hurdles and fences, stays two and a half miles.

Carry On Brendan (IRE)

101 94
11-y-o b g Electric-Jackie's Pet (Strong Gale)
M Mullineaux The Hon Mrs S Pakenham

Placings:*2F/6F3/200-0440* (1076)
2001/02: 20^{0}G, 22^{4}GF, 25^{4}GS, 24^{0}GF

	Starts	1st	2nd	3rd	Win & Pl
Hurdles	1	0	0	0	0
Chases	3	0	0	0	320
Career Total	12	0	2	1	3230

Going: Sf: 0-0 GS: 0-1 Gd: 0-1 GF: - Fm: 0-2
Distance: 2m/2m3: 0-0 2m4-2m7: 0-2 3m+: 0-2
Track: LH: 0-3 RH: 0-1 Tight: 0-3 Gall: 0-0
Aids: Bl: 0-0 Vi: 0-0 Tstrap: 0-0
Best Rating: 124 12/98 Uttx 2m4f gd-sft Ch

Carryonharry (IRE)

110(108h) (132h)143
8-y-o gr g Roselier (FR)-Bluebell Avenue (Boreen Beag)
M C Pipe Drs' D Silk J Castro M Gillard P Walker

Placings:*663113/1133-1110F* (4677)
2001/02: 22^{1}GS, 23^{1}GF, 23^{1}G, 24^{0}GS, 36^{F}G

	Starts	1st	2nd	3rd	Win & Pl
Chases	5	3	0	0	14404
Career Total	15	7	0	4	35719

134	12/01	Extr	2m7f110y	D Ch	GD	£5538
125	11/01	Extr	2m7f110y	D Ch	G-F	£5681
143	11/01	Font	2m6f	E Ch	G-S	£3185
133	11/00	Chep	3m	C(0-130)HHdl	HVY	£5057
130	11/00	Kemp	3m110y	D(0-120)HHdl	SFT	£4212
114	2/00	Wwck	2m4f110y	D Hdl	GD	£3685
106	1/00	Plum	2m5f	E Hdl	SFT	£2415

Total win prize-money £29774

Going: Sf: 0-0 GS: 1-2 Gd: 1-2 GF: - Fm: 1-1
Distance: 2m/2m3: 0-0 2m4-2m7: 1-1 **3m+: 2-4**
Track: LH: 0-2 **RH: 2-2 Tight: 1-2** Gall: 0-1
Aids: Bl: 0-0 Vi: 0-0 Tstrap: 0-0
Best Rating: 143 11/01 Font 2m6f gd-sft Ch

He showed improved form to win twice over hurdles in 2000/2001, but on both occasions had little in reserve. Scored a hat-trick on his first three starts over fences, but was well beaten at Cheltenham in March 2002 and fell at the first in the National. Has won on good and soft ground.

Cartmel Prince

71 37
4-y-o b g Prince Daniel (USA)-Oh My Oh My (Ballacashtal (CAN))
M Todhunter P G Airey, R R Whitton, F G Steel

Placings:*6* (1246)
2001/02: 17^{6}G

	Starts	1st	2nd	3rd	Win & Pl
Hurdles	1	0	0	0	0
Career Total	1	0	0	0	0

Going: Sf: 0-0 GS: 0-0 Gd: 0-1 GF: - Fm: 0-0
Distance: 2m/2m3: 0-1 2m4-2m7: 0-0 3m+: 0-0
Track: LH: 0-1 RH: 0-0 Tight: 0-1 Gall: 0-0
Aids: Bl: 0-0 Vi: 0-0 Tstrap: 0-0
Best Rating: 37 8/01 Ctml 2m1f110y good Hdl

Carway Princess

56f 33f
6-y-o ch m Then Again-Gray Laura (Grey Desire)
B J Llewellyn Carway Racing Club

Placings:*00* (1093)
2001/02: 16^{0}G, 16^{0}GF

	Starts	1st	2nd	3rd	Win & Pl
NH Flat	2	0	0	0	
Career Total	2	0	0	0	

Going: Sf: 0-0 GS: 0-0 Gd: 0-1 GF: - Fm: 0-1
Distance: 2m/2m3: 0-2 2m4-2m7: 0-0 3m+: 0-0
Track: LH: 0-2 RH: 0-0 Tight: 0-0 Gall: 0-0
Aids: Bl: 0-0 Vi: 0-0 Tstrap: 0-0
Best Rating: 33 8/01 Worc 2m gd-fm NHF

Casablanca (IRE)

9-y-o b g Strong Gale-Guess Twice (Deep Run)
D J Caro D J Caro

Placings:*P/P* (0366)
2001/02: 25^{P}G

	Starts	1st	2nd	3rd	Win & Pl
Hurdles	1	0	0	0	
Career Total	2	0	0	0	

Going: Sf: 0-0 GS: 0-0 Gd: 0-1 GF: - Fm: 0-0
Distance: 2m/2m3: 0-0 2m4-2m7: 0-0 3m+: 0-1
Track: LH: 0-0 RH: 0-0 Tight: 0-0 Gall: 0-0
Aids: Bl: 0-0 Vi: 0-0 Tstrap: 0-0
Best Rating:

Case Of Poteen (IRE)

105 90
6-y-o b/br m Witness Box (USA)-On The Hooch (Over The River (FR))
Mrs S C Bradburne J G Bradburne

Placings:*60/3232503-043246* (4745)
2001/02: 22^{0}GS, 22^{4}G, 22^{3}GS, 16^{2}HY, 24^{4}S, 24^{6}G

	Starts	1st	2nd	3rd	Win & Pl
Hurdles	6	0	1	1	1079
Career Total	15	0	3	4	4261

Going: Sf: 0-2 GS: 0-2 Gd: 0-2 GF: - Fm: 0-0
Distance: 2m/2m3: 0-1 2m4-2m7: 0-3 3m+: 0-2
Track: LH: 0-5 RH: 0-1 Tight: 0-2 Gall: 0-0
Aids: Bl: 0-0 Vi: 0-0 Tstrap: 0-0
Best Rating: 103 1/01 Newc 2m4f heavy Hdl

Staying hurdler, she has shown plenty of promise but continues to fall short of the spoils and is proving frustrating. She is fully exposed.

Cash 'N' Credit

86f 50f
4-y-o b f Homo Sapien-Not Enough (Balinger)
R Dickin Mrs J M E Mann

Placings:*00* (4166)
2001/02: 16^{0}HY, 16^{0}GS

	Starts	1st	2nd	3rd	Win & Pl
NH Flat	2	0	0	0	
Career Total	2	0	0	0	

Going: Sf: 0-1 GS: 0-1 Gd: 0-0 GF: - Fm: 0-0
Distance: 2m/2m3: 0-2 2m4-2m7: 0-0 3m+: 0-0
Track: LH: 0-2 RH: 0-0 Tight: 0-0 Gall: 0-0
Aids: Bl: 0-0 Vi: 0-0 Tstrap: 0-0
Best Rating: 50 3/02 Wwck 2m gd-sft NHF

Modest bumper form.

Cash Account

9-y-o b g Lord Bud-Gilzie Bank (New Brig)
R Harvey Mrs V J R Bostock

Placings:F (3653)
2001/02: 24^{F}S

	Starts	1st	2nd	3rd	Win & Pl
Chases	1	0	0	0	
Career Total	**1**	**0**	**0**	**0**	

Going: Sf: 0-1 GS: 0-0 Gd: 0-0 GF: - Fm: 0-0
Distance: 2m/2m3: 0-0 2m4-2m7: 0-0 3m+: 0-1
Track: LH: 0-0 RH: 0-1 Tight: 0-0 Gall: 0-1
Aids: Bl: 0-0 Vi: 0-0 Tstrap: 0-0
Best Rating:

Cash For Questions (IRE)

99 82
10-y-o b g Supreme Leader-Deep Dollar (Deep Run)
R A Fahey P S Cresswell

Placings:*03/41/5016/U0*-P (4908)
2001/02: 21^{P}G

	Starts	1st	2nd	3rd	Win & Pl
Hurdles	1	0	0	0	
Career Total	**11**	**2**	**0**	**1**	**6022**
110 1/00 Donc	2m4f	E(0-115)HHdl		GD	£2951
91 12/98 Catt	2m3f	E Hdl		GD	£2584

Total win prize-money £5535

Going: Sf: 0-0 GS: 0-0 Gd: 0-1 GF: - Fm: 0-0
Distance: 2m/2m3: 0-0 2m4-2m7: 0-1 3m+: 0-0
Track: LH: 0-0 RH: 0-1 Tight: 0-1 Gall: 0-0
Aids: Bl: 0-0 Vi: 0-0 Tstrap: 0-0
Best Rating: **110** 1/00 Donc 2m4f good Hdl

Cashaban

81 70
9-y-o ch g Ballacashtal (CAN)-Portway Anna (Hot Brandy)
J S Smith Michael J Smith

Placings:00UPP3/PP/24-F0P (4898)
2001/02: 17^{F}G, 16^{0}S, 16^{P}G

	Starts	1st	2nd	3rd	Win & Pl
Hurdles	2	0	0	0	0
Chases	1	0	0	0	0
Career Total	**13**	**0**	**1**	**1**	**1210**

Going: Sf: 0-1 GS: 0-0 Gd: 0-2 GF: - Fm: 0-0
Distance: 2m/2m3: 0-3 2m4-2m7: 0-0 3m+: 0-0
Track: LH: 0-0 RH: 0-3 Tight: 0-0 Gall: 0-0
Aids: Bl: 0-0 Vi: 0-0 Tstrap: 0-0
Best Rating: **82** 5/00 Strf 2m110y good Hdl

Cashel Bay (USA)

107 129
4-y-o b c Nureyev (USA)-Madame Premier (USA) (Raja Baba (USA))
Luke Comer Luke Comer

Placings:53356035 (4952a)
2001/02: 16^{5}GY, 16^{3}YS, 16^{3}SH, 16^{5}HY, 16^{6}HY, 17^{0}G, 16^{3}GY, 16^{5}G

	Starts	1st	2nd	3rd	Win & Pl
Hurdles	8	0	0	3	5518
Career Total	**8**	**0**	**0**	**3**	**5518**

Going: Sf: 0-2 GS: 0-0 Gd: 0-2 GF: - Fm: 0-0
Distance: 2m/2m3: 0-8 2m4-2m7: 0-0 3m+: 0-0
Track: LH: 0-4 RH: 0-4 Tight: 0-0 Gall: 0-1
Aids: Bl: 0-0 Vi: 0-0 Tstrap: 0-0
Best Rating: **129** 4/02 Punc 2m good Hdl

Fair Irish hurdler, suited by cut in the ground.

Cashew Kid (IRE)

5-y-o b g Persian Mews-No Honey (Dual)
Miss K Marks Nick Shutts

Placings:*60* (1799)
2001/02: 17^{6}GF, 16^{0}S

	Starts	1st	2nd	3rd	Win & Pl
NH Flat	2	0	0	0	0
Career Total	**2**	**0**	**0**	**0**	**0**

Going: Sf: 0-1 GS: 0-0 Gd: 0-0 GF: - Fm: 0-1
Distance: 2m/2m3: 0-2 2m4-2m7: 0-0 3m+: 0-0
Track: LH: 0-1 RH: 0-1 Tight: 0-0 Gall: 0-0
Aids: Bl: 0-0 Vi: 0-0 Tstrap: 0-0
Best Rating: **55** 9/01 Hrfd 2m1f gd-fm NHF

Cashmere Lady

101 81
10-y-o b m Hubbly Bubbly (USA)-Choir (High Top)
J L Eyre Mrs Sybil Howe

Placings:43/405/0350 (3464)
2001/02: 21^{0}GS, 16^{3}GS, 19^{5}G, 16^{0}S

	Starts	1st	2nd	3rd	Win & Pl
Hurdles	4	0	0	1	478
Career Total	**9**	**0**	**0**	**2**	**746**

Going: Sf: 0-1 GS: 0-2 Gd: 0-1 GF: - Fm: 0-0
Distance: 2m/2m3: 0-3 2m4-2m7: 0-1 3m+: 0-0
Track: LH: 0-3 RH: 0-1 Tight: 0-3 Gall: 0-1
Aids: Bl: 0-0 Vi: 0-0 Tstrap: 0-0
Best Rating: **93** 1/99 Muss 2m gd-sft Hdl

Exposed hurdler, suited by the mud.

Caspar's Date

92f 82f
5-y-o ch g Afzal-Rabdanna (Rabdan)
J Gallagher Smith Wadley Homes Ltd

Placings:*0* (4743)
2001/02: 16^{0}GF

	Starts	1st	2nd	3rd	Win & Pl
NH Flat	1	0	0	0	
Career Total	**1**	**0**	**0**	**0**	

Going: Sf: 0-0 GS: 0-0 Gd: 0-0 GF: - Fm: 0-1
Distance: 2m/2m3: 0-1 2m4-2m7: 0-0 3m+: 0-0
Track: LH: 0-0 RH: 0-1 Tight: 0-0 Gall: 0-0
Aids: Bl: 0-0 Vi: 0-0 Tstrap: 0-0
Best Rating: **78** 4/02 Ludl 2m gd-fm NHF

Cassia

88
8-y-o ch m Be My Native (USA)-Cinnamon Run (Deep Run)
N A Gaselee Club Ten

Placings:*13/02P0/F* (3231)
2001/02: 16^{F}GS

	Starts	1st	2nd	3rd	Win & Pl
Hurdles	1	0	0	0	
Career Total	**7**	**1**	**1**	**1**	**2089**
95 12/98 Hrfd	2m1f	H NHF		GD	£1234

Total win prize-money £123

Going: Sf: 0-0 GS: 0-1 Gd: 0-0 GF: - Fm: 0-0
Distance: 2m/2m3: 0-1 2m4-2m7: 0-0 3m+: 0-0
Track: LH: 0-0 RH: 0-1 Tight: 0-0 Gall: 0-1
Aids: Bl: 0-0 Vi: 0-0 Tstrap: 0-0
Best Rating: **99** 12/99 Winc 2m soft Hdl

Cassia Green

87 99
8-y-o gr g Scallywag-Casa's Star (Top Star)
R N Bevis Mrs J Greenway

Placings:P6 (4843)
2001/02: 24^{P}S, 17^{6}G

	Starts	1st	2nd	3rd	Win & Pl
Chases	2	0	0	0	0
Career Total	**2**	**0**	**0**	**0**	**0**

Going: Sf: 0-1 GS: 0-0 Gd: 0-1 GF: - Fm: 0-0
Distance: 2m/2m3: 0-1 2m4-2m7: 0-0 3m+: 0-1
Track: LH: 0-2 RH: 0-0 Tight: 0-2 Gall: 0-0
Aids: Bl: 0-0 Vi: 0-0 Tstrap: 0-0
Best Rating: **93** 4/02 Bang 2m1f110y good Ch

Winning pointer, held a winning lead when crashing out two out in a modest handicap chase at Uttoxeter in June.

Cassia Heights

108(101h) (79h)111
7-y-o b g Montelimar (USA)-Cloncoose (IRE) (Remainder Man)
S A Brookshaw Mr B Ridge & Mr D Hewitt

Placings:*000/0*200P-0542**U4P311331** (4497)
2001/02: 24^{0}G, 20^{5}G, 21^{4}GF, 20^{2}GF, 20^{U}GF, 17^{4}S, 20^{P}G, 20^{3}G, 24^{1}G, 24^{1}S, 24^{3}S, 24^{3}G, 24^{1}G

	Starts	1st	2nd	3rd	Win & Pl
Hurdles	3	0	0	0	0
Chases	10	3	1	3	18650
Career Total	**21**	**3**	**2**	**3**	**19522**
111 3/02 Hayd	3m	D(0-125)HCh		GD	£7085
101 1/02 Donc	3m	D(0-115)HCh		SFT	£4290
102 1/02 Ludl	3m	E(0-105)HCh		GD	£3581

Total win prize-money £14957

Going: Sf: 1-3 GS: 0-0 Gd: 2-7 GF: - Fm: 0-3
Distance: 2m/2m3: 0-1 2m4-2m7: 0-6 **3m+: 3-6**
Track: **LH: 2-5** RH: 1-8 Tight: 1-8 Gall: 1-1
Aids: Bl: 0-0 Vi: 0-0 **Tstrap: 3-13**
Best Rating: **111** 3/02 Hayd 3m good Ch

He jumped much better when winning at Ludlow in January 2002 and followed up that success when winning at Doncaster in the same month and at Haydock in March. Acts on good and soft ground and stays three miles.

Cassio's Boy

74 60
11-y-o b g Presidium-Cassio Lil (Scottish Rifle)
G M McCourt Lyonshall Racing

Placings:00330050/01P204010U/41264052F14/12F20PP/P0/51145034442/242140P000-0 (0052)
2001/02: 20^{0}G

	Starts	1st	2nd	3rd	Win & Pl
Hurdles	1	0	0	0	0
Career Total	**60**	**8**	**8**	**3**	**35040**
103 9/00 Hrfd	2m3f110y	F(0-110)HHdl		G-S	£3100
103 10/99 Bang	2m4f	F(0-110)HHdl		SFT	£3728

01	9/99	Hrfd	2m3f110y	F(0-110)HHdl	GD	£3452
08	10/97	Worc	2m4f	C(0-130)HHdl	SFT	£3450
03	3/97	Chep	2m4f110y	D(0-125)HHdl	GD	£3160
8	11/96	Bang	2m4f	E(0-110)HHdl	G-S	£2927
9	3/96	Hrfd	2m3f110y	E(0-100)HHdl	SFT	£2752
7	11/95	Chep	2m4f110y	F Hdl	SFT	£2267

Total win prize-money £24841

Going: Sf: 0-0 GS: 0-0 Gd: 0-1 GF: - Fm: 0-0
Distance: 2m/2m3: 0-0 2m4-2m7: 0-1 3m+: 0-0
Track: LH: 0-1 RH: 0-0 Tight: 0-1 Gall: 0-0
Aids: Bl: 0-0 Vi: 0-0 Tstrap: 0-0
Best Rating: 108 10/97 Worc 2m4f good Hdl

Casterbridge

92 **66**

10-y-o ch g Nearly A Hand-G W Supermare (Rymer)
Jedd O'Keeffe Tony Sweetman

Placings:01/5/33104/64P23PP-F45P **(3256)**
2001/02: 25^{F}GS, 26^{4}S, 30^{5}GS, 30^{P}S

	Starts	1st	2nd	3rd	Win & Pl
Chases	4	0	0	0	533
Career Total	**19**	**2**	**1**	**3**	**13095**

131	2/00	Leic	2m7f110y	D Ch	SFT	£4290
105	3/98	Chep	2m4f110y	D Hdl	SFT	£2957

Total win prize-money £7247

Going: Sf: 0-2 GS: 0-2 Gd: 0-0 GF: - Fm: 0-0
Distance: 2m/2m3: 0-0 2m4-2m7: 0-0 3m+: 0-4
Track: LH: 0-3 RH: 0-1 Tight: 0-1 Gall: 0-2
Aids: Bl: 0-2 Vi: 0-0 Tstrap: 0-0
Best Rating: 131 2/00 Leic 2m7f110y soft Ch

Castle Arrow (IRE)

9-y-o b g Mansooj-Soulful (So Blessed)
Graham Richards (J White 24/3) Miss R Williams

Placings:5P03/0**F/2F4/P00P4P2** **(4727)**
2001/02: 21^{P}G, 18^{0}GF, 16^{0}G, 21^{P}GF, 22^{4}GF, 26^{P}GF, 24^{2}GF

	Starts	1st	2nd	3rd	Win & Pl
Hurdles	1	0	0	0	0
Chases	6	0	1	0	1078
Career Total	**16**	**0**	**2**	**1**	**1943**

Going: Sf: 0-0 GS: 0-0 Gd: 0-2 GF: - Fm: 0-5
Distance: 2m/2m3: 0-2 2m4-2m7: 0-3 3m+: 0-2
Track: LH: 0-5 RH: 0-1 Tight: 0-4 Gall: 0-0
Aids: Bl: 0-5 Vi: 0-0 Tstrap: 0-0
Best Rating: 94 5/99 Uttx 2m5f gd-fm Ch

Castle Clear (IRE)

100(110h) (94h)**83+**

9-y-o b g Castle Keep-Rose Of Allendale (Green Shoon)
Mrs S C Bradburne (Mrs M Reveley 22/7) R Hilley

Placings:*1/0320*/F523/UU12P343U014/U560-0663313313 **(4896)**
2001/02: 21^{0}GF, 20^{6}GF, 22^{6}GS, 18^{3}G, 20^{3}GS, 20^{1}S, 20^{3}G, 20^{3}HY, 22^{1}GF, 20^{3}G

	Starts	1st	2nd	3rd	Win & Pl
Hurdles	8	2	0	5	9172
Chases	2	0	0	0	0
Career Total	**35**	**5**	**3**	**9**	**22699**

89	4/02	Kels	2m6f110y	D(0-120)HHdl	G-F	£3465
89	12/01	Ayr	2m4f	F(0-105)HHdl	SFT	£3052
102	1/00	Sthl	2m4f110y	E(0-115)HCh	G-S	£3313
107	6/99	Prth	2m	E Ch	SFT	£3452
110	3/97	Ayr	2m	H NHF	SFT	£1035

Total win prize-money £14319

Going: Sf: 1-2 GS: 0-2 Gd: 0-3 GF: - Fm: 1-3
Distance: 2m/2m3: 0-1 **2m4-2m7: 2-9** 3m+: 0-0
Track: **LH: 2-8** RH: 0-2 **Tight: 1-7** Gall: 0-0
Aids: Bl: 0-1 Vi: 0-0 Tstrap: 0-0
Best Rating: 110 3/97 Ayr 2m soft NHF

A winning chaser, he has looked happier back over hurdles recently. Stays two miles-six, acts on any ground.

Castle Folly (IRE)

94 **91**

10-y-o b g Carlingford Castle-Air Plane (Arratos (FR))
J White Nick Quesnel

Placings:P-0P4 **(3452)**
2001/02: 17^{0}G, 17^{P}S, 20^{4}HY

	Starts	1st	2nd	3rd	Win & Pl
Chases	3	0	0	0	219
Career Total	**4**	**0**	**0**	**0**	**219**

Going: Sf: 0-2 GS: 0-0 Gd: 0-1 GF: - Fm: 0-0
Distance: 2m/2m3: 0-2 2m4-2m7: 0-1 3m+: 0-0
Track: LH: 0-3 RH: 0-0 Tight: 0-3 Gall: 0-0
Aids: Bl: 0-1 Vi: 0-0 Tstrap: 0-0
Best Rating: 79 1/02 Plum 2m4f heavy Ch

Moderate maiden chaser. Likes to force the pace and stays three and a quarter miles.

Castle Friend

98 **78+**

7-y-o b g Durgam (USA)-Furry Friend (USA) (Bold Bidder)
F S Storey F S Storey

Placings:240/04 **(4785)**
2001/02: 21^{0}S, 16^{4}F

	Starts	1st	2nd	3rd	Win & Pl
Hurdles	2	0	0	0	0
Career Total	**5**	**0**	**1**	**0**	**748**

Going: Sf: 0-1 GS: 0-0 Gd: 0-0 GF: - Fm: 0-1
Distance: 2m/2m3: 0-1 2m4-2m7: 0-1 3m+: 0-0
Track: LH: 0-2 RH: 0-0 Tight: 0-1 Gall: 0-1
Aids: Bl: 0-0 Vi: 0-0 Tstrap: 0-0
Best Rating: 90 9/98 Sedg 2m1f gd-fm Hdl

Castle Lynch (IRE)

95 **121**

10-y-o b m Castle Keep-Shirowen (Master Owen)
C Tizzard Mrs Audrey Kley

Placings:*0060/41*/3U11P3FP3-66U500 **(2929)**
2001/02: 19^{6}G, 25^{6}G, 21^{U}G, 19^{5}GS, 16^{0}G, 24^{0}GS

	Starts	1st	2nd	3rd	Win & Pl
Chases	6	0	0	0	0
Career Total	**21**	**3**	**0**	**3**	**11558**

121	11/00	Winc	2m	D Ch	SFT	£4017
116	11/00	Winc	2m5f	E(0-105)HCh	SFT	£4426
108	3/00	Winc	2m5f	H Ch	G-S	£1118

Total win prize-money £9562

Going: Sf: 0-0 GS: 0-2 Gd: 0-4 GF: - Fm: 0-0
Distance: 2m/2m3: 0-2 2m4-2m7: 0-2 3m+: 0-2
Track: LH: 0-0 RH: 0-6 Tight: 0-2 Gall: 0-0
Aids: Bl: 0-0 Vi: 0-0 Tstrap: 0-0
Best Rating: 121 4/01 Winc 3m1f110y soft Ch

Modest handicap chaser, best ridden from the front.

Suited by cut in the ground and goes well at Wincanton. Likes to race prominently.

Castle Prince (IRE)

111(53h) **150**

8-y-o b g Homo Sapien-Lisaleen Lady (Miners Lamp)
R J Hodges Miss R Dobson

Placings:*66000*/2432F2-33144515 **(4912)**
2001/02: 16^{3}G, 16^{3}G, 16^{1}S, 16^{4}S, 16^{4}S, 16^{5}G, 16^{1}G, 16^{5}G

	Starts	1st	2nd	3rd	Win & Pl
Chases	8	2	0	2	11747
Career Total	**19**	**2**	**3**	**3**	**15090**

120	4/02	Winc	2m	D(0-115)HCh	GD	£4368
112	1/02	Folk	2m	E(0-105)HCh	SFT	£3367

Total win prize-money £7735

Going: Sf: 1-3 GS: 0-0 Gd: 1-5 GF: - Fm: 0-0
Distance: **2m/2m3: 2-8** 2m4-2m7: 0-0 3m+: 0-0
Track: LH: 0-0 **RH: 2-8 Tight: 1-4** Gall: 0-0
Aids: Bl: 0-0 Vi: 0-0 Tstrap: 0-0
Best Rating: 150 4/02 Sand 2m good Ch

He was let down by his jumping as a novice during the 2000/2001 season, but got the hang of things in 2001/2002 winning at Folkestone in January. Suited by two miles and acts on soft and fast ground. Thought to be a bit of a short-runner, but made all to score at Wincanton over Easter.

Castle Road (IRE)

7-y-o b g Good Thyne (USA)-Merry Miss (Deep Run)
D R Gandolfo Starlight Racing

Placings:PP **(1669)**
2001/02: 22^{P}GS, 24^{P}G

	Starts	1st	2nd	3rd	Win & Pl
Hurdles	2	0	0	0	
Career Total	**2**	**0**	**0**	**0**	

Going: Sf: 0-0 GS: 0-1 Gd: 0-1 GF: - Fm: 0-0
Distance: 2m/2m3: 0-0 2m4-2m7: 0-1 3m+: 0-1
Track: LH: 0-2 RH: 0-0 Tight: 0-1 Gall: 0-0
Aids: Bl: 0-0 Vi: 0-0 Tstrap: 0-0
Best Rating:

Castle Stephen (IRE)

71 **52**

11-y-o ro g Carlingford Castle-Lucy Platter (FR) (Record Token)
E M Caine Mrs Karen Woodhead

Placings:PP/PP/P0000 **(2683)**
2001/02: 24^{P}GF, 16^{0}G, 16^{0}G, 16^{0}GS, 16^{0}G

	Starts	1st	2nd	3rd	Win & Pl
Hurdles	5	0	0	0	
Career Total	**9**	**0**	**0**	**0**	

Going: Sf: 0-0 GS: 0-1 Gd: 0-3 GF: - Fm: 0-1
Distance: 2m/2m3: 0-4 2m4-2m7: 0-0 3m+: 0-1
Track: LH: 0-4 RH: 0-1 Tight: 0-2 Gall: 0-1
Aids: Bl: 0-0 Vi: 0-0 Tstrap: 0-0
Best Rating: 52 11/01 Weth 2m good Hdl

Castlebridge

65 **18**

5-y-o b g Batshoof-Super Sisters (AUS) (Call Report (USA))

M D I Usher P Sweeting

Placings:3-0 (1755)
2001/02: 16^{0}GS

	Starts	1st	2nd	3rd	Win & Pl
Hurdles	1	0	0	0	
Career Total	**2**	**0**	**0**	**1**	**320**

Going: Sf: 0-0 GS: 0-1 Gd: 0-0 GF: - Fm: 0-0
Distance: 2m/2m3: 0-1 2m4-2m7: 0-0 3m+: 0-0
Track: LH: 0-1 RH: 0-0 Tight: 0-1 Gall: 0-0
Aids: Bl: 0-1 Vi: 0-0 Tstrap: 0-0
Best Rating: 68 8/00 Bang 2m1f good Hdl

Castleshane (IRE)

114 **130**

5-y-o b g Kris-Ahbab (IRE) (Ajdal (USA))
S Gollings W Hobson,J King,G King,P Winfrow

Placings:2340P-F51242053 (4820)
2001/02: 16^{F}G, 19^{5}G, 16^{1}G, 16^{2}G, 16^{4}Y, 16^{2}GS, 16^{0}GS, 16^{5}G, 17^{3}G

	Starts	1st	2nd	3rd	Win & Pl
Hurdles	9	1	2	1	17186
Career Total	**14**	**1**	**3**	**2**	**19262**

106	10/01	Chel	2m110y	D Hdl	GD	£7345

Total win prize-money £7345

Going: Sf: 0-0 GS: 0-2 Gd: 1-6 GF: - Fm: 0-0
Distance: **2m/2m3: 1-8** 2m4-2m7: 0-1 3m+: 0-0
Track: **LH: 1-4** RH: 0-5 Tight: 0-2 Gall: 0-1
Aids: Bl: 0-0 Vi: 0-0 Tstrap: 0-0
Best Rating: 130 2/02 Kemp 2m gd-sft Hdl

He apparently likes his own way out in front, otherwise he can tend to sulk. The tactics worked well when he won at Cheltenham in October 2001 and he has run some fine races otherwise when only one or two have been able to catch him. Connections reckon he is best going right-handed. Suited by two miles and a sound surface.

Castletown Count

94 **100**

10-y-o b g Then Again-Pepeke (Mummy's Pet)
M W Easterby Abbots Salford Caravan Park

Placings:2521UP/21602/F232601-66U50 (2511)
2001/02: 20^{6}G, 21^{6}GS, 25^{U}G, 25^{5}G, 25^{0}S

	Starts	1st	2nd	3rd	Win & Pl
Chases	5	0	0	0	0
Career Total	**23**	**3**	**6**	**1**	**18186**

118	2/01	Catt	2m	E(0-115)HCh	SFT	£3461
117	1/00	Catt	2m3f	E(0-115)HCh	GD	£3542
110	1/99	Catt	2m3f	E(0-105)HCh	SFT	£3912

Total win prize-money £10916

Going: Sf: 0-1 GS: 0-1 Gd: 0-3 GF: - Fm: 0-0
Distance: 2m/2m3: 0-0 2m4-2m7: 0-2 3m+: 0-3
Track: LH: 0-5 RH: 0-0 Tight: 0-3 Gall: 0-0
Aids: Bl: 0-1 Vi: 0-0 Tstrap: 0-0
Best Rating: 118 2/01 Catt 2m soft Ch

A modest handicapper, he seems to reserve his best for Catterick. Suited by trips of around two and a half miles.

Castrato

75 **49**

6-y-o b g Rock City-Vocalist (Crooner)
B N Doran P N Exton

Placings:6-00P000 (3759)
2001/02: 16^{0}GF, 16^{0}GF, 16^{P}S, 16^{0}GF, 19^{0}HY, 17^{0}S

	Starts	1st	2nd	3rd	Win & Pl
Hurdles	6	0	0	0	
Career Total	**7**	**0**	**0**	**0**	**0**

Going: Sf: 0-3 GS: 0-0 Gd: 0-0 GF: - Fm: 0-3
Distance: 2m/2m3: 0-5 2m4-2m7: 0-1 3m+: 0-0
Track: LH: 0-2 RH: 0-4 Tight: 0-1 Gall: 0-0
Aids: Bl: 0-2 Vi: 0-0 Tstrap: 0-2
Best Rating: 49 2/02 Tntn 2m1f soft Hdl

Casual Water (IRE)

91 **73**

11-y-o b g Simply Great (FR)-Top Nurse (High Top)
C N Kellett J T Hunt

Placings:1340P/12/0/0012121F/36P6/U0 (0364)
2001/02: 21^{U}GF, 20^{0}GF

	Starts	1st	2nd	3rd	Win & Pl
Chases	2	0	0	0	
Career Total	**22**	**5**	**3**	**2**	**15928**

113	10/98	Tntn	2m3f	F(0-95)HCh	FRM	£2814
100	8/98	Font	2m2f	E Ch	G-F	£2915
94	7/98	NAbb	2m1f	E(0-110)HHdl	G-F	£2545
88	5/95	Strf	2m110y	F(0-100)HHdl	GD	£2395
70	10/94	Extr	2m1f110y	Hdl	GD	£1905

Total win prize-money £12574

Going: Sf: 0-0 GS: 0-0 Gd: 0-0 GF: - Fm: 0-2
Distance: 2m/2m3: 0-0 2m4-2m7: 0-2 3m+: 0-0
Track: LH: 0-2 RH: 0-0 Tight: 0-2 Gall: 0-0
Aids: Bl: 0-0 Vi: 0-0 Tstrap: 0-0
Best Rating: 113 10/98 Tntn 2m3f firm Ch

Catfish Keith (IRE)

105 **143**

8-y-o b g Be My Native (USA)-Diklers Run (Deep Run)
M C Pipe (G M McCourt 31/1) The Vintage Group

Placings:3/1640/310P153/0146-1046PP (4914)
2001/02: 16^{1}S, 16^{0}G, 16^{4}GF, 16^{6}S, 16^{P}HY, 20^{P}G

	Starts	1st	2nd	3rd	Win & Pl
Chases	6	1	0	0	7880
Career Total	**22**	**5**	**0**	**3**	**39195**

143	10/01	Towc	2m110y	D(0-125)HCh	SFT	£6851
143	12/00	Leic	2m4f110y	C(0-135)HCh	G-S	£11206
127	4/00	Towc	2m110y	D Ch	GD	£3939
143	11/99	Asct	2m	B Ch	GD	£8377
104	11/98	Wind	2m	D Hdl	GD	£2804

Total win prize-money £33177

Going: Sf: 1-3 GS: 0-0 Gd: 0-2 GF: - Fm: 0-1
Distance: **2m/2m3: 1-5** 2m4-2m7: 0-1 3m+: 0-0
Track: LH: 0-1 **RH: 1-5** Tight: 0-0 Gall: 0-0
Aids: Bl: 0-0 Vi: 0-1 Tstrap: 0-0
Best Rating: 143 10/01 Towc 2m110y soft Ch

Best around two and a half miles on right-handed tracks, he is fragile and failed to recapture his form immediately after winning a gruelling contest at Leicester in the middle of the 2000/2001 season. He ran into fourth behind Blowing Wind in the Victor Chandler Handicap Chase at Ascot, but that may have flattered him and his only win since came at Towcester in October 2001. He runs well fresh and has now joined Martin Pipe.

Catherine's Way (IRE)

10-y-o b g Mandalus-Sharp Approach (Crash Course)
Mrs P K J Brightwell Mrs P K J Brightwell

Placings:0/405F/42141/1P/U4-2P5 (4538
2001/02: 21^{2}GS, 20^{P}S, 24^{5}G

	Starts	1st	2nd	3rd	Win & Pl
Chases	3	0	1	0	619
Career Total	**17**	**3**	**2**	**0**	**12875**

130	2/00	MRas	2m6f110y	D(0-125)HCh	G-S	£4538
121	3/99	Leic	2m4f110y	E(0-105)HCh	SFT	£3496
117	12/98	Hntg	2m110y	E(0-105)HCh	SFT	£290

Total win prize-money £1093

Going: Sf: 0-1 GS: 0-1 Gd: 0-1 GF: - Fm: 0-0
Distance: 2m/2m3: 0-0 2m4-2m7: 0-2 3m+: 0-1
Track: LH: 0-2 RH: 0-1 Tight: 0-2 Gall: 0-0
Aids: Bl: 0-0 Vi: 0-0 Tstrap: 0-0
Best Rating: 130 2/00 MRas 2m6f110y gd-sft Ch

Front-running hunter chaser, suited by cut and goes wel fresh.

Cats Cross

73 **51**

7-y-o ch m Riverwise (USA)-Cut Above The Rest (Indiaro)
N R Mitchell Mrs M A Cooke

Placings:000-0P0P (4051
2001/02: 16^{0}S, 22^{P}G, 24^{0}S, 24^{P}G

	Starts	1st	2nd	3rd	Win & Pl
Hurdles	4	0	0	0	
Career Total	**7**	**0**	**0**	**0**	

Going: Sf: 0-2 GS: 0-0 Gd: 0-2 GF: - Fm: 0-0
Distance: 2m/2m3: 0-1 2m4-2m7: 0-1 3m+: 0-2
Track: LH: 0-2 RH: 0-2 Tight: 0-1 Gall: 0-0
Aids: Bl: 0-0 Vi: 0-0 Tstrap: 0-0
Best Rating: 69 2/01 Towc 2m heavy NHF

Catullus

81 **48**

6-y-o b g Prince Sabo-Rive-Jumelle (IRE) (M Double M (USA))
K F Clutterbuck K F Clutterbuck

Placings:30401/233052P0-PP0 (3449)
2001/02: 16^{P}HY, 16^{P}S, 16^{0}GS

	Starts	1st	2nd	3rd	Win & Pl
Hurdles	3	0	0	0	
Career Total	**16**	**1**	**2**	**3**	**5503**

85	4/00	Uttx	2m	E Hdl	HVY	£2747

Total win prize-money £2748

Going: Sf: 0-2 GS: 0-1 Gd: 0-0 GF: - Fm: 0-0
Distance: 2m/2m3: 0-3 2m4-2m7: 0-0 3m+: 0-0
Track: LH: 0-1 RH: 0-2 Tight: 0-1 Gall: 0-0
Aids: Bl: 0-0 Vi: 0-3 Tstrap: 0-0
Best Rating: 95 11/00 Tntn 2m1f good Hdl

Caxton Star

110 **123**

9-y-o ch g Soviet Star (USA)-Fiesta Fun (Welsh Pageant)
C R Egerton P A Mason

Placings:320/152F212P11P (1888)
2001/02: 17^{1}GF, 16^{5}GF, 17^{2}GS, 16^{F}G, 17^{2}GS, 19^{1}GF, 19^{2}GF, 24^{P}G, 17^{1}G, 16^{1}G, 16^{P}G

	Starts	1st	2nd	3rd	Win & Pl
Hurdles	10	4	3	0	14302
Chases	1	0	0	0	0
Career Total	**14**	**4**	**4**	**1**	**15548**

123	10/01	Towc	2m	D Hdl	GD	£3640

123	10/01	Sedg	2m1f	E Hdl	GD	£2541
111	9/01	MRas	2m3f110y	E Hdl	G-F	£2733
117	6/01	MRas	2m1f110y	E Hdl	G-F	£2509

Total win prize-money £11425

Going: Sf: 0-0 GS: 0-2 Gd: 2-5 GF: - Fm: 2-4
Distance: **2m/2m3: 3-8** 2m4-2m7: 1-2 3m+: 0-1
Track: LH: 1-5 **RH: 3-5 Tight: 3-6** Gall: 0-0
Aids: **Bl: 2-4** Vi: 0-0 Tstrap: 0-0
Best Rating: 123 10/01 Towc 2m good Hdl

He gained four all-the-way wins in novice hurdles last season. Suited by fast ground and forcing tactics.

Cead Mile Failte

89 **69**
7-y-o ch g Most Welcome-Avionne (Derrylin)
B J Llewellyn B W Parren

Placings:P0400U0 **(4271)**
2001/02: 16^{P}GS, 16^{0}GS, 16^{4}S, 17^{0}G, 17^{0}G, 16^{U}S, 16^{0}G

	Starts	1st	2nd	3rd	Win & Pl
Hurdles	7	0	0	0	0
Career Total	**7**	**0**	**0**	**0**	**0**

Going: Sf: 0-2 GS: 0-2 Gd: 0-3 GF: - Fm: 0-0
Distance: 2m/2m3: 0-7 2m4-2m7: 0-0 3m+: 0-0
Track: LH: 0-4 RH: 0-3 Tight: 0-3 Gall: 0-0
Aids: Bl: 0-0 Vi: 0-0 Tstrap: 0-0
Best Rating: 69 10/01 Strf 2m110y gd-sft Hdl

Ceanannas Mor (IRE)

114 **142**
8-y-o b/br g Strong Gale-Game Sunset (Menelek)
N J Henderson Major Christopher Hanbury

Placings:033/14FF-164032 **(4192)**
2001/02: 24^{1}GS, 27^{6}G, 23^{4}GF, 24^{0}G, 24^{3}S, 24^{2}GS

	Starts	1st	2nd	3rd	Win & Pl
Chases	6	1	1	1	27372
Career Total	**13**	**2**	**1**	**3**	**31935**

142	10/01	Kemp	3m	B(0-145)HCh	G-S	£17400
130	11/00	Leic	2m7f110y	E Ch	G-S	£3302

Total win prize-money £20702

Going: Sf: 0-1 GS: 1-2 Gd: 0-2 GF: - Fm: 0-1
Distance: 2m/2m3: 0-0 2m4-2m7: 0-0 **3m+: 1-6**
Track: LH: 0-3 **RH: 1-3** Tight: 0-0 Gall: 0-3
Aids: Bl: 0-0 Vi: 0-0 Tstrap: 0-0
Best Rating: 142 3/02 Chel 3m110y gd-sft Ch

He jumped soundly when winning Kempton's Charisma Gold Cup on his reappearance in 2001, but held until runner-up in the Kim Muir at the Cheltenham Festival. Stays three miles. Acts on good/good to soft ground.

Cedar Chief

102(77c) (56c)**85**
5-y-o b g Saddlers' Hall (IRE)-Dame Ashfield (Grundy)
R J O'Sullivan R O S Racing

Placings:24304-4F45410P**F**026 **(4415)**
2001/02: 25^{4}S, 22^{F}GF, 16^{4}GF, 20^{5}GF, 24^{4}GF, 22^{1}HY, 21^{0}GS, 22^{P}HY, 20^{F}G, 17^{0}S, 22^{2}S, 22^{6}S

	Starts	1st	2nd	3rd	Win & Pl
Hurdles	11	1	1	0	2130
Chases	1	0	0	0	0
Career Total	**17**	**1**	**2**	**1**	**3099**

85	10/01	Folk	2m6f110y	G(0-95)HHdl	HVY	£1561

Total win prize-money £1561

Going: Sf: 1-6 GS: 0-1 Gd: 0-1 GF: - Fm: 0-4
Distance: 2m/2m3: 0-2 **2m4-2m7: 1-8** 3m+: 0-2
Track: LH: 0-6 **RH: 1-3 Tight: 1-10** Gall: 0-0
Aids: **Bl: 1-10** Vi: 0-0 Tstrap: 0-0
Best Rating: 85 10/01 Folk 2m6f110y heavy Hdl

Cedar Father (IRE)

(93h) (57h)
8-y-o b g Phardante (FR)-Inger-Lea (Record Run)
R Lee E R Clough

Placings:*00*P56P/66-05P **(1035)**
2001/02: 20^{0}G, 24^{5}S, 21^{P}G

	Starts	1st	2nd	3rd	Win & Pl
Hurdles	2	0	0	0	0
Chases	1	0	0	0	0
Career Total	**11**	**0**	**0**	**0**	**0**

Going: Sf: 0-1 GS: 0-0 Gd: 0-2 GF: - Fm: 0-0
Distance: 2m/2m3: 0-0 2m4-2m7: 0-2 3m+: 0-1
Track: LH: 0-3 RH: 0-0 Tight: 0-1 Gall: 0-0
Aids: Bl: 0-0 Vi: 0-0 Tstrap: 0-3
Best Rating: 86 1/00 Kemp 2m good NHF

Cedar Flag (IRE)

99 **68**
8-y-o br g Jareer (USA)-Sasha Lea (Cawston's Clown)
L A Dace (M R Ewer-Hoad 3/1) Luke Dace

Placings:*0/0/*406 **(4883)**
2001/02: 21^{4}G, 16^{0}GF, 22^{6}GF

	Starts	1st	2nd	3rd	Win & Pl
Hurdles	3	0	0	0	0
Career Total	**5**	**0**	**0**	**0**	**0**

Going: Sf: 0-0 GS: 0-0 Gd: 0-1 GF: - Fm: 0-2
Distance: 2m/2m3: 0-1 2m4-2m7: 0-2 3m+: 0-0
Track: LH: 0-3 RH: 0-0 Tight: 0-3 Gall: 0-0
Aids: Bl: 0-0 Vi: 0-0 Tstrap: 0-1
Best Rating: 74 10/99 Hntg 2m110y gd-fm NHF

Cedar Green

108 **129**
8-y-o br g Bustino-Explosiva (USA) (Explodent (USA))
K C Bailey J Perriss

Placings:*0/***P41R23PP-F12126** **(3793)**
2001/02: 22^{F}S, 26^{1}S, 25^{2}HY, 28^{1}S, 25^{2}HY, 26^{6}S

	Starts	1st	2nd	3rd	Win & Pl
Chases	6	2	2	0	14587
Career Total	**15**	**3**	**3**	**1**	**20976**

129	1/02	Carl	3m4f	C(0-130)Ch	SFT	£7020
119	12/01	Wwck	3m2f	D(0-120)HCh	SFT	£3932
123	12/00	Towc	2m6f	D Ch	HVY	£4130

Total win prize-money £15083

Going: Sf: 2-6 GS: 0-0 Gd: 0-0 GF: - Fm: 0-0
Distance: 2m/2m3: 0-0 2m4-2m7: 0-1 **3m+: 2-5**
Track: **LH: 1-2** RH: 0-3 Tight: 0-0 Gall: 0-0
Aids: **Bl: 2-6** Vi: 0-0 Tstrap: 0-0
Best Rating: 129 1/02 Towc 3m1f heavy Ch

An out-and-out staying chaser, he has scored several times in the mud, but does not always look the most reliable ride. Wears blinkers.

Cedar Square (IRE)

105 **120**
11-y-o b g Dancing Dissident (USA)-Friendly Ann (Artaius (USA))
V R A Dartnall Nick Viney

Placings:0/F/1/1U0P5112/32641/P-P2UP4 **(4658)**
2001/02: 25^{P}G, 22^{2}G, 24^{U}G, 24^{P}GS, 24^{4}G

	Starts	1st	2nd	3rd	Win & Pl
Chases	5	0	1	0	2340
Career Total	**22**	**5**	**3**	**1**	**28806**

138	2/00	Kemp	3m	D(0-125)HCh	GD	£7150
130	4/99	Bang	3m110y	D(0-125)HCh	G-S	£7782
130	4/99	Hntg	3m	D(0-120)HCh	G-F	£4287
120	5/98	Aint	3m1f	H Ch	G-F	£1781
112	4/98	Chel	2m5f	H Ch	GD	£1961

Total win prize-money £22963

Going: Sf: 0-0 GS: 0-1 Gd: 0-4 GF: - Fm: 0-0
Distance: 2m/2m3: 0-0 2m4-2m7: 0-1 3m+: 0-4
Track: LH: 0-2 RH: 0-3 Tight: 0-1 Gall: 0-3
Aids: Bl: 0-0 Vi: 0-0 Tstrap: 0-0
Best Rating: 138 2/00 Kemp 3m good Ch

He is an effective handicap chaser at a modest level. Suited by trips just short of three miles but does stay that trip on an easy track. Acts on good/good to soft ground.

Cede Nullis

11-y-o b m Primitive Rising (USA)-Sweet Mood (Le Johnstan)
Peter Maddison Peter Maddison

Placings:P/UP-0101 **(0556)**
2001/02: 21^{0}G, 20^{1}GF, 16^{0}G, 24^{1}GF

	Starts	1st	2nd	3rd	Win & Pl
Chases	4	2	0	0	2445
Career Total	**7**	**2**	**0**	**0**	**2445**

99	5/01	Hntg	3m	H Ch	G-F	£1346
90	5/01	Hntg	2m4f110y	H Ch	G-F	£1098

Total win prize-money £2446

Going: Sf: 0-0 GS: 0-0 Gd: 0-2 GF: - Fm: 2-2
Distance: 2m/2m3: 0-1 2m4-2m7: 1-2 3m+: 1-1
Track: LH: 0-1 **RH: 2-2** Tight: 0-1 **Gall: 2-2**
Aids: Bl: 0-1 Vi: 0-0 Tstrap: 0-0
Best Rating: 99 5/01 Hntg 3m gd-fm Ch

Ceejayell

9-y-o b m Say Primula-Spring Garden (Silly Prices)
I Emmerson T B Tarn

Placings:*00/*000P00/PP60/P **(0066)**
2001/02: 21^{P}G

	Starts	1st	2nd	3rd	Win & Pl
Chases	1	0	0	0	
Career Total	**13**	**0**	**0**	**0**	**0**

Going: Sf: 0-0 GS: 0-0 Gd: 0-1 GF: - Fm: 0-0
Distance: 2m/2m3: 0-0 2m4-2m7: 0-1 3m+: 0-0
Track: LH: 0-1 RH: 0-0 Tight: 0-1 Gall: 0-0
Aids: Bl: 0-0 Vi: 0-0 Tstrap: 0-0
Best Rating: 62 4/99 Sedg 2m1f gd-sft Hdl

Ceinwen

7-y-o ch m Keen-Drudwen (Sayf El Arab (USA))
A W Carroll C F Basterfield

Placings:0 **(1556)**

2001/02: 16^{0}G

	Starts	1st	2nd	3rd	Win & Pl
Hurdles	1	0	0	0	
Career Total	**1**	**0**	**0**	**0**	

Going: Sf: 0-0 GS: 0-0 Gd: 0-1 GF: - Fm: 0-0
Distance: 2m/2m3: 0-1 2m4-2m7: 0-0 3m+: 0-0
Track: LH: 0-1 RH: 0-0 Tight: 0-0 Gall: 0-0
Aids: Bl: 0-0 Vi: 0-0 Tstrap: 0-0
Best Rating:

Celebration March

90 79

11-y-o b g Sousa-Boundless Grace (Flandre Ii)
M J Coombe J D Roberts

Placings:U-5 (0559)
2001/02: 22^{5}GF

	Starts	1st	2nd	3rd	Win & Pl
Hurdles	1	0	0	0	0
Career Total	**2**	**0**	**0**	**0**	**0**

Going: Sf: 0-0 GS: 0-0 Gd: 0-0 GF: - Fm: 0-1
Distance: 2m/2m3: 0-0 2m4-2m7: 0-1 3m+: 0-0
Track: LH: 0-1 RH: 0-0 Tight: 0-1 Gall: 0-0
Aids: Bl: 0-0 Vi: 0-0 Tstrap: 0-0
Best Rating: 79 5/01 NAbb 2m6f gd-fm Hdl

Celera

7-y-o gr m Petoski-Sarsa (Sassafras (FR))
Simon Earle D V Wakefield

Placings:P-PP (4114)
2001/02: 16^{P}S, 16^{P}G

	Starts	1st	2nd	3rd	Win & Pl
Hurdles	2	0	0	0	
Career Total	**3**	**0**	**0**	**0**	

Going: Sf: 0-1 GS: 0-0 Gd: 0-1 GF: - Fm: 0-0
Distance: 2m/2m3: 0-2 2m4-2m7: 0-0 3m+: 0-0
Track: LH: 0-0 RH: 0-2 Tight: 0-0 Gall: 0-0
Aids: Bl: 0-0 Vi: 0-0 Tstrap: 0-1
Best Rating:

Celias Twink

9-y-o b m Buckley-Celia's Halo (Mountain Call)
Mrs J A Saunders Mrs M E Thompson

Placings:P (1842)
2001/02: 24^{P}S

	Starts	1st	2nd	3rd	Win & Pl
Hurdles	1	0	0	0	
Career Total	**1**	**0**	**0**	**0**	

Going: Sf: 0-1 GS: 0-0 Gd: 0-0 GF: - Fm: 0-0
Distance: 2m/2m3: 0-0 2m4-2m7: 0-0 3m+: 0-1
Track: LH: 0-0 RH: 0-1 Tight: 0-0 Gall: 0-0
Aids: Bl: 0-0 Vi: 0-0 Tstrap: 0-0
Best Rating:

Celibate (IRE)

109(42h) 153

11-y-o ch g Shy Groom (USA)-Dance Alone (USA) (Monteverdi)
C J Mann Stamford Bridge Partnership

Placings:25213664/0521210446F0/2111123F2/15451 24/0231531/33433226B/03P1355265-10403236P (4914)
2001/02: 21^{1}G, 20^{0}G, 24^{4}G, 24^{0}G, 19^{3}G, 21^{2}GS, 19^{3}GS, 36^{6}G, 20^{P}G

	Starts	1st	2nd	3rd	Win & Pl
Chases	9	1	1	2	42192
Career Total	**71**	**13**	**13**	**12**	**264440**

153	10/01	Winc	2m5f	A HCh	GD	£21000
157	12/00	Asct	2m	B HCh	SFT	£9339
163	4/99	Punc	2m	Ch	YLD	£32098
163	2/99	Newb	2m1f	A Ch	G-S	£18503
162	12/97	Asct	2m	B HCh	G-S	£9403
155	10/97	Kemp	2m	B(0-150)HCh	GD	£4429
132	11/96	Chel	2m	A Ch	GD	£11780
118	10/96	Chel	2m	D Ch	FRM	£3701
132	10/96	Kemp	2m	D Ch	GD	£3436
108	9/96	Worc	2m	D Ch	G-F	£3562
118	12/95	Hayd	2m	C(0-135)HHdl	GD	£3728
113	11/95	Towc	2m	D(0-120)HHdl	G-F	£2756
104	11/94	Clon	2m	Hdl	SFT	£2120

Total win prize-money £125857

Going: Sf: 0-0 GS: 0-2 Gd: 1-7 GF: - Fm: 0-0
Distance: 2m/2m3: 0-0 **2m4-2m7: 1-6** 3m+: 0-3
Track: LH: 0-2 **RH: 1-7** Tight: 0-1 Gall: 0-1
Aids: Bl: 0-0 Vi: 0-0 Tstrap: 0-0
Best Rating: 163 2/00 Asct 2m3f110y gd-sft Ch

He is admirably consistent, although not as good as he once was, and he has struggled against the very best two-milers in the last couple of seasons. He stepped up to around two and a half miles in the first half of 2001 and made a winning reappearance over two miles five at Wincanton in October of that year, the furthest he has won over, although he has failed to build on that. Has won on soft and good ground and likes to front-run.

Celioso (IRE)

52

5-y-o b g Celio Rufo-Bettons Rose (Roselier (FR))
A Crook Trevor Hemmings

Placings:00P (3362)
2001/02: 17^{0}G, 19^{0}G, 25^{P}GS

	Starts	1st	2nd	3rd	Win & Pl
NH Flat	1	0	0	0	0
Hurdles	2	0	0	0	0
Career Total	**3**	**0**	**0**	**0**	**0**

Going: Sf: 0-0 GS: 0-1 Gd: 0-2 GF: - Fm: 0-0
Distance: 2m/2m3: 0-2 2m4-2m7: 0-0 3m+: 0-1
Track: LH: 0-3 RH: 0-0 Tight: 0-3 Gall: 0-0
Aids: Bl: 0-0 Vi: 0-0 Tstrap: 0-0
Best Rating: 76 11/01 Sedg 2m1f good NHF

Celony

97 70

5-y-o b m Primitive Rising (USA)-Lapopie (Deep Run)
C P Morlock Dwight Makins

Placings:00P (4586)
2001/02: 16^{0}G, 17^{0}S, 22^{P}G

	Starts	1st	2nd	3rd	Win & Pl
NH Flat	2	0	0	0	0
Hurdles	1	0	0	0	0
Career Total	**3**	**0**	**0**	**0**	**0**

Going: Sf: 0-1 GS: 0-0 Gd: 0-2 GF: - Fm: 0-0
Distance: 2m/2m3: 0-2 2m4-2m7: 0-1 3m+: 0-0
Track: LH: 0-1 RH: 0-1 Tight: 0-1 Gall: 0-0
Aids: Bl: 0-0 Vi: 0-0 Tstrap: 0-0

Best Rating: 75 11/01 Wwck 2m good NHF

Celtic Abbey

14-y-o b g Celtic Cone-Cagaleena (Cagirama)
Mrs Christine Hardinge G J Powell

Placings:F1123F44/2/2P4U1/14PFP/3361033/1/P4 (0271)
2001/02: 25^{P}G, 25^{4}G

	Starts	1st	2nd	3rd	Win & Pl
Chases	2	0	0	0	0
Career Total	**29**	**6**	**3**	**5**	**34824**

121	3/00	Chep	3m	H Ch	GD	£1841
120	3/99	Ludl	3m	H Ch	G-S	£1563
136	5/97	Strf	3m4f	B Ch	GD	£12575
136	4/97	Chel	3m2f110y	H Ch	G-F	£4026
114	6/94	Strf	3m4f	Ch	G-F	£3551
100	5/94	Uttx	2m5f	Ch	G-F	£1881

Total win prize-money £25440

Going: Sf: 0-0 GS: 0-0 Gd: 0-2 GF: - Fm: 0-0
Distance: 2m/2m3: 0-0 2m4-2m7: 0-0 3m+: 0-2
Track: LH: 0-0 RH: 0-2 Tight: 0-0 Gall: 0-0
Aids: Bl: 0-0 Vi: 0-0 Tstrap: 0-0
Best Rating: 138 5/98 Strf 3m good Ch

Celtic Bounty (IRE)

64 37

6-y-o b g Treasure Hunter-Welsh Glen (Furry Glen)
R J Hodges R J Hodges

Placings:0-00 (4485)
2001/02: 16^{0}G, 19^{0}G

	Starts	1st	2nd	3rd	Win & Pl
NH Flat	1	0	0	0	0
Hurdles	1	0	0	0	0
Career Total	**3**	**0**	**0**	**0**	

Going: Sf: 0-0 GS: 0-0 Gd: 0-2 GF: - Fm: 0-0
Distance: 2m/2m3: 0-2 2m4-2m7: 0-0 3m+: 0-0
Track: LH: 0-0 RH: 0-2 Tight: 0-0 Gall: 0-0
Aids: Bl: 0-0 Vi: 0-0 Tstrap: 0-0
Best Rating: 75 12/00 Hntg 2m110y heavy NHF

Celtic Exit (FR)

91 70

8-y-o b g Exit To Nowhere (USA)-Amour Celtique (Northfields (USA))
I A Balding Action Bloodstock

Placings:0 (2063)
2001/02: 16^{0}G

	Starts	1st	2nd	3rd	Win & Pl
Hurdles	1	0	0	0	
Career Total	**1**	**0**	**0**	**0**	

Going: Sf: 0-0 GS: 0-0 Gd: 0-1 GF: - Fm: 0-0
Distance: 2m/2m3: 0-1 2m4-2m7: 0-0 3m+: 0-0
Track: LH: 0-0 RH: 0-1 Tight: 0-0 Gall: 0-1
Aids: Bl: 0-0 Vi: 0-0 Tstrap: 0-0
Best Rating: 70 11/01 Hntg 2m110y good Hdl

Celtic Justice (IRE)

105 113

7-y-o br g Mister Lord (USA)-Just Ginger (The Parson)
R J Hodges Fieldspring Racing

Placings: 5/04016055 **(4403)**
2001/02: 16^{0}S, 16^{4}G, 17^{0}G, 16^{1}S, 20^{6}G, 21^{0}S, 16^{5}GS, 19^{5}S

	Starts	1st	2nd	3rd	Win & Pl
NH Flat	3	0	0	0	0
Hurdles	5	1	0	0	3402
Career Total	**9**	**1**	**0**	**0**	**3402**

113	12/01	Chep	2m110y	D Hdl	SFT	£3402

Total win prize-money £3402

Going: Sf: 1-4 GS: 0-1 Gd: 0-3 GF: - Fm: 0-0
Distance: **2m/2m3: 1-6** 2m4-2m7: 0-2 3m+: 0-0
Track: **LH: 1-6** RH: 0-2 Tight: 0-2 Gall: 0-1
Aids: Bl: 0-0 Vi: 0-0 Tstrap: 0-0
Best Rating: 113 12/01 Chep 2m110y soft Hdl

Winning Irish pointer and fair novice hurdler, winner of a small race at Chepstow on soft ground.

Celtic Land

103 **82**

9-y-o b m Landyap (USA)-Celtic Mist (Celtic Cone)
R G Frost Mrs J R Bastard

Placings: *000*/2440/502**P**2236334/000-4032 **(0920)**
2001/02: 22^{4}GF, 17^{0}G, 22^{3}GF, 27^{2}GF

	Starts	1st	2nd	3rd	Win & Pl
Hurdles	4	0	1	1	1169
Career Total	25	0	5	4	4876

Going: Sf: 0-0 GS: 0-0 Gd: 0-1 GF: - Fm: 0-3
Distance: 2m/2m3: 0-1 2m4-2m7: 0-2 3m+: 0-1
Track: LH: 0-4 RH: 0-0 Tight: 0-4 Gall: 0-0
Aids: Bl: 0-2 Vi: 0-0 Tstrap: 0-0
Best Rating: 91 3/00 NAbb 2m110y good Ch

Celtic Native (IRE)

107(118h) (124h)**126**

7-y-o b/br m Be My Native (USA)-Tarahumara (Soldier Rose)
P J Hobbs Mrs Jill Emery

Placings: *1*1111011/4230-311 **(2774)**
2001/02: 19^{3}GF, 21^{1}G, 19^{1}G

	Starts	1st	2nd	3rd	Win & Pl
Chases	3	2	0	1	10674
Career Total	**16**	**10**	**1**	**2**	**80538**

109	12/01	Extr	2m3f110y	D Ch	GD	£3913
123	11/01	NAbb	2m5f110y	C Ch	GD	£5930
149	4/00	Chel	2m5f110y	B HHdl	SFT	£13650
139	4/00	Chel	2m5f110y	B Hdl	SFT	£16802
149	2/00	Winc	2m6f	B Hdl	G-S	£13000
126	1/00	Tntn	2m3f110y	D Hdl	G-S	£3343
122	12/99	Winc	2m	E Hdl	SFT	£2472
118	12/99	Extr	2m3f110y	D Hdl	G-S	£4077
114	11/99	Extr	2m1f	H NHF	G-S	£1702
113	10/99	Bang	2m1f	H NHF	G-S	£1772

Total win prize-money £66665

Going: Sf: 0-0 GS: 0-0 Gd: 2-2 GF: - Fm: 0-1
Distance: 2m/2m3: 0-0 **2m4-2m7: 2-3** 3m+: 0-0
Track: LH: 1-1 RH: 1-2 **Tight: 1-1** Gall: 0-0
Aids: Bl: 0-0 Vi: 0-0 Tstrap: 0-0
Best Rating: 149 12/00 Asct 3m1f110y heavy Hdl

She carried all before her as a novice hurdler in 1999/200, but found winning difficult when tried against top-class opposition last term. She was switched successfully to fences last season. She has now been retired to stud.

Celtic Pride (IRE)

99 **137**

7-y-o gr g Roselier (FR)-Grannie No (Brave Invader (USA))
J J O'Neill Walters Plant Hire Ltd

Placings: 0110-P10 **(4193)**
2001/02: 21^{P}S, 23^{1}HY, 25^{0}GS

	Starts	1st	2nd	3rd	Win & Pl
Hurdles	3	1	0	0	8783
Career Total	**7**	**3**	**0**	**0**	**20468**

137	2/02	Hayd	2m7f110y	B HHdl	HVY	£8782
125	1/01	Navn	2m6f	Hdl	SFT	£6677
110	1/01	Fair	2m6f	Hdl	HVY	£5008

Total win prize-money £20468

Going: Sf: 1-2 GS: 0-1 Gd: 0-0 GF: - Fm: 0-0
Distance: 2m/2m3: 0-0 2m4-2m7: 0-1 **3m+: 1-2**
Track: **LH: 1-3** RH: 0-0 Tight: 0-1 Gall: 0-1
Aids: Bl: 0-0 Vi: 0-0 Tstrap: 0-0
Best Rating: 137 2/02 Hayd 2m7f110y heavy Hdl

A decent Irish novice hurdler in 2000/200. Lightly raced. Now with Jonjo O'Neill, he won from out of the handicap at Haydock in February 2002, but was very disappointing at Cheltenham in March. Stays three miles and suited by soft ground.

Celtic Revival

94f **71f**

6-y-o b g Current Edition (IRE)-Celtic Remorse (Celtic Cone)
D Brace David Brace

Placings: *050* **(1858)**
2001/02: 17^{0}GF, 16^{5}GF, 17^{0}S

	Starts	1st	2nd	3rd	Win & Pl
NH Flat	3	0	0	0	0
Career Total	**3**	**0**	**0**	**0**	**0**

Going: Sf: 0-1 GS: 0-0 Gd: 0-0 GF: - Fm: 0-2
Distance: 2m/2m3: 0-3 2m4-2m7: 0-0 3m+: 0-0
Track: LH: 0-1 RH: 0-2 Tight: 0-1 Gall: 0-0
Aids: Bl: 0-0 Vi: 0-0 Tstrap: 0-0
Best Rating: 71 10/01 Ludl 2m gd-fm NHF

Celtic Rover

4-y-o b g Celtic Swing-Lady Sabo (Prince Sabo)
R C Spicer Mrs J A Nichols

Placings: PP **(1412)**
2001/02: 16^{P}GF, 16^{P}GF

	Starts	1st	2nd	3rd	Win & Pl
Hurdles	2	0	0	0	
Career Total	**2**	**0**	**0**	**0**	

Going: Sf: 0-0 GS: 0-0 Gd: 0-0 GF: - Fm: 0-2
Distance: 2m/2m3: 0-2 2m4-2m7: 0-0 3m+: 0-0
Track: LH: 0-2 RH: 0-0 Tight: 0-2 Gall: 0-0
Aids: Bl: 0-0 Vi: 0-0 Tstrap: 0-0
Best Rating:

Celtic Season

10-y-o b g Vital Season-Welsh Flower (Welsh Saint)
C W Loggin (Miss H C Knight 1/9) Richard West

Placings: *6*/505/2F1P04/12U14P3/F3PF52P12-P042 **(4054)**
2001/02: 24^{P}G, 24^{0}GF, 25^{4}GF, 20^{2}S

	Starts	1st	2nd	3rd	Win & Pl
Chases	4	0	1	0	951
Career Total	**30**	**4**	**5**	**2**	**22764**

126	3/01	Hntg	3m	F(0-110)HCh	SFT	£2625
126	12/99	Ling	2m4f110y	C(0-130)HCh	SFT	£5766
126	9/99	Hntg	2m4f110y	D(0-125)HCh	GD	£4055
126	1/99	Leic	2m4f110y	F(0-100)HCh	SFT	£2427

Total win prize-money £14873

Going: Sf: 0-1 GS: 0-0 Gd: 0-1 GF: - Fm: 0-2
Distance: 2m/2m3: 0-0 2m4-2m7: 0-1 3m+: 0-3
Track: LH: 0-1 RH: 0-3 Tight: 0-2 Gall: 0-1
Aids: Bl: 0-1 Vi: 0-0 Tstrap: 0-4
Best Rating: 126 4/01 Hntg 3m soft Ch

Consistent staying handicap chaser, when he manages to complete. Not the most reliable jumper, he acts with cut and wears a tongue-tie.

Celtic Star (IRE)

101 **100**

4-y-o b g Celtic Swing-Recherchee (Rainbow Quest (USA))
Nick Williams (M R Channon 10/9) Mrs Jane Kelly

Placings: 3243226 **(4417)**
2001/02: 16^{3}G, 16^{2}GF, 16^{4}G, 16^{3}G, 18^{2}S, 17^{2}S, 16^{6}GS

	Starts	1st	2nd	3rd	Win & Pl
Hurdles	7	0	3	2	4349
Career Total	**7**	**0**	**3**	**2**	**4349**

Going: Sf: 0-2 GS: 0-1 Gd: 0-3 GF: - Fm: 0-1
Distance: 2m/2m3: 0-7 2m4-2m7: 0-0 3m+: 0-0
Track: LH: 0-4 RH: 0-3 Tight: 0-2 Gall: 0-1
Aids: Bl: 0-0 Vi: 0-0 Tstrap: 0-0
Best Rating: 100 1/02 Font 2m2f110y soft Hdl

Celtic Sword

(65h) (17h)

7-y-o ch g Broadsword (USA)-Voolin (Jimmy Reppin)
A G Hobbs Unity Farm Holiday Centre Ltd

Placings: *00*PFP **(1261)**
2001/02: 16^{0}G, 20^{0}GF, 24^{P}GF, 20^{F}GF, 20^{P}GF

	Starts	1st	2nd	3rd	Win & Pl
NH Flat	1	0	0	0	0
Hurdles	1	0	0	0	0
Chases	3	0	0	0	0
Career Total	**5**	**0**	**0**	**0**	

Going: Sf: 0-0 GS: 0-0 Gd: 0-1 GF: - Fm: 0-4
Distance: 2m/2m3: 0-1 2m4-2m7: 0-3 3m+: 0-1
Track: LH: 0-3 RH: 0-2 Tight: 0-1 Gall: 0-2
Aids: Bl: 0-0 Vi: 0-0 Tstrap: 0-0
Best Rating: 61 5/01 Hntg 2m110y good NHF

Celtic Ted

4-y-o b g Celtic Swing-Careful Dancer (Gorytus (USA))
P Butler Mrs E Lucey-Butler

Placings: 0 **(2037)**
2001/02: 16^{0}GS

	Starts	1st	2nd	3rd	Win & Pl
Hurdles	1	0	0	0	
Career Total	**1**	**0**	**0**	**0**	

Going: Sf: 0-0 GS: 0-1 Gd: 0-0 GF: - Fm: 0-0
Distance: 2m/2m3: 0-1 2m4-2m7: 0-0 3m+: 0-0
Track: LH: 0-0 RH: 0-1 Tight: 0-0 Gall: 0-0
Aids: Bl: 0-0 Vi: 0-0 Tstrap: 0-0

Best Rating: mfy

Celtic Token

13-y-o ch g Celtic Cone-Ready Token (SWE) (Record Token)
Miss S Waugh The Stowford Partnership

Placings:0/0F0P/F656U/U (4118)
2001/02: 25^{U}G

	Starts	1st	2nd	3rd	Win & Pl
Chases	1	0	0	0	
Career Total	**11**	**0**	**0**	**0**	

Going: Sf: 0-0 GS: 0-0 Gd: 0-1 GF: - Fm: 0-0
Distance: 2m/2m3: 0-0 2m4-2m7: 0-0 3m+: 0-1
Track: LH: 0-0 RH: 0-1 Tight: 0-0 Gall: 0-0
Aids: Bl: 0-0 Vi: 0-0 Tstrap: 0-0
Best Rating: 83 2/95 Donc 2m3f110y good Ch

Celtic Vision (IRE)

99f 112f

6-y-o b g Be My Native (USA)-Dream Run (Deep Run)
J J O'Neill Mrs J Doyle & Mrs P Shanahan

Placings:3-1020 (4948a)
2001/02: 17^{1}HY, 16^{0}G, 16^{2}S, 16^{0}G

	Starts	1st	2nd	3rd	Win & Pl
NH Flat	4	1	1	0	2813
Career Total	**5**	**1**	**1**	**1**	**3071**

112	12/01	NAbb	2m1f	H NHF	HVY	£2317

Total win prize-money £2317

Going: Sf: 1-2 GS: 0-0 Gd: 0-2 GF: - Fm: 0-0
Distance: **2m/2m3: 1-4** 2m4-2m7: 0-3 3m+: 0-0
Track: **LH: 1-1** RH: 0-3 **Tight: 1-1** Gall: 0-0
Aids: Bl: 0-0 Vi: 0-0 Tstrap: 0-2
Best Rating: 112 2/02 Winc 2m soft NHF

Comfortable bumper winner in heavy ground, struggled on faster ground in a better-class event at Ascot.

Celtic Who (IRE)

101 87

11-y-o br g Strong Gale-Whosview (Fine Blade (USA))
R Ford Mrs C P Lees-Jones

Placings:000/0P00B3/502/4/4 (0092)
2001/02: 16^{4}S

	Starts	1st	2nd	3rd	Win & Pl
Chases	1	0	0	0	0
Career Total	**14**	**0**	**1**	**1**	**1300**

Going: Sf: 0-1 GS: 0-0 Gd: 0-0 GF: - Fm: 0-0
Distance: 2m/2m3: 0-1 2m4-2m7: 0-0 3m+: 0-0
Track: LH: 0-1 RH: 0-0 Tight: 0-0 Gall: 0-0
Aids: Bl: 0-0 Vi: 0-0 Tstrap: 0-0
Best Rating: 91 7/97 Gway 2m1f yield Ch

Cenkos (FR)

113 176

8-y-o ch g Nikos-Vincenza (Grundy)
P F Nicholls Mrs J Stewart

Placings:111/4/PF1F121121/244423P-14444351 (4912)
2001/02: 16^{1}GF, 21^{4}G, 17^{4}GF, 16^{4}GS, 16^{4}G, 16^{3}GS, 21^{5}GF, 16^{1}G

	Starts	1st	2nd	3rd	Win & Pl
Chases	8	2	0	1	130864
Career Total	**29**	**10**	**4**	**2**	**291889**

176	4/02	Sand	2m	B Ch	GD	£44625
164	5/01	Wwck	2m110y	B Ch	G-F	£10952
165	4/00	Aint	2m	A Ch	GD	£36000
168	2/00	Wwck	2m	A Ch	SFT	£14410
162	1/00	Kemp	2m	D Ch	GD	£5908
150	12/99	Sthl	2m	B(0-140)HCh	SFT	£8651
133	12/99	Plum	2m1f	E Ch	GD	£2900
	4/98	Engh	2m1f	Hdl	HVY	£15152
	3/98	Engh	2m2f	Hdl	VS	£10101
	3/98	Engh	2m110y	Hdl	HLD	£10101

Total win prize-money £158802

Going: Sf: 0-0 GS: 0-2 Gd: 1-3 GF: - Fm: 1-3
Distance: **2m/2m3: 2-6** 2m4-2m7: 0-2 3m+: 0-0
Track: LH: 0-1 **RH: 1-5** Tight: 0-0 Gall: 0-1
Aids: Bl: 0-1 Vi: 0-0 Tstrap: 0-0
Best Rating: 176 4/02 Sand 2m good Ch

Best on good ground, he joined Paul Nicholls for whom he won early in the new season. Struggled in decent company afterwards, before running a blinder to finish third in the 2002 Queen Mother Champion Chase, only caught up the hill. Returned from a good run in Japan to take a top-class chase at Sandown in April.

Centaur Express

(90h) (89h)

10-y-o b g Siberian Express (USA)-Gay Twenties (Lord Gayle (USA))
A Streeter Centaur Racing Ltd

Placings:34321F112/11030/526012U3/514311/3U533/05 (4160)
2001/02: 17^{0}HY, 16^{5}GS

	Starts	1st	2nd	3rd	Win & Pl
Hurdles	2	0	0	0	0
Career Total	**35**	**9**	**4**	**8**	**35068**

128	3/99	Leic	2m1f	E(0-115)HCh	HVY	£3548
128	1/99	Leic	2m1f	E(0-115)HCh	SFT	£2768
116	11/98	MRas	2m1f110y	D(0-120)HCh	HVY	£3675
128	3/98	Bang	2m1f110y	D Ch	G-S	£3436
121	12/96	MRas	2m1f110y	D(0-120)HHdl	GD	£2945
120	11/96	Bang	2m1f	E(0-110)HHdl	G-S	£3176
114	3/96	Newb	2m110y	C(0-135)HHdl	HVY	£3395
96	3/96	Catt	2m	E Hdl	GD	£2374
83	1/96	Catt	2m	G(0-90)HHdl	GD	£2392

Total win prize-money £27711

Going: Sf: 0-1 GS: 0-1 Gd: 0-0 GF: - Fm: 0-0
Distance: 2m/2m3: 0-2 2m4-2m7: 0-0 3m+: 0-0
Track: LH: 0-1 RH: 0-1 Tight: 0-0 Gall: 0-0
Aids: Bl: 0-0 Vi: 0-0 Tstrap: 0-0
Best Rating: 128 3/99 Leic 2m1f heavy Ch

Mud-loving front runner at his best but on the decline now.

Centaur Spirit

94 83

5-y-o b g Distant Relative-Winnie Reckless (Local Suitor (USA))
A Streeter Centaur Racing Ltd

Placings:4-54 (1755)
2001/02: 16^{5}GS, 16^{4}GS

	Starts	1st	2nd	3rd	Win & Pl
Hurdles	2	0	0	0	0
Career Total	**3**	**0**	**0**	**0**	**220**

Going: Sf: 0-0 GS: 0-2 Gd: 0-0 GF: - Fm: 0-0
Distance: 2m/2m3: 0-2 2m4-2m7: 0-0 3m+: 0-0
Track: LH: 0-2 RH: 0-0 Tight: 0-1 Gall: 0-0
Aids: Bl: 0-0 Vi: 0-0 Tstrap: 0-0
Best Rating: 90 11/00 Leic 2m heavy Hd

Lightly raced, he has won once on the flat, although he has failed to impress since, both on the flat and over hurdles.

Cento (IRE)

100 98

9-y-o b g Shernazar-Callianire (Sir Gaylord)
Mrs S D Williams Eric Le Ruez

Placings:2333/44520/0033615P43/15500/1232255-034 (1026)
2001/02: 19^{0}G, 22^{3}GF, 22^{4}G

	Starts	1st	2nd	3rd	Win & Pl
Hurdles	3	0	0	1	619
Career Total	**34**	**3**	**5**	**8**	**17877**

106	5/00	Extr	2m3f	E(0-115)HHdl	GD	£3003
106	11/99	Extr	2m3f	D(0-125)HHdl	G-S	£3160
106	12/98	Tntn	2m3f110y	F(0-95)HHdl	G-S	£2616

Total win prize-money £8779

Going: Sf: 0-0 GS: 0-0 Gd: 0-2 GF: - Fm: 0-1
Distance: 2m/2m3: 0-0 2m4-2m7: 0-3 3m+: 0-0
Track: LH: 0-2 RH: 0-1 Tight: 0-2 Gall: 0-0
Aids: Bl: 0-3 Vi: 0-0 Tstrap: 0-0
Best Rating: 106 11/00 Tntn 2m3f110y good Hd

Cerasus Knight (IRE)

7-y-o b g Arctic Lord-Cherry Field (Precipice Wood)
A G Newcombe Lavis Medical Systems

Placings:000/6P0-UP0 (1131)
2001/02: 22^{U}GF, 22^{P}G, 16^{0}GF

	Starts	1st	2nd	3rd	Win & Pl
Hurdles	3	0	0	0	
Career Total	**9**	**0**	**0**	**0**	0

Going: Sf: 0-0 GS: 0-0 Gd: 0-1 GF: - Fm: 0-2
Distance: 2m/2m3: 0-1 2m4-2m7: 0-2 3m+: 0-0
Track: LH: 0-3 RH: 0-0 Tight: 0-2 Gall: 0-0
Aids: Bl: 0-0 Vi: 0-0 Tstrap: 0-0
Best Rating: 80 5/00 Extr 2m1f gd-fm NHF

Cerock

77 15

6-y-o b g Rock City-Uninvited (Be My Guest (USA))
C P Morlock Andrew F Sawyer

Placings:330/P6P0-P0 (1907)
2001/02: 20^{P}G, 16^{0}S

	Starts	1st	2nd	3rd	Win & Pl
Hurdles	2	0	0	0	
Career Total	**9**	**0**	**0**	**2**	**522**

Going: Sf: 0-1 GS: 0-0 Gd: 0-1 GF: - Fm: 0-0
Distance: 2m/2m3: 0-1 2m4-2m7: 0-1 3m+: 0-0
Track: LH: 0-1 RH: 0-1 Tight: 0-1 Gall: 0-1
Aids: Bl: 0-0 Vi: 0-0 Tstrap: 0-1
Best Rating: 88 3/00 Wwck 2m soft NHF

Cerruti (DEN)

7-y-o b h Shernazar-Chalkey Road (Relko)
K R Burke (Niels Petersen 4/10) Mrs Elaine M Burke

Placings:1350P (3395)

2001/02: 17^{1}HY, 16^{3}VS, 17^{5}S, 16^{0}HY, 16^{P}GS

	Starts	1st	2nd	3rd	Win & Pl
Hurdles	5	1	0	1	2647
Career Total	**5**	**1**	**0**	**1**	**2647**

8/01 Ovrl 2m1f Hdl HVY £2111
Total win prize-money £2111

Going: Sf: 1-3 GS: 0-1 Gd: 0-0 GF: - Fm: 0-0
Distance: **2m/2m3: 1-5** 2m4-2m7: 0-0 3m+: 0-0
Track: LH: 0-1 RH: 0-0 Tight: 0-0 Gall: 0-0
Aids: Bl: 0-0 Vi: 0-0 Tstrap: 0-1
Best Rating:

Certain Surprise

91 (89h) (83h) 65
8-y-o b m Grey Desire-Richesse (FR) (Far Away Son (USA))
M Madgwick Mrs H Veal

Placings:46053/255040/43F3/3P6-500 **(0487)**
2001/02: 18^{5}GF, 16^{0}GF, 18^{0}GF

	Starts	1st	2nd	3rd	Win & Pl
Hurdles	1	0	0	0	0
Chases	2	0	0	0	0
Career Total	21	0	1	4	1957

Going: Sf: 0-0 GS: 0-0 Gd: 0-0 GF: - Fm: 0-3
Distance: 2m/2m3: 0-3 2m4-2m7: 0-0 3m+: 0-0
Track: LH: 0-2 RH: 0-0 Tight: 0-3 Gall: 0-0
Aids: Bl: 0-3 Vi: 0-0 Tstrap: 0-0
Best Rating: 83 5/01 Font 2m2f110y gd-fm Hdl

Cesaria (FR)

109 133
5-y-o b m Highest Honor (FR)-Cat Storm (CAN) (Storm Cat (USA))
M C Pipe (J Bertran De Balanda 20/10) Joe Moran

Placings:2310211500 **(4939a)**
2001/02: 17^{2}VS, 18^{3}VS, 18^{1}VS, 18^{0}VS, 16^{2}G, 16^{1}GS, 16^{1}HY, 20^{5}GS, 16^{0}G, 20^{0}Y

	Starts	1st	2nd	3rd	Win & Pl
Hurdles	10	3	2	1	23918
Career Total	**10**	**3**	**2**	**1**	**23918**

126 2/02 Plum 2m E Hdl HVY £2583
133 12/01 Leic 2m E Hdl G-S £3167
9/01 Autl 2m2f Hdl VS £10669
Total win prize-money £16420

Going: Sf: 1-1 GS: 1-2 Gd: 0-2 GF: - Fm: 0-0
Distance: **2m/2m3: 3-8** 2m4-2m7: 0-2 3m+: 0-0
Track: LH: 1-4 RH: 1-2 **Tight: 1-3** Gall: 0-0
Aids: Bl: 0-0 Vi: 0-1 Tstrap: 0-0
Best Rating: 133 12/01 Leic 2m gd-sft Hdl

A French import, she just lost out at Plumpton on her British debut before winning easily at Leicester in December 2001. Fortunate winner at Plumpton next time, she may not want the ground too testing. Well held in Listed company at Aintree in April. Suited by two miles. Has won on soft ground and good.

Cezanne

107 104
13-y-o b g Ajdal (USA)-Reprocolor (Jimmy Reppin)
M J Roberts Mike Roberts

Placings:62/1465235/0F-40 **(2280)**

2001/02: 16^{4}G, 16^{0}GF

	Starts	1st	2nd	3rd	Win & Pl
Hurdles	2	0	0	0	0
Career Total	**13**	**1**	**2**	**1**	**6462**

111 5/99 Hntg 2m110y E Hdl G-F £2880
Total win prize-money £2880

Going: Sf: 0-0 GS: 0-0 Gd: 0-1 GF: - Fm: 0-1
Distance: 2m/2m3: 0-2 2m4-2m7: 0-0 3m+: 0-0
Track: LH: 0-0 RH: 0-2 Tight: 0-0 Gall: 0-0
Aids: Bl: 0-0 Vi: 0-0 Tstrap: 0-0
Best Rating: 114 5/00 Towc 2m gd-fm Hdl

A former winner of the Irish Champion Stakes on the Flat, but a failure at stud, he showed some ability and aptitude in a light campaign over hurdles as a novice. Fair form in useful company since. Off the track for a year and a half, he reappeared in November 2001 and ran well until tiring between the last two flights. Best at two miles. Best on a sound surface.

Chabrol (CAN)

42
9-y-o b g El Gran Senor (USA)-Off The Record (USA) (Chas Conerly (USA))
Ms A E Embiricos Ms A E Embiricos

Placings:44/62150010P/500304/0FP/0-U **(0552)**
2001/02: 21^{U}GF

	Starts	1st	2nd	3rd	Win & Pl
Hurdles	1	0	0	0	
Career Total	**22**	**2**	**1**	**1**	**15340**

112 2/98 Wind 2m6f110y D Hdl G-F £3393
112 11/97 Uttx 2m4f110y A Hdl SFT £9509
Total win prize-money £12903

Going: Sf: 0-0 GS: 0-0 Gd: 0-0 GF: - Fm: 0-1
Distance: 2m/2m3: 0-0 2m4-2m7: 0-1 3m+: 0-0
Track: LH: 0-0 RH: 0-1 Tight: 0-0 Gall: 0-1
Aids: Bl: 0-0 Vi: 0-0 Tstrap: 0-1
Best Rating: 113 5/98 Worc 3m gd-fm Hdl

Chadswell (IRE)

103 (108h) (108h) 115
9-y-o b g Lord Americo-Marita Ann (Crozier)
R Ford Mike Proudfoot Partnership

Placings:543461/10P-24F531142 **(4428)**
2001/02: 24^{2}GS, 24^{4}S, 24^{F}HY, 27^{5}HY, 24^{3}S, 27^{1}S, 28^{1}S, 21^{4}S, 23^{2}HY

	Starts	1st	2nd	3rd	Win & Pl
Hurdles	4	0	1	1	1541
Chases	5	2	1	0	9059
Career Total	**18**	**4**	**2**	**2**	**17039**

114 3/02 Sedg 3m4f D(0-115)HCh SFT £4007
110 2/02 Sedg 3m3f E(0-110)HCh SFT £3297
102 5/00 Ctml 2m6f F(0-95)HHdl G-S £3068
99 4/00 Carl 2m4f110y E Hdl G-S £2562
Total win prize-money £12934

Going: Sf: 2-8 GS: 0-1 Gd: 0-0 GF: - Fm: 0-0
Distance: 2m/2m3: 0-0 2m4-2m7: 0-2 **3m+: 2-7**
Track: **LH: 2-7** RH: 0-2 **Tight: 2-5** Gall: 0-0
Aids: Bl: 0-0 Vi: 0-0 Tstrap: 0-0
Best Rating: 115 3/02 Uttx 2m7f heavy Ch

Twice a winner over hurdles at around two and a half miles and quickly made his mark over fences. Needs three miles over fences.

Chain Line

28
12-y-o br g Relkino-Housemistress (New Member)
J W F Aynsley J W F Aynsley

Placings:0/060/0P0/PP5/400P000/1FP0PFP/00P5P-F5PP **(4858)**
2001/02: 25^{F}S, 16^{5}GF, 16^{P}GF, 16^{P}G

	Starts	1st	2nd	3rd	Win & Pl
Hurdles	3	0	0	0	0
Chases	1	0	0	0	0
Career Total	**33**	**1**	**0**	**0**	**2668**

88 6/99 Hexm 2m E Hdl G-F £2668
Total win prize-money £2668

Going: Sf: 0-1 GS: 0-0 Gd: 0-1 GF: - Fm: 0-2
Distance: 2m/2m3: 0-3 2m4-2m7: 0-0 3m+: 0-1
Track: LH: 0-3 RH: 0-0 Tight: 0-1 Gall: 0-1
Aids: Bl: 0-0 Vi: 0-0 Tstrap: 0-0
Best Rating: 88 6/99 Hexm 2m gd-fm Hdl

Only one win over hurdles back in 1999 to his name. Lightly raced in recent times.

Chalcedony

91 (97h) (100h) 112+
6-y-o ch g Highest Honor (FR)-Sweet Holland (USA) (Alydar (USA))
R Rowe (G L Moore 24/1) R Stillwell

Placings:603136-3F0PP4 **(4508)**
2001/02: 17^{3}HY, 24^{F}G, 22^{0}S, 20^{P}G, 16^{P}HY, 17^{4}G

	Starts	1st	2nd	3rd	Win & Pl
Hurdles	5	0	0	1	417
Chases	1	0	0	0	240
Career Total	**12**	**1**	**0**	**3**	**4833**

102 2/01 Plum 2m E(0-115)HHdl SFT £3526
Total win prize-money £3526

Going: Sf: 0-3 GS: 0-0 Gd: 0-3 GF: - Fm: 0-0
Distance: 2m/2m3: 0-3 2m4-2m7: 0-2 3m+: 0-1
Track: LH: 0-2 RH: 0-4 Tight: 0-3 Gall: 0-0
Aids: Bl: 0-1 Vi: 0-0 Tstrap: 0-0
Best Rating: 109 3/02 Plum 2m1f good Ch

Chalcuchima

9-y-o gr g Reprimand-Ica (Great Nephew)
F E Sutherland Miss H P J Scheffers

Placings:P0PU/5/P/P-PP0 **(0585)**
2001/02: 20^{P}GF, 24^{P}GF, 24^{0}GF

	Starts	1st	2nd	3rd	Win & Pl
Chases	3	0	0	0	
Career Total	**10**	**0**	**0**	**0**	**0**

Going: Sf: 0-0 GS: 0-0 Gd: 0-0 GF: - Fm: 0-3
Distance: 2m/2m3: 0-0 2m4-2m7: 0-1 3m+: 0-2
Track: LH: 0-1 RH: 0-2 Tight: 0-1 Gall: 0-2
Aids: Bl: 0-2 Vi: 0-0 Tstrap: 0-0
Best Rating: 52 1/98 Extr 2m2f heavy Hdl

Chalkie Run (IRE)

91 79
8-y-o b g Commanche Run-Chalk It Down (Cheval)
N J Henderson Sir Peter & Lady Gibbings

Placings:313/4FP-6 **(2717)**
2001/02: 19^{6}G

	Starts	1st	2nd	3rd	Win & Pl
Hurdles	1	0	0	0	0
Career Total	**7**	**1**	**0**	**2**	**4822**

93 4/00 Cork 2m4f NHF Y-S £3864

Total win prize-money £3864

Going: Sf: 0-0 GS: 0-0 Gd: 0-1 GF: - Fm: 0-0
Distance: 2m/2m3: 0-0 2m4-2m7: 0-1 3m+: 0-0
Track: LH: 0-0 RH: 0-1 Tight: 0-0 Gall: 0-0
Aids: Bl: 0-0 Vi: 0-0 Tstrap: 0-0
Best Rating: 122 11/00 Newb 2m5f soft Hdl

Chalmers Place (IRE)

111 **147**

8-y-o b g Mandalus-Bramble Girl (Ovac (ITY))
Miss H C Knight Chalmers Place Partnership

Placings:22121/**4152U6-211F45** **(4819)**
2001/02: 22^{2}GS, 24^{1}G, 25^{1}GF, 24^{F}G, 24^{4}G, 26^{5}GF

	Starts	1st	2nd	3rd	Win & Pl
Chases	6	2	1	0	17343
Career Total	**17**	**5**	**5**	**0**	**34307**

147	11/01	Winc	3m1f110y	C(0-135)HCh	G-F	£7525
147	11/01	Kemp	3m	D(0-120)HCh	GD	£7150
133	11/00	Hntg	2m4f110y	D Ch	GD	£5391
122	3/00	Sand	2m110y	D Hdl	GD	£3623
112	1/00	Winc	2m	E Hdl	G-S	£2205

Total win prize-money £25896

Going: Sf: 0-0 GS: 0-1 Gd: 1-3 GF: - Fm: 1-2
Distance: 2m/2m3: 0-0 2m4-2m7: 0-1 **3m+: 2-5**
Track: LH: 0-1 **RH: 2-4** Tight: 0-1 Gall: 0-1
Aids: Bl: 0-0 Vi: 0-0 Tstrap: 0-0
Best Rating: 147 11/01 Winc 3m1f110y gd-fm Ch

Capable novice chaser in 2000/2001. Won at Kempton in November 2001 over three miles and followed up at Wincanton. Acts on a sound surface. Stays three miles.

Champagne Dawn (IRE)

39

9-y-o br g Orchestra-Bramble Rose (Pals Passage)
Mrs Pippa Bickerton David Bickerton

Placings:P/PP-00 **(0641)**
2001/02: 20^{0}G, 24^{0}GF

	Starts	1st	2nd	3rd	Win & Pl
Hurdles	2	0	0	0	
Career Total	**5**	**0**	**0**	**0**	

Going: Sf: 0-0 GS: 0-0 Gd: 0-1 GF: - Fm: 0-1
Distance: 2m/2m3: 0-0 2m4-2m7: 0-1 3m+: 0-1
Track: LH: 0-1 RH: 0-1 Tight: 0-2 Gall: 0-0
Aids: Bl: 0-0 Vi: 0-0 Tstrap: 0-2
Best Rating:

Champagne Lil

99 **90**

5-y-o gr m Terimon-Sparkling Cinders (Netherkelly)
N A Twiston-Davies Mark Powell

Placings:41U53 **(4048)**
2001/02: 17^{4}GS, 16^{1}G, 19^{U}G, 19^{5}GS, 19^{3}G

	Starts	1st	2nd	3rd	Win & Pl
NH Flat	2	1	0	0	1617
Hurdles	3	0	0	1	587
Career Total	**5**	**1**	**0**	**1**	**2204**

96	10/01	Chep	2m110y	H NHF	GD	£1617

Total win prize-money £1617

Going: Sf: 0-0 GS: 0-2 Gd: 1-3 GF: - Fm: 0-0
Distance: 2m/2m3: **1-4** 2m4-2m7: 0-1 3m+: 0-0
Track: **LH: 1-2** RH: 0-2 Tight: 0-1 Gall: 0-1
Aids: Bl: 0-0 Vi: 0-0 Tstrap: 0-0
Best Rating: 96 10/01 Chep 2m110y good NHF

From a good jumping family, including Razer Blade, Prancing Blade and Roller Blade, got off the mark in a Chepstow bumper. Placed form over hurdles since. Acts on good ground.

Champagne N Dreams

55 **2**

10-y-o b m Rambo Dancer (CAN)-Pink Sensation (Sagaro)
G A Harker Mrs J L Harker

Placings:000/P0 **(3326)**
2001/02: 16^{P}G, 16^{0}S

	Starts	1st	2nd	3rd	Win & Pl
Hurdles	2	0	0	0	
Career Total	**5**	**0**	**0**	**0**	

Going: Sf: 0-1 GS: 0-0 Gd: 0-1 GF: - Fm: 0-0
Distance: 2m/2m3: 0-2 2m4-2m7: 0-0 3m+: 0-0
Track: LH: 0-2 RH: 0-0 Tight: 0-0 Gall: 0-2
Aids: Bl: 0-0 Vi: 0-0 Tstrap: 0-0
Best Rating: 57 11/95 Weth 2m good Hdl

Chan Move

84 **38**

10-y-o b g Move Off-Kanisa (Chantro)
W J Smith W J Smith

Placings:000/0P000F0PP0/PP/P025520/P00-00R **(3328)**
2001/02: 20^{0}GF, 16^{0}GF, 20^{R}S

	Starts	1st	2nd	3rd	Win & Pl
Hurdles	3	0	0	0	
Career Total	**28**	**0**	**2**	**0**	**986**

Going: Sf: 0-1 GS: 0-0 Gd: 0-0 GF: - Fm: 0-2
Distance: 2m/2m3: 0-1 2m4-2m7: 0-2 3m+: 0-0
Track: LH: 0-3 RH: 0-0 Tight: 0-1 Gall: 0-1
Aids: Bl: 0-1 Vi: 0-0 Tstrap: 0-0
Best Rating: 84 4/00 Newc 2m gd-sft Hdl

Chance Investment

86 **70**

5-y-o b m Homo Sapien-Edithmead (IRE) (Shardari)
R Ford D E Harrison

Placings:*00*4P2P **(4919)**
2001/02: 17^{0}GS, 16^{0}GS, 16^{4}G, 17^{P}S, 17^{2}GF, 21^{P}GF

	Starts	1st	2nd	3rd	Win & Pl
NH Flat	2	0	0	0	0
Hurdles	4	0	1	0	772
Career Total	**6**	**0**	**1**	**0**	**772**

Going: Sf: 0-1 GS: 0-2 Gd: 0-1 GF: - Fm: 0-2
Distance: 2m/2m3: 0-5 2m4-2m7: 0-1 3m+: 0-0
Track: LH: 0-5 RH: 0-1 Tight: 0-5 Gall: 0-1
Aids: Bl: 0-0 Vi: 0-0 Tstrap: 0-0
Best Rating: 70 4/02 Sedg 2m1f gd-fm Hdl

Lightly-raced hurdler, seems suited by a sound surface.

Chance Remark (IRE)

81 **54**

4-y-o ch f Goldmark (USA)-Fair Chance (Young Emperor)
M Todhunter (A Berry 8/6) B Batey

Placings:F5 **(1246)**
2001/02: 17^{F}G, 17^{5}G

	Starts	1st	2nd	3rd	Win & Pl
Hurdles	2	0	0	0	0
Career Total	**2**	**0**	**0**	**0**	**0**

Going: Sf: 0-0 GS: 0-0 Gd: 0-2 GF: - Fm: 0-0
Distance: 2m/2m3: 0-2 2m4-2m7: 0-0 3m+: 0-0
Track: LH: 0-2 RH: 0-0 Tight: 0-2 Gall: 0-0
Aids: Bl: 0-0 Vi: 0-0 Tstrap: 0-0
Best Rating: 54 8/01 Ctml 2m1f110y good Hdl

Chancers Dante (IRE)

102 **90**

6-y-o b g Phardante (FR)-Own Acre (Linacre)
Ferdy Murphy (Sean Aherne 2/6) Mrs P B Symes

Placings:/0003 **(3437)**
2001/02: 20^{1}G, 20^{0}G, 20^{0}G, 22^{0}G, 27^{3}HY

	Starts	1st	2nd	3rd	Win & Pl
NH Flat	1	1	0	0	4730
Hurdles	4	0	0	1	350
Career Total	**5**	**1**	**0**	**1**	**5080**

101	6/01	Cork	2m4f	NHF	GD	£4729

Total win prize-money £4730

Going: Sf: 0-1 GS: 0-0 Gd: 1-4 GF: - Fm: 0-0
Distance: 2m/2m3: 0-0 **2m4-2m7: 1-4** 3m+: 0-1
Track: LH: 0-4 RH: 0-0 Tight: 0-3 Gall: 0-1
Aids: Bl: 0-0 Vi: 0-0 Tstrap: 0-0
Best Rating: 101 6/01 Cork 2m4f good NHF

Channahrlie (IRE)

105(107h) (93h)**103**

8-y-o gr g Celio Rufo-Derravarragh Lady (IRE) (Radical)
R Dickin J C Clemmow

Placings:034/2061**0-551224PF**16 **(4817)**
2001/02: 16^{5}G, 20^{5}S, 24^{1}G, 24^{2}GF, 28^{2}GS, 24^{4}GS, 25^{P}S, 23^{F}G, 26^{1}GF, 24^{6}GF

	Starts	1st	2nd	3rd	Win & Pl
Hurdles	2	1	0	0	2912
Chases	8	1	2	0	7610
Career Total	**18**	**3**	**3**	**1**	**15937**

93	4/02	Hrfd	3m2f	E(0-105)HHdl	G-F	£2912
100	8/01	Bang	3m110y	D(0-125)HCh	GD	£5382
100	12/00	Leic	2m	D(0-110)HCh	G-S	£4241

Total win prize-money £12535

Going: Sf: 0-2 GS: 0-2 Gd: 1-3 GF: - Fm: 1-3
Distance: 2m/2m3: 0-1 2m4-2m7: 0-1 **3m+: 2-8**
Track: LH: 1-3 RH: 1-6 **Tight: 1-3** Gall: 0-0
Aids: Bl: 0-0 Vi: 0-0 Tstrap: 0-0
Best Rating: 103 8/01 Uttx 3m gd-fm Ch

Reverted to hurdling when winning an extended three miles Novices' handicap at Hereford April 2002.

Channel Highlander

97(80c) (72c)86

7-y-o b g Jendali (USA)-Young Mary (Young Generation)

L Lungo (Mrs S C Bradburne 9/5) R Flynn

Placings:*600*/0540350U-6604 **(2471)**

2001/02: 16^{6}GF, 20^{6}GS, 20^{0}G, 18^{4}GS

	Starts	1st	2nd	3rd	Win & Pl
Hurdles	3	0	0	0	0
Chases	1	0	0	0	0
Career Total	**15**	**0**	**0**	**1**	**318**

Going: Sf: 0-0 GS: 0-2 Gd: 0-1 GF: - Fm: 0-1
Distance: 2m/2m3: 0-2 2m4-2m7: 0-2 3m+: 0-0
Track: LH: 0-3 RH: 0-0 Tight: 0-1 Gall: 0-1
Aids: Bl: 0-0 Vi: 0-0 Tstrap: 0-0
Best Rating: 86 10/01 Carl 2m4f gd-sft Hdl

Chanticlier

94f 116f

5-y-o b g Roselier (FR)-Cherry Crest (Pollerton)

K C Bailey Mrs Jane Lane

Placings:2 **(4158)**

2001/02: 16^{2}GS

	Starts	1st	2nd	3rd	Win & Pl
NH Flat	1	0	1	0	729
Career Total	**1**	**0**	**1**	**0**	**729**

Going: Sf: 0-0 GS: 0-1 Gd: 0-0 GF: - Fm: 0-0
Distance: 2m/2m3: 0-1 2m4-2m7: 0-0 3m+: 0-0
Track: LH: 0-0 RH: 0-1 Tight: 0-0 Gall: 0-0
Aids: Bl: 0-0 Vi: 0-0 Tstrap: 0-0
Best Rating: 116 3/02 Sand 2m110y gd-sft NHF

He gave a hotpot a real fright on his debut in a Sandown bumper and looks to have a real future.

Chantilly Rose

93 78

10-y-o b m Primitive Rising (USA)-Milly L'Attaque (Military)

Miss R Brewis Miss Rhona Brewis

Placings:0066/0052/P/PP0P-P04446P **(4875)**

2001/02: 22^{P}G, 20^{0}G, 21^{4}HY, 24^{4}GS, 27^{4}S, 22^{6}S, 24^{P}G

	Starts	1st	2nd	3rd	Win & Pl
Hurdles	7	0	0	0	0
Career Total	**20**	**0**	**1**	**0**	**552**

Going: Sf: 0-3 GS: 0-1 Gd: 0-3 GF: - Fm: 0-0
Distance: 2m/2m3: 0-0 2m4-2m7: 0-4 3m+: 0-3
Track: LH: 0-5 RH: 0-2 Tight: 0-5 Gall: 0-1
Aids: Bl: 0-0 Vi: 0-0 Tstrap: 0-0
Best Rating: 80 3/99 Kels 2m6f110y good Hdl

Chaos Theory

105(111h) (111h)127

7-y-o b g Jupiter Island-Indian Orchid (Warpath)

Mrs M Reveley R Burridge

Placings:*U/40*F113/63600-0FP1FP4F **(4556)**

2001/02: 16^{P}G, 21^{F}GS, 16^{P}G, 20^{1}GF, 16^{F}G, 20^{P}S, 20^{4}GF, 17^{F}G

	Starts	1st	2nd	3rd	Win & Pl
Hurdles	3	0	0	0	0
Chases	5	1	0	0	4504
Career Total	**20**	**3**	**0**	**2**	**11842**

127	12/01	Muss	2m4f	D Ch	G-F	£4270
122	1/00	Hntg	2m110y	D Hdl	GD	£3346
104	1/00	Muss	2m	E Hdl	SFT	£2772

Total win prize-money £10389

Going: Sf: 0-1 GS: 0-1 Gd: 0-4 GF: - Fm: 1-2
Distance: 2m/2m3: 0-4 **2m4-2m7: 1-4** 3m+: 0-0
Track: LH: 0-1 **RH: 1-7 Tight: 1-3** Gall: 0-2
Aids: Bl: 0-0 Vi: 0-0 Tstrap: 0-0
Best Rating: 127 12/01 Muss 2m4f gd-fm Ch

Took a crashing fall at Kempton in October 2001, but looked a different horse when racing like a veteran who knows the game to land his chasing debut but has gone the wrong way since.

Chaparro Amargoso (IRE)

112(104h) (86h)120

9-y-o b g Ela-Mana-Mou-Champanera (Top Ville)

B Ellison E J Berry

Placings: 1/3/3P6-12F43446052 **(4920)**

2001/02: 16^{1}GF, 16^{2}GF, 16^{F}GF, 16^{4}G, 21^{3}S, 21^{4}S, 16^{4}S, 20^{6}G, 20^{0}GS, 17^{5}GF, 21^{2}GF

	Starts	1st	2nd	3rd	Win & Pl
Hurdles	2	0	0	0	0
Chases	9	1	2	1	6842
Career Total	**16**	**2**	**2**	**3**	**8756**

118	7/01	Sedg	2m110y	E Ch	G-F	£3152
110	10/97	Hexm	2m	H NHF	G-F	£1187

Total win prize-money £4340

Going: Sf: 0-3 GS: 0-1 Gd: 0-2 GF: - Fm: 1-5
Distance: 2m/2m3: 1-6 2m4-2m7: 0-5 3m+: 0-0
Track: LH: 1-7 RH: 0-4 **Tight: 1-8** Gall: 0-0
Aids: Bl: 0-0 Vi: 0-2 Tstrap: 0-5
Best Rating: 118 7/01 Sedg 2m110y gd-fm Ch

A consistent performer in modest handicap chases, he is best suited by two miles and fast ground.

Chapel Road (IRE)

96 76

12-y-o b g Buckskin (FR)-Lovely Choice (Deep Run)

O O'Neill J A Danahar

Placings:*00/044*400030/4105056/0 **(1189)**

2001/02: 20^{0}G

	Starts	1st	2nd	3rd	Win & Pl
Hurdles	1	0	0	0	
Career Total	**19**	**1**	**0**	**1**	**4636**

99	11/99	Clon	3m	Hdl	Y-S	£3696

Total win prize-money £3696

Going: Sf: 0-0 GS: 0-0 Gd: 0-1 GF: - Fm: 0-0
Distance: 2m/2m3: 0-0 2m4-2m7: 0-1 3m+: 0-0
Track: LH: 0-1 RH: 0-0 Tight: 0-1 Gall: 0-0
Aids: Bl: 0-0 Vi: 0-0 Tstrap: 0-0
Best Rating: 99 12/99 Clon 2m6f sft-hvy Hdl

Chapeltown (IRE)

111 135

10-y-o b g Denel (FR)-Lady Dunsford (Torus)

N J Henderson Newbury Racehorse Owners Group Ii

Placings:*066630/213*/1513-41 **(2125)**

2001/02: 16^{4}G, 19^{1}G

	Starts	1st	2nd	3rd	Win & Pl
Hurdles	2	1	0	0	9625
Career Total	**15**	**4**	**1**	**3**	**24006**

135	11/01	Newb	2m3f	C(0-135)HHdl	GD	£7150
130	3/01	Newb	2m110y	D Hdl	HVY	£4738
135	11/00	Newb	2m110y	C Hdl	HVY	£5720
99	5/98	DRoy	2m	NHF	GD	£1489

Total win prize-money £19098

Going: Sf: 0-0 GS: 0-0 Gd: 1-2 GF: - Fm: 0-0
Distance: 2m/2m3: 1-2 2m4-2m7: 0-0 3m+: 0-0
Track: LH: 1-2 RH: 0-0 Tight: 0-0 **Gall: 1-1**
Aids: Bl: 0-0 Vi: 0-0 Tstrap: 0-0
Best Rating: 135 11/01 Newb 2m3f good Hdl

Proved himself a fan of Newbury, fortunately for the Newbury Racehorse Owners Group II who own him, with three hurdle wins there up to two miles three furlongs.

Charles Spencelayh (IRE)

101 91

6-y-o b g Tenby-Legit (IRE) (Runnett)

M C Pipe (Rune Haugen 4/10) Mick Fletcher

Placings:5P600 **(4033)**

2001/02: 17^{5}S, 18^{P}G, 19^{6}GF, 17^{0}S, 20^{0}S

	Starts	1st	2nd	3rd	Win & Pl
Hurdles	5	0	0	0	0
Career Total	**5**	**0**	**0**	**0**	**0**

Going: Sf: 0-3 GS: 0-0 Gd: 0-1 GF: - Fm: 0-1
Distance: 2m/2m3: 0-4 2m4-2m7: 0-1 3m+: 0-0
Track: LH: 0-0 RH: 0-2 Tight: 0-2 Gall: 0-0
Aids: Bl: 0-0 Vi: 0-0 Tstrap: 0-0
Best Rating: 91 1/02 Tntn 2m1f soft Hdl

Charlestown Lass

88 82

5-y-o b m Bob Back (USA)-Prepare (IRE) (Millfontaine)

J Neville Mrs Margaret Mulligan

Placings:*00*-2065 **(4684)**

2001/02: 17^{2}HY, 16^{0}S, 19^{6}S, 19^{5}GF

	Starts	1st	2nd	3rd	Win & Pl
NH Flat	1	0	1	0	454
Hurdles	3	0	0	0	0
Career Total	**6**	**0**	**1**	**0**	**454**

Going: Sf: 0-3 GS: 0-0 Gd: 0-0 GF: - Fm: 0-1
Distance: 2m/2m3: 0-2 2m4-2m7: 0-2 3m+: 0-0
Track: LH: 0-0 RH: 0-3 Tight: 0-2 Gall: 0-1
Aids: Bl: 0-0 Vi: 0-1 Tstrap: 0-0
Best Rating: 100 12/01 Folk 2m1f110y heavy NHF

Lightly-raced mare, has shown ability in bumpers. Well beaten on hurdles debut but appeared suited by the step up in trip next time. Ran her best race so far on heavy ground.

Charley Lambert (IRE)

106 121

11-y-o b g Strong Gale-Frankford Run (Deep Run)

J Mackie R M Mitchell And Mr D G Savala

Placings:*45/4*042BP0/F12140/51U4/F126/135-2P **(0356)**

2001/02: 21^{2}GF, 20^{P}GS

	Starts	1st	2nd	3rd	Win & Pl
Chases	2	0	1	0	2139
Career Total	**28**	**5**	**4**	**1**	**21621**

120	12/00	Newc	2m4f	D(0-125)HCh	SFT	£3750
117	5/99	Uttx	2m5f	D Ch	G-F	£4182
115	10/98	Carl	2m4f110y	D Ch	GD	£3501

106 12/97 Sedg 2m5f110y E Hdl GD £2022
106 11/97 Newc 2m4f E Hdl G-F £2232
Total win prize-money £15689

Going: Sf: 0-0 GS: 0-1 Gd: 0-0 GF: - Fm: 0-1
Distance: 2m/2m3: 0-0 2m4-2m7: 0-2 3m+: 0-0
Track: LH: 0-2 RH: 0-0 Tight: 0-1 Gall: 0-0
Aids: Bl: 0-0 Vi: 0-0 Tstrap: 0-0
Best Rating: 121 5/01 Ayr 2m5f110y gd-fm Ch

Lightly-raced recently, has yet to prove he stays three miles. Needs a sound surface.

Charlie Banker (IRE)

93 **125**

10-y-o b g Supreme Leader-Hack Along (Little Buskins)
K R Burke David Whyte

Placings:00/P66/1P4131P/**24423F1/1PPF** (3547)
2001/02: 24^{1}S, 24^{P}G, 25^{P}GS, 24^{F}S

	Starts	1st	2nd	3rd	Win & Pl
Chases	4	1	0	0	3126
Career Total	**23**	**5**	**2**	**2**	**18162**

125 12/01 Sthl 3m110y E(0-115)HCh SFT £3125
119 3/00 Hntg 2m4f110y E Ch G-F £3120
110 3/99 Hexm 2m4f110y E(0-105)HHdl G-S £2647
105 2/99 Muss 3m D(0-110)HHdl G-F £3143
110 12/98 Wind 2m4f F(0-105)HHdl G-S £2052
Total win prize-money £14090

Going: Sf: 1-2 GS: 0-1 Gd: 0-1 GF: - Fm: 0-0
Distance: 2m/2m3: 0-0 2m4-2m7: 0-0 **3m+: 1-4**
Track: **LH: 1-3** RH: 0-1 **Tight: 1-1** Gall: 0-1
Aids: Bl: 0-0 Vi: 0-1 Tstrap: 0-0
Best Rating: 125 12/01 Sthl 3m110y soft Ch

Charlie Brownie

78 **60**

8-y-o b g Sula Bula-Peanuts (FR) (Mistigri)
A W Carroll Jolly Boys

Placings:0P (4637)
2001/02: 16^{0}GS, 20^{P}GF

	Starts	1st	2nd	3rd	Win & Pl
Hurdles	2	0	0	0	
Career Total	**2**	**0**	**0**	**0**	

Going: Sf: 0-0 GS: 0-1 Gd: 0-0 GF: - Fm: 0-1
Distance: 2m/2m3: 0-1 2m4-2m7: 0-1 3m+: 0-0
Track: LH: 0-0 RH: 0-2 Tight: 0-0 Gall: 0-0
Aids: Bl: 0-0 Vi: 0-0 Tstrap: 0-0
Best Rating: 60 3/02 Sand 2m110y gd-sft Hdl

Charlie Chang (IRE)

105(82h) (38h)**100**

9-y-o b g Don't Forget Me-East River (FR) (Arctic Tern (USA))
A G Juckes David Workman

Placings:6002/3P001160/0P/004**P14** (4903)
2001/02: 20^{0}G, 16^{0}GF, 20^{4}S, 19^{P}HY, 24^{1}S, 24^{4}G

	Starts	1st	2nd	3rd	Win & Pl
Hurdles	2	0	0	0	0
Chases	4	1	0	0	6043
Career Total	**20**	**3**	**1**	**1**	**10788**

100 3/02 Bang 3m110y D Ch SFT £4410
90 3/99 Wwck 2m F(0-100)HHdl SFT £2110
86 2/99 Folk 2m1f110y G(0-90)HHdl G-S £1660
Total win prize-money £8180

Going: Sf: 1-3 GS: 0-0 Gd: 0-2 GF: - Fm: 0-1
Distance: 2m/2m3: 0-2 2m4-2m7: 0-2 **3m+: 1-2**
Track: **LH: 1-4** RH: 0-2 **Tight: 1-3** Gall: 0-0
Aids: Bl: 0-3 Vi: 0-0 Tstrap: 0-0
Best Rating: 100 3/02 Bang 3m110y soft Ch

Modest novice chaser who won a farcical event at Bangor in 2002 over an extended three miles. Goes well in soft ground.

Charlie Charlie

101 **89**

11-y-o b g Emarati (USA)-Hound Song (Jukebox)
L Wells A Russell & P B Davis Insurance

Placings:0/4/02/22234F202-01P (3277)
2001/02: 22^{0}GS, 21^{1}S, 21^{P}S

	Starts	1st	2nd	3rd	Win & Pl
Hurdles	3	1	0	0	2195
Career Total	**16**	**1**	**6**	**1**	**6439**

89 12/01 Plum 2m5f F Hdl SFT £2194
Total win prize-money £2195

Going: Sf: 1-2 GS: 0-1 Gd: 0-0 GF: - Fm: 0-0
Distance: 2m/2m3: 0-0 **2m4-2m7: 1-3** 3m+: 0-0
Track: **LH: 1-3** RH: 0-0 **Tight: 1-3** Gall: 0-0
Aids: Bl: 0-1 Vi: 0-0 **Tstrap: 1-2**
Best Rating: 89 12/01 Plum 2m5f soft Hdl

Finally broke his duck in a weak claimer in bad ground.

Charlie Collis

62f **47f**

7-y-o b g Deltic (USA)-Oneninefive (Sayyaf)
Mrs E B Scott Mrs E B Scott

Placings:00 (1773)
2001/02: 16^{0}G, 17^{0}GS

	Starts	1st	2nd	3rd	Win & Pl
NH Flat	2	0	0	0	
Career Total	**2**	**0**	**0**	**0**	

Going: Sf: 0-0 GS: 0-1 Gd: 0-1 GF: - Fm: 0-0
Distance: 2m/2m3: 0-2 2m4-2m7: 0-0 3m+: 0-0
Track: LH: 0-1 RH: 0-1 Tight: 0-0 Gall: 0-0
Aids: Bl: 0-0 Vi: 0-0 Tstrap: 0-0
Best Rating: 47 10/01 Chep 2m110y good NHF

Charlie D'Or

9-y-o ch g Le Coq D'Or-Edwards Victoria (IRE) (Buckskin (FR))
J P Dodds E F Brown

Placings:000/05P/0603**P/P** (0802)
2001/02: 16^{P}GF

	Starts	1st	2nd	3rd	Win & Pl
Chases	1	0	0	0	
Career Total	**12**	**0**	**0**	**1**	**422**

Going: Sf: 0-0 GS: 0-0 Gd: 0-0 GF: - Fm: 0-1
Distance: 2m/2m3: 0-1 2m4-2m7: 0-0 3m+: 0-0
Track: LH: 0-0 RH: 0-1 Tight: 0-0 Gall: 0-0
Aids: Bl: 0-0 Vi: 0-0 Tstrap: 0-0
Best Rating: 78 12/97 Muss 2m good NHF

Charlie Siddle

99(96h) (67h)**90**

8-y-o b g Thowra (FR)-Figrant (USA) (L'Emigrant (USA))
Miss K M George A B Parr

Placings:54P/**F5-4546**044**P** (3513)
2001/02: 21^{4}GF, 20^{5}GF, 21^{4}GS, 16^{6}GF, 24^{0}G, 20^{4}GF, 19^{4}G, 16^{P}S

	Starts	1st	2nd	3rd	Win & Pl
Hurdles	3	0	0	0	0
Chases	5	0	0	0	601
Career Total	**13**	**0**	**0**	**0**	**837**

Going: Sf: 0-1 GS: 0-1 Gd: 0-2 GF: - Fm: 0-4
Distance: 2m/2m3: 0-3 2m4-2m7: 0-4 3m+: 0-1
Track: LH: 0-7 RH: 0-1 Tight: 0-6 Gall: 0-0
Aids: Bl: 0-1 Vi: 0-1 Tstrap: 0-0
Best Rating: 90 4/01 Extr 2m3f110y soft Ch

Charlie Strong (IRE)

9-y-o b g Strong Gale-The Village Vixen (Buckskin (FR))
R Kelvin-Hughes R Kelvin-Hughes

Placings:6/1-63 (4865)
2001/02: 23^{6}G, 23^{3}F

	Starts	1st	2nd	3rd	Win & Pl
Chases	2	0	0	1	322
Career Total	**4**	**1**	**0**	**1**	**2112**

119 4/01 Extr 2m7f110y H Ch G-S £1790
Total win prize-money £1791

Going: Sf: 0-0 GS: 0-0 Gd: 0-1 GF: - Fm: 0-1
Distance: 2m/2m3: 0-0 2m4-2m7: 0-0 3m+: 0-2
Track: LH: 0-0 RH: 0-2 Tight: 0-0 Gall: 0-0
Aids: Bl: 0-0 Vi: 0-0 Tstrap: 0-0
Best Rating: 119 4/01 Extr 2m7f110y gd-sft Ch

Charlie Taylor (IRE)

6-y-o ch g Insan (USA)-Gusserane Lark (Napoleon Bonaparte)
C N Kellett Sean A Taylor

Placings:0-0 (1655)
2001/02: 17^{0}G

	Starts	1st	2nd	3rd	Win & Pl
Hurdles	1	0	0	0	
Career Total	**2**	**0**	**0**	**0**	

Going: Sf: 0-0 GS: 0-0 Gd: 0-1 GF: - Fm: 0-0
Distance: 2m/2m3: 0-1 2m4-2m7: 0-0 3m+: 0-0
Track: LH: 0-1 RH: 0-0 Tight: 0-1 Gall: 0-0
Aids: Bl: 0-0 Vi: 0-0 Tstrap: 0-0
Best Rating: 54 10/00 MRas 2m1f110y good NHF

Charlieadams (IRE)

105 **111+**

12-y-o b g Carlingford Castle-Lucy Platter (FR) (Record Token)
J F W Muir J F W Muir

Placings:0/000**P0/2/4U3/50F3-O116UUP** (4692)
2001/02: 21°G, 20^{1}S, 20^{1}GF, 24^{6}S, 21^{U}HY, 21^{U}G, 25^{P}GF

	Starts	1st	2nd	3rd	Win & Pl
Chases	7	2	0	0	3654
Career Total	**21**	**2**	**1**	**2**	**4755**

98 5/01 Hexm 2m4f110y H Ch G-F £1337
98 5/01 Prth 2m4f110y H Ch SFT £2317
Total win prize-money £3654

oing: Sf: 1-3 GS: 0-0 Gd: 0-2 GF: - Fm: 1-2
istance: 2m/2m3: 0-0 **2m4-2m7: 2-5** 3m+: 0-2
rack: LH: 1-5 RH: 1-2 Tight: 0-4 Gall: 0-0
ids: Bl: 0-0 Vi: 0-0 Tstrap: 0-0
est Rating: 105 4/99 DRoy 3m yield Ch

lodest hunter chase winner, he scored on his first outg for professional handling when taking a handicap hase at Sedgefield in July.

Charliemoore

3f **90f**

-y-o ch g Karinga Bay-Your Care (FR) (Caerwent)
L Moore Bryan Pennick

lacings:*01* **(4784)**
001/02: 16^{0}GF, 18^{1}GF

	Starts	1st	2nd	3rd	Win & Pl
H Flat	2	1	0	0	1712
areer Total	**2**	**1**	**0**	**0**	**1712**

4/02	Plum	2m2f	H NHF	G-F	£1711

Total win prize-money £1712

oing: Sf: 0-0 GS: 0-0 Gd: 0-0 GF: - Fm: 1-2
istance: **2m/2m3: 1-2** 2m4-2m7: 0-0 3m+: 0-0
rack: LH: 0-0 RH: 0-1 Tight: 0-0 Gall: 0-0
ids: Bl: 0-0 Vi: 0-0 Tstrap: 0-0
est Rating: 90 4/02 Plum 2m2f gd-fm NHF

lade all to land his second bumper on fast ground.

Charlies Future

9 **93**

-y-o b g Democratic (USA)-Faustelerie (Faustus JSA))
R Rodford Mrs C A Lewis-Jones

lacings:55003 **(4502)**
001/02: 16^{5}GF, 17^{5}S, 16^{0}S, 19^{0}G, 22^{3}G

	Starts	1st	2nd	3rd	Win & Pl
lurdles	5	0	0	1	448
areer Total	**5**	**0**	**0**	**1**	**448**

oing: Sf: 0-2 GS: 0-0 Gd: 0-2 GF: - Fm: 0-1
istance: 2m/2m3: 0-4 2m4-2m7: 0-1 3m+: 0-0
rack: LH: 0-1 RH: 0-4 Tight: 0-2 Gall: 0-0
ids: Bl: 0-0 Vi: 0-0 Tstrap: 0-0
est Rating: 93 3/02 NAbb 2m6f good Hdl

howed improved form when tackling a longer trip in ovices' handicap hurdle at Newton Abbot in March 002.

Charmed

-y-o ch g Savahra Sound-Sweet And Lucky (Lucky Vednesday)
J Gingell Gentlemen Don't Work On Mondays

lacings:P **(0965)**
001/02: 17^{P}GS

	Starts	1st	2nd	3rd	Win & Pl
lurdles	1	0	0	0	
areer Total	**1**	**0**	**0**	**0**	

oing: Sf: 0-0 GS: 0-1 Gd: 0-0 GF: - Fm: 0-0
istance: 2m/2m3: 0-1 2m4-2m7: 0-0 3m+: 0-0
rack: LH: 0-0 RH: 0-0 Tight: 0-0 Gall: 0-0
ids: Bl: 0-0 Vi: 0-0 Tstrap: 0-0
est Rating:

Charming Admiral (IRE)

83(61c) **36**

9-y-o b g Shareef Dancer (USA)-Lilac Charm (Bustino)
Mrs A Duffield The Old Spice Girls

Placings:4312013/3014F2/116P-50 **(2630)**
2001/02: 22^{5}HY, 24^{0}S

	Starts	1st	2nd	3rd	Win & Pl
Hurdles	2	0	0	0	0
Career Total	**19**	**5**	**2**	**3**	**20016**

119	9/00	Sedg	2m5f	E(0-115)HCh	SFT	£4153
119	8/00	Ctml	2m5f110y	F(0-110)HCh	G-S	£3461
106	2/99	Carl	2m4f110y	D Ch	HVY	£3964
126	4/98	Kels	2m110y	D(0-125)HHdl	HVY	£2762
124	1/98	Catt	2m3f	E Hdl	G-S	£2092

Total win prize-money £16434

Going: Sf: 0-2 GS: 0-0 Gd: 0-0 GF: - Fm: 0-0
Distance: 2m/2m3: 0-0 2m4-2m7: 0-1 3m+: 0-1
Track: LH: 0-2 RH: 0-0 Tight: 0-0 Gall: 0-0
Aids: Bl: 0-1 Vi: 0-0 Tstrap: 0-0
Best Rating: 126 4/98 Kels 2m110y heavy Hdl

Charming Tina (IRE)

5-y-o ch m Indian Ridge-Tina's Charm (IRE) (Hatim (USA))
B G Powell Mrs Chris Harrington

Placings:*04P* **(4114)**
2001/02: 17^{0}G, 16^{4}GS, 16^{P}G

	Starts	1st	2nd	3rd	Win & Pl
NH Flat	1	0	0	0	0
Hurdles	2	0	0	0	0
Career Total	**3**	**0**	**0**	**0**	**0**

Going: Sf: 0-0 GS: 0-1 Gd: 0-2 GF: - Fm: 0-0
Distance: 2m/2m3: 0-3 2m4-2m7: 0-0 3m+: 0-0
Track: LH: 0-2 RH: 0-1 Tight: 0-2 Gall: 0-0
Aids: Bl: 0-0 Vi: 0-0 Tstrap: 0-0
Best Rating: 15 10/01 Bang 2m1f good NHF

Charmouth Forest

86 **85**

6-y-o ch g Lir-Crimson Lady (Crimson Beau)
C J Gray D J Staddon

Placings:*00-6*50 **(4114)**
2001/02: 17^{6}HY, 17^{5}S, 16^{0}G

	Starts	1st	2nd	3rd	Win & Pl
NH Flat	1	0	0	0	0
Hurdles	2	0	0	0	0
Career Total	**5**	**0**	**0**	**0**	**0**

Going: Sf: 0-2 GS: 0-0 Gd: 0-1 GF: - Fm: 0-0
Distance: 2m/2m3: 0-3 2m4-2m7: 0-0 3m+: 0-0
Track: LH: 0-1 RH: 0-2 Tight: 0-2 Gall: 0-0
Aids: Bl: 0-0 Vi: 0-0 Tstrap: 0-0
Best Rating: 85 2/02 Tntn 2m1f soft Hdl

Charnwood Jack (USA)

110 (77h)**113**

9-y-o ch g Sanglamore (USA)-Hyroglyph (USA) (Northern Dancer)
M Todhunter Leeds Plywood And Doors Ltd

Placings:5/2143305**F31F0**/11P2U22416663/2U02453 40-41P **(0790)**
2001/02: 17^{4}G, 16^{1}GS, 19^{P}GF

	Starts	1st	2nd	3rd	Win & Pl
Hurdles	1	0	0	0	0
Chases	2	1	0	0	5538
Career Total	**38**	**6**	**6**	**5**	**30220**

113	6/01	Hexm	2m110y	D(0-125)HCh	G-S	£5538
112	10/99	Sedg	2m110y	E(0-115)HCh	G-F	£3072
111	5/99	Ctml	2m1f110y	F(0-100)HCh	GD	£3064
109	5/99	Hexm	2m110y	F(0-105)HCh	SFT	£3262
106	3/99	Hexm	2m110y	E Ch	SFT	£2988
96	6/98	Prth	2m4f110y	E Hdl	G-F	£2655

Total win prize-money £20581

Going: Sf: 0-0 GS: 1-1 Gd: 0-1 GF: - Fm: 0-1
Distance: **2m/2m3: 1-2** 2m4-2m7: 0-1 3m+: 0-0
Track: **LH: 1-1** RH: 0-2 Tight: 0-2 Gall: 0-0
Aids: Bl: 0-0 Vi: 0-0 Tstrap: 0-0
Best Rating: 115 5/00 Hexm 2m110y gd-fm Ch

Charter Ridge (IRE)

9-y-o b g Glacial Storm (USA)-Pure Spec (Fine Blade (USA))
J J O'Neill Anne Duchess Of Westminster

Placings:*1*03611/5BF4/11P312442-PP **(3227)**
2001/02: 24^{P}G, 25^{P}G

	Starts	1st	2nd	3rd	Win & Pl
Chases	2	0	0	0	
Career Total	**21**	**6**	**2**	**2**	**34611**

143	10/00	Aint	3m1f	C Ch	GD	£6870
128	5/00	Aint	3m1f	D(0-120)HCh	G-F	£4228
133	5/00	Weth	3m1f	D(0-110)HCh	G-F	£5265
109	4/99	Bang	3m	E Hdl	G-S	£2990
102	4/99	Bang	2m4f	E Hdl	GD	£2486
102	6/98	Clon	2m4f	NHF	GD	£2382

Total win prize-money £24223

Going: Sf: 0-0 GS: 0-0 Gd: 0-2 GF: - Fm: 0-0
Distance: 2m/2m3: 0-0 2m4-2m7: 0-0 3m+: 0-2
Track: LH: 0-1 RH: 0-1 Tight: 0-0 Gall: 0-1
Aids: Bl: 0-0 Vi: 0-0 Tstrap: 0-0
Best Rating: 145 11/00 Newb 3m gd-sft Ch

A bumper winner in Ireland for Tony Mullins, he has done well for Jonjo O'Neill and developed into a useful novice chaser last season. He has had his problems subsequently. Stays three miles. Acts on good/good to soft ground.

Charter Royal (FR)

102(85h) (50h)**93**

7-y-o gr g Royal Charter (FR)-Tadjmine (FR) (Tadj (FR))
A R Dicken Ron Affleck

Placings:*650*/050300/2241F0F-60145053400U **(4889)**
2001/02: 20^{6}GF, 18^{0}G, 16^{1}S, 16^{4}S, 16^{5}G, 16^{0}S, 20^{5}S, 24^{3}S, 21^{4}S, 20^{0}GS, 20^{0}GF, 26^{U}G

	Starts	1st	2nd	3rd	Win & Pl
Hurdles	3	0	0	0	0
Chases	9	1	0	1	2980
Career Total	**28**	**2**	**2**	**2**	**7584**

90	11/01	Sedg	2m110y	F(0-110)HCh	SFT	£2520
90	1/01	Catt	2m	F(0-100)HCh	G-S	£2401

Total win prize-money £4922

Going: Sf: 1-6 GS: 0-1 Gd: 0-3 GF: - Fm: 0-2
Distance: **2m/2m3: 1-5** 2m4-2m7: 0-5 3m+: 0-2
Track: **LH: 1-7** RH: 0-4 **Tight: 1-7** Gall: 0-1

Aids: Bl: 0-0 Vi: 0-0 Tstrap: 0-0
Best Rating: 94 10/00 Carl 2m gd-sft Ch

Chase Night

9-y-o b g Le Coq D'Or-Royal Question (Grey Ghost)
D W Whillans Chas N Whillans

Placings:P (0783)
2001/02: 16^{P}G

	Starts	1st	2nd	3rd	Win & Pl
Hurdles	1	0	0	0	
Career Total	1	0	0	0	

Going: Sf: 0-0 GS: 0-0 Gd: 0-1 GF: - Fm: 0-0
Distance: 2m/2m3: 0-1 2m4-2m7: 0-0 3m+: 0-0
Track: LH: 0-1 RH: 0-0 Tight: 0-0 Gall: 0-0
Aids: Bl: 0-0 Vi: 0-0 Tstrap: 0-0
Best Rating:

Chasing Bailey's

88(45h) 66

8-y-o b g Neltino-Rosie Oh (Laurence O)
C Grant G R Bailey Ltd (baileys Horse Feeds)

Placings:40/F46/F6-6 (2071)
2001/02: 21^{6}S

	Starts	1st	2nd	3rd	Win & Pl
Chases	1	0	0	0	0
Career Total	8	0	0	0	0

Going: Sf: 0-1 GS: 0-0 Gd: 0-0 GF: - Fm: 0-0
Distance: 2m/2m3: 0-0 2m4-2m7: 0-1 3m+: 0-0
Track: LH: 0-1 RH: 0-0 Tight: 0-1 Gall: 0-0
Aids: Bl: 0-0 Vi: 0-0 Tstrap: 0-0
Best Rating: 92 4/99 Hexm 2m4f110y good Hdl

Chasing Daisy

10-y-o b m Lyphento (USA)-Blue Breeze (USA) (Blue Times (USA))
J W Dufosee I R Snowden & Mrs Sue Condry

Placings:PP (0579)
2001/02: 21^{P}G, 24^{P}GF

	Starts	1st	2nd	3rd	Win & Pl
Chases	2	0	0	0	
Career Total	2	0	0	0	

Going: Sf: 0-0 GS: 0-0 Gd: 0-1 GF: - Fm: 0-1
Distance: 2m/2m3: 0-0 2m4-2m7: 0-1 3m+: 0-1
Track: LH: 0-1 RH: 0-1 Tight: 0-2 Gall: 0-0
Aids: Bl: 0-0 Vi: 0-0 Tstrap: 0-0
Best Rating:

Chasing The Bride

9-y-o b g Gildoran-Bride (Remainder Man)
J W Dufosee Mrs Susan Hooper

Placings:U/22116/22-PU4P (4826)
2001/02: 26^{P}S, 25^{U}G, 24^{4}G, 26^{P}G

	Starts	1st	2nd	3rd	Win & Pl
Chases	4	0	0	0	0
Career Total	12	2	4	0	6850

114	4/00	Asct	3m110y	H Ch	GD	£2697
112	3/00	Winc	3m1f110y	H Ch	G-S	£1557

Total win prize-money £4256

Going: Sf: 0-1 GS: 0-0 Gd: 0-3 GF: - Fm: 0-0
Distance: 2m/2m3: 0-0 2m4-2m7: 0-0 3m+: 0-4
Track: LH: 0-1 RH: 0-2 Tight: 0-2 Gall: 0-1
Aids: Bl: 0-0 Vi: 0-0 Tstrap: 0-4
Best Rating: 127 2/01 Kemp 3m good Ch

Chateau Rose (IRE)

109 107

6-y-o b g Roselier (FR)-Claycastle (IRE) (Carlingford Castle)
N A Gaselee The Southern Set

Placings:*30*-32220 (4154)
2001/02: 16^{3}S, 21^{2}S, 22^{2}S, 25^{2}HY, 20^{0}GS

	Starts	1st	2nd	3rd	Win & Pl
Hurdles	5	0	3	1	3101
Career Total	7	0	3	2	3456

Going: Sf: 0-4 GS: 0-1 Gd: 0-0 GF: - Fm: 0-0
Distance: 2m/2m3: 0-1 2m4-2m7: 0-3 3m+: 0-1
Track: LH: 0-1 RH: 0-2 Tight: 0-1 Gall: 0-0
Aids: Bl: 0-0 Vi: 0-0 Tstrap: 0-0
Best Rating: 107 12/01 Strf 2m6f110y soft Hdl

Placed form in staying novice hurdles. Stays three miles. Acts on soft/heavy ground.

Chater Flair

97 102

5-y-o b g Efisio-Native Flair (Be My Native (USA))
C J Mann (W R Muir 29/1) Bobby Robson And Partners

Placings:2 (4906)
2001/02: 19^{2}G

	Starts	1st	2nd	3rd	Win & Pl
Hurdles	1	0	1	0	1245
Career Total	1	0	1	0	1245

Going: Sf: 0-0 GS: 0-0 Gd: 0-1 GF: - Fm: 0-0
Distance: 2m/2m3: 0-0 2m4-2m7: 0-1 3m+: 0-0
Track: LH: 0-0 RH: 0-1 Tight: 0-1 Gall: 0-0
Aids: Bl: 0-0 Vi: 0-0 Tstrap: 0-0
Best Rating: 102 4/02 MRas 2m3f110y good Hdl

Runner-up in both completed starts over hurdles. Stays well and acts on fast ground.

Chatergold (IRE)

97(110c) (105c)75

10-y-o b g Posen (USA)-Fiodoir (Weavers Hall)
P Wegmann (G M McCourt 5/9) P Wegmann

Placings:00P/**P5P4P53/320UU26/013041U2244155-20S15P425O6PP4** (4265)
2001/02: 25^{2}F, 24^{0}GF, 20^{S}GF, 25^{1}GF, 25^{5}GF, 22^{P}GF, 26^{4}GF, 22^{2}S, 23^{5}GF, 22°S, 25^{6}HY, 25^{P}S, 25^{P}S, 20^{4}S

	Starts	1st	2nd	3rd	Win & Pl
Hurdles	1	0	0	0	0
Chases	13	1	2	0	6968
Career Total	45	4	6	3	20353

105	7/01	Wolv	3m1f	E(0-115)HCh	G-F	£4065
105	12/00	Folk	2m	F(0-95)HCh	SFT	£3042
100	9/00	Font	3m2f110y	E(0-105)HCh	G-S	£3055
89	5/00	Extr	2m3f	H Ch	G-F	£1485

Total win prize-money £11648

Going: Sf: 0-6 GS: 0-0 Gd: 0-0 GF: - Fm: 1-8
Distance: 2m/2m3: 0-0 2m4-2m7: 0-5 **3m+: 1-9**
Track: **LH: 1-3** RH: 0-9 **Tight: 1-5** Gall: 0-1
Aids: **Bl: 1-6** Vi: 0-0 Tstrap: 0-0

Best Rating: 105 11/01 Towc 2m6f soft Cl

A modest chaser suited by three miles and fast ground.

Chaucers Miller

81 57

6-y-o ch g Baron Blakeney-Reine De Rosehill (Shack (USA))
G B Balding H M F McCall

Placings:P-0 (0214
2001/02: 22^{0}GF

	Starts	1st	2nd	3rd	Win & Pl
Hurdles	1	0	0	0	
Career Total	2	0	0	0	

Going: Sf: 0-0 GS: 0-0 Gd: 0-0 GF: - Fm: 0-1
Distance: 2m/2m3: 0-0 2m4-2m7: 0-1 3m+: 0-0
Track: LH: 0-0 RH: 0-1 Tight: 0-0 Gall: 0-0
Aids: Bl: 0-0 Vi: 0-0 Tstrap: 0-0
Best Rating: 57 5/01 Winc 2m6f gd-fm Hd

Chauvinist (IRE)

99 11

7-y-o b g Roselier (FR)-Sacajawea (Tanfirion)
N J Henderson Mrs E Roberts

Placings:*1*-224 (3657
2001/02: 20^{2}G, 20^{2}GS, 22^{4}S

	Starts	1st	2nd	3rd	Win & Pl
Hurdles	3	0	2	0	5530
Career Total	4	1	2	0	8071

118	2/01	Kemp	2m	HNHF	G-S	£254

Total win prize-money £254

Going: Sf: 0-1 GS: 0-1 Gd: 0-1 GF: - Fm: 0-0
Distance: 2m/2m3: 0-0 2m4-2m7: 0-3 3m+: 0-0
Track: LH: 0-0 RH: 0-3 Tight: 0-0 Gall: 0-0
Aids: Bl: 0-0 Vi: 0-0 Tstrap: 0-0
Best Rating: 118 1/02 Asct 2m4f gd-sft Hd

Won his only bumper at Kempton early in 2001, and ran well in novice hurdles last season. Stays two and a half miles. Lacks a turn of foot. Suited by good to soft ground.

Chaweng Beach

76 32

4-y-o ro f Chaddleworth (IRE)-Swallow Bay (Penmarric (USA))
C P Morlock (S Kirk 2/11) C P H Morlock

Placings:0 (2780
2001/02: 16^{0}G

	Starts	1st	2nd	3rd	Win & Pl
Hurdles	1	0	0	0	
Career Total	1	0	0	0	

Going: Sf: 0-0 GS: 0-0 Gd: 0-1 GF: - Fm: 0-0
Distance: 2m/2m3: 0-1 2m4-2m7: 0-0 3m+: 0-0
Track: LH: 0-0 RH: 0-1 Tight: 0-0 Gall: 0-0
Aids: Bl: 0-0 Vi: 0-0 Tstrap: 0-0
Best Rating: 32 12/01 Ludl 2m good Hd

Cheater (IRE)

11-y-o b g Good Thyne (USA)-Cute Play (Salluceva)
Nick Gifford J A C Ayton

Placings:*255*25165P/115P/43PPP3P2PU/PP/3P

(0585)

2001/02: 21[3]GF, 24[P]GF

	Starts	1st	2nd	3rd	Win & Pl
Chases	2	0	0	1	362
Career Total	**27**	**3**	**3**	**3**	**12958**

94	10/97	Sedg	2m5f	E Ch	G-F	£3039
96	9/97	Prth	2m4f110y	F(0-100)HHdl	G-F	£2801
94	1/97	Muss	3m	D(0-125)HHdl	G-F	£3659

Total win prize-money £9500

Going: Sf: 0-0 GS: 0-0 Gd: 0-0 GF: - Fm: 0-2
Distance: 2m/2m3: 0-0 2m4-2m7: 0-1 3m+: 0-1
Track: LH: 0-2 RH: 0-0 Tight: 0-2 Gall: 0-0
Aids: Bl: 0-0 Vi: 0-0 Tstrap: 0-0
Best Rating: 98 9/98 Font 2m3f gd-fm Ch

Cheeka

99 96

13-y-o ch g Dawn Johnny (USA)-Lallax (Laxton)
C Smith David J Thompson

Placings:5P25P433/P3/**FFP242P33/434P/3P5524/P4 350/11P455/FP6P/P-1** (0478)
2001/02: 17[1]G

	Starts	1st	2nd	3rd	Win & Pl
Chases	1	1	0	0	3627
Career Total	**46**	**3**	**4**	**8**	**18485**

96	5/01	MRas	2m1f110y	F(0-100)HCh	GD	£3627
99	5/98	MRas	2m1f110y	E(0-110)HCh	G-F	£3276
97	5/98	Sthl	2m	F(0-95)HCh	GD	£3470

Total win prize-money £10374

Going: Sf: 0-0 GS: 0-0 Gd: 1-1 GF: - Fm: 0-0
Distance: 2m/2m3: 1-1 2m4-2m7: 0-0 3m+: 0-0
Track: LH: 0-0 **RH: 1-1 Tight: 1-1** Gall: 0-0
Aids: Bl: 0-0 Vi: 0-0 Tstrap: 0-0
Best Rating: 102 1/99 Donc 2m110y good Ch

Cheerful Groom (IRE)

11-y-o ch g Shy Groom (USA)-Carange (Known Fact (USA))
Mrs H L Walton Bill Cahill

Placings:P/P/0-P (0432)
2001/02: 20[P]GF

	Starts	1st	2nd	3rd	Win & Pl
Hurdles	1	0	0	0	
Career Total	**4**	**0**	**0**	**0**	

Going: Sf: 0-0 GS: 0-0 Gd: 0-0 GF: - Fm: 0-1
Distance: 2m/2m3: 0-0 2m4-2m7: 0-1 3m+: 0-0
Track: LH: 0-0 RH: 0-1 Tight: 0-1 Gall: 0-0
Aids: Bl: 0-0 Vi: 0-0 Tstrap: 0-0
Best Rating:

Chem's Truce (IRE)

86 103

5-y-o b g Brief Truce (USA)-In The Rigging (USA) (Topsider (USA))
Miss Venetia Williams (W R Muir 27/10) O P Dakin

Placings:P60 (4594)
2001/02: 16[P]S, 16[6]GS, 16[0]G

	Starts	1st	2nd	3rd	Win & Pl
Hurdles	3	0	0	0	0
Career Total	**3**	**0**	**0**	**0**	**0**

Going: Sf: 0-1 GS: 0-1 Gd: 0-1 GF: - Fm: 0-0
Distance: 2m/2m3: 0-3 2m4-2m7: 0-0 3m+: 0-0
Track: LH: 0-1 RH: 0-2 Tight: 0-0 Gall: 0-0
Aids: Bl: 0-0 Vi: 0-0 Tstrap: 0-0
Best Rating: 103 2/02 Winc 2m gd-sft Hdl

A decent middle-distance handicapper on the Flat for William Muir, he travelled well before being pulled up on his hurdling debut when he was reported to have lost his action, but ran better next time. Possibly needs faster ground.

Chequered Flag

(109h) (101h) 110

7-y-o ch m Deploy-Monza (Hotfoot)
P R Webber Mrs D Barnett

Placings:4/46-0125420 (1541)
2001/02: 16[0]GF, 16[1]GS, 16[2]GF, 16[5]GF, 16[4]GF, 20[2]G, 19[0]G

	Starts	1st	2nd	3rd	Win & Pl
Hurdles	7	1	2	0	5637
Career Total	**10**	**1**	**2**	**0**	**5637**

95	7/01	Wolv	2m	E Hdl	G-S	£2374

Total win prize-money £2374

Going: Sf: 0-0 GS: 1-1 Gd: 0-2 GF: - Fm: 0-4
Distance: 2m/2m3: 1-5 2m4-2m7: 0-2 3m+: 0-0
Track: LH: 1-5 RH: 0-2 **Tight: 1-4** Gall: 0-1
Aids: Bl: 0-0 Vi: 0-0 Tstrap: 0-0
Best Rating: 101 9/01 Bang 2m4f good Hdl

Chergale (IRE)

107 95

10-y-o b m Strong Gale-Cherry Sorbet (Torus)
M J Ryan P Picton-Warlow

Placings:5/33/**6-64U22P** (1138)
2001/02: 17[6]GF, 21[4]GF, 21[U]G, 24[2]GF, 24[2]GF, 24[P]G

	Starts	1st	2nd	3rd	Win & Pl
Chases	6	0	2	0	2447
Career Total	**10**	**0**	**2**	**2**	**2769**

Going: Sf: 0-0 GS: 0-0 Gd: 0-2 GF: - Fm: 0-4
Distance: 2m/2m3: 0-1 2m4-2m7: 0-2 3m+: 0-3
Track: LH: 0-5 RH: 0-1 Tight: 0-6 Gall: 0-0
Aids: Bl: 0-0 Vi: 0-0 Tstrap: 0-0
Best Rating: 95 8/01 Strf 3m gd-fm Ch

Chergan (IRE)

112 126

9-y-o b g Yashgan-Cherry Bright (IRE) (Miners Lamp)
Mrs S C Bradburne Copland, Hardie And Steel

Placings:PF3/P35042U222/23P42114P-32P62222214 (4891)
2001/02: 21[3]GF, 25[2]G, 25[P]GS, 20[6]GS, 24[2]GF, 24[2]G, 20[2]G, 20[2]S, 16[2]HY, 16[1]G, 16[4]G

	Starts	1st	2nd	3rd	Win & Pl
Chases	11	1	6	1	17011
Career Total	**33**	**3**	**12**	**4**	**36100**

126	3/02	Hayd	2m	D(0-120)HCh	GD	£7052
126	1/01	Muss	2m4f	F(0-110)HCh	G-S	£4858
116	1/01	Muss	2m4f	F(0-110)HCh	GD	£3601

Total win prize-money £15513

Going: Sf: 0-2 GS: 0-2 Gd: 1-5 GF: - Fm: 0-2
Distance: 2m/2m3: 1-3 2m4-2m7: 0-4 3m+: 0-4
Track: LH: 1-6 RH: 0-5 Tight: 0-7 Gall: 0-1
Aids: Bl: 0-0 Vi: 0-0 Tstrap: 0-0
Best Rating: 126 3/02 Hayd 2m good Ch

A Musselburgh regular, he took time to get the hang of things over fences. He scored twice in the 2000/2001 season and has run some decent races since. Stays three miles on ground no worse than good to soft, but is best over two and a half on soft.

Cherokee Boy

112 134

10-y-o gr g Mirror Boy-Cherry Side (General Ironside)
B J M Ryall Hunt & Co (bournemouth) Ltd

Placings:2433P121/62111R0/05P-1122062 6 (4918)
2001/02: 25[1]G, 25[1]GF, 23[2]GF, 32[2]GS, 25[0]G, 23[6]G, 29[2]GF, 28[6]GF

	Starts	1st	2nd	3rd	Win & Pl
Chases	8	2	3	0	14194
Career Total	**26**	**7**	**6**	**2**	**38233**

133	5/01	Winc	3m1f110y	D(0-120)HCh	G-F	£4699
127	5/01	Hrfd	3m1f110y	F(0-105)HCh	GD	£3900
127	2/00	Wwck	3m5f	F(0-110)HCh	GD	£3048
111	11/99	Tntn	3m3f	D(0-125)HCh	GD	£6937
108	10/99	Winc	3m1f110y	F(0-110)HCh	G-F	£4260
103	4/99	Font	3m2f110y	E Ch	GD	£2867
93	3/99	Font	3m2f110y	E Ch	G-F	£2985

Total win prize-money £28700

Going: Sf: 0-0 GS: 0-1 Gd: 1-3 GF: - Fm: 1-4
Distance: 2m/2m3: 0-0 2m4-2m7: 0-0 **3m+: 2-8**
Track: LH: 0-1 **RH: 2-5** Tight: 0-1 Gall: 0-0
Aids: Bl: 0-0 Vi: 0-0 Tstrap: 0-0
Best Rating: 134 12/01 Extr 4m gd-sft Ch

A decent staying handicap chaser at the minor tracks. Ideally served by fast ground and a right-handed course.

Cherokee Red (IRE)

6-y-o ch g Be My Native (USA)-Sapphire Red (Red Alert)
C P Morlock Pell-Mell Partners

Placings:0P (4854)
2001/02: 16[0]S, 22[P]G

	Starts	1st	2nd	3rd	Win & Pl
NH Flat	1	0	0	0	0
Hurdles	1	0	0	0	0
Career Total	**2**	**0**	**0**	**0**	

Going: Sf: 0-1 GS: 0-0 Gd: 0-1 GF: - Fm: 0-0
Distance: 2m/2m3: 0-1 2m4-2m7: 0-1 3m+: 0-0
Track: LH: 0-2 RH: 0-0 Tight: 0-1 Gall: 0-0
Aids: Bl: 0-0 Vi: 0-0 Tstrap: 0-0
Best Rating:

Cherry Tart (IRE)

104(107h) (100h) 115

8-y-o b m Persian Mews-Cherry Avenue (King's Ride)
R Ford A Eyres D F Price A Woods

Placings:6P3503P205/U4U1023-3112213 (4749)
2001/02: 19[3]G, 20[1]GF, 20[1]GF, 17[2]S, 20[2]G, 16[1]HY, 20[3]GF

	Starts	1st	2nd	3rd	Win & Pl
Hurdles	4	2	2	0	7087
Chases	3	1	0	2	8069
Career Total	**24**	**4**	**4**	**5**	**21119**

98	3/02	Hexm	2m110y	E(0-110)HHdl	HVY	£2425
115	6/01	Prth	2m4f110y	F(0-110)HCh	G-F	£5434
97	5/01	Prth	2m4f110y	F(0-90)HHdl	G-F	£3262
101	1/01	Newc	2m110y	E(0-105)HCh	HVY	£3061

Total win prize-money £14184

Going: Sf: 1-2 GS: 0-0 Gd: 0-2 GF: - Fm: 2-3
Distance: 2m/2m3: 1-2 **2m4-2m7: 2-5** 3m+: 0-0
Track: LH: 1-2 **RH: 2-5** Tight: 0-1 Gall: 0-0
Aids: Bl: 0-0 Vi: 0-0 Tstrap: 0-0
Best Rating: 115 4/02 Carl 2m4f gd-fm Ch

Modest handicap chaser/hurdler. Effective on good/heavy. Stays 2m4f well and likes to front run.

Cherrynut

81(77h) (42h)**70**

13-y-o b g Idiots Delight-Merry Cherry (Deep Run)
M Mullineaux P T Hollins

Placings:21U23/1FP/2P651R/5PP6/114/06P **(0926)**
2001/02: 21°GF, 20^{6}GS, 25^{P}GF

	Starts	1st	2nd	3rd	Win & Pl
Hurdles	1	0	0	0	0
Chases	2	0	0	0	0
Career Total	**24**	**5**	**3**	**1**	**30492**

117	5/99	Weth	2m4f110y	H Ch	GD	£1423
117	5/99	Bang	3m110y	H Ch	GD	£3452
146	3/98	Winc	2m5f	C(0-135)HCh	GD	£6076
133	11/96	Worc	2m7f110y	C(0-135)HCh	GD	£5025
117	10/95	Worc	2m4f110y	D Ch	GD	£4276

Total win prize-money £20254

Going: Sf: 0-0 GS: 0-1 Gd: 0-0 GF: - Fm: 0-2
Distance: 2m/2m3: 0-0 2m4-2m7: 0-2 3m+: 0-1
Track: LH: 0-2 RH: 0-1 Tight: 0-2 Gall: 0-1
Aids: Bl: 0-0 Vi: 0-0 Tstrap: 0-0
Best Rating: 146 3/98 Winc 2m5f good Ch

Cheval De Guerre (IRE)

98 **94**

11-y-o b g Satco (FR)-Treasured Gift (Vivadari)
K C Bailey John Stanley

Placings:1P/2P/PP-0 **(0055)**
2001/02: 20°GS

	Starts	1st	2nd	3rd	Win & Pl
Chases	1	0	0	0	
Career Total	**7**	**1**	**1**	**0**	**7144**

117	1/98	Wwck	2m4f110y	C Ch	SFT	£5472

Total win prize-money £5472

Going: Sf: 0-0 GS: 0-1 Gd: 0-0 GF: - Fm: 0-0
Distance: 2m/2m3: 0-0 2m4-2m7: 0-1 3m+: 0-0
Track: LH: 0-1 RH: 0-0 Tight: 0-1 Gall: 0-0
Aids: Bl: 0-0 Vi: 0-0 Tstrap: 0-0
Best Rating: 141 3/99 Newb 3m soft Ch

Chevalier Bayard (IRE)

101 **96**

9-y-o br g Strong Gale-Flying Pegus (Beau Chapeau)
J R Adam James R Adam

Placings:06P/0433F/32/260-36U **(3859)**
2001/02: 20^{3}GS, 16^{6}S, 19^{U}S

	Starts	1st	2nd	3rd	Win & Pl
Chases	3	0	0	1	599
Career Total	**16**	**0**	**2**	**4**	**4568**

Going: Sf: 0-2 GS: 0-1 Gd: 0-0 GF: - Fm: 0-0
Distance: 2m/2m3: 0-1 2m4-2m7: 0-2 3m+: 0-0
Track: LH: 0-2 RH: 0-1 Tight: 0-2 Gall: 0-1
Aids: Bl: 0-0 Vi: 0-0 Tstrap: 0-0
Best Rating: 106 12/00 Donc 2m110y heavy Ch

Fair novice chaser. Has been lightly raced over the last couple of seasons. Best trip seems to be around two and a half miles. Suited by a sound surface.

Chevalier Errant (IRE)

109 **144**

9-y-o b/br g Strong Gale-Luminous Run (Deep Run)
J R Adam James R Adam

Placings:0531/235333532/24114326-11B **(0969)**
2001/02: 17^{1}GF, 20^{1}GF, 20^{B}GS

	Starts	1st	2nd	3rd	Win & Pl
Chases	3	2	0	0	17341
Career Total	**24**	**5**	**4**	**7**	**44103**

138	6/01	MRas	2m4f	C(0-135)HCh	G-F	£10476
138	6/01	Strf	2m1f110y	C(0-135)HCh	G-F	£6864
130	12/00	Donc	2m110y	C(0-130)HCh	HVY	£6022
129	11/00	Ayr	2m	C(0-130)HCh	SFT	£6118
102	4/99	Kels	2m110y	E Hdl	G-F	£3025

Total win prize-money £32506

Going: Sf: 0-0 GS: 0-1 Gd: 0-0 GF: - Fm: 2-2
Distance: 2m/2m3: 1-1 2m4-2m7: 1-2 3m+: 0-0
Track: LH: 1-1 RH: 1-1 **Tight: 2-2** Gall: 0-0
Aids: Bl: 0-0 Vi: 0-0 Tstrap: 0-0
Best Rating: 138 6/01 MRas 2m4f gd-fm Ch

Decent handicapper at around two and a half miles, effective on fast ground.

Chevet Girl (IRE)

105 **99**

7-y-o ch m Roselier (FR)-Vulcash (IRE) (Callernish)
J Howard Johnson D M Gibbons

Placings:0663-5115510 **(4879)**
2001/02: 20^{5}GF, 17^{1}GS, 16^{1}G, 17^{5}S, 16^{5}S, 16^{1}GF, 16^{0}G

	Starts	1st	2nd	3rd	Win & Pl
Hurdles	7	3	0	0	9085
Career Total	**11**	**3**	**0**	**1**	**9380**

99	4/02	Kels	2m110y	D(0-125)HHdl	G-F	£3591
99	11/01	Weth	2m	E(0-105)HHdl	GD	£3052
85	10/01	Carl	2m1f	E(0-115)HHdl	G-S	£2441

Total win prize-money £9085

Going: Sf: 0-2 GS: 1-1 Gd: 1-2 GF: - Fm: 1-2
Distance: **2m/2m3: 3-6** 2m4-2m7: 0-1 3m+: 0-0
Track: **LH: 2-2** RH: 1-5 **Tight: 1-2** Gall: 0-0
Aids: Bl: 0-0 Vi: 0-0 Tstrap: 0-0
Best Rating: 99 4/02 Kels 2m110y gd-fm Hdl

Chica Holly

7-y-o b m Bold Fox-Chica Mia (Camden Town)
R S Wood R S Wood

Placings:P/P-6 **(2302)**
2001/02: 19^{6}GF

	Starts	1st	2nd	3rd	Win & Pl
Hurdles	1	0	0	0	0
Career Total	**3**	**0**	**0**	**0**	**0**

Going: Sf: 0-0 GS: 0-0 Gd: 0-0 GF: - Fm: 0-1
Distance: 2m/2m3: 0-1 2m4-2m7: 0-0 3m+: 0-0
Track: LH: 0-1 RH: 0-0 Tight: 0-1 Gall: 0-0
Aids: Bl: 0-0 Vi: 0-0 Tstrap: 0-1
Best Rating:

Chicago Bear (IRE)

6-y-o ch g Night Shift (USA)-Last Drama (IRE) (Last Tycoon)
D Brace David Brace

Placings:P001113204/5330-P0 **(1629)**
2001/02: 17^{P}GS, 21^{0}GF

	Starts	1st	2nd	3rd	Win & Pl
Hurdles	2	0	0	0	
Career Total	**16**	**3**	**1**	**3**	**7982**

98	2/00	Chep	2m110y	F(0-95)HHdl	SFT	£1876
98	2/00	Leic	2m	G(0-90)HHdl	G-S	£1865
86	1/00	Leic	2m	G(0-90)HHdl	SFT	£2002

Total win prize-money £5744

Going: Sf: 0-0 GS: 0-1 Gd: 0-0 GF: - Fm: 0-1
Distance: 2m/2m3: 0-1 2m4-2m7: 0-1 3m+: 0-0
Track: LH: 0-0 RH: 0-1 Tight: 0-1 Gall: 0-0
Aids: Bl: 0-0 Vi: 0-0 Tstrap: 0-1
Best Rating: 98 2/00 Chep 2m110y soft Hdl

Chicago Bulls (IRE)

108 **120**

4-y-o b g Darshaan-Celestial Melody (USA) (The Minstrel (CAN))
A King (C F Wall 4/9) J A H West

Placings:54455110 **(4939a)**
2001/02: 16^{5}G, 16^{4}G, 16^{4}G, 16^{5}GS, 16^{5}S, 20^{1}S, 21^{1}S, 20^{0}Y

	Starts	1st	2nd	3rd	Win & Pl
Hurdles	8	2	0	0	6921
Career Total	**8**	**2**	**0**	**0**	**6921**

120	3/02	Ludl	2m5f	E Hdl	SFT	£3125
108	2/02	Donc	2m4f	E Hdl	SFT	£3164

Total win prize-money £6290

Going: Sf: 2-3 GS: 0-1 Gd: 0-3 GF: - Fm: 0-0
Distance: 2m/2m3: 0-5 **2m4-2m7: 2-3** 3m+: 0-0
Track: LH: 1-1 RH: 1-7 Tight: 0-0 **Gall: 1-2**
Aids: Bl: 0-0 Vi: 0-0 Tstrap: 0-0
Best Rating: 120 3/02 Ludl 2m5f soft Hdl

He showed improved form to win novice hurdles in 2002. Suited by two and a half miles and soft ground.

Chicago City (IRE)

106 **128**

9-y-o br g Strong Gale-Orchardstown (Pollerton)
J T Gifford S N J Embiricos

Placings:023/432P/4144134/F6P-5114P **(2764)**
2001/02: 21^{5}GF, 20^{1}GS, 20^{1}G, 25^{4}G, 22^{P}G

	Starts	1st	2nd	3rd	Win & Pl
Chases	5	2	0	0	10532
Career Total	**22**	**4**	**2**	**3**	**24413**

128	11/01	Newb	2m4f	D(0-125)HCh	GD	£7215
125	10/01	Font	2m4f	F(0-105)HCh	G-S	£3010
128	2/00	Sand	2m4f110y	D Ch	G-S	£5096
108	11/99	Folk	2m	E Ch	G-F	£3466

Total win prize-money £18787

Going: Sf: 0-0 GS: 1-1 Gd: 1-3 GF: - Fm: 0-1
Distance: 2m/2m3: 0-0 **2m4-2m7: 2-4** 3m+: 0-1
Track: **LH: 1-3** RH: 0-1 Tight: 1-1 Gall: 1-2
Aids: Bl: 0-0 Vi: 0-0 Tstrap: 0-0
Best Rating: 133 10/00 Chel 2m4f110y good Ch

He seemed to lose confidence after taking a tired fall at Cheltenham in October 2000, but dropped in the weights as a consequence and scored at Fontwell and Newbur, but was only fourth at Wetherby after that. Probably best around two and a half miles, he does not want the ground too soft. Best suited to galloping tracks.

Chicanery (IRE)

68 **27**

5-y-o b g Irish River (FR)-Deceive (Machiavellian (USA))
Mrs L Stubbs F W Swain

Placings:0 **(1943)**
2001/02: 16^{0}GS

	Starts	1st	2nd	3rd	Win & Pl
Hurdles	1	0	0	0	
Career Total	**1**	**0**	**0**	**0**	

Going: Sf: 0-0 GS: 0-1 Gd: 0-0 GF: - Fm: 0-0
Distance: 2m/2m3: 0-1 2m4-2m7: 0-0 3m+: 0-0
Track: LH: 0-1 RH: 0-0 Tight: 0-1 Gall: 0-0
Aids: Bl: 0-0 Vi: 0-0 Tstrap: 0-0
Best Rating: 27 11/01 Plum 2m gd-sft Hdl

Chickasaw Trail

4-y-o ch f Be My Chief (USA)-Maraschino (Lycius (USA))
R Hollinshead Anthony White

Placings:3 **(2794)**
2001/02: 16^{3}S

	Starts	1st	2nd	3rd	Win & Pl
Hurdles	1	0	0	1	271
Career Total	**1**	**0**	**0**	**1**	**271**

Going: Sf: 0-1 GS: 0-0 Gd: 0-0 GF: - Fm: 0-0
Distance: 2m/2m3: 0-1 2m4-2m7: 0-0 3m+: 0-0
Track: LH: 0-1 RH: 0-0 Tight: 0-0 Gall: 0-0
Aids: Bl: 0-0 Vi: 0-0 Tstrap: 0-0
Best Rating:

Chicuelo (FR)

111 **153+**

6-y-o b g Mansonnien (FR)-Dovapas (FR) (Paseo (FR))
Ian Williams Mrs Belinda Harvey

Placings:03/512F023/222433210-225025 **(4901)**
2001/02: 19^{2}G, 20^{2}G, 20^{5}GS, 16^{0}G, 19^{2}GF, 16^{5}G

	Starts	1st	2nd	3rd	Win & Pl
Chases	6	0	3	0	4964
Career Total	**24**	**2**	**9**	**4**	**144252**

	4/01	Autl	2m2f	Hdl	HVY	£14549
	7/99	Autl	1m1f110y	Hdl	HLD	£10764

Total win prize-money £25313

Going: Sf: 0-0 GS: 0-1 Gd: 0-4 GF: - Fm: 0-1
Distance: 2m/2m3: 0-2 2m4-2m7: 0-4 3m+: 0-0
Track: LH: 0-2 RH: 0-3 Tight: 0-1 Gall: 0-2
Aids: Bl: 0-1 Vi: 0-3 Tstrap: 0-0
Best Rating: 143 12/01 Donc 2m3f110y good Ch

A French import who won on heavy ground and wore blinkers in France. Has showed ability in novice chases for Ian Williams in 2001/2, and bolted up in a valuable Market Rasen handicap on his first start for Pipe.

Chief Chippie

81(105h) (78h)**73**

9-y-o b g Mandalus-Little Katrina (Little Buskins)
P Needham P Needham

Placings:00P0/P03PP00/P53P0U5PP/453P5304P/00-P461PP56 **(4786)**
2001/02: 20^{P}S, 20^{4}HY, 24^{6}S, 19^{1}G, 27^{P}HY, 19^{P}GS, 17^{5}S, 20^{6}F

	Starts	1st	2nd	3rd	Win & Pl
Hurdles	8	1	0	0	2023
Career Total	**39**	**1**	**0**	**4**	**4072**

78	12/01	Catt	2m3f	F(0-100)HHdl	GD	£2023

Total win prize-money £2023

Going: Sf: 0-5 GS: 0-1 Gd: 1-1 GF: - Fm: 0-1
Distance: **2m/2m3: 1-3** 2m4-2m7: 0-3 3m+: 0-2
Track: **LH: 1-6** RH: 0-0 **Tight: 1-4** Gall: 0-1
Aids: Bl: 0-4 Vi: 0-0 Tstrap: 0-0
Best Rating: 90 2/00 Carl 2m4f110y heavy Hdl

Chief Monte (IRE)

40

7-y-o b g Montelimar (USA)-Giollaretta (Giolla Mear)
Mrs S J Smith J Henderson (co Durham)

Placings:00-P0 **(4768)**
2001/02: 17^{P}GS, 16^{0}GF

	Starts	1st	2nd	3rd	Win & Pl
Hurdles	2	0	0	0	
Career Total	**4**	**0**	**0**	**0**	

Going: Sf: 0-0 GS: 0-1 Gd: 0-0 GF: - Fm: 0-1
Distance: 2m/2m3: 0-2 2m4-2m7: 0-0 3m+: 0-0
Track: LH: 0-0 RH: 0-1 Tight: 0-0 Gall: 0-0
Aids: Bl: 0-0 Vi: 0-0 Tstrap: 0-0
Best Rating: 67 3/01 MRas 2m1f110y good NHF

Chief Mouse

99(59h) **80**

9-y-o b g Be My Chief (USA)-Top Mouse (High Top)
B D Leavy J A Provan

Placings:12106P111/5634030/P05424310000/PU155/331321-P **(2953)**
2001/02: 17^{P}S

	Starts	1st	2nd	3rd	Win & Pl
Chases	1	0	0	0	
Career Total	**40**	**9**	**3**	**6**	**41214**

114	7/00	Strf	3m	D(0-120)HCh	G-F	£4810
111	6/00	Uttx	2m	D(0-120)HCh	G-F	£3692
99	10/99	Ludl	2m4f	D(0-110)HCh	G-F	£4162
90	9/98	Bang	2m4f	E(0-110)HHdl	GD	£3631
106	4/97	Asct	2m110y	D(0-110)HHdl	G-F	£3420
106	4/97	Chel	2m4f110y	C HHdl	G-F	£4788
88	3/97	Ludl	2m	F Hdl	G-F	£2094
104	11/96	MRas	2m1f110y	D Hdl	GD	£3148
86	8/96	Hrfd	2m1f	E Hdl	G-F	£2444

Total win prize-money £32190

Going: Sf: 0-1 GS: 0-0 Gd: 0-0 GF: - Fm: 0-0
Distance: 2m/2m3: 0-1 2m4-2m7: 0-0 3m+: 0-0
Track: LH: 0-1 RH: 0-0 Tight: 0-1 Gall: 0-0
Aids: Bl: 0-0 Vi: 0-0 Tstrap: 0-0
Best Rating: 114 7/00 Strf 3m gd-fm Ch

Moderate handicap chaser. Acts on good and good to firm ground, he is effective from two miles to three miles.

Chief Predator (USA)

8-y-o ch g Chief's Crown (USA)-Tsavorite (USA) (Halo (USA))
Mrs D C Faulkner (D L Williams 24/3) Mrs I E M Hussey

Placings:463P3/1130004000/0425604550/65400-0 **(4727)**
2001/02: 24^{0}GF

	Starts	1st	2nd	3rd	Win & Pl
Chases	1	0	0	0	
Career Total	**31**	**2**	**1**	**3**	**5986**

83	5/98	Hntg	3m2f	E(0-100)HHdl	G-F	£2460
83	5/98	Towc	2m	G Hdl	GD	£1702

Total win prize-money £4162

Going: Sf: 0-0 GS: 0-0 Gd: 0-0 GF: - Fm: 0-1
Distance: 2m/2m3: 0-0 2m4-2m7: 0-0 3m+: 0-1
Track: LH: 0-1 RH: 0-0 Tight: 0-0 Gall: 0-0
Aids: Bl: 0-0 Vi: 0-0 Tstrap: 0-0
Best Rating: 84 6/00 MRas 2m6f110y gd-fm Ch

Chief Wallah

74 **67**

6-y-o b g Be My Chief (USA)-Arusha (IRE) (Dance Of Life (USA))
N J Henderson Raymond Tooth

Placings:60 **(1406)**
2001/02: 16^{6}GF, 16^{0}GF

	Starts	1st	2nd	3rd	Win & Pl
Hurdles	2	0	0	0	0
Career Total	**2**	**0**	**0**	**0**	**0**

Going: Sf: 0-0 GS: 0-0 Gd: 0-0 GF: - Fm: 0-2
Distance: 2m/2m3: 0-2 2m4-2m7: 0-0 3m+: 0-0
Track: LH: 0-2 RH: 0-0 Tight: 0-0 Gall: 0-0
Aids: Bl: 0-1 Vi: 0-0 Tstrap: 0-0
Best Rating: 67 8/01 Worc 2m gd-fm Hdl

Chief Wardance

100 **104**

8-y-o ch g Profilic-Dolly Wardance (Warpath)
C N Kellett (Mrs S Lamyman 1/7) Mrs Jennifer Woodward

Placings:50/12F4214/4265/14F23-005 **(4869)**
2001/02: 16^{0}GF, 16^{0}G, 20^{5}GF

	Starts	1st	2nd	3rd	Win & Pl
Hurdles	3	0	0	0	0
Career Total	**21**	**3**	**4**	**1**	**12246**

120	5/00	Weth	2m	E(0-115)HHdl	G-F	£2842
106	2/99	Newc	2m	E Hdl	G-S	£2431
95	5/98	Uttx	2m	H NHF	G-F	£1413

Total win prize-money £6687

Going: Sf: 0-0 GS: 0-0 Gd: 0-1 GF: - Fm: 0-2
Distance: 2m/2m3: 0-2 2m4-2m7: 0-1 3m+: 0-0
Track: LH: 0-3 RH: 0-0 Tight: 0-1 Gall: 0-0
Aids: Bl: 0-0 Vi: 0-0 Tstrap: 0-0
Best Rating: 120 7/00 Sthl 2m gd-fm Hdl

Winner of two hurdle races and a bumper.

Chief's Song

99 **148**

12-y-o b g Chief Singer-Tizzy (Formidable (USA))
S Dow Mrs Anne Devine

Placings:F232/1132P160/U01103P/4165200/121514F/2122036U4/613661563206/11050P-5066P **(4635)**
2001/02: 16^{5}GS, 16^{0}G, 20^{6}G, 16^{6}S, 19^{P}GF

	Starts	1st	2nd	3rd	Win & Pl

	Starts	1st	2nd	3rd	Win & Pl
Chases	5	0	0	0	0
Career Total	**65**	**14**	**9**	**6**	**181379**

156	10/00	Kemp	2m	B(0-140)HCh	G-S	£8879
152	9/00	Hntg	2m4f110y	C(0-135)HCh	GD	£6864
147	1/00	Sand	2m	B(0-145)HCh	SFT	£9709
156	10/99	Kemp	2m	B(0-150)HCh	G-F	£9000
150	10/98	Kemp	2m	B(0-150)HCh	GD	£6571
132	12/97	Asct	2m3f110y	A Ch	G-S	£15069
140	11/97	Asct	2m	B Ch	G-S	£6807
130	10/97	Kemp	2m	D Ch	GD	£3720
136	10/96	Kemp	2m	B Hdl	G-F	£4765
138	12/95	Sand	2m110y	B(0-150)HHdl	GD	£35550
132	11/95	Chel	2m110y	B Hdl	GD	£6710
127	1/95	Asct	2m110y	C Hdl	GD	£3745
123	11/94	Chel	2m110y	Hdl	GD	£6645
106	10/94	Font	2m2f	Hdl	GD	£1622

Total win prize-money £125659

Going: Sf: 0-1 GS: 0-1 Gd: 0-2 GF: - Fm: 0-1
Distance: 2m/2m3: 0-3 2m4-2m7: 0-2 3m+: 0-0
Track: LH: 0-0 RH: 0-5 Tight: 0-0 Gall: 0-0
Aids: Bl: 0-0 Vi: 0-0 Tstrap: 0-0
Best Rating: 156 10/00 Kemp 2m gd-sft Ch

A useful performer between two and two and a half miles, he is most effective going right-handed. He won twice in the 2000/2001 season but has been well beaten since when tackling warmer company. Runs well at Kempton. Acts on good and good to soft ground.

Chieftain's Crown (USA)

83 **64**

11-y-o ch g Chief's Crown (USA)-Simple Taste (USA) (Sharpen Up)
Mrs H M Bridges (R Simpson 10/3) Mrs H M Bridges

Placings:5P2111/6564/1244/P **(4327)**
2001/02: 19^{P}S

	Starts	1st	2nd	3rd	Win & Pl
Hurdles	1	0	0	0	
Career Total	**15**	**4**	**2**	**0**	**10986**

92	5/97	Font	2m2f110y	E(0-110)HHdl	G-F	£2241
91	5/96	Plum	2m4f	E(0-115)HHdl	FRM	£2259
91	4/96	Plum	2m4f	E(0-110)HHdl	FRM	£2574
91	4/96	Plum	2m4f	E Hdl	G-F	£2490

Total win prize-money £9565

Going: Sf: 0-1 GS: 0-0 Gd: 0-0 GF: - Fm: 0-0
Distance: 2m/2m3: 0-0 2m4-2m7: 0-1 3m+: 0-0
Track: LH: 0-0 RH: 0-1 Tight: 0-0 Gall: 0-0
Aids: Bl: 0-1 Vi: 0-0 Tstrap: 0-0
Best Rating: 93 9/97 Plum 2m4f gd-fm Hdl

Chill Wind

(84h) (18h)**52**

13-y-o gr g Siberian Express (USA)-Springwell (Miami Springs)
N Bycroft E H Daley

Placings:15P1/652/4P3/0421F3F5/3223P/PPP000-P **(0092)**
2001/02: 16^{P}S

	Starts	1st	2nd	3rd	Win & Pl
Chases	1	0	0	0	
Career Total	**30**	**3**	**4**	**4**	**10359**

95	3/97	Carl	2m	F(0-100)HCh	HVY	£2696
78	3/93	Carl	2m1f	HHdl	GD	£2108
106	9/92	Carl	2m1f	Hdl	G-F	£788

Total win prize-money £5592

Going: Sf: 0-1 GS: 0-0 Gd: 0-0 GF: - Fm: 0-0
Distance: 2m/2m3: 0-1 2m4-2m7: 0-0 3m+: 0-0
Track: LH: 0-1 RH: 0-0 Tight: 0-0 Gall: 0-0
Aids: Bl: 0-0 Vi: 0-0 Tstrap: 0-0
Best Rating: 106 9/92 Carl 2m1f gd-fm Hdl

Chilli Jo

83 **61**

10-y-o b g Latest Model-Arctic Caper (Pardigras)
D D Scott Mrs M Fooks

Placings:PP-P **(2390)**
2001/02: 16^{P}S

	Starts	1st	2nd	3rd	Win & Pl
Chases	1	0	0	0	
Career Total	**3**	**0**	**0**	**0**	

Going: Sf: 0-1 GS: 0-0 Gd: 0-0 GF: - Fm: 0-0
Distance: 2m/2m3: 0-1 2m4-2m7: 0-0 3m+: 0-0
Track: LH: 0-1 RH: 0-0 Tight: 0-0 Gall: 0-0
Aids: Bl: 0-0 Vi: 0-0 Tstrap: 0-0
Best Rating:

Chimes At Midnight (USA)

116 **141**

5-y-o b h Danzig (USA)-Surely Georgies (USA) (Alleged (USA))
Luke Comer Luke Comer

Placings:2045 **(4944a)**
2001/02: 16^{2}HY, 16^{0}GS, 16^{4}GY, 20^{5}G

	Starts	1st	2nd	3rd	Win & Pl
Hurdles	4	0	1	0	3890
Career Total	**4**	**0**	**1**	**0**	**3890**

Going: Sf: 0-1 GS: 0-1 Gd: 0-1 GF: - Fm: 0-0
Distance: 2m/2m3: 0-3 2m4-2m7: 0-1 3m+: 0-0
Track: LH: 0-2 RH: 0-2 Tight: 0-0 Gall: 0-0
Aids: Bl: 0-4 Vi: 0-0 Tstrap: 0-0
Best Rating: 141 4/02 Punc 2m4f good Hdl

A Group Three winner over a mile and six in Ireland in 2001, he was highly tried subsequently and failed to trouble the judge. Finished a fine runner-up on his debut over flights and ran respectably in better company.

China Lal

64 **41**

10-y-o b m Rakaposhi King-Doris Blake (Roscoe Blake)
R Ford J S Swindells

Placings:0/P/0 **(0191)**
2001/02: 23^{0}GF

	Starts	1st	2nd	3rd	Win & Pl
Hurdles	1	0	0	0	
Career Total	**3**	**0**	**0**	**0**	

Going: Sf: 0-0 GS: 0-0 Gd: 0-0 GF: - Fm: 0-1
Distance: 2m/2m3: 0-0 2m4-2m7: 0-0 3m+: 0-1
Track: LH: 0-1 RH: 0-0 Tight: 0-1 Gall: 0-0
Aids: Bl: 0-0 Vi: 0-0 Tstrap: 0-0
Best Rating: 41 5/01 Fknm 2m7f110y gd-fm Hdl

Chirapira

66f **25f**

5-y-o b m Rakaposhi King-Brass Buckle (IRE) (Buckskin (FR))
M A Barnes Miss Alison P Lee

Placings:*0* **(2772)**
2001/02: 16^{0}G

	Starts	1st	2nd	3rd	Win & Pl
NH Flat	1	0	0	0	
Career Total	**1**	**0**	**0**	**0**	

Going: Sf: 0-0 GS: 0-0 Gd: 0-1 GF: - Fm: 0-0
Distance: 2m/2m3: 0-1 2m4-2m7: 0-0 3m+: 0-0
Track: LH: 0-1 RH: 0-0 Tight: 0-1 Gall: 0-0
Aids: Bl: 0-0 Vi: 0-0 Tstrap: 0-0
Best Rating: 25 12/01 Catt 2m good NHF

Chism (IRE)

11-y-o br g Euphemism-Melody Gayle Vii (Damsire Unregistered)
Mrs A L Tory Mrs J R Webber

Placings:324/43132P/PP5/63-P **(0063)**
2001/02: 26^{P}G

	Starts	1st	2nd	3rd	Win & Pl
Chases	1	0	0	0	
Career Total	**15**	**1**	**2**	**4**	**3757**

102	3/99	Winc	2m5f	H Ch	GD	£1203

Total win prize-money £1204

Going: Sf: 0-0 GS: 0-0 Gd: 0-1 GF: - Fm: 0-0
Distance: 2m/2m3: 0-0 2m4-2m7: 0-0 3m+: 0-1
Track: LH: 0-0 RH: 0-1 Tight: 0-1 Gall: 0-0
Aids: Bl: 0-0 Vi: 0-0 Tstrap: 0-0
Best Rating: 102 3/00 Font 2m4f gd-fm Ch

Chives (IRE)

117(56h) **156**

7-y-o b g Good Thyne (USA)-Chatty Actress (Le Bavard (FR))
Miss H C Knight Trevor Hemmings

Placings:*15*/11-31F133 **(4232)**
2001/02: 20^{3}GS, 24^{1}S, 24^{F}G, 25^{1}S, 26^{3}S, 24^{3}GS

	Starts	1st	2nd	3rd	Win & Pl
Chases	6	2	0	3	24981
Career Total	**10**	**5**	**0**	**3**	**33165**

141	2/02	Winc	3m1f110y	D Ch	SFT	£4368
136	12/01	Strf	3m	D Ch	SFT	£5154
130	11/00	Kemp	2m5f	D Hdl	SFT	£3753
105	10/00	Hrfd	2m1f	E Hdl	GD	£2684
116	2/00	Sand	2m110y	H NHF	SFT	£1746

Total win prize-money £17709

Going: Sf: 2-3 GS: 0-2 Gd: 0-1 GF: - Fm: 0-0
Distance: 2m/2m3: 0-0 2m4-2m7: 0-1 **3m+: 2-5**
Track: LH: 1-3 RH: 1-3 **Tight: 1-1** Gall: 0-2
Aids: Bl: 0-0 Vi: 0-0 Tstrap: 0-0
Best Rating: 156 3/02 Chel 3m110y gd-sft Ch

Twice a winner over hurdles in the autumn of 2000 before sustaining an injury that required firing and a year off. He put up a promising effort on his debut over fences on his return despite breaking a blood-vessel, before getting off the mark over the larger obstacles at Stratford towards the end of 2001. Successful at Wincanton since, he also ran a blinder to finish third in the Royal & SunAlliance Chase at the 2002 Festival. Has won on good and soft, stays three miles and is suited by a right-handed track.

Chivvy Charver (IRE)

69 **76**

5-y-o ch g Commanche Run-Claddagh Pride (Bargello)
G A Swinbank Ward And Gartzon

Placings:*46* **(4860)**
2001/02: 17^4G, 16^6G

	Starts	1st	2nd	3rd	Win & Pl
NH Flat	2	0	0	0	0
Career Total	**2**	**0**	**0**	**0**	**0**

Going: Sf: 0-0 GS: 0-0 Gd: 0-2 GF: - Fm: 0-0
Distance: 2m/2m3: 0-2 2m4-2m7: 0-0 3m+: 0-0
Track: LH: 0-0 RH: 0-1 Tight: 0-0 Gall: 0-0
Aids: Bl: 0-0 Vi: 0-0 Tstrap: 0-0
Best Rating: 89 4/02 Carl 2m1f good NHF

Cho Polu (IRE)

81f 78f

5-y-o ch g Un Desperado (FR)-Rainbow Alliance (IRE) (Golden Love)
P J Hobbs M J Tuckey

Placings:*0* **(3503)**
2001/02: 16^0S

	Starts	1st	2nd	3rd	Win & Pl
NH Flat	1	0	0	0	
Career Total	**1**	**0**	**0**	**0**	

Going: Sf: 0-1 GS: 0-0 Gd: 0-0 GF: - Fm: 0-0
Distance: 2m/2m3: 0-1 2m4-2m7: 0-0 3m+: 0-0
Track: LH: 0-0 RH: 0-1 Tight: 0-0 Gall: 0-0
Aids: Bl: 0-0 Vi: 0-0 Tstrap: 0-0
Best Rating: 78 1/02 Kemp 2m soft NHF

Chocolate Bombe (IRE)

5-y-o ch g Un Desperado (FR)-Lady Nerak (Pitpan)
N A Twiston-Davies Alan Parker

Placings:*0*PP **(2950)**
2001/02: 17^0G, 20^PS, 22^PS

	Starts	1st	2nd	3rd	Win & Pl
NH Flat	1	0	0	0	0
Hurdles	2	0	0	0	0
Career Total	**3**	**0**	**0**	**0**	

Going: Sf: 0-2 GS: 0-0 Gd: 0-1 GF: - Fm: 0-0
Distance: 2m/2m3: 0-1 2m4-2m7: 0-2 3m+: 0-0
Track: LH: 0-2 RH: 0-1 Tight: 0-1 Gall: 0-0
Aids: Bl: 0-0 Vi: 0-0 Tstrap: 0-0
Best Rating: 78 5/01 Extr 2m1f good NHF

Chocstaw (IRE)

98 99

5-y-o b g Mtoto-Cwm Deri (IRE) (Alzao (USA))
Mrs P Robeson Sir Evelyn De Rothschild

Placings:3000-02 **(2691)**
2001/02: 16^0G, 16^2S

	Starts	1st	2nd	3rd	Win & Pl
Hurdles	2	0	1	0	1045
Career Total	**6**	**0**	**1**	**1**	**1484**

Going: Sf: 0-1 GS: 0-0 Gd: 0-1 GF: - Fm: 0-0
Distance: 2m/2m3: 0-2 2m4-2m7: 0-0 3m+: 0-0
Track: LH: 0-2 RH: 0-0 Tight: 0-0 Gall: 0-0
Aids: Bl: 0-0 Vi: 0-0 Tstrap: 0-0
Best Rating: 99 12/01 Hayd 2m soft Hdl

Choisty (IRE)

108 130

12-y-o ch g Callernish-Rosemount Rose (Ashmore (FR))
H E Haynes H Edward Haynes

Placings:5**C32/2UF11U/F1FP/4PR041U1/22142F/0-PPP21P3** **(4532)**
2001/02: 26^PS, 25^PG, 29^PGS, 26^2S, 29^1G, 28^PS, 26^3GS

	Starts	1st	2nd	3rd	Win & Pl
Chases	7	1	1	1	9652
Career Total	**36**	**7**	**6**	**2**	**58836**

130	3/02	Wwck	3m5f	C(0-135)HCh	GD	£6857
145	1/00	Wwck	3m5f	B(0-145)HCh	SFT	£14014
132	5/99	Hrfd	3m1f110y	E(0-115)HCh	GD	£3525
137	3/99	Chep	3m	D(0-120)HCh	G-S	£7002
125	3/98	Wwck	3m5f	C(0-135)HCh	SFT	£8550
115	1/97	Weth	3m1f	E Ch	GD	£3077
106	1/97	Carl	3m	D Ch	GD	£3842

Total win prize-money £46871

Going: Sf: 0-3 GS: 0-2 Gd: 1-2 GF: - Fm: 0-0
Distance: 2m/2m3: 0-0 2m4-2m7: 0-0 **3m+: 1-7**
Track: **LH: 1-5** RH: 0-0 Tight: 0-0 Gall: 0-0
Aids: Bl: 0-0 Vi: 0-0 Tstrap: 0-0
Best Rating: 145 3/00 Wwck 3m5f soft Ch

He has enjoyed a fair amount of success in staying handicap chases over the years, but did not take to Aintree when tried in three consecutive Grand Nationals, falling twice and unseating once. Showed his first form for nearly two years when second at Warwick in February 2002 and took the Warwick National for the second time in five years.

Chop-Chop (IRE)

(96h) (84h)

8-y-o b/br g Be My Native (USA)-Arctic Bavard (Le Bavard (FR))
D C Turner Mrs M E Turner

Placings:*0*/P/0PPU4650-030400P3 **(2482)**
2001/02: 17^0G, 17^3G, 17^0GF, 17^4GF, 16^0GF, 19^0GF, 17^PS, 16^3HY

	Starts	1st	2nd	3rd	Win & Pl
Hurdles	7	0	0	1	522
Chases	1	0	0	1	575
Career Total	**18**	**0**	**0**	**2**	**1309**

Going: Sf: 0-2 GS: 0-0 Gd: 0-2 GF: - Fm: 0-4
Distance: 2m/2m3: 0-8 2m4-2m7: 0-0 3m+: 0-1
Track: LH: 0-7 RH: 0-1 Tight: 0-6 Gall: 0-0
Aids: Bl: 0-0 Vi: 0-0 Tstrap: 0-8
Best Rating: 90 10/00 Extr 2m1f good Hdl

Chop-N-Change

105 103

7-y-o b m Michelozzo (USA)-Guinea Feather (Over The River (FR))
D J Wintle David A Hunt

Placings:*6*/5641P33-610 **(3215)**
2001/02: 20^6S, 22^1HY, 24^0GS

	Starts	1st	2nd	3rd	Win & Pl
Hurdles	3	1	0	0	3371
Career Total	**11**	**2**	**0**	**2**	**10509**

103	11/01	Uttx	2m6f110y	D(0-125)HHdl	HVY	£3370
102	2/01	Carl	2m4f110y	D Hdl	HVY	£3510

Total win prize-money £6881

Going: Sf: 1-2 GS: 0-1 Gd: 0-0 GF: - Fm: 0-0
Distance: 2m/2m3: 0-0 **2m4-2m7: 1-2** 3m+: 0-1
Track: LH: 1-3 RH: 0-0 Tight: 0-0 Gall: 0-1
Aids: Bl: 0-0 Vi: 0-0 Tstrap: 0-0
Best Rating: 103 11/01 Uttx 2m6f110y heavy Hdl

Lightly-raced, modest staying hurdler. Gets in excess of three miles but effective at shorter, suited by heavy ground.

Chopin (IRE)

71 31

8-y-o b g Classic Music (USA)-La Toulzanie (FR) (Sanctus Ii)
K G Wingrove First In Racing Partnership

Placings:16P6045/43261400/0/P0P **(3334)**
2001/02: 16^PS, 16^0GF, 16^PG

	Starts	1st	2nd	3rd	Win & Pl
Hurdles	3	0	0	0	
Career Total	**19**	**2**	**1**	**1**	**4516**

83	10/98	Strf	2m110y	G Hdl	G-S	£1618
73	8/97	Font	2m2f110y	E Hdl	GD	£2238

Total win prize-money £3856

Going: Sf: 0-1 GS: 0-0 Gd: 0-1 GF: - Fm: 0-1
Distance: 2m/2m3: 0-3 2m4-2m7: 0-0 3m+: 0-0
Track: LH: 0-1 RH: 0-2 Tight: 0-0 Gall: 0-0
Aids: Bl: 0-2 Vi: 0-0 Tstrap: 0-3
Best Rating: 83 10/98 Strf 2m110y gd-sft Hdl

Chopins Revolution

100

8-y-o b m Rakaposhi King-Sujono (Grey Mirage)
N A Twiston-Davies Mrs Julia Baldanza

Placings:*20*/5P0004/34160-1 **(2778)**
2001/02: 22^1G

	Starts	1st	2nd	3rd	Win & Pl
Hurdles	1	1	0	0	2387
Career Total	**14**	**2**	**1**	**1**	**6335**

100	12/01	Extr	2m6f110y	F(0-100)HHdl	GD	£2387
100	1/01	Extr	2m6f110y	F(0-100)HHdl	HVY	£2762

Total win prize-money £5149

Going: Sf: 0-0 GS: 0-0 Gd: 1-1 GF: - Fm: 0-0
Distance: 2m/2m3: 0-0 **2m4-2m7: 1-1** 3m+: 0-0
Track: LH: 0-0 RH: 0-0 Tight: 0-0 Gall: 0-0
Aids: Bl: 0-0 Vi: 0-0 Tstrap: 0-0
Best Rating: 100 12/01 Extr 2m6f110y good Hdl

Chopneyev (FR)

107 114

4-y-o b g Goldneyev (USA)-Pierre De Soleil (FR) (Jefferson)
R T Phillips (J-L Pelletan 10/5) Mrs Claire Smith

Placings:20 **(4651)**
2001/02: 17^2S, 16^0G

	Starts	1st	2nd	3rd	Win & Pl
Hurdles	2	0	1	0	1100
Career Total	**2**	**0**	**1**	**0**	**1100**

Going: Sf: 0-1 GS: 0-0 Gd: 0-1 GF: - Fm: 0-0
Distance: 2m/2m3: 0-2 2m4-2m7: 0-0 3m+: 0-0
Track: LH: 0-1 RH: 0-1 Tight: 0-1 Gall: 0-0
Aids: Bl: 0-0 Vi: 0-0 Tstrap: 0-0
Best Rating: 114 3/02 Hrfd 2m1f soft Hdl

A winner on the Flat in the mud over 13 furlongs in France, there was plenty of promise on his hurdling debut.

Chopwell Curtains

98 **101**

12-y-o ch g Town And Country-Liquer Candy (Laurence O)

J Howard Johnson Miss Lucy S Johnson

Placings:322/15C1132/**211P1F/3/PP0-65** **(0567)**

2001/02: 27^{6}G, 25^{5}F

	Starts	1st	2nd	3rd	Win & Pl
Chases	2	0	0	0	0
Career Total	**22**	**6**	**4**	**3**	**25739**

122	4/97	Ayr	3m1f	D Ch	GD	£5478
127	3/97	Bang	3m110y	D Ch	GD	£4357
94	11/96	Hexm	3m1f	E Ch	GD	£3479
105	12/95	Hexm	3m	E Hdl	GD	£2598
112	12/95	Weth	2m7f110y	D Hdl	GD	£3150
97	11/95	Carl	2m1f	H NHF	G-F	£1318

Total win prize-money £20383

Going: Sf: 0-0 GS: 0-0 Gd: 0-1 GF: - Fm: 0-1
Distance: 2m/2m3: 0-0 2m4-2m7: 0-0 3m+: 0-2
Track: LH: 0-2 RH: 0-0 Tight: 0-1 Gall: 0-0
Aids: Bl: 0-0 Vi: 0-0 Tstrap: 0-0
Best Rating: 127 3/97 Bang 3m110y good Ch

Chopwell Fabrics (IRE)

4-y-o b g Thatching-Maridana (USA) (Nijinsky (CAN))

J Howard Johnson Durham Drapes Ltd

Placings:PP **(4840)**

2001/02: 17^{P}GS, 16^{P}G

	Starts	1st	2nd	3rd	Win & Pl
Hurdles	2	0	0	0	
Career Total	**2**	**0**	**0**	**0**	

Going: Sf: 0-0 GS: 0-1 Gd: 0-1 GF: - Fm: 0-0
Distance: 2m/2m3: 0-2 2m4-2m7: 0-0 3m+: 0-0
Track: LH: 0-1 RH: 0-1 Tight: 0-1 Gall: 0-0
Aids: Bl: 0-0 Vi: 0-0 Tstrap: 0-0
Best Rating:

Christiansted (IRE)

104 **118**

7-y-o ch g Soviet Lad (USA)-How True (Known Fact (USA))

Ferdy Murphy (K A Ryan 21/9) John Duddy

Placings:406111/0/00030 **(3768)**

2001/02: 16^{0}G, 16^{0}G, 21^{0}G, 24^{3}G, 16^{0}GS

	Starts	1st	2nd	3rd	Win & Pl
Hurdles	5	0	0	1	1605
Career Total	**12**	**3**	**0**	**1**	**9287**

128	2/99	Muss	2m	E(0-105)HHdl	FRM	£2753
124	2/99	Donc	2m4f	E Hdl	G-F	£2302
111	2/99	Catt	2m	E Hdl	GD	£2430

Total win prize-money £7487

Going: Sf: 0-0 GS: 0-1 Gd: 0-4 GF: - Fm: 0-0
Distance: 2m/2m3: 0-3 2m4-2m7: 0-1 3m+: 0-1
Track: LH: 0-4 RH: 0-1 Tight: 0-2 Gall: 0-1
Aids: Bl: 0-0 Vi: 0-0 Tstrap: 0-0
Best Rating: 128 2/99 Muss 2m firm Hdl

A decent hurdler in 1999. He showed his first form for a while when returning to Musselburgh in December 2001. Did not look to get the three miles that day. Suited by a sound surface.

Christmas Morning (IRE)

73 **40**

4-y-o b g Brief Truce (USA)-Maid O'Cannie (Efisio)

M W Easterby Lord & Lady Manton

Placings:5 **(1231)**

2001/02: 16^{5}GF

	Starts	1st	2nd	3rd	Win & Pl
Hurdles	1	0	0	0	0
Career Total	**1**	**0**	**0**	**0**	**0**

Going: Sf: 0-0 GS: 0-0 Gd: 0-0 GF: - Fm: 0-1
Distance: 2m/2m3: 0-1 2m4-2m7: 0-0 3m+: 0-0
Track: LH: 0-1 RH: 0-0 Tight: 0-0 Gall: 0-0
Aids: Bl: 0-0 Vi: 0-0 Tstrap: 0-0
Best Rating: 40 8/01 Uttx 2m gd-fm Hdl

Christopher

105 **116**

5-y-o gr g Arzanni-Forest Nymph (NZ) (Oak Ridge (FR))

P J Hobbs A Stennett

Placings:10263 **(3510)**

2001/02: 17^{1}G, 16^{0}G, 17^{2}HY, 20^{6}S, 17^{3}S

	Starts	1st	2nd	3rd	Win & Pl
NH Flat	2	1	0	0	1957
Hurdles	3	0	1	1	1383
Career Total	**5**	**1**	**1**	**1**	**3340**

101	5/01	Hrfd	2m1f	H NHF	GD	£1956

Total win prize-money £1957

Going: Sf: 0-3 GS: 0-0 Gd: 1-2 GF: - Fm: 0-0
Distance: **2m/2m3: 1-4** 2m4-2m7: 0-1 3m+: 0-0
Track: LH: 0-3 **RH: 1-2** Tight: 0-2 Gall: 0-0
Aids: Bl: 0-0 Vi: 0-0 Tstrap: 0-0
Best Rating: 107 1/02 Tntn 2m1f soft Hdl

Bumper winner, appreciated a sound surface when winning a novices' hurdle at Exeter May 2002. Followed up at Uttoxeter, acts on good ground, stays two and a half miles. Should progress to better things.

Christy's Pride (IRE)

97 **109**

10-y-o ch m Kambalda-Caddy Shack (Precipice Wood)

C Weedon Atlantic Foods Ltd

Placings:05/512321-**P**4 **(2357)**

2001/02: 21^{P}S, 24^{4}S

	Starts	1st	2nd	3rd	Win & Pl
Hurdles	1	0	0	0	413
Chases	1	0	0	0	0
Career Total	**10**	**2**	**2**	**1**	**12458**

109	4/01	Asct	3m	C(0-135)HHdl	HVY	£6288
104	1/01	Font	2m6f110y	F(0-90)HHdl	SFT	£2562

Total win prize-money £8851

Going: Sf: 0-2 GS: 0-0 Gd: 0-0 GF: - Fm: 0-0
Distance: 2m/2m3: 0-0 2m4-2m7: 0-1 3m+: 0-1
Track: LH: 0-1 RH: 0-1 Tight: 0-1 Gall: 0-0
Aids: Bl: 0-0 Vi: 0-0 Tstrap: 0-0
Best Rating: 109 4/01 Asct 3m heavy Hdl

A fair staying handicap hurdler. Loves the mud. Stays three miles. Pulled up on her only chasing start.

Chubby Morton

8-y-o b g Rough Stones-Decoyanne (Decoy Boy)

J E Curry J E Curry

Placings:P **(0338)**

2001/02: 20^{P}S

	Starts	1st	2nd	3rd	Win & Pl
Chases	1	0	0	0	
Career Total	**1**	**0**	**0**	**0**	

Going: Sf: 0-1 GS: 0-0 Gd: 0-0 GF: - Fm: 0-0
Distance: 2m/2m3: 0-0 2m4-2m7: 0-1 3m+: 0-0
Track: LH: 0-0 RH: 0-1 Tight: 0-0 Gall: 0-0
Aids: Bl: 0-0 Vi: 0-0 Tstrap: 0-0
Best Rating:

Chunito

7-y-o b g Beveled (USA)-Wasimah (Caerleon (USA))

D M Lloyd D M Lloyd

Placings:240000/6/4454-P **(0793)**

2001/02: 22^{P}GF

	Starts	1st	2nd	3rd	Win & Pl
Hurdles	1	0	0	0	
Career Total	**12**	**0**	**1**	**0**	**598**

Going: Sf: 0-0 GS: 0-0 Gd: 0-0 GF: - Fm: 0-1
Distance: 2m/2m3: 0-0 2m4-2m7: 0-1 3m+: 0-0
Track: LH: 0-1 RH: 0-0 Tight: 0-1 Gall: 0-0
Aids: Bl: 0-0 Vi: 0-0 Tstrap: 0-0
Best Rating: 90 9/98 NAbb 2m1f gd-fm Hdl

Church Place (IRE)

107 **138**

9-y-o b g Persian Mews-Hurry Miss (Royal Buck)

Noel Meade Church Place Syndicate

Placings:000/**B425**24/**10P22331/P01-13F** **(3955a)**

2001/02: 25^{1}G, 27^{3}S, 24^{F}Y, 25S

	Starts	1st	2nd	3rd	Win & Pl
Chases	4	1	0	1	12734
Career Total	**25**	**5**	**4**	**3**	**39402**

135	9/01	Punc	3m1f	(0-116)HCh	GD	£7233
131	4/01	Leop	3m	HCh	SH	£11008
131	1/00	DRoy	2m4f	Ch	Y-S	£3588
114	5/99	DRoy	2m4f	Ch	G-F	£3989
97	2/98	Naas	2m4f	Hdl	Y-S	£2680

Total win prize-money £28500

Going: Sf: 0-2 GS: 0-0 Gd: 1-1 GF: - Fm: 0-0
Distance: 2m/2m3: 0-0 2m4-2m7: 0-0 **3m+: 1-4**
Track: LH: 0-2 **RH: 1-2** Tight: 0-1 Gall: 0-0
Aids: **Bl: 1-3** Vi: 0-0 Tstrap: 0-0
Best Rating: 138 11/01 Aint 3m3f soft Ch

Irish staying chaser. Acts well in the mud. Likes to front run.

Churchill

7-y-o ch g Carlingford Castle-Hodsock Venture (Major Portion)

M E Sowersby Keith Brown Properties (Hull) Ltd

Placings:00-UP **(0451)**

2001/02: 20^{U}G, 23^{P}F

	Starts	1st	2nd	3rd	Win & Pl
Hurdles	2	0	0	0	
Career Total	**4**	**0**	**0**	**0**	

Going: Sf: 0-0 GS: 0-0 Gd: 0-1 GF: - Fm: 0-1

Distance: 2m/2m3: 0-0 2m4-2m7: 0-2 3m+: 0-0
Track: LH: 0-2 RH: 0-0 Tight: 0-0 Gall: 0-0
Aids: Bl: 0-0 Vi: 0-0 Tstrap: 0-0
Best Rating: 79 4/01 Muss 2m1f gd-fm NHF

Churchtown Glen (IRE)

100 **111**

9-y-o b/br g Be My Native (USA)-Hill Side Glen (Goldhill)
Ian Williams J & C Tipton

Placings:*0*163533/130115002/533133334P/P233F05 0P-31PP26 **(4600)**
2001/02: 25^{3}G, 26^{1}S, 25^{P}G, 25^{P}S, 25^{2}S, 24^{6}GF

	Starts	1st	2nd	3rd	Win & Pl
Chases	6	1	1	1	4720
Career Total	**41**	**6**	**3**	**13**	**40318**

111	11/01	Uttx	3m2f	F(0-95)HCh	SFT	£3031
108	11/99	Newb	2m4f	D Ch	G-F	£5336
117	12/98	Hayd	2m4f	B HHdl	SFT	£6827
117	11/98	Hayd	2m6f	B HHdl	HVY	£5022
118	10/98	Strf	2m3f	C(0-135)HHdl	GD	£3743
97	11/97	Ludl	2m5f110y	E Hdl	GD	£2346

Total win prize-money £26305

Going: Sf: 1-3 GS: 0-0 Gd: 0-2 GF: - Fm: 0-1
Distance: 2m/2m3: 0-0 2m4-2m7: 0-0 **3m+: 1-6**
Track: **LH: 1-2** RH: 0-3 Tight: 0-1 Gall: 0-0
Aids: Bl: 0-0 Vi: 0-0 Tstrap: 0-2
Best Rating: 123 11/99 Hayd 2m4f gd-sft Ch

Modest chaser, stays three miles plus. Acts on soft/heavy ground, but has won on faster.

Cigarillo (IRE)

83f **70f**

4-y-o br g Vestris Abu-Rose-Anore (Roselier (FR))
Noel T Chance C C Shand Kydd

Placings:*6* **(4910)**
2001/02: 17^{6}G

	Starts	1st	2nd	3rd	Win & Pl
NH Flat	1	0	0	0	0
Career Total	**1**	**0**	**0**	**0**	**0**

Going: Sf: 0-0 GS: 0-0 Gd: 0-1 GF: - Fm: 0-0
Distance: 2m/2m3: 0-1 2m4-2m7: 0-0 3m+: 0-0
Track: LH: 0-0 RH: 0-1 Tight: 0-1 Gall: 0-0
Aids: Bl: 0-0 Vi: 0-0 Tstrap: 0-0
Best Rating: 70 4/02 MRas 2m1f110y good NHF

Cill Churnain (IRE)

108(104c) (118c)**108+**

9-y-o b g Arctic Cider (USA)-The Dozer (IRE) (Bulldozer)
Mrs S J Smith (J M Turner 16/5) Keith Middleton

Placings:PO/**PUR2U3U2O24531** **(4195)**
2001/02: 26^{P}G, 27^{U}GF, 23^{R}GF, 24^{2}GF, 26^{U}G, 20^{3}GS, 20^{U}GS, 20^{2}G, 20°GS, 24^{2}S, 24^{4}G, 20^{5}GS, 21^{3}S, 21^{1}S

	Starts	1st	2nd	3rd	Win & Pl
Hurdles	3	0	2	0	1430
Chases	11	1	1	2	5497
Career Total	**16**	**1**	**3**	**2**	**6927**

118	3/02	Sedg	2m5f	E Ch	SFT	£3051

Total win prize-money £3052

Going: Sf: 1-3 GS: 0-4 Gd: 0-4 GF: - Fm: 0-3
Distance: 2m/2m3: 0-0 **2m4-2m7: 1-7** 3m+: 0-7

Track: **LH: 1-11** RH: 0-2 **Tight: 1-10** Gall: 0-1
Aids: Bl: 0-0 Vi: 0-0 Tstrap: 0-0
Best Rating: 118 3/02 Sedg 2m5f soft Ch

Not very big. Has shown signs of temperament but did little wrong when getting off the mark over fences at Sedgefield on soft ground in March. Ready winner of three mile novices hurdle at Worcester June 2002. Dropped back to two miles five to follow up at Sedgefeild. Handles the soft but is considered best on a sounder surface.

Cimarrone Cove (IRE)

103(30h) **137**

7-y-o b g Roselier (FR)-Sugarstown (Sassafras (FR))
M Pitman Philip Matton

Placings:*2*/4124/P4611F3-3606P **(3587)**
2001/02: 24^{3}GS, 29^{6}G, 26^{0}G, 24^{6}G, 28^{P}HY

	Starts	1st	2nd	3rd	Win & Pl
Chases	5	0	0	1	1683
Career Total	**17**	**3**	**2**	**2**	**16948**

140	12/00	Newb	3m	D Ch	SFT	£4348
129	12/00	Donc	3m	D Ch	HVY	£5118
114	12/99	Hntg	3m2f	E Hdl	G-S	£2757

Total win prize-money £12226

Going: Sf: 0-1 GS: 0-1 Gd: 0-3 GF: - Fm: 0-0
Distance: 2m/2m3: 0-0 2m4-2m7: 0-0 3m+: 0-5
Track: LH: 0-3 RH: 0-1 Tight: 0-0 Gall: 0-2
Aids: Bl: 0-1 Vi: 0-1 Tstrap: 0-0
Best Rating: 140 2/01 Newb 3m soft Ch

Handicap chaser, who stays well and suited by soft ground.

Cinder Hills

104 **102**

7-y-o ch m Deploy-Dame Du Moulin (Shiny Tenth)
M W Easterby Winton Bloodstock Ltd

Placings:42P/0P311/36 **(4488)**
2001/02: 16^{3}HY, 20^{6}GS

	Starts	1st	2nd	3rd	Win & Pl
Hurdles	2	0	0	1	347
Career Total	**10**	**2**	**1**	**2**	**6528**

110	4/00	Kels	2m6f110y	D(0-120)HHdl	SFT	£3055
98	2/00	Newc	2m4f	F(0-105)HHdl	SFT	£1939

Total win prize-money £4994

Going: Sf: 0-1 GS: 0-1 Gd: 0-0 GF: - Fm: 0-0
Distance: 2m/2m3: 0-1 2m4-2m7: 0-1 3m+: 0-0
Track: LH: 0-1 RH: 0-0 Tight: 0-0 Gall: 0-0
Aids: Bl: 0-0 Vi: 0-0 Tstrap: 0-0
Best Rating: 110 4/00 Kels 2m6f110y soft Hdl

Modest handicap hurdler, she notched up a couple of wins before a two-year absence. She ran a good race under top weight in testing conditions on her return in March 2002.

Cinder Kopje

9-y-o ch m Mirror Boy-Meall Mhor (Fez)
M A Barnes Miss Alison P Lee

Placings:*00*/P **(4857)**
2001/02: 20^{P}G

	Starts	1st	2nd	3rd	Win & Pl
Hurdles	1	0	0	0	
Career Total	**3**	**0**	**0**	**0**	

Going: Sf: 0-0 GS: 0-0 Gd: 0-1 GF: - Fm: 0-0
Distance: 2m/2m3: 0-0 2m4-2m7: 0-1 3m+: 0-0
Track: LH: 0-1 RH: 0-0 Tight: 0-0 Gall: 0-0
Aids: Bl: 0-0 Vi: 0-0 Tstrap: 0-1
Best Rating:

Cindesti (IRE)

94(69h) (44h)**92**

6-y-o b g Barathea (IRE)-Niamh Cinn Oir (IRE) (King Of Clubs)
J G Given J E Titley

Placings:614/50-4U66 **(1258)**
2001/02: 20^{4}G, 20^{U}GS, 20^{6}GF, 20^{6}GF

	Starts	1st	2nd	3rd	Win & Pl
Hurdles	1	0	0	0	0
Chases	3	0	0	0	421
Career Total	**9**	**1**	**0**	**0**	**2801**

115	2/00	Donc	2m4f	E Hdl	GD	£2380

Total win prize-money £2380

Going: Sf: 0-0 GS: 0-1 Gd: 0-1 GF: - Fm: 0-2
Distance: 2m/2m3: 0-0 2m4-2m7: 0-4 3m+: 0-0
Track: LH: 0-0 RH: 0-3 Tight: 0-2 Gall: 0-1
Aids: Bl: 0-0 Vi: 0-0 Tstrap: 0-0
Best Rating: 115 2/00 Donc 2m4f good Hdl

Cinema Paradiso

97 **114**

8-y-o b g Polar Falcon (USA)-Epure (Bellypha)
D W Chapman (N G Richards 26/7) J M Chapman

Placings:4F4462/23110023/**6F0F-400** **(1020)**
2001/02: 17^{4}GS, 16^{0}GF, 17^{0}GF

	Starts	1st	2nd	3rd	Win & Pl
Hurdles	3	0	0	0	345
Career Total	**21**	**2**	**3**	**2**	**9745**

120	9/99	Prth	2m110y	E Hdl	SFT	£2970
108	8/99	Ctml	2m1f110y	E Hdl	GD	£2880

Total win prize-money £5850

Going: Sf: 0-0 GS: 0-1 Gd: 0-0 GF: - Fm: 0-2
Distance: 2m/2m3: 0-3 2m4-2m7: 0-0 3m+: 0-0
Track: LH: 0-2 RH: 0-1 Tight: 0-2 Gall: 0-0
Aids: Bl: 0-0 Vi: 0-0 Tstrap: 0-0
Best Rating: 126 11/99 Bang 2m1f good Hdl

Cinnamon Line

103 **97**

6-y-o ch g Derrylin-Cinnamon Run (Deep Run)
R H Alner Club Ten

Placings:*24*-3350 **(4400)**
2001/02: 21^{3}HY, 24^{3}HY, 20^{5}GS, 21^{0}S

	Starts	1st	2nd	3rd	Win & Pl
Hurdles	4	0	0	2	928
Career Total	**6**	**0**	**1**	**2**	**1684**

Going: Sf: 0-3 GS: 0-1 Gd: 0-0 GF: - Fm: 0-0
Distance: 2m/2m3: 0-0 2m4-2m7: 0-3 3m+: 0-1
Track: LH: 0-3 RH: 0-1 Tight: 0-0 Gall: 0-1
Aids: Bl: 0-0 Vi: 0-0 Tstrap: 0-0
Best Rating: 110 3/01 Newb 2m110y heavy NHF

A chaser in the making. Has shown promise in bumper and novice hurdle company. Acts on soft/heavy ground.

Circle Of Magic

99 **80**

8-y-o gr m Midyan (USA)-Miss Witch (High Line)
M C Pipe M C Pipe

Placings:521P1133/060/0/120202P4666-05P063P **(1340)**
2001/02: 19^{0}G, 17^{5}G, 22^{P}GF, 22^{0}GF, 20^{6}S, 17^{3}G, 22^{P}GF

	Starts	1st	2nd	3rd	Win & Pl
Hurdles	7	0	0	1	341
Career Total	**30**	**4**	**4**	**3**	**10227**

94	9/00	Extr	2m1f	G(0-95)HHdl	GD	£1792
80	2/98	Plum	2m1f	F Hdl	GD	£2012
73	1/98	Tntn	2m1f	G Hdl	SFT	£1544
64	11/97	Tntn	2m1f	G Hdl	GD	£1784

Total win prize-money £7132

Going: Sf: 0-1 GS: 0-0 Gd: 0-3 GF: - Fm: 0-3
Distance: 2m/2m3: 0-2 2m4-2m7: 0-5 3m+: 0-0
Track: LH: 0-6 RH: 0-1 Tight: 0-5 Gall: 0-0
Aids: Bl: 0-0 Vi: 0-3 Tstrap: 0-3
Best Rating: 97 11/00 Extr 2m1f gd-sft Hdl

Circle Of Wolves

93 **91**

4-y-o ch g Wolfhound (USA)-Misty Halo (High Top)
Bob Jones The Circle Of Wolves Partnership

Placings:5543 **(3492)**
2001/02: 17^{5}GS, 16^{5}GS, 16^{4}GS, 24^{3}S

	Starts	1st	2nd	3rd	Win & Pl
Hurdles	4	0	0	1	2394
Career Total	**4**	**0**	**0**	**1**	**2394**

Going: Sf: 0-1 GS: 0-3 Gd: 0-0 GF: - Fm: 0-0
Distance: 2m/2m3: 0-3 2m4-2m7: 0-0 3m+: 0-1
Track: LH: 0-1 RH: 0-3 Tight: 0-0 Gall: 0-1
Aids: Bl: 0-0 Vi: 0-0 Tstrap: 0-0
Best Rating: 91 1/02 Donc 3m110y soft Hdl

Moderate hurdler over two miles. Most effective when he can get his toe in.

Circuit Breaker (IRE)

11-y-o b g Torus-Lovely Choice (Deep Run)
H W Lavis B J Kelly

Placings:00P/P/P-PP **(0838)**
2001/02: 23^{P}G, 24^{P}G

	Starts	1st	2nd	3rd	Win & Pl
Hurdles	1	0	0	0	0
Chases	1	0	0	0	0
Career Total	**6**	**0**	**0**	**0**	**0**

Going: Sf: 0-0 GS: 0-0 Gd: 0-2 GF: - Fm: 0-0
Distance: 2m/2m3: 0-0 2m4-2m7: 0-0 3m+: 0-2
Track: LH: 0-2 RH: 0-0 Tight: 0-0 Gall: 0-0
Aids: Bl: 0-0 Vi: 0-0 Tstrap: 0-0
Best Rating: 71 3/98 Navn 2m yld-sft NHF

Cisco

90 **59**

4-y-o b g Shambo-School Run (Deep Run)
Andrew Turnell Dr John Hollowood

Placings:050 **(4689)**
2001/02: 16^{0}GS, 16^{5}HY, 16^{0}GF

	Starts	1st	2nd	3rd	Win & Pl
NH Flat	1	0	0	0	0
Hurdles	2	0	0	0	0
Career Total	**3**	**0**	**0**	**0**	**0**

Going: Sf: 0-1 GS: 0-1 Gd: 0-0 GF: - Fm: 0-1
Distance: 2m/2m3: 0-3 2m4-2m7: 0-0 3m+: 0-0
Track: LH: 0-3 RH: 0-0 Tight: 0-1 Gall: 0-2
Aids: Bl: 0-0 Vi: 0-0 Tstrap: 0-0
Best Rating: 64 3/02 Donc 2m110y gd-sft NHF

Cita Verda (FR)

103 **115**

4-y-o b f Take Risks (FR)-Mossita (FR) (Tip Moss (FR))
P Monteith (A Hosselet 17/6) Mr & Mrs Raymond Anderson Green

Placings:1102 **(4840)**
2001/02: 16^{1}S, 16^{1}HY, 16^{0}G, 16^{2}G

	Starts	1st	2nd	3rd	Win & Pl
Hurdles	4	2	1	0	7278
Career Total	**4**	**2**	**1**	**0**	**7278**

115	3/02	Ayr	2m	E Hdl	HVY	£3024
85	2/02	Muss	2m	E Hdl	SFT	£2660

Total win prize-money £5684

Going: Sf: 2-2 GS: 0-0 Gd: 0-2 GF: - Fm: 0-0
Distance: **2m/2m3: 2-4** 2m4-2m7: 0-0 3m+: 0-0
Track: LH: 1-3 RH: 1-1 **Tight: 1-2** Gall: 0-0
Aids: Bl: 0-0 Vi: 0-0 Tstrap: 0-0
Best Rating: 115 3/02 Ayr 2m heavy Hdl

Useful hurdler. Stays two miles and acts well in the mud, but is also effective on a faster surface.

Citius (IRE)

93(112h) (89h)**121**

6-y-o b g Supreme Leader-Fancy Me Not (IRE) (Bulldozer)
R Rowe Tom Perkins

Placings:213-00613 **(3873)**
2001/02: 18^{0}GS, 21^{0}G, 17^{6}GS, 21^{1}GS, 20^{3}GS

	Starts	1st	2nd	3rd	Win & Pl
Hurdles	2	0	0	0	0
Chases	3	1	0	1	5025
Career Total	**8**	**2**	**1**	**2**	**9244**

121	1/02	Winc	2m5f	D Ch	G-S	£4387
115	1/01	Folk	2m1f110y	E Hdl	HVY	£2541

Total win prize-money £6929

Going: Sf: 0-0 GS: 1-4 Gd: 0-1 GF: - Fm: 0-0
Distance: 2m/2m3: 0-2 **2m4-2m7: 1-3** 3m+: 0-0
Track: LH: 0-2 **RH: 1-3** Tight: 0-1 Gall: 0-2
Aids: Bl: 0-0 Vi: 0-0 Tstrap: 0-0
Best Rating: 121 2/02 Hntg 2m4f110y gd-sft Ch

Successful over hurdles in January 2001, he has also been successful over fences. Effective from two to two miles five, he acts on a soft surface.

City Bank Dudley

81 **68**

5-y-o b g Noble Patriarch-Derry's Delight (Mufrij)
N Wilson J B Slatcher

Placings:5 **(0236)**
2001/02: 16^{5}GF

	Starts	1st	2nd	3rd	Win & Pl
Hurdles	1	0	0	0	0
Career Total	**1**	**0**	**0**	**0**	**0**

Going: Sf: 0-0 GS: 0-0 Gd: 0-0 GF: - Fm: 0-1
Distance: 2m/2m3: 0-1 2m4-2m7: 0-0 3m+: 0-0
Track: LH: 0-1 RH: 0-0 Tight: 0-1 Gall: 0-0
Aids: Bl: 0-0 Vi: 0-0 Tstrap: 0-0
Best Rating: 68 5/01 Sthl 2m gd-fm Hdl

City Dispatch

5-y-o b g Safawan-Baladee (Mummy's Pet)
J S Moore C D S Partnership

Placings:0 **(1892)**
2001/02: 16^{0}G

	Starts	1st	2nd	3rd	Win & Pl
NH Flat	1	0	0	0	
Career Total	**1**	**0**	**0**	**0**	

Going: Sf: 0-0 GS: 0-0 Gd: 0-1 GF: - Fm: 0-0
Distance: 2m/2m3: 0-1 2m4-2m7: 0-0 3m+: 0-0
Track: LH: 0-1 RH: 0-0 Tight: 0-0 Gall: 0-0
Aids: Bl: 0-0 Vi: 0-0 Tstrap: 0-0
Best Rating:

City Express

53

7-y-o ch g Rock City-Caroles Express (Scottish Reel)
M Wellings Mrs L A Wellings

Placings:00/0P **(1039)**
2001/02: 16^{0}GF, 20^{P}GF

	Starts	1st	2nd	3rd	Win & Pl
Hurdles	2	0	0	0	
Career Total	**4**	**0**	**0**	**0**	

Going: Sf: 0-0 GS: 0-0 Gd: 0-0 GF: - Fm: 0-2
Distance: 2m/2m3: 0-1 2m4-2m7: 0-1 3m+: 0-0
Track: LH: 0-2 RH: 0-0 Tight: 0-1 Gall: 0-0
Aids: Bl: 0-0 Vi: 0-0 Tstrap: 0-0
Best Rating: 40 2/99 Newb 2m110y good NHF

City Flyer

93 **74**

5-y-o br g Night Shift (USA)-Al Guswa (Shernazar)
Miss J Feilden C Morris

Placings:65 **(2064)**
2001/02: 16^{6}GS, 16^{5}G

	Starts	1st	2nd	3rd	Win & Pl
Hurdles	2	0	0	0	0
Career Total	**2**	**0**	**0**	**0**	**0**

Going: Sf: 0-0 GS: 0-1 Gd: 0-1 GF: - Fm: 0-0
Distance: 2m/2m3: 0-2 2m4-2m7: 0-0 3m+: 0-0
Track: LH: 0-1 RH: 0-1 Tight: 0-1 Gall: 0-1
Aids: Bl: 0-0 Vi: 0-0 Tstrap: 0-0
Best Rating: 74 11/01 Hntg 2m110y good Hdl

City Gent

101(93h) (68h)**108**

8-y-o b g Primitive Rising (USA)-Classy Lassy (Class Distinction)
N Wilson Miss Jean Atkinson

Placings:050SF/PUF535/2364P211-665PP400 **(4908)**
2001/02: 16^{6}G, 16^{6}G, 16^{5}G, 16^{P}S, 19^{P}GF, 16^{4}GF, 17^{0}G,

21^{0}G

	Starts	1st	2nd	3rd	Win & Pl
Hurdles	1	0	0	0	0
Chases	7	0	0	0	0
Career Total	**27**	**2**	**2**	**2**	**12206**

108	4/01	MRas	2m1f110y	E(0-105)HCh	HVY	£3932
108	2/01	Muss	2m	D(0-110)HCh	GD	£4823

Total win prize-money £8756

Going: Sf: 0-1 GS: 0-0 Gd: 0-5 GF: - Fm: 0-2
Distance: 2m/2m3: 0-7 2m4-2m7: 0-1 3m+: 0-0
Track: LH: 0-5 RH: 0-3 Tight: 0-7 Gall: 0-0
Aids: Bl: 0-1 Vi: 0-0 Tstrap: 0-5
Best Rating: 108 4/01 MRas 2m1f110y heavy Ch

City Hall (IRE)

95(104h) (120h)110

8-y-o gr g Generous (IRE)-City Fortress (Troy)
Mrs V C Ward The Late Mrs R F Key & Mrs V C Ward

Placings:2F112/4232032/PF53P3-4P **(2172)**
2001/02: 21^{4}G, 24^{PS}

	Starts	1st	2nd	3rd	Win & Pl
Chases	2	0	0	0	244
Career Total	**20**	**2**	**5**	**4**	**55790**

142	2/98	Sand	2m110y	D Hdl	GD	£3663
118	1/98	Sand	2m110y	D Hdl	SFT	£3696

Total win prize-money £7360

Going: Sf: 0-1 GS: 0-0 Gd: 0-1 GF: - Fm: 0-0
Distance: 2m/2m3: 0-0 2m4-2m7: 0-1 3m+: 0-1
Track: LH: 0-2 RH: 0-0 Tight: 0-1 Gall: 0-0
Aids: Bl: 0-0 Vi: 0-2 Tstrap: 0-0
Best Rating: 156 2/99 Newb 2m110y good Hdl

Formerly a high class hurdler (placed in the Triumph Hurdle and Tote Gold Trophy), he was injured at the end of the 1998-1999 campaign and has not looked the same horse since. Effective up to three miles, he flopped over fences and may need to drop a few pounds before winning a handicap hurdle.

City Poser (IRE)

103 116

7-y-o b g Posen (USA)-Citissima (Simbir)
Simon Earle The Plum Merchants

Placings:0002/41440-50641 **(4599)**
2001/02: 16^{5}GF, 20^{0}S, 21^{6}GS, 24^{4}S, 25^{1}GF

	Starts	1st	2nd	3rd	Win & Pl
Hurdles	5	1	0	0	4585
Career Total	**14**	**2**	**1**	**0**	**9928**

116	4/02	Wwck	3m1f	D(0-115)HHdl	G-F	£4309
96	9/00	Baln	2m	(0-102)HHdl	SFT	£3588

Total win prize-money £7898

Going: Sf: 0-2 GS: 0-1 Gd: 0-0 GF: - Fm: 1-2
Distance: 2m/2m3: 0-1 2m4-2m7: 0-2 **3m+: 1-2**
Track: LH: 0-3 RH: 0-1 Tight: 0-0 Gall: 0-2
Aids: Bl: 0-0 Vi: 0-0 Tstrap: 0-0
Best Rating: 116 4/02 Wwck 3m1f gd-fm Hdl

A fair handicap hurdler, he handles soft ground but is suited by faster. Stays three miles.

City Standard (IRE)

101 98

6-y-o b g Rainbow Quest (USA)-City Fortress (Troy)
M F Harris (R Williams 9/6) M Harris

Placings:546P **(4187)**
2001/02: 16^{5}GF, 20^{4}G, 17^{6}HY, 19^{PS}

	Starts	1st	2nd	3rd	Win & Pl
Hurdles	4	0	0	0	0
Career Total	**4**	**0**	**0**	**0**	**0**

Going: Sf: 0-2 GS: 0-0 Gd: 0-1 GF: - Fm: 0-1
Distance: 2m/2m3: 0-2 2m4-2m7: 0-2 3m+: 0-0
Track: LH: 0-2 RH: 0-2 Tight: 0-3 Gall: 0-0
Aids: Bl: 0-0 Vi: 0-0 Tstrap: 0-0
Best Rating: 98 6/01 Strf 2m110y gd-fm Hdl

A fair lightly-raced staying handicapper on the Flat. Fairly inauspicious start to hurdles so far. Probably best at around two miles.

City Venture

98f 117f

5-y-o ch g Pursuit Of Love-City Of Angels (Woodman (USA))
T H Caldwell R S G Jones

Placings:*01-1* **(0181)**
2001/02: 16^{1}GF

	Starts	1st	2nd	3rd	Win & Pl
NH Flat	1	1	0	0	1638
Career Total	**3**	**2**	**0**	**0**	**4946**

117	5/01	Ayr	2m	H NHF	G-F	£1638
98	4/01	Ayr	2m	H NHF	G-F	£3307

Total win prize-money £4946

Going: Sf: 0-0 GS: 0-0 Gd: 0-0 GF: - Fm: 1-1
Distance: **2m/2m3: 1-1** 2m4-2m7: 0-0 3m+: 0-0
Track: **LH: 1-1** RH: 0-0 Tight: 0-0 Gall: 0-0
Aids: Bl: 0-0 Vi: 0-0 Tstrap: 0-0
Best Rating: 117 5/01 Ayr 2m gd-fm NHF

Civil List (IRE)

6-y-o b g Executive Perk-Ferryforth Lady (IRE) (Royal Fountain)
Mrs P Sly The Craftsmen

Placings:P **(2208)**
2001/02: 16^{P}GS

	Starts	1st	2nd	3rd	Win & Pl
Hurdles	1	0	0	0	
Career Total	**1**	**0**	**0**	**0**	

Going: Sf: 0-0 GS: 0-1 Gd: 0-0 GF: - Fm: 0-0
Distance: 2m/2m3: 0-1 2m4-2m7: 0-0 3m+: 0-0
Track: LH: 0-0 RH: 0-1 Tight: 0-0 Gall: 0-0
Aids: Bl: 0-0 Vi: 0-0 Tstrap: 0-0
Best Rating:

Clair Valley

110 90

8-y-o b m Ardross-Annicombe Run (Deep Run)
Ferdy Murphy Oak Wood Racing

Placings:*3045*/65P-0326 **(0907)**
2001/02: 21^{0}G, 24^{3}GF, 24^{2}F, 24^{6}G

	Starts	1st	2nd	3rd	Win & Pl
Hurdles	4	0	1	1	1224
Career Total	**11**	**0**	**1**	**2**	**1426**

Going: Sf: 0-0 GS: 0-0 Gd: 0-2 GF: - Fm: 0-2
Distance: 2m/2m3: 0-0 2m4-2m7: 0-1 3m+: 0-3
Track: LH: 0-3 RH: 0-1 Tight: 0-1 Gall: 0-0
Aids: Bl: 0-0 Vi: 0-0 Tstrap: 0-0
Best Rating: 90 5/01 Hexm 3m firm Hdl

Some ability in novice hurdles until winning at Wolverhampton in July 2002. Stays three miles and goes on any ground.

Claire's Dancer (IRE)

103 100

9-y-o b g Classic Music (USA)-Midnight Patrol (Ashmore (FR))
Andrew Turnell Mrs Claire Hollowood

Placings:00/31644403/454014/**62/P-41** **(1043)**
2001/02: 16^{4}F, 20^{1}GF

	Starts	1st	2nd	3rd	Win & Pl
Chases	2	1	0	0	3919
Career Total	**21**	**3**	**1**	**2**	**10612**

100	7/01	Uttx	2m4f	E(0-105)HCh	G-F	£3705
93	4/99	Hntg	2m5f110y	F(0-110)HHdl	G-F	£2542
95	10/97	Winc	2m	E(0-100)HHdl	FRM	£2146

Total win prize-money £8393

Going: Sf: 0-0 GS: 0-0 Gd: 0-0 GF: - Fm: 1-2
Distance: 2m/2m3: 0-1 **2m4-2m7: 1-1** 3m+: 0-0
Track: **LH: 1-2** RH: 0-0 Tight: 0-1 Gall: 0-0
Aids: Bl: 0-0 Vi: 0-0 Tstrap: 0-0
Best Rating: 100 7/01 Uttx 2m4f gd-fm Ch

Clandestine

109 129

6-y-o b m Saddlers' Hall (IRE)-Fleeting Affair (Hotfoot)
N J Henderson Brian & Gwen Griffiths

Placings:133210/2040-341010 **(4231)**
2001/02: 19^{3}G, 20^{4}G, 20^{1}S, 21^{0}G, 21^{1}GS, 21^{0}GS

	Starts	1st	2nd	3rd	Win & Pl
Hurdles	6	2	0	1	9605
Career Total	**16**	**4**	**2**	**3**	**24725**

129	1/02	Hntg	2m5f110y	D(0-120)HHdl	G-S	£3486
129	12/01	Folk	2m4f110y	C(0-130)HHdl	SFT	£5148
117	3/00	Folk	2m1f110y	E Hdl	G-F	£2304
109	11/99	Newb	2m110y	C Hdl	GD	£4510

Total win prize-money £15448

Going: Sf: 1-1 GS: 1-2 Gd: 0-3 GF: - Fm: 0-0
Distance: 2m/2m3: 0-0 **2m4-2m7: 2-6** 3m+: 0-0
Track: LH: 0-2 **RH: 2-4** Tight: 1-1 Gall: 1-2
Aids: Bl: 0-1 Vi: 0-0 Tstrap: 0-0
Best Rating: 129 1/02 Hntg 2m5f110y gd-sft Hdl

A winner on the Flat and over hurdles, she had a disappointing 2000/01 season. She runs well fresh and came out after a four-month break to win a decent handicap in December 2001 comfortably, although she was very disappointing next time. Bounced back to form at Huntingdon. Acts on most types of ground and stays two and a half miles.

Clanfluther (IRE)

75 38

12-y-o b g Shernazar-Habanna (Habitat)
N G Ayliffe N G Ayliffe

Placings:35/0/P1000UP/000-0 **(0682)**
2001/02: 22^{0}G

	Starts	1st	2nd	3rd	Win & Pl
Hurdles	1	0	0	0	
Career Total	**14**	**1**	**0**	**1**	**2891**

76	6/99	Clon	2m	(0-95)HHdl	G-F	£2762

Total win prize-money £2762

Going: Sf: 0-0 GS: 0-0 Gd: 0-1 GF: - Fm: 0-0
Distance: 2m/2m3: 0-0 2m4-2m7: 0-1 3m+: 0-0
Track: LH: 0-1 RH: 0-0 Tight: 0-1 Gall: 0-0
Aids: Bl: 0-0 Vi: 0-0 Tstrap: 0-0
Best Rating: 96 9/95 DRoy 2m4f firm Hdl

Claras Pride (IRE)

87 **79**

10-y-o b g Be My Native (USA)-Our Hollow (Wolver Hollow)
M S Wilesmith M S Wilesmith

Placings:00655/0/F **(0255)**
2001/02: 20^{F}GF

	Starts	1st	2nd	3rd	Win & Pl
Chases	1	0	0	0	
Career Total	**7**	**0**	**0**	**0**	

Going: Sf: 0-0 GS: 0-0 Gd: 0-0 GF: - Fm: 0-1
Distance: 2m/2m3: 0-0 2m4-2m7: 0-1 3m+: 0-0
Track: LH: 0-1 RH: 0-0 Tight: 0-1 Gall: 0-0
Aids: Bl: 0-0 Vi: 0-0 Tstrap: 0-0
Best Rating: 88 7/98 Wxfd 2m good NHF

Clarendon (IRE)

106 **125+**

6-y-o ch g Forest Wind (USA)-Sparkish (IRE) (Persian Bold)
P J Hobbs The Plus Fours

Placings:43-11 **(0832)**
2001/02: 16^{1}GF, 17^{1}GF

	Starts	1st	2nd	3rd	Win & Pl
Hurdles	2	2	0	0	6116
Career Total	**4**	**2**	**0**	**1**	**6830**

108	6/01	NAbb	2m1f	D Hdl	G-F	£3554
106	6/01	Worc	2m	E Hdl	G-F	£2562

Total win prize-money £6116

Going: Sf: 0-0 GS: 0-0 Gd: 0-0 GF: - Fm: 2-2
Distance: **2m/2m3: 2-2** 2m4-2m7: 0-0 3m+: 0-0
Track: **LH: 2-2** RH: 0-0 **Tight: 1-1** Gall: 0-0
Aids: Bl: 0-0 Vi: 0-0 Tstrap: 0-0
Best Rating: 108 6/01 NAbb 2m1f gd-fm Hdl

Fair hurdler, returning from a year off when winning at Stratford in July 2002. Likes fast ground.

Clashbridane (IRE)

10-y-o b g Lancastrian-Castleview Rose (Master Buck)
Mrs G B Walford (T D Walford 10/2) Mrs G B Walford

Placings:P-P2043P **(4859)**
2001/02: 25^{P}S, 20^{2}S, 24^{0}GF, 21^{4}S, 26^{3}GS, 25^{P}G

	Starts	1st	2nd	3rd	Win & Pl
Chases	6	0	1	1	993
Career Total	**7**	**0**	**1**	**1**	**993**

Going: Sf: 0-3 GS: 0-1 Gd: 0-1 GF: - Fm: 0-1
Distance: 2m/2m3: 0-0 2m4-2m7: 0-2 3m+: 0-4
Track: LH: 0-4 RH: 0-2 Tight: 0-2 Gall: 0-0
Aids: Bl: 0-0 Vi: 0-0 Tstrap: 0-0
Best Rating: 93 4/02 Carl 3m2f gd-sft Ch

Class Of Ninetytwo (IRE)

13-y-o b g Lancastrian-Lothian Lassie (Precipice Wood)
S Wynne (Allan Wynne 19/5) A Wynne, M Williams, A Mower, Mr & Mrs J E Stockto

Placings:050/65000/P11113/212/PF5P/P-P21 **(4091)**
2001/02: 25^{P}S, 24^{2}GS, 24^{1}S

	Starts	1st	2nd	3rd	Win & Pl
Chases	3	1	1	0	2338
Career Total	**25**	**6**	**3**	**1**	**29504**

102	3/02	Bang	3m110y	H Ch	SFT	£1498
125	11/96	Wwck	3m2f	B(0-145)HCh	GD	£6736
122	2/96	Chep	3m2f110y	D(0-125)HCh	SFT	£4099
117	1/96	Leic	3m	F(0-105)HCh	GD	£3236
108	12/95	Ludl	3m	F(0-100)HCh	G-F	£2775
111	11/95	Wwck	3m2f	D Ch	GD	£3756

Total win prize-money £22100

Going: Sf: 1-2 GS: 0-1 Gd: 0-0 GF: - Fm: 0-0
Distance: 2m/2m3: 0-0 2m4-2m7: 0-0 **3m+: 1-3**
Track: LH: 0-2 RH: 0-0 Tight: 0-1 Gall: 0-0
Aids: Bl: 0-0 Vi: 0-0 Tstrap: 0-0
Best Rating: 125 11/96 Wwck 3m2f good Ch

A one-time fair staying handicapper, he is a modest hunter chaser these days. Likes to dominate.

Classic Affair (FR)

81 **26**

6-y-o b g Always Fair (USA)-Classic Storm (Belfort (FR))
Miss A Stokell Ms Caron Stokell

Placings:F/0P0-0 **(1068)**
2001/02: 17^{0}GF

	Starts	1st	2nd	3rd	Win & Pl
Hurdles	1	0	0	0	
Career Total	**5**	**0**	**0**	**0**	

Going: Sf: 0-0 GS: 0-0 Gd: 0-0 GF: - Fm: 0-1
Distance: 2m/2m3: 0-1 2m4-2m7: 0-0 3m+: 0-0
Track: LH: 0-1 RH: 0-0 Tight: 0-1 Gall: 0-0
Aids: Bl: 0-0 Vi: 0-0 Tstrap: 0-0
Best Rating: 81 4/00 MRas 2m1f110y soft Hdl

Classic Colours (USA)

68 **28**

9-y-o ch g Blushing John (USA)-All Agleam (USA) (Gleaming (USA))
G H Yardley Philip Jones

Placings:05/00/00/0-0 **(1387)**
2001/02: 16^{0}G

	Starts	1st	2nd	3rd	Win & Pl
Hurdles	1	0	0	0	
Career Total	**8**	**0**	**0**	**0**	**0**

Going: Sf: 0-0 GS: 0-0 Gd: 0-1 GF: - Fm: 0-0
Distance: 2m/2m3: 0-1 2m4-2m7: 0-0 3m+: 0-0
Track: LH: 0-1 RH: 0-0 Tight: 0-0 Gall: 0-0
Aids: Bl: 0-0 Vi: 0-0 Tstrap: 0-0
Best Rating: 72 11/98 Wwck 2m good Hdl

Classic Defence (IRE)

69 **49**

9-y-o b g Cyrano De Bergerac-My Alanna (Dalsaan)
B J Llewellyn The Welsh Valleys Syndicate

Placings:1/06/P-P0 **(0596)**
2001/02: 16^{P}GF, 17^{0}G

	Starts	1st	2nd	3rd	Win & Pl
Hurdles	2	0	0	0	
Career Total	**6**	**1**	**0**	**0**	**2915**

102	10/96	Kemp	2m	D Hdl	G-F	£2915

Total win prize-money £2915

Going: Sf: 0-0 GS: 0-0 Gd: 0-1 GF: - Fm: 0-1
Distance: 2m/2m3: 0-2 2m4-2m7: 0-0 3m+: 0-0
Track: LH: 0-1 RH: 0-1 Tight: 0-1 Gall: 0-1
Aids: Bl: 0-0 Vi: 0-1 Tstrap: 0-0
Best Rating: 102 10/96 Kemp 2m gd-fm Hdl

Classic Eagle

76 **63**

9-y-o b g Unfuwain (USA)-La Lutine (My Swallow)
N A Graham (Pat Mitchell 8/8) Steve Rees Racing Classic Eagle

Placings:013102P/42316245/F0/4-00 **(4579)**
2001/02: 16^{0}S, 16^{0}G

	Starts	1st	2nd	3rd	Win & Pl
Hurdles	2	0	0	0	
Career Total	**20**	**3**	**3**	**2**	**13003**

123	11/98	Hntg	2m110y	E(0-115)HHdl	G-S	£2600
115	2/98	Fknm	2m	E(0-115)HHdl	G-F	£2985
120	12/97	Catt	2m	E Hdl	G-S	£2038

Total win prize-money £7623

Going: Sf: 0-1 GS: 0-0 Gd: 0-1 GF: - Fm: 0-0
Distance: 2m/2m3: 0-2 2m4-2m7: 0-0 3m+: 0-0
Track: LH: 0-1 RH: 0-1 Tight: 0-0 Gall: 0-0
Aids: Bl: 0-0 Vi: 0-0 Tstrap: 0-0
Best Rating: 125 3/99 Asct 2m110y gd-fm Hdl

Classic Exhibit

99 **77**

13-y-o b g Tate Gallery (USA)-See The Tops (Cure The Blues (USA))
A L Forbes Principal Racing

Placings:632213F4/3/60012/1651113/45/00P010/0P05F0/0-325000 **(2349)**
2001/02: 19^{3}G, 17^{2}G, 16^{5}GF, 24^{0}GS, 16^{0}GS, 19^{0}GS

	Starts	1st	2nd	3rd	Win & Pl
Hurdles	6	0	1	1	1073
Career Total	**42**	**7**	**4**	**5**	**20263**

87	10/98	Worc	2m	G(0-95)HHdl	GD	£1996
83	8/95	Prth	2m110y	D(0-120)HHdl	G-F	£3014
89	8/95	Strf	2m110y	F(0-105)HHdl	G-F	£2276
83	8/95	Worc	2m	D(0-120)HHdl	G-F	£3397
77	5/95	Newc	2m110y	G(0-95)HHdl	G-F	£1917
71	3/95	Hntg	2m110y	G(0-90)HHdl	G-F	£2304
104	10/92	Uttx	2m	Hdl	GD	£1626

Total win prize-money £16532

Going: Sf: 0-0 GS: 0-3 Gd: 0-2 GF: - Fm: 0-1
Distance: 2m/2m3: 0-4 2m4-2m7: 0-1 3m+: 0-1
Track: LH: 0-4 RH: 0-2 Tight: 0-5 Gall: 0-0
Aids: Bl: 0-0 Vi: 0-0 Tstrap: 0-0
Best Rating: 109 10/92 Bang 2m1f good Hdl

Classic Fable (IRE)

88 **60**

10-y-o b m Lafontaine (USA)-Rathmill Syke (True Song)
J L Needham J L Needham

Placings:*0*/P-P00646PUF4 **(4408)**
2001/02: 26^{P}G, 21^{0}GF, 17^{0}G, 16^{6}GF, 16^{4}S, 16^{6}G, 24^{P}G, 20^{U}GS, 17^{F}G, 17^{4}S

	Starts	1st	2nd	3rd	Win & Pl
Hurdles	7	0	0	0	0
Chases	3	0	0	0	0
Career Total	**12**	**0**	**0**	**0**	**0**

Going: Sf: 0-2 GS: 0-1 Gd: 0-5 GF: - Fm: 0-2
Distance: 2m/2m3: 0-6 2m4-2m7: 0-2 3m+: 0-2
Track: LH: 0-1 RH: 0-8 Tight: 0-3 Gall: 0-0
Aids: Bl: 0-0 Vi: 0-0 Tstrap: 0-6
Best Rating: 60 3/02 Bang 2m1f soft Hdl

Classic Fairy (IRE)

76
10-y-o b m Executive Perk-Amy Fairy (The Parson)
J L Needham J L Needham

Placings:*0*/P0-UP **(0354)**
2001/02: 24^{U}GF, 17^{P}GS

	Starts	1st	2nd	3rd	Win & Pl
Chases	2	0	0	0	
Career Total	**5**	**0**	**0**	**0**	

Going: Sf: 0-0 GS: 0-1 Gd: 0-0 GF: - Fm: 0-1
Distance: 2m/2m3: 0-1 2m4-2m7: 0-0 3m+: 0-1
Track: LH: 0-2 RH: 0-0 Tight: 0-2 Gall: 0-0
Aids: Bl: 0-0 Vi: 0-0 Tstrap: 0-2
Best Rating: 76 4/01 Font 2m6f good Ch

Classic Jazz (NZ)

97 **104**
7-y-o br g Paris Opera (AUS)-Johnny Loves Jazz (NZ) (Virginia Privateer (USA))
N J Henderson Michael Buckley

Placings:1 **(0674)**
2001/02: 16^{1}GF

	Starts	1st	2nd	3rd	Win & Pl
Hurdles	1	1	0	0	2562
Career Total	**1**	**1**	**0**	**0**	**2562**

104 6/01 Worc 2m E Hdl GF £2562
Total win prize-money £2562

Going: Sf: 0-0 GS: 0-0 Gd: 0-0 GF: - Fm: 1-1
Distance: **2m/2m3: 1-1** 2m4-2m7: 0-0 3m+: 0-0
Track: **LH: 1-1** RH: 0-0 Tight: 0-0 Gall: 0-0
Aids: Bl: 0-0 Vi: 0-0 Tstrap: 0-0
Best Rating: 104 6/01 Worc 2m gd-fm Hdl

Classic Lash (IRE)

100 **93**
6-y-o b g Classic Cheer (IRE)-Khaiylasha (IRE) (Kahyasi)
P J Rothwell J McEvoy

Placings:000030216F0300 **(4083a)**
2001/02: 16^{0}GF, 16^{0}GY, 20^{0}G, 20^{0}G, 22^{3}G, 20^{0}GY, 22^{2}GF, 24^{1}F, 24^{6}G, 21^{F}G, 24^{0}Y, 20^{3}S, 20^{0}S, 18^{0}S

	Starts	1st	2nd	3rd	Win & Pl
Hurdles	14	1	1	2	6460
Career Total	**14**	**1**	**1**	**2**	**6460**

93 9/01 DRoy 3m (0-102)HHdl FRM £3895
Total win prize-money £3895

Going: Sf: 0-3 GS: 0-0 Gd: 0-5 GF: - Fm: 1-3
Distance: 2m/2m3: 0-3 2m4-2m7: 0-8 **3m+: 1-3**
Track: LH: 0-1 RH: 0-3 Tight: 0-0 Gall: 0-1
Aids: Bl: 0-1 Vi: 0-0 Tstrap: 0-0
Best Rating: 93 9/01 DRoy 3m firm Hdl

Classic Pal (USA)

88(95h) (72h)**73**
11-y-o b g Danzatore (CAN)-Welsh Garden (Welsh Saint)
M J M Evans M J M Evans

Placings:062/01P/P22F/32310P5P/536253/624P605-0 **(0053)**
2001/02: 17^{0}GS

	Starts	1st	2nd	3rd	Win & Pl
Chases	1	0	0	0	
Career Total	**32**	**2**	**6**	**4**	**9942**

87 6/97 Worc 2m F(0-105)HHdl GD £2197
90 5/95 Worc 2m E Hdl GD £2232
Total win prize-money £4431

Going: Sf: 0-0 GS: 0-1 Gd: 0-0 GF: - Fm: 0-0
Distance: 2m/2m3: 0-1 2m4-2m7: 0-0 3m+: 0-0
Track: LH: 0-1 RH: 0-0 Tight: 0-1 Gall: 0-0
Aids: Bl: 0-0 Vi: 0-0 Tstrap: 0-0
Best Rating: 96 4/95 Chep 2m110y firm Hdl

Classified (IRE)

111 **155**
6-y-o b g Roselier (FR)-Treidlia (Mandalus)
M C Pipe (John Joseph Murphy 13/10) D A Johnson

Placings:*0-11*111141 **(4653)**
2001/02: 20^{1}G, 16^{1}HY, 21^{1}G, 21^{1}G, 21^{1}S, 22^{1}S, 21^{4}GS, 20^{1}G

	Starts	1st	2nd	3rd	Win & Pl
NH Flat	2	2	0	0	7826
Hurdles	6	5	0	0	71920
Career Total	**9**	**7**	**0**	**0**	**79745**

155 4/02 Aint 2m4f A Hdl GD £29000
141 2/02 Sand 2m6f B Hdl SFT £7215
145 1/02 Wwck 2m5f A Hdl SFT £12000
144 12/01 Newb 2m5f A Hdl GD £16660
121 12/01 Plum 2m5f E Hdl GD £2544
124 12/01 Towc 2m H NHF HVY £2261
108 10/01 Gowr 2m4f NHF GD £5564
Total win prize-money £75246

Going: Sf: 3-3 GS: 0-1 Gd: 4-4 GF: - Fm: 0-0
Distance: 2m/2m3: 1-1 **2m4-2m7: 6-7** 3m+: 0-0
Track: **LH: 3-4** RH: 2-2 **Tight: 2-2** Gall: 1-2
Aids: Bl: 0-0 Vi: 0-0 Tstrap: 0-0
Best Rating: 155 4/02 Aint 2m4f good Hdl

Won a bumper at Gowran when trained in Ireland, and added a similar event at Towcester in December 2001 for Martin Pipe. Unbeaten in his first four races over hurdles, including valuable events at Newbury and Warwick, before finishing fourth when favourite for the Royal & SunAlliance Hurdle. Regained the winning thread at Aintree. He stays two miles five and acts on good and heavy. Should make a very useful novice chaser.

Claudius Tertius

100 **75+**
5-y-o b g Rudimentary (USA)-Sanctuary Cove (Habitat)
N B Mason (M E Sowersby 2/8) N B Mason

Placings:050000-0P1P00P **(4908)**
2001/02: 17^{0}GF, 17^{P}G, 21^{1}GF, 24^{P}G, 22^{0}GS, 22^{0}GF, 21^{P}G

	Starts	1st	2nd	3rd	Win & Pl
Hurdles	7	1	0	0	2216
Career Total	**13**	**1**	**0**	**0**	**2216**

67 8/01 Sedg 2m5f110y F(0-100)HHdl G-F £2215
Total win prize-money £2216

Going: Sf: 0-0 GS: 0-1 Gd: 0-3 GF: - Fm: 1-3
Distance: 2m/2m3: 0-2 **2m4-2m7: 1-4** 3m+: 0-1
Track: **LH: 1-3** RH: 0-4 **Tight: 1-6** Gall: 0-0
Aids: Bl: 0-1 Vi: 0-0 Tstrap: 0-2
Best Rating: 67 8/01 Sedg 2m5f110y gd-fm Hdl

Plating-class handicap hurdler. Goes well round Sedgefield. Stays two miles five. Acts on a sound surface.

Clavering (IRE)

79(83h) (76h)**70**
12-y-o br g Good Thyne (USA)-Caffra Mills (Pitpan)
E M Caine Mrs Karen Woodhead

Placings:*2*/P442P/**4FF/0363F4P**P00/02**P**/0-00**50P** **(2687)**
2001/02: 16^{0}G, 16^{0}G, 16^{5}G, 20^{0}GS, 19^{P}G

	Starts	1st	2nd	3rd	Win & Pl
Hurdles	2	0	0	0	0
Chases	3	0	0	0	0
Career Total	**28**	**0**	**3**	**2**	**3681**

Going: Sf: 0-0 GS: 0-1 Gd: 0-4 GF: - Fm: 0-0
Distance: 2m/2m3: 0-3 2m4-2m7: 0-2 3m+: 0-0
Track: LH: 0-5 RH: 0-0 Tight: 0-1 Gall: 0-2
Aids: Bl: 0-0 Vi: 0-0 Tstrap: 0-0
Best Rating: 96 12/98 Catt 2m good Ch

Not the most reliable jumper, his best run to date was a distant second to Auetaler in an Aintree novice hurdle in 1999. He is becoming expensive to follow.

Claymore (IRE)

106 **128**
6-y-o b g Broadsword (USA)-Mazza (Mazilier (USA))
O Sherwood B T Stewart-Brown

Placings:*010*F12P3 **(4890)**
2001/02: 17^{0}G, 18^{1}GS, 16^{0}G, 19^{F}GS, 18^{1}G, 22^{2}S, 20^{P}G, 24^{3}G

	Starts	1st	2nd	3rd	Win & Pl
NH Flat	3	1	0	0	1652
Hurdles	5	1	1	1	7289
Career Total	**8**	**2**	**1**	**1**	**8941**

115 1/02 Font 2m2f110y E Hdl GD £2730
111 11/01 Plum 2m2f H NHF G-S £1652
Total win prize-money £4382

Going: Sf: 0-1 GS: 1-2 Gd: 1-5 GF: - Fm: 0-0
Distance: **2m/2m3: 2-5** 2m4-2m7: 0-2 3m+: 0-1
Track: **LH: 1-4** RH: 0-3 **Tight: 1-2** Gall: 0-1
Aids: Bl: 0-0 Vi: 0-0 Tstrap: 0-0
Best Rating: 128 2/02 Winc 2m6f soft Hdl

Won a bumper in easy fashion on his second start and, falling on his hurdles bow, made amends next time in good style, before a good effort at Wincanton in February 2002 when second. Stays two and a quarter miles. Best on good to soft ground.

Clear Dawn (IRE)

90(104h) (95h)**110**
7-y-o b g Clearly Bust-Cobra Queen (Dawn Review)
J M Jefferson Mr & Mrs J M Davenport

Placings:P66/530331035-331 **(1719)**
2001/02: 20^{3}G, 25^{3}G, 23^{1}G

	Starts	1st	2nd	3rd	Win & Pl
Chases	3	1	0	2	4673
Career Total	**15**	**2**	**0**	**6**	**10069**

110	10/01	Weth	2m7f110y	E(0-105)HCh	GD	£3542
100	1/01	Muss	3m	F(0-105)HHdl	GD	£3721

Total win prize-money £7264

Going: Sf: 0-0 GS: 0-0 Gd: 1-3 GF: - Fm: 0-0
Distance: 2m/2m3: 0-0 2m4-2m7: 0-1 **3m+: 1-2**
Track: LH: 0-2 RH: 0-0 Tight: 0-1 Gall: 0-0
Aids: Bl: 0-0 Vi: 0-0 Tstrap: 0-0
Best Rating: 110 10/01 Weth 2m7f110y good Ch

Won once over hurdles but his future definitely lies over fences. Switched to the major obstacles in May 2001 and got off the mark at his third attempt over two miles seven. Will stay further. Acts on a sound surface.

Clear Skies (IRE)

103 **131**

9-y-o b g Phardante (FR)-Fighting Doleila (Humdoleila)
N A Gaselee Mrs R W S Baker

Placings:0/343/2535/**52-132** **(4516)**
2001/02: 16^{1}S, 16^{3}G, 16^{2}GS

	Starts	1st	2nd	3rd	Win & Pl
Chases	3	1	1	1	6344
Career Total	**13**	**1**	**3**	**4**	**12165**

120	2/02	Leic	2m	E Ch	SFT	£3419

Total win prize-money £3419

Going: Sf: 1-1 GS: 0-1 Gd: 0-1 GF: - Fm: 0-0
Distance: **2m/2m3: 1-3** 2m4-2m7: 0-0 3m+: 0-0
Track: LH: 0-0 **RH: 1-3** Tight: 0-0 Gall: 0-0
Aids: Bl: 0-0 Vi: 0-0 Tstrap: 0-0
Best Rating: 131 3/02 Sand 2m good Ch

A fair novice hurdler. Switched to fences in the winter of 2000 but missed the whole of 2001. Made a winning reappearance in February 2002. Acts on soft ground and is effective at two miles.

Clever Thyne (IRE)

100 **104**

5-y-o b g Good Thyne (USA)-Clever Milly (Precipice Wood)
H D Daly Mrs Geoffrey Churton

Placings:4555 **(4373)**
2001/02: 16^{4}S, 20^{5}S, 16^{5}GS, 21^{5}S

	Starts	1st	2nd	3rd	Win & Pl
NH Flat	1	0	0	0	0
Hurdles	3	0	0	0	0
Career Total	**4**	**0**	**0**	**0**	**0**

Going: Sf: 0-3 GS: 0-1 Gd: 0-0 GF: - Fm: 0-0
Distance: 2m/2m3: 0-2 2m4-2m7: 0-2 3m+: 0-0
Track: LH: 0-2 RH: 0-2 Tight: 0-0 Gall: 0-1
Aids: Bl: 0-0 Vi: 0-0 Tstrap: 0-1
Best Rating: 101 11/01 Hayd 2m soft NHF

Showed promise on his bumper debut over two miles but has looked in need of a test of stamina in novice hurdles at up to two and a half miles. Handles soft ground.

Clifton Mist

97 **85**

6-y-o gr m Lyphento (USA)-Brave Maiden (Three Legs)
H S Howe Richard Garrard

Placings:U5P5/R44-600445600 **(4881)**
2001/02: 16^{6}GS, 17^{0}GS, 17^{0}G, 19^{4}S, 21^{4}S, 24^{5}S, 21^{6}HY, 21^{0}G, 18^{0}GF

	Starts	1st	2nd	3rd	Win & Pl
Hurdles	9	0	0	0	535
Career Total	**16**	**0**	**0**	**0**	**954**

Going: Sf: 0-4 GS: 0-2 Gd: 0-2 GF: - Fm: 0-1
Distance: 2m/2m3: 0-4 2m4-2m7: 0-4 3m+: 0-1
Track: LH: 0-3 RH: 0-6 Tight: 0-4 Gall: 0-0
Aids: Bl: 0-0 Vi: 0-0 Tstrap: 0-0
Best Rating: 85 12/01 Extr 2m1f gd-sft Hdl

Clifton Set

97 **83**

11-y-o b g Northern State (USA)-Brave Maiden (Three Legs)
Noel T Chance Mrs Christine Fennell

Placings:422310551/1433656523/**12**/235/**153123153**/3455/6-0P **(0494)**
2001/02: 25^{0}GF, 25^{P}G

	Starts	1st	2nd	3rd	Win & Pl
Chases	2	0	0	0	
Career Total	**40**	**7**	**6**	**9**	**45089**

125	11/98	Kemp	3m	D(0-120)HCh	SFT	£4045
128	9/98	Worc	2m7f110y	C(0-130)HCh	GD	£7067
134	7/98	Wolv	3m1f	E(0-115)HCh	G-F	£3618
96	8/96	NAbb	3m2f110y	E Ch	GD	£2859
124	9/95	NAbb	3m3f	D(0-120)HHdl	GD	£2595
107	4/95	Hrfd	3m2f	F(0-100)HHdl	FRM	£2388
96	12/94	Kemp	2m5f	Hdl	SFT	£5280

Total win prize-money £27856

Going: Sf: 0-0 GS: 0-0 Gd: 0-1 GF: - Fm: 0-1
Distance: 2m/2m3: 0-0 2m4-2m7: 0-0 3m+: 0-2
Track: LH: 0-0 RH: 0-2 Tight: 0-0 Gall: 0-0
Aids: Bl: 0-2 Vi: 0-0 Tstrap: 0-0
Best Rating: 134 3/00 Chel 3m110y good Ch

Clingstone

91f **68f**

6-y-o b m Henbit (USA)-Linen Leaf (Bold Owl)
T R George Timothy N Chick

Placings:06 **(2480)**
2001/02: 17^{0}G, 17^{6}S

	Starts	1st	2nd	3rd	Win & Pl
NH Flat	2	0	0	0	
Career Total	**2**	**0**	**0**	**0**	

Going: Sf: 0-1 GS: 0-0 Gd: 0-1 GF: - Fm: 0-0
Distance: 2m/2m3: 0-2 2m4-2m7: 0-0 3m+: 0-0
Track: LH: 0-1 RH: 0-1 Tight: 0-1 Gall: 0-0
Aids: Bl: 0-0 Vi: 0-0 Tstrap: 0-0
Best Rating: 68 12/01 Hrfd 2m1f soft NHF

She looked to need a greater test of stamina after her two bumpers and has the scope to make her mark over obstacles.

Clodagh Valley (IRE)

7-y-o b g Doubletour (USA)-Raise A Princess (USA) (Raise A Native)
R J Bevis (R N Bevis 24/3) M Parry

Placings:0344/000000-P **(4846)**
2001/02: 24^{P}G

	Starts	1st	2nd	3rd	Win & Pl
Chases	1	0	0	0	
Career Total	**11**	**0**	**0**	**1**	**680**

Going: Sf: 0-0 GS: 0-0 Gd: 0-1 GF: - Fm: 0-0
Distance: 2m/2m3: 0-0 2m4-2m7: 0-0 3m+: 0-1
Track: LH: 0-1 RH: 0-0 Tight: 0-1 Gall: 0-0
Aids: Bl: 0-0 Vi: 0-0 Tstrap: 0-0
Best Rating: 89 3/00 Thur 2m soft NHF

Clodoald (FR)

109 **109**

5-y-o b g Beaudelaire (USA)-Mint Stick (FR) (Tropular)
M C Pipe (J Remy 22/5) Stef Stefanou

Placings:6/02F032255640132000-302300000P44 **(4847)**
2001/02: 17^{3}HY, 17^{0}GS, 17^{2}G, 16^{3}GF, 17^{0}G, 16^{0}G, 19^{0}GS, 19^{0}GS, 16^{0}S, 16^{P}GS, 16^{4}GF, 20^{4}G

	Starts	1st	2nd	3rd	Win & Pl
Hurdles	10	0	1	1	1923
Chases	2	0	0	1	3492
Career Total	**31**	**1**	**5**	**4**	**28382**

	12/00	Engh	2m1f	Ch	HVY	£6244

Total win prize-money £6244

Going: Sf: 0-2 GS: 0-4 Gd: 0-4 GF: - Fm: 0-2
Distance: 2m/2m3: 0-9 2m4-2m7: 0-3 3m+: 0-0
Track: LH: 0-7 RH: 0-3 Tight: 0-4 Gall: 0-1
Aids: Bl: 0-0 Vi: 0-0 Tstrap: 0-2
Best Rating: 101 8/01 Uttx 2m gd-fm Hdl

Fair form in novice hurdles, he had to drop to a two mile seller to get off the mark here at Uttoxeter in July. Followed up in similar company over two and a half miles at Worcester the following month.

Cloigeann Rua (IRE)

9-y-o ch m Glacial Storm (USA)-Cool Amanda (Prince Hansel)
E M Caine Mrs Karen Woodhead

Placings:000/PPPP-U **(1939)**
2001/02: 16^{U}G

	Starts	1st	2nd	3rd	Win & Pl
Hurdles	1	0	0	0	
Career Total	**8**	**0**	**0**	**0**	

Going: Sf: 0-0 GS: 0-0 Gd: 0-1 GF: - Fm: 0-0
Distance: 2m/2m3: 0-1 2m4-2m7: 0-0 3m+: 0-0
Track: LH: 0-1 RH: 0-0 Tight: 0-0 Gall: 0-0
Aids: Bl: 0-0 Vi: 0-0 Tstrap: 0-0
Best Rating: 60 12/99 Donc 2m110y gd-fm NHF

She is having terrible trouble completing over fences and hurdles.

Clonard Prince (IRE)

101 **112**

8-y-o ch g Over The River (FR)-First Field (IRE) (Forties Field (FR))
Miss Elizabeth Doyle Alec Scallan

Placings:*036*-44140 **(4233)**
2001/02: 20^{4}YS, 25^{4}Y, 20^{1}SH, 20^{4}S, 32^{0}GS

	Starts	1st	2nd	3rd	Win & Pl
Chases	5	1	0	0	6358
Career Total	**8**	**1**	**0**	**1**	**6638**

110 1/02 Tram 2m4f Ch SH £5079
Total win prize-money £5080

Going: Sf: 0-1 GS: 0-1 Gd: 0-0 GF: - Fm: 0-0
Distance: 2m/2m3: 0-0 **2m4-2m7: 1-3** 3m+: 0-2
Track: LH: 0-3 RH: 0-1 Tight: 0-0 Gall: 0-1
Aids: Bl: 0-0 Vi: 0-0 Tstrap: 0-0
Best Rating: 112 11/01 Navn 2m4f yld-sft Ch

Cloney Boy (IRE)

9-y-o b g Brush Aside (USA)-Fairy Island (Prince Hansel)
Michael Smith Michael Smith

Placings:*UOO*-OU **(0473)**
2001/02: 25°G, 20^{U}GF

	Starts	1st	2nd	3rd	Win & Pl
Chases	2	0	0	0	
Career Total	**5**	**0**	**0**	**0**	

Going: Sf: 0-0 GS: 0-0 Gd: 0-1 GF: - Fm: 0-1
Distance: 2m/2m3: 0-0 2m4-2m7: 0-1 3m+: 0-1
Track: LH: 0-2 RH: 0-0 Tight: 0-0 Gall: 0-0
Aids: Bl: 0-0 Vi: 0-0 Tstrap: 0-0
Best Rating:

Clonroche Vinyls (IRE)

102 101

7-y-o ch m Rashar (USA)-Clonroche Beggar (Pauper)
Ferdy Murphy Nicholas Butterly

Placings:*1*3024 **(4198)**
2001/02: 17^{1}HY, 21^{3}HY, 16^{0}S, 21^{2}S, 21^{4}S

	Starts	1st	2nd	3rd	Win & Pl
NH Flat	1	1	0	0	1589
Hurdles	4	0	1	1	1246
Career Total	**5**	**1**	**1**	**1**	**2835**

100 12/01 Folk 2m1f110y H NHF HVY £1589
Total win prize-money £1589

Going: Sf: 1-5 GS: 0-0 Gd: 0-0 GF: - Fm: 0-0
Distance: **2m/2m3: 1-2** 2m4-2m7: 0-3 3m+: 0-0
Track: LH: 0-2 RH: 0-2 **Tight: 1-3** Gall: 0-1
Aids: Bl: 0-0 Vi: 0-0 Tstrap: 0-0
Best Rating: 101 3/02 Towc 2m5f soft Hdl

Acts on a soft surface and stays two miles five furlongs.

Clonshire Paddy (IRE)

88 108d

6-y-o gr g Roselier (FR)-Gusserane Princess (Paddy's Stream)
C Grant Lord Daresbury & J E Greenall

Placings:*64/6*2503-F **(1575)**
2001/02: 25^{F}G

	Starts	1st	2nd	3rd	Win & Pl
Chases	1	0	0	0	

Career Total	**8**	**0**	**1**	**1**	**1335**

Going: Sf: 0-0 GS: 0-0 Gd: 0-1 GF: - Fm: 0-0
Distance: 2m/2m3: 0-0 2m4-2m7: 0-0 3m+: 0-1
Track: LH: 0-1 RH: 0-0 Tight: 0-1 Gall: 0-0
Aids: Bl: 0-0 Vi: 0-0 Tstrap: 0-0
Best Rating: 108 4/01 Hayd 2m6f soft Hdl

Cloth Of Gold

105 122

5-y-o b g Barathea (IRE)-Bustinetta (Bustino)
Lady Herries Mrs H A Cameron-Rose

Placings:461 **(4548)**
2001/02: 19^{4}G, 21^{6}G, 21^{1}GF

	Starts	1st	2nd	3rd	Win & Pl
Hurdles	3	1	0	0	2835
Career Total	**3**	**1**	**0**	**0**	**2835**

96 4/02 Hntg 2m5f110y E Hdl G-F £2835
Total win prize-money £2835

Going: Sf: 0-0 GS: 0-0 Gd: 0-2 GF: - Fm: 1-1
Distance: 2m/2m3: 0-1 **2m4-2m7: 1-2** 3m+: 0-0
Track: LH: 0-0 **RH: 1-3** Tight: 0-0 **Gall: 1-1**
Aids: Bl: 0-0 Vi: 0-0 Tstrap: 0-0
Best Rating: 122 2/02 Kemp 2m5f good Hdl

Cloudkicker (IRE)

94 93

9-y-o b g Dry Dock-Last Sprite (Tug Of War)
Miss Venetia Williams A J Roberts

Placings:*346P/5*2F **(3452)**
2001/02: 16^{5}G, 20^{2}S, 20^{F}HY

	Starts	1st	2nd	3rd	Win & Pl
Chases	3	0	1	0	960
Career Total	**7**	**0**	**1**	**1**	**1198**

Going: Sf: 0-2 GS: 0-0 Gd: 0-1 GF: - Fm: 0-0
Distance: 2m/2m3: 0-1 2m4-2m7: 0-2 3m+: 0-0
Track: LH: 0-2 RH: 0-1 Tight: 0-2 Gall: 0-0
Aids: Bl: 0-0 Vi: 0-0 Tstrap: 0-0
Best Rating: 100 12/99 Uttx 2m soft NHF

Lightly-raced maiden over jumps. Stays two and a half miles on the soft.

Cloudy Creek (IRE)

102 99

8-y-o gr g Roselier (FR)-Jacob's Creek (IRE) (Buckskin (FR))
Miss H C Knight Chamberlain Addiscott Silk Partnership

Placings:10 **(4502)**
2001/02: 21^{1}GS, 22^{0}G

	Starts	1st	2nd	3rd	Win & Pl
Hurdles	2	1	0	0	2489
Career Total	**2**	**1**	**0**	**0**	**2489**

99 3/02 Plum 2m5f E Hdl G-S £2488
Total win prize-money £2489

Going: Sf: 0-0 GS: 1-1 Gd: 0-1 GF: - Fm: 0-0
Distance: 2m/2m3: 0-0 **2m4-2m7: 1-2** 3m+: 0-0
Track: **LH: 1-2** RH: 0-0 **Tight: 1-2** Gall: 0-0
Aids: Bl: 0-0 Vi: 0-0 Tstrap: 0-0
Best Rating: 99 3/02 Plum 2m5f gd-sft Hdl

Former point winner, won his hurdle debut over two miles five on easy ground. Likes to race prominently.

Clownfish

98 92

8-y-o b g Silly Prices-Sea Sand (Sousa)
A R Dicken Mrs C Nisbet

Placings:*0PF5/4*3F-30P **(3283)**
2001/02: 22^{3}GS, 25^{0}G, 20^{P}S

	Starts	1st	2nd	3rd	Win & Pl
Chases	3	0	0	1	510
Career Total	**10**	**0**	**0**	**2**	**1359**

Going: Sf: 0-1 GS: 0-1 Gd: 0-1 GF: - Fm: 0-0
Distance: 2m/2m3: 0-0 2m4-2m7: 0-2 3m+: 0-1
Track: LH: 0-2 RH: 0-1 Tight: 0-2 Gall: 0-0
Aids: Bl: 0-0 Vi: 0-0 Tstrap: 0-0
Best Rating: 92 12/01 Kels 2m6f110y gd-sft Ch

Very moderate placed form over fences.

Co Optimist

84 80

5-y-o b g Homo Sapien-Tapua Taranata (IRE) (Mandalus)
N A Twiston-Davies The Co-Optimistic Partnership

Placings:*1*5064 **(4519)**
2001/02: 17^{1}G, 17^{5}S, 16^{0}S, 24^{6}G, 21^{4}GS

	Starts	1st	2nd	3rd	Win & Pl
NH Flat	3	1	0	0	1540
Hurdles	2	0	0	0	0
Career Total	**5**	**1**	**0**	**0**	**1540**

103 10/01 MRas 2m1f110y H NHF GD £1540
Total win prize-money £1540

Going: Sf: 0-2 GS: 0-1 Gd: 1-2 GF: - Fm: 0-0
Distance: **2m/2m3: 1-3** 2m4-2m7: 0-1 3m+: 0-1
Track: LH: 0-2 **RH: 1-3 Tight: 1-2** Gall: 0-1
Aids: Bl: 0-0 Vi: 0-0 Tstrap: 0-0
Best Rating: 103 10/01 MRas 2m1f110y good NHF

Runaway winner of a bumper at Market Rasen on his debut.

Coastguard (IRE)

113(98h) 117

8-y-o b g Satco (FR)-Godlike (Godswalk (USA))
C J Mann The Coastlyne Partnership

Placings:*526311P*-53UP214651 **(4399)**
2001/02: 20^{5}S, 24^{3}G, 24^{U}G, 22^{P}HY, 20^{2}G, 21^{1}S, 22^{4}S, 24^{6}GS, 24^{5}G, 22^{1}GS

	Starts	1st	2nd	3rd	Win & Pl
Hurdles	1	0	0	0	0
Chases	9	2	1	1	12500
Career Total	**17**	**4**	**2**	**2**	**18967**

117 3/02 Newb 2m6f110y D(0-120)HCh G-S £7247
111 12/01 Strf 2m5f110y F(0-110)HCh SFT £3549
97 3/01 Plum 2m5f F(0-90)Hdl HVY £2320
96 2/01 Folk 2m6f110y F(0-110)HHdl HVY £1985
Total win prize-money £15103

Going: Sf: 1-4 GS: 1-2 Gd: 0-4 GF: - Fm: 0-0
Distance: 2m/2m3: 0-0 **2m4-2m7: 2-6** 3m+: 0-4
Track: **LH: 2-5** RH: 0-4 Tight: 1-4 Gall: 1-3
Aids: **Bl: 2-10** Vi: 0-0 Tstrap: 0-0
Best Rating: 117 3/02 Newb 2m6f110y gd-sft Ch

Suited by two and half to three miles and soft ground. Fortunate winner at Stratford in December 2001, having been unlucky himself the time before, and scored again at Newbury in March 2002. Does not always jump that well.

Cobbet (CZE)

110 **127**

6-y-o b g Favoured Nations (IRE)-Creace (CZE) (Sirano (CZE))

T R George Timothy N Chick

Placings:101122344 **(4157)**

2001/02: 16^{1}GF, 16^{0}GF, 16^{1}GF, 16^{1}G, 16^{2}G, 16^{2}G, 16^{3}GS, 21^{4}G, 16^{4}GS

	Starts	1st	2nd	3rd	Win & Pl
Hurdles	9	3	2	1	13514
Career Total	**9**	**3**	**2**	**1**	**13514**

115	10/01	Winc	2m	F(0-110)HHdl	GD	£3250
104	10/01	Winc	2m	F(0-100)HHdl	G-F	£2485
100	5/01	Fknm	2m	G Hdl	G-F	£1596

Total win prize-money £7331

Going: Sf: 0-0 GS: 0-2 Gd: 1-4 GF: - Fm: 2-3
Distance: **2m/2m3: 3-8** 2m4-2m7: 0-1 3m+: 0-0
Track: LH: 1-2 **RH: 2-7 Tight: 1-1** Gall: 0-1
Aids: Bl: 0-0 Vi: 0-0 Tstrap: 0-0
Best Rating: 127 11/01 Chel 2m110y good Hdl

Ex-Polish-trained, he won a Fakenham seller on his debut. Stepped up on that to land two handicap hurdles at Wincanton in October 2001 and ran perhaps his best race to date when second behind Image De Marque II in a valuable handicap at Cheltenham the following month. Two miles is his trip and he is best on decent ground.

Coble

92 **67**

8-y-o b g Slip Anchor-Main Sail (Blakeney)

D McCain M F Foster

Placings:064P003/006146050/004/0330**R**-00 **(0500)**

2001/02: 16^{0}GF, 16^{0}GF

	Starts	1st	2nd	3rd	Win & Pl
Hurdles	2	0	0	0	
Career Total	**26**	**1**	**0**	**3**	**2821**

83	1/99	Ludl	2m	G(0-95)HHdl	SFT	£1710

Total win prize-money £1711

Going: Sf: 0-0 GS: 0-0 Gd: 0-0 GF: - Fm: 0-2
Distance: 2m/2m3: 0-2 2m4-2m7: 0-0 3m+: 0-0
Track: LH: 0-1 RH: 0-1 Tight: 0-0 Gall: 0-1
Aids: Bl: 0-2 Vi: 0-0 Tstrap: 0-2
Best Rating: 87 2/99 Bang 2m1f good Hdl

Coble Lane

109 **127**

10-y-o ch g Minster Son-Preziosa (Homing)

Ian Williams John Poynton & Jim Brewer

Placings:*2352*/0520/111P/**U**-02F1 **(0980)**

2001/02: 16^{0}GF, 20^{2}GF, 20^{F}GF, 21^{1}G

	Starts	1st	2nd	3rd	Win & Pl
Chases	4	1	1	0	4890
Career Total	**17**	**4**	**4**	**1**	**17406**

112	7/01	Strf	2m5f110y	E Ch	GD	£3705
117	6/99	MRas	2m3f110y	D Hdl	GD	£3140
111	5/99	MRas	2m3f110y	C(0-130)HHdl	G-F	£4432
107	5/99	Extr	2m1f	E(0-115)HHdl	FRM	£3078

Total win prize-money £14356

Going: Sf: 0-0 GS: 0-0 Gd: 1-1 GF: - Fm: 0-3
Distance: 2m/2m3: 0-1 **2m4-2m7: 1-3** 3m+: 0-0
Track: **LH: 1-1** RH: 0-2 **Tight: 1-2** Gall: 0-0
Aids: Bl: 0-0 Vi: 0-0 Tstrap: 0-0
Best Rating: 127 6/01 MRas 2m4f gd-fm Ch

Cock A Hoop

101 **91**

8-y-o b g Roscoe Blake-Rose Delight (Idiots Delight)

C J Mann Mrs M Richardson

Placings:PP/1-P **(3161)**

2001/02: 26^{P}S

	Starts	1st	2nd	3rd	Win & Pl
Hurdles	1	0	0	0	
Career Total	**4**	**1**	**0**	**0**	**2824**

92	6/00	Hrfd	3m2f	E Hdl	G-F	£2824

Total win prize-money £2824

Going: Sf: 0-1 GS: 0-0 Gd: 0-0 GF: - Fm: 0-0
Distance: 2m/2m3: 0-0 2m4-2m7: 0-0 3m+: 0-1
Track: LH: 0-0 RH: 0-1 Tight: 0-0 Gall: 0-0
Aids: Bl: 0-0 Vi: 0-0 Tstrap: 0-0
Best Rating: 92 6/00 Hrfd 3m2f gd-fm Hdl

Lightly raced hurdler, stays three miles and acts on fast ground.

Cocktail Cabinet (IRE)

96 **90**

7-y-o b g Supreme Leader-White Lady Club (Callernish)

Mrs D Haine Mrs Solna Thomson Jones

Placings:*3206*-6510B0 **(4577)**

2001/02: 23^{6}GF, 21^{5}G, 22^{1}G, 20^{0}GS, 24^{B}S, 24^{0}G

	Starts	1st	2nd	3rd	Win & Pl
Hurdles	6	1	0	0	2310
Career Total	**10**	**1**	**1**	**1**	**2952**

90	12/01	Font	2m6f110y	F(0-110)HHdl	GD	£2310

Total win prize-money £2310

Going: Sf: 0-1 GS: 0-1 Gd: 1-3 GF: - Fm: 0-1
Distance: 2m/2m3: 0-0 **2m4-2m7: 1-3** 3m+: 0-3
Track: **LH: 1-3** RH: 0-3 **Tight: 1-2** Gall: 0-1
Aids: Bl: 0-0 Vi: 0-0 Tstrap: 0-0
Best Rating: 103 1/01 Fknm 2m soft NHF

Got off the mark in a conditional jockeys' handicap hurdle at Fontwell in December, though the form amounts to little.

Coconut

71 **30**

6-y-o b g Shirley Heights-Magical Retreat (USA) (Sir Ivor)

W Clay M Braycotton

Placings:40 **(1624)**

2001/02: 17^{4}G, 16^{0}GF

	Starts	1st	2nd	3rd	Win & Pl
Hurdles	2	0	0	0	281
Career Total	**2**	**0**	**0**	**0**	**281**

Going: Sf: 0-0 GS: 0-0 Gd: 0-1 GF: - Fm: 0-1
Distance: 2m/2m3: 0-2 2m4-2m7: 0-0 3m+: 0-0
Track: LH: 0-1 RH: 0-1 Tight: 0-1 Gall: 0-0
Aids: Bl: 0-0 Vi: 0-0 Tstrap: 0-0
Best Rating: 30 10/01 Ludl 2m gd-fm Hdl

Coddington Girl

10-y-o br m Green Adventure (USA)-Emancipated (Mansingh (USA))

Miss H S Chapman E T Chapman

Placings:*0*/F **(0254)**

2001/02: 24^{F}GF

	Starts	1st	2nd	3rd	Win & Pl
Chases	1	0	0	0	
Career Total	**2**	**0**	**0**	**0**	

Going: Sf: 0-0 GS: 0-0 Gd: 0-0 GF: - Fm: 0-1
Distance: 2m/2m3: 0-0 2m4-2m7: 0-0 3m+: 0-1
Track: LH: 0-1 RH: 0-0 Tight: 0-1 Gall: 0-0
Aids: Bl: 0-0 Vi: 0-0 Tstrap: 0-0
Best Rating: 59 3/98 Ludl 2m good NHF

Cold Comfort

97 **74**

10-y-o b g Arctic Lord-Main Brand (Main Reef)

I R Brown I R Brown

Placings:U6 **(4724)**

2001/02: 19^{U}S, 16^{6}GF

	Starts	1st	2nd	3rd	Win & Pl
Hurdles	2	0	0	0	
Career Total	**2**	**0**	**0**	**0**	**0**

Going: Sf: 0-1 GS: 0-0 Gd: 0-0 GF: - Fm: 0-1
Distance: 2m/2m3: 0-1 2m4-2m7: 0-1 3m+: 0-0
Track: LH: 0-1 RH: 0-1 Tight: 0-0 Gall: 0-0
Aids: Bl: 0-0 Vi: 0-0 Tstrap: 0-0
Best Rating: 74 4/02 Chep 2m110y gd-fm Hdl

Cold Encounter (IRE)

110(91h) (88h)**120**

7-y-o ch g Polar Falcon (USA)-Scene Galante (FR) (Sicyos (USA))

R M Stronge Anthony Hibbard And Joe Baker

Placings:3222005P/**454**-122142 **(1255)**

2001/02: 24^{1}GF, 26^{2}GF, 22^{2}GF, 20^{1}GS, 25^{4}GF, 22^{2}GF

	Starts	1st	2nd	3rd	Win & Pl
Hurdles	1	0	1	0	733
Chases	5	2	2	0	9058
Career Total	**17**	**2**	**6**	**1**	**12464**

120	7/01	MRas	2m4f	E Ch	G-S	£3428
98	5/01	Hntg	3m	F(0-100)HCh	G-F	£2824

Total win prize-money £6254

Going: Sf: 0-0 GS: 1-1 Gd: 0-0 GF: - Fm: 1-5
Distance: 2m/2m3: 0-0 2m4-2m7: 1-3 3m+: 1-3
Track: LH: 0-0 **RH: 1-4** Tight: 0-3 **Gall: 1-2**
Aids: Bl: 0-0 Vi: 0-0 Tstrap: 0-0
Best Rating: 120 7/01 MRas 2m4f gd-sft Ch

Coleham

89f **94f**

4-y-o b f Saddlers' Hall (IRE)-Katie Scarlett (Lochnager)

W M Brisbourne John Pugh

Placings:*14* **(4377)**

2001/02: 16^{1}G, 16^{4}S

	Starts	1st	2nd	3rd	Win & Pl
NH Flat	2	1	0	0	2034
Career Total	**2**	**1**	**0**	**0**	**2034**

94	2/02	Ludl	2m	H NHF	GD	£2033

Total win prize-money £2034

Going: Sf: 0-1 GS: 0-0 Gd: 1-1 GF: - Fm: 0-0
Distance: **2m/2m3: 1-2** 2m4-2m7: 0-0 3m+: 0-0
Track: LH: 0-0 **RH: 1-2** Tight: 0-0 Gall: 0-0

Aids: Bl: 0-0 Vi: 0-0 Tstrap: 0-0
Best Rating: 94 3/02 Ludl 2m soft NHF

Ready winner on her bumper debut.

Colette (IRE)

96 101

5-y-o b m Nicolotte-Ascensiontide (Ela-Mana-Mou)
Simon T Lewis (R T Phillips 28/5) Simon T Lewis

Placings:2-34065F023000412 **(4772)**
2001/02: 16^{3}S, 17^{4}G, 17^{0}GF, 19^{6}G, 21^{5}G, 17^{F}S, 17^{0}G, 16^{2}S, 20^{3}S, 16^{0}HY, 16^{0}HY, 16^{0}S, 17^{4}S, 21^{1}G, 21^{2}G

	Starts	1st	2nd	3rd	Win & Pl
Hurdles	15	1	2	2	4127
Career Total	**16**	**1**	**3**	**2**	**4845**

82 3/02 Plum 2m5f G(0-90)HHdl GD £2107
Total win prize-money £2107

Going: Sf: 0-8 GS: 0-0 Gd: 1-6 GF: - Fm: 0-1
Distance: 2m/2m3: 0-10 **2m4-2m7: 1-5** 3m+: 0-0
Track: **LH: 1-5** RH: 0-10 **Tight: 1-6** Gall: 0-0
Aids: Bl: 0-0 Vi: 0-0 Tstrap: 0-0
Best Rating: 101 4/01 Plum 2m heavy Hdl

Modest hurdler, stayed two miles five furlongs. (DEAD)

Colin's Hope

75f

4-y-o b g Then Again-Bahawir Pour (USA) (Green Dancer (USA))
M W Easterby Steve Hull

Placings:*6* **(3257)**
2001/02: 16^{6}G

	Starts	1st	2nd	3rd	Win & Pl
NH Flat	1	0	0	0	0
Career Total	**1**	**0**	**0**	**0**	**0**

Going: Sf: 0-1 GS: 0-0 Gd: 0-0 GF: - Fm: 0-0
Distance: 2m/2m3: 0-1 2m4-2m7: 0-0 3m+: 0-0
Track: LH: 0-0 RH: 0-0 Tight: 0-0 Gall: 0-0
Aids: Bl: 0-0 Vi: 0-0 Tstrap: 0-0
Best Rating: 75 1/02 Newc 2m soft NHF

Collectivity

97 63

4-y-o b f Dr Devious (IRE)-Loch Quest (USA) (Lomond (USA))
J S Moore (B De Haan 3/8) Tidmarsh Racing Club

Placings:656P **(2594)**
2001/02: 17^{6}F, 16^{5}GS, 17^{6}GS, 17^{P}S

	Starts	1st	2nd	3rd	Win & Pl
Hurdles	4	0	0	0	0
Career Total	**4**	**0**	**0**	**0**	**0**

Going: Sf: 0-1 GS: 0-2 Gd: 0-0 GF: - Fm: 0-1
Distance: 2m/2m3: 0-4 2m4-2m7: 0-0 3m+: 0-0
Track: LH: 0-0 RH: 0-4 Tight: 0-3 Gall: 0-0
Aids: Bl: 0-0 Vi: 0-2 Tstrap: 0-0
Best Rating: 63 11/01 Leic 2m gd-sft Hdl

College Rock

71 41

5-y-o ch g Rock Hopper-Sea Aura (Roi Soleil)
R Brotherton Ms Gerardine P O'Reilly

Placings:0 **(2656)**
2001/02: 17^{0}GS

	Starts	1st	2nd	3rd	Win & Pl
Hurdles	1	0	0	0	
Career Total	**1**	**0**	**0**	**0**	

Going: Sf: 0-0 GS: 0-1 Gd: 0-0 GF: - Fm: 0-0
Distance: 2m/2m3: 0-1 2m4-2m7: 0-0 3m+: 0-0
Track: LH: 0-0 RH: 0-1 Tight: 0-1 Gall: 0-0
Aids: Bl: 0-0 Vi: 0-1 Tstrap: 0-0
Best Rating: 41 12/01 Tntn 2m1f gd-sft Hdl

College Superman

86 65

6-y-o ch g Infantry-Deviji (Mansingh (USA))
Miss H C Knight Lynn Partnership

Placings:*0-0* **(4597)**
2001/02: 19^{0}GF

	Starts	1st	2nd	3rd	Win & Pl
Hurdles	1	0	0	0	
Career Total	**2**	**0**	**0**	**0**	

Going: Sf: 0-0 GS: 0-0 Gd: 0-0 GF: - Fm: 0-1
Distance: 2m/2m3: 0-1 2m4-2m7: 0-0 3m+: 0-0
Track: LH: 0-1 RH: 0-0 Tight: 0-0 Gall: 0-0
Aids: Bl: 0-0 Vi: 0-0 Tstrap: 0-0
Best Rating: 65 4/02 Wwck 2m3f gd-fm Hdl

Collier Hill

99f 93f

4-y-o ch g Dr Devious (IRE)-Polar Queen (Polish Precedent (USA))
G A Swinbank R H Hall

Placings:*1* **(4098)**
2001/02: 16^{1}GS

	Starts	1st	2nd	3rd	Win & Pl
NH Flat	1	1	0	0	1722
Career Total	**1**	**1**	**0**	**0**	**1722**

93 3/02 Catt 2m H NHF G-S £1722
Total win prize-money £1722

Going: Sf: 0-0 GS: 1-1 Gd: 0-0 GF: - Fm: 0-0
Distance: **2m/2m3: 1-1** 2m4-2m7: 0-0 3m+: 0-0
Track: **LH: 1-1** RH: 0-0 **Tight: 1-1** Gall: 0-0
Aids: Bl: 0-0 Vi: 0-0 Tstrap: 0-0
Best Rating: 93 3/02 Catt 2m gd-sft NHF

Flat-bred who made a successful bow in bumper company at Catterick in March. Likely to try his hand on the Flat proper before he goes hurdling.

Colline De Feu

95 95

5-y-o b m Sabrehill (USA)-Band Of Fire (USA) (Chief's Crown (USA))
Mrs P Sly David L Bayliss

Placings:061064 **(4536)**
2001/02: 22^{0}S, 16^{6}GS, 20^{1}S, 21^{0}S, 20^{6}S, 16^{4}G

	Starts	1st	2nd	3rd	Win & Pl
Hurdles	6	1	0	0	3392
Career Total	**6**	**1**	**0**	**0**	**3392**

95 1/02 Fknm 2m4f D Hdl SFT £3391
Total win prize-money £3392

Going: Sf: 1-4 GS: 0-1 Gd: 0-1 GF: - Fm: 0-0
Distance: 2m/2m3: 0-2 **2m4-2m7: 1-4** 3m+: 0-0
Track: **LH: 1-4** RH: 0-2 **Tight: 1-3** Gall: 0-0
Aids: Bl: 0-0 Vi: 0-0 Tstrap: 0-0
Best Rating: 95 1/02 Fknm 2m4f soft Hdl

Won a weak Fakenham novices' hurdle in January 2002 on testing ground.

Colombe D'Or

104 73+

5-y-o gr g Petong-Deep Divide (Nashwan (USA))
M C Chapman Rasen Goes Racing

Placings:04-3063050 **(4906)**
2001/02: 16^{3}GS, 17^{0}G, 16^{6}G, 16^{3}G, 16^{0}G, 17^{5}G, 19^{0}G

	Starts	1st	2nd	3rd	Win & Pl
Hurdles	7	0	0	2	847
Career Total	**9**	**0**	**0**	**2**	**847**

Going: Sf: 0-0 GS: 0-1 Gd: 0-6 GF: - Fm: 0-0
Distance: 2m/2m3: 0-6 2m4-2m7: 0-1 3m+: 0-0
Track: LH: 0-4 RH: 0-3 Tight: 0-4 Gall: 0-2
Aids: Bl: 0-0 Vi: 0-0 Tstrap: 0-0
Best Rating: 79 11/01 Hntg 2m110y good Hdl

Little sign of ability over hurdles.

Colombian Green (IRE)

113 123

8-y-o b g Sadler's Wells (USA)-Sharaya (USA) (Youth (USA))
D R Gandolfo Starlight Racing

Placings:0/2F242-1346 **(4515)**
2001/02: 17^{1}S, 16^{3}G, 19^{4}G, 16^{6}GS

	Starts	1st	2nd	3rd	Win & Pl
Hurdles	4	1	0	1	4711
Career Total	**10**	**1**	**3**	**1**	**8182**

123 10/01 Hrfd 2m1f D(0-120)HHdl SFT £3311
Total win prize-money £3311

Going: Sf: 1-1 GS: 0-1 Gd: 0-2 GF: - Fm: 0-0
Distance: **2m/2m3: 1-4** 2m4-2m7: 0-0 3m+: 0-0
Track: LH: 0-1 **RH: 1-3** Tight: 0-0 Gall: 0-1
Aids: Bl: 0-0 Vi: 0-0 Tstrap: 0-0
Best Rating: 123 11/01 Asct 2m110y good Hdl

A winner over hurdles, he acts on soft ground and is suited by around two miles.

Colonel Blazer

100 99

10-y-o b g Jupiter Island-Glen Dancer (Furry Glen)
M W Easterby Miss S Fenwick

Placings:*103*/01P1/44141F/2436062/113450/46-4 **(0068)**
2001/02: 27^{4}G

	Starts	1st	2nd	3rd	Win & Pl
Chases	1	0	0	0	303
Career Total	**29**	**7**	**2**	**3**	**27808**

114	5/99	Towc	2m110y	D(0-125)HCh	G-F	£4027
116	5/99	Extr	2m1f	E(0-115)HCh	G-F	£4342
114	2/98	Leic	2m4f110y	E(0-115)HCh	GD	£3379
114	1/98	Wind	2m	E(0-100)HCh	G-S	£2823
83	4/97	Extr	2m2f	E Hdl	G-F	£2367
102	2/97	Tntn	2m3f110y	D Hdl	G-S	£2567
104	1/96	Kemp	2m	H NHF	GD	£1581

Total win prize-money £21089

Going: Sf: 0-0 GS: 0-0 Gd: 0-1 GF: - Fm: 0-0
Distance: 2m/2m3: 0-0 2m4-2m7: 0-0 3m+: 0-1
Track: LH: 0-1 RH: 0-0 Tight: 0-1 Gall: 0-0
Aids: Bl: 0-1 Vi: 0-0 Tstrap: 0-0

Best Rating: 116 5/99 Extr 2m1f gd-fm Ch

Colonel Braxton (IRE)

111 (151h)153

7-y-o b g Buckskin (FR)-Light The Lamp (Miners Lamp)

D T Hughes Mrs John Magnier

Placings:*162*/6111-B215 **(4232)**

2001/02: 18^{BY}, $24^{2}Y$, $20^{1}HY$, $24^{5}GS$

	Starts	1st	2nd	3rd	Win & Pl
Chases	4	1	1	0	22875
Career Total	**11**	**5**	**2**	**0**	**92481**

153	2/02	Naas	2m4f	Ch	HVY	£15153
151	4/01	Fair	2m4f	Hdl	SFT	£35000
151	2/01	Leop	2m2f	Hdl	HVY	£23588
139	1/01	Naas	2m3f	Hdl	SFT	£5564
125	12/99	Leop	2m	NHF	SH	£4620

Total win prize-money £83928

Going: Sf: 1-1 GS: 0-1 Gd: 0-0 GF: - Fm: 0-0
Distance: 2m/2m3: 0-1 **2m4-2m7: 1-1** 3m+: 0-2
Track: LH: 0-2 RH: 0-1 Tight: 0-0 Gall: 0-1
Aids: Bl: 0-0 Vi: 0-0 Tstrap: 0-0
Best Rating: 153 2/02 Naas 2m4f heavy Ch

A decent hurdler, he switched to fences in December 2001, but was brought down on his debut. Gained compensation two outings later when winning over two and a half miles on unsuitably heavy ground at Naas, but was never a threat in the Royal & SunAlliance Chase at the 2002 Festival.. Acts on a sound surface but handles soft/heavy ground.

Colonel Brown (IRE)

(77h) (96h)109

6-y-o b g Scenic-Musical Smoke (IRE) (Orchestra)

O O'Neill (C F Swan 17/7) R S Lanchbury

Placings:*0*/*0*006000-5201P4 **(1666)**

2001/02: $16^{5}GF$, $16^{2}GY$, $16^{0}GF$, $17^{1}F$, $20^{P}GF$, $16^{4}G$

	Starts	1st	2nd	3rd	Win & Pl
Hurdles	4	0	1	0	903
Chases	2	1	0	0	5266
Career Total	**14**	**1**	**1**	**0**	**6170**

109	7/01	Dund	2m1f	Ch	FRM	£5008

Total win prize-money £5008

Going: Sf: 0-0 GS: 0-0 Gd: 0-1 GF: - Fm: 1-4
Distance: **2m/2m3: 1-5** 2m4-2m7: 0-1 3m+: 0-0
Track: LH: 0-1 RH: 0-1 Tight: 0-1 Gall: 0-1
Aids: Bl: 0-1 Vi: 0-0 **Tstrap: 1-4**
Best Rating: 109 7/01 Dund 2m1f firm Ch

Colonel Ching (IRE)

8-y-o b g Mazaad-Jamie's Lady (Ashmore (FR))

C J Mann Mr D Allport & Mr R B Michaelson

Placings:P **(2696)**

2001/02: $20^{P}S$

	Starts	1st	2nd	3rd	Win & Pl
Hurdles	1	0	0	0	
Career Total	**1**	**0**	**0**	**0**	

Going: Sf: 0-1 GS: 0-0 Gd: 0-0 GF: - Fm: 0-0
Distance: 2m/2m3: 0-0 2m4-2m7: 0-1 3m+: 0-0
Track: LH: 0-1 RH: 0-0 Tight: 0-0 Gall: 0-0
Aids: Bl: 0-0 Vi: 0-0 Tstrap: 0-0
Best Rating:

Colonel Colt

83 53

11-y-o b g Saint Andrews (FR)-Vallee Des Sauges (USA) (Secretariat (USA))

R J Price Pete Holder

Placings:05P/4243/PP3/2/F222/44456P/32405-0P0S **(1625)**

2001/02: $23^{0}GF$, $24^{P}G$, $19^{0}G$, $24^{S}GF$

	Starts	1st	2nd	3rd	Win & Pl
Chases	4	0	0	0	
Career Total	**30**	**0**	**6**	**3**	**7312**

Going: Sf: 0-0 GS: 0-0 Gd: 0-2 GF: - Fm: 0-2
Distance: 2m/2m3: 0-1 2m4-2m7: 0-0 3m+: 0-3
Track: LH: 0-2 RH: 0-2 Tight: 0-2 Gall: 0-0
Aids: Bl: 0-0 Vi: 0-0 Tstrap: 0-0
Best Rating: 91 3/99 Font 3m2f110y gd-fm Ch

Colonel Conca

78 47

7-y-o ch g Milieu-Lorna's Choice (Oats)

G F White F V White

Placings:*00*/60P-0 **(0327)**

2001/02: $20^{0}GS$

	Starts	1st	2nd	3rd	Win & Pl
Hurdles	1	0	0	0	
Career Total	**6**	**0**	**0**	**0**	**0**

Going: Sf: 0-0 GS: 0-1 Gd: 0-0 GF: - Fm: 0-0
Distance: 2m/2m3: 0-0 2m4-2m7: 0-1 3m+: 0-0
Track: LH: 0-0 RH: 0-1 Tight: 0-0 Gall: 0-0
Aids: Bl: 0-0 Vi: 0-0 Tstrap: 0-0
Best Rating: 85 11/99 Hexm 2m good NHF

Colonel Crump (IRE)

10-y-o b g Satco (FR)-Bajan Princess (Head For Heights)

Mrs M B Stephens Mrs M B Stephens

Placings:*0*/000/0/P **(0325)**

2001/02: $21^{P}G$

	Starts	1st	2nd	3rd	Win & Pl
Chases	1	0	0	0	
Career Total	**6**	**0**	**0**	**0**	

Going: Sf: 0-0 GS: 0-0 Gd: 0-1 GF: - Fm: 0-0
Distance: 2m/2m3: 0-0 2m4-2m7: 0-1 3m+: 0-0
Track: LH: 0-0 RH: 0-1 Tight: 0-1 Gall: 0-0
Aids: Bl: 0-0 Vi: 0-0 Tstrap: 0-0
Best Rating: 72 8/97 Rosc 2m good NHF

Colonel Custer

7-y-o ch g Komaite (USA)-Mohican (Great Nephew)

R Brotherton Binding Matters Ltd

Placings:P **(2418)**

2001/02: $16^{P}HY$

	Starts	1st	2nd	3rd	Win & Pl
Hurdles	1	0	0	0	
Career Total	**1**	**0**	**0**	**0**	

Going: Sf: 0-1 GS: 0-0 Gd: 0-0 GF: - Fm: 0-0
Distance: 2m/2m3: 0-1 2m4-2m7: 0-0 3m+: 0-0
Track: LH: 0-1 RH: 0-0 Tight: 0-0 Gall: 0-0
Aids: Bl: 0-0 Vi: 0-0 Tstrap: 0-0
Best Rating:

Colonel Frank

91f 93f

5-y-o b g Toulon-Fit For Firing (FR) (In Fijar (USA))

B G Powell The Hambledon Hunters

Placings:*0* **(3883)**

2001/02: $16^{0}GS$

	Starts	1st	2nd	3rd	Win & Pl
NH Flat	1	0	0	0	
Career Total	**1**	**0**	**0**	**0**	

Going: Sf: 0-0 GS: 0-1 Gd: 0-0 GF: - Fm: 0-0
Distance: 2m/2m3: 0-1 2m4-2m7: 0-0 3m+: 0-0
Track: LH: 0-0 RH: 0-1 Tight: 0-0 Gall: 0-0
Aids: Bl: 0-0 Vi: 0-0 Tstrap: 0-0
Best Rating: 93 2/02 Winc 2m gd-sft NHF

Colonel No (IRE)

75f 70f

5-y-o b g Supreme Leader-No Not (Ovac (ITY))

H D Daly J A Wales

Placings:*0-0* **(0377)**

2001/02: $16^{0}GF$

	Starts	1st	2nd	3rd	Win & Pl
NH Flat	1	0	0	0	
Career Total	**2**	**0**	**0**	**0**	

Going: Sf: 0-0 GS: 0-0 Gd: 0-0 GF: - Fm: 0-1
Distance: 2m/2m3: 0-1 2m4-2m7: 0-0 3m+: 0-0
Track: LH: 0-0 RH: 0-1 Tight: 0-0 Gall: 0-1
Aids: Bl: 0-0 Vi: 0-0 Tstrap: 0-0
Best Rating: 70 4/01 Winc 2m soft NHF

Colonial Rule (USA)

95 94

5-y-o b g Pleasant Colony (USA)-Musicale (USA) (The Minstrel (CAN))

J J O'Neill A K Collins

Placings:022F1P-P **(2001)**

2001/02: $20^{P}S$

	Starts	1st	2nd	3rd	Win & Pl
Hurdles	1	0	0	0	
Career Total	**7**	**1**	**2**	**0**	**2724**

93	2/01	Catt	2m3f	G(0-90)HHdl	SFT	£1708

Total win prize-money £1708

Going: Sf: 0-1 GS: 0-0 Gd: 0-0 GF: - Fm: 0-0
Distance: 2m/2m3: 0-0 2m4-2m7: 0-1 3m+: 0-0
Track: LH: 0-1 RH: 0-0 Tight: 0-0 Gall: 0-0
Aids: Bl: 0-0 Vi: 0-0 Tstrap: 0-1
Best Rating: 93 2/01 Catt 2m3f soft Hdl

Colonial Sunrise (USA)

97 96

5-y-o b g Pleasant Colony (USA)-Dancing Reef (USA) (Danzig (USA))

T D Easterby Elite Racing Club

Placings:*342*-434 **(4431)**

2001/02: 17^{4}GS, 16^{3}HY, 16^{4}HY

	Starts	1st	2nd	3rd	Win & Pl
Hurdles	3	0	0	1	547
Career Total	**6**	**0**	**1**	**2**	**1324**

Going: Sf: 0-2 GS: 0-1 Gd: 0-0 GF: - Fm: 0-0
Distance: 2m/2m3: 0-3 2m4-2m7: 0-0 3m+: 0-0
Track: LH: 0-2 RH: 0-1 Tight: 0-1 Gall: 0-1
Aids: Bl: 0-0 Vi: 0-0 Tstrap: 0-0
Best Rating: 96 3/02 MRas 2m1f110y gd-sft Hdl

Colorado Son

5-y-o ch g Minster Son-Colorado Insight (Green Ruby (USA))
Miss M E Rowland Paul Mayo

Placings:0-P **(1748)**
2001/02: 19^{P}G

	Starts	1st	2nd	3rd	Win & Pl
Hurdles	1	0	0	0	
Career Total	**2**	**0**	**0**	**0**	

Going: Sf: 0-0 GS: 0-0 Gd: 0-1 GF: - Fm: 0-0
Distance: 2m/2m3: 0-0 2m4-2m7: 0-1 3m+: 0-0
Track: LH: 0-0 RH: 0-1 Tight: 0-1 Gall: 0-0
Aids: Bl: 0-0 Vi: 0-0 Tstrap: 0-0
Best Rating: 11 3/01 MRas 2m1f110y gd-sft Hdl

Colourful Life (IRE)

117(106c) (132c)**116**

6-y-o ch g Rainbows For Life (CAN)-Rasmara (Kalaglow)
Mrs M Reveley (A Crook 9/5) Andy Peake & David Jackson

Placings:4225-1**U1F14F**114 **(4418)**
2001/02: 20^{1}G, 23^{U}G, 20^{1}G, 16^{F}G, 16^{1}HY, 16^{4}G, 20^{F}S, 16^{1}S, 16^{1}GS, 16^{4}GS

	Starts	1st	2nd	3rd	Win & Pl
Hurdles	4	3	0	0	24525
Chases	6	2	0	0	10785
Career Total	**14**	**5**	**2**	**0**	**37054**

116	2/02	Kemp	2m	C(0-135)HHdl	G-S	£10920
111	2/02	Newc	2m	B HHdl	SFT	£8489
130	11/01	Uttx	2m	D Ch	HVY	£4944
132	11/01	Weth	2m4f110y	D(0-115)HCh	GD	£5372
96	5/01	Weth	2m4f110y	D Hdl	GD	£4011

Total win prize-money £33736

Going: Sf: 2-3 GS: 1-2 Gd: 2-5 GF: - Fm: 0-0
Distance: **2m/2m3: 3-6** 2m4-2m7: 2-3 3m+: 0-1
Track: **LH: 4-8** RH: 1-1 Tight: 0-0 **Gall: 1-4**
Aids: Bl: 0-0 Vi: 0-0 Tstrap: 0-0
Best Rating: 132 11/01 Weth 2m4f110y good Ch

He won over hurdles before embarking on a chasing career in the autumn of 2001 and won twice from six starts over fences, but he also failed to complete three times and has been a revelation since returning to hurdles. After winning a valuable novice handicap at Newcastle, he followed up under a penalty in a decent handicap at Kempton. He has won over two miles, but looks ideally suited by further. Has won on good ground and heavy.

Columba (IRE)

97 **125**

6-y-o b g Lord Americo-Jackson Miss (Condorcet (FR))
D T Hughes Thomas Winters

Placings:42F2F1333U **(4188)**
2001/02: 16^{4}G, 16^{2}GY, 16^{F}GF, 16^{2}G, 20^{F}S, 16^{1}Y, 20^{3}S, 16^{3}SH, 20^{3}HY, 16^{U}GS

	Starts	1st	2nd	3rd	Win & Pl
NH Flat	1	0	0	0	1210
Hurdles	9	1	2	3	12436
Career Total	**10**	**1**	**2**	**3**	**13646**

125	12/01	Fair	2m	Hdl	YLD	£5564

Total win prize-money £5565

Going: Sf: 0-3 GS: 0-1 Gd: 0-2 GF: - Fm: 0-1
Distance: **2m/2m3: 1-7** 2m4-2m7: 0-3 3m+: 0-0
Track: LH: 0-2 **RH: 1-4** Tight: 0-0 Gall: 0-0
Aids: Bl: 0-0 Vi: 0-0 Tstrap: 0-0
Best Rating: 125 12/01 Fair 2m yield Hdl

Fair Irish hurdler. Acts on any ground.

Colvada

88

6-y-o b m North Col-Prevada (Soldier Rose)
A King The Virtual Partnership

Placings:FPP **(4385)**
2001/02: 19^{F}S, 20^{P}S, 22^{P}S

	Starts	1st	2nd	3rd	Win & Pl
Hurdles	3	0	0	0	
Career Total	**3**	**0**	**0**	**0**	

Going: Sf: 0-3 GS: 0-0 Gd: 0-0 GF: - Fm: 0-0
Distance: 2m/2m3: 0-0 2m4-2m7: 0-3 3m+: 0-0
Track: LH: 0-0 RH: 0-3 Tight: 0-0 Gall: 0-0
Aids: Bl: 0-0 Vi: 0-0 Tstrap: 0-0
Best Rating: 88 1/02 Hrfd 2m3f110y soft Hdl

Comandante (FR)

97 **99**

4-y-o ch g Apple Tree (FR)-Sea Ring (FR) (Bering)
G Macaire Mrs F Montauban

Placings:5-001P5 **(3377)**
2001/02: 17^{0}S, 16^{0}, 16^{1}GS, 17^{P}HY, 16^{5}GS

	Starts	1st	2nd	3rd	Win & Pl
Hurdles	5	1	0	0	3591
Career Total	**6**	**1**	**0**	**0**	**4803**

99	10/01	Kemp	2m	D Hdl	G-S	£3591

Total win prize-money £3591

Going: Sf: 0-2 GS: 1-2 Gd: 0-0 GF: - Fm: 0-0
Distance: **2m/2m3: 1-5** 2m4-2m7: 0-0 3m+: 0-0
Track: LH: 0-0 **RH: 1-2** Tight: 0-0 Gall: 0-0
Aids: Bl: 0-0 Vi: 0-0 Tstrap: 0-0
Best Rating: 99 10/01 Kemp 2m gd-sft Hdl

Ordinary form in France, but landed a moderate juvenile hurdle at Kempton in October over two miles on a sound surface.

Combe Castle

7-y-o gr g Carlingford Castle-Silver Cirrus (General Ironside)
J C McConnochie The Norfolk Neighbours

Placings:*0*-0UPP **(4906)**
2001/02: 20^{0}GS, 20^{U}GS, 21^{P}GS, 19^{P}G

	Starts	1st	2nd	3rd	Win & Pl
Hurdles	4	0	0	0	
Career Total	**5**	**0**	**0**	**0**	

Going: Sf: 0-0 GS: 0-3 Gd: 0-1 GF: - Fm: 0-0
Distance: 2m/2m3: 0-0 2m4-2m7: 0-4 3m+: 0-0
Track: LH: 0-1 RH: 0-3 Tight: 0-2 Gall: 0-0
Aids: Bl: 0-0 Vi: 0-0 Tstrap: 0-0
Best Rating: 25 2/01 Weth 2m soft NHF

Combined Venture (IRE)

6-y-o b h Dolphin Street (FR)-Centinela (Caerleon (USA))
J A Pickering (K A Morgan 23/6) Mrs Joanne Woods

Placings:F002U-P **(1747)**
2001/02: 17^{P}G

	Starts	1st	2nd	3rd	Win & Pl
Hurdles	1	0	0	0	
Career Total	**6**	**0**	**1**	**0**	**446**

Going: Sf: 0-0 GS: 0-0 Gd: 0-1 GF: - Fm: 0-0
Distance: 2m/2m3: 0-1 2m4-2m7: 0-0 3m+: 0-0
Track: LH: 0-0 RH: 0-1 Tight: 0-1 Gall: 0-0
Aids: Bl: 0-0 Vi: 0-0 Tstrap: 0-1
Best Rating: 70 3/01 MRas 2m1f110y good Hdl

Come Home Sober (IRE)

71 **65**

10-y-o b g Be My Native (USA)-Siliferous (Sandy Creek)
Miss A M Newton-Smith Mrs Christine Davies

Placings.0/P-P3F **(1827)**
2001/02: 24^{P}GF, 24^{3}G, 24^{F}G

	Starts	1st	2nd	3rd	Win & Pl
Chases	3	0	0	1	518
Career Total	**5**	**0**	**0**	**1**	**518**

Going: Sf: 0-0 GS: 0-0 Gd: 0-2 GF: - Fm: 0-1
Distance: 2m/2m3: 0-0 2m4-2m7: 0-0 3m+: 0-3
Track: LH: 0-1 RH: 0-2 Tight: 0-1 Gall: 0-2
Aids: Bl: 0-1 Vi: 0-1 Tstrap: 0-0
Best Rating: 74 11/98 Wind 2m4f good Hdl

Come On Penny

79 **69**

11-y-o b m Rakaposhi King-Gokatiego (Huntercombe)
C L Popham Miss S Rudge

Placings:*01024*/031/2F024P5265/F56**123UP62/2533 3P**40402/**F0522033-50U5P** **(1138)**
2001/02: 16^{5}G, 16^{0}GS, 16^{U}GF, 16^{5}G, 24^{P}G

	Starts	1st	2nd	3rd	Win & Pl
Chases	5	0	0	0	0
Career Total	**52**	**3**	**10**	**7**	**19798**

103	10/98	Extr	2m1f	E(0-105)HCh	GD	£3790
80	9/96	Worc	2m	E Hdl	G-F	£2460
99	12/95	Ludl	2m	H NHF	G-F	£1318

Total win prize-money £7569

Going: Sf: 0-0 GS: 0-1 Gd: 0-3 GF: - Fm: 0-1
Distance: 2m/2m3: 0-4 2m4-2m7: 0-0 3m+: 0-1
Track: LH: 0-5 RH: 0-0 Tight: 0-5 Gall: 0-0
Aids: Bl: 0-0 Vi: 0-0 Tstrap: 0-0
Best Rating: 103 5/99 Towc 2m110y gd-fm Ch

Come The Dawn

88f **92f**

6-y-o b m Gunner B-Herald The Dawn (Dubassoff (USA))

Mrs H Dalton The Dawn Raiders

Placings:*46* **(2757)**
2001/02: 17^{4}G, 17^{6}GS

	Starts	1st	2nd	3rd	Win & Pl
NH Flat	2	0	0	0	0
Career Total	**2**	**0**	**0**	**0**	**0**

Going: Sf: 0-0 GS: 0-1 Gd: 0-1 GF: - Fm: 0-0
Distance: 2m/2m3: 0-2 2m4-2m7: 0-0 3m+: 0-0
Track: LH: 0-1 RH: 0-1 Tight: 0-1 Gall: 0-0
Aids: Bl: 0-0 Vi: 0-0 Tstrap: 0-0
Best Rating: 92 11/01 Hrfd 2m1f good NHF

Comedy Gayle

15-y-o b g Lir-Follifoot's Folly (Comedy Star (USA))
Miss D Cole Ms Sue Willcock

Placings:600/**P13/3U2P/21PP/P15P012** **(1151)**
2001/02: 25^{P}G, 22^{1}GF, 23^{5}GF, 21^{P}GF, 23^{0}G, 21^{1}G, 21^{2}GF

	Starts	1st	2nd	3rd	Win & Pl
Chases	7	2	1	0	7656
Career Total	**21**	**4**	**3**	**2**	**14620**

115	8/01	NAbb	2m5f110y	F(0-90)Ch	GD	£2926
115	5/01	Font	2m6f	E(0-115)HCh	G-F	£3500
115	5/99	Strf	3m	H Ch	GD	£3668
115	3/98	NAbb	2m5f110y	H Ch	SFT	£1004

Total win prize-money £11099

Going: Sf: 0-0 GS: 0-0 Gd: 1-3 GF: - Fm: 1-4
Distance: 2m/2m3: 0-0 **2m4-2m7: 2-4** 3m+: 0-3
Track: **LH: 1-5** RH: 0-1 **Tight: 2-4** Gall: 0-0
Aids: Bl: 0-0 Vi: 0-0 Tstrap: 0-0
Best Rating: 115 8/01 NAbb 2m5f110y gd-fm Ch

Modest handicap chase winner. Effective on good to firm ground at around two and a half miles. Has won over three miles but not since 1999.

Comeragh Gale (IRE)

99 **100**
9-y-o br g Strong Gale-Comeragh Princess (Le Moss)
V R A Dartnall Nick Viney

Placings:020-40P6 **(4484)**
2001/02: 22^{4}GS, 22^{0}G, 26^{P}G, 17^{6}G

	Starts	1st	2nd	3rd	Win & Pl
Hurdles	4	0	0	0	0
Career Total	**7**	**0**	**1**	**0**	**712**

Going: Sf: 0-0 GS: 0-1 Gd: 0-3 GF: - Fm: 0-0
Distance: 2m/2m3: 0-1 2m4-2m7: 0-2 3m+: 0-1
Track: LH: 0-1 RH: 0-3 Tight: 0-1 Gall: 0-0
Aids: Bl: 0-1 Vi: 0-0 Tstrap: 0-0
Best Rating: 89 6/00 NAbb 2m1f good Hdl

A point-to-point winner. Wore blinkers when winning 22 furlong Amateur Riders' Novices' Hurdle at Exeter on good ground May 2002.

Comex Flyer (IRE)

113 **135**
5-y-o ch g Prince Of Birds (USA)-Smashing Pet (Mummy's Pet)
P F Nicholls Neil Smith

Placings:F-1243111120 **(2031)**
2001/02: 16^{1}GF, 16^{2}GF, 16^{4}GF, 16^{3}GF, 16^{1}GF, 18^{1}GF, 18^{1}GF, 18^{1}S, 16^{2}G, 20^{0}GS

	Starts	1st	2nd	3rd	Win & Pl
Hurdles	10	5	2	1	27518
Career Total	**11**	**5**	**2**	**1**	**27518**

135	10/01	Font	2m2f110y	B HHdl	SFT	£12342
115	9/01	Font	2m2f110y	E Hdl	G-F	£3150
120	8/01	Font	2m2f110y	E(0-115)HHdl	G-F	£2397
120	8/01	Worc	2m	E Hdl	G-F	£2954
112	5/01	Sthl	2m	E Hdl	G-F	£2527

Total win prize-money £23371

Going: Sf: 1-1 GS: 0-1 Gd: 0-1 GF: - Fm: 4-7
Distance: **2m/2m3: 5-9** 2m4-2m7: 0-1 3m+: 0-0
Track: **LH: 5-9** RH: 0-1 **Tight: 4-6** Gall: 0-0
Aids: Bl: 0-0 Vi: 0-0 Tstrap: 0-0
Best Rating: 135 10/01 Font 2m2f110y soft Hdl

He has taken well to jumping, winning four times over hurdles, including a Class B handicap at Fontwell in October, but came off second-best to Benbyas at Wetherby in November. He has won on soft ground, but most of his wins have come on a firm surface over an extended two miles two furlongs..

Coming Through (IRE)

92 **78**
10-y-o ch g Le Bavard (FR)-Gay Countess (Master Buck)
T Wall D Pugh

Placings:PPPP **(4547)**
2001/02: 20^{P}GF, 20^{P}S, 24^{P}GS, 20^{P}GF

	Starts	1st	2nd	3rd	Win & Pl
Chases	4	0	0	0	
Career Total	**4**	**0**	**0**	**0**	

Going: Sf: 0-1 GS: 0-1 Gd: 0-0 GF: - Fm: 0-2
Distance: 2m/2m3: 0-0 2m4-2m7: 0-3 3m+: 0-1
Track: LH: 0-1 RH: 0-3 Tight: 0-3 Gall: 0-1
Aids: Bl: 0-0 Vi: 0-1 Tstrap: 0-0
Best Rating:

Commanche Bow (IRE)

83 **70**
8-y-o b g Commanche Run-Gale Belle (Strong Gale)
Ian Williams N Jinks & G Edmunds

Placings:*0/00*0PP/**F-PP0F0** **(1241)**
2001/02: 20^{P}G, 23^{P}G, 16^{0}GF, 20^{F}G, 20^{0}GF

	Starts	1st	2nd	3rd	Win & Pl
Chases	5	0	0	0	
Career Total	**12**	**0**	**0**	**0**	

Going: Sf: 0-0 GS: 0-0 Gd: 0-3 GF: - Fm: 0-2
Distance: 2m/2m3: 0-1 2m4-2m7: 0-3 3m+: 0-1
Track: LH: 0-4 RH: 0-1 Tight: 0-3 Gall: 0-0
Aids: Bl: 0-0 Vi: 0-0 Tstrap: 0-0
Best Rating: 79 4/99 Towc 2m good NHF

Commanche Court (IRE)

120(102h) (140h)**184**
9-y-o ch h Commanche Run-Sorceress (FR) (Fabulous Dancer (USA))
T M Walsh D F Desmond

Placings:111/21064/121134/**332B1/1342P-5530242P** **(4705a)**
2001/02: 29^{5}G, 20^{5}Y, 24^{3}YS, 26^{0}S, 20^{2}SH, 16^{4}HY, 26^{2}G, 29^{P}GY

	Starts	1st	2nd	3rd	Win & Pl
Hurdles	2	0	1	0	2564
Chases	6	0	1	1	72185
Career Total	**32**	**9**	**6**	**5**	**339613**

162	5/00	Punc	3m1f	Ch	GD	£59520
174	4/00	Fair	3m5f	HCh	G-Y	£62680
147	12/98	Leop	3m	Hdl	SH	£8445
156	12/98	Navn	2m4f	Hdl	HVY	£14076
153	10/98	Navn	2m4f	Hdl	HVY	£9853
150	12/97	Leop	2m	HHdl	HVY	£6782
133	3/97	Chel	2m1f	A Hdl	GD	£44289
128	2/97	Punc	2m	Hdl	SFT	£6782
128	2/97	Leop	2m	Hdl	G-Y	£6782

Total win prize-money £219211

Going: Sf: 0-2 GS: 0-0 Gd: 0-2 GF: - Fm: 0-0
Distance: 2m/2m3: 0-1 2m4-2m7: 0-2 3m+: 0-5
Track: LH: 0-5 RH: 0-1 Tight: 0-0 Gall: 0-2
Aids: Bl: 0-0 Vi: 0-0 Tstrap: 0-0
Best Rating: 184 3/02 Chel 3m2f110y good Ch

Top-class chaser, versatile and admirably game, he ran some fair races in 2001/2002 without winning, before putting up a career-best display when second in the Cheltenham Gold Cup. Feeling the effects of his Cheltenham exertions when pulled up in the Irish National on his final start.

Commanche Cup (IRE)

75 **33**
9-y-o b g Commanche Run-Royal Cup (Politico (USA))
A P James Jim Tew

Placings:*0/00*F0P/P0/U0P **(1393)**
2001/02: 20^{U}G, 20^{0}G, 24^{P}GF

	Starts	1st	2nd	3rd	Win & Pl
Hurdles	3	0	0	0	
Career Total	**11**	**0**	**0**	**0**	

Going: Sf: 0-0 GS: 0-0 Gd: 0-2 GF: - Fm: 0-1
Distance: 2m/2m3: 0-0 2m4-2m7: 0-2 3m+: 0-1
Track: LH: 0-3 RH: 0-0 Tight: 0-0 Gall: 0-0
Aids: Bl: 0-1 Vi: 0-0 Tstrap: 0-0
Best Rating: 69 3/98 Ludl 2m good NHF

Commanche Drums (IRE)

95 **87**
8-y-o b g Commanche Run-Mabbots Own (Royal Trip)
O Brennan W Wharton

Placings:*50/*340P **(2578)**
2001/02: 16^{3}G, 16^{4}S, 16^{0}G, 20^{P}S

	Starts	1st	2nd	3rd	Win & Pl
Hurdles	4	0	0	1	408
Career Total	**6**	**0**	**0**	**1**	**408**

Going: Sf: 0-2 GS: 0-0 Gd: 0-2 GF: - Fm: 0-0
Distance: 2m/2m3: 0-3 2m4-2m7: 0-1 3m+: 0-0
Track: LH: 0-4 RH: 0-0 Tight: 0-0 Gall: 0-0
Aids: Bl: 0-0 Vi: 0-0 Tstrap: 0-0
Best Rating: 89 5/99 Worc 2m gd-sft NHF

Commanche Fox (IRE)

71 **23**

-y-o ch g Commanche Run-Shalom Joy (Kemal (FR))
J Armson R J Armson

lacings:0PP/P-PPP0P00P (1147)
001/02: 19^{P}G, 20^{P}F, 19^{P}G, 17^{0}GF, 21^{P}GS, 19^{0}GF, 16^{0}GF, 4^{P}GF

	Starts	1st	2nd	3rd	Win & Pl
lurdles	8	0	0	0	
areer Total	**12**	**0**	**0**	**0**	

oing: Sf: 0-0 GS: 0-1 Gd: 0-2 GF: - Fm: 0-5
istance: 2m/2m3: 0-3 2m4-2m7: 0-4 3m+: 0-1
rack: LH: 0-4 RH: 0-3 Tight: 0-3 Gall: 0-0
ids: Bl: 0-0 Vi: 0-0 Tstrap: 0-0
est Rating: 23 6/01 MRas 2m1f110y gd-fm Hdl

Commanche General (IRE)

90f **97f**

-y-o b g Commanche Run-Shannon Amber (IRE) Phardante (FR))
F Panvert J F Panvert

lacings:00 (4423)
001/02: 16^{0}G, 16^{0}GS

	Starts	1st	2nd	3rd	Win & Pl
IH Flat	2	0	0	0	
areer Total	**2**	**0**	**0**	**0**	

oing: Sf: 0-0 GS: 0-1 Gd: 0-1 GF: - Fm: 0-0
istance: 2m/2m3: 0-2 2m4-2m7: 0-0 3m+: 0-0
rack: LH: 0-1 RH: 0-1 Tight: 0-0 Gall: 0-1
ids: Bl: 0-0 Vi: 0-0 Tstrap: 0-0
est Rating: 91 2/02 Kemp 2m good NHF

Commanche Hero (IRE)

105 **89+**

-y-o ch g Cardinal Flower-Fair Bavard (Le Bavard FR))
J Price Pete Holder

lacings:104/64F0043/00/00F3F46334 (4550)
001/02: 20^{0}GF, 16^{0}G, 22^{F}GF, 20^{3}S, 21^{F}GS, 21^{4}G, 20^{6}S, 4^{3}G, 22^{3}G, 21^{4}GF

	Starts	1st	2nd	3rd	Win & Pl
lurdles	10	0	0	3	1283
areer Total	**22**	**1**	**0**	**4**	**3476**

03	1/98	Font	2m2f	H NHF	SFT	£1434

Total win prize-money £1434

oing: Sf: 0-2 GS: 0-1 Gd: 0-4 GF: - Fm: 0-3
istance: 2m/2m3: 0-1 2m4-2m7: 0-8 3m+: 0-1
rack: LH: 0-1 RH: 0-8 Tight: 0-1 Gall: 0-3
ids: Bl: 0-0 Vi: 0-0 Tstrap: 0-0
est Rating: 103 1/98 Font 2m2f soft NHF

le made a successful debut in a bumper in January 998, but has failed to win since and looks very one-aced.

Commanche Jim (IRE)

101 **103**

-y-o b g Commanche Run-On A Dream (Balinger)
H Alner David O Moon

lacings:5/0-0644145P0 (4513)
001/02: 16^{0}GF, 22^{6}GF, 22^{4}G, 24^{4}G, 25^{1}S, 24^{4}GS, 24^{5}S,

26^{P}GF, 24^{0}GS

	Starts	1st	2nd	3rd	Win & Pl
NH Flat	1	0	0	0	0
Hurdles	8	1	0	0	3146
Career Total	**11**	**1**	**0**	**0**	**3146**

101	12/01	Plum	3m1f110y	E(0-105)HHdl	SFT	£2418

Total win prize-money £2419

Going: Sf: 1-2 GS: 0-2 Gd: 0-2 GF: - Fm: 0-3
Distance: 2m/2m3: 0-1 2m4-2m7: 0-2 **3m+: 1-6**
Track: LH: 0-2 RH: 0-6 Tight: 0-0 Gall: 0-2
Aids: Bl: 0-0 Vi: 0-0 Tstrap: 0-0
Best Rating: 103 1/02 Newb 3m110y gd-sft Hdl

Handicap hurdler, who stays well and handles soft ground.

Commanche Law (IRE)

106 **100**

9-y-o b g Commanche Run-Laurenca (Laurence O)
K C Bailey Totteridge Racing

Placings:14/0-5156P305 (4756)
2001/02: 20^{5}GS, 20^{1}HY, 20^{5}S, 26^{6}S, 26^{P}S, 24^{3}G, 26^{0}GF, 20^{5}GF

	Starts	1st	2nd	3rd	Win & Pl
Hurdles	8	1	0	1	3371
Career Total	**11**	**2**	**0**	**1**	**5983**

100	11/01	Uttx	2m4f110y	E Hdl	HVY	£2667
100	3/98	Ludl	2m	H NHF	G-S	£1308

Total win prize-money £3975

Going: Sf: 1-4 GS: 0-1 Gd: 0-1 GF: - Fm: 0-2
Distance: 2m/2m3: 0-0 **2m4-2m7: 1-4** 3m+: 0-4
Track: **LH: 1-2** RH: 0-5 Tight: 0-2 Gall: 0-2
Aids: Bl: 0-2 Vi: 0-2 Tstrap: 0-0
Best Rating: 107 4/98 Fair 2m gd-yld NHF

Has been difficult to train and remains lightly raced. Has won on heavy but thought to prefer better ground.

Commanche Quest (IRE)

99 **104**

6-y-o b g Commanche Run-Conna Dodger (IRE) (Kemal (FR))
Mrs M Reveley The Eleven O'Clock Club

Placings:642534 (4432)
2001/02: 17^{6}S, 20^{4}S, 20^{2}HY, 20^{5}S, 20^{3}HY, 20^{4}HY

	Starts	1st	2nd	3rd	Win & Pl
NH Flat	1	0	0	0	0
Hurdles	5	0	1	1	3428
Career Total	**6**	**0**	**1**	**1**	**3428**

Going: Sf: 0-6 GS: 0-0 Gd: 0-0 GF: - Fm: 0-0
Distance: 2m/2m3: 0-1 2m4-2m7: 0-5 3m+: 0-0
Track: LH: 0-5 RH: 0-1 Tight: 0-0 Gall: 0-1
Aids: Bl: 0-0 Vi: 0-0 Tstrap: 0-0
Best Rating: 104 12/01 Hayd 2m4f heavy Hdl

A chaser in the making, he has looked a stayer so far over hurdles.

Commanche Spirit (IRE)

8-y-o b g Commanche Run-Emmett's Lass (Deep Run)
Mrs Sue Bell (S Gollings 10/2) Mrs Sue Bell

Placings:PPP-4P (4859)
2001/02: 27^{4}GF, 25^{P}G

	Starts	1st	2nd	3rd	Win & Pl
Chases	2	0	0	0	0
Career Total	**5**	**0**	**0**	**0**	**0**

Going: Sf: 0-0 GS: 0-0 Gd: 0-1 GF: - Fm: 0-1
Distance: 2m/2m3: 0-0 2m4-2m7: 0-0 3m+: 0-2
Track: LH: 0-2 RH: 0-0 Tight: 0-1 Gall: 0-0
Aids: Bl: 0-0 Vi: 0-0 Tstrap: 0-0
Best Rating: 64 4/02 Sedg 3m3f gd-fm Ch

Commanche Summer

104 **93**

8-y-o b m Commanche Run-Royal Typhoon (Royal Fountain)
A Robson A Robson

Placings:0U23/6/460**P4-40P40436** (4687)
2001/02: 20^{4}G, 20^{0}S, 21^{P}G, 25^{4}S, 26^{0}HY, 24^{4}GS, 26^{3}GS, 25^{6}GF

	Starts	1st	2nd	3rd	Win & Pl
Chases	8	0	0	1	1615
Career Total	**18**	**0**	**1**	**2**	**3049**

Going: Sf: 0-3 GS: 0-2 Gd: 0-2 GF: - Fm: 0-1
Distance: 2m/2m3: 0-0 2m4-2m7: 0-3 3m+: 0-5
Track: LH: 0-4 RH: 0-4 Tight: 0-3 Gall: 0-0
Aids: Bl: 0-0 Vi: 0-0 Tstrap: 0-0
Best Rating: 93 10/01 Bang 2m4f110y good Ch

Moderate staying chaser, suited by soft ground.

Commanche Whorl (IRE)

105f

7-y-o b g Commanche Run-Cailin Dubh (Le Bavard (FR))
Cecil Mahon Coleman Rooney

Placings:00/56-000000P (4178)
2001/02: 16^{U}G, 16^{0}GF, 20^{0}Y, 22^{0}GY, 24^{0}SH, 19^{0}SH, 16^{P}GS

	Starts	1st	2nd	3rd	Win & Pl
NH Flat	2	0	0	0	0
Hurdles	5	0	0	0	0
Career Total	**11**	**0**	**0**	**0**	

Going: Sf: 0-0 GS: 0-1 Gd: 0-1 GF: - Fm: 0-1
Distance: 2m/2m3: 0-4 2m4-2m7: 0-2 3m+: 0-1
Track: LH: 0-3 RH: 0-2 Tight: 0-1 Gall: 0-0
Aids: Bl: 0-3 Vi: 0-0 Tstrap: 0-0
Best Rating: 101 2/01 Leop 2m heavy NHF

Commanche Wind (IRE)

105 **107**

7-y-o b g Commanche Run-Delko (Decent Fellow)
E W Tuer G Tuer

Placings:0/0060300-5F (1020)
2001/02: 17^{5}GF, 17^{F}GF

	Starts	1st	2nd	3rd	Win & Pl
Hurdles	2	0	0	0	0
Career Total	**10**	**0**	**0**	**1**	**336**

Going: Sf: 0-0 GS: 0-0 Gd: 0-0 GF: - Fm: 0-2
Distance: 2m/2m3: 0-2 2m4-2m7: 0-0 3m+: 0-0

Track: LH: 0-1 RH: 0-1 Tight: 0-2 Gall: 0-0
Aids: Bl: 0-0 Vi: 0-0 Tstrap: 0-0
Best Rating: 107 8/00 Kbgn 2m gd-fm Hdl

Modest hurdler, stays two and a half miles.

Commander Conn

87 63

7-y-o b g Perpendicular-Bonny Bright Eyes (Rarity)
C J Price Nigel Lilley

Placings:6PU000 **(1629)**
2001/02: 17^{6}F, 16^{P}GS, 16^{U}GF, 16^{0}GF, 19^{0}GF, 21^{0}GF

	Starts	1st	2nd	3rd	Win & Pl
Hurdles	6	0	0	0	0
Career Total	**6**	**0**	**0**	**0**	**0**

Going: Sf: 0-0 GS: 0-1 Gd: 0-0 GF: - Fm: 0-5
Distance: 2m/2m3: 0-4 2m4-2m7: 0-2 3m+: 0-0
Track: LH: 0-2 RH: 0-3 Tight: 0-2 Gall: 0-1
Aids: Bl: 0-0 Vi: 0-0 Tstrap: 0-0
Best Rating: 63 8/01 Strf 2m110y gd-fm Hdl

Commander Druce (IRE)

7-y-o ch g Cardinal Flower-Shuil Ar Ais (Quayside)
M A Barnes M Barnes

Placings:*OP* **(1593)**
2001/02: 16°S, 17^{P}GS

	Starts	1st	2nd	3rd	Win & Pl
NH Flat	2	0	0	0	
Career Total	**2**	**0**	**0**	**0**	

Going: Sf: 0-1 GS: 0-1 Gd: 0-0 GF: - Fm: 0-0
Distance: 2m/2m3: 0-2 2m4-2m7: 0-0 3m+: 0-0
Track: LH: 0-1 RH: 0-1 Tight: 0-1 Gall: 0-0
Aids: Bl: 0-0 Vi: 0-0 Tstrap: 0-2
Best Rating:

Commander Glen (IRE)

90 73

10-y-o b g Glenstal (USA)-Une Parisienne (FR) (Bolkonski)
A Crook (J W Hughes 14/4) B & K Associates

Placings:251351/5546366/51406/P101455/22-P4 **(0662)**
2001/02: 24^{P}S, 24^{4}F

	Starts	1st	2nd	3rd	Win & Pl
Chases	2	0	0	0	383
Career Total	**29**	**5**	**3**	**2**	**23992**

111	8/99	Prth	3m	E(0-115)HCh	G-F	£4182
111	6/99	Sthl	3m110y	F(0-105)HCh	G-F	£3074
111	9/98	Prth	2m4f110y	D Ch	GD	£4182
99	12/96	Muss	2m4f	E(0-100)HHdl	G-F	£2542
84	10/96	Kels	2m2f	E Hdl	FRM	£1884

Total win prize-money £15864

Going: Sf: 0-1 GS: 0-0 Gd: 0-0 GF: - Fm: 0-1
Distance: 2m/2m3: 0-0 2m4-2m7: 0-0 3m+: 0-2
Track: LH: 0-0 RH: 0-2 Tight: 0-0 Gall: 0-0
Aids: Bl: 0-1 Vi: 0-1 Tstrap: 0-0
Best Rating: 111 5/00 Sedg 3m3f gd-fm Ch

Committed Schedule (IRE)

107 129

11-y-o b g Saxon Farm-Padykin (Bustino)
N G Richards J M Newbould

Placings:*0/00*0605024633/1121F6F/44242P4/41140/32-P26P **(2448)**
2001/02: 26^{P}GS, 26^{2}GS, 28^{6}GS, 30^{P}GS

	Starts	1st	2nd	3rd	Win & Pl
Chases	4	0	1	0	1070
Career Total	**38**	**5**	**6**	**3**	**30821**

135	10/99	Carl	3m2f	D(0-125)HCh	GD	£4182
133	10/99	Carl	3m2f	D(0-125)HCh	GD	£4492
109	12/97	Carl	3m2f	C(0-130)HCh	SFT	£4546
107	11/97	Catt	3m1f110y	E Ch	GD	£2969
95	11/97	Hexm	3m1f	F Ch	G-F	£2725

Total win prize-money £18916

Going: Sf: 0-0 GS: 0-4 Gd: 0-0 GF: - Fm: 0-0
Distance: 2m/2m3: 0-0 2m4-2m7: 0-0 3m+: 0-4
Track: LH: 0-3 RH: 0-1 Tight: 0-2 Gall: 0-1
Aids: Bl: 0-0 Vi: 0-0 Tstrap: 0-0
Best Rating: 135 10/00 Carl 3m2f good Ch

A useful if lightly raced staying handicap chaser, he goes well at Carlisle and is a sound jumper.

Common Man (IRE)

82 103

9-y-o b g Lafontaine (USA)-Adroit Miss (Quayside)
O Brennan Brian Culley

Placings:4/30*0P*/4/15110-000 **(1474)**
2001/02: 16^{0}G, 19^{0}G, 19^{0}S

	Starts	1st	2nd	3rd	Win & Pl
Hurdles	3	0	0	0	
Career Total	**14**	**3**	**0**	**1**	**15458**

118	10/00	Chel	2m110y	B HHdl	GD	£8346
104	10/00	MRas	2m3f110y	D Hdl	GD	£3656
107	5/00	Aint	2m110y	D Hdl	G-F	£3006

Total win prize-money £15008

Going: Sf: 0-1 GS: 0-0 Gd: 0-2 GF: - Fm: 0-0
Distance: 2m/2m3: 0-1 2m4-2m7: 0-2 3m+: 0-0
Track: LH: 0-1 RH: 0-2 Tight: 0-2 Gall: 0-0
Aids: Bl: 0-0 Vi: 0-0 Tstrap: 0-0
Best Rating: 118 10/00 Chel 2m110y good Hdl

Common View (IRE)

7-y-o b g Scenic-Stony Ground (Relko)
J A Moore J A Moore

Placings:P/P **(1500)**
2001/02: 21^{P}G

	Starts	1st	2nd	3rd	Win & Pl
Hurdles	1	0	0	0	
Career Total	**2**	**0**	**0**	**0**	

Going: Sf: 0-0 GS: 0-0 Gd: 0-1 GF: - Fm: 0-0
Distance: 2m/2m3: 0-0 2m4-2m7: 0-1 3m+: 0-0
Track: LH: 0-1 RH: 0-0 Tight: 0-1 Gall: 0-0
Aids: Bl: 0-0 Vi: 0-0 Tstrap: 0-0
Best Rating:

Commonwealth (IRE)

6-y-o b g Common Grounds-Silver Slipper (Indian Ridge)
K A Morgan J T Summerfield

Placings:20/12225-0 **(2206)**
2001/02: 16^{0}GS

	Starts	1st	2nd	3rd	Win & Pl
Hurdles	1	0	0	0	
Career Total	**8**	**1**	**4**	**0**	**5919**

103	5/00	Kels	2m110y	E Hdl	GD	£2380

Total win prize-money £2380

Going: Sf: 0-0 GS: 0-1 Gd: 0-0 GF: - Fm: 0-0
Distance: 2m/2m3: 0-1 2m4-2m7: 0-0 3m+: 0-0
Track: LH: 0-0 RH: 0-1 Tight: 0-0 Gall: 0-0
Aids: Bl: 0-0 Vi: 0-0 Tstrap: 0-1
Best Rating: 103 2/01 Muss 2m good Hdl

Commuter Country

11-y-o gr g Town And Country-Landed Lady (Realm)
Mrs P K J Brightwell Mrs P K J Brightwell

Placings:*0*/660/2/06/4P **(4534)**
2001/02: 21^{4}G, 21^{P}G

	Starts	1st	2nd	3rd	Win & Pl
Chases	2	0	0	0	156
Career Total	**9**	**0**	**1**	**0**	**786**

Going: Sf: 0-0 GS: 0-0 Gd: 0-2 GF: - Fm: 0-0
Distance: 2m/2m3: 0-0 2m4-2m7: 0-2 3m+: 0-0
Track: LH: 0-2 RH: 0-0 Tight: 0-2 Gall: 0-0
Aids: Bl: 0-0 Vi: 0-0 Tstrap: 0-0
Best Rating: 100 3/00 Fknm 2m5f110y good Ch

Compatriot (IRE)

83 63

6-y-o b g Bigstone (IRE)-Campestral (USA) (Alleged (USA))
J J O'Neill Foreneish Racing

Placings:0 **(1560)**
2001/02: 16^{0}GS

	Starts	1st	2nd	3rd	Win & Pl
Hurdles	1	0	0	0	
Career Total	**1**	**0**	**0**	**0**	

Going: Sf: 0-0 GS: 0-1 Gd: 0-0 GF: - Fm: 0-0
Distance: 2m/2m3: 0-1 2m4-2m7: 0-0 3m+: 0-0
Track: LH: 0-1 RH: 0-0 Tight: 0-0 Gall: 0-0
Aids: Bl: 0-0 Vi: 0-0 Tstrap: 0-1
Best Rating: 63 10/01 Uttx 2m gd-sft Hdl

Compton Amica (IRE)

100 92

6-y-o gr m High Estate-Nephrite (Godswalk (USA))
K Bishop Keith Watkins

Placings:0061P2P-0P20 **(4500)**
2001/02: 20^{0}S, 22^{P}HY, 17^{2}G, 17^{0}G

	Starts	1st	2nd	3rd	Win & Pl
Hurdles	4	0	1	0	608
Career Total	**11**	**1**	**2**	**0**	**3913**

6	12/00	Winc	2m	F(0-95)HHdl	G-S	£2625

Total win prize-money £2625

Going: Sf: 0-2 GS: 0-0 Gd: 0-2 GF: - Fm: 0-0
Distance: 2m/2m3: 0-2 2m4-2m7: 0-2 3m+: 0-0
Track: LH: 0-3 RH: 0-1 Tight: 0-1 Gall: 0-0
Aids: Bl: 0-0 Vi: 0-0 Tstrap: 0-0
Best Rating: 92 3/02 Extr 2m1f good Hdl

Moderate handicap hurdler at around two miles on soft ground. Goes well at Wincanton.

Compton Chick (IRE)

99 92

4-y-o b f Dolphin Street (FR)-Cecina (Welsh Saint)
J W Mullins (G A Butler 25/9) Seamus Mullins

Placings:355 **(4559)**
2001/02: 17^{3}G, 17^{5}S, 16^{5}GF

	Starts	1st	2nd	3rd	Win & Pl
Hurdles	3	0	0	1	298
Career Total	**3**	**0**	**0**	**1**	**298**

Going: Sf: 0-1 GS: 0-0 Gd: 0-1 GF: - Fm: 0-1
Distance: 2m/2m3: 0-3 2m4-2m7: 0-0 3m+: 0-0
Track: LH: 0-1 RH: 0-2 Tight: 0-1 Gall: 0-0
Aids: Bl: 0-0 Vi: 0-0 Tstrap: 0-0
Best Rating: 85 4/02 Plum 2m gd-fm Hdl

Modest form over hurdles so far.

Comtake (IRE)

61 18

6-y-o ch g Denel (FR)-Rainbow Ryde (IRE) (Supreme Leader)
J Howard Johnson Comtake-Welding Engineering Specialists

Placings:0P **(4689)**
2001/02: 16^{0}G, 16^{P}GF

	Starts	1st	2nd	3rd	Win & Pl
Hurdles	2	0	0	0	
Career Total	**2**	**0**	**0**	**0**	

Going: Sf: 0-0 GS: 0-0 Gd: 0-1 GF: - Fm: 0-1
Distance: 2m/2m3: 0-2 2m4-2m7: 0-0 3m+: 0-0
Track: LH: 0-2 RH: 0-0 Tight: 0-1 Gall: 0-0
Aids: Bl: 0-0 Vi: 0-0 Tstrap: 0-0
Best Rating: 18 11/01 Weth 2m good Hdl

Con Tricks

107(97h) (103h)107

9-y-o b g El Conquistador-Dame Nellie (Dominion)
J W Mullins Shildon Racing

Placings:*0/0/*6P45F1/42426243-2 **(4133)**
2001/02: 24^{2}G

	Starts	1st	2nd	3rd	Win & Pl
Chases	1	0	1	0	1776
Career Total	**17**	**1**	**4**	**1**	**10603**

103	4/00	Towc	2m5f	F Hdl	GD	£1922

Total win prize-money £1922

Going: Sf: 0-0 GS: 0-0 Gd: 0-1 GF: - Fm: 0-0
Distance: 2m/2m3: 0-0 2m4-2m7: 0-0 3m+: 0-1
Track: LH: 0-0 RH: 0-1 Tight: 0-0 Gall: 0-0
Aids: Bl: 0-0 Vi: 0-0 Tstrap: 0-0
Best Rating: 113 2/01 Wwck 3m2f soft Ch

A winner over hurdles, he has shown some ability over fences and does not have that many miles on the clock for his age. Stays well.

Concert Pianist

101 127

7-y-o b g Rakaposhi King-Divine Affair (IRE) (The Parson)
P Winkworth Ms J P Segal

Placings: *1/334*/11143-04 **(2759)**
2001/02: 20^{0}GS, 21^{4}GS

	Starts	1st	2nd	3rd	Win & Pl
Hurdles	2	0	0	0	769
Career Total	**11**	**4**	**0**	**3**	**21780**

125	1/01	Asct	2m4f	D Hdl	SFT	£4875
125	11/00	Chep	2m4f	C Hdl	HVY	£5187
118	10/00	Wwck	2m3f	D Hdl	SFT	£3269
92	2/99	Font	2m2f110y	H NHF	SFT	£1451

Total win prize-money £14784

Going: Sf: 0-0 GS: 0-2 Gd: 0-0 GF: - Fm: 0-0
Distance: 2m/2m3: 0-0 2m4-2m7: 0-2 3m+: 0-0
Track: LH: 0-2 RH: 0-0 Tight: 0-0 Gall: 0-1
Aids: Bl: 0-0 Vi: 0-0 Tstrap: 0-0
Best Rating: 151 3/01 Sand 2m4f110y heavy Hdl

He had a fine first season over hurdles in 2000/01, winning three times before making the frame behind Baracouda at Fontwell, and was a gallant third under a big weight in the E.B.F Novices' Handicap Hurdle Final at Sandown. Disappointing in two runs last season. I likely to stay three miles, he may be best employed in novice chases.

Concerto Collonges (FR)

12-y-o br g El Badr-Marlane Collonge (FR) (Cap Martin (FR))
Miss A Armitage O R M Hartley

Placings:1/052-0 **(4892)**
2001/02: 31^{0}G

	Starts	1st	2nd	3rd	Win & Pl
Chases	1	0	0	0	
Career Total	**5**	**1**	**1**	**0**	**2308**

99	4/00	Carl	3m2f	H Ch	G-S	£1363

Total win prize-money £1364

Going: Sf: 0-0 GS: 0-0 Gd: 0-1 GF: - Fm: 0-0
Distance: 2m/2m3: 0-0 2m4-2m7: 0-0 3m+: 0-1
Track: LH: 0-0 RH: 0-0 Tight: 0-0 Gall: 0-0
Aids: Bl: 0-0 Vi: 0-0 Tstrap: 0-0
Best Rating: 99 4/01 Prth 3m7f heavy Ch

Consistent pointer who pays his way. Needs soft ground.

Condoyle (IRE)

98 86

9-y-o b g Rare One-Worthy Gale (Strong Gale)
R J Baker John Warren & Percy Buckingham

Placings:F5B4335056 **(1617)**
2001/02: 22^{F}GF, 22^{5}G, 22^{B}GF, 17^{4}GF, 20^{3}G, 22^{3}G, 22^{5}GF, 17^{0}GF, 19^{5}GF, 17^{6}GF

	Starts	1st	2nd	3rd	Win & Pl
Hurdles	10	0	0	2	1084
Career Total	**10**	**0**	**0**	**2**	**1084**

Going: Sf: 0-0 GS: 0-0 Gd: 0-3 GF: - Fm: 0-7
Distance: 2m/2m3: 0-3 2m4-2m7: 0-7 3m+: 0-0
Track: LH: 0-7 RH: 0-3 Tight: 0-6 Gall: 0-0
Aids: Bl: 0-1 Vi: 0-0 Tstrap: 0-0
Best Rating: 86 7/01 Worc 2m4f good Hdl

Connel's Croft

95 80

10-y-o ch g Rich Charlie-Technology (FR) (Top Ville)
P D Evans P D Evans

Placings:*02/00*P00/FFPPP544623042/1521U20/1001-40 **(1189)**
2001/02: 16^{4}GF, 20^{0}G

	Starts	1st	2nd	3rd	Win & Pl
Hurdles	2	0	0	0	0
Career Total	**34**	**4**	**5**	**1**	**13444**

104	9/00	Worc	2m	G(0-90)HHdl	G-F	£1526
104	5/00	Ludl	2m	F(0-105)HHdl	GD	£3198
87	6/99	Uttx	2m	E(0-105)HHdl	G-S	£3696
88	5/99	Uttx	2m	G(0-95)HHdl	G-F	£1763

Total win prize-money £10183

Going: Sf: 0-0 GS: 0-0 Gd: 0-1 GF: - Fm: 0-1
Distance: 2m/2m3: 0-1 2m4-2m7: 0-1 3m+: 0-0
Track: LH: 0-2 RH: 0-0 Tight: 0-1 Gall: 0-0
Aids: Bl: 0-0 Vi: 0-2 Tstrap: 0-0
Best Rating: 104 9/00 Worc 2m gd-fm Hdl

Connor Macleod (IRE)

112 152

9-y-o ch g Torus-Blackrath Gem (Bargello)
M Pitman Autofour Engineering

Placings:*1503*P1/F2214543/535-2FP **(1407)**
2001/02: 20^{2}GF, 21^{F}GF, 23^{P}GF

	Starts	1st	2nd	3rd	Win & Pl
Chases	3	0	1	0	3320
Career Total	**20**	**3**	**3**	**3**	**53674**

144	11/99	Worc	2m7f110y	A Ch	G-S	£14300
122	4/99	Chel	2m5f110y	B Hdl	GD	£16491
108	6/98	Worc	2m	H NHF	G-F	£1381

Total win prize-money £32173

Going: Sf: 0-0 GS: 0-0 Gd: 0-0 GF: - Fm: 0-3
Distance: 2m/2m3: 0-0 2m4-2m7: 0-2 3m+: 0-1
Track: LH: 0-3 RH: 0-0 Tight: 0-2 Gall: 0-0
Aids: Bl: 0-0 Vi: 0-0 Tstrap: 0-0
Best Rating: 152 5/01 Sthl 2m4f110y gd-fm Ch

A useful chaser, yet to prove that he conclusively stays three miles, he was not at his best in the summer of 2001.

Conora (NZ)

9-y-o b g Conquistarose (USA)-Soundora (NZ) (Sound Reason (CAN))
O O'Neill J Russell

Placings:05/000P/3UPF-P **(0215)**
2001/02: 21^{P}GF

	Starts	1st	2nd	3rd	Win & Pl
Chases	1	0	0	0	
Career Total	**11**	**0**	**0**	**1**	**454**

Going: Sf: 0-0 GS: 0-0 Gd: 0-0 GF: - Fm: 0-1
Distance: 2m/2m3: 0-0 2m4-2m7: 0-1 3m+: 0-0
Track: LH: 0-0 RH: 0-1 Tight: 0-0 Gall: 0-0
Aids: Bl: 0-0 Vi: 0-0 Tstrap: 0-0

Best Rating: 80 5/00 Wwck 2m gd-fm Ch

Conquer (IRE)

102(98h) **115**

7-y-o b g Phardante (FR)-Tullow Performance (Gala Performance (USA))

H D Daly M Ward-Thomas

Placings:334-3 (1379)

2001/02: 25^{3}GF

	Starts	1st	2nd	3rd	Win & Pl
Chases	1	0	0	1	544
Career Total	**4**	**0**	**0**	**3**	**1429**

Going: Sf: 0-0 GS: 0-0 Gd: 0-0 GF: - Fm: 0-1
Distance: 2m/2m3: 0-0 2m4-2m7: 0-0 3m+: 0-1
Track: LH: 0-0 RH: 0-1 Tight: 0-0 Gall: 0-0
Aids: Bl: 0-0 Vi: 0-0 Tstrap: 0-0
Best Rating: 115 9/01 Hrfd 3m1f110y gd-fm Ch

Conquistador (IRE)

89 **68**

6-y-o b g Alphabatim (USA)-Reign Of Terror (IRE) (Orchestra)

Ms A E Embiricos Mrs S N J Embiricos

Placings:54P (3390)

2001/02: 16^{5}S, 21^{4}G, 23^{P}GS

	Starts	1st	2nd	3rd	Win & Pl
Hurdles	3	0	0	0	0
Career Total	**3**	**0**	**0**	**0**	**0**

Going: Sf: 0-1 GS: 0-1 Gd: 0-1 GF: - Fm: 0-0
Distance: 2m/2m3: 0-1 2m4-2m7: 0-2 3m+: 0-0
Track: LH: 0-2 RH: 0-1 Tight: 0-1 Gall: 0-0
Aids: Bl: 0-0 Vi: 0-0 Tstrap: 0-0
Best Rating: 68 10/01 Towc 2m soft Hdl

Conspirito (IRE)

(72h) (48h)

9-y-o b g Orchestra-Fly Fuss (Little Buskins)

R J Hodges R Callow

Placings:*450*/024/P0U (4115)

2001/02: 22^{P}S, 19^{0}GS, 21^{U}G

	Starts	1st	2nd	3rd	Win & Pl
Hurdles	2	0	0	0	0
Chases	1	0	0	0	0
Career Total	**9**	**0**	**1**	**0**	**1005**

Going: Sf: 0-1 GS: 0-1 Gd: 0-1 GF: - Fm: 0-0
Distance: 2m/2m3: 0-1 2m4-2m7: 0-2 3m+: 0-0
Track: LH: 0-1 RH: 0-2 Tight: 0-1 Gall: 0-0
Aids: Bl: 0-0 Vi: 0-0 Tstrap: 0-0
Best Rating: 114 11/99 Worc 2m4f good Hdl

Contes (IRE)

106(81h) (98h)**122**

10-y-o b g Lafontaine (USA)-Dara's Diocese (Bishop Of Orange)

P R Hedger P R Hedger

Placings:353P1P51/0F-2000 (4909)

2001/02: 22^{2}G, 22^{0}S, 24^{0}GS, 20^{0}GF

	Starts	1st	2nd	3rd	Win & Pl
Hurdles	2	0	1	0	660
Chases	2	0	0	0	0
Career Total	**14**	**2**	**1**	**2**	**10640**
124	4/00	Font	2m6f	C Ch	GD £7052
127	2/00	Folk	2m5f	F(0-90)HCh	G-S £2452

Total win prize-money £9506

Going: Sf: 0-1 GS: 0-1 Gd: 0-1 GF: - Fm: 0-1
Distance: 2m/2m3: 0-0 2m4-2m7: 0-3 3m+: 0-1
Track: LH: 0-1 RH: 0-3 Tight: 0-3 Gall: 0-1
Aids: Bl: 0-0 Vi: 0-0 Tstrap: 0-0
Best Rating: 127 2/00 Folk 2m5f gd-sft Ch

Modest chaser at up to three miles, lightly raced in recent years. Improved form since wearing blinkers and was clear when falling at the last over two and a half miles at Bangor May 2002.

Contingency

9-y-o b g Broadsword (USA)-Saucy Linda (Saucy Kit)

Mrs Caroline Bailey Miss Claire Hill

Placings:F-6 (0090)

2001/02: 25^{6}S

	Starts	1st	2nd	3rd	Win & Pl
Chases	1	0	0	0	0
Career Total	**2**	**0**	**0**	**0**	**0**

Going: Sf: 0-1 GS: 0-0 Gd: 0-0 GF: - Fm: 0-0
Distance: 2m/2m3: 0-0 2m4-2m7: 0-0 3m+: 0-1
Track: LH: 0-1 RH: 0-0 Tight: 0-0 Gall: 0-0
Aids: Bl: 0-0 Vi: 0-0 Tstrap: 0-0
Best Rating:

Contra Charge

8-y-o gr g Arzanni-Winter Wonder (Sunyboy)

N A Twiston-Davies Mr F J Mills & Mr W Mills

Placings:*10000*-P (0124)

2001/02: 24^{P}F

	Starts	1st	2nd	3rd	Win & Pl
Hurdles	1	0	0	0	
Career Total	**6**	**1**	**0**	**0**	**1505**
97	10/00	Ludl	2m	H NHF	G-F £1505

Total win prize-money £1505

Going: Sf: 0-0 GS: 0-0 Gd: 0-0 GF: - Fm: 0-1
Distance: 2m/2m3: 0-0 2m4-2m7: 0-0 3m+: 0-1
Track: LH: 0-0 RH: 0-1 Tight: 0-1 Gall: 0-0
Aids: Bl: 0-0 Vi: 0-0 Tstrap: 0-0
Best Rating: 97 10/00 Ludl 2m gd-fm NHF

Contract Scotland (IRE)

103 **94**

7-y-o br g Religiously (USA)-Stroked Again (On Your Mark)

L Lungo Contract Construction (scotland) Ltd

Placings:*000*-520421 (4766)

2001/02: 20^{5}GS, 20^{2}GS, 20^{0}G, 24^{4}S, 24^{2}S, 20^{1}GF

	Starts	1st	2nd	3rd	Win & Pl
Hurdles	6	1	2	0	4976
Career Total	**9**	**1**	**2**	**0**	**4976**
92	4/02	Hexm	2m4f110y	E(0-105)HHdl	G-F £2919

Total win prize-money £2919

Going: Sf: 0-2 GS: 0-2 Gd: 0-1 GF: - Fm: 1-1
Distance: 2m/2m3: 0-0 **2m4-2m7: 1-4** 3m+: 0-2
Track: **LH: 1-3** RH: 0-3 Tight: 0-2 Gall: 0-1
Aids: Bl: 0-0 Vi: 0-0 Tstrap: 0-0
Best Rating: 92 4/02 Hexm 2m4f110y gd-fm Hdl

Handicap hurdler. He stays two and a half miles and likes cut in the ground, but is also effective on a fast surface.

Contrafire (IRE)

94 **6**

10-y-o b g Contract Law (USA)-Fiery Song (Ballad Rock)

A C Whillans John J Elliot

Placings:112/44363F356510/5265621/P/05P0-00 (0517

2001/02: 16^{0}GF, 24^{0}F

	Starts	1st	2nd	3rd	Win & Pl
Hurdles	2	0	0	0	
Career Total	**29**	**4**	**3**	**3**	**16451**
106	1/99	Muss	3m	E(0-115)HHdl	SFT £3668
96	3/98	Hexm	2m	E(0-115)HHdl	GD £2404
111	10/96	Carl	2m1f	E Hdl	GD £2486
113	10/96	Bang	2m1f	E Hdl	G-F £2878

Total win prize-money £1143

Going: Sf: 0-0 GS: 0-0 Gd: 0-0 GF: - Fm: 0-2
Distance: 2m/2m3: 0-1 2m4-2m7: 0-0 3m+: 0-1
Track: LH: 0-2 RH: 0-0 Tight: 0-0 Gall: 0-0
Aids: Bl: 0-0 Vi: 0-2 Tstrap: 0-0
Best Rating: 113 10/96 Bang 2m1f gd-fm Hdl

Conwy Castle

94 **101**

5-y-o b g Sri Pekan (USA)-Dumayla (Shernazar)

Mrs S Lamyman (P R Webber 19/5) David Fravigar And Nigel Underwood

Placings:23523-5 (0365

2001/02: 19^{5}GF

	Starts	1st	2nd	3rd	Win & Pl
Hurdles	1	0	0	0	0
Career Total	**6**	**0**	**2**	**2**	**4263**

Going: Sf: 0-0 GS: 0-0 Gd: 0-0 GF: - Fm: 0-1
Distance: 2m/2m3: 0-0 2m4-2m7: 0-1 3m+: 0-0
Track: LH: 0-1 RH: 0-0 Tight: 0-1 Gall: 0-0
Aids: Bl: 0-0 Vi: 0-0 Tstrap: 0-0
Best Rating: 110 11/00 Newb 2m110y gd-sft Hdl

Cookie Crumble

60 **3**

4-y-o b f Never So Bold-Well Tried (IRE) (Thatching)

D McCain (R Hollinshead 25/10) D McCain

Placings:060 (2780

2001/02: 16^{0}GF, 17^{6}GS, 16^{0}G

	Starts	1st	2nd	3rd	Win & Pl
Hurdles	3	0	0	0	0
Career Total	**3**	**0**	**0**	**0**	**0**

Going: Sf: 0-0 GS: 0-1 Gd: 0-1 GF: - Fm: 0-1
Distance: 2m/2m3: 0-3 2m4-2m7: 0-0 3m+: 0-0
Track: LH: 0-1 RH: 0-2 Tight: 0-1 Gall: 0-0
Aids: Bl: 0-1 Vi: 0-0 Tstrap: 0-0
Best Rating: 3 10/01 Ludl 2m gd-fm Hdl

Cool Archie

9-y-o b g Roscoe Blake-Echo Lake (Tycoon Ii)

M Mullineaux Michael Mullineaux

Placings:P (1191)
2001/02: 20PG

	Starts	1st	2nd	3rd	Win & Pl
Hurdles	1	0	0	0	
Career Total	**1**	**0**	**0**	**0**	

Going: Sf: 0-0 GS: 0-0 Gd: 0-1 GF: - Fm: 0-0
Distance: 2m/2m3: 0-0 2m4-2m7: 0-1 3m+: 0-0
Track: LH: 0-1 RH: 0-0 Tight: 0-1 Gall: 0-0
Aids: Bl: 0-0 Vi: 0-0 Tstrap: 0-0
Best Rating:

Cool Border

98 **98**

7-y-o gr m Grey Desire-Irish Orchid (Free State)
M Bradstock (Mrs M Reveley 30/5) J G St P Burridge

Placings:*65-0*26P (4518)
2001/02: 160GF, 202GS, 196S, 21PGS

	Starts	1st	2nd	3rd	Win & Pl
NH Flat	1	0	0	0	0
Hurdles	3	0	1	0	1108
Career Total	**6**	**0**	**1**	**0**	**1108**

Going: Sf: 0-1 GS: 0-2 Gd: 0-0 GF: - Fm: 0-1
Distance: 2m/2m3: 0-1 2m4-2m7: 0-3 3m+: 0-0
Track: LH: 0-0 RH: 0-3 Tight: 0-1 Gall: 0-1
Aids: Bl: 0-0 Vi: 0-0 Tstrap: 0-0
Best Rating: 98 12/01 Hntg 2m4f110y gd-sft Hdl

Cool Chilli

78f **81f**

4-y-o gr g Gran Alba (USA)-Miss Flossa (FR) (Big John (FR))
N J Pomfret R P Brett

Placings:*500* (4910)
2001/02: 165GF, 160G, 170G

	Starts	1st	2nd	3rd	Win & Pl
NH Flat	3	0	0	0	0
Career Total	**3**	**0**	**0**	**0**	**0**

Going: Sf: 0-0 GS: 0-0 Gd: 0-2 GF: - Fm: 0-1
Distance: 2m/2m3: 0-3 2m4-2m7: 0-0 3m+: 0-0
Track: LH: 0-0 RH: 0-3 Tight: 0-1 Gall: 0-1
Aids: Bl: 0-0 Vi: 0-0 Tstrap: 0-0
Best Rating: 81 3/02 Hntg 2m110y gd-fm NHF

Showed some ability on first start in a bumper.

Cool Gunner

93(74h) (19h)**100**

12-y-o b g Gunner B-Coolek (Menelek)
J S King Miss S Douglas-Pennant

Placings:*00FU/61U4110/142414P/4314/054211P/006*45PP (4602)
2001/02: 190GS, 190G, 166GF, 194S, 245GS, 21PS, 20PGF

	Starts	1st	2nd	3rd	Win & Pl
Hurdles	2	0	0	0	0
Chases	5	0	0	0	271
Career Total	**36**	**8**	**2**	**1**	**31124**

124	3/00	Extr	2m3f	E(0-115)HCh	G-F	£4004
124	3/00	Tntn	2m110y	F(0-105)HCh	GD	£2704
124	11/98	Wwck	2m	C(0-135)HCh	GD	£4760
119	2/98	Winc	2m	D Ch	G-F	£3551
107	11/97	Winc	2m	D(0-125)HHdl	GD	£3415
104	3/97	Extr	2m2f	E(0-115)HHdl	G-F	£2444
95	3/97	Extr	2m3f110y	D(0-120)HHdl	G-S	£2775
88	12/96	Extr	2m2f	D(0-105)HHdl	SFT	£3129

Total win prize-money £26784

Going: Sf: 0-2 GS: 0-2 Gd: 0-1 GF: - Fm: 0-2
Distance: 2m/2m3: 0-4 2m4-2m7: 0-2 3m+: 0-1
Track: LH: 0-2 RH: 0-5 Tight: 0-2 Gall: 0-1
Aids: Bl: 0-0 Vi: 0-0 Tstrap: 0-0
Best Rating: 124 3/00 Extr 2m3f gd-fm Ch

Cool Investment (IRE)

105 **99**

5-y-o b g Prince Of Birds (USA)-Superb Investment (IRE) (Hatim (USA))
R M Stronge (M Johnston 20/10) A P Holland

Placings:4003333 (4011)
2001/02: 194S, 160G, 160G, 193S, 203S, 203HY, 213S

	Starts	1st	2nd	3rd	Win & Pl
Hurdles	7	0	0	4	2483
Career Total	**7**	**0**	**0**	**4**	**2483**

Going: Sf: 0-5 GS: 0-0 Gd: 0-2 GF: - Fm: 0-0
Distance: 2m/2m3: 0-3 2m4-2m7: 0-4 3m+: 0-0
Track: LH: 0-4 RH: 0-3 Tight: 0-1 Gall: 0-3
Aids: Bl: 0-0 Vi: 0-0 Tstrap: 0-5
Best Rating: 99 3/02 Newb 2m5f soft Hdl

Winner on the Flat, he is still a maiden over hurdles but is consistent. Acts on most types of ground.

Cool Kevin

9-y-o b g Sharkskin Suit (USA)-Cool Snipe (Dynastic)
Mrs M A Kendall (Trainer Unknown 10/2) Mrs M A Kendall

Placings:*6640/*P (4859)
2001/02: 25PG

	Starts	1st	2nd	3rd	Win & Pl
Chases	1	0	0	0	
Career Total	**5**	**0**	**0**	**0**	**0**

Going: Sf: 0-0 GS: 0-0 Gd: 0-1 GF: - Fm: 0-0
Distance: 2m/2m3: 0-0 2m4-2m7: 0-0 3m+: 0-1
Track: LH: 0-1 RH: 0-0 Tight: 0-0 Gall: 0-0
Aids: Bl: 0-0 Vi: 0-0 Tstrap: 0-0
Best Rating: 68 2/97 Ayr 2m soft NHF

Cool Million

9-y-o ch g Derrylin-Goldaw (Gala Performance (USA))
Mrs H M Bridges Mrs H M Bridges

Placings:U (4132)
2001/02: 25UG

	Starts	1st	2nd	3rd	Win & Pl
Chases	1	0	0	0	
Career Total	**1**	**0**	**0**	**0**	

Going: Sf: 0-0 GS: 0-0 Gd: 0-1 GF: - Fm: 0-0
Distance: 2m/2m3: 0-0 2m4-2m7: 0-0 3m+: 0-1
Track: LH: 0-0 RH: 0-1 Tight: 0-0 Gall: 0-0
Aids: Bl: 0-0 Vi: 0-0 Tstrap: 0-0
Best Rating:

Cool Miner (IRE)

96 **69**

10-y-o b g Miners Lamp-Coolafinka (IRE) (Strong Statement (USA))
J Wade John Wade

Placings:065P/40P4/21020-0P0P (4869)
2001/02: 210GF, 22PG, 210HY, 20PGF

	Starts	1st	2nd	3rd	Win & Pl
Hurdles	4	0	0	0	
Career Total	**17**	**1**	**2**	**0**	**4273**

89	5/00	Hexm	2m4f110y	E(0-105)HHdl	GD	£2347

Total win prize-money £2347

Going: Sf: 0-1 GS: 0-0 Gd: 0-1 GF: - Fm: 0-2
Distance: 2m/2m3: 0-0 2m4-2m7: 0-4 3m+: 0-0
Track: LH: 0-4 RH: 0-0 Tight: 0-3 Gall: 0-0
Aids: Bl: 0-0 Vi: 0-0 Tstrap: 0-0
Best Rating: 89 5/00 Hexm 2m4f110y good Hdl

Cool Monty (IRE)

101 **122**

8-y-o ch g Montelimar (USA)-Rose Ground (Over The River (FR))
R Rowe Guy Luck

Placings:*0/44*-202 (3382)
2001/02: 162S, 200G, 212GS

	Starts	1st	2nd	3rd	Win & Pl
Hurdles	3	0	2	0	2953
Career Total	**6**	**0**	**2**	**0**	**3425**

Going: Sf: 0-1 GS: 0-1 Gd: 0-1 GF: - Fm: 0-0
Distance: 2m/2m3: 0-1 2m4-2m7: 0-2 3m+: 0-0
Track: LH: 0-0 RH: 0-2 Tight: 0-1 Gall: 0-0
Aids: Bl: 0-0 Vi: 0-0 Tstrap: 0-0
Best Rating: 122 12/01 Sand 2m110y soft Hdl

Has shown ability in novice company and looks capable of winning over two miles plus. Likes soft ground.

Cool Roxy

99

5-y-o b g Environment Friend-Roxy River (Ardross)
A G Blackmore A G Blackmore

Placings:*00*F (4275)
2001/02: 160GS, 160GS, 16FG

	Starts	1st	2nd	3rd	Win & Pl
NH Flat	2	0	0	0	0
Hurdles	1	0	0	0	0
Career Total	**3**	**0**	**0**	**0**	

Going: Sf: 0-0 GS: 0-2 Gd: 0-1 GF: - Fm: 0-0
Distance: 2m/2m3: 0-3 2m4-2m7: 0-0 3m+: 0-0
Track: LH: 0-1 RH: 0-2 Tight: 0-1 Gall: 0-1
Aids: Bl: 0-0 Vi: 0-0 Tstrap: 0-0
Best Rating: 99 3/02 Fknm 2m good Hdl

Cool Runner

12-y-o b g Sunyboy-Nosey's Daughter (Song)
Mrs Susan Nock Gerard Nock

Placings:*40/610563/F0P/3533P/65/P0* (0429)
2001/02: 26PG, 250G

	Starts	1st	2nd	3rd	Win & Pl
Chases	2	0	0	0	
Career Total	**20**	**1**	**0**	**4**	**4694**

104	11/95	Worc	2m4f	E Hdl	SFT	£2862

Total win prize-money £2863

Going: Sf: 0-0 GS: 0-0 Gd: 0-2 GF: - Fm: 0-0
Distance: 2m/2m3: 0-0 2m4-2m7: 0-0 3m+: 0-2

Track: LH: 0-0 RH: 0-1 Tight: 0-1 Gall: 0-0
Aids: Bl: 0-1 Vi: 0-0 Tstrap: 0-0
Best Rating: 104 3/96 Font 2m6f gd-sft Hdl

Cool Song

89f 87f

6-y-o ch g Michelozzo (USA)-Vi's Delight (New Member)
D J Caro D J Caro

Placings:*5* (3236)
2001/02: 16^{5}GS

	Starts	1st	2nd	3rd	Win & Pl
NH Flat	1	0	0	0	0
Career Total	**1**	**0**	**0**	**0**	**0**

Going: Sf: 0-0 GS: 0-1 Gd: 0-0 GF: - Fm: 0-0
Distance: 2m/2m3: 0-1 2m4-2m7: 0-0 3m+: 0-0
Track: LH: 0-0 RH: 0-1 Tight: 0-0 Gall: 0-1
Aids: Bl: 0-0 Vi: 0-0 Tstrap: 0-0
Best Rating: 87 1/02 Hntg 2m110y gd-sft NHF

Cool Wager

82 70

10-y-o br g Arctic Lord-Gamblingway (Gambling Debt)
Mrs H Pudd (B G Powell 15/5) R C Pudd

Placings:*0*/F050/**5P6** (1794)
2001/02: 19^{5}G, 22^{P}S, 19^{6}S

	Starts	1st	2nd	3rd	Win & Pl
Chases	3	0	0	0	0
Career Total	**8**	**0**	**0**	**0**	**0**

Going: Sf: 0-2 GS: 0-0 Gd: 0-1 GF: - Fm: 0-0
Distance: 2m/2m3: 0-1 2m4-2m7: 0-2 3m+: 0-0
Track: LH: 0-1 RH: 0-1 Tight: 0-1 Gall: 0-0
Aids: Bl: 0-0 Vi: 0-0 Tstrap: 0-0
Best Rating: 70 5/01 Hrfd 2m3f good Ch

Coole Abbey (IRE)

10-y-o b g Viteric (FR)-Eleanors Joy (Sheer Grit)
Mrs Clare Moore Mrs Clare Moore

Placings:F12/1622/112/2-2200 (4650)
2001/02: 24^{2}S, 24^{2}GS, 26^{0}G, 21^{0}G

	Starts	1st	2nd	3rd	Win & Pl
Chases	4	0	2	0	1308
Career Total	**15**	**4**	**7**	**0**	**12659**

125	3/00	MRas	3m1f	H Ch	G-F	£1610
126	2/00	Muss	3m	H Ch	G-S	£2310
126	2/99	Muss	3m	H Ch	G-F	£1940
122	3/98	Newc	2m4f	H Ch	G-F	£1023

Total win prize-money £6884

Going: Sf: 0-1 GS: 0-1 Gd: 0-2 GF: - Fm: 0-0
Distance: 2m/2m3: 0-0 2m4-2m7: 0-1 3m+: 0-3
Track: LH: 0-2 RH: 0-2 Tight: 0-3 Gall: 0-1
Aids: Bl: 0-0 Vi: 0-0 Tstrap: 0-0
Best Rating: 126 2/00 Muss 3m gd-sft Ch

A useful hunter chaser, he ran well on his return from a lengthy absence in February 2002, but subsequently well held in better company. Stays three miles. Has won on good to firm and good to soft.

Coole Chief

9-y-o ch g Weld-Beringa Bee (Sunley Builds)
R Ford (W J Warner 12/5) Richard Ford

Placings:5P (0913)
2001/02: 20^{5}GF, 24^{P}G

	Starts	1st	2nd	3rd	Win & Pl
Chases	2	0	0	0	0
Career Total	**2**	**0**	**0**	**0**	**0**

Going: Sf: 0-0 GS: 0-0 Gd: 0-1 GF: - Fm: 0-1
Distance: 2m/2m3: 0-0 2m4-2m7: 0-1 3m+: 0-1
Track: LH: 0-1 RH: 0-1 Tight: 0-1 Gall: 0-1
Aids: Bl: 0-0 Vi: 0-0 Tstrap: 0-0
Best Rating:

Coole Spirit (IRE)

103 133

9-y-o b g All Haste (USA)-Chocolatebiscuit (Biskrah)
Miss E C Lavelle Coole And The Gang

Placings:2105/4323F-11 (2172)
2001/02: 26^{1}GS, 24^{1}S

	Starts	1st	2nd	3rd	Win & Pl
Chases	2	2	0	0	6643
Career Total	**11**	**3**	**2**	**2**	**15238**

133	11/01	Uttx	3m	E Ch	SFT	£3523
122	10/01	Font	3m2f110y	E Ch	G-S	£3120
108	12/99	Leic	2m4f110y	D Hdl	GD	£3665

Total win prize-money £10308

Going: Sf: 1-1 GS: 1-1 Gd: 0-0 GF: - Fm: 0-0
Distance: 2m/2m3: 0-0 2m4-2m7: 0-0 **3m+: 2-2**
Track: **LH: 1-1** RH: 0-0 **Tight: 1-1** Gall: 0-0
Aids: Bl: 0-0 Vi: 0-0 Tstrap: 0-0
Best Rating: 133 11/01 Uttx 3m soft Ch

He showed a decent level of form without winning in novice chases in 2000/1, running well behind Whitenzo and Killusty. Made a winning return at Fontwell. He stays beyond three miles and is sure to win more races over fences.

Coolin River (IRE)

7-y-o b g River Falls-The Coolin (Don)
Mrs H M Bridges Mrs H M Bridges

Placings:0/060P5/0P0 (2140)
2001/02: 22^{0}GF, 22^{P}G, 19^{0}G

	Starts	1st	2nd	3rd	Win & Pl
Hurdles	3	0	0	0	
Career Total	**9**	**0**	**0**	**0**	**0**

Going: Sf: 0-0 GS: 0-0 Gd: 0-2 GF: - Fm: 0-1
Distance: 2m/2m3: 0-0 2m4-2m7: 0-3 3m+: 0-0
Track: LH: 0-0 RH: 0-1 Tight: 0-1 Gall: 0-0
Aids: Bl: 0-0 Vi: 0-0 Tstrap: 0-2
Best Rating: 77 5/99 Uttx 2m good Hdl

Cooling Castle (FR)

92 71

6-y-o ch g Sanglamore (USA)-Syphaly (USA) (Lyphard (USA))
Ronald Thompson B Bruce

Placings:2P/30 (0877)
2001/02: 17^{3}GF, 21^{0}G

	Starts	1st	2nd	3rd	Win & Pl
Hurdles	2	0	0	1	359
Career Total	**4**	**0**	**1**	**1**	**1235**

Going: Sf: 0-0 GS: 0-0 Gd: 0-1 GF: - Fm: 0-1
Distance: 2m/2m3: 0-1 2m4-2m7: 0-1 3m+: 0-0
Track: LH: 0-0 RH: 0-2 Tight: 0-2 Gall: 0-0
Aids: Bl: 0-0 Vi: 0-0 Tstrap: 0-0
Best Rating: 93 11/99 Weth 2m good Hdl

Cooling Off (IRE)

100 102

5-y-o b m Brief Truce (USA)-Lovers' Parlour (Beldale Flutter (USA))
J R Jenkins Christopher Shankland

Placings:214405 (4239)
2001/02: 18^{2}S, 20^{1}S, 16^{4}G, 20^{4}GS, 16^{0}S, 16^{5}GF

	Starts	1st	2nd	3rd	Win & Pl
Hurdles	6	1	1	0	4029
Career Total	**6**	**1**	**1**	**0**	**4029**

102	10/01	Fknm	2m4f	D Hdl	SFT	£3326

Total win prize-money £3326

Going: Sf: 1-3 GS: 0-1 Gd: 0-1 GF: - Fm: 0-1
Distance: 2m/2m3: 0-4 **2m4-2m7: 1-2** 3m+: 0-0
Track: **LH: 1-2** RH: 0-4 **Tight: 1-2** Gall: 0-2
Aids: Bl: 0-0 Vi: 0-0 Tstrap: 0-0
Best Rating: 102 10/01 Fknm 2m4f soft Hdl

Won a two and a half mile soft ground novices' hurdle at Fakenham in December.

Coolnagorna (IRE)

89 89

5-y-o b/br g Warcraft (USA)-Mandalaw (IRE) (Mandalus)
J J O'Neill (T Hogan 22/11) Mrs G Smith

Placings:*P5116* (3773)
2001/02: 16^{P}YS, 16^{5}YS, 16^{1}Y, 16^{1}YS, 16^{6}S

	Starts	1st	2nd	3rd	Win & Pl
NH Flat	4	2	0	0	9181
Hurdles	1	0	0	0	0
Career Total	**5**	**2**	**0**	**0**	**9181**

110	11/01	Cork	2m	NHF	Y-S	£5008
101	11/01	Cork	2m	NHF	YLD	£4173

Total win prize-money £9181

Going: Sf: 0-1 GS: 0-0 Gd: 0-0 GF: - Fm: 0-0
Distance: **2m/2m3: 2-5** 2m4-2m7: 0-0 3m+: 0-0
Track: LH: 0-0 RH: 0-1 Tight: 0-0 Gall: 0-0
Aids: Bl: 0-0 Vi: 0-0 Tstrap: 0-0
Best Rating: 110 11/01 Cork 2m yld-sft NHF

Coolree Lord (IRE)

11-y-o b g Mister Lord (USA)-Margeno's Love (Golden Love)
Jon Trice-Rolph (P Beaumont 10/2) Jon Trice-Rolph

Placings:00*0*00235613/0043P124531PP/4100P0/FP3 62102434/45P-P (3895)
2001/02: 26^{P}HY

	Starts	1st	2nd	3rd	Win & Pl
Chases	1	0	0	0	
Career Total	**45**	**5**	**4**	**6**	**21289**

96	12/99	Catt	3m1f110y	E(0-115)HHdl	GD	£2290
103	5/98	Kbgn	3m1f	(0-116)Ch	G-F	£2531
100	3/98	Leop	3m	Ch	G-Y	£2978
90	10/97	Wxfd	3m	(0-109)HHdl	G-F	£3221
86	3/97	Clon	3m	(0-102)HHdl	GD	£3391

Total win prize-money £14413

Going: Sf: 0-1 GS: 0-0 Gd: 0-0 GF: - Fm: 0-0

Distance: 2m/2m3: 0-0 2m4-2m7: 0-0 3m+: 0-1
Track: LH: 0-1 RH: 0-0 Tight: 0-0 Gall: 0-0
Aids: Bl: 0-0 Vi: 0-0 Tstrap: 0-0
Best Rating: 103 5/98 Kbgn 3m1f gd-fm Ch

Coolsan (IRE)

98 90

7-y-o b g Insan (USA)-Coolreagh Princess (Raise You Ten)
R H Alner M Worcester

Placings: *1-0P3* (4152)
2001/02: 16^{0}G, 24^{P}HY, 20^{3}GS

	Starts	1st	2nd	3rd	Win & Pl
Hurdles	3	0	0		547
Career Total	4	1	0	1	4998

114	4/01	Cork	2m4f	NHF	SFT £4451

Total win prize-money £4452

Going: Sf: 0-1 GS: 0-1 Gd: 0-1 GF: - Fm: 0-0
Distance: 2m/2m3: 0-1 2m4-2m7: 0-1 3m+: 0-1
Track: LH: 0-3 RH: 0-0 Tight: 0-0 Gall: 0-0
Aids: Bl: 0-0 Vi: 0-0 Tstrap: 0-1
Best Rating: 114 4/01 Cork 2m4f soft NHF

He won a Cork bumper for Donal Hassett on his debut in April 2001, and was third in a maiden hurdle in March 2002, his first form in Britain.

Coolteen Hero (IRE)

101 106d

12-y-o b g King Luthier-Running Stream (Paddy's Stream)
R H Alner J Browne,Mrs C Robertson,Mrs E Woodhouse

Placings: 612U5U12212/F11222F3233/315B534FP/F 521203235/431432253-05425113063 (4681)
2001/02: 16^{0}G, 20^{5}GF, 20^{4}GF, 25^{2}GF, 24^{5}GF, 24^{1}GS, 23^{1}GF, 24^{3}S, 24^{0}GS, 21^{6}S, 25^{3}GF

	Starts	1st	2nd	3rd	Win & Pl
Chases	11	2	1	2	8165
Career Total	61	10	14	12	55346

106	11/01	Leic	2m7f110y	F(0-105)HCh	G-F	£3020
106	11/01	Chep	3m	F(0-110)HCh	G-S	£2555
116	11/00	Leic	2m4f110y	F(0-100)HCh	G-S	£2889
120	11/99	Hrfd	2m3f	F(0-110)HCh	GD	£3525
119	11/98	Plum	2m	E(0-115)HCh	SFT	£3452
118	10/97	Bang	2m1f110y	E(0-115)HCh	GD	£4135
114	9/97	Extr	2m1f110y	E(0-115)HCh	G-F	£3436
104	4/97	Extr	2m3f110y	D(0-125)HCh	FRM	£3629
98	2/97	Plum	2m	E Ch	G-S	£3183
78	10/96	Tntn	2m110y	E Ch	G-F	£2828

Total win prize-money £32656

Going: Sf: 0-2 GS: 1-2 Gd: 0-1 GF: - Fm: 1-6
Distance: 2m/2m3: 0-1 2m4-2m7: 0-3 **3m+: 2-7**
Track: LH: 1-3 RH: 1-7 Tight: 0-5 Gall: 0-0
Aids: Bl: 0-0 Vi: 0-0 Tstrap: 0-0
Best Rating: 121 2/00 Font 2m2f soft Ch

A front-running handicapper, he lacks finishing speed and usually finds one or two too good for him, until he finally landed the spoils at Chepstow in November, albeit amongst selling company. Followed up at Leicester. Stays three miles. Acts on a sound surface, handles soft.

Coombe Gold (IRE)

100 75

5-y-o b g Insan (USA)-Augustaeliza (IRE) (Callernish)
J T Gifford D S Norden & R S Norden

Placings: *064* (4730)
2001/02: 16^{0}G, 16^{6}S, 20^{4}GF

	Starts	1st	2nd	3rd	Win & Pl
NH Flat	1	0	0	0	0
Hurdles	2	0	0	0	0
Career Total	3	0	0	0	0

Going: Sf: 0-1 GS: 0-0 Gd: 0-1 GF: - Fm: 0-1
Distance: 2m/2m3: 0-2 2m4-2m7: 0-1 3m+: 0-0
Track: LH: 0-2 RH: 0-1 Tight: 0-0 Gall: 0-0
Aids: Bl: 0-0 Vi: 0-0 Tstrap: 0-0
Best Rating: 75 4/02 Chep 2m4f gd-fm Hdl

Coombs Spinney

75f 53f

5-y-o b g Homo Sapien-Woodram Delight (Idiots Delight)
Mrs P Sly R M Micklethwait

Placings: *00* (4552)
2001/02: 17^{0}GS, 16^{0}GF

	Starts	1st	2nd	3rd	Win & Pl
NH Flat	2	0	0	0	
Career Total	2	0	0	0	

Going: Sf: 0-0 GS: 0-1 Gd: 0-0 GF: - Fm: 0-1
Distance: 2m/2m3: 0-2 2m4-2m7: 0-0 3m+: 0-0
Track: LH: 0-0 RH: 0-2 Tight: 0-1 Gall: 0-1
Aids: Bl: 0-0 Vi: 0-0 Tstrap: 0-0
Best Rating: 53 3/02 MRas 2m1f110y gd-sft NHF

Cootehill Boy (IRE)

(98h) (87h)

8-y-o br g Strong Gale-Orospring (Tesoro Mio)
W Storey John J Maguire

Placings: *0/0500/01133-664* (1351)
2001/02: 20^{6}S, 21^{6}GF, 21^{4}GF

	Starts	1st	2nd	3rd	Win & Pl
Hurdles	3	0	0	0	0
Career Total	13	2	0	2	5825

90	8/00	Prth	3m110y	F(0-100)HHdl	GD	£2990
93	8/00	Sedg	2m5f110y	F(0-100)HHdl	GD	£2226

Total win prize-money £5216

Going: Sf: 0-1 GS: 0-0 Gd: 0-0 GF: - Fm: 0-2
Distance: 2m/2m3: 0-0 2m4-2m7: 0-3 3m+: 0-0
Track: LH: 0-2 RH: 0-1 Tight: 0-2 Gall: 0-0
Aids: Bl: 0-0 Vi: 0-0 Tstrap: 0-3
Best Rating: 95 10/00 Weth 2m7f gd-sft Hdl

Cope With Reality (IRE)

9-y-o b g Danehill (USA)-Reality (Known Fact (USA))
J J O'Neill Miss A Kershaw

Placings: *50121F/PPP121/P* (1469)
2001/02: 24^{P}G

	Starts	1st	2nd	3rd	Win & Pl
Hurdles	1	0	0	0	
Career Total	13	4	2	0	10071

117	2/00	Muss	3m	E(0-115)HHdl	G-S	£2717
107	12/99	Sedg	2m5f110y	F(0-110)HHdl	G-S	£2670
106	11/98	Ayr	2m6f	E Hdl	G-S	£2495
102	10/98	Sedg	2m1f	H NHF	GD	£1161

Total win prize-money £9043

Going: Sf: 0-0 GS: 0-0 Gd: 0-1 GF: - Fm: 0-0
Distance: 2m/2m3: 0-0 2m4-2m7: 0-0 3m+: 0-1
Track: LH: 0-0 RH: 0-1 Tight: 0-0 Gall: 0-0
Aids: Bl: 0-0 Vi: 0-0 Tstrap: 0-0
Best Rating: 117 2/00 Muss 3m gd-sft Hdl

Copeland

119 164

7-y-o b g Generous (IRE)-Whitehaven (Top Ville)
M C Pipe Dr D B A & Mrs Heather Silk

Placings: 211202/3635053-211202U1 (4902)
2001/02: 16^{2}GS, 17^{1}HY, 16^{1}S, 16^{2}GS, 17^{0}G, 16^{2}GS, 16^{U}G, 16^{1}G

	Starts	1st	2nd	3rd	Win & Pl
Hurdles	8	3	3	0	129737
Career Total	21	5	6	3	211700

158	4/02	Sand	2m110y	B Hdl	GD	£35700
164	2/02	Newb	2m110y	A HHdl	SFT	£63800
164	1/02	Chel	2m1f	B(0-145)HHdl	HVY	£10257
143	12/99	Sand	2m110y	B HHdl	G-S	£34900
128	11/99	Wwck	2m2f110y	D Hdl	GD	£4146

Total win prize-money £148803

Going: Sf: 2-2 GS: 0-3 Gd: 1-3 GF: - Fm: 0-0
Distance: **2m/2m3: 3-8** 2m4-2m7: 0-0 3m+: 0-0
Track: **LH: 2-5** RH: 1-3 Tight: 0-0 **Gall: 2-3**
Aids: Bl: 0-0 **Vi: 3-8** Tstrap: 0-0
Best Rating: 164 2/02 Winc 2m gd-sft Hdl

A very useful handicap hurdler at around two miles. He was a comfortable winner at Cheltenham in the 2001/02 season, before following up in the Tote Gold Trophy at Newbury. Ran some fine races in defeat after that, including when a good second behind subsequent Champion Hurdler Hors La Loi III at Wincanton, before scoring narrowly at Sandown in April. Seems to handle any ground and usually wears a visor.

Coppeen Cross (IRE)

(88h) (84h)71

8-y-o b g Phardante (FR)-Greek Opal (Furry Glen)
O Brennan O Brennan

Placings: *60* (3391)
2001/02: 20^{6}G, 23^{0}GS

	Starts	1st	2nd	3rd	Win & Pl
Hurdles	1	0	0	0	0
Chases	1	0	0	0	0
Career Total	2	0	0	0	0

Going: Sf: 0-0 GS: 0-1 Gd: 0-1 GF: - Fm: 0-0
Distance: 2m/2m3: 0-0 2m4-2m7: 0-1 3m+: 0-1
Track: LH: 0-1 RH: 0-0 Tight: 0-0 Gall: 0-0
Aids: Bl: 0-0 Vi: 0-0 Tstrap: 0-0
Best Rating: 84 11/01 Hayd 2m4f good Hdl

Coppeen Sam (IRE)

87 68

7-y-o b g Samhoi (USA)-Castleview Rose (Master Buck)
Miss Jacqueline S Doyle The 1st Flemington Partnership

Placings: *3430-000* (1488)
2001/02: 20^{0}G, 22^{0}F, 20^{0}GF

	Starts	1st	2nd	3rd	Win & Pl
Hurdles	3	0	0	0	
Career Total	7	0	0	2	582

Going: Sf: 0-0 GS: 0-0 Gd: 0-1 GF: - Fm: 0-2
Distance: 2m/2m3: 0-0 2m4-2m7: 0-3 3m+: 0-0
Track: LH: 0-0 RH: 0-2 Tight: 0-0 Gall: 0-2
Aids: Bl: 0-2 Vi: 0-0 Tstrap: 0-0
Best Rating: 100 12/00 Hntg 2m110y heavy NHF

Copper Coil

12-y-o ch g Undulate (USA)-April Rose (Wollow)
Richard J Smith R A Lloyd

Placings:*40*50230520/234251533P/15P6005P5/1104 **U3P0/44U/30-5** **(0077)**
2001/02: 23^{5}G

	Starts	1st	2nd	3rd	Win & Pl
Chases	1	0	0	0	0
Career Total	**43**	**4**	**4**	**6**	**16026**

114 5/98 Extr 2m3f110y E(0-110)HHdl FRM £2791
119 5/98 Hrfd 2m3f110y E(0-115)HHdl GD £2892
95 10/97 Font 2m6f110y E(0-115)HHdl GD £2322
95 12/96 Plum 3m110y E(0-100)HHdl G-S £2364
Total win prize-money £10370

Going: Sf: 0-0 GS: 0-0 Gd: 0-1 GF: - Fm: 0-0
Distance: 2m/2m3: 0-0 2m4-2m7: 0-0 3m+: 0-1
Track: LH: 0-0 RH: 0-1 Tight: 0-0 Gall: 0-0
Aids: Bl: 0-0 Vi: 0-0 Tstrap: 0-0
Best Rating: 119 5/98 Hrfd 2m3f110y good Hdl

Copper Coin (IRE)

108(105h) (74h)128
8-y-o b/br g Mandalus-Two-Penny Rice (Reformed Character)
R N Bevis Miss N C Taylor

Placings:03123/02U6-00**U1** (3321)
2001/02: 21^{0}GS, 20^{0}S, 23^{U}G, 24^{1}GS

	Starts	1st	2nd	3rd	Win & Pl
Hurdles	2	0	0	0	0
Chases	2	1	0	0	3055
Career Total	**13**	**2**	**2**	**2**	**9535**

128 1/02 Hntg 3m E Ch G-S £3055
101 12/98 Wind 2m E Hdl G-S £2092
Total win prize-money £5148

Going: Sf: 0-1 GS: 1-2 Gd: 0-1 GF: - Fm: 0-0
Distance: 2m/2m3: 0-0 2m4-2m7: 0-2 **3m+: 1-2**
Track: LH: 0-1 **RH: 1-3** Tight: 0-0 **Gall: 1-1**
Aids: Bl: 0-0 Vi: 0-0 Tstrap: 0-0
Best Rating: 128 1/02 Hntg 3m gd-sft Ch

Surprise winner of a novice chase in January 2002, jumping well and racing prominently. Stays three miles.

Copper Moss

4-y-o ch g Le Moss-Shiona Anne (Royal Fountain)
J Barclay Kinneston Racing

Placings:*0* (3613)
2001/02: 16^{0}S

	Starts	1st	2nd	3rd	Win & Pl
NH Flat	1	0	0	0	
Career Total	**1**	**0**	**0**	**0**	

Going: Sf: 0-1 GS: 0-0 Gd: 0-0 GF: - Fm: 0-0
Distance: 2m/2m3: 0-1 2m4-2m7: 0-0 3m+: 0-0
Track: LH: 0-0 RH: 0-1 Tight: 0-1 Gall: 0-0
Aids: Bl: 0-0 Vi: 0-0 Tstrap: 0-0
Best Rating:

Copper Shell

103(48h) 117
8-y-o ch g Beveled (USA)-Luly My Love (Hello Gorgeous (USA))
G L Moore Brighton Racing Club

Placings:5P230/400604/504/5**1210-P553P26** **(4495)**
2001/02: 20^{P}GS, 16^{5}S, 17^{5}G, 16^{3}S, 18^{P}HY, 16^{2}S, 16^{6}G

	Starts	1st	2nd	3rd	Win & Pl
Chases	7	0	1	1	1662
Career Total	**26**	**2**	**3**	**2**	**10775**

117 4/01 Plum 2m1f E Ch SFT £3883
110 1/01 Folk 2m E(0-105)HCh HVY £2912
Total win prize-money £6796

Going: Sf: 0-4 GS: 0-1 Gd: 0-2 GF: - Fm: 0-0
Distance: 2m/2m3: 0-6 2m4-2m7: 0-1 3m+: 0-0
Track: LH: 0-3 RH: 0-2 Tight: 0-3 Gall: 0-2
Aids: Bl: 0-0 Vi: 0-0 Tstrap: 0-7
Best Rating: 117 4/01 Plum 2m1f soft Ch

A winner on the Flat and he has also been successful over fences. Wears a tongue strap and acts on a soft surface, he is effective at around two miles.

Copper Thistle (IRE)

14-y-o b g Ovac (ITY)-Phantom Thistle (Deep Run)
Mrs Caroline Bailey R S Hunnisett

Placings:4/2P/10/3/2/1P-2 **(0256)**
2001/02: 28^{2}GF

	Starts	1st	2nd	3rd	Win & Pl
Chases	1	0	1	0	747
Career Total	**10**	**2**	**3**	**1**	**8430**

126 5/00 Towc 3m1f H Ch G-F £4212
93 3/97 Leic 3m H Ch GD £2152
Total win prize-money £6365

Going: Sf: 0-0 GS: 0-0 Gd: 0-0 GF: - Fm: 0-1
Distance: 2m/2m3: 0-0 2m4-2m7: 0-0 3m+: 0-1
Track: LH: 0-1 RH: 0-0 Tight: 0-1 Gall: 0-0
Aids: Bl: 0-0 Vi: 0-0 Tstrap: 0-0
Best Rating: 126 5/00 Towc 3m1f gd-fm Ch

Copperpot (IRE)

76 78
5-y-o ch g Treasure Hunter-Merillion (Touch Paper)
N G Richards Trevor Hemmings

Placings:055 **(4520)**
2001/02: 20^{0}G, 20^{5}HY, 20^{5}G

	Starts	1st	2nd	3rd	Win & Pl
Hurdles	3	0	0	0	0
Career Total	**3**	**0**	**0**	**0**	**0**

Going: Sf: 0-1 GS: 0-0 Gd: 0-2 GF: - Fm: 0-0
Distance: 2m/2m3: 0-0 2m4-2m7: 0-3 3m+: 0-0
Track: LH: 0-1 RH: 0-0 Tight: 0-0 Gall: 0-1
Aids: Bl: 0-0 Vi: 0-0 Tstrap: 0-0
Best Rating: 78 4/02 Carl 2m4f good Hdl

Copplestone (IRE)

92 81
6-y-o b g Second Set (IRE)-Queen Of The Brush (Averof)
W Storey (J R Best 14/12) B P Bradshaw

Placings:44 **(4438)**
2001/02: 16^{4}GS, 16^{4}S

	Starts	1st	2nd	3rd	Win & Pl
Hurdles	2	0	0	0	0
Career Total	**2**	**0**	**0**	**0**	

Going: Sf: 0-1 GS: 0-1 Gd: 0-0 GF: - Fm: 0-0
Distance: 2m/2m3: 0-2 2m4-2m7: 0-0 3m+: 0-0
Track: LH: 0-2 RH: 0-0 Tight: 0-2 Gall: 0-0
Aids: Bl: 0-0 Vi: 0-0 Tstrap: 0-0
Best Rating: 81 3/02 Kels 2m110y soft Hdl

Showed some ability on his first start over hurdles.

Copshaw Road

33
9-y-o b g Teenoso (USA)-Marjoemin (Import)
B Mactaggart Ashleybank Investments Limited

Placings:*0*/**F**-0P00P **(4745)**
2001/02: 20^{0}S, 16^{P}HY, 22^{0}HY, 20^{0}G, 24^{P}G

	Starts	1st	2nd	3rd	Win & Pl
Hurdles	5	0	0	0	
Career Total	**7**	**0**	**0**	**0**	

Going: Sf: 0-3 GS: 0-0 Gd: 0-2 GF: - Fm: 0-0
Distance: 2m/2m3: 0-1 2m4-2m7: 0-3 3m+: 0-1
Track: LH: 0-3 RH: 0-1 Tight: 0-1 Gall: 0-0
Aids: Bl: 0-0 Vi: 0-0 Tstrap: 0-0
Best Rating: 33 4/02 Carl 2m4f good Hdl

Copyforce Girl

6-y-o b m Elmaamul (USA)-Sabaya (USA) (Seattle Dancer (USA))
D Burchell (J K Price 8/1) J K Price

Placings:0/0 **(3157)**
2001/02: 17^{0}S

	Starts	1st	2nd	3rd	Win & Pl
Hurdles	1	0	0	0	
Career Total	**2**	**0**	**0**	**0**	

Going: Sf: 0-1 GS: 0-0 Gd: 0-0 GF: - Fm: 0-0
Distance: 2m/2m3: 0-1 2m4-2m7: 0-0 3m+: 0-0
Track: LH: 0-0 RH: 0-1 Tight: 0-0 Gall: 0-0
Aids: Bl: 0-0 Vi: 0-0 Tstrap: 0-1
Best Rating:

Coq Hardi Dancer (IRE)

12-y-o b g Mandalus-Cut The Cake (Fine Blade (USA))
Mrs S J Smith Mrs S Smith

Placings:*00/55/3434/3/F-P* **(3442)**
2001/02: 16^{P}HY

	Starts	1st	2nd	3rd	Win & Pl
Chases	1	0	0	0	
Career Total	**11**	**0**	**0**	**3**	**1821**

Going: Sf: 0-1 GS: 0-0 Gd: 0-0 GF: - Fm: 0-0
Distance: 2m/2m3: 0-1 2m4-2m7: 0-0 3m+: 0-0
Track: LH: 0-1 RH: 0-0 Tight: 0-1 Gall: 0-0
Aids: Bl: 0-0 Vi: 0-0 Tstrap: 0-0
Best Rating: 90 10/97 Worc 2m7f110y soft Ch

Coquelles (FR)

(110h) (87h)
6-y-o b m In The Wings-La Toja (FR) (Gift Card (FR))

R M Stronge A P Holland

Placings:6/P-50521 **(4187)**
2001/02: 16^{5}S, 20^{0}GS, 21^{5}S, 21^{2}HY, 19^{1}S

	Starts	1st	2nd	3rd	Win & Pl
Hurdles	5	1	1	0	4188
Career Total	**7**	**1**	**1**	**0**	**4188**

87	3/02	Tntn	2m3f110y	E(0-105)HHdl	SFT	£3486

Total win prize-money £3486

Going: Sf: 1-4 GS: 0-1 Gd: 0-0 GF: - Fm: 0-0
Distance: 2m/2m3: 0-1 **2m4-2m7: 1-4** 3m+: 0-0
Track: LH: 0-3 **RH: 1-2 Tight: 1-4** Gall: 0-0
Aids: Bl: 0-0 Vi: 0-0 Tstrap: 0-0
Best Rating: 87 3/02 Tntn 2m3f110y soft Hdl

Modest hurdler, stays two and a half miles and acts on soft ground, and won a modest handicap hurdle in these conditions in March 2002.

Coral Island

104(93h) (93h)**138**
8-y-o b g Charmer-Misowni (Niniski (USA))
R M Stronge Robert Stronge

Placings:1130/00600/F016100/00**1412164**P **(4500)**
2001/02: 18^{0}GS, 22^{0}GS, 16^{1}S, 19^{4}G, 17^{1}G, 17^{2}G, 19^{1}S, 20^{6}GS, 20^{4}S, 17^{P}G

	Starts	1st	2nd	3rd	Win & Pl
Hurdles	3	0	0	0	0
Chases	7	3	1	0	14897
Career Total	**26**	**7**	**1**	**1**	**26913**

138	1/02	Donc	2m3f110y	D Ch	SFT	£4431
127	12/01	Plum	2m1f	D Ch	GD	£4030
124	12/01	Wwck	2m110y	D Ch	SFT	£4004
117	12/99	Font	2m6f110y	C(0-130)HHdl	G-S	£4742
106	10/99	Font	2m6f110y	E(0-115)HHdl	GD	£2285
103	9/97	Sedg	2m1f	E Hdl	G-F	£2320
103	8/97	Prth	2m110y	E Hdl	GD	£2276

Total win prize-money £24089

Going: Sf: 2-3 GS: 0-3 Gd: 1-4 GF: - Fm: 0-0
Distance: **2m/2m3: 2-5** 2m4-2m7: 1-5 3m+: 0-0
Track: **LH: 2-7** RH: 0-2 Tight: 1-4 Gall: 1-3
Aids: Bl: 0-0 Vi: 0-0 Tstrap: 0-0
Best Rating: 138 1/02 Donc 2m3f110y soft Ch

He has gone well fresh in the past and particularly well at Fontwell. He switched successfully to fences at the end of 2001 with wins in modest company and a good second at Newbury in January 2002. His victories over fences have been at shorter trips, but he has won at up to two miles six over hurdles. Handles good ground or softer.

Coral Reef (IRE)

90 **94**
6-y-o ch m Karinga Bay-Mamara Reef (Salse (USA))
W G M Turner David Chown

Placings:443F13/10-603 **(0266)**
2001/02: 16^{6}S, 18^{0}GF, 19^{3}G

	Starts	1st	2nd	3rd	Win & Pl
Hurdles	3	0	0	1	292
Career Total	**11**	**2**	**0**	**3**	**5962**

95	3/01	Strf	2m3f	G Hdl	SFT	£2982
81	1/00	Tntn	2m1f	G Hdl	G-S	£1589

Total win prize-money £4571

Going: Sf: 0-1 GS: 0-0 Gd: 0-1 GF: - Fm: 0-1
Distance: 2m/2m3: 0-2 2m4-2m7: 0-1 3m+: 0-0
Track: LH: 0-2 RH: 0-1 Tight: 0-2 Gall: 0-0
Aids: Bl: 0-0 Vi: 0-1 Tstrap: 0-0
Best Rating: 95 3/01 Strf 2m3f soft Hdl

Coralette (IRE)

(72h) (25h)
12-y-o ch g Le Moss-Myralette (Deep Run)
B P J Baugh Russell Dobney

Placings:420/P/40054053/3/P/P-00 **(0374)**
2001/02: 19^{0}F, 26^{0}GF

	Starts	1st	2nd	3rd	Win & Pl
Hurdles	2	0	0	0	
Career Total	**17**	**0**	**1**	**2**	**1536**

Going: Sf: 0-0 GS: 0-0 Gd: 0-0 GF: - Fm: 0-2
Distance: 2m/2m3: 0-0 2m4-2m7: 0-1 3m+: 0-1
Track: LH: 0-0 RH: 0-2 Tight: 0-1 Gall: 0-1
Aids: Bl: 0-0 Vi: 0-2 Tstrap: 0-0
Best Rating: 104 12/95 Towc 2m soft Hdl

Coralinga

71f
5-y-o b m Terimon-Kintra (Sunyboy)
Miss E C Lavelle Mrs Julien Turner

Placings:2 **(4784)**
2001/02: 18^{2}GF

	Starts	1st	2nd	3rd	Win & Pl
NH Flat	1	0	1	0	489
Career Total	**1**	**0**	**1**	**0**	**489**

Going: Sf: 0-0 GS: 0-0 Gd: 0-0 GF: - Fm: 0-1
Distance: 2m/2m3: 0-1 2m4-2m7: 0-0 3m+: 0-0
Track: LH: 0-0 RH: 0-0 Tight: 0-0 Gall: 0-0
Aids: Bl: 0-0 Vi: 0-0 Tstrap: 0-0
Best Rating: 71 4/02 Plum 2m2f gd-fm NHF

Showed promise on bumper debut.

Corbie Abbey (IRE)

81(99h) (97h)**85**
7-y-o b g Glacial Storm (USA)-Dromoland Lady (Pollerton)
B Mactaggart J Stephenson

Placings:600/0P6P0-300F4 **(2117)**
2001/02: 16^{3}GF, 20^{0}GS, 17^{0}G, 17^{F}G, 16^{4}GS

	Starts	1st	2nd	3rd	Win & Pl
Hurdles	2	0	0	1	429
Chases	3	0	0	0	0
Career Total	**13**	**0**	**0**	**1**	**429**

Going: Sf: 0-0 GS: 0-2 Gd: 0-2 GF: - Fm: 0-1
Distance: 2m/2m3: 0-4 2m4-2m7: 0-1 3m+: 0-0
Track: LH: 0-4 RH: 0-0 Tight: 0-3 Gall: 0-0
Aids: Bl: 0-0 Vi: 0-0 Tstrap: 0-0
Best Rating: 97 4/01 Ayr 2m good Hdl

Corbie's Glen

90 **77**
8-y-o b m Broadsword (USA)-Celestial Bride (Godswalk (USA))
B Mactaggart Mrs M Marshall

Placings:00065/404 **(4830)**
2001/02: 22^{4}GS, 22^{0}GS, 24^{4}G

	Starts	1st	2nd	3rd	Win & Pl
Hurdles	3	0	0	0	558
Career Total	**8**	**0**	**0**	**0**	**558**

Going: Sf: 0-0 GS: 0-2 Gd: 0-1 GF: - Fm: 0-0
Distance: 2m/2m3: 0-0 2m4-2m7: 0-2 3m+: 0-1
Track: LH: 0-3 RH: 0-0 Tight: 0-1 Gall: 0-0
Aids: Bl: 0-0 Vi: 0-0 Tstrap: 0-0
Best Rating: 78 2/00 Muss 2m4f good Hdl

Corehill Countess (IRE)

103 **90**
9-y-o ch m Jamesmead-Miss Allright (Candy Cane)
I A Duncan Mrs B Preston

Placings:P03030310U0/00000/005F0-0200 **(2407)**
2001/02: 17^{0}YS, 20^{2}YS, 20^{0}S, 20^{0}HY

	Starts	1st	2nd	3rd	Win & Pl
Hurdles	4	0	1	0	1290
Career Total	**25**	**1**	**1**	**3**	**3306**

85	9/98	Dpat	2m1f172y	NHF	SFT	£1494

Total win prize-money £1495

Going: Sf: 0-2 GS: 0-0 Gd: 0-0 GF: - Fm: 0-0
Distance: 2m/2m3: 0-1 2m4-2m7: 0-3 3m+: 0-0
Track: LH: 0-0 RH: 0-2 Tight: 0-0 Gall: 0-0
Aids: Bl: 0-3 Vi: 0-0 Tstrap: 0-1
Best Rating: 90 11/01 Punc 2m4f yld-sft Hdl

Corkan (IRE)

111 **101+**
8-y-o b g Torus-Broad Tab (Cantab)
J Cullinan Mrs E Reid

Placings:066P/**533P4-2P441** **(4510)**
2001/02: 26^{2}G, 24^{P}G, 24^{4}G, 26^{4}S, 26^{1}G

	Starts	1st	2nd	3rd	Win & Pl
Chases	5	1	1	0	4254
Career Total	**14**	**1**	**1**	**2**	**5434**

93	3/02	Plum	3m2f	F(0-95)HCh	GD	£2509

Total win prize-money £2509

Going: Sf: 0-1 GS: 0-0 Gd: 1-4 GF: - Fm: 0-0
Distance: 2m/2m3: 0-0 2m4-2m7: 0-0 **3m+: 1-5**
Track: LH: 0-0 RH: 0-2 Tight: 0-2 Gall: 0-0
Aids: Bl: 0-0 Vi: 0-0 Tstrap: 0-0
Best Rating: 95 5/01 Folk 3m2f good Ch

Ex-Irish gelding. Modest chaser at around three and a quarter miles on good ground.

Corket (IRE)

12-y-o b g Orchestra-Tor-Na-Grena (Torus)
S O'Sullivan S O'Sullivan

Placings:*15*000061612/111F0P/**1115F/FPPP6522/P5236/PPPP/P3U0P22143-00** **(0577)**
2001/02: 25^{0}G, 21^{0}GF

	Starts	1st	2nd	3rd	Win & Pl
Chases	2	0	0	0	
Career Total	**51**	**10**	**6**	**3**	**64249**

125	9/00	Strf	3m	D(0-125)HCh	GD	£5712
133	2/97	Naas	2m4f	Ch	SFT	£6782
126	2/97	Navn	2m4f	Ch	Y-S	£4069
115	1/97	Navn	2m1f	Ch	G-Y	£4069
136	11/95	Gowr	2m1f	(0-123)HHdl	Y-S	£2712
126	10/95	Wxfd	2m2f100y	(0-123)HHdl	G-Y	£3221
122	10/95	Navn	2m4f	(0-130)HHdl	GD	£3391
108	4/95	Limk	2m	(0-109)HHdl	GD	£2712
94	3/95	Dpat	2m1f172y	Hdl	HVY	£1356
	10/94	Fair	2m	NHF	SFT	£2935

Total win prize-money £36963

Going: Sf: 0-0 GS: 0-0 Gd: 0-1 GF: - Fm: 0-1
Distance: 2m/2m3: 0-0 2m4-2m7: 0-1 3m+: 0-1

Track: LH: 0-2 RH: 0-0 Tight: 0-1 Gall: 0-0
Aids: Bl: 0-0 Vi: 0-0 Tstrap: 0-1
Best Rating: 152 4/97 Punc 3m1f good Ch

Formerly useful ex-Irish chaser, reaching the veteran stage and now hunter chasing.

Corletto (POL)

109 91

5-y-o b g Professional (IRE)-Cortesia (POL) (Who Knows)
T R George B A Kilpatrick

Placings:P65115 (4908)
2001/02: 16PG, 196S, 165S, 171S, 171GF, 215G

	Starts	1st	2nd	3rd	Win & Pl
Hurdles	6	2	0	0	6830
Career Total	**6**	**2**	**0**	**0**	**6830**

91	4/02	Hrfd	2m1f	D(0-115)HHdl	G-F	£3896
85	3/02	Tntn	2m1f	F(0-95)HHdl	SFT	£2933

Total win prize-money £6830

Going: Sf: 1-3 GS: 0-0 Gd: 0-2 GF: - Fm: 1-1
Distance: **2m/2m3: 2-4** 2m4-2m7: 0-2 3m+: 0-0
Track: LH: 0-2 **RH: 2-4 Tight: 1-3** Gall: 0-0
Aids: Bl: 0-0 Vi: 0-0 Tstrap: 0-0
Best Rating: 91 4/02 Hrfd 2m1f gd-fm Hdl

A strongly-made gelding, back-to-back wins in novice handicaps in spring 2002. Appears to handle any ground.

Corn Bunting

86f 77f

5-y-o b/br m Teenoso (USA)-Annie Kelly (Oats)
Ian Williams Mrs R Hoare

Placings:5 (0678)
2001/02: 165GF

	Starts	1st	2nd	3rd	Win & Pl
NH Flat	1	0	0	0	0
Career Total	**1**	**0**	**0**	**0**	**0**

Going: Sf: 0-0 GS: 0-0 Gd: 0-0 GF: - Fm: 0-1
Distance: 2m/2m3: 0-1 2m4-2m7: 0-0 3m+: 0-0
Track: LH: 0-1 RH: 0-0 Tight: 0-0 Gall: 0-0
Aids: Bl: 0-0 Vi: 0-0 Tstrap: 0-0
Best Rating: 77 6/01 Worc 2m gd-fm NHF

Corniche (IRE)

(111h) (116h)

7-y-o b/br g Marju (IRE)-Far But Near (USA) (Far North (CAN))
B J Llewellyn (N A Twiston-Davies 23/11) John Marks

Placings:21033/0652F3U3/321022U24P-0P614F (4192)
2001/02: 210G, 16PGF, 186G, 241G, 254HY, 24FGS

	Starts	1st	2nd	3rd	Win & Pl
Hurdles	4	1	0	0	7158
Chases	2	0	0	0	0
Career Total	**29**	**3**	**6**	**5**	**45142**

115	12/01	Sthl	3m110y	C(0-130)HHdl	GD	£6873
144	10/00	Chel	2m	C Ch	GD	£5876
117	3/99	Newb	2m3f	D Hdl	SFT	£3532

Total win prize-money £16282

Going: Sf: 0-1 GS: 0-1 Gd: 1-3 GF: - Fm: 0-1
Distance: 2m/2m3: 0-2 2m4-2m7: 0-1 **3m+: 1-3**
Track: **LH: 1-4** RH: 0-1 **Tight: 1-2** Gall: 0-2
Aids: Bl: 0-0 Vi: 0-0 Tstrap: 0-0
Best Rating: 147 1/01 Tntn 2m110y heavy Ch

A keen front-runner, he was a useful hurdler before switching to fences but struggled against some smart rivals and won only once. Changed stables late in 2001 and returned to the smaller obstacles, winning over three miles at Southwell in December 2001. Suited by good ground, although has shown form on an easier surface. Stays three miles.

Cornish Gale (IRE)

103(89h) (85h)149

8-y-o br g Strong Gale-Seanaphobal Lady (Kambalda)
P F Nicholls C G Roach

Placings:0/22P-53111 (2789)
2001/02: 165GF, 203GF, 191GF, 201G, 161G

	Starts	1st	2nd	3rd	Win & Pl
Hurdles	1	0	0	0	0
Chases	4	3	0	1	28836
Career Total	**9**	**3**	**2**	**1**	**29958**

148	12/01	Asct	2m	C(0-125)HCh	GD	£10166
149	11/01	Chel	2m4f110y	B Ch	GD	£12754
133	11/01	Extr	2m3f110y	D Ch	G-F	£5395

Total win prize-money £28315

Going: Sf: 0-0 GS: 0-0 **Gd: 2-2** GF: - Fm: 1-3
Distance: 2m/2m3: 1-2 **2m4-2m7: 2-3** 3m+: 0-0
Track: LH: 1-1 **RH: 2-4** Tight: 0-1 **Gall: 1-1**
Aids: Bl: 0-0 Vi: 0-0 Tstrap: 0-0
Best Rating: 149 11/01 Chel 2m4f110y good Ch

Progressive novice chaser, has had a wind operation and has since won three times over fences. Acts on good and good to firm and is effective at around two and a half miles. Jumps well.

Cornish Hope

8-y-o b g Henbit (USA)-Sleepers (Swing Easy (USA))
C J Gray K F Fisher

Placings:P (3757)
2001/02: 17PS

	Starts	1st	2nd	3rd	Win & Pl
Hurdles	1	0	0	0	
Career Total	**1**	**0**	**0**	**0**	

Going: Sf: 0-1 GS: 0-0 Gd: 0-0 GF: - Fm: 0-0
Distance: 2m/2m3: 0-1 2m4-2m7: 0-0 3m+: 0-0
Track: LH: 0-0 RH: 0-1 Tight: 0-1 Gall: 0-0
Aids: Bl: 0-0 Vi: 0-0 Tstrap: 0-0
Best Rating:

Corrage (IRE)

84 45

5-y-o b g Corrouge (USA)-Cora Gold (Goldhill)
N A Twiston-Davies Michael Gates

Placings:0 (3989)
2001/02: 240S

	Starts	1st	2nd	3rd	Win & Pl
Hurdles	1	0	0	0	
Career Total	**1**	**0**	**0**	**0**	

Going: Sf: 0-1 GS: 0-0 Gd: 0-0 GF: - Fm: 0-0
Distance: 2m/2m3: 0-0 2m4-2m7: 0-0 3m+: 0-1
Track: LH: 0-0 RH: 0-1 Tight: 0-1 Gall: 0-0
Aids: Bl: 0-0 Vi: 0-0 Tstrap: 0-0
Best Rating: 45 2/02 Tntn 3m110y soft Hdl

Corrie Mashie

7-y-o b g North Col-Loch Dirowahn (The Brianstan)
J G Smyth-Osbourne Mrs E T Smyth-Osbourne

Placings:4F (0370)
2001/02: 164G, 16FG

	Starts	1st	2nd	3rd	Win & Pl
NH Flat	1	0	0	0	0
Hurdles	1	0	0	0	0
Career Total	**2**	**0**	**0**	**0**	**0**

Going: Sf: 0-0 GS: 0-0 Gd: 0-2 GF: - Fm: 0-0
Distance: 2m/2m3: 0-2 2m4-2m7: 0-0 3m+: 0-0
Track: LH: 0-1 RH: 0-1 Tight: 0-0 Gall: 0-1
Aids: Bl: 0-0 Vi: 0-0 Tstrap: 0-0
Best Rating: 89 5/01 Hntg 2m110y good NHF

Corroboree (IRE)

95 83

5-y-o b g Corrouge (USA)-Laura's Toi (Quayside)
N A Twiston-Davies The Corroborators

Placings:32000 (4597)
2001/02: 163S, 172GS, 240S, 190S, 190GF

	Starts	1st	2nd	3rd	Win & Pl
NH Flat	2	0	1	1	924
Hurdles	3	0	0	0	0
Career Total	**5**	**0**	**1**	**1**	**924**

Going: Sf: 0-3 GS: 0-1 Gd: 0-0 GF: - Fm: 0-1
Distance: 2m/2m3: 0-4 2m4-2m7: 0-0 3m+: 0-1
Track: LH: 0-3 RH: 0-1 Tight: 0-0 Gall: 0-1
Aids: Bl: 0-0 Vi: 0-0 Tstrap: 0-0
Best Rating: 107 11/01 Aint 2m1f gd-sft NHF

Has shown promise in bumpers.

Cosa Fuair (IRE)

12-y-o b g Roselier (FR)-Bold And True (Sir Herbert)
F E Sutherland Miss H P J Scheffers

Placings:0056/52/03P/45/PP (0430)
2001/02: 20PGF, 16PG

	Starts	1st	2nd	3rd	Win & Pl
Chases	2	0	0	0	
Career Total	**13**	**0**	**1**	**1**	**1206**

Going: Sf: 0-0 GS: 0-0 Gd: 0-1 GF: - Fm: 0-1
Distance: 2m/2m3: 0-1 2m4-2m7: 0-1 3m+: 0-0
Track: LH: 0-0 RH: 0-1 Tight: 0-0 Gall: 0-1
Aids: Bl: 0-1 Vi: 0-0 Tstrap: 0-0
Best Rating: 85 11/96 Wwck 2m3f gd-fm Hdl

Cosmic Buzz

83 74

5-y-o ch g Cosmonaut-G'Ime A Buzz (Electric)
J G Given D M Beresford

Placings:404-00 (0640)
2001/02: 200GS, 190GF

	Starts	1st	2nd	3rd	Win & Pl
Hurdles	2	0	0	0	
Career Total	**5**	**0**	**0**	**0**	**339**

Going: Sf: 0-0 GS: 0-1 Gd: 0-0 GF: - Fm: 0-1
Distance: 2m/2m3: 0-0 2m4-2m7: 0-2 3m+: 0-0
Track: LH: 0-1 RH: 0-1 Tight: 0-2 Gall: 0-0

Aids: Bl: 0-1 Vi: 0-0 Tstrap: 0-0
Best Rating: 74 4/01 MRas 2m3f110y heavy Hdl

Cosmic Dancer

69 **53**

5-y-o b g Cosmonaut-Djanila (Fabulous Dancer (USA))
D J S Ffrench Davis L F Hoare

Placings:00-0 **(0431)**
2001/02: 17^{0}GF

	Starts	1st	2nd	3rd	Win & Pl
Hurdles	1	0	0	0	
Career Total	**3**	**0**	**0**	**0**	

Going: Sf: 0-0 GS: 0-0 Gd: 0-0 GF: - Fm: 0-1
Distance: 2m/2m3: 0-1 2m4-2m7: 0-0 3m+: 0-0
Track: LH: 0-0 RH: 0-1 Tight: 0-1 Gall: 0-0
Aids: Bl: 0-0 Vi: 0-0 Tstrap: 0-0
Best Rating: 53 4/01 Hrfd 2m1f good Hdl

Cosmic Flight (IRE)

85f **84f**

6-y-o b g Torus-Palatine Lady (Pauper)
Noel T Chance Top Flight Racing

Placings:0-50 **(1946)**
2001/02: 16^{5}GF, 18^{0}GS

	Starts	1st	2nd	3rd	Win & Pl
NH Flat	2	0	0	0	0
Career Total	**3**	**0**	**0**	**0**	**0**

Going: Sf: 0-0 GS: 0-1 Gd: 0-0 GF: - Fm: 0-1
Distance: 2m/2m3: 0-2 2m4-2m7: 0-0 3m+: 0-0
Track: LH: 0-1 RH: 0-0 Tight: 0-0 Gall: 0-0
Aids: Bl: 0-0 Vi: 0-0 Tstrap: 0-0
Best Rating: 84 9/01 Worc 2m gd-fm NHF

Cosmo Jack (IRE)

6-y-o b g Balla Cove-Foolish Law (IRE) (Law Society (USA))
S Flook (M C Pipe 10/2) S Flook

Placings:5101110/0PPP0-3PP **(4755)**
2001/02: 16^{3}S, 20^{P}S, 23^{P}GF

	Starts	1st	2nd	3rd	Win & Pl
Chases	3	0	0	1	314
Career Total	**15**	**4**	**0**	**1**	**9191**

96 1/00 Tntn 2m1f E(0-105)HHdl SFT £2601
104 1/00 Leic 2m G Hdl SFT £1904
86 12/99 Ludl 2m F Hdl G-S £2766
85 11/99 Catt 2m G Hdl G-F £1605
Total win prize-money £8877

Going: Sf: 0-2 GS: 0-0 Gd: 0-0 GF: - Fm: 0-1
Distance: 2m/2m3: 0-1 2m4-2m7: 0-2 3m+: 0-0
Track: LH: 0-1 RH: 0-2 Tight: 0-1 Gall: 0-0
Aids: Bl: 0-0 Vi: 0-0 Tstrap: 0-0
Best Rating: 104 1/00 Leic 2m soft Hdl

Fair hurdler in cracking form from 1999 to the start of 2000, but has since lost his way.

Cosmocrat

90 **93**

4-y-o b g Cosmonaut-Bella Coola (Northern State (USA))
C G Cox (M Meade 23/10) S Barrow,A Dawson,G O'Toole,G Whyte

Placings:6F **(3890)**
2001/02: 16^{6}S, 16^{F}HY

	Starts	1st	2nd	3rd	Win & Pl
Hurdles	2	0	0	0	0
Career Total	**2**	**0**	**0**	**0**	**0**

Going: Sf: 0-2 GS: 0-0 Gd: 0-0 GF: - Fm: 0-0
Distance: 2m/2m3: 0-2 2m4-2m7: 0-0 3m+: 0-0
Track: LH: 0-1 RH: 0-1 Tight: 0-0 Gall: 0-0
Aids: Bl: 0-0 Vi: 0-0 Tstrap: 0-0
Best Rating: 93 2/02 Sand 2m110y soft Hdl

Fair miler on the Flat. Has raced too keenly over hurdles to date, needs to learn to settle. Won on soft ground on the level.

Cotten Thistle

93f **70f**

5-y-o b g Beveled (USA)-Try For Gold (Chief Singer)
J M Jefferson J M Jefferson

Placings:5 **(1263)**
2001/02: 16^{5}GF

	Starts	1st	2nd	3rd	Win & Pl
NH Flat	1	0	0	0	0
Career Total	**1**	**0**	**0**	**0**	**0**

Going: Sf: 0-0 GS: 0-0 Gd: 0-0 GF: - Fm: 0-1
Distance: 2m/2m3: 0-1 2m4-2m7: 0-0 3m+: 0-0
Track: LH: 0-0 RH: 0-1 Tight: 0-0 Gall: 0-1
Aids: Bl: 0-0 Vi: 0-0 Tstrap: 0-0
Best Rating: 70 8/01 Hntg 2m110y gd-fm NHF

Cottstown Boy (IRE)

107(100c) (102c)**109**

11-y-o ch g King Luthier-Ballyanihan (Le Moss)
Mrs S C Bradburne The Hon Thomas Cochrane

Placings:003045/3FUF62U32U23111/304146102255/51FP0613653/P40363033-532113253PP60 **(4893)**
2001/02: 24^{5}GS, 20^{3}GF, 20^{2}G, 24^{1}G, 24^{1}G, 22^{3}G, 20^{2}GS, 22^{5}GS, 24^{3}S, 20^{P}GS, 20^{P}HY, 24^{6}G, 20^{0}G

	Starts	1st	2nd	3rd	Win & Pl
Hurdles	9	0	2	2	3623
Chases	4	2	0	1	8740
Career Total	**66**	**9**	**7**	**14**	**53056**

99 10/01 Sthl 3m110y F(0-110)HCh GD £2562
102 9/01 Prth 3m F(0-100)HCh GD £5655
118 12/99 Ayr 2m4f D(0-125)HHdl HVY £2986
105 8/99 Prth 3m D Ch G-F £4401
117 12/98 Ayr 2m4f D(0-125)HHdl HVY £2901
115 11/98 Ayr 2m4f C(0-135)HHdl G-S £4825
108 4/98 Prth 2m4f110y D(0-110)HHdl HVY £4744
107 4/98 Prth 3m110y E(0-110)HHdl GD £3902
101 3/98 Kels 2m6f110y E Hdl GD £2010
Total win prize-money £33988

Going: Sf: 0-2 GS: 0-4 Gd: 2-6 GF: - Fm: 0-1
Distance: 2m/2m3: 0-0 2m4-2m7: 0-8 **3m+: 2-5**
Track: LH: 1-5 RH: 1-8 **Tight: 1-5** Gall: 0-0
Aids: Bl: 0-0 Vi: 0-0 Tstrap: 0-0
Best Rating: 118 11/00 Ayr 2m4f soft Hdl

Modest hurdler/chaser, made a winning return to fences in September 2001 over three miles and followed up the following month at Southwell. Suited by three miles and good ground.

Couloir

103 **88**

6-y-o gr m Gran Alba (USA)-Hollow Creek (Tarqogan)
H Morrison H Morrison

Placings:6-46002166 **(4896)**
2001/02: 16^{4}G, 22^{6}G, 20^{0}S, 21^{0}S, 16^{2}S, 16^{1}G, 17^{6}F, 20^{6}G

	Starts	1st	2nd	3rd	Win & Pl
Hurdles	8	1	1	0	3300
Career Total	**9**	**1**	**1**	**0**	**3300**

85 4/02 Winc 2m E(0-110)HHdl GD £2520
Total win prize-money £2520

Going: Sf: 0-3 GS: 0-0 Gd: 1-4 GF: - Fm: 0-1
Distance: 2m/2m3: 1-4 2m4-2m7: 0-4 3m+: 0-0
Track: LH: 0-1 **RH: 1-6** Tight: 0-1 Gall: 0-1
Aids: Bl: 0-0 Vi: 0-0 Tstrap: 0-0
Best Rating: 88 4/02 Extr 2m1f firm Hdl

Broke her duck at the seventh attempt over hurdles when dropped back to the minimum trip. Effective on good and slightly softer.

Coulthard (IRE)

95(109h) (121h)**127**

9-y-o ch g Glenstal (USA)-Royal Aunt (Martinmas)
Mrs P Sly R Brazier

Placings:033/52332FF4151/612162/0320/000F-234353F0 **(4593)**
2001/02: 16^{2}G, 16^{3}G, 16^{4}G, 16^{3}GS, 19^{5}S, 16^{3}S, 17^{F}GS, 16^{0}G

	Starts	1st	2nd	3rd	Win & Pl
Hurdles	4	0	1	1	3541
Chases	4	0	0	2	1246
Career Total	**36**	**4**	**6**	**8**	**32526**

130 1/99 Wwck 2m D(0-125)HHdl SFT £2838
121 11/98 Towc 2m D(0-125)HHdl SFT £2745
112 4/98 Asct 2m110y D(0-110)HHdl SFT £3647
109 3/98 Limk 2m (0-123)HHdl SFT £3573
Total win prize-money £12806

Going: Sf: 0-2 GS: 0-2 Gd: 0-4 GF: - Fm: 0-0
Distance: 2m/2m3: 0-8 2m4-2m7: 0-0 3m+: 0-0
Track: LH: 0-4 RH: 0-4 Tight: 0-2 Gall: 0-3
Aids: Bl: 0-0 Vi: 0-0 Tstrap: 0-2
Best Rating: 130 1/00 Chel 2m1f gd-sft Hdl

A useful handicap hurdler, he has not won over hurdles since April 1999 and does not produce much under pressure. A bit disappointing over fences. Acts well with cut in the ground and is best over two miles.

Coulton

104 **110**

15-y-o ch g Final Straw-Pontevecchio Due (Welsh Pageant)
O Sherwood M G St Quinton

Placings:P2/13111/4210/1U112FF3P/11P32111/10F0F63U1/12/33UP5U/50/6P111/16UP-40P **(1028)**
2001/02: 21^{4}GF, 23^{0}G, 24^{P}G

	Starts	1st	2nd	3rd	Win & Pl
Chases	3	0	0	0	686
Career Total	**59**	**20**	**5**	**6**	**225399**

139 5/00 Chel 2m5f H Ch GD £3415
139 3/00 Sand 2m4f110y H Ch GD £3406
114 3/00 Donc 2m3f110y H Ch G-S £1253
129 2/00 Sand 2m4f110y H Ch G-S £2072
166 10/96 Winc 2m5f A HCh G-F £18660
166 4/96 Asct 2m B HCh G-F £10357
164 10/95 Winc 2m5f HCh FRM £15700
164 4/95 Sand 2m4f110y A Ch GD £15625

158	4/95	Aint	2m	A HCh	G-F	£26020
155	3/95	Chel	2m5f	B Ch	SFT	£29552
154	11/94	Newb	2m1f	(0-140)HCh	G-S	£5530
148	11/94	Strf	2m1f110y	(0-125)HCh	G-S	£3759
105	11/93	Aint	2m4f	Ch	GD	£7995
108	11/93	Newc	2m110y	Ch	GD	£2884
121	10/93	Weth	2m	Ch	SFT	£2846
150	2/93	Nott	2m	HHdl	GD	£4760
	5/92	Uttx	2m4f	Hdl	GD	£9690
143	4/92	Aint	2m4f	Hdl	GD	£10598
120	1/92	Weth	2m4f	Hdl	SFT	£1870
115	12/91	Newc	2m4f	Hdl	G-F	£1716

Total win prize-money £177712

Going: Sf: 0-0 GS: 0-0 Gd: 0-2 GF: - Fm: 0-1
Distance: 2m/2m3: 0-0 2m4-2m7: 0-1 3m+: 0-2
Track: LH: 0-3 RH: 0-0 Tight: 0-2 Gall: 0-0
Aids: Bl: 0-0 Vi: 0-0 Tstrap: 0-0
Best Rating: 166 10/96 Winc 2m5f gd-fm Ch

A top class hurdler/chaser in his prime, he is now in honourable retirement.

Counsel

102 **77**

7-y-o ch g Most Welcome-My Polished Corner (IRE) (Tate Gallery (USA))
J C Tuck The Japica Partnership

Placings:000P-10020 **(4646)**
2001/02: 20^{1}GF, 19^{0}GF, 19^{0}G, 22^{2}G, 21^{0}G

	Starts	1st	2nd	3rd	Win & Pl
Hurdles	5	1	1	0	2982
Career Total	**9**	**1**	**1**	**0**	**2982**

73	8/01	Font	2m4f	F(0-90)HHdl	G-F	£2299

Total win prize-money £2300

Going: Sf: 0-0 GS: 0-0 Gd: 0-3 GF: - Fm: 1-2
Distance: 2m/2m3: 0-0 **2m4-2m7: 1-5** 3m+: 0-0
Track: LH: 0-0 RH: 0-3 **Tight: 1-1** Gall: 0-0
Aids: Bl: 0-0 Vi: 0-0 Tstrap: 0-0
Best Rating: 77 12/01 Extr 2m6f110y good Hdl

Has won a couple of point to points and has modest form over hurdles. Should have a change of fortune when switched to fences.

Count Campioni (IRE)

85(105h) **114**

8-y-o br g Brush Aside (USA)-Emerald Flair (Flair Path)
M Pitman Garrett - Gibbon

Placings:11132/123330/13345-0 **(0491)**
2001/02: 22^{0}GF

	Starts	1st	2nd	3rd	Win & Pl
Chases	1	0	0	0	
Career Total	**17**	**5**	**2**	**6**	**44050**

136	9/00	Uttx	3m	D Ch	G-S	£4381
147	11/99	Newb	2m110y	B Hdl	G-F	£6453
110	2/99	Fknm	2m4f	D Hdl	G-S	£2666
105	1/99	Ludl	2m	H NHF	SFT	£1598
105	11/98	Ludl	2m	H NHF	GD	£1276

Total win prize-money £16377

Going: Sf: 0-0 GS: 0-0 Gd: 0-0 GF: - Fm: 0-1
Distance: 2m/2m3: 0-0 2m4-2m7: 0-1 3m+: 0-0
Track: LH: 0-0 RH: 0-0 Tight: 0-1 Gall: 0-0
Aids: Bl: 0-0 Vi: 0-0 Tstrap: 0-0
Best Rating: 152 1/00 Chel 2m5f110y gd-sft Hdl

A smart staying hurdler at his best, he went backwards over fences in 2000/01. He cannot be supported at present and seems to lack confidence.

Count Frederick

6-y-o b/br g Anshan-Minteen (Teenoso (USA))
J R Jenkins Mrs Stella Peirce

Placings:0 **(0978)**
2001/02: 16^{0}G

	Starts	1st	2nd	3rd	Win & Pl
Hurdles	1	0	0	0	
Career Total	**1**	**0**	**0**	**0**	

Going: Sf: 0-0 GS: 0-0 Gd: 0-1 GF: - Fm: 0-0
Distance: 2m/2m3: 0-1 2m4-2m7: 0-0 3m+: 0-0
Track: LH: 0-1 RH: 0-0 Tight: 0-1 Gall: 0-0
Aids: Bl: 0-0 Vi: 0-0 Tstrap: 0-0
Best Rating:

Count Karmuski

10-y-o b g Ardross-Trimar Gold (Goldhill)
Ferdy Murphy P E Atkinson

Placings:4/502014/22F5F1134/0P12020/44210-0 **(0202)**
2001/02: 16^{0}G

	Starts	1st	2nd	3rd	Win & Pl
Chases	1	0	0	0	
Career Total	**29**	**5**	**6**	**1**	**27379**

127	2/01	Catt	2m3f	D(0-120)HCh	SFT	£4309
125	11/99	Sedg	2m110y	F(0-110)HCh	GD	£2600
120	2/99	Catt	2m3f	D(0-120)HCh	GD	£4224
111	1/99	Catt	2m	D(0-120)HCh	GD	£4825
116	3/98	Catt	2m	E Hdl	G-S	£2248

Total win prize-money £18207

Going: Sf: 0-0 GS: 0-0 Gd: 0-1 GF: - Fm: 0-0
Distance: 2m/2m3: 0-1 2m4-2m7: 0-0 3m+: 0-0
Track: LH: 0-1 RH: 0-0 Tight: 0-0 Gall: 0-0
Aids: Bl: 0-1 Vi: 0-0 Tstrap: 0-0
Best Rating: 127 2/01 Catt 2m3f soft Ch

Another character, who is prone to mistakes. Needs decent ground to be seen to best effect and could be worth a try over two and half miles plus.

Count Keni

85 **67**

7-y-o ch g Formidable (USA)-Flying Amy (Norwick (USA))
Miss K B Roncoroni Mrs J Roncoroni

Placings:0P/000/00-65 **(4859)**
2001/02: 25^{6}GF, 25^{5}G

	Starts	1st	2nd	3rd	Win & Pl
Chases	2	0	0	0	0
Career Total	**9**	**0**	**0**	**0**	**0**

Going: Sf: 0-0 GS: 0-0 Gd: 0-1 GF: - Fm: 0-1
Distance: 2m/2m3: 0-0 2m4-2m7: 0-0 3m+: 0-2
Track: LH: 0-2 RH: 0-0 Tight: 0-1 Gall: 0-0
Aids: Bl: 0-0 Vi: 0-0 Tstrap: 0-0
Best Rating: 67 4/02 Hexm 3m1f good Ch

Modest pointer, has looked one paced under Rules.

Count Oski

97 **92**

6-y-o b g Petoski-Sea Countess (Ercolano (USA))
M J Ryan The Laodiceans

Placings:0-05500 **(4597)**
2001/02: 16^{0}GS, 16^{5}HY, 20^{5}GS, 20^{0}S, 19^{0}GF

	Starts	1st	2nd	3rd	Win & Pl
NH Flat	2	0	0	0	0
Hurdles	3	0	0	0	0
Career Total	**6**	**0**	**0**	**0**	**0**

Going: Sf: 0-2 GS: 0-2 Gd: 0-0 GF: - Fm: 0-1
Distance: 2m/2m3: 0-3 2m4-2m7: 0-2 3m+: 0-0
Track: LH: 0-3 RH: 0-2 Tight: 0-1 Gall: 0-2
Aids: Bl: 0-0 Vi: 0-0 Tstrap: 0-0
Best Rating: 92 4/02 Wwck 2m3f gd-fm Hdl

Count Tallahassee

74 **59+**

5-y-o ch g Dervish-Give Me An Answer (True Song)
J Parkes Mrs I M Moore

Placings:00-0P **(4314)**
2001/02: 16^{0}S, 20^{P}HY

	Starts	1st	2nd	3rd	Win & Pl
NH Flat	1	0	0	0	0
Hurdles	1	0	0	0	0
Career Total	**4**	**0**	**0**	**0**	

Going: Sf: 0-2 GS: 0-0 Gd: 0-0 GF: - Fm: 0-0
Distance: 2m/2m3: 0-1 2m4-2m7: 0-1 3m+: 0-0
Track: LH: 0-1 RH: 0-0 Tight: 0-1 Gall: 0-0
Aids: Bl: 0-0 Vi: 0-0 Tstrap: 0-0
Best Rating: 54 2/01 Weth 2m soft NHF

Count Tirol (IRE)

63 **24**

5-y-o b g Tirol-Bid High (IRE) (High Estate)
J R Payne J R Payne

Placings:00P **(4654)**
2001/02: 17^{0}G, 17^{0}GS, 17^{P}GS

	Starts	1st	2nd	3rd	Win & Pl
Hurdles	3	0	0	0	
Career Total	**3**	**0**	**0**	**0**	

Going: Sf: 0-0 GS: 0-2 Gd: 0-1 GF: - Fm: 0-0
Distance: 2m/2m3: 0-3 2m4-2m7: 0-0 3m+: 0-0
Track: LH: 0-1 RH: 0-2 Tight: 0-3 Gall: 0-0
Aids: Bl: 0-1 Vi: 0-0 Tstrap: 0-0
Best Rating: 24 12/01 Tntn 2m1f gd-sft Hdl

Count Tony

105 **111**

8-y-o ch g Keen-Turtle Dove (Gyr (USA))
P Bowen Brian Collett

Placings:412165/1200/02210P/2P0-5F0F30 **(4028)**
2001/02: 24^{5}GF, 20^{F}GF, 19^{0}GS, 20^{F}G, 20^{3}S, 21^{0}GS

	Starts	1st	2nd	3rd	Win & Pl
Hurdles	6	0	0	1	864
Career Total	**25**	**4**	**5**	**1**	**22013**

117	6/99	Worc	2m4f	C(0-135)HHdl	G-F	£4705
112	5/98	Prth	2m110y	E Hdl	G-F	£2598
110	2/98	Catt	2m	E Hdl	GD	£2332
108	11/97	Ayr	2m	E Hdl	G-S	£2262

Total win prize-money £11897

Going: Sf: 0-1 GS: 0-2 Gd: 0-1 GF: - Fm: 0-2
Distance: 2m/2m3: 0-0 2m4-2m7: 0-5 3m+: 0-1
Track: LH: 0-5 RH: 0-1 Tight: 0-3 Gall: 0-3
Aids: Bl: 0-0 Vi: 0-0 Tstrap: 0-0
Best Rating: 117 6/99 Worc 2m4f gd-fm Hdl

odest handicap hurdler. Best on fast ground at around
vo and a half miles.

Count Von Knockagh (IRE)

110

y-o br g Ilium-First In (Over The River (FR))
H Alner H Wellstead

lacings:041/2-FP (2127)
001/02: 24^{F}G, 24^{P}G

	Starts	1st	2nd	3rd	Win & Pl
hases	2	0	0	0	
areer Total	**6**	**1**	**1**	**0**	**3700**

5	10/99	Winc	2m6f	E Hdl	G-F	£2080

Total win prize-money £2080

oing: Sf: 0-0 GS: 0-0 Gd: 0-2 GF: - Fm: 0-0
istance: 2m/2m3: 0-0 2m4-2m7: 0-0 3m+: 0-2
rack: LH: 0-1 RH: 0-1 Tight: 0-0 Gall: 0-1
ids: Bl: 0-0 Vi: 0-0 Tstrap: 0-0
est Rating: 110 4/01 Kemp 3m good Ch

Countess Of Chell

34f 71f

y-o b m Gildoran-Chanelle (The Parson)
Miss Venetia Williams Kinnersley Optimists

lacings:2-5 (2480)
001/02: 17^{5}S

	Starts	1st	2nd	3rd	Win & Pl
NH Flat	1	0	0	0	0
areer Total	**2**	**0**	**1**	**0**	**478**

oing: Sf: 0-1 GS: 0-0 Gd: 0-0 GF: - Fm: 0-0
istance: 2m/2m3: 0-1 2m4-2m7: 0-0 3m+: 0-0
rack: LH: 0-0 RH: 0-1 Tight: 0-0 Gall: 0-0
ids: Bl: 0-0 Vi: 0-0 Tstrap: 0-0
est Rating: 102 5/00 Bang 2m1f good NHF

Country Beau

111 127

0-y-o b g Town And Country-Chanelle (The Parson)
S King Mrs J J Peppiatt

lacings:611/21616/511U31P/4P2002/2FFF53P (4851)
001/02: 25^{2}G, 20^{F}G, 20^{F}G, 25^{F}G, 20^{5}GS, 23^{3}G, 20^{P}G

	Starts	1st	2nd	3rd	Win & Pl
hases	7	0	1	1	2424
areer Total	**28**	**7**	**4**	**2**	**29701**

25	2/99	Winc	2m	D Ch	G-S	£5630
34	11/98	Tntn	2m3f	C Ch	GD	£4788
36	10/98	Chel	2m110y	E(0-135)HHdl	GD	£2736
28	2/98	Sand	2m110y	D Hdl	GD	£2866
32	12/97	Sand	2m110y	D Hdl	G-S	£3152
19	3/97	Newb	2m110y	H NHF	G-F	£1320
21	2/97	Kemp	2m	H NHF	GD	£1413

Total win prize-money £21905

oing: Sf: 0-0 GS: 0-1 Gd: 0-6 GF: - Fm: 0-0
istance: 2m/2m3: 0-0 2m4-2m7: 0-4 3m+: 0-3
rack: LH: 0-2 RH: 0-5 Tight: 0-2 Gall: 0-1
ids: Bl: 0-0 Vi: 0-0 Tstrap: 0-0
est Rating: 144 12/99 Chel 3m good Hdl

air chaser, stays three miles, likes good or slightly soft-r ground. Has taken a lot of falls recently and seems to ave lost his confidence.

Country Boy

11-y-o b g Town And Country-Hollomoore (Moorestyle)
J J Bridger Tarragon Racing Ii

Placings:0000/36003/46F624243P/60030-54PP (0837)
2001/02: 16^{5}F, 18^{4}GF, 25^{P}F, 20^{P}G

	Starts	1st	2nd	3rd	Win & Pl
Hurdles	1	0	0	0	0
Chases	3	0	0	0	0
Career Total	**28**	**0**	**2**	**4**	**3326**

Going: Sf: 0-0 GS: 0-0 Gd: 0-1 GF: - Fm: 0-3
Distance: 2m/2m3: 0-2 2m4-2m7: 0-1 3m+: 0-1
Track: LH: 0-2 RH: 0-1 Tight: 0-2 Gall: 0-0
Aids: Bl: 0-1 Vi: 0-0 Tstrap: 0-0
Best Rating: 90 1/01 Kemp 2m soft Ch

Country Bumpkin

6-y-o ch g Village Star (FR)-Malham Tarn (Riverman (USA))
H J Manners (H E Haynes 3/5) Miss L K Hilder

Placings:0P (2712)
2001/02: 20^{0}S, 21^{P}HY

	Starts	1st	2nd	3rd	Win & Pl
Hurdles	2	0	0	0	
Career Total	**2**	**0**	**0**	**0**	

Going: Sf: 0-2 GS: 0-0 Gd: 0-0 GF: - Fm: 0-0
Distance: 2m/2m3: 0-0 2m4-2m7: 0-2 3m+: 0-0
Track: LH: 0-1 RH: 0-1 Tight: 0-0 Gall: 0-0
Aids: Bl: 0-0 Vi: 0-0 Tstrap: 0-0
Best Rating:

Country Chef

58 13

6-y-o b g Henbit (USA)-Witney Girl (Le Bavard (FR))
N G Richards The Highly Sociable Syndicate

Placings:560 (4894)
2001/02: 17^{5}G, 16^{6}GF, 16^{0}G

	Starts	1st	2nd	3rd	Win & Pl
NH Flat	2	0	0	0	0
Hurdles	1	0	0	0	0
Career Total	**3**	**0**	**0**	**0**	**0**

Going: Sf: 0-0 GS: 0-0 Gd: 0-2 GF: - Fm: 0-1
Distance: 2m/2m3: 0-3 2m4-2m7: 0-0 3m+: 0-0
Track: LH: 0-1 RH: 0-2 Tight: 0-1 Gall: 0-0
Aids: Bl: 0-0 Vi: 0-0 Tstrap: 0-0
Best Rating: 83 11/01 Sedg 2m1f good NHF

Country Kris

104 104

10-y-o b g Town And Country-Mariban (Mummy's Pet)
B J M Ryall B J M Ryall

Placings:042/4240/3622/0202PP66/560-020100 (4848)
2001/02: 19^{0}F, 24^{2}G, 22^{0}GF, 16^{1}GS, 19^{0}G, 16^{0}G

	Starts	1st	2nd	3rd	Win & Pl
Hurdles	6	1	1	0	2885
Career Total	**28**	**1**	**7**	**1**	**7484**

104	10/01	Strf	2m110y	F(0-100)HHdl	G-S	£2303

Total win prize-money £2303

Going: Sf: 0-0 GS: 1-1 Gd: 0-3 GF: - Fm: 0-2
Distance: 2m/2m3: 1-2 2m4-2m7: 0-3 3m+: 0-1
Track: LH: 1-4 RH: 0-2 Tight: 1-5 Gall: 0-0
Aids: Bl: 0-0 Vi: 0-1 Tstrap: 0-0
Best Rating: 106 11/99 Extr 2m6f gd-sft Hdl

Returned from nearly four months off to break his duck at the age of nine, at Stratford in October of 2001 over two miles.

Country Minstrel (IRE)

11-y-o b g Black Minstrel-Madamme Highlights (Andretti)
J D J Davies M I Forbes

Placings:0F0/2FP43FFP20/32P030/0/P/P (2034)
2001/02: 24^{P}GS

	Starts	1st	2nd	3rd	Win & Pl
Hurdles	1	0	0	0	
Career Total	**22**	**0**	**3**	**3**	**4718**

Going: Sf: 0-0 GS: 0-1 Gd: 0-0 GF: - Fm: 0-0
Distance: 2m/2m3: 0-0 2m4-2m7: 0-0 3m+: 0-1
Track: LH: 0-1 RH: 0-0 Tight: 0-0 Gall: 0-0
Aids: Bl: 0-0 Vi: 0-0 Tstrap: 0-0
Best Rating: 89 11/97 Chel 2m110y gd-fm Hdl

Country Rose

68 19

6-y-o ch m Carlingford Castle-Clover Song (True Song)
Mrs P Townsley The Village Idiot Partnership

Placings:U00 (4823)
2001/02: 16^{U}S, 16^{0}HY, 17^{0}G

	Starts	1st	2nd	3rd	Win & Pl
NH Flat	3	0	0	0	
Career Total	**3**	**0**	**0**	**0**	

Going: Sf: 0-2 GS: 0-0 Gd: 0-1 GF: - Fm: 0-0
Distance: 2m/2m3: 0-3 2m4-2m7: 0-0 3m+: 0-0
Track: LH: 0-2 RH: 0-1 Tight: 0-0 Gall: 0-1
Aids: Bl: 0-0 Vi: 0-0 Tstrap: 0-1
Best Rating: 42 4/02 Chel 2m1f good NHF

Poor bumper form.

Countrywide Pride (IRE)

93 71

4-y-o ch g Eagle Eyed (USA)-Lady's Dream (Mazilier (USA))
K R Burke Mrs Elaine M Burke

Placings:F05P (4752)
2001/02: 16^{F}G, 16^{0}GF, 16^{5}G, 16^{P}GF

	Starts	1st	2nd	3rd	Win & Pl
Hurdles	4	0	0	0	0
Career Total	**4**	**0**	**0**	**0**	**0**

Going: Sf: 0-0 GS: 0-0 Gd: 0-2 GF: - Fm: 0-2
Distance: 2m/2m3: 0-4 2m4-2m7: 0-0 3m+: 0-0
Track: LH: 0-4 RH: 0-0 Tight: 0-1 Gall: 0-1
Aids: Bl: 0-0 Vi: 0-0 Tstrap: 0-0
Best Rating: 71 12/01 Donc 2m110y good Hdl

Consistently in the frame on sand and turf on the Flat, he has shown little form over hurdles so far.

Countrywide Star (IRE)

4-y-o ch g Common Grounds-Silver Slipper (Indian Ridge)
J G Given (K R Burke 2/1) J E Titley

Placings:0P (4284)
2001/02: 17^{0}GS, 17^{P}GS

	Starts	1st	2nd	3rd	Win & Pl
Hurdles	2	0	0	0	
Career Total	**2**	**0**	**0**	**0**	

Going: Sf: 0-0 GS: 0-2 Gd: 0-0 GF: - Fm: 0-0
Distance: 2m/2m3: 0-2 2m4-2m7: 0-0 3m+: 0-0
Track: LH: 0-0 RH: 0-2 Tight: 0-2 Gall: 0-0
Aids: Bl: 0-0 Vi: 0-0 Tstrap: 0-0
Best Rating:

County Derry

9-y-o b g Derrylin-Colonial Princess (Roscoe Blake)
J Scott G T Lever

Placings:PP-14523 (4826)
2001/02: 28^{1}GF, 33^{4}G, 26^{5}G, 22^{2}GS, 26^{3}G

	Starts	1st	2nd	3rd	Win & Pl
Chases	5	1	1	1	4525
Career Total	**7**	**1**	**1**	**1**	**4525**

110 5/01 Strf 3m4f H Ch G-F £2614
Total win prize-money £2615

Going: Sf: 0-0 GS: 0-1 Gd: 0-3 GF: - Fm: 1-1
Distance: 2m/2m3: 0-0 2m4-2m7: 0-1 **3m+: 1-4**
Track: **LH: 1-4** RH: 0-0 **Tight: 1-1** Gall: 0-3
Aids: Bl: 0-0 Vi: 0-0 Tstrap: 0-0
Best Rating: 129 3/02 Chel 3m2f110y good Ch

Useful pointer who came into his own in 2001/2. He won a hunter chase in May but has since reverted to points and acts on any ground. Has been let down on occasions by his jumping.

County Flyer

101(87h) **105**
9-y-o b g Cruise Missile-Random Select (Random Shot)
J S Smith R J Heathman (county Contractors) Ltd

Placings:*00/P0/*43003-44461 (2545)
2001/02: 19^{4}G, 20^{4}G, 22^{4}G, 20^{6}G, 23^{1}GS

	Starts	1st	2nd	3rd	Win & Pl
Chases	5	1	0	0	4296
Career Total	**14**	**1**	**0**	**2**	**5453**

101 12/01 Extr 2m7f110y E(0-105)HCh G-S £3796
Total win prize-money £3796

Going: Sf: 0-0 GS: 1-1 Gd: 0-4 GF: - Fm: 0-0
Distance: 2m/2m3: 0-1 2m4-2m7: 0-3 **3m+: 1-1**
Track: LH: 0-2 **RH: 1-3** Tight: 0-2 Gall: 0-1
Aids: Bl: 0-1 Vi: 0-0 Tstrap: 0-0
Best Rating: 105 5/01 Bang 2m4f110y good Ch

Finished lame when landing a weak novices' chase at Exeter in December.

Courage Under Fire

110(91h) (90h)**122**
7-y-o b g Risk Me (FR)-Dreamtime Quest (Blakeney)
C C Bealby T P Radford

Placings:0/65P05/01-53P3336122P (4313)
2001/02: 24^{5}GS, 24^{3}S, 24^{P}S, 21^{3}GS, 22^{3}S, 20^{3}GS, 25^{6}GS, 22^{1}S, 24^{2}GS, 22^{2}S, 24^{P}HY

	Starts	1st	2nd	3rd	Win & Pl
Hurdles	3	0	0	1	322
Chases	8	1	2	3	7961
Career Total	**19**	**2**	**2**	**4**	**10484**

122 2/02 MRas 2m6f110y E(0-105)HCh SFT £3444
112 4/01 Fknm 3m110y H Ch G-S £2200
Total win prize-money £5645

Going: Sf: 1-6 GS: 0-5 Gd: 0-0 GF: - Fm: 0-0
Distance: 2m/2m3: 0-0 **2m4-2m7: 1-5** 3m+: 0-6
Track: LH: 0-4 **RH: 1-7 Tight: 1-9** Gall: 0-1
Aids: **Bl: 1-4** Vi: 0-0 Tstrap: 0-0
Best Rating: 122 2/02 MRas 2m6f110y soft Ch

Moderate chaser, stays well and best with cut in the ground.

Course Doctor (IRE)

94(99h) (120h)**113**
10-y-o ch g Roselier (FR)-Faultless Girl (Crash Course)
A Dickman Mike Smallman

Placings:0B612/*F1U1U2F1/1FFF0/*6105F3-0U20 (0834)
2001/02: 28^{0}G, 21^{U}GF, 21^{2}GF, 27^{0}GF

	Starts	1st	2nd	3rd	Win & Pl
Hurdles	2	0	1	0	984
Chases	2	0	0	0	0
Career Total	**28**	**6**	**3**	**1**	**41134**

122 10/00 Aint 3m110y D(0-120)HHdl GD £7143
145 12/99 Weth 2m4f110y B(0-145)HCh G-S £8465
145 2/99 Ayr 2m5f110y D Ch SFT £4890
130 12/98 Ayr 2m5f110y D(0-110)HCh G-S £3756
115 11/98 Ayr 2m4f D Ch G-S £4440
101 4/98 Carl 2m4f110y E(0-105)HHdl SFT £2612
Total win prize-money £31308

Going: Sf: 0-0 GS: 0-0 Gd: 0-1 GF: - Fm: 0-3
Distance: 2m/2m3: 0-0 2m4-2m7: 0-2 3m+: 0-2
Track: LH: 0-3 RH: 0-1 Tight: 0-2 Gall: 0-1
Aids: Bl: 0-0 Vi: 0-0 Tstrap: 0-0
Best Rating: 146 1/99 Newc 2m4f soft Ch

Possibly best when forcing the pace around two and a half miles, he would be a decent handicap chaser if able to get his jumping sorted out.

Course Fishing

64 **26**
11-y-o ch g Squill (USA)-Migoletty (Oats)
G D Bull G D Bull

Placings:P0/P0 (2274)
2001/02: 16^{P}GS, 16^{0}G

	Starts	1st	2nd	3rd	Win & Pl
Hurdles	2	0	0	0	
Career Total	**4**	**0**	**0**	**0**	

Going: Sf: 0-0 GS: 0-1 Gd: 0-1 GF: - Fm: 0-0
Distance: 2m/2m3: 0-2 2m4-2m7: 0-0 3m+: 0-0
Track: LH: 0-2 RH: 0-0 Tight: 0-0 Gall: 0-0
Aids: Bl: 0-0 Vi: 0-0 Tstrap: 0-0
Best Rating: 26 11/01 Wwck 2m good Hdl

Courser's Cove

94f **98f**
5-y-o b g Sir Harry Lewis (USA)-Pearl Cove (Town And Country)
Mrs P Robeson Mrs P Robeson

Placings:*020* (377
2001/02: 16^{0}GS, 16^{2}GS, 16^{0}S

	Starts	1st	2nd	3rd	Win & Pl
NH Flat	3	0	1	0	458
Career Total	**3**	**0**	**1**	**0**	**458**

Going: Sf: 0-1 GS: 0-2 Gd: 0-0 GF: - Fm: 0-0
Distance: 2m/2m3: 0-3 2m4-2m7: 0-0 3m+: 0-0
Track: LH: 0-0 RH: 0-3 Tight: 0-0 Gall: 0-2
Aids: Bl: 0-0 Vi: 0-0 Tstrap: 0-0
Best Rating: 98 1/02 Hntg 2m110y gd-sft NHF

Showed promise in bumpers at Huntingdon over two miles. Should stay further. Acts on good to soft ground.

Coursing Run (IRE)

100 **117**
6-y-o ch g Glacial Storm (USA)-Let The Hare Run (IRE) (Tale Quale)
H D Daly The Hon Mrs A E Heber-Percy

Placings:21P5 (4030
2001/02: 16^{2}S, 20^{1}S, 20^{P}GS, 24^{5}GS

	Starts	1st	2nd	3rd	Win & Pl
Hurdles	4	1	1	0	4614
Career Total	**4**	**1**	**1**	**0**	**4614**

117 11/01 Chep 2m4f D Hdl SFT £349
Total win prize-money £349

Going: Sf: 1-2 GS: 0-2 Gd: 0-0 GF: - Fm: 0-0
Distance: 2m/2m3: 0-1 **2m4-2m7: 1-2** 3m+: 0-1
Track: **LH: 1-3** RH: 0-1 Tight: 0-0 Gall: 0-1
Aids: Bl: 0-0 Vi: 0-0 Tstrap: 0-0
Best Rating: 117 11/01 Chep 2m4f soft Hd

Stayed on well into second on his hurdles debut and went one better next time. Disappointed when pulled up at Ascot in January. Seems suited by give.

Court Alert

18
7-y-o b g Petoski-Banbury Cake (Seaepic (USA))
Lady Connell J E Connell

Placings:0PP (0666)
2001/02: 25^{0}G, 22^{P}GF, 20^{P}G

	Starts	1st	2nd	3rd	Win & Pl
Hurdles	3	0	0	0	
Career Total	**3**	**0**	**0**	**0**	

Going: Sf: 0-0 GS: 0-0 Gd: 0-2 GF: - Fm: 0-1
Distance: 2m/2m3: 0-0 2m4-2m7: 0-2 3m+: 0-1
Track: LH: 0-2 RH: 0-0 Tight: 0-1 Gall: 0-0
Aids: Bl: 0-0 Vi: 0-0 Tstrap: 0-0
Best Rating: 18 5/01 Wwck 3m1f good Hdl

Court Champagne

107 **94**
6-y-o b m Batshoof-Fairfield's Breeze (Buckskin (FR))
R J Price Derek & Cheryl Holder

Placings:611P6-0143 (1597)
2001/02: 17^{0}F, 16^{1}GF, 16^{4}F, 16^{3}G

	Starts	1st	2nd	3rd	Win & Pl
Hurdles	4	1	0	1	3041
Career Total	**9**	**3**	**0**	**1**	**10415**

91 5/01 Wwck 2m E(0-115)HHdl G-F £2625
96 2/01 Ludl 2m E(0-115)HHdl G-S £4124

76	6/00	Strf	2m110y	D Hdl	GD	£3250

Total win prize-money £9999

Going: Sf: 0-0 GS: 0-0 Gd: 0-1 GF: - Fm: 1-3
Distance: **2m/2m3: 1-4** 2m4-2m7: 0-0 3m+: 0-0
Track: **LH: 1-3** RH: 0-1 Tight: 0-2 Gall: 0-0
Aids: Bl: 0-0 Vi: 0-0 Tstrap: 0-0
Best Rating: **96** 2/01 Ludl 2m gd-sft Hdl

Court In The Act (IRE)

93 **80**

6-y-o b m Commanche Run-Princess Andromeda (Corvaro (USA))
J W Mullins Ian F Sandell

Placings: *40060*-6420 **(4181)**
2001/02: 17^{6}G, 22^{4}GF, 22^{2}G, 19^{0}S

	Starts	1st	2nd	3rd	Win & Pl
Hurdles	4	0	1	0	872
Career Total	**9**	**0**	**1**	**0**	**872**

Going: Sf: 0-1 GS: 0-0 Gd: 0-2 GF: - Fm: 0-1
Distance: 2m/2m3: 0-1 2m4-2m7: 0-3 3m+: 0-0
Track: LH: 0-2 RH: 0-2 Tight: 0-3 Gall: 0-0
Aids: Bl: 0-0 Vi: 0-0 Tstrap: 0-0
Best Rating: **80** 6/01 NAbb 2m6f good Hdl

Won poor novices' seller over just short of two and three quarter miles at Southwell July 2002.

Court Leney (IRE)

71 **49**

7-y-o b g Commanche Run-Dont Call Me Lady (Le Bavard (FR))
B J Llewellyn R Mason

Placings: 0 **(0673)**
2001/02: 16^{0}GF

	Starts	1st	2nd	3rd	Win & Pl
Hurdles	1	0	0	0	
Career Total	**1**	**0**	**0**	**0**	

Going: Sf: 0-0 GS: 0-0 Gd: 0-0 GF: - Fm: 0-1
Distance: 2m/2m3: 0-1 2m4-2m7: 0-0 3m+: 0-0
Track: LH: 0-1 RH: 0-0 Tight: 0-0 Gall: 0-0
Aids: Bl: 0-0 Vi: 0-0 Tstrap: 0-0
Best Rating: **49** 6/01 Worc 2m gd-fm Hdl

Court Nanny

8-y-o ch m Nicholas Bill-Tudor Sunset (Sunyboy)
P D Purdy P D Purdy

Placings: *0/0*-FP **(4504)**
2001/02: 19^{F}S, 17^{P}G

	Starts	1st	2nd	3rd	Win & Pl
Hurdles	2	0	0	0	
Career Total	**4**	**0**	**0**	**0**	

Going: Sf: 0-1 GS: 0-0 Gd: 0-1 GF: - Fm: 0-0
Distance: 2m/2m3: 0-1 2m4-2m7: 0-1 3m+: 0-0
Track: LH: 0-1 RH: 0-1 Tight: 0-2 Gall: 0-0
Aids: Bl: 0-0 Vi: 0-0 Tstrap: 0-0
Best Rating: **76** 4/00 Font 2m2f110y good NHF

Court Of Appeal

98 **102**

5-y-o ch g Bering-Hiawatha's Song (USA) (Chief's Crown (USA))
B Ellison (G M McCourt 21/9) Ashley Young

Placings: 105 **(4673)**
2001/02: 16^{1}G, 17^{0}S, 17^{5}GF

	Starts	1st	2nd	3rd	Win & Pl
Hurdles	3	1	0	0	2744
Career Total	**3**	**1**	**0**	**0**	**2744**

102	1/02	Muss	2m	E Hdl	GD	£2744

Total win prize-money £2744

Going: Sf: 0-1 GS: 0-0 Gd: 1-1 GF: - Fm: 0-1
Distance: **2m/2m3: 1-3** 2m4-2m7: 0-0 3m+: 0-0
Track: LH: 0-2 **RH: 1-1 Tight: 1-3** Gall: 0-0
Aids: Bl: 0-0 Vi: 0-0 Tstrap: 0-1
Best Rating: **102** 1/02 Muss 2m good Hdl

A fair Flat handicapper, made a winning hurdles debut at Musselburgh in January 2002 but held since. Suited by good ground and two miles, but may not want it much faster.

Court Of Justice (USA)

101 **117**

6-y-o b g Alleged (USA)-Captive Island (Northfields (USA))
Mrs H Dalton R Simpson, T Pryke, R Simcox

Placings: 142-246 **(4542)**
2001/02: 20^{2}S, 16^{4}S, 17^{6}G

	Starts	1st	2nd	3rd	Win & Pl
Hurdles	3	0	1	0	1450
Career Total	**6**	**1**	**2**	**0**	**6364**

113	11/00	Weth	2m	D Hdl	SFT	£3308

Total win prize-money £3309

Going: Sf: 0-2 GS: 0-0 Gd: 0-1 GF: - Fm: 0-0
Distance: 2m/2m3: 0-2 2m4-2m7: 0-1 3m+: 0-0
Track: LH: 0-2 RH: 0-1 Tight: 0-1 Gall: 0-0
Aids: Bl: 0-0 Vi: 0-0 Tstrap: 0-0
Best Rating: **117** 12/01 Sthl 2m4f110y soft Hdl

Fair, lightly-raced hurdler, stays two and a half miles, has won over two miles, suited by soft ground.

Court Ordeal (IRE)

101(94c) **99**

7-y-o ch g Kris-In Review (Ela-Mana-Mou)
R N Bevis Ewson Contractors And Steve Corbett

Placings: 65304F15/4050P/232**P4F**-530P0 **(4847)**
2001/02: 20^{5}S, 17^{3}GS, 21^{0}HY, 20^{P}GS, 20^{0}G

	Starts	1st	2nd	3rd	Win & Pl
Hurdles	4	0	0	1	298
Chases	1	0	0	0	0
Career Total	**24**	**1**	**2**	**3**	**5191**

93	2/99	Carl	2m1f	E Hdl	HVY	£2346

Total win prize-money £2346

Going: Sf: 0-2 GS: 0-2 Gd: 0-1 GF: - Fm: 0-0
Distance: 2m/2m3: 0-1 2m4-2m7: 0-4 3m+: 0-0
Track: LH: 0-3 RH: 0-1 Tight: 0-3 Gall: 0-0
Aids: Bl: 0-0 Vi: 0-1 Tstrap: 0-0
Best Rating: **101** 12/99 Hrfd 2m3f110y heavy Hdl

Lowly-rated hurdler/chaser. Best at around two miles.

Court Thyne (IRE)

11-y-o b g Good Thyne (USA)-Clonaslee Baby (Konigssee)
P J Millington P J Millington

Placings: P-P **(0229)**
2001/02: 30^{P}GF

	Starts	1st	2nd	3rd	Win & Pl
Chases	1	0	0	0	
Career Total	**2**	**0**	**0**	**0**	

Going: Sf: 0-0 GS: 0-0 Gd: 0-0 GF: - Fm: 0-1
Distance: 2m/2m3: 0-0 2m4-2m7: 0-0 3m+: 0-1
Track: LH: 0-0 RH: 0-1 Tight: 0-0 Gall: 0-1
Aids: Bl: 0-0 Vi: 0-0 Tstrap: 0-0
Best Rating:

Courtledge

105(97h) (78h)**112**

7-y-o b g Unfuwain (USA)-Tremellick (Mummy's Pet)
M J Gingell Going Grey Partnership

Placings: P60504*60116* **(4814)**
2001/02: 18^{P}GS, 20^{6}S, 16^{0}G, 20^{5}S, 16^{0}S, 23^{4}S, 21^{0}HY, 24^{6}GS, 20^{0}G, 24^{1}G, 21^{1}G, 21^{6}GF

	Starts	1st	2nd	3rd	Win & Pl
Hurdles	7	0	0	0	0
Chases	5	2	0	0	8280
Career Total	**12**	**2**	**0**	**0**	**8280**

112	4/02	Fknm	2m5f110y	E(0-110)HCh	GD	£4114
101	3/02	Fknm	3m110y	D Ch	GD	£4165

Total win prize-money £8280

Going: Sf: 0-5 GS: 0-2 Gd: 2-4 GF: - Fm: 0-1
Distance: 2m/2m3: 0-3 2m4-2m7: 1-6 3m+: 1-3
Track: **LH: 2-8** RH: 0-3 **Tight: 2-7** Gall: 0-1
Aids: Bl. 0-0 Vi. 0-0 Tstrap: 0-0
Best Rating: **112** 4/02 Fknm 2m5f110y good Ch

A fair handicap chaser. Effective from two and a half to three miles and the ground good or softer.

Covent Garden

91 **82**

4-y-o b g Sadler's Wells (USA)-Temple Row (Ardross)
J Howard Johnson (Sir Michael Stoute 28/9) Ada Partnership

Placings: U60 **(4651)**
2001/02: 17^{U}GS, 17^{6}GS, 16^{0}G

	Starts	1st	2nd	3rd	Win & Pl
Hurdles	3	0	0	0	0
Career Total	**3**	**0**	**0**	**0**	**0**

Going: Sf: 0-0 GS: 0-2 Gd: 0-1 GF: - Fm: 0-0
Distance: 2m/2m3: 0-3 2m4-2m7: 0-0 3m+: 0-0
Track: LH: 0-1 RH: 0-2 Tight: 0-3 Gall: 0-0
Aids: Bl: 0-0 Vi: 0-0 Tstrap: 0-0
Best Rating: **82** 3/02 MRas 2m1f110y gd-sft Hdl

Useful at his best on the Flat, but yet to show much over hurdles.

Cowanstown Prince

73 **29**

8-y-o ch g Derrylin-Craftsmans Made (Jimsun)
M Sheppard Mrs S Bird

Placings: *000/B06530/025000/0-0* **(0084)**
2001/02: 25^{0}G

	Starts	1st	2nd	3rd	Win & Pl
Chases	1	0	0	0	
Career Total	**17**	**0**	**1**	**1**	**1225**

Going: Sf: 0-0 GS: 0-0 Gd: 0-1 GF: - Fm: 0-0
Distance: 2m/2m3: 0-0 2m4-2m7: 0-0 3m+: 0-1
Track: LH: 0-0 RH: 0-1 Tight: 0-0 Gall: 0-0
Aids: Bl: 0-0 Vi: 0-0 Tstrap: 0-0
Best Rating: 89 10/98 Naas 2m yield NHF

Cowboyboots (IRE)

96f 98f

4-y-o b g Lord Americo-Little Welly (Little Buskins)
L Wells L Wells

Placings:*523* **(4391)**
2001/02: 16^{5}S, 17^{2}GS, 16^{3}S

	Starts	1st	2nd	3rd	Win & Pl
NH Flat	3	0	1	1	777
Career Total	**3**	**0**	**1**	**1**	**777**

Going: Sf: 0-2 GS: 0-1 Gd: 0-0 GF: - Fm: 0-0
Distance: 2m/2m3: 0-3 2m4-2m7: 0-0 3m+: 0-0
Track: LH: 0-1 RH: 0-2 Tight: 0-1 Gall: 0-0
Aids: Bl: 0-0 Vi: 0-0 Tstrap: 0-0
Best Rating: 98 3/02 Winc 2m soft NHF

Coxwell Cossack

101 112

9-y-o ch g Gildoran-Stepout (Sagaro)
S Gollings F S W Partnership

Placings:*3/3P2/0445FF5/412221124045-30052* **(4558)**
2001/02: 16^{3}G, 21^{0}GS, 16^{0}S, 21^{5}GS, 19^{2}GF

	Starts	1st	2nd	3rd	Win & Pl		
Hurdles	5	0	1	1	1347		
Career Total	**28**	**3**	**6**	**3**	**19392**		
116 8/00	MRas	2m3f110y	C(0-130)HHdl		G-F	£5920	
116 7/00	MRas	2m1f110y	D Hdl		G-F	£3421	
104 6/00	MRas	2m1f110y	E Hdl		GD	£2590	

Total win prize-money £11932

Going: Sf: 0-1 GS: 0-2 Gd: 0-1 GF: - Fm: 0-1
Distance: 2m/2m3: 0-2 2m4-2m7: 0-3 3m+: 0-0
Track: LH: 0-1 RH: 0-4 Tight: 0-2 Gall: 0-2
Aids: Bl: 0-0 Vi: 0-0 Tstrap: 0-0
Best Rating: 116 8/00 MRas 2m3f110y gd-fm Hdl

Handicap hurdler. Best on good ground or faster, he has a good record at Market Rasen and is effective from two miles to two miles six furlongs.

Coxwell Footman

78 42

6-y-o b g Infantry-Coxwell Quick Step (Balinger)
Mrs L C Taylor Mrs P A Allsopp

Placings:*0F0P* **(4479)**
2001/02: 16^{0}G, 16^{F}HY, 16^{0}S, 19^{P}G

	Starts	1st	2nd	3rd	Win & Pl
NH Flat	1	0	0	0	0
Hurdles	3	0	0	0	0
Career Total	**4**	**0**	**0**	**0**	

Going: Sf: 0-2 GS: 0-0 Gd: 0-2 GF: - Fm: 0-0
Distance: 2m/2m3: 0-4 2m4-2m7: 0-0 3m+: 0-0
Track: LH: 0-0 RH: 0-4 Tight: 0-0 Gall: 0-1
Aids: Bl: 0-0 Vi: 0-0 Tstrap: 0-0
Best Rating: 83 1/02 Ludl 2m good NHF

Coy Lad (IRE)

94f 106f

5-y-o ch g Be My Native (USA)-Don't Tutch Me (The Parson)
J G Fitzgerald Mr & Mrs Raymond Anderson Green

Placings:*44* **(4180)**
2001/02: 16^{4}S, 16^{4}GS

	Starts	1st	2nd	3rd	Win & Pl
NH Flat	2	0	0	0	825
Career Total	**2**	**0**	**0**	**0**	**825**

Going: Sf: 0-1 GS: 0-1 Gd: 0-0 GF: - Fm: 0-0
Distance: 2m/2m3: 0-2 2m4-2m7: 0-0 3m+: 0-0
Track: LH: 0-1 RH: 0-0 Tight: 0-0 Gall: 0-1
Aids: Bl: 0-0 Vi: 0-0 Tstrap: 0-0
Best Rating: 106 2/02 Newb 2m110y soft NHF

Showed some ability in a Newbury bumper on his debut, but disappointing second time. He is better than that and should make the grade over hurdles.

Crabapple Hill (IRE)

10-y-o gr g Duca Di Busted-Tender Galatea (Tender King)
T H Caldwell W Puddifer

Placings:*3342P/31123F3P/P-0* **(0205)**
2001/02: 25^{0}G

	Starts	1st	2nd	3rd	Win & Pl		
Chases	1	0	0	0			
Career Total	**15**	**2**	**2**	**5**	**11543**		
115 7/98	Bang	3m110y	D Ch		GD	£3720	
110 6/98	Strf	3m	E Ch		G-S	£2823	

Total win prize-money £6545

Going: Sf: 0-0 GS: 0-0 Gd: 0-1 GF: - Fm: 0-0
Distance: 2m/2m3: 0-0 2m4-2m7: 0-0 3m+: 0-1
Track: LH: 0-1 RH: 0-0 Tight: 0-0 Gall: 0-0
Aids: Bl: 0-0 Vi: 0-0 Tstrap: 0-0
Best Rating: 122 9/98 Worc 2m7f110y good Ch

Crack On Dandy (IRE)

78f 86f

5-y-o b g Phardante (FR)-Gray's Ellergy (Oats)
D R Gandolfo Mrs C Skipworth

Placings:*00* **(2648)**
2001/02: 16^{0}GS, 16^{0}GS

	Starts	1st	2nd	3rd	Win & Pl
NH Flat	2	0	0	0	
Career Total	**2**	**0**	**0**	**0**	

Going: Sf: 0-0 GS: 0-2 Gd: 0-0 GF: - Fm: 0-0
Distance: 2m/2m3: 0-2 2m4-2m7: 0-0 3m+: 0-0
Track: LH: 0-0 RH: 0-2 Tight: 0-0 Gall: 0-1
Aids: Bl: 0-0 Vi: 0-0 Tstrap: 0-0
Best Rating: 86 12/01 Hntg 2m110y gd-sft NHF

Crack Regiment (IRE)

101 87

10-y-o b g Lafontaine (USA)-Princess Crack (IRE) (Buckskin (FR))
R H Buckler Twentyman

Placings:*P4/3F2/022F-5P00* **(4131)**
2001/02: 21^{5}G, 24^{P}HY, 22^{0}S, 26^{0}G

	Starts	1st	2nd	3rd	Win & Pl
Hurdles	4	0	0	0	700
Career Total	**13**	**0**	**3**	**1**	**4514**

Going: Sf: 0-2 GS: 0-0 Gd: 0-2 GF: - Fm: 0-0
Distance: 2m/2m3: 0-0 2m4-2m7: 0-2 3m+: 0-2
Track: LH: 0-2 RH: 0-2 Tight: 0-1 Gall: 0-1
Aids: Bl: 0-0 Vi: 0-0 Tstrap: 0-0
Best Rating: 112 11/00 Newb 2m5f soft Hdl

A former winning point to pointer. Still a novice over hurdles. Acts on a sound surface. Stays two miles-six.

Cracking Blade

81f 76f

5-y-o b g Sure Blade (USA)-Norstock (Norwick (USA))
J White The Norstock Partnership

Placings:*000* **(4887)**
2001/02: 16^{0}G, 18^{0}G, 18^{0}GF

	Starts	1st	2nd	3rd	Win & Pl
NH Flat	3	0	0	0	
Career Total	**3**	**0**	**0**	**0**	

Going: Sf: 0-0 GS: 0-0 Gd: 0-2 GF: - Fm: 0-1
Distance: 2m/2m3: 0-3 2m4-2m7: 0-0 3m+: 0-0
Track: LH: 0-2 RH: 0-1 Tight: 0-2 Gall: 0-0
Aids: Bl: 0-0 Vi: 0-0 Tstrap: 0-0
Best Rating: 76 12/01 Ludl 2m good NHF

Cracking Dawn (IRE)

111 132

7-y-o b g Be My Native (USA)-Rare Coin (Kemal (FR))
R H Alner (John J Costello 5/5) Peter Bonner

Placings:*0-012* **(4134)**
2001/02: 16^{0}G, 22^{1}S, 20^{2}GS

	Starts	1st	2nd	3rd	Win & Pl		
NH Flat	1	0	0	0	0		
Hurdles	2	1	1	0	4658		
Career Total	**4**	**1**	**1**	**0**	**4658**		
132 2/02	Font	2m6f110y	E Hdl		SFT	£3332	

Total win prize-money £3332

Going: Sf: 1-1 GS: 0-1 Gd: 0-1 GF: - Fm: 0-0
Distance: 2m/2m3: 0-1 **2m4-2m7: 1-2** 3m+: 0-0
Track: **LH: 1-1** RH: 0-1 **Tight: 1-1** Gall: 0-0
Aids: Bl: 0-0 Vi: 0-0 Tstrap: 0-0
Best Rating: 132 2/02 Font 2m6f110y soft Hdl

A winner of Irish point-to-points, he won a Fontwell novice hurdle on his British debut. Stays well.

Crackrattle (IRE)

8-y-o ch g Montelimar (USA)-Gaye Le Moss (Le Moss)
P J Millington P J Millington

Placings:*6/P* **(0094)**
2001/02: 25^{P}S

	Starts	1st	2nd	3rd	Win & Pl
Chases	1	0	0	0	
Career Total	**2**	**0**	**0**	**0**	**0**

Going: Sf: 0-1 GS: 0-0 Gd: 0-0 GF: - Fm: 0-0
Distance: 2m/2m3: 0-0 2m4-2m7: 0-0 3m+: 0-1
Track: LH: 0-1 RH: 0-0 Tight: 0-0 Gall: 0-0
Aids: Bl: 0-0 Vi: 0-0 Tstrap: 0-0

Best Rating: 66 4/99 Towc 2m good NHF

Cracksman

9-y-o b g Scallywag-Furstin (Furry Glen)
T Wall D Pugh

Placings:*00/0/*PP-P **(0355)**
2001/02: 17^{P}GS

	Starts	1st	2nd	3rd	Win & Pl
Hurdles	1	0	0	0	
Career Total	**6**	**0**	**0**	**0**	

Going: Sf: 0-0 GS: 0-1 Gd: 0-0 GF: - Fm: 0-0
Distance: 2m/2m3: 0-1 2m4-2m7: 0-0 3m+: 0-0
Track: LH: 0-1 RH: 0-0 Tight: 0-1 Gall: 0-0
Aids: Bl: 0-1 Vi: 0-0 Tstrap: 0-0
Best Rating:

Cracow (IRE)

96(91c) (93c)80
5-y-o b g Polish Precedent (USA)-Height Of Secrecy (Shirley Heights)
N J Hawke (J W Hills 2/10) The Cornish 'Crac' Partnership

Placings:00P004 **(4866)**
2001/02: 16^{0}GS, 16^{0}G, 21^{P}S, 16^{0}G, 17^{0}G, 17^{4}F

	Starts	1st	2nd	3rd	Win & Pl
Hurdles	6	0	0	0	0
Career Total	**6**	**0**	**0**	**0**	**0**

Going: Sf: 0-1 GS: 0-1 Gd: 0-3 GF: - Fm: 0-1
Distance: 2m/2m3: 0-5 2m4-2m7: 0-1 3m+: 0-0
Track: LH: 0-0 RH: 0-6 Tight: 0-1 Gall: 0-0
Aids: Bl: 0-2 Vi: 0-0 Tstrap: 0-0
Best Rating: 80 2/02 Winc 2m gd-sft Hdl

Crafty Lad (IRE)

51f 87f
5-y-o b g Warcraft (USA)-Deep Lass (Deep Run)
Mrs M Reveley The Lingdale Optimists

Placings:*0*P **(4790)**
2001/02: 16^{0}HY, 16^{P}F

	Starts	1st	2nd	3rd	Win & Pl
NH Flat	2	0	0	0	
Career Total	**2**	**0**	**0**	**0**	

Going: Sf: 0-1 GS: 0-0 Gd: 0-0 GF: - Fm: 0-1
Distance: 2m/2m3: 0-2 2m4-2m7: 0-0 3m+: 0-0
Track: LH: 0-1 RH: 0-0 Tight: 0-0 Gall: 0-0
Aids: Bl: 0-0 Vi: 0-0 Tstrap: 0-0
Best Rating: 87 3/02 Ayr 2m heavy NHF

Craigary

93(95c) (84c)71
11-y-o b g Dunbeath (USA)-Velvet Pearl (Record Token)
D A Nolan James A Cringan

Placings:00/000064/060/3211406/00F03/6033256/03 P440650-64530300P000 **(3611)**
2001/02: 16^{6}GF, 20^{4}GF, 21^{5}G, 20^{3}G, 22^{0}G, 17^{3}GS, 18^{0}G, 21^{0}G, 25^{P}S, 16^{0}GF, 20^{0}G, 20^{0}S

	Starts	1st	2nd	3rd	Win & Pl
Hurdles	6	0	0	2	885
Chases	6	0	0	0	536
Career Total	**51**	**2**	**2**	**7**	**8999**

92	12/97	Catt	2m3f	E(0-110)HHdl	GD	£2220
92	11/97	Sedg	2m1f	G(0-95)HHdl	GD	£1842

Total win prize-money £4062

Going: Sf: 0-2 GS: 0-1 Gd: 0-6 GF: - Fm: 0-3
Distance: 2m/2m3: 0-4 2m4-2m7: 0-7 3m+: 0-1
Track: LH: 0-5 RH: 0-7 Tight: 0-7 Gall: 0-0
Aids: Bl: 0-0 Vi: 0-0 Tstrap: 0-0
Best Rating: 96 11/00 Ayr 2m soft Ch

Mixes chasing hurdling and Flat racing, but has not won over jumps since 1997.

Craven Hill (IRE)

77 32
8-y-o gr g Pursuit Of Love-Crodelle (IRE) (Formidable (USA))
N A Twiston-Davies The Berryman Lycett Experience

Placings:4R0-00P0 **(1038)**
2001/02: 20^{0}GF, 20^{0}G, 16^{P}G, 17^{0}G

	Starts	1st	2nd	3rd	Win & Pl
Hurdles	4	0	0	0	
Career Total	**7**	**0**	**0**	**0**	**0**

Going: Sf: 0-0 GS: 0-0 Gd: 0-3 GF: - Fm: 0-1
Distance: 2m/2m3: 0-2 2m4-2m7: 0-2 3m+: 0-0
Track: LH: 0-4 RH: 0-0 Tight: 0-1 Gall: 0-0
Aids: Bl: 0-3 Vi: 0-0 Tstrap: 0-0
Best Rating: 70 7/00 Worc 2m4f gd-fm Hdl

Crawfordstowncross (IRE)

(69h) (26h)
10-y-o b g Homo Sapien-Annagarry (Proverb)
Graham Smith Graham Smith

Placings:2/F*0*U-6SP **(1596)**
2001/02: 16^{6}GF, 20^{S}GF, 20^{P}G

	Starts	1st	2nd	3rd	Win & Pl
Hurdles	2	0	0	0	0
Chases	1	0	0	0	0
Career Total	**7**	**0**	**1**	**0**	**640**

Going: Sf: 0-0 GS: 0-0 Gd: 0-1 GF: - Fm: 0-2
Distance: 2m/2m3: 0-1 2m4-2m7: 0-2 3m+: 0-0
Track: LH: 0-3 RH: 0-0 Tight: 0-2 Gall: 0-0
Aids: Bl: 0-0 Vi: 0-0 Tstrap: 0-0
Best Rating: 48 5/00 Dpat 2m4f110y good NHF

Crazy Horse (IRE)

107(98c) 159
9-y-o b g Little Bighorn-Our Dorcet (Condorcet (FR))
L Lungo Ashleybank Investments Limited

Placings:*P101*/2211213/5U2220/3U31-1 **(0079)**
2001/02: 23^{1}G

	Starts	1st	2nd	3rd	Win & Pl
Hurdles	1	1	0	0	10238
Career Total	**22**	**7**	**6**	**3**	**76206**

152	5/01	Hayd	2m7f110y	B Hdl	GD	£10237
159	4/01	Aint	2m4f	B HHdl	SFT	£26000
150	3/99	Kels	2m2f	B Hdl	SFT	£13680
125	1/99	Kels	2m110y	D Hdl	HVY	£2932
133	12/98	Ayr	2m	E Hdl	HVY	£2682
120	4/98	Ayr	2m	H NHF	GD	£3598
128	2/98	Weth	2m	H NHF	GD	£1434

Total win prize-money £60566

Going: Sf: 0-0 GS: 0-0 Gd: 1-1 GF: - Fm: 0-0
Distance: 2m/2m3: 0-0 2m4-2m7: 0-0 **3m+: 1-1**
Track: **LH: 1-1** RH: 0-0 Tight: 0-0 Gall: 0-0
Aids: Bl: 0-0 Vi: 0-0 Tstrap: 0-0
Best Rating: 159 4/01 Aint 2m4f soft Hdl

A very able hurdler , he probably needs at least two and a half miles these days and has to be produced late. Off the track since winning at haydock in May 2001.

Crazy Mazie

97f 83f
5-y-o b m Risk Me (FR)-Post Impressionist (IRE) (Ahonoora)
K A Morgan Mrs S J Storer

Placings:*6663* **(4910)**
2001/02: 17^{6}GS, 16^{6}HY, 16^{6}GF, 17^{3}G

	Starts	1st	2nd	3rd	Win & Pl
NH Flat	4	0	0	1	257
Career Total	**4**	**0**	**0**	**1**	**257**

Going: Sf: 0-1 GS: 0-1 Gd: 0-1 GF: - Fm: 0-1
Distance: 2m/2m3: 0-4 2m4-2m7: 0-0 3m+: 0-0
Track: LH: 0-1 RH: 0-3 Tight: 0-3 Gall: 0-0
Aids: Bl: 0-0 Vi: 0-0 Tstrap: 0-0
Best Rating: 83 4/02 MRas 2m1f110y good NHF

Cream Gorse

97 85
6-y-o ch m Alflora (IRE)-Celtic Slave (Celtic Cone)
H D Daly B G Hellyer

Placings:*5*-55440 **(4577)**
2001/02: 16^{5}G, 16^{5}G, 20^{4}GS, 19^{4}G, 24^{0}G

	Starts	1st	2nd	3rd	Win & Pl
Hurdles	5	0	0	0	571
Career Total	**6**	**0**	**0**	**0**	**571**

Going: Sf: 0-0 GS: 0-1 Gd: 0-4 GF: - Fm: 0-0
Distance: 2m/2m3: 0-3 2m4-2m7: 0-1 3m+: 0-1
Track: LH: 0-2 RH: 0-3 Tight: 0-0 Gall: 0-1
Aids: Bl: 0-0 Vi: 0-0 Tstrap: 0-0
Best Rating: 85 3/02 Extr 2m3f good Hdl

Chasing type who has shown some ability in novice hurdles.

Cream Supreme (IRE)

12-y-o gr g Supreme Leader-Grandpa's River (Over The River (FR))
Evan Williams Mrs J M Hegarty

Placings:*00/000/5/U-00* **(0497)**
2001/02: 24^{0}GS, 25^{0}G

	Starts	1st	2nd	3rd	Win & Pl
Chases	2	0	0	0	
Career Total	**9**	**0**	**0**	**0**	**0**

Going: Sf: 0-0 GS: 0-1 Gd: 0-1 GF: - Fm: 0-0
Distance: 2m/2m3: 0-0 2m4-2m7: 0-0 3m+: 0-2
Track: LH: 0-1 RH: 0-1 Tight: 0-1 Gall: 0-0
Aids: Bl: 0-1 Vi: 0-0 Tstrap: 0-0
Best Rating: 64 5/95 Navn 2m2f firm Hdl

Creative Time (IRE)

100(78h) (66h)116

6-y-o b g Houmayoun (FR)-Creative Princess (IRE) (Creative Plan (USA))

Miss H C Knight Mrs G M Sturges & H Stephen Smith

Placings:3334 **(3776)**

2001/02: 22^{3}S, 23^{3}GF, 23^{3}G, 24^{4}S

	Starts	1st	2nd	3rd	Win & Pl
Hurdles	1	0	0	1	374
Chases	3	0	0	2	1743
Career Total	**4**	**0**	**0**	**3**	**2117**

Going: Sf: 0-2 GS: 0-0 Gd: 0-1 GF: - Fm: 0-1
Distance: 2m/2m3: 0-0 2m4-2m7: 0-1 3m+: 0-3
Track: LH: 0-1 RH: 0-3 Tight: 0-1 Gall: 0-0
Aids: Bl: 0-0 Vi: 0-0 Tstrap: 0-0
Best Rating: 116 2/02 Sand 3m110y soft Ch

Fair efforts in novice company.

Credenza Moment

81 78

4-y-o b c Pyramus (USA)-Mystoski (Petoski)

M Madgwick (R Hannon 9/8) W V Roker

Placings:P5000O **(4507)**

2001/02: 18^{P}GF, 16^{5}GS, 16^{0}G, 18^{0}G, 16^{0}G, 21^{0}G

	Starts	1st	2nd	3rd	Win & Pl
Hurdles	6	0	0	0	0
Career Total	**6**	**0**	**0**	**0**	**0**

Going: Sf: 0-0 GS: 0-1 Gd: 0-4 GF: - Fm: 0-1
Distance: 2m/2m3: 0-5 2m4-2m7: 0-1 3m+: 0-0
Track: LH: 0-3 RH: 0-3 Tight: 0-3 Gall: 0-0
Aids: Bl: 0-1 Vi: 0-0 Tstrap: 0-0
Best Rating: 78 11/01 Sand 2m110y gd-sft Hdl

Credit Controller (IRE)

13-y-o b g Dromod Hill-Fotopan (Polyfoto)

F L Matthews J E Wood

Placings:*0*/0052P/2323644/**PP** **(4685)**

2001/02: 20^{P}S, 16^{P}GF

	Starts	1st	2nd	3rd	Win & Pl
Chases	2	0	0	0	
Career Total	**15**	**0**	**3**	**2**	**2171**

Going: Sf: 0-1 GS: 0-0 Gd: 0-0 GF: - Fm: 0-1
Distance: 2m/2m3: 0-1 2m4-2m7: 0-1 3m+: 0-0
Track: LH: 0-0 RH: 0-2 Tight: 0-1 Gall: 0-0
Aids: Bl: 0-2 Vi: 0-0 Tstrap: 0-0
Best Rating: 57 12/96 Font 2m2f110y good Hdl

Creek Tower

77f 74f

5-y-o b g Rainbow Quest (USA)-Pass The Peace (Alzao (USA))

A Streeter Malt 'N' Hops

Placings:*00* **(4180)**

2001/02: 16^{0}GS, 16^{0}GS

	Starts	1st	2nd	3rd	Win & Pl
NH Flat	2	0	0	0	
Career Total	**2**	**0**	**0**	**0**	

Going: Sf: 0-0 GS: 0-2 Gd: 0-0 GF: - Fm: 0-0
Distance: 2m/2m3: 0-2 2m4-2m7: 0-0 3m+: 0-0
Track: LH: 0-1 RH: 0-0 Tight: 0-0 Gall: 0-1
Aids: Bl: 0-0 Vi: 0-0 Tstrap: 0-0
Best Rating: 74 3/02 Strf 2m110y gd-sft NHF

Cregg House (IRE)

116(101h) (113h)166

7-y-o ch g King Persian-Loyal River (Over The River (FR))

P Mullins (S Donohoe 29/10) Mrs Kathleen Kennedy

Placings:*0223446*/3F421136-PP4024222R **(4705a)**

2001/02: 21^{P}Y, 24^{P}GF, 20^{4}Y, 22^{0}SH, 25^{2}Y, 24^{4}Y, 25^{2}YS, 20^{2}S, 21^{2}G, 29^{R}GY

	Starts	1st	2nd	3rd	Win & Pl	
Chases	10	0	4	0	29538	
Career Total	**25**	**2**	**7**	**3**	**52559**	
126 2/01	Fair	3m1f	HCh		YLD	£10483
114 1/01	Fair	2m5f120y	Ch		HVY	£5564

Total win prize-money £16049

Going: Sf: 0-1 GS: 0-0 Gd: 0-1 GF: - Fm: 0-1
Distance: 2m/2m3: 0-0 2m4-2m7: 0-5 3m+: 0-5
Track: LH: 0-4 RH: 0-5 Tight: 0-0 Gall: 0-1
Aids: Bl: 0-1 Vi: 0-0 Tstrap: 0-1
Best Rating: 166 3/02 Chel 2m5f good Ch

Useful Irish chaser, runner-up in the Cathcart. Refused at the last at Fairyhouse subsequently. Travels well but tends to find little off the bridle. Suited by cut in the ground.

Creon

102(112h) (114h)119

7-y-o b g Saddlers' Hall (IRE)-Creake (Derring Do)

J J O'Neill J P McManus

Placings:004/04P120/0003**F0500**1164-3002430061 **(4889)**

2001/02: 18^{3}Y, 22^{0}YS, 20^{0}Y, 23^{2}G, 23^{4}G, 22^{3}S, 20^{0}S, 24^{0}GS, 22^{6}HY, 26^{1}G

	Starts	1st	2nd	3rd	Win & Pl	
Hurdles	3	0	0	0	0	
Chases	7	1	1	2	8498	
Career Total	**32**	**4**	**2**	**3**	**23478**	
119 4/02	Prth	3m2f110y	F(0-90)HCh		GD	£5330
134 1/01	Kemp	3m110y	D(0-120)HHdl		SFT	£5187
134 12/00	Weth	2m7f	C(0-130)HHdl		SFT	£4992
90 9/99	Baln	2m	Hdl		G-F	£2957

Total win prize-money £18466

Going: Sf: 0-3 GS: 0-1 Gd: 1-3 GF: - Fm: 0-0
Distance: 2m/2m3: 0-1 2m4-2m7: 0-5 **3m+: 1-4**
Track: LH: 0-2 RH: 0-6 Tight: 0-1 Gall: 0-1
Aids: Bl: 0-0 Vi: 0-0 Tstrap: 0-0
Best Rating: 134 1/01 Kemp 3m110y soft Hdl

Acts on soft ground, stays three miles plus, an easy winner when returned to fences at Perth in April.

Crepusculaire (FR)

79 51

5-y-o ch m Hernando (FR)-Guest Performer (Be My Guest (USA))

C R Egerton (N A Callaghan 25/10) Andy J Smith

Placings:0 **(4113)**

2001/02: 16^{0}G

	Starts	1st	2nd	3rd	Win & Pl
Hurdles	1	0	0	0	
Career Total	**1**	**0**	**0**	**0**	

Going: Sf: 0-0 GS: 0-0 Gd: 0-1 GF: - Fm: 0-0
Distance: 2m/2m3: 0-1 2m4-2m7: 0-0 3m+: 0-0
Track: LH: 0-0 RH: 0-1 Tight: 0-0 Gall: 0-0
Aids: Bl: 0-0 Vi: 0-0 Tstrap: 0-0
Best Rating: 54 3/02 Winc 2m good Hdl

Fair French staying handicapper on the Flat, before showing form on soft ground on the level in Britain. Well beaten on her hurdles bow at Wincanton in March 2002 on good ground.

Cresswell Cherry (IRE)

103 93

7-y-o b m Camden Town-Cherry Country (Town And Country)

N A Twiston-Davies James Cheetham

Placings:34P-2021636 **(4572)**

2001/02: 22^{2}GF, 25^{0}G, 19^{2}S, 16^{1}HY, 17^{6}HY, 16^{3}S, 20^{6}G

	Starts	1st	2nd	3rd	Win & Pl	
Hurdles	7	1	2	1	5047	
Career Total	**10**	**1**	**2**	**2**	**5560**	
93 1/02	Towc	2m	E(0-110)HHdl		HVY	£2978

Total win prize-money £2979

Going: Sf: 1-4 GS: 0-0 Gd: 0-2 GF: - Fm: 0-1
Distance: **2m/2m3: 1-3** 2m4-2m7: 0-3 3m+: 0-1
Track: LH: 0-2 **RH: 1-4** Tight: 0-0 Gall: 0-0
Aids: Bl: 0-0 Vi: 0-0 Tstrap: 0-0
Best Rating: 93 3/02 Towc 2m soft Hdl

An ex-pointer, fair handicap hurdler, she acts on heavy ground and is effective over two miles, but stays further.

Cresswell Gold

77f 56f

5-y-o b m Homo Sapien-Running For Gold (Rymer)

P Bowen Bruce McKay

Placings:*0* **(1545)**

2001/02: 17^{0}G

	Starts	1st	2nd	3rd	Win & Pl
NH Flat	1	0	0	0	
Career Total	**1**	**0**	**0**	**0**	

Going: Sf: 0-0 GS: 0-0 Gd: 0-1 GF: - Fm: 0-0
Distance: 2m/2m3: 0-1 2m4-2m7: 0-0 3m+: 0-0
Track: LH: 0-0 RH: 0-1 Tight: 0-0 Gall: 0-0
Aids: Bl: 0-0 Vi: 0-0 Tstrap: 0-0
Best Rating: 49 10/01 Hrfd 2m1f good NHF

Cresswell Native (IRE)

107(110h) (105h)112

8-y-o b m Be My Native (USA)-Nanallac Girl (Deep Run)

P F Nicholls (J Neville 1/5) Mrs Angela Tincknell

Placings:*1024*/21U152-0433U1 **(4412)**

2001/02: 20^{0}G, 22^{4}G, 16^{3}G, 16^{3}S, 21^{U}HY, 20^{1}S

	Starts	1st	2nd	3rd	Win & Pl	
Hurdles	3	0	0	1	826	
Chases	3	1	0	1	3934	
Career Total	**16**	**4**	**3**	**2**	**23274**	
112 3/02	Font	2m4f	E Ch		SFT	£3304
119 1/01	Font	2m2f110y	E Hdl		SFT	£2765
109 11/00	Tntn	2m3f110y	C Hdl		G-S	£5050
122 12/99	Ling	2m110y	H NHF		SFT	£1632

Total win prize-money £12752

Going: Sf: 1-3 GS: 0-0 Gd: 0-3 GF: - Fm: 0-0
Distance: 2m/2m3: 0-2 **2m4-2m7: 1-4** 3m+: 0-0
Track: LH: 0-1 RH: 0-4 **Tight: 1-1** Gall: 0-1
Aids: Bl: 0-0 Vi: 0-0 Tstrap: 0-0
Best Rating: 122 2/00 Font 2m2f110y soft NHF

Twice a winner over hurdles short of two and a half miles, she found the trip on the short side on her first run over fences but got off the mark over the larger obstacles in a weak event at Fontwell. Acts on soft ground.

Cresswell Quay

84

9-y-o ch g Bold Fox-Karatina (FR) (Dilettante Ii)
P Bowen Bruce McKay

Placings:*60*/50650/5/4313-F46P **(2415)**
2001/02: 24^{F}G, 26^{4}GS, 26^{6}S, 26^{P}HY

	Starts	1st	2nd	3rd	Win & Pl
Chases	4	0	0	0	500
Career Total	**16**	**1**	**0**	**2**	**4345**

94 7/00 Wolv 3m1f E Hdl G-S £2293
Total win prize-money £2293

Going: Sf: 0-2 GS: 0-1 Gd: 0-1 GF: - Fm: 0-0
Distance: 2m/2m3: 0-0 2m4-2m7: 0-0 3m+: 0-4
Track: LH: 0-3 RH: 0-0 Tight: 0-1 Gall: 0-0
Aids: Bl: 0-0 Vi: 0-0 Tstrap: 0-0
Best Rating: 108 7/00 Wolv 3m1f good Ch

Crest Wing (USA)

91(70h) (63h)75

9-y-o b g Storm Bird (CAN)-Purify (USA) (Fappiano (USA))
Miss Z C Davison The Secret Circle (1)

Placings:PP0/0/4-66500POU5 **(4562)**
2001/02: 24^{0}G, 24^{6}GF, 22^{5}GF, 21^{0}G, 22^{0}G, 25^{P}G, 21°S, 24^{U}G, 20^{5}GF

	Starts	1st	2nd	3rd	Win & Pl
Hurdles	5	0	0	0	0
Chases	4	0	0	0	0
Career Total	**14**	**0**	**0**	**0**	**0**

Going: Sf: 0-1 GS: 0-0 Gd: 0-5 GF: - Fm: 0-3
Distance: 2m/2m3: 0-0 2m4-2m7: 0-5 3m+: 0-4
Track: LH: 0-4 RH: 0-3 Tight: 0-4 Gall: 0-0
Aids: Bl: 0-0 Vi: 0-1 Tstrap: 0-3
Best Rating: 75 4/02 Plum 2m4f gd-fm Ch

Crime Stopper

9-y-o b m Broadsword (USA)-Sorority (Tap On Wood)
Miss S J Wilton John Pointon And Sons

Placings:*05*PP/PP/U **(1543)**
2001/02: 19^{U}G

	Starts	1st	2nd	3rd	Win & Pl
Chases	1	0	0	0	
Career Total	**7**	**0**	**0**	**0**	**0**

Going: Sf: 0-0 GS: 0-0 Gd: 0-1 GF: - Fm: 0-0
Distance: 2m/2m3: 0-1 2m4-2m7: 0-0 3m+: 0-0
Track: LH: 0-0 RH: 0-1 Tight: 0-0 Gall: 0-0
Aids: Bl: 0-0 Vi: 0-0 Tstrap: 0-0
Best Rating: 71 12/97 Uttx 2m gd-sft NHF

Criminal Silk

89 69

7-y-o b m Tragic Role (USA)-See You In Court (London Gazette)
S J Gilmore L G Kimber

Placings:*060-006* **(4850)**
2001/02: 16^{0}GS, 21^{0}GS, 22^{6}G

	Starts	1st	2nd	3rd	Win & Pl
NH Flat	1	0	0	0	0
Hurdles	2	0	0	0	0
Career Total	**6**	**0**	**0**	**0**	**0**

Going: Sf: 0-0 GS: 0-2 Gd: 0-1 GF: - Fm: 0-0
Distance: 2m/2m3: 0-1 2m4-2m7: 0-2 3m+: 0-0
Track: LH: 0-2 RH: 0-1 Tight: 0-2 Gall: 0-0
Aids: Bl: 0-0 Vi: 0-0 Tstrap: 0-0
Best Rating: 91 12/00 Donc 2m110y heavy NHF

Crimson Bow

12-y-o b m Balinger-Crimson Flag (Kinglet)
Keith Thomas Miss C R Thomas

Placings:P **(4522)**
2001/02: 17^{P}G

	Starts	1st	2nd	3rd	Win & Pl
Hurdles	1	0	0	0	
Career Total	**1**	**0**	**0**	**0**	

Going: Sf: 0-0 GS: 0-0 Gd: 0-1 GF: - Fm: 0-0
Distance: 2m/2m3: 0-1 2m4-2m7: 0-0 3m+: 0-0
Track: LH: 0-0 RH: 0-1 Tight: 0-0 Gall: 0-0
Aids: Bl: 0-0 Vi: 0-0 Tstrap: 0-0
Best Rating:

Crimson Brocade

85 91

11-y-o b m Daring March-Stellaris (Star Appeal)
Mrs K J Tutty N D Tutty

Placings:*50*/4P/55PP **(3391)**
2001/02: 25^{5}G, 27^{5}S, 24^{P}GS, 23^{P}GS

	Starts	1st	2nd	3rd	Win & Pl
Chases	4	0	0	0	0
Career Total	**8**	**0**	**0**	**0**	**248**

Going: Sf: 0-1 GS: 0-2 Gd: 0-1 GF: - Fm: 0-0
Distance: 2m/2m3: 0-0 2m4-2m7: 0-0 3m+: 0-4
Track: LH: 0-3 RH: 0-0 Tight: 0-1 Gall: 0-1
Aids: Bl: 0-0 Vi: 0-0 Tstrap: 0-0
Best Rating: 91 11/01 Weth 3m1f good Ch

Ordinary novice chaser.

Crimson Pirate (IRE)

91f 90f

5-y-o b g Phardante (FR)-Stroked Again (On Your Mark)
B De Haan Duncan Heath

Placings:*0* **(2942)**
2001/02: 16^{0}G

	Starts	1st	2nd	3rd	Win & Pl
NH Flat	1	0	0	0	
Career Total	**1**	**0**	**0**	**0**	

Going: Sf: 0-0 GS: 0-0 Gd: 0-1 GF: - Fm: 0-0
Distance: 2m/2m3: 0-1 2m4-2m7: 0-0 3m+: 0-0
Track: LH: 0-1 RH: 0-0 Tight: 0-0 Gall: 0-1
Aids: Bl: 0-0 Vi: 0-0 Tstrap: 0-0
Best Rating: 90 12/01 Newb 2m110y good NHF

Crisis (IRE)

6-y-o b g Second Set (IRE)-Special Offer (IRE) (Shy Groom (USA))
P T Dalton Mrs R S Perkins

Placings:2433134/331-6 **(4528)**
2001/02: 20^{6}GS

	Starts	1st	2nd	3rd	Win & Pl
Hurdles	1	0	0	0	0
Career Total	**11**	**2**	**1**	**5**	**10879**

108 11/00 Uttx 2m4f110y E(0-115)HHdl HVY £2338
95 1/00 Leic 2m4f110y E Hdl SFT £3588
Total win prize-money £5926

Going: Sf: 0-0 GS: 0-1 Gd: 0-0 GF: - Fm: 0-0
Distance: 2m/2m3: 0-0 2m4-2m7: 0-1 3m+: 0-0
Track: LH: 0-1 RH: 0-0 Tight: 0-0 Gall: 0-0
Aids: Bl: 0-0 Vi: 0-0 Tstrap: 0-0
Best Rating: 108 11/00 Uttx 2m4f110y heavy Hdl

Fair hurdler at around two and a half miles. Acts on soft/heavy ground.

Cristoforo (IRE)

67 20

5-y-o b g Perugino (USA)-Red Barons Lady (IRE) (Electric)
B J Curley P Byrne

Placings:000 **(3319)**
2001/02: 16^{0}G, 16^{0}G, 16^{0}GS

	Starts	1st	2nd	3rd	Win & Pl
Hurdles	3	0	0	0	
Career Total	**3**	**0**	**0**	**0**	

Going: Sf: 0-0 GS: 0-1 Gd: 0-2 GF: - Fm: 0-0
Distance: 2m/2m3: 0-3 2m4-2m7: 0-0 3m+: 0-0
Track: LH: 0-1 RH: 0-2 Tight: 0-0 Gall: 0-2
Aids: Bl: 0-0 Vi: 0-0 Tstrap: 0-0
Best Rating: 20 11/01 Hntg 2m110y good Hdl

Cristophe

87 72

4-y-o b g Kris-Our Shirley (Shirley Heights)
A Crook (S P C Woods 30/8) Million In Mind Partnership (11)

Placings:000P0 **(4786)**
2001/02: 16^{0}S, 16^{0}GS, 16^{0}S, 17^{P}S, 20^{0}F

	Starts	1st	2nd	3rd	Win & Pl
Hurdles	5	0	0	0	
Career Total	**5**	**0**	**0**	**0**	

Going: Sf: 0-3 GS: 0-1 Gd: 0-0 GF: - Fm: 0-1
Distance: 2m/2m3: 0-4 2m4-2m7: 0-1 3m+: 0-0
Track: LH: 0-5 RH: 0-0 Tight: 0-2 Gall: 0-2
Aids: Bl: 0-0 Vi: 0-1 Tstrap: 0-0
Best Rating: 72 1/02 Newc 2m soft Hdl

Moderate maiden on the flat and over hurdles.

Cristys Picnic (IRE)

12-y-o b g Tremblant-My Maizey (Buckskin (FR))
G M Spencer G F Smith

Placings:06/43060/000P412/30P113P/02330400/35P6P665RU/06P-P (4755)
2001/02: 23^{P}GF

	Starts	1st	2nd	3rd	Win & Pl
Chases	1	0	0	0	
Career Total	**43**	**3**	**2**	**6**	**24034**

118	7/97	Tipp	2m4f	HCh	GD	£6782
109	7/97	Kbgn	2m7f	HCh	GD	£8762
86	4/97	Navn	2m4f	Ch	FRM	£3051

Total win prize-money £18596

Going: Sf: 0-0 GS: 0-0 Gd: 0-0 GF: - Fm: 0-1
Distance: 2m/2m3: 0-0 2m4-2m7: 0-1 3m+: 0-0
Track: LH: 0-1 RH: 0-0 Tight: 0-0 Gall: 0-0
Aids: Bl: 0-0 Vi: 0-0 Tstrap: 0-0
Best Rating: 118 7/98 Wxfd 2m4f gd-fm Ch

Modest pointer.

Crocknamohill (IRE)

89 **75**
11-y-o br g Strong Gale-Rusty Iron (General Ironside)
D G Bridgwater Mrs C Kelly

Placings:00/6/602P0343466PP3PP/22P125/P33P006P/00450423-5 (0723)
2001/02: 25^{5}F

	Starts	1st	2nd	3rd	Win & Pl
Chases	1	0	0	0	0
Career Total	**42**	**1**	**5**	**6**	**11353**

94	9/98	MRas	2m6f110y	E Ch	GD	£3231

Total win prize-money £3231

Going: Sf: 0-0 GS: 0-0 Gd: 0-0 GF: - Fm: 0-1
Distance: 2m/2m3: 0-0 2m4-2m7: 0-0 3m+: 0-1
Track: LH: 0-0 RH: 0-1 Tight: 0-0 Gall: 0-0
Aids: Bl: 0-0 Vi: 0-1 Tstrap: 0-0
Best Rating: 94 9/99 MRas 2m4f gd-fm Ch

Croesy Pennant

9-y-o b g Nalchik (USA)-Courtney Pennant (Angus)
R Williams R Williams

Placings:0/6/PP (1906)
2001/02: 22^{P}G, 22^{P}S

	Starts	1st	2nd	3rd	Win & Pl
Hurdles	2	0	0	0	
Career Total	**4**	**0**	**0**	**0**	**0**

Going: Sf: 0-1 GS: 0-0 Gd: 0-1 GF: - Fm: 0-0
Distance: 2m/2m3: 0-0 2m4-2m7: 0-2 3m+: 0-0
Track: LH: 0-1 RH: 0-0 Tight: 0-1 Gall: 0-0
Aids: Bl: 0-0 Vi: 0-0 Tstrap: 0-0
Best Rating: 71 9/99 Worc 2m gd-fm NHF

Pulled up in his first two starts over hurdles.

Croft Court

11-y-o b g Crofthall-Queen Of Dara (Dara Monarch)
D J Wintle D J Renney

Placings:F/4-1P0 (0579)
2001/02: 26^{1}GS, 33^{P}G, 24^{0}GF

	Starts	1st	2nd	3rd	Win & Pl
Chases	3	1	0	0	3315
Career Total	**5**	**1**	**0**	**0**	**3705**

106	4/01	Plum	3m2f	E Ch	G-S	£3315

Total win prize-money £3315

Going: Sf: 0-0 GS: 1-1 Gd: 0-1 GF: - Fm: 0-1
Distance: 2m/2m3: 0-0 2m4-2m7: 0-0 **3m+: 1-3**
Track: LH: 0-1 RH: 0-0 Tight: 0-1 Gall: 0-0
Aids: Bl: 0-1 Vi: 0-0 Tstrap: 0-0
Best Rating: 106 4/01 Plum 3m2f gd-sft Ch

Croker (IRE)

103 **81**
7-y-o ch g Rainbows For Life (CAN)-Almagest (Dike (USA))
Simon T Lewis (J J Bridger 7/5) Simon T Lewis

Placings:4313/3344/P66033P-0001400 (1401)
2001/02: 18^{0}GF, 20^{0}S, 16^{0}G, 17^{1}G, 20^{4}G, 17^{0}GF, 20^{0}G

	Starts	1st	2nd	3rd	Win & Pl
Hurdles	7	1	0	0	2667
Career Total	**22**	**2**	**0**	**6**	**7521**

81	8/01	Bang	2m1f	G(0-95)HHdl	GD	£2383
110	11/98	Uttx	2m	E Hdl	SFT	£2295

Total win prize-money £4679

Going: Sf: 0-1 GS: 0-0 Gd: 1-4 GF: - Fm: 0-2
Distance: **2m/2m3: 1-4** 2m4-2m7: 0-3 3m+: 0-0
Track: **LH: 1-7** RH: 0-0 **Tight: 1-5** Gall: 0-0
Aids: Bl: 0-1 Vi: 0-1 Tstrap: 0-0
Best Rating: 113 12/98 Wwck 2m gd-sft Hdl

Cromer Pier

68 **37**
7-y-o b g Reprimand-Fleur Du Val (Valiyar)
G Fierro G Fierro

Placings:605001/PP0P1002P00-0 (2025)
2001/02: 16^{0}S

	Starts	1st	2nd	3rd	Win & Pl
Hurdles	1	0	0	0	
Career Total	**18**	**2**	**1**	**0**	**3544**

83	10/00	MRas	2m1f110y	G(0-95)HHdl	GD	£1456
93	4/00	MRas	2m1f110y	G Hdl	SFT	£1519

Total win prize-money £2975

Going: Sf: 0-1 GS: 0-0 Gd: 0-0 GF: - Fm: 0-0
Distance: 2m/2m3: 0-1 2m4-2m7: 0-0 3m+: 0-0
Track: LH: 0-1 RH: 0-0 Tight: 0-0 Gall: 0-0
Aids: Bl: 0-0 Vi: 0-0 Tstrap: 0-0
Best Rating: 93 4/00 MRas 2m1f110y soft Hdl

Cromwell (IRE)

102(71h) **123**
7-y-o b g Last Tycoon-Catherine Parr (USA) (Riverman (USA))
M C Chapman Gb Racing

Placings:06054/34411145364064455l/323612441P61410-0236P (1236)
2001/02: 25^{0}GF, 25^{2}F, 20^{3}GF, 22^{6}G, 26^{P}GS

	Starts	1st	2nd	3rd	Win & Pl
Chases	5	0	1	1	2517
Career Total	**43**	**8**	**3**	**5**	**38931**

123	3/01	MRas	3m1f	D Ch	HVY	£5303
117	2/01	Catt	3m1f110y	E Ch	SFT	£3745
117	11/00	MRas	3m1f	E(0-115)HCh	G-S	£4329
112	10/00	MRas	3m1f	D Ch	GD	£5096
107	4/00	MRas	2m3f110y	D Hdl	SFT	£3000
103	8/99	MRas	3m	D Hdl	G-F	£3109
103	7/99	MRas	2m1f110y	D Hdl	G-F	£3070
106	7/99	MRas	2m5f110y	E Hdl	G-F	£2316

Total win prize-money £29970

Going: Sf: 0-0 GS: 0-1 Gd: 0-1 GF: - Fm: 0-3
Distance: 2m/2m3: 0-0 2m4-2m7: 0-2 3m+: 0-3
Track: LH: 0-2 RH: 0-3 Tight: 0-3 Gall: 0-0
Aids: Bl: 0-5 Vi: 0-0 Tstrap: 0-0
Best Rating: 123 5/01 Weth 3m1f firm Ch

A multiple course winner at Market Rasen, he seems to cope with most surfaces.

Crookedstone (IRE)

(86c) **93**
10-y-o br g Brush Aside (USA)-Pops Princess (IRE) (Le Moss)
K C Bailey Major-Gen R L T Burges

Placings:146/622/011222/FPP5U05-P (1952)
2001/02: 22^{P}GF

	Starts	1st	2nd	3rd	Win & Pl
Hurdles	1	0	0	0	
Career Total	**20**	**3**	**5**	**0**	**18357**

125	3/00	Extr	2m3f	D Ch	G-S	£4407
116	2/00	Leic	2m	E Ch	G-S	£3315
108	3/98	Newb	2m110y	H NHF	HVY	£1424

Total win prize-money £9146

Going: Sf: 0-0 GS: 0-0 Gd: 0-0 GF: - Fm: 0-1
Distance: 2m/2m3: 0-0 2m4-2m7: 0-1 3m+: 0-0
Track: LH: 0-0 RH: 0-0 Tight: 0-0 Gall: 0-0
Aids: Bl: 0-0 Vi: 0-0 Tstrap: 0-0
Best Rating: 140 4/00 Sand 2m4f110y soft Ch

Crosaree (IRE)

17
9-y-o b g Celio Rufo-Windmill Road (IRE) (King's Ride)
D J Wintle M Harper

Placings:0-0 (0054)
2001/02: 24^{0}G

	Starts	1st	2nd	3rd	Win & Pl
Hurdles	1	0	0	0	
Career Total	**2**	**0**	**0**	**0**	

Going: Sf: 0-0 GS: 0-0 Gd: 0-1 GF: - Fm: 0-0
Distance: 2m/2m3: 0-0 2m4-2m7: 0-0 3m+: 0-1
Track: LH: 0-1 RH: 0-0 Tight: 0-1 Gall: 0-0
Aids: Bl: 0-0 Vi: 0-0 Tstrap: 0-0
Best Rating: 17 4/01 NAbb 3m3f soft Hdl

Cross River

7-y-o b g Reprimand-River Maiden (USA) (Riverman (USA))
Mrs S J Smith Mrs S Smith

Placings:000/00-0P (3557)
2001/02: 16^{0}G, 19^{P}S

	Starts	1st	2nd	3rd	Win & Pl
Hurdles	2	0	0	0	
Career Total	**7**	**0**	**0**	**0**	

Going: Sf: 0-1 GS: 0-0 Gd: 0-1 GF: - Fm: 0-0
Distance: 2m/2m3: 0-2 2m4-2m7: 0-0 3m+: 0-0
Track: LH: 0-2 RH: 0-0 Tight: 0-1 Gall: 0-1
Aids: Bl: 0-0 Vi: 0-0 Tstrap: 0-0
Best Rating: 63 10/99 Chel 2m110y good NHF

110	3/00	Strf	3m	D(0-120)HCh	GD	£7319
87	4/98	Fknm	2m4f	F(0-100)HHdl	G-S	£3670
89	12/97	Sthl	2m4f110y	F(0-100)HHdl	GD	£2197
89	11/96	Hrfd	2m1f	E Hdl	G-S	£2486

Total win prize-money £15674

Going: Sf: 0-4 GS: 0-0 Gd: 0-1 GF: - Fm: 0-0
Distance: 2m/2m3: 0-0 2m4-2m7: 0-3 3m+: 0-2
Track: LH: 0-1 RH: 0-3 Tight: 0-1 Gall: 0-2
Aids: Bl: 0-0 Vi: 0-0 Tstrap: 0-0
Best Rating: 110 3/00 Strf 3m good Ch

Cross The Rubicon (IRE)

100 85

11-y-o ch g Over The River (FR)-One Way Only (Le Bavard (FR))
G A Harker P I Harker

Placings:0/P334P/P32P/5P3/P-U03P35 **(4856)**
2001/02: 25^{U}GS, 32^{0}HY, 25^{3}HY, 24^{P}G, 25^{3}GF, 25^{5}G

	Starts	1st	2nd	3rd	Win & Pl
Chases	6	0	0	2	1128
Career Total	**20**	**0**	**1**	**6**	**4410**

Going: Sf: 0-2 GS: 0-1 Gd: 0-2 GF: - Fm: 0-1
Distance: 2m/2m3: 0-0 2m4-2m7: 0-0 3m+: 0-6
Track: LH: 0-6 RH: 0-0 Tight: 0-2 Gall: 0-0
Aids: Bl: 0-6 Vi: 0-0 Tstrap: 0-0
Best Rating: 99 3/99 Ayr 3m1f soft Ch

Cross The Suir (IRE)

99(103c) (102c)109

8-y-o b g Decent Fellow-Prime Preacher (Wind Drift)
J J O'Neill Sir Peter O'Sullevan

Placings:4/0133354-3334 **(1762)**
2001/02: 21^{3}G, 24^{3}GF, 22^{3}GF, 25^{4}S

	Starts	1st	2nd	3rd	Win & Pl
Hurdles	3	0	0	2	846
Chases	1	0	0	1	570
Career Total	**12**	**1**	**0**	**6**	**6860**

93	8/00	Cork	3m	Hdl	GD	£3864

Total win prize-money £3864

Going: Sf: 0-1 GS: 0-0 Gd: 0-1 GF: - Fm: 0-2
Distance: 2m/2m3: 0-0 2m4-2m7: 0-2 3m+: 0-2
Track: LH: 0-3 RH: 0-0 Tight: 0-3 Gall: 0-0
Aids: Bl: 0-0 Vi: 0-0 Tstrap: 0-0
Best Rating: 113 3/01 Hntg 3m soft Ch

Crossapol Bay

6-y-o b/br g Skyliner-Vidette (Billion (USA))
Mrs L Wadham Mrs J K Buckle

Placings:0 **(3375)**
2001/02: 16^{0}S

	Starts	1st	2nd	3rd	Win & Pl
NH Flat	1	0	0	0	
Career Total	**1**	**0**	**0**	**0**	

Going: Sf: 0-1 GS: 0-0 Gd: 0-0 GF: - Fm: 0-0
Distance: 2m/2m3: 0-1 2m4-2m7: 0-0 3m+: 0-0
Track: LH: 0-1 RH: 0-0 Tight: 0-0 Gall: 0-0
Aids: Bl: 0-0 Vi: 0-0 Tstrap: 0-0
Best Rating:

Crown And Cushion

100 94

9-y-o b g High Adventure-Soulieana (Manado)
T R Greathead Mrs S Greathead

Placings:10PP/345131/52F1U/P-PU456 **(4568)**
2001/02: 24^{P}S, 21^{U}HY, 20^{4}S, 20^{5}S, 24^{6}G

	Starts	1st	2nd	3rd	Win & Pl
Hurdles	4	0	0	0	0
Chases	1	0	0	0	0
Career Total	**21**	**4**	**1**	**2**	**17450**

Crown Rule (IRE)

7-y-o ch g Be My Native (USA)-Super Deal (IRE) (Yashgan)
H D Daly The Earl Cadogan

Placings:6/2-0 **(0421)**
2001/02: 24^{0}G

	Starts	1st	2nd	3rd	Win & Pl
Hurdles	1	0	0	0	
Career Total	**3**	**0**	**1**	**0**	**710**

Going: Sf: 0-0 GS: 0-0 Gd: 0-1 GF: - Fm: 0-0
Distance: 2m/2m3: 0-0 2m4-2m7: 0-0 3m+: 0-1
Track: LH: 0-1 RH: 0-0 Tight: 0-1 Gall: 0-0
Aids: Bl: 0-0 Vi: 0-0 Tstrap: 0-0
Best Rating: 82 11/00 Uttx 2m6f110y heavy Hdl

Crowning Glory

84 30

8-y-o b m Rakaposhi King-Miss Lizzie (Push On)
Mrs D A Hamer The Tally Ho Partnership

Placings:50/P0 **(3986)**
2001/02: 16^{P}S, 19^{0}S

	Starts	1st	2nd	3rd	Win & Pl
Hurdles	2	0	0	0	
Career Total	**4**	**0**	**0**	**0**	**0**

Going: Sf: 0-2 GS: 0-0 Gd: 0-0 GF: - Fm: 0-0
Distance: 2m/2m3: 0-1 2m4-2m7: 0-1 3m+: 0-0
Track: LH: 0-0 RH: 0-2 Tight: 0-1 Gall: 0-0
Aids: Bl: 0-0 Vi: 0-0 Tstrap: 0-0
Best Rating: 78 12/99 Hrfd 2m1f good NHF

Crozanni

7-y-o gr g Arzanni-Saucy Laura (Crozier)
Mrs P Ford Ray Cawthorn

Placings:P/6 **(1039)**
2001/02: 20^{6}GF

	Starts	1st	2nd	3rd	Win & Pl
Hurdles	1	0	0	0	0
Career Total	**2**	**0**	**0**	**0**	**0**

Going: Sf: 0-0 GS: 0-0 Gd: 0-0 GF: - Fm: 0-1
Distance: 2m/2m3: 0-0 2m4-2m7: 0-1 3m+: 0-0
Track: LH: 0-1 RH: 0-0 Tight: 0-0 Gall: 0-0
Aids: Bl: 0-0 Vi: 0-0 Tstrap: 0-0
Best Rating:

Cruagh Express (IRE)

101 88

6-y-o b g Unblest-Cry In The Dark (Godswalk (USA))
G L Moore E Farncombe

Placings:13P **(2709)**
2001/02: 16^{1}GS, 16^{3}G, 16^{P}G

	Starts	1st	2nd	3rd	Win & Pl
Hurdles	3	1	0	1	2785
Career Total	**3**	**1**	**0**	**1**	**2785**

88	11/01	Plum	2m	F Hdl	G-S	£2331

Total win prize-money £2331

Going: Sf: 0-0 GS: 1-1 Gd: 0-2 GF: - Fm: 0-0
Distance: **2m/2m3: 1-3** 2m4-2m7: 0-0 3m+: 0-0
Track: **LH: 1-3** RH: 0-0 **Tight: 1-3** Gall: 0-0
Aids: Bl: 0-0 Vi: 0-0 **Tstrap: 1-3**
Best Rating: 88 11/01 Plum 2m good Hdl

A fair handicapper at around a mile on the Flat. Had no problem with stamina when he won on his hurdles debut at Plumpton over two miles. Reported to have made a noise though.

Crucara

(81h) 75

9-y-o b m Cruise Missile-Mascara Vii (Damsire Unregistered)
J S Smith R P Taylor

Placings:0/0PP/6005-P **(0501)**
2001/02: 24^{P}GF

	Starts	1st	2nd	3rd	Win & Pl
Chases	1	0	0	0	
Career Total	**9**	**0**	**0**	**0**	**0**

Going: Sf: 0-0 GS: 0-0 Gd: 0-0 GF: - Fm: 0-1
Distance: 2m/2m3: 0-0 2m4-2m7: 0-0 3m+: 0-1
Track: LH: 0-0 RH: 0-1 Tight: 0-0 Gall: 0-1
Aids: Bl: 0-0 Vi: 0-0 Tstrap: 0-0
Best Rating: 75 4/01 Tntn 2m3f gd-fm Ch

Cruise The Fairway (IRE)

107(110h) (112h)140

6-y-o b g Insan (USA)-Tickhill (General Assembly (USA))
B G Powell R J T 290 Limited

Placings:10/1413346-3412 **(3211)**
2001/02: 21^{3}GS, 20^{4}S, 24^{1}G, 22^{2}G

	Starts	1st	2nd	3rd	Win & Pl
Hurdles	1	0	0	1	781
Chases	3	1	1	0	10797
Career Total	**13**	**4**	**1**	**3**	**24384**

135	12/01	Newb	3m	C Ch	GD	£8287
111	1/01	Extr	2m1f	E Hdl	HVY	£2119
113	11/00	Aint	2m110y	D Hdl	G-S	£4309
103	3/00	Newb	2m110y	H NHF	SFT	£2478

Total win prize-money £17196

Going: Sf: 0-1 GS: 0-1 Gd: 1-2 GF: - Fm: 0-0
Distance: 2m/2m3: 0-0 2m4-2m7: 0-3 **3m+: 1-1**
Track: **LH: 1-3** RH: 0-1 Tight: 0-0 **Gall: 1-3**
Aids: Bl: 0-0 Vi: 0-0 Tstrap: 0-0
Best Rating: 140 1/02 Newb 2m6f110y good Ch

A winner of a bumper, over hurdles and over fences, he acts on ground varying from good to heavy. Stays three miles.

Crusoe (IRE)

78 **45**

5-y-o b g Turtle Island (IRE)-Self Reliance (Never So Bold)

A Sadik A Sadik

Placings:P0004P (2952)

2001/02: 16^{P}GS, 16^{0}G, 17^{0}S, 17^{0}G, 17^{4}S, 16^{P}S

	Starts	1st	2nd	3rd	Win & Pl
Hurdles	6	0	0	0	0
Career Total	**6**	**0**	**0**	**0**	**0**

Going: Sf: 0-3 GS: 0-1 Gd: 0-2 GF: - Fm: 0-0
Distance: 2m/2m3: 0-6 2m4-2m7: 0-0 3m+: 0-0
Track: LH: 0-4 RH: 0-2 Tight: 0-3 Gall: 0-0
Aids: Bl: 0-1 Vi: 0-0 Tstrap: 0-2
Best Rating: **45** 12/01 Hrfd 2m1f soft Hdl

Cruz Santa

108 **105+**

9-y-o b m Lord Bud-Linpac Mapleleaf (Dominion)

Mrs M Reveley The Mary Reveley Racing Club

Placings:R/230233453500/23U/10222332-121434 (3775)

2001/02: 17^{1}S, 20^{2}G, 23^{1}G, 20^{4}GS, 20^{3}HY, 20^{4}S

	Starts	1st	2nd	3rd	Win & Pl
Hurdles	6	2	1	1	9018
Career Total	**30**	**3**	**8**	**8**	**19069**

103	11/01	Weth	2m7f	G Hdl	GD	£2338
102	10/01	Carl	2m1f	E(0-115)HHdl	SFT	£2968
85	5/00	Ctml	2m1f110y	G Hdl	G-F	£2436

Total win prize-money £7742

Going: Sf: 1-3 GS: 0-1 Gd: 1-2 GF: - Fm: 0-0
Distance: 2m/2m3: 1-1 2m4-2m7: 1-5 3m+: 0-0
Track: LH: 1-4 RH: 1-2 Tight: 0-0 Gall: 0-1
Aids: Bl: 0-0 Vi: 0-0 Tstrap: 0-0
Best Rating: **105** 12/01 Hayd 2m4f heavy Hdl

She has had such a frustrating career with a plethora of major placings, but very few actual wins. Best held up, she is suited by a good pace and her easy wins in sellers indicate she is slightly better than that grade. Stays two miles seven and acts on any ground.

Crystal Eclipse

64f **5f**

6-y-o gr m Miners Lamp-Crystal Comet (Cosmo)

C Tizzard M W Hoskins

Placings:0 (3811)

2001/02: 18^{0}S

	Starts	1st	2nd	3rd	Win & Pl
NH Flat	1	0	0	0	
Career Total	**1**	**0**	**0**	**0**	

Going: Sf: 0-1 GS: 0-0 Gd: 0-0 GF: - Fm: 0-0
Distance: 2m/2m3: 0-1 2m4-2m7: 0-0 3m+: 0-0
Track: LH: 0-1 RH: 0-0 Tight: 0-1 Gall: 0-0
Aids: Bl: 0-0 Vi: 0-0 Tstrap: 0-0
Best Rating: **5** 2/02 Font 2m2f110y soft NHF

Crystal Gift

104 **121**

10-y-o b g Dominion-Grain Lady (USA) (Greinton)

A C Whillans Mrs L M Whillans

Placings:43221/226/12441/26052F11/004066014-330214 (4496)

2001/02: 16^{3}G, 24^{3}G, 23^{0}HY, 24^{2}GS, 20^{1}S, 22^{4}G

	Starts	1st	2nd	3rd	Win & Pl
Hurdles	6	1	1	2	13656
Career Total	**36**	**7**	**8**	**3**	**57653**

121	3/02	Ayr	2m4f	C(0-135)HHdl	SFT	£6831
121	4/01	Hayd	2m	B(0-140)HHdl	SFT	£10046
125	3/00	Kels	2m2f	C(0-135)HHdl	G-S	£8658
118	3/00	Ayr	2m4f	D(0-125)HHdl	HVY	£3016
111	3/99	Hexm	2m4f110y	D(0-125)HHdl	G-S	£2768
103	1/99	Ayr	2m	C(0-135)HHdl	HVY	£4445
101	5/96	Kels	2m110y	D Hdl	SFT	£3053

Total win prize-money £38818

Going: Sf: 1-2 GS: 0-1 Gd: 0-3 GF: - Fm: 0-0
Distance: 2m/2m3: 0-1 **2m4-2m7: 1-2** 3m+: 0-3
Track: **LH: 1-6** RH: 0-0 Tight: 0-2 Gall: 0-1
Aids: Bl: 0-0 Vi: 0-0 Tstrap: 0-0
Best Rating: **125** 3/00 Kels 2m2f gd-sft Hdl

Useful handicap hurdler. He tends to show his best form in the spring. Effective from two to three miles, but must have soft ground.

Crystal Vein

78f **60f**

4-y-o gr g Miners Lamp-Crystal Comet (Cosmo)

B R Millman Victor G Palmer

Placings:*0U0* (4180)

2001/02: 16^{0}S, 16^{U}GS, 16^{0}GS

	Starts	1st	2nd	3rd	Win & Pl
NH Flat	3	0	0	0	
Career Total	**3**	**0**	**0**	**0**	

Going: Sf: 0-1 GS: 0-2 Gd: 0-0 GF: - Fm: 0-0
Distance: 2m/2m3: 0-3 2m4-2m7: 0-0 3m+: 0-0
Track: LH: 0-1 RH: 0-1 Tight: 0-0 Gall: 0-1
Aids: Bl: 0-0 Vi: 0-0 Tstrap: 0-0
Best Rating: **60** 3/02 Strf 2m110y gd-sft NHF

Cuddle Up

82 **70**

7-y-o b g Nomadic Way (USA)-Grand Queen (Grand Conde (FR))

T D Walford A G Knowles

Placings:*0-6*006P (4871)

2001/02: 17^{6}G, 17^{0}G, 20^{0}S, 17^{6}GS, 25^{P}GF

	Starts	1st	2nd	3rd	Win & Pl
NH Flat	1	0	0	0	0
Hurdles	4	0	0	0	0
Career Total	**6**	**0**	**0**	**0**	**0**

Going: Sf: 0-1 GS: 0-1 Gd: 0-2 GF: - Fm: 0-1
Distance: 2m/2m3: 0-3 2m4-2m7: 0-1 3m+: 0-1
Track: LH: 0-4 RH: 0-1 Tight: 0-2 Gall: 0-1
Aids: Bl: 0-1 Vi: 0-0 Tstrap: 0-0
Best Rating: **70** 3/02 Carl 2m1f gd-sft Hdl

Cudlic Candyfloss

94(100h) (68h)**85**

9-y-o b m Abutammam-Cudlic Cream (No Evil)

P Bowen Mrs L J Williams

Placings:*066*P60P/P3-60504P0 (3763)

2001/02: 20^{6}GF, 22^{0}F, 24^{5}G, 19^{0}G, 20^{4}G, 20^{P}G, 24^{0}S

	Starts	1st	2nd	3rd	Win & Pl
Hurdles	5	0	0	0	0
Chases	2	0	0	0	235
Career Total	**16**	**0**	**0**	**1**	**235**

Going: Sf: 0-1 GS: 0-0 Gd: 0-4 GF: - Fm: 0-2
Distance: 2m/2m3: 0-1 2m4-2m7: 0-4 3m+: 0-2
Track: LH: 0-3 RH: 0-2 Tight: 0-5 Gall: 0-0
Aids: Bl: 0-0 Vi: 0-0 Tstrap: 0-0
Best Rating: **85** 12/01 Font 2m4f good Ch

Cuigiu (IRE)

100 **81**

5-y-o b g Persian Bold-Homosassa (Burslem)

A B Mulholland Toon Partners

Placings:056-44P (1588)

2001/02: 16^{4}GF, 17^{4}GF, 17^{P}GS

	Starts	1st	2nd	3rd	Win & Pl
Hurdles	3	0	0	0	0
Career Total	**6**	**0**	**0**	**0**	**0**

Going: Sf: 0-0 GS: 0-1 Gd: 0-0 GF: - Fm: 0-2
Distance: 2m/2m3: 0-3 2m4-2m7: 0-0 3m+: 0-0
Track: LH: 0-2 RH: 0-1 Tight: 0-2 Gall: 0-0
Aids: Bl: 0-0 Vi: 0-0 Tstrap: 0-3
Best Rating: **81** 9/01 MRas 2m1f110y gd-fm Hdl

Cullen Bay (IRE)

103 **106**

7-y-o b m Supreme Leader-Pollyville (Pollerton)

N J Henderson R R Hetherington

Placings:*1-31* (3397)

2001/02: 17^{3}GS, 20^{1}S

	Starts	1st	2nd	3rd	Win & Pl
NH Flat	1	0	0	1	250
Hurdles	1	1	0	0	3262
Career Total	**3**	**2**	**0**	**1**	**5185**

106	1/02	Font	2m4f	E Hdl	SFT	£3262
117	5/00	Bang	2m1f	H NHF	GD	£1673

Total win prize-money £4935

Going: Sf: 1-1 GS: 0-1 Gd: 0-0 GF: - Fm: 0-0
Distance: 2m/2m3: 0-1 **2m4-2m7: 1-1** 3m+: 0-0
Track: LH: 0-1 RH: 0-0 **Tight: 1-2** Gall: 0-0
Aids: Bl: 0-0 Vi: 0-0 Tstrap: 0-0
Best Rating: **117** 5/00 Bang 2m1f good NHF

Useful bumper form. Won on heavy ground on his hurdles bow at Fontwell. Stays two and a half miles.

Cullian

97f **86f**

5-y-o b m Missed Flight-Diamond Gig (Pitskelly)

Mrs N Smith The Cullian Partnership

Placings:*0504* (3606)

2001/02: 16^{0}G, 18^{5}S, 18^{0}G, 18^{4}HY

	Starts	1st	2nd	3rd	Win & Pl
NH Flat	4	0	0	0	0
Career Total	**4**	**0**	**0**	**0**	**0**

Going: Sf: 0-2 GS: 0-0 Gd: 0-2 GF: - Fm: 0-0
Distance: 2m/2m3: 0-4 2m4-2m7: 0-0 3m+: 0-0
Track: LH: 0-2 RH: 0-1 Tight: 0-2 Gall: 0-0
Aids: Bl: 0-0 Vi: 0-0 Tstrap: 0-0
Best Rating: **86** 2/02 Font 2m2f110y heavy NHF

Culzean (IRE)

75 **71**

6-y-o b g Machiavellian (USA)-Eileen Jenny (IRE) (Kris)

R Hannon Stonethorn Stud Farms Limited

Placings:0 **(2446)**

2001/02: 16^{0}S

Starts		1st	2nd	3rd	Win & Pl
Hurdles	1	0	0	0	
Career Total	**1**	**0**	**0**	**0**	

Going: Sf: 0-1 GS: 0-0 Gd: 0-0 GF: - Fm: 0-0
Distance: 2m/2m3: 0-1 2m4-2m7: 0-0 3m+: 0-0
Track: LH: 0-1 RH: 0-0 Tight: 0-0 Gall: 0-1
Aids: Bl: 0-0 Vi: 0-0 Tstrap: 0-0
Best Rating: 71 12/01 Newb 2m110y soft Hdl

Cumberland Youth

11-y-o b g Town And Country-Key Biscayne (Deep Run)

Mrs E Garley T & Mrs P M George

Placings:00P/PP/**P4PPP5UP3000/PPP/4R-P** **(0227)**

2001/02: 24^{P}GF

Starts		1st	2nd	3rd	Win & Pl
Chases	1	0	0	0	
Career Total	**23**	**0**	**0**	**1**	**626**

Going: Sf: 0-0 GS: 0-0 Gd: 0-0 GF: - Fm: 0-1
Distance: 2m/2m3: 0-0 2m4-2m7: 0-0 3m+: 0-1
Track: LH: 0-0 RH: 0-1 Tight: 0-0 Gall: 0-1
Aids: Bl: 0-0 Vi: 0-0 Tstrap: 0-0
Best Rating: 72 5/00 Towc 2m6f gd-fm Ch

Cumbrian Challenge (IRE)

87 **100**

13-y-o ch g Be My Native (USA)-Sixpenny (English Prince)

T D Easterby Cumbrian Industrials Ltd

Placings:20311645/63103260/**131132341FP/5502125 1/46111101P363/42403410265/02126614062/5PP015 3-0** **(0202)**

2001/02: 16^{0}G

Starts		1st	2nd	3rd	Win & Pl
Chases	1	0	0	0	
Career Total	**77**	**18**	**10**	**10**	**165297**

125	2/01	Sedg	2m110y	F(0-110)HCh	SFT	£3395
154	1/00	Donc	2m110y	B HCh	GD	£10023
154	11/99	Weth	2m	B(0-150)HCh	GD	£8314
154	12/98	Weth	2m	A HCh	SFT	£18424
147	1/98	Donc	2m110y	B HCh	GD	£7053
140	12/97	Weth	2m4f110y	B HCh	SFT	£7022
149	12/97	Weth	2m4f110y	B(0-145)HCh	GD	£6651
138	11/97	Weth	2m	B(0-150)HCh	G-S	£6697
136	10/97	Weth	2m	C(0-135)HCh	G-F	£4419
134	4/97	Asct	2m	B HCh	G-F	£10230
136	12/96	Donc	2m3f110y	B(0-145)HCh	G-F	£4526
126	2/96	Weth	2m	C HCh	G-S	£4500
126	12/95	Weth	2m4f110y	D Ch	GD	£4094
125	11/95	Asct	2m	C Ch	GD	£6760
124	10/95	Weth	2m	D Ch	G-F	£3473
129	11/94	Newc	2m110y	(0-135)HHdl	GD	£6970
127	1/94	Donc	2m110y	Hdl	G-S	£6735
104	12/93	Weth	2m	Hdl	SFT	£2250

Total win prize-money £121541

Going: Sf: 0-0 GS: 0-0 Gd: 0-1 GF: - Fm: 0-0
Distance: 2m/2m3: 0-1 2m4-2m7: 0-0 3m+: 0-0
Track: LH: 0-1 RH: 0-0 Tight: 0-0 Gall: 0-0
Aids: Bl: 0-0 Vi: 0-0 Tstrap: 0-0
Best Rating: 154 1/00 Donc 2m110y good Ch

A real Wetherby specialist, his best days are behind him.

Cupboard Lover

111 **126**

6-y-o ch g Risk Me (FR)-Galejade (Sharrood (USA))

N J Henderson Mrs Lesley Lockwood And Mrs Judy Mihalop

Placings:2150-042201004 **(4818)**

2001/02: 16^{0}GF, 17^{4}G, 16^{2}G, 19^{2}G, 16^{0}S, 21^{1}G, 20^{0}S, 21^{0}GS, 21^{4}GF

Starts		1st	2nd	3rd	Win & Pl
Hurdles	9	1	2	0	11862
Career Total	**13**	**2**	**3**	**0**	**16146**

126	12/01	Kemp	2m5f	C(0-135)HHdl	GD	£7410
120	1/01	Tntn	2m1f	E Hdl	SFT	£2680

Total win prize-money £10090

Going: Sf: 0-2 GS: 0-1 Gd: 1-4 GF: - Fm: 0-2
Distance: 2m/2m3: 0-5 **2m4-2m7: 1-4** 3m+: 0-0
Track: LH: 0-6 **RH: 1-3** Tight: 0-2 Gall: 0-3
Aids: Bl: 0-0 Vi: 0-0 Tstrap: 0-0
Best Rating: 126 12/01 Kemp 2m5f good Hdl

A fair handicapper on the Flat, he got off the mark on his second start over hurdles at Taunton in January 2001. Some good efforts since, including when winning a competitive handicap hurdle at Kempton on Boxing Day 2001, but well held in the showcase handicap hurdle at the Festival. Acts on most types of ground and stays two miles five furlongs. Suited by a sharp, right-handed track. in good form on the Flat in the summer of 2002.

Curiositski

76 **65**

6-y-o b m Petoski-Nosey's Daughter (Song)

M C Pipe D Rees

Placings:0-40405 **(1222)**

2001/02: 17^{4}G, 17^{0}G, 16^{4}S, 16^{0}GF, 18^{5}GF

Starts		1st	2nd	3rd	Win & Pl
NH Flat	2	0	0	0	0
Hurdles	3	0	0	0	0
Career Total	**6**	**0**	**0**	**0**	**0**

Going: Sf: 0-1 GS: 0-0 Gd: 0-2 GF: - Fm: 0-2
Distance: 2m/2m3: 0-5 2m4-2m7: 0-0 3m+: 0-0
Track: LH: 0-5 RH: 0-0 Tight: 0-3 Gall: 0-0
Aids: Bl: 0-0 Vi: 0-0 Tstrap: 0-0
Best Rating: 70 5/01 Bang 2m1f good NHF

Curly Spencer (IRE)

99 **121**

8-y-o br g Yashgan-Tim's Brief (Avocat)

A Parker Mr & Mrs Raymond Anderson Green

Placings:00/543051100/**1U-PF2422** **(4490)**

2001/02: 26^{P}S, 20^{F}GS, 20^{2}S, 20^{4}GS, 20^{2}HY, 20^{2}GS

Starts		1st	2nd	3rd	Win & Pl
Chases	6	0	3	0	4144
Career Total	**19**	**3**	**3**	**1**	**14939**

126	2/01	Carl	2m4f110y	F(0-100)HCh	HVY	£3721
119	3/00	Hexm	2m4f110y	F(0-100)HCh	SFT	£3107
113	3/00	Carl	2m	E(0-115)HCh	HVY	£3380

Total win prize-money £10208

Going: Sf: 0-3 GS: 0-3 Gd: 0-0 GF: - Fm: 0-0
Distance: 2m/2m3: 0-0 2m4-2m7: 0-5 3m+: 0-1
Track: LH: 0-2 RH: 0-4 Tight: 0-1 Gall: 0-1
Aids: Bl: 0-0 Vi: 0-0 Tstrap: 0-0
Best Rating: 126 2/01 Carl 2m4f110y heavy Ch

Inconsistent handicapper over fences, goes well over two and a half miles in bottomless ground.

Curtainsatchopwell (IRE)

(93h) (70h)

8-y-o b g Soviet Lad (USA)-Missquickdecision (IRE) (Master Willie)

T D Walford Mrs J M Newitt

Placings:000456265/000-F **(0066)**

2001/02: 21^{F}G

Starts		1st	2nd	3rd	Win & Pl
Chases	1	0	0	0	
Career Total	**13**	**0**	**1**	**0**	**784**

Going: Sf: 0-0 GS: 0-0 Gd: 0-1 GF: - Fm: 0-0
Distance: 2m/2m3: 0-0 2m4-2m7: 0-1 3m+: 0-0
Track: LH: 0-1 RH: 0-0 Tight: 0-1 Gall: 0-0
Aids: Bl: 0-0 Vi: 0-0 Tstrap: 0-0
Best Rating: 98 3/99 Muss 2m4f good Hdl

Cusin

92 **89**

6-y-o ch g Arazi (USA)-Fairy Tern (Mill Reef (USA))

M E Sowersby M E Sowersby

Placings:355 **(1421)**

2001/02: 17^{3}GF, 17^{5}GF, 17^{5}G

Starts		1st	2nd	3rd	Win & Pl
Hurdles	3	0	0	1	467
Career Total	**3**	**0**	**0**	**1**	**467**

Going: Sf: 0-0 GS: 0-0 Gd: 0-1 GF: - Fm: 0-2
Distance: 2m/2m3: 0-3 2m4-2m7: 0-0 3m+: 0-0
Track: LH: 0-3 RH: 0-0 Tight: 0-3 Gall: 0-0
Aids: Bl: 0-0 Vi: 0-0 Tstrap: 0-3
Best Rating: 89 8/01 Sedg 2m1f gd-fm Hdl

Cut Down The Sound (IRE)

7-y-o ch g Shiel Hill-Carolin Lass (IRE) (Carlingford Castle)

E Haddock E Haddock

Placings:P **(0192)**

2001/02: 24^{P}GF

Starts		1st	2nd	3rd	Win & Pl
Chases	1	0	0	0	
Career Total	**1**	**0**	**0**	**0**	

Going: Sf: 0-0 GS: 0-0 Gd: 0-0 GF: - Fm: 0-1
Distance: 2m/2m3: 0-0 2m4-2m7: 0-0 3m+: 0-1
Track: LH: 0-1 RH: 0-0 Tight: 0-1 Gall: 0-0
Aids: Bl: 0-1 Vi: 0-0 Tstrap: 0-0
Best Rating:

Cut The Deck

80 **50**

6-y-o b g First Trump-Kantikoy (Alzao (USA))
M W Easterby M W Easterby

Placings:*0-000* **(1815)**
2001/02: 17^{0}GS, 17^{0}G, 24^{0}S

	Starts	1st	2nd	3rd	Win & Pl
NH Flat	1	0	0	0	0
Hurdles	2	0	0	0	0
Career Total	**4**	**0**	**0**	**0**	

Going: Sf: 0-1 GS: 0-1 Gd: 0-1 GF: - Fm: 0-0
Distance: 2m/2m3: 0-2 2m4-2m7: 0-0 3m+: 0-1
Track: LH: 0-2 RH: 0-1 Tight: 0-2 Gall: 0-0
Aids: Bl: 0-0 Vi: 0-0 Tstrap: 0-0
Best Rating: 88 12/00 Donc 2m110y heavy NHF

Cut Throat Jake

49

5-y-o ch g Karinga Bay-French Lip (Scorpio (FR))
S J Gilmore Pieces Of Eight

Placings:0 **(4025)**
2001/02: 16^{0}S

	Starts	1st	2nd	3rd	Win & Pl
Hurdles	1	0	0	0	
Career Total	**1**	**0**	**0**	**0**	

Going: Sf: 0-1 GS: 0-0 Gd: 0-0 GF: - Fm: 0-0
Distance: 2m/2m3: 0-1 2m4-2m7: 0-0 3m+: 0-0
Track: LH: 0-0 RH: 0-1 Tight: 0-0 Gall: 0-1
Aids: Bl: 0-0 Vi: 0-0 Tstrap: 0-0
Best Rating:

Cuthill Hope (IRE)

104 **113**

11-y-o gr g Peacock (FR)-Sicilian Princess (Sicilian Prince)
A C Whillans Stephen Gilchrist

Placings:441/**331F6F1/143O/12U-50P1P5** **(4897)**
2001/02: 22^{5}G, 16^{0}S, 25^{P}HY, 25^{1}S, 25^{P}G, 24^{5}G

	Starts	1st	2nd	3rd	Win & Pl
Chases	6	1	0	0	5954
Career Total	**23**	**6**	**1**	**3**	**28615**

129	3/02	Kels	3m1f	D(0-120)HCh	SFT	£5427
128	11/00	Ayr	2m4f	D(0-120)HCh	G-S	£3750
116	5/98	Aint	2m	D(0-125)HCh	G-F	£4622
128	4/98	Kels	2m1f	D Ch	SFT	£3403
128	1/98	Donc	2m3f110y	D Ch	GD	£4237
103	3/97	Plum	2m1f	E Hdl	G-S	£2553

Total win prize-money £23995

Going: Sf: 1-3 GS: 0-0 Gd: 0-3 GF: - Fm: 0-0
Distance: 2m/2m3: 0-1 2m4-2m7: 0-1 **3m+: 1-4**
Track: **LH: 1-5** RH: 0-1 **Tight: 1-3** Gall: 0-1
Aids: Bl: 0-0 **Vi: 1-3** Tstrap: 0-0
Best Rating: 129 3/02 Kels 3m1f soft Ch

Useful handicap chaser. Stays three miles plus. Acts on a sound surface and with cut. Missed all of 1999 and most of 2000 due to injury. Won at Kelso in March 2002. Likes to make the running.

Cutina

92(96h) **79**

8-y-o b m Tina's Pet-Cute Pam (Pamroy)
S A Brookshaw W R J Everall

Placings:*06630-***P44236PP** **(4541)**
2001/02: 22^{P}G, 24^{4}GF, 24^{4}S, 24^{2}S, 26^{3}S, 24^{6}S, 24^{P}S, 25^{P}G

	Starts	1st	2nd	3rd	Win & Pl
Hurdles	1	0	0	0	0
Chases	7	0	1	1	1742
Career Total	**13**	**0**	**1**	**2**	**2134**

Going: Sf: 0-5 GS: 0-0 Gd: 0-2 GF: - Fm: 0-1
Distance: 2m/2m3: 0-0 2m4-2m7: 0-1 3m+: 0-7
Track: LH: 0-4 RH: 0-3 Tight: 0-3 Gall: 0-1
Aids: Bl: 0-0 Vi: 0-0 Tstrap: 0-0
Best Rating: 81 2/01 Bang 2m1f heavy Hdl

Cutthroat Kid (IRE)

95 **80**

12-y-o b g Last Tycoon-Get Ahead (Silly Season)
T R Greathead Mrs S Greathead

Placings:12/12631415/3140/00042/1025/03003-045440 **(3654)**
2001/02: 24^{0}GF, 26^{4}G, 21^{5}HY, 24^{4}GS, 22^{4}S, 26^{0}S

	Starts	1st	2nd	3rd	Win & Pl
Hurdles	6	0	0	0	0
Career Total	**34**	**6**	**4**	**4**	**19089**

93	12/99	Hntg	2m5f110y	F(0-100)HHdl	G-S	£2108
99	3/97	MRas	2m3f110y	F Hdl	GD	£1994
111	1/96	Ayr	2m6f	E(0-115)HHdl	GD	£2631
111	1/96	Sedg	2m5f110y	D(0-120)HHdl	G-F	£2860
88	5/95	Sedg	2m5f110y	E Hdl	FRM	£2318
103	12/94	Donc	2m4f	Hdl	GD	£2485

Total win prize-money £14399

Going: Sf: 0-3 GS: 0-1 Gd: 0-1 GF: - Fm: 0-1
Distance: 2m/2m3: 0-0 2m4-2m7: 0-2 3m+: 0-4
Track: LH: 0-1 RH: 0-5 Tight: 0-2 Gall: 0-2
Aids: Bl: 0-2 Vi: 0-0 Tstrap: 0-0
Best Rating: 114 1/96 Newc 2m4f good Hdl

Veteran, plating-class staying hurdler, suited by a sharp track.

Cwm Aron

7-y-o b m Saxon Farm-Cwm Arctic (Cisto (FR))
Mrs A Price Mrs B Brown

Placings:*0* **(0359)**
2001/02: 17^{0}GS

	Starts	1st	2nd	3rd	Win & Pl
NH Flat	1	0	0	0	
Career Total	**1**	**0**	**0**	**0**	

Going: Sf: 0-0 GS: 0-1 Gd: 0-0 GF: - Fm: 0-0
Distance: 2m/2m3: 0-1 2m4-2m7: 0-0 3m+: 0-0
Track: LH: 0-1 RH: 0-0 Tight: 0-1 Gall: 0-0
Aids: Bl: 0-0 Vi: 0-0 Tstrap: 0-0
Best Rating:

Cyanara

103 **76**

6-y-o b m Jupiter Island-Shamana (Broadsword (USA))
Dr P Pritchard Mrs Grace Ann-Hanney

Placings:*0/*P-P061P00P0 **(4842)**
2001/02: 17^{P}G, 17^{0}S, 17^{6}G, 16^{1}S, 21^{P}G, 19^{0}S, 16^{0}S, 22^{P}G, 20^{0}G

	Starts	1st	2nd	3rd	Win & Pl
Hurdles	9	1	0	0	3234
Career Total	**11**	**1**	**0**	**0**	**3234**

76	11/01	Fknm	2m	E(0-105)HHdl	SFT	£3234

Total win prize-money £3234

Going: Sf: 1-4 GS: 0-0 Gd: 0-5 GF: - Fm: 0-0
Distance: **2m/2m3: 1-5** 2m4-2m7: 0-4 3m+: 0-0
Track: **LH: 1-7** RH: 0-2 **Tight: 1-6** Gall: 0-2
Aids: Bl: 0-0 Vi: 0-0 Tstrap: 0-0
Best Rating: 76 11/01 Fknm 2m soft Hdl

Goes well over two miles and acts on soft ground.

Cybele Eria (FR)

113 **117**

5-y-o b m Johann Quatz (FR)-Money Can't Buy (Thatching)
N J Henderson The Studwell Partnership

Placings:23-2241 **(4326)**
2001/02: 16^{2}S, 16^{2}GS, 16^{4}GS, 17^{1}S

	Starts	1st	2nd	3rd	Win & Pl
Hurdles	4	1	2	0	5036
Career Total	**6**	**1**	**3**	**1**	**6570**

117	3/02	Hrfd	2m1f	E Hdl	SFT	£2849

Total win prize-money £2849

Going: Sf: 1-2 GS: 0-2 Gd: 0-0 GF: - Fm: 0-0
Distance: **2m/2m3: 1-4** 2m4-2m7: 0-0 3m+: 0-0
Track: LH: 0-2 **RH: 1-2** Tight: 0-0 Gall: 0-1
Aids: Bl: 0-0 Vi: 0-0 Tstrap: 0-0
Best Rating: 117 3/02 Hrfd 2m1f soft Hdl

Cyfor Malta (FR)

115 **172**

9-y-o b g Cyborg (FR)-Force Nine (FR) (Luthier)
M C Pipe D A Johnson

Placings:3**2111211/11/3-1402P** **(4839)**
2001/02: 20^{1}S, 25^{4}HY, 26^{0}G, 25^{2}G, 33^{P}G

	Starts	1st	2nd	3rd	Win & Pl
Chases	5	1	1	0	50825
Career Total	**16**	**8**	**3**	**2**	**242361**

172	12/01	Newb	2m4f	B(0-145)HCh	SFT	£20300
175	1/99	Chel	3m1f110y	A Ch	SFT	£18390
169	11/98	Chel	2m4f110y	A HCh	GD	£47260
160	4/98	Aint	2m6f	B(0-145)HCh	SFT	£25072
149	3/98	Chel	2m5f	B Ch	GD	£33500
148	1/98	Sand	2m4f110y	D Ch	G-S	£4485
	11/97	Autl	2m4f110y	Ch	HLD	£22447
	10/97	Autl	2m1f110y	Ch	VS	£13468

Total win prize-money £184923

Going: Sf: 1-2 GS: 0-0 Gd: 0-3 GF: - Fm: 0-0
Distance: 2m/2m3: 0-0 **2m4-2m7: 1-1** 3m+: 0-4
Track: **LH: 1-5** RH: 0-0 Tight: 0-1 **Gall: 1-3**
Aids: Bl: 0-0 Vi: 0-2 Tstrap: 0-0
Best Rating: 175 1/99 Chel 3m1f110y soft Ch

Looked an outstanding prospect when landing the Murphy's Gold Cup and the Pillar Chase in 1998/1999, but a leg injury then kept him off the track for two years. In need of the run when well beaten in the Pillar Chase on his sole run in 2000/2001, but he was fit enough to land a Newbury handicap on his return in 2001/2002. Possibly unsuited by the ground in the Pillar Chase, but was disappointing in the Gold Cup. Wore a visor when chasing home Florida Pearl at Aintree, before pulling up in the Scottish National. Acts on an easy surface and stays three miles.

Cyindien (FR)

103f **104f**

5-y-o b/br g Cyborg (FR)-Indiana Rose (FR) (Cadoudal (FR))
Miss Venetia Williams Sir Robert Ogden

Placings:5 **(3154)**
2001/02: 18^{5}G

	Starts	1st	2nd	3rd	Win & Pl
NH Flat	1	0	0	0	0
Career Total	**1**	**0**	**0**	**0**	**0**

Going: Sf: 0-0 GS: 0-0 Gd: 0-1 GF: - Fm: 0-0
Distance: 2m/2m3: 0-1 2m4-2m7: 0-0 3m+: 0-0
Track: LH: 0-1 RH: 0-0 Tight: 0-1 Gall: 0-0
Aids: Bl: 0-0 Vi: 0-0 Tstrap: 0-0
Best Rating: 104 1/02 Font 2m2f110y good NHF

Cynara

102 **90**

4-y-o b f Imp Society (USA)-Reina (Homeboy)
G M Moore A J Racehorses

Placings:01003 **(4198)**
2001/02: 16^{0}G, 17^{1}S, 16^{0}S, 17^{0}GS, 21^{3}S

	Starts	1st	2nd	3rd	Win & Pl
Hurdles	5	1	0	1	3027
Career Total	**5**	**1**	**0**	**1**	**3027**

90 12/01 MRas 2m1f110y E Hdl SFT £2653
Total win prize-money £2653

Going: Sf: 1-3 GS: 0-1 Gd: 0-1 GF: - Fm: 0-0
Distance: **2m/2m3: 1-4** 2m4-2m7: 0-1 3m+: 0-0
Track: LH: 0-3 **RH: 1-2 Tight: 1-3** Gall: 0-2
Aids: Bl: 0-0 Vi: 0-2 Tstrap: 0-0
Best Rating: 90 3/02 Sedg 2m5f110y soft Hdl

Fair performer on the level at around a mile. She was soundly beaten on her hurdles bow but won next time when left clear at the last, and has run with credit since.

D J Flippance (IRE)

109(104h) (90h) **101**

7-y-o b g Orchestra-Jane Bond (Good Bond)
A Parker Mr & Mrs Raymond Anderson Green

Placings:*006*/503-25312PP **(4889)**
2001/02: 22^{2}GS, 22^{5}GS, 27^{3}HY, 24^{1}S, 28^{2}S, 26^{P}GS, 26^{P}G

Starts	1st	2nd	3rd	Win & Pl
Hurdles	2	0	1	0	860
Chases	5	1	1	1	5090
Career Total	**13**	**1**	**2**	**2**	**6426**

100 2/02 Muss 3m E Ch SFT £3388
Total win prize-money £3388

Going: Sf: 1-3 GS: 0-3 Gd: 0-1 GF: - Fm: 0-0
Distance: 2m/2m3: 0-0 2m4-2m7: 0-2 **3m+: 1-5**
Track: LH: 0-4 **RH: 1-2 Tight: 1-5** Gall: 0-0
Aids: Bl: 0-0 Vi: 0-0 Tstrap: 0-0
Best Rating: 101 3/02 Sedg 3m4f soft Ch

Fair chaser. Suited by three miles and soft ground.

D Judge (IRE)

(87h) (95h) **105**

8-y-o b m Strong Gale-Lady Of Aherlow (Le Bavard (FR))
Thomas Carberry (J R Jenkins 11/7) Robert Burke

Placings:*2000*/0330/30F-00006P53 **(4720a)**
2001/02: 20^{0}GF, 20^{0}G, 16^{0}GF, 20^{0}G, 16^{6}GY, 24^{P}HY, 16^{5}GY, 22^{3}GY

	Starts	1st	2nd	3rd	Win & Pl
Hurdles	6	0	0	0	0
Chases	2	0	0	1	794
Career Total	**19**	**0**	**1**	**4**	**2554**

Going: Sf: 0-1 GS: 0-0 Gd: 0-2 GF: - Fm: 0-2
Distance: 2m/2m3: 0-3 2m4-2m7: 0-4 3m+: 0-1
Track: LH: 0-3 RH: 0-1 Tight: 0-1 Gall: 0-0
Aids: Bl: 0-1 Vi: 0-0 Tstrap: 0-1
Best Rating: 105 4/02 Fair 2m6f100y gd-yld Ch

D'Argent (IRE)

106 **119**

5-y-o gr g Roselier (FR)-Money Galore (IRE) (Monksfield)
A King Nigel Bunter

Placings:*0211* **(4479)**
2001/02: 16^{0}G, 18^{2}HY, 20^{1}S, 19^{1}G

	Starts	1st	2nd	3rd	Win & Pl
NH Flat	1	0	0	0	0
Hurdles	3	2	1	0	6711
Career Total	**4**	**2**	**1**	**0**	**6711**

119 3/02 Extr 2m3f E Hdl GD £2842
119 3/02 Donc 2m4f E Hdl SFT £3122
Total win prize-money £5964

Going: Sf: 1-2 GS: 0-0 Gd: 1-2 GF: - Fm: 0-0
Distance: 2m/2m3: 1-3 2m4-2m7: 1-1 3m+: 0-0
Track: LH: 1-3 RH: 1-1 Tight: 0-1 **Gall: 1-2**
Aids: Bl: 0-0 Vi: 0-0 Tstrap: 0-0
Best Rating: 119 3/02 Extr 2m3f good Hdl

Dabarpour (IRE)

104 **112**

6-y-o b/br g Alzao (USA)-Dabara (IRE) (Shardari)
Ian Williams Terry Warner

Placings:4050/32500-120003124 **(2649)**
2001/02: 16^{1}GF, 16^{2}F, 16^{0}G, 17^{0}GF, 17^{0}G, 16^{3}G, 16^{1}G, 16^{6}G, 16^{4}G

	Starts	1st	2nd	3rd	Win & Pl
Hurdles	9	2	2	1	8056
Career Total	**18**	**2**	**3**	**2**	**9302**

103 11/01 Hntg 2m110y E(0-115)HHdl GD £2429
100 6/01 Strf 2m110y E(0-105)HHdl G-F £3209
Total win prize-money £5639

Going: Sf: 0-0 GS: 0-0 Gd: 1-6 GF: - Fm: 1-3
Distance: **2m/2m3: 2-9** 2m4-2m7: 0-0 3m+: 0-0
Track: LH: 1-3 RH: 1-6 Tight: 1-3 Gall: 1-1
Aids: Bl: 0-0 Vi: 0-0 **Tstrap: 2-8**
Best Rating: 104 11/01 Kemp 2m good Hdl

Moderate novice hurdler, suited by fast ground. Usually wears a tongue tie.

Daddy Dancer (FR)

11-y-o b g Italic (FR)-Tresse D'Or (FR) (Northern Treat (USA))
Martin Jones (Mrs P Ford 10/2) R F Jones

Placings:4/60F362/3F33P3P/643P/6-F **(3984)**
2001/02: 31^{F}GS

	Starts	1st	2nd	3rd	Win & Pl
Chases	1	0	0	0	
Career Total	**20**	**0**	**1**	**6**	**5729**

Going: Sf: 0-0 GS: 0-1 Gd: 0-0 GF: - Fm: 0-0
Distance: 2m/2m3: 0-0 2m4-2m7: 0-0 3m+: 0-1
Track: LH: 0-0 RH: 0-0 Tight: 0-0 Gall: 0-0
Aids: Bl: 0-0 Vi: 0-0 Tstrap: 0-0
Best Rating: 109 2/99 Leic 2m4f110y gd-sft Ch

Dads Lad (IRE)

105 **110**

8-y-o b g Supreme Leader-Furryvale (Furry Glen)
H D Daly Mrs Strachan,Parkinson & Hon Mrs C Cecil

Placings:4334-304514 **(4426)**
2001/02: 28^{3}S, 25^{0}G, 24^{4}HY, 23^{5}S, 24^{1}S, 26^{4}HY

	Starts	1st	2nd	3rd	Win & Pl
Chases	6	1	0	1	5503
Career Total	**10**	**1**	**0**	**3**	**7406**

110 3/02 Bang 3m110y D(0-110)HCh SFT £4231
Total win prize-money £4232

Going: Sf: 1-5 GS: 0-0 Gd: 0-1 GF: - Fm: 0-0
Distance: 2m/2m3: 0-0 2m4-2m7: 0-0 **3m+: 1-6**
Track: **LH: 1-4** RH: 0-2 **Tight: 1-2** Gall: 0-0
Aids: **Bl: 1-2** Vi: 0-0 Tstrap: 0-0
Best Rating: 113 2/01 Tntn 3m heavy Ch

Modest novice chaser, suited by soft ground, stays three miles. Off the mark at Bangor when blinkered for the first time.

Daily Tonic

84 **64**

5-y-o ch g Sanglamore (USA)-Woodwardia (USA) (El Gran Senor (USA))
N A Twiston-Davies Odyssey Racing

Placings:00-60 **(1760)**
2001/02: 16^{6}GS, 16^{0}GS

	Starts	1st	2nd	3rd	Win & Pl
Hurdles	2	0	0	0	0
Career Total	**4**	**0**	**0**	**0**	**0**

Going: Sf: 0-0 GS: 0-2 Gd: 0-0 GF: - Fm: 0-0
Distance: 2m/2m3: 0-2 2m4-2m7: 0-0 3m+: 0-0
Track: LH: 0-2 RH: 0-0 Tight: 0-1 Gall: 0-0
Aids: Bl: 0-0 Vi: 0-0 Tstrap: 0-0
Best Rating: 64 10/01 Uttx 2m gd-sft Hdl

Daisy Dale

62f **40f**

4-y-o gr f Terimon-Quetta's Girl (Orchestra)
Mrs S Lamyman P Lamyman

Placings:*000* **(4539)**
2001/02: 16^{0}GS, 17^{0}GS, 16^{0}G

	Starts	1st	2nd	3rd	Win & Pl
NH Flat	3	0	0	0	
Career Total	**3**	**0**	**0**	**0**	

Going: Sf: 0-0 GS: 0-2 Gd: 0-1 GF: - Fm: 0-0
Distance: 2m/2m3: 0-3 2m4-2m7: 0-0 3m+: 0-0
Track: LH: 0-2 RH: 0-1 Tight: 0-3 Gall: 0-0
Aids: Bl: 0-0 Vi: 0-0 Tstrap: 0-0
Best Rating: 40 2/02 Fknm 2m gd-sft NHF

Dajam Vu

85 **63**

5-y-o ch m Lyphento (USA)-Dancing Diamond (IRE) (Alzao (USA))
J S King Dajam Ltd

Placings:033-50P **(2560)**
2001/02: 22^{5}GF, 20^{0}GS, 20^{P}S

	Starts	1st	2nd	3rd	Win & Pl
Hurdles	3	0	0	0	0
Career Total	**6**	**0**	**0**	**2**	**551**

Going: Sf: 0-1 GS: 0-1 Gd: 0-0 GF: - Fm: 0-1
Distance: 2m/2m3: 0-0 2m4-2m7: 0-3 3m+: 0-0
Track: LH: 0-2 RH: 0-1 Tight: 0-1 Gall: 0-0
Aids: Bl: 0-0 Vi: 0-0 Tstrap: 0-0
Best Rating: 72 10/00 Tntn 2m1f good Hdl

Dajraan (IRE)

88 | 67

13-y-o b g Shirley Heights-Sugarbird (Star Appeal)
R J Smith Mrs Sarah Stafford

Placings:0P4/P210/P/P/04 **(0317)**
2001/02: 19^{0}G, 23^{4}F

	Starts	1st	2nd	3rd	Win & Pl
Chases	2	0	0	0	321
Career Total	**11**	**1**	**1**	**0**	**3529**

96	5/96	Uttx	2m	E(0-100)HHdl	G-S	£2347

Total win prize-money £2348

Going: Sf: 0-0 GS: 0-0 Gd: 0-1 GF: - Fm: 0-1
Distance: 2m/2m3: 0-1 2m4-2m7: 0-0 3m+: 0-1
Track: LH: 0-0 RH: 0-2 Tight: 0-0 Gall: 0-0
Aids: Bl: 0-0 Vi: 0-0 Tstrap: 0-0
Best Rating: 96 5/96 Uttx 2m gd-sft Hdl

Dakisi Royale

5-y-o ch m King's Signet (USA)-Marcroft (Crofthall)
P D Evans P D Evans

Placings:CB **(2649)**
2001/02: 17^{C}S, 16^{B}G

	Starts	1st	2nd	3rd	Win & Pl
Hurdles	2	0	0	0	
Career Total	**2**	**0**	**0**	**0**	

Going: Sf: 0-1 GS: 0-0 Gd: 0-1 GF: - Fm: 0-0
Distance: 2m/2m3: 0-2 2m4-2m7: 0-0 3m+: 0-0
Track: LH: 0-1 RH: 0-1 Tight: 0-1 Gall: 0-0
Aids: Bl: 0-0 Vi: 0-0 Tstrap: 0-1
Best Rating:

Dalametre

96 | 104

15-y-o b g Dutch Treat-Composite (Compensation)
M J M Evans M J M Evans

Placings:62U/3/232/P033104/PP30/441PP1/1254-041 **(2756)**
2001/02: 20^{0}S, 21^{4}S, 20^{1}S

	Starts	1st	2nd	3rd	Win & Pl
Chases	3	1	0	0	3928
Career Total	**31**	**5**	**4**	**5**	**24167**

104	12/01	Bang	2m4f110y	F(0-110)HCh	SFT	£3656
104	10/00	Strf	2m4f	D(0-120)HCh	G-S	£5817
104	3/00	Bang	3m110y	D(0-110)HCh	SFT	£4228
92	11/99	Bang	2m4f110y	E(0-105)HCh	HVY	£3696
85	4/98	Hrfd	2m	H Ch	SFT	£1095

Total win prize-money £18493

Going: Sf: 1-3 GS: 0-0 Gd: 0-0 GF: - Fm: 0-0
Distance: 2m/2m3: 0-0 **2m4-2m7: 1-3** 3m+: 0-0
Track: **LH: 1-3** RH: 0-0 **Tight: 1-2** Gall: 0-0
Aids: Bl: 0-0 Vi: 0-0 Tstrap: 0-0
Best Rating: 104 12/01 Bang 2m4f110y soft Ch

Modest chaser, stays three miles, suited by soft ground. Retired after winning at Bangor in December 2001.

Dalby Carr

7-y-o b m Henbit (USA)-Havenwood Lady (Fair Season)
R H P Williams (P G Murphy 27/1) A Lowrie & Mrs J Lowrie

Placings:3400P-650065U **(4179)**
2001/02: 16^{6}F, 20^{5}GF, 18^{0}GF, 17^{0}GF, 22^{6}GF, 24^{5}GF, 24^{U}GS

	Starts	1st	2nd	3rd	Win & Pl
Hurdles	6	0	0	0	0
Chases	1	0	0	0	0
Career Total	**12**	**0**	**0**	**1**	**221**

Going: Sf: 0-0 GS: 0-1 Gd: 0-0 GF: - Fm: 0-6
Distance: 2m/2m3: 0-3 2m4-2m7: 0-2 3m+: 0-2
Track: LH: 0-4 RH: 0-2 Tight: 0-2 Gall: 0-0
Aids: Bl: 0-0 Vi: 0-0 Tstrap: 0-0
Best Rating: 95 10/00 Bang 2m1f soft NHF

Dalby Of York

6-y-o ch g Polar Falcon (USA)-Miller's Creek (USA) (Star De Naskra (USA))
M E Sowersby M E Sowersby

Placings:P **(0880)**
2001/02: 19^{P}G

	Starts	1st	2nd	3rd	Win & Pl
Hurdles	1	0	0	0	
Career Total	**1**	**0**	**0**	**0**	

Going: Sf: 0-0 GS: 0-0 Gd: 0-1 GF: - Fm: 0-0
Distance: 2m/2m3: 0-0 2m4-2m7: 0-1 3m+: 0-0
Track: LH: 0-0 RH: 0-1 Tight: 0-1 Gall: 0-0
Aids: Bl: 0-0 Vi: 0-0 Tstrap: 0-0
Best Rating:

Dalcassian Buck (IRE)

99(90c) | (75c)93+

8-y-o ch g Buckskin (FR)-Menebeans (IRE) (Duky)
K C Bailey Have Fun Racing Partnership

Placings:F4P6P **(4751)**
2001/02: 21^{F}S, 24^{4}GS, 24^{P}GS, 19^{6}S, 20^{P}GF

	Starts	1st	2nd	3rd	Win & Pl
Hurdles	1	0	0	0	0
Chases	4	0	0	0	235
Career Total	**5**	**0**	**0**	**0**	**235**

Going: Sf: 0-2 GS: 0-2 Gd: 0-0 GF: - Fm: 0-1
Distance: 2m/2m3: 0-1 2m4-2m7: 0-2 3m+: 0-2
Track: LH: 0-3 RH: 0-2 Tight: 0-1 Gall: 0-2
Aids: Bl: 0-0 Vi: 0-0 Tstrap: 0-0
Best Rating: 80 3/02 Newb 2m3f soft Hdl

Modest hurdler/chaser, won a weak novices' hurdle at Towcester in April 2002. Effective at a stiff two miles.

Dalligan (IRE)

108 | 109+

8-y-o b g Executive Perk-Comeragh Queen (The Parson)
N J Pewter N J Pewter

Placings:6U **(0322)**
2001/02: 24^{6}GF, 21^{U}G

	Starts	1st	2nd	3rd	Win & Pl
Chases	2	0	0	0	0
Career Total	**2**	**0**	**0**	**0**	**0**

Going: Sf: 0-0 GS: 0-0 Gd: 0-1 GF: - Fm: 0-1
Distance: 2m/2m3: 0-0 2m4-2m7: 0-1 3m+: 0-1
Track: LH: 0-1 RH: 0-1 Tight: 0-2 Gall: 0-0
Aids: Bl: 0-0 Vi: 0-0 Tstrap: 0-0
Best Rating: 82 5/01 Fknm 3m110y gd-fm Ch

Modest pointer/hunter chaser, is best with cut in the ground.

Dalton Lady

78(84h) | 85

8-y-o b m Roscoe Blake-Drom Lady (Royalty)
B Mactaggart Robert W Armstrong

Placings:000/0/P3-**44FF** **(4439)**
2001/02: 16^{4}S, 16^{4}S, 16^{F}S, 17^{F}S

	Starts	1st	2nd	3rd	Win & Pl
Chases	4	0	0	0	597
Career Total	**10**	**0**	**0**	**1**	**1070**

Going: Sf: 0-4 GS: 0-0 Gd: 0-0 GF: - Fm: 0-0
Distance: 2m/2m3: 0-4 2m4-2m7: 0-0 3m+: 0-0
Track: LH: 0-2 RH: 0-2 Tight: 0-1 Gall: 0-0
Aids: Bl: 0-0 Vi: 0-0 Tstrap: 0-0
Best Rating: 85 3/02 Kels 2m1f soft Ch

Lightly-raced modest novice chaser, runs only when there is cut.

Dalus Park (IRE)

7-y-o b g Mandalus-Pollerton Park (Pollerton)
Mrs Antonia Bealby R E N Gardiner

Placings:2 **(4057)**
2001/02: 23^{2}S

	Starts	1st	2nd	3rd	Win & Pl
Chases	1	0	1	0	658
Career Total	**1**	**0**	**1**	**0**	**658**

Going: Sf: 0-1 GS: 0-0 Gd: 0-0 GF: - Fm: 0-0
Distance: 2m/2m3: 0-0 2m4-2m7: 0-0 3m+: 0-1
Track: LH: 0-0 RH: 0-1 Tight: 0-0 Gall: 0-0
Aids: Bl: 0-0 Vi: 0-0 Tstrap: 0-0
Best Rating: 100 3/02 Leic 2m7f110y soft Ch

Winning pointer, he shaped with promise on his debut over regulation fences. Acts with cut.

Dam The Breeze

111(93h) | (111h)123

9-y-o b g Ikdam-Cool Breeze (Windjammer (USA))
Mrs H Dalton Kevin Glastonbury

Placings:FPP/45F21601-112 **(3227)**
2001/02: 24^{1}G, 26^{1}GF, 25^{2}G

	Starts	1st	2nd	3rd	Win & Pl
Hurdles	1	1	0	0	2520
Chases	2	1	1	0	6046
Career Total	**14**	**4**	**2**	**0**	**17018**

111	5/01	Hntg	3m2f	F(0-95)HHdl	G-F	£2520
121	5/01	Hntg	3m	E(0-115)HCh	GD	£4329
115	4/01	MRas	3m1f	F(0-95)Ch	G-S	£3906
123	8/00	Worc	2m7f110y	E Ch	G-F	£3347

Total win prize-money £14103

Going: Sf: 0-0 GS: 0-0 Gd: 1-2 GF: - Fm: 1-1
Distance: 2m/2m3: 0-0 2m4-2m7: 0-0 **3m+: 2-3**
Track: LH: 0-0 **RH: 2-3** Tight: 0-0 **Gall: 2-2**
Aids: Bl: 0-0 Vi: 0-0 Tstrap: 0-0
Best Rating: 123 1/02 Winc 3m1f110y good Ch

Modest staying hurdler/chaser, in good heart in 2001, appreciates a decent surface.

Damaris

76 **70**

10-y-o ch m Dancing High-Lekuti (Le Coq D'Or)
Mrs K J Tutty N D Tutty

Placings:*42*/400P0/30/4600-**P04P** **(2510)**
2001/02: 21^{P}G, 21^{0}S, 19^{4}GF, 16^{P}S

	Starts	1st	2nd	3rd	Win & Pl
Hurdles	2	0	0	0	0
Chases	2	0	0	0	0
Career Total	**17**	**0**	**1**	**1**	**966**

Going: Sf: 0-2 GS: 0-0 Gd: 0-1 GF: - Fm: 0-1
Distance: 2m/2m3: 0-2 2m4-2m7: 0-2 3m+: 0-0
Track: LH: 0-4 RH: 0-0 Tight: 0-4 Gall: 0-0
Aids: Bl: 0-0 Vi: 0-0 Tstrap: 0-0
Best Rating: 96 4/98 MRas 1m5f110y soft NHF

Dambusters

97 **89**

8-y-o b g Damister (USA)-Key To The River (USA) (Irish River (FR))
Mrs L Williamson Halewood International Ltd

Placings:*0/2*45/P-06400P **(3355)**
2001/02: 20^{0}G, 22^{6}S, 22^{4}S, 25^{0}S, 26^{0}S, 24^{P}HY

	Starts	1st	2nd	3rd	Win & Pl
Hurdles	4	0	0	0	0
Chases	2	0	0	0	408
Career Total	**11**	**0**	**1**	**0**	**866**

Going: Sf: 0-5 GS: 0-0 Gd: 0-1 GF: - Fm: 0-0
Distance: 2m/2m3: 0-0 2m4-2m7: 0-3 3m+: 0-3
Track: LH: 0-4 RH: 0-2 Tight: 0-1 Gall: 0-0
Aids: Bl: 0-2 Vi: 0-0 Tstrap: 0-0
Best Rating: 103 12/99 Donc 2m110y gd-fm NHF

Lightly-raced, he has not cut much ice in hurdling company to date.

Dame Fonteyn

104 **96**

5-y-o b m Suave Dancer (USA)-Her Honour (Teenoso (USA))
C Tizzard (M C Pipe 18/5) Miss Sarah Tizzard

Placings:300-30F245243 **(4881)**
2001/02: 16^{3}G, 17^{0}GF, 16^{F}G, 16^{2}S, 17^{4}S, 21^{5}HY, 22^{2}S, 17^{4}G, 18^{3}GF

	Starts	1st	2nd	3rd	Win & Pl
Hurdles	9	0	2	2	2210
Career Total	**12**	**0**	**2**	**3**	**2580**

Going: Sf: 0-4 GS: 0-0 Gd: 0-3 GF: - Fm: 0-2
Distance: 2m/2m3: 0-7 2m4-2m7: 0-2 3m+: 0-0
Track: LH: 0-6 RH: 0-3 Tight: 0-7 Gall: 0-0
Aids: Bl: 0-1 Vi: 0-0 Tstrap: 0-0
Best Rating: 96 4/02 Font 2m2f110y gd-fm Hdl

Stays two miles six furlongs. Best on easy ground although has yet to lose her maiden tag over hurdles.

Dame Hattie

80 **86**

7-y-o b m Hatim (USA)-Camden Grove (Uncle Pokey)
A Scott G M Abercrombie

Placings:*5/55/5*P00-03PPPP **(4867)**
2001/02: 20^{0}G, 19^{3}GF, 19^{P}S, 24^{P}S, 20^{P}GF, 16^{P}GF

	Starts	1st	2nd	3rd	Win & Pl
Hurdles	6	0	0	1	273
Career Total	**13**	**0**	**0**	**1**	**273**

Going: Sf: 0-2 GS: 0-0 Gd: 0-1 GF: - Fm: 0-3
Distance: 2m/2m3: 0-3 2m4-2m7: 0-2 3m+: 0-1
Track: LH: 0-6 RH: 0-0 Tight: 0-2 Gall: 0-1
Aids: Bl: 0-0 Vi: 0-0 Tstrap: 0-0
Best Rating: 101 4/00 Ayr 2m good NHF

Damien's Choice (IRE)

104(102h) (108h)**118**

10-y-o b g Erin's Hope-Reenoga (Tug Of War)
Ferdy Murphy M Sawers

Placings:*264*/43/525P0**P**240/04126/40**650**-21**P11226** **(4691)**
2001/02: 17^{2}G, 16^{1}G, 16^{P}GS, 16^{1}S, 16^{1}S, 16^{2}GS, 16^{2}GS, 17^{6}GF

	Starts	1st	2nd	3rd	Win & Pl
Hurdles	2	1	1	0	3090
Chases	6	2	2	0	9451
Career Total	**34**	**4**	**7**	**2**	**19407**

112 12/01 Catt 2m F(0-105)HCh SFT £3965
104 11/01 Sedg 2m110y F(0-100)HCh SFT £2884
108 6/01 Hexm 2m E(0-115)HHdl GD £2366
81 11/99 Kels 2m110y F(0-95)HHdl GD £3039
Total win prize-money £12254

Going: Sf: 2-2 GS: 0-3 Gd: 1-2 GF: - Fm: 0-1
Distance: **2m/2m3: 3-8** 2m4-2m7: 0-0 3m+: 0-0
Track: **LH: 3-6** RH: 0-2 **Tight: 2-5** Gall: 0-1
Aids: Bl: 0-0 Vi: 0-0 Tstrap: 0-0
Best Rating: 118 1/02 Catt 2m gd-sft Ch

Not the most consistent over hurdles, he took to fences much better with two wins from his first three starts during 2001. Best over two miles when there is cut in the ground.

Damien's Law

5-y-o b g Contract Law (USA)-Cinderella Derek (Hittite Glory)
A D Smith Pertemps Group Limited

Placings:P **(0734)**
2001/02: 22^{P}G

	Starts	1st	2nd	3rd	Win & Pl
Hurdles	1	0	0	0	
Career Total	**1**	**0**	**0**	**0**	

Going: Sf: 0-0 GS: 0-0 Gd: 0-1 GF: - Fm: 0-0
Distance: 2m/2m3: 0-0 2m4-2m7: 0-1 3m+: 0-0
Track: LH: 0-1 RH: 0-0 Tight: 0-1 Gall: 0-0
Aids: Bl: 0-0 Vi: 0-0 Tstrap: 0-0
Best Rating:

Damiens Pride (IRE)

12-y-o b g Bulldozer-Riopoless (Royal And Regal (USA))
Miss D Cole (Mrs S J Batchelor 31/5) Mrs S J Batchelor

Placings:302P **(0835)**
2001/02: 19^{3}F, 16^{0}G, 26^{2}GF, 26^{P}GF

	Starts	1st	2nd	3rd	Win & Pl
Chases	4	0	1	1	878
Career Total	**4**	**0**	**1**	**1**	**878**

Going: Sf: 0-0 GS: 0-0 Gd: 0-1 GF: - Fm: 0-3
Distance: 2m/2m3: 0-1 2m4-2m7: 0-1 3m+: 0-2
Track: LH: 0-2 RH: 0-1 Tight: 0-2 Gall: 0-0
Aids: Bl: 0-0 Vi: 0-0 Tstrap: 0-0
Best Rating: 100 5/01 NAbb 3m2f110y gd-fm Ch

Fair veteran pointer/hunter who finished good second at the 2002 Cheltenham hunter chase meeting. Suited by a sound surface.

Damoiselle

99 **88**

6-y-o b m Sir Harry Lewis (USA)-Jouvencelle (Rusticaro (FR))
N A Twiston-Davies H R Mould

Placings:*450*/54301-F051P **(4739)**
2001/02: 19^{F}GS, 19^{0}G, 21^{5}GS, 21^{1}GF, 21^{P}GF

	Starts	1st	2nd	3rd	Win & Pl
Hurdles	5	1	0	0	2702
Career Total	**13**	**2**	**0**	**1**	**6808**

88 4/02 Hntg 2m5f110y E(0-110)HHdl G-F £2702
84 4/01 Tntn 2m3f110y D(0-110)HHdl G-F £3517
Total win prize-money £6220

Going: Sf: 0-0 GS: 0-2 Gd: 0-1 GF: - Fm: 1-2
Distance: 2m/2m3: 0-2 **2m4-2m7: 1-3** 3m+: 0-0
Track: LH: 0-1 **RH: 1-3** Tight: 0-0 **Gall: 1-2**
Aids: Bl: 0-0 Vi: 0-0 Tstrap: 0-0
Best Rating: 91 3/00 Uttx 2m good NHF

She is best on fast ground and is suited by trips of around two and a half miles.

Damp Course (IRE)

(73h) (89h)

9-y-o ch g Montelimar (USA)-Running Tide (Deep Run)
N A Twiston-Davies G C Mordaunt

Placings:*625*046223/1124**16P3P**/334**20UP**-00 **(0347)**
2001/02: 24^{0}G, 27^{0}G

	Starts	1st	2nd	3rd	Win & Pl
Hurdles	2	0	0	0	
Career Total	**27**	**3**	**5**	**4**	**15576**

124 12/99 Wwck 3m1f110y F(0-110)HCh SFT £4055
90 10/99 Hexm 3m E Hdl GD £2322
109 9/99 Worc 3m F Hdl G-F £1884
Total win prize-money £8261

Going: Sf: 0-0 GS: 0-0 Gd: 0-2 GF: - Fm: 0-0
Distance: 2m/2m3: 0-0 2m4-2m7: 0-0 3m+: 0-2
Track: LH: 0-1 RH: 0-1 Tight: 0-1 Gall: 0-0
Aids: Bl: 0-1 Vi: 0-0 Tstrap: 0-0
Best Rating: 124 12/99 Wwck 3m1f110y soft Ch

Damus (GER)

114(98h) (118h)**140**

8-y-o br g Surumu (GER)-Dawn Side (CAN) (Bold Forbes (USA))
Ian Williams The Winning Line

Placings:203/132**2U/1311300**-**1221P5** **(4635)**
2001/02: 17^{1}GS, 16^{2}GS, 16^{2}S, 16^{1}G, 16^{P}G, 19^{5}GF

	Starts	1st	2nd	3rd	Win & Pl
Hurdles	1	1	0	0	5551
Chases	5	1	2	0	17804
Career Total	**21**	**6**	**5**	**4**	**46010**

140 12/01 Sthl 2m B(0-140)HCh GD £13848
118 10/01 MRas 2m1f110y D(0-120)HHdl G-S £5551
140 12/00 Fknm 2m110y E Ch G-S £3003
138 7/00 Wolv 2m C(0-135)HCh G-S £7928
125 5/00 Hrfd 2m E Ch G-S £3051

123	10/99	Plum	2m	E(0-105)HHdl	G-F	£3176

Total win prize-money £36559

Going: Sf: 0-1 GS: 1-2 Gd: 1-2 GF: - Fm: 0-1
Distance: **2m/2m3: 2-5** 2m4-2m7: 0-1 3m+: 0-0
Track: LH: 1-2 RH: 1-3 **Tight: 2-2** Gall: 0-1
Aids: Bl: 0-0 Vi: 0-0 Tstrap: 0-0
Best Rating: 140 12/01 Sthl 2m good Ch

Fair handicap chaser, jumps well and won over hurdles on his in 2001 before good efforts over fences. Unlikely to stay much beyond two miles. Acts on good to soft ground.

Dan De Man (IRE)

107(99c) (102c)**96**

11-y-o b g Phardante (FR)-Slave De (Arctic Slave)
Miss L C Siddall David J Poulter Partnership

Placings: *05/0*60F5/3P0151225/41123360/4560404P5 1/040P400-03P100024000 (4872)
2001/02: 16^{0}S, 16^{3}G, 16^{P}GF, 20^{1}S, 20^{0}G, 20^{0}G, 20^{0}G, 16^{2}GS, 17^{4}G, 16^{0}S, 16^{0}GF, 16^{0}GF

	Starts	1st	2nd	3rd	Win & Pl
Hurdles	8	1	1	0	3458
Chases	4	0	0	1	908
Career Total	**53**	**6**	**4**	**4**	**21940**

92	11/01	Hayd	2m4f	F(0-110)HHdl	SFT	£2758
107	4/00	Newc	2m110y	E Ch	G-S	£3458
115	12/98	Newc	2m	E(0-110)HHdl	SFT	£2211
112	11/98	Weth	2m4f110y	E(0-110)HHdl	GD	£2407
97	1/98	Donc	2m110y	F(0-110)HHdl	GD	£2356
84	12/97	Newc	2m	F(0-100)HHdl	GD	£1934

Total win prize-money £15127

Going: Sf: 1-3 GS: 0-1 Gd: 0-5 GF: - Fm: 0-3
Distance: 2m/2m3: 0-8 **2m4-2m7: 1-4** 3m+: 0-0
Track: **LH: 1-11** RH: 0-0 Tight: 0-0 Gall: 0-5
Aids: Bl: 0-0 Vi: 0-0 Tstrap: 0-0
Best Rating: 120 1/99 Donc 2m110y good Ch

Versatile but inconsistent sort, he runs over both hurdles and fences and is effective on a soft surface and stays two miles four furlongs.

Danby's Flyer

6-y-o b m Local Suitor (USA)-Dohty Baby (Hittite Glory)
J M Jefferson D T Todd

Placings: *00*P (4275)
2001/02: 16^{0}G, 16^{0}S, 16^{P}G

	Starts	1st	2nd	3rd	Win & Pl
NH Flat	1	0	0	0	0
Hurdles	2	0	0	0	0
Career Total	**3**	**0**	**0**	**0**	

Going: Sf: 0-1 GS: 0-0 Gd: 0-2 GF: - Fm: 0-0
Distance: 2m/2m3: 0-3 2m4-2m7: 0-0 3m+: 0-0
Track: LH: 0-2 RH: 0-1 Tight: 0-1 Gall: 0-2
Aids: Bl: 0-0 Vi: 0-0 Tstrap: 0-1
Best Rating:

Danbys Gorse

10-y-o ch g Presidium-Dohty Baby (Hittite Glory)
Miss Louise Todd D T Todd

Placings: 10404/4P00221530/5351353F34/25U41133 02/444P1254/120566000-F (3861)
2001/02: 19^{F}S

	Starts	1st	2nd	3rd	Win & Pl
Chases	1	0	0	0	
Career Total	**53**	**7**	**6**	**7**	**34142**

109	5/00	Weth	2m	E(0-115)HCh	G-F	£3620
100	3/00	Towc	2m	D(0-120)HHdl	SFT	£2918
109	2/99	Muss	2m4f	D(0-120)HCh	GD	£4065
107	1/99	Newc	2m4f	E(0-115)HCh	SFT	£3598
102	12/97	Weth	2m4f110y	D(0-110)HCh	SFT	£3881
94	2/97	Weth	2m4f110y	D(0-125)HHdl	SFT	£2792
100	1/96	Towc	2m	E Hdl	SFT	£2897

Total win prize-money £23777

Going: Sf: 0-1 GS: 0-0 Gd: 0-0 GF: - Fm: 0-0
Distance: 2m/2m3: 0-0 2m4-2m7: 0-1 3m+: 0-0
Track: LH: 0-1 RH: 0-0 Tight: 0-0 Gall: 0-1
Aids: Bl: 0-0 Vi: 0-0 Tstrap: 0-0
Best Rating: 109 5/00 MRas 2m1f110y gd-sft Ch

Dance Theatre (IRE)

89 **83**

4-y-o b g Sadler's Wells (USA)-Noora Abu (Ahonoora)
J R Jenkins (J S Bolger 17/6) Miss I Leitendorfa

Placings: 6 (2311)
2001/02: 16^{6}G

	Starts	1st	2nd	3rd	Win & Pl
Hurdles	1	0	0	0	0
Career Total	**1**	**0**	**0**	**0**	**0**

Going: Sf: 0-0 GS: 0-0 Gd: 0-1 GF: - Fm: 0-0
Distance: 2m/2m3: 0-1 2m4-2m7: 0-0 3m+: 0-0
Track: LH: 0-0 RH: 0-1 Tight: 0-0 Gall: 0-1
Aids: Bl: 0-0 Vi: 0-0 Tstrap: 0-0
Best Rating: 83 11/01 Hntg 2m110y good Hdl

An Irish import by Sadler's Wells, he was well beaten on his hurdling debut.

Dancemma

5-y-o ch m Emarati (USA)-Hanglands (Bustino)
H J Collingridge D T Thom

Placings: 6P (1906)
2001/02: 17^{6}GS, 22^{P}S

	Starts	1st	2nd	3rd	Win & Pl
Hurdles	2	0	0	0	0
Career Total	**2**	**0**	**0**	**0**	**0**

Going: Sf: 0-1 GS: 0-1 Gd: 0-0 GF: - Fm: 0-0
Distance: 2m/2m3: 0-1 2m4-2m7: 0-1 3m+: 0-0
Track: LH: 0-2 RH: 0-0 Tight: 0-2 Gall: 0-0
Aids: Bl: 0-0 Vi: 0-0 Tstrap: 0-0
Best Rating:

Dancetillyoudrop (IRE)

103(44h) **124**

11-y-o b g Clearly Bust-Keep Dancing (Lord Gayle (USA))
P F Nicholls Derek Millard

Placings: *1*2522/3F1342FP2/FF2P110446/F24313/P3 13201532-5P122 (4892)
2001/02: 25^{5}F, 27^{P}GF, 26^{1}HY, 26^{2}HY, 31^{2}G

	Starts	1st	2nd	3rd	Win & Pl
Hurdles	1	0	0	0	0
Chases	4	1	2	0	3651
Career Total	**45**	**8**	**11**	**7**	**45935**

122	2/02	Plum	3m2f	H Ch	HVY	£1148
122	11/00	Font	3m2f110y	D(0-125)HCh	HVY	£3955
124	5/00	Font	3m2f110y	F(0-105)HCh	GD	£2990
124	11/99	Winc	3m1f110y	D(0-125)HCh	GD	£7035
113	1/99	Winc	3m1f110y	E(0-115)HCh	SFT	£3454
122	1/99	Font	3m2f110y	D(0-125)HCh	SFT	£4352
107	11/97	Worc	2m4f110y	E(0-105)HCh	SFT	£3125
102	6/96	Naas	2m	NHF	YLD	£2824

Total win prize-money £28886

Going: Sf: 1-2 GS: 0-0 Gd: 0-1 GF: - Fm: 0-2
Distance: 2m/2m3: 0-0 2m4-2m7: 0-0 **3m+: 1-5**
Track: LH: 0-0 RH: 0-0 Tight: 0-1 Gall: 0-0
Aids: Bl: 0-0 Vi: 0-0 Tstrap: 0-0
Best Rating: 124 4/02 Prth 3m7f good Ch

An ordinary staying handicap chaser who successfully switched to hunter chasing in 2002. He stays well and likes the mud, but has won on good and good to firm, and goes well at Fontwell.

Dancing Al

91 **79**

7-y-o br g Alnasr Alwasheek-Lyne Dancer (Be My Native (USA))
J S Moore Miss L D Martin

Placings: 053B5/0PB/3P-4 (1493)
2001/02: 17^{4}GF

	Starts	1st	2nd	3rd	Win & Pl
Hurdles	1	0	0	0	0
Career Total	**11**	**0**	**0**	**2**	**566**

Going: Sf: 0-0 GS: 0-0 Gd: 0-0 GF: - Fm: 0-1
Distance: 2m/2m3: 0-1 2m4-2m7: 0-0 3m+: 0-0
Track: LH: 0-0 RH: 0-1 Tight: 0-0 Gall: 0-0
Aids: Bl: 0-0 Vi: 0-0 Tstrap: 0-0
Best Rating: 79 10/01 Extr 2m1f gd-fm Hdl

Dancing Bay

108 **121**

5-y-o b g Suave Dancer (USA)-Kabayil (Dancing Brave (USA))
N J Henderson (Miss J A Camacho 10/11) Elite Racing Club

Placings: 2F (4034)
2001/02: 17^{2}S, 20^{F}S

	Starts	1st	2nd	3rd	Win & Pl
Hurdles	2	0	1	0	1095
Career Total	**2**	**0**	**1**	**0**	**1095**

Going: Sf: 0-2 GS: 0-0 Gd: 0-0 GF: - Fm: 0-0
Distance: 2m/2m3: 0-1 2m4-2m7: 0-1 3m+: 0-0
Track: LH: 0-0 RH: 0-1 Tight: 0-2 Gall: 0-0
Aids: Bl: 0-0 Vi: 0-0 Tstrap: 0-0
Best Rating: 121 3/02 Font 2m4f soft Hdl

Fair staying handicapper on the level. Shaped with promise when just tapped for toe on his debut over timber by Triumph Hurdle favourite, Londoner, on soft ground. Fell when challenging next time.

Dancing Brook

7-y-o ch g Jasoor-Millbrook Rose (Meadowbrook)
W Storey Mrs E Hall

Placings: *00*P (1927)
2001/02: 17^{0}GS, 17^{0}GS, 22^{P}G

	Starts	1st	2nd	3rd	Win & Pl

	Starts	1st	2nd	3rd	Win & Pl
NH Flat	2	0	0	0	0
Hurdles	1	0	0	0	0
Career Total	3	0	0	0	

Going: Sf: 0-0 GS: 0-2 Gd: 0-1 GF: - Fm: 0-0
Distance: 2m/2m3: 0-2 2m4-2m7: 0-1 3m+: 0-0
Track: LH: 0-2 RH: 0-1 Tight: 0-2 Gall: 0-0
Aids: Bl: 0-0 Vi: 0-0 Tstrap: 0-0
Best Rating:

Dancing Dervish

74

7-y-o b g Shareef Dancer (USA)-Taj Victory (Final Straw)
D Burchell Vivian Guy

Placings:0P042/35506440U006/3400444033-P (0122)
2001/02: 19^{PF}

	Starts	1st	2nd	3rd	Win & Pl
Hurdles	1	0	0	0	
Career Total	28	0	1	4	2555

Going: Sf: 0-0 GS: 0-0 Gd: 0-0 GF: - Fm: 0-1
Distance: 2m/2m3: 0-0 2m4-2m7: 0-1 3m+: 0-0
Track: LH: 0-0 RH: 0-1 Tight: 0-1 Gall: 0-0
Aids: Bl: 0-0 Vi: 0-1 Tstrap: 0-0
Best Rating: 85 5/99 Strf 2m110y good Hdl

Dancing Dill

90

7-y-o b m Dancing High-Some Shiela (Remainder Man)
N G Richards J R Jeffreys

Placings:3/3624-P (0273)
2001/02: 20^{PGF}

	Starts	1st	2nd	3rd	Win & Pl
Hurdles	1	0	0	0	
Career Total	6	0	1	2	1754

Going: Sf: 0-0 GS: 0-0 Gd: 0-0 GF: - Fm: 0-1
Distance: 2m/2m3: 0-0 2m4-2m7: 0-1 3m+: 0-0
Track: LH: 0-0 RH: 0-1 Tight: 0-0 Gall: 0-0
Aids: Bl: 0-0 Vi: 0-0 Tstrap: 0-0
Best Rating: 90 5/01 Prth 2m4f110y gd-fm Hdl

Dancing Fosenby

(88h) (66h)52

6-y-o b g Terimon-Wave Dancer (Dance In Time (CAN))
D McCain D McCain

Placings:4PP0043 (4640)
2001/02: 17^{4}G, 16^{P}S, 16^{P}GS, 17^{0}HY, 16^{0}S, 17^{4}S, 16^{3}G

	Starts	1st	2nd	3rd	Win & Pl
Hurdles	7	0	0	1	500
Career Total	7	0	0	1	500

Going: Sf: 0-4 GS: 0-1 Gd: 0-2 GF: - Fm: 0-0
Distance: 2m/2m3: 0-7 2m4-2m7: 0-0 3m+: 0-0
Track: LH: 0-5 RH: 0-2 Tight: 0-4 Gall: 0-1
Aids: Bl: 0-3 Vi: 0-0 Tstrap: 0-0
Best Rating: 66 4/02 Ludl 2m good Hdl

Dancing King (IRE)

72 33

6-y-o b g Fairy King (USA)-Zariysha (IRE) (Darshaan)
P W Hiatt P W Hiatt

Placings:F-0 (1624)
2001/02: 16^{0}GF

	Starts	1st	2nd	3rd	Win & Pl
Hurdles	1	0	0	0	
Career Total	2	0	0	0	

Going: Sf: 0-0 GS: 0-0 Gd: 0-0 GF: - Fm: 0-1
Distance: 2m/2m3: 0-1 2m4-2m7: 0-0 3m+: 0-0
Track: LH: 0-0 RH: 0-1 Tight: 0-0 Gall: 0-0
Aids: Bl: 0-0 Vi: 0-0 Tstrap: 0-0
Best Rating: 33 10/01 Ludl 2m gd-fm Hdl

Dancing Kris

9-y-o b g Kris-Liska's Dance (USA) (Riverman (USA))
Ian Williams Paul Robson

Placings:040/0-0 (2069)
2001/02: 16^{0}G

	Starts	1st	2nd	3rd	Win & Pl
Hurdles	1	0	0	0	
Career Total	5	0	0	0	0

Going: Sf: 0-0 GS: 0-0 Gd: 0-1 GF: - Fm: 0-0
Distance: 2m/2m3: 0-1 2m4-2m7: 0-0 3m+: 0-0
Track: LH: 0-0 RH: 0-1 Tight: 0-0 Gall: 0-1
Aids: Bl: 0-0 Vi: 0-0 Tstrap: 0-0
Best Rating: 90 2/00 Newc 2m soft Hdl

Dancing Lady

6-y-o b m Dancing High-Lady's Island (IRE) (Over The River (FR))
J I A Charlton Sydney Ramsey & Partners

Placings:0-000 (4198)
2001/02: 16^{0}GS, 16^{0}S, 21^{0}S

	Starts	1st	2nd	3rd	Win & Pl
NH Flat	2	0	0	0	0
Hurdles	1	0	0	0	0
Career Total	4	0	0	0	

Going: Sf: 0-2 GS: 0-1 Gd: 0-0 GF: - Fm: 0-0
Distance: 2m/2m3: 0-2 2m4-2m7: 0-1 3m+: 0-0
Track: LH: 0-2 RH: 0-0 Tight: 0-1 Gall: 0-0
Aids: Bl: 0-0 Vi: 0-0 Tstrap: 0-1
Best Rating: 48 4/01 MRas 2m1f110y heavy NHF

Dancing Laird

105(95h) 123

10-y-o ch g Scottish Reel-Well Connected (Bold And Free)
K C Bailey A N Solomons

Placings:4/15/3/00-224 (2940)
2001/02: 20^{2}S, 20^{2}GS, 22^{4}G

	Starts	1st	2nd	3rd	Win & Pl
Chases	3	0	2	0	2881
Career Total	9	1	2	1	5731

108	11/98	Wind	2m	E Hdl	G-S	£2530

Total win prize-money £2530

Going: Sf: 0-1 GS: 0-1 Gd: 0-1 GF: - Fm: 0-0
Distance: 2m/2m3: 0-0 2m4-2m7: 0-3 3m+: 0-0
Track: LH: 0-2 RH: 0-1 Tight: 0-2 Gall: 0-1
Aids: Bl: 0-0 Vi: 0-0 Tstrap: 0-0
Best Rating: 123 11/01 Strf 2m4f soft Ch

Fair hurdler/novice chaser, stays two miles four furlongs and acts on good to soft ground.

Dancing Ledge (IRE)

9-y-o ch g Over The River (FR)-The Hogget (Cheval)
C R Millington J R Millington

Placings:0/P (0641)
2001/02: 24^{P}GF

	Starts	1st	2nd	3rd	Win & Pl
Hurdles	1	0	0	0	
Career Total	2	0	0	0	

Going: Sf: 0-0 GS: 0-0 Gd: 0-0 GF: - Fm: 0-1
Distance: 2m/2m3: 0-0 2m4-2m7: 0-0 3m+: 0-1
Track: LH: 0-0 RH: 0-1 Tight: 0-1 Gall: 0-0
Aids: Bl: 0-0 Vi: 0-0 Tstrap: 0-0
Best Rating: 47 7/99 Leop 2m4f gd-fm NHF

Dancing Paddy

96 88

14-y-o b g Nordance (USA)-Ninotchka (Niniski (USA))
K O Cunningham-Brown Bychance Racing

Placings:4211F3003/330241F01/51103/5041F3421/2342003/31F2044/2P6/0465241/455P/P435-056 **(2711)**
2001/02: 20^{0}GF, 20^{5}HY, 16^{6}HY

	Starts	1st	2nd	3rd	Win & Pl
Hurdles	3	0	0	0	0
Career Total	67	10	8	10	113287

109	3/99	Font	2m2f110y	E(0-115)HHdl	SFT	£5251
149	12/96	Chel	2m110y	B HCh	G-F	£6714
151	4/95	Ayr	2m	A Ch	G-F	£13736
150	2/95	Asct	2m	C Ch	SFT	£10016
140	3/94	Newb	2m110y	HHdl	GD	£5952
137	1/94	Chel	2m1f	(0-145)HHdl	SFT	£4926
130	4/93	Asct	2m110y	HHdl	HVY	£5106
130	1/93	Chel	2m1f	(0-135)HHdl	SFT	£3752
129	1/92	Font	2m2f	Hdl	G-S	£1165
122	1/92	NAbb	2m150y	Hdl	SFT	£1362

Total win prize-money £57983

Going: Sf: 0-2 GS: 0-0 Gd: 0-0 GF: - Fm: 0-1
Distance: 2m/2m3: 0-1 2m4-2m7: 0-2 3m+: 0-0
Track: LH: 0-1 RH: 0-2 Tight: 0-0 Gall: 0-0
Aids: Bl: 0-0 Vi: 0-0 Tstrap: 0-3
Best Rating: 151 4/95 Ayr 2m gd-fm Ch

Dancing Pearl

100f 106f

4-y-o ch f Dancing Spree (USA)-Elegant Rose (Noalto)
C J Price J E Heymans

Placings:344 (4823)
2001/02: 16^{3}G, 16^{4}G, 17^{4}G

	Starts	1st	2nd	3rd	Win & Pl
NH Flat	3	0	0	1	1684
Career Total	3	0	0	1	1684

Going: Sf: 0-0 GS: 0-0 Gd: 0-3 GF: - Fm: 0-0
Distance: 2m/2m3: 0-3 2m4-2m7: 0-0 3m+: 0-0
Track: LH: 0-2 RH: 0-1 Tight: 0-0 Gall: 0-1
Aids: Bl: 0-0 Vi: 0-0 Tstrap: 0-0
Best Rating: 106 4/02 Chel 2m1f good NHF

Half-sister to useful sprinter Bowden Rose, she has shown some ability in bumpers.

Dancing Phantom

7-y-o b g Darshaan-Dancing Prize (IRE) (Sadler's Wells (USA))
M W Easterby Bernard Bargh & John Walsh

Placings:1/0-P (2318)
2001/02: 20^{P}GS

	Starts	1st	2nd	3rd	Win & Pl
Hurdles	1	0	0	0	
Career Total	**3**	**1**	**0**	**0**	**3168**

127	11/99	Weth	2m	D Hdl	GD	£3168

Total win prize-money £3168

Going: Sf: 0-0 GS: 0-1 Gd: 0-0 GF: - Fm: 0-0
Distance: 2m/2m3: 0-0 2m4-2m7: 0-1 3m+: 0-0
Track: LH: 0-1 RH: 0-0 Tight: 0-1 Gall: 0-0
Aids: Bl: 0-0 Vi: 0-0 Tstrap: 0-0
Best Rating: 127 11/99 Weth 2m good Hdl

He won on his debut over hurdles in 1999 but has been lightly raced since, both on the Flat and over the sticks.

Dancing Shirley

86f 80f

4-y-o b f Dancing Spree (USA)-High Heather (Shirley Heights)
T P McGovern T P McGovern

Placings:40 (4552)
2001/02: 16^{4}GF, 16^{0}GF

	Starts	1st	2nd	3rd	Win & Pl
NH Flat	2	0	0	0	0
Career Total	**2**	**0**	**0**	**0**	**0**

Going: Sf: 0-0 GS: 0-0 Gd: 0-0 GF: - Fm: 0-2
Distance: 2m/2m3: 0-2 2m4-2m7: 0-0 3m+: 0-0
Track: LH: 0-0 RH: 0-2 Tight: 0-0 Gall: 0-2
Aids: Bl: 0-0 Vi: 0-0 Tstrap: 0-0
Best Rating: 80 3/02 Hntg 2m110y gd-fm NHF

Bred for speed rather than stamina. Showed ability on debut.

Dancing Shiva

105 94

7-y-o ch m Michelozzo (USA)-Royal Pam (Pamroy)
Simon Earle Graham Brown

Placings:4/2-13P (4480)
2001/02: 24^{1}S, 22^{3}GS, 22^{P}G

	Starts	1st	2nd	3rd	Win & Pl
Hurdles	3	1	0	1	4566
Career Total	**5**	**1**	**1**	**1**	**5672**

86	10/01	Towc	3m	D Hdl	SFT	£4108

Total win prize-money £4108

Going: Sf: 1-1 GS: 0-1 Gd: 0-1 GF: - Fm: 0-0
Distance: 2m/2m3: 0-0 2m4-2m7: 0-2 **3m+: 1-1**
Track: LH: 0-0 **RH: 1-1** Tight: 0-0 Gall: 0-0
Aids: Bl: 0-0 Vi: 0-0 Tstrap: 0-0
Best Rating: 100 11/00 Wwck 2m5f soft Hdl

An improving sort, she got off the mark at her third attempt in a fair novice hurdle at Towcester. Stays well.

Dande's Rambo

80 100

5-y-o gr g Rambo Dancer (CAN)-Kajetana (FR) (Caro)
P R Hedger Noel Cronin

Placings:5 (0102)
2001/02: 18^{5}GF

	Starts	1st	2nd	3rd	Win & Pl
Hurdles	1	0	0	0	0
Career Total	**1**	**0**	**0**	**0**	**0**

Going: Sf: 0-0 GS: 0-0 Gd: 0-0 GF: - Fm: 0-1
Distance: 2m/2m3: 0-1 2m4-2m7: 0-0 3m+: 0-0
Track: LH: 0-1 RH: 0-0 Tight: 0-1 Gall: 0-0
Aids: Bl: 0-0 Vi: 0-0 Tstrap: 0-0
Best Rating: 100 5/01 Font 2m2f110y gd-fm Hdl

Dandonell (IRE)

(102h) (94h)

8-y-o b g Ajraas (USA)-Courtown Bay (Don)
J C Tuck Mrs Erica Griffiths

Placings:0254/02P662/6-5115P01P3 (4733)
2001/02: 19^{5}G, 22^{1}F, 22^{1}GF, 22^{5}GF, 24^{P}GF, 22^{0}GF, 22^{1}GS, 24^{P}G, 24^{3}F

	Starts	1st	2nd	3rd	Win & Pl
Hurdles	9	3	0	1	9287
Career Total	**20**	**3**	**3**	**1**	**11277**

94	12/01	Extr	2m6f110y	E(0-115)HHdl	G-S	£3206
94	5/01	Font	2m6f110y	E(0-115)HHdl	G-F	£2534
82	5/01	Extr	2m6f110y	F(0-100)HHdl	FRM	£2716

Total win prize-money £8456

Going: Sf: 0-0 GS: 1-1 Gd: 0-2 GF: - Fm: 2-6
Distance: 2m/2m3: 0-1 **2m4-2m7: 3-5** 3m+: 0-3
Track: **LH: 1-3** RH: 0-3 **Tight: 1-2** Gall: 0-0
Aids: Bl: 0-0 Vi: 0-0 Tstrap: 0-0
Best Rating: 94 12/01 Extr 2m6f110y gd-sft Hdl

Three times successful at around two and three-quarter miles over hurdles including two wins at Exeter. Seems to act on anything but extremes of going.

Danea (FR)

8-y-o b m Ambroise (FR)-Dama Alpina (GER) (Alpenkonig (GER))
A G Juckes R T Juckes

Placings:P6P (1386)
2001/02: 16^{P}GS, 19^{6}GF, 16^{P}GF

	Starts	1st	2nd	3rd	Win & Pl
Hurdles	2	0	0	0	0
Chases	1	0	0	0	0
Career Total	**3**	**0**	**0**	**0**	**0**

Going: Sf: 0-0 GS: 0-1 Gd: 0-0 GF: - Fm: 0-2
Distance: 2m/2m3: 0-3 2m4-2m7: 0-0 3m+: 0-0
Track: LH: 0-3 RH: 0-0 Tight: 0-2 Gall: 0-0
Aids: Bl: 0-0 Vi: 0-1 Tstrap: 0-0
Best Rating:

Danegold (IRE)

104 133

10-y-o b g Danehill (USA)-Cistus (Sun Prince)
R T Phillips Graeme Love

Placings:0/2130/11P5P5200/031110000/60020/2P0P-024 (1389)
2001/02: 16^{0}G, 20^{2}GF, 24^{4}G

	Starts	1st	2nd	3rd	Win & Pl
Hurdles	3	0	1	0	945
Career Total	**35**	**6**	**5**	**2**	**35574**

142	9/98	Bang	2m1f	C(0-130)HHdl	GD	£4065
130	8/98	Font	2m2f110y	E(0-110)HHdl	G-F	£2320
118	8/98	Ctml	2m1f110y	D(0-120)HHdl	GD	£2804
126	10/97	Uttx	2m	D(0-120)HHdl	GD	£3347
120	9/97	Bang	2m1f	C(0-130)HHdl	GD	£3468
100	12/96	Wind	2m	E Hdl	GD	£2075

Total win prize-money £18080

Going: Sf: 0-0 GS: 0-0 Gd: 0-2 GF: - Fm: 0-1
Distance: 2m/2m3: 0-1 2m4-2m7: 0-1 3m+: 0-1
Track: LH: 0-3 RH: 0-0 Tight: 0-0 Gall: 0-0
Aids: Bl: 0-0 Vi: 0-0 Tstrap: 0-0
Best Rating: 144 1/01 Hayd 2m soft Hdl

He is capable but unpredictable. Best when held up behind a fast pace, he has yet to prove himself beyond two miles and is not one to rely on.

Danger Flynn (IRE)

61 10

12-y-o b g Boreen (FR)-Stramillian (Furry Glen)
Miss A M Newton-Smith E J Farrant

Placings:0/003005/3004040/405/01210/5F1314P/0PP00 (3602)
2001/02: 25^{0}S, 26^{P}GS, 25^{P}S, 21^{0}HY, 22^{0}HY

	Starts	1st	2nd	3rd	Win & Pl
Hurdles	3	0	0	0	0
Chases	2	0	0	0	0
Career Total	**34**	**4**	**1**	**3**	**14990**

123	1/99	Fknm	3m110y	D Ch	G-S	£3286
125	12/98	Towc	2m6f	D Ch	SFT	£3829
109	12/97	Towc	3m	E(0-115)HHdl	G-S	£2442
113	10/97	Strf	2m6f110y	E Hdl	GD	£2582

Total win prize-money £12141

Going: Sf: 0-4 GS: 0-1 Gd: 0-0 GF: - Fm: 0-0
Distance: 2m/2m3: 0-0 2m4-2m7: 0-2 3m+: 0-3
Track: LH: 0-2 RH: 0-1 Tight: 0-4 Gall: 0-0
Aids: Bl: 0-0 Vi: 0-1 Tstrap: 0-0
Best Rating: 125 12/98 Towc 2m6f soft Ch

Veteran, plating-class hurdler/chaser. Stays three miles. Best on an easy surface.

Dangerous Deploy

100 75

5-y-o b g Deploy-Emily-Mou (IRE) (Cadeaux Genereux)
Miss K M George A M Wellstead

Placings:40554-P4 (1906)
2001/02: 24^{P}GF, 22^{4}S

	Starts	1st	2nd	3rd	Win & Pl
Hurdles	2	0	0	0	0
Career Total	**7**	**0**	**0**	**0**	**235**

Going: Sf: 0-1 GS: 0-0 Gd: 0-0 GF: - Fm: 0-1
Distance: 2m/2m3: 0-0 2m4-2m7: 0-1 3m+: 0-1
Track: LH: 0-2 RH: 0-0 Tight: 0-1 Gall: 0-0
Aids: Bl: 0-0 Vi: 0-0 Tstrap: 0-0
Best Rating: 75 11/01 Strf 2m6f110y soft Hdl

Very moderate form at up to three miles over hurdles.

Daniavi (IRE)

4-y-o ch g Kris-Danishara (IRE) (Slew O'Gold (USA))
J A Glover (Sir Michael Stoute 27/6) P B A (skegness) Ltd

Placings:P (2531)
2001/02: 17^{P}S

	Starts	1st	2nd	3rd	Win & Pl
Hurdles	1	0	0	0	
Career Total	**1**	**0**	**0**	**0**	

Going: Sf: 0-1 GS: 0-0 Gd: 0-0 GF: - Fm: 0-0
Distance: 2m/2m3: 0-1 2m4-2m7: 0-0 3m+: 0-0
Track: LH: 0-0 RH: 0-1 Tight: 0-1 Gall: 0-0
Aids: Bl: 0-0 Vi: 0-0 Tstrap: 0-0
Best Rating:

Daniel Deronda

8-y-o b g Danehill (USA)-Kilvarnet (Furry Glen)
Jean-Rene Auvray Lambourn Racing Limited

Placings:P (4548)
2001/02: 21^{P}GF

	Starts	1st	2nd	3rd	Win & Pl
Hurdles	1	0	0	0	
Career Total	**1**	**0**	**0**	**0**	

Going: Sf: 0-0 GS: 0-0 Gd: 0-0 GF: - Fm: 0-1
Distance: 2m/2m3: 0-0 2m4-2m7: 0-1 3m+: 0-0
Track: LH: 0-0 RH: 0-1 Tight: 0-0 Gall: 0-1
Aids: Bl: 0-0 Vi: 0-0 Tstrap: 0-0
Best Rating:

Danka

69 40
8-y-o gr g Petong-Angel Drummer (Dance In Time (CAN))
J C Fox S J V Construction

Placings:06P (2560)
2001/02: 19^{0}G, 16^{6}S, 20^{P}S

	Starts	1st	2nd	3rd	Win & Pl
Hurdles	3	0	0	0	0
Career Total	**3**	**0**	**0**	**0**	**0**

Going: Sf: 0-2 GS: 0-0 Gd: 0-1 GF: - Fm: 0-0
Distance: 2m/2m3: 0-2 2m4-2m7: 0-1 3m+: 0-0
Track: LH: 0-2 RH: 0-1 Tight: 0-0 Gall: 0-1
Aids: Bl: 0-0 Vi: 0-0 Tstrap: 0-0
Best Rating: 40 11/01 Towc 2m soft Hdl

Dannicus

11-y-o b g Derrylin-Kerris Melody (Furry Glen)
R Barber (Trainer Unknown 24/3) D A Shone

Placings:0/30**P0**/P/P (4735)
2001/02: 23^{P}F

	Starts	1st	2nd	3rd	Win & Pl
Chases	1	0	0	0	
Career Total	**7**	**0**	**0**	**1**	**389**

Going: Sf: 0-0 GS: 0-0 Gd: 0-0 GF: - Fm: 0-1
Distance: 2m/2m3: 0-0 2m4-2m7: 0-0 3m+: 0-1
Track: LH: 0-0 RH: 0-1 Tight: 0-0 Gall: 0-0
Aids: Bl: 0-0 Vi: 0-0 Tstrap: 0-0
Best Rating: 89 12/96 Chep 2m110y soft Hdl

Danny Deever

77 47
6-y-o b g Deploy-Yes (Blakeney)
Mrs T M Gibson Mrs T M Gibson

Placings:55/045 (0801)
2001/02: 16^{0}F, 16^{4}GF, 20^{6}GF

	Starts	1st	2nd	3rd	Win & Pl
Hurdles	3	0	0	0	0
Career Total	**5**	**0**	**0**	**0**	**0**

Going: Sf: 0-0 GS: 0-0 Gd: 0-0 GF: - Fm: 0-3
Distance: 2m/2m3: 0-2 2m4-2m7: 0-1 3m+: 0-0
Track: LH: 0-1 RH: 0-2 Tight: 0-0 Gall: 0-0
Aids: Bl: 0-0 Vi: 0-0 Tstrap: 0-0
Best Rating: 63 9/99 Hntg 2m110y good Hdl

Danny Gale (IRE)

65
11-y-o b g Strong Gale-Mary The Rake (On Your Mark)
R Williams R Williams

Placings:0P6P/1P0040/**05PBPP** (1354)
2001/02: 16^{0}G, 16^{5}G, 16^{P}GF, 24^{B}GF, 23^{P}G, 21^{P}GF

	Starts	1st	2nd	3rd	Win & Pl
Chases	6	0	0	0	0
Career Total	**16**	**1**	**0**	**0**	**2675**

78	9/96	Bang	2m1f	E Hdl	GD	£2472

Total win prize-money £2472

Going: Sf: 0-0 GS: 0-0 Gd: 0-3 GF: - Fm: 0-3
Distance: 2m/2m3: 0-3 2m4-2m7: 0-1 3m+: 0-2
Track: LH: 0-5 RH: 0-1 Tight: 0-3 Gall: 0-0
Aids: Bl: 0-0 Vi: 0-0 Tstrap: 0-5
Best Rating: 78 9/96 Bang 2m1f good Hdl

Dante's Cavalier (IRE)

107 134
12-y-o b g Phardante (FR)-Ring Road (Giolla Mear)
D R Gandolfo M A Dore

Placings:311/22142/**3243211F**/132231021/2230/4-360 (0776)
2001/02: 17^{3}G, 20^{6}G, 20^{0}GF

	Starts	1st	2nd	3rd	Win & Pl
Chases	3	0	0	1	743
Career Total	**33**	**8**	**10**	**7**	**61332**

137	4/99	Chel	2m110y	C(0-135)HCh	GD	£8904
135	2/99	Sand	2m	B(0-145)HCh	GD	£7966
130	11/98	Font	2m2f	D(0-125)HCh	SFT	£3667
125	3/98	Sand	2m	D(0-125)HCh	GD	£4045
126	3/98	Hntg	2m4f110y	E Ch	SFT	£3133
110	12/96	Folk	2m6f110y	F Hdl	G-S	£2411
114	4/95	Aint	2m110y	A NHF	G-F	£7005
108	3/95	Folk	2m1f110y	H NHF	HVY	£1287

Total win prize-money £38421

Going: Sf: 0-0 GS: 0-0 Gd: 0-2 GF: - Fm: 0-1
Distance: 2m/2m3: 0-1 2m4-2m7: 0-2 3m+: 0-0
Track: LH: 0-2 RH: 0-1 Tight: 0-0 Gall: 0-0
Aids: Bl: 0-0 Vi: 0-0 Tstrap: 0-0
Best Rating: 137 12/99 Asct 2m gd-sft Ch

Useful two-mile chaser on his day who goes best on goodish ground but now at the veteran stage. Has slipped down the handicap and been tried over longer trips.

Danteco

97(104h) (94+h)104+
7-y-o gr g Phardante (FR)-Up Cooke (Deep Run)
Miss Kate Milligan Mrs J M L Milligan

Placings:3/6056-P00 (2316)
2001/02: 20^{P}G, 20^{0}G, 20^{0}GS

	Starts	1st	2nd	3rd	Win & Pl
Hurdles	3	0	0	0	
Career Total	**8**	**0**	**0**	**1**	**223**

Going: Sf: 0-0 GS: 0-1 Gd: 0-2 GF: - Fm: 0-0
Distance: 2m/2m3: 0-0 2m4-2m7: 0-3 3m+: 0-0
Track: LH: 0-3 RH: 0-0 Tight: 0-2 Gall: 0-1
Aids: Bl: 0-0 Vi: 0-0 Tstrap: 0-0
Best Rating: 97 12/00 Muss 2m good NHF

Dantes Inpharno (IRE)

81(91c) 54
8-y-o b g Phardante (FR)-Cacador's Magnet (China Town)
H D Daly Mrs A L Wood

Placings:3003F0/0**66-P0** (0587)
2001/02: 19^{P}G, 16^{0}GF

	Starts	1st	2nd	3rd	Win & Pl
Hurdles	2	0	0	0	
Career Total	**11**	**0**	**0**	**2**	**614**

Going: Sf: 0-0 GS: 0-0 Gd: 0-1 GF: - Fm: 0-1
Distance: 2m/2m3: 0-2 2m4-2m7: 0-0 3m+: 0-0
Track: LH: 0-2 RH: 0-0 Tight: 0-1 Gall: 0-0
Aids: Bl: 0-1 Vi: 0-1 Tstrap: 0-0
Best Rating: 101 10/99 Bang 2m1f soft NHF

Dantes Venture (IRE)

89f 87f
5-y-o b g Phardante (FR)-Fast Adventure (Deep Run)
D J Caro Mrs J F Billington

Placings:005 (4571)
2001/02: 16^{0}G, 17^{0}GS, 16^{5}G

	Starts	1st	2nd	3rd	Win & Pl
NH Flat	3	0	0	0	0
Career Total	**3**	**0**	**0**	**0**	**0**

Going: Sf: 0-0 GS: 0-1 Gd: 0-2 GF: - Fm: 0-0
Distance: 2m/2m3: 0-3 2m4-2m7: 0-0 3m+: 0-0
Track: LH: 0-1 RH: 0-2 Tight: 0-1 Gall: 0-1
Aids: Bl: 0-0 Vi: 0-0 Tstrap: 0-0
Best Rating: 87 12/01 Newb 2m110y good NHF

Dantie Boy (IRE)

105 110
6-y-o br g Phardante (FR)-Ballybride Gale (IRE) (Strong Gale)
P J Hobbs Mrs Anona Taylor

Placings:521 (4861)
2001/02: 19^{5}S, 19^{2}G, 22^{1}F

	Starts	1st	2nd	3rd	Win & Pl
Hurdles	3	1	1	0	3884
Career Total	**3**	**1**	**1**	**0**	**3884**

109	4/02	Extr	2m6f110y	E Hdl	FRM	£3071

Total win prize-money £3072

Going: Sf: 0-1 GS: 0-0 Gd: 0-1 GF: - Fm: 1-1
Distance: 2m/2m3: 0-1 **2m4-2m7: 1-2** 3m+: 0-0
Track: LH: 0-0 RH: 0-2 Tight: 0-1 Gall: 0-0
Aids: Bl: 0-0 Vi: 0-0 Tstrap: 0-0
Best Rating: 110 3/02 Extr 2m3f good Hdl

Stepped up in trip when overcoming novicey jumping to win 22 furlong novice hurdle on fast ground at Exeter April 2002.

Danyerman

83 **95**

9-y-o ch g Sylvan Express-Janie-O (Hittite Glory)

J M Jefferson P Nelson

Placings:*20/1*/P5-63F **(2051)**

2001/02: 20^{6}G, 20^{3}S, 20^{F}S

	Starts	1st	2nd	3rd	Win & Pl
Hurdles	3	0	0	1	373
Career Total	**8**	**1**	**1**	**1**	**2642**

101	5/98	Uttx	2m	H NHF	G-S	£1826

Total win prize-money £1826

Going: Sf: 0-2 GS: 0-0 Gd: 0-1 GF: - Fm: 0-0
Distance: 2m/2m3: 0-0 2m4-2m7: 0-3 3m+: 0-0
Track: LH: 0-1 RH: 0-0 Tight: 0-1 Gall: 0-0
Aids: Bl: 0-0 Vi: 0-0 Tstrap: 0-0
Best Rating: 123 2/98 Hayd 2m good NHF

Danzante (IRE)

88(63h) **32**

10-y-o b g Ajraas (USA)-Baliana (CAN) (Riverman (USA))

B G Powell G Irlam

Placings: *1*6P5/00360P0P**4**/**P224P2**/**3P**0**P**23PP2/P**0P**
3312130-P0**0P** **(1443)**

2001/02: 22^{P}GF, 26^{0}GF, 25^{0}G, 26^{P}GF

	Starts	1st	2nd	3rd	Win & Pl
Hurdles	2	0	0	0	0
Chases	2	0	0	0	0
Career Total	**42**	**3**	**6**	**6**	**12486**

85	10/00	Hntg	3m2f	F(0-110)HHdl	G-F	£1806
80	9/00	Worc	3m	E(0-105)HHdl	G-F	£2785
	11/96	Wwck	2m	H NHF	G-F	£1364

Total win prize-money £5955

Going: Sf: 0-0 GS: 0-0 Gd: 0-1 GF: - Fm: 0-3
Distance: 2m/2m3: 0-0 2m4-2m7: 0-1 3m+: 0-3
Track: LH: 0-2 RH: 0-1 Tight: 0-2 Gall: 0-1
Aids: Bl: 0-1 Vi: 0-3 Tstrap: 0-0
Best Rating: 85 10/00 Hntg 3m2f gd-fm Hdl

Danzas

78 **45**

8-y-o b g Polish Precedent (USA)-Dancing Rocks (Green Dancer (USA))

J M Bradley Martyn James, Pete Smith, Neil Jenkins

Placings:006P0/0/0 **(1405)**

2001/02: 16^{0}GF

	Starts	1st	2nd	3rd	Win & Pl
Hurdles	1	0	0	0	
Career Total	**7**	**0**	**0**	**0**	**0**

Going: Sf: 0-0 GS: 0-0 Gd: 0-0 GF: - Fm: 0-1
Distance: 2m/2m3: 0-1 2m4-2m7: 0-0 3m+: 0-0
Track: LH: 0-1 RH: 0-0 Tight: 0-0 Gall: 0-0
Aids: Bl: 0-0 Vi: 0-0 Tstrap: 0-0
Best Rating: 71 10/98 Strf 2m110y good Hdl

Danzig Dancer (IRE)

101 **98**

4-y-o b g Barathea (IRE)-Blueberry Walk (Green Desert (USA))

C A Dwyer (K F O'Brien 6/12) Mrs Shelley Dwyer

Placings:5006002F **(4169)**

2001/02: 16^{5}HY, 16^{0}SH, 16^{0}Y, 16^{6}S, 16^{0}HY, 17^{0}GS, 21^{2}GS, 21^{F}GS

	Starts	1st	2nd	3rd	Win & Pl
Hurdles	8	0	1	0	568
Career Total	**8**	**0**	**1**	**0**	**568**

Going: Sf: 0-3 GS: 0-3 Gd: 0-0 GF: - Fm: 0-0
Distance: 2m/2m3: 0-6 2m4-2m7: 0-2 3m+: 0-0
Track: LH: 0-1 RH: 0-5 Tight: 0-2 Gall: 0-0
Aids: Bl: 0-1 Vi: 0-0 Tstrap: 0-1
Best Rating: 98 11/01 Punc 2m soft Hdl

One-time fairly useful hurdler in Ireland, now only plating-class.

Danzig Flyer (IRE)

90 **65**

7-y-o b g Roi Danzig (USA)-Fenland Express (IRE) (Reasonable (FR))

M Mullineaux Mrs Renee Farrington-Kirkham

Placings:000/6P0/600 **(2134)**

2001/02: 19^{6}GS, 16^{0}S, 21^{0}GF

	Starts	1st	2nd	3rd	Win & Pl
Hurdles	3	0	0	0	0
Career Total	**9**	**0**	**0**	**0**	**0**

Going: Sf: 0-1 GS: 0-1 Gd: 0-0 GF: - Fm: 0-1
Distance: 2m/2m3: 0-1 2m4-2m7: 0-2 3m+: 0-0
Track: LH: 0-1 RH: 0-2 Tight: 0-1 Gall: 0-0
Aids: Bl: 0-0 Vi: 0-0 Tstrap: 0-0
Best Rating: 65 11/01 Strf 2m110y soft Hdl

Danzig Island (IRE)

107(110h) (101h)**111**

11-y-o b g Roi Danzig (USA)-Island Morn (USA) (Our Native (USA))

Mrs H Dalton Mrs S Barber And A B Wood

Placings:443/15013/0**F**/**2P**0P/**2**13/P1-2**010125** **(4738)**

2001/02: 20^{2}G, 25^{0}G, 20^{1}G, 25^{0}G, 20^{1}S, 21^{2}G, 24^{5}GF

	Starts	1st	2nd	3rd	Win & Pl
Hurdles	1	0	1	0	744
Chases	6	2	1	0	8850
Career Total	**26**	**6**	**4**	**3**	**23388**

111	3/02	Leic	2m4f110y	E(0-110)HCh	SFT	£3318
104	6/01	Worc	2m4f110y	D(0-110)HCh	GD	£4290
101	4/01	Weth	2m7f	G(0-90)HHdl	G-S	£2744
101	3/00	Plum	3m1f110y	F(0-100)HHdl	GD	£2268
103	2/96	Ludl	2m5f110y	E Hdl	GD	£2542
96	11/95	Nott	2m5f110y	E Hdl	G-F	£2461

Total win prize-money £17623

Going: Sf: 1-1 GS: 0-0 Gd: 1-5 GF: - Fm: 0-1
Distance: 2m/2m3: 0-0 **2m4-2m7: 2-4** 3m+: 0-3
Track: LH: 1-4 RH: 1-3 Tight: 0-3 Gall: 0-0
Aids: Bl: 0-0 Vi: 0-2 Tstrap: 0-0
Best Rating: 111 3/02 Leic 2m4f110y soft Ch

Winning handicapper over fences on good to soft ground. Has won over three miles, but looks best suited to two and a half of late, particularly when given an uncontested lead. Has had a patchy career due to a series of different injuries, and connections believe he is a horse for a summer campaign.

Dapper Look (NZ)

65 **34**

6-y-o b g Kaaptive Edition (NZ)-Impeccable (NZ) (Palatable (USA))

P R Webber The Alchemists

Placings:0P0 **(4867)**

2001/02: 20^{0}GF, 16^{P}S, 16^{0}GF

	Starts	1st	2nd	3rd	Win & Pl
Hurdles	3	0	0	0	
Career Total	**3**	**0**	**0**	**0**	

Going: Sf: 0-1 GS: 0-0 Gd: 0-0 GF: - Fm: 0-2
Distance: 2m/2m3: 0-2 2m4-2m7: 0-1 3m+: 0-0
Track: LH: 0-3 RH: 0-0 Tight: 0-0 Gall: 0-0
Aids: Bl: 0-0 Vi: 0-0 Tstrap: 0-0
Best Rating: 35 4/02 Weth 2m gd-fm Hdl

Darak (IRE)

92 **81**

6-y-o b g Doyoun-Dararita (IRE) (Halo (USA))

Ferdy Murphy The Ferdy Murphy Racing Club

Placings:0000150F-40000 **(2510)**

2001/02: 16^{4}GF, 16^{0}GS, 17^{0}G, 17^{0}S, 16^{0}S

	Starts	1st	2nd	3rd	Win & Pl
Hurdles	5	0	0	0	
Career Total	**13**	**1**	**0**	**0**	**3299**

92	8/00	Ctml	2m1f110y	G(0-90)HHdl	G-S	£3298

Total win prize-money £3299

Going: Sf: 0-2 GS: 0-1 Gd: 0-1 GF: - Fm: 0-1
Distance: 2m/2m3: 0-5 2m4-2m7: 0-0 3m+: 0-0
Track: LH: 0-4 RH: 0-1 Tight: 0-3 Gall: 0-0
Aids: Bl: 0-0 Vi: 0-0 Tstrap: 0-0
Best Rating: 92 8/00 Ctml 2m1f110y gd-sft Hdl

Darakshan (IRE)

104(61c) **114**

10-y-o b g Akarad (FR)-Dafayna (Habitat)

D W P Arbuthnot Noel Cronin

Placings: *1301*/3223112/35025P/2/0/0**15F6**560P-**U**5011550413P **(3461)**

2001/02: 20^{U}GF, 20^{5}GF, 24^{0}GF, 21^{1}GS, 21^{1}G, 24^{5}F, 21^{5}S, 21^{0}G, 22^{4}GS, 21^{1}HY, 20^{3}S, 25^{P}HY

	Starts	1st	2nd	3rd	Win & Pl
Hurdles	11	3	0	1	7188
Chases	1	0	0	0	0
Career Total	**40**	**8**	**5**	**5**	**27870**

114	12/01	Towc	2m5f	F Hdl	HVY	£2352
108	10/01	Towc	2m5f	G Hdl	GD	£1995
108	9/01	Plum	2m5f	G(0-95)HHdl	G-S	£2394
124	5/00	Strf	2m1f110y	D Ch	G-F	£4238
111	3/97	Bang	2m1f	E Hdl	G-S	£2379
104	2/97	Bang	2m1f	E Hdl	GD	£2836
106	4/96	MRas	1m5f110y	H NHF	G-F	£1434
105	2/96	Punc	2m	NHF	Y-S	£3177

Total win prize-money £20806

Going: Sf: 1-4 GS: 1-2 Gd: 1-2 GF: - Fm: 0-4
Distance: 2m/2m3: 0-0 **2m4-2m7: 3-9** 3m+: 0-3
Track: LH: 1-5 **RH: 2-5 Tight: 1-2** Gall: 0-1
Aids: Bl: 0-0 Vi: 0-1 Tstrap: 0-0
Best Rating: 124 5/00 Strf 2m1f110y gd-fm Ch

A horse who has had his problems over the years, he won his first race for 15 months when taking a Plumpton seller in September 2001. Followed up in the same grade at Towcester the following month and in a claimer there in December. Does not want the ground too soft or too firm. Stays two miles five. Has worn sheepskin cheekpieces.

Daramsan (IRE)

95f **111f**

5-y-o br g Doyoun-Daralaka (IRE) (The Minstrel (CAN))

Denys Smith B Batey

Placings: *14-21* (0550)
2001/02: 16^{2}GF, 16^{1}GF

	Starts	1st	2nd	3rd	Win & Pl
NH Flat	2	1	1	0	2001
Career Total	**4**	**2**	**1**	**0**	**3688**

111	5/01	Newc	2m	H NHF	G-F	£1533
107	4/01	Muss	2m1f	H NHF	G-F	£1687

Total win prize-money £3220

Going: Sf: 0-0 GS: 0-0 Gd: 0-0 GF: - Fm: 1-2
Distance: **2m/2m3: 1-2** 2m4-2m7: 0-0 3m+: 0-0
Track: LH: 0-1 RH: 0-0 Tight: 0-0 Gall: 0-0
Aids: Bl: 0-0 Vi: 0-0 Tstrap: 0-0
Best Rating: **111** 5/01 Newc 2m gd-fm NHF

Twice a winner of bumpers on fast ground in the spring of 2001, but broke down on the Flat subsequently.

Darapour (IRE)

117 **139**

8-y-o b g Fairy King (USA)-Dawala (IRE) (Lashkari)
J J O'Neill (A P O'Brien 13/3) J P McManus

Placings:21034/64420/5404/202F-2311546P (4231)
2001/02: 16^{2}G, 16^{3}GF, 20^{1}GF, 16^{1}GY, 16^{5}S, 25^{4}G, 20^{6}YS, 21^{P}GS

	Starts	1st	2nd	3rd	Win & Pl
Hurdles	8	2	1	1	16876
Career Total	**26**	**3**	**5**	**2**	**37791**

118	8/01	Gway	2m	Hdl	G-Y	£6955
135	5/01	Clon	2m4f	Hdl	G-F	£4173
132	1/98	Leop	2m	Hdl	Y-S	£3573

Total win prize-money £14703

Going: Sf: 0-1 GS: 0-1 Gd: 0-2 GF: - Fm: 1-2
Distance: 2m/2m3: 1-4 2m4-2m7: 1-3 3m+: 0-1
Track: LH: 0-3 RH: 0-0 Tight: 0-0 Gall: 0-2
Aids: Bl: 0-0 Vi: 0-0 Tstrap: 0-0
Best Rating: **139** 11/01 Chel 3m1f110y good Hdl

A smart Irish hurdler. Not really big enough to jump fences, he stays well but does not find much off the bridle. Best with ease in the ground. Has won over two and two and a half miles.

Daraydan (IRE)

10-y-o b g Kahyasi-Delsy (FR) (Abdos)
M C Pipe Martin Pipe Racing Club

Placings:16130321/111400/11P506002/021153003/621-0 (0075)
2001/02: 24^{0}G

	Starts	1st	2nd	3rd	Win & Pl
Hurdles	1	0	0	0	
Career Total	**36**	**11**	**4**	**4**	**73348**

115	4/01	NAbb	3m3f	F Hdl	SFT	£2331
144	10/99	Chel	2m5f	B(0-145)HHdl	GD	£6911
140	6/99	Uttx	2m6f110y	B(0-140)HHdl	GD	£5771
110	7/98	Wolv	2m4f110y	E Ch	G-F	£2959
102	7/98	Worc	2m	E Ch	GD	£3345
151	12/97	Chel	2m4f110y	B Hdl	GD	£10260
125	11/97	Newb	2m5f	B Hdl	GD	£5344
151	10/97	Chel	2m5f	B(0-145)HHdl	G-F	£4751
135	4/97	Asct	2m4f	C Hdl	G-F	£3728
123	12/96	Chel	2m1f	C Hdl	G-F	£3810
119	11/96	Leic	2m	E Hdl	G-S	£2924

Total win prize-money £52138

Going: Sf: 0-0 GS: 0-0 Gd: 0-1 GF: - Fm: 0-0
Distance: 2m/2m3: 0-0 2m4-2m7: 0-0 3m+: 0-1
Track: LH: 0-0 RH: 0-1 Tight: 0-0 Gall: 0-0
Aids: Bl: 0-0 Vi: 0-0 Tstrap: 0-0
Best Rating: **151** 12/97 Chel 2m4f110y good Hdl

A useful staying hurdler in his prime, he now plies his trade in point-to-points. Stays very well. Probably effective on any ground nowadays, he is quirky and not one to place much faith in.

Darcy

96 **80**

8-y-o ch g Miswaki (USA)-Princess Accord (USA) (D'Accord (USA))
D C O'Brien Mrs S Harris

Placings:33525/04/441P-0FP4 (4169)
2001/02: 16^{0}G, 20^{F}S, 20^{P}S, 21^{4}GS

	Starts	1st	2nd	3rd	Win & Pl
Hurdles	3	0	0	0	0
Chases	1	0	0	0	0
Career Total	**15**	**1**	**1**	**2**	**5857**

105	1/01	Plum	2m5f	D(0-125)HHdl	SFT	£3269

Total win prize-money £3269

Going: Sf: 0-2 GS: 0-1 Gd: 0-1 GF: - Fm: 0-0
Distance: 2m/2m3: 0-1 2m4-2m7: 0-3 3m+: 0-0
Track: LH: 0-2 RH: 0-2 Tight: 0-3 Gall: 0-1
Aids: Bl: 0-0 Vi: 0-0 Tstrap: 0-0
Best Rating: **119** 12/97 Kemp 2m soft Hdl

A moderate handicap hurdler who scored a shock win at Plumpton in January 2001, but has shown little worthwhile form since. Stays two miles five. Acts on soft ground.

Darcy Dancer

69 **22**

5-y-o b g Be My Chief (USA)-Little White Star (Mill Reef (USA))
D J S Cosgrove J P Racing

Placings:00 (0365)
2001/02: 16^{0}GF, 19^{0}GF

	Starts	1st	2nd	3rd	Win & Pl
Hurdles	2	0	0	0	
Career Total	**2**	**0**	**0**	**0**	

Going: Sf: 0-0 GS: 0-0 Gd: 0-0 GF: - Fm: 0-2
Distance: 2m/2m3: 0-1 2m4-2m7: 0-1 3m+: 0-0
Track: LH: 0-2 RH: 0-0 Tight: 0-2 Gall: 0-0
Aids: Bl: 0-0 Vi: 0-0 Tstrap: 0-0
Best Rating: **22** 5/01 Ling 2m3f110y gd-fm Hdl

Darcy Jones

83 **85**

6-y-o br g Mahrajan-Small Brook (Brianston Zipper)
B R Millman Mrs Claire Jones

Placings:PP-50P (4051)
2001/02: 16^{5}GS, 17^{0}HY, 24^{P}G

	Starts	1st	2nd	3rd	Win & Pl
Hurdles	3	0	0	0	0
Career Total	**5**	**0**	**0**	**0**	**0**

Going: Sf: 0-1 GS: 0-1 Gd: 0-1 GF: - Fm: 0-0
Distance: 2m/2m3: 0-2 2m4-2m7: 0-0 3m+: 0-1
Track: LH: 0-0 RH: 0-3 Tight: 0-0 Gall: 0-0
Aids: Bl: 0-0 Vi: 0-0 Tstrap: 0-0
Best Rating: **85** 1/02 Winc 2m gd-sft Hdl

Dare

112 **112**

7-y-o b g Beveled (USA)-Run Amber Run (Run The Gantlet (USA))
R Lee (P D Evans 8/11) J E Potter

Placings:0P/014/2222266-0F211024 (4593)
2001/02: 16^{0}G, 16^{F}GF, 18^{2}GS, 16^{1}S, 17^{1}G, 17^{0}HY, 19^{2}G, 16^{4}G

	Starts	1st	2nd	3rd	Win & Pl
Hurdles	7	2	2	0	7655
Chases	1	0	0	0	0
Career Total	**20**	**3**	**7**	**0**	**14329**

107	11/01	NAbb	2m1f	F(0-110)HHdl	GD	£2569
112	11/01	Uttx	2m	F(0-110)HHdl	SFT	£2611
79	1/00	Wwck	2m	E(0-105)HHdl	SFT	£2870

Total win prize-money £8050

Going: Sf: 1-2 GS: 0-1 Gd: 1-4 GF: - Fm: 0-1
Distance: **2m/2m3: 2-7** 2m4-2m7: 0-1 3m+: 0-0
Track: **LH: 2-4** RH: 0-3 **Tight: 1-2** Gall: 0-1
Aids: Bl: 0-0 Vi: 0-3 **Tstrap: 2-7**
Best Rating: **112** 4/02 Uttx 2m good Hdl

A fair handicap hurdler at up to two and a half miles. Has won on good but prefers soft ground. Needs a strong pace.

Dargo

93 **50**

8-y-o b g Formidable (USA)-Mountain Memory (High Top)
D G Bridgwater The Rule Racing Syndicate

Placings:0/61336P/0 (0834)
2001/02: 27^{0}GF

	Starts	1st	2nd	3rd	Win & Pl
Hurdles	1	0	0	0	
Career Total	**8**	**1**	**0**	**2**	**4018**

116	6/99	Worc	2m4f	E Hdl	G-S	£2880

Total win prize-money £2880

Going: Sf: 0-0 GS: 0-0 Gd: 0-0 GF: - Fm: 0-1
Distance: 2m/2m3: 0-0 2m4-2m7: 0-0 3m+: 0-1
Track: LH: 0-1 RH: 0-0 Tight: 0-1 Gall: 0-0
Aids: Bl: 0-0 Vi: 0-0 Tstrap: 0-1
Best Rating: **116** 6/99 Worc 2m4f gd-sft Hdl

Daring King

69 **39**

12-y-o b g King Of Spain-Annacando (Derrylin)
Dr J R J Naylor Mrs S P Elphick

Placings:U/0625/43610641P/4P2P4P/6243P25/63040053/34P/0 (1105)
2001/02: 22^{0}G

	Starts	1st	2nd	3rd	Win & Pl
Hurdles	1	0	0	0	
Career Total	**39**	**2**	**4**	**5**	**10966**

93	3/96	Font	2m6f	E(0-115)HHdl	G-F	£2880
92	11/95	Font	2m6f	E(0-110)HHdl	SFT	£2343

Total win prize-money £5225

Going: Sf: 0-0 GS: 0-0 Gd: 0-1 GF: - Fm: 0-0
Distance: 2m/2m3: 0-0 2m4-2m7: 0-1 3m+: 0-0
Track: LH: 0-1 RH: 0-0 Tight: 0-1 Gall: 0-0
Aids: Bl: 0-0 Vi: 0-0 Tstrap: 0-0
Best Rating: **93** 3/96 Font 2m6f gd-fm Hdl

Daring Native (IRE)

9-y-o b/br g Be My Native (USA)-Scarlet Tina (Dusky Boy)
P J Millington (J Howard Johnson 3/2) P J Millington

Placings:000PP4/033-P (4569)
2001/02: 22^{P}G

	Starts	1st	2nd	3rd	Win & Pl
Chases	1	0	0	0	
Career Total	**10**	**0**	**0**	**2**	**1113**

Going: Sf: 0-0 GS: 0-0 Gd: 0-1 GF: - Fm: 0-0
Distance: 2m/2m3: 0-0 2m4-2m7: 0-1 3m+: 0-0
Track: LH: 0-0 RH: 0-1 Tight: 0-0 Gall: 0-0
Aids: Bl: 0-0 Vi: 0-1 Tstrap: 0-1
Best Rating: 92 2/01 Weth 3m1f soft Ch

Daring News

88 64

7-y-o b g Risk Me (FR)-Hot Sunday Sport (Star Appeal)
O O'Neill Michael J Brown

Placings:01U5/52/0P-6 (3449)
2001/02: 16^{6}GS

	Starts	1st	2nd	3rd	Win & Pl
Hurdles	1	0	0	0	0
Career Total	**9**	**1**	**1**	**0**	**2612**

83 3/99 Towc 2m G Hdl GD £1674
Total win prize-money £1674

Going: Sf: 0-0 GS: 0-1 Gd: 0-0 GF: - Fm: 0-0
Distance: 2m/2m3: 0-1 2m4-2m7: 0-0 3m+: 0-0
Track: LH: 0-1 RH: 0-0 Tight: 0-1 Gall: 0-0
Aids: Bl: 0-0 Vi: 0-0 Tstrap: 0-0
Best Rating: 89 6/99 Worc 2m4f gd-fm Hdl

Daring Thomas

93 96

7-y-o b g Derrylin-Dawn Encounter (Rymer)
Mark Campion Mr Barry & Dame Sheila Noakes

Placings:0455443-5 (0214)
2001/02: 22^{5}GF

	Starts	1st	2nd	3rd	Win & Pl
Hurdles	1	0	0	0	0
Career Total	**8**	**0**	**0**	**1**	**377**

Going: Sf: 0-0 GS: 0-0 Gd: 0-0 GF: - Fm: 0-1
Distance: 2m/2m3: 0-0 2m4-2m7: 0-1 3m+: 0-0
Track: LH: 0-0 RH: 0-1 Tight: 0-0 Gall: 0-0
Aids: Bl: 0-0 Vi: 0-0 Tstrap: 0-0
Best Rating: 96 4/01 Font 2m6f110y good Hdl

Daringly

101 95

13-y-o b g Daring March-Leylandia (Wolver Hollow)
Michael Appleby (M F Barraclough 10/2) Michael Appleby

Placings:0001503P0**P**40**4**/**UPF**24/P000**0P**/6**12**P/**4P**/5**P**/**P**PP00**4P6**/**P5605350-52234**0**P**0**5203P5P0** (4483)
2001/02: 18^{5}GF, 21^{2}GF, 25^{2}F, 20^{3}GF, 20^{4}GF, 22^{0}G, 25^{P}GF, 20^{0}G, 22^{5}GF, 26^{2}GF, 24^{0}GF, 20^{3}GF, 24^{P}GF, 22^{5}GS, 25^{P}G, 19^{0}G

	Starts	1st	2nd	3rd	Win & Pl
Hurdles	1	0	0	0	0
Chases	15	0	3	2	4210
Career Total	**64**	**2**	**5**	**4**	**13960**

86 6/96 MRas 2m6f110y D(0-105)HCh G-F £4107
76 11/93 Uttx 2m Hdl GD £1864
Total win prize-money £5972

Going: Sf: 0-0 GS: 0-1 Gd: 0-4 GF: - Fm: 0-11
Distance: 2m/2m3: 0-1 2m4-2m7: 0-9 3m+: 0-6
Track: LH: 0-6 RH: 0-5 Tight: 0-11 Gall: 0-1
Aids: Bl: 0-0 Vi: 0-0 Tstrap: 0-0
Best Rating: 95 8/01 Font 3m2f110y gd-fm Ch

Moderate, veteran chaser with a poor strike rate. Best on fast ground.

Dark Crusader (IRE)

93(105h) 95

7-y-o br g Cajetano (USA)-Glissade (Furry Glen)
Miss Lucinda V Russell Brahms & Liszt

Placings:42204P/4311PP-44PPP (4122)
2001/02: 22^{4}GS, 16^{4}S, 24^{P}HY, 24^{P}GS, 22^{P}HY

	Starts	1st	2nd	3rd	Win & Pl
Hurdles	1	0	0	0	0
Chases	4	0	0	0	554
Career Total	**17**	**2**	**2**	**1**	**7782**

118 12/00 Folk 2m4f110y E Hdl HVY £2621
118 11/00 Towc 2m5f E Hdl SFT £2275
Total win prize-money £4897

Going: Sf: 0-3 GS: 0-2 Gd: 0-0 GF: - Fm: 0-0
Distance: 2m/2m3: 0-1 2m4-2m7: 0-2 3m+: 0-2
Track: LH: 0-4 RH: 0-1 Tight: 0-2 Gall: 0-0
Aids: Bl: 0-1 Vi: 0-0 Tstrap: 0-0
Best Rating: 118 12/00 Folk 2m4f110y heavy Hdl

A modest hurdler/chaser he showed improved form once tackling two and a half miles plus, winning novice hurdles at Towcester and Folkestone in the winter of 2000. Has shown some ability over fences. Can be a bit of a moody customer and has worn blinkers. Likes to get his toe in.

Dark Fairy

107 118+

4-y-o br f Tragic Role (USA)-Sharp Fairy (Sharpo)
M C Pipe (P W D'Arcy 24/9) D A Johnson

Placings:12403 (4559)
2001/02: 17^{1}GS, 16^{2}G, 17^{4}HY, 16^{0}G, 16^{3}GF

	Starts	1st	2nd	3rd	Win & Pl
Hurdles	5	1	1	1	5194
Career Total	**5**	**1**	**1**	**1**	**5194**

106 10/01 Hrfd 2m1f E Hdl G-S £2593
Total win prize-money £2594

Going: Sf: 0-1 GS: 1-1 Gd: 0-2 GF: - Fm: 0-1
Distance: **2m/2m3: 1-5** 2m4-2m7: 0-0 3m+: 0-0
Track: LH: 0-2 **RH: 1-3** Tight: 0-1 Gall: 0-1
Aids: Bl: 0-0 Vi: 0-0 Tstrap: 0-0
Best Rating: 113 1/02 Chel 2m1f heavy Hdl

Bought for 21,000gns after winning a ten-furlong seller at Leicester in September 2001, she won on her hurdling debut at Hereford, but her limitations have been exposed subsequently. Landed an uncompetitive event when stepped up to 22 furlongs at Newton Abbot July 2002. Seems to handle most types of ground.

Dark Princess (IRE)

96 96

7-y-o b m Good Thyne (USA)-Gardamus (Pauper)
Miss Venetia Williams Kinnersley Optimists

Placings:5345 (3514)
2001/02: 17^{5}G, 20^{3}HY, 22^{4}S, 24^{5}S

	Starts	1st	2nd	3rd	Win & Pl
NH Flat	1	0	0	0	0
Hurdles	3	0	0	1	552
Career Total	**4**	**0**	**0**	**1**	**552**

Going: Sf: 0-3 GS: 0-0 Gd: 0-1 GF: - Fm: 0-0
Distance: 2m/2m3: 0-1 2m4-2m7: 0-2 3m+: 0-1
Track: LH: 0-1 RH: 0-3 Tight: 0-2 Gall: 0-0
Aids: Bl: 0-0 Vi: 0-0 Tstrap: 0-0
Best Rating: 96 12/01 Leic 2m4f110y heavy Hdl

Dark Romance (IRE)

13-y-o b m Sarab-Narnia (Le Moss)
Miss Z C Davison A A Goldson

Placings:4/30504/013553105625/3203P/052P600-PPPP (1840)
2001/02: 22^{P}GF, 17^{P}GF, 16^{P}G, 16^{P}S

	Starts	1st	2nd	3rd	Win & Pl
Hurdles	4	0	0	0	
Career Total	**34**	**2**	**3**	**5**	**10484**

102 2/99 Sand 2m110y E(0-115)HHdl GD £2918
101 11/98 Towc 2m E Hdl SFT £2512
Total win prize-money £5431

Going: Sf: 0-1 GS: 0-0 Gd: 0-1 GF: - Fm: 0-2
Distance: 2m/2m3: 0-3 2m4-2m7: 0-1 3m+: 0-0
Track: LH: 0-0 RH: 0-4 Tight: 0-0 Gall: 0-0
Aids: Bl: 0-0 Vi: 0-1 Tstrap: 0-0
Best Rating: 102 3/00 Towc 2m soft Hdl

Dark Shadows

106 99

7-y-o b g Machiavellian (USA)-Instant Desire (USA) (Northern Dancer)
W Storey D O Cremin

Placings:4020/066 (2683)
2001/02: 20^{0}G, 16^{6}GS, 16^{6}G

	Starts	1st	2nd	3rd	Win & Pl
Hurdles	3	0	0	0	0
Career Total	**7**	**0**	**1**	**0**	**496**

Going: Sf: 0-0 GS: 0-1 Gd: 0-2 GF: - Fm: 0-0
Distance: 2m/2m3: 0-2 2m4-2m7: 0-1 3m+: 0-0
Track: LH: 0-3 RH: 0-0 Tight: 0-0 Gall: 0-3
Aids: Bl: 0-0 Vi: 0-0 Tstrap: 0-0
Best Rating: 106 3/00 MRas 1m5f110y gd-fm NHF

Dark Shell (IRE)

111 135

7-y-o b g Darshaan-Grecian Urn (Ela-Mana-Mou)
N J Henderson Mr & Mrs John Poynton

Placings:210-040 (4939a)
2001/02: 17^{0}G, 16^{4}G, 20^{0}Y

	Starts	1st	2nd	3rd	Win & Pl
Hurdles	3	0	0	0	2000
Career Total	**6**	**1**	**1**	**0**	**5857**

130 3/01 Hntg 2m110y E Hdl SFT £2723
Total win prize-money £2723

Going: Sf: 0-0 GS: 0-0 Gd: 0-2 GF: - Fm: 0-0
Distance: 2m/2m3: 0-2 2m4-2m7: 0-1 3m+: 0-0
Track: LH: 0-2 RH: 0-1 Tight: 0-1 Gall: 0-1
Aids: Bl: 0-0 Vi: 0-0 Tstrap: 0-0
Best Rating: 135 4/02 Aint 2m110y good Hdl

Lightly-raced hurdler, was returning from a very long break when runner-up on his hurdling debut at Wincanton in 2001, before going one better next time at Huntington. Has been competing in hot handicaps since. Acts on a soft surface and suited by two miles.

Dark Silhouette (IRE)

13-y-o br g Good Thyne (USA)-Primrose Walk (Charlottown)
E Haddock E Haddock

Placings:0/0/3021/0/F2F/P0/5-UP (0232)
2001/02: 24^{U}GF, 21^{P}GF

	Starts	1st	2nd	3rd	Win & Pl
Hurdles	1	0	0	0	0
Chases	1	0	0	0	0
Career Total	**15**	**1**	**2**	**1**	**3553**

80	11/94	Hntg	2m5f110y	Hdl	GD	£1847

Total win prize-money £1847

Going: Sf: 0-0 GS: 0-0 Gd: 0-0 GF: - Fm: 0-2
Distance: 2m/2m3: 0-0 2m4-2m7: 0-1 3m+: 0-1
Track: LH: 0-1 RH: 0-1 Tight: 0-1 Gall: 0-1
Aids: Bl: 0-0 Vi: 0-2 Tstrap: 0-0
Best Rating: 81 11/94 MRas 2m3f110y good Hdl

Dark Society

99 87
4-y-o b g Imp Society (USA)-No Candles Tonight (Star Appeal)
A W Carroll (P W Harris 18/9) Group 1 Racing (1994) Ltd

Placings:26523023 (4915)
2001/02: 17^{2}GS, 16^{6}G, 17^{5}S, 16^{2}HY, 16^{3}HY, 16^{0}S, 17^{2}S, 17^{3}GF

	Starts	1st	2nd	3rd	Win & Pl
Hurdles	8	0	3	2	2192
Career Total	**8**	**0**	**3**	**2**	**2192**

Going: Sf: 0-5 GS: 0-1 Gd: 0-1 GF: - Fm: 0-1
Distance: 2m/2m3: 0-8 2m4-2m7: 0-0 3m+: 0-0
Track: LH: 0-5 RH: 0-3 Tight: 0-5 Gall: 0-1
Aids: Bl: 0-0 Vi: 0-0 Tstrap: 0-0
Best Rating: 87 2/02 Plum 2m heavy Hdl

Moderate two-mile hurdler. Can travel well in his races but tends to find little under pressure. Suited by soft ground.

Dark Stranger (FR)

106 151
11-y-o b g Iveday (FR)-Abeille Royale (USA) (Turn To Mars (USA))
M C Pipe Terry Neill

Placings:412F2/34P/11201P1/24P11U/03P3R4-25600032 (4913)
2001/02: 20^{2}GS, 20^{5}G, 25^{6}G, 24^{0}G, 24^{0}G, 20^{0}GS, 26^{3}GF, 29^{2}G

	Starts	1st	2nd	3rd	Win & Pl
Chases	8	0	2	1	32031
Career Total	**35**	**7**	**6**	**4**	**138323**

159	3/00	Chel	2m4f110y	B HCh	GD	£35750
145	2/00	Leic	2m4f110y	D(0-125)HCh	GD	£5135
150	4/99	Sand	2m4f110y	C HCh	GD	£13851
145	4/99	Asct	2m3f110y	C Ch	G-F	£6840
137	1/99	Ling	2m4f110y	D(0-110)HCh	HVY	£3794
133	1/99	Ludl	2m4f	F(0-100)HCh	G-S	£2450
114	2/96	Hayd	2m	D Hdl	SFT	£3235

Total win prize-money £71056

Going: Sf: 0-0 GS: 0-2 Gd: 0-5 GF: - Fm: 0-1
Distance: 2m/2m3: 0-0 2m4-2m7: 0-3 3m+: 0-5
Track: LH: 0-3 RH: 0-5 Tight: 0-0 Gall: 0-3
Aids: Bl: 0-8 Vi: 0-0 Tstrap: 0-0
Best Rating: 159 3/00 Chel 2m4f110y good Ch

Decent handicap chaser, he took the Mildmay of Flete at the 2000 Festival in first-time blinkers, but despite some fine efforts in decent races since, has not managed another victory. He did not enjoy the best of luck in either the 2000 and 2001 Grand Nationals. Ran really well to be second in the Attheraces Gold Cup in April 2002. Stays three and a half miles and appears to need top-of-the-ground these days. His best form in the past has tended to come after the turn of the year.

Dark'n Sharp (GER)

121 (110h) (101h) 161
7-y-o b g Sharpo-Daytona Beach (GER) (Konigsstuhl (GER))
R T Phillips Ascot Five Plus One

Placings:11316-**F2311** (4829)
2001/02: 16^{F}GS, 16^{2}S, 16^{3}G, 16^{1}G, 16^{1}G

	Starts	1st	2nd	3rd	Win & Pl
Chases	5	2	1	1	48263
Career Total	**10**	**5**	**1**	**2**	**63904**

142	4/02	Ayr	2m	C Ch	GD	£6191
161	4/02	Aint	2m	A HCh	GD	£34800
129	2/01	Newc	2m	B HHdl	HVY	£8329
125	12/00	Donc	2m110y	E Hdl	G-S	£2978
109	11/00	Newc	2m	D Hdl	G-S	£3016

Total win prize-money £55316

Going: Sf: 0-1 GS: 0-1 Gd: 2-3 GF: - Fm: 0-0
Distance: **2m/2m3: 2-5** 2m4-2m7: 0-0 3m+: 0-0
Track: **LH: 2-4** RH: 0-1 **Tight: 1-1** Gall: 0-3
Aids: Bl: 0-0 Vi: 0-0 Tstrap: 0-0
Best Rating: 161 4/02 Aint 2m good Ch

Useful novice hurdler in the 2000/2001 season, winning three times. He fell on his chase debut in January 2002 when looking the likely winner and nearly gained compensation next time. A good third against seasoned handicappers at the Festival, he opened his account with a runaway success at Aintree and followed up at Ayr in April 2002. Two miles is his trip. Acts on soft ground.

Darnley

77f 82f
5-y-o b/br g Henbit (USA)-Reeling (Relkino)
J N R Billinge J N R Billinge

Placings:0 (4900)
2001/02: 16^{0}G

	Starts	1st	2nd	3rd	Win & Pl
NH Flat	1	0	0	0	
Career Total	**1**	**0**	**0**	**0**	

Going: Sf: 0-0 GS: 0-0 Gd: 0-1 GF: - Fm: 0-0
Distance: 2m/2m3: 0-1 2m4-2m7: 0-0 3m+: 0-0
Track: LH: 0-0 RH: 0-1 Tight: 0-0 Gall: 0-0
Aids: Bl: 0-0 Vi: 0-0 Tstrap: 0-0
Best Rating: 82 4/02 Prth 2m110y good NHF

Darrell Boy (IRE)

99 74
7-y-o b g Commanche Run-Free For Ever (Little Buskins)
J R Norton L & R Racing

Placings:00-04P50P33P1 (4196)
2001/02: 16^{0}GF, 16^{4}GS, 21^{P}GS, 23^{5}S, 20^{0}S, 25^{P}GS, 20^{3}S, 21^{3}HY, 27^{P}S, 27^{1}S

	Starts	1st	2nd	3rd	Win & Pl
NH Flat	2	0	0	0	0
Hurdles	8	1	0	2	2360
Career Total	**12**	**1**	**0**	**2**	**2360**

74	3/02	Sedg	3m3f110y	G(0-90)HHdl	SFT	£1841

Total win prize-money £1841

Going: Sf: 1-6 GS: 0-3 Gd: 0-0 GF: - Fm: 0-1
Distance: 2m/2m3: 0-2 2m4-2m7: 0-5 **3m+: 1-3**
Track: **LH: 1-8** RH: 0-1 **Tight: 1-4** Gall: 0-1
Aids: Bl: 0-2 **Vi: 1-5** Tstrap: 0-0
Best Rating: 91 5/01 Newc 2m gd-fm NHF

Plating-class hurdler, often wears blinkers or visor. Successful over a marathon trip at Sedgefield in March 2002.

Darwell's Folly (USA)

90 75
7-y-o ch g Blushing John (USA)-Hispanolia (FR) (Kris)
P Monteith G M Cowan

Placings:0P0000 (4898)
2001/02: 17^{0}GS, 16^{P}GS, 16^{0}GS, 16^{0}S, 17^{0}GF, 16^{0}G

	Starts	1st	2nd	3rd	Win & Pl
Hurdles	6	0	0	0	
Career Total	**6**	**0**	**0**	**0**	

Going: Sf: 0-1 GS: 0-3 Gd: 0-1 GF: - Fm: 0-1
Distance: 2m/2m3: 0-6 2m4-2m7: 0-0 3m+: 0-0
Track: LH: 0-3 RH: 0-2 Tight: 0-1 Gall: 0-0
Aids: Bl: 0-0 Vi: 0-0 Tstrap: 0-2
Best Rating: 75 10/01 Carl 2m1f gd-sft Hdl

Darwin Tower

82 48
4-y-o gr g Bin Ajwaad (IRE)-Floria Tosca (Petong)
B W Murray B Murray

Placings:00 (2301)
2001/02: 16^{0}G, 16^{0}GF

	Starts	1st	2nd	3rd	Win & Pl
Hurdles	2	0	0	0	
Career Total	**2**	**0**	**0**	**0**	

Going: Sf: 0-0 GS: 0-0 Gd: 0-1 GF: - Fm: 0-1
Distance: 2m/2m3: 0-2 2m4-2m7: 0-0 3m+: 0-0
Track: LH: 0-2 RH: 0-0 Tight: 0-1 Gall: 0-1
Aids: Bl: 0-0 Vi: 0-0 Tstrap: 0-0
Best Rating: 48 11/01 Newc 2m good Hdl

Dasharan (IRE)

100 100
9-y-o b g Shahrastani (USA)-Delsy (FR) (Abdos)
Ian Williams Mr & Mrs John Poynton

Placings:0/PF/511460/0-3P (1016)
2001/02: 20^{3}G, 24^{P}G

	Starts	1st	2nd	3rd	Win & Pl
Hurdles	2	0	0	1	362
Career Total	**12**	**2**	**0**	**1**	**5912**

114	7/99	MRas	2m5f110y	D(0-120)HHdl	G-F	£2913

114 6/99 NAbb 2m6f D Hdl GD £2437
Total win prize-money £5351

Going: Sf: 0-0 GS: 0-0 Gd: 0-2 GF: - Fm: 0-0
Distance: 2m/2m3: 0-0 2m4-2m7: 0-1 3m+: 0-1
Track: LH: 0-2 RH: 0-0 Tight: 0-1 Gall: 0-0
Aids: Bl: 0-0 Vi: 0-0 Tstrap: 0-0
Best Rating: 114 7/99 MRas 2m5f110y gd-fm Hdl

Dashing Buck (IRE)

109 117

10-y-o b g Buckskin (FR)-El Scarsdale (Furry Glen)
J Wade John Wade

Placings:F/2P3F16P (4233)
2001/02: 22^{2}S, 25^{P}G, 21^{3}S, 28^{F}S, 25^{1}GS, 33^{6}S, 32^{P}GS

	Starts	1st	2nd	3rd	Win & Pl
Chases	7	1	1	1	8439
Career Total	**8**	**1**	**1**	**1**	**8439**

117 1/02 Weth 3m1f D(0-115)HCh G-S £4231
Total win prize-money £4232

Going: Sf: 0-4 GS: 1-2 Gd: 0-1 GF: - Fm: 0-0
Distance: 2m/2m3: 0-0 2m4-2m7: 0-2 **3m+: 1-5**
Track: **LH: 1-5** RH: 0-2 Tight: 0-3 Gall: 0-2
Aids: Bl: 0-0 Vi: 0-0 Tstrap: 0-0
Best Rating: 117 1/02 Weth 3m1f gd-sft Ch

Winning pointer in 1997, lightly raced and modest form since. Won a fair three-mile chase at the start of 2002 on easy ground.

Dashing Chief (IRE)

7-y-o b g Darshaan-Calaloo Sioux (USA) (Our Native (USA))
R Wilman R P Beare

Placings:400/0 (3268)
2001/02: 20^{0}G

	Starts	1st	2nd	3rd	Win & Pl
Hurdles	1	0	0	0	
Career Total	**4**	**0**	**0**	**0**	**0**

Going: Sf: 0-0 GS: 0-0 Gd: 0-1 GF: - Fm: 0-0
Distance: 2m/2m3: 0-0 2m4-2m7: 0-1 3m+: 0-0
Track: LH: 0-1 RH: 0-0 Tight: 0-0 Gall: 0-1
Aids: Bl: 0-0 Vi: 0-0 Tstrap: 0-1
Best Rating: 59 2/99 Plum 2m1f soft Hdl

Lightly-raced over hurdles, he has shown little so far. Tends to pull.

Dashing Dollar (IRE)

104 101

11-y-o b g Lord Americo-Cora Swan (Tarqogan)
J R Payne R J Payne

Placings:*0/061*120/440/1/F00113/0U0065-10P405020 (4480)
2001/02: 22^{1}GS, 24^{0}G, 27^{P}G, 22^{4}HY, 20^{0}G, 24^{5}S, 22^{0}GS, 19^{2}G, 22^{0}G

	Starts	1st	2nd	3rd	Win & Pl
Hurdles	9	1	1	0	4772
Career Total	**32**	**6**	**2**	**1**	**23712**

119 5/01 Extr 2m6f110y E(0-115)HHdl G-S £3346
121 4/00 Extr 2m3f110y D(0-125)HHdl HVY £3753
114 3/00 Extr 2m7f E(0-115)HHdl G-S £3315
116 11/98 Wind 2m6f110y D(0-125)HHdl GD £5303
112 11/96 Clon 2m Hdl Y-S £2295
116 11/96 Clon 2m NHF YLD £2648
Total win prize-money £20661

Going: Sf: 0-2 GS: 1-2 Gd: 0-5 GF: - Fm: 0-0
Distance: 2m/2m3: 0-1 **2m4-2m7: 1-5** 3m+: 0-3
Track: LH: 0-3 RH: 0-4 Tight: 0-2 Gall: 0-1
Aids: Bl: 0-0 Vi: 0-0 Tstrap: 0-0
Best Rating: 121 4/00 Extr 2m3f110y heavy Hdl

Fairly useful handicap hurdler who is versatile as regards ground and stays two miles-six. Goes particularly well at Exeter.

Dashoski (IRE)

5-y-o b m Petoski-Dashing March (Daring March)
M S Saunders M S Saunders

Placings:P (1797)
2001/02: 16^{P}S

	Starts	1st	2nd	3rd	Win & Pl
Hurdles	1	0	0	0	
Career Total	**1**	**0**	**0**	**0**	

Going: Sf: 0-1 GS: 0-0 Gd: 0-0 GF: - Fm: 0-0
Distance: 2m/2m3: 0-1 2m4-2m7: 0-0 3m+: 0-0
Track: LH: 0-1 RH: 0-0 Tight: 0-0 Gall: 0-0
Aids: Bl: 0-0 Vi: 0-0 Tstrap: 0-0
Best Rating:

Dat My Horse (IRE)

104 (102c)122+

8-y-o b g All Haste (USA)-Toposki (FR) (Top Ville)
R H P Williams A Lowrie & Mrs J Lowrie

Placings:F5/P-FF (4727)
2001/02: 25^{F}G, 24^{F}GF

	Starts	1st	2nd	3rd	Win & Pl
Chases	2	0	0	0	
Career Total	**5**	**0**	**0**	**0**	**0**

Going: Sf: 0-0 GS: 0-0 Gd: 0-1 GF: - Fm: 0-1
Distance: 2m/2m3: 0-0 2m4-2m7: 0-0 3m+: 0-2
Track: LH: 0-2 RH: 0-0 Tight: 0-1 Gall: 0-0
Aids: Bl: 0-0 Vi: 0-0 Tstrap: 0-0
Best Rating: 108 5/01 Aint 3m1f good Ch

A winning pointer, he has problems with regulation fences but reverted successfully to hurdles in the new season. Stays well, acts on fast ground.

Datito (IRE)

103 98

7-y-o b g Over The River (FR)-Crash Call (Crash Course)
R T Phillips G Lansbury

Placings:*1*-42 (4874)
2001/02: 20^{4}G, 20^{2}G

	Starts	1st	2nd	3rd	Win & Pl
Hurdles	2	0	1	0	1144
Career Total	**3**	**1**	**1**	**0**	**2852**

126 3/01 Hayd 2m H NHF HVY £1708
Total win prize-money £1708

Going: Sf: 0-0 GS: 0-0 Gd: 0-2 GF: - Fm: 0-0
Distance: 2m/2m3: 0-0 2m4-2m7: 0-2 3m+: 0-0
Track: LH: 0-0 RH: 0-1 Tight: 0-0 Gall: 0-0
Aids: Bl: 0-0 Vi: 0-0 Tstrap: 0-0
Best Rating: 126 3/01 Hayd 2m heavy NHF

An Irish point-to-point winner, made a winning debut under Rules in a bumper at Haydock in March 2001. Beaten twice over hurdles on faster ground after a year's absence.

Daughter In Law (IRE)

98 66

9-y-o b m Law Society (USA)-Colonial Line (USA) (Plenty Old (USA))
Miss C J E Caroe Miss C J E Caroe

Placings:P0040P3/0035P000/33205500/0400600-P2 (4236)
2001/02: 20^{P}S, 21^{2}GF

	Starts	1st	2nd	3rd	Win & Pl
Hurdles	2	0	1	0	488
Career Total	**32**	**0**	**2**	**4**	**2223**

Going: Sf: 0-1 GS: 0-0 Gd: 0-0 GF: - Fm: 0-1
Distance: 2m/2m3: 0-0 2m4-2m7: 0-2 3m+: 0-0
Track: LH: 0-0 RH: 0-2 Tight: 0-0 Gall: 0-1
Aids: Bl: 0-0 Vi: 0-0 Tstrap: 0-2
Best Rating: 81 5/99 Towc 2m soft Hdl

Plating-class hurdler. Best at around two and a half miles, likes fast ground, usually tongue tied.

Daunted (IRE)

6-y-o b g Priolo (USA)-Dauntess (Formidable (USA))
R Wilman (G L Moore 21/7) Century Racing

Placings:5/P (4314)
2001/02: 20^{P}HY

	Starts	1st	2nd	3rd	Win & Pl
Hurdles	1	0	0	0	
Career Total	**2**	**0**	**0**	**0**	**0**

Going: Sf: 0-1 GS: 0-0 Gd: 0-0 GF: - Fm: 0-0
Distance: 2m/2m3: 0-0 2m4-2m7: 0-1 3m+: 0-0
Track: LH: 0-1 RH: 0-0 Tight: 0-1 Gall: 0-0
Aids: Bl: 0-0 Vi: 0-0 Tstrap: 0-0
Best Rating: 73 2/00 Plum 2m heavy Hdl

Dauntless Girl

86 63

7-y-o ch m Derrylin-Battle Fleet (Alias Smith (USA))
B G Powell Mrs Richard Plummer

Placings:*0/0/4*P-40RL (0781)
2001/02: 20^{4}F, 22^{0}GF, 22^{R}G, 20^{L}G

	Starts	1st	2nd	3rd	Win & Pl
Hurdles	4	0	0	0	0
Career Total	**8**	**0**	**0**	**0**	**0**

Going: Sf: 0-0 GS: 0-0 Gd: 0-2 GF: - Fm: 0-2
Distance: 2m/2m3: 0-0 2m4-2m7: 0-4 3m+: 0-0
Track: LH: 0-4 RH: 0-0 Tight: 0-3 Gall: 0-0
Aids: Bl: 0-0 Vi: 0-0 Tstrap: 0-0
Best Rating: 63 5/01 NAbb 2m6f gd-fm Hdl

Daveysfire

90 60

4-y-o b f Gildoran-Doubtfire (Jalmood (USA))
A R Dicken J A Davidson

Placings:00 (2918)
2001/02: 16^{0}G, 16^{0}G

	Starts	1st	2nd	3rd	Win & Pl
Hurdles	2	0	0	0	
Career Total	**2**	**0**	**0**	**0**	

Going: Sf: 0-0 GS: 0-0 Gd: 0-2 GF: - Fm: 0-0
Distance: 2m/2m3: 0-2 2m4-2m7: 0-0 3m+: 0-0
Track: LH: 0-1 RH: 0-1 Tight: 0-1 Gall: 0-1
Aids: Bl: 0-0 Vi: 0-0 Tstrap: 0-0
Best Rating: 60 11/01 Newc 2m good Hdl

Davids Lad (IRE)

113 (91h) **164**

8-y-o b g Yashgan-Cool Nora (IRE) (Lafontaine (USA))
A J Martin Eddie Joe's Racing Syndicate

Placings:0000S501/14F504P5114P6/00110F61-111543F (4677)
2001/02: 29^{1}G, 24^{1}G, 16^{1}Y, 21^{5}SH, 16^{4}YS, 21^{3}G, 36^{F}G

	Starts	1st	2nd	3rd	Win & Pl
Hurdles	1	0	0	0	0
Chases	6	3	0	1	98811
Career Total	**36**	**10**	**0**	**1**	**150516**

157	10/01	Rosc	2m	Ch	YLD	£7862
164	5/01	Navn	3m	HCh	GD	£16693
158	5/01	Fair	3m5f	HCh	GD	£65725
160	4/01	Fair	2m4f	HCh	SFT	£19395
134	11/00	Chel	2m4f110y	D(0-125)HCh	G-S	£11505
121	10/00	Navn	2m4f	(0-116)HCh	YLD	£5520
109	1/00	Fair	2m4f	(0-102)HHdl	SFT	£4416
111	1/00	Muss	3m	F(0-105)HHdl	GD	£3591
97	5/99	Prth	2m4f110y	F(0-110)HHdl	HVY	£3793
91	4/99	DRoy	2m4f	(0-102)HHdl	YLD	£2823

Total win prize-money £141328

Going: Sf: 0-0 GS: 0-0 Gd: 2-4 GF: - Fm: 0-0
Distance: 2m/2m3: 1-2 2m4-2m7: 0-2 **3m+: 2-3**
Track: LH: 0-2 RH: 0-0 Tight: 0-1 Gall: 0-1
Aids: Bl: 0-0 Vi: 0-0 **Tstrap: 3-7**
Best Rating: 164 5/01 Navn 3m good Ch

Useful Irish chaser, he proved a revelation under Tony Martin's astute handling, capping a cracking campaign by winning the Powers Gold Label Irish Grand National at Fairyhouse in 2001. Blessed with speed and stamina, he has form on all sorts of ground. Has won at distances from two miles to three miles five, usually wears a tongue strap.

Davoski

117 **160**

8-y-o b g Niniski (USA)-Pamela Peach (Habitat)
Miss Venetia Williams Sir Robert Ogden

Placings:113132142210/1/16120-34 (3658)
2001/02: 16^{3}G, 21^{4}S

	Starts	1st	2nd	3rd	Win & Pl
Chases	2	0	0	1	7384
Career Total	**20**	**8**	**4**	**3**	**72682**

162	12/00	Chel	2m110y	B HCh	SFT	£13663
150	10/00	Strf	2m5f110y	C(0-135)HCh	SFT	£6890
144	10/99	Fknm	2m5f110y	C Ch	GD	£8135
136	4/99	Uttx	2m	C(0-135)HHdl	G-S	£5083
134	1/99	Kemp	2m	D Hdl	SFT	£2944
121	11/98	NAbb	2m1f	E(0-110)HHdl	SFT	£2684
114	10/98	Uttx	2m	E Hdl	GD	£2431
98	9/98	Hrfd	2m1f	E Hdl	G-F	£2430

Total win prize-money £44262

Going: Sf: 0-1 GS: 0-0 Gd: 0-1 GF: - Fm: 0-0
Distance: 2m/2m3: 0-1 2m4-2m7: 0-1 3m+: 0-0
Track: LH: 0-0 RH: 0-2 Tight: 0-0 Gall: 0-0
Aids: Bl: 0-0 Vi: 0-0 Tstrap: 0-0
Best Rating: 162 12/00 Chel 2m110y soft Ch

Useful chaser, he developed into a very useful handicapper in 2000/2001 before being sidelined for a year with leg trouble. Returned with a good third in the Victor Chandler in January 2002. He stays two miles five, but seems most effective at the minimum trip, handles soft ground and acts well on a sharp left-handed track.

Davy's Dream (IRE)

103 **94**

10-y-o b g Strong Gale-Shuil Liss (Deep Run)
C C Bealby North Lodge Racing

Placings:000630/0P5000/6P0620P/P0242231055-43P (1272)
2001/02: 17^{4}GF, 24^{3}G, 24^{P}GF

	Starts	1st	2nd	3rd	Win & Pl
Chases	3	0	0	1	756
Career Total	**33**	**1**	**4**	**3**	**7274**

97	9/00	Dpat	2m2f	(0-95)HCh	GD	£2760

Total win prize-money £2760

Going: Sf: 0-0 GS: 0-0 Gd: 0-1 GF: - Fm: 0-2
Distance: 2m/2m3: 0-1 2m4-2m7: 0-0 3m+: 0-2
Track: LH: 0-3 RH: 0-0 Tight: 0-3 Gall: 0-0
Aids: Bl: 0-0 Vi: 0-0 Tstrap: 0-0
Best Rating: 97 9/00 Dpat 2m2f good Ch

Davy's Image

8-y-o ch g Milieu-Reigate Head (Timber King)
B Bousfield Mrs D A Bousfield

Placings:0P-PP (4520)
2001/02: 22^{P}HY, 20^{P}G

	Starts	1st	2nd	3rd	Win & Pl
Hurdles	2	0	0	0	
Career Total	**4**	**0**	**0**	**0**	

Going: Sf: 0-1 GS: 0-0 Gd: 0-1 GF: - Fm: 0-0
Distance: 2m/2m3: 0-0 2m4-2m7: 0-2 3m+: 0-0
Track: LH: 0-1 RH: 0-0 Tight: 0-1 Gall: 0-0
Aids: Bl: 0-0 Vi: 0-0 Tstrap: 0-2
Best Rating:

Dawn Court

74f **52f**

5-y-o b m Rakaposhi King-Herald The Dawn (Dubassoff (USA))
R H Alner Mrs U Wainwright

Placings:0 (4887)
2001/02: 18^{0}GF

	Starts	1st	2nd	3rd	Win & Pl
NH Flat	1	0	0	0	
Career Total	**1**	**0**	**0**	**0**	

Going: Sf: 0-0 GS: 0-0 Gd: 0-0 GF: - Fm: 0-1
Distance: 2m/2m3: 0-1 2m4-2m7: 0-0 3m+: 0-0
Track: LH: 0-1 RH: 0-0 Tight: 0-1 Gall: 0-0
Aids: Bl: 0-0 Vi: 0-0 Tstrap: 0-0
Best Rating: 52 4/02 Font 2m2f110y gd-fm NHF

Dawn Fox (IRE)

72 **54**

6-y-o ch m Phardante (FR)-Golden Vixen (Goldhill)
N G Ayliffe D T Hooper

Placings:06 (4861)
2001/02: 17^{0}GS, 22^{6}F

	Starts	1st	2nd	3rd	Win & Pl
NH Flat	1	0	0	0	0
Hurdles	1	0	0	0	0
Career Total	**2**	**0**	**0**	**0**	**0**

Going: Sf: 0-0 GS: 0-1 Gd: 0-0 GF: - Fm: 0-1
Distance: 2m/2m3: 0-1 2m4-2m7: 0-1 3m+: 0-0
Track: LH: 0-0 RH: 0-1 Tight: 0-0 Gall: 0-0
Aids: Bl: 0-0 Vi: 0-0 Tstrap: 0-0
Best Rating:

Dawn Gamble

87 **67**

6-y-o b m Karinga Bay-Tharita (Thatch (USA))
P R Rodford R J Croker

Placings:0P-FP000 (4586)
2001/02: 17^{F}GS, 17^{P}GS, 16^{0}GS, 16^{0}G, 22^{0}G

	Starts	1st	2nd	3rd	Win & Pl
Hurdles	5	0	0	0	
Career Total	**7**	**0**	**0**	**0**	

Going: Sf: 0-0 GS: 0-3 Gd: 0-2 GF: - Fm: 0-0
Distance: 2m/2m3: 0-4 2m4-2m7: 0-1 3m+: 0-0
Track: LH: 0-0 RH: 0-5 Tight: 0-0 Gall: 0-0
Aids: Bl: 0-0 Vi: 0-0 Tstrap: 0-0
Best Rating: 70 3/02 Winc 2m good Hdl

Dawn Leader (IRE)

(105h) (117h)

11-y-o b g Supreme Leader-Tudor Dawn (Deep Run)
A J Lidderdale Bonusprint

Placings:1/10/1132/1213/F20P0/2 (4028)
2001/02: 21^{2}GS

	Starts	1st	2nd	3rd	Win & Pl
Hurdles	1	0	1	0	1760
Career Total	**17**	**6**	**4**	**2**	**39394**

156	2/99	Sand	2m4f110y	D Ch	GD	£3882
133	11/98	Newb	2m1f	D Ch	G-S	£3522
127	1/98	Hntg	2m110y	E Hdl	G-S	£2094
124	12/97	Chel	2m1f	C Hdl	GD	£3663
131	2/97	Sand	2m110y	H NHF	GD	£1448
116	4/96	Worc	2m	H NHF	G-F	£2094

Total win prize-money £16705

Going: Sf: 0-0 GS: 0-1 Gd: 0-0 GF: - Fm: 0-0
Distance: 2m/2m3: 0-0 2m4-2m7: 0-1 3m+: 0-0
Track: LH: 0-1 RH: 0-0 Tight: 0-0 Gall: 0-1
Aids: Bl: 0-0 Vi: 0-0 Tstrap: 0-0
Best Rating: 156 4/99 Aint 2m gd-sft Ch

A formerly useful hurdler/chaser who has had more than his share of injury problems. He had his first outing since April 2000 in March, running well over hurdles at Newbury in March 2002. Talented, he does just seem to think about things, though. Goes well fresh.

Dawn Project (IRE)

96 **101**

7-y-o ch m Project Manager-Mafiosa (Miami Springs)
Miss E C Lavelle J L Walters, E D Hood, S D Watts

Placings:F5F4/422522-4 (0073)
2001/02: 19^{4}G

	Starts	1st	2nd	3rd	Win & Pl
Hurdles	1	0	0	0	0
Career Total	**11**	**0**	**4**	**0**	**2684**

Going: Sf: 0-0 GS: 0-0 Gd: 0-1 GF: - Fm: 0-0
Distance: 2m/2m3: 0-1 2m4-2m7: 0-0 3m+: 0-0
Track: LH: 0-0 RH: 0-1 Tight: 0-0 Gall: 0-0
Aids: Bl: 0-0 Vi: 0-0 Tstrap: 0-0

Best Rating: 101 5/01 Extr 2m3f good Hdl

Modest maiden hurdler who is too consistent for her own good. suited by two and half miles and a sound surface.

Dawn Raider

7-y-o b g Sizzling Melody-Dawn Magic (Cleon)
P Butler Mrs Gill Oakley

Placings:0/P (4411)
2001/02: 18^{PS}

	Starts	1st	2nd	3rd	Win & Pl
Hurdles	1	0	0	0	
Career Total	**2**	**0**	**0**	**0**	

Going: Sf: 0-1 GS: 0-0 Gd: 0-0 GF: - Fm: 0-0
Distance: 2m/2m3: 0-1 2m4-2m7: 0-0 3m+: 0-0
Track: LH: 0-1 RH: 0-0 Tight: 0-1 Gall: 0-0
Aids: Bl: 0-0 Vi: 0-0 Tstrap: 0-0
Best Rating:

Dawn To Dusk (IRE)

11-y-o br g Kambalda-Atlantic Breeze (Strong Gale)
S G Knight Mrs Peter Denning

Placings:00/0S0/60/PP4P6/40165-P (0913)
2001/02: 24^{P}G

	Starts	1st	2nd	3rd	Win & Pl
Chases	1	0	0	0	
Career Total	**18**	**1**	**0**	**0**	**2467**

66 8/00 Font 2m6f110y F(0-100)HHdl G-F £2247
Total win prize-money £2247

Going: Sf: 0-0 GS: 0-0 Gd: 0-1 GF: - Fm: 0-0
Distance: 2m/2m3: 0-0 2m4-2m7: 0-0 3m+: 0-1
Track: LH: 0-1 RH: 0-0 Tight: 0-1 Gall: 0-0
Aids: Bl: 0-0 Vi: 0-0 Tstrap: 0-0
Best Rating: 76 4/97 List 2m gd-yld Hdl

Daytime Dawn (IRE)

85 77
11-y-o b g Rashar (USA)-Ard Clos (Ardoon)
R N C Wale R N C Wale

Placings:*F0*/564/00/**U1**/1/0-4 (4685)
2001/02: 16^{4}GF

	Starts	1st	2nd	3rd	Win & Pl
Chases	1	0	0	0	0
Career Total	**12**	**2**	**0**	**0**	**4455**

118 4/00 Hrfd 2m H Ch GD £2012
94 4/99 Hrfd 2m3f H Ch G-F £2442
Total win prize-money £4455

Going: Sf: 0-0 GS: 0-0 Gd: 0-0 GF: - Fm: 0-1
Distance: 2m/2m3: 0-1 2m4-2m7: 0-0 3m+: 0-0
Track: LH: 0-0 RH: 0-1 Tight: 0-0 Gall: 0-0
Aids: Bl: 0-0 Vi: 0-0 Tstrap: 0-0
Best Rating: 118 4/00 Hrfd 2m good Ch

Dazzling Stone

8-y-o b g Mujtahid (USA)-Lady In Green (Shareef Dancer (USA))
David Thompson David Bartlett

Placings:0443050/**FU-0P** (0473)
2001/02: 20^{0}GF, 20^{P}GF

	Starts	1st	2nd	3rd	Win & Pl
Chases	2	0	0	0	
Career Total	**11**	**0**	**0**	**1**	**308**

Going: Sf: 0-0 GS: 0-0 Gd: 0-0 GF: - Fm: 0-2
Distance: 2m/2m3: 0-0 2m4-2m7: 0-2 3m+: 0-0
Track: LH: 0-1 RH: 0-1 Tight: 0-0 Gall: 0-1
Aids: Bl: 0-0 Vi: 0-0 Tstrap: 0-0
Best Rating: 88 7/99 Sedg 2m1f gd-fm Hdl

De Oralie (IRE)

100 72
9-y-o ch g Tremblant-Tsing Tao (He Loves Me)
A J Lockwood A J Lockwood

Placings:000*0*/*36*0350/00**PF**6**5**/**U0**-PP (4772)
2001/02: 16^{P}GS, 21^{P}G

	Starts	1st	2nd	3rd	Win & Pl
Hurdles	2	0	0	0	
Career Total	**20**	**0**	**0**	**2**	**598**

Going: Sf: 0-0 GS: 0-1 Gd: 0-1 GF: - Fm: 0-0
Distance: 2m/2m3: 0-1 2m4-2m7: 0-1 3m+: 0-0
Track: LH: 0-1 RH: 0-1 Tight: 0-2 Gall: 0-0
Aids: Bl: 0-0 Vi: 0-0 Tstrap: 0-0
Best Rating: 92 5/98 Klny 2m1f yld-sft NHF

Headstrong plater.

De Tramuntana

104(92c) (103c)115
5-y-o b m Alzao (USA)-Glamour Game (Nashwan (USA))
P R Hedger P R Hedger

Placings:22413-04056**240P** (4568)
2001/02: 17^{0}G, 18^{4}S, 20^{0}G, 21^{5}GS, 18^{6}HY, 20^{2}GS, 20^{4}S, 22^{0}S, 24^{P}G

	Starts	1st	2nd	3rd	Win & Pl
Hurdles	7	0	0	0	1064
Chases	2	0	1	0	1584
Career Total	**14**	**1**	**3**	**1**	**6851**

115 3/01 Font 2m2f110y F Hdl SFT £2205
Total win prize-money £2205

Going: Sf: 0-4 GS: 0-2 Gd: 0-3 GF: - Fm: 0-0
Distance: 2m/2m3: 0-3 2m4-2m7: 0-5 3m+: 0-1
Track: LH: 0-4 RH: 0-3 Tight: 0-6 Gall: 0-2
Aids: Bl: 0-1 Vi: 0-0 Tstrap: 0-8
Best Rating: 115 4/01 Newb 2m110y soft Hdl

Modest hurdler/chaser, stays two and a half miles, appreciates soft ground and is usually tongue tied.

Dead-Eyed Dick (IRE)

82 76
6-y-o b g Un Desperado (FR)-Glendale Charmer (Down The Hatch)
P R Webber Mrs J A Chenery

Placings:*00*-05P (4781)
2001/02: 17^{0}G, 16^{5}S, 16^{P}GF

	Starts	1st	2nd	3rd	Win & Pl
Hurdles	3	0	0	0	0
Career Total	**5**	**0**	**0**	**0**	**0**

Going: Sf: 0-1 GS: 0-0 Gd: 0-1 GF: - Fm: 0-1
Distance: 2m/2m3: 0-3 2m4-2m7: 0-0 3m+: 0-0
Track: LH: 0-3 RH: 0-0 Tight: 0-2 Gall: 0-1
Aids: Bl: 0-0 Vi: 0-0 Tstrap: 0-0
Best Rating: 76 12/01 Chel 2m1f good Hdl

Deadly Doris

93 92
8-y-o b m Ron's Victory (USA)-Camp Chair (Ela-Mana-Mou)
N A Smith Stan Hey And Partners

Placings:*540*/55600/5042U25355-15655 (3708)
2001/02: 16^{1}S, 17^{5}GS, 16^{6}HY, 16^{5}HY, 17^{5}HY

	Starts	1st	2nd	3rd	Win & Pl
Hurdles	5	1	0	0	2618
Career Total	**23**	**1**	**2**	**1**	**4195**

92 11/01 Towc 2m E Hdl SFT £2618
Total win prize-money £2618

Going: Sf: 1-4 GS: 0-1 Gd: 0-0 GF: - Fm: 0-0
Distance: **2m/2m3: 1-5** 2m4-2m7: 0-0 3m+: 0-0
Track: LH: 0-2 **RH: 1-3** Tight: 0-1 Gall: 0-0
Aids: Bl: 0-0 Vi: 0-0 Tstrap: 0-0
Best Rating: 94 1/99 Hntg 2m110y soft NHF

Modest hurdler, suited by two miles and soft ground. Has worn blinkers.

Deal A King

85 78
8-y-o ch g Rakaposhi King-Woodford Lady (Mandalus)
Mrs H Dalton Mrs Heather Dalton

Placings:2/**P65** (3737)
2001/02: 24^{P}GS, 20^{6}S, 16^{5}S

	Starts	1st	2nd	3rd	Win & Pl
Chases	3	0	0	0	0
Career Total	**4**	**0**	**1**	**0**	**472**

Going: Sf: 0-2 GS: 0-1 Gd: 0-0 GF: - Fm: 0-0
Distance: 2m/2m3: 0-1 2m4-2m7: 0-1 3m+: 0-1
Track: LH: 0-2 RH: 0-1 Tight: 0-2 Gall: 0-0
Aids: Bl: 0-0 Vi: 0-0 Tstrap: 0-0
Best Rating: 78 2/02 Leic 2m soft Ch

Dealer Del

8-y-o b g Deltic (USA)-No Deal (Sharp Deal)
L G Cottrell Mrs Hazel Leeves

Placings:053 (0774)
2001/02: 24^{0}GF, 26^{5}G, 23^{3}GF

	Starts	1st	2nd	3rd	Win & Pl
Chases	3	0	0	1	491
Career Total	**3**	**0**	**0**	**1**	**491**

Going: Sf: 0-0 GS: 0-0 Gd: 0-1 GF: - Fm: 0-2
Distance: 2m/2m3: 0-0 2m4-2m7: 0-0 3m+: 0-3
Track: LH: 0-3 RH: 0-0 Tight: 0-2 Gall: 0-0
Aids: Bl: 0-0 Vi: 0-0 Tstrap: 0-0
Best Rating: 75 6/01 NAbb 3m2f110y good Ch

Dealer's Choice (IRE)

104(102h) (93h)128
8-y-o gr g Roselier (FR)-Cam Flower Vii (Damsire Unregistered)
G Brown P Duffy, G King, D Roberts, B Savage

Placings:*1*/2**F65F5**/**U-261P1P** (4814)

2001/02: 21^{2}GS, 22^{6}GF, 20^{1}G, 24^{P}G, 20^{1}S, 21^{P}GF

	Starts	1st	2nd	3rd	Win & Pl
Hurdles	2	0	1	0	672
Chases	4	2	0	0	9035
Career Total	**14**	**3**	**2**	**0**	**12570**

128	3/02	Ludl	2m4f	D(0-115)HCh	SFT	£5148
118	12/01	Ludl	2m4f	F(0-95)HCh	GD	£3887
97	4/99	Font	2m2f110y	H NHF	GD	£1567

Total win prize-money £10602

Going: Sf: 1-1 GS: 0-1 Gd: 1-2 GF: - Fm: 0-2
Distance: 2m/2m3: 0-0 **2m4-2m7: 2-5** 3m+: 0-1
Track: LH: 0-2 **RH: 2-3 Tight: 2-3** Gall: 0-1
Aids: Bl: 0-0 Vi: 0-0 Tstrap: 0-0
Best Rating: 128 3/02 Ludl 2m4f soft Ch

Modest hurdler/chaser. Off for 18 months before running a close second on his return over hurdles in November 2001. Won twice over fences at Ludlow subsequently. He stays two miles five furlongs and is suited by an easy surface and a sharp track.

Dean Of Devon (IRE)

100 **106**

7-y-o gr g Roselier (FR)-Miss Pitpan (Pitpan)
L Lungo P E Truscott

Placings:*34*F5/2343-31 **(4063)**
2001/02: 23^{3}GS, 27^{1}S

	Starts	1st	2nd	3rd	Win & Pl
Hurdles	2	1	0	1	2588
Career Total	**10**	**1**	**1**	**4**	**4649**

106	3/02	Sedg	3m3f110y	F Hdl	SFT	£2205

Total win prize-money £2205

Going: Sf: 1-1 GS: 0-1 Gd: 0-0 GF: - Fm: 0-0
Distance: 2m/2m3: 0-0 2m4-2m7: 0-1 **3m+: 1-1**
Track: **LH: 1-2** RH: 0-0 **Tight: 1-1** Gall: 0-0
Aids: Bl: 0-0 Vi: 0-0 Tstrap: 0-0
Best Rating: 106 3/02 Sedg 3m3f110y soft Hdl

Fair novice hurdler, he acts on soft ground and stays three miles three furlongs.

Deano's Beeno

104 **163**

10-y-o b g Far North (CAN)-Sans Dot (Busted)
M C Pipe Axom

Placings:105/111/2105/12215/1210-00 **(4251)**
2001/02: 25^{0}VS, 24^{0}G

	Starts	1st	2nd	3rd	Win & Pl
Hurdles	2	0	0	0	0
Career Total	**21**	**9**	**4**	**0**	**115691**

176	1/01	Donc	3m110y	A Hdl	GD	£15780
176	11/00	Newb	3m110y	A Hdl	SFT	£13800
156	2/00	Newb	3m	C Ch	G-S	£6474
176	11/99	Newb	3m110y	A Hdl	G-S	£13100
174	1/99	Hayd	2m7f110y	A Hdl	SFT	£12440
153	12/97	Bang	3m	B(0-140)HHdl	GD	£4783
154	11/97	Hayd	2m6f	B HHdl	SFT	£4883
148	11/97	NAbb	2m6f	D(0-125)HHdl	SFT	£2762
132	12/96	NAbb	2m1f	D Hdl	SFT	£2911

Total win prize-money £76935

Going: Sf: 0-0 GS: 0-0 Gd: 0-1 GF: - Fm: 0-0
Distance: 2m/2m3: 0-0 2m4-2m7: 0-0 3m+: 0-2
Track: LH: 0-0 RH: 0-0 Tight: 0-0 Gall: 0-0
Aids: Bl: 0-0 Vi: 0-0 Tstrap: 0-0
Best Rating: 176 1/01 Donc 3m110y good Hdl

Best on flat, left-handed tracks, he has an outstanding record under such conditions. He is also best caught fresh, having been successful on his seasonal debut no fewer than four times, but the decision to arrive at the 2002 Stayers' Hurdle fresh did not pay dividends. There is the suspicion that he needs to dominate, but when things go his way he is a high-class staying hurdler.

Dear Deal

108(46h) **131**

9-y-o b g Sharp Deal-The Deer Hound (Cash And Carry)
C Tizzard J A G Meaden

Placings:*665*/2443/11-**32P4** **(4634)**
2001/02: 22^{3}S, 25^{2}S, 22^{P}S, 24^{4}GF

	Starts	1st	2nd	3rd	Win & Pl
Chases	4	0	1	1	2720
Career Total	**13**	**2**	**2**	**2**	**10619**

121	10/00	Winc	2m6f	E Hdl	G-S	£2506
118	9/00	Extr	2m6f110y	E Hdl	GD	£2632

Total win prize-money £5138

Going: Sf: 0-3 GS: 0-0 Gd: 0-0 GF: - Fm: 0-1
Distance: 2m/2m3: 0-0 2m4-2m7: 0-2 3m+: 0-2
Track: LH: 0-1 RH: 0-2 Tight: 0-1 Gall: 0-1
Aids: Bl: 0-0 Vi: 0-0 Tstrap: 0-0
Best Rating: 131 2/02 Winc 3m1f110y soft Ch

Formerly a useful hurdler, he missed the whole of 2001, but has shown ability over fences since returning in January 2002. Stays three miles plus, is suited by soft ground, but has won on faster.

Deb's Son

104 **100**

5-y-o b g Minster Son-Deb's Ball (Glenstal (USA))
D Moffatt Mr & Mrs A G Milligan

Placings:32403-613040 **(2914)**
2001/02: 24^{6}S, 22^{1}GS, 27^{3}GS, 20^{0}G, 24^{4}GS, 23^{0}HY

	Starts	1st	2nd	3rd	Win & Pl
Hurdles	6	1	0	1	3747
Career Total	**11**	**1**	**1**	**3**	**5216**

100	8/01	Ctml	2m6f	E Hdl	G-S	£3115

Total win prize-money £3115

Going: Sf: 0-2 GS: 1-3 Gd: 0-1 GF: - Fm: 0-0
Distance: 2m/2m3: 0-0 **2m4-2m7: 1-2** 3m+: 0-4
Track: **LH: 1-6** RH: 0-0 **Tight: 1-2** Gall: 0-2
Aids: Bl: 0-0 Vi: 0-0 Tstrap: 0-0
Best Rating: 100 8/01 Ctml 2m6f gd-sft Hdl

Modest hurdler, stays two miles-six plus, suited by cut in the ground.

Debonair Boy (IRE)

7-y-o b g Alphabatim (USA)-Hallelujah (The Parson)
Mrs C J Kerr Mrs C J Kerr

Placings:0P **(4892)**
2001/02: 26^{0}GS, 31^{P}G

	Starts	1st	2nd	3rd	Win & Pl
Chases	2	0	0	0	
Career Total	**2**	**0**	**0**	**0**	

Going: Sf: 0-0 GS: 0-1 Gd: 0-1 GF: - Fm: 0-0
Distance: 2m/2m3: 0-0 2m4-2m7: 0-0 3m+: 0-2
Track: LH: 0-0 RH: 0-1 Tight: 0-0 Gall: 0-0
Aids: Bl: 0-0 Vi: 0-0 Tstrap: 0-0
Best Rating:

Decarla

7-y-o ch m Carlingford Castle-Decanna (Decoy Boy)
Mrs P Ford R F Jones

Placings:U-P0PP **(3332)**
2001/02: 26^{P}G, 20^{0}S, 19^{P}S, 21^{P}G

	Starts	1st	2nd	3rd	Win & Pl
Hurdles	4	0	0	0	
Career Total	**5**	**0**	**0**	**0**	

Going: Sf: 0-2 GS: 0-0 Gd: 0-2 GF: - Fm: 0-0
Distance: 2m/2m3: 0-0 2m4-2m7: 0-3 3m+: 0-1
Track: LH: 0-1 RH: 0-3 Tight: 0-0 Gall: 0-0
Aids: Bl: 0-0 Vi: 0-0 Tstrap: 0-0
Best Rating:

Decent Fellow (GER)

107 **127**

7-y-o ch g Esclavo (FR)-Domicella (In Fijar (USA))
Josef Vana Ii Plus Vadu

Placings:221444 **(2665)**
2001/02: 17^{2}G, 18^{2}S, 15^{1}S, 26^{4}GF, 31^{4}G, 31^{4}GS

	Starts	1st	2nd	3rd	Win & Pl
Hurdles	1	1	0	0	361
Chases	5	0	2	0	4182
Career Total	**6**	**1**	**2**	**0**	**4543**

	9/01	Most	1m7f	Hdl	SFT	£361

Total win prize-money £361

Going: Sf: 1-2 GS: 0-1 Gd: 0-2 GF: - Fm: 0-1
Distance: 2m/2m3: 0-2 2m4-2m7: 0-0 3m+: 0-3
Track: LH: 0-2 RH: 0-0 Tight: 0-0 Gall: 0-0
Aids: Bl: 0-1 Vi: 0-0 Tstrap: 0-0
Best Rating: 127 12/01 Chel 3m7f gd-sft Ch

German bred, Czech-trained chaser, usually runs in cross-country chases. He has been there or thereabouts on all starts in Britain.

Decoded

100(89h) **95**

6-y-o ch g Deploy-Golden Panda (Music Boy)
Jedd O'Keeffe Mrs H E Aitkin

Placings:431260/56-**663F65** **(4487)**
2001/02: 21^{6}G, 25^{6}S, 26^{3}HY, 24^{F}S, 32^{6}HY, 26^{5}GS

	Starts	1st	2nd	3rd	Win & Pl
Chases	6	0	0	1	763
Career Total	**14**	**1**	**1**	**2**	**4904**

94	1/00	Ayr	2m4f	E Hdl	SFT	£2723

Total win prize-money £2723

Going: Sf: 0-4 GS: 0-1 Gd: 0-1 GF: - Fm: 0-0
Distance: 2m/2m3: 0-0 2m4-2m7: 0-1 3m+: 0-5
Track: LH: 0-4 RH: 0-2 Tight: 0-0 Gall: 0-1
Aids: Bl: 0-0 Vi: 0-0 Tstrap: 0-0
Best Rating: 95 1/02 Carl 3m2f heavy Ch

Looked set to be a real stayer after his hurdles win at the start of 2000, but has been hard to find a trip with and has not won over jumps since, including over fences. Acts in the mud.

Dee Diamond (USA)

5-y-o b m Eagle Eyed (USA)-Noumea (USA) (Plugged Nickle (USA))

Andrew Turnell Mrs Claire Hollowood

Placings:4003-P (0236)
2001/02: 16PGF

	Starts	1st	2nd	3rd	Win & Pl
Hurdles	1	0	0	0	
Career Total	5	0	0	1	703

Going: Sf: 0-0 GS: 0-0 Gd: 0-0 GF: - Fm: 0-1
Distance: 2m/2m3: 0-1 2m4-2m7: 0-0 3m+: 0-0
Track: LH: 0-1 RH: 0-0 Tight: 0-1 Gall: 0-0
Aids: Bl: 0-0 Vi: 0-0 Tstrap: 0-0
Best Rating: 78 10/00 Kels 2m110y good Hdl

Deedeejay

57 **14**

9-y-o b m Cigar-Miss Patdonna (Starch Reduced)
P M Rich Miss H Lewis

Placings:0 (2139)
2001/02: 170G

	Starts	1st	2nd	3rd	Win & Pl
Hurdles	1	0	0	0	
Career Total	1	0	0	0	

Going: Sf: 0-0 GS: 0-0 Gd: 0-1 GF: - Fm: 0-0
Distance: 2m/2m3: 0-1 2m4-2m7: 0-0 3m+: 0-0
Track: LH: 0-0 RH: 0-1 Tight: 0-1 Gall: 0-0
Aids: Bl: 0-0 Vi: 0-0 Tstrap: 0-0
Best Rating: 14 11/01 Tntn 2m1f good Hdl

Deel Time

82(68c) **53**

9-y-o ch g Gildoran-Milltown Lady (Deep Run)
Ian Williams The Bartley Syndicate

Placings:5/0P4/P0F1F-P00P (1760)
2001/02: 20PGF, 200GF, 160G, 16PGS

	Starts	1st	2nd	3rd	Win & Pl
Hurdles	3	0	0	0	0
Chases	1	0	0	0	0
Career Total	13	1	0	0	2359

94	10/00	Towc	2m110y	F(0-105)HCh	G-S	£2359

Total win prize-money £2359

Going: Sf: 0-0 GS: 0-1 Gd: 0-1 GF: - Fm: 0-2
Distance: 2m/2m3: 0-2 2m4-2m7: 0-2 3m+: 0-0
Track: LH: 0-2 RH: 0-2 Tight: 0-1 Gall: 0-1
Aids: Bl: 0-0 Vi: 0-0 Tstrap: 0-0
Best Rating: 94 10/00 Towc 2m110y gd-sft Ch

Deep Sunset (IRE)

108 **126**

6-y-o b m Supreme Leader-Twinkle Sunset (Deep Run)
N J Henderson R A Ballin

Placings:132-2144 (4420)
2001/02: 162G, 201GS, 214G, 214GS

	Starts	1st	2nd	3rd	Win & Pl
Hurdles	4	1	1	0	8051
Career Total	7	2	2	1	14421

113	12/01	Hntg	2m4f110y	D Hdl	G-S	£3601
103	12/00	Ludl	2m	H NHF	SFT	£1708

Total win prize-money £5309

Going: Sf: 0-0 GS: 1-2 Gd: 0-2 GF: - Fm: 0-0
Distance: 2m/2m3: 0-1 **2m4-2m7: 1-3** 3m+: 0-0
Track: LH: 0-2 **RH: 1-2** Tight: 0-0 **Gall: 1-3**
Aids: Bl: 0-0 Vi: 0-0 Tstrap: 0-0
Best Rating: 126 12/01 Newb 2m5f good Hdl

A winner of a bumper, she got off the mark over hurdles with a fine win at Huntingdon in December 2001, but was held in good company subsequently. Suited by two and a half miles and soft ground.

Deep Water (USA)

110(85c) **130**

8-y-o b g Diesis-Water Course (USA) (Irish River (FR))
L Lungo The County Set

Placings:1121/5/410/0211F0P-03336 (4893)
2001/02: 160G, 203G, 223S, 203S, 206G

	Starts	1st	2nd	3rd	Win & Pl
Hurdles	5	0	0	3	3387
Career Total	20	6	2	3	70773

133	12/00	MRas	2m1f110y	D Ch	SFT	£5421
125	11/00	Catt	2m	D Ch	GD	£4173
140	2/00	Hayd	2m	B Hdl	SFT	£14490
146	4/98	Aint	2m110y	A Hdl	GD	£28334
126	2/98	Kels	2m110y	C Hdl	G-S	£4065
100	1/98	Kels	2m110y	D Hdl	HVY	£3025

Total win prize-money £59508

Going: Sf: 0-2 GS: 0-0 Gd: 0-3 GF: - Fm: 0-0
Distance: 2m/2m3: 0-1 2m4-2m7: 0-4 3m+: 0-0
Track: LH: 0-4 RH: 0-1 Tight: 0-0 Gall: 0-1
Aids: Bl: 0-0 Vi: 0-0 Tstrap: 0-0
Best Rating: 146 4/98 Aint 2m110y good Hdl

A smart hurdler who won the Glenlivet Anniversary Hurdle at Aintree in 1998, he scrambled home in two uncompetitive novice chases at the end of 2000 and was found out when tried in better company. Decent efforts over hurdles for a new yard in 2001/02, stays two and a half miles plus.

Deepritive

86f **73f**

5-y-o b m Primitive Rising (USA)-Last Of The Deep (IRE) (Deep Run)
Ian Williams T A Peake

Placings:000 (4910)
2001/02: 170GS, 160GF, 170G

	Starts	1st	2nd	3rd	Win & Pl
NH Flat	3	0	0	0	
Career Total	3	0	0	0	

Going: Sf: 0-0 GS: 0-1 Gd: 0-1 GF: - Fm: 0-1
Distance: 2m/2m3: 0-3 2m4-2m7: 0-0 3m+: 0-0
Track: LH: 0-0 RH: 0-3 Tight: 0-2 Gall: 0-0
Aids: Bl: 0-0 Vi: 0-0 Tstrap: 0-0
Best Rating: 77 3/02 MRas 2m1f110y gd-sft NHF

Chasing-bred who has shown some ability in bumpers.

Deer Park Lass (IRE)

93(95h) (80h)**92**

10-y-o ch m Mister Lord (USA)-Adare Flore (IRE) (Fairbairn)
R Johnson (S R Bolton 18/5) Mrs C Lawson-Croome

Placings:5B/P/0RP06R02524 (4671)
2001/02: 250G, 25RG, 25PS, 200GS, 166S, 24RS, 240S, 162GS, 215S, 162S, 214GF

	Starts	1st	2nd	3rd	Win & Pl
Hurdles	2	0	0	0	0
Chases	9	0	2	0	2772
Career Total	14	0	2	0	2772

Going: Sf: 0-6 GS: 0-2 Gd: 0-2 GF: - Fm: 0-1
Distance: 2m/2m3: 0-3 2m4-2m7: 0-3 3m+: 0-5
Track: LH: 0-10 RH: 0-1 Tight: 0-6 Gall: 0-2
Aids: Bl: 0-0 Vi: 0-0 Tstrap: 0-1
Best Rating: 92 3/02 Sedg 2m110y soft Ch

Still a maiden over hurdles and fences, but acts on soft ground and is effective over two miles.

Deerhunter

11-y-o b/br g Gunner B-Royal Scarlet (Royal Fountain)
G A Harker G A Harker

Placings:04/0P/0 (3824)
2001/02: 210S

	Starts	1st	2nd	3rd	Win & Pl
Chases	1	0	0	0	
Career Total	5	0	0	0	0

Going: Sf: 0-1 GS: 0-0 Gd: 0-0 GF: - Fm: 0-0
Distance: 2m/2m3: 0-0 2m4-2m7: 0-1 3m+: 0-0
Track: LH: 0-1 RH: 0-0 Tight: 0-1 Gall: 0-0
Aids: Bl: 0-0 Vi: 0-0 Tstrap: 0-0
Best Rating: 84 12/96 Muss 2m gd-fm NHF

Winning pointer.

Defendtherealm

104(102h) (83h)**119**

11-y-o br g Derring Rose-Armagnac Princess (Armagnac Monarch)
R G Frost R G Frost

Placings:503231/3430U122/54F5F1U1/34245/213PP 53-4PU5 (2485)
2001/02: 214GF, 21PGF, 23UGF, 225HY

	Starts	1st	2nd	3rd	Win & Pl
Hurdles	1	0	0	0	0
Chases	3	0	0	0	308
Career Total	38	5	5	7	27197

120	8/00	NAbb	3m2f110y	D(0-120)HCh	G-F	£4284
120	4/99	Extr	2m7f110y	E(0-105)HCh	SFT	£3965
120	3/99	Extr	2m3f	D Ch	SFT	£3710
93	3/98	NAbb	2m6f	D(0-120)HHdl	SFT	£2805
94	3/97	NAbb	2m6f	E Hdl	HVY	£2284

Total win prize-money £17052

Going: Sf: 0-1 GS: 0-0 Gd: 0-0 GF: - Fm: 0-3
Distance: 2m/2m3: 0-0 2m4-2m7: 0-3 3m+: 0-1
Track: LH: 0-3 RH: 0-1 Tight: 0-3 Gall: 0-0
Aids: Bl: 0-1 Vi: 0-0 Tstrap: 0-0
Best Rating: 120 8/00 NAbb 3m2f110y gd-fm Ch

He is an effective sort in modest handicap chases in the West country.

Deferlant (FR)

102(107h) (130h)**122**

5-y-o ch g Bering-Sail Storm (USA) (Topsider (USA))
Mrs H Dalton (M C Pipe 9/2) Mrs G McNeela

Placings:123120-622224300 (4193)
2001/02: 176G, 192GF, 162GF, 202GF, 162GF, 174GS, 183S, 230HY, 250GS

	Starts	1st	2nd	3rd	Win & Pl
Hurdles	9	0	4	1	6125
Career Total	15	2	6	2	16777

115	12/00	Newb	2m110y	D Hdl	SFT	£3786
110	7/00	MRas	2m1f110y	D Hdl	G-F	£3477

Total win prize-money £7264

Going: Sf: 0-2 GS: 0-2 Gd: 0-1 GF: - Fm: 0-4
Distance: 2m/2m3: 0-5 2m4-2m7: 0-2 3m+: 0-2
Track: LH: 0-7 RH: 0-2 Tight: 0-6 Gall: 0-1
Aids: Bl: 0-0 Vi: 0-9 Tstrap: 0-0
Best Rating: 130 8/01 Strf 2m110y gd-fm Hdl

A winner on the Flat in France and over hurdles in England, but has kept on finding one or two too good for him since the end of 2000. Often finishes weakly over fences but got a deserved success at Stratford in July 2002 and had a simple task when following up next time at Perth. Acts on most types of ground and stays in excess of two and a half miles. Usually visored.

Degree Of Power

4-y-o b f Sure Blade (USA)-One Degree (Crooner)
Mrs L Richards (Miss D A McHale 7/5) Manor Boys

Placings:0 **(2409)**
2001/02: 17^{0}GS

	Starts	1st	2nd	3rd	Win & Pl
Hurdles	1	0	0	0	
Career Total	**1**	**0**	**0**	**0**	

Going: Sf: 0-0 GS: 0-1 Gd: 0-0 GF: - Fm: 0-0
Distance: 2m/2m3: 0-1 2m4-2m7: 0-0 3m+: 0-0
Track: LH: 0-0 RH: 0-1 Tight: 0-1 Gall: 0-0
Aids: Bl: 0-0 Vi: 0-0 Tstrap: 0-0
Best Rating:

Delaware (FR)

108(106c) (144c)**112**
6-y-o ch g Garde Royale-L'Indienne (FR) (Le Nain Jaune (FR))
M C Pipe Sandicroft Stud Syndicate Ii

Placings:2/4/005U1B21F-62F **(4664)**
2001/02: 21^{6}G, 21^{2}GS, 21^{F}G

	Starts	1st	2nd	3rd	Win & Pl
Chases	3	0	1	0	2220
Career Total	**14**	**2**	**3**	**0**	**22628**

123	2/01	Ludl	2m4f	E Ch	GD	£3484
	7/00	Autl	2m1f110y	Ch	HVY	£6244

Total win prize-money £9728

Going: Sf: 0-0 GS: 0-1 Gd: 0-2 GF: - Fm: 0-0
Distance: 2m/2m3: 0-0 2m4-2m7: 0-3 3m+: 0-0
Track: LH: 0-1 RH: 0-2 Tight: 0-1 Gall: 0-0
Aids: Bl: 0-0 Vi: 0-3 Tstrap: 0-0
Best Rating: 144 2/02 Winc 2m5f gd-sft Ch

A French import. Effective over fences and hurdles and stays two and three-quarter miles. Has won on all types of ground.

Delayed (FR)

101(114h) **132**
6-y-o b m Fijar Tango (FR)-Antea (FR) (Esprit Du Nord (USA))
N A Twiston-Davies H J M Price

Placings:23113/020501-6 **(2193)**
2001/02: 20^{6}G

	Starts	1st	2nd	3rd	Win & Pl
Chases	1	0	0	0	0
Career Total	**12**	**3**	**2**	**2**	**23390**

125	3/01	Sand	2m	C Ch	SFT	£6890
121	1/00	Kemp	2m	D Hdl	GD	£3477
124	12/99	Kemp	2m	B Hdl	SFT	£7295

Total win prize-money £17663

Going: Sf: 0-0 GS: 0-0 Gd: 0-1 GF: - Fm: 0-0
Distance: 2m/2m3: 0-0 2m4-2m7: 0-1 3m+: 0-0
Track: LH: 0-1 RH: 0-0 Tight: 0-0 Gall: 0-1
Aids: Bl: 0-0 Vi: 0-0 Tstrap: 0-0
Best Rating: 132 11/01 Chel 2m4f110y good Ch

Useful over hurdles, she made a successful chasing debut at Sandown in March 2001. Suited by two miles and good ground or softer.

Deliceo (IRE)

104(70h) **94**
9-y-o br g Roselier (FR)-Grey's Delight (Decent Fellow)
M Sheppard The Blues Partnership

Placings: *1/0*035204/36332412P4P-21462443F **(4514)**
2001/02: 16^{2}GS, 22^{1}S, 20^{4}GS, 25^{6}S, 24^{2}GS, 20^{4}S, 24^{4}G, 25^{3}S, 25^{F}GS

	Starts	1st	2nd	3rd	Win & Pl
Chases	9	1	2	1	6525
Career Total	**28**	**3**	**5**	**5**	**17927**

94	11/01	Towc	2m6f	F(0-105)HCh	SFT	£3753
94	12/00	Ludl	2m4f	D(0-115)HCh	SFT	£5012
92	10/98	Carl	2m1f	H NHF	GD	£1255

Total win prize-money £10022

Going: Sf: 1-4 GS: 0-4 Gd: 0-1 GF: - Fm: 0-0
Distance: 2m/2m3: 0-1 **2m4-2m7: 1-3** 3m+: 0-5
Track: LH: 0-1 **RH: 1-8** Tight: 0-2 Gall: 0-2
Aids: Bl: 0-0 Vi: 0-0 Tstrap: 0-0
Best Rating: 94 11/01 Towc 2m6f soft Ch

Moderate chaser, stays three miles, needs soft ground.

Delilah Blue (NZ)

106(71h) **118**
9-y-o b m High Ice (USA)-Calamity (NZ) (Bally Royal)
S A Brookshaw Brian Davies

Placings:50/004/120P31U0-01FP33 **(1279)**
2001/02: 19^{0}G, 19^{1}F, 20^{F}GS, 22^{P}GY, 20^{3}G, 21^{3}GF

	Starts	1st	2nd	3rd	Win & Pl
Chases	6	1	0	2	5536
Career Total	**19**	**3**	**1**	**3**	**13104**

118	6/01	Hrfd	2m3f	F(0-110)HCh	FRM	£3552
118	11/00	Ludl	2m	E(0-105)HCh	GD	£3406
95	5/00	Chep	2m110y	E(0-105)HHdl	FRM	£2516

Total win prize-money £9475

Going: Sf: 0-0 GS: 0-1 Gd: 0-2 GF: - Fm: 1-2
Distance: **2m/2m3: 1-1** 2m4-2m7: 0-5 3m+: 0-0
Track: LH: 0-3 **RH: 1-2** Tight: 0-2 Gall: 0-0
Aids: Bl: 0-0 Vi: 0-0 Tstrap: 0-0
Best Rating: 118 6/01 Hrfd 2m3f firm Ch

Moderate chaser, stays two and a half miles and acts on a sound surface.

Dellone

104(98c) (72c)**92**
10-y-o b g Gunner B-Coire Vannich (Celtic Cone)
T R George M C Houghton

Placings:R/F4/62U32P32P-6441041F6 **(4327)**
2001/02: 22^{6}S, 19^{4}S, 25^{4}G, 17^{1}S, 19^{0}GS, 16^{4}HY, 17^{1}HY, 17^{F}S, 19^{6}S

	Starts	1st	2nd	3rd	Win & Pl
Hurdles	6	2	0	0	5121
Chases	3	0	0	0	0
Career Total	**21**	**2**	**3**	**2**	**9042**

92	2/02	Hrfd	2m1f	E(0-100)HHdl	HVY	£2702
88	12/01	Hrfd	2m1f	E(0-105)HHdl	SFT	£2418

Total win prize-money £5121

Going: Sf: 2-7 GS: 0-1 Gd: 0-1 GF: - Fm: 0-0
Distance: **2m/2m3: 2-4** 2m4-2m7: 0-4 3m+: 0-1
Track: LH: 0-2 **RH: 2-6** Tight: 0-3 Gall: 0-0
Aids: Bl: 0-0 Vi: 0-0 Tstrap: 0-0
Best Rating: 92 2/02 Folk 2m1f110y soft Hdl

A modest handicapper over fencesand hurdles, is best in the mud. Won two weak hurdle races at Hereford in 2001/02.

Delmo

60 **13**
7-y-o ch g Democratic (USA)-Charlotte Piaf (Morston (FR))
J White Mrs P A White

Placings:OP/0 **(1387)**
2001/02: 16^{0}G

	Starts	1st	2nd	3rd	Win & Pl
Hurdles	1	0	0	0	
Career Total	**3**	**0**	**0**	**0**	

Going: Sf: 0-0 GS: 0-0 Gd: 0-1 GF: - Fm: 0-0
Distance: 2m/2m3: 0-1 2m4-2m7: 0-0 3m+: 0-0
Track: LH: 0-1 RH: 0-0 Tight: 0-0 Gall: 0-0
Aids: Bl: 0-0 Vi: 0-0 Tstrap: 0-0
Best Rating: 13 9/01 Uttx 2m good Hdl

Deltas First

84 **72**
6-y-o b g Nile Delta (IRE)-Shalabia (Fast Topaze (USA))
R D E Woodhouse R Priestley Developments Co Ltd

Placings:0-P6 **(1072)**
2001/02: 17^{P}GS, 17^{6}GF

	Starts	1st	2nd	3rd	Win & Pl
Hurdles	2	0	0	0	0
Career Total	**3**	**0**	**0**	**0**	**0**

Going: Sf: 0-0 GS: 0-1 Gd: 0-0 GF: - Fm: 0-1
Distance: 2m/2m3: 0-2 2m4-2m7: 0-0 3m+: 0-0
Track: LH: 0-1 RH: 0-0 Tight: 0-1 Gall: 0-0
Aids: Bl: 0-0 Vi: 0-0 Tstrap: 0-0
Best Rating: 72 8/01 Sedg 2m1f gd-fm Hdl

Demasta (NZ)

115 **158**
11-y-o ch g Northerly Native (USA)-Hit It Gold (AUS) (Hit It Benny (AUS))
N J Henderson Michael Buckley

Placings:1113/1/114/11611 **(4901)**
2001/02: 16^{1}GF, 20^{1}G, 20^{6}GS, 16^{1}G, 16^{1}G

	Starts	1st	2nd	3rd	Win & Pl
Chases	5	4	0	0	39405
Career Total	**13**	**10**	**0**	**1**	**67575**

155	4/02	Sand	2m	B(0-145)HCh	GD	£17400
150	4/02	Chel	2m110y	C(0-135)HCh	GD	£12662
133	7/01	MRas	2m4f	D Ch	GD	£5466
124	6/01	NAbb	2m110y	D Ch	G-F	£3876
	8/99	Maia	2m1f110y	Hdl	GD	£8201
	8/99	Maia	2m1f110y	Hdl	GD	£7290
	5/99	Elle	1m6f175y	Hdl	SFT	£2381
	9/97	Awap	1m5f	Hdl	SFT	£2048
	9/97	Araw	1m6f	Hdl	SFT	£1775
	8/97	Hast	1m4f110y	Hdl	G-S	£2101

Total win prize-money £63202

Going: Sf: 0-0 GS: 0-1 Gd: 3-3 GF: - Fm: 1-1

Distance: 2m/2m3: **3-3** 2m4-2m7: 1-2 3m+: 0-0
Track: LH: 2-2 RH: 2-2 **Tight: 2-2** Gall: 1-1
Aids: Bl: 0-0 Vi: 0-0 Tstrap: 0-0
Best Rating: 155 4/02 Sand 2m good Ch

A winner in his native New Zealand and Italy prior to coming to Britain, he was an impressive winner of two novice chases in the summer of 2001. He returned from a long absence when easily winning at Cheltenham and Sandown April 2002, and completed the hat-trick early in the new season. Likes to force the pace and is effective at up to two and a half miles on ground good or faster.

Denarii (IRE)

10-y-o ch m Denel (FR)-Troubled Course (Crash Course)
Ms A E Embiricos Ms A E Embiricos

Placings:U-P0 (0254)
2001/02: 26^{P}GS, 24^{0}GF

	Starts	1st	2nd	3rd	Win & Pl
Chases	2	0	0	0	
Career Total	**3**	**0**	**0**	**0**	

Going: Sf: 0-0 GS: 0-1 Gd: 0-0 GF: - Fm: 0-1
Distance: 2m/2m3: 0-0 2m4-2m7: 0-0 3m+: 0-2
Track: LH: 0-1 RH: 0-0 Tight: 0-1 Gall: 0-0
Aids: Bl: 0-0 Vi: 0-0 Tstrap: 0-0
Best Rating: 82 5/01 Strf 3m gd-fm Ch

Denarius (USA)

(115h) (114h)
7-y-o b g Silver Hawk (USA)-Ambrosine (USA) (Mr Prospector (USA))
G A Swinbank Mr S V Rutter

Placings:*11/0/*13PP3-23525**P** (3549)
2001/02: 20^{2}S, 19^{3}G, 20^{5}F, 19^{2}S, 24^{5}GF, 20^{P}S

	Starts	1st	2nd	3rd	Win & Pl
Hurdles	5	0	2	1	2448
Chases	1	0	0	0	0
Career Total	**14**	**3**	**2**	**3**	**8413**

103	11/00	Catt	2m3f	E Hdl	G-S	£1858
111	4/99	Carl	2m1f	H NHF	GD	£1682
96	3/99	Carl	2m1f	H NHF	SFT	£1430

Total win prize-money £4973

Going: Sf: 0-3 GS: 0-0 Gd: 0-1 GF: - Fm: 0-2
Distance: 2m/2m3: 0-1 2m4-2m7: 0-4 3m+: 0-1
Track: LH: 0-4 RH: 0-2 Tight: 0-3 Gall: 0-1
Aids: Bl: 0-0 Vi: 0-0 Tstrap: 0-5
Best Rating: 114 12/01 Catt 2m3f soft Hdl

Modest hurdler/chaser, stays two and a half miles, often wears a tongue tie.

Dene View (IRE)

99(94c) (73c)94
7-y-o br g Good Thyne (USA)-The Furnituremaker (Mandalus)
R A Fahey C H Stevens

Placings:*00/*00-44333**05**P (4772)
2001/02: 20^{4}G, 20^{4}GS, 20^{3}GF, 20^{3}GS, 21^{3}HY, 16^{0}S, 24^{5}HY, 21^{P}G

	Starts	1st	2nd	3rd	Win & Pl
Hurdles	6	0	0	3	1134
Chases	2	0	0	0	0
Career Total	**12**	**0**	**0**	**3**	**1134**

Going: Sf: 0-3 GS: 0-2 Gd: 0-2 GF: - Fm: 0-1

Distance: 2m/2m3: 0-1 2m4-2m7: 0-6 3m+: 0-1
Track: LH: 0-4 RH: 0-3 Tight: 0-4 Gall: 0-2
Aids: Bl: 0-0 Vi: 0-0 Tstrap: 0-0
Best Rating: 94 1/02 Wwck 2m5f heavy Hdl

A slowly-improving hurdler, stays two and a half miles plus.

Deneises Blossom (IRE)

102 81
9-y-o b m Beau Sher-Lindabell (Over The River (FR))
W Storey John J Maguire

Placings:45B/P-602400350 (4491)
2001/02: 20^{6}G, 22^{0}G, 22^{2}GS, 20^{4}S, 21^{0}S, 16^{0}GS, 16^{3}S, 16^{5}S, 20^{0}GS

	Starts	1st	2nd	3rd	Win & Pl
Hurdles	9	0	1	1	1154
Career Total	**13**	**0**	**1**	**1**	**1330**

Going: Sf: 0-4 GS: 0-3 Gd: 0-2 GF: - Fm: 0-0
Distance: 2m/2m3: 0-3 2m4-2m7: 0-6 3m+: 0-0
Track: LH: 0-7 RH: 0-0 Tight: 0-3 Gall: 0-3
Aids: Bl: 0-0 Vi: 0-0 Tstrap: 0-0
Best Rating: 91 4/00 List 3m yld-sft Ch

Moderate hurdler, stays two miles-six, appreciates cut in the ground.

Denise's Profiles

102 101
12-y-o b g Royal Vulcan-Lovelyroseofclare (Torus)
Miss K M George Exterior Profiles Ltd

Placings:*13163/*2/4U132P (1865)
2001/02: 24^{4}G, 24^{U}GF, 27^{1}G, 24^{3}GF, 24^{2}GS, 25^{P}G

	Starts	1st	2nd	3rd	Win & Pl
Hurdles	6	1	1	1	4411
Career Total	**12**	**3**	**2**	**3**	**10156**

94	7/01	Strf	3m3f	F(0-100)HHdl	GD	£3041
117	2/95	Wwck	2m	H NHF	SFT	£1444
100	12/94	Wwck	2m	NHF	HVY	£2184

Total win prize-money £6671

Going: Sf: 0-0 GS: 0-1 Gd: 1-3 GF: - Fm: 0-2
Distance: 2m/2m3: 0-0 2m4-2m7: 0-0 **3m+: 1-6**
Track: **LH: 1-4** RH: 0-2 **Tight: 1-4** Gall: 0-1
Aids: Bl: 0-0 Vi: 0-0 Tstrap: 0-0
Best Rating: 117 4/95 Aint 2m110y gd-fm NHF

Moderate staying hurdler, acts on any ground.

Dennett Lough (IRE)

11-y-o b g Torus-Monica's Pet (Sovereign Gleam)
C Storey Mrs A D Wauchope

Placings:FB/26F/53-52250 (4892)
2001/02: 25^{5}S, 24^{2}GF, 27^{2}GF, 25^{5}GF, 31^{0}G

	Starts	1st	2nd	3rd	Win & Pl
Chases	5	0	2	0	1295
Career Total	**12**	**0**	**3**	**1**	**2187**

Going: Sf: 0-1 GS: 0-0 Gd: 0-1 GF: - Fm: 0-3
Distance: 2m/2m3: 0-0 2m4-2m7: 0-0 3m+: 0-5
Track: LH: 0-3 RH: 0-1 Tight: 0-2 Gall: 0-0
Aids: Bl: 0-0 Vi: 0-0 Tstrap: 0-0
Best Rating: 101 5/00 Ctml 3m2f gd-fm Ch

Modest staying pointer/hunter chaser, suited by fast ground although handles softer.

Deoch An Dorais (IRE)

96 115
7-y-o b g Supreme Leader-General Rain (General Ironside)
N J Henderson Queen Elizabeth

Placings:*6/0053122/*33-3F00 (4028)
2001/02: 16^{3}S, 16^{F}G, 16^{0}S, 21^{0}GS

	Starts	1st	2nd	3rd	Win & Pl
Hurdles	4	0	0	1	1140
Career Total	**14**	**1**	**2**	**4**	**9052**

101	1/00	Naas	2m	NHF	SFT	£3312

Total win prize-money £3312

Going: Sf: 0-2 GS: 0-1 Gd: 0-1 GF: - Fm: 0-0
Distance: 2m/2m3: 0-3 2m4-2m7: 0-1 3m+: 0-0
Track: LH: 0-3 RH: 0-1 Tight: 0-0 Gall: 0-2
Aids: Bl: 0-0 Vi: 0-0 Tstrap: 0-0
Best Rating: 115 12/01 Newb 2m110y soft Hdl

A strong sort who has shown fair form in bumpers and novice hurdles. Best at around two miles on an easy surface.

Dere Lyn

98 78
4-y-o b g Awesome-Our Resolution (Caerleon (USA))
D Burchell Lyn Phillips

Placings:000 (4813)
2001/02: 16^{0}S, 16^{0}G, 17^{0}GF

	Starts	1st	2nd	3rd	Win & Pl
Hurdles	3	0	0	0	
Career Total	**3**	**0**	**0**	**0**	

Going: Sf: 0-1 GS: 0-0 Gd: 0-1 GF: - Fm: 0-1
Distance: 2m/2m3: 0-3 2m4-2m7: 0-0 3m+: 0-0
Track: LH: 0-3 RH: 0-0 Tight: 0-0 Gall: 0-1
Aids: Bl: 0-0 Vi: 0-0 Tstrap: 0-0
Best Rating: 65 3/02 Hayd 2m good Hdl

Moderate form in novice hurdles.

Dereck's-Mi-Dad

95 78
8-y-o b/br g Nomadic Way (USA)-I'm Fine (Fitzwilliam (USA))
A Dickman Mike Smallman

Placings:*50*203/05 (2264)
2001/02: 17^{0}G, 17^{5}S

	Starts	1st	2nd	3rd	Win & Pl
Hurdles	2	0	0	0	0
Career Total	**7**	**0**	**1**	**1**	**1028**

Going: Sf: 0-1 GS: 0-0 Gd: 0-1 GF: - Fm: 0-0
Distance: 2m/2m3: 0-2 2m4-2m7: 0-0 3m+: 0-0
Track: LH: 0-2 RH: 0-0 Tight: 0-2 Gall: 0-0
Aids: Bl: 0-0 Vi: 0-0 Tstrap: 0-0
Best Rating: 92 2/00 Catt 2m3f good Hdl

Derivative (IRE)

100 112
4-y-o b/br g Erin's Isle-Our Hope (Dancing Brave (USA))
Miss Venetia Williams (J S Bolger 1/7) P Ryan

Placings:20 (4651)
2001/02: 16^{2}S, 16^{0}G

	Starts	1st	2nd	3rd	Win & Pl
Hurdles	2	0	1	0	1392
Career Total	**2**	**0**	**1**	**0**	**1392**

Going: Sf: 0-1 GS: 0-0 Gd: 0-1 GF: - Fm: 0-0
Distance: 2m/2m3: 0-2 2m4-2m7: 0-0 3m+: 0-0
Track: LH: 0-2 RH: 0-0 Tight: 0-1 Gall: 0-1
Aids: Bl: 0-0 Vi: 0-0 Tstrap: 0-0
Best Rating: **112** 3/02 Newb 2m110y soft Hdl

He had Mozart behind him when running second in a Listed race on the Flat in Ireland in 2001. Doubts concerning his ability to stay two miles over hurdles were quashed on his debut over timber at Newbury in March 2002 but was most disapointing at Aintree.

Derra Glen (IRE)

80 **32**

8-y-o b g Supreme Leader-Corivia (Over The River (FR))
N A Twiston-Davies The Derra Glen Partnership

Placings:*356*P53/213P03/**20365-FP0** **(1379)**
2001/02: 26^{F}GF, 26^{P}GF, 25^{0}GF

	Starts	1st	2nd	3rd	Win & Pl
Chases	3	0	0	0	
Career Total	**20**	**1**	**2**	**5**	**5543**

87	10/99	Sthl	3m110y	E Hdl	G-S	£2253

Total win prize-money £2253

Going: Sf: 0-0 GS: 0-0 Gd: 0-0 GF: - Fm: 0-3
Distance: 2m/2m3: 0-0 2m4-2m7: 0-0 3m+: 0-3
Track: LH: 0-2 RH: 0-1 Tight: 0-1 Gall: 0-0
Aids: Bl: 0-2 Vi: 0-0 Tstrap: 0-1
Best Rating: **112** 5/00 Towc 2m6f gd-fm Ch

Derring Bridge

101(99c) (107c)**103**

12-y-o b g Derring Rose-Bridge Ash (Normandy)
Mrs S M Johnson I K Johnson

Placings:*0*P51U0F/040055P4/031U654300642/22311 13211436/42**22221143**/400**2113342120F/1244435F-63514R0** **(1395)**
2001/02: 30^{6}G, 32^{3}GF, 26^{5}GF, 24^{1}G, 24^{4}GF, 24^{R}GF, 24^{0}GF

	Starts	1st	2nd	3rd	Win & Pl
Hurdles	3	1	0	0	4430
Chases	4	0	0	1	1550
Career Total	**80**	**14**	**13**	**10**	**79808**

102	7/01	Worc	3m	D(0-125)HHdl	GD	£4017
126	6/00	Worc	2m7f110y	C(0-135)HCh	G-F	£7046
124	9/99	Hntg	3m	E(0-115)HCh	GD	£3601
116	7/99	NAbb	3m2f110y	D(0-125)HCh	G-F	£3543
126	7/99	Worc	2m7f110y	F(0-110)HCh	G-F	£2497
115	9/98	NAbb	3m2f110y	D(0-120)HCh	G-F	£3355
104	8/98	Worc	2m7f110y	E Ch	G-F	£2951
107	9/97	MRas	3m	C(0-130)HHdl	GD	£3717
111	9/97	NAbb	3m3f	D(0-120)HHdl	GD	£2655
104	7/97	Worc	3m	D(0-125)HHdl	G-F	£2756
107	6/97	Uttx	3m110y	D(0-125)HHdl	GD	£3436
111	6/97	Sthl	3m110y	E(0-110)HHdl	G-S	£2390
89	6/96	Sthl	3m110y	E(0-110)HHdl	G-F	£3054
83	3/95	Ludl	2m5f110y	E Hdl	G-S	£2626

Total win prize-money £47647

Going: Sf: 0-0 GS: 0-0 Gd: 1-2 GF: - Fm: 0-5
Distance: 2m/2m3: 0-0 2m4-2m7: 0-0 **3m+: 1-7**
Track: **LH: 1-6** RH: 0-0 Tight: 0-3 Gall: 0-0
Aids: Bl: 0-0 Vi: 0-0 Tstrap: 0-0
Best Rating: **126** 7/00 Uttx 4m110y gd-fm Ch

An out and out stayer, he goes well on fast ground and tends to pick up a race every summer. Worcester specialist.

Derring Dove

81(96c) (99c)**35**

10-y-o b g Derring Rose-Shadey Dove (Deadly Nightshade)
H W Lavis H W Lavis

Placings:*0*/P05/**P**/**4432P-400** **(1240)**
2001/02: 24^{4}GF, 26^{0}GF, 24^{0}GF

	Starts	1st	2nd	3rd	Win & Pl
Hurdles	1	0	0	0	0
Chases	2	0	0	0	147
Career Total	**13**	**0**	**1**	**1**	**1308**

Going: Sf: 0-0 GS: 0-0 Gd: 0-0 GF: - Fm: 0-3
Distance: 2m/2m3: 0-0 2m4-2m7: 0-0 3m+: 0-3
Track: LH: 0-3 RH: 0-0 Tight: 0-2 Gall: 0-0
Aids: Bl: 0-0 Vi: 0-0 Tstrap: 0-0
Best Rating: **109** 2/01 Ludl 3m gd-sft Ch

Derry Ann

94f **91f**

6-y-o b m Derrylin-Ancat Girl (Politico (USA))
G P Kelly Mrs H Ratcliffe

Placings:*040* **(4595)**
2001/02: 16^{0}GF, 17^{4}GS, 16^{0}G

	Starts	1st	2nd	3rd	Win & Pl
NH Flat	3	0	0	0	0
Career Total	**3**	**0**	**0**	**0**	**0**

Going: Sf: 0-0 GS: 0-1 Gd: 0-1 GF: - Fm: 0-1
Distance: 2m/2m3: 0-3 2m4-2m7: 0-0 3m+: 0-0
Track: LH: 0-1 RH: 0-2 Tight: 0-1 Gall: 0-1
Aids: Bl: 0-0 Vi: 0-0 Tstrap: 0-0
Best Rating: **91** 3/02 MRas 2m1f110y gd-sft NHF

Glimmer of ability in bumpers.

Derryair

9-y-o b g Derrylin-Deep Dora (Deep Run)
James Owen (H H G Owen 20/1) Mrs D E S Surman

Placings:5-442P **(4569)**
2001/02: 26^{4}G, 24^{4}GS, 20^{2}S, 22^{P}G

	Starts	1st	2nd	3rd	Win & Pl
Chases	4	0	1	0	650
Career Total	**5**	**0**	**1**	**0**	**650**

Going: Sf: 0-1 GS: 0-1 Gd: 0-2 GF: - Fm: 0-0
Distance: 2m/2m3: 0-0 2m4-2m7: 0-2 3m+: 0-2
Track: LH: 0-0 RH: 0-4 Tight: 0-1 Gall: 0-1
Aids: Bl: 0-0 Vi: 0-0 Tstrap: 0-0
Best Rating: **107** 3/02 Leic 2m4f110y soft Ch

Staying hunter/pointer, his last win came in April 2000. Lacks a turn of foot, and is best on a lively surface.

Derrykin

(76h) (36h)

8-y-o b m Derrylin-Kins Token (Relkino)
Mrs K Lundberg-Young Mrs Kin Lundberg-Young

Placings:PPP-P0P **(2410)**
2001/02: 22^{P}GF, 17^{0}G, 19^{P}GS

Starts	1st	2nd	3rd	Win & Pl	
Hurdles	2	0	0	0	0
Chases	1	0	0	0	0
Career Total	**6**	**0**	**0**	**0**	**0**

Going: Sf: 0-0 GS: 0-1 Gd: 0-1 GF: - Fm: 0-1
Distance: 2m/2m3: 0-2 2m4-2m7: 0-1 3m+: 0-0
Track: LH: 0-0 RH: 0-2 Tight: 0-2 Gall: 0-0
Aids: Bl: 0-0 Vi: 0-0 Tstrap: 0-0
Best Rating: **36** 11/01 Tntn 2m1f good Hdl

Derrymore Mist (IRE)

10-y-o ch g Le Bavard (FR)-Cheribond (Relkino)
P F Nicholls Jeffrey Hordle

Placings:*351*/**11224/3U3-F** **(0068)**
2001/02: 27^{F}G

	Starts	1st	2nd	3rd	Win & Pl
Chases	1	0	0	0	
Career Total	**12**	**3**	**2**	**3**	**21050**

131	11/98	Winc	3m1f110y	E(0-105)HCh	G-S	£5485
123	10/98	Winc	3m1f110y	D Ch	G-S	£3668
113	4/98	Fair	2m2f	NHF	G-Y	£5521

Total win prize-money £14676

Going: Sf: 0-0 GS: 0-0 Gd: 0-1 GF: - Fm: 0-0
Distance: 2m/2m3: 0-0 2m4-2m7: 0-0 3m+: 0-1
Track: LH: 0-1 RH: 0-0 Tight: 0-1 Gall: 0-0
Aids: Bl: 0-0 Vi: 0-0 Tstrap: 0-0
Best Rating: **131** 1/01 Font 3m2f110y soft Ch

Modest staying chaser, took a fatal fall at Sedgefield in May 2001. (DEAD)

Derryrose

9-y-o br g Derrylin-Levantine Rose (Levanter)
R J Kyle (Miss V Haigh 17/3) R J Kyle

Placings:6P526P30U/5P430P0-3 **(4690)**
2001/02: 25^{3}GF

	Starts	1st	2nd	3rd	Win & Pl
Chases	1	0	0	1	398
Career Total	**17**	**0**	**1**	**3**	**1737**

Going: Sf: 0-0 GS: 0-0 Gd: 0-0 GF: - Fm: 0-1
Distance: 2m/2m3: 0-0 2m4-2m7: 0-0 3m+: 0-1
Track: LH: 0-1 RH: 0-0 Tight: 0-1 Gall: 0-0
Aids: Bl: 0-0 Vi: 0-0 Tstrap: 0-0
Best Rating: **99** 5/00 Weth 2m4f110y gd-sft Hdl

Desailly

109 **132**

8-y-o ch g Teamster-G W Superstar (Rymer)
G B Balding The Team

Placings:452/**3U3U1** **(4481)**
2001/02: 17^{3}GS, 20^{U}S, 21^{3}GS, 19^{U}G, 23^{1}G

	Starts	1st	2nd	3rd	Win & Pl
Chases	5	1	0	2	6899
Career Total	**8**	**1**	**1**	**2**	**8479**

132	3/02	Extr	2m7f110y	D(0-125)HCh	GD	£4914

Total win prize-money £4914

Going: Sf: 0-1 GS: 0-2 Gd: 1-2 GF: - Fm: 0-0
Distance: 2m/2m3: 0-1 2m4-2m7: 0-3 **3m+: 1-1**
Track: LH: 0-1 **RH: 1-4** Tight: 0-0 Gall: 0-0
Aids: Bl: 0-0 Vi: 0-0 Tstrap: 0-0
Best Rating: **132** 3/02 Extr 2m7f110y good Ch

Lightly-raced chaser. Showed promise over fences in December 2001 when third in a novice chase, and got off the mark when stepped up to nearly three miles and held up at Exeter in March.

Desert Boot

76 **93**

7-y-o gr g High Kicker (USA)-Desert Mist (Sharrood (USA))
T H Caldwell T H Caldwell

Placings: *60/0/U*-P0PP **(4909)**
2001/02: 23^{P}GS, 20^{0}S, 24^{P}HY, 20^{P}GF

	Starts	1st	2nd	3rd	Win & Pl
Hurdles	3	0	0	0	0
Chases	1	0	0	0	0
Career Total	**8**	**0**	**0**	**0**	**0**

Going: Sf: 0-2 GS: 0-1 Gd: 0-0 GF: - Fm: 0-1
Distance: 2m/2m3: 0-0 2m4-2m7: 0-3 3m+: 0-1
Track: LH: 0-3 RH: 0-1 Tight: 0-1 Gall: 0-1
Aids: Bl: 0-0 Vi: 0-0 Tstrap: 0-0
Best Rating: 64 1/99 Hayd 2m soft NHF

Of no account.

Desert Brave (IRE)

12-y-o b g Commanche Run-Desert Pet (Petingo)
Mrs S J Smith T And B Benson

Placings: *0002605/03U36/3530121021F3/20P50U5/P54/PPP* **(4312)**
2001/02: 19^{P}S, 19^{P}GS, 20^{P}HY

	Starts	1st	2nd	3rd	Win & Pl
Hurdles	1	0	0	0	0
Chases	2	0	0	0	0
Career Total	**37**	**3**	**4**	**5**	**17232**

99	3/98	Donc	2m3f110y	D(0-110)HCh	SFT	£4305
102	1/98	Catt	2m3f	E(0-105)HCh	SFT	£3402
95	12/97	Donc	2m110y	D Ch	GD	£3496

Total win prize-money £11203

Going: Sf: 0-2 GS: 0-1 Gd: 0-0 GF: - Fm: 0-0
Distance: 2m/2m3: 0-1 2m4-2m7: 0-2 3m+: 0-0
Track: LH: 0-3 RH: 0-0 Tight: 0-2 Gall: 0-1
Aids: Bl: 0-0 Vi: 0-0 Tstrap: 0-0
Best Rating: 102 5/98 Hexm 2m110y gd-sft Ch

Desert Devil

10-y-o b g Green Desert (USA)-Jolie Pelouse (USA) (Riverman (USA))
K Robson Mrs M Armstrong

Placings: *00/4/F*-U **(3749)**
2001/02: 24^{U}S

	Starts	1st	2nd	3rd	Win & Pl
Chases	1	0	0	0	
Career Total	**5**	**0**	**0**	**0**	**0**

Going: Sf: 0-1 GS: 0-0 Gd: 0-0 GF: - Fm: 0-0
Distance: 2m/2m3: 0-0 2m4-2m7: 0-0 3m+: 0-1
Track: LH: 0-0 RH: 0-1 Tight: 0-1 Gall: 0-0
Aids: Bl: 0-0 Vi: 0-0 Tstrap: 0-0
Best Rating: 75 10/96 Weth 2m good NHF

Desert Fighter

105 **104**

11-y-o b g Green Desert (USA)-Jungle Rose (Shirley Heights)
Mrs M Reveley A Frame

Placings: 06UU/2140153/143025523F1/43P32/63/043-421334035 **(4094)**
2001/02: 16^{4}G, 16^{2}G, 16^{1}GF, 16^{3}G, 16^{3}GF, 16^{4}GF, 19^{0}G, 20^{3}G, 16^{5}GS

	Starts	1st	2nd	3rd	Win & Pl
Hurdles	9	1	1	3	4036
Career Total	**41**	**5**	**5**	**10**	**23895**

90	10/01	Ludl	2m	G Hdl	G-F	£2149
116	4/97	Weth	2m	D(0-125)HHdl	G-F	£2880
116	10/96	Weth	2m	C(0-135)HHdl	GD	£3574
107	11/95	Catt	2m3f	E(0-110)HHdl	G-F	£2364
98	10/95	Weth	2m4f110y	D Hdl	G-F	£3050

Total win prize-money £14017

Going: Sf: 0-0 GS: 0-1 Gd: 0-5 GF: - Fm: 1-3
Distance: **2m/2m3: 1-8** 2m4-2m7: 0-1 3m+: 0-0
Track: LH: 0-4 **RH: 1-5** Tight: 0-4 Gall: 0-0
Aids: Bl: 0-0 Vi: 0-0 Tstrap: 0-0
Best Rating: 116 10/98 Weth 2m good Hdl

Useful plater over hurdles, he goes well on a sound surface and is effective at around two miles.

Desert Melody (IRE)

10-y-o b g Carlingford Castle-Jasmine Melody (Jasmine Star)
R Rowe Mrs P V Crocker

Placings: *0P/P03420/P1P6*-P **(0107)**
2001/02: 22^{P}GF

	Starts	1st	2nd	3rd	Win & Pl
Hurdles	1	0	0	0	
Career Total	**13**	**1**	**1**	**1**	**3393**

76	10/00	Towc	2m5f	E(0-105)HHdl	G-F	£2390

Total win prize-money £2391

Going: Sf: 0-0 GS: 0-0 Gd: 0-0 GF: - Fm: 0-1
Distance: 2m/2m3: 0-0 2m4-2m7: 0-1 3m+: 0-0
Track: LH: 0-1 RH: 0-0 Tight: 0-1 Gall: 0-0
Aids: Bl: 0-0 Vi: 0-0 Tstrap: 0-0
Best Rating: 76 10/00 Towc 2m5f gd-fm Hdl

Desert Mountain (IRE)

112 **166**

9-y-o b g Alzao (USA)-Curie Point (USA) (Sharpen Up)
P F Nicholls Frank W Golding

Placings: 2101/1050253/01131/251533-26610F **(4649)**
2001/02: 17^{2}GF, 16^{6}GS, 16^{6}G, 16^{1}G, 16^{0}GS, 16^{F}G

	Starts	1st	2nd	3rd	Win & Pl
Chases	6	1	1	0	23810
Career Total	**28**	**8**	**4**	**4**	**75096**

163	2/02	Kemp	2m	B Ch	GD	£14560
158	2/01	Kemp	2m	B Ch	GD	£10383
140	11/98	Wwck	2m	D Ch	SFT	£3470
137	10/98	Hntg	2m110y	E(0-105)HCh	GD	£2959
105	9/98	Hntg	2m110y	E Ch	G-F	£2929
131	10/97	Weth	2m	C(0-135)HHdl	G-F	£4792
109	3/97	Strf	2m110y	C(0-130)HHdl	GD	£4328
114	1/97	Folk	2m1f110y	E Hdl	SFT	£2749

Total win prize-money £46172

Going: Sf: 0-0 GS: 0-2 Gd: 1-3 GF: - Fm: 0-1
Distance: **2m/2m3: 1-6** 2m4-2m7: 0-0 3m+: 0-0
Track: LH: 0-2 **RH: 1-4** Tight: 0-1 Gall: 0-1
Aids: Bl: 0-0 Vi: 0-0 Tstrap: 0-0
Best Rating: 166 4/01 Sand 2m gd-sft Ch

He became a smart chaser over two miles in recent seasons and ran with credit against some of the best over that trip, although just looking held. At his best in small fields, he was sadly killed at Aintree in April. (DEAD)

Desert Music

83 **58**

6-y-o b m Ardkinglass-Musical Princess (Cavo Doro)
J R Weymes John Weymes Racing

Placings: 0 **(2149)**
2001/02: 20^{0}G

	Starts	1st	2nd	3rd	Win & Pl
Hurdles	1	0	0	0	
Career Total	**1**	**0**	**0**	**0**	

Going: Sf: 0-0 GS: 0-0 Gd: 0-1 GF: - Fm: 0-0
Distance: 2m/2m3: 0-0 2m4-2m7: 0-1 3m+: 0-0
Track: LH: 0-1 RH: 0-0 Tight: 0-0 Gall: 0-1
Aids: Bl: 0-0 Vi: 0-0 Tstrap: 0-0
Best Rating: 58 11/01 Newc 2m4f good Hdl

Desert Project (IRE)

7-y-o b m Project Manager-Diandra (Shardari)
Mrs L C Jewell The Bear Swallowers

Placings: *0*P **(0557)**
2001/02: 17^{0}GF, 16^{P}GF

	Starts	1st	2nd	3rd	Win & Pl
NH Flat	1	0	0	0	0
Hurdles	1	0	0	0	0
Career Total	**2**	**0**	**0**	**0**	

Going: Sf: 0-0 GS: 0-0 Gd: 0-0 GF: - Fm: 0-2
Distance: 2m/2m3: 0-2 2m4-2m7: 0-0 3m+: 0-0
Track: LH: 0-0 RH: 0-1 Tight: 0-1 Gall: 0-1
Aids: Bl: 0-0 Vi: 0-0 Tstrap: 0-0
Best Rating:

Desert Storm

92 **66**

6-y-o ch m Distinct Native-Secret Storm (Secret Ace)
L Lungo Mrs T Cunningham-Jardine

Placings: 0 **(3785)**
2001/02: 20^{0}S

	Starts	1st	2nd	3rd	Win & Pl
Hurdles	1	0	0	0	
Career Total	**1**	**0**	**0**	**0**	

Going: Sf: 0-1 GS: 0-0 Gd: 0-0 GF: - Fm: 0-0
Distance: 2m/2m3: 0-0 2m4-2m7: 0-1 3m+: 0-0
Track: LH: 0-1 RH: 0-0 Tight: 0-0 Gall: 0-1
Aids: Bl: 0-0 Vi: 0-0 Tstrap: 0-0
Best Rating: 66 2/02 Newc 2m4f soft Hdl

Desert Traveller (IRE)

79 **45**

4-y-o b g Desert Style (IRE)-Cellatica (USA) (Sir Ivor)
R J Baker R J Baker

Placings: 00P000 **(2780)**
2001/02: 17^{0}GF, 18^{0}GF, 17^{P}GS, 16^{0}GF, 17^{0}GS, 16^{0}G

	Starts	1st	2nd	3rd	Win & Pl

	Starts	1st	2nd	3rd	Win & Pl
urdles	6	0	0	0	
areer Total	6	0	0	0	

oing: Sf: 0-0 GS: 0-2 Gd: 0-1 GF: - Fm: 0-3
istance: 2m/2m3: 0-6 2m4-2m7: 0-0 3m+: 0-0
rack: LH: 0-1 RH: 0-5 Tight: 0-2 Gall: 0-0
ids: Bl: 0-4 Vi: 0-0 Tstrap: 0-0
est Rating: 45 11/01 Tntn 2m1f gd-sft Hdl

Design X Press

53f

-y-o b g Henbit (USA)-Stubbs Daughter (Stubbs iazette)
P McCormack Mrs D McCormack

lacings:*0* **(3550)**
001/02: 16^{0}S

	Starts	1st	2nd	3rd	Win & Pl
H Flat	1	0	0	0	
areer Total	**1**	**0**	**0**	**0**	

oing: Sf: 0-1 GS: 0-0 Gd: 0-0 GF: - Fm: 0-0
istance: 2m/2m3: 0-1 2m4-2m7: 0-0 3m+: 0-0
rack: LH: 0-0 RH: 0-0 Tight: 0-0 Gall: 0-0
ids: Bl: 0-0 Vi: 0-0 Tstrap: 0-0
est Rating: 53 1/02 Newc 2m soft NHF

Designer Label (IRE)

100 **96**

-y-o ch g Insan (USA)-Belle Babillard (IRE) (Le avard (FR))
I Pitman Mrs Sue Venton

lacings:636-63P **(2330)**
001/02: 21^{6}GF, 21^{3}G, 21^{P}G

	Starts	1st	2nd	3rd	Win & Pl
urdles	3	0	0	1	548
areer Total	**6**	**0**	**0**	**2**	**1016**

oing: Sf: 0-0 GS: 0-0 Gd: 0-2 GF: - Fm: 0-1
istance: 2m/2m3: 0-0 2m4-2m7: 0-3 3m+: 0-0
rack: LH: 0-2 RH: 0-1 Tight: 0-2 Gall: 0-0
ids: Bl: 0-0 Vi: 0-0 Tstrap: 0-0
est Rating: 108 11/00 Kemp 2m soft Hdl

nice type for fences, he has shown modest ability in ovice hurdles.

Desmond Tutu (IRE)

97f **113f**

-y-o b g Be My Native (USA)-Amy Fairy (The Parson)
F Nicholls D J Nichols

lacings:*1* **(4887)**
001/02: 18^{1}GF

	Starts	1st	2nd	3rd	Win & Pl
H Flat	1	1	0	0	2065
areer Total	**1**	**1**	**0**	**0**	**2065**

13	4/02	Font	2m2f110y	H NHF	G-F	£2065

Total win prize-money £2065

oing: Sf: 0-0 GS: 0-0 Gd: 0-0 GF: - Fm: 1-1
istance: **2m/2m3: 1-1** 2m4-2m7: 0-0 3m+: 0-0
rack: **LH: 1-1** RH: 0-0 **Tight: 1-1** Gall: 0-0
ids: Bl: 0-0 Vi: 0-0 Tstrap: 0-0
est Rating: 113 4/02 Font 2m2f110y gd-fm NHF

ut of a winner in Ireland, made a winning debut in a ontwell bumper in April 2002.

Desperate Measures

104 **73**

6-y-o ch m Kasakov-Precious Ballerina (Ballacashtal (CAN))
Miss Lucinda V Russell (J Hetherton 17/11) A D Stewart

Placings:*04050* **(4894)**
2001/02: 16^{0}S, 17^{4}GF, 16^{0}S, 16^{5}S, 16^{0}G

	Starts	1st	2nd	3rd	Win & Pl
NH Flat	4	0	0	0	0
Hurdles	1	0	0	0	0
Career Total	**5**	**0**	**0**	**0**	**0**

Going: Sf: 0-3 GS: 0-0 Gd: 0-1 GF: - Fm: 0-1
Distance: 2m/2m3: 0-5 2m4-2m7: 0-0 3m+: 0-0
Track: LH: 0-1 RH: 0-2 Tight: 0-1 Gall: 0-0
Aids: Bl: 0-0 Vi: 0-0 Tstrap: 0-0
Best Rating: 92 12/01 Muss 2m1f gd-fm NHF

Has shown limited ability in bumpers and hurdles. Seems suited by fast ground.

Destiny Calls

95(57h) **105**

12-y-o ch g Lord Avie (USA)-Miss Renege (USA) (Riva Ridge (USA))
N A Gaselee Mrs R W S Baker

Placings:2211/2220U/**1131321/252/44444/51/31L401 R1R/60241-0445** **(4643)**
2001/02: 20^{0}G, 20^{4}G, 21^{4}G, 20^{5}G

	Starts	1st	2nd	3rd	Win & Pl
Chases	4	0	0	0	974
Career Total	**44**	**11**	**9**	**3**	**81758**

143	8/00	Uttx	2m5f	C(0-135)HCh	G-F	£6114
148	11/99	Newb	2m4f	D(0-125)HCh	G-F	£6254
148	8/99	Uttx	2m5f	C(0-135)HCh	G-F	£5772
140	5/99	Strf	2m5f110y	C(0-135)HCh	GD	£5998
131	3/99	Newb	2m4f	C(0-135)HCh	G-F	£7699
127	4/96	Sand	2m4f110y	C HCh	G-F	£13851
112	11/95	Wwck	2m	D Ch	GD	£3802
116	10/95	Bang	2m1f110y	D Ch	GD	£3631
107	5/95	Wwck	2m	C(0-130)HHdl	G-F	£3525
90	4/94	Uttx	2m	Hdl	GD	£1987
85	3/94	Newb	2m110y	Hdl	GD	£2840

Total win prize-money £61477

Going: Sf: 0-0 GS: 0-0 Gd: 0-4 GF: - Fm: 0-0
Distance: 2m/2m3: 0-0 2m4-2m7: 0-4 3m+: 0-0
Track: LH: 0-3 RH: 0-1 Tight: 0-1 Gall: 0-2
Aids: Bl: 0-0 Vi: 0-0 Tstrap: 0-0
Best Rating: 148 11/99 Newb 2m4f gd-fm Ch

Formerly fair chaser, best at two and ahalf miles on fast ground, he has refused to race in his time and is far from straightforward, but did nothing wrong when winning gamely at Uttoxeter in August 2000. Not seen out again for 14 months, he struggled in handicaps since but has taken a big drop in the ratings as a result.

Detachment (USA)

95(88h) (72h)**82**

9-y-o b g Night Shift (USA)-Mumble Peg (General Assembly (USA))
Miss Z C Davison The Secret Circle (1)

Placings:U0PP02/P/00-00**45534**U0000**6** **(4560)**
2001/02: 17^{0}GS, 16^{0}G, 20^{4}GS, 16^{5}G, 17^{5}G, 17^{3}GS, 16^{4}G, 16^{U}GF, 22^{0}S, 16^{0}S, 17^{0}S, 16^{0}G, 17^{6}GF

	Starts	1st	2nd	3rd	Win & Pl
Hurdles	7	0	0	0	0
Chases	6	0	0	1	416
Career Total	**22**	**0**	**1**	**1**	**876**

Going: Sf: 0-3 GS: 0-3 Gd: 0-5 GF: - Fm: 0-2
Distance: 2m/2m3: 0-11 2m4-2m7: 0-2 3m+: 0-0
Track: LH: 0-4 RH: 0-8 Tight: 0-9 Gall: 0-0
Aids: Bl: 0-0 Vi: 0-0 Tstrap: 0-1
Best Rating: 82 11/01 Plum 2m1f gd-sft Ch

Moderate hurdler. Switched to fences in the 2001/2002 season but nothing of note so far. Best over two miles on good ground.

Detonateur (FR)

107 **116**

4-y-o b g Pistolet Bleu (IRE)-Soviet Princess (IRE) (Soviet Lad (USA))
Ian Williams Mr & Mrs John Poynton

Placings:020 **(4188)**
2001/02: 16^{0}GS, 16^{2}HY, 16^{0}GS

	Starts	1st	2nd	3rd	Win & Pl
Hurdles	3	0	1	0	1115
Career Total	**3**	**0**	**1**	**0**	**1115**

Going: Sf: 0-1 GS: 0-2 Gd: 0-0 GF: - Fm: 0-0
Distance: 2m/2m3: 0-3 2m4-2m7: 0-0 3m+: 0-0
Track: LH: 0-2 RH: 0-1 Tight: 0-0 Gall: 0-1
Aids: Bl: 0-0 Vi: 0-0 Tstrap: 0-0
Best Rating: 116 3/02 Chel 2m110y gd-sft Hdl

Placed on the Flat in France. Tailed off on his hurdles bow but appreciated the softer ground on his next start. Suited by two miles and soft ground.

Deva's Way

10-y-o ch g Cigar-Lasses Nightshade (Deadly Nightshade)
Dr P Pritchard J E Tuck

Placings:PP/P-P **(0665)**
2001/02: 20^{P}G

	Starts	1st	2nd	3rd	Win & Pl
Hurdles	1	0	0	0	
Career Total	**4**	**0**	**0**	**0**	

Going: Sf: 0-0 GS: 0-0 Gd: 0-1 GF: - Fm: 0-0
Distance: 2m/2m3: 0-0 2m4-2m7: 0-1 3m+: 0-0
Track: LH: 0-1 RH: 0-0 Tight: 0-0 Gall: 0-0
Aids: Bl: 0-0 Vi: 0-0 Tstrap: 0-0
Best Rating:

Devil's Run (IRE)

106 **112**

6-y-o b g Commanche Run-She Devil (Le Moss)
J Wade John Wade

Placings:004-0331134 **(4488)**
2001/02: 22^{0}G, 27^{3}S, 23^{3}S, 20^{1}GS, 20^{1}S, 20^{3}S, 20^{4}GS

	Starts	1st	2nd	3rd	Win & Pl
Hurdles	7	2	0	3	12427
Career Total	**10**	**2**	**0**	**3**	**12427**

112	2/02	Newc	2m4f	B(0-140)HHdl	SFT	£6753
108	1/02	Weth	2m4f110y	D(0-115)HHdl	G-S	£3500

Total win prize-money £10254

Going: Sf: 1-4 GS: 1-2 Gd: 0-1 GF: - Fm: 0-0
Distance: 2m/2m3: 0-0 **2m4-2m7: 2-6** 3m+: 0-1
Track: **LH: 2-6** RH: 0-0 Tight: 0-2 **Gall: 1-1**
Aids: Bl: 0-0 Vi: 0-0 Tstrap: 0-0

Best Rating: 112 3/02 Ayr 2m4f soft Hdl

Progressive hurdler, suited by the drop back to two and a half miles when winning at Wetherby in January 2002. Followed up at Newcastle, should stay further. Acts on soft/heavy ground.

Devil's Sting (IRE)

13-y-o ch g Henbit (USA)-Hells Mistress (Skymaster)
R C Harper R C Harper

Placings:U0P/P53/4P/PP (0577)
2001/02: 33^{P}G, 21^{P}GF

	Starts	1st	2nd	3rd	Win & Pl
Chases	2	0	0	0	
Career Total	**10**	**0**	**0**	**1**	**612**

Going: Sf: 0-0 GS: 0-0 Gd: 0-1 GF: - Fm: 0-1
Distance: 2m/2m3: 0-0 2m4-2m7: 0-1 3m+: 0-1
Track: LH: 0-1 RH: 0-0 Tight: 0-1 Gall: 0-0
Aids: Bl: 0-0 Vi: 0-0 Tstrap: 0-0
Best Rating: 77 7/98 Wolv 2m4f110y good Ch

Devils Dingle

49 26

6-y-o ch g Broadsword (USA)-Macusla (Lighter)
Mrs P Sly R M Micklethwait

Placings:030 (3465)
2001/02: 16^{0}S, 20^{3}S, 20^{0}S

	Starts	1st	2nd	3rd	Win & Pl
NH Flat	1	0	0	0	0
Hurdles	2	0	0	1	548
Career Total	**3**	**0**	**0**	**1**	**548**

Going: Sf: 0-3 GS: 0-0 Gd: 0-0 GF: - Fm: 0-0
Distance: 2m/2m3: 0-1 2m4-2m7: 0-2 3m+: 0-0
Track: LH: 0-2 RH: 0-1 Tight: 0-0 Gall: 0-1
Aids: Bl: 0-0 Vi: 0-0 Tstrap: 0-0
Best Rating: 41 12/01 Wwck 2m soft NHF

Devon View (IRE)

106 133

8-y-o b g Jolly Jake (NZ)-Skipaside (Quayside)
P F Nicholls Jeffrey Hordle

Placings:P-212122 (4891)
2001/02: 16^{2}S, 16^{1}S, 20^{2}S, 19^{1}S, 19^{2}GS, 16^{2}G

	Starts	1st	2nd	3rd	Win & Pl
Chases	6	2	4	0	12650
Career Total	**7**	**2**	**4**	**0**	**12650**

123 3/02 Chep 2m3f110y E Ch SFT £3081
133 2/02 Leic 2m E Ch SFT £3406
Total win prize-money £6487

Going: Sf: 2-4 GS: 0-1 Gd: 0-1 GF: - Fm: 0-0
Distance: 2m/2m3: 1-3 2m4-2m7: 1-3 3m+: 0-0
Track: LH: 1-2 RH: 1-3 Tight: 0-2 Gall: 0-0
Aids: Bl: 0-0 Vi: 0-0 Tstrap: 0-0
Best Rating: 133 4/02 Prth 2m good Ch

Fair chaser, lightly raced. He acts on soft ground and is effective over two to two and a half miles.

Devote

106 95

4-y-o b g Pennekamp (USA)-Radiant Bride (USA) (Blushing Groom (FR))
B J Llewellyn The Welsh Valleys Syndicate

Placings:35420213 (4052)
2001/02: 18^{3}GF, 17^{5}G, 16^{4}G, 17^{2}S, 16^{0}GS, 17^{2}S, 19^{1}S, 19^{3}G

	Starts	1st	2nd	3rd	Win & Pl
Hurdles	8	1	2	2	6072
Career Total	**8**	**1**	**2**	**2**	**6072**

95 2/02 Tntn 2m3f110y E(0-110)HHdl SFT £3388
Total win prize-money £3388

Going: Sf: 1-3 GS: 0-1 Gd: 0-3 GF: - Fm: 0-1
Distance: 2m/2m3: 0-7 **2m4-2m7: 1-1** 3m+: 0-0
Track: LH: 0-4 **RH: 1-4 Tight: 1-5** Gall: 0-0
Aids: **Bl: 1-6** Vi: 0-0 Tstrap: 0-0
Best Rating: 95 3/02 Extr 2m3f good Hdl

Not the most fluent jumper, he has a mischievous streak in him but stays all day and won his debut in handicap company.

Diamanikos (FR)

70f 63f

6-y-o b g Nikos-Diamarella (FR) (Rose Laurel)
Miss H C Knight Mrs B J Lockhart

Placings:0 (3777)
2001/02: 16^{0}S

	Starts	1st	2nd	3rd	Win & Pl
NH Flat	1	0	0	0	
Career Total	**1**	**0**	**0**	**0**	

Going: Sf: 0-1 GS: 0-0 Gd: 0-0 GF: - Fm: 0-0
Distance: 2m/2m3: 0-1 2m4-2m7: 0-0 3m+: 0-0
Track: LH: 0-0 RH: 0-1 Tight: 0-0 Gall: 0-0
Aids: Bl: 0-0 Vi: 0-0 Tstrap: 0-0
Best Rating: 63 2/02 Sand 2m110y soft NHF

Diamond Beach

90 67

9-y-o b g Lugana Beach-Cannon Boy (USA) (Canonero (USA))
B J Llewellyn (M J M Evans 10/5) Miss Emily Jane Jones

Placings:0U0212/5433/206250/0530-00 (1347)
2001/02: 17^{0}G, 17^{0}GF

	Starts	1st	2nd	3rd	Win & Pl
Hurdles	2	0	0	0	
Career Total	**22**	**1**	**4**	**3**	**5675**

89 3/97 Hexm 2m E(0-110)HHdl SFT £2311
Total win prize-money £2312

Going: Sf: 0-0 GS: 0-0 Gd: 0-1 GF: - Fm: 0-1
Distance: 2m/2m3: 0-2 2m4-2m7: 0-0 3m+: 0-0
Track: LH: 0-1 RH: 0-1 Tight: 0-1 Gall: 0-0
Aids: Bl: 0-0 Vi: 0-0 Tstrap: 0-0
Best Rating: 103 11/99 Hexm 2m good Hdl

Diamond Cottage (IRE)

107 86

7-y-o b g Peacock (FR)-Sea Bright (IRE) (King's Ride)
R Johnson J L Gledson

Placings:0/00P2 (4443)
2001/02: 25^{0}GS, 20^{0}S, 20^{P}GS, 27^{2}S

	Starts	1st	2nd	3rd	Win & Pl
Hurdles	4	0	1	0	857
Career Total	**5**	**0**	**1**	**0**	**857**

Going: Sf: 0-2 GS: 0-2 Gd: 0-0 GF: - Fm: 0-0
Distance: 2m/2m3: 0-0 2m4-2m7: 0-2 3m+: 0-2
Track: LH: 0-4 RH: 0-0 Tight: 0-2 Gall: 0-2
Aids: Bl: 0-0 Vi: 0-0 Tstrap: 0-0
Best Rating: 74 3/02 Kels 3m3f soft Hdl

Lightly-raced hurdler who showed improved form when faced with an extreme test in March 2002.

Diamond Crown (IRE)

107 90

11-y-o ch g Kris-State Treasure (USA) (Secretariat (USA))
Denys Smith Mr B R Bradbury

Placings:00035/031340P-02202221 (1419)
2001/02: 16^{0}GF, 16^{2}F, 16^{2}GS, 20^{0}G, 17^{2}GF, 17^{2}GF, 17^{2}GF, 21^{1}G

	Starts	1st	2nd	3rd	Win & Pl
Hurdles	8	1	5	0	4803
Career Total	**20**	**2**	**5**	**3**	**7412**

90 9/01 Sedg 2m5f110y G(0-95)HHdl GD £1918
83 8/00 Sedg 2m1f G(0-90)HHdl GD £1855
Total win prize-money £3773

Going: Sf: 0-0 GS: 0-1 Gd: 1-2 GF: - Fm: 0-5
Distance: 2m/2m3: 0-6 **2m4-2m7: 1-2** 3m+: 0-0
Track: **LH: 1-8** RH: 0-0 **Tight: 1-4** Gall: 0-0
Aids: Bl: 0-0 Vi: 0-0 Tstrap: 0-0
Best Rating: 90 9/01 Sedg 2m5f110y good Hdl

Veteran selling hurdler, stays two miles-five plus, acts on a sound surface.

Diamond Dynasty

5-y-o b g Son Pardo-Reperage (USA) (Key To Content (USA))
J N R Billinge J N R Billinge

Placings:000PP (4880)
2001/02: 16^{0}G, 16^{0}S, 17^{0}G, 16^{P}G, 20^{P}G

	Starts	1st	2nd	3rd	Win & Pl
NH Flat	3	0	0	0	0
Hurdles	2	0	0	0	0
Career Total	**5**	**0**	**0**	**0**	

Going: Sf: 0-1 GS: 0-0 Gd: 0-4 GF: - Fm: 0-0
Distance: 2m/2m3: 0-4 2m4-2m7: 0-1 3m+: 0-0
Track: LH: 0-2 RH: 0-3 Tight: 0-0 Gall: 0-0
Aids: Bl: 0-0 Vi: 0-0 Tstrap: 0-0
Best Rating: 54 3/02 Ayr 2m soft NHF

Diamond Hall

97(100h) (102h)102

9-y-o b g Lapierre-Willitwin (Majestic Maharaj)
K R Burke (Ian Williams 19/10) R D Tudor

Placings:51/1200/3/1/40P633F (1736)
2001/02: 17^{4}G, 16^{0}GF, 17^{P}GF, 16^{6}GF, 16^{3}G, 16^{3}G, 19^{F}S

	Starts	1st	2nd	3rd	Win & Pl
Hurdles	2	0	0	0	0
Chases	5	0	0	2	1048
Career Total	**15**	**3**	**1**	**3**	**7671**

102 5/99 Strf 2m110y F(0-100)HHdl G-S £2682
91 10/97 Ludl 2m H NHF G-F £1213
84 4/97 Chep 2m110y H NHF FRM £1686
Total win prize-money £5582

Going: Sf: 0-1 GS: 0-0 Gd: 0-3 GF: - Fm: 0-3
Distance: 2m/2m3: 0-7 2m4-2m7: 0-0 3m+: 0-0
Track: LH: 0-4 RH: 0-3 Tight: 0-3 Gall: 0-1
Aids: Bl: 0-0 Vi: 0-0 Tstrap: 0-0
Best Rating: 102 9/01 Uttx 2m gd-fm Ch

Fair hurdler, moderate novice chaser, handles fast ground.

Diamond Joshua (IRE)

107 **131**

4-y-o b g Mujadil (USA)-Elminya (IRE) (Sure Blade (USA))
John Berry Diamond Racing Ltd

Placings:1333P **(4813)**
2001/02: 16^{1}G, 16^{3}G, 16^{3}G, 17^{3}G, 17^{P}GF

	Starts	1st	2nd	3rd	Win & Pl
Hurdles	5	1	0	3	15906
Career Total	**5**	**1**	**0**	**3**	**15906**

101	10/01	Weth	2m	D Hdl	GD	£3843

Total win prize-money £3843

Going: Sf: 0-0 GS: 0-0 Gd: 1-4 GF: - Fm: 0-1
Distance: **2m/2m3: 1-5** 2m4-2m7: 0-0 3m+: 0-0
Track: **LH: 1-5** RH: 0-0 Tight: 0-0 Gall: 0-2
Aids: Bl: 0-0 Vi: 0-0 Tstrap: 0-0
Best Rating: 131 3/02 Chel 2m1f good Hdl

A maiden on the Flat, he won on his hurdles debut at Wetherby over two miles on good ground, and then ran a very good race back at Wetherby in November when third in Listed company. Stepped up on his previous efforts when a staying-on third in the Triumph Hurdle. Suited by two miles on a sound surface, will stay further.

Diamond Rose

101 **94**

8-y-o br m Ardross-Scarlet Dymond (Rymer)
Mrs H Pudd (B G Powell 2/5) Mrs H Pudd

Placings:*2/20*04506/130-0041P **(3983)**
2001/02: 22^{0}GS, 16^{0}G, 24^{4}S, 24^{1}S, 24^{P}G

	Starts	1st	2nd	3rd	Win & Pl
Hurdles	5	1	0	0	3017
Career Total	**16**	**2**	**2**	**1**	**7013**

94	2/02	Tntn	3m110y	F(0-100)HHdl	SFT	£3017
97	11/00	Extr	2m6f110y	F(0-100)HHdl	G-S	£2777

Total win prize-money £5795

Going: Sf: 1-2 GS: 0-1 Gd: 0-2 GF: - Fm: 0-0
Distance: 2m/2m3: 0-1 2m4-2m7: 0-1 **3m+: 1-3**
Track: LH: 0-0 **RH: 1-4 Tight: 1-2** Gall: 0-0
Aids: Bl: 0-0 Vi: 0-0 Tstrap: 0-0
Best Rating: 103 10/98 Bang 2m1f good NHF

Modest staying handicap hurdler, she acts with cut.

Diamond Run

6-y-o ch m Gildoran-Mermaid Bay (Jupiter Island)
A King All The King's Men

Placings:*0*-P **(0797)**
2001/02: 17^{P}GF

	Starts	1st	2nd	3rd	Win & Pl
Hurdles	1	0	0	0	
Career Total	**2**	**0**	**0**	**0**	

Going: Sf: 0-0 GS: 0-0 Gd: 0-0 GF: - Fm: 0-1
Distance: 2m/2m3: 0-1 2m4-2m7: 0-0 3m+: 0-0
Track: LH: 0-1 RH: 0-0 Tight: 0-1 Gall: 0-0
Aids: Bl: 0-0 Vi: 0-0 Tstrap: 0-0
Best Rating: 31 12/00 Ludl 2m soft NHF

Dibea Times (FR)

113 **140**

5-y-o b g Sheyrann-Cerise Royale (FR) (Garde Royale)
J M Jefferson Mr & Mrs Raymond Anderson Green

Placings:1111P-4FP3 **(4837)**
2001/02: 16^{4}GS, 16^{F}G, 20^{P}G, 16^{3}G

	Starts	1st	2nd	3rd	Win & Pl
Hurdles	4	0	0	1	5025
Career Total	**9**	**4**	**0**	**1**	**25807**

131	2/01	Kels	2m2f	D Hdl	SFT	£4173
128	1/01	Newc	2m	E Hdl	SFT	£2604
122	12/00	Newc	2m	E Hdl	SFT	£2478
	5/00	Autl	1m7f	Hdl	VS	£11527

Total win prize-money £20782

Going: Sf: 0-0 GS: 0-1 Gd: 0-3 GF: - Fm: 0-0
Distance: 2m/2m3: 0-3 2m4-2m7: 0-1 3m+: 0-0
Track: LH: 0-3 RH: 0-1 Tight: 0-1 Gall: 0-1
Aids: Bl: 0-0 Vi: 0-0 Tstrap: 0-0
Best Rating: 140 12/01 Newc 2m gd-sft Hdl

A winner over hurdles in France, he won his first three in this country, but was subsequently found out in much better company, including when third in the Scottish National at Ayr in April 2002. Prefers soft ground and two miles. Reportedly returned to France to join Guillaime Macaire.

Diceman (IRE)

80 **52**

7-y-o b g Supreme Leader-Henry's Gamble (IRE) (Carlingford Castle)
Mrs H Dalton Trevor Hemmings

Placings:332/3-0 **(4494)**
2001/02: 22^{0}G

	Starts	1st	2nd	3rd	Win & Pl
Hurdles	1	0	0	0	
Career Total	**5**	**0**	**1**	**3**	**1677**

Going: Sf: 0-0 GS: 0-0 Gd: 0-1 GF: - Fm: 0-0
Distance: 2m/2m3: 0-0 2m4-2m7: 0-1 3m+: 0-0
Track: LH: 0-1 RH: 0-0 Tight: 0-0 Gall: 0-0
Aids: Bl: 0-0 Vi: 0-0 Tstrap: 0-0
Best Rating: 104 4/00 Carl 2m1f gd-sft NHF

Dick McCarthy (IRE)

106 **116**

10-y-o b g Lancastrian-Waltzing Shoon (Green Shoon)
R Rowe Exors Of The Late Mr I Kerman

Placings:*50050/0222/003/132162310/2360-*424226322 **(4882)**
2001/02: 20^{4}GF, 22^{2}GF, 22^{4}S, 25^{2}G, 24^{2}GS, 25^{6}S, 26^{3}S, 22^{2}G, 26^{2}GF

	Starts	1st	2nd	3rd	Win & Pl
Chases	9	0	5	1	6352
Career Total	**34**	**3**	**11**	**5**	**31445**

125	3/00	Newb	2m6f110y	D(0-120)HCh	G-F	£7247
125	12/99	Plum	2m1f	E Ch	SFT	£3895
116	10/99	Plum	2m4f	D(0-115)HCh	G-F	£5365

Total win prize-money £16509

Going: Sf: 0-3 GS: 0-1 Gd: 0-2 GF: - Fm: 0-3
Distance: 2m/2m3: 0-0 2m4-2m7: 0-4 3m+: 0-5
Track: LH: 0-0 RH: 0-5 Tight: 0-7 Gall: 0-0
Aids: Bl: 0-0 Vi: 0-0 Tstrap: 0-0
Best Rating: 128 1/00 Plum 2m4f soft Ch

Fair chaser, stays three miles plus, acts on any ground. Consistently placed but difficult to win with.

Dick The Taxi

93 **130**

8-y-o b g Karlinsky (USA)-Another Galaxy (IRE) (Anita's Prince)
R J Smith R Hibberd,Mrs J Jackson,Miss G Eager

Placings:*101/0*321P1-0P6 **(4688)**
2001/02: 16^{0}G, 16^{P}S, 16^{6}GF

	Starts	1st	2nd	3rd	Win & Pl
Hurdles	3	0	0	0	0
Career Total	**12**	**4**	**1**	**1**	**10342**

130	4/01	Fknm	2m	D(0-110)HHdl	G-S	£3291
117	2/01	Tntn	2m1f	E Hdl	HVY	£2702
122	4/00	MRas	1m5f110y	H NHF	SFT	£1533
119	5/99	Worc	2m	H NHF	G-S	£1735

Total win prize-money £9261

Going: Sf: 0-1 GS: 0-0 Gd: 0-1 GF: - Fm: 0-1
Distance: 2m/2m3: 0-3 2m4-2m7: 0-0 3m+: 0-0
Track: LH: 0-3 RH: 0-0 Tight: 0-1 Gall: 0-1
Aids: Bl: 0-0 Vi: 0-0 Tstrap: 0-0
Best Rating: 130 4/01 Fknm 2m gd-sft Hdl

A winner of bumpers and hurdle races, he has also shown form on the Polytrackon the Flat. Suited by two miles and soft ground.

Dick'n Mick

5-y-o b g Secret Appeal-Gilboa (Shirley Heights)
J G Smyth-Osbourne (Lady Connell 19/5) Sir Michael Connell

Placings:*0*P **(0370)**
2001/02: 17^{0}GS, 16^{P}G

	Starts	1st	2nd	3rd	Win & Pl
NH Flat	1	0	0	0	0
Hurdles	1	0	0	0	0
Career Total	**2**	**0**	**0**	**0**	

Going: Sf: 0-0 GS: 0-1 Gd: 0-1 GF: - Fm: 0-0
Distance: 2m/2m3: 0-2 2m4-2m7: 0-0 3m+: 0-0
Track: LH: 0-1 RH: 0-0 Tight: 0-1 Gall: 0-0
Aids: Bl: 0-0 Vi: 0-0 Tstrap: 0-0
Best Rating:

Dicks Darlin'

(75h) (39h)

9-y-o b m My Richard-Hi Darlin' (Prince De Galles)
H J Manners H J Manners

Placings:*00/00060/40*-0P **(0774)**
2001/02: 16^{0}G, 23^{P}GF

	Starts	1st	2nd	3rd	Win & Pl
Hurdles	1	0	0	0	0
Chases	1	0	0	0	0
Career Total	**11**	**0**	**0**	**0**	**250**

Going: Sf: 0-0 GS: 0-0 Gd: 0-1 GF: - Fm: 0-1
Distance: 2m/2m3: 0-1 2m4-2m7: 0-0 3m+: 0-1
Track: LH: 0-2 RH: 0-0 Tight: 0-0 Gall: 0-0
Aids: Bl: 0-0 Vi: 0-0 Tstrap: 0-0
Best Rating: 52 6/00 Strf 2m110y good Hdl

Didntcostalotbut

5-y-o b m Whittingham (IRE)-Homemaker (Homeboy)
M J Wilkinson Wontcostalot Partnership

Placings:P-P (0236)
2001/02: 16^{P}GF

	Starts	1st	2nd	3rd	Win & Pl
Hurdles	1	0	0	0	
Career Total	**2**	**0**	**0**	**0**	

Going: Sf: 0-0 GS: 0-0 Gd: 0-0 GF: - Fm: 0-1
Distance: 2m/2m3: 0-1 2m4-2m7: 0-0 3m+: 0-0
Track: LH: 0-1 RH: 0-0 Tight: 0-1 Gall: 0-0
Aids: Bl: 0-0 Vi: 0-0 Tstrap: 0-0
Best Rating:

Die Fledermaus (IRE)

107(85h) (89+h)120+

8-y-o b g Batshoof-Top Mouse (High Top)
D J Wintle L & P Partnership

Placings:60F0/23440/3113124/141231200-363024105 (2715)
2001/02: 21^{3}GF, 20^{6}G, 20^{3}GF, 22^{0}G, 24^{2}G, 24^{4}S, 24^{1}G, 25^{0}S, 16^{5}HY

	Starts	1st	2nd	3rd	Win & Pl
Hurdles	1	0	0	0	0
Chases	8	1	1	2	5626
Career Total	**34**	**7**	**5**	**6**	**35389**

119	11/01	Tntn	3m	F(0-105)HCh	GD	£3080
118	8/00	Sthl	3m110y	E(0-115)HCh	GD	£4357
115	7/00	Wolv	2m4f110y	D(0-125)HHdl	GD	£6711
115	6/00	NAbb	2m5f110y	D Ch	G-F	£3760
111	10/99	Chep	2m4f	D(0-125)HHdl	SFT	£3062
106	8/99	Ctml	2m6f	E Hdl	GD	£2915
104	8/99	Bang	2m4f	E Hdl	GD	£1882

Total win prize-money £25769

Going: Sf: 0-3 GS: 0-0 Gd: 1-4 GF: - Fm: 0-2
Distance: 2m/2m3: 0-1 2m4-2m7: 0-4 **3m+: 1-4**
Track: LH: 0-5 **RH: 1-4 Tight: 1-7** Gall: 0-0
Aids: Bl: 0-3 Vi: 0-0 Tstrap: 0-0
Best Rating: 124 9/00 NAbb 2m5f110y gd-fm Ch

Useful hurdler, equally effective over fences. Suited by two and a half over hurdles and three miles over fences. Acts on most surfaces.

Dig For Gold

89(96h) (72h)62

9-y-o ch g Digamist (USA)-Formidable Task (Formidable (USA))
R D E Woodhouse R D E Woodhouse

Placings:*040*/23540/P100/032P3/F-P50 (1068)
2001/02: 20^{P}G, 20^{5}GS, 17^{0}GF

	Starts	1st	2nd	3rd	Win & Pl
Hurdles	1	0	0	0	0
Chases	2	0	0	0	0
Career Total	**21**	**1**	**2**	**3**	**5126**

80	1/99	Catt	2m	F(0-95)HHdl	GD	£2024

Total win prize-money £2024

Going: Sf: 0-0 GS: 0-1 Gd: 0-1 GF: - Fm: 0-1
Distance: 2m/2m3: 0-1 2m4-2m7: 0-2 3m+: 0-0
Track: LH: 0-2 RH: 0-0 Tight: 0-2 Gall: 0-0
Aids: Bl: 0-0 Vi: 0-0 Tstrap: 0-1
Best Rating: 90 7/99 Sedg 2m110y gd-fm Ch

Digital Signal (IRE)

93 82

9-y-o b g Moscow Society (USA)-Air Rina (USA) (Lear Fan (USA))
G M O'Neill Emmet's Syndicate

Placings:L*44/32*0002240220/*33*512B4361/60000P-00F5B (3418a)
2001/02: 16^{0}Y, 20^{0}YS, 21^{F}G, 20^{5}S, 16^{B}SH

	Starts	1st	2nd	3rd	Win & Pl
Hurdles	5	0	0	0	
Career Total	**36**	**2**	**6**	**4**	**11579**

101	1/99	Tram	2m	(0-95)HHdl	HVY	£2608
93	8/98	Tral	2m4f	(0-109)HHdl	GD	£2989

Total win prize-money £5598

Going: Sf: 0-1 GS: 0-0 Gd: 0-1 GF: - Fm: 0-0
Distance: 2m/2m3: 0-2 2m4-2m7: 0-3 3m+: 0-0
Track: LH: 0-1 RH: 0-3 Tight: 0-0 Gall: 0-1
Aids: Bl: 0-0 Vi: 0-0 Tstrap: 0-0
Best Rating: 101 12/00 Cork 2m soft Hdl

Digup St Edmunds

(38h)

9-y-o br g Bustino-Sharp Glance (IRE) (Deep Run)
Miss Venetia Williams Sir Clement Freud

Placings:*0/21*U51/0-PF (3471)
2001/02: 21^{P}S, 21^{F}S

	Starts	1st	2nd	3rd	Win & Pl
Hurdles	1	0	0	0	0
Chases	1	0	0	0	0
Career Total	**9**	**2**	**1**	**0**	**6363**

107	4/00	Chep	2m4f	E Hdl	SFT	£2170
107	1/00	Tntn	3m110y	D Hdl	G-S	£3705

Total win prize-money £5875

Going: Sf: 0-2 GS: 0-0 Gd: 0-0 GF: - Fm: 0-0
Distance: 2m/2m3: 0-0 2m4-2m7: 0-2 3m+: 0-0
Track: LH: 0-1 RH: 0-1 Tight: 0-2 Gall: 0-0
Aids: Bl: 0-0 Vi: 0-0 Tstrap: 0-0
Best Rating: 107 4/00 Chep 2m4f soft Hdl

A winner twice over hurdles, he fell on his chasing debut. Stays well and is suited by soft ground.

Dihatjum

102 108

5-y-o b g Mujtahid (USA)-Rosie Potts (Shareef Dancer (USA))
R M Flower M Lickert

Placings:21P001 (4782)
2001/02: 16^{2}GF, 16^{1}GS, 18^{P}S, 17^{0}G, 16^{0}G, 16^{1}GF

	Starts	1st	2nd	3rd	Win & Pl
Hurdles	6	2	1	0	6636
Career Total	**6**	**2**	**1**	**0**	**6636**

104	4/02	Plum	2m	E(0-110)HHdl	G-F	£3374
104	9/01	Plum	2m	E Hdl	G-S	£2506

Total win prize-money £5880

Going: Sf: 0-1 GS: 1-1 Gd: 0-2 GF: - Fm: 1-2
Distance: **2m/2m3: 2-6** 2m4-2m7: 0-0 3m+: 0-0
Track: **LH: 2-4** RH: 0-2 **Tight: 2-4** Gall: 0-0
Aids: Bl: 0-0 Vi: 0-0 Tstrap: 0-0
Best Rating: 104 4/02 Plum 2m gd-fm Hdl

A moderate handicapper on the Flat, ran really well on his hurdling debut at Plumpton in September and got off the mark at the same track two weeks later. Also won his first race of 2002 there.

Diletia

100 102

5-y-o b m Dilum (USA)-Miss Laetitia (IRE) (Entitled)
R H Alner T H Chadney

Placings:25246-656262F (4854)
2001/02: 20^{6}S, 17^{5}S, 21^{6}S, 20^{2}S, 22^{6}S, 19^{2}GF, 22^{F}G

	Starts	1st	2nd	3rd	Win & Pl
Hurdles	7	0	2	0	1603
Career Total	**12**	**0**	**4**	**0**	**3861**

Going: Sf: 0-5 GS: 0-0 Gd: 0-1 GF: - Fm: 0-1
Distance: 2m/2m3: 0-1 2m4-2m7: 0-6 3m+: 0-0
Track: LH: 0-1 RH: 0-5 Tight: 0-4 Gall: 0-0
Aids: Bl: 0-0 Vi: 0-0 Tstrap: 0-0
Best Rating: 104 11/00 Hrfd 2m1f gd-sft Hdl

Has been running well over hurdles. Best coming with a late run. Found just under two and a half miles on fast ground inadequate when runner-up in a maiden hurdle at Hereford in April 2002. May have been a shade unlucky when falling at the last over 22 furlongs at Stratford next time.

Dilkusha (IRE)

77 62

7-y-o b g Indian Ridge-Crimson Glen (Glenstal (USA))
B A Pearce Trevor Painting

Placings:5P (1260)
2001/02: 16^{5}GF, 16^{P}GF

	Starts	1st	2nd	3rd	Win & Pl
Hurdles	2	0	0	0	0
Career Total	**2**	**0**	**0**	**0**	**0**

Going: Sf: 0-0 GS: 0-0 Gd: 0-0 GF: - Fm: 0-2
Distance: 2m/2m3: 0-2 2m4-2m7: 0-0 3m+: 0-0
Track: LH: 0-1 RH: 0-1 Tight: 0-0 Gall: 0-1
Aids: Bl: 0-0 Vi: 0-0 Tstrap: 0-0
Best Rating: 62 6/01 Worc 2m gd-fm Hdl

Dinar (USA)

92 69

7-y-o b h Dixieland Band (USA)-Bold Jessie (Never So Bold)
B J Llewellyn (R Brotherton 11/5) J Rees

Placings:0 (1260)
2001/02: 16^{0}GF

	Starts	1st	2nd	3rd	Win & Pl
Hurdles	1	0	0	0	
Career Total	**1**	**0**	**0**	**0**	

Going: Sf: 0-0 GS: 0-0 Gd: 0-0 GF: - Fm: 0-1
Distance: 2m/2m3: 0-1 2m4-2m7: 0-0 3m+: 0-0
Track: LH: 0-0 RH: 0-1 Tight: 0-0 Gall: 0-1
Aids: Bl: 0-0 Vi: 0-0 Tstrap: 0-0
Best Rating: 69 8/01 Hntg 2m110y gd-fm Hdl

Dingo Dancer

106(80h) 111

9-y-o b g Dancing High-Some Shiela (Remainder Man)
J P Dodds J R Jeffreys

Placings:4000054/11P00-PP12 (4905)

2001/02: 24^{P}S, 16^{P}S, 17^{1}GF, 17^{2}GF

	Starts	1st	2nd	3rd	Win & Pl
Hurdles	1	0	0	0	0
Chases	3	1	1	0	5572
Career Total	**16**	**3**	**1**	**0**	**11617**

106	4/02	Kels	2m1f	E(0-110)HCh	G-F	£4407
86	5/00	Prth	2m110y	E(0-105)HHdl	G-S	£3454
78	5/00	Newc	2m4f	E(0-105)HHdl	G-F	£2590

Total win prize-money £10452

Going: Sf: 0-2 GS: 0-0 Gd: 0-0 GF: - Fm: 1-2
Distance: **2m/2m3: 1-3** 2m4-2m7: 0-0 3m+: 0-1
Track: **LH: 1-2** RH: 0-2 **Tight: 1-3** Gall: 0-1
Aids: Bl: 0-0 Vi: 0-0 Tstrap: 0-0
Best Rating: 106 4/02 Kels 2m1f gd-fm Ch

Modest handicap chaser.

Dinky Dora

100 **87**

9-y-o ch m Gunner B-Will Be Wanton (Palm Track)
J K Cresswell J K S Cresswell

Placings: *020*/4000/61555PP326/5065/05455-136 **(0846)**
2001/02: 19^{1}GF, 19^{3}GF, 22^{6}GF

	Starts	1st	2nd	3rd	Win & Pl
Hurdles	3	1	0	1	2157
Career Total	**29**	**2**	**2**	**2**	**6577**

87	6/01	MRas	2m3f110y	G(0-90)HHdl	G-F	£1736
93	5/98	Worc	2m4f	E(0-100)HHdl	G-F	£2862

Total win prize-money £4598

Going: Sf: 0-0 GS: 0-0 Gd: 0-0 GF: - Fm: 1-3
Distance: 2m/2m3: 0-0 **2m4-2m7: 1-3** 3m+: 0-0
Track: LH: 0-1 **RH: 1-2 Tight: 1-3** Gall: 0-0
Aids: Bl: 0-0 Vi: 0-0 Tstrap: 0-0
Best Rating: 99 12/97 Uttx 2m gd-sft NHF

Dion Dee

69 **32**

6-y-o ch m Anshan-Jade Mistress (Damister (USA))
Dr J R J Naylor B C Mills

Placings: 0 **(0341)**
2001/02: 16^{0}G

	Starts	1st	2nd	3rd	Win & Pl
Hurdles	1	0	0	0	
Career Total	**1**	**0**	**0**	**0**	

Going: Sf: 0-0 GS: 0-0 Gd: 0-1 GF: - Fm: 0-0
Distance: 2m/2m3: 0-1 2m4-2m7: 0-0 3m+: 0-0
Track: LH: 0-1 RH: 0-0 Tight: 0-1 Gall: 0-0
Aids: Bl: 0-0 Vi: 0-0 Tstrap: 0-0
Best Rating: 32 5/01 Aint 2m110y good Hdl

Direct Access (IRE)

103(114h) **146**

7-y-o ch g Roselier (FR)-Spanish Flame (IRE) (Spanish Place (USA))
L Lungo Ashleybank Investments Limited

Placings: 1111-11F24 **(4835)**
2001/02: 16^{1}S, 20^{1}HY, 25^{F}G, 22^{2}S, 25^{4}G

	Starts	1st	2nd	3rd	Win & Pl
Chases	5	2	1	0	14570
Career Total	**9**	**6**	**1**	**0**	**41663**

146	11/01	Carl	2m4f	D Ch	HVY	£5187
123	11/01	Carl	2m	D Ch	SFT	£4823
143	3/01	Sand	2m4f110y	A HHdl	HVY	£18560
143	2/01	Kels	2m6f110y	E Hdl	SFT	£2730
142	1/01	Ayr	2m4f	D Hdl	G-S	£3423
122	12/00	Ayr	2m4f	E Hdl	SFT	£2380

Total win prize-money £37103

Going: Sf: 2-3 GS: 0-0 Gd: 0-2 GF: - Fm: 0-0
Distance: 2m/2m3: 1-1 2m4-2m7: 1-2 3m+: 0-2
Track: LH: 0-2 **RH: 2-2** Tight: 0-0 Gall: 0-1
Aids: Bl: 0-0 Vi: 0-0 Tstrap: 0-0
Best Rating: 146 11/01 Carl 2m4f heavy Ch

A winning point-to-pointer who is unbeaten over hurdles and won his first two over fences before falling at Cheltenham in December 2001. Lost his way a little afterwards but has time on his side. Acts on soft ground, should stay three miles.

Direct Bearing (IRE)

106 **126**

5-y-o b g Polish Precedent (USA)-Uncertain Affair (IRE) (Darshaan)
D K Weld Michael W J Smurfit

Placings: *1*-1024 **(4943a)**
2001/02: 16^{1}HY, 21^{0}GS, 16^{2}Y, 16^{4}G

	Starts	1st	2nd	3rd	Win & Pl
Hurdles	4	1	1	0	11135
Career Total	**5**	**2**	**1**	**0**	**15587**

117	1/02	Leop	2m	Hdl	HVY	£7619
113	1/01	Fair	2m	NHF	SFT	£4451

Total win prize-money £12072

Going: Sf: 1-1 GS: 0-1 Gd: 0-1 GF: - Fm: 0-0
Distance: **2m/2m3: 1-3** 2m4-2m7: 0-1 3m+: 0-0
Track: **LH: 1-2** RH: 0-2 Tight: 0-0 Gall: 0-1
Aids: Bl: 0-0 Vi: 0-0 Tstrap: 0-0
Best Rating: 126 4/02 Fair 2m yield Hdl

Decent stayer on the Flat, made a winning debut over hurdles on heavy ground in January 2002. His limitations were exposed afterwards. Likely to get further than two miles in time.

Direct Hit

7-y-o ch m Gunner B-Sweet Canyon (NZ) (Headland (USA))
J R Jenkins Mrs Jean Powell

Placings: *50U05*/P00-P **(0588)**
2001/02: 16^{P}GF

	Starts	1st	2nd	3rd	Win & Pl
Hurdles	1	0	0	0	
Career Total	**9**	**0**	**0**	**0**	**0**

Going: Sf: 0-0 GS: 0-0 Gd: 0-0 GF: - Fm: 0-1
Distance: 2m/2m3: 0-1 2m4-2m7: 0-0 3m+: 0-0
Track: LH: 0-1 RH: 0-0 Tight: 0-1 Gall: 0-0
Aids: Bl: 0-1 Vi: 0-0 Tstrap: 0-0
Best Rating: 85 1/00 Donc 2m110y good Hdl

Direction

97f **89f**

4-y-o b f Lahib (USA)-Theme (IRE) (Sadler's Wells (USA))
K A Morgan John Sheridan

Placings: *1* **(4289)**
2001/02: 17^{1}GS

	Starts	1st	2nd	3rd	Win & Pl
NH Flat	1	1	0	0	1617
Career Total	**1**	**1**	**0**	**0**	**1617**

93	3/02	MRas	2m1f110y	H NHF	G-S	£1617

Total win prize-money £1617

Going: Sf: 0-0 GS: 1-1 Gd: 0-0 GF: - Fm: 0-0
Distance: **2m/2m3: 1-1** 2m4-2m7: 0-0 3m+: 0-0
Track: LH: 0-0 **RH: 1-1 Tight: 1-1** Gall: 0-0
Aids: Bl: 0-0 Vi: 0-0 Tstrap: 0-0
Best Rating: 93 3/02 MRas 2m1f110y gd-sft NHF

Half-sister to bumper and hurdle winner Sea Drifting. Took a mares' bumper by a decisive margin on her debut at Market Rasen in March.

Dirk Cove (IRE)

105(116h) **118**

8-y-o ch g Montelimar (USA)-Another Miller (Gala Performance (USA))
R Rowe Dr B Alexander

Placings: 543/11205-36 **(4133)**
2001/02: 20^{3}S, 24^{6}G

	Starts	1st	2nd	3rd	Win & Pl
Chases	2	0	0	1	959
Career Total	**10**	**2**	**1**	**2**	**8739**

107	12/00	Tntn	3m110y	D(0-120)HHdl	SFT	£3575
104	11/00	Towc	2m5f	E(0-115)HHdl	SFT	£2240

Total win prize-money £5815

Going: Sf: 0-1 GS: 0-0 Gd: 0-1 GF: - Fm: 0-0
Distance: 2m/2m3: 0-0 2m4-2m7: 0-1 3m+: 0-1
Track: LH: 0-0 RH: 0-1 Tight: 0-1 Gall: 0-0
Aids: Bl: 0-0 Vi: 0-0 Tstrap: 0-0
Best Rating: 118 3/02 Sand 3m110y good Ch

Fair staying hurdler, suited by soft ground and stays three miles. Yet to convince over fences.

Discus

63

8-y-o b g Syrtos-Hilly Path (Brave Invader (USA))
Ian Williams Cockbury Court Partnership

Placings: P-0 **(0352)**
2001/02: 22^{0}G

	Starts	1st	2nd	3rd	Win & Pl
Hurdles	1	0	0	0	
Career Total	**2**	**0**	**0**	**0**	

Going: Sf: 0-0 GS: 0-0 Gd: 0-1 GF: - Fm: 0-0
Distance: 2m/2m3: 0-0 2m4-2m7: 0-1 3m+: 0-0
Track: LH: 0-1 RH: 0-0 Tight: 0-1 Gall: 0-0
Aids: Bl: 0-0 Vi: 0-0 Tstrap: 0-0
Best Rating:

Dishabille

6-y-o b m Dilum (USA)-Swagger Lady (Tate Gallery (USA))
I Park Mrs C Park

Placings: P000/0-PPP0P **(4919)**
2001/02: 24^{P}S, 24^{P}S, 20^{P}S, 16^{0}GS, 21^{P}GF

	Starts	1st	2nd	3rd	Win & Pl
Hurdles	5	0	0	0	
Career Total	**10**	**0**	**0**	**0**	

Going: Sf: 0-3 GS: 0-1 Gd: 0-0 GF: - Fm: 0-1
Distance: 2m/2m3: 0-1 2m4-2m7: 0-2 3m+: 0-2
Track: LH: 0-5 RH: 0-0 Tight: 0-1 Gall: 0-3
Aids: Bl: 0-0 Vi: 0-0 Tstrap: 0-3
Best Rating: 48 4/00 Sedg 2m1f good Hdl

Lightly raced and well held in modest hurdling company. Has worn a tongue strap.

Dispol Miss Chief

32 **9**

5-y-o ch m Be My Chief (USA)-Tino-Ella (Bustino)
I W McInnes I W McInnes

Placings:P-0P **(0236)**
2001/02: 16^{0}S, 16^{P}GF

	Starts	1st	2nd	3rd	Win & Pl
Hurdles	2	0	0	0	
Career Total	**3**	**0**	**0**	**0**	

Going: Sf: 0-1 GS: 0-0 Gd: 0-0 GF: - Fm: 0-1
Distance: 2m/2m3: 0-2 2m4-2m7: 0-0 3m+: 0-0
Track: LH: 0-2 RH: 0-0 Tight: 0-1 Gall: 0-0
Aids: Bl: 0-0 Vi: 0-0 Tstrap: 0-0
Best Rating: 9 5/01 Hexm 2m soft Hdl

Dissington Me

77(78h) (36h)**41**

7-y-o gr m Presidium-Zam's Slave (Zambrano)
R Johnson Da & W Wyllie

Placings:*30/0*PP/6PP-P0PUP006**0P** **(1470)**
2001/02: 24^{P}S, 16^{0}GF, 16^{P}GS, 16^{U}F, 20^{P}GF, 19^{0}G, 21^{0}GF, 24^{6}G, 21^{0}GF, 20^{P}G

	Starts	1st	2nd	3rd	Win & Pl
Hurdles	8	0	0	0	0
Chases	2	0	0	0	0
Career Total	**18**	**0**	**0**	**1**	**192**

Going: Sf: 0-1 GS: 0-1 Gd: 0-3 GF: - Fm: 0-5
Distance: 2m/2m3: 0-3 2m4-2m7: 0-5 3m+: 0-2
Track: LH: 0-4 RH: 0-6 Tight: 0-3 Gall: 0-0
Aids: Bl: 0-0 Vi: 0-0 Tstrap: 0-3
Best Rating: 57 2/99 Ayr 2m soft NHF

Distant Storm

107 **106**

9-y-o ch g Pharly (FR)-Candle In The Wind (Thatching)
B J Llewellyn D H Driscoll

Placings:23/5435PP111222313/5233423P233502/33 24021232165333/336546056-31P3232P3 **(2293)**
2001/02: 21^{3}GF, 19^{1}GF, 20^{P}GF, 22^{3}G, 18^{2}GF, 19^{3}GF, 19^{2}GS, 22^{P}G, 19^{3}GF

	Starts	1st	2nd	3rd	Win & Pl		
Hurdles	9	1	2	4	6988		
Career Total	**65**	**7**	**14**	**21**	**47254**		
106	6/01	MRas	2m3f110y	D(0-120)HHdl		G-F	£3598
117	12/99	Chep	2m110y	C(0-135)HHdl		HVY	£8247
102	10/99	Winc	2m6f	F(0-105)HHdl		GD	£2892
102	3/98	Hntg	2m110y	E(0-110)HHdl		GD	£2250
90	11/97	Winc	2m	E(0-100)HHdl		GD	£2248
93	11/97	Uttx	2m	E(0-100)HHdl		GD	£2449
78	10/97	Extr	2m1f110y	G(0-95)HHdl		GD	£1812

Total win prize-money £23496

Going: Sf: 0-0 GS: 0-1 Gd: 0-2 GF: - Fm: 1-6
Distance: 2m/2m3: 0-4 **2m4-2m7: 1-5** 3m+: 0-0
Track: LH: 0-3 **RH: 1-6 Tight: 1-4** Gall: 0-1
Aids: Bl: 1-9 Vi: 0-0 Tstrap: 1-9
Best Rating: 117 6/00 Strf 2m110y good Hdl

Modest hurdler, he is effective at various trips and handles most surfaces. Usually wears blinkers and a tongue tie. Goes well for Emily Jones.

Distinct (IRE)

9-y-o b g Distinctly North (USA)-Shy Jinks (Shy Groom (USA))
W M Scott (A C Whillans 20/1) Mrs Murray Scott

Placings:05405/33**P6FP**/**5P5P**/**6P** **(4892)**
2001/02: 21^{6}S, 31^{P}G

	Starts	1st	2nd	3rd	Win & Pl
Chases	2	0	0	0	0
Career Total	**17**	**0**	**0**	**2**	**632**

Going: Sf: 0-1 GS: 0-0 Gd: 0-1 GF: - Fm: 0-0
Distance: 2m/2m3: 0-0 2m4-2m7: 0-1 3m+: 0-1
Track: LH: 0-1 RH: 0-0 Tight: 0-1 Gall: 0-0
Aids: Bl: 0-0 Vi: 0-0 Tstrap: 0-0
Best Rating: 74 3/98 Carl 2m4f110y heavy Hdl

Selling-class hurdler and winning pointer.

Distinctive (IRE)

13-y-o ch g Orchestra-Zimuletta (Distinctly (USA))
Mrs Caroline Chadney Mrs D J Jackson

Placings:*54*/F0300/06**F315**/**1P62135**/**31U11P4**/**5P4**/**6 FPP**/**40**/**23-11** **(4846)**
2001/02: 20^{1}GF, 24^{1}G

	Starts	1st	2nd	3rd	Win & Pl		
Chases	2	2	0	0	3164		
Career Total	**40**	**8**	**2**	**5**	**29577**		
111	4/02	Bang	3m110y	H Ch		GD	£1883
118	5/01	Wwck	2m4f110y	H Ch		G-F	£1281
	2/97	Hntg	2m4f110y	D(0-120)HCh		GD	£3582
	2/97	Strf	2m5f110y	D(0-125)HCh		GD	£3582
	12/96	Bang	2m4f110y	D(0-120)HCh		GD	£4065
	2/96	Leic	3m	E(0-110)HCh		G-S	£3479
	12/95	Bang	2m4f110y	D(0-120)HCh		G-S	£3793
	3/95	Nott	2m5f110y	E Ch		G-S	£2846

Total win prize-money £24514

Going: Sf: 0-0 GS: 0-0 Gd: 1-1 GF: - Fm: 1-1
Distance: 2m/2m3: 0-0 2m4-2m7: 1-1 3m+: 1-1
Track: **LH: 2-2** RH: 0-0 **Tight: 1-1** Gall: 0-0
Aids: Bl: 0-0 Vi: 0-0 Tstrap: 0-0
Best Rating: 118 5/01 Wwck 2m4f110y gd-fm Ch

Sprightly veteran hunter chaser, very tough and needs fast ground.

Distinctly East (IRE)

88 **77**

5-y-o b g Distinctly North (USA)-Raggy (Smoggy)
Miss S J Wilton John Pointon And Sons

Placings:3600-0040 **(1439)**
2001/02: 16^{0}GF, 16^{0}GF, 17^{4}GF, 18^{0}GF

	Starts	1st	2nd	3rd	Win & Pl
Hurdles	4	0	0	0	0
Career Total	**8**	**0**	**0**	**1**	**429**

Going: Sf: 0-0 GS: 0-0 Gd: 0-0 GF: - Fm: 0-4
Distance: 2m/2m3: 0-4 2m4-2m7: 0-0 3m+: 0-0
Track: LH: 0-3 RH: 0-1 Tight: 0-1 Gall: 0-0
Aids: Bl: 0-1 Vi: 0-2 Tstrap: 0-0
Best Rating: 81 8/00 Worc 2m gd-fm Hdl

Diva

100 **101**

5-y-o b m Exit To Nowhere (USA)-Opera Lover (IRE) (Sadler's Wells (USA))
A King Mrs Joy Fenton And Partners

Placings:1324-40 **(0241)**
2001/02: 17^{4}G, 16^{0}GF

	Starts	1st	2nd	3rd	Win & Pl		
Hurdles	2	0	0	0	0		
Career Total	**6**	**1**	**1**	**1**	**4348**		
119	10/00	Hrfd	2m1f	E Hdl		GD	£2583

Total win prize-money £2583

Going: Sf: 0-0 GS: 0-0 Gd: 0-1 GF: - Fm: 0-1
Distance: 2m/2m3: 0-2 2m4-2m7: 0-0 3m+: 0-0
Track: LH: 0-1 RH: 0-1 Tight: 0-0 Gall: 0-0
Aids: Bl: 0-0 Vi: 0-0 Tstrap: 0-0
Best Rating: 119 10/00 Hrfd 2m1f good Hdl

Fairly useful hurdler on her day but has stamina limitations and needs a sharp track and good ground or faster to shine.

Diva's Delight

94 **92**

8-y-o b g Takachiho-L'Oraz (Ile De Bourbon (USA))
Mrs S Lamyman Queens Head Racing Club

Placings:*0600*/FP020-3P2P **(3625)**
2001/02: 24^{3}G, 29^{P}S, 24^{2}S, 22^{P}S

	Starts	1st	2nd	3rd	Win & Pl
Chases	4	0	1	1	1674
Career Total	**13**	**0**	**2**	**1**	**2833**

Going: Sf: 0-3 GS: 0-0 Gd: 0-1 GF: - Fm: 0-0
Distance: 2m/2m3: 0-0 2m4-2m7: 0-1 3m+: 0-3
Track: LH: 0-2 RH: 0-1 Tight: 0-3 Gall: 0-0
Aids: Bl: 0-0 Vi: 0-0 Tstrap: 0-0
Best Rating: 92 1/02 Fknm 3m110y soft Ch

Moderate novice chaser, stays three miles.

Divertimiento

97(90h) **104**

11-y-o b g Night Shift (USA)-Aunt Jemima (Busted)
J Mackie A J Wall

Placings:5/5412B3310/3/50/06044-42056 **(1192)**
2001/02: 17^{4}GS, 17^{2}G, 20^{0}G, 16^{5}GF, 20^{6}G

	Starts	1st	2nd	3rd	Win & Pl		
Chases	5	0	1	0	1341		
Career Total	**23**	**2**	**2**	**3**	**22534**		
122	3/96	Chep	2m110y	C Hdl		G-S	£13745
117	11/95	Leic	2m	E Hdl		G-S	£3225

Total win prize-money £16970

Going: Sf: 0-0 GS: 0-1 Gd: 0-3 GF: - Fm: 0-1
Distance: 2m/2m3: 0-3 2m4-2m7: 0-2 3m+: 0-0
Track: LH: 0-5 RH: 0-0 Tight: 0-4 Gall: 0-0
Aids: Bl: 0-0 Vi: 0-1 Tstrap: 0-0
Best Rating: 122 3/96 Chep 2m110y gd-sft Hdl

Very moderate handicap chaser, best at around two miles, does not want the ground too soft.

Divet Hill

106(109c) (134c)**104+**

8-y-o b g Milieu-Bargello's Lady (Bargello)
Mrs A Hamilton Ian Hamilton

Placings:*5*P-4O12221133 **(4692)**
2001/02: 25^{4}S, 20°GF, 24^{1}GF, 24^{2}GF, 20^{2}G, 16^{2}GF, 16^{1}G, 21^{1}GF, 21^{3}G, 25^{3}GF

	Starts	1st	2nd	3rd	Win & Pl
Chases	10	3	3	2	15387

Career Total	**12**	**3**	**3**	**2**		**15387**

131 9/01 Sedg 2m5f E Ch G-F £3282
108 8/01 Prth 2m D Ch GD £4056
125 5/01 Newc 3m E Ch G-F £3668
Total win prize-money £11007

Going: Sf: 0-1 GS: 0-0 Gd: 1-3 GF: - Fm: 2-6
Distance: 2m/2m3: 1-2 2m4-2m7: 1-4 3m+: 1-4
Track: LH: 2-8 RH: 1-2 Tight: 1-4 Gall: 1-1
Aids: Bl: 0-0 Vi: 0-0 Tstrap: 0-0
Best Rating: 131 9/01 Sedg 2m5f gd-fm Ch

A fair front-running chaser, effective at two and a half to three miles plus. A good jumper, he is suited by fast ground. Genuine sort, he took a modest satyrs' novices' hurdle at Sedgefield in July.

Divine Mist (IRE)

87f **88f**

5-y-o br g Roselier (FR)-Tate Divinity (IRE) (Tate Gallery (USA))
Miss H C Knight Trevor Hemmings

Placings:00 **(3798)**
2001/02: 16^{0}G, 16^{0}S

	Starts	1st	2nd	3rd	Win & Pl
NH Flat	2	0	0	0	
Career Total	**2**	**0**	**0**	**0**	

Going: Sf: 0-1 GS: 0-0 Gd: 0-1 GF: - Fm: 0-0
Distance: 2m/2m3: 0-2 2m4-2m7: 0-0 3m+: 0-0
Track: LH: 0-1 RH: 0-1 Tight: 0-0 Gall: 0-0
Aids: Bl: 0-0 Vi: 0-0 Tstrap: 0-0
Best Rating: 88 12/01 Ludl 2m good NHF

Divorce Action (IRE)

113(77c) (75c)**117**

6-y-o b g Common Grounds-Overdue Reaction (Be My Guest (USA))
R M Stronge Kevin Elliott

Placings:26510/406-413456 **(1398)**
2001/02: 16^{4}GF, 16^{1}GF, 17^{3}G, 16^{4}GF, 16^{5}GF, 16^{6}GF

	Starts	1st	2nd	3rd	Win & Pl
Hurdles	5	1	0	1	6357
Chases	1	0	0	0	0
Career Total	**14**	**2**	**1**	**1**	**12566**

117 7/01 Sthl 2m D(0-120)HHdl G-F £5395
99 3/00 Newb 2m110y D(0-120)HHdl G-F £5362
Total win prize-money £10758

Going: Sf: 0-0 GS: 0-0 Gd: 0-1 GF: - Fm: 1-5
Distance: 2m/2m3: 1-6 2m4-2m7: 0-0 3m+: 0-0
Track: LH: 1-6 RH: 0-0 **Tight: 1-5** Gall: 0-0
Aids: Bl: 0-0 Vi: 0-0 Tstrap: 0-0
Best Rating: 117 7/01 Sthl 2m gd-fm Hdl

Fair handicap hurdler at the minimum trip on fast ground.

Divulge (USA)

105 **91**

5-y-o b g Diesis-Avira (Dancing Brave (USA))
P J Hobbs (K A Morgan 2/6) Jay Dee Bloodstock Limited

Placings:000-03F6 **(3228)**
2001/02: 16^{0}GF, 16^{3}S, 16^{F}G, 16^{6}G

	Starts	1st	2nd	3rd	Win & Pl
Hurdles	4	0	0	1	395
Career Total	**7**	**0**	**0**	**1**	**395**

Going: Sf: 0-1 GS: 0-0 Gd: 0-2 GF: - Fm: 0-1
Distance: 2m/2m3: 0-4 2m4-2m7: 0-0 3m+: 0-0
Track: LH: 0-2 RH: 0-2 Tight: 0-2 Gall: 0-0
Aids: Bl: 0-0 Vi: 0-0 Tstrap: 0-0
Best Rating: 91 11/01 Strf 2m110y soft Hdl

Having shown little previously he has not been disgraced on last two starts but stamina looks strictly limited.

Dix Bay

104 **111**

7-y-o b g Teenoso (USA)-Cooks Lawn (The Parson)
M W Easterby Mrs E J Wright And Mr A D Bairstow

Placings:042/1213-2061 **(4869)**
2001/02: 16^{2}G, 20^{0}G, 16^{6}S, 20^{1}GF

	Starts	1st	2nd	3rd	Win & Pl
Hurdles	4	1	1	0	5337
Career Total	**11**	**3**	**3**	**1**	**12649**

111 4/02 Weth 2m4f110y D(0-115)HHdl G-F £4277
106 1/01 Weth 2m4f110y D Hdl G-S £3759
108 10/00 MRas 2m1f110y H NHF GD £1554
Total win prize-money £9590

Going: Sf: 0-1 GS: 0-0 Gd: 0-2 GF: - Fm: 1-1
Distance: 2m/2m3: 0-2 **2m4-2m7: 1-2** 3m+: 0-0
Track: LH: 1-4 RH: 0-0 Tight: 0-0 Gall: 0-0
Aids: Bl: 0-0 Vi: 0-0 Tstrap: 0-0
Best Rating: 111 4/02 Weth 2m4f110y gd fm Hdl

Modest hurdler, he is effective at up to two and a half miles and acts on most going. Can go well fresh and was reappearing after a break when successful at Wetherby in April 2002.

Dizzy Tilly

94 **109**

8-y-o b m Anshan-Nadema (Artaius (USA))
A J Martin J H Lowry

Placings:000/4030 **(2167)**
2001/02: 16^{4}G, 16^{0}G, 16^{3}G, 16^{0}G

	Starts	1st	2nd	3rd	Win & Pl
Hurdles	4	0	0	1	802
Career Total	**7**	**0**	**0**	**1**	**802**

Going: Sf: 0-0 GS: 0-0 Gd: 0-4 GF: - Fm: 0-0
Distance: 2m/2m3: 0-4 2m4-2m7: 0-0 3m+: 0-0
Track: LH: 0-1 RH: 0-0 Tight: 0-0 Gall: 0-0
Aids: Bl: 0-1 Vi: 0-0 Tstrap: 0-2
Best Rating: 109 7/01 Tipp 2m good Hdl

A winner at middle distances on the Flat, has shown ability in a few runs over hurdles in Ireland.

Djeddah (FR)

113 **146**

11-y-o b g Shafoun (FR)-Union Jack Iii (FR) (Mister Jack (FR))
F Doumen Roger Barby

Placings:3244/11130P1132/53405PR2P6/453P14/F1 13050/6P0440UP-03R0106U **(4677)**
2001/02: 29^{0}S, 25^{3}G, 34^{R}GF, 25^{0}HY, 24^{1}G, 31^{0}GS, 24^{6}S, 36^{U}G

Starts		1st	2nd	3rd	Win & Pl
Chases	8	1	0	1	18444
Career Total	**53**	**9**	**3**	**7**	**366437**

146 11/01 Asct 3m110y B(0-150)HCh GD £10198
9/99 Autl 2m5f110y Ch SFT £26911
7/99 Autl 2m6f Ch SFT £32293
4/99 Nanc 2m5f Ch SFT £10764
2/97 Asct 3m110y A Ch G-F £15875
12/96 Kemp 3m Ch G-F £23100
9/96 Autl 2m2f HHdl VS £31620
6/96 Autl 2m5f110y Ch SFT £19762
Total win prize-money £183699

Going: Sf: 0-3 GS: 0-1 Gd: 1-3 GF: - Fm: 0-1
Distance: 2m/2m3: 0-0 2m4-2m7: 0-0 **3m+: 1-8**
Track: LH: 0-4 **RH: 1-2** Tight: 0-1 Gall: 0-0
Aids: Bl: 1-6 Vi: 0-0 Tstrap: 0-0
Best Rating: 153 2/00 Kemp 3m gd-sft Ch

He had not won in this country since his novice season until winning at Ascot in November. Needs a sound surface to produce his best. Stays three miles. Normally runs in blinkers.

Do It On Dani

102 **95**

7-y-o br m Weld-Dark City (Sweet Monday)
Mrs A M Thorpe Mrs A M Thorpe

Placings:3405-06042342 **(1393)**
2001/02: 16^{0}S, 17^{6}F, 19^{0}GF, 25^{4}GF, 27^{2}G, 24^{3}GF, 22^{4}GF, 24^{2}GF

	Starts	1st	2nd	3rd	Win & Pl
Hurdles	8	0	2	1	1662
Career Total	**12**	**0**	**2**	**2**	**1898**

Going: Sf: 0-1 GS: 0-0 Gd: 0-1 GF: - Fm: 0-6
Distance: 2m/2m3: 0-3 2m4-2m7: 0-1 3m+: 0-4
Track: LH: 0-7 RH: 0-1 Tight: 0-5 Gall: 0-0
Aids: Bl: 0-0 Vi: 0-0 Tstrap: 0-0
Best Rating: 96 11/00 Hrfd 2m1f soft NHF

Stays well and won three mile three furlong handicap at Newton Abbot June 2002. Acts on fast ground.

Do Keep Up

60f **37f**

5-y-o b g Missed Flight-Aimee Jane (USA) (Our Native (USA))
N P Littmoden W R Hornby

Placings:00 **(3784)**
2001/02: 16^{0}S, 16^{0}S

	Starts	1st	2nd	3rd	Win & Pl
NH Flat	2	0	0	0	
Career Total	**2**	**0**	**0**	**0**	

Going: Sf: 0-2 GS: 0-0 Gd: 0-0 GF: - Fm: 0-0
Distance: 2m/2m3: 0-2 2m4-2m7: 0-0 3m+: 0-0
Track: LH: 0-0 RH: 0-2 Tight: 0-0 Gall: 0-0
Aids: Bl: 0-0 Vi: 0-0 Tstrap: 0-0
Best Rating: 37 1/02 Kemp 2m soft NHF

Do Me A Favour (IRE)

104(93h) (87h)**108**

8-y-o b g Classic Memory-Ice Pearl (Flatbush)
J T Gifford D G Trangmar

Placings:3/46/6363P42P **(4849)**
2001/02: 16^{6}G, 24^{3}G, 24^{6}S, 23^{3}S, 22^{P}S, 26^{4}GS, 25^{2}GS, 24^{P}G

	Starts	1st	2nd	3rd	Win & Pl
Hurdles	2	0	0	1	752
Chases	6	0	1	1	1752
Career Total	**11**	**0**	**1**	**3**	**2911**

Going: Sf: 0-3 GS: 0-2 Gd: 0-3 GF: - Fm: 0-0
Distance: 2m/2m3: 0-1 2m4-2m7: 0-1 3m+: 0-6
Track: LH: 0-3 RH: 0-4 Tight: 0-2 Gall: 0-1
Aids: Bl: 0-1 Vi: 0-0 Tstrap: 0-0
Best Rating: 108 3/02 Towc 3m1f gd-sft Ch

Novice hurdler/chaser. Stays three miles. Acts on good to soft/soft ground.

Do Ye Know Wha (IRE)

102 **122**

10-y-o b g Ajraas (USA)-Norton Princess (Wolver Hollow)
R Curtis Eddie Gloyne

Placings: *21230*/0/1124/**1442PP**4/313-P4340 **(4231)**
2001/02: 19^{P}GF, 22^{4}S, 24^{3}G, 24^{4}S, 21^{0}GS

	Starts	1st	2nd	3rd	Win & Pl
Hurdles	5	0	0	1	2064
Career Total	**25**	**5**	**4**	**4**	**33245**

125	10/00	Ludl	3m	E(0-115)HHdl	G-F	£4485
117	9/99	Hntg	3m	E Ch	GD	£2968
118	10/98	Chep	2m4f110y	E Hdl	G-S	£1996
115	10/98	Bang	2m4f	E Hdl	GD	£2358
117	10/96	Naas	2m	NHF	GD	£3530

Total win prize-money £15338

Going: Sf: 0-2 GS: 0-1 Gd: 0-1 GF: - Fm: 0-1
Distance: 2m/2m3: 0-0 2m4-2m7: 0-3 3m+: 0-2
Track: LH: 0-2 RH: 0-3 Tight: 0-1 Gall: 0-1
Aids: Bl: 0-1 Vi: 0-0 Tstrap: 0-0
Best Rating: 132 12/98 Sand 2m6f good Hdl

Fair hurdler, stays three miles and acts on a sound surface.

Docklands Limo

110 **143**

9-y-o b h Most Welcome-Bugle Sound (Bustino)
N A Twiston-Davies John Marks

Placings: 2102/4365501-2 **(0080)**
2001/02: 16^{2}G

	Starts	1st	2nd	3rd	Win & Pl
Hurdles	1	0	1	0	10350
Career Total	**12**	**2**	**3**	**1**	**46365**

143	4/01	Aint	2m110y	B HHdl	HVY	£26000
124	3/00	Newb	2m110y	D Hdl	G-F	£3867

Total win prize-money £29868

Going: Sf: 0-0 GS: 0-0 Gd: 0-1 GF: - Fm: 0-0
Distance: 2m/2m3: 0-1 2m4-2m7: 0-0 3m+: 0-0
Track: LH: 0-1 RH: 0-0 Tight: 0-0 Gall: 0-0
Aids: Bl: 0-0 Vi: 0-0 Tstrap: 0-0
Best Rating: 143 5/01 Hayd 2m good Hdl

A useful handicap hurdler who gained his biggest victory at Aintree on Grand National day 2001 when winning a valuable handicap hurdle over two miles in desperate conditions, and ran a very good race at Haydock after that when second. Not seen since the spring of 2001.

Doctor Bravious (IRE)

9-y-o b g Priolo (USA)-Sharp Slipper (Sharpo)
Jamie Poulton Chris Steward & Christian Taylor

Placings: 033P0/0402440115342/P1253/0P-P5 **(4169)**
2001/02: 20^{P}HY, 21^{5}GS

	Starts	1st	2nd	3rd	Win & Pl
Hurdles	1	0	0	0	0
Chases	1	0	0	0	0
Career Total	**27**	**3**	**3**	**4**	**13168**

98	12/99	Plum	2m5f	E(0-115)HHdl	GD	£2320
97	2/99	Plum	2m1f	E(0-115)HHdl	SFT	£5199
86	1/99	Tntn	2m1f	G Hdl	SFT	£1509

Total win prize-money £9028

Going: Sf: 0-1 GS: 0-1 Gd: 0-0 GF: - Fm: 0-0
Distance: 2m/2m3: 0-0 2m4-2m7: 0-2 3m+: 0-0
Track: LH: 0-2 RH: 0-0 Tight: 0-2 Gall: 0-0
Aids: Bl: 0-2 Vi: 0-0 Tstrap: 0-0
Best Rating: 100 4/99 Plum 2m4f good Hdl

Doctor Dove

75 **44**

8-y-o ch g St Enodoc-Saucy Dove (Saucy Kit)
Miss Venetia Williams Mrs H Spencer

Placings: *33/5*-0 **(0370)**
2001/02: 16^{0}G

	Starts	1st	2nd	3rd	Win & Pl
Hurdles	1	0	0	0	
Career Total	**4**	**0**	**0**	**2**	**471**

Going: Sf: 0-0 GS: 0-0 Gd: 0-1 GF: - Fm: 0-0
Distance: 2m/2m3: 0-1 2m4-2m7: 0-0 3m+: 0-0
Track: LH: 0-1 RH: 0-0 Tight: 0-0 Gall: 0-0
Aids: Bl: 0-0 Vi: 0-0 Tstrap: 0-0
Best Rating: 90 4/00 NAbb 2m1f heavy NHF

Doctor Goddard

(116h) (131h)

7-y-o b g Niniski (USA)-Kamada (USA) (Blushing Groom (FR))
P J Hobbs Allan Stennett & Terry Warner

Placings: 2/2134/3330020-F **(1555)**
2001/02: 19^{F}G

	Starts	1st	2nd	3rd	Win & Pl
Chases	1	0	0	0	
Career Total	**13**	**1**	**3**	**4**	**33031**

123	1/00	Uttx	2m	D Hdl	SFT	£3786

Total win prize-money £3786

Going: Sf: 0-0 GS: 0-0 Gd: 0-1 GF: - Fm: 0-0
Distance: 2m/2m3: 0-0 2m4-2m7: 0-1 3m+: 0-0
Track: LH: 0-1 RH: 0-0 Tight: 0-0 Gall: 0-0
Aids: Bl: 0-0 Vi: 0-0 Tstrap: 0-0
Best Rating: 140 1/01 Asct 2m110y soft Hdl

Had only won one race over hurdles but continually showed up well in hot handicaps last season. Effective up to two and a half miles, he enjoyed soft ground. Killed on chasing debut at Chepstow.

Doctor Green (FR)

98 **99**

9-y-o b g Green Desert (USA)-Highbrow (Shirley Heights)
M C Pipe M C Pipe

Placings: 1114354P/561406154021/2542-3634320F5530 **(4657)**
2001/02: 17^{3}GF, 19^{6}GF, 17^{3}GF, 19^{4}GF, 19^{3}GS, 17^{2}GF, 19^{0}GS, 17^{F}GS, 19^{5}S, 17^{5}S, 16^{3}GS, 24^{0}G

	Starts	1st	2nd	3rd	Win & Pl
Hurdles	12	0	1	4	2218
Career Total	**36**	**6**	**4**	**5**	**19663**

113	4/00	Extr	2m1f110y	G(0-95)HHdl	HVY	£2044
98	12/99	Tntn	2m3f110y	G Hdl	G-S	£1523
106	10/99	Strf	2m110y	G Hdl	G-S	£1744
109	10/96	Chel	2m110y	C Hdl	G-F	£3468
107	10/96	Wwck	2m	D Hdl	FRM	£3109
101	10/96	Extr	2m1f110y	E Hdl	GD	£1969

Total win prize-money £13858

Going: Sf: 0-2 GS: 0-4 Gd: 0-1 GF: - Fm: 0-5
Distance: 2m/2m3: 0-8 2m4-2m7: 0-3 3m+: 0-1
Track: LH: 0-1 RH: 0-11 Tight: 0-6 Gall: 0-0
Aids: Bl: 0-0 Vi: 0-12 Tstrap: 0-0
Best Rating: 119 5/00 Uttx 2m4f110y good Hdl

Fair plater, likes to front-run, suited by cut in the ground. Has won from two miles to two miles three furlongs.

Doctor Hicks

8-y-o b g Seymour Hicks (FR)-Miss Malleret (Netherkelly)
J C McConnochie Dingley Dell Racing Ltd

Placings: V0P/P00/P0P0 **(3765)**
2001/02: 23^{P}S, 20^{0}GS, 21^{P}S, 16^{0}GS

	Starts	1st	2nd	3rd	Win & Pl
Hurdles	4	0	0	0	
Career Total	**10**	**0**	**0**	**0**	

Going: Sf: 0-2 GS: 0-2 Gd: 0-0 GF: - Fm: 0-0
Distance: 2m/2m3: 0-1 2m4-2m7: 0-2 3m+: 0-1
Track: LH: 0-2 RH: 0-2 Tight: 0-2 Gall: 0-1
Aids: Bl: 0-1 Vi: 0-0 Tstrap: 0-0
Best Rating:

Doctor John

90 **75**

5-y-o ch g Handsome Sailor-Bollin Sophie (Efisio)
Andrew Turnell Dr John Hollowood

Placings: 6 **(0827)**
2001/02: 16^{6}GF

	Starts	1st	2nd	3rd	Win & Pl
Hurdles	1	0	0	0	0
Career Total	**1**	**0**	**0**	**0**	**0**

Going: Sf: 0-0 GS: 0-0 Gd: 0-0 GF: - Fm: 0-1
Distance: 2m/2m3: 0-1 2m4-2m7: 0-0 3m+: 0-0
Track: LH: 0-1 RH: 0-0 Tight: 0-1 Gall: 0-0
Aids: Bl: 0-0 Vi: 0-0 Tstrap: 0-0
Best Rating: 75 6/01 Strf 2m110y gd-fm Hdl

Doctor Wood

80 **66**

7-y-o b g Joligeneration-Ladywood (Doctor Wall)
Miss V A Stephens D G Stephens

Placings: *10*P **(3339)**
2001/02: 17^{1}G, 17^{0}HY, 19^{P}S

	Starts	1st	2nd	3rd	Win & Pl
NH Flat	2	1	0	0	2384
Hurdles	1	0	0	0	0
Career Total	**3**	**1**	**0**	**0**	**2384**

92	11/01	Tntn	2m1f	H NHF	GD	£2383

Total win prize-money £2384

Going: Sf: 0-2 GS: 0-0 Gd: 1-1 GF: - Fm: 0-0
Distance: **2m/2m3: 1-2** 2m4-2m7: 0-1 3m+: 0-0

Track: LH: 0-1 RH: 0-1 Tight: 0-2 Gall: 0-0
Aids: Bl: 0-0 Vi: 0-0 Tstrap: 0-0
Best Rating: 92 11/01 Tntn 2m1f good NHF

Caused a bit of an upset when winning a Taunton bumper at 33/1 in November.

Dolly Dove

88 **41**

7-y-o b m Gran Alba (USA)-Celtic Dove (Celtic Cone)
C J Price Ryan Price

Placings:00-00 **(1907)**
2001/02: 20^{0}G, 16^{0}S

	Starts	1st	2nd	3rd	Win & Pl
Hurdles	2	0	0	0	
Career Total	**4**	**0**	**0**	**0**	

Going: Sf: 0-1 GS: 0-0 Gd: 0-1 GF: - Fm: 0-0
Distance: 2m/2m3: 0-1 2m4-2m7: 0-1 3m+: 0-0
Track: LH: 0-2 RH: 0-0 Tight: 0-1 Gall: 0-0
Aids: Bl: 0-0 Vi: 0-0 Tstrap: 0-0
Best Rating: 41 7/01 Worc 2m4f good Hdl

Dolly Mop

76f **69f**

6-y-o b m Nearly A Hand-Roving Seal (Privy Seal)
B J M Ryall D R Bell

Placings:0 **(1773)**
2001/02: 17^{0}GS

	Starts	1st	2nd	3rd	Win & Pl
NH Flat	1	0	0	0	
Career Total	**1**	**0**	**0**	**0**	

Going: Sf: 0-0 GS: 0-1 Gd: 0-0 GF: - Fm: 0-0
Distance: 2m/2m3: 0-1 2m4-2m7: 0-0 3m+: 0-0
Track: LH: 0-0 RH: 0-1 Tight: 0-0 Gall: 0-0
Aids: Bl: 0-0 Vi: 0-0 Tstrap: 0-0
Best Rating: 69 10/01 Extr 2m1f gd-sft NHF

Dolphinelle (IRE)

99 **85**

6-y-o b g Dolphin Street (FR)-Mamie's Joy (Prince Tenderfoot (USA))
Jamie Poulton Mrs G M Temmerman

Placings:050-34P0003 **(4509)**
2001/02: 16^{3}GF, 16^{4}GS, 16^{P}S, 16^{0}G, 16^{0}G, 16^{0}S, 16^{3}G

	Starts	1st	2nd	3rd	Win & Pl
Hurdles	7	0	0	2	668
Career Total	**10**	**0**	**0**	**2**	**668**

Going: Sf: 0-2 GS: 0-1 Gd: 0-3 GF: - Fm: 0-1
Distance: 2m/2m3: 0-7 2m4-2m7: 0-0 3m+: 0-0
Track: LH: 0-6 RH: 0-1 Tight: 0-6 Gall: 0-0
Aids: Bl: 0-2 Vi: 0-0 Tstrap: 0-0
Best Rating: 93 12/00 Kemp 2m gd-sft Hdl

Dom Pilippe (FR)

5-y-o b/br g Saint Cyrien (FR)-Moomaw (Akarad (FR))
M C Pipe Malcolm B Jones

Placings:0-00P **(4726)**
2001/02: 17^{0}G, 18^{0}G, 20^{P}GF

	Starts	1st	2nd	3rd	Win & Pl
NH Flat	2	0	0	0	0
Hurdles	1	0	0	0	0
Career Total	**4**	**0**	**0**	**0**	

Going: Sf: 0-0 GS: 0-0 Gd: 0-2 GF: - Fm: 0-1
Distance: 2m/2m3: 0-2 2m4-2m7: 0-1 3m+: 0-0
Track: LH: 0-2 RH: 0-1 Tight: 0-1 Gall: 0-0
Aids: Bl: 0-0 Vi: 0-0 Tstrap: 0-0
Best Rating: 61 4/01 Newb 2m110y soft NHF

Domappel

111 **114**

10-y-o b g Domynsky-Appelania (Star Appeal)
M C Banks M C Banks

Placings:5106/153213/004/633230/243-42 **(4814)**
2001/02: 20^{4}GF, 21^{2}GF

	Starts	1st	2nd	3rd	Win & Pl
Chases	2	0	1	0	4004
Career Total	**24**	**3**	**4**	**6**	**27639**
117 3/97	Uttx	2m4f110y	B HHdl	GD	£10065
116 11/96	Wwck	2m3f	D(0-125)HHdl	GD	£2908
112 12/95	Hayd	2m	D Hdl	GD	£2957

Total win prize-money £15931

Going: Sf: 0-0 GS: 0-0 Gd: 0-0 GF: - Fm: 0-2
Distance: 2m/2m3: 0-0 2m4-2m7: 0-2 3m+: 0-0
Track: LH: 0-2 RH: 0-0 Tight: 0-0 Gall: 0-1
Aids: Bl: 0-0 Vi: 0-0 Tstrap: 0-0
Best Rating: 122 12/98 Donc 2m4f good Hdl

Modest hurdler/chaser, on a long losing run and lightly-raced of late. Suited by a sound surface.

Dome

92 **89**

4-y-o b/br g Be My Chief (USA)-Round Tower (High Top)
S Dow (R Charlton 9/7) Troubleshooters

Placings:4P6 **(4559)**
2001/02: 16^{4}S, 16^{P}GS, 16^{6}GF

	Starts	1st	2nd	3rd	Win & Pl
Hurdles	3	0	0	0	271
Career Total	**3**	**0**	**0**	**0**	**271**

Going: Sf: 0-1 GS: 0-1 Gd: 0-0 GF: - Fm: 0-1
Distance: 2m/2m3: 0-3 2m4-2m7: 0-0 3m+: 0-0
Track: LH: 0-2 RH: 0-1 Tight: 0-1 Gall: 0-1
Aids: Bl: 0-0 Vi: 0-0 Tstrap: 0-1
Best Rating: 59 12/01 Sand 2m110y soft Hdl

Domenico (IRE)

100 **98**

4-y-o b g Sadler's Wells (USA)-Russian Ballet (USA) (Nijinsky (CAN))
P R Webber (Charles O'Brien 14/10) Mrs Mary O'Connor

Placings:02 **(4263)**
2001/02: 16^{0}G, 16^{2}S

	Starts	1st	2nd	3rd	Win & Pl
Hurdles	2	0	1	0	762
Career Total	**2**	**0**	**1**	**0**	**762**

Going: Sf: 0-1 GS: 0-0 Gd: 0-1 GF: - Fm: 0-0
Distance: 2m/2m3: 0-2 2m4-2m7: 0-0 3m+: 0-0
Track: LH: 0-1 RH: 0-1 Tight: 0-0 Gall: 0-0
Aids: Bl: 0-0 Vi: 0-0 Tstrap: 0-0
Best Rating: 99 3/02 Chep 2m110y soft Hdl

Irish maiden winner on the Flat. Highly tried on his hurdles debut on his debut in this country. Dropped to a more realistic grade when runner-up at Chepstow next time. Suited by two miles. Acts on good ground, handles soft.

Dominikus

107(105h) (105h)**125**

5-y-o b g Second Set (IRE)-Dolce Vita (GER) (Windwurf (GER))
Ferdy Murphy The Aarons Archer Partnership

Placings:405-116066420 **(4947a)**
2001/02: 16^{1}F, 16^{1}G, 16^{6}G, 16^{0}G, 21^{6}S, 21^{6}G, 16^{4}GS, 20^{2}GF, 18^{0}G

	Starts	1st	2nd	3rd	Win & Pl
Hurdles	9	2	1	0	6466
Career Total	**12**	**2**	**1**	**0**	**6787**
89 6/01	Hexm	2m	D Hdl	GD	£3353
89 5/01	Hexm	2m	F(0-95)HHdl	FRM	£2017

Total win prize-money £5370

Going: Sf: 0-1 GS: 0-1 Gd: 1-5 GF: - Fm: 1-2
Distance: **2m/2m3: 2-6** 2m4-2m7: 0-3 3m+: 0-0
Track: **LH: 2-8** RH: 0-0 Tight: 0-1 Gall: 0-2
Aids: Bl: 0-0 Vi: 0-0 Tstrap: 0-0
Best Rating: 113 4/02 Hexm 2m4f110y gd-fm Hdl

Fair hurdler who goes well at Hexham. Won two and a half miles novice chase at Market Rasen July 2002. Likes the ground good or faster.

Domirome (FR)

(114h) (121h)

4-y-o b g Roi De Rome (USA)-Bold Senorita (IRE) (Pennine Walk)
G Macaire Mlle Y Shen

Placings:233-31221 **(3668)**
2001/02: 17^{3}VS, 17^{1}VS, 17^{2}HO, 16^{2}GS, 16^{1}S

	Starts	1st	2nd	3rd	Win & Pl
Hurdles	2	1	1	0	5772
Chases	3	1	1	1	24976
Career Total	**8**	**2**	**3**	**3**	**36073**
121 2/02	Kemp	2m	D Hdl	SFT	£4446
10/01	Nanc	2m1f	Ch	VS	£4365

Total win prize-money £8811

Going: Sf: 1-1 GS: 0-1 Gd: 0-0 GF: - Fm: 0-0
Distance: **2m/2m3: 2-5** 2m4-2m7: 0-0 3m+: 0-0
Track: LH: 0-0 **RH: 1-2** Tight: 0-0 Gall: 0-0
Aids: Bl: 0-0 Vi: 0-0 Tstrap: 0-0
Best Rating: 121 2/02 Kemp 2m soft Hdl

A winner over fences in France, with placed form over hurdles, he was runner-up over the smaller obstacles at Kempton in January before winning at the same course in February. Acts on soft ground.

Domquista D'Or

106 **82**

5-y-o b g Superpower-Gild The Lily (Ile De Bourbon (USA))
G A Ham Colin B Taylor

Placings:P0653035 **(4601)**
2001/02: 16^{P}GF, 16^{0}S, 17^{6}S, 16^{5}S, 16^{3}G, 16^{0}HY, 17^{3}S, 16^{5}GF

	Starts	1st	2nd	3rd	Win & Pl

Hurdles	8	0	0	2	846
Career Total	**8**	**0**	**0**	**2**	**846**

Going: Sf: 0-5 GS: 0-0 Gd: 0-1 GF: - Fm: 0-2
Distance: 2m/2m3: 0-8 2m4-2m7: 0-0 3m+: 0-0
Track: LH: 0-6 RH: 0-2 Tight: 0-2 Gall: 0-0
Aids: Bl: 0-0 Vi: 0-0 Tstrap: 0-0
Best Rating: 82 4/02 Wwck 2m gd-fm Hdl

Still a maiden over jumps. Best efforts have come at around two miles on soft ground.

Don Bosco (IRE)

84 **75**

6-y-o ch g Grand Lodge (USA)-Suyayeb (USA) (The Minstrel (CAN))
E Stanners Mrs Patricia E Cunningham

Placings:F5 **(1014)**
2001/02: 16^{F}GS, 16^{5}G

	Starts	1st	2nd	3rd	Win & Pl
Hurdles	2	0	0	0	0
Career Total	**2**	**0**	**0**	**0**	**0**

Going: Sf: 0-0 GS: 0-1 Gd: 0-1 GF: - Fm: 0-0
Distance: 2m/2m3: 0-2 2m4-2m7: 0-0 3m+: 0-0
Track: LH: 0-2 RH: 0-0 Tight: 0-1 Gall: 0-0
Aids: Bl: 0-0 Vi: 0-0 Tstrap: 0-0
Best Rating: 79 7/01 Worc 2m good Hdl

Don Ido (ARG)

6-y-o b g Lazy Boy (ARG)-She's Goy You (ARG) (Indalecio (ARG))
J A B Old W E Sturt

Placings:U **(4655)**
2001/02: 17^{U}GS

	Starts	1st	2nd	3rd	Win & Pl
Hurdles	1	0	0	0	
Career Total	**1**	**0**	**0**	**0**	

Going: Sf: 0-0 GS: 0-1 Gd: 0-0 GF: - Fm: 0-0
Distance: 2m/2m3: 0-1 2m4-2m7: 0-0 3m+: 0-0
Track: LH: 0-0 RH: 0-1 Tight: 0-1 Gall: 0-0
Aids: Bl: 0-0 Vi: 0-0 Tstrap: 0-0
Best Rating:

Don't Tell Deb

62 **28**

6-y-o b m Henbit (USA)-Blue Point (IRE) (On Your Mark)
R N Bevis Mr B Ridge & Mr D Hewitt

Placings:5PP-0 **(0674)**
2001/02: 16^{0}GF

	Starts	1st	2nd	3rd	Win & Pl
Hurdles	1	0	0	0	
Career Total	**4**	**0**	**0**	**0**	**0**

Going: Sf: 0-0 GS: 0-0 Gd: 0-0 GF: - Fm: 0-1
Distance: 2m/2m3: 0-1 2m4-2m7: 0-0 3m+: 0-0
Track: LH: 0-1 RH: 0-0 Tight: 0-0 Gall: 0-0
Aids: Bl: 0-0 Vi: 0-0 Tstrap: 0-0
Best Rating: 28 6/01 Worc 2m gd-fm Hdl

Don't Tell Jr (IRE)

73 **112**

8-y-o b g Mister Lord (USA)-Middle Third (Miners Lamp)
Ferdy Murphy Exors Of The Late Mr G A Hubbard

Placings:0PP6/65-321 **(3712)**
2001/02: 25^{3}G, 26^{2}S, 26^{1}HY

	Starts	1st	2nd	3rd	Win & Pl
Chases	3	1	1	1	4519
Career Total	**9**	**1**	**1**	**1**	**4519**

112 2/02 Plum 3m2f E Ch HVY £3055
Total win prize-money £3055

Going: Sf: 1-2 GS: 0-0 Gd: 0-1 GF: - Fm: 0-0
Distance: 2m/2m3: 0-0 2m4-2m7: 0-0 **3m+: 1-3**
Track: LH: 0-0 RH: 0-1 Tight: 0-1 Gall: 0-0
Aids: Bl: 0-0 Vi: 0-0 Tstrap: 0-0
Best Rating: 112 2/02 Plum 3m2f heavy Ch

Pulled up in two from three starts over hurdles. Proceeded to improve with every run when put over fences and shows his best over marathon trips on soft ground.

Dona Ferentis (IRE)

7-y-o b m Homo Sapien-Greek Tan (Pitpan)
S Flook (H D Daly 20/1) S Flook

Placings:PP-40FP **(4735)**
2001/02: 16^{4}GF, 16^{0}F, 19^{F}G, 23^{P}F

	Starts	1st	2nd	3rd	Win & Pl
Hurdles	2	0	0	0	0
Chases	2	0	0	0	0
Career Total	**6**	**0**	**0**	**0**	**0**

Going: Sf: 0-0 GS: 0-0 Gd: 0-1 GF: - Fm: 0-3
Distance: 2m/2m3: 0-3 2m4-2m7: 0-0 3m+: 0-1
Track: LH: 0-0 RH: 0-4 Tight: 0-0 Gall: 0-1
Aids: Bl: 0-0 Vi: 0-0 Tstrap: 0-0
Best Rating: 88 5/01 Hntg 2m110y gd-fm Hdl

Donald D

6-y-o b g Nomination-Duck Soup (Decoy Boy)
Brendan W Duke Susan Livsey, Ian Griffiths

Placings:0P **(3514)**
2001/02: 16^{0}G, 24^{P}S

	Starts	1st	2nd	3rd	Win & Pl
NH Flat	1	0	0	0	0
Hurdles	1	0	0	0	0
Career Total	**2**	**0**	**0**	**0**	

Going: Sf: 0-1 GS: 0-0 Gd: 0-1 GF: - Fm: 0-0
Distance: 2m/2m3: 0-1 2m4-2m7: 0-0 3m+: 0-1
Track: LH: 0-1 RH: 0-1 Tight: 0-1 Gall: 0-0
Aids: Bl: 0-0 Vi: 0-0 Tstrap: 0-0
Best Rating:

Donald Whasyrtrous

6-y-o b g Alflora (IRE)-Polly Verry (Politico (USA))
J R Adam James R Adam

Placings:0/000-P **(2175)**
2001/02: 16^{P}G

	Starts	1st	2nd	3rd	Win & Pl
Hurdles	1	0	0	0	
Career Total	**5**	**0**	**0**	**0**	

Going: Sf: 0-0 GS: 0-0 Gd: 0-1 GF: - Fm: 0-0
Distance: 2m/2m3: 0-1 2m4-2m7: 0-0 3m+: 0-0
Track: LH: 0-1 RH: 0-0 Tight: 0-0 Gall: 0-0
Aids: Bl: 0-0 Vi: 0-0 Tstrap: 0-0
Best Rating: 49 2/01 Kels 2m110y soft Hdl

Donallach Mor (IRE)

125

10-y-o b g Phardante (FR)-Panalee (Pitpan)
Miss Venetia Williams Mrs Charles Sample

Placings:1/11P0/2-2P **(3392)**
2001/02: 26^{2}G, 25^{P}GS

	Starts	1st	2nd	3rd	Win & Pl
Chases	2	0	1	0	1205
Career Total	**8**	**3**	**2**	**0**	**13041**

121 10/99 Towc 2m6f E Ch GD £2739
132 5/99 Strf 3m4f H Ch GD £6414
110 4/99 Hntg 3m H Ch GD £1475
Total win prize-money £10628

Going: Sf: 0-0 GS: 0-1 Gd: 0-1 GF: - Fm: 0-0
Distance: 2m/2m3: 0-0 2m4-2m7: 0-0 3m+: 0-2
Track: LH: 0-1 RH: 0-0 Tight: 0-0 Gall: 0-0
Aids: Bl: 0-0 Vi: 0-0 Tstrap: 0-0
Best Rating: 135 5/00 Aint 3m1f gd-fm Ch

A former hunter chaser, he acts on good ground and goes well over two miles and six furlongs plus. Lightly raced in recent seasons.

Donatus (IRE)

97 **103**

6-y-o b g Royal Academy (USA)-La Dame Du Lac (USA) (Round Table)
S Dow Michael A J Hall & Miss M Shields

Placings:22240/41P-0SPP3 **(4782)**
2001/02: 19^{0}G, 21^{S}GF, 20^{P}G, 16^{P}GS, 16^{3}GF

	Starts	1st	2nd	3rd	Win & Pl
Hurdles	5	0	0	1	482
Career Total	**13**	**1**	**3**	**1**	**7721**

111 10/00 Fknm 2m4f D Hdl GD £2990
Total win prize-money £2990

Going: Sf: 0-0 GS: 0-1 Gd: 0-2 GF: - Fm: 0-2
Distance: 2m/2m3: 0-2 2m4-2m7: 0-3 3m+: 0-0
Track: LH: 0-3 RH: 0-2 Tight: 0-3 Gall: 0-0
Aids: Bl: 0-0 Vi: 0-1 Tstrap: 0-0
Best Rating: 130 3/00 Chel 2m1f gd-fm Hdl

Frustrating sort over hurdles, often there or thereabouts but on a long losing run. Still better than he was on the Flat.

Donnegale (IRE)

103(111h) (107h)**105**

10-y-o b g Strong Gale-Marys Gift (Monksfield)
T D Walford J Eddings

Placings:60406/4/P31140/1P/F0123-PP142430P **(4523)**
2001/02: 27^{P}G, 24^{P}S, 27^{1}GS, 27^{4}G, 25^{2}S, 25^{4}GS, 27^{3}S, 26^{0}GF, 26^{P}GS

	Starts	1st	2nd	3rd	Win & Pl
Hurdles	2	0	0	0	0
Chases	7	1	1	1	5417
Career Total	**28**	**5**	**2**	**3**	**19790**

105 10/01 Sedg 3m3f F(0-100)HCh G-S £3626
107 2/01 Catt 3m1f110y E(0-115)HHdl SFT £5307
103 3/00 Catt 3m1f110y H Ch G-F £1553
101 2/99 Catt 3m1f110y E(0-105)HHdl GD £2444
89 12/98 Sedg 3m3f110y E Hdl GD £2460
Total win prize-money £15391

Going: Sf: 0-3 GS: 1-3 Gd: 0-2 GF: - Fm: 0-1
Distance: 2m/2m3: 0-0 2m4-2m7: 0-0 **3m+: 1-9**
Track: **LH: 1-6** RH: 0-3 **Tight: 1-7** Gall: 0-1
Aids: **Bl: 1-7** Vi: 0-2 Tstrap: 0-0
Best Rating: 107 4/01 Muss 3m gd-fm Hdl

Moderate dual-purpose stayer, his jumping is not always up to scratch. Acts on a soft surface.

Donnington (IRE)

(98h) (93h)
12-y-o b g Good Thyne (USA)-Eljay (Double U Jay)
T P Tate B T Stewart-Brown

Placings: *1/5154P2/***P4UFF/0** **(2433)**
2001/02: 20^{0}GS

	Starts	1st	2nd	3rd	Win & Pl
Hurdles	1	0	0	0	
Career Total	**13**	**2**	**1**	**0**	**6702**

115	1/97	Uttx	2m	E Hdl	GD	£2463
111	4/95	Asct	2m110y	H NHF	FRM	£2347

Total win prize-money £4811

Going: Sf: 0-0 GS: 0-1 Gd: 0-0 GF: - Fm: 0-0
Distance: 2m/2m3: 0-0 2m4-2m7: 0-1 3m+: 0-0
Track: LH: 0-1 RH: 0-0 Tight: 0-0 Gall: 0-0
Aids: Bl: 0-0 Vi: 0-0 Tstrap: 0-0
Best Rating: 122 1/98 Folk 2m5f good Ch

Fell twice on his last two starts in 1998 and was subsequently absent for nearly four years before returning in a claiming hurdle in December 2001.

Donnybrook (IRE)

113 126
9-y-o ch g Riot Helmet-Evening Bun (Baragoi)
R D E Woodhouse R Smith,D Hall,D Thompson,Mrs C Clarke

Placings: *00/***433P042/151144300/3221315/P40240-503403410** **(4691)**
2001/02: 16^{5}G, 16^{0}G, 19^{3}GF, 22^{4}S, 19^{0}G, 19^{3}S, 16^{4}S, 16^{1}HY, 17^{0}GF

	Starts	1st	2nd	3rd	Win & Pl
Chases	9	1	0	2	7231
Career Total	**40**	**6**	**4**	**7**	**46758**

126	3/02	Newc	2m110y	D(0-125)HCh	HVY	£4728
131	1/00	Newc	2m4f	A Ch	SFT	£19500
125	12/99	Uttx	2m	D Ch	SFT	£4182
102	10/98	Weth	2m	E(0-105)HHdl	SFT	£3174
93	10/98	MRas	2m3f110y	E Hdl	SFT	£2845
95	5/98	Hexm	2m	E Hdl	GD	£2033

Total win prize-money £36465

Going: Sf: 1-4 GS: 0-0 Gd: 0-3 GF: - Fm: 0-2
Distance: **2m/2m3: 1-7** 2m4-2m7: 0-2 3m+: 0-0
Track: **LH: 1-7** RH: 0-2 Tight: 0-4 **Gall: 1-3**
Aids: **Bl: 1-5** Vi: 0-0 Tstrap: 0-0
Best Rating: 131 1/00 Newc 2m4f soft Ch

Fair handicap chaser. He jumps well and is best on soft ground. Stays two and a half miles.

Dont Forget Curtis (IRE)

73 29
10-y-o b g Don't Forget Me-Norse Lady (Viking (USA))
Mrs K M Lamb Mrs K M Lamb

Placings:0064/F304540040/4553351225P/P40406P/P00560/0300-0P00P0 **(2770)**
2001/02: 20^{0}GF, 22^{P}G, 20^{0}G, 20^{0}HY, 24^{P}S, 25^{0}G

	Starts	1st	2nd	3rd	Win & Pl
Hurdles	6	0	0	0	
Career Total	**48**	**1**	**2**	**4**	**5801**

78	10/97	Hexm	3m	F(0-100)HHdl	GD	£2167

Total win prize-money £2167

Going: Sf: 0-2 GS: 0-0 Gd: 0-3 GF: - Fm: 0-1
Distance: 2m/2m3: 0-0 2m4-2m7: 0-4 3m+: 0-2
Track: LH: 0-5 RH: 0-0 Tight: 0-2 Gall: 0-1
Aids: Bl: 0-0 Vi: 0-0 Tstrap: 0-0
Best Rating: 105 5/98 Hexm 3m firm Hdl

Dont Say That (IRE)

(82h) (42h)
10-y-o ch g Phardante (FR)-Kix (King Emperor (USA))
J P Dodds The Four Farmers

Placings:*0P0/***P0PFP** **(4769)**
2001/02: 20^{P}GF, 19^{0}G, 21^{P}GF, 22^{F}GS, 25^{P}GF

	Starts	1st	2nd	3rd	Win & Pl
Hurdles	3	0	0	0	0
Chases	2	0	0	0	0
Career Total	**8**	**0**	**0**	**0**	

Going: Sf: 0-0 GS: 0-1 Gd: 0-1 GF: - Fm: 0-3
Distance: 2m/2m3: 0-0 2m4-2m7: 0-4 3m+: 0-1
Track: LH: 0-3 RH: 0-2 Tight: 0-3 Gall: 0-0
Aids: Bl: 0-0 Vi: 0-0 Tstrap: 0-3
Best Rating: 42 7/01 MRas 2m3f110y good Hdl

Doodle Bug

79
5-y-o b m Missed Flight-Kaiserlinde (GER) (Frontal)
Miss K Marks Nick Shults

Placings:0U1-BP **(0837)**
2001/02: 17^{B}G, 20^{P}G

	Starts	1st	2nd	3rd	Win & Pl
Hurdles	2	0	0	0	
Career Total	**5**	**1**	**0**	**0**	**2065**

79	4/01	Hrfd	2m1f	G Hdl	GD	£2065

Total win prize-money £2065

Going: Sf: 0-0 GS: 0-0 Gd: 0-2 GF: - Fm: 0-0
Distance: 2m/2m3: 0-1 2m4-2m7: 0-1 3m+: 0-0
Track: LH: 0-1 RH: 0-1 Tight: 0-0 Gall: 0-0
Aids: Bl: 0-0 Vi: 0-0 Tstrap: 0-0
Best Rating: 87 2/01 Donc 2m110y good Hdl

Dook's Delight (IRE)

91(115h) (87h)112
11-y-o b g Satco (FR)-Mar Del Plata (Crowned Prince (USA))
R A Fahey Mike Caulfield

Placings:*5/04***10546/6560403/41PP5300/65520132PP P1B02/1431/5114452133-04P4** **(4059)**
2001/02: 20^{0}G, 30^{4}S, 24^{P}S, 27^{4}S

	Starts	1st	2nd	3rd	Win & Pl
Hurdles	2	0	0	0	0
Chases	2	0	0	0	316
Career Total	**56**	**9**	**4**	**6**	**34513**

105	2/01	Sedg	3m3f110y	F(0-110)HHdl	G-S	£5284
116	11/00	Carl	2m4f110y	F(0-95)HCh	SFT	£2726
115	11/00	Sedg	3m3f	F(0-105)HCh	SFT	£2808
105	11/99	Hexm	2m4f110y	F(0-105)HCh	GD	£2962
101	5/99	Kels	3m3f	E(0-115)HHdl	G-F	£2668
97	3/99	Hexm	2m4f110y	F(0-100)HCh	SFT	£3236
97	9/98	Dpat	2m2f	(0-102)HCh	SFT	£1494
89	5/97	Tipp	2m4f	(0-116)HHdl	Y-S	£2712
103	12/95	Thur	2m	NHF	GD	£3391

Total win prize-money £27286

Going: Sf: 0-3 GS: 0-0 Gd: 0-1 GF: - Fm: 0-0
Distance: 2m/2m3: 0-0 2m4-2m7: 0-1 3m+: 0-3
Track: LH: 0-4 RH: 0-0 Tight: 0-1 Gall: 0-3
Aids: Bl: 0-0 Vi: 0-0 Tstrap: 0-0
Best Rating: 116 11/00 Carl 2m4f110y soft Ch

Modest staying chaser, suited by extreme distances and soft ground.

Doonerin (IRE)

8-y-o ch g Persian Mews-Miss Leeway (Tarboosh (USA))
N G Ayliffe Mrs M A Barrett

Placings:*000P/PP-P* **(4387)**
2001/02: 16^{P}S

	Starts	1st	2nd	3rd	Win & Pl
Hurdles	1	0	0	0	
Career Total	**7**	**0**	**0**	**0**	

Going: Sf: 0-1 GS: 0-0 Gd: 0-0 GF: - Fm: 0-0
Distance: 2m/2m3: 0-1 2m4-2m7: 0-0 3m+: 0-0
Track: LH: 0-0 RH: 0-1 Tight: 0-0 Gall: 0-0
Aids: Bl: 0-0 Vi: 0-0 Tstrap: 0-0
Best Rating: 35 8/99 Rosc 2m gd-yld NHF

Doran's Day (IRE)

96 90
5-y-o b g Gildoran-Inverdonan (Our Mirage)
Mrs H Dalton Trevor Hemmings

Placings:*005* **(4180)**
2001/02: 17^{0}S, 16^{0}GS, 16^{5}GS

	Starts	1st	2nd	3rd	Win & Pl
NH Flat	3	0	0	0	0
Career Total	**3**	**0**	**0**	**0**	**0**

Going: Sf: 0-1 GS: 0-2 Gd: 0-0 GF: - Fm: 0-0
Distance: 2m/2m3: 0-3 2m4-2m7: 0-0 3m+: 0-0
Track: LH: 0-1 RH: 0-0 Tight: 0-2 Gall: 0-0
Aids: Bl: 0-0 Vi: 0-0 Tstrap: 0-0
Best Rating: 90 3/02 Strf 2m110y gd-sft NHF

Dorans Gold

117 139
8-y-o b g Gildoran-Cindie Girl (Orchestra)
P F Nicholls Mel Fordham S Fisher M Harper H Johnson

Placings:*2/***1P50/11F2F42-12P** **(2165)**
2001/02: 20^{1}GS, 24^{2}GS, 20^{P}G

	Starts	1st	2nd	3rd	Win & Pl
Chases	3	1	1	0	43897
Career Total	**15**	**4**	**4**	**0**	**59686**

134	7/01	MRas	2m4f	B(0-140)HCh	G-S	£37297
128	10/00	Hntg	2m4f110y	E Ch	G-F	£2951
113	5/00	Extr	2m3f	E(0-105)HCh	GD	£3136
112	11/99	Aint	2m110y	D Hdl	GD	£3993

Total win prize-money £47378

Going: Sf: 0-0 GS: 1-2 Gd: 0-1 GF: - Fm: 0-0
Distance: 2m/2m3: 0-0 **2m4-2m7: 1-2** 3m+: 0-1
Track: LH: 0-1 RH: 0-1 Tight: 0-0 Gall: 0-1
Aids: Bl: 0-0 Vi: 0-0 Tstrap: 0-0
Best Rating: 139 10/01 Kemp 3m gd-sft Ch

He made a bright start to his career over fences in the

autumn of 2000, but seemed to lose confidence in mid-season and became prone to mistakes. Moved to Paul Nicholls and landed a touch at Market Rasen in July 2001. Good effort next time, when runner-up in the Charisma at Kempton before pulling up in the Thomas Pink. Suited by two and a half miles and a sound surface.

Dorans Grove

104 **90**

8-y-o b m Gildoran-Binny Grove (Sunyboy)
J S King Miss J Cunningham

Placings: *01/220*/40**P**50/40P-3466**F**0 **(4152)**
2001/02: 20^{3}S, 24^{4}GS, 21^{6}S, 26^{6}S, 23^{F}S, 20^{0}GS

	Starts	1st	2nd	3rd	Win & Pl
Hurdles	4	0	0	1	367
Chases	2	0	0	0	0
Career Total	**19**	**1**	**2**	**1**	**2530**

96	3/98	Wwck	2m	H NHF	SFT	£1497

Total win prize-money £1497

Going: Sf: 0-4 GS: 0-2 Gd: 0-0 GF: - Fm: 0-0
Distance: 2m/2m3: 0-0 2m4-2m7: 0-3 3m+: 0-3
Track: LH: 0-4 RH: 0-2 Tight: 0-0 Gall: 0-0
Aids: Bl: 0-0 Vi: 0-0 Tstrap: 0-0
Best Rating: 99 12/98 Ling 2m110y soft NHF

A bumper winner, she has failed to get her head in front since then.

Dorans Magic

104(110h) (114h)**119**

7-y-o b g Gildoran-Mearlin (Giolla Mear)
Mrs S J Smith Trevor Hemmings

Placings: *64/0*2241-054102P **(4767)**
2001/02: 20^{0}S, 20^{5}GS, 20^{4}S, 20^{1}HY, 20^{0}G, 24^{2}S, 25^{P}GF

	Starts	1st	2nd	3rd	Win & Pl
Chases	7	1	1	0	5565
Career Total	**14**	**2**	**3**	**0**	**11715**

119	2/02	Wwck	2m4f110y	D Ch	HVY	£4069
114	4/01	Hayd	2m6f	D Hdl	SFT	£3877

Total win prize-money £7946

Going: Sf: 1-4 GS: 0-1 Gd: 0-1 GF: - Fm: 0-1
Distance: 2m/2m3: 0-0 **2m4-2m7: 1-5** 3m+: 0-2
Track: **LH: 1-6** RH: 0-1 Tight: 0-1 Gall: 0-2
Aids: Bl: 0-0 Vi: 0-0 Tstrap: 0-0
Best Rating: 119 2/02 Wwck 2m4f110y heavy Ch

A winner over hurdles and fences. Acts on soft ground, stays three miles.

Dorans Pride (IRE)

95(103h) (131h)**161**

13-y-o ch g Orchestra-Marians Pride (Pry)
Michael Hourigan T J Doran

Placings: *1*/1222111F/12211142/11/**11111F31**/111513 4/112103/421P12236/B21323333-40 **(4913)**
2001/02: 20^{4}Y, 29^{0}G

	Starts	1st	2nd	3rd	Win & Pl
Hurdles	1	0	0	0	907
Chases	1	0	0	0	0
Career Total	**60**	**27**	**12**	**9**	**630772**

157	11/00	Clon	2m4f	Ch	SFT	£15600
150	1/00	Navn	2m4f	HHdl	SFT	£5520
157	11/99	Clon	2m4f	Ch	Y-S	£17410
177	12/98	Leop	3m	Ch	SH	£45217
177	11/98	Clon	2m4f	Ch	SFT	£11956
168	10/98	Gowr	2m4f	Ch	SFT	£16891
170	2/98	Leop	3m	Ch	Y-S	£50434
170	12/97	Fair	2m4f	Ch	GD	£23564
177	11/97	Clon	2m4f	Ch	SFT	£13564
177	9/97	List	3m	HCh	YLD	£30693
151	4/97	Fair	2m4f	Ch	G-F	£22871
162	2/97	Leop	2m5f	Ch	G-Y	£9653
140	12/96	Leop	3m	Ch	G-Y	£7061
157	12/96	Fair	2m4f	Ch	YLD	£23453
136	11/96	Punc	2m4f	Ch	YLD	£7123
144	12/95	Fair	2m4f	Hdl	YLD	£27722
143	11/95	Navn	2m4f	Hdl	GD	£6782
163	3/95	Chel	3m	A Hdl	SFT	£47422
153	2/95	Punc	3m	Hdl	HVY	£9579
154	12/94	Leop	2m6f	Hdl	HVY	£6523
144	11/94	Navn	2m4f	Hdl	G-Y	£6523
135	2/94	Punc	2m2f110y	Hdl	SFT	£6571
138	2/94	Fair	2m2f	Hdl	HVY	£3942
127	1/94	Naas	2m3f	HHdl	HVY	£6571
106	9/93	List	2m	Hdl	SFT	£4134
	4/93	Baln	2m	NHF	SFT	£2411

Total win prize-money £429202

Going: Sf: 0-0 GS: 0-0 Gd: 0-1 GF: - Fm: 0-0
Distance: 2m/2m3: 0-0 2m4-2m7: 0-1 3m+: 0-1
Track: LH: 0-1 RH: 0-1 Tight: 0-0 Gall: 0-0
Aids: Bl: 0-0 Vi: 0-0 Tstrap: 0-0
Best Rating: 177 12/98 Leop 3m sft-hvy Ch

A marvellous veteran, he was top class over both hurdles and fences, and even in 2001 was a versatile and useful chaser and hurdler whol picked up plenty of prize-money for making the frame in some of the best races in Ireland. A credit to connections, he was honourably retired in summer of 2002.

Dormston Boyo

12-y-o b g Sula Bula-March At Dawn (Nishapour (FR))
T Wall D B Roberts

Placings: 0465/F300F3/**3**003P6/2/0342331242403/32 000PPP/0 **(0189)**
2001/02: 16^{0}GF

	Starts	1st	2nd	3rd	Win & Pl
Hurdles	1	0	0	0	
Career Total	**39**	**1**	**5**	**9**	**11184**

82	8/98	Worc	2m	E(0-100)HCh	G-F	£3020

Total win prize-money £3020

Going: Sf: 0-0 GS: 0-0 Gd: 0-0 GF: - Fm: 0-1
Distance: 2m/2m3: 0-1 2m4-2m7: 0-0 3m+: 0-0
Track: LH: 0-1 RH: 0-0 Tight: 0-1 Gall: 0-0
Aids: Bl: 0-1 Vi: 0-0 Tstrap: 0-0
Best Rating: 84 5/99 Ctml 2m1f110y good Ch

Dorset Fern (IRE)

95 **67**

6-y-o b m Tirol-La Duse (Junius (USA))
G B Balding Miss M Lane

Placings: *060*/00-00000003UP0 **(4484)**
2001/02: 17^{0}GS, 16^{0}G, 17^{0}GF, 20^{0}GS, 18^{0}GS, 17^{0}G, 19^{0}GS, 19^{3}GS, 16^{U}G, 16^{P}GS, 17^{0}G

	Starts	1st	2nd	3rd	Win & Pl
Hurdles	11	0	0	1	228
Career Total	**16**	**0**	**0**	**1**	**228**

Going: Sf: 0-0 GS: 0-6 Gd: 0-4 GF: - Fm: 0-1
Distance: 2m/2m3: 0-9 2m4-2m7: 0-2 3m+: 0-0
Track: LH: 0-3 RH: 0-7 Tight: 0-3 Gall: 0-0
Aids: Bl: 0-0 Vi: 0-0 Tstrap: 0-0
Best Rating: 67 12/01 Tntn 2m3f110y gd-sft Hdl

Plating-class maiden. Looks slow.

Dos Desperados (IRE)

6-y-o b g Un Desperado (FR)-Ballycahan Girl (Bargello)
Miss E C Lavelle R J Lavelle

Placings: P **(3702)**
2001/02: 19^{P}HY

	Starts	1st	2nd	3rd	Win & Pl
Hurdles	1	0	0	0	
Career Total	**1**	**0**	**0**	**0**	

Going: Sf: 0-1 GS: 0-0 Gd: 0-0 GF: - Fm: 0-0
Distance: 2m/2m3: 0-0 2m4-2m7: 0-1 3m+: 0-0
Track: LH: 0-0 RH: 0-1 Tight: 0-0 Gall: 0-0
Aids: Bl: 0-0 Vi: 0-0 Tstrap: 0-0
Best Rating:

Double Account (FR)

105 (105h)**112**

7-y-o b g Sillery (USA)-Fabulous Account (USA) (Private Account (USA))
C J Mann (A L T Moore 2/8) M J & C G Cruddace

Placings: 3/120500165/3024**0**40-103321 **(1480)**
2001/02: 18^{1}G, 20^{0}G, 21^{3}F, 17^{3}GY, 22^{2}GF, 20^{1}GS

	Starts	1st	2nd	3rd	Win & Pl
Hurdles	1	0	0	0	0
Chases	5	2	1	2	8550
Career Total	**23**	**4**	**3**	**4**	**26838**

106	5/01	Clon	2m2f	Ch	GD	£5286
108	1/00	Punc	2m	(0-137)HHdl	Y-S	£4968
104	5/99	Navn	2m	Hdl	GD	£5524

Total win prize-money £15779

Going: Sf: 0-0 GS: 1-1 Gd: 1-2 GF: - Fm: 0-2
Distance: 2m/2m3: 1-2 2m4-2m7: 1-4 3m+: 0-0
Track: **LH: 1-1** RH: 0-1 **Tight: 1-2** Gall: 0-0
Aids: Bl: 0-0 Vi: 0-0 Tstrap: 0-0
Best Rating: 122 12/00 Fair 2m yld-sft Hdl

An ex-Irish novice chaser, appreciated two and a half miles and easy ground when staying on late to dead-heat at Plumpton in September.

Double Agent

95 **100**

9-y-o ch g Niniski (USA)-Rexana (Relko)
Miss A M Newton-Smith E J Farrant

Placings: 611F03/50315360/300**2**562/3/0P5013 **(4415)**
2001/02: 22^{0}GF, 25^{P}G, 22^{5}HY, 24^{0}GS, 22^{1}S, 22^{3}S

	Starts	1st	2nd	3rd	Win & Pl
Hurdles	5	1	0	1	2634
Chases	1	0	0	0	0
Career Total	**28**	**4**	**2**	**6**	**14670**

100	1/02	Folk	2m6f110y	G Hdl	SFT	£2275
103	12/97	Newc	2m4f	C(0-135)HHdl	GD	£3273
103	2/97	Muss	2m	E(0-105)HHdl	GD	£2560
101	2/97	Muss	2m	E Hdl	G-F	£2399

Total win prize-money £10508

Going: Sf: 1-3 GS: 0-1 Gd: 0-1 GF: - Fm: 0-1
Distance: 2m/2m3: 0-0 **2m4-2m7: 1-4** 3m+: 0-2
Track: LH: 0-2 **RH: 1-4 Tight: 1-4** Gall: 0-1
Aids: Bl: 0-0 Vi: 0-0 Tstrap: 0-0
Best Rating: 106 1/99 Muss 2m4f gd-sft Ch

A fair hurdler on good ground a few years ago, he has suffered with injury and had little racing recently. Made most to win at Folkestone in January 2002. Acts on a sound surface but has won in heavy ground.

Double Baileys

6-y-o b g Robellino (USA)-Thimblerigger (Sharpen Up)
C P Morlock The Trogs

Placings:0 **(2022)**
2001/02: 22^{0}S

	Starts	1st	2nd	3rd	Win & Pl
Hurdles	1	0	0	0	
Career Total	**1**	**0**	**0**	**0**	

Going: Sf: 0-1 GS: 0-0 Gd: 0-0 GF: - Fm: 0-0
Distance: 2m/2m3: 0-0 2m4-2m7: 0-1 3m+: 0-0
Track: LH: 0-1 RH: 0-0 Tight: 0-0 Gall: 0-0
Aids: Bl: 0-0 Vi: 0-0 Tstrap: 0-0
Best Rating:

Double Bid

90 **76**

5-y-o b g Rudimentary (USA)-Bidweaya (USA) (Lear Fan (USA))
Mrs N S Sharpe (Miss K Marks 3/6) K Morgan

Placings:3F01P0-6P000U **(4542)**
2001/02: 19^{6}G, 16^{P}GF, 16^{0}G, 20^{0}S, 19^{0}S, 17^{U}G

	Starts	1st	2nd	3rd	Win & Pl
Hurdles	6	0	0	0	0
Career Total	**12**	**1**	**0**	**1**	**2461**

92 2/01 Donc 2m110y G Hdl GD £1985
Total win prize-money £1985

Going: Sf: 0-2 GS: 0-0 Gd: 0-3 GF: - Fm: 0-1
Distance: 2m/2m3: 0-3 2m4-2m7: 0-3 3m+: 0-0
Track: LH: 0-1 RH: 0-5 Tight: 0-2 Gall: 0-0
Aids: Bl: 0-0 Vi: 0-0 Tstrap: 0-1
Best Rating: **92** 2/01 Donc 2m110y good Hdl

Double Blade

102 **128**

7-y-o b g Kris-Sesame (Derrylin)
Mrs M Reveley The Mary Reveley Racing Club

Placings:11110/4300-313 **(2685)**
2001/02: 16^{3}G, 16^{1}G, 16^{3}G

	Starts	1st	2nd	3rd	Win & Pl
Hurdles	3	1	0	2	7479
Career Total	**12**	**5**	**0**	**3**	**23650**

123 11/01 Weth 2m C(0-135)HHdl GD £5395
130 11/99 Sedg 2m1f C Hdl GD £4696
130 10/99 Weth 2m C Hdl GD £4955
119 10/99 Sedg 2m1f E Hdl G-F £2635
106 9/99 Sedg 2m1f E Hdl G-F £2407
Total win prize-money £20090

Going: Sf: 0-0 GS: 0-0 Gd: 1-3 GF: - Fm: 0-0
Distance: **2m/2m3: 1-3** 2m4-2m7: 0-0 3m+: 0-0
Track: **LH: 1-3** RH: 0-0 Tight: 0-0 Gall: 0-1
Aids: Bl: 0-0 Vi: 0-0 Tstrap: 0-0
Best Rating: **130** 10/00 Weth 2m gd-sft Hdl

A useful novice hurdler back in 1999, he lost his way afterwards and looked to have his own ideas about the game, but was given a peach of a ride to win at Wetherby in November 2001. Suited by two miles and a sound surface.

Double Bogey Blues (IRE)

93 (108h)**114**

6-y-o b g Celio Rufo-Belmount Star (IRE) (Good Thyne (USA))
M F Morris F-One Syndicate

Placings:05-41F6**054**P03 **(4934a)**
2001/02: 20^{4}S, 22^{1}YS, 21^{F}G, 22^{6}HY, 19^{0}Y, 21^{5}YS, 24^{4}S, 24^{P}HY, 24^{0}GF, 24^{3}YS

	Starts	1st	2nd	3rd	Win & Pl
Hurdles	6	1	0	0	5952
Chases	4	0	0	1	1184
Career Total	**12**	**1**	**0**	**1**	**7136**

105 11/01 Thur 2m6f Hdl Y-S £5564
Total win prize-money £5565

Going: Sf: 0-4 GS: 0-0 Gd: 0-1 GF: - Fm: 0-1
Distance: 2m/2m3: 0-1 **2m4-2m7: 1-5** 3m+: 0-4
Track: LH: 0-4 **RH: 1-3** Tight: 0-0 Gall: 0-1
Aids: Bl: 0-0 Vi: 0-0 Tstrap: 0-0
Best Rating: **114** 4/02 Cork 3m yld-sft Ch

A winner over hurdles in November 2001, he has yet to show much aptitude for fences.

Double Irish (NZ)

11-y-o ch g Mcginty (NZ)-Coober Princess (NZ) (Coober Prince)
B De Haan Mrs D Vaughan

Placings:24PPFP0PP/0 **(0793)**
2001/02: 22^{0}GF

	Starts	1st	2nd	3rd	Win & Pl
Hurdles	1	0	0	0	
Career Total	**10**	**0**	**1**	**0**	**1349**

Going: Sf: 0-0 GS: 0-0 Gd: 0-0 GF: - Fm: 0-1
Distance: 2m/2m3: 0-0 2m4-2m7: 0-1 3m+: 0-0
Track: LH: 0-1 RH: 0-0 Tight: 0-1 Gall: 0-0
Aids: Bl: 0-0 Vi: 0-0 Tstrap: 0-0
Best Rating: **87** 10/99 Towc 2m6f good Ch

Double Red (IRE)

114

5-y-o b m Thatching-Local Custom (IRE) (Be My Native (USA))
A King J Brown, S Faccenda, S Hughes, R Benton

Placings:2P1115-P0P **(3894)**
2001/02: 19^{P}G, 20^{0}S, 21^{P}HY

	Starts	1st	2nd	3rd	Win & Pl
Hurdles	3	0	0	0	
Career Total	**9**	**3**	**1**	**0**	**14296**

118 3/01 Hayd 2m D(0-125)HHdl HVY £5609
103 3/01 Newb 2m110y D(0-120)HHdl HVY £5216
89 2/01 Hntg 2m110y E Hdl G-S £2553
Total win prize-money £13380

Going: Sf: 0-2 GS: 0-0 Gd: 0-1 GF: - Fm: 0-0
Distance: 2m/2m3: 0-0 2m4-2m7: 0-3 3m+: 0-0
Track: LH: 0-1 RH: 0-1 Tight: 0-0 Gall: 0-0
Aids: Bl: 0-1 Vi: 0-0 Tstrap: 0-0
Best Rating: **118** 3/01 Hayd 2m heavy Hdl

Fair handicap hurdler, notched up a hat-trick of wins early in 2001. He has been a little disappointing since then. Effective at around two miles and is suited by a soft surface.

Double Star

93 **80**

11-y-o b g Soviet Star (USA)-Startino (Bustino)
John A Harris (Exors Of The Late J L Harris 1/7) J South

Placings:*32/51*330P6/0/3P2325/2PP0-0F405200 **(1840)**
2001/02: 16^{0}GF, 22^{F}GF, 21^{4}G, 21^{0}GS, 17^{5}GF, 20^{2}GF, 20^{0}GF, 16^{0}S

	Starts	1st	2nd	3rd	Win & Pl
Hurdles	8	0	1	0	443
Career Total	**28**	**1**	**5**	**5**	**6874**

97 6/97 MRas 1m5f110y H NHF G-F £1245
Total win prize-money £1245

Going: Sf: 0-1 GS: 0-1 Gd: 0-1 GF: - Fm: 0-5
Distance: 2m/2m3: 0-3 2m4-2m7: 0-5 3m+: 0-0
Track: LH: 0-1 RH: 0-6 Tight: 0-3 Gall: 0-3
Aids: Bl: 0-0 Vi: 0-0 Tstrap: 0-0
Best Rating: **105** 4/97 MRas 1m5f110y good NHF

Double Tee (IRE)

91 (92c) (45c)**77**

6-y-o br g Jurado (USA)-Monkeylane (Monksfield)
N J Hawke Mrs June Dodd

Placings:*6*0-000660U**P** **(4732)**
2001/02: 20^{0}GF, 17^{0}G, 19^{0}GF, 22^{6}G, 22^{6}G, 19^{U}S, 17^{U}G, 23^{P}F

	Starts	1st	2nd	3rd	Win & Pl
Hurdles	7	0	0	0	0
Chases	1	0	0	0	0
Career Total	**10**	**0**	**0**	**0**	**0**

Going: Sf: 0-1 GS: 0-0 Gd: 0-4 GF: - Fm: 0-3
Distance: 2m/2m3: 0-3 2m4-2m7: 0-4 3m+: 0-1
Track: LH: 0-1 RH: 0-6 Tight: 0-1 Gall: 0-0
Aids: Bl: 0-0 Vi: 0-0 Tstrap: 0-0
Best Rating: **77** 12/01 Winc 2m6f good Hdl

Double Timer (IRE)

109 **110**

7-y-o ch g Doubletour (USA)-Midnightattheoasis (IRE) (King Persian)
J J O'Neill J P McManus

Placings:*1-16*4211 **(3499)**
2001/02: 16^{1}G, 16^{6}G, 20^{4}S, 22^{2}S, 24^{1}S, 24^{1}S

	Starts	1st	2nd	3rd	Win & Pl
NH Flat	2	1	0	0	2282
Hurdles	4	2	1	0	8245
Career Total	**7**	**4**	**1**	**0**	**12189**

110 1/02 Kemp 3m110y D(0-120)HHdl SFT £5050
105 12/01 Sthl 3m110y E Hdl SFT £2436
102 9/01 Prth 2m110y H NHF GD £2282
111 10/00 Sedg 2m1f H NHF G-S £1662
Total win prize-money £11432

Going: Sf: 2-4 GS: 0-0 Gd: 1-2 GF: - Fm: 0-0
Distance: 2m/2m3: 1-2 2m4-2m7: 0-2 **3m+: 2-2**
Track: LH: 1-4 **RH: 2-2 Tight: 1-1** Gall: 0-0
Aids: Bl: 0-0 Vi: 0-0 Tstrap: 0-0
Best Rating: **111** 10/00 Sedg 2m1f gd-sft NHF

A dual bumper winner, he is a progressive handicap hurdler with wins at Southwell in December 2001 and at Kempton the following month. Effective over three miles in soft ground.

Double Whirl

6-y-o ch g Destroyer-Priceless Peril (Silly Prices)
M Todhunter Mrs David Marshall

Placings:*P* **(1593)**
2001/02: 17^{P}GS

	Starts	1st	2nd	3rd	Win & Pl
NH Flat	1	0	0	0	
Career Total	**1**	**0**	**0**	**0**	

Going: Sf: 0-0 GS: 0-1 Gd: 0-0 GF: - Fm: 0-0
Distance: 2m/2m3: 0-1 2m4-2m7: 0-0 3m+: 0-0
Track: LH: 0-1 RH: 0-0 Tight: 0-1 Gall: 0-0
Aids: Bl: 0-0 Vi: 0-0 Tstrap: 0-0
Best Rating:

Double You Cubed

8-y-o b g Destroyer-Bright Suggestion (Magnate)
J S Goldie J S Goldie

Placings:P5PP **(3677)**
2001/02: 22^{P}GS, 20^{5}S, 24^{P}S, 20^{P}HY

	Starts	1st	2nd	3rd	Win & Pl
Hurdles	4	0	0	0	0
Career Total	**4**	**0**	**0**	**0**	**0**

Going: Sf: 0-3 GS: 0-1 Gd: 0-0 GF: - Fm: 0-0
Distance: 2m/2m3: 0-0 2m4-2m7: 0-3 3m+: 0-1
Track: LH: 0-4 RH: 0-0 Tight: 0-0 Gall: 0-1
Aids: Bl: 0-0 Vi: 0-0 Tstrap: 0-0
Best Rating:

Well held in modest hurdling company.

Doublet

107 **110**

7-y-o ch g Bustino-Pas De Deux (Nijinsky (CAN))
B R Millman Pine Crest Racing

Placings:311/13/222550 **(3389)**
2001/02: 17^{2}GF, 24^{2}F, 22^{2}G, 22^{5}S, 20^{5}G, 22^{0}GS

	Starts	1st	2nd	3rd	Win & Pl
Hurdles	6	0	3	0	3335
Career Total	**11**	**3**	**3**	**2**	**11888**

111	5/99	Extr	2m1f	E Hdl	G-F	£2512
104	4/99	Ludl	2m	E Hdl	G-S	£2560
105	4/99	Tntn	2m1f	E Hdl	FRM	£2514

Total win prize-money £7587

Going: Sf: 0-1 GS: 0-1 Gd: 0-2 GF: - Fm: 0-2
Distance: 2m/2m3: 0-1 2m4-2m7: 0-4 3m+: 0-1
Track: LH: 0-0 RH: 0-6 Tight: 0-1 Gall: 0-0
Aids: Bl: 0-0 Vi: 0-0 Tstrap: 0-0
Best Rating: 111 5/99 Extr 2m1f gd-fm Hdl

Completed a hat-trick of novice hurdle wins in the spring of 1999, but missed nearly two years with an injury. Fit from the Flat when returning to hurdles, he ran well on good ground in the autumn of 2001.

Douceur Des Songes (FR)

104 (77c)**112**

5-y-o b m Art Francais (USA)-Ma Poetesse (FR) (Sorrento (FR))
M C Pipe (F Danloux 22/6) Yvonne & The Toy Boys

Placings:4004-P002331 **(4881)**
2001/02: 18^{P}HO, 18^{0}GS, 18^{0}VS, 17^{2}VS, 16^{3}S, 20^{3}S, 18^{1}GF

	Starts	1st	2nd	3rd	Win & Pl
Hurdles	4	1	0	1	3071
Chases	3	0	1	1	3676
Career Total	**11**	**1**	**1**	**2**	**11765**

105	4/02	Font	2m2f110y	E Hdl	G-F	£2709

Total win prize-money £2709

Going: Sf: 0-2 GS: 0-1 Gd: 0-0 GF: - Fm: 1-1
Distance: **2m/2m3: 1-6** 2m4-2m7: 0-1 3m+: 0-0
Track: **LH: 1-1** RH: 0-1 **Tight: 1-2** Gall: 0-0
Aids: Bl: 0-0 Vi: 0-0 Tstrap: 0-0
Best Rating: 105 4/02 Font 2m2f110y gd-fm Hdl

Fair form in France over hurdles and fences, she won a maiden hurdle at Fontwell in April 2002. Acts on any ground.

Doukash (FR)

112(104h) (104h)**112**

5-y-o b/br g Cadoudal (FR)-Paris Kash (FR) (Kashtan (FR))
C A Dwyer (M C Pipe 20/2) Mrs Shelley Dwyer

Placings:3/2245-20P5511B1P6 **(4895)**
2001/02: 20^{2}G, 21^{0}G, 25^{P}S, 22^{5}G, 23^{5}G, 19^{1}HY, 21^{1}GS, 20^{B}GS, 20^{1}G, 21^{P}G, 20^{6}G

	Starts	1st	2nd	3rd	Win & Pl
Hurdles	5	2	1	0	5693
Chases	6	1	0	0	2744
Career Total	**16**	**3**	**3**	**1**	**18431**

112	3/02	Plum	2m4f	F(0-100)HCh	GD	£2744
104	2/02	Ludl	2m5f	G Hdl	G-S	£1988
103	2/02	Hrfd	2m3f110y	F Hdl	HVY	£2373

Total win prize-money £7105

Going: Sf: 1-2 GS: 1-2 Gd: 1-7 GF: - Fm: 0-0
Distance: 2m/2m3: 0-0 **2m4-2m7: 3-9** 3m+: 0-2
Track: LH: 1-5 **RH: 2-5 Tight: 1-3** Gall: 0-2
Aids: Bl: 0-0 Vi: 0-0 Tstrap: 0-0
Best Rating: 112 3/02 Plum 2m4f good Ch

Disappointed over fences before winning a weak event over hurdles at Hereford in February 2002. Followed up in a seller. Landed a handicap chase for new connections in March. Stays two miles five furlongs and acts on good and heavy ground.

Dove From Above

95 **67**

9-y-o b g Henbit (USA)-Sally's Dove (Celtic Cone)
R J Price Mrs Chris Davies

Placings:*0400*/0P06/40200416F/P-F06F **(0828)**
2001/02: 19^{F}F, 17^{0}G, 20^{6}GF, 24^{F}GF

	Starts	1st	2nd	3rd	Win & Pl
Chases	4	0	0	0	0
Career Total	**22**	**1**	**1**	**0**	**3828**

79	10/99	Ludl	2m5f	E(0-105)HHdl	G-F	£2766

Total win prize-money £2766

Going: Sf: 0-0 GS: 0-0 Gd: 0-1 GF: - Fm: 0-3
Distance: 2m/2m3: 0-2 2m4-2m7: 0-1 3m+: 0-1
Track: LH: 0-2 RH: 0-2 Tight: 0-3 Gall: 0-1
Aids: Bl: 0-4 Vi: 0-0 Tstrap: 0-0
Best Rating: 90 9/97 Hntg 2m110y gd-fm NHF

Dove's Dominion

70 **21**

5-y-o b g Primo Dominie-Dame Helene (USA) (Sir Ivor)
A J Chamberlain (D N Carey 10/6) D N Carey

Placings:0-000 **(0674)**
2001/02: 17^{0}GS, 19^{0}G, 16^{0}GF

	Starts	1st	2nd	3rd	Win & Pl
Hurdles	3	0	0	0	
Career Total	**4**	**0**	**0**	**0**	

Going: Sf: 0-0 GS: 0-1 Gd: 0-1 GF: - Fm: 0-1
Distance: 2m/2m3: 0-2 2m4-2m7: 0-1 3m+: 0-0
Track: LH: 0-2 RH: 0-1 Tight: 0-1 Gall: 0-0
Aids: Bl: 0-0 Vi: 0-1 Tstrap: 0-0
Best Rating: 41 11/00 Hrfd 2m1f gd-sft Hdl

Dovetto

98 **97**

13-y-o ch g Riberetto-Shadey Dove (Deadly Nightshade)
C J Price Mrs M Price

Placings:*0*/555/0/0/30/0464102422/3544442312/0635 3P1255/50200031-3420P36P5 **(4505)**
2001/02: 21^{3}GF, 20^{4}GF, 20^{2}GF, 21^{0}G, 24^{P}G, 20^{3}S, 16^{6}S, 20^{P}HY, 21^{5}G

	Starts	1st	2nd	3rd	Win & Pl
Chases	9	0	1	2	1642
Career Total	**55**	**4**	**8**	**8**	**26088**

97	4/01	Plum	2m4f	F(0-100)HCh	SFT	£3542
95	3/00	Hrfd	2m	E(0-115)HCh	GD	£4381
92	3/99	Chep	2m3f110y	D(0-110)HCh	G-S	£3772
86	1/98	Extr	2m2f	E(0-100)HHdl	HVY	£2565

Total win prize-money £14261

Going: Sf: 0-3 GS: 0-0 Gd: 0-3 GF: - Fm: 0-3
Distance: 2m/2m3: 0-1 2m4-2m7: 0-7 3m+: 0-1
Track: LH: 0-5 RH: 0-4 Tight: 0-5 Gall: 0-0
Aids: Bl: 0-0 Vi: 0-0 Tstrap: 0-0
Best Rating: 97 4/01 Plum 2m4f soft Ch

A half-brother to Flakey Dove, he is an ordinary handicap chaser at around two and a half miles, effective in soft ground.

Down To Business (IRE)

7-y-o b m Good Thyne (USA)-Dark Foam (Bustineto)
D Burchell Mrs D L Smith-Hopper

Placings:*0* **(0359)**
2001/02: 17^{0}GS

	Starts	1st	2nd	3rd	Win & Pl
NH Flat	1	0	0	0	
Career Total	**1**	**0**	**0**	**0**	

Going: Sf: 0-0 GS: 0-1 Gd: 0-0 GF: - Fm: 0-0
Distance: 2m/2m3: 0-1 2m4-2m7: 0-0 3m+: 0-0
Track: LH: 0-1 RH: 0-0 Tight: 0-1 Gall: 0-0
Aids: Bl: 0-0 Vi: 0-0 Tstrap: 0-0
Best Rating:

Downpour (USA)

101 **100**

4-y-o b g Torrential (USA)-Juliac (USA) (Accipiter (USA))
Ian Williams (Sir Mark Prescott 11/10) Favourites Racing Ltd

Placings:0 **(4006)**
2001/02: 16^{0}S

	Starts	1st	2nd	3rd	Win & Pl
Hurdles	1	0	0	0	
Career Total	**1**	**0**	**0**	**0**	

Going: Sf: 0-1 GS: 0-0 Gd: 0-0 GF: - Fm: 0-0
Distance: 2m/2m3: 0-1 2m4-2m7: 0-0 3m+: 0-0
Track: LH: 0-1 RH: 0-0 Tight: 0-0 Gall: 0-1
Aids: Bl: 0-0 Vi: 0-0 Tstrap: 0-0
Best Rating: 81 3/02 Newb 2m110y soft Hdl

Dr Bones (IRE)

9-y-o b/br g Durgam (USA)-Rose Deer (Whistling Deer)
L Lungo Mrs Ann Fortune

Placings:0101/241461121/42140/5P0F/PP-P **(0179)**
2001/02: 21^{P}GF

	Starts	1st	2nd	3rd	Win & Pl
Chases	1	0	0	0	
Career Total	**25**	**7**	**3**	**0**	**41061**

139	12/98	Weth	2m4f110y	B(0-145)HCh	GD	£7223
139	4/98	Prth	2m4f110y	C Ch	GD	£7220
100	2/98	Catt	2m	D Ch	GD	£3548
110	2/98	Muss	2m	E Ch	GD	£3374
124	12/97	Weth	2m	C(0-135)HHdl	GD	£3574
117	3/97	Limk	2m	Hdl	Y-S	£2712
114	1/97	Leop	2m	Hdl	G-Y	£4069

Total win prize-money £31722

Going: Sf: 0-0 GS: 0-0 Gd: 0-0 GF: - Fm: 0-1
Distance: 2m/2m3: 0-0 2m4-2m7: 0-1 3m+: 0-0
Track: LH: 0-1 RH: 0-0 Tight: 0-0 Gall: 0-0
Aids: Bl: 0-1 Vi: 0-0 Tstrap: 0-0
Best Rating: 139 3/99 Chel 2m4f110y gd-sft Ch

Dr Charlie

103 **101**

4-y-o ch g Dr Devious (IRE)-Miss Toot (Ardross)
C J Mann Martin Myers

Placings:61 **(4597)**
2001/02: 16^{6}S, 19^{1}GF

	Starts	1st	2nd	3rd	Win & Pl
Hurdles	2	1	0	0	2923
Career Total	**2**	**1**	**0**	**0**	**2923**

101	4/02	Wwck	2m3f	E Hdl	G-F	£2922

Total win prize-money £2923

Going: Sf: 0-1 GS: 0-0 Gd: 0-0 GF: - Fm: 1-1
Distance: **2m/2m3: 1-2** 2m4-2m7: 0-0 3m+: 0-0
Track: **LH: 1-2** RH: 0-0 Tight: 0-0 Gall: 0-1
Aids: Bl: 0-0 Vi: 0-0 Tstrap: 0-0
Best Rating: 101 4/02 Wwck 2m3f gd-fm Hdl

Well bred expensive yearling who failed to make the grade on the Flat, despite showing definite promise on only start. Shaped well in soft ground on novice hurdle debut and followed that up with success in a two mile-three novice hurdle at Warwick in April 2002 on a quick surface.

Dr Jazz (NZ)

93(78c) **113d**

10-y-o ch g First Norman (USA)-Almacenista (NZ) (Nuage D'Or (USA))
M C Pipe P A Deal

Placings:21F1236/**424221**/56300-0PP65P **(3342)**
2001/02: 16^{0}GF, 18^{P}GF, 17^{P}GF, 16^{6}HY, 24^{5}GS, 19^{P}S

	Starts	1st	2nd	3rd	Win & Pl
Hurdles	6	0	0	0	0
Career Total	**24**	**3**	**5**	**2**	**20683**

135	4/00	Uttx	2m	C(0-135)HHdl	HVY	£5245
123	1/99	Folk	2m1f110y	E Hdl	HVY	£2488
	7/98	Puke	1m5f110y	Hdl	HVY	£1144

Total win prize-money £8878

Going: Sf: 0-2 GS: 0-1 Gd: 0-0 GF: - Fm: 0-3
Distance: 2m/2m3: 0-4 2m4-2m7: 0-1 3m+: 0-1
Track: LH: 0-3 RH: 0-3 Tight: 0-4 Gall: 0-0
Aids: Bl: 0-1 Vi: 0-0 Tstrap: 0-0
Best Rating: 135 4/00 Uttx 2m heavy Hdl

Dr Saddler

86f **67f**

6-y-o b g Saddlers' Hall (IRE)-Dama De Noche (Rusticaro (FR))
D Mullarkey Dune Racing

Placings:*00* **(4166)**
2001/02: 16^{0}GS, 16^{0}GS

	Starts	1st	2nd	3rd	Win & Pl
NH Flat	2	0	0	0	
Career Total	**2**	**0**	**0**	**0**	

Going: Sf: 0-0 GS: 0-2 Gd: 0-0 GF: - Fm: 0-0
Distance: 2m/2m3: 0-2 2m4-2m7: 0-0 3m+: 0-0
Track: LH: 0-1 RH: 0-1 Tight: 0-0 Gall: 0-0
Aids: Bl: 0-0 Vi: 0-0 Tstrap: 0-0
Best Rating: 67 2/02 Winc 2m gd-sft NHF

Poor bumper form.

Dr Strangelove (IRE)

4-y-o ch g Dr Devious (IRE)-Renzola (Dragonara Palace (USA))
A Crook (B W Hills 31/8) Andy Crook Racing Jumps Partnership

Placings:PP **(4044)**
2001/02: 16^{P}S, 17^{P}GS

	Starts	1st	2nd	3rd	Win & Pl
Hurdles	2	0	0	0	
Career Total	**2**	**0**	**0**	**0**	

Going: Sf: 0-1 GS: 0-1 Gd: 0-0 GF: - Fm: 0-0
Distance: 2m/2m3: 0-2 2m4-2m7: 0-0 3m+: 0-0
Track: LH: 0-1 RH: 0-1 Tight: 0-2 Gall: 0-0
Aids: Bl: 0-1 Vi: 0-0 Tstrap: 0-0
Best Rating:

Dragon Hunter (IRE)

103 **110**

7-y-o b g Welsh Term-Sahob (Roselier (FR))
C R Egerton J Douglas & T Davis

Placings:421P **(4373)**
2001/02: 19^{4}S, 24^{2}S, 27^{1}S, 21^{P}S

	Starts	1st	2nd	3rd	Win & Pl
Hurdles	4	1	1	0	3783
Career Total	**4**	**1**	**1**	**0**	**3783**

110	3/02	Font	3m3f	E Hdl	SFT	£2509

Total win prize-money £2510

Going: Sf: 1-4 GS: 0-0 Gd: 0-0 GF: - Fm: 0-0
Distance: 2m/2m3: 0-0 2m4-2m7: 0-2 **3m+: 1-2**
Track: LH: 0-0 RH: 0-3 **Tight: 1-3** Gall: 0-0
Aids: Bl: 0-0 Vi: 0-0 Tstrap: 0-0
Best Rating: 110 3/02 Font 3m3f soft Hdl

Novice hurdler, stays extreme distances.

Dragon Island

90 **68**

7-y-o b g Jupiter Island-Dragon Fire (Dragonara Palace (USA))
D R Gandolfo The Fools Day Partnership

Placings:*4/04060-0P* **(1397)**
2001/02: 17^{0}GF, 24^{P}GF

	Starts	1st	2nd	3rd	Win & Pl
Hurdles	2	0	0	0	
Career Total	**8**	**0**	**0**	**0**	**0**

Going: Sf: 0-0 GS: 0-0 Gd: 0-0 GF: - Fm: 0-2
Distance: 2m/2m3: 0-1 2m4-2m7: 0-0 3m+: 0-1
Track: LH: 0-2 RH: 0-0 Tight: 0-1 Gall: 0-0
Aids: Bl: 0-0 Vi: 0-2 Tstrap: 0-0
Best Rating: 92 3/00 Newb 2m110y soft NHF

Dragon King

109 **102**

10-y-o b g Rakaposhi King-Dunsilly Bell (London Bells (CAN))
P Bowen (M Mullineaux 6/6) R Greenway

Placings:*2/05*0046110/032031353302/5P**3323131130 330453U440220/22253250400-04131103** **(1489)**
2001/02: 22^{0}GF, 20^{4}GS, 20^{1}S, 26^{3}GF, 26^{1}GF, 25^{1}GF, 24^{0}GF, 24^{3}GF

	Starts	1st	2nd	3rd	Win & Pl
Chases	8	3	0	2	11334
Career Total	**66**	**9**	**10**	**16**	**46073**

102	9/01	MRas	3m1f	F(0-110)HCh	G-F	£4114
102	8/01	NAbb	3m2f110y	F(0-100)HCh	G-F	£2947
96	7/01	Worc	2m4f110y	F(0-100)HCh	SFT	£2975
121	9/99	Sedg	2m5f	D(0-120)HCh	G-F	£3699
121	9/99	NAbb	2m5f110y	D(0-125)HCh	G-F	£3765
100	8/99	NAbb	2m110y	D Ch	GD	£3838
98	11/98	Wind	2m	E(0-110)HHdl	G-S	£2880
94	3/98	Tntn	2m1f	F(0-95)HHdl	G-S	£2050
84	3/98	Tntn	2m1f	F(0-105)HHdl	G-S	£1903

Total win prize-money £28172

Going: Sf: 1-1 GS: 0-1 Gd: 0-0 GF: - Fm: 2-6
Distance: 2m/2m3: 0-0 2m4-2m7: 1-3 **3m+: 2-5**
Track: **LH: 2-5** RH: 1-3 **Tight: 2-5** Gall: 0-1
Aids: Bl: 0-0 Vi: 0-0 Tstrap: 0-0
Best Rating: 121 9/99 Sedg 2m5f gd-fm Ch

Modest chaser, he ended a long losing run over two and a half miles at Worcester in July 2001, and subsequently scored twice on fast ground over distances beyond three miles at Newton Abbot and Market Rasen. Won extended 21 furlong Class F classified chase at Newton Abbot July 2002 and has now scored four times at that course.

Dragon Stout

94 **91**

9-y-o ch g Forzando-La Belle Princesse (Royal Match)
R E Barr (Miss C L Dennis 26/5) R T Dennis

Placings:6U564 **(0972)**
2001/02: 21^{6}G, 20^{U}GF, 20^{5}G, 20^{6}G, 24^{4}GF

	Starts	1st	2nd	3rd	Win & Pl
Chases	5	0	0	0	262
Career Total	**5**	**0**	**0**	**0**	**262**

Going: Sf: 0-0 GS: 0-0 Gd: 0-3 GF: - Fm: 0-2
Distance: 2m/2m3: 0-0 2m4-2m7: 0-4 3m+: 0-1

Track: LH: 0-4 RH: 0-1 Tight: 0-3 Gall: 0-0
Aids: Bl: 0-0 Vi: 0-0 Tstrap: 0-3
Best Rating: 91 5/01 Sedg 2m5f good Ch

Dragons Bay (IRE)

13-y-o b g Radical-Logical View (Mandalus)
Paul Morgan Paul Morgan

Placings:3PP6266U223/13P6U31121/162343P/0P-0P (4376)
2001/02: 19^{0}S, 20^{P}S

	Starts	1st	2nd	3rd	Win & Pl
Chases	2	0	0	0	
Career Total	**32**	**5**	**5**	**6**	**26641**

131	5/99	MRas	2m1f110y	E(0-115)HCh	G-F	£3132
128	4/99	MRas	2m1f110y	E(0-105)HCh	SFT	£3912
114	3/99	MRas	2m1f110y	F(0-110)HCh	G-S	£3626
118	3/99	Donc	2m3f110y	D(0-110)HCh	G-S	£4565
98	9/98	Carl	2m	F(0-105)HCh	GD	£2762

Total win prize-money £17997

Going: Sf: 0-2 GS: 0-0 Gd: 0-0 GF: - Fm: 0-0
Distance: 2m/2m3: 0-0 2m4-2m7: 0-2 3m+: 0-0
Track: LH: 0-1 RH: 0-1 Tight: 0-1 Gall: 0-1
Aids: Bl: 0-2 Vi: 0-0 Tstrap: 0-0
Best Rating: 131 12/99 Sedg 2m110y soft Ch

Drakestone

106 105

11-y-o b g Motivate-Lyricist (Averof)
R L Brown R L Brown

Placings:_06034/030033/52/306/_**F3U54P0113/2-4013440P2** (2719)
2001/02: 16^{4}G, 22^{0}GF, 20^{1}GF, 20^{3}GF, 20^{4}GF, 20^{4}G, 21^{0}G, 24^{P}S, 17^{2}G

	Starts	1st	2nd	3rd	Win & Pl
Hurdles	9	1	1	1	3786
Career Total	**36**	**3**	**3**	**8**	**13895**

103	8/01	Worc	2m4f	F Hdl	G-F	£1897
97	2/00	Bang	2m1f	F(0-110)HHdl	G-S	£3623
75	1/00	Hrfd	2m1f	F Hdl	G-S	£2324

Total win prize-money £7845

Going: Sf: 0-1 GS: 0-0 Gd: 0-4 GF: - Fm: 1-4
Distance: 2m/2m3: 0-2 **2m4-2m7: 1-6** 3m+: 0-1
Track: **LH: 1-8** RH: 0-1 Tight: 0-1 Gall: 0-1
Aids: Bl: 0-1 Vi: 0-0 Tstrap: 0-0
Best Rating: 105 10/01 Chep 2m4f good Hdl

Plating-class hurdler, stays two and a half miles, suited by a sound surface although has won with cut in the ground.

Drama King

105 96d

10-y-o b g Tragic Role (USA)-Consistent Queen (Queens Hussar)
B J Llewellyn Alan J Williams

Placings:F5142/0612/501/00P-36416500P (4173)
2001/02: 21^{3}G, 16^{6}S, 16^{4}S, 20^{1}S, 16^{6}GS, 19^{5}S, 21^{0}HY, 24^{0}G, 25^{P}GS

	Starts	1st	2nd	3rd	Win & Pl
Hurdles	9	1	0	1	2191
Career Total	**24**	**4**	**2**	**1**	**10942**

96	12/01	Folk	2m4f110y	F(0-100)HHdl	SFT	£1820
96	1/00	Uttx	2m4f110y	G(0-95)HHdl	SFT	£2191
100	7/98	Worc	2m4f	E(0-115)HHdl	G-F	£2337
95	3/98	Strf	2m3f	G Hdl	GD	£2901

Total win prize-money £9251

Going: Sf: 1-5 GS: 0-2 Gd: 0-2 GF: - Fm: 0-0
Distance: 2m/2m3: 0-3 **2m4-2m7: 1-4** 3m+: 0-2
Track: LH: 0-2 **RH: 1-4 Tight: 1-2** Gall: 0-0
Aids: **Bl: 1-8** Vi: 0-0 Tstrap: 0-0
Best Rating: 100 7/98 Strf 2m6f110y gd-fm Hdl

A plating-class hurdler, acts on any ground and stays two and a half miles. Has a tendency to find little off the bridle.

Dramatic Miss

71f 54f

7-y-o b m Deploy-Stos (IRE) (Bluebird (USA))
R J Price Stephen J Fletcher

Placings:_00_ (0911)
2001/02: 17^{0}GF, 16^{0}G

	Starts	1st	2nd	3rd	Win & Pl
NH Flat	2	0	0	0	
Career Total	**2**	**0**	**0**	**0**	

Going: Sf: 0-0 GS: 0-0 Gd: 0-1 GF: - Fm: 0-1
Distance: 2m/2m3: 0-2 2m4-2m7: 0-0 3m+: 0-0
Track: LH: 0-1 RH: 0-1 Tight: 0-1 Gall: 0-0
Aids: Bl: 0-0 Vi: 0-0 Tstrap: 0-0
Best Rating: 54 6/01 MRas 2m1f110y gd-fm NHF

Dramatic Quest

102 113

5-y-o b g Zafonic (USA)-Ultra Finesse (USA) (Rahy (USA))
Ian Williams (M Johnston 5/10) M Murphy

Placings:4106 (4126)
2001/02: 16^{4}G, 16^{1}S, 20^{0}S, 19^{6}G

	Starts	1st	2nd	3rd	Win & Pl
Hurdles	4	1	0	0	3472
Career Total	**4**	**1**	**0**	**0**	**3472**

113	1/02	Donc	2m110y	D Hdl	SFT	£3472

Total win prize-money £3472

Going: Sf: 1-2 GS: 0-0 Gd: 0-2 GF: - Fm: 0-0
Distance: **2m/2m3: 1-2** 2m4-2m7: 0-2 3m+: 0-0
Track: **LH: 1-1** RH: 0-3 Tight: 0-0 **Gall: 1-2**
Aids: Bl: 0-0 Vi: 0-0 Tstrap: 0-0
Best Rating: 113 1/02 Donc 2m110y soft Hdl

Listed class on the Flat, he got off the mark over hurdles at Doncaster in January 2002, but disappointed over a longer trip next time. Effective over two miles and he goes well on soft ground.

Dream Of Nurmi

113(108h) (121h)142

8-y-o ch g Pursuit Of Love-Finlandaise (FR) (Arctic Tern (USA))
Mrs S J Smith Mrs Jacqueline Conroy

Placings:11/R21R05/0600-51115U44P31 (4876)
2001/02: 21^{5}G, 20^{1}F, 20^{1}G, 21^{1}GF, 20^{5}GS, 19^{U}G, 19^{4}S, 24^{4}GS, 21^{P}G, 20^{3}G, 20^{1}G

	Starts	1st	2nd	3rd	Win & Pl
Hurdles	2	0	0	1	1828
Chases	9	4	0	0	20933
Career Total	**23**	**7**	**1**	**1**	**32942**

142	4/02	Prth	2m4f110y	D(0-125)HCh	GD	£8684
125	7/01	Strf	2m5f110y	D Ch	G-F	£4147
125	6/01	Hexm	2m4f110y	E Ch	GD	£3243
123	5/01	Weth	2m4f110y	D Ch	FRM	£4368
132	12/99	Wwck	2m	D(0-125)HHdl	SFT	£3899
112	4/99	Hntg	2m110y	E Hdl	GD	£2757
112	4/99	Ludl	2m	E Hdl	GD	£2640

Total win prize-money £29740

Going: Sf: 0-1 GS: 0-2 Gd: 2-6 GF: - Fm: 2-2
Distance: 2m/2m3: 0-0 **2m4-2m7: 4-10** 3m+: 0-1
Track: **LH: 3-9** RH: 1-1 **Tight: 1-2** Gall: 0-4
Aids: Bl: 0-0 Vi: 0-0 Tstrap: 0-0
Best Rating: 142 4/02 Prth 2m4f110y good Ch

A capable hurdler on his day, he refused to jump off on several occasions in the past, but his new yard seem to have sweetened him up. Took well to fences during the summer of 2001, completing a hat-trick, although he was well held until winning at Perth in April. Best on a sound surface.

Dream On Me

52

6-y-o b m Prince Sabo-Helens Dreamgirl (Caerleon (USA))
H J Manners H J Manners

Placings:U6F0/0 (0976)
2001/02: 16^{0}GF

	Starts	1st	2nd	3rd	Win & Pl
Hurdles	1	0	0	0	
Career Total	**5**	**0**	**0**	**0**	**0**

Going: Sf: 0-0 GS: 0-0 Gd: 0-0 GF: - Fm: 0-1
Distance: 2m/2m3: 0-1 2m4-2m7: 0-0 3m+: 0-0
Track: LH: 0-1 RH: 0-0 Tight: 0-1 Gall: 0-0
Aids: Bl: 0-0 Vi: 0-0 Tstrap: 0-0
Best Rating: 49 9/99 Hntg 2m110y good Hdl

Dream With Me (FR)

101 121+

5-y-o b g Johann Quatz (FR)-Midnight Ride (FR) (Fast Topaze (USA))
C R Egerton Dr G Madan Mohan

Placings:256 (4040)
2001/02: 16^{2}HY, 16^{5}GS, 17^{6}GS

	Starts	1st	2nd	3rd	Win & Pl
Hurdles	3	0	1	0	780
Career Total	**3**	**0**	**1**	**0**	**780**

Going: Sf: 0-1 GS: 0-2 Gd: 0-0 GF: - Fm: 0-0
Distance: 2m/2m3: 0-3 2m4-2m7: 0-0 3m+: 0-0
Track: LH: 0-1 RH: 0-2 Tight: 0-1 Gall: 0-0
Aids: Bl: 0-1 Vi: 0-0 Tstrap: 0-0
Best Rating: 105 2/02 Winc 2m gd-sft Hdl

A winner on the Flat in France, he was a well beaten favourite when second at Uttoxeter on his hurdling debut and looked a doubtful stayer on both his next starts. Has since joined Martin Pipe.

Dreamie Battle

92 83

4-y-o br f Makbul-Highland Rossie (Pablond)
R Hollinshead Tim Leadbeater

Placings:00 (4594)
2001/02: 16^{0}G, 16^{0}G

	Starts	1st	2nd	3rd	Win & Pl
Hurdles	2	0	0	0	
Career Total	**2**	**0**	**0**	**0**	

Going: Sf: 0-0 GS: 0-0 Gd: 0-2 GF: - Fm: 0-0
Distance: 2m/2m3: 0-2 2m4-2m7: 0-0 3m+: 0-0
Track: LH: 0-1 RH: 0-1 Tight: 0-0 Gall: 0-0

Aids: Bl: 0-0 Vi: 0-0 Tstrap: 0-0
Best Rating: 83 2/02 Ludl 2m good Hdl

Little form to get excited about over hurdles so far.

Dress Dance (IRE)

78

12-y-o b g Nordance (USA)-Pitaya (Princely Gift)
N R Mitchell Mrs J R Powell

Placings:F434350/P02P6342/20446164P0/0**5464FFP**/PP56/26640/**55PP05-P** (0215)
2001/02: 21^{P}GF

	Starts	1st	2nd	3rd	Win & Pl
Chases	1	0	0	0	
Career Total	**49**	**1**	**4**	**3**	**8053**

97	1/96	Tntn	2m1f	D(0-120)HHdl	G-S	£2883

Total win prize-money £2884

Going: Sf: 0-0 GS: 0-0 Gd: 0-0 GF: - Fm: 0-1
Distance: 2m/2m3: 0-0 2m4-2m7: 0-1 3m+: 0-0
Track: LH: 0-0 RH: 0-1 Tight: 0-0 Gall: 0-0
Aids: Bl: 0-1 Vi: 0-0 Tstrap: 0-0
Best Rating: 97 3/96 Sand 2m110y gd-sft Hdl

Drift

96 72

8-y-o b g Slip Anchor-Norgabie (Northfields (USA))
J M Bradley (B J Llewellyn 26/5) Miss S Howell

Placings:00/4/00-042U6 (2546)
2001/02: 17^{0}S, 17^{4}G, 19^{2}GS, 16^{U}HY, 19^{6}GS

	Starts	1st	2nd	3rd	Win & Pl
Hurdles	5	0	1	0	466
Career Total	**10**	**0**	**1**	**0**	**466**

Going: Sf: 0-2 GS: 0-2 Gd: 0-1 GF: - Fm: 0-0
Distance: 2m/2m3: 0-4 2m4-2m7: 0-1 3m+: 0-0
Track: LH: 0-2 RH: 0-3 Tight: 0-3 Gall: 0-0
Aids: Bl: 0-0 Vi: 0-0 Tstrap: 0-0
Best Rating: 72 11/01 MRas 2m3f110y gd-sft Hdl

Selling-class hurdler who regularly runs on the level for a pipe-opener between jump races, he is best with juice in the ground.

Droit De Seigneur (USA)

7-y-o b g Chief's Crown (USA)-Slydamsel (USA) (Damascus (USA))
J R Norton J Norton

Placings:50/26U/00-P (1833)
2001/02: 20^{P}G

	Starts	1st	2nd	3rd	Win & Pl
Hurdles	1	0	0	0	
Career Total	**8**	**0**	**1**	**0**	**493**

Going: Sf: 0-0 GS: 0-0 Gd: 0-1 GF: - Fm: 0-0
Distance: 2m/2m3: 0-0 2m4-2m7: 0-1 3m+: 0-0
Track: LH: 0-1 RH: 0-0 Tight: 0-1 Gall: 0-0
Aids: Bl: 0-0 Vi: 0-0 Tstrap: 0-0
Best Rating: 93 5/99 Uttx 2m gd-fm NHF

Drom Wood (IRE)

99 98

6-y-o ch g Be My Native (USA)-Try Your Case (Proverb)
C J Mann (Anthony Mullins 4/7) Mrs M Devine

Placings:*0104* (4030)
2001/02: 16^{0}HY, 17^{1}GF, 20^{0}G, 24^{4}GS

	Starts	1st	2nd	3rd	Win & Pl
NH Flat	2	1	0	0	3756
Hurdles	2	0	0	0	357
Career Total	**4**	**1**	**0**	**0**	**4113**

100	7/01	Bell	2m1f	NHF	G-F	£3756

Total win prize-money £3756

Going: Sf: 0-1 GS: 0-1 Gd: 0-1 GF: - Fm: 1-1
Distance: **2m/2m3: 1-2** 2m4-2m7: 0-1 3m+: 0-1
Track: LH: 0-1 RH: 0-1 Tight: 0-0 Gall: 0-1
Aids: Bl: 0-0 Vi: 0-0 **Tstrap: 1-1**
Best Rating: 100 7/01 Bell 2m1f gd-fm NHF

An Irish bumper winner, has disappointed on his runs over hurdles since coming to Britain.

Druid's Glen (IRE)

102 114

6-y-o br g Un Desperado (FR)-Fais Vite (USA) (Sharpen Up)
J J O'Neill (Miss F M Crowley 6/5) J P McManus

Placings:*253*411 (4854)
2001/02: 18^{2}G, 16^{5}G, 20^{3}GS, 20^{4}HY, 22^{1}GS, 22^{1}G

	Starts	1st	2nd	3rd	Win & Pl
NH Flat	2	0	1	0	1677
Hurdles	3	2	0	1	8209
Chases	1	0	0	0	212
Career Total	**6**	**2**	**1**	**1**	**10199**

114	4/02	Strf	2m6f110y	E Hdl	GD	£3220
113	3/02	Strf	2m6f110y	D Hdl	G-S	£4173

Total win prize-money £7393

Going: Sf: 0-1 GS: 1-2 Gd: 1-3 GF: - Fm: 0-0
Distance: 2m/2m3: 0-2 **2m4-2m7: 2-4** 3m+: 0-0
Track: **LH: 2-3** RH: 0-2 **Tight: 2-2** Gall: 0-0
Aids: Bl: 0-0 Vi: 0-0 Tstrap: 0-0
Best Rating: 119 5/01 Fair 2m2f good NHF

Won an Irish point and finished placed in a bumper. Showed ability over hurdles before winning at Stratford in March 2002 when stepped up in trip. May have been a shade fortunate to follow-up over course and distance the following month. Looks a nice chasing type. Acts on good/good to soft ground.

Drum Battle

103 115

10-y-o ch g Bold Arrangement-Cannon Boy (USA) (Canonero (USA))
W G M Turner David Chown

Placings:4233/P61422/52P300351/6**5211/PPU300**4P/**U4F23F21PP** (4783)
2001/02: 26^{U}G, 26^{4}GS, 27^{F}GS, 26^{2}S, 24^{3}GS, 26^{F}S, 26^{2}S, 29^{1}HY, 34^{P}HY, 29^{P}GF

	Starts	1st	2nd	3rd	Win & Pl
Chases	10	1	2	1	7603
Career Total	**42**	**5**	**7**	**6**	**24721**

115	2/02	Wwck	3m5f	E(0-110)HCh	HVY	£4506
125	1/99	Font	3m2f110y	E Ch	SFT	£2802
120	12/98	Hrfd	3m1f110y	D Ch	SFT	£3728
101	4/98	Plum	2m4f	E(0-115)HHdl	G-S	£2490
90	2/97	Ludl	2m5f110y	E Hdl	GD	£2444

Total win prize-money £15972

Going: Sf: 1-5 GS: 0-3 Gd: 0-1 GF: - Fm: 0-1
Distance: 2m/2m3: 0-0 2m4-2m7: 0-0 **3m+: 1-10**
Track: **LH: 1-3** RH: 0-3 Tight: 0-4 Gall: 0-0
Aids: Bl: 0-0 Vi: 0-0 **Tstrap: 1-6**
Best Rating: 125 1/99 Font 3m2f110y soft Ch

Stays well and handles heavy ground, but not the best of jumpers.

Drum Majorette

93f 98f

7-y-o ch m Infantry-Smart Chick (True Song)
L G Cottrell A J Cottrell

Placings:*44* (2294)
2001/02: 17^{4}GS, 17^{4}GF

	Starts	1st	2nd	3rd	Win & Pl
NH Flat	2	0	0	0	0
Career Total	**2**	**0**	**0**	**0**	**0**

Going: Sf: 0-0 GS: 0-1 Gd: 0-0 GF: - Fm: 0-1
Distance: 2m/2m3: 0-2 2m4-2m7: 0-0 3m+: 0-0
Track: LH: 0-0 RH: 0-2 Tight: 0-0 Gall: 0-0
Aids: Bl: 0-0 Vi: 0-0 Tstrap: 0-0
Best Rating: 98 11/01 Extr 2m1f gd-fm NHF

Drumdoney (IRE)

7-y-o br g Dromod Hill-Stradbally Bay (Shackleton)
R H Alner J P M & J W Cook

Placings:*6*F (0322)
2001/02: 18^{6}GF, 21^{F}G

	Starts	1st	2nd	3rd	Win & Pl
NH Flat	1	0	0	0	0
Chases	1	0	0	0	0
Career Total	**2**	**0**	**0**	**0**	**0**

Going: Sf: 0-0 GS: 0-0 Gd: 0-1 GF: - Fm: 0-1
Distance: 2m/2m3: 0-1 2m4-2m7: 0-1 3m+: 0-0
Track: LH: 0-1 RH: 0-1 Tight: 0-2 Gall: 0-0
Aids: Bl: 0-0 Vi: 0-0 Tstrap: 0-0
Best Rating: 93 5/01 Font 2m2f110y gd-fm NHF

Drumlin (IRE)

7-y-o b g Glacial Storm (USA)-Shannon Lough (IRE) (Deep Run)
J M Turner J M Turner

Placings:*54O21*/525P-6 (4274)
2001/02: 21^{6}G

	Starts	1st	2nd	3rd	Win & Pl
Chases	1	0	0	0	0
Career Total	**10**	**1**	**2**	**0**	**4330**

114	1/00	Plum	2m	E Hdl	SFT	£2747

Total win prize-money £2748

Going: Sf: 0-0 GS: 0-0 Gd: 0-1 GF: - Fm: 0-0
Distance: 2m/2m3: 0-0 2m4-2m7: 0-1 3m+: 0-0
Track: LH: 0-1 RH: 0-0 Tight: 0-1 Gall: 0-0
Aids: Bl: 0-0 Vi: 0-0 Tstrap: 0-0
Best Rating: 124 12/99 Uttx 2m soft Hdl

Druridge Bay (IRE)

6-y-o b g Turtle Island (IRE)-Lady Of Shalott (King's Lake (USA))
D G Bridgwater Mrs Mary Bridgwater

Placings:F00-P (1755)
2001/02: 16^{P}GS

	Starts	1st	2nd	3rd	Win & Pl
Hurdles	1	0	0	0	
Career Total	**4**	**0**	**0**	**0**	

Going: Sf: 0-0 GS: 0-1 Gd: 0-0 GF: - Fm: 0-0
Distance: 2m/2m3: 0-1 2m4-2m7: 0-0 3m+: 0-0
Track: LH: 0-1 RH: 0-0 Tight: 0-1 Gall: 0-0
Aids: Bl: 0-0 Vi: 0-0 Tstrap: 0-0
Best Rating: 30 10/00 Strf 2m110y soft Hdl

Dry Highline (IRE)

10-y-o b g Dry Dock-Fandango Girl (Last Fandango)
Mrs Ruth Hayter Mrs A Villar

Placings:*0/05/P44/***PF** (4534)
2001/02: 26^{P}G, 21^{F}G

	Starts	1st	2nd	3rd	Win & Pl
Chases	2	0	0	0	
Career Total	**8**	**0**	**0**	**0**	**268**

Going: Sf: 0-0 GS: 0-0 Gd: 0-2 GF: - Fm: 0-0
Distance: 2m/2m3: 0-0 2m4-2m7: 0-1 3m+: 0-1
Track: LH: 0-2 RH: 0-0 Tight: 0-1 Gall: 0-1
Aids: Bl: 0-0 Vi: 0-0 Tstrap: 0-0
Best Rating: 95 4/99 Clon 2m4f heavy Hdl

Front-running pointer/hunter chaser who has won on good and heavy ground. Not a totally reliable jumper but has a good record when completing.

Dry Hill Lad

11-y-o b g Cruise Missile-Arctic Lee (Arctic Judge)
Miss E Morton Miss E Morton

Placings:2FFP555/245/U1330PF/P4 (4846)
2001/02: 27^{P}GF, 24^{4}G

	Starts	1st	2nd	3rd	Win & Pl
Chases	2	0	0	0	0
Career Total	**19**	**1**	**2**	**2**	**4450**

102	5/99	Fknm	3m110y	H Ch	G-F	£2224

Total win prize-money £2225

Going: Sf: 0-0 GS: 0-0 Gd: 0-1 GF: - Fm: 0-1
Distance: 2m/2m3: 0-0 2m4-2m7: 0-0 3m+: 0-2
Track: LH: 0-2 RH: 0-0 Tight: 0-2 Gall: 0-0
Aids: Bl: 0-0 Vi: 0-0 Tstrap: 0-0
Best Rating: 102 2/00 Weth 3m1f soft Ch

Poor hunter chaser who usually makes jumping errors.

Dubai Seven Stars

111 124
4-y-o ch f Suave Dancer (USA)-Her Honour (Teenoso (USA))
M C Pipe Mrs Alison C Farrant

Placings:1P10 (4188)
2001/02: 16^{1}G, 19^{P}S, 17^{1}S, 16^{0}GS

	Starts	1st	2nd	3rd	Win & Pl
Hurdles	4	2	0	0	5071
Career Total	**4**	**2**	**0**	**0**	**5071**

103	1/02	Tntn	2m1f	E Hdl	SFT	£2631
115	12/01	Plum	2m	E Hdl	GD	£2439

Total win prize-money £5071

Going: Sf: 1-2 GS: 0-1 Gd: 1-1 GF: - Fm: 0-0
Distance: **2m/2m3: 2-3** 2m4-2m7: 0-1 3m+: 0-0
Track: LH: 1-2 RH: 1-2 **Tight: 2-2** Gall: 0-0
Aids: Bl: 0-0 Vi: 0-0 Tstrap: 0-0
Best Rating: 124 3/02 Chel 2m110y gd-sft Hdl

Got off the mark on her debut over hurdles at Plumpton in December 2001. Pulled too hard on her next outing. Won next time out at Taunton in heavy ground. Goes well over two miles. Has won on good ground and heavy.

Dublin Lights (IRE)

(72c) (54c)
7-y-o b/br g Electric-Whosview (Fine Blade (USA))
J I A Charlton J I A Charlton

Placings:*0*-**P00** (4591)
2001/02: 20^{P}HY, 16^{0}GS, 16^{0}G

	Starts	1st	2nd	3rd	Win & Pl
Hurdles	1	0	0	0	0
Chases	2	0	0	0	0
Career Total	**4**	**0**	**0**	**0**	

Going: Sf: 0-1 GS: 0-1 Gd: 0-1 GF: - Fm: 0-0
Distance: 2m/2m3: 0-2 2m4-2m7: 0-1 3m+: 0-0
Track: LH: 0-3 RH: 0-0 Tight: 0-1 Gall: 0-0
Aids: Bl: 0-0 Vi: 0-0 Tstrap: 0-0
Best Rating: 70 5/00 Dpat 2m1f172y gd-fm NHF

Lightly-raced and well held in a bumper and chases.

Duc De Coigny

7-y-o b g Damister (USA)-Shercol (Monseigneur (USA))
M Mullineaux Major W R Paton-Smith And Partners

Placings:*0* (2757)
2001/02: 17^{0}GS

	Starts	1st	2nd	3rd	Win & Pl
NH Flat	1	0	0	0	
Career Total	**1**	**0**	**0**	**0**	

Going: Sf: 0-0 GS: 0-1 Gd: 0-0 GF: - Fm: 0-0
Distance: 2m/2m3: 0-1 2m4-2m7: 0-0 3m+: 0-0
Track: LH: 0-1 RH: 0-0 Tight: 0-1 Gall: 0-0
Aids: Bl: 0-0 Vi: 0-0 Tstrap: 0-0
Best Rating:

Duchamp (USA)

110(104h) (110h)131
5-y-o b g Pine Bluff (USA)-Higher Learning (USA) (Fappiano (USA))
I A Balding Exors Of The Late Robert Hitchins

Placings:35-21213132F (4192)
2001/02: 16^{2}GF, 18^{1}GF, 16^{2}GF, 16^{1}S, 16^{3}G, 19^{1}G, 22^{3}G, 24^{2}G, 24^{F}GS

	Starts	1st	2nd	3rd	Win & Pl
Hurdles	3	1	2	0	3873
Chases	6	2	1	2	12208
Career Total	**11**	**3**	**3**	**3**	**16439**

141	12/01	Donc	2m3f110y	D Ch	GD	£4407
120	11/01	Towc	2m110y	E Ch	SFT	£3822
110	5/01	Font	2m2f110y	E Hdl	G-F	£2418

Total win prize-money £10648

Going: Sf: 1-1 GS: 0-1 Gd: 1-4 GF: - Fm: 1-3
Distance: **2m/2m3: 2-5** 2m4-2m7: 1-2 3m+: 0-2
Track: **LH: 2-6** RH: 1-2 Tight: 1-2 Gall: 1-3
Aids: Bl: 0-0 **Vi: 2-6** Tstrap: 0-0
Best Rating: 141 12/01 Donc 2m3f110y good Ch

A winner on the Flat, over hurdles and fences, he stays two miles three furlongs and acts on most ground. In the process of running a decent race when falling in the Kim Muir at the Festival.

Dudeen (IRE)

103 87
7-y-o br m Anshan-Pipers Pool (IRE) (Mtoto)
R Ford David Bostock

Placings:24F/53P/334022-1 (0806)
2001/02: 20^{1}GF

	Starts	1st	2nd	3rd	Win & Pl
Hurdles	1	1	0	0	
Career Total	**13**	**1**	**3**	**3**	**3098**

Going: Sf: 0-0 GS: 0-0 Gd: 0-0 GF: - Fm: 1-1
Distance: 2m/2m3: 0-0 **2m4-2m7: 1-1** 3m+: 0-0
Track: LH: 0-0 **RH: 1-1** Tight: 0-0 Gall: 0-0
Aids: Bl: 0-0 Vi: 0-0 Tstrap: 0-0
Best Rating: 91 9/00 Hntg 2m4f110y gd-fm Hdl

Duello

101 89
11-y-o b g Sure Blade (USA)-Royal Loft (Homing)
M C Pipe M C Pipe

Placings:0P/30/4102/P0/34220P00-53U51 (4047)
2001/02: 16^{5}G, 20^{3}HY, 22^{U}G, 16^{5}S, 17^{1}G

	Starts	1st	2nd	3rd	Win & Pl
Hurdles	5	1	0	1	2412
Career Total	**23**	**2**	**3**	**3**	**7892**

89	3/02	Extr	2m1f	F(0-95)HHdl	GD	£2128
106	11/98	Ludl	2m	E(0-105)HHdl	GD	£2549

Total win prize-money £4677

Going: Sf: 0-2 GS: 0-0 Gd: 1-3 GF: - Fm: 0-0
Distance: **2m/2m3: 1-3** 2m4-2m7: 0-2 3m+: 0-0
Track: LH: 0-2 **RH: 1-2** Tight: 0-2 Gall: 0-0
Aids: Bl: 0-0 **Vi: 1-5** Tstrap: 0-0
Best Rating: 109 5/00 Worc 2m gd-fm Hdl

Goes well over two miles and is effective on most types of ground, but is best on a sound surface. A character, he won under his amateur pilot at Exeter in March 2002.

Duet For One

94 72
10-y-o ch g Nearly A Hand-Grey Receipt (Rugantino)
N R Mitchell David House

Placings:*3/2/***PFP6/5PPPP** (3149)
2001/02: 22^{5}S, 25^{P}G, 26^{P}GS, 23^{P}G, 22^{P}G

	Starts	1st	2nd	3rd	Win & Pl
Chases	5	0	0	0	0
Career Total	**11**	**0**	**1**	**1**	**585**

Going: Sf: 0-1 GS: 0-1 Gd: 0-3 GF: - Fm: 0-0
Distance: 2m/2m3: 0-0 2m4-2m7: 0-2 3m+: 0-3
Track: LH: 0-0 RH: 0-2 Tight: 0-3 Gall: 0-0
Aids: Bl: 0-1 Vi: 0-0 Tstrap: 0-0
Best Rating: 91 5/98 Extr 2m2f good NHF

Duke Of Buckingham (IRE)

100f 104f
6-y-o b g Phardante (FR)-Deselby's Choice (Crash Course)
P R Webber C W Booth

Placings:*3-3* (0108)
2001/02: 18^{3}GF

	Starts	1st	2nd	3rd	Win & Pl

NH Flat	1	0	0	1	281
Career Total	**2**	**0**	**0**	**2**	**505**

Going: Sf: 0-0 GS: 0-0 Gd: 0-0 GF: - Fm: 0-1
Distance: 2m/2m3: 0-1 2m4-2m7: 0-0 3m+: 0-0
Track: LH: 0-1 RH: 0-0 Tight: 0-1 Gall: 0-0
Aids: Bl: 0-0 Vi: 0-0 Tstrap: 0-0
Best Rating: **104** 5/01 Font 2m2f110y gd-fm NHF

Modest form in bumpers before winning a point in the spring of 2002. Acts on a sound surface.

Duke Of Modena

73 45

5-y-o ch g Salse (USA)-Palace Street (USA) (Secreto (USA))
G B Balding Miss B Swire

Placings:0 **(2656)**
2001/02: 17^{0}GS

	Starts	1st	2nd	3rd	Win & Pl
Hurdles	1	0	0	0	
Career Total	**1**	**0**	**0**	**0**	

Going: Sf: 0-0 GS: 0-1 Gd: 0-0 GF: - Fm: 0-0
Distance: 2m/2m3: 0-1 2m4-2m7: 0-0 3m+: 0-0
Track: LH: 0-0 RH: 0-1 Tight: 0-1 Gall: 0-0
Aids: Bl: 0-0 Vi: 0-0 Tstrap: 0-0
Best Rating: **45** 12/01 Tntn 2m1f gd-sft Hdl

Dulas Bay

118 136

8-y-o b g Selkirk (USA)-Ivory Gull (USA) (Storm Bird (CAN))
M Pitman Mrs M A Hoffman

Placings:23313/P36P0/6/1F1F30-61314400 **(4664)**
2001/02: 20^{6}G, 20^{1}GS, 20^{3}G, 20^{1}S, 21^{4}HY, 24^{4}G, 24^{0}GS, 21^{0}G

	Starts	1st	2nd	3rd	Win & Pl
Chases	8	2	0	1	23887
Career Total	**25**	**5**	**1**	**6**	**40147**

136	1/02	Wwck	2m4f110y	C(0-135)HCh	SFT	£7312
130	11/01	Sand	2m4f110y	C(0-135)HCh	G-S	£8190
130	1/01	Kemp	2m4f110y	D(0-115)HCh	SFT	£5164
122	1/01	Ludl	2m4f	E(0-105)HCh	SFT	£3464
108	4/98	Weth	2m	D Hdl	G-S	£3125

Total win prize-money £27257

Going: Sf: 1-2 GS: 1-2 Gd: 0-4 GF: - Fm: 0-0
Distance: 2m/2m3: 0-0 **2m4-2m7: 2-6** 3m+: 0-2
Track: LH: 1-5 RH: 1-3 Tight: 0-1 Gall: 0-3
Aids: Bl: 0-0 Vi: 0-0 Tstrap: 0-0
Best Rating: **136** 1/02 Wwck 2m4f110y soft Ch

A useful handicap chaser, he goes well fresh and stays two and a half miles plus. Successful at Warwick in January 2002. Although unable to add to that subsequently. Usually held up.

Duma Tau (IRE)

6-y-o gr g Executive Perk-Di's Wag (Scallywag)
J T Gifford Mrs S N J Embiricos

Placings:P **(4422)**
2001/02: 16^{P}GS

	Starts	1st	2nd	3rd	Win & Pl
Hurdles	1	0	0	0	
Career Total	**1**	**0**	**0**	**0**	

Going: Sf: 0-0 GS: 0-1 Gd: 0-0 GF: - Fm: 0-0
Distance: 2m/2m3: 0-1 2m4-2m7: 0-0 3m+: 0-0
Track: LH: 0-1 RH: 0-0 Tight: 0-0 Gall: 0-1
Aids: Bl: 0-0 Vi: 0-0 Tstrap: 0-0
Best Rating:

Dumadic

85 56

5-y-o b g Nomadic Way (USA)-Duright (Dubassoff (USA))
T D Walford Peter Sawney

Placings:*0-30*P **(4857)**
2001/02: 16^{3}HY, 17^{0}G, 20^{P}G

	Starts	1st	2nd	3rd	Win & Pl
NH Flat	2	0	0	1	253
Hurdles	1	0	0	0	0
Career Total	**4**	**0**	**0**	**1**	**253**

Going: Sf: 0-1 GS: 0-0 Gd: 0-2 GF: - Fm: 0-0
Distance: 2m/2m3: 0-2 2m4-2m7: 0-1 3m+: 0-0
Track: LH: 0-2 RH: 0-1 Tight: 0-1 Gall: 0-0
Aids: Bl: 0-0 Vi: 0-0 Tstrap: 0-0
Best Rating: **88** 3/02 Sthl 2m heavy NHF

Dun Distinctly (IRE)

83(92h) (66h)81

5-y-o b g Distinctly North (USA)-Dunbally (Dunphy)
P C Haslam Lady Kitson

Placings:310P-5000 **(3363)**
2001/02: 17^{5}GS, 16^{0}G, 20^{0}G, 16^{0}GS

	Starts	1st	2nd	3rd	Win & Pl
Hurdles	4	0	0	0	0
Career Total	**8**	**1**	**0**	**1**	**1899**

95	11/00	Catt	2m	G Hdl	GD	£1554

Total win prize-money £1554

Going: Sf: 0-0 GS: 0-2 Gd: 0-2 GF: - Fm: 0-0
Distance: 2m/2m3: 0-3 2m4-2m7: 0-1 3m+: 0-0
Track: LH: 0-3 RH: 0-1 Tight: 0-1 Gall: 0-1
Aids: Bl: 0-0 Vi: 0-0 Tstrap: 0-0
Best Rating: **95** 11/00 Catt 2m good Hdl

Duncrievie Gale

79f 80f

5-y-o gr g Gildoran-The Whirlie Weevil (Scallywag)
Mrs L B Normile Robertson McCallum

Placings:*0* **(4841)**
2001/02: 16^{0}G

	Starts	1st	2nd	3rd	Win & Pl
NH Flat	1	0	0	0	
Career Total	**1**	**0**	**0**	**0**	

Going: Sf: 0-0 GS: 0-0 Gd: 0-1 GF: - Fm: 0-0
Distance: 2m/2m3: 0-1 2m4-2m7: 0-0 3m+: 0-0
Track: LH: 0-1 RH: 0-0 Tight: 0-0 Gall: 0-0
Aids: Bl: 0-0 Vi: 0-0 Tstrap: 0-0
Best Rating: **80** 4/02 Ayr 2m good NHF

Dunethna (IRE)

78 80

9-y-o b g Phardante (FR)-Portia's Delight (IRE) (The Parson)
Mrs W D Sykes D E Edwards

Placings:PP3 **(0566)**
2001/02: 24^{P}GS, 24^{P}GF, 25^{3}F

	Starts	1st	2nd	3rd	Win & Pl
Hurdles	1	0	0	1	492
Chases	2	0	0	0	0
Career Total	**3**	**0**	**0**	**1**	**492**

Going: Sf: 0-0 GS: 0-1 Gd: 0-0 GF: - Fm: 0-2
Distance: 2m/2m3: 0-0 2m4-2m7: 0-0 3m+: 0-3
Track: LH: 0-3 RH: 0-0 Tight: 0-2 Gall: 0-0
Aids: Bl: 0-0 Vi: 0-0 Tstrap: 0-0
Best Rating: **80** 5/01 Weth 3m1f firm Hdl

A winning pointer who has been well beaten under Rules.

Dungarvans Choice (IRE)

100 126

7-y-o ch g Orchestra-Marys Gift (Monksfield)
N J Henderson Elite Racing Club

Placings:*2014*-2110 **(4188)**
2001/02: 20^{2}S, 16^{1}GS, 16^{1}HY, 16^{0}GS

	Starts	1st	2nd	3rd	Win & Pl
Hurdles	4	2	1	0	8302
Career Total	**8**	**3**	**2**	**0**	**10907**

123	2/02	Sand	2m110y	D Hdl	HVY	£4660
126	1/02	Hntg	2m110y	E Hdl	G-S	£2569
109	1/01	Chep	2m110y	H NHF	G-S	£1401

Total win prize-money £8721

Going: Sf: 1-2 GS: 1-2 Gd: 0-0 GF: - Fm: 0-0
Distance: **2m/2m3: 2-3** 2m4-2m7: 0-1 3m+: 0-0
Track: LH: 0-2 **RH: 2-2** Tight: 0-0 **Gall: 1-1**
Aids: Bl: 0-0 Vi: 0-0 Tstrap: 0-0
Best Rating: **126** 1/02 Hntg 2m110y gd-sft Hdl

Promising form in bumpers and novice hurdles. Effective at up to two and a half miles and appreciates cut in the ground. Should make a chaser.

Dunkerron

100 88

5-y-o b g Pursuit Of Love-Top Berry (High Top)
J Joseph (P L Gilligan 16/10) Jack Joseph

Placings:3P053 **(4601)**
2001/02: 16^{3}S, 16^{P}S, 16^{0}S, 20^{5}S, 16^{3}GF

	Starts	1st	2nd	3rd	Win & Pl
Hurdles	5	0	0	2	914
Career Total	**5**	**0**	**0**	**2**	**914**

Going: Sf: 0-4 GS: 0-0 Gd: 0-0 GF: - Fm: 0-1
Distance: 2m/2m3: 0-4 2m4-2m7: 0-1 3m+: 0-0
Track: LH: 0-2 RH: 0-2 Tight: 0-1 Gall: 0-0
Aids: Bl: 0-0 Vi: 0-0 Tstrap: 0-0
Best Rating: **88** 12/01 Chep 2m110y soft Hdl

Modest hurdler, suited by a sound surface and a positive ride.

Dunmail Raise

8-y-o b m Milieu-Miss Apollo (Apollo Eight)
J L Goulding Mrs M Goulding

Placings:*00*/P-P **(0222)**
2001/02: 20^{P}GF

	Starts	1st	2nd	3rd	Win & Pl
Hurdles	1	0	0	0	

	Starts	1st	2nd	3rd	Win & Pl
Career Total	4	0	0	0	

Going: Sf: 0-0 GS: 0-0 Gd: 0-0 GF: - Fm: 0-1
Distance: 2m/2m3: 0-0 2m4-2m7: 0-1 3m+: 0-0
Track: LH: 0-1 RH: 0-0 Tight: 0-0 Gall: 0-0
Aids: Bl: 0-0 Vi: 0-0 Tstrap: 0-0
Best Rating:

Dunnellie

9-y-o b m Dunbeath (USA)-Miss Gallant (Gallo Gallante)
Paul Morris P B R Abrasives (w'Ton) Ltd

Placings: *00*/P (0358)
2001/02: 24^{P}GS

	Starts	1st	2nd	3rd	Win & Pl
Chases	1	0	0	0	
Career Total	3	0	0	0	

Going: Sf: 0-0 GS: 0-1 Gd: 0-0 GF: - Fm: 0-0
Distance: 2m/2m3: 0-0 2m4-2m7: 0-0 3m+: 0-1
Track: LH: 0-1 RH: 0-0 Tight: 0-1 Gall: 0-0
Aids: Bl: 0-0 Vi: 0-0 Tstrap: 0-0
Best Rating: 52 4/97 Hexm 2m firm NHF

Dunnicks Chance

55
7-y-o b m Greensmith-Field Chance (Whistlefield)
P R Rodford F G Tucker

Placings: *0*F50-60 (1038)
2001/02: 22^{6}GF, 17^{0}G

	Starts	1st	2nd	3rd	Win & Pl
Hurdles	2	0	0	0	0
Career Total	6	0	0	0	0

Going: Sf: 0-0 GS: 0-0 Gd: 0-1 GF: - Fm: 0-1
Distance: 2m/2m3: 0-1 2m4-2m7: 0-1 3m+: 0-0
Track: LH: 0-2 RH: 0-0 Tight: 0-2 Gall: 0-0
Aids: Bl: 0-0 Vi: 0-0 Tstrap: 0-0
Best Rating: 67 12/00 Tntn 2m1f soft NHF

Dunnicks Country

92 75
12-y-o ch m Town And Country-Celtic Beauty (Celtic Cone)
F G Tucker F G Tucker

Placings: *00*/*000*/4440/PP50/0PUFPPP/54354P536/32P/5343P-53535PP5P (4482)
2001/02: 24^{5}S, 16^{3}G, 23^{5}GF, 19^{3}G, 26^{5}S, 22^{P}HY, 19^{P}HY, 25^{5}G, 25^{P}G

	Starts	1st	2nd	3rd	Win & Pl
Chases	9	0	0	2	1056
Career Total	46	0	1	7	5421

Going: Sf: 0-4 GS: 0-0 Gd: 0-4 GF: - Fm: 0-1
Distance: 2m/2m3: 0-2 2m4-2m7: 0-2 3m+: 0-5
Track: LH: 0-1 RH: 0-6 Tight: 0-1 Gall: 0-0
Aids: Bl: 0-5 Vi: 0-0 Tstrap: 0-0
Best Rating: 87 11/98 Tntn 2m3f good Ch

A modest staying chaser, she has a habit of pulling up and is best suited to an easy surface.

Dunnicks Field

82 55
6-y-o b g Greensmith-Field Chance (Whistlefield)
P R Rodford F G Tucker

Placings: *000* (4007)
2001/02: 17^{0}HY, 16^{0}S, 19^{0}S

	Starts	1st	2nd	3rd	Win & Pl
NH Flat	2	0	0	0	0
Hurdles	1	0	0	0	0
Career Total	3	0	0	0	

Going: Sf: 0-3 GS: 0-0 Gd: 0-0 GF: - Fm: 0-0
Distance: 2m/2m3: 0-3 2m4-2m7: 0-0 3m+: 0-0
Track: LH: 0-2 RH: 0-1 Tight: 0-1 Gall: 0-1
Aids: Bl: 0-0 Vi: 0-0 Tstrap: 0-0
Best Rating: 90 2/02 Asct 2m110y soft NHF

Dunnicks Head

6-y-o b m Greensmith-Country Magic (National Trust)
P R Rodford F G Tucker

Placings: *0* (3345)
2001/02: 17^{0}S

	Starts	1st	2nd	3rd	Win & Pl
NH Flat	1	0	0	0	
Career Total	1	0	0	0	

Going: Sf: 0-1 GS: 0-0 Gd: 0-0 GF: - Fm: 0-0
Distance: 2m/2m3: 0-1 2m4-2m7: 0-0 3m+: 0-0
Track: LH: 0-0 RH: 0-0 Tight: 0-0 Gall: 0-0
Aids: Bl: 0-0 Vi: 0-0 Tstrap: 0-0
Best Rating:

Dunnicks Town

10-y-o b g Town And Country-Country Magic (National Trust)
F G Tucker F G Tucker

Placings: *5*/P0/005446PU5/0P4P54450/645P4-P50P (3224)
2001/02: 25^{P}G, 19^{5}GF, 19^{0}GS, 21^{P}G

	Starts	1st	2nd	3rd	Win & Pl
Chases	4	0	0	0	0
Career Total	30	0	0	0	2810

Going: Sf: 0-0 GS: 0-1 Gd: 0-2 GF: - Fm: 0-1
Distance: 2m/2m3: 0-1 2m4-2m7: 0-2 3m+: 0-1
Track: LH: 0-0 RH: 0-4 Tight: 0-1 Gall: 0-0
Aids: Bl: 0-3 Vi: 0-0 Tstrap: 0-0
Best Rating: 94 5/00 Extr 2m1f good Ch

Dunnicks View

108 97
13-y-o b g Sula Bula-Country Magic (National Trust)
F G Tucker F G Tucker

Placings: 55/6050/P0P02/P43/3U3403P/F4F34622435/4562165P33/6521026-000222536 (4532)
2001/02: 24^{0}G, 19^{0}GS, 24^{0}GS, 25^{2}S, 26^{2}S, 24^{2}S, 26^{5}S, 24^{3}S, 26^{6}GS

	Starts	1st	2nd	3rd	Win & Pl
Chases	9	0	3	1	4047
Career Total	58	2	9	9	23074

97	12/00	Tntn	3m	F(0-105)HCh	SFT	£3461
101	1/00	Tntn	3m	F(0-95)HCh	SFT	£3077

Total win prize-money £6539

Going: Sf: 0-5 GS: 0-3 Gd: 0-1 GF: - Fm: 0-0
Distance: 2m/2m3: 0-1 2m4-2m7: 0-0 3m+: 0-8
Track: LH: 0-2 RH: 0-6 Tight: 0-6 Gall: 0-0
Aids: Bl: 0-0 Vi: 0-0 Tstrap: 0-0
Best Rating: 101 4/00 Winc 3m1f110y gd-sft Ch

Modest staying chaser, tends to reserve his best for Taunton. Stays three and a quarter miles. Acts on soft ground.

Dunraven

95 85
7-y-o b g Perpendicular-Politique (Politico (USA))
M J Gingell (T D Easterby 18/1) Fare Dealing Partnerhsip

Placings: *6F6*/0503P50 (4772)
2001/02: 16^{0}G, 16^{5}GS, 19^{0}S, 20^{3}G, 24^{P}HY, 16^{5}G, 21^{0}G

	Starts	1st	2nd	3rd	Win & Pl
Hurdles	7	0	0	1	354
Career Total	10	0	0	1	354

Going: Sf: 0-2 GS: 0-1 Gd: 0-4 GF: - Fm: 0-0
Distance: 2m/2m3: 0-4 2m4-2m7: 0-2 3m+: 0-1
Track: LH: 0-6 RH: 0-1 Tight: 0-5 Gall: 0-0
Aids: Bl: 0-0 Vi: 0-0 Tstrap: 0-0
Best Rating: 85 12/01 Sthl 2m4f110y good Hdl

He has shown little in bumpers, and over hurdles.

Dunsdon (IRE)

83 44
10-y-o b g Beau Sher-Decent Vulgan (Decent Fellow)
Mrs L B Normile L B N Racing Club

Placings: 5-54P (0806)
2001/02: 24^{5}S, 24^{4}GF, 20^{P}GF

	Starts	1st	2nd	3rd	Win & Pl
Hurdles	3	0	0	0	0
Career Total	4	0	0	0	0

Going: Sf: 0-1 GS: 0-0 Gd: 0-0 GF: - Fm: 0-2
Distance: 2m/2m3: 0-0 2m4-2m7: 0-1 3m+: 0-2
Track: LH: 0-0 RH: 0-3 Tight: 0-0 Gall: 0-0
Aids: Bl: 0-0 Vi: 0-0 Tstrap: 0-0
Best Rating: 44 6/01 Prth 3m110y gd-fm Hdl

Dunsfold Duchess (IRE)

6-y-o b m Bustino-Rositary (FR) (Trenel)
P Winkworth The Dunsfold Dollies

Placings: *6000*-UP (2112)
2001/02: 17^{U}S, 20^{P}S

	Starts	1st	2nd	3rd	Win & Pl
Hurdles	2	0	0	0	
Career Total	6	0	0	0	0

Going: Sf: 0-2 GS: 0-0 Gd: 0-0 GF: - Fm: 0-0
Distance: 2m/2m3: 0-1 2m4-2m7: 0-1 3m+: 0-0
Track: LH: 0-1 RH: 0-1 Tight: 0-2 Gall: 0-0
Aids: Bl: 0-0 Vi: 0-0 Tstrap: 0-0
Best Rating:

Dunster Castle

99(86c) (70c)106
7-y-o ch g Carlingford Castle-Gay Edition (New Member)
P J Hobbs Mrs D L Whateley

Placings: *1*/25F-32631 (4586)
2001/02: 20^{3}G, 22^{2}G, 23^{6}G, 22^{3}G, 22^{1}G

	Starts	1st	2nd	3rd	Win & Pl
Hurdles	4	1	1	2	4547
Chases	1	0	0	0	0
Career Total	**9**	**2**	**2**	**2**	**7364**

106	4/02	Winc	2m6f	E Hdl	GD	£3052
105	3/00	Chep	2m110y	H NHF	GD	£1757

Total win prize-money £4809

Going: Sf: 0-0 GS: 0-0 Gd: 1-5 GF: - Fm: 0-0
Distance: 2m/2m3: 0-0 **2m4-2m7: 1-4** 3m+: 0-1
Track: LH: 0-1 **RH: 1-4** Tight: 0-1 Gall: 0-0
Aids: Bl: 0-0 Vi: 0-0 Tstrap: 0-0
Best Rating: 106 4/02 Winc 2m6f good Hdl

Has shown plenty of ability in novice hurdles but progress has been governed by jumping problems. Made all to land an overdue victory in a novices' hurdle in April. Has looked a tricky ride, stays well and handles soft.

Dunston Ace

8-y-o b g Sizzling Melody-Miss Vaigly Blue (Vaigly Great)
B D Leavy Paul Hollinshead

Placings:0PPP **(4574)**
2001/02: 16^{0}S, 16^{P}HY, 20^{P}G, 21^{P}GS

	Starts	1st	2nd	3rd	Win & Pl
Hurdles	3	0	0	0	0
Chases	1	0	0	0	0
Career Total	**4**	**0**	**0**	**0**	

Going: Sf: 0-2 GS: 0-1 Gd: 0-1 GF: - Fm: 0-0
Distance: 2m/2m3: 0-2 2m4-2m7: 0-2 3m+: 0-0
Track: LH: 0-4 RH: 0-0 Tight: 0-1 Gall: 0-0
Aids: Bl: 0-0 Vi: 0-0 Tstrap: 0-0
Best Rating:

Of no account over hurdles and seems unlikely to prove any better over fences.

Dunston Bill

108(81h) (73h)**129**

8-y-o b g Sizzling Melody-Fardella (ITY) (Molvedo)
C J Mann Rod & Mandy Bransgrove

Placings:624/20P31/325P041/642144124F **(4407)**
2001/02: 16^{6}GS, 20^{4}G, 21^{2}S, 21^{1}HY, 22^{4}G, 19^{4}S, 20^{1}S, 20^{2}S, 20^{4}GS, 20^{F}S

	Starts	1st	2nd	3rd	Win & Pl
Hurdles	1	0	0	0	0
Chases	9	2	2	0	13975
Career Total	**25**	**4**	**5**	**2**	**22978**

129	1/02	Kemp	2m4f110y	D(0-115)HCh	SFT	£5096
122	12/01	NAbb	2m5f110y	E(0-105)HCh	HVY	£3427
106	4/00	Hrfd	2m1f	E(0-115)HHdl	GD	£4082
98	4/99	Towc	2m	F(0-105)HHdl	SFT	£1933

Total win prize-money £14538

Going: Sf: 2-6 GS: 0-2 Gd: 0-2 GF: - Fm: 0-0
Distance: 2m/2m3: 0-2 **2m4-2m7: 2-8** 3m+: 0-0
Track: LH: 1-6 RH: 1-4 **Tight: 1-5** Gall: 0-2
Aids: **Bl: 2-9** Vi: 0-0 Tstrap: 0-0
Best Rating: 129 2/02 Kemp 2m4f110y soft Ch

A winner over fences and hurdles, he enjoyed a productive season over fences in 2001/02. Goes well on a sharp track and likes Kempton, seems best on a soft surface and stays two miles five furlongs.

Dunston Gold

94(84h) (59h)**74+**

8-y-o ch g Risk Me (FR)-Maria Whittaker (Cure The Blues (USA))
G Barnett T Walker

Placings:50 **(1387)**
2001/02: 20^{5}G, 16^{0}G

	Starts	1st	2nd	3rd	Win & Pl
Hurdles	2	0	0	0	0
Career Total	**2**	**0**	**0**	**0**	**0**

Going: Sf: 0-0 GS: 0-0 Gd: 0-2 GF: - Fm: 0-0
Distance: 2m/2m3: 0-1 2m4-2m7: 0-1 3m+: 0-0
Track: LH: 0-2 RH: 0-0 Tight: 0-1 Gall: 0-0
Aids: Bl: 0-0 Vi: 0-0 Tstrap: 0-0
Best Rating: 59 8/01 Bang 2m4f good Hdl

Modest pointer, has shown little under Rules.

Dunston Heath (IRE)

103 **71**

9-y-o b g Durgam (USA)-Yola (IRE) (Last Tycoon)
B D Leavy Barry Leavy

Placings:0P40000/500163/60020241P/4004P **(4316)**
2001/02: 17^{4}GS, 21^{0}GS, 20^{0}S, 24^{4}G, 24^{P}HY

	Starts	1st	2nd	3rd	Win & Pl
Hurdles	5	0	0	0	626
Career Total	**27**	**2**	**2**	**1**	**10092**

87	4/00	Bang	2m4f	F(0-100)HHdl	G-S	£5167
84	3/99	Hntg	2m5f110y	G(0-90)HHdl	G-S	£2458

Total win prize-money £7626

Going: Sf: 0-2 GS: 0-2 Gd: 0-1 GF: - Fm: 0-0
Distance: 2m/2m3: 0-1 2m4-2m7: 0-2 3m+: 0-2
Track: LH: 0-2 RH: 0-3 Tight: 0-2 Gall: 0-2
Aids: Bl: 0-0 Vi: 0-0 Tstrap: 0-1
Best Rating: 87 4/00 Bang 2m4f gd-sft Hdl

Dunston Reel

8-y-o b g Scottish Reel-Mindblowing (Pongee (ZIM))
W Clay T Walker

Placings:P **(1139)**
2001/02: 22^{P}G

	Starts	1st	2nd	3rd	Win & Pl
Hurdles	1	0	0	0	
Career Total	**1**	**0**	**0**	**0**	

Going: Sf: 0-0 GS: 0-0 Gd: 0-1 GF: - Fm: 0-0
Distance: 2m/2m3: 0-0 2m4-2m7: 0-1 3m+: 0-0
Track: LH: 0-1 RH: 0-0 Tight: 0-1 Gall: 0-0
Aids: Bl: 0-0 Vi: 0-0 Tstrap: 0-1
Best Rating:

Dunston Slick

91(91c) (93c)**64**

9-y-o ch g Weld-Havrin Princess (Scallywag)
W Clay T Walker

Placings:0/P/005000U60000 **(2785)**
2001/02: 17^{0}G, 20^{0}G, 16^{5}GS, 19^{0}G, 20^{0}GF, 16^{0}GF, 19^{U}G, 16^{6}S, 16^{0}GF, 26^{0}G, 16^{0}G, 20^{0}G

	Starts	1st	2nd	3rd	Win & Pl
Hurdles	7	0	0	0	0
Chases	5	0	0	0	0
Career Total	**14**	**0**	**0**	**0**	**0**

Going: Sf: 0-1 GS: 0-1 Gd: 0-7 GF: - Fm: 0-3
Distance: 2m/2m3: 0-8 2m4-2m7: 0-3 3m+: 0-1
Track: LH: 0-6 RH: 0-6 Tight: 0-5 Gall: 0-1
Aids: Bl: 0-0 Vi: 0-3 Tstrap: 0-5
Best Rating: 93 12/01 Ludl 2m good Ch

Not the cleanest of jumpers, he has not cut much ice over jumps to date.

Durham

11-y-o ch g Caerleon (USA)-Sanctuary (Welsh Pageant)
J Neville Shark Racing

Placings:525120/PU66P/U/4P **(1479)**
2001/02: 20^{4}GF, 21^{P}GS

	Starts	1st	2nd	3rd	Win & Pl
Hurdles	2	0	0	0	
Career Total	**14**	**1**	**2**	**0**	**3509**

80	11/94	MRas	2m1f110y	Hdl	GD	£2199

Total win prize-money £2199

Going: Sf: 0-0 GS: 0-1 Gd: 0-0 GF: - Fm: 0-1
Distance: 2m/2m3: 0-0 2m4-2m7: 0-2 3m+: 0-0
Track: LH: 0-2 RH: 0-0 Tight: 0-1 Gall: 0-0
Aids: Bl: 0-1 Vi: 0-0 Tstrap: 0-1
Best Rating: 80 11/94 MRas 2m1f110y good Hdl

Durham Dandy

6-y-o b g Inchinor-Disco Girl (FR) (Green Dancer (USA))
Miss J E Foster John Dwyer

Placings:43022/54-4P **(0497)**
2001/02: 24^{4}GF, 25^{P}G

	Starts	1st	2nd	3rd	Win & Pl
Chases	2	0	0	0	133
Career Total	**9**	**0**	**2**	**1**	**2039**

Going: Sf: 0-0 GS: 0-0 Gd: 0-1 GF: - Fm: 0-1
Distance: 2m/2m3: 0-0 2m4-2m7: 0-0 3m+: 0-2
Track: LH: 0-1 RH: 0-1 Tight: 0-1 Gall: 0-0
Aids: Bl: 0-0 Vi: 0-0 Tstrap: 0-0
Best Rating: 85 12/99 Catt 2m gd-fm Hdl

Durlston Bay

103 **104**

5-y-o b g Welsh Captain-Nelliellamay (Super Splash (USA))
S Dow Sandbaggers Club

Placings:4P5P6 **(4764)**
2001/02: 22^{4}GS, 22^{P}S, 22^{5}G, 24^{P}S, 16^{6}GF

	Starts	1st	2nd	3rd	Win & Pl
Hurdles	5	0	0	0	0
Career Total	**5**	**0**	**0**	**0**	**0**

Going: Sf: 0-2 GS: 0-1 Gd: 0-1 GF: - Fm: 0-1
Distance: 2m/2m3: 0-1 2m4-2m7: 0-3 3m+: 0-1
Track: LH: 0-2 RH: 0-3 Tight: 0-3 Gall: 0-0
Aids: Bl: 0-0 Vi: 0-0 Tstrap: 0-0
Best Rating: 98 1/02 Font 2m6f110y good Hdl

Modest hurdler, stays well and acts on fast ground.

Dushaan

105 96

7-y-o ch g Anshan-Soon To Be (Hot Spark)
J J O'Neill A K Collins

Placings:5/3400405P1-10P (3652)
2001/02: 16^{1}S, 16^{0}GS, 20^{P}S

	Starts	1st	2nd	3rd	Win & Pl
Hurdles	3	1	0	0	3445
Career Total	**13**	**2**	**0**	**1**	**6333**

96	5/01	Prth	2m110y	E(0-105)HHdl	SFT	£3445
96	4/01	Weth	2m	F(0-100)HHdl	G-S	£2614

Total win prize-money £6060

Going: Sf: 1-2 GS: 0-1 Gd: 0-0 GF: - Fm: 0-0
Distance: **2m/2m3: 1-2** 2m4-2m7: 0-1 3m+: 0-0
Track: LH: 0-1 **RH: 1-2** Tight: 0-1 Gall: 0-1
Aids: Bl: 0-0 Vi: 0-0 Tstrap: 0-0
Best Rating: 101 5/00 Prth 2m110y gd-sft NHF

Moderate hurdler, showed progressive form in the spring of 2001, winning at Wetherby and Perth. Suited by soft ground.

Dusk Duel (USA)

114 159

7-y-o b g Kris-Night Secret (Nijinsky (CAN))
N J Henderson Anthony Speelman

Placings:10/2110/3112-30 (2801)
2001/02: 19^{3}G, 24^{0}G

	Starts	1st	2nd	3rd	Win & Pl
Chases	2	0	0	1	5750
Career Total	**12**	**5**	**2**	**2**	**53891**

149	12/00	Kemp	2m	B Ch	G-S	£8437
158	12/00	Chel	2m5f	B Ch	SFT	£11340
141	2/00	Weth	2m	A Hdl	SFT	£9600
149	1/00	Asct	2m110y	C Hdl	SFT	£4914
107	3/99	Sand	2m110y	H NHF	SFT	£1619

Total win prize-money £35911

Going: Sf: 0-0 GS: 0-0 Gd: 0-2 GF: - Fm: 0-0
Distance: 2m/2m3: 0-0 2m4-2m7: 0-1 3m+: 0-1
Track: LH: 0-0 RH: 0-2 Tight: 0-0 Gall: 0-0
Aids: Bl: 0-0 Vi: 0-0 Tstrap: 0-0
Best Rating: 159 11/01 Asct 2m3f110y good Ch

A smart hurdler, he won novice chases at Cheltenham and Kempton in the winter of 2000. Good return at Ascot in November 2001, but beaten over three miles next time and missed the rest of the season. Acts on soft ground.

Dusky Diva (IRE)

88 78

7-y-o b m Be My Native (USA)-Brownskin (Buckskin (FR))
N A Twiston-Davies Bunkers Hill Racing (1)

Placings:30-66464 (1724)
2001/02: 17^{6}GS, 17^{6}G, 22^{4}G, 16^{6}GF, 25^{4}G

	Starts	1st	2nd	3rd	Win & Pl
NH Flat	1	0	0	0	0
Hurdles	4	0	0	0	0
Career Total	**7**	**0**	**0**	**1**	**216**

Going: Sf: 0-0 GS: 0-1 Gd: 0-3 GF: - Fm: 0-1
Distance: 2m/2m3: 0-3 2m4-2m7: 0-1 3m+: 0-1
Track: LH: 0-4 RH: 0-1 Tight: 0-2 Gall: 0-0
Aids: Bl: 0-0 Vi: 0-0 Tstrap: 0-0
Best Rating: 101 11/00 Hrfd 2m1f soft NHF

Dusty Carpet

78 63

4-y-o ch g Pivotal-Euridice (IRE) (Woodman (USA))
M J Weeden (C A Dwyer 15/10) Mrs M C M Walters

Placings:04F (4736)
2001/02: 16^{0}GS, 17^{4}GS, 17^{F}F

	Starts	1st	2nd	3rd	Win & Pl
Hurdles	3	0	0	0	0
Career Total	**3**	**0**	**0**	**0**	**0**

Going: Sf: 0-0 GS: 0-2 Gd: 0-0 GF: - Fm: 0-1
Distance: 2m/2m3: 0-3 2m4-2m7: 0-0 3m+: 0-0
Track: LH: 0-0 RH: 0-3 Tight: 0-1 Gall: 0-0
Aids: Bl: 0-0 Vi: 0-0 Tstrap: 0-0
Best Rating: 66 4/02 Tntn 2m1f gd-sft Hdl

A winner on the sand, he has shown little over hurdles.

Dusty Democrat

96 68

4-y-o b g Democratic (USA)-Two Shots (Dom Racine (FR))
W G M Turner T.O.C.S. Ltd

Placings:0005656P (3709)
2001/02: 17^{0}G, 16^{0}G, 17^{0}GF, 17^{5}F, 16^{6}GS, 17^{5}GS, 16^{6}G, 16^{P}HY

	Starts	1st	2nd	3rd	Win & Pl
Hurdles	8	0	0	0	0
Career Total	**8**	**0**	**0**	**0**	**0**

Going: Sf: 0-1 GS: 0-2 Gd: 0-3 GF: - Fm: 0-2
Distance: 2m/2m3: 0-8 2m4-2m7: 0-0 3m+: 0-0
Track: LH: 0-3 RH: 0-5 Tight: 0-5 Gall: 0-0
Aids: Bl: 0-0 Vi: 0-7 Tstrap: 0-1
Best Rating: 68 11/01 Tntn 2m1f gd-sft Hdl

Dusty Princess

4-y-o gr f Aragon-Lady Seren (IRE) (Doulab (USA))
Mrs J R Buckley Miss Sarah Buckley

Placings:P (2324)
2001/02: 16^{P}S

	Starts	1st	2nd	3rd	Win & Pl
Hurdles	1	0	0	0	
Career Total	**1**	**0**	**0**	**0**	

Going: Sf: 0-1 GS: 0-0 Gd: 0-0 GF: - Fm: 0-0
Distance: 2m/2m3: 0-1 2m4-2m7: 0-0 3m+: 0-0
Track: LH: 0-1 RH: 0-0 Tight: 0-1 Gall: 0-0
Aids: Bl: 0-0 Vi: 0-0 Tstrap: 0-0
Best Rating:

Dutch Dyane

95 85

9-y-o b m Midyan (USA)-Double Dutch (Nicholas Bill)
G P Enright L Fuller, Miss P Ross, Neil Kenworthy

Placings:0024/4331/1531F2/34040P-3P0 (4136)
2001/02: 22^{3}S, 20^{P}G, 22^{0}GS

	Starts	1st	2nd	3rd	Win & Pl
Hurdles	3	0	0	1	483
Career Total	**25**	**3**	**3**	**5**	**16470**

108	1/00	Leic	2m4f110y	E(0-115)HHdl	SFT	£5492
96	11/99	Font	2m6f110y	F(0-110)HHdl	GD	£2320
94	11/98	Leic	2m4f110y	E(0-100)HHdl	SFT	£2882

Total win prize-money £10695

Going: Sf: 0-1 GS: 0-1 Gd: 0-1 GF: - Fm: 0-0
Distance: 2m/2m3: 0-0 2m4-2m7: 0-3 3m+: 0-0
Track: LH: 0-1 RH: 0-2 Tight: 0-1 Gall: 0-0
Aids: Bl: 0-0 Vi: 0-0 Tstrap: 0-0
Best Rating: 112 11/00 Newb 2m3f soft Hdl

Very moderate hurdler, stays two miles-six and appreciates soft ground.

Dutch Nightingale

92 80

8-y-o b m Warrshan (USA)-Double Dutch (Nicholas Bill)
G P Enright The Aedean Partnership

Placings:6/50U/P0-00 (0679)
2001/02: 19^{0}GF, 17^{0}G

	Starts	1st	2nd	3rd	Win & Pl
Hurdles	2	0	0	0	
Career Total	**8**	**0**	**0**	**0**	**0**

Going: Sf: 0-0 GS: 0-0 Gd: 0-1 GF: - Fm: 0-1
Distance: 2m/2m3: 0-1 2m4-2m7: 0-1 3m+: 0-0
Track: LH: 0-2 RH: 0-0 Tight: 0-2 Gall: 0-0
Aids: Bl: 0-2 Vi: 0-0 Tstrap: 0-0
Best Rating: 80 5/01 Ling 2m3f110y gd-fm Hdl

Dutchess

3

7-y-o b m Lord Americo-Lady Vulmid (Sir Lark)
Mrs H Pudd Mrs H Pudd

Placings:0P60-PP (1952)
2001/02: 24^{P}GF, 22^{P}GF

	Starts	1st	2nd	3rd	Win & Pl
Hurdles	2	0	0	0	
Career Total	**6**	**0**	**0**	**0**	**0**

Going: Sf: 0-0 GS: 0-0 Gd: 0-0 GF: - Fm: 0-2
Distance: 2m/2m3: 0-0 2m4-2m7: 0-1 3m+: 0-1
Track: LH: 0-0 RH: 0-1 Tight: 0-0 Gall: 0-0
Aids: Bl: 0-0 Vi: 0-0 Tstrap: 0-0
Best Rating: 62 2/01 Tntn 2m1f heavy Hdl

Duxey's Shadow (IRE)

56f 67f

4-y-o ch g Fourstars Allstar (USA)-Island Shadow (IRE) (Nearly A Nose (USA))
G A Ham Corey M Gardner

Placings:0 (4603)
2001/02: 16^{0}GF

	Starts	1st	2nd	3rd	Win & Pl
NH Flat	1	0	0	0	
Career Total	**1**	**0**	**0**	**0**	

Going: Sf: 0-0 GS: 0-0 Gd: 0-0 GF: - Fm: 0-1
Distance: 2m/2m3: 0-1 2m4-2m7: 0-0 3m+: 0-0
Track: LH: 0-1 RH: 0-0 Tight: 0-0 Gall: 0-0
Aids: Bl: 0-0 Vi: 0-0 Tstrap: 0-0
Best Rating: 67 4/02 Wwck 2m gd-fm NHF

Dynamic Lord (IRE)

8-y-o b/br g Mister Lord (USA)-Hill Side Glen (Goldhill)
J M Turner J M Turner

Placings:260B0/413FP/UP-00 (0229)
2001/02: 26^{0}G, 30^{0}GF

	Starts	1st	2nd	3rd	Win & Pl
Chases	2	0	0	0	
Career Total	**14**	**1**	**1**	**1**	**4506**

113 12/99 Sedg 2m5f E Ch G-S £3109
Total win prize-money £3110

Going: Sf: 0-0 GS: 0-0 Gd: 0-1 GF: - Fm: 0-1
Distance: 2m/2m3: 0-0 2m4-2m7: 0-0 3m+: 0-2
Track: LH: 0-0 RH: 0-2 Tight: 0-1 Gall: 0-1
Aids: Bl: 0-0 Vi: 0-0 Tstrap: 0-0
Best Rating: **113** 12/99 Sedg 2m5f gd-sft Ch

Eagle Canyon (IRE)

95 **73**
9-y-o b/br g Persian Bold-Chrism (Baptism)
D M Lloyd (R T Phillips 31/5) D M Lloyd

Placings:0P/050032/0F05P-035P (0953)
2001/02: 20^{0}G, 21^{3}GF, 22^{5}GF, 20^{P}S

	Starts	1st	2nd	3rd	Win & Pl
Hurdles	4	0	0	1	270
Career Total	**17**	**0**	**1**	**2**	**1874**

Going: Sf: 0-1 GS: 0-0 Gd: 0-1 GF: - Fm: 0-2
Distance: 2m/2m3: 0-0 2m4-2m7: 0-4 3m+: 0-0
Track: LH: 0-3 RH: 0-1 Tight: 0-2 Gall: 0-1
Aids: Bl: 0-2 Vi: 0-0 Tstrap: 0-0
Best Rating: **89** 4/99 Bang 2m1f good Hdl

Earl Sigurd (IRE)

106 **103**
4-y-o ch g High Kicker (USA)-My Kind (Mon Tresor)
L Lungo William Jardine

Placings:3131 (2512)
2001/02: 16^{3}G, 16^{1}G, 16^{3}G, 16^{1}S

	Starts	1st	2nd	3rd	Win & Pl
Hurdles	4	2	0	2	7409
Career Total	**4**	**2**	**0**	**2**	**7409**

103 12/01 Catt 2m D Hdl SFT £3997
88 10/01 Kels 2m110y E Hdl GD £2618
Total win prize-money £6616

Going: Sf: 1-1 GS: 0-0 Gd: 1-3 GF: - Fm: 0-0
Distance: **2m/2m3: 2-4** 2m4-2m7: 0-0 3m+: 0-0
Track: **LH: 2-3** RH: 0-1 **Tight: 2-2** Gall: 0-1
Aids: Bl: 0-0 Vi: 0-0 Tstrap: 0-0
Best Rating: **103** 12/01 Catt 2m soft Hdl

A maiden on the Flat. Has scored twice from four starts over hurdles. Has won on a sound surface and soft ground.

Earls Seat (IRE)

7-y-o b g Lord Americo-Merry Love (Golden Love)
J I A Charlton M H Walton

Placings:*01*-24F (2916)
2001/02: 16^{2}G, 16^{4}G, 20^{F}HY

	Starts	1st	2nd	3rd	Win & Pl
NH Flat	2	0	1	0	1893
Hurdles	1	0	0	0	0
Career Total	**5**	**1**	**1**	**0**	**4035**

111 4/01 Hntg 2m110y H NHF SFT £2142
Total win prize-money £2142

Going: Sf: 0-1 GS: 0-0 Gd: 0-2 GF: - Fm: 0-0
Distance: 2m/2m3: 0-2 2m4-2m7: 0-1 3m+: 0-0

Track: LH: 0-3 RH: 0-0 Tight: 0-0 Gall: 0-0
Aids: Bl: 0-0 Vi: 0-0 Tstrap: 0-0
Best Rating: **111** 11/01 Chel 2m110y good NHF

Looked a promising sort in bumpers before taking a fatal fall on his hurdling debut.

Early Dawn

110 **85**
8-y-o ch m Rakaposhi King-Early Run (Deep Run)
C Grant Peter Dowson

Placings:PP (4915)
2001/02: 16^{P}GF, 17^{P}GF

	Starts	1st	2nd	3rd	Win & Pl
Hurdles	2	0	0	0	
Career Total	**2**	**0**	**0**	**0**	

Going: Sf: 0-0 GS: 0-0 Gd: 0-0 GF: - Fm: 0-2
Distance: 2m/2m3: 0-2 2m4-2m7: 0-0 3m+: 0-0
Track: LH: 0-2 RH: 0-0 Tight: 0-1 Gall: 0-0
Aids: Bl: 0-0 Vi: 0-0 Tstrap: 0-0
Best Rating:

Early Morning Call (IRE)

10-y-o ch g Henbit (USA)-Golonig (Goldhill)
Paul Keane (Ms A E Embiricos 20/1) The It's My Job Partnership

Placings:3/232/2P (3817)
2001/02: 25^{2}HY, 21^{P}S

	Starts	1st	2nd	3rd	Win & Pl
Chases	2	0	1	0	533
Career Total	**6**	**0**	**3**	**2**	**3283**

Going: Sf: 0-2 GS: 0-0 Gd: 0-0 GF: - Fm: 0-0
Distance: 2m/2m3: 0-0 2m4-2m7: 0-1 3m+: 0-1
Track: LH: 0-0 RH: 0-2 Tight: 0-1 Gall: 0-0
Aids: Bl: 0-0 Vi: 0-0 Tstrap: 0-0
Best Rating: **88** 2/00 Fknm 3m110y good Ch

Modest pointer/hunter chaser, best on good ground or softer.

Early Riser

4-y-o b f Primitive Rising (USA)-Coneygree (Northern State (USA))
C C Bealby P M Bradley

Placings:*00* (4910)
2001/02: 17^{0}GS, 17^{0}G

	Starts	1st	2nd	3rd	Win & Pl
NH Flat	2	0	0	0	
Career Total	**2**	**0**	**0**	**0**	

Going: Sf: 0-0 GS: 0-1 Gd: 0-1 GF: - Fm: 0-0
Distance: 2m/2m3: 0-2 2m4-2m7: 0-0 3m+: 0-0
Track: LH: 0-0 RH: 0-2 Tight: 0-2 Gall: 0-0
Aids: Bl: 0-0 Vi: 0-0 Tstrap: 0-0
Best Rating: **50** 3/02 MRas 2m1f110y gd-sft NHF

Earthmover (IRE)

116(116h) **162**
11-y-o ch g Mister Lord (USA)-Clare's Crystal (Tekoah)
P F Nicholls R M Penny

Placings:11111/FU0P/511536F/112233U0-1342P3 (4815)
2001/02: 24^{1}G, 27^{3}G, 25^{4}G, 26^{2}S, 24^{P}GS, 21^{3}GF

	Starts	1st	2nd	3rd	Win & Pl
Chases	6	1	1	2	34798
Career Total	**30**	**10**	**3**	**5**	**126210**

160 10/01 Chep 3m B(0-145)HCh GD £9937
162 5/00 Weth 3m1f B(0-145)HCh G-S £9486
158 5/00 Chep 3m B(0-145)HCh FRM £8703
151 11/99 Chep 3m B(0-150)HHdl SFT £6824
141 10/99 Chel 3m1f110y D Hdl GD £4531
161 3/98 Chel 3m2f110y B Ch GD £18957
135 3/98 Newb 3m H Ch SFT £1576
129 2/98 Wwck 3m2f H Ch GD £1086
117 5/97 Strf 3m4f H Ch GD £4272
110 5/97 Chep 3m H Ch G-S £3434
Total win prize-money £68811

Going: Sf: 0-1 GS: 0-1 Gd: 1-3 GF: - Fm: 0-1
Distance: 2m/2m3: 0-0 2m4-2m7: 0-1 **3m+: 1-5**
Track: **LH: 1-6** RH: 0-0 Tight: 0-0 Gall: 0-4
Aids: Bl: 0-0 Vi: 0-0 Tstrap: 0-0
Best Rating: **162** 1/02 Wwck 3m2f soft Ch

He won at Chepstow under top weight in October 2001 and has run with credit since. He stays well and acts on any going, but probably best on a sound surface and his jumping this term has been much improved. Goes well fresh and is game.

Easby Blue

110(91h) (79h)**89**
10-y-o b g Teenoso (USA)-Mellie (Impecunious)
J A Pickering S Kitching

Placings:*513/5*/20P/1F434/000**4F5534334F3P** (4602)
2001/02: 16^{0}GF, 16^{0}GF, 16^{0}GF, 16^{4}G, 21^{F}G, 24^{5}G, 17^{5}S, 16^{3}GF, 16^{4}G, 20^{3}S, 16^{3}S, 20^{4}S, 20^{F}HY, 16^{3}HY, 20^{P}GF

	Starts	1st	2nd	3rd	Win & Pl
Hurdles	3	0	0	0	0
Chases	12	0	0	4	2360
Career Total	**27**	**2**	**1**	**6**	**7561**

97 6/99 Prth 2m110y E Hdl G-S £2724
103 3/97 Catt 2m H NHF G-S £1175
Total win prize-money £3899

Going: Sf: 0-6 GS: 0-0 Gd: 0-4 GF: - Fm: 0-5
Distance: 2m/2m3: 0-9 2m4-2m7: 0-5 3m+: 0-1
Track: LH: 0-8 RH: 0-6 Tight: 0-4 Gall: 0-2
Aids: Bl: 0-0 Vi: 0-0 Tstrap: 0-3
Best Rating: **104** 4/97 Prth 2m110y good NHF

Modest novice chaser, best at two miles.

East Hill (IRE)

100 **107**
6-y-o b g Satco (FR)-Sharmalyne (FR) (Melyno)
G B Balding Mr & Mrs Tony Geake

Placings:*341*-2240 (3483)
2001/02: 17^{2}G, 21^{2}G, 21^{4}S, 17^{0}HY

	Starts	1st	2nd	3rd	Win & Pl
Hurdles	4	0	2	0	2399
Career Total	**7**	**1**	**2**	**1**	**4554**

106 4/01 Font 2m2f110y H NHF GD £1914
Total win prize-money £1915

Going: Sf: 0-2 GS: 0-0 Gd: 0-2 GF: - Fm: 0-0
Distance: 2m/2m3: 0-2 2m4-2m7: 0-2 3m+: 0-0
Track: LH: 0-1 RH: 0-2 Tight: 0-0 Gall: 0-1
Aids: Bl: 0-0 Vi: 0-0 Tstrap: 0-0
Best Rating: **107** 11/01 Kemp 2m5f good Hdl

Made a promising hurdling debut, having shown form in

bumpers in 2000/01. Running well over hurdles but looks a future chaser.

Eastdon Gold Dust

104 **113**

9-y-o b g Gold Dust-Aunt Etty (Record Token)

R J Baker M A Swift

Placings:3O3P0/04F055P6/535**342112/016-242P** **(1153)**

2001/02: 26^{2}GF, 26^{4}GF, 21^{2}G, 26^{P}GF

	Starts	1st	2nd	3rd	Win & Pl
Chases	4	0	2	0	2472
Career Total	**29**	**3**	**4**	**4**	**15731**

113	5/00	NAbb	2m5f110y	D(0-120)HCh	G-F	£3779
95	9/99	NAbb	2m110y	F(0-100)HCh	G-F	£2583
106	8/99	NAbb	2m5f110y	F(0-105)HCh	GD	£2962

Total win prize-money £9325

Going: Sf: 0-0 GS: 0-0 Gd: 0-1 GF: - Fm: 0-3
Distance: 2m/2m3: 0-0 2m4-2m7: 0-1 3m+: 0-3
Track: LH: 0-4 RH: 0-0 Tight: 0-4 Gall: 0-0
Aids: Bl: 0-0 Vi: 0-0 Tstrap: 0-0
Best Rating: 113 7/01 NAbb 2m5f110y good Ch

Moderate West Country chaser, a regular at newton abbot where he goes well. Stays three miles plus and acts on a sound surface.

Easter Bonnet

4-y-o ch f My Generation-Flower Othe Forest (Indian Forest (USA))

N M Babbage B Babbage

Placings:P **(4682)**

2001/02: 17^{P}GF

	Starts	1st	2nd	3rd	Win & Pl
Hurdles	1	0	0	0	
Career Total	**1**	**0**	**0**	**0**	

Going: Sf: 0-0 GS: 0-0 Gd: 0-0 GF: - Fm: 0-1
Distance: 2m/2m3: 0-1 2m4-2m7: 0-0 3m+: 0-0
Track: LH: 0-0 RH: 0-1 Tight: 0-0 Gall: 0-0
Aids: Bl: 0-0 Vi: 0-0 Tstrap: 0-0
Best Rating:

Eastern Project (IRE)

99 **104**

8-y-o b g Project Manager-Diandra (Shardari)

A Crook Steve Semple

Placings:546533/312321333/331**122254P/500-3F0456** **(0970)**

2001/02: 16^{3}GF, 16^{F}F, 16^{0}GS, 16^{4}GF, 16^{5}GS, 17^{6}GS

	Starts	1st	2nd	3rd	Win & Pl
Hurdles	1	0	0	0	0
Chases	5	0	0	1	1058
Career Total	**34**	**4**	**5**	**10**	**27167**

123	6/99	Sthl	2m	B(0-145)HHdl	G-F	£8676
117	6/99	Prth	2m110y	E(0-115)HHdl	SFT	£2749
114	11/98	Ayr	2m	E Hdl	G-S	£2600
96	6/98	Prth	2m110y	E(0-100)HHdl	G-F	£2634

Total win prize-money £16660

Going: Sf: 0-0 GS: 0-3 Gd: 0-0 GF: - Fm: 0-3
Distance: 2m/2m3: 0-6 2m4-2m7: 0-0 3m+: 0-0
Track: LH: 0-3 RH: 0-2 Tight: 0-1 Gall: 0-0
Aids: Bl: 0-6 Vi: 0-0 Tstrap: 0-0
Best Rating: 123 6/99 Sthl 2m gd-fm Hdl

Eastern Red

4-y-o b f Contract Law (USA)-Gagajulu (Al Hareb (USA))

Miss M Bragg (Ronald Thompson 25/6) Miss M Bragg

Placings:PF **(2535)**

2001/02: 17^{P}G, 16^{F}G

	Starts	1st	2nd	3rd	Win & Pl
Hurdles	2	0	0	0	
Career Total	**2**	**0**	**0**	**0**	

Going: Sf: 0-0 GS: 0-0 Gd: 0-2 GF: - Fm: 0-0
Distance: 2m/2m3: 0-2 2m4-2m7: 0-0 3m+: 0-0
Track: LH: 0-0 RH: 0-2 Tight: 0-0 Gall: 0-0
Aids: Bl: 0-0 Vi: 0-0 Tstrap: 0-0
Best Rating:

Eastern Tribute (USA)

107 **116**

6-y-o b g Affirmed (USA)-Mia Duchessa (USA) (Nijinsky (CAN))

A C Whillans John J Elliot

Placings:33F44/51410202-033225P42 **(4879)**

2001/02: 20^{0}S, 16^{3}S, 20^{3}GS, 20^{2}HY, 20^{2}S, 20^{5}HY, 20^{P}HY, 18^{4}HY, 16^{2}G

	Starts	1st	2nd	3rd	Win & Pl
Hurdles	9	0	3	2	6437
Career Total	**22**	**2**	**5**	**4**	**17497**

110	1/01	Ayr	2m	D(0-125)HHdl	SFT	£3388
98	11/00	Ayr	2m	E Hdl	SFT	£1974

Total win prize-money £5362

Going: Sf: 0-7 GS: 0-1 Gd: 0-1 GF: - Fm: 0-0
Distance: 2m/2m3: 0-3 2m4-2m7: 0-6 3m+: 0-0
Track: LH: 0-7 RH: 0-1 Tight: 0-1 Gall: 0-0
Aids: Bl: 0-0 Vi: 0-0 Tstrap: 0-0
Best Rating: 112 12/01 Hayd 2m4f heavy Hdl

A winner over hurdles, he is suited by a soft surface and goes well between two miles and two miles four furlongs.

Easthorpe

14-y-o b g Sweet Monday-Crammond Brig (New Brig)

Mrs J Fitzgerald Mrs J Fitzgerald

Placings:6P20126/5131203/**12U51231221/11111126/20422P/P546115/6366045U35/4235U3/6** **(0227)**

2001/02: 24^{6}GF

	Starts	1st	2nd	3rd	Win & Pl
Chases	1	0	0	0	0
Career Total	**63**	**15**	**12**	**7**	**112965**

136	3/98	Donc	2m3f110y	C(0-135)HCh	SFT	£14530
136	2/98	MRas	2m4f	C(0-135)HCh	GD	£10406
135	1/96	Winc	2m	(0-135)HCh	GD	£6760
136	1/96	Sand	2m	B HCh	G-S	£7230
126	12/95	Hayd	2m	B(0-140)HCh	GD	£8013
131	11/95	Hayd	2m	B(0-140)HCh	G-F	£7210
127	10/95	Chel	2m110y	B HCh	G-F	£6807
116	9/95	NAbb	2m110y	C(0-130)HCh	G-S	£4372
115	4/95	MRas	2m1f110y	D(0-120)HCh	G-F	£3910
107	3/95	Donc	2m110y	D Ch	GD	£3470
107	12/94	Ludl	2m	Ch	GD	£2573
94	9/94	Tntn	2m110y	Ch	G-F	£2788
112	1/94	Nott	2m	(0-120)HHdl	SFT	£2226
100	11/93	Wind	2m	(0-130)HHdl	GD	£3132
98	2/93	Wolv	2m110y	Hdl	GD	£1484

Total win prize-money £84913

Going: Sf: 0-0 GS: 0-0 Gd: 0-0 GF: - Fm: 0-1
Distance: 2m/2m3: 0-0 2m4-2m7: 0-0 3m+: 0-1
Track: LH: 0-0 RH: 0-1 Tight: 0-0 Gall: 0-1
Aids: Bl: 0-0 Vi: 0-0 Tstrap: 0-0
Best Rating: 140 1/97 Hayd 2m gd-fm Ch

Eastlands Hi-Light

13-y-o ch g Saxon Farm-Light O' Love (Lighter)

J G Staveley J G Staveley

Placings:24/6/U254232/66P/0 **(4690)**

2001/02: 25^{0}GF

	Starts	1st	2nd	3rd	Win & Pl
Chases	1	0	0	0	
Career Total	**14**	**0**	**4**	**1**	**2847**

Going: Sf: 0-0 GS: 0-0 Gd: 0-0 GF: - Fm: 0-1
Distance: 2m/2m3: 0-0 2m4-2m7: 0-0 3m+: 0-1
Track: LH: 0-1 RH: 0-0 Tight: 0-1 Gall: 0-0
Aids: Bl: 0-0 Vi: 0-0 Tstrap: 0-0
Best Rating: 102 4/98 Ayr 3m3f110y good Ch

Easton Gale

99 **133**

8-y-o b g Strong Gale-Laurello (Bargello)

Ferdy Murphy Exors Of The Late Mr G A Hubbard

Placings:05252/1PPP/1113F-16 **(2686)**

2001/02: 24^{1}S, 26^{6}G

	Starts	1st	2nd	3rd	Win & Pl
Chases	2	1	0	0	4669
Career Total	**16**	**5**	**2**	**1**	**27822**

133	11/01	Fknm	3m110y	D(0-120)HCh	SFT	£4669
133	10/00	Fknm	2m5f110y	C Ch	GD	£6548
128	6/00	Fknm	3m110y	E(0-115)HCh	GD	£5271
114	5/00	Towc	2m6f	E Ch	G-F	£2983
120	10/99	Uttx	2m6f110y	C Hdl	G-S	£5204

Total win prize-money £24678

Going: Sf: 1-1 GS: 0-0 Gd: 0-1 GF: - Fm: 0-0
Distance: 2m/2m3: 0-0 2m4-2m7: 0-0 **3m+: 1-2**
Track: **LH: 1-2** RH: 0-0 **Tight: 1-1** Gall: 0-1
Aids: Bl: 0-0 Vi: 0-0 Tstrap: 0-0
Best Rating: 133 11/01 Fknm 3m110y soft Ch

Fair chaser, lightly-raced of late. Goes well at Fakenham, acts on any ground.

Eastwell Hall

91 **105**

7-y-o b g Saddlers' Hall (IRE)-Kinchenjunga (Darshaan)

T P McGovern Eastwell Manor Racing

Placings:F41246213/644PP-5 **(0476)**

2001/02: 19^{5}G

	Starts	1st	2nd	3rd	Win & Pl
Hurdles	1	0	0	0	0
Career Total	**15**	**2**	**2**	**1**	**13989**

138	4/00	Asct	2m4f	C Hdl	GD	£5005
106	12/99	Wwck	2m	E Hdl	SFT	£2784

Total win prize-money £7789

Going: Sf: 0-0 GS: 0-0 Gd: 0-1 GF: - Fm: 0-0
Distance: 2m/2m3: 0-0 2m4-2m7: 0-1 3m+: 0-0

Track: LH: 0-0 RH: 0-1 Tight: 0-1 Gall: 0-0
Aids: Bl: 0-0 Vi: 0-0 Tstrap: 0-0
Best Rating: 139 3/00 Chel 2m110y good Hdl

A decent novice hurdler in 2000, he has lost his way and been lightly-raced since.

Eastwell Manor

93 **80**

4-y-o b g Dancing Spree (USA)-Kinchenjunga (Darshaan)
Miss M Bragg (T P McGovern 22/8) George Standing

Placings:PP **(4530)**
2001/02: 17^{P}GS, 20^{P}GS

	Starts	1st	2nd	3rd	Win & Pl
Hurdles	2	0	0	0	
Career Total	**2**	**0**	**0**	**0**	

Going: Sf: 0-0 GS: 0-2 Gd: 0-0 GF: - Fm: 0-0
Distance: 2m/2m3: 0-1 2m4-2m7: 0-1 3m+: 0-0
Track: LH: 0-1 RH: 0-0 Tight: 0-0 Gall: 0-0
Aids: Bl: 0-1 Vi: 0-0 Tstrap: 0-0
Best Rating:

Eastwood Drifter (USA)

92 **70**

5-y-o ch g Woodman (USA)-Mandarina (USA) (El Gran Senor (USA))
B G Powell The Late Carmine Giannini And Son

Placings:0P5-05 **(0552)**
2001/02: 16^{0}F, 21^{5}GF

	Starts	1st	2nd	3rd	Win & Pl
Hurdles	2	0	0	0	0
Career Total	**5**	**0**	**0**	**0**	**0**

Going: Sf: 0-0 GS: 0-0 Gd: 0-0 GF: - Fm: 0-2
Distance: 2m/2m3: 0-1 2m4-2m7: 0-1 3m+: 0-0
Track: LH: 0-1 RH: 0-1 Tight: 0-1 Gall: 0-1
Aids: Bl: 0-0 Vi: 0-0 Tstrap: 0-1
Best Rating: 70 5/01 Hntg 2m5f110y gd-fm Hdl

Easy Baron

8-y-o gr g Baron Blakeney-Flying Easy (Swing Easy (USA))
R J Baker Mrs N S Farley

Placings:PP/0-R **(1035)**
2001/02: 21^{R}G

	Starts	1st	2nd	3rd	Win & Pl
Chases	1	0	0	0	
Career Total	**4**	**0**	**0**	**0**	

Going: Sf: 0-0 GS: 0-0 Gd: 0-1 GF: - Fm: 0-0
Distance: 2m/2m3: 0-0 2m4-2m7: 0-1 3m+: 0-0
Track: LH: 0-1 RH: 0-0 Tight: 0-1 Gall: 0-0
Aids: Bl: 0-0 Vi: 0-0 Tstrap: 0-0
Best Rating:

Easy Tiger (FR)

91f **76f**

4-y-o ch g Sillery (USA)-Extreme Dream (FR) (Zino)
N J Henderson Team Tiger

Placings:0 **(4032)**
2001/02: 16^{0}GS

	Starts	1st	2nd	3rd	Win & Pl
NH Flat	1	0	0	0	
Career Total	**1**	**0**	**0**	**0**	

Going: Sf: 0-0 GS: 0-1 Gd: 0-0 GF: - Fm: 0-0
Distance: 2m/2m3: 0-1 2m4-2m7: 0-0 3m+: 0-0
Track: LH: 0-1 RH: 0-0 Tight: 0-0 Gall: 0-1
Aids: Bl: 0-0 Vi: 0-0 Tstrap: 0-0
Best Rating: 56 3/02 Newb 2m110y gd-sft NHF

Eaton Dove

93 **61**

9-y-o gr g Little Wolf-Another Dove (Grey Love)
C J Price Mrs M Price

Placings:0/P/P00/PP-00560 **(1239)**
2001/02: 16^{0}GF, 16^{0}GF, 17^{5}F, 20^{6}GF, 20^{0}GF

	Starts	1st	2nd	3rd	Win & Pl
Hurdles	5	0	0	0	0
Career Total	**12**	**0**	**0**	**0**	**0**

Going: Sf: 0-0 GS: 0-0 Gd: 0-0 GF: - Fm: 0-5
Distance: 2m/2m3: 0-3 2m4-2m7: 0-2 3m+: 0-0
Track: LH: 0-3 RH: 0-2 Tight: 0-1 Gall: 0-1
Aids: Bl: 0-0 Vi: 0-0 Tstrap: 0-0
Best Rating: 74 2/00 Ludl 2m good Hdl

Eau De Cologne

120 **159**

10-y-o b g Persian Bold-No More Rosies (Warpath)
Mrs L Richards Ms M Evans

Placings:3212/1F2342611/42/**2116**/42113-20P32UP **(4913)**
2001/02: 21^{2}G, 20^{0}G, 25^{P}G, 21^{3}S, 24^{2}G, 25^{U}C, 29^{P}G

	Starts	1st	2nd	3rd	Win & Pl
Chases	7	0	2	1	29418
Career Total	**31**	**8**	**9**	**4**	**107153**

159	3/01	Asct	2m3f110y	B HCh	SFT	£10088
153	12/00	Kemp	3m	C(0-130)HCh	G-S	£11310
154	3/00	Newb	3m	C(0-140)HCh	G-F	£10520
147	3/00	Winc	2m5f	D Ch	G-S	£4387
138	4/98	Asct	3m	B HHdl	SFT	£5193
141	2/98	Newb	3m110y	C(0-130)HHdl	GD	£4130
113	5/97	Hrfd	2m3f110y	E Hdl	GD	£2070
107	3/97	Plum	2m4f	E Hdl	G-F	£2826

Total win prize-money £50526

Going: Sf: 0-1 GS: 0-0 Gd: 0-6 GF: - Fm: 0-0
Distance: 2m/2m3: 0-0 2m4-2m7: 0-3 3m+: 0-4
Track: LH: 0-3 RH: 0-4 Tight: 0-1 Gall: 0-2
Aids: Bl: 0-1 Vi: 0-0 Tstrap: 0-0
Best Rating: 159 2/02 Kemp 3m good Ch

Useful handicap chaser. He is effective at two and a half to three miles and acts on most types of ground, but does not want it too heavy. He is apparently a lazy horse and is difficult to get ready at home.

Eau Pure (FR)

(50h) (46h)

5-y-o b m Epervier Bleu-Eau De Nuit (King's Lake (USA))
B A Pearce (Jack Barbe 3/10) Trevor Painting

Placings:005-0FP4613000 **(2515)**
2001/02: 17^{0}S, 15^{F}, 17^{P}, 17^{4}, 18^{6}, 17^{1}S, 17^{3}VS, 19^{0}VS, 17^{0}VS, 16^{0}S

	Starts	1st	2nd	3rd	Win & Pl
Hurdles	3	0	0	0	0
Chases	7	1	0	1	7953
Career Total	**13**	**1**	**0**	**1**	**8340**

	8/01	Diep	2m1f110y	Ch	SFT	£3686

Total win prize-money £3686

Going: Sf: 1-3 GS: 0-0 Gd: 0-0 GF: - Fm: 0-0
Distance: **2m/2m3: 1-9** 2m4-2m7: 0-0 3m+: 0-0
Track: LH: 0-1 RH: 0-0 Tight: 0-1 Gall: 0-0
Aids: Bl: 0-0 Vi: 0-0 Tstrap: 0-0
Best Rating: 46 12/01 Plum 2m soft Hdl

Winner of a chase in France on soft ground, well beaten on British debut over hurdles.

Eau So Sloe

11-y-o b g Baron Blakeney-Final Attraction (Jalmood (USA))
F L Matthews Mrs L Danton

Placings:5/0PF4F4P/2/PP0P/PPPP/PPPUP **(4376)**
2001/02: 25^{P}G, 16^{P}G, 21^{P}GS, 16^{U}S, 20^{P}S

	Starts	1st	2nd	3rd	Win & Pl
Chases	5	0	0	0	
Career Total	**22**	**0**	**1**	**0**	**1075**

Going: Sf: 0-2 GS: 0-1 Gd: 0-2 GF: - Fm: 0-0
Distance: 2m/2m3: 0-2 2m4-2m7: 0-2 3m+: 0-1
Track: LH: 0-1 RH: 0-3 Tight: 0-2 Gall: 0-0
Aids: Bl: 0-4 Vi: 0-0 Tstrap: 0-0
Best Rating: 86 12/95 Folk 2m1f110y good NHF

Eaux Les Coeurs (FR)

103 **104**

5-y-o b m Saint Cyrien (FR)-Lamakara (FR) (Akarad (FR))
A M Hales Andrew L Cohen

Placings:023-R1FP **(4267)**
2001/02: 24^{R}GS, 22^{1}S, 21^{F}HY, 24^{P}S

	Starts	1st	2nd	3rd	Win & Pl
Hurdles	3	1	0	0	2646
Chases	1	0	0	0	0
Career Total	**7**	**1**	**1**	**1**	**7659**

100	2/02	Folk	2m6f110y	E Hdl	SFT	£2646

Total win prize-money £2646

Going: Sf: 1-3 GS: 0-1 Gd: 0-0 GF: - Fm: 0-0
Distance: 2m/2m3: 0-0 **2m4-2m7: 1-2** 3m+: 0-2
Track: LH: 0-3 **RH: 1-1 Tight: 1-3** Gall: 0-0
Aids: Bl: 0-0 Vi: 0-0 Tstrap: 0-0
Best Rating: 104 2/02 Plum 2m5f heavy Hdl

Placed over fences in France, but a casualty on her British debut when falling twice in the farcical race at Southwell. Facile victory over an extended two miles-six over hurdles on the soft next time, but struggled subsequently.

Ebinzayd (IRE)

107 **126**

6-y-o b g Tenby-Sharakawa (IRE) (Darshaan)
L Lungo Miss S Blumberg

Placings:0/12113-2U0 **(4667)**
2001/02: 20^{2}GF, 16^{U}S, 20^{0}G

	Starts	1st	2nd	3rd	Win & Pl
Hurdles	2	0	1	0	1048
Chases	1	0	0	0	0
Career Total	**9**	**3**	**2**	**1**	**11926**

119	4/01	Muss	2m1f	D Hdl		G-F	£3822
109	1/01	Muss	2m	E Hdl		G-S	£2254
116	11/00	Kels	2m110y	E Hdl		SFT	£2964

Total win prize-money £9040

Going: Sf: 0-1 GS: 0-0 Gd: 0-1 GF: - Fm: 0-1
Distance: 2m/2m3: 0-1 2m4-2m7: 0-2 3m+: 0-0
Track: LH: 0-1 RH: 0-2 Tight: 0-2 Gall: 0-0
Aids: Bl: 0-0 Vi: 0-0 Tstrap: 0-0
Best Rating: 126 4/02 Aint 2m4f good Hdl

Useful on the Flat for Ed Dunlop, he finished lame on his hurdles debut and jumped poorly first time over fences. He ran with promise on his return to hurdles at Aintree. Stays two and a half miles.

Ebony Light (IRE)

102 **100**

6-y-o br g Buckskin (FR)-Amelioras Daughter (General Ironside)
D McCain Roger Bellamy

Placings: *40213* **(4842)**
2001/02: 17^{4}GS, 16^{0}S, 27^{2}S, 24^{1}HY, 20^{3}G

	Starts	1st	2nd	3rd	Win & Pl
NH Flat	2	0	0	0	0
Hurdles	3	1	1	1	3898
Career Total	**5**	**1**	**1**	**1**	**3898**

100	3/02	Uttx	3m110y	E Hdl		HVY	£2702

Total win prize-money £2702

Going: Sf: 1-3 GS: 0-1 Gd: 0-1 GF: - Fm: 0-0
Distance: 2m/2m3: 0-2 2m4-2m7: 0-1 **3m+: 1-2**
Track: **LH: 1-5** RH: 0-0 Tight: 0-3 Gall: 0-0
Aids: Bl: 0-0 Vi: 0-0 Tstrap: 0-0
Best Rating: 100 4/02 Bang 2m4f good Hdl

Big sort, novice hurdler he is effective at three miles plus and recorded his win in soft ground at Uttoxeter.

Echo Du Lac (FR)

113 **113**

6-y-o b g Matahawk-Love Dream (FR) (Platonic Love)
A King (P R Webber 12/5) Jerry Wright

Placings: 46/3P10-P3 **(2788)**
2001/02: 21^{P}GF, 20^{3}G

	Starts	1st	2nd	3rd	Win & Pl
Hurdles	2	0	0	1	1075
Career Total	**8**	**1**	**0**	**2**	**4647**

110	3/01	Ling	2m110y	E(0-105)HHdl		HVY	£2933

Total win prize-money £2933

Going: Sf: 0-0 GS: 0-0 Gd: 0-1 GF: - Fm: 0-1
Distance: 2m/2m3: 0-0 2m4-2m7: 0-2 3m+: 0-0
Track: LH: 0-0 RH: 0-1 Tight: 0-0 Gall: 0-0
Aids: Bl: 0-0 Vi: 0-0 Tstrap: 0-1
Best Rating: 113 12/01 Asct 2m4f good Hdl

He cannot have the ground too soft and relished the bottomless ground when winning at Lingfield in March 2001.

Echo's Of Dawn (IRE)

108 **134**

10-y-o ch g Duky-Nicenames (IRE) (Decent Fellow)
John R Upson Middleham Park Racing Xvii

Placings: UP532/4112U153/1626P **(4414)**
2001/02: 24^{1}S, 24^{6}G, 24^{2}GS, 24^{6}GS, 28^{P}S

	Starts	1st	2nd	3rd	Win & Pl
Chases	5	1	1	0	16002
Career Total	**18**	**4**	**3**	**2**	**32855**

134	11/01	Bang	3m110y	C(0-130)HCh		SFT	£6955
134	1/00	Ludl	3m	E(0-105)HCh		GD	£3818
127	11/99	Uttx	2m5f	E(0-115)HCh		G-S	£4182
119	11/99	Uttx	2m4f	E(0-105)HCh		SFT	£2957

Total win prize-money £17913

Going: Sf: 1-2 GS: 0-2 Gd: 0-1 GF: - Fm: 0-0
Distance: 2m/2m3: 0-0 2m4-2m7: 0-0 **3m+: 1-5**
Track: **LH: 1-3** RH: 0-1 **Tight: 1-1** Gall: 0-2
Aids: Bl: 0-0 Vi: 0-0 Tstrap: 0-0
Best Rating: 134 2/02 Sand 3m110y gd-sft Ch

Fair three-mile chaser. Goes on good ground or softer. Returned from a long absence with a win at Bangor in November 2001, and was a good second to Billingsgate in the Agfa Diamond Handicap at Sandown. Stays three miles, acts on soft ground but has won on good.

Eco Warrior (IRE)

9-y-o ch g Be My Native (USA)-Kerry Minstrel (Black Minstrel)
Mrs A Bell (D J G Murray Smith 10/2) Mrs A Bell

Placings: 05/522P/3-2 **(4777)**
2001/02: 25^{2}G

	Starts	1st	2nd	3rd	Win & Pl
Chases	1	0	1	0	336
Career Total	**8**	**0**	**3**	**1**	**2511**

Going: Sf: 0-0 GS: 0-0 Gd: 0-1 GF: - Fm: 0-0
Distance: 2m/2m3: 0-0 2m4-2m7: 0-0 3m+: 0-1
Track: LH: 0-0 RH: 0-1 Tight: 0-1 Gall: 0-0
Aids: Bl: 0-0 Vi: 0-0 Tstrap: 0-0
Best Rating: 107 1/00 Sthl 3m110y gd-sft Ch

Moderate hunter chaser/pointer, acts on good or softer. Not the best of jumpers.

Ecuyer Du Roi (FR)

107 **123**

6-y-o b g Roi De Rome (USA)-Mill's Cambric (FR) (Iron Duke (FR))
M C Pipe R Stanley

Placings: 1522F6P/**2P121** **(4783)**
2001/02: 21^{2}GF, 20^{P}G, 26^{1}GF, 24^{2}G, 29^{1}GF

	Starts	1st	2nd	3rd	Win & Pl
Chases	5	2	2	0	10368
Career Total	**12**	**3**	**4**	**0**	**26245**

123	4/02	Plum	3m5f	D(0-115)HCh		G-F	£4875
117	6/01	NAbb	3m2f110y	F(0-110)HCh		G-F	£3010
	5/99	Engh	1m7f	Hdl		VS	£6997

Total win prize-money £14882

Going: Sf: 0-0 GS: 0-0 Gd: 0-2 GF: - Fm: 2-3
Distance: 2m/2m3: 0-0 2m4-2m7: 0-2 **3m+: 2-3**
Track: **LH: 1-4** RH: 0-0 **Tight: 1-3** Gall: 0-0
Aids: Bl: 0-0 Vi: 0-0 **Tstrap: 2-5**
Best Rating: 123 4/02 Plum 3m5f gd-fm Ch

Lightly raced staying chaser up to three miles five. Likes a sound surface.

Eddie (IRE)

10-y-o b g Orchestra-Bavette (Le Bavard (FR))
P England (Mrs John Harrington 3/3) P England

Placings: P4/062P32/5/0310424/U **(4288)**
2001/02: 25^{U}GS

	Starts	1st	2nd	3rd	Win & Pl
Chases	1	0	0	0	
Career Total	**17**	**1**	**3**	**2**	**7511**

104	1/00	Punc	3m	Ch		SFT	£3864

Total win prize-money £3864

Going: Sf: 0-0 GS: 0-1 Gd: 0-0 GF: - Fm: 0-0
Distance: 2m/2m3: 0-0 2m4-2m7: 0-0 3m+: 0-1
Track: LH: 0-0 RH: 0-1 Tight: 0-1 Gall: 0-0
Aids: Bl: 0-0 Vi: 0-0 Tstrap: 0-0
Best Rating: 111 1/00 Punc 2m yld-sft Ch

Modest winning pointer who has stamina limitations.

Eddie Rombo

7-y-o b g Aragon-Jolimo (Fortissimo)
Mrs S M Odell W J Odell

Placings: P055000P060/0/**50-003P** **(4057)**
2001/02: 20^{0}GF, 21^{0}GF, 24^{3}S, 23^{P}S

	Starts	1st	2nd	3rd	Win & Pl
Chases	4	0	0	1	165
Career Total	**18**	**0**	**0**	**1**	**165**

Going: Sf: 0-2 GS: 0-0 Gd: 0-0 GF: - Fm: 0-2
Distance: 2m/2m3: 0-0 2m4-2m7: 0-2 3m+: 0-2
Track: LH: 0-1 RH: 0-3 Tight: 0-1 Gall: 0-2
Aids: Bl: 0-0 Vi: 0-0 Tstrap: 0-0
Best Rating: 90 2/02 Hntg 3m soft Ch

Modest hunter chaser. Stays three miles in the mud.

Eddy's Son (IRE)

10-y-o b g Brush Aside (USA)-Light The Lamp (Miners Lamp)
I McMath (R T Phillips 20/1) Mrs A J McMath

Placings: 1/142/20/05-24 **(3749)**
2001/02: 24^{2}G, 24^{4}S

	Starts	1st	2nd	3rd	Win & Pl
Hurdles	1	0	1	0	976
Chases	1	0	0	0	0
Career Total	**10**	**2**	**3**	**0**	**5520**

125	11/98	Wwck	2m	H NHF		SFT	£1465
111	11/97	Wwck	2m	H NHF		G-S	£1035

Total win prize-money £2501

Going: Sf: 0-1 GS: 0-0 Gd: 0-1 GF: - Fm: 0-0
Distance: 2m/2m3: 0-0 2m4-2m7: 0-0 3m+: 0-2
Track: LH: 0-1 RH: 0-1 Tight: 0-2 Gall: 0-0
Aids: Bl: 0-0 Vi: 0-0 Tstrap: 0-0
Best Rating: 125 12/98 Chep 2m110y heavy NHF

Ede'Iff

87 **67**

5-y-o b m Tragic Role (USA)-Flying Amy (Norwick (USA))
W G M Turner Hawks And Doves Racing Syndicate

Placings: P400-5 **(4589)**
2001/02: 16^{5}G

	Starts	1st	2nd	3rd	Win & Pl
Hurdles	1	0	0	0	0
Career Total	**5**	**0**	**0**	**0**	**0**

Going: Sf: 0-0 GS: 0-0 Gd: 0-1 GF: - Fm: 0-0
Distance: 2m/2m3: 0-1 2m4-2m7: 0-0 3m+: 0-0
Track: LH: 0-0 RH: 0-1 Tight: 0-0 Gall: 0-0

Aids: Bl: 0-0 Vi: 0-0 Tstrap: 0-0
Best Rating: 81 11/00 Tntn 2m1f gd-sft Hdl

Eden Dancer

105(94h) (98h)137

10-y-o b g Shareef Dancer (USA)-Dash (Connaught)
M C Pipe Geoffrey Hamilton

Placings:32241/1333003/21124**FF5**06/64P0/1011412/310**11234-01156PP** **(3467)**
2001/02: 16^{0}GF, 20^{1}G, 20^{1}G, 16^{5}GF, 20^{6}G, 20^{P}S, 19^{P}S

	Starts	1st	2nd	3rd	Win & Pl
Hurdles	1	0	0	0	0
Chases	6	2	0	0	13894
Career Total	**48**	**13**	**6**	**7**	**65068**

137	8/01	Bang	2m4f110y	D(0-125)HCh	GD	£7020
133	6/01	Worc	2m4f110y	C(0-130)HCh	GD	£6873
133	9/00	Plum	2m1f	E Ch	GD	£3780
125	9/00	Sedg	2m110y	E Ch	GD	£3607
137	6/00	MRas	2m1f110y	D Ch	G-F	£5992
127	10/99	Ludl	2m	D(0-120)HHdl	G-F	£3680
125	7/99	MRas	2m1f110y	B(0-140)HHdl	G-F	£10220
121	7/99	MRas	2m1f110y	F(0-105)HHdl	G-F	£1928
114	5/99	Extr	2m1f	G(0-95)HHdl	G-F	£1968
105	9/97	Prth	2m110y	F Hdl	G-F	£2283
104	8/97	Sedg	2m1f	F Hdl	G-F	£2020
100	5/96	Prth	2m110y	D Hdl	G-F	£2736
106	2/96	Muss	2m	E Hdl	G-F	£2630

Total win prize-money £54741

Going: Sf: 0-2 GS: 0-0 Gd: 2-3 GF: - Fm: 0-2
Distance: 2m/2m3: 0-2 **2m4-2m7: 2-5** 3m+: 0-0
Track: **LH: 2-6** RH: 0-1 **Tight: 1-3** Gall: 0-2
Aids: Bl: 0-0 Vi: 0-0 Tstrap: 0-0
Best Rating: 137 8/01 Bang 2m4f110y good Ch

A tough front runner, he is suited by fast ground and had a successful time summer jumping in 2001, but failed to build on that during the winter months. Best around at two and a half miles, he is useful when allowed to bully inferior opposition.

Edgar Gink (IRE)

101 (92h)102

8-y-o ch g Step Together (USA)-Turbo Run (Deep Run)
S E H Sherwood The For Example Partnership

Placings:5P-4P53 **(4162)**
2001/02: 25^{4}G, 25^{P}G, 24^{5}S, 20^{3}G

	Starts	1st	2nd	3rd	Win & Pl
Hurdles	1	0	0	0	0
Chases	3	0	0	1	623
Career Total	**6**	**0**	**0**	**1**	**623**

Going: Sf: 0-1 GS: 0-0 Gd: 0-3 GF: - Fm: 0-0
Distance: 2m/2m3: 0-0 2m4-2m7: 0-1 3m+: 0-3
Track: LH: 0-1 RH: 0-2 Tight: 0-0 Gall: 0-0
Aids: Bl: 0-0 Vi: 0-0 Tstrap: 0-1
Best Rating: 102 3/02 Wwck 2m4f110y good Ch

Limited ability in novice chases. Best at distances short of three miles.

Edgatorius (IRE)

62f 91f

6-y-o b g Phardante (FR)-Silent Shot (Random Shot)
B Smart Mrs Julie Martin

Placings:0 **(4499)**
2001/02: 16^{0}G

	Starts	1st	2nd	3rd	Win & Pl
NH Flat	1	0	0	0	
Career Total	**1**	**0**	**0**	**0**	

Going: Sf: 0-0 GS: 0-0 Gd: 0-1 GF: - Fm: 0-0
Distance: 2m/2m3: 0-1 2m4-2m7: 0-0 3m+: 0-0
Track: LH: 0-1 RH: 0-0 Tight: 0-0 Gall: 0-0
Aids: Bl: 0-0 Vi: 0-0 Tstrap: 0-0
Best Rating: 91 3/02 Hayd 2m good NHF

Irish pointer. Looked headstrong and difficult to steer on his bumper debut here.

Edgely (IRE)

7-y-o b g Warcraft (USA)-Clodagh's Treasure (Tarqogan)
K G Wingrove K O Warner

Placings:0 **(4842)**
2001/02: 20^{0}G

	Starts	1st	2nd	3rd	Win & Pl
Hurdles	1	0	0	0	
Career Total	**1**	**0**	**0**	**0**	

Going: Sf: 0-0 GS: 0-0 Gd: 0-1 GF: - Fm: 0-0
Distance: 2m/2m3: 0-0 2m4-2m7: 0-1 3m+: 0-0
Track: LH: 0-1 RH: 0-0 Tight: 0-1 Gall: 0-0
Aids: Bl: 0-0 Vi: 0-0 Tstrap: 0-0
Best Rating:

Edifice (JPN)

6-y-o ch g Carroll House-Moon Tosho (JPN) (Steel Heart)
B Ellison Keith Middleton

Placings:0P **(1676)**
2001/02: 17^{0}GS, 17^{P}G

	Starts	1st	2nd	3rd	Win & Pl
Hurdles	2	0	0	0	
Career Total	**2**	**0**	**0**	**0**	

Going: Sf: 0-0 GS: 0-1 Gd: 0-1 GF: - Fm: 0-0
Distance: 2m/2m3: 0-2 2m4-2m7: 0-0 3m+: 0-0
Track: LH: 0-2 RH: 0-0 Tight: 0-2 Gall: 0-0
Aids: Bl: 0-0 Vi: 0-0 Tstrap: 0-0
Best Rating:

Edipo Re

104 93

10-y-o b g Slip Anchor-Lady Barrister (Law Society (USA))
Ian Williams Tony Eaves

Placings:0/6001/2-1165 **(1398)**
2001/02: 16^{1}GF, 16^{1}F, 17^{6}F, 16^{5}GF

	Starts	1st	2nd	3rd	Win & Pl
Hurdles	4	2	0	0	4568
Career Total	**10**	**3**	**1**	**0**	**6704**

93	5/01	Weth	2m	F(0-100)HHdl	FRM	£2100
90	5/01	Hntg	2m110y	F(0-100)HHdl	G-F	£2467
79	4/00	Hntg	2m110y	G(0-95)HHdl	GD	£1666

Total win prize-money £6234

Going: Sf: 0-0 GS: 0-0 Gd: 0-0 GF: - Fm: 2-4
Distance: **2m/2m3: 2-4** 2m4-2m7: 0-0 3m+: 0-0
Track: LH: 1-2 RH: 1-2 Tight: 0-0 **Gall: 1-1**
Aids: Bl: 0-0 Vi: 0-0 Tstrap: 0-0
Best Rating: 93 5/01 Weth 2m firm Hdl

Very moderate handicap hurdler, suited by two miles and fast ground.

Edmond (FR)

108 143

10-y-o b g Video Rock (FR)-Galia Iii (FR) (Baraban)
H D Daly Lady Knutsford

Placings:2/2F111/**1133F1/1112P/033PF-403P** **(4299)**
2001/02: 26^{4}HY, 29^{0}GS, 28^{3}HY, 34^{P}HY

	Starts	1st	2nd	3rd	Win & Pl
Chases	4	0	0	1	8230
Career Total	**26**	**9**	**3**	**5**	**113161**

156	12/99	Chep	3m5f110y	A HCh	HVY	£40300
143	12/99	Chep	3m2f110y	C(0-130)HCh	SFT	£10796
139	11/99	Chep	3m	D(0-125)HCh	SFT	£3818
133	4/99	Uttx	3m2f	E Ch	G-S	£3582
140	12/98	Towc	2m6f	D Ch	SFT	£4175
135	11/98	Extr	2m6f110y	D Ch	SFT	£3782
130	3/98	Newb	3m110y	D Hdl	G-S	£3078
130	3/98	Extr	3m2f	E Hdl	SFT	£2574
117	12/97	Hntg	3m2f	E Hdl	G-S	£2582

Total win prize-money £74691

Going: Sf: 0-3 GS: 0-1 Gd: 0-0 GF: - Fm: 0-0
Distance: 2m/2m3: 0-0 2m4-2m7: 0-0 3m+: 0-4
Track: LH: 0-3 RH: 0-1 Tight: 0-0 Gall: 0-0
Aids: Bl: 0-3 Vi: 0-0 Tstrap: 0-0
Best Rating: 156 2/00 Uttx 3m4f soft Ch

He won the Welsh National in 1999 but has found life tougher off higher marks since. Very genuine at his best, he looked mulish when pulled up in the Northern National in February 2001 and was ridden too aggressively before trying to refuse at the Chair in the 2001 Grand National when blinkered. Now has something to prove. Suited by soft or heavy ground.

Edredon Bleu (FR)

115 178

10-y-o b g Grand Tresor (FR)-Nuit Bleue Iii (FR) (Le Pontet (FR))
Miss H C Knight Jim Lewis

Placings:1520P/41111F/41212/51331/3161-1243 **(4912)**
2001/02: 20^{1}GS, 16^{2}GS, 16^{4}GS, 16^{3}G

	Starts	1st	2nd	3rd	Win & Pl
Chases	4	1	1	1	66850
Career Total	**29**	**12**	**4**	**4**	**423288**

178	11/01	Hntg	2m4f110y	A Ch	G-S	£30000
177	4/01	Sand	2m	A Ch	G-S	£49300
178	11/00	Hntg	2m4f110y	A Ch	G-S	£27000
176	3/00	Chel	2m	A Ch	GD	£107300
173	11/99	Hntg	2m4f110y	A Ch	G-F	£23750
173	2/99	Sand	2m	B HCh	GD	£8036
170	11/98	Hntg	2m4f110y	A Ch	GD	£18211
156	3/98	Chel	2m110y	B HCh	GD	£29611
154	2/98	Sand	2m	B(0-145)HCh	G-F	£7578
144	12/97	Kemp	2m4f110y	B HCh	SFT	£12741
140	12/97	Leic	2m4f110y	C(0-130)HCh	GD	£4945

Total win prize-money £318474

Going: Sf: 0-0 GS: 1-3 Gd: 0-1 GF: - Fm: 0-0
Distance: 2m/2m3: 0-3 **2m4-2m7: 1-1** 3m+: 0-0
Track: LH: 0-1 **RH: 1-3** Tight: 0-0 **Gall: 1-2**
Aids: Bl: 0-0 Vi: 0-0 **Tstrap: 1-4**
Best Rating: 178 11/01 Hntg 2m4f110y gd-sft Ch

Top-class chaser, winner of the Queen Mother Champion Chase in 2000, he was denied the chance to defend his crown in 2001 by the loss of the Festival and was not helped by the softish ground when fourth in the 2002 running. He stays two and a half miles and has won four successive runnings of the Peterborough Chase at Huntingdon. A good jumper, he has won on soft ground, but his attacking style of racing is best suited to fast conditions.

Edwarda

96(92h) (106h)**107**

7-y-o ch m Safawan-Edraianthus (Windjammer (USA))

M C Pipe Roger Stanley & Yvonne Reynolds

Placings:3152P/122124/22**323**-F434 **(1340)**

2001/02: 23^{F}G, 20^{4}GF, 20^{3}GF, 22^{4}GF

	Starts	1st	2nd	3rd	Win & Pl
Hurdles	2	0	0	1	271
Chases	2	0	0	0	260
Career Total	**20**	**3**	**7**	**4**	**24265**

132	3/00	Newb	2m110y	D(0-125)HHdl	SFT	£5343
104	5/99	Ctml	2m1f110y	D Hdl	GD	£2892
107	11/98	Wwck	2m	D Hdl	SFT	£3276

Total win prize-money £11511

Going: Sf: 0-0 GS: 0-0 Gd: 0-1 GF: - Fm: 0-3
Distance: 2m/2m3: 0-0 2m4-2m7: 0-3 3m+: 0-1
Track: LH: 0-4 RH: 0-0 Tight: 0-2 Gall: 0-0
Aids: Bl: 0-0 Vi: 0-4 Tstrap: 0-0
Best Rating: 134 6/00 Strf 2m110y good Hdl

Fair hurdler, has looked less effective over fences. Acts on any ground, usually wears a visor

Effectual

103 **134**

9-y-o b g Efisio-Moharabuiee (Pas De Seul)

Miss Venetia Williams B C Dice

Placings:311211145/3311564/201255343/20-6600 **(4647)**

2001/02: 21^{6}HY, 24^{6}GS, 24^{0}G, 24^{0}G

	Starts	1st	2nd	3rd	Win & Pl
Hurdles	4	0	0	0	0
Career Total	**31**	**8**	**4**	**5**	**85961**

156	12/99	Chel	3m	B HHdl	GD	£6911
140	1/99	Font	2m2f110y	C(0-130)HHdl	SFT	£4735
138	12/98	Donc	2m110y	B HHdl	GD	£5020
136	3/98	Chep	2m110y	B Hdl	SFT	£13745
132	3/98	Donc	2m110y	C(0-135)Hdl	SFT	£4090
130	2/98	Weth	2m	B(0-145)HHdl	GD	£5455
127	12/97	Tntn	2m1f	D Hdl	GD	£3018
125	12/97	NAbb	2m1f	E Hdl	HVY	£2148

Total win prize-money £45125

Going: Sf: 0-1 GS: 0-1 Gd: 0-2 GF: - Fm: 0-0
Distance: 2m/2m3: 0-0 2m4-2m7: 0-1 3m+: 0-3
Track: LH: 0-2 RH: 0-1 Tight: 0-1 Gall: 0-1
Aids: Bl: 0-0 Vi: 0-0 Tstrap: 0-0
Best Rating: 159 5/00 Punc 3m good Hdl

A smart hurdler at his best, he has not always looked a straightforward ride. Fourth to Bacchanal in the 2000 Stayers' Hurdle at the Cheltenham Festival, he only ran twice in the early part of the 2000/2001 season. Absent for over a year with a tendon injury, he reappeared in January 2002 and has been well held. Stays three miles. Has won on good and soft ground. Needs good ground over three miles.

Egypt

104 **87**

4-y-o b g Green Desert (USA)-Just You Wait (Nonoalco (USA))

Miss K Marks (Sir Mark Prescott 30/10) Nick Shutts

Placings:P66554 **(4601)**

2001/02: 16^{P}S, 16^{6}S, 17^{6}S, 16^{5}S, 16^{5}GS, 16^{4}GF

	Starts	1st	2nd	3rd	Win & Pl
Hurdles	6	0	0	0	0
Career Total	**6**	**0**	**0**	**0**	**0**

Going: Sf: 0-4 GS: 0-1 Gd: 0-0 GF: - Fm: 0-1
Distance: 2m/2m3: 0-6 2m4-2m7: 0-0 3m+: 0-0
Track: LH: 0-4 RH: 0-2 Tight: 0-2 Gall: 0-1
Aids: Bl: 0-0 Vi: 0-0 Tstrap: 0-0
Best Rating: 87 1/02 Catt 2m soft Hdl

Successful at around a mile on the Flat, he has shown only moderate form over hurdles, winning at Uttoxeter in heavy ground in June.

Egypt Point (IRE)

82f **72f**

5-y-o b g Jurado (USA)-Cherry Jubilee (Le Bavard (FR))

D G Bridgwater Long Hill Partnership

Placings:*0* **(4910)**

2001/02: 17^{0}G

	Starts	1st	2nd	3rd	Win & Pl
NH Flat	1	0	0	0	
Career Total	**1**	**0**	**0**	**0**	

Going: Sf: 0-0 GS: 0-0 Gd: 0-1 GF: - Fm: 0-0
Distance: 2m/2m3: 0-1 2m4-2m7: 0-0 3m+: 0-0
Track: LH: 0-0 RH: 0-1 Tight: 0-1 Gall: 0-0
Aids: Bl: 0-0 Vi: 0-0 Tstrap: 0-0
Best Rating: 72 4/02 MRas 2m1f110y good NHF

Ehtefaal (USA)

93 **88**

11-y-o b g Alysheba (USA)-Bolt From The Blue (USA) (Blue Times (USA))

J S King Mrs Marygold O'Kelly

Placings:1BF004/452/3242233/12530/006425/21/000-4645 **(1147)**

2001/02: 22^{4}GS, 22^{6}GF, 21^{4}GF, 24^{5}GF

	Starts	1st	2nd	3rd	Win & Pl
Hurdles	4	0	0	0	0
Career Total	**36**	**3**	**7**	**4**	**14878**

100	5/99	Extr	2m6f	E(0-115)HHdl	G-F	£3322
103	5/97	Towc	2m5f	D(0-125)HHdl	G-F	£2819
82	7/94	NAbb	2m1f	Hdl	G-F	£1838

Total win prize-money £7981

Going: Sf: 0-0 GS: 0-1 Gd: 0-0 GF: - Fm: 0-3
Distance: 2m/2m3: 0-0 2m4-2m7: 0-3 3m+: 0-1
Track: LH: 0-1 RH: 0-2 Tight: 0-1 Gall: 0-1
Aids: Bl: 0-0 Vi: 0-0 Tstrap: 0-0
Best Rating: 103 5/97 Chep 2m4f110y gd-sft Hdl

Ei Ei

112(105h) (101h)**138**

7-y-o b g North Briton-Branitska (Mummy's Pet)

M C Chapman (M Hill 15/7) Mrs S M Richards

Placings:0641121111540246032 **(4851)**

2001/02: 16^{0}GF, 17^{6}G, 17^{4}GS, 16^{1}GF, 16^{1}GF, 17^{2}GS, 17^{1}GF, 20^{1}S, 16^{1}G, 16^{1}G, 16^{5}GS, 16^{4}G, 16^{0}GS, 16^{2}G, 16^{4}G, 16^{6}S, 16^{0}GS, 17^{3}G, 20^{2}G

	Starts	1st	2nd	3rd	Win & Pl
Hurdles	7	1	0	1	3044
Chases	12	5	3	0	23457
Career Total	**19**	**6**	**3**	**1**	**26500**

138	10/01	Sthl	2m	E(0-115)HCh	GD	£3386
122	10/01	Sedg	2m110y	E(0-115)HCh	GD	£3265
137	9/01	MRas	2m4f	F(0-110)HCh	SFT	£3916
134	9/01	Strf	2m1f110y	D(0-120)HCh	G-F	£4127
102	8/01	Sthl	2m	F(0-100)HCh	G-F	£2775
91	7/01	Strf	2m110y	G Hdl	G-F	£1967

Total win prize-money £19440

Going: Sf: 1-2 GS: 0-5 Gd: 2-8 GF: - Fm: 3-4
Distance: 2m/2m3: 5-17 2m4-2m7: 1-2 3m+: 0-0
Track: LH: 5-13 RH: 1-6 **Tight: 6-12** Gall: 0-4
Aids: Bl: 0-0 Vi: 0-0 Tstrap: 0-0
Best Rating: 138 10/01 Sthl 2m good Ch

A plating-class hurdler. Much better over fences where his front-running tactics have proved to be effective. Best at around two miles.

Eight (IRE)

6-y-o ch g Thatching-Up To You (Sallust)

C G Cox Charles Curtis

Placings:P **(2684)**

2001/02: 16^{P}G

	Starts	1st	2nd	3rd	Win & Pl
Hurdles	1	0	0	0	
Career Total	**1**	**0**	**0**	**0**	

Going: Sf: 0-0 GS: 0-0 Gd: 0-1 GF: - Fm: 0-0
Distance: 2m/2m3: 0-1 2m4-2m7: 0-0 3m+: 0-0
Track: LH: 0-1 RH: 0-0 Tight: 0-0 Gall: 0-1
Aids: Bl: 0-0 Vi: 0-0 Tstrap: 0-0
Best Rating:

Eightsome

86 **53**

6-y-o b m Broadsword (USA)-Glen Dancer (Furry Glen)

E L James Nicholas Cowan & Mrs R V James

Placings:*0-0*0000 **(4048)**

2001/02: 17^{0}G, 17^{0}S, 16^{0}GS, 16^{0}S, 19^{0}G

	Starts	1st	2nd	3rd	Win & Pl
NH Flat	2	0	0	0	0
Hurdles	3	0	0	0	0
Career Total	**6**	**0**	**0**	**0**	

Going: Sf: 0-2 GS: 0-1 Gd: 0-2 GF: - Fm: 0-0
Distance: 2m/2m3: 0-5 2m4-2m7: 0-0 3m+: 0-0
Track: LH: 0-1 RH: 0-4 Tight: 0-1 Gall: 0-2
Aids: Bl: 0-0 Vi: 0-0 Tstrap: 0-0
Best Rating: 65 12/01 Hrfd 2m1f soft NHF

Eileen Alanna (IRE)

101 **84**

10-y-o b m Rashar (USA)-Kilcotty Wonder (Peacock (FR))

G F Edwards G F Edwards

Placings:*02244244FP0P/4621660P*-00124 **(2778)**

2001/02: 21^{0}GF, 21^{0}GS, 27^{1}G, 27^{2}S, 22^{4}G

	Starts	1st	2nd	3rd	Win & Pl
Hurdles	5	1	1	0	2640
Career Total	**25**	**2**	**5**	**0**	**8065**

78	11/01	Sedg	3m3f110y	F(0-100)HHdl	GD	£2198
98	11/00	MRas	2m5f110y	F Hdl	G-S	£1951

Total win prize-money £4150

Going: Sf: 0-1 GS: 0-1 Gd: 1-2 GF: - Fm: 0-1
Distance: 2m/2m3: 0-0 2m4-2m7: 0-3 **3m+: 1-2**
Track: LH: 1-3 RH: 0-1 **Tight: 1-3** Gall: 0-1
Aids: Bl: 0-0 Vi: 0-0 Tstrap: 0-0
Best Rating: 98 11/00 MRas 2m5f110y gd-sft Hdl

A fustrating sort, she has been placed numerous times and, bar two modest hurdle wins, has proved short of toe at the business end. She prefers to be held up, stays three miles three furlongs and is suited by cut in the ground.

Eirawe (FR)

29

9-y-o b g Lashkari-Ederiya (FR) (Top Ville)
M J M Evans Mrs J Z Munday

Placings: *60235/06030/05/54500-0* **(0241)**
2001/02: 16^{0}GF

	Starts	1st	2nd	3rd	Win & Pl
Hurdles	1	0	0	0	
Career Total	**18**	**0**	**1**	**2**	**687**

Going: Sf: 0-0 GS: 0-0 Gd: 0-0 GF: - Fm: 0-1
Distance: 2m/2m3: 0-1 2m4-2m7: 0-0 3m+: 0-0
Track: LH: 0-1 RH: 0-0 Tight: 0-0 Gall: 0-0
Aids: Bl: 0-0 Vi: 0-0 Tstrap: 0-0
Best Rating: 88 9/97 MRas 1m5f110y good NHF

Eirienne (IRE)

88(79h) (49h)**68**

7-y-o ch m Be My Native (USA)-Donegal Star (Quayside)
R H Alner Pell-Mell Partners

Placings: *2P*-006U **(2138)**
2001/02: 17^{0}GF, 22^{0}G, 21^{6}G, 19^{U}G

	Starts	1st	2nd	3rd	Win & Pl
Hurdles	2	0	0	0	0
Chases	2	0	0	0	0
Career Total	**6**	**0**	**1**	**0**	**472**

Going: Sf: 0-0 GS: 0-0 Gd: 0-3 GF: - Fm: 0-1
Distance: 2m/2m3: 0-2 2m4-2m7: 0-2 3m+: 0-0
Track: LH: 0-1 RH: 0-3 Tight: 0-4 Gall: 0-0
Aids: Bl: 0-0 Vi: 0-0 Tstrap: 0-0
Best Rating: 108 11/00 Extr 2m1f gd-sft NHF

Ekeus (IRE)

12-y-o ch g Henbit (USA)-Flying Early (Ballyciptic)
P Greenwood (J S King 17/2) Mrs G Greenwood

Placings: *0006/03*P42/11PP3P/543251544/552P35P/0-P **(4659)**
2001/02: 24^{P}G

	Starts	1st	2nd	3rd	Win & Pl
Chases	1	0	0	0	
Career Total	**33**	**3**	**3**	**4**	**18136**

98	11/98	Winc	2m5f	E(0-115)HCh	G-S	£4240
88	11/97	Wind	3m	E(0-100)HCh	G-F	£3507
84	11/97	Tntn	2m3f	E(0-100)HCh	GD	£4279

Total win prize-money £12029

Going: Sf: 0-0 GS: 0-0 Gd: 0-1 GF: - Fm: 0-0
Distance: 2m/2m3: 0-0 2m4-2m7: 0-0 3m+: 0-1
Track: LH: 0-0 RH: 0-1 Tight: 0-1 Gall: 0-0
Aids: Bl: 0-0 Vi: 0-0 Tstrap: 0-0
Best Rating: 98 10/99 Winc 3m1f110y gd-fm Ch

El Bandito (IRE)

83(97h) (87h)**76**

8-y-o ch g Un Desperado (FR)-Red Marble (Le Bavard (FR))
J Howard Johnson J Coupe

Placings: *52/13*30-4P55F00 **(4898)**
2001/02: 20^{4}G, 17^{P}GS, 24^{5}GS, 19^{5}G, 20^{F}G, 24^{0}G, 16^{0}G

	Starts	1st	2nd	3rd	Win & Pl
Hurdles	5	0	0	0	0
Chases	2	0	0	0	0
Career Total	**13**	**1**	**1**	**2**	**2964**

105	5/00	Extr	2m1f	H NHF	G-F	£1767

Total win prize-money £1768

Going: Sf: 0-0 GS: 0-2 Gd: 0-5 GF: - Fm: 0-0
Distance: 2m/2m3: 0-3 2m4-2m7: 0-2 3m+: 0-2
Track: LH: 0-3 RH: 0-4 Tight: 0-3 Gall: 0-1
Aids: Bl: 0-0 Vi: 0-0 Tstrap: 0-0
Best Rating: 111 5/00 Worc 2m good NHF

El Blade

106 **120**

5-y-o b g Dashing Blade-Elisha (GER) (Konigsstuhl (GER))
B G Powell The Winning Line

Placings: F2151 **(4128)**
2001/02: 17^{F}G, 19^{2}S, 19^{1}G, 21^{5}S, 19^{1}G

	Starts	1st	2nd	3rd	Win & Pl
Hurdles	5	2	1	0	6731
Career Total	**5**	**2**	**1**	**0**	**6731**

120	3/02	Hrfd	2m3f110y	D(0-120)HHdl	GD	£3454
107	12/01	Hrfd	2m3f110y	E Hdl	GD	£2513

Total win prize-money £5968

Going: Sf: 0-2 GS: 0-0 Gd: 2-3 GF: - Fm: 0-0
Distance: 2m/2m3: 0-1 **2m4-2m7: 2-4** 3m+: 0-0
Track: LH: 0-1 **RH: 2-4** Tight: 0-1 Gall: 0-0
Aids: Bl: 0-0 Vi: 0-0 Tstrap: 0-0
Best Rating: 120 3/02 Hrfd 2m3f110y good Hdl

Front-running hurdler, stays two and a half miles, goes well at Hereford.

El Cordobes (IRE)

101 **108**

11-y-o b g Torus-Queens Tricks (Le Bavard (FR))
Mrs J R Buckley Mrs J R Buckley

Placings: *3/005000/0/2*P55445/13154213/32010-6654P400 **(4872)**
2001/02: 17^{6}GS, 16^{6}S, 16^{5}GS, 19^{4}S, 20^{P}GS, 17^{4}G, 17^{0}G, 16^{0}GF

	Starts	1st	2nd	3rd	Win & Pl
Chases	8	0	0	0	361
Career Total	**36**	**4**	**3**	**4**	**20899**

108	10/00	Fknm	2m5f110y	F(0-100)HCh	GD	£3563
104	3/00	Donc	2m110y	D(0-110)HCh	G-S	£4134
102	9/99	Hntg	2m110y	E(0-115)HCh	G-F	£3109
100	5/99	Hntg	2m4f110y	F(0-100)HCh	G-F	£3406

Total win prize-money £14214

Going: Sf: 0-2 GS: 0-3 Gd: 0-2 GF: - Fm: 0-1
Distance: 2m/2m3: 0-6 2m4-2m7: 0-2 3m+: 0-0
Track: LH: 0-3 RH: 0-5 Tight: 0-5 Gall: 0-2
Aids: Bl: 0-0 Vi: 0-0 Tstrap: 0-0
Best Rating: 108 12/01 Hntg 2m110y gd-sft Ch

Headstrong front-runner. Effective from two miles to two miles five furlongs. Acts on a sound surface, but also effective with cut in the ground.

El Divino (GER)

89 **93**

7-y-o b g Platini (GER)-Eivissa (GER) (Frontal)
P F Nicholls The Winning Line

Placings: F55 **(4591)**
2001/02: 16^{F}S, 16^{5}G, 16^{5}G

	Starts	1st	2nd	3rd	Win & Pl
Hurdles	3	0	0	0	0
Career Total	**3**	**0**	**0**	**0**	**0**

Going: Sf: 0-1 GS: 0-0 Gd: 0-2 GF: - Fm: 0-0
Distance: 2m/2m3: 0-3 2m4-2m7: 0-0 3m+: 0-0
Track: LH: 0-2 RH: 0-1 Tight: 0-0 Gall: 0-0
Aids: Bl: 0-0 Vi: 0-0 Tstrap: 0-0
Best Rating: 93 3/02 Winc 2m good Hdl

Group winner on the Flat in Germany but has yet to show anything like that level of ability over hurdles. Capable of better and will be interesting when qualified for handicaps. Goes well in soft ground.

El Don

84 **60**

10-y-o b g High Kicker (USA)-Madam Gerard (Brigadier Gerard)
C L Popham El Don Partnership

Placings: 0/12214P13/55142/P0F/FP600/**F5F0-00** **(0562)**
2001/02: 18^{0}GF, 22^{0}GF

	Starts	1st	2nd	3rd	Win & Pl
Hurdles	2	0	0	0	
Career Total	**28**	**4**	**3**	**1**	**18037**

111	10/97	Font	2m2f110y	D(0-125)HHdl	GD	£3416
111	4/97	Chep	2m4f110y	C(0-135)HHdl	FRM	£3533
102	11/96	Weth	2m	B(0-145)HHdl	GD	£4825
100	5/96	Font	2m2f	E Hdl	G-F	£2427

Total win prize-money £14202

Going: Sf: 0-0 GS: 0-0 Gd: 0-0 GF: - Fm: 0-2
Distance: 2m/2m3: 0-1 2m4-2m7: 0-1 3m+: 0-0
Track: LH: 0-2 RH: 0-0 Tight: 0-2 Gall: 0-0
Aids: Bl: 0-0 Vi: 0-0 Tstrap: 0-0
Best Rating: 114 4/99 Fknm 2m4f good Hdl

El Fuerte

98 **42**

7-y-o b g Perpendicular-Sleekit (Blakeney)
W Clay Lee Heath

Placings: 3P540/USP/0P0-0 **(0372)**
2001/02: 16^{0}GF

	Starts	1st	2nd	3rd	Win & Pl
Hurdles	1	0	0	0	
Career Total	**12**	**0**	**0**	**1**	**305**

Going: Sf: 0-0 GS: 0-0 Gd: 0-0 GF: - Fm: 0-1
Distance: 2m/2m3: 0-1 2m4-2m7: 0-0 3m+: 0-0
Track: LH: 0-0 RH: 0-1 Tight: 0-0 Gall: 0-1
Aids: Bl: 0-0 Vi: 0-1 Tstrap: 0-0
Best Rating: 74 3/99 Bang 2m1f gd-sft Hdl

El Hombre Del Rio (IRE)

91f **106f**

5-y-o ch g Over The River (FR)-Hug In A Fog (IRE) (Strong Gale)
R H Alner Perpetual Pub's Lazy Punters Black Book

Placings: *0P* **(4887)**
2001/02: 16^{0}GS, 18^{P}GF

	Starts	1st	2nd	3rd	Win & Pl
NH Flat	2	0	0	0	
Career Total	**2**	**0**	**0**	**0**	

Going: Sf: 0-0 GS: 0-1 Gd: 0-0 GF: - Fm: 0-1
Distance: 2m/2m3: 0-2 2m4-2m7: 0-0 3m+: 0-0
Track: LH: 0-2 RH: 0-0 Tight: 0-1 Gall: 0-1
Aids: Bl: 0-0 Vi: 0-0 Tstrap: 0-0
Best Rating: 106 3/02 Newb 2m110y gd-sft NHF

El Karim (USA)

6-y-o ch h Storm Cat (USA)-Gmaasha (IRE) (Kris)
R Ford R Burgess

Placings:P (0912)
2001/02: 16^{P}GF

	Starts	1st	2nd	3rd	Win & Pl
Hurdles	1	0	0	0	
Career Total	**1**	**0**	**0**	**0**	

Going: Sf: 0-0 GS: 0-0 Gd: 0-0 GF: - Fm: 0-1
Distance: 2m/2m3: 0-1 2m4-2m7: 0-0 3m+: 0-0
Track: LH: 0-1 RH: 0-0 Tight: 0-1 Gall: 0-0
Aids: Bl: 0-0 Vi: 0-0 Tstrap: 0-1
Best Rating:

El Monty (IRE)

103 **126**

7-y-o b g Montelimar (USA)-Tax Code (Workboy)
R H Alner The Collars And Cuffs Partnership

Placings:*25/46*/12 (4149)
2001/02: 17^{1}S, 20^{2}GS

	Starts	1st	2nd	3rd	Win & Pl
Hurdles	2	1	1	0	4099
Career Total	**6**	**1**	**2**	**0**	**4539**

111	12/01	Folk	2m1f110y	E Hdl	SFT	£2555

Total win prize-money £2555

Going: Sf: 1-1 GS: 0-1 Gd: 0-0 GF: - Fm: 0-0
Distance: **2m/2m3: 1-1** 2m4-2m7: 0-1 3m+: 0-0
Track: LH: 0-1 **RH: 1-1 Tight: 1-1** Gall: 0-0
Aids: Bl: 0-0 Vi: 0-0 Tstrap: 0-0
Best Rating: 126 3/02 Chep 2m4f gd-sft Hdl

The booking of McCoy was noteworthy when he beat a long odds-on favourite after a two-year break in December 2001. Good run next time. Acts on soft ground.

El Rubio

(44c) **67**

11-y-o b g Tuam-Woodland Promise (Philemon)
M J Gingell M J Gingell

Placings:*0030*/0415P0/**P50P0F4**/**P0P0-P** (0189)
2001/02: 16^{P}GF

	Starts	1st	2nd	3rd	Win & Pl
Hurdles	1	0	0	0	
Career Total	**22**	**1**	**0**	**1**	**3460**

100	1/96	Hayd	2m	D Hdl	SFT	£3061

Total win prize-money £3061

Going: Sf: 0-0 GS: 0-0 Gd: 0-0 GF: - Fm: 0-1
Distance: 2m/2m3: 0-1 2m4-2m7: 0-0 3m+: 0-0
Track: LH: 0-1 RH: 0-0 Tight: 0-1 Gall: 0-0
Aids: Bl: 0-0 Vi: 0-1 Tstrap: 0-0
Best Rating: 100 2/96 Hayd 2m soft Hdl

El Viejo (IRE)

108 **120**

5-y-o b g Norwich-Shuil Na Gale (Strong Gale)
L Wells Mrs Carrie Zetter-Wells

Placings:*33-311*P2P (4229)
2001/02: 17^{3}GS, 16^{1}GS, 20^{1}G, 20^{P}S, 21^{2}G, 21^{P}GS

	Starts	1st	2nd	3rd	Win & Pl
NH Flat	2	1	0	1	2684
Hurdles	4	1	1	0	9256
Career Total	**8**	**2**	**1**	**3**	**12719**

120	11/01	Asct	2m4f	C Hdl	GD	£4966
110	11/01	Sand	2m110y	H NHF	G-S	£2425

Total win prize-money £7392

Going: Sf: 0-1 GS: 1-3 Gd: 1-2 GF: - Fm: 0-0
Distance: 2m/2m3: 1-2 2m4-2m7: 1-4 3m+: 0-0
Track: LH: 0-1 **RH: 2-5** Tight: 0-0 Gall: 0-1
Aids: Bl: 0-0 Vi: 0-0 Tstrap: 0-0
Best Rating: 120 2/02 Kemp 2m5f good Hdl

Bred to stay. Placed in some decent bumpers before winning one in good style at Sandown in November. Followed up with hurdles debut win in decent company, but pulled up with breathing problems when upped in class next time. Suited by at least two and a half miles over hurdles, he ran really well in a handicap at Kempton after a break. Will make a chaser.

El Zito (IRE)

106 **122**

5-y-o b g Mukaddamah (USA)-Samite (FR) (Tennyson (FR))
M G Quinlan Mario Lanfranchi

Placings:16245-1 (0062)
2001/02: 17^{1}GS

	Starts	1st	2nd	3rd	Win & Pl
Hurdles	1	1	0	0	3621
Career Total	**6**	**2**	**1**	**0**	**7713**

122	5/01	Folk	2m1f110y	F(0-110)HHdl	G-S	£3620
107	12/00	Folk	2m1f110y	E Hdl	HVY	£2730

Total win prize-money £6351

Going: Sf: 0-0 GS: 1-1 Gd: 0-0 GF: - Fm: 0-0
Distance: **2m/2m3: 1-1** 2m4-2m7: 0-0 3m+: 0-0
Track: LH: 0-0 **RH: 1-1 Tight: 1-1** Gall: 0-0
Aids: Bl: 0-0 Vi: 0-0 **Tstrap: 1-1**
Best Rating: 122 5/01 Folk 2m1f110y gd-sft Hdl

Modest hurdler, suited by soft ground, usually wears a tongue tie.

Ela Agapi Mou (USA)

(110h) (92h)

9-y-o b g Storm Bird (CAN)-Vaguar (USA) (Vaguely Noble)
R S Brookhouse R S Brookhouse

Placings:2511/1031001003/1310P330/U4000P3/3305 5420P2334-2606 (4599)
2001/02: 20^{2}S, 25^{6}HY, 21^{0}GS, 25^{6}GF

	Starts	1st	2nd	3rd	Win & Pl
Hurdles	4	0	1	0	748
Career Total	**46**	**7**	**4**	**10**	**35112**

134	11/98	Newb	2m5f	C(0-135)HHdl	G-S	£4958
130	10/98	Plum	2m4f	E(0-115)HHdl	G-F	£2802
125	2/98	Kemp	2m5f	D(0-125)HHdl	GD	£3420
129	11/97	Asct	2m110y	B(0-145)HHdl	SFT	£6664
99	5/97	Font	2m2f110y	E Hdl	G-F	£2302
126	3/97	Ling	2m3f110y	D Hdl	G-S	£3400
113	3/97	Font	2m2f110y	D Hdl	GD	£2906

Total win prize-money £26456

Going: Sf: 0-2 GS: 0-1 Gd: 0-0 GF: - Fm: 0-1
Distance: 2m/2m3: 0-0 2m4-2m7: 0-2 3m+: 0-2
Track: LH: 0-1 RH: 0-1 Tight: 0-1 Gall: 0-0
Aids: Bl: 0-2 Vi: 0-0 Tstrap: 0-0
Best Rating: 134 11/98 Newb 2m5f gd-sft Hdl

Modest hurdler, not as good as he was. Seems to handle any ground and stays three miles.

Ela Agori Mou (IRE)

87f **103f**

5-y-o ch g Ela-Mana-Mou-La Courant (USA) (Little Current (USA))
D Eddy Brian Chicken

Placings:*0-2010* (4235)
2001/02: 16^{2}GF, 17^{0}GF, 17^{1}GF, 16^{0}GS

	Starts	1st	2nd	3rd	Win & Pl
NH Flat	4	1	1	0	2006
Career Total	**5**	**1**	**1**	**0**	**2006**

82	9/01	Hrfd	2m1f	H NHF	G-F	£1568

Total win prize-money £1568

Going: Sf: 0-0 GS: 0-1 Gd: 0-0 GF: - Fm: 1-3
Distance: **2m/2m3: 1-4** 2m4-2m7: 0-0 3m+: 0-0
Track: LH: 0-1 **RH: 1-2** Tight: 0-1 Gall: 0-0
Aids: Bl: 0-0 Vi: 0-0 Tstrap: 0-0
Best Rating: 103 5/01 Newc 2m gd-fm NHF

Moderate bumper winner on fast ground.

Elaando

(101h) (105h)

7-y-o b g Darshaan-Evocatrice (Persepolis (FR))
Mrs Merrita Jones Speed 2911 Ltd

Placings:561/1314504351/0-2 (4731)
2001/02: 17^{2}F

	Starts	1st	2nd	3rd	Win & Pl
Hurdles	1	0	1	0	820
Career Total	**15**	**4**	**1**	**2**	**12740**

115	4/00	Towc	2m	D(0-125)HHdl	GD	£3133
112	6/99	MRas	2m3f110y	F(0-105)HHdl	G-F	£2442
110	5/99	Extr	2m1f	F(0-100)HHdl	FRM	£2810
94	4/99	Folk	2m1f110y	E Hdl	G-F	£2264

Total win prize-money £10651

Going: Sf: 0-0 GS: 0-0 Gd: 0-0 GF: - Fm: 0-1
Distance: 2m/2m3: 0-1 2m4-2m7: 0-0 3m+: 0-0
Track: LH: 0-0 RH: 0-1 Tight: 0-0 Gall: 0-0
Aids: Bl: 0-0 Vi: 0-0 Tstrap: 0-0
Best Rating: 115 4/00 Towc 2m good Hdl

Fair hurdler, best on a sound surface. He has had injury problems, but is particularly effective in the summer and is suited by two miles plus.

Electric Avenue (IRE)

10-y-o b/br m Electric-Pride 'N' Poverty (Boreen (FR))
A J Wilson Tim Leadbeater

Placings:*50*/P/PP/4P56-PPP (3741)
2001/02: 22^{P}G, 24^{P}GS, 23^{P}S

	Starts	1st	2nd	3rd	Win & Pl
Hurdles	1	0	0	0	0

Chases	2	0	0	0	0
Career Total	**12**	**0**	**0**	**0**	**0**

Going: Sf: 0-1 GS: 0-1 Gd: 0-1 GF: - Fm: 0-0
Distance: 2m/2m3: 0-0 2m4-2m7: 0-1 3m+: 0-2
Track: LH: 0-0 RH: 0-3 Tight: 0-0 Gall: 0-1
Aids: Bl: 0-0 Vi: 0-0 Tstrap: 0-0
Best Rating: 89 3/98 Gowr 2m4f yld-sft NHF

Elegant City

90 **86**

8-y-o ch m Scallywag-City's Sister (Maystreak)
N G Richards E Briggs

Placings: *2013*/16/6 **(2154)**
2001/02: 20^{6}G

	Starts	1st	2nd	3rd	Win & Pl
Hurdles	1	0	0	0	0
Career Total	**7**	**2**	**1**	**1**	**5259**

105	11/99	Hayd	2m	D Hdl	GD	£3111
102	2/99	Bang	2m1f	H NHF	GD	£1588

Total win prize-money £4699

Going: Sf: 0-0 GS: 0-0 Gd: 0-1 GF: - Fm: 0-0
Distance: 2m/2m3: 0-0 2m4-2m7: 0-1 3m+: 0-0
Track: LH: 0-1 RH: 0-0 Tight: 0-0 Gall: 0-1
Aids: Bl: 0-0 Vi: 0-0 Tstrap: 0-0
Best Rating: 105 11/99 Hayd 2m good Hdl

Former bumper winner, she has been lightly-raced over hurdles since.

Elegant Des Cosses (FR)

100 **111**

10-y-o b g Missolonghi (USA)-Quintaine Aulmes (FR) (Faunus (FR))
P J Hobbs R J B Partners

Placings: 31103544/P12342023/1542-4 **(1766)**
2001/02: 20^{4}S

	Starts	1st	2nd	3rd	Win & Pl
Chases	1	0	0	0	316
Career Total	**22**	**4**	**4**	**4**	**21760**

116	8/00	NAbb	2m5f110y	D(0-120)HCh	GD	£4046
116	8/99	NAbb	2m5f110y	F(0-110)HCh	GD	£5784
106	12/98	NAbb	2m1f	E(0-100)HHdl	SFT	£2211
106	11/98	Extr	2m1f	E Hdl	SFT	£2637

Total win prize-money £14678

Going: Sf: 0-1 GS: 0-0 Gd: 0-0 GF: - Fm: 0-0
Distance: 2m/2m3: 0-0 2m4-2m7: 0-1 3m+: 0-0
Track: LH: 0-1 RH: 0-0 Tight: 0-1 Gall: 0-0
Aids: Bl: 0-1 Vi: 0-0 Tstrap: 0-0
Best Rating: 116 8/00 NAbb 2m5f110y good Ch

Fair ex-French chaser, best at around two and a half miles. Acts on good or softer, likes Newton Abbot.

Elegant Fan (USA)

68 **29**

7-y-o b/br g Lear Fan (USA)-Elegance (USA) (Providential)
Mrs K M Lamb Mrs K M Lamb

Placings: 000/00P00/P44640000P-P6PPP0 **(3440)**
2001/02: 20^{P}GS, 16^{6}G, 21^{P}GF, 16^{P}GS, 20^{P}G, 17^{0}HY

	Starts	1st	2nd	3rd	Win & Pl
Hurdles	6	0	0	0	0
Career Total	**24**	**0**	**0**	**0**	**212**

Going: Sf: 0-1 GS: 0-2 Gd: 0-2 GF: - Fm: 0-1
Distance: 2m/2m3: 0-3 2m4-2m7: 0-3 3m+: 0-0
Track: LH: 0-5 RH: 0-1 Tight: 0-3 Gall: 0-1
Aids: Bl: 0-2 Vi: 0-0 Tstrap: 0-1
Best Rating: 70 4/99 Sedg 2m1f firm Hdl

Elegant Man

6-y-o b g Elegant Monarch-Man Maid (Mandamus)
H D Daly Ludlow Racing Partnership

Placings: 0-P **(0054)**
2001/02: 24^{P}G

	Starts	1st	2nd	3rd	Win & Pl
Hurdles	1	0	0	0	
Career Total	**2**	**0**	**0**	**0**	

Going: Sf: 0-0 GS: 0-0 Gd: 0-1 GF: - Fm: 0-0
Distance: 2m/2m3: 0-0 2m4-2m7: 0-0 3m+: 0-1
Track: LH: 0-1 RH: 0-0 Tight: 0-1 Gall: 0-0
Aids: Bl: 0-0 Vi: 0-0 Tstrap: 0-0
Best Rating: 68 2/01 Ludl 2m5f gd-sft Hdl

Elegant Maud (IRE)

62 **29**

8-y-o b m Shardari-Maud Gonne (Laser Light)
Graeme Roe Graeme Roe

Placings: *U60/U0*-0P **(3156)**
2001/02: 16^{0}G, 19^{P}S

	Starts	1st	2nd	3rd	Win & Pl
Hurdles	2	0	0	0	
Career Total	**7**	**0**	**0**	**0**	**0**

Going: Sf: 0-1 GS: 0-0 Gd: 0-1 GF: - Fm: 0-0
Distance: 2m/2m3: 0-1 2m4-2m7: 0-1 3m+: 0-0
Track: LH: 0-0 RH: 0-2 Tight: 0-0 Gall: 0-0
Aids: Bl: 0-0 Vi: 0-0 Tstrap: 0-0
Best Rating: 89 3/99 Ludl 2m good NHF

Elegant Piper

6-y-o b g Northern Elegance-Denby Wood (Lord Bud)
Miss A Stokell Tony Longbottom

Placings: *0P*/00P **(2179)**
2001/02: 16^{0}G, 16^{0}S, 23^{P}G

	Starts	1st	2nd	3rd	Win & Pl
NH Flat	2	0	0	0	0
Hurdles	1	0	0	0	0
Career Total	**5**	**0**	**0**	**0**	

Going: Sf: 0-1 GS: 0-0 Gd: 0-2 GF: - Fm: 0-0
Distance: 2m/2m3: 0-2 2m4-2m7: 0-1 3m+: 0-0
Track: LH: 0-2 RH: 0-1 Tight: 0-0 Gall: 0-1
Aids: Bl: 0-0 Vi: 0-0 Tstrap: 0-0
Best Rating: 38 11/01 Hayd 2m soft NHF

Elegant Sprite

102(82h) **106**

9-y-o ch g Remezzo-Elfin Elegance (Remainder Man)
D J Wintle Lady Blyth

Placings: B00P4-6311PP **(4109)**
2001/02: 16^{6}S, 24^{3}G, 25^{1}G, 25^{1}S, 26^{P}S, 25^{P}S

	Starts	1st	2nd	3rd	Win & Pl
Chases	6	2	0	1	7647
Career Total	**11**	**2**	**0**	**1**	**7951**

106	1/02	Hrfd	3m1f110y	F(0-95)HCh	SFT	£4407
106	12/01	Folk	3m1f	F(0-95)HCh	GD	£2860

Total win prize-money £7267

Going: Sf: 1-4 GS: 0-0 Gd: 1-2 GF: - Fm: 0-0
Distance: 2m/2m3: 0-1 2m4-2m7: 0-0 **3m+: 2-5**
Track: LH: 0-0 **RH: 2-5 Tight: 1-2** Gall: 0-0
Aids: Bl: 0-0 Vi: 0-0 Tstrap: 0-0
Best Rating: 106 1/02 Hrfd 3m1f110y soft Ch

Unsuccessful over hurdles, he won modest handicap chases in the winter of 2001/02. Suited by good ground or softer and a right-handed track.

Elegantissime (FR)

68 **62**

5-y-o b g Nashwan (USA)-Riviere D'Argent (USA) (Nijinsky (CAN))
K C Bailey Racing Club Kcb

Placings: PP-0 **(0236)**
2001/02: 16^{0}GF

	Starts	1st	2nd	3rd	Win & Pl
Hurdles	1	0	0	0	
Career Total	**3**	**0**	**0**	**0**	

Going: Sf: 0-0 GS: 0-0 Gd: 0-0 GF: - Fm: 0-1
Distance: 2m/2m3: 0-1 2m4-2m7: 0-0 3m+: 0-0
Track: LH: 0-1 RH: 0-0 Tight: 0-1 Gall: 0-0
Aids: Bl: 0-0 Vi: 0-0 Tstrap: 0-1
Best Rating: 62 5/01 Sthl 2m gd-fm Hdl

Elenas River (IRE)

108(106c) (127c)**106**

6-y-o br g Over The River (FR)-Elena's Beauty (Tarqogan)
Miss H C Knight Ian David Limited

Placings: 556-02213 **(4762)**
2001/02: 21^{0}G, 21^{2}G, 19^{2}GS, 21^{1}G, 20^{3}GF

	Starts	1st	2nd	3rd	Win & Pl
Hurdles	4	1	1	1	9303
Chases	1	0	1	0	1825
Career Total	**8**	**1**	**2**	**1**	**11128**

99	2/02	Ludl	2m5f	D(0-120)HHdl	GD	£5187

Total win prize-money £5187

Going: Sf: 0-0 GS: 0-1 Gd: 1-3 GF: - Fm: 0-1
Distance: 2m/2m3: 0-0 **2m4-2m7: 1-5** 3m+: 0-0
Track: LH: 0-1 **RH: 1-4** Tight: 0-2 Gall: 0-0
Aids: Bl: 0-0 Vi: 0-0 Tstrap: 0-0
Best Rating: 127 11/01 NAbb 2m5f110y good Ch

Put up a promising fight with Celtic Native on his chasing debut and was runner-up back over hurdles next time before winning over the smaller obstacles at Ludlow. Likes good ground, stays two miles five furlongs well.

Elgar

99 **105**

5-y-o ch g Alflora (IRE)-School Run (Deep Run)
N A Twiston-Davies Mrs S Tainton

Placings: *02* **(4494)**
2001/02: 16^{0}S, 22^{2}G

	Starts	1st	2nd	3rd	Win & Pl
NH Flat	1	0	0	0	0
Hurdles	1	0	1	0	1568
Career Total	**2**	**0**	**1**	**0**	**1568**

Going: Sf: 0-1 GS: 0-0 Gd: 0-1 GF: - Fm: 0-0
Distance: 2m/2m3: 0-1 2m4-2m7: 0-1 3m+: 0-0
Track: LH: 0-2 RH: 0-0 Tight: 0-0 Gall: 0-0

Aids: Bl: 0-0 Vi: 0-0 Tstrap: 0-0
Best Rating: **109** 3/02 Hayd 2m6f good Hdl

Chasing-type, runner up on his first outing over hurdles at Haydock in March.

Eliipop

72 **49**

4-y-o b g First Trump-Hasty Key (USA) (Key To The Mint (USA))
R J Price (J R Fanshawe 27/10) Fox And Cub Partnership

Placings:00 (2311)
2001/02: 16^{0}GS, 16^{0}G

	Starts	1st	2nd	3rd	Win & Pl
Hurdles	2	0	0	0	
Career Total	**2**	**0**	**0**	**0**	

Going: Sf: 0-0 GS: 0-1 Gd: 0-1 GF: - Fm: 0-0
Distance: 2m/2m3: 0-2 2m4-2m7: 0-0 3m+: 0-0
Track: LH: 0-0 RH: 0-2 Tight: 0-0 Gall: 0-1
Aids: Bl: 0-0 Vi: 0-0 Tstrap: 0-0
Best Rating: **49** 10/01 Kemp 2m gd-sft Hdl

Eliza Dolittle

7-y-o b m Bandmaster (USA)-Eskimo Slave (New Member)
C P Morlock Mrs Z S Clark

Placings:*0/0*-P (0370)
2001/02: 16^{P}G

	Starts	1st	2nd	3rd	Win & Pl
Hurdles	1	0	0	0	
Career Total	**3**	**0**	**0**	**0**	

Going: Sf: 0-0 GS: 0-0 Gd: 0-1 GF: - Fm: 0-0
Distance: 2m/2m3: 0-1 2m4-2m7: 0-0 3m+: 0-0
Track: LH: 0-1 RH: 0-0 Tight: 0-0 Gall: 0-0
Aids: Bl: 0-0 Vi: 0-0 Tstrap: 0-0
Best Rating:

Eljutan (IRE)

101 **102**

4-y-o b g Namaqualand (USA)-Camarat (Ahonoora)
R J O'Sullivan Jack Joseph

Placings:134 (2311)
2001/02: 16^{1}GF, 16^{3}G, 16^{4}G

	Starts	1st	2nd	3rd	Win & Pl
Hurdles	3	1	0	1	4163
Career Total	**3**	**1**	**0**	**1**	**4163**

102	9/01	Plum	2m	E Hdl	G-F	£2478

Total win prize-money £2478

Going: Sf: 0-0 GS: 0-0 Gd: 0-2 GF: - Fm: 1-1
Distance: **2m/2m3: 1-3** 2m4-2m7: 0-0 3m+: 0-0
Track: **LH: 1-2** RH: 0-1 **Tight: 1-1** Gall: 0-1
Aids: Bl: 0-0 Vi: 0-0 Tstrap: 0-0
Best Rating: **102** 9/01 Plum 2m gd-fm Hdl

Comfortable winner on his hurdles debut at Plumpton, was found out in better class and may need further.

Ell Gee

12-y-o ch m Ra Nova-Evening Song (True Song)
Mrs P Townsley Paul Townsley

Placings:*0/0000/*F65FP/PPPP/P-P3 (0322)
2001/02: 26^{P}G, 21^{3}G

	Starts	1st	2nd	3rd	Win & Pl
Chases	2	0	0	1	336
Career Total	**17**	**0**	**0**	**1**	**336**

Going: Sf: 0-0 GS: 0-0 Gd: 0-2 GF: - Fm: 0-0
Distance: 2m/2m3: 0-0 2m4-2m7: 0-1 3m+: 0-1
Track: LH: 0-0 RH: 0-2 Tight: 0-2 Gall: 0-0
Aids: Bl: 0-0 Vi: 0-0 Tstrap: 0-0
Best Rating: **86** 5/01 Folk 2m5f good Ch

Moderate pointer/hunter chaser, suited by fast ground.

Ell-Emm-Ess

7-y-o b m Golden Heights-Four M'S (Majestic Maharaj)
P M Rich L W Jones & M D Jones

Placings:*0/*P (0906)
2001/02: 20^{P}G

	Starts	1st	2nd	3rd	Win & Pl
Hurdles	1	0	0	0	
Career Total	**2**	**0**	**0**	**0**	

Going: Sf: 0-0 GS: 0-0 Gd: 0-1 GF: - Fm: 0-0
Distance: 2m/2m3: 0-0 2m4-2m7: 0-1 3m+: 0-0
Track: LH: 0-1 RH: 0-0 Tight: 0-0 Gall: 0-0
Aids: Bl: 0-0 Vi: 0-0 Tstrap: 0-0
Best Rating: **20** 2/00 Wwck 2m good NHF

Ella Falls (IRE)

85(87h) (66h)**89**

7-y-o b m Dancing Dissident (USA)-Over Swing (FR) (Saint Cyrien (FR))
Mrs H Dalton Ray Bailey

Placings:F0P/0/1350-0U (0791)
2001/02: 22^{0}GF, 22^{U}GF

	Starts	1st	2nd	3rd	Win & Pl
Chases	2	0	0	0	
Career Total	**10**	**1**	**0**	**1**	**2223**

88	7/00	Worc	3m	F(0-100)HHdl	G-F	£1897

Total win prize-money £1897

Going: Sf: 0-0 GS: 0-0 Gd: 0-0 GF: - Fm: 0-2
Distance: 2m/2m3: 0-0 2m4-2m7: 0-2 3m+: 0-0
Track: LH: 0-0 RH: 0-2 Tight: 0-2 Gall: 0-0
Aids: Bl: 0-0 Vi: 0-0 Tstrap: 0-0
Best Rating: **89** 6/01 MRas 2m6f110y gd-fm Ch

Ella Pee-Elle

53 **16**

7-y-o b m Elmaamul (USA)-Alipampa (IRE) (Glenstal (USA))
R J Price Rock Racing Club

Placings:*34P0F*-P0P (1733)
2001/02: 16^{P}GS, 16^{0}GF, 19^{P}GS

	Starts	1st	2nd	3rd	Win & Pl
Hurdles	3	0	0	0	
Career Total	**8**	**0**	**0**	**1**	**209**

Going: Sf: 0-0 GS: 0-2 Gd: 0-0 GF: - Fm: 0-1
Distance: 2m/2m3: 0-2 2m4-2m7: 0-1 3m+: 0-0
Track: LH: 0-2 RH: 0-1 Tight: 0-1 Gall: 0-0
Aids: Bl: 0-0 Vi: 0-0 Tstrap: 0-0
Best Rating: **84** 7/00 Worc 2m good NHF

Ellamine

103(90c) (98c)**105**

8-y-o b m Warrshan (USA)-Anhaar (Ela-Mana-Mou)
M C Pipe (J Neville 20/10) Orchard Partnership

Placings:621322/3/0400440122143F00 (3927)
2001/02: 22^{0}GS, 21^{4}GF, 19^{0}G, 22^{0}GF, 22^{4}G, 20^{4}GF, 24^{0}GF, 18^{1}GF, 17^{2}GF, 19^{2}GF, 16^{1}GS, 16^{4}S, 23^{3}GS, 19^{F}GS, 19^{0}S, 21^{0}HY

	Starts	1st	2nd	3rd	Win & Pl
Hurdles	14	2	2	0	5815
Chases	2	0	0	1	584
Career Total	**23**	**3**	**5**	**3**	**11715**

98	10/01	Strf	2m110y	G Hdl	G-S	£2023
98	9/01	Font	2m2f110y	G(0-95)HHdl	G-F	£2436
94	7/98	Wolv	2m	E Hdl	GD	£2207

Total win prize-money £6666

Going: Sf: 0-3 GS: 1-4 Gd: 0-2 GF: - Fm: 1-7
Distance: **2m/2m3: 2-6** 2m4-2m7: 0-8 3m+: 0-2
Track: **LH: 2-8** RH: 0-6 **Tight: 2-7** Gall: 0-0
Aids: Bl: 0-0 Vi: 0-0 **Tstrap: 2-11**
Best Rating: **98** 12/01 Extr 2m7f110y gd-sft Ch

Selling-class hurdler, stays two miles-six. Acts on most surfaces, often tongue tied. Did not take to fences when tried in December 2001.

Ellemford

7-y-o b m Broadsword (USA)-Spandulay (USA) (Arts And Letters (USA))
R Ford Richard Ford

Placings:P (1833)
2001/02: 20^{P}G

	Starts	1st	2nd	3rd	Win & Pl
Hurdles	1	0	0	0	
Career Total	**1**	**0**	**0**	**0**	

Going: Sf: 0-0 GS: 0-0 Gd: 0-1 GF: - Fm: 0-0
Distance: 2m/2m3: 0-0 2m4-2m7: 0-1 3m+: 0-0
Track: LH: 0-1 RH: 0-0 Tight: 0-1 Gall: 0-0
Aids: Bl: 0-0 Vi: 0-0 Tstrap: 0-0
Best Rating:

Ellie Opter

72 **34**

6-y-o ch m Gold Dust-Penhill Flame (Main Reef)
N R Mitchell Miss D Sargent

Placings:*0*-00 (3340)
2001/02: 17^{0}G, 17^{0}S

	Starts	1st	2nd	3rd	Win & Pl
NH Flat	1	0	0	0	0
Hurdles	1	0	0	0	0
Career Total	**3**	**0**	**0**	**0**	

Going: Sf: 0-1 GS: 0-0 Gd: 0-1 GF: - Fm: 0-0
Distance: 2m/2m3: 0-2 2m4-2m7: 0-0 3m+: 0-0
Track: LH: 0-1 RH: 0-1 Tight: 0-2 Gall: 0-0
Aids: Bl: 0-0 Vi: 0-0 Tstrap: 0-0
Best Rating: **86** 4/01 Tntn 2m1f gd-fm NHF

Ellieberry (IRE)

4-y-o ch f Lucky Guest-Persian Flower (Persian Heights)
I W McInnes (B Ellison 4/8) Ian McInnes

lacings:PP (2150)
001/02: 16^{P}G, 16^{P}G

	Starts	1st	2nd	3rd	Win & Pl
urdles	2	0	0	0	
areer Total	**2**	**0**	**0**	**0**	

oing: Sf: 0-0 GS: 0-0 Gd: 0-2 GF: - Fm: 0-0
istance: 2m/2m3: 0-2 2m4-2m7: 0-0 3m+: 0-0
rack: LH: 0-2 RH: 0-0 Tight: 0-0 Gall: 0-1
ids: Bl: 0-0 Vi: 0-0 Tstrap: 0-0
est Rating:

Ello Ollie (IRE)

05(105c) (101c)**94**
-y-o b g Roselier (FR)-Kayanna (Torenaga)
ndrew Turnell Dr John Hollowood

lacings:3022U50/**06P1F22** **(4745)**
001/02: 16^{0}GF, 20^{6}GS, 24^{P}S, 23^{1}G, 22^{F}S, 26^{2}G, 24^{2}G

	Starts	1st	2nd	3rd	Win & Pl
urdles	2	0	2	0	1605
hases	5	1	0	0	3913
areer Total	**14**	**1**	**4**	**1**	**7681**

1 1/02 Leic 2m7f110y F(0-95)HCh GD £3913
Total win prize-money £3913

oing: Sf: 0-2 GS: 0-1 Gd: 1-3 GF: - Fm: 0-1
istance: 2m/2m3: 0-1 2m4-2m7: 0-2 **3m+: 1-4**
rack: LH: 0-2 **RH: 1-5** Tight: 0-1 Gall: 0-1
ids: **Bl: 1-3** Vi: 0-0 Tstrap: 0-0
est Rating: 101 1/02 Leic 2m7f110y good Ch

andicap hurdler/chaser, effective over three miles and cts on good ground. Has won in blinkers.

Ellora Mill

-y-o b m Elegant Monarch-Jim's Mushroom (Skyliner)
liss D Cole Mrs Marilyn Cook

lacings:0PP6/P **(1378)**
001/02: 19^{P}GF

	Starts	1st	2nd	3rd	Win & Pl
lurdles	1	0	0	0	
areer Total	**5**	**0**	**0**	**0**	**0**

oing: Sf: 0-0 GS: 0-0 Gd: 0-0 GF: - Fm: 0-1
istance: 2m/2m3: 0-0 2m4-2m7: 0-1 3m+: 0-0
rack: LH: 0-0 RH: 0-1 Tight: 0-0 Gall: 0-0
ids: Bl: 0-0 Vi: 0-0 Tstrap: 0-0
est Rating:

Eloi Ii (FR)

0-y-o ch g Video Rock (FR)-Judelle (FR) (Laniste)
R Summers Tony Eaves

Placings:122F4364/162133442/60P545F605P3202/0
4/P4 **(4545)**
001/02: 24^{P}GF, 19^{4}G

	Starts	1st	2nd	3rd	Win & Pl
hases	2	0	0	0	0
areer Total	**37**	**3**	**6**	**4**	**103568**

8/97 Claf 2m1f Hdl GD £6713
5/97 Engh 2m3f Ch VS £11223
9/96 Autl 2m2f Hdl SFT £13175
Total win prize-money £31111

oing: Sf: 0-0 GS: 0-0 Gd: 0-1 GF: - Fm: 0-1
istance: 2m/2m3: 0-1 2m4-2m7: 0-0 3m+: 0-1
rack: LH: 0-1 RH: 0-1 Tight: 0-1 Gall: 0-0

Aids: Bl: 0-0 Vi: 0-0 Tstrap: 0-0
Best Rating: 66 4/02 Hrfd 2m3f good Ch

Elsa's Pride

83(57h) **54**
7-y-o b g Mon Tresor-Elsa (Green Ruby (USA))
J M Jefferson Mrs M E Dixon

Placings:*650605*/506412**424U23P-0** **(0221)**
2001/02: 20^{0}GF

	Starts	1st	2nd	3rd	Win & Pl
Chases	1	0	0	0	
Career Total	**20**	**1**	**3**	**1**	**6441**

79 7/00 Sedg 2m5f110y E Hdl G-F £2282
Total win prize-money £2282

Going: Sf: 0-0 GS: 0-0 Gd: 0-0 GF: - Fm: 0-1
Distance: 2m/2m3: 0-0 2m4-2m7: 0-1 3m+: 0-0
Track: LH: 0-1 RH: 0-0 Tight: 0-0 Gall: 0-0
Aids: Bl: 0-0 Vi: 0-0 Tstrap: 0-0
Best Rating: 105 9/00 Sedg 2m110y good Ch

Elsaroni

96(98h) (92h)**75**
8-y-o ch g Primitive Rising (USA)-Malmo (Free State)
P Beaumont Mrs E Dixon

Placings:*0*/00P/56454P **(4896)**
2001/02: 20^{5}G, 25^{6}GS, 20^{4}G, 20^{5}G, 20^{4}G, 20^{P}G

	Starts	1st	2nd	3rd	Win & Pl
Hurdles	6	0	0	0	0
Career Total	**10**	**0**	**0**	**0**	**0**

Going: Sf: 0-1 GS: 0-1 Gd: 0-4 GF: - Fm: 0-0
Distance: 2m/2m3: 0-0 2m4-2m7: 0-5 3m+: 0-1
Track: LH: 0-5 RH: 0-1 Tight: 0-0 Gall: 0-3
Aids: Bl: 0-2 Vi: 0-0 Tstrap: 0-0
Best Rating: 92 1/02 Donc 2m4f good Hdl

Showed little over hurdles but looks more of a chaser.

Eluna

111 **124**
4-y-o ch f Unfuwain (USA)-Elisha (GER) (Konigsstuhl (GER))
Ian Williams (C Von Der Recke 22/2) Mr & Mrs John Poynton

Placings:21100 **(4952a)**
2001/02: 16^{2}HY, 16^{1}HY, 16^{1}HY, 17^{0}G, 16^{0}G

	Starts	1st	2nd	3rd	Win & Pl
Hurdles	5	2	1	0	5695
Career Total	**5**	**2**	**1**	**0**	**5695**

124 2/02 Wwck 2m E Hdl HVY £2954
118 1/02 Wwck 2m E Hdl HVY £2740
Total win prize-money £5695

Going: Sf: 2-3 GS: 0-0 Gd: 0-2 GF: - Fm: 0-0
Distance: **2m/2m3: 2-5** 2m4-2m7: 0-0 3m+: 0-0
Track: **LH: 2-3** RH: 0-1 Tight: 0-0 Gall: 0-1
Aids: Bl: 0-0 Vi: 0-0 Tstrap: 0-0
Best Rating: 124 2/02 Wwck 2m heavy Hdl

A former German-trained filly who won on the level over nine furlongs, she won twice at Warwick at the start of 2002, but then joined Ian Williams and was well beaten in the Triumph. Acts on heavy ground.

Elvis

102(99h) (101h)**107**
9-y-o b g Southern Music-Tyqueen (Tycoon Ii)
L Wells The Chap Quartet

Placings:*60*/P0P/660511/003-233F **(0910)**
2001/02: 17^{2}GF, 17^{3}GF, 16^{3}GF, 16^{F}G

	Starts	1st	2nd	3rd	Win & Pl
Hurdles	2	0	1	1	1600
Chases	2	0	0	1	596
Career Total	**18**	**2**	**1**	**3**	**8529**

98 12/99 Font 2m2f110y D(0-120)HHdl G-S £3070
101 12/99 Font 2m2f110y G Hdl GD £2867
Total win prize-money £5939

Going: Sf: 0-0 GS: 0-0 Gd: 0-1 GF: - Fm: 0-3
Distance: 2m/2m3: 0-4 2m4-2m7: 0-0 3m+: 0-0
Track: LH: 0-4 RH: 0-0 Tight: 0-3 Gall: 0-0
Aids: Bl: 0-0 Vi: 0-0 Tstrap: 0-0
Best Rating: 107 6/01 NAbb 2m110y gd-fm Ch

Does not find much for pressure.

Elvis Reigns

105(85h) (92h)**116**
6-y-o b g Rock City-Free Rein (Sagaro)
Ferdy Murphy A G Chappell

Placings:231UPP00/P-004 **(4858)**
2001/02: 16^{0}G, 16^{0}GS, 16^{4}G

	Starts	1st	2nd	3rd	Win & Pl
Hurdles	3	0	0	0	0
Career Total	**12**	**1**	**1**	**1**	**21851**

7/99 Autl 2m1f110y Hdl SFT £11840
Total win prize-money £11840

Going: Sf: 0-0 GS: 0-1 Gd: 0-2 GF: - Fm: 0-0
Distance: 2m/2m3: 0-3 2m4-2m7: 0-0 3m+: 0-0
Track: LH: 0-2 RH: 0-0 Tight: 0-1 Gall: 0-0
Aids: Bl: 0-0 Vi: 0-0 Tstrap: 0-0
Best Rating: 82 4/02 Hexm 2m110y good Hdl

Elysian Hawk

88 **99**
9-y-o ch g Heavenly Manna-Honeybuzzard (FR) (Sea Hawk II)
R J Hodges R A Ford

Placings:*5/3*/P-224 **(3702)**
2001/02: 22^{2}S, 22^{2}HY, 19^{4}HY

	Starts	1st	2nd	3rd	Win & Pl
Hurdles	3	0	2	0	1202
Career Total	**6**	**0**	**2**	**1**	**1922**

Going: Sf: 0-3 GS: 0-0 Gd: 0-0 GF: - Fm: 0-0
Distance: 2m/2m3: 0-0 2m4-2m7: 0-3 3m+: 0-0
Track: LH: 0-1 RH: 0-2 Tight: 0-2 Gall: 0-0
Aids: Bl: 0-0 Vi: 0-0 Tstrap: 0-0
Best Rating: 102 5/98 Towc 2m good NHF

Lightly-raced injury-prone hurdler. Ran well in sellers in early 2002 over two miles-six. Acts on soft ground.

Em's Light

7-y-o b g Lighter-Gaelic Empress (Regular Guy)
A Parker J John Paterson

Placings:PP **(4259)**
2001/02: 24^{P}HY, 24^{P}HY

	Starts	1st	2nd	3rd	Win & Pl
Hurdles	2	0	0	0	

	Starts	1st	2nd	3rd	Win & Pl
Career Total	2	0	0	0	

Going: Sf: 0-2 GS: 0-0 Gd: 0-0 GF: - Fm: 0-0
Distance: 2m/2m3: 0-0 2m4-2m7: 0-0 3m+: 0-2
Track: LH: 0-2 RH: 0-0 Tight: 0-0 Gall: 0-0
Aids: Bl: 0-0 Vi: 0-0 Tstrap: 0-0
Best Rating:

Em-T-Inch

71 **52**

6-y-o ch m Emarati (USA)-Three Inches (Nearly A Hand)
Jane Southcombe P L Southcombe

Placings:00-00P (1769)
2001/02: 16^{0}GF, 17^{0}G, 17^{P}G

	Starts	1st	2nd	3rd	Win & Pl
Hurdles	3	0	0	0	
Career Total	5	0	0	0	

Going: Sf: 0-0 GS: 0-0 Gd: 0-2 GF: - Fm: 0-1
Distance: 2m/2m3: 0-3 2m4-2m7: 0-0 3m+: 0-0
Track: LH: 0-0 RH: 0-3 Tight: 0-0 Gall: 0-0
Aids: Bl: 0-0 Vi: 0-0 Tstrap: 0-0
Best Rating: 67 5/00 Extr 2m1f gd-fm NHF

Emali

5-y-o b g Emarati (USA)-Princess Poquito (Hard Fought)
J S Moore The Country Life Partnership

Placings:P-P (0007)
2001/02: 16^{P}S

	Starts	1st	2nd	3rd	Win & Pl
Hurdles	1	0	0	0	
Career Total	2	0	0	0	

Going: Sf: 0-1 GS: 0-0 Gd: 0-0 GF: - Fm: 0-0
Distance: 2m/2m3: 0-1 2m4-2m7: 0-0 3m+: 0-0
Track: LH: 0-1 RH: 0-0 Tight: 0-1 Gall: 0-0
Aids: Bl: 0-0 Vi: 0-0 Tstrap: 0-1
Best Rating:

Ember

9-y-o b m Nicholas (USA)-Cinderwench (Crooner)
C J Hemsley The Ember Partnership

Placings:6P/2440/0P (0850)
2001/02: 17^{0}F, 16^{P}GF

	Starts	1st	2nd	3rd	Win & Pl
Hurdles	2	0	0	0	
Career Total	8	0	1	0	672

Going: Sf: 0-0 GS: 0-0 Gd: 0-0 GF: - Fm: 0-2
Distance: 2m/2m3: 0-2 2m4-2m7: 0-0 3m+: 0-0
Track: LH: 0-1 RH: 0-1 Tight: 0-1 Gall: 0-0
Aids: Bl: 0-0 Vi: 0-0 Tstrap: 0-0
Best Rating: 82 10/97 Strf 2m110y good Hdl

Emencee

5-y-o b g Lucky Wednesday-Nattfari (Tyrnavos)
A Bailey Morris Nicholson Cartwright Ltd

Placings:0 (4410)
2001/02: 17^{0}S

	Starts	1st	2nd	3rd	Win & Pl
NH Flat	1	0	0	0	
Career Total	1	0	0	0	

Going: Sf: 0-1 GS: 0-0 Gd: 0-0 GF: - Fm: 0-0
Distance: 2m/2m3: 0-1 2m4-2m7: 0-0 3m+: 0-0
Track: LH: 0-1 RH: 0-0 Tight: 0-1 Gall: 0-0
Aids: Bl: 0-0 Vi: 0-0 Tstrap: 0-0
Best Rating:

Emerald Hunter (USA)

70 **30**

7-y-o b/br g Quest For Fame-In Jubilation (USA) (Isgala)
K O Cunningham-Brown Miss C Berry

Placings:P4/0 (0778)
2001/02: 20^{0}GF

	Starts	1st	2nd	3rd	Win & Pl
Hurdles	1	0	0	0	
Career Total	3	0	0	0	195

Going: Sf: 0-0 GS: 0-0 Gd: 0-0 GF: - Fm: 0-1
Distance: 2m/2m3: 0-0 2m4-2m7: 0-1 3m+: 0-0
Track: LH: 0-1 RH: 0-0 Tight: 0-0 Gall: 0-0
Aids: Bl: 0-0 Vi: 0-0 Tstrap: 0-0
Best Rating: 66 8/99 Hntg 2m4f110y gd-fm Hdl

Emerald Palm

4-y-o b f Green Desert (USA)-Opus One (Slip Anchor)
P J Hobbs (J Noseda 13/6) Sir Robert Ogden

Placings:P (1188)
2001/02: 17^{P}G

	Starts	1st	2nd	3rd	Win & Pl
Hurdles	1	0	0	0	
Career Total	1	0	0	0	

Going: Sf: 0-0 GS: 0-0 Gd: 0-1 GF: - Fm: 0-0
Distance: 2m/2m3: 0-1 2m4-2m7: 0-0 3m+: 0-0
Track: LH: 0-1 RH: 0-0 Tight: 0-1 Gall: 0-0
Aids: Bl: 0-0 Vi: 0-0 Tstrap: 0-0
Best Rating:

Emily Skye

65f

5-y-o bl m Almoojid-Skye Duck (Adonijah)
A D Smith Duckhaven Stud

Placings:0 (3345)
2001/02: 17^{0}S

	Starts	1st	2nd	3rd	Win & Pl
NH Flat	1	0	0	0	
Career Total	1	0	0	0	

Going: Sf: 0-1 GS: 0-0 Gd: 0-0 GF: - Fm: 0-0
Distance: 2m/2m3: 0-1 2m4-2m7: 0-0 3m+: 0-0
Track: LH: 0-0 RH: 0-0 Tight: 0-0 Gall: 0-0
Aids: Bl: 0-0 Vi: 0-0 Tstrap: 0-0
Best Rating: 65 1/02 Tntn 2m1f soft NHF

Eminence (IRE)

4-y-o b g Machiavellian (USA)-Divine Danse (FR) (Kris)
P R Webber Paul Webber

Placings:P (3210
2001/02: 16^{P}GS

	Starts	1st	2nd	3rd	Win & Pl
Hurdles	1	0	0	0	
Career Total	1	0	0	0	

Going: Sf: 0-0 GS: 0-1 Gd: 0-0 GF: - Fm: 0-0
Distance: 2m/2m3: 0-1 2m4-2m7: 0-0 3m+: 0-0
Track: LH: 0-1 RH: 0-0 Tight: 0-0 Gall: 0-1
Aids: Bl: 0-0 Vi: 0-0 Tstrap: 0-0
Best Rating:

Emmas Hope

62 **32**

5-y-o b m Emarati (USA)-Ray Of Hope (Rainbow Quest (USA))
B P J Baugh Mrs Joan M Chrimes

Placings:5-00 (1194
2001/02: 16^{0}GF, 20^{0}GS

	Starts	1st	2nd	3rd	Win & Pl
Hurdles	2	0	0	0	
Career Total	3	0	0	0	0

Going: Sf: 0-0 GS: 0-1 Gd: 0-0 GF: - Fm: 0-1
Distance: 2m/2m3: 0-1 2m4-2m7: 0-1 3m+: 0-0
Track: LH: 0-2 RH: 0-0 Tight: 0-1 Gall: 0-0
Aids: Bl: 0-0 Vi: 0-0 Tstrap: 0-0
Best Rating: 32 7/01 Uttx 2m gd-fm Hd

Emperor Hili (IRE)

8-y-o b g Montelimar (USA)-Winterville (Rusticaro (FR))
N J Pomfret Miss Hannah Walsgrove

Placings:6-0 (0226
2001/02: 20^{0}GF

	Starts	1st	2nd	3rd	Win & Pl
Chases	1	0	0	0	
Career Total	2	0	0	0	0

Going: Sf: 0-0 GS: 0-0 Gd: 0-0 GF: - Fm: 0-1
Distance: 2m/2m3: 0-0 2m4-2m7: 0-1 3m+: 0-0
Track: LH: 0-0 RH: 0-1 Tight: 0-0 Gall: 0-1
Aids: Bl: 0-0 Vi: 0-0 Tstrap: 0-0
Best Rating: 66 4/01 MRas 2m1f110y gd-sft Ch

Emperor Ross (IRE)

110(99h) (106h)**142**

7-y-o b/br g Roselier (FR)-Gilded Empress (Menelek)
N G Richards J Hales

Placings:30-33 (3267)
2001/02: 24^{3}S, 24^{3}G

	Starts	1st	2nd	3rd	Win & Pl
Hurdles	1	0	0	1	384
Chases	1	0	0	1	658
Career Total	4	0	0	3	1578

Going: Sf: 0-1 GS: 0-0 Gd: 0-1 GF: - Fm: 0-0
Distance: 2m/2m3: 0-0 2m4-2m7: 0-0 3m+: 0-2
Track: LH: 0-2 RH: 0-0 Tight: 0-0 Gall: 0-1
Aids: Bl: 0-0 Vi: 0-0 Tstrap: 0-2
Best Rating: 107 1/01 Donc 3m110y good Hdl

Placed in points, hurdles and chases, he has reportedly had breathing problems. Improved form over fences in 2002. Stays three and a half miles, acts on any ground.

Emperor's Magic (IRE)

105 **124**

11-y-o ch g Over The River (FR)-Sengirrefcha (Reformed Character)

N B Mason N B Mason

Placings:63/2/**33523/512404-1U13421F3** **(4775)**

2001/02: 20^{1}S, 19^{U}GF, 25^{1}S, 20^{3}G, 20^{4}S, 24^{2}GS, 22^{1}S, 24^{F}GS, 22^{3}G

	Starts	1st	2nd	3rd	Win & Pl
Chases	9	3	1	2	20698
Career Total	**23**	**4**	**4**	**6**	**29349**

121 3/02 MRas 2m6f110y D(0-120)HCh SFT £4771
120 12/01 Catt 3m1f110y F(0-110)HCh SFT £4290
108 11/01 Carl 2m4f E(0-115)HCh SFT £6955
107 2/01 Carl 2m4f110y F(0-105)HCh SFT £3575
Total win prize-money £19591

Going: Sf: 3-4 GS: 0-2 Gd: 0-2 GF: - Fm: 0-1
Distance: 2m/2m3: 0-1 **2m4-2m7: 2-5** 3m+: 1-3
Track: LH: 1-3 **RH: 2-6 Tight: 2-5** Gall: 0-0
Aids: Bl: 0-0 Vi: 0-0 Tstrap: 0-2
Best Rating: 124 3/02 Strf 3m gd-sft Ch

Fair chaser. Stays three miles one. Acts on soft ground. Has worn a tongue tie.

Empire Gold (USA)

86(92h) (70h)**70**

7-y-o ch g Strike The Gold (USA)-Careless Halo (USA) (Sunny's Halo (CAN))

K C Bailey Mrs E A Kellar

Placings:4010/063/F0U0 **(2925)**

2001/02: 16^{F}S, 19^{0}G, 16^{U}GF, 19^{0}GS

	Starts	1st	2nd	3rd	Win & Pl
Hurdles	2	0	0	0	0
Chases	2	0	0	0	0
Career Total	**11**	**1**	**0**	**1**	**3070**

103 2/99 Muss 2m E Hdl FRM £2075
Total win prize-money £2075

Going: Sf: 0-1 GS: 0-1 Gd: 0-1 GF: - Fm: 0-1
Distance: 2m/2m3: 0-4 2m4-2m7: 0-0 3m+: 0-0
Track: LH: 0-2 RH: 0-2 Tight: 0-1 Gall: 0-0
Aids: Bl: 0-2 Vi: 0-0 Tstrap: 0-0
Best Rating: 113 11/99 Catt 2m gd-fm Ch

Empire Park

108 (101c)**120**

7-y-o b g Tragic Role (USA)-Millaine (Formidable (USA))

C R Egerton Elite Racing Club

Placings:12/**F**512311214P3520 **(4572)**

2001/02: 16^{F}GF, 21^{5}GF, 16^{1}G, 17^{2}G, 21^{3}G, 19^{1}GS, 16^{1}S, 22^{2}HY, 19^{1}G, 20^{4}S, 18^{P}HY, 20^{3}S, 21^{5}GS, 16^{2}GS, 20^{0}G

	Starts	1st	2nd	3rd	Win & Pl
Hurdles	14	4	3	2	14328
Chases	1	0	0	0	0
Career Total	**17**	**5**	**4**	**2**	**16450**

120 12/01 Newb 2m3f F(0-110)HHdl GD £3276
120 11/01 Towc 2m G Hdl SFT £1946
100 10/01 Hrfd 2m3f110y G Hdl G-S £1949
109 9/01 Prth 2m110y F Hdl GD £2975
93 7/99 MRas 2m1f110y F Hdl G-F £1452
Total win prize-money £11599

Going: Sf: 1-5 GS: 1-3 Gd: 2-5 GF: - Fm: 0-2
Distance: **2m/2m3: 3-7** 2m4-2m7: 1-8 3m+: 0-0
Track: LH: 1-9 **RH: 3-6** Tight: 0-5 **Gall: 1-3**
Aids: **Bl: 4-14** Vi: 0-1 Tstrap: 0-0
Best Rating: 120 3/02 Donc 2m4f soft Hdl

A consistent sort in modest handicap hurdles, he stays two miles three furlongs and acts on most types of ground.

Empress Alice

5-y-o b m Petoski-Blue Empress (Blue Cashmere)

R E Peacock Three Of A Kind Racing

Placings:0 **(1759)**

2001/02: 16^{0}GS

	Starts	1st	2nd	3rd	Win & Pl
Hurdles	1	0	0	0	
Career Total	**1**	**0**	**0**	**0**	

Going: Sf: 0-0 GS: 0-1 Gd: 0-0 GF: - Fm: 0-0
Distance: 2m/2m3: 0-1 2m4-2m7: 0-0 3m+: 0-0
Track: LH: 0-1 RH: 0-0 Tight: 0-1 Gall: 0-0
Aids: Bl: 0-0 Vi: 0-0 Tstrap: 0-0
Best Rating:

Empress Emmilline

6-y-o ch m My Generation-Over The Mill (Milford)

M Mullineaux F H F Garth Ormond

Placings:PPP **(3856)**

2001/02: 16^{P}GS, 16^{P}HY, 16^{P}S

	Starts	1st	2nd	3rd	Win & Pl
Hurdles	3	0	0	0	
Career Total	**3**	**0**	**0**	**0**	

Going: Sf: 0-2 GS: 0-1 Gd: 0-0 GF: - Fm: 0-0
Distance: 2m/2m3: 0-3 2m4-2m7: 0-0 3m+: 0-0
Track: LH: 0-3 RH: 0-0 Tight: 0-1 Gall: 0-1
Aids: Bl: 0-0 Vi: 0-0 Tstrap: 0-0
Best Rating:

En El Em (IRE)

77 **60**

4-y-o b f Namaqualand (USA)-Banaiyka (IRE) (Shernazar)

J J Quinn U K Letterbox Marketing Ltd (n L M)

Placings:54 **(1141)**

2001/02: 17^{5}GS, 16^{4}G

	Starts	1st	2nd	3rd	Win & Pl
Hurdles	2	0	0	0	0
Career Total	**2**	**0**	**0**	**0**	**0**

Going: Sf: 0-0 GS: 0-1 Gd: 0-1 GF: - Fm: 0-0
Distance: 2m/2m3: 0-2 2m4-2m7: 0-0 3m+: 0-0
Track: LH: 0-1 RH: 0-0 Tight: 0-1 Gall: 0-0
Aids: Bl: 0-0 Vi: 0-0 Tstrap: 0-0
Best Rating: 60 8/01 Strf 2m110y good Hdl

En El Em Flyer

88 **68**

7-y-o b g Seymour Hicks (FR)-Sound 'N' Rhythm (Tudor Rhythm)

R Curtis Keith J Bradley/Gordon Houldsworth

Placings:60000P **(4131)**

2001/02: 16^{6}GF, 16^{0}G, 21^{0}G, 19^{0}GS, 20^{0}GS, 26^{P}G

	Starts	1st	2nd	3rd	Win & Pl
NH Flat	2	0	0	0	0
Hurdles	4	0	0	0	0
Career Total	**6**	**0**	**0**	**0**	**0**

Going: Sf: 0-0 GS: 0-2 Gd: 0-3 GF: - Fm: 0-1
Distance: 2m/2m3: 0-3 2m4-2m7: 0-2 3m+: 0-1
Track: LH: 0-5 RH: 0-1 Tight: 0-3 Gall: 0-1
Aids: Bl: 0-0 Vi: 0-0 Tstrap: 0-0
Best Rating: 81 6/01 Worc 2m gd-fm NHF

Enchanted Cottage

100 **80**

10-y-o b g Governor General-Mitsubishi Colour (Cut Above)

D M Grissell Pleisure Ltd

Placings:00P535/12216/F30/0P6364P55/60-62410P3 **(4561)**

2001/02: 17^{6}GS, 21^{2}GF, 21^{4}GS, 20^{1}GS, 22^{0}GS, 21^{P}S, 21^{3}GF

	Starts	1st	2nd	3rd	Win & Pl
Hurdles	6	1	1	1	3265
Chases	1	0	0	0	0
Career Total	**32**	**3**	**3**	**4**	**10776**

80 10/01 Font 2m4f G(0-95)HHdl G-S £2299
95 3/97 Hexm 2m4f110y E(0-100)HHdl SFT £2794
79 2/97 Catt 2m3f E(0-105)HHdl GD £2211
Total win prize-money £7306

Going: Sf: 0-1 GS: 1-4 Gd: 0-0 GF: - Fm: 0-2
Distance: 2m/2m3: 0-1 **2m4-2m7: 1-0** 3m+: 0-0
Track: LH: 0-3 RH: 0-3 **Tight: 1-6** Gall: 0-1
Aids: Bl: 0-0 Vi: 0-0 Tstrap: 0-0
Best Rating: 95 3/97 Hexm 2m4f110y soft Hdl

Plating-class hurdler, stays two and a half miles plus. Suited by fast ground but handles some cut.

Encima Del Rio (IRE)

9-y-o ch g Over The River (FR)-Spanish Royale (Royal Buck)

C L Popham C L Popham

Placings:P/PP **(1144)**

2001/02: 26^{P}G, 24^{P}GF

	Starts	1st	2nd	3rd	Win & Pl
Chases	2	0	0	0	
Career Total	**3**	**0**	**0**	**0**	

Going: Sf: 0-0 GS: 0-0 Gd: 0-1 GF: - Fm: 0-1
Distance: 2m/2m3: 0-0 2m4-2m7: 0-0 3m+: 0-2
Track: LH: 0-2 RH: 0-0 Tight: 0-2 Gall: 0-0
Aids: Bl: 0-0 Vi: 0-0 Tstrap: 0-0
Best Rating:

Encore Cadoudal (FR)

96f **107f**

4-y-o b g Cadoudal (FR)-Maousse (FR) (Labus (FR))

M C Pipe D A Johnson

Placings:20 **(3784)**

2001/02: 16^{2}S, 16^{0}S

	Starts	1st	2nd	3rd	Win & Pl
NH Flat	2	0	1	0	668
Career Total	**2**	**0**	**1**	**0**	**668**

Going: Sf: 0-2 GS: 0-0 Gd: 0-0 GF: - Fm: 0-0

Distance: 2m/2m3: 0-2 2m4-2m7: 0-0 3m+: 0-0
Track: LH: 0-1 RH: 0-1 Tight: 0-0 Gall: 0-0
Aids: Bl: 0-0 Vi: 0-0 Tstrap: 0-0
Best Rating: 107 1/02 Hayd 2m soft NHF

A half-brother to dual winning hurdler Mauosse Honor. Made an encouraging bumper debut at Haydock in January.

Enfilade

6-y-o b g Deploy-Bargouzine (Hotfoot)
K A Morgan Mrs J M Penney

Placings:PP **(1500)**
2001/02: 20^{P}G, 21^{P}G

	Starts	1st	2nd	3rd	Win & Pl
Hurdles	2	0	0	0	
Career Total	**2**	**0**	**0**	**0**	

Going: Sf: 0-0 GS: 0-0 Gd: 0-2 GF: - Fm: 0-0
Distance: 2m/2m3: 0-0 2m4-2m7: 0-2 3m+: 0-0
Track: LH: 0-2 RH: 0-0 Tight: 0-2 Gall: 0-0
Aids: Bl: 0-0 Vi: 0-0 Tstrap: 0-2
Best Rating:

Engaged

7-y-o b g St Ninian-Betrothed (Aglojo)
T D Walford John A Cooper

Placings:P-F **(1722)**
2001/02: 25^{F}G

	Starts	1st	2nd	3rd	Win & Pl
Chases	1	0	0	0	
Career Total	2	**0**	**0**	**0**	

Going: Sf: 0-0 GS: 0-0 Gd: 0-1 GF: - Fm: 0-0
Distance: 2m/2m3: 0-0 2m4-2m7: 0-0 3m+: 0-1
Track: LH: 0-1 RH: 0-0 Tight: 0-0 Gall: 0-0
Aids: Bl: 0-0 Vi: 0-0 Tstrap: 0-0
Best Rating:

Engstrum (IRE)

83 **72**
4-y-o ch g Grand Lodge (USA)-Gentle Guest (IRE) (Be My Guest (USA))
C J Mann (H Morrison 4/10) The Whitcoombe Partnership

Placings:0002P **(4152)**
2001/02: 18^{0}G, 16^{0}GS, 16^{0}GS, 21^{2}HY, 20^{P}GS

	Starts	1st	2nd	3rd	Win & Pl
Hurdles	5	0	1	0	744
Career Total	**5**	**0**	**1**	**0**	**744**

Going: Sf: 0-1 GS: 0-3 Gd: 0-1 GF: - Fm: 0-0
Distance: 2m/2m3: 0-3 2m4-2m7: 0-2 3m+: 0-0
Track: LH: 0-5 RH: 0-0 Tight: 0-2 Gall: 0-2
Aids: Bl: 0-5 Vi: 0-0 Tstrap: 0-0
Best Rating: 72 12/01 Newb 2m110y gd-sft Hdl

A modest stayer on the Flat, his looked suited by being upped to two miles-five on heavy ground. Usually wears blinkers.

Enhancer

97f **99f**
4-y-o b c Zafonic (USA)-Ypha (USA) (Lyphard (USA))
G A Swinbank K Elliott

Placings:*1* **(3613)**
2001/02: 16^{1}S

	Starts	1st	2nd	3rd	Win & Pl
NH Flat	1	1	0	0	1866
Career Total	**1**	**1**	**0**	**0**	**1866**

99	2/02	Muss	2m	H NHF	SFT	£1865

Total win prize-money £1866

Going: Sf: 1-1 GS: 0-0 Gd: 0-0 GF: - Fm: 0-0
Distance: **2m/2m3: 1-1** 2m4-2m7: 0-0 3m+: 0-0
Track: LH: 0-0 **RH: 1-1 Tight: 1-1** Gall: 0-0
Aids: Bl: 0-0 Vi: 0-0 Tstrap: 0-0
Best Rating: 99 2/02 Muss 2m soft NHF

A half-brother to useful jumper Redemption, he won a weak bumper on his debut at Musselburgh.

Ennel Boy (IRE)

101 **100**
9-y-o ch g Torus-Golden Symphony (Le Moss)
N M Babbage (K A Morgan 31/5) B Babbage

Placings:*0*/0/PP**04**/312 **(1150)**
2001/02: 23^{3}GF, 26^{1}GF, 22^{2}GF

	Starts	1st	2nd	3rd	Win & Pl
Hurdles	3	1	1	1	3749
Career Total	**9**	**1**	**1**	**1**	**3995**

100	5/01	Hntg	3m2f	E(0-105)HHdl	G-F	£2565

Total win prize-money £2566

Going: Sf: 0-0 GS: 0-0 Gd: 0-0 GF: - Fm: 1-3
Distance: 2m/2m3: 0-0 2m4-2m7: 0-1 **3m+: 1-2**
Track: LH: 0-2 **RH: 1-1** Tight: 0-2 **Gall: 1-1**
Aids: Bl: 0-0 Vi: 0-0 Tstrap: 0-0
Best Rating: 100 8/01 NAbb 2m6f gd-fm Hdl

Unsuccessful over fences, he ran well over hurdles in the summer of 2001. Stays three miles plus, acts on fast ground.

Enrique (GER)

113(97h) **151**
7-y-o ch g Niniski (USA)-Eicidora (GER) (Surumu (GER))
P J Hobbs Sir Robert Ogden

Placings:1220113/5**211F-4P125** **(4839)**
2001/02: 25^{4}G, 24^{P}S, 25^{1}G, 25^{2}G, 33^{5}G

	Starts	1st	2nd	3rd	Win & Pl
Chases	5	1	1	0	19149
Career Total	**17**	**6**	**4**	**1**	**52144**

147	12/01	Winc	3m1f110y	D(0-125)HCh	GD	£9148
151	11/00	Ludl	3m	D Ch	GD	£4446
138	11/00	Ludl	2m4f	E Ch	GD	£3552
137	3/00	Ling	2m3f110y	C(0-135)HHdl	GD	£14885
133	3/00	Sand	2m110y	E(0-115)HHdl	GD	£4212
113	11/99	NAbb	2m1f	E Hdl	SFT	£2422

Total win prize-money £38667

Going: Sf: 0-1 GS: 0-0 Gd: 1-4 GF: - Fm: 0-0
Distance: 2m/2m3: 0-0 2m4-2m7: 0-0 **3m+: 1-5**
Track: LH: 0-3 **RH: 1-2** Tight: 0-2 Gall: 0-0
Aids: Bl: 0-0 Vi: 0-0 Tstrap: 0-0
Best Rating: 151 4/02 Aint 3m1f good Ch

Useful handicap chaser. Stays beyond three miles and is effective on good and soft ground.

Ensign (IRE)

92 **65**
7-y-o b g Mandalus-Le Tricolore Token (Damsire Unregistered)
B I Case Case Racing Partnership

Placings:*00*/P5-FPP600 **(1580)**
2001/02: 26^{F}GF, 23^{P}G, 25^{P}GS, 22^{6}GF, 22^{0}GF, 24^{0}GS

	Starts	1st	2nd	3rd	Win & Pl
Hurdles	4	0	0	0	0
Chases	2	0	0	0	0
Career Total	**10**	**0**	**0**	**0**	**0**

Going: Sf: 0-0 GS: 0-2 Gd: 0-1 GF: - Fm: 0-3
Distance: 2m/2m3: 0-0 2m4-2m7: 0-2 3m+: 0-4
Track: LH: 0-4 RH: 0-1 Tight: 0-5 Gall: 0-0
Aids: Bl: 0-0 Vi: 0-0 Tstrap: 0-0
Best Rating: 79 3/00 Hntg 2m110y gd-fm NHF

Entertainer (IRE)

113(74c) (72c)**135**
6-y-o b g Be My Guest (USA)-Green Wings (General Assembly (USA))
P F Nicholls Malcom Pearce & Gerry Mizel

Placings:22/1F2401-001 **(0840)**
2001/02: 16^{0}G, 16^{0}GF, 20^{1}G

	Starts	1st	2nd	3rd	Win & Pl
Hurdles	2	1	0	0	5520
Chases	1	0	0	0	0
Career Total	**11**	**3**	**3**	**0**	**15035**

135	6/01	Worc	2m4f	C(0-135)HHdl	GD	£5519
126	4/01	Winc	2m	E Hdl	SFT	£3493
126	5/00	Font	2m2f110y	E Hdl	GD	£2450

Total win prize-money £11463

Going: Sf: 0-0 GS: 0-0 Gd: 1-2 GF: - Fm: 0-1
Distance: 2m/2m3: 0-2 **2m4-2m7: 1-1** 3m+: 0-0
Track: **LH: 1-3** RH: 0-0 Tight: 0-1 Gall: 0-0
Aids: Bl: 0-0 Vi: 0-0 Tstrap: 0-0
Best Rating: 135 6/01 Worc 2m4f good Hdl

He travels really well in his races, but, as he showed on the Flat, does not find a great deal off the bridle. Acts on good but has won on softer.

Epicure (FR)

106 **134+**
5-y-o b/br g Northern Crystal-L'Epicurienne (FR) (Rex Magna (FR))
Ian Williams Mrs Belinda Harvey

Placings:*00*00 **(4894)**
2001/02: 17^{0}GS, 18^{0}G, 16^{0}GS, 16^{0}G

	Starts	1st	2nd	3rd	Win & Pl
NH Flat	2	0	0	0	0
Hurdles	2	0	0	0	0
Career Total	**4**	**0**	**0**	**0**	**0**

Going: Sf: 0-0 GS: 0-2 Gd: 0-2 GF: - Fm: 0-0
Distance: 2m/2m3: 0-4 2m4-2m7: 0-0 3m+: 0-0
Track: LH: 0-1 RH: 0-2 Tight: 0-1 Gall: 0-0
Aids: Bl: 0-0 Vi: 0-0 Tstrap: 0-0
Best Rating: 85 1/02 Font 2m2f110y good NHF

Showed marked improvement since joining Martin Pipe and completed a hat-trick during the summer of 2002. Handles most types of ground.

Eponine

97(113h) (122h)**120**
8-y-o ch m Sharpo-Norska (Northfields (USA))
E A Elliott Eric A Elliott

Placings:211/43103064/22212235213/03300-541423UPP2 **(4581)**

2001/02: 17^{5}G, 20^{4}GS, 17^{1}G, 17^{4}G, 16^{2}GF, 20^{3}S, 19^{U}GS, 20^{P}GS, 21^{P}HY, 20^{2}G

	Starts	1st	2nd	3rd	Win & Pl
Hurdles	3	0	1	0	2072
Chases	7	1	1	1	5367
Career Total	**37**	**6**	**9**	**7**	**37412**

120	10/01	Kels	2m1f	E Ch	GD	£3120
128	2/00	Wwck	2m	C(0-135)HHdl	SFT	£4871
128	10/99	Kels	2m2f	E(0-115)HHdl	GD	£2290
118	12/98	Weth	2m	C(0-135)HHdl	SFT	£3540
95	11/97	Newc	2m	E Hdl	G-F	£2190
96	10/97	Hexm	2m	E Hdl	GD	£2385

Total win prize-money £18397

Going: Sf: 0-2 GS: 0-3 Gd: 1-4 GF: - Fm: 0-1
Distance: **2m/2m3: 1-5** 2m4-2m7: 0-5 3m+: 0-0
Track: **LH: 1-9** RH: 0-1 **Tight: 1-6** Gall: 0-0
Aids: Bl: 0-3 Vi: 0-0 Tstrap: 0-0
Best Rating: 128 10/00 Weth 2m gd-sft Hdl

Has won on the Flat, over hurdles, and over fences, although she has found one or two too good subsequently. Acts on most types of ground, and is very effective at around two miles. Has had problems with her jumping.

Epsilo De La Ronce (FR)

10-y-o b/br g Le Riverain (FR)-India Rosa (FR) (Carnaval)
S Flook S Flook

Placings:61440PF**250/4/56210-215F2P40P** **(4865)**
2001/02: 20^{2}GF, 24^{1}GS, 21^{5}GF, 22^{F}HY, 19^{2}S, 26^{P}G, 22^{4}GS, 21^{0}G, 23^{P}F

	Starts	1st	2nd	3rd	Win & Pl
Chases	9	1	2	0	4345
Career Total	**25**	**3**	**4**	**0**	**12305**

119	5/01	Strf	3m	H Ch	G-S	£3523
119	4/01	Asct	2m3f110y	H Ch	SFT	£3227
	9/98	Pmnl	2m2f110y	Ch	GD	£2727

Total win prize-money £9477

Going: Sf: 0-2 GS: 1-2 Gd: 0-2 GF: - Fm: 0-3
Distance: 2m/2m3: 0-0 2m4-2m7: 0-6 **3m+: 1-3**
Track: **LH: 1-7** RH: 0-1 **Tight: 1-3** Gall: 0-3
Aids: Bl: 0-0 Vi: 0-0 Tstrap: 0-0
Best Rating: 119 5/01 Strf 3m gd-sft Ch

Fair hunter chaser. Acts on fast and yielding ground. Stays three miles, perhaps more effective over shorter.

Equiname

89f **104f**

5-y-o b g Rock Hopper-Bayrouge (IRE) (Gorytus (USA))
D Eddy Mrs Karen McLintock

Placings:*0200* **(3680)**
2001/02: 16^{0}G, 16^{2}S, 16^{0}S, 16^{0}HY

	Starts	1st	2nd	3rd	Win & Pl
NH Flat	4	0	1	0	568
Career Total	**4**	**0**	**1**	**0**	**568**

Going: Sf: 0-3 GS: 0-0 Gd: 0-1 GF: - Fm: 0-0
Distance: 2m/2m3: 0-4 2m4-2m7: 0-0 3m+: 0-0
Track: LH: 0-2 RH: 0-1 Tight: 0-0 Gall: 0-0
Aids: Bl: 0-0 Vi: 0-0 Tstrap: 0-0
Best Rating: 104 1/02 Hayd 2m soft NHF

Improved on debut effort to finish second in a bumper at Newcastle. Acts on soft ground and is effective at two miles.

Equiname's Fancy

106 **98**

6-y-o ch g Minster Son-Joe's Fancy (Apollo Eight)
A Dickman Mike Smallman

Placings:*5221*/0-062225 **(4747)**
2001/02: 20^{0}HY, 24^{6}S, 17^{2}S, 19^{2}GS, 20^{2}HY, 20^{5}G

	Starts	1st	2nd	3rd	Win & Pl
Hurdles	6	0	3	0	2109
Career Total	**11**	**1**	**5**	**0**	**4928**

94	4/00	Newc	2m	H NHF	G-S	£1743

Total win prize-money £1743

Going: Sf: 0-4 GS: 0-1 Gd: 0-1 GF: - Fm: 0-0
Distance: 2m/2m3: 0-2 2m4-2m7: 0-3 3m+: 0-1
Track: LH: 0-5 RH: 0-0 Tight: 0-2 Gall: 0-2
Aids: Bl: 0-0 Vi: 0-0 Tstrap: 0-0
Best Rating: 98 3/02 Catt 2m3f gd-sft Hdl

Lightly raced bumper winner, improving steadily over hurdles.

Equiname's Reward

80f **73f**

7-y-o br g Henbit (USA)-Impressive Reward (USA) (Impressive)
D Eddy Equiname Ltd

Placings:*460/0* **(0181)**
2001/02: 10^{0}F

	Starts	1st	2nd	3rd	Win & Pl
NH Flat	1	0	0	0	
Career Total	**4**	**0**	**0**	**0**	**0**

Going: Sf: 0-0 GS: 0-0 Gd: 0-0 GF: - Fm: 0-1
Distance: 2m/2m3: 0-1 2m4-2m7: 0-0 3m+: 0-0
Track: LH: 0-1 RH: 0-0 Tight: 0-0 Gall: 0-0
Aids: Bl: 0-0 Vi: 0-0 Tstrap: 0-0
Best Rating: 97 1/00 Muss 2m soft NHF

Equity's Darling (IRE)

95 **75**

10-y-o b m Law Society (USA)-Curie Abu (Crofter (USA))
D C O'Brien D C O'Brien

Placings:004032L2/6B01P40/0323P5/0011132/00500/P-P50 **(4136)**
2001/02: 22^{P}HY, 22^{5}S, 22^{0}GS

	Starts	1st	2nd	3rd	Win & Pl
Hurdles	3	0	0	0	0
Career Total	**37**	**4**	**4**	**4**	**18329**

105	3/99	Sand	2m6f	D(0-120)HHdl	G-S	£5485
94	2/99	Folk	2m6f110y	E(0-115)HHdl	G-S	£2264
96	2/99	Ling	2m3f110y	F(0-110)HHdl	SFT	£2192
89	1/97	Ling	2m3f110y	E(0-100)HHdl	SFT	£2419

Total win prize-money £12362

Going: Sf: 0-2 GS: 0-1 Gd: 0-0 GF: - Fm: 0-0
Distance: 2m/2m3: 0-0 2m4-2m7: 0-3 3m+: 0-0
Track: LH: 0-0 RH: 0-3 Tight: 0-2 Gall: 0-0
Aids: Bl: 0-3 Vi: 0-0 Tstrap: 0-0
Best Rating: 105 3/99 Asct 3m gd-fm Hdl

Fair handicap hurdler. Best form was in the spring of 1999 but has struggled to recapture that since and has her own ideas about the game. Suited by two and a half to three miles with give underfoot.

Eric's Bett

94 **69**

9-y-o ro g Chilibang-Mira Lady (Henbit (USA))
J D J Davies M I Forbes

Placings:602/1150P/5/P/00060-053F **(2288)**
2001/02: 17^{0}GF, 17^{5}GF, 19^{3}GF, 17^{F}GF

	Starts	1st	2nd	3rd	Win & Pl
Hurdles	4	0	0	1	256
Career Total	**19**	**2**	**1**	**1**	**5356**

86	8/97	NAbb	2m1f	E Hdl	G-F	£2190
81	8/97	Strf	2m110y	E Hdl	G-F	£2262

Total win prize-money £4452

Going: Sf: 0-0 GS: 0-0 Gd: 0-0 GF: - Fm: 0-4
Distance: 2m/2m3: 0-4 2m4-2m7: 0-0 3m+: 0-0
Track: LH: 0-1 RH: 0-3 Tight: 0-1 Gall: 0-0
Aids: Bl: 0-0 Vi: 0-0 Tstrap: 0-0
Best Rating: 93 12/96 Catt 2m good Hdl

Has had his problems and been lightly-raced in recent seasons.

Erics Way

5-y-o b g Man Among Men (IRE)-Gypsy Crystal (USA) (Flying Saucer)
P R Rodford E T Wey

Placings:*000* **(2487)**
2001/02: 16^{0}G, 17^{0}G, 17^{0}HY

	Starts	1st	2nd	3rd	Win & Pl
NH Flat	3	0	0	0	
Career Total	**3**	**0**	**0**	**0**	

Going: Sf: 0-1 GS: 0-0 Gd: 0-2 GF: - Fm: 0-0
Distance: 2m/2m3: 0-3 2m4-2m7: 0-0 3m+: 0-0
Track: LH: 0-3 RH: 0-0 Tight: 0-2 Gall: 0-0
Aids: Bl: 0-0 Vi: 0-0 Tstrap: 0-0
Best Rating: 73 10/01 Chel 2m110y good NHF

Erin Alley (IRE)

101 **95**

9-y-o ch g Be My Native (USA)-Cousin Flo (True Song)
D J Wintle Lavender Hill Stud L L C

Placings:*55005*/P3P/**P-022F1P** **(4162)**
2001/02: 16^{0}GF, 19^{2}S, 21^{2}G, 21^{F}S, 20^{1}HY, 20^{P}G

	Starts	1st	2nd	3rd	Win & Pl
Chases	6	1	2	0	4291
Career Total	**15**	**1**	**2**	**1**	**4851**

95	1/02	Plum	2m4f	F(0-90)HCh	HVY	£2847

Total win prize-money £2847

Going: Sf: 1-3 GS: 0-0 Gd: 0-2 GF: - Fm: 0-1
Distance: 2m/2m3: 0-1 **2m4-2m7: 1-5** 3m+: 0-0
Track: **LH: 1-5** RH: 0-1 **Tight: 1-4** Gall: 0-0
Aids: Bl: 0-0 Vi: 0-0 Tstrap: 0-0
Best Rating: 104 12/97 Towc 2m soft NHF

Modest chaser, stays two and a half miles and acts in the mud.

Erin's Surprise (IRE)

6-y-o b g Erin's Hope-Ballinlassa (IRE) (Mandalus)
P J Millington P J Millington

Placings:UPP **(0340)**
2001/02: 25^{U}G, 21^{P}GF, 25^{P}G

	Starts	1st	2nd	3rd	Win & Pl
Chases	3	0	0	0	

	Starts	1st	2nd	3rd
Career Total	3	0	0	0

Going: Sf: 0-0 GS: 0-0 Gd: 0-2 GF: - Fm: 0-1
Distance: 2m/2m3: 0-0 2m4-2m7: 0-1 3m+: 0-2
Track: LH: 0-3 RH: 0-0 Tight: 0-2 Gall: 0-0
Aids: Bl: 0-0 Vi: 0-0 Tstrap: 0-0
Best Rating:

Erins Lass (IRE)

106 **79+**

5-y-o b m Erin's Isle-Amative (Beau Charmeur (FR))
R Dickin Stratford Members Club

Placings:00P6 **(4540)**
2001/02: 16^{0}G, 17^{0}G, 16^{P}S, 19^{6}G

	Starts	1st	2nd	3rd	Win & Pl
Hurdles	4	0	0	0	0
Career Total	**4**	**0**	**0**	**0**	**0**

Going: Sf: 0-1 GS: 0-0 Gd: 0-3 GF: - Fm: 0-0
Distance: 2m/2m3: 0-3 2m4-2m7: 0-1 3m+: 0-0
Track: LH: 0-3 RH: 0-1 Tight: 0-1 Gall: 0-1
Aids: Bl: 0-0 Vi: 0-0 Tstrap: 0-0
Best Rating: 69 4/02 Hrfd 2m3f110y good Hdl

Plating class hurdler at up to two miles three. In good heart this summer, making the frame twice.

Eriny (USA)

13-y-o b g Erin's Isle-Memorable Girl (USA) (Iron Ruler (USA))
J J Quinn Lady Anne Bentinck

Placings:3U05/41032021/F6P0426/PP0/2014600125/3625F6/0P-0 **(2509)**
2001/02: 19^{0}S

	Starts	1st	2nd	3rd	Win & Pl
Hurdles	1	0	0	0	
Career Total	**41**	**4**	**6**	**3**	**14345**

88	3/99	Hexm	2m	E(0-115)HHdl	G-S	£2363
88	11/98	Hexm	2m	F(0-105)HHdl	HVY	£1974
97	4/96	Hexm	2m	E(0-115)HHdl	G-F	£2553
78	6/95	Prth	2m110y	E Hdl	G-S	£2232

Total win prize-money £9124

Going: Sf: 0-1 GS: 0-0 Gd: 0-0 GF: - Fm: 0-0
Distance: 2m/2m3: 0-1 2m4-2m7: 0-0 3m+: 0-0
Track: LH: 0-1 RH: 0-0 Tight: 0-1 Gall: 0-0
Aids: Bl: 0-0 Vi: 0-0 Tstrap: 0-0
Best Rating: 97 4/96 Hexm 2m gd-fm Hdl

Eriskay (IRE)

100 **107**

6-y-o b g Montelimar (USA)-Little Peach (Ragapan)
L Lungo Colonel D C Greig

Placings:*0*UPU12 **(4857)**
2001/02: 16^{0}S, 20^{U}S, 16^{P}HY, 24^{U}S, 22^{1}S, 20^{2}G

	Starts	1st	2nd	3rd	Win & Pl
NH Flat	1	0	0	0	0
Hurdles	5	1	1	0	3659
Career Total	**6**	**1**	**1**	**0**	**3659**

107	3/02	Kels	2m6f110y	E Hdl	SFT	£2723

Total win prize-money £2723

Going: Sf: 1-5 GS: 0-0 Gd: 0-1 GF: - Fm: 0-0
Distance: 2m/2m3: 0-2 **2m4-2m7: 1-3** 3m+: 0-1
Track: **LH: 1-6** RH: 0-0 **Tight: 1-1** Gall: 0-1
Aids: Bl: 0-0 Vi: 0-0 Tstrap: 0-0
Best Rating: 107 3/02 Kels 2m6f110y soft Hdl

Was the victim of bad luck when failing to complete on first three starts over hurdles. Showed improved form when winning at Kelso in March and running well after. Stays two miles-six and looks a potential chaser.

Ernest William (IRE)

105(95h) (115h)**134**

10-y-o b/br g Phardante (FR)-Minerstown (IRE) (Miners Lamp)
Ferdy Murphy Exors Of The Late Mr G A Hubbard

Placings:*0*/0F450/11F141/1-**52311U** **(4876)**
2001/02: 20^{5}HY, 16^{2}G, 19^{3}S, 17^{1}G, 22^{1}G, 20^{U}G

	Starts	1st	2nd	3rd	Win & Pl
Chases	6	2	1	1	12902
Career Total	**19**	**7**	**1**	**1**	**31651**

134	4/02	MRas	2m6f110y	D(0-120)HCh	GD	£6890
105	4/02	MRas	2m1f110y	D Ch	GD	£4088
115	4/01	Prth	2m4f110y	C(0-130)HHdl	HVY	£5882
117	3/98	Ling	2m3f110y	C(0-135)HHdl	GD	£4889
115	2/98	Hntg	2m5f110y	E(0-110)HHdl	GD	£2652
100	12/97	Hntg	2m5f110y	F(0-100)HHdl	G-S	£2244
93	12/97	Wwck	2m3f	E(0-100)HHdl	GD	£2640

Total win prize-money £29290

Going: Sf: 0-2 GS: 0-0 Gd: 2-4 GF: - Fm: 0-0
Distance: 2m/2m3: 1-2 2m4-2m7: 1-4 3m+: 0-0
Track: LH: 0-1 **RH: 2-5 Tight: 2-3** Gall: 0-1
Aids: Bl: 0-0 Vi: 0-0 Tstrap: 0-0
Best Rating: 134 4/02 MRas 2m6f110y good Ch

Comfortable winner of a novices' chase and a handicap at Market Rasen in April 2002. Stays two-and-three-quarter miles, acts on a sound surface.

Ernford Tommygun

7-y-o b g Terimon-Wicklewood (Ovac (ITY))
M J Wilkinson Mrs M McInnes Skinner

Placings:P **(1845)**
2001/02: 16^{P}S

	Starts	1st	2nd	3rd	Win & Pl
Hurdles	1	0	0	0	
Career Total	**1**	**0**	**0**	**0**	

Going: Sf: 0-1 GS: 0-0 Gd: 0-0 GF: - Fm: 0-0
Distance: 2m/2m3: 0-1 2m4-2m7: 0-0 3m+: 0-0
Track: LH: 0-0 RH: 0-1 Tight: 0-0 Gall: 0-0
Aids: Bl: 0-0 Vi: 0-0 Tstrap: 0-0
Best Rating:

Erni (FR)

10-y-o b g Un Numide (FR)-Quianoa (FR) (Beaugency (FR))
W M Burnell W M Burnell

Placings:363/52/**0-FP** **(4859)**
2001/02: 25^{F}GS, 25^{P}G

	Starts	1st	2nd	3rd	Win & Pl
Chases	2	0	0	0	
Career Total	**8**	**0**	**1**	**2**	**1448**

Going: Sf: 0-0 GS: 0-1 Gd: 0-1 GF: - Fm: 0-0
Distance: 2m/2m3: 0-0 2m4-2m7: 0-0 3m+: 0-2
Track: LH: 0-1 RH: 0-0 Tight: 0-0 Gall: 0-0
Aids: Bl: 0-0 Vi: 0-0 Tstrap: 0-0
Best Rating: 82 5/97 Towc 3m good Hdl

Errand Boy

108 **134**

8-y-o b g Ardross-Love Match (USA) (Affiliate (USA))
Mrs S J Smith Trevor Hemmings

Placings:*12*/161F115/**F422U0-2U4222344** **(4652)**
2001/02: 17^{2}G, 25^{U}G, 25^{4}GS, 20^{2}S, 21^{2}S, 20^{2}S, 21^{3}HY, 19^{4}GS, 20^{4}G

	Starts	1st	2nd	3rd	Win & Pl
Chases	9	0	4	1	17082
Career Total	**24**	**5**	**7**	**1**	**53045**

132	3/00	Sand	2m4f110y	A HHdl	GD	£16800
132	2/00	Newc	2m	C HHdl	HVY	£7085
103	12/99	Catt	2m3f	E Hdl	G-F	£1940
105	10/99	Sthl	2m	E Hdl	G-S	£2192
119	3/99	Catt	2m	H NHF	SFT	£1525

Total win prize-money £29542

Going: Sf: 0-4 GS: 0-2 Gd: 0-3 GF: - Fm: 0-0
Distance: 2m/2m3: 0-1 2m4-2m7: 0-6 3m+: 0-2
Track: LH: 0-8 RH: 0-1 Tight: 0-4 Gall: 0-3
Aids: Bl: 0-0 Vi: 0-0 Tstrap: 0-0
Best Rating: 148 4/00 Aint 3m110y good Hdl

A winner of a bumper and four novice hurdles including the 2000 EBF Final, he has some fair form over fences, but keeps on finding one or two too good. Acts on most types of ground and is effective at up to two miles four furlongs. Not the best of jumpers and likes to dominate.

Errigal (FR)

90(93c) **86**

7-y-o ch g Murmure (FR)-Miss Big John (FR) (Big John (FR))
R T Phillips The Wild Rovers Racing Partnership

Placings:4245104/34P4PF45-00 **(0371)**
2001/02: 19^{0}G, 21^{0}G

	Starts	1st	2nd	3rd	Win & Pl
Hurdles	2	0	0	0	
Career Total	**17**	**1**	**1**	**1**	**5232**

91	1/99	Fknm	2m4f	D Hdl	G-S	£2692

Total win prize-money £2693

Going: Sf: 0-0 GS: 0-0 Gd: 0-2 GF: - Fm: 0-0
Distance: 2m/2m3: 0-1 2m4-2m7: 0-1 3m+: 0-0
Track: LH: 0-0 RH: 0-1 Tight: 0-0 Gall: 0-0
Aids: Bl: 0-0 Vi: 0-0 Tstrap: 0-0
Best Rating: 106 11/00 Wwck 3m110y heavy Ch

Erro Codigo

92 **78**

7-y-o b g Formidable (USA)-Home Wrecker (DEN) (Affiliation Order (USA))
F P Murtagh Mrs Anna Kenny

Placings:0500660-26 **(0742)**
2001/02: 16^{2}F, 16^{6}GS

	Starts	1st	2nd	3rd	Win & Pl
Hurdles	2	0	1	0	576
Career Total	**9**	**0**	**1**	**0**	**576**

Going: Sf: 0-0 GS: 0-1 Gd: 0-0 GF: - Fm: 0-1
Distance: 2m/2m3: 0-2 2m4-2m7: 0-0 3m+: 0-0
Track: LH: 0-2 RH: 0-0 Tight: 0-0 Gall: 0-0
Aids: Bl: 0-0 Vi: 0-0 Tstrap: 0-0
Best Rating: 63 6/01 Hexm 2m gd-sft Hdl

Errol Glamohr

103(106h) (83h)99

6-y-o b m Sir Harry Lewis (USA)-Steel Typhoon (General Ironside)

Mrs S C Bradburne James Glass

Placings:00U50-34512443 **(4442)**

2001/02: 24^{3}G, 20^{4}GS, 22^{5}GS, 22^{1}GS, 24^{2}G, 25^{4}GS, 20^{4}HY, 25^{3}S

	Starts	1st	2nd	3rd	Win & Pl
Hurdles	3	0	0	1	424
Chases	5	1	1	1	6455
Career Total	**13**	**1**	**1**	**2**	**6879**

99	12/01	Kels	2m6f110y	E Ch	G-S	£3315

Total win prize-money £3315

Going: Sf: 0-2 GS: 1-4 Gd: 0-2 GF: - Fm: 0-0
Distance: 2m/2m3: 0-0 **2m4-2m7: 1-4** 3m+: 0-4
Track: **LH: 1-5** RH: 0-2 **Tight: 1-4** Gall: 0-0
Aids: Bl: 0-0 Vi: 0-0 Tstrap: 0-0
Best Rating: 99 12/01 Kels 2m6f110y gd-sft Ch

Made a winning chase debut at Kelso in November 2001. Has won at up to two miles six furlongs on good to soft ground, does not want it too testing.

Erzadjan (IRE)

12-y-o b g Kahyasi-Ezana (Ela-Mana-Mou)

Mrs Sarah L Dent John Mackley

Placings:15234005/U1U111/024U03/0-3F **(0259)**

2001/02: 25^{3}S, 21^{F}GF

	Starts	1st	2nd	3rd	Win & Pl
Chases	2	0	0	1	384
Career Total	**23**	**5**	**2**	**3**	**22243**

134	4/96	Weth	2m4f110y	C(0-135)HHdl	GD	£4115
129	4/96	Kels	2m6f110y	D(0-120)HHdl	G-F	£2827
115	3/96	Uttx	3m110y	B(0-140)HHdl	GD	£4947
104	3/96	Kels	2m2f	D(0-120)HHdl	G-S	£2853
85	10/93	Newc	2m110y	Hdl	GD	£2280

Total win prize-money £17022

Going: Sf: 0-1 GS: 0-0 Gd: 0-0 GF: - Fm: 0-1
Distance: 2m/2m3: 0-0 2m4-2m7: 0-1 3m+: 0-1
Track: LH: 0-2 RH: 0-0 Tight: 0-1 Gall: 0-0
Aids: Bl: 0-0 Vi: 0-0 Tstrap: 0-0
Best Rating: 134 2/97 Sand 2m6f gd-fm Hdl

Formerly decent hurdler, showed form in hunter chases in 2001. Acts on any ground.

Es Elle (IRE)

73 53

4-y-o ch g Prince Of Birds (USA)-Bebe Auction (IRE) (Auction Ring (USA))

H M Kavanagh (J J O'Neill 15/9) Mrs S Kavanagh

Placings:4P **(1558)**

2001/02: 17^{4}G, 16^{P}G

	Starts	1st	2nd	3rd	Win & Pl
Hurdles	2	0	0	0	0
Career Total	**2**	**0**	**0**	**0**	**0**

Going: Sf: 0-0 GS: 0-0 Gd: 0-2 GF: - Fm: 0-0
Distance: 2m/2m3: 0-2 2m4-2m7: 0-0 3m+: 0-0
Track: LH: 0-2 RH: 0-0 Tight: 0-1 Gall: 0-0
Aids: Bl: 0-0 Vi: 0-0 Tstrap: 0-0
Best Rating: 53 9/01 Bang 2m1f good Hdl

Escartefigue (FR)

10-y-o b g Start Fast (FR)-Dona Clara (Crystal Palace (FR))

T Long (P F Nicholls 24/2) K W Biggins

Placings:1531432/533512/**121121/4232202F/4524UP/6P-25** **(4659)**

2001/02: 24^{2}S, 24^{5}G

	Starts	1st	2nd	3rd	Win & Pl
Chases	2	0	1	0	868
Career Total	**37**	**7**	**10**	**5**	**221492**

171	4/98	Aint	3m1f	A Ch	G-S	£37648
158	2/98	Chep	3m	B Ch	G-S	£7457
147	1/98	Weth	3m1f	A Ch	SFT	£11720
131	12/97	Worc	2m4f110y	E Ch	SFT	£3395
158	4/97	Aint	3m110y	B HHdl	GD	£11088
125	2/96	Ling	2m110y	D Hdl	HVY	£4012
	11/95	Autl	1m7f	HHdl	HVY	£17964

Total win prize-money £93287

Going: Sf: 0-1 GS: 0-0 Gd: 0-1 GF: - Fm: 0-0
Distance: 2m/2m3: 0-0 2m4-2m7: 0-0 3m+: 0-2
Track: LH: 0-0 RH: 0-2 Tight: 0-2 Gall: 0-0
Aids: Bl: 0-0 Vi: 0-0 Tstrap: 0-0
Best Rating: 171 2/99 Leop 3m soft Ch

A top-class chaser in his day for David Nicholson and later Paul Nicholls, he rather lost his way and is now showing ordinary form in hunter chases. Not the most straightforward of individuals.

Escondido (IRE)

8-y-o br g Mandalus-Lilly's Pride (IRE) (Long Pond)

Miss Lucinda V Russell Mrs L R Joughin

Placings:P **(1575)**

2001/02: 25^{P}G

	Starts	1st	2nd	3rd	Win & Pl
Chases	1	0	0	0	
Career Total	**1**	**0**	**0**	**0**	

Going: Sf: 0-0 GS: 0-0 Gd: 0-1 GF: - Fm: 0-0
Distance: 2m/2m3: 0-0 2m4-2m7: 0-0 3m+: 0-1
Track: LH: 0-1 RH: 0-0 Tight: 0-1 Gall: 0-0
Aids: Bl: 0-0 Vi: 0-0 Tstrap: 0-0
Best Rating:

Escort

103 100

6-y-o b g Most Welcome-Benazir (High Top)

W Clay The Escort Partnership

Placings:2P4/06512533-303P **(4572)**

2001/02: 24^{3}F, 16^{0}S, 21^{3}GS, 20^{P}G

	Starts	1st	2nd	3rd	Win & Pl
Hurdles	4	0	0	2	866
Career Total	**15**	**1**	**2**	**4**	**6541**

94	12/00	Weth	2m4f110y	D(0-110)HHdl	SFT	£3250

Total win prize-money £3250

Going: Sf: 0-1 GS: 0-1 Gd: 0-1 GF: - Fm: 0-1
Distance: 2m/2m3: 0-1 2m4-2m7: 0-2 3m+: 0-1
Track: LH: 0-3 RH: 0-0 Tight: 0-1 Gall: 0-1
Aids: Bl: 0-0 Vi: 0-2 Tstrap: 0-0
Best Rating: 100 5/01 Sthl 3m110y firm Hdl

A winner on the Flat, he has been successful over hurdles on soft ground and is effective over two miles four.

Esendi

98 98

7-y-o b g Buckley-Cagaleena (Cagirama)

G M McCourt Mrs Kathy Stuart

Placings:0-P445 **(2327)**

2001/02: 24^{P}GF, 22^{4}GS, 17^{4}S, 16^{5}S

	Starts	1st	2nd	3rd	Win & Pl
Hurdles	4	0	0	0	375
Career Total	**5**	**0**	**0**	**0**	**375**

Going: Sf: 0-2 GS: 0-1 Gd: 0-0 GF: - Fm: 0-1
Distance: 2m/2m3: 0-2 2m4-2m7: 0-1 3m+: 0-1
Track: LH: 0-3 RH: 0-1 Tight: 0-1 Gall: 0-0
Aids: Bl: 0-0 Vi: 0-0 Tstrap: 0-0
Best Rating: 98 10/01 Hrfd 2m1f soft Hdl

Eskleybrook

105(101h) (88h)155

9-y-o b g Arzanni-Crystal Run Vii (Damsire Unregistered)

N A Twiston-Davies V Y Gethin

Placings:00/P54PP111/1132/11F-4F30U6 **(4824)**

2001/02: 19^{4}S, 21^{F}HY, 17^{3}S, 16^{0}G, 21^{U}G, 16^{6}G

	Starts	1st	2nd	3rd	Win & Pl
Hurdles	1	0	0	0	0
Chases	5	0	0	1	3960
Career Total	**23**	**7**	**1**	**2**	**42624**

159	2/01	Sand	2m	C(0-135)HCh	SFT	£8580
149	1/01	Kemp	2m	D(0-120)HCh	SFT	£5668
133	10/99	Extr	2m1f	E(0-115)HCh	GD	£4143
125	5/99	Strf	2m1f110y	C(0-130)HCh	GD	£5725
117	4/99	Bang	2m1f110y	F(0-100)HCh	G-S	£4260
140	4/99	Wwck	2m	E(0-115)HCh	SFT	£3028
105	4/99	Hrfd	2m	F(0-110)HCh	G-F	£3550

Total win prize-money £34954

Going: Sf: 0-3 GS: 0-0 Gd: 0-3 GF: - Fm: 0-0
Distance: 2m/2m3: 0-3 2m4-2m7: 0-3 3m+: 0-0
Track: LH: 0-5 RH: 0-1 Tight: 0-1 Gall: 0-4
Aids: Bl: 0-1 Vi: 0-0 Tstrap: 0-0
Best Rating: 159 2/01 Sand 2m soft Ch

Decent front-running handicap chaser. Suited by two miles and, though he has won on good ground, looks especially suited by soft.

Esperanza Iv (FR)

107 109

10-y-o b m Quart De Vin (FR)-Relizane Iii (FR) (Diaghilev)

M J Roberts Mike Roberts

Placings:6501P3133P/3/2U221434/51243-P26 **(4760)**

2001/02: 24^{P}G, 24^{2}S, 24^{6}GF

	Starts	1st	2nd	3rd	Win & Pl
Hurdles	1	0	0	0	450
Chases	2	0	1	0	893
Career Total	**27**	**4**	**5**	**6**	**25510**

115	11/00	Leic	2m7f110y	F(0-110)HCh	G-S	£2687
100	2/00	Fknm	3m110y	F(0-100)HCh	GD	£4270
101	2/98	Plum	3m1f110y	E Ch	GD	£3263
87	11/97	Towc	3m	D Hdl	GD	£2714

Total win prize-money £12936

Going: Sf: 0-1 GS: 0-0 Gd: 0-1 GF: - Fm: 0-1
Distance: 2m/2m3: 0-0 2m4-2m7: 0-0 3m+: 0-3
Track: LH: 0-1 RH: 0-2 Tight: 0-1 Gall: 0-1
Aids: Bl: 0-0 Vi: 0-0 Tstrap: 0-0
Best Rating: 115 12/00 Leic 2m7f110y gd-sft Ch

Consistent if modest handicap chaser. Stays three miles and acts on good to soft ground.

Established

5-y-o b g Not In Doubt (USA)-Copper Trader (Faustus (USA))
J R Best Teapot Lane Partnership

Placings:0-P **(2949)**
2001/02: 22^{PS}

	Starts	1st	2nd	3rd	Win & Pl
Hurdles	1	0	0	0	
Career Total	**2**	**0**	**0**	**0**	

Going: Sf: 0-1 GS: 0-0 Gd: 0-0 GF: - Fm: 0-0
Distance: 2m/2m3: 0-0 2m4-2m7: 0-1 3m+: 0-0
Track: LH: 0-1 RH: 0-0 Tight: 0-1 Gall: 0-0
Aids: Bl: 0-0 Vi: 0-0 Tstrap: 0-0
Best Rating:

Estacado (IRE)

109 **121**
6-y-o b m Dolphin Street (FR)-Raubritter (Levmoss)
J W Mullins Woodford Valley Racing

Placings:10112202B04/40FF0-4220150F0 **(2664)**
2001/02: 24^{4}G, 27^{2}GF, 27^{2}GF, 21^{0}YS, 22^{1}GF, 20^{5}G, 21^{0}G, 22^{F}G, 24^{0}G

	Starts	1st	2nd	3rd	Win & Pl
Hurdles	9	1	2	0	6312
Career Total	**25**	**4**	**5**	**0**	**23692**

121	8/01	NAbb	2m6f	D(0-125)HHdl	G-F	£3250
113	12/99	Font	2m2f110y	E Hdl	GD	£2337
113	12/99	Winc	2m	E Hdl	GD	£2347
94	10/99	Winc	2m	F Hdl	GD	£2274

Total win prize-money £10211

Going: Sf: 0-0 GS: 0-0 Gd: 0-5 GF: - Fm: 1-3
Distance: 2m/2m3: 0-0 **2m4-2m7: 1-5** 3m+: 0-4
Track: **LH: 1-6** RH: 0-1 **Tight: 1-4** Gall: 0-1
Aids: Bl: 0-0 Vi: 0-1 Tstrap: 0-0
Best Rating: 121 8/01 NAbb 2m6f gd-fm Hdl

Fairly useful form as a juvenile hurdler but has only won once in handicap company since at Newton Abbot in August 2001. Stays well and best on a sound surface. Would not want it too soft.

Estrela Candente

6-y-o ch m Carlton (GER)-Soleil Etoile (Roi Soleil)
M D I Usher Mrs J Gawthorpe

Placings:00-0 **(0320)**
2001/02: 17^{0}F

	Starts	1st	2nd	3rd	Win & Pl
NH Flat	1	0	0	0	
Career Total	**3**	**0**	**0**	**0**	

Going: Sf: 0-0 GS: 0-0 Gd: 0-0 GF: - Fm: 0-1
Distance: 2m/2m3: 0-1 2m4-2m7: 0-0 3m+: 0-0
Track: LH: 0-0 RH: 0-1 Tight: 0-0 Gall: 0-0
Aids: Bl: 0-0 Vi: 0-0 Tstrap: 0-0
Best Rating:

Estuary (USA)

101 **91**
7-y-o ch g Riverman (USA)-Ocean Ballad (Grundy)
Ms A E Embiricos D W Haggie

Placings:6/300 **(3319)**
2001/02: 16^{3}G, 20^{0}G, 16^{0}GS

	Starts	1st	2nd	3rd	Win & Pl
Hurdles	3	0	0	1	347
Career Total	**4**	**0**	**0**	**1**	**347**

Going: Sf: 0-0 GS: 0-1 Gd: 0-2 GF: - Fm: 0-0
Distance: 2m/2m3: 0-2 2m4-2m7: 0-1 3m+: 0-0
Track: LH: 0-1 RH: 0-2 Tight: 0-0 Gall: 0-3
Aids: Bl: 0-0 Vi: 0-0 Tstrap: 0-0
Best Rating: 91 11/01 Hntg 2m110y good Hdl

He has shown some ability in a bumper and over hurdles, and should be able to make his mark when the ground is fast.

Estupendo (IRE)

63
5-y-o b g Tidaro (USA)-Spendapromise (Goldhill)
L Wells David Cox

Placings:00 **(4883)**
2001/02: 16^{0}GF, 22^{0}GF

	Starts	1st	2nd	3rd	Win & Pl
NH Flat	1	0	0	0	0
Hurdles	1	0	0	0	0
Career Total	**2**	**0**	**0**	**0**	

Going: Sf: 0-0 GS: 0-0 Gd: 0-0 GF: - Fm: 0-2
Distance: 2m/2m3: 0-1 2m4-2m7: 0-1 3m+: 0-0
Track: LH: 0-1 RH: 0-1 Tight: 0-1 Gall: 0-1
Aids: Bl: 0-0 Vi: 0-0 Tstrap: 0-0
Best Rating: 80 4/02 Hntg 2m110y gd-fm NHF

Eternal Spring (IRE)

112 **149**
5-y-o b g Persian Bold-Emerald Waters (King's Lake (USA))
J R Fanshawe Paul Green

Placings:043-2142 **(4653)**
2001/02: 17^{2}HY, 16^{1}S, 16^{4}GS, 20^{2}G

	Starts	1st	2nd	3rd	Win & Pl
Hurdles	4	1	2	0	24724
Career Total	**7**	**1**	**2**	**1**	**25726**

144	2/02	Newb	2m110y	C Hdl	SFT	£6344

Total win prize-money £6344

Going: Sf: 1-2 GS: 0-1 Gd: 0-1 GF: - Fm: 0-0
Distance: **2m/2m3: 1-3** 2m4-2m7: 0-1 3m+: 0-0
Track: **LH: 1-4** RH: 0-0 Tight: 0-1 **Gall: 1-2**
Aids: Bl: 0-0 Vi: 0-0 Tstrap: 0-0
Best Rating: 149 4/02 Aint 2m4f good Hdl

A decent stayer on the level, he is a useful novice hurdler, successful at Newbury in February before a good fourth in the Supreme Novices' Hurdle at the Festival and was runner-up to Classified at Aintree.. Suited by soft ground.

Etoile Dancer

96 **97**
7-y-o ch g Suave Dancer (USA)-Padelia (Thatching)
Miss Venetia Williams M B Roberts

Placings:P/F-2 **(0489)**
2001/02: 20^{2}GF

	Starts	1st	2nd	3rd	Win & Pl
Chases	1	0	1	0	915
Career Total	**3**	**0**	**1**	**0**	**915**

Going: Sf: 0-0 GS: 0-0 Gd: 0-0 GF: - Fm: 0-1
Distance: 2m/2m3: 0-0 2m4-2m7: 0-1 3m+: 0-0
Track: LH: 0-0 RH: 0-0 Tight: 0-1 Gall: 0-0
Aids: Bl: 0-0 Vi: 0-0 Tstrap: 0-0
Best Rating: 97 5/01 Font 2m4f gd-fm Ch

Lightly-raced chaser, looks best on fast ground.

Eton (GER)

102 **97**
6-y-o ch g Suave Dancer (USA)-Ermione (Surumu (GER))
D Nicholls (Miss Venetia Williams 4/5) V Greaves

Placings:4/2 **(0058)**
2001/02: 17^{2}GS

	Starts	1st	2nd	3rd	Win & Pl
Hurdles	1	0	1	0	880
Career Total	**2**	**0**	**1**	**0**	**880**

Going: Sf: 0-0 GS: 0-1 Gd: 0-0 GF: - Fm: 0-0
Distance: 2m/2m3: 0-1 2m4-2m7: 0-0 3m+: 0-0
Track: LH: 0-0 RH: 0-1 Tight: 0-1 Gall: 0-0
Aids: Bl: 0-0 Vi: 0-0 Tstrap: 0-0
Best Rating: 98 3/00 Ludl 2m gd-sft Hdl

Has respectable form on the level in Germany. He showed ability in two outings over hurdles for Venetia Williams. Now with Dandy Nicholls and racing on the Flat.

Etourneau Ii (FR)

10-y-o ch g Brezzo (FR)-Rose Marie Iii (FR) (Saumon (FR))
M C Pipe M C Pipe

Placings:1141/33/30/P3405/P **(1762)**
2001/02: 25^{P}S

	Starts	1st	2nd	3rd	Win & Pl
Hurdles	1	0	0	0	
Career Total	**14**	**3**	**0**	**4**	**30967**

4/97	Comp	2m1f110y	Hdl	VS	£3928
6/96	LE L	2m4f	Ch	GD	£3923
5/96	Fntb	2m3f	Ch	VS	£4216

Total win prize-money £12067

Going: Sf: 0-1 GS: 0-0 Gd: 0-0 GF: - Fm: 0-0
Distance: 2m/2m3: 0-0 2m4-2m7: 0-0 3m+: 0-1
Track: LH: 0-0 RH: 0-0 Tight: 0-0 Gall: 0-0
Aids: Bl: 0-0 Vi: 0-0 Tstrap: 0-0
Best Rating: 103 8/99 MRas 2m3f110y gd-fm Hdl

Ettrick (NZ)

108 **94**
7-y-o b g Hereward The Wake (USA)-Kardinia (NZ) (Creag-An-Sgor)
Mrs Barbara Waring (P J Hobbs 4/10) Hugh J Shapter

Placings:3P5-445PP6P0 **(4853)**
2001/02: 16^{4}GF, 20^{4}GF, 17^{5}GF, 16^{P}G, 20^{P}S, 16^{6}G, 16^{P}GS, 16^{0}G

	Starts	1st	2nd	3rd	Win & Pl
Hurdles	7	0	0	0	263
Chases	1	0	0	0	0
Career Total	**11**	**0**	**0**	**1**	**976**

Going: Sf: 0-1 GS: 0-1 Gd: 0-3 GF: - Fm: 0-3

Distance: 2m/2m3: 0-6 2m4-2m7: 0-2 3m+: 0-0
Track: LH: 0-6 RH: 0-1 Tight: 0-4 Gall: 0-1
Aids: Bl: 0-1 Vi: 0-0 Tstrap: 0-0
Best Rating: **94** 8/01 Worc 2m gd-fm Hdl

Modest hurdler, suited by two miles and fast ground. Not the most consistent.

Eurolinkhellraiser (IRE)

11-y-o b/br g Mandalus-Lady Lucifer (Lucifer (USA))
K A Nelmes (Trainer Unknown 17/2) Ms T Bather

Placings: *60/0* (4132)
2001/02: 25^{0}G

	Starts	1st	2nd	3rd	Win & Pl
Chases	1	0	0	0	
Career Total	**3**	**0**	**0**	**0**	

Going: Sf: 0-0 GS: 0-0 Gd: 0-1 GF: - Fm: 0-0
Distance: 2m/2m3: 0-0 2m4-2m7: 0-0 3m+: 0-1
Track: LH: 0-0 RH: 0-1 Tight: 0-0 Gall: 0-0
Aids: Bl: 0-0 Vi: 0-0 Tstrap: 0-0
Best Rating: **80** 2/96 Towc 2m heavy NHF

Europa

110(101h) 153

6-y-o b g Jupiter Island-Dublin Ferry (Celtic Cone)
T P Tate D T Otewart Drown

Placings: *15/1*112-1312FP2 (4899)
2001/02: 16^{1}S, 18^{3}G, 19^{1}GS, 20^{2}S, 24^{F}GS, 25^{P}G, 16^{2}G

	Starts	1st	2nd	3rd	Win & Pl
Chases	7	2	2	1	14014
Career Total	**13**	**6**	**3**	**1**	**24633**

147	1/02	Catt	2m3f	D Ch	G-S	£6279
127	12/01	Hexm	2m110y	E Ch	SFT	£3003
131	2/01	Bang	2m1f	E Hdl	HVY	£2744
143	1/01	Donc	2m4f	D Hdl	GD	£4007
112	11/00	Wwck	2m	H NHF	HVY	£1575
119	3/00	Donc	2m110y	H NHF	GD	£1631

Total win prize-money £19240

Going: Sf: 1-2 GS: 1-2 Gd: 0-3 GF: - Fm: 0-0
Distance: **2m/2m3: 2-4** 2m4-2m7: 0-1 3m+: 0-2
Track: **LH: 2-5** RH: 0-2 **Tight: 1-2** Gall: 0-2
Aids: Bl: 0-0 Vi: 0-0 Tstrap: 0-0
Best Rating: **153** 12/01 Newb 2m2f110y good Ch

Useful chaser who has a fine win-to-run ratio over hurdles and fences. Stays two and half miles but may prove better over shorter, handles any going.

Europrime Games

71 48

4-y-o b c Mind Games-Flower Princess (Slip Anchor)
John A Harris (R J Smith 25/7) Robin Hood Racing

Placings: 6 (1399)
2001/02: 17^{6}G

	Starts	1st	2nd	3rd	Win & Pl
Hurdles	1	0	0	0	0
Career Total	**1**	**0**	**0**	**0**	**0**

Going: Sf: 0-0 GS: 0-0 Gd: 0-1 GF: - Fm: 0-0
Distance: 2m/2m3: 0-1 2m4-2m7: 0-0 3m+: 0-0
Track: LH: 0-1 RH: 0-0 Tight: 0-1 Gall: 0-0
Aids: Bl: 0-0 Vi: 0-0 Tstrap: 0-0
Best Rating: **48** 9/01 Bang 2m1f good Hdl

Eurotrek (IRE)

102 127

6-y-o ch g Eurobus-Orient Jewel (Pollerton)
R H Alner Paul Green

Placings: *2612* (3262)
2001/02: 16^{2}S, 16^{6}G, 19^{1}GS, 21^{2}S

	Starts	1st	2nd	3rd	Win & Pl
NH Flat	2	0	1	0	620
Hurdles	2	1	1	0	9183
Career Total	**4**	**1**	**2**	**0**	**9803**

120	12/01	Newb	2m3f	D Hdl	G-S	£4582

Total win prize-money £4583

Going: Sf: 0-2 GS: 1-1 Gd: 0-1 GF: - Fm: 0-0
Distance: **2m/2m3: 1-3** 2m4-2m7: 0-1 3m+: 0-0
Track: **LH: 1-3** RH: 0-0 Tight: 0-0 **Gall: 1-1**
Aids: Bl: 0-0 Vi: 0-0 Tstrap: 0-0
Best Rating: **127** 1/02 Wwck 2m5f soft Hdl

Promising efforts in a couple of bumpers, before getting off the mark over hurdles at the first time of asking. Good effort behind Classified next time. Acts on soft ground and is effective over two and a half miles.

Eurotwist

89(85h) (70h)71

13-y-o b g Viking (USA)-Orange Bowl (General Assembly (USA))
Dr P Pritchard Dominic Ryan

Placings: 221/004/1160/525FP/53030/30/060F0/5600/00056 (1015)
2001/02: 16^{0}GF, 19^{0}GF, 16^{0}GF, 16^{5}G, 23^{6}G

	Starts	1st	2nd	3rd	Win & Pl
Hurdles	3	0	0	0	0
Chases	2	0	0	0	0
Career Total	**36**	**3**	**3**	**3**	**10496**

107	12/94	Weth	2m	(0-130)HHdl	GD	£3496
104	11/94	Sedg	2m1f110y	(0-100)HHdl	GD	£2339
96	2/93	Catt	2m	Hdl	G-S	£1910

Total win prize-money £7745

Going: Sf: 0-0 GS: 0-0 Gd: 0-2 GF: - Fm: 0-3
Distance: 2m/2m3: 0-4 2m4-2m7: 0-0 3m+: 0-1
Track: LH: 0-5 RH: 0-0 Tight: 0-2 Gall: 0-0
Aids: Bl: 0-0 Vi: 0-0 Tstrap: 0-0
Best Rating: **110** 11/95 Kels 2m2f gd-sft Hdl

Evan's Collier Boy (IRE)

9-y-o b g Supreme Leader-Little Treat (Miners Lamp)
D Brace David Brace

Placings: U-P (1502)
2001/02: 21^{P}G

	Starts	1st	2nd	3rd	Win & Pl
Chases	1	0	0	0	
Career Total	**2**	**0**	**0**	**0**	

Going: Sf: 0-0 GS: 0-0 Gd: 0-1 GF: - Fm: 0-0
Distance: 2m/2m3: 0-0 2m4-2m7: 0-1 3m+: 0-0
Track: LH: 0-1 RH: 0-0 Tight: 0-1 Gall: 0-0
Aids: Bl: 0-0 Vi: 0-0 Tstrap: 0-0
Best Rating:

Eveies Boy (IRE)

7-y-o b g Shardari-Bloomfield (IRE) (Alzao (USA))
B I Case Paul Rackham

Placings: *00/040S/FP* (0360)
2001/02: 18^{F}GF, 16^{P}GF

	Starts	1st	2nd	3rd	Win & Pl
Chases	2	0	0	0	
Career Total	**8**	**0**	**0**	**0**	**167**

Going: Sf: 0-0 GS: 0-0 Gd: 0-0 GF: - Fm: 0-2
Distance: 2m/2m3: 0-2 2m4-2m7: 0-0 3m+: 0-0
Track: LH: 0-1 RH: 0-0 Tight: 0-2 Gall: 0-0
Aids: Bl: 0-0 Vi: 0-0 Tstrap: 0-0
Best Rating: **56** 7/99 Tipp 2m gd-fm Hdl

Even Flow (IRE)

88 125

13-y-o b g Mandalus-Mariners Chain (Walshford)
T Casey A T A Wates

Placings: *04/44411263/1/131132/1330/P402F3/05200*
6161-5 (0011)
2001/02: 20^{5}GS

	Starts	1st	2nd	3rd	Win & Pl
Chases	1	0	0	0	0
Career Total	**37**	**9**	**4**	**6**	**81085**

125	4/01	Newb	3m	D(0-125)HCh	SFT	£5447
119	2/01	Font	3m2f110y	D(0-125)HCh	G-S	£4173
141	12/98	Kemp	2m4f110y	B HCh	SFT	£10960
140	2/98	Hayd	2m4f	B(0-145)HCh	GD	£14083
134	1/98	Kemp	2m4f110y	B(0-145)HCh	G-S	£7531
113	12/97	Wwck	2m4f110y	C(0-130)HCh	GD	£4378
109	11/95	Kemp	2m4f110y	D Ch	G F	£3100
112	1/95	Kemp	2m5f	D Hdl	HVY	£2960
107	12/94	Sthl	2m4f110y	(0-100)HHdl	SFT	£1815

Total win prize-money £54843

Going: Sf: 0-0 GS: 0-1 Gd: 0-0 GF: - Fm: 0-0
Distance: 2m/2m3: 0-0 2m4-2m7: 0-1 3m+: 0-0
Track: LH: 0-1 RH: 0-0 Tight: 0-1 Gall: 0-0
Aids: Bl: 0-0 Vi: 0-0 Tstrap: 0-0
Best Rating: **141** 2/99 Kemp 3m soft Ch

Formerly smart, he is not the force of old but remains competitive over three miles in ordinary company.

Evening Chorus (USA)

106 101

7-y-o b g Shadeed (USA)-Evening Air (USA) (J O Tobin (USA))
P Wegmann P Wegmann

Placings: 36/P4102635/010111343600F0-542210540300 (1492)
2001/02: 17^{5}F, 21^{4}G, 20^{2}GF, 20^{2}GF, 22^{1}GF, 22^{0}GF, 22^{5}G, 20^{4}G, 20^{0}GF, 20^{3}GF, 24^{0}GF, 26^{0}G

	Starts	1st	2nd	3rd	Win & Pl
Hurdles	12	1	2	1	3921
Career Total	**36**	**6**	**3**	**5**	**17186**

101	6/01	NAbb	2m6f	F(0-105)HHdl	G-F	£2401
108	7/00	Worc	3m	D(0-125)HHdl	G-F	£4043
100	7/00	Worc	2m4f	G(0-90)HHdl	G-F	£1519
91	6/00	Hexm	2m4f110y	G(0-95)HHdl	G-F	£1951
91	5/00	Towc	2m	G Hdl	G-F	£1533
88	9/99	Worc	2m	G(0-95)HHdl	G-F	£1744

Total win prize-money £13192

Going: Sf: 0-0 GS: 0-0 Gd: 0-4 GF: - Fm: 1-8
Distance: 2m/2m3: 0-1 **2m4-2m7: 1-9** 3m+: 0-2
Track: **LH: 1-9** RH: 0-2 **Tight: 1-5** Gall: 0-1
Aids: Bl: 0-1 Vi: 0-2 Tstrap: 0-0
Best Rating: **108** 7/00 Worc 3m gd-fm Hdl

Evening Splash (IRE)

55f **89f**

6-y-o b m Royal Fountain-Red Dusk (Deep Run)
Mrs J K M Oliver The Bank Partnership

Placings:*5* **(4145)**
2001/02: 16^{5}HY

	Starts	1st	2nd	3rd	Win & Pl
NH Flat	1	0	0	0	0
Career Total	**1**	**0**	**0**	**0**	**0**

Going: Sf: 0-1 GS: 0-0 Gd: 0-0 GF: - Fm: 0-0
Distance: 2m/2m3: 0-1 2m4-2m7: 0-0 3m+: 0-0
Track: LH: 0-1 RH: 0-0 Tight: 0-0 Gall: 0-0
Aids: Bl: 0-0 Vi: 0-0 Tstrap: 0-0
Best Rating: 89 3/02 Ayr 2m heavy NHF

A chasing type, proved green on hurdle debut.

Ever Blessed (IRE)

10-y-o b g Lafontaine (USA)-Sanctify (Joshua)
M Pitman Stewart Andrew

Placings:*12/3/232/*2111F/11P/P **(3493)**
2001/02: 24^{P}S

	Starts	1st	2nd	3rd	Win & Pl
Chases	1	0	0	0	
Career Total	**15**	**6**	**4**	**2**	**77457**

165	11/99	Newb	3m2f110y	A HCh	G-S	£48880
147	10/99	Chep	3m	B(0-145)HCh	SFT	£8533
140	3/99	Bang	3m110y	D Ch	SFT	£4548
116	3/99	Towc	2m6f	E Ch	SFT	£3028
138	1/99	Leic	2m7f110y	F Ch	SFT	£2212
113	2/96	Asct	2m110y	H NHF	SFT	£2851

Total win prize-money £70054

Going: Sf: 0-1 GS: 0-0 Gd: 0-0 GF: - Fm: 0-0
Distance: 2m/2m3: 0-0 2m4-2m7: 0-0 3m+: 0-1
Track: LH: 0-1 RH: 0-0 Tight: 0-0 Gall: 0-1
Aids: Bl: 0-0 Vi: 0-0 Tstrap: 0-0
Best Rating: 165 11/99 Newb 3m2f110y gd-sft Ch

A smart handicapper, he won the 1999 Hennessy. Never easy to train, he was deliberately sent to the 2000 Gold Cup without a prep race, but found conditions too fast and was pulled up, reportedly injuring his off-fore knee. Pulled up on his return after nearly two years off. Acts on soft ground and stays three and a quarter miles. He has reportedly joined Philip Hobbs.

Everbold

5-y-o b m Never So Bold-Out Of Hours (Lochnager)
D McCain Mrs D McCain

Placings:P **(0332)**
2001/02: 16^{P}GS

	Starts	1st	2nd	3rd	Win & Pl
Hurdles	1	0	0	0	
Career Total	**1**	**0**	**0**	**0**	

Going: Sf: 0-0 GS: 0-1 Gd: 0-0 GF: - Fm: 0-0
Distance: 2m/2m3: 0-1 2m4-2m7: 0-0 3m+: 0-0
Track: LH: 0-0 RH: 0-1 Tight: 0-0 Gall: 0-0
Aids: Bl: 0-0 Vi: 0-0 Tstrap: 0-0
Best Rating:

Eviyrn (IRE)

102 **85**

6-y-o b g In The Wings-Evrana (USA) (Nureyev (USA))
J R Jenkins Home Counties Finance Limited

Placings:65056/0143500P-32FP **(2114)**
2001/02: 24^{3}G, 20^{2}G, 16^{F}S, 17^{P}S

	Starts	1st	2nd	3rd	Win & Pl
Hurdles	4	0	1	1	1350
Career Total	**17**	**1**	**1**	**2**	**4497**

86	10/00	Plum	2m	E(0-105)HHdl	SFT	£2576

Total win prize-money £2576

Going: Sf: 0-2 GS: 0-0 Gd: 0-2 GF: - Fm: 0-0
Distance: 2m/2m3: 0-2 2m4-2m7: 0-1 3m+: 0-1
Track: LH: 0-2 RH: 0-2 Tight: 0-2 Gall: 0-0
Aids: Bl: 0-0 Vi: 0-2 Tstrap: 0-0
Best Rating: 90 12/00 Donc 2m110y heavy Hdl

A fair hurdler over the minimum trip. Has looked a bit quirky in the past. Suited by soft ground.

Evolution (IRE)

98 **73**

5-y-o b m Phardante (FR)-Cape Breeze (IRE) (Strong Gale)
N A Twiston-Davies Mrs S Tainton

Placings:*56*-40034 **(4577)**
2001/02: 21^{4}G, 21^{0}S, 21^{0}G, 26^{3}G, 24^{4}G

	Starts	1st	2nd	3rd	Win & Pl
Hurdles	5	0	0	1	636
Career Total	**7**	**0**	**0**	**1**	**636**

Going: Sf: 0-1 GS: 0-0 Gd: 0-4 GF: - Fm: 0-0
Distance: 2m/2m3: 0-0 2m4-2m7: 0-3 3m+: 0-2
Track: LH: 0-1 RH: 0-2 Tight: 0-0 Gall: 0-0
Aids: Bl: 0-3 Vi: 0-0 Tstrap: 0-0
Best Rating: 79 2/01 Wwck 2m soft NHF

Poor form, best in blinkers over hurdles.

Evolution Lad (IRE)

72 **57**

6-y-o b g Sharp Charter-Neatly Does It (IRE) (Camden Town)
N A Twiston-Davies Evolution Films Limited

Placings:*1*300P **(4842)**
2001/02: 16^{1}GF, 16^{3}GF, 20^{0}HY, 16^{0}G, 20^{P}G

	Starts	1st	2nd	3rd	Win & Pl
NH Flat	2	1	0	1	1995
Hurdles	3	0	0	0	0
Career Total	**5**	**1**	**0**	**1**	**1995**

91	10/01	Ludl	2m	H NHF	G-F	£1750

Total win prize-money £1750

Going: Sf: 0-1 GS: 0-0 Gd: 0-2 GF: - Fm: 1-2
Distance: **2m/2m3: 1-3** 2m4-2m7: 0-2 3m+: 0-0
Track: LH: 0-2 **RH: 1-3** Tight: 0-1 Gall: 0-0
Aids: Bl: 0-0 Vi: 0-0 Tstrap: 0-0
Best Rating: 91 10/01 Ludl 2m gd-fm NHF

Winner of a Ludlow bumper but held over hurdles subsequently.

Ewar Bold

102 **90**

9-y-o b g Bold Arrangement-Monaneigue Lady (Julio Mariner)
K G Wingrove A F Maiden

Placings:U06655P43/0/P/F/03F0 **(4847)**
2001/02: 25^{0}GS, 21^{3}GS, 17^{F}GF, 20^{0}G

	Starts	1st	2nd	3rd	Win & Pl
Hurdles	4	0	0	1	279
Career Total	**16**	**0**	**0**	**2**	**534**

Going: Sf: 0-0 GS: 0-2 Gd: 0-1 GF: - Fm: 0-1
Distance: 2m/2m3: 0-1 2m4-2m7: 0-2 3m+: 0-1
Track: LH: 0-1 RH: 0-2 Tight: 0-1 Gall: 0-0
Aids: Bl: 0-0 Vi: 0-0 Tstrap: 0-4
Best Rating: 90 3/02 Towc 2m5f gd-sft Hdl

Selling-class hurdler, suited by cut in the ground.

Exact (FR)

10-y-o ch g Beyssac (FR)-Valse De Sienne (FR) (Petit Montmorency (USA))
N P Williams N P Williams

Placings:PPP4/U655034/1/P35 **(4692)**
2001/02: 24^{P}S, 27^{3}GF, 25^{5}GF

	Starts	1st	2nd	3rd	Win & Pl
Chases	3	0	0	1	216
Career Total	**15**	**1**	**0**	**2**	**3971**

103	5/99	Chep	3m	E(0-115)HHdl	GD	£2542

Total win prize-money £2542

Going: Sf: 0-1 GS: 0-0 Gd: 0-0 GF: - Fm: 0-2
Distance: 2m/2m3: 0-0 2m4-2m7: 0-0 3m+: 0-3
Track: LH: 0-2 RH: 0-1 Tight: 0-3 Gall: 0-0
Aids: Bl: 0-2 Vi: 0-0 Tstrap: 0-2
Best Rating: 112 4/99 Uttx 2m4f gd-sft Ch

Modest pointer/hunter chaser. Suited by good ground or faster and front-running tactics. Wears blinkers and has worn a tongue tie.

Exalted (IRE)

103 **117**

9-y-o b g High Estate-Heavenward (USA) (Conquistador Cielo (USA))
T A K Cuthbert Mrs Elva Maxwell & Roy Thorburn

Placings:240/12046R30/56506423235126/03202104/40256-45035F **(4834)**
2001/02: 20^{4}GS, 20^{5}GS, 20^{0}S, 20^{3}HY, 20^{5}S, 22^{F}G

	Starts	1st	2nd	3rd	Win & Pl
Hurdles	6	0	0	1	896
Career Total	**44**	**3**	**8**	**5**	**24116**

118	1/00	Ayr	2m4f	B(0-145)HHdl	SFT	£6899
106	2/99	Ayr	2m4f	F(0-95)HHdl	SFT	£2878
109	10/97	Hrfd	2m1f	E Hdl	G-F	£2290

Total win prize-money £12068

Going: Sf: 0-3 GS: 0-2 Gd: 0-1 GF: - Fm: 0-0
Distance: 2m/2m3: 0-0 2m4-2m7: 0-6 3m+: 0-0
Track: LH: 0-5 RH: 0-0 Tight: 0-0 Gall: 0-1
Aids: Bl: 0-0 Vi: 0-0 Tstrap: 0-0
Best Rating: 119 1/01 Ayr 2m4f gd-sft Hdl

He is a bit of a character and not the most reliable of sorts. Stays well and acts in soft ground. Mixes turf Flat racing with hurdling. Suited by a strong pace.

Excise Man

97 **93**

14-y-o ch g Import-Super Satin (Lord Of Verona)
J B Walton F T Walton

Placings:*6*/P0/34004/0P56044/331F/5/0353F3P65000/12/00-0520 **(0803)**

2001/02: 25^{0}S, 20^{5}F, 20^{2}GS, 24^{0}GF

	Starts	1st	2nd	3rd	Win & Pl
Chases	4	0	1	0	998
Career Total	**40**	**2**	**2**	**6**	**11193**

93 6/99 Hexm 2m4f110y F(0-105)HCh G-F £3088
76 5/96 Hexm 2m110y E Ch G-F £2134
Total win prize-money £5224

Going: Sf: 0-1 GS: 0-1 Gd: 0-0 GF: - Fm: 0-2
Distance: 2m/2m3: 0-0 2m4-2m7: 0-2 3m+: 0-2
Track: LH: 0-3 RH: 0-1 Tight: 0-0 Gall: 0-0
Aids: Bl: 0-0 Vi: 0-0 Tstrap: 0-2
Best Rating: 94 12/94 Newc 2m110y good Ch

Veteran pointer/hunter chaser, acts on any ground.

Executive Choice (IRE)

103 **103**

8-y-o b g Don't Forget Me-Shadia (USA) (Naskra (USA))
Miss V Haigh (B Ellison 18/1) Tune Pack Produce Ltd

Placings:26/12142400/3061U12405-05405UPP0B **(4917)**
2001/02: 17^{0}G, 17^{5}G, 17^{4}GF, 17^{0}G, 17^{5}GS, 20^{U}G, 17^{P}GS, 24^{P}G, 17^{0}GS, 21^{B}GF

	Starts	1st	2nd	3rd	Win & Pl
Hurdles	10	0	0	0	0
Career Total	**30**	**4**	**4**	**1**	**11666**

109 12/00 Fknm 2m G(0-95)HHdl G-S £1802
102 11/00 Sedg 2m1f G(0-95)HHdl SFT £1631
105 8/99 Ctml 2m1f110y E(0-105)HHdl GD £2302
100 7/99 Sedg 2m1f E Hdl G-F £2512
Total win prize-money £8250

Going: Sf: 0-0 GS: 0-3 Gd: 0-5 GF: - Fm: 0-2
Distance: 2m/2m3: 0-7 2m4-2m7: 0-2 3m+: 0-1
Track: LH: 0-8 RH: 0-2 Tight: 0-9 Gall: 0-1
Aids: Bl: 0-0 Vi: 0-1 Tstrap: 0-9
Best Rating: 109 12/00 Fknm 2m gd-sft Hdl

Executive Decision (IRE)

(109h) (121h)**117**

8-y-o ch g Classic Music (USA)-Bengala (FR) (Hard To Beat)
P J Hobbs E Gutner & M Krysztofiak Racing

Placings:116/2055150/**14/F-6U26** **(3880)**
2001/02: 16^{6}GS, 16^{U}S, 16^{2}HY, 21^{6}GS

	Starts	1st	2nd	3rd	Win & Pl
Hurdles	1	0	0	0	0
Chases	3	0	1	0	1564
Career Total	**17**	**4**	**2**	**0**	**20200**

139 11/99 NAbb 2m110y E Ch SFT £3156
133 3/99 Chep 2m110y C(0-130)HHdl HVY £4417
117 2/98 Navn 2m Hdl SFT £5956
119 12/97 Leop 2m Hdl HVY £4069
Total win prize-money £17600

Going: Sf: 0-2 GS: 0-2 Gd: 0-0 GF: - Fm: 0-0
Distance: 2m/2m3: 0-3 2m4-2m7: 0-1 3m+: 0-0
Track: LH: 0-1 RH: 0-3 Tight: 0-0 Gall: 0-0
Aids: Bl: 0-1 Vi: 0-2 Tstrap: 0-0
Best Rating: 139 11/99 Chep 2m110y good Ch

Fair hurdler/chaser. Best over two miles on a soft surface. Has worn blinkers and a visor.

Executive Office (IRE)

(67c)

9-y-o bl g Executive Perk-Lilly's Pride (IRE) (Long Pond)
Simon T Lewis Simon T Lewis

Placings:000*0*/6/**5230435-P**PF **(4108)**
2001/02: 21^{P}G, 24^{P}S, 24^{F}S

	Starts	1st	2nd	3rd	Win & Pl
Hurdles	2	0	0	0	0
Chases	1	0	0	0	0
Career Total	**15**	**0**	**1**	**2**	**2073**

Going: Sf: 0-2 GS: 0-0 Gd: 0-1 GF: - Fm: 0-0
Distance: 2m/2m3: 0-0 2m4-2m7: 0-1 3m+: 0-2
Track: LH: 0-0 RH: 0-2 Tight: 0-1 Gall: 0-0
Aids: Bl: 0-0 Vi: 0-0 Tstrap: 0-0
Best Rating: 103 10/00 Extr 2m7f110y good Ch

Exellent Adventure

4-y-o ch g Gold Dust-Freedom Weekend (USA) (Shahrastani (USA))
D Burchell Mrs D L Smith-Hopper

Placings:F **(3157)**
2001/02: 17^{F}S

	Starts	1st	2nd	3rd	Win & Pl
Hurdles	1	0	0	0	
Career Total	**1**	**0**	**0**	**0**	

Going: Sf: 0-1 GS: 0-0 Gd: 0-0 GF: - Fm: 0-0
Distance: 2m/2m3: 0-1 2m4-2m7: 0-0 3m+: 0-0
Track: LH: 0-0 RH: 0-1 Tight: 0-0 Gall: 0-0
Aids: Bl: 0-0 Vi: 0-0 Tstrap: 0-0
Best Rating:

Exhibition Girl (IRE)

72 **40**

5-y-o ch m Perugino (USA)-Shy Jinks (Shy Groom (USA))
Andrew Turnell Mrs Kate Dalton

Placings:66 **(3448)**
2001/02: 16^{6}GF, 16^{6}GS

	Starts	1st	2nd	3rd	Win & Pl
Hurdles	2	0	0	0	0
Career Total	**2**	**0**	**0**	**0**	**0**

Going: Sf: 0-0 GS: 0-1 Gd: 0-0 GF: - Fm: 0-1
Distance: 2m/2m3: 0-2 2m4-2m7: 0-0 3m+: 0-0
Track: LH: 0-2 RH: 0-0 Tight: 0-2 Gall: 0-0
Aids: Bl: 0-0 Vi: 0-0 Tstrap: 0-0
Best Rating: 40 8/01 Sthl 2m gd-fm Hdl

Existential (FR)

96(56h) **112**

7-y-o b g Exit To Nowhere (USA)-Lyceana (USA) (Super Concorde (USA))
P F Nicholls H B Geddes

Placings:5/32P3P/2-4 **(1896)**
2001/02: 20^{4}GS

	Starts	1st	2nd	3rd	Win & Pl
Chases	1	0	0	0	0
Career Total	**8**	**0**	**2**	**2**	**2549**

Going: Sf: 0-0 GS: 0-1 Gd: 0-0 GF: - Fm: 0-0
Distance: 2m/2m3: 0-0 2m4-2m7: 0-1 3m+: 0-0
Track: LH: 0-0 RH: 0-0 Tight: 0-1 Gall: 0-0
Aids: Bl: 0-0 Vi: 0-0 Tstrap: 0-0
Best Rating: 112 10/01 Font 2m4f gd-sft Ch

Exit Swinger (FR)

117(99h) (139h)**165**

7-y-o b g Exit To Nowhere (USA)-Morganella (FR) (D'Arras (FR))
M C Pipe Sandicroft Stud Syndicate

Placings:26/5**F3064**3122105**1/263F-316420** **(4827a)**
2001/02: 20^{3}G, 17^{1}S, 16^{6}G, 16^{4}G, 16^{2}G, 21^{0}GF

	Starts	1st	2nd	3rd	Win & Pl
Hurdles	1	0	0	0	1500
Chases	5	1	1	1	35510
Career Total	**26**	**4**	**5**	**4**	**104749**

165 12/01 Newb 2m1f C(0-135)HCh SFT £9510
146 4/00 Sand 2m4f110y C HCh SFT £17517
136 2/00 Chep 2m4f D Hdl SFT £3334
12/99 Autl 2m1f110y Ch HLD £6997
Total win prize-money £37360

Going: Sf: 1-1 GS: 0-0 Gd: 0-4 GF: - Fm: 0-1
Distance: **2m/2m3: 1-4** 2m4-2m7: 0-2 3m+: 0-0
Track: **LH: 1-3** RH: 0-2 Tight: 0-0 **Gall: 1-3**
Aids: Bl: 0-0 Vi: 0-0 Tstrap: 0-0
Best Rating: 165 3/02 Chel 2m110y good Ch

A winner over fences in France, he made a successful chasing debut in Britain at Sandown and started 2000/01 off with a brave second in the Thomas Pink Gold Cup. Third to Shooting Light in this season's Thomas Pink, he won a competitive handicap at the Hennessy meeting on a tight rein, before decent efforts off a higher mark. Unproven beyond two and a half miles, he likes to get his toe in.

Exit To Wave (FR)

107 **160**

6-y-o ch g Exit To Nowhere (USA)-Hereke (Blakeney)
P F Nicholls Malcolm Pearce & Gerry Mizel Ii

Placings:11111P344/P**1F1P142U-440** **(4234)**
2001/02: 20^{4}G, 19^{4}GS, 20^{0}GS

	Starts	1st	2nd	3rd	Win & Pl
Chases	3	0	0	0	4070
Career Total	**21**	**8**	**1**	**1**	**70668**

155 3/01 Wwck 2m110y B HCh HVY £10717
146 1/01 Asct 2m A Ch G-S £15000
135 11/00 Wwck 2m110y D Ch HVY £4039
12/99 Cagn 2m2f Hdl SFT £7685
12/99 Bord 2m2f Hdl GD £3842
11/99 Bord 2m2f Hdl VS £3445
10/99 Bord 2m110y Hdl HVY £3767
10/99 Mtbn 2m1f110y Hdl SFT £2368
Total win prize-money £50863

Going: Sf: 0-0 GS: 0-2 Gd: 0-1 GF: - Fm: 0-0
Distance: 2m/2m3: 0-0 2m4-2m7: 0-3 3m+: 0-0
Track: LH: 0-2 RH: 0-1 Tight: 0-0 Gall: 0-1
Aids: Bl: 0-0 Vi: 0-0 Tstrap: 0-3
Best Rating: 160 11/01 Weth 2m4f110y good Ch

Decent handicap chaser. He was held in good handicaps in 2001/02. Best on a soft surface and has worn a tongue tie.

Exjaysix

69 **35**

4-y-o b g Chocolat De Meguro (USA)-Secret Chant (Silly Prices)
M A Barnes M Barnes

Placings:0 **(1418)**
2001/02: 17^{0}G

	Starts	1st	2nd	3rd	Win & Pl
Hurdles	1	0	0	0	
Career Total	**1**	**0**	**0**	**0**	

Going: Sf: 0-0 GS: 0-0 Gd: 0-1 GF: - Fm: 0-0
Distance: 2m/2m3: 0-1 2m4-2m7: 0-0 3m+: 0-0
Track: LH: 0-1 RH: 0-0 Tight: 0-1 Gall: 0-0
Aids: Bl: 0-0 Vi: 0-0 Tstrap: 0-0
Best Rating: 35 9/01 Sedg 2m1f good Hdl

Exodous (ARG)

94 **97**

6-y-o ch g Equalize (USA)-Empire Glory (ARG) (Good Manners (USA))
J A B Old W E Sturt

Placings:65 **(4422)**
2001/02: 16^{6}G, 16^{5}GS

	Starts	1st	2nd	3rd	Win & Pl
Hurdles	2	0	0	0	0
Career Total	**2**	**0**	**0**	**0**	**0**

Going: Sf: 0-0 GS: 0-1 Gd: 0-1 GF: - Fm: 0-0
Distance: 2m/2m3: 0-2 2m4-2m7: 0-0 3m+: 0-0
Track: LH: 0-1 RH: 0-1 Tight: 0-0 Gall: 0-1
Aids: Bl: 0-0 Vi: 0-0 Tstrap: 0-0
Best Rating: 97 3/02 Newb 2m110y gd-sft Hdl

Won six times on the Flat in Argentina at up to a mile and a half. Now with Jim Old but was reported to have made a noise on his hurdles bow at Wincanton in March 2002.

Exotic Hawk (USA)

6-y-o b m Silver Hawk (USA)-Seeking The Stars (USA) (Seeking The Gold (USA))
G M Moore Mrs A Roddis

Placings:*0/P* **(4873)**
2001/02: 16^{P}GF

	Starts	1st	2nd	3rd	Win & Pl
NH Flat	1	0	0	0	
Career Total	**2**	**0**	**0**	**0**	

Going: Sf: 0-0 GS: 0-0 Gd: 0-0 GF: - Fm: 0-1
Distance: 2m/2m3: 0-1 2m4-2m7: 0-0 3m+: 0-0
Track: LH: 0-1 RH: 0-0 Tight: 0-0 Gall: 0-0
Aids: Bl: 0-0 Vi: 0-0 Tstrap: 0-0
Best Rating: 48 1/00 Donc 2m110y gd-fm NHF

Expense Account (IRE)

(96h) (67h)

8-y-o b m Executive Perk-Cranagh Lady (Le Bavard (FR))
Mrs H Dalton Paul O'Connell & Aidan Walls

Placings:*00*-50PB **(4590)**
2001/02: 21^{5}S, 20^{0}GS, 22^{P}HY, 24^{B}G

Starts	1st	2nd	3rd	Win & Pl
Hurdles	2	0	0	0	0
Chases	2	0	0	0	0
Career Total	**6**	**0**	**0**	**0**	**0**

Going: Sf: 0-2 GS: 0-1 Gd: 0-1 GF: - Fm: 0-0
Distance: 2m/2m3: 0-0 2m4-2m7: 0-3 3m+: 0-1
Track: LH: 0-1 RH: 0-3 Tight: 0-0 Gall: 0-1
Aids: Bl: 0-0 Vi: 0-0 Tstrap: 0-0
Best Rating: 67 11/01 Towc 2m5f soft Hdl

Expensive Gale

77f **60f**

7-y-o b g Tirley Gale-Expensive Lark (Sir Lark)
J S Smith Donald Smith

Placings:*0* **(3563)**
2001/02: 16^{0}HY

	Starts	1st	2nd	3rd	Win & Pl
NH Flat	1	0	0	0	
Career Total	**1**	**0**	**0**	**0**	

Going: Sf: 0-1 GS: 0-0 Gd: 0-0 GF: - Fm: 0-0
Distance: 2m/2m3: 0-1 2m4-2m7: 0-0 3m+: 0-0
Track: LH: 0-0 RH: 0-1 Tight: 0-0 Gall: 0-0
Aids: Bl: 0-0 Vi: 0-0 Tstrap: 0-0
Best Rating: 60 1/02 Towc 2m heavy NHF

Expensive Presant (IRE)

74f **48f**

6-y-o ch g Dry Dock-Skylin (Skyliner)
A M Hales Andrew L Cohen

Placings:*00* **(1832)**
2001/02: 16^{0}G, 16^{0}G

	Starts	1st	2nd	3rd	Win & Pl
NH Flat	2	0	0	0	
Career Total	**2**	**0**	**0**	**0**	

Going: Sf: 0-0 GS: 0-0 Gd: 0-2 GF: - Fm: 0-0
Distance: 2m/2m3: 0-2 2m4-2m7: 0-0 3m+: 0-0
Track: LH: 0-1 RH: 0-1 Tight: 0-1 Gall: 0-1
Aids: Bl: 0-0 Vi: 0-0 Tstrap: 0-0
Best Rating: 48 10/01 Sthl 2m good NHF

Explosive

4-y-o b g Saddlers' Hall (IRE)-Pursuit Of Glory (Shirley Heights)
P J Hobbs (C A Cyzer 1/10) P J Hobbs

Placings:P **(3641)**
2001/02: 16^{P}S

	Starts	1st	2nd	3rd	Win & Pl
Hurdles	1	0	0	0	
Career Total	**1**	**0**	**0**	**0**	

Going: Sf: 0-1 GS: 0-0 Gd: 0-0 GF: - Fm: 0-0
Distance: 2m/2m3: 0-1 2m4-2m7: 0-0 3m+: 0-0
Track: LH: 0-0 RH: 0-1 Tight: 0-0 Gall: 0-0
Aids: Bl: 0-0 Vi: 0-0 Tstrap: 0-0
Best Rating:

Exstoto

110 **108**

5-y-o b g Mtoto-Stoproveritate (Scorpio (FR))
R A Fahey J D Clark And Partners

Placings:*4-1*01313F241 **(4581)**
2001/02: 16^{1}GF, 16^{0}GF, 17^{1}GF, 17^{3}G, 19^{1}GS, 22^{3}G, 20^{F}GS, 20^{2}HY, 20^{4}GS, 20^{1}G

	Starts	1st	2nd	3rd	Win & Pl
NH Flat	3	2	0	0	3101
Hurdles	7	2	1	2	12227
Career Total	**11**	**4**	**1**	**2**	**15328**

108	4/02	Weth	2m4f110y	B(0-145)HHdl	GD	£5109
108	10/01	MRas	2m3f110y	D Hdl	G-S	£3430
97	7/01	Sedg	2m1f	H NHF	G-F	£1536
97	5/01	Sthl	2m	H NHF	G-F	£1564

Total win prize-money £11641

Going: Sf: 0-1 GS: 1-3 Gd: 1-3 GF: - Fm: 2-3
Distance: 2m/2m3: 2-4 2m4-2m7: 2-6 3m+: 0-0
Track: **LH: 3-6** RH: 1-2 **Tight: 3-5** Gall: 0-0
Aids: Bl: 0-0 Vi: 0-0 Tstrap: 0-0
Best Rating: 108 4/02 Weth 2m4f110y good Hdl

A dual bumper winner on fast ground, he got off the mark on his second start over hurdles at Market Rasen in October 2001 and possibly ran his best race when fourth in the EBF Final at Sandown. He has plenty of stamina and looks to need three miles.

Exterior Profiles (IRE)

110 **100**

12-y-o b g Good Thyne (USA)-Best Of Kin (Pry)
Miss K M George Stableline

Placings: *1/1*21550F3/1**F4U3F**/F/P150552**U**43263604234 **(4657)**
2001/02: 20^{P}G, 20^{1}GF, 19^{5}GF, 22^{0}GF, 21^{5}GF, 27^{5}GF, 24^{2}GF, 24^{U}GF, 26^{4}GF, 21^{3}GS, 22^{2}GF, 24^{6}F, 18^{3}GS, 24^{6}GF, 17^{0}G, 22^{4}S, 19^{2}S, 19^{3}S, 24^{4}G

	Starts	1st	2nd	3rd	Win & Pl
Hurdles	18	1	3	3	4948
Chases	1	0	0	0	0
Career Total	**35**	**5**	**4**	**5**	**16069**

100	5/01	Hexm	2m4f110y	E(0-115)HHdl	G-F	£1949
110	5/96	Uttx	2m4f110y	D Hdl	G-F	£2871
111	11/95	Kemp	2m	D Hdl	GD	£2780
107	5/95	Wwck	2m	H NHF	G-F	£1602
107	4/95	Ayr	2m	H NHF	G-F	£1329

Total win prize-money £10532

Going: Sf: 0-3 GS: 0-2 Gd: 0-3 GF: - Fm: 1-11
Distance: 2m/2m3: 0-2 **2m4-2m7: 1-10** 3m+: 0-7
Track: **LH: 1-9** RH: 0-10 Tight: 0-14 Gall: 0-0
Aids: Bl: 0-0 Vi: 0-0 Tstrap: 0-0
Best Rating: 125 3/97 Wwck 2m4f110y good Ch

Plating-class hurdler, suited by two and a half miles and stays three. Likes to make the running.

Extra Cache (NZ)

(109h) (121h)**95**

9-y-o br g Cache Of Gold (USA)-Gizmo (NZ) (Jubilee Wine (USA))
O Brennan Lady Anne Bentinck

Placings:3/1432-114643 **(4776)**
2001/02: 16^{1}G, 16^{1}F, 20^{4}F, 21^{6}G, 16^{4}GS, 17^{3}G

	Starts	1st	2nd	3rd	Win & Pl
Hurdles	6	2	0	1	6696
Career Total	**11**	**3**	**1**	**3**	**10572**

121	5/01	Weth	2m	E(0-115)HHdl	FRM	£2562
114	5/01	Weth	2m	E(0-115)HHdl	GD	£2632
108	5/00	Towc	2m	E Hdl	G-F	£2534

Total win prize-money £7728

Going: Sf: 0-0 GS: 0-1 Gd: 1-3 GF: - Fm: 1-2
Distance: **2m/2m3: 2-4** 2m4-2m7: 0-2 3m+: 0-0
Track: **LH: 2-3** RH: 0-3 Tight: 0-2 Gall: 0-0
Aids: Bl: 0-0 Vi: 0-0 Tstrap: 0-0
Best Rating: 121 5/01 Weth 2m firm Hdl

Extra Jack (FR)

115 **161**

10-y-o b g Neustrien (FR)-Union Jack Iii (FR) (Mister Jack (FR))

P F Nicholls Sir Robert Ogden

Placings:511/P/0450/12061011031231/0PF1-511420 **(4664)**

2001/02: 20^{5}GS, 19^{1}S, 19^{1}GS, 16^{4}GS, 19^{2}GS, 21^{0}G

	Starts	1st	2nd	3rd	Win & Pl
Chases	6	2	1	0	21712
Career Total	**32**	**11**	**3**	**2**	**128543**

161	12/01	Chep	2m3f110y	C(0-135)HCh	G-S	£10270
157	11/01	Chep	2m3f110y	C(0-130)HCh	SFT	£7322
154	4/01	Prth	2m	B(0-150)HCh	HVY	£9818
123	4/00	Strf	2m6f110y	E Hdl	GD	£2646
	12/99	Cagn	2m5f110y	Hdl	GD	£6459
	11/99	Autl	2m3f	Ch	HLD	£6997
	10/99	Autl	2m3f	Ch	HVY	£6997
	9/99	Autl	2m2f110y	Ch	VS	£6997
	6/99	Autl	2m2f110y	Ch	VS	£6997
	4/97	Autl	2m5f110y	HCh	VS	£22447
	3/97	Autl	2m6f	Ch	VS	£11223

Total win prize-money £98175

Going: Sf: 1-1 GS: 1-4 Gd: 0-1 GF: - Fm: 0-0
Distance: 2m/2m3: 0-1 **2m4-2m7: 2-5** 3m+: 0-0
Track: **LH: 2-4** RH: 0-2 Tight: 0-1 Gall: 0-1
Aids: **Bl: 2-6** Vi: 0-0 Tstrap: 0-0
Best Rating: **161** 3/02 Donc 2m3f110y gd-sft Ch

Decent handicap chaser. Probably best at around two and a half miles these days, he goes well in testing conditions and usually wears blinkers.

Extra Proud

105(104h) (95h)**120+**

8-y-o ch g Dancing High-Spring Onion (King Sitric)

W Amos W Amos

Placings:6F62/60-2PF102 **(4908)**

2001/02: 22^{2}G, 22^{P}GS, 18^{F}G, 20^{1}G, 20^{0}G, 21^{2}G

	Starts	1st	2nd	3rd	Win & Pl
Hurdles	6	1	2	0	4705
Career Total	**12**	**1**	**3**	**0**	**5353**

95	12/01	Muss	2m4f	E Hdl	GD	£3052

Total win prize-money £3052

Going: Sf: 0-0 GS: 0-1 Gd: 1-5 GF: - Fm: 0-0
Distance: 2m/2m3: 0-1 **2m4-2m7: 1-5** 3m+: 0-0
Track: LH: 0-3 **RH: 1-3 Tight: 1-6** Gall: 0-0
Aids: Bl: 0-0 Vi: 0-0 **Tstrap: 1-6**
Best Rating: **95** 4/02 MRas 2m5f110y good Hdl

Fair novice chaser at around two and a half miles on a sound surface. Not the most fluent of jumpers.

Extra Stout (IRE)

10-y-o ch g Buckskin (FR)-Bold Strike (FR) (Bold Lad (USA))

Miss J M Furness J C Clark

Placings:*0*/060P/**F/114/4PP/P-05B0** **(4692)**

2001/02: 25^{0}G, 24^{5}GF, 20^{B}GF, 25^{0}GF

	Starts	1st	2nd	3rd	Win & Pl
Chases	4	0	0	0	0
Career Total	**17**	**2**	**0**	**0**	**11337**

107	4/99	Aint	3m1f	B Ch	GD	£8537
103	3/99	Sand	3m110y	H Ch	GD	£2042

Total win prize-money £10580

Going: Sf: 0-0 GS: 0-0 Gd: 0-1 GF: - Fm: 0-3
Distance: 2m/2m3: 0-0 2m4-2m7: 0-1 3m+: 0-3
Track: LH: 0-3 RH: 0-1 Tight: 0-1 Gall: 0-0
Aids: Bl: 0-0 Vi: 0-0 Tstrap: 0-1
Best Rating: **107** 4/99 Aint 3m1f good Ch

Extravagant Lady (IRE)

68 **51**

7-y-o b m Cataldi-Energance (IRE) (Salmon Leap (USA))

P R Webber J A H West

Placings:*6/50-0*0P **(1087)**

2001/02: 17^{0}GF, 16^{0}S, 16^{P}GF

	Starts	1st	2nd	3rd	Win & Pl
NH Flat	1	0	0	0	0
Hurdles	2	0	0	0	0
Career Total	**6**	**0**	**0**	**0**	**0**

Going: Sf: 0-1 GS: 0-0 Gd: 0-0 GF: - Fm: 0-2
Distance: 2m/2m3: 0-3 2m4-2m7: 0-0 3m+: 0-0
Track: LH: 0-2 RH: 0-0 Tight: 0-1 Gall: 0-0
Aids: Bl: 0-0 Vi: 0-0 Tstrap: 0-0
Best Rating: **79** 5/00 Worc 2m good NHF

Eyes Dont Lie (IRE)

93 **69**

4-y-o b g Namaqualand (USA)-Avidal Park (Horage)

D A Nolan (I Semple 21/9) Mrs J McFadyen-Murray

Placings:54034P **(4840)**

2001/02: 16^{5}G, 16^{4}GS, 16^{0}S, 16^{3}G, 16^{4}S, 16^{P}G

	Starts	1st	2nd	3rd	Win & Pl
Hurdles	6	0	0	1	456
Career Total	**6**	**0**	**0**	**1**	**456**

Going: Sf: 0-2 GS: 0-1 Gd: 0-3 GF: - Fm: 0-0
Distance: 2m/2m3: 0-6 2m4-2m7: 0-0 3m+: 0-0
Track: LH: 0-4 RH: 0-2 Tight: 0-4 Gall: 0-0
Aids: Bl: 0-3 Vi: 0-0 Tstrap: 0-5
Best Rating: **69** 12/01 Muss 2m good Hdl

Modest hurdler, usually wears a tongue tie, has worn blinkers.

Eyeshigher

83f **71f**

5-y-o b g Keen-Miss Nosey Oats (Oats)

K R Burke P A Matthews

Placings:*000* **(4552)**

2001/02: 16^{0}G, 16^{0}S, 16^{0}GF

	Starts	1st	2nd	3rd	Win & Pl
NH Flat	3	0	0	0	
Career Total	**3**	**0**	**0**	**0**	

Going: Sf: 0-1 GS: 0-0 Gd: 0-1 GF: - Fm: 0-1
Distance: 2m/2m3: 0-3 2m4-2m7: 0-0 3m+: 0-0
Track: LH: 0-1 RH: 0-1 Tight: 0-0 Gall: 0-2
Aids: Bl: 0-0 Vi: 0-0 Tstrap: 0-0
Best Rating: **71** 12/01 Donc 2m110y good NHF

Face The Class (IRE)

101 **94**

6-y-o ch m Up And At 'Em-Siva (FR) (Bellypha)

M C Pipe S A Helaissi

Placings:1221440043/0054PP040-325P **(0640)**

2001/02: 16^{3}S, 19^{2}G, 19^{5}G, 19^{P}GF

	Starts	1st	2nd	3rd	Win & Pl
Hurdles	4	0	1	1	962
Career Total	**23**	**2**	**3**	**2**	**9377**

110	12/99	Folk	2m1f110y	E Hdl	SFT	£2460
88	11/99	Leic	2m	G Hdl	G-S	£2094

Total win prize-money £4554

Going: Sf: 0-1 GS: 0-0 Gd: 0-2 GF: - Fm: 0-1
Distance: 2m/2m3: 0-1 2m4-2m7: 0-3 3m+: 0-0
Track: LH: 0-1 RH: 0-3 Tight: 0-2 Gall: 0-0
Aids: Bl: 0-0 Vi: 0-0 Tstrap: 0-3
Best Rating: **110** 4/00 Uttx 2m heavy Hdl

Selling hurdler, suited by soft ground, has worn a tongue tie.

Fact Cat

78f **66f**

4-y-o ch g So Factual (USA)-Zealous Kitten (USA) (The Minstrel (CAN))

R J Price Mrs K Oseman

Placings:*000* **(4180)**

2001/02: 16^{0}G, 16^{0}S, 16^{0}GS

	Starts	1st	2nd	3rd	Win & Pl
NH Flat	3	0	0	0	
Career Total	**3**	**0**	**0**	**0**	

Going: Sf: 0-1 GS: 0-1 Gd: 0-1 GF: - Fm: 0-0
Distance: 2m/2m3: 0-3 2m4-2m7: 0-0 3m+: 0-0
Track: LH: 0-1 RH: 0-1 Tight: 0-0 Gall: 0-0
Aids: Bl: 0-0 Vi: 0-0 Tstrap: 0-0
Best Rating: **66** 2/02 Wwck 2m soft NHF

Factor Ten (IRE)

14-y-o b g Kemal (FR)-Kissowen (Pitpan)

Mrs S Richardson James Richardson

Placings:*536*3131/**2PP/22/6P/111P12/P2P/34/425-40** **(0427)**

2001/02: 30^{4}GF, 33^{0}G

	Starts	1st	2nd	3rd	Win & Pl
Chases	2	0	0	0	0
Career Total	**30**	**6**	**6**	**4**	**28171**

123	10/96	Bang	3m110y	D(0-120)HCh	G-F	£4507
114	6/96	Uttx	2m5f	C Ch	G-F	£5174
120	5/96	Uttx	2m5f	D Ch	G-F	£3517
118	5/96	Worc	2m7f	E Ch	G-F	£3468
104	4/93	Ludl	2m5f110y	Hdl	GD	£1475
99	2/93	Kemp	2m	Hdl	GD	£2162

Total win prize-money £20307

Going: Sf: 0-0 GS: 0-0 Gd: 0-1 GF: - Fm: 0-1
Distance: 2m/2m3: 0-0 2m4-2m7: 0-0 3m+: 0-2
Track: LH: 0-0 RH: 0-1 Tight: 0-0 Gall: 0-1
Aids: Bl: 0-0 Vi: 0-0 Tstrap: 0-0
Best Rating: **125** 5/97 Strf 3m good Ch

Fadalko (FR)

116 **178**

9-y-o b g Cadoudal (FR)-Kalliste (FR) (Calicot (FR))

P F Nicholls Sir Robert Ogden

Placings:2111/25P6210/**11512U2F/122112-33620314** (4912)
2001/02: 17^{3}GF, 16^{3}GS, 24^{6}G, 17^{2}S, 16^{0}GS, 20^{3}G, 21^{1}GF, 16^{4}G

	Starts	1st	2nd	3rd	Win & Pl
Chases	8	1	1	3	64508
Career Total	**33**	**11**	**9**	**3**	**341258**

176	4/02	Chel	2m5f	A Ch	G-F	£24562
178	4/01	Aint	2m4f	A Ch	SFT	£74400
171	12/00	Winc	2m5f	B Ch	G-S	£9642
167	10/00	Winc	2m5f	A HCh	G-S	£21000
172	2/00	Uttx	2m	C HCh	SFT	£7020
155	11/99	Chel	2m	A Ch	GD	£13100
150	10/99	Bang	2m1f110y	D Ch	SFT	£4130
145	4/99	Ayr	2m	A HHdl	SFT	£15385
	3/98	Autl	2m2f	Hdl	VS	£30303
	12/97	Autl	2m1f110y	Hdl	HLD	£16835
	11/97	Autl	2m1f110y	Hdl	VS	£11223

Total win prize-money £227602

Going: Sf: 0-1 GS: 0-2 Gd: 0-3 GF: - Fm: 1-2
Distance: 2m/2m3: 0-5 **2m4-2m7: 1-2** 3m+: 0-1
Track: **LH: 1-4** RH: 0-4 Tight: 0-1 **Gall: 1-3**
Aids: Bl: 0-0 Vi: 0-0 Tstrap: 0-0
Best Rating: 178 4/01 Sand 2m gd-sft Ch

Established himself amongst the top chasers in 2000/2001 and played a full role in one of the races of the season when losing out by a nostril to Edredon Bleu at Sandown after a pulsating battle. He was not at his best in 2001/2002 but finished an excellent third in the Martell Cup at Aintree before winning a nice prize at Cheltenham. A genuine sort, versatile in terms of trip and ground.

Faddad (USA)

95 85

6-y-o b g Irish River (FR)-Miss Mistletoes (IRE) (The Minstrel (CAN))
D C O'Brien Mrs S Harris

Placings:0-0 (4564)
2001/02: 16^{0}GF

	Starts	1st	2nd	3rd	Win & Pl
Hurdles	1	0	0	0	
Career Total	**2**	**0**	**0**	**0**	

Going: Sf: 0-0 GS: 0-0 Gd: 0-0 GF: - Fm: 0-1
Distance: 2m/2m3: 0-1 2m4-2m7: 0-0 3m+: 0-0
Track: LH: 0-1 RH: 0-0 Tight: 0-1 Gall: 0-0
Aids: Bl: 0-0 Vi: 0-0 Tstrap: 0-0
Best Rating: 79 4/02 Plum 2m gd-fm Hdl

Fadhel (USA)

6-y-o b g Zilzal (USA)-Nice Life (USA) (Sportin' Life (USA))
E W Tuer E Tuer

Placings:P (1197)
2001/02: 16^{P}G

	Starts	1st	2nd	3rd	Win & Pl
Hurdles	1	0	0	0	
Career Total	**1**	**0**	**0**	**0**	

Going: Sf: 0-0 GS: 0-0 Gd: 0-1 GF: - Fm: 0-0
Distance: 2m/2m3: 0-1 2m4-2m7: 0-0 3m+: 0-0
Track: LH: 0-0 RH: 0-1 Tight: 0-0 Gall: 0-0
Aids: Bl: 0-0 Vi: 0-0 Tstrap: 0-0
Best Rating:

Fadoudal Du Cochet (FR)

109 (140h) 153

9-y-o b g Cadoudal (FR)-Eau De Vie (FR) (Dhaudevi (FR))
A L T Moore Sir Anthony O'Reilly

Placings:0023/2131134/**14312/0115-321133** (4938a)
2001/02: 16^{3}Y, 16^{2}YS, 16^{1}S, 16^{1}G, 16^{3}GY, 16^{3}YS

	Starts	1st	2nd	3rd	Win & Pl
Hurdles	1	1	0	0	23926
Chases	5	1	1	3	50849
Career Total	**26**	**9**	**4**	**7**	**123643**

153	3/02	Chel	2m110y	A HCh	GD	£39000
140	2/02	Gowr	2m	Hdl	SFT	£23926
153	1/01	Navn	2m1f	(0-123)HCh	SFT	£6677
138	12/00	Punc	2m	(0-123)HCh	SH	£6072
135	2/00	Punc	2m	Ch	SFT	£10400
121	10/99	Navn	2m1f	Ch	Y-S	£4312
134	1/99	Naas	2m	Hdl	HVY	£6138
134	1/99	Thur	2m	Hdl	HVY	£4296
106	11/98	Cork	2m	Hdl	SFT	£2391

Total win prize-money £103214

Going: Sf: 1-1 GS: 0-0 Gd: 1-1 GF: - Fm: 0-0
Distance: **2m/2m3: 2-6** 2m4-2m7: 0-0 3m+: 0-0
Track: **LH: 1-1** RH: 0-1 Tight: 0-0 **Gall: 1-1**
Aids: Bl: 0-0 Vi: 0-0 Tstrap: 0-0
Best Rating: 153 3/02 Chel 2m110y good Ch

A winner over hurdles and fences in Ireland, he acts well on a soft surface and is effective at around two miles. Game winner of the Grand Annual Chase at the Cheltenham Festival.

Fair Finnish (IRE)

91 75

8-y-o b g Commanche Run-Karelia (USA) (Sir Ivor)
A Streeter (W Clay 16/7) Capricorn Hospitality

Placings:0540652P0/060002565644004030**1**/010454 64306P463002-0065500 (4578)
2001/02: 22^{0}GF, 25^{0}GF, 23^{6}HY, 20^{5}S, 21^{5}HY, 21^{0}GF, 23^{0}G

	Starts	1st	2nd	3rd	Win & Pl
Hurdles	7	0	0	0	
Career Total	**53**	**2**	**3**	**3**	**6715**

80	5/00	Hntg	3m2f	E(0-105)HHdl	G-F	£2441
75	4/00	Uttx	2m4f110y	G(0-95)HHdl	SFT	£1708

Total win prize-money £4150

Going: Sf: 0-3 GS: 0-0 Gd: 0-1 GF: - Fm: 0-3
Distance: 2m/2m3: 0-0 2m4-2m7: 0-5 3m+: 0-2
Track: LH: 0-5 RH: 0-2 Tight: 0-3 Gall: 0-1
Aids: Bl: 0-1 Vi: 0-2 Tstrap: 0-0
Best Rating: 82 3/99 MRas 2m1f110y gd-sft Hdl

Fair Prospect

103f 104f

6-y-o b g Sir Harry Lewis (USA)-Fair Sara (Mcindoe)
J A Glover Fourstar Partners

Placings:15 (0843)
2001/02: 16^{1}GS, 16^{5}G

	Starts	1st	2nd	3rd	Win & Pl
NH Flat	2	1	0	0	1610
Career Total	**2**	**1**	**0**	**0**	**1610**

102	6/01	Hexm	2m	H NHF	G-S	£1610

Total win prize-money £1610

Going: Sf: 0-0 GS: 1-1 Gd: 0-1 GF: - Fm: 0-0
Distance: **2m/2m3: 1-2** 2m4-2m7: 0-0 3m+: 0-0
Track: **LH: 1-2** RH: 0-0 Tight: 0-0 Gall: 0-0
Aids: Bl: 0-0 Vi: 0-0 Tstrap: 0-0
Best Rating: 104 6/01 Worc 2m good NHF

A bumper winner on easy ground in the summer of 2001.

Fair Wind (IRE)

10-y-o b g Strong Gale-Corcomroe (Busted)
Mrs H Bartlett (Miss Rachel David 23/5) Mrs H Bartlett

Placings:31-P164 (4826)
2001/02: 33^{P}G, 26^{1}HY, 26^{6}G, 26^{4}G

	Starts	1st	2nd	3rd	Win & Pl
Chases	4	1	0	0	1776
Career Total	**6**	**2**	**0**	**1**	**4513**

125	2/02	Wwck	3m2f	H Ch	HVY	£1330
125	4/01	Extr	2m7f110y	H Ch	SFT	£2271

Total win prize-money £3602

Going: Sf: 1-1 GS: 0-0 Gd: 0-3 GF: - Fm: 0-0
Distance: 2m/2m3: 0-0 2m4-2m7: 0-0 **3m+: 1-4**
Track: **LH: 1-3** RH: 0-0 Tight: 0-0 Gall: 0-2
Aids: Bl: 0-0 Vi: 0-0 Tstrap: 0-0
Best Rating: 125 3/02 Chel 3m2f110y good Ch

Useful hunter chaser, acts in most types of ground.

Fairmead Princess

4-y-o b f Rudimentary (USA)-Lessons Lass (IRE) (Doyoun)
M J Gingell (C F Wall 8/10) C N & Mrs A V Roberts

Placings:00 (4813)
2001/02: 16^{0}G, 17^{0}GF

	Starts	1st	2nd	3rd	Win & Pl
Hurdles	2	0	0	0	
Career Total	**2**	**0**	**0**	**0**	

Going: Sf: 0-0 GS: 0-0 Gd: 0-1 GF: - Fm: 0-1
Distance: 2m/2m3: 0-2 2m4-2m7: 0-0 3m+: 0-0
Track: LH: 0-2 RH: 0-0 Tight: 0-0 Gall: 0-1
Aids: Bl: 0-0 Vi: 0-0 Tstrap: 0-0
Best Rating:

Fairmile Star

82 47

6-y-o gr g Weld-Damsong (Petong)
J M Jefferson Tom Mowbray

Placings:2-00P6 (2920)
2001/02: 17^{0}GS, 17^{0}S, 24^{P}S, 20^{6}G

	Starts	1st	2nd	3rd	Win & Pl
NH Flat	2	0	0	0	0
Hurdles	2	0	0	0	0
Career Total	**5**	**0**	**1**	**0**	**546**

Going: Sf: 0-2 GS: 0-1 Gd: 0-1 GF: - Fm: 0-0
Distance: 2m/2m3: 0-2 2m4-2m7: 0-1 3m+: 0-1
Track: LH: 0-1 RH: 0-3 Tight: 0-3 Gall: 0-0
Aids: Bl: 0-0 Vi: 0-0 Tstrap: 0-0
Best Rating: 98 5/00 Prth 2m110y gd-sft NHF

Fairtoto

100 110

6-y-o b g Mtoto-Fairy Feet (Sadler's Wells (USA))

D J Wintle Mrs Joan L Egan

Placings:650/51222-22203 **(3894)**
2001/02: 22^{2}GS, 22^{2}GF, 22^{2}G, 21^{0}GS, 21^{3}HY

	Starts	1st	2nd	3rd	Win & Pl
Hurdles	5	0	3	1	3164
Career Total	**13**	**1**	**6**	**1**	**9039**

106	7/00	Strf	2m6f110y	D Hdl	G-F	£3266

Total win prize-money £3266

Going: Sf: 0-1 GS: 0-2 Gd: 0-1 GF: - Fm: 0-1
Distance: 2m/2m3: 0-0 2m4-2m7: 0-5 3m+: 0-0
Track: LH: 0-2 RH: 0-1 Tight: 0-2 Gall: 0-1
Aids: Bl: 0-0 Vi: 0-0 Tstrap: 0-4
Best Rating: 110 5/01 NAbb 2m6f gd-fm Hdl

Fair dual-purpose stayer, stays two miles-six, appreciates fast ground and a sharp track.

Fairy Hill

70 **41**

6-y-o b g Henbit (USA)-Starch Brook (Starch Reduced)
H D Daly (R Dickin 29/6) The United Partnership

Placings:P-POPP **(2755)**
2001/02: 16^{P}GF, 17^{0}F, 16^{P}GF, 17^{P}GS

	Starts	1st	2nd	3rd	Win & Pl
Hurdles	4	0	0	0	
Career Total	**5**	**0**	**0**	**0**	

Going: Sf: 0-0 GS: 0-1 Gd: 0-0 GF: - Fm: 0-3
Distance: 2m/2m3: 0-4 2m4-2m7: 0-0 3m+: 0-0
Track: LH: 0-3 RH: 0-1 Tight: 0-0 Gall: 0-0
Aids: Bl: 0-0 Vi: 0-0 Tstrap: 0-2
Best Rating: 41 6/01 Hrfd 2m1f firm Hdl

Fait Le Jojo (FR)

111 **148**

5-y-o b g Pistolet Bleu (IRE)-Pretty Davis (USA) (Trempolino (USA))
P J Hobbs Jay Dee Bloodstock Limited

Placings:12F26-0322501 **(4758)**
2001/02: 16^{0}G, 16^{3}S, 16^{2}G, 16^{2}G, 16^{5}S, 16^{0}GS, 16^{1}GF

	Starts	1st	2nd	3rd	Win & Pl
Hurdles	7	1	2	1	37153
Career Total	**12**	**2**	**4**	**1**	**49764**

145	4/02	Asct	2m110y	B(0-140)HHdl	G-F	£7156
135	11/00	Asct	2m110y	B Hdl	SFT	£8073

Total win prize-money £15230

Going: Sf: 0-2 GS: 0-1 Gd: 0-3 GF: - Fm: 1-1
Distance: 2m/2m3: 1-7 2m4-2m7: 0-0 3m+: 0-0
Track: LH: 0-4 **RH: 1-3** Tight: 0-0 Gall: 0-3
Aids: Bl: 0-0 Vi: 0-0 Tstrap: 0-0
Best Rating: 148 12/01 Asct 2m110y good Hdl

A decent staying handicapper on the Flat, he is a useful handicapper over hurdles. Running respectably this season, he is dangerous when given an uncontested lead, as he proved when scoring at Ascot in April. He has won on soft ground and good to firm.

Faith Again (IRE)

100 **91**

6-y-o b m Namaqualand (USA)-Intricacy (Formidable (USA))
A Streeter Centaur Racing Ltd

Placings:P111430/0F00-0534440 **(4908)**
2001/02: 20^{0}GF, 19^{5}G, 21^{3}GF, 19^{4}GS, 20^{4}S, 20^{4}G, 21^{0}G

	Starts	1st	2nd	3rd	Win & Pl
Hurdles	7	0	0	1	382
Career Total	**18**	**3**	**0**	**2**	**10080**

96	10/99	Ludl	2m	E Hdl	G-F	£2724
96	9/99	Tntn	2m1f	E Hdl	G-F	£2558
111	9/99	Bang	2m1f	D Hdl	G-F	£3290

Total win prize-money £8572

Going: Sf: 0-1 GS: 0-1 Gd: 0-3 GF: - Fm: 0-2
Distance: 2m/2m3: 0-0 2m4-2m7: 0-7 3m+: 0-0
Track: LH: 0-3 RH: 0-3 Tight: 0-3 Gall: 0-1
Aids: Bl: 0-0 Vi: 0-1 Tstrap: 0-0
Best Rating: 111 7/00 Worc 2m4f good Hdl

She showed good juvenile form over hurdles, but was found out when upped in class. Essentially a plater, she likes to be held up and races at around two and a half miles these days.

Falchion

105 **110**

7-y-o b g Broadsword (USA)-Fastlass (Celtic Cone)
J R Bewley R Bewley

Placings:6/56025-1352 **(3690)**
2001/02: 22^{1}GS, 20^{3}HY, 20^{5}S, 20^{2}HY

	Starts	1st	2nd	3rd	Win & Pl
Hurdles	4	1	1	1	6409
Career Total	**10**	**1**	**2**	**1**	**7207**

106	11/01	Ayr	2m6f	E Hdl	G-S	£2597

Total win prize-money £2597

Going: Sf: 0-3 GS: 1-1 Gd: 0-0 GF: - Fm: 0-0
Distance: 2m/2m3: 0-0 **2m4-2m7: 1-4** 3m+: 0-0
Track: LH: 1-3 RH: 0-0 Tight: 0-0 Gall: 0-0
Aids: Bl: 0-0 Vi: 0-0 **Tstrap: 1-4**
Best Rating: 110 12/01 Hayd 2m4f soft Hdl

Moderate novice hurdler, he showed stamina was his strong suit when accounting for an in-form rival on his seasonal debut. Fair efforts over shorter trips on softer ground subsequently. Usually wears a tongue tie.

Falcon Du Coteau (FR)

111 **125**

9-y-o b g Apeldoorn (FR)-Ifrika (FR) (Bamako Iii)
A J Martin Lyreen Syndicate

Placings:000460/102/60-03131213F **(4664)**
2001/02: 16^{0}YS, 24^{3}G, 17^{1}Y, 20^{3}GS, 16^{1}S, 16^{2}YS, 19^{1}HY, 16^{3}S, 21^{F}G

	Starts	1st	2nd	3rd	Win & Pl
Chases	9	3	1	3	31479
Career Total	**20**	**4**	**2**	**3**	**35834**

125	1/02	Leop	2m3f	(0-130)HCh	HVY	£13957
120	12/01	Punc	2m	(0-116)HCh	SFT	£7862
111	11/01	Clon	2m1f	(0-102)HCh	YLD	£5008
87	5/99	Gowr	2m	(0-102)HHdl	GD	£3069

Total win prize-money £29897

Going: Sf: 2-3 GS: 0-1 Gd: 0-2 GF: - Fm: 0-0
Distance: 2m/2m3: 3-6 2m4-2m7: 0-2 3m+: 0-1
Track: LH: 1-3 RH: 1-3 Tight: 0-2 Gall: 0-0
Aids: Bl: 3-7 Vi: 0-0 Tstrap: 0-0
Best Rating: 125 1/02 Leop 2m3f heavy Ch

Fair handicap chaser, he is effective at around two miles and acts well with cut in the ground. Winner of a Listed event at Leopardstown in the mud at the start of this year. Likes to make the running.

Falcon Ridge

98 **97**

8-y-o ch g Seven Hearts-Glen Kella Manx (Tickled Pink)
Miss E C Lavelle J R Lavelle

Placings:6454133/244/P-P42 **(1149)**
2001/02: 21^{P}G, 21^{4}G, 16^{2}GF

	Starts	1st	2nd	3rd	Win & Pl
Chases	3	0	1	0	1029
Career Total	**14**	**1**	**2**	**2**	**4925**

102	3/99	Tntn	2m1f	F(0-105)HHdl	SFT	£1962

Total win prize-money £1963

Going: Sf: 0-0 GS: 0-0 Gd: 0-2 GF: - Fm: 0-1
Distance: 2m/2m3: 0-1 2m4-2m7: 0-2 3m+: 0-0
Track: LH: 0-3 RH: 0-0 Tight: 0-3 Gall: 0-0
Aids: Bl: 0-0 Vi: 0-0 Tstrap: 0-0
Best Rating: 102 5/99 Worc 2m4f gd-fm Hdl

Modest chaser, stays two miles-five and acts on a sound surface.

Falcon Spirit

97 **89**

6-y-o b g Polar Falcon (USA)-Amina (Brigadier Gerard)
John G Carr (Mrs M Reveley 2/8) A-One Syndicate

Placings:FO/U4U06 **(1446a)**
2001/02: 16^{U}GF, 16^{4}GF, 16^{U}GF, 17^{0}GF, 20^{6}F

	Starts	1st	2nd	3rd	Win & Pl
Hurdles	5	0	0	0	0
Career Total	**7**	**0**	**0**	**0**	**0**

Going: Sf: 0-0 GS: 0-0 Gd: 0-0 GF: - Fm: 0-5
Distance: 2m/2m3: 0-4 2m4-2m7: 0-1 3m+: 0-0
Track: LH: 0-4 RH: 0-1 Tight: 0-2 Gall: 0-0
Aids: Bl: 0-1 Vi: 0-4 Tstrap: 0-0
Best Rating: 89 9/01 Fair 2m4f firm Hdl

Falcon's Flame (USA)

9-y-o b/br g Hawkster (USA)-Staunch Flame (USA) (Bold Forbes (USA))
V Thompson V Thompson

Placings:233400/0036336533/6036445333/0/P **(4692)**
2001/02: 25^{P}GF

	Starts	1st	2nd	3rd	Win & Pl
Chases	1	0	0	0	
Career Total	**28**	**0**	**1**	**11**	**6410**

Going: Sf: 0-0 GS: 0-0 Gd: 0-0 GF: - Fm: 0-1
Distance: 2m/2m3: 0-0 2m4-2m7: 0-0 3m+: 0-1
Track: LH: 0-1 RH: 0-0 Tight: 0-1 Gall: 0-0
Aids: Bl: 0-0 Vi: 0-0 Tstrap: 0-0
Best Rating: 94 3/99 Hexm 2m4f110y soft Ch

Falmouth Bay (IRE)

101(108h) (103h)**116**

13-y-o b g Miners Lamp-Vita Veritas (Linacre)
E L James Tantivy Racing Partnership

Placings:15/410P/1PF2UP/PPFP5402/11001036/213 21/02-3P1PF **(3870)**
2001/02: 20^{3}G, 25^{P}G, 21^{1}GS, 22^{P}GS, 24^{F}GS

	Starts	1st	2nd	3rd	Win & Pl
Hurdles	2	1	0	0	1967
Chases	3	0	0	1	1043
Career Total	**40**	**9**	**5**	**3**	**35887**

103	12/01	Hntg	2m5f110y	F Hdl	G-S	£1967
123	4/00	Tntn	3m	D(0-120)HCh	G-S	£5473
121	11/99	Winc	2m6f	D(0-120)HHdl	GD	£4104
118	1/99	Folk	2m1f110y	F(0-105)HHdl	HVY	£1807
118	11/98	Winc	2m6f	D(0-120)HHdl	G-S	£3582
106	10/98	Extr	2m3f	E(0-110)HHdl	GD	£2853
112	11/95	Tntn	2m3f	C Ch	GD	£4690
98	12/94	Towc	2m	Hdl	SFT	£2040
110	3/94	Sand	2m110y	NHF	G-S	£1954

Total win prize-money £28473

Going: Sf: 0-0 GS: 1-3 Gd: 0-2 GF: - Fm: 0-0
Distance: 2m/2m3: 0-0 **2m4-2m7: 1-3** 3m+: 0-2
Track: LH: 0-0 **RH: 1-5** Tight: 0-1 **Gall: 1-3**
Aids: Bl: 0-0 Vi: 0-0 Tstrap: 0-1
Best Rating: 123 4/00 Tntn 3m gd-sft Ch

He mixes hurdling and chasing these days and is at the veteran stage. He was a fortunate winner of a claiming hurdle at Huntingdon in December 2001. Suited by cut in the ground.

Famfoni (FR)

113(98h) (96h)**120**

9-y-o b g Pamponi (FR)-India Rosa (FR) (Carnaval)
K C Bailey The Propelers Partnership

Placings:322/424/43452/2-15 **(4951a)**
2001/02: 24^{1}GS, 31^{5}G

	Starts	1st	2nd	3rd	Win & Pl
Chases	2	1	0	0	4037
Career Total	**14**	**1**	**5**	**2**	**19338**

120	3/02	Ludl	3m	D Ch	G-S	£4036

Total win prize-money £4037

Going: Sf: 0-0 GS: 1-1 Gd: 0-1 GF: - Fm: 0-0
Distance: 2m/2m3: 0-0 2m4-2m7: 0-0 **3m+: 1-2**
Track: LH: 0-0 **RH: 1-2 Tight: 1-1** Gall: 0-0
Aids: Bl: 0-0 Vi: 0-0 Tstrap: 0-0
Best Rating: 126 4/00 Asct 3m110y soft Ch

Useful staying chaser. Has worn blinkers and visor but won without them in spring of 2002. Acts on soft/heavy ground.

Fami (FR)

97 **104**

9-y-o ch g Le Nain Jaune (FR)-Quimie Ii (FR) (Barbotan (FR))
Miss Venetia Williams Len Jakeman

Placings:U310/024UUU13F/1F5-035U **(4313)**
2001/02: 24^{0}S, 25^{3}S, 26^{5}S, 24^{U}HY

	Starts	1st	2nd	3rd	Win & Pl
Chases	4	0	0	1	678
Career Total	**20**	**3**	**1**	**3**	**12088**

117	11/00	Hrfd	2m3f	E(0-115)HCh	SFT	£3731
110	1/00	Font	3m2f110y	F(0-100)HCh	GD	£2843
99	4/99	Bang	2m4f	E Hdl	GD	£2486

Total win prize-money £9061

Going: Sf: 0-4 GS: 0-0 Gd: 0-0 GF: - Fm: 0-0
Distance: 2m/2m3: 0-0 2m4-2m7: 0-0 3m+: 0-4
Track: LH: 0-2 RH: 0-1 Tight: 0-3 Gall: 0-0
Aids: Bl: 0-0 Vi: 0-0 Tstrap: 0-0
Best Rating: 117 11/00 Hrfd 2m3f soft Ch

Modest staying chaser, suited by soft ground.

Familie Footsteps

104 **106**

8-y-o b g Primitive Rising (USA)-Ramilie (Rambah)
G A Swinbank Miss A H Sykes

Placings:0/4/3500-311F2 **(1421)**
2001/02: 16^{3}GS, 17^{1}GF, 17^{1}GF, 16^{F}GF, 17^{2}G

	Starts	1st	2nd	3rd	Win & Pl
Hurdles	5	2	1	1	6831
Career Total	**11**	**2**	**1**	**2**	**7444**

102	8/01	Sedg	2m1f	D Hdl	G-F	£3265
94	7/01	Sedg	2m1f	E Hdl	G-F	£2523

Total win prize-money £5790

Going: Sf: 0-0 GS: 0-1 Gd: 0-1 GF: - Fm: 2-3
Distance: **2m/2m3: 2-5** 2m4-2m7: 0-0 3m+: 0-0
Track: **LH: 2-5** RH: 0-0 **Tight: 2-3** Gall: 0-0
Aids: Bl: 0-0 Vi: 0-0 Tstrap: 0-0
Best Rating: 106 9/01 Sedg 2m1f good Hdl

Successfull in two hurdle races on fast ground.

Family Business (IRE)

107(92h) (94h)**142**

6-y-o ch g Over The River (FR)-Morego (Way Up North)
M C Pipe P J Finn

Placings:20-4121203 **(4884)**
2001/02: 21^{4}G, 23^{1}G, 24^{2}GS, 24^{1}GS, 24^{2}S, 32^{0}GS, 22^{3}GF

	Starts	1st	2nd	3rd	Win & Pl
Hurdles	1	0	0	0	672
Chases	6	2	2	1	12064
Career Total	**9**	**2**	**3**	**1**	**13704**

	1/02	Sthl	3m110y	E Ch	G-S	£4824
142	12/01	Leic	2m7f110y	E Ch	GD	£3146

Total win prize-money £7970

Going: Sf: 0-1 GS: 1-3 Gd: 1-2 GF: - Fm: 0-1
Distance: 2m/2m3: 0-0 2m4-2m7: 0-2 **3m+: 2-5**
Track: LH: 1-3 RH: 1-3 **Tight: 1-4** Gall: 0-2
Aids: Bl: 0-0 Vi: 0-0 Tstrap: 0-0
Best Rating: 142 12/01 Leic 2m7f110y good Ch

Fair chaser, acts on good or easy ground and is effective at around three miles. Won on his chasing debut, but had to be remounted on his next two runs, coming home alone in a farce of a race at Southwell. Held subsequently.

Fancy A Buck

93 **53**

7-y-o b m Buckley-Fortune's Fancy (Workboy)
N J Pomfret Tony Mills

Placings:0000660 **(4578)**
2001/02: 17^{0}GS, 16^{0}S, 21^{0}S, 16^{0}S, 21^{6}GF, 17^{6}S, 23^{0}G

	Starts	1st	2nd	3rd	Win & Pl
NH Flat	1	0	0	0	0
Hurdles	6	0	0	0	0
Career Total	**7**	**0**	**0**	**0**	**0**

Going: Sf: 0-4 GS: 0-1 Gd: 0-1 GF: - Fm: 0-1
Distance: 2m/2m3: 0-4 2m4-2m7: 0-3 3m+: 0-0
Track: LH: 0-2 RH: 0-5 Tight: 0-2 Gall: 0-2
Aids: Bl: 0-0 Vi: 0-0 Tstrap: 0-4
Best Rating: 53 3/02 Hntg 2m5f110y gd-fm Hdl

Has achieved very little over hurdles to date including in selling company.

Fandango De Chassy (FR)

110(105h) (116h)**117**

9-y-o b g Brezzo (FR)-Laita De Mercurey (FR) (Dom Luc (FR))
Mrs L Wadham C J Hays

Placings:0000/35FU052/21112221 1P6/PPP-3451110321 **(4514)**
2001/02: 24^{3}G, 25^{4}G, 26^{5}G, 24^{1}S, 24^{1}S, 24^{1}HY, 22^{0}G, 25^{3}HY, 25^{2}S, 25^{1}GS

	Starts	1st	2nd	3rd	Win & Pl
Hurdles	5	3	0	1	13541
Chases	5	1	1	1	5920
Career Total	**35**	**9**	**6**	**3**	**47745**

117	3/02	Towc	3m1f	F(0-100)HCh	G-S	£3559
113	12/01	Towc	3m	E(0-115)HHdl	HVY	£5248
110	11/01	Towc	3m	D(0-120)HHdl	SFT	£5362
108	11/01	Towc	3m	F(0-90)Hdl	SFT	£2362
110	1/00	Naas	3m	(0-116)HCh	SH	£6072
105	1/00	Fair	3m1f	(0-123)HCh	SFT	£8320
103	6/99	Prth	3m110y	F(0-110)HHdl	SFT	£2879
101	6/99	Prth	2m4f110y	F(0-95)HCh	G-S	£3582
109	5/99	DRoy	3m	Hdl	SFT	£3069

Total win prize-money £40458

Going: Sf: 3-5 GS: 1-1 Gd: 0-4 GF: - Fm: 0-0
Distance: 2m/2m3: 0-0 2m4-2m7: 0-1 **3m+: 4-9**
Track: LH: 0-0 **RH: 4-8** Tight: 0-1 Gall: 0-2
Aids: Bl: 0-0 Vi: 0-0 Tstrap: 0-3
Best Rating: 117 3/02 Towc 3m1f gd-sft Ch

Showed consistent form in Ireland and was successful in hunter chases and point-to-points in this country. He won three times over hurdles at Towcester in late 2001 having lost his confidence in the Foxhunters' at Aintree in the spring of 2001, and returned successfully to fences in the spring of 2002. A real stayer, he is suited to soft ground and likes Towcester.

Fanfaron (FR)

9-y-o b g Sarpedon (FR)-Ocana Iv (FR) (Monsieur X)
Paul Phillips (C R Egerton 3/2) Edwin Phillips

Placings:3/21/123R22/25251/2366R4-1B5 **(4402)**
2001/02: 24^{1}S, 24^{B}S, 22^{5}GS

	Starts	1st	2nd	3rd	Win & Pl
Chases	3	1	0	0	3094
Career Total	**23**	**4**	**7**	**3**	**26539**

123	2/02	Tntn	3m	H Ch	SFT	£3094
146	4/00	Plum	2m4f	F(0-110)HCh	SFT	£3250
146	11/98	MRas	2m4f	E Ch	HVY	£3093
	9/97	Bord	2m2f	Hdl	SFT	£3367

Total win prize-money £12804

Going: Sf: 1-2 GS: 0-1 Gd: 0-0 GF: - Fm: 0-0
Distance: 2m/2m3: 0-0 2m4-2m7: 0-1 **3m+: 1-2**
Track: LH: 0-1 **RH: 1-2 Tight: 1-2** Gall: 0-1
Aids: Bl: 0-0 Vi: 0-0 Tstrap: 0-0
Best Rating: 146 4/00 Plum 2m4f soft Ch

Modest hunter chaser/pointer. Stays three miles. Acts on good ground but best on soft.

Fanion De Nourry (FR)

9-y-o ch g Bad Conduct (USA)-Ottomane (FR) (Quart De Vin (FR))
E Haddock Miss H M Newell

Placings:4FF/OP040O/0P5/12P0-00P **(3984)**
2001/02: 25^{0}G, 33^{0}G, 31^{P}GS

	Starts	1st	2nd	3rd	Win & Pl
Chases	3	0	0	0	
Career Total	**19**	**1**	**1**	**0**	**2464**

111	5/00	Towc	3m1f	H Ch	G-F	£1568

Total win prize-money £1568

Going: Sf: 0-0 GS: 0-1 Gd: 0-2 GF: - Fm: 0-0
Distance: 2m/2m3: 0-0 2m4-2m7: 0-0 3m+: 0-3
Track: LH: 0-0 RH: 0-1 Tight: 0-0 Gall: 0-0
Aids: Bl: 0-0 Vi: 0-0 Tstrap: 0-0
Best Rating: 118 5/00 Uttx 4m2f gd-fm Ch

Fantasmic

97f 99f

6-y-o ch g Broadsword (USA)-Squeaky Cottage (True Song)
A M Hales Andrew L Cohen

Placings:*40* **(4019)**
2001/02: 16^{4}HY, 16^{0}GS

	Starts	1st	2nd	3rd	Win & Pl
NH Flat	2	0	0	0	0
Career Total	**2**	**0**	**0**	**0**	**0**

Going: Sf: 0-1 GS: 0-1 Gd: 0-0 GF: - Fm: 0-0
Distance: 2m/2m3: 0-2 2m4-2m7: 0-0 3m+: 0-0
Track: LH: 0-1 RH: 0-1 Tight: 0-0 Gall: 0-1
Aids: Bl: 0-0 Vi: 0-0 Tstrap: 0-0
Best Rating: 99 1/02 Towc 2m heavy NHF

Fantasy Park

98 84

5-y-o b g Sanglamore (USA)-Fantasy Flyer (USA) (Lear Fan (USA))
G M McCourt Elizabeth Lewis & McCourt Fine Meats Ltd

Placings:PP4-00200420 **(2035)**
2001/02: 17^{0}G, 20^{0}GS, 20^{2}GS, 20^{0}GF, 20^{0}GF, 16^{4}GS, 21^{2}GF, 22^{0}GS

	Starts	1st	2nd	3rd	Win & Pl
Hurdles	8	0	2	0	1513
Career Total	**11**	**0**	**2**	**0**	**1513**

Going: Sf: 0-0 GS: 0-4 Gd: 0-1 GF: 0-1 Fm: 0-3
Distance: 2m/2m3: 0-2 2m4-2m7: 0-6 3m+: 0-0
Track: LH: 0-4 RH: 0-4 Tight: 0-1 Gall: 0-1
Aids: Bl: 0-1 Vi: 0-1 Tstrap: 0-0
Best Rating: 84 6/01 Hexm 2m4f110y gd-sft Hdl

Plating-class hurdler, acts on fast ground and with cut. Has worn a visor and blinkers

Far Bridge (IRE)

(78h) (57h)

7-y-o ch g Phardante (FR)-Droichidin (Good Thyne (USA))
P Wegmann (E Stanners 1/5) P Wegmann

Placings:6-00P **(1909)**
2001/02: 20^{0}G, 20^{0}GF, 20^{P}S

	Starts	1st	2nd	3rd	Win & Pl
Hurdles	2	0	0	0	0
Chases	1	0	0	0	0
Career Total	**4**	**0**	**0**	**0**	**0**

Going: Sf: 0-1 GS: 0-0 Gd: 0-1 GF: - Fm: 0-1
Distance: 2m/2m3: 0-0 2m4-2m7: 0-3 3m+: 0-0
Track: LH: 0-2 RH: 0-1 Tight: 0-1 Gall: 0-1
Aids: Bl: 0-0 Vi: 0-0 Tstrap: 0-0
Best Rating: 57 5/01 Hntg 2m4f110y good Hdl

Far Glen (IRE)

101 89

7-y-o b g Phardante (FR)-Asigh Glen (Furry Glen)
R D E Woodhouse R D E Woodhouse

Placings:FPP-553P50063 **(4857)**
2001/02: 17^{5}G, 20^{5}G, 23^{3}G, 24^{P}S, 25^{5}GF, 20^{0}G, 25^{0}GS, 24^{6}G, 20^{3}G

	Starts	1st	2nd	3rd	Win & Pl
Hurdles	9	0	0	2	826
Career Total	**12**	**0**	**0**	**2**	**826**

Going: Sf: 0-1 GS: 0-1 Gd: 0-6 GF: - Fm: 0-1
Distance: 2m/2m3: 0-1 2m4-2m7: 0-4 3m+: 0-4
Track: LH: 0-8 RH: 0-1 Tight: 0-2 Gall: 0-1
Aids: Bl: 0-0 Vi: 0-0 Tstrap: 0-3
Best Rating: 89 4/02 Hexm 2m4f110y good Hdl

Moderate form over hurdles to date. Stays two and a half miles plus, acts on fast ground.

Faraway Look (USA)

5-y-o br g Distant View (USA)-Summer Trip (USA) (L'Emigrant (USA))
P J Hobbs (J R Fanshawe 19/10) Mrs David Thompson

Placings:P **(3223)**
2001/02: 16^{P}G

	Starts	1st	2nd	3rd	Win & Pl
Hurdles	1	0	0	0	
Career Total	**1**	**0**	**0**	**0**	

Going: Sf: 0-0 GS: 0-0 Gd: 0-1 GF: - Fm: 0-0
Distance: 2m/2m3: 0-1 2m4-2m7: 0-0 3m+: 0-0
Track: LH: 0-0 RH: 0-1 Tight: 0-0 Gall: 0-0
Aids: Bl: 0-0 Vi: 0-0 Tstrap: 0-0
Best Rating:

Farceur Du Mesnil (FR)

96 94

9-y-o b g Pharly (FR)-Grundygold (FR) (Grundy)
K A Morgan The French Experience

Placings:2F4P/44341052/1102P-45P00 **(1306)**
2001/02: 16^{4}GF, 16^{5}G, 16^{P}GF, 17^{0}GF, 17^{0}GF

	Starts	1st	2nd	3rd	Win & Pl
Hurdles	4	0	0	0	0
Chases	1	0	0	0	0
Career Total	**22**	**3**	**3**	**1**	**7164**

101	5/00	Hntg	2m110y	G(0-95)HHdl	G-S	£1589
101	5/00	Newc	2m	G(0-95)HHdl	G-F	£1683
96	12/99	Leic	2m	G Hdl	G-S	£1618

Total win prize-money £4891

Going: Sf: 0-0 GS: 0-0 Gd: 0-1 GF: - Fm: 0-4
Distance: 2m/2m3: 0-5 2m4-2m7: 0-0 3m+: 0-0
Track: LH: 0-2 RH: 0-3 Tight: 0-3 Gall: 0-1
Aids: Bl: 0-4 Vi: 0-0 Tstrap: 0-0
Best Rating: 101 5/00 Hntg 2m110y gd-sft Hdl

Fard Du Moulin Mas (FR)

92(81h) (92h)118

9-y-o b/br g Morespeed-Soiree D'Ex (FR) (Kashtan (FR))
M E D Francis Mrs Merrick Francis Iii

Placings:13/1P3P/0054PP6/6325116F/0PP-4P50 **(4636)**
2001/02: 24^{4}G, 24^{P}GS, 24^{5}S, 24^{0}GF

	Starts	1st	2nd	3rd	Win & Pl
Hurdles	2	0	0	0	0
Chases	2	0	0	0	764
Career Total	**28**	**4**	**1**	**3**	**71065**

146	11/99	Sand	2m4f110y	C(0-130)HCh	GD	£7002
137	10/99	Worc	2m4f	C(0-135)HHdl	G-F	£5084
	9/97	Autl	2m2f	Ch	SFT	£13468
	3/97	Autl	2m1f110y	Hdl	VS	£11223

Total win prize-money £36778

Going: Sf: 0-1 GS: 0-1 Gd: 0-1 GF: - Fm: 0-1
Distance: 2m/2m3: 0-0 2m4-2m7: 0-0 3m+: 0-4
Track: LH: 0-2 RH: 0-2 Tight: 0-1 Gall: 0-0
Aids: Bl: 0-0 Vi: 0-0 Tstrap: 0-0
Best Rating: 146 12/99 Asct 3m110y gd-sft Ch

Ex-French, he was going like a winner when falling in the valuable Tote Silver Cup at Ascot in December 1999, suffering a career-threatening injury. Showed signs of a return to form at Chepstow in October 2001 over three miles. Best trip around two and a half miles. Has done most of his winning on good to soft.

Fardross

57

16-y-o b g Fidel-Miss Maraise (Orange Melody)
Mrs L Williamson G W Briscoe

Placings:*505*/1FF1255P/32F/U2/PP4-P **(0054)**
2001/02: 24^{P}G

	Starts	1st	2nd	3rd	Win & Pl
Hurdles	1	0	0	0	
Career Total	**20**	**2**	**3**	**1**	**10054**

113	11/93	Leic	3m	Ch	GD	£2528
98	10/93	Uttx	2m7f	Ch	GD	£3306

Total win prize-money £5834

Going: Sf: 0-0 GS: 0-0 Gd: 0-1 GF: - Fm: 0-0
Distance: 2m/2m3: 0-0 2m4-2m7: 0-0 3m+: 0-1
Track: LH: 0-1 RH: 0-0 Tight: 0-1 Gall: 0-0
Aids: Bl: 0-0 Vi: 0-0 Tstrap: 0-0
Best Rating: 113 11/93 Leic 3m good Ch

Fare Dealing (IRE)

105 102

9-y-o b g Tremblant-Charming Whisper (Deep Run)
M J Gingell (T R George 31/10) Fare Dealing Partnerhsip

Placings:*34*B450/FF-4312P032 **(4535)**
2001/02: 20^{4}GS, 21^{3}GS, 20^{1}G, 20^{2}GS, 21^{P}HY, 22^{0}GS, 18^{3}S, 20^{2}G

	Starts	1st	2nd	3rd	Win & Pl
Hurdles	8	1	2	2	5169
Career Total	**16**	**1**	**2**	**3**	**5390**

97	12/01	Sthl	2m4f110y	E(0-105)HHdl	GD	£2478

Total win prize-money £2478

Going: Sf: 0-2 GS: 0-4 Gd: 1-2 GF: - Fm: 0-0
Distance: 2m/2m3: 0-1 **2m4-2m7: 1-7** 3m+: 0-0
Track: **LH: 1-5** RH: 0-2 **Tight: 1-6** Gall: 0-1
Aids: Bl: 0-0 Vi: 0-0 Tstrap: 0-0
Best Rating: 102 1/02 Sthl 2m4f110y gd-sft Hdl

Modest hurdler, won an ordinary novices' handicap hurdle at Southwell in December 2001, and ran some fair races subsequently. Suited by good ground.

Farebit

88(92h) (68h)69

8-y-o b m Henbit (USA)-Ina's Farewell (Random Shot)

Miss S E Forster C Storey

Placings:6/6030600U (1814)

2001/02: 21^{6}G, 16^{0}GF, 16^{3}GS, 20^{0}G, 20^{6}GF, 22^{0}GS, 21^{0}GF, 20^{U}S

	Starts	1st	2nd	3rd	Win & Pl
Hurdles	6	0	0	1	426
Chases	2	0	0	0	0
Career Total	**9**	**0**	**0**	**1**	**426**

Going: Sf: 0-1 GS: 0-2 Gd: 0-2 GF: - Fm: 0-3
Distance: 2m/2m3: 0-2 2m4-2m7: 0-6 3m+: 0-0
Track: LH: 0-5 RH: 0-3 Tight: 0-3 Gall: 0-0
Aids: Bl: 0-0 Vi: 0-0 Tstrap: 0-1
Best Rating: 69 9/01 Sedg 2m5f gd-fm Ch

Farfields Prince

89(102c) (117c)73

10-y-o b g Weldnaas (USA)-Coca (Levmoss)

M J Wilkinson City Living

Placings:2115230/05U4/F1422255-P16F (2513)

2001/02: 19^{P}GF, 17^{1}GF, 16^{6}G, 16^{F}S

	Starts	1st	2nd	3rd	Win & Pl
Hurdles	1	0	0	0	0
Chases	3	1	0	0	3308
Career Total	**23**	**4**	**5**	**1**	**17750**

117	9/01	Plum	2m1f	F(0-110)HCh	G-F	£3307
106	5/00	Hexm	2m110y	E Ch	GD	£2204
117	10/98	Weth	2m	C Hdl	GD	£4081
112	10/98	Hexm	2m	E Hdl	GD	£2490

Total win prize-money £12084

Going: Sf: 0-1 GS: 0-0 Gd: 0-1 GF: - Fm: 1-2
Distance: **2m/2m3: 1-3** 2m4-2m7: 0-1 3m+: 0-0
Track: **LH: 1-3** RH: 0-1 **Tight: 1-4** Gall: 0-0
Aids: **Bl: 1-2** Vi: 0-1 Tstrap: 0-0
Best Rating: 117 9/01 Plum 2m1f gd-fm Ch

Farinel

113 134

6-y-o b g In The Wings-Dame De L'Oise (USA) (Riverman (USA))

A L T Moore J P McManus

Placings:0/3004-4512212P (4939a)

2001/02: 16^{4}G, 18^{5}GY, 19^{1}G, 20^{2}GF, 20^{2}YS, 24^{1}YS, 20^{2}G, 20^{P}Y

	Starts	1st	2nd	3rd	Win & Pl
Hurdles	8	2	3	0	40009
Career Total	**13**	**2**	**3**	**1**	**40634**

123	1/02	Leop	3m	HHdl	Y-S	£15950
106	8/01	Kbgn	2m3f	(0-116)HHdl	GD	£7233

Total win prize-money £23185

Going: Sf: 0-0 GS: 0-0 Gd: 1-3 GF: - Fm: 0-1
Distance: 2m/2m3: 1-3 2m4-2m7: 0-4 3m+: 1-1
Track: **LH: 1-3** RH: 0-1 Tight: 0-1 Gall: 0-0
Aids: Bl: 0-0 Vi: 0-0 Tstrap: 0-0
Best Rating: 134 4/02 Aint 2m4f good Hdl

Useful Irish handicap hurdler. Rewarded for his consistency with a comfortable win over two miles three at Kilbeggan in summer of 2001, and easily won a Pertemps qualifier at Leopardstown in January 2002. Good effort at Aintree. Stays three miles.

Farmer Jack

115 135

6-y-o b g Alflora (IRE)-Cheryls Pet (IRE) (General Ironside)

J W Mullins (N R Mitchell 23/10) Peter Partridge

Placings:1-4511420 (4229)

2001/02: 16^{4}GF, 17^{5}G, 19^{1}G, 20^{1}GS, 22^{4}S, 20^{2}S, 21^{0}GS

	Starts	1st	2nd	3rd	Win & Pl
Hurdles	7	2	1	0	17587
Career Total	**8**	**3**	**1**	**0**	**19155**

135	1/02	Asct	2m4f	C Hdl	G-S	£5304
110	12/01	Extr	2m3f	E Hdl	GD	£2922
105	4/01	Tntn	2m1f	H NHF	G-F	£1568

Total win prize-money £9795

Going: Sf: 0-2 GS: 1-2 Gd: 1-2 GF: - Fm: 0-1
Distance: 2m/2m3: 1-3 2m4-2m7: 1-4 3m+: 0-0
Track: LH: 0-1 **RH: 2-6** Tight: 0-0 Gall: 0-1
Aids: Bl: 0-0 Vi: 0-0 Tstrap: 0-0
Best Rating: 135 1/02 Asct 2m4f gd-sft Hdl

Won a Taunton bumper in the spring of 2001 and got off the mark over hurdles at Exeter in December. Followed up with the minimum of fuss over further at Ascot in January 2002. Decent efforts subsequently. Best with give in the ground. Stays two and a half miles.

Fas

64

6-y-o ch g Weldnaas (USA)-Polly's Teahouse (Shack (USA))

C W Fairhurst (J D Bethell 28/5) F & T Walton

Placings:4 (4673)

2001/02: 17^{4}GF

	Starts	1st	2nd	3rd	Win & Pl
Hurdles	1	0	0	0	0
Career Total	**1**	**0**	**0**	**0**	**0**

Going: Sf: 0-0 GS: 0-0 Gd: 0-0 GF: - Fm: 0-1
Distance: 2m/2m3: 0-1 2m4-2m7: 0-0 3m+: 0-0
Track: LH: 0-1 RH: 0-0 Tight: 0-1 Gall: 0-0
Aids: Bl: 0-0 Vi: 0-0 Tstrap: 0-0
Best Rating: 64 4/02 Sedg 2m1f gd-fm Hdl

Fasgo (IRE)

106(84h) (110h)126

7-y-o b g Montelimar (USA)-Action Plan (Creative Plan (USA))

P F Nicholls F A Smith

Placings:1P31P0 (4532)

2001/02: 24^{1}GS, 23^{P}GS, 24^{3}S, 24^{1}S, 32^{P}GS, 26^{0}GS

	Starts	1st	2nd	3rd	Win & Pl
Hurdles	1	1	0	0	1918
Chases	5	1	0	1	6060
Career Total	**6**	**2**	**0**	**1**	**7978**

126	2/02	Sand	3m110y	D(0-115)HCh	SFT	£5005
110	11/01	Chep	3m	F Hdl	G-S	£1918

Total win prize-money £6923

Going: Sf: 1-2 GS: 1-4 Gd: 0-0 GF: - Fm: 0-0
Distance: 2m/2m3: 0-0 2m4-2m7: 0-0 **3m+: 2-6**
Track: LH: 1-3 RH: 1-3 Tight: 0-0 Gall: 0-2
Aids: Bl: 0-0 Vi: 0-0 Tstrap: 0-0
Best Rating: 126 2/02 Sand 3m110y soft Ch

A winning point to pointer, he won on his debut over hurdles in November 2001 and scored under Rules over fences in February 2002. Acts on good and soft ground. Stays three miles.

Fashion Day

68f

5-y-o br m Environment Friend-Daffodil (Welsh Pageant)

Mrs L C Taylor T N Siviter

Placings:0 (1630)

2001/02: 16^{0}GF

	Starts	1st	2nd	3rd	Win & Pl
NH Flat	1	0	0	0	
Career Total	**1**	**0**	**0**	**0**	

Going: Sf: 0-0 GS: 0-0 Gd: 0-0 GF: - Fm: 0-1
Distance: 2m/2m3: 0-1 2m4-2m7: 0-0 3m+: 0-0
Track: LH: 0-0 RH: 0-1 Tight: 0-0 Gall: 0-0
Aids: Bl: 0-0 Vi: 0-0 Tstrap: 0-0
Best Rating: 68 10/01 Ludl 2m gd-fm NHF

Fashion House

85 78+

6-y-o b m Homo Sapien-High Heels (IRE) (Supreme Leader)

S Pike Stewart Pike

Placings:50 (2487)

2001/02: 17^{5}G, 17^{0}HY

	Starts	1st	2nd	3rd	Win & Pl
NH Flat	2	0	0	0	0
Career Total	**2**	**0**	**0**	**0**	**0**

Going: Sf: 0-1 GS: 0-0 Gd: 0-1 GF: - Fm: 0-0
Distance: 2m/2m3: 0-2 2m4-2m7: 0-0 3m+: 0-0
Track: LH: 0-1 RH: 0-0 Tight: 0-1 Gall: 0-0
Aids: Bl: 0-0 Vi: 0-0 Tstrap: 0-0
Best Rating: 80 11/01 Tntn 2m1f good NHF

Fashion Victim

103 91

7-y-o b g High Estate-Kirkby Belle (Bay Express)

M Tate J A Simpson

Placings:00/464F550-400150 (2211)

2001/02: 17^{4}G, 20^{0}GF, 16^{0}GF, 17^{1}G, 16^{5}S, 19^{0}G

	Starts	1st	2nd	3rd	Win & Pl
Hurdles	6	1	0	0	2499
Career Total	**15**	**1**	**0**	**0**	**2499**

91	10/01	Hrfd	2m1f	F(0-100)HHdl	GD	£2499

Total win prize-money £2499

Going: Sf: 0-1 GS: 0-0 Gd: 1-3 GF: - Fm: 0-2
Distance: **2m/2m3: 1-4** 2m4-2m7: 0-2 3m+: 0-0
Track: LH: 0-3 **RH: 1-3** Tight: 0-2 Gall: 0-0
Aids: Bl: 0-0 Vi: 0-0 Tstrap: 0-0
Best Rating: 91 10/01 Hrfd 2m1f good Hdl

Modest handicap hurdler, he has won over two miles and is a fan of the Hereford track.

Fasil (IRE)

96 99

9-y-o ch g Polish Patriot (USA)-Apple Peel (Pall Mall)

Mrs S D Williams Alan Chatfield

Placings:0314/0/31P/5302 (1383)

2001/02: 22^{5}GF, 22^{3}GF, 27^{0}G, 26^{2}GF

	Starts	1st	2nd	3rd	Win & Pl
Hurdles	4	0	1	1	1346
Career Total	**12**	**2**	**1**	**3**	**7266**

4	12/99	Font	2m6f110y	F(0-110)HHdl	GD	£2495
3	3/97	Tntn	2m3f110y	F Hdl	GD	£2249

Total win prize-money £4745

oing: Sf: 0-0 GS: 0-0 Gd: 0-1 GF: - Fm: 0-3
stance: 2m/2m3: 0-0 2m4-2m7: 0-2 3m+: 0-2
ack: LH: 0-3 RH: 0-1 Tight: 0-3 Gall: 0-0
ids: Bl: 0-1 Vi: 0-0 Tstrap: 0-0
est Rating: 108 2/97 Ludl 2m good Hdl

oderate, lightly-raced hurdler, stays three miles plus nd suited by a sound surface.

Fassan (IRE)

06 **91**

)-y-o br g Contract Law (USA)-Persian Susan (USA) Herbager)
Crook Mrs Anne Lavelle

acings:F232/523024/03222166/**34224/12321P/5466 5643-PP5424P** **(4855)**
)01/02: 25^{P}G, 22^{P}G, 22^{5}S, 20^{4}HY, 21^{2}S, 21^{4}GF, 20^{P}G

	Starts	1st	2nd	3rd	Win & Pl
hases	7	0	1	0	1818
areer Total	**45**	**3**	**12**	**7**	**36782**

4	2/00	Hayd	2m	C HCh	SFT	£6041
4	11/99	Aint	2m	D(0-115)HCh	GD	£9187
0	3/98	Catt	2m	E Hdl	SFT	£2598

Total win prize-money £17828

oing: Sf: 0-3 GS: 0-0 Gd: 0-3 GF: - Fm: 0-1
istance: 2m/2m3: 0-0 2m4-2m7: 0-6 3m+: 0-1
rack: LH: 0-5 RH: 0-1 Tight: 0-4 Gall: 0-0
ids: Bl: 0-4 Vi: 0-1 Tstrap: 0-0
est Rating: 114 2/00 Hayd 2m soft Ch

loderate chaser, his last win came at Haydock in ebruary 2000 and he does not appear to relish a strugle. Suited by small fields and soft ground, often wears eadgear.

Fast King (FR)

)7 **94**

-y-o b g Housamix (FR)-Fast Girl (FR) (Gay Minstrel FR))
J Hobbs (Y De Nicolay 17/8) The Kingpins

lacings:3105 **(3167)**
001/02: 16^{3}G, 17^{1}GS, 18^{0}G, 16^{5}S

	Starts	1st	2nd	3rd	Win & Pl
lurdles	4	1	0	1	3442
areer Total	**4**	**1**	**0**	**1**	**3442**

)	11/01	Bang	2m1f	E Hdl	G-S	£2691

Total win prize-money £2692

oing: Sf: 0-1 GS: 1-1 Gd: 0-2 GF: - Fm: 0-0
istance: **2m/2m3: 1-4** 2m4-2m7: 0-0 3m+: 0-0
rack: **LH: 1-2** RH: 0-2 **Tight: 1-2** Gall: 0-0
ids: **Bl: 1-2** Vi: 0-0 Tstrap: 0-0
est Rating: 94 11/01 Asct 2m110y good Hdl

lodest ex-French hurdler, suited by soft ground.

Fast Lane (IRE)

103 **103**

-y-o b/br g Montelimar (USA)-Toretta (Torus)
P McGovern C R H Racing

lacings:6-4313 **(1923)**
001/02: 22^{4}G, 22^{3}GF, 21^{1}G, 20^{3}G

	Starts	1st	2nd	3rd	Win & Pl
lurdles	4	1	0	2	4602
areer Total	**5**	**1**	**0**	**2**	**4602**

102	10/01	Towc	2m5f	E(0-105)HHdl	GD	£3052

Total win prize-money £3052

Going: Sf: 0-0 GS: 0-0 Gd: 1-3 GF: - Fm: 0-1
Distance: 2m/2m3: 0-0 **2m4-2m7: 1-4** 3m+: 0-0
Track: LH: 0-2 **RH: 1-2** Tight: 0-2 Gall: 0-0
Aids: Bl: 0-0 Vi: 0-0 Tstrap: 0-0
Best Rating: 103 11/01 Asct 2m4f good Hdl

A winning pointer, he showed the right attitude to win a handicap hurdle at Towcester in October.

Fast Track (IRE)

91 **85**

5-y-o b/br h Doyoun-Manntika (Kalamoun)
G M McCourt Mccourt Fine Meats,D J Rushen,E Lewis

Placings:006 **(2691)**
2001/02: 16^{0}GS, 16^{0}S, 16^{6}S

	Starts	1st	2nd	3rd	Win & Pl
Hurdles	3	0	0	0	0
Career Total	**3**	**0**	**0**	**0**	**0**

Going: Sf: 0-2 GS: 0-1 Gd: 0-0 GF: - Fm: 0-0
Distance: 2m/2m3: 0-3 2m4-2m7: 0-0 3m+: 0-0
Track: LH: 0-2 RH: 0-1 Tight: 0-1 Gall: 0-0
Aids: Bl: 0-0 Vi: 0-0 Tstrap: 0-0
Best Rating: 85 12/01 Hayd 2m soft Hdl

Fataliste (FR)

8-y-o b g Nikos-Faracha (FR) (Kenmare (FR))
B A Pearce Trevor Painting

Placings:501144211/50/F/P **(0676)**
2001/02: 16^{P}GF

	Starts	1st	2nd	3rd	Win & Pl
Hurdles	1	0	0	0	
Career Total	**13**	**4**	**1**	**0**	**36618**

138	4/98	Aint	2m110y	A Hdl	GD	£17180
138	2/98	Kemp	2m	A Hdl	G-F	£9509
118	9/97	Strf	2m110y	E Hdl	GD	£2176
	9/97	Autl	1m7f	Hdl	SFT	£6295

Total win prize-money £35161

Going: Sf: 0-0 GS: 0-0 Gd: 0-0 GF: - Fm: 0-1
Distance: 2m/2m3: 0-1 2m4-2m7: 0-0 3m+: 0-0
Track: LH: 0-1 RH: 0-0 Tight: 0-0 Gall: 0-0
Aids: Bl: 0-0 Vi: 0-0 Tstrap: 0-0
Best Rating: 138 2/99 Winc 2m gd-sft Hdl

Fatehalkhair (IRE)

109(113c) (145c)**125**

10-y-o ch g Kris-Midway Lady (USA) (Alleged (USA))
B Ellison R Wagner

Placings:3232/11021134F1F/163301P0/04/011F5214 64-010P5421 **(4918)**
2001/02: 21^{0}G, 21^{1}S, 16^{0}G, 16^{P}G, 16^{5}S, 16^{4}S, 21^{2}S, 28^{1}GF

	Starts	1st	2nd	3rd	Win & Pl
Hurdles	5	1	0	0	9591
Chases	3	1	1	0	15332
Career Total	**43**	**12**	**5**	**5**	**74416**

145	4/02	Sedg	3m4f	D(0-125)HCh	G-F	£14105
125	11/01	Sedg	2m5f110y	B HHdl	SFT	£8438
135	12/00	Sedg	2m5f	E Ch	SFT	£3168
135	8/00	Sedg	2m110y	E Ch	GD	£3042
116	7/00	Sedg	2m110y	E Ch	FRM	£3168
131	2/99	Sedg	2m1f	D(0-125)HHdl	GD	£5836
120	7/98	Sedg	2m5f110y	D(0-120)HHdl	G-F	£2843
117	2/98	Sedg	2m1f	D(0-125)HHdl	GD	£2952
105	10/97	Sedg	2m5f110y	D(0-125)HHdl	G-F	£3685
106	9/97	Sedg	2m1f	E Hdl	G-F	£2320
99	5/97	Sedg	2m1f	F(0-100)HHdl	G-F	£2248
94	5/97	Sedg	2m1f	E Hdl	G-F	£2320

Total win prize-money £54129

Going: Sf: 1-4 GS: 0-0 Gd: 0-3 GF: - Fm: 1-1
Distance: 2m/2m3: 0-4 2m4-2m7: 1-3 3m+: 1-1
Track: **LH: 2-8** RH: 0-0 **Tight: 2-5** Gall: 0-1
Aids: Bl: 0-0 Vi: 0-0 Tstrap: 0-0
Best Rating: 145 4/02 Sedg 3m4f gd-fm Ch

Difficult to beat at Sedgefield where he has gained all of his wins over hurdles and fences. Effective up to three and a half miles. A tidy jumper he prefers a sound surface. A winner on the Flat too.

Father D (IRE)

98 **100**

7-y-o b g Mister Lord (USA)-Abrahams Cross (IRE) (Bustomi)
R H Buckler Samways Fish Merchants & Transporters

Placings:03P2401 **(4594)**
2001/02: 17^{0}GS, 17^{3}HY, 24^{P}HY, 16^{2}HY, 19^{4}G, 16^{0}S, 16^{1}G

	Starts	1st	2nd	3rd	Win & Pl
NH Flat	2	0	0	1	331
Hurdles	5	1	1	0	3491
Career Total	**7**	**1**	**1**	**1**	**3822**

100	4/02	Uttx	2m	E Hdl	GD	£2702

Total win prize-money £2702

Going: Sf: 0-4 GS: 0-1 Gd: 1-2 GF: - Fm: 0-0
Distance: **2m/2m3: 1-5** 2m4-2m7: 0-1 3m+: 0-1
Track: **LH: 1-4** RH: 0-3 Tight: 0-2 Gall: 0-0
Aids: Bl: 0-0 Vi: 0-0 Tstrap: 0-0
Best Rating: 105 12/01 NAbb 2m1f heavy NHF

Keen front-running novice hurdler, best at two miles, won at Uttoxeter in April 2002.

Father McCarten (IRE)

105 **143**

9-y-o ch g Be My Native (USA)-Mossiness (Le Moss)
M Pitman Malcolm C Denmark

Placings:3/21/3-152P **(4232)**
2001/02: 19^{1}G, 20^{5}S, 24^{2}GS, 24^{P}GS

	Starts	1st	2nd	3rd	Win & Pl
Chases	4	1	1	0	12473
Career Total	**8**	**2**	**2**	**2**	**14996**

143	11/01	Asct	2m3f110y	D Ch	GD	£4368
110	10/98	Hntg	2m110y	H NHF	GD	£1213

Total win prize-money £5582

Going: Sf: 0-1 GS: 0-2 Gd: 1-1 GF: - Fm: 0-0
Distance: 2m/2m3: 0-0 **2m4-2m7: 1-2** 3m+: 0-2
Track: LH: 0-2 **RH: 1-2** Tight: 0-0 Gall: 0-2
Aids: Bl: 0-0 Vi: 0-0 Tstrap: 0-0
Best Rating: 143 2/02 Asct 3m110y gd-sft Ch

A bumper winner and has also won over fences, acts on good ground.

Father Mulcahy

102 **100**

6-y-o b g Safawan-Constant Delight (Never So Bold)
D McCain Mrs D McCain

Placings:43/3020 (4572)
2001/02: 16^{3}HY, 16^{0}S, 20^{2}HY, 20^{0}G

	Starts	1st	2nd	3rd	Win & Pl
Hurdles	4	0	1	1	1541
Career Total	**6**	**0**	**1**	**2**	**2338**

Going: Sf: 0-3 GS: 0-0 Gd: 0-1 GF: - Fm: 0-0
Distance: 2m/2m3: 0-2 2m4-2m7: 0-2 3m+: 0-0
Track: LH: 0-2 RH: 0-2 Tight: 0-0 Gall: 0-0
Aids: Bl: 0-0 Vi: 0-0 Tstrap: 0-0
Best Rating: 100 3/02 Uttx 2m4f110y heavy Hdl

Novice hurdler, returned from 684 days off to run a creditable third at Towcester in January 2002. Suited by heavy ground.

Father Paddy

99 89
7-y-o ch g Minster Son-Sister Claire (Quayside)
J G Fitzgerald P McMahon

Placings:321/6-5063 (4583)
2001/02: 24^{5}S, 20^{0}G, 20^{6}G, 20^{3}G

	Starts	1st	2nd	3rd	Win & Pl
Hurdles	4	0	0	1	449
Career Total	**8**	**1**	**1**	**2**	**5614**

107	3/00	Carl	2m1f	H NHF	G-S	£4446

Total win prize-money £4446

Going: Sf: 0-1 GS: 0-0 Gd: 0-3 GF: - Fm: 0-0
Distance: 2m/2m3: 0-0 2m4-2m7: 0-3 3m+: 0-1
Track: LH: 0-4 RH: 0-0 Tight: 0-1 Gall: 0-1
Aids: Bl: 0-0 Vi: 0-0 Tstrap: 0-0
Best Rating: 107 3/00 Carl 2m1f gd-sft NHF

Lightly-raced bumper winner who has shown only moderate form over hurdles.

Father Rector (IRE)

111 126
13-y-o b g The Parson-Mwanamio (Sole Mio (USA))
R Tate The Hon Robert Hanson

Placings:05/5056112U350/504303P/6426321146101 6/13F/111P/240141550/5-41043 (0960)
2001/02: 20^{4}GF, 22^{1}G, 24^{0}GF, 22^{4}G, 21^{3}GF

	Starts	1st	2nd	3rd	Win & Pl
Chases	5	1	0	1	4255
Career Total	**56**	**13**	**4**	**6**	**58728**

123	5/01	MRas	2m6f110y	H Ch	GD	£2460
136	10/99	Strf	2m5f110y	C(0-135)HCh	G-F	£8008
135	6/99	Worc	2m4f110y	D(0-120)HCh	G-F	£3923
135	10/98	Winc	2m5f	E(0-115)HCh	G-F	£4580
126	5/98	MRas	2m6f110y	H Ch	G-F	£2052
119	5/98	Hrfd	2m3f	H Ch	GD	£1830
124	2/98	Hntg	3m	H Ch	GD	£1213
102	3/97	Thur	2m6f	Ch	GD	£2712
115	9/96	List	3m	HHdl	G-F	£7371
115	8/96	Tram	2m4f	(0-109)HHdl	GD	£2824
108	8/96	Gway	2m5f190y	HHdl	G-F	£9974
110	11/94	Clon	2m	Hdl	HVY	£2120
	11/94	Clon	2m	NHF	Y-S	£2446

Total win prize-money £51518

Going: Sf: 0-0 GS: 0-0 Gd: 1-2 GF: - Fm: 0-3
Distance: 2m/2m3: 0-0 **2m4-2m7: 1-4** 3m+: 0-1
Track: LH: 0-3 **RH: 1-2 Tight: 1-5** Gall: 0-0
Aids: Bl: 0-0 Vi: 0-0 Tstrap: 0-0
Best Rating: 136 10/99 Strf 2m5f110y gd-fm Ch

Veteran pointer/hunter chaser, suited by fast ground. Stays three miles plus, but looks better at shorter.

Father Seamus

4-y-o b g Bin Ajwaad (IRE)-Merry Rous (Rousillon (USA))
P Butler P Butler

Placings:0P0 (4559)
2001/02: 16^{0}GS, 16^{P}G, 16^{0}GF

	Starts	1st	2nd	3rd	Win & Pl
Hurdles	3	0	0	0	
Career Total	**3**	**0**	**0**	**0**	

Going: Sf: 0-0 GS: 0-1 Gd: 0-1 GF: - Fm: 0-1
Distance: 2m/2m3: 0-3 2m4-2m7: 0-0 3m+: 0-0
Track: LH: 0-2 RH: 0-1 Tight: 0-2 Gall: 0-0
Aids: Bl: 0-0 Vi: 0-0 Tstrap: 0-0
Best Rating:

Fathereilly

96f 90f
7-y-o b g Syrtos-Water-Zade (Cruise Missile)
O O'Neill Miss H Smith

Placings:6U34 (1154)
2001/02: 17^{6}GF, 16^{U}G, 16^{3}GF, 17^{4}GF

	Starts	1st	2nd	3rd	Win & Pl
NH Flat	4	0	0	1	207
Career Total	**4**	**0**	**0**	**1**	**207**

Going: Sf: 0-0 GS: 0-0 Gd: 0-1 GF: - Fm: 0-3
Distance: 2m/2m3: 0-4 2m4-2m7: 0-0 3m+: 0-0
Track: LH: 0-3 RH: 0-1 Tight: 0-2 Gall: 0-0
Aids: Bl: 0-0 Vi: 0-0 Tstrap: 0-0
Best Rating: 90 6/01 MRas 2m1f110y gd-fm NHF

Moderate bumper form in the summer of 2001.

Faustino

109 99
10-y-o br g Faustus (USA)-Hot Case (Upper Case (USA))
D M Grissell The Rooster Club

Placings:501631/142010022/43F12323/4B5/U35332F /51PPP-236 (4886)
2001/02: 16^{2}S, 20^{3}G, 18^{6}GF

	Starts	1st	2nd	3rd	Win & Pl
Chases	3	0	1	1	1643
Career Total	**41**	**6**	**7**	**8**	**29888**

95	6/00	Prth	2m4f110y	F(0-110)HCh	SFT	£4771
81	9/97	Extr	2m3f	D Ch	G-F	£3501
111	8/96	Hrfd	2m3f110y	D(0-125)HHdl	G-F	£2864
104	5/96	Ludl	2m	E Hdl	G-F	£2285
113	4/96	Asct	2m110y	D(0-110)HHdl	G-F	£3517
101	3/96	Winc	2m	E Hdl	G-F	£2232

Total win prize-money £19172

Going: Sf: 0-1 GS: 0-0 Gd: 0-1 GF: - Fm: 0-1
Distance: 2m/2m3: 0-2 2m4-2m7: 0-1 3m+: 0-0
Track: LH: 0-1 RH: 0-1 Tight: 0-3 Gall: 0-0
Aids: Bl: 0-0 Vi: 0-0 Tstrap: 0-0
Best Rating: 113 4/96 Asct 2m110y gd-fm Hdl

Formerly a useful chaser on firm ground, he has since proved himself on easy going and is versatile as regards trip. He is reported to have had breathing problems.

Faustnluce Lady

87 59
13-y-o b m Faustus (USA)-Miss Friendly (Status Seeker)
W J Smith W J Smith

Placings:0P/0/P/6021/55/00**PU**00**PR**0/PP00523/00C 000 (457
2001/02: 16^{0}GF, 20^F, 21^{0}GF, 20^{0}G, 17^{0}S, 21^{0}S, 20^{0}G

	Starts	1st	2nd	3rd	Win & P
Hurdles	7	0	0	0	
Career Total	**33**	**1**	**2**	**1**	**3581**

79	5/96	Ctml	2m1f110y	E Hdl	SFT	£238

Total win prize-money £238

Going: Sf: 0-2 GS: 0-0 Gd: 0-2 GF: - Fm: 0-3
Distance: 2m/2m3: 0-2 2m4-2m7: 0-5 3m+: 0-0
Track: LH: 0-6 RH: 0-1 Tight: 0-2 Gall: 0-1
Aids: Bl: 0-4 Vi: 0-0 Tstrap: 0-1
Best Rating: 79 5/96 Ctml 2m1f110y soft Hc

Favoured Option (IRE)

110(99h) (20h)116
7-y-o ch g Glacial Storm (USA)-Hot House Flower (Derring Rose)
Ian Williams K A Cosby

Placings:006/P20351-0F634321 (4748
2001/02: 22^{0}GS, 22^{F}HY, 24^{6}GS, 24^{3}S, 24^{4}S, 24^{3}GF, 24^{2}GF, 26^{1}GF

	Starts	1st	2nd	3rd	Win & Pl
Hurdles	2	0	0	0	0
Chases	6	1	1	2	9372
Career Total	**17**	**2**	**2**	**3**	**12970**

116	4/02	Carl	3m2f	D(0-115)HCh	G-F	£700
97	2/01	Folk	2m6f110y	E Hdl	HVY	£254

Total win prize-money £954

Going: Sf: 0-3 GS: 0-2 Gd: 0-0 GF: - Fm: 1-3
Distance: 2m/2m3: 0-0 2m4-2m7: 0-2 **3m+: 1-6**
Track: LH: 0-3 **RH: 1-5** Tight: 0-1 Gall: 0-4
Aids: Bl: 0-0 Vi: 0-0 Tstrap: 0-0
Best Rating: 116 4/02 Carl 3m2f gd-fm Ch

Took a long-distance novice hurdle in the mud in February 2001, but his first victory over fences at Carlisle in April 2002 came on fast ground.

Fawn Prince (IRE)

100(85c) (83c)87
9-y-o b g Electric-Regent Star (Prince Regent (FR))
M J Gingell Alec Lochore

Placings:10/6000/10/530/02630P66 (1807
2001/02: 16^{0}GF, 16^{2}GF, 16^{6}F, 16^{3}GF, 16^{0}GF, 17^{P}GF, 16^{6}G, 16^{6}S

	Starts	1st	2nd	3rd	Win & Pl
Hurdles	7	0	1	1	799
Chases	1	0	0	0	0
Career Total	**19**	**2**	**1**	**2**	**6544**

103	7/98	Bell	2m1f	Hdl	G-F	£2391
104	1/97	Leop	2m	NHF	G-Y	£3051

Total win prize-money £5443

Going: Sf: 0-1 GS: 0-0 Gd: 0-1 GF: - Fm: 0-6
Distance: 2m/2m3: 0-8 2m4-2m7: 0-0 3m+: 0-0
Track: LH: 0-6 RH: 0-2 Tight: 0-5 Gall: 0-0
Aids: Bl: 0-0 Vi: 0-1 Tstrap: 0-0
Best Rating: 104 1/97 Leop 2m gd-yld NHF

Selling hurdler, suited by fast ground.

Fayrway Rhythm (IRE)

104 103
5-y-o b g Fayruz-The Way She Moves (North Stoke)
I Emmerson (P J Hobbs 15/11) Ms Josie Swinburn

Placings:06-3446031230 (3821)
2001/02: 20^3GS, 18^4GF, 20^4GF, 20^6GS, 17^0G, 16^3GS, 17^1G, 17^2HY, 16^3S, 17^0S

	Starts	1st	2nd	3rd	Win & Pl
Hurdles	10	1	1	3	4555
Career Total	**12**	**1**	**1**	**3**	**4555**

103 11/01 Tntn 2m1f G(0-90)HHdl GD £1732
Total win prize-money £1733

Going: Sf: 0-3 GS: 0-3 Gd: 1-2 GF: - Fm: 0-2
Distance: **2m/2m3: 1-7** 2m4-2m7: 0-3 3m+: 0-0
Track: LH: 0-6 **RH: 1-4 Tight: 1-5** Gall: 0-0
Aids: Bl: 0-3 **Vi: 1-5** Tstrap: 0-2
Best Rating: 103 11/01 Carl 2m1f heavy Hdl

Placed form over hurdles. Has become disappointing and dropped to claiming company to get off the mark at the ninth attempt at Taunton in November. Good effort for new yard next time. Runs in blinkers or a visor.

Feanor

103 **95**
4-y-o b f Presidium-Nouvelle Cuisine (Yawa)
G M Moore Major E J Watt

Placings:5F653P133 (4092)
2001/02: 17^5G, 16^FG, 16^6G, 16^5GF, 16^3S, 16^PG, 16^1S, 16^3S, 16^3GS

	Starts	1st	2nd	3rd	Win & Pl
Hurdles	9	1	0	3	4372
Career Total	**9**	**1**	**0**	**3**	**4372**

95 1/02 Catt 2m E Hdl SFT £2723
Total win prize-money £2723

Going: Sf: 1-3 GS: 0-1 Gd: 0-4 GF: - Fm: 0-1
Distance: **2m/2m3: 1-9** 2m4-2m7: 0-0 3m+: 0-0
Track: **LH: 1-7** RH: 0-2 **Tight: 1-8** Gall: 0-1
Aids: Bl: 0-0 Vi: 0-0 Tstrap: 0-0
Best Rating: 95 1/02 Catt 2m soft Hdl

Moderate form shown over hurdles, before getting off the mark at Catterick in January 2002. Acts on soft ground and is effective over two miles. Seems to like Catterick.

Fear Siuil (IRE)

111 **120**
9-y-o b g Strong Gale-Astral River (Over The River (FR))
D M Forster D M Forster

Placings:0P0/54P/P-P1FPP3 (4920)
2001/02: 21^PG, 19^1GF, 19^FG, 20^PG, 21^PGF, 21^3GF

	Starts	1st	2nd	3rd	Win & Pl
Chases	6	1	0	1	5655
Career Total	**13**	**1**	**0**	**1**	**5920**

120 11/01 Catt 2m3f E(0-115)HCh G-F £5027
Total win prize-money £5028

Going: Sf: 0-0 GS: 0-0 Gd: 0-3 GF: - Fm: 1-3
Distance: **2m/2m3: 1-1** 2m4-2m7: 0-5 3m+: 0-0
Track: **LH: 1-6** RH: 0-0 **Tight: 1-4** Gall: 0-2
Aids: Bl: 0-0 Vi: 0-0 **Tstrap: 1-4**
Best Rating: 120 11/01 Catt 2m3f gd-fm Ch

Handicap chaser, stays two and a half miles. Best on a sound surface, has worn a tongue tie.

Felix Randal (IRE)

103 **98**
6-y-o ch g Be My Native (USA)-Odd Sox (FR) (Main Reef)
J J O'Neill Anne Duchess Of Westminster

Placings:06P0P12 (4847)
2001/02: 17^0GS, 22^6S, 20^PG, 25^0GS, 24^PS, 21^1G, 20^2G

	Starts	1st	2nd	3rd	Win & Pl
NH Flat	1	0	0	0	0
Hurdles	5	1	1	0	5514
Chases	1	0	0	0	0
Career Total	**7**	**1**	**1**	**0**	**5514**

96 4/02 Ludl 2m5f E(0-105)HHdl GD £3900
Total win prize-money £3900

Going: Sf: 0-2 GS: 0-2 Gd: 1-3 GF: - Fm: 0-0
Distance: 2m/2m3: 0-1 **2m4-2m7: 1-4** 3m+: 0-2
Track: LH: 0-4 **RH: 1-3** Tight: 0-3 Gall: 0-2
Aids: Bl: 0-0 Vi: 0-0 Tstrap: 0-0
Best Rating: 98 4/02 Bang 2m4f good Hdl

Had shown modest form in first five starts until taking advantage of move into handicap company with comfortable success at Ludlow in April 2002. Decent ground seems to suit and two mile four plus.

Felixrdotcom

103 **106**
6-y-o ch g Gran Alba (USA)-Golden Curd (FR) (Nice Havrais (USA))
J T Gifford Felix Rosenstiel's Widow & Son

Placings:6-5P42 (4411)
2001/02: 16^5G, 20^PG, 16^4G, 18^2S

	Starts	1st	2nd	3rd	Win & Pl
Hurdles	4	0	1	0	1008
Career Total	**5**	**0**	**1**	**0**	**1008**

Going: Sf: 0-1 GS: 0-0 Gd: 0-3 GF: - Fm: 0-0
Distance: 2m/2m3: 0-3 2m4-2m7: 0-1 3m+: 0-0
Track: LH: 0-1 RH: 0-3 Tight: 0-1 Gall: 0-0
Aids: Bl: 0-0 Vi: 0-0 Tstrap: 0-0
Best Rating: 106 3/02 Font 2m2f110y soft Hdl

Looks to be getting the hang of things over hurdles. Acts with cut.

Felony (IRE)

7-y-o ch g Pharly (FR)-Scales Of Justice (Final Straw)
L P Grassick Baskerville Racing Club

Placings:P0063/1/P (0371)
2001/02: 21^PG

	Starts	1st	2nd	3rd	Win & Pl
Hurdles	1	0	0	0	
Career Total	**7**	**1**	**0**	**1**	**1865**

82 5/99 Hrfd 2m3f110y G Hdl G-S £1658
Total win prize-money £1658

Going: Sf: 0-0 GS: 0-0 Gd: 0-1 GF: - Fm: 0-0
Distance: 2m/2m3: 0-0 2m4-2m7: 0-1 3m+: 0-0
Track: LH: 0-0 RH: 0-0 Tight: 0-0 Gall: 0-0
Aids: Bl: 0-0 Vi: 0-0 Tstrap: 0-1
Best Rating: 82 5/99 Hrfd 2m3f110y gd-sft Hdl

Fergus No

70 **17**
8-y-o ch g Be My Chief (USA)-Secret Freedom (USA) (Secreto (USA))
B G Powell Mrs Rachel A Powell

Placings:66-00 (0907)
2001/02: 16^0GF, 24^0G

	Starts	1st	2nd	3rd	Win & Pl
Hurdles	2	0	0	0	
Career Total	**4**	**0**	**0**	**0**	**0**

Going: Sf: 0-0 GS: 0-0 Gd: 0-1 GF: - Fm: 0-1
Distance: 2m/2m3: 0-1 2m4-2m7: 0-0 3m+: 0-1
Track: LH: 0-2 RH: 0-0 Tight: 0-1 Gall: 0-0
Aids: Bl: 0-0 Vi: 0-0 Tstrap: 0-0
Best Rating: 71 5/00 Winc 2m firm Hdl

Fermoy Lady (IRE)

85 **47**
7-y-o b m Riot Helmet-Ballybrack (Golden Love)
W W Dennis Mrs Jill Dennis

Placings:0-6 (2411)
2001/02: 19^6GS

	Starts	1st	2nd	3rd	Win & Pl
Hurdles	1	0	0	0	0
Career Total	**2**	**0**	**0**	**0**	**0**

Going: Sf: 0-0 GS: 0-1 Gd: 0-0 GF: - Fm: 0-0
Distance: 2m/2m3: 0-0 2m4-2m7: 0-1 3m+: 0-0
Track: LH: 0-0 RH: 0-1 Tight: 0-1 Gall: 0-0
Aids: Bl: 0-0 Vi: 0-0 Tstrap: 0-0
Best Rating: 64 11/00 Extr 2m1f gd-sft NHF

Fern Leader (IRE)

12-y-o b g Supreme Leader-Mossbrook (Le Moss)
Miss L Blackford R C Skinner

Placings:32U/3224U41F4222F/4P12/F/U-F (0259)
2001/02: 21^FGF

	Starts	1st	2nd	3rd	Win & Pl
Chases	1	0	0	0	
Career Total	**23**	**2**	**7**	**2**	**14222**

100 5/98 Ctml 2m5f110y E Ch G-F £3079
100 1/98 Muss 3m E(0-105)HCh G-S £2882
Total win prize-money £5962

Going: Sf: 0-0 GS: 0-0 Gd: 0-0 GF: - Fm: 0-1
Distance: 2m/2m3: 0-0 2m4-2m7: 0-1 3m+: 0-0
Track: LH: 0-1 RH: 0-0 Tight: 0-1 Gall: 0-0
Aids: Bl: 0-0 Vi: 0-0 Tstrap: 0-0
Best Rating: 100 5/98 Ctml 2m5f110y gd-fm Ch

Ferrers

113(112h) (121h)**131**
11-y-o b g Homeboy-Gay Twenties (Lord Gayle (USA))
Mrs P Sly J L Burt

Placings:401/05300F645/22203/124146P/12324/1000-64031253310 (4635)
2001/02: 20^6GS, 16^4G, 16^0G, 20^3GS, 23^1GF, 20^2G, 24^5GS, 20^3S, 19^3GS, 21^1HY, 19^0GF

	Starts	1st	2nd	3rd	Win & Pl
Hurdles	2	0	0	0	553
Chases	9	2	1	3	16933
Career Total	**44**	**7**	**7**	**6**	**56311**

131 3/02 Uttx 2m5f C(0-135)HCh HVY £7297
121 12/01 Leic 2m7f110y D(0-125)HCh G-F £4241
126 12/00 Chel 2m1f C(0-135)HHdl SFT £15210
113 11/99 Towc 2m D(0-120)HHdl GD £2856
125 1/99 Hntg 2m110y D Ch SFT £3951
110 12/98 Towc 2m G(0-95)HHdl SFT £1716
97 2/96 Sedg 2m1f110y H NHF GD £1800

Total win prize-money £37072

Going: Sf: 1-2 GS: 0-4 Gd: 0-3 GF: - Fm: 1-2
Distance: 2m/2m3: 0-2 2m4-2m7: 1-7 3m+: 1-2
Track: LH: 1-5 RH: 1-6 Tight: 0-1 Gall: 0-3
Aids: Bl: 0-0 Vi: 0-0 Tstrap: 0-0
Best Rating: 131 3/02 Uttx 2m5f heavy Ch

Fairly useful hurdler/chaser, he relished the testing conditions when winning at Uttoxeter in March 2002. Effective at up to three miles.

Ferrets Hill (IRE)

79 **67**

6-y-o br g Good Thyne (USA)-Doolin Lake (IRE) (Salluceva)
N J Henderson Mrs T H Barclay/mrs F D McInnes Skinner

Placings:*20* **(2282)**
2001/02: 16^{2}S, 20^{0}G

	Starts	1st	2nd	3rd	Win & Pl
NH Flat	1	0	1	0	415
Hurdles	1	0	0	0	0
Career Total	**2**	**0**	**1**	**0**	**415**

Going: Sf: 0-1 GS: 0-0 Gd: 0-1 GF: - Fm: 0-0
Distance: 2m/2m3: 0-1 2m4-2m7: 0-1 3m+: 0-0
Track: LH: 0-1 RH: 0-1 Tight: 0-1 Gall: 0-0
Aids: Bl: 0-0 Vi: 0-0 Tstrap: 0-0
Best Rating: 96 10/01 Fknm 2m soft NHF

Ran well on his debut in a bumper, but tailed off over hurdles next time.

Ferryhill (IRE)

71 **43**

9-y-o b g Over The River (FR)-Eden Valley (Kambalda)
B J M Ryall J J Boulter

Placings:30/6B/5P **(4328)**
2001/02: 22^{5}HY, 25^{P}S

	Starts	1st	2nd	3rd	Win & Pl
Chases	2	0	0	0	0
Career Total	**6**	**0**	**0**	**1**	**176**

Going: Sf: 0-2 GS: 0-0 Gd: 0-0 GF: - Fm: 0-0
Distance: 2m/2m3: 0-0 2m4-2m7: 0-1 3m+: 0-1
Track: LH: 0-0 RH: 0-1 Tight: 0-1 Gall: 0-0
Aids: Bl: 0-0 Vi: 0-0 Tstrap: 0-0
Best Rating: 99 1/98 Ludl 2m gd-sft NHF

Festival Flyer

98 **90**

7-y-o b g Alhijaz-Odilese (Mummy's Pet)
Miss M Bragg W H Whitley

Placings:P/4541-P34 **(4119)**
2001/02: 22^{P}GS, 26^{3}GS, 22^{4}G

	Starts	1st	2nd	3rd	Win & Pl
Hurdles	3	0	0	1	568
Career Total	**8**	**1**	**0**	**1**	**3478**

98 8/00 NAbb 2m6f D Hdl G-F £2910
Total win prize-money £2911

Going: Sf: 0-0 GS: 0-2 Gd: 0-1 GF: - Fm: 0-0
Distance: 2m/2m3: 0-0 2m4-2m7: 0-2 3m+: 0-1
Track: LH: 0-0 RH: 0-2 Tight: 0-0 Gall: 0-0
Aids: Bl: 0-0 Vi: 0-0 Tstrap: 0-0
Best Rating: 98 8/00 NAbb 2m6f gd-fm Hdl

Staying hurdler, acts well on good or faster ground.

Ffrancasal (IRE)

8-y-o b m Cataldi-Goolamoss (Le Moss)
P S McEntee The Ffrancasal Partnership

Placings:*0P/UP* **(0641)**
2001/02: 20^{U}GF, 24^{P}GF

	Starts	1st	2nd	3rd	Win & Pl
Hurdles	2	0	0	0	
Career Total	**4**	**0**	**0**	**0**	

Going: Sf: 0-0 GS: 0-0 Gd: 0-0 GF: - Fm: 0-2
Distance: 2m/2m3: 0-0 2m4-2m7: 0-1 3m+: 0-1
Track: LH: 0-0 RH: 0-2 Tight: 0-1 Gall: 0-1
Aids: Bl: 0-0 Vi: 0-0 Tstrap: 0-0
Best Rating:

Fiddlers Hill

10-y-o br g Macmillion-Clanwilla (Pauper)
A King Mrs Diane M Curtis

Placings:5/4P **(4386)**
2001/02: 20^{4}S, 16^{P}S

	Starts	1st	2nd	3rd	Win & Pl
Chases	2	0	0	0	238
Career Total	**3**	**0**	**0**	**0**	**238**

Going: Sf: 0-2 GS: 0-0 Gd: 0-0 GF: - Fm: 0-0
Distance: 2m/2m3: 0-1 2m4-2m7: 0-1 3m+: 0-0
Track: LH: 0-0 RH: 0-2 Tight: 0-0 Gall: 0-0
Aids: Bl: 0-0 Vi: 0-0 Tstrap: 0-0
Best Rating:

Field Master (IRE)

106 **90**

5-y-o ch g Foxhound (USA)-Bold Avril (IRE) (Persian Bold)
C J Gray A P Smith

Placings:425-5O0U4656216040 **(4484)**
2001/02: 18^{5}GF, 17°GF, 17^{0}GF, 19^{U}G, 19^{4}GF, 19^{6}GF, 16^{5}GF, 20^{6}S, 19^{2}G, 19^{1}GS, 19^{6}GS, 21^{0}S, 19^{4}S, 17^{0}G

	Starts	1st	2nd	3rd	Win & Pl
Hurdles	14	1	1	0	3184
Career Total	**17**	**1**	**2**	**0**	**4049**

90 12/01 Extr 2m3f F(0-95)HHdl G-S £2464
Total win prize-money £2464

Going: Sf: 0-3 GS: 1-2 Gd: 0-3 GF: - Fm: 0-6
Distance: **2m/2m3: 1-8** 2m4-2m7: 0-6 3m+: 0-0
Track: LH: 0-5 **RH: 1-9** Tight: 0-7 Gall: 0-0
Aids: Bl: 0-0 Vi: 0-0 Tstrap: 0-0
Best Rating: 90 12/01 Extr 2m3f gd-sft Hdl

Modest form in novice hurdle events, winning a weak handicap at Exeter in December.

Fielding's Hay (IRE)

102 **85**

6-y-o b m Supreme Leader-Kates Fling (USA) (Quiet Fling (USA))
A Streeter Green Card Golfers

Placings:*0-134*U55 **(2782)**
2001/02: 16^{1}GF, 17^{3}G, 17^{4}G, 20^{U}G, 20^{5}HY, 21^{5}G

	Starts	1st	2nd	3rd	Win & Pl
NH Flat	3	1	0	1	1887
Hurdles	3	0	0	0	0
Career Total	**7**	**1**	**0**	**1**	**1887**

108 5/01 Sthl 2m H NHF G-F £1561
Total win prize-money £1561

Going: Sf: 0-1 GS: 0-0 Gd: 0-4 GF: - Fm: 1-1
Distance: **2m/2m3: 1-3** 2m4-2m7: 0-3 3m+: 0-0
Track: **LH: 1-5** RH: 0-1 **Tight: 1-3** Gall: 0-0
Aids: Bl: 0-0 Vi: 0-3 Tstrap: 0-0
Best Rating: 108 5/01 Sthl 2m gd-fm NHF

Fair form in bumpers, not as good over hurdles.

Fierce Money

100f **93f**

6-y-o b g Nicholas Bill-Nut Tree (King Of Spain)
R T Phillips Richard Phillips

Placings:*4* **(4743)**
2001/02: 16^{4}GF

	Starts	1st	2nd	3rd	Win & Pl
NH Flat	1	0	0	0	0
Career Total	**1**	**0**	**0**	**0**	**0**

Going: Sf: 0-0 GS: 0-0 Gd: 0-0 GF: - Fm: 0-1
Distance: 2m/2m3: 0-1 2m4-2m7: 0-0 3m+: 0-0
Track: LH: 0-0 RH: 0-1 Tight: 0-0 Gall: 0-0
Aids: Bl: 0-0 Vi: 0-0 Tstrap: 0-0
Best Rating: 93 4/02 Ludl 2m gd-fm NHF

Fiery Creek

83f **89f**

5-y-o ch m Moscow Society (USA)-Deep Creek (Deep Run)
D J Wintle John W Egan

Placings:*30* **(4235)**
2001/02: 16^{3}HY, 16^{0}GS

	Starts	1st	2nd	3rd	Win & Pl
NH Flat	2	0	0	1	271
Career Total	**2**	**0**	**0**	**1**	**271**

Going: Sf: 0-1 GS: 0-1 Gd: 0-0 GF: - Fm: 0-0
Distance: 2m/2m3: 0-2 2m4-2m7: 0-0 3m+: 0-0
Track: LH: 0-2 RH: 0-0 Tight: 0-0 Gall: 0-0
Aids: Bl: 0-0 Vi: 0-0 Tstrap: 0-0
Best Rating: 89 2/02 Wwck 2m heavy NHF

Promising bumper debut after pulling hard.

Fiery Furnace (IRE)

29

7-y-o ch g Abednego-Five Cherries (Cantab)
D Moffatt Mrs D H Clyde

Placings:6U **(3362)**
2001/02: 20^{6}HY, 25^{U}GS

	Starts	1st	2nd	3rd	Win & Pl
Hurdles	2	0	0	0	0
Career Total	**2**	**0**	**0**	**0**	**0**

Going: Sf: 0-1 GS: 0-1 Gd: 0-0 GF: - Fm: 0-0
Distance: 2m/2m3: 0-0 2m4-2m7: 0-1 3m+: 0-1
Track: LH: 0-1 RH: 0-0 Tight: 0-1 Gall: 0-0
Aids: Bl: 0-0 Vi: 0-0 Tstrap: 0-0
Best Rating: 29 11/01 Carl 2m4f heavy Hdl

Fiery Peace

5-y-o ch g Tina's Pet-Burning Mirage (Pamroy)
H D Daly R M Kirkland

Placings:*5P0* (4762)
2001/02: 16^{5}G, 16^{P}GS, 20^{0}GF

	Starts	1st	2nd	3rd	Win & Pl
NH Flat	1	0	0	0	0
Hurdles	2	0	0	0	0
Career Total	**3**	**0**	**0**	**0**	**0**

Going: Sf: 0-0 GS: 0-1 Gd: 0-1 GF: - Fm: 0-1
Distance: 2m/2m3: 0-2 2m4-2m7: 0-1 3m+: 0-0
Track: LH: 0-0 RH: 0-3 Tight: 0-0 Gall: 0-1
Aids: Bl: 0-0 Vi: 0-0 Tstrap: 0-0
Best Rating: 96 12/01 Ludl 2m good NHF

Fiesta

4-y-o ch f Most Welcome-Taza (Persian Bold)
O Sherwood (C W Thornton 15/8) Ledwidge Best Dellal Forde

Placings:*P* (2535)
2001/02: 16^{P}G

	Starts	1st	2nd	3rd	Win & Pl
Hurdles	1	0	0	0	
Career Total	**1**	**0**	**0**	**0**	

Going: Sf: 0-0 GS: 0-0 Gd: 0-1 GF: - Fm: 0-0
Distance: 2m/2m3: 0-1 2m4-2m7: 0-0 3m+: 0-0
Track: LH: 0-0 RH: 0-1 Tight: 0-0 Gall: 0-0
Aids: Bl: 0-0 Vi: 0-0 Tstrap: 0-0
Best Rating:

Fife And Drum (USA)

75 **42**
5-y-o b/br g Rahy (USA)-Fife (IRE) (Lomond (USA))
J Akehurst Last Order's Partnership

Placings:*000* (2773)
2001/02: 16^{0}G, 19^{0}S, 19^{0}G

	Starts	1st	2nd	3rd	Win & Pl
Hurdles	3	0	0	0	
Career Total	**3**	**0**	**0**	**0**	

Going: Sf: 0-1 GS: 0-0 Gd: 0-2 GF: - Fm: 0-0
Distance: 2m/2m3: 0-3 2m4-2m7: 0-0 3m+: 0-0
Track: LH: 0-1 RH: 0-2 Tight: 0-0 Gall: 0-1
Aids: Bl: 0-0 Vi: 0-0 Tstrap: 0-0
Best Rating: 42 12/01 Extr 2m3f good Hdl

Fair handicapper at around nine furlongs on the Flat. Has been unlucky in running on last two starts over hurdles. Best suited by a sound surface.

Fifteen Reds

103 **90+**
7-y-o b g Jumbo Hirt (USA)-Dominance (Dominion)
F S Storey F S Storey

Placings:*20/56/460-60635* (4788)
2001/02: 21^{6}GF, 17^{0}GF, 21^{6}G, 17^{3}G, 20^{5}F

	Starts	1st	2nd	3rd	Win & Pl
Hurdles	5	0	0	1	364
Career Total	**12**	**0**	**1**	**1**	**762**

Going: Sf: 0-0 GS: 0-0 Gd: 0-2 GF: - Fm: 0-3
Distance: 2m/2m3: 0-2 2m4-2m7: 0-3 3m+: 0-0
Track: LH: 0-5 RH: 0-0 Tight: 0-4 Gall: 0-1
Aids: Bl: 0-0 Vi: 0-0 Tstrap: 0-0

Best Rating: 90 1/99 MRas 1m5f110y soft NHF

Modest, staying novice hurdler.

Fifth Generation (IRE)

111(106c) (95c)**96**
12-y-o b g Bulldozer-Fragrant's Last (Little Buskins)
Dr P Pritchard Matthew Vick

Placings:*40/24***U4***/6335***F***/01111/30***F***/6***U***00026***F***00/***P***5 44254010-05***P***524***P***0***U***2131O44303 (4680)
2001/02: 20^{0}G, 22^{5}G, 22^{P}GF, 26^{5}GF, 20^{2}S, 20^{4}GF, 26^{P}GF, 24^{0}GS, 24^{U}S, 16^{2}GS, 20^{1}HY, 26^{3}S, 16^{1}HY, 20°S, 16^{4}S, 16^{4}S, 21^{3}GS, 17^{0}G, 17^{3}GF

	Starts	1st	2nd	3rd	Win & Pl
Hurdles	13	2	1	3	7029
Chases	6	0	1	0	850
Career Total	**58**	**7**	**5**	**6**	**27547**

96	1/02	Uttx	2m	F(0-90)Hdl	HVY	£1946
90	12/01	Leic	2m4f110y	G(0-90)HHdl	HVY	£1988
96	4/01	NAbb	2m6f	E(0-105)HHdl	SFT	£3136
116	12/97	Limk	2m4f	(0-123)HCh	HVY	£3391
109	12/97	Clon	2m4f	(0-102)HCh	HVY	£3899
97	12/97	Thur	2m2f	(0-109)HCh	SFT	£2204
95	11/97	Clon	2m4f	(0-109)HCh	HVY	£3391

Total win prize-money £19956

Going: Sf: 2-8 GS: 0-3 Gd: 0-3 GF: - Fm: 0-5
Distance: 2m/2m3: 1-6 2m4-2m7: 1-8 3m+: 0-5
Track: LH: 1-12 RH: 1-7 Tight: 0-9 Gall: 0-2
Aids: Bl: 0-0 Vi: 0-0 Tstrap: 0-0
Best Rating: 116 1/99 Punc 2m5f heavy Ch

Veteran front-running hurdler/chaser, best suited by a soft surface and appears to be most effective at up to two miles four furlongs in moderate company, but has won over two miles.

Fiftysevenchannels (IRE)

13-y-o b g Bustineto-Allitess (Mugatpura)
Miss A Armitage John A Cooper

Placings:1224/2111P2444/510301P/2521533/0521/3/ P0 (4833)
2001/02: 25^{P}GS, 27^{0}G

	Starts	1st	2nd	3rd	Win & Pl
Chases	2	0	0	0	
Career Total	**34**	**8**	**7**	**4**	**62981**

133	11/98	Fair	2m	HCh	Y-S	£5978
112	11/97	Chel	3m7f	B Ch	G-F	£17668
129	2/97	Fair	2m	HCh	G-Y	£6782
128	11/96	Leop	2m1f	HCh	YLD	£4546
123	1/96	Fair	2m	(0-120)HCh	Y-S	£3177
128	1/96	Tram	2m6f	Ch	YLD	£3712
103	5/95	Weth	2m4f110y	H Ch	GD	£2010
105	2/95	Hrfd	3m1f110y	H Ch	HVY	£1968

Total win prize-money £45844

Going: Sf: 0-0 GS: 0-1 Gd: 0-1 GF: - Fm: 0-0
Distance: 2m/2m3: 0-0 2m4-2m7: 0-0 3m+: 0-2
Track: LH: 0-1 RH: 0-1 Tight: 0-1 Gall: 0-0
Aids: Bl: 0-0 Vi: 0-0 Tstrap: 0-0
Best Rating: 137 11/98 Chel 3m7f gd-sft Ch

Once smart hunter now a veteran. Acts on any ground.

Figale

68f **18f**
5-y-o b m Buckley-Greggina (Tina's Pet)
J C Tuck Luckley Partnership

Placings:*0* (0108)
2001/02: 18^{0}GF

	Starts	1st	2nd	3rd	Win & Pl
NH Flat	1	0	0	0	
Career Total	**1**	**0**	**0**	**0**	

Going: Sf: 0-0 GS: 0-0 Gd: 0-0 GF: - Fm: 0-1
Distance: 2m/2m3: 0-1 2m4-2m7: 0-0 3m+: 0-0
Track: LH: 0-1 RH: 0-0 Tight: 0-1 Gall: 0-0
Aids: Bl: 0-0 Vi: 0-0 Tstrap: 0-0
Best Rating: 18 5/01 Font 2m2f110y gd-fm NHF

Figawin

100 **103**
7-y-o b g Rudimentary (USA)-Dear Person (Rainbow Quest (USA))
Mrs H L Walton A E Walton

Placings:5540066/625F3453/230U060363F1-52 (1808)
2001/02: 24^{5}F, 24^{2}S

	Starts	1st	2nd	3rd	Win & Pl
Chases	2	0	1	0	1465
Career Total	**29**	**1**	**3**	**5**	**9095**

100	4/01	Fknm	2m5f110y	F(0-110)HCh	G-S	£4231

Total win prize-money £4232

Going: Sf: 0-1 GS: 0-0 Gd: 0-0 GF: - Fm: 0-1
Distance: 2m/2m3: 0-0 2m4-2m7: 0-0 3m+: 0-2
Track: LH: 0-2 RH: 0-0 Tight: 0-2 Gall: 0-0
Aids: Bl: 0-0 Vi: 0-0 Tstrap: 0-0
Best Rating: 103 10/01 Fknm 3m110y soft Ch

Moderate chaser, suited by soft ground. Goes well at Fakenham.

Fighting Times

84 **42**
10-y-o b g Good Times (ITY)-Duellist (Town Crier)
Miss K Marks Nick Shutts

Placings:06012/021043/2050F/0 (0081)
2001/02: 17^{0}G

	Starts	1st	2nd	3rd	Win & Pl
Hurdles	1	0	0	0	
Career Total	**17**	**2**	**3**	**1**	**6592**

87	2/99	NAbb	2m110y	E Ch	HVY	£2697
78	2/98	Tntn	2m1f	G(0-95)HHdl	G-F	£1495

Total win prize-money £4192

Going: Sf: 0-0 GS: 0-0 Gd: 0-1 GF: - Fm: 0-0
Distance: 2m/2m3: 0-1 2m4-2m7: 0-0 3m+: 0-0
Track: LH: 0-0 RH: 0-1 Tight: 0-0 Gall: 0-0
Aids: Bl: 0-0 Vi: 0-1 Tstrap: 0-0
Best Rating: 88 6/99 Worc 2m gd-fm Hdl

Filial (IRE)

90(94c) (84c)**83**
9-y-o b g Danehill (USA)-Sephira (Luthier)
Mrs A Duffield Mrs Ann Swinbank

Placings:F6210P/F3P-6436 (2264)
2001/02: 17^{6}G, 16^{4}G, 17^{3}G, 17^{6}S

	Starts	1st	2nd	3rd	Win & Pl
Hurdles	3	0	0	1	237
Chases	1	0	0	0	0
Career Total	**13**	**1**	**1**	**2**	**3460**

96	7/99	Worc	2m4f	E Hdl	G-F	£2600

Total win prize-money £2600

Going: Sf: 0-1 GS: 0-0 Gd: 0-3 GF: - Fm: 0-0
Distance: 2m/2m3: 0-4 2m4-2m7: 0-0 3m+: 0-0
Track: LH: 0-4 RH: 0-0 Tight: 0-4 Gall: 0-0
Aids: Bl: 0-0 Vi: 0-0 Tstrap: 0-2
Best Rating: 99 8/00 Ctml 2m1f110y good Ch

Lightly-raced selling hurdler, suited by good ground, has worn a tongue tie.

Fils De Cresson (IRE)

105 **108**

12-y-o b g Torus-Hellfire Hostess (Lucifer (USA))
J R Adam James R Adam

Placings:63/F54P34/F/P33124136/5P3344/05-5221 **(4872)**
2001/02: 17^{5}GS, 17^{2}G, 17^{2}GF, 16^{1}GF

	Starts	1st	2nd	3rd	Win & Pl
Chases	4	1	2	0	6287
Career Total	**30**	**3**	**3**	**7**	**20543**

108	4/02	Weth	2m	F(0-100)HCh	G-F	£3486
125	3/99	Ayr	2m	D(0-125)HCh	SFT	£4337
113	12/98	Catt	2m	E Ch	GD	£2753

Total win prize-money £10578

Going: Sf: 0-0 GS: 0-1 Gd: 0-1 GF: - Fm: 1-2
Distance: **2m/2m3: 1-4** 2m4-2m7: 0-0 3m+: 0-0
Track: **LH: 1-2** RH: 0-1 Tight: 0-2 Gall: 0-0
Aids: Bl: 0-0 Vi: 0-0 **Tstrap: 1-3**
Best Rating: 125 3/99 Ayr 2m soft Ch

Moderate two-mile chaser, acts on any ground.

Filscot

107 (80h)**110**

10-y-o b g Scottish Reel-Fililode (Mossberry)
C P Morlock P J Morgan

Placings:*261*/F443/31400124/2542224023/5F212443 03P-5030P3 **(4602)**
2001/02: 25^{5}G, 21^{0}GF, 22^{3}GF, 21^{0}G, 21^{P}S, 20^{3}GF

	Starts	1st	2nd	3rd	Win & Pl
Hurdles	1	0	0	0	0
Chases	5	0	0	2	960
Career Total	**42**	**4**	**9**	**7**	**24598**

123	10/00	Ludl	2m4f	E Ch	G-F	£3081
105	2/99	Kemp	2m5f	D(0-120)HHdl	GD	£3680
108	5/98	Hntg	2m4f110y	E Hdl	G-F	£2530
101	4/97	NAbb	2m1f	H NHF	FRM	£1278

Total win prize-money £10569

Going: Sf: 0-1 GS: 0-0 Gd: 0-2 GF: - Fm: 0-3
Distance: 2m/2m3: 0-0 2m4-2m7: 0-5 3m+: 0-1
Track: LH: 0-2 RH: 0-2 Tight: 0-2 Gall: 0-0
Aids: Bl: 0-0 Vi: 0-0 Tstrap: 0-0
Best Rating: 126 11/99 Leic 2m7f110y gd-fm Ch

He has a modest strike rate over hurdles and fences. Best on a sound surface, stays well.

Fin Bec (FR)

106 **118**

9-y-o b g Tip Moss (FR)-Tourbrune (FR) (Pamponi (FR))
A P Jones P Newell

Placings:*30*/235332/3411PU/35125621UP-35P24046 **(4419)**
2001/02: 23^{3}G, 23^{5}G, 24^{P}GF, 24^{2}G, 25^{4}S, 24^{0}GS, 24^{4}GS, 24^{6}GS

	Starts	1st	2nd	3rd	Win & Pl
Chases	8	0	1	1	5657
Career Total	**32**	**4**	**5**	**7**	**26262**

116	1/01	Folk	3m2f	F(0-100)HCh	HVY	£2520
111	10/00	Sthl	3m110y	E Hdl	HVY	£2710
116	3/00	Sand	3m110y	D(0-115)HCh	GD	£5027
116	2/00	Leic	2m4f110y	F(0-95)HCh	SFT	£3526

Total win prize-money £13785

Going: Sf: 0-1 GS: 0-3 Gd: 0-3 GF: - Fm: 0-1
Distance: 2m/2m3: 0-0 2m4-2m7: 0-0 3m+: 0-8
Track: LH: 0-6 RH: 0-2 Tight: 0-2 Gall: 0-4
Aids: Bl: 0-2 Vi: 0-0 Tstrap: 0-0
Best Rating: 118 3/02 Newb 3m gd-sft Ch

Fair staying chaser. Suited by soft ground. Likes to make the running.

Final Chance

84 **70**

8-y-o ch m Nader-Milly's Chance (Mljet)
C Tizzard L G Tizzard

Placings:*000*/6/60 **(1439)**
2001/02: 17^{6}GF, 18^{0}GF

	Starts	1st	2nd	3rd	Win & Pl
Hurdles	2	0	0	0	0
Career Total	**6**	**0**	**0**	**0**	**0**

Going: Sf: 0-0 GS: 0-0 Gd: 0-0 GF: - Fm: 0-2
Distance: 2m/2m3: 0-2 2m4-2m7: 0-0 3m+: 0-0
Track: LH: 0-2 RH: 0-0 Tight: 0-2 Gall: 0-0
Aids: Bl: 0-0 Vi: 0-0 Tstrap: 0-0
Best Rating: 74 1/99 Font 2m2f110y soft NHF

Final Command

102f **101f**

5-y-o ch g Gildoran-Fine Fettle (Final Straw)
J C Tuck The Fine Gild Racing Partnership

Placings:2 **(4571)**
2001/02: 16^{2}G

	Starts	1st	2nd	3rd	Win & Pl
NH Flat	1	0	1	0	492
Career Total	**1**	**0**	**1**	**0**	**492**

Going: Sf: 0-0 GS: 0-0 Gd: 0-1 GF: - Fm: 0-0
Distance: 2m/2m3: 0-1 2m4-2m7: 0-0 3m+: 0-0
Track: LH: 0-0 RH: 0-1 Tight: 0-0 Gall: 0-0
Aids: Bl: 0-0 Vi: 0-0 Tstrap: 0-0
Best Rating: 101 4/02 Towc 2m good NHF

Defied big odds by running a cracking race on his debut, pulling right away from the remainder of the field with the winner in a Towcester bumper . He should go one better in due course.

Final Escapade

9-y-o ch g St Columbus-Country Princess (Country Retreat)
P R Webber Mrs E M Wharton

Placings:P **(1754)**
2001/02: 24^{P}GS

	Starts	1st	2nd	3rd	Win & Pl
Chases	1	0	0	0	
Career Total	**1**	**0**	**0**	**0**	

Going: Sf: 0-0 GS: 0-1 Gd: 0-0 GF: - Fm: 0-0
Distance: 2m/2m3: 0-0 2m4-2m7: 0-0 3m+: 0-1
Track: LH: 0-1 RH: 0-0 Tight: 0-1 Gall: 0-0
Aids: Bl: 0-0 Vi: 0-0 Tstrap: 0-0
Best Rating:

Final Lap

98 **72**

6-y-o b g Batshoof-Lap Of Honour (Final Straw)
Simon T Lewis (G M McCourt 5/8) Simon T Lewis

Placings:0P-P6U000P040 **(4904)**
2001/02: 16^{P}S, 16^{6}GF, 20^{U}GF, 17^{0}G, 16^{0}G, 16^{0}GS, 16^{P}S, 17^{0}G, 17^{4}GF, 17^{0}G

	Starts	1st	2nd	3rd	Win & Pl
Hurdles	10	0	0	0	0
Career Total	**12**	**0**	**0**	**0**	**0**

Going: Sf: 0-2 GS: 0-1 Gd: 0-4 GF: - Fm: 0-3
Distance: 2m/2m3: 0-9 2m4-2m7: 0-1 3m+: 0-0
Track: LH: 0-6 RH: 0-4 Tight: 0-6 Gall: 0-0
Aids: Bl: 0-0 Vi: 0-0 Tstrap: 0-0
Best Rating: 74 6/01 Worc 2m gd-fm Hdl

Has had extensive treatment for back problems and sprang a surprise when 25/1 winner of Stratford seller August 2002. Acts on soft ground.

Final Settlement (IRE)

7-y-o b g Soviet Lad (USA)-Tender Time (Tender King)
J R Jenkins T H Ounsley

Placings:13/0-P **(1647)**
2001/02: 16^{P}G

	Starts	1st	2nd	3rd	Win & Pl
Hurdles	1	0	0	0	
Career Total	**4**	**1**	**0**	**1**	**5626**

115	1/00	Kemp	2m	D Hdl	GD	£3786

Total win prize-money £3786

Going: Sf: 0-0 GS: 0-0 Gd: 0-1 GF: - Fm: 0-0
Distance: 2m/2m3: 0-1 2m4-2m7: 0-0 3m+: 0-0
Track: LH: 0-0 RH: 0-1 Tight: 0-0 Gall: 0-1
Aids: Bl: 0-0 Vi: 0-0 Tstrap: 0-0
Best Rating: 117 2/00 Weth 2m soft Hdl

Made a winning hurdles debut at Kempton in January 2001, showing the right attitude under McCoy, but died after breaking down at Huntingdon in October 2001. (DEAD)

Finbar (IRE)

77f **62f**

6-y-o b g Good Thyne (USA)-Shuil Eile (Deep Run)
P J Hobbs R A S Offer

Placings:*0* **(4639)**
2001/02: 16^{0}GF

	Starts	1st	2nd	3rd	Win & Pl
NH Flat	1	0	0	0	
Career Total	**1**	**0**	**0**	**0**	

Going: Sf: 0-0 GS: 0-0 Gd: 0-0 GF: - Fm: 0-1
Distance: 2m/2m3: 0-1 2m4-2m7: 0-0 3m+: 0-0
Track: LH: 0-0 RH: 0-1 Tight: 0-0 Gall: 0-0
Aids: Bl: 0-0 Vi: 0-0 Tstrap: 0-0
Best Rating: 62 4/02 Asct 2m110y gd-fm NHF

Finbar's Law

5-y-o b g Contract Law (USA)-De Valera (Faustus (USA))

Grant Mrs June Quinn

acings:*P-O6* (0545)
01/02: 16°S, 16^{6}GF

	Starts	1st	2nd	3rd	Win & Pl
I Flat	1	0	0	0	0
urdles	1	0	0	0	0
areer Total	3	0	0	0	0

oing: Sf: 0-1 GS: 0-0 Gd: 0-0 GF: - Fm: 0-1
istance: 2m/2m3: 0-2 2m4-2m7: 0-0 3m+: 0-0
ack: LH: 0-1 RH: 0-1 Tight: 0-0 Gall: 0-1
ds: Bl: 0-0 Vi: 0-0 Tstrap: 0-0
est Rating:

Finbar's Revenge

7 (103h) (105h) 120
y-o b g Gildoran-Grotto Princess (Pollerton)
E H Sherwood K A Price

acings:3251-F05652 (4849)
001/02: 20^{F}G, 22^{0}G, 24^{5}G, 24^{6}S, 22^{5}G, 24^{2}G

	Starts	1st	2nd	3rd	Win & Pl
urdles	2	0	0	0	0
hases	4	0	1	0	1330
areer Total	10	1	2	1	6089

5 4/01 Hrfd 2m3f110y E(0-105)HHdl GD £3514
Total win prize-money £3514

oing: Sf: 0-1 GS: 0-0 Gd: 0-5 GF: - Fm: 0-0
istance: 2m/2m3: 0-0 2m4-2m7: 0-3 3m+: 0-3
rack: LH: 0-2 RH: 0-4 Tight: 0-3 Gall: 0-1
ids: Bl: 0-1 Vi: 0-0 Tstrap: 0-0
est Rating: 120 4/02 Strf 3m good Ch

ghtly-raced modest handicapper over both hurdles and nces. Has won over timber over the extended two iles three on good ground.

Finches Lane (IRE)

33 67
y-o b g Le Bavard (FR)-Alice Mann (Mandalus)
Brown Gary Brown

acings:*0-56* (4548)
001/02: 20^{5}HY, 21^{6}GF

	Starts	1st	2nd	3rd	Win & Pl
urdles	2	0	0	0	0
areer Total	3	0	0	0	0

oing: Sf: 0-1 GS: 0-0 Gd: 0-0 GF: - Fm: 0-1
istance: 2m/2m3: 0-0 2m4-2m7: 0-2 3m+: 0-0
rack: LH: 0-1 RH: 0-1 Tight: 0-1 Gall: 0-1
ids: Bl: 0-0 Vi: 0-0 Tstrap: 0-0
est Rating: 99 9/00 Fair 2m gd-fm NHF

Find The King (IRE)

106 125
-y-o b h King's Theatre (IRE)-Undiscovered (Tap On Wood)
J O'Grady (D W P Arbuthnot 8/9) J S Gutkin

lacings:110B (4952a)
001/02: 16^{1}SH, 16^{1}S, 16^{0}G, 16^{B}G

	Starts	1st	2nd	3rd	Win & Pl
urdles	4	2	0	0	13623
areer Total	4	2	0	0	13623

19 3/02 Limk 2m Hdl SFT £9171
25 12/01 Clon 2m Hdl SH £4451
Total win prize-money £13624

Going: Sf: 1-1 GS: 0-0 Gd: 0-2 GF: - Fm: 0-0
Distance: **2m/2m3: 2-4** 2m4-2m7: 0-0 3m+: 0-0
Track: LH: 0-1 RH: 0-1 Tight: 0-1 Gall: 0-0
Aids: Bl: 0-0 Vi: 0-0 **Tstrap: 2-4**
Best Rating: 125 12/01 Clon 2m sft-hvy Hdl

Useful staying handicapper on the Flat, he won his hurdles debut with the minimum of fuss at Clonmel in December 2001 and followed up against older horses but ran a moody race when well beaten at Aintree.

Finder Keeps (USA)

75 83
7-y-o b g Discover (USA)-Stark Home (USA) (Graustark)
Mrs Merrita Jones Exors Of The Late F J Sainsbury

Placings:*00-6* (0026)
2001/02: 20^{6}G

	Starts	1st	2nd	3rd	Win & Pl
Hurdles	1	0	0	0	0
Career Total	3	0	0	0	0

Going: Sf: 0-0 GS: 0-0 Gd: 0-1 GF: - Fm: 0-0
Distance: 2m/2m3: 0-0 2m4-2m7: 0-1 3m+: 0-0
Track: LH: 0-0 RH: 0-1 Tight: 0-0 Gall: 0-1
Aids: Bl: 0-0 Vi: 0-0 Tstrap: 0-0
Best Rating: 83 5/01 Hntg 2m4f110y good Hdl

Fine And Dandy (IRE)

73
6-y-o b g Roselier (FR)-Hawthorn Dandy (Deep Run)
Mrs H Dalton Trevor Hemmings

Placings:*0-P4P* (2631)
2001/02: 20^{P}G, 20^{4}HY, 16^{P}S

	Starts	1st	2nd	3rd	Win & Pl
Hurdles	3	0	0	0	0
Career Total	4	0	0	0	0

Going: Sf: 0-2 GS: 0-0 Gd: 0-1 GF: - Fm: 0-0
Distance: 2m/2m3: 0-1 2m4-2m7: 0-2 3m+: 0-0
Track: LH: 0-2 RH: 0-0 Tight: 0-1 Gall: 0-0
Aids: Bl: 0-0 Vi: 0-0 Tstrap: 0-0
Best Rating: 73 11/01 Carl 2m4f heavy Hdl

Fine Attitude (IRE)

98 96
9-y-o b g Castle Keep-Big Polly (Pollerton)
M A Allen M Morley

Placings:*042/5000/P30* (0839)
2001/02: 26^{P}GS, 20^{3}GF, 23^{0}G

	Starts	1st	2nd	3rd	Win & Pl
Chases	3	0	0	1	460
Career Total	10	0	1	1	1537

Going: Sf: 0-0 GS: 0-1 Gd: 0-1 GF: - Fm: 0-1
Distance: 2m/2m3: 0-0 2m4-2m7: 0-1 3m+: 0-2
Track: LH: 0-1 RH: 0-1 Tight: 0-0 Gall: 0-1
Aids: Bl: 0-0 Vi: 0-0 Tstrap: 0-3
Best Rating: 100 12/99 Font 2m4f gd-sft Hdl

Moderate hurdler/chaser, acts on any ground.

Fine Point (IRE)

(70h) (44h)
8-y-o b/br g Cataldi-Oak Tavern Lady (Dublin Taxi)
C R Barwell The Fine Pointers

Placings:006F/02500600-PPP0F (1342)
2001/02: 17^{P}GF, 21^{P}GF, 16^{P}G, 17^{0}GF, 16^{F}GF

	Starts	1st	2nd	3rd	Win & Pl
Hurdles	2	0	0	0	0
Chases	3	0	0	0	0
Career Total	17	0	1	0	768

Going: Sf: 0-0 GS: 0-0 Gd: 0-1 GF: - Fm: 0-4
Distance: 2m/2m3: 0-4 2m4-2m7: 0-1 3m+: 0-0
Track: LH: 0-5 RH: 0-0 Tight: 0-4 Gall: 0-0
Aids: Bl: 0-0 Vi: 0-1 Tstrap: 0-0
Best Rating: 85 10/00 Extr 2m1f good Hdl

Fine Times

8-y-o b g Timeless Times (USA)-Marfen (Lochnager)
Milson Robinson Milson Robinson

Placings:0P/0P-1 (4777)
2001/02: 25^{1}G

	Starts	1st	2nd	3rd	Win & Pl
Chases	1	1	0	0	1091
Career Total	5	1	0	0	1091

97 4/02 MRas 3m1f H Ch GD £1090
Total win prize-money £1091

Going: Sf: 0-0 GS: 0-0 Gd: 1-1 GF: - Fm: 0-0
Distance: 2m/2m3: 0-0 2m4-2m7: 0-0 **3m+: 1-1**
Track: LH: 0-0 **RH: 1-1 Tight: 1-1** Gall: 0-0
Aids: Bl: 0-0 Vi: 0-0 **Tstrap: 1-1**
Best Rating: 97 4/02 MRas 3m1f good Ch

Modest pointer, won a hunter chase at Market Rasen in April 2002. Acts on a sound surface.

Finest Of Men

6-y-o b g Tina's Pet-Merry Missus (Bargello)
J B Walton F T Walton

Placings:*0-305* (4439)
2001/02: 16^{3}S, 16^{0}GS, 17^{5}S

	Starts	1st	2nd	3rd	Win & Pl
NH Flat	2	0	0	1	267
Chases	1	0	0	0	0
Career Total	4	0	0	1	267

Going: Sf: 0-2 GS: 0-1 Gd: 0-0 GF: - Fm: 0-0
Distance: 2m/2m3: 0-3 2m4-2m7: 0-0 3m+: 0-0
Track: LH: 0-2 RH: 0-1 Tight: 0-3 Gall: 0-0
Aids: Bl: 0-0 Vi: 0-0 Tstrap: 0-0
Best Rating: 80 2/02 Muss 2m soft NHF

A half-brother to the useful staying chaser Merry Master. He will not come into his own until he tackles fences.

Finn McCool (IRE)

4-y-o b g Blues Traveller (IRE)-Schonbein (IRE) (Persian Heights)
R A Fahey Yorkshire Racing Club Owners Group 1990

Placings:F (2156)
2001/02: 16^{F}GS

	Starts	1st	2nd	3rd	Win & Pl

	Starts	1st	2nd	3rd	Win & Pl
Hurdles	1	0	0	0	
Career Total	**1**	**0**	**0**	**0**	

Going: Sf: 0-0 GS: 0-1 Gd: 0-0 GF: - Fm: 0-0
Distance: 2m/2m3: 0-1 2m4-2m7: 0-0 3m+: 0-0
Track: LH: 0-1 RH: 0-0 Tight: 0-0 Gall: 0-0
Aids: Bl: 0-0 Vi: 0-0 Tstrap: 0-0
Best Rating:

Finner Cottage (IRE)

9-y-o ch g Torus-Deep Pine (Deep Run)
B J Llewellyn R W J Willcox

Placings:*0P*/P (1258)
2001/02: 20^{P}GF

	Starts	1st	2nd	3rd	Win & Pl
Hurdles	1	0	0	0	
Career Total	**3**	**0**	**0**	**0**	

Going: Sf: 0-0 GS: 0-0 Gd: 0-0 GF: - Fm: 0-1
Distance: 2m/2m3: 0-0 2m4-2m7: 0-1 3m+: 0-0
Track: LH: 0-0 RH: 0-1 Tight: 0-0 Gall: 0-1
Aids: Bl: 0-0 Vi: 0-0 Tstrap: 0-0
Best Rating:

Finnow Thyne (IRE)

12-y-o br g Good Thyne (USA)-Mother Cluck (Energist)
Nick Gifford Mrs Sarah Dunsdon

Placings:113/P5BP-P (0063)
2001/02: 26^{P}G

	Starts	1st	2nd	3rd	Win & Pl
Chases	1	0	0	0	
Career Total	**8**	**2**	**0**	**1**	**4792**

101	3/00	Strf	3m	H Ch	GD	£2353
113	2/00	Folk	2m5f	H Ch	G-S	£1046

Total win prize-money £3400

Going: Sf: 0-0 GS: 0-0 Gd: 0-1 GF: - Fm: 0-0
Distance: 2m/2m3: 0-0 2m4-2m7: 0-0 3m+: 0-1
Track: LH: 0-0 RH: 0-1 Tight: 0-1 Gall: 0-0
Aids: Bl: 0-0 Vi: 0-0 Tstrap: 0-0
Best Rating: 136 4/00 Aint 3m1f good Ch

A profilic winning point to pointer, he has struggled somewhat in hunter chasers and is best at his own game. Prefers cut in the ground.

Finnure (IRE)

103 **109**
10-y-o ch g Lancastrian-Wayward Express (Pony Express)
G M Moore M K Roddis

Placings:04030/P**124P2**/**PP34-3431F51P05** (4260)
2001/02: 27^{3}G, 27^{4}G, 27^{3}S, 28^{1}S, 29^{F}S, 30^{5}S, 24^{1}GS, 25^{P}HY, 25^{0}S, 32^{5}HY

	Starts	1st	2nd	3rd	Win & Pl
Chases	10	2	0	2	6438
Career Total	**25**	**3**	**2**	**4**	**12951**

109	1/02	Sthl	3m110y	F(0-90)HCh	G-S	£2632
109	12/01	MRas	3m4f110y	F(0-110)HCh	SFT	£3024
95	1/00	Sedg	3m3f	E Ch	SFT	£2678

Total win prize-money £8334

Going: Sf: 1-7 GS: 1-1 Gd: 0-2 GF: - Fm: 0-0
Distance: 2m/2m3: 0-0 2m4-2m7: 0-0 **3m+: 2-10**
Track: LH: 1-8 RH: 1-2 **Tight: 2-6** Gall: 0-1
Aids: Bl: 0-0 **Vi: 2-8** Tstrap: 0-0
Best Rating: 109 1/02 Sthl 3m110y gd-sft Ch

Moderate staying chaser, suited by marathon trips and easy ground.

Fintino

8-y-o gr m Neltino-Finkin (Fine Blue)
Ian Williams The Duck Racing Partnership

Placings:*0*/*0*-P (4373)
2001/02: 21^{P}S

	Starts	1st	2nd	3rd	Win & Pl
Hurdles	1	0	0	0	
Career Total	**3**	**0**	**0**	**0**	

Going: Sf: 0-1 GS: 0-0 Gd: 0-0 GF: - Fm: 0-0
Distance: 2m/2m3: 0-0 2m4-2m7: 0-1 3m+: 0-0
Track: LH: 0-0 RH: 0-1 Tight: 0-0 Gall: 0-0
Aids: Bl: 0-0 Vi: 0-0 Tstrap: 0-0
Best Rating: 43 5/00 Font 2m2f110y good NHF

Fintona Boy (IRE)

13-y-o b g Royal Fountain-Clonbanin Vulvic (Kitsos)
Mrs Caroline Chadney Derek Tyler

Placings:336-3R (0254)
2001/02: 24^{3}GS, 24^{R}GF

	Starts	1st	2nd	3rd	Win & Pl
Chases	2	0	0	1	235
Career Total	**5**	**0**	**0**	**3**	**793**

Going: Sf: 0-0 GS: 0-1 Gd: 0-0 GF: - Fm: 0-1
Distance: 2m/2m3: 0-0 2m4-2m7: 0-0 3m+: 0-2
Track: LH: 0-2 RH: 0-0 Tight: 0-2 Gall: 0-0
Aids: Bl: 0-0 Vi: 0-0 Tstrap: 0-2
Best Rating: 95 5/01 Bang 3m110y gd-sft Ch

Veteran pointer/hunter chaser, acts on any ground.

Fiolino (FR)

107(81h) (94h)**109**
9-y-o b g Bayolidaan (FR)-Vellea (FR) (Cap Martin (FR))
M W Easterby Mrs M E Curtis

Placings:*0440*/04062/**P61P55323** (4443)
2001/02: 20^{P}GS, 20^{6}S, 24^{1}S, 23^{P}G, 20^{5}S, 24^{5}S, 25^{3}S, 32^{2}HY, 27^{3}S

	Starts	1st	2nd	3rd	Win & Pl
Hurdles	1	0	0	1	429
Chases	8	1	1	1	4797
Career Total	**18**	**1**	**2**	**2**	**5781**

105	12/01	Uttx	3m	E(0-105)HCh	SFT	£3159

Total win prize-money £3159

Going: Sf: 1-7 GS: 0-1 Gd: 0-1 GF: - Fm: 0-0
Distance: 2m/2m3: 0-0 2m4-2m7: 0-3 **3m+: 1-6**
Track: **LH: 1-4** RH: 0-5 Tight: 0-3 Gall: 0-1
Aids: Bl: 0-0 Vi: 0-0 Tstrap: 0-0
Best Rating: 109 3/02 Hexm 4m heavy Ch

Moderate staying chaser, acts on soft ground. Makes mistakes, best held up.

Fionnula's Rainbow (IRE)

110(103h) (113h)**10**
7-y-o ch m Rainbows For Life (CAN)-Bon Retour (Sallust)
Simon T Lewis (Noel T Chance 16/3) Simon T Lewi

Placings:052526631/2202/14435-**2141140P3P4** (490
2001/02: 21^{2}GF, 20^{1}G, 21^{4}G, 21^{1}S, 20^{1}GS, 20^{4}HY, 22^{0}S, 21^{P}HY, 22^{3}G, 19^{P}GF, 20^{4}GF

	Starts	1st	2nd	3rd	Win & P
Hurdles	4	1	1	0	555
Chases	7	2	0	1	944
Career Total	**29**	**5**	**6**	**3**	**2623**

135	12/01	Hntg	2m4f110y	D Ch	G-S	£39
135	11/01	Fknm	2m5f110y	D Ch	SFT	£37
113	9/01	Hntg	2m4f110y	D(0-120)HHdl	GD	£41
113	11/00	Winc	2m	E(0-115)HHdl	SFT	£36
92	4/99	Wxfd	2m	Hdl	Y-S	£24

Total win prize-money £180

Going: Sf: 1-4 GS: 1-1 Gd: 1-3 GF: - Fm: 0-3
Distance: 2m/2m3: 0-0 **2m4-2m7: 3-11** 3m+: 0-0
Track: LH: 1-5 **RH: 2-6** Tight: 1-5 **Gall: 2-2**
Aids: Bl: 0-0 Vi: 0-0 Tstrap: 0-0
Best Rating: 135 12/01 Hntg 2m4f110y gd-sft C

Consistent ex-Irish hurdler, she took well to fences in 2001/02. Best with cut in the ground. Stays two miles five, suited by cut in the ground.

Fiori

109 **13**
6-y-o b g Anshan-Fen Princess (IRE) (Trojan Fen)
P C Haslam Wilson Imports I

Placings:2/13211-40061610 (425
2001/02: 17^{4}G, 24^{0}S, 16^{0}G, 16^{6}G, 17^{1}HY, 20^{6}S, 16^{1}S, 17^{0}G

	Starts	1st	2nd	3rd	Win & P
Hurdles	8	2	0	0	407
Career Total	**14**	**5**	**2**	**1**	**1696**

130	11/01	Carl	2m1f	D(0-120)HHdl	HVY	£331
130	3/01	MRas	2m1f110y	D Hdl	G-S	£382
122	2/01	Uttx	2m	D Hdl	SFT	£285
134	12/00	Hayd	2m	D Hdl	HVY	£325

Total win prize-money £132

Going: Sf: 2-4 GS: 0-0 Gd: 0-4 GF: - Fm: 0-0
Distance: **2m/2m3: 2-6** 2m4-2m7: 0-1 3m+: 0-1
Track: LH: 1-6 RH: 1-2 Tight: 0-2 Gall: 0-1
Aids: Bl: 0-0 Vi: 0-0 Tstrap: 0-0
Best Rating: 134 2/02 Wwck 2m soft H

A stayer on the Flat, he took well to hurdles last season but had become disappointing until making all at Carlisle in November 2001. He scored again at Warwick in February. Goes well in testing ground and is best at around two miles.

Fire On Ice (IRE)

10-y-o b g Sadler's Wells (USA)-Foolish Lady (USA) (Foolish Pleasure (USA))
Neil King Neil King

Placings:6323/2/**P** (0063
2001/02: 26^{P}G

Starts	1st	2nd	3rd	Win & Pl	
Chases	1	0	0	0	
Career Total	**6**	**0**	**2**	**2**	**2242**

Going: Sf: 0-0 GS: 0-0 Gd: 0-1 GF: - Fm: 0-0
Distance: 2m/2m3: 0-0 2m4-2m7: 0-0 3m+: 0-1
Track: LH: 0-0 RH: 0-1 Tight: 0-1 Gall: 0-0
Aids: Bl: 0-0 Vi: 0-0 Tstrap: 0-0
Best Rating: 111 3/98 Fknm 2m good Hdl

Fireaway

106 **117**

8-y-o b g Infantry-Handymouse (Nearly A Hand)
O Brennan Mrs Pat Brennan

Placings: *1132*-12362 **(4637)**
2001/02: 16^{1}G, 16^{2}G, 16^{3}S, 20^{6}GS, 20^{2}GF

	Starts	1st	2nd	3rd	Win & Pl
Hurdles	5	1	2	1	6364
Career Total	**9**	**3**	**3**	**2**	**12368**

104	12/01	Donc	2m110y	E Hdl		GD	£3276
126	12/00	Donc	2m110y	H NHF		HVY	£1736
114	5/00	Chep	2m110y	H NHF		FRM	£1662

Total win prize-money £6675

Going: Sf: 0-1 GS: 0-1 Gd: 1-2 GF: - Fm: 0-1
Distance: **2m/2m3: 1-3** 2m4-2m7: 0-2 3m+: 0-0
Track: **LH: 1-4** RH: 0-1 Tight: 0-0 **Gall: 1-4**
Aids: Bl: 0-0 Vi: 0-0 Tstrap: 0-0
Best Rating: 126 12/00 Chep 2m110y soft NHF

A decent bumper horse turned novice hurdler, but has not built on his victory at Doncaster in December 2001.

Fireball Macnamara (IRE)

106 **113**

6-y-o b g Lord Americo-Glint Of Baron (Glint Of Gold)
M Pitman J C Hitchins

Placings: *56/4*-01421024100 **(4188)**
2001/02: 16^{0}G, 16^{1}GF, 16^{4}GF, 22^{2}GF, 16^{1}GF, 17^{0}GF, 16^{2}GS, 16^{4}G, 16^{1}G, 17^{0}G, 16^{0}GS

	Starts	1st	2nd	3rd	Win & Pl
Hurdles	11	3	2	0	21805
Career Total	**14**	**3**	**2**	**0**	**21805**

113	11/01	Chel	2m110y	A Hdl		GD	£15000
112	8/01	Sthl	2m	E Hdl		C-F	£2450
103	5/01	Hntg	2m110y	E Hdl		G-F	£2429

Total win prize-money £19879

Going: Sf: 0-0 GS: 0-2 Gd: 1-4 GF: - Fm: 2-5
Distance: **2m/2m3: 3-10** 2m4-2m7: 0-1 3m+: 0-0
Track: **LH: 2-9** RH: 1-2 Tight: 1-4 Gall: 1-2
Aids: Bl: 0-0 Vi: 0-0 Tstrap: 0-0
Best Rating: 113 11/01 Chel 2m110y good Hdl

A winner twice over hurdles on fast ground during the summer of 2001. Ran with credit on easier ground at Plumpton in September. Disappointed due to a back problem next time but came out and caused a surprise at Cheltenham in November.

Firechick

86 **41**

7-y-o b m Teenoso (USA)-Mirthful (Will Somers)
Mrs D A Hamer Mrs J Mathias

Placings: *600/0*-0 **(1239)**
2001/02: 20^{0}GF

	Starts	1st	2nd	3rd	Win & Pl
Hurdles	1	0	0	0	
Career Total	**5**	**0**	**0**	**0**	**0**

Going: Sf: 0-0 GS: 0-0 Gd: 0-0 GF: - Fm: 0-1
Distance: 2m/2m3: 0-0 2m4-2m7: 0-1 3m+: 0-0
Track: LH: 0-1 RH: 0-0 Tight: 0-0 Gall: 0-0
Aids: Bl: 0-0 Vi: 0-0 Tstrap: 0-0
Best Rating: 89 4/00 Hntg 2m110y good NHF

Fireside Girl (IRE)

102(92c) **100**

8-y-o br m Strong Gale-Colleen Glen (Furry Glen)
D M Forster D M Forster

Placings: *60/0625/1146FU0P*-4553P0P **(3821)**
2001/02: 21^{4}G, 21^{5}G, 16^{5}S, 17^{3}HY, 16^{P}S, 16^{0}S, 17^{P}S

	Starts	1st	2nd	3rd	Win & Pl
Hurdles	7	0	0	1	473
Career Total	**21**	**2**	**1**	**1**	**7872**

101	10/00	Sedg	2m1f	D Hdl		G-S	£3152
101	10/00	Hexm	2m	E Hdl		HVY	£2938

Total win prize-money £6091

Going: Sf: 0-5 GS: 0-0 Gd: 0-2 GF: - Fm: 0-0
Distance: 2m/2m3: 0-5 2m4-2m7: 0-2 3m+: 0-0
Track: LH: 0-4 RH: 0-3 Tight: 0-4 Gall: 0-0
Aids: Bl: 0-0 Vi: 0-0 Tstrap: 0-0
Best Rating: 101 11/00 Chel 2m110y gd-sft Hdl

Handicap hurdler, suited by soft ground.

Firestone (GER)

111 **103**

5-y-o b g Dictator's Song (USA)-Fatinizza (IRE) (Niniski (USA))
A W Carroll K Marshall

Placings: 50P24131 **(4147)**
2001/02: 16^{5}S, 16^{0}G, 20^{P}HY, 16^{2}G, 16^{4}GS, 16^{1}HY, 17^{3}S, 16^{1}GS

	Starts	1st	2nd	3rd	Win & Pl
Hurdles	8	2	1	1	10249
Career Total	**8**	**2**	**1**	**1**	**10249**

103	3/02	Chep	2m110y	C(0-130)HHdl		G-S	£6825
88	2/02	Plum	2m	F(0-90)HHdl		HVY	£1949

Total win prize-money £8775

Going: Sf: 1-4 GS: 1-2 Gd: 0-2 GF: - Fm: 0-0
Distance: **2m/2m3: 2-7** 2m4-2m7: 0-1 3m+: 0-0
Track: **LH: 2-4** RH: 0-4 **Tight: 1-4** Gall: 0-2
Aids: Bl: 0-0 Vi: 0-0 Tstrap: 0-0
Best Rating: 103 3/02 Chep 2m110y gd-sft Hdl

Moderate hurdler, suited by soft ground. Likes to be held up. Best at two miles.

Firetree (IRE)

102 **117**

7-y-o b g Supreme Leader-Upshepops (IRE) (The Parson)
J J O'Neill Miss A Kershaw

Placings: 14F13 **(4480)**
2001/02: 22^{1}S, 26^{4}S, 26^{F}GS, 26^{1}S, 22^{3}G

	Starts	1st	2nd	3rd	Win & Pl
Hurdles	5	2	0	1	7003
Career Total	**5**	**2**	**0**	**1**	**7003**

117	3/02	Hntg	3m2f	D(0-115)HHdl		SFT	£3318
109	12/01	Strf	2m6f110y	E Hdl		SFT	£3115

Total win prize-money £6433

Going: Sf: 2-3 GS: 0-1 Gd: 0-1 GF: - Fm: 0-0
Distance: 2m/2m3: 0-0 2m4-2m7: 1-2 3m+: 1-3
Track: LH: 1-1 RH: 1-3 Tight: 1-1 Gall: 1-2
Aids: Bl: 0-0 Vi: 0-0 **Tstrap: 2-4**
Best Rating: 117 3/02 Hntg 3m2f soft Hdl

Decent staying handicapper over hurdles. Acts with cut. Wears a tongue-strap.

First Alliance (IRE)

97 **67**

5-y-o b g Caerleon (USA)-Lady Liberty (NZ) (Noble Bijou (USA))
K A Morgan Mrs P A L Butler

Placings: *55*-050050 **(4646)**
2001/02: 16^{0}S, 17^{5}GS, 16^{0}GS, 20^{0}S, 19^{5}GS, 21^{0}G

	Starts	1st	2nd	3rd	Win & Pl
Hurdles	6	0	0	0	0
Career Total	**8**	**0**	**0**	**0**	**0**

Going: Sf: 0-2 GS: 0-3 Gd: 0-1 GF: - Fm: 0-0
Distance: 2m/2m3: 0-4 2m4-2m7: 0-2 3m+: 0-0
Track: LH: 0-3 RH: 0-3 Tight: 0-3 Gall: 0-0
Aids: Bl: 0-0 Vi: 0-2 Tstrap: 0-1
Best Rating: 81 3/01 MRas 2m1f110y good NHF

First And Fourmost (IRE)

88 **86**

5-y-o b/br g Alphabatim (USA)-Molly Owen (IRE) (Kambalda)
Miss H C Knight The Incorrigibles

Placings: 400 **(3225)**
2001/02: 16^{4}G, 19^{0}GS, 22^{0}G

	Starts	1st	2nd	3rd	Win & Pl
Hurdles	3	0	0	0	263
Career Total	**3**	**0**	**0**	**0**	**263**

Going: Sf: 0-0 GS: 0-1 Gd: 0-2 GF: - Fm: 0-0
Distance: 2m/2m3: 0-2 2m4-2m7: 0-1 3m+: 0-0
Track: LH: 0-1 RH: 0-2 Tight: 0-0 Gall: 0-1
Aids: Bl: 0-0 Vi: 0-0 Tstrap: 0-0
Best Rating: 86 11/01 Kemp 2m good Hdl

First Back (IRE)

5-y-o b g Fourstars Allstar (USA)-Par Un Nez (IRE) (Cyrano De Bergerac)
C W Fairhurst Twinacre Nurseries Ltd

Placings: P **(1590)**
2001/02: 17^{P}GS

	Starts	1st	2nd	3rd	Win & Pl
Hurdles	1	0	0	0	
Career Total	**1**	**0**	**0**	**0**	

Going: Sf: 0-0 GS: 0-1 Gd: 0-0 GF: - Fm: 0-0
Distance: 2m/2m3: 0-1 2m4-2m7: 0-0 3m+: 0-0
Track: LH: 0-1 RH: 0-0 Tight: 0-1 Gall: 0-0
Aids: Bl: 0-0 Vi: 0-0 Tstrap: 0-0
Best Rating:

First Ballot (IRE)

117 **134**

6-y-o b g Perugino (USA)-Election Special (Chief Singer)
D R C Elsworth J C Smith

Placings: 61P-300 **(4231)**

2001/02: 16[3]S, 16[0]G, 21[0]GS

	Starts	1st	2nd	3rd	Win & Pl
Hurdles	3	0	0	1	6050
Career Total	**6**	**1**	**0**	**1**	**12186**

140 2/01 Kemp 2m5f C Hdl G-S £6136

Total win prize-money £6136

Going: Sf: 0-1 GS: 0-1 Gd: 0-1 GF: - Fm: 0-0
Distance: 2m/2m3: 0-2 2m4-2m7: 0-1 3m+: 0-0
Track: LH: 0-1 RH: 0-2 Tight: 0-0 Gall: 0-1
Aids: Bl: 0-0 Vi: 0-0 Tstrap: 0-0
Best Rating: 140 2/01 Kemp 2m5f gd-sft Hdl

A stayer on the Flat, he got off the mark over hurdles when stepped up to two miles five furlongs at Kempton on good to soft ground, but was biting off more than he could chew in the Martell Aintree Hurdle in 2001. Lightly-raced in good company in 2001/02 . Does not want the ground too soft.

First Bash (IRE)

88(95h) **105**

12-y-o ch g Ragabash-Colette's First (Buckskin (FR))
B G Powell A S Jones

Placings:FF/6F60-530 **(0501)**
2001/02: 24[5]F, 25[3]F, 24[0]GF

	Starts	1st	2nd	3rd	Win & Pl
Chases	3	0	0	1	720
Career Total	**9**	**0**	**0**	**1**	**720**

Going: Sf: 0-0 GS: 0-0 Gd: 0-0 GF: - Fm: 0-3
Distance: 2m/2m3: 0-0 2m4-2m7: 0-0 3m+: 0-3
Track: LH: 0-0 RH: 0-2 Tight: 0-1 Gall: 0-1
Aids: Bl: 0-0 Vi: 0-0 Tstrap: 0-0
Best Rating: 105 5/01 Extr 3m1f110y firm Ch

Very moderate, veteran handicap chaser, acts on fast and easy ground.

First Class

12-y-o b g Sulaafah (USA)-Salvo Star (Salvo)
G N Alford G N Alford

Placings:0PPU30/144P55253F/3PB/53/2/42P-P **(1076)**
2001/02: 24[P]GF

	Starts	1st	2nd	3rd	Win & Pl
Chases	1	0	0	0	
Career Total	**26**	**1**	**3**	**4**	**6920**

5/96 Hrfd 2m3f110y E Hdl FRM £2415

Total win prize-money £2415

Going: Sf: 0-0 GS: 0-0 Gd: 0-0 GF: - Fm: 0-1
Distance: 2m/2m3: 0-0 2m4-2m7: 0-0 3m+: 0-1
Track: LH: 0-1 RH: 0-0 Tight: 0-1 Gall: 0-0
Aids: Bl: 0-0 Vi: 0-0 Tstrap: 0-0
Best Rating: 94 8/00 Strf 3m gd-fm Ch

First Day Cover (IRE)

91f **97f**

6-y-o b g Toulon-Bilberry (Nicholas Bill)
Noel T Chance A D Weller

Placings:51 **(2521)**
2001/02: 17[5]G, 18[1]S

	Starts	1st	2nd	3rd	Win & Pl
NH Flat	2	1	0	0	1558
Career Total	**2**	**1**	**0**	**0**	**1558**

97 12/01 Plum 2m2f H NHF SFT £1557

Total win prize-money £1558

Going: Sf: 1-1 GS: 0-0 Gd: 0-1 GF: - Fm: 0-0
Distance: 2m/2m3: 1-2 2m4-2m7: 0-0 3m+: 0-0
Track: LH: 0-1 RH: 0-0 Tight: 0-1 Gall: 0-0
Aids: Bl: 0-0 Vi: 0-0 Tstrap: 0-0
Best Rating: 97 12/01 Plum 2m2f soft NHF

Benefited from his debut to land a Plumpton bumper. Looks a staying type.

First Embrace

99 **91**

6-y-o b g Faustus (USA)-Legal Embrace (CAN) (Legal Bid (USA))
K Bell North Farm Stud

Placings:2226-24U5055 **(3325)**
2001/02: 16[2]G, 22[4]G, 19[U]GF, 19[5]GF, 16[0]GF, 19[5]GS, 20[5]GS

	Starts	1st	2nd	3rd	Win & Pl
Hurdles	7	0	1	0	703
Career Total	**11**	**0**	**4**	**0**	**2052**

Going: Sf: 0-0 GS: 0-2 Gd: 0-2 GF: - Fm: 0-3
Distance: 2m/2m3: 0-4 2m4-2m7: 0-3 3m+: 0-0
Track: LH: 0-3 RH: 0-4 Tight: 0-2 Gall: 0-2
Aids: Bl: 0-0 Vi: 0-0 Tstrap: 0-1
Best Rating: 108 5/00 Hntg 2m110y gd-sft NHF

Moderate form in bumpers and hurdles at around two miles.

First Flight

107 **114**

6-y-o br g Neltino-The Beginning (Goldhill)
K C Bailey Major Basil Heaton

Placings:3-4220 **(4154)**
2001/02: 22[4]S, 19[2]GS, 24[2]S, 20[0]GS

	Starts	1st	2nd	3rd	Win & Pl
Hurdles	4	0	2	0	2844
Career Total	**5**	**0**	**2**	**1**	**3083**

Going: Sf: 0-2 GS: 0-2 Gd: 0-0 GF: - Fm: 0-0
Distance: 2m/2m3: 0-1 2m4-2m7: 0-2 3m+: 0-1
Track: LH: 0-2 RH: 0-2 Tight: 0-0 Gall: 0-1
Aids: Bl: 0-0 Vi: 0-0 Tstrap: 0-0
Best Rating: 114 2/02 Kemp 3m110y soft Hdl

Has shown plenty of promise in a handful of novice hurdles without winning but should not be long in rectifying that. Acts with cut and stays three miles.

First Gold (FR)

107(121h) (151h)**188**

9-y-o b g Shafoun (FR)-Nuit D'Or Ii (FR) (Pot D'Or (FR))
F Doumen J P McManus

Placings:6242111F/1/F2/32111121U-534 **(2848)**
2001/02: 29[5]S, 24[3]S, 24[4]G

	Starts	1st	2nd	3rd	Win & Pl
Hurdles	1	0	0	1	2750
Chases	2	0	0	0	23795
Career Total	**23**	**9**	**5**	**2**	**596892**

188 4/01 Aint 3m1f A Ch SFT £71400
188 12/00 Kemp 3m A Ch G-S £87000
180 11/00 Autl 3m3f110y Ch HVY £84534
10/00 Autl 2m6f Ch VS £38425
9/00 Autl 2m4f110y Hdl VS £10567
5/98 Autl 3m5f Ch SFT £121212
3/98 Autl 2m5f110y HCh VS £35353
2/98 Autl 2m2f110y Ch VS £10101
1/98 Pau 2m4f110y Ch SFT £5051

Total win prize-money £463643

Going: Sf: 0-2 GS: 0-0 Gd: 0-1 GF: - Fm: 0-0
Distance: 2m/2m3: 0-0 2m4-2m7: 0-0 3m+: 0-3
Track: LH: 0-1 RH: 0-1 Tight: 0-0 Gall: 0-1
Aids: Bl: 0-0 Vi: 0-0 Tstrap: 0-0
Best Rating: 188 4/01 Aint 3m1f soft Ch

He first came to the attention of British racefans in 2000 when beating the legendary Al Capone II in the Prix la Haye Jousselin at Auteuil, and went on to provide Francois Doumen with his fifth winner of the King George VI Chase, jumping superbly to slam Florida Pearl by ten lengths. He became a short-priced favourite for the Gold Cup, but confidence was dented somewhat when he was beaten by the novice Shotgun Willy at Newbury. With the Festival having fallen by the wayside, First Gold was re-routed to Aintree, where he impressed in landing the Martell Cup. He was sent off at odds-on for his final appearance in Sandown's Tote Gold Trophy, but he parted company with Thierry Doumen after an error at the tenth. Beaten by new star Kotkijet early in the new season in France, he performed with credit over hurdles at Newbury on his return from a break. Disappointed when well beaten in the King George. The jury is out on his ability to act on fast ground, he jumps fast and low and there is no doubting his brilliance when conditions are right.

First Judgement (IRE)

81f **84f**

6-y-o b g Leading Counsel (USA)-Star Gold (Bonne Noel)
J W Mullins Adam Day

Placings:00 **(3154)**
2001/02: 17[0]GS, 18[0]G

	Starts	1st	2nd	3rd	Win & Pl
NH Flat	2	0	0	0	
Career Total	**2**	**0**	**0**	**0**	

Going: Sf: 0-0 GS: 0-1 Gd: 0-1 GF: - Fm: 0-0
Distance: 2m/2m3: 0-2 2m4-2m7: 0-0 3m+: 0-0
Track: LH: 0-1 RH: 0-1 Tight: 0-1 Gall: 0-0
Aids: Bl: 0-0 Vi: 0-0 Tstrap: 0-0
Best Rating: 84 10/01 Extr 2m1f gd-sft NHF

First Light

110 **112**

10-y-o b g Lord Bud-New Dawning (Deep Run)
J J Quinn Four Wise Men

Placings:2252/5F00/1/36532/010063020-22135P **(4178)**
2001/02: 16[2]HY, 19[2]G, 16[1]GS, 16[3]S, 17[5]S, 16[P]GS

	Starts	1st	2nd	3rd	Win & Pl
Hurdles	6	1	2	1	4514
Career Total	**29**	**3**	**7**	**4**	**13695**

112 12/01 Weth 2m E(0-115)HHdl G-S £2450
103 11/00 Sedg 2m1f E(0-115)HHdl SFT £2348
92 9/98 Strf 2m110y E Hdl GD £2220

Total win prize-money £7019

Going: Sf: 0-3 GS: 1-2 Gd: 0-1 GF: - Fm: 0-0
Distance: **2m/2m3: 1-6** 2m4-2m7: 0-0 3m+: 0-0
Track: **LH: 1-5** RH: 0-1 Tight: 0-3 Gall: 0-1
Aids: Bl: 0-0 Vi: 0-0 Tstrap: 0-0
Best Rating: 112 12/01 Weth 2m gd-sft Hdl

Acts on good and soft ground and is effective at around two miles. He wins in his turn.

First Love

109 **138**

6-y-o br g Bustino-First Romance (Royalty)
N J Henderson Queen Elizabeth

Placings:*2121*-1221 **(4138)**
2001/02: 16^{1}S, 16^{2}GS, 20^{2}S, 16^{1}GS

	Starts	1st	2nd	3rd	Win & Pl
Hurdles	4	2	2	0	13880
Career Total	**8**	**4**	**4**	**0**	**19338**

116	3/02	Sand	2m110y	D Hdl	G-S	£4524
138	12/01	Sand	2m110y	D Hdl	SFT	£4524
128	4/01	Asct	2m110y	H NHF	HVY	£2583
123	2/01	Towc	2m	H NHF	HVY	£1575

Total win prize-money £13206

Going: Sf: 1-2 GS: 1-2 Gd: 0-0 GF: - Fm: 0-0
Distance: **2m/2m3: 2-3** 2m4-2m7: 0-1 3m+: 0-0
Track: LH: 0-0 **RH: 2-4** Tight: 0-0 Gall: 0-1
Aids: Bl: 0-0 Vi: 0-0 Tstrap: 0-0
Best Rating: 138 12/01 Sand 2m110y soft Hdl

A big, strong gelding whose future lies over fences. Showed plenty of ability to win two bumpers and got off the mark in fine style over hurdles at Sandown in December 2001. Ran well in decent novice events subsequently and completed a straightforward task back at Sandown. Should stay at least two and a half miles and appears to appreciate cut in the ground.

First Son (IRE)

5-y-o ch g Barathea (IRE)-Turban (Glint Of Gold)
J A B Old (John M Oxx 3/8) W E Sturt

Placings:U **(4684)**
2001/02: 19^{U}GF

	Starts	1st	2nd	3rd	Win & Pl
Hurdles	1	0	0	0	
Career Total	**1**	**0**	**0**	**0**	

Going: Sf: 0-0 GS: 0-0 Gd: 0-0 GF: - Fm: 0-1
Distance: 2m/2m3: 0-0 2m4-2m7: 0-1 3m+: 0-0
Track: LH: 0-0 RH: 0-1 Tight: 0-0 Gall: 0-0
Aids: Bl: 0-0 Vi: 0-0 Tstrap: 0-0
Best Rating:

First Tenor (IRE)

100(80h) (37h)**92**

8-y-o b g Glacial Storm (USA)-Rustic Path (Proverb)
D Brace David Brace

Placings:PB01P **(1585)**
2001/02: 20^{P}GF, 20^{B}GF, 22^{0}GF, 24^{1}G, 28^{P}GS

	Starts	1st	2nd	3rd	Win & Pl
Hurdles	1	0	0	0	0
Chases	4	1	0	0	5233
Career Total	**5**	**1**	**0**	**0**	**5233**

92	9/01	Bang	3m110y	F(0-100)HCh	GD	£5232

Total win prize-money £5233

Going: Sf: 0-0 GS: 0-1 Gd: 1-1 GF: - Fm: 0-3
Distance: 2m/2m3: 0-0 2m4-2m7: 0-3 **3m+: 1-2**
Track: **LH: 1-4** RH: 0-1 **Tight: 1-4** Gall: 0-0
Aids: Bl: 0-0 Vi: 0-0 Tstrap: 0-0
Best Rating: 92 9/01 Bang 3m110y good Ch

Modest ex-pointer/chaser, stays three miles and acts on good or softer.

First Truth

110 **111+**

5-y-o b g Rudimentary (USA)-Pursuit Of Truth (USA) (Irish River (FR))
Mrs H Dalton Ray Bailey

Placings:20063 **(3768)**
2001/02: 16^{2}S, 16^{0}HY, 17^{0}GS, 16^{6}S, 16^{3}GS

	Starts	1st	2nd	3rd	Win & Pl
Hurdles	5	0	1	1	1264
Career Total	**5**	**0**	**1**	**1**	**1264**

Going: Sf: 0-3 GS: 0-2 Gd: 0-0 GF: - Fm: 0-0
Distance: 2m/2m3: 0-5 2m4-2m7: 0-0 3m+: 0-0
Track: LH: 0-4 RH: 0-1 Tight: 0-2 Gall: 0-1
Aids: Bl: 0-0 Vi: 0-0 Tstrap: 0-0
Best Rating: 95 11/01 Uttx 2m soft Hdl

Fair efforts over hurdles to date at around two miles. Gives the impression a stiffer test would suit. Acts on soft ground.

Fisher Street

100(89h) (59h)**107+**

7-y-o gr g Tigani-Pricket Walk (Amboise)
Mrs S C Bradburne Mrs C J Kerr

Placings:*00*/025**0440130**31PP **(4889)**
2001/02: 20^{0}GS, 24^{0}GF, 20^{0}G, 16^{0}G, 20^{1}GS, 20^{1}HY, 24^{0}S, 16^{1}GF, 16^{3}G, 16^{0}S, 24^{3}GS, 20^{1}HY, 20^{P}GF, 26^{P}G

	Starts	1st	2nd	3rd	Win & Pl
Hurdles	4	0	1	0	828
Chases	10	2	0	2	8639
Career Total	**16**	**2**	**1**	**2**	**9467**

98	3/02	Newc	2m4f	E Ch	HVY	£3415
98	12/01	Muss	2m	F(0-95)HCh	G-F	£3052

Total win prize-money £6468

Going: Sf: 1-4 GS: 0-3 Gd: 0-4 GF: - Fm: 1-3
Distance: 2m/2m3: 1-4 2m4-2m7: 1-6 3m+: 0-4
Track: LH: 1-2 RH: 1-10 Tight: 1-4 Gall: 1-1
Aids: Bl: 0-0 Vi: 0-0 Tstrap: 0-0
Best Rating: 98 3/02 Newc 2m4f heavy Ch

A fair novice hurdler in 2001/2. Switched his attentions to fencing this term, proving best at two and a half miles. Jumps soundly.

Fishki's Lad

102(98c) **102+**

7-y-o b g Casteddu-Fishki (Niniski (USA))
A Crook Sunstar Racing Ltd

Placings:*3310*/2061512/04432-00P0P **(4856)**
2001/02: 20^{0}GS, 24^{0}GF, 24^{P}S, 20^{0}S, 25^{P}G

	Starts	1st	2nd	3rd	Win & Pl
Hurdles	4	0	0	0	0
Chases	1	0	0	0	0
Career Total	**21**	**3**	**3**	**3**	**11651**

103	4/00	Hexm	2m4f110y	D(0-125)HHdl	GD	£3172
102	2/00	Muss	3m	E Hdl	GD	£2450
97	3/99	Hexm	2m	H NHF	G-S	£1556

Total win prize-money £7179

Going: Sf: 0-2 GS: 0-1 Gd: 0-1 GF: - Fm: 0-1
Distance: 2m/2m3: 0-0 2m4-2m7: 0-2 3m+: 0-3
Track: LH: 0-4 RH: 0-1 Tight: 0-1 Gall: 0-2
Aids: Bl: 0-5 Vi: 0-0 Tstrap: 0-0
Best Rating: 107 1/01 Muss 3m gd-sft Hdl

Acts on good ground and stays three miles. Has been fitted with blinkers and a visor.

Five Minutes

84f **69f**

6-y-o b m Syrtos-Florence May (Grange Melody)
J W Tudor J W Tudor

Placings:*0* **(0078)**
2001/02: 17^{0}G

	Starts	1st	2nd	3rd	Win & Pl
NH Flat	1	0	0	0	
Career Total	**1**	**0**	**0**	**0**	

Going: Sf: 0-0 GS: 0-0 Gd: 0-1 GF: - Fm: 0-0
Distance: 2m/2m3: 0-1 2m4-2m7: 0-0 3m+: 0-0
Track: LH: 0-0 RH: 0-1 Tight: 0-0 Gall: 0-0
Aids: Bl: 0-0 Vi: 0-0 Tstrap: 0-0
Best Rating: 69 5/01 Extr 2m1f good NHF

Flag Fen (USA)

102 **100**

11-y-o b/br g Riverman (USA)-Damascus Flag (USA) (Damascus (USA))
H J Collingridge Mrs Carol Dolan

Placings:310-4F602 **(3768)**
2001/02: 16^{4}GF, 16^{F}G, 16^{6}S, 16^{0}S, 16^{2}GS

	Starts	1st	2nd	3rd	Win & Pl
Hurdles	5	0	1	0	1225
Career Total	**8**	**1**	**1**	**1**	**3292**

110	12/00	Fknm	2m	E Hdl	G-S	£1764

Total win prize-money £1764

Going: Sf: 0-2 GS: 0-1 Gd: 0-1 GF: - Fm: 0-1
Distance: 2m/2m3: 0-5 2m4-2m7: 0-0 3m+: 0-0
Track: LH: 0-4 RH: 0-1 Tight: 0-3 Gall: 0-2
Aids: Bl: 0-0 Vi: 0-0 Tstrap: 0-0
Best Rating: 110 12/00 Fknm 2m gd-sft Hdl

He made a late transition to the jumping game but came good at the second attempt when a battling winner of a moderate novice hurdle at Fakenham in December 2000. Has mixed hurdling with runs on the Flat since but with little reward. Best at two miles with give in the ground.

Flagship Colm (IRE)

105 **128**

7-y-o ch g Accordion-Maryland Flagship (Persian Bold)
R J Baker P Slade

Placings:*3334*41235305/413100-0 **(0080)**
2001/02: 16^{0}G

	Starts	1st	2nd	3rd	Win & Pl
Hurdles	1	0	0	0	
Career Total	**19**	**3**	**1**	**6**	**21204**

132	12/00	Kemp	2m	B(0-140)HHdl	G-S	£10744
121	8/00	NAbb	2m6f	F(0-110)HHdl	G-F	£2691
110	1/00	Extr	2m1f110y	E Hdl	HVY	£3269

Total win prize-money £16705

Going: Sf: 0-0 GS: 0-0 Gd: 0-1 GF: - Fm: 0-0
Distance: 2m/2m3: 0-1 2m4-2m7: 0-0 3m+: 0-0
Track: LH: 0-1 RH: 0-0 Tight: 0-0 Gall: 0-0
Aids: Bl: 0-0 Vi: 0-0 Tstrap: 0-0
Best Rating: 132 12/00 Kemp 2m gd-sft Hdl

Flagship Uberalles (IRE)

117 **182**

8-y-o br g Accordion-Fourth Degree (Oats)
P J Hobbs E Gutner & M Krysztofiak Racing

Placings:113/22121111/11213PP/1244-112 **(4912)**
2001/02: 16^{1}GS, 16^{1}GS, 16^{2}G

	Starts	1st	2nd	3rd	Win & Pl
Chases	3	2	1	0	190500
Career Total	**25**	**13**	**6**	**2**	**486376**

180	3/02	Chel	2m	A Ch	G-S	£127600
182	12/01	Sand	2m	A Ch	G-S	£46400
183	12/00	Chel	2m110y	A Ch	SFT	£31900
177	2/00	Newb	2m1f	A Ch	G-S	£25350
176	12/99	Sand	2m	A Ch	GD	£38700
168	11/99	Extr	2m1f	A HCh	G-S	£19050
157	4/99	Aint	2m	A Ch	G-S	£32725
163	3/99	Chel	2m	A Ch	G-S	£57300
150	2/99	Wwck	2m	A Ch	G-S	£16224
137	1/99	Kemp	2m	D Ch	SFT	£4810
137	12/98	Extr	2m1f110y	C Ch	GD	£5114
99	3/98	Limk	2m	Hdl	YLD	£3573
113	3/98	Navn	2m	Hdl	Y-S	£2680

Total win prize-money £411428

Going: Sf: 0-0 GS: 2-2 Gd: 0-1 GF: - Fm: 0-0
Distance: **2m/2m3: 2-3** 2m4-2m7: 0-0 3m+: 0-0
Track: LH: 1-1 RH: 1-2 Tight: 0-0 **Gall: 1-1**
Aids: Bl: 0-0 Vi: 0-0 Tstrap: 0-0
Best Rating: 183 12/00 Chel 2m110y soft Ch

Top-class two-mile chaser. Formerly with Paul Nicholls, he joined Noel Chance before the 2000/01 season, but moved to the Philip Hobbs yard for the 2001/2002 season and gained his third Tingle Creek Chase impressively on his return. An effective performer fresh, he was deliberately roughed off after that and gained a famous victory in the Queen Mother Champion Chase. Best on soft ground, he was beaten on good at Sandown in April.

Flahive's First

103(108h) (89h)**102**

8-y-o ch g Interrex (CAN)-Striking Image (IRE) (Flash Of Steel)
D Burchell (R J Price 9/3) Don Gould

Placings:F043206/00002033141004033 6F44U0255/3 4130P/P502P-PF0420 **(4908)**
2001/02: 17^{P}HY, 16^{F}S, 16^{0}GS, 20^{4}G, 17^{2}GF, 21^{0}G

	Starts	1st	2nd	3rd	Win & Pl
Hurdles	5	0	1	0	1199
Chases	1	0	0	0	0
Career Total	**50**	**3**	**5**	**7**	**13263**

87	6/99	Worc	2m	F(0-105)HHdl	G-S	£1957
84	8/98	Ctml	2m1f110y	G(0-90)HHdl	G-F	£2432
80	8/98	Worc	2m	G Hdl	GD	£1520

Total win prize-money £5910

Going: Sf: 0-2 GS: 0-1 Gd: 0-2 GF: - Fm: 0-1
Distance: 2m/2m3: 0-4 2m4-2m7: 0-2 3m+: 0-0
Track: LH: 0-2 RH: 0-4 Tight: 0-2 Gall: 0-0
Aids: Bl: 0-0 Vi: 0-0 Tstrap: 0-0
Best Rating: 97 2/02 Tntn 2m110y soft Ch

Moderate handicap hurdler, best over the minimum trip on a sound surface. Has the ability to win a minor race over fences but needs to brush up his jumping.

Flaked Oats

(39h) (113h)

13-y-o b g Oats-Polly Toodle (Kabale)
P F Nicholls P Swaffield, C Thistlethwaite, S Frost

Placings:1F1/1/3UF404P/14522FU/315510P-3 **(1767)**
2001/02: 22^{3}G

	Starts	1st	2nd	3rd	Win & Pl
Hurdles	1	0	0	1	388
Career Total	**26**	**6**	**2**	**3**	**123560**

139	2/01	Uttx	3m4f	B HCh	HVY	£38675
143	11/00	Winc	3m1f110y	B(0-150)HCh	G-S	£22750
143	11/99	Winc	3m1f110y	B(0-150)HCh	GD	£20875
132	11/97	Font	3m2f110y	D(0-120)HCh	G-S	£4240
113	2/97	Font	3m2f110y	(0-120)HCh	SFT	£3770
107	12/96	Font	3m2f110y	E Ch	GD	£3080

Total win prize-money £93390

Going: Sf: 0-0 GS: 0-0 Gd: 0-1 GF: - Fm: 0-0
Distance: 2m/2m3: 0-0 2m4-2m7: 0-1 3m+: 0-0
Track: LH: 0-0 RH: 0-0 Tight: 0-0 Gall: 0-0
Aids: Bl: 0-1 Vi: 0-0 Tstrap: 0-0
Best Rating: 143 11/00 Winc 3m1f110y gd-sft Ch

Veteran staying chaser. He collected two valuable staying handicaps in 200/01, notably the Singer & Friedlander National Trial at Uttoxeter in February. Stays three and a half miles and is suited by testing ground. Had one run last season in a hurdle race.

Flame Creek (IRE)

109 **135+**

6-y-o b g Shardari-Sheila's Pet (IRE) (Welsh Term)
Noel T Chance Martin Wesson Partners

Placings:*1*-21 **(4820)**
2001/02: 17^{2}HY, 17^{1}G

	Starts	1st	2nd	3rd	Win & Pl
Hurdles	2	1	1	0	9793
Career Total	**3**	**2**	**1**	**0**	**11466**

133	4/02	Chel	2m1f	B Hdl	GD	£9009
119	4/01	Winc	2m	H NHF	SFT	£1673

Total win prize-money £10682

Going: Sf: 0-1 GS: 0-0 Gd: 1-1 GF: - Fm: 0-0
Distance: **2m/2m3: 1-2** 2m4-2m7: 0-0 3m+: 0-0
Track: **LH: 1-1** RH: 0-1 Tight: 0-1 **Gall: 1-1**
Aids: Bl: 0-0 Vi: 0-0 Tstrap: 0-0
Best Rating: 133 4/02 Chel 2m1f good Hdl

Won a Wincanton bumper in good style on his debut, but was beaten at odds-on on his hurdling debut at Folkestone. Probably does not want the ground too soft and may need to go left-handed. Won an uncompetitive Class B novices' hurdle at Cheltenham in April 2002. Considered to be a chaser in the making.

Flame Dancer

71f **73f**

4-y-o b c Dancing Spree (USA)-Madam Taylor (Free State)
M Mullineaux Frank Chadwick

Placings:*00* **(4679)**
2001/02: 16^{0}GF, 17^{0}G

	Starts	1st	2nd	3rd	Win & Pl
NH Flat	2	0	0	0	
Career Total	**2**	**0**	**0**	**0**	

Going: Sf: 0-0 GS: 0-0 Gd: 0-1 GF: - Fm: 0-1
Distance: 2m/2m3: 0-2 2m4-2m7: 0-0 3m+: 0-0
Track: LH: 0-0 RH: 0-1 Tight: 0-0 Gall: 0-1
Aids: Bl: 0-0 Vi: 0-0 Tstrap: 0-0
Best Rating: 73 3/02 Hntg 2m110y gd-fm NHF

Flamengo (FR)

9-y-o b g Bayolidaan (FR)-Raiatea (FR) (Quart De Vin (FR))
R G Miles (O Sherwood 3/2) R G Miles

Placings:*5/01*P2/P **(4727)**
2001/02: 24^{P}GF

	Starts	1st	2nd	3rd	Win & Pl
Chases	1	0	0	0	
Career Total	**6**	**1**	**1**	**0**	**3322**

101	12/98	Hrfd	2m3f110y	E Hdl	GD	£2612

Total win prize-money £2612

Going: Sf: 0-0 GS: 0-0 Gd: 0-0 GF: - Fm: 0-1
Distance: 2m/2m3: 0-0 2m4-2m7: 0-0 3m+: 0-1
Track: LH: 0-1 RH: 0-0 Tight: 0-0 Gall: 0-0
Aids: Bl: 0-0 Vi: 0-0 Tstrap: 0-0
Best Rating: 102 1/98 Hntg 2m110y gd-sft NHF

Flamme De La Vie

4-y-o b g Blushing Flame (USA)-La Belle Vie (Indian King (USA))
J K Price (G A Butler 5/7) J K Price

Placings:0 **(1080)**
2001/02: 17^{0}G

	Starts	1st	2nd	3rd	Win & Pl
Hurdles	1	0	0	0	
Career Total	**1**	**0**	**0**	**0**	

Going: Sf: 0-0 GS: 0-0 Gd: 0-1 GF: - Fm: 0-0
Distance: 2m/2m3: 0-1 2m4-2m7: 0-0 3m+: 0-0
Track: LH: 0-1 RH: 0-0 Tight: 0-1 Gall: 0-0
Aids: Bl: 0-0 Vi: 0-0 Tstrap: 0-0
Best Rating:

Flash Gordon

112 **119**

8-y-o ch g Gildoran-Florence May (Grange Melody)
Mrs S Richardson R G Fairbarns

Placings:*0/*1-51 **(4129)**
2001/02: 16^{5}GS, 16^{1}G

	Starts	1st	2nd	3rd	Win & Pl
Chases	2	1	0	0	4524
Career Total	**4**	**2**	**0**	**0**	**7670**

119	3/02	Hrfd	2m	D(0-115)HCh	GD	£4524
109	4/01	Tntn	2m3f	E Ch	G-F	£3146

Total win prize-money £7670

Going: Sf: 0-0 GS: 0-1 Gd: 1-1 GF: - Fm: 0-0
Distance: **2m/2m3: 1-2** 2m4-2m7: 0-0 3m+: 0-0
Track: LH: 0-0 **RH: 1-2** Tight: 0-0 Gall: 0-1
Aids: Bl: 0-0 Vi: 0-0 Tstrap: 0-0
Best Rating: 119 3/02 Hrfd 2m good Ch

Bold chaser, effective at two miles, sometimes gives problems at the start.

Flash Of Memory

90f **99f**

5-y-o b m Rock Hopper-Mystic Memory (Ela-Mana-Mou)
R A Fahey Carnoustie Racing Club Ltd

Placings:*5212* **(3750)**
2001/02: 16^{5}GF, 17^{2}G, 17^{1}GF, 16^{2}S

	Starts	1st	2nd	3rd	Win & Pl

	Starts	1st	2nd	3rd	Win & Pl
NH Flat	4	1	2	0	2711
Career Total	**4**	**1**	**2**	**0**	**2711**

99	12/01	Muss	2m1f	H NHF	G-F	£1582

Total win prize-money £1582

Going: Sf: 0-1 GS: 0-0 Gd: 0-1 GF: - Fm: 1-2
Distance: **2m/2m3: 1-4** 2m4-2m7: 0-0 3m+: 0-0
Track: LH: 0-0 RH: 0-2 Tight: 0-1 Gall: 0-0
Aids: Bl: 0-0 Vi: 0-0 Tstrap: 0-0
Best Rating: 99 2/02 Muss 2m soft NHF

Second in a bumper on her second start, she got off the mark in a similar race at Musselburgh. Runner-up there under her penalty.

Flashant

87 **48**

7-y-o ch g Henbit (USA)-La Furze (Winden)
A W Carroll A Bayman

Placings:*000*/4001/P0-0 **(4096)**
2001/02: 19^{0}GS

	Starts	1st	2nd	3rd	Win & Pl
Hurdles	1	0	0	0	
Career Total	**10**	**1**	**0**	**0**	**2562**

84	3/00	Sedg	2m1f	E(0-105)HHdl	G-F	£2282

Total win prize-money £2282

Going: Sf: 0-0 GS: 0-1 Gd: 0-0 GF: - Fm: 0-0
Distance: 2m/2m3: 0-1 2m4-2m7: 0-0 3m+: 0-0
Track: LH: 0-1 RH: 0-0 Tight: 0-1 Gall: 0-0
Aids: Bl: 0-0 Vi: 0-0 Tstrap: 0-0
Best Rating: 84 3/00 Sedg 2m1f gd-fm Hdl

Flat Top

110 **127**

11-y-o b g Blakeney-New Edition (Great Nephew)
M W Easterby Major M Watson

Placings:21F4/P6200P/**F4P042P4/2P5F2P1113/U213 443112/P353/12253302FP-522P0313** **(4489)**
2001/02: 20^{5}G, 24^{2}G, 25^{2}S, 24^{P}HY, 20^{0}S, 24^{3}S, 24^{1}GS, 26^{3}GS

	Starts	1st	2nd	3rd	Win & Pl
Chases	8	1	2	2	21213
Career Total	**62**	**9**	**12**	**9**	**71462**

127	3/02	Newb	3m	C(0-135)HCh	G-S	£15636
123	10/00	Hexm	2m4f110y	E(0-115)HCh	HVY	£2847
127	3/99	Newc	3m	E(0-115)HCh	GD	£2788
127	3/99	Newc	3m	D(0-125)HCh	SFT	£8609
110	12/98	Catt	3m1f110y	E(0-115)HHdl	GD	£2486
127	4/98	Hexm	3m1f	E Ch	HVY	£3154
127	4/98	Chel	2m5f	D(0-115)HCh	HVY	£5402
115	4/98	Weth	2m4f110y	D Ch	G-S	£3684
	3/95	Hexm	3m	E Hdl	HVY	£2304

Total win prize-money £46912

Going: Sf: 0-4 GS: 1-2 Gd: 0-2 GF: - Fm: 0-0
Distance: 2m/2m3: 0-0 2m4-2m7: 0-2 **3m+: 1-6**
Track: **LH: 1-5** RH: 0-3 Tight: 0-1 **Gall: 1-2**
Aids: Bl: 0-0 Vi: 0-0 Tstrap: 0-0
Best Rating: 127 3/02 Carl 3m2f gd-sft Ch

Fair chaser, stays three miles and suited by soft ground. Benefited from strong handling when winning at Newbury in March 2002.

Flaxen Pride (IRE)

98(89h) (80h)**102**

7-y-o ch m Pips Pride-Fair Chance (Young Emperor)
Mrs M Reveley A Evans, M Bailey, D Playforth, J Snaith

Placings:520/0124-060**21000** **(2771)**
2001/02: 16^{0}F, 16^{6}F, 17^{0}GF, 16^{2}G, 16^{1}GS, 19^{0}GF, 16^{0}S, 16^{0}G

	Starts	1st	2nd	3rd	Win & Pl
Hurdles	3	0	0	0	0
Chases	5	1	1	0	4502
Career Total	**15**	**2**	**3**	**0**	**7997**

102	10/01	Sedg	2m110y	F(0-100)HCh	G-S	£3445
100	7/00	Sedg	2m1f	E Hdl	FRM	£2317

Total win prize-money £5762

Going: Sf: 0-1 GS: 1-1 Gd: 0-2 GF: - Fm: 0-4
Distance: **2m/2m3: 1-8** 2m4-2m7: 0-0 3m+: 0-0
Track: **LH: 1-7** RH: 0-1 **Tight: 1-6** Gall: 0-0
Aids: Bl: 0-0 Vi: 0-0 Tstrap: 0-0
Best Rating: 102 10/01 Sedg 2m110y gd-sft Ch

Her hurdling career has been interspersed with regular pipe-openers on the Flat, and she built on her chasing debut with a win at Sedgefield in October. Acts on any ground and is best at around two miles.

Flaxley Abbey

91f **78f**

5-y-o gr m Arzanni-Dunbrody Abbey (Proverb)
J D Frost David G Jones

Placings:*0* **(4410)**
2001/02: 17^{0}S

	Starts	1st	2nd	3rd	Win & Pl
NH Flat	1	0	0	0	
Career Total	**1**	**0**	**0**	**0**	

Going: Sf: 0-1 GS: 0-0 Gd: 0-0 GF: - Fm: 0-0
Distance: 2m/2m3: 0-1 2m4-2m7: 0-0 3m+: 0-0
Track: LH: 0-1 RH: 0-0 Tight: 0-1 Gall: 0-0
Aids: Bl: 0-0 Vi: 0-0 Tstrap: 0-0
Best Rating:

Flaxley Wood

110(88h) **139**

11-y-o b/br g Kambalda-Coolbawn Run (Deep Run)
R H Buckler Mrs D A La Trobe

Placings:*50*/6541P/134132126/**1112P4/1**12F4P-504 **(2518)**
2001/02: 20^{5}G, 27^{0}G, 20^{4}S

	Starts	1st	2nd	3rd	Win & Pl
Chases	3	0	0	0	293
Career Total	**31**	**9**	**4**	**2**	**54244**

138	10/00	Chel	2m4f110y	C(0-135)HCh	GD	£10676
125	10/00	Sthl	2m4f110y	C(0-130)HHdl	HVY	£6873
136	1/99	Chel	2m5f	C HCh	SFT	£7360
109	8/98	Worc	2m7f110y	D Ch	GD	£3767
109	7/98	Worc	2m7f110y	E Ch	G-F	£3257
108	2/98	Font	2m6f110y	D(0-120)HHdl	GD	£3080
	12/97	Font	2m6f110y	D(0-120)HHdl	SFT	£3021
	10/97	Strf	2m6f110y	D(0-125)HHdl	GD	£2784
	1/97	Plum	2m4f	E(0-110)HHdl	GD	£2490

Total win prize-money £43312

Going: Sf: 0-1 GS: 0-0 Gd: 0-2 GF: - Fm: 0-0
Distance: 2m/2m3: 0-0 2m4-2m7: 0-2 3m+: 0-1
Track: LH: 0-3 RH: 0-0 Tight: 0-1 Gall: 0-2
Aids: Bl: 0-0 Vi: 0-0 Tstrap: 0-0
Best Rating: 145 1/01 Chel 2m5f soft Ch

He is a useful chaser and effective from two and a half to three miles on any ground. Best when ridden aggressively, he goes well when fresh and has recorded four of his successes after a break of 120 days or longer.

Fleet Lad (USA)

88 **67**

7-y-o b g Afleet (CAN)-Temperence Cordial (USA) (Temperence Hill (USA))
R G Frost J E Blake

Placings:*31*PP/500 **(2275)**
2001/02: 17^{5}GF, 17^{0}G, 16^{0}GF

	Starts	1st	2nd	3rd	Win & Pl
Hurdles	3	0	0	0	0
Career Total	**7**	**1**	**0**	**1**	**3377**

80	8/99	Tral	2m1f	NHF	YLD	£3080

Total win prize-money £3080

Going: Sf: 0-0 GS: 0-0 Gd: 0-1 GF: - Fm: 0-2
Distance: 2m/2m3: 0-3 2m4-2m7: 0-0 3m+: 0-0
Track: LH: 0-0 RH: 0-3 Tight: 0-0 Gall: 0-0
Aids: Bl: 0-0 Vi: 0-0 Tstrap: 0-0
Best Rating: 80 8/99 Tral 2m1f yield NHF

Fleur

65 **39**

6-y-o b m Petoski-Mizzie Lizzie (Netherkelly)
J Gallagher M K Florey

Placings:*5* **(4603)**
2001/02: 16^{5}GF

	Starts	1st	2nd	3rd	Win & Pl
NH Flat	1	0	0	0	0
Career Total	**1**	**0**	**0**	**0**	**0**

Going: Sf: 0-0 GS: 0-0 Gd: 0-0 GF: - Fm: 0-1
Distance: 2m/2m3: 0-1 2m4-2m7: 0-0 3m+: 0-0
Track: LH: 0-1 RH: 0-0 Tight: 0-0 Gall: 0-0
Aids: Bl: 0-0 Vi: 0-0 Tstrap: 0-0
Best Rating: 79 4/02 Wwck 2m gd-fm NHF

Fleur De Marechal

98(97h) (74h)**87**

7-y-o br m Greensmith-Welsh Flower (Welsh Saint)
J W Mullins Patrick Everard

Placings:*05300*/34404P-553U3 **(4562)**
2001/02: 17^{5}G, 16^{5}GF, 25^{3}G, 20^{U}S, 20^{3}GF

	Starts	1st	2nd	3rd	Win & Pl
Hurdles	2	0	0	0	0
Chases	3	0	0	2	910
Career Total	**16**	**0**	**0**	**4**	**1744**

Going: Sf: 0-1 GS: 0-0 Gd: 0-2 GF: - Fm: 0-2
Distance: 2m/2m3: 0-2 2m4-2m7: 0-2 3m+: 0-1
Track: LH: 0-3 RH: 0-1 Tight: 0-3 Gall: 0-0
Aids: Bl: 0-0 Vi: 0-0 Tstrap: 0-0
Best Rating: 93 11/99 Hrfd 2m1f good NHF

Modest novice chaser. May be best at trips short of three miles.

Flexible Concience (IRE)

101 **93**

7-y-o br g Glacial Storm (USA)-Philly Athletic (Sit In The Corner (USA))
J A B Old Willie Robertson/nigel Dempster

Placings:*004* **(4518)**
2001/02: 17^{0}G, 20^{0}G, 21^{4}GS

	Starts	1st	2nd	3rd	Win & Pl
NH Flat	1	0	0	0	0
Hurdles	2	0	0	0	0
Career Total	**3**	**0**	**0**	**0**	**0**

Going: Sf: 0-0 GS: 0-1 Gd: 0-2 GF: - Fm: 0-0
Distance: 2m/2m3: 0-1 2m4-2m7: 0-2 3m+: 0-0
Track: LH: 0-0 RH: 0-3 Tight: 0-0 Gall: 0-0
Aids: Bl: 0-0 Vi: 0-0 Tstrap: 0-0
Best Rating: 93 3/02 Towc 2m5f gd-sft Hdl

Lightly-raced individual at up to two miles five, modest form to date.

Flight For Freedom

91 **76**

7-y-o b m Saddlers' Hall (IRE)-Anatroccolo (Ile De Bourbon (USA))
Ferdy Murphy B Harrison-Burcombe

Placings:12/25P/530P233445-060 **(0927)**
2001/02: 24^{0}GF, 20^{6}G, 25^{0}GF

	Starts	1st	2nd	3rd	Win & Pl
Hurdles	3	0	0	0	0
Career Total	**18**	**1**	**3**	**3**	**5818**

77 8/98 Prth 2m110y D Hdl G-F £2668
Total win prize-money £2668

Going: Sf: 0-0 GS: 0-0 Gd: 0-1 GF: - Fm: 0-2
Distance: 2m/2m3: 0-0 2m4-2m7: 0-1 3m+: 0-2
Track: LH: 0-3 RH: 0-0 Tight: 0-1 Gall: 0-0
Aids: Bl: 0-0 Vi: 0-0 Tstrap: 0-0
Best Rating: 95 5/99 Hexm 2m gd-fm Hdl

Flighty Leader (IRE)

99(103c) **58**

10-y-o b g Supreme Leader-Flighty Ann (The Parson)
P Spottiswood (L Lungo 12/5) P Spottiswood

Placings:033044/140533/46423F5-30600 **(4786)**
2001/02: 24^{3}GF, 20^{0}G, 24^{6}S, 23^{0}G, 20^{0}F

	Starts	1st	2nd	3rd	Win & Pl
Hurdles	5	0	0	1	319
Career Total	**24**	**1**	**1**	**6**	**5789**

101 10/99 Kels 2m6f110y G Hdl GD £1954
Total win prize-money £1954

Going: Sf: 0-1 GS: 0-0 Gd: 0-2 GF: - Fm: 0-2
Distance: 2m/2m3: 0-0 2m4-2m7: 0-3 3m+: 0-2
Track: LH: 0-4 RH: 0-1 Tight: 0-1 Gall: 0-2
Aids: Bl: 0-0 Vi: 0-0 Tstrap: 0-0
Best Rating: 101 10/99 Kels 2m6f110y good Hdl

Flinders

108(96h) (81h)**88**

7-y-o b m Henbit (USA)-Stupid Cupid (Idiots Delight)
R Rowe Leith Hill Chasers

Placings:363/4300-3054550 **(4511)**
2001/02: 20^{3}GF, 20^{0}GF, 20^{5}G, 16^{4}G, 20^{5}G, 16^{5}S, 20^{0}G

	Starts	1st	2nd	3rd	Win & Pl
Hurdles	4	0	0	1	266
Chases	3	0	0	0	0
Career Total	**14**	**0**	**0**	**4**	**1060**

Going: Sf: 0-1 GS: 0-0 Gd: 0-4 GF: - Fm: 0-2
Distance: 2m/2m3: 0-2 2m4-2m7: 0-5 3m+: 0-0
Track: LH: 0-2 RH: 0-4 Tight: 0-5 Gall: 0-0
Aids: Bl: 0-0 Vi: 0-0 Tstrap: 0-0
Best Rating: 97 1/00 Folk 2m1f110y soft NHF

Flinders Chase

(109h) **116**

7-y-o gr g Terimon-Proverbial Rose (Proverb)
C J Mann P M Warren

Placings:41-3U **(2795)**
2001/02: 20^{3}S, 21^{U}S

	Starts	1st	2nd	3rd	Win & Pl
Chases	2	0	0	1	585
Career Total	**4**	**1**	**0**	**1**	**4400**

113 11/00 MRas 2m1f110y D Hdl SFT £3225
Total win prize-money £3225

Going: Sf: 0-2 GS: 0-0 Gd: 0-0 GF: - Fm: 0-0
Distance: 2m/2m3: 0-0 2m4-2m7: 0-2 3m+: 0-0
Track: LH: 0-2 RH: 0-0 Tight: 0-1 Gall: 0-0
Aids: Bl: 0-0 Vi: 0-0 Tstrap: 0-0
Best Rating: 123 11/00 Chel 2m110y gd-sft NHF

Promising chaser, lightly raced.

Flinders Range (USA)

78 **59**

4-y-o b g Pleasant Colony (USA)-Ixtapa (USA) (Chief's Crown (USA))
R M H Cowell (T R George 1/3) Mr & Mrs D A Gamble

Placings:00 **(4006)**
2001/02: 17^{0}S, 16^{0}S

	Starts	1st	2nd	3rd	Win & Pl
Hurdles	2	0	0	0	
Career Total	**2**	**0**	**0**	**0**	

Going: Sf: 0-2 GS: 0-0 Gd: 0-0 GF: - Fm: 0-0
Distance: 2m/2m3: 0-2 2m4-2m7: 0-0 3m+: 0-0
Track: LH: 0-1 RH: 0-1 Tight: 0-1 Gall: 0-1
Aids: Bl: 0-0 Vi: 0-0 Tstrap: 0-0
Best Rating: 59 2/02 Tntn 2m1f soft Hdl

Flip The Lid (IRE)

102 **80**

13-y-o b/br m Orchestra-Punters Gold (Yankee Gold)
Miss J Sawney Peter Sawney

Placings:000/06F3600/P20/P5P4 **(2263)**
2001/02: 25^{P}G, 27^{5}G, 27^{P}G, 27^{4}S

	Starts	1st	2nd	3rd	Win & Pl
Chases	4	0	0	0	0
Career Total	**17**	**0**	**1**	**1**	**1238**

Going: Sf: 0-1 GS: 0-0 Gd: 0-3 GF: - Fm: 0-0
Distance: 2m/2m3: 0-0 2m4-2m7: 0-0 3m+: 0-4
Track: LH: 0-4 RH: 0-0 Tight: 0-4 Gall: 0-0
Aids: Bl: 0-0 Vi: 0-0 Tstrap: 0-0
Best Rating: 85 10/99 Sedg 2m5f gd-fm Ch

Fliquet Bay (IRE)

103 **87**

5-y-o b g Namaqualand (USA)-Thatcherite (Final Straw)
G M McCourt A J Ballantyne

Placings:1500-4322P0 **(1353)**
2001/02: 19^{4}G, 17^{3}GF, 20^{2}S, 21^{2}GS, 24^{P}GF, 22^{0}GF

	Starts	1st	2nd	3rd	Win & Pl
Hurdles	6	0	2	1	1167
Career Total	**10**	**1**	**2**	**1**	**3127**

85 12/00 Donc 2m110y G Hdl HVY £1960
Total win prize-money £1960

Going: Sf: 0-1 GS: 0-1 Gd: 0-1 GF: - Fm: 0-3
Distance: 2m/2m3: 0-1 2m4-2m7: 0-4 3m+: 0-1
Track: LH: 0-3 RH: 0-2 Tight: 0-3 Gall: 0-0
Aids: Bl: 0-2 Vi: 0-2 Tstrap: 0-0
Best Rating: 87 7/01 MRas 2m5f110y gd-sft Hdl

Selling hurdler, stays two miles-five, acts on any ground. Has worn a visor or blinkers.

Flora Bright

103f **92f**

6-y-o b m Alflora (IRE)-Oh So Bright (Celtic Cone)
J J O'Neill Mrs A E Goodwin

Placings:0-6 **(4873)**
2001/02: 16^{6}GF

	Starts	1st	2nd	3rd	Win & Pl
NH Flat	1	0	0	0	0
Career Total	**2**	**0**	**0**	**0**	**0**

Going: Sf: 0-0 GS: 0-0 Gd: 0-0 GF: - Fm: 0-1
Distance: 2m/2m3: 0-1 2m4-2m7: 0-0 3m+: 0-0
Track: LH: 0-1 RH: 0-0 Tight: 0-0 Gall: 0-0
Aids: Bl: 0-0 Vi: 0-0 Tstrap: 0-0
Best Rating: 92 4/02 Weth 2m gd-fm NHF

Glimmer of ability in bumper company.

Flora Muck

96 **82**

6-y-o b m Alflora (IRE)-Muckertoo (Sagaro)
N A Twiston-Davies The 'Yes' - 'No' - Wait'....Sorries

Placings:46060 **(4577)**
2001/02: 17^{4}G, 21^{6}G, 24^{0}S, 21^{6}S, 24^{0}G

	Starts	1st	2nd	3rd	Win & Pl
NH Flat	1	0	0	0	0
Hurdles	4	0	0	0	0
Career Total	**5**	**0**	**0**	**0**	**0**

Going: Sf: 0-2 GS: 0-0 Gd: 0-3 GF: - Fm: 0-0
Distance: 2m/2m3: 0-1 2m4-2m7: 0-2 3m+: 0-2
Track: LH: 0-2 RH: 0-3 Tight: 0-2 Gall: 0-0
Aids: Bl: 0-0 Vi: 0-0 Tstrap: 0-0
Best Rating: 88 10/01 Bang 2m1f good NHF

Flora Poste

94 **63**

6-y-o ch m Alflora (IRE)-Preachers Popsy (The Parson)
Miss Venetia Williams Piers F Dibben

Placings:6-40 **(2883)**
2001/02: 18^{4}S, 20^{0}GS

	Starts	1st	2nd	3rd	Win & Pl
NH Flat	1	0	0	0	0
Hurdles	1	0	0	0	0
Career Total	**3**	**0**	**0**	**0**	**0**

Going: Sf: 0-1 GS: 0-1 Gd: 0-0 GF: - Fm: 0-0
Distance: 2m/2m3: 0-1 2m4-2m7: 0-1 3m+: 0-0
Track: LH: 0-1 RH: 0-0 Tight: 0-0 Gall: 0-0
Aids: Bl: 0-0 Vi: 0-0 Tstrap: 0-0
Best Rating: 77 3/01 Newb 2m110y heavy NHF

Flora Princess

98 **94**

5-y-o b m Alflora (IRE)-Rakaposhi Queen (Rakaposhi King)
A King Mrs D J Hues

Placings:0-550333 (4575)
2001/02: 17^{5}GS, 19^{5}G, 22^{0}S, 16^{3}GS, 19^{3}S, 20^{3}G

	Starts	1st	2nd	3rd	Win & Pl
Hurdles	6	0	0	3	1702
Career Total	7	0	0	3	1702

Going: Sf: 0-2 GS: 0-2 Gd: 0-2 GF: - Fm: 0-0
Distance: 2m/2m3: 0-3 2m4-2m7: 0-3 3m+: 0-0
Track: LH: 0-2 RH: 0-4 Tight: 0-0 Gall: 0-1
Aids: Bl: 0-0 Vi: 0-0 Tstrap: 0-0
Best Rating: 94 3/02 Hrfd 2m3f110y soft Hdl

Modest form over hurdles, stays two and a half miles.

Floral Leader

6-y-o b m Alflora (IRE)-Inch Ahead (IRE) (Over The River (FR))
C N Kellett (J A Pickering 22/2) Mrs Helen Herrick

Placings:000P (4597)
2001/02: 16^{0}HY, 16^{0}HY, 16^{0}HY, 19^{P}GF

	Starts	1st	2nd	3rd	Win & Pl
NH Flat	3	0	0	0	0
Hurdles	1	0	0	0	0
Career Total	4	0	0	0	0

Going: Sf: 0-3 GS: 0-0 Gd: 0-0 GF: - Fm: 0-1
Distance: 2m/2m3: 0-4 2m4-2m7: 0-0 3m+: 0-0
Track: LH: 0-3 RH: 0-1 Tight: 0-1 Gall: 0-0
Aids: Bl: 0-0 Vi: 0-0 Tstrap: 0-0
Best Rating: 49 1/02 Towc 2m heavy NHF

Floranz

83f 69f
6-y-o br m Afzal-Tuesday Member (New Member)
Mrs M Evans W J Evans

Placings:0 (0253)
2001/02: 17^{0}GF

	Starts	1st	2nd	3rd	Win & Pl
NH Flat	1	0	0	0	0
Career Total	1	0	0	0	0

Going: Sf: 0-0 GS: 0-0 Gd: 0-0 GF: - Fm: 0-1
Distance: 2m/2m3: 0-1 2m4-2m7: 0-0 3m+: 0-0
Track: LH: 0-1 RH: 0-0 Tight: 0-1 Gall: 0-0
Aids: Bl: 0-0 Vi: 0-0 Tstrap: 0-0
Best Rating: 69 5/01 NAbb 2m1f gd-fm NHF

Florida (IRE)

4-y-o b f Sri Pekan (USA)-Florinda (CAN) (Vice Regent (CAN))
I A Wood Neardown Stables

Placings:P5 (2704)
2001/02: 17^{P}S, 16^{5}G

	Starts	1st	2nd	3rd	Win & Pl
Hurdles	2	0	0	0	0
Career Total	2	0	0	0	0

Going: Sf: 0-1 GS: 0-0 Gd: 0-1 GF: - Fm: 0-0
Distance: 2m/2m3: 0-2 2m4-2m7: 0-0 3m+: 0-0
Track: LH: 0-1 RH: 0-1 Tight: 0-2 Gall: 0-0
Aids: Bl: 0-0 Vi: 0-0 Tstrap: 0-0
Best Rating: mfy

Moderate maiden over hurdles.

Florida Pearl (IRE)

119 184
10-y-o b g Florida Son-Ice Pearl (Flatbush)
W P Mullins Mrs Violet O'Leary

Placings:*11/111/F132/12112/42212-3114011* (4945a)
2001/02: 24^{3}YS, 20^{1}S, 24^{1}G, 24^{4}HY, 26^{0}G, 25^{1}G, 25^{1}G

	Starts	1st	2nd	3rd	Win & Pl
Chases	7	4	0	1	265142
Career Total	26	14	6	2	787175

180	4/02	Punc	3m1f	Ch	GD	£60858
184	4/02	Aint	3m1f	A Ch	GD	£69600
182	12/01	Kemp	3m	A Ch	GD	£87000
176	12/01	Punc	2m4f	Ch	SFT	£36693
173	2/01	Leop	3m	Ch	HVY	£55443
174	2/00	Leop	3m	Ch	YLD	£53680
171	1/00	Leop	2m3f	HCh	YLD	£7800
170	11/99	DRoy	3m1f	Ch	SFT	£55803
174	2/99	Leop	3m	Ch	SFT	£54464
173	3/98	Chel	3m110y	A Ch	GD	£54817
152	2/98	Leop	2m5f	Ch	Y-S	£28260
157	12/97	Leop	2m3f	Ch	HVY	£4069
134	3/97	Chel	2m110y	A NHF	G-F	£18760
132	12/96	Leop	2m	NHF	YLD	£4237

Total win prize-money £591489

Going: Sf: 1-2 GS: 0-0 Gd: 3-4 GF: - Fm: 0-0
Distance: 2m/2m3: 0-0 2m4-2m7: 1-1 3m+: 3-6
Track: LH: 1-3 RH: 3-3 Tight: 1-1 Gall: 0-1
Aids: Bl: 0-0 Vi: 0-0 Tstrap: 0-0
Best Rating: 184 4/02 Aint 3m1f good Ch

Ireland's best chaser, he seems destined never to win a Cheltenham Gold Cup, his second to Looks Like Trouble in 2000 emphasising that the final hill is just beyond him. He disappointed on his return in 2001/02, but came back to form when beating Native Upmanship at Punchestown before taking a good renewal of the King George. He disappointed when attempting to win his fourth Hennessy and his stamina once again gave out in the Gold Cup Back to his best at Aintree in the Martell Cup. He stays three miles, acts on any ground but looks especially effective on soft. Ideally suited by flat, galloping tracks.

Florida Rain (IRE)

104f 95f
6-y-o b g Florida Son-Ameretto (Stetchworth (USA))
Mrs M Reveley Andy Peake & David Jackson

Placings:*00-34* (4019)
2001/02: 16^{3}GS, 16^{4}GS

	Starts	1st	2nd	3rd	Win & Pl
NH Flat	2	0	0	1	247
Career Total	4	0	0	1	247

Going: Sf: 0-0 GS: 0-2 Gd: 0-0 GF: - Fm: 0-0
Distance: 2m/2m3: 0-2 2m4-2m7: 0-0 3m+: 0-0
Track: LH: 0-2 RH: 0-0 Tight: 0-1 Gall: 0-1
Aids: Bl: 0-0 Vi: 0-0 Tstrap: 0-0
Best Rating: 95 3/02 Donc 2m110y gd-sft NHF

A chaser in the making. Best effort when third in a bumper on good to soft on his third start.

Floruceva (IRE)

12-y-o ch m Florida Son-Lluceva Bay (Salluceva)
T P Tate T P Tate

Placings:*63/2211P/F3/3-5S0* (0428)
2001/02: 21^{5}G, 21^{S}GF, 21^{0}G

	Starts	1st	2nd	3rd	Win & Pl
Chases	3	0	0	0	0
Career Total	13	2	2	3	5603

108	4/99	Sedg	2m5f	H Ch	G-F	£1632
104	4/99	Kels	3m1f	H Ch	G-F	£2149

Total win prize-money £3782

Going: Sf: 0-0 GS: 0-0 Gd: 0-2 GF: - Fm: 0-1
Distance: 2m/2m3: 0-0 2m4-2m7: 0-3 3m+: 0-0
Track: LH: 0-2 RH: 0-0 Tight: 0-2 Gall: 0-0
Aids: Bl: 0-0 Vi: 0-0 Tstrap: 0-0
Best Rating: 108 4/99 Sedg 2m5f gd-fm Ch

Flossy Tops

73f 83f
4-y-o b f Gildoran-Right You Be (Sunyboy)
R D E Woodhouse David Scott

Placings:*20* (3999)
2001/02: 16^{2}S, 16^{0}S

	Starts	1st	2nd	3rd	Win & Pl
NH Flat	2	0	1	0	552
Career Total	2	0	1	0	552

Going: Sf: 0-2 GS: 0-0 Gd: 0-0 GF: - Fm: 0-0
Distance: 2m/2m3: 0-2 2m4-2m7: 0-0 3m+: 0-0
Track: LH: 0-1 RH: 0-0 Tight: 0-0 Gall: 0-1
Aids: Bl: 0-0 Vi: 0-0 Tstrap: 0-0
Best Rating: 83 1/02 Newc 2m soft NHF

Ran well on her debut in a soft-ground Newcastle bumper.but was edgy when disappointing next time.

Fluff 'N' Puff

98(111h) (66h)105
8-y-o ch g Nicholas Bill-Puff Puff (All Systems Go)
J S King Dajam Ltd

Placings:*003/062-0*PF32F53 (4264)
2001/02: 17^{0}G, 20^{P}S, 20^{F}G, 23^{3}G, 19^{2}GS, 21^{F}GS, 24^{5}GS, 19^{3}S

	Starts	1st	2nd	3rd	Win & Pl
Hurdles	1	0	0	0	0
Chases	7	0	1	2	1937
Career Total	14	0	2	3	3025

Going: Sf: 0-2 GS: 0-3 Gd: 0-3 GF: - Fm: 0-0
Distance: 2m/2m3: 0-2 2m4-2m7: 0-4 3m+: 0-2
Track: LH: 0-2 RH: 0-6 Tight: 0-3 Gall: 0-1
Aids: Bl: 0-1 Vi: 0-0 Tstrap: 0-0
Best Rating: 105 3/02 Chep 2m3f110y soft Ch

Modest performer, has placed form over hurrdles and fences. Best on a decent surface.

Flutterbud

10-y-o b m Lord Bud-Spartan Flutter (Spartan General)
Miss V Haigh Miss V Haigh

Placings:55/140/5P00-P (1353)
2001/02: 22^{P}GF

	Starts	1st	2nd	3rd	Win & Pl
Hurdles	1	0	0	0	
Career Total	10	1	0	0	2867

90	11/97	Chep	2m4f110y	D Hdl	G-S	£2596

Total win prize-money £2596

Going: Sf: 0-0 GS: 0-0 Gd: 0-0 GF: - Fm: 0-1
Distance: 2m/2m3: 0-0 2m4-2m7: 0-1 3m+: 0-0

Track: LH: 0-1 RH: 0-0 Tight: 0-1 Gall: 0-0
Aids: Bl: 0-0 Vi: 0-0 Tstrap: 0-0
Best Rating: 90 11/97 Chep 2m4f110y gd-sft Hdl

Fly Executive

11-y-o b g Executive Perk-March Fly (Sousa)
T Wall Mrs Tracey Mactaggart

Placings:*00*/PP **(0566)**
2001/02: 19^{P}G, 25^{P}F

	Starts	1st	2nd	3rd	Win & Pl
Hurdles	1	0	0	0	0
Chases	1	0	0	0	0
Career Total	**4**	**0**	**0**	**0**	**0**

Going: Sf: 0-0 GS: 0-0 Gd: 0-1 GF: - Fm: 0-1
Distance: 2m/2m3: 0-1 2m4-2m7: 0-0 3m+: 0-1
Track: LH: 0-1 RH: 0-1 Tight: 0-0 Gall: 0-0
Aids: Bl: 0-0 Vi: 0-0 Tstrap: 0-0
Best Rating: 30 12/96 Newc 2m gd-sft NHF

Fly For Paddy

84f 78f
4-y-o b g Michelozzo (USA)-Tirley Pop Eye (Cruise Missile)
Mrs H Dalton B Perkins

Placings:*30* **(3883)**
2001/02: 16^{3}G, 16^{0}GS

	Starts	1st	2nd	3rd	Win & Pl
NH Flat	2	0	0	1	316
Career Total	**2**	**0**	**0**	**1**	**316**

Going: Sf: 0-0 GS: 0-1 Gd: 0-1 GF: - Fm: 0-0
Distance: 2m/2m3: 0-2 2m4-2m7: 0-0 3m+: 0-0
Track: LH: 0-0 RH: 0-2 Tight: 0-0 Gall: 0-0
Aids: Bl: 0-0 Vi: 0-0 Tstrap: 0-0
Best Rating: 78 1/02 Ludl 2m good NHF

Third in bumper on racecourse debut.

Flying Bold (IRE)

99 85
7-y-o ch g Persian Bold-Princess Reema (USA) (Affirmed (USA))
N G Ayliffe (L Lungo 16/5) Mrs M A Barrett

Placings:0/33103120/0530-304000 **(3987)**
2001/02: 16^{3}GS, 17^{0}G, 17^{4}S, 16^{0}S, 17^{0}S, 19^{0}S

	Starts	1st	2nd	3rd	Win & Pl
Hurdles	6	0	0	1	424
Career Total	**19**	**2**	**1**	**5**	**5936**

89	1/00	Catt	2m3f	G(0-90)HHdl	GD	£1620
86	10/99	Kels	2m110y	G Hdl	GD	£2010

Total win prize-money £3631

Going: Sf: 0-4 GS: 0-1 Gd: 0-1 GF: - Fm: 0-0
Distance: 2m/2m3: 0-5 2m4-2m7: 0-1 3m+: 0-0
Track: LH: 0-3 RH: 0-3 Tight: 0-4 Gall: 0-0
Aids: Bl: 0-0 Vi: 0-0 Tstrap: 0-0
Best Rating: 94 2/00 Catt 2m3f good Hdl

Selling hurdler, suited by two miles-three on good ground.

Flying Dante (IRE)

78 41
8-y-o ch g Phardante (FR)-Flying Finch (Deep Run)
Miss L C Siddall Miss L C Siddall

Placings:00/PPPP-PP0PP **(4519)**
2001/02: 20^{P}G, 16^{P}S, 17^{0}S, 24^{P}HY, 21^{P}GS

	Starts	1st	2nd	3rd	Win & Pl
Hurdles	5	0	0	0	
Career Total	**11**	**0**	**0**	**0**	

Going: Sf: 0-3 GS: 0-1 Gd: 0-1 GF: - Fm: 0-0
Distance: 2m/2m3: 0-2 2m4-2m7: 0-2 3m+: 0-1
Track: LH: 0-2 RH: 0-3 Tight: 0-1 Gall: 0-0
Aids: Bl: 0-0 Vi: 0-0 Tstrap: 0-0
Best Rating: 65 4/00 Hexm 2m good Hdl

Flying Eagle

88 94
11-y-o b g Shaadi (USA)-Fly Me (FR) (Luthier)
P J Hobbs D Charlesworth

Placings:4/211242/0/314064/UP/126/12530-30 **(0582)**
2001/02: 18^{3}GF, 19^{0}GF

	Starts	1st	2nd	3rd	Win & Pl
Hurdles	2	0	0	1	368
Career Total	**26**	**5**	**5**	**3**	**22399**

124	5/00	Font	2m2f110y	F Hdl	GD	£2033
109	10/99	Plum	2m	F Hdl	G-F	£2582
118	11/97	Sand	2m110y	B(0-145)HHdl	GD	£5002
101	7/95	Strf	2m110y	Hdl	G-F	£2234
93	6/95	Uttx	2m	D Hdl	G-F	£2931

Total win prize-money £14784

Going: Sf: 0-0 GS: 0-0 Gd: 0-0 GF: - Fm: 0-2
Distance: 2m/2m3: 0-2 2m4-2m7: 0-0 3m+: 0-0
Track: LH: 0-2 RH: 0-0 Tight: 0-2 Gall: 0-0
Aids: Bl: 0-0 Vi: 0-0 Tstrap: 0-0
Best Rating: 124 5/00 Wwck 2m gd-fm Hdl

Won nicely on his return to hurdles at Plumpton in October, having landed the a decent event on the Flat at Epsom in August. Best on a decent surface.

Flying Fiddler (IRE)

11-y-o ch g Orchestra-Rambling Ivy (Mandalus)
M J Roberts Mike Roberts

Placings:*5044/3244126/130/5/405/2* **(4534)**
2001/02: 21^{2}G

	Starts	1st	2nd	3rd	Win & Pl
Chases	1	0	1	0	632
Career Total	**19**	**2**	**3**	**2**	**10975**

110	10/97	Kemp	2m5f	C(0-135)HHdl	GD	£3517
104	2/97	Asct	2m4f	E(0-120)HHdl	G-F	£3533

Total win prize-money £7052

Going: Sf: 0-0 GS: 0-0 Gd: 0-1 GF: - Fm: 0-0
Distance: 2m/2m3: 0-0 2m4-2m7: 0-1 3m+: 0-0
Track: LH: 0-1 RH: 0-0 Tight: 0-1 Gall: 0-0
Aids: Bl: 0-0 Vi: 0-0 Tstrap: 0-0
Best Rating: 110 3/00 Font 2m4f gd-sft Ch

Formerly fair hurdler, now at veteran stage and running in hunter chases.

Flying Footsie

75(91h) (62h)47
9-y-o b m Scottish Reel-Drom Lady (Royalty)
M J Roberts Mike Roberts

Placings: 100P/20602/320/P4R-0P5 **(3275)**
2001/02: 24^{0}G, 24^{P}S, 20^{5}S

	Starts	1st	2nd	3rd	Win & Pl
Hurdles	2	0	0	0	0

Chases	1	0	0	0	0
Career Total	**18**	**1**	**3**	**1**	**4278**

92	1/98	Folk	2m1f110y	H NHF	G-S	£1276

Total win prize-money £1277

Going: Sf: 0-2 GS: 0-0 Gd: 0-1 GF: - Fm: 0-0
Distance: 2m/2m3: 0-0 2m4-2m7: 0-1 3m+: 0-2
Track: LH: 0-2 RH: 0-1 Tight: 0-2 Gall: 0-0
Aids: Bl: 0-0 Vi: 0-0 Tstrap: 0-0
Best Rating: 108 1/00 Font 2m6f110y gd-sft Hdl

Flying Fortress

76 74
5-y-o b g Petoski-Misty Fort (Menelek)
H D Daly J B Sumner

Placings:*06* **(3869)**
2001/02: 16^{0}S, 16^{6}GS

	Starts	1st	2nd	3rd	Win & Pl
NH Flat	1	0	0	0	0
Hurdles	1	0	0	0	0
Career Total	**2**	**0**	**0**	**0**	**0**

Going: Sf: 0-1 GS: 0-1 Gd: 0-0 GF: - Fm: 0-0
Distance: 2m/2m3: 0-2 2m4-2m7: 0-0 3m+: 0-0
Track: LH: 0-1 RH: 0-1 Tight: 0-0 Gall: 0-0
Aids: Bl: 0-0 Vi: 0-0 Tstrap: 0-0
Best Rating: 74 2/02 Ludl 2m gd-sft Hdl

Flying Fortune (IRE)

102 102
6-y-o b g Jolly Jake (NZ)-Dynamite Flyer (USA) (Explodent (USA))
N M Babbage Colin Rashbrook

Placings:*00*354 **(4007)**
2001/02: 16^{0}G, 18^{0}G, 16^{3}GS, 16^{5}S, 19^{4}S

	Starts	1st	2nd	3rd	Win & Pl
NH Flat	2	0	0	0	0
Hurdles	3	0	0	1	829
Career Total	**5**	**0**	**0**	**1**	**829**

Going: Sf: 0-2 GS: 0-1 Gd: 0-2 GF: - Fm: 0-0
Distance: 2m/2m3: 0-5 2m4-2m7: 0-0 3m+: 0-0
Track: LH: 0-3 RH: 0-2 Tight: 0-1 Gall: 0-2
Aids: Bl: 0-0 Vi: 0-0 Tstrap: 0-0
Best Rating: 102 3/02 Newb 2m3f soft Hdl

Well held in bumpers. Ran on well on hurdle debut. Likes cut in the ground.

Flying Gunner

96 110
11-y-o ch g Gunner B-Dans Le Vent (Pollerton)
A King Mrs R J Skan

Placings:632F3/2212215/5P4B34035/1121100/64041 P4/3205-00 **(2029)**
2001/02: 24^{0}G, 24^{0}GS

	Starts	1st	2nd	3rd	Win & Pl
Hurdles	2	0	0	0	
Career Total	**41**	**7**	**7**	**5**	**53829**

140	2/00	Newb	3m110y	C(0-130)HHdl	G-S	£5947
135	2/99	Newb	3m110y	C(0-130)HHdl	G-S	£4731
132	1/99	Uttx	3m110y	C(0-135)HHdl	SFT	£7545
128	11/98	Chep	3m	C(0-130)HHdl	G-S	£5199
122	11/98	Newb	3m110y	C(0-135)HHdl	G-S	£5021
109	2/97	Hntg	3m2f	E Hdl	G-S	£2600
112	11/96	Chep	3m	D Hdl	G-S	£2823

Total win prize-money £33868

Going: Sf: 0-0 GS: 0-1 Gd: 0-1 GF: - Fm: 0-0
Distance: 2m/2m3: 0-0 2m4-2m7: 0-0 3m+: 0-2
Track: LH: 0-2 RH: 0-0 Tight: 0-1 Gall: 0-0
Aids: Bl: 0-0 Vi: 0-0 Tstrap: 0-0
Best Rating: **140** 11/00 Chel 3m1f110y gd-sft Hdl

Particularly lazy, he needs plenty of driving. Once a decent staying handicap hurdler, he has been lightly raced of late. Best over three miles with cut in the ground and has a good record at Newbury.

Flying High (IRE)

106(98h) (87h)**100**

7-y-o b g Fayruz-Shayista (Tap On Wood)
M Todhunter B Batey

Placings:00/0P-054246201362 **(1680)**
2001/02: 16^{0}GF, 16^{5}GS, 20^{4}F, 20^{2}F, 19^{4}GF, 20^{6}GS, 17^{2}GF, 16^{0}GF, 16^{1}GF, 17^{3}GS, 16^{6}G, 16^{2}G

	Starts	1st	2nd	3rd	Win & Pl
Hurdles	7	0	2	0	1146
Chases	5	1	1	1	4271
Career Total	**16**	**1**	**3**	**1**	**5417**

94	8/01	Sedg	2m110y	E Ch	G-F	£2912

Total win prize-money £2912

Going: Sf: 0-0 GS: 0-3 Gd: 0-2 GF: - Fm: 1-7
Distance: **2m/2m3: 1-8** 2m4-2m7: 0-4 3m+: 0-0
Track: **LH: 1-8** RH: 0-4 **Tight: 1-6** Gall: 0-0
Aids: Bl: 0-0 Vi: 0-0 Tstrap: 0-0
Best Rating: **100** 10/01 Sedg 2m110y good Ch

Flying Instructor

116 **158**

12-y-o gr g Neltino-Flying Mistress (Lear Jet)
P R Webber Mrs John Webber

Placings:60/301611/P03143F3/1326143525/135101/6414232/455P104P-16046521P3 **(4845)**
2001/02: 25^{1}F, 24^{6}GF, 25^{0}G, 24^{4}G, 20^{6}S, 25^{5}GS, 20^{2}HY, 19^{1}GS, 21^{P}HY, 24^{3}G

	Starts	1st	2nd	3rd	Win & Pl
Chases	10	2	1	1	29220
Career Total	**57**	**13**	**5**	**9**	**188985**

162	3/02	Dono	2m3f110y	B(0 140)HCh	G S	£10842
158	5/01	Weth	3m1f	B(0-145)HCh	FRM	£9083
160	2/01	Hayd	2m4f	B HCh	SFT	£14170
163	12/99	Weth	2m4f110y	B HCh	G-S	£10338
159	4/99	Aint	2m	A HCh	GD	£26775
163	2/99	Newb	2m4f	B(0-145)HCh	G-S	£10934
162	12/98	Chel	2m110y	B HCh	GD	£8563
156	1/98	Hayd	2m	B HCh	SFT	£7067
116	5/97	Bang	2m1f110y	D Ch	GD	£3355
130	2/97	Hayd	2m	C Ch	GD	£4485
126	4/96	Asct	2m110y	C(0-135)HHdl	G-F	£5152
122	3/96	Uttx	2m	C Hdl	G-S	£3891
86	11/95	Nott	2m	D Hdl	G-F	£3202

Total win prize-money £117860

Going: Sf: 0-3 GS: 1-2 Gd: 0-3 GF: - Fm: 1-2
Distance: 2m/2m3: 0-0 2m4-2m7: 1-4 3m+: 1-6
Track: **LH: 2-10** RH: 0-0 Tight: 0-1 **Gall: 1-1**
Aids: Bl: 0-0 Vi: 0-0 Tstrap: 0-0
Best Rating: **163** 5/00 Punc 2m yield Ch

A useful chaser between two and a half and three miles nowadays, he has not been disgraced in some decent races this season. He stays three miles on fast ground, is best when allowed to dominate and is suited by flat left-handed tracks. Won at Doncaster in March 2002, 10lb lower than his last win 10 months earlier.

Flying Maria

11-y-o gr m Neltino-Flying Mistress (Lear Jet)
J S Papworth J S Papworth

Placings:2F5242P/113/UP-P **(4376)**
2001/02: 20^{P}S

	Starts	1st	2nd	3rd	Win & Pl
Chases	1	0	0	0	
Career Total	**13**	**2**	**3**	**1**	**5865**

110	3/00	NAbb	2m5f110y	H Ch	GD	£1482
123	3/00	Ludl	2m4f	H Ch	SFT	£2436

Total win prize-money £3918

Going: Sf: 0-1 GS: 0-0 Gd: 0-0 GF: - Fm: 0-0
Distance: 2m/2m3: 0-0 2m4-2m7: 0-1 3m+: 0-0
Track: LH: 0-0 RH: 0-1 Tight: 0-1 Gall: 0-0
Aids: Bl: 0-0 Vi: 0-0 Tstrap: 0-0
Best Rating: **123** 3/00 Ludl 2m4f soft Ch

Flying Pennant (IRE)

84 **63**

9-y-o gr g Waajib-Flying Beckee (IRE) (Godswalk (USA))
J M Bradley E A Hayward

Placings:360435/0 **(1405)**
2001/02: 16^{0}GF

	Starts	1st	2nd	3rd	Win & Pl
Hurdles	1	0	0	0	
Career Total	**7**	**0**	**0**	**2**	**597**

Going: Sf: 0-0 GS: 0-0 Gd: 0-0 GF: - Fm: 0-1
Distance: 2m/2m3: 0-1 2m4-2m7: 0-0 3m+: 0-0
Track: LH: 0-1 RH: 0-0 Tight: 0-0 Gall: 0-0
Aids: Bl: 0-0 Vi: 0-0 Tstrap: 0-0
Best Rating: **80** 11/99 Tntn 2m1f good Hdl

Flying Trix (IRE)

96(109h) (109h)**116**

6-y-o b g Lord Americo-Bannow Drive (IRE) (Miners Lamp)
M Pitman Patrick Bancroft

Placings:*35*/43113PP-00643 **(3888)**
2001/02: 21^{0}G, 24^{0}GS, 24^{6}S, 26^{4}HY, 24^{3}GS

	Starts	1st	2nd	3rd	Win & Pl
Hurdles	3	0	0	0	0
Chases	2	0	0	1	1312
Career Total	**14**	**2**	**0**	**4**	**10085**

113	1/01	Uttx	3m110y	D Hdl	HVY	£3612
119	12/00	Towc	2m5f	D Hdl	HVY	£3055

Total win prize-money £6667

Going: Sf: 0-2 GS: 0-2 Gd: 0-1 GF: - Fm: 0-0
Distance: 2m/2m3: 0-0 2m4-2m7: 0-1 3m+: 0-4
Track: LH: 0-4 RH: 0-1 Tight: 0-0 Gall: 0-1
Aids: Bl: 0-0 Vi: 0-0 Tstrap: 0-0
Best Rating: **126** 2/01 Asct 3m heavy Hdl

A progressive sort in 2000/01, he struggled for form last season over hurdles and fences.

Flying Veil

8-y-o gr g Neltino-Take The Veil (Monksfield)
D M Grissell Chartwell Racing

Placings:*60*/P-0 **(0058)**
2001/02: 17^{0}GS

	Starts	1st	2nd	3rd	Win & Pl
Hurdles	1	0	0	0	
Career Total	**4**	**0**	**0**	**0**	**0**

Going: Sf: 0-0 GS: 0-1 Gd: 0-0 GF: - Fm: 0-0
Distance: 2m/2m3: 0-1 2m4-2m7: 0-0 3m+: 0-0
Track: LH: 0-0 RH: 0-1 Tight: 0-1 Gall: 0-0
Aids: Bl: 0-0 Vi: 0-0 Tstrap: 0-0
Best Rating: **69** 5/01 Folk 2m1f110y gd-sft Hdl

Flyoff (IRE)

90 **69**

5-y-o b g Mtoto-Flyleaf (FR) (Persian Bold)
K A Morgan Harmer Personal Care Ltd

Placings:6 **(4486)**
2001/02: 17^{6}GS

	Starts	1st	2nd	3rd	Win & Pl
Hurdles	1	0	0	0	0
Career Total	**1**	**0**	**0**	**0**	**0**

Going: Sf: 0-0 GS: 0-1 Gd: 0-0 GF: - Fm: 0-0
Distance: 2m/2m3: 0-1 2m4-2m7: 0-0 3m+: 0-0
Track: LH: 0-0 RH: 0-1 Tight: 0-0 Gall: 0-0
Aids: Bl: 0-0 Vi: 0-0 Tstrap: 0-0
Best Rating: **69** 3/02 Carl 2m1f gd-sft Hdl

Fnan

79(114h) (138h)**111**

6-y-o b g Generous (IRE)-Rafha (Kris)
Noel Meade D P Sharkey

Placings:21112P-42000153 **(4954a)**
2001/02: 20^{4}GY, 24^{2}YS, 24^{0}Y, 16^{0}S, 21^{0}GS, 18^{1}GY, 20^{5}G, 24^{3}G

	Starts	1st	2nd	3rd	Win & Pl
Hurdles	5	1	0	1	14070
Chases	3	0	1	0	1419
Career Total	**14**	**4**	**3**	**1**	**29695**

138	3/02	Fair	2m2f	I Hdl	G-Y	£7975
125	6/00	Wxfd	2m4f	Hdl	G-Y	£3588
114	5/00	Fair	2m	Hdl	G-Y	£3864
114	5/00	Navn	2m2f	Hdl	G-Y	£3588

Total win prize-money £19015

Going: Sf: 0-1 GS: 0-1 Gd: 0-2 GF: - Fm: 0-0
Distance: **2m/2m3: 1-2** 2m4-2m7: 0-3 3m+: 0-3
Track: LH: 0-3 **RH: 1-3** Tight: 0-1 Gall: 0-1
Aids: Bl: 0-0 Vi: 0-0 Tstrap: 0-2
Best Rating: **138** 4/02 Punc 3m good Hdl

Handicap hurdler. Stays two and a half miles, often wears a tongue strap.

Foggy (IRE)

80 (80c)**71**

9-y-o gr g Merrymount-Rosy Waters (Roselier (FR))
J R Norton Miss A J Hurst

Placings:0000061/2451/040-UPP060 **(4573)**
2001/02: 20^{U}GS, 24^{P}S, 24^{P}S, 20^{0}HY, 24^{6}HY, 20^{0}G

	Starts	1st	2nd	3rd	Win & Pl
Hurdles	4	0	0	0	0
Chases	2	0	0	0	0
Career Total	**20**	**2**	**1**	**0**	**6006**

101	3/00	Hexm	3m	F(0-100)HHdl	SFT	£2159
89	4/99	Towc	2m5f	E(0-105)HHdl	SFT	£2862

Total win prize-money £5023

Going: Sf: 0-4 GS: 0-1 Gd: 0-1 GF: - Fm: 0-0
Distance: 2m/2m3: 0-0 2m4-2m7: 0-3 3m+: 0-3
Track: LH: 0-6 RH: 0-0 Tight: 0-1 Gall: 0-2
Aids: Bl: 0-0 Vi: 0-2 Tstrap: 0-0
Best Rating: 101 3/00 Hexm 3m soft Hdl

Folk Hero (IRE)

10-y-o b g Brush Aside (USA)-Highway Mistress (Royal Highway)
M A Allen M Morley

Placings: *00/020360/01050*P/P **(0104)**
2001/02: 18^{P}GF

	Starts	1st	2nd	3rd	Win & Pl
Hurdles	1	0	0	0	
Career Total	**15**	**1**	**1**	**1**	**3203**

97	5/98	Slig	2m	NHF	GD	£2382

Total win prize-money £2383

Going: Sf: 0-0 GS: 0-0 Gd: 0-0 GF: - Fm: 0-1
Distance: 2m/2m3: 0-1 2m4-2m7: 0-0 3m+: 0-0
Track: LH: 0-1 RH: 0-0 Tight: 0-1 Gall: 0-0
Aids: Bl: 0-0 Vi: 0-0 Tstrap: 0-1
Best Rating: 101 9/97 Clon 2m yld-sft NHF

Folliday (FR)

109 129

9-y-o b g Sharken (FR)-Oliday (FR) (Djarvis (FR))
A L T Moore F Cruess-Callaghan

Placings: *243/32/241*311/0U45F56F **(4664)**
2001/02: 16^{0}S, 19^{U}YS, 25^{4}Y, 24^{5}Y, 24^{F}HY, 19^{5}HY, 16^{6}S, 21^{F}G

	Starts	1st	2nd	3rd	Win & Pl
Hurdles	1	0	0	0	0
Chases	7	0	0	0	3065
Career Total	**19**	**3**	**3**	**3**	**19283**

136	11/99	Dpat	2m6f	Ch	YLD	£3696
133	11/99	DRoy	2m4f	Ch	SFT	£6517
104	9/99	Dund	2m4f153y	Hdl	YLD	£2217

Total win prize-money £12432

Going: Sf: 0-4 GS: 0-0 Gd: 0-1 GF: - Fm: 0-0
Distance: 2m/2m3: 0-4 2m4-2m7: 0-1 3m+: 0-3
Track: LH: 0-4 RH: 0-3 Tight: 0-1 Gall: 0-0
Aids: Bl: 0-0 Vi: 0-0 Tstrap: 0-0
Best Rating: 136 11/99 Dpat 2m6f yield Ch

Irish chaser, stays three miles and suited by cut.

Follow De Call

12-y-o b g Callernish-Designer (Celtic Cone)
Michael Blake Staverton Owners Group

Placings: *00/003F00003/54202325110632/553543324 4F14/40646000/60P-P03* **(4545)**
2001/02: 20^{P}GF, 21^{0}G, 19^{3}G

	Starts	1st	2nd	3rd	Win & Pl
Chases	3	0	0	1	329
Career Total	**52**	**3**	**5**	**8**	**16557**

91	1/99	Uttx	2m	F(0-110)HCh	SFT	£2710
91	10/97	Bang	2m1f	E Hdl	GD	£2274
89	9/97	Bang	2m1f	D Hdl	GD	£2788

Total win prize-money £7772

Going: Sf: 0-0 GS: 0-0 Gd: 0-2 GF: - Fm: 0-1
Distance: 2m/2m3: 0-1 2m4-2m7: 0-2 3m+: 0-0
Track: LH: 0-1 RH: 0-1 Tight: 0-0 Gall: 0-0
Aids: Bl: 0-0 Vi: 0-0 Tstrap: 0-2
Best Rating: 96 10/99 Bang 2m1f110y soft Ch

A modest hunter chaser these days, he has the tendency to throw in the odd slow jump.

Follow Freddy

4-y-o ch g Factual (USA)-Forgiving (Jellaby)
R S Brookhouse (M Johnston 15/8) Mrs S J Brookhouse

Placings: P **(4642)**
2001/02: 16^{P}G

	Starts	1st	2nd	3rd	Win & Pl
Hurdles	1	0	0	0	
Career Total	**1**	**0**	**0**	**0**	

Going: Sf: 0-0 GS: 0-0 Gd: 0-1 GF: - Fm: 0-0
Distance: 2m/2m3: 0-1 2m4-2m7: 0-0 3m+: 0-0
Track: LH: 0-0 RH: 0-1 Tight: 0-0 Gall: 0-0
Aids: Bl: 0-0 Vi: 0-0 Tstrap: 0-0
Best Rating:

Follow Jean

6-y-o b m Perpendicular-Ask Jean (Ascertain (USA))
M E Sowersby M E Sowersby

Placings: *00* **(3750)**
2001/02: 17^{0}S, 16^{0}S

	Starts	1st	2nd	3rd	Win & Pl
NH Flat	2	0	0	0	
Career Total	**2**	**0**	**0**	**0**	

Going: Sf: 0-2 GS: 0-0 Gd: 0-0 GF: - Fm: 0-0
Distance: 2m/2m3: 0-2 2m4-2m7: 0-0 3m+: 0-0
Track: LH: 0-1 RH: 0-1 Tight: 0-2 Gall: 0-0
Aids: Bl: 0-0 Vi: 0-0 Tstrap: 0-0
Best Rating: 68 2/02 Muss 2m soft NHF

Follow Lammtarra (IRE)

93 119

5-y-o ch g Lammtarra (USA)-Felawnah (USA) (Mr Prospector (USA))
Miss Venetia Williams (M R Channon 26/10) The 1961 Partnership

Placings: 11F **(4888)**
2001/02: 16^{1}GS, 16^{1}HY, 16^{F}G

	Starts	1st	2nd	3rd	Win & Pl
Hurdles	3	2	0	0	6251
Career Total	**3**	**2**	**0**	**0**	**6251**

117	1/02	Towc	2m	E Hdl	HVY	£3283
119	1/02	Weth	2m	E Hdl	G-S	£2968

Total win prize-money £6251

Going: Sf: 1-1 GS: 1-1 Gd: 0-1 GF: - Fm: 0-0
Distance: 2m/2m3: 2-3 2m4-2m7: 0-0 3m+: 0-0
Track: LH: 1-1 RH: 1-2 Tight: 0-0 Gall: 0-0
Aids: Bl: 0-0 Vi: 0-0 Tstrap: 0-0
Best Rating: 119 1/02 Weth 2m gd-sft Hdl

A useful stayer on the Flat, he made a winning debut over hurdles at Wetherby in January 2002 and followed up in good style at Towcester before falling at Perth in April. Suited by cut in the ground.

Follow Me

106 110

6-y-o ch g Keen-Fairlead (Slip Anchor)
J J O'Neill D O'Connor

Placings: 4034/2211P6-1002230 **(4963a)**
2001/02: 24^{1}G, 24^{0}HY, 20^{0}G, 20^{2}S, 24^{2}GS, 24^{3}S, 24^{0}GY

	Starts	1st	2nd	3rd	Win & Pl
Hurdles	7	1	2	1	6684
Career Total	**17**	**3**	**4**	**2**	**14780**

104	10/01	Sthl	3m110y	D(0-120)HHdl	GD	£3474
110	11/00	Hayd	2m4f	F(0-110)HHdl	HVY	£2590
100	10/00	Carl	2m1f	E(0-115)HHdl	G-S	£2664

Total win prize-money £8728

Going: Sf: 0-3 GS: 0-1 Gd: 1-2 GF: - Fm: 0-0
Distance: 2m/2m3: 0-0 2m4-2m7: 0-2 **3m+: 1-5**
Track: LH: 1-3 RH: 0-4 **Tight: 1-2** Gall: 0-0
Aids: Bl: 0-0 Vi: 0-0 Tstrap: 0-0
Best Rating: 110 3/02 Bang 3m soft Hdl

Fairly useful handicap hurdler who does not do anything quickly, stays three miles, acts on most types of ground.

Follow The Trend (IRE)

102 108

8-y-o br g Beau Sher-Newgate Princess (Prince Regent (FR))
Miss A M Newton-Smith The Murray, Smith And Wilson Partnership

Placings: 503405/63U1U1UF-P5544112P **(4287)**
2001/02: 21^{P}GF, 24^{5}GF, 21^{5}G, 24^{4}G, 21^{4}G, 21^{1}S, 20^{1}S, 21^{2}S, 20^{P}GS

	Starts	1st	2nd	3rd	Win & Pl
Chases	9	2	1	0	7319
Career Total	**23**	**4**	**1**	**2**	**12983**

106	2/02	Hntg	2m4f110y	F(0-95)HCh	SFT	£2688
99	1/02	Folk	2m5f	F(0-95)HCh	SFT	£3376
99	2/01	Folk	2m5f	F(0-90)HCh	SFT	£2520
98	1/01	Folk	2m5f	G(0-90)HCh	SFT	£1929

Total win prize-money £10514

Going: Sf: 2-3 GS: 0-1 Gd: 0-3 GF: - Fm: 0-2
Distance: 2m/2m3: 0-0 **2m4-2m7: 2-7** 3m+: 0-2
Track: LH: 0-1 **RH: 2-7** Tight: 1-5 Gall: 1-2
Aids: Bl: 0-0 Vi: 0-0 Tstrap: 0-0
Best Rating: 108 2/02 Folk 2m5f soft Ch

Fair handicap chaser. Best over two miles five on soft ground. Wears sheepskin sideburns due to lack of concentration, according to his trainer. Hits form at the beginning of the year and goes well at Folkestone.

Followeroffashion (IRE)

5-y-o b g Unfuwain (USA)-Al Theraab (USA) (Roberto (USA))
B G Powell R Barrs And Mrs Diana Adams

Placings: P **(0102)**
2001/02: 18^{P}GF

	Starts	1st	2nd	3rd	Win & Pl
Hurdles	1	0	0	0	
Career Total	**1**	**0**	**0**	**0**	

Going: Sf: 0-0 GS: 0-0 Gd: 0-0 GF: - Fm: 0-1
Distance: 2m/2m3: 0-1 2m4-2m7: 0-0 3m+: 0-0
Track: LH: 0-1 RH: 0-0 Tight: 0-1 Gall: 0-0
Aids: Bl: 0-0 Vi: 0-0 Tstrap: 0-0

Best Rating:

Folly Road (IRE)

103(41h) **128**

12-y-o b g Mister Lord (USA)-Lady Can (Cantab)
D L Williams Miss B W Palmer

Placings:541015FF/0/23115/P353U13412/404PPP20 2P0-0S4240P4U513 **(4388)**
2001/02: 28^{0}G, 24^{S}F, 24^{4}S, 24^{2}GS, 27^{4}GS, 26^{0}S, 29^{P}GS, 24^{4}S, 26^{U}HY, 24^{5}GS, 24^{1}G, 25^{3}S

	Starts	1st	2nd	3rd	Win & Pl
Chases	12	1	1	1	9853
Career Total	**47**	**7**	**5**	**5**	**70212**

124	3/02	Sand	3m110y	E Ch	GD	£7182
128	4/00	Chep	3m	E(0-115)HCh	SFT	£3324
128	2/00	MRas	3m4f110y	D(0-120)HCh	G-S	£4192
128	12/98	Folk	3m2f	D(0-125)HCh	G-S	£7580
124	11/98	Wwck	3m2f	C(0-130)HCh	SFT	£4926
116	1/97	Punc	3m	Ch	YLD	£3051
97	11/96	Naas	2m4f	Hdl	YLD	£3177

Total win prize-money £33437

Going: Sf: 0-5 GS: 0-4 Gd: 1-2 GF: - Fm: 0-1
Distance: 2m/2m3: 0-0 2m4-2m7: 0-0 **3m+: 1-12**
Track: LH: 0-5 **RH: 1-6** Tight: 0-5 Gall: 0-0
Aids: Bl: 0-0 Vi: 0-5 Tstrap: 0-0
Best Rating: 128 11/01 Chep 3m gd-sft Ch

He finished second to Beau in the 2000 Whitbread Gold Cup, but was beaten a distance and may have been flat tered, a view backed up by the fact he did not win again until landing the 2002 Grand Military Gold Cup at Sandown. He stays extreme distances in his own time, but is not a great jumper and has worn blinkers and a visor in the past.

Foly Pleasant (FR)

123 **177**

8-y-o ch g Vaguely Pleasant (FR)-Jeffologie (FR) (Jefferson)
Miss H C Knight Jim Lewis & Friends

Placings:1/111P1/122/22-1210P **(4663)**
2001/02: 21^{1}GS, 20^{2}G, 21^{1}HY, 20^{0}GS, 20^{P}G

	Starts	1st	2nd	3rd	Win & Pl
Chases	5	2	1	0	61338
Career Total	**16**	**8**	**5**	**0**	**107360**

177	1/02	Chel	2m5f	A HCh	HVY	£32500
155	10/01	Strf	2m5f110y	C(0-135)HCh	G-S	£6838
	5/99	Dax	2m1f110y	Hdl	SFT	£4306
	4/99	Pau	2m4f110y	Hdl	VS	£4306
	1/99	Pau	2m2f	Hdl	VS	£15070
	1/99	Pau	2m2f	Hdl	HVY	£7535
	12/98	Pau	2m2f110y	Ch	SFT	£5382
	4/98	Pau	2m2f110y	Ch	SFT	£4

Total win prize-money £75941

Going: Sf: 1-1 GS: 1-2 Gd: 0-2 GF: - Fm: 0-0
Distance: 2m/2m3: 0-0 **2m4-2m7: 2-5** 3m+: 0-0
Track: **LH: 2-5** RH: 0-0 Tight: 1-2 Gall: 1-3
Aids: Bl: 0-0 Vi: 0-0 **Tstrap: 2-5**
Best Rating: 177 1/02 Chel 2m5f heavy Ch

A winner four times over fences and twice over hurdles in France, he finished runner-up on each of his four starts for his new stable in 2000/1. He showed improvement on each outing and ran his best race when chasing home Shooting Light at Cheltenham in November 2001. Won a valuable handicap there in January 2002, but disappointed slightly at the Festival. He is suited by two and a half miles plus and soft ground.

Fond Farewell (IRE)

96 **92**

7-y-o b m Phardante (FR)-Doorslammer (Avocat)
K C Bailey Mrs J Way

Placings:*00/6*-6343640 **(4568)**
2001/02: 19^{6}G, 25^{3}G, 22^{4}G, 25^{3}GS, 24^{6}S, 25^{4}GS, 24^{0}G

	Starts	1st	2nd	3rd	Win & Pl
Hurdles	7	0	0	2	788
Career Total	**10**	**0**	**0**	**2**	**788**

Going: Sf: 0-1 GS: 0-2 Gd: 0-4 GF: - Fm: 0-0
Distance: 2m/2m3: 0-0 2m4-2m7: 0-2 3m+: 0-5
Track: LH: 0-1 RH: 0-3 Tight: 0-1 Gall: 0-0
Aids: Bl: 0-0 Vi: 0-0 Tstrap: 0-0
Best Rating: 92 3/02 Wwck 3m1f gd-sft Hdl

Lightly-raced, yet to get off the mark. Stays three miles plus.

Fond Memories (IRE)

5-y-o b m Air Display (USA)-Short Memories (Quisling)
Simon T Lewis Simon T Lewis

Placings:*0P* **(2194)**
2001/02: 17^{0}G, 16^{P}G

	Starts	1st	2nd	3rd	Win & Pl
NH Flat	2	0	0	0	
Career Total	**2**	**0**	**0**	**0**	

Going: Sf: 0-0 GS: 0-0 Gd: 0-2 GF: - Fm: 0-0
Distance: 2m/2m3: 0-2 2m4-2m7: 0-0 3m+: 0-0
Track: LH: 0-2 RH: 0-0 Tight: 0-1 Gall: 0-0
Aids: Bl: 0-0 Vi: 0-0 Tstrap: 0-0
Best Rating:

Fondmort (FR)

115(115h) **161**

6-y-o b g Cyborg (FR)-Hansie (FR) (Sukawa (FR))
N J Henderson W J Brown

Placings:30/214132P-1P1153 **(4675)**
2001/02: 16^{1}GS, 16^{P}G, 16^{1}GS, 16^{1}G, 16^{5}GS, 16^{3}G

	Starts	1st	2nd	3rd	Win & Pl
Chases	6	3	0	1	45577
Career Total	**15**	**5**	**2**	**3**	**85013**

156	12/01	Kemp	2m	B Ch	GD	£11287
160	12/01	Sand	2m	A Ch	G-S	£18000
150	10/01	Kemp	2m	D Ch	G-S	£4914
130	12/00	Kemp	2m	B Hdl	G-S	£7215
	9/00	Autl	2m2f	Hdl	VS	£14409

Total win prize-money £55826

Going: Sf: 0-0 GS: 2-3 Gd: 1-3 GF: - Fm: 0-0
Distance: **2m/2m3: 3-6** 2m4-2m7: 0-0 3m+: 0-0
Track: LH: 0-3 **RH: 3-3** Tight: 0-1 Gall: 0-2
Aids: Bl: 0-0 Vi: 0-0 Tstrap: 0-0
Best Rating: 161 11/01 Chel 2m good Ch

A French import, he made an impressive chasing debut at Kempton in October 2001 and won in style at Sandown. Battled hard to follow up at Kempton over Christmas, but was not seen again until finishing lame in the Arkle at Cheltenham in March 2002. Below form when well beaten at Aintree. Partial to soft ground, he looks a decent chaser in the making and could be one to follow in handicap company next term. Suited to two miles and good/good to soft ground.

Fools Errand (IRE)

12-y-o b g Fool's Holme (USA)-Zalazula (Lord Gayle (USA))
Miss S Waugh (R Ford 17/2) The Stowford Partnership

Placings:1S4/042256/25**413431/21125P314/5345P/3 P06/620/1624P-0** **(4650)**
2001/02: 21^{0}G

	Starts	1st	2nd	3rd	Win & Pl
Chases	1	0	0	0	
Career Total	**44**	**7**	**7**	**5**	**36047**

111	6/00	Uttx	3m2f	E(0-115)HCh	GD	£3016
118	3/97	Winc	3m1f110y	D(0-120)Ch	G-F	£4120
116	11/96	Towc	2m6f	D(0-120)HCh	GD	£3591
118	11/96	Extr	2m6f110y	C(0-135)HCh	G-S	£4856
106	4/96	Chep	2m3f110y	E Ch	SFT	£3031
108	2/96	Ling	2m4f110y	D Ch	HVY	£4424
85	1/94	Folk	2m1f110y	Hdl	HVY	£1543

Total win prize-money £24583

Going: Sf: 0-0 GS: 0-0 Gd: 0-1 GF: - Fm: 0-0
Distance: 2m/2m3: 0-0 2m4-2m7: 0-1 3m+: 0-0
Track: LH: 0-1 RH: 0-0 Tight: 0-1 Gall: 0-0
Aids: Bl: 0-0 Vi: 0-0 Tstrap: 0-0
Best Rating: 118 3/97 Winc 3m1f110y gd-fm Ch

Modest handicap chaser, he won over three miles two in June 2000. Lightly-raced and well held since then. Best when avoiding heavy ground.

Fools Perks

78 **54**

8-y-o ch m Executive Perk-Coumenole (Beau Chapeau)
M Madgwick M Madgwick

Placings:0P **(2330)**
2001/02: 16^{0}G, 21^{P}G

	Starts	1st	2nd	3rd	Win & Pl
Hurdles	2	0	0	0	
Career Total	**2**	**0**	**0**	**0**	

Going: Sf: 0-0 GS: 0-0 Gd: 0-2 GF: - Fm: 0-0
Distance: 2m/2m3: 0-1 2m4-2m7: 0-1 3m+: 0-0
Track: LH: 0-1 RH: 0-1 Tight: 0-1 Gall: 0-0
Aids: Bl: 0-0 Vi: 0-0 Tstrap: 0-0
Best Rating: 54 10/01 Winc 2m good Hdl

For Cathal (IRE)

11-y-o b g Legal Circles (USA)-Noble For Stamps (Deep Run)
Mrs Sarah L Dent John Mackley

Placings:231/1211/44F2326/P-622P24 **(4833)**
2001/02: 25^{6}S, 25^{2}G, 24^{2}GF, 28^{P}GF, 25^{2}GF, 27^{4}G

	Starts	1st	2nd	3rd	Win & Pl
Chases	6	0	3	0	2307
Career Total	**21**	**4**	**7**	**2**	**25745**

118	4/98	Newc	3m	E Hdl	SFT	£2274
119	3/98	Sedg	3m4f	C(0-130)HCh	G-S	£10601
104	11/97	Newc	3m	E Hdl	GD	£2253
98	2/97	Newc	3m	E Ch	GD	£2901

Total win prize-money £18030

Going: Sf: 0-1 GS: 0-0 Gd: 0-2 GF: - Fm: 0-3
Distance: 2m/2m3: 0-0 2m4-2m7: 0-0 3m+: 0-6
Track: LH: 0-6 RH: 0-0 Tight: 0-3 Gall: 0-0
Aids: Bl: 0-0 Vi: 0-0 Tstrap: 0-0
Best Rating: 119 3/98 Sedg 3m4f gd-sft Ch

One-time useful chaser but in his dottage is a slow hunter chaser.

For Your Ears Only (IRE)

89f 96f

6-y-o b g Be My Native (USA)-Sister Ida (Bustino)
A Parker Mr & Mrs Raymond Anderson Green

Placings:*3-00* (4900)
2001/02: 16^{0}GS, 16^{0}G

	Starts	1st	2nd	3rd	Win & Pl
NH Flat	2	0	0	0	
Career Total	**3**	**0**	**0**	**1**	**473**

Going: Sf: 0-0 GS: 0-1 Gd: 0-1 GF: - Fm: 0-0
Distance: 2m/2m3: 0-2 2m4-2m7: 0-0 3m+: 0-0
Track: LH: 0-1 RH: 0-1 Tight: 0-0 Gall: 0-0
Aids: Bl: 0-0 Vi: 0-0 Tstrap: 0-0
Best Rating: 96 4/02 Prth 2m110y good NHF

Forbes Park

89

7-y-o b g Alzao (USA)-Rose Alto (Adonijah)
B G Powell J Coombe

Placings:0 (4850)
2001/02: 22^{0}G

	Starts	1st	2nd	3rd	Win & Pl
Hurdles	1	0	0	0	
Career Total	**1**	**0**	**0**	**0**	

Going: Sf: 0-0 GS: 0-0 Gd: 0-1 GF: - Fm: 0-0
Distance: 2m/2m3: 0-0 2m4-2m7: 0-1 3m+: 0-0
Track: LH: 0-1 RH: 0-0 Tight: 0-1 Gall: 0-0
Aids: Bl: 0-0 Vi: 0-0 Tstrap: 0-0
Best Rating:

Forbidden Waters (IRE)

11-y-o b g Over The River (FR)-Monalee Stream (Paddy's Stream)
A J Tizzard A J Tizzard

Placings:*001*/3/P-P (0077)
2001/02: 23^{P}G

	Starts	1st	2nd	3rd	Win & Pl
Chases	1	0	0	0	
Career Total	**6**	**1**	**0**	**1**	**3002**

80	4/97	Sthl	2m4f110y	E Hdl	GD	£2679

Total win prize-money £2679

Going: Sf: 0-0 GS: 0-0 Gd: 0-1 GF: - Fm: 0-0
Distance: 2m/2m3: 0-0 2m4-2m7: 0-0 3m+: 0-1
Track: LH: 0-0 RH: 0-1 Tight: 0-0 Gall: 0-0
Aids: Bl: 0-0 Vi: 0-0 Tstrap: 0-0
Best Rating: 80 4/97 Sthl 2m4f110y good Hdl

Foreshore Man

100 (34h)95

11-y-o b g Derrylin-Royal Birthday (St Paddy)
B S Rothwell Premier Protection Services Ltd

Placings:60/420**B3U/332U4/0541314440-0366P526** (4490)
2001/02: 20^{0}S, 22^{3}G, 24^{6}GS, 24^{6}HY, 20^{P}S, 24^{5}S, 20^{2}HY, 20^{6}GS

	Starts	1st	2nd	3rd	Win & Pl
Hurdles	1	0	0	0	0
Chases	7	0	1	1	1445
Career Total	**31**	**2**	**3**	**5**	**18729**

103	12/00	Hayd	2m6f	D(0-115)HCh	HVY	£6058
95	11/00	Weth	2m4f110y	D(0-110)HCh	HVY	£5291

Total win prize-money £11349

Going: Sf: 0-5 GS: 0-2 Gd: 0-1 GF: - Fm: 0-0
Distance: 2m/2m3: 0-0 2m4-2m7: 0-5 3m+: 0-3
Track: LH: 0-4 RH: 0-2 Tight: 0-1 Gall: 0-2
Aids: Bl: 0-0 Vi: 0-7 Tstrap: 0-0
Best Rating: 108 1/00 Weth 2m4f110y soft Ch

Fair handicap chaser, effective at up to two miles-six. Suited by plenty of cut.

Forest Dante (IRE)

104 122

9-y-o ch g Phardante (FR)-Mossy Mistress (IRE) (Le Moss)
F Kirby Fred Kirby

Placings:6000F/602F1043/S1131PF-435231FP2 (4775)
2001/02: 21^{4}GS, 20^{3}G, 17^{5}G, 19^{2}GF, 20^{3}G, 19^{1}S, 22^{F}S, 20^{P}GS, 22^{2}G

	Starts	1st	2nd	3rd	Win & Pl
Chases	9	1	2	2	9717
Career Total	**29**	**5**	**3**	**4**	**34438**

122	1/02	Catt	2m3f	D(0-120)HCh	SFT	£4062
119	11/00	Catt	2m3f	E(0-115)HCh	GD	£5005
122	10/00	Sthl	2m4f110y	D(0-120)HCh	HVY	£6808
115	9/00	MRas	2m4f	F(0-110)HCh	G-F	£4251
97	1/00	Catt	2m	E(0-105)HCh	GD	£4264

Total win prize-money £24392

Going: Sf: 1-2 GS: 0-2 Gd: 0-4 GF: - Fm: 0-1
Distance: **2m/2m3: 1-3** 2m4-2m7: 0-6 3m+: 0-0
Track: **LH: 1-5** RH: 0-4 **Tight: 1-8** Gall: 0-0
Aids: Bl: 0-0 Vi: 0-0 Tstrap: 0-0
Best Rating: 122 4/02 MRas 2m6f110y good Ch

A big, able jumper. Best at around two and a half miles, he acts on any ground. Goes well at Catterick.

Forest Feather (IRE)

14-y-o b g Arapahos (FR)-Mistress Boreen (Boreen (FR))
Miss J E Mathias Miss J E Mathias

Placings:225P121/16553403425/03020/*22430P*/246P 50/0/1/030425-P (0218)
2001/02: 21^{P}GF

	Starts	1st	2nd	3rd	Win & Pl
Chases	1	0	0	0	
Career Total	**44**	**4**	**9**	**5**	**21651**

106	4/00	MRas	3m1f	H Ch	G-F	£1197
116	5/94	Strf	2m6f110y	Hdl	GD	£2108
116	4/94	Weth	2m4f110y	Hdl	GD	£2250
113	3/94	Newb	2m5f	Hdl	GD	£3142

Total win prize-money £8698

Going: Sf: 0-0 GS: 0-0 Gd: 0-0 GF: - Fm: 0-1
Distance: 2m/2m3: 0-0 2m4-2m7: 0-1 3m+: 0-0
Track: LH: 0-0 RH: 0-1 Tight: 0-0 Gall: 0-0
Aids: Bl: 0-0 Vi: 0-0 Tstrap: 0-0
Best Rating: 124 1/96 Kemp 2m5f good Hdl

Forest Flora

93(50h) 87

8-y-o b m King's Ride-Celtic Flora (Celtic Cone)
J W Mullins New Forest Racing Partnership

Placings:*00*U460/B2312P34442362/030P-**60F0** (4415)
2001/02: 24^{6}G, 26^{0}G, 23^{F}GF, 22^{0}S

	Starts	1st	2nd	3rd	Win & Pl
Hurdles	1	0	0	0	0
Chases	3	0	0	0	0
Career Total	**28**	**1**	**4**	**4**	**6997**

86	9/99	Worc	3m	E(0-105)HHdl	G-F	£2425

Total win prize-money £2425

Going: Sf: 0-1 GS: 0-0 Gd: 0-2 GF: - Fm: 0-1
Distance: 2m/2m3: 0-0 2m4-2m7: 0-1 3m+: 0-3
Track: LH: 0-3 RH: 0-0 Tight: 0-2 Gall: 0-0
Aids: Bl: 0-0 Vi: 0-0 Tstrap: 0-0
Best Rating: 88 4/00 NAbb 2m6f heavy Hdl

Forest Fountain (IRE)

11-y-o b/br g Royal Fountain-Forest Gale (Strong Gale)
Mrs H L Needham J D Callow

Placings:P/P/35B/31-4330P510 (4826)
2001/02: 24^{4}G, 28^{3}GF, 33^{3}G, 24^{0}G, 32^{P}GS, 25^{5}GS, 24^{1}GF, 26^{0}G

	Starts	1st	2nd	3rd	Win & Pl
Chases	8	1	0	2	4186
Career Total	**15**	**2**	**0**	**4**	**8843**

100	4/02	Ludl	3m	H Ch	G-F	£2628
117	5/00	Strf	3m	H Ch	G-F	£2951

Total win prize-money £5580

Going: Sf: 0-0 GS: 0-2 Gd: 0-4 GF: - Fm: 1-2
Distance: 2m/2m3: 0-0 2m4-2m7: 0-0 **3m+: 1-8**
Track: LH: 0-3 **RH: 1-4 Tight: 1-3** Gall: 0-3
Aids: Bl: 0-0 Vi: 0-0 Tstrap: 0-0
Best Rating: 117 5/00 Strf 3m gd-fm Ch

A winner of point-to-points and over fences, he acts on most types of ground and is effective at around three miles.

Forest Green Flyer

93 80

6-y-o b m Syrtos-Bolton Flyer (Aragon)
O O'Neill T Horsley

Placings:60000/046-406255P0 (4752)
2001/02: 19^{4}G, 17^{0}G, 16^{6}GS, 16^{2}S, 17^{5}S, 17^{5}S, 17^{P}G, 16^{0}GF

	Starts	1st	2nd	3rd	Win & Pl
Hurdles	8	0	1	0	589
Career Total	**16**	**0**	**1**	**0**	**589**

Going: Sf: 0-3 GS: 0-1 Gd: 0-3 GF: - Fm: 0-1
Distance: 2m/2m3: 0-7 2m4-2m7: 0-1 3m+: 0-0
Track: LH: 0-3 RH: 0-5 Tight: 0-4 Gall: 0-0
Aids: Bl: 0-0 Vi: 0-1 Tstrap: 0-3
Best Rating: 80 2/02 Ludl 2m soft Hdl

Selling-class hurdler.

Forest Gunner

107 **123**

8-y-o ch g Gunner B-Gouly Duff (Party Mink)

R Ford John Gilsenan

Placings: *40*/36-1213125 **(4890)**

2001/02: 20^{1}G, 22^{2}G, 21^{1}GS, 24^{3}S, 23^{1}GS, 24^{2}GS, 24^{5}G

	Starts	1st	2nd	3rd	Win & Pl
Hurdles	7	3	2	1	11579
Career Total	**11**	**3**	**2**	**2**	**11905**

123	1/02	Weth	2m7f	E Hdl	G-S	£2681
123	11/01	MRas	2m5f110y	F Hdl	G-S	£2254
120	5/01	Aint	2m4f	D Hdl	GD	£3584

Total win prize-money £8519

Going: Sf: 0-1 GS: 2-3 Gd: 1-3 GF: - Fm: 0-0
Distance: 2m/2m3: 0-0 **2m4-2m7: 3-4** 3m+: 0-3
Track: **LH: 2-5** RH: 1-2 **Tight: 2-3** Gall: 0-1
Aids: Bl: 0-0 Vi: 0-0 Tstrap: 0-0
Best Rating: 123 1/02 Weth 2m7f gd-sft Hdl

A fair hurdler who has had his problems with injury, he showed what he is capable of in 2001/02. Well suited by sharp tracks, and appreciates good ground or slightly softer. Likes to front run and stays two miles seven.

Forest Heath (IRE)

63 **73**

5-y-o gr g Common Grounds-Caroline Lady (JPN) (Caro)

H J Collingridge Forest Heath Partnership

Placings: 5 **(4275)**

2001/02: 16^{5}G

	Starts	1st	2nd	3rd	Win & Pl
Hurdles	1	0	0	0	0
Career Total	**1**	**0**	**0**	**0**	**0**

Going: Sf: 0-0 GS: 0-0 Gd: 0-1 GF: - Fm: 0-0
Distance: 2m/2m3: 0-1 2m4-2m7: 0-0 3m+: 0-0
Track: LH: 0-1 RH: 0-0 Tight: 0-1 Gall: 0-0
Aids: Bl: 0-0 Vi: 0-0 Tstrap: 0-0
Best Rating: 73 3/02 Fknm 2m good Hdl

Forest Ivory (NZ)

101 **134**

11-y-o ch g Ivory Hunter (USA)-Fair And Square (NZ) (Crown Lease)

R D Wylie (R T Phillips 5/5) B Collier

Placings: *1220*/11241/F112/4333460/53235/30-00P3600 **(4647)**

2001/02: 23^{0}G, 24^{0}S, 28^{P}S, 23^{3}HY, 24^{6}GS, 25^{0}GS, 24^{0}G

	Starts	1st	2nd	3rd	Win & Pl
Hurdles	6	0	0	1	1351
Chases	1	0	0	0	0
Career Total	**34**	**6**	**5**	**7**	**94070**

143	11/97	Bang	3m110y	D Ch	SFT	£3842
117	11/97	Weth	3m1f	D Ch	G-S	£3600
142	4/97	Aint	3m110y	A Hdl	GD	£21532
120	12/96	Worc	2m4f	E Hdl	G-S	£2915
117	11/96	Towc	2m5f	F Hdl	GD	£1849
117	11/95	Worc	2m	H NHF	SFT	£1455

Total win prize-money £35194

Going: Sf: 0-3 GS: 0-2 Gd: 0-2 GF: - Fm: 0-0
Distance: 2m/2m3: 0-0 2m4-2m7: 0-0 3m+: 0-7
Track: LH: 0-6 RH: 0-0 Tight: 0-1 Gall: 0-2
Aids: Bl: 0-0 Vi: 0-1 Tstrap: 0-0
Best Rating: 147 12/98 Chep 3m5f110y heavy Ch

Capable of smart form in marathon chases, he has been campaigned mainly over hurdles in 2001/2002 without much success. Suited by testing conditions and distances around three miles. Lacks pace and is difficult to win with nowadays.

Forest Jump (IRE)

8-y-o ch g Accordion-Mandy's Last (Krayyan)

P F Nicholls M Fordham S Fisher B Davies G Richardson

Placings: *5/33*31P42/31331-PPP **(4501)**

2001/02: 24^{P}S, 24^{P}S, 27^{P}G

	Starts	1st	2nd	3rd	Win & Pl
Hurdles	1	0	0	0	0
Chases	2	0	0	0	0
Career Total	**16**	**3**	**1**	**6**	**13778**

132	2/01	Tntn	3m	E(0-115)HCh	HVY	£4329
110	11/00	Font	2m6f	E Ch	HVY	£3120
112	1/00	Hrfd	2m3f110y	E Hdl	G-S	£2814

Total win prize-money £10263

Going: Sf: 0-2 GS: 0-0 Gd: 0-1 GF: - Fm: 0-0
Distance: 2m/2m3: 0-0 2m4-2m7: 0-0 3m+: 0-3
Track: LH: 0-2 RH: 0-1 Tight: 0-3 Gall: 0-0
Aids: Bl: 0-2 Vi: 0-0 Tstrap: 0-0
Best Rating: 132 2/01 Tntn 3m heavy Ch

Fair staying chaser, suited by soft ground and stays three miles. Has worn blinkers and is suited by a positive ride.

Forest Maze

40f

6-y-o b m Arzanni-Forest Nymph (NZ) (Oak Ridge (FR))

M F Barraclough M F Barraclough

Placings: *06* **(1731)**

2001/02: 17^{0}S, 17^{6}F

	Starts	1st	2nd	3rd	Win & Pl
NH Flat	2	0	0	0	0
Career Total	**2**	**0**	**0**	**0**	**0**

Going: Sf: 0-1 GS: 0-0 Gd: 0-0 GF: - Fm: 0-1
Distance: 2m/2m3: 0-2 2m4-2m7: 0-0 3m+: 0-0
Track: LH: 0-0 RH: 0-1 Tight: 0-1 Gall: 0-0
Aids: Bl: 0-0 Vi: 0-0 Tstrap: 0-0
Best Rating: 40 10/01 Tntn 2m1f firm NHF

Forest Rider (IRE)

92 **89**

6-y-o b g King's Ride-Forest Pride (IRE) (Be My Native (USA))

Miss H C Knight Trevor Hemmings

Placings: *22*-6 **(1833)**

2001/02: 20^{6}G

	Starts	1st	2nd	3rd	Win & Pl
Hurdles	1	0	0	0	0
Career Total	**3**	**0**	**2**	**0**	**1138**

Going: Sf: 0-0 GS: 0-0 Gd: 0-1 GF: - Fm: 0-0
Distance: 2m/2m3: 0-0 2m4-2m7: 0-1 3m+: 0-0
Track: LH: 0-1 RH: 0-0 Tight: 0-1 Gall: 0-0
Aids: Bl: 0-0 Vi: 0-0 Tstrap: 0-0
Best Rating: 101 12/00 Ludl 2m soft NHF

Forest Run Forest

98 **95**

10-y-o b g Supreme Leader-Laurello (Bargello)

C J Mann Mrs L G Turner

Placings: *0/3*554040/64/463451/533021621000-6P06 **(4128)**

2001/02: 19^{6}GS, 21^{P}GS, 19^{0}S, 19^{6}G

	Starts	1st	2nd	3rd	Win & Pl
Hurdles	4	0	0	0	0
Career Total	**32**	**3**	**2**	**4**	**15730**

106	1/01	Leic	2m4f110y	D(0-120)HHdl	HVY	£4923
104	12/00	Leic	2m4f110y	D(0-120)HHdl	HVY	£3484
107	12/99	Tntn	2m3f110y	F(0-95)HHdl	SFT	£2604

Total win prize-money £11013

Going: Sf: 0-1 GS: 0-2 Gd: 0-1 GF: - Fm: 0-0
Distance: 2m/2m3: 0-0 2m4-2m7: 0-4 3m+: 0-0
Track: LH: 0-0 RH: 0-4 Tight: 0-3 Gall: 0-0
Aids: Bl: 0-4 Vi: 0-0 Tstrap: 0-0
Best Rating: 107 12/99 Tntn 2m3f110y soft Hdl

Forest Thyne (IRE)

95(92h) (68h)**78**

8-y-o ch g Good Thyne (USA)-Tullow Performance (Gala Performance (USA))

J R Jenkins (Ferdy Murphy 20/2) Jack McGrath

Placings: *320*/023450/5-PPFP0P4 **(4316)**

2001/02: 24^{P}F, 20^{P}G, 20^{F}GS, 23^{P}G, 26^{0}HY, 19^{F}S, 24^{4}HY

	Starts	1st	2nd	3rd	Win & Pl
Hurdles	1	0	0	0	0
Chases	6	0	0	0	0
Career Total	**17**	**0**	**2**	**2**	**2352**

Going: Sf: 0-3 GS: 0-1 Gd: 0-2 GF: - Fm: 0-1
Distance: 2m/2m3: 0-0 2m4-2m7: 0-3 3m+: 0-4
Track: LH: 0-3 RH: 0-3 Tight: 0-1 Gall: 0-3
Aids: Bl: 0-0 Vi: 0-1 Tstrap: 0-0
Best Rating: 101 11/98 Worc 2m heavy NHF

Forever Grey (IRE)

97(91c) (61c)**86**

10-y-o gr m Celio Rufo-Princess Moy (Gleason (USA))

R Johnson Jack Thornton

Placings: P403P0/2360000/02P262434166636236/46 12413456062654-02410F060 **(4332)**

2001/02: 24^{0}GF, 16^{2}GF, 16^{4}F, 16^{1}GS, 21^{0}GF, 20^{F}GF, 27^{0}GF, 19^{6}GS, 21^{0}S

	Starts	1st	2nd	3rd	Win & Pl
Hurdles	7	1	1	0	2583
Chases	2	0	0	0	0
Career Total	**56**	**4**	**8**	**6**	**20713**

86	6/01	Hexm	2m	F(0-105)HHdl	G-S	£2054
102	9/00	Hntg	3m2f	F(0-90)HHdl	GD	£2007
103	5/00	Hexm	2m4f110y	F(0-105)HCh	GD	£2832
93	11/99	Sedg	2m5f110y	F(0-105)HHdl	GD	£1912

Total win prize-money £8808

Going: Sf: 0-1 GS: 1-2 Gd: 0-0 GF: - Fm: 0-6
Distance: **2m/2m3: 1-4** 2m4-2m7: 0-3 3m+: 0-2
Track: **LH: 1-8** RH: 0-1 Tight: 0-5 Gall: 0-0
Aids: Bl: 0-0 Vi: 0-0 **Tstrap: 1-9**
Best Rating: 103 6/00 MRas 2m4f gd-sft Ch

Versatile mare, equally effective over hurdles and fences. Does not always find as much as expected off the bridle.

Forever Noble (IRE)

108 **102**

9-y-o b g Forzando-Pagan Queen (Vaguely Noble)

O Sherwood Mrs Florence C Ratter

Placings:32/620/1P222241/F352U3/1-6505 **(4576)**
2001/02: 25^{6}G, 24^{5}G, 24^{0}GS, 26^{5}GS

	Starts	1st	2nd	3rd	Win & Pl
Chases	4	0	0	0	0
Career Total	**24**	**3**	**7**	**3**	**19116**

135	10/00	Fknm	3m110y	F(0-110)HCh	GD	£4602
116	4/99	Weth	2m4f110y	D Hdl	G-F	£3436
103	11/98	Hntg	2m110y	E Hdl	G-S	£2110

Total win prize-money £10148

Going: Sf: 0-0 GS: 0-2 Gd: 0-2 GF: - Fm: 0-0
Distance: 2m/2m3: 0-0 2m4-2m7: 0-0 3m+: 0-4
Track: LH: 0-2 RH: 0-2 Tight: 0-0 Gall: 0-1
Aids: Bl: 0-1 Vi: 0-0 Tstrap: 0-0
Best Rating: **135** 10/00 Fknm 3m110y good Ch

Off the track for a long time after winning at Fakenham in October 2000, and well held on his return to action. Stays three miles. Acts on good/good to soft ground.

Formal Bid (USA)

106 **115**

5-y-o b/br g Dynaformer (USA)-Fantastic Bid (USA) (Auction Ring (USA))
C C Bealby Michael Hill

Placings:2522P **(4515)**
2001/02: 20^{2}S, 16^{5}HY, 17^{2}GS, 20^{2}HY, 16^{P}GS

	Starts	1st	2nd	3rd	Win & Pl
Hurdles	5	0	3	0	2675
Career Total	**5**	**0**	**3**	**0**	**2675**

Going: Sf: 0-3 GS: 0-2 Gd: 0-0 GF: - Fm: 0-0
Distance: 2m/2m3: 0-3 2m4-2m7: 0-2 3m+: 0-0
Track: LH: 0-2 RH: 0-3 Tight: 0-3 Gall: 0-0
Aids: Bl: 0-0 Vi: 0-0 Tstrap: 0-0
Best Rating: **115** 3/02 MRas 2m1f110y gd-sft Hdl

Modest form when runner-up in novice hurdles, acts in soft ground.

Formal Invitation (IRE)

13-y-o ch g Be My Guest (USA)-Clarista (USA) (Riva Ridge (USA))
David Maybury Back To The Bar (syndicate)

Placings:322114/211/112/2PP/P4/0 **(4645)**
2001/02: 24^{0}G

	Starts	1st	2nd	3rd	Win & Pl
Chases	1	0	0	0	
Career Total	**18**	**6**	**5**	**1**	**21737**

131	5/97	Strf	2m5f110y	D Ch	GD	£3548
124	5/97	Uttx	2m4f	D(0-125)HCh	G-S	£3517
125	4/97	Chel	2m5f	D Ch	G-F	£3397
123	3/97	MRas	2m4f	D Ch	G-F	£3773
91	3/93	Wolv	2m110y	Hdl	G-F	£1484
85	3/93	Ludl	2m	Hdl	G-F	£1475

Total win prize-money £17196

Going: Sf: 0-0 GS: 0-0 Gd: 0-1 GF: - Fm: 0-0
Distance: 2m/2m3: 0-0 2m4-2m7: 0-0 3m+: 0-1
Track: LH: 0-0 RH: 0-1 Tight: 0-1 Gall: 0-0
Aids: Bl: 0-0 Vi: 0-0 Tstrap: 0-0
Best Rating: **131** 5/97 Strf 2m5f110y good Ch

Formidable Partner

(95h) (91h)

9-y-o b g Formidable (USA)-Brush Away (Ahonoora)
Mrs V C Ward The Late Mrs R F Key & Mrs V C Ward

Placings:63534/24204P5P/0P0112014/364P-005 **(3765)**
2001/02: 19^{0}GS, 19^{0}S, 16^{5}GS

	Starts	1st	2nd	3rd	Win & Pl
Hurdles	1	0	0	0	0
Chases	2	0	0	0	0
Career Total	**29**	**3**	**3**	**3**	**8771**

105	2/00	Catt	2m3f	G(0-95)HHdl	GD	£2058
105	12/99	Catt	2m	G(0-95)HHdl	G-F	£1558
91	10/99	Towc	2m	G Hdl	GD	£1870

Total win prize-money £5486

Going: Sf: 0-1 GS: 0-2 Gd: 0-0 GF: - Fm: 0-0
Distance: 2m/2m3: 0-3 2m4-2m7: 0-0 3m+: 0-0
Track: LH: 0-3 RH: 0-0 Tight: 0-3 Gall: 0-0
Aids: Bl: 0-2 Vi: 0-0 Tstrap: 0-0
Best Rating: **105** 2/00 Catt 2m3f good Hdl

Had a good season over hurdles in 1999/2000, but then had a lay-off and has struggled since returning.

Fornaught Alliance (IRE)

107(103h) (97h)**107**

9-y-o br g Zaffaran (USA)-Carrick Shannon (Green Shoon)
Ferdy Murphy R & G Leonard

Placings:5335050356/52223522B23005/2142253-006R61145 **(4918)**
2001/02: 25^{0}G, 31^{0}G, 30^{6}GS, 31^{R}GS, 20^{6}GS, 27^{1}S, 21^{1}S, 22^{4}G, 28^{5}GF

	Starts	1st	2nd	3rd	Win & Pl
Hurdles	2	1	0	0	5488
Chases	7	1	0	0	4392
Career Total	**40**	**3**	**9**	**6**	**32973**

107	3/02	Sedg	2m5f	D(0-120)HCh	SFT	£3987
97	2/02	Sedg	3m3f110y	E(0-110)HHdl	SFT	£5488
124	11/00	Hayd	2m6f	D(0-120)HCh	SFT	£8060

Total win prize-money £17536

Going: Sf: 2-2 GS: 0-3 Gd: 0-3 GF: - Fm: 0-1
Distance: 2m/2m3: 0-0 2m4-2m7: 1-3 3m+: 1-6
Track: **LH: 2-7** RH: 0-2 **Tight: 2-5** Gall: 0-1
Aids: **Bl: 2-5** Vi: 0-2 Tstrap: 0-0
Best Rating: **124** 1/01 Fknm 3m110y soft Ch

Versatile, if quirky, sort who is suited by three miles.

Forrest Tribe (IRE)

110 **108**

9-y-o b/br g Be My Native (USA)-Island Bridge (Mandalus)
W Jenks (Eugene M O'Sullivan 13/5) Mrs Douglas Graham

Placings:0644/140/234143P4/55020PF-500636232 **(4184)**
2001/02: 20^{5}YS, 20^{0}G, 20^{0}GF, 25^{6}G, 24^{3}GF, 20^{6}G, 24^{2}G, 23^{3}G, 24^{2}S

	Starts	1st	2nd	3rd	Win & Pl
Chases	9	0	2	2	3340
Career Total	**31**	**2**	**4**	**4**	**18725**

122	2/00	Kels	2m6f110y	C(0-130)HCh	G-S	£7621
121	3/99	Ayr	2m4f	E Ch	SFT	£2898

Total win prize-money £10519

Going: Sf: 0-1 GS: 0-0 Gd: 0-5 GF: - Fm: 0-2
Distance: 2m/2m3: 0-0 2m4-2m7: 0-4 3m+: 0-5
Track: LH: 0-1 RH: 0-6 Tight: 0-3 Gall: 0-0
Aids: Bl: 0-8 Vi: 0-0 Tstrap: 0-1
Best Rating: **122** 2/00 Kels 2m6f110y gd-sft Ch

Ex-Irish chaser, effective over three miles and best with a bit of cut.

Fort Knox (IRE)

83 **61**

11-y-o b g Treasure Kay-Single Viking (Viking (USA))
Jamie Poulton Mrs D M Hickling

Placings:0001/35F20606/365FU3362U0/406010PR-06 **(0492)**
2001/02: 16^{0}S, 18^{6}GF

	Starts	1st	2nd	3rd	Win & Pl
Hurdles	2	0	0	0	0
Career Total	**33**	**2**	**2**	**4**	**10453**

85	11/00	Plum	2m	F(0-110)HHdl	HVY	£3493
99	4/98	Plum	2m1f	E Hdl	SFT	£2598

Total win prize-money £6093

Going: Sf: 0-1 GS: 0-0 Gd: 0-0 GF: - Fm: 0-1
Distance: 2m/2m3: 0-2 2m4-2m7: 0-0 3m+: 0-0
Track: LH: 0-2 RH: 0-0 Tight: 0-2 Gall: 0-0
Aids: Bl: 0-0 Vi: 0-0 Tstrap: 0-0
Best Rating: **105** 5/98 Hntg 2m110y gd-fm Hdl

Fort Sumter (USA)

90 **81**

6-y-o b g Sea Hero (USA)-Gray And Red (USA) (Wolf Power (SAF))
P R Hedger E Whelan

Placings:0/0-4 **(0431)**
2001/02: 17^{4}GF

	Starts	1st	2nd	3rd	Win & Pl
Hurdles	1	0	0	0	0
Career Total	**3**	**0**	**0**	**0**	**0**

Going: Sf: 0-0 GS: 0-0 Gd: 0-0 GF: - Fm: 0-1
Distance: 2m/2m3: 0-1 2m4-2m7: 0-0 3m+: 0-0
Track: LH: 0-0 RH: 0-1 Tight: 0-1 Gall: 0-0
Aids: Bl: 0-0 Vi: 0-0 Tstrap: 0-0
Best Rating: **81** 5/01 Folk 2m1f110y gd-fm Hdl

Fort William

(103h) (77h)

6-y-o b g Ezzoud (IRE)-Lovely Noor (USA) (Fappiano (USA))
Ian Williams Willsford Racing Incorporated

Placings:400/P246-006P **(0972)**
2001/02: 24^{0}G, 21^{0}G, 23^{6}GF, 24^{P}GF

	Starts	1st	2nd	3rd	Win & Pl
Hurdles	2	0	0	0	0
Chases	2	0	0	0	0
Career Total	**11**	**0**	**1**	**0**	**1357**

Going: Sf: 0-0 GS: 0-0 Gd: 0-2 GF: - Fm: 0-2
Distance: 2m/2m3: 0-0 2m4-2m7: 0-1 3m+: 0-3
Track: LH: 0-3 RH: 0-0 Tight: 0-2 Gall: 0-0
Aids: Bl: 0-3 Vi: 0-0 Tstrap: 0-0
Best Rating: **96** 12/00 Weth 2m4f110y soft Hdl

Forthechop

88 **52**

5-y-o b g Minshaanshu Amad (USA)-Cousin Jenny (Midyan (USA))
R C Harper (Mrs H L Walton 20/6) R C Harper

Placings:4P000 (4533)
2001/02: 20^{4}S, 17^{P}S, 16^{0}S, 16^{0}G, 16^{0}G

	Starts	1st	2nd	3rd	Win & Pl
Hurdles	5	0	0	0	274
Career Total	5	0	0	0	274

Going: Sf: 0-3 GS: 0-0 Gd: 0-2 GF: - Fm: 0-0
Distance: 2m/2m3: 0-4 2m4-2m7: 0-1 3m+: 0-0
Track: LH: 0-2 RH: 0-3 Tight: 0-2 Gall: 0-0
Aids: Bl: 0-0 Vi: 0-0 Tstrap: 0-0
Best Rating: 52 3/02 Fknm 2m good Hdl

Fortius (IRE)

90 100

8-y-o ch g Over The River (FR)-Dream Daisy (Choral Society)
Miss E C Lavelle The Frisky Fillies

Placings:04136P/3145P302-5P30 (3654)
2001/02: 20^{5}GS, 26^{P}S, 26^{3}S, 26^{0}S

	Starts	1st	2nd	3rd	Win & Pl
Hurdles	1	0	0	0	0
Chases	3	0	0	1	474
Career Total	18	2	1	4	8872

114 12/00 Font 3m2f110y E Ch SFT £3107
104 11/99 Uttx 2m6f110y E Hdl SFT £2505
Total win prize-money £5612

Going: Sf: 0-3 GS: 0-1 Gd: 0-0 GF: - Fm: 0-0
Distance: 2m/2m3: 0-0 2m4-2m7: 0-1 3m+: 0-0
Track: LH: 0-1 RH: 0-2 Tight: 0-2 Gall: 0-1
Aids: Bl: 0-0 Vi: 0-2 Tstrap: 0-3
Best Rating: 114 12/00 Font 3m2f110y soft Ch

Forto (GER)

100 112

6-y-o ch h Acatenango (GER)-Flunder (Nebos (GER))
D L Williams (A Wohler 24/8) N F Dawe

Placings:33011 (4883)
2001/02: 16^{3}S, 16^{3}G, 16^{0}GS, 24^{1}GF, 22^{1}GF

	Starts	1st	2nd	3rd	Win & Pl
Hurdles	5	2	0	2	6513
Career Total	5	2	0	2	6513

112 4/02 Font 2m6f110y E Hdl G-F £2719
107 4/02 Ludl 3m E Hdl G-F £2618
Total win prize-money £5338

Going: Sf: 0-1 GS: 0-1 Gd: 0-1 GF: - Fm: 2-2
Distance: 2m/2m3: 0-3 2m4-2m7: 1-1 3m+: 1-1
Track: LH: 1-2 RH: 1-3 **Tight: 1-1** Gall: 0-0
Aids: Bl: 0-0 Vi: 0-0 Tstrap: 0-0
Best Rating: 112 4/02 Font 2m6f110y gd-fm Hdl

A two-time winner on the Flat over middle distances in Germany, he won two small novice hurdles in April 2002. Acts on fast ground, stays three miles.

Fortune Hunter (IRE)

85 69

8-y-o ch g Lycius (USA)-Cardomine (Dom Racine (FR))
Jedd O'Keeffe M J Norman

Placings:P35240F/5 (0467)
2001/02: 20^{5}GF

	Starts	1st	2nd	3rd	Win & Pl
Chases	1	0	0	0	0
Career Total	8	0	1	1	871

Going: Sf: 0-0 GS: 0-0 Gd: 0-0 GF: - Fm: 0-1
Distance: 2m/2m3: 0-0 2m4-2m7: 0-1 3m+: 0-0
Track: LH: 0-1 RH: 0-0 Tight: 0-0 Gall: 0-0
Aids: Bl: 0-0 Vi: 0-0 Tstrap: 0-0
Best Rating: 74 11/97 Catt 2m good Hdl

Fortune Point (IRE)

96 86

4-y-o ch g Cadeaux Genereux-Mountains Of Mist (IRE) (Shirley Heights)
M C Pipe (J Noseda 19/10) Lucayan Stud

Placings:6505 (4782)
2001/02: 16^{6}S, 16^{5}HY, 16^{0}S, 16^{5}GF

	Starts	1st	2nd	3rd	Win & Pl
Hurdles	4	0	0	0	0
Career Total	4	0	0	0	0

Going: Sf: 0-3 GS: 0-0 Gd: 0-0 GF: - Fm: 0-1
Distance: 2m/2m3: 0-4 2m4-2m7: 0-0 3m+: 0-0
Track: LH: 0-3 RH: 0-1 Tight: 0-1 Gall: 0-1
Aids: Bl: 0-0 Vi: 0-0 Tstrap: 0-0
Best Rating: 86 4/02 Plum 2m gd-fm Hdl

A maiden on the Flat, he has shown only moderate ability over hurdles.

Fortunes Flight (IRE)

(82h) (54h)

9-y-o b g Tremblant-Night Rose (Sovereign Gleam)
R M Carson (J S King 11/5) R M Carson

Placings:*20/0/0PPR/PU0-00* (1567)
2001/02: 21^{0}GF, 20^{0}GS

	Starts	1st	2nd	3rd	Win & Pl
Hurdles	1	0	0	0	0
Chases	1	0	0	0	0
Career Total	12	0	1	0	391

Going: Sf: 0-0 GS: 0-1 Gd: 0-0 GF: - Fm: 0-1
Distance: 2m/2m3: 0-0 2m4-2m7: 0-2 3m+: 0-0
Track: LH: 0-0 RH: 0-1 Tight: 0-1 Gall: 0-0
Aids: Bl: 0-1 Vi: 0-0 Tstrap: 0-0
Best Rating: 100 3/97 Sand 2m110y good NHF

Fortytwo Dee (IRE)

74

12-y-o b m Amazing Bust-Maggie's Way (Decent Fellow)
A W Carroll Triumph International Limited

Placings:06P3/5563026PP3U04/5F13P/P663P3/3216 336-0P (0675)
2001/02: 21^{0}GF, 23^{P}GF

	Starts	1st	2nd	3rd	Win & Pl
Chases	2	0	0	0	
Career Total	37	2	2	9	12025

88 10/00 Chep 2m3f110y G(0-90)HCh G-S £1904
100 12/98 Uttx 2m5f E(0-105)HCh SFT £3745
Total win prize-money £5649

Going: Sf: 0-0 GS: 0-0 Gd: 0-0 GF: - Fm: 0-2
Distance: 2m/2m3: 0-0 2m4-2m7: 0-1 3m+: 0-1
Track: LH: 0-2 RH: 0-0 Tight: 0-1 Gall: 0-0
Aids: Bl: 0-0 Vi: 0-0 Tstrap: 0-0
Best Rating: 100 12/98 Uttx 2m5f soft Ch

Fosse Hill

95 93

5-y-o b g Bustino-Amber's Image (Billion (USA))
Miss H C Knight Lord Vestey

Placings:*10* (4235)
2001/02: 16^{1}GF, 16^{0}GS

	Starts	1st	2nd	3rd	Win & Pl
NH Flat	2	1	0	0	1712
Career Total	2	1	0	0	1712

106 11/01 Ludl 2m H NHF G-F £1711
Total win prize-money £1712

Going: Sf: 0-0 GS: 0-1 Gd: 0-0 GF: - Fm: 1-1
Distance: **2m/2m3: 1-2** 2m4-2m7: 0-0 3m+: 0-0
Track: LH: 0-1 **RH: 1-1** Tight: 0-0 Gall: 0-0
Aids: Bl: 0-0 Vi: 0-0 Tstrap: 0-0
Best Rating: 106 11/01 Ludl 2m gd-fm NHF

Made a winning bumper debut at Ludlow, but well beaten on hurdling debut subsequently.

Foston Second (IRE)

100 68

5-y-o ch m Lycius (USA)-Gentle Guest (IRE) (Be My Guest (USA))
C Weedon Atlantic Foods Ltd

Placings:36 (4176)
2001/02: 16^{3}G, 19^{6}GS

	Starts	1st	2nd	3rd	Win & Pl
Hurdles	2	0	0	1	283
Career Total	2	0	0	1	283

Going: Sf: 0-0 GS: 0-1 Gd: 0-1 GF: - Fm: 0-0
Distance: 2m/2m3: 0-2 2m4-2m7: 0-0 3m+: 0-0
Track: LH: 0-1 RH: 0-1 Tight: 0-1 Gall: 0-0
Aids: Bl: 0-0 Vi: 0-0 Tstrap: 0-0
Best Rating: 68 12/01 Leic 2m good Hdl

Maiden on the Flat, beaten in a seller on hurdling debut.

Fou Doux (FR)

(88h) (70h)

6-y-o b g Le Grillon Ii (FR)-Folie Douce (FR) (Fast (FR))
D G Bridgwater Paul Porter

Placings:4221/2-PP (4640)
2001/02: 19^{P}GS, 16^{P}G

	Starts	1st	2nd	3rd	Win & Pl
Hurdles	2	0	0	0	
Career Total	7	1	3	0	12624

12/99 Pau 2m110y Hdl VS £5920
Total win prize-money £5920

Going: Sf: 0-0 GS: 0-1 Gd: 0-1 GF: - Fm: 0-0
Distance: 2m/2m3: 0-2 2m4-2m7: 0-0 3m+: 0-0
Track: LH: 0-1 RH: 0-1 Tight: 0-1 Gall: 0-0
Aids: Bl: 0-1 Vi: 0-1 Tstrap: 0-1
Best Rating:

Fouette

76 59

4-y-o b f Saddlers' Hall (IRE)-Tight Spin (High Top)
J Howard Johnson (N A Graham 29/10) J Howard Johnson

Placings:004F **(4785)**
2001/02: 16^{0}S, 16^{0}S, 18^{4}HY, 16^{F}F

	Starts	1st	2nd	3rd	Win & Pl
Hurdles	4	0	0	0	0
Career Total	**4**	**0**	**0**	**0**	**0**

Going: Sf: 0-3 GS: 0-0 Gd: 0-0 GF: - Fm: 0-1
Distance: 2m/2m3: 0-4 2m4-2m7: 0-0 3m+: 0-0
Track: LH: 0-3 RH: 0-1 Tight: 0-3 Gall: 0-1
Aids: Bl: 0-0 Vi: 0-0 Tstrap: 0-0
Best Rating: 59 3/02 Kels 2m2f heavy Hdl

Foundation North

8-y-o b m Reesh-Isolationist (Welsh Pageant)
Jedd O'Keeffe Colin Edney & David Robson

Placings:*0/00*-PP **(0651)**
2001/02: 17^{P}G, 16^{P}GF

	Starts	1st	2nd	3rd	Win & Pl
Hurdles	2	0	0	0	
Career Total	**5**	**0**	**0**	**0**	

Going: Sf: 0-0 GS: 0-0 Gd: 0-1 GF: - Fm: 0-1
Distance: 2m/2m3: 0-2 2m4-2m7: 0-0 3m+: 0-0
Track: LH: 0-0 RH: 0-2 Tight: 0-1 Gall: 0-0
Aids: Bl: 0-0 Vi: 0-0 Tstrap: 0-0
Best Rating: 52 1/01 Catt 2m gd-sft NHF

Foundry Lane

86 **125**
11-y-o b g Mtoto-Eider (Niniski (USA))
Mrs M Reveley Mrs T E Sharratt

Placings:12210/**U2F140/1611/1F-F4** **(1491)**
2001/02: 20^{F}GS, 20^{4}G

	Starts	1st	2nd	3rd	Win & Pl
Chases	2	0	0	0	515
Career Total	**19**	**7**	**3**	**0**	**70481**

161	7/00	MRas	2m4f	B(0-140)HCh	G-F	£34222
152	2/00	Catt	2m3f	D(0-120)HCh	GD	£4134
147	1/00	Hntg	2m110y	E(0-115)HCh	GD	£2958
152	11/99	Aint	2m4f	C(0-135)HHdl	GD	£9480
125	1/99	Weth	2m	D Ch	SFT	£3580
146	2/98	Weth	2m	A Hdl	GD	£8918
108	11/97	Hayd	2m	D Hdl	GD	£2941

Total win prize-money £66236

Going: Sf: 0-0 GS: 0-1 Gd: 0-1 GF: - Fm: 0-0
Distance: 2m/2m3: 0-0 2m4-2m7: 0-2 3m+: 0-0
Track: LH: 0-0 RH: 0-1 Tight: 0-0 Gall: 0-1
Aids: Bl: 0-0 Vi: 0-0 Tstrap: 0-0
Best Rating: 161 7/00 MRas 2m4f gd-fm Ch

He is not a natural chaser but warmed up on the Flat prior to winning a valuable chase at Market Rasen in the summer of 2000. Has fallen in his two chases since, including the same race at the Lincolnshire track, but stayed on his feet at Huntingdon in September. Suited by good or faster, and stays two and a half miles.

Fountain Bank (IRE)

106(104h) (109h)**114+**
9-y-o b g Lafontaine (USA)-Clogrecon Lass (Raise You Ten)
M J Gingell Dr Tom Alexander

Placings:*30*/4046/P3-F21112441P4660 **(4817)**
2001/02: 25^{F}S, 23^{2}GF, 23^{1}GF, 20^{1}GF, 22^{1}GF, 20^{2}S, 24^{4}GF, 21^{4}GF, 22^{1}GF, 22^{P}S, 24^{4}G, 21^{6}G, 16^{6}G, 24^{0}GF

	Starts	1st	2nd	3rd	Win & Pl
Hurdles	14	4	2	0	12983
Career Total	**22**	**4**	**2**	**2**	**13808**

109	9/01	Font	2m6f110y	F(0-110)HHdl	G-F	£2688
108	6/01	Strf	2m6f110y	F(0-95)HHdl	G-F	£2443
101	6/01	Worc	2m4f	F(0-110)HHdl	G-F	£2562
95	6/01	Fknm	2m7f110y	F(0-100)HHdl	G-F	£3003

Total win prize-money £10696

Going: Sf: 0-3 GS: 0-0 Gd: 0-3 GF: - Fm: 4-8
Distance: 2m/2m3: 0-1 **2m4-2m7: 3-7** 3m+: 1-6
Track: **LH: 4-12** RH: 0-0 **Tight: 3-8** Gall: 0-1
Aids: Bl: 0-0 **Vi: 4-14** Tstrap: 0-0
Best Rating: 109 9/01 Font 2m6f110y gd-fm Hdl

Four times a winner on good to firm ground at between two and a half and three miles over hurdles. Lost his way after winning at Fontwell in August 2001. Landed Class E beginners' chase at Worcester August 2002.

Fountain Brig

97 **70**
6-y-o b/br g Royal Fountain-Lillie's Brig (New Brig)
J Barclay Alexander Family

Placings:*06053* **(4125)**
2001/02: 16^{0}GS, 20^{6}S, 24^{0}S, 20^{5}HY, 16^{3}HY

	Starts	1st	2nd	3rd	Win & Pl
NH Flat	1	0	0	0	0
Hurdles	4	0	0	1	496
Career Total	**5**	**0**	**0**	**1**	**496**

Going: Sf: 0-4 GS: 0-1 Gd: 0-0 GF: - Fm: 0-0
Distance: 2m/2m3: 0-2 2m4-2m7: 0-2 3m+: 0-1
Track: LH: 0-5 RH: 0-0 Tight: 0-0 Gall: 0-1
Aids: Bl: 0-0 Vi: 0-0 Tstrap: 0-0
Best Rating: 70 3/02 Ayr 2m heavy Hdl

Little sign of ability so far.

Four Eagles (USA)

91 **95**
4-y-o b g Lear Fan (USA)-Bloomingly (ARG) (Candy Stripes (USA))
D R C Elsworth Mcdowell Racing

Placings:P354 **(2758)**
2001/02: 16^{P}G, 16^{3}G, 18^{5}G, 16^{4}GS

	Starts	1st	2nd	3rd	Win & Pl
Hurdles	4	0	0	1	1179
Career Total	**4**	**0**	**0**	**1**	**1179**

Going: Sf: 0-0 GS: 0-1 Gd: 0-3 GF: - Fm: 0-0
Distance: 2m/2m3: 0-4 2m4-2m7: 0-0 3m+: 0-0
Track: LH: 0-4 RH: 0-0 Tight: 0-1 Gall: 0-3
Aids: Bl: 0-0 Vi: 0-0 Tstrap: 0-0
Best Rating: 95 12/01 Newb 2m110y gd-sft Hdl

In the frame over hurdles, but his form does not add up to much.

Four Men (IRE)

5-y-o b g Nicolotte-Sound Pet (Runnett)
Miss K M George (A Berry 17/1) Nigel Gooding

Placings:P **(4127)**
2001/02: 17^{P}G

	Starts	1st	2nd	3rd	Win & Pl
Hurdles	1	0	0	0	
Career Total	**1**	**0**	**0**	**0**	

Going: Sf: 0-0 GS: 0-0 Gd: 0-1 GF: - Fm: 0-0
Distance: 2m/2m3: 0-1 2m4-2m7: 0-0 3m+: 0-0
Track: LH: 0-0 RH: 0-1 Tight: 0-0 Gall: 0-0
Aids: Bl: 0-0 Vi: 0-0 Tstrap: 0-0
Best Rating: 2 3/02 Hrfd 2m1f good Hdl

Four Mile Clump

101(91h) (96h)**117**
8-y-o b g Petoski-Rare Luck (Rare One)
P J Jones P J Jones

Placings:0P0**R3/PP**-23**P11** **(2720)**
2001/02: 26^{2}GF, 25^{3}GS, 24^{P}G, 25^{1}G, 25^{1}G

	Starts	1st	2nd	3rd	Win & Pl
Hurdles	1	0	1	0	720
Chases	4	2	0	1	10297
Career Total	**12**	**2**	**1**	**2**	**11417**

117	12/01	Hrfd	3m1f110y	F(0-100)HCh	GD	£7068
105	11/01	Hrfd	3m1f110y	F(0-90)HCh	GD	£2796

Total win prize-money £9866

Going: Sf: 0-0 GS: 0-1 Gd: 2-3 GF: - Fm: 0-1
Distance: 2m/2m3: 0-0 2m4-2m7: 0-0 **3m+: 2-5**
Track: LH: 0-1 **RH: 2-3** Tight: 0-0 Gall: 0-2
Aids: Bl: 0-0 Vi: 0-0 Tstrap: 0-0
Best Rating: 117 12/01 Hrfd 3m1f110y good Ch

A modest dual-purpose performer who had a tendency not to complete, responded well to forcing tactics when bolting up at Hereford in November and followed up at the same track the following month.

Four Of A Kind

77f **71f**
4-y-o b g Most Welcome-Pegs (Mandrake Major)
C W Thornton Guy Reed

Placings:*00* **(4841)**
2001/02: 16^{0}GS, 16^{0}G

	Starts	1st	2nd	3rd	Win & Pl
NH Flat	2	0	0	0	
Career Total	**2**	**0**	**0**	**0**	

Going: Sf: 0-0 GS: 0-1 Gd: 0-1 GF: - Fm: 0-0
Distance: 2m/2m3: 0-2 2m4-2m7: 0-0 3m+: 0-0
Track: LH: 0-2 RH: 0-0 Tight: 0-1 Gall: 0-0
Aids: Bl: 0-0 Vi: 0-0 Tstrap: 0-0
Best Rating: 71 4/02 Ayr 2m good NHF

Four To Win (IRE)

94 **88**
6-y-o b g Tremblant-Ballybeg Rose (IRE) (Roselier (FR))
Miss Jacqueline S Doyle Cover Point Racing

Placings:*0*460P **(4387)**
2001/02: 16^{0}GS, 16^{4}GS, 16^{6}HY, 19^{0}S, 16^{P}S

	Starts	1st	2nd	3rd	Win & Pl
NH Flat	1	0	0	0	0
Hurdles	4	0	0	0	0
Career Total	**5**	**0**	**0**	**0**	**0**

Going: Sf: 0-3 GS: 0-2 Gd: 0-0 GF: - Fm: 0-0
Distance: 2m/2m3: 0-5 2m4-2m7: 0-0 3m+: 0-0
Track: LH: 0-1 RH: 0-4 Tight: 0-0 Gall: 0-3
Aids: Bl: 0-0 Vi: 0-0 Tstrap: 0-0
Best Rating: 88 1/02 Hntg 2m110y gd-sft Hdl

Fourdaned (IRE)

9-y-o b g Danehill (USA)-Pro Patria (Petingo)
Mrs L C Jewell The Lively Lads

Placings:255/00/5 (1254)
2001/02: 20^{5}GF

	Starts	1st	2nd	3rd	Win & Pl
Hurdles	1	0	0	0	0
Career Total	**6**	**0**	**1**	**0**	**554**

Going: Sf: 0-0 GS: 0-0 Gd: 0-0 GF: - Fm: 0-1
Distance: 2m/2m3: 0-0 2m4-2m7: 0-1 3m+: 0-0
Track: LH: 0-0 RH: 0-0 Tight: 0-1 Gall: 0-0
Aids: Bl: 0-0 Vi: 0-1 Tstrap: 0-0
Best Rating: 98 1/98 Folk 2m1f110y gd-sft Hdl

Fours Are Wild (IRE)

84 **75**

9-y-o ch g Montelimar (USA)-Lousion (Lucifer (USA))
K C Bailey Mrs Amelia Dalton

Placings:0/0011P2/P-P0PU4 (4864)
2001/02: 25^{P}G, 20^{0}G, 26^{P}HY, 24^{U}GF, 25^{4}F

	Starts	1st	2nd	3rd	Win & Pl
Chases	5	0	0	0	400
Career Total	**13**	**2**	**1**	**0**	**10122**

133	11/99	Weth	2m4f110y	D(0-110)HCh	GD	£3899
120	11/99	Kemp	2m4f110y	D Ch	GD	£4611

Total win prize-money £8510

Going: Sf: 0-1 GS: 0-0 Gd: 0-2 GF: - Fm: 0-2
Distance: 2m/2m3: 0-0 2m4-2m7: 0-1 3m+: 0-4
Track: LH: 0-2 RH: 0-1 Tight: 0-0 Gall: 0-1
Aids: Bl: 0-0 Vi: 0-0 Tstrap: 0-0
Best Rating: 133 11/99 Weth 2m4f110y good Ch

Fox In The Box

90f **104f**

5-y-o gr g Supreme Leader-Charlotte Gray (Rolfe (USA))
R H Alner Peter Bonner

Placings:046 (4158)
2001/02: 16^{0}G, 16^{4}S, 16^{6}GS

	Starts	1st	2nd	3rd	Win & Pl
NH Flat	3	0	0	0	0
Career Total	**3**	**0**	**0**	**0**	**0**

Going: Sf: 0-1 GS: 0-1 Gd: 0-1 GF: - Fm: 0-0
Distance: 2m/2m3: 0-3 2m4-2m7: 0-0 3m+: 0-0
Track: LH: 0-0 RH: 0-3 Tight: 0-0 Gall: 0-0
Aids: Bl: 0-0 Vi: 0-0 Tstrap: 0-0
Best Rating: 104 3/02 Sand 2m110y gd-sft NHF

Fox Island (IRE)

80

9-y-o b g Ashmolean (USA)-My First Lady (Ballymore)
J J O'Neill Mrs Peter S Thompson

Placings:PP5/6-U3 (1639)
2001/02: 20^{U}G, 20^{3}GS

	Starts	1st	2nd	3rd	Win & Pl
Hurdles	2	0	0	1	301
Career Total	**6**	**0**	**0**	**1**	**301**

Going: Sf: 0-0 GS: 0-1 Gd: 0-1 GF: - Fm: 0-0
Distance: 2m/2m3: 0-0 2m4-2m7: 0-2 3m+: 0-0
Track: LH: 0-0 RH: 0-1 Tight: 0-0 Gall: 0-0
Aids: Bl: 0-0 Vi: 0-0 Tstrap: 0-0
Best Rating: 80 10/01 Carl 2m4f gd-sft Hdl

Foxbow (IRE)

93 **74**

12-y-o b g Mandalus-Lady Bow (Deep Run)
P Wegmann R Koniger

Placings:3/2/01036/F/F4/P/41P52/62P6PPP-545U6P (0971)
2001/02: 16^{5}GF, 16^{4}GS, 16^{5}GF, 17^{U}G, 16^{6}GF, 20^{P}GF

	Starts	1st	2nd	3rd	Win & Pl
Chases	6	0	0	0	0
Career Total	**29**	**2**	**3**	**2**	**11743**

107	7/99	NAbb	2m5f110y	D(0-120)HCh	G-S	£4280
98	11/95	Asct	3m	C Hdl	GD	£3582

Total win prize-money £7863

Going: Sf: 0-0 GS: 0-1 Gd: 0-1 GF: - Fm: 0-4
Distance: 2m/2m3: 0-5 2m4-2m7: 0-1 3m+: 0-0
Track: LH: 0-4 RH: 0-1 Tight: 0-5 Gall: 0-0
Aids: Bl: 0-0 Vi: 0-0 Tstrap: 0-0
Best Rating: 107 7/99 NAbb 2m5f110y gd-sft Ch

Foxchapel King (IRE)

119 **170**

9-y-o b g Jolly Jake (NZ)-Monatrim (Le Moss)
M F Morris Sir Anthony O'Reilly

Placings:11166P/122FF114/0314322/2610P2-61110U (4945a)
2001/02: 29^{6}G, 24^{1}Y, 24^{1}YS, 24^{1}Y, 26^{0}G, 25^{U}G

	Starts	1st	2nd	3rd	Win & Pl
Chases	6	3	0	0	140121
Career Total	**33**	**11**	**6**	**2**	**276225**

170	12/01	Leop	3m	Ch	YLD	£60282
161	11/01	DRoy	3m	Ch	Y-S	£53225
161	10/01	Limk	3m	HCh	YLD	£26209
161	11/00	Chel	3m3f110y	B HCh	G-S	£32500
153	11/99	Navn	3m	HCh	YLD	£29017
139	4/99	Cork	3m	Ch	SFT	£11562
123	2/99	Clon	2m4f	Ch	SFT	£4296
113	10/98	Thur	2m6f	Ch	GD	£3138
137	12/97	Leop	2m4f	Hdl	HVY	£4069
121	11/97	Naas	2m	Hdl	SH	£3051
98	11/97	Clon	2m	Hdl	G-Y	£2543

Total win prize-money £229899

Going: Sf: 0-0 GS: 0-0 Gd: 0-3 GF: - Fm: 0-0
Distance: 2m/2m3: 0-0 2m4-2m7: 0-0 **3m+: 3-6**
Track: LH: 1-2 RH: 1-2 Tight: 0-0 Gall: 0-1
Aids: Bl: 0-0 Vi: 0-0 Tstrap: 0-0
Best Rating: 170 12/01 Leop 3m yield Ch

Runner-up in the 2000 Irish National, he was a wide-margin winner of a competitive handicap at Cheltenham in November 2000, but was well beaten subsequently until scoring at Limerick in October 2001. His jumping still has room for improvement. Stays three and a half miles. Likes to get his toe in but has never won on heavy ground over fences. Made all to win the Champion Chase at Down Royal in November 2001 and the Ericcson Chase the following month.

Foxmead Flight

5-y-o b g Lyphento (USA)-Toscana (Town And Country)
P C Ritchens Mrs A E Morton

Placings:0P0 (1556)
2001/02: 16^{0}G, 20^{P}GF, 16^{0}G

	Starts	1st	2nd	3rd	Win & Pl
NH Flat	1	0	0	0	0
Hurdles	2	0	0	0	0
Career Total	**3**	**0**	**0**	**0**	

Going: Sf: 0-0 GS: 0-0 Gd: 0-2 GF: - Fm: 0-1
Distance: 2m/2m3: 0-2 2m4-2m7: 0-1 3m+: 0-0
Track: LH: 0-3 RH: 0-0 Tight: 0-0 Gall: 0-0
Aids: Bl: 0-0 Vi: 0-0 Tstrap: 0-0
Best Rating: 20 6/01 Worc 2m good NHF

Foxy Dawn

91 **82**

11-y-o ch g Gabitat-Serious Affair (Valiyar)
Mrs L C Jewell Mrs A Greengrow

Placings:PR-00555P45504B (2592)
2001/02: 18^{0}GF, 24^{0}GF, 25^{5}GF, 26^{5}GF, 26^{5}GF, 21^{P}GF, 20^{4}GF, 26^{5}S, 26^{5}GS, 21^{0}G, 29^{4}S, 25^{B}G

	Starts	1st	2nd	3rd	Win & Pl
Hurdles	1	0	0	0	0
Chases	11	0	0	0	631
Career Total	**14**	**0**	**0**	**0**	**631**

Going: Sf: 0-2 GS: 0-1 Gd: 0-2 GF: - Fm: 0-7
Distance: 2m/2m3: 0-1 2m4-2m7: 0-3 3m+: 0-8
Track: LH: 0-3 RH: 0-4 Tight: 0-9 Gall: 0-1
Aids: Bl: 0-3 Vi: 0-3 Tstrap: 0-0
Best Rating: 82 10/01 Font 3m2f110y gd-sft Ch

Foxy Lad

6-y-o ch g Bob's Return (IRE)-Shy Hiker (Netherkelly)
Graeme Roe M J Lilley

Placings:0-500 (4570)
2001/02: 16^{5}GF, 16^{0}GF, 16^{0}G

	Starts	1st	2nd	3rd	Win & Pl
NH Flat	3	0	0	0	0
Career Total	**4**	**0**	**0**	**0**	**0**

Going: Sf: 0-0 GS: 0-0 Gd: 0-1 GF: - Fm: 0-2
Distance: 2m/2m3: 0-3 2m4-2m7: 0-0 3m+: 0-0
Track: LH: 0-2 RH: 0-1 Tight: 0-0 Gall: 0-0
Aids: Bl: 0-0 Vi: 0-1 Tstrap: 0-0
Best Rating: 67 8/01 Worc 2m gd-fm NHF

Foxy Royale

78 **42**

6-y-o b g Bold Fox-Celtic Royale (Celtic Cone)
Mrs A Price Mrs A Price

Placings:00 (0355)
2001/02: 19^{0}G, 17^{0}GS

	Starts	1st	2nd	3rd	Win & Pl
Hurdles	2	0	0	0	
Career Total	**2**	**0**	**0**	**0**	

Going: Sf: 0-0 GS: 0-1 Gd: 0-1 GF: - Fm: 0-0
Distance: 2m/2m3: 0-1 2m4-2m7: 0-1 3m+: 0-0
Track: LH: 0-1 RH: 0-1 Tight: 0-1 Gall: 0-0
Aids: Bl: 0-0 Vi: 0-0 Tstrap: 0-0
Best Rating: 42 5/01 Bang 2m1f gd-sft Hdl

Fragrant Rose

100f **116f**

6-y-o b m Alflora (IRE)-Levantine Rose (Levanter)
Miss H C Knight Exors Of The Late Mrs B A Jenks

Placings: *1316* (4823)
2001/02: 17^{1}G, 16^{3}G, 17^{1}S, 17^{6}G

	Starts	1st	2nd	3rd	Win & Pl
NH Flat	4	2	0	1	4128
Career Total	**4**	**2**	**0**	**1**	**4128**

116	1/02	Tntn	2m1f	H NHF	SFT	£2114
110	11/01	Hrfd	2m1f	H NHF	GD	£1631

Total win prize-money £3745

Going: Sf: 1-1 GS: 0-0 Gd: 1-3 GF: - Fm: 0-0
Distance: **2m/2m3: 2-4** 2m4-2m7: 0-0 3m+: 0-0
Track: LH: 0-2 **RH: 1-1** Tight: 0-0 Gall: 0-2
Aids: Bl: 0-0 Vi: 0-0 Tstrap: 0-0
Best Rating: **116** 1/02 Tntn 2m1f soft NHF

Dual bumper winner, acts on good and soft ground and is effective at around two miles.

Francis Bay (USA)

88 (135h) 135

7-y-o b g Alleged (USA)-Montage (USA) (Alydar (USA))
D K Weld M Magowan

Placings:3123/153016/0110106-440P00 (4960a)
2001/02: 22^{4}GY, 16^{4}GF, 20^{0}S, 16^{P}G, 16^{0}GY, 16^{0}GY

	Starts	1st	2nd	3rd	Win & Pl
Hurdles	1	0	0	0	419
Chases	5	0	0	0	2621
Career Total	**23**	**6**	**1**	**3**	**33508**

135	8/00	Gway	2m1f	HCh	GD	£8560
122	7/00	Klny	2m1f	(0-123)HCh	G-F	£4416
115	6/00	Baln	2m1f	(0-102)HCh	GD	£4002
91	3/00	DRoy	2m	Ch	G-Y	£3312
115	7/99	Gway	2m	Hdl	G-F	£4296
96	2/99	Naas	2m	Hdl	SFT	£3069

Total win prize-money £27656

Going: Sf: 0-1 GS: 0-0 Gd: 0-1 GF: - Fm: 0-1
Distance: 2m/2m3: 0-4 2m4-2m7: 0-2 3m+: 0-0
Track: LH: 0-2 RH: 0-2 Tight: 0-0 Gall: 0-1
Aids: Bl: 0-5 Vi: 0-0 Tstrap: 0-0
Best Rating: **135** 9/01 Gway 2m gd-fm Hdl

Suited by decent ground, he hacked up in a valuable handicap at Galway in August 2000 before struggling on a soft surface in the spring. Not so effective in 2001/02.

Francolino (FR)

94(93c) 82

9-y-o b g Useful (FR)-Quintefeuille Ii (FR) (Kashtan (FR))
N A Gaselee Barry Marsden

Placings:4321350/45314/2P442/2541512/41PP04P-P040 (1497)
2001/02: 21^{P}GF, 20^{0}G, 20^{4}G, 19^{0}GF

	Starts	1st	2nd	3rd	Win & Pl
Hurdles	3	0	0	0	0
Chases	1	0	0	0	0
Career Total	**35**	**5**	**5**	**3**	**59831**

140	10/00	Plum	2m4f	D(0-125)HCh	SFT	£4480
	4/00	Pmnl	2m3f	Ch	SFT	£2882
	2/00	Pau	2m3f	Ch	SFT	£3842
	11/97	Ange	2m5f	Ch	VS	£9540
	1/97	Pau	2m2f110y	Ch	VS	£5612

Total win prize-money £26356

Going: Sf: 0-0 GS: 0-0 Gd: 0-2 GF: - Fm: 0-2
Distance: 2m/2m3: 0-1 2m4-2m7: 0-3 3m+: 0-0
Track: LH: 0-3 RH: 0-1 Tight: 0-1 Gall: 0-0
Aids: Bl: 0-1 Vi: 0-0 Tstrap: 0-0
Best Rating: **140** 10/00 Plum 2m4f soft Ch

Francophile (IRE)

11-y-o ch g Caribo-French Miss (Golden Love)
S R Bolton Mrs Margaret R Dunning

Placings:P (0205)
2001/02: 25^{P}G

	Starts	1st	2nd	3rd	Win & Pl
Chases	1	0	0	0	
Career Total	**1**	**0**	**0**	**0**	

Going: Sf: 0-0 GS: 0-0 Gd: 0-1 GF: - Fm: 0-0
Distance: 2m/2m3: 0-0 2m4-2m7: 0-0 3m+: 0-1
Track: LH: 0-1 RH: 0-0 Tight: 0-0 Gall: 0-0
Aids: Bl: 0-0 Vi: 0-0 Tstrap: 0-0
Best Rating:

Frank Byrne

(66h)

10-y-o b g Rakaposhi King-Polarita (Arctic Kanda)
J A B Old J Fishpool

Placings:*20*/32P/454451/33P43P-4 (0366)
2001/02: 25^{4}G

	Starts	1st	2nd	3rd	Win & Pl
Hurdles	1	0	0	0	0
Career Total	**18**	**1**	**2**	**4**	**8266**

120	4/00	Uttx	2m4f	E(0-115)HCh	HVY	£4013

Total win prize-money £4014

Going: Sf: 0-0 GS: 0-0 Gd: 0-1 GF: - Fm: 0-0
Distance: 2m/2m3: 0-0 2m4-2m7: 0-0 3m+: 0-1
Track: LH: 0-0 RH: 0-0 Tight: 0-0 Gall: 0-0
Aids: Bl: 0-1 Vi: 0-0 Tstrap: 0-0
Best Rating: **120** 4/00 Uttx 2m4f heavy Ch

Frank Knows

96 90

12-y-o ch g Chilibang-Chance Match (Royal Match)
Capt J A George Captain & Mrs J A George

Placings:6P/0P0/24/22/P3P0U/P5P13-05P04 (2707)
2001/02: 16^{0}G, 16^{5}S, 21^{P}G, 16^{0}GS, 20^{4}G

	Starts	1st	2nd	3rd	Win & Pl
Chases	5	0	0	0	294
Career Total	**24**	**1**	**3**	**2**	**6445**

90	4/01	Plum	2m1f	G(0-90)HCh	SFT	£2478

Total win prize-money £2478

Going: Sf: 0-1 GS: 0-1 Gd: 0-3 GF: - Fm: 0-0
Distance: 2m/2m3: 0-3 2m4-2m7: 0-2 3m+: 0-0
Track: LH: 0-2 RH: 0-2 Tight: 0-2 Gall: 0-1
Aids: Bl: 0-0 Vi: 0-0 Tstrap: 0-0
Best Rating: **90** 4/01 Plum 2m1f soft Ch

Frankie Anson

89f 80f

5-y-o b g Anshan-Smilingatstrangers (Macmillion)
Mrs Barbara Waring Frank Hanson

Placings:*50* (1799)
2001/02: 17^{5}G, 16^{0}S

	Starts	1st	2nd	3rd	Win & Pl
NH Flat	2	0	0	0	0
Career Total	**2**	**0**	**0**	**0**	**0**

Going: Sf: 0-1 GS: 0-0 Gd: 0-1 GF: - Fm: 0-0
Distance: 2m/2m3: 0-2 2m4-2m7: 0-0 3m+: 0-0
Track: LH: 0-1 RH: 0-1 Tight: 0-0 Gall: 0-0
Aids: Bl: 0-0 Vi: 0-0 Tstrap: 0-0
Best Rating: **80** 10/01 Hrfd 2m1f good NHF

Frankie Willow (IRE)

100 99

9-y-o ch g Lanfranco-Winnie Willow (Kambalda)
J R Jenkins Mrs B McAtamney

Placings:*104*/2020323/0506234-126 (0775)
2001/02: 20^{1}G, 20^{2}GF, 20^{6}GF

	Starts	1st	2nd	3rd	Win & Pl
Hurdles	3	1	1	0	3698
Career Total	**20**	**2**	**5**	**3**	**8217**

99	5/01	Hntg	2m4f110y	F(0-105)HHdl	GD	£2870
89	1/97	DRoy	2m	NHF	G-Y	£1356

Total win prize-money £4226

Going: Sf: 0-0 GS: 0-0 Gd: 1-1 GF: - Fm: 0-2
Distance: 2m/2m3: 0-0 **2m4-2m7: 1-3** 3m+: 0-0
Track: LH: 0-2 **RH: 1-1** Tight: 0-1 **Gall: 1-1**
Aids: Bl: 0-0 Vi: 0-1 Tstrap: 0-0
Best Rating: **99** 5/01 Hntg 2m4f110y good Hdl

Frankie's River

101 92

5-y-o b g Over The River (FR)-Up The Junction (IRE) (Treasure Kay)
R H Alner Paul Murphy& Frank Watson

Placings:*462* (4756)
2001/02: 16^{4}S, 21^{6}S, 20^{2}GF

	Starts	1st	2nd	3rd	Win & Pl
NH Flat	1	0	0	0	0
Hurdles	2	0	1	0	1143
Career Total	**3**	**0**	**1**	**0**	**1143**

Going: Sf: 0-2 GS: 0-0 Gd: 0-0 GF: - Fm: 0-1
Distance: 2m/2m3: 0-1 2m4-2m7: 0-2 3m+: 0-0
Track: LH: 0-3 RH: 0-0 Tight: 0-1 Gall: 0-0
Aids: Bl: 0-0 Vi: 0-0 Tstrap: 0-0
Best Rating: **107** 12/01 Wwck 2m soft NHF

Appeared on the upgrade when well beaten second to odds-on favourite under tender handling at Uttoxeter in April. Stays two and a half miles.

Frankincense (IRE)

94 92

6-y-o gr g Paris House-Mistral Wood (USA) (Far North (CAN))
N Tinkler (C Von Der Recke 19/11) Colin Tinkler Snr

Placings:6230 (4127)
2001/02: 16^{6}GS, 16^{2}GS, 16^{3}G, 17^{0}G

	Starts	1st	2nd	3rd	Win & Pl
Hurdles	4	0	1	1	1297
Career Total	**4**	**0**	**1**	**1**	**1297**

Going: Sf: 0-0 GS: 0-2 Gd: 0-2 GF: - Fm: 0-0
Distance: 2m/2m3: 0-4 2m4-2m7: 0-0 3m+: 0-0
Track: LH: 0-1 RH: 0-3 Tight: 0-1 Gall: 0-0
Aids: Bl: 0-0 Vi: 0-0 Tstrap: 0-0
Best Rating: **92** 12/01 Ludl 2m good Hdl

A winner on the Flat in Germany, he has shown a little

over hurdles.

Frantic Tan (IRE)

10-y-o ch g Zaffaran (USA)-Brownskin (Buckskin (FR))
N A Twiston-Davies The Bunkers Hill Mob

Placings:*613*/4/012/**U211U6-6PUUP** **(4839)**
2001/02: 24^{6}G, 26^{P}S, 34^{U}HY, 36^{U}G, 33^{P}G

	Starts	1st	2nd	3rd	Win & Pl
Chases	5	0	0	0	0
Career Total	**18**	**4**	**2**	**1**	**87664**

167	2/01	Hayd	3m4f110y	A HCh	SFT	£58000
157	2/01	Newb	3m	C Ch	SFT	£6972
116	2/00	Hayd	2m6f	D Hdl	SFT	£3412
131	2/98	Newb	2m110y	H NHF	GD	£6937

Total win prize-money £75323

Going: Sf: 0-2 GS: 0-0 Gd: 0-3 GF: - Fm: 0-0
Distance: 2m/2m3: 0-0 2m4-2m7: 0-0 3m+: 0-5
Track: LH: 0-5 RH: 0-0 Tight: 0-1 Gall: 0-1
Aids: Bl: 0-0 Vi: 0-0 Tstrap: 0-0
Best Rating: 167 2/01 Hayd 3m4f110y soft Ch

A leading bumper performer and a useful novice hurdler, he put in a fine performance when beating Behrajan at Newbury and when winning the De Vere Gold Cup Chase at Haydock in the 2000/2001 season. Disappointing this term, although he was going well when departing at Uttoxeter. Unseated in the Grand National and pulled up in the Scottish version. He has won at up to three and a half miles and acts on soft ground. Has been tubed.

Frazer Island (IRE)

13-y-o br g Phardante (FR)-Avransha (Random Shot)
Nick Gifford (R Rowe 3/2) L J & Mrs I Sherwood

Placings:*505F0/22122U1/1U4F0344/P4420BF/2253/***4** **(3810)**
2001/02: 26^{4}S

	Starts	1st	2nd	3rd	Win & Pl
Chases	1	0	0	0	533
Career Total	**32**	**3**	**7**	**2**	**31975**

133	10/97	Chep	2m3f110y	C(0-130)HCh	GD	£4393
130	4/97	Plum	3m1f110y	E Ch	G-F	£3176
130	2/97	Hntg	2m4f110y	E Ch	G-S	£3023

Total win prize-money £10593

Going: Sf: 0-1 GS: 0-0 Gd: 0-0 GF: - Fm: 0-0
Distance: 2m/2m3: 0-0 2m4-2m7: 0-0 3m+: 0-1
Track: LH: 0-0 RH: 0-0 Tight: 0-1 Gall: 0-0
Aids: Bl: 0-0 Vi: 0-0 Tstrap: 0-0
Best Rating: 138 11/99 Asct 3m110y good Ch

Frazer's Lad

101 **84**
5-y-o b g Whittingham (IRE)-Loch Tain (Lochnager)
M E Sowersby (A Bailey 21/8) A Milner

Placings:P000P **(4871)**
2001/02: 17^{P}S, 17^{0}GS, 16^{0}GS, 21^{0}GF, 25^{P}GF

	Starts	1st	2nd	3rd	Win & Pl
Hurdles	5	0	0	0	
Career Total	**5**	**0**	**0**	**0**	

Going: Sf: 0-1 GS: 0-2 Gd: 0-0 GF: - Fm: 0-2
Distance: 2m/2m3: 0-3 2m4-2m7: 0-1 3m+: 0-1
Track: LH: 0-4 RH: 0-1 Tight: 0-4 Gall: 0-0
Aids: Bl: 0-0 Vi: 0-2 Tstrap: 0-0
Best Rating: 67 4/02 Sedg 2m5f110y gd-fm Hdl

Plating-class hurdler, in good heart in the summer of 2002.

Fred's In The Know

104 **124**
7-y-o ch g Interrex (CAN)-Lady Vynz (Whitstead)
N Waggott N Waggott

Placings:52/23212300-54222P **(4306)**
2001/02: 20^{5}GS, 17^{4}S, 21^{2}GS, 20^{2}HY, 21^{2}GS, 20^{P}S

	Starts	1st	2nd	3rd	Win & Pl
Hurdles	6	0	3	0	3362
Career Total	**16**	**1**	**7**	**2**	**12566**

131	12/00	Leic	2m4f110y	D Hdl	HVY	£3848

Total win prize-money £3848

Going: Sf: 0-3 GS: 0-3 Gd: 0-0 GF: - Fm: 0-0
Distance: 2m/2m3: 0-1 2m4-2m7: 0-5 3m+: 0-0
Track: LH: 0-3 RH: 0-3 Tight: 0-2 Gall: 0-0
Aids: Bl: 0-0 Vi: 0-0 Tstrap: 0-0
Best Rating: 131 1/01 Newc 2m4f soft Hdl

Moderate hurdler at the start of 2000/2001, he was disappointing until beginning of 2002 when dropped in trip. Best at around two and a half miles in soft ground.

Freddie Muck

(82h)
12-y-o b g Idiots Delight-Muckertoo (Sagaro)
N A Twiston-Davies Mrs C Twiston-Davies

Placings:*0/23042244402/5212031/11213630/***31412/3135P62/2P0/13442UP-6** **(1090)**
2001/02: 24^{6}GF

	Starts	1st	2nd	3rd	Win & Pl
Hurdles	1	0	0	0	0
Career Total	**50**	**9**	**11**	**8**	**72089**

131	7/00	NAbb	3m2f110y	C(0-135)HCh	G-F	£5642
138	11/98	NAbb	3m2f110y	B HCh	SFT	£8612
127	3/98	Uttx	3m2f	C HCh	GD	£13615
123	12/97	Hrfd	3m1f110y	E Ch	SFT	£3368
131	12/96	Bang	3m	B(0-140)HHdl	GD	£4765
125	10/96	MRas	3m	C(0-130)HHdl	GD	£3371
119	9/96	Worc	2m4f	B(0-140)HHdl	G-F	£4922
111	11/95	Carl	2m4f110y	F(0-105)HHdl	GD	£2178
80	8/95	Uttx	2m4f110y	D Hdl	FRM	£2556

Total win prize-money £49030

Going: Sf: 0-0 GS: 0-0 Gd: 0-0 GF: - Fm: 0-1
Distance: 2m/2m3: 0-0 2m4-2m7: 0-0 3m+: 0-1
Track: LH: 0-1 RH: 0-0 Tight: 0-0 Gall: 0-0
Aids: Bl: 0-1 Vi: 0-0 Tstrap: 0-0
Best Rating: 138 11/98 NAbb 3m2f110y soft Ch

Freddie Taylor

73 **42**
5-y-o b g Sula Bula-Clowater Lady (IRE) (Orchestra)
J C McConnochie (H S Howe 5/5) J C McConnochie

Placings:*40F0-*0P **(4316)**
2001/02: 17^{0}G, 24^{P}HY

	Starts	1st	2nd	3rd	Win & Pl
Hurdles	2	0	0	0	
Career Total	**6**	**0**	**0**	**0**	**0**

Going: Sf: 0-1 GS: 0-0 Gd: 0-1 GF: - Fm: 0-0
Distance: 2m/2m3: 0-1 2m4-2m7: 0-0 3m+: 0-1
Track: LH: 0-1 RH: 0-1 Tight: 0-1 Gall: 0-0
Aids: Bl: 0-0 Vi: 0-0 Tstrap: 0-0
Best Rating: 84 2/01 Winc 2m good NHF

He has jumped poorly on all starts over flights so far.

Freddie's Comet (IRE)

100 **92**
6-y-o b g Freddie's Star-Baltimore Bay (Bishop Of Orange)
John R Upson Middleham Park Racing Vii

Placings:*U0-*PP43 **(4906)**
2001/02: 17^{P}G, 21^{P}GS, 17^{4}G, 19^{3}G

	Starts	1st	2nd	3rd	Win & Pl
Hurdles	4	0	0	1	623
Career Total	**6**	**0**	**0**	**1**	**623**

Going: Sf: 0-0 GS: 0-1 Gd: 0-3 GF: - Fm: 0-0
Distance: 2m/2m3: 0-2 2m4-2m7: 0-2 3m+: 0-0
Track: LH: 0-0 RH: 0-4 Tight: 0-2 Gall: 0-0
Aids: Bl: 0-0 Vi: 0-0 Tstrap: 0-0
Best Rating: 97 11/00 Ludl 2m good NHF

Modest hurdler, stays two and a half miles, not an easy ride.

Freddy B

7-y-o b g North Col-Honiara (Pitcairn)
M F Barraclough M F Barraclough

Placings:*P* **(1813)**
2001/02: 10^{P}O

	Starts	1st	2nd	3rd	Win & Pl
NH Flat	1	0	0	0	
Career Total	**1**	**0**	**0**	**0**	

Going: Sf: 0-1 GS: 0-0 Gd: 0-0 GF: - Fm: 0-0
Distance: 2m/2m3: 0-1 2m4-2m7: 0-0 3m+: 0-0
Track: LH: 0-1 RH: 0-0 Tight: 0-1 Gall: 0-0
Aids: Bl: 0-0 Vi: 0-0 Tstrap: 0-0
Best Rating:

Freddy Flintstone

95 **85**
5-y-o b g Bigstone (IRE)-Daring Ditty (Daring March)
O Sherwood (R Hannon 30/8) Lady Whent And Friends

Placings:62 **(1617)**
2001/02: 16^{6}GF, 17^{2}GF

	Starts	1st	2nd	3rd	Win & Pl
Hurdles	2	0	1	0	790
Career Total	**2**	**0**	**1**	**0**	**790**

Going: Sf: 0-0 GS: 0-0 Gd: 0-0 GF: - Fm: 0-2
Distance: 2m/2m3: 0-2 2m4-2m7: 0-0 3m+: 0-0
Track: LH: 0-1 RH: 0-1 Tight: 0-1 Gall: 0-0
Aids: Bl: 0-0 Vi: 0-0 Tstrap: 0-0
Best Rating: 85 10/01 Extr 2m1f gd-fm Hdl

Fair effort on second appearance over hurdles at Exeter in October. Handles fast ground.

Frederic Forever (IRE)

99 **112**
4-y-o b g Exit To Nowhere (USA)-Sarooh's Love (USA) (Nureyev (USA))
P J Hobbs (F Head 26/5) Mrs D A Winton

Placings:11215225 **(3260)**

2001/02: 18^{1}GF, 17^{1}GF, 17^{2}G, 16^{1}G, 16^{5}G, 16^{2}G, 16^{2}S, 16^{5}S

	Starts	1st	2nd	3rd	Win & Pl
Hurdles	8	3	3	0	13229
Career Total	**8**	**3**	**3**	**0**	**13229**

107	10/01	Chep	2m110y	D Hdl	GD	£3464
108	9/01	NAbb	2m1f	E Hdl	G-F	£2863
96	8/01	Font	2m2f110y	E Hdl	G-F	£2324

Total win prize-money £8652

Going: Sf: 0-2 GS: 0-0 Gd: 1-4 GF: - Fm: 2-2
Distance: **2m/2m3: 3-8** 2m4-2m7: 0-0 3m+: 0-0
Track: **LH: 3-6** RH: 0-2 **Tight: 2-3** Gall: 0-1
Aids: Bl: 0-1 Vi: 0-0 Tstrap: 0-0
Best Rating: 112 12/01 Sand 2m110y soft Hdl

Useful juvenile hurdler in the autumn of 2001, he has faced some tough opposition since in ground that does not suit him and he has been well held. Suited by good ground or faster.

Free

107(106c) (137c)118

7-y-o ch g Gone West (USA)-Bemissed (USA) (Nijinsky (CAN))
Mrs M Reveley P D Savill

Placings:212315/**U113**/5232-3P110351F60 **(4265)**
2001/02: 21^{3}GF, 23^{P}GF, 26^{1}GS, 21^{1}G, 25^{0}G, 25^{3}S, 24^{5}GS, 25^{1}GF, 21^{F}GS, 20^{6}S, 20^{0}S

	Starts	1st	2nd	3rd	Win & Pl
Hurdles	7	1	0	2	3741
Chases	4	2	0	0	7979
Career Total	**25**	**7**	**4**	**5**	**30916**

110	11/01	Catt	3m1f110y	E(0-115)HHdl	G-F	£2730
137	9/01	Sedg	2m5f	D(0-120)HCh	GD	£3766
137	8/01	Ctml	3m2f	D(0-120)HCh	G-S	£4212
129	11/99	Sedg	2m5f	E Ch	GD	£3051
130	10/99	Carl	2m4f110y	E Ch	GD	£3680
116	12/98	Catt	2m	E Hdl	GD	£2430
94	10/98	Kels	2m110y	F Hdl	G-S	£2010

Total win prize-money £21880

Going: Sf: 0-3 GS: 1-3 Gd: 1-2 GF: - Fm: 1-3
Distance: 2m/2m3: 0-0 2m4-2m7: 1-5 **3m+: 2-6**
Track: **LH: 3-9** RH: 0-1 **Tight: 3-5** Gall: 0-2
Aids: **Bl: 1-1** Vi: 0-3 Tstrap: 0-0
Best Rating: 137 9/01 Sedg 2m5f good Ch

Fair chaser, stays three miles plus but effective at shorter. Likes to front-run, but his victories in the late summer of 2001 were gained with a measure of restraint employed. Seems most effective on good ground. Reverted to hurdles in October and scored a month later at Catterick.

Free Kevin

98 82

6-y-o b g Midyan (USA)-Island Desert (IRE) (Green Desert (USA))
Dr J R J Naylor R Cheetham

Placings:650060 **(3342)**
2001/02: 17^{6}F, 16^{5}GS, 16^{0}G, 16^{0}G, 16^{6}G, 19^{0}S

	Starts	1st	2nd	3rd	Win & Pl
Hurdles	6	0	0	0	0
Career Total	**6**	**0**	**0**	**0**	**0**

Going: Sf: 0-1 GS: 0-1 Gd: 0-3 GF: - Fm: 0-1
Distance: 2m/2m3: 0-5 2m4-2m7: 0-1 3m+: 0-0
Track: LH: 0-2 RH: 0-4 Tight: 0-3 Gall: 0-0
Aids: Bl: 0-0 Vi: 0-0 Tstrap: 0-0
Best Rating: 82 10/01 Tntn 2m1f firm Hdl

Free To Conker (IRE)

9-y-o b g Executive Perk-Golden Chestnut (Green Shoon)
B I Case Mrs Elizabeth Young & Mrs Hilary Pye

Placings:0/P/P **(2456)**
2001/02: 21^{P}S

	Starts	1st	2nd	3rd	Win & Pl
Hurdles	1	0	0	0	
Career Total	**3**	**0**	**0**	**0**	

Going: Sf: 0-1 GS: 0-0 Gd: 0-0 GF: - Fm: 0-0
Distance: 2m/2m3: 0-0 2m4-2m7: 0-1 3m+: 0-0
Track: LH: 0-0 RH: 0-0 Tight: 0-0 Gall: 0-0
Aids: Bl: 0-0 Vi: 0-0 Tstrap: 0-0
Best Rating: 56 11/98 Ludl 2m good NHF

Free To Run (IRE)

103 (43h)113+

8-y-o b g Satco (FR)-Lady Oats (Oats)
Mrs S J Smith Mrs S Smith

Placings:00040/100/40030044F-0045344 **(3439)**
2001/02: 20^{0}GS, 21^{0}G, 20^{4}GS, 25^{5}S, 20^{3}S, 26^{4}HY, 27^{4}HY

	Starts	1st	2nd	3rd	Win & Pl
Hurdles	1	0	0	0	0
Chases	6	0	0	1	1490
Career Total	**24**	**1**	**0**	**2**	**4546**

80	5/99	Dpat	2m1f172y	NHF	GD	£1994

Total win prize-money £1995

Going: Sf: 0-4 GS: 0-2 Gd: 0-1 GF: - Fm: 0-0
Distance: 2m/2m3: 0-0 2m4-2m7: 0-4 3m+: 0-3
Track: LH: 0-5 RH: 0-1 Tight: 0-3 Gall: 0-1
Aids: Bl: 0-0 Vi: 0-0 Tstrap: 0-0
Best Rating: 95 11/00 Dpat 2m6f soft Hdl

Free Will

92 92

5-y-o ch g Indian Ridge-Free Guest (Be My Guest (USA))
A Scott A & J Scott Ltd

Placings:20P **(2182)**
2001/02: 16^{2}GS, 17^{0}S, 16^{P}GS

	Starts	1st	2nd	3rd	Win & Pl
Hurdles	3	0	1	0	697
Career Total	**3**	**0**	**1**	**0**	**697**

Going: Sf: 0-1 GS: 0-2 Gd: 0-0 GF: - Fm: 0-0
Distance: 2m/2m3: 0-3 2m4-2m7: 0-0 3m+: 0-0
Track: LH: 0-3 RH: 0-0 Tight: 0-2 Gall: 0-0
Aids: Bl: 0-0 Vi: 0-0 Tstrap: 0-0
Best Rating: 92 10/01 Kels 2m110y gd-sft Hdl

Free-Valley-Mou (IRE)

70

6-y-o b g Ela-Mana-Mou-Kilcoy (USA) (Secreto (USA))
R Johnson Robert Johnson

Placings:P/44-P6 **(1195)**
2001/02: 17^{P}GS, 20^{6}G

	Starts	1st	2nd	3rd	Win & Pl
Hurdles	2	0	0	0	0
Career Total	**5**	**0**	**0**	**0**	**234**

Going: Sf: 0-0 GS: 0-1 Gd: 0-1 GF: - Fm: 0-0
Distance: 2m/2m3: 0-1 2m4-2m7: 0-1 3m+: 0-0
Track: LH: 0-0 RH: 0-1 Tight: 0-0 Gall: 0-0
Aids: Bl: 0-0 Vi: 0-0 Tstrap: 0-0
Best Rating: 73 5/00 Kels 2m110y good Hdl

Freebrough

8-y-o gr g Scallywag-Miss Anax (Anax)
M Tate M Tate

Placings:0-PP **(0370)**
2001/02: 19^{P}G, 16^{P}G

	Starts	1st	2nd	3rd	Win & Pl
Hurdles	2	0	0	0	
Career Total	**3**	**0**	**0**	**0**	

Going: Sf: 0-0 GS: 0-0 Gd: 0-2 GF: - Fm: 0-0
Distance: 2m/2m3: 0-1 2m4-2m7: 0-1 3m+: 0-0
Track: LH: 0-1 RH: 0-1 Tight: 0-0 Gall: 0-0
Aids: Bl: 0-0 Vi: 0-0 Tstrap: 0-0
Best Rating:

Freedom Fighter

11-y-o b g Fearless Action (USA)-Zuleika Hill (Yellow River)
Mrs Rosemary Gasson Mrs Rosemary Gasson

Placings:1PF2P/P303P-52PP43C **(4826)**
2001/02: 25^{5}G, 30^{2}GF, 26^{P}G, 28^{P}GF, 26^{4}HY, 23^{3}S, 26^{C}G

	Starts	1st	2nd	3rd	Win & Pl
Chases	7	0	1	1	1246
Career Total	**17**	**1**	**2**	**3**	**5792**

96	5/99	Strf	3m	H Ch	G-S	£3184

Total win prize-money £3184

Going: Sf: 0-2 GS: 0-0 Gd: 0-3 GF: - Fm: 0-2
Distance: 2m/2m3: 0-0 2m4-2m7: 0-0 3m+: 0-7
Track: LH: 0-3 RH: 0-3 Tight: 0-1 Gall: 0-2
Aids: Bl: 0-0 Vi: 0-0 Tstrap: 0-0
Best Rating: 107 5/00 Strf 3m gd-fm Ch

Winning pointer, prefers a sound surface.

Freedom Road (IRE)

8-y-o b g Mandalus-Cash Discount (Deep Run)
G A Swinbank Leading Star Racing

Placings:P0OP/50P0-P **(2179)**
2001/02: 23^{P}G

	Starts	1st	2nd	3rd	Win & Pl
Hurdles	1	0	0	0	
Career Total	**9**	**0**	**0**	**0**	**0**

Going: Sf: 0-0 GS: 0-0 Gd: 0-1 GF: - Fm: 0-0
Distance: 2m/2m3: 0-0 2m4-2m7: 0-1 3m+: 0-0
Track: LH: 0-1 RH: 0-0 Tight: 0-0 Gall: 0-0
Aids: Bl: 0-0 Vi: 0-0 Tstrap: 0-0
Best Rating: 81 11/00 Newc 2m4f soft Hdl

Freeline Fantasy (IRE)

87f 101f

5-y-o ch g Shernazar-Lollia Paulina (IRE) (Phardante (FR))

P R Webber Irving Struel & Geoffrey Thomas

Placings:3 **(4570)**
2001/02: 16^{3}G

	Starts	1st	2nd	3rd	Win & Pl
NH Flat	1	0	0	1	247
Career Total	**1**	**0**	**0**	**1**	**247**

Going: Sf: 0-0 GS: 0-0 Gd: 0-1 GF: - Fm: 0-0
Distance: 2m/2m3: 0-1 2m4-2m7: 0-0 3m+: 0-0
Track: LH: 0-0 RH: 0-1 Tight: 0-0 Gall: 0-0
Aids: Bl: 0-0 Vi: 0-0 Tstrap: 0-0
Best Rating: 101 4/02 Towc 2m good NHF

Out of a mare who placed in a fast-ground bumper, ran a promising race on his racecourse bow in a Towcester bumper.

Freestyler (IRE)

94 **91**

10-y-o b/br g Phardante (FR)-Financial Burden (Mandalus)
R Hollinshead Mrs B L Shaw

Placings:*40000/0/00/*UP-5 **(0053)**
2001/02: 17^{5}GS

	Starts	1st	2nd	3rd	Win & Pl
Chases	1	0	0	0	0
Career Total	**13**	**0**	**0**	**0**	**139**

Going: Sf: 0-0 GS: 0-1 Gd: 0-0 GF: - Fm: 0-0
Distance: 2m/2m3: 0-1 2m4-2m7: 0-0 3m+: 0-0
Track: LH: 0-1 RH: 0-0 Tight: 0-1 Gall: 0-0
Aids: Bl: 0-0 Vi: 0-0 Tstrap: 0-1
Best Rating: 91 5/01 Bang 2m1f110y gd-sft Ch

Freetown (IRE)

111(101c) (120c)**154**

6-y-o b g Shirley Heights-Pageantry (Welsh Pageant)
L Lungo Miss S Blumberg & R Nairn

Placings:32/111123-34113 **(4647)**
2001/02: 21^{3}GS, 16^{4}S, 20^{1}HY, 25^{1}GS, 24^{3}G

	Starts	1st	2nd	3rd	Win & Pl
Hurdles	3	1	0	2	38155
Chases	2	1	0	0	9047
Career Total	**13**	**6**	**2**	**4**	**64843**

154	3/02	Chel	3m1f110y	A HHdl	G-S	£32500
123	2/02	Ayr	2m4f	C Ch	HVY	£8807
136	12/00	Weth	2m7f	D Hdl	SFT	£3250
114	11/00	Carl	3m110y	E Hdl	HVY	£2396
121	10/00	Carl	3m110y	E Hdl	SFT	£2475
120	6/00	Prth	3m110y	E Hdl	SFT	£2933

Total win prize-money £52363

Going: Sf: 1-2 GS: 1-2 Gd: 0-1 GF: - Fm: 0-0
Distance: 2m/2m3: 0-1 2m4-2m7: 1-2 3m+: 1-2
Track: **LH: 2-4** RH: 0-1 Tight: 0-2 **Gall: 1-2**
Aids: Bl: 0-0 Vi: 0-0 Tstrap: 0-0
Best Rating: 154 4/02 Aint 3m110y good Hdl

His big pay day came when successful in the Pertemps Final at the Cheltenham Festival in March 2002. As effective over hurdles as fences, he stays beyond three miles and acts well with cut in the ground.

French Cedar

63 **88**

6-y-o b g Jupiter Island-Another Rumour (The Parson)
Mrs John Harrington (N J Henderson 18/1) Kevin Lee

Placings:*0-0*P4 **(4791a)**
2001/02: 20^{0}S, 24^{P}HY, 20^{4}Y

	Starts	1st	2nd	3rd	Win & Pl
Hurdles	3	0	0	0	331
Career Total	**4**	**0**	**0**	**0**	**331**

Going: Sf: 0-2 GS: 0-0 Gd: 0-0 GF: - Fm: 0-0
Distance: 2m/2m3: 0-0 2m4-2m7: 0-2 3m+: 0-1
Track: LH: 0-2 RH: 0-0 Tight: 0-0 Gall: 0-0
Aids: Bl: 0-0 Vi: 0-0 Tstrap: 0-0
Best Rating: 86 4/02 Gowr 2m4f yield Hdl

French Connection

92(105h) (81h)**71+**

7-y-o b g Tirol-Heaven-Liegh-Grey (Grey Desire)
B D Leavy S H Riley

Placings:4/5410631-500000005 **(4905)**
2001/02: 17^{5}GF, 20^{0}S, 16^{0}GF, 16^{0}GF, 19^{0}G, 17^{0}G, 16^{0}S, 17^{0}G, 17^{5}GF

	Starts	1st	2nd	3rd	Win & Pl
Hurdles	7	0	0	0	0
Chases	2	0	0	0	0
Career Total	**17**	**2**	**0**	**1**	**3938**

81	4/01	MRas	2m1f110y	G(0-95)HHdl	HVY	£1820
81	8/00	Uttx	2m	G(0-95)HHdl	G-F	£1904

Total win prize-money £3724

Going: Sf: 0-2 GS: 0-0 Gd: 0-3 GF: - Fm: 0-4
Distance: 2m/2m3: 0-8 2m4-2m7: 0-1 3m+: 0-0
Track: LH: 0-4 RH: 0-5 Tight: 0-3 Gall: 0-0
Aids: Bl: 0-7 Vi: 0-0 Tstrap: 0-1
Best Rating: 81 4/01 MRas 2m1f110y heavy Hdl

Plating-class hurdler, best at around two miles, acts on any ground.

French Executive (IRE)

102 **109**

7-y-o br g Beau Sher-Executive Move (IRE) (Executive Perk)
P F Nicholls T Chappell,R Eddy,Mrs Jackson,Mrs Solman

Placings:43-223216332 **(4883)**
2001/02: 22^{2}GF, 22^{2}GS, 22^{3}GF, 22^{2}HY, 19^{1}S, 17^{6}S, 19^{3}S, 22^{3}G, 22^{2}GF

	Starts	1st	2nd	3rd	Win & Pl
Hurdles	9	1	4	3	7907
Career Total	**11**	**1**	**4**	**4**	**8609**

109	1/02	Tntn	2m3f110y	E(0-105)HHdl	SFT	£2870

Total win prize-money £2870

Going: Sf: 1-4 GS: 0-1 Gd: 0-1 GF: - Fm: 0-3
Distance: 2m/2m3: 0-1 **2m4-2m7: 1-8** 3m+: 0-0
Track: LH: 0-3 **RH: 1-6 Tight: 1-6** Gall: 0-0
Aids: Bl: 0-1 Vi: 0-0 Tstrap: 0-0
Best Rating: 109 1/02 Tntn 2m3f110y soft Hdl

Quite a keen sort, he had been placed several times in novice hurdles, before getting off the mark over hurdles at Taunton in January 2002. Acts on any ground and is effective over two miles three, although he stays further.

French Fancy (IRE)

62 **25**

5-y-o gr m Paris House-Clipping (Kris)
B A Pearce J Salter

Placings:0 **(0674)**
2001/02: 16^{0}GF

	Starts	1st	2nd	3rd	Win & Pl
Hurdles	1	0	0	0	
Career Total	**1**	**0**	**0**	**0**	

Going: Sf: 0-0 GS: 0-0 Gd: 0-0 GF: - Fm: 0-1
Distance: 2m/2m3: 0-1 2m4-2m7: 0-0 3m+: 0-0
Track: LH: 0-1 RH: 0-0 Tight: 0-0 Gall: 0-0
Aids: Bl: 0-0 Vi: 0-0 Tstrap: 0-0
Best Rating: 25 6/01 Worc 2m gd-fm Hdl

French Master (IRE)

84 **59**

5-y-o b g Petardia-Reasonably French (Reasonable (FR))
A Crook (Jedd O'Keeffe 2/9) Ms Karen McNish

Placings:400-00 **(4283)**
2001/02: 17^{0}GF, 17^{0}GS

	Starts	1st	2nd	3rd	Win & Pl
Hurdles	2	0	0	0	
Career Total	**5**	**0**	**0**	**0**	**268**

Going: Sf: 0-0 GS: 0-1 Gd: 0-0 GF: - Fm: 0-1
Distance: 2m/2m3: 0-2 2m4-2m7: 0-0 3m+: 0-0
Track: LH: 0-0 RH: 0-2 Tight: 0-2 Gall: 0-0
Aids: Bl: 0-0 Vi: 0-0 Tstrap: 0-0
Best Rating: 52 3/02 MRas 2m1f110y gd-sft Hdl

French Style (IRE)

54 (107h)**110**

6-y-o b m Archway (IRE)-Rustic Stile (Rusticaro (FR))
D T Hughes B P Macmahon

Placings:4322/0211056-0P4FF5 **(4476a)**
2001/02: 20^{0}GY, 20^{P}YS, 16^{4}Y, 20^{F}HY, 20^{F}GS, 17^{5}SH

	Starts	1st	2nd	3rd	Win & Pl
Hurdles	2	0	0	0	0
Chases	4	0	0	0	387
Career Total	**17**	**2**	**3**	**1**	**15663**

114	12/00	Punc	2m	Hdl	SH	£6072
110	9/00	List	2m	Hdl	HVY	£4968

Total win prize-money £11040

Going: Sf: 0-1 GS: 0-1 Gd: 0-0 GF: - Fm: 0-0
Distance: 2m/2m3: 0-2 2m4-2m7: 0-4 3m+: 0-0
Track: LH: 0-2 RH: 0-2 Tight: 0-1 Gall: 0-0
Aids: Bl: 0-0 Vi: 0-0 Tstrap: 0-0
Best Rating: 116 1/01 Naas 2m3f soft Hdl

Frenchman's Creek

118 **168**

8-y-o b g Emperor Fountain-Hollow Creek (Tarqogan)
H Morrison Rory Sweet & Panda Wilson

Placings:3/231/5F222143-13313 **(4913)**
2001/02: 20^{1}G, 25^{3}G, 24^{3}S, 24^{1}GS, 29^{3}G

	Starts	1st	2nd	3rd	Win & Pl
Chases	5	2	0	3	82430
Career Total	**17**	**4**	**4**	**6**	**103324**

168	3/02	Chel	3m110y	A HCh	G-S	£45500
148	11/01	Chel	2m4f110y	D(0-125)HCh	GD	£12662
145	3/01	Asct	2m3f110y	C Ch	SFT	£6191
122	1/00	Ludl	2m5f	F Hdl	G-S	£2380

Total win prize-money £66733

Going: Sf: 0-1 GS: 1-1 Gd: 1-3 GF: - Fm: 0-0
Distance: 2m/2m3: 0-0 2m4-2m7: 1-1 3m+: 1-4
Track: **LH: 2-4** RH: 0-1 Tight: 0-0 **Gall: 2-4**
Aids: Bl: 0-0 Vi: 0-0 Tstrap: 0-0

Best Rating: 168 3/02 Chel 3m110y gd-sft Ch

He has taken well to fences and met some decent sorts before breaking his duck in a novice chase at Ascot in March 2001. Made a wining return at Cheltenham in November of 2001 and ran some fair races in defeat after that before posting a top class performance when successful in the Ritz Club at Cheltenham in March 2002. He stays three miles and is often held up. Has won on good and soft ground.

Fresh Prince

14-y-o b g Balinger-Lasses Nightshade (Deadly Nightshade)
Miss A Nolan Mrs Vanessa Ramm

Placings:P/P (0497)
2001/02: 25^{P}G

	Starts	1st	2nd	3rd	Win & Pl
Chases	1	0	0	0	
Career Total	**2**	**0**	**0**	**0**	

Going: Sf: 0-0 GS: 0-0 Gd: 0-1 GF: - Fm: 0-0
Distance: 2m/2m3: 0-0 2m4-2m7: 0-0 3m+: 0-1
Track: LH: 0-0 RH: 0-1 Tight: 0-0 Gall: 0-0
Aids: Bl: 0-0 Vi: 0-0 Tstrap: 0-0
Best Rating:

Friar Waddon

9-y-o b g Pablond-Looking Swell (Simbir)
K Cumings (R J Baker 20/1) P J Clarke

Placings:F6P3 (4735)
2001/02: 24^{F}GF, 22^{6}GF, 26^{P}G, 23^{3}F

	Starts	1st	2nd	3rd	Win & Pl
Hurdles	1	0	0	0	0
Chases	3	0	0	1	271
Career Total	**4**	**0**	**0**	**1**	**271**

Going: Sf: 0-0 GS: 0-0 Gd: 0-1 GF: - Fm: 0-3
Distance: 2m/2m3: 0-0 2m4-2m7: 0-1 3m+: 0-3
Track: LH: 0-3 RH: 0-1 Tight: 0-3 Gall: 0-0
Aids: Bl: 0-0 Vi: 0-0 Tstrap: 0-0
Best Rating: 105 4/02 Extr 2m7f110y firm Ch

Fair pointer/hunter, handles any ground.

Friedhelmo (GER)

71 **75**

6-y-o ch g Dashing Blade-Fox For Gold (Glint Of Gold)
Miss Venetia Williams G H Leatham

Placings:03/1-0 (4879)
2001/02: 16^{0}G

	Starts	1st	2nd	3rd	Win & Pl
Hurdles	1		0	0	0
Career Total	**4**	**1**	**0**	**1**	**2773**

109 5/00 Worc 2m E Hdl G-F £2401
Total win prize-money £2401

Going: Sf: 0-0 GS: 0-0 Gd: 0-1 GF: - Fm: 0-0
Distance: 2m/2m3: 0-1 2m4-2m7: 0-0 3m+: 0-0
Track: LH: 0-0 RH: 0-1 Tight: 0-0 Gall: 0-0
Aids: Bl: 0-0 Vi: 0-0 Tstrap: 0-0
Best Rating: 109 5/00 Worc 2m gd-fm Hdl

Friendly Dancer

79f **58f**

7-y-o b m Environment Friend-Harvest Dance (Mill Reef (USA))
T P McGovern Mrs Sally Rowe

Placings:00 (4595)
2001/02: 16^{0}S, 16^{0}G

	Starts	1st	2nd	3rd	Win & Pl
NH Flat	2	0	0	0	
Career Total	**2**	**0**	**0**	**0**	

Going: Sf: 0-1 GS: 0-0 Gd: 0-1 GF: - Fm: 0-0
Distance: 2m/2m3: 0-2 2m4-2m7: 0-0 3m+: 0-0
Track: LH: 0-1 RH: 0-1 Tight: 0-0 Gall: 0-0
Aids: Bl: 0-0 Vi: 0-0 Tstrap: 0-0
Best Rating: 58 4/02 Uttx 2m good NHF

Friendly George (IRE)

6-y-o b g Febrino-Deepfry (Deep Run)
D J Caro Mrs J F Billington

Placings:00P (3355)
2001/02: 16^{0}S, 17^{0}GS, 24^{P}HY

	Starts	1st	2nd	3rd	Win & Pl
NH Flat	2	0	0	0	0
Hurdles	1	0	0	0	0
Career Total	**3**	**0**	**0**	**0**	

Going: Sf: 0-2 GS: 0-1 Gd: 0-0 GF: - Fm: 0-0
Distance: 2m/2m3: 0-2 2m4-2m7: 0-0 3m+: 0-1
Track: LH: 0-3 RH: 0-0 Tight: 0-1 Gall: 0-0
Aids: Bl: 0-0 Vi: 0-0 Tstrap: 0-0
Best Rating:

Frileux Royal (FR)

109(101c) (107c)**96**

9-y-o br g Sarpedon (FR)-La Frileuse (FR) (El Toro (FR))
T R George Nelson Morrison Underwriting Agency

Placings:F/12411PU0/443RPP-2R0RR0120P (4889)
2001/02: 24^{2}GF, 34^{R}GF, 31^{0}G, 26^{R}HY, 31^{R}GS, 21^{0}GS, 26^{1}GS, 24^{2}G, 24^{0}G, 26^{P}G

	Starts	1st	2nd	3rd	Win & Pl
Hurdles	4	1	1	0	5097
Chases	6	0	1	0	850
Career Total	**25**	**4**	**3**	**1**	**23621**

96 2/02 Ludl 3m2f110y E(0-110)HHdl G-S £3688
12/99 Seic 3m110y Ch SFT £6459
11/99 Agtn 2m6f110y Ch HVY £3445
9/99 Chag 2m6f110y Ch SFT £2153
Total win prize-money £15746

Going: Sf: 0-1 GS: 1-3 Gd: 0-4 GF: - Fm: 0-2
Distance: 2m/2m3: 0-0 2m4-2m7: 0-1 **3m+: 1-9**
Track: LH: 0-5 **RH: 1-4** Tight: 0-0 Gall: 0-2
Aids: Bl: 0-0 Vi: 0-1 Tstrap: 0-0
Best Rating: 139 11/00 Chel 3m7f soft Ch

Won three times in France. Largely disappointing in Britain, but was sweetened up by a spell of hunting to win a handicap hurdle in February 2002. Stays well and acts well with cut in the ground.

Frog Street (IRE)

8-y-o b m Orchestra-Credora Bay (Orange Bay)
P R Webber Henry T Cole

Placings:0FPP-P (0044)
2001/02: 17^{P}GS

	Starts	1st	2nd	3rd	Win & Pl
Hurdles	1	0	0	0	
Career Total	**5**	**0**	**0**	**0**	

Going: Sf: 0-0 GS: 0-1 Gd: 0-0 GF: - Fm: 0-0
Distance: 2m/2m3: 0-1 2m4-2m7: 0-0 3m+: 0-0
Track: LH: 0-0 RH: 0-1 Tight: 0-0 Gall: 0-0
Aids: Bl: 0-0 Vi: 0-0 Tstrap: 0-0
Best Rating: 66 11/00 Extr 2m1f gd-sft NHF

Frogman (IRE)

8-y-o b g Mandalus-Le Tricolore Token (Damsire Unregistered)
R T Phillips D J Hillyard

Placings:055250/P (4588)
2001/02: 22^{P}G

	Starts	1st	2nd	3rd	Win & Pl
Hurdles	1	0	0	0	
Career Total	**7**	**0**	**1**	**0**	**1368**

Going: Sf: 0-0 GS: 0-0 Gd: 0-1 GF: - Fm: 0-0
Distance: 2m/2m3: 0-0 2m4-2m7: 0-1 3m+: 0-0
Track: LH: 0-0 RH: 0-1 Tight: 0-0 Gall: 0-0
Aids: Bl: 0-0 Vi: 0-0 Tstrap: 0-0
Best Rating: 97 2/00 Leic 2m4f110y gd-sft Hdl

Frogmarch (USA)

107 **127**

12-y-o ch g Diesis-La Francaise (USA) (Jim French (USA))
K Bell John E Mills

Placings:511121/55/P5/2F33/2240-245 (4193)
2001/02: 22^{2}S, 25^{4}S, 25^{5}GS

	Starts	1st	2nd	3rd	Win & Pl
Hurdles	3	0	1	0	2964
Career Total	**21**	**4**	**5**	**2**	**22248**

128 4/96 NAbb 2m1f C(0-130)HHdl G-S £3468
124 3/96 Wind 2m E Hdl SFT £2617
111 3/96 Newb 2m110y D(0-110)HHdl G-S £3826
104 2/96 Sand 2m110y F Hdl SFT £2883
Total win prize-money £12797

Going: Sf: 0-2 GS: 0-1 Gd: 0-0 GF: - Fm: 0-0
Distance: 2m/2m3: 0-0 2m4-2m7: 0-1 3m+: 0-2
Track: LH: 0-1 RH: 0-1 Tight: 0-0 Gall: 0-1
Aids: Bl: 0-0 Vi: 0-0 Tstrap: 0-0
Best Rating: 128 4/96 NAbb 2m1f gd-sft Hdl

Lightly-raced staying hurdler. Suited by soft ground and stays three miles.

From Little Acorns (IRE)

100 **104**

6-y-o b g Denel (FR)-Mount Gawn (Harwell)
Ferdy Murphy Mrs A T B Kearney

Placings:00-2005 (3690)
2001/02: 20^{2}G, 20^{0}S, 16^{0}GS, 20^{5}HY

	Starts	1st	2nd	3rd	Win & Pl
Hurdles	4	0	1	0	1571
Career Total	**6**	**0**	**1**	**0**	**1571**

Going: Sf: 0-2 GS: 0-1 Gd: 0-1 GF: - Fm: 0-0
Distance: 2m/2m3: 0-1 2m4-2m7: 0-3 3m+: 0-0
Track: LH: 0-4 RH: 0-0 Tight: 0-0 Gall: 0-0
Aids: Bl: 0-0 Vi: 0-0 Tstrap: 0-0
Best Rating: 101 11/01 Hayd 2m4f good Hdl

Ex-Irish, has shown ability over hurdles on fast ground and got off the mark under those conditions at Hexham in May 2002.

Frontier Flight (USA)

88 **57**

12-y-o b g Flying Paster (USA)-Sly Charmer (USA) (Valdez (USA))
P W Hiatt S F Holder

Placings:645/2/42152213P00/52FF1F5642**P15/3P64** 641225411246F00/00PP0P/2**PPP**/412F3P0-00P (1275)
2001/02: 19^{0}G, 18^{0}VS, 20^{P}GF

	Starts	1st	2nd	3rd	Win & Pl
Hurdles	3	0	0	0	
Career Total	**67**	**8**	**11**	**3**	**30941**

89	7/00	Wolv	2m4f110y	F(0-110)HHdl	G-S	£3081
100	11/97	Tntn	2m3f110y	D(0-120)HHdl	GD	£2937
101	11/97	Wwck	2m3f	G(0-100)HHdl	G-S	£1638
88	8/97	Sthl	2m4f110y	G(0-95)HHdl	G-F	£1[illegible]
85	12/96	Tntn	2m3f	E(0-100)HCh	GD	£3036
101	8/96	Sthl	2m4f110y	E(0-115)HHdl	GD	£2924
89	11/95	Worc	2m	F(0-105)HHdl	G-F	£2477
80	9/95	Worc	2m	G(0-95)HHdl	G-F	£1982

Total win prize-money £19938

Going: Sf: 0-0 GS: 0-0 Gd: 0-1 GF: - Fm: 0-1
Distance: 2m/2m3: 0-2 2m4-2m7: 0-1 3m+: 0-0
Track: LH: 0-2 RH: 0-0 Tight: 0-2 Gall: 0-0
Aids: Bl: 0-0 Vi: 0-0 Tstrap: 0-0
Best Rating: 101 12/97 Fknm 2m4f gd-sft Hdl

Frontis

79 **45**

5-y-o ch g Be My Chief (USA)-Heavy Rock (IRE) (Ballad Rock)
J G Fitzgerald Marquesa De Moratalla

Placings:*0-3300* (4874)
2001/02: 17^{3}G, 16^{3}S, 20^{0}G, 20^{0}G

	Starts	1st	2nd	3rd	Win & Pl
NH Flat	2	0	0	2	503
Hurdles	2	0	0	0	0
Career Total	**5**	**0**	**0**	**2**	**503**

Going: Sf: 0-1 GS: 0-0 Gd: 0-3 GF: - Fm: 0-0
Distance: 2m/2m3: 0-2 2m4-2m7: 0-2 3m+: 0-0
Track: LH: 0-3 RH: 0-1 Tight: 0-1 Gall: 0-1
Aids: Bl: 0-0 Vi: 0-0 Tstrap: 0-0
Best Rating: 91 11/01 Uttx 2m soft NHF

Well beaten in a soft-ground bumper at Haydock on his debut back in February 2001, he shaped well on a sounder surface at Sedgefield in November.

Frosty Canyon

113(112h) **159**

9-y-o b g Arctic Lord-Rose Ravine (Deep Run)
P R Webber Mrs P Sherwood

Placings:*1210*/1564/P041144-122114 (4232)
2001/02: 24^{1}GS, 24^{2}G, 24^{2}G, 22^{1}G, 24^{1}S, 24^{4}GS

	Starts	1st	2nd	3rd	Win & Pl
Chases	6	3	2	0	30931
Career Total	**21**	**8**	**3**	**0**	**62308**

159	2/02	Newb	3m	C Ch	SFT	£7150
146	1/02	Newb	2m6f110y	D Ch	GD	£5525
146	10/01	Strf	3m	D Ch	G-S	£4127
151	1/01	Wwck	3m1f	B HHdl	SFT	£8632
136	12/00	Kemp	3m110y	C(0-135)HHdl	G-S	£7410
115	11/99	Hayd	2m	D Hdl	GD	£3403
123	2/99	Sand	2m110y	H NHF	G-S	£1588
118	11/98	Chep	2m110y	H NHF	G-S	£1660

Total win prize-money £39497

Going: Sf: 1-1 GS: 1-2 Gd: 1-3 GF: - Fm: 0-0
Distance: 2m/2m3: 0-0 2m4-2m7: 1-1 **3m+: 2-5**
Track: **LH: 3-5** RH: 0-1 Tight: 1-1 **Gall: 2-4**
Aids: Bl: 1-3 **Vi: 2-3** Tstrap: 0-0
Best Rating: 159 2/02 Newb 3m soft Ch

A very useful novice chaser, he is a decent performer when able to go his own pace in a small field, but struggled with the strong pace before staying on to finish fourth in the Royal & SunAlliance Chase at the 2002 Festival. Stays three miles and usually wears a visor or blinkers. Acts on good and soft ground and is a consistent sort.

Frosty Carol

8-y-o b m Arctic Lord-Chic Carolyn (Red Sunset)
M C Pipe M C Pipe

Placings:P0P (2483)
2001/02: 22^{P}GF, 19^{0}GS, 17^{P}HY

	Starts	1st	2nd	3rd	Win & Pl
Hurdles	3	0	0	0	
Career Total	**3**	**0**	**0**	**0**	

Going: Sf: 0-1 GS: 0-1 Gd: 0-0 GF: - Fm: 0-1
Distance: 2m/2m3: 0-1 2m4-2m7: 0-2 3m+: 0-0
Track: LH: 0-2 RH: 0-1 Tight: 0-3 Gall: 0-0
Aids: Bl: 0-0 Vi: 0-0 Tstrap: 0-0
Best Rating: mfy

Frosty Mistress

100 **104**

6-y-o b m Arctic Lord-Mistress Caramore (IRE) (Moscow Society (USA))
Mrs Susan Nock Gerard Nock

Placings:*00*-2P0 (3874)
2001/02: 16^{2}GS, 22^{P}S, 16^{0}S

	Starts	1st	2nd	3rd	Win & Pl
Hurdles	3	0	1	0	704
Career Total	**5**	**0**	**1**	**0**	**704**

Going: Sf: 0-2 GS: 0-1 Gd: 0-0 GF: - Fm: 0-0
Distance: 2m/2m3: 0-2 2m4-2m7: 0-1 3m+: 0-0
Track: LH: 0-1 RH: 0-2 Tight: 0-1 Gall: 0-1
Aids: Bl: 0-0 Vi: 0-0 Tstrap: 0-0
Best Rating: 104 1/02 Sthl 2m gd-sft Hdl

Stayed on into second in a modest race on her hurdling debut but held subsequently.

Frozen Assets (IRE)

88f **90f**

5-y-o br g Shardari-Frost Bound (Hawaiian Return (USA))
M Pitman The Nicky Watts Partnership

Placings:*5* (4887)
2001/02: 18^{5}GF

	Starts	1st	2nd	3rd	Win & Pl
NH Flat	1	0	0	0	0
Career Total	**1**	**0**	**0**	**0**	**0**

Going: Sf: 0-0 GS: 0-0 Gd: 0-0 GF: - Fm: 0-1
Distance: 2m/2m3: 0-1 2m4-2m7: 0-0 3m+: 0-0
Track: LH: 0-1 RH: 0-0 Tight: 0-1 Gall: 0-0
Aids: Bl: 0-0 Vi: 0-0 Tstrap: 0-0
Best Rating: 90 4/02 Font 2m2f110y gd-fm NHF

Some ability on his bumper debut.

Fruitcase

4-y-o b f Alderbrook-Nutcase (Idiots Delight)
Miss K Marks Nick Shutts

Placings:*0* (3985)
2001/02: 16^{0}G

	Starts	1st	2nd	3rd	Win & Pl
NH Flat	1	0	0	0	
Career Total	**1**	**0**	**0**	**0**	

Going: Sf: 0-0 GS: 0-0 Gd: 0-1 GF: - Fm: 0-0
Distance: 2m/2m3: 0-1 2m4-2m7: 0-0 3m+: 0-0
Track: LH: 0-0 RH: 0-1 Tight: 0-0 Gall: 0-0
Aids: Bl: 0-0 Vi: 0-0 Tstrap: 0-0
Best Rating:

Fuegian

7-y-o ch g Arazi (USA)-Well Beyond (IRE) (Don't Forget Me)
M Madgwick W V Roker

Placings:F/P (1221)
2001/02: 18^{P}GF

	Starts	1st	2nd	3rd	Win & Pl
Hurdles	1	0	0	0	
Career Total	**2**	**0**	**0**	**0**	

Going: Sf: 0-0 GS: 0-0 Gd: 0-0 GF: - Fm: 0-1
Distance: 2m/2m3: 0-1 2m4-2m7: 0-0 3m+: 0-0
Track: LH: 0-1 RH: 0-0 Tight: 0-1 Gall: 0-0
Aids: Bl: 0-0 Vi: 0-0 Tstrap: 0-0
Best Rating:

Fuero Real (FR)

(81h) (61h)

7-y-o b g Highest Honor (FR)-Highest Pleasure (USA) (Foolish Pleasure (USA))
Simon T Lewis (R J Hodges 16/5) Simon T Lewis

Placings:0P2P/0UP0/0P-006U0P (4565)
2001/02: 16^{0}G, 16^{0}S, 17^{6}S, 21^{U}GS, 21^{0}GF, 16^{P}G

	Starts	1st	2nd	3rd	Win & Pl
Hurdles	6	0	0	0	0
Career Total	**16**	**0**	**1**	**0**	**704**

Going: Sf: 0-2 GS: 0-1 Gd: 0-2 GF: - Fm: 0-1
Distance: 2m/2m3: 0-4 2m4-2m7: 0-2 3m+: 0-0
Track: LH: 0-0 RH: 0-6 Tight: 0-1 Gall: 0-1
Aids: Bl: 0-0 Vi: 0-0 Tstrap: 0-0
Best Rating: 81 4/99 Tntn 2m1f firm Hdl

Fujiyama II (FR)

103(65c) (86c)125

9-y-o gr g Royal Charter (FR)-Seville (FR) (Quart De Vin (FR))

Mrs L C Taylor (S & W Kalley 2/7) Mrs L C Taylor

Placings:0121/P5/5FP/10P0-13P4P0P0 (4572)

2001/02: 21^{1}S, 18^{3}VS, 18^{P}GS, 17^{4}S, 20^{P}S, 16^{0}S, 20^{P}S, 20^{0}G

	Starts	1st	2nd	3rd	Win & Pl
Hurdles	6	1	0	1	6045
Chases	2	0	0	0	236
Career Total	**21**	**4**	**1**	**1**	**39448**

125	4/01	Plum	2m5f	E(0-115)HHdl	SFT	£2408
125	1/01	Plum	2m	E(0-115)HHdl	HVY	£3493
	11/97	Autl	2m2f	Hdl	HLD	£16835
	9/97	Autl	2m2f	Hdl	SFT	£11223

Total win prize-money £33960

Going: Sf: 1-5 GS: 0-1 Gd: 0-1 GF: - Fm: 0-0
Distance: 2m/2m3: 0-4 2m4-2m7: 1-4 3m+: 0-0
Track: LH: 1-5 RH: 0-1 Tight: 1-2 Gall: 0-0
Aids: Bl: 0-0 Vi: 0-0 Tstrap: 0-1
Best Rating: 125 4/01 Plum 2m5f soft Hdl

Full Ahead (IRE)

103 117

5-y-o b g Slip Anchor-Foulard (IRE) (Sadler's Wells (USA))

A King Nigel Bunter

Placings:562-210 (4633)

2001/02: 18^{2}GF, 19^{1}GF, 20^{0}GF

	Starts	1st	2nd	3rd	Win & Pl
Hurdles	3	1	1	0	3593
Career Total	**6**	**1**	**2**	**0**	**4309**

104	5/01	Ling	2m3f110y	E Hdl	G-F	£2838

Total win prize-money £2839

Going: Sf: 0-0 GS: 0-0 Gd: 0-0 GF: - Fm: 1-3
Distance: 2m/2m3: 0-1 2m4-2m7: 1-2 3m+: 0-0
Track: LH: 1-2 RH: 0-1 Tight: 1-2 Gall: 0-0
Aids: Bl: 0-0 Vi: 0-0 Tstrap: 0-0
Best Rating: 117 4/02 Asct 2m4f gd-fm Hdl

He got off the mark over hurdles in a novice event at Lingfield in May 2001, but went missing afterwards. Suited by two and a half miles and fast ground.

Full Egalite

93 69

6-y-o gr g Ezzoud (IRE)-Milva (Jellaby)

B R Johnson Miss Julie Reeves

Placings:U6 (4512)

2001/02: 17^{U}S, 21^{6}G

	Starts	1st	2nd	3rd	Win & Pl
Hurdles	2	0	0	0	0
Career Total	**2**	**0**	**0**	**0**	**0**

Going: Sf: 0-1 GS: 0-0 Gd: 0-1 GF: - Fm: 0-0
Distance: 2m/2m3: 0-1 2m4-2m7: 0-1 3m+: 0-0
Track: LH: 0-1 RH: 0-1 Tight: 0-2 Gall: 0-0
Aids: Bl: 0-1 Vi: 0-0 Tstrap: 0-0
Best Rating: 69 2/02 Folk 2m1f110y soft Hdl

Full Irish (IRE)

105 137

6-y-o ch g Rashar (USA)-Ross Gale (Strong Gale)

L Lungo D Stronach

Placings:2-11F111 (4888)

2001/02: 17^{1}G, 16^{1}S, 16^{F}GS, 17^{1}HY, 20^{1}GS, 16^{1}G

	Starts	1st	2nd	3rd	Win & Pl
NH Flat	2	2	0	0	3745
Hurdles	4	3	0	0	12987
Career Total	**7**	**5**	**1**	**0**	**17544**

127	4/02	Prth	2m110y	D Hdl	GD	£3874
137	3/02	Donc	2m4f	C Hdl	G-S	£5648
115	1/02	Sedg	2m1f	D Hdl	HVY	£3464
121	11/01	Hayd	2m	H NHF	SFT	£2170
120	10/01	Sedg	2m1f	H NHF	GD	£1575

Total win prize-money £16733

Going: Sf: 2-2 GS: 1-2 Gd: 2-2 GF: - Fm: 0-0
Distance: 2m/2m3: 4-5 2m4-2m7: 1-1 3m+: 0-0
Track: LH: 4-5 RH: 1-1 Tight: 2-2 Gall: 1-2
Aids: Bl: 0-0 Vi: 0-0 Tstrap: 0-0
Best Rating: 137 3/02 Donc 2m4f gd-sft Hdl

Easy winner of bumpers in the autumn of 2001, benefited from intensive schooling to score on his second run over hurdles and followed up at Doncaster in March. Looks a decent prospect. Acts on an easy surface. Suited by distances around two miles.

Full On

69f 54f

5-y-o b g Le Moss-Flighty Dove (Cruise Missile)

A M Hales Andrew L Cohen

Placings:0 (4269)

2001/02: 16^{0}S

	Starts	1st	2nd	3rd	Win & Pl
NH Flat	1	0	0	0	
Career Total	**1**	**0**	**0**	**0**	

Going: Sf: 0-1 GS: 0-0 Gd: 0-0 GF: - Fm: 0-0
Distance: 2m/2m3: 0-1 2m4-2m7: 0-0 3m+: 0-0
Track: LH: 0-1 RH: 0-0 Tight: 0-0 Gall: 0-0
Aids: Bl: 0-0 Vi: 0-0 Tstrap: 0-0
Best Rating: 54 3/02 Chep 2m110y soft NHF

Full Suit

6-y-o b m Local Suitor (USA)-Dereks Daughter (Derek H)

C E N Smith Mrs J Smith

Placings:00 (4873)

2001/02: 17^{0}GS, 16^{0}GF

	Starts	1st	2nd	3rd	Win & Pl
NH Flat	2	0	0	0	
Career Total	**2**	**0**	**0**	**0**	

Going: Sf: 0-0 GS: 0-1 Gd: 0-0 GF: - Fm: 0-1
Distance: 2m/2m3: 0-2 2m4-2m7: 0-0 3m+: 0-0
Track: LH: 0-1 RH: 0-1 Tight: 0-1 Gall: 0-0
Aids: Bl: 0-0 Vi: 0-0 Tstrap: 0-0
Best Rating:

Fullopep

106 144

8-y-o b g Dunbeath (USA)-Suggia (Alzao (USA))

Mrs M Reveley Mr & Mrs W J Williams

Placings:112/1155/PP-113350 (2688)

2001/02: 16^{1}G, 16^{1}GF, 20^{3}G, 20^{3}G, 16^{5}G, 19^{0}G

	Starts	1st	2nd	3rd	Win & Pl
Chases	6	2	0	2	11076
Career Total	**15**	**6**	**1**	**2**	**27515**

144	5/01	Newc	2m110y	D(0-125)HCh	G-F	£4696
135	5/01	Weth	2m	E(0-115)HCh	GD	£3346
135	11/99	Sedg	2m5f	C Ch	GD	£6937
132	10/99	Sedg	2m5f	E Ch	GD	£3436
118	9/98	Sedg	2m1f	E Hdl	GD	£2687
104	9/98	Sedg	2m1f	E Hdl	G-F	£2337

Total win prize-money £23442

Going: Sf: 0-0 GS: 0-0 Gd: 1-5 GF: - Fm: 1-1
Distance: 2m/2m3: 2-3 2m4-2m7: 0-3 3m+: 0-0
Track: LH: 2-6 RH: 0-0 Tight: 0-0 Gall: 1-2
Aids: Bl: 0-0 Vi: 0-0 Tstrap: 0-0
Best Rating: 144 10/01 Weth 2m4f110y good Ch

Notched up two wins on the trot in May of 2001, both of which over two miles, on good and good to firm ground. Stays two and a half miles.

Funcheon Gale

15-y-o b g Strong Gale-Funcheon Breeze (Deep Run)

Mrs A E Lee W J Lee

Placings:60PF23/11U031P1/14F33/33P/PP-P (0326)

2001/02: 21^{P}G

	Starts	1st	2nd	3rd	Win & Pl
Chases	1	0	0	0	
Career Total	**25**	**5**	**1**	**6**	**23425**

111	5/97	Chep	3m	C(0-130)HCh	GD	£4601
103	3/97	Towc	2m6f	C(0-130)HCh	G-F	£4647
89	11/96	Folk	3m2f	F(0-100)HCh	GD	£4302
105	6/96	Worc	2m7f	E(0-100)HCh	GD	£3104
84	5/96	Towc	2m6f	E(0-100)HCh	G-S	£3172

Total win prize-money £19829

Going: Sf: 0-0 GS: 0-0 Gd: 0-1 GF: - Fm: 0-0
Distance: 2m/2m3: 0-0 2m4-2m7: 0-1 3m+: 0-0
Track: LH: 0-0 RH: 0-1 Tight: 0-1 Gall: 0-0
Aids: Bl: 0-0 Vi: 0-0 Tstrap: 0-0
Best Rating: 111 5/97 Chep 3m good Ch

Fundy (IRE)

99(101c) (90c)88

13-y-o b g Arapahos (FR)-S T Blue (Blue Rullah)

Mrs H Dalton A J Brazier

Placings:1-P00 (0671)

2001/02: 25^{P}G, 20^{0}GS, 24^{0}G

	Starts	1st	2nd	3rd	Win & Pl
Hurdles	2	0	0	0	0
Chases	1	0	0	0	0
Career Total	**4**	**1**	**0**	**0**	**2655**

90	4/01	Plum	2m4f	F Ch	SFT	£2655

Total win prize-money £2655

Going: Sf: 0-0 GS: 0-1 Gd: 0-2 GF: - Fm: 0-0
Distance: 2m/2m3: 0-0 2m4-2m7: 0-1 3m+: 0-2
Track: LH: 0-2 RH: 0-1 Tight: 0-1 Gall: 0-0
Aids: Bl: 0-0 Vi: 0-0 Tstrap: 0-0
Best Rating: 90 4/01 Plum 2m4f soft Ch

Funky

97 78

9-y-o ch m Classic Music (USA)-Foreno (Formidable (USA))

J Mackie The Higham Partnership

Placings:005004/214P/03P/4310-60 (0419)
2001/02: 17^{6}G, 20^{0}G

	Starts	1st	2nd	3rd	Win & Pl
Hurdles	2	0	0	0	0
Career Total	**19**	**2**	**1**	**2**	**4308**

88	11/00	Uttx	2m	G(0-90)HHdl	HVY	£1498
77	5/98	Hexm	2m	G(0-95)HHdl	FRM	£1897

Total win prize-money £3395

Going: Sf: 0-0 GS: 0-0 Gd: 0-2 GF: - Fm: 0-0
Distance: 2m/2m3: 0-1 2m4-2m7: 0-1 3m+: 0-0
Track: LH: 0-1 RH: 0-1 Tight: 0-1 Gall: 0-0
Aids: Bl: 0-0 Vi: 0-0 Tstrap: 0-0
Best Rating: 88 11/00 Uttx 2m heavy Hdl

Funny Farm

12-y-o ch g Funny Man-Ba Ba Belle (Petit Instant)
Alan Walter Mrs Jane Walter

Placings:3/P (3984)
2001/02: 31^{P}GS

	Starts	1st	2nd	3rd	Win & Pl
Chases	1	0	0	0	
Career Total	**2**	**0**	**0**	**1**	**413**

Going: Sf: 0-0 GS: 0-1 Gd: 0-0 GF: - Fm: 0-0
Distance: 2m/2m3: 0-0 2m4-2m7: 0-0 3m+: 0-1
Track: LH: 0-0 RH: 0-0 Tight: 0-0 Gall: 0-0
Aids: Bl: 0-0 Vi: 0-0 Tstrap: 0-0
Best Rating: 81 4/00 Thrn 3m gd-sft Ch

Funny Genie (FR)

87 90
9-y-o b g Genereux Genie-Sauteuse De Retz (FR) (Funny Hobby)
Mrs L C Taylor Mrs L C Taylor

Placings:P/P0PP11/P62331P/P-5U4 (0599)
2001/02: 21^{5}GF, 16^{U}GF, 16^{4}G

	Starts	1st	2nd	3rd	Win & Pl
Chases	3	0	0	0	0
Career Total	**18**	**3**	**1**	**2**	**9148**

103	3/00	Folk	2m	F(0-90)HCh	G-F	£2452
88	2/98	Folk	2m1f110y	F(0-95)HHdl	G-F	£2136
90	2/98	Hrfd	2m1f	F(0-90)HHdl	GD	£2570

Total win prize-money £7159

Going: Sf: 0-0 GS: 0-0 Gd: 0-1 GF: - Fm: 0-2
Distance: 2m/2m3: 0-2 2m4-2m7: 0-1 3m+: 0-0
Track: LH: 0-2 RH: 0-1 Tight: 0-2 Gall: 0-1
Aids: Bl: 0-0 Vi: 0-3 Tstrap: 0-0
Best Rating: 103 3/00 Folk 2m gd-fm Ch

Furry Fox (IRE)

14-y-o b g Furry Glen-Pillow Chat (Le Bavard (FR))
T Jewitt T Jewitt

Placings:0/036153/P2P/6-6P (4826)
2001/02: 26^{6}HY, 26^{P}G

	Starts	1st	2nd	3rd	Win & Pl
Chases	2	0	0	0	0
Career Total	**13**	**1**	**1**	**2**	**5016**

79	2/97	Font	3m2f110y	E(0-100)HCh	SFT	£3183

Total win prize-money £3184

Going: Sf: 0-1 GS: 0-0 Gd: 0-1 GF: - Fm: 0-0
Distance: 2m/2m3: 0-0 2m4-2m7: 0-0 3m+: 0-2
Track: LH: 0-2 RH: 0-0 Tight: 0-0 Gall: 0-1
Aids: Bl: 0-0 Vi: 0-0 Tstrap: 0-0
Best Rating: 86 5/97 Ludl 3m gd-fm Ch

Fursan (USA)

9-y-o b g Fred Astaire (USA)-Ancient Art (USA) (Tell (USA))
Paul Phillips Edwin Phillips

Placings:PP/0/3230P-PP (0561)
2001/02: 21^{P}GF, 21^{P}GF

	Starts	1st	2nd	3rd	Win & Pl
Chases	2	0	0	0	
Career Total	**10**	**0**	**1**	**2**	**1337**

Going: Sf: 0-0 GS: 0-0 Gd: 0-0 GF: - Fm: 0-2
Distance: 2m/2m3: 0-0 2m4-2m7: 0-2 3m+: 0-0
Track: LH: 0-1 RH: 0-1 Tight: 0-1 Gall: 0-0
Aids: Bl: 0-0 Vi: 0-0 Tstrap: 0-2
Best Rating: 106 5/00 Uttx 2m5f good Ch

Further Risk

7-y-o ch g Risk Me (FR)-Farinara (Dragonara Palace (USA))
Mrs H L Walton A E Walton

Placings:0/R (2326)
2001/02: 21^{R}S

	Starts	1st	2nd	3rd	Win & Pl
Chases	1	0	0	0	
Career Total	**2**	**0**	**0**	**0**	

Going: Sf: 0-1 GS: 0-0 Gd: 0-0 GF: - Fm: 0-0
Distance: 2m/2m3: 0-0 2m4-2m7: 0-1 3m+: 0-0
Track: LH: 0-1 RH: 0-0 Tight: 0-1 Gall: 0-0
Aids: Bl: 0-0 Vi: 0-0 Tstrap: 0-0
Best Rating:

A poor performer in all disciplines to date.

Fusul (USA)

88
6-y-o ch g Miswaki (USA)-Silent Turn (USA) (Silent Cal (USA))
G L Moore Dave Allen,Barry Prichard,Wayne Russell

Placings:F (0209)
2001/02: 16^{F}F

	Starts	1st	2nd	3rd	Win & Pl
Hurdles	1	0	0	0	
Career Total	**1**	**0**	**0**	**0**	

Going: Sf: 0-0 GS: 0-0 Gd: 0-0 GF: - Fm: 0-1
Distance: 2m/2m3: 0-1 2m4-2m7: 0-0 3m+: 0-0
Track: LH: 0-1 RH: 0-0 Tight: 0-1 Gall: 0-0
Aids: Bl: 0-0 Vi: 0-0 Tstrap: 0-1
Best Rating: 88 5/01 Sthl 2m firm Hdl

Futona

87(83h) (58h)69
10-y-o ch m Fearless Action (USA)-Chaise Longue (Full Of Hope)
A J Wilson Mrs T D Pilkington

Placings:00/006/06P20661P/40PP-02 (0505)
2001/02: 22^{0}GF, 20^{2}GF

	Starts	1st	2nd	3rd	Win & Pl
Hurdles	1	0	0	0	0
Chases	1	0	1	0	932
Career Total	**20**	**1**	**2**	**0**	**4843**

105	3/00	Winc	2m6f	E Hdl	GD	£2751

Total win prize-money £2751

Going: Sf: 0-0 GS: 0-0 Gd: 0-0 GF: - Fm: 0-2
Distance: 2m/2m3: 0-0 2m4-2m7: 0-2 3m+: 0-0
Track: LH: 0-0 RH: 0-2 Tight: 0-0 Gall: 0-1
Aids: Bl: 0-0 Vi: 0-0 Tstrap: 0-0
Best Rating: 105 3/00 Winc 2m6f good Hdl

G-And-T

9-y-o b m Gildoran-Littledrunkgirl (Carlingford Castle)
Mrs J M Mann Mrs J M E Mann

Placings:0F-F (4057)
2001/02: 23^{F}S, ^^

	Starts	1st	2nd	3rd	Win & Pl
Chases	1	0	0	0	
Career Total	**3**	**0**	**0**	**0**	

Going: Sf: 0-1 GS: 0-0 Gd: 0-0 GF: - Fm: 0-0
Distance: 2m/2m3: 0-0 2m4-2m7: 0-0 3m+: 0-1
Track: LH: 0-0 RH: 0-1 Tight: 0-0 Gall: 0-0
Aids: Bl: 0-0 Vi: 0-0 Tstrap: 0-0
Best Rating:

Gabby Hayes (IRE)

(87h) (73h)
6-y-o b g Tirol-All Laughter (Vision (USA))
Ferdy Murphy (B G Powell 26/9) Access Computer Consulting Plc

Placings:2032354251044/64404FP-04U (1828)
2001/02: 24^{0}GF, 16^{4}G, 16^{U}G

	Starts	1st	2nd	3rd	Win & Pl
Hurdles	2	0	0	0	0
Chases	1	0	0	0	0
Career Total	**23**	**1**	**3**	**2**	**9163**

102	3/00	Navn	2m	Hdl	Y-S	£3588

Total win prize-money £3588

Going: Sf: 0-0 GS: 0-0 Gd: 0-2 GF: - Fm: 0-1
Distance: 2m/2m3: 0-2 2m4-2m7: 0-0 3m+: 0-1
Track: LH: 0-2 RH: 0-1 Tight: 0-1 Gall: 0-0
Aids: Bl: 0-0 Vi: 0-2 Tstrap: 0-1
Best Rating: 115 4/00 Fair 2m gd-yld Hdl

Gablesea

93 53
8-y-o b g Beveled (USA)-Me Spede (Valiyar)
B P J Baugh Messrs Chrimes, Winn & Wilson

Placings:P/0-000 (2399)
2001/02: 16^{0}G, 16^{0}S, 16^{0}G

	Starts	1st	2nd	3rd	Win & Pl
Hurdles	3	0	0	0	
Career Total	**5**	**0**	**0**	**0**	

Going: Sf: 0-1 GS: 0-0 Gd: 0-2 GF: - Fm: 0-0
Distance: 2m/2m3: 0-3 2m4-2m7: 0-0 3m+: 0-0
Track: LH: 0-3 RH: 0-0 Tight: 0-1 Gall: 0-0
Aids: Bl: 0-0 Vi: 0-2 Tstrap: 0-0
Best Rating: 53 10/01 Aint 2m110y good Hdl

Gadz'Art (FR)

112 **146**

8-y-o b g Art Bleu-Naftane (FR) (Trac)

A King (J-P Totain 19/6) Michael Gates

Placings:11313/144264/531P2245/0PP45-623FP02U **(4664)**

2001/02: 22^{6}HY, 20^{2}S, 20^{3}GS, 24^{F}G, 19^{P}G, 20^{0}GS, 21^{2}HY, 21^{U}G

	Starts	1st	2nd	3rd	Win & Pl
Hurdles	1	0	1	0	4850
Chases	7	0	1	1	6259
Career Total	**32**	**5**	**5**	**4**	**192414**

10/99	Autl	2m7f110y	HCh		VS	£53821
6/98	Autl	2m1f110y	Ch		VS	£12121
3/98	Pau	2m2f110y	Ch		GD	£7071
1/98	Pau	2m2f110y	Ch		HVY	£4803
1/98	Pau	2m110y	Hdl		HVY	£5050

Total win prize-money £82866

Going: Sf: 0-3 GS: 0-2 Gd: 0-3 GF: - Fm: 0-0
Distance: 2m/2m3: 0-0 2m4-2m7: 0-7 3m+: 0-1
Track: LH: 0-3 RH: 0-3 Tight: 0-1 Gall: 0-1
Aids: Bl: 0-8 Vi: 0-0 Tstrap: 0-1
Best Rating: 146 12/01 Sand 2m4f110y gd-sft Ch

Formerly a useful chaser in France, he showed little in two runs for Kim Bailey in December 2000 and is now with Alan King. Fair efforts without winning and seems best when fitted with blinkers. Looks best over two and a half miles with plenty of cut in the ground.

Gaelic Probe (IRE)

89 **76**

8-y-o b g Roi Danzig (USA)-Scottish Gaelic (USA) (Highland Park (USA))

John A Harris Probe Racing Syndicate

Placings:652/3306400/03/4P **(2898)**

2001/02: 16^{4}G, 16^{P}G

	Starts	1st	2nd	3rd	Win & Pl
Chases	2	0	0	0	327
Career Total	**14**	**0**	**1**	**3**	**1535**

Going: Sf: 0-0 GS: 0-0 Gd: 0-2 GF: - Fm: 0-0
Distance: 2m/2m3: 0-2 2m4-2m7: 0-0 3m+: 0-0
Track: LH: 0-1 RH: 0-1 Tight: 0-0 Gall: 0-1
Aids: Bl: 0-0 Vi: 0-0 Tstrap: 0-0
Best Rating: 103 2/98 Naas 2m yield Hdl

Gaia Grey

101 **97**

6-y-o gr m Environment Friend-Princess David (USA) (Irish River (FR))

T P Tate Mrs Sylvia Clegg

Placings: *1-300* **(2675)**

2001/02: 16^{3}G, 16^{0}G, 16^{0}G

	Starts	1st	2nd	3rd	Win & Pl
NH Flat	3	0	0	1	223
Career Total	**4**	**1**	**0**	**1**	**1882**

105	2/01	Donc	2m110y	H NHF	GD	£1659

Total win prize-money £1659

Going: Sf: 0-0 GS: 0-0 Gd: 0-3 GF: - Fm: 0-0
Distance: 2m/2m3: 0-3 2m4-2m7: 0-0 3m+: 0-0
Track: LH: 0-3 RH: 0-0 Tight: 0-0 Gall: 0-1
Aids: Bl: 0-0 Vi: 0-0 Tstrap: 0-0
Best Rating: 105 11/01 Wwck 2m good NHF

Runaway bumper winner on her debut but has taken time to find her feet over hurdles. Eventually got off the mark over timber in three mile novice hurdle at Worcester July 2002. Has given problems at the start.

Gala Du Moulin Mas (FR)

97(96h) (57h)**94**

8-y-o b g Le Riverain (FR)-Soiree D'Ex (FR) (Kashtan (FR))

M E D Francis Mrs Merrick Francis Iii

Placings:12/344P-PP53 **(4909)**

2001/02: 22^{P}S, 20^{P}HY, 21^{5}G, 20^{3}GF

	Starts	1st	2nd	3rd	Win & Pl
Hurdles	3	0	0	0	0
Chases	1	0	0	1	576
Career Total	**10**	**1**	**1**	**2**	**9723**

7/98	Diep	2m1f110y	Ch	SFT	£3535

Total win prize-money £3535

Going: Sf: 0-2 GS: 0-0 Gd: 0-1 GF: - Fm: 0-1
Distance: 2m/2m3: 0-0 2m4-2m7: 0-4 3m+: 0-0
Track: LH: 0-2 RH: 0-2 Tight: 0-2 Gall: 0-0
Aids: Bl: 0-0 Vi: 0-0 Tstrap: 0-0
Best Rating: 76 4/02 MRas 2m4f gd-fm Ch

Ex-French chaser, returned from an absence in 2002. Showed his best form on fast ground in the spring.

Galant Moss (FR)

115(113c) (149c)**145**

8-y-o b/br g Tip Moss (FR)-Tchela (FR) (Le Nain Jaune (FR))

M C Pipe C M , B J & R F Batterham Ii

Placings:213222323311/6P2400/01P414P3-12F65030401 **(4744a)**

2001/02: 18^{1}VS, 20^{2}GF, 20^{F}GS, 20^{6}GS, 25^{5}G, 24^{0}G, 25^{3}S, 22^{0}S, 20^{4}S, 25^{0}GS, 18^{1}VS

	Starts	1st	2nd	3rd	Win & Pl
Hurdles	9	2	0	1	29774
Chases	2	0	1	0	1816
Career Total	**37**	**7**	**7**	**6**	**188155**

133	4/02	Autl	2m2f	Hdl	VS	£14723
	6/01	Autl	2m2f	Hdl	VS	£12124
152	12/00	Asct	2m3f110y	A Ch	SFT	£13200
130	10/00	Sedg	2m5f	E Ch	G-S	£3282
151	5/99	Hayd	2m7f110y	B Hdl	GD	£6905
144	4/99	Asct	3m	A Hdl	G-F	£18750
	6/98	Autl	2m2f	HHdl	VS	£19192

Total win prize-money £88177

Going: Sf: 0-3 GS: 0-3 Gd: 0-2 GF: - Fm: 0-1
Distance: **2m/2m3: 2-2** 2m4-2m7: 0-5 3m+: 0-4
Track: LH: 0-4 RH: 0-2 Tight: 0-1 Gall: 0-2
Aids: Bl: 0-0 Vi: 0-0 Tstrap: 0-0
Best Rating: 152 12/00 Asct 2m3f110y soft Ch

A winner of some competitive races over both hurdles and fences, including when beating Shooting Light at Ascot in 2000. Probably best at distances short of three miles although he stays that trip, he does not want the ground too fast. Made a return to high-grade handicap hurdling in 2001, in which he has been inconsistent. Loves Auteuil, and now remains in France under the guidance of Stephane Kalley.

Galapiat Du Mesnil (FR)

111 **150**

8-y-o b g Sarpedon (FR)-Polka De Montrin (FR) (Danoso)

P F Nicholls Mel Fordham B Fulton S Fisher T Hayward

Placings:3210/4131513/31F25-102412210 **(4664)**

2001/02: 24^{1}GS, 24^{0}GF, 23^{2}GF, 24^{4}GF, 19^{1}S, 31^{2}G, 31^{2}GS, 19^{1}GS, 21^{0}G

	Starts	1st	2nd	3rd	Win & Pl
Chases	9	3	3	0	41704
Career Total	**25**	**8**	**5**	**4**	**81089**

146	3/02	Chep	2m3f110y	C(0-135)HCh	G-S	£10029
146	10/01	Chep	2m3f110y	C(0-130)HCh	SFT	£9150
140	5/01	Strf	3m	C(0-135)HCh	G-S	£6942
140	9/00	Worc	2m7f110y	C(0-135)HCh	G-F	£8127
118	3/00	Fknm	3m110y	D Ch	GD	£3906
140	11/99	Asct	3m110y	C HCh	GD	£6840
133	10/99	Worc	2m7f110y	D Ch	G-F	£4109
112	1/99	Plum	2m4f	E Hdl	HVY	£2215

Total win prize-money £51320

Going: Sf: 1-1 GS: 2-3 Gd: 0-2 GF: - Fm: 0-3
Distance: 2m/2m3: 0-0 **2m4-2m7: 2-3** 3m+: 1-6
Track: **LH: 3-8** RH: 0-1 **Tight: 1-2** Gall: 0-0
Aids: Bl: 0-0 Vi: 0-0 Tstrap: 0-0
Best Rating: 146 3/02 Chep 2m3f110y gd-sft Ch

Useful chaser, versatile when it comes to trip and especially suited by soft ground. A good fourth in the Kerry National in September 2001, he finished alone at Chepstow next time. Finished second twice over Cheltenham's cross country course before scoring back at Chepstow, where he has a good record.

Galapino

95 **89**

9-y-o b g Charmer-Carousella (Rousillon (USA))

Jamie Poulton Glendale Partnership Ltd

Placings:F/213/436100/26400000-0555 **(4509)**

2001/02: 18^{0}GF, 22^{5}S, 16^{5}HY, 16^{5}G

	Starts	1st	2nd	3rd	Win & Pl
Hurdles	4	0	0	0	0
Career Total	**22**	**2**	**2**	**2**	**10982**

123	1/00	Font	2m2f110y	D(0-125)HHdl	GD	£4095
111	10/98	Font	2m2f110y	E Hdl	GD	£2530

Total win prize-money £6625

Going: Sf: 0-2 GS: 0-0 Gd: 0-1 GF: - Fm: 0-1
Distance: 2m/2m3: 0-3 2m4-2m7: 0-1 3m+: 0-0
Track: LH: 0-4 RH: 0-0 Tight: 0-4 Gall: 0-0
Aids: Bl: 0-4 Vi: 0-0 Tstrap: 0-0
Best Rating: 123 1/00 Font 2m2f110y good Hdl

He is on the downgrade and, although kept very busy, is currently on a very long losing run. His best form in recent seasons has come on a tight track such as Fontwell.

Gale Force (IRE)

93 **70**

11-y-o b g Strong Gale-Stay As You Are (Buckskin (FR))

P Beaumont Mrs J M Plummer

Placings: *600/60*U00011/4563216134/4P5456/513P2332-0 **(0068)**

2001/02: 27^{0}G

	Starts	1st	2nd	3rd	Win & Pl
Chases	1	0	0	0	
Career Total	**36**	**5**	**3**	**5**	**26000**

110	5/00	Kels	3m1f	E(0-115)HCh	G-F	£4329
112	4/99	Carl	3m2f	E(0-115)HCh	GD	£3793
115	2/99	Muss	3m	F(0-110)HCh	G-F	£2775
111	5/98	Sedg	2m5f110y	E Ch	GD	£3254

86	4/98	Carl	2m4f110y	E(0-100)HCh	GD	£2957

Total win prize-money £17109

Going: Sf: 0-0 GS: 0-0 Gd: 0-1 GF: - Fm: 0-0
Distance: 2m/2m3: 0-0 2m4-2m7: 0-0 3m+: 0-1
Track: LH: 0-1 RH: 0-0 Tight: 0-1 Gall: 0-0
Aids: Bl: 0-0 Vi: 0-0 Tstrap: 0-0
Best Rating: 115 2/99 Muss 3m gd-fm Ch

Gale On The Lake (IRE)

37 **22**

8-y-o b m Strong Gale-By The Lake (Tyrant (USA))
N B Mason N B Mason

Placings: *566*/P-0 **(0089)**
2001/02: 16[0]S

	Starts	1st	2nd	3rd	Win & Pl
Hurdles	1	0	0	0	
Career Total	**5**	**0**	**0**	**0**	**0**

Going: Sf: 0-1 GS: 0-0 Gd: 0-0 GF: - Fm: 0-0
Distance: 2m/2m3: 0-1 2m4-2m7: 0-0 3m+: 0-0
Track: LH: 0-1 RH: 0-0 Tight: 0-0 Gall: 0-0
Aids: Bl: 0-0 Vi: 0-0 Tstrap: 0-0
Best Rating: 79 9/99 Carl 2m1f gd-fm NHF

Galeaway (IRE)

8-y-o b g Strong Gale-Geeaway (Gala Performance (USA))
M J Roberts Mike Roberts

Placings: 0/415-PF4 **(4537)**
2001/02: 25[P]G, 26[F]G, 21[4]G

	Starts	1st	2nd	3rd	Win & Pl
Chases	3	0	0	0	317
Career Total	**7**	**1**	**0**	**0**	**1896**
95 5/00	Folk	3m2f	H Ch	GD	£1456

Total win prize-money £1456

Going: Sf: 0-0 GS: 0-0 Gd: 0-3 GF: - Fm: 0-0
Distance: 2m/2m3: 0-0 2m4-2m7: 0-1 3m+: 0-2
Track: LH: 0-1 RH: 0-1 Tight: 0-2 Gall: 0-0
Aids: Bl: 0-0 Vi: 0-0 Tstrap: 0-1
Best Rating: 95 5/00 Folk 3m2f good Ch

Galen (IRE)

108 **113**

11-y-o br g Roselier (FR)-Gaye Le Moss (Le Moss)
Mrs S J Smith David Campbell

Placings: *440*/45063/25140153/53P011P0/P61143116 4/06564P32-151232 **(1563)**
2001/02: 24[1]F, 20[5]GS, 23[1]G, 25[2]GF, 25[3]GF, 26[2]GS

	Starts	1st	2nd	3rd	Win & Pl
Chases	6	2	2	1	12451
Career Total	**48**	**10**	**4**	**6**	**51780**

113	6/01	Worc	2m7f110y	F(0-110)HCh	GD	£4761
109	5/01	Sthl	3m110y	F(0-110)HCh	FRM	£3805
123	1/00	Towc	2m6f	D(0-120)HCh	HVY	£7020
123	12/99	Uttx	3m	D(0-120)HCh	SFT	£5408
123	11/99	Towc	2m6f	D(0-125)HCh	GD	£4655
111	10/99	Sthl	2m4f110y	F(0-110)HCh	G-S	£3485
108	2/99	Catt	3m6f	C(0-130)HCh	GD	£6937
108	1/99	Catt	3m1f110y	F(0-110)HCh	SFT	£2840
101	11/97	Sedg	3m3f110y	E Hdl	GD	£2285

Total win prize-money £41199

Going: Sf: 0-0 GS: 0-2 Gd: 1-1 GF: - Fm: 1-3
Distance: 2m/2m3: 0-0 2m4-2m7: 0-1 **3m+: 2-5**
Track: **LH: 2-5** RH: 0-1 **Tight: 1-3** Gall: 0-0
Aids: Bl: 0-0 Vi: 0-0 Tstrap: 0-0
Best Rating: 123 3/00 Towc 3m1f good Ch

Fair handicap chaser at around three miles. Has won on fast ground and softer.

Gales Cavalier (IRE)

111 **142**

14-y-o b g Strong Gale-Ring Road (Giolla Mear)
D R Gandolfo Starlight Racing

Placings: 24211P/11112P/22P11/2322302/1330/U3P4 /1 **(0435)**
2001/02: 21[1]GF

	Starts	1st	2nd	3rd	Win & Pl
Chases	1	1	0	0	4431
Career Total	**33**	**10**	**9**	**5**	**130947**

142	5/01	Folk	2m5f	D(0-125)HCh	G-F	£4431
163	10/97	Winc	2m5f	A HCh	GD	£18660
158	4/96	Chel	2m5f	A Ch	GD	£20286
152	3/96	Extr	2m2f	B(0-145)HCh	G-S	£7155
142	1/95	Asct	2m	A Ch	GD	£13760
140	12/94	Kemp	2m	Ch	SFT	£10091
119	11/94	Nott	2m	Ch	SFT	£2748
120	10/94	Bang	2m1f110y	Ch	G-S	£3663
109	1/94	Hntg	2m110y	Hdl	SFT	£2156
99	1/94	Winc	2m	Hdl	G-S	£2495

Total win prize-money £85118

Going: Sf: 0-0 GS: 0-0 Gd: 0-0 GF: - Fm: 1-1
Distance: 2m/2m3: 0-0 **2m4-2m7: 1-1** 3m+: 0-0
Track: LH: 0-0 **RH: 1-1 Tight: 1-1** Gall: 0-0
Aids: Bl: 0-0 Vi: 0-0 Tstrap: 0-0
Best Rating: 163 10/97 Winc 2m5f good Ch

Former useful chaser at around two and a half miles, he came back from retirement in 2001 to win at Folkestone, during which time he had been hunting.

Galevanter (IRE)

77 **36**

8-y-o b g Strong Gale-Cherry Crest (Pollerton)
H D Daly Mrs Jane Lane

Placings: *0*/0 **(0352)**
2001/02: 22[0]G

	Starts	1st	2nd	3rd	Win & Pl
Hurdles	1	0	0	0	
Career Total	**2**	**0**	**0**	**0**	

Going: Sf: 0-0 GS: 0-0 Gd: 0-1 GF: - Fm: 0-0
Distance: 2m/2m3: 0-0 2m4-2m7: 0-1 3m+: 0-0
Track: LH: 0-1 RH: 0-0 Tight: 0-1 Gall: 0-0
Aids: Bl: 0-0 Vi: 0-0 Tstrap: 0-0
Best Rating: 77 5/99 Worc 2m gd-fm NHF

Galileo (POL)

111 **154**

6-y-o b g Jape (USA)-Goldika (POL) (Dakota)
T R George (S Walotek 28/10) Mrs S Nelson,Allan Stennett,Terry Warner

Placings: 11 **(4229)**
2001/02: 21[1]G, 21[1]GS

	Starts	1st	2nd	3rd	Win & Pl
Hurdles	2	2	0	0	59870
Career Total	**2**	**2**	**0**	**0**	**59870**

154	3/02	Chel	2m5f	A Hdl	G-S	£52200
142	2/02	Kemp	2m5f	C Hdl	GD	£7670

Total win prize-money £59870

Going: Sf: 0-0 GS: 1-1 Gd: 1-1 GF: - Fm: 0-0
Distance: 2m/2m3: 0-0 **2m4-2m7: 2-2** 3m+: 0-0
Track: LH: 1-1 RH: 1-1 Tight: 0-0 **Gall: 1-1**
Aids: Bl: 0-0 Vi: 0-0 Tstrap: 0-0
Best Rating: 154 3/02 Chel 2m5f gd-sft Hdl

Winner of the Polish St Leger and Listed placed on the Flat in Germany, bolted up on his hurdling debut at Kempton in February 2002, and followed up in the Royal & SunAlliance Hurdle the following month.

Galindo

94 **92**

8-y-o b g Rakaposhi King-Edwina's Dawn (Space King)
J Howard Johnson J Howard Johnson

Placings: *5/560224*/03P **(3328)**
2001/02: 22[0]GS, 20[3]G, 20[P]S

	Starts	1st	2nd	3rd	Win & Pl
Hurdles	3	0	0	1	287
Career Total	**10**	**0**	**2**	**1**	**1629**

Going: Sf: 0-1 GS: 0-1 Gd: 0-1 GF: - Fm: 0-0
Distance: 2m/2m3: 0-0 2m4-2m7: 0-3 3m+: 0-0
Track: LH: 0-3 RH: 0-0 Tight: 0-1 Gall: 0-2
Aids: Bl: 0-0 Vi: 0-0 Tstrap: 0-0
Best Rating: 96 5/99 Hexm 2m4f110y good Hdl

A half-brother to My Shenandoah, he went missing for two years, but made an encouraging return to hurdles when just found wanting over two and a half miles at Newcastle towards the end of 2001.

Gallant Major

10-y-o ch g Infantry-Miss Gallant (Gallo Gallante)
K F Clutterbuck K F Clutterbuck

Placings: *0/P/0/4*/P **(0106)**
2001/02: 18[P]GF

	Starts	1st	2nd	3rd	Win & Pl
Chases	1	0	0	0	
Career Total	**5**	**0**	**0**	**0**	**191**

Going: Sf: 0-0 GS: 0-0 Gd: 0-0 GF: - Fm: 0-1
Distance: 2m/2m3: 0-1 2m4-2m7: 0-0 3m+: 0-0
Track: LH: 0-0 RH: 0-0 Tight: 0-1 Gall: 0-0
Aids: Bl: 0-0 Vi: 0-0 Tstrap: 0-0
Best Rating: 70 10/98 Sedg 2m1f gd-sft Hdl

Galleon Beach

5-y-o b g Shirley Heights-Music In My Life (IRE) (Law Society (USA))
J W Hills Christopher Wright

Placings: 3 **(2517)**
2001/02: 21[3]S

	Starts	1st	2nd	3rd	Win & Pl
Hurdles	1	0	0	1	314
Career Total	**1**	**0**	**0**	**1**	**314**

Going: Sf: 0-1 GS: 0-0 Gd: 0-0 GF: - Fm: 0-0
Distance: 2m/2m3: 0-0 2m4-2m7: 0-1 3m+: 0-0

Track: LH: 0-1 RH: 0-0 Tight: 0-1 Gall: 0-0
Aids: Bl: 0-0 Vi: 0-1 Tstrap: 0-1
Best Rating: mfy

He became unreliable on the Flat, and is not one to trust judged on his sole outing over hurdles.

Galley Gap (IRE)

77f 55f

6-y-o b m Northern Park (USA)-Al Faraa (USA) (Slew O'Gold (USA))
I W McInnes I W McInnes

Placings:*0-0* **(0240)**
2001/02: 16^{0}GF

	Starts	1st	2nd	3rd	Win & Pl
NH Flat	1	0	0	0	
Career Total	**2**	**0**	**0**	**0**	

Going: Sf: 0-0 GS: 0-0 Gd: 0-0 GF: - Fm: 0-1
Distance: 2m/2m3: 0-1 2m4-2m7: 0-0 3m+: 0-0
Track: LH: 0-1 RH: 0-0 Tight: 0-1 Gall: 0-0
Aids: Bl: 0-0 Vi: 0-0 Tstrap: 0-0
Best Rating: 55 5/01 Sthl 2m gd-fm NHF

Gallileo Strike (IRE)

92 99

6-y-o b g Magical Strike (USA)-Dame Daffodil (IRE) (Petorius)
Thomas Cooper Thornbirds Syndicate

Placings:000/1100 **(4950a)**
2001/02: 16^{1}G, 16^{1}GF, 16^{0}G, 16^{0}G

	Starts	1st	2nd	3rd	Win & Pl
Hurdles	4	2	0	0	11407
Career Total	**7**	**2**	**0**	**0**	**11407**

99	9/01	List	2m	(0-109)HHdl	G-F	£6399
99	9/01	Tral	2m	(0-109)HHdl	GD	£5008

Total win prize-money £11407

Going: Sf: 0-0 GS: 0-0 Gd: 1-3 GF: - Fm: 1-1
Distance: **2m/2m3: 2-4** 2m4-2m7: 0-0 3m+: 0-0
Track: **LH: 1-2** RH: 0-1 Tight: 0-0 Gall: 0-0
Aids: Bl: 0-0 Vi: 0-0 Tstrap: 0-0
Best Rating: 99 9/01 List 2m gd-fm Hdl

An Irish-trained dual purpose gelding. He won on the Flat before scoring twice over hurdles in September 2001. Suited by a good/fast surface.

Gallion's Reach (IRE)

111(109h) (87h)104+

7-y-o b g Good Thyne (USA)-Raise Our Hopes (IRE) (Salluceva)
N A Twiston-Davies H R Mould

Placings:*3505*/62P1003-**42PP2P** **(4889)**
2001/02: 26^{4}S, 20^{2}HY, 25^{P}S, 20^{P}G, 20^{2}G, 26^{P}G

	Starts	1st	2nd	3rd	Win & Pl
Chases	6	0	2	0	1634
Career Total	**17**	**1**	**3**	**2**	**8979**

94	2/01	Hayd	2m	C(0-125)HHdl	HVY	£5083

Total win prize-money £5083

Going: Sf: 0-3 GS: 0-0 Gd: 0-3 GF: - Fm: 0-0
Distance: 2m/2m3: 0-0 2m4-2m7: 0-3 3m+: 0-3
Track: LH: 0-4 RH: 0-1 Tight: 0-1 Gall: 0-0
Aids: Bl: 0-0 Vi: 0-0 Tstrap: 0-1
Best Rating: 100 12/99 Uttx 2m soft NHF

Won two mile novices handicap hurdle in February 2001 and three mile novices handicap chase in August 2002. Likes soft ground.

Gallop Rhythm (IRE)

88 94

6-y-o ch g Mister Lord (USA)-Kiltannon (Dalsaan)
R J Baker St Bartholomews & The Royal London Turf

Placings:*0-00***2** **(4726)**
2001/02: 16^{0}G, 19^{0}G, 20^{2}GF

	Starts	1st	2nd	3rd	Win & Pl
NH Flat	1	0	0	0	0
Hurdles	2	0	1	0	766
Career Total	**4**	**0**	**1**	**0**	**766**

Going: Sf: 0-0 GS: 0-0 Gd: 0-2 GF: - Fm: 0-1
Distance: 2m/2m3: 0-2 2m4-2m7: 0-1 3m+: 0-0
Track: LH: 0-1 RH: 0-2 Tight: 0-0 Gall: 0-0
Aids: Bl: 0-0 Vi: 0-0 Tstrap: 0-0
Best Rating: 94 4/02 Chep 2m4f gd-fm Hdl

Novice hurdler, stays two and a half miles.

Galloping Guns (IRE)

98(95c) (65c)79

10-y-o b g Conquering Hero (USA)-Jillette (Fine Blade (USA))
B J Llewellyn Patrick Harrington

Placings:50236000/6001521303F21F/P50054403653502/50122052B42306U6/330636**543123**-0**05**520P **(1405)**
2001/02: 22^{0}G, 23^{0}G, 25^{5}GF, 27^{5}G, 16^{2}GF, 22^{0}GF, 16^{P}GF

	Starts	1st	2nd	3rd	Win & Pl
Hurdles	5	0	1	0	460
Chases	2	0	0	0	0
Career Total	**72**	**5**	**10**	**11**	**21034**

89	9/00	Hrfd	3m1f110y	E(0-105)HCh	G-F	£3376
88	7/99	Worc	2m4f	G(0-95)HHdl	G-F	£2010
74	12/97	Ludl	2m	F(0-105)HHdl	GD	£2801
74	9/97	Plum	2m1f	G(0-90)HHdl	G-F	£1832
71	8/97	Worc	2m	G(0-95)HHdl	G-F	£1922

Total win prize-money £11944

Going: Sf: 0-0 GS: 0-0 Gd: 0-3 GF: - Fm: 0-4
Distance: 2m/2m3: 0-2 2m4-2m7: 0-2 3m+: 0-3
Track: LH: 0-7 RH: 0-0 Tight: 0-4 Gall: 0-0
Aids: Bl: 0-0 Vi: 0-0 Tstrap: 0-0
Best Rating: 89 10/00 Sthl 3m110y heavy Ch

Galway (IRE)

9-y-o b g Jurado (USA)-Solanum (Green Shoon)
N A Twiston-Davies Mrs J K Powell

Placings:*00*/605F60/0P0*03*/**152U-0** **(0577)**
2001/02: 21^{0}GF

	Starts	1st	2nd	3rd	Win & Pl
Chases	1	0	0	0	
Career Total	**18**	**1**	**1**	**1**	**3450**

127	2/01	Muss	3m	H Ch	GD	£2352

Total win prize-money £2352

Going: Sf: 0-0 GS: 0-0 Gd: 0-0 GF: - Fm: 0-1
Distance: 2m/2m3: 0-0 2m4-2m7: 0-1 3m+: 0-0
Track: LH: 0-1 RH: 0-0 Tight: 0-1 Gall: 0-0
Aids: Bl: 0-0 Vi: 0-0 Tstrap: 0-0
Best Rating: 127 2/01 Muss 3m good Ch

Placed form in Irish novice hurdles. Won a point to point and a Hunter Chase at the beginning of 2001. Stays three miles. Acts on good and heavy ground.

Galy Bay

95 77

4-y-o b f Bin Ajwaad (IRE)-Sylhall (Sharpo)
A Bailey J A Bianchi

Placings:U53 **(1800)**
2001/02: 17^{U}G, 16^{5}G, 16^{3}GF

	Starts	1st	2nd	3rd	Win & Pl
Hurdles	3	0	0	1	383
Career Total	**3**	**0**	**0**	**1**	**383**

Going: Sf: 0-0 GS: 0-0 Gd: 0-2 GF: - Fm: 0-1
Distance: 2m/2m3: 0-3 2m4-2m7: 0-0 3m+: 0-0
Track: LH: 0-1 RH: 0-2 Tight: 0-1 Gall: 0-0
Aids: Bl: 0-0 Vi: 0-0 Tstrap: 0-0
Best Rating: 77 10/01 Ludl 2m gd-fm Hdl

A minor winner on the Flat, she looks to have stamina limitations over hurdles.

Game Endeavour (IRE)

89f 85f

6-y-o ch g Naheez (USA)-Jemma's Gold (IRE) (Buckskin (FR))
E Stanners Team George Iii

Placings:*0* **(0078)**
2001/02: 17^{0}G

	Starts	1st	2nd	3rd	Win & Pl
NH Flat	1	0	0	0	
Career Total	**1**	**0**	**0**	**0**	

Going: Sf: 0-0 GS: 0-0 Gd: 0-1 GF: - Fm: 0-0
Distance: 2m/2m3: 0-1 2m4-2m7: 0-0 3m+: 0-0
Track: LH: 0-0 RH: 0-1 Tight: 0-0 Gall: 0-0
Aids: Bl: 0-0 Vi: 0-0 Tstrap: 0-0
Best Rating: 85 5/01 Extr 2m1f good NHF

Game Gunner

104 105

10-y-o b g Gunner B-The Waiting Game (Cruise Missile)
John Allen Miss B Lewis

Placings:14U4P2 **(3998)**
2001/02: 24^{1}GF, 24^{4}G, 22^{U}S, 24^{4}G, 24^{P}S, 19^{2}S

	Starts	1st	2nd	3rd	Win & Pl
Chases	6	1	1	0	5227
Career Total	**6**	**1**	**1**	**0**	**5227**

105	6/01	Strf	3m	H Ch	G-F	£3705

Total win prize-money £3705

Going: Sf: 0-3 GS: 0-0 Gd: 0-2 GF: - Fm: 1-1
Distance: 2m/2m3: 0-0 2m4-2m7: 0-2 **3m+: 1-4**
Track: **LH: 1-3** RH: 0-3 **Tight: 1-3** Gall: 0-1
Aids: Bl: 0-0 Vi: 0-0 Tstrap: 0-0
Best Rating: 105 3/02 Donc 2m3f110y soft Ch

Winning Hunter who likes fast ground.

Game On (IRE)

99 **90**

6-y-o b g Terimon-Nun So Game (The Parson)
C R Egerton Mrs Janette Yeomans

Placings:2P24P **(4502)**
2001/02: 17^{2}GS, 20^{P}HY, 19^{2}S, 16^{4}S, 22^{P}G

	Starts	1st	2nd	3rd	Win & Pl
NH Flat	1	0	1	0	544
Hurdles	4	0	1	0	814
Career Total	**5**	**0**	**2**	**0**	**1358**

Going: Sf: 0-3 GS: 0-1 Gd: 0-1 GF: - Fm: 0-0
Distance: 2m/2m3: 0-2 2m4-2m7: 0-3 3m+: 0-0
Track: LH: 0-2 RH: 0-2 Tight: 0-2 Gall: 0-1
Aids: Bl: 0-0 Vi: 0-0 Tstrap: 0-1
Best Rating: 109 5/01 Folk 2m1f110y gd-sft NHF

Showed promise on his bumper debut in May 2001 and placed form over hurdles since. Acts on good and soft ground.

Gamitas

4-y-o b f Dolphin Street (FR)-Driftholme (Safawan)
G M McCourt (A P Jarvis 1/8) Graham McCourt

Placings:F0P **(4682)**
2001/02: 17^{F}G, 16^{0}S, 17^{P}GF

	Starts	1st	2nd	3rd	Win & Pl
Hurdles	3	0	0	0	
Career Total	**3**	**0**	**0**	**0**	

Going: Sf: 0-1 GS: 0-0 Gd: 0-1 GF: - Fm: 0-1
Distance: 2m/2m3: 0-3 2m4-2m7: 0-0 3m+: 0-0
Track: LH: 0-1 RH: 0-2 Tight: 0-0 Gall: 0-0
Aids: Bl: 0-0 Vi: 0-0 Tstrap: 0-0
Best Rating: 2 3/02 Hrfd 2m1f good Hdl

Gandon

92 **73**

5-y-o ch g Hernando (FR)-Severine (USA) (Trempolino (USA))
P G Murphy On The Move

Placings:00000 **(4601)**
2001/02: 16^{0}S, 16^{0}G, 20^{0}HY, 17^{0}S, 16^{0}GF

	Starts	1st	2nd	3rd	Win & Pl
Hurdles	5	0	0	0	
Career Total	**5**	**0**	**0**	**0**	

Going: Sf: 0-3 GS: 0-0 Gd: 0-1 GF: - Fm: 0-1
Distance: 2m/2m3: 0-4 2m4-2m7: 0-1 3m+: 0-0
Track: LH: 0-3 RH: 0-2 Tight: 0-1 Gall: 0-0
Aids: Bl: 0-0 Vi: 0-0 Tstrap: 0-0
Best Rating: 73 11/01 Wwck 2m good Hdl

Gangster

97

8-y-o b g Gunner B-Moll (Rugantino)
Lady Connell Sir Michael Connell

Placings:0-3 **(0009)**
2001/02: 26^{3}GS

	Starts	1st	2nd	3rd	Win & Pl
Chases	1	0	0	1	510
Career Total	**2**	**0**	**0**	**1**	**510**

Going: Sf: 0-0 GS: 0-1 Gd: 0-0 GF: - Fm: 0-0
Distance: 2m/2m3: 0-0 2m4-2m7: 0-0 3m+: 0-1
Track: LH: 0-0 RH: 0-0 Tight: 0-0 Gall: 0-0
Aids: Bl: 0-0 Vi: 0-0 Tstrap: 0-0
Best Rating: 97 4/01 Plum 3m2f gd-sft Ch

Gangsters R Us (IRE)

93 **91**

6-y-o br g Treasure Hunter-Our Mare Mick (Choral Society)
A Parker J B Purefoy

Placings:P-536 **(4125)**
2001/02: 22^{5}GS, 17^{3}S, 16^{6}HY

	Starts	1st	2nd	3rd	Win & Pl
Hurdles	3	0	0	1	369
Career Total	**4**	**0**	**0**	**1**	**369**

Going: Sf: 0-2 GS: 0-1 Gd: 0-0 GF: - Fm: 0-0
Distance: 2m/2m3: 0-2 2m4-2m7: 0-1 3m+: 0-0
Track: LH: 0-3 RH: 0-0 Tight: 0-1 Gall: 0-0
Aids: Bl: 0-0 Vi: 0-0 Tstrap: 0-0
Best Rating: 91 2/02 Sedg 2m1f soft Hdl

Lightly-raced chasing type, he shaped with promise on his third start over hurdles. Appreciates patient tactics.

Garden Party Ii (FR)

103(42h) **110**

8-y-o br g Argument (FR)-Betty Royale (FR) (Royal Charter (FR))
Mrs D Thomson Area Eight

Placings:*2604*/0060F0/0P62F50-30032454 **(4829)**
2001/02: 17^{3}G, 17^{0}G, 21^{0}G, 16^{3}S, 16^{2}HY, 17^{4}S, 17^{5}GF, 16^{4}G

	Starts	1st	2nd	3rd	Win & Pl
Chases	8	0	1	2	2802
Career Total	**25**	**0**	**3**	**2**	**4208**

Going: Sf: 0-3 GS: 0-0 Gd: 0-4 GF: - Fm: 0-1
Distance: 2m/2m3: 0-7 2m4-2m7: 0-1 3m+: 0-0
Track: LH: 0-8 RH: 0-0 Tight: 0-4 Gall: 0-0
Aids: Bl: 0-0 Vi: 0-0 Tstrap: 0-0
Best Rating: 110 4/02 Ayr 2m good Ch

Still a maiden over both hurdles and fences.

Gardor (FR)

103 **102**

4-y-o b g Kendor (FR)-Garboesque (Priolo (USA))
J G Fitzgerald Halewood International Ltd

Placings:452 **(4284)**
2001/02: 16^{4}G, 16^{5}S, 17^{2}GS

	Starts	1st	2nd	3rd	Win & Pl
Hurdles	3	0	1	0	1130
Career Total	**3**	**0**	**1**	**0**	**1130**

Going: Sf: 0-1 GS: 0-1 Gd: 0-1 GF: - Fm: 0-0
Distance: 2m/2m3: 0-3 2m4-2m7: 0-0 3m+: 0-0
Track: LH: 0-2 RH: 0-1 Tight: 0-2 Gall: 0-1
Aids: Bl: 0-0 Vi: 0-0 Tstrap: 0-0
Best Rating: 102 3/02 MRas 2m1f110y gd-sft Hdl

Disappointing on the Flat but looks like making a better hurdler.

Gare Hill (IRE)

101 **108**

8-y-o ch g Aristocracy-Morning Jane (IRE) (Over The River (FR))
J T Gifford Michael S Wilson

Placings:500/P/U-5F1413P **(4233)**
2001/02: 20^{5}G, 22^{F}S, 21^{1}G, 25^{4}G, 26^{1}S, 22^{3}HY, 32^{P}GS

	Starts	1st	2nd	3rd	Win & Pl
Chases	7	2	0	1	6629
Career Total	**12**	**2**	**0**	**1**	**6629**

108	1/02	Plum	3m2f	F(0-90)HCh	SFT	£3150
91	12/01	Folk	2m5f	F(0-95)HCh	GD	£2814

Total win prize-money £5965

Going: Sf: 1-3 GS: 0-1 Gd: 1-3 GF: - Fm: 0-0
Distance: 2m/2m3: 0-0 2m4-2m7: 1-4 3m+: 1-3
Track: LH: 0-1 **RH: 1-4 Tight: 1-3** Gall: 0-2
Aids: Bl: 0-0 Vi: 0-0 Tstrap: 0-0
Best Rating: 108 1/02 Plum 3m2f soft Ch

Lightly-raced individual. Moderate form over hurdles. Finished lame in October 1999 and missed all of 2000. Unseated on chasing debut in spring of 2001. Improved to score a couple of times at up to three and a quarter miles. Acts on any ground.

Garethson (IRE)

11-y-o b g Cataldi-Tartan Sash (Crofter (USA))
O W King (A King 20/1) A King

Placings:3233/30613/1U40FP5/2U/133 **(4416)**
2001/02: 19^{1}S, 20^{3}S, 20^{3}S

	Starts	1st	2nd	3rd	Win & Pl
Chases	3	1	0	2	2231
Career Total	**21**	**3**	**2**	**7**	**14668**

108	2/02	Donc	2m3f110y	H Ch	SFT	£1596
130	5/98	Towc	2m6f	E Ch	GD	£3065
129	3/98	Extr	2m3f110y	D Ch	SFT	£3906

Total win prize-money £8568

Going: Sf: 1-3 GS: 0-0 Gd: 0-0 GF: - Fm: 0-0
Distance: 2m/2m3: 0-0 **2m4-2m7: 1-3** 3m+: 0-0
Track: **LH: 1-1** RH: 0-1 Tight: 0-1 **Gall: 1-1**
Aids: Bl: 0 0 Vi: 0-0 Tstrap: 0-0
Best Rating: 130 5/98 Towc 2m6f good Ch

He appears to be enjoying something of a renaissance this season having looked a light of his former self last season. Best over two and a half miles with cut.

Gargoyle Girl

101 **84+**

5-y-o b m Be My Chief (USA)-May Hills Legacy (IRE) (Be My Guest (USA))
J S Goldie Mrs C Brown

Placings:0502 **(4898)**
2001/02: 16^{0}GS, 19^{5}GF, 16^{0}S, 16^{2}G

	Starts	1st	2nd	3rd	Win & Pl
Hurdles	4	0	1	0	1136
Career Total	**4**	**0**	**1**	**0**	**1136**

Going: Sf: 0-1 GS: 0-1 Gd: 0-1 GF: - Fm: 0-1
Distance: 2m/2m3: 0-4 2m4-2m7: 0-0 3m+: 0-0
Track: LH: 0-3 RH: 0-1 Tight: 0-1 Gall: 0-0
Aids: Bl: 0-0 Vi: 0-0 Tstrap: 0-0
Best Rating: 81 4/02 Prth 2m110y good Hdl

Moderate hurdler, seems suited by a sound surface.

Garolo (FR)

12-y-o b g Garde Royale-Valgoya (FR) (Valdingran (FR))
Mrs F Browne (M R Bosley 27/1) Miss S L Samworth

Placings:F25/13020/**3121022PF**/3P453/3323655/**P**-P15 **(4517)**
2001/02: 22^{P}GS, 25^{1}S, 22^{5}GS

	Starts	1st	2nd	3rd	Win & Pl
Hurdles	1	0	0	0	0
Chases	2	1	0	0	2174
Career Total	**33**	**4**	**6**	**7**	**29029**

108	3/02	Towc	3m1f	H Ch	SFT	£2173
115	12/96	Uttx	2m	D Ch	G-S	£3598
	1/96	Cagn	2m55y	Hdl	SFT	£7905

Total win prize-money £13678

Going: Sf: 1-1 GS: 0-2 Gd: 0-0 GF: - Fm: 0-0
Distance: 2m/2m3: 0-0 2m4-2m7: 0-2 **3m+: 1-1**
Track: LH: 0-0 **RH: 1-2** Tight: 0-0 Gall: 0-0
Aids: **Bl: 1-2** Vi: 0-0 Tstrap: 0-1
Best Rating: 130 2/96 Kemp 2m soft Hdl

A formerly decent hurdler/chaser, improved for the re-application of blinkers and completed a hat-trick in a moderate Towcester hunter chase in March 2002, having won two earlier points. Suited by good ground or slightly easier.

Garolsa (FR)

106 **120**

8-y-o b g Rivelago (FR)-Rols Du Chatelier (FR) (Diaghilev)
C Tizzard R G And C L Tizzard

Placings:02/1/**2P4**/**P2P**-**026PP** **(3712)**
2001/02: 24^{0}GS, 24^{2}GF, 20^{6}GS, 26^{P}G, 26^{P}HY

	Starts	1st	2nd	3rd	Win & Pl
Chases	5	0	1	0	2045
Career Total	**14**	**1**	**4**	**0**	**13127**

105	3/99	Chep	2m4f110y	D Hdl	SFT	£2996

Total win prize-money £2996

Going: Sf: 0-1 GS: 0-2 Gd: 0-1 GF: - Fm: 0-1
Distance: 2m/2m3: 0-0 2m4-2m7: 0-1 3m+: 0-4
Track: LH: 0-1 RH: 0-2 Tight: 0-1 Gall: 0-0
Aids: Bl: 0-0 Vi: 0-0 Tstrap: 0-1
Best Rating: 121 4/00 Asct 3m110y soft Ch

Mainly disappointing over fences but ran well enough at Ascot in December when encountering fast ground for the first time. Stays three miles.

Garruth (IRE)

107(113h) (150h)**136**

8-y-o gr g Good Thyne (USA)-Lady Sipash (Erin's Hope)
P F Nicholls A Bloom

Placings:*6/405331*/00113221141-**14363251** **(4916)**
2001/02: 26^{1}G, 24^{4}G, 26^{3}HY, 28^{6}HY, 26^{3}HY, 28^{2}S, 25^{5}G, 27^{1}GF

	Starts	1st	2nd	3rd	Win & Pl
Chases	8	2	1	2	16772
Career Total	**26**	**8**	**3**	**5**	**79731**

112	4/02	Sedg	3m3f	D Ch	G-F	£4378
118	11/01	Plum	3m2f	D Ch	GD	£4322
150	4/01	Aint	3m110y	A Hdl	SFT	£29000
135	1/01	Uttx	3m110y	C(0-135)HHdl	HVY	£5239
127	12/00	Chel	3m	A Hdl	SFT	£12000
126	10/00	Kels	2m6f110y	E Hdl	G-S	£2422
104	9/00	Sedg	2m5f110y	E Hdl	SFT	£2716
91	4/00	List	2m4f	NHF	SH	£3588

Total win prize-money £63667

Going: Sf: 0-4 GS: 0-0 Gd: 1-3 GF: - Fm: 1-1
Distance: 2m/2m3: 0-0 2m4-2m7: 0-0 **3m+: 2-8**
Track: **LH: 1-5** RH: 0-0 **Tight: 1-1** Gall: 0-1
Aids: **Bl: 1-3** Vi: 0-0 Tstrap: 0-1
Best Rating: 150 4/01 Aint 3m110y soft Hdl

A bumper winner in Ireland, he has won at up to three miles over hurdles and handled the bottomless conditions really well when winning the 2001 Sefton Novices' Hurdle at Aintree by a distance. Made a workmanlike start to his career over fences at Plumpton, but subsequently went backwards. Stays really well, but does not always look an easy ride.

Garryspillane (IRE)

10-y-o b g Royal Fountain-Lucylet (Kinglet)
P Jones M Mann

Placings:00/35-**3233** **(4678)**
2001/02: 21^{3}G, 28^{2}GF, 20^{3}S, 25^{3}G

	Starts	1st	2nd	3rd	Win & Pl
Chases	4	0	1	3	4930
Career Total	**8**	**0**	**1**	**4**	**5463**

Going: Sf: 0-1 GS: 0-0 Gd: 0-2 GF: - Fm: 0-1
Distance: 2m/2m3: 0-0 2m4-2m7: 0-2 3m+: 0-2
Track: LH: 0-2 RH: 0-1 Tight: 0-2 Gall: 0-0
Aids: Bl: 0-0 Vi: 0-0 Tstrap: 0-0
Best Rating: 116 4/02 Aint 3m1f good Ch

Winning pointer, has plenty of stamina but tends to find little under pressure. Acts on any going. Appreciates patient tactics.

Garyhaloo (IRE)

119

9-y-o b g Mississippi-Fairway Lady (Miami Springs)
Miss Venetia Williams W E Prichard

Placings:*3/22640*/**212-FPPPP** **(4889)**
2001/02: 27^{F}S, 24^{P}S, 25^{P}S, 23^{P}G, 26^{P}G

	Starts	1st	2nd	3rd	Win & Pl
Chases	5	0	0	0	
Career Total	**14**	**1**	**4**	**1**	**7728**

119	3/01	Extr	2m3f110y	E(0-105)HCh	HVY	£3971

Total win prize-money £3972

Going: Sf: 0-3 GS: 0-0 Gd: 0-2 GF: - Fm: 0-0
Distance: 2m/2m3: 0-0 2m4-2m7: 0-0 3m+: 0-5
Track: LH: 0-0 RH: 0-4 Tight: 0-2 Gall: 0-0
Aids: Bl: 0-3 Vi: 0-0 Tstrap: 0-0
Best Rating: 119 4/01 MRas 3m1f gd-sft Ch

Modest chaser, he acts on heavy ground and is effective from two miles-three to three miles plus.

Gastornis

95f **68f**

4-y-o ch g Primitive Rising (USA)-Meggies Dene (Apollo Eight)
M W Easterby Lord Daresbury

Placings:*5* **(4019)**
2001/02: 16^{5}GS

	Starts	1st	2nd	3rd	Win & Pl
NH Flat	1	0	0	0	0
Career Total	**1**	**0**	**0**	**0**	**0**

Going: Sf: 0-0 GS: 0-1 Gd: 0-0 GF: - Fm: 0-0
Distance: 2m/2m3: 0-1 2m4-2m7: 0-0 3m+: 0-0
Track: LH: 0-1 RH: 0-0 Tight: 0-0 Gall: 0-1
Aids: Bl: 0-0 Vi: 0-0 Tstrap: 0-0
Best Rating: 68 3/02 Donc 2m110y gd-sft NHF

Bred to be a chaser, he showed ability on his bumper debut at Doncaster in March 2002.

Gate Expectations

51f **15f**

4-y-o b f Alflora (IRE)-Dorazine (Kalaglow)
R J Price Englands Gate Limited

Placings:*0* **(3896)**
2001/02: 16^{0}HY

	Starts	1st	2nd	3rd	Win & Pl
NH Flat	1	0	0	0	
Career Total	**1**	**0**	**0**	**0**	

Going: Sf: 0-1 GS: 0-0 Gd: 0-0 GF: - Fm: 0-0
Distance: 2m/2m3: 0-1 2m4-2m7: 0-0 3m+: 0-0
Track: LH: 0-1 RH: 0-0 Tight: 0-0 Gall: 0-0
Aids: Bl: 0-0 Vi: 0-0 Tstrap: 0-0
Best Rating: 15 2/02 Wwck 2m heavy NHF

Gate Of Dreams

7-y-o b h Exit To Nowhere (USA)-Picnicing (Good Times (ITY))
A W Carroll Michael Gates

Placings:*0*-*P* **(1649)**
2001/02: 16^{P}G

	Starts	1st	2nd	3rd	Win & Pl
NH Flat	1	0	0	0	
Career Total	**2**	**0**	**0**	**0**	

Going: Sf: 0-0 GS: 0-0 Gd: 0-1 GF: - Fm: 0-0
Distance: 2m/2m3: 0-1 2m4-2m7: 0-0 3m+: 0-0
Track: LH: 0-0 RH: 0-1 Tight: 0-0 Gall: 0-1
Aids: Bl: 0-0 Vi: 0-0 Tstrap: 0-0
Best Rating: 73 3/01 Hntg 2m110y soft NHF

Gatflax (IRE)

112(98h) (98h)**106**

10-y-o b g Supreme Leader-Polly's Slipper (Pollerton)
Andrew Turnell Dr John Hollowood

Placings:*1*/*1*6312135/030P/**552RP**/**PP24564**-**51352133065** **(4551)**
2001/02: 16^{5}GS, 16^{1}G, 16^{3}GF, 20^{5}GF, 16^{2}S, 16^{1}S, 16^{3}G, 16^{3}G, 16^{0}S, 16^{6}S, 16^{5}GF

	Starts	1st	2nd	3rd	Win & Pl
Hurdles	1	0	0	0	0
Chases	10	2	1	3	8193
Career Total	**36**	**6**	**4**	**6**	**31672**

106	12/01	Sthl	2m	F(0-110)HCh	SFT	£2884
104	6/01	Worc	2m	F(0-95)HCh	GD	£2782
129	2/98	Chep	2m110y	E Hdl	G-S	£2612
135	1/98	Asct	2m110y	D Hdl	SFT	£3728
115	10/97	Hntg	2m110y	H NHF	GD	£1381
114	3/97	Asct	2m110y	H NHF	GD	£1955

Total win prize-money £15345

Going: Sf: 1-4 GS: 0-1 Gd: 1-3 GF: - Fm: 0-3
Distance: **2m/2m3: 2-10** 2m4-2m7: 0-1 3m+: 0-0

Track: LH: 2-8 RH: 0-3 **Tight: 1-4** Gall: 0-2
Aids: Bl: 0-0 Vi: 0-0 Tstrap: 0-0
Best Rating: 146 3/98 Chel 2m1f110y good Hdl

A smart novice hurdler in the 1997/1998 campaign, he cost his current connections a massive 200,000 guineas. Landed low grade soft ground handicap chases as Southwell in December 2001 and Stratford August 2002. Best at around two miles.

Gatorade (NZ)

113(63h) **125**

10-y-o ch g Dahar (USA)-Ribena (NZ) (Battle-Waggon)
G M McCourt D Metcalf

Placings:046/0112201212P-**421245P** **(1561)**
2001/02: 21^{4}GF, 20^{2}G, 17^{1}G, 20^{2}GF, 18^{4}GF, 16^{5}GF, 20^{P}GS

	Starts	1st	2nd	3rd	Win & Pl
Hurdles	1	0	0	0	0
Chases	6	1	2	0	6832
Career Total	**21**	**5**	**6**	**0**	**28182**

122	7/01	Strf	2m1f110y	E Ch	GD	£3055
121	9/00	Uttx	2m4f110y	B(0-140)HHdl	G-S	£6721
104	8/00	NAbb	2m1f	D Hdl	GD	£2879
113	6/00	Worc	2m4f	F(0-110)HHdl	G-F	£2348
105	6/00	Uttx	2m4f110y	D Hdl	G-F	£3237

Total win prize-money £18242

Going: Sf: 0-0 GS: 0-1 Gd: 1-2 GF: - Fm: 0-4
Distance: **2m/2m3: 1-3** 2m4-2m7: 0-4 3m+: 0-0
Track: **LH: 1-4** RH: 0-2 **Tight: 1-5** Gall: 0-0
Aids: Bl: 0-0 Vi: 0-0 Tstrap: 0-0
Best Rating: 122 7/01 Strf 2m1f110y good Ch

Has won six times and is the epitome of a summer jumper. Acts on most types of ground, and seems best between two miles and two miles four. Successful on first outing for Ian Williams at Worcester in June 2002.

Gatsby (IRE)

100 **99**

6-y-o gr g Roselier (FR)-Burren Gale (IRE) (Strong Gale)
N A Twiston-Davies Mrs J K Powell

Placings:630 **(4398)**
2001/02: 16^{6}G, 24^{3}GS, 24^{0}S

	Starts	1st	2nd	3rd	Win & Pl
NH Flat	1	0	0	0	0
Hurdles	2	0	0	1	714
Career Total	**3**	**0**	**0**	**1**	**714**

Going: Sf: 0-1 GS: 0-1 Gd: 0-1 GF: - Fm: 0-0
Distance: 2m/2m3: 0-1 2m4-2m7: 0-0 3m+: 0-2
Track: LH: 0-2 RH: 0-1 Tight: 0-0 Gall: 0-2
Aids: Bl: 0-0 Vi: 0-0 Tstrap: 0-0
Best Rating: 99 3/02 Newb 3m110y gd-sft Hdl

Gaucho

73 **30**

5-y-o b g Rambo Dancer (CAN)-Sioux Be It (Warpath)
T H Caldwell T H Caldwell

Placings:460-00PP **(4842)**
2001/02: 16^{0}G, 20^{0}G, 21^{P}S, 20^{P}G

	Starts	1st	2nd	3rd	Win & Pl
NH Flat	1	0	0	0	0
Hurdles	3	0	0	0	0
Career Total	**7**	**0**	**0**	**0**	**0**

Going: Sf: 0-1 GS: 0-0 Gd: 0-3 GF: - Fm: 0-0
Distance: 2m/2m3: 0-1 2m4-2m7: 0-3 3m+: 0-0
Track: LH: 0-3 RH: 0-1 Tight: 0-2 Gall: 0-1
Aids: Bl: 0-0 Vi: 0-0 Tstrap: 0-0
Best Rating: 74 4/01 Muss 2m1f gd-fm NHF

Gaultier Gale (IRE)

102 **104**

8-y-o b g Ajraas (USA)-David's Pleasure (Welsh Saint)
Mrs L B Normile (Ian Williams 24/1) Steve Whiting,John Beaton,Alison Kendall

Placings:15060/500/**00B0351206P44/342014144F0-10P50PPP** **(4909)**
2001/02: 21^{1}GF, 24^{0}GF, 21^{P}GF, 20^{5}GS, 20^{0}G, 21^{P}S, 20^{P}S, 20^{P}GF

	Starts	1st	2nd	3rd	Win & Pl
Chases	8	1	0	0	2537
Career Total	**40**	**5**	**2**	**2**	**19111**

104	5/01	Fknm	2m5f110y	F(0-90)HCh	G-F	£2536
104	8/00	Sthl	2m4f110y	F(0-105)HCh	GD	£3406
95	7/00	Sthl	2m4f110y	F(0-95)HCh	G-F	£2808
89	9/99	Dpat	2m2f	(0-95)HCh	GD	£2464
113	12/97	Clon	2m	Hdl	HVY	£2712

Total win prize-money £13928

Going: Sf: 0-2 GS: 0-1 Gd: 0-1 GF: - Fm: 1-4
Distance: 2m/2m3: 0-0 **2m4-2m7: 1-7** 3m+: 0-1
Track: **LH: 1-5** RH: 0-3 **Tight: 1-5** Gall: 0-1
Aids: Bl: 0-1 Vi: 0-2 Tstrap: 0-0
Best Rating: 113 12/97 Clon 2m heavy Hdl

Moderate handicap chaser. Stays two and a half miles. Acts on a sound surface.

Gavroche Collonges (FR)

100(86h) (59h)**83**

8-y-o b g Video Rock (FR)-Amazone Collonges (FR) (Olmeto)
Mrs H Dalton Beaverfast Ltd

Placings:P/P0416/03F0F005/0P00-0 **(0059)**
2001/02: 16^{0}G

	Starts	1st	2nd	3rd	Win & Pl
Chases	1	0	0	0	
Career Total	**19**	**1**	**0**	**1**	**21496**

3/99	Engh	2m3f	Ch	HVY	£10764

Total win prize-money £10764

Going: Sf: 0-0 GS: 0-0 Gd: 0-1 GF: - Fm: 0-0
Distance: 2m/2m3: 0-1 2m4-2m7: 0-0 3m+: 0-0
Track: LH: 0-0 RH: 0-1 Tight: 0-1 Gall: 0-0
Aids: Bl: 0-1 Vi: 0-0 Tstrap: 0-0
Best Rating: 83 5/01 Folk 2m good Ch

Gay Arctic

9-y-o b m Arctic Lord-Gay Edition (New Member)
P J Hobbs A L Hobbs

Placings:0/F5P/4/PP **(1189)**
2001/02: 20^{P}GF, 20^{P}G

	Starts	1st	2nd	3rd	Win & Pl
Hurdles	2	0	0	0	
Career Total	**7**	**0**	**0**	**0**	**0**

Going: Sf: 0-0 GS: 0-0 Gd: 0-1 GF: - Fm: 0-1
Distance: 2m/2m3: 0-0 2m4-2m7: 0-2 3m+: 0-0
Track: LH: 0-2 RH: 0-0 Tight: 0-1 Gall: 0-0
Aids: Bl: 0-0 Vi: 0-0 Tstrap: 0-1
Best Rating: 40 12/98 Uttx 2m soft Hdl

Gay Cavalier

75 **53**

8-y-o b g Almoojid-Indomitable (FR) (Indian King (USA))
G F H Charles-Jones R G Gay

Placings:0P **(0914)**
2001/02: 17^{0}G, 22^{P}GF

	Starts	1st	2nd	3rd	Win & Pl
Hurdles	2	0	0	0	
Career Total	**2**	**0**	**0**	**0**	

Going: Sf: 0-0 GS: 0-0 Gd: 0-1 GF: - Fm: 0-1
Distance: 2m/2m3: 0-1 2m4-2m7: 0-1 3m+: 0-0
Track: LH: 0-2 RH: 0-0 Tight: 0-2 Gall: 0-0
Aids: Bl: 0-0 Vi: 0-0 Tstrap: 0-0
Best Rating: 53 6/01 NAbb 2m1f good Hdl

Gay Lover

85 **64**

5-y-o gr m Environment Friend-Gay Ming (Gay Meadow)
Dr J R J Naylor Mrs S Clifford

Placings:0 **(2289)**
2001/02: 17^{0}GF

	Starts	1st	2nd	3rd	Win & Pl
Hurdles	1	0	0	0	
Career Total	**1**	**0**	**0**	**0**	

Going: Sf: 0-0 GS: 0-0 Gd: 0-0 GF: - Fm: 0-1
Distance: 2m/2m3: 0-1 2m4-2m7: 0-0 3m+: 0-0
Track: LH: 0-0 RH: 0-1 Tight: 0-0 Gall: 0-0
Aids: Bl: 0-0 Vi: 0-0 Tstrap: 0-0
Best Rating: 64 11/01 Extr 2m1f gd-fm Hdl

Gayles And Showers (IRE)

105 **116**

8-y-o b g Lord Americo-Decent Shower (Decent Fellow)
Mrs S C Bradburne Copland, Hardie And Steel

Placings:0364/3050**46F50P/51416141520U3-50560P124P** **(4897)**
2001/02: 21^{5}GS, 20^{0}G, 20^{5}GS, 20^{6}GS, 16^{0}S, 25^{P}HY, 20^{1}HY, 24^{2}HY, 20^{4}G, 24^{P}G

	Starts	1st	2nd	3rd	Win & Pl
Chases	10	1	1	0	5373
Career Total	**37**	**5**	**2**	**3**	**27373**

111	3/02	Ayr	2m4f	E(0-110)HCh	HVY	£3851
122	1/01	Ayr	2m4f	C(0-130)HCh	SFT	£6103
117	11/00	Newc	2m110y	E(0-115)HCh	SFT	£2938
112	10/00	Hexm	2m110y	F(0-90)Ch	HVY	£2716
112	5/00	Prth	2m	D Ch	G-S	£4108

Total win prize-money £19717

Going: Sf: 1-4 GS: 0-3 Gd: 0-3 GF: - Fm: 0-0
Distance: 2m/2m3: 0-1 **2m4-2m7: 1-6** 3m+: 0-3
Track: **LH: 1-8** RH: 0-2 Tight: 0-1 Gall: 0-3
Aids: Bl: 0-0 Vi: 0-2 Tstrap: 0-0
Best Rating: 122 2/01 Newc 2m4f heavy Ch

A winner several times over fences in both novice and handicap company, he acts on a soft surface and stays three miles.

Gaynor

89(100h) (83h)86

6-y-o b m Almoojid-High Kabour (Kabour)
P J Hobbs R G Gay

Placings:41-55 **(3645)**
2001/02: 19^{5}S, 16^{5}S

	Starts	1st	2nd	3rd	Win & Pl
Hurdles	2	0	0	0	0
Career Total	**4**	**1**	**0**	**0**	**3523**

89 9/00 Chep 2m110y D Hdl GD £3523
Total win prize-money £3523

Going: Sf: 0-2 GS: 0-0 Gd: 0-0 GF: - Fm: 0-0
Distance: 2m/2m3: 0-1 2m4-2m7: 0-1 3m+: 0-0
Track: LH: 0-0 RH: 0-2 Tight: 0-0 Gall: 0-0
Aids: Bl: 0-0 Vi: 0-0 Tstrap: 0-0
Best Rating: 89 9/00 Chep 2m110y good Hdl

Gaysun

109(98h) (107h)128

10-y-o b g Lir-Indomitable (FR) (Indian King (USA))
P J Hobbs R G Gay

Placings:54/110221F33/43212354-211163222 **(2133)**
2001/02: 20^{2}G, 24^{1}GF, 24^{1}S, 22^{1}GF, 23^{6}GF, 23^{3}GF, 24^{2}F, 24^{2}G, 24^{2}GF

	Starts	1st	2nd	3rd	Win & Pl
Hurdles	2	2	0	0	5366
Chases	7	1	4	1	13791
Career Total	**28**	**7**	**8**	**5**	**44600**

107 8/01 Strf 2m6f110y E Hdl G-F £2957
107 7/01 Worc 3m E Hdl SFT £2408
128 6/01 Strf 3m D(0-125)HCh G-F £4403
128 8/00 Uttx 2m4f D(0-125)HCh G-F £4030
115 10/99 Winc 2m5f E(0-115)HCh GD £5225
102 8/99 NAbb 2m5f110y D(0-125)HCh G-S £3710
104 5/99 Extr 2m3f H Ch FRM £1567
Total win prize-money £24304

Going: Sf: 1-1 GS: 0-0 Gd: 0-2 GF: - Fm: 2-6
Distance: 2m/2m3: 0-0 2m4-2m7: 1-2 **3m+: 2-7**
Track: **LH: 3-6** RH: 0-3 **Tight: 2-4** Gall: 0-0
Aids: Bl: 0-0 Vi: 0-0 Tstrap: 0-0
Best Rating: 128 11/01 Ludl 3m gd-fm Ch

A former hunter chaser, he was in fine form during the summer, scoring once over fences and taking advantage of novice status to score twice over hurdles. Stays three miles and acts on fast ground. Looks set for a successful summer campaign.

Gee A Two (IRE)

75f 52f

5-y-o gr h Roselier (FR)-Miss Doogles (Beau Charmeur (FR))
Ferdy Murphy S L & M A Hubbard Rodwell

Placings:0 **(4552)**
2001/02: 16^{0}GF

	Starts	1st	2nd	3rd	Win & Pl
NH Flat	1	0	0	0	
Career Total	**1**	**0**	**0**	**0**	

Going: Sf: 0-0 GS: 0-0 Gd: 0-0 GF: - Fm: 0-1
Distance: 2m/2m3: 0-1 2m4-2m7: 0-0 3m+: 0-0
Track: LH: 0-0 RH: 0-1 Tight: 0-0 Gall: 0-1
Aids: Bl: 0-0 Vi: 0-0 Tstrap: 0-0
Best Rating: 52 4/02 Hntg 2m110y gd-fm NHF

Gee Aker Malayo (IRE)

101f 103f

6-y-o b g Phardante (FR)-Flying Silver (Master Buck)
R T Phillips Old Grammarians Partnership

Placings:530 **(4526)**
2001/02: 18^{5}S, 16^{3}S, 17^{0}G

	Starts	1st	2nd	3rd	Win & Pl
NH Flat	3	0	0	1	234
Career Total	**3**	**0**	**0**	**1**	**234**

Going: Sf: 0-2 GS: 0-0 Gd: 0-1 GF: - Fm: 0-0
Distance: 2m/2m3: 0-3 2m4-2m7: 0-0 3m+: 0-0
Track: LH: 0-2 RH: 0-1 Tight: 0-1 Gall: 0-0
Aids: Bl: 0-0 Vi: 0-0 Tstrap: 0-0
Best Rating: 103 3/02 Chep 2m110y soft NHF

Has shown promise in bumpers on soft/heavy ground, disappointed on faster.

Gee Bee Boy

100(92c) (73c)66

8-y-o ch g Beveled (USA)-Blue And White (Busted)
D G Bridgwater (G M McCourt 17/1) Daltagh Construction Ltd

Placings:23/361U4PP020/323413106-0U045034600040 **(4680)**
2001/02: 16^{0}GF, 16^{U}S, 16^{0}GF, 17^{4}GS, 16^{5}G, 16^{0}GS, 20^{3}GS, 16^{4}G, 17^{6}G, 16^{0}S, 16^{0}S, 16^{0}G, 16^{4}GF, 17^{0}GF

	Starts	1st	2nd	3rd	Win & Pl
Hurdles	12	0	0	1	329
Chases	2	0	0	0	241
Career Total	**35**	**3**	**3**	**6**	**12620**

100 10/00 Strf 2m110y F(0-100)HHdl SFT £2310
100 8/00 Worc 2m G Hdl G-F £1498
105 6/99 Uttx 2m D Hdl G-S £3793
Total win prize-money £7602

Going: Sf: 0-3 GS: 0-3 Gd: 0-4 GF: - Fm: 0-4
Distance: 2m/2m3: 0-13 2m4-2m7: 0-1 3m+: 0-0
Track: LH: 0-6 RH: 0-7 Tight: 0-5 Gall: 0-3
Aids: Bl: 0-0 Vi: 0-3 Tstrap: 0-2
Best Rating: 105 6/99 Uttx 2m gd-sft Hdl

Plating-class front-running hurdler. Last win over hurdles was in October 2000. Acts on most types of ground, and best at around two miles.

Geisha

106 106

10-y-o b m Royal Vulcan-Maycrest (Imperial Fling (USA))
N A Twiston-Davies Mrs J K Powell

Placings:0/600/O21 **(2035)**
2001/02: 24°G, 24^{2}GF, 22^{1}GS

	Starts	1st	2nd	3rd	Win & Pl
Hurdles	3	1	1	0	4573
Career Total	**7**	**1**	**1**	**0**	**4573**

106 11/01 Sand 2m6f F(0-105)HHdl G-S £3656
Total win prize-money £3656

Going: Sf: 0-0 GS: 1-1 Gd: 0-1 GF: - Fm: 0-1
Distance: 2m/2m3: 0-0 **2m4-2m7: 1-1** 3m+: 0-2
Track: LH: 0-1 **RH: 1-2** Tight: 0-0 Gall: 0-0
Aids: Bl: 0-0 Vi: 0-0 Tstrap: 0-0
Best Rating: 106 11/01 Sand 2m6f gd-sft Hdl

Just caught in a Ludlow handicap hurdle in October 2001 but went one better when making all in a modest event at Sandown the following month. Stays well and looks best going right-handed.

Gem Of Holly

98 68

9-y-o b m Holly Buoy-Stuart's Gem (Meldrum)
R S Wood R S Wood

Placings:0/003/00P/54006F1P6/06-0300660 **(4786)**
2001/02: 17^{0}S, 19^{3}S, 19^{0}G, 21^{0}HY, 17^{6}S, 23^{6}G, 20^{0}F

	Starts	1st	2nd	3rd	Win & Pl
Hurdles	7	0	0	1	225
Career Total	**25**	**1**	**0**	**2**	**2122**

76 1/00 Sedg 2m5f110y G(0-90)Hdl SFT £1736
Total win prize-money £1736

Going: Sf: 0-4 GS: 0-0 Gd: 0-2 GF: - Fm: 0-1
Distance: 2m/2m3: 0-3 2m4-2m7: 0-4 3m+: 0-0
Track: LH: 0-6 RH: 0-1 Tight: 0-5 Gall: 0-1
Aids: Bl: 0-0 Vi: 0-0 Tstrap: 0-7
Best Rating: 76 1/00 Sedg 2m5f110y soft Hdl

Winning hurdler but looks to have lost the plot.

Gemi Bed (FR)

99 98

7-y-o b g Double Bed (FR)-Gemia (FR) (King Of Macedon)
G L Moore (J-M Capitte 8/11) Mrs J Moore

Placings:6 **(4564)**
2001/02: 16^{6}GF

	Starts	1st	2nd	3rd	Win & Pl
Hurdles	1	0	0	0	0
Career Total	**1**	**0**	**0**	**0**	**0**

Going: Sf: 0-0 GS: 0-0 Gd: 0-0 GF: - Fm: 0-1
Distance: 2m/2m3: 0-1 2m4-2m7: 0-0 3m+: 0-0
Track: LH: 0-1 RH: 0-0 Tight: 0-1 Gall: 0-0
Aids: Bl: 0-0 Vi: 0-0 Tstrap: 0-0
Best Rating: 85 4/02 Plum 2m gd-fm Hdl

A French import, has shown ability over hurdles.

Gemolly (IRE)

95(101h) (54h)77

9-y-o b m Be My Native (USA)-Hayhurst (Sandhurst Prince)
T Needham T Needham

Placings:P00P4/35P4P0UP/P6466-04P0 **(3763)**
2001/02: 22^{0}GF, 19^{4}GS, 20^{P}S, 24^{0}S

	Starts	1st	2nd	3rd	Win & Pl
Hurdles	2	0	0	0	0
Chases	2	0	0	0	320
Career Total	**22**	**0**	**0**	**1**	**770**

Going: Sf: 0-2 GS: 0-1 Gd: 0-0 GF: - Fm: 0-1
Distance: 2m/2m3: 0-0 2m4-2m7: 0-3 3m+: 0-1
Track: LH: 0-3 RH: 0-1 Tight: 0-2 Gall: 0-0
Aids: Bl: 0-1 Vi: 0-0 Tstrap: 0-0
Best Rating: 71 10/98 MRas 3m gd-sft Hdl

Genepi

5-y-o ch m Gildoran-Tamergale (IRE) (Strong Gale)
Mrs A J Perrett Mrs R Vaughan

Placings: *0-3*PP **(4881)**
2001/02: 17^{3}HY, 16^{P}GS, 18^{P}GF

	Starts	1st	2nd	3rd	Win & Pl
NH Flat	1	0	0	1	227
Hurdles	2	0	0	0	0
Career Total	**4**	**0**	**0**	**1**	**227**

Going: Sf: 0-1 GS: 0-1 Gd: 0-0 GF: - Fm: 0-1
Distance: 2m/2m3: 0-3 2m4-2m7: 0-0 3m+: 0-0
Track: LH: 0-1 RH: 0-1 Tight: 0-2 Gall: 0-0
Aids: Bl: 0-0 Vi: 0-0 Tstrap: 0-0
Best Rating: 97 12/01 Folk 2m1f110y heavy NHF

General

114 **120**

5-y-o b g Cadeaux Genereux-Bareilly (USA) (Lyphard (USA))
Mrs N Smith Tony Hayward

Placings: *05*-301151 **(4171)**
2001/02: 17^{3}S, 16^{0}S, 16^{1}HY, 16^{1}S, 20^{5}HY, 16^{1}GS

	Starts	1st	2nd	3rd	Win & Pl
Hurdles	6	3	0	1	9405
Career Total	**8**	**3**	**0**	**1**	**9405**

120	3/02	Plum	2m	E Hdl	G-S	£2457
120	1/02	Leic	2m	E Hdl	SFT	£3451
115	12/01	Towc	2m	E Hdl	HVY	£3073

Total win prize-money £8981

Going: Sf: 2-5 GS: 1-1 Gd: 0-0 GF: - Fm: 0-0
Distance: **2m/2m3: 3-5** 2m4-2m7: 0-1 3m+: 0-0
Track: LH: 1-4 **RH: 2-2 Tight: 1-3** Gall: 0-0
Aids: Bl: 0-0 Vi: 0-0 Tstrap: 0-0
Best Rating: 120 3/02 Plum 2m gd-sft Hdl

He acts well in testing ground and won novice hurdles at Towcester, Leicester and Plumpton. Suited by two miles and soft/heavy ground.

General Claremont (IRE)

109(58h) **137**

9-y-o gr g Strong Gale-Kasam (General Ironside)
P F Nicholls K G Manley

Placings: *0/3*00305/**2F1F**0/5**1243-P1224U4** **(2652)**
2001/02: 25^{P}GF, 26^{1}G, 32^{2}GF, 26^{2}GF, 24^{4}G, 25^{U}GF, 27^{4}G

	Starts	1st	2nd	3rd	Win & Pl
Chases	7	1	2	0	10193
Career Total	**24**	**3**	**4**	**3**	**21094**

136	6/01	NAbb	3m2f110y	D(0-120)HCh	GD	£4124
130	11/00	Tntn	3m	F(0-105)HCh	GD	£2925
122	1/00	Leic	2m4f110y	E Ch	GD	£3042

Total win prize-money £10091

Going: Sf: 0-0 GS: 0-0 Gd: 1-3 GF: - Fm: 0-4
Distance: 2m/2m3: 0-0 2m4-2m7: 0-0 **3m+: 1-7**
Track: **LH: 1-3** RH: 0-3 **Tight: 1-3** Gall: 0-1
Aids: Bl: 0-0 Vi: 0-0 Tstrap: 0-0
Best Rating: 138 7/01 NAbb 3m2f110y gd-fm Ch

Fair staying chaser on good ground or faster. Not always the best of jumpers.

General Crack (IRE)

90 **48**

13-y-o ch g Lancastrian-Barna Havna (Crash Course)
Mrs Merrita Jones (P Williams 26/5) Mrs D J Hughes

Placings: *16UP/1063***U1F1/1111P/3PP/FU/P5P** **(1276)**
2001/02: 22^{P}G, 26^{5}G, 24^{P}GF

	Starts	1st	2nd	3rd	Win & Pl
Chases	3	0	0	0	0
Career Total	**25**	**8**	**0**	**2**	**39937**

143	10/96	Kemp	3m	B(0-150)HCh	GD	£10260
148	10/96	Chep	3m	B(0-145)HCh	GD	£7103
128	5/96	Strf	3m	C(0-135)HCh	G-F	£5182
	5/96	Winc	3m1f110y	D(0-120)HCh	FRM	£3769
111	4/96	Winc	3m1f110y	E Ch	G-F	£3457
109	3/96	Winc	2m5f	D Ch	G-F	£3873
104	11/95	Chep	2m4f110y	D Hdl	G-S	£2845
	7/94	Kbgn	2m3f	NHF	GD	£2122

Total win prize-money £38612

Going: Sf: 0-0 GS: 0-0 Gd: 0-2 GF: - Fm: 0-1
Distance: 2m/2m3: 0-0 2m4-2m7: 0-1 3m+: 0-2
Track: LH: 0-2 RH: 0-1 Tight: 0-2 Gall: 0-0
Aids: Bl: 0-0 Vi: 0-0 Tstrap: 0-0
Best Rating: 148 10/96 Chep 3m good Ch

General Custer (IRE)

77(99c) **80**

8-y-o b g Buckskin (FR)-Cottage Theme (Brave Invader (USA))
Andrew Turnell Dr John Hollowood

Placings: 04523/**F2P505-0** **(0374)**
2001/02: 26^{0}GF

	Starts	1st	2nd	3rd	Win & Pl
Hurdles	1	0	0	0	
Career Total	**12**	**0**	**2**	**1**	**2596**

Going: Sf: 0-0 GS: 0-0 Gd: 0-0 GF: - Fm: 0-1
Distance: 2m/2m3: 0-0 2m4-2m7: 0-0 3m+: 0-1
Track: LH: 0-0 RH: 0-1 Tight: 0-0 Gall: 0-1
Aids: Bl: 0-1 Vi: 0-0 Tstrap: 0-0
Best Rating: 113 11/00 Kelo 2m6f110y soft Ch

General Dominion

93 **88**

5-y-o b g Governor General-Innocent Princess (NZ) (Full On Aces (AUS))
G A Swinbank (F P Murtagh 7/8) Mrs L Irving

Placings: 50 **(4785)**
2001/02: 17^{5}GF, 16^{0}F

	Starts	1st	2nd	3rd	Win & Pl
Hurdles	2	0	0	0	0
Career Total	**2**	**0**	**0**	**0**	**0**

Going: Sf: 0-0 GS: 0-0 Gd: 0-0 GF: - Fm: 0-2
Distance: 2m/2m3: 0-2 2m4-2m7: 0-0 3m+: 0-0
Track: LH: 0-1 RH: 0-1 Tight: 0-1 Gall: 0-1
Aids: Bl: 0-0 Vi: 0-0 Tstrap: 0-0
Best Rating: 88 4/02 MRas 2m1f110y gd-fm Hdl

General Duroc (IRE)

97f **95f**

6-y-o ch g Un Desperado (FR)-Satula (Deep Run)
R T Phillips (Edward U Hales 30/5) Graeme Love

Placings: *26* **(3502)**
2001/02: 16^{2}F, 16^{6}S

	Starts	1st	2nd	3rd	Win & Pl
NH Flat	2	0	1	0	1032
Career Total	**2**	**0**	**1**	**0**	**1032**

Going: Sf: 0-1 GS: 0-0 Gd: 0-0 GF: - Fm: 0-1
Distance: 2m/2m3: 0-2 2m4-2m7: 0-0 3m+: 0-0
Track: LH: 0-0 RH: 0-1 Tight: 0-0 Gall: 0-0
Aids: Bl: 0-0 Vi: 0-0 Tstrap: 0-0
Best Rating: 95 1/02 Kemp 2m soft NHF

Ex-Irish, sold for 36,000gns after finishing second in a Fairyhouse bumper in May 2001.

General Flight

(98h) (90h)

8-y-o b g Governor General-Tarka (Deep Run)
Mrs L Richards Brian Seal & Roger Rees

Placings: *5/6*561P0/350-6P **(2925)**
2001/02: 16^{6}G, 19^{P}GS

	Starts	1st	2nd	3rd	Win & Pl
Hurdles	1	0	0	0	0
Chases	1	0	0	0	0
Career Total	**12**	**1**	**0**	**1**	**2351**

90	12/98	Catt	2m	E Hdl	GD	£2024

Total win prize-money £2024

Going: Sf: 0-0 GS: 0-1 Gd: 0-1 GF: - Fm: 0-0
Distance: 2m/2m3: 0-2 2m4-2m7: 0-0 3m+: 0-0
Track: LH: 0-0 RH: 0-2 Tight: 0-1 Gall: 0-0
Aids: Bl: 0-0 Vi: 0-0 Tstrap: 0-0
Best Rating: 95 12/00 Folk 2m1f110y heavy Hdl

Modest hurdler, seems to act on any ground.

General Gleeson (IRE)

102 **86**

10-y-o ch g Jackson's Drift (USA)-Lady General (General Ironside)
J F Panvert J F Panvert

Placings: *40*/450/P004-3004423 **(0907)**
2001/02: 16^{3}GF, 19^{0}GF, 16^{0}GF, 23^{4}GF, 16^{4}GF, 20^{2}G, 24^{3}G

	Starts	1st	2nd	3rd	Win & Pl
Hurdles	7	0	1	2	1230
Career Total	**16**	**0**	**1**	**2**	**1369**

Going: Sf: 0-0 GS: 0-0 Gd: 0-2 GF: - Fm: 0-5
Distance: 2m/2m3: 0-3 2m4-2m7: 0-2 3m+: 0-2
Track: LH: 0-6 RH: 0-1 Tight: 0-3 Gall: 0-1
Aids: Bl: 0-0 Vi: 0-0 Tstrap: 0-0
Best Rating: 88 7/97 Kbgn 2m3f good NHF

General Gossip (IRE)

93 **95**

6-y-o b/br g Supreme Leader-Sno-Sleigh (Bargello)
J A B Old The Early Birds

Placings:052 (4138)
2001/02: 16^{0}S, 16^{5}S, 16^{2}GS

	Starts	1st	2nd	3rd	Win & Pl
NH Flat	2	0	0	0	0
Hurdles	1	0	1	0	1392
Career Total	**3**	**0**	**1**	**0**	**1392**

Going: Sf: 0-2 GS: 0-1 Gd: 0-0 GF: - Fm: 0-0
Distance: 2m/2m3: 0-3 2m4-2m7: 0-0 3m+: 0-0
Track: LH: 0-0 RH: 0-3 Tight: 0-0 Gall: 0-0
Aids: Bl: 0-0 Vi: 0-0 Tstrap: 0-0
Best Rating: 113 2/02 Asct 2m110y soft NHF

Fair form in novice hurdles and looks to need a test of stamina.

General Haven

81 **48**
9-y-o ch g Hadeer-Verchinina (Star Appeal)
J S Wainwright T W Heseltine

Placings:0P3/660/0/00 (1094)
2001/02: 21^{0}G, 17^{0}GF

	Starts	1st	2nd	3rd	Win & Pl
Hurdles	2	0	0	0	
Career Total	**9**	**0**	**0**	**1**	**405**

Going: Sf: 0-0 GS: 0-0 Gd: 0-1 GF: - Fm: 0-1
Distance: 2m/2m3: 0-1 2m4-2m7: 0-1 3m+: 0-0
Track: LH: 0-0 RH: 0-2 Tight: 0-2 Gall: 0-0
Aids: Bl: 0-0 Vi: 0-1 Tstrap: 0-0
Best Rating: 112 12/97 Donc 2m110y good Hdl

General Wolfe

13-y-o ch g Rolfe (USA)-Pillbox (Spartan General)
Miss Venetia Williams The Winning Line

Placings:6/4141/U411/211F2/140/261/1F60P/24B5-521 (4892)
2001/02: 21^{5}G, 26^{2}G, 31^{1}G

	Starts	1st	2nd	3rd	Win & Pl
Chases	3	1	1	0	5970
Career Total	**32**	**10**	**5**	**0**	**122000**

135	4/02	Prth	3m7f	H Ch	GD	£4186
172	1/99	Hayd	3m	A HCh	SFT	£25300
154	1/98	Hayd	3m	A HCh	SFT	£25408
150	2/97	Hayd	3m	C(0-135)HCh	G-S	£4531
145	2/96	Hayd	3m	C(0-135)HCh	G-S	£4508
125	1/96	Carl	3m	B(0-140)HCh	G-S	£7185
116	3/95	Worc	2m7f	F(0-100)HCh	G-S	£3315
118	1/95	Leic	3m	E(0-110)HCh	G-S	£3522
122	2/94	Folk	2m6f110y	Hdl	HVY	£1896
102	12/93	Towc	2m5f	Hdl	SFT	£2041

Total win prize-money £81895

Going: Sf: 0-0 GS: 0-0 Gd: 1-3 GF: - Fm: 0-0
Distance: 2m/2m3: 0-0 2m4-2m7: 0-1 **3m+: 1-2**
Track: LH: 0-2 RH: 0-0 Tight: 0-1 Gall: 0-1
Aids: Bl: 0-0 Vi: 0-0 Tstrap: 0-0
Best Rating: 172 1/99 Hayd 3m soft Ch

He has had his problems and has been very lightly raced in recent years. Best when fresh, he put up a splendid display under twelve stone on his reappearance at Sandown and may have been feeling the effects when below-par at Wincanton. He has not had much luck in the National, as he did not have the soft ground he needs in 1997 or 1999, and was brought down in the race in 2001.

Genereux

9-y-o ch g Generous (IRE)-Flo Russell (USA) (Round Table)
Mrs A Price (T Morton 4/10) Mrs A Price

Placings:P43/33334/0PPP (4645)
2001/02: 19^{0}GF, 19^{P}G, 25^{P}G, 24^{P}G

	Starts	1st	2nd	3rd	Win & Pl
Hurdles	2	0	0	0	0
Chases	2	0	0	0	0
Career Total	**12**	**0**	**0**	**5**	**1570**

Going: Sf: 0-0 GS: 0-0 Gd: 0-3 GF: - Fm: 0-1
Distance: 2m/2m3: 0-0 2m4-2m7: 0-2 3m+: 0-2
Track: LH: 0-0 RH: 0-4 Tight: 0-1 Gall: 0-0
Aids: Bl: 0-0 Vi: 0-2 Tstrap: 0-1
Best Rating: 79 5/97 Extr 2m3f110y good Hdl

Generosity

83 **53**
7-y-o ch h Generous (IRE)-Pageantry (Welsh Pageant)
Dr P Pritchard Steven R Hanney

Placings:0 (1615)
2001/02: 17^{0}GF

	Starts	1st	2nd	3rd	Win & Pl
Hurdles	1	0	0	0	
Career Total	**1**	**0**	**0**	**0**	

Going: Sf: 0-0 GS: 0-0 Gd: 0-0 GF: - Fm: 0-1
Distance: 2m/2m3: 0-1 2m4-2m7: 0-0 3m+: 0-0
Track: LH: 0-0 RH: 0-1 Tight: 0-0 Gall: 0-0
Aids: Bl: 0-0 Vi: 0-0 Tstrap: 0-0
Best Rating: 53 10/01 Extr 2m1f gd-fm Hdl

Generous Deal (IRE)

(87h) (46h)
8-y-o ch g Generous (IRE)-Honor To Her (USA) (Sir Ivor)
J Gallagher B P Jones

Placings:5516/06305-PP6 (0451)
2001/02: 26^{P}GS, 24^{P}F, 23^{6}F

	Starts	1st	2nd	3rd	Win & Pl
Hurdles	1	0	0	0	0
Chases	2	0	0	0	0
Career Total	**12**	**1**	**0**	**1**	**1719**

94	12/98	Ling	2m110y	H NHF	SFT	£1203

Total win prize-money £1203

Going: Sf: 0-0 GS: 0-1 Gd: 0-0 GF: - Fm: 0-2
Distance: 2m/2m3: 0-0 2m4-2m7: 0-1 3m+: 0-2
Track: LH: 0-2 RH: 0-0 Tight: 0-1 Gall: 0-0
Aids: Bl: 0-1 Vi: 0-0 Tstrap: 0-0
Best Rating: 94 12/98 Ling 2m110y soft NHF

Genetic

85(99h) **107**
7-y-o b g Syrtos-Abdera (Ahonoora)
D G Bridgwater Mrs S A Macechern

Placings:00430/20-P1P (2592)
2001/02: 24^{P}G, 24^{1}GF, 25^{P}G

	Starts	1st	2nd	3rd	Win & Pl
Chases	3	1	0	0	4979
Career Total	**10**	**1**	**1**	**1**	**6070**

107	11/01	Ludl	3m	D Ch	G-F	£4979

Total win prize-money £4979

Going: Sf: 0-0 GS: 0-0 Gd: 0-2 GF: - Fm: 1-1
Distance: 2m/2m3: 0-0 2m4-2m7: 0-0 **3m+: 1-3**
Track: LH: 0-1 **RH: 1-2 Tight: 1-2** Gall: 0-1
Aids: Bl: 0-0 Vi: 0-0 Tstrap: 0-0
Best Rating: 107 11/01 Ludl 3m gd-fm Ch

Effective at three miles, he acts on good to firm ground.

Genetic George (IRE)

87 **101**
10-y-o b g King's Ride-Ballyea Jacki (Straight Lad)
Dr P Pritchard A J Whiting

Placings:513/B06/3U-3 (1410)
2001/02: 16^{3}GF

	Starts	1st	2nd	3rd	Win & Pl
Chases	1	0	0	1	604
Career Total	**9**	**1**	**0**	**3**	**5157**

99	4/99	Cork	2m4f	Hdl	SFT	£3683

Total win prize-money £3683

Going: Sf: 0-0 GS: 0-0 Gd: 0-0 GF: - Fm: 0-1
Distance: 2m/2m3: 0-1 2m4-2m7: 0-0 3m+: 0-0
Track: LH: 0-1 RH: 0-0 Tight: 0-0 Gall: 0-0
Aids: Bl: 0-0 Vi: 0-0 Tstrap: 0-0
Best Rating: 101 9/01 Worc 2m gd-fm Ch

Won a maiden hurdle in Ireland in 1999 but held since over hurdles. Better efforts in novice chases at around two miles. Has won on soft, handles faster ground.

Genscher

88(107h) (95h)**81**
6-y-o b g Cadeaux Genereux-Marienbad (FR) (Darshaan)
R Allan Robert Miller-Bakewell

Placings:145P44/3S-04144605 (3351)
2001/02: 17^{0}G, 16^{4}GF, 16^{1}GF, 16^{4}G, 17^{4}GF, 16^{6}G, 16^{0}S, 16^{5}G

	Starts	1st	2nd	3rd	Win & Pl
Hurdles	7	1	0	0	4797
Chases	1	0	0	0	0
Career Total	**16**	**2**	**0**	**1**	**7448**

95	6/01	Prth	2m110y	E(0-115)HHdl	G-F	£4225
84	11/99	Ayr	2m	E Hdl	GD	£2355

Total win prize-money £6580

Going: Sf: 0-1 GS: 0-0 Gd: 0-4 GF: - Fm: 1-3
Distance: **2m/2m3: 1-8** 2m4-2m7: 0-0 3m+: 0-0
Track: LH: 0-4 **RH: 1-4** Tight: 0-3 Gall: 0-1
Aids: Bl: 0-0 Vi: 0-0 Tstrap: 0-1
Best Rating: 95 6/01 Prth 2m110y gd-fm Hdl

Gentle Buck (IRE)

13-y-o ch g Buckskin (FR)-Announcement (Laurence O)
Mrs P Smith Terry E G Smith

Placings:013/1212/63P/F134/0FP03/00-P (4402)
2001/02: 22^{P}GS

	Starts	1st	2nd	3rd	Win & Pl
Chases	1	0	0	0	0
Career Total	**22**	**4**	**2**	**4**	**32859**

102	11/97	Limk	2m6f	Ch	HVY	£4069
128	3/96	Navn	3m	Hdl	SFT	£9974

121	11/95	Gowr	2m6f	Hdl	Y-S	£3391
116	4/95	Gowr	2m1f	NHF	Y-S	£2712

Total win prize-money £20147

Going: Sf: 0-0 GS: 0-1 Gd: 0-0 GF: - Fm: 0-0
Distance: 2m/2m3: 0-0 2m4-2m7: 0-1 3m+: 0-0
Track: LH: 0-1 RH: 0-0 Tight: 0-0 Gall: 0-1
Aids: Bl: 0-0 Vi: 0-0 Tstrap: 0-0
Best Rating: 129 4/96 Punc 2m4f soft Hdl

Gentle Rivage (FR)

100 **132**

8-y-o b g Rose Laurel-Silverado Trail (USA) (Greinton)
N A Twiston-Davies Geoffrey And Donna Keeys

Placings:*3212422341/112213234/***2U2FF4** **(3692)**
2001/02: 20^{2}G, 24^{U}S, 19^{2}GS, 24^{F}G, 16^{F}HY, 22^{4}HY

	Starts	1st	2nd	3rd	Win & Pl
Chases	6	0	2	0	7431
Career Total	**25**	**5**	**9**	**4**	**52083**

140	11/99	Uttx	2m4f110y	A Hdl	SFT	£9525
123	9/99	Prth	3m110y	E Hdl	SFT	£2775
116	9/99	Worc	2m4f	E Hdl	G-F	£2407
114	5/99	Uttx	2m6f110y	E Hdl	GD	£2599
110	11/98	Hayd	2m	H NHF	SFT	£1215

Total win prize-money £18523

Going: Sf: 0-3 GS: 0-1 Gd: 0-2 GF: - Fm: 0-0
Distance: 2m/2m3: 0-1 2m4-2m7: 0-3 3m+: 0-2
Track: LH: 0-4 RH: 0-1 Tight: 0-1 Gall: 0-1
Aids: Bl: 0-0 Vi: 0-0 Tstrap: 0-0
Best Rating: 149 4/00 Aint 3m110y good Hdl

He was a very useful novice hurdler in 1999/2000, finishing third to Monsignor at the Festival. He missed the following season, but has shown promise over fences since returning. He looks to need three miles and his jumping has room for improvement.

Gentry (IRE)

97 **75**

11-y-o b g Aristocracy-Remember Don (Don)
D McCain Champ Chicken Co Ltd

Placings:*2P/4/PPP/6/14F323PP-6P55P4330* **(1837)**
2001/02: 26^{6}GF, 20^{P}GS, 20^{5}GF, 26^{5}GF, 24^{P}GF, 24^{4}GF, 19^{3}GF, 19^{3}G, 25^{0}G

	Starts	1st	2nd	3rd	Win & Pl
Hurdles	1	0	0	0	0
Chases	8	0	0	2	1062
Career Total	**24**	**1**	**2**	**4**	**7289**

94	5/00	Towc	2m110y	E(0-105)HCh	G-F	£2944

Total win prize-money £2945

Going: Sf: 0-0 GS: 0-1 Gd: 0-2 GF: - Fm: 0-6
Distance: 2m/2m3: 0-2 2m4-2m7: 0-2 3m+: 0-5
Track: LH: 0-6 RH: 0-2 Tight: 0-4 Gall: 0-0
Aids: Bl: 0-4 Vi: 0-0 Tstrap: 0-0
Best Rating: 98 6/97 Rosc 2m gd-yld NHF

Genuine Article (IRE)

106 **106**

6-y-o ch g Insan (USA)-Rosemount Rose (Ashmore (FR))
M Pitman Malcolm C Denmark

Placings:*10/*34400-3311 **(0916)**
2001/02: 22^{3}GF, 23^{3}GF, 16^{1}GF, 16^{1}GF

	Starts	1st	2nd	3rd	Win & Pl
Hurdles	4	2	0	2	6650
Career Total	**11**	**3**	**0**	**3**	**9597**

106	7/01	Strf	2m110y	D(0-125)HHdl	G-F	£3393
104	7/01	Strf	2m110y	E(0-105)HHdl	G-F	£2471
91	2/00	Wwck	2m	H NHF	SFT	£1956

Total win prize-money £7821

Going: Sf: 0-0 GS: 0-0 Gd: 0-0 GF: - Fm: 2-4
Distance: **2m/2m3: 2-2** 2m4-2m7: 0-1 3m+: 0-1
Track: **LH: 2-4** RH: 0-0 **Tight: 2-4** Gall: 0-0
Aids: Bl: 0-0 Vi: 0-0 Tstrap: 0-0
Best Rating: 106 7/01 Strf 2m110y gd-fm Hdl

Good winner on his debut in a Warwick bumper, he failed to build on that until scoring back to back wins in the summer of 2001.

Genuine John (IRE)

9-y-o b g High Estate-Fiscal Folly (USA) (Foolish Pleasure (USA))
J Parkes Mrs G M Z Spink

Placings:0/P0360/6-P **(1724)**
2001/02: 25^{P}G

	Starts	1st	2nd	3rd	Win & Pl
Hurdles	1	0	0	0	
Career Total	**8**	**0**	**0**	**1**	**334**

Going: Sf: 0-0 GS: 0-0 Gd: 0-1 GF: - Fm: 0-0
Distance: 2m/2m3: 0-0 2m4-2m7: 0-0 3m+: 0-1
Track: LH: 0-1 RH: 0-0 Tight: 0-0 Gall: 0-0
Aids: Bl: 0-0 Vi: 0-0 Tstrap: 0-1
Best Rating: 83 1/00 Donc 2m110y gd-fm Hdl

Geordies Express

10-y-o b g Tina's Pet-Maestroes Beauty (Music Maestro)
G T Bewley G T Bewley

Placings:5/33U261 **(4690)**
2001/02: 24^{3}S, 21^{3}S, 21^{U}HY, 27^{2}S, 25^{6}HY, 25^{1}GF

	Starts	1st	2nd	3rd	Win & Pl
Chases	6	1	1	2	3566
Career Total	**7**	**1**	**1**	**2**	**3566**

109	4/02	Kels	3m1f	H Ch	G-F	£2587

Total win prize-money £2587

Going: Sf: 0-5 GS: 0-0 Gd: 0-0 GF: - Fm: 1-1
Distance: 2m/2m3: 0-0 2m4-2m7: 0-2 **3m+: 1-4**
Track: **LH: 1-5** RH: 0-1 **Tight: 1-5** Gall: 0-0
Aids: Bl: 0-0 Vi: 0-0 Tstrap: 0-0
Best Rating: 109 4/02 Kels 3m1f gd-fm Ch

Winning pointer and Hunter Chaser. Acts on a sound surface. Handles soft ground.

George Ashford (IRE)

92(87h) (24h)**65**

12-y-o b g Ashford (USA)-Running Feud (Prince Tenderfoot (USA))
P R Johnson P Johnson

Placings:*02344000/26024344414143P0P/031324606/44/***56P6-5P0P06** **(4590)**
2001/02: 16^{5}GF, 26^{P}S, 20^{0}HY, 24^{P}GS, 24^{0}S, 24^{6}G

	Starts	1st	2nd	3rd	Win & Pl
Hurdles	1	0	0	0	0
Chases	5	0	0	0	0
Career Total	**46**	**3**	**4**	**5**	**12745**

94	8/96	Sthl	3m110y	E(0-100)HCh	GD	£3812
90	11/95	Hexm	2m4f110y	E Hdl	G-F	£2422
91	8/95	Dpat	2m1f172y	Hdl	FRM	£1356

Total win prize-money £7591

Going: Sf: 0-3 GS: 0-1 Gd: 0-1 GF: - Fm: 0-1
Distance: 2m/2m3: 0-1 2m4-2m7: 0-1 3m+: 0-4
Track: LH: 0-3 RH: 0-3 Tight: 0-2 Gall: 0-1
Aids: Bl: 0-1 Vi: 0-0 Tstrap: 0-0
Best Rating: 96 12/95 Weth 2m4f110y good Hdl

Acts well on a sound surface, but has not won since August 1996.

George Dillingham

12-y-o b g Top Ville-Premier Rose (Sharp Edge)
M J Jackson David Yeomans

Placings:25/0214214/2/5/**533-2FF** **(4376)**
2001/02: 24^{2}S, 19^{F}S, 20^{F}S

	Starts	1st	2nd	3rd	Win & Pl
Chases	3	0	1	0	330
Career Total	**17**	**2**	**5**	**2**	**11955**

114	3/98	Donc	2m110y	E(0-105)HHdl	SFT	£2721
100	1/98	Muss	2m	E Hdl	G-S	£2057

Total win prize-money £4778

Going: Sf: 0-3 GS: 0-0 Gd: 0-0 GF: - Fm: 0-0
Distance: 2m/2m3: 0-0 2m4-2m7: 0-2 3m+: 0-1
Track: LH: 0-1 RH: 0-2 Tight: 0-1 Gall: 0-2
Aids: Bl: 0-0 Vi: 0-0 Tstrap: 0-0
Best Rating: 114 3/98 Donc 2m110y soft Hdl

A fairly useful stayer on the Flat, he was successful over hurdles and has been paying his way over fences. Has been pointing aswell. Appreciates cut in the ground.

Georgia Peach (IRE)

96 **84**

4-y-o b g Pennekamp (USA)-Across The Ice (USA) (General Holme (USA))
L Lungo (D K Weld 26/9) Miss S Blumberg

Placings:50 **(4494)**
2001/02: 18^{5}HY, 22^{0}G

	Starts	1st	2nd	3rd	Win & Pl
Hurdles	2	0	0	0	0
Career Total	**2**	**0**	**0**	**0**	**0**

Going: Sf: 0-1 GS: 0-0 Gd: 0-1 GF: - Fm: 0-0
Distance: 2m/2m3: 0-1 2m4-2m7: 0-1 3m+: 0-0
Track: LH: 0-2 RH: 0-0 Tight: 0-1 Gall: 0-0
Aids: Bl: 0-0 Vi: 0-0 Tstrap: 0-0
Best Rating: 67 3/02 Kels 2m2f heavy Hdl

Georgian Harry (IRE)

102 **103**

5-y-o b g Warcraft (USA)-Solo Player (Blue Refrain)
R T Phillips (S A Brookshaw 12/5) Dawn And Mark Dennis

Placings:*0-*06442 **(4597)**
2001/02: 16^{0}GF, 16^{6}G, 16^{4}G, 19^{4}S, 19^{2}GF

	Starts	1st	2nd	3rd	Win & Pl
NH Flat	2	0	0	0	0
Hurdles	3	0	1	0	835
Career Total	**6**	**0**	**1**	**0**	**835**

Going: Sf: 0-1 GS: 0-0 Gd: 0-2 GF: - Fm: 0-2
Distance: 2m/2m3: 0-5 2m4-2m7: 0-0 3m+: 0-0
Track: LH: 0-4 RH: 0-1 Tight: 0-2 Gall: 0-1
Aids: Bl: 0-0 Vi: 0-0 Tstrap: 0-0
Best Rating: 103 4/02 Wwck 2m3f gd-fm Hdl

No real promise in bumpers, but better over hurdles.Stays two miles-three, acts on a sound surface. Looks as though three miles will suit.

Georgic Blaze

99 **91**

8-y-o b g Petoski-Pooka (Dominion)
G A Ham E Simmons

Placings:*60*P/000-P1PU0U0F **(4047)**
2001/02: 20^{P}S, 17^{1}S, 19^{P}G, 19^{U}GS, 17^{0}G, 19^{U}S, 19^{0}S, 17^{F}G

	Starts	1st	2nd	3rd	Win & Pl
Hurdles	8	1	0	0	2289
Career Total	**14**	**1**	**0**	**0**	**2289**

91	11/01	NAbb	2m1f	G Hdl	SFT	£2289

Total win prize-money £2289

Going: Sf: 1-4 GS: 0-1 Gd: 0-3 GF: - Fm: 0-0
Distance: **2m/2m3: 1-4** 2m4-2m7: 0-4 3m+: 0-0
Track: **LH: 1-2** RH: 0-6 **Tight: 1-3** Gall: 0-0
Aids: Bl: 0-0 Vi: 0-0 Tstrap: 0-0
Best Rating: 91 11/01 NAbb 2m1f soft Hdl

Looked of little ability until winning a seller at Newton Abbot in November 2001.

Geos (FR)

113(113c) (163c)**167**

7-y-o b g Pistolet Bleu (IRE)-Kaprika (FR) (Cadoudal (FR))
N J Henderson Thurloe Finsbury

Placings:12111/063132102/31132-264P **(4676)**
2001/02: 20^{2}GS, 16^{6}HY, 16^{4}GS, 20^{P}G

	Starts	1st	2nd	3rd	Win & Pl
Hurdles	3	0	0	0	13500
Chases	1	0	1	0	11500
Career Total	**23**	**8**	**5**	**4**	**223312**

154	12/00	Kemp	2m	A Hdl	G-S	£29000
167	12/00	Chel	2m1f	A Hdl	SFT	£24000
164	2/00	Newb	2m110y	A HHdl	G-S	£58000
135	11/99	Leic	2m	C(0-130)HHdl	G-S	£7200
	3/99	Lyrh	2m1f	Ch	HLD	£4306
	12/98	Engh	2m1f110y	Hdl	HLD	£11111
	12/98	Engh	2m1f110y	Hdl	VS	£10101
	6/98	Vitr	1m7f	Hdl	SFT	£2626

Total win prize-money £146344

Going: Sf: 0-1 GS: 0-2 Gd: 0-1 GF: - Fm: 0-0
Distance: 2m/2m3: 0-2 2m4-2m7: 0-2 3m+: 0-0
Track: LH: 0-3 RH: 0-1 Tight: 0-1 Gall: 0-1
Aids: Bl: 0-0 Vi: 0-0 Tstrap: 0-0
Best Rating: 167 4/01 Sand 2m110y soft Hdl

A high-class hurdler who enjoyed a very successful year in 2000, but has not quite gone on to the type of success that seemed likely and has kept finding one or two too good in the 2001/2002 season. He won over fences in France in his younger days and is not eligible for novice chases, but did well when chasing home Edredon Bleu on his first attempt over British fences in the autumn of 2001. Suited by cut in the ground and two miles.

Gerej (POL)

87 **57**

12-y-o ch g Unoaprile-Gerda (POL) (Damon (POL))
Mrs P Sly (Miss Katie Thory 21/4) Miss Katie Thory

Placings:04 **(0450)**
2001/02: 24^{0}GF, 23^{4}F

	Starts	1st	2nd	3rd	Win & Pl
Chases	2	0	0	0	316
Career Total	**2**	**0**	**0**	**0**	**316**

Going: Sf: 0-0 GS: 0-0 Gd: 0-0 GF: - Fm: 0-2
Distance: 2m/2m3: 0-0 2m4-2m7: 0-0 3m+: 0-2
Track: LH: 0-1 RH: 0-0 Tight: 0-1 Gall: 0-0
Aids: Bl: 0-0 Vi: 0-0 Tstrap: 0-0
Best Rating: 57 5/01 Fknm 3m110y gd-fm Ch

German Legend

79 **49**

12-y-o br g Faustus (USA)-Fairfields (Sharpen Up)
D A Lamb D G Pryde

Placings:0006055/543363/10335550F30/04**13603P/3**
3/23U045FF0/0**P/45-00** **(0960)**
2001/02: 20^{0}GS, 21^{0}GF

	Starts	1st	2nd	3rd	Win & Pl
Chases	2	0	0	0	
Career Total	**49**	**2**	**1**	**11**	**10051**

78	9/96	Carl	3m	E Ch	FRM	£2060
76	5/95	Hexm	3m	G(0-100)HHdl	FRM	£2176

Total win prize-money £4237

Going: Sf: 0-0 GS: 0-1 Gd: 0-0 GF: - Fm: 0-1
Distance: 2m/2m3: 0-0 2m4-2m7: 0-2 3m+: 0-0
Track: LH: 0-2 RH: 0-0 Tight: 0-1 Gall: 0-0
Aids: Bl: 0-0 Vi: 0-0 Tstrap: 0-0
Best Rating: 92 5/98 Hexm 3m1f gd-fm Ch

Gerry And Tom (IRE)

12-y-o ch g Strong Statement (USA)-Clare's Hansel (Prince Hansel)
C J Hemsley Miss A K Hope

Placings:*0*/**03025P**05300/**05655PP4/3245/P4** **(1394)**
2001/02: 23^{P}GF, 23^{4}GF

	Starts	1st	2nd	3rd	Win & Pl
Chases	2	0	0	0	300
Career Total	**26**	**0**	**2**	**3**	**3760**

Going: Sf: 0-0 GS: 0-0 Gd: 0-0 GF: - Fm: 0-2
Distance: 2m/2m3: 0-0 2m4-2m7: 0-0 3m+: 0-2
Track: LH: 0-2 RH: 0-0 Tight: 0-0 Gall: 0-0
Aids: Bl: 0-0 Vi: 0-0 Tstrap: 0-0
Best Rating: 93 11/97 Clon 2m4f gd-yld Ch

Get Real (IRE)

108(85h) (85h)**164**

11-y-o br g Executive Perk-Lisa's Music (Abwah)
N J Henderson Pioneer Heat-Treatment

Placings:*42*/654/**1112/212/11P15/1224224-206P**
(4759)
2001/02: 16^{2}G, 16^{0}G, 16^{6}G, 19^{P}GF

	Starts	1st	2nd	3rd	Win & Pl
Hurdles	1	0	0	0	0
Chases	3	0	1	0	5177
Career Total	**28**	**8**	**9**	**0**	**121102**

165	5/00	Punc	2m	Ch	YLD	£29920
170	12/99	Asct	2m	B HCh	G-S	£9403
160	11/99	Asct	2m	B HCh	GD	£10756
157	10/99	Asct	2m	B HCh	GD	£16758
149	12/98	Asct	2m	B HCh	G-S	£9339
136	4/98	Ludl	2m	D Ch	GD	£3582
129	12/97	Hntg	2m110y	E(0-105)HCh	GD	£3731
125	11/97	Ludl	2m	E Ch	GD	£2918

Total win prize-money £86411

Going: Sf: 0-0 GS: 0-0 Gd: 0-3 GF: - Fm: 0-1
Distance: 2m/2m3: 0-3 2m4-2m7: 0-1 3m+: 0-0
Track: LH: 0-0 RH: 0-4 Tight: 0-4 Gall: 0-0
Aids: Bl: 0-0 Vi: 0-0 Tstrap: 0-0
Best Rating: 170 2/01 Kemp 2m good Ch

A front-runner who is far better going right-handed, he only just gets the two miles and is something of an Ascot regular. He won the valuable B.M.W Chase at Punchestown in May 2000 but endured a rather frustrating campaign thereafter, being a beaten favourite on no fewer than five of his six starts. He returned to action after a break at Ascot in December 2001, where he was once again a beaten favourite, after being caught close home by Wahiba Sands. Held on his return to hurdles in April.

Get The Gist (IRE)

89 **75**

9-y-o b g Ore-Rare Picture (Pollerton)
Mrs D A Hamer Mrs D A Hamer

Placings:4 **(1393)**
2001/02: 24^{4}GF

	Starts	1st	2nd	3rd	Win & Pl
Hurdles	1	0	0	0	0
Career Total	**1**	**0**	**0**	**0**	**0**

Going: Sf: 0-0 GS: 0-0 Gd: 0-0 GF: - Fm: 0-1
Distance: 2m/2m3: 0-0 2m4-2m7: 0-0 3m+: 0-1
Track: LH: 0-1 RH: 0-0 Tight: 0-1 Gall: 0-0
Aids: Bl: 0-0 Vi: 0-0 Tstrap: 0-0
Best Rating: 75 9/01 Worc 3m gd-fm Hdl

Geyserville

4-y-o ch g Mujtahid (USA)-Pennsylvania (USA) (Northjet)
Brendan W Duke (P W D'Arcy 11/6) Brendan W Duke Racing

Placings:P **(1735)**
2001/02: 17^{P}GS

	Starts	1st	2nd	3rd	Win & Pl
Hurdles	1	0	0	0	
Career Total	**1**	**0**	**0**	**0**	

Going: Sf: 0-0 GS: 0-1 Gd: 0-0 GF: - Fm: 0-0
Distance: 2m/2m3: 0-1 2m4-2m7: 0-0 3m+: 0-0
Track: LH: 0-0 RH: 0-1 Tight: 0-0 Gall: 0-0
Aids: Bl: 0-0 Vi: 0-0 Tstrap: 0-0
Best Rating:

Ghaazi

95(102h) (94h)88

6-y-o ch g Lahib (USA)-Shurooq (USA) (Affirmed (USA))

M Hill Martin Hill

Placings:4233405-34043 **(2661)**

2001/02: 16^{3}GF, 16^{4}G, 16^{0}G, 17^{4}GS, 19^{3}GS

	Starts	1st	2nd	3rd	Win & Pl
Hurdles	5	0	0	2	1555
Career Total	**12**	**0**	**1**	**4**	**3796**

Going: Sf: 0-0 GS: 0-2 Gd: 0-2 GF: - Fm: 0-1
Distance: 2m/2m3: 0-4 2m4-2m7: 0-1 3m+: 0-0
Track: LH: 0-1 RH: 0-4 Tight: 0-2 Gall: 0-0
Aids: Bl: 0-0 Vi: 0-1 Tstrap: 0-0
Best Rating: 94 12/01 Tntn 2m3f110y gd-sft Hdl

Moderate, free-running novice hurdler, best suited by good or fast ground and a good gallop. Has worn head-gear.

Ghadames (FR)

109(44h) 130+

8-y-o b g Synefos (USA)-Ouargla (FR) (Armos)

M Todhunter Sir Robert Ogden

Placings:50/0P12/6152-11 **(1086)**

2001/02: 20^{1}F, 20^{1}G

	Starts	1st	2nd	3rd	Win & Pl
Chases	2	2	0	0	5811
Career Total	**12**	**4**	**2**	**0**	**14413**

130	8/01	Bang	2m4f110y	F(0-95)HCh	GD	£2996
118	5/01	Hexm	2m4f110y	F(0-105)HCh	FRM	£2814
112	10/00	Ludl	2m5f	E(0-105)HHdl	G-F	£2695
102	3/00	Bang	2m1f110y	D Ch	GD	£3867

Total win prize-money £12374

Going: Sf: 0-0 GS: 0-0 Gd: 1-1 GF: - Fm: 1-1
Distance: 2m/2m3: 0-0 **2m4-2m7: 2-2** 3m+: 0-0
Track: **LH: 2-2** RH: 0-0 **Tight: 1-1** Gall: 0-0
Aids: Bl: 0-0 Vi: 0-0 Tstrap: 0-0
Best Rating: 130 8/01 Bang 2m4f110y good Ch

Progressive chaser, he is a keen sort who is effective at two and a half miles. Appears to act on most types of ground. Needs a decent pace.

Ghali (USA)

69 76

7-y-o b g Alleged (USA)-Kareema (USA) (Coastal (USA))

J F Coupland J F Coupland

Placings:0054/P45400P400/0P000-P0 **(4906)**

2001/02: 21^{P}G, 19^{0}G

	Starts	1st	2nd	3rd	Win & Pl
Hurdles	2	0	0	0	
Career Total	**21**	**0**	**0**	**0**	**382**

Going: Sf: 0-0 GS: 0-0 Gd: 0-2 GF: - Fm: 0-0
Distance: 2m/2m3: 0-0 2m4-2m7: 0-2 3m+: 0-0
Track: LH: 0-0 RH: 0-2 Tight: 0-2 Gall: 0-0
Aids: Bl: 0-0 Vi: 0-0 Tstrap: 0-2
Best Rating: 90 3/00 Sedg 2m5f110y gd-fm Hdl

Ghost

8-y-o gr m Formidable (USA)-Genie Spirit (Nishapour (FR))

Mrs D Thomson Mrs Dorothy Thomson

Placings:*600*/P **(4689)**

2001/02: 16^{P}GF

	Starts	1st	2nd	3rd	Win & Pl
Hurdles	1	0	0	0	
Career Total	**4**	**0**	**0**	**0**	**0**

Going: Sf: 0-0 GS: 0-0 Gd: 0-0 GF: - Fm: 0-1
Distance: 2m/2m3: 0-1 2m4-2m7: 0-0 3m+: 0-0
Track: LH: 0-1 RH: 0-0 Tight: 0-1 Gall: 0-0
Aids: Bl: 0-0 Vi: 0-0 Tstrap: 0-0
Best Rating: 78 9/98 Hntg 2m110y gd-fm NHF

Ghost Moon

(68h)

7-y-o b g Cadeaux Genereux-Sickle Moon (Shirley Heights)

N J Hawke Mrs J B Jenkins

Placings:30/F02/PP00-0 **(0082)**

2001/02: 19^{0}G

	Starts	1st	2nd	3rd	Win & Pl
Chases	1	0	0	0	
Career Total	**10**	**0**	**1**	**1**	**300**

Going: Sf: 0-0 GS: 0-0 Gd: 0-1 GF: - Fm: 0-0
Distance: 2m/2m3: 0-1 2m4-2m7: 0-0 3m+: 0-0
Track: LH: 0-0 RH: 0-1 Tight: 0-0 Gall: 0-0
Aids: Bl: 0-0 Vi: 0-0 Tstrap: 0-0
Best Rating: 79 1/99 MRas 1m5f110y soft NHF

Ghutah

107(105h) (88h)110

8-y-o ch g Lycius (USA)-Barada (USA) (Damascus (USA))

Mrs A M Thorpe (G A Swinbank 7/9) Three A's Caravan

Placings:0F0PP/U23046P-6F1115450433 **(4917)**

2001/02: 16^{6}GF, 16^{F}GF, 17^{1}GF, 16^{1}GF, 17^{1}GF, 16^{5}S, 16^{4}GF, 19^{5}GS, 16^{0}G, 16^{4}GS, 16^{3}F, 21^{3}GF

	Starts	1st	2nd	3rd	Win & Pl
Hurdles	12	3	0	2	7855
Career Total	**24**	**3**	**1**	**3**	**8674**

88	9/01	Sedg	2m1f	G(0-95)HHdl	G-F	£2033
83	8/01	Uttx	2m	G(0-95)HHdl	G-F	£2009
83	8/01	Sedg	2m1f	G(0-90)HHdl	G-F	£1981

Total win prize-money £6024

Going: Sf: 0-1 GS: 0-2 Gd: 0-1 GF: - Fm: 3-8
Distance: **2m/2m3: 3-11** 2m4-2m7: 0-1 3m+: 0-0
Track: **LH: 3-8** RH: 0-4 **Tight: 2-4** Gall: 0-2
Aids: Bl: 0-1 Vi: 0-0 Tstrap: 0-0
Best Rating: 88 4/02 Newc 2m firm Hdl

It took him time to find his feet over hurdles, but he eventually came good with a hat-trick on firm ground in the late summer of 2001. Held off higher marks subsequently.

Gianluca (IRE)

98 101

8-y-o br g Un Desperado (FR)-Belwood Girl (Ballymore)

C R Egerton M E T Davies

Placings: 1/1 **(2208)**

2001/02: 16^{1}GS

	Starts	1st	2nd	3rd	Win & Pl
Hurdles	1	1	0	0	3231
Career Total	**2**	**2**	**0**	**0**	**4868**

101	11/01	Leic	2m	E Hdl	G-S	£3230
115	12/99	Ludl	2m	H NHF	GD	£1637

Total win prize-money £4868

Going: Sf: 0-0 GS: 1-1 Gd: 0-0 GF: - Fm: 0-0
Distance: **2m/2m3: 1-1** 2m4-2m7: 0-0 3m+: 0-0
Track: LH: 0-0 **RH: 1-1** Tight: 0-0 Gall: 0-0
Aids: Bl: 0-0 Vi: 0-0 Tstrap: 0-0
Best Rating: 115 12/99 Ludl 2m good NHF

He won a bumper at Ludlow on his racecourse debut in December 1999. Absent until winning his hurdles debut on his reappearance in November 2001.

Gielgud

97 95

5-y-o b g Faustus (USA)-Shirl (Shirley Heights)

P R Webber Mrs J K Powell

Placings:20032 **(4842)**

2001/02: 17^{2}S, 16^{0}G, 17^{6}G, 16^{3}HY, 20^{2}G

	Starts	1st	2nd	3rd	Win & Pl
NH Flat	2	0	1	0	493
Hurdles	3	0	1	1	1657
Career Total	**5**	**0**	**2**	**1**	**2150**

Going: Sf: 0-2 GS: 0-0 Gd: 0-3 GF: - Fm: 0-0
Distance: 2m/2m3: 0-4 2m4-2m7: 0-1 3m+: 0-0
Track: LH: 0-5 RH: 0-0 Tight: 0-2 Gall: 0-1
Aids: Bl: 0-0 Vi: 0-0 Tstrap: 0-0
Best Rating: 98 10/01 Bang 2m1f soft NHF

Just touched off in a bumper on his debut in October and appreciated the better ground when runner-up in a novices' hurdle at Bangor in April. A potential chaser.

Gigi Beach (IRE)

98 (105h)113

11-y-o ch g Roselier (FR)-Cranagh Lady (Le Bavard (FR))

Ian Williams (P F Nicholls 30/6) Mrs Rosemary Paterson

Placings:54U11/23P4121/25223F0/F2P2340-P6P2535 **(3457)**

2001/02: 28^{P}G, 28^{6}GF, 26^{P}GF, 25^{2}G, 30^{5}GS, 27^{3}G, 26^{5}S

	Starts	1st	2nd	3rd	Win & Pl
Hurdles	1	0	1	0	978
Chases	6	0	0	1	1224
Career Total	**33**	**4**	**8**	**4**	**45516**

131	4/99	Chel	3m2f110y	C(0-135)HCh	GD	£8247
126	3/99	Extr	3m6f	D(0-125)HCh	SFT	£7415
125	4/98	Font	3m2f110y	E Ch	SFT	£3353
96	3/98	Font	3m2f110y	E Ch	G-F	£2768

Total win prize-money £21783

Going: Sf: 0-1 GS: 0-1 Gd: 0-3 GF: - Fm: 0-2
Distance: 2m/2m3: 0-0 2m4-2m7: 0-0 3m+: 0-7
Track: LH: 0-4 RH: 0-2 Tight: 0-4 Gall: 0-1
Aids: Bl: 0-3 Vi: 0-1 Tstrap: 0-0
Best Rating: 134 11/00 Chel 3m110y gd-sft Ch

He lacks pace and is most effective forcing the issue over extreme distances. Disappointing in 2000/2001 and has changed stables since. Seems best on good ground. Has worn blinkers unsuccessfully but ran better in a visor.

Gigolo Gerry (IRE)

9-y-o b g Mandalus-Some Madam (Some Hand)
R Rowe Nicholas Cooper

Placings:36233/22-P (3323)
2001/02: 16^{P}GS

	Starts	1st	2nd	3rd	Win & Pl
Chases	1	0	0	0	
Career Total	**8**	**0**	**3**	**3**	**7636**

Going: Sf: 0-0 GS: 0-1 Gd: 0-0 GF: - Fm: 0-0
Distance: 2m/2m3: 0-1 2m4-2m7: 0-0 3m+: 0-0
Track: LH: 0-0 RH: 0-1 Tight: 0-0 Gall: 0-1
Aids: Bl: 0-0 Vi: 0-0 Tstrap: 0-0
Best Rating: 130 12/00 Kemp 2m4f110y gd-sft Ch

Still a maiden under Rules, he ran two promising races in novice chases and will break his duck before long. He promises to stay three miles and goes well on good ground.

Gigs Gambit (IRE)

91f 99f
5-y-o ch g Hubbly Bubbly (USA)-Music Slipper (IRE) (Orchestra)
M Pitman J Barson

Placings:*350* (4166)
2001/02: 16^{3}S, 16^{5}S, 16^{0}GS

	Starts	1st	2nd	3rd	Win & Pl
NH Flat	3	0	0	1	286
Career Total	**3**	**0**	**0**	**1**	**286**

Going: Sf: 0-2 GS: 0-1 Gd: 0-0 GF: - Fm: 0-0
Distance: 2m/2m3: 0-3 2m4-2m7: 0-0 3m+: 0-0
Track: LH: 0-1 RH: 0-2 Tight: 0-0 Gall: 0-0
Aids: Bl: 0-0 Vi: 0-0 Tstrap: 0-0
Best Rating: 99 2/02 Sand 2m110y soft NHF

Modest bumper form.

Giko

75 56
8-y-o b g Arazi (USA)-Gayane (Nureyev (USA))
Jane Southcombe V R V Partnership

Placings:0 (2139)
2001/02: 17^{0}G

	Starts	1st	2nd	3rd	Win & Pl
Hurdles	1	0	0	0	
Career Total	**1**	**0**	**0**	**0**	

Going: Sf: 0-0 GS: 0-0 Gd: 0-1 GF: - Fm: 0-0
Distance: 2m/2m3: 0-1 2m4-2m7: 0-0 3m+: 0-0
Track: LH: 0-0 RH: 0-1 Tight: 0-1 Gall: 0-0
Aids: Bl: 0-0 Vi: 0-0 Tstrap: 0-0
Best Rating: 56 11/01 Tntn 2m1f good Hdl

Gilbert White

88 66
9-y-o b g Little Wolf-Caribs Love (Caliban)
J Barclay Mrs G Rowan-Hamilton

Placings:*4P/P3/*0-00F (3347)
2001/02: 16^{0}GS, 16^{0}GS, 16^{F}G

	Starts	1st	2nd	3rd	Win & Pl
Hurdles	3	0	0	0	
Career Total	**8**	**0**	**0**	**1**	**503**

Going: Sf: 0-0 GS: 0-2 Gd: 0-1 GF: - Fm: 0-0
Distance: 2m/2m3: 0-3 2m4-2m7: 0-0 3m+: 0-0
Track: LH: 0-2 RH: 0-1 Tight: 0-3 Gall: 0-0
Aids: Bl: 0-0 Vi: 0-0 Tstrap: 0-0
Best Rating: 99 3/99 Chep 2m110y gd-sft NHF

Gilded Lily

72 38
7-y-o b m Gildoran-Fit For A King (Royalty)
J Neville Ron Bartlett

Placings:*000/*00PP-0 (0122)
2001/02: 19^{0}F

	Starts	1st	2nd	3rd	Win & Pl
Hurdles	1	0	0	0	
Career Total	**8**	**0**	**0**	**0**	

Going: Sf: 0-0 GS: 0-0 Gd: 0-0 GF: - Fm: 0-1
Distance: 2m/2m3: 0-0 2m4-2m7: 0-1 3m+: 0-0
Track: LH: 0-0 RH: 0-1 Tight: 0-1 Gall: 0-0
Aids: Bl: 0-0 Vi: 0-0 Tstrap: 0-0
Best Rating: 67 5/00 Hntg 2m110y gd-fm Hdl

Gilded Way

8-y-o b g Gildoran-Gamblingway (Gambling Debt)
E Haddock E Haddock

Placings:*0-*P (0366)
2001/02: 25^{P}G

	Starts	1st	2nd	3rd	Win & Pl
Hurdles	1	0	0	0	
Career Total	**2**	**0**	**0**	**0**	

Going: Sf: 0-0 GS: 0-0 Gd: 0-1 GF: - Fm: 0-0
Distance: 2m/2m3: 0-0 2m4-2m7: 0-0 3m+: 0-1
Track: LH: 0-0 RH: 0-0 Tight: 0-0 Gall: 0-0
Aids: Bl: 0-0 Vi: 0-0 Tstrap: 0-0
Best Rating: 11 1/01 Catt 2m gd-sft NHF

Gildrom

8-y-o b g Gildoran-Drombay (Relkino)
Mrs M Elliot M T Elliot

Placings:1P2-12 (0429)
2001/02: 24^{1}GF, 25^{2}G

	Starts	1st	2nd	3rd	Win & Pl
Chases	2	1	1	0	2858
Career Total	**5**	**2**	**2**	**0**	**4767**

118	5/01	Strf	3m	H Ch	G-F	£1722
130	2/01	Hntg	3m	H Ch	G-S	£1201

Total win prize-money £2925

Going: Sf: 0-0 GS: 0-0 Gd: 0-1 GF: - Fm: 1-1
Distance: 2m/2m3: 0-0 2m4-2m7: 0-0 **3m+: 1-2**
Track: **LH: 1-1** RH: 0-0 **Tight: 1-1** Gall: 0-0
Aids: Bl: 0-0 Vi: 0-0 Tstrap: 0-0
Best Rating: 130 2/01 Hntg 3m gd-sft Ch

Useful Hunter Chaser. Effective over three miles with give underfoot.

Gilfoot Breeze (IRE)

81 64
5-y-o b g Forest Wind (USA)-Ma Bella Luna (Jalmood (USA))
A Robson (J R Norton 27/11) A Robson

Placings:3006-0600 (4491)
2001/02: 23^{0}G, 20^{6}S, 19^{0}GS, 20^{0}GS

	Starts	1st	2nd	3rd	Win & Pl
Hurdles	4	0	0	0	0
Career Total	**8**	**0**	**0**	**1**	**362**

Going: Sf: 0-1 GS: 0-2 Gd: 0-1 GF: - Fm: 0-0
Distance: 2m/2m3: 0-0 2m4-2m7: 0-4 3m+: 0-0
Track: LH: 0-1 RH: 0-1 Tight: 0-1 Gall: 0-0
Aids: Bl: 0-0 Vi: 0-0 Tstrap: 0-0
Best Rating: 86 11/00 MRas 2m1f110y soft Hdl

Gillone

10-y-o b g Gildoran-Speakalone (Articulate)
J H Docker J H Docker

Placings:F (4053)
2001/02: 20^{F}S

	Starts	1st	2nd	3rd	Win & Pl
Chases	1	0	0	0	
Career Total	**1**	**0**	**0**	**0**	

Going: Sf: 0-1 GS: 0-0 Gd: 0-0 GF: - Fm: 0-0
Distance: 2m/2m3: 0-0 2m4-2m7: 0-1 3m+: 0-0
Track: LH: 0-0 RH: 0-1 Tight: 0-0 Gall: 0-0
Aids: Bl: 0-0 Vi: 0-0 Tstrap: 0-0
Best Rating:

Gilly Weet

91 69
6-y-o b m Almoojid-Sindos (Busted)
R Hollinshead Mrs G A Weetman

Placings:00/P-422005 (2212)
2001/02: 16^{4}GS, 17^{2}G, 20^{2}G, 16^{0}GF, 17^{0}G, 17^{5}G

	Starts	1st	2nd	3rd	Win & Pl
Hurdles	6	0	2	0	1773
Career Total	**9**	**0**	**2**	**0**	**1773**

Going: Sf: 0-0 GS: 0-1 Gd: 0-4 GF: - Fm: 0-1
Distance: 2m/2m3: 0-5 2m4-2m7: 0-1 3m+: 0-0
Track: LH: 0-4 RH: 0-2 Tight: 0-3 Gall: 0-0
Aids: Bl: 0-0 Vi: 0-0 Tstrap: 0-0
Best Rating: 69 8/01 Bang 2m4f good Hdl

Plating-class hurdler, he goes well at Bangor on good ground.

Gillymoss

71
8-y-o b/br m Gildoran-Mossy Morning (Le Moss)
J C Tuck Mrs J M F Dibben

Placings: 0PP-6P3 (2778)
2001/02: 22^6GF, 20^PGS, 22^3G

	Starts	1st	2nd	3rd	Win & Pl
Hurdles	2	0	0	1	341
Chases	1	0	0	0	0
Career Total	**6**	**0**	**0**	**1**	**341**

Going: Sf: 0-0 GS: 0-1 Gd: 0-1 GF: - Fm: 0-1
Distance: 2m/2m3: 0-0 2m4-2m7: 0-3 3m+: 0-0
Track: LH: 0-0 RH: 0-0 Tight: 0-1 Gall: 0-0
Aids: Bl: 0-0 Vi: 0-0 Tstrap: 0-0
Best Rating: 71 12/01 Extr 2m6f110y good Hdl

Gilzine

91 66

6-y-o b g Gildoran-Sherzine (Gorytus (USA))
M Hill Better Late Than Never

Placings: 34-6U (3986)
2001/02: 17^6GS, 19US

	Starts	1st	2nd	3rd	Win & Pl
NH Flat	1	0	0	0	0
Hurdles	1	0	0	0	0
Career Total	**4**	**0**	**0**	**1**	**253**

Going: Sf: 0-1 GS: 0-1 Gd: 0-0 GF: - Fm: 0-0
Distance: 2m/2m3: 0-1 2m4-2m7: 0-1 3m+: 0-0
Track: LH: 0-0 RH: 0-2 Tight: 0-1 Gall: 0-0
Aids: Bl: 0-0 Vi: 0-0 Tstrap: 0-0
Best Rating: 89 5/00 Extr 2m1f gd-fm NHF

Gimme Shelter (IRE)

8-y-o ch m Glacial Storm (USA)-Glen Dieu (Furry Glen)
S J Marshall S J Marshall

Placings: 004042P/4-F (2634)
2001/02: 25^FS

	Starts	1st	2nd	3rd	Win & Pl
Chases	1	0	0	0	
Career Total	**9**	**0**	**1**	**0**	**615**

Going: Sf: 0-1 GS: 0-0 Gd: 0-0 GF: - Fm: 0-0
Distance: 2m/2m3: 0-0 2m4-2m7: 0-0 3m+: 0-1
Track: LH: 0-1 RH: 0-0 Tight: 0-0 Gall: 0-0
Aids: Bl: 0-0 Vi: 0-0 Tstrap: 0-0
Best Rating: 76 1/00 Sedg 2m5f110y soft Hdl

Gin N Ice (IRE)

103(83h) (54h)73

9-y-o gr g Glacial Storm (USA)-Theo's Gin (Teofane)
J R Cornwall (Mrs D Haine 21/7) J R Cornwall

Placings: 026010050/4P03F0-000P40PP4PU42 (4574)
2001/02: 22^0GF, 21^0G, 21^0GS, 16^PS, 16^4G, 20^0G, 24^PG, 22^PS, 20^4G, 24^PGS, 24US, 25^4S, 21^2GS

	Starts	1st	2nd	3rd	Win & Pl
Hurdles	3	0	0	0	0
Chases	10	0	1	0	1312
Career Total	**28**	**1**	**2**	**1**	**5052**

79	8/99	Kbgn	2m3f	Hdl	G-Y	£2464

Total win prize-money £2464

Going: Sf: 0-4 GS: 0-3 Gd: 0-5 GF: - Fm: 0-1
Distance: 2m/2m3: 0-2 2m4-2m7: 0-7 3m+: 0-4
Track: LH: 0-4 RH: 0-6 Tight: 0-6 Gall: 0-2
Aids: Bl: 0-4 Vi: 0-2 Tstrap: 0-0
Best Rating: 91 9/00 Gowr 2m good Hdl

Poor novice chaser.

Gin Palace (IRE)

110 109

4-y-o gr g King's Theatre (IRE)-Ikala (Lashkari)
G L Moore Mrs Patricia Gilmore

Placings: 42 (3668)
2001/02: 16^4G, 16^2S

	Starts	1st	2nd	3rd	Win & Pl
Hurdles	2	0	1	0	1743
Career Total	**2**	**0**	**1**	**0**	**1743**

Going: Sf: 0-1 GS: 0-0 Gd: 0-1 GF: - Fm: 0-0
Distance: 2m/2m3: 0-2 2m4-2m7: 0-0 3m+: 0-0
Track: LH: 0-0 RH: 0-2 Tight: 0-0 Gall: 0-0
Aids: Bl: 0-0 Vi: 0-0 Tstrap: 0-0
Best Rating: 109 2/02 Kemp 2m soft Hdl

Fairly useful middle-distance performer on the Flat, put disappointing hurdle debut behind him when finishing runner-up in Kempton juvenile hurdle in February. Well capable of success over hurdles, effective on soft ground or faster. Suited by two miles.

Ginger Fox (USA)

71 96

9-y-o ch g Diesis-Over Your Shoulder (USA) (Graustark)
M Pitman Martin Van Doorne

Placings: 4P/312P10P/2FP3100/522/030 (3165)
2001/02: 16^0G, 17^3S, 23^0G

	Starts	1st	2nd	3rd	Win & Pl
Hurdles	1	0	0	0	0
Chases	2	0	0	1	472
Career Total	**22**	**3**	**4**	**3**	**23510**

136	2/99	Donc	2m110y	B(0-140)HHdl	G-F	£5884
123	1/98	Donc	2m4f	A Hdl	GD	£9475
91	11/97	Wwck	2m	E Hdl	G-S	£2749

Total win prize-money £18110

Going: Sf: 0-1 GS: 0-0 Gd: 0-2 GF: - Fm: 0-0
Distance: 2m/2m3: 0-2 2m4-2m7: 0-0 3m+: 0-1
Track: LH: 0-1 RH: 0-2 Tight: 0-1 Gall: 0-0
Aids: Bl: 0-1 Vi: 0-1 Tstrap: 0-0
Best Rating: 136 2/99 Donc 2m110y gd-fm Hdl

A one-time useful hurdler, he has not shown a great deal over fences following a lay-off.

Ginger Rogers

96 89

8-y-o ch m Gildoran-Axe Valley (Royben)
R E Peacock P Ponting

Placings: 3/0-2 (0045)
2001/02: 17^2GS

	Starts	1st	2nd	3rd	Win & Pl
Hurdles	1	0	1	0	639
Career Total	**3**	**0**	**1**	**1**	**1002**

Going: Sf: 0-0 GS: 0-1 Gd: 0-0 GF: - Fm: 0-0
Distance: 2m/2m3: 0-1 2m4-2m7: 0-0 3m+: 0-0
Track: LH: 0-0 RH: 0-1 Tight: 0-0 Gall: 0-0
Aids: Bl: 0-0 Vi: 0-0 Tstrap: 0-0
Best Rating: 89 5/01 Extr 2m1f gd-sft Hdl

Gingerbread Man

7-y-o ch g Derrylin-Red Rambler (Rymer)
F Kirby Fred Kirby

Placings: 000-PP (1564)
2001/02: 17^PG, 16^PGS

	Starts	1st	2nd	3rd	Win & Pl
Hurdles	2	0	0	0	
Career Total	**5**	**0**	**0**	**0**	

Going: Sf: 0-0 GS: 0-1 Gd: 0-1 GF: - Fm: 0-0
Distance: 2m/2m3: 0-2 2m4-2m7: 0-0 3m+: 0-0
Track: LH: 0-2 RH: 0-0 Tight: 0-1 Gall: 0-0
Aids: Bl: 0-0 Vi: 0-0 Tstrap: 0-0
Best Rating: 68 7/00 Worc 2m good NHF

Ginski

69 34

6-y-o b g Petoski-Upham Lass (Sula Bula)
C J Drewe Mrs J Strange

Placings: 0-0000 (4519)
2001/02: 17^0GF, 16^0GS, 16^0GS, 21^0GS

	Starts	1st	2nd	3rd	Win & Pl
NH Flat	1	0	0	0	0
Hurdles	3	0	0	0	0
Career Total	**5**	**0**	**0**	**0**	

Going: Sf: 0-0 GS: 0-3 Gd: 0-0 GF: - Fm: 0-1
Distance: 2m/2m3: 0-3 2m4-2m7: 0-1 3m+: 0-0
Track: LH: 0-0 RH: 0-3 Tight: 0-1 Gall: 0-1
Aids: Bl: 0-0 Vi: 0-0 Tstrap: 0-1
Best Rating: 34 1/02 Hntg 2m110y gd-sft Hdl

Giocomo (IRE)

106 127

4-y-o ch g Indian Ridge-Karri Valley (USA) (Storm Bird (CAN))
J J O'Neill (Charles O'Brien 27/10) Euan & Bernardine Roger

Placings: 4311P0 (4952a)
2001/02: 16^4GS, 16^3HY, 16^1S, 16^1G, 17^PG, 16^0G

	Starts	1st	2nd	3rd	Win & Pl
Hurdles	6	2	0	1	21384
Career Total	**6**	**2**	**0**	**1**	**21384**

127	2/02	Kemp	2m	A Hdl	GD	£12000
117	2/02	Hntg	2m110y	B Hdl	SFT	£8671

Total win prize-money £20671

Going: Sf: 1-2 GS: 0-1 Gd: 1-3 GF: - Fm: 0-0
Distance: **2m/2m3: 2-6** 2m4-2m7: 0-0 3m+: 0-0
Track: LH: 0-3 **RH: 2-3** Tight: 0-0 **Gall: 1-3**
Aids: Bl: 0-1 Vi: 0-0 Tstrap: 0-0
Best Rating: 127 2/02 Kemp 2m good Hdl

Maiden on the Flat in Ireland. Joined Jonjo O'Neill in the winter of 2001 and improved to score twice over hurdles in February 2002 including a Grade Two at Kempton. Handles heavy ground.

Giolla Valley (IRE)

102(84h) (59h)108

8-y-o b g Boyne Valley-Bean Giolla (Giolla Mear)
Mrs M Reveley The Mary Reveley Racing Club

Placings:_06_F640-**2PU242** (4596)
2001/02: 20^{2}S, 21^{P}G, 20^{U}GS, 16^{2}S, 16^{4}HY, 20^{2}G

	Starts	1st	2nd	3rd	Win & Pl
Chases	6	0	3	0	3403
Career Total	**12**	**0**	**3**	**0**	**3403**

Going: Sf: 0-3 GS: 0-1 Gd: 0-2 GF: - Fm: 0-0
Distance: 2m/2m3: 0-2 2m4-2m7: 0-4 3m+: 0-0
Track: LH: 0-6 RH: 0-0 Tight: 0-0 Gall: 0-1
Aids: Bl: 0-0 Vi: 0-0 Tstrap: 0-0
Best Rating: 108 4/02 Uttx 2m4f good Ch

He failed to trouble the judges when tried over hurdles, but is running better over fences.

Gipsy Cricketer

98(78h) (51h)96+

6-y-o b g Anshan-Tinkers Fairy (Myjinski (USA))
N A Twiston-Davies (Mrs Marilyn Scudamore 6/4)
The 'Yes' - 'No' - Wait'....Sorries

Placings:_006P/53003600-0P_ (0927)
2001/02: 16^{0}GF, 25^{P}GF

	Starts	1st	2nd	3rd	Win & Pl
Hurdles	2	0	0	0	
Career Total	**14**	**0**	**0**	**2**	**689**

Going: Sf: 0-0 GS: 0-0 Gd: 0-0 GF: - Fm: 0-2
Distance: 2m/2m3: 0-1 2m4-2m7: 0-0 3m+: 0-1
Track: LH: 0-2 RH: 0-0 Tight: 0-1 Gall: 0-0
Aids: Bl: 0-0 Vi: 0-0 Tstrap: 0-2
Best Rating: 79 10/00 Extr 2m3f good Hdl

A useful pointer. Has taken time to get the hang of jumping regulation fences. Looked ahead of the Handicapper when winning two mile novices handicap at Worcester July 2002. Unsuited by soft ground after being raised 12lb next time.

Gipsy Geof (IRE)

112(104h) (107h)109

11-y-o b g Miners Lamp-Princess Menelek (Menelek)
Ferdy Murphy Exors Of The Late Mr G A Hubbard

Placings:_605/43/FP3152_**P1**_/34F25/P6F/452FU-_**42P43112O** (4869)
2001/02: 21^{4}GF, 16^{2}S, 21^{P}S, 16^{4}GS, 16^{3}S, 17^{1}GS, 16^{1}G, 17^{2}G, 20°GF

	Starts	1st	2nd	3rd	Win & Pl
Hurdles	6	2	1	1	5954
Chases	3	0	1	0	1336
Career Total	**35**	**4**	**5**	**4**	**18594**

107	4/02	Weth	2m	F(0-100)HHdl	GD	£2345
107	3/02	MRas	2m1f110y	G(0-95)HHdl	G-S	£1722
111	3/98	Sand	2m	D Ch	GD	£3692
108	11/97	Leic	2m	E Hdl	G-S	£2616

Total win prize-money £10376

Going: Sf: 0-3 GS: 1-2 Gd: 1-2 GF: - Fm: 0-2
Distance: **2m/2m3: 2-6** 2m4-2m7: 0-3 3m+: 0-0
Track: LH: 1-5 RH: 1-4 **Tight: 1-6** Gall: 0-1
Aids: Bl: 0-0 Vi: 0-0 Tstrap: 0-0
Best Rating: 120 3/99 Folk 2m good Ch

A half-brother to Imperial Call, he can make mistakes. Effective at the lowest level these days, he stays two and a half miles and acts in soft ground.

Girl Band (IRE)

4-y-o b f Bluebird (USA)-Bandit Girl (Robellino (USA))
E A Elliott Mrs Anne E Elliott

Placings:P (2449)
2001/02: 16^{P}GS

	Starts	1st	2nd	3rd	Win & Pl
Hurdles	1	0	0	0	
Career Total	**1**	**0**	**0**	**0**	

Going: Sf: 0-0 GS: 0-1 Gd: 0-0 GF: - Fm: 0-0
Distance: 2m/2m3: 0-1 2m4-2m7: 0-0 3m+: 0-0
Track: LH: 0-1 RH: 0-0 Tight: 0-0 Gall: 0-1
Aids: Bl: 0-0 Vi: 0-0 Tstrap: 0-0
Best Rating:

Girl's Best Friend

79 24

5-y-o b m Nicolotte-Diamond Princess (Horage)
N J Henderson (D W P Arbuthnot 27/11) Stephen Crown

Placings:5-P (4504)
2001/02: 17^{P}G

	Starts	1st	2nd	3rd	Win & Pl
Hurdles	1	0	0	0	
Career Total	**2**	**0**	**0**	**0**	0

Going: Sf: 0-0 GS: 0-0 Gd: 0-1 GF: - Fm: 0-0
Distance: 2m/2m3: 0-1 2m4-2m7: 0-0 3m+: 0-0
Track: LH: 0-1 RH: 0-0 Tight: 0-1 Gall: 0-0
Aids: Bl: 0-0 Vi: 0-0 Tstrap: 0-0
Best Rating:

Girlzone (IRE)

102 87

7-y-o ch m Orchestra-Blue Rainbow (Balinger)
J M Jefferson Mrs K S Gaffney & Mrs Alix Stevenson

Placings:_160/06_P-4 (0203)
2001/02: 20^{4}G

	Starts	1st	2nd	3rd	Win & Pl
Hurdles	1	0	0	0	0
Career Total	**7**	**1**	**0**	**0**	**1589**

97	2/00	Donc	2m110y	H NHF	GD	£1589

Total win prize-money £1589

Going: Sf: 0-0 GS: 0-0 Gd: 0-1 GF: - Fm: 0-0
Distance: 2m/2m3: 0-0 2m4-2m7: 0-1 3m+: 0-0
Track: LH: 0-1 RH: 0-0 Tight: 0-0 Gall: 0-0
Aids: Bl: 0-0 Vi: 0-0 Tstrap: 0-0
Best Rating: 97 2/00 Donc 2m110y good NHF

Gismo

94f 87f

5-y-o ch g Arazi (USA)-Gisarne (USA) (Diesis)
Miss Jacqueline S Doyle Tom Ford

Placings:_00-10_ (0678)
2001/02: 17^{1}GF, 16^{0}GF

	Starts	1st	2nd	3rd	Win & Pl
NH Flat	2	1	0	0	1572
Career Total	**4**	**1**	**0**	**0**	**1572**

87	5/01	Folk	2m1f110y	H NHF	G-F	£1571

Total win prize-money £1572

Going: Sf: 0-0 GS: 0-0 Gd: 0-0 GF: - Fm: 1-2
Distance: **2m/2m3: 1-2** 2m4-2m7: 0-0 3m+: 0-0
Track: LH: 0-1 RH: 0-0 **Tight: 1-1** Gall: 0-0
Aids: Bl: 0-0 Vi: 0-0 Tstrap: 0-0
Best Rating: 87 5/01 Folk 2m1f110y gd-fm NHF

Give Me Roses

86 45

8-y-o b m Ardross-Give Me Credit (Le Bavard (FR))
P Beaumont Julia Lloyd & G E Leech

Placings:6PPP0 (4486)
2001/02: 23^{6}S, 24^{P}S, 25^{P}GS, 16^{P}S, 17^{0}GS

	Starts	1st	2nd	3rd	Win & Pl
Hurdles	5	0	0	0	0
Career Total	**5**	**0**	**0**	**0**	**0**

Going: Sf: 0-3 GS: 0-2 Gd: 0-0 GF: - Fm: 0-0
Distance: 2m/2m3: 0-2 2m4-2m7: 0-1 3m+: 0-2
Track: LH: 0-4 RH: 0-1 Tight: 0-1 Gall: 0-2
Aids: Bl: 0-0 Vi: 0-0 Tstrap: 0-0
Best Rating: 45 12/01 Weth 2m7f soft Hdl

Not very big, she showed nothing on her belated racecourse debut over hurdles at the end of 2001.

Give Over (IRE)

107(66h) (131h)151

9-y-o b g Lord Americo-Romany River (Over The River (FR))
Edward U Hales Mrs E Queally

Placings:_06/2632312500/030131010-_**05211UB6P2** (4705a)
2001/02: 22^{0}GF, 22^{5}G, 22^{2}Y, 25^{1}Y, 24^{1}Y, 21^{U}YS, 24^{B}SH, 21^{6}HY, 24^{P}GS, 29^{2}GY

	Starts	1st	2nd	3rd	Win & Pl
Hurdles	1	0	0	0	0
Chases	9	2	2	0	44443
Career Total	**31**	**6**	**5**	**4**	**74975**

141	12/01	Leop	3m	Ch	YLD	£15725
129	12/01	Fair	3m1f	Ch	YLD	£6677
131	4/01	Cork	2m4f	(0-130)HHdl	Y-S	£13104
124	2/01	Naas	3m	(0-116)HHdl	SH	£5008
138	11/00	Clon	3m	(0-116)HHdl	SH	£3312
118	1/00	Punc	3m	Hdl	Y-S	£4416

Total win prize-money £48244

Going: Sf: 0-1 GS: 0-1 Gd: 0-1 GF: - Fm: 0-1
Distance: 2m/2m3: 0-0 2m4-2m7: 0-5 **3m+: 2-5**
Track: LH: 1-5 RH: 1-3 Tight: 0-0 Gall: 0-1
Aids: Bl: 0-0 Vi: 0-0 Tstrap: 0-0
Best Rating: 151 4/02 Fair 3m5f gd-yld Ch

He has taken well to fences and scored twice in December 2001. An early casualty on his next two starts, he was well beaten in the Sun Alliance at Cheltenham. Stays well.

Give Us A Price

7-y-o b m Silly Prices-Give Us A Treat (Cree Song)
John A Harris I R Bennett

Placings:P0 (4555)
2001/02: 16^{P}HY, 19^{0}GF

	Starts	1st	2nd	3rd	Win & Pl
Hurdles	2	0	0	0	

	Starts	1st	2nd	3rd	Win & Pl
Career Total	2	0	0	0	

Going: Sf: 0-1 GS: 0-0 Gd: 0-0 GF: - Fm: 0-1
Distance: 2m/2m3: 0-1 2m4-2m7: 0-1 3m+: 0-0
Track: LH: 0-1 RH: 0-1 Tight: 0-2 Gall: 0-0
Aids: Bl: 0-0 Vi: 0-0 Tstrap: 0-0
Best Rating:

Giveaway

(108h) (94h)
7-y-o ch g Generous (IRE)-Radiant Bride (USA) (Blushing Groom (FR))
D J Wintle The Lavender Hill Mob

Placings:6/1600/000-P3400430 **(4908)**
2001/02: 20^{P}G, 20^{3}S, 16^{4}G, 16^{0}S, 21^{0}HY, 16^{4}S, 20^{3}G, 21^{0}G

	Starts	1st	2nd	3rd	Win & Pl
Hurdles	8	0	0	2	995
Career Total	**16**	**1**	**0**	**2**	**3695**

101 5/99 Gowr 2m Hdl GD £2700
Total win prize-money £2701

Going: Sf: 0-4 GS: 0-0 Gd: 0-4 GF: - Fm: 0-0
Distance: 2m/2m3: 0-3 2m4-2m7: 0-5 3m+: 0-0
Track: LH: 0-5 RH: 0-2 Tight: 0-3 Gall: 0-0
Aids: Bl: 0-0 Vi: 0-0 Tstrap: 0-7
Best Rating: 109 5/00 Punc 2m good Hdl

Ex-Irish, he ran well when third over hurdles at Chepstow in October. Acts on soft ground but suited by good. Has worn a tongue tie.

Givre (IRE)

103 91
4-y-o b g Houmayoun (FR)-Interj (Salmon Leap (USA))
R A Fahey (J E Mulhern 27/5) P D Smith Holdings Ltd

Placings:5100 **(4785)**
2001/02: 16^{5}G, 16^{1}GF, 16^{0}S, 16^{0}F

	Starts	1st	2nd	3rd	Win & Pl
Hurdles	4	1	0	0	1883
Career Total	**4**	**1**	**0**	**0**	**1883**

88 11/01 Catt 2m G Hdl G-F £1883
Total win prize-money £1883

Going: Sf: 0-1 GS: 0-0 Gd: 0-1 GF: - Fm: 1-2
Distance: **2m/2m3: 1-4** 2m4-2m7: 0-0 3m+: 0-0
Track: **LH: 1-4** RH: 0-0 **Tight: 1-1** Gall: 0-3
Aids: Bl: 0-0 Vi: 0-0 Tstrap: 0-0
Best Rating: 91 11/01 Newc 2m good Hdl

A poor performer on the level, he proved he prefers the jumping game when winning at Catterick on his second attempt over hurdles, although he has been held since, on both the flat and over hurdles. Best on a sound surface.

Givry (IRE)

12-y-o b g Remainder Man-Beyond The Rainbow (Royal Palace)
N Parker Mrs R E Parker

Placings:P50FP/4/UP0 **(0579)**
2001/02: 24^{U}GF, 33^{P}G, 24^{0}GF

	Starts	1st	2nd	3rd	Win & Pl
Chases	3	0	0	0	
Career Total	**9**	**0**	**0**	**0**	**214**

Going: Sf: 0-0 GS: 0-0 Gd: 0-1 GF: - Fm: 0-2
Distance: 2m/2m3: 0-0 2m4-2m7: 0-0 3m+: 0-3
Track: LH: 0-2 RH: 0-0 Tight: 0-2 Gall: 0-0
Aids: Bl: 0-0 Vi: 0-3 Tstrap: 0-0
Best Rating: 75 2/97 Tntn 2m1f good Hdl

Givus A Hand

12-y-o ch g Nearly A Hand-Chanelle (The Parson)
Mrs J M Bailey Mrs J M Bailey

Placings:4P **(0425)**
2001/02: 24^{4}GF, 21^{P}G

	Starts	1st	2nd	3rd	Win & Pl
Chases	2	0	0	0	156
Career Total	**2**	**0**	**0**	**0**	**156**

Going: Sf: 0-0 GS: 0-0 Gd: 0-1 GF: - Fm: 0-1
Distance: 2m/2m3: 0-0 2m4-2m7: 0-1 3m+: 0-1
Track: LH: 0-0 RH: 0-1 Tight: 0-0 Gall: 0-1
Aids: Bl: 0-0 Vi: 0-0 Tstrap: 0-0
Best Rating: 81 5/01 Hntg 3m gd-fm Ch

Glacial Dancer (IRE)

100 121
9-y-o b g Glacial Storm (USA)-Castleblagh (General Ironside)
L Lungo A S Lyburn

Placings:6234421/13/P-323 **(2396)**
2001/02: 20^{3}G, 20^{2}GS, 25^{3}G

	Starts	1st	2nd	3rd	Win & Pl
Chases	3	0	1	2	2723
Career Total	**13**	**2**	**3**	**4**	**10266**

112 1/00 Ayr 3m110y D(0-110)HHdl SFT £3152
99 5/99 Hexm 3m F(0-100)HHdl GD £2220
Total win prize-money £5374

Going: Sf: 0-0 GS: 0-1 Gd: 0-2 GF: - Fm: 0-0
Distance: 2m/2m3: 0-0 2m4-2m7: 0-2 3m+: 0-1
Track: LH: 0-3 RH: 0-0 Tight: 0-0 Gall: 0-0
Aids: Bl: 0-0 Vi: 0-0 Tstrap: 0-0
Best Rating: 121 11/01 Ayr 2m4f gd-sft Ch

Won two hurdle races in a row, the first of which came in May 1999, and the second in January of 2000, both over three miles, although he was disappointing dropped in trip after that, and was not seen again for over a year. Not so good over fences so far. Acts on good ground or softer.

Glacial Enterprise (IRE)

105(79h) (67h)121
9-y-o ch g Glacial Storm (USA)-Miss Shamrock (Saritamer (USA))
P J Hobbs Colin Brown Racing Ii

Placings:22/1520-32P10 **(4414)**
2001/02: 25^{3}G, 26^{2}S, 27^{P}S, 26^{1}HY, 28^{0}S

	Starts	1st	2nd	3rd	Win & Pl
Chases	5	1	1	1	5652
Career Total	**11**	**2**	**4**	**1**	**13997**

121 2/02 Font 3m2f110y D Ch HVY £3965
110 11/00 Tntn 3m110y C Hdl GD £5284
Total win prize-money £9250

Going: Sf: 1-4 GS: 0-0 Gd: 0-1 GF: - Fm: 0-0
Distance: 2m/2m3: 0-0 2m4-2m7: 0-0 **3m+: 1-5**
Track: LH: 0-1 RH: 0-2 **Tight: 1-2** Gall: 0-0
Aids: **Bl: 1-3** Vi: 0-0 Tstrap: 0-0
Best Rating: 127 1/01 Font 3m2f110y soft Ch

Winner of an Irish point to point. He ran twice over hurdles in this country before scoring over three miles at Taunton. Has mixed chasing and hurdling since. Stays three miles. Has won on good ground.

Glacial King (IRE)

99 98
10-y-o br g Glacial Storm (USA)-Doorslammer (Avocat)
K Bishop Mrs E K Ellis

Placings:0PF2/PP32/26 **(3762)**
2001/02: 23^{2}GS, 24^{6}S

	Starts	1st	2nd	3rd	Win & Pl
Chases	2	0	1	0	1168
Career Total	**10**	**0**	**3**	**1**	**3925**

Going: Sf: 0-1 GS: 0-1 Gd: 0-0 GF: - Fm: 0-0
Distance: 2m/2m3: 0-0 2m4-2m7: 0-0 3m+: 0-2
Track: LH: 0-0 RH: 0-2 Tight: 0-1 Gall: 0-0
Aids: Bl: 0-0 Vi: 0-0 Tstrap: 0-0
Best Rating: 98 12/01 Extr 2m7f110y gd-sft Ch

Promising return to the fray following a long absence.

Glacial Missile (IRE)

100(100h) (01h)117
9-y-o ch m Glacial Storm (USA)-Trident Missile (Vulgan Slave)
P Bowen R Owen

Placings:2233P3332P/05P1111344P/P3UP-1F **(1582)**
2001/02: 20^{1}GF, 22^{F}GS

	Starts	1st	2nd	3rd	Win & Pl
Chases	2	1	0	0	3848
Career Total	**27**	**5**	**3**	**7**	**20257**

117 8/01 Worc 2m4f110y D Ch G-F £3848
109 8/99 MRas 2m3f110y E Hdl G-F £2705
99 7/99 MRas 2m3f110y D Hdl G-F £3857
97 7/99 Worc 2m4f E Hdl G-F £2318
96 6/99 Worc 2m4f E Hdl G-F £2652
Total win prize-money £15381

Going: Sf: 0-0 GS: 0-1 Gd: 0-0 GF: - Fm: 1-1
Distance: 2m/2m3: 0-0 **2m4-2m7: 1-2** 3m+: 0-0
Track: **LH: 1-1** RH: 0-1 Tight: 0-1 Gall: 0-0
Aids: Bl: 0-0 Vi: 0-0 Tstrap: 0-0
Best Rating: 117 8/01 Worc 2m4f110y gd-fm Ch

Completed a four-timer in novice hurdles in the summer of 1999. Landed a novice chase in July 2001. Likes fast ground. Effective at two and a half miles.

Glacial Pearl (IRE)

77 58
7-y-o ch g Glacial Storm (USA)-Hopeful Dawn (Prince Hansel)
P F Nicholls Mr & Mrs F Golding

Placings:15-06 **(4654)**
2001/02: 20^{0}S, 17^{6}GS

	Starts	1st	2nd	3rd	Win & Pl
Hurdles	2	0	0	0	0
Career Total	**4**	**1**	**0**	**0**	**1547**

109 7/00 Sedg 2m1f H NHF G-F £1547
Total win prize-money £1547

Going: Sf: 0-1 GS: 0-1 Gd: 0-0 GF: - Fm: 0-0

Distance: 2m/2m3: 0-1 2m4-2m7: 0-1 3m+: 0-0
Track: LH: 0-1 RH: 0-1 Tight: 0-1 Gall: 0-0
Aids: Bl: 0-0 Vi: 0-0 Tstrap: 0-0
Best Rating: 109 7/00 Sedg 2m1f gd-fm NHF

Glacial River (IRE)

96 **85**

9-y-o ch g Glacial Storm (USA)-Lucky Trout (Beau Charmeur (FR))
D J Caro D J Caro

Placings: *60/6*03U/6350/322 **(1240)**
2001/02: 25^{3}S, 23^{2}GF, 24^{2}GF

	Starts	1st	2nd	3rd	Win & Pl
Hurdles	3	0	2	1	1775
Career Total	**13**	**0**	**2**	**3**	**2383**

Going: Sf: 0-1 GS: 0-0 Gd: 0-0 GF: - Fm: 0-2
Distance: 2m/2m3: 0-0 2m4-2m7: 0-0 3m+: 0-3
Track: LH: 0-2 RH: 0-0 Tight: 0-1 Gall: 0-0
Aids: Bl: 0-0 Vi: 0-0 Tstrap: 0-0
Best Rating: 95 2/98 Wwck 2m good NHF

Glacial Sunset (IRE)

97 **120+**

7-y-o ch g Glacial Storm (USA)-Twinkle Sunset (Deep Run)
A J Lidderdale (E Stanners 15/5) George Ward

Placings: *4/1*0-34 **(3994)**
2001/02: 17^{3}G, 20^{4}S

	Starts	1st	2nd	3rd	Win & Pl
Hurdles	2	0	0	1	468
Career Total	**5**	**1**	**0**	**1**	**2204**

111	5/00	Font	2m2f110y	H NHF	GD	£1736

Total win prize-money £1736

Going: Sf: 0-1 GS: 0-0 Gd: 0-1 GF: - Fm: 0-0
Distance: 2m/2m3: 0-1 2m4-2m7: 0-1 3m+: 0-0
Track: LH: 0-1 RH: 0-1 Tight: 0-0 Gall: 0-1
Aids: Bl: 0-0 Vi: 0-0 Tstrap: 0-0
Best Rating: 112 5/01 Hrfd 2m1f good Hdl

A lightly-raced bumper winner. Appreciated the combination of fast ground and a step up in distance when impressive winner of Class F handicap over 22 furlongs at Wincanton May 2002. Appears on the upgrade.

Glacial Tabhairne (IRE)

93 **73**

8-y-o ch g Glacial Storm (USA)-Taberna Lady (Paddy's Stream)
K C Bailey J Perriss

Placings: F0 **(4874)**
2001/02: 22^{F}GS, 20^{0}G

	Starts	1st	2nd	3rd	Win & Pl
Hurdles	2	0	0	0	
Career Total	**2**	**0**	**0**	**0**	

Going: Sf: 0-0 GS: 0-1 Gd: 0-1 GF: - Fm: 0-0
Distance: 2m/2m3: 0-0 2m4-2m7: 0-2 3m+: 0-0
Track: LH: 0-1 RH: 0-1 Tight: 0-1 Gall: 0-0
Aids: Bl: 0-0 Vi: 0-0 Tstrap: 0-0
Best Rating: 72 4/02 Prth 2m4f110y good Hdl

Gladiateur Iv (FR)

112(98h) (97h)**155**

8-y-o b g Useful (FR)-Friga (FR) (Montevideo)
P J Hobbs The Cobra Partnership

Placings: 3315/323P01313/15125231P-431013 **(4739)**
2001/02: 20^{4}G, 23^{3}GF, 20^{1}GF, 20^{0}GS, 21^{1}GF, 21^{3}GF

	Starts	1st	2nd	3rd	Win & Pl
Hurdles	1	0	0	1	620
Chases	5	2	0	1	11663
Career Total	**28**	**8**	**3**	**9**	**52549**

141	8/01	NAbb	2m5f110y	D(0-120)HCh	G-F	£3997
142	7/01	Strf	2m4f	C(0-135)HCh	G-F	£5902
139	10/00	Tntn	3m	D(0-120)HCh	GD	£5694
133	6/00	Worc	2m4f110y	D(0-120)HCh	G-F	£3721
140	5/00	Worc	2m4f110y	D(0-125)HCh	GD	£3835
126	3/00	Ludl	2m4f	D Ch	GD	£4127
126	2/00	Ludl	2m4f	E Ch	GD	£3250
110	1/99	Ling	2m110y	E Hdl	HVY	£2256

Total win prize-money £32785

Going: Sf: 0-0 GS: 0-1 Gd: 0-1 GF: - Fm: 2-4
Distance: 2m/2m3: 0-0 **2m4-2m7: 2-5** 3m+: 0-1
Track: **LH: 2-4** RH: 0-1 **Tight: 2-2** Gall: 0-0
Aids: Bl: 0-0 Vi: 0-0 **Tstrap: 1-1**
Best Rating: 142 7/01 Strf 2m4f gd-fm Ch

A respectable fast ground chaser, he is effective from two and a half to three miles and is usually held up.

Gladys May (IRE)

5-y-o b m Moscow Society (USA)-Cashla (IRE) (Duky)
P J Hobbs R J B Partners

Placings: *0*3 **(4743)**
2001/02: 17^{0}GF, 16^{3}GF

	Starts	1st	2nd	3rd	Win & Pl
NH Flat	2	0	0	1	318
Career Total	**2**	**0**	**0**	**1**	**318**

Going: Sf: 0-0 GS: 0-0 Gd: 0-0 GF: - Fm: 0-2
Distance: 2m/2m3: 0-2 2m4-2m7: 0-0 3m+: 0-0
Track: LH: 0-0 RH: 0-2 Tight: 0-0 Gall: 0-0
Aids: Bl: 0-0 Vi: 0-0 Tstrap: 0-0
Best Rating: 90 4/02 Ludl 2m gd-fm NHF

Has shown ability in bumpers.

Glamanglitz

105 **123**

12-y-o ch g Town And Country-Pretty Useful (Firestreak)
P T Dalton Mrs Julie Martin

Placings: *20065/PFU433F3U/12135214P1/10212454/ 00P4313352303*2/U14021225-342P300 **(4495)**
2001/02: 16^{3}G, 20^{4}GF, 16^{2}GF, 20^{P}G, 16^{3}S, 16^{0}G, 16^{0}G

	Starts	1st	2nd	3rd	Win & Pl
Chases	7	0	1	2	3772
Career Total	**62**	**9**	**11**	**11**	**70778**

128	9/00	Worc	2m	C(0-135)HCh	G-F	£6745
115	5/00	Aint	2m	D(0-125)HCh	G-F	£4498
115	10/99	Worc	2m	D(0-125)HCh	G-F	£3744
128	9/98	Uttx	2m5f	C(0-130)HCh	G-F	£5105
125	5/98	Uttx	2m4f	D(0-125)HCh	GD	£3501
121	2/98	Donc	2m3f110y	E(0-105)HCh	G-F	£3496
121	11/97	Uttx	2m5f	E(0-105)HCh	GD	£2963
106	6/97	Uttx	2m5f	C Ch	GD	£5363
104	5/97	Uttx	2m7f	E Ch	GD	£2914

Total win prize-money £38334

Going: Sf: 0-1 GS: 0-0 Gd: 0-4 GF: - Fm: 0-2
Distance: 2m/2m3: 0-5 2m4-2m7: 0-2 3m+: 0-0
Track: LH: 0-7 RH: 0-0 Tight: 0-2 Gall: 0-1
Aids: Bl: 0-0 Vi: 0-0 Tstrap: 0-0
Best Rating: 135 11/00 Chel 2m gd-sft Ch

Successful over fences, he is best when racing prominently on good ground or faster. Most effective at up to two and a half miles.

Glamour Girl

97 **74**

6-y-o b m Lord Americo-Money Galore (IRE) (Monksfield)
M J Wilkinson D R Bateman

Placings: *0/*000 **(4048)**
2001/02: 19^{0}S, 16^{0}S, 19^{0}G

	Starts	1st	2nd	3rd	Win & Pl
Hurdles	3	0	0	0	
Career Total	**4**	**0**	**0**	**0**	

Going: Sf: 0-2 GS: 0-0 Gd: 0-1 GF: - Fm: 0-0
Distance: 2m/2m3: 0-2 2m4-2m7: 0-1 3m+: 0-0
Track: LH: 0-0 RH: 0-3 Tight: 0-0 Gall: 0-1
Aids: Bl: 0-0 Vi: 0-0 Tstrap: 0-0
Best Rating: 74 2/02 Hntg 2m110y soft Hdl

Glanamana (IRE)

(100h) (95h)

6-y-o b g Be My Native (USA)-Brides Choice (Cheval)
J S King Mrs Marygold O'Kelly

Placings: *31-0*300PP **(4115)**
2001/02: 16^{0}G, 20^{3}S, 20^{0}GS, 21^{0}S, 20^{P}HY, 21^{P}G

	Starts	1st	2nd	3rd	Win & Pl
NH Flat	1	0	0	0	0
Hurdles	3	0	0	1	536
Chases	2	0	0	0	0
Career Total	**8**	**1**	**0**	**2**	**3423**

111	3/01	Newb	2m110y	H NHF	HVY	£2646

Total win prize-money £2646

Going: Sf: 0-3 GS: 0-1 Gd: 0-2 GF: - Fm: 0-0
Distance: 2m/2m3: 0-1 2m4-2m7: 0-5 3m+: 0-0
Track: LH: 0-4 RH: 0-2 Tight: 0-0 Gall: 0-0
Aids: Bl: 0-0 Vi: 0-0 Tstrap: 0-0
Best Rating: 111 3/01 Newb 2m110y heavy NHF

Winning form in bumpers at the back end of the 2000/2001 season on heavy ground. Third on hurdles bow.

Glanmerin (IRE)

109 **119**

11-y-o b g Lomond (USA)-Abalvina (FR) (Abdos)
R Lee Rex Norton And Michael Sprake

Placings: 113/0/5024/02P/**U2114/503-U624P01** **(4312)**
2001/02: 20^{U}GS, 19^{6}S, 19^{2}G, 24^{4}GS, 22^{P}S, 24^{0}GS, 20^{1}HY

	Starts	1st	2nd	3rd	Win & Pl
Chases	7	1	1	0	4383
Career Total	**26**	**5**	**4**	**2**	**24338**

112	3/02	Sthl	2m4f110y	F(0-90)HCh	HVY	£3119
133	3/00	Hntg	2m110y	D(0-125)HCh	SFT	£4396
133	2/00	Hntg	2m110y	D(0-125)HCh	SFT	£4420
109	3/95	Worc	2m	E Hdl	G-S	£2320
102	2/95	Nott	2m	D Hdl	G-S	£3662

Total win prize-money £17918

Going: Sf: 1-3 GS: 0-3 Gd: 0-1 GF: - Fm: 0-0

Distance: 2m/2m3: 0-2 **2m4-2m7: 1-3** 3m+: 0-2
Track: **LH: 1-2** RH: 0-5 **Tight: 1-3** Gall: 0-2
Aids: Bl: 0-0 Vi: 0-0 Tstrap: 0-0
Best Rating: 133 3/00 Hntg 2m110y soft Ch

Modest chaser, dropped to a decent mark before winning in bad ground at Southwell.

Glebe Beauty (IRE)

67 **32**

6-y-o b m Good Thyne (USA)-Le Bavellen (Le Bavard (FR))
Mrs L B Normile (John F Gleeson 10/5) The Friday Agreement

Placings:00P (4875)
2001/02: 18^{0}HY, 18^{0}GF, 16^{0}GS, 24^{P}G

	Starts	1st	2nd	3rd	Win & Pl
NH Flat	2	0	0	0	0
Hurdles	2	0	0	0	0
Career Total	**4**	**0**	**0**	**0**	

Going: Sf: 0-1 GS: 0-1 Gd: 0-1 GF: - Fm: 0-1
Distance: 2m/2m3: 0-3 2m4-2m7: 0-0 3m+: 0-1
Track: LH: 0-1 RH: 0-1 Tight: 0-0 Gall: 0-0
Aids: Bl: 0-0 Vi: 0-0 Tstrap: 0-0
Best Rating: 83 5/01 Thur 2m2f gd-fm NHF

Glemot (IRE)

114 **128**

14-y-o br g Strong Gale-Lady Nethertown (Windjammer (USA))
P R Webber Dennis Yardy

Placings:0P/6031524/F01144/2121U23/1112323/241 2232U0/P1F33322004/5/56152P145/61P5355-51PP31 (1229)
2001/02: 24^{5}GF, 21^{1}GF, 20^{P}GF, 20^{P}G, 21^{3}GF, 20^{1}GF

	Starts	1st	2nd	3rd	Win & Pl
Chases	6	2	0	1	13521
Career Total	**72**	**15**	**13**	**10**	**117163**

128	8/01	Uttx	2m4f	D(0-125)HCh	G-F	£3987
126	6/01	Strf	2m5f110y	B(0-140)HCh	G-F	£8918
134	6/00	Strf	2m5f110y	B(0-140)HCh	GD	£8424
138	12/99	Leic	2m4f110y	C(0-135)HCh	GD	£11405
136	11/99	Hntg	2m4f110y	C(0-130)HCh	GD	£5930
136	5/97	Weth	3m1f	C(0-135)HCh	G-F	£4730
136	10/96	Kemp	2m4f110y	C(0-135)HCh	GD	£4459
134	9/95	Uttx	2m5f	D(0-125)HCh	GD	£3477
127	5/95	Towc	2m110y	D(0-125)HCh	G-F	£3444
130	5/95	Bang	2m4f110y	D(0-125)HCh	G-F	£3477
123	11/94	Sand	2m4f110y	HCh	G-S	£4417
122	10/94	Strf	2m1f110y	(0-125)HCh	GD	£3387
99	12/93	Muss	2m	Ch	GD	£2455
92	11/93	Carl	2m	Ch	G-F	£2976
80	11/92	Kels	2m110y	HHdl	SFT	£1996

Total win prize-money £73488

Going: Sf: 0-0 GS: 0-0 Gd: 0-1 GF: - Fm: 2-5
Distance: 2m/2m3: 0-0 **2m4-2m7: 2-5** 3m+: 0-1
Track: **LH: 2-5** RH: 0-1 **Tight: 1-5** Gall: 0-0
Aids: Bl: 0-0 Vi: 0-0 Tstrap: 0-0
Best Rating: 136 12/99 Leic 2m4f110y good Ch

A grand veteran, he has never been a strong finisher but always wins a race or two on his favoured fast ground.

Glen Mist (IRE)

(82h) (93h)

7-y-o b g Maelstrom Lake-Zamana (Ya Zaman (USA))
Ferdy Murphy Tony Lynch

Placings:0/P46U (4107)
2001/02: 20^{P}G, 20^{4}S, 19^{6}S, 22^{U}S

	Starts	1st	2nd	3rd	Win & Pl
Hurdles	1	0	0	0	280
Chases	3	0	0	0	0
Career Total	**5**	**0**	**0**	**0**	**280**

Going: Sf: 0-3 GS: 0-0 Gd: 0-1 GF: - Fm: 0-0
Distance: 2m/2m3: 0-1 2m4-2m7: 0-3 3m+: 0-0
Track: LH: 0-2 RH: 0-2 Tight: 0-1 Gall: 0-1
Aids: Bl: 0-1 Vi: 0-0 Tstrap: 0-0
Best Rating: 93 12/01 Hayd 2m4f soft Hdl

Glen Parker (IRE)

9-y-o ch g Bluebird (USA)-Trina's Girl (Nonoalco (USA))
R F Marvin (D A Lamb 18/9) Mrs M A Marvin

Placings:P/060PP/P0P (1421)
2001/02: 16^{P}GS, 16^{0}GF, 17^{P}G

	Starts	1st	2nd	3rd	Win & Pl
Hurdles	3	0	0	0	
Career Total	**9**	**0**	**0**	**0**	**0**

Going: Sf: 0-0 GS: 0-1 Gd: 0-1 GF: - Fm: 0-1
Distance: 2m/2m3: 0-3 2m4-2m7: 0-0 3m+: 0-0
Track: LH: 0-2 RH: 0-1 Tight: 0-1 Gall: 0-0
Aids: Bl: 0-0 Vi: 0-0 Tstrap: 0-0
Best Rating: 88 7/99 Sedg 2m1f gd-fm Hdl

Glen Warrior

87 **74**

6-y-o b g Michelozzo (USA)-Mascara Vii (Damsire Unregistered)
J S Smith Donald Smith

Placings:0U (4874)
2001/02: 16^{0}S, 20^{U}G

	Starts	1st	2nd	3rd	Win & Pl
NH Flat	1	0	0	0	0
Hurdles	1	0	0	0	0
Career Total	**2**	**0**	**0**	**0**	

Going: Sf: 0-1 GS: 0-0 Gd: 0-1 GF: - Fm: 0-0
Distance: 2m/2m3: 0-1 2m4-2m7: 0-1 3m+: 0-0
Track: LH: 0-0 RH: 0-2 Tight: 0-0 Gall: 0-0
Aids: Bl: 0-0 Vi: 0-0 Tstrap: 0-0
Best Rating: 84 2/02 Winc 2m soft NHF

Glenalla Braes (IRE)

72 **62**

9-y-o b g Roi Guillaume (FR)-Willowho Pride (Arapaho)
M J Gingell Robert Barr

Placings:P-04 (0566)
2001/02: 23^{0}GF, 25^{4}F

	Starts	1st	2nd	3rd	Win & Pl
Hurdles	2	0	0	0	0
Career Total	**3**	**0**	**0**	**0**	**0**

Going: Sf: 0-0 GS: 0-0 Gd: 0-0 GF: - Fm: 0-2
Distance: 2m/2m3: 0-0 2m4-2m7: 0-0 3m+: 0-2
Track: LH: 0-2 RH: 0-0 Tight: 0-1 Gall: 0-0
Aids: Bl: 0-0 Vi: 0-0 Tstrap: 0-0
Best Rating: 62 5/01 Weth 3m1f firm Hdl

Glencove

(74h) (23h)

8-y-o ch m Derrylin-Velda (Thatch (USA))
W Clay S Taberner

Placings:6443/600P (1084)
2001/02: 16^{6}F, 20^{0}G, 24^{0}G, 20^{P}G

	Starts	1st	2nd	3rd	Win & Pl
Hurdles	3	0	0	0	0
Chases	1	0	0	0	0
Career Total	**8**	**0**	**0**	**1**	**187**

Going: Sf: 0-0 GS: 0-0 Gd: 0-3 GF: - Fm: 0-1
Distance: 2m/2m3: 0-1 2m4-2m7: 0-2 3m+: 0-1
Track: LH: 0-4 RH: 0-0 Tight: 0-2 Gall: 0-0
Aids: Bl: 0-0 Vi: 0-0 Tstrap: 0-0
Best Rating: 89 6/99 Worc 2m gd-fm NHF

Glendamah (IRE)

101 **87**

5-y-o b g Mukaddamah (USA)-Sea Glen (IRE) (Glenstal (USA))
J R Weymes White Rose Poultry Ltd

Placings:650026 (4917)
2001/02: [illegible]

	Starts	1st	2nd	3rd	Win & Pl
Hurdles	6	0	1	0	558
Career Total	**6**	**0**	**1**	**0**	**558**

Going: Sf: 0-2 GS: 0-2 Gd: 0-0 GF: - Fm: 0-2
Distance: 2m/2m3: 0-4 2m4-2m7: 0-2 3m+: 0-0
Track: LH: 0-4 RH: 0-2 Tight: 0-4 Gall: 0-2
Aids: Bl: 0-0 Vi: 0-0 Tstrap: 0-0
Best Rating: 78 4/02 Sedg 2m5f110y gd-fm Hdl

Plating-class hurdler, winner of two sellers at Hexham in May 2002. Suited by a sound surface.

Glendari (IRE)

82(85h) (67h)**63**

7-y-o b g Shardari-Beautiful Glen (Furry Glen)
Mrs M Reveley The Believers

Placings:0/0504-0006P (2768)
2001/02: 17^{0}GF, 17^{0}GF, 16^{0}GF, 16^{6}G, 19^{P}G

	Starts	1st	2nd	3rd	Win & Pl
Hurdles	3	0	0	0	0
Chases	2	0	0	0	0
Career Total	**10**	**0**	**0**	**0**	**0**

Going: Sf: 0-0 GS: 0-0 Gd: 0-2 GF: - Fm: 0-3
Distance: 2m/2m3: 0-5 2m4-2m7: 0-0 3m+: 0-0
Track: LH: 0-5 RH: 0-0 Tight: 0-4 Gall: 0-1
Aids: Bl: 0-0 Vi: 0-0 Tstrap: 0-0
Best Rating: 95 12/00 Muss 2m good NHF

Glendoe (IRE)

11-y-o b/br g Lord Americo-Jazz Bavard (Le Bavard (FR))
R H Buckler Mr K C B Mackenzie & Mr L G Kimber

Placings:P0F/556F/P1FU342/F6P4F/P-P (0060)
2001/02: 17^{P}GS

	Starts	1st	2nd	3rd	Win & Pl
Hurdles	1	0	0	0	
Career Total	**21**	**1**	**1**	**1**	**5069**
108 12/97 Font 2m2f E(0-100)HCh SFT					£3023

Total win prize-money £3024

Going: Sf: 0-0 GS: 0-1 Gd: 0-0 GF: - Fm: 0-0
Distance: 2m/2m3: 0-1 2m4-2m7: 0-0 3m+: 0-0
Track: LH: 0-0 RH: 0-1 Tight: 0-1 Gall: 0-0
Aids: Bl: 0-0 Vi: 0-0 Tstrap: 0-0
Best Rating: 116 10/98 Strf 2m1f110y good Ch

Glenelly Gale (IRE)

116 **142**

8-y-o b/br g Strong Gale-Smart Fashion (Carlburg)
A L T Moore F Bradley

Placings:0/2F140/5124U13-5035103 (4649)
2001/02: 20^{5}G, 16^{0}G, 19^{3}YS, 16^{5}Y, 16^{1}YS, 20^{0}S, 16^{3}G

	Starts	1st	2nd	3rd	Win & Pl
Chases	7	1	0	2	15165
Career Total	**20**	**4**	**2**	**3**	**49712**
129 1/02 Thur 2m Ch Y-S					£7831
132 2/01 Fair 2m100y Ch HVY					£18346
129 10/00 Gowr 2m1f Ch SFT					£4692
123 1/00 Punc 2m Hdl SFT					£3312

Total win prize-money £34182

Going: Sf: 0-1 GS: 0-0 Gd: 0-3 GF: - Fm: 0-0
Distance: **2m/2m3: 1-5** 2m4-2m7: 0-2 3m+: 0-0
Track: LH: 0-3 RH: 0-0 Tight: 0-1 Gall: 0-0
Aids: Bl: 0-0 Vi: 0-0 Tstrap: 0-0
Best Rating: 142 4/02 Aint 2m good Ch

Fair two-mile Irish handicap chaser. Acts on soft/heavy ground.

Glenfarclas Boy (IRE)

103(100h) (78h)**105**

6-y-o b g Montelimar (USA)-Fairy Blaze (IRE) (Good Thyne (USA))
Miss Lucinda V Russell Mrs Ishbel Grant

Placings:600F-0F4P46 (4874)
2001/02: 20^{0}G, 20^{F}GS, 20^{4}HY, 24^{P}S, 17^{4}GS, 20^{6}G

	Starts	1st	2nd	3rd	Win & Pl
Hurdles	6	0	0	0	0
Career Total	**10**	**0**	**0**	**0**	**0**

Going: Sf: 0-2 GS: 0-2 Gd: 0-2 GF: - Fm: 0-0
Distance: 2m/2m3: 0-1 2m4-2m7: 0-4 3m+: 0-1
Track: LH: 0-3 RH: 0-3 Tight: 0-0 Gall: 0-0
Aids: Bl: 0-0 Vi: 0-0 Tstrap: 0-0
Best Rating: 84 5/00 Prth 2m110y gd-sft NHF

Uninspiring over hurdles to date.

Glengolden (IRE)

99 **87**

9-y-o ch m Glenstal (USA)-Talk Is Cheap (Le Bavard (FR))
Mrs S C Bradburne Timothy Hardie

Placings:50/54 (4878)
2001/02: 25^{5}GF, 24^{4}G

	Starts	1st	2nd	3rd	Win & Pl
Chases	2	0	0	0	557
Career Total	4	0	0	0	557

Going: Sf: 0-0 GS: 0-0 Gd: 0-1 GF: - Fm: 0-1
Distance: 2m/2m3: 0-0 2m4-2m7: 0-0 3m+: 0-2
Track: LH: 0-1 RH: 0-1 Tight: 0-1 Gall: 0-0
Aids: Bl: 0-0 Vi: 0-0 Tstrap: 0-0
Best Rating: 87 4/02 Kels 3m1f gd-fm Ch

Glenmore

78f

5-y-o ch g Michelozzo (USA)-Random Select (Random Shot)
Noel T Chance Mike Browne

Placings:*0* (3257)
2001/02: 16^{0}S

	Starts	1st	2nd	3rd	Win & Pl
NH Flat	1	0	0	0	
Career Total	**1**	**0**	**0**	**0**	

Going: Sf: 0-1 GS: 0-0 Gd: 0-0 GF: - Fm: 0-0
Distance: 2m/2m3: 0-1 2m4-2m7: 0-0 3m+: 0-0
Track: LH: 0-0 RH: 0-0 Tight: 0-0 Gall: 0-0
Aids: Bl: 0-0 Vi: 0-0 Tstrap: 0-0
Best Rating: 78 1/02 Newc 2m soft NHF

Glenmoss Tara (IRE)

102f **127f**

4-y-o b f Zaffaran (USA)-Majestic Run (Deep Run)
N G Richards West Coast Fiddlers

Placings:*112* (4823)
2001/02: 16^{1}S, 16^{1}G, 17^{2}G

	Starts	1st	2nd	3rd	Win & Pl
NH Flat	3	2	1	0	7577
Career Total	**3**	**2**	**1**	**0**	**7577**
98 2/02 Donc 2m110y H NHF SFT					£2002

Total win prize-money £2002

Going: Sf: 1-1 GS: 0-0 Gd: 1-2 GF: - Fm: 0-0
Distance: **2m/2m3: 2-3** 2m4-2m7: 0-0 3m+: 0-0
Track: **LH: 2-3** RH: 0-0 Tight: 0-0 **Gall: 1-2**
Aids: Bl: 0-0 Vi: 0-0 Tstrap: 0-0
Best Rating: 127 4/02 Chel 2m1f good NHF

Won her first two bumpers, dead-heating in the second of them. Has a turn of foot and swishes her tail under pressure.

Glensan (IRE)

5-y-o b g Insan (USA)-Strikes Glen (Le Moss)
Mrs H Dalton A J Brazier

Placings:4P (3271)
2001/02: 16^{4}GS, 16^{P}G

	Starts	1st	2nd	3rd	Win & Pl
NH Flat	1	0	0	0	0
Hurdles	1	0	0	0	0
Career Total	**2**	**0**	**0**	**0**	**0**

Going: Sf: 0-0 GS: 0-1 Gd: 0-1 GF: - Fm: 0-0
Distance: 2m/2m3: 0-2 2m4-2m7: 0-0 3m+: 0-0
Track: LH: 0-1 RH: 0-1 Tight: 0-0 Gall: 0-2
Aids: Bl: 0-0 Vi: 0-0 Tstrap: 0-0
Best Rating: 92 12/01 Hntg 2m110y gd-sft NHF

Glenwhargen (IRE)

105 **78**

5-y-o b m Polar Falcon (USA)-La Veine (USA) (Diesis)
Miss Sheena West The Happy Hour Partnership

Placings:3-P14430544 (4565)
2001/02: 22^{P}S, 16^{1}S, 16^{4}S, 16^{4}S, 17^{3}HY, 18^{0}HY, 19^{5}S, 16^{4}GS, 16^{4}G

	Starts	1st	2nd	3rd	Win & Pl
Hurdles	9	1	0	1	2814
Career Total	**10**	**1**	**0**	**2**	**3129**
76 11/01 Towc 2m G Hdl SFT					£1946

Total win prize-money £1946

Going: Sf: 1-7 GS: 0-1 Gd: 0-1 GF: - Fm: 0-0
Distance: **2m/2m3: 1-7** 2m4-2m7: 0-2 3m+: 0-0
Track: LH: 0-4 **RH: 1-5** Tight: 0-6 Gall: 0-0
Aids: Bl: 0-0 Vi: 0-0 **Tstrap: 1-9**
Best Rating: 78 4/02 Towc 2m good Hdl

Has arthritic joints and a wind problem, she is only plating class and acts on soft ground and is effective over two miles.

Glevum

10-y-o gr m Town And Country-Peggy Wig (Counsel)
Mrs Marilyn Scudamore Mrs J K Powell

Placings:*06*/6400/3P000F354/3P3P-F52 (0579)
2001/02: 25^{F}S, 24^{5}GF, 24^{2}GF

	Starts	1st	2nd	3rd	Win & Pl
Chases	3	0	1	0	382
Career Total	**22**	**0**	**1**	**4**	**2643**

Going: Sf: 0-1 GS: 0-0 Gd: 0-0 GF: - Fm: 0-2
Distance: 2m/2m3: 0-0 2m4-2m7: 0-0 3m+: 0-3
Track: LH: 0-3 RH: 0-0 Tight: 0-2 Gall: 0-0
Aids: Bl: 0-1 Vi: 0-0 Tstrap: 0-0
Best Rating: 103 6/01 Strf 3m gd-fm Ch

Glinger (IRE)

101 (59h)**104**

9-y-o b g Remainder Man-Harilla (Sir Herbert)
N G Richards James Westoll

Placings:6650/FP-4422 (4895)
2001/02: 22^{4}GS, 20^{4}G, 20^{2}GF, 20^{2}G

	Starts	1st	2nd	3rd	Win & Pl
Hurdles	1	0	0	0	0
Chases	3	0	2	0	3271
Career Total	**10**	**0**	**2**	**0**	**3271**

Going: Sf: 0-0 GS: 0-1 Gd: 0-2 GF: 0-1 Fm: 0-1
Distance: 2m/2m3: 0-0 2m4-2m7: 0-4 3m+: 0-0
Track: LH: 0-1 RH: 0-3 Tight: 0-1 Gall: 0-0
Aids: Bl: 0-0 Vi: 0-0 Tstrap: 0-0
Best Rating: 104 4/02 Prth 2m4f110y good Ch

Glitter Isle (IRE)

108 **124**

12-y-o gr g Roselier (FR)-Decent Dame (Decent Fellow)
J T Gifford Mrs Timothy Pilkington

Placings:624434/2116/34322/051204/P/63545110-03P4P6 (4038)
2001/02: 24^{0}G, 26^{3}GS, 30^{P}GS, 24^{4}S, 23^{P}S, 26^{6}S

	Starts	1st	2nd	3rd	Win & Pl

	Starts	1st	2nd	3rd	Win & Pl
Chases	6	0	0	1	1143
Career Total	**36**	**5**	**5**	**5**	**57552**

130	3/01	Font	3m4f	D(0-120)HCh	HVY	£4251
122	2/01	Winc	2m5f	D(0-120)HCh	GD	£7098
140	12/98	Winc	3m1f110y	B(0-145)HCh	SFT	£9117
133	2/97	Ling	2m4f110y	D Ch	HVY	£3996
121	1/97	Ling	2m	D Ch	G-S	£3597

Total win prize-money £28061

Going: Sf: 0-3 GS: 0-2 Gd: 0-1 GF: - Fm: 0-0
Distance: 2m/2m3: 0-0 2m4-2m7: 0-0 3m+: 0-6
Track: LH: 0-1 RH: 0-3 Tight: 0-2 Gall: 0-2
Aids: Bl: 0-1 Vi: 0-0 Tstrap: 0-0
Best Rating: **143** 1/99 Sand 3m5f110y gd-sft Ch

He was a very decent handicap chaser a few seasons ago, but lost his way and dropped a huge amount in the handicap. He won a couple of modest events last season but struggled again when upped in class.

Global Draw (IRE)

(51h)
6-y-o ch g Be My Guest (USA)-Almost A Lady (IRE) (Entitled)
Mrs A M Thorpe Mrs A M Thorpe

Placings:3/0506P**P-PP** **(0317)**
2001/02: 18^{P}GF, 23^{P}F

	Starts	1st	2nd	3rd	Win & Pl
Chases	2	0	0	0	
Career Total	**9**	**0**	**0**	**1**	**410**

Going: Sf: 0-0 GS: 0-0 Gd: 0-0 GF: - Fm: 0-2
Distance: 2m/2m3: 0-1 2m4-2m7: 0-0 3m+: 0-1
Track: LH: 0-0 RH: 0-1 Tight: 0-1 Gall: 0-0
Aids: Bl: 0-2 Vi: 0-0 Tstrap: 0-0
Best Rating: **85** 6/00 Uttx 2m4f110y good Hdl

Global Search (FR)

88(83h) (116h)**103**
8-y-o b g Green Dancer (USA)-Merry Quest (USA) (Gay Mecene (USA))
L Lungo Elite Racing Club

Placings:032/2/112**13F-U44P** **(3556)**
2001/02: 16^{U}G, 16^{4}S, 16^{4}S, 19^{P}S

	Starts	1st	2nd	3rd	Win & Pl
Hurdles	1	0	0	0	0
Chases	3	0	0	0	696
Career Total	**14**	**3**	**3**	**2**	**14053**

130	11/00	Ayr	2m	D Ch	SFT	£3887
93	6/00	Prth	2m110y	E Hdl	SFT	£2756
111	5/00	Weth	2m	D Hdl	G-S	£3016

Total win prize-money £9659

Going: Sf: 0-3 GS: 0-0 Gd: 0-1 GF: - Fm: 0-0
Distance: 2m/2m3: 0-4 2m4-2m7: 0-0 3m+: 0-0
Track: LH: 0-4 RH: 0-0 Tight: 0-2 Gall: 0-0
Aids: Bl: 0-0 Vi: 0-0 Tstrap: 0-0
Best Rating: **130** 1/01 Ayr 2m gd-sft Ch

A winner twice over hurdles as a novice, he jumped well when winning on his chasing debut at Ayr in November 2000, but did not build on that and his jumping deteriorated. Has had breathing problems and two miles in soft ground looks right on the edge of his stamina.

Globe Runner

94 **106**
9-y-o b g Adbass (USA)-Scenic Villa (Top Ville)
J J O'Neill G & P Barker Ltd/globe Engineering

Placings:242P12/21042/4322145/56310/010PP-04FF **(4869)**
2001/02: 20^{0}HY, 20^{4}S, 21^{F}GF, 20^{F}GF

	Starts	1st	2nd	3rd	Win & Pl
Hurdles	4	0	0	0	271
Career Total	**32**	**5**	**7**	**2**	**33634**

128	1/01	Ayr	2m4f	B(0-145)HHdl	G-S	£7083
125	3/00	Weth	2m4f110y	D(0-125)HHdl	G-S	£3172
130	12/98	Hayd	2m4f	C(0-135)HHdl	SFT	£3896
123	11/97	Ayr	2m4f	C(0-135)HHdl	G-S	£4793
93	2/97	Uttx	2m	E(0-105)HHdl	GD	£2347

Total win prize-money £21293

Going: Sf: 0-2 GS: 0-0 Gd: 0-0 GF: - Fm: 0-2
Distance: 2m/2m3: 0-0 2m4-2m7: 0-4 3m+: 0-0
Track: LH: 0-3 RH: 0-0 Tight: 0-0 Gall: 0-1
Aids: Bl: 0-1 Vi: 0-0 Tstrap: 0-0
Best Rating: **130** 2/99 Asct 2m4f gd-sft Hdl

Decent handicap hurdler, he was a model of consistency over hurdles. (DEAD)

Glorious Welcome

71 **53**
4-y-o b g Past Glories-Rest And Welcome (Town And Country)
Jane Southcombe Mrs V H Nicholas

Placings:004P **(3396)**
2001/02: 16^{0}G, 17^{0}HY, 16^{4}G, 18^{P}S

	Starts	1st	2nd	3rd	Win & Pl
Hurdles	4	0	0	0	0
Career Total	**4**	**0**	**0**	**0**	**0**

Going: Sf: 0-2 GS: 0-0 Gd: 0-2 GF: - Fm: 0-0
Distance: 2m/2m3: 0-4 2m4-2m7: 0-0 3m+: 0-0
Track: LH: 0-4 RH: 0-0 Tight: 0-3 Gall: 0-1
Aids: Bl: 0-0 Vi: 0-0 Tstrap: 0-3
Best Rating: **53** 12/01 Plum 2m good Hdl

Glory Of Love

60 **75**
7-y-o b g Belmez (USA)-Princess Lieven (Royal Palace)
Mrs A M Naughton Miss Lorna Preston

Placings:5P/2 **(0089)**
2001/02: 16^{2}S

	Starts	1st	2nd	3rd	Win & Pl
Hurdles	1	0	1	0	541
Career Total	**3**	**0**	**1**	**0**	**541**

Going: Sf: 0-1 GS: 0-0 Gd: 0-0 GF: - Fm: 0-0
Distance: 2m/2m3: 0-1 2m4-2m7: 0-0 3m+: 0-0
Track: LH: 0-1 RH: 0-0 Tight: 0-0 Gall: 0-0
Aids: Bl: 0-0 Vi: 0-0 Tstrap: 0-0
Best Rating: **75** 5/01 Hexm 2m soft Hdl

Glory Quest (USA)

84 **81**
5-y-o b g Quest For Fame-Sonseri (Prince Tenderfoot (USA))
Miss Gay Kelleway (M Pitman 2/4) Miss Gay Kelleway

Placings:0 **(4591)**
2001/02: 16^{0}G

	Starts	1st	2nd	3rd	Win & Pl
Hurdles	1	0	0	0	0
Career Total	**1**	**0**	**0**	**0**	

Going: Sf: 0-0 GS: 0-0 Gd: 0-1 GF: - Fm: 0-0
Distance: 2m/2m3: 0-1 2m4-2m7: 0-0 3m+: 0-0
Track: LH: 0-1 RH: 0-0 Tight: 0-0 Gall: 0-0
Aids: Bl: 0-0 Vi: 0-0 Tstrap: 0-0
Best Rating: **83** 4/02 Uttx 2m good Hdl

Glory Storey (IRE)

112(85h) (82h)**114**
8-y-o b g Tremblant-Boule De Soie (The Parson)
K C Bailey I M S Racing

Placings:403-0**U455213** **(4863)**
2001/02: 22^{0}GS, 24^{U}G, 25^{4}G, 24^{5}GS, 24^{5}G, 16^{2}G, 24^{1}GF, 19^{3}F

	Starts	1st	2nd	3rd	Win & Pl
Hurdles	1	0	0	0	0
Chases	7	1	1	1	6892
Career Total	**11**	**1**	**1**	**2**	**7246**

114	4/02	Ludl	3m	D(0-110)HCh	G-F	£4498

Total win prize-money £4498

Going: Sf: 0-0 GS: 0-2 Gd: 0-4 GF: - Fm: 1-2
Distance: 2m/2m3: 0-1 2m4-2m7: 0-2 **3m+: 1-5**
Track: LH: 0-0 **RH: 1-7 Tight: 1-2** Gall: 0-1
Aids: Bl: 0-0 Vi: 0-0 Tstrap: 0-0
Best Rating: **114** 4/02 Ludl 3m gd-fm Ch

Winner of an Irish point to point. He has made the frame in bumpers, hurdles and over fences before landing a Ludlow novice chase. Stays three miles, handles a sound surface.

Glory Trail (IRE)

8-y-o b g Supreme Leader-Death Or Glory (Hasdrubal)
D M Grissell R Griffiths

Placings:*00-6* **(0580)**
2001/02: 22^{6}GF

	Starts	1st	2nd	3rd	Win & Pl
Hurdles	1	0	0	0	0
Career Total	**3**	**0**	**0**	**0**	**0**

Going: Sf: 0-0 GS: 0-0 Gd: 0-0 GF: - Fm: 0-1
Distance: 2m/2m3: 0-0 2m4-2m7: 0-1 3m+: 0-0
Track: LH: 0-1 RH: 0-0 Tight: 0-1 Gall: 0-0
Aids: Bl: 0-0 Vi: 0-0 Tstrap: 0-0
Best Rating: **76** 6/01 Strf 2m6f110y gd-fm Hdl

Glucose (FR)

103 **135**
5-y-o b g Double Bed (FR)-Sclos (FR) (Direct Flight)
F Doumen R Britten-Long

Placings:P6F46P-P04213060
2001/02: 18^{P}HY, 18^{0}VS, 18^{4}S, 17^{2}G, 19^{1}S, 17^{3}HY, 18^{0}HO, 16^{6}S, 19^{0}HY

	Starts	1st	2nd	3rd	Win & Pl
Hurdles	9	1	1	1	26674
Career Total	**15**	**1**	**1**	**1**	**28787**

	9/01	Stra	2m3f	Hdl	SFT	£10669

Total win prize-money £10669

Going: Sf: 1-6 GS: 0-0 Gd: 0-1 GF: - Fm: 0-0
Distance: **2m/2m3: 1-8** 2m4-2m7: 0-1 3m+: 0-0
Track: LH: 0-2 RH: 0-0 Tight: 0-0 Gall: 0-1

Aids: Bl: 0-0 Vi: 0-0 Tstrap: 0-0
Best Rating: 135 2/02 Newb 2m110y soft Hdl

Go Ballistic

112(99h) 175
13-y-o br g Celtic Cone-National Clover (National Trust)
Miss H C Knight Mrs B J Lockhart

Placings: 1232/50313P41P/124F42BF461/4121F4P/P 54U410B/5P224/222P/102-03P0 (4913)
2001/02: 24^{0}G, 25^{3}HY, 26^{P}G, 29^{0}G

	Starts	1st	2nd	3rd	Win & Pl
Chases	4	0	0	1	8625
Career Total	**55**	**9**	**11**	**4**	**245843**

140	12/00	Chel	3m	B HHdl	SFT	£8923
173	2/98	Winc	3m1f110y	B Ch	G-F	£11925
144	12/96	Asct	3m110y	B HCh	G-F	£24378
131	11/96	Asct	3m110y	B HCh	G-F	£8013
126	4/96	Asct	3m110y	C Ch	G-F	£11464
117	10/95	Worc	2m4f	C(0-130)HHdl	GD	£3416
112	3/95	Donc	2m4f	E Hdl	GD	£2845
108	12/94	Leic	2m	Hdl	HVY	£2249
114	2/94	Sand	2m110y	NHF	G-S	£1926

Total win prize-money £75142

Going: Sf: 0-1 GS: 0-0 Gd: 0-3 GF: - Fm: 0-0
Distance: 2m/2m3: 0-0 2m4-2m7: 0-0 3m+: 0-4
Track: LH: 0-2 RH: 0-2 Tight: 0-0 Gall: 0-2
Aids: Bl: 0-0 Vi: 0-0 Tstrap: 0-0
Best Rating: 177 3/99 Chel 3m2f110y gd-sft Ch

A fine servant, he was runner-up to See More Business in the Gold Cup of 1999, but was reported to have a wind problem after pulling up in the same race in 2000. He bounced back with a winning reappearance over hurdles in December of that year but, after trailing home well beaten in the King George, his days as a major player seemed behind him. However, he still runs his heart out against the best and is capable of decent efforts in small-field conditions events.

Go Boy

76f 65f
4-y-o b g Sovereign Water (FR)-Tinkle (Petoski)
R D E Woodhouse Go Racing

Placings: 00 (3777)
2001/02: 16^{0}S, 16^{0}S

	Starts	1st	2nd	3rd	Win & Pl
NH Flat	2	0	0	0	
Career Total	**2**	**0**	**0**	**0**	

Going: Sf: 0-2 GS: 0-0 Gd: 0-0 GF: - Fm: 0-0
Distance: 2m/2m3: 0-2 2m4-2m7: 0-0 3m+: 0-0
Track: LH: 0-0 RH: 0-1 Tight: 0-0 Gall: 0-0
Aids: Bl: 0-0 Vi: 0-0 Tstrap: 0-0
Best Rating: 65 2/02 Sand 2m110y soft NHF

Go For It Sweetie (IRE)

9-y-o b m Brush Aside (USA)-Arctic Mistress (Quayside)
B D Leavy Barry Leavy

Placings: 0/0/PP0FS/06P-F (0232)
2001/02: 21^{F}GF

	Starts	1st	2nd	3rd	Win & Pl
Hurdles	1	0	0	0	
Career Total	**11**	**0**	**0**	**0**	**0**

Going: Sf: 0-0 GS: 0-0 Gd: 0-0 GF: - Fm: 0-1
Distance: 2m/2m3: 0-0 2m4-2m7: 0-1 3m+: 0-0
Track: LH: 0-0 RH: 0-1 Tight: 0-0 Gall: 0-1
Aids: Bl: 0-1 Vi: 0-0 Tstrap: 0-1
Best Rating: 65 9/97 MRas 1m5f110y good NHF

Go Man (IRE)

89 83
8-y-o b g Mandalus-Cherry Park (Netherkelly)
R Lee J E Potter

Placings: 00/P/06 (4820)
2001/02: 16^{0}G, 17^{6}G

	Starts	1st	2nd	3rd	Win & Pl
Hurdles	2	0	0	0	0
Career Total	**5**	**0**	**0**	**0**	**0**

Going: Sf: 0-0 GS: 0-0 Gd: 0-2 GF: - Fm: 0-0
Distance: 2m/2m3: 0-2 2m4-2m7: 0-0 3m+: 0-0
Track: LH: 0-2 RH: 0-0 Tight: 0-0 Gall: 0-1
Aids: Bl: 0-0 Vi: 0-0 Tstrap: 0-0
Best Rating: 83 4/02 Uttx 2m good Hdl

Go Nomadic

8-y-o br g Nomadic Way (USA)-Dreamago (Sir Mago)
D G Atkinson (Trainer Unknown 10/2) D G Atkinson

Placings: 210 (4678)
2001/02: 25^{2}GS, 25^{1}HY, 25^{0}G

	Starts	1st	2nd	3rd	Win & Pl
Chases	3	1	1	0	3146
Career Total	**3**	**1**	**1**	**0**	**3146**

113	3/02	Kels	3m1f	H Ch	HVY	£2691

Total win prize-money £2692

Going: Sf: 1-1 GS: 0-1 Gd: 0-1 GF: - Fm: 0-0
Distance: 2m/2m3: 0-0 2m4-2m7: 0-0 **3m+: 1-3**
Track: **LH: 1-2** RH: 0-0 **Tight: 1-2** Gall: 0-0
Aids: Bl: 0-0 Vi: 0-0 **Tstrap: 1-3**
Best Rating: 113 3/02 Kels 3m1f heavy Ch

Hunter chaser. Acts on a soft surface and is effective at around three miles.

Go Positive

96 65
7-y-o b m Profilic-Rather Gorgeous (Billion (USA))
Mark Campion Mrs J Greaves

Placings: 40/6-0000 (2429)
2001/02: 16^{0}GF, 16^{0}S, 19^{0}G, 24^{0}G

	Starts	1st	2nd	3rd	Win & Pl
Hurdles	4	0	0	0	
Career Total	**7**	**0**	**0**	**0**	**213**

Going: Sf: 0-1 GS: 0-0 Gd: 0-2 GF: - Fm: 0-1
Distance: 2m/2m3: 0-3 2m4-2m7: 0-0 3m+: 0-1
Track: LH: 0-3 RH: 0-1 Tight: 0-1 Gall: 0-2
Aids: Bl: 0-0 Vi: 0-0 Tstrap: 0-0
Best Rating: 65 10/01 Towc 2m soft Hdl

Moderate hurdler.

Go Thunder (IRE)

8-y-o b g Nordico (USA)-Moving Off (Henbit (USA))
D A Nolan Miss G Joughin

Placings: 00005/00/P (2723)
2001/02: 17^{P}GF

	Starts	1st	2nd	3rd	Win & Pl
Hurdles	1	0	0	0	
Career Total	**8**	**0**	**0**	**0**	

Going: Sf: 0-0 GS: 0-0 Gd: 0-0 GF: - Fm: 0-1
Distance: 2m/2m3: 0-1 2m4-2m7: 0-0 3m+: 0-0
Track: LH: 0-0 RH: 0-0 Tight: 0-0 Gall: 0-0
Aids: Bl: 0-0 Vi: 0-0 Tstrap: 0-1
Best Rating: 68 5/98 Clon 2m gd-fm Hdl

Go White Lightning (IRE)

95 91
7-y-o gr g Zaffaran (USA)-Rosy Posy (IRE) (Roselier (FR))
M Bradstock Fishtank Racing

Placings: U1/1-0U (4479)
2001/02: 19^{0}S, 19^{U}G

	Starts	1st	2nd	3rd	Win & Pl
Hurdles	2	0	0	0	
Career Total	**5**	**2**	**0**	**0**	**3423**

107	5/00	Hrfd	2m1f	H NHF	GD	£1841
107	4/00	MRas	2m1f110y	H NHF	SFT	£1582

Total win prize-money £3423

Going: Sf: 0-1 GS: 0-0 Gd: 0-1 GF: - Fm: 0-0
Distance: 2m/2m3: 0-2 2m4-2m7: 0-0 3m+: 0-0
Track: LH: 0-1 RH: 0-1 Tight: 0-0 Gall: 0-1
Aids: Bl: 0-0 Vi: 0-0 Tstrap: 0-0
Best Rating: 107 5/00 Hrfd 2m1f good NHF

An excitable type, he was a dual bumper winner in the spring of 2001, beating a decent sort on the second occasion. Handles good ground and softer.

Go-Onmyson

106 110
9-y-o b g Primitive Rising (USA)-Ice Lass (Heroic Air)
M Tate J A Simpson

Placings: 5/40360F1/1PP64346460/31304350-0231P0 (2664)
2001/02: 20^{0}G, 20^{2}GF, 20^{3}GF, 24^{1}GF, 21^{P}S, 24^{0}G

	Starts	1st	2nd	3rd	Win & Pl
Hurdles	6	1	1	1	6579
Career Total	**33**	**4**	**1**	**6**	**16724**

110	10/01	Ludl	3m	E(0-115)HHdl	G-F	£4420
104	6/00	Worc	2m4f	F(0-100)HHdl	G-F	£2093
99	5/99	Chep	2m110y	E(0-105)HHdl	GD	£2528
73	3/99	Chep	2m110y	G Hdl	G-S	£1604

Total win prize-money £10645

Going: Sf: 0-1 GS: 0-0 Gd: 0-2 GF: - Fm: 1-3
Distance: 2m/2m3: 0-0 2m4-2m7: 0-4 **3m+: 1-2**
Track: LH: 0-3 RH: 0-1 Tight: 0-0 Gall: 0-0
Aids: **Bl: 1-6** Vi: 0-0 Tstrap: 0-0
Best Rating: 110 10/01 Ludl 3m gd-fm Hdl

Goes well between two and three miles and acts on most types of ground.

Goawayoutofthat (IRE)

8-y-o b g Carefree Dancer (USA)-Creative Princess (IRE) (Creative Plan (USA))
Miss A Nolan Mrs P Duncan

Placings:4P-P (0090)
2001/02: 25^{PS}

	Starts	1st	2nd	3rd	Win & Pl
Chases	1	0	0	0	
Career Total	**3**	**0**	**0**	**0**	**0**

Going: Sf: 0-1 GS: 0-0 Gd: 0-0 GF: - Fm: 0-0
Distance: 2m/2m3: 0-0 2m4-2m7: 0-0 3m+: 0-1
Track: LH: 0-1 RH: 0-0 Tight: 0-0 Gall: 0-0
Aids: Bl: 0-0 Vi: 0-0 Tstrap: 0-0
Best Rating: 101 3/01 MRas 3m1f gd-sft Ch

Goddess

85 83
8-y-o b m River God (USA)-Deaconess (The Parson)
P R Webber W H Carson

Placings:52 (0838)
2001/02: 20^{5}GF, 24^{2}G

	Starts	1st	2nd	3rd	Win & Pl
Hurdles	2	0	1	0	732
Career Total	**2**	**0**	**1**	**0**	**732**

Going: Sf: 0-0 GS: 0-0 Gd: 0-1 GF: - Fm: 0-1
Distance: 2m/2m3: 0-0 2m4-2m7: 0-1 3m+: 0-1
Track: LH: 0-1 RH: 0-1 Tight: 0-0 Gall: 0-1
Aids: Bl: 0-0 Vi: 0-0 Tstrap: 0-0
Best Rating: 83 6/01 Worc 3m good Hdl

Gofagold

102 88
7-y-o ch g Tina's Pet-Golden Della (Glint Of Gold)
A C Whillans Mrs L M Whillans

Placings:40/53-0432 (4894)
2001/02: 16^{0}HY, 17^{4}S, 17^{3}S, 16^{2}G

	Starts	1st	2nd	3rd	Win & Pl
Hurdles	4	0	1	1	1515
Career Total	**8**	**0**	**1**	**2**	**1939**

Going: Sf: 0-3 GS: 0-0 Gd: 0-1 GF: - Fm: 0-0
Distance: 2m/2m3: 0-4 2m4-2m7: 0-0 3m+: 0-0
Track: LH: 0-3 RH: 0-1 Tight: 0-2 Gall: 0-0
Aids: Bl: 0-0 Vi: 0-0 Tstrap: 0-0
Best Rating: 88 4/02 Prth 2m110y good Hdl

Placed at a low level in novices' hurdles.

Goguenard (FR)

110 146d
8-y-o b g Gaspard De La Nuit (FR)-Laika Iii (FR) (El Toro (FR))
N J Henderson Trevor Hemmings

Placings:012113/3214/0412F331500/415421-00P0F6 (4914)
2001/02: 20^{0}S, 24^{0}S, 24^{P}G, 24^{0}GS, 36^{F}G, 20^{6}G

	Starts	1st	2nd	3rd	Win & Pl
Chases	6	0	0	0	450
Career Total	**33**	**8**	**4**	**4**	**98433**

151	4/01	Sand	2m4f110y	B(0-150)HCh	SFT	£19500
	11/00	Toul	2m5f110y	Hdl	SFT	£6244
	1/00	Pau	2m4f110y	HCh	SFT	£9606
	9/99	Nior	2m3f	Hdl	VS	£3229
	4/99	Toul	2m1f110y	Ch		£3767
	3/98	Engh	2m1f110y	Ch	SFT	£10101
	1/98	Pau	2m1f	Ch	HVY	£5051

Total win prize-money £61426

Going: Sf: 0-2 GS: 0-1 Gd: 0-3 GF: - Fm: 0-0
Distance: 2m/2m3: 0-0 2m4-2m7: 0-2 3m+: 0-4
Track: LH: 0-4 RH: 0-2 Tight: 0-1 Gall: 0-2
Aids: Bl: 0-0 Vi: 0-1 Tstrap: 0-0
Best Rating: 151 4/01 Sand 2m4f110y soft Ch

A prolific winner in France, now with Nicky Henderson. Best at around two and a half miles.

Gohh

101 97
6-y-o ch g Alflora (IRE)-Lavenham's Last (Rymer)
M W Easterby Mrs P A H Hartley

Placings:45-1021P (3546)
2001/02: 17^{1}GS, 17^{0}G, 17^{2}GS, 17^{1}S, 20^{P}S

	Starts	1st	2nd	3rd	Win & Pl
NH Flat	2	1	0	0	1582
Hurdles	3	1	1	0	4300
Career Total	**7**	**2**	**1**	**0**	**5882**

97	12/01	MRas	2m1f110y	D Hdl	SFT	£3444
97	10/01	MRas	2m1f110y	H NHF	G-S	£1582

Total win prize-money £5026

Going: Sf: 1-2 GS: 1-2 Gd: 0-1 GF: - Fm: 0-0
Distance: **2m/2m3: 2-4** 2m4-2m7: 0-1 3m+: 0-0
Track: LH: 0-2 **RH: 2-3 Tight: 2-4** Gall: 0-1
Aids: Bl: 0-0 Vi: 0-0 Tstrap: 0-2
Best Rating: 97 12/01 MRas 2m1f110y soft Hdl

A bumper winner at Market Rasen, he won a novice hurdle over the same course and distance in December 2001. Likes to front run. His real future lies over fences.

Going For Broke

101 122
8-y-o b g Simply Great (FR)-Empty Purse (Pennine Walk)
C J Mann Royal Racing

Placings:333F/3122144113/6002/2133 (1132)
2001/02: 16^{2}GF, 16^{1}GF, 16^{3}GF, 20^{3}GF

	Starts	1st	2nd	3rd	Win & Pl
Chases	4	1	1	2	8892
Career Total	**22**	**5**	**4**	**7**	**25346**

108	6/01	Prth	2m	C Ch	G-F	£6812
122	10/98	Bang	2m1f	E(0-110)HHdl	GD	£3598
120	9/98	Worc	2m	E(0-115)HHdl	G-F	£2337
105	7/98	Strf	2m110y	E Hdl	G-F	£2374
100	5/98	Bang	2m1f	D(0-120)HHdl	GD	£3517

Total win prize-money £18641

Going: Sf: 0-0 GS: 0-0 Gd: 0-0 GF: - Fm: 1-4
Distance: **2m/2m3: 1-3** 2m4-2m7: 0-1 3m+: 0-0
Track: LH: 0-3 **RH: 1-1** Tight: 0-1 Gall: 0-0
Aids: Bl: 0-0 Vi: 0-0 Tstrap: 0-0
Best Rating: 122 8/01 Worc 2m4f110y gd-fm Ch

Ran well at Worcester in June 2001 and scored next time out at Perth.

Going Global (IRE)

109 112
5-y-o ch g Bob Back (USA)-Ukraine Girl (Targowice (USA))
G L Moore Mike Charlton And Rodger Sargent

Placings:000-3310 (4147)
2001/02: 16^{3}G, 20^{3}G, 21^{1}HY, 16^{0}GS

	Starts	1st	2nd	3rd	Win & Pl
Hurdles	4	1	0	2	4196
Career Total	**7**	**1**	**0**	**2**	**4196**

112	2/02	Plum	2m5f	E Hdl	HVY	£2604

Total win prize-money £2604

Going: Sf: 1-1 GS: 0-1 Gd: 0-2 GF: - Fm: 0-0
Distance: 2m/2m3: 0-2 **2m4-2m7: 1-2** 3m+: 0-0
Track: **LH: 1-3** RH: 0-0 **Tight: 1-3** Gall: 0-0
Aids: Bl: 0-0 Vi: 0-0 Tstrap: 0-2
Best Rating: 112 2/02 Plum 2m5f heavy Hdl

Useful on the Flat, he has not looked a natural over hurdles and has undergone a soft palate operation. Landed a novice hurdle in bad ground in February 2002.

Going Native (IRE)

73 39
8-y-o b m Be My Native (USA)-French Class (The Parson)
Miss Venetia Williams The Down South Syndicate

Placings:0/0 (4094)
2001/02: 16^{0}G

	Starts	1st	2nd	3rd	Win & Pl
Hurdles	1	0	0	0	
Career Total	**2**	**0**	**0**	**0**	

Going: Sf: 0-0 GS: 0-0 Gd: 0-1 GF: - Fm: 0-0
Distance: 2m/2m3: 0-1 2m4-2m7: 0-0 3m+: 0-0
Track: LH: 0-0 RH: 0-1 Tight: 0-0 Gall: 0-0
Aids: Bl: 0-0 Vi: 0-0 Tstrap: 0-0
Best Rating: 39 4/02 Prth 2m110y good Hdl

Going Primitive

11-y-o b g Primitive Rising (USA)-Good Going Girl (Import)
R Lancaster (Mrs P Grainger 3/2) R J Lancaster

Placings:243/32/P (3817)
2001/02: 21^{P}S

	Starts	1st	2nd	3rd	Win & Pl
Chases	1	0	0	0	
Career Total	**6**	**0**	**2**	**2**	**1475**

Going: Sf: 0-1 GS: 0-0 Gd: 0-0 GF: - Fm: 0-0
Distance: 2m/2m3: 0-0 2m4-2m7: 0-1 3m+: 0-0
Track: LH: 0-0 RH: 0-1 Tight: 0-1 Gall: 0-0
Aids: Bl: 0-0 Vi: 0-0 Tstrap: 0-0
Best Rating: 97 5/97 Worc 2m gd-sft NHF

Going Solo

6-y-o ch m Sula Bula-Little Beaver (Privy Seal)
Mrs S Gardner D V Gardner

Placings:00 (2142)
2001/02: 17^{0}GF, 17^{0}G

	Starts	1st	2nd	3rd	Win & Pl

NH Flat	2	0	0	0
Career Total	**2**	**0**	**0**	**0**

Going: Sf: 0-0 GS: 0-0 Gd: 0-1 GF: - Fm: 0-1
Distance: 2m/2m3: 0-2 2m4-2m7: 0-0 3m+: 0-0
Track: LH: 0-1 RH: 0-0 Tight: 0-1 Gall: 0-0
Aids: Bl: 0-0 Vi: 0-0 Tstrap: 0-0
Best Rating: 35 8/01 NAbb 2m1f gd-fm NHF

Gola Cher (IRE)

104(101h) **142**

8-y-o b g Beau Sher-Owen Money (Master Owen)
A King Mr & Mrs F C Welch

Placings:11212-1210 **(4191)**
2001/02: 19¹GS, 25²G, 24¹S, 24⁰GS

	Starts	1st	2nd	3rd	Win & Pl
Chases	4	2	1	0	22813
Career Total	**9**	**5**	**3**	**0**	**47862**

128	1/02	Kemp	3m	D Ch	SFT	£4114
141	11/01	Chep	2m3f110y	A Ch	G-S	£15000
126	2/01	Sand	2m6f	B Hdl	HVY	£7182
132	11/00	Asct	3m	C Hdl	SFT	£4836
113	10/00	Strf	2m6f110y	E Hdl	G-S	£2681

Total win prize-money £33815

Going: Sf: 1-1 GS: 1-2 Gd: 0-1 GF: - Fm: 0-0
Distance: 2m/2m3: 0-0 2m4-2m7: 1-1 3m+: 1-3
Track: LH: 1-3 RH: 1-1 Tight: 0-0 Gall: 0-2
Aids: Bl: 0-0 Vi: 0-0 Tstrap: 0-0
Best Rating: 142 12/01 Chel 3m1f110y good Ch

A big, chasing type, he did really well over hurdles in 2000/2001, winning three times, and looks to be an exciting prospect over fences with wins at Chepstow and Kempton. Stays really well and loves the mud.

Gola Supreme (IRE)

98 **103**

7-y-o gr g Supreme Leader-Coal Burn (King Sitric)
A King Jerry Wright & Peter Smith

Placings:1P **(3262)**
2001/02: 24¹G, 21ᴾS

	Starts	1st	2nd	3rd	Win & Pl
Hurdles	2	1	0	0	4888
Career Total	**2**	**1**	**0**	**0**	**4888**

103	11/01	Asct	3m	C Hdl	GD	£4888

Total win prize-money £4888

Going: Sf: 0-1 GS: 0-0 Gd: 1-1 GF: - Fm: 0-0
Distance: 2m/2m3: 0-0 2m4-2m7: 0-1 **3m+: 1-1**
Track: LH: 0-0 **RH: 1-1** Tight: 0-0 Gall: 0-0
Aids: Bl: 0-0 Vi: 0-0 Tstrap: 0-0
Best Rating: 103 11/01 Asct 3m good Hdl

A winner of a point to point in Ireland, he is a staying chaser in the making. Scored on his hurdles debut at Ascot, but was disappointing after that at Warwick in January 2002. Stays three miles. Acts on an easy surface.

Gold Kriek

92 **80**

5-y-o b g High Kicker (USA)-Ship Of Gold (Glint Of Gold)
M E Sowersby The Southwold Set

Placings:0F-604000 **(2264)**
2001/02: 16⁶S, 16⁰G, 20⁴F, 22⁰GF, 16⁰G, 17⁰S

	Starts	1st	2nd	3rd	Win & Pl
Hurdles	6	0	0	0	0
Career Total	**8**	**0**	**0**	**0**	**0**

Going: Sf: 0-2 GS: 0-0 Gd: 0-2 GF: - Fm: 0-2
Distance: 2m/2m3: 0-4 2m4-2m7: 0-2 3m+: 0-0
Track: LH: 0-6 RH: 0-0 Tight: 0-3 Gall: 0-0
Aids: Bl: 0-0 Vi: 0-0 Tstrap: 0-0
Best Rating: 80 4/01 Hayd 2m soft Hdl

Gold Quest (IRE)

104 **114**

5-y-o ch g Rainbow Quest (USA)-My Potters (USA) (Irish River (FR))
C J Mann The Tramp Partnership

Placings:0P105P **(4818)**
2001/02: 16⁰GF, 19ᴾS, 21¹S, 21⁰GS, 20⁵GF, 21ᴾGF

	Starts	1st	2nd	3rd	Win & Pl
Hurdles	6	1	0	0	3035
Career Total	**6**	**1**	**0**	**0**	**3035**

114	2/02	Ludl	2m5f	E Hdl	SFT	£3034

Total win prize-money £3035

Going: Sf: 1-2 GS: 0-1 Gd: 0-0 GF: - Fm: 0-3
Distance: 2m/2m3: 0-2 **2m4-2m7: 1-4** 3m+: 0-0
Track: LH: 0-3 **RH: 1-3** Tight: 0-0 Gall: 0-2
Aids: Bl: 0-0 Vi: 0-0 **Tstrap: 1-6**
Best Rating: 114 4/02 Asct 2m4f gd-fm Hdl

Formerly decent on the Flat, he showed nothing on his first two runs over hurdles but, following a soft palate operation, he sprung a 50/1 surprise at Ludlow in January 2002. Stays two miles five furlongs, acts on soft ground.

Gold Standard (IRE)

77 **74**

4-y-o ch g Goldmark (USA)-Miss Audimar (USA) (Mr. Leader (USA))
D R C Elsworth R Black, J Stott, L Ferraris, D Watson

Placings:6 **(2427)**
2001/02: 16⁶G

	Starts	1st	2nd	3rd	Win & Pl
Hurdles	1	0	0	0	0
Career Total	**1**	**0**	**0**	**0**	**0**

Going: Sf: 0-0 GS: 0-0 Gd: 0-1 GF: - Fm: 0-0
Distance: 2m/2m3: 0-1 2m4-2m7: 0-0 3m+: 0-0
Track: LH: 0-1 RH: 0-0 Tight: 0-0 Gall: 0-1
Aids: Bl: 0-0 Vi: 0-0 Tstrap: 0-0
Best Rating: 74 11/01 Newb 2m110y good Hdl

Gold Statuette (IRE)

4-y-o ch g Caerleon (USA)-Nawara (Welsh Pageant)
T P McGovern (J W Hills 27/8) B & M McHugh Ltd Civil Engineering

Placings:F **(3210)**
2001/02: 16ᶠGS

	Starts	1st	2nd	3rd	Win & Pl
Hurdles	1	0	0	0	
Career Total	**1**	**0**	**0**	**0**	

Going: Sf: 0-0 GS: 0-1 Gd: 0-0 GF: - Fm: 0-0
Distance: 2m/2m3: 0-1 2m4-2m7: 0-0 3m+: 0-0
Track: LH: 0-1 RH: 0-0 Tight: 0-0 Gall: 0-1
Aids: Bl: 0-0 Vi: 0-0 Tstrap: 0-0
Best Rating: mfy

Goldanzig (IRE)

99 **124**

7-y-o b g Posen (USA)-Sharp Invite (Sharpo)
T P McGovern Wellpool Cleaning Services Ltd

Placings:22211/6P/50U2-0 **(0080)**
2001/02: 16⁰G

	Starts	1st	2nd	3rd	Win & Pl
Hurdles	1	0	0	0	
Career Total	**12**	**2**	**4**	**0**	**10754**

114	10/98	Navn	2m	Hdl	SH	£3586
112	10/98	Gowr	2m	Hdl	SFT	£3586

Total win prize-money £7174

Going: Sf: 0-0 GS: 0-0 Gd: 0-1 GF: - Fm: 0-0
Distance: 2m/2m3: 0-1 2m4-2m7: 0-0 3m+: 0-0
Track: LH: 0-1 RH: 0-0 Tight: 0-0 Gall: 0-0
Aids: Bl: 0-0 Vi: 0-0 Tstrap: 0-1
Best Rating: 124 4/01 Newb 2m3f soft Hdl

Goldbridge (IRE)

102(64h) **106**

7-y-o b g Distinctly North (USA)-Bold Kate (Bold Lad (IRE))
T P McGovern Alan W Clarke

Placings:413000/255034/622112124-3P23 **(4547)**
2001/02: 17³G, 21ᴾG, 20²GF, 20³GF

	Starts	1st	2nd	3rd	Win & Pl
Chases	4	0	1	2	1868
Career Total	**25**	**4**	**6**	**4**	**18055**

120	8/00	Sthl	2m4f110y	E(0-115)HHdl	G-F	£2352
115	7/00	Strf	2m6f110y	F(0-110)HHdl	G-F	£2310
118	6/00	MRas	2m3f110y	F(0-105)HHdl	G-F	£2747
95	8/98	Tram	2m	Hdl	G-F	£2391

Total win prize-money £9801

Going: Sf: 0-0 GS: 0-0 Gd: 0-2 GF: - Fm: 0-2
Distance: 2m/2m3: 0-1 2m4-2m7: 0-3 3m+: 0-0
Track: LH: 0-1 RH: 0-3 Tight: 0-2 Gall: 0-2
Aids: Bl: 0-0 Vi: 0-0 Tstrap: 0-0
Best Rating: 120 9/00 Hntg 2m4f110y gd-fm Hdl

Fast ground staying hurdler. In the frame over fences.

Golden (FR)

101 **77+**

4-y-o ch f Sanglamore (USA)-Golden Sea (FR) (Saint Cyrien (FR))
N A Gaselee (Mme C Head-Maarek 5/10) K V Stenborg

Placings:001 **(4655)**
2001/02: 16⁰S, 16⁰G, 17¹GS

	Starts	1st	2nd	3rd	Win & Pl
Hurdles	3	1	0	0	2800
Career Total	**3**	**1**	**0**	**0**	**2800**

70	4/02	Tntn	2m1f	E Hdl	G-S	£2800

Total win prize-money £2800

Going: Sf: 0-1 GS: 1-1 Gd: 0-1 GF: - Fm: 0-0
Distance: **2m/2m3: 1-3** 2m4-2m7: 0-0 3m+: 0-0
Track: LH: 0-0 **RH: 1-3 Tight: 1-1** Gall: 0-1
Aids: Bl: 0-0 Vi: 0-0 Tstrap: 0-0
Best Rating: 70 4/02 Tntn 2m1f gd-sft Hdl

Shrewdly placed to land very modest hurdle at Taunton in April 2002. Handles good or softer.

Golden Air

9-y-o ch g Buckley-Havon Air (Celtic Cone)
J L Spearing Mrs Peter Badger

Placings:P/P (0641)
2001/02: 24^{P}GF

	Starts	1st	2nd	3rd	Win & Pl
Hurdles	1	0	0	0	
Career Total	**2**	**0**	**0**	**0**	

Going: Sf: 0-0 GS: 0-0 Gd: 0-0 GF: - Fm: 0-1
Distance: 2m/2m3: 0-0 2m4-2m7: 0-0 3m+: 0-1
Track: LH: 0-0 RH: 0-1 Tight: 0-1 Gall: 0-0
Aids: Bl: 0-0 Vi: 0-0 Tstrap: 0-0
Best Rating: mfy

Golden Alpha (IRE)

107(109h) (137h)**134+**
8-y-o b g Alphabatim (USA)-Gina's Love (Golden Love)
M C Pipe D A Johnson

Placings:*1/120/*131064 (4832)
2001/02: 16^{1}S, 16^{3}G, 16^{1}GS, 21^{0}GS, 16^{6}G, 20^{4}G

	Starts	1st	2nd	3rd	Win & Pl
Hurdles	6	2	0	1	8333
Career Total	**10**	**4**	**1**	**1**	**23921**

120	1/02	Winc	2m	F Hdl	G-S	£3136
128	12/01	Chep	2m110y	D Hdl	SFT	£3412
128	2/99	Newb	2m110y	H NHF	GD	£2931
121	4/98	Punc	2m	NHF	HVY	£5956

Total win prize-money £15437

Going: Sf: 1-1 GS: 1-2 Gd: 0-3 GF: - Fm: 0-0
Distance: **2m/2m3: 2-4** 2m4-2m7: 0-2 3m+: 0-0
Track: LH: 1-5 RH: 1-1 Tight: 0-1 Gall: 0-2
Aids: Bl: 0-0 Vi: 0-3 Tstrap: 0-0
Best Rating: **137** 4/02 Aint 2m110y good Hdl

Second in the Weatherbys Champion Bumper at the 1999 Cheltenham Festival, he returned after over two years off to score on his hurdling debut at Chepstow in December 2001 and won a small race at Wincanton early the following year, only to then disappoint. He has been found some easy opportunities to rack up a string of victories over fences in the summer of 2002 and it will be interesting to too how he fares when the better horses appear.

Golden Bar (IRE)

11-y-o ch g Phardante (FR)-Take Me Home (Amoristic (USA))
R J Rowsell (Bernard Jones 22/6) R J Rowsell

Placings:*6/000/060/00P600/*265-2FP (4402)
2001/02: 24^{2}F, 20^{F}F, 22^{P}GS

	Starts	1st	2nd	3rd	Win & Pl
Chases	3	0	1	0	677
Career Total	**19**	**0**	**2**	**0**	**1221**

Going: Sf: 0-0 GS: 0-1 Gd: 0-0 GF: - Fm: 0-2
Distance: 2m/2m3: 0-0 2m4-2m7: 0-2 3m+: 0-1
Track: LH: 0-1 RH: 0-0 Tight: 0-0 Gall: 0-1
Aids: Bl: 0-0 Vi: 0-0 Tstrap: 0-0
Best Rating: **88** 9/00 Dpat 2m1f172y good Hdl

Golden Chance (IRE)

5-y-o b g Unfuwain (USA)-Golden Digger (USA) (Mr Prospector (USA))
M W Easterby The Shooting Syndicate

Placings:5 (2348)
2001/02: 21^{5}GS

	Starts	1st	2nd	3rd	Win & Pl
Hurdles	1	0	0	0	0
Career Total	**1**	**0**	**0**	**0**	**0**

Going: Sf: 0-0 GS: 0-1 Gd: 0-0 GF: - Fm: 0-0
Distance: 2m/2m3: 0-0 2m4-2m7: 0-1 3m+: 0-0
Track: LH: 0-0 RH: 0-1 Tight: 0-1 Gall: 0-0
Aids: Bl: 0-0 Vi: 0-0 Tstrap: 0-0
Best Rating: mfy

Golden Chimes (USA)

103 **116**
7-y-o ch g Woodman (USA)-Russian Ballet (USA) (Nijinsky (CAN))
E W Tuer G Tuer

Placings:P222/1000-14 (1023)
2001/02: 21^{1}GF, 21^{1}GF

	Starts	1st	2nd	3rd	Win & Pl
Hurdles	2	1	0	0	3255
Career Total	**10**	**2**	**3**	**0**	**8032**

116	7/01	Sedg	2m5f110y	D(0-120)HHdl	G-F	£3255
114	5/00	Sedg	2m5f110y	E Hdl	G-F	£2646

Total win prize-money £5901

Going: Sf: 0-0 GS: 0-0 Gd: 0-0 GF: - Fm: 1-2
Distance: 2m/2m3: 0-0 **2m4-2m7: 1-2** 3m+: 0-0
Track: **LH: 1-2** RH: 0-0 **Tight: 1-2** Gall: 0-0
Aids: Bl: 0-0 Vi: 0-0 Tstrap: 0-0
Best Rating: **116** 7/01 Sedg 2m5f110y gd-fm Hdl

Golden Coin

97f **116f**
6-y-o ch g St Ninian-Legal Coin (Official)
W M Brisbourne Bob Moseley

Placings:*6* (2173)
2001/02: 16^{6}S

	Starts	1st	2nd	3rd	Win & Pl
NH Flat	1	0	0	0	0
Career Total	**1**	**0**	**0**	**0**	**0**

Going: Sf: 0-1 GS: 0-0 Gd: 0-0 GF: - Fm: 0-0
Distance: 2m/2m3: 0-1 2m4-2m7: 0-0 3m+: 0-0
Track: LH: 0-1 RH: 0-0 Tight: 0-0 Gall: 0-0
Aids: Bl: 0-0 Vi: 0-0 Tstrap: 0-0
Best Rating: **84** 11/01 Uttx 2m soft NHF

Dual bumper winner on an easy surface but probably handles faster ground.

Golden Crusader

72 **48**
5-y-o b g Gildoran-Pusey Street (Native Bazaar)
J W Mullins First Impressions Racing Group

Placings:*00-30*5P00 (4584)
2001/02: 16^{3}G, 16^{0}S, 16^{5}GS, 16^{P}G, 16^{0}GS, 16^{0}G

	Starts	1st	2nd	3rd	Win & Pl
NH Flat	2	0	0	1	230
Hurdles	4	0	0	0	313
Career Total	**8**	**0**	**0**	**1**	**543**

Going: Sf: 0-1 GS: 0-2 Gd: 0-3 GF: - Fm: 0-0
Distance: 2m/2m3: 0-6 2m4-2m7: 0-0 3m+: 0-0
Track: LH: 0-3 RH: 0-3 Tight: 0-0 Gall: 0-2
Aids: Bl: 0-0 Vi: 0-0 Tstrap: 0-0
Best Rating: **91** 11/01 Winc 2m good NHF

Golden Dawn

90(77h) (69h)**64**
5-y-o gr g Gran Alba (USA)-Golden Curd (FR) (Nice Havrais (USA))
G M Moore Mrs Alurie O'Sullivan

Placings:00P4 (4768)
2001/02: 20^{0}S, 20^{0}G, 20^{P}S, 16^{4}GF

	Starts	1st	2nd	3rd	Win & Pl
Hurdles	4	0	0	0	0
Career Total	**4**	**0**	**0**	**0**	**0**

Going: Sf: 0-2 GS: 0-0 Gd: 0-1 GF: - Fm: 0-1
Distance: 2m/2m3: 0-1 2m4-2m7: 0-3 3m+: 0-0
Track: LH: 0-2 RH: 0-1 Tight: 0-0 Gall: 0-1
Aids: Bl: 0-0 Vi: 0-0 Tstrap: 0-0
Best Rating: **69** 4/02 Hexm 2m110y gd-fm Hdl

Modest hurdle form.

Golden Dragonfly (IRE)

4-y-o ch g Eagle Eyed (USA)-Shanna (BEL) (River Smile (USA))
P C Haslam (D Nicholls 1/9) T S Palin & Barbara Cunningham

Placings:F (1188)
2001/02: 17^{F}G

	Starts	1st	2nd	3rd	Win & Pl
Hurdles	1	0	0	0	
Career Total	**1**	**0**	**0**	**0**	

Going: Sf: 0-0 GS: 0-0 Gd: 0-1 GF: - Fm: 0-0
Distance: 2m/2m3: 0-1 2m4-2m7: 0-0 3m+: 0-0
Track: LH: 0-1 RH: 0-0 Tight: 0-1 Gall: 0-0
Aids: Bl: 0-0 Vi: 0-0 Tstrap: 0-1
Best Rating:

Golden Goal (GER)

110(111h) (132h)**148**
6-y-o br g Nebos (GER)-Goralin (GER) (La Tour (GER))
Miss Venetia Williams The Winning Line

Placings:3102202/032P-6131114 (4255)
2001/02: 16^{6}G, 22^{1}G, 20^{3}S, 20^{1}S, 20^{1}GS, 20^{1}G, 21^{4}G

	Starts	1st	2nd	3rd	Win & Pl
Hurdles	1	0	0	0	0
Chases	6	4	0	1	58250
Career Total	**18**	**5**	**4**	**3**	**68902**

148	2/02	Kemp	2m4f110y	A Ch	GD	£16375
148	2/02	Sand	2m4f110y	A Ch	G-S	£24000

141	1/02	Plum	2m4f	E Ch	SFT	£3250
135	11/01	Hayd	2m6f	C Ch	GD	£8855
122	12/99	Fknm	2m	D Hdl	GD	£2777

Total win prize-money £55257

Going: Sf: 1-2 GS: 1-1 Gd: 2-4 GF: - Fm: 0-0
Distance: 2m/2m3: 0-1 **2m4-2m7: 4-6** 3m+: 0-0
Track: LH: 1-4 **RH: 2-2 Tight: 1-1** Gall: 0-1
Aids: Bl: 0-0 Vi: 0-0 Tstrap: 0-0
Best Rating: 148 2/02 Kemp 2m4f110y good Ch

He posted some decent efforts over hurdles but won only once. He jumped well when making a winning debut over fences at Haydock and added to that at Plumpton early in 2002. Landed decent events at Sandown and Kempton before finishing fourth in the Cathcart at Cheltenham. Suited by good ground or softer and a flat track. Stays two miles six and should get further in time.

Golden Gravel (IRE)

9-y-o ch g Domynsky-Whimbrel (Dara Monarch)
Simon T Lewis Simon T Lewis

Placings: 0P/05-0RP (3814)
2001/02: 21^{0}G, 24^{R}G, 17^{P}S

	Starts	1st	2nd	3rd	Win & Pl
Hurdles	3	0	0	0	
Career Total	**7**	**0**	**0**	**0**	**0**

Going: Sf: 0-1 GS: 0-0 Gd: 0-2 GF: - Fm: 0-0
Distance: 2m/2m3: 0-1 2m4-2m7: 0-1 3m+: 0-1
Track: LH: 0-1 RH: 0-2 Tight: 0-1 Gall: 0-1
Aids: Bl: 0-0 Vi: 0-0 Tstrap: 0-0
Best Rating: 63 10/99 Carl 2m1f good NHF

Golden Hawk (USA)

104 **81**

7-y-o ch g Silver Hawk (USA)-Crockadore (USA) (Nijinsky (CAN))
Mrs D M Ewart Mrs J A Niven

Placings: 40/1/60-055 (4898)
2001/02: 16^{0}S, 16^{5}S, 16^{5}G

	Starts	1st	2nd	3rd	Win & Pl
Hurdles	3	0	0	0	0
Career Total	**8**	**1**	**0**	**0**	**2373**

100	9/99	Hntg	2m110y	E Hdl	G-F	£2372

Total win prize-money £2373

Going: Sf: 0-2 GS: 0-0 Gd: 0-1 GF: - Fm: 0-0
Distance: 2m/2m3: 0-3 2m4-2m7: 0-0 3m+: 0-0
Track: LH: 0-1 RH: 0-2 Tight: 0-2 Gall: 0-0
Aids: Bl: 0-0 Vi: 0-0 Tstrap: 0-0
Best Rating: 103 12/98 Leic 2m gd-sft Hdl

Moderate hurdler, may benefit from further than the minimum trip.

Golden Lily

81(56c) **60**

9-y-o ch m Interrex (CAN)-Gold Risk (Mansingh (USA))
R J Hodges Mrs M Fairbairn

Placings: 300/05500225/0123621U6360P54/100351P P/04PP0-00 (0562)
2001/02: 17^{0}GS, 22^{0}GF

	Starts	1st	2nd	3rd	Win & Pl
Hurdles	2	0	0	0	
Career Total	**41**	**4**	**4**	**4**	**11619**

98	1/00	Ludl	2m4f	F(0-100)HCh	GD	£2574
81	5/99	Chep	2m4f110y	G(0-95)HHdl	GD	£1954
80	11/98	Uttx	2m4f110y	G Hdl	SFT	£1626
72	7/98	Worc	2m4f	G(0-90)HHdl	G-F	£1912

Total win prize-money £8067

Going: Sf: 0-0 GS: 0-1 Gd: 0-0 GF: - Fm: 0-1
Distance: 2m/2m3: 0-1 2m4-2m7: 0-1 3m+: 0-0
Track: LH: 0-1 RH: 0-1 Tight: 0-2 Gall: 0-0
Aids: Bl: 0-1 Vi: 0-0 Tstrap: 0-0
Best Rating: 98 1/00 Ludl 2m4f good Ch

Golden Lisa

50 **13**

7-y-o b m Golden Heights-Girl In Green (Connaught)
F Jordan Tim Powell

Placings: 000P (1393)
2001/02: 17^{0}GS, 16^{0}GF, 16^{0}GF, 24^{P}GF

	Starts	1st	2nd	3rd	Win & Pl
NH Flat	1	0	0	0	0
Hurdles	3	0	0	0	0
Career Total	**4**	**0**	**0**	**0**	

Going: Sf: 0-0 GS: 0-1 Gd: 0-0 GF: - Fm: 0-3
Distance: 2m/2m3: 0-3 2m4-2m7: 0-0 3m+: 0-1
Track: LH: 0-4 RH: 0-0 Tight: 0-1 Gall: 0-0
Aids: Bl: 0-0 Vi: 0-0 Tstrap: 0-0
Best Rating: 13 8/01 Worc 2m gd-fm Hdl

Golden Orion (IRE)

103 **87**

7-y-o ch g Phardante (FR)-Raise The Bells (Belfalas)
Mrs D Thomson Discounted Cashflow

Placings: 65606233550 (4874)
2001/02: 16^{6}G, 22^{5}GS, 22^{6}GS, 16^{0}GS, 20^{6}G, 20^{2}G, 20^{3}S, 16^{3}GS, 16^{5}S, 20^{5}GF, 20^{0}G

	Starts	1st	2nd	3rd	Win & Pl
NH Flat	1	0	0	0	0
Hurdles	10	0	1	2	1752
Career Total	**11**	**0**	**1**	**2**	**1752**

Going: Sf: 0-2 GS: 0-4 Gd: 0-4 GF: - Fm: 0-1
Distance: 2m/2m3: 0-4 2m4-2m7: 0-7 3m+: 0-0
Track: LH: 0-5 RH: 0-6 Tight: 0-7 Gall: 0-0
Aids: Bl: 0-0 Vi: 0-0 Tstrap: 0-0
Best Rating: 87 2/02 Muss 2m gd-sft Hdl

Modest novice hurdler, stays two and a half miles.

Golden Rambler (IRE)

99 **129**

6-y-o br g Roselier (FR)-Goldiyana (FR) (Glint Of Gold)
J J O'Neill Exors Of The Late Robert Hitchins

Placings: 5-24211 (3369)
2001/02: 16^{2}G, 16^{4}GS, 20^{2}S, 20^{1}HY, 20^{1}S

	Starts	1st	2nd	3rd	Win & Pl
NH Flat	2	0	1	0	451
Hurdles	3	2	1	0	8508
Career Total	**6**	**2**	**2**	**0**	**8959**

129	1/02	Hayd	2m4f	E Hdl	SFT	£3500
115	12/01	Hayd	2m4f	D Hdl	HVY	£3848

Total win prize-money £7348

Going: Sf: 2-3 GS: 0-1 Gd: 0-1 GF: - Fm: 0-0
Distance: 2m/2m3: 0-2 **2m4-2m7: 2-3** 3m+: 0-0
Track: **LH: 2-4** RH: 0-1 Tight: 0-1 Gall: 0-0
Aids: Bl: 0-0 Vi: 0-0 Tstrap: 0-0
Best Rating: 129 1/02 Hayd 2m4f soft Hdl

Fair efforts in bumpers, before getting off the mark over hurdles at the second attempt at Haydock in December 2001 and followed up the following month. Acts on heavy ground and stays two miles four furlongs.

Golden Rose (IRE)

99(107h) (91h)**103**

10-y-o br m Roselier (FR)-Lady Nethertown (Windjammer (USA))
T P McGovern Ahmed Abdel-Khaleq

Placings: 25/P1/F350FP42U3/P15114P-5023U0 (4814)
2001/02: 20^{5}S, 21^{0}S, 22^{2}HY, 21^{3}HY, 21^{U}HY, 21^{0}GF

	Starts	1st	2nd	3rd	Win & Pl
Hurdles	3	0	0	1	351
Chases	3	0	1	0	1670
Career Total	**27**	**4**	**3**	**3**	**13008**

115	1/01	Font	2m4f	E Hdl	SFT	£3178
110	12/00	Hntg	2m5f110y	F(0-100)HHdl	HVY	£2095
113	11/00	Plum	2m5f	E(0-115)HHdl	HVY	£2317
99	3/99	Towc	2m	H NHF	SFT	£1451

Total win prize-money £9043

Going: Sf: 0-5 GS: 0-0 Gd: 0-0 GF: - Fm: 0-1
Distance: 2m/2m3: 0-0 2m4-2m7: 0-6 3m+: 0-0
Track: LH: 0-4 RH: 0-2 Tight: 0-3 Gall: 0-1
Aids: Bl: 0-0 Vi: 0-0 Tstrap: 0-0
Best Rating: 115 1/01 Font 2m4f soft Hdl

A game handicap hurdler who loves cut in the ground, the majority of her successes have come over two miles five furlongs. Made a creditable start over fences in January 2002, acts on a soft surface.

Golden Thunderbolt (FR)

102(90c) (105c)**103**

9-y-o b g Persian Bold-Carmita (Caerleon (USA))
H Alexander Phil Lever

Placings: 2205/34523232/35244533/3624226P2415-5520PPP0123144 (4869)
2001/02: 16^{5}S, 16^{5}F, 16^{2}F, 16^{0}GF, 17^{P}G, 16^{P}G, 21^{P}S, 16^{0}GS, 19^{1}S, 16^{2}GS, 16^{3}G, 20^{1}G, 20^{4}GF, 20^{4}GF

	Starts	1st	2nd	3rd	Win & Pl
Hurdles	7	2	1	1	6609
Chases	7	0	1	0	1288
Career Total	**46**	**3**	**12**	**8**	**20331**

103	4/02	Fknm	2m4f	E(0-105)HHdl	GD	£3003
95	1/02	Catt	2m3f	G(0-90)HHdl	SFT	£1904
100	2/01	Fknm	2m	G(0-90)HHdl	SFT	£1877

Total win prize-money £6784

Going: Sf: 1-3 GS: 0-2 Gd: 1-4 GF: - Fm: 0-5
Distance: 2m/2m3: 1-10 2m4-2m7: 1-4 3m+: 0-0
Track: **LH: 2-10** RH: 0-4 **Tight: 2-8** Gall: 0-0
Aids: Bl: 0-0 Vi: 0-0 Tstrap: 0-0
Best Rating: 105 6/01 Prth 2m firm Ch

Modest front-running hurdler. Acts on good and soft ground, he is effective at up to two miles three furlongs and likes a sharp track, particularly Fakenham.

Goldengirlmichelle (IRE)

103 **104**

7-y-o b m Project Manager-Arbour Day (Artaius (USA))
J J O'Neill (F P Murtagh 27/9) The Cartmel Syndicate

Placings:036120/223P044F21/2266-144200650P00 **(2058)**
2001/02: 17^{1}G, 24^{4}GF, 16^{4}GF, 20^{2}GS, 21^{0}GF, 27^{0}GF, 17^{6}GS, 24^{5}G, 20^{0}G, 21^{P}GF, 21^{0}G, 22^{0}GS

	Starts	1st	2nd	3rd	Win & Pl
Hurdles	12	1	1	0	3501
Career Total	**32**	**3**	**7**	**2**	**15073**

99 5/01 Sedg 2m1f F(0-100)HHdl GD £2534
90 3/00 Sedg 3m3f110y G(0-95)HHdl G-F £1557
87 3/99 Muss 2m E Hdl GD £2374
Total win prize-money £6466

Going: Sf: 0-0 GS: 0-3 Gd: 1-4 GF: - Fm: 0-5
Distance: **2m/2m3: 1-3** 2m4-2m7: 0-6 3m+: 0-3
Track: **LH: 1-10** RH: 0-1 **Tight: 1-7** Gall: 0-0
Aids: Bl: 0-0 Vi: 0-0 Tstrap: 0-1
Best Rating: 104 7/01 Wolv 2m4f110y gd-sft Hdl

Golders Green

71f **66f**

5-y-o b g Gildoran-Mayfair Minx (St Columbus)
H Morrison Mrs M D W Wilson

Placings:*0* **(4391)**
2001/02: 16^{0}S

	Starts	1st	2nd	3rd	Win & Pl
NH Flat	1	0	0	0	
Career Total	**1**	**0**	**0**	**0**	

Going: Sf: 0-1 GS: 0-0 Gd: 0-0 GF: - Fm: 0-0
Distance: 2m/2m3: 0-1 2m4-2m7: 0-0 3m+: 0-0
Track: LH: 0-0 RH: 0-1 Tight: 0-0 Gall: 0-0
Aids: Bl: 0-0 Vi: 0-0 Tstrap: 0-0
Best Rating: 66 3/02 Winc 2m soft NHF

Goldoak

87 **69**

7-y-o ch g Sunley Builds-Indian Election (Sula Bula)
R E Pocock T E Pocock

Placings:*006*U6P **(4762)**
2001/02: 16^{0}G, 17^{0}G, 20^{6}S, 24^{U}S, 24^{6}S, 20^{P}GF

	Starts	1st	2nd	3rd	Win & Pl
NH Flat	2	0	0	0	0
Hurdles	4	0	0	0	0
Career Total	**6**	**0**	**0**	**0**	**0**

Going: Sf: 0-3 GS: 0-0 Gd: 0-2 GF: - Fm: 0-1
Distance: 2m/2m3: 0-2 2m4-2m7: 0-2 3m+: 0-2
Track: LH: 0-3 RH: 0-3 Tight: 0-3 Gall: 0-0
Aids: Bl: 0-0 Vi: 0-0 Tstrap: 0-0
Best Rating: 91 10/01 Chep 2m110y good NHF

Goldstone

10-y-o b g Precious Metal-Moon Chant (Humdoleila)
S Flook Mrs S E Vaughan

Placings:P **(4741)**
2001/02: 24^{P}GF

	Starts	1st	2nd	3rd	Win & Pl
Chases	1	0	0	0	
Career Total	**1**	**0**	**0**	**0**	

Going: Sf: 0-0 GS: 0-0 Gd: 0-0 GF: - Fm: 0-1
Distance: 2m/2m3: 0-0 2m4-2m7: 0-0 3m+: 0-1
Track: LH: 0-0 RH: 0-1 Tight: 0-1 Gall: 0-0
Aids: Bl: 0-0 Vi: 0-0 Tstrap: 0-0
Best Rating:

Gollaccia

102 **73**

8-y-o gr m Mystiko (USA)-Millie Grey (Grey Ghost)
J I A Charlton Mrs H I S Calzini

Placings:0/06/633/0520 **(4871)**
2001/02: 17^{0}GS, 24^{5}HY, 23^{2}G, 25^{0}GF

	Starts	1st	2nd	3rd	Win & Pl
Hurdles	4	0	1	0	662
Career Total	**10**	**0**	**1**	**2**	**1184**

Going: Sf: 0-1 GS: 0-1 Gd: 0-1 GF: - Fm: 0-1
Distance: 2m/2m3: 0-1 2m4-2m7: 0-1 3m+: 0-2
Track: LH: 0-3 RH: 0-1 Tight: 0-1 Gall: 0-0
Aids: Bl: 0-0 Vi: 0-0 Tstrap: 0-0
Best Rating: 73 3/02 MRas 2m1f110y gd-sft Hdl

Golly It's Molly

6-y-o b m Majed (IRE)-Faithful Image (Jolly Lolly)
J C McConnochie Mrs R E Stocks

Placings:*00*-P **(0594)**
2001/02: 20^{P}GF

	Starts	1st	2nd	3rd	Win & Pl
Hurdles	1	0	0	0	
Career Total	**3**	**0**	**0**	**0**	

Going: Sf: 0-0 GS: 0-0 Gd: 0-0 GF: - Fm: 0-1
Distance: 2m/2m3: 0-0 2m4-2m7: 0-1 3m+: 0-0
Track: LH: 0-1 RH: 0-0 Tight: 0-1 Gall: 0-0
Aids: Bl: 0-0 Vi: 0-0 Tstrap: 0-0
Best Rating: 10 2/01 Donc 2m110y good NHF

Gollyhott (IRE)

91 **72**

7-y-o gr g Roselier (FR)-Liffey Lady (Camden Town)
N J Henderson Gollyhott Trading Ltd

Placings:*02*P-0 **(0058)**
2001/02: 17^{0}GS

	Starts	1st	2nd	3rd	Win & Pl
Hurdles	1	0	0	0	
Career Total	**4**	**0**	**1**	**0**	**424**

Going: Sf: 0-0 GS: 0-1 Gd: 0-0 GF: - Fm: 0-0
Distance: 2m/2m3: 0-1 2m4-2m7: 0-0 3m+: 0-0
Track: LH: 0-0 RH: 0-1 Tight: 0-1 Gall: 0-0
Aids: Bl: 0-0 Vi: 0-0 Tstrap: 0-0
Best Rating: 107 1/01 Chep 2m110y gd-sft NHF

Gone Far (USA)

112 **125**

5-y-o b g Gone West (USA)-Vallee Dansante (USA) (Lyphard (USA))
M C Pipe (C Laffon-Parias 8/9) Matt Archer & Miss Jean Broadhurst

Placings:134 **(4404)**
2001/02: 17^{1}S, 16^{3}GS, 17^{4}S

	Starts	1st	2nd	3rd	Win & Pl
Hurdles	3	1	0	1	4943
Career Total	**3**	**1**	**0**	**1**	**4943**

119 1/02 Tntn 2m1f E Hdl SFT £2643
Total win prize-money £2643

Going: Sf: 1-2 GS: 0-1 Gd: 0-0 GF: - Fm: 0-0
Distance: **2m/2m3: 1-3** 2m4-2m7: 0-0 3m+: 0-0
Track: LH: 0-1 **RH: 1-2 Tight: 1-2** Gall: 0-0
Aids: Bl: 0-0 Vi: 0-0 Tstrap: 0-0
Best Rating: 125 2/02 Kemp 2m gd-sft Hdl

A useful stayer on the Flat in France. Made a winning debut over hurdle for new connections at Taunton in January 2002 and may have been unlucky not to follow-up in a Grade Two at Kempton before flopping in a weak race next time. Suited by two miles and soft ground.

Gone Too Far

99 **80**

4-y-o b g Reprimand-Blue Nile (IRE) (Bluebird (USA))
M Dods D J Orr

Placings:2202 **(2918)**
2001/02: 16^{2}G, 16^{2}GF, 16^{0}S, 16^{2}G

	Starts	1st	2nd	3rd	Win & Pl
Hurdles	4	0	3	0	2590
Career Total	**4**	**0**	**3**	**0**	**2590**

Going: Sf: 0-1 GS: 0-0 Gd: 0-2 GF: - Fm: 0-1
Distance: 2m/2m3: 0-4 2m4-2m7: 0-0 3m+: 0-0
Track: LH: 0-1 RH: 0-3 Tight: 0-1 Gall: 0-0
Aids: Bl: 0-0 Vi: 0-0 Tstrap: 0-0
Best Rating: 80 12/01 Muss 2m good Hdl

A modest handicapper on the Flat, has shown ability over hurdles and looks capable of winning a race given a sound surface.

Good Day

(95h) (61h)**72**

8-y-o gr g Petong-Courtesy Call (Northfields (USA))
A Robson A Robson

Placings:2020/1244/540P/06-0UP3P **(3353)**
2001/02: 22^{0}G, 21^{U}G, 18^{P}GS, 24^{3}G, 20^{P}G

	Starts	1st	2nd	3rd	Win & Pl
Hurdles	2	0	0	0	0
Chases	3	0	0	1	651
Career Total	**19**	**1**	**3**	**1**	**5253**

95 8/98 Prth 2m4f110y E Hdl G-F £2608
Total win prize-money £2608

Going: Sf: 0-0 GS: 0-1 Gd: 0-4 GF: - Fm: 0-0
Distance: 2m/2m3: 0-1 2m4-2m7: 0-3 3m+: 0-1
Track: LH: 0-3 RH: 0-2 Tight: 0-5 Gall: 0-0
Aids: Bl: 0-0 Vi: 0-0 Tstrap: 0-0
Best Rating: 100 9/98 Sedg 2m5f110y good Hdl

Moderate form since winning a novice hurdle in 1998.

Good Fun

8-y-o b g Good Thyne (USA)-The Bean-Goose (King Sitric)
Miss S E Forster Mrs S A Sutton

Placings:P-S (0467)
2001/02: 20^{S}GF

	Starts	1st	2nd	3rd	Win & Pl
Chases	1	0	0	0	
Career Total	**2**	**0**	**0**	**0**	

Going: Sf: 0-0 GS: 0-0 Gd: 0-0 GF: - Fm: 0-1
Distance: 2m/2m3: 0-0 2m4-2m7: 0-1 3m+: 0-0
Track: LH: 0-1 RH: 0-0 Tight: 0-0 Gall: 0-0
Aids: Bl: 0-0 Vi: 0-0 Tstrap: 0-1
Best Rating:

Good Good (IRE)

8-y-o ch m Good Thyne (USA)-Pinata (Deep Run)
F J Brennan (A J Chamberlain 24/3) F J Brennan

Placings:*260*/0-2 (4569)
2001/02: 22^{2}G

	Starts	1st	2nd	3rd	Win & Pl
Chases	1	0	1	0	642
Career Total	**5**	**0**	**2**	**0**	**1114**

Going: Sf: 0-0 GS: 0-0 Gd: 0-1 GF: - Fm: 0-0
Distance: 2m/2m3: 0-0 2m4-2m7: 0-1 3m+: 0-0
Track: LH: 0-0 RH: 0-1 Tight: 0-0 Gall: 0-0
Aids: Bl: 0-0 Vi: 0-0 Tstrap: 0-1
Best Rating: 100 3/00 Towc 2m soft NHF

Winning pointer at a minor level, ran a sound race on his hunter chase debut at Towcester in April 2002.

Good Heart (IRE)

91 **84**

7-y-o ch g Be My Native (USA)-Johnstown Love (IRE) (Golden Love)
T P Tate The Clegg Family

Placings:*1*/06/43-06 (1404)
2001/02: 16^{0}G, 17^{6}G

	Starts	1st	2nd	3rd	Win & Pl
Hurdles	2	0	0	0	0
Career Total	**7**	**1**	**0**	**1**	**2201**

119	2/99	Hayd	2m	H NHF	SFT	£1495

Total win prize-money £1495

Going: Sf: 0-0 GS: 0-0 Gd: 0-2 GF: - Fm: 0-0
Distance: 2m/2m3: 0-2 2m4-2m7: 0-0 3m+: 0-0
Track: LH: 0-2 RH: 0-0 Tight: 0-1 Gall: 0-0
Aids: Bl: 0-0 Vi: 0-1 Tstrap: 0-0
Best Rating: 119 2/99 Hayd 2m soft NHF

Good Looking Guy

102 **99**

13-y-o ch g Cruise Missile-Saxon Belle (Deep Run)
Mrs J A Young Mrs Judy Young

Placings:00P/U/3/334F4P/3P40U2P-0553P0 (3149)
2001/02: 23^{0}G, 25^{5}G, 24^{5}GF, 24^{3}G, 21^{P}G, 22^{0}G

	Starts	1st	2nd	3rd	Win & Pl
Chases	6	0	0	1	876
Career Total	**24**	**0**	**1**	**5**	**4292**

Going: Sf: 0-0 GS: 0-0 Gd: 0-5 GF: - Fm: 0-1
Distance: 2m/2m3: 0-0 2m4-2m7: 0-2 3m+: 0-4
Track: LH: 0-3 RH: 0-1 Tight: 0-2 Gall: 0-2
Aids: Bl: 0-0 Vi: 0-0 Tstrap: 0-2
Best Rating: 102 5/00 Extr 2m6f110y gd-fm Ch

Often in the frame, but getting on now and not difficult to beat.

Good Lord Murphy (IRE)

108 **146**

10-y-o br g Montelimar (USA)-Semiwild (USA) (Rumbo (USA))
P J Hobbs The Country Side

Placings:*2*/0211214/P50P/1212/10P-30 (3752)
2001/02: 24^{3}G, 24^{0}S

	Starts	1st	2nd	3rd	Win & Pl
Chases	2	0	0	1	1569
Career Total	**21**	**6**	**5**	**1**	**45351**

164	11/00	Asct	3m110y	B(0-150)HCh	SFT	£10296
145	12/99	Hrfd	3m1f110y	E Ch	HVY	£4340
138	11/99	Towc	3m1f	D Ch	GD	£4086
127	3/98	Sand	2m6f	D Hdl	SFT	£3663
127	2/98	Sand	2m6f	D Hdl	GD	£3598
108	1/98	Wwck	2m4f110y	E Hdl	SFT	£3352

Total win prize-money £29338

Going: Sf: 0-1 GS: 0-0 Gd: 0-1 GF: - Fm: 0-0
Distance: 2m/2m3: 0-0 2m4-2m7: 0-0 3m+: 0-2
Track: LH: 0-0 RH: 0-2 Tight: 0-0 Gall: 0-0
Aids: Bl: 0-0 Vi: 0-0 Tstrap: 0-0
Best Rating: 164 11/00 Asct 3m110y soft Ch

He took well to fences in his novice season, running his best race when chasing Beau home at Ascot. However, he has clearly had his training problems and was restricted to just three starts in the 2001/2002 season. Best on easy ground, he stays well and is one to note in long distance handicaps.

Good Morning

83 **46**

8-y-o b m Current Edition (IRE)-Havenod (Tom Noddy)
J W Tudor J W Tudor

Placings:6400 (1240)
2001/02: 17^{6}G, 24^{4}S, 22^{0}GF, 24^{0}GF

	Starts	1st	2nd	3rd	Win & Pl
Hurdles	4	0	0	0	0
Career Total	**4**	**0**	**0**	**0**	**0**

Going: Sf: 0-1 GS: 0-0 Gd: 0-1 GF: - Fm: 0-2
Distance: 2m/2m3: 0-1 2m4-2m7: 0-1 3m+: 0-2
Track: LH: 0-3 RH: 0-1 Tight: 0-1 Gall: 0-0
Aids: Bl: 0-0 Vi: 0-0 Tstrap: 0-0
Best Rating: 46 8/01 Strf 2m6f110y gd-fm Hdl

Good Potential (IRE)

98 **90**

6-y-o b g Petardia-Steel Duchess (IRE) (Yashgan)
D J Wintle Brigadier Racing 2000

Placings:00400446/5246126P0-P331 (4415)
2001/02: 20^{P}S, 20^{3}S, 20^{3}S, 22^{1}S

	Starts	1st	2nd	3rd	Win & Pl
Hurdles	4	1	0	2	3368
Career Total	**21**	**2**	**2**	**2**	**8228**

90	3/02	Font	2m6f110y	F(0-100)HHdl	SFT	£2509
96	1/01	Sthl	2m	F(0-95)HHdl	HVY	£2443

Total win prize-money £4953

Going: Sf: 1-4 GS: 0-0 Gd: 0-0 GF: - Fm: 0-0
Distance: 2m/2m3: 0-0 **2m4-2m7: 1-4** 3m+: 0-0
Track: **LH: 1-2** RH: 0-2 **Tight: 1-1** Gall: 0-1
Aids: Bl: 0-0 Vi: 0-0 **Tstrap: 1-2**
Best Rating: 96 2/01 Carl 2m1f heavy Hdl

Acts on soft ground. Easy winner from a poor field at Fontwell in March. Stays two miles six.

Good Thyne Guy (IRE)

90(99h) (59h)**106**

7-y-o b g Good Thyne (USA)-Mourne Trix (Golden Love)
C Tizzard The Wakehill Partnership

Placings:*23010*-F0 (2216)
2001/02: 24^{F}S, 26^{0}G

	Starts	1st	2nd	3rd	Win & Pl
Chases	2	0	0	0	
Career Total	**7**	**1**	**1**	**1**	**3692**

103	3/01	Font	2m2f110y	D Hdl	HVY	£2982

Total win prize-money £2982

Going: Sf: 0-1 GS: 0-0 Gd: 0-1 GF: - Fm: 0-0
Distance: 2m/2m3: 0-0 2m4-2m7: 0-0 3m+: 0-2
Track: LH: 0-2 RH: 0-0 Tight: 0-1 Gall: 0-0
Aids: Bl: 0-0 Vi: 0-0 Tstrap: 0-0
Best Rating: 106 10/01 Chep 3m soft Ch

Lightly-raced, he has won on heavy ground over two miles two furlongs but has shown nothing since being switched to fences.

Good Thyne Murphy (IRE)

6-y-o b g Good Thyne (USA)-Early Pace (Black Minstrel)
R N Bevis Time & Leisure Ltd

Placings:*0*-0 (0054)
2001/02: 24^{0}G

	Starts	1st	2nd	3rd	Win & Pl
Hurdles	1	0	0	0	
Career Total	**2**	**0**	**0**	**0**	

Going: Sf: 0-0 GS: 0-0 Gd: 0-1 GF: - Fm: 0-0
Distance: 2m/2m3: 0-0 2m4-2m7: 0-0 3m+: 0-1
Track: LH: 0-1 RH: 0-0 Tight: 0-1 Gall: 0-0
Aids: Bl: 0-0 Vi: 0-0 Tstrap: 0-1
Best Rating: 73 3/01 Hayd 2m heavy NHF

Good Time Abbey (IRE)

92 **109**

9-y-o b/br g Good Thyne (USA)-Rose Abbey (Irish Love)
J G Portman M E Chamberlayne,D H Smyly,W R B Webb

Placings:452/*41P*/2-06PPP (4502)
2001/02: 19^{0}G, 20^{6}G, 20^{P}G, 24^{P}G, 22^{P}G

	Starts	1st	2nd	3rd	Win & Pl
Hurdles	3	0	0	0	0
Chases	2	0	0	0	0
Career Total	**12**	**1**	**2**	**0**	**4639**

96	6/99	Clon	2m4f	NHF	G-F	£2762

Total win prize-money £2762

Going: Sf: 0-0 GS: 0-0 Gd: 0-5 GF: - Fm: 0-0
Distance: 2m/2m3: 0-0 2m4-2m7: 0-4 3m+: 0-1
Track: LH: 0-2 RH: 0-2 Tight: 0-3 Gall: 0-0
Aids: Bl: 0-0 Vi: 0-0 Tstrap: 0-0
Best Rating: 109 4/01 Font 2m4f good Hdl

Good Time Bobby

71

5-y-o b g Primitive Rising (USA)-Goodreda (Good Times (ITY))
G A Swinbank Mrs K Morrell

Placings:_0-00_PU3 **(4673)**
2001/02: 16^{0}GF, 16^{0}G, 17^{P}HY, 19^{U}S, 17^{3}GF

	Starts	1st	2nd	3rd	Win & Pl
NH Flat	2	0	0	0	0
Hurdles	3	0	0	1	386
Career Total	**6**	**0**	**0**	**1**	**386**

Going: Sf: 0-2 GS: 0-0 Gd: 0-1 GF: - Fm: 0-2
Distance: 2m/2m3: 0-5 2m4-2m7: 0-0 3m+: 0-0
Track: LH: 0-5 RH: 0-0 Tight: 0-4 Gall: 0-0
Aids: Bl: 0-0 Vi: 0-0 Tstrap: 0-0
Best Rating: 87 4/01 MRas 1m5f110y gd-sft NHF

Modest hurdler, seems better on a sound surface.

Good Time Melody (IRE)

106 (95h) **145**

9-y-o b g Good Thyne (USA)-Raashideah (Dancer's Image (USA))
J W Mullins (A King 24/1) Miss Suzannah Cotterill

Placings:_2/22400/_**22121P-14005P** **(4135)**
2001/02: 23^{1}GS, 24^{4}G, 24^{0}G, 28^{0}S, 25^{5}HY, 24^{P}G

	Starts	1st	2nd	3rd	Win & Pl
Hurdles	1	0	0	0	0
Chases	5	1	0	0	7330
Career Total	**18**	**3**	**6**	**0**	**25052**

145	5/01	Extr	2m7f110y	C(0-135)HCh	G-S	£6571
139	1/01	Sthl	3m110y	E Ch	HVY	£3182
140	11/00	Winc	3m1f110y	D(0-120)HCh	SFT	£5206

Total win prize-money £14961

Going: Sf: 0-2 GS: 1-1 Gd: 0-3 GF: - Fm: 0-0
Distance: 2m/2m3: 0-0 2m4-2m7: 0-0 **3m+: 1-6**
Track: LH: 0-2 **RH: 1-3** Tight: 0-0 Gall: 0-1
Aids: **Bl: 1-2** Vi: 0-0 Tstrap: 0-0
Best Rating: 145 5/01 Extr 2m7f110y gd-sft Ch

A tough stayer, he responded well to first-time blinkers when winning a handicap chase at Exeter in May 2001. Acts on soft ground.

Good Vibes

101 **109**

10-y-o b g Ardross-Harmoney Jane (Hard Boy)
O Sherwood M G St Quinton

Placings:_221_123213/11/**2/13213542/0PP6** **(3671)**
2001/02: 24^{0}GS, 20^{P}G, 20^{P}GS, 20^{6}S

	Starts	1st	2nd	3rd	Win & Pl

	Starts	1st	2nd	3rd	Win & Pl
Chases	4	0	0	0	0
Career Total	**24**	**7**	**7**	**4**	**52888**

148	1/00	Hntg	2m110y	D Ch	GD	£4810
136	12/99	Sand	2m4f110y	D Ch	GD	£4162
138	11/97	Aint	2m110y	C(0-135)HHdl	G-S	£10406
132	11/97	Weth	2m	C(0-135)HHdl	G-F	£3444
112	3/97	Weth	2m	D Hdl	GD	£2985
112	12/96	MRas	2m1f110y	D Hdl	GD	£3115
110	11/96	Aint	2m110y	H NHF	GD	£1934

Total win prize-money £30858

Going: Sf: 0-1 GS: 0-2 Gd: 0-1 GF: - Fm: 0-0
Distance: 2m/2m3: 0-0 2m4-2m7: 0-3 3m+: 0-1
Track: LH: 0-1 RH: 0-3 Tight: 0-0 Gall: 0-1
Aids: Bl: 0-1 Vi: 0-0 Tstrap: 0-0
Best Rating: 148 1/00 Hntg 2m110y good Ch

A successful hurdler in1996/1997, he has enjoyed a decent first season over fences, although he steered a somewhat wayward course when winning at Huntingdon in 2000. Held when tackling the better novices. Absent between April 2000 and October 2001, he has been well held since. Stays three miles. Most of his wins came on soft ground.

Goodbye Goldstone

83 **69**

6-y-o b g Mtoto-Shareehan (Dancing Brave (USA))
T P McGovern Ashley Carr

Placings:_04_ **(3814)**
2001/02: 16^{0}G, 17^{4}S

	Starts	1st	2nd	3rd	Win & Pl
Hurdles	2	0	0	0	0
Career Total	**2**	**0**	**0**	**0**	**0**

Going: Sf: 0-1 GS: 0-0 Gd: 0-1 GF: - Fm: 0-0
Distance: 2m/2m3: 0-2 2m4-2m7: 0-0 3m+: 0-0
Track: LH: 0-1 RH: 0-1 Tight: 0-2 Gall: 0-0
Aids: Bl: 0-0 Vi: 0-0 Tstrap: 0-0
Best Rating: 69 2/02 Folk 2m1f110y soft Hdl

Goodie Girl (IRE)

7-y-o b m Good Thyne (USA)-Kalanshoe (Random Shot)
N A Twiston-Davies N A Twiston-Davies

Placings:_0444_P **(1618)**
2001/02: 16^{0}G, 16^{4}GF, 17^{4}GF, 17^{4}GF, 21^{P}G

	Starts	1st	2nd	3rd	Win & Pl
NH Flat	4	0	0	0	0
Hurdles	1	0	0	0	0
Career Total	**5**	**0**	**0**	**0**	**0**

Going: Sf: 0-0 GS: 0-0 Gd: 0-2 GF: - Fm: 0-3
Distance: 2m/2m3: 0-4 2m4-2m7: 0-1 3m+: 0-0
Track: LH: 0-3 RH: 0-2 Tight: 0-1 Gall: 0-0
Aids: Bl: 0-0 Vi: 0-0 Tstrap: 0-3
Best Rating: 72 8/01 NAbb 2m1f gd-fm NHF

Goodlooking Broad

6-y-o b m Broadsword (USA)-Goodlooking Bird (Golden Love)
D M Grissell Magellan Partnership

Placings:_0_ **(0108)**

2001/02: 18^{0}GF

	Starts	1st	2nd	3rd	Win & Pl
NH Flat	1	0	0	0	
Career Total	**1**	**0**	**0**	**0**	

Going: Sf: 0-0 GS: 0-0 Gd: 0-0 GF: - Fm: 0-1
Distance: 2m/2m3: 0-1 2m4-2m7: 0-0 3m+: 0-0
Track: LH: 0-1 RH: 0-0 Tight: 0-1 Gall: 0-0
Aids: Bl: 0-0 Vi: 0-0 Tstrap: 0-0
Best Rating: mfy

Goodnightgodbless (IRE)

7-y-o b m King's Ride-Lady Of Aherlow (Le Bavard (FR))
Thomas Carberry (J R Jenkins 11/7) Robert Burke

Placings:_000_ **(1779a)**
2001/02: 17^{0}GF, 16^{0}G, 17^{0}YS

	Starts	1st	2nd	3rd	Win & Pl
NH Flat	2	0	0	0	0
Hurdles	1	0	0	0	0
Career Total	**3**	**0**	**0**	**0**	

Going: Sf: 0-0 GS: 0-0 Gd: 0-1 GF: - Fm: 0-1
Distance: 2m/2m3: 0-3 2m4-2m7: 0-0 3m+: 0-0
Track: LH: 0-1 RH: 0-2 Tight: 0-1 Gall: 0-0
Aids: Bl: 0-0 Vi: 0-0 Tstrap: 0-0
Best Rating: 67 6/01 MRas 2m1f110y gd-fm NHF

Goodtimelady (IRE)

(87c) **100**

8-y-o b/br m Good Thyne (USA)-Peppardstownlady (Gleason (USA))
R T Phillips Cheltenham Racing Ltd

Placings:_00_400/66**621-103** **(3823)**
2001/02: 25^{1}S, 21^{0}HY, 27^{3}S

	Starts	1st	2nd	3rd	Win & Pl
Hurdles	3	1	0	1	3308
Career Total	**13**	**2**	**1**	**1**	**6644**

100	4/01	Plum	3m1f110y	E(0-105)HHdl	SFT	£2523
91	4/01	Plum	2m5f	G(0-90)HHdl	HVY	£2180

Total win prize-money £4705

Going: Sf: 1-3 GS: 0-0 Gd: 0-0 GF: - Fm: 0-0
Distance: 2m/2m3: 0-0 2m4-2m7: 0-1 **3m+: 1-2**
Track: LH: 0-1 RH: 0-0 Tight: 0-1 Gall: 0-0
Aids: Bl: 0-0 Vi: 0-0 Tstrap: 0-0
Best Rating: 100 4/01 Plum 3m1f110y soft Hdl

Scored a Plumpton double over hurdles in April 2001 on soft/heavy ground.

Goolds Cross (IRE)

9-y-o b g Un Desperado (FR)-Aunt Moll (Brave Invader (USA))
Miss L C Siddall A Emmerson

Placings:FP0-P **(2152)**
2001/02: 20^{P}G

	Starts	1st	2nd	3rd	Win & Pl
Hurdles	1	0	0	0	
Career Total	**4**	**0**	**0**	**0**	

Going: Sf: 0-0 GS: 0-0 Gd: 0-1 GF: - Fm: 0-0
Distance: 2m/2m3: 0-0 2m4-2m7: 0-1 3m+: 0-0
Track: LH: 0-1 RH: 0-0 Tight: 0-0 Gall: 0-1
Aids: Bl: 0-0 Vi: 0-0 Tstrap: 0-0
Best Rating: mfy

Gordi (USA)

86 **76**

9-y-o ch g Theatrical-Royal Alydar (USA) (Alydar (USA))

Miss L Bower Miss Lindsay Bower

Placings:0/01/050F (4415)

2001/02: 18^{0}G, 16^{5}GS, 17^{0}G, 22^{F}S

	Starts	1st	2nd	3rd	Win & Pl
Hurdles	4	0	0	0	0
Career Total	**7**	**1**	**0**	**0**	**2002**

118 10/99 Dpat 2m1f87y Hdl Y-S £2002

Total win prize-money £2002

Going: Sf: 0-1 GS: 0-1 Gd: 0-2 GF: - Fm: 0-0
Distance: 2m/2m3: 0-3 2m4-2m7: 0-1 3m+: 0-0
Track: LH: 0-3 RH: 0-1 Tight: 0-3 Gall: 0-0
Aids: Bl: 0-0 Vi: 0-0 Tstrap: 0-0
Best Rating: 118 10/99 Dpat 2m1f87y yld-sft Hdl

Gorsey Bank (IRE)

10-y-o b g Lancastrian-Yankee's Princess (Yankee Gold)

E A Thomas (C J Price 23/5) E A Thomas

Placings:PP-4P40 (4179)

2001/02: 24^{4}G, 20^{P}G, 25^{4}HY, 24^{0}GS

	Starts	1st	2nd	3rd	Win & Pl
Chases	4	0	0	0	287
Career Total	**6**	**0**	**0**	**0**	**287**

Going: Sf: 0-1 GS: 0-1 Gd: 0-2 GF: - Fm: 0-0
Distance: 2m/2m3: 0-0 2m4-2m7: 0-1 3m+: 0-3
Track: LH: 0-2 RH: 0-2 Tight: 0-2 Gall: 0-1
Aids: Bl: 0-0 Vi: 0-0 Tstrap: 0-0
Best Rating: 76 3/02 Strf 3m gd-sft Ch

Gortmore Mews (IRE)

100(103h) (113h)**126**

8-y-o b g Persian Mews-Flat Out (Random Shot)

Ferdy Murphy John McMullen W F-Clenell Susan Sample

Placings:*51/1*52010/02**103-U550143P** (4891)

2001/02: 20^{U}G, 20^{5}G, 20^{5}G, 20^{0}GS, 19^{1}G, 20^{4}S, 21^{3}G, 16^{P}G

	Starts	1st	2nd	3rd	Win & Pl
Hurdles	1	0	0	0	0
Chases	7	1	0	1	4305
Career Total	**21**	**5**	**2**	**2**	**19103**

126 12/01 Hrfd 2m3f F(0-105)HCh GD £3349
6/00 Tral 2m Ch Y-S £3312
99 3/00 Leop 2m Hdl GD £3588
119 5/99 Gowr 2m NHF YLD £3069
106 3/99 Wxfd 2m2f NHF Y-S £2608

Total win prize-money £15928

Going: Sf: 0-1 GS: 0-1 Gd: 1-6 GF: - Fm: 0-0
Distance: **2m/2m3: 1-2** 2m4-2m7: 0-6 3m+: 0-0
Track: LH: 0-4 **RH: 1-4** Tight: 0-4 Gall: 0-1
Aids: Bl: 0-2 Vi: 0-0 Tstrap: 0-0
Best Rating: 126 12/01 Hrfd 2m3f good Ch

Formerly trained in Ireland, he won three times over hurdles and on his chasing debut at Tralee in June 2000. Went missing after July of that year until joining Ferdy Murphy in the autumn of 2001. Suited by two miles to two miles-three and good or softer ground.

Gortroe Guy (IRE)

83 **68**

10-y-o b g Carlingford Castle-Calfstown Night (Bargello)

J F Panvert J F Panvert

Placings:06030206626/00F/00F6FP-400UPPU (4854)

2001/02: 20^{4}S, 22^{0}GS, 22^{0}GS, 24^{U}GS, 24^{P}S, 24^{P}S, 22^{U}G

	Starts	1st	2nd	3rd	Win & Pl
Hurdles	5	0	0	0	0
Chases	2	0	0	0	0
Career Total	**27**	**0**	**2**	**1**	**2129**

Going: Sf: 0-3 GS: 0-3 Gd: 0-1 GF: - Fm: 0-0
Distance: 2m/2m3: 0-0 2m4-2m7: 0-4 3m+: 0-3
Track: LH: 0-4 RH: 0-3 Tight: 0-4 Gall: 0-1
Aids: Bl: 0-0 Vi: 0-0 Tstrap: 0-0
Best Rating: 101 1/99 Punc 3m heavy Hdl

Ex-Irish import. Has shown only ordinary form in this country. Has yet to prove he stays three miles. Has raced mainly on an easy surface.

Gospel Song

102 **92**

10-y-o ch g King Among Kings-Market Blues (Porto Bello)

A C Whillans Chas N Whillans

Placings:432/023/416415/2453415/6025/02620005-P0003 (4432)

2001/02: 17^{P}HY, 16^{0}S, 20^{0}S, 17^{0}S, 20^{3}HY

	Starts	1st	2nd	3rd	Win & Pl
Hurdles	5	0	0	1	538
Career Total	**36**	**3**	**6**	**4**	**15543**

114 3/99 Ayr 2m4f C(0-130)HHdl SFT £2804
111 3/98 Ayr 2m D(0-110)HHdl SFT £2910
109 1/98 Muss 2m F Hdl G-S £2185

Total win prize-money £7899

Going: Sf: 0-5 GS: 0-0 Gd: 0-0 GF: - Fm: 0-0
Distance: 2m/2m3: 0-3 2m4-2m7: 0-2 3m+: 0-0
Track: LH: 0-3 RH: 0-2 Tight: 0-2 Gall: 0-2
Aids: Bl: 0-0 Vi: 0-0 Tstrap: 0-0
Best Rating: 114 11/00 Newc 2m soft Hdl

Fair handicap hurdler, best at two miles but stays further.

Got Alot On (USA)

62 **36**

4-y-o b/br g Charnwood Forest (IRE)-Fleety Belle (GER) (Assert)

Miss M Bragg Mrs Anne Standing & Gordon Gout

Placings:0 (2535)

2001/02: 16^{0}G

	Starts	1st	2nd	3rd	Win & Pl
Hurdles	1	0	0	0	
Career Total	**1**	**0**	**0**	**0**	

Going: Sf: 0-0 GS: 0-0 Gd: 0-1 GF: - Fm: 0-0
Distance: 2m/2m3: 0-1 2m4-2m7: 0-0 3m+: 0-0
Track: LH: 0-0 RH: 0-1 Tight: 0-0 Gall: 0-0
Aids: Bl: 0-0 Vi: 0-0 Tstrap: 0-0
Best Rating: 36 12/01 Winc 2m good Hdl

Got News For You

101(102h) **120**

8-y-o gr g Positive Statement (USA)-Madame Ruby (FR) (Homing)

N J Hawke Mrs D A Wetherall

Placings:*56/6/*F010020-**F1PP6** (4849)

2001/02: 22^{F}S, 20^{1}G, 20^{P}S, 20^{P}G, 24^{6}G

	Starts	1st	2nd	3rd	Win & Pl
Chases	5	1	0	0	3073
Career Total	**15**	**2**	**1**	**0**	**6685**

120 10/01 Sthl 2m4f110y E Ch GD £3073
109 11/00 Hrfd 2m3f110y E Hdl SFT £2870

Total win prize-money £5943

Going: Sf: 0-2 GS: 0-0 Gd: 1-3 GF: - Fm: 0-0
Distance: 2m/2m3: 0-0 **2m4-2m7: 1-4** 3m+: 0-1
Track: **LH: 1-4** RH: 0-1 **Tight: 1-4** Gall: 0-0
Aids: Bl: 0-0 Vi: 0-0 Tstrap: 0-0
Best Rating: 120 10/01 Sthl 2m4f110y good Ch

A fair hurdler, he made amends for falling on his chasing debut at Market Rasen in September 2001 by making a quick winning reappearance at Southwell ten days later. Suited by two and a half miles and especially suited by soft ground.

Got One Too (FR)

115 **148**

5-y-o ch g Green Tune (USA)-Gloria Mundi (FR) (Saint Cyrien (FR))

N J Henderson Mary-Anne Parker & Sir Eric Parker

Placings:202-**1115140** (4188)

2001/02: 17^{1}G, 19^{1}G, 16^{1}S, 16^{5}G, 16^{1}GS, 16^{4}S, 16^{0}GS

	Starts	1st	2nd	3rd	Win & Pl
Hurdles	7	4	0	0	40904
Career Total	**10**	**4**	**2**	**0**	**43430**

148 1/02 Asct 2m110y B HHdl G-S £10179
145 12/01 Newb 2m110y A(0-145)HHdl SFT £15500
120 11/01 Newb 2m3f D Hdl GD £3952
125 5/01 Hrfd 2m1f E Hdl GD £3272

Total win prize-money £32904

Going: Sf: 1-2 GS: 1-2 Gd: 2-3 GF: - Fm: 0-0
Distance: **2m/2m3: 4-7** 2m4-2m7: 0-0 3m+: 0-0
Track: LH: 2-4 RH: 2-3 Tight: 0-0 **Gall: 2-3**
Aids: Bl: 0-0 Vi: 0-0 Tstrap: 0-0
Best Rating: 148 1/02 Asct 2m110y gd-sft Hdl

A useful stayer on the Flat, he has progressed well over hurdles, completing a hat-trick in the Gerry Feilden at Newbury. Likes to make the running, and stays two miles three, but was held up when scoring at Ascot in January 2002. Fourth in the Tote Gold Trophy at Newbury. Possibly does not want the ground too soft.

Gotha (FR)

87(105c) (114c)**76**

8-y-o ch g Royal Charter (FR)-Royaute (FR) (Signani (FR))

Mrs L C Taylor Mrs L C Taylor

Placings:*000/*66**3F3**/10**16F-P02362F0P00** (4509)

2001/02: 24^{P}G, 20^{0}S, 20^{2}GS, 19^{3}G, 16^{6}GS, 21^{2}S, 20^{F}S, 20^{0}S, 19^{P}S, 21^{0}GF, 16^{0}G

	Starts	1st	2nd	3rd	Win & Pl
Hurdles	4	0	0	0	0
Chases	7	0	2	1	2969

Career Total	24	2	2	3	11635

123	12/00	Hrfd	2m3f	D(0-110)HCh	HVY	£4970
91	5/00	Strf	2m6f110y	E Hdl	GD	£2898

Total win prize-money £7868

Going: Sf: 0-5 GS: 0-2 Gd: 0-3 GF: - Fm: 0-1
Distance: 2m/2m3: 0-3 2m4-2m7: 0-7 3m+: 0-1
Track: LH: 0-6 RH: 0-5 Tight: 0-4 Gall: 0-4
Aids: Bl: 0-1 Vi: 0-5 Tstrap: 0-1
Best Rating: **123** 12/00 Hrfd 2m3f heavy Ch

An ex-Irish dual-purpose contender over jumps, he made no impact until his second run in this country in May 2000 where he landed a weak hurdle at Stratford. Following his only other win in a novice chase at Hereford at the end of that year, he fell whilst in touch in a competitive chase at Ayr. Has gone the wrong way since and has even failed to make an impact in selling company when reverting to hurdles.

Gotham (IRE)

79 **38**

5-y-o gr g Gothland (FR)-Inchriver (IRE) (Over The River (FR))
R H Alner Pell-Mell Partners

Placings:00 (3339)
2001/02: 16^{0}G, 19^{0}S

	Starts	1st	2nd	3rd	Win & Pl
NH Flat	1	0	0	0	0
Hurdles	1	0	0	0	0
Career Total	**2**	**0**	**0**	**0**	

Going: Sf: 0-1 GS: 0-0 Gd: 0-1 GF: - Fm: 0-0
Distance: 2m/2m3: 0-1 2m4-2m7: 0-1 3m+: 0-0
Track: LH: 0-0 RH: 0-2 Tight: 0-1 Gall: 0-0
Aids: Bl: 0-0 Vi: 0-0 Tstrap: 0-0
Best Rating: **78** 11/01 Winc 2m good NHF

Gottabe

106(107h) (115h)**125+**

9-y-o ch g Gunner B-Topsy Bee (Be Friendly)
Mrs S J Smith Keith Nicholson

Placings:02U46134-2600153430 (4893)
2001/02: 20^{2}G, 22^{6}G, 21^{0}S, 21^{0}G, 20^{1}S, 16^{5}S, 20^{3}S, 24^{4}S, 20^{3}GS, 20^{0}G

	Starts	1st	2nd	3rd	Win & Pl
Hurdles	6	1	1	0	4577
Chases	4	0	0	2	1215
Career Total	**18**	**2**	**2**	**3**	**10540**

115	12/01	Sthl	2m4f110y	D(0-125)HHdl	SFT	£3464
108	2/01	Sedg	2m5f110y	E Hdl	SFT	£2548

Total win prize-money £6013

Going: Sf: 1-5 GS: 0-1 Gd: 0-4 GF: - Fm: 0-0
Distance: 2m/2m3: 0-1 **2m4-2m7: 1-8** 3m+: 0-1
Track: **LH: 1-7** RH: 0-3 **Tight: 1-4** Gall: 0-5
Aids: Bl: 0-0 Vi: 0-0 Tstrap: 0-1
Best Rating: **115** 12/01 Sthl 2m4f110y soft Hdl

He gained his first win over hurdles in an ordinary novice event at Sedgefield in February 2001. Held afterwards, but a drop in the handicap helped him return to winning ways at Southwell in December. Suited by two and a half miles he won easily over fences at Wetherby in May and should continue to give a good account.

Governor Daniel

95(97h) (91+h)**106**

11-y-o b g Governor General-Princess Semele (Imperial Fling (USA))

Ian Williams Dsm Demolition Limited

Placings:2/0306/1U44/4P50/42131/11PF111P-P5P0 (1441)
2001/02: 21^{P}G, 20^{5}GF, 20^{P}GF, 20^{0}GF

	Starts	1st	2nd	3rd	Win & Pl
Chases	4	0	0	0	0
Career Total	**30**	**8**	**2**	**2**	**32003**

115	9/00	Plum	2m5f	D(0-125)HHdl	G-F	£3103
115	9/00	Hrfd	2m3f110y	F(0-100)HHdl	G-F	£2877
115	8/00	Sthl	2m4f110y	F(0-110)HHdl	GD	£2891
122	6/00	MRas	2m4f	C(0-135)HCh	G-F	£10481
125	6/00	NAbb	2m110y	F(0-105)HCh	G-F	£3454
112	9/99	Sedg	2m5f	E Ch	G-F	£3254
95	8/99	MRas	2m1f110y	G(0-95)HHdl	G-F	£1679
101	5/96	Sthl	2m2f	E Hdl	G-F	£2658

Total win prize-money £30399

Going: Sf: 0-0 GS: 0-0 Gd: 0-1 GF: - Fm: 0-3
Distance: 2m/2m3: 0-0 2m4-2m7: 0-4 3m+: 0-0
Track: LH: 0-3 RH: 0-0 Tight: 0-3 Gall: 0-0
Aids: Bl: 0-0 Vi: 0-0 Tstrap: 0-4
Best Rating: **125** 6/00 NAbb 2m110y gd-fm Ch

Won three times over hurdles in the summer of 2000 but is not so good over fences.

Gower-Slave

105 **145**

10-y-o b g Mandalus-Slave's Bangle (Prince Rheingold)
P J Hobbs Bob Bevan

Placings:42005/3123U31P/221111102P6/212/1411-6P3PF (4664)
2001/02: 27^{6}S, 24^{P}G, 24^{3}HY, 20^{P}GS, 21^{F}G

	Starts	1st	2nd	3rd	Win & Pl
Chases	5	0	0	1	2235
Career Total	**36**	**11**	**7**	**4**	**84240**

145	4/01	Aint	2m5f110y	B(0-150)HCh	SFT	£32500
145	2/01	Ludl	2m4f	D(0-125)HCh	G-S	£5135
130	12/00	Newb	2m6f110y	C(0-130)HCh	SFT	£6610
133	7/99	Bang	3m110y	D(0-125)HCh	G-F	£4810
127	7/98	Sedg	2m5f	D(0-125)HCh	G-F	£4224
124	6/98	Worc	2m7f110y	E(0-110)HCh	GD	£3133
120	6/98	Worc	2m4f110y	D(0-120)HCh	GD	£3926
115	6/98	Worc	2m7f110y	E(0-110)HCh	G-F	£3179
106	5/98	Ctml	3m2f	E Ch	G-F	£2784
92	11/97	Wwck	3m2f	D Ch	G-F	£4161
85	5/97	Strf	2m6f110y	E Hdl	GD	£1996

Total win prize-money £72462

Going: Sf: 0-2 GS: 0-1 Gd: 0-2 GF: - Fm: 0-0
Distance: 2m/2m3: 0-0 2m4-2m7: 0-2 3m+: 0-3
Track: LH: 0-5 RH: 0-0 Tight: 0-2 Gall: 0-2
Aids: Bl: 0-0 Vi: 0-0 Tstrap: 0-0
Best Rating: **145** 11/01 Aint 3m3f soft Ch

A fair hurdler and very useful chaser, he produced a career-best effort to win the John Hughes Trophy at Aintree in April 2001. Best at two and a half miles, he has a cracking strike-rate over fences. Best with give in the ground.

Graceful Dancer

92f **98f**

5-y-o b m Old Vic-Its My Turn (Palm Track)
C P Morlock The Fairway Connection

Placings:20 (4595)
2001/02: 16^{2}S, 16^{0}G

	Starts	1st	2nd	3rd	Win & Pl
NH Flat	2	0	1	0	476
Career Total	**2**	**0**	**1**	**0**	**476**

Going: Sf: 0-1 GS: 0-0 Gd: 0-1 GF: - Fm: 0-0
Distance: 2m/2m3: 0-2 2m4-2m7: 0-0 3m+: 0-0
Track: LH: 0-2 RH: 0-0 Tight: 0-0 Gall: 0-1
Aids: Bl: 0-0 Vi: 0-0 Tstrap: 0-0
Best Rating: **98** 3/02 Donc 2m110y soft NHF

Runner-up in a mares' only bumper at Doncaster in March on her debut.

Gracie Grey

7-y-o gr m Terimon-Passage To Freedom (Pals Passage)
Mrs S Lamyman Rowland Hill

Placings:053302/P/23300-P (0451)
2001/02: 23^{P}F

	Starts	1st	2nd	3rd	Win & Pl
Hurdles	1	0	0	0	
Career Total	**13**	**0**	**2**	**4**	**3596**

Going: Sf: 0-0 GS: 0-0 Gd: 0-0 GF: - Fm: 0-1
Distance: 2m/2m3: 0-0 2m4-2m7: 0-1 3m+: 0-0
Track: LH: 0-1 RH: 0-0 Tight: 0-0 Gall: 0-0
Aids: Bl: 0-0 Vi: 0-1 Tstrap: 0-0
Best Rating: **94** 4/99 MRas 2m3f110y soft Hdl

Gradient

12-y-o b g Shirley Heights-Grimpola (GER) (Windwurf (GER))
N J Dawe N J Dawe

Placings:U0 (0430)
2001/02: 19^{U}F, 16^{0}G

	Starts	1st	2nd	3rd	Win & Pl
Chases	2	0	0	0	
Career Total	**2**	**0**	**0**	**0**	

Going: Sf: 0-0 GS: 0-0 Gd: 0-1 GF: - Fm: 0-1
Distance: 2m/2m3: 0-1 2m4-2m7: 0-1 3m+: 0-0
Track: LH: 0-0 RH: 0-1 Tight: 0-0 Gall: 0-0
Aids: Bl: 0-0 Vi: 0-0 Tstrap: 0-0
Best Rating: **28** 5/01 Chel 2m110y good Ch

Grafton Truce (IRE)

102 **99**

5-y-o ch g Brief Truce (USA)-Grafton Street (GER) (Pentathlon)
Miss Lucinda V Russell (C Von Der Recke 19/11) A R Trotter

Placings:21236P0F (4492)
2001/02: 16^{2}G, 16^{1}G, 16^{2}GS, 16^{3}S, 16^{6}G, 16^{P}S, 16^{0}HY, 17^{F}GS

	Starts	1st	2nd	3rd	Win & Pl
Hurdles	8	1	2	1	2233
Career Total	**8**	**1**	**2**	**1**	**2233**

Going: Sf: 0-3 GS: 0-2 Gd: 1-3 GF: - Fm: 0-0
Distance: **2m/2m3: 1-8** 2m4-2m7: 0-0 3m+: 0-0
Track: LH: 0-3 RH: 0-3 Tight: 0-1 Gall: 0-1
Aids: Bl: 0-0 Vi: 0-0 Tstrap: 0-0
Best Rating: **99** 12/01 Ayr 2m soft Hdl

Ex-German, he has been placed in ordinary company

over hurdles in this country.

Graig Hill Rose

88(84c) (89c)**62**

7-y-o b m Rustingo-Lyricist (Averof)
P D Evans S R Brown

Placings:*00P-5P0* **(3332)**
2001/02: 16^{5}GF, 19^{P}S, 21^{0}G

	Starts	1st	2nd	3rd	Win & Pl
Hurdles	2	0	0	0	0
Chases	1	0	0	0	0
Career Total	**6**	**0**	**0**	**0**	**0**

Going: Sf: 0-1 GS: 0-0 Gd: 0-1 GF: - Fm: 0-1
Distance: 2m/2m3: 0-1 2m4-2m7: 0-2 3m+: 0-0
Track: LH: 0-1 RH: 0-2 Tight: 0-0 Gall: 0-0
Aids: Bl: 0-0 Vi: 0-0 Tstrap: 0-0
Best Rating: 89 9/01 Worc 2m gd-fm Ch

Grain Storm (IRE)

96 **71**

4-y-o b f Marju (IRE)-Zuhal (Busted)
P C Haslam T Palin/s Hatchard/p Dalton

Placings:21 **(2780)**
2001/02: 17^{2}S, 16^{1}G

	Starts	1st	2nd	3rd	Win & Pl
Hurdles	2	1	1	0	3127
Career Total	**2**	**1**	**1**	**0**	**3127**

71	12/01	Ludl	2m	G Hdl	GD	£2681

Total win prize-money £2681

Going: Sf: 0-1 GS: 0-0 Gd: 1-1 GF: - Fm: 0-0
Distance: **2m/2m3: 1-2** 2m4-2m7: 0-0 3m+: 0-0
Track: LH: 0-0 **RH: 1-2** Tight: 0-1 Gall: 0-0
Aids: Bl: 0-0 Vi: 0-0 Tstrap: 0-0
Best Rating: 71 12/01 Ludl 2m good Hdl

A fast-ground performer on the Flat, she won in selling grade at Ludlow in December, displaying fine battling qualities.

Gralmano (IRE)

115 **135**

7-y-o b g Scenic-Llangollen (IRE) (Caerleon (USA))
K A Ryan Coleorton Moor Racing

Placings:111 **(2583)**
2001/02: 16^{1}G, 16^{1}GS, 16^{1}S

	Starts	1st	2nd	3rd	Win & Pl
Hurdles	3	3	0	0	10919
Career Total	**3**	**3**	**0**	**0**	**10919**

130	12/01	Weth	2m	C(0-135)HHdl	SFT	£5343
126	11/01	Kels	2m110y	E Hdl	G-S	£3125
121	10/01	Kels	2m110y	E Hdl	GD	£2450

Total win prize-money £10919

Going: Sf: 1-1 GS: 1-1 Gd: 1-1 GF: - Fm: 0-0
Distance: **2m/2m3: 3-3** 2m4-2m7: 0-0 3m+: 0-0
Track: **LH: 3-3** RH: 0-0 **Tight: 2-2** Gall: 0-0
Aids: Bl: 0-0 Vi: 0-0 Tstrap: 0-0
Best Rating: 130 12/01 Weth 2m soft Hdl

A useful handicapper on the Flat, he took to hurdles well in 2001/2002, winning all his three starts. Good second when just out of the handicap in the Swinton Hurdle. Suited by good or slightly easier ground.

Gran Maestro

100f **90f**

6-y-o bl g Gran Alba (USA)-Deauville Duchess (Ballad Rock)
P J Hobbs Rod Hamilton

Placings:*30* **(1559)**
2001/02: 17^{3}GF, 16^{0}G

	Starts	1st	2nd	3rd	Win & Pl
NH Flat	2	0	0	1	311
Career Total	**2**	**0**	**0**	**1**	**311**

Going: Sf: 0-0 GS: 0-0 Gd: 0-1 GF: - Fm: 0-1
Distance: 2m/2m3: 0-2 2m4-2m7: 0-0 3m+: 0-0
Track: LH: 0-2 RH: 0-0 Tight: 0-1 Gall: 0-0
Aids: Bl: 0-0 Vi: 0-0 Tstrap: 0-0
Best Rating: 90 10/01 Chep 2m110y good NHF

Gran Statement

68f **52f**

5-y-o b g Gran Alba (USA)-State Lady (IRE) (Strong Statement (USA))
Ferdy Murphy C W Cooper

Placings:*0* **(0377)**
2001/02: 16^{0}GF

	Starts	1st	2nd	3rd	Win & Pl
NH Flat	1	0	0	0	
Career Total	**1**	**0**	**0**	**0**	

Going: Sf: 0-0 GS: 0-0 Gd: 0-0 GF: - Fm: 0-1
Distance: 2m/2m3: 0-1 2m4-2m7: 0-0 3m+: 0-0
Track: LH: 0-0 RH: 0-1 Tight: 0-0 Gall: 0-1
Aids: Bl: 0-0 Vi: 0-0 Tstrap: 0-0
Best Rating: 52 5/01 Hntg 2m110y gd-fm NHF

Gran Times

6-y-o b m Gran Alba (USA)-Times Lady (Good Times (ITY))
M Madgwick Mrs J E M Powell

Placings:*0* **(1946)**
2001/02: 18^{0}GS

	Starts	1st	2nd	3rd	Win & Pl
NH Flat	1	0	0	0	
Career Total	**1**	**0**	**0**	**0**	

Going: Sf: 0-0 GS: 0-1 Gd: 0-0 GF: - Fm: 0-0
Distance: 2m/2m3: 0-1 2m4-2m7: 0-0 3m+: 0-0
Track: LH: 0-0 RH: 0-0 Tight: 0-0 Gall: 0-0
Aids: Bl: 0-0 Vi: 0-0 Tstrap: 0-0
Best Rating:

Gran Turismo (IRE)

106 **121**

9-y-o br g Sovereign Water (FR)-Granalice (Giolla Mear)
R Rowe Dr B Alexander

Placings:*15432/14/***0U4/F5F12U466-10** **(2331)**
2001/02: 24^{1}GF, 29^{0}G

	Starts	1st	2nd	3rd	Win & Pl
Chases	2	1	0	0	7410
Career Total	**21**	**4**	**2**	**1**	**18320**

121	5/01	Ling	3m	D(0-120)HCh	G-F	£7410
118	1/01	Font	3m2f110y	E(0-115)HCh	SFT	£3510
104	5/98	Chep	2m4f110y	E Hdl	G-F	£1996
87	6/97	Slig	2m	NHF	G-F	£2712

Total win prize-money £15629

Going: Sf: 0-0 GS: 0-0 Gd: 0-1 GF: - Fm: 1-1
Distance: 2m/2m3: 0-0 2m4-2m7: 0-0 **3m+: 1-2**
Track: **LH: 1-1** RH: 0-0 **Tight: 1-1** Gall: 0-0
Aids: Bl: 0-0 Vi: 0-0 Tstrap: 0-0
Best Rating: 121 5/01 Ling 3m gd-fm Ch

Has won over hurdles and fences, acts on most types of ground and stays three miles two furlongs.

Granby Bell

103 **123**

11-y-o b g Ballacashtal (CAN)-Betbellof (Averof)
Miss E C Lavelle (P Hayward 14/1) H A Watton

Placings:00P230/04133260/**0B434121P/6F10P-P30P2P4124** **(4643)**
2001/02: 20^{P}GF, 20^{3}GF, 21^{0}GF, 25^{P}GS, 19^{2}GS, 20^{P}G, 20^{4}S, 20^{1}GS, 20^{2}S, 20^{4}G

	Starts	1st	2nd	3rd	Win & Pl
Chases	10	1	2	1	6916
Career Total	**38**	**5**	**5**	**5**	**30837**

123	3/02	Plum	2m4f	E(0-110)HCh	G-S	£3234
123	11/00	Hrfd	2m3f	E(0-115)HCh	G-S	£4114
120	3/00	Newb	2m2f110y	D(0-110)HCh	G-F	£5564
123	2/00	Kemp	2m4f110y	D(0-115)HCh	GD	£5118
94	12/98	Hrfd	2m3f110y	F(0-100)HHdl	G-S	£2206

Total win prize-money £20238

Going: Sf: 0-2 GS: 1-3 Gd: 0-2 GF: - Fm: 0-3
Distance: 2m/2m3: 0-1 **2m4-2m7: 1-8** 3m+: 0-1
Track: **LH: 1-4** RH: 0-5 **Tight: 1-6** Gall: 0-0
Aids: Bl: 0-0 **Vi: 1-7** Tstrap: 0-0
Best Rating: 123 3/02 Plum 2m4f gd-sft Ch

A modest front-running chaser, he stays two and a half miles, but does not want the ground too soft. Often wears a visor and has broken blood-vessels.

Grand Ambition (USA)

(98h) (94h)**85**

6-y-o b g Lear Fan (USA)-Longing To Dance (USA) (Nureyev (USA))
Michael Hourigan (T H Caldwell 19/12) R J Mills

Placings:0-30063P0P3 **(4209a)**
2001/02: 16^{3}GF, 16^{0}GF, 17^{0}F, 16^{6}G, 17^{3}G, 22^{P}GS, 19^{0}GF, 17^{P}GS, 16^{3}SH

	Starts	1st	2nd	3rd	Win & Pl
Hurdles	9	0	0	3	1374
Career Total	**10**	**0**	**0**	**3**	**1374**

Going: Sf: 0-0 GS: 0-2 Gd: 0-2 GF: - Fm: 0-4
Distance: 2m/2m3: 0-7 2m4-2m7: 0-2 3m+: 0-0
Track: LH: 0-5 RH: 0-3 Tight: 0-5 Gall: 0-1
Aids: Bl: 0-0 Vi: 0-0 Tstrap: 0-0
Best Rating: 94 5/01 Hntg 2m110y gd-fm Hdl

He has shown snippets of form over hurdles, but looks no world-beater. Suited by fast ground.

Grand Commanche

89 **62**

7-y-o b g Gran Alba (USA)-Bella Run (Commanche Run)
N R Mitchell Percy J Harris

Placings:*060/0*40P/050PP004 **(4733)**

2001/02: 16^{0}G, 20^{5}S, 17^{0}G, 22^{P}G, 18^{P}HY, 16^{0}S, 16^{0}G, 24^{4}F

	Starts	1st	2nd	3rd	Win & Pl
Hurdles	8	0	0	0	416
Career Total	**15**	**0**	**0**	**0**	**416**

Going: Sf: 0-3 GS: 0-0 Gd: 0-4 GF: - Fm: 0-1
Distance: 2m/2m3: 0-5 2m4-2m7: 0-2 3m+: 0-1
Track: LH: 0-2 RH: 0-6 Tight: 0-1 Gall: 0-0
Aids: Bl: 0-1 Vi: 0-0 Tstrap: 0-0
Best Rating: 89 11/99 Ludl 2m5f good Hdl

Little ability over hurdles.

Grand Fougeray (FR)

91(81h) (56h)**100**

8-y-o b g Port Etienne (FR)-Poupee Du Fougeray (FR) (Rigolo Iv)
A W Carroll (K C Bailey 15/10) R T C Racing

Placings:134/1F10-PFP**P2FP** **(3335)**

2001/02: 20^{P}S, 24^{F}G, 22^{P}HY, 16^{P}GS, 16^{2}G, 16^{F}S, 20^{P}G

	Starts	1st	2nd	3rd	Win & Pl
Hurdles	1	0	0	0	0
Chases	6	0	1	0	1652
Career Total	**14**	**3**	**1**	**1**	**9856**

Date	Course	Distance	Race	Going	Prize
9/00	PLOE	2m4f	Ch	GD	£2305
8/00	Blng	2m4f	Ch	GD	£2498
6/00	[illegible]	2m0f	Ch	GD	[illegible]

Total win prize-money £7171

Going: Sf: 0-3 GS: 0-1 Gd: 0-3 GF: - Fm: 0-0
Distance: 2m/2m3: 0-3 2m4-2m7: 0-3 3m+: 0-1
Track: LH: 0-2 RH: 0-5 Tight: 0-6 Gall: 0-1
Aids: Bl: 0-1 Vi: 0-0 Tstrap: 0-0
Best Rating: 100 12/01 Ludl 2m good Ch

Three times a winner over fences in the French Provinces, he has shown little since moving to Britain.

Grand Prairie (SWE)

91 **71**

6-y-o b g Prairie-Platonica (ITY) (Primo Dominie)
N B Mason N B Mason

Placings:5U **(4867)**

2001/02: 17^{5}GS, 16^{U}GF

	Starts	1st	2nd	3rd	Win & Pl
Hurdles	2	0	0	0	0
Career Total	**2**	**0**	**0**	**0**	**0**

Going: Sf: 0-0 GS: 0-1 Gd: 0-0 GF: - Fm: 0-1
Distance: 2m/2m3: 0-2 2m4-2m7: 0-0 3m+: 0-0
Track: LH: 0-1 RH: 0-1 Tight: 0-0 Gall: 0-0
Aids: Bl: 0-0 Vi: 0-0 Tstrap: 0-0
Best Rating: 71 3/02 Carl 2m1f gd-sft Hdl

Multiple scorer on the Flat in Sweden. Has shown some ability over here.

Grand Slam (IRE)

96(89c) (101c)**104**

7-y-o b g Second Set (IRE)-Lady In The Park (IRE) (Last Tycoon)
L Lungo R J Gilbert

Placings:00/312-120045P0 **(4688)**

2001/02: 16^{1}GF, 17^{2}G, 16^{0}GF, 16^{0}G, 16^{4}GF, 16^{5}GS, 16^{P}S, 16^{0}GF

	Starts	1st	2nd	3rd	Win & Pl
Hurdles	7	1	1	0	3611
Chases	1	0	0	0	320
Career Total	**13**	**2**	**2**	**1**	**7602**

Rating	Date	Course	Distance	Race	Going	Prize
98	5/01	Ayr	2m	E Hdl	G-F	£2999
88	1/01	Muss	2m	E Hdl	G-S	£2254

Total win prize-money £5254

Going: Sf: 0-1 GS: 0-1 Gd: 0-2 GF: - Fm: 1-4
Distance: **2m/2m3: 1-8** 2m4-2m7: 0-0 3m+: 0-0
Track: **LH: 1-6** RH: 0-2 Tight: 0-4 Gall: 0-2
Aids: Bl: 0-0 Vi: 0-0 Tstrap: 0-0
Best Rating: 104 5/01 MRas 2m1f110y good Hdl

Acts on most types of ground and is effective at around two miles. Creditable effort on his chasing debut.

Grandee Line

89 **95**

7-y-o gr g Gran Alba (USA)-Judys Line (Capricorn Line)
R H Alner Cliff Gaylard

Placings:*0/*1P **(4883)**

2001/02: 20^{1}GF, 22^{P}GF

	Starts	1st	2nd	3rd	Win & Pl
Hurdles	2	1	0	0	2681
Career Total	**3**	**1**	**0**	**0**	**2681**

Rating	Date	Course	Distance	Race	Going	Prize
95	4/02	Chep	2m4f	E Hdl	G-F	£2681

Total win prize-money £2681

Going: Sf: 0-0 GS: 0-0 Gd: 0-0 GF: - Fm: 1-2
Distance: 2m/2m3: 0-0 **2m4-2m7: 1-2** 3m+: 0-0
Track: **LH: 1-2** RH: 0-0 Tight: 0-1 Gall: 0-0
Aids: Bl: 0-0 Vi: 0-0 Tstrap: 0-0
Best Rating: 95 4/02 Chep 2m4f gd-fm Hdl

Won an ordinary novices' event on his hurdling bow. Stays two and a half miles.

Grandma Griffiths

47

4-y-o b f Eagle Eyed (USA)-Buck Comtess (USA) (Spend A Buck (USA))
P G Murphy (Mrs L Stubbs 30/5) Harold Winton

Placings:00 **(2780)**

2001/02: 16^{0}HY, 16^{0}G

	Starts	1st	2nd	3rd	Win & Pl
Hurdles	2	0	0	0	
Career Total	**2**	**0**	**0**	**0**	

Going: Sf: 0-1 GS: 0-0 Gd: 0-1 GF: - Fm: 0-0
Distance: 2m/2m3: 0-2 2m4-2m7: 0-0 3m+: 0-0
Track: LH: 0-0 RH: 0-2 Tight: 0-0 Gall: 0-0
Aids: Bl: 0-0 Vi: 0-0 Tstrap: 0-0
Best Rating:

Grandma Lily (IRE)

4-y-o b f Bigstone (IRE)-Mrs Fisher (IRE) (Salmon Leap (USA))
S Gollings (Sir Mark Prescott 18/8) David Fravigar,Alan Mann,David Marshall

Placings:0P **(4315)**

2001/02: 17^{0}GS, 16^{P}HY

	Starts	1st	2nd	3rd	Win & Pl
Hurdles	2	0	0	0	
Career Total	**2**	**0**	**0**	**0**	

Going: Sf: 0-1 GS: 0-1 Gd: 0-0 GF: - Fm: 0-0
Distance: 2m/2m3: 0-2 2m4-2m7: 0-0 3m+: 0-0
Track: LH: 0-1 RH: 0-1 Tight: 0-2 Gall: 0-0
Aids: Bl: 0-0 Vi: 0-0 Tstrap: 0-0
Best Rating:

Grangewick Flight

96 **93**

8-y-o b g Lighter-Feathery (Le Coq D'Or)
N Wilson Mrs H D Marks

Placings:F4463 **(4868)**

2001/02: 16^{F}S, 21^{4}S, 26^{4}GS, 20^{6}GF, 20^{3}GF

	Starts	1st	2nd	3rd	Win & Pl
Chases	5	0	0	1	1148
Career Total	**5**	**0**	**0**	**1**	**1148**

Going: Sf: 0-2 GS: 0-1 Gd: 0-0 GF: - Fm: 0-2
Distance: 2m/2m3: 0-1 2m4-2m7: 0-3 3m+: 0-1
Track: LH: 0-3 RH: 0-2 Tight: 0-2 Gall: 0-0
Aids: Bl: 0-0 Vi: 0-0 Tstrap: 0-0
Best Rating: 95 3/02 Carl 3m2f gd-sft Ch

Placed in points but is very moderate under Rules.

Granham Charm (IRE)

95 **70**

7-y-o ch m Phardante (FR)-Deadly Charm (USA) (Bates Motel (USA))
M A Barnes A Smithson

Placings:*00/*R00300-43F04 **(1021)**

2001/02: 16^{4}F, 16^{3}F, 16^{F}GF, 17^{0}G, 21^{4}GF

	Starts	1st	2nd	3rd	Win & Pl
Hurdles	5	0	0	1	429
Career Total	**13**	**0**	**0**	**2**	**955**

Going: Sf: 0-0 GS: 0-0 Gd: 0-1 GF: - Fm: 0-4
Distance: 2m/2m3: 0-4 2m4-2m7: 0-1 3m+: 0-0
Track: LH: 0-2 RH: 0-3 Tight: 0-2 Gall: 0-0
Aids: Bl: 0-0 Vi: 0-0 Tstrap: 0-4
Best Rating: 70 5/01 Hexm 2m firm Hdl

Granit D'Estruval (FR)

113(107h) (120h)**153**

8-y-o b g Quart De Vin (FR)-Jalousie (FR) (Blockhaus)
Ferdy Murphy W J Gott

Placings:*5/2/***211F-12P**1 **(3592)**

2001/02: 26^{1}S, 24^{2}GS, 24^{P}Y, 24^{1}HY

	Starts	1st	2nd	3rd	Win & Pl
Hurdles	1	1	0	0	3650
Chases	3	1	1	0	9627
Career Total	**10**	**4**	**3**	**0**	**21000**

Rating	Date	Course	Distance	Race	Going	Prize
120	2/02	Uttx	3m110y	D Hdl	HVY	£3649
153	11/01	Carl	3m2f	C(0-130)HCh	SFT	£6922
130	12/00	Newc	3m	E Ch	SFT	£3120
114	11/00	Carl	3m2f	F Ch	SFT	£2353

Total win prize-money £16046

Going: Sf: 2-2 GS: 0-1 Gd: 0-0 GF: - Fm: 0-0
Distance: 2m/2m3: 0-0 2m4-2m7: 0-0 **3m+: 2-4**
Track: LH: 1-2 RH: 1-2 Tight: 0-0 Gall: 0-0
Aids: Bl: 0-0 Vi: 0-0 Tstrap: 0-0

Best Rating: 153 11/01 Carl 3m2f soft Ch

A smart novice chaser in 2000/2001, he made an impressive start to the following season, but then faced some stiff tasks and was not up to it. Gained a confidence booster over hurdles at Uttoxeter in February 2002. Likes to get his toe in and is suited by a test of stamina.

Granite Steps

107 **108**

6-y-o gr g Gran Alba (USA)-Pablena (Pablond)
Ferdy Murphy Mrs T H Barclay/mrs F D McInnes Skinner

Placings:_0_-22231 **(4518)**
2001/02: 20^{2}S, 19^{2}GS, 20^{2}S, 25^{3}GS, 21^{1}GS

	Starts	1st	2nd	3rd	Win & Pl
Hurdles	5	1	3	1	4967
Career Total	**6**	**1**	**3**	**1**	**4967**

103 3/02 Towc 2m5f F Hdl G-S £1953
Total win prize-money £1953

Going: Sf: 0-2 GS: 1-3 Gd: 0-0 GF: - Fm: 0-0
Distance: 2m/2m3: 0-0 **2m4-2m7: 1-4** 3m+: 0-1
Track: LH: 0-1 **RH: 1-3** Tight: 0-1 Gall: 0-1
Aids: Bl: 0-0 Vi: 0-0 Tstrap: 0-0
Best Rating: 108 2/02 Newc 2m4f soft Hdl

Runner-up several times in novice hurdles and should find a race before he eventually goes chasing.

Granny Dick

93 **90**

7-y-o ch m Broadsword (USA)-Penny's Colours (Hornet)
J L Spearing B Dowling

Placings:_35354_-P0F0P4 **(4682)**
2001/02: 22^{P}GF, 19^{0}G, 20^{F}GS, 20^{0}S, 26^{P}GS, 17^{4}GF

	Starts	1st	2nd	3rd	Win & Pl
Hurdles	6	0	0	0	0
Career Total	**11**	**0**	**0**	**2**	**998**

Going: Sf: 0-1 GS: 0-2 Gd: 0-1 GF: - Fm: 0-2
Distance: 2m/2m3: 0-1 2m4-2m7: 0-4 3m+: 0-1
Track: LH: 0-0 RH: 0-6 Tight: 0-0 Gall: 0-1
Aids: Bl: 0-1 Vi: 0-0 Tstrap: 0-0
Best Rating: 90 4/01 Asct 2m4f heavy Hdl

Found the trip inadequate when dropped into a seller over an extended two miles.

Granny Rich

100 **102d**

8-y-o ch m Ardross-Weareagrandmother (Prince Tenderfoot (USA))
P M Rich P M Rich

Placings:_30_/0P0/411115F/4FP4-0015F21 **(4528)**
2001/02: 17^{0}GS, 16^{0}G, 16^{1}S, 19^{5}GS, 19^{F}S, 19^{2}S, 20^{1}GS

	Starts	1st	2nd	3rd	Win & Pl
Hurdles	7	2	1	0	6913
Career Total	**23**	**6**	**1**	**1**	**17928**

102 4/02 Chep 2m4f D(0-125)HHdl G-S £3465
94 11/01 Chep 2m110y F(0-90)Hdl SFT £2324
118 1/00 Hrfd 2m3f110y F(0-110)HHdl G-S £3331
115 12/99 Wwck 2m2f110y E(0-105)HHdl SFT £2402
96 12/99 Hrfd 2m1f E(0-105)HHdl GD £2640
99 11/99 Uttx 2m G(0-90)HHdl G-S £1647
Total win prize-money £15810

Going: Sf: 1-3 GS: 1-3 Gd: 0-1 GF: - Fm: 0-0
Distance: 2m/2m3: 1-3 2m4-2m7: 1-4 3m+: 0-0
Track: **LH: 2-2** RH: 0-5 Tight: 0-2 Gall: 0-0
Aids: Bl: 0-0 Vi: 0-0 Tstrap: 0-0
Best Rating: 118 1/00 Hrfd 2m3f110y gd-sft Hdl

Modest handicap hurdler, suited by soft ground. Stays two and a half miles, tends to come from behind.

Grasp The Nettle (IRE)

10-y-o b g Henbit (USA)-Euroville Lady (Light Brigade)
K C Bailey K C Bailey

Placings:1/_603_/PP **(3390)**
2001/02: 21^{P}HY, 23^{P}GS

	Starts	1st	2nd	3rd	Win & Pl
Hurdles	2	0	0	0	
Career Total	**6**	**1**	**0**	**1**	**2346**

106 4/98 Baln 2m NHF SFT £1935
Total win prize-money £1936

Going: Sf: 0-1 GS: 0-1 Gd: 0-0 GF: - Fm: 0-0
Distance: 2m/2m3: 0-0 2m4-2m7: 0-2 3m+: 0-0
Track: LH: 0-1 RH: 0-1 Tight: 0-0 Gall: 0-0
Aids: Bl: 0-1 Vi: 0-0 Tstrap: 0-0
Best Rating: 106 4/98 Baln 2m soft NHF

Grass Island (IRE)

91 **107**

13-y-o b g The Parson-Helenium (Khalkis)
T P McGovern B & M McHugh Ltd Civil Engineering

Placings:0P/2/45/013111/UP633PU-40 **(1665)**
2001/02: 20^{4}S, 20^{0}G

	Starts	1st	2nd	3rd	Win & Pl
Chases	2	0	0	0	301
Career Total	**20**	**4**	**1**	**3**	**22953**

124 4/00 Chel 2m5f D(0-115)HCh SFT £8482
113 4/00 Plum 2m4f E(0-115)HCh G-S £3542
104 2/00 Hntg 3m D(0-110)HCh SFT £4598
105 1/00 Font 2m6f F(0-90)HCh G-S £2847
Total win prize-money £19472

Going: Sf: 0-1 GS: 0-0 Gd: 0-1 GF: - Fm: 0-0
Distance: 2m/2m3: 0-0 2m4-2m7: 0-2 3m+: 0-0
Track: LH: 0-1 RH: 0-1 Tight: 0-2 Gall: 0-0
Aids: Bl: 0-1 Vi: 0-0 Tstrap: 0-0
Best Rating: 124 5/00 Punc 2m4f good Ch

Grate Deel (IRE)

107 **111**

12-y-o ch g The Parson-Cahernane Girl (Bargello)
Mrs S J Smith Mrs M Ashby

Placings:_6/05_014/5632/4**224P/3P0P11622P/36550/34 351410-0P5** **(4870)**
2001/02: 24^{0}F, 25^{P}G, 23^{5}GF

	Starts	1st	2nd	3rd	Win & Pl
Chases	3	0	0	0	0
Career Total	**41**	**5**	**5**	**5**	**30098**

114 10/00 MRas 3m4f110y F(0-100)HCh GD £3667
114 8/00 MRas 3m1f F(0-110)HCh G-F £7377
114 11/98 Hayd 2m4f D Ch SFT £4335
114 10/98 Weth 3m1f E(0-105)HCh GD £3493
89 2/96 Sedg 2m5f110y E Hdl GD £2407
Total win prize-money £21281

Going: Sf: 0-0 GS: 0-0 Gd: 0-1 GF: - Fm: 0-2
Distance: 2m/2m3: 0-0 2m4-2m7: 0-0 3m+: 0-3
Track: LH: 0-1 RH: 0-1 Tight: 0-2 Gall: 0-0
Aids: Bl: 0-0 Vi: 0-0 Tstrap: 0-0
Best Rating: 114 10/00 MRas 3m4f110y good Ch

Modest handicap chaser, effective at three miles. In good form in the summer of 2002.

Grate Spark (IRE)

92 **74**

6-y-o b g Posen (USA)-Linda's Fantasy (Raga Navarro (ITY))
J F Coupland J F Coupland

Placings:50/0-6505 **(2947)**
2001/02: 20^{6}G, 20^{5}F, 16^{0}G, 20^{5}G

	Starts	1st	2nd	3rd	Win & Pl
Hurdles	4	0	0	0	0
Career Total	**7**	**0**	**0**	**0**	**0**

Going: Sf: 0-0 GS: 0-0 Gd: 0-3 GF: - Fm: 0-1
Distance: 2m/2m3: 0-1 2m4-2m7: 0-3 3m+: 0-0
Track: LH: 0-4 RH: 0-0 Tight: 0-2 Gall: 0-1
Aids: Bl: 0-0 Vi: 0-0 Tstrap: 0-1
Best Rating: 74 5/01 Weth 2m4f110y firm Hdl

Gratomi (IRE)

99(87h) **106**

12-y-o b g Bustomi-Granny Grumble (Politico (USA))
P C Ritchens John Pearl

Placings:S/P/216**62F112221/3FU224212/30**304304/0 **66503F5**03**-31006** **(1259)**
2001/02: 20^{3}GF, 16^{1}GF, 16^{0}G, 20^{0}GF, 16^{6}GF

	Starts	1st	2nd	3rd	Win & Pl
Chases	5	1	0	1	3410
Career Total	**46**	**6**	**9**	**7**	**35319**

106 5/01 Hntg 2m110y F(0-105)HCh G-F £2912
123 4/99 Ludl 2m4f D(0-125)HCh GD £4143
117 4/98 Extr 2m3f110y D(0-125)HCh SFT £3818
103 2/98 Folk 2m F(0-100)HCh G-F £2691
93 2/98 Hrfd 2m3f E(0-100)HCh GD £3009
100 6/97 Worc 2m4f E Hdl GD £2617
Total win prize-money £19191

Going: Sf: 0-0 GS: 0-0 Gd: 0-1 GF: - Fm: 1-4
Distance: **2m/2m3: 1-3** 2m4-2m7: 0-2 3m+: 0-0
Track: LH: 0-3 **RH: 1-2** Tight: 0-3 **Gall: 1-2**
Aids: Bl: 0-0 Vi: 0-0 Tstrap: 0-0
Best Rating: 127 10/99 Towc 2m110y good Ch

Grattan Lodge (IRE)

93 **74**

5-y-o gr g Roselier (FR)-Shallow Run (Deep Run)
J Howard Johnson W M G Black

Placings:P0P **(4392)**
2001/02: 24^{P}S, 20^{0}S, 22^{P}HY

	Starts	1st	2nd	3rd	Win & Pl
Hurdles	3	0	0	0	
Career Total	**3**	**0**	**0**	**0**	

Going: Sf: 0-3 GS: 0-0 Gd: 0-0 GF: - Fm: 0-0
Distance: 2m/2m3: 0-0 2m4-2m7: 0-2 3m+: 0-1
Track: LH: 0-3 RH: 0-0 Tight: 0-1 Gall: 0-1
Aids: Bl: 0-0 Vi: 0-0 Tstrap: 0-0
Best Rating: 74 2/02 Newc 2m4f soft Hdl

Grave Doubts

91 **75**

6-y-o ch g Karinga Bay-Redgrave Girl (Deep Run)

K Bishop Diana Kirkman & Bill Davies

Placings: *1302* **(4743)**

2001/02: 17^{1}G, 16^{3}G, 17^{0}G, 16^{2}GF

	Starts	1st	2nd	3rd	Win & Pl
NH Flat	4	1	1	1	3134
Career Total	**4**	**1**	**1**	**1**	**3134**

110	6/01	NAbb	2m1f	H NHF	GD	£2282

Total win prize-money £2282

Going: Sf: 0-0 GS: 0-0 Gd: 1-3 GF: - Fm: 0-1
Distance: **2m/2m3: 1-4** 2m4-2m7: 0-0 3m+: 0-0
Track: **LH: 1-2** RH: 0-2 **Tight: 1-1** Gall: 0-0
Aids: Bl: 0-0 Vi: 0-0 Tstrap: 0-0
Best Rating: 110 6/01 Worc 2m good NHF

Fair bumper performer on a sound surface.

Gray Knight (IRE)

103 **86**

5-y-o gr g Insan (USA)-Moohono (IRE) (Roselier (FR))

Miss H C Knight Ramp Partnership

Placings: *5-40* **(2717)**

2001/02: 17^{4}G, 19^{0}G

	Starts	1st	2nd	3rd	Win & Pl
Hurdles	2	0	0	0	0
Career Total	**0**	**0**	**0**	**0**	**0**

Going: Sf: 0-0 GS: 0-0 Gd: 0-2 GF: - Fm: 0-0
Distance: 2m/2m3: 0-1 2m4-2m7: 0-1 3m+: 0-0
Track: LH: 0-1 RH: 0-1 Tight: 0-1 Gall: 0-0
Aids: Bl: 0-0 Vi: 0-0 Tstrap: 0-0
Best Rating: 86 11/01 NAbb 2m1f good Hdl

Great Crusader

88(94h) (78h)**94**

10-y-o ch g Deploy-Shannon Princess (Connaught)

M J Hogan Mrs Barbara Hogan

Placings: *32/44P***3FP** **(2329)**

2001/02: 22^{4}G, 20^{4}GF, 18^{P}S, 16^{3}G, 16^{F}S, 26^{P}G

	Starts	1st	2nd	3rd	Win & Pl
Hurdles	3	0	0	0	271
Chases	3	0	0	1	524
Career Total	**8**	**0**	**1**	**2**	**4318**

Going: Sf: 0-2 GS: 0-0 Gd: 0-3 GF: - Fm: 0-1
Distance: 2m/2m3: 0-3 2m4-2m7: 0-2 3m+: 0-1
Track: LH: 0-3 RH: 0-2 Tight: 0-3 Gall: 0-0
Aids: Bl: 0-0 Vi: 0-0 Tstrap: 0-0
Best Rating: 133 1/99 Sand 2m110y soft Hdl

Whose staggered career includes lay-offs from 1995-1999 and 1999-2001, has not had a win for seven years. His good form over hurdles in 1999 seems to have eluded him nowadays. Connections have embarked on a steeplechase campaign with him.

Great Hopper

84 **56**

7-y-o b m Rock Hopper-Spun Gold (Thatch (USA))

F Watson F Watson

Placings: 4 **(1592)**

2001/02: 17^{4}GS

	Starts	1st	2nd	3rd	Win & Pl
Hurdles	1	0	0	0	0
Career Total	**1**	**0**	**0**	**0**	**0**

Going: Sf: 0-0 GS: 0-1 Gd: 0-0 GF: - Fm: 0-0
Distance: 2m/2m3: 0-1 2m4-2m7: 0-0 3m+: 0-0
Track: LH: 0-1 RH: 0-0 Tight: 0-1 Gall: 0-0
Aids: Bl: 0-0 Vi: 0-0 Tstrap: 0-0
Best Rating: 56 10/01 Sedg 2m1f gd-sft Hdl

Great Leveler (IRE)

72

11-y-o b g Satco (FR)-Bramble Lane (Boreen (FR))

Gerard Keane Braveheart Syndicate

Placings: 3000630-P00 **(2488a)**

2001/02: 24^{P}F, 21^{0}G, 18^{0}YS

	Starts	1st	2nd	3rd	Win & Pl
Hurdles	2	0	0	0	0
Chases	1	0	0	0	0
Career Total	**10**	**0**	**0**	**2**	**844**

Going: Sf: 0-0 GS: 0-0 Gd: 0-1 GF: - Fm: 0-1
Distance: 2m/2m3: 0-1 2m4-2m7: 0-1 3m+: 0-1
Track: LH: 0-1 RH: 0-1 Tight: 0-0 Gall: 0-1
Aids: Bl: 0-1 Vi: 0-0 Tstrap: 0-3
Best Rating: 109 6/00 Naas 2m3f yield NHF

Grecian Star

10-y-o b g Crested Lark-Grecian Lace (Spartan General)

G J Tarry R John White

Placings: 512 **(4763)**

2001/02: 23^{5}S, 22^{1}GS, 24^{2}GF

	Starts	1st	2nd	3rd	Win & Pl
Chases	3	1	1	0	3072
Career Total	**3**	**1**	**1**	**0**	**3072**

115	3/02	Towc	2m6f	H Ch	G-S	£2226

Total win prize-money £2226

Going: Sf: 0-1 GS: 1-1 Gd: 0-0 GF: - Fm: 0-1
Distance: 2m/2m3: 0-0 **2m4-2m7: 1-1** 3m+: 0-2
Track: LH: 0-0 **RH: 1-3** Tight: 0-0 Gall: 0-0
Aids: Bl: 0-0 Vi: 0-0 Tstrap: 0-0
Best Rating: 115 4/02 Asct 3m110y gd-fm Ch

Green Card (USA)

106 **140**

8-y-o br h Green Dancer (USA)-Dunkellin (USA) (Irish River (FR))

S P C Woods P Pottinger/n Thomas/n Yardy

Placings: 111P-120 **(0964)**

2001/02: 16^{1}GF, 16^{2}GF, 17^{0}GS

	Starts	1st	2nd	3rd	Win & Pl
Hurdles	3	1	1	0	7296
Career Total	**7**	**4**	**1**	**0**	**14269**

136	6/01	Strf	2m110y	C(0-135)HHdl	G-F	£5791
132	10/00	Font	2m2f110y	E Hdl	GD	£1858
136	8/00	Font	2m2f110y	E Hdl	G-F	£2306
120	7/00	Strf	2m110y	E Hdl	G-F	£2808

Total win prize-money £12766

Going: Sf: 0-0 GS: 0-1 Gd: 0-0 GF: - Fm: 1-2
Distance: **2m/2m3: 1-3** 2m4-2m7: 0-0 3m+: 0-0
Track: **LH: 1-2** RH: 0-0 **Tight: 1-2** Gall: 0-0
Aids: Bl: 0-0 Vi: 0-0 Tstrap: 0-0
Best Rating: 140 7/01 Strf 2m110y gd-fm Hdl

Green Crusader

93 **68**

11-y-o b g Green Desert (USA)-Hysterical (High Top)

Mrs V C Ward Mrs V C Ward

Placings: 610453/5/01341300/211330/04664**564/0-2** **(4270)**

2001/02: 24^{2}G

	Starts	1st	2nd	3rd	Win & Pl
Chases	1	0	1	0	1190
Career Total	**31**	**5**	**2**	**5**	**20524**

125	6/98	Uttx	3m110y	D(0-125)HHdl	GD	£3438
125	5/98	Ctml	2m6f	D(0-120)HHdl	G-F	£3452
111	2/98	Hayd	2m4f	D(0-120)HHdl	GD	£3011
100	1/98	Wind	2m4f	F(0-105)HHdl	G-S	£2407
100	2/96	Plum	2m1f	F Hdl	SFT	£2116

Total win prize-money £14426

Going: Sf: 0-0 GS: 0-0 Gd: 0-1 GF: - Fm: 0-0
Distance: 2m/2m3: 0-0 2m4-2m7: 0-0 3m+: 0-1
Track: LH: 0-1 RH: 0-0 Tight: 0-1 Gall: 0-0
Aids: Bl: 0-0 Vi: 0-0 Tstrap: 0-0
Best Rating: 125 3/99 Uttx 2m6f110y gd-sft Hdl

Green Ideal

99 **121**

4-y-o b c Mark Of Esteem (IRE)-Emerald (USA) (El Gran Senor (USA))

N J Henderson (Mrs A J Perrett 25/8) Thurloe Thoroughbreds Viii

Placings: 1P0 **(4651)**

2001/02: 16^{1}GS, 17^{P}HY, 16^{0}G

	Starts	1st	2nd	3rd	Win & Pl
Hurdles	3	1	0	0	4427
Career Total	**3**	**1**	**0**	**0**	**4427**

121	12/01	Newb	2m110y	D Hdl	G-S	£4426

Total win prize-money £4427

Going: Sf: 0-1 GS: 1-1 Gd: 0-1 GF: - Fm: 0-0
Distance: **2m/2m3: 1-3** 2m4-2m7: 0-0 3m+: 0-0
Track: **LH: 1-3** RH: 0-0 Tight: 0-1 **Gall: 1-2**
Aids: Bl: 0-0 Vi: 0-0 Tstrap: 0-1
Best Rating: 121 12/01 Newb 2m110y gd-sft Hdl

Lightly-raced on the Flat, he made a good start over hurdles when winning a decent race at Newbury in December 2001, but was pulled up at Cheltenham next time when he reportedly made a noise.

Green Jacket

78 **29**

7-y-o b g Green Desert (USA)-Select Sale (Auction Ring (USA))

J Joseph Jack Joseph

Placings: 000P2/00/05PBP-60 **(4546)**

2001/02: 21^{6}GS, 16^{0}GF

	Starts	1st	2nd	3rd	Win & Pl
Hurdles	2	0	0	0	0
Career Total	**14**	**0**	**1**	**0**	**660**

Going: Sf: 0-0 GS: 0-1 Gd: 0-0 GF: - Fm: 0-1
Distance: 2m/2m3: 0-1 2m4-2m7: 0-1 3m+: 0-0
Track: LH: 0-1 RH: 0-1 Tight: 0-1 Gall: 0-1
Aids: Bl: 0-0 Vi: 0-0 Tstrap: 0-0
Best Rating: 74 5/99 Extr 2m1f firm Hdl

Green Magical (IRE)

98 **99**

6-y-o ch m Magical Strike (USA)-Green Legend (IRE) (Montekin)

T Hogan (J Cullinan 1/7) John M Carroll

Placings:0F/3-222300 **(1868a)**

2001/02: 22^{2}GF, 24^{2}G, 20^{2}YS, 20^{3}SH, 20^{0}SH, 20^{0}Y

	Starts	1st	2nd	3rd	Win & Pl
Hurdles	6	0	3	1	3240
Career Total	**9**	**0**	**3**	**2**	**3629**

Going: Sf: 0-0 GS: 0-0 Gd: 0-1 GF: - Fm: 0-1
Distance: 2m/2m3: 0-0 2m4-2m7: 0-5 3m+: 0-1
Track: LH: 0-1 RH: 0-1 Tight: 0-1 Gall: 0-0
Aids: Bl: 0-0 Vi: 0-0 Tstrap: 0-0
Best Rating: 99 7/01 Baln 2m4f yld-sft Hdl

Green Missile

83 **47**

7-y-o b g Green Ruby (USA)-Amber Missile Vii (Damsire Unregistered)

G B Balding Mrs P D Gulliver

Placings:*000*-00 **(0906)**

2001/02: 17^{0}G, 20^{0}G

	Starts	1st	2nd	3rd	Win & Pl
Hurdles	2	0	0	0	
Career Total	**5**	**0**	**0**	**0**	

Going: Sf: 0-0 GS: 0-0 Gd: 0-2 GF: - Fm: 0-0
Distance: 2m/2m3: 0-1 2m4-2m7: 0-1 3m+: 0-0
Track: LH: 0-1 RH: 0-1 Tight: 0-0 Gall: 0-0
Aids: Bl: 0-0 Vi: 0-1 Tstrap: 0-0
Best Rating: 88 10/00 Extr 2m1f good NHF

Green Pursuit

6-y-o b g Green Desert (USA)-Vayavaig (Damister (USA))

J G M O'Shea (J A Osborne 14/8) Gary Roberts

Placings:0/P **(2476)**

2001/02: 17^{P}S

	Starts	1st	2nd	3rd	Win & Pl
Hurdles	1	0	0	0	
Career Total	**2**	**0**	**0**	**0**	

Going: Sf: 0-1 GS: 0-0 Gd: 0-0 GF: - Fm: 0-0
Distance: 2m/2m3: 0-1 2m4-2m7: 0-0 3m+: 0-0
Track: LH: 0-0 RH: 0-1 Tight: 0-1 Gall: 0-0
Aids: Bl: 0-0 Vi: 0-1 Tstrap: 0-0
Best Rating:

Green Sheen (IRE)

100 **78**

14-y-o ch g Green Shoon-Hill Sixty (Slippered)

Miss S E Forster Miss Sandra Forster

Placings:046/3P/P/5/P/46 **(0782)**

2001/02: 20^{4}GF, 20^{6}G

	Starts	1st	2nd	3rd	Win & Pl
Chases	2	0	0	0	162
Career Total	**10**	**0**	**0**	**1**	**412**

Going: Sf: 0-0 GS: 0-0 Gd: 0-1 GF: - Fm: 0-1
Distance: 2m/2m3: 0-0 2m4-2m7: 0-2 3m+: 0-0
Track: LH: 0-2 RH: 0-0 Tight: 0-0 Gall: 0-0
Aids: Bl: 0-0 Vi: 0-0 Tstrap: 0-0
Best Rating: 86 11/92 Sedg 3m3f110y good Hdl

Green Smoke

105 **82**

6-y-o gr g Green Adventure (USA)-Smoke (Rusticaro (FR))

J M Jefferson Mrs J U Hales

Placings:*U000*-20325 **(2909)**

2001/02: 20^{2}GS, 21^{0}G, 22^{3}GS, 22^{2}GS, 25^{5}GS

	Starts	1st	2nd	3rd	Win & Pl
Hurdles	5	0	2	1	2236
Career Total	**9**	**0**	**2**	**1**	**2236**

Going: Sf: 0-0 GS: 0-4 Gd: 0-1 GF: - Fm: 0-0
Distance: 2m/2m3: 0-0 2m4-2m7: 0-4 3m+: 0-1
Track: LH: 0-4 RH: 0-1 Tight: 0-3 Gall: 0-0
Aids: Bl: 0-0 Vi: 0-0 Tstrap: 0-0
Best Rating: 83 1/01 Newc 2m soft NHF

Modest novice hurdler, probably stays three miles.

Green-Lavel (IRE)

6-y-o b g Phardante (FR)-Credora Bay (Orange Bay)

A King C W Lane

Placings:*00*-P **(0214)**

2001/02: 22^{P}GF

	Starts	1st	2nd	3rd	Win & Pl
Hurdles	1	0	0	0	
Career Total	**3**	**0**	**0**	**0**	

Going: Sf: 0-0 GS: 0-0 Gd: 0-0 GF: - Fm: 0-1
Distance: 2m/2m3: 0-0 2m4-2m7: 0-1 3m+: 0-0
Track: LH: 0-0 RH: 0-1 Tight: 0-0 Gall: 0-0
Aids: Bl: 0-0 Vi: 0-0 Tstrap: 0-0
Best Rating: 91 11/00 Ludl 2m good NHF

Greenacres Miss

66f **30f**

5-y-o b m Michelozzo (USA)-Royal Cause (Le Bavard (FR))

C N Kellett Geoffrey Arthur Probin

Placings:*00* **(1586)**

2001/02: 17^{0}GF, 17^{0}GS

	Starts	1st	2nd	3rd	Win & Pl
NH Flat	2	0	0	0	
Career Total	**2**	**0**	**0**	**0**	

Going: Sf: 0-0 GS: 0-1 Gd: 0-0 GF: - Fm: 0-1
Distance: 2m/2m3: 0-2 2m4-2m7: 0-0 3m+: 0-0
Track: LH: 0-0 RH: 0-2 Tight: 0-1 Gall: 0-0
Aids: Bl: 0-0 Vi: 0-0 Tstrap: 0-0
Best Rating: 30 9/01 Hrfd 2m1f gd-fm NHF

Greenback (BEL)

106 **106**

11-y-o b g Absalom-Batalya (BEL) (Boulou)

R G Frost Jack Joseph

Placings:U2112122111100/1/**23F1113313/50400544 3/233110** **(2661)**

2001/02: 17^{2}F, 22^{3}GS, 16^{3}GF, 16^{1}GF, 16^{1}GF, 19^{0}GS

	Starts	1st	2nd	3rd	Win & Pl
Hurdles	6	2	1	2	5880
Career Total	**40**	**14**	**6**	**7**	**68127**

100	11/01	Ludl	2m	G Hdl	G-F	£2107
90	11/01	Ludl	2m	G Hdl	G-F	£2096
128	4/97	Asct	2m3f110y	C Ch	G-F	£5654
128	12/96	Kemp	2m4f110y	B Ch	G-F	£10308
119	12/96	Folk	2m	E Ch	G-S	£3305
113	11/96	Tntn	2m3f	C Ch	G-F	£4531
120	5/95	Towc	2m	D(0-125)HHdl	G-F	£2883
120	2/95	Kemp	2m	A Hdl	HVY	£9780
100	12/94	Sand	2m110y	Hdl	GD	£3129
114	11/94	Kemp	2m	Hdl	GD	£2448
108	11/94	Sand	2m110y	Hdl	SFT	£3192
100	9/94	Tntn	2m1f	Hdl	G-F	£1733
77	8/94	Extr	2m1f110y	Hdl	FRM	£2263
87	8/94	NAbb	2m1f	Hdl	G-S	£1818

Total win prize-money £55254

Going: Sf: 0-0 GS: 0-2 Gd: 0-0 GF: - Fm: 2-4
Distance: **2m/2m3: 2-4** 2m4-2m7: 0-2 3m+: 0-0
Track: LH: 0-1 **RH: 2-5** Tight: 0-2 Gall: 0-0
Aids: Bl: 0-0 Vi: 0-0 Tstrap: 0-0
Best Rating: 128 4/97 Asct 2m3f110y gd-fm Ch

Plating-class hurdler nowadays. Likes fast ground and stays two miles four furlongs. Genuine sort.

Greenfire (FR)

4-y-o ch g Ashkalani (IRE)-Greenvera (USA) (Riverman (USA))

Mrs Dianne Sayer Andrew Sayer

Placings:0 **(4900)**

2001/02: 16^{0}G

	Starts	1st	2nd	3rd	Win & Pl
NH Flat	1	0	0	0	
Career Total	**1**	**0**	**0**	**0**	

Going: Sf: 0-0 GS: 0-0 Gd: 0-1 GF: - Fm: 0-0
Distance: 2m/2m3: 0-1 2m4-2m7: 0-0 3m+: 0-0
Track: LH: 0-0 RH: 0-1 Tight: 0-0 Gall: 0-0
Aids: Bl: 0-0 Vi: 0-0 Tstrap: 0-0
Best Rating:

Greenhope (IRE)

108 **124**

4-y-o b g Definite Article-Unbidden Melody (USA) (Chieftain Ii)

N J Henderson (J A Osborne 16/8) Lynn Wilson,Giles Wilson

Placings:1110 **(4952a)**

2001/02: 16^{1}G, 16^{1}G, 16^{1}G, 16^{0}G

	Starts	1st	2nd	3rd	Win & Pl
Hurdles	4	3	0	0	20547
Career Total	**4**	**3**	**0**	**0**	**20547**

124	12/01	Kemp	2m	B Hdl	GD	£7052
118	11/01	Chel	2m110y	B Hdl	GD	£8619
111	11/01	Asct	2m110y	C Hdl	GD	£4875

Total win prize-money £20547

Going: Sf: 0-0 GS: 0-0 Gd: 3-4 GF: - Fm: 0-0
Distance: **2m/2m3: 3-4** 2m4-2m7: 0-0 3m+: 0-0
Track: LH: 1-1 **RH: 2-3** Tight: 0-0 Gall: 0-0
Aids: Bl: 0-0 Vi: 0-0 Tstrap: 0-0
Best Rating: 124 12/01 Kemp 2m good Hdl

A winner of his first three starts over hurdles against some decent juvenile novices, he struggled in the third of those and was given a break afterwards. Does not want the ground too soft and is seen to best effect when making the running.

Greenkeys (AUS)

88 67

8-y-o b g Bonhomie (USA)-Cindy Doll (AUS) (Cindy's Son)
N B Mason N B Mason

Placings:*6000/0* **(0220)**
2001/02: 16^{0}GF

	Starts	1st	2nd	3rd	Win & Pl
Hurdles	1	0	0	0	
Career Total	**5**	**0**	**0**	**0**	**0**

Going: Sf: 0-0 GS: 0-0 Gd: 0-0 GF: - Fm: 0-1
Distance: 2m/2m3: 0-1 2m4-2m7: 0-0 3m+: 0-0
Track: LH: 0-1 RH: 0-0 Tight: 0-0 Gall: 0-0
Aids: Bl: 0-0 Vi: 0-0 Tstrap: 0-0
Best Rating: 71 3/00 Uttx 2m4f110y good Hdl

Greenlees

4-y-o b f Greensmith-Scawsby Lees (Stanford)
W G M Turner Hawks And Doves Racing Syndicate

Placings:RP **(2794)**
2001/02: 17^{R}GS, 16^{P}S

	Starts	1st	2nd	3rd	Win & Pl
Hurdles	2	0	0	0	
Career Total	**2**	**0**	**0**	**0**	

Going: Sf: 0-1 GS: 0-1 Gd: 0-0 GF: - Fm: 0-0
Distance: 2m/2m3: 0-2 2m4-2m7: 0-0 3m+: 0-0
Track: LH: 0-1 RH: 0-1 Tight: 0-1 Gall: 0-0
Aids: Bl: 0-0 Vi: 0-0 Tstrap: 0-0
Best Rating:

Greensmith Lane

86 80

6-y-o br g Greensmith-Handy Lane (Nearly A Hand)
N J Hawke M L Stoddart

Placings:*26F* **(4736)**
2001/02: 17^{2}G, 17^{6}G, 17^{F}F

	Starts	1st	2nd	3rd	Win & Pl
NH Flat	2	0	1	0	681
Hurdles	1	0	0	0	0
Career Total	**3**	**0**	**1**	**0**	**681**

Going: Sf: 0-0 GS: 0-0 Gd: 0-2 GF: - Fm: 0-1
Distance: 2m/2m3: 0-3 2m4-2m7: 0-0 3m+: 0-0
Track: LH: 0-1 RH: 0-1 Tight: 0-1 Gall: 0-0
Aids: Bl: 0-0 Vi: 0-0 Tstrap: 0-0
Best Rating: 91 11/01 Tntn 2m1f good NHF

Has shown ability over hurdles.

Greenwich

102 113

8-y-o br g Handsome Sailor-Praise The Lord (Lord Gayle (USA))
N A Twiston-Davies (Mrs Marilyn Scudamore 7/4) Mrs J K Powell

Placings:*60/2045540/6*34PF-2B35 **(0848)**
2001/02: 23^{2}G, 28^{B}GF, 28^{3}GF, 32^{5}GF

	Starts	1st	2nd	3rd	Win & Pl
Chases	4	0	1	1	1765
Career Total	**18**	**0**	**2**	**2**	**3207**

Going: Sf: 0-0 GS: 0-0 Gd: 0-1 GF: - Fm: 0-3
Distance: 2m/2m3: 0-0 2m4-2m7: 0-0 3m+: 0-4
Track: LH: 0-2 RH: 0-1 Tight: 0-2 Gall: 0-0
Aids: Bl: 0-0 Vi: 0-0 Tstrap: 0-0
Best Rating: 113 6/01 Strf 3m4f gd-fm Ch

Modest maiden hurdler/hunter. Capable of winning a hunter chase when things go his way.

Gregale

102 90

6-y-o b m Gildoran-Minigale (Strong Gale)
J Neville (J Milton 15/5) J Milton

Placings:F140 **(1029)**
2001/02: 25^{F}G, 22^{1}G, 24^{4}G, 19^{0}G

	Starts	1st	2nd	3rd	Win & Pl
Hurdles	3	1	0	0	3108
Chases	1	0	0	0	0
Career Total	**4**	**1**	**0**	**0**	**3108**

90 6/01 NAbb 2m6f E Hdl GD £3108
Total win prize-money £3108

Going: Sf: 0-0 GS: 0-0 Gd: 1-4 GF: - Fm: 0-0
Distance: 2m/2m3: 0-1 **2m4-2m7: 1-1** 3m+: 0-2
Track: **LH: 1-3** RH: 0-1 **Tight: 1-2** Gall: 0-0
Aids: Bl: 0-0 Vi: 0-0 **Tstrap: 1-1**
Best Rating: 90 6/01 NAbb 2m6f good Hdl

Gregorio

77 26

12-y-o b g Strong Gale-Cala Conta (Deep Run)
Mark Campion The Wellington Partnership

Placings:3/0600/P42/5-P6P2PP **(2463)**
2001/02: 19^{P}G, 24^{6}GF, 20^{P}GF, 24^{2}GF, 22^{P}G, 21^{P}G

	Starts	1st	2nd	3rd	Win & Pl
Hurdles	1	0	0	0	0
Chases	5	0	1	0	1155
Career Total	**15**	**0**	**2**	**1**	**2272**

Going: Sf: 0-0 GS: 0-0 Gd: 0-3 GF: - Fm: 0-3
Distance: 2m/2m3: 0-0 2m4-2m7: 0-4 3m+: 0-2
Track: LH: 0-2 RH: 0-3 Tight: 0-4 Gall: 0-2
Aids: Bl: 0-0 Vi: 0-0 Tstrap: 0-0
Best Rating: 97 5/96 Extr 2m2f gd-fm NHF

A moderate novice. Has reportedly made a noise when pulled up in the past. Races on a sound surface.

Gregorio (FR)

107 148

8-y-o b/br g Passing Sale (FR)-Apside (FR) (Mistigri)
Mrs S A Bramall Miss Anna Bramall

Placings:43/4*123/22*-1316330 **(3955a)**
2001/02: 18^{1}G, 19^{3}Y, 17^{1}S, 18^{6}YS, 20^{3}Y, 19^{3}Y, 25^{0}S

	Starts	1st	2nd	3rd	Win & Pl
Chases	7	2	0	3	18884
Career Total	**15**	**3**	**3**	**5**	**38360**

146 10/01 Bang 2m1f110y C(0-130)HCh SFT £7288
132 5/01 Fair 2m2f Ch GD £7862
116 10/99 Wxfd 2m NHF SFT £3080
Total win prize-money £18231

Going: Sf: 1-2 GS: 0-0 Gd: 1-1 GF: - Fm: 0-0
Distance: **2m/2m3: 2-5** 2m4-2m7: 0-1 3m+: 0-1
Track: **LH: 1-3** RH: 0-1 **Tight: 1-1** Gall: 0-0
Aids: Bl: 0-0 Vi: 0-0 Tstrap: 0-0
Best Rating: 146 10/01 Bang 2m1f110y soft Ch

He did well from limited opportunities in novice chases in 2000/2001, finishing second to Red Striker at Newcastle in January and won well at Bangor in October. Suited by easy ground, he is a useful handicapper in the making.

Gregorio

77 26

12-y-o b g Strong Gale-Cala Conta (Deep Run)
Mark Campion The Wellington Partnership

Placings:3/0600/P42/5-P6P2PP **(2463)**
2001/02: 19^{P}G, 24^{6}GF, 20^{P}GF, 24^{2}GF, 22^{P}G, 21^{P}G

	Starts	1st	2nd	3rd	Win & Pl
Hurdles	1	0	0	0	0
Chases	5	0	1	0	1155
Career Total	**15**	**0**	**2**	**1**	**2272**

Going: Sf: 0-0 GS: 0-0 Gd: 0-3 GF: - Fm: 0-3
Distance: 2m/2m3: 0-0 2m4-2m7: 0-4 3m+: 0-2
Track: LH: 0-2 RH: 0-3 Tight: 0-4 Gall: 0-2
Aids: Bl: 0-0 Vi: 0-0 Tstrap: 0-0
Best Rating: 97 5/96 Extr 2m2f gd-fm NHF

A moderate novice. Has reportedly made a noise when pulled up in the past. Races on a sound surface.

Gregs Way

99(110h) (88h)94

8-y-o br g Nomadic Way (USA)-Gregory's Lady (Meldrum)
Mrs S J Smith Keith Nicholson

Placings:*4/050*-F3360 **(1488)**
2001/02: 16^{F}GF, 17^{3}GS, 19^{3}GF, 17^{6}GS, 20^{0}GF

	Starts	1st	2nd	3rd	Win & Pl
Hurdles	5	0	0	2	1059
Career Total	**9**	**0**	**0**	**2**	**1059**

Going: Sf: 0-0 GS: 0-2 Gd: 0-0 GF: - Fm: 0-3
Distance: 2m/2m3: 0-3 2m4-2m7: 0-2 3m+: 0-0
Track: LH: 0-2 RH: 0-2 Tight: 0-2 Gall: 0-1
Aids: Bl: 0-0 Vi: 0-0 Tstrap: 0-0
Best Rating: 88 8/01 MRas 2m3f110y gd-fm Hdl

Modest novice hurdler who scored decisively at Stratford over two miles three in July. Well suited by forcing tactics, he has looked short of stamina over three miles. Yet to impress over fences.

Gremlin One

5-y-o ch g Democratic (USA)-Calcutta Queen (Night Shift (USA))
W Storey Gremlin Racing

Placings:PP **(1590)**

2001/02: 17^{P}G, 17^{P}GS

	Starts	1st	2nd	3rd	Win & Pl
Hurdles	2	0	0	0	
Career Total	**2**	**0**	**0**	**0**	

Going: Sf: 0-0 GS: 0-1 Gd: 0-1 GF: - Fm: 0-0
Distance: 2m/2m3: 0-2 2m4-2m7: 0-0 3m+: 0-0
Track: LH: 0-2 RH: 0-0 Tight: 0-2 Gall: 0-0
Aids: Bl: 0-0 Vi: 0-0 Tstrap: 0-1
Best Rating:

Grenadier (IRE)

97 **80**

5-y-o b g Sadler's Wells (USA)-Sandhurst Goddess (Sandhurst Prince)
Miss L C Siddall (W R Muir 18/10) Podso Racing

Placings:00 **(4040)**
2001/02: 17^{0}F, 17^{0}GS

	Starts	1st	2nd	3rd	Win & Pl
Hurdles	2	0	0	0	
Career Total	**2**	**0**	**0**	**0**	

Going: Sf: 0-0 GS: 0-1 Gd: 0-0 GF: - Fm: 0-1
Distance: 2m/2m3: 0-2 2m4-2m7: 0-0 3m+: 0-0
Track: LH: 0-0 RH: 0-2 Tight: 0-2 Gall: 0-0
Aids: Bl: 0-0 Vi: 0-0 Tstrap: 0-1
Best Rating: 80 10/01 Tntn 2m1f firm Hdl

Gretton

91f

5-y-o b m Terimon-Gulsha (Glint Of Gold)
N A Twiston-Davies Mrs Marilyn Scudamore

Placings:*0* **(4679)**
2001/02: 17^{0}G

	Starts	1st	2nd	3rd	Win & Pl
NH Flat	1	0	0	0	
Career Total	**1**	**0**	**0**	**0**	

Going: Sf: 0-0 GS: 0-0 Gd: 0-1 GF: - Fm: 0-0
Distance: 2m/2m3: 0-1 2m4-2m7: 0-0 3m+: 0-0
Track: LH: 0-0 RH: 0-0 Tight: 0-0 Gall: 0-0
Aids: Bl: 0-0 Vi: 0-0 Tstrap: 0-0
Best Rating: 91 4/02 Aint 2m1f good NHF

Grey Abbey (IRE)

120 **165**

8-y-o gr g Nestor-Tacovaon (Avocat)
F P Murtagh Ken Roper,Elinor M Roper,Norman Furness

Placings:*50*/P0P11153/**4F62F11121-51F4P0314** **(4839)**
2001/02: 20^{5}G, 25^{1}GS, 26^{F}S, 20^{4}S, 25^{P}GS, 20^{0}HY, 26^{3}GS, 25^{1}G, 33^{4}G

	Starts	1st	2nd	3rd	Win & Pl
Chases	9	2	0	1	27252
Career Total	**29**	**9**	**2**	**2**	**65326**

165	4/02	Weth	3m1f	B(0-150)HCh	GD	£10962
154	11/01	Ayr	3m1f	C(0-135)HCh	G-S	£6812
145	4/01	Ayr	2m4f	A Ch	G-F	£15600
143	2/01	Kels	2m1f	D Ch	SFT	£3867
135	1/01	Ayr	2m	D Ch	G-S	£4134
138	1/01	Ayr	2m5f110y	D Ch	SFT	£4108
116	2/00	Newc	2m4f	F(0-90)HHdl	SFT	£1974
108	2/00	Newc	2m	F(0-100)HHdl	SFT	£1939
85	12/99	Ayr	2m	E(0-105)HHdl	HVY	£2654

Total win prize-money £52051

Going: Sf: 0-3 GS: 1-3 Gd: 1-3 GF: - Fm: 0-0
Distance: 2m/2m3: 0-0 2m4-2m7: 0-3 **3m+: 2-6**
Track: **LH: 2-9** RH: 0-0 Tight: 0-0 Gall: 0-2
Aids: Bl: 0-0 Vi: 0-0 **Tstrap: 1-2**
Best Rating: 165 4/02 Weth 3m1f good Ch

Useful novice chaser. A bold jumper, he is best when forcing the pace and seems to act on any ground. He stays beyond four miles and goes very well at Ayr.

Grey Expectations

100 **87**

7-y-o gr g Terimon-Flammable (IRE) (Prince Rupert (FR))
D Eddy (A Crook 15/6) Equiname Ltd

Placings:*4/10*3042U0/0P2505-6P**PP**046 **(3821)**
2001/02: 17^{6}G, 16^{P}GS, 21^{P}G, 24^{P}GS, 17^{0}S, 16^{4}S, 17^{6}S

	Starts	1st	2nd	3rd	Win & Pl
Hurdles	5	0	0	0	0
Chases	2	0	0	0	0
Career Total	**22**	**1**	**2**	**1**	**4208**

93	5/99	Prth	2m110y	H NHF	HVY	£1997

Total win prize-money £1998

Going: Sf: 0-3 GS: 0-2 Gd: 0-2 GF: - Fm: 0-0
Distance: 2m/2m3: 0-5 2m4-2m7: 0-1 3m+: 0-1
Track: LH: 0-4 RH: 0-3 Tight: 0-3 Gall: 0-1
Aids: Bl: 0-0 Vi: 0-0 Tstrap: 0-0
Best Rating: 94 10/00 Strf 2m110y gd-sft Hdl

Won a bumper in 1999 but yet to score over hurdles or fences.

Grey Finch

13-y-o gr g Nishapour (FR)-Swiftsand (Sharpen Up)
J A T De Giles J A T De Giles

Placings:*065P5/20500***U/P/P** **(0212)**
2001/02: 20^{P}F

	Starts	1st	2nd	3rd	Win & Pl
Hurdles	1	0	0	0	
Career Total	**13**	**0**	**1**	**0**	**636**

Going: Sf: 0-0 GS: 0-0 Gd: 0-0 GF: - Fm: 0-1
Distance: 2m/2m3: 0-0 2m4-2m7: 0-1 3m+: 0-0
Track: LH: 0-1 RH: 0-0 Tight: 0-1 Gall: 0-0
Aids: Bl: 0-0 Vi: 0-0 Tstrap: 0-0
Best Rating: 78 11/95 Folk 2m1f110y gd-fm Hdl

Grey Friars

8-y-o gr g Neltino-Queen Of The Nile (Hittite Glory)
Mrs L Williamson R A Hughes

Placings:*040*-PP **(2129)**
2001/02: 16^{P}S, 16^{P}GF

	Starts	1st	2nd	3rd	Win & Pl
Hurdles	2	0	0	0	0
Career Total	**5**	**0**	**0**	**0**	**0**

Going: Sf: 0-1 GS: 0-0 Gd: 0-0 GF: - Fm: 0-1
Distance: 2m/2m3: 0-2 2m4-2m7: 0-0 3m+: 0-0
Track: LH: 0-1 RH: 0-1 Tight: 0-0 Gall: 0-0
Aids: Bl: 0-0 Vi: 0-0 Tstrap: 0-0
Best Rating: 95 9/00 Worc 2m gd-fm NHF

Grey Leader

76 **34**

7-y-o gr g Baron Blakeney-Aingers Green (Nicky's Double)
D E Cantillon D H Gibbon

Placings:*00***PP0** **(3321)**
2001/02: 17^{0}GS, 16^{0}G, 24^{P}G, 23^{P}G, 24^{0}GS

	Starts	1st	2nd	3rd	Win & Pl
NH Flat	2	0	0	0	0
Chases	3	0	0	0	0
Career Total	**5**	**0**	**0**	**0**	

Going: Sf: 0-0 GS: 0-2 Gd: 0-3 GF: - Fm: 0-0
Distance: 2m/2m3: 0-2 2m4-2m7: 0-0 3m+: 0-3
Track: LH: 0-0 RH: 0-4 Tight: 0-1 Gall: 0-2
Aids: Bl: 0-0 Vi: 0-0 Tstrap: 0-0
Best Rating: 71 5/01 Folk 2m1f110y gd-sft NHF

Grey Shot

10-y-o gr g Sharrood (USA)-Optaria (Song)
I A Balding Exors Of The Late Robert Hitchins

Placings:121/1126100/1/10F-F **(3658)**
2001/02: 21^{F}S

	Starts	1st	2nd	3rd	Win & Pl
Chases	1	0	0	0	
Career Total	**15**	**7**	**2**	**0**	**98021**

161	1/01	Asct	2m3f110y	B HCh	G-S	£9860
147	9/99	Extr	2m1f	E Ch	G-S	£3517
150	2/99	Winc	2m	A Hdl	G-S	£19340
159	11/98	Chel	2m110y	B HHdl	G-S	£29654
159	11/98	Winc	2m	A HHdl	G-S	£13720
133	2/98	Asct	2m110y	D Hdl	GD	£3663
134	12/97	Tntn	2m1f	C Hdl	GD	£4039

Total win prize-money £83798

Going: Sf: 0-1 GS: 0-0 Gd: 0-0 GF: - Fm: 0-0
Distance: 2m/2m3: 0-0 2m4-2m7: 0-1 3m+: 0-0
Track: LH: 0-0 RH: 0-1 Tight: 0-0 Gall: 0-0
Aids: Bl: 0-0 Vi: 0-0 Tstrap: 0-0
Best Rating: 161 1/01 Asct 2m3f110y gd-sft Ch

A winner of two `Cup' races on the Flat, he has taken well to fences and, having won his first chase at Exeter in 1999, returned from a year off to score at Ascot in 2001, but disappointed on much softer ground at Huntingdon before taking a heavy fall at Sandown at the end of last term. He has won from behind, but seems happiest when bowling along in front, and will always be difficult to beat when winging around the likes of Wincanton. Stays two and a half miles. Acts on good to soft ground.

Grey Spirit

69 **53**

6-y-o gr g Terimon-Genie Spirit (Nishapour (FR))
P F Nicholls Hunt & Co (bournemouth) Ltd

Placings:*50* **(3150)**
2001/02: 17^{5}GS, 18^{0}G

	Starts	1st	2nd	3rd	Win & Pl
NH Flat	1	0	0	0	0
Hurdles	1	0	0	0	0
Career Total	**2**	**0**	**0**	**0**	**0**

Going: Sf: 0-0 GS: 0-1 Gd: 0-1 GF: - Fm: 0-0
Distance: 2m/2m3: 0-2 2m4-2m7: 0-0 3m+: 0-0
Track: LH: 0-2 RH: 0-0 Tight: 0-2 Gall: 0-0

Aids: Bl: 0-0 Vi: 0-0 Tstrap: 0-0
Best Rating: **86** 12/01 Bang 2m1f gd-sft NHF

Greycoat

91 **83**

4-y-o ch g Lion Cavern (USA)-It's Academic (Royal Academy (USA))
Jean-Rene Auvray (Mrs J R Ramsden 7/5) Lambourn Racing Limited

Placings:350U (4546)
2001/02: 16^{3}GF, 16^{5}GF, 17^{0}F, 16^{U}GF

	Starts	1st	2nd	3rd	Win & Pl
Hurdles	4	0	0	1	354
Career Total	**4**	**0**	**0**	**1**	**354**

Going: Sf: 0-0 GS: 0-0 Gd: 0-0 GF: - Fm: 0-4
Distance: 2m/2m3: 0-4 2m4-2m7: 0-0 3m+: 0-0
Track: LH: 0-1 RH: 0-3 Tight: 0-2 Gall: 0-1
Aids: Bl: 0-0 Vi: 0-0 Tstrap: 0-0
Best Rating: **83** 9/01 Plum 2m gd-fm Hdl

Greyfield (IRE)

102(85h) (100h)**118**

6-y-o b g Persian Bold-Noble Dust (USA) (Dust Commander (USA))
K Bishop Slabs And Lucan

Placings:531F5/354-024 (2410)
2001/02: 16^{0}GF, 19^{2}F, 19^{4}GS

	Starts	1st	2nd	3rd	Win & Pl
Hurdles	1	0	0	0	0
Chases	2	0	1	0	2224
Career Total	**11**	**1**	**1**	**2**	**11443**

120	3/00	Winc	2m	E Hdl	G-S	£2247

Total win prize-money £2247

Going: Sf: 0-0 GS: 0-1 Gd: 0-0 GF: - Fm: 0-2
Distance: 2m/2m3: 0-3 2m4-2m7: 0-0 3m+: 0-0
Track: LH: 0-1 RH: 0-2 Tight: 0-2 Gall: 0-0
Aids: Bl: 0-0 Vi: 0-0 Tstrap: 0-0
Best Rating: **136** 9/00 Chep 2m110y good Hdl

He was a useful juvenile in 1999/2000 and ran creditably in the face of stiff tasks last season. Raced around two miles, he has been running creditably back on the Flat and ran well when runner-up on his chasing debut.

Greyton (IRE)

99 **108**

9-y-o gr g Zaffaran (USA)-Rosy Posy (IRE) (Roselier (FR))
R Rowe Tim Clowes

Placings:352045/34154-2 (0373)
2001/02: 24^{2}GF

	Starts	1st	2nd	3rd	Win & Pl
Chases	1	0	1	0	1084
Career Total	**12**	**1**	**2**	**2**	**7541**

108	1/01	Winc	3m1f110y	E(0-115)HCh	SFT	£4173

Total win prize-money £4173

Going: Sf: 0-0 GS: 0-0 Gd: 0-0 GF: - Fm: 0-1
Distance: 2m/2m3: 0-0 2m4-2m7: 0-0 3m+: 0-1
Track: LH: 0-0 RH: 0-1 Tight: 0-0 Gall: 0-1
Aids: Bl: 0-0 Vi: 0-0 Tstrap: 0-0
Best Rating: **108** 5/01 Hntg 3m gd-fm Ch

Grilse Run (IRE)

(78h)

6-y-o b g Ilium-Miss Cynthia (Dawn Review)
C C Bealby Mrs Robert Bingley

Placings:060P-P3 (2672)
2001/02: 23^{P}G, 24^{3}G

	Starts	1st	2nd	3rd	Win & Pl
Chases	2	0	0	1	753
Career Total	**6**	**0**	**0**	**1**	**753**

Going: Sf: 0-0 GS: 0-0 Gd: 0-2 GF: - Fm: 0-0
Distance: 2m/2m3: 0-0 2m4-2m7: 0-0 3m+: 0-2
Track: LH: 0-1 RH: 0-1 Tight: 0-0 Gall: 0-1
Aids: Bl: 0-0 Vi: 0-0 Tstrap: 0-0
Best Rating: **81** 2/01 Towc 2m heavy Hdl

Grimaldi Lad (IRE)

96(56h) **112**

8-y-o b g Lord Americo-Carousel Zingira (Reesh)
A Crook A Saccomando

Placings:251556/P633P3412/211F51-4U5F (0803)
2001/02: 21^{4}GF, 25^{U}F, 20^{5}G, 24^{F}GF

	Starts	1st	2nd	3rd	Win & Pl
Chases	4	0	0	0	535
Career Total	**25**	**5**	**3**	**3**	**26077**

137	9/00	MRas	2m6f110y	C Ch	G-F	£6942
171	7/00	MRas	2m1f	D Ch	GD	£[illegible]
101	6/00	Prth	2m	D Ch	GD	£5512
99	3/00	Muss	2m4f	F(0-100)HHdl	G-F	£2632
92	9/98	Prth	2m110y	H NHF	GD	£1870

Total win prize-money £22309

Going: Sf: 0-0 GS: 0-0 Gd: 0-1 GF: - Fm: 0-3
Distance: 2m/2m3: 0-0 2m4-2m7: 0-2 3m+: 0-2
Track: LH: 0-3 RH: 0-1 Tight: 0-0 Gall: 0-0
Aids: Bl: 0-0 Vi: 0-0 Tstrap: 0-0
Best Rating: **137** 9/00 MRas 2m6f110y gd-fm Ch

Suited by a decent surface, he did well over fences in the summer of 2000. Stays two and three-quarter miles, acts on good and fast ground. All his wins have been on right-handed tracks.

Grimes

114(105h) (167h)**151**

9-y-o b g Reprimand-Diva Madonna (Chief Singer)
C Roche J P McManus

Placings:01021/10044/2/4532/114-51112232 (4676)
2001/02: 16^{5}G, 17^{1}G, 16^{1}G, 22^{1}GY, 16^{2}S, 16^{2}Y, 16^{3}S, 20^{2}G

	Starts	1st	2nd	3rd	Win & Pl
Hurdles	5	2	2	0	76803
Chases	3	1	1	1	54274
Career Total	**26**	**8**	**6**	**2**	**271894**

151	8/01	Gway	2m6f	HCh	G-Y	£49395
167	7/01	Tipp	2m	Hdl	GD	£22096
165	5/01	Klny	2m1f	HHdl	GD	£18346
167	5/00	Klny	2m1f	HHdl	GD	£13000
167	5/00	Punc	2m	Hdl	GD	£52800
146	10/97	Leop	2m	HHdl	G-Y	£8138
138	4/97	Punc	2m	Hdl	GD	£30693
118	12/96	Leop	2m	Hdl	YLD	£9974

Total win prize-money £204445

Going: Sf: 0-2 GS: 0-0 Gd: 2-4 GF: - Fm: 0-0
Distance: **2m/2m3: 2-6** 2m4-2m7: 1-2 3m+: 0-0
Track: LH: 0-1 RH: 0-2 Tight: 0-1 Gall: 0-0
Aids: Bl: 0-0 Vi: 0-0 Tstrap: 0-0
Best Rating: **167** 7/01 Tipp 2m good Hdl

A versatile and talented performer, he landed the Shell Champion Hurdle at Punchestown in May 2000. He won his first race over fences in August 2001 and remains open to improvement over the larger obstacles, but to run to his best he needs fast ground. Has won at distances from two miles to two miles six.

Griselina (IRE)

92(82c) (89c)**71**

7-y-o b m Mandalus-Thistletopper (Le Bavard (FR))
B G Powell Mrs Linda Goddard

Placings:005/64-UP4005PP (4657)
2001/02: 26^{U}GS, 24^{P}F, 21^{4}GS, 20^{0}GS, 24^{0}S, 20^{5}GS, 25^{P}G, 24^{P}G

	Starts	1st	2nd	3rd	Win & Pl
Hurdles	4	0	0	0	0
Chases	4	0	0	0	0
Career Total	**13**	**0**	**0**	**0**	**396**

Going: Sf: 0-1 GS: 0-4 Gd: 0-2 GF: - Fm: 0-1
Distance: 2m/2m3: 0-0 2m4-2m7: 0-3 3m+: 0-5
Track: LH: 0-2 RH: 0-5 Tight: 0-4 Gall: 0-2
Aids: Bl: 0-0 Vi: 0-1 Tstrap: 0-0
Best Rating: **89** 2/02 Ludl 2m4f gd-sft Ch

Only moderate form over hurdles and fences.

Grizzly Activewear (IRE)

109 **104**

8-y-o ch g Camden Town-Boro Cent (Little Buskins)
G M Moore (Eugene M O'Sullivan 12/5) Mrs Alurie O'Sullivan

Placings:0-00323110406 (3216)
2001/02: 16^{0}GF, 20^{0}G, 25^{3}GF, 24^{2}G, 22^{3}GS, 24^{1}G, 27^{1}GS, 24^{0}G, 27^{4}S, 24^{0}GF, 20^{6}GS

	Starts	1st	2nd	3rd	Win & Pl
Hurdles	11	2	1	2	7301
Career Total	**12**	**2**	**1**	**2**	**7301**

104	10/01	Sedg	3m3f110y	E Hdl	G-S	£2565
104	9/01	Prth	3m110y	E Hdl	GD	£2968

Total win prize-money £5534

Going: Sf: 0-1 GS: 1-3 Gd: 1-4 GF: - Fm: 0-3
Distance: 2m/2m3: 0-1 2m4-2m7: 0-3 **3m+: 2-7**
Track: LH: 1-7 RH: 1-3 **Tight: 1-6** Gall: 0-0
Aids: Bl: 0-0 Vi: 0-0 Tstrap: 0-0
Best Rating: **104** 10/01 Sedg 3m3f110y gd-sft Hdl

Modest staying hurdler. Stays three miles plus and is suited by good ground or slightly softer.

Grizzly Bear (IRE)

99 **100**

12-y-o b g Orchestra-Grilse (Raga Navarro (ITY))
R M Stronge G B Barlow

Placings:0061P/32/B11FP5/124B343/24P-56 (1859)
2001/02: 27^{5}G, 24^{6}S

	Starts	1st	2nd	3rd	Win & Pl
Chases	2	0	0	0	0
Career Total	**25**	**4**	**3**	**3**	**26317**

135	11/99	Uttx	3m2f	E(0-115)HCh	SFT	£4640
130	1/99	Ling	3m	F(0-105)HCh	HVY	£7295
121	1/99	Wwck	3m2f	E(0-115)HCh	SFT	£3353
92	3/97	Uttx	3m2f	E Ch	G-F	£2918

Total win prize-money £18206

Going: Sf: 0-1 GS: 0-0 Gd: 0-1 GF: - Fm: 0-0
Distance: 2m/2m3: 0-0 2m4-2m7: 0-0 3m+: 0-2
Track: LH: 0-2 RH: 0-0 Tight: 0-2 Gall: 0-0
Aids: Bl: 0-0 Vi: 0-0 Tstrap: 0-0
Best Rating: 135 11/99 Uttx 3m2f soft Ch

Fair handicap chaser at three miles on soft/heavy ground.

Grizzly Golfwear (IRE)

101(50h) **66**

8-y-o b g Commanche Run-Dunwellan (Tekoah)
K R Pearce Keith R Pearce

Placings:FP/5P500-**P06** **(0681)**
2001/02: 26^{P}GF, 25^{0}G, 26^{0}G

	Starts	1st	2nd	3rd	Win & Pl
Chases	3	0	0	0	0
Career Total	**10**	**0**	**0**	**0**	**0**

Going: Sf: 0-0 GS: 0-0 Gd: 0-2 GF: - Fm: 0-1
Distance: 2m/2m3: 0-0 2m4-2m7: 0-0 3m+: 0-3
Track: LH: 0-1 RH: 0-1 Tight: 0-2 Gall: 0-0
Aids: Bl: 0-0 Vi: 0-0 Tstrap: 0-0
Best Rating: 84 10/00 MRas 2m3f110y good Hdl

Groovy Grace (IRE)

87 **70**

6-y-o ch m Glacial Storm (USA)-Winnie Wumpkins (IRE) (Roselier (FR))
G L Moore Paul Stamp

Placings:*0-0* **(0365)**
2001/02: 19^{0}GF

	Starts	1st	2nd	3rd	Win & Pl
Hurdles	1	0	0	0	
Career Total	**2**	**0**	**0**	**0**	

Going: Sf: 0-0 GS: 0-0 Gd: 0-0 GF: - Fm: 0-1
Distance: 2m/2m3: 0-0 2m4-2m7: 0-1 3m+: 0-0
Track: LH: 0-1 RH: 0-0 Tight: 0-1 Gall: 0-0
Aids: Bl: 0-0 Vi: 0-0 Tstrap: 0-0
Best Rating: 70 5/01 Ling 2m3f110y gd-fm Hdl

Grosvenor Flyer (IRE)

6-y-o ch g Dolphin Street (FR)-Kilcsem Eile (IRE) (Commanche Run)
T D McCarthy A D Spence

Placings:505/P **(0107)**
2001/02: 22^{P}GF

	Starts	1st	2nd	3rd	Win & Pl
Hurdles	1	0	0	0	
Career Total	**4**	**0**	**0**	**0**	**0**

Going: Sf: 0-0 GS: 0-0 Gd: 0-0 GF: - Fm: 0-1
Distance: 2m/2m3: 0-0 2m4-2m7: 0-1 3m+: 0-0
Track: LH: 0-1 RH: 0-0 Tight: 0-1 Gall: 0-0
Aids: Bl: 0-1 Vi: 0-0 Tstrap: 0-0
Best Rating: 98 11/99 Newb 2m110y good Hdl

Ground Ball (IRE)

109 **124**

5-y-o b/br g Bob's Return (IRE)-Bettyhill (Ardross)
C F Swan J P McManus

Placings:*1-42105* **(4629a)**
2001/02: 20^{4}Y, 16^{2}Y, 16^{1}YS, 16^{0}GS, 18^{5}GY

	Starts	1st	2nd	3rd	Win & Pl
Hurdles	5	1	1	0	10138
Career Total	**6**	**2**	**1**	**0**	**14312**

121	1/02	Navn	2m	Hdl	Y-S	£8009
123	4/01	Cork	2m	NHF	Y-S	£4173

Total win prize-money £12182

Going: Sf: 0-0 GS: 0-1 Gd: 0-0 GF: - Fm: 0-0
Distance: **2m/2m3: 1-4** 2m4-2m7: 0-1 3m+: 0-0
Track: **LH: 1-2** RH: 0-3 Tight: 0-0 Gall: 0-0
Aids: Bl: 0-0 Vi: 0-0 Tstrap: 0-0
Best Rating: 124 2/02 Kemp 2m gd-sft Hdl

Got off the mark on his debut in a Cork bumper, before a couple of good efforts in maiden hurdle events. Scored over hurdles at Navan in January 2002. Well held in Kempton Grade Two. Effective over two miles, he appreciates cut in the ground.

Group One's Hope

6-y-o b m Absalom-Hopeful Waters (Forlorn River)
A W Carroll Group 1 Racing (1994) Ltd

Placings:*0-0* **(2215)**
2001/02: 17^{0}G

	Starts	1st	2nd	3rd	Win & Pl
NH Flat	1	0	0	0	
Career Total	**2**	**0**	**0**	**0**	

Going: Sf: 0-0 GS: 0-0 Gd: 0-1 GF: - Fm: 0-0
Distance: 2m/2m3: 0-1 2m4-2m7: 0-0 3m+: 0-0
Track: LH: 0-0 RH: 0-1 Tight: 0-0 Gall: 0-0
Aids: Bl: 0-0 Vi: 0-0 Tstrap: 0-0
Best Rating:

Grouse Hall

90

8-y-o ch g Primitive Rising (USA)-Em-Kay-Em (Slim Jim)
G M Moore P E Sowerby

Placings:*10*/6U0026/4-4 **(1719)**
2001/02: 23^{4}G

	Starts	1st	2nd	3rd	Win & Pl
Chases	1	0	0	0	273
Career Total	**10**	**1**	**1**	**0**	**2421**

103	3/99	Ayr	2m	H NHF	SFT	£1346

Total win prize-money £1347

Going: Sf: 0-0 GS: 0-0 Gd: 0-1 GF: - Fm: 0-0
Distance: 2m/2m3: 0-0 2m4-2m7: 0-0 3m+: 0-1
Track: LH: 0-0 RH: 0-0 Tight: 0-0 Gall: 0-0
Aids: Bl: 0-0 Vi: 0-0 Tstrap: 0-0
Best Rating: 103 3/99 Ayr 2m soft NHF

Grove Dancer

71 **34**

4-y-o b f Reprimand-Brisighella (IRE) (Al Hareb (USA))
B G Powell P H Betts

Placings:0P **(2209)**
2001/02: 16^{0}G, 17^{P}G

	Starts	1st	2nd	3rd	Win & Pl
Hurdles	2	0	0	0	
Career Total	**2**	**0**	**0**	**0**	

Going: Sf: 0-0 GS: 0-0 Gd: 0-2 GF: - Fm: 0-0
Distance: 2m/2m3: 0-2 2m4-2m7: 0-0 3m+: 0-0
Track: LH: 0-1 RH: 0-1 Tight: 0-0 Gall: 0-0
Aids: Bl: 0-0 Vi: 0-0 Tstrap: 0-0
Best Rating: 34 11/01 Wwck 2m good Hdl

Grove House

83 **67**

6-y-o b g Hatim (USA)-Camden Grove (Uncle Pokey)
A Scott Andy Scott

Placings:*3420* **(4860)**
2001/02: 16^{3}G, 17^{4}GS, 16^{2}GF, 16^{0}G

	Starts	1st	2nd	3rd	Win & Pl
NH Flat	4	0	1	1	1024
Career Total	**4**	**0**	**1**	**1**	**1024**

Going: Sf: 0-0 GS: 0-1 Gd: 0-2 GF: - Fm: 0-1
Distance: 2m/2m3: 0-4 2m4-2m7: 0-0 3m+: 0-0
Track: LH: 0-1 RH: 0-1 Tight: 0-1 Gall: 0-0
Aids: Bl: 0-0 Vi: 0-0 Tstrap: 0-0
Best Rating: 103 4/02 Hexm 2m110y gd-fm NHF

Fair form in bumpers and hurdles, stays three miles and acts on a fast surface.

Grumpy Stumpy

92(91h) (81h)**106**

7-y-o ch g Gunner B-Moaning Jenny (Privy Seal)
N A Twiston-Davies The 'Yes' - 'No' - Wait'....Sorries

Placings:*23*-36F33 **(2012)**
2001/02: 26^{3}G, 24^{6}G, 16^{F}G, 25^{3}G, 22^{3}S

	Starts	1st	2nd	3rd	Win & Pl
Hurdles	2	0	0	1	400
Chases	3	0	0	2	930
Career Total	**7**	**0**	**1**	**4**	**2440**

Going: Sf: 0-1 GS: 0-0 Gd: 0-4 GF: - Fm: 0-0
Distance: 2m/2m3: 0-1 2m4-2m7: 0-1 3m+: 0-3
Track: LH: 0-1 RH: 0-4 Tight: 0-0 Gall: 0-0
Aids: Bl: 0-0 Vi: 0-0 Tstrap: 0-0
Best Rating: 112 3/01 Newb 2m110y heavy NHF

Guard A Dream (IRE)

68 **58**

8-y-o ch g Durgam (USA)-Adarenna (FR) (Mill Reef (USA))
B G Powell Miss K Mundy

Placings:5-P4 **(0490)**
2001/02: 19^{P}G, 27^{4}GF

	Starts	1st	2nd	3rd	Win & Pl
Hurdles	2	0	0	0	0
Career Total	**3**	**0**	**0**	**0**	**0**

Going: Sf: 0-0 GS: 0-0 Gd: 0-1 GF: - Fm: 0-1
Distance: 2m/2m3: 0-0 2m4-2m7: 0-1 3m+: 0-1
Track: LH: 0-0 RH: 0-1 Tight: 0-1 Gall: 0-0
Aids: Bl: 0-1 Vi: 0-0 Tstrap: 0-0

Best Rating: 58 5/01 Font 3m3f gd-fm Hdl

Guard Duty

110 131

5-y-o b g Deploy-Hymne D'Amour (USA) (Dixieland Band (USA))

M C Pipe Neil Edwards And Malcolm Jones

Placings:211114-2000 (4667)

2001/02: 22^{2}HY, 24^{0}G, 25^{0}GS, 20^{0}G

	Starts	1st	2nd	3rd	Win & Pl
Hurdles	4	0	1	0	1656
Career Total	**10**	**4**	**2**	**0**	**14754**

131	2/01	Wwck	2m5f	E(0-115)HHdl	SFT	£3818
125	2/01	Tntn	2m3f110y	F(0-110)HHdl	HVY	£3540
134	1/01	Tntn	2m3f110y	F(0-100)HHdl	HVY	£2381
112	1/01	Tntn	2m1f	G Hdl	SFT	£1631

Total win prize-money £11372

Going: Sf: 0-1 GS: 0-1 Gd: 0-2 GF: - Fm: 0-0
Distance: 2m/2m3: 0-0 2m4-2m7: 0-2 3m+: 0-2
Track: LH: 0-3 RH: 0-0 Tight: 0-2 Gall: 0-1
Aids: Bl: 0-0 Vi: 0-0 Tstrap: 0-4
Best Rating: **134** 1/01 Tntn 2m3f110y heavy Hdl

A winner on the Flat and over hurdles, he acts well on a soft surface and goes well over two miles to two miles five furlongs, but stays three miles.

Gudlage (USA)

92(103h) (101h)111

6-y-o b g Gulch (USA)-Triple Kiss (Shareef Dancer (USA))

M W Easterby Lord Daresbury

Placings:0-1P3003 (4899)

2001/02: 16^{1}G, 20^{P}GS, 16^{3}G, 16^{0}GS, 16^{0}GS, 16^{3}G

	Starts	1st	2nd	3rd	Win & Pl
Hurdles	5	1	0	1	3595
Chases	1	0	0	1	1096
Career Total	**7**	**1**	**0**	**2**	**4691**

96	10/01	Aint	2m110y	E Hdl	GD	£3248

Total win prize-money £3248

Going: Sf: 0-0 GS: 0-3 Gd: 1-3 GF: - Fm: 0-0
Distance: **2m/2m3: 1-5** 2m4-2m7: 0-1 3m+: 0-0
Track: **LH: 1-5** RH: 0-1 **Tight: 1-3** Gall: 0-2
Aids: Bl: 0-0 Vi: 0-0 **Tstrap: 1-6**
Best Rating: **111** 4/02 Prth 2m good Ch

Had shown little over hurdles until getting off the mark at Aintree in October 2001. Best over two miles. Usually tongue tied.

Gue Au Loup (FR)

106 130

8-y-o gr g Royal Charter (FR)-Arche D'Alliance (FR) (Pamponi (FR))

H D Daly Mr & Mrs M P Wiggin

Placings:2552/F5/2-12 (0424)

2001/02: 17^{1}GS, 20^{2}G

	Starts	1st	2nd	3rd	Win & Pl
Chases	2	1	1	0	5521
Career Total	**9**	**1**	**4**	**0**	**14158**

119	5/01	Bang	2m1f110y	F(0-100)HCh	G-S	£4485

Total win prize-money £4485

Going: Sf: 0-0 GS: 1-1 Gd: 0-1 GF: - Fm: 0-0
Distance: **2m/2m3: 1-1** 2m4-2m7: 0-1 3m+: 0-0
Track: **LH: 1-2** RH: 0-0 **Tight: 1-2** Gall: 0-0
Aids: Bl: 0-0 Vi: 0-0 Tstrap: 0-0
Best Rating: **130** 5/01 Bang 2m4f110y good Ch

Ex-French recruit. Started off in novice chases in this country, then went pointing successfully before winning a novice event at Bangor in April 2001. Suited by two and a half miles. Acts on most ground.

Guid Willie Waught (IRE)

109(103h) (85h)112+

7-y-o ch g Montelimar (USA)-Drumdeels Star (IRE) (Le Bavard (FR))

J R Adam J W Hazeldine

Placings:5506-32604654 (4895)

2001/02: 16^{3}GF, 17^{2}GF, 17^{6}GS, 16^{0}G, 16^{4}G, 16^{6}GF, 17^{5}G, 20^{4}G

	Starts	1st	2nd	3rd	Win & Pl
Hurdles	4	0	1	1	1288
Chases	4	0	0	0	771
Career Total	**12**	**0**	**1**	**1**	**2058**

Going: Sf: 0-0 GS: 0-1 Gd: 0-4 GF: - Fm: 0-3
Distance: 2m/2m3: 0-7 2m4-2m7: 0-1 3m+: 0-0
Track: LH: 0-3 RH: 0-4 Tight: 0-4 Gall: 0-0
Aids: Bl: 0-0 Vi: 0-0 Tstrap: 0-0
Best Rating: **92** 4/02 Prth 2m4f110y good Ch

Fair novice chaser, suited by fast ground and two and a half miles.

Guido (IRE)

90 125

11-y-o b g Supreme Leader-Cool Amanda (Prince Hansel)

Miss Venetia Williams P Tompsett

Placings:*012*/0533/311/F53311-3 (1910)

2001/02: 17^{3}S

	Starts	1st	2nd	3rd	Win & Pl
Chases	1	0	0	1	935
Career Total	**17**	**5**	**1**	**6**	**24558**

125	4/01	Prth	2m4f110y	D(0-115)HCh	HVY	£7566
125	4/01	Hntg	2m110y	D(0-115)HCh	SFT	£4186
115	11/99	Nowb	2m3f	D(0-110)HHdl	G-F	£5147
114	5/99	Ctml	2m1f110y	D Hdl	G-F	£3009
107	12/96	Folk	2m1f110y	H NHF	G-S	£1322

Total win prize-money £21230

Going: Sf: 0-1 GS: 0-0 Gd: 0-0 GF: - Fm: 0-0
Distance: 2m/2m3: 0-1 2m4-2m7: 0-0 3m+: 0-0
Track: LH: 0-1 RH: 0-0 Tight: 0-1 Gall: 0-0
Aids: Bl: 0-0 Vi: 0-0 Tstrap: 0-0
Best Rating: **125** 4/01 Prth 2m4f110y heavy Ch

Three times a winner over hurdles, he progressed well over fences in the early part of 2001 and ended up with victories at Huntingdon and Perth. Stays two and a half miles and goes very well on soft ground.

Guilder

99 121

8-y-o b g Groom Dancer (USA)-Guillem (USA) (Nijinsky (CAN))

P R Webber Economic Security

Placings:5222/13P51/**3P52F53/111UP0-3240** (1766)

2001/02: 17^{3}GS, 20^{2}GF, 23^{4}GF, 20^{0}S

	Starts	1st	2nd	3rd	Win & Pl
Chases	4	0	1	1	2560
Career Total	**26**	**5**	**5**	**4**	**29462**

131	11/00	Plum	2m4f	D(0-125)HCh	SFT	£5145
113	10/00	Towc	2m110y	D(0-125)HCh	GD	£3718
125	6/00	Worc	2m	E Ch	G-F	£3029
115	2/99	Bang	2m1f	E Hdl	GD	£2808
110	10/98	Bang	2m1f	E Hdl	GD	£2284

Total win prize-money £16985

Going: Sf: 0-1 GS: 0-1 Gd: 0-0 GF: - Fm: 0-2
Distance: 2m/2m3: 0-1 2m4-2m7: 0-2 3m+: 0-1
Track: LH: 0-2 RH: 0-1 Tight: 0-2 Gall: 0-0
Aids: Bl: 0-0 Vi: 0-0 Tstrap: 0-0
Best Rating: **131** 11/00 Plum 2m4f heavy Ch

Has won over hurdles and fences, but last win came in 2000.

Guilsborough Gorse

108 111

7-y-o b g Past Glories-Buckby Folly (Netherkelly)

T D Walford Mrs E C York

Placings:32P3-525F31 (4868)

2001/02: 20^{5}S, 23^{2}G, 25^{5}G, 24^{F}GS, 25^{3}G, 20^{1}GF

	Starts	1st	2nd	3rd	Win & Pl
Chases	6	1	1	1	5360
Career Total	**10**	**1**	**2**	**3**	**7026**

106	4/02	Weth	2m4f110y	E Ch	G-F	£3503

Total win prize-money £3504

Going: Sf: 0-1 GS: 0-1 Gd: 0-3 GF: - Fm: 1-1
Distance: 2m/2m3: 0-0 **2m4-2m7: 1-2** 3m+: 0-4
Track: **LH: 1-4** RH: 0-1 Tight: 0-2 Gall: 0-1
Aids: Bl: 0-0 Vi: 0-0 Tstrap: 0-0
Best Rating: **106** 4/02 Weth 2m4f110y gd-fm Ch

Winner of a point-to-point in Febuary 2000, he has shown moderate form over fences and eventually won under Rules in a modest event at Wetherby in April 2002. Acts well with cut in the ground and runs over two miles four furlongs to three miles two furlongs.

Guilt Of A Sinner (IRE)

(97h) (109h)

9-y-o b g Spanish Place (USA)-Riseaway (Raise You Ten)

Miss Venetia Williams Mrs Gill Harrison

Placings:055/P215-U (1851)

2001/02: 25^{U}G

	Starts	1st	2nd	3rd	Win & Pl
Chases	1	0	0	0	
Career Total	**8**	**1**	**1**	**0**	**4830**

109	4/01	Extr	2m6f110y	D(0-120)HHdl	G-S	£3705

Total win prize-money £3705

Going: Sf: 0-0 GS: 0-0 Gd: 0-1 GF: - Fm: 0-0
Distance: 2m/2m3: 0-0 2m4-2m7: 0-0 3m+: 0-1
Track: LH: 0-0 RH: 0-1 Tight: 0-0 Gall: 0-0
Aids: Bl: 0-0 Vi: 0-0 Tstrap: 0-0
Best Rating: **109** 4/01 Extr 2m6f110y gd-sft Hdl

Guilty Suspect

58 28

5-y-o b m Reprimand-Island Desert (IRE) (Green Desert (USA))

Mrs S J Smith Mrs S Smith

Placings:0P0 (1409)

2001/02: 16^{0}GF, 16^{P}GF, 16^{0}GF

	Starts	1st	2nd	3rd	Win & Pl

	Starts	1st	2nd	3rd	Win & Pl
Hurdles	3	0	0	0	
Career Total	**3**	**0**	**0**	**0**	

Going: Sf: 0-0 GS: 0-0 Gd: 0-0 GF: - Fm: 0-3
Distance: 2m/2m3: 0-3 2m4-2m7: 0-0 3m+: 0-0
Track: LH: 0-3 RH: 0-0 Tight: 0-1 Gall: 0-0
Aids: Bl: 0-0 Vi: 0-0 Tstrap: 0-0
Best Rating: 28 8/01 Worc 2m gd-fm Hdl

Gulch King (USA)

62 **57**

4-y-o b g Gulch (USA)-Crockadore (USA) (Nijinsky (CAN))
G L Moore (D K Weld 8/10) Paul Chapman

Placings:0P0 **(3751)**
2001/02: 16^{0}GS, 18^{P}S, 16^{0}HY

	Starts	1st	2nd	3rd	Win & Pl
Hurdles	3	0	0	0	
Career Total	**3**	**0**	**0**	**0**	

Going: Sf: 0-2 GS: 0-1 Gd: 0-0 GF: - Fm: 0-0
Distance: 2m/2m3: 0-3 2m4-2m7: 0-0 3m+: 0-0
Track: LH: 0-2 RH: 0-1 Tight: 0-1 Gall: 0-1
Aids: Bl: 0-0 Vi: 0-0 Tstrap: 0-0
Best Rating: 57 2/02 Sand 2m110y heavy Hdl

Gulshan

113(112h) **136**

8-y-o b m Batshoof-Gulsha (Glint Of Gold)
N A Twiston-Davies Mrs J K Powell

Placings:*3602*/54033513/0UF3-1104222635 **(4192)**
2001/02: 19^{1}G, 20^{1}GF, 24^{0}GF, 20^{4}GS, 20^{2}G, 20^{2}G, 20^{2}G, 19^{6}G, 20^{3}GS, 24^{5}GS

	Starts	1st	2nd	3rd	Win & Pl
Chases	10	2	3	1	38783
Career Total	**26**	**3**	**4**	**6**	**65472**

131	5/01	Prth	2m4f110y	D Ch	G-F	£10920
136	5/01	Extr	2m3f110y	A HCh	GD	£13585
125	3/00	Newb	2m5f	C HHdl	G-F	£17290

Total win prize-money £41795

Going: Sf: 0-0 GS: 0-3 Gd: 1-5 GF: - Fm: 1-2
Distance: 2m/2m3: 0-0 **2m4-2m7: 2-8** 3m+: 0-2
Track: LH: 0-4 **RH: 2-5** Tight: 0-1 Gall: 0-3
Aids: Bl: 0-0 Vi: 0-0 **Tstrap: 2-10**
Best Rating: 136 11/01 Chel 2m4f110y good Ch

A winner over hurdles and fences, she had the misfortune to come up against some very smart young chasers towards the end of 2001. She is a front-runner and does not want the ground too soft. Regularly wears a tongue strap. Best at around two and a half miles.

Gumair (USA)

75 **35**

9-y-o ch g Summer Squall (USA)-Finisterre (AUS) (Biscay (AUS))
A J K Dunn A J K Dunn

Placings:C663/F3P/0132-0P **(0979)**
2001/02: 20^{0}GF, 27^{P}G

	Starts	1st	2nd	3rd	Win & Pl
Hurdles	2	0	0	0	
Career Total	**13**	**1**	**1**	**3**	**5153**

98	8/00	Strf	2m6f110y	D Hdl	G-F	£3233

Total win prize-money £3234

Going: Sf: 0-0 GS: 0-0 Gd: 0-1 GF: - Fm: 0-1
Distance: 2m/2m3: 0-0 2m4-2m7: 0-1 3m+: 0-1
Track: LH: 0-2 RH: 0-0 Tight: 0-1 Gall: 0-0
Aids: Bl: 0-0 Vi: 0-0 Tstrap: 0-0
Best Rating: 98 8/00 Strf 2m6f110y gd-fm Hdl

Gumley Gale

114 **121**

7-y-o b g Greensmith-Clodaigh Gale (Strong Gale)
K Bishop Portcullis Racing

Placings:*34*/0-2631F512 **(2788)**
2001/02: 16^{2}GF, 16^{6}GF, 17^{3}GF, 20^{1}S, 19^{F}G, 19^{5}GF, 22^{1}G, 20^{2}G

	Starts	1st	2nd	3rd	Win & Pl
Hurdles	8	2	2	1	10245
Career Total	**11**	**2**	**2**	**2**	**10449**

121	11/01	NAbb	2m6f	D(0-125)HHdl	GD	£3267
110	7/01	Worc	2m4f	E(0-115)HHdl	SFT	£3510

Total win prize-money £6778

Going: Sf: 1-1 GS: 0-0 Gd: 1-3 GF: - Fm: 0-4
Distance: 2m/2m3: 0-4 **2m4-2m7: 2-4** 3m+: 0-0
Track: **LH: 2-4** RH: 0-4 **Tight: 1-3** Gall: 0-0
Aids: Bl: 0-0 Vi: 0-0 Tstrap: 0-0
Best Rating: 121 11/01 NAbb 2m6f good Hdl

Fair handicap hurdler, handles any ground and stays two miles six.

Gun Hill (IRE)

37

5-y-o b g Ridgewood Ben-Lils Fairy (Fairy King (USA))
Mrs S J Smith (M C Chapman 4/6) Reg Racing

Placings:*0*-0 **(1136)**
2001/02: 16^{0}GF

	Starts	1st	2nd	3rd	Win & Pl
Hurdles	1	0	0	0	
Career Total	**2**	**0**	**0**	**0**	

Going: Sf: 0-0 GS: 0-0 Gd: 0-0 GF: - Fm: 0-1
Distance: 2m/2m3: 0-1 2m4-2m7: 0-0 3m+: 0-0
Track: LH: 0-1 RH: 0-0 Tight: 0-0 Gall: 0-0
Aids: Bl: 0-0 Vi: 0-0 Tstrap: 0-0
Best Rating:

Gun Shot

105 **99**

7-y-o ch m Gunner B-Real Beauty (Kinglet)
N M Babbage B & M Babbage & Co Ltd

Placings:*002*/6P0-006113102 **(4108)**
2001/02: 24^{0}G, 20^{0}GF, 27^{6}GF, 24^{1}GF, 24^{1}GF, 22^{3}GF, 21^{1}S, 24^{0}HY, 24^{2}S

	Starts	1st	2nd	3rd	Win & Pl
Hurdles	9	3	1	1	14678
Career Total	**15**	**3**	**2**	**1**	**15494**

99	11/01	Towc	2m5f	D(0-125)HHdl	SFT	£6994
99	8/01	MRas	3m	D Hdl	G-F	£4241
89	7/01	Sthl	3m110y	F(0-90)HHdl	G-F	£2296

Total win prize-money £13531

Going: Sf: 1-3 GS: 0-0 Gd: 0-1 GF: - Fm: 2-5
Distance: 2m/2m3: 0-0 2m4-2m7: 1-3 **3m+: 2-6**
Track: LH: 1-5 **RH: 2-4 Tight: 2-4** Gall: 0-0
Aids: Bl: 0-0 Vi: 0-0 Tstrap: 0-0
Best Rating: 99 3/02 Towc 3m soft Hdl

Fair handicap hurdler. She stays well and landed a brace of novice hurdles in the summer.

Gun'n Roses II (FR)

107 **153**

8-y-o gr g Royal Charter (FR)-Offenbach Ii (FR) (Ermitage (FR))
M C Pipe Mrs H J Clarke

Placings:11P32/12P0/3P/1P11P-3F516F **(4677)**
2001/02: 24^{3}G, 19^{F}S, 20^{5}S, 19^{1}S, 17^{6}S, 36^{F}G

	Starts	1st	2nd	3rd	Win & Pl
Chases	6	1	0	1	7721
Career Total	**22**	**7**	**2**	**3**	**51955**

153	1/02	Donc	2m3f110y	C(0-130)HCh	SFT	£6376
144	3/01	Hayd	2m6f	D Ch	HVY	£5671
155	2/01	Wwck	2m4f110y	C(0-130)HCh	SFT	£6695
148	12/00	Chep	2m3f110y	D(0-125)HCh	SFT	£6776
116	5/98	Uttx	2m	E Hdl	G-S	£2263
	1/98	Pau	2m2f	Hdl	SFT	£6061
	12/97	Pau	2m110y	Hdl	VS	£6734

Total win prize-money £40578

Going: Sf: 1-4 GS: 0-0 Gd: 0-2 GF: - Fm: 0-0
Distance: 2m/2m3: 0-1 **2m4-2m7: 1-3** 3m+: 0-2
Track: **LH: 1-6** RH: 0-0 Tight: 0-1 **Gall: 1-3**
Aids: Bl: 0-0 Vi: 0-0 Tstrap: 0-0
Best Rating: 155 2/01 Wwck 2m4f110y soft Ch

Formerly with Micky Hammond, he did well for the Pipe yard in 2000/2001, winning at Chepstow, Warwick and Haydock. He had looked held since then until returning to form at Doncaster in January 2002, winning a competitive handicap chase. Suited by around two and a half to two and three-quarter miles and soft ground, disappointed when dropped to two miles.

Gunner B Special

101 **86**

9-y-o ch g Gunner B-Sola Mia (Tolomeo)
R Lee (D Burchell 10/11) The Eagle Racing Partnership

Placings:04P/0400/P-0102566 **(4268)**
2001/02: 21^{0}GS, 16^{1}S, 20^{0}G, 17^{2}GS, 16^{5}GS, 16^{6}GS, 16^{6}S

	Starts	1st	2nd	3rd	Win & Pl
Chases	7	1	1	0	3721
Career Total	**15**	**1**	**1**	**0**	**3721**

83	7/01	Worc	2m	F(0-95)HCh	SFT	£2756

Total win prize-money £2756

Going: Sf: 1-2 GS: 0-4 Gd: 0-1 GF: - Fm: 0-0
Distance: **2m/2m3: 1-5** 2m4-2m7: 0-2 3m+: 0-0
Track: **LH: 1-6** RH: 0-1 Tight: 0-3 Gall: 0-0
Aids: Bl: 0-0 Vi: 0-0 Tstrap: 0-1
Best Rating: 85 9/01 Plum 2m1f gd-sft Ch

Fair novice chaser, suited by easy ground and two miles. Good efforts given those conditions in the summer of 2001.

Gunner Boon

80 **66**

12-y-o b g Gunner B-Miss Boon (Road House Ii)
D Brace David Brace

Placings:U/3/6P-00P3 **(1040)**
2001/02: 16^{0}G, 22^{0}G, 24^{P}GF, 23^{3}GF

	Starts	1st	2nd	3rd	Win & Pl
Chases	4	0	0	1	643
Career Total	**8**	**0**	**0**	**2**	**977**

Going: Sf: 0-0 GS: 0-0 Gd: 0-2 GF: - Fm: 0-2
Distance: 2m/2m3: 0-1 2m4-2m7: 0-2 3m+: 0-1
Track: LH: 0-3 RH: 0-1 Tight: 0-2 Gall: 0-0
Aids: Bl: 0-1 Vi: 0-0 Tstrap: 0-0
Best Rating: 101 3/00 Leic 2m4f110y gd-sft Ch

Gunner Marc

92 **91**

8-y-o b m Gunner B-Pugilistic (Hard Fought)
Miss Lucinda V Russell Masons Arms Racing Club

Placings: *40145/52F523F/P*36F31PP-0P6P (4877)
2001/02: 19^{0}G, 24^{P}GF, 20^{6}S, 24^{P}G

	Starts	1st	2nd	3rd	Win & Pl
Hurdles	2	0	0	0	0
Chases	2	0	0	0	0
Career Total	24	2	2	3	8641

109	2/01	Kels	2m6f110y	D Ch	SFT	£3802
89	2/99	Muss	2m	E Hdl	GD	£2056

Total win prize-money £5859

Going: Sf: 0-1 GS: 0-0 Gd: 0-2 GF: - Fm: 0-1
Distance: 2m/2m3: 0-0 2m4-2m7: 0-2 3m+: 0-2
Track: LH: 0-1 RH: 0-3 Tight: 0-0 Gall: 0-0
Aids: Bl: 0-0 Vi: 0-0 Tstrap: 0-0
Best Rating: 115 12/00 Hntg 2m4f110y soft Ch

Gunner Welburn

10-y-o ch g Gunner B-Vedra (IRE) (Carlingford Castle)
Mrs J A Saunders (Mrs Caroline Bailey 14/3) W A Ritson

Placings: 1/111/F121-5122 (4650)
2001/02: 26^{5}G, 22^{1}HY, 26^{2}G, 21^{2}G

	Starts	1st	2nd	3rd	Win & Pl
Chases	4	1	2	0	21550
Career Total	12	7	3	0	58479

129	2/02	Hayd	2m6f	H Ch	HVY	£6890
154	4/01	Aint	2m5f110y	B Ch	SFT	£18460
150	2/01	Hayd	3m	H Ch	HVY	£6857
138	4/00	Bang	3m110y	H Ch	G-S	£1715
138	2/00	Font	3m2f110y	H Ch	SFT	£3591
120	2/00	Wwck	3m1f110y	H Ch	GD	£1270
111	4/99	Chel	3m1f110y	H Ch	G-S	£2775

Total win prize-money £41560

Going: Sf: 1-1 GS: 0-0 Gd: 0-3 GF: - Fm: 0-0
Distance: 2m/2m3: 0-0 **2m4-2m7: 1-2** 3m+: 0-2
Track: LH: 0-2 RH: 0-0 Tight: 0-1 Gall: 0-1
Aids: Bl: 0-0 Vi: 0-0 Tstrap: 0-0
Best Rating: 154 4/01 Aint 2m5f110y soft Ch

A top hunter, put in a superb round of jumping under Julian Pritchard to beat stablemate Secret Bay in the Martell Fox Hunters' Chase at Aintree in 2001. He revels in the mud. Found only Last Option too good in the Foxhunters' at Cheltenham 2002 and was then runner-up at Aintree.

Gunnerbe Posh

80(92h) (84h)**56**

8-y-o ch g Rakaposhi King-Triggered (Gunner B)
Noel T Chance Mrs S Maxse & J Maxse

Placings: *23/P*00240 (3649)
2001/02: 19^{P}GS, 16^{0}G, 19^{0}G, 19^{2}GS, 20^{4}GS, 20^{0}S

	Starts	1st	2nd	3rd	Win & Pl
Hurdles	5	0	1	0	704
Chases	1	0	0	0	0
Career Total	8	0	2	1	1407

Going: Sf: 0-1 GS: 0-3 Gd: 0-2 GF: - Fm: 0-0
Distance: 2m/2m3: 0-3 2m4-2m7: 0-3 3m+: 0-0
Track: LH: 0-1 RH: 0-5 Tight: 0-1 Gall: 0-3
Aids: Bl: 0-0 Vi: 0-0 Tstrap: 0-0
Best Rating: 105 3/99 Newb 2m110y soft NHF

Gunnerblong

108(87h) **135**

9-y-o ch g Gunner B-At Long Last (John French)
D R Gandolfo Mrs John Lee

Placings: *1404/*32131/242-P21243 (4498)
2001/02: 20^{P}GS, 17^{2}S, 22^{1}G, 22^{2}HY, 19^{4}GS, 22^{3}G

	Starts	1st	2nd	3rd	Win & Pl
Hurdles	1	0	0	0	0
Chases	5	1	2	1	10229
Career Total	18	4	5	3	29649

135	11/01	Newb	2m6f110y	D Ch	GD	£5876
125	3/00	Newb	2m3f	D Hdl	SFT	£4127
116	12/99	Uttx	2m4f110y	E Hdl	SFT	£2704
105	11/98	NAbb	2m1f	H NHF	SFT	£1236

Total win prize-money £13945

Going: Sf: 0-2 GS: 0-2 Gd: 1-2 GF: - Fm: 0-0
Distance: 2m/2m3: 0-1 **2m4-2m7: 1-5** 3m+: 0-0
Track: **LH: 1-4** RH: 0-0 Tight: 0-1 **Gall: 1-2**
Aids: Bl: 0-0 Vi: 0-0 Tstrap: 0-0
Best Rating: 135 2/02 Hayd 2m6f heavy Ch

A three-time winner over hurdles who stays two miles six, he progressed to win a novice chase at Newbury on good ground in November 2001. Suited by soft ground, he does not always produce a great deal in a finish. Needs holding up and producing late.

Gunpowder Square (IRE)

69f **51f**

5-y-o b g Hamas (IRE)-Lovely Ali (IRE) (Dunbeath (USA))
M Pitman The Leaflet Company Ltd

Placings: *0*-0 (2041)
2001/02: 16^{0}GS

	Starts	1st	2nd	3rd	Win & Pl
NH Flat	1	0	0	0	
Career Total	2	0	0	0	

Going: Sf: 0-0 GS: 0-1 Gd: 0-0 GF: - Fm: 0-0
Distance: 2m/2m3: 0-1 2m4-2m7: 0-0 3m+: 0-0
Track: LH: 0-0 RH: 0-1 Tight: 0-0 Gall: 0-0
Aids: Bl: 0-0 Vi: 0-0 Tstrap: 0-0
Best Rating: 63 1/01 Font 2m2f110y soft NHF

Gunther McBride (IRE)

126(115h) (117h)**156**

7-y-o b g Glacial Storm (USA)-What Side (General Ironside)
P J Hobbs M J Tuckey

Placings: 1/3P1-12221163 (4839)
2001/02: 22^{1}G, 25^{2}G, 26^{2}G, 24^{2}GS, 24^{1}S, 24^{1}G, 24^{6}GS, 33^{3}G

	Starts	1st	2nd	3rd	Win & Pl
Hurdles	3	1	2	0	6310
Chases	5	2	1	1	74374
Career Total	12	5	3	2	90288

156	2/02	Kemp	3m	A HCh	GD	£52200
135	1/02	Kemp	3m	D(0-125)HCh	SFT	£7215
117	10/01	Extr	2m6f110y	E Hdl	GD	£2716
116	4/01	Leop	3m	Ch	SH	£5564
88	4/00	Cork	3m	Ch	Y-S	£3588

Total win prize-money £71284

Going: Sf: 1-1 GS: 0-2 Gd: 2-5 GF: - Fm: 0-0
Distance: 2m/2m3: 0-0 2m4-2m7: 1-1 **3m+: 2-7**
Track: LH: 0-5 **RH: 2-2** Tight: 0-0 Gall: 0-4
Aids: Bl: 0-0 Vi: 0-0 Tstrap: 0-0
Best Rating: 156 2/02 Kemp 3m good Ch

A successful hunter chaser in Ireland, he made a good start to his career in this country with a win in an amateur novices' hurdle at Exeter in October 2001. Runner-up on his next three starts before landing a Kempton handicap chase. Followed up with a clear-cut win in the Racing Post Chase, but was a little disappointing at Cheltenham in March 2002. However, he returned to form when third in the Scottish National in April 2002. Acts on good and soft ground. Stays three miles.

Guru

100 **103**

4-y-o b g Slip Anchor-Ower (IRE) (Lomond (USA))
S Dow (I A Balding 17/10) Will Bennett, Thomas Cox & Geoff Brain

Placings: 164 (4417)
2001/02: 17^{1}G, 16^{6}GS, 16^{4}GS

	Starts	1st	2nd	3rd	Win & Pl
Hurdles	3	1	0	0	3213
Career Total	3	1	0	0	3213

101	12/01	Folk	2m1f110y	E Hdl	SFT	£2894

Total win prize-money £2895

Going: Sf: 1-1 GS: 0-2 Gd: 0-0 GF: - Fm: 0-0
Distance: **2m/2m3: 1-3** 2m4-2m7: 0-0 3m+: 0-0
Track: LH: 0-2 **RH: 1-1 Tight: 1-1** Gall: 0-2
Aids: Bl: 0-0 Vi: 0-0 Tstrap: 0-0
Best Rating: 103 3/02 Newb 2m110y gd-sft Hdl

Winner of a weak race on his hurdles debut, acts on soft ground and is effective at around two miles.

Guru Rinpoche

93 **82**

10-y-o ch g Scallywag-Ishkhara (Hittite Glory)
R G Frost P A Tylor

Placings: *20/6*60F301/326F1/F45PP-0PP0 (3515)
2001/02: 19^{0}G, 22^{P}GF, 22^{P}GS, 19^{0}S

	Starts	1st	2nd	3rd	Win & Pl
Hurdles	4	0	0	0	
Career Total	23	2	2	2	7541

95	1/00	Tntn	3m110y	F(0-110)HHdl	SFT	£3623
84	3/99	Extr	2m1f110y	G Hdl	GD	£1786

Total win prize-money £5410

Going: Sf: 0-1 GS: 0-1 Gd: 0-1 GF: - Fm: 0-1
Distance: 2m/2m3: 0-1 2m4-2m7: 0-3 3m+: 0-0
Track: LH: 0-1 RH: 0-3 Tight: 0-2 Gall: 0-0
Aids: Bl: 0-0 Vi: 0-0 Tstrap: 0-0
Best Rating: 100 5/98 Chep 2m110y gd-fm NHF

Gus Berry (IRE)

98 **104**

9-y-o ch g Montelimar (USA)-Eurolink Sea Baby (Deep Run)
D M Forster D M Forster

Placings: *10P/P2520*/**FPP145/6P11P-U4240** (3366)
2001/02: 27^{U}G, 25^{4}G, 27^{2}S, 30^{4}GS, 25^{0}GS

	Starts	1st	2nd	3rd	Win & Pl
Chases	5	0	1	0	1397
Career Total	**24**	**4**	**3**	**0**	**17710**

106	2/01	Sedg	3m3f	F(0-110)HCh	G-S	£4026
113	12/00	Sedg	3m3f	F(0-95)HCh	SFT	£3978
106	2/00	Sedg	3m3f110y	F(0-110)HHdl	G-S	£5239
84	12/97	Catt	2m	H NHF	G-S	£1213

Total win prize-money £14458

Going: Sf: 0-1 GS: 0-2 Gd: 0-2 GF: - Fm: 0-0
Distance: 2m/2m3: 0-0 2m4-2m7: 0-0 3m+: 0-5
Track: LH: 0-5 RH: 0-0 Tight: 0-4 Gall: 0-1
Aids: Bl: 0-5 Vi: 0-0 Tstrap: 0-0
Best Rating: 113 12/00 Sedg 3m3f soft Ch

He has a good record at Sedgefield and stays well. Best on ground with cut in it.

Gutsy Dalton (IRE)

85 73

8-y-o b g Good Thyne (USA)-No Not (Ovac (ITY))
Noel T Chance C Green & J Dennis

Placings:0-565 (2461)
2001/02: 22^{5}GS, 20^{6}GS, 20^{5}HY

	Starts	1st	2nd	3rd	Win & Pl
Hurdles	3	0	0	0	0
Career Total	**4**	**0**	**0**	**0**	**0**

Going: Sf: 0-1 GS: 0-2 Gd: 0-0 GF: - Fm: 0-0
Distance: 2m/2m3: 0-0 2m4-2m7: 0-3 3m+: 0-0
Track: LH: 0-1 RH: 0-1 Tight: 0-3 Gall: 0-0
Aids: Bl: 0-0 Vi: 0-0 Tstrap: 0-0
Best Rating: 73 10/01 Font 2m6f110y gd-sft Hdl

Gwen's A Singer

8-y-o ch m Fearless Action (USA)-Air Streak (Air Trooper)
A W Carroll R Clarke

Placings:PPP (3336)
2001/02: 24^{P}S, 20^{P}GS, 20^{P}G

	Starts	1st	2nd	3rd	Win & Pl
Chases	3	0	0	0	
Career Total	**3**	**0**	**0**	**0**	

Going: Sf: 0-1 GS: 0-1 Gd: 0-1 GF: - Fm: 0-0
Distance: 2m/2m3: 0-0 2m4-2m7: 0-2 3m+: 0-1
Track: LH: 0-1 RH: 0-2 Tight: 0-2 Gall: 0-1
Aids: Bl: 0-0 Vi: 0-0 Tstrap: 0-1
Best Rating:

Gwylan

76f 63f

7-y-o b g Crested Lark-Flopsy Mopsy (Full Of Hope)
J S King W J Lee

Placings:*0* (2786)
2001/02: 16^{0}G

	Starts	1st	2nd	3rd	Win & Pl
NH Flat	1	0	0	0	
Career Total	**1**	**0**	**0**	**0**	

Going: Sf: 0-0 GS: 0-0 Gd: 0-1 GF: - Fm: 0-0
Distance: 2m/2m3: 0-1 2m4-2m7: 0-0 3m+: 0-0
Track: LH: 0-0 RH: 0-1 Tight: 0-0 Gall: 0-0
Aids: Bl: 0-0 Vi: 0-0 Tstrap: 0-0
Best Rating: 63 12/01 Ludl 2m good NHF

Gymcrak Jester

63

8-y-o b g Derrylin-Emerin (King Emperor (USA))
D Moffatt (M A Barnes 24/6) A A Bland

Placings:660400/0/**F00FP-P00** (4520)
2001/02: 20^{P}GF, 17^{0}HY, 20^{0}G

	Starts	1st	2nd	3rd	Win & Pl
Hurdles	3	0	0	0	
Career Total	**15**	**0**	**0**	**0**	**0**

Going: Sf: 0-1 GS: 0-0 Gd: 0-1 GF: - Fm: 0-1
Distance: 2m/2m3: 0-1 2m4-2m7: 0-2 3m+: 0-0
Track: LH: 0-0 RH: 0-2 Tight: 0-0 Gall: 0-0
Aids: Bl: 0-0 Vi: 0-0 Tstrap: 0-0
Best Rating: 81 10/00 Kels 2m1f soft Ch

Gypsy (IRE)

114 101+

6-y-o b g Distinctly North (USA)-Winscarlet North (Garland Knight)
Miss Venetia Williams (N B Mason 11/3) Favourites Racing Ltd

Placings:5333015 (4540)
2001/02: 16^{5}S, 20^{3}S, 17^{3}HY, 16^{3}S, 16^{0}GS, 19^{1}GS, 19^{5}G

	Starts	1st	2nd	3rd	Win & Pl
Hurdles	7	1	0	3	5245
Career Total	**7**	**1**	**0**	**3**	**5245**

96	3/02	Strf	2m3f	G Hdl	G-S	£2912

Total win prize-money £2912

Going: Sf: 0-4 GS: 1-2 Gd: 0-1 GF: - Fm: 0-0
Distance: **2m/2m3: 1-5** 2m4-2m7: 0-2 3m+: 0-0
Track: **LH: 1-5** RH: 0-2 **Tight: 1-2** Gall: 0-3
Aids: Bl: 0-0 Vi: 0-0 Tstrap: 0-0
Best Rating: 100 2/02 Newc 2m soft Hdl

Had to be dropped into a seller to get off the mark at Stratford in March 2002. Added a modest handicap hurdle at Wolverhampton in July. Suited by two miles and easy ground.

Gypsy Song (IRE)

87 71

5-y-o b g Turtle Island (IRE)-Kate Labelle (Teenoso (USA))
J A Glover Boston R S

Placings:0500 (4271)
2001/02: 20^{0}S, 16^{5}S, 20^{0}S, 16^{0}G

	Starts	1st	2nd	3rd	Win & Pl
Hurdles	4	0	0	0	0
Career Total	**4**	**0**	**0**	**0**	**0**

Going: Sf: 0-3 GS: 0-0 Gd: 0-1 GF: - Fm: 0-0
Distance: 2m/2m3: 0-2 2m4-2m7: 0-2 3m+: 0-0
Track: LH: 0-4 RH: 0-0 Tight: 0-1 Gall: 0-2
Aids: Bl: 0-1 Vi: 0-0 Tstrap: 0-0
Best Rating: 71 2/02 Donc 2m110y soft Hdl

Haafel (USA)

94 111

5-y-o ch g Diesis-Dish Dash (Bustino)
G L Moore D R Hunnisett

Placings:0-1P66 (3756)
2001/02: 20^{1}GS, 20^{P}HY, 22^{6}G, 20^{6}HY

	Starts	1st	2nd	3rd	Win & Pl
Hurdles	4	1	0	0	2387
Career Total	**5**	**1**	**0**	**0**	**2387**

111	11/01	Font	2m4f	E Hdl	G-S	£2387

Total win prize-money £2387

Going: Sf: 0-2 GS: 1-1 Gd: 0-1 GF: - Fm: 0-0
Distance: 2m/2m3: 0-0 **2m4-2m7: 1-4** 3m+: 0-0
Track: LH: 0-1 RH: 0-2 **Tight: 1-3** Gall: 0-0
Aids: Bl: 0-0 Vi: 0-0 Tstrap: 0-0
Best Rating: 111 11/01 Font 2m4f gd-sft Hdl

He got off the mark in a maiden hurdle at Fontwell in November 2001, winning easily. Acts in soft ground.

Hachley (FR)

91 76

7-y-o b/br g Grand Tresor (FR)-Tess Bowl (FR) (Rolling Bowl (FR))
C P Morlock W F Caudwell

Placings:0 (0370)
2001/02: 16^{0}G

	Starts	1st	2nd	3rd	Win & Pl
Hurdles	1	0	0	0	
Career Total	**1**	**0**	**0**	**0**	

Going: Sf: 0-0 GS: 0-0 Gd: 0-1 GF: - Fm: 0-0
Distance: 2m/2m3: 0-1 2m4-2m7: 0-0 3m+: 0-0
Track: LH: 0-1 RH: 0-0 Tight: 0-0 Gall: 0-0
Aids: Bl: 0-0 Vi: 0-0 Tstrap: 0-0
Best Rating: 76 5/01 Wwck 2m good Hdl

Hachty Boy (FR)

104(106h) (104h)121

6-y-o br g Cadoudal (FR)-Hachty Girl (FR) (Ashtar)
Miss H C Knight David Zeffman

Placings:55606/015344-**32324** (4761)
2001/02: 19^{3}G, 16^{2}G, 20^{3}S, 20^{2}GF, 19^{4}GF

	Starts	1st	2nd	3rd	Win & Pl
Chases	5	0	2	2	3955
Career Total	**16**	**1**	**2**	**3**	**7658**

111	11/00	Hrfd	2m3f110y	F(0-100)HHdl	G-S	£2733

Total win prize-money £2734

Going: Sf: 0-1 GS: 0-0 Gd: 0-2 GF: - Fm: 0-2
Distance: 2m/2m3: 0-2 2m4-2m7: 0-3 3m+: 0-0
Track: LH: 0-1 RH: 0-4 Tight: 0-1 Gall: 0-1
Aids: Bl: 0-0 Vi: 0-0 Tstrap: 0-0
Best Rating: 121 11/01 Strf 2m4f soft Ch

He showed fair form in novice hurdles and was placed on his first three starts over fences and appreciated the step up to three miles when opening his account at Wetherby in May.

Hackbridge

(86h) (70h)

6-y-o b g Petoski-Air Streak (Air Trooper)
J Howard Johnson Sutton Business Centre

Placings:*20*-00UPPP (3822)

2001/02: 16^{0}GS, 17^{0}G, 27^{U}S, 25^{P}GS, 24^{P}S, 21^{P}S

	Starts	1st	2nd	3rd	Win & Pl
Hurdles	5	0	0	0	0
Chases	1	0	0	0	0
Career Total	**8**	**0**	**1**	**0**	**454**

Going: Sf: 0-3 GS: 0-2 Gd: 0-1 GF: - Fm: 0-0
Distance: 2m/2m3: 0-2 2m4-2m7: 0-1 3m+: 0-3
Track: LH: 0-6 RH: 0-0 Tight: 0-5 Gall: 0-1
Aids: Bl: 0-0 Vi: 0-0 Tstrap: 0-0
Best Rating: 96 2/01 Sedg 2m1f soft NHF

Failed to complete four times from his first six starts over hurdles/fences.

Hacketts Cross (IRE)

(83h) (40h)
14-y-o b g Rusticaro (FR)-Anglesea Market (Sea Hawk II)
Mrs L Williamson G W Briscoe

Placings:3/110600/432/04331B/22/06P52311430250P/1233211P/FP/P/P-0F **(0723)**
2001/02: 19^{0}GF, 25^{F}F

	Starts	1st	2nd	3rd	Win & Pl
Hurdles	1	0	0	0	0
Chases	1	0	0	0	0
Career Total	**47**	**8**	**7**	**8**	**25626**

96	8/97	NAbb	2m5f110y	E Ch	G-F	£2832
93	8/97	Bang	2m4f	D(0-120)HHdl	GD	£3387
93	5/97	Ctml	2m1f110y	G(0-90)HHdl	G-F	£2402
91	9/96	NAbb	2m1f	G Hdl	GD	£1965
85	9/96	Plum	2m4f	G Hdl	G-F	£1859
108	6/94	Wxfd	2m2f	(0-109)HHdl	G-F	£2611
	6/92	Rosc	2m	NHF	GD	£3224

Total win prize-money £18283

Going: Sf: 0-0 GS: 0-0 Gd: 0-0 GF: - Fm: 0-2
Distance: 2m/2m3: 0-0 2m4-2m7: 0-1 3m+: 0-1
Track: LH: 0-0 RH: 0-2 Tight: 0-1 Gall: 0-0
Aids: Bl: 0-0 Vi: 0-0 Tstrap: 0-0
Best Rating: 108 6/94 Wxfd 2m2f gd-fm Hdl

Hada Barney

63 **13**
7-y-o b g Glacial Storm (USA)-Northwood Star (IRE) (Henbit (USA))
M W Easterby C N Barnes

Placings:0-06 **(3557)**
2001/02: 16^{0}G, 19^{6}S

	Starts	1st	2nd	3rd	Win & Pl
NH Flat	1	0	0	0	0
Hurdles	1	0	0	0	0
Career Total	**3**	**0**	**0**	**0**	**0**

Going: Sf: 0-1 GS: 0-0 Gd: 0-1 GF: - Fm: 0-0
Distance: 2m/2m3: 0-2 2m4-2m7: 0-0 3m+: 0-0
Track: LH: 0-2 RH: 0-0 Tight: 0-2 Gall: 0-0
Aids: Bl: 0-0 Vi: 0-0 Tstrap: 0-0
Best Rating: 71 12/01 Catt 2m good NHF

Hadaani

85 **49**
4-y-o b f Mtoto-Trude (GER) (Windwurf (GER))
P G Murphy (W J Haggas 16/8) P G Murphy

Placings:0000 **(3210)**
2001/02: 16^{0}GS, 16^{0}G, 16^{0}G, 16^{0}GS

	Starts	1st	2nd	3rd	Win & Pl
Hurdles	4	0	0	0	
Career Total	**4**	**0**	**0**	**0**	

Going: Sf: 0-0 GS: 0-2 Gd: 0-2 GF: - Fm: 0-0
Distance: 2m/2m3: 0-4 2m4-2m7: 0-0 3m+: 0-0
Track: LH: 0-2 RH: 0-2 Tight: 0-0 Gall: 0-2
Aids: Bl: 0-0 Vi: 0-0 Tstrap: 0-0
Best Rating: 49 12/01 Ludl 2m good Hdl

Hadeqa

93 **68**
6-y-o ch g Hadeer-Heavenly Queen (Scottish Reel)
F Jordan The French Connection

Placings:13P0/P000-0400 **(1380)**
2001/02: 17^{0}GF, 22^{4}G, 17^{0}GF, 19^{0}GF

	Starts	1st	2nd	3rd	Win & Pl
Hurdles	4	0	0	0	0
Career Total	**12**	**1**	**0**	**1**	**3183**

82	7/99	MRas	2m1f110y	E Hdl	G-F	£2765

Total win prize-money £2765

Going: Sf: 0-0 GS: 0-0 Gd: 0-1 GF: - Fm: 0-3
Distance: 2m/2m3: 0-2 2m4-2m7: 0-2 3m+: 0-0
Track: LH: 0-2 RH: 0-2 Tight: 0-3 Gall: 0-0
Aids: Bl: 0-0 Vi: 0-0 Tstrap: 0-1
Best Rating: 92 9/00 NAbb 2m1f gd-sft Hdl

Hades De Sienne (FR)

111 (96h) (76h) **115**
7-y-o b g Concorde Jr (USA)-Aube De Slenne (FR) (Cupids Dew)
A Parker Mr & Mrs Raymond Anderson Green

Placings:PF454/22P13-4232F2 **(4394)**
2001/02: 22^{4}GS, 28^{2}GS, 25^{3}S, 25^{2}HY, 32^{F}HY, 32^{2}HY

	Starts	1st	2nd	3rd	Win & Pl
Hurdles	1	0	0	0	0
Chases	5	0	3	1	13798
Career Total	**16**	**1**	**5**	**2**	**20693**

104	1/01	Ayr	3m1f	E(0-105)HCh	SFT	£3256

Total win prize-money £3257

Going: Sf: 0-4 GS: 0-2 Gd: 0-0 GF: - Fm: 0-0
Distance: 2m/2m3: 0-0 2m4-2m7: 0-1 3m+: 0-5
Track: LH: 0-6 RH: 0-0 Tight: 0-3 Gall: 0-0
Aids: Bl: 0-0 Vi: 0-1 Tstrap: 0-0
Best Rating: 115 3/02 Kels 4m heavy Ch

Consistent handicap chaser. Stays three miles. Acts on soft ground.

Haditovski

110 **131**
6-y-o b g Hatim (USA)-Grand Occasion (Great Nephew)
J Mackie Mrs Sue Adams

Placings:U641005662/20111140303126-220153206 **(4418)**
2001/02: 16^{2}G, 16^{2}GS, 16^{0}S, 16^{1}S, 16^{5}GS, 17^{3}HY, 16^{2}S, 16^{0}GS, 16^{6}GS

	Starts	1st	2nd	3rd	Win & Pl
Hurdles	9	1	3	1	14149
Career Total	**33**	**7**	**6**	**3**	**42901**

131	12/01	Uttx	2m	C(0-130)HHdl	SFT	£4992
122	3/01	Newb	2m110y	C(0-130)HHdl	HVY	£5902
129	11/00	Hntg	2m110y	D(0-120)HHdl	G-S	£7117
120	11/00	Weth	2m	D(0-125)HHdl	HVY	£3601
110	11/00	Uttx	2m	F(0-100)HHdl	HVY	£2324
115	10/00	Sthl	2m	F(0-105)HHdl	SFT	£1808
111	11/99	Uttx	2m	E Hdl	SFT	£2337

Total win prize-money £28083

Going: Sf: 1-4 GS: 0-4 Gd: 0-1 GF: - Fm: 0-0
Distance: **2m/2m3: 1-9** 2m4-2m7: 0-0 3m+: 0-0
Track: **LH: 1-6** RH: 0-3 Tight: 0-0 Gall: 0-5
Aids: Bl: 0-0 **Vi: 1-9** Tstrap: 0-0
Best Rating: 131 3/02 Newb 2m110y soft Hdl

A useful handicap hurdler, he is suited by around two miles and a soft surface. Usually races prominently.

Hag's Way (IRE)

12-y-o ch g Roselier (FR)-Lucifer's Way (Lucifer (USA))
Lady Susan Brooke Lady Susan Brooke

Placings:00/31P413P/53FPP/6210U325/224/0P-PPUP **(4091)**
2001/02: 25^{P}G, 33^{P}G, 24^{U}GS, 24^{P}S

	Starts	1st	2nd	3rd	Win & Pl
Chases	4	0	0	0	
Career Total	**31**	**3**	**4**	**4**	**15680**

107	12/98	Catt	3m1f110y	D(0-120)HCh	GD	£3769
97	2/96	Chep	3m2f110y	E(0-100)HCh	SFT	£3070
94	1/96	Font	2m3f	Ch	SFT	£3260

Total win prize-money £10100

Going: Sf: 0-1 GS: 0-1 Gd: 0-2 GF: - Fm: 0-0
Distance: 2m/2m3: 0-0 2m4-2m7: 0-0 3m+: 0-4
Track: LH: 0-0 RH: 0-2 Tight: 0-1 Gall: 0-0
Aids: Bl: 0-1 Vi: 0-0 Tstrap: 0-0
Best Rating: 107 12/98 Catt 3m1f110y good Ch

Haikal

102 **88**
5-y-o b g Owington-Magic Milly (Simply Great (FR))
E W Tuer E Tuer

Placings:P45-52430021P **(4896)**
2001/02: 17^{5}GF, 17^{2}GF, 20^{4}G, 17^{3}GS, 16^{0}GS, 16^{0}S, 20^{2}HY, 20^{1}G, 20^{P}G

	Starts	1st	2nd	3rd	Win & Pl
Hurdles	9	1	2	1	5354
Career Total	**12**	**1**	**2**	**1**	**5354**

88	4/02	Carl	2m4f	E(0-110)HHdl	GD	£2982

Total win prize-money £2982

Going: Sf: 0-2 GS: 0-2 Gd: 1-3 GF: - Fm: 0-2
Distance: 2m/2m3: 0-5 **2m4-2m7: 1-4** 3m+: 0-0
Track: LH: 0-6 RH: 0-2 Tight: 0-4 Gall: 0-2
Aids: Bl: 0-0 Vi: 0-0 Tstrap: 0-0
Best Rating: 93 2/01 Muss 2m good Hdl

Modest hurdler, stays two miles-four, acts on any ground.

Hail Sheeva

5-y-o ch m Democratic (USA)-Sun Storm (Sunyboy)
Miss K M George R J Matthews

Placings:OP **(1996)**
2001/02: 17°F, 17^{P}S

	Starts	1st	2nd	3rd	Win & Pl

	Starts	1st	2nd	3rd	Win & Pl
Hurdles	2	0	0	0	
Career Total	**2**	**0**	**0**	**0**	

Going: Sf: 0-1 GS: 0-0 Gd: 0-0 GF: - Fm: 0-1
Distance: 2m/2m3: 0-2 2m4-2m7: 0-0 3m+: 0-0
Track: LH: 0-1 RH: 0-1 Tight: 0-2 Gall: 0-0
Aids: Bl: 0-0 Vi: 0-0 Tstrap: 0-0
Best Rating:

Hailstorm (IRE)

100 **105**

9-y-o ch g Glacial Storm (USA)-Sindys Gale (Strong Gale)
Miss Lucinda V Russell Peter K Dale Ltd

Placings: *064*222100/4/64**22/6P02143-1UFPP60** **(4876)**
2001/02: 20^{1}GF, 20^{U}S, 25^{F}GS, 22^{P}S, 20^{P}HY, 25^{6}S, 20^{0}G

	Starts	1st	2nd	3rd	Win & Pl
Chases	7	1	0	0	4479
Career Total	**28**	**3**	**6**	**1**	**17284**

105	9/01	MRas	2m4f	D(0-120)HCh	G-F	£4478
108	12/00	Ayr	2m5f110y	D(0-110)HCh	SFT	£4046
111	2/98	Ludl	2m5f110y	E Hdl	GD	£2500

Total win prize-money £11025

Going: Sf: 0-4 GS: 0-1 Gd: 0-1 GF: - Fm: 1-1
Distance: 2m/2m3: 0-0 **2m4-2m7: 1-5** 3m+: 0-2
Track: LH: 0-3 **RH: 1-4 Tight: 1-5** Gall: 0-0
Aids: Bl: 0-0 Vi: 0-0 Tstrap: 0-0
Best Rating: **127** 2/00 Ludl 2m4f good Ch

He got off the mark over fences in soft ground at Ayr in 2000, but showed he could act on fast ground when winning at Market Rasen in September 2001. Probably needs further than two and a half miles.

Haithem (IRE)

5-y-o b g Mtoto-Wukk (IRE) (Glow (USA))
R Wilman (D Shaw 3/11) Century Racing

Placings: 0 **(1759)**
2001/02: 16^{0}GS

	Starts	1st	2nd	3rd	Win & Pl
Hurdles	1	0	0	0	
Career Total	**1**	**0**	**0**	**0**	

Going: Sf: 0-0 GS: 0-1 Gd: 0-0 GF: - Fm: 0-0
Distance: 2m/2m3: 0-1 2m4-2m7: 0-0 3m+: 0-0
Track: LH: 0-1 RH: 0-0 Tight: 0-1 Gall: 0-0
Aids: Bl: 0-0 Vi: 0-0 Tstrap: 0-1
Best Rating:

Hakim (NZ)

95 **97**

8-y-o ch g Half Iced (USA)-Topitup (NZ) (Little Brown Jug (NZ))
G M McCourt T N Siviter

Placings: 2 **(0209)**
2001/02: 16^{2}F

	Starts	1st	2nd	3rd	Win & Pl
Hurdles	1	0	1	0	1046
Career Total	**1**	**0**	**1**	**0**	**1046**

Going: Sf: 0-0 GS: 0-0 Gd: 0-0 GF: - Fm: 0-1
Distance: 2m/2m3: 0-1 2m4-2m7: 0-0 3m+: 0-0

Track: LH: 0-1 RH: 0-0 Tight: 0-1 Gall: 0-0
Aids: Bl: 0-0 Vi: 0-0 Tstrap: 0-0
Best Rating: **97** 5/01 Sthl 2m firm Hdl

Hal Hoo Yaroom

(103h) (105h)

9-y-o b g Belmez (USA)-Princess Nawaal (USA) (Seattle Slew (USA))
J R Jenkins The East India Dock Partnership

Placings: 3/1325/5541331601/2233661/35**F** **(2326)**
2001/02: 21^{3}GF, 20^{5}G, 21^{F}S

	Starts	1st	2nd	3rd	Win & Pl
Hurdles	2	0	0	1	478
Chases	1	0	0	0	0
Career Total	**25**	**5**	**3**	**7**	**18580**

110	3/00	Font	2m2f110y	E(0-115)HHdl	G-F	£2464
112	4/99	Plum	2m4f	E(0-115)HHdl	GD	£2285
108	11/98	Plum	2m1f	E(0-110)HHdl	SFT	£2670
108	9/98	Plum	2m4f	D(0-120)HHdl	G-F	£2802
101	11/97	Plum	2m1f	G Hdl	G-F	£1908

Total win prize-money £12130

Going: Sf: 0-1 GS: 0-0 Gd: 0-1 GF: - Fm: 0-1
Distance: 2m/2m3: 0-0 2m4-2m7: 0-3 3m+: 0-0
Track: LH: 0-3 RH: 0-0 Tight: 0-3 Gall: 0-0
Aids: Bl: 0-0 Vi: 0-0 Tstrap: 0-0
Best Rating: **112** 9/99 Plum 2m5f gd-fm Hdl

Halexy (FR)

7-y-o b g Iron Duke (FR)-Tartifume Ii (FR) (Mistigri)
Miss Venetia Williams Sir Robert Ogden

Placings: *10*116/4144-P **(0344)**
2001/02: 25^{P}G

	Starts	1st	2nd	3rd	Win & Pl
Chases	1	0	0	0	
Career Total	**10**	**4**	**0**	**0**	**13454**

138	12/00	Sthl	3m110y	E Ch	SFT	£2866
119	2/00	MRas	2m3f110y	D Hdl	G-S	£3282
128	1/00	Hayd	2m	D Hdl	SFT	£3266
110	11/99	NAbb	2m1f	H NHF	SFT	£1565

Total win prize-money £10981

Going: Sf: 0-0 GS: 0-0 Gd: 0-1 GF: - Fm: 0-0
Distance: 2m/2m3: 0-0 2m4-2m7: 0-0 3m+: 0-1
Track: LH: 0-1 RH: 0-0 Tight: 0-1 Gall: 0-0
Aids: Bl: 0-0 Vi: 0-0 Tstrap: 0-0
Best Rating: **138** 12/00 Sthl 3m110y soft Ch

He looked a decent prospect when winning a novice chase in December 2000, but jumped moderately and appeared unenthusiastic on his three remaining starts. He stays well but is one to have reservations about for the time being.

Half An Hour

97f **119f**

5-y-o b g Alflora (IRE)-Country Mistress (Town And Country)
A King C W Lane

Placings: *136* **(4499)**
2001/02: 16^{1}S, 16^{3}S, 16^{6}G

	Starts	1st	2nd	3rd	Win & Pl
NH Flat	3	1	0	1	3616
Career Total	**3**	**1**	**0**	**1**	**3616**

119	1/02	Hayd	2m	H NHF	SFT	£2338

Total win prize-money £2338

Going: Sf: 1-2 GS: 0-0 Gd: 0-1 GF: - Fm: 0-0
Distance: **2m/2m3: 1-3** 2m4-2m7: 0-0 3m+: 0-0
Track: **LH: 1-3** RH: 0-0 Tight: 0-0 Gall: 0-0
Aids: Bl: 0-0 Vi: 0-0 Tstrap: 0-0
Best Rating: **119** 1/02 Hayd 2m soft NHF

A half-brother to winning pointer and novice chaser Libido. An old-fashioned chasing type, he won his bumper debut in good style at Haydock. Acts on soft ground.

Half Nelson

86 **75**

4-y-o br g Be My Chief (USA)-Petindia (Petong)
T R George Mrs Sharon C Nelson

Placings: 0 **(4894)**
2001/02: 16^{0}G

	Starts	1st	2nd	3rd	Win & Pl
Hurdles	1	0	0	0	
Career Total	**1**	**0**	**0**	**0**	

Going: Sf: 0-0 GS: 0-0 Gd: 0-1 GF: - Fm: 0-0
Distance: 2m/2m3: 0-1 2m4-2m7: 0-0 3m+: 0-0
Track: LH: 0-0 RH: 0-1 Tight: 0-0 Gall: 0-0
Aids: Bl: 0-0 Vi: 0-0 Tstrap: 0-0
Best Rating: **31** 4/02 Prth 2m110y good Hdl

Half The Pot (IRE)

113 **121**

7-y-o b g Homo Sapien-Deep Green (Deep Run)
R Rowe Mrs P V Crocker

Placings: *52P*/46B0-B421111P **(3809)**
2001/02: 22^{B}GF, 20^{4}GF, 16^{2}S, 20^{1}S, 22^{1}HY, 21^{1}S, 18^{1}S, 22^{P}S

	Starts	1st	2nd	3rd	Win & Pl
Hurdles	8	4	1	0	12463
Career Total	**15**	**4**	**2**	**0**	**13231**

121	1/02	Font	2m2f110y	D(0-125)HHdl	SFT	£4108
120	1/02	Plum	2m5f	D(0-125)HHdl	SFT	£3444
96	12/01	Folk	2m6f110y	F(0-105)HHdl	HVY	£2259
117	11/01	Folk	2m4f110y	F(0-100)HHdl	SFT	£1897

Total win prize-money £11709

Going: Sf: 4-6 GS: 0-0 Gd: 0-0 GF: - Fm: 0-2
Distance: 2m/2m3: 1-2 **2m4-2m7: 3-6** 3m+: 0-0
Track: LH: 2-5 RH: 2-3 **Tight: 4-8** Gall: 0-0
Aids: Bl: 0-0 Vi: 0-0 Tstrap: 0-0
Best Rating: **121** 1/02 Font 2m2f110y soft Hdl

Moderate novice hurdler, seems suited by forcing tactics and used them successfully to score four times in a row between November 2001 and January 2002. Suited by soft ground. Stays two miles six.

Halham Tarn (IRE)

82 **53**

12-y-o b g Pennine Walk-Nouniya (Vayrann)
Miss G Browne Mrs M L Luck

Placings: 145/PPP/34300**5233**12/U5**FP**526P04/533**53** **PU4**P**P3PP/P53**4P**22U1/5200/53-P60** **(2647)**
2001/02: 19^{P}S, 16^{6}G, 16^{0}GS

	Starts	1st	2nd	3rd	Win & Pl
Chases	3	0	0	0	0
Career Total	**58**	**3**	**6**	**10**	**14925**

86	4/99	Chel	2m110y	H Ch	G-S	£2400
95	3/96	Leic	2m1f	H Ch	G-S	£2040
96	1/94	Kemp	2m	Hdl	G-S	£2784

Total win prize-money £7224

Going: Sf: 0-1 GS: 0-1 Gd: 0-1 GF: - Fm: 0-0
Distance: 2m/2m3: 0-2 2m4-2m7: 0-1 3m+: 0-0
Track: LH: 0-1 RH: 0-2 Tight: 0-1 Gall: 0-1
Aids: Bl: 0-0 Vi: 0-0 Tstrap: 0-3
Best Rating: 96 1/94 Kemp 2m gd-sft Hdl

Halidon Hill (IRE)

6-y-o b g Commanche Run-Baladine (Black Minstrel)
B Mactaggart J Stephenson

Placings:P-PP (1815)
2001/02: 22^{P}GF, 24^{P}S

	Starts	1st	2nd	3rd	Win & Pl
Hurdles	2	0	0	0	
Career Total	**3**	**0**	**0**	**0**	

Going: Sf: 0-1 GS: 0-0 Gd: 0-0 GF: - Fm: 0-1
Distance: 2m/2m3: 0-0 2m4-2m7: 0-1 3m+: 0-1
Track: LH: 0-1 RH: 0-1 Tight: 0-0 Gall: 0-0
Aids: Bl: 0-0 Vi: 0-0 Tstrap: 0-0
Best Rating:

Hall's Mill (IRE)

13-y-o ch g Buckskin (FR)-Grainne Geal (General Ironside)
Miss S Waugh Rupert C Irving

Placings:6/U/U23/456/1-F (4650)
2001/02: 21^{F}G

	Starts	1st	2nd	3rd	Win & Pl
Chases	1	0	0	0	
Career Total	**10**	**1**	**1**	**1**	**2974**
111 5/00 Chel	2m5f	H Ch		GD	£2262

Total win prize-money £2262

Going: Sf: 0-0 GS: 0-0 Gd: 0-1 GF: - Fm: 0-0
Distance: 2m/2m3: 0-0 2m4-2m7: 0-1 3m+: 0-0
Track: LH: 0-1 RH: 0-0 Tight: 0-1 Gall: 0-0
Aids: Bl: 0-0 Vi: 0-0 Tstrap: 0-0
Best Rating: 111 5/00 Chel 2m5f good Ch

Winning pointer/hunter chaser, he acts on most ground bar extremes of going.

Hallyards Gael (IRE)

103(112h) (113h)**117**
8-y-o br g Strong Gale-Secret Ocean (Most Secret)
Mrs M Reveley G M Mair

Placings:4/411-32323 (4893)
2001/02: 16^{3}GS, 16^{2}GS, 16^{3}S, 18^{2}GS, 20^{3}G

	Starts	1st	2nd	3rd	Win & Pl
Hurdles	1	0	0	1	913
Chases	4	0	2	2	4300
Career Total	**9**	**2**	**2**	**3**	**11154**
116 10/00 Kels	2m110y	E Hdl		G-S	£2506
96 6/00 Prth	2m110y	D Hdl		GD	£3435

Total win prize-money £5941

Going: Sf: 0-1 GS: 0-3 Gd: 0-1 GF: - Fm: 0-0
Distance: 2m/2m3: 0-4 2m4-2m7: 0-1 3m+: 0-0
Track: LH: 0-4 RH: 0-1 Tight: 0-0 Gall: 0-2
Aids: Bl: 0-0 Vi: 0-0 Tstrap: 0-0
Best Rating: 117 3/02 Newb 2m2f110y gd-sft Ch

A winner twice over hurdles, he has yet to show the same level of form over fences though enjoyed a bloodless first win at Wetherby in May 2002. Acts on good and good to soft ground.

Ham Stone

53f **16f**
4-y-o b g Picea-Blushing Belle (Local Suitor (USA))
B J M Ryall S N Burfield

Placings:0 (4032)
2001/02: 16^{0}GS

	Starts	1st	2nd	3rd	Win & Pl
NH Flat	1	0	0	0	
Career Total	**1**	**0**	**0**	**0**	

Going: Sf: 0-0 GS: 0-1 Gd: 0-0 GF: - Fm: 0-0
Distance: 2m/2m3: 0-1 2m4-2m7: 0-0 3m+: 0-0
Track: LH: 0-1 RH: 0-0 Tight: 0-0 Gall: 0-1
Aids: Bl: 0-0 Vi: 0-0 Tstrap: 0-0
Best Rating: 16 3/02 Newb 2m110y gd-sft NHF

Hamadeenah

100 **93**
4-y-o ch f Alhijaz-Mahbob Dancer (FR) (Groom Dancer (USA))
K C Bailey (K A Ryan 6/10) Mrs N L Spence

Placings:5416 (4737)
2001/02: 16^{5}G, 16^{4}G, 16^{1}GF, 16^{6}GF

	Starts	1st	2nd	3rd	Win & Pl
Hurdles	4	1	0	0	2758
Career Total	**4**	**1**	**0**	**0**	**2758**
93 3/02 Hntg	2m110y	E Hdl		G-F	£2758

Total win prize-money £2758

Going: Sf: 0-0 GS: 0-0 Gd: 0-2 GF: - Fm: 1-2
Distance: **2m/2m3: 1-4** 2m4-2m7: 0-0 3m+: 0-0
Track: LH: 0-0 **RH: 1-4** Tight: 0-0 **Gall: 1-1**
Aids: Bl: 0-0 Vi: 0-0 Tstrap: 0-0
Best Rating: 93 3/02 Hntg 2m110y gd-fm Hdl

Opened her account over hurdles at Huntingdon in March 2002. Likes fast ground.

Hamba Kashle

69 **36**
6-y-o ch g Phountzi (USA)-Plectrum (Adonijah)
O O'Neill Mrs Carol J Welch

Placings:00P (0906)
2001/02: 16^{0}GF, 17^{0}F, 20^{P}G

	Starts	1st	2nd	3rd	Win & Pl
NH Flat	1	0	0	0	0
Hurdles	2	0	0	0	0
Career Total	**3**	**0**	**0**	**0**	

Going: Sf: 0-0 GS: 0-0 Gd: 0-1 GF: - Fm: 0-2
Distance: 2m/2m3: 0-2 2m4-2m7: 0-1 3m+: 0-0
Track: LH: 0-2 RH: 0-1 Tight: 0-1 Gall: 0-0
Aids: Bl: 0-0 Vi: 0-0 Tstrap: 0-0
Best Rating: 62 5/01 Sthl 2m gd-fm NHF

Hamish

82 **80**
8-y-o b g Rakaposhi King-Kellamba (Netherkelly)
B I Case Edward Harvey

Placings:4/PP03P (0907)
2001/02: 24^{P}GF, 25^{P}G, 20^{0}GF, 24^{3}G, 24^{P}G

	Starts	1st	2nd	3rd	Win & Pl
Hurdles	4	0	0	1	366
Chases	1	0	0	0	0
Career Total	**6**	**0**	**0**	**1**	**366**

Going: Sf: 0-0 GS: 0-0 Gd: 0-3 GF: - Fm: 0-2
Distance: 2m/2m3: 0-0 2m4-2m7: 0-1 3m+: 0-4
Track: LH: 0-4 RH: 0-0 Tight: 0-1 Gall: 0-0
Aids: Bl: 0-0 Vi: 0-0 Tstrap: 0-3
Best Rating: 80 6/01 Worc 3m good Hdl

Hanakham (IRE)

100(107h) (94h)**117**
13-y-o b g Phardante (FR)-Evas Charm (Carlburg)
D McCain Army Air Corps

Placings:1U31/3/1/F0F-2604 (4135)
2001/02: 24^{2}S, 26^{6}HY, 24^{0}S, 24^{4}G

	Starts	1st	2nd	3rd	Win & Pl
Hurdles	1	0	1	0	790
Chases	3	0	0	0	553
Career Total	**13**	**3**	**1**	**2**	**75534**
163 11/99 Chel	3m3f110y	B HCh		GD	£10250
157 3/97 Chel	3m110y	A Ch		G-F	£57282
138 10/96 Winc	3m1f110y	D Ch		G-F	£3658

Total win prize-money £71191

Going: Sf: 0-3 GS: 0-0 Gd: 0-1 GF: - Fm: 0-0
Distance: 2m/2m3: 0-0 2m4-2m7: 0-0 3m+: 0-4
Track: LH: 0-1 RH: 0-3 Tight: 0-0 Gall: 0-0
Aids: Bl: 0-0 Vi: 0-0 Tstrap: 0-0
Best Rating: 166 2/99 Sand 3m110y good Ch

He has had numerous problems since winning the Sun Alliance Chase in 1997. Made a belated hurdles debut at Carlisle over three miles in November 2001 on soft ground, staying on well for second. Has decent form on fast ground. Stays three and a half miles but looks a light of former days.

Hand Care (IRE)

11-y-o br m Hollow Hand-Aughramunn (Kambalda)
R Wilman R Wilman

Placings:0P/0P (1273)
2001/02: 24^{0}GF, 24^{P}GF

	Starts	1st	2nd	3rd	Win & Pl
Hurdles	2	0	0	0	
Career Total	**4**	**0**	**0**	**0**	

Going: Sf: 0-0 GS: 0-0 Gd: 0-0 GF: - Fm: 0-2
Distance: 2m/2m3: 0-0 2m4-2m7: 0-0 3m+: 0-2
Track: LH: 0-1 RH: 0-1 Tight: 0-2 Gall: 0-0
Aids: Bl: 0-0 Vi: 0-0 Tstrap: 0-1
Best Rating: 48 7/96 Gowr 2m gd-yld NHF

Hand Inn Hand

105 **133**
6-y-o b g Alflora (IRE)-Deep Line (Deep Run)
H D Daly Patrick Burling Developments Ltd

Placings:141-015 (4178)
2001/02: 19^{0}G, 16^{1}S, 16^{5}GS

	Starts	1st	2nd	3rd	Win & Pl
Hurdles	3	1	0	0	4836
Career Total	**6**	**3**	**0**	**0**	**12974**
133 2/02 Asct	2m110y	D(0-120)HHdl		SFT	£4836

124	3/01	MRas	2m1f110y	D Hdl	G-S	£3822
118	1/01	Tntn	2m3f110y	D Hdl	SFT	£3626

Total win prize-money £12284

Going: Sf: 1-1 GS: 0-1 Gd: 0-1 GF: - Fm: 0-0
Distance: **2m/2m3: 1-3** 2m4-2m7: 0-0 3m+: 0-0
Track: LH: 0-2 **RH: 1-1** Tight: 0-1 Gall: 0-1
Aids: Bl: 0-0 Vi: 0-0 Tstrap: 0-0
Best Rating: 133 2/02 Asct 2m110y soft Hdl

Related to Morley Street and Granville Again. A lovely big chasing type. Decent novice hurdler in the 2000/2001 season and opened the New Year in fine style with a handicap victory. Stays two and a half miles, has won over two. Acts on easy ground.

Handsome Henry

97(102c) (103c)105

9-y-o b g Handsome Sailor-Pendil's Niece (Roscoe Blake)
N G Richards David Wesley Yates

Placings:*00*/050/125313-64523405 **(1817)**
2001/02: 16^{6}GF, 16^{4}GS, 20^{5}GS, 20^{2}GF, 20^{3}G, 20^{4}GF, 16^{0}G, 17^{5}S

	Starts	1st	2nd	3rd	Win & Pl
Hurdles	6	0	0	0	0
Chases	2	0	1	1	1681
Career Total	**19**	**2**	**2**	**3**	**8131**

101	9/00	Sedg	2m1f	E Hdl	GD	£1862
96	5/00	Hexm	2m	E Hdl	GD	£2450

Total win prize-money £4312

Going: Sf: 0-1 GS: 0-2 Gd: 0-2 GF: - Fm: 0-3
Distance: 2m/2m3: 0-4 2m4-2m7: 0-4 3m+: 0-0
Track: LH: 0-7 RH: 0-1 Tight: 0-5 Gall: 0-0
Aids: Bl: 0-1 Vi: 0-0 Tstrap: 0-0
Best Rating: 105 4/01 Muss 2m1f gd-fm Hdl

Handsome Lad (IRE)

53 34

4-y-o b g Inzar (USA)-Elite Exhibition (Exhibitioner)
A Scott Andy Scott

Placings:P00P **(4766)**
2001/02: 17^{P}G, 17^{0}G, 17^{0}GF, 20^{P}GF

	Starts	1st	2nd	3rd	Win & Pl
Hurdles	4	0	0	0	
Career Total	**4**	**0**	**0**	**0**	

Going: Sf: 0-0 GS: 0-0 Gd: 0-2 GF: - Fm: 0-2
Distance: 2m/2m3: 0-3 2m4-2m7: 0-1 3m+: 0-0
Track: LH: 0-4 RH: 0-0 Tight: 0-3 Gall: 0-0
Aids: Bl: 0-0 Vi: 0-0 Tstrap: 0-0
Best Rating: 34 4/02 Sedg 2m1f gd-fm Hdl

Has raced with no enthusiasm over hurdles.

Handy Boy

90f 90f

7-y-o b g Arzanni-Handymouse (Nearly A Hand)
J Gallagher Horses Away Racing Club

Placings:*6* **(0685)**
2001/02: 17^{6}G

	Starts	1st	2nd	3rd	Win & Pl
NH Flat	1	0	0	0	0
Career Total	**1**	**0**	**0**	**0**	**0**

Going: Sf: 0-0 GS: 0-0 Gd: 0-1 GF: - Fm: 0-0
Distance: 2m/2m3: 0-1 2m4-2m7: 0-0 3m+: 0-0
Track: LH: 0-1 RH: 0-0 Tight: 0-1 Gall: 0-0
Aids: Bl: 0-0 Vi: 0-0 Tstrap: 0-0
Best Rating: 90 6/01 NAbb 2m1f good NHF

Handy Money

88f 94f

5-y-o b g Imperial Frontier (USA)-Cryptic Gold (Glint Of Gold)
M J Ryan William Dixon

Placings:*000* **(3784)**
2001/02: 16^{0}S, 16^{0}S, 16^{0}S

	Starts	1st	2nd	3rd	Win & Pl
NH Flat	3	0	0	0	
Career Total	**3**	**0**	**0**	**0**	

Going: Sf: 0-3 GS: 0-0 Gd: 0-0 GF: - Fm: 0-0
Distance: 2m/2m3: 0-3 2m4-2m7: 0-0 3m+: 0-0
Track: LH: 0-1 RH: 0-2 Tight: 0-0 Gall: 0-1
Aids: Bl: 0-0 Vi: 0-0 Tstrap: 0-0
Best Rating: 94 1/02 Kemp 2m soft NHF

Handyman (IRE)

111 137

8-y-o b g Hollow Hand-Shady Ahan (Mon Capitaine)
P J Hobbs Elizabeth Hodgson And Denise Shefras

Placings:*2/2421*/**U12P36-126U22** **(4481)**
2001/02: 25^{1}GS, 25^{2}GF, 24^{6}GS, 24^{U}S, 26^{2}S, 23^{2}G

	Starts	1st	2nd	3rd	Win & Pl
Chases	6	1	3	0	7650
Career Total	**17**	**3**	**7**	**1**	**18659**

137	10/01	Extr	3m1f110y	F(0-105)HCh	G-S	£3024
137	11/00	Uttx	3m	D Ch	HVY	£3740
106	3/00	NAbb	2m6f	E Hdl	GD	£2359

Total win prize-money £9124

Going: Sf: 0-2 GS: 1-2 Gd: 0-1 GF: - Fm: 0-1
Distance: 2m/2m3: 0-0 2m4-2m7: 0-0 **3m+: 1-6**
Track: LH: 0-0 RH: 0-4 Tight: 0-1 Gall: 0-1
Aids: Bl: 0-0 Vi: 0-0 Tstrap: 0-0
Best Rating: 137 10/01 Extr 3m1f110y gd-sft Ch

Fair staying chaser, suited by three miles plus and soft ground.

Hang'Em Out To Dry (IRE)

105 116

11-y-o b g Executive Perk-Obsession (Wolver Hollow)
E L James Mrs S M Russell & Mr A Walls

Placings:60P/P/42113P/12/FP50P-16P0 **(2526)**
2001/02: 17^{1}G, 16^{6}G, 20^{P}G, 20^{0}G

	Starts	1st	2nd	3rd	Win & Pl
Chases	4	1	0	0	4846
Career Total	**21**	**4**	**2**	**1**	**20341**

116	10/01	Bang	2m1f110y	F(0-110)HCh	GD	£4845
118	11/99	Kemp	2m	D(0-120)HCh	GD	£4674
105	1/99	Donc	2m110y	E(0-105)HCh	G-S	£3935
101	1/99	Leic	2m1f	E(0-105)HCh	G-S	£3496

Total win prize-money £16951

Going: Sf: 0-0 GS: 0-0 Gd: 1-4 GF: - Fm: 0-0
Distance: **2m/2m3: 1-2** 2m4-2m7: 0-2 3m+: 0-0
Track: **LH: 1-3** RH: 0-1 **Tight: 1-1** Gall: 0-0
Aids: Bl: 0-0 Vi: 0-0 Tstrap: 0-1
Best Rating: 125 11/99 Wwck 2m good Ch

Showed little in 2000/1, but landed a weak Bangor handicap first time out in 2001/2002. Likes good ground.

Hannah Park (IRE)

113 104

6-y-o b m Lycius (USA)-Wassl This Then (IRE) (Wassl)
P Monteith The Dregs Of Humanity

Placings:5-P1451 **(4896)**
2001/02: 16^{P}GS, 17^{1}G, 17^{4}GS, 17^{5}GS, 20^{1}G

	Starts	1st	2nd	3rd	Win & Pl
Hurdles	5	2	0	0	7647
Career Total	**6**	**2**	**0**	**0**	**7647**

104	4/02	Prth	2m4f110y	D(0-110)HHdl	GD	£4602
97	8/01	Ctml	2m1f110y	E Hdl	GD	£3045

Total win prize-money £7647

Going: Sf: 0-0 GS: 0-3 Gd: 2-2 GF: - Fm: 0-0
Distance: 2m/2m3: 1-4 2m4-2m7: 1-1 3m+: 0-0
Track: LH: 1-2 RH: 1-3 **Tight: 1-2** Gall: 0-0
Aids: Bl: 0-0 Vi: 0-0 Tstrap: 0-0
Best Rating: 104 4/02 Prth 2m4f110y good Hdl

Hannigan's Lodger (IRE)

102(99h) (109h)142

8-y-o b m Be My Native (USA)-Angolass (Al Sirat (USA))
N A Twiston-Davies The Lodgers

Placings:*22265142*/**12123420-PP65045UP** **(4729)**
2001/02: 24^{P}G, 24^{P}GS, 22^{6}S, 24^{5}G, 20^{0}S, 24^{4}GS, 24^{5}GS, 24^{U}G, 24^{P}GF

	Starts	1st	2nd	3rd	Win & Pl
Hurdles	2	0	0	0	0
Chases	7	0	0	0	545
Career Total	**25**	**3**	**7**	**1**	**35607**

136	12/00	Hntg	2m4f110y	D Ch	SFT	£3737
130	9/00	Extr	2m1f110y	E Ch	GD	£3526
121	3/00	Bang	2m4f	D(0-110)HHdl	G-S	£5395

Total win prize-money £12659

Going: Sf: 0-2 GS: 0-3 Gd: 0-3 GF: - Fm: 0-1
Distance: 2m/2m3: 0-0 2m4-2m7: 0-2 3m+: 0-7
Track: LH: 0-5 RH: 0-4 Tight: 0-1 Gall: 0-0
Aids: Bl: 0-0 Vi: 0-0 Tstrap: 0-0
Best Rating: 142 4/01 Aint 2m4f soft Ch

A winner over hurdles and fences, she acts on good and soft ground and is suited by two/two and a half miles.

Hanoi Hanna

6-y-o b m Lancastrian-Farm Track (Saxon Farm)
R Johnson Harry Humble

Placings:P **(4875)**
2001/02: 24^{P}G

	Starts	1st	2nd	3rd	Win & Pl
Hurdles	1	0	0	0	
Career Total	**1**	**0**	**0**	**0**	

Going: Sf: 0-0 GS: 0-0 Gd: 0-1 GF: - Fm: 0-0
Distance: 2m/2m3: 0-0 2m4-2m7: 0-0 3m+: 0-1
Track: LH: 0-0 RH: 0-1 Tight: 0-0 Gall: 0-0
Aids: Bl: 0-0 Vi: 0-0 Tstrap: 0-0
Best Rating:

Hanover Square

104 **91**

6-y-o b g Le Moss-Hilly-Down Lass (Deep Run)
N A Twiston-Davies The Oriental Partnership Iii

Placings: *60*-U20P **(3654)**
2001/02: 20^U^G, 24^2^S, 21^0^HY, 26^P^S

	Starts	1st	2nd	3rd	Win & Pl
Hurdles	4	0	1	0	1264
Career Total	**6**	**0**	**1**	**0**	**1264**

Going: Sf: 0-3 GS: 0-0 Gd: 0-1 GF: - Fm: 0-0
Distance: 2m/2m3: 0-0 2m4-2m7: 0-2 3m+: 0-2
Track: LH: 0-1 RH: 0-3 Tight: 0-1 Gall: 0-1
Aids: Bl: 0-0 Vi: 0-0 Tstrap: 0-0
Best Rating: 91 10/01 Towc 3m soft Hdl

Good form in novice hurdles. Acts on soft ground.

Happicat (IRE)

81(109h) (119h)**91+**

7-y-o gr g Cataldi-Gladonia (Godswalk (USA))
P R Webber D A Beaumont

Placings: *O6*/0P00/23552-122120 **(4853)**
2001/02: 17^1^G, 17^2^GF, 16^2^GF, 16^1^GF, 16^2^GF, 16^0^G

	Starts	1st	2nd	3rd	Win & Pl
Hurdles	6	2	3	0	10761
Career Total	**17**	**2**	**5**	**1**	**12598**

115	7/01	Strf	2m110y	C(0-130)HHdl	G-F	£4888
99	5/01	Hrfd	2m1f	D(0-110)HHdl	GD	£3150

Total win prize-money £8038

Going: Sf: 0-0 GS: 0-0 Gd: 1-2 GF: - Fm: 1-4
Distance: **2m/2m3: 2-6** 2m4-2m7: 0-0 3m+: 0-0
Track: LH: 1-4 RH: 1-2 **Tight: 1-4** Gall: 0-0
Aids: Bl: 0-0 Vi: 0-0 Tstrap: 0-0
Best Rating: 119 8/01 Uttx 2m gd-fm Hdl

Fair hurdler who goes well on fast ground and a tight track. Has won on a right-handed track but apparently prefers to go in the other direction

Happy Change (GER)

98(95h) (86h)**100**

8-y-o ch g Surumu (GER)-Happy Gini (USA) (Ginistrelli (USA))
Miss Venetia Williams (M Johnston 20/7) The Winning Line

Placings: 1/0-0 **(4893)**
2001/02: 20^0^G

	Starts	1st	2nd	3rd	Win & Pl
Hurdles	1	0	0	0	
Career Total	**3**	**1**	**0**	**0**	**3631**

117	10/99	Uttx	2m	D Hdl	G-S	£3631

Total win prize-money £3631

Going: Sf: 0-0 GS: 0-0 Gd: 0-1 GF: - Fm: 0-0
Distance: 2m/2m3: 0-0 2m4-2m7: 0-1 3m+: 0-0
Track: LH: 0-0 RH: 0-1 Tight: 0-0 Gall: 0-0
Aids: Bl: 0-0 Vi: 0-0 Tstrap: 0-0
Best Rating: 117 10/99 Uttx 2m gd-sft Hdl

Placed in a Group One on the Flat. Has been lightly raced over jumps. Acts on most types of ground.

Happy Days

107 **87**

7-y-o b g Primitive Rising (USA)-Miami Dolphin (Derrylin)
D Moffatt J W Barrett

Placings: 050F333/30/45-64005 **(4670)**
2001/02: 17^6^HY, 19^4^S, 25^0^GS, 19^0^S, 21^5^GF

	Starts	1st	2nd	3rd	Win & Pl
Hurdles	5	0	0	0	0
Career Total	**16**	**0**	**0**	**4**	**1442**

Going: Sf: 0-3 GS: 0-1 Gd: 0-0 GF: - Fm: 0-1
Distance: 2m/2m3: 0-3 2m4-2m7: 0-1 3m+: 0-1
Track: LH: 0-4 RH: 0-1 Tight: 0-3 Gall: 0-0
Aids: Bl: 0-0 Vi: 0-1 Tstrap: 0-0
Best Rating: 92 3/99 Kels 2m110y soft Hdl

Happy Hussar (IRE)

104 **98**

9-y-o b g Balinger-Merry Mirth (Menelek)
Dr P Pritchard Dr J J Kabler

Placings: *1*30P/**U03PBP/02P5U-2401343546604** **(4753)**
2001/02: 21^2^GF, 24^4^GF, 25^0^GF, 25^1^G, 26^3^S, 24^4^G, 26^3^HY, 25^5^G, 25^4^S, 23^6^S, 24^6^G, 32^0^GS, 26^4^GF

	Starts	1st	2nd	3rd	Win & Pl
Chases	13	1	1	2	6949
Career Total	**28**	**2**	**2**	**4**	**10228**

98	10/01	Hrfd	3m1f110y	E Ch	GD	£3100
101	12/98	Ludl	2m	H NHF	G-S	£1350

Total win prize-money £4451

Going: Sf: 0-4 GS: 0-1 Gd: 1-4 GF: - Fm: 0-4
Distance: 2m/2m3: 0-0 2m4-2m7: 0-1 **3m+: 1-12**
Track: LH: 0-7 **RH: 1-5** Tight: 0-4 Gall: 0-3
Aids: Bl: 0-0 Vi: 0-0 Tstrap: 0-0
Best Rating: 101 12/98 Ludl 2m gd-sft NHF

Handicap chaser. Stays well, acts on most ground

Harapour (FR)

97 **105**

4-y-o b g Valanour (IRE)-Haratiyna (Top Ville)
P F Nicholls (A De Royer Dupre 22/7) Mrs Jan Smith

Placings: 3P **(4326)**
2001/02: 16^3^S, 17^P^S

	Starts	1st	2nd	3rd	Win & Pl
Hurdles	2	0	0	1	696
Career Total	**2**	**0**	**0**	**1**	**696**

Going: Sf: 0-2 GS: 0-0 Gd: 0-0 GF: - Fm: 0-0
Distance: 2m/2m3: 0-2 2m4-2m7: 0-0 3m+: 0-0
Track: LH: 0-1 RH: 0-1 Tight: 0-0 Gall: 0-1
Aids: Bl: 0-0 Vi: 0-0 Tstrap: 0-0
Best Rating: 105 3/02 Newb 2m110y soft Hdl

A middle-distance winner on the Flat in France, he ran a promising race at Newbury on his hurdling debut.

Harbour Island

89 **108**

10-y-o b g Rainbow Quest (USA)-Quay Line (High Line)
B J Llewellyn Miss Emily Jane Jones

Placings: 1U66/50P0/0PP/0/P1-P4P **(4733)**
2001/02: 27^P^GF, 27^4^G, 24^P^F

	Starts	1st	2nd	3rd	Win & Pl
Hurdles	3	0	0	0	0
Career Total	**17**	**2**	**0**	**0**	**7202**

108	4/01	Font	3m3f	D(0-125)HHdl	GD	£3570
115	1/97	Hayd	2m4f	E Hdl	G-F	£2778

Total win prize-money £6348

Going: Sf: 0-0 GS: 0-0 Gd: 0-1 GF: - Fm: 0-2
Distance: 2m/2m3: 0-0 2m4-2m7: 0-0 3m+: 0-3
Track: LH: 0-2 RH: 0-1 Tight: 0-2 Gall: 0-0
Aids: Bl: 0-3 Vi: 0-0 Tstrap: 0-0
Best Rating: 125 3/97 Chel 2m5f gd-fm Hdl

Harbour Pilot (IRE)

115 (128h)**160**

7-y-o b g Be My Native (USA)-Las-Cancellas (Monksfield)
Noel Meade Kays Syndicate

Placings: *110*/2S11534-1161U2 **(4711a)**
2001/02: 22^1^SH, 20^1^Y, 24^6^Y, 21^1^HY, 24^U^GS, 20^2^Y

	Starts	1st	2nd	3rd	Win & Pl
Chases	6	3	1	0	93350
Career Total	**16**	**7**	**2**	**1**	**122561**

160	2/02	Leop	2m5f	Ch	HVY	£43865
151	12/01	Fair	2m4f	Ch	YLD	£31451
154	10/01	Gway	2m6f	Ch	SH	£8125
141	12/00	Navn	2m4f	Hdl	HVY	£13000
127	11/00	Naas	2m3f	Hdl	SH	£4416
111	3/00	Navn	2m	NHF	Y-S	£3588
97	1/00	Naas	2m	NHF	[illegible]	£3312

Total win prize-money £107758

Going: Sf: 1-1 GS: 0-1 Gd: 0-0 GF: - Fm: 0-0
Distance: 2m/2m3: 0-0 **2m4-2m7: 3-4** 3m+: 0-2
Track: LH: 1-3 **RH: 2-3** Tight: 0-0 Gall: 0-1
Aids: Bl: 0-0 Vi: 0-0 Tstrap: 0-0
Best Rating: 160 2/02 Leop 2m5f heavy Ch

A useful novice, he has won three times over fences, bouncing back from a poor run at Leopardstown over Christmas to win well there next time. Has won at up to two miles six and should stay further. Has won on soft, but acts on heavy.

Harbour Point (IRE)

79f **78f**

6-y-o b g Glacial Storm (USA)-Forest Jem (Croghan Hill)
D J Caro D J Caro

Placings: *0* **(3338)**
2001/02: 16^0^G

	Starts	1st	2nd	3rd	Win & Pl
NH Flat	1	0	0	0	
Career Total	**1**	**0**	**0**	**0**	

Going: Sf: 0-0 GS: 0-0 Gd: 0-1 GF: - Fm: 0-0
Distance: 2m/2m3: 0-1 2m4-2m7: 0-0 3m+: 0-0
Track: LH: 0-0 RH: 0-1 Tight: 0-0 Gall: 0-0
Aids: Bl: 0-0 Vi: 0-0 Tstrap: 0-0
Best Rating: 78 1/02 Ludl 2m good NHF

Harcamone (FR)

94(115h) (48h)**118**

7-y-o br g Passing Sale (FR)-Raise A Baby (FR) (Albert De Vongy)
M Sheppard R W Guilding

Placings: F3/FF00/002P115P-0**FU34404** **(4264)**

2001/02: 16^{0}G, 16^{F}G, 16^{U}S, 20^{3}S, 16^{4}HY, 16^{4}HY, 20^{0}G, 19^{4}S

	Starts	1st	2nd	3rd	Win & Pl
Hurdles	1	0	0	0	0
Chases	7	0	0	1	1489
Career Total	**22**	**2**	**1**	**2**	**10336**

110	2/01	Bang	2m1f	F(0-110)HHdl	HVY	£3623
96	1/01	Wwck	2m	E(0-105)HHdl	SFT	£3653

Total win prize-money £7277

Going: Sf: 0-5 GS: 0-0 Gd: 0-3 GF: - Fm: 0-0
Distance: 2m/2m3: 0-5 2m4-2m7: 0-3 3m+: 0-0
Track: LH: 0-4 RH: 0-4 Tight: 0-2 Gall: 0-0
Aids: Bl: 0-0 Vi: 0-0 Tstrap: 0-8
Best Rating: 118 12/01 Hrfd 2m soft Ch

Picked up a couple of weak hurdle races in the mud in 2000/01, but unable to add to that last season and is described by his trainer as an unpredictable character. Two miles suits him well.

Harcelante (FR)

5-y-o br m Balleroy (USA)-Hekabe (GER) (Surumu (GER))
P W Hiatt S F Holder

Placings:P (2755)
2001/02: 17^{P}GS

	Starts	1st	2nd	3rd	Win & Pl
Hurdles	1	0	0	0	
Career Total	**1**	**0**	**0**	**0**	

Going: Sf: 0-0 GS: 0-1 Gd: 0-0 GF: - Fm: 0-0
Distance: 2m/2m3: 0-1 2m4-2m7: 0-0 3m+: 0-0
Track: LH: 0-1 RH: 0-0 Tight: 0-1 Gall: 0-0
Aids: Bl: 0-0 Vi: 0-0 Tstrap: 0-0
Best Rating:

Hard Days Night (IRE)

68 42

5-y-o b g Mujtahid (USA)-Oiche Mhaith (Night Shift (USA))
M Blanshard David Sykes

Placings:P0P (2340)
2001/02: 16^{P}GS, 17^{0}G, 21^{P}GF

	Starts	1st	2nd	3rd	Win & Pl
Hurdles	3	0	0	0	
Career Total	**3**	**0**	**0**	**0**	

Going: Sf: 0-0 GS: 0-1 Gd: 0-1 GF: - Fm: 0-1
Distance: 2m/2m3: 0-2 2m4-2m7: 0-1 3m+: 0-0
Track: LH: 0-1 RH: 0-2 Tight: 0-1 Gall: 0-0
Aids: Bl: 0-0 Vi: 0-0 Tstrap: 0-0
Best Rating: 42 11/01 Tntn 2m1f good Hdl

Hard Lines (USA)

104 94

6-y-o b g Silver Hawk (USA)-Arctic Eclipse (USA) (Northern Dancer)
A Crook Turner Technology Ltd

Placings:4FPU-140P (3231)
2001/02: 17^{1}GS, 17^{4}G, 16^{0}G, 16^{P}GS

	Starts	1st	2nd	3rd	Win & Pl
Hurdles	4	1	0	0	2632
Career Total	**8**	**1**	**0**	**0**	**2632**

94	8/01	Ctml	2m1f110y	E(0-105)HHdl	G-S	£2632

Total win prize-money £2632

Going: Sf: 0-0 GS: 1-2 Gd: 0-2 GF: - Fm: 0-0
Distance: **2m/2m3: 1-4** 2m4-2m7: 0-0 3m+: 0-0
Track: **LH: 1-3** RH: 0-1 **Tight: 1-2** Gall: 0-1
Aids: Bl: 0-0 Vi: 0-0 Tstrap: 0-0
Best Rating: **94** 8/01 Ctml 2m1f110y gd-sft Hdl

A dual winner on the Flat in 2001, he won a handicap on his seasonal debut, but was well beaten in better company subsequently.

Hard Rain

74f 42f

5-y-o ch g Rock Hopper-Rainy Day Woman (Sure Blade (USA))
R Williams R Williams

Placings:*00* (4743)
2001/02: 17^{0}G, 16^{0}GF

	Starts	1st	2nd	3rd	Win & Pl
NH Flat	2	0	0	0	
Career Total	**2**	**0**	**0**	**0**	

Going: Sf: 0-0 GS: 0-0 Gd: 0-1 GF: - Fm: 0-1
Distance: 2m/2m3: 0-2 2m4-2m7: 0-0 3m+: 0-0
Track: LH: 0-1 RH: 0-1 Tight: 0-1 Gall: 0-0
Aids: Bl: 0-0 Vi: 0-0 Tstrap: 0-0
Best Rating: 42 4/02 Ludl 2m gd-fm NHF

Hard To Know (IRE)

100 103+

4-y-o b g Common Grounds-Lady Fern (Old Vic)
P J Hobbs (D J S Cosgrove 11/12) Ms C Hehir

Placings:0002 (4866)
2001/02: 16^{0}S, 16^{0}HY, 16^{0}S, 17^{2}F

	Starts	1st	2nd	3rd	Win & Pl
Hurdles	4	0	1	0	844
Career Total	**4**	**0**	**1**	**0**	**844**

Going: Sf: 0-3 GS: 0-0 Gd: 0-0 GF: - Fm: 0-1
Distance: 2m/2m3: 0-4 2m4-2m7: 0-0 3m+: 0-0
Track: LH: 0-2 RH: 0-2 Tight: 0-0 Gall: 0-1
Aids: Bl: 0-0 Vi: 0-0 Tstrap: 0-0
Best Rating: 93 4/02 Extr 2m1f firm Hdl

Showed improved form when runner-up on firm ground in novices' handicap at Exeter April 2002. Scored at Ludlow the following month.

Hard To Start (IRE)

112 133

7-y-o b g Supreme Leader-Sea Skin (Buckskin (FR))
P J Hobbs Ms C Hehir

Placings:*2310*/112166 (4647)
2001/02: 22^{1}GS, 21^{1}G, 21^{2}G, 24^{1}S, 21^{6}GS, 24^{6}G

	Starts	1st	2nd	3rd	Win & Pl
Hurdles	6	3	1	0	20006
Career Total	**10**	**4**	**2**	**1**	**25254**

127	2/02	Kemp	3m110y	D Hdl	SFT	£4660
126	10/01	Chel	2m5f	B Hdl	GD	£7182
114	10/01	Uttx	2m6f110y	C Hdl	G-S	£4875
122	2/00	Kemp	2m	H NHF	SFT	£3068

Total win prize-money £19787

Going: Sf: 1-1 GS: 1-2 Gd: 1-3 GF: - Fm: 0-0
Distance: 2m/2m3: 0-0 **2m4-2m7: 2-4** 3m+: 1-2
Track: **LH: 2-5** RH: 1-1 Tight: 0-1 **Gall: 1-3**
Aids: **Bl: 1-3** Vi: 0-0 Tstrap: 0-0
Best Rating: **133** 3/02 Chel 2m5f gd-sft Hdl

A decent bumper horse a few seasons ago, he won three times in 2001/2002 including at Kempton over three miles, winning with something in hand in a fair contest, although he was well held after that in the Coral Cup at Cheltenham in March 2002. Effective on good or a softer surface.

Harden Glen

11-y-o b g Respect-Polly Peril (Politico (USA))
C Storey (Miss S E Forster 20/10) M H Walton

Placings:63/2032054312/63SPP0P/52503UPP-050 (4692)
2001/02: 25^{0}G, 25^{5}GS, 25^{0}GF

	Starts	1st	2nd	3rd	Win & Pl
Chases	3	0	0	0	0
Career Total	**30**	**1**	**4**	**5**	**10723**

103	4/99	Kels	3m1f	D Ch	G-F	£3837

Total win prize-money £3838

Going: Sf: 0-0 GS: 0-1 Gd: 0-1 GF: - Fm: 0-1
Distance: 2m/2m3: 0-0 2m4-2m7: 0-0 3m+: 0-3
Track: LH: 0-3 RH: 0-0 Tight: 0-3 Gall: 0-0
Aids: Bl: 0-0 Vi: 0-0 Tstrap: 0-0
Best Rating: 103 5/99 Weth 3m1f good Ch

Hardi De Chalamont (FR)

86 121

7-y-o gr g Royal Charter (FR)-Naita Ii (FR) (Dom Luc (FR))
A Parker Mr & Mrs Raymond Anderson Green

Placings:14/1FP2-F3P (4879)
2001/02: 16^{F}GF, 20^{3}F, 16^{P}G

	Starts	1st	2nd	3rd	Win & Pl
Hurdles	1	0	0	0	0
Chases	2	0	0	1	606
Career Total	**9**	**2**	**1**	**1**	**12151**

5/00	Fntb	2m3f	Ch	GD	£3074
1/00	Pau	2m2f	Hdl	SFT	£5764

Total win prize-money £8838

Going: Sf: 0-0 GS: 0-0 Gd: 0-1 GF: - Fm: 0-2
Distance: 2m/2m3: 0-2 2m4-2m7: 0-1 3m+: 0-0
Track: LH: 0-2 RH: 0-1 Tight: 0-0 Gall: 0-0
Aids: Bl: 0-0 Vi: 0-0 Tstrap: 0-0
Best Rating: 121 4/01 Ayr 2m good Ch

Hardi Guichois (FR)

(102c) (84c)72

7-y-o b g Montorselli-Lady Belle (FR) (Or De Chine)
A Crook Jay Dee Bloodstock Limited

Placings:12P/1663PPP3-3P (0825)
2001/02: 18^{3}GF, 22^{P}GF

	Starts	1st	2nd	3rd	Win & Pl
Hurdles	1	0	0	0	0
Chases	1	0	0	1	341
Career Total	**13**	**2**	**1**	**3**	**9852**

5/00	Mtne	2m6f110y	Ch	GD	£2402
11/99	Agtn	2m4f	Ch	GD	£3444

Total win prize-money £5846

Going: Sf: 0-0 GS: 0-0 Gd: 0-0 GF: - Fm: 0-2
Distance: 2m/2m3: 0-1 2m4-2m7: 0-1 3m+: 0-0
Track: LH: 0-1 RH: 0-0 Tight: 0-2 Gall: 0-0
Aids: Bl: 0-0 Vi: 0-0 Tstrap: 0-0

Best Rating: **84** 5/01 Font 2m2f gd-fm Ch

Hardly (IRE)

91(84h) (69h)94

9-y-o ch g Good Thyne (USA)-Monks Lass (IRE) (Monksfield)

R M Stronge (Miss H C Knight 1/5) Peter J Douglas Engineering

Placings:4123/20/P214F3-PF02 **(1390)**

2001/02: 23^{P}GF, 20^{F}GS, 20^{0}GF, 21^{2}G

	Starts	1st	2nd	3rd	Win & Pl
Hurdles	1	0	0	0	0
Chases	3	0	1	0	1230
Career Total	**16**	**2**	**4**	**2**	**11748**

128	11/00	MRas	2m4f	E Ch	G-S	£3146
119	1/99	Winc	2m	E Hdl	SFT	£2514

Total win prize-money £5660

Going: Sf: 0-0 GS: 0-1 Gd: 0-1 GF: - Fm: 0-2
Distance: 2m/2m3: 0-0 2m4-2m7: 0-3 3m+: 0-1
Track: LH: 0-4 RH: 0-0 Tight: 0-2 Gall: 0-0
Aids: Bl: 0-0 Vi: 0-0 Tstrap: 0-1
Best Rating: **128** 11/00 MRas 2m4f gd-sft Ch

Hardwick Lodge

79 43

6-y-o ch m Grand Lodge (USA)-Mrs Musgrove (Jalmood (USA))

T D Easterby Ms Chantelle Dodson

Placings:205/0 **(2176)**

2001/02: 20^{0}G

	Starts	1st	2nd	3rd	Win & Pl
Hurdles	1	0	0	0	
Career Total	**4**	**0**	**1**	**0**	**1608**

Going: Sf: 0-0 GS: 0-0 Gd: 0-1 GF: - Fm: 0-0
Distance: 2m/2m3: 0-0 2m4-2m7: 0-1 3m+: 0-0
Track: LH: 0-1 RH: 0-0 Tight: 0-0 Gall: 0-0
Aids: Bl: 0-0 Vi: 0-0 Tstrap: 0-0
Best Rating: **80** 11/99 Hntg 2m110y gd-fm Hdl

Hardy Breeze (IRE)

97 (55h)88

11-y-o b g Henbit (USA)-Chake-Chake (Goldhill)

Miss A M Newton-Smith Mrs John Grist

Placings:P5606/5P656/02P30051/56P2-5000552 **(4563)**

2001/02: 25^{5}S, 25^{0}S, 26^{0}G, 29^{0}G, 26^{5}S, 25^{5}GS, 26^{2}GF

	Starts	1st	2nd	3rd	Win & Pl
Hurdles	3	0	0	0	0
Chases	4	0	1	0	808
Career Total	**29**	**1**	**3**	**1**	**5629**

93	4/00	Plum	3m2f	F(0-90)HCh	GD	£2898

Total win prize-money £2898

Going: Sf: 0-3 GS: 0-1 Gd: 0-2 GF: - Fm: 0-1
Distance: 2m/2m3: 0-0 2m4-2m7: 0-0 3m+: 0-7
Track: LH: 0-1 RH: 0-0 Tight: 0-0 Gall: 0-0
Aids: Bl: 0-0 Vi: 0-0 Tstrap: 0-0
Best Rating: **93** 4/00 Plum 3m2f good Ch

Moderate staying chaser. Seems to handle any ground.

Hardycomestohardy (IRE)

9-y-o b g Be My Native (USA)-Bid For Fun (IRE) (Auction Ring (USA))

Miss Maria D Myco (M F Morris 20/1) Miss Maria D Myco

Placings:0/550/04015/044P/5400-P **(3824)**

2001/02: 21^{P}S

	Starts	1st	2nd	3rd	Win & Pl
Chases	1	0	0	0	
Career Total	**18**	**1**	**0**	**0**	**4682**

101	9/98	List	2m	Hdl	GD	£3929

Total win prize-money £3929

Going: Sf: 0-1 GS: 0-0 Gd: 0-0 GF: - Fm: 0-0
Distance: 2m/2m3: 0-0 2m4-2m7: 0-1 3m+: 0-0
Track: LH: 0-1 RH: 0-0 Tight: 0-1 Gall: 0-0
Aids: Bl: 0-0 Vi: 0-0 Tstrap: 0-0
Best Rating: **101** 9/98 List 2m good Hdl

Harebelle

79 48

5-y-o b m Almoojid-Velvet Heart (IRE) (Damister (USA))

A D Smith David M Williams

Placings:00P-60 **(1996)**

2001/02: 22^{6}G, 17^{0}S

	Starts	1st	2nd	3rd	Win & Pl
Hurdles	2	0	0	0	0
Career Total	**5**	**0**	**0**	**0**	**0**

Going: Sf: 0-1 GS: 0-0 Gd: 0-1 GF: - Fm: 0-0
Distance: 2m/2m3: 0-1 2m4-2m7: 0-1 3m+: 0-0
Track: LH: 0-1 RH: 0-1 Tight: 0-1 Gall: 0-0
Aids: Bl: 0-0 Vi: 0-0 Tstrap: 0-0
Best Rating: **55** 2/01 Wwck 2m soft NHF

Harem Scarem (IRE)

106(99h) (64h)96

11-y-o b g Lord Americo-River Rescue (Over The River (FR))

Mrs L Williamson Halewood International Ltd

Placings:014/06PB30F6/O003410622120F2-0P535136P52 **(4855)**

2001/02: 16^{0}S, 16^{P}HY, 16^{5}S, 16^{3}S, 16^{5}HY, 16^{1}HY, 16^{3}S, 16^{6}S, 16^{P}HY, 16^{5}HY, 20^{2}G

	Starts	1st	2nd	3rd	Win & Pl
Hurdles	2	0	0	0	0
Chases	9	1	1	2	6054
Career Total	**37**	**4**	**5**	**4**	**19069**

96	2/02	Hrfd	2m	F(0-100)HCh	HVY	£3848
94	3/01	Ling	2m	F(0-95)HCh	HVY	£2947
83	1/01	Leic	2m	G(0-90)HHdl	HVY	£1932
102	8/97	Tral	2m1f	NHF	SFT	£3391

Total win prize-money £12118

Going: Sf: 1-10 GS: 0-0 Gd: 0-1 GF: - Fm: 0-0
Distance: **2m/2m3: 1-10** 2m4-2m7: 0-1 3m+: 0-0
Track: LH: 0-7 **RH: 1-4** Tight: 0-3 Gall: 0-1
Aids: Bl: 0-0 Vi: 0-0 Tstrap: 0-0
Best Rating: **102** 8/97 Tral 2m1f soft NHF

Modest two-mile chaser, although stays further, likes to front run and effective in testing ground.

Harfdecent

98 137

11-y-o b g Primitive Rising (USA)-Grand Queen (Grand Conde (FR))

Mrs M Reveley A G Knowles

Placings:0/030P413/453112/F314P/332112P/P0-3P26F **(4015)**

2001/02: 20^{3}GS, 19^{P}S, 19^{2}S, 20^{6}GS, 19^{F}GS

	Starts	1st	2nd	3rd	Win & Pl
Chases	5	0	1	1	1879
Career Total	**33**	**6**	**4**	**7**	**33888**

134	1/00	Donc	2m3f110y	C(0-130)HCh	G-F	£5993
124	1/00	Muss	3m	E(0-115)HCh	SFT	£3575
119	2/99	Donc	2m3f110y	E(0-115)HCh	G-F	£2960
110	4/98	Sedg	2m5f	E(0-115)HCh	G-S	£4055
110	3/98	Catt	2m3f	D Ch	SFT	£3574
86	3/97	Sedg	2m5f110y	E Hdl	G-F	£2253

Total win prize-money £22410

Going: Sf: 0-2 GS: 0-3 Gd: 0-0 GF: - Fm: 0-0
Distance: 2m/2m3: 0-1 2m4-2m7: 0-4 3m+: 0-0
Track: LH: 0-4 RH: 0-1 Tight: 0-2 Gall: 0-3
Aids: Bl: 0-0 Vi: 0-0 Tstrap: 0-0
Best Rating: **137** 1/02 Catt 2m3f soft Ch

Fair chaser, stays three miles but possibly most effective at shorter. Handles soft ground but probably best on a sound surface.

Harik

106 122

8-y-o ch g Persian Bold-Yaqut (USA) (Northern Dancer)

G L Moore The Best Beech Partnership

Placings:P/32F36331/53436/21136-306212P23P **(4886)**

2001/02: 16^{3}GF, 16^{0}GF, 17^{6}GF, 16^{2}GF, 20^{1}GF, 20^{2}G, 20^{P}G, 18^{2}GS, 16^{3}G, 18^{P}GF

	Starts	1st	2nd	3rd	Win & Pl
Chases	10	1	3	2	8066
Career Total	**29**	**4**	**5**	**9**	**20829**

119	9/01	Font	2m4f	F(0-105)HCh	G-F	£3167
115	5/00	Font	2m4f	F Ch	GD	£2843
115	5/00	Hntg	2m110y	E Ch	G-F	£2880
113	4/99	Font	2m2f110y	E Hdl	GD	£2215

Total win prize-money £11107

Going: Sf: 0-0 GS: 0-1 Gd: 0-3 GF: - Fm: 1-6
Distance: 2m/2m3: 0-7 **2m4-2m7: 1-3** 3m+: 0-0
Track: LH: 0-5 RH: 0-2 **Tight: 1-8** Gall: 0-1
Aids: Bl: 0-1 **Vi: 1-5** Tstrap: 0-9
Best Rating: **122** 4/02 Winc 2m good Ch

A very versatile performer, he splits his time between racing on sand and over fences these days and is successful under both codes. Suited by fast ground over fences and stays two and a half miles. Has a good record at Fontwell.

Hariymi (IRE)

7-y-o gr g Woodman (USA)-Harouniya (Siberian Express (USA))

R Rowe Mrs Jean R Bishop

Placings:33210/0F0-P **(1647)**

2001/02: 16^{P}G

	Starts	1st	2nd	3rd	Win & Pl
Hurdles	1	0	0	0	
Career Total	**9**	**1**	**1**	**2**	**11512**

124	2/00	Kemp	2m	A Hdl	SFT	£9600

Total win prize-money £9600

Going: Sf: 0-0 GS: 0-0 Gd: 0-1 GF: - Fm: 0-0
Distance: 2m/2m3: 0-1 2m4-2m7: 0-0 3m+: 0-0
Track: LH: 0-0 RH: 0-1 Tight: 0-0 Gall: 0-1
Aids: Bl: 0-0 Vi: 0-0 Tstrap: 0-0
Best Rating: **124** 2/00 Kemp 2m soft Hdl

One-time decent hurdler. Died after breaking down at Huntingdon in October 2001. (DEAD)

Harjach

75 **65**

5-y-o b g Sir Harry Lewis (USA)-Acolyn (Derrylin)
P J Hobbs (B G Powell 28/1) Mrs J Chesney

Placings:0000 **(4584)**
2001/02: 17^{0}G, 17^{0}F, 16^{0}S, 16^{0}G

	Starts	1st	2nd	3rd	Win & Pl
NH Flat	3	0	0	0	0
Hurdles	1	0	0	0	0
Career Total	**4**	**0**	**0**	**0**	

Going: Sf: 0-1 GS: 0-0 Gd: 0-2 GF: - Fm: 0-1
Distance: 2m/2m3: 0-4 2m4-2m7: 0-0 3m+: 0-0
Track: LH: 0-0 RH: 0-4 Tight: 0-0 Gall: 0-0
Aids: Bl: 0-0 Vi: 0-0 Tstrap: 0-0
Best Rating: **87** 5/01 Extr 2m1f good NHF

Harleidalus (IRE)

107 **107**

8-y-o b g Mandalus-Spartan Park (Scorpio (FR))
Mrs L B Normile K J Fehilly

Placings:50/**0-P31** **(0648)**
2001/02: 24^{P}GS, 23^{3}F, 24^{1}GF

	Starts	1st	2nd	3rd	Win & Pl
Chases	3	1	0	1	4727
Career Total	**6**	**1**	**0**	**1**	**4727**

107 6/01 Prth 3m D Ch G-F £4095
Total win prize-money £4095

Going: Sf: 0-0 GS: 0-1 Gd: 0-0 GF: - Fm: 1-2
Distance: 2m/2m3: 0-0 2m4-2m7: 0-0 **3m+: 1-3**
Track: LH: 0-0 **RH: 1-2** Tight: 0-0 Gall: 0-0
Aids: Bl: 0-0 Vi: 0-0 Tstrap: 0-0
Best Rating: **107** 6/01 Prth 3m gd-fm Ch

Harlequin Boy

91(85h) (85h)**81**

9-y-o b g Roscoe Blake-Gain The Day (Bivouac)
C Tizzard R P & S H Richards

Placings:0-006 **(0796)**
2001/02: 16^{0}GF, 22^{0}G, 16^{6}GF

	Starts	1st	2nd	3rd	Win & Pl
Hurdles	2	0	0	0	0
Chases	1	0	0	0	0
Career Total	**4**	**0**	**0**	**0**	**0**

Going: Sf: 0-0 GS: 0-0 Gd: 0-1 GF: - Fm: 0-2
Distance: 2m/2m3: 0-2 2m4-2m7: 0-1 3m+: 0-0
Track: LH: 0-2 RH: 0-1 Tight: 0-2 Gall: 0-0
Aids: Bl: 0-1 Vi: 0-0 Tstrap: 0-0
Best Rating: **85** 5/01 Winc 2m gd-fm Hdl

Harlequin Chorus

12-y-o ch g Jester-Raise The Dawn (Rymer)
F E Sutherland Miss H P J Scheffers

Placings:*240*55/0526/3**F**11**2F**2/232P6**2**/**P5**54/**PP** **(0556)**
2001/02: 20^{P}GF, 24^{P}GF

	Starts	1st	2nd	3rd	Win & Pl
Chases	2	0	0	0	
Career Total	**28**	**2**	**7**	**2**	**16017**

89 12/97 MRas 2m1f110y D Hdl G-S £3106
111 11/97 Wwck 2m C Hdl G-S £4256
Total win prize-money £7363

Going: Sf: 0-0 GS: 0-0 Gd: 0-0 GF: - Fm: 0-2
Distance: 2m/2m3: 0-0 2m4-2m7: 0-1 3m+: 0-1
Track: LH: 0-0 RH: 0-2 Tight: 0-0 Gall: 0-2
Aids: Bl: 0-0 Vi: 0-0 Tstrap: 0-0
Best Rating: **121** 1/99 Donc 2m4f good Hdl

Harleyburn

99 **71**

10-y-o b g Wonderful Surprise-Miss Anax (Anax)
Mrs A C Hamilton (Mrs J K M Oliver 3/12) Mrs M A Bowie

Placings:0F040P **(4745)**
2001/02: 17^{0}GS, 22^{F}GS, 22^{0}G, 22^{4}GS, 22^{0}GS, 24^{P}G

	Starts	1st	2nd	3rd	Win & Pl
Hurdles	6	0	0	0	0
Career Total	**6**	**0**	**0**	**0**	**0**

Going: Sf: 0-0 GS: 0-4 Gd: 0-2 GF: - Fm: 0-0
Distance: 2m/2m3: 0-1 2m4-2m7: 0-4 3m+: 0-1
Track: LH: 0-4 RH: 0-2 Tight: 0-4 Gall: 0-0
Aids: Bl: 0-4 Vi: 0-0 Tstrap: 0-0
Best Rating: **71** 11/01 Kels 2m6f110y gd-sft Hdl

Harlov (FR)

106(114h) (104h)**114**

7-y-o ch g Garde Royale-Paulownia (FR) (Montevideo)
A Parker Mr & Mrs Raymond Anderson Green

Placings:00/3030313/2**F**22-**F**2660**2131** **(4856)**
2001/02: 20^{F}S, 24^{2}GS, 20^{6}HY, 27^{6}HY, 27^{0}S, 27^{2}S, 26^{1}GS, 26^{3}GF, 25^{1}G

	Starts	1st	2nd	3rd	Win & Pl
Hurdles	5	0	2	0	2003
Chases	4	2	0	1	9619
Career Total	**22**	**3**	**5**	**5**	**19681**

114 4/02 Hexm 3m1f E Ch GD £3672
103 3/02 Carl 3m2f D Ch G-S £4868
91 3/00 Ayr 3m110y D(0-115)HHdl HVY £3614
Total win prize-money £12156

Going: Sf: 0-5 GS: 1-2 Gd: 1-1 GF: - Fm: 0-1
Distance: 2m/2m3: 0-0 2m4-2m7: 0-2 **3m+: 2-7**
Track: LH: 1-5 RH: 1-3 Tight: 0-3 Gall: 0-0
Aids: Bl: 0-0 Vi: 0-0 Tstrap: 0-0
Best Rating: **114** 4/02 Hexm 3m1f good Ch

Fair handicap hurdler at around three miles on a soft surface.

Harmonic (USA)

107 **95**

5-y-o b m Shadeed (USA)-Running Melody (Rheingold)
Mrs L Wadham (D R C Elsworth 25/10) J J W Wadham

Placings:P224522 **(4564)**
2001/02: 19^{P}GF, 16^{2}S, 16^{2}GS, 16^{4}S, 16^{5}S, 16^{2}GF, 16^{2}GF

	Starts	1st	2nd	3rd	Win & Pl
Hurdles	7	0	4	0	3039
Career Total	**7**	**0**	**4**	**0**	**3039**

Going: Sf: 0-3 GS: 0-1 Gd: 0-0 GF: - Fm: 0-3
Distance: 2m/2m3: 0-7 2m4-2m7: 0-0 3m+: 0-0
Track: LH: 0-4 RH: 0-3 Tight: 0-4 Gall: 0-2
Aids: Bl: 0-0 Vi: 0-0 Tstrap: 0-0
Best Rating: **95** 4/02 Plum 2m gd-fm Hdl

Keeps finding one or two to beat her on the Flat and over hurdles. Suited by fast ground.

Harpasgon De L'Ombre (FR)

102 **106**

7-y-o b g Mbaiki (FR)-Undress (FR) (Signani (FR))
O Sherwood It Wasn't Us

Placings:464F42 **(4909)**
2001/02: 23^{4}G, 24^{6}GS, 20^{4}S, 20^{F}GS, 16^{4}G, 20^{2}GF

	Starts	1st	2nd	3rd	Win & Pl
Chases	6	0	1	0	2058
Career Total	**6**	**0**	**1**	**0**	**2058**

Going: Sf: 0-1 GS: 0-2 Gd: 0-2 GF: - Fm: 0-1
Distance: 2m/2m3: 0-1 2m4-2m7: 0-3 3m+: 0-2
Track: LH: 0-2 RH: 0-4 Tight: 0-2 Gall: 0-1
Aids: Bl: 0-0 Vi: 0-0 Tstrap: 0-0
Best Rating: **106** 4/02 MRas 2m4f gd-fm Ch

Lightly raced novice chaser who has looked headstrong on occasion. Has shown modest form around two and a half miles.

Harppy (FR)

60 **37**

7-y-o b g Kedellic (FR)-Flute De Pan (FR) (Saint Estephe (FR))
M C Pipe P A Deal

Placings:00P**0/1000**312S**P**PP-0 **(0266)**
2001/02: 19^{0}G

	Starts	1st	2nd	3rd	Win & Pl
Hurdles	1	0	0	0	
Career Total	**16**	**2**	**1**	**1**	**7395**

91 8/00 Uttx 3m110y E Hdl G-F £2723
5/00 Fntb 2m3f Ch SFT £3074
Total win prize-money £5797

Going: Sf: 0-0 GS: 0-0 Gd: 0-1 GF: - Fm: 0-0
Distance: 2m/2m3: 0-0 2m4-2m7: 0-1 3m+: 0-0
Track: LH: 0-0 RH: 0-1 Tight: 0-0 Gall: 0-0
Aids: Bl: 0-0 Vi: 0-1 Tstrap: 0-1
Best Rating: **91** 9/00 Plum 2m5f good Hdl

Harrovian

95f **107f**

5-y-o b g Deploy-Homeoftheclassics (Tate Gallery (USA))
Ferdy Murphy Major & Mrs Ivan Straker

Placings:*2* **(3701)**
2001/02: 16^{2}S

	Starts	1st	2nd	3rd	Win & Pl
NH Flat	1	0	1	0	3450
Career Total	**1**	**0**	**1**	**0**	**3450**

Going: Sf: 0-1 GS: 0-0 Gd: 0-0 GF: - Fm: 0-0
Distance: 2m/2m3: 0-1 2m4-2m7: 0-0 3m+: 0-0

Track: LH: 0-1 RH: 0-0 Tight: 0-0 Gall: 0-1
Aids: Bl: 0-0 Vi: 0-0 Tstrap: 0-0
Best Rating: 107 2/02 Newb 2m110y soft NHF

Promising debut in a Newbury bumper.

Harry Harestone

102(108h) **123**
7-y-o b g Miners Lamp-Slipalong (Slippered)
P J Jones Mrs A H Jones

Placings:000/45140-322FP (4009)
2001/02: 16^{3}S, 19^{2}GS, 21^{2}HY, 24^{F}S, 22^{P}S

	Starts	1st	2nd	3rd	Win & Pl
Chases	5	0	2	1	5721
Career Total	13	1	2	1	14533

113 1/01 Chel 2m1f D(0-120)HHdl SFT £7442
Total win prize-money £7443

Going: Sf: 0-4 GS: 0-1 Gd: 0-0 GF: - Fm: 0-0
Distance: 2m/2m3: 0-1 2m4-2m7: 0-3 3m+: 0-1
Track: LH: 0-4 RH: 0-1 Tight: 0-0 Gall: 0-3
Aids: Bl: 0-0 Vi: 0-0 Tstrap: 0-0
Best Rating: 123 1/02 Chel 2m5f heavy Ch

Winning hurdler who has shown promise so far over fences. Acts on soft ground. Stays two miles five.

Harry Hooly

109 **101**
7-y-o b g Lithgie-Brig-Drummond Lass (Peacock (FR))
Mrs H O Graham Mrs H O Graham

Placings:0030P4101U31 (4261)
2001/02: 22^{0}G, 22^{0}GS, 24^{3}S, 24^{0}S, 27^{P}S, 22^{4}GS, 24^{1}S, 24^{0}S, 27^{1}HY, 27^{U}S, 27^{3}S, 24^{1}HY

	Starts	1st	2nd	3rd	Win & Pl
Hurdles	12	3	0	2	7465
Career Total	12	3	0	2	7465

93 3/02 Hexm 3m F(0-100)HHdl HVY £2044
90 1/02 Sedg 3m3f110y E(0-105)HHdl HVY £2450
88 12/01 Hexm 3m F(0-105)HHdl SFT £2138
Total win prize-money £6633

Going: Sf: 3-9 GS: 0-2 Gd: 0-1 GF: - Fm: 0-0
Distance: 2m/2m3: 0-0 2m4-2m7: 0-3 **3m+: 3-9**
Track: **LH: 3-10** RH: 0-2 **Tight: 1-7** Gall: 0-1
Aids: Bl: 0-0 Vi: 0-0 Tstrap: 0-0
Best Rating: 93 3/02 Hexm 3m heavy Hdl

Modest handicap hurdler. He is effective at around three miles and acts on soft ground.

Harry Hotspur (IRE)

113 **91**
9-y-o gr g Celio Rufo-Midsummer Blends (IRE) (Duky)
Ian Williams The Five Nations Partnership

Placings:0040/5023P/PP31 (4238)
2001/02: 24^{P}HY, 23^{P}S, 24^{3}S, 24^{1}GF

	Starts	1st	2nd	3rd	Win & Pl
Hurdles	1	0	0	0	0
Chases	3	1	0	1	3052
Career Total	13	1	1	2	4613

91 3/02 Hntg 3m F(0-95)HCh G-F £2674
Total win prize-money £2674

Going: Sf: 0-3 GS: 0-0 Gd: 0-0 GF: - Fm: 1-1
Distance: 2m/2m3: 0-0 2m4-2m7: 0-0 **3m+: 1-4**
Track: LH: 0-1 **RH: 1-3** Tight: 0-0 **Gall: 1-2**
Aids: Bl: 0-0 **Vi: 1-2** Tstrap: 0-0
Best Rating: 91 3/02 Hntg 3m gd-fm Ch

Modest staying chaser, he appreciates a positive ride and off the mark at Huntingdon in March improving for the fitting of a visor. Likes fast ground.

Harry Welsh (IRE)

10-y-o gr g Treasure Kay-Excelling Miss (USA) (Exceller (USA))
J E Collinson Mrs E M Collinson

Placings:600000000/0/006P0/00/PP (1189)
2001/02: 19^{P}GF, 20^{P}G

	Starts	1st	2nd	3rd	Win & Pl
Hurdles	2	0	0	0	
Career Total	19	0	0	0	0

Going: Sf: 0-0 GS: 0-0 Gd: 0-1 GF: - Fm: 0-1
Distance: 2m/2m3: 0-1 2m4-2m7: 0-1 3m+: 0-0
Track: LH: 0-2 RH: 0-0 Tight: 0-2 Gall: 0-0
Aids: Bl: 0-1 Vi: 0-0 Tstrap: 0-0
Best Rating: 84 9/96 Clon 2m good Hdl

Harvest Home (IRE)

69 **55**
10-y-o b g Dromod Hill-Carlys Bank (Saucy Kit)
Miss D Cole W P Harper

Placings:F4 (0831)
2001/02: 21^{F}GS, 21^{4}GF

	Starts	1st	2nd	3rd	Win & Pl
Chases	2	0	0	0	295
Career Total	2	0	0	0	295

Going: Sf: 0-0 GS: 0-1 Gd: 0-0 GF: - Fm: 0-1
Distance: 2m/2m3: 0-0 2m4-2m7: 0-2 3m+: 0-0
Track: LH: 0-2 RH: 0-0 Tight: 0-2 Gall: 0-0
Aids: Bl: 0-0 Vi: 0-0 Tstrap: 0-0
Best Rating: 55 6/01 NAbb 2m5f110y gd-fm Ch

Harveysinahurry

9-y-o b g Push On-Shylyn (Hay Chas)
D Burchell Mrs D L Smith-Hopper

Placings:0/P-P (0778)
2001/02: 20^{P}GF

	Starts	1st	2nd	3rd	Win & Pl
Hurdles	1	0	0	0	
Career Total	3	0	0	0	

Going: Sf: 0-0 GS: 0-0 Gd: 0-0 GF: - Fm: 0-1
Distance: 2m/2m3: 0-0 2m4-2m7: 0-1 3m+: 0-0
Track: LH: 0-1 RH: 0-0 Tight: 0-0 Gall: 0-0
Aids: Bl: 0-1 Vi: 0-0 Tstrap: 0-0
Best Rating:

Harvis (FR)

106(103h) **143**
7-y-o b g Djarvis (FR)-Tirana (FR) (Over)
Miss Venetia Williams P Richardson & J M Kinnear

Placings:6302233/4111FF0-12422 (4843)
2001/02: 20^{1}HY, 16^{2}GS, 16^{4}HY, 20^{2}G, 17^{2}G

	Starts	1st	2nd	3rd	Win & Pl
Chases	5	1	3	0	17130
Career Total	19	4	5	3	56814

139 12/01 Hayd 2m4f C Ch HVY £6435
136 12/00 Chep 2m110y D(0-120)HHdl SFT £10400
130 11/00 Leic 2m4f110y D Hdl HVY £3367
110 11/00 Towc 2m E Hdl SFT £2324
Total win prize-money £22526

Going: Sf: 1-2 GS: 0-1 Gd: 0-2 GF: - Fm: 0-0
Distance: 2m/2m3: 0-3 **2m4-2m7: 1-2** 3m+: 0-0
Track: **LH: 1-3** RH: 0-2 Tight: 0-2 Gall: 0-1
Aids: Bl: 0-0 Vi: 0-0 Tstrap: 0-0
Best Rating: 143 4/02 Aint 2m4f good Ch

Ex-French, he jumped well when winning at Haydock on his debut over British fences and ran with credit subsequently. Stays two and a half miles.

Hasard Saisi (FR)

104(93h) (89h)**124**
6-y-o ch g Mill Pond (FR)-Askja (FR) (Jefferson)
P F Nicholls Jeffrey Hordle

Placings:PP3456/53163510124-P305 (2878)
2001/02: 17^{P}GS, 16^{3}GF, 16^{0}S, 16^{5}G

	Starts	1st	2nd	3rd	Win & Pl
Chases	4	0	0	1	627
Career Total	21	3	1	4	20677

1/01 Pau 2m3f110y Ch HVY £6305
11/00 Seic 2m1f110y Ch HLD £2882
6/00 Lrsy 2m1f Ch GD £2690
Total win prize-money £11877

Going: Sf: 0-1 GS: 0-1 Gd: 0-1 GF: - Fm: 0-1
Distance: 2m/2m3: 0-4 2m4-2m7: 0-0 3m+: 0-0
Track: LH: 0-1 RH: 0-2 Tight: 0-1 Gall: 0-0
Aids: Bl: 0-0 Vi: 0-0 Tstrap: 0-3
Best Rating: 124 11/01 Winc 2m gd-fm Ch

Good chaser in France, he made his debut in England in April of 2001, and ran with some promise, but was very disappointing in 2001/02.

Hastate

7-y-o b g Persian Bold-Gisarne (USA) (Diesis)
Mrs R M Lampard The Red Lion Racing Club

Placings:536U23213/2-P43 (4402)
2001/02: 26^{P}HY, 20^{4}G, 22^{3}GS

	Starts	1st	2nd	3rd	Win & Pl
Chases	3	0	0	1	555
Career Total	13	1	3	4	9611

106 3/00 Newb 2m3f E(0-110)HHdl G-F £3981
Total win prize-money £3981

Going: Sf: 0-1 GS: 0-1 Gd: 0-1 GF: - Fm: 0-0
Distance: 2m/2m3: 0-0 2m4-2m7: 0-2 3m+: 0-1
Track: LH: 0-2 RH: 0-1 Tight: 0-0 Gall: 0-1
Aids: Bl: 0-0 Vi: 0-0 Tstrap: 0-0
Best Rating: 116 3/02 Newb 2m6f110y gd-sft Ch

Hasten Bak

96(98c) (91c)**82**
9-y-o ch g Shaab-Kirstins Pride (Silly Prices)
Mrs S Gardner D V Gardner

Placings:032/4P13P5/323PFF5-00P0F4F0040U0 (4657)
2001/02: 22^{0}GS, 22^{0}GF, 23^{P}GF, 22^{0}GS, 25^{F}S, 24^{4}S, 24^{F}S, 19^{0}S, 17^{0}G, 26^{4}G, 22^{0}G, 27^{U}G, 24^{0}G

	Starts	1st	2nd	3rd	Win & Pl
Hurdles	10	0	0	0	0
Chases	3	0	0	0	280
Career Total	29	1	2	4	7028

108 1/00 Extr 2m1f110y E(0-105)HCh HVY £3298

Total win prize-money £3299

Going: Sf: 0-4 GS: 0-2 Gd: 0-5 GF: - Fm: 0-2
Distance: 2m/2m3: 0-1 2m4-2m7: 0-5 3m+: 0-7
Track: LH: 0-2 RH: 0-8 Tight: 0-5 Gall: 0-0
Aids: Bl: 0-0 Vi: 0-0 Tstrap: 0-0
Best Rating: 108 1/00 Tntn 2m3f gd-sft Ch

Hatcham Boy (IRE)

12-y-o br g Roselier (FR)-Auling (Tarqogan)
Mrs Ruth Hayter A Howland Jackson

Placings:20S12/**1U2P2/23FUU**02/**3/21P2-232** **(4538)**
2001/02: 26^{2}G, 31^{3}G, 24^{2}G

	Starts	1st	2nd	3rd	Win & Pl
Chases	3	0	2	1	1541
Career Total	**25**	**3**	**10**	**3**	**20758**

116	5/00	Uttx	4m2f	H Ch	G-F	£2912
126	11/96	Newb	3m	C Ch	G-S	£4627
116	1/96	Hayd	2m6f	D Hdl	SFT	£3035

Total win prize-money £10574

Going: Sf: 0-0 GS: 0-0 Gd: 0-3 GF: - Fm: 0-0
Distance: 2m/2m3: 0-0 2m4-2m7: 0-0 3m+: 0-3
Track: LH: 0-1 RH: 0-2 Tight: 0-3 Gall: 0-0
Aids: Bl: 0-2 Vi: 0-0 Tstrap: 0-0
Best Rating: 128 10/97 Strf 3m4f good Ch

Veteran hunter chaser, suited by marathon trips and a sound surface.

Hati Roy (IRE)

118 **157**

9-y-o b m Lafontaine (USA)-Stage Debut (Decent Fellow)
Miss H C Knight Mrs R A Humphries

Placings:113100/**1113-3105P** **(4191)**
2001/02: 24^{3}G, 27^{1}G, 26^{0}S, 26^{5}S, 24^{P}GS

	Starts	1st	2nd	3rd	Win & Pl
Chases	5	1	0	1	34029
Career Total	**15**	**7**	**0**	**3**	**76609**

157	11/01	Chel	3m3f110y	B HCh	GD	£32500
157	12/00	Chel	3m1f110y	C Ch	SFT	£8463
136	10/00	Chel	3m110y	C Ch	GD	£6792
131	10/00	Bang	2m4f110y	D Ch	SFT	£5232
130	1/00	Donc	3m110y	D Hdl	G-F	£3331
107	12/99	Hntg	2m5f110y	D Hdl	GD	£3826
109	11/99	Wwck	2m4f110y	D Hdl	GD	£3647

Total win prize-money £63792

Going: Sf: 0-2 GS: 0-1 Gd: 1-2 GF: - Fm: 0-0
Distance: 2m/2m3: 0-0 2m4-2m7: 0-0 **3m+: 1-5**
Track: **LH: 1-5** RH: 0-0 Tight: 0-0 **Gall: 1-3**
Aids: Bl: 0-0 Vi: 0-0 Tstrap: 0-0
Best Rating: 157 11/01 Chel 3m3f110y good Ch

An Irish point to point winner, she jumped soundly to land her first three novice chases in the 2000/2001season, but was tailed off when last of three finishers behind What's Up Boys at Aintree. A creditable third behind Earthmover in a handicap at Chepstow on her reappearance, she reversed that form at Cheltenham, but failed to go on from that. Acts on any ground. Stays three and a half miles.

Hatties Fortune

84 **60**

6-y-o b m Alhaatmi-Sweet Fortune (Dubassoff (USA))
K A Morgan K G Kitchen

Placings:*00/0*P0P0-00 **(0591)**
2001/02: 20^{0}GF, 23^{0}GF

	Starts	1st	2nd	3rd	Win & Pl
Hurdles	2	0	0	0	
Career Total	**9**	**0**	**0**	**0**	

Going: Sf: 0-0 GS: 0-0 Gd: 0-0 GF: - Fm: 0-2
Distance: 2m/2m3: 0-0 2m4-2m7: 0-1 3m+: 0-1
Track: LH: 0-2 RH: 0-0 Tight: 0-2 Gall: 0-0
Aids: Bl: 0-0 Vi: 0-0 Tstrap: 0-0
Best Rating: 67 4/00 MRas 1m5f110y soft NHF

Hatton Farm Babe

11-y-o b m Lochnager-Hatton Farm Girl (Humdoleila)
Mrs Susan Norbury Mrs Susan Norbury

Placings:P/F/3PP **(4288)**
2001/02: 20^{3}GF, 21^{P}G, 25^{P}GS

	Starts	1st	2nd	3rd	Win & Pl
Chases	3	0	0	1	169
Career Total	**5**	**0**	**0**	**1**	**169**

Going: Sf: 0-0 GS: 0-1 Gd: 0-1 GF: - Fm: 0-1
Distance: 2m/2m3: 0-0 2m4-2m7: 0-2 3m+: 0-1
Track: LH: 0-0 RH: 0-2 Tight: 0-1 Gall: 0-1
Aids: Bl: 0-0 Vi: 0-0 Tstrap: 0-0
Best Rating: 87 5/01 Hntg 2m4f110y gd-fm Ch

Modest hunter chaser, stepped up on previous form when winning at Uttoxeter in May.

Haughty Lady

40

6-y-o b m Sizzling Melody-Juris Prudence (IRE) (Law Society (USA))
Ronald Thompson Mrs P J Dobson

Placings:P-0 **(0451)**
2001/02: 23^{0}F

	Starts	1st	2nd	3rd	Win & Pl
Hurdles	1	0	0	0	
Career Total	**2**	**0**	**0**	**0**	

Going: Sf: 0-0 GS: 0-0 Gd: 0-0 GF: - Fm: 0-1
Distance: 2m/2m3: 0-0 2m4-2m7: 0-1 3m+: 0-0
Track: LH: 0-1 RH: 0-0 Tight: 0-0 Gall: 0-0
Aids: Bl: 0-0 Vi: 0-0 Tstrap: 0-0
Best Rating: 40 5/01 Weth 2m7f firm Hdl

Haut Cercy (FR)

103 **133**

7-y-o b g Roi De Rome (USA)-Mamoussia (FR) (Laniste)
H D Daly The Wiggin Partnership

Placings:*3*/213221/**2-3325F** **(4849)**
2001/02: 20^{3}S, 24^{3}S, 24^{2}S, 32^{5}GS, 24^{F}G

	Starts	1st	2nd	3rd	Win & Pl
Chases	5	0	1	2	2955
Career Total	**13**	**2**	**5**	**4**	**13200**

120	3/00	Tntn	3m110y	E Hdl	GD	£2459
119	12/99	Hrfd	2m3f110y	E Hdl	SFT	£2206

Total win prize-money £4666

Going: Sf: 0-3 GS: 0-1 Gd: 0-1 GF: - Fm: 0-0
Distance: 2m/2m3: 0-0 2m4-2m7: 0-1 3m+: 0-4
Track: LH: 0-4 RH: 0-1 Tight: 0-1 Gall: 0-2
Aids: Bl: 0-0 Vi: 0-0 Tstrap: 0-0
Best Rating: 140 10/00 Winc 3m1f110y gd-sft Ch

A progressive novice hurdler in 1999/2000, he made a promising start to his chasing career when second behind Shotgun Willy at Wincanton in October 2000. Not seen again until January 2002, he has shown he retains his ability. Stays well. Has won on good and soft ground.

Havana (IRE)

100 **80**

6-y-o b m Dolphin Street (FR)-Royaltess (Royal And Regal (USA))
R Ford Gary Williams

Placings:00-643PP43P44 **(4917)**
2001/02: 16^{6}S, 20^{4}F, 24^{3}G, 21^{P}S, 20^{P}GS, 17^{4}GS, 16^{3}S, 19^{P}S, 17^{4}S, 21^{4}GF

	Starts	1st	2nd	3rd	Win & Pl
Hurdles	10	0	0	2	1430
Career Total	**12**	**0**	**0**	**2**	**1430**

Going: Sf: 0-5 GS: 0-2 Gd: 0-1 GF: - Fm: 0-2
Distance: 2m/2m3: 0-5 2m4-2m7: 0-4 3m+: 0-1
Track: LH: 0-8 RH: 0-2 Tight: 0-7 Gall: 0-0
Aids: Bl: 0-0 Vi: 0-0 Tstrap: 0-9
Best Rating: 80 5/01 Hexm 2m4f110y firm Hdl

Often placed, but has yet to win a race of any sort and looks a mare without a trip.

Have A Break

7-y-o b g Most Welcome-Miss Tealeaf (USA) (Lear Fan (USA))
J White Nick Quesnel

Placings:4/B **(0254)**
2001/02: 24^{B}GF

	Starts	1st	2nd	3rd	Win & Pl
Chases	1	0	0	0	
Career Total	**2**	**0**	**0**	**0**	**0**

Going: Sf: 0-0 GS: 0-0 Gd: 0-0 GF: - Fm: 0-1
Distance: 2m/2m3: 0-0 2m4-2m7: 0-0 3m+: 0-1
Track: LH: 0-1 RH: 0-0 Tight: 0-1 Gall: 0-0
Aids: Bl: 0-0 Vi: 0-0 Tstrap: 0-0
Best Rating: 73 10/98 Worc 2m good Hdl

Have-No-Doubt (IRE)

8-y-o b g Glacial Storm (USA)-Lady Kas (Pollerton)
L A Dace Luke Dace

Placings:F5/2 **(3817)**
2001/02: 21^{2}S

	Starts	1st	2nd	3rd	Win & Pl
Chases	1	0	1	0	332
Career Total	**3**	**0**	**1**	**0**	**332**

Going: Sf: 0-1 GS: 0-0 Gd: 0-0 GF: - Fm: 0-0
Distance: 2m/2m3: 0-0 2m4-2m7: 0-1 3m+: 0-0
Track: LH: 0-0 RH: 0-1 Tight: 0-1 Gall: 0-0
Aids: Bl: 0-0 Vi: 0-0 Tstrap: 0-0
Best Rating: 109 2/02 Folk 2m5f soft Ch

Lightly-raced, he won a three-mile point at the start of 2001 and shaped with promise in a hunter chase a year later.

Havetwotaketwo (IRE)

8-y-o b g Phardante (FR)-Arctic Tartan (Deep Run)
J Howard Johnson J Howard Johnson

Placings: *000/P* (1587)
2001/02: 27^{P}GS

	Starts	1st	2nd	3rd	Win & Pl
Hurdles	1	0	0	0	
Career Total	**4**	**0**	**0**	**0**	

Going: Sf: 0-0 GS: 0-1 Gd: 0-0 GF: - Fm: 0-0
Distance: 2m/2m3: 0-0 2m4-2m7: 0-0 3m+: 0-1
Track: LH: 0-1 RH: 0-0 Tight: 0-1 Gall: 0-0
Aids: Bl: 0-0 Vi: 0-0 Tstrap: 0-0
Best Rating: 72 3/00 Leop 2m good Hdl

Havre De Thaix (FR)

(94h) (91h)
7-y-o b g Roi De Rome (USA)-Une Amie (FR) (Prove It Baby (USA))
C Diard C Diard

Placings: 115111FO/2U1F1OF-13F5511P330 (4231)
2001/02: 17^{1}S, 20^{3}S, 19^{F}, 20^{5}VS, 19^{5}S, 18^{1}S, 18^{1}VS, 20^{P}S, 19^{3}HY, 21^{3}HO, 21^{0}GS

	Starts	1st	2nd	3rd	Win & Pl
Hurdles	7	1	0	1	7856
Chases	4	2	0	2	16763
Career Total	**26**	**10**	**1**	**3**	**75200**

1/02	Pau	2m2f110y	Ch		VS	£7596
12/01	Pau	2m2f110y	Ch		SFT	£6888
9/01	Chat	2m1f	Hdl		SFT	£3395
1/01	Pau	2m110y	Hdl		SFT	£6305
12/00	Pau	2m3f110y	Ch		VS	£6244
1/00	Pau	2m3f	Ch		SFT	£5764
12/99	Pau	2m1f	Ch		SFT	£6459
12/99	Autl	2m2f	Hdl		HLD	£10764
11/99	Nant	2m1f110y	Hdl		HLD	£3767
10/99	Sabl	2m1f	Hdl		VS	£3842

Total win prize-money £61024

Going: Sf: 2-6 GS: 0-1 Gd: 0-0 GF: - Fm: 0-0
Distance: **2m/2m3: 3-3** 2m4-2m7: 0-8 3m+: 0-0
Track: LH: 0-2 RH: 0-0 Tight: 0-0 Gall: 0-1
Aids: **Bl: 3-8** Vi: 0-0 Tstrap: 0-1
Best Rating: 91 3/02 Chel 2m5f gd-sft Hdl

A winner over hurdles and fences in France, he handles testing conditions. Unproven beyond two and a half miles.

Hawadeth

106 121
7-y-o ch g Machiavellian (USA)-Ghzaalh (USA) (Northern Dancer)
V R A Dartnall (Gerard Stack 17/5) Nick Viney

Placings: 3023-424121612 (4853)
2001/02: 16^{4}HY, 16^{2}S, 20^{4}GS, 17^{1}HY, 16^{2}S, 16^{1}S, 17^{6}HY, 17^{1}G, 16^{2}G

	Starts	1st	2nd	3rd	Win & Pl
Hurdles	9	3	3	0	15808
Career Total	**13**	**3**	**4**	**2**	**17796**

116	3/02	NAbb	2m1f	D(0-115)HHdl	GD	£5720
119	1/02	Plum	2m	E Hdl	SFT	£2688
109	12/01	NAbb	2m1f	D Hdl	HVY	£3519

Total win prize-money £11928

Going: Sf: 2-6 GS: 0-1 Gd: 1-2 GF: - Fm: 0-0
Distance: **2m/2m3: 3-8** 2m4-2m7: 0-1 3m+: 0-0
Track: **LH: 3-7** RH: 0-0 **Tight: 3-5** Gall: 0-1
Aids: Bl: 0-1 Vi: 0-0 Tstrap: 0-0
Best Rating: **119** 4/02 Strf 2m110y good Hdl

A winner on the level, he was placed a number of times in novice hurdles in Ireland and has proved a fair two-mile handicapper.Has won twice in the mud in this country but is considered to appreciate better ground by his trainer.

Hawaiian Sam (IRE)

12-y-o b g Hawaiian Return (USA)-Thomastown Girl (Tekoah)
Miss G Browne Brig C K Price

Placings: P32/0102FU342/232106/F551P55/310P/4F-50 (0428)
2001/02: 24^{5}GF, 21^{0}G

	Starts	1st	2nd	3rd	Win & Pl
Chases	2	0	0	0	0
Career Total	**33**	**4**	**5**	**4**	**18727**

115	6/99	Worc	2m7f110y	F(0-110)HCh	G-S	£3042
115	12/98	Hntg	2m4f110y	E(0-110)HCh	SFT	£2921
112	2/97	Sand	3m110y	D(0-120)HCh	GD	£3437
96	11/95	Wind	2m	E Hdl	G-F	£2320

Total win prize-money £11722

Going: Sf: 0-0 GS: 0-0 Gd: 0-1 GF: - Fm: 0-1
Distance: 2m/2m3: 0-0 2m4-2m7: 0-1 3m+: 0-1
Track: LH: 0-0 RH: 0-1 Tight: 0-0 Gall: 0-1
Aids: Bl: 0-0 Vi: 0-0 Tstrap: 0-0
Best Rating: 115 6/99 Worc 2m7f110y gd-sft Ch

Hawkes Run

112 132
4-y-o b g Hernando (FR)-Wise Speculation (USA) (Mr Prospector (USA))
C J Mann (B J Meehan 17/6) The Baron Rouge Partnership

Placings: 11213P0 (4250)
2001/02: 17^{1}GS, 16^{1}G, 16^{2}G, 16^{1}G, 16^{3}GS, 17^{P}HY, 17^{0}G

	Starts	1st	2nd	3rd	Win & Pl
Hurdles	7	3	1	1	19814
Career Total	**7**	**3**	**1**	**1**	**19814**

116	11/01	Hntg	2m110y	B Hdl	GD	£8190
94	8/01	Strf	2m110y	E Hdl	GD	£2989
95	7/01	MRas	2m1f110y	D Hdl	G-S	£3835

Total win prize-money £15014

Going: Sf: 0-1 GS: 1-2 Gd: 2-4 GF: - Fm: 0-0
Distance: **2m/2m3: 3-7** 2m4-2m7: 0-0 3m+: 0-0
Track: LH: 1-4 RH: 1-2 Tight: 1-1 Gall: 1-3
Aids: Bl: 0-1 Vi: 0-0 Tstrap: 0-0
Best Rating: **132** 12/01 Chep 2m110y gd-sft Hdl

Useful juvenile hurdler, suited by two miles and good ground but likes to get his toe in. Has been unsuccessfully tried in blinkers.

Hawthorn

63 21
6-y-o ch g Primo Dominie-Starr Danias (USA) (Sensitive Prince (USA))
J G Fitzgerald Marquesa De Moratalla

Placings: *36/0-0* (2399)
2001/02: 16^{0}G

	Starts	1st	2nd	3rd	Win & Pl
Hurdles	1	0	0	0	
Career Total	**4**	**0**	**0**	**1**	**243**

Going: Sf: 0-0 GS: 0-0 Gd: 0-1 GF: - Fm: 0-0
Distance: 2m/2m3: 0-1 2m4-2m7: 0-0 3m+: 0-0
Track: LH: 0-1 RH: 0-0 Tight: 0-0 Gall: 0-0
Aids: Bl: 0-0 Vi: 0-0 Tstrap: 0-0
Best Rating: 95 4/00 Ayr 2m good NHF

Hayaain

107 118
9-y-o b g Shirley Heights-Littlefield (Bay Express)
J Barclay (P G Murphy 13/11) Kinneston Racing

Placings: 1451/1024400/0050B2112P0 (4893)
2001/02: 17^{0}G, 22^{0}GF, 24^{5}GF, 24^{0}GF, 27^{B}G, 24^{2}S, 24^{1}GF, 24^{1}G, 24^{2}G, 24^{P}S, 20^{0}G

	Starts	1st	2nd	3rd	Win & Pl
Hurdles	11	2	2	0	15035
Career Total	**22**	**5**	**3**	**0**	**32561**

110	12/01	Muss	3m	D(0-125)HHdl	GD	£8465
105	12/01	Muss	3m	D(0-125)HHdl	G-F	£4891
132	9/99	Hntg	2m4f110y	D(0-125)HHdl	GD	£7002
95	3/97	Uttx	2m4f110y	E Hdl	G-F	£2200
106	2/97	Sand	2m110y	C Hdl	G-F	£3517

Total win prize-money £26078

Going: Sf: 0-2 GS: 0-0 Gd: 1-5 GF: - Fm: 1-4
Distance: 2m/2m3: 0-1 2m4-2m7: 0-2 **3m+: 2-8**
Track: LH: 0-5 **RH: 2-6 Tight: 2-7** Gall: 0-0
Aids: Bl: 0-0 Vi: 0-0 Tstrap: 0-0
Best Rating: 132 11/99 Asct 3m good Hdl

A fair hurdler at one time, he lost his way until a change of stable jolted him back to winning form for his new trainer Jim Barclay, scoring twice at Musselburgh in December 2001. He looks to need three miles and a sound surface.

Haydens Field

114 137+
8-y-o b g Bedford (USA)-Releta (Relkino)
P M Rich Miss H Lewis

Placings: *63623*-21 (4530)
2001/02: 24^{2}HY, 20^{1}GS

	Starts	1st	2nd	3rd	Win & Pl
Hurdles	2	1	1	0	4084
Career Total	**7**	**1**	**2**	**2**	**5534**

120	4/02	Chep	2m4f	E Hdl	G-S	£2961

Total win prize-money £2961

Going: Sf: 0-1 GS: 1-1 Gd: 0-0 GF: - Fm: 0-0
Distance: 2m/2m3: 0-0 **2m4-2m7: 1-1** 3m+: 0-1
Track: **LH: 1-2** RH: 0-0 Tight: 0-0 Gall: 0-0
Aids: Bl: 0-0 Vi: 0-0 Tstrap: 0-0
Best Rating: **124** 3/01 Strf 2m6f110y soft Hdl

Completed a four-timer of front-running victories in the spring of 2002. Stays three miles and handles soft and good ground.

Haydn James (USA)

107(101h) (116h)135
8-y-o ch g Danzig Connection (USA)-Royal Fi Fi (USA) (Conquistador Cielo (USA))
P J Hobbs Mrs Ann Painter

Placings: 14102112-F1064065 (2293)
2001/02: 20^{F}G, 20^{1}G, 20^{0}G, 20^{6}GF, 17^{4}GF, 21^{0}G, 19^{6}G, 19^{5}GF

	Starts	1st	2nd	3rd	Win & Pl
Hurdles	6	1	0	0	4358

	Starts	1st	2nd	3rd	Win & Pl
Chases	2	0	0	0	0
Career Total	**16**	**5**	**2**	**0**	**18310**

116	8/01	Bang	2m4f	E(0-115)HHdl	GD	£4095
116	8/00	Font	2m2f	E Ch	G-F	£3580
118	8/00	Font	2m4f	E Ch	G-F	£3097
98	6/00	NAbb	2m1f	F(0-100)HHdl	G-F	£2282
98	5/00	Hrfd	2m3f110y	E Hdl	GD	£2600

Total win prize-money £15655

Going: Sf: 0-0 GS: 0-0 Gd: 1-5 GF: - Fm: 0-3
Distance: 2m/2m3: 0-2 **2m4-2m7: 1-6** 3m+: 0-0
Track: **LH: 1-4** RH: 0-4 **Tight: 1-4** Gall: 0-0
Aids: Bl: 0-0 Vi: 0-0 Tstrap: 0-0
Best Rating: 133 7/01 Strf 2m4f good Ch

Fair hurdler/chaser, suited by good or fast ground with his best form in the last couple of seasons coming in the summer months. Best over two and a half miles.

Haystacks (IRE)

104 **102**

6-y-o b g Contract Law (USA)-Florissa (FR) (Persepolis (FR))
D Moffatt Mr & Mrs A G Milligan

Placings:0225F14/413050-05634 **(2196)**
2001/02: 20^{0}GF, 17^{5}GS, 20^{6}G, 22^{3}GS, 23^{4}G

	Starts	1st	2nd	3rd	Win & Pl
Hurdles	5	0	0	1	676
Career Total	**18**	**2**	**2**	**2**	**9423**

104	5/00	Ctml	2m6f	D(0-120)HHdl	G-F	£3721
97	3/00	Kels	2m2f	E Hdl	G-S	£2366

Total win prize-money £6087

Going: Sf: 0-0 GS: 0-2 Gd: 0-2 GF: - Fm: 0-1
Distance: 2m/2m3: 0-1 2m4-2m7: 0-3 3m+: 0-1
Track: LH: 0-5 RH: 0-0 Tight: 0-3 Gall: 0-0
Aids: Bl: 0-0 Vi: 0-1 Tstrap: 0-0
Best Rating: 105 10/00 Kels 2m6f110y soft Hdl

Fair staying hurdler, handles any ground.

Hazard A Guess (IRE)

91 **115**

12-y-o ch g Digamist (USA)-Guess Who (Be My Guest (USA))
B S Rothwell Mike Gosse

Placings:302/130/**2U2** **(4556)**
2001/02: 20^{2}G, 20^{U}GF, 17^{2}G

	Starts	1st	2nd	3rd	Win & Pl
Chases	3	0	2	0	2534
Career Total	**9**	**1**	**3**	**2**	**6975**

119	12/97	Donc	2m110y	E Hdl	GD	£3015

Total win prize-money £3015

Going: Sf: 0-0 GS: 0-0 Gd: 0-2 GF: - Fm: 0-1
Distance: 2m/2m3: 0-1 2m4-2m7: 0-2 3m+: 0-0
Track: LH: 0-1 RH: 0-2 Tight: 0-1 Gall: 0-1
Aids: Bl: 0-0 Vi: 0-0 Tstrap: 0-0
Best Rating: 119 12/97 Donc 2m110y good Hdl

Hazel Reilly (IRE)

11-y-o b m Mister Lord (USA)-Vickies Gold (Golden Love)
Mrs Sarah L Dent John Mackley

Placings:6243-3422 **(4525)**
2001/02: 25^{3}S, 25^{4}GS, 25^{2}HY, 26^{2}GS

	Starts	1st	2nd	3rd	Win & Pl
Chases	4	0	2	1	1705
Career Total	**8**	**0**	**3**	**2**	**2699**

Going: Sf: 0-2 GS: 0-2 Gd: 0-0 GF: - Fm: 0-0
Distance: 2m/2m3: 0-0 2m4-2m7: 0-0 3m+: 0-4
Track: LH: 0-2 RH: 0-1 Tight: 0-1 Gall: 0-0
Aids: Bl: 0-0 Vi: 0-0 Tstrap: 0-0
Best Rating: 104 3/02 Kels 3m1f heavy Ch

Out-and-out stayer in points and hunter chases.

Hazeljack

95 **96**

7-y-o b g Sula Bula-Hazelwain (Hard Fact)
Dr P Pritchard A J Whiting

Placings:0/065F4 **(2948)**
2001/02: 19^{0}G, 21^{6}G, 20^{5}S, 21^{F}G, 20^{4}G

	Starts	1st	2nd	3rd	Win & Pl
Hurdles	5	0	0	0	0
Career Total	**6**	**0**	**0**	**0**	**0**

Going: Sf: 0-1 GS: 0-0 Gd: 0-4 GF: - Fm: 0-0
Distance: 2m/2m3: 0-0 2m4-2m7: 0-5 3m+: 0-0
Track: LH: 0-4 RH: 0-1 Tight: 0-2 Gall: 0-1
Aids: Bl: 0-0 Vi: 0-0 Tstrap: 0-0
Best Rating: 96 12/01 Plum 2m5f good Hdl

Has shown fair form in novice hurdles. Stays two and a half miles. Acts on a sound surface.

Hazy Sea (IRE)

43

10-y-o b g Supreme Leader-Sea Castle (Carlingford Castle)
J A Pickering J A Pickering

Placings:0/060040/0UP5/P0P **(2572)**
2001/02: 24^{P}S, 24^{0}G, 25^{P}HY

	Starts	1st	2nd	3rd	Win & Pl
Hurdles	1	0	0	0	0
Chases	2	0	0	0	0
Career Total	**14**	**0**	**0**	**0**	**201**

Going: Sf: 0-2 GS: 0-0 Gd: 0-1 GF: - Fm: 0-0
Distance: 2m/2m3: 0-0 2m4-2m7: 0-0 3m+: 0-3
Track: LH: 0-0 RH: 0-2 Tight: 0-0 Gall: 0-0
Aids: Bl: 0-0 Vi: 0-0 Tstrap: 0-0
Best Rating: 80 3/99 Limk 3m soft Hdl

He Knows The Rules

107 **93**

10-y-o b g Tirol-Falls Of Lora (Scottish Rifle)
R H Buckler Samways Fish Merchants & Transporters

Placings:P/562/55113104/44444/**4S225-5460335** **(1415)**
2001/02: 16^{5}G, 17^{4}G, 21^{6}GF, 23^{0}G, 20^{3}GF, 20^{3}GF, 20^{5}GF

	Starts	1st	2nd	3rd	Win & Pl
Chases	7	0	0	2	1050
Career Total	**29**	**3**	**3**	**3**	**12774**

100	10/97	Extr	2m1f110y	D(0-125)HHdl	GD	£2697
98	9/97	Font	2m2f110y	F Hdl	GD	£2194
85	8/97	Font	2m2f110y	G Hdl	GD	£1908

Total win prize-money £6799

Going: Sf: 0-0 GS: 0-0 Gd: 0-3 GF: - Fm: 0-4
Distance: 2m/2m3: 0-2 2m4-2m7: 0-4 3m+: 0-1
Track: LH: 0-5 RH: 0-1 Tight: 0-5 Gall: 0-0
Aids: Bl: 0-0 Vi: 0-0 Tstrap: 0-2
Best Rating: 100 10/97 Extr 2m1f110y good Hdl

He's My Uncle

7-y-o ch g Phardante (FR)-Red Dusk (Deep Run)
Mrs J K M Oliver Mrs J K M Oliver

Placings:0P **(3785)**
2001/02: 17^{0}S, 20^{P}S

	Starts	1st	2nd	3rd	Win & Pl
NH Flat	1	0	0	0	0
Hurdles	1	0	0	0	0
Career Total	**2**	**0**	**0**	**0**	

Going: Sf: 0-2 GS: 0-0 Gd: 0-0 GF: - Fm: 0-0
Distance: 2m/2m3: 0-1 2m4-2m7: 0-1 3m+: 0-0
Track: LH: 0-1 RH: 0-1 Tight: 0-0 Gall: 0-1
Aids: Bl: 0-0 Vi: 0-0 Tstrap: 0-0
Best Rating: 63 11/01 Carl 2m1f soft NHF

He's The Boss (IRE)

97f **109f**

5-y-o b g Supreme Leader-Attykee (IRE) (Le Moss)
R H Buckler M J Hallett

Placings:01 **(4180)**
2001/02: 16^{0}G, 16^{1}GS

	Starts	1st	2nd	3rd	Win & Pl
NH Flat	2	1	0	0	3101
Career Total	**2**	**1**	**0**	**0**	**3101**

109	3/02	Strf	2m110y	H NHF	G-S	£3101

Total win prize-money £3101

Going: Sf: 0-0 GS: 1-1 Gd: 0-1 GF: - Fm: 0-0
Distance: **2m/2m3: 1-2** 2m4-2m7: 0-0 3m+: 0-0
Track: LH: 0-1 RH: 0-0 Tight: 0-0 Gall: 0-1
Aids: Bl: 0-0 Vi: 0-0 Tstrap: 0-0
Best Rating: 109 3/02 Strf 2m110y gd-sft NHF

Won a Stratford bumper in great style on his second start and looks a useful prospect.

Head For Heaven

79(84h) **73**

12-y-o b g Persian Heights-Believer (Blakeney)
M R Ewer-Hoad Foray Racing & J E Taylor

Placings:234110**F2/62202/452143F03/13P341P11/P4 P5P0-0** **(0105)**
2001/02: 20^{0}GF

	Starts	1st	2nd	3rd	Win & Pl
Chases	1	0	0	0	
Career Total	**38**	**7**	**6**	**5**	**34752**

117	3/00	Ling	2m	D(0-120)HCh	GD	£6955
117	2/00	Font	2m2f	F(0-105)HCh	SFT	£2957
113	1/00	Plum	2m1f	D(0-125)HCh	SFT	£7150
117	9/99	Font	2m2f	F(0-105)HCh	GD	£2770
101	3/99	Font	2m3f	E Ch	SFT	£2737
96	12/95	Plum	2m1f	G(0-90)HHdl	SFT	£1790
94	11/95	Font	2m2f	F Hdl	SFT	£2139

Total win prize-money £26501

Going: Sf: 0-0 GS: 0-0 Gd: 0-0 GF: - Fm: 0-1
Distance: 2m/2m3: 0-0 2m4-2m7: 0-1 3m+: 0-0
Track: LH: 0-0 RH: 0-0 Tight: 0-1 Gall: 0-0
Aids: Bl: 0-0 Vi: 0-0 Tstrap: 0-0
Best Rating: 117 3/00 Ling 2m good Ch

Head For Home (IRE)

5-y-o ch m Executive Perk-Lancastrian Rose (IRE) (Lancastrian)
Mrs Dianne Sayer Mrs Dianne Sayer

Placings: P00P (4875)
2001/02: 17^{PS}, 16^{0S}, 17^{0G}, 24^{PG}

	Starts	1st	2nd	3rd	Win & Pl
NH Flat	3	0	0	0	0
Hurdles	1	0	0	0	0
Career Total	**4**	**0**	**0**	**0**	

Going: Sf: 0-2 GS: 0-0 Gd: 0-2 GF: - Fm: 0-0
Distance: 2m/2m3: 0-3 2m4-2m7: 0-0 3m+: 0-1
Track: LH: 0-1 RH: 0-3 Tight: 0-2 Gall: 0-0
Aids: Bl: 0-0 Vi: 0-0 Tstrap: 0-0
Best Rating: 65 2/02 Muss 2m soft NHF

Head Gardener (IRE)

93(84c) 72
8-y-o b g Be My Chief (USA)-Silk Petal (Petorius)
R Lee Richard Lee

Placings: 0/00014030/31U2PF/032UP-00406 (1618)
2001/02: $24^{0}F$, $22^{0}GF$, $22^{4}GF$, $24^{0}GS$, $21^{6}G$

	Starts	1st	2nd	3rd	Win & Pl
Hurdles	5	0	0	0	0
Career Total	**25**	**2**	**2**	**3**	**8416**

95 1/00 Hrfd 3m1f110y F(0-95)HCh G-S £3640
75 12/98 Chep 2m4f110y G Hdl GD £2066
Total win prize-money £5706

Going: Sf: 0-0 GS: 0-1 Gd: 0-1 GF: - Fm: 0-3
Distance: 2m/2m3: 0-0 2m4-2m7: 0-3 3m+: 0-2
Track: LH: 0-3 RH: 0-2 Tight: 0-4 Gall: 0-0
Aids: Bl: 0-2 Vi: 0-3 Tstrap: 0-0
Best Rating: 102 3/00 NAbb 3m2f110y good Ch

Head Lady

6-y-o ch m Headin' Up-Lady Gail (Sharrood (USA))
J L Needham J L Needham

Placings: 00P-P (3869)
2001/02: 16^{PGS}

	Starts	1st	2nd	3rd	Win & Pl
Hurdles	1	0	0	0	
Career Total	**4**	**0**	**0**	**0**	

Going: Sf: 0-0 GS: 0-1 Gd: 0-0 GF: - Fm: 0-0
Distance: 2m/2m3: 0-1 2m4-2m7: 0-0 3m+: 0-0
Track: LH: 0-0 RH: 0-1 Tight: 0-0 Gall: 0-0
Aids: Bl: 0-0 Vi: 0-0 Tstrap: 0-0
Best Rating:

Headwrecker (IRE)

102 94
6-y-o br g Good Thyne (USA)-Sallowglen Gale (IRE) (Strong Gale)
N J Henderson Gollyhott Trading Ltd

Placings: 52540 (4842)
2001/02: $17^{5}GS$, $18^{2}G$, $18^{5}HY$, $21^{4}S$, $20^{0}G$

Starts	1st	2nd	3rd	Win & Pl

	Starts	1st	2nd	3rd	Win & Pl
NH Flat	2	0	1	0	480
Hurdles	3	0	0	0	0
Career Total	**5**	**0**	**1**	**0**	**480**

Going: Sf: 0-2 GS: 0-1 Gd: 0-2 GF: - Fm: 0-0
Distance: 2m/2m3: 0-3 2m4-2m7: 0-2 3m+: 0-0
Track: LH: 0-3 RH: 0-1 Tight: 0-4 Gall: 0-0
Aids: Bl: 0-0 Vi: 0-0 Tstrap: 0-0
Best Rating: 114 1/02 Font 2m2f110y good NHF

Showed plenty of promise in bumpers but well held in heavy ground on novice hurdle debut.

Hear My Song (IRE)

83(85h) (72h)73
6-y-o b g Commanche Run-Pampered Finch Vii (Damsire Unregistered)
J S King Turville Racing Partnership

Placings: 000PP (4484)
2001/02: $16^{0}GS$, $20^{0}HY$, $16^{0}G$, $18^{P}HY$, $17^{P}G$

	Starts	1st	2nd	3rd	Win & Pl
NH Flat	1	0	0	0	0
Hurdles	4	0	0	0	0
Career Total	**5**	**0**	**0**	**0**	

Going: Sf: 0-2 GS: 0-1 Gd: 0-2 GF: - Fm: 0-0
Distance: 2m/2m3: 0-4 2m4-2m7: 0-1 3m+: 0-0
Track: LH: 0-1 RH: 0-4 Tight: 0-1 Gall: 0-0
Aids: Bl: 0-0 Vi: 0-0 Tstrap: 0-0
Best Rating: 73 1/02 Winc 2m good Hdl

Heart Full Of Soul

8-y-o ch g Primo Dominie-Scales Of Justice (Final Straw)
C R Cox (Miss H M Irving 3/3) C R Cox

Placings: 00/00/P34066/306F4-P (4376)
2001/02: 20^{PS}

	Starts	1st	2nd	3rd	Win & Pl
Chases	1	0	0	0	
Career Total	**16**	**0**	**0**	**2**	**2350**

Going: Sf: 0-1 GS: 0-0 Gd: 0-0 GF: - Fm: 0-0
Distance: 2m/2m3: 0-0 2m4-2m7: 0-1 3m+: 0-0
Track: LH: 0-0 RH: 0-1 Tight: 0-1 Gall: 0-0
Aids: Bl: 0-1 Vi: 0-0 Tstrap: 0-1
Best Rating: 90 2/00 Font 2m2f soft Ch

Heart Of The Sun (IRE)

93 91
7-y-o b g Castle Keep-Damberee (Deep Run)
Miss Z C Davison (Noel T Chance 28/7) The Friday Night Racing Club

Placings: 300/000-30605 (4779)
2001/02: $16^{3}GF$, $20^{0}G$, $19^{6}G$, $16^{0}G$, $21^{5}GF$

	Starts	1st	2nd	3rd	Win & Pl
Hurdles	5	0	0	1	366
Career Total	**11**	**0**	**0**	**2**	**622**

Going: Sf: 0-0 GS: 0-0 Gd: 0-3 GF: - Fm: 0-2
Distance: 2m/2m3: 0-3 2m4-2m7: 0-2 3m+: 0-0
Track: LH: 0-5 RH: 0-0 Tight: 0-3 Gall: 0-0
Aids: Bl: 0-0 Vi: 0-0 Tstrap: 0-0
Best Rating: 105 1/00 Font 2m2f110y gd-sft NHF

Heartache

5-y-o b g Jurado (USA)-Heresy (IRE) (Black Minstrel)
R Mathew Robin Mathew

Placings: P (2950)
2001/02: 22^{PS}

	Starts	1st	2nd	3rd	Win & Pl
Hurdles	1	0	0	0	
Career Total	**1**	**0**	**0**	**0**	

Going: Sf: 0-1 GS: 0-0 Gd: 0-0 GF: - Fm: 0-0
Distance: 2m/2m3: 0-0 2m4-2m7: 0-1 3m+: 0-0
Track: LH: 0-1 RH: 0-0 Tight: 0-1 Gall: 0-0
Aids: Bl: 0-0 Vi: 0-0 Tstrap: 0-0
Best Rating:

Heathman (IRE)

6-y-o b g Common Grounds-Dul Dul (USA) (Shadeed (USA))
R J Baker S M McCausland

Placings: P (1996)
2001/02: 17^{PS}

	Starts	1st	2nd	3rd	Win & Pl
Hurdles	1	0	0	0	
Career Total	**1**	**0**	**0**	**0**	

Going: Sf: 0-1 GS: 0-0 Gd: 0-0 GF: - Fm: 0-0
Distance: 2m/2m3: 0-1 2m4-2m7: 0-0 3m+: 0-0
Track: LH: 0-1 RH: 0-0 Tight: 0-1 Gall: 0-0
Aids: Bl: 0-0 Vi: 0-0 Tstrap: 0-0
Best Rating:

Heathyards Element

100 (73c)84
6-y-o ch g Henbit (USA)-Moment's Pleasure (USA) (What A Pleasure (USA))
D McCain L A Morgan

Placings: 2043/0F005-25543530 (1752)
2001/02: $20^{2}F$, $20^{5}GF$, $21^{5}GF$, $17^{4}GS$, $17^{3}GS$, $17^{5}G$, $16^{3}GS$, $22^{0}G$

	Starts	1st	2nd	3rd	Win & Pl
Hurdles	6	0	1	1	1222
Chases	2	0	0	1	750
Career Total	**17**	**0**	**2**	**3**	**3128**

Going: Sf: 0-0 GS: 0-3 Gd: 0-2 GF: - Fm: 0-3
Distance: 2m/2m3: 0-4 2m4-2m7: 0-4 3m+: 0-0
Track: LH: 0-5 RH: 0-3 Tight: 0-5 Gall: 0-0
Aids: Bl: 0-0 Vi: 0-0 Tstrap: 0-0
Best Rating: 86 1/00 Ludl 2m good NHF

Heathyards Guest (IRE)

92 80
4-y-o ch g Be My Guest (USA)-Noble Nadia (Thatching)
Mrs K Walton (R Hollinshead 15/10) G M Marshall

Placings: 04 (4915)
2001/02: $17^{0}G$, $17^{4}GF$

	Starts	1st	2nd	3rd	Win & Pl
Hurdles	2	0	0	0	0

	Starts	1st	2nd	3rd	Win & Pl
Career Total	2	0	0	0	0

Going: Sf: 0-0 GS: 0-0 Gd: 0-1 GF: - Fm: 0-1
Distance: 2m/2m3: 0-2 2m4-2m7: 0-0 3m+: 0-0
Track: LH: 0-1 RH: 0-1 Tight: 0-2 Gall: 0-0
Aids: Bl: 0-0 Vi: 0-0 Tstrap: 0-0
Best Rating: 80 4/02 Sedg 2m1f gd-fm Hdl

A maiden under both codes.

Heathyards Lad (IRE)

79 **52**

5-y-o b g Petardia-Maiden's Dance (Hotfoot)
Dr P Pritchard (M Wigham 5/11) Norwester Racing Club

Placings:50PPP0P00P (4757)
2001/02: 18^{5}S, 16^{0}G, 16^{P}GS, 17^{P}HY, 19^{P}HY, 17^{0}S, 16^{P}G, 17^{0}S, 17^{0}G, 16^{P}GF

	Starts	1st	2nd	3rd	Win & Pl
Hurdles	10	0	0	0	0
Career Total	10	0	0	0	0

Going: Sf: 0-5 GS: 0-1 Gd: 0-3 GF: - Fm: 0-1
Distance: 2m/2m3: 0-9 2m4-2m7: 0-1 3m+: 0-0
Track: LH: 0-5 RH: 0-5 Tight: 0-5 Gall: 0-1
Aids: Bl: 0-0 Vi: 0-0 Tstrap: 0-2
Best Rating: 52 10/01 Font 2m2f110y soft Hdl

Only has a 50% completion ratio in his hurdle races.

Heathyards Tipple (IRE)

100 **91**

6-y-o b m Marju (IRE)-Nikki's Groom (Shy Groom (USA))
D McCain Mrs D McCain

Placings:114223P316/06-00355002400 (2653)
2001/02: 17^{0}G, 16^{0}GS, 16^{3}GF, 16^{5}F, 16^{5}GF, 17^{0}GF, 17^{0}GF, 16^{2}G, 19^{4}F, 20^{0}GS, 16^{0}G

	Starts	1st	2nd	3rd	Win & Pl
Hurdles	11	0	1	1	1096
Career Total	23	3	3	3	11912

91	3/00	Sedg	2m1f	E(0-105)HHdl	G-F	£2282
88	9/99	Sedg	2m1f	E Hdl	G-F	£2425
86	8/99	Ctml	2m1f110y	E Hdl	GD	£2635

Total win prize-money £7342

Going: Sf: 0-0 GS: 0-2 Gd: 0-3 GF: - Fm: 0-6
Distance: 2m/2m3: 0-9 2m4-2m7: 0-2 3m+: 0-0
Track: LH: 0-6 RH: 0-5 Tight: 0-6 Gall: 0-0
Aids: Bl: 0-8 Vi: 0-0 Tstrap: 0-0
Best Rating: 91 5/01 Hexm 2m gd-fm Hdl

Fair juvenile in 1999/2000, he returned to winning ways at Hexham in June 2002.

Heavenly Hill

77f **71f**

5-y-o b m Nomadic Way (USA)-Tees Gazette Girl (Kalaglow)
Mrs M Reveley Mrs M B Thwaites

Placings:*0* (3862)
2001/02: 16^{0}S

	Starts	1st	2nd	3rd	Win & Pl
NH Flat	1	0	0	0	
Career Total	1	0	0	0	

Going: Sf: 0-1 GS: 0-0 Gd: 0-0 GF: - Fm: 0-0
Distance: 2m/2m3: 0-1 2m4-2m7: 0-0 3m+: 0-0
Track: LH: 0-1 RH: 0-0 Tight: 0-0 Gall: 0-1
Aids: Bl: 0-0 Vi: 0-0 Tstrap: 0-0
Best Rating: 71 2/02 Donc 2m110y soft NHF

Heavenly Stride

101(88h) (111h)**121**

6-y-o b g Karinga Bay-Chapel Hill (IRE) (The Parson)
D McCain Eamonn O'Malley

Placings:121/2051 (4086)
2001/02: 16^{2}S, 17^{0}HY, 16^{5}HY, 17^{1}S

	Starts	1st	2nd	3rd	Win & Pl
Hurdles	2	0	1	0	985
Chases	2	1	0	0	4134
Career Total	7	3	2	0	10761

121	3/02	Bang	2m1f110y	D Ch	SFT	£4134
111	4/00	Carl	2m1f	E Hdl	G-S	£2548
102	3/00	Ayr	2m	E Hdl	HVY	£2310

Total win prize-money £8992

Going: Sf: 1-4 GS: 0-0 Gd: 0-0 GF: - Fm: 0-0
Distance: **2m/2m3: 1-4** 2m4-2m7: 0-0 3m+: 0-0
Track: **LH: 1-3** RH: 0-1 **Tight: 1-1** Gall: 0-0
Aids: Bl: 0-0 Vi: 0-0 Tstrap: 0-0
Best Rating: 121 3/02 Bang 2m1f110y soft Ch

A winning novice hurdler in 1999/2000, he missed the next season but shaped well on his return. Out of sorts until winning a weakly-contested novice chase in March. Acts on soft ground.

Heavens Above

10-y-o br g Celestial Storm (USA)-Regal Wonder (Stupendous)
Ferdy Murphy R & G Leonard

Placings:3000/P63313/32/32F20/22P032P/PP (4197)
2001/02: 25^{P}S, 21^{P}S

	Starts	1st	2nd	3rd	Win & Pl
Chases	2	0	0	0	
Career Total	26	1	6	7	11729

78	1/97	Muss	2m4f	E(0-100)HHdl	G-F	£2616

Total win prize-money £2616

Going: Sf: 0-2 GS: 0-0 Gd: 0-0 GF: - Fm: 0-0
Distance: 2m/2m3: 0-0 2m4-2m7: 0-1 3m+: 0-1
Track: LH: 0-2 RH: 0-0 Tight: 0-2 Gall: 0-0
Aids: Bl: 0-0 Vi: 0-0 Tstrap: 0-0
Best Rating: 116 2/00 Sedg 3m3f gd-sft Ch

Looks a light of other days.

Hedante (IRE)

8-y-o b g Phardante (FR)-Hedmareth (Green Shoon)
Miss A M Newton-Smith John Grist

Placings:U3/PP64U-PP4 (3474)
2001/02: 26^{P}GS, 26^{P}G, 26^{4}S

	Starts	1st	2nd	3rd	Win & Pl
Chases	3	0	0	0	0
Career Total	10	0	0	1	1135

Going: Sf: 0-1 GS: 0-1 Gd: 0-1 GF: - Fm: 0-0
Distance: 2m/2m3: 0-0 2m4-2m7: 0-0 3m+: 0-3
Track: LH: 0-0 RH: 0-1 Tight: 0-1 Gall: 0-0
Aids: Bl: 0-0 Vi: 0-0 Tstrap: 0-3
Best Rating: 76 2/01 Plum 3m2f soft Ch

Hee's A Dancer

10-y-o b g Rambo Dancer (CAN)-Heemee (On Your Mark)
R W J Willcox R W J Willcox

Placings:1F41/6402F5/2/F1/U63/26P5P-P (4376)
2001/02: 20^{P}S

	Starts	1st	2nd	3rd	Win & Pl
Chases	1	0	0	0	
Career Total	22	3	3	1	8148

106	4/99	Ludl	2m4f	H Ch	GD	£1725
94	11/95	Catt	2m	G Hdl	G-F	£1856
94	9/95	Kels	2m110y	E Hdl	FRM	£1716

Total win prize-money £5297

Going: Sf: 0-1 GS: 0-0 Gd: 0-0 GF: - Fm: 0-0
Distance: 2m/2m3: 0-0 2m4-2m7: 0-1 3m+: 0-0
Track: LH: 0-0 RH: 0-1 Tight: 0-1 Gall: 0-0
Aids: Bl: 0-0 Vi: 0-0 Tstrap: 0-0
Best Rating: 106 5/00 Ludl 3m good Ch

Heezapistol (FR)

111 **126**

4-y-o b g Pistolet Bleu (IRE)-Strictly Cool (USA) (Bering)
W P Mullins (Mme C Head-Maarek 14/5) Amber Syndicate

Placings:1610F (4952a)
2001/02: 16^{1}Y, 16^{6}Y, 16^{1}SH, 17^{0}G, 16^{F}G

	Starts	1st	2nd	3rd	Win & Pl
Hurdles	5	2	0	0	19438
Career Total	5	2	0	0	19438

126	1/02	Punc	2m	Hdl	SH	£12760
126	11/01	DRoy	2m	Hdl	YLD	£6677

Total win prize-money £19438

Going: Sf: 0-0 GS: 0-0 Gd: 0-2 GF: - Fm: 0-0
Distance: **2m/2m3: 2-5** 2m4-2m7: 0-0 3m+: 0-0
Track: LH: 0-1 **RH: 1-3** Tight: 0-0 Gall: 0-1
Aids: Bl: 0-0 Vi: 0-0 Tstrap: 0-0
Best Rating: 126 1/02 Punc 2m sft-hvy Hdl

Won on his hurdling debut at Down Royal but suffered some muscle damage in his back when disappointing on his next start. Bounced back to form at Punchestown. Goes well in soft ground.

Heidi Iii (FR)

114(75h) **136**

7-y-o b g Bayolidaan (FR)-Irlandaise (FR) (Or De Chine)
A Crook Turner Technology Ltd

Placings:01/21/11222110-52PP2 (4582)
2001/02: 25^{5}GS, 25^{2}GS, 24^{P}S, 26^{P}GS, 25^{2}G

	Starts	1st	2nd	3rd	Win & Pl
Chases	5	0	2	0	10359
Career Total	17	6	6	0	73273

148	2/01	Newc	2m4f	B(0-140)HCh	HVY	£8684
148	1/01	Donc	3m	B(0-145)HCh	GD	£31850
128	6/00	Prth	2m4f110y	E Hdl	HVY	£2691
113	5/00	Weth	2m	E Hdl	G-F	£2772
117	4/00	Carl	2m1f	E Hdl	SFT	£2786
	1/99	Pau	2m1f	Ch	HLD	£5382

Total win prize-money £54166

Going: Sf: 0-1 GS: 0-3 Gd: 0-1 GF: - Fm: 0-0
Distance: 2m/2m3: 0-0 2m4-2m7: 0-0 3m+: 0-5
Track: LH: 0-5 RH: 0-0 Tight: 0-0 Gall: 0-2
Aids: Bl: 0-0 Vi: 0-0 Tstrap: 0-0

Best Rating: 148 2/01 Newc 2m4f heavy Ch

Tough and consistent, he enjoyed a cracking 2000/2001 season highlighted by a brave win in the Great Yorkshire Chase at Doncaster in 2001. Sruggled somewhat in 2001/02. Acts on soft/heavy. Has won at two and a half and three miles.

Heiress Of Meath (IRE)

90 77

7-y-o ch m Imperial Frontier (USA)-Rich Heiress (IRE) (Last Tycoon)

M J Weeden Dr Ian R Shenkin

Placings:P/P645P-04 **(1268)**

2001/02: 17^0G, 17^4GF

	Starts	1st	2nd	3rd	Win & Pl
Hurdles	2	0	0	0	0
Career Total	**8**	**0**	**0**	**0**	**0**

Going: Sf: 0-0 GS: 0-0 Gd: 0-1 GF: - Fm: 0-1
Distance: 2m/2m3: 0-2 2m4-2m7: 0-0 3m+: 0-0
Track: LH: 0-2 RH: 0-0 Tight: 0-2 Gall: 0-0
Aids: Bl: 0-0 Vi: 0-0 Tstrap: 0-0
Best Rating: 90 10/00 Tntn 2m1f good Hdl

Helali Manor

80 53

4-y-o b f Muhtarram (USA)-Royal Mazi (King's Lake (USA))

G P Kelly G P Kelly

Placings:0PPP **(3552)**

2001/02: 16^0G, 16^PG, 16^PG, 16^PS

	Starts	1st	2nd	3rd	Win & Pl
Hurdles	4	0	0	0	
Career Total	**4**	**0**	**0**	**0**	

Going: Sf: 0-1 GS: 0-0 Gd: 0-3 GF: - Fm: 0-0
Distance: 2m/2m3: 0-4 2m4-2m7: 0-0 3m+: 0-0
Track: LH: 0-4 RH: 0-0 Tight: 0-1 Gall: 0-2
Aids: Bl: 0-0 Vi: 0-0 Tstrap: 0-0
Best Rating: 53 10/01 Weth 2m good Hdl

Helixir Du Theil (FR)

(106h) (107h)

7-y-o ch g Aelan Hapi (USA)-Manolette (FR) (Signani (FR))

R H Buckler The Robbers Dog

Placings:0/4P-0400222 **(4844)**

2001/02: 19^0G, 22^4G, 24^0G, 21^0S, 24^2S, 26^2G, 24^2G

	Starts	1st	2nd	3rd	Win & Pl
Hurdles	7	0	3	0	3682
Career Total	**10**	**0**	**3**	**0**	**3960**

Going: Sf: 0-2 GS: 0-0 Gd: 0-5 GF: - Fm: 0-0
Distance: 2m/2m3: 0-0 2m4-2m7: 0-3 3m+: 0-4
Track: LH: 0-4 RH: 0-3 Tight: 0-2 Gall: 0-1
Aids: Bl: 0-0 Vi: 0-0 Tstrap: 0-0
Best Rating: 111 4/02 Bang 3m good Hdl

Modest hurdler, needs a stamina test. Runner-up on his last three starts of 2001/02.

Hell-Of-A-Shindy (IRE)

101 119

8-y-o b g Phardante (FR)-Tonto's Girl (Strong Gale)

J J O'Neill (E Bolger 10/6) J P McManus

Placings:4F/F3-P15324 **(4421)**

2001/02: 24^PG, 24^1F, 20^5S, 21^3GS, 22^2S, 18^4GS

	Starts	1st	2nd	3rd	Win & Pl
Chases	6	1	1	1	8209
Career Total	**10**	**1**	**1**	**2**	**9016**
105 6/01 Clon 3m	Ch			FRM	£3895

Total win prize-money £3895

Going: Sf: 0-2 GS: 0-2 Gd: 0-1 GF: - Fm: 1-1
Distance: 2m/2m3: 0-1 2m4-2m7: 0-3 **3m+: 1-2**
Track: LH: 0-2 RH: 0-2 Tight: 0-0 Gall: 0-2
Aids: Bl: 0-0 Vi: 0-0 **Tstrap: 1-1**
Best Rating: 119 3/02 Newb 2m6f110y soft Ch

Won a Clonmel hunter chase in June 2001, and has shown ability since coming to Britain. Stays three miles. Acts on a sound surface.

Hello De Vauxbuin (FR)

99(60h) 107

7-y-o b g Le Nain Jaune (FR)-Quadrille De Cuy (FR) (Baraban)

R Ford (Miss H C Knight 17/1) Mick Coulson

Placings:P0P/35-0P0 **(4748)**

2001/02: 16^0G, 19^PS, 26^0GF

	Starts	1st	2nd	3rd	Win & Pl
Chases	3	0	0	0	
Career Total	**8**	**0**	**0**	**1**	**425**

Going: Sf: 0-1 GS: 0-0 Gd: 0-1 GF: - Fm: 0-1
Distance: 2m/2m3: 0-2 2m4-2m7: 0-0 3m+: 0-1
Track: LH: 0-0 RH: 0-3 Tight: 0-2 Gall: 0-0
Aids: Bl: 0-0 Vi: 0-0 Tstrap: 0-0
Best Rating: 97 5/00 Hrfd 2m1f good Hdl

Lightly-raced gelding with modest form to date over hurdles and fences. Successful at Newcastle in April 2002. Suited by good ground.

Hellodock (IRE)

102 94

7-y-o b g Dry Dock-Hello October (Callernish)

Ferdy Murphy Getjar Limited

Placings:FF26 **(4494)**

2001/02: 20^FS, 20^FS, 16^2S, 22^6G

	Starts	1st	2nd	3rd	Win & Pl
Hurdles	4	0	1	0	756
Career Total	**4**	**0**	**1**	**0**	**756**

Going: Sf: 0-3 GS: 0-0 Gd: 0-1 GF: - Fm: 0-0
Distance: 2m/2m3: 0-1 2m4-2m7: 0-3 3m+: 0-0
Track: LH: 0-3 RH: 0-1 Tight: 0-0 Gall: 0-3
Aids: Bl: 0-0 Vi: 0-0 Tstrap: 0-0
Best Rating: 94 3/02 Hntg 2m110y soft Hdl

Showed promise on his third start over hurdles.

Help Yourself (IRE)

54

6-y-o gr m Roselier (FR)-Sweet Run (Deep Run)

L Lungo Alistair Duncan

Placings:16 **(3331)**

2001/02: 16^1G, 16^6S

	Starts	1st	2nd	3rd	Win & Pl
NH Flat	2	1	0	0	1526
Career Total	**2**	**1**	**0**	**0**	**1526**
98 11/01 Weth 2m	H NHF			GD	£1526

Total win prize-money £1526

Going: Sf: 0-1 GS: 0-0 Gd: 1-1 GF: - Fm: 0-0
Distance: **2m/2m3: 1-2** 2m4-2m7: 0-0 3m+: 0-0
Track: **LH: 1-1** RH: 0-0 Tight: 0-0 Gall: 0-0
Aids: Bl: 0-0 Vi: 0-0 Tstrap: 0-0
Best Rating: 98 11/01 Weth 2m good NHF

Won an ordinary Wetherby bumper on her debut.

Helvetius

95(102h) (99h)106

6-y-o b g In The Wings-Hejraan (USA) (Alydar (USA))

P C Ritchens John Pearl

Placings:0-44221324420 **(2941)**

2001/02: 17^4F, 17^4GF, 20^2G, 20^2G, 22^1G, 22^3G, 22^2GF, 19^4GF, 20^4HY, 19^2G, 19^0G

	Starts	1st	2nd	3rd	Win & Pl
Hurdles	11	1	4	1	7165
Career Total	**12**	**1**	**4**	**1**	**7165**
82 8/01 NAbb 2m6f	D Hdl			GD	£3210

Total win prize-money £3211

Going: Sf: 0-1 GS: 0-0 Gd: 1-6 GF: - Fm: 0-4
Distance: 2m/2m3: 0-4 **2m4-2m7: 1-7** 3m+: 0-0
Track: **LH: 1-6** RH: 0-4 **Tight: 1-4** Gall: 0-1
Aids: Bl: 0-0 Vi: 0-0 Tstrap: 0-0
Best Rating: 99 12/01 Hrfd 2m3f110y good Hdl

Moderate hurdler, suited by two and three-quarter miles and good ground. May have been a shade fortunate to make winning debut over fences at Newton Abbot July 2002.

Henbit's Party

85f 67f

5-y-o ch m Henbit (USA)-Bantol Bouquet (Red Regent)

B A McMahon T E Wardall

Placings:000 **(2007)**

2001/02: 17^0G, 17^0G, 16^0S

	Starts	1st	2nd	3rd	Win & Pl
NH Flat	3	0	0	0	
Career Total	**3**	**0**	**0**	**0**	

Going: Sf: 0-1 GS: 0-0 Gd: 0-2 GF: - Fm: 0-0
Distance: 2m/2m3: 0-3 2m4-2m7: 0-0 3m+: 0-0
Track: LH: 0-1 RH: 0-2 Tight: 0-1 Gall: 0-0
Aids: Bl: 0-0 Vi: 0-0 Tstrap: 0-0
Best Rating: 67 10/01 Hrfd 2m1f good NHF

Henbridge

92 63

6-y-o ch m Henbit (USA)-Celtic Bridge (Celtic Cone)

Mrs S M Johnson E J Praill

Placings:000-P500P0 **(3758)**

2001/02: 20^PF, 17^5G, 20^0GS, 20^0GS, 17^PHY, 17^0S

	Starts	1st	2nd	3rd	Win & Pl
Hurdles	6	0	0	0	0
Career Total	**9**	**0**	**0**	**0**	**0**

Going: Sf: 0-2 GS: 0-2 Gd: 0-1 GF: - Fm: 0-1

Distance: 2m/2m3: 0-3 2m4-2m7: 0-3 3m+: 0-0
Track: LH: 0-1 RH: 0-5 Tight: 0-2 Gall: 0-1
Aids: Bl: 0-0 Vi: 0-0 Tstrap: 0-0
Best Rating: 63 2/02 Tntn 2m1f soft Hdl

Henbury (IRE)

91 100

9-y-o b g Henbit (USA)-Lady Trissie (Politico (USA))
P Beaumont J N Yeadon

Placings:*004/0/0020423/***P3F5-4P3P** (0670)
2001/02: 20^{4}G, 20^{P}F, 20^{3}F, 23^{P}G

	Starts	1st	2nd	3rd	Win & Pl
Chases	4	0	0	1	991
Career Total	**19**	**0**	**2**	**3**	**3351**

Going: Sf: 0-0 GS: 0-0 Gd: 0-2 GF: - Fm: 0-2
Distance: 2m/2m3: 0-0 2m4-2m7: 0-3 3m+: 0-1
Track: LH: 0-4 RH: 0-0 Tight: 0-0 Gall: 0-0
Aids: Bl: 0-2 Vi: 0-0 Tstrap: 0-0
Best Rating: 122 12/00 Muss 2m4f good Ch

Henbury Dancer

89 62

6-y-o br m Teamster-Record Flight (Record Token)
R J Hodges Frank E Crumpler

Placings:0P00FP0P (4385)
2001/02: 17^{0}GS, 17^{P}G, 17^{0}GF, 20^{0}S, 19^{F}S, 22^{P}G, 19^{0}S, 22^{P}S

	Starts	1st	2nd	3rd	Win & Pl
Hurdles	7	0	0	0	0
Chases	1	0	0	0	0
Career Total	**8**	**0**	**0**	**0**	

Going: Sf: 0-4 GS: 0-1 Gd: 0-2 GF: - Fm: 0-1
Distance: 2m/2m3: 0-4 2m4-2m7: 0-4 3m+: 0-0
Track: LH: 0-1 RH: 0-7 Tight: 0-2 Gall: 0-0
Aids: Bl: 0-0 Vi: 0-0 Tstrap: 0-0
Best Rating: 62 3/02 Tntn 2m3f110y soft Hdl

Hendra Chieftain

8-y-o ch g Shaab-Strumpetus (Bold As Brass)
Miss D Cole D G Congdon

Placings:P-05 (0794)
2001/02: 24^{0}F, 22^{5}GF

	Starts	1st	2nd	3rd	Win & Pl
Hurdles	2	0	0	0	0
Career Total	**3**	**0**	**0**	**0**	**0**

Going: Sf: 0-0 GS: 0-0 Gd: 0-0 GF: - Fm: 0-2
Distance: 2m/2m3: 0-0 2m4-2m7: 0-1 3m+: 0-1
Track: LH: 0-1 RH: 0-1 Tight: 0-2 Gall: 0-0
Aids: Bl: 0-0 Vi: 0-0 Tstrap: 0-0
Best Rating:

Hennerwood Ivy

7-y-o b m Tina's Pet-Come On Clover (Oats)
R J Price Cyril Thomas

Placings:*0* (2135)
2001/02: 16^{0}GF

	Starts	1st	2nd	3rd	Win & Pl
NH Flat	1	0	0	0	
Career Total	**1**	**0**	**0**	**0**	

Going: Sf: 0-0 GS: 0-0 Gd: 0-0 GF: - Fm: 0-1
Distance: 2m/2m3: 0-1 2m4-2m7: 0-0 3m+: 0-0
Track: LH: 0-0 RH: 0-1 Tight: 0-0 Gall: 0-0
Aids: Bl: 0-0 Vi: 0-0 Tstrap: 0-0
Best Rating:

Henrianjames

84(92h) (90+h)104

7-y-o b g Tina's Pet-Real Claire (Dreams To Reality (USA))
Mrs M Reveley K Benson

Placings:*0-0*061 (4789)
2001/02: 16^{0}S, 16^{0}S, 16^{6}GS, 16^{1}F

	Starts	1st	2nd	3rd	Win & Pl
NH Flat	1	0	0	0	0
Hurdles	1	0	0	0	0
Chases	2	1	0	0	3329
Career Total	**5**	**1**	**0**	**0**	**3329**

104 4/02 Newc 2m110y E Ch FRM £3328
Total win prize-money £3329

Going: Sf: 0-2 GS: 0-1 Gd: 0-0 GF: - Fm: 1-1
Distance: **2m/2m3: 1-4** 2m4-2m7: 0-0 3m+: 0-0
Track: **LH: 1-4** RH: 0-0 Tight: 0-1 **Gall: 1-2**
Aids: Bl: 0-0 Vi: 0-0 Tstrap: 0-0
Best Rating: 104 4/02 Newc 2m110y firm Ch

Achieved next to nothing until landing a three-runner novice chase on fast ground at Newcastle in spring of 2002. Handles good to soft.

Henrietta Holmes (IRE)

81

6-y-o gr m Persian Bold-Faakirah (Dragonara Palace (USA))
Mrs L Richards The Henrietta Partnership

Placings:56/65U3442-5B0 (3401)
2001/02: 21^{5}G, 24^{B}G, 22^{0}S

	Starts	1st	2nd	3rd	Win & Pl
Hurdles	3	0	0	0	0
Career Total	**12**	**0**	**1**	**1**	**1225**

Going: Sf: 0-1 GS: 0-0 Gd: 0-2 GF: - Fm: 0-0
Distance: 2m/2m3: 0-0 2m4-2m7: 0-2 3m+: 0-1
Track: LH: 0-2 RH: 0-0 Tight: 0-1 Gall: 0-0
Aids: Bl: 0-0 Vi: 0-0 Tstrap: 0-0
Best Rating: 82 10/00 Plum 2m5f soft Hdl

Only moderate form over hurdles. Suited by fast ground.

Henry Harber (IRE)

45 26

4-y-o b g Dilum (USA)-Marguerite Bay (IRE) (Darshaan)
G L Moore (T E Powell 11/9) Lawrence Pratt

Placings:0 (2547)
2001/02: 16^{0}S

	Starts	1st	2nd	3rd	Win & Pl
Hurdles	1	0	0	0	
Career Total	**1**	**0**	**0**	**0**	

Going: Sf: 0-1 GS: 0-0 Gd: 0-0 GF: - Fm: 0-0
Distance: 2m/2m3: 0-1 2m4-2m7: 0-0 3m+: 0-0
Track: LH: 0-0 RH: 0-1 Tight: 0-0 Gall: 0-0
Aids: Bl: 0-0 Vi: 0-0 Tstrap: 0-0
Best Rating: 26 12/01 Sand 2m110y soft Hdl

Henry Isaiah (IRE)

5-y-o b g Corrouge (USA)-Maid In The Mist (Pry)
R H Alner Alvin Trowbridge

Placings:PP0BP (4730)
2001/02: 24^{P}S, 17^{P}S, 16^{0}HY, 22^{B}G, 20^{P}GF

	Starts	1st	2nd	3rd	Win & Pl
Hurdles	5	0	0	0	
Career Total	**5**	**0**	**0**	**0**	

Going: Sf: 0-3 GS: 0-0 Gd: 0-1 GF: - Fm: 0-1
Distance: 2m/2m3: 0-2 2m4-2m7: 0-2 3m+: 0-1
Track: LH: 0-2 RH: 0-3 Tight: 0-3 Gall: 0-0
Aids: Bl: 0-0 Vi: 0-0 Tstrap: 0-0
Best Rating:

Henry Island (IRE)

106 114

9-y-o ch g Sharp Victor (USA)-Monterana (Sallust)
Mrs A J Bowlby J G Hickford

Placings:RP/3R1531/2200-4 (2148)
2001/02: 21^{4}G

	Starts	1st	2nd	3rd	Win & Pl
Hurdles	1	0	0	0	726
Career Total	**13**	**2**	**2**	**2**	**9487**

119 4/00 Hntg 2m5f110y F(0-110)HHdl GD £2102
116 2/00 Hntg 2m4f110y F(0-95)HHdl SFT £3038
Total win prize-money £5141

Going: Sf: 0-0 GS: 0-0 Gd: 0-1 GF: - Fm: 0-0
Distance: 2m/2m3: 0-0 2m4-2m7: 0-1 3m+: 0-0
Track: LH: 0-1 RH: 0-0 Tight: 0-0 Gall: 0-1
Aids: Bl: 0-0 Vi: 0-0 Tstrap: 0-0
Best Rating: 119 10/00 Sthl 2m4f110y heavy Hdl

Henry Pearson (USA)

64 41

4-y-o ch g Distant View (USA)-Lady Ellen (USA) (Explosive Bid (USA))
T H Caldwell Hogarth Racing

Placings:0 (3460)
2001/02: 16^{0}HY

	Starts	1st	2nd	3rd	Win & Pl
Hurdles	1	0	0	0	
Career Total	**1**	**0**	**0**	**0**	

Going: Sf: 0-1 GS: 0-0 Gd: 0-0 GF: - Fm: 0-0
Distance: 2m/2m3: 0-1 2m4-2m7: 0-0 3m+: 0-0
Track: LH: 0-1 RH: 0-0 Tight: 0-0 Gall: 0-0
Aids: Bl: 0-0 Vi: 0-0 Tstrap: 0-0
Best Rating: 41 1/02 Wwck 2m heavy Hdl

Maiden on the Flat. No show on hurdles debut.

Hensil

92f 79f

6-y-o br m Henbit (USA)-Silver Thorn (Record Run)
A W Carroll (Ian Williams 10/6) Wellesbourne Property Ltd

Placings:*06* (1832)
2001/02: 16^{0}GF, 16^{6}G

	Starts	1st	2nd	3rd	Win & Pl
NH Flat	2	0	0	0	0
Career Total	**2**	**0**	**0**	**0**	**0**

Going: Sf: 0-0 GS: 0-0 Gd: 0-1 GF: - Fm: 0-1
Distance: 2m/2m3: 0-2 2m4-2m7: 0-0 3m+: 0-0
Track: LH: 0-2 RH: 0-0 Tight: 0-1 Gall: 0-0
Aids: Bl: 0-0 Vi: 0-0 Tstrap: 0-0
Best Rating: 79 10/01 Sthl 2m good NHF

Her Royal Highness

79f **77f**

5-y-o b/br m Rock City-Dutch Princess (Royalty)
M J Ryan Peter P Scott

Placings:*0* **(3777)**
2001/02: 16^{0}S

	Starts	1st	2nd	3rd	Win & Pl
NH Flat	1	0	0	0	
Career Total	**1**	**0**	**0**	**0**	

Going: Sf: 0-1 GS: 0-0 Gd: 0-0 GF: - Fm: 0-0
Distance: 2m/2m3: 0-1 2m4-2m7: 0-0 3m+: 0-0
Track: LH: 0-0 RH: 0-1 Tight: 0-0 Gall: 0-0
Aids: Bl: 0-0 Vi: 0-0 Tstrap: 0-0
Best Rating: 77 2/02 Sand 2m110y soft NHF

Heracles

110(108h) (120h)**130**

6-y-o b g Unfuwain (USA)-La Masse (High Top)
B G Powell Mrs D A La Trobe

Placings:*022*/1135-524P **(2763)**
2001/02: 21^{5}G, 20^{2}GS, 21^{4}G, 19^{P}GS

	Starts	1st	2nd	3rd	Win & Pl
Hurdles	2	0	0	0	0
Chases	2	0	1	0	1663
Career Total	**11**	**2**	**3**	**1**	**12144**

116	1/01	Kemp	2m5f	D Hdl	SFT	£3851
125	1/01	Kemp	2m	D Hdl	SFT	£4738

Total win prize-money £8590

Going: Sf: 0-0 GS: 0-2 Gd: 0-2 GF: - Fm: 0-0
Distance: 2m/2m3: 0-1 2m4-2m7: 0-3 3m+: 0-0
Track: LH: 0-2 RH: 0-2 Tight: 0-1 Gall: 0-3
Aids: Bl: 0-0 Vi: 0-0 Tstrap: 0-0
Best Rating: 127 2/01 Kemp 2m5f gd-sft Hdl

Landed his first two starts over hurdles, both at Kempton, but beaten in better company afterwards. Won minor novice chase at Southwell May 2002. Stays two and a half miles plus, acts on soft ground, and is suited by a flat, right-handed track.

Herbisahead (IRE)

10-y-o b g Supreme Leader-Emmett's Lass (Deep Run)
Miss E M England Miss E M V England

Placings:*0/60/00/PP-P0P* **(2522)**
2001/02: 25^{P}S, 26^{0}G, 23^{P}G

	Starts	1st	2nd	3rd	Win & Pl
Chases	3	0	0	0	
Career Total	**10**	**0**	**0**	**0**	**0**

Going: Sf: 0-1 GS: 0-0 Gd: 0-2 GF: - Fm: 0-0
Distance: 2m/2m3: 0-0 2m4-2m7: 0-0 3m+: 0-3
Track: LH: 0-1 RH: 0-2 Tight: 0-0 Gall: 0-0
Aids: Bl: 0-0 Vi: 0-0 Tstrap: 0-0
Best Rating: 92 9/97 Worc 2m good NHF

Here Comes Henry

123

8-y-o ch g Dortino-Epryana (English Prince)
R H Alner A D & Mrs S A Old

Placings:136-P **(2939)**
2001/02: 24^{P}G

	Starts	1st	2nd	3rd	Win & Pl
Chases	1	0	0	0	
Career Total	**4**	**1**	**0**	**1**	**3944**

137	3/01	Strf	3m	H Ch	SFT	£2249

Total win prize-money £2249

Going: Sf: 0-0 GS: 0-0 Gd: 0-1 GF: - Fm: 0-0
Distance: 2m/2m3: 0-0 2m4-2m7: 0-0 3m+: 0-1
Track: LH: 0-1 RH: 0-0 Tight: 0-0 Gall: 0-1
Aids: Bl: 0-0 Vi: 0-0 Tstrap: 0-0
Best Rating: 137 3/01 Strf 3m soft Ch

Unbeaten in five point to points in 2000, he won on his debut over regulation fences at Stratford in March 2001 but has not gone on from that. Stays three miles. Acts on a sound surface.

Here Comes Steve

74f **66f**

5-y-o b g Primitive Rising (USA)-Keldholme (Derek H)
A Crook Steve Semple

Placings:*00* **(4309)**
2001/02: 16^{0}S, 16^{0}S

	Starts	1st	2nd	3rd	Win & Pl
NH Flat	2	0	0	0	
Career Total	**2**	**0**	**0**	**0**	

Going: Sf: 0-2 GS: 0-0 Gd: 0-0 GF: - Fm: 0-0
Distance: 2m/2m3: 0-2 2m4-2m7: 0-0 3m+: 0-0
Track: LH: 0-1 RH: 0-0 Tight: 0-0 Gall: 0-0
Aids: Bl: 0-0 Vi: 0-0 Tstrap: 0-0
Best Rating: 66 3/02 Ayr 2m soft NHF

Here's To Howie (USA)

95 **85**

8-y-o b g Hermitage (USA)-Choice Comment (USA) (Rich Cream (USA))
M R Bosley M F Cartwright

Placings:F/32441U/213043416/32423-55 **(1232)**
2001/02: 16^{5}G, 16^{5}GF

	Starts	1st	2nd	3rd	Win & Pl
Hurdles	2	0	0	0	0
Career Total	**23**	**3**	**4**	**5**	**19485**

110	3/00	Fknm	2m	D(0-120)HHdl	GD	£5261
108	6/99	Strf	2m110y	D(0-120)HHdl	G-F	£3938
106	4/99	Tntn	2m1f	E Hdl	FRM	£2514

Total win prize-money £11714

Going: Sf: 0-0 GS: 0-0 Gd: 0-1 GF: - Fm: 0-1
Distance: 2m/2m3: 0-2 2m4-2m7: 0-0 3m+: 0-0
Track: LH: 0-2 RH: 0-0 Tight: 0-1 Gall: 0-0
Aids: Bl: 0-0 Vi: 0-0 Tstrap: 0-0
Best Rating: 119 7/00 Strf 2m110y gd-fm Hdl

Herman Sherman (IRE)

92(85h) (59h)**87**

7-y-o b g Mandalus-Glory Hunter (Le Bavard (FR))
Mrs L Williamson Halewood International Ltd

Placings:13O0/020P20/0F60U0 **(4240)**
2001/02: 20^{0}G, 24^{F}G, 20^{6}GS, 24^{0}GS, 24^{U}G, 26^{0}GF

	Starts	1st	2nd	3rd	Win & Pl
Hurdles	3	0	0	0	0
Chases	3	0	0	0	0
Career Total	**16**	**1**	**2**	**1**	**5183**

103	3/99	Bang	2m1f	E Hdl	SFT	£2654

Total win prize-money £2654

Going: Sf: 0-0 GS: 0-2 Gd: 0-3 GF: - Fm: 0-1
Distance: 2m/2m3: 0-0 2m4-2m7: 0-2 3m+: 0-4
Track: LH: 0-3 RH: 0-3 Tight: 0-2 Gall: 0-3
Aids: Bl: 0-0 Vi: 0-0 Tstrap: 0-0
Best Rating: 110 1/00 Ludl 3m good Hdl

Hermes Iii (FR)

110 **123+**

7-y-o b g Quart De Vin (FR)-Queenly (FR) (Pot D'Or (FR))
N J Henderson Thurloe Thoroughbreds Iv

Placings:1/52 **(3773)**
2001/02: 16^{5}G, 16^{2}G

	Starts	1st	2nd	3rd	Win & Pl
Hurdles	2	0	1	0	1398
Career Total	**3**	**1**	**1**	**0**	**4472**

4/00	Fntb	2m1f110y	Ch	SFT	£3074

Total win prize-money £3074

Going: Sf: 0-1 GS: 0-0 Gd: 0-1 GF: - Fm: 0-0
Distance: 2m/2m3: 0-2 2m4-2m7: 0-0 3m+: 0-0
Track: LH: 0-1 RH: 0-1 Tight: 0-0 Gall: 0-1
Aids: Bl: 0-0 Vi: 0-0 Tstrap: 0-0
Best Rating: 112 2/02 Sand 2m110y soft Hdl

A winner in France over fences, he has shown ability in novice hurdles in this country. Goes well in soft ground.

Hernandita

103 **113**

4-y-o b f Hernando (FR)-Dara Dee (Dara Monarch)
M C Pipe (J L Dunlop 25/10) P Clarke

Placings:1145 **(4842)**
2001/02: 16^{1}G, 16^{1}GS, 16^{4}G, 20^{5}G

	Starts	1st	2nd	3rd	Win & Pl
Hurdles	4	2	0	0	5407
Career Total	**4**	**2**	**0**	**0**	**5407**

110	1/02	Sthl	2m	E Hdl	G-S	£2464
113	12/01	Winc	2m	E Hdl	GD	£2569

Total win prize-money £5033

Going: Sf: 0-0 GS: 1-1 Gd: 1-3 GF: - Fm: 0-0
Distance: **2m/2m3: 2-3** 2m4-2m7: 0-1 3m+: 0-0
Track: LH: 1-3 RH: 1-1 **Tight: 1-2** Gall: 0-0
Aids: Bl: 0-0 Vi: 0-1 Tstrap: 0-0
Best Rating: 113 12/01 Winc 2m good Hdl

Made a good start to her hurdling career with two wins in modest company, but jumped poorly when flopping on her third start. Suited by two miles and has won on good and heavy ground.

Hero's Son (FR)

(64h) **69**

6-y-o ch g Hero's Honor (USA)-Happy Waki (USA) (Miswaki (USA))

J J O'Neill Darren C Mercer

Placings:5P3/120F23-F (0275)

2001/02: 20^{F}GF

	Starts	1st	2nd	3rd	Win & Pl
Chases	1	0	0	0	
Career Total	**10**	**1**	**2**	**2**	**6996**

100 10/00 Carl 2m1f E Hdl G-S £2542

Total win prize-money £2542

Going: Sf: 0-0 GS: 0-0 Gd: 0-0 GF: - Fm: 0-1
Distance: 2m/2m3: 0-0 2m4-2m7: 0-1 3m+: 0-0
Track: LH: 0-0 RH: 0-1 Tight: 0-0 Gall: 0-0
Aids: Bl: 0-0 Vi: 0-0 Tstrap: 0-0
Best Rating: 112 1/01 Donc 2m3f110y good Ch

Won a novice hurdle at Carlisle on his return and was by no means disgraced on his chase debut next time.

Heroicus (NZ)

5-y-o ch g Heroicity (AUS)-Glenford (NZ) (Sackford (USA))

F Kirby (N J Henderson 15/11) Fred Kirby

Placings:04FPPP (4858)

2001/02: 17^{0}G, 16^{4}GF, 16^{F}GS, 20^{P}HY, 17^{P}GF, 16^{P}G

	Starts	1st	2nd	3rd	Win & Pl
NH Flat	2	0	0	0	0
Hurdles	4	0	0	0	0
Career Total	**6**	**0**	**0**	**0**	**0**

Going: Sf: 0-1 GS: 0-1 Gd: 0-2 GF: - Fm: 0-2
Distance: 2m/2m3: 0-5 2m4-2m7: 0-1 3m+: 0-0
Track: LH: 0-3 RH: 0-2 Tight: 0-3 Gall: 0-0
Aids: Bl: 0-0 Vi: 0-0 Tstrap: 0-0
Best Rating: 76 11/01 Ludl 2m gd-fm NHF

Heros Collonges (FR)

108 **160**

7-y-o b g Dom Alco (FR)-Carmen Collonges (FR) (Olmeto)

G Macaire J Hales

Placings:231111 (3379)

2001/02: 18^{2}, 17^{3}, 21^{1}S, 20^{1}G, 21^{1}VS, 24^{1}G

	Starts	1st	2nd	3rd	Win & Pl
Chases	6	4	1	1	46297
Career Total	**6**	**4**	**1**	**1**	**46297**

160 1/02 Kemp 3m C Ch GD £7315
11/01 Autl 2m5f110y HCh VS £21339
9/01 Autl 2m4f110y Ch GD £11639
8/01 Diep 2m5f Ch SFT £3686

Total win prize-money £43979

Going: Sf: 1-1 GS: 0-0 Gd: 2-2 GF: - Fm: 0-0
Distance: 2m/2m3: 0-2 **2m4-2m7: 3-3** 3m+: 1-1
Track: LH: 0-0 **RH: 1-1** Tight: 0-0 Gall: 0-0
Aids: Bl: 0-0 Vi: 0-0 Tstrap: 0-0
Best Rating: 160 1/02 Kemp 3m good Ch

A very useful French novice chaser, he impressed on his British debut at Kempton. Stays three miles and jumps well.

Heros Fatal (FR)

151

8-y-o ch g Hero's Honor (USA)-Femme Fatale (FR) (Garde Royale)

M C Pipe Frank A Farrant

Placings:24140/111600/F-F (2297)

2001/02: 24^{F}G

	Starts	1st	2nd	3rd	Win & Pl
Hurdles	1	0	0	0	
Career Total	**13**	**4**	**1**	**0**	**38376**

147 12/99 Chel 2m4f110y B Hdl G-S £10897
143 11/99 MRas 2m5f110y B HHdl G-S £6853
137 11/99 Chel 2m5f C(0-135)HHdl GD £17750
117 2/99 Ling 2m110y F Hdl SFT £1905

Total win prize-money £37406

Going: Sf: 0-0 GS: 0-0 Gd: 0-1 GF: - Fm: 0-0
Distance: 2m/2m3: 0-0 2m4-2m7: 0-0 3m+: 0-1
Track: LH: 0-0 RH: 0-1 Tight: 0-0 Gall: 0-0
Aids: Bl: 0-0 Vi: 0-0 Tstrap: 0-0
Best Rating: 151 11/01 Asct 3m good Hdl

The winner of the Cesarewitch on the Flat, he returned to the jumping scene in February but took a nasty fall on his chasing debut. Fell fatally over hurdles at Ascot in November 2001. (DEAD)

Herself

108 **108**

5-y-o b m Hernando (FR)-Kirsten (Kris)

J Mackie Ms Caroline F Breay

Placings:352-446313252 (4572)

2001/02: 19^{4}G, 20^{4}GS, 20^{6}G, 22^{3}S, 20^{1}GS, 22^{3}HY, 20^{2}GS, 20^{5}S, 20^{2}G

	Starts	1st	2nd	3rd	Win & Pl
Hurdles	9	1	2	2	5938
Career Total	**12**	**1**	**3**	**3**	**7011**

106 11/01 Leic 2m4f110y E(0-105)HHdl G-S £2989

Total win prize-money £2989

Going: Sf: 0-3 GS: 1-3 Gd: 0-3 GF: - Fm: 0-0
Distance: 2m/2m3: 0-0 **2m4-2m7: 1-9** 3m+: 0-0
Track: LH: 0-5 **RH: 1-4** Tight: 0-1 Gall: 0-0
Aids: Bl: 0-0 Vi: 0-0 **Tstrap: 1-8**
Best Rating: 108 4/02 Uttx 2m4f110y good Hdl

A consistent performer. She relishes the mud, stays two miles six. Lost her maiden tag at Leicester in November and has continued to run well since then.

Hersilia (IRE)

100(102c) (97+c)**92**

11-y-o br m Mandalus-Milan Pride (Northern Guest (USA))

R Ford L A E Hopkins

Placings:0/5564533214604/035064450212/F00F3620425/5 (0193)

2001/02: 20^{5}GF

	Starts	1st	2nd	3rd	Win & Pl
Hurdles	1	0	0	0	0
Career Total	**38**	**2**	**5**	**4**	**9503**

93 3/97 DRoy 2m Ch G-Y £2373
98 1/96 Tram 2m4f Hdl YLD £2648

Total win prize-money £5022

Going: Sf: 0-0 GS: 0-0 Gd: 0-0 GF: - Fm: 0-1
Distance: 2m/2m3: 0-0 2m4-2m7: 0-1 3m+: 0-0
Track: LH: 0-1 RH: 0-0 Tight: 0-1 Gall: 0-0
Aids: Bl: 0-0 Vi: 0-0 Tstrap: 0-0
Best Rating: 107 3/97 Dpat 3m gd-yld Ch

Winning pointer, third over hurdles in May 2002.

Hersov (IRE)

106 **123**

6-y-o gr g Roselier (FR)-Higher Again (Strong Gale)

N J Henderson Michael H Watt

Placings:352 (4398)

2001/02: 20^{3}G, 21^{5}G, 24^{2}S

	Starts	1st	2nd	3rd	Win & Pl
Hurdles	3	0	1	1	2996
Career Total	**3**	**0**	**1**	**1**	**2996**

Going: Sf: 0-1 GS: 0-0 Gd: 0-2 GF: - Fm: 0-0
Distance: 2m/2m3: 0-0 2m4-2m7: 0-2 3m+: 0-1
Track: LH: 0-1 RH: 0-2 Tight: 0-0 Gall: 0-1
Aids: Bl: 0-0 Vi: 0-0 Tstrap: 0-0
Best Rating: 123 2/02 Kemp 2m5f good Hdl

From the family of Morley Street and Granville Again, made an encouraging debut over hurdles at Ascot in December 2001. He looks a stayer and is a chaser in the making.

Hescondido (FR)

111 **159**

7-y-o gr g Dadarissime (FR)-Vahine De Prairie (FR) (Brezzo (FR))

Miss Venetia Williams Major-Gen R L T Burges

Placings:311413321/6236P-F21146 (4897)

2001/02: 25^{F}G, 26^{2}GS, 22^{1}G, 20^{1}S, 24^{4}S, 24^{6}G

	Starts	1st	2nd	3rd	Win & Pl
Chases	6	2	1	0	16282
Career Total	**20**	**6**	**3**	**4**	**45203**

159 2/02 Kemp 2m4f110y C(0-135)HCh SFT £7182
145 12/01 Newb 2m6f110y C(0-130)HCh GD £6786
135 4/00 Weth 2m4f110y D Ch SFT £4134
8/99 Mesl 2m1f110y Ch SFT £6997
6/99 Segr 2m3f Ch GD £2906
6/99 Stma 2m1f Hdl GD £3229

Total win prize-money £31235

Going: Sf: 1-2 GS: 0-1 Gd: 1-3 GF: - Fm: 0-0
Distance: 2m/2m3: 0-0 **2m4-2m7: 2-2** 3m+: 0-4
Track: LH: 1-1 RH: 1-4 Tight: 0-2 **Gall: 1-1**
Aids: Bl: 0-0 Vi: 0-0 Tstrap: 0-0
Best Rating: 159 2/02 Kemp 2m4f110y soft Ch

Front-running chaser, stays two miles-six. Has had his jumping problems but proved a revelation in 2001/2002 and may just have taken time to acclimatise. Suited by soft ground, he really impressed when winning over two and a half miles at Kempton in February.

Hetra Hawk

89 **62**

6-y-o ch g Be My Guest (USA)-Silver Ore (FR) (Silver Hawk (USA))

W J Musson K L West

Placings:0 (4021)

2001/02: 16^{0}S

	Starts	1st	2nd	3rd	Win & Pl
Hurdles	1	0	0	0	
Career Total	**1**	**0**	**0**	**0**	

Going: Sf: 0-1 GS: 0-0 Gd: 0-0 GF: - Fm: 0-0
Distance: 2m/2m3: 0-1 2m4-2m7: 0-0 3m+: 0-0
Track: LH: 0-0 RH: 0-1 Tight: 0-0 Gall: 0-1
Aids: Bl: 0-0 Vi: 0-0 Tstrap: 0-0
Best Rating: 62 3/02 Hntg 2m110y soft Hdl

Hever Golf Charmer

77 26

8-y-o b g Precocious-Callas Star (Chief Singer)
N Rossiter Mrs E Rossiter

Placings:3045/550F0/00 **(2669)**
2001/02: 20^{0}S, 16^{0}G

	Starts	1st	2nd	3rd	Win & Pl
Hurdles	2	0	0	0	
Career Total	**11**	**0**	**0**	**1**	**268**

Going: Sf: 0-1 GS: 0-0 Gd: 0-1 GF: - Fm: 0-0
Distance: 2m/2m3: 0-1 2m4-2m7: 0-1 3m+: 0-0
Track: LH: 0-2 RH: 0-0 Tight: 0-1 Gall: 0-1
Aids: Bl: 0-0 Vi: 0-0 Tstrap: 0-0
Best Rating: **66** 8/98 Worc 2m gd-fm Hdl

Hever Golf Diamond

81 60

9-y-o b g Nomination-Cadi Ha (Welsh Pageant)
J R Best Seamus And Matt Racing

Placings:1435005P/4123054011P0/1215106/404U2/0 36P6-00 **(0966)**
2001/02: 21^{0}GF, 21^{0}GS

	Starts	1st	2nd	3rd	Win & Pl
Hurdles	2	0	0	0	
Career Total	**39**	**7**	**3**	**3**	**21274**

109	12/98	Font	2m6f110y	E(0-110)HHdl	G-S	£2372
109	11/98	Font	2m6f110y	E(0-110)HHdl	SFT	£2302
100	10/98	MRas	2m1f110y	G(0-95)HHdl	GD	£1702
93	12/97	MRas	2m3f110y	G(0-95)HHdl	G-S	£1838
82	11/97	MRas	2m3f110y	G(0-90)HHdl	G-S	£1773
80	5/97	Fknm	2m	G(0-95)HHdl	GD	£2746
80	10/96	Ludl	2m	E Hdl	FRM	£2451

Total win prize-money £15188

Going: Sf: 0-0 GS: 0-1 Gd: 0-0 GF: - Fm: 0-1
Distance: 2m/2m3: 0-0 2m4-2m7: 0-2 3m+: 0-0
Track: LH: 0-0 RH: 0-1 Tight: 0-0 Gall: 0-1
Aids: Bl: 0-0 Vi: 0-1 Tstrap: 0-0
Best Rating: **109** 3/00 Font 2m2f110y gd-sft Hdl

Hever Golf Glory

86 69

8-y-o b g Efisio-Zaius (Artaius (USA))
C N Kellett D H & Mrs R E Muir

Placings:600-05 **(0375)**
2001/02: 16^{0}GF, 16^{5}GF

	Starts	1st	2nd	3rd	Win & Pl
Hurdles	2	0	0	0	0
Career Total	**5**	**0**	**0**	**0**	**0**

Going: Sf: 0-0 GS: 0-0 Gd: 0-0 GF: - Fm: 0-2
Distance: 2m/2m3: 0-2 2m4-2m7: 0-0 3m+: 0-0
Track: LH: 0-1 RH: 0-1 Tight: 0-1 Gall: 0-1
Aids: Bl: 0-0 Vi: 0-0 Tstrap: 0-0
Best Rating: **69** 5/01 Hntg 2m110y gd-fm Hdl

Hey Ref (IRE)

80f 51f

5-y-o b g King's Ride-Jeanarie (Reformed Character)
J J O'Neill J P McManus

Placings:*0* **(4166)**
2001/02: 16^{0}GS

	Starts	1st	2nd	3rd	Win & Pl
NH Flat	1	0	0	0	
Career Total	**1**	**0**	**0**	**0**	

Going: Sf: 0-0 GS: 0-1 Gd: 0-0 GF: - Fm: 0-0
Distance: 2m/2m3: 0-1 2m4-2m7: 0-0 3m+: 0-0
Track: LH: 0-1 RH: 0-0 Tight: 0-0 Gall: 0-0
Aids: Bl: 0-0 Vi: 0-0 Tstrap: 0-0
Best Rating: **51** 3/02 Wwck 2m gd-sft NHF

Hi Buddy

91 90

5-y-o br g High Kicker (USA)-Star Thyme (Point North)
J Mackie R M Mitchell

Placings:400 **(2418)**
2001/02: 16^{4}S, 16^{0}G, 16^{0}HY

	Starts	1st	2nd	3rd	Win & Pl
Hurdles	3	0	0	0	280
Career Total	**3**	**0**	**0**	**0**	**280**

Going: Sf: 0-2 GS: 0-0 Gd: 0-1 GF: - Fm: 0-0
Distance: 2m/2m3: 0-3 2m4-2m7: 0-0 3m+: 0-0
Track: LH: 0-3 RH: 0-0 Tight: 0-0 Gall: 0-0
Aids: Bl: 0-0 Vi: 0-2 Tstrap: 0-0
Best Rating: **83** 11/01 Hayd 2m soft Hdl

Hi Lily

100 94

6-y-o b m Jupiter Island-By Line (High Line)
C J Mann Granville J Harper

Placings:*0-05* **(2135)**
2001/02: 16^{0}G, 16^{5}GF

	Starts	1st	2nd	3rd	Win & Pl
NH Flat	2	0	0	0	0
Career Total	**3**	**0**	**0**	**0**	**0**

Going: Sf: 0-0 GS: 0-0 Gd: 0-1 GF: - Fm: 0-1
Distance: 2m/2m3: 0-2 2m4-2m7: 0-0 3m+: 0-0
Track: LH: 0-1 RH: 0-1 Tight: 0-0 Gall: 0-0
Aids: Bl: 0-0 Vi: 0-0 Tstrap: 0-0
Best Rating: **77** 10/01 Chel 2m110y good NHF

Hi Rudolf

103(78h) (76h)91

7-y-o b g Ballet Royal (USA)-Hi Darlin' (Prince De Galles)
H J Manners H J Manners

Placings:053P/0P/P-53P3 **(4738)**
2001/02: 19^{5}G, 21^{3}S, 16^{P}GS, 24^{3}GF

	Starts	1st	2nd	3rd	Win & Pl
Hurdles	1	0	0	0	0
Chases	3	0	0	2	858
Career Total	**11**	**0**	**0**	**3**	**1067**

Going: Sf: 0-1 GS: 0-1 Gd: 0-1 GF: - Fm: 0-1
Distance: 2m/2m3: 0-1 2m4-2m7: 0-2 3m+: 0-1
Track: LH: 0-0 RH: 0-4 Tight: 0-2 Gall: 0-0
Aids: Bl: 0-0 Vi: 0-0 Tstrap: 0-0
Best Rating: **90** 2/02 Folk 2m5f soft Ch

Modest hunter/novice chaser, best at around two and a half miles. Not the best of jumpers.

Hi Tek

86 61

7-y-o ch m Arzanni-Storm Foot (Import)
M Tate Hi Tek Group

Placings:*00000/40-P400400* **(1806)**
2001/02: 26^{P}G, 19^{4}G, 20^{0}G, 16^{0}GF, 22^{4}GF, 21^{0}G, 24^{0}GF

	Starts	1st	2nd	3rd	Win & Pl
Hurdles	7	0	0	0	0
Career Total	**14**	**0**	**0**	**0**	**233**

Going: Sf: 0-0 GS: 0-0 Gd: 0-4 GF: - Fm: 0-3
Distance: 2m/2m3: 0-2 2m4-2m7: 0-3 3m+: 0-2
Track: LH: 0-3 RH: 0-3 Tight: 0-0 Gall: 0-0
Aids: Bl: 0-1 Vi: 0-0 Tstrap: 0-0
Best Rating: **71** 1/00 Ludl 2m good NHF

Hibernate (IRE)

8-y-o ch g Lahib (USA)-Ministra (USA) (Deputy Minister (CAN))
K R Burke Platinum Racing Club Limited

Placings:6040/055/P **(2902)**
2001/02: 16^{P}S

	Starts	1st	2nd	3rd	Win & Pl
Hurdles	1	0	0	0	
Career Total	**8**	**0**	**0**	**0**	**0**

Going: Sf: 0-1 GS: 0-0 Gd: 0-0 GF: - Fm: 0-0
Distance: 2m/2m3: 0-1 2m4-2m7: 0-0 3m+: 0-0
Track: LH: 0-0 RH: 0-1 Tight: 0-0 Gall: 0-0
Aids: Bl: 0-0 Vi: 0-0 Tstrap: 0-0
Best Rating: **79** 12/98 Catt 2m good Hdl

Hiblissimo

99 79

8-y-o ch m Noblissimo (FR)-Hivally (High Line)
B W Murray Mrs M Lingwood

Placings:*00-0560206* **(2349)**
2001/02: 16^{0}GF, 17^{5}G, 19^{6}G, 19^{0}GF, 24^{2}GS, 25^{0}G, 19^{6}GS

	Starts	1st	2nd	3rd	Win & Pl
Hurdles	7	0	1	0	775
Career Total	**9**	**0**	**1**	**0**	**775**

Going: Sf: 0-0 GS: 0-2 Gd: 0-3 GF: - Fm: 0-2
Distance: 2m/2m3: 0-2 2m4-2m7: 0-3 3m+: 0-2
Track: LH: 0-2 RH: 0-5 Tight: 0-5 Gall: 0-0
Aids: Bl: 0-0 Vi: 0-0 Tstrap: 0-0
Best Rating: **79** 10/01 MRas 3m gd-sft Hdl

Hickey's Gift (IRE)

91

6-y-o ch g Over The River (FR)-Chorabelle (Choral Society)
R H Alner R Alner

Placings:*05P* **(4544)**
2001/02: 16^{0}GS, 17^{5}S, 26^{P}G

	Starts	1st	2nd	3rd	Win & Pl
NH Flat	2	0	0	0	0
Hurdles	1	0	0	0	0
Career Total	**3**	**0**	**0**	**0**	**0**

Going: Sf: 0-1 GS: 0-1 Gd: 0-1 GF: - Fm: 0-0
Distance: 2m/2m3: 0-2 2m4-2m7: 0-0 3m+: 0-1
Track: LH: 0-1 RH: 0-2 Tight: 0-0 Gall: 0-0
Aids: Bl: 0-0 Vi: 0-0 Tstrap: 0-0
Best Rating: **81** 3/02 Hrfd 2m1f soft NHF

Showed little before landing a weak Warwick novice hurdle on firm ground in May. A chasing type.

Hidden Bounty (IRE)

96 109

6-y-o b g Generous (IRE)-Sought Out (IRE) (Rainbow Quest (USA))

Mrs M Reveley M E Foxton

Placings:006121 **(4817)**

2001/02: 16^0GS, 16^0G, 23^6GS, 20^1S, 21^2S, 24^1GF

	Starts	1st	2nd	3rd	Win & Pl
Hurdles	6	2	1	0	12347
Career Total	**6**	**2**	**1**	**0**	**12347**

104	4/02	Chel	3m	D(0-120)HHdl	G-F	£9243
109	2/02	Hntg	2m4f110y	F(0-95)HHdl	SFT	£2063

Total win prize-money £11307

Going: Sf: 1-2 GS: 0-2 Gd: 0-1 GF: - Fm: 1-1
Distance: 2m/2m3: 0-2 2m4-2m7: 1-3 3m+: 1-1
Track: LH: 0-4 **RH: 1-1** Tight: 0-1 **Gall: 1-2**
Aids: Bl: 0-0 Vi: 0-0 Tstrap: 0-0
Best Rating: 109 2/02 Hntg 2m4f110y soft Hdl

Won on his handicap debut at Huntingdon but was beaten by a slow pace in his attempt to defy a penalty next time. Bounced back when upped in trip in a competitive race at Cheltenham.

Hidden Exit

63f 75f

6-y-o b m Landyap (USA)-Queen Of The Nile (Hittite Glory)

Mrs L Williamson R A Hughes

Placings:000 **(4377)**

2001/02: 17^0S, 16^0G, 16^0S

	Starts	1st	2nd	3rd	Win & Pl
NH Flat	3	0	0	0	
Career Total	**3**	**0**	**0**	**0**	

Going: Sf: 0-2 GS: 0-0 Gd: 0-1 GF: - Fm: 0-0
Distance: 2m/2m3: 0-3 2m4-2m7: 0-0 3m+: 0-0
Track: LH: 0-1 RH: 0-2 Tight: 0-1 Gall: 0-0
Aids: Bl: 0-0 Vi: 0-0 Tstrap: 0-0
Best Rating: 51 1/02 Sedg 2m1f soft NHF

Hidden Lake (IRE)

80 61

4-y-o b g Lake Coniston (IRE)-Valmarana (USA) (Danzig Connection (USA))

Mrs A J Bowlby Mrs Amanda Bowlby

Placings:6 **(1444)**

2001/02: 18^6GF

	Starts	1st	2nd	3rd	Win & Pl
Hurdles	1	0	0	0	0
Career Total	**1**	**0**	**0**	**0**	**0**

Going: Sf: 0-0 GS: 0-0 Gd: 0-0 GF: - Fm: 0-1
Distance: 2m/2m3: 0-1 2m4-2m7: 0-0 3m+: 0-0
Track: LH: 0-1 RH: 0-0 Tight: 0-1 Gall: 0-0
Aids: Bl: 0-0 Vi: 0-0 Tstrap: 0-1
Best Rating: 61 9/01 Font 2m2f110y gd-fm Hdl

Hidden Pearl (IRE)

91 68

6-y-o b g Posen (USA)-Cockney Miss (Camden Town)

Ferdy Murphy Exors Of The Late Mr G A Hubbard

Placings:P0P0 **(4774)**

2001/02: 17^PHY, 16^0G, 20^PG, 17^0G

	Starts	1st	2nd	3rd	Win & Pl
Hurdles	4	0	0	0	
Career Total	**4**	**0**	**0**	**0**	

Going: Sf: 0-1 GS: 0-0 Gd: 0-3 GF: - Fm: 0-0
Distance: 2m/2m3: 0-3 2m4-2m7: 0-1 3m+: 0-0
Track: LH: 0-2 RH: 0-2 Tight: 0-2 Gall: 0-1
Aids: Bl: 0-0 Vi: 0-0 Tstrap: 0-0
Best Rating: 51 4/02 MRas 2m1f110y good Hdl

Hidden Valley

114(109h) (127h)121

10-y-o b g St Columbus-Leven Valley (Ragstone)

J D Frost (R G Frost 21/2) G G A Gregson

Placings:0/0/05112F62/011F11-544024 **(4481)**

2001/02: 21^5G, 23^4S, 21^4GS, 24^0G, 20^2S, 23^4G

	Starts	1st	2nd	3rd	Win & Pl
Chases	6	0	1	0	3623
Career Total	**22**	**6**	**3**	**0**	**27738**

127	4/01	Extr	2m3f	D(0-125)HHdl	SFT	£3969
127	3/01	Extr	2m6f110y	D(0-125)HHdl	HVY	£3656
119	1/01	Extr	2m1f110y	F(0-100)HCh	HVY	£3132
113	11/00	NAbb	2m5f110y	F(0-110)HCh	HVY	£5404
80	11/99	Extr	2m6f	E(0-105)HHdl	G-S	£2921
90	8/99	NAbb	2m1f	F(0-100)HHdl	G-F	£2862

Total win prize-money £21945

Going: Sf: 0-2 GS: 0-1 Gd: 0-3 GF: - Fm: 0-0
Distance: 2m/2m3: 0-0 2m4-2m7: 0-3 3m+: 0-3
Track: LH: 0-1 RH: 0-5 Tight: 0-1 Gall: 0-0
Aids: Bl: 0-0 Vi: 0-0 Tstrap: 0-0
Best Rating: 127 4/01 Extr 2m3f soft Hdl

Fair handicapper over both hurdles and fences who stays two miles-seven in the mud and loves Exeter.

Hiers De Brouage (FR)

89 106

7-y-o b g Neustrien (FR)-Thalandrezienne (FR) (Le Correzien (FR))

J G Portman Seddon - Brown Partnership

Placings:0300/PP16 **(4421)**

2001/02: 24^PG, 24^PS, 19^1GS, 18^6GS

	Starts	1st	2nd	3rd	Win & Pl
Chases	4	1	0	0	3998
Career Total	**8**	**1**	**0**	**1**	**5727**

106	3/02	Chep	2m3f110y	D Ch	G-S	£3997

Total win prize-money £3998

Going: Sf: 0-1 GS: 1-2 Gd: 0-1 GF: - Fm: 0-0
Distance: 2m/2m3: 0-1 **2m4-2m7: 1-1** 3m+: 0-2
Track: **LH: 1-4** RH: 0-0 Tight: 0-0 Gall: 0-3
Aids: Bl: 0-0 Vi: 0-0 Tstrap: 0-0
Best Rating: 106 3/02 Chep 2m3f110y gd-sft Ch

Ex-French, he had luck on his side when winning a Chepstow novice chase in March 2002.

Hifinanba

102 71

6-y-o gr m Gran Alba (USA)-High Finesse (High Line)

J W Mullins Miss C A James

Placings:6-06R6P00 **(4588)**

2001/02: 17^0G, 17^6GF, 17^RGF, 21^6G, 22^PS, 16^0G, 22^0G

	Starts	1st	2nd	3rd	Win & Pl
NH Flat	3	0	0	0	0
Hurdles	4	0	0	0	0
Career Total	**8**	**0**	**0**	**0**	**0**

Going: Sf: 0-1 GS: 0-0 Gd: 0-4 GF: - Fm: 0-2
Distance: 2m/2m3: 0-4 2m4-2m7: 0-3 3m+: 0-0
Track: LH: 0-2 RH: 0-4 Tight: 0-3 Gall: 0-0
Aids: Bl: 0-0 Vi: 0-0 Tstrap: 0-0
Best Rating: 90 4/01 Tntn 2m1f gd-fm NHF

High Cheviot

99 100

5-y-o b h Shirley Heights-Cutleaf (Kris)

Ferdy Murphy High Cheviot Racing Partnership

Placings:22 **(4594)**

2001/02: 16^2GS, 16^2G

	Starts	1st	2nd	3rd	Win & Pl
Hurdles	2	0	2	0	1728
Career Total	**2**	**0**	**2**	**0**	**1728**

Going: Sf: 0-0 GS: 0-1 Gd: 0-1 GF: - Fm: 0-0
Distance: 2m/2m3: 0-2 2m4-2m7: 0-0 3m+: 0-0
Track: LH: 0-2 RH: 0-0 Tight: 0-1 Gall: 0-0
Aids: Bl: 0-0 Vi: 0-0 Tstrap: 0-0
Best Rating: 100 4/02 Uttx 2m good Hdl

Having his first run since his two-year-old days when runner-up in a Kelso novices' hurdle. Filled the same position next time.

High Cotton (IRE)

110(110h) (114h)142

7-y-o gr g Ala Hounak-Planalife (Beau Charmeur (FR))

D R C Elsworth R Burridge

Placings:62522-243543 **(3778)**

2001/02: 24^2G, 24^4G, 25^3G, 24^5G, 24^4S, 24^3GS

	Starts	1st	2nd	3rd	Win & Pl
Hurdles	1	0	1	0	1812
Chases	5	0	0	2	8999
Career Total	**11**	**0**	**4**	**2**	**14638**

Going: Sf: 0-1 GS: 0-1 Gd: 0-4 GF: - Fm: 0-0
Distance: 2m/2m3: 0-0 2m4-2m7: 0-0 3m+: 0-6
Track: LH: 0-3 RH: 0-3 Tight: 0-1 Gall: 0-3
Aids: Bl: 0-0 Vi: 0-0 Tstrap: 0-0
Best Rating: 142 12/01 Kemp 3m good Ch

Fair form in novice hurdles and novice chases. Acts on good ground but appreciates very soft ground. Stays three miles, has worn sheepskin cheekpieces.

High Danby (IRE)

8-y-o b g Millfontaine-Lakeroad (Boreen (FR))

V R A Dartnall Nick Viney

Placings:3/0-P **(1793)**

2001/02: 20^PS

	Starts	1st	2nd	3rd	Win & Pl
Hurdles	1	0	0	0	
Career Total	**3**	**0**	**0**	**1**	**248**

Going: Sf: 0-1 GS: 0-0 Gd: 0-0 GF: - Fm: 0-0
Distance: 2m/2m3: 0-0 2m4-2m7: 0-1 3m+: 0-0
Track: LH: 0-1 RH: 0-0 Tight: 0-0 Gall: 0-0
Aids: Bl: 0-0 Vi: 0-0 Tstrap: 0-0
Best Rating: 102 3/99 Chep 2m110y gd-sft NHF

High Expectations (IRE)

7-y-o ch g Over The River (FR)-Andy's Fancy (IRE) (Andretti)
J S Haldane (T P Tate 10/3) J S Haldane

Placings:0/U (4690)
2001/02: 25^{U}GF

	Starts	1st	2nd	3rd	Win & Pl
Chases	1	0	0	0	
Career Total	**2**	**0**	**0**	**0**	

Going: Sf: 0-0 GS: 0-0 Gd: 0-0 GF: - Fm: 0-1
Distance: 2m/2m3: 0-0 2m4-2m7: 0-0 3m+: 0-1
Track: LH: 0-1 RH: 0-0 Tight: 0-1 Gall: 0-0
Aids: Bl: 0-0 Vi: 0-0 Tstrap: 0-0
Best Rating: 84 4/99 Towc 2m good NHF

High Gale (IRE)

10-y-o b g Strong Gale-High Board (High Line)
T Wall (P F Nicholls 28/5) D B Roberts

Placings:0/0U630/FF11/P/FF-PPP (1802)
2001/02: 16^{P}GF, 16^{P}GF, 16^{P}GF

	Starts	1st	2nd	3rd	Win & Pl
Hurdles	1	0	0	0	0
Chases	2	0	0	0	0
Career Total	**16**	**2**	**0**	**1**	**7866**

124	4/99	Folk	2m	E(0-100)HCh	G-F	£2898
116	4/99	Tntn	2m110y	D Ch	FRM	£4713

Total win prize-money £7611

Going: Sf: 0-0 GS: 0-0 Gd: 0-0 GF: - Fm: 0-3
Distance: 2m/2m3: 0-3 2m4-2m7: 0-0 3m+: 0-0
Track: LH: 0-0 RH: 0-3 Tight: 0-1 Gall: 0-1
Aids: Bl: 0-0 Vi: 0-0 Tstrap: 0-0
Best Rating: 124 4/99 Folk 2m gd-fm Ch

He won a couple of novice chases in April 1999, but has been lightly-raced since and has had problems completing. Suited by fast ground.

High Green

69

10-y-o b g Green Adventure (USA)-High Affair (High Line)
J L Spearing Mrs Peter Badger

Placings:PP5 (3224)
2001/02: 22^{P}S, 20^{P}S, 21^{5}G

	Starts	1st	2nd	3rd	Win & Pl
Chases	3	0	0	0	0
Career Total	**3**	**0**	**0**	**0**	**0**

Going: Sf: 0-2 GS: 0-0 Gd: 0-1 GF: - Fm: 0-0
Distance: 2m/2m3: 0-0 2m4-2m7: 0-3 3m+: 0-0
Track: LH: 0-1 RH: 0-2 Tight: 0-1 Gall: 0-0
Aids: Bl: 0-1 Vi: 0-0 Tstrap: 0-0
Best Rating: 69 1/02 Winc 2m5f good Ch

High Hoyland

100 95

6-y-o b g High Estate-Waffling (Lomond (USA))
Jedd O'Keeffe Mrs L J Gennard

Placings:P25-30 (0587)
2001/02: 16^{3}GF, 16^{0}GF

	Starts	1st	2nd	3rd	Win & Pl
Hurdles	2	0	0	1	528
Career Total	**5**	**0**	**1**	**1**	**1172**

Going: Sf: 0-0 GS: 0-0 Gd: 0-0 GF: - Fm: 0-2
Distance: 2m/2m3: 0-2 2m4-2m7: 0-0 3m+: 0-0
Track: LH: 0-1 RH: 0-1 Tight: 0-1 Gall: 0-0
Aids: Bl: 0-0 Vi: 0-0 Tstrap: 0-0
Best Rating: 95 5/01 Prth 2m110y gd-fm Hdl

High In The Clouds (IRE)

98 116

10-y-o b g Scenic-Miracle Drug (USA) (Seattle Slew (USA))
H D Daly (C J B Barlow 7/4) Mrs Richard Strachan & Mrs David Lewis

Placings:2123/23/0232221/223U12/60 (0494)
2001/02: 24^{6}G, 25^{0}G

	Starts	1st	2nd	3rd	Win & Pl
Chases	2	0	0	0	0
Career Total	**21**	**3**	**10**	**4**	**24456**

130	11/99	Hntg	3m	D(0-120)HCh	GD	£3847
113	3/99	Ludl	2m4f	E Ch	GD	£3501
110	2/97	Ludl	2m	E Hdl	GD	£2542

Total win prize-money £9890

Going: Sf: 0-0 GS: 0-0 Gd: 0-2 GF: - Fm: 0-0
Distance: 2m/2m3: 0-0 2m4-2m7: 0-0 3m+: 0-2
Track: LH: 0-0 RH: 0-2 Tight: 0-0 Gall: 0-1
Aids: Bl: 0-2 Vi: 0-0 Tstrap: 0-0
Best Rating: 137 4/97 Aint 2m110y good Hdl

High Learie

12-y-o b g Petoski-Lady Doubloon (Pieces Of Eight)
Mrs D M Grissell Major J R D Barnard

Placings:44/16F46/1222/F414322B/3451P/FPP/5-3P0 (4135)
2001/02: 21^{3}G, 24^{P}GF, 24^{0}G

	Starts	1st	2nd	3rd	Win & Pl
Chases	3	0	0	1	273
Career Total	**31**	**4**	**5**	**3**	**21330**

108	3/99	Hntg	3m	E(0-115)HCh	SFT	£3782
107	11/97	Hntg	3m	E(0-110)HCh	GD	£3023
93	2/97	Plum	3m1f110y	E Ch	G-S	£3290
102	12/95	Extr	2m2f	E Hdl	G-S	£4111

Total win prize-money £14207

Going: Sf: 0-0 GS: 0-0 Gd: 0-2 GF: - Fm: 0-1
Distance: 2m/2m3: 0-0 2m4-2m7: 0-1 3m+: 0-2
Track: LH: 0-1 RH: 0-2 Tight: 0-2 Gall: 0-0
Aids: Bl: 0-0 Vi: 0-0 Tstrap: 0-0
Best Rating: 108 3/99 Hntg 3m soft Ch

High Mood

114

12-y-o b g Jalmood (USA)-Copt Hall Princess (Crowned Prince (USA))
T R George John French

Placings:00/UP/004U/141F6/235243F6/U312164/216 44-4 (2200)
2001/02: 22^{4}G

	Starts	1st	2nd	3rd	Win & Pl
Chases	1	0	0	0	277
Career Total	**34**	**5**	**4**	**3**	**28561**

134	11/00	Newb	2m6f110y	E(0-115)HCh	G-S	£5200
117	2/00	Newc	2m4f	D(0-125)HCh	SFT	£3721
104	12/99	Sedg	2m5f	F(0-105)HCh	SFT	£2901
102	12/97	Uttx	2m5f	E(0-105)HCh	SFT	£3522
102	11/97	Weth	2m	D(0-110)HCh	GD	£3600

Total win prize-money £18945

Going: Sf: 0-0 GS: 0-0 Gd: 0-1 GF: - Fm: 0-0
Distance: 2m/2m3: 0-0 2m4-2m7: 0-1 3m+: 0-0
Track: LH: 0-0 RH: 0-0 Tight: 0-0 Gall: 0-0
Aids: Bl: 0-0 Vi: 0-0 Tstrap: 0-0
Best Rating: 134 11/00 Newb 2m6f110y gd-sft Ch

Best around two and a half miles on testing ground, he has always been prone to mistakes.

High Peak

92 89

5-y-o b g Alflora (IRE)-High Heels (IRE) (Supreme Leader)
C Grant Lord Daresbury

Placings:00354 (4888)
2001/02: 17^{0}S, 17^{0}GS, 16^{3}G, 16^{5}G, 16^{4}G

	Starts	1st	2nd	3rd	Win & Pl
NH Flat	3	0	0	1	222
Hurdles	2	0	0	0	298
Career Total	**5**	**0**	**0**	**1**	**520**

Going: Sf: 0-1 GS: 0-1 Gd: 0-3 GF: - Fm: 0-0
Distance: 2m/2m3: 0-5 2m4-2m7: 0-0 3m+: 0-0
Track: LH: 0-2 RH: 0-2 Tight: 0-2 Gall: 0-0
Aids: Bl: 0-0 Vi: 0-0 Tstrap: 0-0
Best Rating: 89 4/02 Uttx 2m good Hdl

Showed his first sign of form when third in a Musselburgh bumper.

High Places

102f 103f

4-y-o b g Shirley Heights-Fajjoura (IRE) (Fairy King (USA))
G A Swinbank Derek Hyde

Placings:2 (4552)
2001/02: 16^{2}GF

	Starts	1st	2nd	3rd	Win & Pl
NH Flat	1	0	1	0	512
Career Total	**1**	**0**	**1**	**0**	**512**

Going: Sf: 0-0 GS: 0-0 Gd: 0-0 GF: - Fm: 0-1
Distance: 2m/2m3: 0-1 2m4-2m7: 0-0 3m+: 0-0
Track: LH: 0-0 RH: 0-1 Tight: 0-0 Gall: 0-1
Aids: Bl: 0-0 Vi: 0-0 Tstrap: 0-0
Best Rating: 103 4/02 Hntg 2m110y gd-fm NHF

High Ranger

82 61

7-y-o b g High Lodge-Hydrangea (Warpath)
I W McInnes Ian McInnes

Placings:50/06-00P (0591)
2001/02: 16^{0}S, 20^{0}F, 23^{P}GF

	Starts	1st	2nd	3rd	Win & Pl
Hurdles	3	0	0	0	
Career Total	**7**	**0**	**0**	**0**	**0**

Going: Sf: 0-1 GS: 0-0 Gd: 0-0 GF: - Fm: 0-2
Distance: 2m/2m3: 0-1 2m4-2m7: 0-1 3m+: 0-1
Track: LH: 0-3 RH: 0-0 Tight: 0-1 Gall: 0-0
Aids: Bl: 0-0 Vi: 0-0 Tstrap: 0-0
Best Rating: 68 5/00 Sedg 2m5f110y gd-fm Hdl

High Ratio (NZ)

92 **96**

6-y-o b g Classic Fame (USA)-Ginevra (NZ) (Alvaro)
A King Nigel Bunter

Placings:0-040 **(2777)**
2001/02: 16^{0}G, 16^{4}S, 17^{0}G

	Starts	1st	2nd	3rd	Win & Pl
Hurdles	3	0	0	0	0
Career Total	**4**	**0**	**0**	**0**	**0**

Going: Sf: 0-1 GS: 0-0 Gd: 0-2 GF: - Fm: 0-0
Distance: 2m/2m3: 0-3 2m4-2m7: 0-0 3m+: 0-0
Track: LH: 0-2 RH: 0-1 Tight: 0-1 Gall: 0-0
Aids: Bl: 0-0 Vi: 0-0 Tstrap: 0-0
Best Rating: 90 10/01 Chel 2m110y good Hdl

High Seas (IRE)

94 **78**

7-y-o b g Pips Pride-Summit Talk (Head For Heights)
Ferdy Murphy W H Winlow

Placings:00P05-0P **(4646)**
2001/02: 16^{0}G, 21^{P}G

	Starts	1st	2nd	3rd	Win & Pl
Hurdles	2	0	0	0	
Career Total	**7**	**0**	**0**	**0**	**0**

Going: Sf: 0-0 GS: 0-0 Gd: 0-2 GF: - Fm: 0-0
Distance: 2m/2m3: 0-1 2m4-2m7: 0-1 3m+: 0-0
Track: LH: 0-1 RH: 0-1 Tight: 0-1 Gall: 0-0
Aids: Bl: 0-0 Vi: 0-0 Tstrap: 0-0
Best Rating: 78 10/01 Aint 2m110y good Hdl

High Sun

74 **48**

6-y-o b g High Estate-Clyde Goddess (IRE) (Scottish Reel)
P Monteith Mrs V Nyberg

Placings:00 **(1931)**
2001/02: 16^{0}G, 16^{0}G

	Starts	1st	2nd	3rd	Win & Pl
Hurdles	2	0	0	0	
Career Total	**2**	**0**	**0**	**0**	

Going: Sf: 0-0 GS: 0-0 Gd: 0-2 GF: - Fm: 0-0
Distance: 2m/2m3: 0-2 2m4-2m7: 0-0 3m+: 0-0
Track: LH: 0-2 RH: 0-0 Tight: 0-2 Gall: 0-0
Aids: Bl: 0-0 Vi: 0-0 Tstrap: 0-0
Best Rating: 48 10/01 Kels 2m110y good Hdl

Highbank

101 **103**

10-y-o b g Puissance-Highland Daisy (He Loves Me)
Mrs M Reveley D H & C Thrower

Placings:03114412/522/0P300/**010P**/0032301002212/2415-04061040B30 **(4908)**
2001/02: 16^{0}G, 17^{4}GS, 16^{0}S, 16^{6}GS, 20^{1}G, 20^{0}G, 16^{4}S, 20^{0}GS, 19^{B}GS, 16^{3}G, 21^{0}G

	Starts	1st	2nd	3rd	Win & Pl
Hurdles	11	1	0	1	3933
Career Total	**48**	**8**	**8**	**5**	**27902**

103	12/01	Donc	2m4f	E(0-115)HHdl	GD	£3178
114	12/00	Newc	2m	F(0-105)HHdl	SFT	£2380
93	12/99	Muss	2m	G(0-95)HHdl	G-S	£2668
93	8/99	Hntg	2m4f110y	G(0-90)HHdl	G-F	£1618
82	5/98	Hexm	2m110y	E Ch	G-F	£2310
106	4/96	Weth	2m	F(0-100)HHdl	GD	£2547
93	1/96	Newc	2m	G Hdl	GD	£2099
95	12/95	Donc	2m110y	G Hdl	G-F	£2176

Total win prize-money £18978

Going: Sf: 0-2 GS: 0-4 Gd: 1-5 GF: - Fm: 0-0
Distance: 2m/2m3: 0-7 **2m4-2m7: 1-4** 3m+: 0-0
Track: **LH: 1-7** RH: 0-4 Tight: 0-3 **Gall: 1-5**
Aids: Bl: 0-3 Vi: 0-0 Tstrap: 0-0
Best Rating: 114 12/00 Newc 2m soft Hdl

Been around a bit, he is still effective every so often in modest hurdle company. Best at up to two and a half miles on good to soft ground.

Highbeath

95 **115**

11-y-o b g Dunbeath (USA)-Singing High (Julio Mariner)
N Wilson Mrs K Jackson

Placings:5/030450/13105311/12500/3212313/001254531/63P-0010F **(0960)**
2001/02: 16^{0}G, 17^{0}G, 22^{1}GF, 22^{0}G, 21^{F}GF

	Starts	1st	2nd	3rd	Win & Pl
Chases	5	1	0	0	3766
Career Total	**44**	**10**	**4**	**8**	**45678**

115	6/01	MRas	2m6f110y	E(0-100)HCh	G-F	£3766
129	12/99	Hntg	2m110y	E(0-110)HCh	GD	£2864
129	9/99	MRas	2m4f	D(0-120)HCh	G-F	£4384
122	10/98	Ludl	2m4f	E(0-115)HCh	G-F	£2762
122	8/98	MRas	2m6f110y	E(0-115)HCh	G-F	£3094
117	9/97	MRas	2m4f	D(0-120)HCh	GD	£4042
95	4/97	MRas	2m4f	E(0-115)HCh	GD	£3299
106	3/97	Donc	2m3f110y	D(0-110)HCh	G-F	£4305
94	10/96	Weth	2m7f	C Hdl	GD	£3860
103	5/96	MRas	2m1f110y	D Hdl	GD	£3164

Total win prize-money £35542

Going: Sf: 0-0 GS: 0-0 Gd: 0-3 GF: - Fm: 1-2
Distance: 2m/2m3: 0-2 **2m4-2m7: 1-3** 3m+: 0-0
Track: LH: 0-2 **RH: 1-3 Tight: 1-4** Gall: 0-0
Aids: Bl: 0-0 Vi: 0-0 Tstrap: 0-0
Best Rating: 138 9/98 MRas 2m4f good Ch

Moderate chaser, stays two miles-six and suited by a sharp, right-handed track and a sound surface. Likes Market Rasen.

Highcroft Boy

95(93h) (110+h)**98+**

7-y-o gr g Silver Owl-Caroline Ranger (Pony Express)
P J Hobbs Mrs Ann Weston

Placings:2 **(0253)**
2001/02: 17^{2}GF

	Starts	1st	2nd	3rd	Win & Pl
NH Flat	1	0	1	0	484
Career Total	**1**	**0**	**1**	**0**	**484**

Going: Sf: 0-0 GS: 0-0 Gd: 0-0 GF: - Fm: 0-1
Distance: 2m/2m3: 0-1 2m4-2m7: 0-0 3m+: 0-0
Track: LH: 0-1 RH: 0-0 Tight: 0-1 Gall: 0-0
Aids: Bl: 0-0 Vi: 0-0 Tstrap: 0-0
Best Rating: 102 5/01 NAbb 2m1f gd-fm NHF

Promising second in fast ground bumper. Appreciated the stamina test when winning over 22 furlongs on hurdling debut in May 2002. Jumped right-handed on his chasing debut. Acts on fast ground.

Highfield Gent (IRE)

(44h)

9-y-o gr g Nestor-Tim's Brief (Avocat)
J White Nick Quesnel

Placings:00F0/3PP/5/6-P **(0774)**
2001/02: 23^{P}GF

	Starts	1st	2nd	3rd	Win & Pl
Chases	1	0	0	0	
Career Total	**10**	**0**	**0**	**1**	**340**

Going: Sf: 0-0 GS: 0-0 Gd: 0-0 GF: - Fm: 0-1
Distance: 2m/2m3: 0-0 2m4-2m7: 0-0 3m+: 0-1
Track: LH: 0-1 RH: 0-0 Tight: 0-0 Gall: 0-0
Aids: Bl: 0-0 Vi: 0-0 Tstrap: 0-0
Best Rating: 83 12/97 Hntg 2m110y good NHF

Highland (IRE)

97(103h) (129h)**133**

8-y-o gr g Supreme Leader-Precipienne (Precipice Wood)
A M Hales (S E H Sherwood 23/5) Andrew L Cohen

Placings:11P124/**U36560-11F** **(0848)**
2001/02: 25^{1}GF, 23^{1}G, 32^{F}GF

	Starts	1st	2nd	3rd	Win & Pl
Chases	3	2	0	0	7593
Career Total	**15**	**5**	**1**	**1**	**18801**

133	6/01	Worc	2m7f110y	D Ch	GD	£4426
120	5/01	Folk	3m1f	E Ch	G-F	£3166
129	1/00	Font	2m6f110y	E Hdl	G-S	£2660
129	11/99	Newb	3m110y	C Hdl	GD	£4510
111	10/99	Worc	2m	H NHF	G-F	£1786

Total win prize-money £16550

Going: Sf: 0-0 GS: 0-0 Gd: 1-1 GF: - Fm: 1-2
Distance: 2m/2m3: 0-0 2m4-2m7: 0-0 **3m+: 2-3**
Track: LH: 1-1 RH: 1-1 **Tight: 1-1** Gall: 0-0
Aids: Bl: 0-0 Vi: 0-0 Tstrap: 0-0
Best Rating: 133 6/01 Worc 2m7f110y good Ch

A decent hurdler, scored twice over fences in the summer of 2001 on a sound surface.

Highland Monarch

9-y-o b g Super Sunrise-Highland Chance (Bronze Hill)
C Storey Mrs A D Wauchope

Placings:P **(0070)**
2001/02: 21^{P}G

	Starts	1st	2nd	3rd	Win & Pl
Chases	1	0	0	0	
Career Total	**1**	**0**	**0**	**0**	

Going: Sf: 0-0 GS: 0-0 Gd: 0-1 GF: - Fm: 0-0
Distance: 2m/2m3: 0-0 2m4-2m7: 0-1 3m+: 0-0
Track: LH: 0-1 RH: 0-0 Tight: 0-1 Gall: 0-0
Aids: Bl: 0-0 Vi: 0-0 Tstrap: 0-0
Best Rating:

Highland Rose (IRE)

103 **90**

6-y-o b m Roselier (FR)-Carrick Grinder (Sheer Grit)
Ms A E Embiricos S N J Embiricos

Placings:0010 **(4854)**
2001/02: 18^{0}GF, 16^{0}GS, 16^{1}S, 22^{0}G

	Starts	1st	2nd	3rd	Win & Pl
NH Flat	1	0	0	0	0

	Starts	1st	2nd	3rd	Win & Pl
Hurdles	3	1	0	0	2646
Career Total	**4**	**1**	**0**	**0**	**2646**

90	3/02	Hntg	2m110y	E Hdl	SFT	£2646

Total win prize-money £2646

Going: Sf: 1-1 GS: 0-1 Gd: 0-1 GF: - Fm: 0-1
Distance: **2m/2m3: 1-3** 2m4-2m7: 0-1 3m+: 0-0
Track: LH: 0-2 **RH: 1-2** Tight: 0-2 **Gall: 1-2**
Aids: Bl: 0-0 Vi: 0-0 Tstrap: 0-0
Best Rating: 90 3/02 Hntg 2m110y soft Hdl

Showed decent improvement on her hurdles debut to win next time at Huntingdon.

Highland Tracker (IRE)

110(99h) 107

7-y-o ch g Indian Ridge-Track Twenty Nine (IRE) (Standaan (FR))
Ferdy Murphy Mrs Katrina Paling

Placings:63563/3052-62 (0472)
2001/02: 16^{6}F, 20^{2}GF

	Starts	1st	2nd	3rd	Win & Pl
Chases	2	0	1	0	648
Career Total	**11**	**0**	**2**	**3**	**3203**

Going: Sf: 0-0 GS: 0-0 Gd: 0-0 GF: - Fm: 0-2
Distance: 2m/2m3: 0-1 2m4-2m7: 0-1 3m+: 0-0
Track: LH: 0-2 RH: 0-0 Tight: 0-1 Gall: 0-0
Aids: Bl: 0-0 Vi: 0-0 Tstrap: 0-0
Best Rating: 107 5/01 Hexm 2m4f110y gd-fm Ch

Highland Wonder

7-y-o ch g Highlands-Friendly Wonder (Be Friendly)
C Grant Henry Bell

Placings:00P (2635)
2001/02: 17^{0}G, 17^{0}S, 24^{P}S

	Starts	1st	2nd	3rd	Win & Pl
NH Flat	2	0	0	0	0
Hurdles	1	0	0	0	0
Career Total	**3**	**0**	**0**	**0**	

Going: Sf: 0-2 GS: 0-0 Gd: 0-1 GF: - Fm: 0-0
Distance: 2m/2m3: 0-2 2m4-2m7: 0-0 3m+: 0-1
Track: LH: 0-2 RH: 0-1 Tight: 0-1 Gall: 0-0
Aids: Bl: 0-0 Vi: 0-0 Tstrap: 0-0
Best Rating: 59 10/01 Sedg 2m1f good NHF

Highlands (FR)

73f 50f

7-y-o b g Shirley Heights-Riosamba (USA) (Caerleon (USA))
C P Morlock M G Hazell

Placings:6/00 (1946)
2001/02: 16^{0}G, 18^{0}GS

	Starts	1st	2nd	3rd	Win & Pl
NH Flat	2	0	0	0	
Career Total	**3**	**0**	**0**	**0**	**0**

Going: Sf: 0-0 GS: 0-1 Gd: 0-1 GF: - Fm: 0-0
Distance: 2m/2m3: 0-2 2m4-2m7: 0-0 3m+: 0-0
Track: LH: 0-1 RH: 0-0 Tight: 0-0 Gall: 0-0
Aids: Bl: 0-0 Vi: 0-0 Tstrap: 0-1
Best Rating: 74 5/99 Worc 2m gd-fm NHF

Highlands Ii (FR)

7-y-o ch g Murmure (FR)-Oland (FR) (Saumon (FR))
P F Nicholls C G Roach

Placings:P-P (0249)
2001/02: 22^{P}GF

	Starts	1st	2nd	3rd	Win & Pl
Hurdles	1	0	0	0	
Career Total	**2**	**0**	**0**	**0**	

Going: Sf: 0-0 GS: 0-0 Gd: 0-0 GF: - Fm: 0-1
Distance: 2m/2m3: 0-0 2m4-2m7: 0-1 3m+: 0-0
Track: LH: 0-1 RH: 0-0 Tight: 0-1 Gall: 0-0
Aids: Bl: 0-0 Vi: 0-0 Tstrap: 0-0
Best Rating:

Hightown Cavalier

95(81c) (64c)83

11-y-o b g Thowra (FR)-Hightown Fontana (Gunner B)
R J Hodges Miss R Dobson

Placings:60P/5431151/**06P42**/0031**P45**/01/00634-0 (0081)
2001/02: 17^{0}G

	Starts	1st	2nd	3rd	Win & Pl
Hurdles	1	0	0	0	
Career Total	**30**	**5**	**1**	**3**	**14824**

95	12/99	Hrfd	2m1f	G Hdl	SFT	£2024
81	1/00	Tntn	2m0f	D(0-110)Ch	SFT	£3870
87	1/96	Tntn	2m3f110y	E(0-115)HHdl	G-S	£2499
89	12/95	Hrfd	2m3f110y	G(0-95)HHdl	GD	£1940
85	12/95	Extr	2m2f	F(0-105)HHdl	G-S	£2176

Total win prize-money £12509

Going: Sf: 0-0 GS: 0-0 Gd: 0-1 GF: - Fm: 0-0
Distance: 2m/2m3: 0-1 2m4-2m7: 0-0 3m+: 0-0
Track: LH: 0-0 RH: 0-1 Tight: 0-0 Gall: 0-0
Aids: Bl: 0-0 Vi: 0-0 Tstrap: 0-0
Best Rating: 95 12/99 Hrfd 2m1f soft Hdl

Hikari San (IRE)

7-y-o b/br g Zaffaran (USA)-Carrick Shannon (Green Shoon)
Noel T Chance Mrs M C Sweeney

Placings:20P (1646)
2001/02: 17^{2}F, 16^{0}GF, 20^{P}G

	Starts	1st	2nd	3rd	Win & Pl
NH Flat	2	0	1	0	625
Hurdles	1	0	0	0	0
Career Total	**3**	**0**	**1**	**0**	**625**

Going: Sf: 0-0 GS: 0-0 Gd: 0-1 GF: - Fm: 0-2
Distance: 2m/2m3: 0-2 2m4-2m7: 0-1 3m+: 0-0
Track: LH: 0-0 RH: 0-3 Tight: 0-0 Gall: 0-2
Aids: Bl: 0-0 Vi: 0-0 Tstrap: 0-0
Best Rating: 96 5/01 Extr 2m1f firm NHF

Hill Charm

4-y-o ch f Minster Son-Snarry Hill (Vitiges (FR))
C Grant Roy Robinson

Placings:6 (4790)
2001/02: 16^{6}F

	Starts	1st	2nd	3rd	Win & Pl
NH Flat	1	0	0	0	0
Career Total	**1**	**0**	**0**	**0**	**0**

Going: Sf: 0-0 GS: 0-0 Gd: 0-0 GF: - Fm: 0-1
Distance: 2m/2m3: 0-1 2m4-2m7: 0-0 3m+: 0-0
Track: LH: 0-0 RH: 0-0 Tight: 0-0 Gall: 0-0
Aids: Bl: 0-0 Vi: 0-0 Tstrap: 0-0
Best Rating: 60 4/02 Newc 2m firm NHF

Hill Track

8-y-o b g Royal Match-Win Green Hill (National Trust)
E Stanners George Ward

Placings:0-P (0914)
2001/02: 22^{P}GF

	Starts	1st	2nd	3rd	Win & Pl
Hurdles	1	0	0	0	
Career Total	**2**	**0**	**0**	**0**	

Going: Sf: 0-0 GS: 0-0 Gd: 0-0 GF: - Fm: 0-1
Distance: 2m/2m3: 0-0 2m4-2m7: 0-1 3m+: 0-0
Track: LH: 0-1 RH: 0-0 Tight: 0-1 Gall: 0-0
Aids: Bl: 0-0 Vi: 0-0 Tstrap: 0-0
Best Rating: 45 11/00 Hrfd 2m3f110y soft Hdl

Hill's Electric (IRE)

(82h) (45h)

10-y-o br g Electric-Turvey (Royal Buck)
A G Hobbs Hill Fuels Limited

Placings:504/0PP (3336)
2001/02: 22^{0}S, 24^{P}S, 20^{P}G

	Starts	1st	2nd	3rd	Win & Pl
Hurdles	2	0	0	0	0
Chases	1	0	0	0	0
Career Total	**6**	**0**	**0**	**0**	**0**

Going: Sf: 0-2 GS: 0-0 Gd: 0-1 GF: - Fm: 0-0
Distance: 2m/2m3: 0-0 2m4-2m7: 0-2 3m+: 0-1
Track: LH: 0-2 RH: 0-1 Tight: 0-2 Gall: 0-0
Aids: Bl: 0-0 Vi: 0-0 Tstrap: 0-0
Best Rating: 99 5/97 Uttx 2m gd-fm NHF

Hillcrest Manor (IRE)

88 97

8-y-o b g Topanoora-Grassed (Busted)
A W Carroll Jolly Boys

Placings:4130/02234/P5PP-62 (2461)
2001/02: 16^{6}G, 20^{2}HY

	Starts	1st	2nd	3rd	Win & Pl
Hurdles	2	0	1	0	528
Career Total	**15**	**1**	**3**	**2**	**6266**

103	11/98	Punc	2m	NHF	HVY	£2989

Total win prize-money £2989

Going: Sf: 0-1 GS: 0-0 Gd: 0-1 GF: - Fm: 0-0
Distance: 2m/2m3: 0-1 2m4-2m7: 0-1 3m+: 0-0
Track: LH: 0-0 RH: 0-2 Tight: 0-1 Gall: 0-0
Aids: Bl: 0-0 Vi: 0-0 Tstrap: 0-0
Best Rating: 121 2/00 Naas 2m4f yield Hdl

Hillesley Henry

7-y-o gr g Zambrano-Diddy Girl (Comedy Star (USA))
Dr P Pritchard Three Of A Kind Racing

Placings: *00-0* **(0320)**
2001/02: 17^{0}F

	Starts	1st	2nd	3rd	Win & Pl
NH Flat	1	0	0	0	
Career Total	**3**	**0**	**0**	**0**	

Going: Sf: 0-0 GS: 0-0 Gd: 0-0 GF: - Fm: 0-1
Distance: 2m/2m3: 0-1 2m4-2m7: 0-0 3m+: 0-0
Track: LH: 0-0 RH: 0-1 Tight: 0-0 Gall: 0-0
Aids: Bl: 0-0 Vi: 0-0 Tstrap: 0-0
Best Rating: 6 3/01 MRas 2m1f110y good NHF

Hillswick

72 **33**

11-y-o ch g Norwick (USA)-Quite Lucky (Precipice Wood)
J S King M G A Court

Placings:0F0PP/211/1/0 **(2115)**
2001/02: 21^{0}G

	Starts	1st	2nd	3rd	Win & Pl
Chases	1	0	0	0	
Career Total	**10**	**3**	**1**	**0**	**8154**

98	8/99	Font	2m4f	F(0-110)HHdl	G-F	£2407
99	11/97	Newb	3m110y	D(0-110)HHdl	GD	£2765
73	10/97	Ludl	2m5f110y	E(0-100)HHdl	G-F	£2360

Total win prize-money £7533

Going: Sf: 0-0 GS: 0-0 Gd: 0-1 GF: - Fm: 0-0
Distance: 2m/2m3: 0-0 2m4-2m7: 0-1 3m+: 0-0
Track: LH: 0-0 RH: 0-1 Tight: 0-1 Gall: 0-0
Aids: Bl: 0-0 Vi: 0-0 Tstrap: 0-0
Best Rating: 99 11/97 Newb 3m110y good Hdl

Veteran staying hurdler, lightly-raced of late, suited by a sound surface.

Hilltopper (IRE)

103 **130**

6-y-o b g Mandalus-Thistletopper (Le Bavard (FR))
F Doumen P-H Vogt

Placings:41F/00042453006-0313025
2001/02: 21^{0}, 18^{3}S, 18^{1}VS, 21^{3}S, 20^{0}VS, 24^{2}G, 17^{5}VS

	Starts	1st	2nd	3rd	Win & Pl
Chases	7	1	1	2	21219
Career Total	**21**	**2**	**2**	**3**	**44893**

	7/01	Autl	2m2f110y	Ch	VS	£12124

Total win prize-money £22690

Going: Sf: 0-2 GS: 0-0 Gd: 0-1 GF: - Fm: 0-0
Distance: **2m/2m3: 1-3** 2m4-2m7: 0-3 3m+: 0-1
Track: LH: 0-1 RH: 0-0 Tight: 0-0 Gall: 0-1
Aids: **Bl: 1-6** Vi: 0-0 Tstrap: 0-0
Best Rating: 130 12/01 Newb 3m good Ch

Hillvalley Fairway

52f

7-y-o b g Thethingaboutitis (USA)-Sovereign Love (He Loves Me)
B P J Baugh Dave Arrowsmith

Placings: *0* **(2321)**
2001/02: 17^{0}GS

	Starts	1st	2nd	3rd	Win & Pl
NH Flat	1	0	0	0	
Career Total	**1**	**0**	**0**	**0**	

Going: Sf: 0-0 GS: 0-1 Gd: 0-0 GF: - Fm: 0-0
Distance: 2m/2m3: 0-1 2m4-2m7: 0-0 3m+: 0-0
Track: LH: 0-0 RH: 0-0 Tight: 0-0 Gall: 0-0

Aids: Bl: 0-0 Vi: 0-0 Tstrap: 0-0
Best Rating: 52 11/01 Aint 2m1f gd-sft NHF

Him Of Praise (IRE)

97 **113**

12-y-o b g Paean-Tamed (Rusticaro (FR))
R M Stronge M G St Quinton

Placings:1/331/111132R/502135/2/004536-6 **(0069)**
2001/02: 28^{6}G

	Starts	1st	2nd	3rd	Win & Pl
Chases	1	0	0	0	0
Career Total	**25**	**7**	**3**	**5**	**138123**

152	2/99	Uttx	3m4f	B HCh	HVY	£32455
137	1/98	Sand	3m5f110y	B HCh	G-S	£20734
133	12/97	Hayd	4m110y	B(0-145)HCh	SFT	£6729
129	11/97	Hayd	3m4f110y	B(0-140)HCh	SFT	£10123
134	11/97	Towc	3m1f	C(0-135)HCh	GD	£4289
104	3/97	Towc	2m6f	E Ch	G-S	£3483
109	3/96	Sand	2m6f	D Hdl	G-S	£2983

Total win prize-money £80799

Going: Sf: 0-0 GS: 0-0 Gd: 0-1 GF: - Fm: 0-0
Distance: 2m/2m3: 0-0 2m4-2m7: 0-0 3m+: 0-1
Track: LH: 0-1 RH: 0-0 Tight: 0-1 Gall: 0-0
Aids: Bl: 0-0 Vi: 0-0 Tstrap: 0-0
Best Rating: 152 11/99 Aint 3m3f good Ch

A nightmare ride, he stays any trip but takes a deal of driving and is not one to trust.

Himalayan Blue

96 **106+**

10-y-o b g Hallgate-Orange Parade (Dara Monarch)
Mrs E H Heath Mrs E H Heath

Placings:6/P5P/PFPU **(4285)**
2001/02: 21^{P}GS, 24^{F}S, 19^{P}GS, 17^{U}GS

	Starts	1st	2nd	3rd	Win & Pl
Hurdles	1	0	0	0	0
Chases	3	0	0	0	0
Career Total	**8**	**0**	**0**	**0**	**0**

Going: Sf: 0-1 GS: 0-3 Gd: 0-0 GF: - Fm: 0-0
Distance: 2m/2m3: 0-1 2m4-2m7: 0-2 3m+: 0-1
Track: LH: 0-2 RH: 0-2 Tight: 0-2 Gall: 0-2
Aids: Bl: 0-0 Vi: 0-0 Tstrap: 0-0
Best Rating: 91 2/98 Sand 2m110y good Hdl

Hindi

101 **93**

6-y-o b g Indian Ridge-Tootsiepop (USA) (Robellino (USA))
N A Graham Douglas Guyer, Norman Fish & Paul Jacobs

Placings:6436-3PP0P **(4090)**
2001/02: 20^{3}GS, 20^{P}S, 20^{P}S, 17^{0}S, 20^{P}S

	Starts	1st	2nd	3rd	Win & Pl
Hurdles	4	0	0	1	516
Chases	1	0	0	0	0
Career Total	**9**	**0**	**0**	**2**	**988**

Going: Sf: 0-4 GS: 0-1 Gd: 0-0 GF: - Fm: 0-0
Distance: 2m/2m3: 0-1 2m4-2m7: 0-4 3m+: 0-0
Track: LH: 0-3 RH: 0-2 Tight: 0-3 Gall: 0-0
Aids: Bl: 0-2 Vi: 0-0 Tstrap: 0-0
Best Rating: 93 5/01 Bang 2m4f gd-sft Hdl

Stays two and a half miles and likes good ground.

Hindiana (FR)

111(114h) (135h)**147**

7-y-o ch g Quart De Vin (FR)-La Salamandre (FR) (Pot D'Or (FR))
Ferdy Murphy Paul Green

Placings:BF22/2136/3011133-4040P0 **(4394)**
2001/02: 24^{4}YS, 26^{0}S, 24^{4}S, 24^{0}S, 24^{P}GS, 32^{0}HY

	Starts	1st	2nd	3rd	Win & Pl
Chases	6	0	0	0	4911
Career Total	**21**	**4**	**3**	**4**	**92570**

145	3/01	Hntg	2m4f110y	E Hdl	SFT	£2317
135	2/01	Asct	3m	D Hdl	HVY	£4771
126	12/00	Muss	2m4f	E Hdl	GD	£2359
	6/99	Autl	2m4f110y	Ch	VS	£32293

Total win prize-money £41740

Going: Sf: 0-4 GS: 0-1 Gd: 0-0 GF: - Fm: 0-0
Distance: 2m/2m3: 0-0 2m4-2m7: 0-0 3m+: 0-6
Track: LH: 0-5 RH: 0-0 Tight: 0-1 Gall: 0-2
Aids: Bl: 0-0 Vi: 0-0 Tstrap: 0-2
Best Rating: 147 1/02 Hayd 3m soft Ch

Useful handicap chaser who faced some stiff tasks in 2001/2. Stays three miles and handles soft ground.

Hint Of Magic

5-y-o b g Magic Ring (IRE)-Thames Glow (Kalaglow)
J G Portman J G B Portman

Placings:P **(2719)**
2001/02: 17^{P}G

	Starts	1st	2nd	3rd	Win & Pl
Hurdles	1	0	0	0	
Career Total	**1**	**0**	**0**	**0**	

Going: Sf: 0-0 GS: 0-0 Gd: 0-1 GF: - Fm: 0-0
Distance: 2m/2m3: 0-1 2m4-2m7: 0-0 3m+: 0-0
Track: LH: 0-0 RH: 0-1 Tight: 0-0 Gall: 0-0
Aids: Bl: 0-0 Vi: 0-0 Tstrap: 0-0
Best Rating:

His Nibs (IRE)

93f **116f**

5-y-o b g Alflora (IRE)-Mrs Jennifer (River Knight (FR))
Miss Venetia Williams John Galvanoni

Placings: *150* **(4679)**
2001/02: 17^{1}GS, 16^{5}GS, 17^{0}G

	Starts	1st	2nd	3rd	Win & Pl
NH Flat	3	1	0	0	1904
Career Total	**3**	**1**	**0**	**0**	**1904**

105	5/01	Folk	2m1f110y	H NHF	G-S	£1904

Total win prize-money £1904

Going: Sf: 0-0 GS: 1-2 Gd: 0-1 GF: - Fm: 0-0
Distance: **2m/2m3: 1-3** 2m4-2m7: 0-0 3m+: 0-0
Track: LH: 0-1 RH: 0-0 **Tight: 1-1** Gall: 0-1
Aids: Bl: 0-0 Vi: 0-0 Tstrap: 0-0
Best Rating: 116 3/02 Newb 2m110y gd-sft NHF

His Song (IRE)

87 **72**

9-y-o ch g Accordion-Pampered Finch Vii (Damsire Unregistered)
N J Henderson (M F Morris 13/1) David Lloyd

Placings:111221/112115U/32341P0/6P-4000 **(3908)**
2001/02: 20^{4}Y, 24^{0}Y, 24^{0}YS, 21^{0}G

	Starts	1st	2nd	3rd	Win & Pl
Hurdles	4	0	0	0	484
Career Total	**26**	**9**	**4**	**2**	**144949**

143	2/00	Naas	2m	Ch	SFT	£15600
150	1/99	Leop	2m1f	Ch	HVY	£16187
151	12/98	Leop	2m1f	Ch	SFT	£22608
138	10/98	Punc	2m	Ch	SFT	£3586
132	10/98	Tipp	2m	Ch	SH	£3586
146	4/98	Punc	2m	Hdl	HVY	£22826
136	12/97	Leop	2m	Hdl	HVY	£9579
120	11/97	Fair	2m2f	Hdl	Y-S	£3391
109	11/97	Naas	2m	Hdl	Y-S	£3730

Total win prize-money £101097

Going: Sf: 0-0 GS: 0-0 Gd: 0-1 GF: - Fm: 0-0
Distance: 2m/2m3: 0-0 2m4-2m7: 0-2 3m+: 0-2
Track: LH: 0-3 RH: 0-1 Tight: 0-0 Gall: 0-0
Aids: Bl: 0-0 Vi: 0-0 Tstrap: 0-3
Best Rating: 151 12/98 Leop 2m1f soft Ch

A big, imposing ex-Irish gelding, he has not reached the heights expected of him over fences and has reverted, unsuccessfully, to hurdling. Now with Nicky Henderson, he was well beaten on his first run for new connections in Britain. Lacks a turn of foot, suited by soft ground, and two and a half miles looks his best trip.

Hisar (IRE)

108(79h) (89h)**138**

9-y-o br g Doyoun-Himaya (IRE) (Mouktar)
P C Ritchens R Catton

Placings:002/21U2/F2P2201/2122226212/3600 42211111540 **(4824)**
2001/02: 16^{4}GF, 16^{2}GF, 19^{2}F, 16^{1}GF, 16^{1}GS, 16^{1}G, 17^{1}G, 16^{1}GF, 16^{5}G, 17^{4}G, 16^{0}G

	Starts	1st	2nd	3rd	Win & Pl
Hurdles	2	0	0	0	0
Chases	9	5	2	0	29006
Career Total	**39**	**9**	**12**	**4**	**53392**

138	9/01	Worc	2m	C(0-135)HCh	G-F	£6679
138	8/01	Strf	2m1f110y	D(0-125)HCh	GD	£5434
138	8/01	NAbb	2m110y	D(0-125)HCh	GD	£3721
127	7/01	Wolv	2m	C(0-135)HCh	G-S	£8080
124	6/01	NAbb	2m110y	F(0-105)HCh	G-F	£2947
132	11/99	Wwck	2m	D(0-125)HCh	GD	£3822
114	5/99	Hrfd	2m	E Ch	GD	£3257
112	4/99	Hrfd	2m1f	E(0-115)HHdl	G-F	£2931
103	10/97	Uttx	2m	E Hdl	GD	£2337

Total win prize-money £39212

Going: Sf: 0-0 GS: 1-1 Gd: 2-5 GF: - Fm: 2-5
Distance: **2m/2m3: 5-11** 2m4-2m7: 0-0 3m+: 0-0
Track: **LH: 5-9** RH: 0-2 **Tight: 4-8** Gall: 0-1
Aids: Bl: 0-0 Vi: 0-0 Tstrap: 0-0
Best Rating: 138 9/01 Worc 2m gd-fm Ch

Likes forcing the pace which offsets his lack of a turn of foot. Completed a fine five-timer over fences in the summer of 2001. Best on fast ground.

Historg (FR)

107(106h) **138**

7-y-o b g Cyborg (FR)-Kalliste (FR) (Calicot (FR))
Ferdy Murphy Jim McCarthy

Placings:40/4300/0212-**P1F1P2** **(4746)**
2001/02: 16^{P}G, 17^{1}S, 22^{F}S, 22^{1}HY, 24^{P}GS, 20^{2}GF

	Starts	1st	2nd	3rd	Win & Pl
Chases	6	2	1	0	9856
Career Total	**16**	**3**	**3**	**1**	**20853**

134	2/02	Hayd	2m6f	D Ch	HVY	£4611
113	12/01	MRas	2m1f110y	E Ch	SFT	£3094
119	1/01	Newc	2m4f	E Hdl	HVY	£2702

Total win prize-money £10408

Going: Sf: 2-3 GS: 0-1 Gd: 0-1 GF: - Fm: 0-1
Distance: 2m/2m3: 1-2 2m4-2m7: 1-3 3m+: 0-1
Track: LH: 0-2 **RH: 1-2 Tight: 1-1** Gall: 0-1
Aids: Bl: 0-0 Vi: 0-0 Tstrap: 0-0
Best Rating: 138 1/02 Hayd 2m6f soft Ch

A winner at Market Rasen and Haydock in 2001/2002, but generally either wins or fails to complete and has been known to suffer from a fibrillating heart. Suited by soft ground and stays two miles six.

Historic (IRE)

122 **157**

6-y-o b g Sadler's Wells (USA)-Urjwan (USA) (Seattle Slew (USA))
T R George Mrs R E R Rumbold

Placings:3312-3F15650 **(4193)**
2001/02: 25^{3}G, 25^{F}G, 24^{1}S, 25^{5}G, 23^{6}S, 23^{5}HY, 25^{0}GS

	Starts	1st	2nd	3rd	Win & Pl
Hurdles	7	1	0	1	17420
Career Total	**11**	**2**	**1**	**3**	**45121**

157	12/01	Newb	3m110y	A Hdl	SFT	£14500
142	2/01	Hayd	2m7f110y	A Hdl	SFT	£15000

Total win prize-money £29500

Going: Sf: 1-3 GS: 0-1 Gd: 0-3 GF: - Fm: 0-0
Distance: 2m/2m3: 0-0 2m4-2m7: 0-0 **3m+: 1-7**
Track: **LH: 1-6** RH: 0-1 Tight: 0-0 **Gall: 1-3**
Aids: Bl: 0-1 Vi: 0-0 Tstrap: 0-0
Best Rating: 157 12/01 Newb 3m110y soft Hdl

Showed useful form as a novice and made a good return at Wetherby in November 2001 when third to Boss Doyle. Made all in a valuable staying event at Newbury in December, but did not repeat that form on his next few starts. Best when able to dominate at a decent pace, stays three miles plus and handles testing ground.

Hit And Run (FR)

110(116h) **145**

7-y-o ch g River Mist (USA)-La Dunanerie (FR) (Guadanini (FR))
M C Pipe Gerry Scanlon & Miss J Kirk

Placings:11112351/5230/0243P-1130 **(4649)**
2001/02: 17^{1}G, 16^{1}S, 16^{3}S, 16^{0}G

	Starts	1st	2nd	3rd	Win & Pl
Chases	4	2	0	1	10892
Career Total	**21**	**7**	**3**	**4**	**57255**

145	1/02	Donc	2m110y	D Ch	SFT	£4452
138	11/01	Plum	2m1f	F Ch	GD	£2990
143	4/99	Wwck	2m	C(0-135)HHdl	SFT	£4789
128	12/98	Sand	2m110y	D Hdl	GD	£2775
119	10/98	Chel	2m110y	C Hdl	GD	£4260
122	9/98	Sedg	2m1f	E Hdl	G-F	£2390
100	9/98	NAbb	2m1f	E Hdl	G-F	£2130

Total win prize-money £23787

Going: Sf: 1-2 GS: 0-0 Gd: 1-2 GF: - Fm: 0-0
Distance: **2m/2m3: 2-4** 2m4-2m7: 0-0 3m+: 0-0
Track: **LH: 2-3** RH: 0-0 Tight: 1-2 Gall: 1-1
Aids: Bl: 0-0 Vi: 0-0 Tstrap: 0-0
Best Rating: 158 2/01 Newb 2m110y soft Hdl

A smart front-running handicap hurdler, he made a successful chasing debut at Plumpton, before following up Doncaster in January 2002. Held in better company before landing the odds in a small race at Hereford. He has won on fast ground but seems better on a yielding surface. Effective at around two miles. He is not the biggest to be running over fences.

Hit Royal (FR)

109(105h) (95h)**113**

7-y-o ch g Montorselli-Valse Royale (FR) (Cap Martin (FR))
G M McCourt David Czarnetzki

Placings:066/515P-241F32F6 **(4643)**
2001/02: 20^{2}GF, 19^{4}S, 16^{1}GF, 20^{F}G, 17^{3}S, 16^{2}HY, 16^{F}S, 20^{6}G

	Starts	1st	2nd	3rd	Win & Pl
Hurdles	1	0	1	0	842
Chases	7	1	1	1	6922
Career Total	**15**	**2**	**2**	**1**	**9563**

113	11/01	Ludl	2m	E(0-105)HCh	G-F	£3760
103	8/00	Worc	3m	F(0-95)HHdl	G-F	£1799

Total win prize-money £5559

Going: Sf: 0-4 GS: 0-0 Gd: 0-2 GF: - Fm: 1-2
Distance: **2m/2m3: 1-5** 2m4-2m7: 0-3 3m+: 0-0
Track: LH: 0-4 **RH: 1-4 Tight: 1-5** Gall: 0-1
Aids: Bl: 0-0 Vi: 0-0 Tstrap: 0-0
Best Rating: 113 11/01 Ludl 2m gd-fm Ch

Effective at up to three miles and best on fast ground, he won a Ludlow novice chase in November 2001.

Hitchhiker

89

8-y-o b g Picea-Lady Lax (Henbit (USA))
R Ford (Miss Venetia Williams 28/1) The Winning Line

Placings:0000000/6022144320/240122P1P/F5-UPF6 **(4489)**
2001/02: 21^{U}G, 24^{P}GS, 24^{F}S, 26^{6}GS

	Starts	1st	2nd	3rd	Win & Pl
Chases	4	0	0	0	0
Career Total	**32**	**3**	**6**	**1**	**17717**

118	3/00	Newc	3m	E(0-115)HCh	GD	£5421
112	12/99	Hntg	3m	E(0-105)HCh	GD	£3446
90	10/98	Weth	3m1f	E(0-105)HHdl	GD	£2903

Total win prize-money £11771

Going: Sf: 0-1 GS: 0-2 Gd: 0-1 GF: - Fm: 0-0
Distance: 2m/2m3: 0-0 2m4-2m7: 0-1 3m+: 0-3
Track: LH: 0-1 RH: 0-3 Tight: 0-0 Gall: 0-2
Aids: Bl: 0-0 Vi: 0-0 Tstrap: 0-0
Best Rating: 118 3/00 Newc 3m good Ch

He did well over fences in the 1999/2000 season, but was off the track for ten months after April 2000 and has not jumped with any fluency since returning.

Hitman (IRE)

115 **136**

7-y-o b g Contract Law (USA)-Loveville (USA) (Assert)
M Pitman The Paper Boys

Placings:P/46-401410P **(4665)**
2001/02: 16^{4}S, 16^{0}G, 16^{1}GS, 16^{4}S, 16^{1}GS, 16^{0}GS, 24^{P}G

	Starts	1st	2nd	3rd	Win & Pl
Hurdles	7	2	0	0	18600
Career Total	**10**	**2**	**0**	**0**	**20800**

134	2/02	Kemp	2m	A Hdl	G-S	£12000
136	1/02	Asct	2m110y	C Hdl	G-S	£5200

Total win prize-money £17200

Going: Sf: 0-2 GS: 2-3 Gd: 0-2 GF: - Fm: 0-0
Distance: **2m/2m3: 2-6** 2m4-2m7: 0-0 3m+: 0-1
Track: LH: 0-5 **RH: 2-2** Tight: 0-1 Gall: 0-1
Aids: Bl: 0-0 Vi: 0-0 Tstrap: 0-0
Best Rating: 154 12/00 Chel 2m1f soft Hdl

A smart performer on the Flat, he is also very useful over hurdles, but has had more than his fair share of problems. He finally showed what he is capable of by winning decent events at Ascot and Kempton early in 2002, but he was well held at the Cheltenham Festival in March. Effective over two miles, but gives the impression he would get further and is suited by a sound surface.

Hobart Junction (IRE)

103 **84**

7-y-o ch g Classic Secret (USA)-Art Duo (Artaius (USA))
J A T De Giles Gavin Macechern

Placings:PU/002540/04325-14305065000 **(4731)**
2001/02: 17^{1}G, 17^{4}GF, 16^{3}GF, 16^{0}GF, 16^{5}G, 17^{0}GF, 16^{6}GF, 18^{5}GF, 19^{0}F, 17^{0}G, 17^{0}F

	Starts	1st	2nd	3rd	Win & Pl
Hurdles	11	1	0	1	2733
Career Total	**24**	**1**	**2**	**2**	**4428**

84	6/01	NAbb	2m1f	G(0-95)HHdl	GD	£2380

Total win prize-money £2380

Going: Sf: 0-0 GS: 0-0 Gd: 1-3 GF: - Fm: 0-8
Distance: **2m/2m3: 1-10** 2m4-2m7: 0-1 3m+: 0-0
Track: **LH: 1-8** RH: 0-3 **Tight: 1-9** Gall: 0-0
Aids: Bl: 0-0 Vi: 0-0 Tstrap: 0-0
Best Rating: 84 8/01 Strf 2m110y good Hdl

Hobbycyr (FR)

7-y-o b g Saint Cyrien (FR)-Sauteuse De Retz (FR) (Funny Hobby)
R Kelvin-Hughes (Miss H C Knight 3/2) R G Kelvin-Hughes

Placings:0/010/0-1 **(4179)**
2001/02: 24^{1}GS

	Starts	1st	2nd	3rd	Win & Pl
Chases	1	1	0	0	2808
Career Total	**6**	**2**	**0**	**0**	**5028**

111	3/02	Strf	3m	H Ch	G-S	£2808
112	12/99	Hrfd	2m3f110y	E Hdl	SFT	£2220

Total win prize-money £5028

Going: Sf: 0-0 GS: 1-1 Gd: 0-0 GF: - Fm: 0-0
Distance: 2m/2m3: 0-0 2m4-2m7: 0-0 **3m+: 1-1**
Track: **LH: 1-1** RH: 0-0 **Tight: 1-1** Gall: 0-0
Aids: Bl: 0-0 Vi: 0-0 Tstrap: 0-0
Best Rating: 112 12/99 Hrfd 2m3f110y soft Hdl

Landed a novice hunter chase at Stratford in March 2002.

Hobo

4-y-o b g Timeless Times (USA)-Skiddaw Bird (Bold Owl)
D W Barker Miss A Clift

Placings:P **(2449)**
2001/02: 16^{P}GS

	Starts	1st	2nd	3rd	Win & Pl
Hurdles	1	0	0	0	
Career Total	**1**	**0**	**0**	**0**	

Going: Sf: 0-0 GS: 0-1 Gd: 0-0 GF: - Fm: 0-0
Distance: 2m/2m3: 0-1 2m4-2m7: 0-0 3m+: 0-0
Track: LH: 0-1 RH: 0-0 Tight: 0-0 Gall: 0-1
Aids: Bl: 0-0 Vi: 0-0 Tstrap: 0-0
Best Rating:

Hoh Express

111

10-y-o b g Waajib-Tissue Paper (Touch Paper)
P R Webber Mrs Joan L Egan

Placings:6314/F2212110/F-PF **(0826)**
2001/02: 20^{P}G, 20^{F}GF

	Starts	1st	2nd	3rd	Win & Pl
Chases	2	0	0	0	
Career Total	**15**	**4**	**3**	**1**	**45633**

147	2/99	Sand	2m4f110y	A Ch	GD	£22505
147	12/98	Kemp	2m4f110y	B Ch	SFT	£12585
140	12/98	Hrfd	2m3f	E Ch	GD	£2814
105	2/98	Muss	2m	E Hdl	GD	£2595

Total win prize-money £40499

Going: Sf: 0-0 GS: 0-0 Gd: 0-1 GF: - Fm: 0-1
Distance: 2m/2m3: 0-0 2m4-2m7: 0-2 3m+: 0-0
Track: LH: 0-2 RH: 0-0 Tight: 0-1 Gall: 0-0
Aids: Bl: 0-0 Vi: 0-0 Tstrap: 0-0
Best Rating: 147 2/99 Sand 2m4f110y good Ch

Hoh Hoh Seven (IRE)

91 **66**

6-y-o b g College Chapel-Fighting Run (Runnett)
I W McInnes I W McInnes

Placings:0P-60P605 **(1075)**
2001/02: 16^{6}GF, 17^{0}GF, 16^{P}GS, 19^{6}G, 21^{0}GF, 19^{5}GF

	Starts	1st	2nd	3rd	Win & Pl
Hurdles	6	0	0	0	0
Career Total	**8**	**0**	**0**	**0**	**0**

Going: Sf: 0-0 GS: 0-1 Gd: 0-1 GF: - Fm: 0-4
Distance: 2m/2m3: 0-4 2m4-2m7: 0-2 3m+: 0-0
Track: LH: 0-4 RH: 0-2 Tight: 0-6 Gall: 0-0
Aids: Bl: 0-1 Vi: 0-0 Tstrap: 0-0
Best Rating: 66 8/01 Strf 2m3f gd-fm Hdl

Hoh No

91(101h) (91h)**83**

6-y-o b g Efisio-Primetta (Precocious)
R M Stronge (M L W Bell 27/8) Berkshire Commercial Components Ltd

Placings:0/F0-3 **(1763)**
2001/02: 16^{3}S

	Starts	1st	2nd	3rd	Win & Pl
Hurdles	1	0	0	1	377
Career Total	**4**	**0**	**0**	**1**	**377**

Going: Sf: 0-1 GS: 0-0 Gd: 0-0 GF: - Fm: 0-0
Distance: 2m/2m3: 0-1 2m4-2m7: 0-0 3m+: 0-0
Track: LH: 0-1 RH: 0-0 Tight: 0-1 Gall: 0-0
Aids: Bl: 0-0 Vi: 0-0 Tstrap: 0-0
Best Rating: 91 10/01 Plum 2m soft Hdl

A dual Flat winner, showed his first hurdling form in a moderate Plumpton novice handicap in October 2001. Won on a sound surface on the level.

Holbeck (IRE)

4-y-o b f Efisio-Autumn Fall (USA) (Sanglamore (USA))
R Wilman (M Johnston 27/7) Mrs Joanna Hughes

Placings:P **(1355)**
2001/02: 16^{P}GF

	Starts	1st	2nd	3rd	Win & Pl
Hurdles	1	0	0	0	
Career Total	**1**	**0**	**0**	**0**	

Going: Sf: 0-0 GS: 0-0 Gd: 0-0 GF: - Fm: 0-1
Distance: 2m/2m3: 0-1 2m4-2m7: 0-0 3m+: 0-0
Track: LH: 0-1 RH: 0-0 Tight: 0-1 Gall: 0-0
Aids: Bl: 0-0 Vi: 0-0 Tstrap: 0-0
Best Rating:

Holborn Hill (IRE)

111

10-y-o gr g Riberetto-Grey Tor (Ahonoora)
C J Mann J E Brown

Placings:06/13P0434/12FF51/1-60 **(3582)**
2001/02: 25^{6}S, 22^{0}S

	Starts	1st	2nd	3rd	Win & Pl
Hurdles	2	0	0	0	0
Career Total	**18**	**4**	**1**	**2**	**30193**

138	5/00	Uttx	3m110y	B(0-140)HHdl	GD	£10757
136	4/00	Chel	2m5f110y	B HHdl	SFT	£10036
120	5/99	Strf	2m6f110y	D Hdl	G-S	£3486
100	11/98	Asct	3m	C Hdl	G-S	£3810

Total win prize-money £28091

Going: Sf: 0-2 GS: 0-0 Gd: 0-0 GF: - Fm: 0-0
Distance: 2m/2m3: 0-0 2m4-2m7: 0-1 3m+: 0-1
Track: LH: 0-0 RH: 0-1 Tight: 0-0 Gall: 0-0
Aids: Bl: 0-0 Vi: 0-0 Tstrap: 0-0
Best Rating: 138 5/00 Uttx 3m110y good Hdl

Fair staying hurdler who did not take to fences in 1999/2000, he returned successfully to hurdles in the spring of 2000 but was then absent until January 2002. Suited by good ground or softer.

Holdimclose

12-y-o b g Teamwork-Holdmetight (New Brig)
Paul O J Hosgood Miss V M Tremlett

Placings:4033151/42F1/402034/32121F4/F2/05-0 **(0077)**
2001/02: 23^{0}G

	Starts	1st	2nd	3rd	Win & Pl
Chases	1	0	0	0	
Career Total	**29**	**5**	**5**	**4**	**23737**

127	2/99	Font	2m3f	E Ch	GD	£2965
114	1/99	Extr	2m7f110y	E Ch	HVY	£3156
	3/97	NAbb	2m6f	D(0-125)HHdl	FRM	£3346
117	5/96	Extr	2m2f	E Hdl	G-S	£2014
108	3/96	NAbb	2m6f	E Hdl	SFT	£2582

Total win prize-money £14065

Going: Sf: 0-0 GS: 0-0 Gd: 0-1 GF: - Fm: 0-0
Distance: 2m/2m3: 0-0 2m4-2m7: 0-0 3m+: 0-1
Track: LH: 0-0 RH: 0-1 Tight: 0-0 Gall: 0-0
Aids: Bl: 0-0 Vi: 0-0 Tstrap: 0-0
Best Rating: 127 2/99 Font 2m3f good Ch

Holding The Fort (IRE)

8-y-o b g Moscow Society (USA)-Lady Of Desmond (Menelek)

I Anderson Ian Anderson

Placings:0-F (0255)
2001/02: 20FGF

	Starts	1st	2nd	3rd	Win & Pl
Chases	1	0	0	0	
Career Total	2	0	0	0	

Going: Sf: 0-0 GS: 0-0 Gd: 0-0 GF: - Fm: 0-1
Distance: 2m/2m3: 0-0 2m4-2m7: 0-1 3m+: 0-0
Track: LH: 0-1 RH: 0-0 Tight: 0-1 Gall: 0-0
Aids: Bl: 0-0 Vi: 0-0 Tstrap: 0-0
Best Rating: 37 4/01 MRas 2m3f110y gd-sft Hdl

Holland's Nephew

5-y-o b g Nearly A Hand-Our Mrs'P (Idiots Delight)
P R Chamings L R Attrill

Placings:000 (4269)
2001/02: 160G, 160G, 160S

	Starts	1st	2nd	3rd	Win & Pl
NH Flat	3	0	0	0	
Career Total	3	0	0	0	

Going: Sf: 0-1 GS: 0-0 Gd: 0-2 GF: - Fm: 0-0
Distance: 2m/2m3: 0-3 2m4-2m7: 0-0 3m+: 0-0
Track: LH: 0-2 RH: 0-1 Tight: 0-0 Gall: 0-1
Aids: Bl: 0-0 Vi: 0-0 Tstrap: 0-0
Best Rating:

Hollington Coral

84 69
8-y-o ro g Belfort (FR)-Littleton Lullaby (Milford)
P C Ritchens Ms Jenny Kitzing

Placings:40 (3223)
2001/02: 164HY, 160G

	Starts	1st	2nd	3rd	Win & Pl
Hurdles	2	0	0	0	0
Career Total	2	0	0	0	0

Going: Sf: 0-1 GS: 0-0 Gd: 0-1 GF: - Fm: 0-0
Distance: 2m/2m3: 0-2 2m4-2m7: 0-0 3m+: 0-0
Track: LH: 0-0 RH: 0-2 Tight: 0-0 Gall: 0-0
Aids: Bl: 0-0 Vi: 0-0 Tstrap: 0-0
Best Rating: 69 1/02 Winc 2m good Hdl

Holloa Away (IRE)

108 74
10-y-o b g Red Sunset-Lili Bengam (Welsh Saint)
J A T De Giles J A T De Giles

Placings:140/354P/0-04163000 (3325)
2001/02: 170F, 224GF, 221GF, 216GS, 213GF, 210GS, 240GF, 200GS

	Starts	1st	2nd	3rd	Win & Pl
Hurdles	8	1	0	1	2328
Career Total	16	2	0	2	4068

70 9/01 Strf 2m6f110y G(0-95)HHdl G-F £1946
99 5/97 Worc 2m H NHF G-S £1402
Total win prize-money £3349

Going: Sf: 0-0 GS: 0-3 Gd: 0-0 GF: - Fm: 1-5
Distance: 2m/2m3: 0-1 2m4-2m7: 1-6 3m+: 0-1
Track: LH: 1-4 RH: 0-4 Tight: 1-5 Gall: 0-1
Aids: Bl: 0-1 Vi: 0-0 Tstrap: 0-0
Best Rating: 99 5/97 Worc 2m gd-sft NHF

Hollow Legs

100 78
6-y-o ch m Alflora (IRE)-Sayshar (Sayfar)
M W Easterby Steve Hull

Placings:006500-320 (4013)
2001/02: 163S, 162GS, 160GS

	Starts	1st	2nd	3rd	Win & Pl
Hurdles	3	0	1	1	1218
Career Total	9	0	1	1	1218

Going: Sf: 0-1 GS: 0-2 Gd: 0-0 GF: - Fm: 0-0
Distance: 2m/2m3: 0-3 2m4-2m7: 0-0 3m+: 0-0
Track: LH: 0-2 RH: 0-1 Tight: 0-1 Gall: 0-2
Aids: Bl: 0-0 Vi: 0-0 Tstrap: 0-0
Best Rating: 79 1/01 Weth 2m heavy NHF

Modest hurdler, showed improvement early in 2002.

Hollows Mill

98 80
6-y-o b g Rudimentary (USA)-Strawberry Song (Final Straw)
F P Murtagh The Great Expectations Sporting Club

Placings:0004 (4894)
2001/02: 160GS, 160HY, 160GF, 164G

	Starts	1st	2nd	3rd	Win & Pl
NH Flat	2	0	0	0	0
Hurdles	2	0	0	0	288
Career Total	4	0	0	0	288

Going: Sf: 0-1 GS: 0-1 Gd: 0-1 GF: - Fm: 0-1
Distance: 2m/2m3: 0-4 2m4-2m7: 0-0 3m+: 0-0
Track: LH: 0-2 RH: 0-1 Tight: 0-2 Gall: 0-0
Aids: Bl: 0-0 Vi: 0-0 Tstrap: 0-0
Best Rating: 77 4/02 Prth 2m110y good Hdl

Hollybush Hybrid

89f 78f
6-y-o ch m Risk Me (FR)-Absent Lover (Nearly A Hand)
S E H Sherwood Hollybush Nurseries Ltd

Placings:0 (4595)
2001/02: 160G

	Starts	1st	2nd	3rd	Win & Pl
NH Flat	1	0	0	0	
Career Total	1	0	0	0	

Going: Sf: 0-0 GS: 0-0 Gd: 0-1 GF: - Fm: 0-0
Distance: 2m/2m3: 0-1 2m4-2m7: 0-0 3m+: 0-0
Track: LH: 0-1 RH: 0-0 Tight: 0-0 Gall: 0-0
Aids: Bl: 0-0 Vi: 0-0 Tstrap: 0-0
Best Rating: 78 4/02 Uttx 2m good NHF

Hollyfield

77
7-y-o b m Holly Buoy-Stuart's Gem (Meldrum)
R S Wood R S Wood

Placings:000/0P0/00 (4332)
2001/02: 270S, 210S

	Starts	1st	2nd	3rd	Win & Pl
Hurdles	2	0	0	0	
Career Total	8	0	0	0	

Going: Sf: 0-2 GS: 0-0 Gd: 0-0 GF: - Fm: 0-0
Distance: 2m/2m3: 0-0 2m4-2m7: 0-1 3m+: 0-1
Track: LH: 0-2 RH: 0-0 Tight: 0-2 Gall: 0-0
Aids: Bl: 0-0 Vi: 0-0 Tstrap: 0-2
Best Rating: 52 4/99 Hexm 2m good NHF

Holywell Girl

85f 58f
5-y-o b m Alhaatmi-Merry Maggie (Stanford)
John A Harris Christopher Morris

Placings:000 (4539)
2001/02: 160GS, 160HY, 160G

	Starts	1st	2nd	3rd	Win & Pl
NH Flat	3	0	0	0	
Career Total	3	0	0	0	

Going: Sf: 0-1 GS: 0-1 Gd: 0-1 GF: - Fm: 0-0
Distance: 2m/2m3: 0-3 2m4-2m7: 0-0 3m+: 0-0
Track: LH: 0-2 RH: 0-1 Tight: 0-2 Gall: 0-0
Aids: Bl: 0-0 Vi: 0-0 Tstrap: 0-0
Best Rating: 58 1/02 Catt 2m gd-sft NHF

Hombre

87 67
7-y-o ch g Shernazar-Delray Jet (USA) (Northjet)
A Crook R D Bickenson

Placings:F05P/245601P-0PP005 (4287)
2001/02: 200GS, 24PHY, 20PS, 190S, 200S, 205GS

	Starts	1st	2nd	3rd	Win & Pl
Chases	6	0	0	0	0
Career Total	17	1	1	0	3889

105 1/01 Weth 2m4f110y E(0-105)HCh HVY £3133
Total win prize-money £3133

Going: Sf: 0-4 GS: 0-2 Gd: 0-0 GF: - Fm: 0-0
Distance: 2m/2m3: 0-1 2m4-2m7: 0-4 3m+: 0-1
Track: LH: 0-3 RH: 0-3 Tight: 0-2 Gall: 0-1
Aids: Bl: 0-1 Vi: 0-0 Tstrap: 0-0
Best Rating: 105 1/01 Weth 2m4f110y heavy Ch

Unreliable and remains out of sorts.

Home James (IRE)

91f 103f
5-y-o b g Commanche Run-Take Me Home (Amoristic (USA))
A King Aiden Murphy

Placings:1 (4317)
2001/02: 161HY

	Starts	1st	2nd	3rd	Win & Pl
NH Flat	1	1	0	0	1771
Career Total	1	1	0	0	1771

103 3/02 Sthl 2m H NHF HVY £1771
Total win prize-money £1771

Going: Sf: 1-1 GS: 0-0 Gd: 0-0 GF: - Fm: 0-0
Distance: 2m/2m3: 1-1 2m4-2m7: 0-0 3m+: 0-0
Track: LH: 1-1 RH: 0-0 Tight: 1-1 Gall: 0-0
Aids: Bl: 0-0 Vi: 0-0 Tstrap: 0-0
Best Rating: 103 3/02 Sthl 2m heavy NHF

Successful debut in a bumper, looking a stayer.

Home Made

72f 58f
4-y-o b g Homo Sapien-Inch Maid (Le Moss)
S A Brookshaw Miss H Brookshaw

Placings:*0* **(4377)**
2001/02: 16^{0}S

	Starts	1st	2nd	3rd	Win & Pl
NH Flat	1	0	0	0	
Career Total	**1**	**0**	**0**	**0**	

Going: Sf: 0-1 GS: 0-0 Gd: 0-0 GF: - Fm: 0-0
Distance: 2m/2m3: 0-1 2m4-2m7: 0-0 3m+: 0-0
Track: LH: 0-0 RH: 0-1 Tight: 0-0 Gall: 0-0
Aids: Bl: 0-0 Vi: 0-0 Tstrap: 0-0
Best Rating:

Home Talk (IRE)

8-y-o b m Euphemism-Home And Dry (Crash Course)
Mrs C J Robinson Jeremy Beasley

Placings:0 **(0246)**
2001/02: 21^{0}GF

	Starts	1st	2nd	3rd	Win & Pl
Hurdles	1	0	0	0	
Career Total	**1**	**0**	**0**	**0**	

Going: Sf: 0-0 GS: 0-0 Gd: 0-0 GF: - Fm: 0-1
Distance: 2m/2m3: 0-0 2m4-2m7: 0-1 3m+: 0-0
Track: LH: 0-0 RH: 0-0 Tight: 0-0 Gall: 0-0
Aids: Bl: 0-0 Vi: 0-0 Tstrap: 0-0
Best Rating:

Homer (IRE)

101 **114**
5-y-o b g Sadler's Wells (USA)-Gravieres (FR) (Saint Estephe (FR))
N M Babbage (Gerard Cully 8/11) B Babbage

Placings:6001002220 **(3152)**
2001/02: 16^{6}HY, 16^{0}GF, 17^{0}GF, 19^{1}G, 17^{0}G, 22^{0}YS, 16^{2}GS, 16^{2}S, 20^{2}G, 20^{0}G

	Starts	1st	2nd	3rd	Win & Pl
Hurdles	10	1	3	0	9380
Career Total	**10**	**1**	**3**	**0**	**9380**

114 7/01 Naas 2m3f Hdl GD £6677
Total win prize-money £6677

Going: Sf: 0-2 GS: 0-1 Gd: 1-4 GF: - Fm: 0-2
Distance: **2m/2m3: 1-7** 2m4-2m7: 0-3 3m+: 0-0
Track: LH: 0-2 RH: 0-2 Tight: 0-1 Gall: 0-1
Aids: Bl: 0-0 Vi: 0-0 Tstrap: 0-0
Best Rating: **114** 12/01 Donc 2m4f good Hdl

A winning hurdler in Ireland who was trained by Aidan O'Brien as a juvenile. Form at a modest level since coming to Britain. stays two and ahalf miles, acts on any ground.

Homestead

108 **105**
8-y-o ch g Indian Ridge-Bertrade (Homeboy)
E McNamara Dooradoyle Syndicate

Placings:0/340343020-0F460412320036 **(4808a)**
2001/02: 16^{0}GF, 17^{F}G, 20^{4}GF, 16^{6}HY, 16^{0}G, 20^{4}YS, 20^{1}YS, 20^{2}S, 20^{3}YS, 20^{2}SH, 20^{0}S, 19^{0}HY, 22^{3}S, 24^{6}GF

	Starts	1st	2nd	3rd	Win & Pl
Hurdles	14	1	2	2	12838
Career Total	**24**	**1**	**3**	**5**	**15277**

101 12/01 Punc 2m4f (0-95)HHdl Y-S £5564
Total win prize-money £5565

Going: Sf: 0-5 GS: 0-0 Gd: 0-2 GF: - Fm: 0-3
Distance: 2m/2m3: 0-5 **2m4-2m7: 1-8** 3m+: 0-1
Track: LH: 0-3 **RH: 1-5** Tight: 0-0 Gall: 0-0
Aids: Bl: 0-0 Vi: 0-0 Tstrap: 0-0
Best Rating: **105** 3/02 Dpat 2m6f soft Hdl

An All-Weather winner who has shown some form over hurdles at a modest level in Ireland.

Homme De Fer

112 **123**
10-y-o b g Arctic Lord-Florence May (Grange Melody)
K C Bailey The Hon C Leigh

Placings:*66*/*623*/1211045/**2113/4022-01124P** **(4753)**
2001/02: 25^{0}G, 21^{1}G, 24^{1}GF, 25^{2}G, 25^{4}G, 26^{P}GF

	Starts	1st	2nd	3rd	Win & Pl
Chases	6	2	1	0	12240
Career Total	**26**	**7**	**6**	**2**	**33298**

123 11/01 Ludl 3m F(0-110)HCh G-F £3672
117 11/01 Winc 2m5f E(0-115)HCh GD £5323
121 7/99 NAbb 2m5f110y E Ch G-F £3403
121 6/99 NAbb 2m5f110y E Ch GD £3156
119 1/99 Font 2m2f110y D Hdl SFT £3062
121 12/98 Hrfd 2m3f110y E Hdl SFT £3060
118 10/98 Plum 2m4f E Hdl G-F £2302
Total win prize-money £23983

Going: Sf: 0-0 GS: 0-0 Gd: 1-4 GF: - Fm: 1-2
Distance: 2m/2m3: 0-0 2m4-2m7: 1-1 3m+: 1-5
Track: LH: 0-1 **RH: 2-5 Tight: 1-1** Gall: 0-0
Aids: Bl: 0-0 Vi: 0-0 Tstrap: 0-0
Best Rating: **123** 12/01 Winc 3m1f110y good Ch

Fair chaser, stays three miles. Acts on most types of ground.

Honest Herbert (IRE)

71 **65**
9-y-o b g Salluceva-Bold And True (Sir Herbert)
K F Clutterbuck (H Alexander 9/5) K F Clutterbuck

Placings:P030/**P2** **(1648)**
2001/02: 24^{P}GF, 24^{2}G

	Starts	1st	2nd	3rd	Win & Pl
Chases	2	0	1	0	1036
Career Total	**6**	**0**	**1**	**1**	**1311**

Going: Sf: 0-0 GS: 0-0 Gd: 0-1 GF: - Fm: 0-1
Distance: 2m/2m3: 0-0 2m4-2m7: 0-0 3m+: 0-2
Track: LH: 0-1 RH: 0-1 Tight: 0-1 Gall: 0-1
Aids: Bl: 0-0 Vi: 0-0 Tstrap: 0-0
Best Rating: **75** 2/99 Muss 2m firm Hdl

Honest Villain (USA)

5-y-o b g St Jovite (USA)-Villandry (USA) (Lyphard's Wish (FR))
J G Given (I A Balding 27/7) Colin G R Booth

Placings:PP **(1564)**
2001/02: 19^{P}GF, 16^{P}GS

	Starts	1st	2nd	3rd	Win & Pl
Hurdles	2	0	0	0	
Career Total	**2**	**0**	**0**	**0**	

Going: Sf: 0-0 GS: 0-1 Gd: 0-0 GF: - Fm: 0-1
Distance: 2m/2m3: 0-1 2m4-2m7: 0-1 3m+: 0-0
Track: LH: 0-1 RH: 0-1 Tight: 0-1 Gall: 0-0
Aids: Bl: 0-1 Vi: 0-0 Tstrap: 0-0
Best Rating:

Honey Honey (FR)

7-y-o gr g Djarvis (FR)-Urta (FR) (Le Pontet (FR))
P J Hobbs R F L Steels Ltd

Placings:1P/P3/1360-0 **(0432)**
2001/02: 20^{0}GF

	Starts	1st	2nd	3rd	Win & Pl
Hurdles	1	0	0	0	
Career Total	**9**	**2**	**0**	**2**	**7667**

6/00 Vich 2m5f110y Ch GD £2882
4/99 Fntb 2m3f Ch VS £3445
Total win prize-money £6327

Going: Sf: 0-0 GS: 0-0 Gd: 0-0 GF: - Fm: 0-1
Distance: 2m/2m3: 0-0 2m4-2m7: 0-1 3m+: 0-0
Track: LH: 0-0 RH: 0-1 Tight: 0-1 Gall: 0-0
Aids: Bl: 0-0 Vi: 0-0 Tstrap: 0-0
Best Rating: **81** 9/00 Worc 2m4f gd-fm Hdl

Honey Mount

103 **127**
11-y-o b g Shirley Heights-Honeybeta (Habitat)
R H Alner Paul Green

Placings:45/1541/20231/12**1234113/61PP0-40** **(0675)**
2001/02: 24^{4}GS, 23^{0}GF

	Starts	1st	2nd	3rd	Win & Pl
Chases	2	0	0	0	534
Career Total	**27**	**8**	**4**	**3**	**57688**

145 10/00 Chel 3m110y E(0-125)HCh GD £4657
145 3/00 Chel 3m110y B(0-140)HCh GD £22750
138 3/00 Ludl 3m D(0-125)HCh SFT £6841
120 10/99 Hrfd 3m1f110y E Ch G-F £3680
106 5/99 Towc 2m5f D(0-125)HHdl G-F £2929
106 4/99 Font 3m3f E(0-115)HHdl GD £2495
99 4/97 Font 3m3f E Hdl G-F £2448
91 11/96 Tntn 3m110y D Hdl G-F £2801
Total win prize-money £48601

Going: Sf: 0-0 GS: 0-1 Gd: 0-0 GF: - Fm: 0-1
Distance: 2m/2m3: 0-0 2m4-2m7: 0-0 3m+: 0-2
Track: LH: 0-2 RH: 0-0 Tight: 0-1 Gall: 0-0
Aids: Bl: 0-0 Vi: 0-0 Tstrap: 0-0
Best Rating: **145** 10/00 Chel 3m110y good Ch

He won the Fulke Walwyn Kim Muir Chase at the Cheltenham Festival in 2000 and scored back there in October of the same year. Lightly raced since, he stays well and is best on good ground or faster.

Honey Thyme

4-y-o ch f Palais De Danse-Forever Honey (Palm Track)
R D Wylie Trevor Barnes

Placings:*0*P **(4486)**
2001/02: 16^{0}S, 17^{P}GS

	Starts	1st	2nd	3rd	Win & Pl
NH Flat	1	0	0	0	0
Hurdles	1	0	0	0	0
Career Total	**2**	**0**	**0**	**0**	

Going: Sf: 0-1 GS: 0-1 Gd: 0-0 GF: - Fm: 0-0
Distance: 2m/2m3: 0-2 2m4-2m7: 0-0 3m+: 0-0
Track: LH: 0-1 RH: 0-1 Tight: 0-0 Gall: 0-0
Aids: Bl: 0-0 Vi: 0-0 Tstrap: 0-0
Best Rating:

Honey Trader

93(98h) (86h)**90**

10-y-o b g Beveled (USA)-Lizzie Bee (Kind Of Hush)

C L Popham T J Hawkins

Placings:3003400/2441160422202256**3200**/1542442 2F4310506/024**11003122F5**/362460PBPP-0P412060**P43** **(4734)**

2001/02: 17^{0}GF, 16^{P}GF, 16^{4}GS, 17^{1}G, 16^{2}G, 17^{0}GF, 17^{6}GF, 16^{0}GF, 19^{P}G, 16^{4}GF, 19^{3}F

	Starts	1st	2nd	3rd	Win & Pl
Hurdles	6	1	0	0	2317
Chases	5	0	1	1	1826
Career Total	**77**	**8**	**15**	**7**	**49235**

79	7/01	NAbb	2m1f	F(0-90)Hdl	GD	£2317
122	11/99	DRoy	2m	(0-116)HCh	SFT	£6160
122	7/99	Klny	2m1f	(0-123)HCh	GD	£4296
120	6/99	Tral	2m	Ch	GD	£2915
117	11/98	Clon	2m	(88-116)HHdl	SFT	£2690
115	5/98	Tral	2m	(0-116)Hdl	GD	£3573
94	6/97	Limk	2m	(0-102)HHdl	FRM	£3391
91	5/97	Baln	2m	Hdl	GD	£2204

Total win prize-money £27550

Going: Sf: 0-0 GS: 0-1 Gd: 1-3 GF: - Fm: 0-7
Distance: **2m/2m3: 1-10** 2m4-2m7: 0-1 3m+: 0-0
Track: **LH: 1-8** RH: 0-3 **Tight: 1-8** Gall: 0-0
Aids: Bl: 0-1 Vi: 0-0 Tstrap: 0-1
Best Rating: 134 11/99 Newb 2m1f gd-sft Ch

Modest hurdler/chaser. Suited by a sound surface and the minimum trip. Seems most effective when held up.

Honky Tonk

6-y-o ch m Brianston Spirit-Brickyard Loopy Lou Vii (Damsire Unregistered)

Miss M Bragg Miss S A Edwards

Placings:*0* **(0253)**

2001/02: 17^{0}GF

	Starts	1st	2nd	3rd	Win & Pl
NH Flat	1	0	0	0	
Career Total	**1**	**0**	**0**	**0**	

Going: Sf: 0-0 GS: 0-0 Gd: 0-0 GF: - Fm: 0-1
Distance: 2m/2m3: 0-1 2m4-2m7: 0-0 3m+: 0-0
Track: LH: 0-1 RH: 0-0 Tight: 0-1 Gall: 0-0
Aids: Bl: 0-0 Vi: 0-0 Tstrap: 0-0
Best Rating:

Hoodwinker (IRE)

79 **75**

13-y-o b g Supreme Leader-Merrybash (Pinzari)

W Jenks Michael Stoddart

Placings:*0*/040622/3103113/P0P/140P**4131**/**451FR22** 330/55/P0F6-0 **(0052)**

2001/02: 20^{0}G

	Starts	1st	2nd	3rd	Win & Pl
Hurdles	1	0	0	0	
Career Total	**42**	**7**	**4**	**6**	**31370**

118	11/98	Worc	2m7f110y	E(0-115)HCh	HVY	£3659
116	4/98	Uttx	3m	D(0-125)HCh	SFT	£3825
114	3/98	Bang	3m110y	D(0-110)HCh	G-S	£3712
111	11/97	Uttx	3m110y	F(0-100)HHdl	GD	£2326
108	2/96	Ludl	2m5f110y	E(0-110)HHdl	GD	£2905
109	1/96	Ludl	3m2f110y	F(0-100)HHdl	GD	£2780
93	11/95	Hayd	2m4f	C Hdl	GD	£3761

Total win prize-money £22970

Going: Sf: 0-0 GS: 0-0 Gd: 0-1 GF: - Fm: 0-0
Distance: 2m/2m3: 0-0 2m4-2m7: 0-1 3m+: 0-0
Track: LH: 0-1 RH: 0-0 Tight: 0-1 Gall: 0-0
Aids: Bl: 0-0 Vi: 0-0 Tstrap: 0-0
Best Rating: 118 4/99 Uttx 3m gd-sft Ch

Hopbine

111 **118**

6-y-o ch m Gildoran-Haraka Sasa (Town And Country)

J L Spearing Mrs P L Aldersey

Placings:*50*-0**25511225** **(4653)**

2001/02: 16^{0}GF, 21^{2}G, 20^{5}HY, 19^{5}S, 20^{1}GS, 21^{1}HY, 20^{2}GS, 21^{2}GS, 20^{5}G

	Starts	1st	2nd	3rd	Win & Pl
NH Flat	1	0	0	0	0
Hurdles	8	2	3	0	25910
Career Total	**11**	**2**	**3**	**0**	**25910**

105	2/02	Wwck	2m5f	D Hdl	HVY	£4077
99	1/02	Sthl	2m4f110y	E(0-105)HHdl	G-S	£2534

Total win prize-money £6612

Going: Sf: 1-3 GS: 1-3 Gd: 0-2 GF: - Fm: 0-1
Distance: 2m/2m3: 0-1 **2m4-2m7: 2-8** 3m+: 0-0
Track: **LH: 1-3** RH: 0-4 **Tight: 1-2** Gall: 0-1
Aids: Bl: 0-0 Vi: 0-0 Tstrap: 0-0
Best Rating: 118 3/02 Newb 2m5f gd-sft Hdl

A fair novice hurdler, winner of a Southwell handicap and a Warwick novices' event at the start of 2002, she ran a blinder to finish runner up in the EBF Final at Sandown. Stays well and looks best on soft ground, though she does handle faster conditions.

Hope Value

76(48h) (61h)**60**

7-y-o b g Rock City-Folle Idee (USA) (Foolish Pleasure (USA))

G F Edwards G F Edwards

Placings:02/614P4FP-U00 **(1995)**

2001/02: 19^{U}F, 19^{0}G, 16^{0}S

	Starts	1st	2nd	3rd	Win & Pl
Hurdles	1	0	0	0	0
Chases	2	0	0	0	0
Career Total	**12**	**1**	**1**	**0**	**3502**

99	8/00	NAbb	2m1f	D Hdl	G-S	£2848

Total win prize-money £2848

Going: Sf: 0-1 GS: 0-0 Gd: 0-1 GF: - Fm: 0-1
Distance: 2m/2m3: 0-1 2m4-2m7: 0-2 3m+: 0-0
Track: LH: 0-2 RH: 0-1 Tight: 0-2 Gall: 0-0
Aids: Bl: 0-0 Vi: 0-0 Tstrap: 0-0
Best Rating: 99 11/00 Tntn 2m3f110y good Hdl

Hopeful Chance (IRE)

107 **90**

5-y-o b g Machiavellian (USA)-Don't Rush (USA) (Alleged (USA))

J R Turner Mrs Sylvia Blakeley

Placings:*2*-0000012P **(4896)**

2001/02: 17^{0}GS, 16^{0}G, 17^{0}S, 16^{0}G, 20^{0}S, 20^{1}G, 20^{2}S, 20^{P}G

	Starts	1st	2nd	3rd	Win & Pl
NH Flat	1	0	0	0	0
Hurdles	7	1	1	0	4046
Career Total	**9**	**1**	**2**	**0**	**4534**

87	1/02	Muss	2m4f	E(0-100)HHdl	GD	£3262

Total win prize-money £3262

Going: Sf: 0-3 GS: 0-1 Gd: 1-4 GF: - Fm: 0-0
Distance: 2m/2m3: 0-4 **2m4-2m7: 1-4** 3m+: 0-0
Track: LH: 0-4 **RH: 1-4 Tight: 1-3** Gall: 0-0
Aids: Bl: 0-0 Vi: 0-0 **Tstrap: 1-3**
Best Rating: 114 3/01 Hayd 2m heavy NHF

Modest hurdler, effective at two and a half miles.

Hopeful Lord (IRE)

95(105h) (100h)**102**

10-y-o b g Lord Americo-Billie Gibb (Cavo Doro)

Dr P Pritchard (J J O'Neill 18/5) Mrs T Pritchard

Placings:F05/2512445**325**/**21132**/315/2F3-P0150PU **(3673)**

2001/02: 25^{P}G, 26^{0}G, 22^{1}S, 25^{5}S, 24^{0}G, 21^{P}HY, 24^{U}S

	Starts	1st	2nd	3rd	Win & Pl
Hurdles	3	1	0	0	3378
Chases	4	0	0	0	0
Career Total	**31**	**5**	**6**	**4**	**33278**

100	10/01	Font	2m6f110y	D(0-120)HHdl	SFT	£3377
129	12/99	Towc	3m1f	D(0-125)HCh	SFT	£7002
116	11/98	MRas	3m1f	E(0-105)HCh	HVY	£3072
107	9/98	Uttx	3m	E(0-100)HCh	G-F	£2749
110	10/97	Weth	2m4f110y	D Hdl	G-F	£3090

Total win prize-money £19292

Going: Sf: 1-4 GS: 0-0 Gd: 0-3 GF: - Fm: 0-0
Distance: 2m/2m3: 0-0 **2m4-2m7: 1-2** 3m+: 0-5
Track: **LH: 1-4** RH: 0-2 **Tight: 1-2** Gall: 0-3
Aids: Bl: 0-0 Vi: 0-0 Tstrap: 0-0
Best Rating: 129 12/99 Towc 3m1f soft Ch

A lightly-raced chaser in recent seasons when with Jonjo O'Neill, he landed a weak handicap hurdle at Fontwell in October 2001 on his second start for his new yard, but has not sparkled over fences. Stays well and acts on all types of ground.

Hopies Delight

9-y-o gr g Genuine Gift (CAN)-Georgias Fancy (Montreal Boy)

G H D Hopes G H D Hopes

Placings:U4/0 **(3824)**

2001/02: 21^{0}S

	Starts	1st	2nd	3rd	Win & Pl
Chases	1	0	0	0	
Career Total	**3**	**0**	**0**	**0**	**121**

Going: Sf: 0-1 GS: 0-0 Gd: 0-0 GF: - Fm: 0-0
Distance: 2m/2m3: 0-0 2m4-2m7: 0-1 3m+: 0-0
Track: LH: 0-1 RH: 0-0 Tight: 0-1 Gall: 0-0
Aids: Bl: 0-0 Vi: 0-0 Tstrap: 0-0
Best Rating: 72 3/99 Newc 2m4f soft Ch

Winning pointer.

Hoping

86f **50f**

4-y-o b f Kris-Shimmering (IRE) (Royal Academy (USA))

A W Carroll W F Hawkings

Placings:*000* **(4166)**

2001/02: 16^{0}G, 16^{0}G, 16^{0}GS

	Starts	1st	2nd	3rd	Win & Pl
NH Flat	3	0	0	0	
Career Total	**3**	**0**	**0**	**0**	

Going: Sf: 0-0 GS: 0-1 Gd: 0-2 GF: - Fm: 0-0

Distance: 2m/2m3: 0-3 2m4-2m7: 0-0 3m+: 0-0
Track: LH: 0-1 RH: 0-2 Tight: 0-0 Gall: 0-0
Aids: Bl: 0-0 Vi: 0-0 Tstrap: 0-0
Best Rating: 50 3/02 Wwck 2m gd-sft NHF

Poor bumper form.

Hoppertree

6-y-o b g Rock Hopper-Snow Tree (Welsh Pageant)
R S Brookhouse R S Brookhouse

Placings:*5-04F* **(3754)**
2001/02: 17^{0}G, 18^{4}G, 16^{F}HY

	Starts	1st	2nd	3rd	Win & Pl
NH Flat	2	0	0	0	0
Hurdles	1	0	0	0	0
Career Total	**4**	**0**	**0**	**0**	**0**

Going: Sf: 0-1 GS: 0-0 Gd: 0-2 GF: - Fm: 0-0
Distance: 2m/2m3: 0-3 2m4-2m7: 0-0 3m+: 0-0
Track: LH: 0-2 RH: 0-1 Tight: 0-2 Gall: 0-0
Aids: Bl: 0-0 Vi: 0-0 Tstrap: 0-0
Best Rating: 105 1/02 Font 2m2f110y good NHF

Horizon (FR)

5-y-o ch g Arctic Tern (USA)-Furtchella (FR) (Dancing Spree (USA))
P C Ritchens (E Lellouche 28/10) R Catton

Placings:00042540-000**151P0** **(4656)**
2001/02: 18^{0}HY, 18^{0}VS, 17^{0}VS, 18^{1}HO, 19^{5}VS, 20^{1}GS, 20^{P}HY, 19^{0}GS

	Starts	1st	2nd	3rd	Win & Pl
Hurdles	2	0	0	0	0
Chases	6	2	0	0	6499
Career Total	**16**	**2**	**1**	**0**	**19422**

	10/01	Saum	2m4f	Ch	G-S	£3104
	10/01	LePe	2m2f110y	Ch	HLD	£2910

Total win prize-money £6014

Going: Sf: 0-2 GS: 1-2 Gd: 0-0 GF: - Fm: 0-0
Distance: 2m/2m3: 1-6 2m4-2m7: 1-2 3m+: 0-0
Track: LH: 0-1 RH: 0-1 Tight: 0-2 Gall: 0-0
Aids: Bl: 0-0 Vi: 0-0 Tstrap: 0-0
Best Rating:

Hors La Loi Iii (FR)

121 **166**

7-y-o b g Cyborg (FR)-Quintessence Iii (FR) (El Condor (FR))
J R Fanshawe Paul Green

Placings:11111/30124/PP2P-**23311** **(4190)**
2001/02: 20^{2}G, 16^{3}GS, 16^{3}G, 16^{1}GS, 16^{1}GS

	Starts	1st	2nd	3rd	Win & Pl
Hurdles	5	2	1	2	192424
Career Total	**19**	**8**	**3**	**3**	**390120**

166	3/02	Chel	2m110y	A Hdl	G-S	£156600
165	2/02	Winc	2m	A Hdl	G-S	£21000
148	2/00	Winc	2m	A Hdl	GD	£21000
155	4/99	Aint	2m110y	A Hdl	G-S	£23750
159	3/99	Chel	2m110y	A Hdl	G-S	£45960
151	1/99	Chel	2m1f	A Hdl	SFT	£9645
137	12/98	Ling	2m110y	A Hdl	SFT	£9002
	11/98	Autl	2m2f	Hdl	VS	£10101

Total win prize-money £297058

Going: Sf: 0-0 GS: 2-3 Gd: 0-2 GF: - Fm: 0-0
Distance: **2m/2m3: 2-4** 2m4-2m7: 0-1 3m+: 0-0
Track: LH: 1-2 RH: 1-3 Tight: 0-0 Gall: 0-1
Aids: Bl: 0-0 Vi: 0-0 **Tstrap: 2-3**
Best Rating: 166 3/02 Chel 2m110y gd-sft Hdl

He has been around a bit in his short life, having had spells with Francois Doumen (twice), Martin Pipe and now with James Fanshawe. A brilliant winner of the 1999 Supreme Novices' Hurdle and runner-up to Istabraq in the 2000 Champion Hurdle, he has struggled for form until taking his second Axminster Carpets (Kingwell) Hurdle in February 2002. Winner of the 2002 Champion Hurdle, with Istabraq and Valiramix failing to finish. Fast ground over two miles is the key to him, and he has worn a tongue strap recently to winning effect. Has broken blood vessels in the past.

Horton Dancer

96 **86**

5-y-o b g Rambo Dancer (CAN)-Horton Lady (Midyan (USA))
D W Barker Robert E Cook

Placings:1603P **(4096)**
2001/02: 17^{1}GS, 17^{6}G, 16^{0}G, 17^{3}GF, 19^{P}GS

	Starts	1st	2nd	3rd	Win & Pl
Hurdles	5	1	0	1	2911
Career Total	**5**	**1**	**0**	**1**	**2911**

86	10/01	Sedg	2m1f	E Hdl	G-S	£2576

Total win prize-money £2576

Going: Sf: 0-0 GS: 1-2 Gd: 0-2 GF: - Fm: 0-1
Distance: **2m/2m3: 1-5** 2m4-2m7: 0-0 3m+: 0-0
Track: **LH: 1-4** RH: 0-0 **Tight: 1-3** Gall: 0-0
Aids: Bl: 0-0 Vi: 0-0 Tstrap: 0-0
Best Rating: 86 12/01 Muss 2m1f gd-fm Hdl

Acts on most types of ground and goes well at around two miles.

Horton-Cum-Peel (IRE)

11-y-o b g Swan's Rock-Lady Beecham (Laurence O)
T R Kinsey Mrs T R Kinsey

Placings:F3F-P **(4057)**
2001/02: 23^{P}S

	Starts	1st	2nd	3rd	Win & Pl
Chases	1	0	0	0	
Career Total	**4**	**0**	**0**	**1**	**302**

Going: Sf: 0-1 GS: 0-0 Gd: 0-0 GF: - Fm: 0-0
Distance: 2m/2m3: 0-0 2m4-2m7: 0-0 3m+: 0-1
Track: LH: 0-0 RH: 0-1 Tight: 0-0 Gall: 0-0
Aids: Bl: 0-0 Vi: 0-0 Tstrap: 0-0
Best Rating: 64 5/00 Ctml 3m2f gd-sft Ch

Horus (IRE)

103 **139**

7-y-o b g Teenoso (USA)-Jennie's First (Idiots Delight)
D Pipe B A Kilpatrick

Placings:1P **(4253)**
2001/02: 25^{1}S, 26^{P}G

	Starts	1st	2nd	3rd	Win & Pl
Chases	2	1	0	0	1352
Career Total	**2**	**1**	**0**	**0**	**1352**

139	2/02	Winc	3m1f110y	H Ch	SFT	£1352

Total win prize-money £1352

Going: Sf: 1-1 GS: 0-0 Gd: 0-1 GF: - Fm: 0-0
Distance: 2m/2m3: 0-0 2m4-2m7: 0-0 **3m+: 1-2**
Track: LH: 0-1 **RH: 1-1** Tight: 0-0 Gall: 0-1
Aids: Bl: 0-0 Vi: 0-0 Tstrap: 0-0
Best Rating: 139 2/02 Winc 3m1f110y soft Ch

A smart point to pointer who has won five of his seven starts between the flags. Made a winning debut over the regulation fences at Wincanton in February 2002. Disappointed in the Foxhunters' at Cheltenham but won there in less exalted company. Not the best of jumpers, but did little wrong on that score when winning a handicap chase in June 2002.

Hot Move

11-y-o ch g Move Off-Hotwave (Hotfoot)
Miss G T Lee (Trainer Unknown 10/2) Miss G T Lee

Placings:P **(3824)**
2001/02: 21^{P}S

	Starts	1st	2nd	3rd	Win & Pl
Chases	1	0	0	0	
Career Total	**1**	**0**	**0**	**0**	

Going: Sf: 0-1 GS: 0-0 Gd: 0-0 GF: - Fm: 0-0
Distance: 2m/2m3: 0-0 2m4-2m7: 0-1 3m+: 0-0
Track: LH: 0-1 RH: 0-0 Tight: 0-1 Gall: 0-0
Aids: Bl: 0-0 Vi: 0-0 Tstrap: 0-0
Best Rating:

Weak pointer.

Hot Plunge

89 **71**

6-y-o b g Bustino-Royal Seal (Privy Seal)
N J Henderson Queen Elizabeth

Placings:*1-244* **(1039)**
2001/02: 16^{2}GF, 16^{4}G, 20^{4}GF

	Starts	1st	2nd	3rd	Win & Pl
NH Flat	2	0	1	0	439
Hurdles	1	0	0	0	0
Career Total	**4**	**1**	**1**	**0**	**1902**

100	6/00	Worc	2m	H NHF	GD	£1463

Total win prize-money £1463

Going: Sf: 0-0 GS: 0-0 Gd: 0-1 GF: - Fm: 0-2
Distance: 2m/2m3: 0-2 2m4-2m7: 0-1 3m+: 0-0
Track: LH: 0-3 RH: 0-0 Tight: 0-0 Gall: 0-0
Aids: Bl: 0-0 Vi: 0-0 Tstrap: 0-0
Best Rating: 109 6/01 Worc 2m good NHF

Hot Shots (FR)

107 **148**

7-y-o b g Passing Sale (FR)-Uguette Iv (FR) (Chamberlin (FR))
M Pitman (A L T Moore 2/8) Mrs Jill Eynon & Mr Robin Eynon

Placings:343210/6300-**213416220P** **(4254)**
2001/02: 17^{2}F, 17^{1}G, 20^{3}YS, 17^{4}GY, 16^{1}GF, 19^{6}G, 16^{2}GS, 16^{2}GS, 16^{0}GS, 16^{P}G

	Starts	1st	2nd	3rd	Win & Pl
Chases	10	2	3	1	14856
Career Total	**20**	**3**	**4**	**4**	**22669**

126	9/01	Worc	2m	D Ch	G-F	£3926
118	6/01	Baln	2m1f	Ch	GD	£5564
110	2/00	Punc	2m	Hdl	Y-S	£4140

Total win prize-money £13631

Going: Sf: 0-0 GS: 0-3 Gd: 1-3 GF: - Fm: 1-2

Distance: **2m/2m3: 2-8** 2m4-2m7: 0-2 3m+: 0-0
Track: **LH: 1-3** RH: 0-3 Tight: 0-0 Gall: 0-1
Aids: Bl: 0-0 Vi: 0-0 Tstrap: 0-0
Best Rating: 148 11/01 Sand 2m gd-sft Ch

A winner over fences in Ireland, he made a successful British debut at Worcester in September 2001. Decent effort two runs later at Kempton and was caught on the line at Sandown next time. Suited by two miles and a sound surface.

Hot To Trot (IRE)

102 **103**

9-y-o b g Yashgan-La Tante (Bold Lad (IRE))
C J Mann Roger Maggs

Placings:211P/P/0P0P0-3PF **(4844)**
2001/02: 24^{3}G, 24^{P}GS, 24^{F}G

	Starts	1st	2nd	3rd	Win & Pl
Hurdles	3	0	0	1	684
Career Total	**13**	**2**	**1**	**1**	**8198**

125	2/99	Folk	2m6f110y	E Hdl	G-S	£2386
125	11/98	Newb	3m110y	C Hdl	GD	£4032

Total win prize-money £6420

Going: Sf: 0-0 GS: 0-1 Gd: 0-2 GF: - Fm: 0-0
Distance: 2m/2m3: 0-0 2m4-2m7: 0-0 3m+: 0-3
Track: LH: 0-1 RH: 0-2 Tight: 0-2 Gall: 0-0
Aids: Bl: 0-1 Vi: 0-0 Tstrap: 0-0
Best Rating: 125 2/99 Folk 2m6f110y gd-sft Hdl

Staying hurdler. Acts on most types of ground. Finished lame in a claimer in August 2002.

Hotpot

9-y-o br g Hotfoot-Miss Polly Peck (March Past)
C J Hemsley W E Dudley

Placings:*000*/0P **(4519)**
2001/02: 16^{0}S, 21^{P}GS

	Starts	1st	2nd	3rd	Win & Pl
Hurdles	2	0	0	0	
Career Total	**5**	**0**	**0**	**0**	

Going: Sf: 0-1 GS: 0-1 Gd: 0-0 GF: - Fm: 0-0
Distance: 2m/2m3: 0-1 2m4-2m7: 0-1 3m+: 0-0
Track: LH: 0-1 RH: 0-1 Tight: 0-1 Gall: 0-0
Aids: Bl: 0-0 Vi: 0-0 Tstrap: 0-0
Best Rating: 71 2/98 Kemp 2m gd-fm NHF

Hotscent (IRE)

88 **61**

11-y-o br m Creative Plan (USA)-North Rose Vii (Damsire Unregistered)
R J Price M A Hill

Placings:0000/400/**U-550PPP** **(3864)**
2001/02: 24^{5}G, 23^{5}F, 24^{0}GF, 23^{P}GF, 20^{P}S, 24^{P}G

	Starts	1st	2nd	3rd	Win & Pl
Chases	6	0	0	0	0
Career Total	**14**	**0**	**0**	**0**	**139**

Going: Sf: 0-1 GS: 0-0 Gd: 0-2 GF: - Fm: 0-3
Distance: 2m/2m3: 0-0 2m4-2m7: 0-1 3m+: 0-5
Track: LH: 0-1 RH: 0-5 Tight: 0-1 Gall: 0-3
Aids: Bl: 0-1 Vi: 0-0 Tstrap: 0-0
Best Rating: 78 6/97 Tipp 2m good NHF

Hotspur Street

105 **80**

10-y-o b g Cadeaux Genereux-Excellent Alibi (USA) (Exceller (USA))
E L James Mrs D C Samworth

Placings:04/445U04/060406650056612/066433550/235356/025253P **(4565)**
2001/02: 19^{0}G, 20^{2}HY, 16^{5}HY, 16^{2}S, 16^{5}S, 22^{3}S, 16^{P}G

	Starts	1st	2nd	3rd	Win & Pl
Hurdles	7	0	2	1	1487
Career Total	**45**	**1**	**4**	**5**	**6086**

77	3/98	Towc	2m	G Hdl	G-S	£1576

Total win prize-money £1576

Going: Sf: 0-5 GS: 0-0 Gd: 0-2 GF: - Fm: 0-0
Distance: 2m/2m3: 0-5 2m4-2m7: 0-2 3m+: 0-0
Track: LH: 0-1 RH: 0-6 Tight: 0-1 Gall: 0-0
Aids: Bl: 0-7 Vi: 0-0 Tstrap: 0-0
Best Rating: 89 12/99 Leic 2m soft Hdl

Appears to act on most types of ground, but is best on a soft surface and effective at two miles. Has a poor strike rate.

Hotters (IRE)

104 **98**

7-y-o b g Be My Native (USA)-Siul Currach (Deep Run)
M Pitman Gollyhott Trading Ltd

Placings:*0-100554* **(3981)**
2001/02: 16^{1}G, 16^{0}G, 19^{0}GS, 18^{5}G, 21^{5}GS, 21^{4}G

	Starts	1st	2nd	3rd	Win & Pl
NH Flat	2	1	0	0	1453
Hurdles	4	0	0	0	399
Career Total	**7**	**1**	**0**	**0**	**1852**

82	10/01	Hntg	2m110y	H NHF	GD	£1452

Total win prize-money £1453

Going: Sf: 0-0 GS: 0-2 Gd: 1-4 GF: - Fm: 0-0
Distance: **2m/2m3: 1-4** 2m4-2m7: 0-2 3m+: 0-0
Track: LH: 0-2 **RH: 1-4** Tight: 0-1 **Gall: 1-2**
Aids: Bl: 0-0 Vi: 0-0 Tstrap: 0-0
Best Rating: 98 1/02 Font 2m2f110y good Hdl

Landed a bumper at Huntingdon in October and should find races over hurdles.

Houghton Bay (IRE)

110 **125**

7-y-o b g Camden Town-Royal Bavard (Le Bavard (FR))
J G Portman Mrs William Hall

Placings:*533*203/10133*504*-1153000 **(4028)**
2001/02: 19^{1}G, 20^{1}S, 21^{5}G, 22^{3}S, 22^{0}S, 16^{0}S, 21^{0}GS

	Starts	1st	2nd	3rd	Win & Pl
Hurdles	7	2	0	1	7594
Career Total	**21**	**4**	**1**	**6**	**16026**

120	10/01	Chep	2m4f	D(0-120)HHdl	SFT	£3391
110	10/01	Hrfd	2m3f110y	F(0-110)HHdl	GD	£3062
120	11/00	NAbb	2m1f	D Hdl	HVY	£3347
117	10/00	Bang	2m4f	E Hdl	SFT	£2348

Total win prize-money £12152

Going: Sf: 1-4 GS: 0-1 Gd: 1-2 GF: - Fm: 0-0
Distance: 2m/2m3: 0-1 **2m4-2m7: 2-6** 3m+: 0-0
Track: LH: 1-3 RH: 1-4 Tight: 0-0 Gall: 0-2
Aids: Bl: 0-0 Vi: 0-0 Tstrap: 0-0
Best Rating: 125 12/01 Sand 2m6f soft Hdl

Fair handicap hurdler. In fine form in the autumn of 2001, winning handicap hurdles at Hereford and Chepstow, although he has been held since then. Acts very well with cut in the ground and is effective at up to two and a half miles.

Hougoumont

72 **34**

6-y-o b g Formidable (USA)-Sure Victory (IRE) (Stalker)
N A Dunger N A Dunger

Placings:0 **(0365)**
2001/02: 19^{0}GF

	Starts	1st	2nd	3rd	Win & Pl
Hurdles	1	0	0	0	
Career Total	**1**	**0**	**0**	**0**	

Going: Sf: 0-0 GS: 0-0 Gd: 0-0 GF: - Fm: 0-1
Distance: 2m/2m3: 0-0 2m4-2m7: 0-1 3m+: 0-0
Track: LH: 0-1 RH: 0-0 Tight: 0-1 Gall: 0-0
Aids: Bl: 0-0 Vi: 0-0 Tstrap: 0-0
Best Rating: 34 5/01 Ling 2m3f110y gd-fm Hdl

Houlihans Choice

61f **85f**

5-y-o ch g Norton Challenger-Model Lady (Le Bavard (FR))
Ferdy Murphy Paddy O'Donnell

Placings:*0* **(4499)**
2001/02: 16^{0}G

	Starts	1st	2nd	3rd	Win & Pl
NH Flat	1	0	0	0	
Career Total	**1**	**0**	**0**	**0**	

Going: Sf: 0-0 GS: 0-0 Gd: 0-1 GF: - Fm: 0-0
Distance: 2m/2m3: 0-1 2m4 2m7: 0-0 3m+: 0-0
Track: LH: 0-1 RH: 0-0 Tight: 0-0 Gall: 0-0
Aids: Bl: 0-0 Vi: 0-0 Tstrap: 0-0
Best Rating: 85 3/02 Hayd 2m good NHF

House Of Dreams

103 **96**

10-y-o b g Darshaan-Helens Dreamgirl (Caerleon (USA))
Mrs M Reveley J & M Leisure / Unos Restaurant

Placings:606/11/22221062/31066U5/3402153F/63 **(1501)**
2001/02: 17^{6}GF, 17^{3}G

	Starts	1st	2nd	3rd	Win & Pl
Hurdles	2	0	0	1	282
Career Total	**30**	**5**	**6**	**4**	**25840**

144	1/00	Weth	2m	C(0-130)HHdl	SFT	£4875
119	5/98	Ctml	2m1f110y	E(0-115)HHdl	G-F	£2814
121	2/98	Catt	2m	C(0-130)HHdl	GD	£4176
101	5/96	Ctml	2m1f110y	D Hdl	GD	£2584
101	5/96	Sedg	2m1f	E Hdl	GD	£2600

Total win prize-money £17050

Going: Sf: 0-0 GS: 0-0 Gd: 0-1 GF: - Fm: 0-1
Distance: 2m/2m3: 0-2 2m4-2m7: 0-0 3m+: 0-0
Track: LH: 0-1 RH: 0-1 Tight: 0-2 Gall: 0-0
Aids: Bl: 0-0 Vi: 0-0 Tstrap: 0-0
Best Rating: 144 1/00 Weth 2m soft Hdl

A one-time useful hurdler, he is not the force of old.

How Friendly

12-y-o ch g Gabitat-Bucks Fizz Music (Be Friendly)
Mrs B Ansell Mrs B Ansell

Placings:*0/F/5-P* **(0322)**
2001/02: 21^{P}G

	Starts	1st	2nd	3rd	Win & Pl
Chases	1	0	0	0	
Career Total	4	0	0	0	0

Going: Sf: 0-0 GS: 0-0 Gd: 0-1 GF: - Fm: 0-0
Distance: 2m/2m3: 0-0 2m4-2m7: 0-1 3m+: 0-0
Track: LH: 0-0 RH: 0-1 Tight: 0-1 Gall: 0-0
Aids: Bl: 0-0 Vi: 0-0 Tstrap: 0-0
Best Rating: 52 5/00 Folk 2m5f good Ch

How Great Thou Art

86f **82f**

6-y-o b g Almoojid-Mamamere (Tres Gate)
R J Baker D R Walsh

Placings:*0-03* **(0911)**
2001/02: 17^{0}G, 16^{3}G

	Starts	1st	2nd	3rd	Win & Pl
NH Flat	2	0	0	1	214
Career Total	3	0	0	1	214

Going: Sf: 0-0 GS: 0-0 Gd: 0-2 GF: - Fm: 0-0
Distance: 2m/2m3: 0-2 2m4-2m7: 0-0 3m+: 0-0
Track: LH: 0-2 RH: 0-0 Tight: 0-1 Gall: 0-0
Aids: Bl: 0-0 Vi: 0-0 Tstrap: 0-0
Best Rating: 82 7/01 Worc 2m good NHF

How Ran On (IRE)

104 **94+**

11-y-o b/br g Mandalus-Kelly's Bridge (Netherkelly)
Mrs L Williamson Halewood International Ltd

Placings:*41/20010/***F0F0254P22/P115F3***/0P0-*
0O51026523400 **(4909)**
2001/02: 20^{0}GS, 16^{0}GF, 17^{5}G, 16^{1}G, 16^{0}GS, 16^{2}GF, 17^{6}G, 16^{5}GF, 20^{2}GF, 16^{3}GF, 17^{4}GF, 16^{0}GS, 20^{0}GF

	Starts	1st	2nd	3rd	Win & Pl
Chases	13	1	2	1	5303
Career Total	39	5	6	2	22901

109	6/01	NAbb	2m110y	F(0-100)HCh	GD	£2982
126	6/99	Gowr	2m5f	(0-109)HCh	GD	£4296
115	5/99	Wxfd	2m4f	(0-109)HCh	Y-S	£3376
99	4/98	Navn	2m	Hdl	SH	£2680
107	4/97	List	2m4f	NHF	G-Y	£3391

Total win prize-money £16726

Going: Sf: 0-0 GS: 0-3 Gd: 1-3 GF: - Fm: 0-7
Distance: **2m/2m3: 1-10** 2m4-2m7: 0-3 3m+: 0-0
Track: **LH: 1-10** RH: 0-3 **Tight: 1-11** Gall: 0-0
Aids: Bl: 0-0 Vi: 0-0 Tstrap: 0-1
Best Rating: 126 6/99 Gowr 2m5f good Ch

Once a fair handicap chaser in Ireland. Won over two miles at Newton Abbot June 2001. Acts on ground good or softer.

How To Run (IRE)

94 **92**

9-y-o b g Commanche Run-How Hostile (Tumble Wind (USA))
D J Wintle C E Barry

Placings:*0603/P00/3P160/***4B34PU-040** **(0908)**
2001/02: 21^{0}G, 24^{4}GF, 23^{0}G

	Starts	1st	2nd	3rd	Win & Pl
Hurdles	1	0	0	0	0

	Starts	1st	2nd	3rd	Win & Pl
Chases	2	0	0	0	256
Career Total	21	1	0	3	4186

90	11/99	Sedg	3m3f110y	E Hdl	GD	£2232

Total win prize-money £2233

Going: Sf: 0-0 GS: 0-0 Gd: 0-2 GF: - Fm: 0-1
Distance: 2m/2m3: 0-0 2m4-2m7: 0-1 3m+: 0-2
Track: LH: 0-2 RH: 0-0 Tight: 0-1 Gall: 0-0
Aids: Bl: 0-0 Vi: 0-0 Tstrap: 0-0
Best Rating: 92 6/01 Strf 3m gd-fm Ch

Howaboys Quest (USA)

94 **74**

5-y-o b g Quest For Fame-Doctor Black (USA) (Family Doctor (USA))
Ferdy Murphy Winlow Brothers

Placings:0345044 **(4772)**
2001/02: 16^{0}GF, 20^{3}GF, 16^{4}G, 16^{5}S, 17^{0}GF, 16^{4}GF, 21^{4}G

	Starts	1st	2nd	3rd	Win & Pl
Hurdles	7	0	0	1	413
Career Total	7	0	0	1	413

Going: Sf: 0-1 GS: 0-0 Gd: 0-2 GF: - Fm: 0-4
Distance: 2m/2m3: 0-5 2m4-2m7: 0-2 3m+: 0-0
Track: LH: 0-3 RH: 0-3 Tight: 0-2 Gall: 0-1
Aids: Bl: 0-0 Vi: 0-0 Tstrap: 0-0
Best Rating: 74 4/02 Hntg 2m110y gd-fm Hdl

Howards Dream (IRE)

50 **19**

4-y-o b g King's Theatre (IRE)-Keiko (Generous (IRE))
D A Nolan (I Semple 22/8) Mrs J McFadyen-Murray

Placings:0 **(1574)**
2001/02: 16^{0}G

	Starts	1st	2nd	3rd	Win & Pl
Hurdles	1	0	0	0	
Career Total	1	0	0	0	

Going: Sf: 0-0 GS: 0-0 Gd: 0-1 GF: - Fm: 0-0
Distance: 2m/2m3: 0-1 2m4-2m7: 0-0 3m+: 0-0
Track: LH: 0-1 RH: 0-0 Tight: 0-1 Gall: 0-0
Aids: Bl: 0-0 Vi: 0-0 Tstrap: 0-1
Best Rating: 19 10/01 Kels 2m110y good Hdl

Howe Timely

85 **68**

5-y-o b g Timeless Times (USA)-Adder Howe (Amboise)
N Bycroft Mrs Susan Johnson

Placings:00P **(3856)**
2001/02: 16^{0}G, 16^{0}GS, 16^{P}S

	Starts	1st	2nd	3rd	Win & Pl
Hurdles	3	0	0	0	
Career Total	3	0	0	0	

Going: Sf: 0-1 GS: 0-1 Gd: 0-1 GF: - Fm: 0-0
Distance: 2m/2m3: 0-3 2m4-2m7: 0-0 3m+: 0-0
Track: LH: 0-3 RH: 0-0 Tight: 0-0 Gall: 0-2
Aids: Bl: 0-0 Vi: 0-0 Tstrap: 0-0
Best Rating: 68 12/01 Donc 2m110y good Hdl

Howey In The Hills (IRE)

69 **40**

6-y-o b g Phardante (FR)-Tacova (Avocat)
D McCain D McCain

Placings:*00* **(3819)**
2001/02: 16^{0}S, 17^{0}S

	Starts	1st	2nd	3rd	Win & Pl
NH Flat	1	0	0	0	0
Hurdles	1	0	0	0	0
Career Total	2	0	0	0	

Going: Sf: 0-2 GS: 0-0 Gd: 0-0 GF: - Fm: 0-0
Distance: 2m/2m3: 0-2 2m4-2m7: 0-0 3m+: 0-0
Track: LH: 0-2 RH: 0-0 Tight: 0-1 Gall: 0-0
Aids: Bl: 0-0 Vi: 0-0 Tstrap: 0-0
Best Rating: 71 1/02 Hayd 2m soft NHF

Well held in novice event on hurdle debut.

Hubbly Bubbly

68f **44f**

4-y-o b g Gildoran-Spinayab (King Of Spain)
J W Mullins J H Mead

Placings:*000* **(4887)**
2001/02: 16^{0}S, 17^{0}G, 18^{0}GF

	Starts	1st	2nd	3rd	Win & Pl
NH Flat	3	0	0	0	
Career Total	3	0	0	0	

Going: Sf: 0-1 GS: 0-0 Gd: 0-1 GF: - Fm: 0-1
Distance: 2m/2m3: 0-3 2m4-2m7: 0-0 3m+: 0-0
Track: LH: 0-3 RH: 0-0 Tight: 0-2 Gall: 0-0
Aids: Bl: 0-0 Vi: 0-0 Tstrap: 0-0
Best Rating: 44 3/02 Chep 2m110y soft NHF

Hubert

97 **102**

12-y-o b g Rolfe (USA)-Pilicina (Milesian)
T R George Three Of A Kind Racing

Placings:U00/0454/303/320/1241**2U3F**4/031220-2 **(1795)**
2001/02: 20^{2}S

	Starts	1st	2nd	3rd	Win & Pl
Hurdles	1	0	1	0	969
Career Total	29	3	6	5	16929

100	1/01	Wwck	2m5f	F(0-90)Hdl	HVY	£2212
115	12/99	Hrfd	2m3f	E(0-115)HCh	GD	£3598
100	9/99	Hrfd	2m3f110y	F(0-100)HHdl	GD	£2815

Total win prize-money £8626

Going: Sf: 0-1 GS: 0-0 Gd: 0-0 GF: - Fm: 0-0
Distance: 2m/2m3: 0-0 2m4-2m7: 0-1 3m+: 0-0
Track: LH: 0-1 RH: 0-0 Tight: 0-0 Gall: 0-0
Aids: Bl: 0-0 Vi: 0-0 Tstrap: 0-0
Best Rating: 116 12/99 Hrfd 2m3f heavy Ch

Versatile sort, effective in modest company over hurdles and fences. Likes soft ground.

Hubert D'Alene (FR)

7-y-o b g Luchiroverte (IRE)-Moldau (FR) (Francois Saubaber)
M De Montfort (F Doumen 25/2) M De Montfort

Placings:P/0260P530340-44PPP
2001/02: 21^{4}VS, 21^{4}HO, 21^{P}HY, 24^{P}S, 22^{P}HY

	Starts	1st	2nd	3rd	Win & Pl
Chases	5	0	0	0	6208
Career Total	**17**	**0**	**1**	**2**	**18678**

Going: Sf: 0-3 GS: 0-0 Gd: 0-0 GF: - Fm: 0-0
Distance: 2m/2m3: 0-0 2m4-2m7: 0-4 3m+: 0-1
Track: LH: 0-2 RH: 0-0 Tight: 0-0 Gall: 0-1
Aids: Bl: 0-0 Vi: 0-0 Tstrap: 0-0
Best Rating:

Hugh Daniels

14-y-o b g Adonijah-Golden Realm (Red Regent)
C J Hemsley Brett Hemsley

Placings:6323360/6331000/05002403230/FU022250 5P5/066PPP/364445444P/0U03P34556/P34606/0066-0 **(1760)**
2001/02: 16^{0}GS

	Starts	1st	2nd	3rd	Win & Pl
Hurdles	1	0	0	0	
Career Total	**73**	**1**	**6**	**11**	**12001**

100	8/93	Wxfd	2m2f	Hdl	GD	£2969

Total win prize-money £2970

Going: Sf: 0-0 GS: 0-1 Gd: 0-0 GF: - Fm: 0-0
Distance: 2m/2m3: 0-1 2m4-2m7: 0-0 3m+: 0-0
Track: LH: 0-1 RH: 0-0 Tight: 0-1 Gall: 0-0
Aids: Bl: 0-0 Vi: 0-0 Tstrap: 0-0
Best Rating: 100 8/93 Wxfd 2m2f good Hdl

Hugo De Grez (FR)

118 **137**

7-y-o b g Useful (FR)-Piqua Des Gres (FR) (Waylay)
A Parker Mr & Mrs Raymond Anderson Green

Placings:01P0/223111/1240-21P5 **(4831)**
2001/02: 25^{2}GS, 26^{1}HY, 33^{P}S, 20^{5}G

	Starts	1st	2nd	3rd	Win & Pl
Chases	4	1	1	0	8986
Career Total	**18**	**6**	**4**	**1**	**47251**

137	11/01	Carl	3m2f	C(0-130)HCh	HVY	£6890
137	11/00	Carl	3m2f	C(0-130)HCh	SFT	£7020
122	4/00	Carl	3m2f	E Ch	SFT	£3542
127	3/00	Carl	3m2f	D(0-115)HCh	G-S	£14495
112	2/00	Carl	2m4f110y	F(0-105)HCh	HVY	£3558
72	2/99	Ayr	3m110y	E Hdl	SFT	£2670

Total win prize-money £38177

Going: Sf: 1-2 GS: 0-1 Gd: 0-1 GF: - Fm: 0-0
Distance: 2m/2m3: 0-0 2m4-2m7: 0-1 **3m+: 1-3**
Track: LH: 0-3 **RH: 1-1** Tight: 0-0 Gall: 0-1
Aids: Bl: 0-0 Vi: 0-0 **Tstrap: 1-4**
Best Rating: 137 11/01 Carl 3m2f heavy Ch

Handicap chaser. Stays three miles two furlongs and is effective on a soft surface.

Hugo De Perro (FR)

104(106c) (125c)**129**

7-y-o b g Perrault-Fontaine Aux Faons (FR) (Nadjar (FR))
P Monteith (M C Pipe 22/10) J W D Campbell

Placings:*52501414*/5304-1F36432 **(4143)**
2001/02: 20^{1}G, 20^{F}GF, 17^{3}GF, 20^{6}G, 19^{4}GF, 16^{3}S, 20^{2}HY

	Starts	1st	2nd	3rd	Win & Pl
Hurdles	4	0	1	1	1590
Chases	3	1	0	1	5639
Career Total	**19**	**3**	**2**	**3**	**17342**

123	5/01	MRas	2m4f	D Ch	GD	£5096
136	2/00	Wwck	2m4f110y	E(0-115)HHdl	SFT	£2632
124	1/00	Leic	2m	E Hdl	SFT	£3042

Total win prize-money £10770

Going: Sf: 0-2 GS: 0-0 Gd: 1-2 GF: - Fm: 0-3
Distance: 2m/2m3: 0-3 **2m4-2m7: 1-4** 3m+: 0-0
Track: LH: 0-3 **RH: 1-4 Tight: 1-3** Gall: 0-0
Aids: Bl: 0-0 Vi: 0-0 Tstrap: 0-0
Best Rating: 136 2/00 Wwck 2m4f110y soft Hdl

Won twice over hurdles early in 2000, but looked short of pace afterwards. Off the mark on his chasing debut in May 2001, he has struggled with his jumping on fast ground since and reverted to hurdles in the autumn.

Huic Holloa (IRE)

93f **86f**

6-y-o b g Denel (FR)-Buckalgo (IRE) (Buckskin (FR))
J A T De Giles V W H Hunt Partnership

Placings:*0*-036 **(2460)**
2001/02: 16^{0}GF, 17^{3}G, 16^{6}S

	Starts	1st	2nd	3rd	Win & Pl
NH Flat	3	0	0	1	341
Career Total	**4**	**0**	**0**	**1**	**341**

Going: Sf: 0-1 GS: 0-0 Gd: 0-1 GF: - Fm: 0-1
Distance: 2m/2m3: 0-3 2m4-2m7: 0-0 3m+: 0-0
Track: LH: 0-1 RH: 0-1 Tight: 0-0 Gall: 0-1
Aids: Bl: 0-0 Vi: 0-0 Tstrap: 0-0
Best Rating: 86 12/01 Wwck 2m soft NHF

Unplaced in two bumpers in the spring, he was staying on strongly in a Taunton bumper in November on good ground.

Huis Clos Ii (FR)

7-y-o b g Quart De Vin (FR)-Pasiphae (FR) (Signani (FR))
Mrs L C Taylor Mrs W Morrell

Placings:010F036/0501PFP5-P **(0011)**
2001/02: 20^{P}GS

	Starts	1st	2nd	3rd	Win & Pl
Chases	1	0	0	0	
Career Total	**16**	**2**	**0**	**1**	**9916**

7/00	Leto	2m3f110y	Ch	GD	£2786
12/99	Pau	2m110y	Hdl	HVY	£5920

Total win prize-money £8706

Going: Sf: 0-0 GS: 0-1 Gd: 0-0 GF: - Fm: 0-0
Distance: 2m/2m3: 0-0 2m4-2m7: 0-1 3m+: 0-0
Track: LH: 0-1 RH: 0-0 Tight: 0-1 Gall: 0-0
Aids: Bl: 0-0 Vi: 0-1 Tstrap: 0-0
Best Rating:

Huish (IRE)

69

11-y-o br g Orchestra-Lysanders Lady (Saulingo)
Mrs N Macauley W Murdoch

Placings:*U0*/006P/06604/3 **(0212)**
2001/02: 20^{3}F

	Starts	1st	2nd	3rd	Win & Pl
Hurdles	1	0	0	1	319
Career Total	**12**	**0**	**0**	**1**	**319**

Going: Sf: 0-0 GS: 0-0 Gd: 0-0 GF: - Fm: 0-1
Distance: 2m/2m3: 0-0 2m4-2m7: 0-1 3m+: 0-0
Track: LH: 0-1 RH: 0-0 Tight: 0-1 Gall: 0-0
Aids: Bl: 0-0 Vi: 0-0 Tstrap: 0-0
Best Rating: 79 3/97 Sand 2m110y good Hdl

Hulla Hoop (FR)

113(87h) **114**

7-y-o b g Alesso (USA)-Ursala (FR) (Toujours Pret (USA))
J J O'Neill Ian G M Dalgleish

Placings:11335/UP550-0P613210 **(1241)**
2001/02: 26^{0}GF, 20^{P}F, 22^{6}GF, 20^{1}GS, 16^{3}GF, 20^{2}G, 20^{1}G, 20^{0}GF

	Starts	1st	2nd	3rd	Win & Pl
Chases	8	2	1	1	10233
Career Total	**18**	**4**	**1**	**3**	**23688**

114	8/01	Prth	2m4f110y	E(0-115)HCh	GD	£4771
101	7/01	Wolv	2m4f110y	F(0-105)HCh	G-S	£4192
	6/99	Csma	2m1f	Ch	GD	£3014
	5/99	Loud	2m4f	Ch	G-F	£3014

Total win prize-money £14992

Going: Sf: 0-0 GS: 1-1 Gd: 1-2 GF: - Fm: 0-5
Distance: 2m/2m3: 0-1 **2m4-2m7: 2-6** 3m+: 0-1
Track: LH: 1-5 RH: 1-2 **Tight: 1-4** Gall: 0-0
Aids: Bl: 0-2 **Vi: 2-6** Tstrap: 0-0
Best Rating: 114 8/01 Prth 2m4f110y good Ch

Fair chaser, stayed two and a half miles. (DEAD)

Hulysse Royal (FR)

100 **131**

7-y-o ch g Garde Royale-Ulysse Moriniere (FR) (Mbaiki (FR))
O Sherwood R K Carvill

Placings:1F2/1203P-5 **(0079)**
2001/02: 23^{5}G

	Starts	1st	2nd	3rd	Win & Pl
Hurdles	1	0	0	0	0
Career Total	**9**	**2**	**2**	**1**	**41845**

144	11/00	Chel	2m110y	B HHdl	G-S	£32500
111	11/99	Wwck	2m	E Hdl	GD	£2805

Total win prize-money £35305

Going: Sf: 0-0 GS: 0-0 Gd: 0-1 GF: - Fm: 0-0
Distance: 2m/2m3: 0-0 2m4-2m7: 0-0 3m+: 0-1
Track: LH: 0-1 RH: 0-0 Tight: 0-0 Gall: 0-0
Aids: Bl: 0-0 Vi: 0-0 Tstrap: 0-0
Best Rating: 150 12/00 Newb 2m110y soft Hdl

He developed into a smart handicap hurdler in 2000/01, winning a valuable event at Cheltenham on his reappearance. From a stable that was largely out of form last term, he remains open to improvement over timber but will be even more interesting if switched to fences. Likely to stay beyond two and a half miles, he has a useful turn of foot.

Hum 'N' Haw (IRE)

91 **60**

11-y-o b g Creative Plan (USA)-Woody Hill (Precipice Wood)
C L Popham Peter Williams

Placings:221P53/U02/650P2/1P5P54PP-60PP0 **(1104)**
2001/02: 21^{6}GF, 18^{0}GF, 22^{P}GF, 20^{P}GF, 26^{0}G

	Starts	1st	2nd	3rd	Win & Pl
Hurdles	1	0	0	0	0
Chases	4	0	0	0	0
Career Total	**27**	**2**	**4**	**1**	**9870**

101	5/00	Fknm	2m5f110y	F(0-90)HCh	FRM	£2299
103	1/98	Leic	2m4f110y	F Ch	SFT	£3132

Total win prize-money £5432

Going: Sf: 0-0 GS: 0-0 Gd: 0-1 GF: - Fm: 0-4

Distance: 2m/2m3: 0-1 2m4-2m7: 0-3 3m+: 0-1
Track: LH: 0-4 RH: 0-0 Tight: 0-5 Gall: 0-0
Aids: Bl: 0-1 Vi: 0-0 Tstrap: 0-1
Best Rating: 103 1/98 Leic 2m4f110y soft Ch

Humming

89f **85f**

5-y-o b g Bluebird (USA)-Risanda (Kris)
Miss M E Rowland Miss M E Rowland

Placings: *0-50* **(3236)**
2001/02: 16^{5}G, 16^{0}GS

	Starts	1st	2nd	3rd	Win & Pl
NH Flat	2	0	0	0	0
Career Total	**3**	**0**	**0**	**0**	**0**

Going: Sf: 0-0 GS: 0-1 Gd: 0-1 GF: - Fm: 0-0
Distance: 2m/2m3: 0-2 2m4-2m7: 0-0 3m+: 0-0
Track: LH: 0-1 RH: 0-1 Tight: 0-0 Gall: 0-2
Aids: Bl: 0-0 Vi: 0-0 Tstrap: 0-0
Best Rating: 85 12/01 Donc 2m110y good NHF

Hunter Gold (FR)

96 **81**

7-y-o br g Chamberlin (FR)-Une de Mai IV (FR) (Ice Light (FR))
T R George Stanley W Clarke

Placings: P5213/24P-3 **(1623)**
2001/02: 21^{3}G

	Starts	1st	2nd	3rd	Win & Pl
Hurdles	1	0	0	1	436
Career Total	**9**	**1**	**2**	**2**	**8248**

12/99 Ange 2m3f Ch HVY £3842
Total win prize-money £3842

Going: Sf: 0-0 GS: 0-0 Gd: 0-1 GF: - Fm: 0-0
Distance: 2m/2m3: 0-0 2m4-2m7: 0-1 3m+: 0-0
Track: LH: 0-0 RH: 0-1 Tight: 0-0 Gall: 0-0
Aids: Bl: 0-0 Vi: 0-0 Tstrap: 0-0
Best Rating: 98 3/00 Bang 2m1f110y soft Ch

A winning chaser in France, he has shown promise over hurdles in this country.

Hunters Creek (IRE)

108 **130**

8-y-o b g Persian Mews-Creek's Sister (King's Ride)
Mrs M Reveley Bewley's Hotels, Glasgow (bsh Ltd)

Placings: *20-33F1213F* **(4652)**
2001/02: 20^{3}G, 21^{3}G, 20^{F}GS, 19^{1}G, 19^{2}GS, 19^{1}S, 22^{3}S, 20^{F}G

	Starts	1st	2nd	3rd	Win & Pl
Chases	8	2	1	3	11534
Career Total	**10**	**2**	**2**	**3**	**12430**

130 1/02 Catt 2m3f D Ch SFT £4179
122 12/01 Catt 2m3f F Ch GD £2886
Total win prize-money £7066

Going: Sf: 1-2 GS: 0-2 Gd: 1-4 GF: - Fm: 0-0
Distance: **2m/2m3: 2-3** 2m4-2m7: 0-5 3m+: 0-0
Track: **LH: 2-8** RH: 0-0 **Tight: 2-6** Gall: 0-1
Aids: Bl: 0-0 Vi: 0-0 Tstrap: 0-0
Best Rating: 130 1/02 Catt 2m3f soft Ch

He has been successful over fences in Britain and is effective at two miles three. He acts on a soft surface and goes well at Catterick. Appeared not to stay two miles six and a half furlongs at Newbury in March.

Hunters Tweed

102(118h) (134h)**127+**

6-y-o ch g Nashwan (USA)-Zorette (USA) (Zilzal (USA))
P Beaumont Robert Gibbons

Placings: 113022-03634000 **(4893)**
2001/02: 16^{0}G, 20^{3}GS, 16^{6}S, 16^{3}S, 23^{4}HY, 21^{0}GS, 24^{0}G, 20^{0}G

	Starts	1st	2nd	3rd	Win & Pl
Hurdles	8	0	0	2	5421
Career Total	**14**	**2**	**2**	**3**	**28118**

134 2/01 Kels 2m110y D Hdl SFT £4013
126 12/00 Weth 2m D Hdl SFT £3679
Total win prize-money £7693

Going: Sf: 0-3 GS: 0-2 Gd: 0-3 GF: - Fm: 0-0
Distance: 2m/2m3: 0-3 2m4-2m7: 0-3 3m+: 0-2
Track: LH: 0-7 RH: 0-1 Tight: 0-2 Gall: 0-1
Aids: Bl: 0-0 Vi: 0-0 Tstrap: 0-0
Best Rating: 134 1/02 Hayd 2m soft Hdl

A useful hurdler, he showed fair form in handicap company. Got off the mark on his chasing debut when stepped up to three miles on fast ground at Perth in May 2002.

Hunters Wood (IRE)

7-y-o gr g Wood Chanter-Barnmeen Lass (IRE) (Floriferous)
R J Baker David Heath

Placings: P-5 **(0249)**
2001/02: 22^{5}GF

	Starts	1st	2nd	3rd	Win & Pl
Hurdles	1	0	0	0	0
Career Total	**2**	**0**	**0**	**0**	**0**

Going: Sf: 0-0 GS: 0-0 Gd: 0-0 GF: - Fm: 0-1
Distance: 2m/2m3: 0-0 2m4-2m7: 0-1 3m+: 0-0
Track: LH: 0-1 RH: 0-0 Tight: 0-1 Gall: 0-0
Aids: Bl: 0-0 Vi: 0-0 Tstrap: 0-0
Best Rating:

Hunting Slane

94(102h) **108**

10-y-o b g Move Off-Singing Slane (Cree Song)
C Grant J H Richardson

Placings: *000P0/00023/31316403131145106/4/P40F4* 20PP-3 **(0221)**
2001/02: 20^{3}GF

	Starts	1st	2nd	3rd	Win & Pl
Chases	1	0	0	1	538
Career Total	**38**	**6**	**2**	**6**	**24925**

123 3/99 Kels 2m2f C(0-135)HHdl GD £7337
114 1/99 Catt 2m3f F(0-110)HHdl SFT £1912
113 12/98 Muss 3m D(0-125)HHdl GD £3330
118 11/98 Catt 3m1f110y E(0-115)HHdl GD £2617
104 6/98 MRas 2m3f110y F(0-105)HHdl G-F £2722
103 5/98 Hexm 2m4f110y E Hdl G-F £1632
Total win prize-money £19552

Going: Sf: 0-0 GS: 0-0 Gd: 0-0 GF: - Fm: 0-1
Distance: 2m/2m3: 0-0 2m4-2m7: 0-1 3m+: 0-0
Track: LH: 0-1 RH: 0-0 Tight: 0-0 Gall: 0-0
Aids: Bl: 0-0 Vi: 0-0 Tstrap: 0-0
Best Rating: 123 3/99 Kels 2m2f good Hdl

Hurdante (IRE)

12-y-o ch g Phardante (FR)-Hurry (Deep Run)
Mrs L A Parker D W Parker

Placings: *24/1201603/2/5/P415*UPP-P6 **(4727)**
2001/02: 25^{P}HY, 24^{6}GF

	Starts	1st	2nd	3rd	Win & Pl
Chases	2	0	0	0	0
Career Total	**20**	**3**	**3**	**1**	**19657**

121 12/00 Newb 2m3f D(0-125)HHdl SFT £5398
110 1/97 Leic 2m4f110y E Hdl G-S £2329
108 5/96 Dund 2m135y NHF YLD £2295
Total win prize-money £10022

Going: Sf: 0-1 GS: 0-0 Gd: 0-0 GF: - Fm: 0-1
Distance: 2m/2m3: 0-0 2m4-2m7: 0-0 3m+: 0-2
Track: LH: 0-1 RH: 0-1 Tight: 0-0 Gall: 0-0
Aids: Bl: 0-0 Vi: 0-0 Tstrap: 0-0
Best Rating: 125 11/97 Chep 2m3f110y gd-sft Ch

Hurlyburly (IRE)

90f **88f**

5-y-o ch g Hubbly Bubbly (USA)-Swans Leap (Swan's Rock)
M Pitman B R H Burrough

Placings: *40* **(1813)**
2001/02: 17^{4}GF, 16^{0}S

	Starts	1st	2nd	3rd	Win & Pl
NH Flat	2	0	0	0	0
Career Total	**2**	**0**	**0**	**0**	**0**

Going: Sf: 0-1 GS: 0-0 Gd: 0-0 GF: - Fm: 0-1
Distance: 2m/2m3: 0-2 2m4-2m7: 0-0 3m+: 0-0
Track: LH: 0-2 RH: 0-0 Tight: 0-2 Gall: 0-0
Aids: Bl: 0-0 Vi: 0-0 Tstrap: 0-0
Best Rating: 88 5/01 NAbb 2m1f gd-fm NHF

Hurricane Bay

74(96h) (77h)

6-y-o ch g Karinga Bay-Clodaigh Gale (Strong Gale)
J J O'Neill Ian G M Dalgleish

Placings: 500 **(1087)**
2001/02: 20^{5}G, 20^{0}G, 16^{0}GF

	Starts	1st	2nd	3rd	Win & Pl
Hurdles	3	0	0	0	0
Career Total	**3**	**0**	**0**	**0**	**0**

Going: Sf: 0-0 GS: 0-0 Gd: 0-2 GF: - Fm: 0-1
Distance: 2m/2m3: 0-1 2m4-2m7: 0-2 3m+: 0-0
Track: LH: 0-3 RH: 0-0 Tight: 0-0 Gall: 0-0
Aids: Bl: 0-0 Vi: 0-0 Tstrap: 0-0
Best Rating: 63 8/01 Worc 2m gd-fm Hdl

Hurricane Dawn (IRE)

100(55h) **101**

8-y-o b m Strong Gale-Aillwee Dawn (Deep Run)
Miss H C Knight Martin Broughton

Placings: *30050/1150*-54P **(0670)**
2001/02: 16^{5}GF, 21^{4}GF, 23^{P}G

	Starts	1st	2nd	3rd	Win & Pl
Chases	3	0	0	0	341
Career Total	**12**	**2**	**0**	**1**	**6331**

108 8/00 Uttx 2m4f110y D Hdl G-F £3022

5/00	Wwck	2m4f110y	E Hdl	G-F	£2755

Total win prize-money £5778

oing: Sf: 0-0 GS: 0-0 Gd: 0-1 GF: - Fm: 0-2
istance: 2m/2m3: 0-1 2m4-2m7: 0-1 3m+: 0-1
rack: LH: 0-2 RH: 0-0 Tight: 0-1 Gall: 0-0
ids: Bl: 0-0 Vi: 0-0 Tstrap: 0-0
est Rating: 108 8/00 Uttx 2m4f110y gd-fm Hdl

Hurricane Georges

)4f 91f

-y-o b g Milieu-Miss Colonnette (Flatbush)
rs L B Normile The Drysdale Family

lacings:*040* **(2188)**
001/02: 17^{0}GS, 17^{4}G, 16^{0}GS

	Starts	1st	2nd	3rd	Win & Pl
H Flat	3	0	0	0	0
areer Total	**3**	**0**	**0**	**0**	**0**

oing: Sf: 0-0 GS: 0-2 Gd: 0-1 GF: - Fm: 0-0
istance: 2m/2m3: 0-3 2m4-2m7: 0-0 3m+: 0-0
rack: LH: 0-2 RH: 0-1 Tight: 0-1 Gall: 0-0
ids: Bl: 0-0 Vi: 0-0 Tstrap: 0-0
est Rating: 91 11/01 Sedg 2m1f good NHF

Hurricane Lamp

17 154

1-y-o b g Derrylin-Lampstone (Ragstone)
King & Mrs F C Welch & Partners

Placings:*16*/112F/**6U1230**/126143F/12523/144F0-133411PP0 **(4914)**
001/02: 16^{4}GF, 20^{1}G, 21^{3}GF, 21^{3}GS, 20^{4}G, 20^{1}G, 20^{1}GS, ^{P}G, 19^{P}GF, 20^{0}G

	Starts	1st	2nd	3rd	Win & Pl
hases	10	3	0	2	26683
areer Total	**39**	**11**	**5**	**5**	**90754**

54	12/01	Sand	2m4f110y	C(0-135)HCh	G-S	£6955
52	11/01	Hntg	2m4f110y	C(0-130)HCh	GD	£6776
54	5/01	Wwck	2m4f110y	C(0-135)HCh	GD	£8684
54	5/00	Wwck	2m	B Ch	G-F	£8743
50	10/99	Weth	2m	C(0-135)HCh	GD	£5735
40	1/99	Sand	2m	B HCh	G-S	£8130
24	5/98	Uttx	2m	D Ch	G-S	£3533
29	1/98	Ludl	2m	E Ch	SFT	£3004
19	12/96	Sand	2m110y	D Hdl	GD	£2970
08	11/96	Wwck	2m	E Hdl	GD	£2721
10	2/96	Sand	2m110y	H NHF	SFT	£2304

Total win prize-money £59557

oing: Sf: 0-0 GS: 1-2 Gd: 2-5 GF: - Fm: 0-3
istance: 2m/2m3: 0-1 **2m4-2m7: 3-9** 3m+: 0-0
rack: LH: 1-4 **RH: 2-5** Tight: 0-2 **Gall: 1-2**
ids: Bl: 0-0 Vi: 0-0 Tstrap: 0-0
est Rating: 154 12/01 Sand 2m4f110y gd-sft Ch

ecent handicap chaser. Acts on most types of ground nd is effective from two miles to two miles four furlongs.

Hurricane Pete (IRE)

105 105

-y-o gr g Roselier (FR)-Hurricane Hattie (Strong Gale)
H Buckler Twentyman

lacings:235-30042130 **(4502)**
001/02: 22^{3}GF, 21^{0}S, 22^{0}GF, 25^{4}S, 24^{2}HY, 22^{1}S, 21^{3}GS, $^{2}0$G

	Starts	1st	2nd	3rd	Win & Pl
Hurdles	8	1	1	2	6568
Career Total	**11**	**1**	**2**	**3**	**7942**

103	2/02	Font	2m6f110y	D(0-125)HHdl	SFT	£5284

Total win prize-money £5285

Going: Sf: 1-4 GS: 0-1 Gd: 0-1 GF: - Fm: 0-2
Distance: 2m/2m3: 0-0 **2m4-2m7: 1-6** 3m+: 0-2
Track: **LH: 1-5** RH: 0-0 **Tight: 1-4** Gall: 0-0
Aids: Bl: 0-0 Vi: 0-0 Tstrap: 0-0
Best Rating: 105 3/02 Plum 2m5f gd-sft Hdl

A former Irish pointer, he landed a handicap hurdle at Fontwell in February 2002. Likes soft ground, may not stay three miles.

Hussard (FR)

112(95h) 108

7-y-o b g Concorde Jr (USA)-Cerise De Totes (FR) (Champ Libre (FR))
O Sherwood H M Heyman

Placings:*061*/26P-**0U1PP6** **(4889)**
2001/02: 20^{0}G, 24^{U}G, 24^{1}GS, 26^{P}G, 24^{P}GF, 26^{6}G

	Starts	1st	2nd	3rd	Win & Pl
Chases	6	1	0	0	3107
Career Total	**12**	**2**	**1**	**0**	**6287**

108	12/01	Hntg	3m	E(0-105)HCh	G-S	£3107
92	4/00	Font	2m2f110y	E Hdl	GD	£2226

Total win prize-money £5333

Going: Sf: 0-0 GS: 1-1 Gd: 0-4 GF: - Fm: 0-1
Distance: 2m/2m3: 0-0 2m4-2m7: 0-1 **3m+: 1-5**
Track: LH: 0-0 **RH: 1-4** Tight: 0-1 **Gall: 1-3**
Aids: Bl: 0-1 Vi: 0-0 Tstrap: 0-0
Best Rating: 108 12/01 Hntg 3m gd-sft Ch

Showed some promise before making almost all the running to win a novice handicap chase at Huntingdon in December 2001. Stays three miles. Has won on good and soft ground.

Hussard Collonges (FR)

119(110h) (122h)161

7-y-o b g Video Rock (FR)-Ariane Collonges (FR) (Quart De Vin (FR))
P Beaumont N W A Bannister

Placings:*00012*-21F21 **(4232)**
2001/02: 24^{2}GS, 20^{1}GS, 20^{F}S, 24^{2}S, 24^{1}GS

	Starts	1st	2nd	3rd	Win & Pl
Chases	5	2	2	0	80638
Career Total	**10**	**3**	**3**	**0**	**86745**

161	3/02	Chel	3m110y	A Ch	G-S	£72500
151	12/01	Weth	2m4f110y	D(0-110)HCh	G-S	£4446
122	4/01	Weth	2m4f110y	D Hdl	G-S	£3395

Total win prize-money £80341

Going: Sf: 0-2 GS: 2-3 Gd: 0-0 GF: - Fm: 0-0
Distance: 2m/2m3: 0-0 2m4-2m7: 1-2 3m+: 1-3
Track: **LH: 2-4** RH: 0-1 Tight: 0-1 **Gall: 1-3**
Aids: Bl: 0-0 Vi: 0-0 Tstrap: 0-0
Best Rating: 161 3/02 Chel 3m110y gd-sft Ch

A winner over two and a half miles over hurdles, he is built to jump fences and soon showed plenty of ability when tried over them including winning at Wetherby, but surpassed all of his previous performances when running out a game winner of the Royal & SunAlliance Chase at the 2002 Festival. Usually jumps well and stays. Suited by soft ground and forcing tactics.

Hussy

94 66

8-y-o b m Broadsword (USA)-Smart Chick (True Song)
Mrs Sarah Horner-Harker Mrs Sarah Horner-Harker

Placings:0P/30P4/PP6P03-P540P **(4770)**
2001/02: 24^{P}GF, 22^{5}G, 21^{4}G, 23^{0}G, 20^{P}GF

	Starts	1st	2nd	3rd	Win & Pl
Hurdles	5	0	0	0	0
Career Total	**17**	**0**	**0**	**2**	**835**

Going: Sf: 0-0 GS: 0-0 Gd: 0-3 GF: - Fm: 0-2
Distance: 2m/2m3: 0-0 2m4-2m7: 0-4 3m+: 0-1
Track: LH: 0-5 RH: 0-0 Tight: 0-3 Gall: 0-0
Aids: Bl: 0-0 Vi: 0-0 Tstrap: 0-0
Best Rating: 91 11/99 Wwck 2m good Hdl

Hyderabad

110 127

4-y-o ch c Deploy-Ajuga (USA) (The Minstrel (CAN))
M F Morris (B W Hills 6/10) Sir Anthony O'Reilly

Placings:4124510 **(4952a)**
2001/02: 16^{4}YS, 16^{1}HY, 16^{2}YS, 16^{4}SH, 17^{5}G, 16^{1}GY, 16^{0}G

	Starts	1st	2nd	3rd	Win & Pl
Hurdles	7	2	1	0	19775
Career Total	**7**	**2**	**1**	**0**	**19775**

127	4/02	Fair	2m	Hdl	G-Y	£9371
110	12/01	Thur	2m	Hdl	HVY	£5008

Total win prize-money £14379

Going: Sf: 1-1 GS: 0-0 Gd: 0-2 GF: - Fm: 0-0
Distance: **2m/2m3: 2-7** 2m4-2m7: 0-0 3m+: 0-0
Track: LH: 0-2 **RH: 2-5** Tight: 0-0 Gall: 0-1
Aids: Bl: 0-0 Vi: 0-0 Tstrap: 0-0
Best Rating: 127 4/02 Fair 2m gd-yld Hdl

Irish-trained juvenile hurdler. Won twice and ran well in good company. Acts in testing conditions.

Hylters Chance (IRE)

11-y-o ch g Zaffaran (USA)-Stickey Stream (Paddy's Stream)
Miss Polly Curling (Ms Kay Rees 14/4) P C Browne

Placings:*000004PP*/21P250/51F/P **(4865)**
2001/02: 23^{P}F

	Starts	1st	2nd	3rd	Win & Pl
Chases	1	0	0	0	
Career Total	**18**	**2**	**2**	**0**	**6722**

88	8/98	Worc	2m7f110y	E(0-100)HCh	GD	£2960
85	10/96	Towc	3m	E(0-100)HHdl	G-F	£2262

Total win prize-money £5222

Going: Sf: 0-0 GS: 0-0 Gd: 0-0 GF: - Fm: 0-1
Distance: 2m/2m3: 0-0 2m4-2m7: 0-0 3m+: 0-1
Track: LH: 0-0 RH: 0-1 Tight: 0-0 Gall: 0-0
Aids: Bl: 0-0 Vi: 0-0 Tstrap: 0-0
Best Rating: 88 8/98 Worc 2m7f110y good Ch

Hyperactive (IRE)

89 85

6-y-o b g Perugino (USA)-Hyannis (FR) (Esprit Du Nord (USA))
B Ellison Hyperactive Partnership

Placings:560 **(1387)**

2001/02: 17^{5}GF, 17^{6}GF, 16^{0}G

	Starts	1st	2nd	3rd	Win & Pl
Hurdles	3	0	0	0	0
Career Total	**3**	**0**	**0**	**0**	**0**

Going: Sf: 0-0 GS: 0-0 Gd: 0-1 GF: - Fm: 0-2
Distance: 2m/2m3: 0-3 2m4-2m7: 0-0 3m+: 0-0
Track: LH: 0-3 RH: 0-0 Tight: 0-2 Gall: 0-0
Aids: Bl: 0-0 Vi: 0-0 Tstrap: 0-0
Best Rating: 85 8/01 Sedg 2m1f gd-fm Hdl

Hyperion Du Moulin Ii (FR)

97 **90**

7-y-o b g Kedellic (FR)-Mipour (FR) (Shakapour)
Lady Herries Lady Sarah Clutton

Placings:0/0-0 **(4411)**
2001/02: 18^{0}S

	Starts	1st	2nd	3rd	Win & Pl
Hurdles	1	0	0	0	
Career Total	**3**	**0**	**0**	**0**	

Going: Sf: 0-1 GS: 0-0 Gd: 0-0 GF: - Fm: 0-0
Distance: 2m/2m3: 0-1 2m4-2m7: 0-0 3m+: 0-0
Track: LH: 0-1 RH: 0-0 Tight: 0-1 Gall: 0-0
Aids: Bl: 0-0 Vi: 0-0 Tstrap: 0-0
Best Rating: 108 3/00 Sand 2m110y good NHF

Hypersonic

99 **65**

5-y-o b g Marju (IRE)-Hi-Li (High Top)
C L Popham H J W Davies

Placings:0FP-PF3P00 **(4565)**
2001/02: 17^{P}G, 20^{F}S, 16^{3}S, 16^{P}S, 17^{0}S, 16^{0}G

	Starts	1st	2nd	3rd	Win & Pl
Hurdles	6	0	0	1	277
Career Total	**9**	**0**	**0**	**1**	**277**

Going: Sf: 0-4 GS: 0-0 Gd: 0-2 GF: - Fm: 0-0
Distance: 2m/2m3: 0-5 2m4-2m7: 0-1 3m+: 0-0
Track: LH: 0-1 RH: 0-5 Tight: 0-2 Gall: 0-0
Aids: Bl: 0-0 Vi: 0-0 Tstrap: 0-0
Best Rating: 65 1/02 Leic 2m soft Hdl

Hypothesis (IRE)

90 **84**

5-y-o b g Sadler's Wells (USA)-Surmise (USA) (Alleged (USA))
Ian Williams (A Bailey 3/11) G Ferrigno

Placings:0-630P0P **(4540)**
2001/02: 16^{6}G, 16^{3}G, 19^{0}S, 20^{P}S, 16^{0}GS, 19^{P}G

	Starts	1st	2nd	3rd	Win & Pl
Hurdles	6	0	0	1	386
Career Total	**7**	**0**	**0**	**1**	**386**

Going: Sf: 0-2 GS: 0-1 Gd: 0-3 GF: - Fm: 0-0
Distance: 2m/2m3: 0-3 2m4-2m7: 0-3 3m+: 0-0
Track: LH: 0-2 RH: 0-4 Tight: 0-1 Gall: 0-1
Aids: Bl: 0-1 Vi: 0-2 Tstrap: 0-3
Best Rating: 84 11/01 Kels 2m110y good Hdl

Modest hurdler.

I Can Imagine (IRE)

114 **133**

7-y-o b m Husyan (USA)-Cyn Alley (The Parson)
Robert Tyner Keep It Quiet Syndicate

Placings:0501231-1214U **(4192)**
2001/02: 21^{1}HY, 28^{2}Y, 24^{1}Y, 24^{4}HY, 24^{U}GS

	Starts	1st	2nd	3rd	Win & Pl
Chases	5	2	1	0	72968
Career Total	**12**	**4**	**2**	**1**	**84775**

133	12/01	Leop	3m	(0-140)HCh	YLD	£59919
111	10/01	Tipp	2m5f	(0-102)HCh	HVY	£6120
97	4/01	Tram	2m4f	(0-95)HCh	SFT	£5564
92	12/00	Clon	2m4f	Ch	SH	£3864

Total win prize-money £75469

Going: Sf: 1-2 GS: 0-1 Gd: 0-0 GF: - Fm: 0-0
Distance: 2m/2m3: 0-0 2m4-2m7: 1-1 3m+: 1-4
Track: **LH: 1-2** RH: 0-1 Tight: 0-0 Gall: 0-1
Aids: Bl: 0-0 Vi: 0-0 **Tstrap: 2-5**
Best Rating: 133 12/01 Leop 3m yield Ch

Useful Irish handicap chaser. Improved for the application of a tongue tie. Stays three miles. Acts on soft/heavy ground.

I Can't Remember

62 **54**

8-y-o gr g Petong-Glenfield Portion (Mummy's Pet)
Miss Lucinda V Russell (S R Bowring 16/6) The Gypsy King Partnership

Placings:0P5 **(4888)**
2001/02: 16^{0}S, 16^{P}F, 16^{5}G

	Starts	1st	2nd	3rd	Win & Pl
Hurdles	3	0	0	0	0
Career Total	**3**	**0**	**0**	**0**	**0**

Going: Sf: 0-1 GS: 0-0 Gd: 0-1 GF: - Fm: 0-1
Distance: 2m/2m3: 0-3 2m4-2m7: 0-0 3m+: 0-0
Track: LH: 0-2 RH: 0-1 Tight: 0-1 Gall: 0-1
Aids: Bl: 0-0 Vi: 0-0 Tstrap: 0-0
Best Rating: 54 4/02 Prth 2m110y good Hdl

I Got Rhythm

102 **101**

4-y-o gr f Lycius (USA)-Eurythmic (Pharly (FR))
Mrs M Reveley G Thomson

Placings:516 **(2907)**
2001/02: 16^{5}S, 16^{1}G, 16^{6}GS

	Starts	1st	2nd	3rd	Win & Pl
Hurdles	3	1	0	0	3696
Career Total	**3**	**1**	**0**	**0**	**3696**

101	11/01	Weth	2m	D Hdl	GD	£3696

Total win prize-money £3696

Going: Sf: 0-1 GS: 0-1 Gd: 1-1 GF: - Fm: 0-0
Distance: **2m/2m3: 1-3** 2m4-2m7: 0-0 3m+: 0-0
Track: **LH: 1-3** RH: 0-0 Tight: 0-0 Gall: 0-0
Aids: Bl: 0-0 Vi: 0-0 Tstrap: 0-0
Best Rating: 101 11/01 Weth 2m good Hdl

Plating-class stayer on the Flat, she has already proved much better over hurdles. Suited by good ground or faster.

I Move Earth

5-y-o b m Bandmaster (USA)-Lady Of Milton (Old Jocus)
P F Nicholls Fred Champion

Placings:0-45P **(2136)**
2001/02: 16^{4}G, 17^{5}GS, 24^{P}G

	Starts	1st	2nd	3rd	Win & Pl
NH Flat	2	0	0	0	0
Hurdles	1	0	0	0	0
Career Total	**4**	**0**	**0**	**0**	**0**

Going: Sf: 0-0 GS: 0-1 Gd: 0-2 GF: - Fm: 0-0
Distance: 2m/2m3: 0-2 2m4-2m7: 0-0 3m+: 0-1
Track: LH: 0-1 RH: 0-2 Tight: 0-1 Gall: 0-0
Aids: Bl: 0-0 Vi: 0-0 Tstrap: 0-0
Best Rating: 89 10/01 Chep 2m110y good NHF

I Up

7-y-o ch g Interrex (CAN)-Secret Stolen (USA) (Sassafras (FR))
B L Lay B L Lay

Placings:P **(4518)**
2001/02: 21^{P}GS

	Starts	1st	2nd	3rd	Win & Pl
Hurdles	1	0	0	0	
Career Total	**1**	**0**	**0**	**0**	

Going: Sf: 0-0 GS: 0-1 Gd: 0-0 GF: - Fm: 0-0
Distance: 2m/2m3: 0-0 2m4-2m7: 0-1 3m+: 0-0
Track: LH: 0-0 RH: 0-1 Tight: 0-0 Gall: 0-0
Aids: Bl: 0-0 Vi: 0-0 Tstrap: 0-0
Best Rating:

I Will Survive (IRE)

7-y-o ch g Good Thyne (USA)-Borgina (Boreen (FR))
H A N Orde-Powlett H A N Orde-Powlett

Placings:0000/F **(1470)**
2001/02: 20^{F}G

	Starts	1st	2nd	3rd	Win & Pl
Chases	1	0	0	0	
Career Total	**5**	**0**	**0**	**0**	

Going: Sf: 0-0 GS: 0-0 Gd: 0-1 GF: - Fm: 0-0
Distance: 2m/2m3: 0-0 2m4-2m7: 0-1 3m+: 0-0
Track: LH: 0-0 RH: 0-1 Tight: 0-0 Gall: 0-0
Aids: Bl: 0-0 Vi: 0-0 Tstrap: 0-0
Best Rating: 80 2/00 Catt 2m good NHF

I'm A Bargain

(103h) (120h) **144**

10-y-o b g Meadowbrook-Super Valu (Golden Love)
N G Richards It's A Bargain Syndicate

Placings:52FPP/1612/11F-P **(0350)**
2001/02: 24^{P}GS

	Starts	1st	2nd	3rd	Win & Pl
Chases	1	0	0	0	
Career Total	**13**	**4**	**2**	**0**	**23308**

120	4/01	Muss	3m	D Hdl	G-F	£3710
143	5/00	Newc	3m	D(0-120)HCh	G-F	£3887
135	1/00	Muss	2m4f	E(0-115)HCh	GD	£4153
127	11/99	Ayr	2m5f110y	D(0-110)HCh	GD	£3925

Total win prize-money £15676

Going: Sf: 0-0 GS: 0-1 Gd: 0-0 GF: - Fm: 0-0
Distance: 2m/2m3: 0-0 2m4-2m7: 0-0 3m+: 0-1
Track: LH: 0-1 RH: 0-0 Tight: 0-1 Gall: 0-0
Aids: Bl: 0-0 Vi: 0-0 Tstrap: 0-1

Best Rating: 144 4/01 Ayr 2m4f good Ch

A huge individual, he has a good record over fences and is genuine despite thrashing his tail on occasions. Best on fast ground.

I'm A Lady

9-y-o gr m Scallywag-Compasita (Old Jocus)
G D Bull G D Bull

Placings:R/PPP (4404)
2001/02: 16^{P}S, 16^{P}GS, 17^{P}S

	Starts	1st	2nd	3rd	Win & Pl
Hurdles	3	0	0	0	
Career Total	**4**	**0**	**0**	**0**	

Going: Sf: 0-2 GS: 0-1 Gd: 0-0 GF: - Fm: 0-0
Distance: 2m/2m3: 0-3 2m4-2m7: 0-0 3m+: 0-0
Track: LH: 0-2 RH: 0-1 Tight: 0-1 Gall: 0-0
Aids: Bl: 0-1 Vi: 0-0 Tstrap: 0-0
Best Rating:

I'm Convinced

65 **40**

8-y-o b g Petoski-Childhay (Roi Soleil)
P F Nicholls T C Frost

Placings:0 (0104)
2001/02: 18^{0}GF

	Starts	1st	2nd	3rd	Win & Pl
Hurdles	1	0	0	0	
Career Total	**1**	**0**	**0**	**0**	

Going: Sf: 0-0 GS: 0-0 Gd: 0-0 GF: - Fm: 0-1
Distance: 2m/2m3: 0-1 2m4-2m7: 0-0 3m+: 0-0
Track: LH: 0-1 RH: 0-0 Tight: 0-1 Gall: 0-0
Aids: Bl: 0-0 Vi: 0-0 Tstrap: 0-0
Best Rating: 40 5/01 Font 2m2f110y gd-fm Hdl

I'm Dreaming (IRE)

8-y-o ch g White Christmas-Suffolk Bells (London Bells (CAN))
Andrew J Martin Andrew J Martin

Placings:0240/P00PP-0P (3653)
2001/02: 24^{0}GF, 24^{P}S

	Starts	1st	2nd	3rd	Win & Pl
Chases	2	0	0	0	
Career Total	**11**	**0**	**1**	**0**	**1024**

Going: Sf: 0-1 GS: 0-0 Gd: 0-0 GF: - Fm: 0-1
Distance: 2m/2m3: 0-0 2m4-2m7: 0-0 3m+: 0-2
Track: LH: 0-1 RH: 0-1 Tight: 0-1 Gall: 0-1
Aids: Bl: 0-0 Vi: 0-0 Tstrap: 0-0
Best Rating: 81 3/00 Tram 2m6f yld-sft Ch

I'm For Waiting

93 **71**

6-y-o ch g Democratic (USA)-Faustelerie (Faustus (USA))
J C McConnochie J C McConnochie

Placings:0550006P6/060145-430 (1940)
2001/02: 20^{4}G, 16^{3}G, 21^{0}GS

	Starts	1st	2nd	3rd	Win & Pl
Hurdles	3	0	0	1	320
Career Total	**18**	**1**	**0**	**1**	**1818**

76	11/00	MRas	2m3f110y	G(0-90)HHdl	G-S	£1498

Total win prize-money £1498

Going: Sf: 0-0 GS: 0-1 Gd: 0-2 GF: - Fm: 0-0
Distance: 2m/2m3: 0-1 2m4-2m7: 0-2 3m+: 0-0
Track: LH: 0-2 RH: 0-1 Tight: 0-2 Gall: 0-1
Aids: Bl: 0-0 Vi: 0-0 Tstrap: 0-0
Best Rating: 76 11/00 MRas 2m3f110y gd-sft Hdl

I'm Imposin (IRE)

93f **103f**

6-y-o b g Posen (USA)-Mrs Doeskin (IRE) (Buckskin (FR))
Mrs A J Perrett Nicholas Cooper

Placings:663 (4887)
2001/02: 16^{6}G, 16^{6}G, 18^{3}GF

	Starts	1st	2nd	3rd	Win & Pl
NH Flat	3	0	0	1	295
Career Total	**3**	**0**	**0**	**1**	**295**

Going: Sf: 0-0 GS: 0-0 Gd: 0-2 GF: - Fm: 0-1
Distance: 2m/2m3: 0-3 2m4-2m7: 0-0 3m+: 0-0
Track: LH: 0-1 RH: 0-2 Tight: 0-1 Gall: 0-0
Aids: Bl: 0-0 Vi: 0-0 Tstrap: 0-0
Best Rating: 103 2/02 Kemp 2m good NHF

Fair form in bumpers on a sound surface.

I'm The Man

103(106h) (105h)**106**

11-y-o ro g Say Primula-Vinovia (Ribston)
Mrs Dianne Sayer (Mrs E Slack 12/1) A Slack

Placings:*60/0*5403/**434143/1220U21F505**3130/**P**P013 **11/4313F**-45P**0P3P63F01** (3746)
2001/02: 20^{4}S, 24^{5}GF, 24^{P}F, 20^{0}GS, 24^{P}GF, 26^{3}GS, 24^{P}G, 26^{6}GS, 25^{3}S, 24^{F}G, 30^{0}S, 24^{1}S

	Starts	1st	2nd	3rd	Win & Pl
Hurdles	3	0	0	0	0
Chases	9	1	0	2	4528
Career Total	**52**	**9**	**3**	**10**	**43611**

106	2/02	Muss	3m	F(0-95)HCh	SFT	£3220
121	5/00	Ctml	3m6f	C(0-130)HCh	G-S	£7117
120	4/00	Carl	3m2f	F(0-95)HCh	G-S	£3851
113	4/00	Carl	2m4f110y	F(0-110)HCh	SFT	£3328
121	3/00	Muss	3m	E(0-115)HCh	G-F	£3657
97	2/99	Muss	3m	E(0-115)HHdl	GD	£2827
110	10/98	Sedg	3m3f	E(0-110)HCh	G-S	£4320
89	5/98	Hexm	3m1f	E(0-115)HCh	G-F	£2490
92	3/98	Hexm	2m4f110y	F(0-100)HCh	SFT	£3288

Total win prize-money £34101

Going: Sf: 1-4 GS: 0-3 Gd: 0-2 GF: - Fm: 0-3
Distance: 2m/2m3: 0-0 2m4-2m7: 0-2 **3m+: 1-10**
Track: LH: 0-7 **RH: 1-5 Tight: 1-4** Gall: 0-1
Aids: Bl: 0-0 Vi: 0-0 Tstrap: 0-0
Best Rating: 121 6/00 Prth 3m good Ch

A winner at staying trips over hurdles and fences, he appreciates a decent surface. Had been out of form for a while before winning at Musselburgh in February 2002. Races prominently.

I'Ve No Say (IRE)

108(89h) (77h)**115**

9-y-o ch g Rising-Mon Democrat (Tanfirion)
Mrs P Sly G A Libson

Placings:400/10602**2U4**-0**3P44155150** (4814)
2001/02: 20^{0}GF, 22^{3}GF, 22^{P}G, 20^{4}G, 20^{4}S, 20^{1}GS, 20^{5}G, 20^{5}GS, 21^{1}S, 19^{5}S, 21^{0}GF

	Starts	1st	2nd	3rd	Win & Pl
Hurdles	1	0	0	0	0
Chases	10	2	0	1	7091
Career Total	**22**	**3**	**2**	**1**	**12520**

115	1/02	Fknm	2m5f110y	E(0-100)HCh	SFT	£2970
115	11/01	Hntg	2m4f110y	F(0-110)HCh	G-S	£3003
111	5/00	Strf	2m6f110y	D Hdl	G-F	£3428

Total win prize-money £9403

Going: Sf: 1-3 GS: 1-2 Gd: 0-3 GF: - Fm: 0-3
Distance: 2m/2m3: 0-0 **2m4-2m7: 2-11** 3m+: 0-0
Track: LH: 1-6 RH: 1-5 Tight: 1-3 Gall: 1-4
Aids: Bl: 0-0 Vi: 0-1 Tstrap: 0-0
Best Rating: 115 1/02 Fknm 2m5f110y soft Ch

Moderate chaser, he acts on most types of ground and is suited by positive tactics.

Iacacia (FR)

(101h)

6-y-o b/br g Silver Rainbow-Palencia (FR) (Taj Dewan)
Miss Venetia Williams J Williams & Mrs G Galvin

Placings:B4/U54-2 (0039)
2001/02: 22^{2}GS

	Starts	1st	2nd	3rd	Win & Pl
Hurdles	1	0	1	0	796
Career Total	**6**	**0**	**1**	**0**	**8481**

Going: Sf: 0-0 GS: 0-1 Gd: 0-0 GF: - Fm: 0-0
Distance: 2m/2m3: 0-0 2m4-2m7: 0-1 3m+: 0-0
Track: LH: 0-0 RH: 0-0 Tight: 0-0 Gall: 0-0
Aids: Bl: 0-0 Vi: 0-0 Tstrap: 0-0
Best Rating: 101 5/01 Extr 2m6f110y gd-sft Hdl

Iadora

90 **96**

7-y-o br m Gildoran-Combe Hill (Crozier)
J A B Old Mrs J A Fowler/the Kentish Men

Placings:*20*-U330 (3406)
2001/02: 17^{U}GS, 16^{3}S, 20^{3}GS, 20^{0}S

	Starts	1st	2nd	3rd	Win & Pl
Hurdles	4	0	0	2	928
Career Total	**6**	**0**	**1**	**2**	**1358**

Going: Sf: 0-2 GS: 0-2 Gd: 0-0 GF: - Fm: 0-0
Distance: 2m/2m3: 0-2 2m4-2m7: 0-2 3m+: 0-0
Track: LH: 0-0 RH: 0-4 Tight: 0-0 Gall: 0-1
Aids: Bl: 0-0 Vi: 0-0 Tstrap: 0-0
Best Rating: 100 11/00 Folk 2m1f110y heavy NHF

Iambe De La See (FR)

108 **119**

6-y-o b m Useful (FR)-Reine Mati (SWI) (Matahawk)
N J Henderson Elite Racing Club

Placings:412-1 (0493)
2001/02: 17^{1}G

	Starts	1st	2nd	3rd	Win & Pl
Hurdles	1	1	0	0	2765
Career Total	**4**	**2**	**1**	**0**	**7320**

119	5/01	Hrfd	2m1f	E Hdl	GD	£2765
109	4/01	NAbb	2m1f	E Hdl	SFT	£3192

Total win prize-money £5957

Going: Sf: 0-0 GS: 0-0 Gd: 1-1 GF: - Fm: 0-0
Distance: **2m/2m3: 1-1** 2m4-2m7: 0-0 3m+: 0-0

Track: LH: 0-0 **RH: 1-1** Tight: 0-0 Gall: 0-0
Aids: Bl: 0-0 Vi: 0-0 Tstrap: 0-0
Best Rating: 119 5/01 Hrfd 2m1f good Hdl

Ibal (FR)

81(105c) (137c)**144**
6-y-o b g Balsamo (FR)-Quart D'Hekla (FR) (Quart De Vin (FR))
Mrs N Smith Tony Hayward And Barry Fulton

Placings:3335/0F21312-24020P **(4301)**
2001/02: 16^{2}S, 16^{4}S, 16^{0}G, 16^{2}HY, 16^{0}S, 22^{P}HY

	Starts	1st	2nd	3rd	Win & Pl
Hurdles	3	0	0	0	0
Chases	3	0	2	0	5606
Career Total	**17**	**2**	**4**	**4**	**48101**

141 3/01 Sand 2m110y B HHdl HVY £23200
125 1/01 Leic 2m E Hdl HVY £3209
Total win prize-money £26410

Going: Sf: 0-5 GS: 0-0 Gd: 0-1 GF: - Fm: 0-0
Distance: 2m/2m3: 0-5 2m4-2m7: 0-1 3m+: 0-0
Track: LH: 0-4 RH: 0-2 Tight: 0-1 Gall: 0-1
Aids: Bl: 0-0 Vi: 0-0 Tstrap: 0-0
Best Rating: 144 4/01 Aint 2m110y heavy Hdl

Ex-French, he has a high cruising speed. Very much at home on bottomless ground, so conditions were ideal when he landed the 2001 Imperial Cup in good style and when runner-up in a valuable handicap at Aintree. Held in novice chases and in a couple of warm handicap hurdles in 2001/02.

Ibin St James

94(88h) (90h)**89**
8-y-o b g Salse (USA)-St James's Antigua (IRE) (Law Society (USA))
M Bradstock (J S Moore 20/2) Dave Breakspear

Placings:04/P11301001/P0P0P-P04P **(4849)**
2001/02: 27^{P}G, 24^{0}G, 26^{4}GS, 24^{P}G

	Starts	1st	2nd	3rd	Win & Pl
Hurdles	3	0	0	0	284
Chases	1	0	0	0	0
Career Total	**20**	**4**	**0**	**1**	**11301**

117 3/00 Hntg 3m2f E(0-115)HHdl SFT £2887
115 12/99 Towc 3m E(0-115)HHdl GD £2547
109 9/99 Hrfd 3m2f E(0-115)HHdl GD £3113
93 8/99 Worc 3m F(0-95)HHdl SFT £2045
Total win prize-money £10594

Going: Sf: 0-0 GS: 0-1 Gd: 0-3 GF: - Fm: 0-0
Distance: 2m/2m3: 0-0 2m4-2m7: 0-0 3m+: 0-4
Track: LH: 0-2 RH: 0-2 Tight: 0-2 Gall: 0-0
Aids: Bl: 0-0 Vi: 0-0 Tstrap: 0-0
Best Rating: 117 3/00 Hntg 3m2f soft Hdl

Ibis Rochelais (FR)

111(108h) (115h)**133**
6-y-o b g Passing Sale (FR)-Ta Rochelaise (FR) (Carmont (FR))
A Ennis (T Casey 4/5) A T A Wates

Placings:F2/3P-134252F **(4115)**
2001/02: 17^{1}GS, 16^{3}G, 20^{4}G, 16^{2}G, 16^{5}HY, 20^{2}S, 21^{F}G

	Starts	1st	2nd	3rd	Win & Pl
Hurdles	3	1	0	1	4224
Chases	4	0	2	0	2579
Career Total	**11**	**1**	**3**	**2**	**9093**

115 5/01 Folk 2m1f110y E Hdl G-S £3080
Total win prize-money £3080

Going: Sf: 0-2 GS: 1-1 Gd: 0-4 GF: - Fm: 0-0
Distance: 2m/2m3: 1-4 2m4-2m7: 0-3 3m+: 0-0
Track: LH: 0-0 **RH: 1-7 Tight: 1-1** Gall: 0-0
Aids: Bl: 0-0 Vi: 0-0 Tstrap: 0-0
Best Rating: 133 2/02 Sand 2m4f110y soft Ch

A decent performer over hurdles, he promises to be better over fences. Will stay two and a half miles.

Icare D'Oudairies (FR)

98 **108**
6-y-o ch g Port Etienne (FR)-Vellea (FR) (Cap Martin (FR))
A Dickman Mike Smallman

Placings:*100*/2400-1500 **(3785)**
2001/02: 20^{1}S, 20^{5}HY, 24^{0}S, 20^{0}S

	Starts	1st	2nd	3rd	Win & Pl
Hurdles	4	1	0	0	2926
Career Total	**11**	**2**	**1**	**0**	**5715**

108 12/01 Weth 2m4f110y E(0-105)HHdl SFT £2926
102 1/00 Hayd 2m H NHF SFT £1771
Total win prize-money £4697

Going: Sf: 1-4 GS: 0-0 Gd: 0-0 GF: - Fm: 0-0
Distance: 2m/2m3: 0-0 **2m4-2m7: 1-3** 3m+: 0-1
Track: LH: 1-4 RH: 0-0 Tight: 0-0 Gall: 0-2
Aids: Bl: 0-0 Vi: 0-0 Tstrap: 0-0
Best Rating: 108 12/01 Weth 2m4f110y soft Hdl

Best caught fresh. He has been successful in a bumper and over hurdles. Acts on a soft surface and stays two miles four furlongs.

Ice

105 **119**
6-y-o b g Polar Falcon (USA)-Sarabah (IRE) (Ela-Mana-Mou)
S E Kettlewell (M Johnston 2/9) Uncle Jacks Pub

Placings:113F **(2755)**
2001/02: 16^{1}G, 17^{1}S, 17^{3}HY, 17^{F}GS

	Starts	1st	2nd	3rd	Win & Pl
Hurdles	4	2	0	1	6963
Career Total	**4**	**2**	**0**	**1**	**6963**

100 11/01 Sedg 2m1f D Hdl SFT £3584
119 9/01 Prth 2m110y E Hdl GD £3017
Total win prize-money £6601

Going: Sf: 1-2 GS: 0-1 Gd: 1-1 GF: - Fm: 0-0
Distance: 2m/2m3: 2-4 2m4-2m7: 0-0 3m+: 0-0
Track: LH: 1-2 RH: 1-2 **Tight: 1-2** Gall: 0-0
Aids: Bl: 0-0 Vi: 0-2 Tstrap: 0-0
Best Rating: 119 9/01 Prth 2m110y good Hdl

Won on his debut over hurdles and followed up under a penalty at Sedgefield. Has won on good and soft ground, both on the Flat and over hurdles. Fell fatally at Bangor in December. (DEAD)

Ice Cool Lad (IRE)

109 **104**
8-y-o b g Glacial Storm (USA)-My Serena (No Argument)
R Rowe Ann & John Symes

Placings:*0*/065PP/15PP-032FP10 **(4511)**
2001/02: 20^{0}GF, 21^{3}G, 20^{2}GS, 21^{F}G, 21^{P}S, 18^{1}HY, 20^{0}G

	Starts	1st	2nd	3rd	Win & Pl
Chases	7	1	1	1	4618
Career Total	**17**	**2**	**1**	**1**	**7790**

104 2/02 Font 2m2f E(0-105)HCh HVY £3234
104 12/00 Font 2m4f F(0-100)HCh SFT £3172
Total win prize-money £6406

Going: Sf: 1-2 GS: 0-1 Gd: 0-3 GF: - Fm: 0-1
Distance: 2m/2m3: 1-1 2m4-2m7: 0-6 3m+: 0-0
Track: LH: 0-2 RH: 0-3 **Tight: 1-7** Gall: 0-0
Aids: Bl: 0-0 Vi: 0-0 Tstrap: 0-0
Best Rating: 104 2/02 Font 2m2f heavy Ch

A low-grade handicapper, he stays two and a half miles and likes to get his toe in. Goes well at Fontwell.

Ice Crystal

98 **115**
5-y-o b g Slip Anchor-Crystal Fountain (Great Nephew)
S Woodman Fortune Racing

Placings:R42411-2PP **(2850)**
2001/02: 21^{2}GS, 22^{P}S, 21^{P}G

	Starts	1st	2nd	3rd	Win & Pl
Hurdles	3	0	1	0	1561
Career Total	**9**	**2**	**2**	**0**	**9073**

109 4/01 Font 2m6f110y E Hdl GD £2639
96 4/01 Plum 2m5f E Hdl HVY £3528
Total win prize-money £6167

Going: Sf: 0-1 GS: 0-1 Gd: 0-1 GF: - Fm: 0-0
Distance: 2m/2m3: 0-0 2m4-2m7: 0-3 3m+: 0-0
Track: LH: 0-0 RH: 0-3 Tight: 0-0 Gall: 0-0
Aids: Bl: 0-0 Vi: 0-0 Tstrap: 0-0
Best Rating: 115 10/01 Kemp 2m5f gd-sft Hdl

Scored a double over hurdles on two starts in the spring of 2001. A shade unlucky not to make a winning seasonal debut, hedisappointed subsequently. He is suited by two and a half miles and cut in the ground.

Ice Cube

92(99h) (86h)**86**
6-y-o b g Rakaposhi King-Arctic Rymes (Rymer)
Mrs L Williamson Miss Judy Eaton

Placings:F000302003250/300530-P00350100 **(4843)**
2001/02: 21^{P}S, 20^{0}GS, 20^{0}G, 20^{3}G, 20^{5}HY, 21^{0}S, 16^{1}S, 16^{0}S, 17^{0}G

	Starts	1st	2nd	3rd	Win & Pl
Hurdles	2	0	0	0	0
Chases	7	1	0	1	3921
Career Total	**28**	**1**	**2**	**5**	**6480**

86 2/02 Tntn 2m110y E(0-100)HCh SFT £3428
Total win prize-money £3429

Going: Sf: 1-5 GS: 0-1 Gd: 0-3 GF: - Fm: 0-0
Distance: 2m/2m3: 1-3 2m4-2m7: 0-6 3m+: 0-0
Track: LH: 0-7 **RH: 1-2 Tight: 1-8** Gall: 0-0
Aids: Bl: 0-0 Vi: 0-0 Tstrap: 0-0
Best Rating: 86 4/02 Bang 2m1f110y good Ch

Modest hurdler/chaser. Acts with cut.

Icealion

67 **43**
4-y-o b g Lion Cavern (USA)-Icecapped (Caerleon (USA))
M W Easterby J W P Curtis

Placings:0 **(3251)**
2001/02: 16^{0}S

	Starts	1st	2nd	3rd	Win & Pl
Hurdles	1	0	0	0	
Career Total	**1**	**0**	**0**	**0**	

Going: Sf: 0-1 GS: 0-0 Gd: 0-0 GF: - Fm: 0-0
Distance: 2m/2m3: 0-1 2m4-2m7: 0-0 3m+: 0-0
Track: LH: 0-1 RH: 0-0 Tight: 0-0 Gall: 0-1
Aids: Bl: 0-0 Vi: 0-0 Tstrap: 0-0
Best Rating: 43 1/02 Newc 2m soft Hdl

Iceberge (IRE)

103f 97f

6-y-o b g Glacial Storm (USA)-Laura Daisy (Buckskin (FR))
Ian Williams Mcmahon (contractors Services) Ltd

Placings:*622* **(4499)**
2001/02: 16^{6}GS, 16^{2}GS, 16^{2}G

	Starts	1st	2nd	3rd	Win & Pl
NH Flat	3	0	2	0	1118
Career Total	**3**	**0**	**2**	**0**	**1118**

Going: Sf: 0-0 GS: 0-2 Gd: 0-1 GF: - Fm: 0-0
Distance: 2m/2m3: 0-3 2m4-2m7: 0-0 3m+: 0-0
Track: LH: 0-2 RH: 0-1 Tight: 0-0 Gall: 0-0
Aids: Bl: 0-0 Vi: 0-0 Tstrap: 0-0
Best Rating: 97 3/02 Hayd 2m good NHF

Runner-up in a bumper on only his second start at Warwick in March and second again at Haydock three weeks later.

Icefire Dancer

78 50

9-y-o b m Arctic Lord-Super Gambler (Lighter)
N Waggott Mrs J Waggott

Placings:P056/P/4100-0 **(4332)**
2001/02: 21^{0}S

	Starts	1st	2nd	3rd	Win & Pl
Hurdles	1	0	0	0	
Career Total	**10**	**1**	**0**	**0**	**1907**

82 5/00 Hexm 2m4f110y E Hdl GD £1906
Total win prize-money £1907

Going: Sf: 0-1 GS: 0-0 Gd: 0-0 GF: - Fm: 0-0
Distance: 2m/2m3: 0-0 2m4-2m7: 0-1 3m+: 0-0
Track: LH: 0-1 RH: 0-0 Tight: 0-1 Gall: 0-0
Aids: Bl: 0-0 Vi: 0-0 Tstrap: 0-1
Best Rating: 82 5/00 Hexm 2m4f110y good Hdl

Icelandic Lord

9-y-o b g Arctic Lord-Arctic Ander (Leander)
Mrs L B Normile (N G Richards 17/3) Mrs L Normile

Placings:FP/P-PP **(4907)**
2001/02: 20^{P}GF, 20^{P}GF

	Starts	1st	2nd	3rd	Win & Pl
Hurdles	1	0	0	0	0
Chases	1	0	0	0	0
Career Total	**5**	**0**	**0**	**0**	

Going: Sf: 0-0 GS: 0-0 Gd: 0-0 GF: - Fm: 0-2
Distance: 2m/2m3: 0-0 2m4-2m7: 0-2 3m+: 0-0
Track: LH: 0-0 RH: 0-2 Tight: 0-1 Gall: 0-0
Aids: Bl: 0-0 Vi: 0-0 Tstrap: 0-0
Best Rating:

Icenfriendly (IRE)

9-y-o b g Lancastrian-No Ice (Laurence O)
D Brace David Brace

Placings:P **(0972)**
2001/02: 24^{P}GF

	Starts	1st	2nd	3rd	Win & Pl
Chases	1	0	0	0	
Career Total	**1**	**0**	**0**	**0**	

Going: Sf: 0-0 GS: 0-0 Gd: 0-0 GF: - Fm: 0-1
Distance: 2m/2m3: 0-0 2m4-2m7: 0-0 3m+: 0-1
Track: LH: 0-1 RH: 0-0 Tight: 0-1 Gall: 0-0
Aids: Bl: 0-0 Vi: 0-0 Tstrap: 0-0
Best Rating:

Iceni Queen

4-y-o b f Formidable (USA)-Queen Warrior (Daring March)
D J Minty (W McKeown 15/10) D J Minty

Placings:P **(4183)**
2001/02: 17^{P}S

	Starts	1st	2nd	3rd	Win & Pl
Hurdles	1	0	0	0	
Career Total	**1**	**0**	**0**	**0**	

Going: Sf: 0-1 GS: 0-0 Gd: 0-0 GF: - Fm: 0-0
Distance: 2m/2m3: 0-1 2m4-2m7: 0-0 3m+: 0-0
Track: LH: 0-0 RH: 0-1 Tight: 0-1 Gall: 0-0
Aids: Bl: 0-0 Vi: 0-0 Tstrap: 0-0
Best Rating:

Ichi Beau (IRE)

114(101h) (116h)154

8-y-o b g Convinced-May As Well (Kemal (FR))
Ferdy Murphy Mrs Fiona Butterly

Placings:*0000/0/504/*11F52312-351233264 **(4838)**
2001/02: 16^{3}G, 16^{5}G, 16^{1}G, 16^{2}G, 16^{3}GS, 16^{3}S, 16^{2}G, 16^{6}G, 16^{4}G

	Starts	1st	2nd	3rd	Win & Pl
Hurdles	1	0	0	1	1120
Chases	8	1	2	2	19131
Career Total	**25**	**4**	**4**	**4**	**53172**

154 12/01 Donc 2m110y C(0-135)HCh GD £6097
138 4/01 Ayr 2m C Ch GD £6301
131 11/00 Aint 2m D(0-115)HCh G-S £10383
128 10/00 Carl 2m F(0-100)HCh G-S £2886
Total win prize-money £25669

Going: Sf: 0-1 GS: 0-1 Gd: 1-7 GF: - Fm: 0-0
Distance: **2m/2m3: 1-9** 2m4-2m7: 0-0 3m+: 0-0
Track: **LH: 1-8** RH: 0-1 Tight: 0-3 **Gall: 1-3**
Aids: Bl: 0-0 Vi: 0-0 **Tstrap: 1-9**
Best Rating: 154 2/02 Kemp 2m good Ch

He improved hand over fist as a chaser in 2000/01 and is now a formidable front runner. Best over two miles, he is suited by a flat, left-handed track and is often tongue tied these days.

Ickford Okey

10-y-o b g Broadsword (USA)-Running Kiss (Deep Run)
Mrs S S Harbour P J Morgan

Placings:*00*/50U/2P6 **(4763)**
2001/02: 24^{2}GS, 22^{P}GS, 24^{6}GF

	Starts	1st	2nd	3rd	Win & Pl
Chases	3	0	1	0	864
Career Total	**8**	**0**	**1**	**0**	**864**

Going: Sf: 0-0 GS: 0-2 Gd: 0-0 GF: - Fm: 0-1
Distance: 2m/2m3: 0-0 2m4-2m7: 0-1 3m+: 0-2
Track: LH: 0-2 RH: 0-1 Tight: 0-1 Gall: 0-1
Aids: Bl: 0-0 Vi: 0-0 Tstrap: 0-0
Best Rating: 111 3/02 Strf 3m gd-sft Ch

A winning pointer, he was narrowly beaten in a novice hunter chase at Stratford and Huntingdon in the spring of 2002 and ought to have won on both occasions. One to be wary of.

Iconic

8-y-o b g Reprimand-Miami Melody (Miami Springs)
Darren Page Darren Page

Placings:*0/64/0206P/4*-P **(4416)**
2001/02: 20^{P}S

	Starts	1st	2nd	3rd	Win & Pl
Chases	1	0	0	0	
Career Total	**10**	**0**	**1**	**0**	**1068**

Going: Sf: 0-1 GS: 0-0 Gd: 0-0 GF: - Fm: 0-0
Distance: 2m/2m3: 0-0 2m4-2m7: 0-1 3m+: 0-0
Track: LH: 0-0 RH: 0-0 Tight: 0-1 Gall: 0-0
Aids: Bl: 0-0 Vi: 0-0 Tstrap: 0-0
Best Rating: 00 7/00 [illegible] 2m110y gd-fm Ch

Idaho D'Ox (FR)

113 138

6-y-o b g Bad Conduct (USA)-Queseda (FR) (Quart De Vin (FR))
M C Pipe (T Civel 6/6) The Dionysius Partnership

Placings:4F00F462F66-O4131232001 20 **(4950a)**
2001/02: 20°GS, 20^{4}VS, 22^{1}GF, 21^{3}G, 16^{1}S, 21^{2}S, 17^{3}HY, 16^{2}S, 20^{0}GS, 17^{0}G, 16^{1}G, 16^{2}G, 16^{0}G

	Starts	1st	2nd	3rd	Win & Pl
Hurdles	11	3	3	2	25310
Chases	2	0	0	0	2125
Career Total	**24**	**3**	**4**	**2**	**36164**

125 4/02 Winc 2m E Hdl GD £2884
120 12/01 Sand 2m110y D(0-110)HHdl SFT £7117
93 10/01 Extr 2m6f110y E Hdl G-F £2450
Total win prize-money £12452

Going: Sf: 1-4 GS: 0-2 Gd: 1-5 GF: - Fm: 1-1
Distance: **2m/2m3: 2-7** 2m4-2m7: 1-6 3m+: 0-0
Track: LH: 0-5 **RH: 2-5** Tight: 0-3 Gall: 0-2
Aids: Bl: 0-3 **Vi: 3-10** Tstrap: 0-0
Best Rating: 138 4/02 Aint 2m110y good Hdl

Won a small novice event on his British debut in the autumn of 2001 when equipped with a visor, and subsequently won a Sandown handicap. Held when upped in class, but when dropped back to novice company, he won with ease before running well at Aintree. Stays two miles-six but effective at shorter trips, and seems to handle any ground.

Idalgo De Guye (FR)

110 125

6-y-o b g Luchiroverte (IRE)-Victoire De Guye (FR) (Brezzo (FR))
G A Harker (H A N Orde-Powlett 29/11) Lord Bolton

Placings:03360F43-PP021PP **(4233)**

2001/02: 20^{P}G, 21^{P}G, 20^{0}G, 20^{2}HY, 25^{1}S, 25^{P}GS, 32^{P}GS

	Starts	1st	2nd	3rd	Win & Pl
Chases	7	1	1	0	8330
Career Total	**15**	**1**	**1**	**3**	**11483**

125 12/01 Ayr 3m1f D(0-125)HCh SFT £6734

Total win prize-money £6734

Going: Sf: 1-2 GS: 0-2 Gd: 0-3 GF: - Fm: 0-0
Distance: 2m/2m3: 0-0 2m4-2m7: 0-4 **3m+: 1-3**
Track: **LH: 1-6** RH: 0-1 Tight: 0-2 Gall: 0-2
Aids: Bl: 0-0 Vi: 0-0 Tstrap: 0-0
Best Rating: 125 12/01 Ayr 3m1f soft Ch

An ex-French import, he was not at all disgraced when runner-up to Direct Access at Carlisle and won readily at Ayr.

Ideal Collonges (FR)

76 58

6-y-o br g Video Rock (FR)-Queen Collonges (FR) (Danoso)
A C Wilson Cooper Wilson

Placings:454-PP4 **(4668)**
2001/02: 20^{P}GF, 16^{P}S, 17^{4}GF

	Starts	1st	2nd	3rd	Win & Pl
Hurdles	3	0	0	0	0
Career Total	**6**	**0**	**0**	**0**	**0**

Going: Sf: 0-1 GS: 0-0 Gd: 0-0 GF: - Fm: 0-2
Distance: 2m/2m3: 0-2 2m4-2m7: 0-1 3m+: 0-0
Track: LH: 0-2 RH: 0-1 Tight: 0-2 Gall: 0-1
Aids: Bl: 0-0 Vi: 0-0 Tstrap: 0-0
Best Rating: 84 11/00 Tntn 2m1f good Hdl

Moderate hurdler who has not progressed with racing.

Ideal De L'Ile (FR)

92 73

6-y-o ch g Aelan Hapi (USA)-Ad Vitam Eternam (FR) (Cap Martin (FR))
H D Daly Stephen Lambert

Placings:5P **(3357)**
2001/02: 20^{5}S, 24^{P}HY

	Starts	1st	2nd	3rd	Win & Pl
Hurdles	2	0	0	0	0
Career Total	**2**	**0**	**0**	**0**	**0**

Going: Sf: 0-2 GS: 0-0 Gd: 0-0 GF: - Fm: 0-0
Distance: 2m/2m3: 0-0 2m4-2m7: 0-1 3m+: 0-1
Track: LH: 0-2 RH: 0-0 Tight: 0-0 Gall: 0-0
Aids: Bl: 0-0 Vi: 0-0 Tstrap: 0-0
Best Rating: 73 12/01 Uttx 2m4f110y soft Hdl

Ideal De Vie (FR)

93 97

6-y-o b g Chef De Clan Ii (FR)-Qualite De La Vie (FR) (Carmarthen (FR))
R H Alner P M De Wilde

Placings:330-5524353 **(4641)**
2001/02: 17^{5}GS, 21^{5}G, 21^{2}G, 20^{4}S, 17^{3}HY, 19^{5}G, 24^{3}G

	Starts	1st	2nd	3rd	Win & Pl
Chases	7	0	1	2	3910
Career Total	**10**	**0**	**1**	**4**	**4918**

Going: Sf: 0-2 GS: 0-1 Gd: 0-4 GF: - Fm: 0-0
Distance: 2m/2m3: 0-2 2m4-2m7: 0-4 3m+: 0-1
Track: LH: 0-2 RH: 0-2 Tight: 0-3 Gall: 0-0
Aids: Bl: 0-0 Vi: 0-0 Tstrap: 0-0
Best Rating: 97 2/02 Plum 2m1f heavy Ch

Ex-French recruit with placed form over hurdles and fences. Placed over fences in this country. Best at around two miles in soft ground.

Ideal Du Bois Beury (FR)

113 134

6-y-o b/br g Useful (FR)-Pampa Star (FR) (Pampabird)
M C Pipe (P Chemin 2/6) D A Johnson

Placings:5-132110P **(4667)**
2001/02: 16^{1}S, 17^{3}GS, 20^{2}GS, 20^{1}S, 20^{1}S, 25^{0}GS, 20^{P}G

	Starts	1st	2nd	3rd	Win & Pl
Hurdles	7	3	1	1	33202
Career Total	**8**	**3**	**1**	**1**	**34259**

134 2/02 Asct 2m4f B(0-150)HHdl SFT £18087
116 1/02 Leic 2m4f110y E(0-110)HHdl SFT £5648
120 12/01 Newb 2m110y B Hdl SFT £7410

Total win prize-money £31146

Going: Sf: 3-3 GS: 0-3 Gd: 0-1 GF: - Fm: 0-0
Distance: 2m/2m3: 1-2 **2m4-2m7: 2-4** 3m+: 0-1
Track: LH: 1-4 **RH: 2-3** Tight: 0-2 **Gall: 1-2**
Aids: Bl: 0-0 Vi: 0-0 Tstrap: 0-0
Best Rating: 134 2/02 Asct 2m4f soft Hdl

Progressive hurdler, who scored a double at the start of 2002, the second of which was a valuable Ascot handicap, but did not appear to stay three miles one when well beaten at Cheltenham next time. Stays two and a half miles and handles soft ground.

Idealko (FR)

(75h)

6-y-o b g Kadalko (FR)-Belfaster (FR) (Royal Charter (FR))
Ian Williams Mrs Maggie Bull

Placings:62/4/1111-0 **(1957)**
2001/02: 25^{0}G

	Starts	1st	2nd	3rd	Win & Pl
Hurdles	1	0	0	0	
Career Total	**8**	**4**	**1**	**0**	**12462**

4/01 Lrsy 2m1f Ch GD £3201
6/00 Diep 2m1f110y Ch GD £2882
6/00 Roya 2m2f Ch GD £2690
6/00 Gemz 2m3f Ch GD £1537

Total win prize-money £10310

Going: Sf: 0-0 GS: 0-0 Gd: 0-1 GF: - Fm: 0-0
Distance: 2m/2m3: 0-0 2m4-2m7: 0-0 3m+: 0-1
Track: LH: 0-0 RH: 0-0 Tight: 0-0 Gall: 0-0
Aids: Bl: 0-0 Vi: 0-0 Tstrap: 0-0
Best Rating: 75 11/01 Wwck 3m1f good Hdl

Winner of four chases in France, but was well beaten on his British debut at Warwick in November of 2001. Acts on good ground.

Ideas Man (IRE)

6-y-o b g Executive Perk-Emmodee (Bowling Pin)
W M Brisbourne Id Technology Group Plc

Placings:50 **(2786)**
2001/02: 16^{5}GF, 16^{0}G

	Starts	1st	2nd	3rd	Win & Pl
NH Flat	2	0	0	0	0
Career Total	**2**	**0**	**0**	**0**	**0**

Going: Sf: 0-0 GS: 0-0 Gd: 0-1 GF: - Fm: 0-1
Distance: 2m/2m3: 0-2 2m4-2m7: 0-0 3m+: 0-0
Track: LH: 0-0 RH: 0-2 Tight: 0-0 Gall: 0-0
Aids: Bl: 0-0 Vi: 0-0 Tstrap: 0-0
Best Rating: 81 12/01 Ludl 2m good NHF

Idiome (FR)

105(98c) (126c)121

6-y-o b g Djarvis (FR)-Asterie L'Ermitage (FR) (Hamster (FR))
Mrs L C Taylor (S & W Kalley 16/6) Mrs L C Taylor

Placings:43/P32-2062F2416333 **(4828)**
2001/02: 17^{2}G, 20^{0}VS, 17^{6}VS, 19^{2}S, 16^{F}G, 19^{2}S, 16^{4}GS, 18^{1}HY, 20^{6}S, 20^{3}GS, 16^{3}GS, 16^{3}G

	Starts	1st	2nd	3rd	Win & Pl
Hurdles	7	1	2	3	10163
Chases	5	0	1	0	1409
Career Total	**17**	**1**	**4**	**5**	**18976**

121 2/02 Font 2m2f110y D(0-115)HHdl HVY £5352

Total win prize-money £5353

Going: Sf: 1-4 GS: 0-3 Gd: 0-3 GF: - Fm: 0-0
Distance: **2m/2m3: 1-9** 2m4-2m7: 0-3 3m+: 0-0
Track: **LH: 1-6** RH: 0-4 **Tight: 1-1** Gall: 0-4
Aids: Bl: 0-0 Vi: 0-0 Tstrap: 0-0
Best Rating: 126 1/02 Hrfd 2m3f soft Ch

Fair hurdler/chaser, acts on soft ground. Has won at up to two and a quarter miles, needs to learn to settle to get two and a half.

Idiot's Star

89 89

10-y-o b g Idiots Delight-Trikkala Star (Tachypous)
Noel T Chance Enda Hunston

Placings:5F000/5014P0/62PP2-0P **(3462)**
2001/02: 17^{0}G, 20^{P}S

	Starts	1st	2nd	3rd	Win & Pl
Chases	2	0	0	0	
Career Total	**18**	**1**	**2**	**0**	**9885**

94 2/00 Thur 3m Ch HVY £3588

Total win prize-money £3588

Going: Sf: 0-1 GS: 0-0 Gd: 0-1 GF: - Fm: 0-0
Distance: 2m/2m3: 0-1 2m4-2m7: 0-1 3m+: 0-0
Track: LH: 0-2 RH: 0-0 Tight: 0-0 Gall: 0-1
Aids: Bl: 0-0 Vi: 0-0 Tstrap: 0-0
Best Rating: 105 1/01 Leop 2m5f soft Ch

Idlewild (IRE)

7-y-o br g Phardante (FR)-Delia Murphy (Golden Love)
Miss A Nolan Mrs Vanessa Ramm

Placings:P **(0094)**
2001/02: 25^{P}S

	Starts	1st	2nd	3rd	Win & Pl
Chases	1	0	0	0	
Career Total	**1**	**0**	**0**	**0**	

Going: Sf: 0-1 GS: 0-0 Gd: 0-0 GF: - Fm: 0-0
Distance: 2m/2m3: 0-0 2m4-2m7: 0-0 3m+: 0-1
Track: LH: 0-1 RH: 0-0 Tight: 0-0 Gall: 0-0
Aids: Bl: 0-0 Vi: 0-0 Tstrap: 0-0
Best Rating:

Idole Des Fontaines (FR)

104 **122**

6-y-o b g Le Riverain (FR)-Dame D'Avril (FR) (Brezzo (FR))

C Diard S Gabbour

Placings:2402132131-10**4031406**

2001/02: 19^{1}HY, 19^{0}VS, 20^{4}S, 26^{0}VS, 23^{3}VS, 21^{1}HO, 21^{4}HY, 24^{0}GS, 23^{6}VS

	Starts	1st	2nd	3rd	Win & Pl
Hurdles	2	1	0	0	9699
Chases	7	1	0	1	26499
Career Total	**19**	**5**	**3**	**3**	**84638**

2/02	Ange	2m5f	Ch	HLD	£9056
5/01	Nant	2m3f110y	Hdl	HVY	£9699
4/01	Autl	2m1f110y	Hdl	HVY	£9699
2/01	Ange	2m5f	Ch	VS	£9214
12/00	Autl	2m4f110y	Ch	HVY	£11527

Total win prize-money £49195

Going: Sf: 1-3 GS: 0-1 Gd: 0-0 GF: - Fm: 0-0
Distance: 2m/2m3: 0-0 **2m4-2m7: 2-6** 3m+: 0-3
Track: LH: 0-2 RH: 0-0 Tight: 0-0 Gall: 0-1
Aids: Bl: 0-3 Vi: 0-0 Tstrap: 0-1
Best Rating: 122 3/02 Chel 3m110y gd-sft Ch

Successful stayer on the Flat in France. He has won over fences and hurdles at distances ranging from two miles one to two miles five furlongs. Acts on heavy ground.

If And But (IRE)

97 **81**

9-y-o ch g Capitano-Stormy Night (Deep Run)

D J Wintle D J Wintle

Placings:*00500*/336F5340256/13151P3**FP**/0004605 0 **(3876)**

2001/02: 20^{0}G, 20^{0}GF, 16^{0}GF, 20^{4}S, 17^{6}GF, 16^{0}HY, 22^{5}G, 20^{0}S

	Starts	1st	2nd	3rd	Win & Pl
Hurdles	8	0	0	0	0
Career Total	**34**	**3**	**1**	**5**	**10365**

104	9/99	Worc	2m	E(0-115)HHdl	SFT	£2308
104	7/99	Dang	2m1f	D Hdl	G-F	£3452
96	7/99	Wolv	2m	E Hdl	G-S	£2189

Total win prize-money £7951

Going: Sf: 0-3 GS: 0-0 Gd: 0-2 GF: - Fm: 0-3
Distance: 2m/2m3: 0-3 2m4-2m7: 0-5 3m+: 0-0
Track: LH: 0-5 RH: 0-2 Tight: 0-2 Gall: 0-1
Aids: Bl: 0-0 Vi: 0-0 Tstrap: 0-0
Best Rating: 104 9/99 Worc 2m soft Hdl

Ifni Du Luc (FR)

108(109h) (120h)**143**

6-y-o b/br m Chamberlin (FR)-Acca Du Luc (FR) (Djarvis (FR))

N J Henderson P J White

Placings:1224/10200-**2121P** **(4297)**

2001/02: 22^{2}GS, 16^{1}G, 20^{2}G, 22^{1}S, 21^{P}HY

	Starts	1st	2nd	3rd	Win & Pl
Chases	5	2	2	0	19760
Career Total	**14**	**4**	**5**	**0**	**36491**

143	1/02	Hayd	2m6f	B Ch	SFT	£10185
114	12/01	Winc	2m	D Ch	GD	£4095
121	12/00	Font	2m2f110y	C(0-130)HHdl	SFT	£7046
109	12/99	Sand	2m110y	D Hdl	G-S	£3046

Total win prize-money £24372

Going: Sf: 1-2 GS: 0-1 Gd: 1-2 GF: - Fm: 0-0
Distance: 2m/2m3: 1-1 2m4-2m7: 1-4 3m+: 0-0
Track: LH: 0-1 **RH: 1-2** Tight: 0-1 Gall: 0-0
Aids: Bl: 0-0 Vi: 0-0 Tstrap: 0-0
Best Rating: 143 1/02 Hayd 2m6f soft Ch

A moderate handicapper over hurdles, she made a pleasing start to her chasing career over the minimum trip late in 2001 and won over two miles six at Haydock. Acts on good ground and soft.

Ifrane Balima (FR)

102 **78**

6-y-o ch g Video Rock (FR)-Balima Des Saccart (FR) (Quart De Vin (FR))

J C Tuck The Kermit Klub

Placings:000F00 **(3812)**

2001/02: 16^{0}GS, 17^{0}S, 17^{0}HY, 16^{F}S, 16^{0}GS, 17^{0}S

	Starts	1st	2nd	3rd	Win & Pl
Hurdles	6	0	0	0	
Career Total	**6**	**0**	**0**	**0**	

Going: Sf: 0-4 GS: 0-2 Gd: 0-0 GF: - Fm: 0-0
Distance: 2m/2m3: 0-6 2m4-2m7: 0-0 3m+: 0-0
Track: LH: 0-3 RH: 0-3 Tight: 0-4 Gall: 0-1
Aids: Bl: 0-0 Vi: 0-0 Tstrap: 0-0
Best Rating: 78 12/01 Leic 2m soft Hdl

Igloo D'Estruval (FR)

100(106c) (110c)**104**

6-y-o br g Garde Royale-Jalousie (FR) (Blockhaus)

Mrs L C Taylor Mrs L C Taylor

Placings:0/01P21U-F3454044P **(4599)**

2001/02: 25^{F}GF, 21^{3}S, 21^{4}G, 22^{5}S, 29^{4}G, 26^{0}G, 24^{4}G, 22^{4}G, 25^{P}GF

	Starts	1st	2nd	3rd	Win & Pl
Hurdles	6	0	0	1	1192
Chases	3	0	0	0	1150
Career Total	**16**	**2**	**1**	**1**	**19147**

114	1/01	Donc	3m	D Ch	GD	£4420
	6/00	Autl	2m1f110y	Ch	HLD	£11527

Total win prize-money £15947

Going: Sf: 0-2 GS: 0-0 Gd: 0-5 GF: - Fm: 0-2
Distance: 2m/2m3: 0-0 2m4-2m7: 0-4 3m+: 0-5
Track: LH: 0-3 RH: 0-2 Tight: 0-2 Gall: 0-2
Aids: Bl: 0-0 Vi: 0-4 Tstrap: 0-0
Best Rating: 114 1/01 Donc 3m good Ch

Fair ex-French chaser, won a novice chase at Doncaster in January 2001, but has had jumping problems since and has mixed chasing and hurdling. Stays three miles. Looks best suited by good to soft/soft ground. Has worn a visor.

Igloux Royal (FR)

6-y-o b g Lights Out (FR)-Onde Royale (FR) (Danoso)

Mrs J A Saunders Mr & Mrs S E Bown, D Yard, A Boughen

Placings:*0* **(2460)**

2001/02: 16^{0}S

	Starts	1st	2nd	3rd	Win & Pl
NH Flat	1	0	0	0	
Career Total	**1**	**0**	**0**	**0**	

Going: Sf: 0-1 GS: 0-0 Gd: 0-0 GF: - Fm: 0-0
Distance: 2m/2m3: 0-1 2m4-2m7: 0-0 3m+: 0-0
Track: LH: 0-1 RH: 0-0 Tight: 0-0 Gall: 0-0
Aids: Bl: 0-0 Vi: 0-0 Tstrap: 0-0
Best Rating:

Ijika (FR)

108 **100**

6-y-o ch g Aelan Hapi (USA)-Belle Des Airs (FR) (Saumon (FR))

H D Daly Brian Luby & Roy Van Gelder

Placings:*00*-26033 **(4848)**

2001/02: 22^{2}S, 21^{6}HY, 24^{0}S, 16^{3}GS, 16^{3}G

	Starts	1st	2nd	3rd	Win & Pl
Hurdles	5	0	1	2	2383
Career Total	**7**	**0**	**1**	**2**	**2383**

Going: Sf: 0-3 GS: 0-1 Gd: 0-1 GF: - Fm: 0-0
Distance: 2m/2m3: 0-2 2m4-2m7: 0-2 3m+: 0-1
Track: LH: 0-3 RH: 0-2 Tight: 0-2 Gall: 0-0
Aids: Bl: 0-0 Vi: 0-0 Tstrap: 0-0
Best Rating: 104 4/02 Strf 2m110y good Hdl

From the family of Edmond, he showed nothing in the mud in bumpers, but made a much more pleasing effort in his debut over hurdles at Stratford in November. Held since, he is effective at up to an extended two miles six furlongs.

Ikemba (IRE)

5-y-o b g Executive Perk-Ardglass Pride (Golden Love)

B P J Baugh M W & A N Harris

Placings:*00*P **(4300)**

2001/02: 16^{0}S, 16^{0}S, 20^{P}HY

	Starts	1st	2nd	3rd	Win & Pl
NH Flat	2	0	0	0	0
Hurdles	1	0	0	0	0
Career Total	**3**	**0**	**0**	**0**	

Going: Sf: 0-3 GS: 0-0 Gd: 0-0 GF: - Fm: 0-0
Distance: 2m/2m3: 0-2 2m4-2m7: 0-1 3m+: 0-0
Track: LH: 0-2 RH: 0-1 Tight: 0-0 Gall: 0-0
Aids: Bl: 0-0 Vi: 0-0 Tstrap: 0-0
Best Rating: 95 1/02 Hayd 2m soft NHF

Il Capitano

109(110h) (116h)**125**

5-y-o ch g Be My Chief (USA)-Taza (Persian Bold)

P F Nicholls Mark Tincknell

Placings:25-152363621 **(4885)**

2001/02: 17^{1}F, 16^{5}G, 17^{2}GS, 20^{3}S, 17^{6}GS, 16^{3}S, 20^{6}GS, 19^{2}F, 27^{1}GF

	Starts	1st	2nd	3rd	Win & Pl
Hurdles	9	2	2	2	13272
Career Total	**11**	**2**	**3**	**2**	**14076**

116	4/02	Font	3m3f	D(0-125)HHdl	G-F	£3482
95	10/01	Tntn	2m1f	E Hdl	FRM	£3276

Total win prize-money £6759

Going: Sf: 0-2 GS: 0-3 Gd: 0-1 GF: - Fm: 2-3
Distance: 2m/2m3: 1-6 2m4-2m7: 0-2 3m+: 1-1
Track: LH: 0-3 **RH: 1-5 Tight: 2-4** Gall: 0-0
Aids: Bl: 0-0 Vi: 0-0 Tstrap: 0-0
Best Rating: 116 4/02 Font 3m3f gd-fm Hdl

Fair novice hurdler, won an ordinary novice on fast ground at Taunton in October and has found life a bit tougher in handicap company before stepping up successfully to three miles-three at Fontwell in April 2002. Handles an easy surface, but possibly best on faster.

Il Cavaliere

99 **120**

7-y-o b g Mtoto-Kalmia (Miller's Mate)
Mrs M Reveley The Thoughtful Partnership

Placings: *15214*/322 **(4014)**
2001/02: 20^{3}G, 16^{2}S, 20^{2}GS

	Starts	1st	2nd	3rd	Win & Pl
Hurdles	3	0	2	1	3216
Career Total	**8**	**2**	**3**	**1**	**7805**

117	10/99	Sedg	2m1f	H NHF	GD	£1647
115	6/99	MRas	1m5f110y	H NHF	G-F	£1493

Total win prize-money £3142

Going: Sf: 0-1 GS: 0-1 Gd: 0-1 GF: - Fm: 0-0
Distance: 2m/2m3: 0-1 2m4-2m7: 0-2 3m+: 0-0
Track: LH: 0-3 RH: 0-0 Tight: 0-0 Gall: 0-3
Aids: Bl: 0-0 Vi: 0-0 Tstrap: 0-0
Best Rating: 126 4/00 Aint 2m110y good NHF

A winner of bumpers before being successful on the Flat. He has shown fair form over hurdles, including when second at Doncaster in January 2002.

Il Destino

80 **63**

7-y-o b g Casteddu-At First Sight (He Loves Me)
J G M O'Shea K W Bell

Placings: P-5U **(0827)**
2001/02: 17^{5}G, 16^{U}GF

	Starts	1st	2nd	3rd	Win & Pl
Hurdles	2	0	0	0	0
Career Total	**3**	**0**	**0**	**0**	**0**

Going: Sf: 0-0 GS: 0-0 Gd: 0-1 GF: - Fm: 0-1
Distance: 2m/2m3: 0-2 2m4-2m7: 0-0 3m+: 0-0
Track: LH: 0-1 RH: 0-1 Tight: 0-1 Gall: 0-0
Aids: Bl: 0-0 Vi: 0-0 Tstrap: 0-0
Best Rating: 68 5/01 Hrfd 2m1f good Hdl

Il Falco (FR)

97 **68**

8-y-o ch g Polar Falcon (USA)-Scimitarlia (USA) (Diesis)
R Curtis Mrs R A Smith

Placings: 4/P0-3 **(0060)**
2001/02: 17^{3}GS

	Starts	1st	2nd	3rd	Win & Pl
Hurdles	1	0	0	1	238
Career Total	**4**	**0**	**0**	**1**	**238**

Going: Sf: 0-0 GS: 0-1 Gd: 0-0 GF: - Fm: 0-0
Distance: 2m/2m3: 0-1 2m4-2m7: 0-0 3m+: 0-0
Track: LH: 0-0 RH: 0-1 Tight: 0-1 Gall: 0-0
Aids: Bl: 0-0 Vi: 0-0 Tstrap: 0-0
Best Rating: 105 3/98 Plum 2m1f good Hdl

Il'Athou (FR)

112(107h) (95h)**145**

6-y-o b g Lute Antique (FR)-Va Thou Line (FR) (El Badr)
S E H Sherwood Lady Thompson

Placings: 2/011P0-111P **(4189)**
2001/02: 17^{1}S, 20^{1}G, 16^{1}G, 16^{P}GS

	Starts	1st	2nd	3rd	Win & Pl
Chases	4	3	0	0	25164
Career Total	**10**	**5**	**1**	**0**	**31873**

145	1/02	Asct	2m	A Ch	GD	£16750
142	11/01	Hntg	2m4f110y	D Ch	GD	£4280
142	10/01	Bang	2m1f110y	D Ch	SFT	£4134
116	1/01	Folk	2m1f110y	F(0-105)HHdl	HVY	£2226
109	12/00	Folk	2m1f110y	E Hdl	HVY	£3042

Total win prize-money £30432

Going: Sf: 1-1 GS: 0-1 Gd: 2-2 GF: - Fm: 0-0
Distance: **2m/2m3: 2-3** 2m4-2m7: 1-1 3m+: 0-0
Track: LH: 1-2 **RH: 2-2** Tight: 1-1 Gall: 1-2
Aids: Bl: 0-0 Vi: 0-0 Tstrap: 0-0
Best Rating: 145 1/02 Asct 2m good Ch

Impressed on his chasing debut at Bangor in October, jumping well and making all. Followed up in similar fashion at Huntingdon and completed the hat-trick at Ascot in January 2002, but he pulled up in the Arkle at Cheltenham in March 2002. Suited by soft ground. Has won from two miles to two and a half. Jumps well.

Ile De Librate

105(100h) (97h)**111**

8-y-o b g Librate-Little Missile (Ile De Bourbon (USA))
R J O'Sullivan Skampcargo Racing Partnership

Placings: 222F02214/4360/**22**/5-421212 **(1443)**
2001/02: 22^{4}GF, 22^{2}GF, 24^{1}G, 23^{2}GF, 23^{1}GF, 26^{2}GF

	Starts	1st	2nd	3rd	Win & Pl
Hurdles	2	0	1	0	724
Chases	4	2	2	0	10313
Career Total	**22**	**3**	**10**	**1**	**19701**

111	9/01	Worc	2m7f110y	D Ch	G-F	£3900
111	7/01	Strf	3m	D Ch	GD	£4338
98	3/98	Plum	2m4f	E Hdl	GD	£2763

Total win prize-money £11002

Going: Sf: 0-0 GS: 0-0 Gd: 1-1 GF: - Fm: 1-5
Distance: 2m/2m3: 0-0 2m4-2m7: 0-2 **3m+: 2-4**
Track: **LH: 2-5** RH: 0-0 **Tight: 1-4** Gall: 0-0
Aids: Bl: 0-0 Vi: 0-0 Tstrap: 0-0
Best Rating: 111 9/01 Font 3m2f110y gd-fm Ch

Fair chaser, stays three miles, acts on a sound surface.

Ile Distinct (IRE)

91(99h) (79h)**76+**

8-y-o b g Dancing Dissident (USA)-Golden Sunlight (Ile De Bourbon (USA))
K R Pearce Keith R Pearce

Placings: 2/40-FF0454 **(1544)**
2001/02: 19^{F}G, 20^{F}GF, 20^{0}GF, 20^{4}GF, 20^{5}GF, 17^{4}G

	Starts	1st	2nd	3rd	Win & Pl
Hurdles	4	0	0	0	0
Chases	2	0	0	0	0
Career Total	**9**	**0**	**1**	**0**	**668**

Going: Sf: 0-0 GS: 0-0 Gd: 0-2 GF: - Fm: 0-4
Distance: 2m/2m3: 0-2 2m4-2m7: 0-4 3m+: 0-0
Track: LH: 0-4 RH: 0-2 Tight: 0-2 Gall: 0-0
Aids: Bl: 0-0 Vi: 0-0 Tstrap: 0-0
Best Rating: 96 9/99 Kels 2m2f gd-fm Hdl

Ilewin Janine (IRE)

101(99h) (94h)**95**

11-y-o b m Soughaan (USA)-Mystery Queen (Martinmas)
G Brown Tom Segrue

Placings: *604*/560F4P2/22/216/0PP/002111513-052P41P **(4312)**
2001/02: 17^{0}G, 16^{5}S, 20^{2}G, 16^{P}HY, 16^{4}HY, 16^{1}S, 20^{P}HY

	Starts	1st	2nd	3rd	Win & Pl
Hurdles	2	0	0	0	0
Chases	5	1	1	0	5241
Career Total	**34**	**6**	**6**	**1**	**18831**

95	2/02	Folk	2m	F(0-90)HCh	SFT	£4065
99	1/01	Leic	2m	G(0-90)HHdl	HVY	£1981
93	9/00	Hrfd	2m3f	G(0-95)HCh	G-S	£2795
80	9/00	Font	2m2f110y	G(0-95)HHdl	GD	£2352
78	9/00	Sedg	2m1f	G(0-95)HHdl	GD	£1547
99	5/98	Uttx	2m	G(0-95)HHdl	G-F	£1595

Total win prize-money £14336

Going: Sf: 1-5 GS: 0-0 Gd: 0-2 GF: - Fm: 0-0
Distance: **2m/2m3: 1-5** 2m4-2m7: 0-2 3m+: 0-0
Track: LH: 0-5 **RH: 1-2 Tight: 1-5** Gall: 0-0
Aids: Bl: 0-0 Vi: 0-0 Tstrap: 0-0
Best Rating: 99 1/01 Leic 2m heavy Hdl

Moderate dual -purpose performer, she was in good heart in the 2000/01 season winning four times on firm ground. She has since proved she can handle the mud, winning over the minimum distance in a Folkestone hurdle in February 2002.

Ilico Ii (FR)

(115h) (140h)

6-y-o b g Trebrook (FR)-Tulipp D'Avril (FR) (Saumon (FR))
P J Hobbs Terry Warner

Placings: 216214-BF **(1768)**
2001/02: 16^{B}G, 17^{F}G

	Starts	1st	2nd	3rd	Win & Pl
Hurdles	1	0	0	0	0
Chases	1	0	0	0	0
Career Total	**8**	**2**	**2**	**0**	**52321**

140	4/01	Aint	2m110y	A Hdl	SFT	£29000
	9/00	Autl	2m2f	Hdl	VS	£10567

Total win prize-money £39567

Going: Sf: 0-0 GS: 0-0 Gd: 0-2 GF: - Fm: 0-0
Distance: 2m/2m3: 0-2 2m4-2m7: 0-0 3m+: 0-0
Track: LH: 0-1 RH: 0-1 Tight: 0-0 Gall: 0-0
Aids: Bl: 0-0 Vi: 0-0 Tstrap: 0-0
Best Rating: 140 4/01 Ayr 2m gd-fm Hdl

Useful ex-French hurdler/chaser. (DEAD)

Illineylad (IRE)

101(91h) (83h)**91**

8-y-o b g Whitehall Bridge-Illiney Girl (Lochnager)
Mrs N S Sharpe The Illiney Group

Placings: 064/60/PF03443P **(2781)**
2001/02: 23^{P}GF, 24^{F}GF, 20^{0}GF, 24^{3}GF, 25^{4}G, 25^{4}S, 25^{3}G, 24^{P}G

	Starts	1st	2nd	3rd	Win & Pl
Hurdles	2	0	0	1	269
Chases	6	0	0	1	864
Career Total	**13**	**0**	**0**	**2**	**1133**

Going: Sf: 0-1 GS: 0-0 Gd: 0-3 GF: - Fm: 0-4
Distance: 2m/2m3: 0-0 2m4-2m7: 0-1 3m+: 0-7
Track: LH: 0-4 RH: 0-4 Tight: 0-2 Gall: 0-0
Aids: Bl: 0-0 Vi: 0-0 Tstrap: 0-0
Best Rating: 91 10/01 Hrfd 3m1f110y good Ch

Former point winner, he stays three miles and is better on a sounder surface.

Ilnamar (FR)

107(119h) (160h)**149**

6-y-o b g Officiel (FR)-Quillemare (FR) (Le Pontet (FR))

M C Pipe Joe Moran

Placings:22F1323/P0121-54U11 **(4676)**

2001/02: 20^5S, 19^4G, 16US, 21^1GS, 20^1G

	Starts	1st	2nd	3rd	Win & Pl
Hurdles	2	2	0	0	111600
Chases	3	0	0	0	2209
Career Total	**17**	**5**	**4**	**2**	**182503**

160	4/02	Aint	2m4f	A Hdl	GD	£69600
157	3/02	Chel	2m5f	A HHdl	G-S	£42000
	12/00	Autl	2m2f	Hdl	HVY	£14409
	10/00	Autl	2m1f110y	Ch	HVY	£10567
	2/00	Pau	2m2f	Hdl	HVY	£4803

Total win prize-money £141379

Going: Sf: 0-2 GS: 1-1 Gd: 1-2 GF: - Fm: 0-0
Distance: 2m/2m3: 0-1 **2m4-2m7: 2-4** 3m+: 0-0
Track: **LH: 2-4** RH: 0-1 Tight: 1-1 Gall: 1-3
Aids: Bl: 0-0 Vi: 0-0 Tstrap: 0-0
Best Rating: 160 4/02 Aint 2m4f good Hdl

Another French-trained import for the Pipe yard, he won twice over two miles in heavy ground at Auteuil over both types of obstacle. Showed promise on his British debut at Newbury behind Cyfor Malta, but failed to build on that and was returned to hurdles for a sparkling victory in the Coral Cup at the 2002 Festival and followed up in the Aintree Hurdle. Acts on soft ground. Suited by distances around two and a half miles.

Image

5-y-o b m Seymour Hicks (FR)-Sugar Owl (Bold Owl)

C J Drewe Mrs Jane Murfett

Placings:0 **(4391)**

2001/02: 16^0S

	Starts	1st	2nd	3rd	Win & Pl
NH Flat	1	0	0	0	
Career Total	**1**	**0**	**0**	**0**	

Going: Sf: 0-1 GS: 0-0 Gd: 0-0 GF: - Fm: 0-0
Distance: 2m/2m3: 0-1 2m4-2m7: 0-0 3m+: 0-0
Track: LH: 0-0 RH: 0-1 Tight: 0-0 Gall: 0-0
Aids: Bl: 0-0 Vi: 0-0 Tstrap: 0-0
Best Rating: mfy

Image De Marque II (FR)

120 **141**

6-y-o b m Royal Charter (FR)-Tourbrune (FR) (Pamponi (FR))

M C Pipe D A Johnson

Placings:2F/210222FF-PP041111223 **(3244)**

2001/02: 17^PGF, 17^PGF, 19^0GF, 17^4GF, 16^1G, 16^1GF, 17^1GS, 21^1GS, 16^2S, 16^2G, 16^3GS

	Starts	1st	2nd	3rd	Win & Pl
Hurdles	11	4	2	1	37705
Career Total	**21**	**5**	**7**	**1**	**63205**

131	11/01	Newb	2m5f	D(0-110)HHdl	G-S	£3696
128	11/01	Tntn	2m1f	D(0-120)HHdl	G-S	£4777
116	11/01	Winc	2m	F(0-100)HHdl	G-F	£2527
117	11/01	Chel	2m110y	D(0-110)HHdl	GD	£9204
	6/00	Autl	2m4f110y	Ch	VS	£11527

Total win prize-money £31732

Going: Sf: 0-1 GS: 2-3 Gd: 1-2 GF: - Fm: 1-5
Distance: **2m/2m3: 3-10** 2m4-2m7: 1-1 3m+: 0-0
Track: LH: 2-4 **RH: 2-7** Tight: 1-3 Gall: 1-1
Aids: Bl: 0-0 Vi: 0-0 **Tstrap: 4-7**
Best Rating: 141 12/01 Sand 2m110y soft Hdl

Ex-French hurdler who took advantage of a lenient handicap mark and the addition of a tongue tie to complete a fine four-timer in the autumn of 2001. Ran arguably her best race when beaten in a valuable Sandown handicap and has contuned to run well since. Effective from two miles to two miles five.

Imaginaire (USA)

111(103h) **139**

7-y-o b g Quest For Fame-Hail The Dancer (USA) (Green Dancer (USA))

Miss Venetia Williams Favourites Racing Ltd

Placings:P66/00**243406P/02200125-33214F** **(4835)**

2001/02: 22^3HY, 16^3G, 16^2S, 20^1GS, 16^4GS, 25^FG

	Starts	1st	2nd	3rd	Win & Pl
Chases	6	1	1	2	16189
Career Total	**26**	**2**	**5**	**3**	**62928**

139	3/02	Strf	2m4f	D Ch	G-S	£5284
120	1/01	Folk	2m6f110y	E Hdl	HVY	£2744

Total win prize-money £8029

Going: Sf: 0-2 GS: 1-2 Gd: 0-2 GF: - Fm: 0-0
Distance: 2m/2m3: 0-3 **2m4-2m7: 1-2** 3m+: 0-1
Track: **LH: 1-2** RH: 0-3 **Tight: 1-1** Gall: 0-0
Aids: Bl: 0-0 Vi: 0-0 Tstrap: 0-2
Best Rating: 139 3/02 Strf 2m4f gd-sft Ch

Decent chaser, failed to win in France, but has been successful in this country. He has had wind problems. Suited by two and a half miles and soft ground.

Imaginative

91 **90**

5-y-o b g Last Tycoon-Imaginary (IRE) (Dancing Brave (USA))

W Jenks The Glazeley Partnership

Placings:00-5100000 **(4573)**

2001/02: 16^5G, 21^1GF, 16^0S, 20^0S, 24^0G, 21^0S, 20^0G

	Starts	1st	2nd	3rd	Win & Pl
Hurdles	7	1	0	0	2671
Career Total	**9**	**1**	**0**	**0**	**2671**

90	10/01	Ludl	2m5f	E(0-105)HHdl	G-F	£2670

Total win prize-money £2671

Going: Sf: 0-3 GS: 0-0 Gd: 0-3 GF: - Fm: 1-1
Distance: 2m/2m3: 0-2 **2m4-2m7: 1-4** 3m+: 0-1
Track: LH: 0-3 **RH: 1-4** Tight: 0-1 Gall: 0-0
Aids: **Bl: 1-5** Vi: 0-0 Tstrap: 0-0
Best Rating: 90 10/01 Ludl 2m5f gd-fm Hdl

A somewhat quirky sort, he won a small race at Ludlow in October. Has a turn of foot.

Imago Ii (FR)

96 **102**

6-y-o b g Chamberlin (FR)-Pensee D'Amour (FR) (Porto Rafti (FR))

Ferdy Murphy Tony Eaves

Placings:1-340 **(3696)**

2001/02: 20^3G, 20^4S, 16^0S

	Starts	1st	2nd	3rd	Win & Pl
Hurdles	3	0	0	1	594
Career Total	**4**	**1**	**0**	**1**	**2754**

110	2/01	Hayd	2m	H NHF	SFT	£2159

Total win prize-money £2160

Going: Sf: 0-2 GS: 0-0 Gd: 0-1 GF: - Fm: 0-0
Distance: 2m/2m3: 0-1 2m4-2m7: 0-2 3m+: 0-0
Track: LH: 0-3 RH: 0-0 Tight: 0-0 Gall: 0-2
Aids: Bl: 0-0 Vi: 0-0 Tstrap: 0-0
Best Rating: 110 2/01 Hayd 2m soft NHF

Winner of a soft-ground Haydock bumper in early 2001, made a fair start over hurdles at the same track in the autumn.

Imari

5-y-o gr m Rock City-Misty Goddess (IRE) (Godswalk (USA))

R G Frost J F O'Donovan

Placings:P **(1994)**

2001/02: 17^PS

	Starts	1st	2nd	3rd	Win & Pl
Hurdles	1	0	0	0	
Career Total	**1**	**0**	**0**	**0**	

Going: Sf: 0-1 GS: 0-0 Gd: 0-0 GF: - Fm: 0-0
Distance: 2m/2m3: 0-1 2m4-2m7: 0-0 3m+: 0-0
Track: LH: 0-1 RH: 0-0 Tight: 0-1 Gall: 0-0
Aids: Bl: 0-0 Vi: 0-0 Tstrap: 0-0
Best Rating:

Imlight (FR)

90 **128**

6-y-o b h Lights Out (FR)-Star Dancer (FR) (Mitsoupam (FR))

G Macaire Mrs Ying Shen

Placings:11-14F14 **(3376)**

2001/02: 17^1S, 17^4HY, 19^FHO, 20^1HO, 16^4G

	Starts	1st	2nd	3rd	Win & Pl
Chases	5	2	0	0	18571
Career Total	**7**	**4**	**0**	**0**	**26255**

11/01	Autl	2m4f110y	Ch	HLD	£11639
10/01	Comp	2m1f110y	Ch	SFT	£4074
8/00	Vich	2m110y	Hdl	VS	£3842
8/00	Vich	2m110y	Hdl	HLD	£3842

Total win prize-money £23397

Going: Sf: 1-2 GS: 0-0 Gd: 0-1 GF: - Fm: 0-0
Distance: 2m/2m3: 1-4 2m4-2m7: 1-1 3m+: 0-0
Track: LH: 0-0 RH: 0-1 Tight: 0-0 Gall: 0-0
Aids: Bl: 0-0 Vi: 0-0 Tstrap: 0-1
Best Rating: 128 1/02 Kemp 2m good Ch

A winner on the Flat, over hurdles and over fences in France. Fourth on his British debut at Kempton over two miles. He acts on a soft surface and probably best suited to two and a half miles.

Immaterial (IRE)

5-y-o b g Barathea (IRE)-La Maree (Tumble Wind (USA))

N J Henderson W V M W & Mrs E S Robins

Placings:213-P **(0026)**

2001/02: 20^PG

	Starts	1st	2nd	3rd	Win & Pl
Hurdles	1	0	0	0	
Career Total	**4**	**1**	**1**	**1**	**6104**

111	11/00	Newb	2m110y	C Hdl	G-S	£4550

Total win prize-money £4550

Going: Sf: 0-0 GS: 0-0 Gd: 0-1 GF: - Fm: 0-0
Distance: 2m/2m3: 0-0 2m4-2m7: 0-1 3m+: 0-0
Track: LH: 0-0 RH: 0-1 Tight: 0-0 Gall: 0-1
Aids: Bl: 0-0 Vi: 0-0 Tstrap: 0-0
Best Rating: 111 11/00 Newb 2m110y gd-sft Hdl

Imnotalady

40f 64f

4-y-o ch f Shalford (IRE)-Lissahane Lass (Daring March)
P R Hedger J J Whelan

Placings:*4* (3290)
2001/02: 17^{4}S

	Starts	1st	2nd	3rd	Win & Pl
NH Flat	1	0	0	0	0
Career Total	**1**	**0**	**0**	**0**	**0**

Going: Sf: 0-1 GS: 0-0 Gd: 0-0 GF: - Fm: 0-0
Distance: 2m/2m3: 0-1 2m4-2m7: 0-0 3m+: 0-0
Track: LH: 0-0 RH: 0-0 Tight: 0-1 Gall: 0-0
Aids: Bl: 0-0 Vi: 0-0 Tstrap: 0-0
Best Rating: 64 1/02 Folk 2m1f110y soft NHF

Impek (FR)

106(122h) (153h)134++

6-y-o b g Lute Antique (FR)-Attualita (FR) (Master Thatch)
Miss H C Knight Jim Lewis

Placings:2150-24423 (4902)
2001/02: 16^{2}GS, 16^{4}G, 16^{4}S, 16^{2}GS, 16^{3}G

	Starts	1st	2nd	3rd	Win & Pl
Hurdles	5	0	2	1	22370
Career Total	**9**	**1**	**3**	**1**	**28847**

131	2/01	Ludl	2m	E Hdl	G-S	£3006

Total win prize-money £3007

Going: Sf: 0-1 GS: 0-2 Gd: 0-2 GF: - Fm: 0-0
Distance: 2m/2m3: 0-5 2m4-2m7: 0-0 3m+: 0-0
Track: LH: 0-2 RH: 0-3 Tight: 0-0 Gall: 0-1
Aids: Bl: 0-1 Vi: 0-0 Tstrap: 0-0
Best Rating: 153 4/02 Sand 2m110y good Hdl

A French import, he showed useful form in novice hurdles in 2000/2001 and has since continued to run well without winning, as when just touched off in the 2002 Imperial Cup. Seems well suited by a right-handed track and good to soft ground.Scored on chasing debut early in the new season.

Impenny

71 44

9-y-o br m Impecunious-My Molly (Averof)
J White G Ivall

Placings:*00*F0/0 (0348)
2001/02: 16^{0}G

	Starts	1st	2nd	3rd	Win & Pl
Hurdles	1	0	0	0	
Career Total	**5**	**0**	**0**	**0**	

Going: Sf: 0-0 GS: 0-0 Gd: 0-1 GF: - Fm: 0-0
Distance: 2m/2m3: 0-1 2m4-2m7: 0-0 3m+: 0-0
Track: LH: 0-1 RH: 0-0 Tight: 0-1 Gall: 0-0
Aids: Bl: 0-0 Vi: 0-0 Tstrap: 0-0
Best Rating: 60 12/98 Ludl 2m gd-sft NHF

Imperial De Thaix (FR)

(104h) (130h)

6-y-o b g Roi De Rome (USA)-Soiree D'Ete (FR) (Prove It Baby (USA))
M C Pipe J S Lammiman

Placings:16411PF-F1 (4818)
2001/02: 20^{F}S, 21^{1}GF

	Starts	1st	2nd	3rd	Win & Pl
Hurdles	1	1	0	0	10452
Chases	1	0	0	0	0
Career Total	**9**	**4**	**0**	**0**	**22918**

130	4/02	Chel	2m5f110y	B HHdl	G-F	£10452
130	1/01	Chep	3m	E Ch	G-S	£2960
151	12/00	Chep	2m3f110y	D Ch	SFT	£3838
	10/00	Nant	2m1f110y	Hdl	HVY	£3362

Total win prize-money £20613

Going: Sf: 0-1 GS: 0-0 Gd: 0-0 GF: - Fm: 1-1
Distance: 2m/2m3: 0-0 **2m4-2m7: 1-2** 3m+: 0-0
Track: **LH: 1-1** RH: 0-1 Tight: 0-0 **Gall: 1-1**
Aids: Bl: 0-0 Vi: 0-0 **Tstrap: 1-2**
Best Rating: 151 12/00 Chep 2m3f110y soft Ch

He looked a star in the making after recording two easy wins at Chepstow on his first outings in this country. Finished lame when beaten at Cheltenham in late January 2001, and was still in contention when falling in Aintree's John Hughes Trophy on his final start of the 2000/01 season. Took a heavy fall on his reappearance in 2002, but reverted successfully to hurdles at Cheltenham. Likely to stay beyond three miles, he acts on any ground.

Imperial Man (IRE)

90(72c) (70c)65

7-y-o b g Mandalus-The Foalicule (Imperial Fling (USA))
M J Gingell (John Paul Berry 20/7) Dr Tom Alexander

Placings:*3*/0000000*450-060*060**F**45**F**05P (2947)
2001/02: 17^{0}G, 20^{6}GF, 16^{0}G, 22^{0}G, 24^{6}GF, 16^{0}GF, 22^{F}S, 24^{4}G, 16^{5}S, 21^{F}G, 26^{0}G, 21^{5}GS, 20^{P}G

	Starts	1st	2nd	3rd	Win & Pl
NH Flat	3	0	0	0	0
Hurdles	6	0	0	0	0
Chases	4	0	0	0	0
Career Total	**24**	**0**	**0**	**1**	**440**

Going: Sf: 0-2 GS: 0-1 Gd: 0-7 GF: - Fm: 0-3
Distance: 2m/2m3: 0-4 2m4-2m7: 0-6 3m+: 0-3
Track: LH: 0-5 RH: 0-3 Tight: 0-5 Gall: 0-2
Aids: Bl: 0-0 Vi: 0-0 Tstrap: 0-1
Best Rating: 92 12/00 Clon 2m sft-hvy NHF

Imperial Rocket (USA)

88 120

5-y-o b/br g Northern Flagship (USA)-Starsawhirl (USA) (Star De Naskra (USA))
N J Henderson The Royal Ascot Racing Club

Placings:05-1 (0102)
2001/02: 18^{1}GF

	Starts	1st	2nd	3rd	Win & Pl
Hurdles	1	1	0	0	2639
Career Total	**3**	**1**	**0**	**0**	**2639**

120	5/01	Font	2m2f110y	E Hdl	G-F	£2639

Total win prize-money £2639

Going: Sf: 0-0 GS: 0-0 Gd: 0-0 GF: - Fm: 1-1
Distance: **2m/2m3: 1-1** 2m4-2m7: 0-0 3m+: 0-0
Track: **LH: 1-1** RH: 0-0 **Tight: 1-1** Gall: 0-0
Aids: Bl: 0-0 Vi: 0-0 Tstrap: 0-0
Best Rating: 120 5/01 Font 2m2f110y gd-fm Hdl

Impero

86 69

4-y-o b g Emperor Jones (USA)-Fight Right (FR) (Crystal Glitters (USA))
R J Armson (Miss B Sanders 7/8) R J Armson

Placings:565P0 (2397)
2001/02: 16^{5}GF, 16^{6}G, 16^{5}G, 16^{P}G, 16^{0}G

	Starts	1st	2nd	3rd	Win & Pl
Hurdles	5	0	0	0	0
Career Total	**5**	**0**	**0**	**0**	**0**

Going: Sf: 0-0 GS: 0-0 Gd: 0-4 GF: - Fm: 0-1
Distance: 2m/2m3: 0-5 2m4-2m7: 0-0 3m+: 0-0
Track: LH: 0-3 RH: 0-2 Tight: 0-0 Gall: 0-2
Aids: Bl: 0-0 Vi: 0-0 Tstrap: 0-0
Best Rating: 69 10/01 Weth 2m good Hdl

Impertio

107 124

8-y-o b g Primitive Rising (USA)-Silly Beggar (Silly Prices)
P Beaumont Mrs S Sunter

Placings:*4542/366326***33233/422F22331-0322U31U20P** (4897)
2001/02: 16^{0}S, 20^{3}S, 25^{2}GS, 28^{2}S, 25^{U}GS, 24^{3}S, 23^{1}S, 22^{U}S, 24^{2}HY, 21^{0}G, 24^{P}G

	Starts	1st	2nd	3rd	Win & Pl
Chases	11	1	3	2	12026
Career Total	**35**	**2**	**10**	**10**	**27293**

124	2/02	Leic	2m7f110y	D(0-125)HCh	SFT	£7150
124	4/01	Prth	2m	D Ch	HVY	£3698

Total win prize-money £10849

Going: Sf: 1-7 GS: 0-2 Gd: 0-2 GF: - Fm: 0-0
Distance: 2m/2m3: 0-1 2m4-2m7: 0-3 **3m+: 1-7**
Track: LH: 0-5 **RH: 1-6** Tight: 0-5 Gall: 0-1
Aids: Bl: 0-1 Vi: 0-0 Tstrap: 0-0
Best Rating: 124 3/02 Sthl 3m110y heavy Ch

He often makes the frame, but usually flatters to deceive and is totally untrustworthy. He was successful over fences at Leicester in February 2002, but has been held since. Acts on soft ground.

Impetuosity (IRE)

80 66

8-y-o ch m Imp Society (USA)-Catherine Clare (Sallust)
W J Reed W J Reed

Placings:06/0/040P (1340)
2001/02: 22^{0}G, 22^{4}GF, 22^{0}GF, 22^{P}GF

	Starts	1st	2nd	3rd	Win & Pl
Hurdles	4	0	0	0	0
Career Total	**7**	**0**	**0**	**0**	**0**

Going: Sf: 0-0 GS: 0-0 Gd: 0-1 GF: - Fm: 0-3
Distance: 2m/2m3: 0-0 2m4-2m7: 0-4 3m+: 0-0
Track: LH: 0-4 RH: 0-0 Tight: 0-4 Gall: 0-0
Aids: Bl: 0-0 Vi: 0-0 Tstrap: 0-0
Best Rating: 66 6/01 NAbb 2m6f gd-fm Hdl

Impetus (GER)

96 79

6-y-o b g Lomitas-Ile De Re (GER) (Readily (ARG))

P Wegmann P Wegmann

Placings:22P000-3 (0355)

2001/02: 17³GS

	Starts	1st	2nd	3rd	Win & Pl
Hurdles	1	0	0	1	410
Career Total	7	0	2	1	1700

Going: Sf: 0-0 GS: 0-1 Gd: 0-0 GF: - Fm: 0-0
Distance: 2m/2m3: 0-1 2m4-2m7: 0-0 3m+: 0-0
Track: LH: 0-1 RH: 0-0 Tight: 0-1 Gall: 0-0
Aids: Bl: 0-0 Vi: 0-0 Tstrap: 0-0
Best Rating: 79 5/01 Bang 2m1f gd-sft Hdl

Impish Lad

88 66

4-y-o b g Imp Society (USA)-Madonna Da Rossi (Mtoto)

D W Whillans (M J Polglase 16/10) Chas N Whillans

Placings:4F5PP (4898)

2001/02: 17⁴S, 16ᶠS, 16⁵S, 16ᴾHY, 16ᴾG

	Starts	1st	2nd	3rd	Win & Pl
Hurdles	5	0	0	0	0
Career Total	5	0	0	0	0

Going: Sf: 0-4 GS: 0-0 Gd: 0-1 GF: - Fm: 0-0
Distance: 2m/2m3: 0-5 2m4-2m7: 0-0 3m+: 0-0
Track: LH: 0-2 RH: 0-3 Tight: 0-2 Gall: 0-1
Aids: Bl: 0-0 Vi: 0-0 Tstrap: 0-0
Best Rating: 66 2/02 Muss 2m soft Hdl

Imprevu (FR)

6-y-o b g Roi De Rome (USA)-Badrapette (FR) (Bad Conduct (USA))

M C Pipe Stef Stefanou

Placings:*00*FP-P (0736)

2001/02: 17ᴾGS

	Starts	1st	2nd	3rd	Win & Pl
Hurdles	1	0	0	0	
Career Total	5	0	0	0	

Going: Sf: 0-0 GS: 0-1 Gd: 0-0 GF: - Fm: 0-0
Distance: 2m/2m3: 0-1 2m4-2m7: 0-0 3m+: 0-0
Track: LH: 0-1 RH: 0-0 Tight: 0-1 Gall: 0-0
Aids: Bl: 0-0 Vi: 0-0 Tstrap: 0-0
Best Rating: 86 10/00 Extr 2m1f good NHF

Imprevue (IRE)

102 74+

8-y-o ch m Priolo (USA)-Las Bela (Welsh Pageant)

R J O'Sullivan (Andrew Reid 18/8) P W Saunders

Placings:60/0 (3929)

2001/02: 16⁰HY

	Starts	1st	2nd	3rd	Win & Pl
Hurdles	1	0	0	0	
Career Total	3	0	0	0	0

Going: Sf: 0-1 GS: 0-0 Gd: 0-0 GF: - Fm: 0-0
Distance: 2m/2m3: 0-1 2m4-2m7: 0-0 3m+: 0-0
Track: LH: 0-1 RH: 0-0 Tight: 0-1 Gall: 0-0
Aids: Bl: 0-0 Vi: 0-0 Tstrap: 0-0
Best Rating: 74 2/00 Folk 2m1f110y gd-sft Hdl

Appreciated a combination of a drop in class and fast ground when winning a two and a half mile selling hurdle at Worcester July 2002.

Imps Reflection

99f 104f

5-y-o gr g Terimon-Carousella (Rousillon (USA))

N J Henderson Mrs C Bailey

Placings:*03* (4552)

2001/02: 17⁰G, 16³GF

	Starts	1st	2nd	3rd	Win & Pl
NH Flat	2	0	0	1	256
Career Total	2	0	0	1	256

Going: Sf: 0-0 GS: 0-0 Gd: 0-1 GF: - Fm: 0-1
Distance: 2m/2m3: 0-2 2m4-2m7: 0-0 3m+: 0-0
Track: LH: 0-1 RH: 0-1 Tight: 0-1 Gall: 0-1
Aids: Bl: 0-0 Vi: 0-0 Tstrap: 0-0
Best Rating: 104 4/02 Hntg 2m110y gd-fm NHF

Imps Way

7-y-o br m Nomadic Way (USA)-Dalton's Delight (Wonderful Surprise)

C Grant Roy Robinson

Placings:P0P (3996)

2001/02: 19ᴾGO, 21⁰G, 21ᴾG

	Starts	1st	2nd	3rd	Win & Pl
Chases	3	0	0	0	
Career Total	3	0	0	0	

Going: Sf: 0-2 GS: 0-1 Gd: 0-0 GF: - Fm: 0-0
Distance: 2m/2m3: 0-1 2m4-2m7: 0-1 3m+: 0-1
Track: LH: 0-3 RH: 0-0 Tight: 0-2 Gall: 0-1
Aids: Bl: 0-0 Vi: 0-0 Tstrap: 0-0
Best Rating:

Modest pointer. Well held in novice chases.

Imustgeton

78 45

8-y-o b m North Col-Double Stitch (Wolver Hollow)

H W Lavis C H Warner

Placings:*00*/05305P-P0 (0493)

2001/02: 19ᴾG, 17⁰G

	Starts	1st	2nd	3rd	Win & Pl
Hurdles	2	0	0	0	
Career Total	10	0	0	1	207

Going: Sf: 0-0 GS: 0-0 Gd: 0-2 GF: - Fm: 0-0
Distance: 2m/2m3: 0-1 2m4-2m7: 0-1 3m+: 0-0
Track: LH: 0-0 RH: 0-2 Tight: 0-0 Gall: 0-0
Aids: Bl: 0-0 Vi: 0-0 Tstrap: 0-2
Best Rating: 75 5/98 Worc 2m gd-fm NHF

In Contrast (IRE)

123 151

6-y-o b/br g Be My Native (USA)-Ballinamona Lady (IRE) (Le Bavard (FR))

P J Hobbs Peter Emery

Placings:*2/2110*-211F311 (4816)

2001/02: 16²G, 17¹G, 16¹G, 16ᶠGS, 16³GS, 16¹G, 21¹GF

	Starts	1st	2nd	3rd	Win & Pl
Hurdles	7	4	1	1	74271
Career Total	12	6	3	1	86505

144	4/02	Chel	2m5f110y	B Hdl	G-F	£19500
151	4/02	Aint	2m110y	A Hdl	GD	£29000
137	12/01	Newb	2m110y	D Hdl	GD	£4914
117	12/01	Chel	2m1f	B Hdl	GD	£8697
142	11/00	Chel	2m110y	B NHF	G-S	£7670
113	10/00	Chel	2m110y	H NHF	GD	£2964

Total win prize-money £72745

Going: Sf: 0-0 GS: 0-2 Gd: 3-4 GF: - Fm: 1-1
Distance: **2m/2m3: 3-6** 2m4-2m7: 1-1 3m+: 0-0
Track: **LH: 4-6** RH: 0-1 Tight: 1-1 **Gall: 3-3**
Aids: Bl: 0-0 Vi: 0-0 Tstrap: 0-0
Best Rating: 151 4/02 Aint 2m110y good Hdl

Placed in his two bumpers in Ireland, he joined Philip Hobbs and scored twice in the autumn of 2000, including a valuable event at Cheltenham. He was far from fluent and rather green when a beaten favourite on his hurdles bow at Cheltenham in October 2001, but won at that venue in December and followed up at Newbury towards the end of 2001. Did not look happy going right-handed at Ascot early in 2002. Third in the Supreme Novices' at the Cheltenham Festival, he returned to winning form at Aintree and followed up in a valuable affair at Cheltenham. Has a tendency to hang left.

In Extremis Ii (FR)

100(74c) (68c)95

6-y-o b g Useful (FR)-Princesa Real (FR) (Garde Royale)

G M Moore Mrs I I Plumb

Placings:*25/540P*-5P6P0F2 (4871)

2001/02: 16⁵S, 17ᴾS, 16⁶G, 19ᴾGS, 20⁰G, 24ᶠG, 25²GF

	Starts	1st	2nd	3rd	Win & Pl
Hurdles	3	0	1	0	698
Chases	4	0	0	0	0
Career Total	13	0	2	0	1481

Going: Sf: 0-2 GS: 0-1 Gd: 0-3 GF: - Fm: 0-1
Distance: 2m/2m3: 0-4 2m4-2m7: 0-1 3m+: 0-2
Track: LH: 0-5 RH: 0-2 Tight: 0-2 Gall: 0-1
Aids: Bl: 0-0 Vi: 0-0 Tstrap: 0-2
Best Rating: 95 11/00 Newc 2m gd-sft NHF

Modest hurdler, stays three miles, but may be better at slightly shorter. Acts on fast ground.

In Question

103(102h) (121h)138

8-y-o b g Deploy-Questionable (Rainbow Quest (USA))

Ian Williams The Winning Line

Placings:116F/1F/1F2P-012P (4643)

2001/02: 20⁰GF, 20¹G, 20²G, 20ᴾG

	Starts	1st	2nd	3rd	Win & Pl
Chases	4	1	1	0	8776
Career Total	14	5	2	0	25173

131	9/01	Hntg	2m4f110y	C(0-135)HCh	GD	£6691
127	12/00	Ludl	2m4f	E(0-115)HCh	G-S	£5590
110	11/99	Leic	2m	E Ch	G-F	£3327
140	2/99	Ludl	2m	E Hdl	GD	£2052
99	10/98	Kels	2m2f	E Hdl	G-S	£2430

Total win prize-money £20090

Going: Sf: 0-0 GS: 0-0 Gd: 1-3 GF: - Fm: 0-1
Distance: 2m/2m3: 0-0 **2m4-2m7: 1-4** 3m+: 0-0
Track: LH: 0-1 **RH: 1-3** Tight: 0-2 **Gall: 1-2**
Aids: Bl: 0-0 Vi: 0-0 Tstrap: 0-0
Best Rating: 140 2/99 Ludl 2m good Hdl

Best when fresh, he is at his best on good ground or

faster. He has had his jumping problems.

In Spirit (IRE)

105 **91**

4-y-o b g Distinctly North (USA)-June Goddess (Junius (USA))

D J S Cosgrove Crown Pkg & Mailing Svs Ltd

Placings:15 **(2066)**

2001/02: 16^{1}GF, 16^{5}G

	Starts	1st	2nd	3rd	Win & Pl
Hurdles	2	1	0	0	2415
Career Total	**2**	**1**	**0**	**0**	**2415**

93	9/01	Hntg	2m110y	E Hdl	G-F	£2415

Total win prize-money £2415

Going: Sf: 0-0 GS: 0-0 Gd: 0-1 GF: - Fm: 1-1
Distance: **2m/2m3: 1-2** 2m4-2m7: 0-0 3m+: 0-0
Track: LH: 0-0 **RH: 1-2** Tight: 0-0 **Gall: 1-2**
Aids: Bl: 0-0 Vi: 0-0 Tstrap: 0-0
Best Rating: 93 9/01 Hntg 2m110y gd-fm Hdl

Lightly raced on the Flat, winning twice, he made a successful debut over hurdles at Huntingdon over two miles on good to firm.

In The Arena (USA)

93 **72**

5-y-o ch g Cadeaux Genereux-Tajfah (USA) (Shadeed (USA))

D Shaw Lee Westwood

Placings:0000 **(2751)**

2001/02: 16^{0}GS, 16^{0}G, 16^{0}G, 17^{0}GS

	Starts	1st	2nd	3rd	Win & Pl
Hurdles	4	0	0	0	
Career Total	**4**	**0**	**0**	**0**	

Going: Sf: 0-0 GS: 0-2 Gd: 0-2 GF: - Fm: 0-0
Distance: 2m/2m3: 0-4 2m4-2m7: 0-0 3m+: 0-0
Track: LH: 0-4 RH: 0-0 Tight: 0-2 Gall: 0-0
Aids: Bl: 0-0 Vi: 0-0 Tstrap: 0-0
Best Rating: 72 11/01 Weth 2m good Hdl

He has shown little over hurdles so far.

In The Blood (IRE)

92 **147**

11-y-o b g Henbit (USA)-Polly's Slipper (Pollerton)

P J Hobbs I L Shaw

Placings:6/22231/1111F/5124310/4PF4-2UFP **(3488)**

2001/02: 19^{2}S, 19^{U}GS, 24^{F}G, 21^{P}HY

	Starts	1st	2nd	3rd	Win & Pl
Chases	4	0	1	0	2075
Career Total	**26**	**7**	**5**	**2**	**62486**

116	3/00	Tntn	2m3f110y	D Hdl	SFT	£3991
157	12/99	Wwck	2m4f	C(0-130)HCh	SFT	£7058
150	4/99	Chep	2m3f110y	C(0-135)HCh	SFT	£6232
143	3/99	Chep	2m3f110y	B HCh	SFT	£13511
137	3/99	Chep	2m3f110y	D(0-125)HCh	HVY	£3538
130	2/99	Font	2m2f	F(0-110)HCh	SFT	£2835
115	1/98	Extr	2m2f	E(0-115)HCh	HVY	£3912

Total win prize-money £41080

Going: Sf: 0-2 GS: 0-1 Gd: 0-1 GF: - Fm: 0-0
Distance: 2m/2m3: 0-0 2m4-2m7: 0-3 3m+: 0-1
Track: LH: 0-4 RH: 0-0 Tight: 0-0 Gall: 0-2
Aids: Bl: 0-0 Vi: 0-0 Tstrap: 0-0
Best Rating: 157 1/00 Uttx 2m4f soft Ch

He is a decent handicapper, but has become somewhat inconsistent. Suited by two and a half miles and soft ground.

In The Flow (USA)

108 **106**

5-y-o b g Irish River (FR)-In The Mood (USA) (Lyphard (USA))

P J Hobbs Aramis Racing Syndicate

Placings:000440-102103 **(1079)**

2001/02: 16^{1}F, 17^{0}GF, 17^{2}G, 16^{1}GF, 16^{0}GF, 16^{3}GF

	Starts	1st	2nd	3rd	Win & Pl
Hurdles	6	2	1	1	7198
Career Total	**12**	**2**	**1**	**1**	**7198**

106	6/01	Strf	2m110y	D(0-120)HHdl	G-F	£3536
106	5/01	Sthl	2m	F(0-95)HHdl	FRM	£2380

Total win prize-money £5916

Going: Sf: 0-0 GS: 0-0 Gd: 0-1 GF: - Fm: 2-5
Distance: **2m/2m3: 2-6** 2m4-2m7: 0-0 3m+: 0-0
Track: **LH: 2-6** RH: 0-0 **Tight: 2-6** Gall: 0-0
Aids: Bl: 0-0 Vi: 0-0 Tstrap: 0-0
Best Rating: 106 6/01 Strf 2m110y gd-fm Hdl

Decent hurdler, suited by fast ground and two miles.

In The Rough (IRE)

106(103h) (98h)**127**

11-y-o b g Strong Gale-Cherry Dawn (Pollerton)

J A B Old Mrs L R Lovell

Placings:1/4/0U/214/1531F-13U62 **(4163)**

2001/02: 26^{1}G, 25^{3}G, 25^{U}HY, 24^{6}GS, 29^{2}G

	Starts	1st	2nd	3rd	Win & Pl
Chases	5	1	1	1	9731
Career Total	**17**	**5**	**2**	**2**	**25380**

127	11/01	NAbb	3m2f110y	C(0-130)HCh	GD	£5944
112	2/01	Weth	3m1f	C(0-130)HHdl	SFT	£5411
103	5/00	Towc	3m	D Hdl	SFT	£3009
134	3/00	Chep	2m3f110y	D Ch	G-S	£3737
89	3/96	Ludl	2m	H NHF	GD	£1346

Total win prize-money £19451

Going: Sf: 0-1 GS: 0-1 Gd: 1-3 GF: - Fm: 0-0
Distance: 2m/2m3: 0-0 2m4-2m7: 0-0 **3m+: 1-5**
Track: **LH: 1-2** RH: 0-2 **Tight: 1-1** Gall: 0-0
Aids: Bl: 0-0 Vi: 0-0 Tstrap: 0-0
Best Rating: 134 3/00 Chep 2m3f110y gd-sft Ch

Useful handicap hurdler and chaser. Stays three and a quarter miles. Acts on soft ground, but handles good.

In Your Interest (IRE)

7-y-o ch g Buckskin (FR)-Officer's Lady (General Ironside)

Mrs H Dalton Kevin Glastonbury

Placings:P/345-P **(4425)**

2001/02: 24^{P}HY

	Starts	1st	2nd	3rd	Win & Pl
Hurdles	1	0	0	0	
Career Total	**5**	**0**	**0**	**1**	**389**

Going: Sf: 0-1 GS: 0-0 Gd: 0-0 GF: - Fm: 0-0
Distance: 2m/2m3: 0-0 2m4-2m7: 0-0 3m+: 0-1
Track: LH: 0-1 RH: 0-0 Tight: 0-0 Gall: 0-0
Aids: Bl: 0-1 Vi: 0-0 Tstrap: 0-0
Best Rating: 92 1/01 Ludl 2m5f soft Hdl

Failed to get round pointing and very limited ability under Rules.

Inaki (FR)

104 **101**

5-y-o b g Dounba (FR)-Incredule (FR) (Concertino (FR))

P Winkworth (M Nicolau 28/11) P Winkworth

Placings:P0P046F13F00F-005F43444 **(4430)**

2001/02: 17^{0}VS, 17^{0}VS, 17^{5}, 18^{F}G, 19^{4}S, 17^{3}HY, 16^{4}HY, 16^{4}GS, 16^{4}HY

	Starts	1st	2nd	3rd	Win & Pl
Chases	9	0	0	1	4590
Career Total	**22**	**1**	**0**	**2**	**11078**

1/01	Pau	2m1f	Ch	HLD	£3880

Total win prize-money £3880

Going: Sf: 0-4 GS: 0-1 Gd: 0-1 GF: - Fm: 0-0
Distance: 2m/2m3: 0-8 2m4-2m7: 0-1 3m+: 0-0
Track: LH: 0-1 RH: 0-2 Tight: 0-0 Gall: 0-1
Aids: Bl: 0-4 Vi: 0-0 Tstrap: 0-0
Best Rating: 101 2/02 Hntg 2m110y gd-sft Ch

Inch Bridge

7-y-o b g Gildoran-Deep Halo (Deep Run)

J Neville Jim McCarthy

Placings:*0P*-P **(4850)**

2001/02: 22^{P}G

	Starts	1st	2nd	3rd	Win & Pl
Hurdles	1	0	0	0	
Career Total	**3**	**0**	**0**	**0**	

Going: Sf: 0-0 GS: 0-0 Gd: 0-1 GF: - Fm: 0-0
Distance: 2m/2m3: 0-0 2m4-2m7: 0-1 3m+: 0-0
Track: LH: 0-1 RH: 0-0 Tight: 0-1 Gall: 0-0
Aids: Bl: 0-0 Vi: 0-0 Tstrap: 0-0
Best Rating: 67 10/00 MRas 2m1f110y good NHF

Inch Champion (IRE)

10-y-o b g Down The Hatch-Little Enda (Little Buskins)

A W Carroll Gordon W Day

Placings:*0*53P02/0PP0P0PP/533115/RPP-PP **(1018)**

2001/02: 24^{P}GF, 23^{P}G

	Starts	1st	2nd	3rd	Win & Pl
Chases	2	0	0	0	
Career Total	**25**	**2**	**1**	**3**	**7839**

88	11/99	Plum	3m2f	E(0-105)HCh	GD	£3533
82	10/99	Chep	2m3f110y	G(0-95)HCh	G-F	£1940

Total win prize-money £5474

Going: Sf: 0-0 GS: 0-0 Gd: 0-1 GF: - Fm: 0-1
Distance: 2m/2m3: 0-0 2m4-2m7: 0-0 3m+: 0-2
Track: LH: 0-1 RH: 0-1 Tight: 0-0 Gall: 0-1
Aids: Bl: 0-0 Vi: 0-0 Tstrap: 0-0
Best Rating: 88 11/99 Plum 3m2f good Ch

Inch Cross (IRE)

11-y-o b g Supreme Leader-Glenaveel (Furry Glen)

Mrs Caroline Bailey R S Hunnisett

Placings:40-66 **(0425)**

2001/02: 24^{6}GS, 21^{6}G

	Starts	1st	2nd	3rd	Win & Pl

	Starts	1st	2nd	3rd	Win & Pl
Chases	2	0	0	0	0
Career Total	**4**	**0**	**0**	**0**	**269**

Going: Sf: 0-0 GS: 0-1 Gd: 0-1 GF: - Fm: 0-0
Distance: 2m/2m3: 0-0 2m4-2m7: 0-1 3m+: 0-1
Track: LH: 0-1 RH: 0-0 Tight: 0-1 Gall: 0-0
Aids: Bl: 0-0 Vi: 0-0 Tstrap: 0-1
Best Rating: 99 5/00 Hntg 3m good Ch

Inch Fountain (IRE)

97 **104**

11-y-o br g Royal Fountain-The Priory (Oats)
Mrs L Wadham (R Curtis 6/12) Cohen Glazer Green Harriers

Placings:335P0F **(3561)**
2001/02: 24^{3}G, 26^{3}GS, 24^{5}G, 28^{P}S, 23^{0}G, 25^{F}HY

	Starts	1st	2nd	3rd	Win & Pl
Chases	6	0	0	2	982
Career Total	**6**	**0**	**0**	**2**	**982**

Going: Sf: 0-2 GS: 0-1 Gd: 0-3 GF: - Fm: 0-0
Distance: 2m/2m3: 0-0 2m4-2m7: 0-0 3m+: 0-6
Track: LH: 0-0 RH: 0-4 Tight: 0-2 Gall: 0-0
Aids: Bl: 0-0 Vi: 0-1 Tstrap: 0-0
Best Rating: 104 11/01 Kemp 3m good Ch

Inch Loss Island

5-y-o ch m Inchinor-Island Mead (Pharly (FR))
W G M Turner D R Tucker

Placings:*0-0P* **(0777)**
2001/02: 17^{0}F, 16^{P}GF

	Starts	1st	2nd	3rd	Win & Pl
NH Flat	1	0	0	0	0
Hurdles	1	0	0	0	0
Career Total	**3**	**0**	**0**	**0**	

Going: Sf: 0-0 GS: 0-0 Gd: 0-0 GF: - Fm: 0-2
Distance: 2m/2m3: 0-2 2m4-2m7: 0-0 3m+: 0-0
Track: LH: 0-1 RH: 0-1 Tight: 0-0 Gall: 0-0
Aids: Bl: 0-0 Vi: 0-0 Tstrap: 0-2
Best Rating: 85 4/01 Tntn 2m1f gd-fm NHF

Inch Way (IRE)

89 **79**

10-y-o br g Kambalda-Glenaveel (Furry Glen)
A J Lockwood Highgreen Partnership

Placings:*20/60***52306/455531/2202P-PPU4** **(3327)**
2001/02: 21^{P}GF, 24^{P}GF, 24^{U}GS, 24^{4}S

	Starts	1st	2nd	3rd	Win & Pl
Chases	4	0	0	0	0
Career Total	**24**	**1**	**5**	**2**	**6582**

95 4/00 Uttx 3m G(0-90)HCh HVY £1946
Total win prize-money £1946

Going: Sf: 0-1 GS: 0-1 Gd: 0-0 GF: - Fm: 0-2
Distance: 2m/2m3: 0-0 2m4-2m7: 0-1 3m+: 0-3
Track: LH: 0-4 RH: 0-0 Tight: 0-1 Gall: 0-3
Aids: Bl: 0-0 Vi: 0-0 Tstrap: 0-0
Best Rating: 95 1/01 Sthl 3m110y heavy Ch

Moderate handicap chaser. Stays three miles, suited by soft ground.

Inching Closer

105 **129**

5-y-o b g Inchinor-Maiyaasah (Kris)
Ferdy Murphy (N A Callaghan 30/6) Mrs N L Spence

Placings:6-14010 **(4229)**
2001/02: 22^{1}S, 16^{4}G, 16^{0}G, 27^{1}S, 21^{0}GS

	Starts	1st	2nd	3rd	Win & Pl
Hurdles	5	2	0	0	5919
Career Total	**6**	**2**	**0**	**0**	**5919**

129 3/02 Sedg 3m3f110y D(0-120)HHdl SFT £3265
117 11/01 Uttx 2m6f110y E Hdl SFT £2653
Total win prize-money £5919

Going: Sf: 2-2 GS: 0-1 Gd: 0-2 GF: - Fm: 0-0
Distance: 2m/2m3: 0-2 2m4-2m7: 1-2 3m+: 1-1
Track: **LH: 2-5** RH: 0-0 **Tight: 1-1** Gall: 0-2
Aids: Bl: 0-0 Vi: 0-0 Tstrap: 0-0
Best Rating: 129 3/02 Sedg 3m3f110y soft Hdl

A fair performer at up to a mile and a half on the level on fast ground. He has shown good form over hurdles from two miles to two miles six furlongs. Won on his handicap debut at Sedgefield in March 2002. A chaser in the making. Acts on soft/heavy ground.

Inchinnan

97 **99**

5-y-o b m Inchinor-Westering (Auction Ring (USA))
C Weedon Atlantic Foods Ltd

Placings:043U **(4147)**
2001/02: 16^{0}G, 17^{4}S, 16^{3}HY, 16^{U}GS

	Starts	1st	2nd	3rd	Win & Pl
Hurdles	4	0	0	1	369
Career Total	**4**	**0**	**0**	**1**	**369**

Going: Sf: 0-2 GS: 0-1 Gd: 0-1 GF: - Fm: 0-0
Distance: 2m/2m3: 0-4 2m4-2m7: 0-0 3m+: 0-0
Track: LH: 0-2 RH: 0-2 Tight: 0-2 Gall: 0-0
Aids: Bl: 0-0 Vi: 0-0 Tstrap: 0-0
Best Rating: 99 1/02 Tntn 2m1f soft Hdl

Lightly raced novice hurdler, suited by soft ground and two miles.

Indalo (IRE)

111 **134**

7-y-o b g Lord Americo-Parsons Princess (The Parson)
Miss Venetia Williams (P J Rothwell 5/5) Roa Arkle Partnership

Placings:*301/5236245*44-3131135 **(4893)**
2001/02: 16^{3}YS, 20^{1}S, 21^{3}S, 19^{1}G, 22^{1}G, 20^{3}G, 20^{5}G

	Starts	1st	2nd	3rd	Win & Pl
Hurdles	7	3	0	3	16184
Career Total	**19**	**4**	**2**	**5**	**23411**

134 3/02 Hayd 2m6f D Hdl GD £5096
127 3/02 Hrfd 2m3f110y E Hdl GD £2807
110 1/02 Leic 2m4f110y E Hdl SFT £3052
95 11/99 Fair 2m NHF SFT £3850
Total win prize-money £14805

Going: Sf: 1-2 GS: 0-0 Gd: 2-4 GF: - Fm: 0-0
Distance: 2m/2m3: 0-1 **2m4-2m7: 3-6** 3m+: 0-0
Track: LH: 1-2 **RH: 2-4** Tight: 0-1 Gall: 0-0
Aids: Bl: 0-0 Vi: 0-0 Tstrap: 0-0
Best Rating: 134 4/02 Aint 2m4f good Hdl

A bumper winner and placed over hurdles in Ireland, he has won three novice hurdles in this country and ran well in an Aintree handicap. A keen sort, he stays two and a half miles and has a high cruising speed.

Indecisive

74 **55**

7-y-o ch m Then Again-Nine Hans (Prince Hansel)
M J Coombe Mrs N M Coombe

Placings:0 **(4485)**
2001/02: 19^{0}G

	Starts	1st	2nd	3rd	Win & Pl
Hurdles	1	0	0	0	
Career Total	**1**	**0**	**0**	**0**	

Going: Sf: 0-0 GS: 0-0 Gd: 0-1 GF: - Fm: 0-0
Distance: 2m/2m3: 0-1 2m4-2m7: 0-0 3m+: 0-0
Track: LH: 0-0 RH: 0-1 Tight: 0-0 Gall: 0-0
Aids: Bl: 0-0 Vi: 0-0 Tstrap: 0-0
Best Rating: 55 3/02 Extr 2m3f good Hdl

Indeed (IRE)

105 **109**

7-y-o ch g Camden Town-Pamrina (Pamroy)
J T Gifford Pell-Mell Partners

Placings:4F1 **(4134)**
2001/02: 16^{4}S, 22^{F}G, 20^{1}GS

	Starts	1st	2nd	3rd	Win & Pl
Hurdles	3	1	0	0	4880
Career Total	**3**	**1**	**0**	**0**	**4880**

109 3/02 Sand 2m4f110y D Hdl G-S £4309
Total win prize-money £4310

Going: Sf: 0-1 GS: 1-1 Gd: 0-1 GF: - Fm: 0-0
Distance: 2m/2m3: 0-1 **2m4-2m7: 1-2** 3m+: 0-0
Track: LH: 0-1 **RH: 1-2** Tight: 0-0 Gall: 0-1
Aids: Bl: 0-0 Vi: 0-0 Tstrap: 0-0
Best Rating: 109 3/02 Sand 2m4f110y gd-sft Hdl

Showed ability before getting off the mark at Sandown in March 2002. Suited by two and a half miles.

Indeed To Goodness (IRE)

104 **105**

7-y-o b m Welsh Term-Clare's Sheen (Choral Society)
J W Mullins Ian M McGready

Placings:*0/43*3P43-013U3106 **(4816)**
2001/02: 22^{0}G, 22^{1}GS, 24^{3}G, 22^{U}G, 21^{3}G, 21^{1}S, 21^{0}GS, 21^{6}GF

	Starts	1st	2nd	3rd	Win & Pl
Hurdles	8	2	0	2	10945
Career Total	**15**	**2**	**0**	**5**	**11809**

105 2/02 Kemp 2m5f B HHdl SFT £6955
102 10/01 Font 2m6f110y E Hdl G-S £2513
Total win prize-money £9468

Going: Sf: 1-1 GS: 1-2 Gd: 0-4 GF: - Fm: 0-1
Distance: 2m/2m3: 0-0 **2m4-2m7: 2-7** 3m+: 0-1
Track: LH: 1-4 RH: 1-4 **Tight: 1-3** Gall: 0-2
Aids: Bl: 0-0 Vi: 0-0 Tstrap: 0-0
Best Rating: 105 2/02 Kemp 2m5f soft Hdl

Developing into a conistent novice hurdler in 2001/2002, posting a solid effort when winning a mares' only handicap hurdle at Kempton in February. Stays well and goes well on soft ground.

Independent Dancer

88f 84f

5-y-o b g Shareef Dancer (USA)-Ecologically Kind (Alleged (USA))
Mrs A Duffield S & G Scaffolding

Placings:*000* (2321)
2001/02: 16^{0}GF, 17^{0}G, 17^{0}GS

	Starts	1st	2nd	3rd	Win & Pl
NH Flat	3	0	0	0	
Career Total	3	0	0	0	

Going: Sf: 0-0 GS: 0-1 Gd: 0-1 GF: - Fm: 0-1
Distance: 2m/2m3: 0-3 2m4-2m7: 0-0 3m+: 0-0
Track: LH: 0-2 RH: 0-0 Tight: 0-1 Gall: 0-0
Aids: Bl: 0-0 Vi: 0-0 Tstrap: 0-0
Best Rating: 84 5/01 Ayr 2m gd-fm NHF

Independent Grey

88 84

11-y-o gr g Grey Ghost-Harsley Suprise (Meldrum)
D M Grissell The Hudson Racing Group

Placings:005332U544/5 (3149)
2001/02: 22^{5}G

	Starts	1st	2nd	3rd	Win & Pl
Chases	1	0	0	0	0
Career Total	11	0	1	2	2414

Going: Sf: 0-0 GS: 0-0 Gd: 0-1 GF: - Fm: 0-0
Distance: 2m/2m3: 0-0 2m4-2m7: 0-1 3m+: 0-0
Track: LH: 0-0 RH: 0-0 Tight: 0-1 Gall: 0-0
Aids: Bl: 0-0 Vi: 0-0 Tstrap: 0-0
Best Rating: 100 1/99 Weth 2m soft Ch

Independent Lady

88 58

6-y-o b m Meadowbrook-Sister Juana (Owen Anthony)
J S Smith Independent Partnership

Placings:*0-00*PP0 (4181)
2001/02: 17^{0}G, 19^{0}S, 20^{P}S, 16^{P}HY, 19^{0}S

	Starts	1st	2nd	3rd	Win & Pl
NH Flat	2	0	0	0	0
Hurdles	4	0	0	0	0
Career Total	6	0	0	0	

Going: Sf: 0-4 GS: 0-0 Gd: 0-1 GF: - Fm: 0-0
Distance: 2m/2m3: 0-2 2m4-2m7: 0-3 3m+: 0-0
Track: LH: 0-1 RH: 0-4 Tight: 0-2 Gall: 0-0
Aids: Bl: 0-0 Vi: 0-0 Tstrap: 0-0
Best Rating: 83 4/01 Tntn 2m1f gd-fm NHF

Indian Beat

84 71

5-y-o ch g Indian Ridge-Rappa Tap Tap (FR) (Tap On Wood)
C L Popham (Mrs L Stubbs 25/8) Mrs C R Hayton

Placings:0 (3757)
2001/02: 17^{0}S

	Starts	1st	2nd	3rd	Win & Pl
Hurdles	1	0	0	0	
Career Total	1	0	0	0	

Going: Sf: 0-1 GS: 0-0 Gd: 0-0 GF: - Fm: 0-0
Distance: 2m/2m3: 0-1 2m4-2m7: 0-0 3m+: 0-0
Track: LH: 0-0 RH: 0-1 Tight: 0-1 Gall: 0-0
Aids: Bl: 0-0 Vi: 0-0 Tstrap: 0-0
Best Rating: 71 2/02 Tntn 2m1f soft Hdl

Indian Chance

106 126

8-y-o b g Teenoso (USA)-Icy Miss (Random Shot)
Dr J R J Naylor Mrs Stella Watson And Jock Cullen

Placings:*00*/3F6131 (4388)
2001/02: 24^{3}GS, 22^{F}HY, 23^{6}G, 23^{1}S, 26^{3}S, 25^{1}S

	Starts	1st	2nd	3rd	Win & Pl
Chases	6	2	0	2	9912
Career Total	8	2	0	2	9912

116	3/02	Winc	3m1f110y	E(0-110)HCh	SFT	£5375
116	2/02	Leic	2m7f110y	E(0-105)HCh	SFT	£3263

Total win prize-money £8639

Going: Sf: 2-4 GS: 0-1 Gd: 0-1 GF: - Fm: 0-0
Distance: 2m/2m3: 0-0 2m4-2m7: 0-1 **3m+: 2-5**
Track: LH: 0-1 **RH: 2-4** Tight: 0-2 Gall: 0-0
Aids: Bl: 0-0 Vi: 0-0 Tstrap: 0-0
Best Rating: 116 3/02 Winc 3m1f110y soft Ch

A fair staying chaser, he stays three miles and acts on soft ground.

Indian Crown

12-y-o b m Welsh Captain-Indian Cash (Indian Ruler)
N B Thomson Miss T R Johnson

Placings:6P054/OOO06/P05P0P/PUPP (2774)
2001/02: 21^{P}GF, 16^{U}G, 20^{P}G, 19^{P}G

	Starts	1st	2nd	3rd	Win & Pl
Chases	4	0	0	0	
Career Total	20	0	0	0	0

Going: Sf: 0-0 GS: 0-0 Gd: 0-3 GF: - Fm: 0-1
Distance: 2m/2m3: 0-1 2m4-2m7: 0-3 3m+: 0-0
Track: LH: 0-0 RH: 0-4 Tight: 0-1 Gall: 0-0
Aids: Bl: 0-0 Vi: 0-0 Tstrap: 0-0
Best Rating: 74 11/95 Winc 2m gd-fm NHF

Indian Gunner

115 99

9-y-o b g Gunner B-Icy Miss (Random Shot)
Dr J R J Naylor Mrs S P Elphick

Placings:54/260P/21U (3286)
2001/02: 16^{2}GF, 16^{1}G, 16^{U}S

	Starts	1st	2nd	3rd	Win & Pl
Chases	3	1	1	0	5096
Career Total	9	1	2	0	6031

96	12/01	Leic	2m	D(0-110)HCh	GD	£4127

Total win prize-money £4128

Going: Sf: 0-1 GS: 0-0 Gd: 1-1 GF: - Fm: 0-1
Distance: **2m/2m3: 1-3** 2m4-2m7: 0-0 3m+: 0-0
Track: LH: 0-0 **RH: 1-3** Tight: 0-1 Gall: 0-0
Aids: Bl: 0-0 Vi: 0-0 Tstrap: 0-0
Best Rating: 99 12/01 Leic 2m gd-fm Ch

Good run in a novice handicap chase in December 2001 after a lengthy absence and followed that up with a win. Acts on good ground.

Indian Jiva (IRE)

8-y-o b m Commanche Run-She's A Dancer (IRE) (Alzao (USA))
B Llewellyn Mrs M Llewellyn

Placings:*520*-0P (3402)
2001/02: 19^{0}G, 20^{P}S

	Starts	1st	2nd	3rd	Win & Pl
Hurdles	2	0	0	0	
Career Total	5	0	1	0	430

Going: Sf: 0-1 GS: 0-0 Gd: 0-1 GF: - Fm: 0-0
Distance: 2m/2m3: 0-0 2m4-2m7: 0-2 3m+: 0-0
Track: LH: 0-0 RH: 0-2 Tight: 0-0 Gall: 0-0
Aids: Bl: 0-0 Vi: 0-0 Tstrap: 0-0
Best Rating: 97 11/00 Chep 2m110y heavy NHF

Indian Miller

37

11-y-o ch g Gildoran-Milltown Lady (Deep Run)
J W Mullins M S Green

Placings:0/0P (1767)
2001/02: 22^{0}GF, 22^{P}G

	Starts	1st	2nd	3rd	Win & Pl
Hurdles	2	0	0	0	
Career Total	3	0	0	0	

Going: Sf: 0-0 GS: 0-0 Gd: 0-1 GF: - Fm: 0-1
Distance: 2m/2m3: 0-0 2m4-2m7: 0-2 3m+: 0-0
Track: LH: 0-0 RH: 0-0 Tight: 0-0 Gall: 0-0
Aids: Bl: 0-0 Vi: 0-0 Tstrap: 0-0
Best Rating: 37 10/01 Extr 2m6f110y gd-fm Hdl

Indian Miss

10-y-o b m Idiots Delight-Icy Miss (Random Shot)
Dr J R J Naylor The Kings Troop Royal Horse Artillery

Placings:*00*/12/4F4/0P (3753)
2001/02: 24^{0}S, 24^{P}S

	Starts	1st	2nd	3rd	Win & Pl
Chases	2	0	0	0	
Career Total	9	1	1	0	5968

107	12/98	Extr	2m3f	D Ch	SFT	£3622

Total win prize-money £3623

Going: Sf: 0-2 GS: 0-0 Gd: 0-0 GF: - Fm: 0-0
Distance: 2m/2m3: 0-0 2m4-2m7: 0-0 3m+: 0-2
Track: LH: 0-0 RH: 0-2 Tight: 0-1 Gall: 0-0
Aids: Bl: 0-0 Vi: 0-0 Tstrap: 0-0
Best Rating: 120 2/99 Tntn 3m gd-sft Ch

Indian Renegade (IRE)

22f 11f

4-y-o b f Commanche Run-Tarary (Boreen (FR))
J S Haldane J S Haldane

Placings:*0* (3750)
2001/02: 16^{0}S

	Starts	1st	2nd	3rd	Win & Pl
NH Flat	1	0	0	0	
Career Total	1	0	0	0	

Going: Sf: 0-1 GS: 0-0 Gd: 0-0 GF: - Fm: 0-0

Distance: 2m/2m3: 0-1 2m4-2m7: 0-0 3m+: 0-0
Track: LH: 0-0 RH: 0-1 Tight: 0-1 Gall: 0-0
Aids: Bl: 0-0 Vi: 0-0 Tstrap: 0-0
Best Rating: 11 2/02 Muss 2m soft NHF

Indian Rope Trick

103(81c) (63c)71
6-y-o ch g Kris-Lassoo (Caerleon (USA))
M W Easterby Mrs J M Jones

Placings:600**P63** (4908)
2001/02: 20^{6}G, 16^{0}G, 20^{0}G, 16^{P}G, 16^{6}GS, 21^{3}G

	Starts	1st	2nd	3rd	Win & Pl
Hurdles	4	0	0	1	369
Chases	2	0	0	0	0
Career Total	**6**	**0**	**0**	**1**	**369**

Going: Sf: 0-0 GS: 0-1 Gd: 0-5 GF: - Fm: 0-0
Distance: 2m/2m3: 0-3 2m4-2m7: 0-3 3m+: 0-0
Track: LH: 0-5 RH: 0-1 Tight: 0-2 Gall: 0-2
Aids: Bl: 0-0 Vi: 0-0 Tstrap: 0-3
Best Rating: 71 4/02 MRas 2m5f110y good Hdl

Maiden jumper, did not jump well on his chasing debut.

Indian Sun

75 17
5-y-o ch g Indian Ridge-Star Tulip (Night Shift (USA))
P D Evans Treble Chance Partnership

Placings:0 (2056)
2001/02: 18^{U}GS

	Starts	1st	2nd	3rd	Win & Pl
Hurdles	1	0	0	0	
Career Total	**1**	**0**	**0**	**0**	

Going: Sf: 0-0 GS: 0-1 Gd: 0-0 GF: - Fm: 0-0
Distance: 2m/2m3: 0-1 2m4-2m7: 0-0 3m+: 0-0
Track: LH: 0-1 RH: 0-0 Tight: 0-1 Gall: 0-0
Aids: Bl: 0-0 Vi: 0-0 Tstrap: 0-1
Best Rating: 17 11/01 Font 2m2f110y gd-sft Hdl

Indian Temple

99(71h) (42h)82
11-y-o ch g Minster Son-Indian Flower (Mansingh (USA))
K Bishop Derek Clarke

Placings:052F0204/2455/002643/421263PF2/221325451P4P5/4P5/0-00650 (2273)
2001/02: 22^{0}GF, 21^{0}GS, 26^{6}G, 24^{5}G, 24^{0}G

	Starts	1st	2nd	3rd	Win & Pl
Hurdles	2	0	0	0	
Chases	3	0	0	0	
Career Total	**49**	**3**	**10**	**3**	**21378**

95	10/98	Tntn	3m	D(0-120)HCh	FRM	£3857
95	5/98	Extr	2m3f110y	E(0-110)HCh	FRM	£3178
83	10/97	Tntn	2m3f	F(0-95)HCh	FRM	£2595

Total win prize-money £9631

Going: Sf: 0-0 GS: 0-1 Gd: 0-3 GF: - Fm: 0-1
Distance: 2m/2m3: 0-0 2m4-2m7: 0-2 3m+: 0-3
Track: LH: 0-3 RH: 0-1 Tight: 0-3 Gall: 0-0
Aids: Bl: 0-0 Vi: 0-0 Tstrap: 0-0
Best Rating: 95 10/98 Tntn 3m firm Ch

Indian Venture (IRE)

109 116
8-y-o b g Commanche Run-Believe It Or Not (Quayside)
N G Richards Dr K S Frasier & Ashleybank Investments

Placings:*10*/0-31102321 (4879)
2001/02: 16^{3}G, 17^{1}GS, 18^{1}G, 16^{0}GS, 16^{2}G, 16^{3}S, 16^{2}GS, 16^{1}G

	Starts	1st	2nd	3rd	Win & Pl
Hurdles	8	3	2	2	14830
Career Total	**11**	**4**	**2**	**2**	**16406**

116	4/02	Prth	2m110y	D(0-120)HHdl	GD	£5746
105	11/01	Kels	2m2f	F(0-110)HHdl	GD	£2257
96	10/01	Carl	2m1f	E Hdl	G-S	£2654
105	12/99	Muss	2m	H NHF	G-S	£1576

Total win prize-money £12234

Going: Sf: 0-1 GS: 1-3 Gd: 2-4 GF: - Fm: 0-0
Distance: **2m/2m3: 3-8** 2m4-2m7: 0-0 3m+: 0-0
Track: LH: 1-3 **RH: 2-5 Tight: 1-5** Gall: 0-0
Aids: Bl: 0-0 Vi: 0-0 Tstrap: 0-0
Best Rating: 116 4/02 Prth 2m110y good Hdl

A bumper winner, he was third on his reappearance at Perth in September 2001. Scored twice on the bounce after that at Carlisle and Kelso and, despite a hike up the handicap, scored again at perth in April. Looks to need further than two miles.

Indian Viceroy

108 95
9-y-o b g Lord Bud-Poppadom (Rapid River)
P Winkworth Bill Naylor

Placings:*0600000/04600/036/213*-RU5 (4511)
2001/02: 21^{R}G, 20^{U}GS, 20^{5}G

	Starts	1st	2nd	3rd	Win & Pl
Chases	3	0	0	0	0
Career Total	**21**	**1**	**1**	**2**	**4759**

100	11/00	Hntg	2m4f110y	F(0-110)HCh	G-S	£2834

Total win prize-money £2834

Going: Sf: 0-0 GS: 0-1 Gd: 0-2 GF: - Fm: 0-0
Distance: 2m/2m3: 0-0 2m4-2m7: 0-3 3m+: 0-0
Track: LH: 0-1 RH: 0-2 Tight: 0-2 Gall: 0-1
Aids: Bl: 0-0 Vi: 0-0 Tstrap: 0-0
Best Rating: 100 11/00 Hntg 2m4f110y gd-sft Ch

Indian Winger (IRE)

9-y-o ch g Commanche Run-On The Blindside (Martinmas)
J Neville Philip A Davies

Placings:P-P (0087)
2001/02: 26^{P}G

	Starts	1st	2nd	3rd	Win & Pl
Hurdles	1	0	0	0	
Career Total	**2**	**0**	**0**	**0**	

Going: Sf: 0-0 GS: 0-0 Gd: 0-1 GF: - Fm: 0-0
Distance: 2m/2m3: 0-0 2m4-2m7: 0-0 3m+: 0-1
Track: LH: 0-0 RH: 0-1 Tight: 0-0 Gall: 0-0
Aids: Bl: 0-0 Vi: 0-0 Tstrap: 0-0
Best Rating:

Indian Wings (IRE)

109(51c) 117
9-y-o b g Commanche Run-Got To Fly (IRE) (Kemal (FR))
A Scott Andy Scott

Placings:P62**P**0P-0P2112P5PP536 (4491)
2001/02: 24^{0}S, 24^{P}S, 20^{2}S, 22^{1}G, 20^{1}S, 22^{2}GS, 22^{P}GS, 24^{5}S, 20^{P}G, 24^{P}G, 20^{5}GS, 21^{3}S, 20^{6}GS

	Starts	1st	2nd	3rd	Win & Pl
Hurdles	13	2	2	1	7965
Career Total	**19**	**2**	**3**	**1**	**8745**

117	11/01	Carl	2m4f	F(0-100)HHdl	SFT	£2802
107	11/01	Kels	2m6f110y	D(0-125)HHdl	GD	£3307

Total win prize-money £6111

Going: Sf: 1-6 GS: 0-4 Gd: 1-3 GF: - Fm: 0-0
Distance: 2m/2m3: 0-0 **2m4-2m7: 2-9** 3m+: 0-4
Track: **LH: 1-7** RH: 0-3 **Tight: 1-5** Gall: 0-1
Aids: Bl: 0-0 Vi: 0-0 Tstrap: 0-0
Best Rating: 117 11/01 Carl 2m4f soft Hdl

An Irish point winner. Lightly-raced. Ran an encouraging race when reappearing at Carlisle in October 2002 and scored two back-to-back wins at Kelso and Carlisle in November, making all both times. Acts on decent ground, handles soft. Should stay further.

Indiana Journey (IRE)

(97h) (106h)93
7-y-o b m Eurobus-Indiana Dancer (Hallgate)
A J Martin J H Lowry

Placings:63*14*-032124**003** (2365a)
2001/02: 20^{0}G, 16^{3}GF, 20^{2}F, 16^{1}F, 16^{2}G, 16^{4}G, 18^{0}GY, 16^{0}Y, 22^{3}S

	Starts	1st	2nd	3rd	Win & Pl
Hurdles	6	1	2	1	6800
Chases	3	0	0	1	621
Career Total	**13**	**2**	**2**	**3**	**10225**

98	7/01	DRoy	2m	Hdl	FRM	£3895
102	8/00	Dpat	2m1f172y	NHF	G-F	£2345

Total win prize-money £6241

Going: Sf: 0-1 GS: 0-0 Gd: 0-3 GF: - Fm: 1-3
Distance: **2m/2m3: 1-6** 2m4-2m7: 0-3 3m+: 0-0
Track: LH: 0-0 RH: 0-1 Tight: 0-0 Gall: 0-0
Aids: Bl: 0-0 Vi: 0-0 Tstrap: 0-0
Best Rating: 106 6/01 DRoy 2m gd-fm Hdl

Indle Rock

86 77
12-y-o b g Hadeer-Song Test (USA) (The Minstrel (CAN))
R Tate R Tate

Placings:5F02/2412633/62/44/F/0BP0 (0879)
2001/02: 20^{0}G, 20^{B}G, 24^{P}GF, 20^{0}G

	Starts	1st	2nd	3rd	Win & Pl
Chases	4	0	0	0	
Career Total	**20**	**1**	**4**	**2**	**5578**

90	6/95	Strf	2m110y	E Hdl	GD	£2360

Total win prize-money £2360

Going: Sf: 0-0 GS: 0-0 Gd: 0-3 GF: - Fm: 0-1
Distance: 2m/2m3: 0-0 2m4-2m7: 0-3 3m+: 0-1
Track: LH: 0-2 RH: 0-2 Tight: 0-3 Gall: 0-0
Aids: Bl: 0-0 Vi: 0-0 Tstrap: 0-0
Best Rating: 93 5/98 Weth 2m4f110y gd-fm Ch

Indien Du Boulay (FR)

100(100h) (102h)124
6-y-o ch g Chef De Clan Ii (FR)-Radesgirl (FR) (Radetzky Marsch (USA))

P Monteith Major General C A Ramsay

Placings:6-21112F3 **(4829)**
2001/02: 16^{2}GF, 20^{1}GS, 20^{1}GF, 16^{1}G, 16^{2}S, 20^{F}GF, 16^{3}G

	Starts	1st	2nd	3rd	Win & Pl
Hurdles	3	2	1	0	6993
Chases	4	1	1	1	6276
Career Total	**8**	**3**	**2**	**1**	**13269**

124	11/01	Ayr	2m	D Ch	GD	£4127
102	5/01	Newc	2m4f	E Hdl	G-F	£2894
100	5/01	Prth	2m4f110y	E Hdl	G-S	£3241

Total win prize-money £10264

Going: Sf: 0-1 GS: 1-1 Gd: 1-2 GF: - Fm: 1-3
Distance: 2m/2m3: 1-4 **2m4-2m7: 2-3** 3m+: 0-0
Track: **LH: 2-5** RH: 1-2 Tight: 0-1 **Gall: 1-1**
Aids: Bl: 0-0 Vi: 0-0 Tstrap: 0-0
Best Rating: 124 11/01 Ayr 2m good Ch

Indigo Baby

85 **30**

7-y-o b/br m Handsome Sailor-Albaciyna (Hotfoot)
N B Mason N B Mason

Placings:_030_000P-00 **(1347)**
2001/02: 17^{0}G, 17^{0}GF

	Starts	1st	2nd	3rd	Win & Pl
Hurdles	2	0	0	0	
Career Total	**9**	**0**	**0**	**1**	**317**

Going: Sf: 0-0 GS: 0-0 Gd: 0-1 GF: - Fm: 0-1
Distance: 2m/2m3: 0-2 2m4-2m7: 0-0 3m+: 0-0
Track: LH: 0-2 RH: 0-0 Tight: 0-2 Gall: 0-0
Aids: Bl: 0-0 Vi: 0-0 Tstrap: 0-2
Best Rating: 85 10/00 MRas 2m1f110y good NHF

Indigo Beach (IRE)

105 **93**

6-y-o b g Rainbows For Life (CAN)-Sandy Maid (Sandy Creek)
P S McEntee Mrs R L McEntee

Placings:P224/303004-0155 **(4772)**
2001/02: 16^{0}G, 16^{1}G, 16^{5}GF, 21^{5}G

	Starts	1st	2nd	3rd	Win & Pl
Hurdles	4	1	0	0	1887
Career Total	**14**	**1**	**2**	**2**	**4029**

70	4/02	Fknm	2m	G(0-90)HHdl	GD	£1887

Total win prize-money £1887

Going: Sf: 0-0 GS: 0-0 Gd: 1-3 GF: - Fm: 0-1
Distance: **2m/2m3: 1-3** 2m4-2m7: 0-1 3m+: 0-0
Track: **LH: 1-3** RH: 0-1 **Tight: 1-3** Gall: 0-0
Aids: **Bl: 1-4** Vi: 0-0 Tstrap: 0-1
Best Rating: 103 10/00 Font 2m4f good Hdl

Selling grade hurdler. Acts on a sound surface and is effective at around two miles.

Indio

83 **61**

7-y-o br g Formidable (USA)-Washita (Valiyar)
B J M Ryall B J M Ryall

Placings:_00_/6P/0P **(0735)**
2001/02: 18^{0}GF, 21^{P}GS

	Starts	1st	2nd	3rd	Win & Pl
Chases	2	0	0	0	
Career Total	**6**	**0**	**0**	**0**	**0**

Going: Sf: 0-0 GS: 0-1 Gd: 0-0 GF: - Fm: 0-1
Distance: 2m/2m3: 0-1 2m4-2m7: 0-1 3m+: 0-0
Track: LH: 0-1 RH: 0-0 Tight: 0-2 Gall: 0-0
Aids: Bl: 0-0 Vi: 0-0 Tstrap: 0-0
Best Rating: 72 3/99 MRas 1m5f110y gd-sft NHF

Indiscret (FR)

49

6-y-o b g Garde Royale-Please (FR) (Le Pontet (FR))
F Jordan (J F C Maxwell 21/11) Tony Cocum, Mark Doyle, Stephen Green

Placings:_60_P **(4519)**
2001/02: 17^{6}S, 16^{0}S, 21^{P}GS

	Starts	1st	2nd	3rd	Win & Pl
NH Flat	2	0	0	0	0
Hurdles	1	0	0	0	0
Career Total	**3**	**0**	**0**	**0**	

Going: Sf: 0-2 GS: 0-1 Gd: 0-0 GF: - Fm: 0-0
Distance: 2m/2m3: 0-2 2m4-2m7: 0-1 3m+: 0-0
Track: LH: 0-1 RH: 0-1 Tight: 0-0 Gall: 0-0
Aids: Bl: 0-0 Vi: 0-0 Tstrap: 0-0
Best Rating: 67 3/02 Chep 2m110y soft NHF

Indium

106 **111+**

8-y-o b g Groom Dancer (USA)-Gold Bracelet (Golden Fleece (USA))
D E Cantillon Mrs Edward Cantillon

Placings:0 **(3463)**
2001/02: 16^{0}S

	Starts	1st	2nd	3rd	Win & Pl
Hurdles	1	0	0	0	
Career Total	1	0	0	0	

Going: Sf: 0-1 GS: 0-0 Gd: 0-0 GF: - Fm: 0-0
Distance: 2m/2m3: 0-1 2m4-2m7: 0-0 3m+: 0-0
Track: LH: 0-1 RH: 0-0 Tight: 0-0 Gall: 0-1
Aids: Bl: 0-0 Vi: 0-0 Tstrap: 0-0
Best Rating: 33 1/02 Donc 2m110y soft Hdl

Fair Flat handicapper, got off the mark over hurdles in May 2002. Suited by fast ground and a flat track.

Indoux (FR)

92 **81**

6-y-o b g Useful (FR)-Pin'Hup (FR) (Signani (FR))
R J Hodges Frank E Crumpler

Placings:_300_-5 **(0124)**
2001/02: 24^{5}F

	Starts	1st	2nd	3rd	Win & Pl
Hurdles	1	0	0	0	0
Career Total	**4**	**0**	**0**	**1**	**215**

Going: Sf: 0-0 GS: 0-0 Gd: 0-0 GF: - Fm: 0-1
Distance: 2m/2m3: 0-0 2m4-2m7: 0-0 3m+: 0-1
Track: LH: 0-0 RH: 0-1 Tight: 0-1 Gall: 0-0
Aids: Bl: 0-0 Vi: 0-0 Tstrap: 0-0
Best Rating: 91 11/00 Chep 2m110y heavy NHF

Inducement

113 **123**

6-y-o ch g Sabrehill (USA)-Verchinina (Star Appeal)
Mrs A J Perrett J B Dale

Placings:4/15641-P350P53 **(4758)**
2001/02: 19^{P}GF, 19^{3}GS, 16^{5}GS, 16^{0}S, 16^{P}G, 16^{5}GS, 16^{3}GF

	Starts	1st	2nd	3rd	Win & Pl
Hurdles	6	0	0	2	1949
Chases	1	0	0	0	0
Career Total	**13**	**2**	**0**	**2**	**10300**

121	4/01	Extr	2m1f	E Hdl	G-S	£2153
117	12/00	Tntn	2m1f	C Hdl	SFT	£5573

Total win prize-money £7727

Going: Sf: 0-1 GS: 0-3 Gd: 0-1 GF: - Fm: 0-2
Distance: 2m/2m3: 0-6 2m4-2m7: 0-1 3m+: 0-0
Track: LH: 0-2 RH: 0-5 Tight: 0-2 Gall: 0-0
Aids: Bl: 0-0 Vi: 0-0 Tstrap: 0-0
Best Rating: 123 4/02 Asct 2m110y gd-fm Hdl

A fair handicapper on the Flat, he has developed into a fair sort over hurdles, but currently looks held by the Handicapper. Acts on fast ground, but looks better with some cut.

Inediana (FR)

6-y-o gr m Badolato (USA)-Cordoba Ii (FR) (Tanlas (FR))
Mrs P Sly R Brazier

Placings:0P-55450P **(1830)**
2001/02: 20^{5}, 22^{5}, 17^{4}, 19^{5}, 20^{0}, 20^{P}G

	Starts	1st	2nd	3rd	Win & Pl
Hurdles	1	0	0	0	0
Chases	5	0	0	0	1483
Career Total	**8**	**0**	**0**	**0**	**1483**

Going: Sf: 0-0 GS: 0-0 Gd: 0-1 GF: - Fm: 0-0
Distance: 2m/2m3: 0-2 2m4-2m7: 0-4 3m+: 0-0
Track: LH: 0-1 RH: 0-0 Tight: 0-1 Gall: 0-0
Aids: Bl: 0-0 Vi: 0-0 Tstrap: 0-0
Best Rating:

Infamelia

84 **70**

6-y-o b m Infantry-Incamelia (St Columbus)
N J Henderson Mrs D A Henderson

Placings:_00_00P **(0873)**
2001/02: 17^{0}GS, 17^{0}G, 22^{0}GF, 20^{0}GF, 25^{P}GS

	Starts	1st	2nd	3rd	Win & Pl
NH Flat	2	0	0	0	0
Hurdles	3	0	0	0	0
Career Total	**5**	**0**	**0**	**0**	

Going: Sf: 0-0 GS: 0-2 Gd: 0-1 GF: - Fm: 0-2
Distance: 2m/2m3: 0-2 2m4-2m7: 0-2 3m+: 0-1
Track: LH: 0-4 RH: 0-0 Tight: 0-4 Gall: 0-0
Aids: Bl: 0-0 Vi: 0-0 Tstrap: 0-0
Best Rating: 88 5/01 Folk 2m1f110y gd-sft NHF

Infini (FR)

100(105c) (118c)**112**

6-y-o gr g Le Nain Jaune (FR)-Contessina (FR) (Mistigri)
M C Pipe (Jack Barbe 27/5) Roa Arkle Partnership

Placings:00/0PP01-541110P23 **(4883)**
2001/02: 18^{5}S, 19^{4}S, 17^{1}GS, 16^{1}GF, 20^{1}GS, 16^{0}G, 17^{P}S, 16^{2}GF, 22^{3}GF

	Starts	1st	2nd	3rd	Win & Pl
Hurdles	5	1	1	1	6455
Chases	4	2	0	0	4144
Career Total	**16**	**4**	**1**	**1**	**14479**

118	9/01	NAbb	2m110y	E Ch	G-F	£3368

108	7/01	MRas	2m1f110y	D Hdl	G-S	£3997
	4/01	Fntb	2m1f110y	Ch	VS	£3880

Total win prize-money £11246

Going: Sf: 0-3 GS: 2-2 Gd: 0-1 GF: - Fm: 1-3
Distance: **2m/2m3: 2-6** 2m4-2m7: 1-3 3m+: 0-0
Track: **LH: 2-6** RH: 0-0 **Tight: 2-5** Gall: 0-0
Aids: Bl: 0-0 Vi: 0-0 Tstrap: 0-0
Best Rating: 118 9/01 Plum 2m4f gd-sft Ch

Fair hurdler/chaser who handles fast and soft ground and may be best at two miles, although has won over two and a half.

Inflation (FR)

103 91

6-y-o b m Port Etienne (FR)-Ravenna Iii (FR) (Unoaprile)
M C Pipe Paul Murphy

Placings:1-200601 **(4779)**
2001/02: 16^{2}S, 21^{0}G, 17^{0}S, 22^{6}S, 21^{0}GS, 21^{1}GF

	Starts	1st	2nd	3rd	Win & Pl
Hurdles	6	1	1	0	3545
Career Total	**7**	**2**	**1**	**0**	**5480**

68	4/02	Plum	2m5f	E Hdl	G-F	£2796
108	2/01	Wwck	2m	H NHF	SFT	£1935

Total win prize-money £4733

Going: Sf: 0-3 GS: 0-1 Gd: 0-1 GF: - Fm: 1-1
Distance: 2m/2m3: 0-2 **2m4-2m7: 1-4** 3m+: 0-0
Track: **LH: 1-2** RH: 0-4 **Tight: 1-2** Gall: 0-1
Aids: Bl: 0-0 **Vi: 1-2** Tstrap: 0-0
Best Rating: 108 2/01 Wwck 2m soft NHF

Made a winning bumper debut in February 2001on soft ground, but is not a natural jumper over hurdles and had to be galvanised by McCoy to win a weak event at Plumpton in April 2002.

Influence Pedler

108 109

9-y-o b g Keen-La Vie En Primrose (Henbit (USA))
Miss K M George Exterior Profiles Ltd

Placings:61203/3253063/213P14411PP/033121242/P4052223422P1 **(4864)**
2001/02: 25^{P}G, 22^{4}GF, 26^{0}GF, 24^{5}G, 24^{2}GF, 27^{2}GF, 25^{2}GF, 24^{3}F, 26^{4}G, 24^{2}G, 24^{2}GF, 24^{P}G, 25^{1}F

	Starts	1st	2nd	3rd	Win & Pl
Chases	13	1	5	1	11854
Career Total	**45**	**8**	**11**	**8**	**52227**

109	4/02	Extr	3m1f110y	D(0-115)HCh	FRM	£5193
115	9/99	Sedg	3m3f	E(0-115)HCh	G-F	£3470
115	8/99	Strf	3m	F(0-105)HCh	GD	£3018
115	12/98	Hrfd	2m3f	E(0-110)HCh	GD	£3430
114	11/98	Ludl	2m4f	D Ch	GD	£3972
97	8/98	MRas	2m4f	D Ch	GD	£3418
94	6/98	MRas	2m1f110y	D Ch	G-F	£4176
112	2/97	Wwck	2m4f110y	B Hdl	GD	£7100

Total win prize-money £33781

Going: Sf: 0-0 GS: 0-0 Gd: 0-5 GF: - Fm: 1-8
Distance: 2m/2m3: 0-0 2m4-2m7: 0-1 **3m+: 1-12**
Track: LH: 0-5 RH: 0-6 Tight: 0-9 Gall: 0-0
Aids: Bl: 0-0 Vi: 0-0 Tstrap: 0-0
Best Rating: 121 11/97 NAbb 2m6f gd-fm Hdl

Won first race since 1999 when making virtually all in an extended three-mile chase at Exeter April 2002. Likes ground conditions good or faster, consistent and often makes the frame.

Inforone (IRE)

96(93h) (73h)116

8-y-o b g Montelimar (USA)-Fisalmar Isle Vii (Damsire Unregistered)
D Magnier (Mrs S J Smith 24/11) D Magnier

Placings:54/52006F-210306 **(4926a)**
2001/02: 20^{2}GS, 22^{1}GF, 24^{0}GF, 23^{3}G, 19^{0}GF, 20^{6}Y

	Starts	1st	2nd	3rd	Win & Pl
Hurdles	1	0	1	0	648
Chases	5	1	0	1	4745
Career Total	**14**	**1**	**2**	**1**	**6520**

101	9/01	MRas	2m6f110y	E Ch	G-F	£4200

Total win prize-money £4200

Going: Sf: 0-0 GS: 0-1 Gd: 0-1 GF: - Fm: 1-3
Distance: 2m/2m3: 0-1 **2m4-2m7: 1-3** 3m+: 0-2
Track: LH: 0-2 **RH: 1-3 Tight: 1-3** Gall: 0-1
Aids: Bl: 0-0 Vi: 0-0 Tstrap: 0-0
Best Rating: 116 10/01 Weth 2m7f110y good Ch

Got off the mark in September 2001 in a two mile and six furlong novice chase at Market Rasen, having previously been well beaten in all his other tries.

Infrasonique (FR)

109 142

6-y-o b g Teresio-Quatalina Iii (FR) (Chateau Du Diable (FR))
Mrs L C Taylor (F-M Louit 19/6) Miss M Talbot

Placings:43225-2412324204221 **(4835)**
2001/02: 17^{2}S, 20^{4}GS, 20^{1}S, 21^{2}S, 22^{3}G, 20^{2}G, 19^{4}S, 20^{2}HY, 24^{0}G, 18^{4}GS, 20^{2}GS, 22^{2}G, 25^{1}G

	Starts	1st	2nd	3rd	Win & Pl
Hurdles	1	0	1	0	1940
Chases	12	2	5	1	46315
Career Total	**18**	**2**	**8**	**2**	**54337**

142	4/02	Ayr	3m1f	B HCh	GD	£21450
	6/01	Autl	2m4f110y	Ch	SFT	£12124

Total win prize-money £33574

Going: Sf: 1-5 GS: 0-3 Gd: 1-5 GF: - Fm: 0-0
Distance: 2m/2m3: 0-2 2m4-2m7: 1-9 3m+: 1-2
Track: **LH: 1-9** RH: 0-0 Tight: 0-2 Gall: 0-4
Aids: Bl: 0-0 Vi: 0-0 Tstrap: 0-0
Best Rating: 142 4/02 Ayr 3m1f good Ch

A sound jumper, he stays three miles and is usually in the frame. Acts on an easy surface.

Ingenu (FR)

104 125

6-y-o b g Royal Charter (FR)-Una Volta (FR) (Toujours Pret (USA))
R H Alner G L Porter

Placings:403/1423522-352P6 **(4177)**
2001/02: 20^{3}S, 21^{5}G, 20^{2}S, 20^{P}HY, 24^{6}GS

	Starts	1st	2nd	3rd	Win & Pl
Chases	5	0	1	1	1803
Career Total	**15**	**1**	**4**	**3**	**21478**

8/00	Diep	2m1f110y	Ch	SFT	£3362

Total win prize-money £3362

Going: Sf: 0-3 GS: 0-1 Gd: 0-1 GF: - Fm: 0-0
Distance: 2m/2m3: 0-0 2m4-2m7: 0-4 3m+: 0-1
Track: LH: 0-4 RH: 0-1 Tight: 0-4 Gall: 0-0
Aids: Bl: 0-0 Vi: 0-0 Tstrap: 0-0
Best Rating: 125 12/01 Plum 2m4f soft Ch

Ex-French chaser, has shown enough to suggest he can win his share of ordinary events. Likes soft ground.

Ingle Dene

9-y-o b g Skyliner-Dreamy Desire (Palm Track)
B Mactaggart Souter Racing

Placings:000/0005/0P045/4305P-0PPP **(0970)**
2001/02: 16^{0}GF, 20^{P}GS, 20^{P}GF, 17^{P}GS

	Starts	1st	2nd	3rd	Win & Pl
Hurdles	1	0	0	0	0
Chases	3	0	0	0	0
Career Total	**21**	**0**	**0**	**1**	**927**

Going: Sf: 0-0 GS: 0-2 Gd: 0-0 GF: - Fm: 0-2
Distance: 2m/2m3: 0-2 2m4-2m7: 0-2 3m+: 0-0
Track: LH: 0-1 RH: 0-2 Tight: 0-0 Gall: 0-0
Aids: Bl: 0-0 Vi: 0-0 Tstrap: 0-0
Best Rating: 106 11/99 Ayr 2m good Ch

Ingletonian

105 120

13-y-o b g Doc Marten-Dreamy Desire (Palm Track)
B Mactaggart Mrs Hilary Mactaggart

Placings:05030/6022431123/445333P/411124/001402F32/46P416/P140/640-2011122 **(2119)**
2001/02: 16^{2}GF, 17^{0}GS, 16^{1}G, 16^{1}G, 16^{1}G, 16^{2}G, 16^{2}GS

	Starts	1st	2nd	3rd	Win & Pl
Hurdles	7	3	3	0	18240
Career Total	**57**	**11**	**9**	**7**	**57252**

116	10/01	Kels	2m110y	D(0-120)HHdl	GD	[illegible]
114	9/01	Prth	2m110y	D(0-125)HHdl	GD	£5421
96	8/01	Prth	2m110y	G Hdl	GD	£2905
122	11/99	Kels	2m110y	D(0-125)HHdl	GD	£3495
126	4/99	Kels	2m1f	D(0-120)HCh	G-F	£3636
117	12/97	Carl	2m	E(0-105)HCh	SFT	£3186
125	3/97	Ayr	2m4f	D(0-125)HHdl	SFT	£2924
119	2/97	Kels	2m2f	D(0-120)HHdl	G-S	£2892
110	2/97	Kels	2m110y	E(0-115)HHdl	GD	£2316
108	1/95	Catt	2m3f	E Hdl	SFT	£2574
91	12/94	Catt	2m	Hdl	G-S	£1976

Total win prize-money £38183

Going: Sf: 0-0 GS: 0-2 Gd: 3-4 GF: - Fm: 0-1
Distance: **2m/2m3: 3-7** 2m4-2m7: 0-0 3m+: 0-0
Track: LH: 1-3 **RH: 2-3 Tight: 1-3** Gall: 0-0
Aids: Bl: 0-0 Vi: 0-0 Tstrap: 0-0
Best Rating: 138 4/97 Ayr 2m good Hdl

A regular at the Scottish tracks, he is well into the veteran stage now, but still knows what it takes to win and completed a hat trick over hurdles during the autumn. Suited by two miles and being able to dominate.

Inigo Jones (IRE)

103 120

6-y-o b g Alzao (USA)-Kindjal (Kris)
G Brown (P W Harris 27/10) Mrs Amanda Killick

Placings:3U15 **(4915)**
2001/02: 17^{3}S, 16^{U}GF, 17^{1}GF, 17^{5}GF

	Starts	1st	2nd	3rd	Win & Pl
Hurdles	4	1	0	1	3071
Career Total	**4**	**1**	**0**	**1**	**3071**

120	4/02	Sedg	2m1f	E Hdl	G-F	£2702

Total win prize-money £2702

Going: Sf: 0-1 GS: 0-0 Gd: 0-0 GF: - Fm: 1-3
Distance: **2m/2m3: 1-4** 2m4-2m7: 0-0 3m+: 0-0
Track: **LH: 1-3** RH: 0-1 **Tight: 1-3** Gall: 0-1
Aids: **Bl: 1-2** Vi: 0-0 Tstrap: 0-0
Best Rating: 120 4/02 Sedg 2m1f gd-fm Hdl

Above average middle-distance handicapper on the Flat. Free-running novice hurdler, got off the mark when blinkered at Sedgefield in April 2002. Suited by fast ground but the type to need everything his own way.

Inigo Montoya

10-y-o b g Liberated-Darklands (Feelings (FR))
C P Dennis Mrs A W Scott-Harden

Placings:4 **(4859)**
2001/02: 25^{4}G

	Starts	1st	2nd	3rd	Win & Pl
Chases	1	0	0	0	121
Career Total	**1**	**0**	**0**	**0**	**121**

Going: Sf: 0-0 GS: 0-0 Gd: 0-1 GF: - Fm: 0-0
Distance: 2m/2m3: 0-0 2m4-2m7: 0-0 3m+: 0-1
Track: LH: 0-1 RH: 0-0 Tight: 0-0 Gall: 0-0
Aids: Bl: 0-0 Vi: 0-0 Tstrap: 0-1
Best Rating: 70 4/02 Hexm 3m1f good Ch

Fair pointer who has returned in 2002 after almost three years off.

Inis Cara (IRE)

105 **122**

10-y-o b g Carlingford Castle-Good Sailing (Scorpio (FR))
Miss Venetia Williams Nancy Hogan Syndicate

Placings: 1/026051161106/113F1232264/023310664/34350F-04P **(4677)**
2001/02: 25^{0}G, 20^{4}S, 36^{P}G

	Starts	1st	2nd	3rd	Win & Pl
Chases	3	0	0	0	535
Career Total	**42**	**9**	**5**	**6**	**126593**

142	12/99	Leop	3m	(0-140)HCh	SFT	£63616
129	1/99	Tram	2m4f	Ch	HVY	£4296
133	11/98	Fair	2m5f110y	Ch	Y-S	£3586
138	10/98	Gowr	2m6f	Ch	SH	£4782
133	2/98	Clon	2m4f	(0-116)HHdl	Y-S	£2680
122	1/98	Leop	2m6f	(0-130)HHdl	Y-S	£3573
112	12/97	Thur	2m6f110y	Hdl	SFT	£2204
111	11/97	Dpat	2m6f	Hdl	SH	£2712
104	4/97	Slig	2m	NHF	HVY	£2204

Total win prize-money £89658

Going: Sf: 0-1 GS: 0-0 Gd: 0-2 GF: - Fm: 0-0
Distance: 2m/2m3: 0-0 2m4-2m7: 0-1 3m+: 0-2
Track: LH: 0-2 RH: 0-1 Tight: 0-2 Gall: 0-0
Aids: Bl: 0-0 Vi: 0-0 Tstrap: 0-0
Best Rating: 150 11/00 DRoy 3m gd-yld Ch

Formerly a useful hurdler and smart chaser in Ireland, where he landed the valuable Paddy Power Chase at Leopardstown in 1999. Has not seen much action since falling in the 2001 Grand National on his first start for Venetia Williams. Best over three miles. Acts on soft ground.

Inis Eile (IRE)

90(80c) (46c)**85**

7-y-o b g Peacock (FR)-Slippery Bell (No Argument)
Mrs S J Smith Worcester Racing Club

Placings: 0-00003 **(2770)**
2001/02: 17^{0}G, 24^{0}S, 22^{0}S, 20^{0}S, 25^{3}G

	Starts	1st	2nd	3rd	Win & Pl
Hurdles	5	0	0	1	350
Career Total	**6**	**0**	**0**	**1**	**350**

Going: Sf: 0-3 GS: 0-0 Gd: 0-2 GF: - Fm: 0-0
Distance: 2m/2m3: 0-1 2m4-2m7: 0-2 3m+: 0-2
Track: LH: 0-4 RH: 0-1 Tight: 0-2 Gall: 0-0
Aids: Bl: 0-0 Vi: 0-0 Tstrap: 0-0
Best Rating: 85 12/01 Hayd 2m4f soft Hdl

Placed form in bumpers and hurdles so far. Stays three miles.

Initiative

78 **49**

6-y-o ch g Arazi (USA)-Dance Quest (FR) (Green Dancer (USA))
J Hetherton (B W Murray 22/7) Frank Reay

Placings:0 **(2070)**
2001/02: 17^{0}S

	Starts	1st	2nd	3rd	Win & Pl
Hurdles	1	0	0	0	
Career Total	**1**	**0**	**0**	**0**	

Going: Sf: 0-1 GS: 0-0 Gd: 0-0 GF: - Fm: 0-0
Distance: 2m/2m3: 0-1 2m4-2m7: 0-0 3m+: 0-0
Track: LH: 0-1 RH: 0-0 Tight: 0-1 Gall: 0-0
Aids: Bl: 0-0 Vi: 0-0 Tstrap: 0-0
Best Rating: 49 11/01 Sedg 2m1f soft Hdl

Inlet (IRE)

84f **93f**

5-y-o ch g Insan (USA)-River Rescue (Over The River (FR))
J T Gifford Pell-Mell Partners

Placings: 0 **(4158)**
2001/02: 16^{0}GS

	Starts	1st	2nd	3rd	Win & Pl
NH Flat	1	0	0	0	
Career Total	**1**	**0**	**0**	**0**	

Going: Sf: 0-0 GS: 0-1 Gd: 0-0 GF: - Fm: 0-0
Distance: 2m/2m3: 0-1 2m4-2m7: 0-0 3m+: 0-0
Track: LH: 0-0 RH: 0-1 Tight: 0-0 Gall: 0-0
Aids: Bl: 0-0 Vi: 0-0 Tstrap: 0-0
Best Rating: 93 3/02 Sand 2m110y gd-sft NHF

Inn Antique (FR)

104(104c) **115+**

6-y-o b g Lute Antique (FR)-Taghera (FR) (Toujours Pret (USA))
P F Nicholls C G Roach

Placings: 0P1P1FP-4P2F **(4838)**
2001/02: 16^{4}G, 16^{P}G, 16^{2}G, 16^{F}G

	Starts	1st	2nd	3rd	Win & Pl
Hurdles	3	0	1	0	1097
Chases	1	0	0	0	0
Career Total	**11**	**2**	**1**	**0**	**16914**

126	1/01	Kemp	2m	D Ch	SFT	£4290
	9/00	Autl	2m2f	Ch	VS	£11527

Total win prize-money £15817

Going: Sf: 0-0 GS: 0-0 Gd: 0-4 GF: - Fm: 0-0
Distance: 2m/2m3: 0-4 2m4-2m7: 0-0 3m+: 0-0
Track: LH: 0-2 RH: 0-2 Tight: 0-0 Gall: 0-0
Aids: Bl: 0-0 Vi: 0-0 Tstrap: 0-0
Best Rating: 126 1/01 Kemp 2m soft Ch

A free-running sort, got off the mark in this country in a novice chase at Kempton in January 2001. However, proved an unreliable jumper subsequently. Had things his own way when making all on return to hurdles at Wincanton May 2002.

Inn At The Top

10-y-o b g Top Ville-Woolpack (Golden Fleece (USA))
J R Turner Mrs Sylvia Blakeley

Placings: 21211/0506/23141/232P131/022P-PFP **(4839)**
2001/02: 24^{P}S, 36^{F}G, 33^{P}G

	Starts	1st	2nd	3rd	Win & Pl
Chases	3	0	0	0	
Career Total	**28**	**7**	**7**	**3**	**73976**

156	4/00	Ayr	2m4f	B HCh	GD	£10366
157	3/00	Donc	2m3f110y	C(0-135)HCh	GD	£10578
141	4/99	Chel	2m5f	C Ch	GD	£6840
130	12/98	Donc	2m3f110y	D Ch	GD	£3834
121	1/97	Donc	2m4f	A Hdl	GD	£9883
120	12/96	Donc	2m4f	E Hdl	G-F	£2847
121	10/96	Hntg	2m4f110y	E Hdl	GD	£2617

Total win prize-money £46968

Going: Sf: 0-1 GS: 0-0 Gd: 0-2 GF: - Fm: 0-0
Distance: 2m/2m3: 0-0 2m4-2m7: 0-0 3m+: 0-3
Track: LH: 0-3 RH: 0-0 Tight: 0-1 Gall: 0-0
Aids: Bl: 0-0 Vi: 0-0 Tstrap: 0-0
Best Rating: 168 1/01 Donc 3m good Ch

Two and a half miles on good or faster ground are his ideal conditions, but he proved he gets three when going down with all guns blazing on soft ground in the Great Yorkshire at Doncaster in 2001. Ran poorly in the Whitbread on his final start of 2000/2001 season. Having only his second run of the season when falling at the first in the Grand National, before pulling up in the Scottish version.

Inn From The Cold (IRE)

85 **55**

6-y-o ch g Glacial Storm (USA)-Silver Apollo (General Ironside)
L Lungo Mrs Barbara Lungo

Placings:0 **(4431)**
2001/02: 16^{0}HY

	Starts	1st	2nd	3rd	Win & Pl
Hurdles	1	0	0	0	
Career Total	**1**	**0**	**0**	**0**	

Going: Sf: 0-1 GS: 0-0 Gd: 0-0 GF: - Fm: 0-0
Distance: 2m/2m3: 0-1 2m4-2m7: 0-0 3m+: 0-0
Track: LH: 0-1 RH: 0-0 Tight: 0-0 Gall: 0-1
Aids: Bl: 0-0 Vi: 0-0 Tstrap: 0-0
Best Rating:

Innes

83 **69**

6-y-o b m Inchinor-Trachelium (Formidable (USA))
Miss S E Hall C Platts

Placings: 2114/0 **(0449)**
2001/02: 20^{0}F

	Starts	1st	2nd	3rd	Win & Pl
Hurdles	1	0	0	0	
Career Total	**5**	**2**	**1**	**0**	**5438**

98	12/99	Sedg	2m1f	F(0-100)HHdl	SFT	£1912
75	10/99	Hexm	2m	E Hdl	GD	£2616

Total win prize-money £4528

Going: Sf: 0-0 GS: 0-0 Gd: 0-0 GF: - Fm: 0-1
Distance: 2m/2m3: 0-0 2m4-2m7: 0-1 3m+: 0-0
Track: LH: 0-1 RH: 0-0 Tight: 0-0 Gall: 0-0

Aids: Bl: 0-0 Vi: 0-0 Tstrap: 0-0
Best Rating: 98 12/99 Sedg 2m1f soft Hdl

Innovate (IRE)

95

10-y-o b m Posen (USA)-Innate (Be My Native (USA))
Miss Lucinda V Russell Peter K Dale

Placings: *00*P350/5PPF02/5144P/6113P-P4 (0277)
2001/02: 25^{PG}, $26^{4}GF$

	Starts	1st	2nd	3rd	Win & Pl
Chases	2	0	0	0	290
Career Total	**24**	**3**	**1**	**2**	**11682**

101 10/00 Towc 3m1f F(0-90)HCh G-F £2821
101 8/00 Uttx 3m F(0-100)HCh G-F £2710
98 6/99 Hexm 2m4f110y F Ch G-F £2909
Total win prize-money £8442

Going: Sf: 0-0 GS: 0-0 Gd: 0-1 GF: - Fm: 0-1
Distance: 2m/2m3: 0-0 2m4-2m7: 0-0 3m+: 0-2
Track: LH: 0-0 RH: 0-1 Tight: 0-0 Gall: 0-0
Aids: Bl: 0-0 Vi: 0-0 Tstrap: 0-2
Best Rating: 105 10/00 Aint 3m1f good Ch

Innox (FR)

113 149

6-y-o b g Lute Antique (FR)-Savane Iii (FR) (Quart De Vin (FR))
F Doumen Marquise De Moratella

Placings: 0F/324F-62512F321P2
2001/02: $21^{6}HY$, $20^{2}S$, $20^{5}G$, $21^{1}VS$, $23^{2}VS$, $27^{F}VS$, $20^{3}S$, $24^{2}G$, $26^{1}S$, $24^{P}GS$, $23^{2}VS$

	Starts	1st	2nd	3rd	Win & Pl
Chases	11	2	4	1	92134
Career Total	**17**	**2**	**5**	**2**	**100926**

144 2/02 Wwck 3m2f C Ch SFT £6812
9/01 Autl 2m5f110y HCh VS £10699
Total win prize-money £17511

Going: Sf: 1-4 GS: 0-1 Gd: 0-2 GF: - Fm: 0-0
Distance: 2m/2m3: 0-0 2m4-2m7: 1-5 3m+: 1-6
Track: **LH: 1-3** RH: 0-1 Tight: 0-0 Gall: 0-2
Aids: Bl: 0-0 Vi: 0-0 Tstrap: 0-0
Best Rating: 149 12/01 Kemp 3m good Ch

Useful French novice chaser, given too much to do when third at Newbury in December 2001. Decent efforts since, winning at Warwick. Needs a stamina test. Loves the mud. Apparently a laid-back individual.

Ino Iii (FR)

104 94

6-y-o b g Bayolidaan (FR)-Belle Gambette (FR) (Quart De Vin (FR))
C R Egerton Mrs C N Weatherby

Placings: 4/0-F2FP (1681)
2001/02: $22^{F}GF$, $26^{2}GF$, $24^{F}G$, $21^{P}G$

	Starts	1st	2nd	3rd	Win & Pl
Chases	4	0	1	0	927
Career Total	**6**	**0**	**1**	**0**	**2079**

Going: Sf: 0-0 GS: 0-0 Gd: 0-2 GF: - Fm: 0-2
Distance: 2m/2m3: 0-0 2m4-2m7: 0-2 3m+: 0-2
Track: LH: 0-2 RH: 0-2 Tight: 0-2 Gall: 0-0
Aids: Bl: 0-0 Vi: 0-0 Tstrap: 0-0
Best Rating: 94 9/01 Uttx 3m2f gd-fm Ch

Insane Lark (IRE)

74 49

8-y-o b g Insan (USA)-Gusserane Lark (Napoleon Bonaparte)
J A B Old Mrs Janet Dacey

Placings: *0*P5-P0P (1393)
2001/02: $24^{P}S$, $20^{0}G$, $24^{P}GF$

	Starts	1st	2nd	3rd	Win & Pl
Hurdles	3	0	0	0	
Career Total	**6**	**0**	**0**	**0**	**0**

Going: Sf: 0-1 GS: 0-0 Gd: 0-1 GF: - Fm: 0-1
Distance: 2m/2m3: 0-0 2m4-2m7: 0-1 3m+: 0-2
Track: LH: 0-3 RH: 0-0 Tight: 0-0 Gall: 0-0
Aids: Bl: 0-2 Vi: 0-0 Tstrap: 0-0
Best Rating: 49 4/01 Tntn 3m110y good Hdl

Instant Justice (IRE)

87 86

6-y-o gr g Roselier (FR)-Montekova (IRE) (Montekin)
D M Grissell Pepin Racing

Placings: 0-5 (1442)
2001/02: $18^{5}GF$

	Starts	1st	2nd	3rd	Win & Pl
Hurdles	1	0	0	0	0
Career Total	**2**	**0**	**0**	**0**	**0**

Going: Sf: 0-0 GS: 0-0 Gd: 0-0 GF: - Fm: 0-1
Distance: 2m/2m3: 0-1 2m4-2m7: 0-0 3m+: 0-0
Track: LH: 0-1 RH: 0-0 Tight: 0-1 Gall: 0-0
Aids: Bl: 0-0 Vi: 0-0 Tstrap: 0-0
Best Rating: 86 9/01 Font 2m2f110y gd-fm Hdl

Inter Rock (FR)

(95h) 91

6-y-o b g Video Rock (FR)-Aniste (FR) (Brezzo (FR))
R C Harper (A King 22/10) R C Harper

Placings: 055/61043-P4P (4568)
2001/02: $24^{P}F$, $26^{4}G$, $24^{P}G$

	Starts	1st	2nd	3rd	Win & Pl
Hurdles	2	0	0	0	0
Chases	1	0	0	0	315
Career Total	**11**	**1**	**0**	**1**	**2904**

108 12/00 Fknm 2m7f110y E Hdl G-S £2261
Total win prize-money £2261

Going: Sf: 0-1 GS: 0-0 Gd: 0-1 GF: - Fm: 0-1
Distance: 2m/2m3: 0-0 2m4-2m7: 0-0 3m+: 0-3
Track: LH: 0-1 RH: 0-1 Tight: 0-1 Gall: 0-0
Aids: Bl: 0-1 Vi: 0-0 Tstrap: 0-0
Best Rating: 108 1/01 Donc 3m110y good Hdl

Interdit (FR)

102(100h) (107h)122+

6-y-o b/br g Shafoun (FR)-Solaine (FR) (Pot D'Or (FR))
P J Hobbs Sir Robert Ogden

Placings: 4120-F55426 (4738)
2001/02: $21^{F}GF$, $17^{5}GS$, $19^{5}S$, $20^{4}G$, $19^{2}G$, $24^{6}GF$

	Starts	1st	2nd	3rd	Win & Pl
Chases	6	0	1	0	1643
Career Total	**10**	**1**	**2**	**0**	**4528**

100 12/00 Extr 2m1f E Hdl HVY £2275
Total win prize-money £2275

Going: Sf: 0-1 GS: 0-1 Gd: 0-2 GF: - Fm: 0-2
Distance: 2m/2m3: 0-3 2m4-2m7: 0-2 3m+: 0-1
Track: LH: 0-1 RH: 0-5 Tight: 0-3 Gall: 0-0
Aids: Bl: 0-1 Vi: 0-0 Tstrap: 0-0
Best Rating: 114 1/01 Extr 2m1f heavy Hdl

Rather in-and-out chaser. Seemed to appreciate the refitting of blinkers when winning at Exeter May 2002. Stays three miles two, acts on any ground.

Intersky Falcon

121 159

5-y-o ch g Polar Falcon (USA)-I'Ll Try (Try My Best (USA))
J J O'Neill Interskyracingcom & Mrs Jonjo O'Neill

Placings: *32*-2312111612 (4902)
2001/02: $16^{2}G$, $16^{3}G$, $19^{1}GF$, $19^{2}GF$, $17^{1}G$, $17^{1}G$, $16^{1}S$, $20^{6}GS$, $16^{1}G$, $16^{2}G$

	Starts	1st	2nd	3rd	Win & Pl
NH Flat	1	0	1	0	427
Hurdles	9	5	2	1	52921
Career Total	**12**	**5**	**4**	**2**	**54526**

149 4/02 Aint 2m110y A HHdl GD £23200
116 2/02 Donc 2m110y C(0-130)HHdl SFT £5876
108 11/01 Sedg 2m1f D Hdl GD £3328
121 9/01 Sedg 2m1f E Hdl GD £2380
102 8/01 MRas 2m3f110y E Hdl G-F £3104
Total win prize-money £37890

Going: Sf: 1-1 GS: 0-1 Gd: [illegible] GF: [illegible] Fm: 1-[illegible]
Distance: **2m/2m3: 4-7** 2m4-2m7: 1-3 3m+: 0-0
Track: **LH: 4-6** RH: 1-4 **Tight: 4-6** Gall: 1-1
Aids: **Bl: 4-6** Vi: 0-0 Tstrap: 0-0
Best Rating: 159 4/02 Sand 2m110y good Hdl

A highly progressive hurdler, he won five times over distances up to two and a half miles during the 2001/2002 season and was especially impressive when winning a Listed handicap hurdle at Aintree, before being touched off at Sandown. Defied a 30lb hike in the ratings when carrying top weight to a hard fought victory in the Swinton Hurdle. Acts on good ground or faster, but has won on soft. Usually wears blinkers and is suited by positive tactics.

Intersky Native (IRE)

101f 106f

6-y-o ch g Be My Native (USA)-Creative Music (Creative Plan (USA))
N G Richards Interskyracing.Com

Placings: *25* (4900)
2001/02: $17^{2}GS$, $16^{5}G$

	Starts	1st	2nd	3rd	Win & Pl
NH Flat	2	0	1	0	499
Career Total	**2**	**0**	**1**	**0**	**499**

Going: Sf: 0-0 GS: 0-1 Gd: 0-1 GF: - Fm: 0-0
Distance: 2m/2m3: 0-2 2m4-2m7: 0-0 3m+: 0-0
Track: LH: 0-1 RH: 0-1 Tight: 0-1 Gall: 0-0
Aids: Bl: 0-0 Vi: 0-0 Tstrap: 0-0
Best Rating: 106 4/02 Prth 2m110y good NHF

Into Battle

101 84

8-y-o b g Daring March-Mischievous Miss (Niniski (USA))
J J Quinn Lady Anne Bentinck

Placings:20/5P003/2P-041 (2669)
2001/02: 17^{0}G, 16^{4}G, 16^{1}G

	Starts	1st	2nd	3rd	Win & Pl
Hurdles	3	1	0	0	2426
Career Total	**12**	**1**	**2**	**1**	**4106**

83	12/01	Donc	2m110y	F(0-100)HHdl	GD	£2425

Total win prize-money £2426

Going: Sf: 0-0 GS: 0-0 Gd: 1-3 GF: - Fm: 0-0
Distance: **2m/2m3: 1-3** 2m4-2m7: 0-0 3m+: 0-0
Track: **LH: 1-3** RH: 0-0 Tight: 0-1 **Gall: 1-1**
Aids: Bl: 0-0 Vi: 0-0 Tstrap: 0-0
Best Rating: 96 2/98 Wwck 2m good NHF

Intox Iii (FR)

104 **125**

6-y-o ch g Garde Royale-Naftane (FR) (Trac)
M C Pipe Stef Stefanou

Placings:10/2156P0P-15611F3 (3343)
2001/02: 17^{1}G, 19^{5}GF, 16^{6}GF, 17^{1}GF, 17^{1}GF, 16^{F}GF, 17^{3}S

	Starts	1st	2nd	3rd	Win & Pl
Hurdles	7	3	0	1	7987
Career Total	**16**	**5**	**1**	**1**	**13243**

120	9/01	NAbb	2m1f	E(0-115)HHdl	G-F	£2639
115	8/01	NAbb	2m1f	F(0-100)HHdl	G-F	£2667
108	5/01	MRas	2m1f110y	F(0-105)HHdl	GD	£2138
108	7/00	NAbb	2m1f	D Hdl	G-F	£3088
99	1/00	Towc	2m	H NHF	HVY	£1641

Total win prize-money £12176

Going: Sf: 0-1 GS: 0-0 Gd: 1-1 GF: - Fm: 2-5
Distance: **2m/2m3: 3-7** 2m4-2m7: 0-0 3m+: 0-0
Track: **LH: 2-5** RH: 1-2 **Tight: 3-6** Gall: 0-0
Aids: Bl: 0-0 **Vi: 3-7** Tstrap: 0-0
Best Rating: 125 1/02 Tntn 2m1f soft Hdl

Handicap hurdler, he acts on most types of ground and is effective over two miles.

Intrepid Gal

97 **92**

7-y-o b m Terimon-Padrigal (Paddy's Stream)
N J Pomfret Nick Pomfret

Placings:5P/P-534 (0504)
2001/02: 20^{5}G, 16^{3}G, 20^{4}GF

	Starts	1st	2nd	3rd	Win & Pl
Hurdles	3	0	0	1	352
Career Total	**6**	**0**	**0**	**1**	**352**

Going: Sf: 0-0 GS: 0-0 Gd: 0-2 GF: - Fm: 0-1
Distance: 2m/2m3: 0-1 2m4-2m7: 0-2 3m+: 0-0
Track: LH: 0-1 RH: 0-2 Tight: 0-0 Gall: 0-2
Aids: Bl: 0-0 Vi: 0-0 Tstrap: 0-0
Best Rating: 92 5/01 Hntg 2m4f110y gd-fm Hdl

Intrepid Mogal

91 **91**

5-y-o b g Terimon-Padrigal (Paddy's Stream)
N J Pomfret J N Cheatle

Placings:00P53 (4684)
2001/02: 17^{0}G, 16^{0}GS, 20^{P}S, 22^{5}GS, 19^{3}GF

	Starts	1st	2nd	3rd	Win & Pl
NH Flat	2	0	0	0	0
Hurdles	3	0	0	1	440
Career Total	**5**	**0**	**0**	**1**	**440**

Going: Sf: 0-1 GS: 0-2 Gd: 0-1 GF: - Fm: 0-1
Distance: 2m/2m3: 0-2 2m4-2m7: 0-3 3m+: 0-0
Track: LH: 0-1 RH: 0-4 Tight: 0-2 Gall: 0-1
Aids: Bl: 0-0 Vi: 0-0 Tstrap: 0-0
Best Rating: 91 4/02 Hrfd 2m3f110y gd-fm Hdl

Showed improved form over hurdles on fast ground.

Intymcginty (IRE)

99f **109f**

5-y-o b g Port Lucaya-Mother Tongue (Montelimar (USA))
Noel T Chance Let's Get Ready To Rumble Partnership

Placings:56 (3784)
2001/02: 16^{5}G, 16^{6}S

	Starts	1st	2nd	3rd	Win & Pl
NH Flat	2	0	0	0	0
Career Total	**2**	**0**	**0**	**0**	**0**

Going: Sf: 0-1 GS: 0-0 Gd: 0-1 GF: - Fm: 0-0
Distance: 2m/2m3: 0-2 2m4-2m7: 0-0 3m+: 0-0
Track: LH: 0-1 RH: 0-1 Tight: 0-0 Gall: 0-1
Aids: Bl: 0-0 Vi: 0-0 Tstrap: 0-0
Best Rating: 109 12/01 Newb 2m110y good NHF

Has shown ability in bumpers.

Invest Wisely

10-y-o ch g Dashing Blade-Saniette (Crystal Palace (FR))
P Beaumont O R M Hartley

Placings:14/34411/54P21/P5FP/P3PP-P5 (0579)
2001/02: 28^{P}GF, 24^{5}GF

	Starts	1st	2nd	3rd	Win & Pl
Chases	2	0	0	0	0
Career Total	**22**	**4**	**1**	**2**	**17541**

119	4/99	Weth	3m5f	C HCh	G-F	£5842
104	3/98	Newc	3m	C(0-130)HHdl	GD	£3998
98	3/98	Newc	3m	D(0-125)HHdl	G-F	£2885
88	12/96	Muss	2m4f	E Hdl	FRM	£2263

Total win prize-money £14989

Going: Sf: 0-0 GS: 0-0 Gd: 0-0 GF: - Fm: 0-2
Distance: 2m/2m3: 0-0 2m4-2m7: 0-0 3m+: 0-2
Track: LH: 0-2 RH: 0-0 Tight: 0-2 Gall: 0-0
Aids: Bl: 0-0 Vi: 0-0 Tstrap: 0-0
Best Rating: 119 4/99 Weth 3m5f gd-fm Ch

Investor Relations (IRE)

101 **89**

4-y-o b g Goldmark (USA)-Debach Delight (Great Nephew)
N J Hawke (B J Meehan 7/5) N J McMullan

Placings:4453 (1725)
2001/02: 17^{4}GF, 16^{4}GF, 18^{5}GF, 17^{3}F

	Starts	1st	2nd	3rd	Win & Pl
Hurdles	4	0	0	1	377
Career Total	**4**	**0**	**0**	**1**	**377**

Going: Sf: 0-0 GS: 0-0 Gd: 0-0 GF: - Fm: 0-4
Distance: 2m/2m3: 0-4 2m4-2m7: 0-0 3m+: 0-0
Track: LH: 0-3 RH: 0-1 Tight: 0-4 Gall: 0-0
Aids: Bl: 0-0 Vi: 0-0 Tstrap: 0-0
Best Rating: 81 10/01 Tntn 2m1f firm Hdl

Won amateur riders selling handicap over 17 furlongs on good ground June 2002.

Invictress (DEN)

100 **98**

7-y-o b m Prince Mab (FR)-Joe's Lake (DEN) (King's Lake (USA))
P J Hobbs Alan Stevens & Denise Winton

Placings:50P/U4122F23-3404 (1380)
2001/02: 19^{3}G, 20^{4}GF, 22^{0}G, 19^{4}GF

	Starts	1st	2nd	3rd	Win & Pl
Hurdles	4	0	0	1	521
Career Total	**15**	**1**	**3**	**2**	**5203**

97	7/00	Worc	2m4f	E(0-105)HHdl	GD	£2408

Total win prize-money £2408

Going: Sf: 0-0 GS: 0-0 Gd: 0-2 GF: - Fm: 0-2
Distance: 2m/2m3: 0-0 2m4-2m7: 0-4 3m+: 0-0
Track: LH: 0-2 RH: 0-2 Tight: 0-1 Gall: 0-0
Aids: Bl: 0-1 Vi: 0-0 Tstrap: 0-0
Best Rating: 98 6/01 Worc 2m4f gd-fm Hdl

Inviramental

106 **93**

6-y-o b g Pursuit Of Love-Corn Futures (Nomination)
Mrs L C Jewell The Likely Bunch

Placings:360U-24 (0434)
2001/02: 16^{2}G, 17^{4}GF

	Starts	1st	2nd	3rd	Win & Pl
Hurdles	2	0	1	0	835
Career Total	**6**	**0**	**1**	**1**	**1161**

Going: Sf: 0-0 GS: 0-0 Gd: 0-1 GF: - Fm: 0-1
Distance: 2m/2m3: 0-2 2m4-2m7: 0-0 3m+: 0-0
Track: LH: 0-0 RH: 0-2 Tight: 0-1 Gall: 0-1
Aids: Bl: 0-0 Vi: 0-0 Tstrap: 0-0
Best Rating: 93 5/01 Hntg 2m110y good Hdl

Invisible Force (IRE)

69 **39**

5-y-o b g Imperial Frontier (USA)-Virginia Cottage (Lomond (USA))
B S Rothwell The Action Racing Club Ltd

Placings:00P (3280)
2001/02: 17^{0}S, 16^{0}S, 17^{P}HY

	Starts	1st	2nd	3rd	Win & Pl
Hurdles	3	0	0	0	
Career Total	**3**	**0**	**0**	**0**	

Going: Sf: 0-3 GS: 0-0 Gd: 0-0 GF: - Fm: 0-0
Distance: 2m/2m3: 0-3 2m4-2m7: 0-0 3m+: 0-0
Track: LH: 0-2 RH: 0-1 Tight: 0-1 Gall: 0-0
Aids: Bl: 0-0 Vi: 0-0 Tstrap: 0-0
Best Rating: 39 12/01 Hayd 2m soft Hdl

Inzamaam (IRE)

81 **52**

6-y-o b m Zaffaran (USA)-Rosy Posy (IRE) (Roselier (FR))
N A Twiston-Davies The 'Yes' - 'No' - Wait'....Sorries

Placings:300-05 (0720)
2001/02: 17^{0}G, 26^{5}F

	Starts	1st	2nd	3rd	Win & Pl
Hurdles	2	0	0	0	0
Career Total	**5**	**0**	**0**	**1**	**239**

Going: Sf: 0-0 GS: 0-0 Gd: 0-1 GF: - Fm: 0-1
Distance: 2m/2m3: 0-1 2m4-2m7: 0-0 3m+: 0-1
Track: LH: 0-0 RH: 0-2 Tight: 0-0 Gall: 0-0
Aids: Bl: 0-0 Vi: 0-0 Tstrap: 0-0
Best Rating: 94 1/01 Kemp 2m soft NHF

Ioga (FR)

97 **87**

6-y-o b/br g Video Rock (FR)-Valentia (FR) (Brezzo (FR))
Miss Venetia Williams Tony Eaves

Placings:P00-5 **(0346)**
2001/02: 20^{5}G

	Starts	1st	2nd	3rd	Win & Pl
Hurdles	1	0	0	0	0
Career Total	**4**	**0**	**0**	**0**	**0**

Going: Sf: 0-0 GS: 0-0 Gd: 0-1 GF: - Fm: 0-0
Distance: 2m/2m3: 0-0 2m4-2m7: 0-1 3m+: 0-0
Track: LH: 0-1 RH: 0-0 Tight: 0-1 Gall: 0-0
Aids: Bl: 0-0 Vi: 0-0 Tstrap: 0-0
Best Rating: 87 5/01 Aint 2m4f good Hdl

Winning chaser for Francois Doumen in France, subsequently disqualified. Showed promise in a two and a half mile novice hurdle on British debut, held since.

Iorana (FR)

103(100c) (110c)**108**

6-y-o ch g Marignan (USA)-Fareham (FR) (Fast Topaze (USA))
M C Pipe Mrs Alison C Farrant

Placings:3/F111502/14**121U5-PP** **(4256)**
2001/02: 20^{P}G, 17^{P}G

	Starts	1st	2nd	3rd	Win & Pl
Hurdles	1	0	0	0	0
Chases	1	0	0	0	0
Career Total	**17**	**6**	**2**	**1**	**31501**

115	2/01	Uttx	2m	D Ch	SFT	£3718
130	9/00	Chep	2m110y	B HHdl	GD	£9821
130	8/00	Uttx	2m4f110y	D(0-125)HHdl	G-F	£3090
115	9/99	Font	2m2f110y	E Hdl	GD	£2232
105	8/99	Worc	2m	E Hdl	G-S	£2355
	6/99	Autl	1m7f	Hdl	VS	£6997

Total win prize-money £28216

Going: Sf: 0-0 GS: 0-0 Gd: 0-2 GF: - Fm: 0-0
Distance: 2m/2m3: 0-1 2m4-2m7: 0-1 3m+: 0-0
Track: LH: 0-1 RH: 0-1 Tight: 0-1 Gall: 0-1
Aids: Bl: 0-0 Vi: 0-0 Tstrap: 0-0
Best Rating: 130 9/00 Chep 2m110y good Hdl

One time decent hurdler, bounced back to form when winning Class D handicap at Worcester August 2002. Could be well handicapped based on that showing.

Ipledgeallegiance (USA)

111 **104**

6-y-o b g Alleged (USA)-Yafill (USA) (Nureyev (USA))
K A Morgan Michael Hill

Placings:2U-43520125U403 **(4879)**
2001/02: 17^{4}GS, 17^{3}GF, 19^{5}GF, 16^{2}G, 16^{0}G, 16^{1}S, 16^{2}S, 16^{5}GS, 16^{U}GS, 16^{4}S, 16^{0}GS, 16^{3}G

	Starts	1st	2nd	3rd	Win & Pl
Hurdles	12	1	2	2	5329
Career Total	**14**	**1**	**3**	**2**	**6155**

104	12/01	Hayd	2m	F(0-110)HHdl	SFT	£2702

Total win prize-money £2702

Going: Sf: 1-3 GS: 0-4 Gd: 0-3 GF: - Fm: 0-2
Distance: **2m/2m3: 1-11** 2m4-2m7: 0-1 3m+: 0-0
Track: **LH: 1-8** RH: 0-4 Tight: 0-6 Gall: 0-4
Aids: Bl: 0-0 Vi: 0-0 **Tstrap: 1-12**
Best Rating: 104 1/02 Fknm 2m soft Hdl

Suited by soft ground and two miles, he won at Haydock in December 2001 and has run well in defeat since. Regularly wears a tongue strap.

Iranoo (IRE)

94 **74**

5-y-o b g Persian Bold-Rose Of Summer (IRE) (Taufan (USA))
R Allan The Banana Bunch

Placings:06-25 **(0800)**
2001/02: 16^{2}GF, 16^{5}GF

	Starts	1st	2nd	3rd	Win & Pl
Hurdles	2	0	1	0	858
Career Total	**4**	**0**	**1**	**0**	**858**

Going: Sf: 0-0 GS: 0-0 Gd: 0-0 GF: - Fm: 0-2
Distance: 2m/2m3: 0-2 2m4-2m7: 0-0 3m+: 0-0
Track: LH: 0-0 RH: 0-2 Tight: 0-0 Gall: 0-0
Aids: Bl: 0-0 Vi: 0-0 Tstrap: 0-0
Best Rating: 74 6/01 Prth 2m110y gd-fm Hdl

Irbee

109(94h) (116h)**152**

10-y-o b g Gunner B-Cupids Bower (Owen Dudley)
P F Nicholls Mrs Bunty Millard

Placings:5/**11PF21123**/2**233115**/**1F-43523044** **(4901)**
2001/02: 16^{4}GS, 20^{3}S, 20^{5}S, 16^{2}S, 16^{3}G, 20^{0}GS, 20^{4}GS, 16^{4}G

	Starts	1st	2nd	3rd	Win & Pl
Hurdles	1	0	0	0	0
Chases	7	0	1	2	11239
Career Total	**27**	**7**	**5**	**5**	**84549**

108	10/00	Chep	2m110y	D Hdl	G-S	£2996
158	2/00	Kemp	2m	B Ch	SFT	£10042
155	1/00	Hayd	2m	B(0-145)HCh	SFT	£8649
150	3/99	Uttx	2m5f	C(0-135)HCh	G-S	£7132
154	3/99	Chep	2m3f110y	D Ch	SFT	£4030
140	11/98	Chep	2m3f110y	A(0-115)Ch	G-S	£12680
136	10/98	Worc	2m4f110y	D Ch	SFT	£3738

Total win prize-money £49271

Going: Sf: 0-3 GS: 0-3 Gd: 0-2 GF: - Fm: 0-0
Distance: 2m/2m3: 0-4 2m4-2m7: 0-4 3m+: 0-0
Track: LH: 0-3 RH: 0-5 Tight: 0-0 Gall: 0-2
Aids: Bl: 0-8 Vi: 0-0 Tstrap: 0-0
Best Rating: 158 2/00 Kemp 2m soft Ch

He was off the track for a year before reappearing in October 2001 and has shown creditable form since returning, if looking hard to win with. Suited by trips ranging from two to two and a half miles, he must have soft ground and is usually blinkered.

Ireland's Eye (IRE)

106 **113**

7-y-o b g Shareef Dancer (USA)-So Romantic (IRE) (Teenoso (USA))
J R Norton Ejam Connection

Placings:*1214*/651431 **(4434)**
2001/02: 17^{6}S, 16^{5}GS, 16^{1}S, 17^{4}HY, 20^{3}S, 20^{1}HY

	Starts	1st	2nd	3rd	Win & Pl
Hurdles	6	2	0	1	7059
Career Total	**10**	**4**	**1**	**1**	**11273**

113	3/02	Newc	2m4f	E Hdl	HVY	£2702
96	12/01	Hexm	2m	D Hdl	SFT	£3705
111	3/99	Newc	2m	H NHF	SFT	£1710
99	1/99	Catt	2m	H NHF	SFT	£1842

Total win prize-money £9960

Going: Sf: 2-5 GS: 0-1 Gd: 0-0 GF: - Fm: 0-0
Distance: 2m/2m3: 1-4 2m4-2m7: 1-2 3m+: 0-0
Track: **LH: 2-5** RH: 0-1 Tight: 0-1 **Gall: 1-3**
Aids: Bl: 0-0 Vi: 0-0 Tstrap: 0-0
Best Rating: 118 4/99 Ayr 2m soft NHF

Fair novice hurdler, stays two and a half miles and acts on soft ground.

Irenie

70f **96f**

7-y-o ch m Nicholas Bill-Porto Irene (Porto Bello)
W G M Turner Donald C Tucker

Placings:*4-0* **(0064)**
2001/02: 17^{0}GS

	Starts	1st	2nd	3rd	Win & Pl
NH Flat	1	0	0	0	
Career Total	**2**	**0**	**0**	**0**	**0**

Going: Sf: 0-0 GS: 0-1 Gd: 0-0 GF: - Fm: 0-0
Distance: 2m/2m3: 0-1 2m4-2m7: 0-0 3m+: 0-0
Track: LH: 0-0 RH: 0-0 Tight: 0-1 Gall: 0-0
Aids: Bl: 0-0 Vi: 0-0 Tstrap: 0-0
Best Rating: 96 4/01 Tntn 2m1f gd-fm NHF

Iris Bleu (FR)

113 **149**

6-y-o ch g Beyssac (FR)-Dear Blue (FR) (Cyborg (FR))
M C Pipe D A Johnson

Placings:011/**12446-3222223PF5** **(4913)**
2001/02: 19^{3}F, 20^{2}S, 16^{2}G, 16^{2}G, 21^{2}G, 19^{2}GS, 24^{3}GS, 26^{P}S, 36^{F}G, 29^{5}G

	Starts	1st	2nd	3rd	Win & Pl
Chases	10	0	5	2	26501
Career Total	**18**	**3**	**6**	**2**	**61170**

131	5/00	Autl	2m1f110y	Ch	VS	£11527
	4/00	Autl	2m2f	Hdl	HLD	£10567
	4/00	Autl	2m1f110y	Hdl	HLD	£9606

Total win prize-money £31700

Going: Sf: 0-2 GS: 0-2 Gd: 0-5 GF: - Fm: 0-1
Distance: 2m/2m3: 0-3 2m4-2m7: 0-3 3m+: 0-4
Track: LH: 0-6 RH: 0-4 Tight: 0-3 Gall: 0-2
Aids: Bl: 0-0 Vi: 0-0 Tstrap: 0-0
Best Rating: 149 12/01 Chep 2m3f110y gd-sft Ch

An ex-French import, he had won his last three hurdle races in his home country before joining Martin Pipe during 2000. Consistently placed over fences, but is becoming frustrating. Handles good or softer and stays three miles.

Iris Collonges (FR)

103(102c) (119c)**115**

6-y-o b g Luchiroverte (IRE)-Soubrette Collonge (FR) (Saumon (FR))
N J Henderson The Barrow Boys Ii

Placings:*0*/2312-6446 **(2431)**
2001/02: 17^{6}GS, 16^{4}S, 16^{4}G, 16^{6}GS

	Starts	1st	2nd	3rd	Win & Pl
Hurdles	2	0	0	0	0
Chases	2	0	0	0	609
Career Total	**9**	**1**	**2**	**1**	**5958**

113 1/01 Winc 2m E Hdl G-S £2037
Total win prize-money £2037

Going: Sf: 0-1 GS: 0-2 Gd: 0-1 GF: - Fm: 0-0
Distance: 2m/2m3: 0-4 2m4-2m7: 0-0 3m+: 0-0
Track: LH: 0-2 RH: 0-2 Tight: 0-1 Gall: 0-1
Aids: Bl: 0-0 Vi: 0-0 Tstrap: 0-0
Best Rating: 120 3/01 Asct 2m110y heavy Hdl

A winner over hurdles on good to soft ground and is suited by around two miles.

Iris Du Butel (FR)

6-y-o b g Passing Sale (FR)-Tigresse De L'Isle (FR) (Quart De Vin (FR))
Ian Williams Mr And Mrs J D Cotton

Placings:06P-P (4869)
2001/02: 20^{P}GF

	Starts	1st	2nd	3rd	Win & Pl
Hurdles	1	0	0	0	
Career Total	**4**	**0**	**0**	**0**	**0**

Going: Sf: 0-0 GS: 0-0 Gd: 0-0 GF: - Fm: 0-1
Distance: 2m/2m3: 0-0 2m4-2m7: 0-1 3m+: 0-0
Track: LH: 0-1 RH: 0-0 Tight: 0-0 Gall: 0-0
Aids: Bl: 0-0 Vi: 0-0 Tstrap: 0-0
Best Rating: 99 12/00 Donc 2m4f heavy Hdl

Iris Royal (FR)

117 136

6-y-o b g Garde Royale-Tchela (FR) (Le Nain Jaune (FR))
N J Henderson Sir Robert Ogden

Placings:41521/1PPP-231022 (4821)
2001/02: 22^{2}G, 21^{3}GS, 22^{1}S, 25^{0}GS, 24^{2}G, 24^{2}G

	Starts	1st	2nd	3rd	Win & Pl
Hurdles	6	1	3	1	44884
Career Total	**15**	**4**	**4**	**1**	**61661**

131 2/02 Sand 2m6f A HHdl SFT £29000
129 1/01 Font 2m4f C(0-135)HHdl SFT £5382
121 4/00 Ayr 2m4f C HHdl GD £4881
119 1/00 Wwck 2m D Hdl SFT £4543
Total win prize-money £43808

Going: Sf: 1-1 GS: 0-2 Gd: 0-3 GF: - Fm: 0-0
Distance: 2m/2m3: 0-0 **2m4-2m7: 1-3** 3m+: 0-3
Track: LH: 0-2 **RH: 1-3** Tight: 0-1 Gall: 0-1
Aids: Bl: 0-0 Vi: 0-0 Tstrap: 0-0
Best Rating: 136 4/02 Chel 3m good Hdl

Useful handicap hurdler, fought hard to get his head in front at Sandown in February, but was held at Cheltenham in March. Just held at Aintree over three miles. Acts on most surfaces, well suited by two and three-quarter miles. Has run well fresh.

Iris's Gift

109f 135f

5-y-o gr g Gunner B-Shirley's Gift (Scallywag)
J J O'Neill Robert Lester

Placings:11152 (4679)
2001/02: 16^{1}GF, 16^{1}GF, 16^{1}S, 16^{5}GS, 17^{2}G

	Starts	1st	2nd	3rd	Win & Pl
NH Flat	5	3	1	0	18910
Career Total	5	3	1	0	18910

116 2/02 Newb 2m110y A NHF SFT £9000
102 9/01 Worc 2m H NHF G-F £1515
95 8/01 Worc 2m H NHF G-F £1494
Total win prize-money £12011

Going: Sf: 1-1 GS: 0-1 Gd: 0-1 GF: - Fm: 2-2
Distance: **2m/2m3: 3-5** 2m4-2m7: 0-0 3m+: 0-0
Track: **LH: 3-4** RH: 0-0 Tight: 0-0 **Gall: 1-1**
Aids: Bl: 0-0 Vi: 0-0 Tstrap: 0-0
Best Rating: 135 4/02 Aint 2m1f good NHF

Won two bumpers on fast ground at Worcester in late summer of 2001 and completed the hat-trick in very different ground at Newbury in February. Ran well in the Festival bumpers at Cheltenham and Aintree and should make a very useful staying novice hurdler.

Irish Blessing (USA)

64 30

5-y-o b g Ghazi (USA)-Win For Leah (USA) (His Majesty (USA))
F Jordan The Bhiss Partnership

Placings:05P (4300)
2001/02: 17^{0}G, 20^{5}G, 20^{P}HY

	Starts	1st	2nd	3rd	Win & Pl
Hurdles	3	0	0	0	0
Career Total	3	0	0	0	0

Going: Sf: 0-1 GS: 0-0 Gd: 0-2 GF: - Fm: 0-0
Distance: 2m/2m3: 0-1 2m4-2m7: 0-2 3m+: 0-0
Track: LH: 0-2 RH: 0-1 Tight: 0-1 Gall: 0-1
Aids: Bl: 0-0 Vi: 0-0 Tstrap: 0-0
Best Rating: 30 8/01 Ctml 2m1f110y good Hdl

Irish Buzz (IRE)

10-y-o b g Satco (FR)-Brisbee (Prince Bee)
Mrs Jane Clifford Mrs Jane Clifford

Placings:0P000/60P/PP/PR (4638)
2001/02: 19^{P}F, 19^{R}GF

	Starts	1st	2nd	3rd	Win & Pl
Chases	2	0	0	0	
Career Total	**12**	**0**	**0**	**0**	**0**

Going: Sf: 0-0 GS: 0-0 Gd: 0-0 GF: - Fm: 0-2
Distance: 2m/2m3: 0-0 2m4-2m7: 0-2 3m+: 0-0
Track: LH: 0-0 RH: 0-2 Tight: 0-0 Gall: 0-0
Aids: Bl: 0-0 Vi: 0-0 Tstrap: 0-0
Best Rating: 71 12/96 Sedg 2m5f110y good Hdl

Irish Chapel (IRE)

72f 53f

6-y-o b g College Chapel-Heart Of Flame (Top Ville)
H E Haynes Miss Sally R Haynes

Placings:00 (1545)
2001/02: 16^{0}G, 17^{0}G

	Starts	1st	2nd	3rd	Win & Pl
NH Flat	2	0	0	0	
Career Total	2	0	0	0	

Going: Sf: 0-0 GS: 0-0 Gd: 0-2 GF: - Fm: 0-0
Distance: 2m/2m3: 0-2 2m4-2m7: 0-0 3m+: 0-0
Track: LH: 0-1 RH: 0-1 Tight: 0-0 Gall: 0-0
Aids: Bl: 0-0 Vi: 0-0 Tstrap: 0-0
Best Rating: 53 7/01 Worc 2m good NHF

Irish Cream (IRE)

95 78

6-y-o b m Petong-Another Baileys (Deploy)
J L Spearing Masonaires

Placings:33002-005P4 (4176)
2001/02: 16^{0}S, 20^{0}GS, 21^{5}S, 20^{P}S, 19^{4}GS

	Starts	1st	2nd	3rd	Win & Pl
Hurdles	5	0	0	0	0
Career Total	**10**	**0**	**1**	**2**	**1645**

Going: Sf: 0-3 GS: 0-2 Gd: 0-0 GF: - Fm: 0-0
Distance: 2m/2m3: 0-2 2m4-2m7: 0-3 3m+: 0-0
Track: LH: 0-2 RH: 0-2 Tight: 0-2 Gall: 0-0
Aids: Bl: 0-2 Vi: 0-0 Tstrap: 0-0
Best Rating: 95 11/00 Uttx 2m heavy Hdl

Irish Fashion (USA)

104 113

7-y-o ch g Nashwan (USA)-L'Irlandaise (USA) (Irish River (FR))
Dr P Pritchard (Noel T Chance 19/5) A J Whiting

Placings:4030531/000-60312120634 (3930)
2001/02: 17^{6}GS, 21^{0}G, 16^{3}S, 16^{1}S, 16^{2}G, 16^{1}G, 16^{2}GS, 20^{0}G, 16^{6}GS, 16^{3}S, 16^{4}HY

	Starts	1st	2nd	3rd	Win & Pl
Hurdles	11	2	2	2	8760
Career Total	**21**	**3**	**2**	**4**	**11979**

106 12/01 Plum 2m F(0-110)HHdl GD £3542
103 12/01 Wwck 2m F(0-100)HHdl SFT £2000
113 4/00 Plum 2m F(0-90)Hdl HVY £2394
Total win prize-money £7938

Going: Sf: 1-4 GS: 0-3 Gd: 1-4 GF: - Fm: 0-0
Distance: **2m/2m3: 2-9** 2m4-2m7: 0-2 3m+: 0-0
Track: **LH: 2-5** RH: 0-4 **Tight: 1-4** Gall: 0-0
Aids: Bl: 0-0 Vi: 0-0 Tstrap: 0-0
Best Rating: 113 2/02 Asct 2m110y soft Hdl

Fair hurdler, if slightly one-paced, he likes the mud and is suited by positive tactics. Made a return to form in December 2001, winning at Warwick and Plumpton, before finishing a fair second at Chepstow, although he was beaten a fair way in a better race at Fontwell in January 2001.

Irish Frolic (IRE)

86 99

10-y-o b g Jareer (USA)-Grey Marble (Realm)
R Rowe The Nicky Watts Partnership

Placings:0/000/66523/132/124-5 (0234)
2001/02: 16^{5}GF

	Starts	1st	2nd	3rd	Win & Pl
Chases	1	0	0	0	0
Career Total	**16**	**2**	**3**	**2**	**9661**

129 9/00 Font 2m4f F(0-105)HCh G-S £2827
112 5/99 Font 2m2f F Ch FRM £2282
Total win prize-money £5111

Going: Sf: 0-0 GS: 0-0 Gd: 0-0 GF: - Fm: 0-1
Distance: 2m/2m3: 0-1 2m4-2m7: 0-0 3m+: 0-0
Track: LH: 0-1 RH: 0-0 Tight: 0-1 Gall: 0-0
Aids: Bl: 0-0 Vi: 0-0 Tstrap: 0-1
Best Rating: 129 10/00 Font 2m6f good Ch

Irish Hussar (IRE)

110 141

6-y-o b g Supreme Leader-Shuil Ard (Quayside)

N J Henderson Major Christopher Hanbury

Placings: *1*-210 **(4229)**
2001/02: 16^{2}S, 19^{1}S, 21^{0}GS

	Starts	1st	2nd	3rd	Win & Pl
Hurdles	3	1	1	0	6905
Career Total	**4**	**2**	**1**	**0**	**9709**

125	3/02	Newb	2m3f	D Hdl	SFT	£4953
127	3/01	Sand	2m110y	H NHF	HVY	£2803

Total win prize-money £7757

Going: Sf: 1-2 GS: 0-1 Gd: 0-0 GF: - Fm: 0-0
Distance: **2m/2m3: 1-2** 2m4-2m7: 0-1 3m+: 0-0
Track: **LH: 1-3** RH: 0-0 Tight: 0-0 **Gall: 1-3**
Aids: Bl: 0-0 Vi: 0-0 Tstrap: 0-0
Best Rating: 141 2/02 Newb 2m110y soft Hdl

Made a winning debut in a bumper at Sandown in March 2001, a race that has worked out well. Promising hurdles debut almost a year later and won easily next time, but well held at the Festival. Looks a smart recruit.

Irish Native (IRE)

5-y-o br g Be My Native (USA)-Thats Irish (Furry Glen)
Miss H C Knight Martin Broughton

Placings: *0*P **(2765)**
2001/02: 16^{0}G, 19^{P}GS

	Starts	1st	2nd	3rd	Win & Pl
NH Flat	1	0	0	0	0
Hurdles	1	0	0	0	0
Career Total	**2**	**0**	**0**	**0**	

Going: Sf: 0-0 GS: 0-1 Gd: 0-1 GF: - Fm: 0-0
Distance: 2m/2m3: 0-2 2m4-2m7: 0-0 3m+: 0-0
Track: LH: 0-1 RH: 0-1 Tight: 0-0 Gall: 0-1
Aids: Bl: 0-0 Vi: 0-0 Tstrap: 0-0
Best Rating: 69 11/01 Winc 2m good NHF

Irish Nougat (IRE)

84f **89f**

6-y-o b g Montelimar (USA)-Solo Girl (IRE) (Le Bavard (FR))
J A B Old The Early Birds

Placings: *0* **(4032)**
2001/02: 16^{0}GS

	Starts	1st	2nd	3rd	Win & Pl
NH Flat	1	0	0	0	
Career Total	**1**	**0**	**0**	**0**	

Going: Sf: 0-0 GS: 0-1 Gd: 0-0 GF: - Fm: 0-0
Distance: 2m/2m3: 0-1 2m4-2m7: 0-0 3m+: 0-0
Track: LH: 0-1 RH: 0-0 Tight: 0-0 Gall: 0-1
Aids: Bl: 0-0 Vi: 0-0 Tstrap: 0-0
Best Rating: 89 3/02 Newb 2m110y gd-sft NHF

Irish Pleasure (IRE)

104 **97**

6-y-o b/br g Grand Plaisir (IRE)-Killegney (Reformed Character)
K Bishop J Stephenson

Placings: *30035* **(4479)**
2001/02: 16^{3}GF, 16^{0}GS, 24^{0}S, 19^{3}G, 19^{5}G

	Starts	1st	2nd	3rd	Win & Pl
NH Flat	2	0	0	1	220
Hurdles	3	0	0	1	401
Career Total	**5**	**0**	**0**	**2**	**621**

Going: Sf: 0-1 GS: 0-1 Gd: 0-2 GF: - Fm: 0-1
Distance: 2m/2m3: 0-3 2m4-2m7: 0-1 3m+: 0-1
Track: LH: 0-1 RH: 0-4 Tight: 0-1 Gall: 0-1
Aids: Bl: 0-0 Vi: 0-0 Tstrap: 0-0
Best Rating: 97 3/02 Hrfd 2m3f110y good Hdl

Irish Raider (NZ)

50

8-y-o b g Epidaurus (USA)-On The Move (AUS) (Bending Away (USA))
G M McCourt T N Siviter

Placings: 0 **(0674)**
2001/02: 16^{0}GF

	Starts	1st	2nd	3rd	Win & Pl
Hurdles	1	0	0	0	
Career Total	**1**	**0**	**0**	**0**	

Going: Sf: 0-0 GS: 0-0 Gd: 0-0 GF: - Fm: 0-1
Distance: 2m/2m3: 0-1 2m4-2m7: 0-0 3m+: 0-0
Track: LH: 0-1 RH: 0-0 Tight: 0-0 Gall: 0-0
Aids: Bl: 0-0 Vi: 0-0 Tstrap: 0-0
Best Rating:

Irish Sea (USA)

9-y-o b g Zilzal (USA)-Dunkellin (USA) (Irish River (FR))
S Flook (B J Llewellyn 10/2) D F Quinlan

Placings: 050P/6622F10U556011/B12/P-3P13 **(4846)**
2001/02: 17^{3}GS, 17^{P}GF, 23^{1}GF, 24^{3}G

	Starts	1st	2nd	3rd	Win & Pl
Hurdles	2	0	0	1	557
Chases	2	1	0	1	1900
Career Total	**26**	**5**	**3**	**2**	**11561**

91	4/02	Uttx	2m7f	H Ch	G-F	£1631
91	7/99	Worc	2m2f	E(0-115)HHdl	G-F	£2372
85	4/99	Folk	2m1f110y	G(0-95)HHdl	G-F	£1660
74	4/99	Tntn	2m3f110y	G(0-90)HHdl	G-S	£1509
84	10/98	MRas	2m1f110y	G(0-95)HHdl	SFT	£1576

Total win prize-money £8749

Going: Sf: 0-0 GS: 0-1 Gd: 0-1 GF: - Fm: 1-2
Distance: 2m/2m3: 0-2 **2m4-2m7: 1-1** 3m+: 0-1
Track: **LH: 1-3** RH: 0-1 Tight: 0-3 Gall: 0-0
Aids: Bl: 0-0 Vi: 0-0 Tstrap: 0-0
Best Rating: 91 4/02 Bang 3m110y good Ch

Took advantage of the misfortune of two rivals when springing a surprise in a 23-furlong hunters' chase at Uttoxeter in April 2002.

Irish Stamp (IRE)

13-y-o b g Niniski (USA)-Bayazida (Bustino)
Ferdy Murphy Paddy O'Donnell

Placings: 0/23/13405213/P20/P222/25P6/B5P/4F/4R **(1732a)**
2001/02: 26^{4}GS, 34^{R}GF

	Starts	1st	2nd	3rd	Win & Pl
Chases	2	0	0	0	324
Career Total	**29**	**2**	**7**	**3**	**40758**

103	4/95	Asct	3m110y	C Ch	FRM	£10308
98	10/94	NAbb	3m3f	(0-115)HHdl	G-S	£2897

Total win prize-money £13207

Going: Sf: 0-0 GS: 0-1 Gd: 0-0 GF: - Fm: 0-1
Distance: 2m/2m3: 0-0 2m4-2m7: 0-0 3m+: 0-2
Track: LH: 0-2 RH: 0-0 Tight: 0-1 Gall: 0-0
Aids: Bl: 0-0 Vi: 0-0 Tstrap: 0-1
Best Rating: 121 11/97 Asct 3m110y good Ch

Irisio (FR)

6-y-o b g Chef De Clan Ii (FR)-Irisiana (FR) (Le Pontet (FR))
R H Alner Lady Talbot Of Malahide

Placings: 20042066-U3PPP **(3738)**
2001/02: 25^{U}G, 25^{3}S, 20^{P}S, 20^{P}G, 20^{P}S

	Starts	1st	2nd	3rd	Win & Pl
Chases	5	0	0	1	489
Career Total	**13**	**0**	**2**	**1**	**777**

Going: Sf: 0-3 GS: 0-0 Gd: 0-2 GF: - Fm: 0-0
Distance: 2m/2m3: 0-0 2m4-2m7: 0-3 3m+: 0-2
Track: LH: 0-1 RH: 0-4 Tight: 0-2 Gall: 0-0
Aids: Bl: 0-2 Vi: 0-0 Tstrap: 0-0
Best Rating:

Irlandais Ii (FR)

95(86h) (85h)**110**

6-y-o ch g Moon Madness-Platine Iii (FR) (Iveday (FR))
G A Harker (H A N Orde-Powlett 24/11) Lord Bolton

Placings: *0*PP4-0654606P **(4847)**
2001/02: 16^{0}G, 16^{6}G, 16^{5}GF, 16^{4}S, 16^{6}GF, 16^{0}GS, 16^{6}G, 20^{P}G

	Starts	1st	2nd	3rd	Win & Pl
Hurdles	2	0	0	0	0
Chases	6	0	0	0	305
Career Total	**12**	**0**	**0**	**0**	**790**

Going: Sf: 0-1 GS: 0-1 Gd: 0-4 GF: - Fm: 0-2
Distance: 2m/2m3: 0-7 2m4-2m7: 0-1 3m+: 0-0
Track: LH: 0-7 RH: 0-1 Tight: 0-6 Gall: 0-0
Aids: Bl: 0-0 Vi: 0-0 Tstrap: 0-3
Best Rating: 110 4/01 Ayr 2m good Ch

Yet to cut much ice over fences.

Iron Express

82

6-y-o b g Teenoso (USA)-Sylvia Beach (The Parson)
G M Moore David Parker

Placings: *30*/433210-P **(0213)**
2001/02: 24^{P}F

	Starts	1st	2nd	3rd	Win & Pl
Hurdles	1	0	0	0	
Career Total	**9**	**1**	**1**	**3**	**3718**

90	1/01	Donc	2m4f	E Hdl	GD	£2254

Total win prize-money £2254

Going: Sf: 0-0 GS: 0-0 Gd: 0-0 GF: - Fm: 0-1
Distance: 2m/2m3: 0-0 2m4-2m7: 0-0 3m+: 0-1
Track: LH: 0-1 RH: 0-0 Tight: 0-1 Gall: 0-0
Aids: Bl: 0-0 Vi: 0-0 Tstrap: 0-0
Best Rating: 91 11/00 Catt 2m3f gd-sft Hdl

Iron N Gold

106(79h) **113**

10-y-o b g Heights Of Gold-Southern Dynasty (Gunner B)
B G Powell D C T Partnership

Placings:023/12P03145/5/22235-2425311 (2419)
2001/02: 20^{2}GF, 20^{4}G, 25^{2}G, 24^{5}G, 19^{3}S, 20^{1}S, 20^{1}HY

	Starts	1st	2nd	3rd	Win & Pl
Chases	7	2	2	1	9371
Career Total	**24**	**4**	**7**	**4**	**20606**

113	11/01	Uttx	2m4f	F(0-110)HCh	HVY	£3400
103	11/01	Uttx	2m4f	E(0-105)HCh	SFT	£3120
97	3/97	Hntg	2m110y	E(0-110)HHdl	G-F	£2267
92	10/96	Strf	2m110y	E Hdl	GD	£2757

Total win prize-money £11546

Going: Sf: 2-3 GS: 0-0 Gd: 0-3 GF: - Fm: 0-1
Distance: 2m/2m3: 0-1 **2m4-2m7: 2-4** 3m+: 0-2
Track: **LH: 2-5** RH: 0-2 Tight: 0-1 Gall: 0-0
Aids: Bl: 0-0 Vi: 0-0 Tstrap: 0-0
Best Rating: 113 11/01 Uttx 2m4f heavy Ch

Fair chaser, suited by two and ahalf miles and soft ground.

Iron Princess (IRE)

6-y-o b m Insan (USA)-Mrs Cullen (Over The River (FR))
G M Moore David Parker

Placings:0-P30PP (4745)
2001/02: 24^{P}S, 16^{3}S, 21^{0}HY, 20^{P}G, 24^{P}G

	Starts	1st	2nd	3rd	Win & Pl
Hurdles	5	0	0	1	358
Career Total	**6**	**0**	**0**	**1**	**358**

Going: Sf: 0-3 GS: 0-0 Gd: 0-2 GF: - Fm: 0-0
Distance: 2m/2m3: 0-1 2m4-2m7: 0-2 3m+: 0-2
Track: LH: 0-4 RH: 0-1 Tight: 0-2 Gall: 0-0
Aids: Bl: 0-0 Vi: 0-1 Tstrap: 0-0
Best Rating: 18 4/01 Fknm 2m gd-sft NHF

Ironbridge

7-y-o gr g Scallywag-Bahama (Bali Dancer)
M Mullineaux John R Wilson

Placings:0-P (0778)
2001/02: 20^{P}GF

	Starts	1st	2nd	3rd	Win & Pl
Hurdles	1	0	0	0	
Career Total	**2**	**0**	**0**	**0**	

Going: Sf: 0-0 GS: 0-0 Gd: 0-0 GF: - Fm: 0-1
Distance: 2m/2m3: 0-0 2m4-2m7: 0-1 3m+: 0-0
Track: LH: 0-1 RH: 0-0 Tight: 0-0 Gall: 0-0
Aids: Bl: 0-0 Vi: 0-0 Tstrap: 0-0
Best Rating: 46 4/01 MRas 2m1f110y heavy NHF

Irouleguy Iii (FR)

6-y-o ch g Quart De Vin (FR)-Linea (FR) (Laniste)
J R Best H J Jarvis

Placings:00/PP (0968)
2001/02: 23^{P}GF, 17^{P}GS

	Starts	1st	2nd	3rd	Win & Pl
Hurdles	2	0	0	0	
Career Total	**4**	**0**	**0**	**0**	

Going: Sf: 0-0 GS: 0-1 Gd: 0-0 GF: - Fm: 0-1
Distance: 2m/2m3: 0-1 2m4-2m7: 0-0 3m+: 0-1
Track: LH: 0-1 RH: 0-0 Tight: 0-1 Gall: 0-0
Aids: Bl: 0-0 Vi: 0-0 Tstrap: 0-0
Best Rating: 32 3/00 Folk 2m1f110y good NHF

Irrefutable

68f 31f

5-y-o b m Greensmith-Express Edition (Comedy Star (USA))
Jane Southcombe Major R P Thorman

Placings:0 (1019)
2001/02: 16^{0}G

	Starts	1st	2nd	3rd	Win & Pl
NH Flat	1	0	0	0	
Career Total	**1**	**0**	**0**	**0**	

Going: Sf: 0-0 GS: 0-0 Gd: 0-1 GF: - Fm: 0-0
Distance: 2m/2m3: 0-1 2m4-2m7: 0-0 3m+: 0-0
Track: LH: 0-1 RH: 0-0 Tight: 0-0 Gall: 0-0
Aids: Bl: 0-0 Vi: 0-0 Tstrap: 0-0
Best Rating: 31 7/01 Worc 2m good NHF

Is Wonderful (USA)

89 94

4-y-o ch g Diesis-Falling In Love (IRE) (Sadler's Wells (USA))
Mrs A J Perrett Seymour Cohn

Placings:2 (2066)
2001/02: 16^{2}G

	Starts	1st	2nd	3rd	Win & Pl
Hurdles	1	0	1	0	1081
Career Total	**1**	**0**	**1**	**0**	**1081**

Going: Sf: 0-0 GS: 0-0 Gd: 0-1 GF: - Fm: 0-0
Distance: 2m/2m3: 0-1 2m4-2m7: 0-0 3m+: 0-0
Track: LH: 0-0 RH: 0-1 Tight: 0-0 Gall: 0-1
Aids: Bl: 0-0 Vi: 0-0 Tstrap: 0-1
Best Rating: 94 11/01 Hntg 2m110y good Hdl

Looked in need of further when runner-up over two miles on his debut over hurdles.

Isam Top (FR)

101(98c) (105c)105

6-y-o b g Siam (USA)-Miss Sic Top (FR) (Mister Sic Top (FR))
M J Hogan (Miss S Edwards 27/8) Mrs Barbara Hogan

Placings:60/P6022246P0-422300324 (4862)
2001/02: 18^{4}GF, 16^{2}G, 16^{2}F, 17^{3}G, 20^{0}GF, 16^{0}GF, 16^{3}GF, 16^{2}GF, 19^{4}F

	Starts	1st	2nd	3rd	Win & Pl
Hurdles	4	0	1	1	1628
Chases	5	0	2	1	2558
Career Total	**21**	**0**	**6**	**2**	**9205**

Going: Sf: 0-0 GS: 0-0 Gd: 0-2 GF: - Fm: 0-7
Distance: 2m/2m3: 0-8 2m4-2m7: 0-1 3m+: 0-0
Track: LH: 0-4 RH: 0-5 Tight: 0-6 Gall: 0-1
Aids: Bl: 0-1 Vi: 0-0 Tstrap: 0-0
Best Rating: 106 10/00 Kemp 2m gd-sft Hdl

Modest hurdler/chaser, suited by a sound surface.

Isambard Kingdom

87f 79f

5-y-o b g Perpendicular-Calder Rose (Derring Rose)
E L James Alan Brackley

Placings:0 (4423)
2001/02: 16^{0}GS

	Starts	1st	2nd	3rd	Win & Pl
NH Flat	1	0	0	0	
Career Total	**1**	**0**	**0**	**0**	

Going: Sf: 0-0 GS: 0-1 Gd: 0-0 GF: - Fm: 0-0
Distance: 2m/2m3: 0-1 2m4-2m7: 0-0 3m+: 0-0
Track: LH: 0-1 RH: 0-0 Tight: 0-0 Gall: 0-1
Aids: Bl: 0-0 Vi: 0-0 Tstrap: 0-0
Best Rating: 79 3/02 Newb 2m110y gd-sft NHF

Isard Du Buard (FR)

87f 108f

6-y-o b g April Night (FR)-Upsala Du Buard (FR) (Un Numide (FR))
E L James Lady Thompson

Placings:1-2 (1559)
2001/02: 16^{2}G

	Starts	1st	2nd	3rd	Win & Pl
NH Flat	1	0	1	0	462
Career Total	**2**	**1**	**1**	**0**	**1932**

108	1/01	Fknm	2m	H NHF	SFT	£1470

Total win prize-money £1470

Going: Sf: 0-0 GS: 0-0 Gd: 0-1 GF: - Fm: 0-0
Distance: 2m/2m3: 0-1 2m4-2m7: 0-0 3m+: 0-0
Track: LH: 0-1 RH: 0-0 Tight: 0-0 Gall: 0-0
Aids: Bl: 0-0 Vi: 0-0 Tstrap: 0-0
Best Rating: 108 10/01 Chep 2m110y good NHF

Stayed on strongly in the testing ground at Fakenham to win, followed this performance with a brave effort under a penalty. A promising sort.

Isca Maiden

(109h) (80h)

8-y-o b m Full Extent (USA)-Sharp N' Easy (Swing Easy (USA))
J C Fox (P Hayward 1/12) Mrs C A Davies

Placings:660P00/01B306/46565P-P100P (4602)
2001/02: 19^{P}G, 16^{1}S, 17^{0}S, 16^{0}S, 20^{P}GF

	Starts	1st	2nd	3rd	Win & Pl
Hurdles	4	1	0	0	4407
Chases	1	0	0	0	0
Career Total	**23**	**2**	**0**	**1**	**6425**

80	10/01	Towc	2m	F(0-100)HHdl	SFT	£4407
87	12/99	Towc	2m	G(0-95)HHdl	SFT	£1660

Total win prize-money £6067

Going: Sf: 1-3 GS: 0-0 Gd: 0-1 GF: - Fm: 0-1
Distance: **2m/2m3: 1-3** 2m4-2m7: 0-2 3m+: 0-0
Track: LH: 0-2 **RH: 1-3** Tight: 0-1 Gall: 0-0
Aids: Bl: 0-0 Vi: 0-0 Tstrap: 0-0
Best Rating: 87 5/00 Towc 2m gd-fm Hdl

A winner twice at Towcester over two miles on soft ground. She favours being ridden prominently.

Isful (FR)

100 114

6-y-o b g Useful (FR)-Contesty (FR) (Sicyos (USA))
M C Pipe D A Johnson

Placings:32143-000P40 (4028)
2001/02: 21^{0}G, 24^{0}S, 24^{0}G, 21^{P}GS, 25^{4}S, 21^{0}GS

	Starts	1st	2nd	3rd	Win & Pl
Hurdles	6	0	0	0	400
Career Total	**11**	**1**	**1**	**2**	**9211**

131	1/01	Tntn	3m110y	D Hdl	HVY	£4066

Total win prize-money £4066

Going: Sf: 0-2 GS: 0-2 Gd: 0-2 GF: - Fm: 0-0
Distance: 2m/2m3: 0-0 2m4-2m7: 0-3 3m+: 0-3
Track: LH: 0-3 RH: 0-1 Tight: 0-0 Gall: 0-2
Aids: Bl: 0-0 Vi: 0-1 Tstrap: 0-0
Best Rating: 131 1/01 Tntn 3m110y heavy Hdl

Won twice on the Flat in France over 12 furlongs, he joined Martin Pipe in 2000. He won a maiden hurdle at Taunton in January 2001, but has been held since. Acts with cut in the ground.

Isio (FR)

117 **135**

6-y-o b g Silver Rainbow-Swifty (FR) (Le Riverain (FR))
N J Henderson (F-M Louit 24/5) Sir Peter & Lady Gibbings

Placings:221211 **(4828)**
2001/02: 16^{2}G, 17^{2}S, 16^{1}S, 16^{2}GS, 16^{1}GS, 16^{1}G

	Starts	1st	2nd	3rd	Win & Pl
Hurdles	6	3	3	0	19670
Career Total	**6**	**3**	**3**	**0**	**19670**

135	4/02	Ayr	2m	C Hdl	GD	£5183
133	3/02	Newb	2m110y	D Hdl	G-S	£4504
118	2/02	Ludl	2m	E Hdl	SFT	£3003

Total win prize-money £12692

Going: Sf: 1-2 GS: 1-2 Gd: 1-2 GF: - Fm: 0-0
Distance: **2m/2m3: 3-6** 2m4-2m7: 0-0 3m+: 0-0
Track: **LH: 2-3** RH: 1-3 Tight: 0-1 **Gall: 1-2**
Aids: Bl: 0-0 Vi: 0-0 Tstrap: 0-0
Best Rating: 135 4/02 Ayr 2m good Hdl

He got off the mark in a modest Ludlow novice hurdle, but his true worth is measured by his defeats behind three very useful sorts at Newbury, Taunton and Kempton. Scored again at Newbury in March, before gaining another success at in novice company at Ayr. Looks a decent long-term prospect. Two miles on soft ground seems ideal.

Iskan (GER)

98 **95**

7-y-o b g Perceive Arrogance (USA)-Ifakara (GER) (Athenagoras (GER))
F P Murtagh (J J O'Neill 24/6) H Henderson

Placings:31P/P000-304PP**F**PP **(4261)**
2001/02: 20^{3}S, 16^{0}F, 16^{4}F, 16^{P}GF, 20^{P}S, 19^{F}S, 19^{P}GS, 24^{P}HY

	Starts	1st	2nd	3rd	Win & Pl
Hurdles	7	0	0	1	817
Chases	1	0	0	0	0
Career Total	**15**	**1**	**0**	**2**	**3746**

98	3/00	Carl	2m4f110y	E Hdl	HVY	£2562

Total win prize-money £2562

Going: Sf: 0-4 GS: 0-1 Gd: 0-0 GF: - Fm: 0-3
Distance: 2m/2m3: 0-5 2m4-2m7: 0-2 3m+: 0-1
Track: LH: 0-4 RH: 0-3 Tight: 0-2 Gall: 0-0
Aids: Bl: 0-0 Vi: 0-2 Tstrap: 0-0
Best Rating: 98 3/00 Carl 2m4f110y heavy Hdl

Island Faith (IRE)

98f **119f**

5-y-o b g Turtle Island (IRE)-Keep The Faith (Furry Glen)
Ferdy Murphy K Lee

Placings:*10* **(4948a)**
2001/02: 17^{1}G, 16^{0}G

	Starts	1st	2nd	3rd	Win & Pl
NH Flat	2	1	0	0	1834
Career Total	**2**	**1**	**0**	**0**	**1834**

119	4/02	Carl	2m1f	H NHF	GD	£1834

Total win prize-money £1834

Going: Sf: 0-0 GS: 0-0 Gd: 1-2 GF: - Fm: 0-0
Distance: **2m/2m3: 1-2** 2m4-2m7: 0-0 3m+: 0-0
Track: LH: 0-0 **RH: 1-2** Tight: 0-0 Gall: 0-0
Aids: Bl: 0-0 Vi: 0-0 Tstrap: 0-0
Best Rating: 119 4/02 Carl 2m1f good NHF

Made a winning debut in a Carlisle bumper in April 2002, but well beaten in a good race at Punchestown.

Island Mirage

9-y-o b m Jupiter Island-Petite Mirage (Hittite Glory)
M R Bosley Mrs Jean M O'Connor

Placings:*00*P/0P-PO **(0555)**
2001/02: 19^{P}G, 20°GF

	Starts	1st	2nd	3rd	Win & Pl
Chases	2	0	0	0	
Career Total	**7**	**0**	**0**	**0**	

Going: Sf: 0-0 GS: 0-0 Gd: 0-1 GF: - Fm: 0-1
Distance: 2m/2m3: 0-1 2m4-2m7: 0-1 3m+: 0-0
Track: LH: 0-0 RH: 0-2 Tight: 0-0 Gall: 0-1
Aids: Bl: 0-0 Vi: 0-0 Tstrap: 0-0
Best Rating: 77 5/00 Extr 3m6f good Hdl

Island Mist

101 **124**

9-y-o gr m Jupiter Island-Misty Fort (Menelek)
H D Daly J B Sumner

Placings:*20*/520403/**232213-24453** **(4374)**
2001/02: 19^{2}G, 16^{4}S, 19^{4}G, 16^{5}GS, 20^{3}S

	Starts	1st	2nd	3rd	Win & Pl
Chases	5	0	1	1	5763
Career Total	**19**	**1**	**6**	**4**	**18364**

124	2/01	Hayd	2m	C(0-125)HCh	SFT	£6136

Total win prize-money £6136

Going: Sf: 0-2 GS: 0-1 Gd: 0-2 GF: - Fm: 0-0
Distance: 2m/2m3: 0-3 2m4-2m7: 0-2 3m+: 0-0
Track: LH: 0-0 RH: 0-5 Tight: 0-1 Gall: 0-1
Aids: Bl: 0-0 Vi: 0-0 Tstrap: 0-0
Best Rating: 124 5/01 Extr 2m3f110y good Ch

Modest chaser, effective from 2m-2m4f on good/heavy.

Island Princess (IRE)

96 **62**

5-y-o b m Turtle Island (IRE)-Classic Dilemma (Sandhurst Prince)
H W Lavis (K O Cunningham-Brown 8/12) G Lavis

Placings:0500P **(3702)**
2001/02: 16^{0}S, 18^{5}GS, 24^{0}G, 20^{0}S, 19^{P}HY

	Starts	1st	2nd	3rd	Win & Pl
Hurdles	5	0	0	0	0
Career Total	**5**	**0**	**0**	**0**	**0**

Going: Sf: 0-3 GS: 0-1 Gd: 0-1 GF: - Fm: 0-0
Distance: 2m/2m3: 0-2 2m4-2m7: 0-2 3m+: 0-1
Track: LH: 0-4 RH: 0-1 Tight: 0-2 Gall: 0-1
Aids: Bl: 0-0 Vi: 0-0 Tstrap: 0-0

Best Rating: 62 11/01 Font 2m2f110y gd-sft Hdl

Moderate on the Flat and over hurdles.

Island Sound

108 **126**

5-y-o b g Turtle Island (IRE)-Ballet (Sharrood (USA))
D R C Elsworth Mrs Michael Meredith

Placings:412P5 **(3979)**
2001/02: 17^{4}G, 17^{1}GS, 16^{2}G, 16^{P}S, 16^{5}G

	Starts	1st	2nd	3rd	Win & Pl
Hurdles	5	1	1	0	8033
Career Total	**5**	**1**	**1**	**0**	**8033**

125	12/01	Tntn	2m1f	C Hdl	G-S	£5853

Total win prize-money £5853

Going: Sf: 0-1 GS: 1-1 Gd: 0-3 GF: - Fm: 0-0
Distance: **2m/2m3: 1-5** 2m4-2m7: 0-0 3m+: 0-0
Track: LH: 0-1 **RH: 1-4 Tight: 1-2** Gall: 0-1
Aids: Bl: 0-0 Vi: 0-0 Tstrap: 0-0
Best Rating: 126 12/01 Kemp 2m good Hdl

A smart front-running sort on the Flat, he was suited by positive tactics when scoring easily at Taunton on easy ground.

Island Thymes

89 **78**

5-y-o br g Alhijaz-Harmonious Sound (Auction Ring (USA))
R Dickin Double Eight Ltd

Placings:00-46 **(0850)**
2001/02: 16^{4}GF, 16^{6}GF

	Starts	1st	2nd	3rd	Win & Pl
Hurdles	2	0	0	0	0
Career Total	**4**	**0**	**0**	**0**	**0**

Going: Sf: 0-0 GS: 0-0 Gd: 0-0 GF: - Fm: 0-2
Distance: 2m/2m3: 0-2 2m4-2m7: 0-0 3m+: 0-0
Track: LH: 0-2 RH: 0-0 Tight: 0-1 Gall: 0-0
Aids: Bl: 0-0 Vi: 0-0 Tstrap: 0-0
Best Rating: 78 7/01 Strf 2m110y gd-fm Hdl

Island Vision (IRE)

74 **66**

12-y-o b g Vision (USA)-Verandah (Jaazeiro (USA))
Mrs H L Walton Mrs Joanna Hughes

Placings:600/51/632412400/3121/00465/435/**P**-0P **(0232)**
2001/02: 19^{0}F, 21^{P}GF

	Starts	1st	2nd	3rd	Win & Pl
Hurdles	2	0	0	0	
Career Total	**29**	**4**	**3**	**3**	**11195**

102	7/96	Sthl	2m	F(0-100)HHdl	G-F	£2589
102	6/96	Sthl	2m	F(0-105)HHdl	G-F	£2211
105	10/95	DRoy	2m4f	Hdl	G-F	£1356
91	8/94	Slig	2m	Hdl	GD	£2120

Total win prize-money £8276

Going: Sf: 0-0 GS: 0-0 Gd: 0-0 GF: - Fm: 0-2
Distance: 2m/2m3: 0-0 2m4-2m7: 0-2 3m+: 0-0
Track: LH: 0-0 RH: 0-2 Tight: 0-1 Gall: 0-1
Aids: Bl: 0-1 Vi: 0-0 Tstrap: 0-0
Best Rating: 109 10/95 Tipp 2m gd-yld Hdl

Island Warrior (IRE)

92(102h) (78h)55

7-y-o b g Warcraft (USA)-Only Flower (Warpath)
F Jordan (B P J Baugh 17/10) M N Dennis

Placings:00/006200-045PPP0P121F (4917)
2001/02: 17^{0}G, 22^{4}GF, 22^{5}G, 24^{P}GF, 19^{P}GF, 25^{P}G, 24^{0}G, 24^{P}GS, 21^{1}GF, 21^{2}G, 21^{1}GF, 21^{F}GF

	Starts	1st	2nd	3rd	Win & Pl
Hurdles	10	2	1	0	4545
Chases	2	0	0	0	0
Career Total	**20**	**2**	**2**	**0**	**5089**

78	4/02	Sedg	2m5f110y	G(0-100)HHdl	G-F	£1953
72	3/02	Hntg	2m5f110y	G(0-90)HHdl	G-F	£1708

Total win prize-money £3661

Going: Sf: 0-0 GS: 0-1 Gd: 0-5 GF: - Fm: 2-6
Distance: 2m/2m3: 0-1 **2m4-2m7: 2-7** 3m+: 0-4
Track: LH: 1-8 RH: 1-4 Tight: 1-9 Gall: 1-1
Aids: Bl: 0-1 Vi: 0-0 Tstrap: 0-2
Best Rating: 84 11/00 Dpat 2m1f172y soft NHF

Showed first worthwhile form when a shock winner of a selling handicap hurdle at Huntingdon in March 2002, and added to that the following month. Suited by two miles-five, a sharp track and fast ground.

Isle Beeavenue (IRE)

7-y-o b h Erin's Isle-Copper Breeze (IRE) (Strong Gale)
K C Bailey K C Bailey

Placings:0 (4152)
2001/02: 20^{0}GS

	Starts	1st	2nd	3rd	Win & Pl
Hurdles	1	0	0	0	
Career Total	**1**	**0**	**0**	**0**	

Going: Sf: 0-0 GS: 0-1 Gd: 0-0 GF: - Fm: 0-0
Distance: 2m/2m3: 0-0 2m4-2m7: 0-1 3m+: 0-0
Track: LH: 0-1 RH: 0-0 Tight: 0-0 Gall: 0-0
Aids: Bl: 0-0 Vi: 0-0 Tstrap: 0-0
Best Rating:

Isle Of Rhum

85 83

10-y-o ch g Jupiter Island-Carribean Sound (Good Times (ITY))
P Monteith Hamilton House Limited

Placings:44/0PP553/330/F4F0036-566 (0660)
2001/02: 16^{5}GF, 16^{6}F, 16^{6}F

	Starts	1st	2nd	3rd	Win & Pl
Chases	3	0	0	0	0
Career Total	**21**	**0**	**0**	**4**	**2291**

Going: Sf: 0-0 GS: 0-0 Gd: 0-0 GF: - Fm: 0-3
Distance: 2m/2m3: 0-3 2m4-2m7: 0-0 3m+: 0-0
Track: LH: 0-2 RH: 0-1 Tight: 0-0 Gall: 0-0
Aids: Bl: 0-0 Vi: 0-0 Tstrap: 0-1
Best Rating: 91 1/98 Ayr 2m soft Hdl

Ismene (FR)

105 108+

6-y-o b m Bad Conduct (USA)-Athena De L'Isle (FR) (Quart De Vin (FR))
Miss Venetia Williams Alan Parker

Placings:263-31F5 (4875)
2001/02: 19^{3}G, 21^{1}G, 21^{F}S, 24^{5}G

	Starts	1st	2nd	3rd	Win & Pl
Hurdles	4	1	0	1	3168
Career Total	**7**	**1**	**1**	**2**	**4298**

103	1/02	Ludl	2m5f	E Hdl	GD	£2807

Total win prize-money £2807

Going: Sf: 0-1 GS: 0-0 Gd: 1-3 GF: - Fm: 0-0
Distance: 2m/2m3: 0-0 **2m4-2m7: 1-3** 3m+: 0-1
Track: LH: 0-0 **RH: 1-4** Tight: 0-0 Gall: 0-0
Aids: Bl: 0-0 Vi: 0-0 Tstrap: 0-0
Best Rating: 107 10/00 Strf 2m6f110y gd-sft Hdl

Fair novice hurdler. She let her supporters down on a few occasions before making amends at Ludlow in January 2002 and added another victory at Uttoxeter in June. Stays two and a half miles.

Iso Bald (FR)

97 98

6-y-o ch g Cyborg (FR)-Renny (FR) (Diaghilev)
P J Hobbs H R C Catherwood

Placings:61502 (4733)
2001/02: 16^{6}G, 20^{1}G, 22^{5}GF, 22^{0}G, 24^{2}F

	Starts	1st	2nd	3rd	Win & Pl
NH Flat	1	0	0	0	0
Hurdles	4	1	1	0	4154
Career Total	**5**	**1**	**1**	**0**	**4154**

98	6/01	Worc	2m4f	E Hdl	GD	£2492

Total win prize-money £2492

Going: Sf: 0-0 GS: 0-0 Gd: 1-3 GF: - Fm: 0-2
Distance: 2m/2m3: 0-1 **2m4-2m7: 1-3** 3m+: 0-1
Track: **LH: 1-1** RH: 0-3 Tight: 0-0 Gall: 0-1
Aids: Bl: 0-0 Vi: 0-0 Tstrap: 0-0
Best Rating: 98 11/01 Extr 2m6f110y gd-fm Hdl

Made hard work of winning a weak maiden hurdle in June 2001 and looks to have been harshly rated on that.

Isotop (FR)

101 95

6-y-o b g Port Etienne (FR)-Clorane (FR) (Rahotep (FR))
John Allen Avon Estates Ltd

Placings:4-0024400 (4577)
2001/02: 17^{0}G, 16^{0}GS, 20^{2}S, 19^{4}GS, 22^{4}S, 22^{0}GS, 24^{0}G

	Starts	1st	2nd	3rd	Win & Pl
NH Flat	2	0	0	0	0
Hurdles	5	0	1	0	872
Career Total	**8**	**0**	**1**	**0**	**872**

Going: Sf: 0-2 GS: 0-3 Gd: 0-2 GF: - Fm: 0-0
Distance: 2m/2m3: 0-2 2m4-2m7: 0-4 3m+: 0-1
Track: LH: 0-2 RH: 0-5 Tight: 0-3 Gall: 0-1
Aids: Bl: 0-0 Vi: 0-0 Tstrap: 0-0
Best Rating: 95 2/02 MRas 2m3f110y gd-sft Hdl

Showed some ability in ordinary company over hurdles.

Isotope Ii (FR)

90 71

6-y-o b/br m Royal Charter (FR)-Biblos (FR) (Vorias (USA))
M C Pipe C R Fleet

Placings:1/05-0 (0370)
2001/02: 16^{0}G

	Starts	1st	2nd	3rd	Win & Pl
Hurdles	1	0	0	0	
Career Total	**4**	**1**	**0**	**0**	**1509**

94	4/00	Fknm	2m	H NHF	GD	£1508

Total win prize-money £1509

Going: Sf: 0-0 GS: 0-0 Gd: 0-1 GF: - Fm: 0-0
Distance: 2m/2m3: 0-1 2m4-2m7: 0-0 3m+: 0-0
Track: LH: 0-1 RH: 0-0 Tight: 0-0 Gall: 0-0
Aids: Bl: 0-0 Vi: 0-0 Tstrap: 0-0
Best Rating: 94 4/00 Fknm 2m good NHF

Isou (FR)

105 114

6-y-o ch g Dom Alco (FR)-Aghate De Saisy (FR) (Rhapsodien)
V R A Dartnall The Isou Partnership

Placings:6505-212F0 (4480)
2001/02: 19^{2}GF, 22^{1}HY, 20^{2}S, 22^{F}S, 22^{0}G

	Starts	1st	2nd	3rd	Win & Pl
Hurdles	5	1	2	0	5381
Career Total	**9**	**1**	**2**	**0**	**5381**

114	12/01	NAbb	2m6f	E(0-105)HHdl	HVY	£2863

Total win prize-money £2863

Going: Sf: 1-3 GS: 0-0 Gd: 0-1 GF: - Fm: 0-1
Distance: 2m/2m3: 0-1 **2m4-2m7: 1-4** 3m+: 0-0
Track: **LH: 1-2** RH: 0-2 **Tight: 1-2** Gall: 0-0
Aids: Bl: 0-0 Vi: 0-0 Tstrap: 0-0
Best Rating: 114 2/02 Font 2m6f110y soft Hdl

Fair novice hurdler, has shown ability on fast and heavy ground. Stays two miles six.

Istabraq (IRE)

118 173

10-y-o b g Sadler's Wells (USA)-Betty's Secret (USA) (Secretariat (USA))
A P O'Brien J P McManus

Placings:211111/111112/1111111/12111/F1F-1P (4190)
2001/02: 16^{1}Y, 16^{P}GS

	Starts	1st	2nd	3rd	Win & Pl
Hurdles	2	1	0	0	26210
Career Total	**29**	**23**	**3**	**0**	**1035440**

163	12/01	Leop	2m	Hdl	YLD	£26209
173	1/01	Leop	2m	Hdl	SFT	£53629
171	3/00	Chel	2m110y	A Hdl	GD	£145000
173	1/00	Leop	2m	Hdl	YLD	£40200
172	12/99	Leop	2m	Hdl	Y-S	£16250
179	10/99	Tipp	2m	Hdl	SH	£34821
181	4/99	Punc	2m	Hdl	GD	£58928
173	4/99	Aint	2m4f	A Hdl	GD	£47600
170	3/99	Chel	2m110y	A Hdl	G-S	£138000
176	1/99	Leop	2m	Hdl	HVY	£33258
162	12/98	Leop	2m	Hdl	HVY	£11956
164	11/98	Fair	2m4f	Hdl	Y-S	£22608
152	11/98	Cork	2m	Hdl	SH	£33782
174	3/98	Chel	2m110y	A Hdl	GD	£137420
153	1/98	Leop	2m	Hdl	Y-S	£30000
156	12/97	Leop	2m	Hdl	HVY	£12772
162	11/97	Fair	2m4f	Hdl	YLD	£25742
159	10/97	Tipp	2m	Hdl	SH	£32178
148	4/97	Punc	2m4f	Hdl	GD	£18415
147	3/97	Chel	2m5f	A Hdl	G-F	£49585
145	2/97	Leop	2m2f	Hdl	G-Y	£12871
137	12/96	Leop	2m2f	Hdl	YLD	£9974
141	12/96	Fair	2m	Hdl	YLD	£16752

Total win prize-money £1007959

Going: Sf: 0-0 GS: 0-1 Gd: 0-0 GF: - Fm: 0-0

Distance: 2m/2m3: 1-2 2m4-2m7: 0-0 3m+: 0-0
Track: LH: 1-2 RH: 0-0 Tight: 0-0 Gall: 0-0
Aids: Bl: 0-0 Vi: 0-0 Tstrap: 0-0
Best Rating: 181 4/99 Punc 2m good Hdl

One of the all-time hurdling greats, he landed his third Champion Hurdle with another brilliant display in 2000. Things went badly wrong for him in 2000/01, however. Making his reappearance at Leopardstown in December, he looked beaten when taking a nasty-looking fall.. He looked back to very near his best, however, in winning the AIG Europe Champion Hurdle at Leopardstown for the fourth time and was odds-on to retain his crown at Cheltenham in 2001. Foot-and-mouth intervened, and the Festival was abandoned. His final outing came in the Shell Champion Hurdle, switched to Leopardstown after Punchestown was cancelled, and remarkably he took another crashing fall at the same flight of hurdles with the race at his mercy. Restricted to one prep race in 2001/02, he was unimpressive in beating Bust Out at Leopardstown, but his problems finally caught up with him when he was pulled up after only jumping a couple of flights in the 2002 Champion Hurdle and was subsequently retired. A fine jumper with a devastating turn of foot, he was effective at up to two and a half miles.

It Takes Time (IRE)

119 158

8-y-o b g Montelimar (USA)-Dysart Lady (King's Ride)
M C Pipe D A Johnson

Placings: *2110*/111-1113331 (4911)
2001/02: 22^{1}S, 25^{1}G, 24^{1}G, 23^{3}S, 24^{3}G, 20^{3}G, 24^{1}G

	Starts	1st	2nd	3rd	Win & Pl
Hurdles	7	4	0	3	99919
Career Total	**14**	**9**	**1**	**3**	**121220**

153	4/02	Sand	3m	B Hdl	GD	£29000
155	12/01	Chel	3m	B HHdl	GD	£8572
139	11/01	Chel	3m1f110y	B HHdl	GD	£27716
138	11/01	NAbb	2m6f	C(0-130)HHdl	SFT	£4820
134	2/01	Font	2m6f110y	D(0-125)HHdl	G-S	£5489
123	1/01	Donc	3m110y	D Hdl	GD	£3752
104	10/00	Extr	2m3f	D Hdl	SFT	£3445
128	1/00	Leop	2m2f	NHF	YLD	£3588
120	12/99	Leop	2m	NHF	SH	£4312

Total win prize-money £90695

Going: Sf: 1-2 GS: 0-0 Gd: 3-5 GF: - Fm: 0-0
Distance: 2m/2m3: 0-0 2m4-2m7: 1-2 **3m+: 3-5**
Track: **LH: 2-4** RH: 0-0 Tight: 1-2 Gall: 1-1
Aids: Bl: 0-0 Vi: 0-0 Tstrap: 0-0
Best Rating: 158 4/02 Aint 2m4f good Hdl

Progressive form once stepped up in trip before a good effort behind Jair Du Cochet in Graded company at Haydock in January 2002. Better effort when third in both the Cheltenham Stayers and in the Martell Aintree Hurdle and got his reward at Sandown in April. He has not always found a lot off the bridle, but should continue to enjoy success. Stays three miles. Has won on good ground and soft.

It's All A Chance (IRE)

106 93

7-y-o ch g Eve's Error-Butlers Pier (Good Thyne (USA))
J Howard Johnson J Howard Johnson

Placings: 0*60*/050P62-4U522F431 (4770)
2001/02: 20^{4}GS, 20^{U}GF, 20^{5}G, 17^{2}GS, 21^{2}G, 25^{F}GS, 25^{4}S, 19^{3}GS, 20^{1}GF

	Starts	1st	2nd	3rd	Win & Pl
Hurdles	7	1	2	1	5418
Chases	2	0	0	0	0
Career Total	**18**	**1**	**3**	**1**	**6408**

93	4/02	Hexm	2m4f110y	D(0-125)HHdl	G-F	£3535

Total win prize-money £3535

Going: Sf: 0-1 GS: 0-4 Gd: 0-2 GF: - Fm: 1-2
Distance: 2m/2m3: 0-2 **2m4-2m7: 1-5** 3m+: 0-2
Track: **LH: 1-7** RH: 0-2 Tight: 0-5 Gall: 0-0
Aids: Bl: 0-0 Vi: 0-0 Tstrap: 0-0
Best Rating: 93 4/02 Hexm 2m4f110y gd-fm Hdl

Handicap hurdler. Suited by two and a half miles and soft ground. Also effective on a fast surface.

It's All Good Fun (IRE)

(92c)

7-y-o b g Top Of The World-Cherry Moss (IRE) (Le Moss)
M Pitman Just Good Fun Club

Placings: *53*/222003/**43FU**20-P (0010)
2001/02: 25^{P}S

	Starts	1st	2nd	3rd	Win & Pl
Hurdles	1	0	0	0	
Career Total	**15**	**0**	**4**	**3**	**3743**

Going: Sf: 0-1 GS: 0-0 Gd: 0-0 GF: - Fm: 0-0
Distance: 2m/2m3: 0-0 2m4-2m7: 0-0 3m+: 0-1
Track: LH: 0-0 RH: 0-0 Tight: 0-0 Gall: 0-0
Aids: Bl: 0-1 Vi: 0-0 Tstrap: 0-0
Best Rating: 108 3/00 Donc 2m4f gd-sft Hdl

It's Beyond Belief (IRE)

106 130

8-y-o b g Supreme Leader-Rossacurra (Deep Run)
P F Nicholls J G Crumpler

Placings: 22 (2522)
2001/02: 26^{2}GS, 23^{2}G

	Starts	1st	2nd	3rd	Win & Pl
Chases	2	0	2	0	1928
Career Total	**2**	**0**	**2**	**0**	**1928**

Going: Sf: 0-0 GS: 0-1 Gd: 0-1 GF: - Fm: 0-0
Distance: 2m/2m3: 0-0 2m4-2m7: 0-0 3m+: 0-2
Track: LH: 0-0 RH: 0-1 Tight: 0-1 Gall: 0-0
Aids: Bl: 0-0 Vi: 0-0 Tstrap: 0-0
Best Rating: 130 12/01 Leic 2m7f110y good Ch

A winning pointer, he has run well in novice chases in England. Stays well.

It's Himself

115 143

10-y-o b g Rakaposhi King-Coole Pilate (Celtic Cone)
A J Martin P M Barrett

Placings: 00P4/**104**/**2F**-025F21 (4961a)
2001/02: 22^{0}SH, 19^{2}YS, 25^{5}Y, 24^{F}Y, 28^{2}HY, 25^{1}GY

	Starts	1st	2nd	3rd	Win & Pl
Chases	6	1	2	0	53212
Career Total	**15**	**2**	**3**	**0**	**62490**

140	4/02	Punc	3m1f	HCh	G-Y	£36134
142	2/00	Hayd	3m	H Ch	HVY	£7475

Total win prize-money £43610

Going: Sf: 0-1 GS: 0-0 Gd: 0-0 GF: - Fm: 0-0
Distance: 2m/2m3: 0-1 2m4-2m7: 0-1 **3m+: 1-4**
Track: LH: 0-3 **RH: 1-3** Tight: 0-0 Gall: 0-0
Aids: Bl: 0-0 Vi: 0-0 **Tstrap: 1-6**
Best Rating: 143 2/02 Uttx 3m4f heavy Ch

A useful hunter chaser in the 2000/2001 season. Seemed to lose his way slightly afterwards but was back to form when second to Streamstown in the National Trial at Uttoxeter in February 2002 and won a valuable handicap at Punchestown in April. Stays three and a half miles. Acts on soft ground.

It's Just Harry

101f 109f

5-y-o b g Tragic Role (USA)-Nipotina (Simply Great (FR))
C R Egerton James Blackshaw

Placings: *3* (4423)
2001/02: 16^{3}GS

	Starts	1st	2nd	3rd	Win & Pl
NH Flat	1	0	0	1	368
Career Total	**1**	**0**	**0**	**1**	**368**

Going: Sf: 0-0 GS: 0-1 Gd: 0-0 GF: - Fm: 0-0
Distance: 2m/2m3: 0-1 2m4-2m7: 0-0 3m+: 0-0
Track: LH: 0-1 RH: 0-0 Tight: 0-0 Gall: 0-1
Aids: Bl: 0-0 Vi: 0-0 Tstrap: 0-0
Best Rating: 109 3/02 Newb 2m110y gd-sft NHF

It's Just Sally

86f 86f

5-y-o b m Kylian (USA)-Hush It Up (Tina's Pet)
C R Egerton James Blackshaw

Placings: *36* (4289)
2001/02: 17^{3}S, 17^{6}GS

	Starts	1st	2nd	3rd	Win & Pl
NH Flat	2	0	0	1	230
Career Total	**2**	**0**	**0**	**1**	**230**

Going: Sf: 0-1 GS: 0-1 Gd: 0-0 GF: - Fm: 0-0
Distance: 2m/2m3: 0-2 2m4-2m7: 0-0 3m+: 0-0
Track: LH: 0-0 RH: 0-1 Tight: 0-2 Gall: 0-0
Aids: Bl: 0-0 Vi: 0-0 Tstrap: 0-0
Best Rating: 86 1/02 Folk 2m1f110y soft NHF

A half-sister to Shadow Leader. Staying on third in a Folkestone bumper on her debut on soft ground. Looks like better ground will suit.

It's Pingu

5-y-o b g Fraam-Pingin (Corvaro (USA))
Miss Sheena West Gerald West

Placings: *0*-4P (3453)
2001/02: 21^{4}S, 21^{P}HY

	Starts	1st	2nd	3rd	Win & Pl
Hurdles	2	0	0	0	0
Career Total	**3**	**0**	**0**	**0**	**0**

Going: Sf: 0-2 GS: 0-0 Gd: 0-0 GF: - Fm: 0-0
Distance: 2m/2m3: 0-0 2m4-2m7: 0-2 3m+: 0-0
Track: LH: 0-2 RH: 0-0 Tight: 0-2 Gall: 0-0
Aids: Bl: 0-0 Vi: 0-0 Tstrap: 0-0
Best Rating: 12 4/01 Asct 2m110y heavy NHF

It's Wallace

99 130

9-y-o b g Bedford (USA)-Rua Batric (Energist)
Miss Sheena West Grand Day Out Partnership

Placings: *45*P2301/P50F2146611/61126/2330-5F**P**05 **(3215)**
2001/02: 21^{5}GF, 19^{F}GF, 29^{P}G, 22^{0}S, 24^{5}GS

	Starts	1st	2nd	3rd	Win & Pl
Hurdles	4	0	0	0	0
Chases	1	0	0	0	0
Career Total	**32**	**6**	**4**	**3**	**24482**

126	1/00	Plum	2m	E(0-115)HHdl	HVY	£2811
122	12/99	Plum	2m	F(0-110)HHdl	HVY	£2867
112	3/99	Plum	2m1f	B HHdl	HVY	£5714
108	2/99	Plum	2m4f	F(0-105)HHdl	G-S	£2425
104	11/98	Plum	2m4f	F(0-100)HHdl	SFT	£2792
91	12/97	Extr	2m2f	F(0-105)HHdl	SFT	£2176

Total win prize-money £18787

Going: Sf: 0-1 GS: 0-1 Gd: 0-1 GF: - Fm: 0-2
Distance: 2m/2m3: 0-0 2m4-2m7: 0-3 3m+: 0-2
Track: LH: 0-2 RH: 0-2 Tight: 0-1 Gall: 0-2
Aids: Bl: 0-0 Vi: 0-0 Tstrap: 0-0
Best Rating: 130 4/01 Sand 3m gd-sft Hdl

He loves soft ground and became something of a Plumpton specialist during the 1999-2000 season, winning five times at the course. Runs his best races when racing prominently at distances up to two and a half miles.

Italian Rose

88 **56**

7-y-o ch m Aragon-Cayla (Tumble Wind (USA))
H W Lavis H W Lavis

Placings: 0P0/00-6 **(1150)**
2001/02: 22^{6}GF

	Starts	1st	2nd	3rd	Win & Pl
Hurdles	1	0	0	0	0
Career Total	**6**	**0**	**0**	**0**	**0**

Going: Sf: 0-0 GS: 0-0 Gd: 0-0 GF: - Fm: 0-1
Distance: 2m/2m3: 0-0 2m4-2m7: 0-1 3m+: 0-0
Track: LH: 0-1 RH: 0-0 Tight: 0-1 Gall: 0-0
Aids: Bl: 0-0 Vi: 0-0 Tstrap: 0-0
Best Rating: 67 5/00 Strf 2m110y gd-fm Hdl

Italko (FR)

88(93h) (55h)**71**

6-y-o b g Kadalko (FR)-Colharienne (FR) (Italic (FR))
Mrs L C Taylor Mrs L C Taylor

Placings: FP/P6**P**-60020 **(1940)**
2001/02: 18^{6}GF, 20^{0}GF, 21^{0}G, 16^{2}S, 21^{0}GS

	Starts	1st	2nd	3rd	Win & Pl
Hurdles	2	0	1	0	532
Chases	3	0	0	0	0
Career Total	**10**	**0**	**1**	**0**	**532**

Going: Sf: 0-1 GS: 0-1 Gd: 0-1 GF: - Fm: 0-2
Distance: 2m/2m3: 0-2 2m4-2m7: 0-3 3m+: 0-0
Track: LH: 0-3 RH: 0-1 Tight: 0-5 Gall: 0-0
Aids: Bl: 0-1 Vi: 0-0 Tstrap: 0-0
Best Rating: 71 5/01 Font 2m2f gd-fm Ch

Itop Du Moulin Mas (FR)

89 **93**

6-y-o b g Useful (FR)-La Malnoue (FR) (Lou Piguet (FR))
B G Powell Swan Horse Racing

Placings: 352031P03-03P **(0375)**
2001/02: 16^{0}G, 16^{3}GF, 16^{P}GF

	Starts	1st	2nd	3rd	Win & Pl
Hurdles	3	0	0	1	298
Career Total	**12**	**1**	**1**	**4**	**4833**

	9/00	Fntb	2m3f	Ch	GD	£3362

Total win prize-money £3362

Going: Sf: 0-0 GS: 0-0 Gd: 0-1 GF: - Fm: 0-2
Distance: 2m/2m3: 0-3 2m4-2m7: 0-0 3m+: 0-0
Track: LH: 0-1 RH: 0-2 Tight: 0-1 Gall: 0-2
Aids: Bl: 0-0 Vi: 0-0 Tstrap: 0-0
Best Rating: 93 5/01 Sthl 2m gd-fm Hdl

Its All Too Much

84f **68f**

4-y-o b f Chaddleworth (IRE)-Nelliellamay (Super Splash (USA))
R Ingram Roger Ingram

Placings: *0* **(4639)**
2001/02: 16^{0}GF

	Starts	1st	2nd	3rd	Win & Pl
NH Flat	1	0	0	0	
Career Total	**1**	**0**	**0**	**0**	

Going: Sf: 0-0 GS: 0-0 Gd: 0-0 GF: - Fm: 0-1
Distance: 2m/2m3: 0-1 2m4-2m7: 0-0 3m+: 0-0
Track: LH: 0-0 RH: 0-1 Tight: 0-0 Gall: 0-0
Aids: Bl: 0-0 Vi: 0-0 Tstrap: 0-0
Best Rating: 68 4/02 Asct 2m110y gd-fm NHF

Its Gotta Be Alfie (IRE)

99(91h) (77h)**92**

7-y-o ch g Zaffaran (USA)-Nimbi (Orchestra)
N A Twiston-Davies Mrs S Tainton

Placings: *0/0*P0-053 **(4510)**
2001/02: 22^{0}G, 20^{5}G, 26^{3}G

	Starts	1st	2nd	3rd	Win & Pl
Hurdles	1	0	0	0	0
Chases	2	0	0	1	386
Career Total	**7**	**0**	**0**	**1**	**386**

Going: Sf: 0-0 GS: 0-0 Gd: 0-3 GF: - Fm: 0-0
Distance: 2m/2m3: 0-0 2m4-2m7: 0-2 3m+: 0-1
Track: LH: 0-1 RH: 0-1 Tight: 0-0 Gall: 0-0
Aids: Bl: 0-0 Vi: 0-0 Tstrap: 0-0
Best Rating: 92 3/02 Plum 3m2f good Ch

Lightly-raced, has shown a glimmer of ability over both hurdles and fences.

Its Meant To Be

85 **69**

6-y-o b m Gunner B-Edwina's Dawn (Space King)
J A B Old W D Hockenhull

Placings: *400*-0P **(3705)**
2001/02: 16^{0}GS, 19^{P}HY

	Starts	1st	2nd	3rd	Win & Pl
Hurdles	2	0	0	0	
Career Total	**5**	**0**	**0**	**0**	**0**

Going: Sf: 0-1 GS: 0-1 Gd: 0-0 GF: - Fm: 0-0
Distance: 2m/2m3: 0-1 2m4-2m7: 0-1 3m+: 0-0
Track: LH: 0-0 RH: 0-2 Tight: 0-0 Gall: 0-0
Aids: Bl: 0-0 Vi: 0-0 Tstrap: 0-0
Best Rating: 98 12/00 Tntn 2m1f soft NHF

Its Only Polite (IRE)

104 **108**

6-y-o b g Roselier (FR)-Decent Debbie (Decent Fellow)
A J Lidderdale (E Stanners 28/11) Bonusprint

Placings: *0*-4433 **(4398)**
2001/02: 18^{4}GS, 20^{4}S, 22^{3}S, 24^{3}S

	Starts	1st	2nd	3rd	Win & Pl
NH Flat	1	0	0	0	0
Hurdles	3	0	0	2	1348
Career Total	**5**	**0**	**0**	**2**	**1348**

Going: Sf: 0-3 GS: 0-1 Gd: 0-0 GF: - Fm: 0-0
Distance: 2m/2m3: 0-1 2m4-2m7: 0-2 3m+: 0-1
Track: LH: 0-2 RH: 0-1 Tight: 0-1 Gall: 0-1
Aids: Bl: 0-0 Vi: 0-0 Tstrap: 0-0
Best Rating: 108 3/02 Newb 3m110y soft Hdl

By Roselier, he looks to be progressing over hurdles and stays well.

Its Time For A Win (IRE)

114 **159**

10-y-o b g Lord Bud-Autumn Gift (Martinmas)
W P Mullins John Kenny

Placings: *112263221301F*/**F11F0F242/6-5FF22131** **(4664)**
2001/02: 24^{5}YS, 20^{F}YS, 21^{F}Y, 19^{2}Y, 19^{2}HY, 20^{1}S, 20^{3}GS, 21^{1}G

	Starts	1st	2nd	3rd	Win & Pl
Chases	8	2	2	1	58690
Career Total	**31**	**8**	**8**	**3**	**109932**

159	4/02	Aint	2m5f110y	B(0-150)HCh	GD	£32500
149	2/02	Navn	2m4f	HCh	SFT	£11963
136	10/99	Tipp	2m6f	Ch	SH	£14508
136	10/99	Dund	2m1f	Ch	Y-S	£4937
119	2/99	Naas	2m	HHdl	SFT	£6138
112	12/98	Navn	2m2f	Hdl	HVY	£3586
113	6/98	Tipp	2m	NHF	Y-S	£2382
114	5/98	Navn	2m	NHF	Y-S	£2680

Total win prize-money £78698

Going: Sf: 1-2 GS: 0-1 Gd: 1-1 GF: - Fm: 0-0
Distance: 2m/2m3: 0-2 **2m4-2m7: 2-5** 3m+: 0-1
Track: **LH: 2-8** RH: 0-0 **Tight: 1-1** Gall: 0-1
Aids: Bl: 0-0 Vi: 0-0 Tstrap: 0-0
Best Rating: 159 4/02 Aint 2m5f110y good Ch

A tough individual, he lost his way after a couple of long absences, but bounced back well during the spring of 2002, including running a good third in the Mildmay of Flete. Jumped really when over the Grand National fences when landing the Topham. Possibly best at distances short of three miles.

Its-On-The-Cards (IRE)

82(84h) (61h)**77**

8-y-o gr g House Of Cards-Summerello (Bargello)

J R Cornwall J R Cornwall

Placings:*006/05244F/050UP*-065040 **(1094)**
2001/02: 16^{0}GF, 16^{6}GF, 17^{5}GF, 24^{0}G, 24^{4}GF, 17^{0}GF

	Starts	1st	2nd	3rd	Win & Pl
Hurdles	2	0	0	0	0
Chases	4	0	0	0	261
Career Total	**20**	**0**	**1**	**0**	**928**

Going: Sf: 0-0 GS: 0-0 Gd: 0-1 GF: - Fm: 0-5
Distance: 2m/2m3: 0-4 2m4-2m7: 0-0 3m+: 0-2
Track: LH: 0-4 RH: 0-2 Tight: 0-5 Gall: 0-0
Aids: Bl: 0-0 Vi: 0-0 Tstrap: 0-0
Best Rating: **95** 8/99 Sthl 2m gd-fm Hdl

Itsallaboutcharm (IRE)

96 **81**

8-y-o b m Sovereign Water (FR)-Welsh Charmer (Welsh Captain)
R T Phillips Mrs Claire Smith

Placings:*015*-2 **(0421)**
2001/02: 24^{2}G

	Starts	1st	2nd	3rd	Win & Pl
Hurdles	1	0	1	0	854
Career Total	**4**	**1**	**1**	**0**	**4718**

108 10/00 Navn 2m2f NHF YLD £3864
Total win prize-money £3864

Going: Sf: 0-0 GS: 0-0 Gd: 0-1 GF: - Fm: 0-0
Distance: 2m/2m3: 0-0 2m4-2m7: 0-0 3m+: 0-1
Track: LH: 0-1 RH: 0-0 Tight: 0-1 Gall: 0-0
Aids: Bl: 0-0 Vi: 0-0 Tstrap: 0-0
Best Rating: **108** 10/00 Navn 2m2f yield NHF

Itsforu

10-y-o b g Itsu (USA)-Game Trust (National Trust)
Mrs J Fitzgerald Mrs S Nash

Placings:*P/3PF*-0 **(0429)**
2001/02: 25^{0}G

	Starts	1st	2nd	3rd	Win & Pl
Chases	1	0	0	0	
Career Total	**5**	**0**	**0**	**1**	**536**

Going: Sf: 0-0 GS: 0-0 Gd: 0-1 GF: - Fm: 0-0
Distance: 2m/2m3: 0-0 2m4-2m7: 0-0 3m+: 0-1
Track: LH: 0-0 RH: 0-0 Tight: 0-0 Gall: 0-0
Aids: Bl: 0-0 Vi: 0-0 Tstrap: 0-0
Best Rating: **97** 5/00 Chel 3m1f110y good Ch

Itsfreddie

10-y-o ch g Itsu (USA)-Pensham's Lawyer (Spanish Lawyer)
P Bowen John Jones

Placings:FU4 **(2388)**
2001/02: 24^{F}G, 24^{U}S, 20^{4}S

	Starts	1st	2nd	3rd	Win & Pl
Hurdles	1	0	0	0	269
Chases	2	0	0	0	0
Career Total	**3**	**0**	**0**	**0**	**269**

Going: Sf: 0-2 GS: 0-0 Gd: 0-1 GF: - Fm: 0-0
Distance: 2m/2m3: 0-0 2m4-2m7: 0-1 3m+: 0-2
Track: LH: 0-3 RH: 0-0 Tight: 0-1 Gall: 0-0
Aids: Bl: 0-0 Vi: 0-0 Tstrap: 0-0
Best Rating: mfy

Itsonlyme (IRE)

107 **136+**

9-y-o b g Broken Hearted-Over The Arctic (Over The River (FR))
Miss Venetia Williams Mel Davies

Placings:*13110/11561/P*-F2 **(3321)**
2001/02: 24^{F}G, 24^{2}GS

	Starts	1st	2nd	3rd	Win & Pl
Chases	2	0	1	0	940
Career Total	**13**	**6**	**1**	**1**	**15712**

126 4/00 Font 2m6f110y E Hdl GD £2702
126 11/99 Bang 2m1f E Hdl SFT £2752
118 11/99 Wwck 2m2f110y D Hdl GD £4198
116 3/99 Hntg 2m110y H NHF G-S £1462
116 1/99 Folk 2m1f110y H NHF HVY £1457
107 11/98 Aint 2m110y H NHF G-S £2029
Total win prize-money £14601

Going: Sf: 0-0 GS: 0-1 Gd: 0-1 GF: - Fm: 0-0
Distance: 2m/2m3: 0-0 2m4-2m7: 0-0 3m+: 0-2
Track: LH: 0-0 RH: 0-2 Tight: 0-0 Gall: 0-1
Aids: Bl: 0-0 Vi: 0-0 Tstrap: 0-0
Best Rating: **133** 1/02 Hntg 3m gd-sft Ch

A three-time soft-ground bumper winner, he was a useful novice hurdler in the 1999/2000 season. Pulled-up in May 2000, he fell on his return over a year later on his first run over fences and was just beaten next time. Scored at Towcester early in the new season. Acts on good and soft ground.

Ivanoph (FR)

105(92h) (111h)**134**

6-y-o b g Roi De Rome (USA)-Veronique Iv (FR) (Mont Basile (FR))
P F Nicholls Neil Smith

Placings:06F/62142-F132F3P **(4649)**
2001/02: 16^{F}G, 16^{1}S, 16^{3}GS, 17^{2}S, 16^{F}S, 17^{3}S, 16^{P}G

	Starts	1st	2nd	3rd	Win & Pl
Hurdles	1	1	0	0	3455
Chases	6	0	1	2	5261
Career Total	**15**	**2**	**3**	**2**	**31072**

111 10/01 Chep 2m110y D Hdl SFT £3454
10/00 Autl 2m1f110y Ch HLD £11527
Total win prize-money £14982

Going: Sf: 1-4 GS: 0-1 Gd: 0-2 GF: - Fm: 0-0
Distance: **2m/2m3: 1-7** 2m4-2m7: 0-0 3m+: 0-0
Track: **LH: 1-6** RH: 0-1 Tight: 0-1 Gall: 0-3
Aids: Bl: 0-0 Vi: 0-0 Tstrap: 0-0
Best Rating: **134** 3/02 Newb 2m1f soft Ch

A winner over fences in France, he reverted to hurdles to win first time out in 2001/2002 at Chepstow. Decent efforts over fences following that without managing to force his head in front. Goes well in soft ground over two miles.

Iverain (FR)

106 **136**

6-y-o b g Le Riverain (FR)-Ursala (FR) (Toujours Pret (USA))
P F Nicholls C G Roach

Placings:0004-11P **(4229)**
2001/02: 20^{1}S, 22^{1}GS, 21^{P}GS

	Starts	1st	2nd	3rd	Win & Pl
Hurdles	3	2	0	0	11947
Career Total	**7**	**2**	**0**	**0**	**14275**

136 2/02 Winc 2m6f C(0-135)HHdl G-S £8463
112 11/01 Chep 2m4f D Hdl SFT £3484
Total win prize-money £11947

Going: Sf: 1-1 GS: 1-2 Gd: 0-0 GF: - Fm: 0-0
Distance: 2m/2m3: 0-0 **2m4-2m7: 2-3** 3m+: 0-0
Track: LH: 1-2 RH: 1-1 Tight: 0-0 Gall: 0-1
Aids: Bl: 0-0 Vi: 0-0 Tstrap: 0-0
Best Rating: **136** 2/02 Winc 2m6f gd-sft Hdl

Lightly raced in France, he won a Chepstow novice hurdle on his British debut. Returned from a bout of coughing to score in a handicap at Wincanton early in 2002. Stays two miles-six and handles soft ground.

Ivor's Dream (IRE)

6-y-o b/br g Borovoe-Almea's Dream (Pauper)
B J Eckley Brian Eckley

Placings:P **(4684)**
2001/02: 19^{P}GF

	Starts	1st	2nd	3rd	Win & Pl
Hurdles	1	0	0	0	
Career Total	**1**	**0**	**0**	**0**	

Going: Sf: 0-0 GS: 0-0 Gd: 0-0 GF: - Fm: 0-1
Distance: 2m/2m3: 0-0 2m4-2m7: 0-1 3m+: 0-0
Track: LH: 0-0 RH: 0-1 Tight: 0-0 Gall: 0-0
Aids: Bl: 0-0 Vi: 0-0 Tstrap: 0-0
Best Rating:

Ivory Coaster (NZ)

(87h) (74h)

11-y-o b g Ivory Hunter (USA)-Rajah's Girl (NZ) (Indian Order)
P R Hedger Jay Dee Bloodstock Limited

Placings:*3/304322/22P4432/56253404/2154613/15P5P*-0 **(0107)**
2001/02: 22^{0}GF

	Starts	1st	2nd	3rd	Win & Pl
Hurdles	1	0	0	0	
Career Total	**35**	**3**	**7**	**6**	**16907**

106 10/00 Hexm 3m1f E Ch HVY £2834
101 11/99 Folk 2m6f110y F(0-105)HHdl SFT £2374
87 6/99 Hrfd 3m2f D Hdl GD £2814
Total win prize-money £8022

Going: Sf: 0-0 GS: 0-0 Gd: 0-0 GF: - Fm: 0-1
Distance: 2m/2m3: 0-0 2m4-2m7: 0-1 3m+: 0-0
Track: LH: 0-1 RH: 0-0 Tight: 0-1 Gall: 0-0
Aids: Bl: 0-0 Vi: 0-0 Tstrap: 0-0
Best Rating: **106** 10/00 Hexm 3m1f heavy Ch

Ivory Gleam

5-y-o b m Be My Chief (USA)-Brillyant Glen (IRE) (Glenstal (USA))
C W Fairhurst David Hawes

Placings:0 **(1643)**
2001/02: 17^{0}GS

	Starts	1st	2nd	3rd	Win & Pl
NH Flat	1	0	0	0	
Career Total	**1**	**0**	**0**	**0**	

Going: Sf: 0-0 GS: 0-1 Gd: 0-0 GF: - Fm: 0-0

Distance: 2m/2m3: 0-1 2m4-2m7: 0-0 3m+: 0-0
Track: LH: 0-0 RH: 0-1 Tight: 0-0 Gall: 0-0
Aids: Bl: 0-0 Vi: 0-0 Tstrap: 0-0
Best Rating:

Iznogoud (FR)

118(116h) (70h)159

6-y-o b/br g Shafoun (FR)-Vancia (FR) (Top Dancer)
M C Pipe County Stores-Avalon Surfacing

Placings:21140-312F (4666)
2001/02: 16³G, 19¹GS, 24²GS, 25ᶠG

	Starts	1st	2nd	3rd	Win & Pl
Chases	4	1	1	1	39368
Career Total	**9**	**3**	**2**	**1**	**56731**

159	2/02	Asct	2m3f110y	B Ch	G-S	£10808
144	1/01	Asct	2m110y	A Hdl	SFT	£12000
117	12/00	Chep	2m110y	D Hdl	HVY	£3383

Total win prize-money £26191

Going: Sf: 0-0 GS: 1-2 Gd: 0-2 GF: - Fm: 0-0
Distance: 2m/2m3: 0-1 **2m4-2m7: 1-1** 3m+: 0-2
Track: LH: 0-2 **RH: 1-2** Tight: 0-1 Gall: 0-1
Aids: Bl: 0-0 Vi: 0-1 Tstrap: 0-0
Best Rating: 159 3/02 Chel 3m110y gd-sft Ch

A French import, he showed very useful form in novice hurdles in 2000/1. Disappointed on his chasing debut in January 2002 but showed the right attitude to win a three-runner race at Ascot next time. Stepped up to three miles, he ran an absolute blinder to finish runner-up in the Royal & SunAlliance Chase at the 2002 Festival but was soon on the deck at Aintree. Well suited by soft ground.

J Dee

102 88

9-y-o ch g Rakaposhi King-Just Pam (Pamroy)
J C McConnochie A Don Mrs J Abbs R Wilson J McConnochie

Placings:0/P000P-450321PP3P (4537)
2001/02: 24⁴GF, 24⁵GF, 23⁰G, 24³GF, 23²GF, 24¹GF, 24ᴾGF, 26ᴾGS, 24³G, 21ᴾG

	Starts	1st	2nd	3rd	Win & Pl
Chases	10	1	1	2	5963
Career Total	**16**	**1**	**1**	**2**	**5963**

88	8/01	Sthl	3m110y	E Ch	G-F	£3555

Total win prize-money £3555

Going: Sf: 0-0 GS: 0-1 Gd: 0-3 GF: - Fm: 1-6
Distance: 2m/2m3: 0-0 2m4-2m7: 0-1 **3m+: 1-9**
Track: **LH: 1-7** RH: 0-2 **Tight: 1-5** Gall: 0-2
Aids: Bl: 0-0 Vi: 0-0 Tstrap: 0-0
Best Rating: 88 8/01 Sthl 3m110y gd-fm Ch

J'Accuse (IRE)

12-y-o ch g Torus-Glens Princess (Prince Hansel)
Mrs E Kulbicki (D L Williams 7/5) Mrs E Kulbicki

Placings:005003/4P4-0P (0425)
2001/02: 26⁰GF, 21ᴾG

	Starts	1st	2nd	3rd	Win & Pl
Chases	2	0	0	0	
Career Total	**11**	**0**	**0**	**1**	**1007**

Going: Sf: 0-0 GS: 0-0 Gd: 0-1 GF: - Fm: 0-1
Distance: 2m/2m3: 0-0 2m4-2m7: 0-1 3m+: 0-1
Track: LH: 0-0 RH: 0-0 Tight: 0-1 Gall: 0-0
Aids: Bl: 0-0 Vi: 0-0 Tstrap: 0-0

Best Rating: 94 4/96 Carl 2m4f110y firm Hdl

Jabiru (IRE)

9-y-o b/br g Lafontaine (USA)-Country Glen (Furry Glen)
Mrs K M Sanderson Mrs K M Sanderson

Placings:200/335F6/P/1 (4735)
2001/02: 23¹F

	Starts	1st	2nd	3rd	Win & Pl
Chases	1	1	0	0	1762
Career Total	**10**	**1**	**1**	**2**	**2946**

107	4/02	Extr	2m7f110y	H Ch	FRM	£1761

Total win prize-money £1762

Going: Sf: 0-0 GS: 0-0 Gd: 0-0 GF: - Fm: 1-1
Distance: 2m/2m3: 0-0 2m4-2m7: 0-0 **3m+: 1-1**
Track: LH: 0-0 **RH: 1-1** Tight: 0-0 Gall: 0-0
Aids: Bl: 0-0 Vi: 0-0 Tstrap: 0-0
Best Rating: 107 4/02 Extr 2m7f110y firm Ch

Useful pointer/hunter chaser. Stays three miles, handles any ground.

Jabo Origny (FR)

87f 85f

5-y-o gr g Royal Charter (FR)-Coralline (FR) (Iron Duke (FR))
Miss Venetia Williams B Moore

Placings:5 (2786)
2001/02: 16⁵G

	Starts	1st	2nd	3rd	Win & Pl
NH Flat	1	0	0	0	0
Career Total	**1**	**0**	**0**	**0**	**0**

Going: Sf: 0-0 GS: 0-0 Gd: 0-1 GF: - Fm: 0-0
Distance: 2m/2m3: 0-1 2m4-2m7: 0-0 3m+: 0-0
Track: LH: 0-0 RH: 0-1 Tight: 0-0 Gall: 0-0
Aids: Bl: 0-0 Vi: 0-0 Tstrap: 0-0
Best Rating: 85 12/01 Ludl 2m good NHF

Jaboune (FR)

108 131+

5-y-o ch g Johann Quatz (FR)-Seasonal Pleasure (USA) (Graustark)
A King (C Boutin 8/10) Mrs R J Skan

Placings:2323 (3340)
2001/02: 16²S, 16³G, 17²GS, 17³S

	Starts	1st	2nd	3rd	Win & Pl
Hurdles	4	0	2	2	6714
Career Total	**4**	**0**	**2**	**2**	**6714**

Going: Sf: 0-2 GS: 0-1 Gd: 0-1 GF: - Fm: 0-0
Distance: 2m/2m3: 0-4 2m4-2m7: 0-0 3m+: 0-0
Track: LH: 0-1 RH: 0-3 Tight: 0-2 Gall: 0-1
Aids: Bl: 0-0 Vi: 0-0 Tstrap: 0-0
Best Rating: 115 12/01 Tntn 2m1f gd-sft Hdl

A decent performer on the Flat in France, he showed plenty of promise over hurdles, but kept on finding one or two too good until completing a hat-trick in June 2002. Acts on any ground.

Jac An Ree (IRE)

91f 80f

6-y-o b g Supreme Leader-Nic An Ree (IRE) (King's Ride)

D M Grissell C Newport, J Draper & T Edmonds

Placings:2 (1650)
2001/02: 16²G

	Starts	1st	2nd	3rd	Win & Pl
NH Flat	1	0	1	0	415
Career Total	**1**	**0**	**1**	**0**	**415**

Going: Sf: 0-0 GS: 0-0 Gd: 0-1 GF: - Fm: 0-0
Distance: 2m/2m3: 0-1 2m4-2m7: 0-0 3m+: 0-0
Track: LH: 0-0 RH: 0-1 Tight: 0-0 Gall: 0-1
Aids: Bl: 0-0 Vi: 0-0 Tstrap: 0-0
Best Rating: 80 10/01 Hntg 2m110y good NHF

Jacdor (IRE)

106(117c) 107

8-y-o b g Be My Native (USA)-Bellalma (Belfalas)
R Dickin Jackie Matthews & Doreen Evans

Placings:45220/3016P/153FFP-PF41305414 (4413)
2001/02: 20ᴾGS, 17ᶠG, 21⁴S, 17¹GS, 20³GS, 24⁰GS, 17⁵S, 16⁴S, 16¹S, 18⁴S

	Starts	1st	2nd	3rd	Win & Pl
Hurdles	7	2	0	1	8194
Chases	3	0	0	0	0
Career Total	**26**	**4**	**2**	**3**	**19275**

106	3/02	Towc	2m	E(0-110)HHdl	SFT	£2628
105	11/01	Bang	2m1f	F(0-110)HHdl	G-S	£3558
129	11/00	Wwck	2m110y	D(0-125)HCh	SFT	£4192
135	3/00	Bang	2m1f110y	E Ch	SFT	£3412

Total win prize-money £13794

Going: Sf: 1-5 GS: 1-4 Gd: 0-1 GF: - Fm: 0-0
Distance: **2m/2m3: 2-6** 2m4-2m7: 0-3 3m+: 0-1
Track: LH: 1-6 RH: 1-4 **Tight: 1-5** Gall: 0-1
Aids: **Bl: 1-3** Vi: 0-0 Tstrap: 0-0
Best Rating: 135 3/00 Bang 2m1f110y soft Ch

He won twice over fences during 2000, but his jumping was never convincing and went totally to pieces in the early part of 2001. Successfully returned to hurdles in 2001/02. Suited by two miles and easy ground.

Jack (IRE)

105 93

10-y-o br g Be My Native (USA)-Martialette (Welsh Saint)
J C Tuck The Cat And Custard Pot

Placings:06/4U60/0452532P/0303P/0001232326 (1988)
2001/02: 17⁰G, 17⁰GF, 17⁰GF, 16¹GF, 16²GF, 16³GF, 16²GF, 16³GS, 16²GF, 16⁶G

	Starts	1st	2nd	3rd	Win & Pl
Hurdles	10	1	3	2	4920
Career Total	**29**	**1**	**5**	**5**	**8717**

73	8/01	Worc	2m	G(0-90)HHdl	G-F	£1608

Total win prize-money £1609

Going: Sf: 0-0 GS: 0-1 Gd: 0-2 GF: - Fm: 1-7
Distance: **2m/2m3: 1-10** 2m4-2m7: 0-0 3m+: 0-0
Track: **LH: 1-6** RH: 0-4 Tight: 0-3 Gall: 0-0
Aids: Bl: 0-0 Vi: 0-0 Tstrap: 0-0
Best Rating: 106 3/99 Ludl 2m4f good Ch

Got off the mark in a seller at Worcester in August of 2001 over two miles on good to firm, and has continued to run well since in handicap hurdles.

Jack Be Smart

97(82h) 71

7-y-o ch g Henbit (USA)-Trimar Gold (Goldhill)

Ferdy Murphy John Smart

Placings:250/360-**04PFP53** **(4916)**
2001/02: 20^{0}G, 25^{4}G, 25^{P}S, 25^{F}G, 27^{P}HY, 20^{5}GF, 27^{3}GF

	Starts	1st	2nd	3rd	Win & Pl
Chases	7	0	0	1	939
Career Total	**13**	**0**	**1**	**2**	**1767**

Going: Sf: 0-2 GS: 0-0 Gd: 0-3 GF: - Fm: 0-2
Distance: 2m/2m3: 0-2 2m4-2m7: 0-2 3m+: 0-5
Track: LH: 0-5 RH: 0-2 Tight: 0-2 Gall: 0-1
Aids: Bl: 0-2 Vi: 0-0 Tstrap: 0-0
Best Rating: 99 2/00 Sedg 2m1f gd-sft NHF

Poor form so far.

Jack Dawson (IRE)

5-y-o b g Persian Bold-Dream Of Jenny (Caerleon (USA))
John Berry The Premier Cru

Placings:P **(2134)**
2001/02: 21^{P}GF

	Starts	1st	2nd	3rd	Win & Pl
Hurdles	1	0	0	0	
Career Total	**1**	**0**	**0**	**0**	

Going: Sf: 0-0 GS: 0-0 Gd: 0-0 GF: - Fm: 0-1
Distance: 2m/2m3: 0-0 2m4-2m7: 0-1 3m+: 0-0
Track: LH: 0-0 RH: 0-1 Tight: 0-0 Gall: 0-0
Aids: Bl: 0-0 Vi: 0-0 Tstrap: 0-0
Best Rating:

Jack Doyle (IRE)

11-y-o ch g Be My Native (USA)-Sister Ida (Bustino)
N A Twiston-Davies Melton Pets Direct Ltd

Placings:0/3214/3FP2P/1114/6P6PP0/P **(1991)**
2001/02: 24^{P}G

	Starts	1st	2nd	3rd	Win & Pl
Chases	1	0	0	0	
Career Total	**21**	**4**	**2**	**2**	**37658**

149	2/98	Sand	2m4f110y	A Ch	GD	£20752
144	1/98	Chel	2m5f	C HCh	G-S	£5576
125	1/98	Ludl	2m4f	E Ch	G-S	£3022
107	10/95	Tipp	2m	Hdl	G-Y	£3221

Total win prize-money £32572

Going: Sf: 0-0 GS: 0-0 Gd: 0-1 GF: - Fm: 0-0
Distance: 2m/2m3: 0-0 2m4-2m7: 0-0 3m+: 0-1
Track: LH: 0-0 RH: 0-1 Tight: 0-0 Gall: 0-0
Aids: Bl: 0-0 Vi: 0-0 Tstrap: 0-0
Best Rating: 149 2/98 Sand 2m4f110y good Ch

He was a high-class novice chaser who completed a hat-trick in the 1997/98 season when beating Cyfor Malta at Sandown. He sadly finished lame when fourth in the Cathcart later that term and was also reported to have a heart murmur. Off the track since March 2000, he was running well at Kempton in November 2001 but landed awkwardly and was again pulled-up lame.

Jack Flush (IRE)

104 85

8-y-o b g Broken Hearted-Clubhouse Turn (IRE) (King Of Clubs)
M E Sowersby M E Sowersby

Placings:015300P/33345612-440P63 **(4332)**
2001/02: 17^{4}G, 27^{4}S, 16^{0}GS, 19^{P}S, 16^{6}GS, 21^{3}S

	Starts	1st	2nd	3rd	Win & Pl
Hurdles	6	0	0	1	252
Career Total	**21**	**2**	**1**	**5**	**5699**

84	2/01	Catt	2m3f	G(0-90)HHdl	SFT	£1939
92	12/98	Catt	2m3f	G Hdl	GD	£1495

Total win prize-money £3434

Going: Sf: 0-3 GS: 0-2 Gd: 0-1 GF: - Fm: 0-0
Distance: 2m/2m3: 0-4 2m4-2m7: 0-1 3m+: 0-1
Track: LH: 0-6 RH: 0-0 Tight: 0-6 Gall: 0-0
Aids: Bl: 0-1 Vi: 0-2 Tstrap: 0-6
Best Rating: 92 12/98 Catt 2m3f good Hdl

Modest selling hurdler. Suited by two and a half miles.

Jack Fry (IRE)

87f 84f

5-y-o gr g Lashkari-Most Of All (Absalom)
Noel T Chance Louisville Syndicate

Placings:0 **(4639)**
2001/02: 16^{0}GF

	Starts	1st	2nd	3rd	Win & Pl
NH Flat	1	0	0	0	
Career Total	**1**	**0**	**0**	**0**	

Going: Sf: 0-0 GS: 0-0 Gd: 0-0 GF: - Fm: 0-1
Distance: 2m/2m3: 0-1 2m4-2m7: 0-0 3m+: 0-0
Track: LH: 0-0 RH: 0-1 Tight: 0-0 Gall: 0-0
Aids: Bl: 0-0 Vi: 0-0 Tstrap: 0-0
Best Rating: 84 4/02 Asct 2m110y gd-fm NHF

Jack Miller

81f

4-y-o b g Forzando-Norvi (Viking (USA))
R A Fahey Exors Of The Late D A Read

Placings:4 **(4790)**
2001/02: 16^{4}F

	Starts	1st	2nd	3rd	Win & Pl
NH Flat	1	0	0	0	0
Career Total	**1**	**0**	**0**	**0**	**0**

Going: Sf: 0-0 GS: 0-0 Gd: 0-0 GF: - Fm: 0-1
Distance: 2m/2m3: 0-1 2m4-2m7: 0-0 3m+: 0-0
Track: LH: 0-0 RH: 0-0 Tight: 0-0 Gall: 0-0
Aids: Bl: 0-0 Vi: 0-0 Tstrap: 0-0
Best Rating: 81 4/02 Newc 2m firm NHF

Jack Reef

7-y-o gr g Mystiko (USA)-Lady Reef (Mill Reef (USA))
D McCain L A Morgan

Placings:0406/0000F/400-P **(0420)**
2001/02: 17^{P}G

	Starts	1st	2nd	3rd	Win & Pl
Chases	1	0	0	0	
Career Total	**13**	**0**	**0**	**0**	**285**

Going: Sf: 0-0 GS: 0-0 Gd: 0-1 GF: - Fm: 0-0
Distance: 2m/2m3: 0-1 2m4-2m7: 0-0 3m+: 0-0
Track: LH: 0-1 RH: 0-0 Tight: 0-1 Gall: 0-0
Aids: Bl: 0-0 Vi: 0-0 Tstrap: 0-0
Best Rating: 90 5/00 Uttx 2m good Ch

Jack Yeats (IRE)

104 101

10-y-o b g Don't Forget Me-Petty Session (Blakeney)

Ferdy Murphy Leeds Plywood And Doors Ltd

Placings:0/20P04420/64F22315234/0P3FF/26300-21PPPPP346 **(4769)**
2001/02: 27^{2}G, 26^{1}GF, 24^{P}GF, 24^{P}GS, 22^{P}S, 24^{P}S, 20^{P}HY, 21^{3}S, 24^{4}G, 25^{6}GF

	Starts	1st	2nd	3rd	Win & Pl
Chases	10	1	1	1	5592
Career Total	**40**	**2**	**7**	**5**	**16031**

101	5/01	Prth	3m2f110y	F(0-95)HCh	G-F	£3770
110	10/97	Fair	2m2f	(0-102)HCh	GD	£3051

Total win prize-money £6822

Going: Sf: 0-4 GS: 0-1 Gd: 0-2 GF: - Fm: 1-3
Distance: 2m/2m3: 0-0 2m4-2m7: 0-3 **3m+: 1-7**
Track: LH: 0-7 RH: 0-2 Tight: 0-5 Gall: 0-1
Aids: Bl: 0-0 Vi: 0-0 Tstrap: 0-0
Best Rating: 110 3/98 Carl 2m heavy Ch

Infrequent finisher and a light of other days.

Jackem (IRE)

103 106

8-y-o b/br g Lord Americo-Laurence Lady (Laurence O)
Ian Williams (P A Fahy 21/2) Ian Williams

Placings:U4*1*BFP0-UF5*363**5*0S0 **(4161)**
2001/02: 17^{U}Y, 16^{F}Y, 18^{5}HY, 16^{3}S, 18^{6}YS, 24^{3}SH, 16^{5}HY, 20^{0}S, 24^{S}HY, 25^{0}GS

	Starts	1st	2nd	3rd	Win & Pl
NH Flat	2	0	0	1	101
Hurdles	6	0	0	1	666
Chases	2	0	0	0	0
Career Total	**17**	**1**	**0**	**2**	**4160**

108	11/00	Tram	2m	NHF	HVY	£2760

Total win prize-money £2760

Going: Sf: 0-5 GS: 0-1 Gd: 0-0 GF: - Fm: 0-0
Distance: 2m/2m3: 0-6 2m4-2m7: 0-1 3m+: 0-3
Track: LH: 0-1 RH: 0-1 Tight: 0-0 Gall: 0-0
Aids: Bl: 0-0 Vi: 0-0 Tstrap: 0-0
Best Rating: 108 11/00 Tram 2m heavy NHF

Has a very poor finishing record over fences. Has been kept busy this year between hurdles and bumpers. Eventually broke his duck in a novices' hurdle at Fakenham in May.

Jackie C (IRE)

103 (106h)125

7-y-o b g Supreme Leader-Gloria St Julien (Duky)
T R George (Peter McCreery 11/6) R J McAlpine

Placings:0440-210F23 **(3165)**
2001/02: 16^{2}YS, 16^{1}G, 17^{0}G, 20^{F}HY, 20^{2}S, 23^{3}G

	Starts	1st	2nd	3rd	Win & Pl
Hurdles	2	1	1	0	5484
Chases	4	0	1	1	2165
Career Total	**10**	**1**	**2**	**1**	**8113**

106	6/01	Slig	2m	Hdl	GD	£4451

Total win prize-money £4452

Going: Sf: 0-2 GS: 0-0 Gd: 1-3 GF: - Fm: 0-0
Distance: **2m/2m3: 1-3** 2m4-2m7: 0-2 3m+: 0-1
Track: LH: 0-2 RH: 0-1 Tight: 0-1 Gall: 0-0
Aids: Bl: 0-0 Vi: 0-0 Tstrap: 0-0
Best Rating: 125 1/02 Leic 2m7f110y good Ch

Moderate Irish hurdler, he is now with Tom George. He is improving over fences but still has something to learn.

Jackie Jarvis (IRE)

5-y-o b m Alphabatim (USA)-Miss Brantridge (Riboboy (USA))
J S Moore Ernie Houghton

Placings:00-R (0684)
2001/02: 17^{R}G

	Starts	1st	2nd	3rd	Win & Pl
NH Flat	1	0	0	0	
Career Total	**3**	**0**	**0**	**0**	

Going: Sf: 0-0 GS: 0-0 Gd: 0-1 GF: - Fm: 0-0
Distance: 2m/2m3: 0-1 2m4-2m7: 0-0 3m+: 0-0
Track: LH: 0-1 RH: 0-0 Tight: 0-1 Gall: 0-0
Aids: Bl: 0-0 Vi: 0-0 Tstrap: 0-0
Best Rating: 50 2/01 Donc 2m110y good NHF

Jacklighte Bellevue (FR)

99 114
5-y-o b g Saint Cyrien (FR)-Kalighte (FR) (Light Butterfly)
A King (Y Fouin 1/11) Million In Mind Partnership (11)

Placings:033124 (4494)
2001/02: 18^{0}VS, 18^{3}VS, 18^{3}G, 21^{1}S, 21^{2}HY, 22^{4}G

	Starts	1st	2nd	3rd	Win & Pl
Hurdles	6	1	1	2	9113
Career Total	**6**	**1**	**1**	**2**	**9113**

114 1/02 Kemp 2m5f D Hdl SFT £3965
Total win prize-money £3965

Going: Sf: 1-2 GS: 0-0 Gd: 0-2 GF: - Fm: 0-0
Distance: 2m/2m3: 0-3 **2m4-2m7: 1-3** 3m+: 0-0
Track: LH: 0-2 **RH: 1-1** Tight: 0-1 Gall: 0-0
Aids: Bl: 0-0 Vi: 0-0 Tstrap: 0-0
Best Rating: 114 2/02 Wwck 2m5f heavy Hdl

Ex-French, he won a novice hurdle at Kempton in January but was a bit disappointing under a penalty. Stays two miles five furlongs. Acts on soft/heavy ground.

Jacks Birthday (IRE)

88 81
4-y-o b g Mukaddamah (USA)-High Concept (IRE) (Thatching)
R J O'Sullivan Jack Joseph

Placings:53 (1632)
2001/02: 16^{5}GF, 16^{3}GF

	Starts	1st	2nd	3rd	Win & Pl
Hurdles	2	0	0	1	469
Career Total	**2**	**0**	**0**	**1**	**469**

Going: Sf: 0-0 GS: 0-0 Gd: 0-0 GF: - Fm: 0-2
Distance: 2m/2m3: 0-2 2m4-2m7: 0-0 3m+: 0-0
Track: LH: 0-1 RH: 0-1 Tight: 0-1 Gall: 0-0
Aids: Bl: 0-0 Vi: 0-0 Tstrap: 0-0
Best Rating: 81 10/01 Winc 2m gd-fm Hdl

Jackson (FR)

75f 68f
5-y-o b g Passing Sale (FR)-Tynia (FR) (Djarvis (FR))
Miss Venetia Williams C B Brookes

Placings:0-0 (2222)
2001/02: 17^{0}G

	Starts	1st	2nd	3rd	Win & Pl
NH Flat	1	0	0	0	
Career Total	**2**	**0**	**0**	**0**	

Going: Sf: 0-0 GS: 0-0 Gd: 0-1 GF: - Fm: 0-0
Distance: 2m/2m3: 0-1 2m4-2m7: 0-0 3m+: 0-0
Track: LH: 0-1 RH: 0-0 Tight: 0-1 Gall: 0-0
Aids: Bl: 0-0 Vi: 0-0 Tstrap: 0-0
Best Rating: 68 4/01 Asct 2m110y heavy NHF

Jackson Court

(90h)
8-y-o ch g Nearly A Hand-Last House (Vital Season)
B G Powell Mrs A Marshall

Placings:06/0600P-F (0190)
2001/02: 21^{F}GF

	Starts	1st	2nd	3rd	Win & Pl
Chases	1	0	0	0	
Career Total	**8**	**0**	**0**	**0**	**0**

Going: Sf: 0-0 GS: 0-0 Gd: 0-0 GF: - Fm: 0-1
Distance: 2m/2m3: 0-0 2m4-2m7: 0-1 3m+: 0-0
Track: LH: 0-1 RH: 0-0 Tight: 0-1 Gall: 0-0
Aids: Bl: 0-0 Vi: 0-0 Tstrap: 0-0
Best Rating: 102 2/99 Newb 2m110y good Hdl

Jackson's Hole

99(97h) (101h)110
9-y-o b g Brush Aside (USA)-Jack's The Girl (IRE) (Supreme Leader)
M W Easterby Michael A Proudfoot

Placings:4/050U/0/F2P-35563 (4313)
2001/02: 19^{3}S, 24^{5}S, 19^{5}GS, 16^{6}S, 24^{3}HY

	Starts	1st	2nd	3rd	Win & Pl
Hurdles	2	0	0	1	356
Chases	3	0	0	1	632
Career Total	**14**	**0**	**1**	**2**	**1976**

Going: Sf: 0-4 GS: 0-1 Gd: 0-0 GF: - Fm: 0-0
Distance: 2m/2m3: 0-3 2m4-2m7: 0-0 3m+: 0-2
Track: LH: 0-5 RH: 0-0 Tight: 0-3 Gall: 0-2
Aids: Bl: 0-0 Vi: 0-0 Tstrap: 0-0
Best Rating: 110 3/02 Sthl 3m110y heavy Ch

Out of a half-sister to Lean Ar Aghaidh, he scored four times out of five between the flags in 2000 but has yet to translate this form to hurdles or fences. Tends to fade badly in the closing stages.

Jacksonville (FR)

98 102
5-y-o b g Petit Montmorency (USA)-Quinine Des Aulnes (FR) (Air Du Nord (USA))
A Parker Mr & Mrs Raymond Anderson Green

Placings:0-0223P (4877)
2001/02: 17^{0}S, 20^{2}HY, 24^{2}GS, 22^{3}HY, 24^{P}G

	Starts	1st	2nd	3rd	Win & Pl
NH Flat	1	0	0	0	0
Hurdles	4	0	2	1	2146
Career Total	**6**	**0**	**2**	**1**	**2146**

Going: Sf: 0-3 GS: 0-1 Gd: 0-1 GF: - Fm: 0-0
Distance: 2m/2m3: 0-1 2m4-2m7: 0-2 3m+: 0-2
Track: LH: 0-2 RH: 0-3 Tight: 0-2 Gall: 0-0
Aids: Bl: 0-0 Vi: 0-0 Tstrap: 0-0
Best Rating: 102 2/02 Ayr 2m4f heavy Hdl

Fair hurdler, stays three miles, suited by soft ground.

Jacopo (FR)

56 24
5-y-o b g Grand Tresor (FR)-Qolombine (FR) (Damsire Unregistered)
R Dickin Fairfields Flyer

Placings:0006 (4655)
2001/02: 17^{0}G, 16^{0}GS, 17^{0}S, 17^{6}GS

	Starts	1st	2nd	3rd	Win & Pl
NH Flat	3	0	0	0	0
Hurdles	1	0	0	0	0
Career Total	**4**	**0**	**0**	**0**	**0**

Going: Sf: 0-1 GS: 0-2 Gd: 0-1 GF: - Fm: 0-0
Distance: 2m/2m3: 0-4 2m4-2m7: 0-0 3m+: 0-0
Track: LH: 0-0 RH: 0-3 Tight: 0-1 Gall: 0-0
Aids: Bl: 0-0 Vi: 0-0 Tstrap: 0-0
Best Rating: 80 5/01 Hrfd 2m1f good NHF

Jade Tiger

84 70
6-y-o ch g Lion Cavern (USA)-Precious Jade (Northfields (USA))
F Jordan Miss Laura Jordan

Placings:FF05/00-0 (1131)
2001/02: 16^{0}GF

	Starts	1st	2nd	3rd	Win & Pl
Hurdles	1	0	0	0	
Career Total	**7**	**0**	**0**	**0**	**0**

Going: Sf: 0-0 GS: 0-0 Gd: 0-0 GF: - Fm: 0-1
Distance: 2m/2m3: 0-1 2m4-2m7: 0-0 3m+: 0-0
Track: LH: 0-1 RH: 0-0 Tight: 0-0 Gall: 0-0
Aids: Bl: 0-0 Vi: 0-0 Tstrap: 0-0
Best Rating: 82 11/99 Hrfd 2m1f good Hdl

Jaffa

108 120
10-y-o ch g Kind Of Hush-Sip Of Orange (Celtic Cone)
Miss J Wormall Mrs R Wormall

Placings:00/4P5/FF-P121 (4907)
2001/02: 24^{P}GF, 20^{1}S, 21^{2}GF, 20^{1}GF

	Starts	1st	2nd	3rd	Win & Pl
Chases	4	2	1	0	8290
Career Total	**11**	**2**	**1**	**0**	**8564**

120 4/02 MRas 2m4f D Ch G-F £4982
112 3/02 Leic 2m4f110y H Ch SFT £2112
Total win prize-money £7095

Going: Sf: 1-1 GS: 0-0 Gd: 0-0 GF: - Fm: 1-3
Distance: 2m/2m3: 0-0 **2m4-2m7: 2-3** 3m+: 0-1
Track: LH: 0-1 **RH: 2-3 Tight: 1-2** Gall: 0-1
Aids: Bl: 0-0 Vi: 0-0 Tstrap: 0-0
Best Rating: 120 4/02 MRas 2m4f gd-fm Ch

Winning pointer/hunter chaser, tends to break blood-vessels. Not the most fluent over his fences.

Jaffeg Storm (IRE)

80 39
6-y-o b g Glacial Storm (USA)-She's A Monkey (Monksfield)
Miss Lucinda V Russell A A Bissett

Placings:0 (4689)

2001/02: 16⁰GF

	Starts	1st	2nd	3rd	Win & Pl
Hurdles	1	0	0	0	
Career Total	**1**	**0**	**0**	**0**	

Going: Sf: 0-0 GS: 0-0 Gd: 0-0 GF: - Fm: 0-1
Distance: 2m/2m3: 0-1 2m4-2m7: 0-0 3m+: 0-0
Track: LH: 0-1 RH: 0-0 Tight: 0-1 Gall: 0-0
Aids: Bl: 0-0 Vi: 0-0 Tstrap: 0-0
Best Rating: 49 4/02 Kels 2m110y gd-fm Hdl

Jaguar (NZ)

105(71c) (86+c)100
9-y-o b g St Hilarion (USA)-Saab (NZ) (Three Legs)
P J Hobbs Sir Robert Ogden

Placings:12/1-53 **(4877)**
2001/02: 24⁵S, 24³G

	Starts	1st	2nd	3rd	Win & Pl
Hurdles	2	0	0	1	716
Career Total	**5**	**2**	**1**	**1**	**7083**
118 10/00 Extr 3m110y E(0-115)HHdl				SFT	£3250
102 11/99 Newc 2m4f E Hdl				GD	£2379

Total win prize-money £5629

Going: Sf: 0-1 GS: 0-0 Gd: 0-1 GF: - Fm: 0-0
Distance: 2m/2m3: 0-0 2m4-2m7: 0-0 3m+: 0-2
Track: LH: 0-1 RH: 0-1 Tight: 0-0 Gall: 0-0
Aids: Bl: 0-1 Vi: 0-0 Tstrap: 0-0
Best Rating: 118 10/00 Extr 3m110y soft Hdl

A winner on the Flat in New Zealand. He has had his problems since coming to Britain and has been lightly-raced. Stays three miles. Acts on good ground or softer.

Jaguar

107 105
6-y-o b g Barathea (IRE)-Oasis (Valiyar)
N A Twiston-Davies Mr F J Mills & Mr W Mills

Placings:12442503/06P000-64F0UP **(4596)**
2001/02: 17⁶GF, 16⁴GS, 17ᶠG, 16⁰GS, 16ᵁHY, 20ᴾG

	Starts	1st	2nd	3rd	Win & Pl
Hurdles	4	0	0	0	750
Chases	2	0	0	0	0
Career Total	**20**	**1**	**2**	**1**	**7313**
120 9/99 Extr 2m1f E Hdl				G-S	£2373

Total win prize-money £2373

Going: Sf: 0-1 GS: 0-2 Gd: 0-2 GF: - Fm: 0-1
Distance: 2m/2m3: 0-5 2m4-2m7: 0-1 3m+: 0-0
Track: LH: 0-4 RH: 0-2 Tight: 0-1 Gall: 0-2
Aids: Bl: 0-1 Vi: 0-0 Tstrap: 0-0
Best Rating: 120 1/00 Wwck 2m soft Hdl

A winner over hurdles, he acts well on good to soft ground and suited by trips around two miles. Has not won since September 1999.

Jail Break (IRE)

83 89
6-y-o ch g Persian Mews-Miss Leeway (Tarboosh (USA))
E McNamara C Maune

Placings:0000-6100P00 **(4630a)**
2001/02: 20⁶GF, 20¹GY, 20⁰GF, 24⁰HY, 16ᴾG, 20⁰S, 20⁰GY

	Starts	1st	2nd	3rd	Win & Pl
Hurdles	7	1	0	0	4452
Career Total	**11**	**1**	**0**	**0**	**4452**
89 8/01 Tral 2m4f (0-102)HHdl				G-Y	£4451

Total win prize-money £4452

Going: Sf: 0-2 GS: 0-0 Gd: 0-1 GF: - Fm: 0-2
Distance: 2m/2m3: 0-1 **2m4-2m7: 1-5** 3m+: 0-1
Track: LH: 0-2 RH: 0-2 Tight: 0-0 Gall: 0-0
Aids: Bl: 0-0 Vi: 0-0 Tstrap: 0-0
Best Rating: 89 8/01 Tral 2m4f gd-yld Hdl

Winner of an easy ground handicap hurdle at Tralee in the summer of 2001.

Jair Du Cochet (FR)

113 165
5-y-o b g Rahotep (FR)-Dilaure (FR) (Rose Laurel)
G Macaire Mrs F Montauban

Placings:C111211-4130 **(4251)**
2001/02: 16⁴GS, 23¹S, 20³S, 24⁰G

	Starts	1st	2nd	3rd	Win & Pl
Hurdles	4	1	0	1	18240
Career Total	**11**	**6**	**1**	**1**	**84623**
165 1/02 Hayd 2m7f110y A Hdl				SFT	£15080
165 1/01 Chel 2m1f A Hdl				SFT	£12000
156 12/00 Chep 2m110y A Hdl				SFT	£17400
11/00 Engh 2m110y Hdl				HVY	£9606
10/00 Engh 2m110y Hdl				HLD	£9606
10/00 Comp 2m Hdl				VS	£3362

Total win prize-money £67054

Going: Sf: 1-2 GS: 0-1 Gd: 0-1 GF: - Fm: 0-0
Distance: 2m/2m3: 0-1 2m4-2m7: 0-1 **3m+: 1-2**
Track: **LH: 1-1** RH: 0-1 Tight: 0-1 Gall: 0-0
Aids: Bl: 0-0 Vi: 0-0 Tstrap: 0-0
Best Rating: 165 1/02 Hayd 2m7f110y soft Hdl

High-class French-trained hurdler. He made a winning debut in this country at Chepstow in December 2000, where all but Bilboa were a distance behind him, and went on to annihilate a decent field at Cheltenham, making all the running in testing conditions. He jumps particularly well and is clearly well suited to soft ground. Disappointed on his return at Kempton, but produced decent staying performance in a Grade Two hurdle at Haydock in January and had excuses for a defeat at Fontwell before being unplaced in the Stayers' Hurdle. Stays three miles.

Jakari (FR)

109 107
5-y-o b g Apeldoorn (FR)-Tartifume Ii (FR) (Mistigri)
H D Daly The Earl Cadogan

Placings:5-1 **(2023)**
2001/02: 16¹S

	Starts	1st	2nd	3rd	Win & Pl
Hurdles	1	1	0	0	2688
Career Total	**2**	**1**	**0**	**0**	**2688**
107 11/01 Uttx 2m E Hdl				SFT	£2688

Total win prize-money £2688

Going: Sf: 1-1 GS: 0-0 Gd: 0-0 GF: - Fm: 0-0
Distance: **2m/2m3: 1-1** 2m4-2m7: 0-0 3m+: 0-0
Track: **LH: 1-1** RH: 0-0 Tight: 0-0 Gall: 0-0
Aids: Bl: 0-0 Vi: 0-0 Tstrap: 0-0
Best Rating: 107 11/01 Uttx 2m soft Hdl

He gave his connections enough to like when landing his hurdling debut at Uttoxeter in November 2001.

Jake The Jumper (IRE)

89 90
5-y-o b g Jolly Jake (NZ)-Princess Tino (IRE) (Rontino)
Miss G Browne Mrs Rosalinde Elsbury

Placings:5045 **(4816)**
2001/02: 17⁵S, 21⁰S, 16⁴HY, 21⁵GF

	Starts	1st	2nd	3rd	Win & Pl
NH Flat	1	0	0	0	0
Hurdles	3	0	0	0	359
Career Total	**4**	**0**	**0**	**0**	**359**

Going: Sf: 0-3 GS: 0-0 Gd: 0-0 GF: - Fm: 0-1
Distance: 2m/2m3: 0-2 2m4-2m7: 0-2 3m+: 0-0
Track: LH: 0-1 RH: 0-2 Tight: 0-1 Gall: 0-1
Aids: Bl: 0-0 Vi: 0-0 Tstrap: 0-0
Best Rating: 90 4/02 Chel 2m5f110y gd-fm Hdl

Lightly-raced individual, with only moderate form to date on soft and firm ground.

Jakes Progress (IRE)

77(106h) (105h)90
8-y-o b g Jolly Jake (NZ)-Coteri Run (Deep Run)
L Lungo Ashleybank Investments Limited

Placings:5664/21-35P4 **(4580)**
2001/02: 17³G, 16⁵G, 19ᴾS, 16⁴G

	Starts	1st	2nd	3rd	Win & Pl
Hurdles	2	0	0	1	362
Chases	2	0	0	0	236
Career Total	**10**	**1**	**1**	**1**	**3584**
84 2/01 Sedg 2m1f E Hdl				G-S	£2058

Total win prize-money £2058

Going: Sf: 0-1 GS: 0-0 Gd: 0-3 GF: - Fm: 0-0
Distance: 2m/2m3: 0-4 2m4-2m7: 0-0 3m+: 0-0
Track: LH: 0-4 RH: 0-0 Tight: 0-2 Gall: 0-0
Aids: Bl: 0-0 Vi: 0-0 Tstrap: 0-0
Best Rating: 109 11/00 Newc 2m gd-sft Hdl

Jalb (IRE)

111 95
8-y-o b g Robellino (USA)-Adjacent (IRE) (Doulab (USA))
P G Murphy Family And Friends

Placings:P/0042122/26200 **(3337)**
2001/02: 22²S, 20⁶S, 19²G, 20⁰G, 24⁰G

	Starts	1st	2nd	3rd	Win & Pl
Hurdles	5	0	2	0	1553
Career Total	**13**	**1**	**5**	**0**	**6925**
90 4/99 Ludl 2m5f110y E(0-105)HHdl				GD	£3022

Total win prize-money £3022

Going: Sf: 0-2 GS: 0-0 Gd: 0-3 GF: - Fm: 0-0
Distance: 2m/2m3: 0-1 2m4-2m7: 0-3 3m+: 0-1
Track: LH: 0-3 RH: 0-2 Tight: 0-1 Gall: 0-0
Aids: Bl: 0-0 Vi: 0-0 Tstrap: 0-1
Best Rating: 95 11/01 Wwck 2m3f good Hdl

Modest hurdler, acts on good or softer.

Jallastep (FR)

94 77
5-y-o b g Boston Two Step (USA)-Balladine (FR) (Rivelago (FR))
J S Goldie Mr & Mrs Raymond Anderson Green

Placings:60P51 **(4765)**
2001/02: 16⁶GS, 16⁰S, 17ᴾHY, 16⁵G, 16¹GF

	Starts	1st	2nd	3rd	Win & Pl
Hurdles	5	1	0	0	2772

	Starts	1st	2nd	3rd	Win & Pl
Career Total	**5**	**1**	**0**	**0**	**2772**

77 4/02 Hexm 2m110y E(0-105)HHdl G-F £2772
Total win prize-money £2772

Going: Sf: 0-2 GS: 0-1 Gd: 0-1 GF: - Fm: 1-1
Distance: **2m/2m3: 1-5** 2m4-2m7: 0-0 3m+: 0-0
Track: LH: 0-3 RH: 0-1 Tight: 0-0 Gall: 0-0
Aids: Bl: 0-0 Vi: 0-0 Tstrap: 0-0
Best Rating: 77 4/02 Hexm 2m110y gd-fm Hdl

Lightly-raced hurdler, acts on a fast surface and is effective over two miles.

Jalons Star (IRE)

106 **107**

4-y-o b g Eagle Eyed (USA)-Regina St Cyr (IRE) (Doulab (USA))
G M McCourt (M Quinn 3/8) Jalons Partnership 2

Placings:4435204012 **(4417)**
2001/02: 17^{4}GS, 17^{4}G, 16^{3}G, 16^{5}G, 16^{2}G, 16^{0}GS, 16^{4}S, 16^{0}S, 17^{1}S, 16^{2}GS

	Starts	1st	2nd	3rd	Win & Pl
Hurdles	10	1	2	1	7309
Career Total	**10**	**1**	**2**	**1**	**7309**

105 3/02 Sedg 2m1f D(0-115)HHdl SFT £3297
Total win prize-money £3297

Going: Sf: 1-3 GS: 0-3 Gd: 0-4 GF: - Fm: 0-0
Distance: **2m/2m3: 1-10** 2m4-2m7: 0-0 3m+: 0-0
Track: **LH: 1-8** RH: 0-1 **Tight: 1-3** Gall: 0-4
Aids: Bl: 0-0 Vi: 0-0 Tstrap: 0-0
Best Rating: 107 3/02 Newb 2m110y gd-sft Hdl

Finally opened his account over hurdles in a low-grade affair at Sedgefield in March. Runner-up under a penalty.

Jaloux D'Estruval (FR)

(86h) (73h)

5-y-o b g Kadalko (FR)-Pommette Iii (FR) (Trac)
Mrs L C Taylor Mrs W Morrell

Placings:05-40P **(2687)**
2001/02: 24^{4}G, 22^{0}S, 19^{P}G

	Starts	1st	2nd	3rd	Win & Pl
Hurdles	2	0	0	0	0
Chases	1	0	0	0	0
Career Total	**5**	**0**	**0**	**0**	**0**

Going: Sf: 0-1 GS: 0-0 Gd: 0-2 GF: - Fm: 0-0
Distance: 2m/2m3: 0-0 2m4-2m7: 0-2 3m+: 0-1
Track: LH: 0-3 RH: 0-0 Tight: 0-2 Gall: 0-1
Aids: Bl: 0-0 Vi: 0-0 Tstrap: 0-0
Best Rating: 80 3/01 Newb 2m110y heavy NHF

Was too headstrong to stay the three-mile distance on his hurdling debut at Southwell.

Jamaican Flight (USA)

104 **109**

9-y-o b h Sunshine Forever (USA)-Kalamona (USA) (Hawaii)
Mrs S Lamyman P Lamyman

Placings:UO52/11111326/31213400/62P24/50F-44604 **(4286)**
2001/02: 21^{4}GS, 20^{4}GS, 24^{6}G, 22^{0}GS, 21^{4}GS

	Starts	1st	2nd	3rd	Win & Pl
Hurdles	5	0	0	0	1160
Career Total	**33**	**7**	**5**	**3**	**35465**

132 11/98 MRas 2m5f110y B HHdl HVY £6716
131 10/98 MRas 2m3f110y C(0-130)HHdl GD £4445
128 9/97 MRas 2m3f110y D(0-120)HHdl GD £2745
105 7/97 MRas 2m3f110y D Hdl GD £2882
113 6/97 MRas 2m3f110y D Hdl GD £2872
107 5/97 MRas 2m3f110y D(0-120)HHdl G-F £2951
100 5/97 Towc 2m E Hdl GD £2407
Total win prize-money £25022

Going: Sf: 0-0 GS: 0-4 Gd: 0-1 GF: - Fm: 0-0
Distance: 2m/2m3: 0-0 2m4-2m7: 0-4 3m+: 0-1
Track: LH: 0-1 RH: 0-4 Tight: 0-3 Gall: 0-0
Aids: Bl: 0-0 Vi: 0-0 Tstrap: 0-0
Best Rating: 132 12/99 MRas 2m3f110y good Hdl

A natural front-runner, this smashing dual-purpose horse has given his connections tremendous value for money on the Flat and over hurdles. Goes particularly well at Market Rasen. Unraced over fences, his last hurdle win was November 1998.

Jambo Bwana

9-y-o ch g Henbit (USA)-Four Friends (Quayside)
P J Millington P J Millington

Placings:040/0P/0/F0 **(0430)**
2001/02: 25^{F}G, 16^{0}G

	Starts	1st	2nd	3rd	Win & Pl
Chases	2	0	0	0	
Career Total	**8**	**0**	**0**	**0**	**0**

Going: Sf: 0-0 GS: 0-0 Gd: 0-2 GF: - Fm: 0-0
Distance: 2m/2m3: 0-1 2m4-2m7: 0-0 3m+: 0-1
Track: LH: 0-1 RH: 0-0 Tight: 0-0 Gall: 0-0
Aids: Bl: 0-0 Vi: 0-0 Tstrap: 0-0
Best Rating: 88 4/99 Uttx 2m gd-sft Hdl

Jamerosier (FR)

101(101c) (102c)**109**

5-y-o b g The Wonder (FR)-Teuphaine (FR) (Barbotan (FR))
Mrs L C Taylor Mrs L C Taylor

Placings:5326 **(4398)**
2001/02: 16^{5}S, 24^{3}S, 22^{2}GS, 24^{6}S

	Starts	1st	2nd	3rd	Win & Pl
NH Flat	1	0	0	0	0
Hurdles	2	0	1	0	1284
Chases	1	0	0	1	508
Career Total	**4**	**0**	**1**	**1**	**1792**

Going: Sf: 0-3 GS: 0-1 Gd: 0-0 GF: - Fm: 0-0
Distance: 2m/2m3: 0-1 2m4-2m7: 0-1 3m+: 0-2
Track: LH: 0-3 RH: 0-1 Tight: 0-1 Gall: 0-2
Aids: Bl: 0-0 Vi: 0-0 Tstrap: 0-0
Best Rating: 109 3/02 Strf 2m6f110y gd-sft Hdl

Half-brother to his trainer's Scottish National winner Gingembre. He has shown enough ability over hurdles and fences to suggest he will be winning races too. Looks a potential out-and-out stayer and just needs experience.

Jameson (IRE)

106 **113**

6-y-o b g Broken Hearted-Seyona (Seymour Hicks (FR))
M Pitman Mrs T Brown

Placings:1/060-3 **(3600)**
2001/02: 18^{3}HY

	Starts	1st	2nd	3rd	Win & Pl
Hurdles	1	0	0	1	374
Career Total	**5**	**1**	**0**	**1**	**2089**

113 3/00 Sand 2m110y H NHF GD £1715
Total win prize-money £1715

Going: Sf: 0-1 GS: 0-0 Gd: 0-0 GF: - Fm: 0-0
Distance: 2m/2m3: 0-1 2m4-2m7: 0-0 3m+: 0-0
Track: LH: 0-1 RH: 0-0 Tight: 0-1 Gall: 0-0
Aids: Bl: 0-0 Vi: 0-0 Tstrap: 0-0
Best Rating: 113 2/02 Font 2m2f110y heavy Hdl

Jamie Ann

54

5-y-o b m Son Pardo-Taine Sands (Record Run)
Miss Sheena West Gerald West

Placings:0 **(2328)**
2001/02: 16^{0}G

	Starts	1st	2nd	3rd	Win & Pl
Hurdles	1	0	0	0	
Career Total	**1**	**0**	**0**	**0**	

Going: Sf: 0-0 GS: 0-0 Gd: 0-0 GF: 0-1 Fm: 0-0
Distance: 2m/2m3: 0-1 2m4-2m7: 0-0 3m+: 0-0
Track: LH: 0-1 RH: 0-0 Tight: 0-1 Gall: 0-0
Aids: Bl: 0-0 Vi: 0-0 Tstrap: 0-0
Best Rating:

Jamorin Dancer

97(98h) (77h)**84**

7-y-o b g Charmer-Geryea (USA) (Desert Wine (USA))
N B Mason N B Mason

Placings:0P0V40/5/0003426005 **(4872)**
2001/02: 17^{0}S, 16^{0}G, 17^{0}S, 16^{3}S, 17^{4}GF, 16^{2}GS, 16^{6}HY, 16^{0}G, 16^{0}G, 16^{5}GF

	Starts	1st	2nd	3rd	Win & Pl
Hurdles	8	0	1	1	780
Chases	2	0	0	0	0
Career Total	**17**	**0**	**1**	**1**	**981**

Going: Sf: 0-4 GS: 0-1 Gd: 0-3 GF: - Fm: 0-2
Distance: 2m/2m3: 0-10 2m4-2m7: 0-0 3m+: 0-0
Track: LH: 0-8 RH: 0-1 Tight: 0-7 Gall: 0-0
Aids: Bl: 0-0 Vi: 0-0 Tstrap: 0-0
Best Rating: 84 4/02 Weth 2m gd-fm Ch

Took some time to get the hang of hurdles and is now trying his hand over fences.

Jan's Dream (IRE)

106(78h) **110**

8-y-o ch m Executive Perk-Aunty Babs (Sexton Blake)
P R Webber Mrs J A Chenery

Placings:46/01/300-4PUR225 **(4508)**
2001/02: 16^{4}G, 20^{P}S, 20^{U}G, 22^{R}HY, 20^{2}S, 20^{2}S, 17^{5}G

	Starts	1st	2nd	3rd	Win & Pl
Chases	7	0	2	0	2609
Career Total	**14**	**1**	**2**	**1**	**5530**

100 4/00 NAbb 2m1f E Hdl HVY £2555
Total win prize-money £2555

Going: Sf: 0-4 GS: 0-0 Gd: 0-3 GF: - Fm: 0-0
Distance: 2m/2m3: 0-2 2m4-2m7: 0-5 3m+: 0-0
Track: LH: 0-2 RH: 0-4 Tight: 0-4 Gall: 0-0
Aids: Bl: 0-0 Vi: 0-0 Tstrap: 0-0

Best Rating: 110 3/02 Font 2m4f soft Ch

Winner of a maiden hurdle in the spring of 2000 in bottomless ground. Well held since over hurdles. Has moderate form over fences. Stays two and a half miles. Acts on soft/heavy ground.

Jandal

102 **80**

8-y-o ch g Arazi (USA)-Littlefield (Bay Express)
Jane Southcombe R A Bown

Placings:0054/60F/0-4P042 **(4682)**
2001/02: 19^{4}GS, 22^{P}S, 17^{0}S, 17^{4}G, 17^{2}GF

	Starts	1st	2nd	3rd	Win & Pl
Hurdles	5	0	1	0	602
Career Total	13	0	1	0	602

Going: Sf: 0-2 GS: 0-1 Gd: 0-1 GF: - Fm: 0-1
Distance: 2m/2m3: 0-3 2m4-2m7: 0-2 3m+: 0-0
Track: LH: 0-1 RH: 0-4 Tight: 0-3 Gall: 0-0
Aids: Bl: 0-0 Vi: 0-0 Tstrap: 0-0
Best Rating: 80 4/02 Hrfd 2m1f gd-fm Hdl

Improved form on fast ground including when narrowly beaten in a Hereford seller in April 2002.

Jane Lechat

105 **75**

7-y-o b m Teenoso (USA)-Richards Kate (Fidel)
Simon T Lewis (Mrs A J Perrett 15/7) Simon T Lewis

Placings:*12600*/4-4P030530PPP **(4657)**
2001/02: 16^{4}S, 17^{P}GF, 16^{0}GF, 16^{3}GF, 17^{0}GS, 16^{5}GF, 22^{3}GF, 17^{0}GF, 24^{P}G, 19^{P}F, 24^{P}G

	Starts	1st	2nd	3rd	Win & Pl
Hurdles	11	0	0	2	559
Career Total	17	1	1	2	2483

94 5/99 Font 2m2f110y H NHF FRM £1493
Total win prize-money £1494

Going: Sf: 0-1 GS: 0-1 Gd: 0-2 GF: - Fm: 0-7
Distance: 2m/2m3: 0-7 2m4-2m7: 0-2 3m+: 0-2
Track: LH: 0-7 RH: 0-4 Tight: 0-9 Gall: 0-0
Aids: Bl: 0-0 Vi: 0-0 Tstrap: 0-0
Best Rating: 105 2/00 Newb 2m110y gd-sft NHF

Janey Kate (IRE)

9-y-o gr m Roselier (FR)-Deep Serve (Quayside)
G M McCourt Racingclubcouk

Placings:2P/3-P **(4871)**
2001/02: 25^{P}GF

	Starts	1st	2nd	3rd	Win & Pl
Hurdles	1	0	0	0	
Career Total	4	0	1	1	1206

Going: Sf: 0-0 GS: 0-0 Gd: 0-0 GF: - Fm: 0-1
Distance: 2m/2m3: 0-0 2m4-2m7: 0-0 3m+: 0-1
Track: LH: 0-1 RH: 0-0 Tight: 0-0 Gall: 0-0
Aids: Bl: 0-0 Vi: 0-0 Tstrap: 0-0
Best Rating: 96 2/00 Font 2m6f110y gd-sft Hdl

Janglynyve

83 **84**

8-y-o ch m Sharpo-Wollow Maid (Wollow)
C A Dwyer D Farrow

Placings:43/146136/220230/030-0 **(1274)**
2001/02: 16^{0}GF

	Starts	1st	2nd	3rd	Win & Pl
Hurdles	1	0	0	0	
Career Total	18	2	3	4	10196

91 2/99 Bang 2m1f F(0-110)HHdl GD £3582
81 5/98 Strf 2m110y G Hdl G-F £1731
Total win prize-money £5315

Going: Sf: 0-0 GS: 0-0 Gd: 0-0 GF: - Fm: 0-1
Distance: 2m/2m3: 0-1 2m4-2m7: 0-0 3m+: 0-0
Track: LH: 0-1 RH: 0-0 Tight: 0-1 Gall: 0-0
Aids: Bl: 0-0 Vi: 0-0 Tstrap: 0-0
Best Rating: 112 2/00 Leic 2m heavy Hdl

Janiture (FR)

93(101h) (112h)**90**

5-y-o gr m Turgeon (USA)-Majaway (FR) (Timmy's Way (FR))
P F Nicholls Malcom Pearce & Gerry Mizel

Placings:46P111-P23 **(4589)**
2001/02: 19^{P}GS, 16^{2}S, 16^{3}G

	Starts	1st	2nd	3rd	Win & Pl
Hurdles	2	0	1	1	1440
Chases	1	0	0	0	0
Career Total	9	3	1	1	11517

4/01 Nant 2m1f110y Hdl VS £3492
4/01 Loud 2m1f Hdl VS £2716
3/01 Seno 1m7f Hdl HVY £0710
Total win prize-money £8924

Going: Sf: 0-1 GS: 0-1 Gd: 0-1 GF: - Fm: 0-0
Distance: 2m/2m3: 0-2 2m4-2m7: 0-1 3m+: 0-0
Track: LH: 0-1 RH: 0-2 Tight: 0-0 Gall: 0-0
Aids: Bl: 0-0 Vi: 0-0 Tstrap: 0-2
Best Rating: 112 3/02 Winc 2m soft Hdl

Successful over hurdles in France three times, she has struggled in a couple of chases and looked one pace over hurdles. Possibly needs a longer trip. Acts on a soft surface.

Janoramic (FR)

90 **98**

5-y-o b g Panoramic-Victoire V (FR) (Nellio (FR))
J G Fitzgerald Mrs Jane Dwyer

Placings:*332*U22 **(4555)**
2001/02: 16^{3}GF, 16^{3}G, 16^{2}G, 16^{U}S, 16^{2}GS, 19^{2}GF

	Starts	1st	2nd	3rd	Win & Pl
NH Flat	3	0	1	2	1033
Hurdles	2	0	2	0	2032
Chases	1	0	0	0	0
Career Total	6	0	3	2	3065

Going: Sf: 0-1 GS: 0-1 Gd: 0-2 GF: - Fm: 0-2
Distance: 2m/2m3: 0-5 2m4-2m7: 0-1 3m+: 0-0
Track: LH: 0-3 RH: 0-3 Tight: 0-4 Gall: 0-1
Aids: Bl: 0-0 Vi: 0-0 Tstrap: 0-0
Best Rating: 101 3/02 Catt 2m gd-sft Hdl

Modest novice hurdler at around two and a half miles.

January Sixteenth

82 **57**

6-y-o b g Presidium-Espanita (Riboboy (USA))
D C O'Brien Mrs S Harris

Placings:*0*/0500 **(4533)**
2001/02: 16^{0}G, 17^{5}S, 18^{0}S, 16^{0}G

	Starts	1st	2nd	3rd	Win & Pl
Hurdles	4	0	0	0	0
Career Total	5	0	0	0	0

Going: Sf: 0-2 GS: 0-0 Gd: 0-2 GF: - Fm: 0-0
Distance: 2m/2m3: 0-4 2m4-2m7: 0-0 3m+: 0-0
Track: LH: 0-3 RH: 0-1 Tight: 0-4 Gall: 0-0
Aids: Bl: 0-0 Vi: 0-0 Tstrap: 0-0
Best Rating: 57 3/02 Font 2m2f110y soft Hdl

Janus Du Cochet (FR)

97 **149**

5-y-o b g Rahotep (FR)-Qualite Du Cochet (FR) (Illustrator (FR))
M C Pipe Terry Neill

Placings:121424-42 **(2664)**
2001/02: 16^{4}G, 24^{2}G

	Starts	1st	2nd	3rd	Win & Pl
Hurdles	2	0	1	0	4013
Career Total	8	2	3	0	64087

11/00 Autl 2m2f HHdl HVY £33622
10/00 Autl 1m7f Hdl HLD £13449
Total win prize-money £47071

Going: Sf: 0-0 GS: 0-0 Gd: 0-2 GF: - Fm: 0-0
Distance: 2m/2m3: 0-1 2m4-2m7: 0-0 3m+: 0-1
Track: LH: 0-0 RH: 0-1 Tight: 0-0 Gall: 0-0
Aids: Bl: 0-0 Vi: 0-0 Tstrap: 0-0
Best Rating: 149 12/01 Chel 3m good Hdl

Ex-French and a dual hurdles winner at Auteuil, he had his limitations exposed in top juvenile events here by his ex-compatriots in 2000/2001. Reappeared at Wincanton over a trip short of his best, but ran much better when stepped up to three miles at Cheltenham.

Japhet (FR)

109 **146**

5-y-o b g Perrault-Una Volta (FR) (Toujours Pret (USA))
G Macaire J-C Audry

Placings:11-1111121F3 **(4666)**
2001/02: 17^{1}HY, 17^{1}GS, 20^{1}G, 20^{1}VS, 22^{1}VS, 24^{2}S, 24^{1}GS, 24^{F}GS, 25^{3}G

	Starts	1st	2nd	3rd	Win & Pl
Hurdles	3	3	0	0	10669
Chases	8	5	1	1	133812
Career Total	11	8	1	1	164849

125 2/02 Kemp 3m C Ch G-S £7455
11/01 Autl 2m6f Ch VS £58196
9/01 Autl 2m4f110y Ch VS £31038
9/01 Autl 2m4f110y Ch GD £14549
5/01 Autl 2m1f110y Ch G-S £12124
5/01 Nant 2m1f110y Hdl HVY £10669
3/01 Autl 2m2f Hdl HVY £9699
2/01 Autl 2m1f110y Hdl VS £10669
Total win prize-money £154399

Going: Sf: 1-2 GS: 2-3 Gd: 1-2 GF: - Fm: 0-0
Distance: 2m/2m3: 2-2 **2m4-2m7: 3-3** 3m+: 1-4
Track: LH: 1-4 RH: 1-1 Tight: 0-1 Gall: 0-2
Aids: Bl: 0-0 Vi: 0-0 Tstrap: 0-0
Best Rating: 146 4/02 Aint 3m1f good Ch

Unbeaten on the Flat, over hurdles and over fences in France, he lost out to Frosty Canyon on his British debut, but might have blown up and made no mistake against two rivals at Kempton. A faller at Cheltenham, he was not at his best when third at Aintree. Remains a bright prospect.

Jaraab

11-y-o b g Sure Blade (USA)-Ostora (USA) (Blushing Groom (FR))
J A Moore J A Moore

Placings:266/P/316/0/P **(0329)**
2001/02: 16^{P}GS

	Starts	1st	2nd	3rd	Win & Pl
Hurdles	1	0	0	0	
Career Total	**9**	**1**	**1**	**1**	**3784**

102	3/99	Sedg	2m1f	E(0-105)HHdl	SFT	£2425

Total win prize-money £2425

Going: Sf: 0-0 GS: 0-1 Gd: 0-0 GF: - Fm: 0-0
Distance: 2m/2m3: 0-1 2m4-2m7: 0-0 3m+: 0-0
Track: LH: 0-0 RH: 0-1 Tight: 0-0 Gall: 0-0
Aids: Bl: 0-0 Vi: 0-0 Tstrap: 0-1
Best Rating: 102 3/99 Sedg 2m1f soft Hdl

Jardin De Beaulieu (FR)

127

5-y-o ch g Rough Magic (FR)-Emblem (FR) (Siberian Express (USA))
Ian Williams Mr & Mrs John Poynton

Placings:2-2P3F **(4189)**
2001/02: 20^{2}GS, 20^{P}GS, 18^{3}GS, 16^{F}GS

	Starts	1st	2nd	3rd	Win & Pl
Hurdles	1	0	0	0	0
Chases	3	0	1	1	3242
Career Total	**5**	**0**	**2**	**1**	**5182**

Going: Sf: 0-0 GS: 0-4 Gd: 0-0 GF: - Fm: 0-0
Distance: 2m/2m3: 0-2 2m4-2m7: 0-2 3m+: 0-0
Track: LH: 0-2 RH: 0-1 Tight: 0-0 Gall: 0-2
Aids: Bl: 0-0 Vi: 0-0 Tstrap: 0-0
Best Rating: 127 3/02 Newb 2m2f110y gd-sft Ch

Placed twice in two starts over fences in France over two and a half miles, but was pulled up over hurdles on his British debut. Showed plenty of promise on his British chase debut at Newbury. He fell when outclassed in the Arkle at Cheltenham in March 2002. Acts on soft/heavy ground.

Jarro (FR)

96 128

6-y-o b g Pistolet Bleu (IRE)-Junta (FR) (Cariellor (FR))
Miss Venetia Williams Mrs David Thompson

Placings:1PF135/5-31513 **(4907)**
2001/02: 20^{3}G, 16^{1}S, 16^{5}S, 17^{1}G, 20^{3}GF

	Starts	1st	2nd	3rd	Win & Pl
Chases	5	2	0	2	9214
Career Total	**12**	**4**	**0**	**3**	**43843**

123	3/02	Plum	2m1f	E Ch	GD	£3120
128	1/02	Tntn	2m110y	D Ch	SFT	£4823
	1/00	Pau	2m2f	Hdl	GD	£13449
	10/99	Autl	1m7f	Hdl	HLD	£7535

Total win prize-money £28927

Going: Sf: 1-2 GS: 0-0 Gd: 1-2 GF: - Fm: 0-1
Distance: **2m/2m3: 2-3** 2m4-2m7: 0-2 3m+: 0-0
Track: LH: 1-2 RH: 1-2 **Tight: 2-5** Gall: 0-0
Aids: Bl: 0-0 Vi: 0-0 Tstrap: 0-0
Best Rating: 128 1/02 Tntn 2m110y soft Ch

A winning hurdler in his native France. Jumped moderately on his early starts over fences in Britain, but put in a better round when winning at Plumpton in March 2002. Acts on good ground or softer.

Jaseur (USA)

87(115h) (113h)57

9-y-o b g Lear Fan (USA)-Spur Wing (USA) (Storm Bird (CAN))
G Barnett J C Bradbury

Placings:2U220-2456 **(4633)**
2001/02: 20^{2}G, 21^{4}S, 24^{5}GS, 20^{6}GF

	Starts	1st	2nd	3rd	Win & Pl
Hurdles	4	0	1	0	1832
Career Total	**9**	**0**	**4**	**0**	**7656**

Going: Sf: 0-1 GS: 0-1 Gd: 0-1 GF: - Fm: 0-1
Distance: 2m/2m3: 0-0 2m4-2m7: 0-3 3m+: 0-1
Track: LH: 0-2 RH: 0-1 Tight: 0-1 Gall: 0-1
Aids: Bl: 0-0 Vi: 0-4 Tstrap: 0-0
Best Rating: 125 12/00 Asct 2m110y heavy Hdl

A decent staying handicapper on the Flat, he was runner-up in a graded event at Ascot at the end of 2000, but is not proving easy to win with due to his lack of fight at the business end. Likes the mud and stays two and a half miles, usually wears a visor.

Jaskini

83 72

6-y-o b g Lion Cavern (USA)-Sharka (Shareef Dancer (USA))
M J Ephgrave (A G Juckes 29/7) M Ephgrave

Placings:P/PP-061 **(1552a)**
2001/02: 16^{0}GF, 17^{6}G, 20^{1}GF

	Starts	1st	2nd	3rd	Win & Pl
Hurdles	3	1	0	0	1100
Career Total	**6**	**1**	**0**	**0**	**1100**

9/01	LES	2m4f	HHdl	G-F	£1100

Total win prize-money £1100

Going: Sf: 0-0 GS: 0-0 Gd: 0-1 GF: - Fm: 1-2
Distance: 2m/2m3: 0-2 **2m4-2m7: 1-1** 3m+: 0-0
Track: **LH: 1-3** RH: 0-0 Tight: 0-1 Gall: 0-0
Aids: Bl: 0-0 Vi: 0-0 Tstrap: 0-0
Best Rating: 72 6/01 Worc 2m gd-fm Hdl

Jasmin D'Anjou (FR)

83 70

5-y-o b g Useful (FR)-Royalla (FR) (Garde Royale)
P Monteith Mr & Mrs Raymond Anderson Green

Placings:*000066* **(4438)**
2001/02: 17^{0}GF, 16^{0}G, 16^{0}HY, 16^{0}HY, 16^{6}S, 16^{6}S

	Starts	1st	2nd	3rd	Win & Pl
NH Flat	3	0	0	0	0
Hurdles	3	0	0	0	0
Career Total	**6**	**0**	**0**	**0**	**0**

Going: Sf: 0-4 GS: 0-0 Gd: 0-1 GF: - Fm: 0-1
Distance: 2m/2m3: 0-6 2m4-2m7: 0-0 3m+: 0-0
Track: LH: 0-4 RH: 0-1 Tight: 0-2 Gall: 0-0
Aids: Bl: 0-0 Vi: 0-0 Tstrap: 0-0
Best Rating: 70 3/02 Kels 2m110y soft Hdl

Poor bumper horse, showed little on his hurdles debut.

Jasmin Guichois (FR)

5-y-o ch g Dom Alco (FR)-Lady Belle (FR) (Or De Chine)
Miss Venetia Williams (F Nicolle 19/6) Seasons Holidays

Placings:4-FP **(3262)**
2001/02: 17^{F}S, 21^{P}S

	Starts	1st	2nd	3rd	Win & Pl
Hurdles	1	0	0	0	0
Chases	1	0	0	0	0
Career Total	**3**	**0**	**0**	**0**	**1940**

Going: Sf: 0-2 GS: 0-0 Gd: 0-0 GF: - Fm: 0-0
Distance: 2m/2m3: 0-1 2m4-2m7: 0-1 3m+: 0-0
Track: LH: 0-0 RH: 0-0 Tight: 0-0 Gall: 0-0
Aids: Bl: 0-0 Vi: 0-0 Tstrap: 0-0
Best Rating:

Ex French, was fourth on his hurdling debut there, before falling on his chase debut. Pulled up over hurdles on his British debut.

Jasper Lad

6-y-o ch g Fearless Action (USA)-Last Shower (Town And Country)
J Gallagher Horses Away Racing Club

Placings:*0-0* **(0843)**
2001/02: 16^{0}G

	Starts	1st	2nd	3rd	Win & Pl
NH Flat	1	0	0	0	
Career Total	**2**	**0**	**0**	**0**	

Going: Sf: 0-0 GS: 0-0 Gd: 0-1 GF: - Fm: 0-0
Distance: 2m/2m3: 0-1 2m4-2m7: 0-0 3m+: 0-0
Track: LH: 0-1 RH: 0-0 Tight: 0-0 Gall: 0-0
Aids: Bl: 0-0 Vi: 0-0 Tstrap: 0-0
Best Rating: 45 6/01 Worc 2m good NHF

Jato Dancer (IRE)

100 88

7-y-o b m Mukaddamah (USA)-Que Tranquila (Dominion)
R Hollinshead Mrs Norman Hill

Placings:323F0 **(3334)**
2001/02: 16^{3}GS, 16^{2}S, 16^{3}S, 17^{F}S, 16^{0}G

	Starts	1st	2nd	3rd	Win & Pl
Hurdles	5	0	1	2	1151
Career Total	**5**	**0**	**1**	**2**	**1151**

Going: Sf: 0-3 GS: 0-1 Gd: 0-1 GF: - Fm: 0-0
Distance: 2m/2m3: 0-5 2m4-2m7: 0-0 3m+: 0-0
Track: LH: 0-2 RH: 0-3 Tight: 0-2 Gall: 0-0
Aids: Bl: 0-0 Vi: 0-0 Tstrap: 0-0
Best Rating: 88 11/01 Strf 2m110y soft Hdl

She won twice on the Flat and ran well over hurdles in November when second at Stratford in a relatively competitive seller over two miles.

Java Sea

105 111

6-y-o br g Warning-Sarah Siddons (FR) (Le Levanstell)
J J O'Neill John B Sunley,A K Collins,J P Carrington

Placings: *34/034*P6-02111 (4090)
2001/02: 23^{0}G, 22^{2}GS, 20^{1}S, 20^{1}GS, 20^{1}S

	Starts	1st	2nd	3rd	Win & Pl
Hurdles	5	3	1	0	11856
Career Total	**12**	**3**	**1**	**2**	**12330**

111	3/02	Bang	2m4f	D(0-110)HHdl	SFT	£5187
99	1/02	Weth	2m4f110y	E(0-105)HHdl	G-S	£2898
91	11/01	Uttx	2m4f110y	E(0-105)HHdl	SFT	£2646

Total win prize-money £10731

Going: Sf: 2-2 GS: 1-2 Gd: 0-1 GF: - Fm: 0-0
Distance: 2m/2m3: 0-0 **2m4-2m7: 3-5** 3m+: 0-0
Track: **LH: 3-4** RH: 0-1 **Tight: 1-1** Gall: 0-0
Aids: Bl: 0-0 Vi: 0-0 Tstrap: 0-0
Best Rating: 111 3/02 Bang 2m4f soft Hdl

Modest handicap hurdler, progressing in 2001/02, stays two and a half miles, suited by front-running tactics.

Javelin

108 **115**

6-y-o ch g Generous (IRE)-Moss (Alzao (USA))
Ian Williams Cockbury Court Partnership

Placings:006F111225 (1888)
2001/02: 16^{0}GF, 17^{0}G, 17^{6}GF, 16^{F}GF, 16^{1}G, 17^{1}G, 16^{1}GF, 17^{2}GF, 16^{2}G, 16^{5}G

	Starts	1st	2nd	3rd	Win & Pl
Hurdles	10	3	2	0	11883
Career Total	**10**	**3**	**2**	**0**	**11883**

115	8/01	Worc	2m	E(0-115)HHdl	G-F	£3415
109	8/01	NAbb	2m1f	F(0-100)HHdl	GD	[illegible]
107	7/01	Worc	2m	F(0-110)HHdl	GD	£1869

Total win prize-money £8225

Going: Sf: 0-0 GS: 0-0 Gd: 2-5 GF: - Fm: 1-5
Distance: **2m/2m3: 3-10** 2m4-2m7: 0-0 3m+: 0-0
Track: **LH: 3-7** RH: 0-3 **Tight: 1-5** Gall: 0-0
Aids: Bl: 0-0 Vi: 0-0 Tstrap: 0-0
Best Rating: 115 8/01 Worc 2m gd-fm Hdl

Completed a summer hat-trick over hurdles and has not been disgraced in defeat. Likes fast ground and left-handed tracks.

Jawrjik (IRE)

95 **71**

4-y-o b g Blues Traveller (IRE)-Eva Fay (IRE) (Fayruz)
B S Rothwell Richard Brown

Placings:000 (2397)
2001/02: 16^{0}G, 16^{0}S, 16^{0}G

	Starts	1st	2nd	3rd	Win & Pl
Hurdles	3	0	0	0	
Career Total	**3**	**0**	**0**	**0**	

Going: Sf: 0-1 GS: 0-0 Gd: 0-2 GF: - Fm: 0-0
Distance: 2m/2m3: 0-3 2m4-2m7: 0-0 3m+: 0-0
Track: LH: 0-3 RH: 0-0 Tight: 0-0 Gall: 0-0
Aids: Bl: 0-0 Vi: 0-0 Tstrap: 0-0
Best Rating: 71 11/01 Hayd 2m soft Hdl

Jay Bee Ell

106 **91**

5-y-o b g Pursuit Of Love-On Request (IRE) (Be My Guest (USA))
A King J M & A L Longman

Placings: *40* (4032)
2001/02: 16^{4}G, 16^{0}GS

	Starts	1st	2nd	3rd	Win & Pl
NH Flat	2	0	0	0	0
Career Total	**2**	**0**	**0**	**0**	**0**

Going: Sf: 0-0 GS: 0-1 Gd: 0-1 GF: - Fm: 0-0
Distance: 2m/2m3: 0-2 2m4-2m7: 0-0 3m+: 0-0
Track: LH: 0-2 RH: 0-0 Tight: 0-0 Gall: 0-2
Aids: Bl: 0-0 Vi: 0-0 Tstrap: 0-0
Best Rating: 110 12/01 Newb 2m110y good NHF

Novice hurdler. Won a slowly run 22 furlong novice hurdle at Stratford in May 2002. Acts on a sound surface.

Jayas (FR)

(101h) (76h)

5-y-o b/br g Rasi Brasak-Rigolette (FR) (Lychee (FR))
M C Pipe Clive D Smith

Placings:021160-0P (3659)
2001/02: 21^{0}GF, 16^{P}S

	Starts	1st	2nd	3rd	Win & Pl
Hurdles	2	0	0	0	
Career Total	**8**	**2**	**1**	**0**	**8227**

92	2/01	Ludl	2m	E Hdl	GD	£2222
	8/00	Stma	2m	Hdl	VS	£4323

Total win prize-money £6546

Going: Sf: 0-1 GS: 0-0 Gd: 0-0 GF: - Fm: 0-1
Distance: 2m/2m3: 0-1 2m4-2m7: 0-1 3m+: 0-0
Track: LH: 0-0 RH: 0-1 Tight: 0-0 Gall: 0-0
Aids: Bl: 0-0 Vi: 0-1 Tstrap: 0-0
Best Rating: 92 2/01 Ludl 2m good Hdl

Jaybeedee

99 **111**

6-y-o b g Rudimentary (USA)-Meavy (Kalaglow)
K C Bailey (Denis P Murphy 22/11) Major-Gen R L T Burges

Placings: *36/32*30514 (4411)
2001/02: 16^{3}G, 16^{2}YS, 16^{3}YS, 21^{0}S, 20^{5}S, 16^{1}HY, 18^{4}S

	Starts	1st	2nd	3rd	Win & Pl
NH Flat	2	0	1	1	1169
Hurdles	5	1	0	1	4230
Career Total	**9**	**1**	**1**	**3**	**5763**

111	3/02	Uttx	2m	D Hdl	HVY	£3552

Total win prize-money £3552

Going: Sf: 1-4 GS: 0-0 Gd: 0-1 GF: - Fm: 0-0
Distance: **2m/2m3: 1-5** 2m4-2m7: 0-2 3m+: 0-0
Track: **LH: 1-2** RH: 0-3 Tight: 0-1 Gall: 0-1
Aids: Bl: 0-0 Vi: 0-0 Tstrap: 0-0
Best Rating: 111 3/02 Uttx 2m heavy Hdl

Placed in bumpers and on his hurdling debut in Ireland, he put up respectable efforts on first two runs in Britain and won well in very testing conditions at Uttoxeter in March 2002. Should have no problem staying two and a half miles.

Jaybejay (NZ)

103 **126**

7-y-o b g High Ice (USA)-Galaxy Light (NZ) (Balios)
M C Pipe (P McKenzie 22/8) Mrs H J Clarke

Placings:310 (4188)
2001/02: 16^{3}S, 16^{1}GS, 16^{0}GS

	Starts	1st	2nd	3rd	Win & Pl
Hurdles	3	1	0	1	4483
Career Total	**3**	**1**	**0**	**1**	**4483**

116	2/02	Winc	2m	D Hdl	G-S	£3990

Total win prize-money £3990

Going: Sf: 0-1 GS: 1-2 Gd: 0-0 GF: - Fm: 0-0
Distance: **2m/2m3: 1-3** 2m4-2m7: 0-0 3m+: 0-0
Track: LH: 0-1 **RH: 1-2** Tight: 0-0 Gall: 0-0
Aids: Bl: 0-0 Vi: 0-0 Tstrap: 0-0
Best Rating: 126 3/02 Chel 2m110y gd-sft Hdl

A useful performer on the Flat in New Zealand, he was a little disappointing on his hurdles debut on soft ground, but got off the mark on a faster surface next time. Looks a keen sort.

Jaywalker (IRE)

(88h) (74h)

8-y-o b g Lord Americo-Jazz Bavard (Le Bavard (FR))
J Howard Johnson Gordon Brown/bert Watson

Placings:22F/PF40/3FF0-P (0221)
2001/02: 20^{P}GF

	Starts	1st	2nd	3rd	Win & Pl
Chases	1	0	0	0	
Career Total	**12**	**0**	**2**	**1**	**2208**

Going: Sf: 0-0 GS: 0-0 Gd: 0-0 GF: - Fm: 0-1
Distance: 2m/2m3: 0-0 2m4-2m7: 0-1 3m+: 0-0
Track: LH: 0-1 RH: 0-0 Tight: 0-0 Gall: 0-0
Aids: Bl: 0-0 Vi: 0-0 Tstrap: 0-0
Best Rating: 99 9/00 Prth 2m4f110y heavy Ch

Jazil

94(97c) **110**

7-y-o b g Nashwan (USA)-Gracious Beauty (USA) (Nijinsky (CAN))
K A Morgan The Jazil Partnership

Placings:12/3FFP-23P (4286)
2001/02: 19^{2}GF, 19^{3}GF, 21^{P}GS

	Starts	1st	2nd	3rd	Win & Pl
Hurdles	3	0	1	1	2242
Career Total	**9**	**1**	**2**	**2**	**6274**

118	3/00	Hrfd	2m3f110y	E Hdl	GD	£2828

Total win prize-money £2828

Going: Sf: 0-0 GS: 0-1 Gd: 0-0 GF: - Fm: 0-2
Distance: 2m/2m3: 0-0 2m4-2m7: 0-3 3m+: 0-0
Track: LH: 0-0 RH: 0-3 Tight: 0-3 Gall: 0-0
Aids: Bl: 0-0 Vi: 0-1 Tstrap: 0-3
Best Rating: 120 11/00 MRas 2m4f gd-sft Ch

Above average on the Flat, he is a fair front-running hurdler at around two and a half miles. An attempt at a chasing campaign proved disastrous.

Jazz Du Forez (FR)

79 **45**

5-y-o b g Video Rock (FR)-Ophyr Du Forez (FR) (Fin Bon)
John Allen Avon Estates Ltd

Placings: *0*0000 (4573)
2001/02: 16^{0}GF, 18^{0}HY, 20^{0}S, 19^{0}GS, 20^{0}G

	Starts	1st	2nd	3rd	Win & Pl
NH Flat	1	0	0	0	0
Hurdles	4	0	0	0	0
Career Total	**5**	**0**	**0**	**0**	

Going: Sf: 0-2 GS: 0-1 Gd: 0-1 GF: - Fm: 0-1
Distance: 2m/2m3: 0-3 2m4-2m7: 0-2 3m+: 0-0
Track: LH: 0-4 RH: 0-1 Tight: 0-2 Gall: 0-1
Aids: Bl: 0-1 Vi: 0-0 Tstrap: 0-0
Best Rating: 57 11/01 Ludl 2m gd-fm NHF

Jazz Duke

99 **112**

9-y-o ch g Rising-Gone (Whistling Wind)
M J Weeden M J Weeden

Placings:0/320PP/F16P04/**3344230-2543U** (4184)
2001/02: 26^{2}GS, 26^{5}G, 25^{4}HY, 26^{3}S, 24^{U}S

	Starts	1st	2nd	3rd	Win & Pl
Chases	5	0	1	1	1911
Career Total	**24**	**1**	**3**	**5**	**11455**

110	12/99	Tntn	3m110y	D(0-120)HHdl	G-S	£3631

Total win prize-money £3631

Going: Sf: 0-3 GS: 0-1 Gd: 0-1 GF: - Fm: 0-0
Distance: 2m/2m3: 0-0 2m4-2m7: 0-0 3m+: 0-5
Track: LH: 0-1 RH: 0-2 Tight: 0-3 Gall: 0-0
Aids: Bl: 0-0 Vi: 0-1 Tstrap: 0-0
Best Rating: **112** 4/01 Asct 3m110y soft Ch

An error-prone novice over hurdles, he showed better form over fences and has repeatedly made the frame. He stays three miles and is suited to cut in the ground.

Jazz Night

88 **75**

5-y-o b g Alhijaz-Hen Night (Mummy's Game)
N A Twiston-Davies The Berryman Lycett Experience

Placings:6 (2924)
2001/02: 17^{6}GS

	Starts	1st	2nd	3rd	Win & Pl
Hurdles	1	0	0	0	0
Career Total	**1**	**0**	**0**	**0**	**0**

Going: Sf: 0-0 GS: 0-1 Gd: 0-0 GF: - Fm: 0-0
Distance: 2m/2m3: 0-1 2m4-2m7: 0-0 3m+: 0-0
Track: LH: 0-0 RH: 0-1 Tight: 0-1 Gall: 0-0
Aids: Bl: 0-0 Vi: 0-0 Tstrap: 0-0
Best Rating: **75** 12/01 Tntn 2m1f gd-sft Hdl

Jazzman (IRE)

10-y-o b g Black Minstrel-Carbery Star (Kemal (FR))
Miss J M Du Plessis Miss J Du Plessis

Placings:0614/2/22F333111/0132543P2/**4U4P-0** (0077)
2001/02: 23^{0}G

	Starts	1st	2nd	3rd	Win & Pl
Chases	1	0	0	0	
Career Total	**28**	**5**	**5**	**5**	**33350**

123	10/99	Worc	2m4f110y	C(0-130)HCh	G-F	£5772
117	4/99	MRas	2m4f	D Ch	SFT	£4765
111	4/99	Plum	2m5f	F Ch	G-S	£2575
111	3/99	MRas	2m4f	D Ch	G-S	£5130
101	2/97	Wind	2m6f110y	D Hdl	GD	£2658

Total win prize-money £20901

Going: Sf: 0-0 GS: 0-0 Gd: 0-1 GF: - Fm: 0-0
Distance: 2m/2m3: 0-0 2m4-2m7: 0-0 3m+: 0-1
Track: LH: 0-0 RH: 0-1 Tight: 0-0 Gall: 0-0
Aids: Bl: 0-0 Vi: 0-0 Tstrap: 0-0
Best Rating: **123** 1/00 Wwck 2m4f soft Ch

Je Suis (IRE)

63f **33f**

6-y-o b m Le Bavard (FR)-La Tortue (Lafontaine (USA))
B J Eckley Brian Eckley

Placings:*0-00* (3985)
2001/02: 17^{0}S, 16^{0}G

	Starts	1st	2nd	3rd	Win & Pl
NH Flat	2	0	0	0	
Career Total	**3**	**0**	**0**	**0**	

Going: Sf: 0-1 GS: 0-0 Gd: 0-1 GF: - Fm: 0-0
Distance: 2m/2m3: 0-2 2m4-2m7: 0-0 3m+: 0-0
Track: LH: 0-0 RH: 0-2 Tight: 0-0 Gall: 0-0
Aids: Bl: 0-0 Vi: 0-0 Tstrap: 0-0
Best Rating: **33** 2/02 Ludl 2m good NHF

Jean D'Auteuil (FR)

98(96h) **133**

6-y-o b g River Sand (FR)-Santa Marta (FR) (Cadmus Ii)
M C Pipe Terry Neill

Placings:164-**233** (3891)
2001/02: 19^{2}GS, 20^{3}G, 20^{3}HY

	Starts	1st	2nd	3rd	Win & Pl
Chases	3	0	1	2	3383
Career Total	**6**	**1**	**1**	**2**	**6575**

103	11/00	Tntn	2m1f	E Hdl	GD	£3192

Total win prize-money £3192

Going: Sf: 0-1 GS: 0-1 Gd: 0-1 GF: - Fm: 0-0
Distance: 2m/2m3: 0-1 2m4-2m7: 0-2 3m+: 0-0
Track: LH: 0-1 RH: 0-2 Tight: 0-1 Gall: 0-0
Aids: Bl: 0-0 Vi: 0-0 Tstrap: 0-0
Best Rating: **133** 11/01 Tntn 2m3f gd-sft Ch

A French import, he made a winning British debut at Taunton in November 2000, but was off the track for ten months before an adequate effort on his chasing debut, although he disappointed after that. Stays two and a half miles. Acts on a sound surface.

Jean Guy (FR)

103 **112**

5-y-o b g Passing Sale (FR)-Umea Iv (FR) (Maiymad)
P J Hobbs (M Rolland 10/8) M Double H

Placings:PP6-3214F45 (4009)
2001/02: 17^{3}GS, 17^{2}VS, 20^{1}S, 20^{4}GS, 21^{F}G, 20^{4}S, 22^{5}S

	Starts	1st	2nd	3rd	Win & Pl
Chases	7	1	1	1	22798
Career Total	**10**	**1**	**1**	**1**	**22798**

	6/01	Autl	2m4f110y	Ch	SFT	£12124

Total win prize-money £12124

Going: Sf: 1-3 GS: 0-2 Gd: 0-1 GF: - Fm: 0-0
Distance: 2m/2m3: 0-2 **2m4-2m7: 1-5** 3m+: 0-0
Track: LH: 0-2 RH: 0-2 Tight: 0-0 Gall: 0-2
Aids: Bl: 0-1 Vi: 0-0 Tstrap: 0-0
Best Rating: **112** 11/01 Hntg 2m4f110y gd-sft Ch

A winning chaser in France over two and a half miles, he has yet to show much in Britain. Acts on soft ground.

Jeanann

9-y-o b m Primitive Rising (USA)-Jean Jeanie (Roman Warrior)
J G Given Tony Evans

Placings:*000*/P0PP/**UPP-5** (1584)
2001/02: 19^{5}GS

	Starts	1st	2nd	3rd	Win & Pl
Hurdles	1	0	0	0	0
Career Total	**11**	**0**	**0**	**0**	**0**

Going: Sf: 0-0 GS: 0-1 Gd: 0-0 GF: - Fm: 0-0
Distance: 2m/2m3: 0-0 2m4-2m7: 0-1 3m+: 0-0
Track: LH: 0-0 RH: 0-1 Tight: 0-1 Gall: 0-0
Aids: Bl: 0-0 Vi: 0-0 Tstrap: 0-0
Best Rating: **74** 12/97 Hntg 2m110y gd-sft NHF

Jeannot De Beauchene (FR)

109 **111**

5-y-o b g En Calcat (FR)-Chipie D'Angron (FR) (Grand Tresor (FR))
R H Alner M Short

Placings:11P (4406)
2001/02: 22^{1}HY, 20^{1}GS, 24^{P}S

	Starts	1st	2nd	3rd	Win & Pl
Hurdles	3	2	0	0	6102
Career Total	**3**	**2**	**0**	**0**	**6102**

111	12/01	Chep	2m4f	D Hdl	G-S	£3757
95	10/01	Folk	2m6f110y	E Hdl	HVY	£2345

Total win prize-money £6102

Going: Sf: 1-2 GS: 1-1 Gd: 0-0 GF: - Fm: 0-0
Distance: 2m/2m3: 0-0 **2m4-2m7: 2-2** 3m+: 0-1
Track: LH: 1-2 RH: 1-1 **Tight: 1-2** Gall: 0-0
Aids: Bl: 0-0 Vi: 0-0 Tstrap: 0-0
Best Rating: **111** 12/01 Chep 2m4f gd-sft Hdl

Put in an impressive performance to win in gruelling conditions on his hurdling debut, over 2m6f, at Folkestone. Followed up in a better race at Chepstow, before being pulled up on his handicap debut on sticky ground.

Jefferies

13-y-o br g Sunyboy-Scotch Princess (Murrayfield)
R H Alner Dr S G F Cave

Placings:25/1P/12612/3122/6105/46/0F-0P (0427)
2001/02: 25^{0}GF, 33^{P}G

	Starts	1st	2nd	3rd	Win & Pl
Chases	2	0	0	0	
Career Total	**23**	**5**	**5**	**1**	**26443**

125	11/98	Tntn	3m	D(0-125)HCh	GD	£4667
125	11/97	Tntn	2m3f	C Ch	GD	£5083
106	2/97	Tntn	2m3f110y	D(0-120)HHdl	GD	£2814
96	11/96	Towc	2m	D(0-120)HHdl	GD	£2910
84	3/96	Tntn	2m3f110y	E Hdl	GD	£2542

Total win prize-money £18018

Going: Sf: 0-0 GS: 0-0 Gd: 0-1 GF: - Fm: 0-1
Distance: 2m/2m3: 0-0 2m4-2m7: 0-0 3m+: 0-2
Track: LH: 0-0 RH: 0-1 Tight: 0-0 Gall: 0-0
Aids: Bl: 0-0 Vi: 0-0 Tstrap: 0-0
Best Rating: **125** 11/98 Tntn 3m good Ch

Jem-A-Dar

64f **47f**

5-y-o b g Mistertopogigo (IRE)-Indian Wells (Reliance Ii)
B G Powell Paul Stamp

Placings:*0* (1773)
2001/02: 17^{0}GS

	Starts	1st	2nd	3rd	Win & Pl
NH Flat	1	0	0	0	
Career Total	**1**	**0**	**0**	**0**	

Going: Sf: 0-0 GS: 0-1 Gd: 0-0 GF: - Fm: 0-0

Distance: 2m/2m3: 0-1 2m4-2m7: 0-0 3m+: 0-0
Track: LH: 0-0 RH: 0-1 Tight: 0-0 Gall: 0-0
Aids: Bl: 0-0 Vi: 0-0 Tstrap: 0-0
Best Rating: 47 10/01 Extr 2m1f gd-sft NHF

Jendee (IRE)

84 **39**
14-y-o b g Dara Monarch-Bunch Of Blue (Martinmas)
J P Dodds T Batey

Placings:42335/23/603614155/54P1/5U52FP5P/4P13 P4P55/3/P-PP0 **(1045)**
2001/02: 20^{P}GF, 27^{P}GF, 26^{0}GF

	Starts	1st	2nd	3rd	Win & Pl
Hurdles	1	0	0	0	0
Chases	2	0	0	0	0
Career Total	**42**	**4**	**3**	**6**	**14230**

93	10/96	Sedg	3m3f	F(0-100)HCh	G-F	£2823
90	12/94	Sedg	3m3f	(0-110)HCh	G-S	£2747
93	1/94	Sedg	3m3f110y	(0-135)HHdl	G-S	£2217
92	12/93	Sedg	3m3f110y	(0-125)HHdl	G-S	£2022

Total win prize-money £9811

Going: Sf: 0-0 GS: 0-0 Gd: 0-0 GF: - Fm: 0-3
Distance: 2m/2m3: 0-0 2m4-2m7: 0-1 3m+: 0-2
Track: LH: 0-3 RH: 0-0 Tight: 0-1 Gall: 0-0
Aids: Bl: 0-0 Vi: 0-0 Tstrap: 0-0
Best Rating: 95 2/96 Sedg 3m3f good Ch

Jenko (FR)

93 **83**
5-y-o b g Cadoubel (FR)-Maika D'Ores (FR) (Gaur)
M C Pipe Network Training Ii

Placings:4-605P **(4731)**
2001/02: 17^{6}S, 16^{0}GS, 17^{5}S, 17^{P}F

	Starts	1st	2nd	3rd	Win & Pl
Hurdles	4	0	0	0	0
Career Total	**5**	**0**	**0**	**0**	**258**

Going: Sf: 0-2 GS: 0-1 Gd: 0-0 GF: - Fm: 0-1
Distance: 2m/2m3: 0-4 2m4-2m7: 0-0 3m+: 0-0
Track: LH: 0-0 RH: 0-4 Tight: 0-2 Gall: 0-0
Aids: Bl: 0-0 Vi: 0-0 Tstrap: 0-2
Best Rating: 83 3/02 Tntn 2m1f soft Hdl

Jennifer Jenkins

4-y-o b f Komaite (USA)-Joemlujen (Forzando)
P D Evans J Powell-Tuck

Placings:P **(1800)**
2001/02: 16^{P}GF

	Starts	1st	2nd	3rd
Hurdles	1	0	0	0
Career Total	**1**	**0**	**0**	**0**

Going: Sf: 0-0 GS: 0-0 Gd: 0-0 GF: - Fm: 0-1
Distance: 2m/2m3: 0-1 2m4-2m7: 0-0 3m+: 0-0
Track: LH: 0-0 RH: 0-1 Tight: 0-0 Gall: 0-0
Aids: Bl: 0-0 Vi: 0-0 Tstrap: 0-0
Best Rating:

Jenniferjo (IRE)

107 **124**
5-y-o b/br m Witness Box (USA)-Sweet Tune (Welsh Chanter)
P A Fahy J B Fahy

Placings:0-5022242131100 **(4944a)**
2001/02: 16^{5}GF, 16^{0}YS, 18^{2}YS, 16^{2}S, 16^{2}Y, 16^{4}YS, 16^{2}Y, 16^{1}S, 16^{3}HY, 16^{1}S, 16^{1}HY, 20^{0}G, 20^{0}G

	Starts	1st	2nd	3rd	Win & Pl
NH Flat	7	1	3	1	7301
Hurdles	6	2	1	0	14349
Career Total	**14**	**3**	**4**	**1**	**21650**

124	3/02	Leop	2m	Hdl	HVY	£7407
95	2/02	Gowr	2m	Hdl	SFT	£5714
96	1/02	DRoy	2m	NHF	SFT	£3386

Total win prize-money £16510

Going: Sf: 3-5 GS: 0-0 Gd: 0-2 GF: - Fm: 0-1
Distance: **2m/2m3: 3-11** 2m4-2m7: 0-2 3m+: 0-0
Track: **LH: 1-2** RH: 0-3 Tight: 0-1 Gall: 0-0
Aids: Bl: 0-0 Vi: 0-0 Tstrap: 0-0
Best Rating: 124 3/02 Leop 2m heavy Hdl

Jenny Rocket

102 **90**
6-y-o b m Minster Son-Jane's Affair (Alleging (USA))
Miss K Marks Nick Shutts

Placings:5222410PP-552P15 **(4919)**
2001/02: 16^{5}G, 16^{5}G, 16^{2}S, 20^{P}S, 17^{1}G, 21^{5}GF

	Starts	1st	2nd	3rd	Win & Pl
Hurdles	6	1	1	0	3219
Career Total	**15**	**2**	**4**	**0**	**6228**

73	4/02	Hrfd	2m1f	G Hdl	GD	£1970
91	11/00	Catt	2m3f	F Hdl	GD	£1438

Total win prize-money £3410

Going: Sf: 0-2 GS: 0-0 Gd: 1-3 GF: - Fm: 0-1
Distance: **2m/2m3: 1-4** 2m4-2m7: 0-2 3m+: 0-0
Track: LH: 0-1 **RH: 1-5** Tight: 0-1 Gall: 0-1
Aids: Bl: 0-0 Vi: 0-0 Tstrap: 0-0
Best Rating: 94 10/00 MRas 2m1f110y good NHF

Moderate hurdler, stays two and a quarter miles. Successful in a seller at Easter 2002.

Jenski

99 **89**
7-y-o b g Petoski-Mrs Jennifer (River Knight (FR))
R J Hodges Mrs R A Vickery

Placings:60/5 **(3339)**
2001/02: 19^{5}S

	Starts	1st	2nd	3rd	Win & Pl
Hurdles	1	0	0	0	0
Career Total	**3**	**0**	**0**	**0**	**0**

Going: Sf: 0-1 GS: 0-0 Gd: 0-0 GF: - Fm: 0-0
Distance: 2m/2m3: 0-0 2m4-2m7: 0-1 3m+: 0-0
Track: LH: 0-0 RH: 0-1 Tight: 0-1 Gall: 0-0
Aids: Bl: 0-0 Vi: 0-0 Tstrap: 0-0
Best Rating: 89 1/02 Tntn 2m3f110y soft Hdl

Moderate ability shown over hurdles so far.

Jentar Equilibra (IRE)

101 **110**
10-y-o b m Miners Lamp-Cora Gold (Goldhill)
P F Nicholls Mr Tony Fear & Mr Patrick Quinn

Placings:00/41114 **(0847)**
2001/02: 24^{4}F, 16^{1}G, 17^{1}G, 17^{1}F, 16^{4}GF

	Starts	1st	2nd	3rd	Win & Pl
Hurdles	5	3	0	0	7761
Career Total	**7**	**3**	**0**	**0**	**7761**

110	6/01	Hrfd	2m1f	E Hdl	FRM	£2723
110	5/01	Hrfd	2m1f	E Hdl	GD	£2765
107	5/01	Strf	2m110y	G Hdl	GD	£1897

Total win prize-money £7385

Going: Sf: 0-0 GS: 0-0 Gd: 2-2 GF: - Fm: 1-3
Distance: **2m/2m3: 3-4** 2m4-2m7: 0-0 3m+: 0-1
Track: LH: 1-2 **RH: 2-3 Tight: 1-3** Gall: 0-0
Aids: Bl: 0-0 Vi: 0-0 Tstrap: 0-0
Best Rating: 110 6/01 Hrfd 2m1f firm Hdl

Jeremy Spider

107 **125**
9-y-o b g Nearly A Hand-Lucibella (Comedy Star (USA))
C Tizzard R G Tizzard

Placings:4152U221/4-P22P1 **(3988)**
2001/02: 24^{P}G, 20^{2}S, 26^{2}HY, 26^{P}HY, 24^{1}S

	Starts	1st	2nd	3rd	Win & Pl
Chases	5	1	2	0	5588
Career Total	**14**	**3**	**5**	**0**	**13342**

125	2/02	Tntn	3m	E Ch	SFT	£3656
110	4/00	Extr	2m7f	E Hdl	HVY	£2254
110	12/99	Plum	2m5f	E Hdl	HVY	£2040

Total win prize-money £7951

Going: Sf: 1-4 GS: 0-0 Gd: 0-1 GF: - Fm: 0-0
Distance: 2m/2m3: 0-0 2m4-2m7: 0-1 **3m+: 1-4**
Track: LH: 0-3 **RH: 1-1 Tight: 1-2** Gall: 0-1
Aids: Bl: 0-0 Vi: 0-0 Tstrap: 0-0
Best Rating: 125 2/02 Tntn 3m soft Ch

Staying novice chaser. Winner of a point-to-point and has also been successful over hurdles, acts well with cut in the ground. Likes to make all. Stays three miles.

Jericho Iii (FR)

104 **106**
5-y-o b g Lute Antique (FR)-La Salamandre (FR) (Pot D'Or (FR))
N J Henderson Sir Robert Ogden

Placings:141P **(4890)**
2001/02: 16^{1}G, 17^{4}G, 16^{1}GS, 24^{P}G

	Starts	1st	2nd	3rd	Win & Pl
NH Flat	1	1	0	0	1610
Hurdles	3	1	0	0	4313
Career Total	**4**	**2**	**0**	**0**	**5923**

106	1/02	Hntg	2m110y	D Hdl	G-S	£3643
97	11/01	Winc	2m	H NHF	GD	£1610

Total win prize-money £5254

Going: Sf: 0-0 GS: 1-1 Gd: 1-3 GF: - Fm: 0-0
Distance: **2m/2m3: 2-3** 2m4-2m7: 0-0 3m+: 0-1
Track: LH: 0-1 **RH: 2-3** Tight: 0-0 **Gall: 1-2**
Aids: Bl: 0-0 Vi: 0-0 Tstrap: 0-0
Best Rating: 106 1/02 Hntg 2m110y gd-sft Hdl

Made a winning debut in a Wincanton bumper and won on his second start over hurdles at Huntingdon. Suited by two miles and good to good to soft ground. Does not look a straightforward ride though.

Jerom De Vindecy (FR)

5-y-o ch g Roi De Rome (USA)-Preves Du Forez (FR) (Quart De Vin (FR))

A R Dicken (Y Fouin 12/6) Ron Affleck

Placings:P6224-640 **(1927)**
2001/02: 17^{6}GS, 17^{4}VS, 22^{0}G

	Starts	1st	2nd	3rd	Win & Pl
Hurdles	1	0	0	0	0
Chases	2	0	0	0	2425
Career Total	**8**	**0**	**2**	**0**	**8729**

Going: Sf: 0-0 GS: 0-1 Gd: 0-1 GF: - Fm: 0-0
Distance: 2m/2m3: 0-2 2m4-2m7: 0-1 3m+: 0-0
Track: LH: 0-1 RH: 0-0 Tight: 0-1 Gall: 0-0
Aids: Bl: 0-1 Vi: 0-0 Tstrap: 0-0
Best Rating:

Jerome Jerome

10-y-o b g Arctic Lord-Polaris Song (True Song)
Mrs Christine Hardinge Peter Gent

Placings:26/0-0P **(0429)**
2001/02: 24^{0}GF, 25^{P}G

	Starts	1st	2nd	3rd	Win & Pl
Chases	2	0	0	0	
Career Total	**5**	**0**	**1**	**0**	**568**

Going: Sf: 0-0 GS: 0-0 Gd: 0-1 GF: - Fm: 0-1
Distance: 2m/2m3: 0-0 2m4-2m7: 0-0 3m+: 0-2
Track: LH: 0-0 RH: 0-1 Tight: 0-0 Gall: 0-1
Aids: Bl: 0-0 Vi: 0-0 Tstrap: 0-0
Best Rating: 76 9/98 Worc 3m gd-fm Hdl

Jerroboam (FR)

78 **47**
5-y-o b g Luchiroverte (IRE)-Banouda (FR) (Crin Noir Ii (FR))
S E H Sherwood The Hon Mrs S Sherwood

Placings:*0* **(4166)**
2001/02: 16^{0}GS

	Starts	1st	2nd	3rd	Win & Pl
NH Flat	1	0	0	0	
Career Total	**1**	**0**	**0**	**0**	

Going: Sf: 0-0 GS: 0-1 Gd: 0-0 GF: - Fm: 0-0
Distance: 2m/2m3: 0-1 2m4-2m7: 0-0 3m+: 0-0
Track: LH: 0-1 RH: 0-0 Tight: 0-0 Gall: 0-0
Aids: Bl: 0-0 Vi: 0-0 Tstrap: 0-0
Best Rating: 62 3/02 Wwck 2m gd-sft NHF

Jeruflo (IRE)

102 **109**
7-y-o b m Glacial Storm (USA)-Martiness (Martinmas)
P R Webber Raymond Anderson Green

Placings:*310*/PP-11 **(0470)**
2001/02: 16^{1}S, 20^{1}GF

	Starts	1st	2nd	3rd	Win & Pl
Hurdles	2	2	0	0	5401
Career Total	**7**	**3**	**0**	**1**	**7272**

109	5/01	Hexm	2m4f110y	E Hdl	G-F	£1900
97	4/01	Plum	2m	D Hdl	SFT	£3500
103	3/00	Towc	2m	H NHF	SFT	£1652

Total win prize-money £7053

Going: Sf: 1-1 GS: 0-0 Gd: 0-0 GF: - Fm: 1-1
Distance: 2m/2m3: 1-1 2m4-2m7: 1-1 3m+: 0-0
Track: **LH: 2-2** RH: 0-0 **Tight: 1-1** Gall: 0-0
Aids: Bl: 0-0 Vi: 0-0 **Tstrap: 2-2**
Best Rating: 109 5/01 Hexm 2m4f110y gd-fm Hdl

A bumper winner, she had a wind operation before finding her form in the spring of 2001. Stays two and a half miles, acts on any ground.

Jessolle

102(106h) (122h)**107**
10-y-o gr m Scallywag-Dark City (Sweet Monday)
N G Richards C R Fleet

Placings:*050031P/112/65***3103***3***10**/3213***2***00P/151564-24* **(0740)**
2001/02: 20^{2}G, 16^{4}GS

	Starts	1st	2nd	3rd	Win & Pl
Hurdles	1	0	1	0	1700
Chases	1	0	0	0	426
Career Total	**35**	**8**	**4**	**6**	**41431**

122	6/00	Prth	2m4f110y	E(0-105)HCh	GD	£6955
122	5/00	Uttx	2m4f	E(0-105)HCh	GD	£3721
132	11/99	Hayd	2m4f	C(0-135)HHdl	GD	£6840
118	4/99	Carl	2m4f110y	D(0-125)HHdl	G-S	£2814
111	1/99	Muss	2m4f	E(0-115)HHdl	G-S	£2851
108	5/97	Bang	2m4f	E(0-105)HHdl	GD	£2738
96	5/97	Hayd	2m4f	F Hdl	G-F	£2015
95	4/97	Kels	2m110y	D Hdl	G-F	£2871

Total win prize-money £30805

Going: Sf: 0-0 GS: 0-1 Gd: 0-1 GF: - Fm: 0-0
Distance: 2m/2m3: 0-1 2m4-2m7: 0-1 3m+: 0-0
Track: LH: 0-2 RH: 0-0 Tight: 0-0 Gall: 0-0
Aids: Bl: 0-0 Vi: 0-0 Tstrap: 0-0
Best Rating: 132 11/99 Hayd 2m4f good Hdl

A versatile sort, she is effective over two and a half miles over hurdles, but has also shown ability over fences.

Jestastar

11-y-o b g Jester-Mickley Spacetrail (Space King)
Mrs J M Bush Mrs J M Bush

Placings:0/PP **(0429)**
2001/02: 24^{P}GF, 25^{P}G

	Starts	1st	2nd	3rd	Win & Pl
Chases	2	0	0	0	
Career Total	**3**	**0**	**0**	**0**	

Going: Sf: 0-0 GS: 0-0 Gd: 0-1 GF: - Fm: 0-1
Distance: 2m/2m3: 0-0 2m4-2m7: 0-0 3m+: 0-2
Track: LH: 0-0 RH: 0-1 Tight: 0-0 Gall: 0-1
Aids: Bl: 0-0 Vi: 0-0 Tstrap: 0-0
Best Rating: 72 5/99 Extr 2m3f firm Ch

Jet Boys (IRE)

75
12-y-o b g Le Bavard (FR)-Fast Adventure (Deep Run)
M Pitman Jet Uk Limited

Placings:*0204/253/021550/11F3P0/532P135/0-0P6* **(1065)**
2001/02: 25^{0}F, 25^{P}GF, 27^{6}G

	Starts	1st	2nd	3rd	Win & Pl
Hurdles	1	0	0	0	0
Chases	2	0	0	0	0
Career Total	**30**	**4**	**4**	**4**	**21334**

126	11/99	Hntg	3m6f110y	C(0-130)HCh	G-F	£6840
123	10/98	Hntg	3m2f	E(0-110)HHdl	GD	£2826
119	5/98	Strf	3m3f	E(0-115)HHdl	GD	£2290
123	11/97	Newb	3m110y	C Hdl	SFT	£3649

Total win prize-money £15605

Going: Sf: 0-0 GS: 0-0 Gd: 0-1 GF: - Fm: 0-2
Distance: 2m/2m3: 0-0 2m4-2m7: 0-0 3m+: 0-3
Track: LH: 0-2 RH: 0-0 Tight: 0-2 Gall: 0-0
Aids: Bl: 0-0 Vi: 0-0 Tstrap: 0-0
Best Rating: 126 11/99 Hntg 3m6f110y gd-fm Ch

Jet Files (IRE)

112 **119**
11-y-o ro g Roselier (FR)-Deepdecending (Deep Run)
M Pitman Jet Uk Limited

Placings:*450P/21020P/P21* **(4814)**
2001/02: 24^{P}S, 20^{2}G, 21^{1}GF

	Starts	1st	2nd	3rd	Win & Pl
Chases	3	1	1	0	14258
Career Total	**13**	**2**	**3**	**0**	**19042**

119	4/02	Chel	2m5f	D(0-115)HCh	G-F	£13013
91	12/97	Towc	2m5f	D Hdl	G-S	£3008

Total win prize-money £16021

Going: Sf: 0-1 GS: 0-0 Gd: 0-1 GF: - Fm: 1-1
Distance: 2m/2m3: 0-0 **2m4-2m7: 1-2** 3m+: 0-1
Track: **LH: 1-2** RH: 0-1 Tight: 0-0 **Gall: 1-1**
Aids: Bl: 0-0 Vi: 0-0 Tstrap: 0-0
Best Rating: 119 4/02 Chel 2m5f gd-fm Ch

Back to form when reappearing in 2002 after missing three seasons, and landed a competitive novices' handicap at Cheltenham. Stays three miles. Acts on soft and fast ground.

Jetowa Du Bois Hue (FR)

98 **103**
5-y-o b g Kadrou (FR)-Vaika (FR) (Cosmopolitan (FR))
T R George B A Kilpatrick

Placings:260 **(4138)**
2001/02: 16^{2}GS, 16^{6}GS, 16^{0}GS

	Starts	1st	2nd	3rd	Win & Pl
Hurdles	3	0	1	0	896
Career Total	**3**	**0**	**1**	**0**	**896**

Going: Sf: 0-0 GS: 0-3 Gd: 0-0 GF: - Fm: 0-0
Distance: 2m/2m3: 0-3 2m4-2m7: 0-0 3m+: 0-0
Track: LH: 0-0 RH: 0-3 Tight: 0-0 Gall: 0-0
Aids: Bl: 0-0 Vi: 0-0 Tstrap: 0-0
Best Rating: 103 1/02 Winc 2m gd-sft Hdl

Promising hurdle debut on soft ground.

Jewel Fighter

97 **64**
8-y-o br m Good Times (ITY)-Duellist (Town Crier)
J L Spearing Fighting Chance Syndicate

Placings:0/0/P02F **(4881)**
2001/02: 16^{P}HY, 17^{0}G, 16^{2}GF, 18^{F}GF

	Starts	1st	2nd	3rd	Win & Pl
Hurdles	4	0	1	0	495
Career Total	**6**	**0**	**1**	**0**	**495**

Going: Sf: 0-1 GS: 0-0 Gd: 0-1 GF: - Fm: 0-2
Distance: 2m/2m3: 0-4 2m4-2m7: 0-0 3m+: 0-0
Track: LH: 0-2 RH: 0-2 Tight: 0-2 Gall: 0-1
Aids: Bl: 0-0 Vi: 0-0 Tstrap: 0-0
Best Rating: 65 3/02 Hrfd 2m1f good Hdl

Jexel (FR)

105 **106+**

5-y-o b g Video Rock (FR)-Siesta (FR) (Prove It Baby (USA))

J S Goldie Mr & Mrs Raymond Anderson Green

Placings: *0-3*22 (4145)

2001/02: 16^{3}GS, 16^{2}HY, 16^{2}HY

	Starts	1st	2nd	3rd	Win & Pl
NH Flat	3	0	2	1	1264
Career Total	4	0	2	1	1264

Going: Sf: 0-2 GS: 0-1 Gd: 0-0 GF: - Fm: 0-0
Distance: 2m/2m3: 0-3 2m4-2m7: 0-0 3m+: 0-0
Track: LH: 0-3 RH: 0-0 Tight: 0-0 Gall: 0-0
Aids: Bl: 0-0 Vi: 0-0 Tstrap: 0-0
Best Rating: 106 3/02 Ayr 2m heavy NHF

In the frame in bumpers at Ayr.

Jilly

75f **45f**

5-y-o b m Ballet Royal (USA)-Shafayif (Ela-Mana-Mou)

H J Manners H J Manners

Placings: *00* (1731)

2001/02: 17^{0}G, 17^{0}F

	Starts	1st	2nd	3rd	Win & Pl
NH Flat	2	0	0	0	
Career Total	2	0	0	0	

Going: Sf: 0-0 GS: 0-0 Gd: 0-1 GF: - Fm: 0-1
Distance: 2m/2m3: 0-2 2m4-2m7: 0-0 3m+: 0-0
Track: LH: 0-0 RH: 0-1 Tight: 0-0 Gall: 0-0
Aids: Bl: 0-0 Vi: 0-0 Tstrap: 0-0
Best Rating: 45 10/01 Hrfd 2m1f good NHF

Jim Bell (IRE)

97 **77**

7-y-o br g Supreme Leader-Mightyatom (Black Minstrel)

J G M O'Shea K W Bell

Placings: *4/00*30P6 (4011)

2001/02: 16^{0}S, 16^{0}S, 20^{3}S, 20^{0}GS, 24^{P}HY, 21^{6}S

	Starts	1st	2nd	3rd	Win & Pl
NH Flat	2	0	0	0	0
Hurdles	4	0	0	1	538
Career Total	7	0	0	1	538

Going: Sf: 0-5 GS: 0-1 Gd: 0-0 GF: - Fm: 0-0
Distance: 2m/2m3: 0-2 2m4-2m7: 0-3 3m+: 0-1
Track: LH: 0-6 RH: 0-0 Tight: 0-0 Gall: 0-1
Aids: Bl: 0-0 Vi: 0-0 Tstrap: 0-0
Best Rating: 91 11/01 Hayd 2m soft NHF

Jim Jam Joey (IRE)

104 **119**

9-y-o ch g Big Sink Hope (USA)-Ascot Princess (Prince Hansel)

D M Grissell The Hon Mrs C Cameron

Placings: 2315226/**6F**123/3-4420 (4136)

2001/02: 21^{4}S, 21^{4}HY, 26^{2}S, 22^{0}GS

	Starts	1st	2nd	3rd	Win & Pl
Hurdles	4	0	1	0	1358
Career Total	17	2	5	3	14031

125	2/00	Folk	2m6f110y	F(0-110)HHdl	SFT	£2395
105	12/98	Font	2m6f110y	E Hdl	SFT	£2775

Total win prize-money £5170

Going: Sf: 0-3 GS: 0-1 Gd: 0-0 GF: - Fm: 0-0
Distance: 2m/2m3: 0-0 2m4-2m7: 0-3 3m+: 0-1
Track: LH: 0-2 RH: 0-2 Tight: 0-2 Gall: 0-1
Aids: Bl: 0-0 Vi: 0-0 Tstrap: 0-0
Best Rating: 125 4/00 Chel 3m soft Hdl

Handicap hurdler, has been lightly raced since winning at Folkestone in February 2000. Acts on soft ground and is effective at around two miles six furlongs.

Jimal

97 **80**

5-y-o b g Reprimand-Into The Fire (Dominion)

J W Mullins Woodmarsh Racing

Placings: 000-4604 (1101)

2001/02: 17^{4}GF, 17^{6}GF, 19^{0}G, 22^{4}G

	Starts	1st	2nd	3rd	Win & Pl
Hurdles	4	0	0	0	0
Career Total	7	0	0	0	0

Going: Sf: 0-0 GS: 0-0 Gd: 0-2 GF: - Fm: 0-2
Distance: 2m/2m3: 0-3 2m4-2m7: 0-1 3m+: 0-0
Track: LH: 0-4 RH: 0-0 Tight: 0-4 Gall: 0-0
Aids: Bl: 0-0 Vi: 0-0 Tstrap: 0-0
Best Rating: 80 4/01 Kemp 2m good Hdl

Jimmy Blues

96(84h) (86h)**78**

7-y-o b g Durgam (USA)-Tibbi Blues (Cure The Blues (USA))

Ferdy Murphy Miss Barbara Spittal

Placings: 4/00-46066 (4768)

2001/02: 16^{4}GF, 17^{6}GS, 16^{0}G, 16^{6}S, 16^{6}GF

	Starts	1st	2nd	3rd	Win & Pl
Hurdles	5	0	0	0	0
Career Total	8	0	0	0	0

Going: Sf: 0-1 GS: 0-1 Gd: 0-1 GF: - Fm: 0-2
Distance: 2m/2m3: 0-5 2m4-2m7: 0-0 3m+: 0-0
Track: LH: 0-1 RH: 0-3 Tight: 0-3 Gall: 0-0
Aids: Bl: 0-0 Vi: 0-0 Tstrap: 0-0
Best Rating: 86 5/01 Ayr 2m gd-fm Hdl

Jimmy Jumbo (IRE)

9-y-o ch g Dragon Palace (USA)-Sail On Lady (New Member)

R Ford J S Swindells

Placings: *0/06-P* (0009)

2001/02: 26^{P}GS

	Starts	1st	2nd	3rd	Win & Pl
Chases	1	0	0	0	
Career Total	4	0	0	0	

Going: Sf: 0-0 GS: 0-1 Gd: 0-0 GF: - Fm: 0-0
Distance: 2m/2m3: 0-0 2m4-2m7: 0-0 3m+: 0-1
Track: LH: 0-0 RH: 0-0 Tight: 0-0 Gall: 0-0
Aids: Bl: 0-0 Vi: 0-0 Tstrap: 0-0
Best Rating: 72 5/00 Dpat 3m gd-fm Ch

Jimmy Swift (IRE)

91 **76**

7-y-o b g Petardia-Grade A Star (IRE) (Alzao (USA))

P R Hedger P R Hedger

Placings: 44S00200P4/02063-000 (0588)

2001/02: 17^{0}GS, 18^{0}GF, 16^{0}GF

	Starts	1st	2nd	3rd	Win & Pl
Hurdles	3	0	0	0	
Career Total	18	0	2	1	1640

Going: Sf: 0-0 GS: 0-1 Gd: 0-0 GF: - Fm: 0-2
Distance: 2m/2m3: 0-3 2m4-2m7: 0-0 3m+: 0-0
Track: LH: 0-2 RH: 0-1 Tight: 0-3 Gall: 0-0
Aids: Bl: 0-0 Vi: 0-0 Tstrap: 0-0
Best Rating: 97 5/99 Navn 2m2f yld-sft Hdl

Jimmy Tennis (FR)

106 **141**

5-y-o b/br g Video Rock (FR)-Via Tennise (FR) (Brezzo (FR))

Miss Venetia Williams (T Civel 29/9) Mr Derek D & Mrs Jean P Clee

Placings: 35-**2131PP** (4878)

2001/02: 17^{2}GS, 17^{1}VS, 17^{3}VS, 24^{1}GS, 24^{P}GS, 24^{P}G

	Starts	1st	2nd	3rd	Win & Pl
Chases	6	2	1	1	42648
Career Total	8	2	1	2	46819

141	2/02	Asct	3m110y	A Ch	G-S	£20825
	6/01	Autl	2m1f110y	Ch	VS	£12124

Total win prize-money £32949

Going: Sf: 0-0 GS: 1-3 Gd: 0-1 GF: - Fm: 0-0
Distance: 2m/2m3: 1-3 2m4-2m7: 0-0 3m+: 1-3
Track: LH: 0-1 **RH: 1-2** Tight: 0-0 Gall: 0-1
Aids: **Bl: 1-3** Vi: 0-0 Tstrap: 0-0
Best Rating: 141 2/02 Asct 3m110y yld-sft Ch

Ex-French winning chaser, he is suited by soft ground and usually wears blinkers. Impressive winner of the Reynoldstown at Ascot in February, but was pulled up in the Royal & SunAlliance.

Jimmy Wiskers (IRE)

97 **97**

7-y-o b g Insan (USA)-Jackson Miss (Condorcet (FR))

Ferdy Murphy Richard Wheeler

Placings: 50-446023 (3557)

2001/02: 23^{4}GF, 16^{4}GS, 16^{6}S, 20^{0}G, 17^{2}HY, 19^{3}S

	Starts	1st	2nd	3rd	Win & Pl
Hurdles	6	0	1	1	1870
Career Total	8	0	1	1	1870

Going: Sf: 0-3 GS: 0-1 Gd: 0-1 GF: - Fm: 0-1
Distance: 2m/2m3: 0-4 2m4-2m7: 0-1 3m+: 0-1
Track: LH: 0-6 RH: 0-0 Tight: 0-4 Gall: 0-1
Aids: Bl: 0-0 Vi: 0-0 Tstrap: 0-0
Best Rating: 97 11/01 Aint 2m110y gd-sft Hdl

Well held in moderate hurdle company.

Jimmy's Cross (IRE)

12-y-o ch g Phardante (FR)-Foredefine (Bonne Noel)

Mrs Sue Maude Mrs Sue Maude

Placings: *131*B21225/P/**24U**/441**24P**0/0433**P4431444** 566P/**235F6** (4865)

2001/02: 21^{2}GF, 25^{3}G, 19^{5}G, 19^{F}GF, 23^{6}F

	Starts	1st	2nd	3rd	Win & Pl
Chases	5	0	1	1	999
Career Total	41	5	6	5	27018

93	9/99	Hrfd	2m3f	G(0-95)HCh	GD	£2948
99	6/98	NAbb	2m5f110y	D Ch	GD	£3485

105	3/96	Hntg	2m4f110y	E Hdl	G-F	£2010
103	10/95	Font	2m2f	Hdl	GD	£2069
94	6/95	Worc	2m	H NHF	G-F	£1688

Total win prize-money £12201

Going: Sf: 0-0 GS: 0-0 Gd: 0-2 GF: - Fm: 0-3
Distance: 2m/2m3: 0-0 2m4-2m7: 0-3 3m+: 0-2
Track: LH: 0-1 RH: 0-4 Tight: 0-1 Gall: 0-0
Aids: Bl: 0-0 Vi: 0-0 Tstrap: 0-0
Best Rating: 118 4/96 Chel 2m5f110y gd-sft Hdl

Jineful (FR)

(89h) (69h)**56**

5-y-o b g Useful (FR)-Finegrila (FR) (Fin Bon)
N J Henderson The Barrow Boys Iii

Placings:4-05 **(4134)**
2001/02: 16^{0}S, 20^{5}GS

	Starts	1st	2nd	3rd	Win & Pl
Hurdles	2	0	0	0	0
Career Total	**3**	**0**	**0**	**0**	**0**

Going: Sf: 0-1 GS: 0-1 Gd: 0-0 GF: - Fm: 0-0
Distance: 2m/2m3: 0-1 2m4-2m7: 0-1 3m+: 0-0
Track: LH: 0-0 RH: 0-2 Tight: 0-0 Gall: 0-0
Aids: Bl: 0-0 Vi: 0-0 Tstrap: 0-0
Best Rating: 69 3/02 Sand 2m4f110y gd-sft Hdl

Chasing type.

Jingle Rose (FR)

(103h) (108h)

5-y-o b g Missolonghi (USA)-Quelle Etoile V (FR) (Mitsoupam (FR))
Miss Venetia Williams (P J Hobbs 2/8) Mrs R J Skan

Placings:P1P430-36P1U **(1220a)**
2001/02: 22^{3}GF, 19^{6}G, 20^{P}GF, 19^{1}GF, 18^{U}S

	Starts	1st	2nd	3rd	Win & Pl
Hurdles	5	1	0	1	2221
Career Total	**11**	**2**	**0**	**2**	**5006**

108	8/01	Strf	2m3f	G Hdl	G-F	£1841
108	11/00	Winc	2m	E Hdl	SFT	£2453

Total win prize-money £4295

Going: Sf: 0-1 GS: 0-0 Gd: 0-1 GF: - Fm: 1-3
Distance: 2m/2m3: 1-2 2m4-2m7: 0-3 3m+: 0-0
Track: LH: 1-3 RH: 0-1 **Tight: 1-2** Gall: 0-0
Aids: Bl: 0-1 Vi: 0-0 Tstrap: 0-0
Best Rating: 108 8/01 Strf 2m3f gd-fm Hdl

Has won twice over hurdles at two miles and two miles three furlongs. Showed better attitude than Kuwait Millennium to land a seller at Stratford. Had not appeared to stay two miles six earlier in the year. Acts on fast ground.

Jivaros (FR)

92 **106**

5-y-o br g Video Rock (FR)-Rives (FR) (Reasonable Choice (USA))
H D Daly Mrs G Leigh

Placings:001 **(4161)**
2001/02: 16^{0}S, 21^{0}S, 25^{1}GS

	Starts	1st	2nd	3rd	Win & Pl
NH Flat	1	0	0	0	0
Hurdles	2	1	0	0	2604
Career Total	**3**	**1**	**0**	**0**	**2604**

106	3/02	Wwck	3m1f	E Hdl	G-S	£2604

Total win prize-money £2604

Going: Sf: 0-2 GS: 1-1 Gd: 0-0 GF: - Fm: 0-0
Distance: 2m/2m3: 0-1 2m4-2m7: 0-1 **3m+: 1-1**
Track: LH: 0-1 RH: 0-1 Tight: 0-0 Gall: 0-0
Aids: Bl: 0-0 Vi: 0-0 Tstrap: 0-0
Best Rating: 106 3/02 Wwck 3m1f gd-sft Hdl

Took a three-mile novices' hurdle at Warwick in March on only his third start.

Job Rage (IRE)

104 **94**

8-y-o b/br g Yashgan-Snatchingly (Thatch (USA))
A Bailey Sandybrow Stables Ltd

Placings:215/P5/U-4036 **(2509)**
2001/02: 20^{4}S, 16^{0}G, 17^{3}G, 19^{6}S

	Starts	1st	2nd	3rd	Win & Pl
Hurdles	4	0	0	1	537
Career Total	**10**	**1**	**1**	**1**	**3448**

102	3/98	Ayr	2m	E Hdl	G-S	£2259

Total win prize-money £2259

Going: Sf: 0-2 GS: 0-0 Gd: 0-2 GF: - Fm: 0-0
Distance: 2m/2m3: 0-3 2m4-2m7: 0-1 3m+: 0-0
Track: LH: 0-3 RH: 0-1 Tight: 0-2 Gall: 0-0
Aids: Bl: 0-1 Vi: 0-0 Tstrap: 0-0
Best Rating: 102 3/98 Ayr 2m gd-sft Hdl

Lightly-raced handicap hurdler who needs cut in the ground and a left-handed track.

Jocko Glasses

102 **119**

5-y-o ch g Inchinor-Corinthia (USA) (Empery (USA))
N J Henderson David J Jackson

Placings:4150-640P0 **(4116)**
2001/02: 16^{6}G, 16^{4}G, 16^{0}GS, 16^{P}GS, 16^{0}G

	Starts	1st	2nd	3rd	Win & Pl
Hurdles	5	0	0	0	418
Career Total	**9**	**1**	**0**	**0**	**8345**

121	12/00	Kemp	2m	B Hdl	G-S	£7377

Total win prize-money £7378

Going: Sf: 0-0 GS: 0-2 Gd: 0-3 GF: - Fm: 0-0
Distance: 2m/2m3: 0-5 2m4-2m7: 0-0 3m+: 0-0
Track: LH: 0-2 RH: 0-3 Tight: 0-0 Gall: 0-0
Aids: Bl: 0-1 Vi: 0-0 Tstrap: 0-0
Best Rating: 122 2/01 Kemp 2m gd-sft Hdl

A fair performer on the Flat, he got off the mark over hurdles at Kempton in December 2000, but was well beaten in a couple of Graded hurdles afterwards and has struggled in the 2001/2002 season in handicap company. Continues to disappoint and joined Mary Reveley in the summer of 2002. Suited by two miles and a sound surface.

Jocks Cross (IRE)

116 **162**

11-y-o ch g Riberetto-Shuil Le Dia (Kabale)
Miss Venetia Williams Mrs Gill Harrison

Placings:2215410/11400/15/**2111F31**/2252P1PU/421 P2F-502F3 **(4148)**
2001/02: 27^{5}G, 26^{0}S, 29^{2}GS, 28^{F}HY, 26^{3}GS

	Starts	1st	2nd	3rd	Win & Pl
Chases	5	0	1	1	18039
Career Total	**40**	**11**	**9**	**2**	**178049**

159	12/00	Chep	3m5f110y	A HCh	SFT	£43500
145	3/00	Chep	3m2f110y	B(0-145)HCh	G-S	£10062
143	4/99	Punc	3m1f	HCh	GD	£33214
118	3/99	Strf	2m4f	D Ch	HVY	£4524
140	2/99	Font	3m2f110y	E Ch	GD	£2802
135	2/99	Font	3m2f110y	D Ch	SFT	£4506
124	4/98	Carl	2m4f110y	D(0-125)HHdl	SFT	£2829
123	11/96	Newc	3m	C(0-135)HHdl	GD	£3355
112	10/96	Carl	3m110y	E(0-115)HHdl	GD	£2290
114	3/96	Bang	2m1f	E Hdl	G-S	£2290
103	1/96	Carl	2m1f	E Hdl	G-S	£2598

Total win prize-money £111971

Going: Sf: 0-2 GS: 0-2 Gd: 0-1 GF: - Fm: 0-0
Distance: 2m/2m3: 0-0 2m4-2m7: 0-0 3m+: 0-5
Track: LH: 0-5 RH: 0-0 Tight: 0-0 Gall: 0-2
Aids: Bl: 0-0 Vi: 0-0 Tstrap: 0-0
Best Rating: 162 12/01 Chep 3m5f110y gd-sft Ch

Small but tough, he likes soft ground and goes well at Chepstow, where he won the Welsh National in 2000 and was runner-up in 2001.

Jodante (IRE)

87f **92f**

5-y-o ch g Phardante (FR)-Crashtown Lucy (Crash Course)
P Beaumont Trevor Hemmings

Placings:0 **(4750)**
2001/02: 17^{0}G

	Starts	1st	2nd	3rd	Win & Pl
NH Flat	1	0	0	0	
Career Total	**1**	**0**	**0**	**0**	

Going: Sf: 0-0 GS: 0-0 Gd: 0-1 GF: - Fm: 0-0
Distance: 2m/2m3: 0-1 2m4-2m7: 0-0 3m+: 0-0
Track: LH: 0-0 RH: 0-1 Tight: 0-0 Gall: 0-0
Aids: Bl: 0-0 Vi: 0-0 Tstrap: 0-0
Best Rating: 85 4/02 Carl 2m1f good NHF

Joe Blake (IRE)

7-y-o b g Jurado (USA)-I'Ve No Idea (Nishapour (FR))
I R Ferguson R A Bartlett

Placings:F141F **(4949a)**
2001/02: 24^{F}HY, 25^{1}S, 26^{4}G, 25^{1}Y, 25^{F}G

	Starts	1st	2nd	3rd	Win & Pl
Chases	5	2	0	0	13006
Career Total	**5**	**2**	**0**	**0**	**13006**

131	4/02	Fair	3m1f	Ch	YLD	£6349
116	2/02	Fair	3m1f	Ch	SFT	£4656

Total win prize-money £11006

Going: Sf: 1-2 GS: 0-0 Gd: 0-2 GF: - Fm: 0-0
Distance: 2m/2m3: 0-0 2m4-2m7: 0-0 **3m+: 2-5**
Track: LH: 0-2 **RH: 2-3** Tight: 0-0 Gall: 0-1
Aids: Bl: 0-0 Vi: 0-0 Tstrap: 0-0
Best Rating: 138 3/02 Chel 3m2f110y good Ch

A decent point-to-pointer, he had the measure of Sheltering in a Leopardstown hunter chase only to fall at the last. Gained compensation with the minimum of fuss at Fairyhouse on his next start, and ran well in defeat at Cheltenham. Stays three miles. Has won on soft but prefers a sounder surface.

Joe Buzz (IRE)

98(97c) (114c)**99**

10-y-o b g Phardante (FR)-Dosie Deegan (Bulldozer)
A Crook Joe Buzzeo

Placings:225101/2325/**F60-12F602** **(4553)**
2001/02: 20^{1}GF, 23^{2}F, 20^{F}G, 20^{6}GS, 20^{0}S, 17^{2}GF

	Starts	1st	2nd	3rd	Win & Pl
Hurdles	3	0	1	0	496
Chases	3	1	1	0	4761
Career Total	**19**	**3**	**6**	**1**	**13989**

114	5/01	Hexm	2m4f110y	E(0-105)HCh	G-F	£3497
108	3/98	Newc	2m4f	E Hdl	GD	£2368
107	2/98	MRas	2m3f110y	D Hdl	GD	£2979

Total win prize-money £8846

Going: Sf: 0-1 GS: 0-1 Gd: 0-1 GF: - Fm: 1-3
Distance: 2m/2m3: 0-1 **2m4-2m7: 1-4** 3m+: 0-1
Track: **LH: 1-3** RH: 0-2 Tight: 0-3 Gall: 0-1
Aids: Bl: 0-0 Vi: 0-0 Tstrap: 0-0
Best Rating: 114 5/01 Hexm 2m4f110y gd-fm Ch

Fair handicap hurdler, managed to score over fences on fast ground in May 2001. He does not quite stay three miles, and has had problems with his jumping. Regularly on his toes before his races.

Joe Crump

94 119

8-y-o ch g Interrex (CAN)-Nellie O'Dowd (USA) (Diesis)
J Mackie Welbeck Hotel/pickering Properties Ltd

Placings:*6/624P/P41111P50-30* **(1561)**
2001/02: 20³G, 20⁰GS

	Starts	1st	2nd	3rd	Win & Pl
Hurdles	2	0	0	1	636
Career Total	**16**	**4**	**1**	**1**	**18435**

123	12/00	Donc	2m4f	E(0-115)HHdl	G-S	£3094
118	11/00	Uttx	2m6f110y	D(0-125)HHdl	HVY	£2879
115	11/00	Chel	2m5f	E(0-115)HHdl	G-S	£8742
111	10/00	Towc	2m5f	F(0-100)HHdl	G-S	£1939

Total win prize-money £16656

Going: Sf: 0-0 GS: 0-1 Gd: 0-1 GF: - Fm: 0-0
Distance: 2m/2m3: 0-0 2m4-2m7: 0-2 3m+: 0-0
Track: LH: 0-1 RH: 0-1 Tight: 0-0 Gall: 0-1
Aids: Bl: 0-0 Vi: 0-2 Tstrap: 0-2
Best Rating: 123 12/00 Donc 2m4f gd-sft Hdl

Won four on the trot in 2000, but has found life tougher this year, looking well held on each occasion. Is suited by cut in the ground.

Joe Cullen (IRE)

110 142

7-y-o ch g River Falls-Moycullen (Le Moss)
W P Mullins Mark F Sheasby

Placings:*11/13-42105000* **(4712a)**
2001/02: 16⁴G, 16²Y, 16¹S, 16⁰YS, 16⁵HY, 16⁰S, 17⁰G, 16⁰Y

	Starts	1st	2nd	3rd	Win & Pl
Hurdles	8	1	1	0	11081
Career Total	**12**	**4**	**1**	**1**	**42029**

137	11/01	Punc	2m	Hdl	SFT	£7233
137	2/01	Fair	2m	Hdl	HVY	£5008
149	3/00	Chel	2m110y	A NHF	GD	£18000
118	6/99	Tral	2m	NHF	GD	£3222

Total win prize-money £33465

Going: Sf: 1-3 GS: 0-0 Gd: 0-2 GF: - Fm: 0-0
Distance: **2m/2m3: 1-8** 2m4-2m7: 0-0 3m+: 0-0
Track: LH: 0-4 **RH: 1-2** Tight: 0-0 Gall: 0-2
Aids: Bl: 0-0 Vi: 0-0 Tstrap: 0-0
Best Rating: 149 3/00 Chel 2m110y good NHF

A former Cheltenham bumper winner. He has shown fair form in handicaps including winning at Punchestown in November 2001. Seems suited by soft ground.

Joe Di Capo (IRE)

100 94

7-y-o b g Phardante (FR)-Supreme Glen (IRE) (Supreme Leader)
A Crook Joe Buzzeo

Placings:432P-01PP **(4817)**
2001/02: 22⁰G, 20¹G, 24ᴾS, 24ᴾGF

	Starts	1st	2nd	3rd	Win & Pl
Hurdles	4	1	0	0	2618
Career Total	**8**	**1**	**1**	**1**	**3780**

94	11/01	Newc	2m4f	E Hdl	GD	£2618

Total win prize-money £2618

Going: Sf: 0-1 GS: 0-0 Gd: 1-2 GF: - Fm: 0-1
Distance: 2m/2m3: 0-0 **2m4-2m7: 1-2** 3m+: 0-2
Track: **LH: 1-3** RH: 0-0 Tight: 0-1 **Gall: 1-2**
Aids: Bl: 0-0 Vi: 0-0 Tstrap: 0-0
Best Rating: 106 12/00 Newc 3m soft Hdl

Plating-class hurdler.

Joe Luke (IRE)

104(104h) (122h)131

10-y-o b g Satco (FR)-Garden County (Ragapan)
G M Moore (J J O'Neill 7/12) Ms M Winter

Placings:*5/000/66/11/P245-14FF2U* **(3445)**
2001/02: 24¹GS, 20⁴G, 24ᶠG, 24ᶠS, 24²S, 24ᵁGS

	Starts	1st	2nd	3rd	Win & Pl
Hurdles	1	0	1	0	1000
Chases	5	1	0	0	4677
Career Total	**18**	**3**	**2**	**0**	**15158**

131	5/01	Prth	3m	D Ch	G-S	£4264
122	4/00	Uttx	3m110y	F(0-100)HHdl	SFT	£3146
110	3/00	Carl	3m110y	E(0-105)HHdl	G-S	£4680

Total win prize-money £12090

Going: Sf: 0-2 GS: 1-2 Gd: 0-2 GF: - Fm: 0-0
Distance: 2m/2m3: 0-0 2m4-2m7: 0-1 **3m+: 1-5**
Track: LH: 0-5 **RH: 1-1** Tight: 0-2 Gall: 0-2
Aids: Bl: 0-0 Vi: 0-0 Tstrap: 0-1
Best Rating: 131 11/01 Newb 3m good Ch

A winner over hurdles and of a novice chase. He stays three miles and is effective on a soft surface.

Joe The Bread (IRE)

7-y-o b g Erdelistan (FR)-Dawning Glory (Hittite Glory)
M Pitman Rolfe East Racing Partnership

Placings:*U0/0* **(2521)**
2001/02: 18⁰S

	Starts	1st	2nd	3rd	Win & Pl
NH Flat	1	0	0	0	
Career Total	**3**	**0**	**0**	**0**	

Going: Sf: 0-1 GS: 0-0 Gd: 0-0 GF: - Fm: 0-0
Distance: 2m/2m3: 0-1 2m4-2m7: 0-0 3m+: 0-0
Track: LH: 0-0 RH: 0-0 Tight: 0-0 Gall: 0-0
Aids: Bl: 0-0 Vi: 0-0 Tstrap: 0-0
Best Rating: 104 1/00 Font 2m2f110y gd-sft NHF

Joely Green

103 93

5-y-o b g Binary Star (USA)-Comedy Lady (Comedy Star (USA))
N P Littmoden Paul J Dixon

Placings:0 **(2683)**
2001/02: 16⁰G

	Starts	1st	2nd	3rd	Win & Pl
Hurdles	1	0	0	0	
Career Total	**1**	**0**	**0**	**0**	

Going: Sf: 0-0 GS: 0-0 Gd: 0-1 GF: - Fm: 0-0
Distance: 2m/2m3: 0-1 2m4-2m7: 0-0 3m+: 0-0
Track: LH: 0-1 RH: 0-0 Tight: 0-0 Gall: 0-1
Aids: Bl: 0-0 Vi: 0-0 Tstrap: 0-0
Best Rating: 93 12/01 Donc 2m110y good Hdl

Joes Edge (IRE)

93f 103f

5-y-o b/br g Supreme Leader-Right Dark (Buckskin (FR))
Ferdy Murphy Chemipetro Limited

Placings:*10* **(4841)**
2001/02: 17¹G, 16⁰G

	Starts	1st	2nd	3rd	Win & Pl
NH Flat	2	1	0	0	2499
Career Total	**2**	**1**	**0**	**0**	**2499**

103	4/02	Carl	2m1f	H NHF	GD	£2499

Total win prize-money £2499

Going: Sf: 0-0 GS: 0-0 Gd: 1-2 GF: - Fm: 0-0
Distance: **2m/2m3: 1-2** 2m4-2m7: 0-0 3m+: 0-0
Track: LH: 0-1 **RH: 1-1** Tight: 0-0 Gall: 0-0
Aids: Bl: 0-0 Vi: 0-0 Tstrap: 0-0
Best Rating: 103 1/02 Ayr 2m good NHF

Joey The Schnoze

101 94

4-y-o ch g Zilzal (USA)-Linda's Design (Persian Bold)
S Magnier Fergus Jones

Placings:02604P **(4565)**
2001/02: 16⁰G, 16²GS, 16⁶S, 17⁰GS, 17⁴S, 16ᴾG

	Starts	1st	2nd	3rd	Win & Pl
Hurdles	6	0	1	0	1042
Career Total	**6**	**0**	**1**	**0**	**1042**

Going: Sf: 0-2 GS: 0-2 Gd: 0-2 GF: - Fm: 0-0
Distance: 2m/2m3: 0-6 2m4-2m7: 0-0 3m+: 0-0
Track: LH: 0-4 RH: 0-2 Tight: 0-2 Gall: 0-3
Aids: Bl: 0-0 Vi: 0-0 Tstrap: 0-0
Best Rating: 94 12/01 Newc 2m gd-sft Hdl

Headstrong juvenile hurdler.

Johann De Vonnas (FR)

94f 100f

5-y-o b g Cadoudal (FR)-Diana De Vonnas (FR) (El Badr)
N J Henderson B T M Racing

Placings:*0* **(4158)**
2001/02: 16⁰GS

	Starts	1st	2nd	3rd	Win & Pl
NH Flat	1	0	0	0	
Career Total	**1**	**0**	**0**	**0**	

Going: Sf: 0-0 GS: 0-1 Gd: 0-0 GF: - Fm: 0-0
Distance: 2m/2m3: 0-1 2m4-2m7: 0-0 3m+: 0-0
Track: LH: 0-0 RH: 0-1 Tight: 0-0 Gall: 0-0
Aids: Bl: 0-0 Vi: 0-0 Tstrap: 0-0
Best Rating: 78 3/02 Sand 2m110y gd-sft NHF

Fair form in bumpers on varying ground.

Johdamar (NZ)

71 12

10-y-o ch g J O Dahlia (USA)-Ewar Star (Grundy)
B G Powell G Irlam

Placings:P4630/52P/0PP (0780)
2001/02: 22^{0}GF, 22^{P}GF, 20^{P}G

	Starts	1st	2nd	3rd	Win & Pl
Hurdles	3	0	0	0	
Career Total	**11**	**0**	**1**	**1**	**975**

Going: Sf: 0-0 GS: 0-0 Gd: 0-1 GF: - Fm: 0-2
Distance: 2m/2m3: 0-0 2m4-2m7: 0-3 3m+: 0-0
Track: LH: 0-2 RH: 0-1 Tight: 0-1 Gall: 0-0
Aids: Bl: 0-1 Vi: 0-0 Tstrap: 0-0
Best Rating: 79 6/99 NAbb 2m6f good Hdl

John Foley (IRE)

97 99

4-y-o b g Petardia-Fast Bay (Bay Express)
Mrs H Dalton (J W Unett 8/12) Foley Steelstock

Placings:4530 (4848)
2001/02: 16^{4}G, 17^{5}G, 16^{3}G, 16^{0}G

	Starts	1st	2nd	3rd	Win & Pl
Hurdles	4	0	0	1	1260
Career Total	**4**	**0**	**0**	**1**	**1260**

Going: Sf: 0-0 GS: 0-0 Gd: 0-4 GF: - Fm: 0-0
Distance: 2m/2m3: 0-4 2m4-2m7: 0-0 3m+: 0-0
Track: LH: 0-2 RH: 0-2 Tight: 0-1 Gall: 0-1
Aids: Bl: 0-0 Vi: 0-0 Tstrap: 0-0
Best Rating: 99 11/01 Hntg 2m110y good Hdl

Fair form in juvenile hurdles in the autumn of 2001 at around two miles on a sound surface.

John Hunter (IRE)

100 104

5-y-o b g Unfuwain (USA)-Aigue (High Top)
M C Pipe (B W Hills 12/10) Lucayan Stud

Placings:31 (4564)
2001/02: 16^{3}HY, 16^{1}GF

	Starts	1st	2nd	3rd	Win & Pl
Hurdles	2	1	0	1	3114
Career Total	**2**	**1**	**0**	**1**	**3114**

104 4/02 Plum 2m E Hdl G-F £2719
Total win prize-money £2720

Going: Sf: 0-1 GS: 0-0 Gd: 0-0 GF: - Fm: 1-1
Distance: **2m/2m3: 1-2** 2m4-2m7: 0-0 3m+: 0-0
Track: **LH: 1-2** RH: 0-0 **Tight: 1-2** Gall: 0-0
Aids: Bl: 0-0 Vi: 0-0 **Tstrap: 1-2**
Best Rating: 104 4/02 Plum 2m gd-fm Hdl

Above average ten-furlong performer on the Flat who won on fast ground, found the heavy ground against him on his hurdling debut, but got off the mark on fast ground in April 2002. Wears a tongue tie.

John Steed (IRE)

100 83

5-y-o b g Thatching-Trinity Hall (Hallgate)
N A Dunger (C Weedon 24/8) N A Dunger

Placings:P2004 (3715)
2001/02: 20^{P}GS, 16^{2}GS, 16^{0}G, 16^{0}GS, 16^{4}HY

	Starts	1st	2nd	3rd	Win & Pl
Hurdles	5	0	1	0	666
Career Total	**5**	**0**	**1**	**0**	**666**

Going: Sf: 0-1 GS: 0-3 Gd: 0-1 GF: - Fm: 0-0
Distance: 2m/2m3: 0-4 2m4-2m7: 0-1 3m+: 0-0
Track: LH: 0-3 RH: 0-1 Tight: 0-4 Gall: 0-1
Aids: Bl: 0-0 Vi: 0-0 Tstrap: 0-0
Best Rating: 83 11/01 Plum 2m gd-sft Hdl

Moderate on the Flat, he was pulled up on his hurdles debut but fared better in claiming company next time when runner-up, moderate form subsequently.

John The Greek (IRE)

77(77h) 88

6-y-o b/br g Aristocracy-Lucky Minstrel (IRE) (Black Minstrel)
M Pitman G C Stevens

Placings:604/500031350-03F3 (1388)
2001/02: 21^{0}GF, 20^{3}GF, 24^{F}GF, 26^{3}GF

	Starts	1st	2nd	3rd	Win & Pl
Chases	4	0	0	2	930
Career Total	**16**	**1**	**0**	**4**	**4348**

92 11/00 Plum 2m5f E(0-105)HHdl HVY £2704
Total win prize-money £2704

Going: Sf: 0-0 GS: 0-0 Gd: 0-0 GF: - Fm: 0-4
Distance: 2m/2m3: 0-0 2m4-2m7: 0-2 3m+: 0-2
Track: LH: 0-2 RH: 0-2 Tight: 0-0 Gall: 0-1
Aids: Bl: 0-0 Vi: 0-2 Tstrap: 0-0
Best Rating: 92 11/00 Plum 2m5f heavy Hdl

John The Mole (IRE)

95f 98f

4-y-o ch g Glacial Storm (USA)-City Dame (Golden Love)
A Crook The Adbrokes Partnership

Placings:430 (4900)
2001/02: 16^{4}G, 17^{3}GS, 16^{0}G

	Starts	1st	2nd	3rd	Win & Pl
NH Flat	3	0	0	1	249
Career Total	**3**	**0**	**0**	**1**	**249**

Going: Sf: 0-0 GS: 0-1 Gd: 0-2 GF: - Fm: 0-0
Distance: 2m/2m3: 0-3 2m4-2m7: 0-0 3m+: 0-0
Track: LH: 0-0 RH: 0-3 Tight: 0-2 Gall: 0-0
Aids: Bl: 0-0 Vi: 0-0 Tstrap: 0-0
Best Rating: 98 3/02 MRas 2m1f110y gd-sft NHF

Johnlegood

106 112

6-y-o ch g Karinga Bay-Dancing Years (USA) (Fred Astaire (USA))
G L Moore Bryan Pennick

Placings:004-4F43P13 (4584)
2001/02: 18^{4}G, 16^{F}GS, 18^{4}HY, 16^{3}HY, 20^{P}GS, 18^{1}S, 16^{3}G

	Starts	1st	2nd	3rd	Win & Pl
Hurdles	7	1	0	2	4657
Career Total	**10**	**1**	**0**	**2**	**4657**

112 3/02 Font 2m2f110y D Hdl SFT £3528
Total win prize-money £3528

Going: Sf: 1-3 GS: 0-2 Gd: 0-2 GF: - Fm: 0-0
Distance: **2m/2m3: 1-6** 2m4-2m7: 0-1 3m+: 0-0
Track: **LH: 1-3** RH: 0-4 **Tight: 1-3** Gall: 0-0
Aids: Bl: 0-0 Vi: 0-0 Tstrap: 0-0
Best Rating: 112 3/02 Font 2m2f110y soft Hdl

Ordinary form in novice hurdles, but gradually getting the hang of things in the early part of 2002. Stays two and a quarter miles, promises to stay further. Acts on soft ground, handles good ground.

Johnnie The Joker

93 99

11-y-o gr g Absalom-Magic Tower (Tower Walk)
O Brennan Miss M Carrington Smith

Placings:24/2114016-56 (1809)
2001/02: 16^{5}GF, 16^{6}S

	Starts	1st	2nd	3rd	Win & Pl
Hurdles	2	0	0	0	0
Career Total	**11**	**3**	**2**	**0**	**9955**

109 8/00 Hntg 2m4f110y E Hdl G-F £2580
106 6/00 Fknm 2m4f E Hdl GD £2658
109 5/00 MRas 2m1f110y E Hdl G-S £2935
Total win prize-money £8176

Going: Sf: 0-1 GS: 0-0 Gd: 0-0 GF: - Fm: 0-1
Distance: 2m/2m3: 0-2 2m4-2m7: 0-0 3m+: 0-0
Track: LH: 0-1 RH: 0-1 Tight: 0-1 Gall: 0-1
Aids: Bl: 0-0 Vi: 0-0 Tstrap: 0-0
Best Rating: 109 8/00 Hntg 2m4f110y gd-fm Hdl

Johnny Staccato

85 55

8-y-o b g Statoblest-Frasquita (Song)
C Drew C Drew

Placings:0 (2683)
2001/02: 16^{0}G

	Starts	1st	2nd	3rd	Win & Pl
Hurdles	1	0	0	0	
Career Total	**1**	**0**	**0**	**0**	

Going: Sf: 0-0 GS: 0-0 Gd: 0-1 GF: - Fm: 0-0
Distance: 2m/2m3: 0-1 2m4-2m7: 0-0 3m+: 0-0
Track: LH: 0-1 RH: 0-0 Tight: 0-0 Gall: 0-1
Aids: Bl: 0-0 Vi: 0-0 Tstrap: 0-0
Best Rating: 55 12/01 Donc 2m110y good Hdl

Johnny-K (IRE)

88 88

11-y-o b g King's Ride-Queen Kate (Queens Hussar)
C R Barwell (Mrs S Prouse 1/6) Mrs S Prouse

Placings:216/15/254P/06P (0796)
2001/02: 16^{0}G, 21^{6}GF, 16^{P}GF

	Starts	1st	2nd	3rd	Win & Pl
Chases	3	0	0	0	0
Career Total	**12**	**2**	**2**	**0**	**4390**

118 11/96 Bang 2m1f H NHF G-S £1721
108 3/96 Hrfd 2m1f H NHF HVY £1409
Total win prize-money £3131

Going: Sf: 0-0 GS: 0-0 Gd: 0-1 GF: - Fm: 0-2
Distance: 2m/2m3: 0-2 2m4-2m7: 0-1 3m+: 0-0
Track: LH: 0-2 RH: 0-0 Tight: 0-2 Gall: 0-0
Aids: Bl: 0-0 Vi: 0-0 Tstrap: 0-0
Best Rating: 118 11/96 Bang 2m1f gd-sft NHF

Johnston's Art (IRE)

107(87c) 103

9-y-o b g Law Society (USA)-Mirror Of Flowers (Artaius (USA))

Mrs D Thomson The Coutts McGregor Clan

Placings:350/13312/P3FPP5/100300-P45052061P40 (4893)

2001/02: 24^{P}G, 22^{4}G, 22^{5}GS, 21^{0}G, 20^{5}S, 24^{2}GF, 24^{0}G, 24^{6}G, 24^{1}S, 24^{P}HY, 22^{4}GF, 20^{0}G

	Starts	1st	2nd	3rd	Win & Pl
Hurdles	12	1	1	0	4893
Career Total	**32**	**4**	**2**	**5**	**14939**

103	1/02	Muss	3m	E(0-110)HHdl	SFT	£3388
116	10/00	Font	2m6f110y	D(0-120)HHdl	GD	£3168
115	3/99	Plum	2m4f	E Hdl	SFT	£2285
114	1/99	Ling	2m110y	H NHF	HVY	£1327

Total win prize-money £10169

Going: Sf: 1-3 GS: 0-1 Gd: 0-6 GF: - Fm: 0-2
Distance: 2m/2m3: 0-0 2m4-2m7: 0-6 **3m+: 1-6**
Track: LH: 0-6 **RH: 1-6 Tight: 1-7** Gall: 0-1
Aids: **Bl: 1-11** Vi: 0-0 Tstrap: 0-0
Best Rating: 120 4/99 Plum 2m4f gd-sft Hdl

Modest hurdler, stays three miles and acts on any ground. Likes to force the pace.

Johnston's Ville (IRE)

92 93

9-y-o b g Commanche Run-Slavesville (Charlottesvilles Flyer)

C Grant (Mrs M B Stephens 3/2) Miss C C Raw

Placings:255/0502/2354/34 (0467)

2001/02: 24^{3}GS, 20^{4}GF

	Starts	1st	2nd	3rd	Win & Pl
Chases	2	0	0	1	819
Career Total	**13**	**0**	**3**	**2**	**3199**

Going: Sf: 0-0 GS: 0-1 Gd: 0-0 GF: - Fm: 0-1
Distance: 2m/2m3: 0-0 2m4-2m7: 0-1 3m+: 0-1
Track: LH: 0-1 RH: 0-1 Tight: 0-0 Gall: 0-0
Aids: Bl: 0-0 Vi: 0-0 Tstrap: 0-0
Best Rating: 105 12/97 Thur 2m sft-hvy NHF

Join The Parade

85 56

6-y-o b m Elmaamul (USA)-Summer Pageant (Chief's Crown (USA))

Mrs P Sly (P Howling 20/10) Peter Curtis

Placings:00 (2683)

2001/02: 16^{0}G, 16^{0}G

	Starts	1st	2nd	3rd	Win & Pl
Hurdles	2	0	0	0	
Career Total	**2**	**0**	**0**	**0**	

Going: Sf: 0-0 GS: 0-0 Gd: 0-2 GF: - Fm: 0-0
Distance: 2m/2m3: 0-2 2m4-2m7: 0-0 3m+: 0-0
Track: LH: 0-2 RH: 0-0 Tight: 0-0 Gall: 0-1
Aids: Bl: 0-0 Vi: 0-0 Tstrap: 0-0
Best Rating: 56 11/01 Weth 2m good Hdl

Joint Account

110 145

12-y-o ch g Sayyaf-Dancing Clara (Billion (USA))

R Tate (Mrs F E Needham 20/2) K Needham

Placings:00/U/14221/132PF1/24-15U3FP11 (4870)

2001/02: 25^{1}G, 25^{5}F, 28^{U}GF, 24^{3}GF, 25^{F}GF, 19^{P}S, 20^{1}GS, 23^{1}GF

	Starts	1st	2nd	3rd	Win & Pl
Chases	8	3	0	1	11588
Career Total	**24**	**7**	**4**	**2**	**20408**

134	4/02	Weth	2m7f110y	D(0-120)HCh	G-F	£5492
126	3/02	MRas	2m4f	E(0-110)HCh	G-S	£3388
125	5/01	Weth	3m1f	H Ch	GD	£2030
112	4/00	Sedg	3m3f	H Ch	GD	£1578
115	5/99	MRas	3m1f	H Ch	G-F	£1062
122	4/99	Hntg	3m	H Ch	GD	£1623
107	5/98	Uttx	2m5f	H Ch	G-F	£1127

Total win prize-money £16304

Going: Sf: 0-1 GS: 1-1 Gd: 1-1 GF: - Fm: 1-5
Distance: 2m/2m3: 0-0 2m4-2m7: 1-2 **3m+: 2-6**
Track: LH: 1-5 RH: 1-2 **Tight: 1-4** Gall: 0-1
Aids: Bl: 0-0 Vi: 0-0 Tstrap: 0-0
Best Rating: 134 4/02 Weth 2m7f110y gd-fm Ch

He has a problem completing, but is capable when things go his way and returned to winning form at Market Rasen in March 2002 and has since scored twice at Wetherby. Suited by three miles and a sound surface.

Jojo (IRE)

12-y-o ch g Buckskin (FR)-Autumn Queen (Menelek)

D M Grissell Mrs John Grist

Placings:06/356F15/3P56/U-P (0326)

2001/02: 21^{P}G

	Starts	1st	2nd	3rd	Win & Pl
Chases	1	0	0	0	
Career Total	**14**	**1**	**0**	**2**	**3333**

93	3/96	Plum	2m4f	E Hdl	SFT	£2406

Total win prize-money £2406

Going: Sf: 0-0 GS: 0-0 Gd: 0-1 GF: - Fm: 0-0
Distance: 2m/2m3: 0-0 2m4-2m7: 0-1 3m+: 0-0
Track: LH: 0-0 RH: 0-1 Tight: 0-1 Gall: 0-0
Aids: Bl: 0-1 Vi: 0-0 Tstrap: 0-0
Best Rating: 93 3/96 Plum 2m4f soft Hdl

Jokers Charm

101 118

11-y-o b g Idiots Delight-By The Lake (Tyrant (USA))

N B Mason N B Mason

Placings:50P/05303/531000422533014440/413665113 0442206-35245 (1527a)

2001/02: 17^{3}G, 17^{5}GF, 17^{2}GF, 16^{4}GF, 19^{5}GF

	Starts	1st	2nd	3rd	Win & Pl
Chases	5	0	1	1	2153
Career Total	**46**	**5**	**5**	**8**	**27603**

119	12/00	Muss	2m	F(0-95)HCh	GD	£2821
119	12/00	Fknm	2m110y	F(0-100)HCh	G-S	£4072
119	9/00	Sedg	2m5f	D(0-120)HCh	GD	£3851
113	11/99	Hexm	2m110y	F(0-95)HCh	GD	£2748
104	7/99	Sedg	2m110y	E Ch	G-F	£3285

Total win prize-money £16778

Going: Sf: 0-0 GS: 0-0 Gd: 0-1 GF: - Fm: 0-4
Distance: 2m/2m3: 0-5 2m4-2m7: 0-0 3m+: 0-0
Track: LH: 0-4 RH: 0-0 Tight: 0-3 Gall: 0-0
Aids: Bl: 0-5 Vi: 0-0 Tstrap: 0-5
Best Rating: 119 2/01 Sedg 2m110y soft Ch

Joking Aside (IRE)

100 123

10-y-o b g Brush Aside (USA)-Primrose Forest (Menelek)

Miss V Haigh (G T Hourigan 13/5) Miss V Haigh

Placings:6/13F2110/4F/24/P5P0020-3400P (3145)

2001/02: 16^{3}YS, 17^{4}G, 16^{0}GS, 16^{0}GS, 16^{P}S

	Starts	1st	2nd	3rd	Win & Pl
Hurdles	5	0	0	1	1327
Career Total	**24**	**3**	**3**	**2**	**17649**

139	4/98	Fair	2m	Hdl	G-Y	£5956
120	3/98	Uttx	2m	D Hdl	GD	£3615
116	12/97	Thur	2m2f	NHF	SH	£2712

Total win prize-money £12285

Going: Sf: 0-1 GS: 0-2 Gd: 0-1 GF: - Fm: 0-0
Distance: 2m/2m3: 0-5 2m4-2m7: 0-0 3m+: 0-0
Track: LH: 0-2 RH: 0-1 Tight: 0-1 Gall: 0-1
Aids: Bl: 0-0 Vi: 0-0 Tstrap: 0-0
Best Rating: 139 4/98 Fair 2m gd-yld Hdl

Goes well at around two miles and acts on ground ranging from good to heavy.

Joli Jazz

87f 54f

4-y-o b f Alhijaz-Thulium (Mansingh (USA))

P F Nicholls Joli Racing

Placings:00 (4743)

2001/02: 18^{0}S, 16^{0}GF

	Starts	1st	2nd	3rd	Win & Pl
NH Flat	2	0	0	0	
Career Total	**2**	**0**	**0**	**0**	

Going: Sf: 0-1 GS: 0-0 Gd: 0-0 GF: - Fm: 0-1
Distance: 2m/2m3: 0-2 2m4-2m7: 0-0 3m+: 0-0
Track: LH: 0-1 RH: 0-1 Tight: 0-1 Gall: 0-0
Aids: Bl: 0-0 Vi: 0-0 Tstrap: 0-0
Best Rating: 54 4/02 Ludl 2m gd-fm NHF

Joli Saddlers

87 95

6-y-o b m Saddlers' Hall (IRE)-Vitality (Young Generation)

P F Nicholls Joli Racing

Placings:2-1 (0680)

2001/02: 22^{1}G

	Starts	1st	2nd	3rd	Win & Pl
Hurdles	1	1	0	0	3052
Career Total	**2**	**1**	**1**	**0**	**3806**

85	6/01	NAbb	2m6f	E Hdl	GD	£3052

Total win prize-money £3052

Going: Sf: 0-0 GS: 0-0 Gd: 1-1 GF: - Fm: 0-0
Distance: 2m/2m3: 0-0 **2m4-2m7: 1-1** 3m+: 0-0
Track: **LH: 1-1** RH: 0-0 **Tight: 1-1** Gall: 0-0
Aids: Bl: 0-0 Vi: 0-0 Tstrap: 0-0
Best Rating: 95 4/01 Font 2m6f110y good Hdl

Jolification

11-y-o b g Joli Wasfi (USA)-Lillylee Lady (USA) (Shecky Greene (USA))

J Honeyball John Honeyball

Placings:PP-P (0231)

2001/02: 24^{P}GF

	Starts	1st	2nd	3rd	Win & Pl

	Starts	1st	2nd	3rd	Win & Pl
Chases	1	0	0	0	
Career Total	3	0	0	0	

Going: Sf: 0-0 GS: 0-0 Gd: 0-0 GF: - Fm: 0-1
Distance: 2m/2m3: 0-0 2m4-2m7: 0-0 3m+: 0-1
Track: LH: 0-0 RH: 0-1 Tight: 0-0 Gall: 0-1
Aids: Bl: 0-1 Vi: 0-0 Tstrap: 0-0
Best Rating:

Jolika (FR)

102f 100f

5-y-o b m Grand Tresor (FR)-Unika Ii (FR) (Rolling Bowl (FR))
L Lungo Dr Kenneth S Fraser

Placings: *4-13* (1657)
2001/02: 16^{1}S, 17^{3}G

	Starts	1st	2nd	3rd	Win & Pl
NH Flat	2	1	0	1	2542
Career Total	3	1	0	1	2542
100 5/01 Prth 2m110y H NHF				SFT	£2289

Total win prize-money £2289

Going: Sf: 1-1 GS: 0-0 Gd: 0-1 GF: - Fm: 0-0
Distance: **2m/2m3: 1-2** 2m4-2m7: 0-0 3m+: 0-0
Track: LH: 0-1 **RH: 1-1** Tight: 0-1 Gall: 0-0
Aids: Bl: 0-0 Vi: 0-0 Tstrap: 0-0
Best Rating: 100 5/01 Prth 2m110y soft NHF

Landed a farcical bumper at Perth in May and was third next time out in October.

Jolirose

81f 59f

7-y-o b m Joligeneration-Rose Red City (Relkino)
Miss V A Stephens D G Stephens

Placings: *0* (1019)
2001/02: 16^{0}G

	Starts	1st	2nd	3rd	Win & Pl
NH Flat	1	0	0	0	
Career Total	1	0	0	0	

Going: Sf: 0-0 GS: 0-0 Gd: 0-1 GF: - Fm: 0-0
Distance: 2m/2m3: 0-1 2m4-2m7: 0-0 3m+: 0-0
Track: LH: 0-1 RH: 0-0 Tight: 0-0 Gall: 0-0
Aids: Bl: 0-0 Vi: 0-0 Tstrap: 0-0
Best Rating: 59 7/01 Worc 2m good NHF

Jollie Bollie (IRE)

115 114

7-y-o b m Husyan (USA)-Jet Travel (Deep Run)
Miss Venetia Williams Mrs Liz Cooper-Mitchell & Mrs Ann Hawke

Placings: *632/1-2P210* (4420)
2001/02: 22^{2}G, 21^{P}G, 20^{2}S, 19^{1}S, 21^{0}GS

	Starts	1st	2nd	3rd	Win & Pl
Hurdles	5	1	2	0	5114
Career Total	9	2	3	1	7482
114 1/02 Hrfd 2m3f110y E Hdl				SFT	£2838
119 4/01 Winc 2m H NHF				SFT	£1673

Total win prize-money £4512

Going: Sf: 1-2 GS: 0-1 Gd: 0-2 GF: - Fm: 0-0
Distance: 2m/2m3: 0-0 **2m4-2m7: 1-5** 3m+: 0-0
Track: LH: 0-3 **RH: 1-1** Tight: 0-1 Gall: 0-1
Aids: Bl: 0-0 Vi: 0-0 Tstrap: 0-0
Best Rating: 119 4/01 Winc 2m soft NHF

A half-sister to useful Storm Alert, she showed useful form in bumpers in the 1999/2000 season. Placed form over hurdles until easily landing a Hereford novice event in January 2002. Stays two miles six and best on soft ground.

Jolly Giant (IRE)

96 79

6-y-o b g Jolly Jake (NZ)-Reve Clair (Deep Run)
P F Nicholls Derek Millard

Placings: 4P (3656)
2001/02: 23^{4}G, 25^{P}S

	Starts	1st	2nd	3rd	Win & Pl
Chases	2	0	0	0	426
Career Total	2	0	0	0	426

Going: Sf: 0-1 GS: 0-0 Gd: 0-1 GF: - Fm: 0-0
Distance: 2m/2m3: 0-0 2m4-2m7: 0-0 3m+: 0-2
Track: LH: 0-0 RH: 0-2 Tight: 0-0 Gall: 0-0
Aids: Bl: 0-0 Vi: 0-0 Tstrap: 0-0
Best Rating: 79 12/01 Extr 2m7f110y good Ch

Jolly Green Giant (IRE)

9-y-o b g Glacial Storm (USA)-Rambling Love (Golden Love)
P R Webber Paul Green

Placings: 2010/1111P-PPP (4016)
2001/02: 20^{P}S, 25^{P}G, 26^{P}GS

	Starts	1st	2nd	3rd	Win & Pl
Chases	3	0	0	0	
Career Total	12	5	1	0	28596
153 3/01 Wwck 3m110y C Ch				HVY	£7392
155 2/01 Hayd 2m6f C Ch				HVY	£7150
159 1/01 Wwck 2m4f110y C Ch				SFT	£6968
133 12/00 Chep 2m3f110y D Ch				HVY	£3789
109 2/00 Sedg 2m5f110y E Hdl				G-S	£2534

Total win prize-money £27834

Going: Sf: 0-1 GS: 0-1 Gd: 0-1 GF: - Fm: 0-0
Distance: 2m/2m3: 0-0 2m4-2m7: 0-1 3m+: 0-2
Track: LH: 0-3 RH: 0-0 Tight: 0-0 Gall: 0-3
Aids: Bl: 0-0 Vi: 0-0 Tstrap: 0-0
Best Rating: 159 1/01 Wwck 2m4f110y soft Ch

Well named, he took to fences wellin 2000/01, winning four times, his most notable scalp being that of Frantic Tan at Warwick. His jumping let him down when favourite against experienced handicappers at Aintree on his final start and he has been pulled up on each of his starts this season. He is effective between two and a half and three miles on soft/heavy ground.

Jolly Hopeful (IRE)

88 92

5-y-o b g Glacial Storm (USA)-Tudor Lady (Green Shoon)
C P Morlock Michael Padfield

Placings: *03* (4726)
2001/02: 16^{0}G, 20^{3}GF

	Starts	1st	2nd	3rd	Win & Pl
NH Flat	1	0	0	0	0
Hurdles	1	0	0	1	383
Career Total	2	0	0	1	383

Going: Sf: 0-0 GS: 0-0 Gd: 0-1 GF: - Fm: 0-1
Distance: 2m/2m3: 0-1 2m4-2m7: 0-1 3m+: 0-0
Track: LH: 0-1 RH: 0-1 Tight: 0-0 Gall: 0-0
Aids: Bl: 0-0 Vi: 0-0 Tstrap: 0-0
Best Rating: 99 2/02 Kemp 2m good NHF

Jolly Jack (IRE)

84 68

11-y-o b g Jolly Jake (NZ)-Hay Party (Party Mink)
Simon T Lewis Simon T Lewis

Placings: P/PPPP50P (4316)
2001/02: 24^{P}G, 24^{P}S, 21^{P}HY, 24^{P}HY, 19^{5}HY, 22^{0}S, 24^{P}HY

	Starts	1st	2nd	3rd	Win & Pl
Hurdles	7	0	0	0	0
Career Total	8	0	0	0	0

Going: Sf: 0-6 GS: 0-0 Gd: 0-1 GF: - Fm: 0-0
Distance: 2m/2m3: 0-0 2m4-2m7: 0-3 3m+: 0-4
Track: LH: 0-4 RH: 0-3 Tight: 0-4 Gall: 0-0
Aids: Bl: 0-0 Vi: 0-0 Tstrap: 0-0
Best Rating: 68 2/02 Hrfd 2m3f110y heavy Hdl

Jolly Joe (IRE)

86f 69f

5-y-o b g Jolly Jake (NZ)-The Bread Robber (Mandalus)
Simon T Lewis Simon T Lewis

Placings: *6* (4571)
2001/02: 16^{6}G

	Starts	1st	2nd	3rd	Win & Pl
NH Flat	1	0	0	0	0
Career Total	1	0	0	0	0

Going: Sf: 0-0 GS: 0-0 Gd: 0-1 GF: - Fm: 0-0
Distance: 2m/2m3: 0-1 2m4-2m7: 0-0 3m+: 0-0
Track: LH: 0-0 RH: 0-1 Tight: 0-0 Gall: 0-0
Aids: Bl: 0-0 Vi: 0-0 Tstrap: 0-0
Best Rating: 69 4/02 Towc 2m good NHF

Jolly John (IRE)

99 (97c) 94

11-y-o b g Jolly Jake (NZ)-Golden Seekers (Manado)
C J Mann (M F Morris 13/5) E P F De Plumpton Hunter

Placings: 00/440U/B50303/603042P6/0P1UF0/065365-4433235P (4588)
2001/02: 20^{4}G, 20^{4}G, 22^{3}HY, 20^{3}GS, 20^{2}S, 20^{3}S, 20^{5}S, 22^{P}G

	Starts	1st	2nd	3rd	Win & Pl
Hurdles	7	0	1	3	1976
Chases	1	0	0	0	355
Career Total	40	1	2	7	8337
103 11/99 Thur 2m2f Ch				Y-S	£3850

Total win prize-money £3850

Going: Sf: 0-4 GS: 0-1 Gd: 0-3 GF: - Fm: 0-0
Distance: 2m/2m3: 0-0 2m4-2m7: 0-8 3m+: 0-0
Track: LH: 0-3 RH: 0-4 Tight: 0-3 Gall: 0-2
Aids: Bl: 0-0 Vi: 0-0 Tstrap: 0-0
Best Rating: 107 10/97 Gowr 2m2f gd-fm Ch

Ex-Irish dual-purpose individual, he has been extremely uninspiring over both hurdles and fences, scoring just once from 38 attempts. He returned to hurdles after joining Charlie Mann's yard in October.

Jolly Minster

8-y-o b g Minster Son-Dash Cascade (Absalom)
D G Atkinson (Mrs M Reveley 20/1) D G Atkinson

Placings: *46*/043442/112 (4335)
2001/02: 21^{1}S, 27^{1}S, 27^{2}S

	Starts	1st	2nd	3rd	Win & Pl
Chases	3	2	1	0	3355
Career Total	**11**	**2**	**2**	**1**	**4483**

106 3/02 Sedg 3m3f H Ch SFT £1484
99 2/02 Sedg 2m5f H Ch SFT £1443
Total win prize-money £2927

Going: Sf: 2-3 GS: 0-0 Gd: 0-0 GF: - Fm: 0-0
Distance: 2m/2m3: 0-0 2m4-2m7: 1-1 3m+: 1-2
Track: **LH: 2-3** RH: 0-0 **Tight: 2-3** Gall: 0-0
Aids: Bl: 0-0 Vi: 0-0 Tstrap: 0-0
Best Rating: 106 3/02 Sedg 3m3f soft Ch

Point winner who has quickly made his mark in Hunter Chases admittedly at a modest level. Doesn't look a real stayer.

Jolly Red (FR)

83f

5-y-o ch g Cyborg (FR)-Orne Ii (FR) (Beau Fixe)
M C Pipe Terry Neill

Placings: *0* (2142)
2001/02: 17^{0}G

	Starts	1st	2nd	3rd	Win & Pl
NH Flat	1	0	0	0	
Career Total	**1**	**0**	**0**	**0**	

Going: Sf: 0-0 GS: 0-0 Gd: 0-1 GF: - Fm: 0-0
Distance: 2m/2m3: 0-1 2m4-2m7: 0-0 3m+: 0-0
Track: LH: 0-0 RH: 0-0 Tight: 0-0 Gall: 0-0
Aids: Bl: 0-0 Vi: 0-0 Tstrap: 0-0
Best Rating: 83 11/01 Tntn 2m1f good NHF

Jolly Rich

8-y-o gr m My Richard-Jolly Girl (Jolly Me)
J Neville Mrs P K Chick

Placings: *26/03/5*-PPSP (4173)
2001/02: 21^{P}G, 22^{P}G, 24^{S}S, 25^{P}GS

	Starts	1st	2nd	3rd	Win & Pl
Hurdles	4	0	0	0	
Career Total	**9**	**0**	**1**	**1**	**637**

Going: Sf: 0-1 GS: 0-1 Gd: 0-2 GF: - Fm: 0-0
Distance: 2m/2m3: 0-0 2m4-2m7: 0-2 3m+: 0-2
Track: LH: 0-1 RH: 0-2 Tight: 0-2 Gall: 0-0
Aids: Bl: 0-0 Vi: 0-1 Tstrap: 0-0
Best Rating: 104 4/00 Asct 2m110y soft NHF

Joly Bey (FR)

5-y-o ch g Beyssac (FR)-Rivolie (FR) (Mistigri)
G Macaire A M Chiche

Placings: *052*
2001/02: 18^{0}S, 17^{5}HY, 22^{2}VS

	Starts	1st	2nd	3rd	Win & Pl
NH Flat	1	0	0	0	0
Hurdles	1	0	0	0	1534
Chases	1	0	1	0	6184
Career Total	**3**	**0**	**1**	**0**	**7718**

Going: Sf: 0-2 GS: 0-0 Gd: 0-0 GF: - Fm: 0-0
Distance: 2m/2m3: 0-2 2m4-2m7: 0-1 3m+: 0-0
Track: LH: 0-1 RH: 0-0 Tight: 0-1 Gall: 0-0
Aids: Bl: 0-0 Vi: 0-0 Tstrap: 0-0
Best Rating: 69 2/02 Font 2m2f110y soft NHF

Joly Bois (FR)

91 78

5-y-o ch g Mister Sicy (FR)-Brindille Jolie (FR) (Lee (FR))
M C Pipe B A Kilpatrick

Placings: PP4 (4654)
2001/02: 16^{P}S, 16^{P}G, 17^{4}GS

	Starts	1st	2nd	3rd	Win & Pl
Hurdles	3	0	0	0	0
Career Total	**3**	**0**	**0**	**0**	**0**

Going: Sf: 0-1 GS: 0-1 Gd: 0-1 GF: - Fm: 0-0
Distance: 2m/2m3: 0-3 2m4-2m7: 0-0 3m+: 0-0
Track: LH: 0-1 RH: 0-2 Tight: 0-1 Gall: 0-1
Aids: Bl: 0-0 Vi: 0-0 Tstrap: 0-0
Best Rating: 78 4/02 Tntn 2m1f gd-sft Hdl

French import who has been disappointing over hurdles to date.

Jona Holley

77 38

9-y-o b g Sharpo-Spurned (USA) (Robellino (USA))
A Streeter Malt 'N' Hops

Placings: 44/0040/P156/060 (3164)
2001/02: 16^{0}S, 16^{6}HY, 16^{0}S

	Starts	1st	2nd	3rd	Win & Pl
Hurdles	3	0	0	0	0
Career Total	**13**	**1**	**0**	**0**	**2495**

98 11/99 Uttx 2m F(0-100)HHdl SFT £2253
Total win prize-money £2253

Going: Sf: 0-3 GS: 0-0 Gd: 0-0 GF: - Fm: 0-0
Distance: 2m/2m3: 0-3 2m4-2m7: 0-0 3m+: 0-0
Track: LH: 0-2 RH: 0-1 Tight: 0-0 Gall: 0-1
Aids: Bl: 0-2 Vi: 0-1 Tstrap: 0-0
Best Rating: 98 11/99 Uttx 2m soft Hdl

Jonaem (IRE)

100(102c) (81c)70

12-y-o b g Mazaad-Priors Mistress (Sallust)
Mrs E Slack Mrs Evelyn Slack

Placings: 00P0/25000236/55412600063/F502/P11/F0 06/3-P00 (4855)
2001/02: 24^{P}G, 25^{0}GF, 20^{0}G

	Starts	1st	2nd	3rd	Win & Pl
Chases	3	0	0	0	
Career Total	**38**	**3**	**4**	**3**	**14024**

104 4/99 Sedg 3m3f F(0-110)HCh G-F £3852
99 4/99 Sedg 3m3f D Ch G-S £3606
82 10/96 Carl 2m4f110y E(0-100)HHdl FRM £2332
Total win prize-money £9791

Going: Sf: 0-0 GS: 0-0 Gd: 0-2 GF: - Fm: 0-1
Distance: 2m/2m3: 0-0 2m4-2m7: 0-1 3m+: 0-2
Track: LH: 0-3 RH: 0-0 Tight: 0-0 Gall: 0-0
Aids: Bl: 0-0 Vi: 0-0 Tstrap: 0-0
Best Rating: 104 4/99 Sedg 3m3f gd-fm Ch

Moderate staying chaser, appreciates a sound surface.

Jones Lad (IRE)

100(101h) (85h)106

7-y-o b g Posen (USA)-Dame's Folly (IRE) (King's Lake (USA))
R H Buckler The Crop Circle

Placings: 0063/005010500/62P-0500520 (4847)
2001/02: 19^{0}G, 19^{5}GS, 19^{0}G, 22^{0}G, 17^{5}G, 21^{2}GF, 20^{0}G

	Starts	1st	2nd	3rd	Win & Pl
Hurdles	7	0	1	0	850
Career Total	**23**	**1**	**2**	**1**	**4045**

85 9/99 Clon 2m4f Hdl G-F £2217
Total win prize-money £2218

Going: Sf: 0-0 GS: 0-1 Gd: 0-5 GF: - Fm: 0-1
Distance: 2m/2m3: 0-2 2m4-2m7: 0-5 3m+: 0-0
Track: LH: 0-2 RH: 0-4 Tight: 0-3 Gall: 0-0
Aids: Bl: 0-0 Vi: 0-0 Tstrap: 0-0
Best Rating: 92 10/00 Ludl 2m5f gd-fm Hdl

Moderate hurdler, suited by good/fast ground and is suited by being ridden positively. Respectable debut over fences at Newton Abbot June 2002 despite being no match for the useful Golden Alpha. Narrowly beaten on handicap debut over same course and distance the following month.

Jongleur Collonges (FR)

99f 104f

5-y-o gr g Royal Charter (FR)-Soubrette Collonge (FR) (Saumon (FR))
R H Alner Andrew Wiles

Placings: *345* (4158)
2001/02: 17^{3}S, 16^{4}S, 16^{5}GS

	Starts	1st	2nd	3rd	Win & Pl
NH Flat	3	0	0	1	224
Career Total	**3**	**0**	**0**	**1**	**224**

Going: Sf: 0-2 GS: 0-1 Gd: 0-0 GF: - Fm: 0-0
Distance: 2m/2m3: 0-3 2m4-2m7: 0-0 3m+: 0-0
Track: LH: 0-0 RH: 0-2 Tight: 0-1 Gall: 0-0
Aids: Bl: 0-0 Vi: 0-0 Tstrap: 0-0
Best Rating: 104 3/02 Sand 2m110y gd-sft NHF

Some ability in bumpers and should make a nice novice hurdler over two and a half miles.

Jonmar (IRE)

78(96h) (68h)55

9-y-o b/br g Mandalus-Queens Tricks (Le Bavard (FR))
K Bell North Farm Partnership

Placings: *0/3/30*-00035 (1223)
2001/02: 22^{0}GF, 21^{0}G, 24^{0}G, 24^{3}GF, 20^{5}GF

	Starts	1st	2nd	3rd	Win & Pl
Hurdles	3	0	0	0	0
Chases	2	0	0	1	523
Career Total	**9**	**0**	**0**	**3**	**1270**

Going: Sf: 0-0 GS: 0-0 Gd: 0-2 GF: - Fm: 0-3
Distance: 2m/2m3: 0-0 2m4-2m7: 0-3 3m+: 0-2
Track: LH: 0-2 RH: 0-1 Tight: 0-2 Gall: 0-0
Aids: Bl: 0-0 Vi: 0-0 Tstrap: 0-1
Best Rating: 89 2/01 Ludl 2m5f gd-sft Hdl

Jordan's Ridge (IRE)

107(110h) (99h)118

6-y-o b/br g Indian Ridge-Sadie Jordan (USA) (Hail The Pirates (USA))

P Monteith Allan W Melville

Placings:0/05002442200-33525341 **(4786)**

2001/02: 16^{3}S, 16^{3}S, 20^{5}S, 16^{2}GS, 16^{5}HY, 24^{3}S, 22^{4}S, 20^{1}F

	Starts	1st	2nd	3rd	Win & Pl
Hurdles	8	1	1	3	3600
Career Total	**20**	**1**	**4**	**3**	**6121**

102	4/02	Newc	2m4f	G(0-95)HHdl	FRM	£1792

Total win prize-money £1792

Going: Sf: 0-6 GS: 0-1 Gd: 0-0 GF: - Fm: 1-1
Distance: 2m/2m3: 0-4 **2m4-2m7: 1-3** 3m+: 0-1
Track: **LH: 1-5** RH: 0-3 Tight: 0-4 **Gall: 1-1**
Aids: Bl: 0-0 Vi: 0-0 Tstrap: 0-0
Best Rating: 102 4/02 Newc 2m4f firm Hdl

Plating-class hurdler, perhaps not the heartiest of battlers. Stays two and a half miles.

Jorn Du Soleil (FR)

88 95

5-y-o ch g Murmure (FR)-Ina Du Soleil (FR) (Or De Chine)

P F Nicholls (G Macaire 21/9) D J & F A Jackson

Placings:200 **(3696)**

2001/02: 16^{2}, 18^{0}VS, 16^{0}S

	Starts	1st	2nd	3rd	Win & Pl
Hurdles	3	0	1	0	1939
Career Total	**3**	**0**	**1**	**0**	**1939**

Going: Sf: 0-1 GS: 0-0 Gd: 0-0 GF: - Fm: 0-0
Distance: 2m/2m3: 0-3 2m4-2m7: 0-0 3m+: 0-0
Track: LH: 0-1 RH: 0-0 Tight: 0-0 Gall: 0-1
Aids: Bl: 0-0 Vi: 0-0 Tstrap: 0-0
Best Rating: 95 2/02 Newb 2m110y soft Hdl

Jorodama King

102 93

8-y-o b g Lighter-Princess Hecate (Autre Prince)

O Sherwood (Mrs P Ford 5/5) Sabrinarchie Partnership

Placings:*200*U/5**6PF**-P**20U0** **(2273)**

2001/02: 26^{P}G, 24^{2}G, 22^{0}S, 26^{U}G, 24^{0}G

	Starts	1st	2nd	3rd	Win & Pl
Hurdles	1	0	0	0	0
Chases	4	0	1	0	1610
Career Total	**13**	**0**	**2**	**0**	**2066**

Going: Sf: 0-1 GS: 0-0 Gd: 0-4 GF: - Fm: 0-0
Distance: 2m/2m3: 0-0 2m4-2m7: 0-1 3m+: 0-4
Track: LH: 0-2 RH: 0-1 Tight: 0-2 Gall: 0-0
Aids: Bl: 0-0 Vi: 0-0 Tstrap: 0-0
Best Rating: 93 9/01 Bang 3m110y good Ch

Wide-margin winner of a poor novices' chase at Plumpton in late April 2002, has looked unenthusiastic since.

Jorodec (IRE)

87 79

11-y-o br g Over The River (FR)-Augusta Victoria (Callernish)

Mrs W D Sykes D E Edwards

Placings:P/06-66 **(0494)**

2001/02: 20^{6}G, 25^{6}G

	Starts	1st	2nd	3rd	Win & Pl
Chases	2	0	0	0	0
Career Total	**5**	**0**	**0**	**0**	**0**

Going: Sf: 0-0 GS: 0-0 Gd: 0-2 GF: - Fm: 0-0
Distance: 2m/2m3: 0-0 2m4-2m7: 0-1 3m+: 0-1
Track: LH: 0-1 RH: 0-1 Tight: 0-0 Gall: 0-0
Aids: Bl: 0-0 Vi: 0-0 Tstrap: 0-0
Best Rating: 79 5/01 Weth 2m4f110y good Ch

Josanjamic

89f 89f

5-y-o b m King Luthier-Ndita (Be My Native (USA))

W S Kittow Kenneth Heard

Placings:*23* **(1559)**

2001/02: 16^{2}GF, 16^{3}G

	Starts	1st	2nd	3rd	Win & Pl
NH Flat	2	0	1	1	664
Career Total	**2**	**0**	**1**	**1**	**664**

Going: Sf: 0-0 GS: 0-0 Gd: 0-1 GF: - Fm: 0-1
Distance: 2m/2m3: 0-2 2m4-2m7: 0-0 3m+: 0-0
Track: LH: 0-2 RH: 0-0 Tight: 0-0 Gall: 0-0
Aids: Bl: 0-0 Vi: 0-0 Tstrap: 0-0
Best Rating: 89 10/01 Chep 2m110y good NHF

Whose dam won twice over a mile as a three-year-old, has made a promising start to her career.

Joshua's Bay

85f 90f

4-y-o b g Karinga Bay-Bonita Blakeney (Baron Blakeney)

J R Jenkins Mr & Mrs Leon Shack

Placings:2 **(4242)**

2001/02: 16^{2}GF

	Starts	1st	2nd	3rd	Win & Pl
NH Flat	1	0	1	0	454
Career Total	**1**	**0**	**1**	**0**	**454**

Going: Sf: 0-0 GS: 0-0 Gd: 0-0 GF: - Fm: 0-1
Distance: 2m/2m3: 0-1 2m4-2m7: 0-0 3m+: 0-0
Track: LH: 0-0 RH: 0-1 Tight: 0-0 Gall: 0-1
Aids: Bl: 0-0 Vi: 0-0 Tstrap: 0-0
Best Rating: 90 3/02 Hntg 2m110y gd-fm NHF

Runner-up on his debut in a bumper at Huntingdon in March.

Joshua's Vision (IRE)

11-y-o b g Vision (USA)-Perle's Fashion (Sallust)

Lady Susan Brooke (R Lee 17/2) Lady Susan Brooke

Placings:*25/32*P02/02/**FF**/0566**P3**/P404523F-5 **(4132)**

2001/02: 25^{5}G

	Starts	1st	2nd	3rd	Win & Pl
Chases	1	0	0	0	0
Career Total	**26**	**0**	**5**	**3**	**4249**

Going: Sf: 0-0 GS: 0-0 Gd: 0-1 GF: - Fm: 0-0
Distance: 2m/2m3: 0-0 2m4-2m7: 0-0 3m+: 0-1
Track: LH: 0-0 RH: 0-1 Tight: 0-0 Gall: 0-0
Aids: Bl: 0-0 Vi: 0-0 Tstrap: 0-0
Best Rating: 98 4/96 Worc 2m gd-fm Hdl

Joss (FR)

66 34

5-y-o b g Kadalko (FR)-Pasiphae (FR) (Signani (FR))

Ian Williams Sir Robert Ogden

Placings:*0*-F0 **(3225)**

2001/02: 17^{F}GS, 22^{0}G

	Starts	1st	2nd	3rd	Win & Pl
Hurdles	2	0	0	0	
Career Total	**3**	**0**	**0**	**0**	

Going: Sf: 0-0 GS: 0-1 Gd: 0-1 GF: - Fm: 0-0
Distance: 2m/2m3: 0-1 2m4-2m7: 0-1 3m+: 0-0
Track: LH: 0-0 RH: 0-2 Tight: 0-0 Gall: 0-0
Aids: Bl: 0-0 Vi: 0-0 Tstrap: 0-0
Best Rating: 52 4/01 Newb 2m110y soft NHF

Joss Bay

69 40

10-y-o ch g Nearly A Hand-Maranzi (Jimmy Reppin)

M A Barnes (T P Tate 20/1) Gordon E Davidson

Placings:F/400/**F**/0 **(3819)**

2001/02: 17^{0}S

	Starts	1st	2nd	3rd	Win & Pl
Hurdles	1	0	0	0	
Career Total	**6**	**0**	**0**	**0**	**0**

Going: Sf: 0-1 GS: 0-0 Gd: 0-0 GF: - Fm: 0-0
Distance: 2m/2m3: 0-1 2m4-2m7: 0-0 3m+: 0-0
Track: LH: 0-1 RH: 0-0 Tight: 0-1 Gall: 0-0
Aids: Bl: 0-0 Vi: 0-0 Tstrap: 0-0
Best Rating: 69 12/97 Catt 2m3f good Hdl

Well held in novice hurdles. Failed to complete on his four starts between the flags.

Joss Naylor (IRE)

115 148

7-y-o b g Be My Native (USA)-Sister Ida (Bustino)

J J O'Neill Darren C Mercer

Placings:*15-1*351125 **(4665)**

2001/02: 17^{1}GS, 20^{3}G, 21^{5}S, 20^{1}S, 21^{1}S, 21^{2}GS, 24^{5}G

	Starts	1st	2nd	3rd	Win & Pl
NH Flat	1	1	0	0	1687
Hurdles	6	2	1	1	32311
Career Total	**9**	**4**	**1**	**1**	**35587**

148	2/02	Wwck	2m5f	B Hdl	SFT	£10497
125	1/02	Donc	2m4f	D Hdl	SFT	£3727
119	10/01	Carl	2m1f	H NHF	G-S	£1687
117	10/00	Chep	2m110y	H NHF	G-S	£1589

Total win prize-money £17502

Going: Sf: 2-3 GS: 1-2 Gd: 0-2 GF: - Fm: 0-0
Distance: 2m/2m3: 1-1 **2m4-2m7: 2-5** 3m+: 0-1
Track: LH: 1-4 RH: 1-1 Tight: 0-2 **Gall: 1-2**
Aids: Bl: 0-0 Vi: 0-0 Tstrap: 0-0
Best Rating: 148 2/02 Wwck 2m5f soft Hdl

Winner of two bumpers, he has developed into a very useful novice hurdler and ran a blinder in the Coral Cup at the 2002 Festival. Acts on good to soft/soft ground and is effective at around two miles four furlongs.

Jour J (FR)

105 145

5-y-o gr g Royal Charter (FR)-Ability (FR) (Olmeto)

M C Pipe (G Cherel 5/11) Stef Stefanou

Placings:331F12P (4264)
2001/02: 18^{3}VS, 18^{3}VS, 21^{1}VS, 22^{F}G, 20^{1}S, 20^{2}S, 19^{P}S

	Starts	1st	2nd	3rd	Win & Pl
Hurdles	2	0	0	2	6402
Chases	5	2	1	0	14588
Career Total	**7**	**2**	**1**	**2**	**20990**

145	1/02	Wwck	2m4f110y	D Ch	SFT	£4426
	11/01	Nant	2m5f110y	Ch	VS	£8244

Total win prize-money £12671

Going: Sf: 1-3 GS: 0-0 Gd: 0-1 GF: - Fm: 0-0
Distance: 2m/2m3: 0-2 **2m4-2m7: 2-5** 3m+: 0-0
Track: **LH: 1-3** RH: 0-0 Tight: 0-1 Gall: 0-1
Aids: Bl: 0-0 Vi: 0-0 Tstrap: 0-0
Best Rating: 145 1/02 Wwck 2m4f110y soft Ch

A winner over fences in France, he fell at the first on his British debut but made all at Warwick next time over two miles four and a half furlongs. Just touched off at Fontwell. A keen sort, he likes soft ground. Not the safest of conveyances.

Jowoody

108(93h) (101h)121

9-y-o ch m Gunner B-Maskwood (Precipice Wood)
E W Tuer (Mrs M Reveley 22/3) Tagwood Syndicate

Placings:0/34322564/454111/**463P-31UF3346** (4748)
2001/02: 28^{3}GS, 29^{1}S, 28^{U}S, 26^{F}HY, 26^{3}S, 21^{3}HY, 32^{4}HY, 26^{6}GF

	Starts	1st	2nd	3rd	Win & Pl
Hurdles	1	0	0	1	474
Chases	7	1	0	2	8621
Career Total	**27**	**4**	**2**	**6**	**19064**

121	12/01	Ayr	3m5f	E(0-115)HCh	SFT	£3178
106	2/99	Newc	3m	F(0-105)HHdl	G-S	£2155
98	1/99	Ayr	3m110y	D(0-110)HHdl	HVY	£2862
93	1/99	MRas	3m	F(0-100)HHdl	SFT	£1821

Total win prize-money £10017

Going: Sf: 1-6 GS: 0-1 Gd: 0-0 GF: - Fm: 0-1
Distance: 2m/2m3: 0-0 2m4-2m7: 0-1 **3m+: 1-7**
Track: **LH: 1-5** RH: 0-2 Tight: 0-2 Gall: 0-1
Aids: Bl: 0-0 Vi: 0-0 Tstrap: 0-0
Best Rating: 121 12/01 Ayr 3m5f soft Ch

Fair staying chaser, suited by soft ground but handles faster.

Joy De Disse (FR)

5-y-o b g Grand Tresor (FR)-Surprise De L'Isle (FR) (Rubloff (USA))
N G Richards Ashleybank Investments Limited

Placings:0 (4499)
2001/02: 16^{0}G

	Starts	1st	2nd	3rd	Win & Pl
NH Flat	1	0	0	0	
Career Total	**1**	**0**	**0**	**0**	

Going: Sf: 0-0 GS: 0-0 Gd: 0-1 GF: - Fm: 0-0
Distance: 2m/2m3: 0-1 2m4-2m7: 0-0 3m+: 0-0
Track: LH: 0-1 RH: 0-0 Tight: 0-0 Gall: 0-0
Aids: Bl: 0-0 Vi: 0-0 Tstrap: 0-0
Best Rating:

Joy For Life (IRE)

101 100

11-y-o b m Satco (FR)-Joy's Toy (Wolverlife)

R M Stronge Robert Stronge

Placings:05U4/P20064/**PP2213/5023/2P0P3F/3-P510** (4503)
2001/02: 24^{P}G, 26^{5}G, 24^{1}HY, 26^{0}G

	Starts	1st	2nd	3rd	Win & Pl
Chases	4	1	0	0	4108
Career Total	**31**	**2**	**5**	**4**	**14361**

100	3/02	Sthl	3m110y	D(0-115)HCh	HVY	£4108
112	4/98	Asct	3m110y	H Ch	G-S	£2736

Total win prize-money £6844

Going: Sf: 1-1 GS: 0-0 Gd: 0-3 GF: - Fm: 0-0
Distance: 2m/2m3: 0-0 2m4-2m7: 0-0 **3m+: 1-4**
Track: **LH: 1-2** RH: 0-0 **Tight: 1-2** Gall: 0-0
Aids: Bl: 0-0 Vi: 0-0 Tstrap: 0-0
Best Rating: 112 3/00 Hrfd 3m1f110y good Ch

Modest chaser, stays three miles plus and acts on soft ground.

Joyeux Royal (FR)

102 103

5-y-o b g Cyborg (FR)-Samba Du Cochet (FR) (Tanlas (FR))
P F Nicholls Barry Fulton, Liam Brady, Tony Hayward

Placings:40-02125 (4644)
2001/02: 22^{0}G, 16^{2}S, 16^{1}G, 16^{2}G, 16^{5}G

	Starts	1st	2nd	3rd	Win & Pl
Hurdles	5	1	2	0	5753
Career Total	**7**	**1**	**2**	**0**	**5753**

103	12/01	Winc	2m	F(0-95)HHdl	GD	£2709

Total win prize-money £2709

Going: Sf: 0-1 GS: 0-0 Gd: 1-4 GF: - Fm: 0-0
Distance: **2m/2m3: 1-4** 2m4-2m7: 0-1 3m+: 0-0
Track: LH: 0-0 **RH: 1-5** Tight: 0-0 Gall: 0-0
Aids: Bl: 0-0 Vi: 0-0 **Tstrap: 1-4**
Best Rating: 103 1/02 Winc 2m good Hdl

An ex-French novice hurdler, has been lightly-raced and showed his first sign of form in a modest handicap at Sandown in the autumn of 2001, then went one better in a Wincanton novice hurdle two months later. Suited by two miles and a sound surface and a tongue tie.

Judaic Ways

106(99h) (72h)116

8-y-o b g Rudimentary (USA)-Judeah (Great Nephew)
H D Daly D Sandells & T Broderick

Placings:604/5004F0P0/**6FF14-P1P12PP0** (4686)
2001/02: 25^{P}G, 23^{1}G, 24^{P}GF, 24^{1}GF, 27^{2}G, 25^{P}GS, 24^{P}GS, 26^{0}GF

	Starts	1st	2nd	3rd	Win & Pl
Hurdles	1	0	0	0	0
Chases	7	2	1	0	10468
Career Total	**24**	**3**	**1**	**0**	**15598**

115	11/01	Ludl	3m	E(0-115)HCh	G-F	£4810
105	7/01	Worc	2m7f110y	F(0-100)HCh	GD	£3209
104	2/01	Ludl	3m	F(0-95)HCh	GD	£4634

Total win prize-money £12655

Going: Sf: 0-0 GS: 0-2 Gd: 1-3 GF: - Fm: 1-3
Distance: 2m/2m3: 0-0 2m4-2m7: 0-0 **3m+: 2-8**
Track: LH: 1-2 RH: 1-6 **Tight: 1-4** Gall: 0-0
Aids: Bl: 0-0 Vi: 0-0 Tstrap: 0-0
Best Rating: 116 12/01 Ludl 3m3f110y good Ch

Useful handicap chaser, suited by fast ground. Goes well at Ludlow.

Judicious (IRE)

65 16

5-y-o b g Fairy King (USA)-Kama Tashoof (Mtoto)
C J Mann (G Wragg 12/7) P M Warren

Placings:P (4724)
2001/02: 16^{P}GF

	Starts	1st	2nd	3rd	Win & Pl
Hurdles	1	0	0	0	
Career Total	**1**	**0**	**0**	**0**	

Going: Sf: 0-0 GS: 0-0 Gd: 0-0 GF: - Fm: 0-1
Distance: 2m/2m3: 0-1 2m4-2m7: 0-0 3m+: 0-0
Track: LH: 0-1 RH: 0-0 Tight: 0-0 Gall: 0-0
Aids: Bl: 0-0 Vi: 0-0 Tstrap: 0-0
Best Rating:

Judicious Norman (IRE)

11-y-o br g Strong Gale-Smart Fashion (Carlburg)
Ms K J Self E O Steward

Placings:60/U05P/**F3F35/5P4/P0/F40** (0426)
2001/02: 21^{F}GF, 21^{4}G, 26^{0}G

	Starts	1st	2nd	3rd	Win & Pl
Chases	3	0	0	0	115
Career Total	**19**	**0**	**0**	**2**	**1219**

Going: Sf: 0-0 GS: 0-0 Gd: 0-2 GF: - Fm: 0-1
Distance: 2m/2m3: 0-0 2m4-2m7: 0-2 3m+: 0-1
Track: LH: 0-1 RH: 0-1 Tight: 0-2 Gall: 0-0
Aids: Bl: 0-0 Vi: 0-0 Tstrap: 0-3
Best Rating: 92 3/96 Newb 2m110y gd-sft Hdl

Judo Roses (FR)

72 16

5-y-o gr g Royal Charter (FR)-Catty Des Roses (FR) (Vorias (USA))
G Macaire G Ghilardi

Placings:30 (3805)
2001/02: 17^{3}G, 22^{0}S

	Starts	1st	2nd	3rd	Win & Pl
Hurdles	2	0	0	1	1018
Career Total	**2**	**0**	**0**	**1**	**1018**

Going: Sf: 0-1 GS: 0-0 Gd: 0-1 GF: - Fm: 0-0
Distance: 2m/2m3: 0-1 2m4-2m7: 0-1 3m+: 0-0
Track: LH: 0-1 RH: 0-0 Tight: 0-1 Gall: 0-0
Aids: Bl: 0-0 Vi: 0-0 Tstrap: 0-0
Best Rating: 16 2/02 Font 2m6f110y soft Hdl

Juke Box Billy (IRE)

14-y-o ch g Kemal (FR)-Friendly Circle (Crash Course)
Miss V J Parvin J H Hewitt

Placings:00/04100O0/4035420/221F232P/5425540/1231/F400/65/46-P0 (0585)
2001/02: 22^{P}G, 24^{0}GF

	Starts	1st	2nd	3rd	Win & Pl
Chases	2	0	0	0	
Career Total	**45**	**4**	**7**	**3**	**18847**

100	3/98	Newc	3m	E(0-115)HCh	G-F	£3032
97	11/97	Hexm	2m4f110y	F(0-105)HCh	G-F	£2976
89	12/95	Sedg	2m5f	F(0-105)HCh	GD	£2860
80	12/93	Muss	2m4f	HHdl	G-F	£1882

Total win prize-money £10751

Going: Sf: 0-0 GS: 0-0 Gd: 0-1 GF: - Fm: 0-1
Distance: 2m/2m3: 0-0 2m4-2m7: 0-1 3m+: 0-1
Track: LH: 0-1 RH: 0-1 Tight: 0-2 Gall: 0-0
Aids: Bl: 0-0 Vi: 0-0 Tstrap: 0-2
Best Rating: 100 4/99 Sedg 2m5f firm Ch

Julie's Leader (IRE)

99(111h) (125h)112

8-y-o b g Supreme Leader-Parkavoureen (Deep Run)
P F Nicholls T And J A Curry

Placings:0/U4F14/1U33-32041 (4641)
2001/02: 24^{3}GF, 24^{2}GS, 24^{0}S, 24^{4}S, 24^{1}G

	Starts	1st	2nd	3rd	Win & Pl
Hurdles	3	0	1	1	2983
Chases	2	1	0	0	5517
Career Total	**15**	**3**	**1**	**3**	**16300**

97	4/02	Ludl	3m	D Ch	GD	£5200
125	1/01	Tntn	3m110y	F(0-110)HHdl	HVY	£3262
105	3/00	Tntn	3m110y	E Hdl	GD	£2472

Total win prize-money £10934

Going: Sf: 0-2 GS: 0-1 Gd: 1-1 GF: - Fm: 0-1
Distance: 2m/2m3: 0-0 2m4-2m7: 0-0 **3m+: 1-5**
Track: LH: 0-3 **RH: 1-2 Tight: 1-2** Gall: 0-0
Aids: Bl: 0-0 Vi: 0-0 Tstrap: 0-0
Best Rating: 125 11/01 Chep 3m gd-sft Hdl

Out of an Irish bumper winner. Won twice at Taunton over hurdles over three miles. Tried over fences, he scored at Ludlow in April 2002. Acts on most types of ground bar a fast surface, appreciates a sharp, right-handed track.

Jultara (IRE)

(55h)

13-y-o ch g Strong Statement (USA)-La Bise (Callernish)
Ian Williams Alan C Elliot

Placings:3135/013522P/U2211/FU3P/633342/1132/4 P-P (0217)
2001/02: 25^{P}GF

	Starts	1st	2nd	3rd	Win & Pl
Chases	1	0	0	0	
Career Total	**33**	**6**	**6**	**8**	**48107**

133	6/99	MRas	3m1f	D(0-120)HCh	GD	£3764
136	5/99	Winc	3m1f110y	D(0-120)HCh	FRM	£4377
133	4/97	Asct	3m110y	C HCh	G-F	£7230
120	3/97	Asct	3m110y	B Ch	GD	£10892
103	1/96	Font	2m6f	E Hdl	SFT	£2678
94	1/95	Towc	2m	H NHF	HVY	£2005

Total win prize-money £30946

Going: Sf: 0-0 GS: 0-0 Gd: 0-0 GF: - Fm: 0-1
Distance: 2m/2m3: 0-0 2m4-2m7: 0-0 3m+: 0-1
Track: LH: 0-0 RH: 0-1 Tight: 0-0 Gall: 0-0
Aids: Bl: 0-1 Vi: 0-0 Tstrap: 0-0
Best Rating: 136 6/99 MRas 2m4f good Ch

Jumbo Star

80(61h) 54

12-y-o ch g Jumbo Hirt (USA)-Joyful Star (Rubor)
J E Dixon Mrs E M Dixon

Placings:5P/5/44160/46/306450P/0/30062PPP/553P U5-00P (2634)
2001/02: 21^{0}G, 21^{0}G, 25^{P}S

	Starts	1st	2nd	3rd	Win & Pl
Chases	3	0	0	0	
Career Total	**35**	**1**	**1**	**3**	**3965**

80	9/95	Carl	2m1f	F(0-100)HHdl	FRM	£1744

Total win prize-money £1744

Going: Sf: 0-1 GS: 0-0 Gd: 0-2 GF: - Fm: 0-0
Distance: 2m/2m3: 0-0 2m4-2m7: 0-2 3m+: 0-1
Track: LH: 0-3 RH: 0-0 Tight: 0-2 Gall: 0-0
Aids: Bl: 0-1 Vi: 0-0 Tstrap: 0-0
Best Rating: 95 1/00 Sedg 2m5f soft Ch

Jumbo's Dream

99 65

11-y-o b g Jumbo Hirt (USA)-Joyful Star (Rubor)
J E Dixon Mrs E M Dixon

Placings:00/23065/10000/421000/006336-000P0 (4747)
2001/02: 22^{0}GS, 21^{0}G, 23^{0}G, 24^{P}S, 20^{0}G

	Starts	1st	2nd	3rd	Win & Pl
Hurdles	5	0	0	0	
Career Total	**29**	**2**	**2**	**3**	**7450**

88	6/99	Hexm	3m	F(0-105)HHdl	G-F	£2658
78	10/98	Hexm	3m	E Hdl	GD	£2238

Total win prize-money £4896

Going: Sf: 0-1 GS: 0-1 Gd: 0-3 GF: - Fm: 0-0
Distance: 2m/2m3: 0-0 2m4-2m7: 0-3 3m+: 0-2
Track: LH: 0-4 RH: 0-0 Tight: 0-2 Gall: 0-0
Aids: Bl: 0-0 Vi: 0-0 Tstrap: 0-0
Best Rating: 89 5/99 Ctml 3m2f gd-fm Hdl

Jumbo's Flyer

80 27

5-y-o ch g Jumbo Hirt (USA)-Fragrant Princess (Germont)
F P Murtagh T H Littleton

Placings:0P0F (2117)
2001/02: 17^{0}G, 16^{P}G, 16^{0}G, 16^{F}GS

	Starts	1st	2nd	3rd	Win & Pl
Hurdles	4	0	0	0	
Career Total	**4**	**0**	**0**	**0**	

Going: Sf: 0-0 GS: 0-1 Gd: 0-3 GF: - Fm: 0-0
Distance: 2m/2m3: 0-4 2m4-2m7: 0-0 3m+: 0-0
Track: LH: 0-3 RH: 0-1 Tight: 0-3 Gall: 0-0
Aids: Bl: 0-0 Vi: 0-0 Tstrap: 0-0
Best Rating: 27 10/01 Aint 2m110y good Hdl

Jump (USA)

91 77

5-y-o b g Trempolino (USA)-Professional Dance (USA) (Nijinsky (CAN))
A W Carroll Dennis Deacon

Placings:05524-02004 (1075)
2001/02: 17^{0}G, 19^{2}G, 19^{0}GF, 22^{0}GF, 19^{4}GF

	Starts	1st	2nd	3rd	Win & Pl
Hurdles	5	0	1	0	760
Career Total	**10**	**0**	**2**	**0**	**1411**

Going: Sf: 0-0 GS: 0-0 Gd: 0-2 GF: - Fm: 0-3
Distance: 2m/2m3: 0-3 2m4-2m7: 0-2 3m+: 0-0
Track: LH: 0-3 RH: 0-2 Tight: 0-3 Gall: 0-0
Aids: Bl: 0-0 Vi: 0-0 Tstrap: 0-0
Best Rating: 79 10/00 Tntn 2m1f good Hdl

Jumpty Dumpty (FR)

85 90

5-y-o b/br g Chamberlin (FR)-Caryatide (FR) (Maiymad)
J C Tuck (G Macaire 14/10) James R Tuck

Placings:0-3323160P (3816)
2001/02: 16^{3}, 16^{3}, 17^{2}G, 19^{3}VS, 20^{1}S, 16^{6}S, 16^{0}GS, 22^{P}S

	Starts	1st	2nd	3rd	Win & Pl
Hurdles	6	0	1	2	3781
Chases	2	1	0	1	4704
Career Total	**9**	**1**	**1**	**3**	**8485**

10/01	Pina	2m4f110y	Ch	SFT	£3395

Total win prize-money £3395

Going: Sf: 1-3 GS: 0-1 Gd: 0-1 GF: - Fm: 0-0
Distance: 2m/2m3: 0-6 **2m4-2m7: 1-2** 3m+: 0-0
Track: LH: 0-1 RH: 0-2 Tight: 0-2 Gall: 0-0
Aids: Bl: 0-0 Vi: 0-0 Tstrap: 0-0
Best Rating: 63 1/02 Winc 2m gd-sft Hdl

An ex-French gelding who has won over fences in his native country on soft ground. Appeared to appreciate sounder surface when winning 22 furlong novices' handicap hurdle at Exeter May 2002.

June's River (IRE)

108 126

9-y-o ch g Over The River (FR)-June Bug (Welsh Saint)
Mrs M Reveley A Flannigan

Placings:002/444011/F/F251U210-U4 (4435)
2001/02: 16^{U}GS, 16^{4}HY

	Starts	1st	2nd	3rd	Win & Pl
Chases	2	0	0	0	364
Career Total	**20**	**4**	**3**	**0**	**15833**

122	2/01	Carl	2m	F(0-105)HCh	HVY	£3477
116	12/00	Hntg	2m110y	F(0-105)HCh	SFT	£2616
116	3/99	Carl	2m	F(0-110)HCh	SFT	£2723
104	2/99	Carl	2m	E(0-105)HCh	HVY	£2931

Total win prize-money £11749

Going: Sf: 0-1 GS: 0-1 Gd: 0-0 GF: - Fm: 0-0
Distance: 2m/2m3: 0-2 2m4-2m7: 0-0 3m+: 0-0
Track: LH: 0-1 RH: 0-1 Tight: 0-0 Gall: 0-1
Aids: Bl: 0-0 Vi: 0-0 Tstrap: 0-0
Best Rating: 126 3/02 Newc 2m110y heavy Ch

Four times a winner over fences, he is best over two miles in soft ground. His jumping can let him down.

Jungle Jinks (IRE)

105 120

7-y-o b g Proud Panther (FR)-Three Ladies (Menelek)
G M Moore Mrs Mary And Miss Susan Hatfield

Placings:6114 (4890)
2001/02: 16^{6}GS, 24^{1}S, 20^{1}G, 24^{4}G

	Starts	1st	2nd	3rd	Win & Pl
Hurdles	4	2	0	0	6630
Career Total	**4**	**2**	**0**	**0**	**6630**

101	4/02	Carl	2m4f	E Hdl	GD	£3143
115	3/02	Ayr	3m110y	E Hdl	SFT	£2712

Total win prize-money £5856

Going: Sf: 1-1 GS: 0-1 Gd: 1-2 GF: - Fm: 0-0
Distance: 2m/2m3: 0-1 2m4-2m7: 1-1 3m+: 1-2
Track: **LH: 1-2** RH: 0-1 Tight: 0-1 Gall: 0-0
Aids: Bl: 0-0 Vi: 0-0 Tstrap: 0-0
Best Rating: 120 4/02 Prth 3m110y good Hdl

Showed some ability on his belated first racecourse appearance in a novices' hurdle at Catterick in March 2002, and followed up with wins at Ayr and Carlisle. Stays three miles, handles good and soft ground.

Jungli (IRE)

108(102h) (132h)161

9-y-o b g Be My Native (USA)-Simple Mind (Decent Fellow)

P R Webber Mrs P Starkey

Placings: *243*/312410/1213311/1221U6-563324 (3697)

2001/02: 16^{5}G, 16^{6}G, 16^{3}G, 16^{3}GS, 16^{2}S, 17^{4}S

	Starts	1st	2nd	3rd	Win & Pl
Hurdles	1	0	0	0	0
Chases	5	0	1	2	8939
Career Total	**28**	**8**	**6**	**6**	**95865**

161	1/01	Donc	2m110y	B(0-150)HCh	GD	£10413
150	10/00	Weth	2m	C(0-135)HCh	G-S	£6405
150	4/00	Aint	2m	A HCh	GD	£30000
150	3/00	Newb	2m1f	C(0-135)HCh	SFT	£6244
140	12/99	Wwck	2m	D Ch	SFT	£4816
126	10/99	Weth	2m	E Ch	GD	£2908
130	3/99	Uttx	2m4f110y	C Hdl	G-S	£5537
130	12/98	Uttx	2m	E Hdl	SFT	£2431

Total win prize-money £68756

Going: Sf: 0-2 GS: 0-1 Gd: 0-3 GF: - Fm: 0-0
Distance: 2m/2m3: 0-6 2m4-2m7: 0-0 3m+: 0-0
Track: LH: 0-6 RH: 0-0 Tight: 0-0 Gall: 0-3
Aids: Bl: 0-0 Vi: 0-0 Tstrap: 0-0
Best Rating: 161 12/01 Weth 2m gd-sft Ch

A game performer, he jumps well and is a credit to connections. He won four of his first seven races in his first season over fences and continues to give a good account. Best suited by two miles and good, good/soft ground but acts on soft. Races prominently.

Junior Collonges (FR)

72 25

5-y-o b g Lute Antique (FR)-Amazone Collonges (FR) (Olmeto)

M Todhunter Sir Robert Ogden

Placings: *40*-5000 (3821)

2001/02: 17^{5}G, 20^{0}G, 16^{0}G, 17^{0}S

	Starts	1st	2nd	3rd	Win & Pl
Hurdles	4	0	0	0	0
Career Total	**6**	**0**	**0**	**0**	**0**

Going: Sf: 0-1 GS: 0-0 Gd: 0-3 GF: - Fm: 0-0
Distance: 2m/2m3: 0-3 2m4-2m7: 0-1 3m+: 0-0
Track: LH: 0-4 RH: 0-0 Tight: 0-3 Gall: 0-1
Aids: Bl: 0-0 Vi: 0-0 Tstrap: 0-0
Best Rating: 86 1/01 Ayr 2m gd-sft NHF

Modest novice hurdler. Best with cut.

Junkanoo

106 111

6-y-o ch g Generous (IRE)-Lupescu (Dixieland Band (USA))

Mrs M Reveley Lucayan Stud

Placings: *51*/*110*-1P3P (4136)

2001/02: 23^{1}S, 24^{P}S, 20^{3}S, 22^{P}GS

	Starts	1st	2nd	3rd	Win & Pl
Hurdles	4	1	0	1	5207
Career Total	**9**	**4**	**0**	**1**	**10065**

111	12/01	Weth	2m7f	D Hdl	SFT	£3591
130	12/00	Newc	2m	H NHF	SFT	£1575
125	12/00	Hntg	2m110y	H NHF	SFT	£1694
110	4/00	MRas	2m1f110y	H NHF	SFT	£1589

Total win prize-money £8449

Going: Sf: 1-3 GS: 0-1 Gd: 0-0 GF: - Fm: 0-0
Distance: 2m/2m3: 0-0 **2m4-2m7: 1-3** 3m+: 0-1
Track: **LH: 1-2** RH: 0-2 Tight: 0-0 Gall: 0-2
Aids: Bl: 0-0 Vi: 0-0 Tstrap: 0-0
Best Rating: 130 12/00 Newc 2m soft NHF

Boasts some decent bumper form and shaped with plenty of promise when scoring on his hurdling debut, but has run too badly too be true on a couple of occasions and may have a problem.

Jupiter De Bussy (FR)

91f 107f

5-y-o b/br g Silver Rainbow-Tosca De Bussy (FR) (Le Riverain (FR))

L Lungo Ashleybank Investments Limited

Placings: *65* (3680)

2001/02: 16^{6}S, 16^{5}HY

	Starts	1st	2nd	3rd	Win & Pl
NH Flat	2	0	0	0	0
Career Total	**2**	**0**	**0**	**0**	**0**

Going: Sf: 0-2 GS: 0-0 Gd: 0-0 GF: - Fm: 0-0
Distance: 2m/2m3: 0-2 2m4-2m7: 0-0 3m+: 0-0
Track: LH: 0-2 RH: 0-0 Tight: 0-0 Gall: 0-0
Aids: Bl: 0-0 Vi: 0-0 Tstrap: 0-0
Best Rating: 107 1/02 Hayd 2m soft NHF

Jupiter Diamond

105 81

7-y-o b g Jupiter Island-Noire Small (USA) (Elocutionist (USA))

Ian Williams M Murphy

Placings: *4*-060003 (4686)

2001/02: 16^{0}S, 20^{6}S, 20^{0}G, 20^{0}3, 26^{0}G, 26^{3}GF

	Starts	1st	2nd	3rd	Win & Pl
NH Flat	1	0	0	0	0
Hurdles	5	0	0	1	416
Career Total	**7**	**0**	**0**	**1**	**416**

Going: Sf: 0-3 GS: 0-0 Gd: 0-2 GF: - Fm: 0-1
Distance: 2m/2m3: 0-1 2m4-2m7: 0-3 3m+: 0-2
Track: LH: 0-3 RH: 0-3 Tight: 0-0 Gall: 0-2
Aids: Bl: 0-0 Vi: 0-0 Tstrap: 0-0
Best Rating: 81 4/02 Hrfd 3m2f gd-fm Hdl

Adopted front running tactics when third over an extended three miles in novices' handicap at Hereford April 2002.

Jupiter Jo

88 83

6-y-o b g Jupiter Island-Marejo (Creetown)

J B Walton F T Walton

Placings: *00* (0744)

2001/02: 16^{0}GF, 16^{0}GS

	Starts	1st	2nd	3rd	Win & Pl
NH Flat	2	0	0	0	
Career Total	**2**	**0**	**0**	**0**	

Going: Sf: 0-0 GS: 0-1 Gd: 0-0 GF: - Fm: 0-1
Distance: 2m/2m3: 0-2 2m4-2m7: 0-0 3m+: 0-0
Track: LH: 0-1 RH: 0-0 Tight: 0-0 Gall: 0-0
Aids: Bl: 0-0 Vi: 0-0 Tstrap: 0-0
Best Rating: 90 5/01 Newc 2m gd-fm NHF

Jupiter's Fancy

84 45

7-y-o ch m Jupiter Island-Joe's Fancy (Apollo Eight)

F P Murtagh Alan Kirtley

Placings: *4300*P (4063)

2001/02: 17^{4}GF, 16^{3}G, 16^{0}GS, 20^{0}S, 27^{P}S

	Starts	1st	2nd	3rd	Win & Pl
NH Flat	3	0	0	1	233
Hurdles	2	0	0	0	0
Career Total	**5**	**0**	**0**	**1**	**233**

Going: Sf: 0-2 GS: 0-1 Gd: 0-1 GF: - Fm: 0-1
Distance: 2m/2m3: 0-3 2m4-2m7: 0-1 3m+: 0-1
Track: LH: 0-5 RH: 0-0 Tight: 0-4 Gall: 0-1
Aids: Bl: 0-0 Vi: 0-0 Tstrap: 0-0
Best Rating: 82 12/01 Catt 2m good NHF

Jupon Vert (FR)

95 92

5-y-o b g Lights Out (FR)-Danse Verte (FR) (Brezzo (FR))

P F Nicholls (Mme I Pacault 13/5) Hawkins, Fear And Quinn

Placings: P5-2P42 (3737)

2001/02: 19^{2}G, 21^{P}S, 20^{4}G, 16^{2}S

	Starts	1st	2nd	3rd	Win & Pl
Hurdles	1	0	0	0	0
Chases	3	0	2	0	3244
Career Total	**6**	**0**	**2**	**0**	**3632**

Going: Sf: 0-2 GS: 0-0 Gd: 0-2 GF: - Fm: 0-0
Distance: 2m/2m3: 0-2 2m4-2m7: 0-2 3m+: 0-0
Track: LH: 0-0 RH: 0-1 Tight: 0-1 Gall: 0-0
Aids: Bl: 0-0 Vi: 0-0 Tstrap: 0-1
Best Rating: 92 2/02 Leic 2m soft Ch

Best effort when second at Leicester in February 2002. That effort was on soft ground over two miles.

Juralan (IRE)

103(96h) (93h)137

7-y-o b g Jurado (USA)-Boylan (Buckskin (FR))

Miss H C Knight Hogarth Racing

Placings: *624*-511P (4255)

2001/02: 19^{5}G, 19^{1}GS, 21^{1}G, 21^{P}G

	Starts	1st	2nd	3rd	Win & Pl
Hurdles	1	0	0	0	0
Chases	3	2	0	0	11359
Career Total	**7**	**2**	**1**	**0**	**11803**

137	1/02	Winc	2m5f	D Ch	GD	£4602
134	11/01	Tntn	2m3f	C Ch	G-S	£6756

Total win prize-money £11359

Going: Sf: 0-0 GS: 1-1 Gd: 1-3 GF: - Fm: 0-0
Distance: 2m/2m3: 1-1 2m4-2m7: 1-3 3m+: 0-0
Track: LH: 0-1 **RH: 2-3 Tight: 1-1** Gall: 0-1
Aids: Bl: 0-0 Vi: 0-0 Tstrap: 0-0
Best Rating: 137 1/02 Winc 2m5f good Ch

A point-to-point winner in Ireland. He showed promise in two bumpers before tackling hurdles. Reported to have finished distressed after his Hereford run in May 2001.

Returned after a six-month break to score at Taunton on his chasing bow, and followed up at Wincanton in January. Jumps well, stays two miles five, and acts on a sound surface.

Jurancon Ii (FR)

105 112

5-y-o b g Scooter Bleu (IRE)-Volniste (FR) (Olmeto)

M C Pipe D A Johnson

Placings:456011P **(4817)**

2001/02: 16^{4}S, 17^{5}S, 17^{6}HY, 19^{0}S, 21^{1}GS, 21^{1}HY, 24^{P}GF

	Starts	1st	2nd	3rd	Win & Pl
Hurdles	7	2	0	0	7973
Career Total	**7**	**2**	**0**	**0**	**7973**

112 2/02 Plum 2m5f D(0-115)HHdl HVY £5330

112 2/02 MRas 2m5f110y E(0-110)HHdl G-S £2642

Total win prize-money £7973

Going: Sf: 1-5 GS: 1-1 Gd: 0-0 GF: - Fm: 0-1
Distance: 2m/2m3: 0-3 **2m4-2m7: 2-3** 3m+: 0-1
Track: LH: 1-4 RH: 1-2 **Tight: 2-5** Gall: 0-0
Aids: Bl: 0-0 Vi: 0-0 Tstrap: 0-0
Best Rating: 112 2/02 Plum 2m5f heavy Hdl

A Flat winner in France, he has won twice over hurdles in this country over two miles five. Has raced mainly on soft and heavy ground.

Jurassic Scratch (IRE)

100 81

6-y-o b g Jurado (USA)-On The Scratch (Le Bavard (FR))

R Rowe Tim Clowes

Placings:6462530P **(4568)**

2001/02: 21^{6}S, 21^{4}GS, 21^{6}G, 20^{2}S, 21^{5}GS, 22^{3}S, 22^{0}S, 24^{P}G

	Starts	1st	2nd	3rd	Win & Pl
Hurdles	8	0	1	1	852
Career Total	**8**	**0**	**1**	**1**	**852**

Going: Sf: 0-4 GS: 0-2 Gd: 0-2 GF: - Fm: 0-0
Distance: 2m/2m3: 0-0 2m4-2m7: 0-7 3m+: 0-1
Track: LH: 0-4 RH: 0-4 Tight: 0-6 Gall: 0-1
Aids: Bl: 0-0 Vi: 0-0 Tstrap: 0-0
Best Rating: 81 12/01 Folk 2m4f110y soft Hdl

Unlucky not to win at Folkestone in December and looks to have a race in him.

Jurist

84(99h) (83h)71

8-y-o b g Then Again-Forest Frolic (Celtic Cone)

B S Rothwell J T Brown

Placings:2/60U5 **(1030)**

2001/02: 20^{6}G, 20^{0}GF, 24^{U}GF, 17^{5}G

	Starts	1st	2nd	3rd	Win & Pl
Hurdles	1	0	0	0	0
Chases	3	0	0	0	0
Career Total	**5**	**0**	**1**	**0**	**421**

Going: Sf: 0-0 GS: 0-0 Gd: 0-2 GF: - Fm: 0-2
Distance: 2m/2m3: 0-1 2m4-2m7: 0-2 3m+: 0-1
Track: LH: 0-3 RH: 0-1 Tight: 0-3 Gall: 0-0
Aids: Bl: 0-0 Vi: 0-0 Tstrap: 0-0
Best Rating: 108 4/99 MRas 1m5f110y soft NHF

Just A Diamond

89(103c) (104c)62

9-y-o ch m Primitive Rising (USA)-Just Diamonds (Laurence O)

R Johnson The Border Terriers

Placings:51F0 **(4875)**

2001/02: 21^{5}HY, 20^{1}S, 21^{F}HY, 24^{0}G

	Starts	1st	2nd	3rd	Win & Pl
Hurdles	2	0	0	0	0
Chases	2	1	0	0	4388
Career Total	**4**	**1**	**0**	**0**	**4388**

104 2/02 MRas 2m4f D Ch SFT £4387

Total win prize-money £4388

Going: Sf: 1-3 GS: 0-0 Gd: 0-1 GF: - Fm: 0-0
Distance: 2m/2m3: 0-0 **2m4-2m7: 1-3** 3m+: 0-1
Track: LH: 0-2 **RH: 1-2 Tight: 1-2** Gall: 0-0
Aids: Bl: 0-0 Vi: 0-0 Tstrap: 0-0
Best Rating: 104 2/02 MRas 2m4f soft Ch

Finished alone when winning a point to point in April 2000. Lightly-raced under Rules. Won a weak event on her debut over fences under Rules in February 2002. Stays three miles. Acts on soft/heavy ground.

Just A Minute (FR)

107 104

5-y-o b m Le Nain Jaune (FR)-Brave Again (FR) (Pot D'Or (FR))

R H Alner H V Perry

Placings:00524 **(4680)**

2001/02: 22^{0}G, 16^{0}G, 17^{5}S, 19^{2}S, 17^{4}GF

	Starts	1st	2nd	3rd	Win & Pl
Hurdles	5	0	1	0	1342
Career Total	**5**	**0**	**1**	**0**	**1342**

Going: Sf: 0-2 GS: 0-0 Gd: 0-2 GF: - Fm: 0-1
Distance: 2m/2m3: 0-3 2m4-2m7: 0-2 3m+: 0-0
Track: LH: 0-0 RH: 0-4 Tight: 0-2 Gall: 0-0
Aids: Bl: 0-0 Vi: 0-0 Tstrap: 0-0
Best Rating: 100 4/02 Hrfd 2m1f gd-fm Hdl

Modest hurdler, stays two and a half miles. Won Mares' Only Novices' Hurdle at Exeter May 2002. Acts on soft ground.

Just A Touch

101 82

6-y-o ch g Rakaposhi King-Minim (Rymer)

P Winkworth David A Turnbull

Placings:000-F014 **(4387)**

2001/02: 16^{F}GS, 16^{0}HY, 17^{1}S, 16^{4}S

	Starts	1st	2nd	3rd	Win & Pl
Hurdles	4	1	0	0	2688
Career Total	**7**	**1**	**0**	**0**	**2688**

82 2/02 Folk 2m1f110y F(0-90)HHdl SFT £2688

Total win prize-money £2688

Going: Sf: 1-3 GS: 0-1 Gd: 0-0 GF: - Fm: 0-0
Distance: **2m/2m3: 1-4** 2m4-2m7: 0-0 3m+: 0-0
Track: LH: 0-0 **RH: 1-4 Tight: 1-1** Gall: 0-1
Aids: Bl: 0-0 Vi: 0-0 Tstrap: 0-0
Best Rating: 82 2/02 Folk 2m1f110y soft Hdl

Just Adam

104(84h) (78h)105

7-y-o b g Primitive Rising (USA)-Mildame (Milford)

R H Buckler The Deadly Sins Partnership

Placings:00/5P-P014P22P **(4886)**

2001/02: 18^{P}GS, 16^{0}G, 24^{1}G, 22^{4}G, 25^{P}G, 22^{2}G, 26^{2}GF, 18^{P}GF

	Starts	1st	2nd	3rd	Win & Pl
Hurdles	2	0	0	0	0
Chases	6	1	2	0	9535
Career Total	**12**	**1**	**2**	**0**	**9535**

105 11/01 Newb 3m D(0-110)HCh GD £6132

Total win prize-money £6132

Going: Sf: 0-0 GS: 0-1 Gd: 1-5 GF: - Fm: 0-2
Distance: 2m/2m3: 0-3 2m4-2m7: 0-2 **3m+: 1-3**
Track: **LH: 1-6** RH: 0-1 Tight: 0-2 **Gall: 1-3**
Aids: Bl: 0-0 Vi: 0-0 Tstrap: 0-0
Best Rating: 105 12/01 Newb 2m6f110y good Ch

Modest chaser, stays three miles. Acts on good ground.

Just An Excuse (IRE)

87 64

9-y-o b g Project Manager-Over The Seas (North Summit)

J J O'Neill Peter Thompson Mark Derry Mark O'Connor

Placings:460/12P0/6 **(1897)**

2001/02: 26^{6}GS

	Starts	1st	2nd	3rd	Win & Pl
Chases	1	0	0	0	0
Career Total	**8**	**1**	**1**	**0**	**3049**

89 11/98 Carl 3m110y E Hdl SFT £2304

Total win prize-money £2304

Going: Sf: 0-0 GS: 0-1 Gd: 0-0 GF: - Fm: 0-0
Distance: 2m/2m3: 0-0 2m4-2m7: 0-0 3m+: 0-1
Track: LH: 0-0 RH: 0-0 Tight: 0-1 Gall: 0-0
Aids: Bl: 0-0 Vi: 0-0 Tstrap: 0-0
Best Rating: 95 11/97 Ayr 2m gd-sft NHF

A fair staying hurdler. Lightly raced. Well beaten on chase debut. Best on an easy surface.

Just Another Punt (IRE)

7-y-o b g Be My Native (USA)-Merapi (Roi Guillaume (FR))

C R Egerton R K Carvill

Placings:0-0 **(0734)**

2001/02: 22^{0}G

	Starts	1st	2nd	3rd	Win & Pl
Hurdles	1	0	0	0	
Career Total	**2**	**0**	**0**	**0**	

Going: Sf: 0-0 GS: 0-0 Gd: 0-1 GF: - Fm: 0-0
Distance: 2m/2m3: 0-0 2m4-2m7: 0-1 3m+: 0-0
Track: LH: 0-1 RH: 0-0 Tight: 0-1 Gall: 0-0
Aids: Bl: 0-0 Vi: 0-0 Tstrap: 0-0
Best Rating: 71 2/01 Asct 2m110y heavy NHF

Just Anything (NZ)

88 57

11-y-o b g Truly Vain (AUS)-Young Margot (NZ) (Hermes)

P G Murphy Miss J Collison

Placings:0P/006F-P6P **(1907)**

2001/02: 17^{P}HY, 16^{8}S, 16^{P}S

	Starts	1st	2nd	3rd	Win & Pl
Hurdles	3	0	0	0	0
Career Total	**9**	**0**	**0**	**0**	**0**

Going: Sf: 0-3 GS: 0-0 Gd: 0-0 GF: - Fm: 0-0
Distance: 2m/2m3: 0-3 2m4-2m7: 0-0 3m+: 0-0
Track: LH: 0-2 RH: 0-1 Tight: 0-3 Gall: 0-0
Aids: Bl: 0-0 Vi: 0-0 Tstrap: 0-3
Best Rating: 77 1/00 Kemp 2m good Hdl

Just Barney Boy

(83h) (48h)
5-y-o b g Past Glories-Pablena (Pablond)
R Nixon G R S Nixon

Placings:44005F (4121)
2001/02: 16^{4}GS, 20^{4}S, 20^{0}G, 20^{0}S, 24^{5}GS, 20^{F}HY

	Starts	1st	2nd	3rd	Win & Pl
Hurdles	4	0	0	0	0
Chases	2	0	0	0	0
Career Total	**6**	**0**	**0**	**0**	**0**

Going: Sf: 0-3 GS: 0-2 Gd: 0-1 GF: - Fm: 0-0
Distance: 2m/2m3: 0-1 2m4-2m7: 0-4 3m+: 0-1
Track: LH: 0-4 RH: 0-2 Tight: 0-3 Gall: 0-1
Aids: Bl: 0-0 Vi: 0-0 Tstrap: 0-0
Best Rating: 48 12/01 Kels 2m110y gd-sft Hdl

Showed no sign of ability so far.

Just Because (IRE)

81 48
10-y-o ch g Sharp Charter-Lakefield Lady (Over The River (FR))
G E Jones G Elwyn Jones

Placings:*0/00F0/0/P0-*0000 (1383)
2001/02: 24^{0}G, 22^{0}G, 20^{0}G, 26^{0}GF

	Starts	1st	2nd	3rd	Win & Pl
Hurdles	4	0	0	0	
Career Total	**12**	**0**	**0**	**0**	

Going: Sf: 0-0 GS: 0-0 Gd: 0-3 GF: - Fm: 0-1
Distance: 2m/2m3: 0-0 2m4-2m7: 0-2 3m+: 0-2
Track: LH: 0-3 RH: 0-1 Tight: 0-2 Gall: 0-0
Aids: Bl: 0-0 Vi: 0-0 Tstrap: 0-0
Best Rating: 48 7/01 Strf 2m6f110y good Hdl

Just Beth

52 64
6-y-o ch m Carlingford Castle-One For The Road (Warpath)
G Fierro G Fierro

Placings:*00440*-05 (0246)
2001/02: 20^{0}G, 21^{5}GF

	Starts	1st	2nd	3rd	Win & Pl
Hurdles	2	0	0	0	0
Career Total	**7**	**0**	**0**	**0**	**0**

Going: Sf: 0-0 GS: 0-0 Gd: 0-1 GF: - Fm: 0-1
Distance: 2m/2m3: 0-0 2m4-2m7: 0-2 3m+: 0-0
Track: LH: 0-0 RH: 0-1 Tight: 0-0 Gall: 0-1
Aids: Bl: 0-0 Vi: 0-0 Tstrap: 0-0
Best Rating: 98 3/01 Hntg 2m110y soft NHF

Just Billy (IRE)

81 58
7-y-o b g Supreme Leader-One Way Only (Le Bavard (FR))
J S King N A Gill

Placings:*0*-000 (4152)
2001/02: 16^{0}GS, 16^{0}S, 20^{0}GS

	Starts	1st	2nd	3rd	Win & Pl
Hurdles	3	0	0	0	
Career Total	**4**	**0**	**0**	**0**	

Going: Sf: 0-1 GS: 0-2 Gd: 0-0 GF: - Fm: 0-0
Distance: 2m/2m3: 0-2 2m4-2m7: 0-1 3m+: 0-0
Track: LH: 0-2 RH: 0-1 Tight: 0-0 Gall: 0-2
Aids: Bl: 0-0 Vi: 0-0 Tstrap: 0-0
Best Rating: 58 1/02 Hntg 2m110y gd-sft Hdl

Just Caramel

103 92
6-y-o b m Montelimar (USA)-Cream By Post (Torus)
P F Nicholls Ridge Racing

Placings:*2-02P*2402 (4861)
2001/02: 18^{0}GF, 17^{2}F, 21^{P}G, 19^{2}GS, 19^{4}S, 17^{0}G, 22^{2}F

	Starts	1st	2nd	3rd	Win & Pl
NH Flat	2	0	1	0	657
Hurdles	5	0	2	0	2539
Career Total	**8**	**0**	**4**	**0**	**3644**

Going: Sf: 0-1 GS: 0-1 Gd: 0-2 GF: - Fm: 0-3
Distance: 2m/2m3: 0-3 2m4-2m7: 0-4 3m+: 0-0
Track: LH: 0-2 RH: 0-2 Tight: 0-4 Gall: 0-0
Aids: Bl: 0-0 Vi: 0-0 Tstrap: 0-0
Best Rating: 100 4/01 Tntn 2m1f gd-fm NHF

Out of a useful point-to-pointer, she has a habit of coming second due to an apparent lack of toe at the business end. Acts on any ground. May do better over fences.

Just Del

6-y-o b m Petoski-Fragrant Hackotto (Simply Great (FR))
R Nixon G R S Nixon

Placings:*0*-000P (2631)
2001/02: 16^{0}G, 16^{0}GS, 16^{0}G, 16^{P}S

	Starts	1st	2nd	3rd	Win & Pl
NH Flat	1	0	0	0	0
Hurdles	3	0	0	0	0
Career Total	**5**	**0**	**0**	**0**	

Going: Sf: 0-1 GS: 0-1 Gd: 0-2 GF: - Fm: 0-0
Distance: 2m/2m3: 0-4 2m4-2m7: 0-0 3m+: 0-0
Track: LH: 0-3 RH: 0-1 Tight: 0-2 Gall: 0-0
Aids: Bl: 0-0 Vi: 0-0 Tstrap: 0-0
Best Rating: 29 10/00 Carl 2m1f gd-sft NHF

Just Ed

100 76
6-y-o ch g Greensmith-Sovereign Maiden (Nearly A Hand)
R Nixon G R S Nixon

Placings:*0*0P50 (4894)
2001/02: 16^{0}G, 16^{0}HY, 22^{P}HY, 16^{5}GF, 16^{0}G

	Starts	1st	2nd	3rd	Win & Pl
NH Flat	1	0	0	0	0
Hurdles	4	0	0	0	0
Career Total	**5**	**0**	**0**	**0**	**0**

Going: Sf: 0-2 GS: 0-0 Gd: 0-2 GF: - Fm: 0-1
Distance: 2m/2m3: 0-4 2m4-2m7: 0-1 3m+: 0-0
Track: LH: 0-4 RH: 0-1 Tight: 0-3 Gall: 0-0
Aids: Bl: 0-0 Vi: 0-0 Tstrap: 0-0
Best Rating: 73 4/02 Kels 2m110y gd-fm Hdl

Just Fluster

61 26
6-y-o ch g Triune-Flamber (Hot Brandy)
Lady Susan Watson Lady Susan Watson

Placings:*0*5P0 (4867)
2001/02: 16^{0}GS, 21^{5}S, 20^{P}HY, 16^{0}GF

	Starts	1st	2nd	3rd	Win & Pl
NH Flat	1	0	0	0	0
Hurdles	3	0	0	0	0
Career Total	**4**	**0**	**0**	**0**	**0**

Going: Sf: 0-2 GS: 0-1 Gd: 0-0 GF: - Fm: 0-1
Distance: 2m/2m3: 0-2 2m4-2m7: 0-2 3m+: 0-0
Track: LH: 0-4 RH: 0-0 Tight: 0-3 Gall: 0-0
Aids: Bl: 0-0 Vi: 0-0 Tstrap: 0-0
Best Rating: 27 4/02 Weth 2m gd-fm Hdl

Has shown little enthusiasm for the game so far.

Just For Ger (IRE)

106 111
8-y-o b g Beau Sher-Reasonar (Reasonable (FR))
J S Goldie (J M Brown 15/5) Strathayr Publishing Ltd

Placings:*000/100000*-53U334132 (3914)
2001/02: 25^{5}S, 24^{3}GF, 23^{U}G, 17^{3}G, 21^{3}G, 16^{4}G, 20^{1}S, 16^{3}S, 20^{2}GS

	Starts	1st	2nd	3rd	Win & Pl
Chases	9	1	1	4	8956
Career Total	**18**	**2**	**1**	**4**	**11302**

111	1/02	Muss	2m4f	E(0-110)HCh	SFT	£4192
86	5/00	Dpat	2m1f172y	Hdl	GD	£2345

Total win prize-money £6539

Going: Sf: 1-3 GS: 0-1 Gd: 0-4 GF: - Fm: 0-1
Distance: 2m/2m3: 0-3 **2m4-2m7: 1-3** 3m+: 0-3
Track: LH: 0-4 **RH: 1-4 Tight: 1-4** Gall: 0-1
Aids: Bl: 0-0 Vi: 0-0 Tstrap: 0-0
Best Rating: 111 1/02 Muss 2m4f soft Ch

Ex-Irish hurdler. Opened his chasing account over two and a half miles at the beginning of the new year on soft ground, and has run with credit subsequently.

Just George

96 81
8-y-o b g Primitive Rising (USA)-Just Jessica (State Diplomacy (USA))
Ms Liz Harrison David Alan Harrison

Placings:PP66PF (3609)
2001/02: 22^{P}GS, 24^{P}GS, 24^{6}S, 26^{6}HY, 27^{P}HY, 24^{F}S

	Starts	1st	2nd	3rd	Win & Pl
Hurdles	3	0	0	0	0
Chases	3	0	0	0	0
Career Total	**6**	**0**	**0**	**0**	**0**

Going: Sf: 0-4 GS: 0-2 Gd: 0-0 GF: - Fm: 0-0
Distance: 2m/2m3: 0-0 2m4-2m7: 0-1 3m+: 0-5
Track: LH: 0-4 RH: 0-2 Tight: 0-2 Gall: 0-1
Aids: Bl: 0-0 Vi: 0-0 Tstrap: 0-0

Best Rating: 81 1/02 Carl 3m2f heavy Ch

Just Good Friends (IRE)

85 **65**

5-y-o b g Shalford (IRE)-Sinfonietta (Foolish Pleasure (USA))

Denys Smith B Batey

Placings:606-6PP05636 **(1746)**

2001/02: 21^{6}GF, 21^{P}GF, 22^{P}GS, 21^{0}GF, 17^{5}G, 17^{6}G, 17^{3}GS, 16^{6}GS

	Starts	1st	2nd	3rd	Win & Pl
Hurdles	8	0	0	1	368
Career Total	**11**	**0**	**0**	**1**	**368**

Going: Sf: 0-0 GS: 0-3 Gd: 0-2 GF: - Fm: 0-3
Distance: 2m/2m3: 0-4 2m4-2m7: 0-4 3m+: 0-0
Track: LH: 0-8 RH: 0-0 Tight: 0-8 Gall: 0-0
Aids: Bl: 0-2 Vi: 0-0 Tstrap: 0-0
Best Rating: 75 10/00 Kels 2m110y good Hdl

Just Good Fun (IRE)

91 **99**

8-y-o br g Good Thyne (USA)-Killonerry (Croghan Hill)

M Pitman Just Good Fun Club

Placings:*40223*/2113221/2P **(1144)**

2001/02: 24^{2}GF, 24^{P}GF

	Starts	1st	2nd	3rd	Win & Pl
Chases	2	0	1	0	1024
Career Total	**14**	**3**	**6**	**2**	**25544**

128	1/00	Asct	3m	B(0-140)HHdl	G-S	£10335
128	10/99	Chep	2m4f	D HHdl	SFT	£3420
104	8/99	Uttx	2m4f110y	D Hdl	G-F	£2963

Total win prize-money £16719

Going: Sf: 0-0 GS: 0-0 Gd: 0-0 GF: - Fm: 0-2
Distance: 2m/2m3: 0-0 2m4-2m7: 0-0 3m+: 0-2
Track: LH: 0-2 RH: 0-0 Tight: 0-2 Gall: 0-0
Aids: Bl: 0-0 Vi: 0-0 Tstrap: 0-0
Best Rating: 128 1/00 Asct 3m gd-sft Hdl

Just Grand (IRE)

86 **54**

8-y-o b g Green Desert (USA)-Aljood (Kris)

J A Moore J A Moore

Placings:0/0P/UF-06P0 **(2723)**

2001/02: 17^{0}GF, 18^{6}G, 20^{P}S, 17^{0}GF

	Starts	1st	2nd	3rd	Win & Pl
Hurdles	4	0	0	0	0
Career Total	**9**	**0**	**0**	**0**	**0**

Going: Sf: 0-1 GS: 0-0 Gd: 0-1 GF: - Fm: 0-2
Distance: 2m/2m3: 0-3 2m4-2m7: 0-1 3m+: 0-0
Track: LH: 0-2 RH: 0-1 Tight: 0-3 Gall: 0-0
Aids: Bl: 0-1 Vi: 0-0 Tstrap: 0-0
Best Rating: 83 9/98 Hntg 2m110y gd-fm Hdl

Just Henry

76f **69f**

5-y-o b g Arzanni-Silk Touch (Lochnager)

A King Roger Allsop

Placings:*0* **(4329)**

2001/02: 17^{0}S

	Starts	1st	2nd	3rd	Win & Pl
NH Flat	1	0	0	0	
Career Total	**1**	**0**	**0**	**0**	

Going: Sf: 0-1 GS: 0-0 Gd: 0-0 GF: - Fm: 0-0
Distance: 2m/2m3: 0-1 2m4-2m7: 0-0 3m+: 0-0
Track: LH: 0-0 RH: 0-1 Tight: 0-0 Gall: 0-0
Aids: Bl: 0-0 Vi: 0-0 Tstrap: 0-0
Best Rating: 69 3/02 Hrfd 2m1f soft NHF

Just Hoping

107 **106**

9-y-o b g Primitive Rising (USA)-Happy Penny (Tower Joy)

Lady Susan Watson Lady Susan Watson

Placings:P4U10 **(4872)**

2001/02: 19^{P}GS, 19^{4}S, 16^{U}S, 16^{1}G, 16^{0}GF

	Starts	1st	2nd	3rd	Win & Pl
Chases	5	1	0	0	3393
Career Total	**5**	**1**	**0**	**0**	**3393**

101	4/02	Weth	2m	E Ch	GD	£3071

Total win prize-money £3071

Going: Sf: 0-2 GS: 0-1 Gd: 1-1 GF: - Fm: 0-1
Distance: **2m/2m3: 1-5** 2m4-2m7: 0-0 3m+: 0-0
Track: **LH: 1-5** RH: 0-0 Tight: 0-2 Gall: 0-1
Aids: Bl: 0-0 Vi: 0-0 Tstrap: 0-0
Best Rating: 101 4/02 Weth 2m good Ch

Novice chaser. Effective with cut in the ground and also acts on good ground. Best at around two miles.

Just In Business

111 **119**

9-y-o b g Lyphento (USA)-Flippit (Dairialatan)

P F Nicholls Tony Fear & Tim Hawkins

Placings:FF-1125 **(3151)**

2001/02: 26^{1}GF, 25^{1}GF, 25^{2}G, 26^{5}G

	Starts	1st	2nd	3rd	Win & Pl
Chases	4	2	1	0	8637
Career Total	**6**	**2**	**1**	**0**	**8637**

119	10/01	Winc	3m1f110y	F(0-95)HCh	G-F	£3445
119	5/01	NAbb	3m2f110y	E Ch	G-F	£3836

Total win prize-money £7281

Going: Sf: 0-0 GS: 0-0 Gd: 0-2 GF: - Fm: 2-2
Distance: 2m/2m3: 0-0 2m4-2m7: 0-0 **3m+: 2-4**
Track: LH: 1-1 RH: 1-2 **Tight: 1-2** Gall: 0-0
Aids: Bl: 0-0 Vi: 0-0 Tstrap: 0-0
Best Rating: 119 10/01 Winc 3m1f110y good Ch

Dour stayer who needs to be allowed to bowl along to be seen to best effect. Acts on fast ground. Prone to errors.

Just In Time

103(108h) (134h)**126**

7-y-o b g Night Shift (USA)-Future Past (USA) (Super Concorde (USA))

P J Hobbs B K Peppiatt

Placings:130-113043 **(4818)**

2001/02: 17^{1}G, 16^{1}GF, 16^{3}GF, 17^{0}G, 20^{4}G, 21^{3}GF

	Starts	1st	2nd	3rd	Win & Pl
Hurdles	6	2	0	2	13089
Career Total	**9**	**3**	**0**	**3**	**18666**

132	5/01	Prth	2m110y	D Hdl	G-F	£3432
128	5/01	Extr	2m1f	D Hdl	GD	£3836
118	12/00	Tntn	2m1f	D Hdl	SFT	£5211

Total win prize-money £12480

Going: Sf: 0-0 GS: 0-0 Gd: 1-3 GF: - Fm: 1-3
Distance: **2m/2m3: 2-4** 2m4-2m7: 0-2 3m+: 0-0
Track: LH: 0-4 **RH: 2-2** Tight: 0-1 Gall: 0-2
Aids: Bl: 0-0 Vi: 0-0 Tstrap: 0-0
Best Rating: 134 6/01 Worc 2m gd-fm Hdl

A useful handicapper on turf and sand on the Flat, has been successful over hurdles but will need to jump better if he is to make his mark in decent company. Made a successful chasing debut at Exeter in May 2002 in what was probably a decent race for the time of year and followed up at Stratford. Effective on good to firm/soft and two miles.

Just Jasmine

119 **146**

10-y-o ch m Nicholas Bill-Linguistic (Porto Bello)

K Bishop Mrs E K Ellis

Placings:*64/354/*3301F4334/35022111/162/5153P-5432323 **(4901)**

2001/02: 20^{5}G, 20^{4}S, 19^{3}G, 19^{2}G, 21^{3}HY, 19^{2}GF, 16^{3}G

	Starts	1st	2nd	3rd	Win & Pl
Chases	7	0	2	3	24672
Career Total	**37**	**6**	**5**	**10**	**76742**

150	1/01	Tntn	2m3f	D(0-125)HCh	HVY	£6987
140	1/00	Tntn	2m3f	D(0-125)HCh	SFT	£6987
127	4/99	Extr	2m1f110y	D(0-120)HCh	SFT	£4138
125	3/99	Uttx	2m5f	C HCh	G-S	£18156
116	2/99	Uttx	2m4f	D Ch	HVY	£5558
94	12/97	Worc	2m	E Hdl	SFT	£2425

Total win prize-money £44253

Going: Sf: 0-2 GS: 0-0 Gd: 0-4 GF: - Fm: 0-1
Distance: 2m/2m3: 0-1 2m4-2m7: 0-6 3m+: 0-0
Track: LH: 0-3 RH: 0-4 Tight: 0-0 Gall: 0-3
Aids: Bl: 0-0 Vi: 0-0 Tstrap: 0-0
Best Rating: 150 1/01 Tntn 2m3f heavy Ch

A useful mare over two and a half miles particularly in testing conditions, she has run some good races in useful company during the 2001/2002 season, but looks in the grip of the Handicapper. Suited by the ground good or softer and is usually held up.

Just Lizzie

112 **117**

9-y-o b m Rakaposhi King-Kilglass (Fidel)

R Nixon G R S Nixon

Placings:*66/0*61561341100/063/FF2305P010-600041244 **(4893)**

2001/02: 20^{6}S, 16^{0}GS, 22^{0}GS, 16^{0}S, 20^{4}S, 20^{1}HY, 20^{2}S, 20^{4}G, 20^{4}G

	Starts	1st	2nd	3rd	Win & Pl
Hurdles	9	1	1	0	6971
Career Total	**36**	**6**	**2**	**3**	**28766**

112	3/02	Ayr	2m4f	D(0-125)HHdl	HVY	£3500
117	4/01	Weth	2m4f110y	B(0-145)HHdl	G-S	£5421
101	2/99	Carl	2m1f	D(0-125)HHdl	HVY	£5706
100	1/99	Catt	2m	F(0-110)HHdl	SFT	£2374
97	11/98	Hexm	2m	F(0-100)HHdl	HVY	£2193
83	6/98	Hexm	2m	E Hdl	HVY	£2469

Total win prize-money £21663

Going: Sf: 1-5 GS: 0-2 Gd: 0-2 GF: - Fm: 0-0
Distance: 2m/2m3: 0-2 **2m4-2m7: 1-7** 3m+: 0-0
Track: **LH: 1-8** RH: 0-1 Tight: 0-2 Gall: 0-1
Aids: Bl: 0-0 Vi: 0-0 Tstrap: 0-0
Best Rating: 117 4/01 Weth 2m4f110y gd-sft Hdl

A useful handicap hurdler. Suited by two and a half miles and testing conditions. Does not want firm ground.

Just Magical

85f **80f**

5-y-o b m Emperor Jones (USA)-Magnetic Point (USA) (Bering)

A B Coogan A B Coogan

Placings:*50* **(2460)**

2001/02: 16^{5}G, 16^{0}S

	Starts	1st	2nd	3rd	Win & Pl
NH Flat	2	0	0	0	0
Career Total	**2**	**0**	**0**	**0**	**0**

Going: Sf: 0-1 GS: 0-0 Gd: 0-1 GF: - Fm: 0-0
Distance: 2m/2m3: 0-2 2m4-2m7: 0-0 3m+: 0-0
Track: LH: 0-2 RH: 0-0 Tight: 0-0 Gall: 0-0
Aids: Bl: 0-0 Vi: 0-0 Tstrap: 0-0
Best Rating: 80 11/01 Wwck 2m good NHF

Just Maybe (IRE)

102 **97**

8-y-o b g Glacial Storm (USA)-Purlace (Realm)

R Johnson C Gwin

Placings:*0/0U40P/5F022* **(4392)**

2001/02: 24^{5}S, 24^{F}S, 24^{0}S, 24^{2}HY, 22^{2}HY

	Starts	1st	2nd	3rd	Win & Pl
Hurdles	5	0	2	0	1637
Career Total	**11**	**0**	**2**	**0**	**1912**

Going: Sf: 0-5 GS: 0-0 Gd: 0-0 GF: - Fm: 0-0
Distance: 2m/2m3: 0-0 2m4-2m7: 0-1 3m+: 0-4
Track: LH: 0-4 RH: 0-1 Tight: 0-1 Gall: 0-1
Aids: Bl: 0-2 Vi: 0-0 Tstrap: 0-1
Best Rating: 97 3/02 Kels 2m6f110y heavy Hdl

Moderate stayer, he acts on soft ground.

Just Midas

92 **70**

4-y-o b g Merdon Melody-Thabeh (Shareef Dancer (USA))

K R Burke D G & D J Robinson

Placings:06 **(2301)**

2001/02: 16^{0}S, 16^{6}GF

	Starts	1st	2nd	3rd	Win & Pl
Hurdles	2	0	0	0	0
Career Total	**2**	**0**	**0**	**0**	**0**

Going: Sf: 0-1 GS: 0-0 Gd: 0-0 GF: - Fm: 0-1
Distance: 2m/2m3: 0-2 2m4-2m7: 0-0 3m+: 0-0
Track: LH: 0-2 RH: 0-0 Tight: 0-1 Gall: 0-0
Aids: Bl: 0-0 Vi: 0-0 Tstrap: 0-0
Best Rating: 70 11/01 Catt 2m gd-fm Hdl

Just Muckin Around (IRE)

86 **78**

6-y-o gr g Celio Rufo-Cousin Muck (IRE) (Henbit (USA))

R H Buckler E H Crawshaw

Placings:*05PP* **(3212)**

2001/02: 16^{0}G, 16^{5}G, 21^{P}HY, 19^{P}GS

	Starts	1st	2nd	3rd	Win & Pl
NH Flat	1	0	0	0	0
Hurdles	3	0	0	0	0
Career Total	**4**	**0**	**0**	**0**	**0**

Going: Sf: 0-1 GS: 0-1 Gd: 0-2 GF: - Fm: 0-0
Distance: 2m/2m3: 0-3 2m4-2m7: 0-1 3m+: 0-0
Track: LH: 0-2 RH: 0-2 Tight: 0-0 Gall: 0-1
Aids: Bl: 0-0 Vi: 0-0 Tstrap: 0-0
Best Rating: 82 10/01 Chel 2m110y good NHF

Just Murphy (IRE)

109 **119**

4-y-o b g Namaqualand (USA)-Bui-Doi (IRE) (Dance Of Life (USA))

N J Henderson (G A Swinbank 27/9) Raymond Tooth

Placings:4513 **(4813)**

2001/02: 17^{4}GS, 16^{5}G, 17^{1}S, 17^{3}GF

	Starts	1st	2nd	3rd	Win & Pl
Hurdles	4	1	0	1	4889
Career Total	**4**	**1**	**0**	**1**	**4889**

116 3/02 Hrfd 2m1f D Hdl SFT £3575

Total win prize-money £3575

Going: Sf: 1-1 GS: 0-1 Gd: 0-1 GF: - Fm: 0-1
Distance: **2m/2m3: 1-4** 2m4-2m7: 0-0 3m+: 0-0
Track: LH: 0-1 **RH: 1-3** Tight: 0-1 Gall: 0-1
Aids: Bl: 0-0 Vi: 0-0 Tstrap: 0-0
Best Rating: 119 4/02 Chel 2m1f gd-fm Hdl

Not a very big sort, he was let down by his jumping on his hurdles debut. Has a slightly awkward head carriage, but that did not stop him running fifth in the Adonis Hurdle and scoring at Hereford in March. Did most of his winning on the level on a sound surface but handles soft ground.

Just One Question (IRE)

103(81h) **87**

12-y-o b g Torus-Stormy Night (Deep Run)

Brendan W Duke (S E H Sherwood 28/5) Mrs Richard Pilkington

Placings:*10/00P2/46***P2F4/6/00-F6P** **(2214)**

2001/02: 21^{F}GF, 24^{6}GF, 25^{P}G

	Starts	1st	2nd	3rd	Win & Pl
Chases	3	0	0	0	0
Career Total	**18**	**1**	**2**	**0**	**5047**

96 11/95 Naas 2m NHF GD £3051

Total win prize-money £3052

Going: Sf: 0-0 GS: 0-0 Gd: 0-1 GF: - Fm: 0-2
Distance: 2m/2m3: 0-0 2m4-2m7: 0-1 3m+: 0-2
Track: LH: 0-0 RH: 0-3 Tight: 0-0 Gall: 0-1
Aids: Bl: 0-0 Vi: 0-0 Tstrap: 0-0
Best Rating: 96 11/95 Naas 2m good NHF

Just Reuben (IRE)

88 **85**

7-y-o gr g Roselier (FR)-Sharp Mama Vii (Damsire Unregistered)

C Tizzard Alvin Trowbridge

Placings:F04P2345 **(4884)**

2001/02: 26^{F}G, 23^{0}G, 21^{4}G, 26^{P}S, 20^{2}HY, 26^{3}GS, 25^{4}G, 22^{5}GF

	Starts	1st	2nd	3rd	Win & Pl
Chases	8	0	1	1	2016
Career Total	**8**	**0**	**1**	**1**	**2016**

Going: Sf: 0-2 GS: 0-1 Gd: 0-4 GF: - Fm: 0-1
Distance: 2m/2m3: 0-0 2m4-2m7: 0-3 3m+: 0-5
Track: LH: 0-1 RH: 0-3 Tight: 0-4 Gall: 0-0
Aids: Bl: 0-0 Vi: 0-0 Tstrap: 0-0
Best Rating: 85 3/02 Plum 3m2f gd-sft Ch

A modest pointer, he was in front when falling on his debut under Rules at Fontwell, but has been well held subsequently.

Just Ruffled

13-y-o b g Rough Lad-Deep Harmony (White Hart Lane)

Miss J Gill (Mrs P A Hooper 24/3) Ms P A Williams

Placings:0 **(4727)**

2001/02: 24^{0}GF

	Starts	1st	2nd	3rd	Win & Pl
Chases	1	0	0	0	
Career Total	1	**0**	**0**	**0**	

Going: Sf: 0-0 GS: 0-0 Gd: 0-0 GF: - Fm: 0-1
Distance: 2m/2m3: 0-0 2m4-2m7: 0-0 3m+: 0-1
Track: LH: 0-1 RH: 0-0 Tight: 0-0 Gall: 0-0
Aids: Bl: 0-0 Vi: 0-0 Tstrap: 0-0
Best Rating:

Just Sal

91 **77**

6-y-o b m Silly Prices-Hanim (IRE) (Hatim (USA))

R Nixon G R S Nixon

Placings:*5030P00* **(4875)**

2001/02: 17^{5}S, 16^{0}S, 16^{3}S, 16^{0}HY, 16^{P}S, 16^{0}GF, 24^{0}G

	Starts	1st	2nd	3rd	Win & Pl
NH Flat	4	0	0	1	224
Hurdles	3	0	0	0	0
Career Total	7	**0**	**0**	**1**	**224**

Going: Sf: 0-5 GS: 0-0 Gd: 0-1 GF: - Fm: 0-1
Distance: 2m/2m3: 0-6 2m4-2m7: 0-0 3m+: 0-1
Track: LH: 0-2 RH: 0-2 Tight: 0-0 Gall: 0-0
Aids: Bl: 0-0 Vi: 0-0 Tstrap: 0-0
Best Rating: 88 11/01 Carl 2m1f soft NHF

Modest form on novice hurdles.

Just Sally

80f **47f**

4-y-o b f Afzal-Hatherley (Deep Run)

J D Frost Mrs G A Robarts

Placings:0 **(4269)**

2001/02: 16^{0}S

	Starts	1st	2nd	3rd	Win & Pl
NH Flat	1	0	0	0	
Career Total	1	**0**	**0**	**0**	

Going: Sf: 0-1 GS: 0-0 Gd: 0-0 GF: - Fm: 0-0
Distance: 2m/2m3: 0-1 2m4-2m7: 0-0 3m+: 0-0
Track: LH: 0-1 RH: 0-0 Tight: 0-0 Gall: 0-0
Aids: Bl: 0-0 Vi: 0-0 Tstrap: 0-0
Best Rating: 40 3/02 Chep 2m110y soft NHF

Just Sooty

99 **92**

7-y-o br g Be My Native (USA)-March Fly (Sousa)

N G Richards David Wesley Yates

Placings:*0/3-62F5* **(4583)**

2001/02: 22^{6}G, 20^{2}G, 19^{F}G, 20^{5}G

	Starts	1st	2nd	3rd	Win & Pl
Hurdles	3	0	1	0	748
Chases	1	0	0	0	0
Career Total	**6**	**0**	**1**	**1**	**1070**

Going: Sf: 0-0 GS: 0-0 Gd: 0-4 GF: - Fm: 0-0
Distance: 2m/2m3: 0-0 2m4-2m7: 0-4 3m+: 0-0
Track: LH: 0-4 RH: 0-0 Tight: 0-1 Gall: 0-2
Aids: Bl: 0-0 Vi: 0-0 Tstrap: 0-0
Best Rating: **92** 11/01 Newc 2m4f good Hdl

Lightly-raced plating-class hurdler, he favours holding-up tactics.

Just Steffi

81(93h) **101**

9-y-o b m El Conquistador-Glen Wise (Fair Decision)
J W Mullins Mrs C White

Placings:*634*P/**F114**04**31**/435303-0444 **(3273)**
2001/02: 26^{0}S, 25^{4}S, 26^{4}HY, 26^{4}S

	Starts	1st	2nd	3rd	Win & Pl
Chases	4	0	0	0	294
Career Total	**22**	**3**	**0**	**5**	**15541**

108	4/00	NAbb	3m2f110y	E(0-115)HCh	HVY	£4173
98	11/99	NAbb	2m5f110y	E(0-105)HCh	SFT	£3205
87	11/99	NAbb	2m5f110y	E(0-105)HCh	G-S	£4685

Total win prize-money £12063

Going: Sf: 0-4 GS: 0-0 Gd: 0-0 GF: - Fm: 0-0
Distance: 2m/2m3: 0-0 2m4-2m7: 0-0 3m+: 0-4
Track: LH: 0-2 RH: 0-1 Tight: 0-2 Gall: 0-0
Aids: Bl: 0-0 Vi: 0-0 Tstrap: 0-0
Best Rating: **108** 4/00 NAbb 3m2f110y heavy Ch

Just Strong (IRE)

106 **107**

9-y-o b/br g Strong Gale-Just Dont Know (Buckskin (FR))
Mrs A M Naughton Miss J M Thompson

Placings:301/P-44PPP14 **(4855)**
2001/02: 24^{4}F, 25^{4}F, 25^{P}GS, 24^{P}GF, 24^{P}HY, 20^{1}GF, 20^{4}G

	Starts	1st	2nd	3rd	Win & Pl
Chases	7	1	0	0	3835
Career Total	**11**	**2**	**0**	**1**	**8850**

107	4/02	Carl	2m4f	E(0-110)HCh	G-F	£3542
88	4/00	MRas	3m1f	D Ch	G-F	£4371

Total win prize-money £7914

Going: Sf: 0-1 GS: 0-1 Gd: 0-1 GF: - Fm: 1-4
Distance: 2m/2m3: 0-0 **2m4-2m7: 1-2** 3m+: 0-5
Track: LH: 0-4 **RH: 1-3** Tight: 0-4 Gall: 0-0
Aids: Bl: 0-0 Vi: 0-0 Tstrap: 0-0
Best Rating: **107** 4/02 Carl 2m4f gd-fm Ch

Modest and inconsistent chaser, stays three miles, best on fast ground in the spring.

Just The Job Too (IRE)

85 **67**

5-y-o b/br g Prince Of Birds (USA)-Bold Encounter (IRE) (Persian Bold)
P C Haslam A Stancliffe & J Trevillion

Placings:000 **(4304)**
2001/02: 16^{0}G, 16^{0}GS, 16^{0}S

	Starts	1st	2nd	3rd	Win & Pl
Hurdles	3	0	0	0	-
Career Total	**3**	**0**	**0**	**0**	

Going: Sf: 0-1 GS: 0-1 Gd: 0-1 GF: - Fm: 0-0
Distance: 2m/2m3: 0-3 2m4-2m7: 0-0 3m+: 0-0
Track: LH: 0-3 RH: 0-0 Tight: 0-0 Gall: 0-0
Aids: Bl: 0-0 Vi: 0-0 Tstrap: 0-0
Best Rating: **67** 5/01 Weth 2m good Hdl

Just Tom

92 **97**

7-y-o ch g Primitive Rising (USA)-Edenburt (Bargello)
Jedd O'Keeffe Mrs A J Findlay

Placings:*630*/006 **(3395)**
2001/02: 20^{0}G, 20^{0}S, 16^{0}GS

	Starts	1st	2nd	3rd	Win & Pl
Hurdles	3	0	0	0	0
Career Total	**6**	**0**	**0**	**1**	**180**

Going: Sf: 0-1 GS: 0-1 Gd: 0-1 GF: - Fm: 0-0
Distance: 2m/2m3: 0-1 2m4-2m7: 0-2 3m+: 0-0
Track: LH: 0-3 RH: 0-0 Tight: 0-0 Gall: 0-1
Aids: Bl: 0-0 Vi: 0-0 Tstrap: 0-0
Best Rating: **97** 1/02 Weth 2m gd-sft Hdl

Just Whiskey (IRE)

92(95h) (64h)**110**

9-y-o b g Satco (FR)-Illinois Belle (Le Bavard (FR))
N A Twiston-Davies Mrs R Vaughan

Placings:*0/3*/0P/44-**21** **(1764)**
2001/02: 25^{2}GF, 26^{1}S

	Starts	1st	2nd	3rd	Win & Pl
Chases	2	1	1	0	5069
Career Total	**8**	**1**	**1**	**1**	**5834**

110	10/01	Plum	3m2f	D(0-110)HCh	SFT	£4095

Total win prize-money £4095

Going: Sf: 1-1 GS: 0-0 Gd: 0-0 GF: - Fm: 0-1
Distance: 2m/2m3: 0-0 2m4-2m7: 0-0 **3m+: 1-2**
Track: LH: 0-0 RH: 0-1 Tight: 0-1 Gall: 0-0
Aids: Bl: 0-0 Vi: 0-0 Tstrap: 0-1
Best Rating: **115** 4/99 Ayr 2m soft NHF

Improved for the switch to fences and longer trips in the autumn of 2001, winning at Plumpton. Handles any ground.

Just Woody (IRE)

84 **70**

4-y-o br g Charnwood Forest (IRE)-Zalamera (Rambo Dancer (CAN))
P Monteith (A Berry 16/11) E Nisbet

Placings:0020 **(3744)**
2001/02: 16^{0}S, 16^{0}S, 16^{2}S, 16^{0}S

	Starts	1st	2nd	3rd	Win & Pl
Hurdles	4	0	1	0	760
Career Total	**4**	**0**	**1**	**0**	**760**

Going: Sf: 0-4 GS: 0-0 Gd: 0-0 GF: - Fm: 0-0
Distance: 2m/2m3: 0-4 2m4-2m7: 0-0 3m+: 0-0
Track: LH: 0-2 RH: 0-2 Tight: 0-3 Gall: 0-1
Aids: Bl: 0-0 Vi: 0-0 Tstrap: 0-0
Best Rating: **70** 2/02 Muss 2m soft Hdl

Little form over hurdles so far.

Justabbi

8-y-o b m Henbit (USA)-Some Dream (Vitiges (FR))
N J Hawke C G Newman

Placings:*6*/P/PP **(0665)**
2001/02: 17^{P}G, 20^{P}G

	Starts	1st	2nd	3rd	Win & Pl
Hurdles	2	0	0	0	
Career Total	**4**	**0**	**0**	**0**	

Going: Sf: 0-0 GS: 0-0 Gd: 0-2 GF: - Fm: 0-0
Distance: 2m/2m3: 0-1 2m4-2m7: 0-1 3m+: 0-0
Track: LH: 0-1 RH: 0-1 Tight: 0-0 Gall: 0-0
Aids: Bl: 0-0 Vi: 0-0 Tstrap: 0-0
Best Rating:

Justenough

72f **61f**

5-y-o b g Alflora (IRE)-Mistress Ross (Impecunious)
R A Fahey R A Fahey

Placings:*0* **(0377)**
2001/02: 16^{0}GF

	Starts	1st	2nd	3rd	Win & Pl
NH Flat	1	0	0	0	
Career Total	**1**	**0**	**0**	**0**	

Going: Sf: 0-0 GS: 0-0 Gd: 0-0 GF: - Fm: 0-1
Distance: 2m/2m3: 0-1 2m4-2m7: 0-0 3m+: 0-0
Track: LH: 0-0 RH: 0-1 Tight: 0-0 Gall: 0-1
Aids: Bl: 0-0 Vi: 0-0 Tstrap: 0-0
Best Rating: **61** 5/01 Hntg 2m110y gd-fm NHF

Justin Mac (IRE)

106 **120+**

11-y-o br g Satco (FR)-Quantas (Roan Rocket)
Mrs H Dalton (A N Dalton 5/3) Mrs Caroline Shaw

Placings:*121*143/P14350P/51**2F**4P0/**1RP-6U1P** **(4376)**
2001/02: 16^{6}G, 19^{U}S, 16^{1}S, 20^{P}S

	Starts	1st	2nd	3rd	Win & Pl
Chases	4	1	0	0	2198
Career Total	**27**	**7**	**2**	**2**	**22909**

115	3/02	Leic	2m	H Ch	SFT	£2198
110	2/01	Fknm	2m5f110y	H Ch	SFT	£2256
118	11/99	Carl	2m1f	F(0-110)HHdl	SFT	£5281
132	11/98	Kels	2m110y	D(0-125)HHdl	SFT	£2731
114	12/97	Weth	2m	D Hdl	SFT	£3323
113	11/97	Aint	2m110y	H NHF	G-S	£1987
113	10/97	Sedg	2m1f	H NHF	G-F	£1213

Total win prize-money £18992

Going: Sf: 1-3 GS: 0-0 Gd: 0-1 GF: - Fm: 0-0
Distance: **2m/2m3: 1-2** 2m4-2m7: 0-2 3m+: 0-0
Track: LH: 0-1 **RH: 1-2** Tight: 0-1 Gall: 0-1
Aids: Bl: 0-1 Vi: 0-0 Tstrap: 0-0
Best Rating: **132** 11/98 Kels 2m110y soft Hdl

Appears to go on any ground. Won the 21 furlong handicap hunter chase on soft ground at Newton Abbot May 2002. Does not quite get three miles.

Justjim

110(42h) **123**

10-y-o b g Derring Rose-Crystal Run Vii (Damsire Unregistered)
N A Twiston-Davies E T Clarke

Placings:000/P0650/6/**1411**/62012B6PF2P-23P4PP (2764)
2001/02: 23^{2}GF, 26^{3}GF, 24^{P}G, 20^{4}G, 24^{P}GS, 22^{P}G

	Starts	1st	2nd	3rd	Win & Pl
Chases	6	0	1	1	3246
Career Total	**30**	**4**	**4**	**1**	**22810**

120	8/00	Bang	3m110y	D(0-125)HCh	GD	£4914
116	8/99	Worc	2m7f110y	E(0-105)HCh	SFT	£2966
95	8/99	Bang	2m4f110y	F(0-100)HCh	GD	£4338
97	7/99	Worc	2m	F(0-100)HCh	G-F	£2672

Total win prize-money £14891

Going: Sf: 0-0 GS: 0-1 Gd: 0-3 GF: - Fm: 0-2
Distance: 2m/2m3: 0-0 2m4-2m7: 0-2 3m+: 0-4
Track: LH: 0-5 RH: 0-1 Tight: 0-2 Gall: 0-2
Aids: Bl: 0-0 Vi: 0-0 Tstrap: 0-3
Best Rating: 123 11/01 Newb 2m4f good Ch

He is not all that consistent, but shows fair form in modest staying chases. He has won on soft ground, but looks better on fast and shows his best form in the summer.

Justuce Alone (IRE)

9-y-o ch g Over The River (FR)-Another Dutchess (Master Buck)
Ferdy Murphy The Poppet Partnership

Placings:000/P52F303/501333PP/46-PPPP (3366)
2001/02: 24^{P}F, 24^{P}GS, 24^{P}S, 25^{P}GS

	Starts	1st	2nd	3rd	Win & Pl
Chases	4	0	0	0	
Career Total	**24**	**1**	**1**	**5**	**6530**

110	11/99	Hexm	3m1f	F Ch	GD	£2772

Total win prize-money £2772

Going: Sf: 0-1 GS: 0-2 Gd: 0-0 GF: - Fm: 0-1
Distance: 2m/2m3: 0-0 2m4-2m7: 0-0 3m+: 0-4
Track: LH: 0-4 RH: 0-0 Tight: 0-2 Gall: 0-2
Aids: Bl: 0-3 Vi: 0-1 Tstrap: 0-0
Best Rating: 110 11/99 Hexm 3m1f good Ch

Justupyourstreet (IRE)

102 107

6-y-o b g Dolphin Street (FR)-Sure Flyer (IRE) (Sure Blade (USA))
Ms Liz Harrison David Alan Harrison

Placings:224F41 (4492)
2001/02: 20^{2}G, 17^{2}HY, 17^{4}HY, 16^{F}S, 16^{4}HY, 17^{1}GS

	Starts	1st	2nd	3rd	Win & Pl
Hurdles	6	1	2	0	5318
Career Total	**6**	**1**	**2**	**0**	**5318**

107	3/02	Carl	2m1f	E Hdl	G-S	£3094

Total win prize-money £3094

Going: Sf: 0-4 GS: 1-1 Gd: 0-1 GF: - Fm: 0-0
Distance: **2m/2m3: 1-5** 2m4-2m7: 0-1 3m+: 0-0
Track: LH: 0-3 **RH: 1-3** Tight: 0-2 Gall: 0-1
Aids: Bl: 0-0 Vi: 0-0 Tstrap: 0-1
Best Rating: 107 3/02 Carl 2m1f gd-sft Hdl

A miler on the Flat, he ran well over hurdles in 2001/02 after a two and a half-year absence, winning at Carlisle in March. He handles testing ground.

Juvantique (FR)

96f 118f

5-y-o b g Lute Antique (FR)-Vivaldy (FR) (Quart De Vin (FR))
M C Pipe M C Pipe

Placings:2 (1773)
2001/02: 17^{2}GS

	Starts	1st	2nd	3rd	Win & Pl
NH Flat	1	0	1	0	517
Career Total	**1**	**0**	**1**	**0**	**517**

Going: Sf: 0-0 GS: 0-1 Gd: 0-0 GF: - Fm: 0-0
Distance: 2m/2m3: 0-1 2m4-2m7: 0-0 3m+: 0-0
Track: LH: 0-0 RH: 0-1 Tight: 0-0 Gall: 0-0
Aids: Bl: 0-0 Vi: 0-0 Tstrap: 0-0
Best Rating: 118 10/01 Extr 2m1f gd-sft NHF

A half-brother to French Listed winner Golden Boy II, was unlucky not to score on his debut in an Exeter bumper, was out in front a long time and just got collared close home.

Juventa (FR)

105 104

5-y-o b m Chef De Clan Ii (FR)-Koutoubia (FR) (Rex Magna (FR))
G Macaire P De Maleissye Melun

Placings:53410-261311130 (3390)
2001/02: 17^{2}GS, 18^{6}VS, 17^{1}G, 17^{3}, 17^{1}GS, 20^{1}VS, 18^{1}G, 20^{3}GS, 23^{0}GS

	Starts	1st	2nd	3rd	Win & Pl
Hurdles	4	2	0	1	7853
Chases	5	2	1	1	10223
Career Total	**14**	**5**	**1**	**3**	**24728**

10/01	Bord	2m2f	Hdl	GD	£3880
10/01	Saum	2m4f	Ch	VS	£3104
9/01	Comp	2m1f110y	Ch	G-S	£4074
8/01	Stma	2m1f	Hdl	GD	£3395
4/01	Comp	2m1f110y	Ch	HVY	£3880

Total win prize-money £18333

Going: Sf: 0-0 GS: 1-4 Gd: 2-2 GF: - Fm: 0-0
Distance: **2m/2m3: 3-6** 2m4-2m7: 1-3 3m+: 0-0
Track: LH: 0-2 RH: 0-0 Tight: 0-0 Gall: 0-0
Aids: Bl: 0-0 Vi: 0-0 Tstrap: 0-0
Best Rating: 104 12/01 Chep 2m4f gd-sft Hdl

A winner over hurdles and fences in France, she was third in a Chepstow novices' hurdle over Christmas.

Juyush (USA)

91(108c) (127c)104

10-y-o b g Silver Hawk (USA)-Silken Doll (USA) (Chieftain Ii)
R M Stronge Robert Stronge

Placings:1111/440/135P/422P121F/0PPP-0P566 (4265)
2001/02: 23^{0}G, 24^{P}S, 23^{5}GF, 27^{6}S, 20^{6}S

	Starts	1st	2nd	3rd	Win & Pl
Hurdles	3	0	0	0	0
Chases	2	0	0	0	0
Career Total	**28**	**7**	**3**	**1**	**55437**

134	3/00	Tntn	3m	E Ch	SFT	£3445
137	2/00	Font	3m2f110y	D Ch	SFT	£4186
158	11/98	Asct	2m4f	A Hdl	G-S	£15699
155	2/97	Hayd	2m	B Hdl	GD	£10065
124	2/97	Sand	2m110y	D Hdl	G-S	£2905
122	1/97	Towc	2m	E Hdl	G-S	£2810
125	1/97	NAbb	2m1f	F Hdl	HVY	£2344

Total win prize-money £41456

Going: Sf: 0-3 GS: 0-0 Gd: 0-1 GF: - Fm: 0-1
Distance: 2m/2m3: 0-0 2m4-2m7: 0-1 3m+: 0-4
Track: LH: 0-3 RH: 0-2 Tight: 0-1 Gall: 0-1
Aids: Bl: 0-0 Vi: 0-0 Tstrap: 0-0
Best Rating: 158 11/98 Asct 2m4f gd-sft Hdl

Moderate chaser, he acts on most types of ground and stays three miles two furlongs.

Jymjam Johnny (IRE)

95 114

13-y-o b g Torus-Inventus (Pitpan)
M J Gingell T Pickett

Placings:0/03200P/5201F/001S0/**P435620**/32112PP/52255/4/P25-04 (0590)
2001/02: 21^{0}GF, 24^{4}GF

	Starts	1st	2nd	3rd	Win & Pl
Chases	2	0	0	0	475
Career Total	**42**	**4**	**8**	**3**	**27415**

122	1/98	Ayr	2m5f110y	E Ch	SFT	£3190
131	12/97	Bang	2m4f110y	D(0-120)HCh	G-S	£4104
100	11/95	Kels	2m2f	D(0-125)HHdl	G-S	£2584
102	3/95	Sand	2m110y	F(0-105)HHdl	G-S	£2997

Total win prize-money £12876

Going: Sf: 0-0 GS: 0-0 Gd: 0-0 GF: - Fm: 0-2
Distance: 2m/2m3: 0-0 2m4-2m7: 0-1 3m+: 0-1
Track: LH: 0-2 RH: 0-0 Tight: 0-2 Gall: 0-0
Aids: Bl: 0-0 Vi: 0-0 Tstrap: 0-0
Best Rating: 131 1/98 Newc 2m4f gd-sft Ch

Ka Rose (FR)

70f 50f

4-y-o b g Missolonghi (USA)-Quelle Etoile V (FR) (Mitsoupam (FR))
Ferdy Murphy J N Anthony

Placings:0 (4750)
2001/02: 17^{0}G

	Starts	1st	2nd	3rd	Win & Pl
NH Flat	1	0	0	0	
Career Total	**1**	**0**	**0**	**0**	

Going: Sf: 0-0 GS: 0-0 Gd: 0-1 GF: - Fm: 0-0
Distance: 2m/2m3: 0-1 2m4-2m7: 0-0 3m+: 0-0
Track: LH: 0-0 RH: 0-1 Tight: 0-0 Gall: 0-0
Aids: Bl: 0-0 Vi: 0-0 Tstrap: 0-0
Best Rating: 50 4/02 Carl 2m1f good NHF

Kabal Of Life (IRE)

84(43h) 104

8-y-o b g Montelimar (USA)-Mystery Of Life (Wolverlife)
A M Hales Andrew L Cohen

Placings:16126-6 (3889)
2001/02: 24^{6}GS

	Starts	1st	2nd	3rd	Win & Pl
Chases	1	0	0	0	0
Career Total	**6**	**2**	**1**	**0**	**7561**

129	12/00	Donc	2m3f110y	D Ch	G-S	£4101
97	10/00	Winc	2m6f	E Hdl	G-S	£2275

Total win prize-money £6377

Going: Sf: 0-0 GS: 0-1 Gd: 0-0 GF: - Fm: 0-0
Distance: 2m/2m3: 0-0 2m4-2m7: 0-0 3m+: 0-1
Track: LH: 0-0 RH: 0-1 Tight: 0-0 Gall: 0-0
Aids: Bl: 0-0 Vi: 0-0 Tstrap: 0-0
Best Rating: 129 12/00 Folk 2m5f soft Ch

Progressed well in 2000/01 but lightly-raced recently. His wins have come on yielding ground.

Kadarann (IRE)

119(116h) **152**

5-y-o b g Bigstone (IRE)-Kadassa (IRE) (Shardari)
P F Nicholls Notalotterry

Placings:121P-**1101211** **(4899)**
2001/02: 16^{1}G, 16^{1}GS, 16^{0}GS, 16^{1}S, 16^{2}G, 16^{1}G, 16^{1}G

	Starts	1st	2nd	3rd	Win & Pl
Chases	7	5	1	0	39608
Career Total	**11**	**7**	**2**	**0**	**49522**

149	4/02	Prth	2m	C Ch	GD	£7124
152	4/02	Ayr	2m	B HCh	GD	£13403
143	3/02	Winc	2m	D Ch	SFT	£4134
146	2/02	Winc	2m	C Ch	G-S	£6288
138	11/01	Wwck	2m110y	C Ch	GD	£6753
128	12/00	Fknm	2m	E Hdl	G-S	£2257
120	10/00	Chel	2m110y	C Hdl	GD	£5486

Total win prize-money £45448

Going: Sf: 1-1 GS: 1-2 Gd: 3-4 GF: - Fm: 0-0
Distance: **2m/2m3: 5-7** 2m4-2m7: 0-0 3m+: 0-0
Track: LH: 1-3 **RH: 3-3** Tight: 0-0 Gall: 0-1
Aids: Bl: 0-0 Vi: 0-0 Tstrap: 0-0
Best Rating: 152 4/02 Ayr 2m good Ch

Ex-French Flat performer, has won twice over hurdles for Nicky Henderson and had a soft palate operation before joining Paul Nicholls, who he won for on his chasing debut. He then came back to score from a three-month absence, but was well beaten in the Arkle at Cheltenham in March 2002. He returned a week later to win an ordinary novice chase at Wincanton, but was held in a more competitive event at Ayr next time before winning the next day and following up at Perth. Effective over two miles on good and good to soft ground. Has shown signs of temperament.

Kaddor (FR)

99 **109**

4-y-o ch g Luchiroverte (IRE)-Cartly (FR) (Quart De Vin (FR))
F Doumen Jim McCarthy

Placings:3 **(2295)**
2001/02: 16^{3}G

	Starts	1st	2nd	3rd	Win & Pl
Hurdles	1	0	0	1	1263
Career Total	**1**	**0**	**0**	**1**	**1263**

Going: Sf: 0-0 GS: 0-0 Gd: 0-1 GF: - Fm: 0-0
Distance: 2m/2m3: 0-1 2m4-2m7: 0-0 3m+: 0-0
Track: LH: 0-0 RH: 0-1 Tight: 0-0 Gall: 0-0
Aids: Bl: 0-0 Vi: 0-0 Tstrap: 0-0
Best Rating: 109 11/01 Asct 2m110y good Hdl

Placed form on the level in France. Third in an Ascot juvenile hurdle and was not knocked about.

Kadito

99 **98**

6-y-o b g Petoski-Kadastra (FR) (Stradavinsky)
R Dickin A P Paton

Placings:4-02500U0450 **(4601)**
2001/02: 17^{0}G, 17^{2}S, 16^{5}S, 19^{0}G, 19^{0}S, 17^{U}HY, 16^{0}GS, 16^{4}GS, 16^{5}S, 16^{0}GF

	Starts	1st	2nd	3rd	Win & Pl
NH Flat	1	0	0	0	0
Hurdles	9	0	1	0	951
Career Total	**11**	**0**	**1**	**0**	**951**

Going: Sf: 0-5 GS: 0-2 Gd: 0-2 GF: - Fm: 0-1
Distance: 2m/2m3: 0-8 2m4-2m7: 0-2 3m+: 0-0
Track: LH: 0-4 RH: 0-6 Tight: 0-0 Gall: 0-1
Aids: Bl: 0-0 Vi: 0-0 Tstrap: 0-0
Best Rating: 98 10/01 Hrfd 2m1f soft Hdl

Modest performer over hurdles. Likes to be held up and is suited to cut in the ground and trips around two miles.

Kadou Nonantais (FR)

112 **142**

9-y-o b g Cadoudal (FR)-Belle Nonantaise (FR) (Charonville (FR))
O Sherwood D & G Mercer

Placings:/1511/0**111211F/PP**P/P**P54-33534P3F** **(4027)**
2001/02: 23^{3}GS, 24^{3}GS, 28^{5}S, 28^{3}S, 24^{4}S, 28^{P}HY, 25^{3}GS, 24^{F}GS

	Starts	1st	2nd	3rd	Win & Pl
Chases	8	0	0	4	8877
Career Total	**28**	**9**	**1**	**4**	**54778**

157	2/99	Newb	3m	C Ch	G-S	£5995
154	1/99	Weth	3m1f	A Ch	HVY	£13720
149	12/98	Ling	2m4f110y	C(0-135)HCh	SFT	£4889
125	11/98	Uttx	2m	D Ch	SFT	£3737
132	11/98	Uttx	2m	D Ch	SFT	£3566
132	4/98	Ayr	2m	C Hdl	GD	£4380
137	3/98	Bang	2m1f	E Hdl	G-S	£2285
116	12/97	Wwck	2m	E Hdl	SFT	£2962
108	12/97	Hrfd	2m1f	H NHF	GD	£1030

Total win prize-money £42568

Going: Sf: 0-4 GS: 0-4 Gd: 0-0 GF: - Fm: 0-0
Distance: 2m/2m3: 0-0 2m4-2m7: 0-0 3m+: 0-8
Track: LH: 0-6 RH: 0-2 Tight: 0-2 Gall: 0-1
Aids: Bl: 0-4 Vi: 0-4 Tstrap: 0-0
Best Rating: 157 2/99 Newb 3m gd-sft Ch

He has failed to recapture the promise of his early performances since taking a crashing fall in the William Hill Handicap Chase at the 1999 Cheltenham Festival. Best around three miles, he showed slight signs of a recovery in 2001 and ran his best race this year in the Peter Marsh Chase, but he remains one to treat with caution. Runs in blinkers or visor these days and suited by an easy surface.

Kadouko (FR)

99 **120**

9-y-o b g Cadoudal (FR)-Perle Bleue (FR) (Iron Duke (FR))
J Howard Johnson (A L T Moore 2/5) G F Bear

Placings:33/33160/**26F25/11545-365453P** **(4490)**
2001/02: 17^{3}YS, 16^{6}G, 16^{5}S, 16^{4}S, 20^{5}S, 21^{3}S, 20^{P}GS

	Starts	1st	2nd	3rd	Win & Pl
Chases	7	0	0	2	1702
Career Total	**24**	**3**	**2**	**6**	**17993**

128	12/00	Thur	2m2f	(0-109)HCh	HVY	£5520
124	11/00	Thur	2m2f	Ch	HVY	£4140
104	1/99	Fair	2m2f	Hdl	HVY	£3069

Total win prize-money £12729

Going: Sf: 0-4 GS: 0-1 Gd: 0-1 GF: - Fm: 0-0
Distance: 2m/2m3: 0-4 2m4-2m7: 0-3 3m+: 0-0
Track: LH: 0-5 RH: 0-1 Tight: 0-1 Gall: 0-3
Aids: Bl: 0-0 Vi: 0-0 Tstrap: 0-2
Best Rating: 128 12/00 Thur 2m2f heavy Ch

A winner over hurdles and fences in Ireland, he is suited by heavy ground and is possibly best going right-handed.

Kafi (USA)

88(92h) (54h)**66**

6-y-o b g Gulch (USA)-Nonoalca (FR) (Nonoalco (USA))
A Streeter Racing For You Limited

Placings:00P/005-**F00000** **(1276)**
2001/02: 16^{F}GF, 17^{0}G, 16^{0}G, 20^{0}GF, 20^{0}G, 24^{0}GF

	Starts	1st	2nd	3rd	Win & Pl
Hurdles	1	0	0	0	0
Chases	5	0	0	0	0
Career Total	**12**	**0**	**0**	**0**	**0**

Going: Sf: 0-0 GS: 0-0 Gd: 0-3 GF: - Fm: 0-3
Distance: 2m/2m3: 0-3 2m4-2m7: 0-2 3m+: 0-1
Track: LH: 0-5 RH: 0-1 Tight: 0-3 Gall: 0-0
Aids: Bl: 0-0 Vi: 0-2 Tstrap: 0-0
Best Rating: 84 11/00 Ludl 2m good Hdl

Kahtan

103 **111**

7-y-o b h Nashwan (USA)-Harmless Albatross (Pas De Seul)
N J Henderson Trevor Hemmings

Placings:006-311 **(1651)**
2001/02: 16^{3}G, 20^{1}G, 20^{1}G

	Starts	1st	2nd	3rd	Win & Pl
Hurdles	3	2	0	1	6065
Career Total	**6**	**2**	**0**	**1**	**6065**

111	10/01	Bang	2m4f	E Hdl	GD	£3052
100	6/01	Worc	2m4f	E Hdl	GD	£2499

Total win prize-money £5551

Going: Sf: 0-0 GS: 0-0 Gd: 2-3 GF: - Fm: 0-0
Distance: 2m/2m3: 0-1 **2m4-2m7: 2-2** 3m+: 0-0
Track: **LH: 2-3** RH: 0-0 **Tight: 1-2** Gall: 0-0
Aids: Bl: 0-0 Vi: 0-0 Tstrap: 0-0
Best Rating: 111 10/01 Bang 2m4f good Hdl

Runner-up in the Queen Alexandra Stakes on the Flat, he landed a novices' hurdle at Bangor and should improve.

Kaid (IRE)

97(98h) (71h)**103**

7-y-o b g Alzao (USA)-Very Charming (USA) (Vaguely Noble)
R Lee Jon Waldman And John Jackson

Placings:6/452/021264-004**526P0** **(3864)**
2001/02: 17^{0}G, 17^{0}G, 16^{4}G, 21^{5}HY, 20^{2}G, 20^{6}G, 23^{P}G, 24^{0}G

	Starts	1st	2nd	3rd	Win & Pl
Hurdles	3	0	0	0	0
Chases	5	0	1	0	1304
Career Total	**18**	**1**	**4**	**0**	**6669**

106	11/00	Hrfd	2m1f	E(0-105)HHdl	SFT	£2607

Total win prize-money £2608

Going: Sf: 0-1 GS: 0-0 Gd: 0-7 GF: - Fm: 0-0
Distance: 2m/2m3: 0-3 2m4-2m7: 0-3 3m+: 0-2
Track: LH: 0-4 RH: 0-4 Tight: 0-7 Gall: 0-0
Aids: Bl: 0-0 Vi: 0-1 Tstrap: 0-0
Best Rating: 112 11/00 Weth 2m heavy Hdl

A winner over hurdles, he has shown regressive form over fences recently. Effective over two miles one, looked a non-stayer over three miles. Suited by soft ground.

Kaikovra (IRE)

103 **106**

6-y-o ch g Toulon-Dreffiane Supreme (Rusticaro (FR))
Noel T Chance Maxse Family P'Ship P Rowley & D Archard

Placings: *02134*-P6265F6 **(3244)**
2001/02: 16^{P}GS, 16^{6}G, 16^{2}G, 16^{6}G, 17^{5}GS, 16^{F}G, 16^{6}GS

	Starts	1st	2nd	3rd	Win & Pl
Hurdles	7	0	1	0	3210
Career Total	**12**	**1**	**2**	**1**	**5785**

103	10/00	Fknm	2m	H NHF	GD	£1463

Total win prize-money £1463

Going: Sf: 0-0 GS: 0-3 Gd: 0-4 GF: - Fm: 0-0
Distance: 2m/2m3: 0-7 2m4-2m7: 0-0 3m+: 0-0
Track: LH: 0-3 RH: 0-4 Tight: 0-2 Gall: 0-0
Aids: Bl: 0-0 Vi: 0-0 Tstrap: 0-0
Best Rating: 106 11/01 Chel 2m110y good Hdl

Ex-Irish, he won his bumper in good style and showed useful form in novice hurdles but was unlucky to come up against Westender at Cheltenham in October. Suited by fast ground and two miles.

Kailan Scamp

73 **25**

9-y-o gr m Palm Track-Noble Scamp (Scallywag)
J Parkes Mrs G M Z Spink

Placings: 4/0/0-00 **(1307)**
2001/02: 19^{0}GF, 16^{0}G

	Starts	1st	2nd	3rd	Win & Pl
Hurdles	2	0	0	0	
Career Total	**5**	**0**	**0**	**0**	**0**

Going: Sf: 0-0 GS: 0-0 Gd: 0-1 GF: - Fm: 0-1
Distance: 2m/2m3: 0-1 2m4-2m7: 0-1 3m+: 0-0
Track: LH: 0-1 RH: 0-1 Tight: 0-1 Gall: 0-0
Aids: Bl: 0-0 Vi: 0-0 Tstrap: 0-2
Best Rating: 80 11/97 Catt 2m good NHF

Kaiserstolz (GER)

100(107c) **91**

9-y-o b g Sure Blade (USA)-Kaisertreue (GER) (Luciano)
Ian Williams The Winning Line

Placings: 351P13/1002F5UP-00 **(1578)**
2001/02: 16^{0}G, 16^{0}G

	Starts	1st	2nd	3rd	Win & Pl
Hurdles	2	0	0	0	
Career Total	**16**	**3**	**1**	**2**	**14269**

127	5/00	Aint	2m110y	B(0-145)HHdl	G-F	£7039
109	4/00	Sedg	2m1f	E Hdl	GD	£2492
116	2/00	Sedg	2m1f	E Hdl	G-S	£2537

Total win prize-money £12070

Going: Sf: 0-0 GS: 0-0 Gd: 0-2 GF: - Fm: 0-0
Distance: 2m/2m3: 0-2 2m4-2m7: 0-0 3m+: 0-0
Track: LH: 0-2 RH: 0-0 Tight: 0-2 Gall: 0-0
Aids: Bl: 0-0 Vi: 0-0 Tstrap: 0-2
Best Rating: 128 12/00 MRas 2m1f110y soft Ch

Kaizen

98f **97f**

5-y-o ch g Lion Cavern (USA)-Legend's Daughter (USA) (Alleged (USA))
Andrew Turnell (M W Easterby 27/10) Dr John Hollowood

Placings: *10-40* **(2321)**
2001/02: 16^{4}G, 17^{0}GS

	Starts	1st	2nd	3rd	Win & Pl
NH Flat	2	0	0	0	0
Career Total	**4**	**1**	**0**	**0**	**1603**

90	1/01	Catt	2m	H NHF	G-S	£1603

Total win prize-money £1603

Going: Sf: 0-0 GS: 0-1 Gd: 0-1 GF: - Fm: 0-0
Distance: 2m/2m3: 0-2 2m4-2m7: 0-0 3m+: 0-0
Track: LH: 0-1 RH: 0-0 Tight: 0-1 Gall: 0-0
Aids: Bl: 0-0 Vi: 0-0 Tstrap: 0-0
Best Rating: 97 10/01 Sthl 2m good NHF

Kaki Crazy (FR)

109(111h) **146**

7-y-o b g Passing Sale (FR)-Radiante Rose (FR) (Akarad (FR))
M C Pipe Archie Gooch

Placings: 15P311F1034P/V515526FP104/64P54F0-412PU4503 **(4049)**
2001/02: 25^{4}GF, 30^{1}G, 28^{2}GF, 32^{P}GF, 29^{U}G, 32^{4}GS, 25^{5}G, 27^{0}S, 30^{3}G

	Starts	1st	2nd	3rd	Win & Pl
Chases	9	1	1	1	9198
Career Total	**40**	**7**	**2**	**3**	**84928**

137	5/01	Bang	3m6f	D(0-125)HCh	GD	£5551
	2/00	Autl	2m5f	HCh	HVY	£14409
	7/00	Claf	2m1f	HCh	GD	£5030
	12/98	Autl	2m2f	Hdl	HVY	£6566
	11/98	Autl	2m2f	Hdl	HVY	£6566
	10/98	Autl	2m2f	Hdl	HLD	£6566
	8/98	Claf	2m	Hdl	VS	£4040

Total win prize-money £49618

Going: Sf: 0-1 GS: 0-1 Gd: 1-4 GF: - Fm: 0-3
Distance: 2m/2m3: 0-0 2m4-2m7: 0-0 **3m+: 1-9**
Track: **LH: 1-2** RH: 0-2 **Tight: 1-3** Gall: 0-0
Aids: Bl: 0-0 **Vi: 1-9** Tstrap: 0-0
Best Rating: 146 6/01 Strf 3m4f gd-fm Ch

A winner of four hurdles and two chases in France, he has not looked entirely straightforward since joining Martin Pipe. A thorough stayer, he races lazily and needs a deal of driving. Seems best on good ground or faster.

Kalahari Ferrari

6-y-o ch g Clantime-Royal Agnes (Royal Palace)
A G Hobbs Furnish With Abbey

Placings: U0P/00-0 **(1260)**
2001/02: 16^{0}GF

	Starts	1st	2nd	3rd	Win & Pl
Hurdles	1	0	0	0	
Career Total	**6**	**0**	**0**	**0**	

Going: Sf: 0-0 GS: 0-0 Gd: 0-0 GF: - Fm: 0-1
Distance: 2m/2m3: 0-1 2m4-2m7: 0-0 3m+: 0-0
Track: LH: 0-0 RH: 0-1 Tight: 0-0 Gall: 0-1
Aids: Bl: 0-0 Vi: 0-0 Tstrap: 0-0
Best Rating: 53 6/00 Worc 2m gd-fm Hdl

Kalahari Sunset (IRE)

7-y-o gr g Warcraft (USA)-Castletown Rose (Roselier (FR))
G Brown Simmonds & Walters

Placings: *P0P*/P **(2113)**
2001/02: 25^{P}G

	Starts	1st	2nd	3rd	Win & Pl
Chases	1	0	0	0	
Career Total	**4**	**0**	**0**	**0**	

Going: Sf: 0-0 GS: 0-0 Gd: 0-1 GF: - Fm: 0-0
Distance: 2m/2m3: 0-0 2m4-2m7: 0-0 3m+: 0-1
Track: LH: 0-0 RH: 0-1 Tight: 0-1 Gall: 0-0
Aids: Bl: 0-0 Vi: 0-0 Tstrap: 0-1
Best Rating: 35 7/99 Sedg 2m1f gd-fm NHF

Kalante (IRE)

(100h) **(84h)**

9-y-o ch g Phardante (FR)-Relkal (Kalaglow)
J G Fitzgerald Mrs G M Sturges

Placings: 306365/2/0FP0-2 **(0640)**
2001/02: 19^{2}GF

	Starts	1st	2nd	3rd	Win & Pl
Hurdles	1	0	1	0	496
Career Total	**12**	**0**	**2**	**2**	**1711**

Going: Sf: 0-0 GS: 0-0 Gd: 0-0 GF: - Fm: 0-1
Distance: 2m/2m3: 0-0 2m4-2m7: 0-1 3m+: 0-0
Track: LH: 0-0 RH: 0-1 Tight: 0-1 Gall: 0-0
Aids: Bl: 0-0 Vi: 0-1 Tstrap: 0-0
Best Rating: 98 10/99 Weth 3m1f gd-fm Hdl

Kalasara (IRE)

69f **93f**

4-y-o b g Darshaan-Kumta (IRE) (Priolo (USA))
C J Mann Mrs Susan Roy

Placings: *1* **(4603)**
2001/02: 16^{1}GF

	Starts	1st	2nd	3rd	Win & Pl
NH Flat	1	1	0	0	2153
Career Total	**1**	**1**	**0**	**0**	**2153**

93	4/02	Wwck	2m	H NHF	G-F	£2152

Total win prize-money £2153

Going: Sf: 0-0 GS: 0-0 Gd: 0-0 GF: - Fm: 1-1
Distance: **2m/2m3: 1-1** 2m4-2m7: 0-0 3m+: 0-0
Track: **LH: 1-1** RH: 0-0 Tight: 0-0 Gall: 0-0
Aids: Bl: 0-0 Vi: 0-0 Tstrap: 0-0
Best Rating: 93 4/02 Wwck 2m gd-fm NHF

A half-brother to decent hurdler Kadoun, won well on his debut in a Warwick bumper.

Kalingalinga

77 **56**

5-y-o b g Zafonic (USA)-Bell Toll (High Line)
B J Curley Mrs B J Curley

Placings: P0 **(4237)**
2001/02: 16^{P}G, 16^{0}GF

	Starts	1st	2nd	3rd	Win & Pl
Hurdles	2	0	0	0	
Career Total	**2**	**0**	**0**	**0**	

Going: Sf: 0-0 GS: 0-0 Gd: 0-1 GF: - Fm: 0-1
Distance: 2m/2m3: 0-2 2m4-2m7: 0-0 3m+: 0-0
Track: LH: 0-0 RH: 0-2 Tight: 0-0 Gall: 0-2
Aids: Bl: 0-0 Vi: 0-0 Tstrap: 0-0
Best Rating: 56 3/02 Hntg 2m110y gd-fm Hdl

Kalisko (FR)

85(78h) (14h)**52**

12-y-o b g Cadoudal (FR)-Mista (FR) (Misti Iv)
Miss L V Davis Miss Louise Davis

Placings:*5U5000/05/1/P3/0***45/1PP-0U35** (3462)
2001/02: 24^{0}GF, 26^{U}S, 26^{3}HY, 20^{5}S

	Starts	1st	2nd	3rd	Win & Pl
Hurdles	1	0	0	0	0
Chases	3	0	0	1	426
Career Total	**21**	**2**	**0**	**2**	**8006**

80	11/00	Uttx	2m4f	E(0-105)HCh	HVY	£4485
93	1/97	Muss	2m4f	E(0-100)HHdl	G-F	£2637

Total win prize-money £7122

Going: Sf: 0-3 GS: 0-0 Gd: 0-0 GF: - Fm: 0-1
Distance: 2m/2m3: 0-0 2m4-2m7: 0-1 3m+: 0-3
Track: LH: 0-3 RH: 0-1 Tight: 0-0 Gall: 0-0
Aids: Bl: 0-0 Vi: 0-0 Tstrap: 0-0
Best Rating: **93** 1/97 Muss 2m4f gd-fm Hdl

Kalivar

93f **79f**

4-y-o ch f Gunner B-Promitto (Roaring Riva)
J L Spearing Nick Shutts

Placings:*400* (4743)
2001/02: 17^{4}S, 16^{0}HY, 16^{0}GF

	Starts	1st	2nd	3rd	Win & Pl
NH Flat	3	0	0	0	0
Career Total	**3**	**0**	**0**	**0**	**0**

Going: Sf: 0-2 GS: 0-0 Gd: 0-0 GF: - Fm: 0-1
Distance: 2m/2m3: 0-3 2m4-2m7: 0-0 3m+: 0-0
Track: LH: 0-1 RH: 0-1 Tight: 0-0 Gall: 0-0
Aids: Bl: 0-0 Vi: 0-0 Tstrap: 0-0
Best Rating: **79** 1/02 Tntn 2m1f soft NHF

Fair debut effort in a bumper at Taunton.

Kalko Du Charmil (FR)

5-y-o b g Kadalko (FR)-Licada (FR) (A Tempo (FR))
Mrs M Reveley Mr And Mrs J D Cotton

Placings:*00***F6** (4832)
2001/02: 16^{0}G, 16^{0}GS, 20^{F}S, 20^{6}G

	Starts	1st	2nd	3rd	Win & Pl
NH Flat	2	0	0	0	0
Hurdles	2	0	0	0	0
Career Total	**4**	**0**	**0**	**0**	**0**

Going: Sf: 0-1 GS: 0-1 Gd: 0-2 GF: - Fm: 0-0
Distance: 2m/2m3: 0-2 2m4-2m7: 0-2 3m+: 0-0
Track: LH: 0-4 RH: 0-0 Tight: 0-0 Gall: 0-1
Aids: Bl: 0-0 Vi: 0-0 Tstrap: 0-0
Best Rating: **96** 10/01 Chel 2m110y good NHF

Kallassor (FR)

100 **77**

4-y-o b g Assessor (IRE)-Balladine (FR) (Rivelago (FR))
P C Ritchens Alan Kidd And Mr Andrew Johnson

Placings:05 (4724)
2001/02: 16^{0}S, 16^{5}GF

	Starts	1st	2nd	3rd	Win & Pl
Hurdles	2	0	0	0	0
Career Total	**2**	**0**	**0**	**0**	**0**

Going: Sf: 0-1 GS: 0-0 Gd: 0-0 GF: - Fm: 0-1
Distance: 2m/2m3: 0-2 2m4-2m7: 0-0 3m+: 0-0
Track: LH: 0-2 RH: 0-0 Tight: 0-0 Gall: 0-1
Aids: Bl: 0-0 Vi: 0-0 Tstrap: 0-0
Best Rating: **71** 4/02 Chep 2m110y gd-fm Hdl

Kaluga (IRE)

97 **82**

4-y-o ch f Tagula (IRE)-Another Baileys (Deploy)
P R Rodford (I A Balding 11/5) Mrs Christine Priest

Placings:600053 (4385)
2001/02: 16^{6}G, 16^{0}G, 16^{0}GS, 21^{0}HY, 24^{5}S, 22^{3}S

	Starts	1st	2nd	3rd	Win & Pl
Hurdles	6	0	0	1	392
Career Total	**6**	**0**	**0**	**1**	**392**

Going: Sf: 0-3 GS: 0-1 Gd: 0-2 GF: - Fm: 0-0
Distance: 2m/2m3: 0-3 2m4-2m7: 0-2 3m+: 0-1
Track: LH: 0-1 RH: 0-4 Tight: 0-1 Gall: 0-2
Aids: Bl: 0-0 Vi: 0-0 Tstrap: 0-0
Best Rating: **82** 3/02 Winc 2m6f soft Hdl

By Tagula, good effort when third over two miles six furlongs at Wincanton in March.

Kamactay (IRE)

108 **104**

10-y-o b g Kambalda-Miss Aglojo (Aglojo)
D T Hughes H A Campbell

Placings:0/*1P*0F0/221163/0006000F/**51500-00030406** (4963a)
2001/02: 16^{0}YS, 22^{0}GY, 22^{0}HY, 16^{3}GS, 20^{0}GY, 20^{4}Y, 20^{0}Y, 24^{6}GY

	Starts	1st	2nd	3rd	Win & Pl
Hurdles	8	0	0	1	1549
Career Total	**33**	**4**	**2**	**2**	**21108**

	6/00	Dund	2m4f153y	(0-123)HHdl	G-Y	£4692
108	1/99	Fair	2m	HHdl	HVY	£6138
101	11/98	Fair	2m	Hdl	Y-S	£4483
103	9/97	Dund	2m135y	NHF	Y-S	£2204

Total win prize-money £17518

Going: Sf: 0-1 GS: 0-1 Gd: 0-0 GF: - Fm: 0-0
Distance: 2m/2m3: 0-2 2m4-2m7: 0-5 3m+: 0-1
Track: LH: 0-3 RH: 0-4 Tight: 0-1 Gall: 0-0
Aids: Bl: 0-1 Vi: 0-0 Tstrap: 0-0
Best Rating: **112** 11/98 Navn 2m sft-hvy Hdl

A fairly useful Irish handicap hurdler in 1998/99, he has been well below that form this term.

Kandy Four (NZ)

105(100h) **117+**

7-y-o ch g Zeditave (AUS)-Executive Suite (NZ) (Western Symphony (USA))
A Crook David J Jackson

Placings:3/0324**032-23P2362F** (4872)
2001/02: 16^{2}G, 16^{3}GF, 16^{P}G, 16^{2}G, 16^{3}G, 16^{6}GS, 16^{2}G, 16^{F}GF

	Starts	1st	2nd	3rd	Win & Pl
Chases	8	0	3	2	4556
Career Total	**16**	**0**	**5**	**5**	**8464**

Going: Sf: 0-0 GS: 0-1 Gd: 0-5 GF: - Fm: 0-2
Distance: 2m/2m3: 0-8 2m4-2m7: 0-0 3m+: 0-0
Track: LH: 0-7 RH: 0-1 Tight: 0-1 Gall: 0-3
Aids: Bl: 0-0 Vi: 0-0 Tstrap: 0-0
Best Rating: **116** 5/01 Weth 2m good Ch

Placed in novice chases before being gifted one at Market Rasen in July. Followed up by a wide margin at Perth and should now stay three miles.

Kandyson

97 **88**

11-y-o gr g Neltino-Kandy Belle (Hot Brandy)
J R Jenkins M J Allingham

Placings:*3/4P5/PF52-***4036** (1623)
2001/02: 16^{4}F, 16^{0}GF, 16^{3}GS, 21^{6}G

	Starts	1st	2nd	3rd	Win & Pl
Hurdles	4	0	0	1	358
Career Total	**12**	**0**	**1**	**2**	**1466**

Going: Sf: 0-0 GS: 0-1 Gd: 0-1 GF: - Fm: 0-2
Distance: 2m/2m3: 0-3 2m4-2m7: 0-1 3m+: 0-0
Track: LH: 0-3 RH: 0-1 Tight: 0-3 Gall: 0-0
Aids: Bl: 0-0 Vi: 0-0 Tstrap: 0-0
Best Rating: **95** 10/00 Towc 2m gd-fm Hdl

Moderate novice hurdler who seems best on fast ground.

Kanisa Diamond

7-y-o ch g Minster Son-Scotto's Regret (Celtic Cone)
Ferdy Murphy L G M Racing

Placings:*0-***6F** (0470)
2001/02: 16^{6}GF, 20^{F}GF

	Starts	1st	2nd	3rd	Win & Pl
NH Flat	1	0	0	0	0
Hurdles	1	0	0	0	0
Career Total	**3**	**0**	**0**	**0**	**0**

Going: Sf: 0-0 GS: 0-0 Gd: 0-0 GF: - Fm: 0-2
Distance: 2m/2m3: 0-1 2m4-2m7: 0-1 3m+: 0-0
Track: LH: 0-2 RH: 0-0 Tight: 0-0 Gall: 0-0
Aids: Bl: 0-0 Vi: 0-0 Tstrap: 0-0
Best Rating: **93** 5/01 Ayr 2m gd-fm NHF

Kanz Wood (USA)

6-y-o ch g Woodman (USA)-Kanz (USA) (The Minstrel (CAN))
A W Carroll (W R Muir 8/9) P J Wilmott

Placings:P (1797)
2001/02: 16^{P}S

	Starts	1st	2nd	3rd	Win & Pl
Hurdles	1	0	0	0	
Career Total	**1**	**0**	**0**	**0**	

Going: Sf: 0-1 GS: 0-0 Gd: 0-0 GF: - Fm: 0-0
Distance: 2m/2m3: 0-1 2m4-2m7: 0-0 3m+: 0-0
Track: LH: 0-1 RH: 0-0 Tight: 0-0 Gall: 0-0
Aids: Bl: 0-0 Vi: 0-0 Tstrap: 0-0
Best Rating:

Kapok (FR)

113 **127**

6-y-o b g Kaldoun (FR)-Karannja (USA) (Shahrastani (USA))
E J O'Grady Mrs Stewart Catherwood

Placings:6/331031045-**36004320100** (4950a)

2001/02: 16^{3}G, 16^{6}G, 16^{0}SH, 16^{0}G, 16^{4}Y, 16^{3}Y, 16^{2}GY, 16^{0}YS, 16^{1}S, 16^{0}Y, 16^{0}G

	Starts	1st	2nd	3rd	Win & Pl
Hurdles	11	1	1	2	15824
Career Total	**21**	**3**	**1**	**5**	**33672**

127 3/02 Limk 2m Hdl SFT £8042
132 1/01 Fair 2m HHdl HVY £7862
112 10/00 Wxfd 2m2f Hdl HVY £4140
Total win prize-money £20046

Going: Sf: 1-1 GS: 0-0 Gd: 0-4 GF: - Fm: 0-0
Distance: **2m/2m3: 1-11** 2m4-2m7: 0-0 3m+: 0-0
Track: LH: 0-3 RH: 0-5 Tight: 0-0 Gall: 0-0
Aids: Bl: 0-4 Vi: 0-0 Tstrap: 0-0
Best Rating: 132 1/01 Fair 2m heavy Hdl

Fair Irish hurdler, acts on a soft surface. Is effective over two miles.

Kappelhoff (IRE)

95f **88f**
5-y-o b g Mukaddamah (USA)-Miss Penguin (General Assembly (USA))
Mrs L Richards (P J Hobbs 7/5) Mrs Lydia Richards

Placings: *000* **(4887)**
2001/02: 18^{0}GF, 16^{0}GS, 18^{0}GF

	Starts	1st	2nd	3rd	Win & Pl
NH Flat	3	0	0	0	
Career Total	**3**	**0**	**0**	**0**	

Going: Sf: 0-0 GS: 0-1 Gd: 0-0 GF: - Fm: 0-2
Distance: 2m/2m3: 0-3 2m4-2m7: 0-0 3m+: 0-0
Track: LH: 0-3 RH: 0-0 Tight: 0-2 Gall: 0-1
Aids: Bl: 0-0 Vi: 0-0 Tstrap: 0-0
Best Rating: 88 5/01 Font 2m2f110y gd-fm NHF

Kara Queen

8-y-o ch m Silver Kite (USA)-Darakah (Doulab (USA))
W J Reed W J Reed

Placings: P **(1268)**
2001/02: 17^{P}GF

	Starts	1st	2nd	3rd	Win & Pl
Hurdles	1	0	0	0	
Career Total	**1**	**0**	**0**	**0**	

Going: Sf: 0-0 GS: 0-0 Gd: 0-0 GF: - Fm: 0-1
Distance: 2m/2m3: 0-1 2m4-2m7: 0-0 3m+: 0-0
Track: LH: 0-1 RH: 0-0 Tight: 0-1 Gall: 0-0
Aids: Bl: 0-0 Vi: 0-0 Tstrap: 0-0
Best Rating:

Karadin (FR)

99(100h) (105h)**111**
8-y-o b g Akarad (FR)-In River (FR) (In Fijar (USA))
R H Buckler Mrs D A La Trobe

Placings: 6004013212/4-0200 **(2889)**
2001/02: 17^{0}S, 17^{2}G, 16^{0}G, 16^{0}GS

	Starts	1st	2nd	3rd	Win & Pl
Hurdles	4	0	1	0	734
Career Total	**15**	**2**	**3**	**1**	**10655**

105 3/00 Winc 2m D(0-125)HHdl G-S £5213
105 1/00 Sthl 2m F(0-95)HHdl G-S £2509
Total win prize-money £7723

Going: Sf: 0-1 GS: 0-1 Gd: 0-2 GF: - Fm: 0-0
Distance: 2m/2m3: 0-4 2m4-2m7: 0-0 3m+: 0-0
Track: LH: 0-2 RH: 0-2 Tight: 0-1 Gall: 0-0
Aids: Bl: 0-0 Vi: 0-0 Tstrap: 0-0
Best Rating: 105 11/01 NAbb 2m1f good Hdl

Fair hurdler, both of his wins over hurdles have come when the ground has been on the soft side of good, but his trainer believes he needs genuinely good ground and his good effort on his second run back after a long layoff came on that surface.

Karajan (IRE)

103 **102**
5-y-o b g Fairy King (USA)-Dernier Cri (Slip Anchor)
G M Moore J R F (management Consultants) Ltd

Placings: 5434241222550 **(4110)**
2001/02: 16^{5}F, 16^{4}GF, 19^{3}G, 17^{4}GF, 20^{2}G, 21^{4}GF, 20^{1}G, 17^{2}GS, 20^{2}S, 17^{2}HY, 17^{5}HY, 21^{5}GS, 16^{0}S

	Starts	1st	2nd	3rd	Win & Pl
Hurdles	13	1	4	1	7086
Career Total	**13**	**1**	**4**	**1**	**7086**

102 9/01 Prth 2m4f110y E Hdl GD £3157
Total win prize-money £3157

Going: Sf: 0-4 GS: 0-2 Gd: 1-3 GF: - Fm: 0-4
Distance: 2m/2m3: 0-7 **2m4-2m7: 1-6** 3m+: 0-0
Track: LH: 0-3 **RH: 1-9** Tight: 0-4 Gall: 0-0
Aids: Bl: 0-0 Vi: 0-0 Tstrap: 0-0
Best Rating: 102 2/02 MRas 2m5f110y gd-sft Hdl

Modest hurdler. Stays two and a half miles, suited by good ground but handles soft.

Karen's Typhoon (IRE)

97(96c) (82c)**66**
11-y-o b g Strong Gale-Pops Girl (Deep Run)
Miss K M George Stableline

Placings: *04S/005430S45/SF110***PUP***0P/0*UFU53/5B0 453/6-6U6F0P **(0958)**
2001/02: 26^{6}GF, 25^{U}GF, 27^{6}G, 22^{F}GF, 21^{0}G, 27^{P}GF

	Starts	1st	2nd	3rd	Win & Pl
Hurdles	4	0	0	0	0
Chases	2	0	0	0	0
Career Total	**41**	**2**	**0**	**3**	**5614**

79 10/97 Towc 2m5f E(0-100)HHdl G-F £2461
74 10/97 Towc 3m E(0-100)HHdl GD £2181
Total win prize-money £4644

Going: Sf: 0-0 GS: 0-0 Gd: 0-2 GF: - Fm: 0-4
Distance: 2m/2m3: 0-0 2m4-2m7: 0-2 3m+: 0-4
Track: LH: 0-4 RH: 0-1 Tight: 0-5 Gall: 0-0
Aids: Bl: 0-1 Vi: 0-0 Tstrap: 0-0
Best Rating: 89 9/99 Sedg 2m5f gd-fm Ch

Karinga City

88 **93**
5-y-o ch g Karinga Bay-Panicaly (Rock City)
Miss M Bragg Edward Retter

Placings: *3605*P **(4762)**
2001/02: 16^{3}S, 16^{6}GS, 16^{0}GS, 19^{5}G, 20^{P}GF

	Starts	1st	2nd	3rd	Win & Pl
NH Flat	3	0	0	1	1725
Hurdles	2	0	0	0	0
Career Total	**5**	**0**	**0**	**1**	**1725**

Going: Sf: 0-1 GS: 0-2 Gd: 0-1 GF: - Fm: 0-1
Distance: 2m/2m3: 0-4 2m4-2m7: 0-1 3m+: 0-0
Track: LH: 0-3 RH: 0-2 Tight: 0-0 Gall: 0-2
Aids: Bl: 0-0 Vi: 0-0 Tstrap: 0-0
Best Rating: 106 3/02 Newb 2m110y gd-sft NHF

Promising debut in a Newbury bumper before beaten in decent company. Ran well on hurdling debut at Exeter in March 2002.

Karinga Prince

100(82h) **97**
6-y-o gr g Karinga Bay-Silent Sister (Kind Of Hush)
G L Moore Mrs Charles Sparrowhawk

Placings: 230/3233-15 **(2309)**
2001/02: 18^{1}GF, 20^{5}GS

	Starts	1st	2nd	3rd	Win & Pl
Chases	2	1	0	0	2678
Career Total	**9**	**1**	**2**	**4**	**6005**

97 5/01 Font 2m2f F Ch G-F £2678
Total win prize-money £2678

Going: Sf: 0-0 GS: 0-1 Gd: 0-0 GF: - Fm: 1-1
Distance: **2m/2m3: 1-1** 2m4-2m7: 0-1 3m+: 0-0
Track: LH: 0-0 RH: 0-1 **Tight: 1-1** Gall: 0-1
Aids: Bl: 0-0 Vi: 0-0 Tstrap: 0-1
Best Rating: 102 11/00 Kemp 2m soft Hdl

Modest hurdler/chaser, handles any ground.

Karolena Bay

106 **94+**
5-y-o ch m Karinga Bay-Owena Deep (Deep Run)
N A Twiston-Davies The Yes - No - Wait ....Sorries

Placings: *06* **(4329)**
2001/02: 16^{0}GS, 17^{6}S

	Starts	1st	2nd	3rd	Win & Pl
NH Flat	2	0	0	0	0
Career Total	**2**	**0**	**0**	**0**	**0**

Going: Sf: 0-1 GS: 0-1 Gd: 0-0 GF: - Fm: 0-0
Distance: 2m/2m3: 0-2 2m4-2m7: 0-0 3m+: 0-0
Track: LH: 0-1 RH: 0-1 Tight: 0-0 Gall: 0-0
Aids: Bl: 0-0 Vi: 0-0 Tstrap: 0-0
Best Rating: 79 3/02 Wwck 2m gd-sft NHF

Won two mile novices' seller at Stratford in May 2002. Improved form when stepped up to three and a quarter miles to win Class F novices handicap at Southwell in July. Acts on the top of the ground.

Karolina (FR)

94 **130**
5-y-o b m Pistolet Bleu (IRE)-Katevana (FR) (Cadoudal (FR))
N J Henderson (J Bertran De Balanda 14/10) Robert Waley-Cohen

Placings: 3252-21**U**430 **(4653)**
2001/02: 18^{2}HY, 18^{1}VS, 17^{U}HO, 17^{4}VS, 16^{3}GS, 20^{0}G

	Starts	1st	2nd	3rd	Win & Pl
Hurdles	4	1	1	1	32360
Chases	2	0	0	0	1164
Career Total	**10**	**1**	**3**	**2**	**46587**

6/01 Autl 2m2f HHdl VS £21339
Total win prize-money £21339

Going: Sf: 0-1 GS: 0-1 Gd: 0-1 GF: - Fm: 0-0
Distance: **2m/2m3: 1-5** 2m4-2m7: 0-1 3m+: 0-0
Track: LH: 0-2 RH: 0-0 Tight: 0-2 Gall: 0-0
Aids: Bl: 0-1 Vi: 0-0 Tstrap: 0-0
Best Rating: 130 5/01 Autl 2m2f heavy Hdl

A winner over hurdles in France, this sister to Katarino disappointed on her British debut.

Karowna

103 112

6-y-o ch m Karinga Bay-Misowni (Niniski (USA))
Ian Williams (S A Brookshaw 4/8) The M28 Partnership

Placings:0266/22F0203P1-363506 **(2433)**
2001/02: 20³GY, 21⁶YS, 21³GF, 24⁵G, 21⁰G, 20⁶GS

	Starts	1st	2nd	3rd	Win & Pl
Hurdles	6	0	0	2	1130
Career Total	**19**	**1**	**4**	**3**	**8521**

112	4/01	Hntg	2m5f110y	E Hdl	SFT	£2489

Total win prize-money £2489

Going: Sf: 0-0 GS: 0-1 Gd: 0-2 GF: - Fm: 0-1
Distance: 2m/2m3: 0-0 2m4-2m7: 0-5 3m+: 0-1
Track: LH: 0-4 RH: 0-0 Tight: 0-2 Gall: 0-1
Aids: Bl: 0-0 Vi: 0-0 Tstrap: 0-0
Best Rating: 112 8/01 Gway 2m4f gd-yld Hdl

Highly tried, she was dropped in grade to get off the mark over hurdles over two miles five at Huntingdon at the end of last season, but she has looked held since then. Acts on easy ground.

Karowna Cove

72f 31f

6-y-o ch m Karinga Bay-Quarry Machine (Laurence O)
B P J Baugh M N Dennis

Placings:0 **(4166)**
2001/02: 16⁰GS

	Starts	1st	2nd	3rd	Win & Pl
NH Flat	1	0	0	0	
Career Total	**1**	**0**	**0**	**0**	

Going: Sf: 0-0 GS: 0-1 Gd: 0-0 GF: - Fm: 0-0
Distance: 2m/2m3: 0-1 2m4-2m7: 0-0 3m+: 0-0
Track: LH: 0-1 RH: 0-0 Tight: 0-0 Gall: 0-0
Aids: Bl: 0-0 Vi: 0-0 Tstrap: 0-0
Best Rating: 31 3/02 Wwck 2m gd-sft NHF

Karratha (IRE)

107(105c) (126c)122

7-y-o b g Supreme Leader-View Of The Hills (Croghan Hill)
P J Hobbs Mrs R J Skan

Placings:232/P16252102-12P0511 **(4480)**
2001/02: 23¹GF, 23²GS, 24ᴾGS, 21⁰G, 22⁵GS, 24¹GS, 22¹G

	Starts	1st	2nd	3rd	Win & Pl
Hurdles	3	2	0	0	7062
Chases	4	1	1	0	5424
Career Total	**19**	**5**	**6**	**1**	**23656**

122	3/02	Extr	2m6f110y	D(0-125)HHdl	GD	£3705
112	3/02	Chep	3m	D(0-125)HHdl	G-S	£3357
124	10/01	Extr	2m7f110y	D Ch	G-F	£4134
114	2/01	Wwck	2m5f	D(0-120)HHdl	SFT	£3416
122	10/00	Chep	2m4f	E Hdl	G-S	£2558

Total win prize-money £17171

Going: Sf: 0-0 GS: 1-4 Gd: 1-2 GF: - Fm: 1-1
Distance: 2m/2m3: 0-0 2m4-2m7: 1-3 **3m+: 2-4**
Track: LH: 1-2 RH: 1-4 Tight: 0-1 Gall: 0-0
Aids: Bl: 0-1 Vi: 0-0 Tstrap: 0-0
Best Rating: 126 10/01 Extr 2m7f110y gd-sft Ch

A fair handicap hurdler at two and a half to three miles on soft ground. Made a successful chasing debut, but rather lost his way over fences, and returned successfully to hurdles in the spring of 2002.

Karzhang

10-y-o b g Rakaposhi King-Smokey Baby (Sagaro)
Mrs C J Robinson (W Jenks 17/2) Jeremy Beasley

Placings:*000*/5P0/3040/24-F **(4416)**
2001/02: 20ᶠS

	Starts	1st	2nd	3rd	Win & Pl
Chases	1	0	0	0	
Career Total	**13**	**0**	**1**	**1**	**1474**

Going: Sf: 0-1 GS: 0-0 Gd: 0-0 GF: - Fm: 0-0
Distance: 2m/2m3: 0-0 2m4-2m7: 0-1 3m+: 0-0
Track: LH: 0-0 RH: 0-0 Tight: 0-1 Gall: 0-0
Aids: Bl: 0-0 Vi: 0-0 Tstrap: 0-0
Best Rating: 88 5/00 Bang 2m1f good Hdl

Kasid (IRE)

96 90

7-y-o b g Caerleon (USA)-Headrest (Habitat)
C J Mann Mr C L Sturgeon & Mrs P A Sturgeon

Placings:5521/406/3-0052 **(4509)**
2001/02: 21⁰GS, 20⁰S, 22⁵G, 16²G

	Starts	1st	2nd	3rd	Win & Pl
Hurdles	4	0	1	0	669
Career Total	**12**	**1**	**2**	**1**	**4641**

106	5/99	Uttx	2m	E Hdl	GD	£2389

Total win prize-money £2390

Going: Sf: 0-1 GS: 0-1 Gd: 0-2 GF: - Fm: 0-0
Distance: 2m/2m3: 0-1 2m4-2m7: 0-3 3m+: 0-0
Track: LH: 0-1 RH: 0-3 Tight: 0-1 Gall: 0-2
Aids: Bl: 0-1 Vi: 0-0 Tstrap: 0-0
Best Rating: 106 5/99 Uttx 2m good Hdl

Lightly raced hurdler, effective at up to two miles five.

Kassala (FR)

106 124

6-y-o b m Phantom Breeze-Tip Land (FR) (Tip Moss (FR))
A King Jules Sigler

Placings:301F2100/3FP-P44F162 **(4587)**
2001/02: 16ᴾGF, 17⁴G, 17⁴G, 17ᶠGS, 16¹GF, 16⁶S, 16²G

	Starts	1st	2nd	3rd	Win & Pl
Hurdles	1	0	0	0	0
Chases	6	1	1	0	6210
Career Total	**18**	**3**	**2**	**2**	**41431**

121	11/01	Winc	2m	D(0-120)HCh	G-F	£4075
	3/00	Engh	2m1f	Ch	HLD	£11527
	10/99	Engh	2m110y	Hdl	VS	£10764

Total win prize-money £26367

Going: Sf: 0-1 GS: 0-1 Gd: 0-3 GF: - Fm: 1-2
Distance: **2m/2m3: 1-7** 2m4-2m7: 0-0 3m+: 0-0
Track: LH: 0-4 **RH: 1-2** Tight: 0-4 Gall: 0-0
Aids: Bl: 0-0 Vi: 0-0 Tstrap: 0-0
Best Rating: 124 4/02 Winc 2m good Ch

A winner over hurdles and fences in France, she was very unlucky when falling at the penultimate fence at Stratford in October when looking all over the winner. Appreciated fast ground when winning over and extended two miles at Stratford June 2002.

Kasserine Pass (IRE)

12-y-o b g Euphemism-Cooliney Queen (General Ironside)
H W Lavis Mrs S John

Placings:*0*/400/66/P **(0666)**
2001/02: 20ᴾG

	Starts	1st	2nd	3rd	Win & Pl
Hurdles	1	0	0	0	
Career Total	**7**	**0**	**0**	**0**	**162**

Going: Sf: 0-0 GS: 0-0 Gd: 0-1 GF: - Fm: 0-0
Distance: 2m/2m3: 0-0 2m4-2m7: 0-1 3m+: 0-0
Track: LH: 0-1 RH: 0-0 Tight: 0-0 Gall: 0-0
Aids: Bl: 0-0 Vi: 0-1 Tstrap: 0-0
Best Rating: 95 9/96 Fair 2m2f gd-fm NHF

Katarino (FR)

112(108h) 156

7-y-o b g Pistolet Bleu (IRE)-Katevana (FR) (Cadoudal (FR))
N J Henderson Robert Waley-Cohen

Placings:4P311111/25400/4-13 **(2846)**
2001/02: 20¹S, 24³G

	Starts	1st	2nd	3rd	Win & Pl
Chases	2	1	0	1	14890
Career Total	**16**	**6**	**1**	**2**	**160083**

156	12/01	Newb	2m4f	A Ch	SFT	£9390
144	4/99	Punc	2m	Hdl	YLD	£38750
155	3/99	Chel	2m1f	A Hdl	G-S	£45960
158	2/99	Kemp	2m	A Hdl	SFT	£9555
145	11/98	Chel	2m110y	B Hdl	GD	£7067
126	11/98	Newb	2m110y	C Hdl	G-S	£3847

Total win prize-money £114570

Going: Sf: 1-1 GS: 0-0 Gd: 0-1 GF: - Fm: 0-0
Distance: 2m/2m3: 0-0 **2m4-2m7: 1-1** 3m+: 0-1
Track: **LH: 1-1** RH: 0-1 Tight: 0-0 **Gall: 1-1**
Aids: Bl: 0-0 Vi: 0-0 Tstrap: 0-0
Best Rating: 158 3/00 Chel 2m110y good Hdl

He has suffered breathing difficulties since winning the Triumph Hurdle in 1999 and faded tamely on his only start in 2000/01. Reportedly operated on again during the close season, he was impressive on his chasing debut at Newbury in December 2001 before being held in a grade One at Kempton, where his breathing problem may have returned. Jumps well. Should stay three miles. Acts on an easy surface.

Kate's Cottage

85f 79f

6-y-o b m Faustus (USA)-Try G'S (Hotfoot)
R Ford Richard Ford

Placings:*60* **(4289)**
2001/02: 16⁶S, 17⁰GS

	Starts	1st	2nd	3rd	Win & Pl
NH Flat	2	0	0	0	0
Career Total	**2**	**0**	**0**	**0**	**0**

Going: Sf: 0-1 GS: 0-1 Gd: 0-0 GF: - Fm: 0-0
Distance: 2m/2m3: 0-2 2m4-2m7: 0-0 3m+: 0-0
Track: LH: 0-1 RH: 0-1 Tight: 0-1 Gall: 0-1
Aids: Bl: 0-0 Vi: 0-0 Tstrap: 0-0
Best Rating: 79 2/02 Donc 2m110y soft NHF

Kates Charm (IRE)

121(100c) (141c)157

9-y-o b m Glacial Storm (USA)-Lil's Charm (Free State)

R H Alner Mrs Norma Kelly

Placings:*3351*/1531110/01**F**1**F**2/21P064-341413 **(3887)**

2001/02: 16^{3}GS, 20^{4}G, 20^{1}S, 20^{4}S, 21^{1}HY, 24^{3}GS

	Starts	1st	2nd	3rd	Win & Pl
Hurdles	5	2	0	1	50520
Chases	1	0	0	1	1378
Career Total	**29**	**10**	**2**	**5**	**115452**

157	1/02	Chel	2m5f110y	A Hdl	HVY	£30000
157	12/01	Chep	2m4f	B(0-140)HHdl	SFT	£15298
146	11/00	Asct	2m4f	A Hdl	SFT	£15600
137	1/00	Hrfd	2m3f	E Ch	G-S	£3185
144	12/99	Winc	2m	D Ch	GD	£3779
131	3/99	Chep	3m	A Hdl	HVY	£9555
132	2/99	Uttx	2m6f110y	C(0-135)HHdl	HVY	£10796
123	1/99	Ling	2m3f110y	D Hdl	HVY	£3138
111	10/98	Winc	2m6f	E Hdl	G-S	£2080
106	4/98	Asct	2m110y	H NHF	GD	£2092

Total win prize-money £95523

Going: Sf: 2-3 GS: 0-2 Gd: 0-1 GF: - Fm: 0-0
Distance: 2m/2m3: 0-1 **2m4-2m7: 2-4** 3m+: 0-1
Track: **LH: 2-3** RH: 0-3 Tight: 0-0 **Gall: 1-1**
Aids: Bl: 0-0 Vi: 0-0 Tstrap: 0-0
Best Rating: 157 1/02 Chel 2m5f110y heavy Hdl

She showed plenty of promise in novice chases during 1999/2000, but stayed hurdling the following season. She won a Grade 2 event at Ascot in November 2000, but was held afterwards until winning a valuable handicap at Chepstow in December 2001. Has since added the Grade One Cleeve Hurdle at Cheltenham and ran well at Kempton after which she was retired. Suited by two and a half miles and soft ground.

Kates Fancy

89f 73f

6-y-o br m Jupiter Island-Richards Kate (Fidel)

Mrs A J Perrett S P Tindall

Placings:*0*-4 **(0436)**

2001/02: 17^{4}GF

	Starts	1st	2nd	3rd	Win & Pl
NH Flat	1	0	0	0	0
Career Total	**2**	**0**	**0**	**0**	**0**

Going: Sf: 0-0 GS: 0-0 Gd: 0-0 GF: - Fm: 0-1
Distance: 2m/2m3: 0-1 2m4-2m7: 0-0 3m+: 0-0
Track: LH: 0-0 RH: 0-0 Tight: 0-1 Gall: 0-0
Aids: Bl: 0-0 Vi: 0-0 Tstrap: 0-0
Best Rating: 73 5/01 Folk 2m1f110y gd-fm NHF

Kates Ivy Hill (IRE)

87(78h) (44h)60

8-y-o b m King Of Shannon-Raj Kumari (Vitiges (FR))

C J Price M W Jones

Placings:0000/0005**P** **(1244)**

2001/02: 17^{0}GS, 17^{0}G, 16^{0}GF, 20^{5}G, 23^{P}GF

	Starts	1st	2nd	3rd	Win & Pl
Hurdles	3	0	0	0	0
Chases	2	0	0	0	0
Career Total	**9**	**0**	**0**	**0**	**0**

Going: Sf: 0-0 GS: 0-1 Gd: 0-2 GF: - Fm: 0-2
Distance: 2m/2m3: 0-3 2m4-2m7: 0-1 3m+: 0-1
Track: LH: 0-3 RH: 0-2 Tight: 0-1 Gall: 0-0
Aids: Bl: 0-0 Vi: 0-0 Tstrap: 0-0
Best Rating: 60 8/01 Bang 2m4f110y good Ch

Kates Son (IRE)

74 22

5-y-o ch g Fayruz-Kates Choice (IRE) (Taufan (USA))

Noel T Chance Fizzgigg Partnership

Placings:00P-0 **(1907)**

2001/02: 16^{0}S

	Starts	1st	2nd	3rd	Win & Pl
Hurdles	1	0	0	0	
Career Total	**4**	**0**	**0**	**0**	

Going: Sf: 0-1 GS: 0-0 Gd: 0-0 GF: - Fm: 0-0
Distance: 2m/2m3: 0-1 2m4-2m7: 0-0 3m+: 0-0
Track: LH: 0-1 RH: 0-0 Tight: 0-1 Gall: 0-0
Aids: Bl: 0-0 Vi: 0-0 Tstrap: 0-0
Best Rating: 69 12/00 Folk 2m1f110y heavy Hdl

Kathella (IRE)

78 63

5-y-o b m Fourstars Allstar (USA)-Niat Supreme (IRE) (Supreme Leader)

N G Ayliffe R Allatt

Placings:*00* **(4887)**

2001/02: 17^{0}S, 18^{0}GF

	Starts	1st	2nd	3rd	Win & Pl
NH Flat	2	0	0	0	
Career Total	**2**	**0**	**0**	**0**	

Going: Sf: 0-1 GS: 0-0 Gd: 0-0 GF: - Fm: 0-1
Distance: 2m/2m3: 0-2 2m4-2m7: 0-0 3m+: 0-0
Track: LH: 0-1 RH: 0-0 Tight: 0-1 Gall: 0-0
Aids: Bl: 0-0 Vi: 0-0 Tstrap: 0-0
Best Rating: 40 4/02 Font 2m2f110y gd-fm NHF

Kathies Pet

88 77

7-y-o b m Tina's Pet-Unveiled (Sayf El Arab (USA))

R J Hodges Mrs E A Tucker

Placings:00303465/1 **(0122)**

2001/02: 19^{1}F

	Starts	1st	2nd	3rd	Win & Pl
Hurdles	1	1	0	0	1624
Career Total	**9**	**1**	**0**	**2**	**2088**

77	5/01	Tntn	2m3f110y	G(0-90)HHdl	FRM	£1624

Total win prize-money £1624

Going: Sf: 0-0 GS: 0-0 Gd: 0-0 GF: - Fm: 1-1
Distance: 2m/2m3: 0-0 **2m4-2m7: 1-1** 3m+: 0-0
Track: LH: 0-0 **RH: 1-1 Tight: 1-1** Gall: 0-0
Aids: Bl: 0-0 Vi: 0-0 Tstrap: 0-0
Best Rating: 77 5/01 Tntn 2m3f110y firm Hdl

Katie Buckers (IRE)

109(86h) 114

8-y-o ch m Yashgan-Glenkins (Furry Glen)

K C Bailey K C Bailey

Placings: *f*03PP-43411 **(4426)**

2001/02: 23^{4}G, 24^{3}GS, 22^{4}HY, 25^{1}G, 26^{1}HY

	Starts	1st	2nd	3rd	Win & Pl
Chases	5	2	0	1	8726
Career Total	**10**	**3**	**0**	**2**	**10686**

114	3/02	Uttx	3m2f	E(0-105)HCh	HVY	£4095
106	3/02	Hrfd	3m1f110y	E Ch	GD	£3357
100	11/00	Chep	2m110y	H NHF	HVY	£1505

Total win prize-money £8957

Going: Sf: 1-2 GS: 0-1 Gd: 1-2 GF: - Fm: 0-0
Distance: 2m/2m3: 0-0 2m4-2m7: 0-1 **3m+: 2-4**
Track: LH: 1-1 RH: 1-4 Tight: 0-0 Gall: 0-1
Aids: Bl: 0-0 Vi: 0-0 Tstrap: 0-0
Best Rating: 114 3/02 Uttx 3m2f heavy Ch

Fair form in novice chases so far. Acts on good and heavy ground. Stays three miles and relished test of stamina when winning at Hereford and Uttoxeter in the spring.

Katies Tight Jeans

43 22

8-y-o b m Green Adventure (USA)-Haraka Sasa (Town And Country)

R E Peacock M F Harris

Placings:*05/0/0*0-P6 **(2565)**

2001/02: 16^{P}GF, 16^{6}S

	Starts	1st	2nd	3rd	Win & Pl
Hurdles	2	0	0	0	0
Career Total	**7**	**0**	**0**	**0**	**0**

Going: Sf: 0-1 GS: 0-0 Gd: 0-0 GF: - Fm: 0-1
Distance: 2m/2m3: 0-2 2m4-2m7: 0-0 3m+: 0-0
Track: LH: 0-1 RH: 0-1 Tight: 0-0 Gall: 0-0
Aids: Bl: 0-0 Vi: 0-0 Tstrap: 0-0
Best Rating: 65 5/00 Worc 2m gd-fm NHF

Katinka

9-y-o b m Rymer-Millymeeta (New Brig)

A M Thomson A M Thomson

Placings:F4-06 **(2473)**

2001/02: 22^{0}GS, 16^{6}GS

	Starts	1st	2nd	3rd	Win & Pl
Hurdles	2	0	0	0	0
Career Total	**4**	**0**	**0**	**0**	**450**

Going: Sf: 0-0 GS: 0-2 Gd: 0-0 GF: - Fm: 0-0
Distance: 2m/2m3: 0-1 2m4-2m7: 0-1 3m+: 0-0
Track: LH: 0-2 RH: 0-0 Tight: 0-1 Gall: 0-0
Aids: Bl: 0-0 Vi: 0-0 Tstrap: 0-0
Best Rating:

Katiypour (IRE)

96 94

5-y-o ch g Be My Guest (USA)-Katiyfa (Auction Ring (USA))

P R Webber Mr & Mrs J S Dale

Placings:66 **(3463)**

2001/02: 16^{6}GF, 16^{6}S

	Starts	1st	2nd	3rd	Win & Pl
Hurdles	2	0	0	0	0
Career Total	**2**	**0**	**0**	**0**	**0**

Going: Sf: 0-1 GS: 0-0 Gd: 0-0 GF: - Fm: 0-1
Distance: 2m/2m3: 0-2 2m4-2m7: 0-0 3m+: 0-0
Track: LH: 0-2 RH: 0-0 Tight: 0-1 Gall: 0-1
Aids: Bl: 0-0 Vi: 0-0 Tstrap: 0-0
Best Rating: 72 1/02 Donc 2m110y soft Hdl

Yet to prove he stays two miles over hurdles.

Katsar (IRE)

96 **74**

10-y-o b g Castle Keep-Welsh Partner (Welsh Saint)
Jedd O'Keeffe Derek Gennard

Placings:0/5F4P0P0/0**PU61U/2U40/256-5** **(0650)**
2001/02: 16^{5}GF

	Starts	1st	2nd	3rd	Win & Pl
Chases	1	0	0	0	0
Career Total	**22**	**1**	**2**	**0**	**5289**

80	9/98	Worc	2m	E(0-100)HCh	G-F	£2974

Total win prize-money £2975

Going: Sf: 0-0 GS: 0-0 Gd: 0-0 GF: - Fm: 0-1
Distance: 2m/2m3: 0-1 2m4-2m7: 0-0 3m+: 0-0
Track: LH: 0-0 RH: 0-1 Tight: 0-0 Gall: 0-0
Aids: Bl: 0-0 Vi: 0-0 Tstrap: 0-0
Best Rating: 91 8/00 Ctml 2m1f110y gd-sft Ch

Kattegat

89(112h) (112h)**105**

6-y-o b g Slip Anchor-Kirsten (Kris)
J A B Old W E Sturt

Placings:220/04-100**353P** **(4514)**
2001/02: 16^{1}GS, 17^{0}G, 21^{0}GS, 16^{3}S, 18^{5}GS, 19^{3}G, 25^{P}GS

	Starts	1st	2nd	3rd	Win & Pl
Hurdles	3	1	0	0	5395
Chases	4	0	0	2	1360
Career Total	**12**	**1**	**2**	**2**	**10427**

112	11/01	Leic	2m	C(0-130)HHdl	G-S	£5395

Total win prize-money £5395

Going: Sf: 0-1 GS: 1-4 Gd: 0-2 GF: - Fm: 0-0
Distance: **2m/2m3: 1-4** 2m4-2m7: 0-2 3m+: 0-1
Track: LH: 0-2 **RH: 1-5** Tight: 0-1 Gall: 0-3
Aids: Bl: 0-0 Vi: 0-0 Tstrap: 0-0
Best Rating: 115 2/00 Hntg 2m4f110y soft Hdl

Lightly-raced hurdler who showed plenty of ability as a juvenile early in 2000. Had foot problems last term. Made a winning return in November 2001. Best at around two miles on an easy surface. He has yet to make his mark over fences.

Katy The Duck (IRE)

105 **73**

7-y-o br m Over The River (FR)-Zagliarelle (FR) (Rose Laurel)
R J Price R J Price

Placings:0P6-0U0 **(4546)**
2001/02: 22^{0}GS, 24^{U}G, 16^{0}GF

	Starts	1st	2nd	3rd	Win & Pl
Hurdles	3	0	0	0	
Career Total	**6**	**0**	**0**	**0**	**0**

Going: Sf: 0-0 GS: 0-1 Gd: 0-1 GF: - Fm: 0-1
Distance: 2m/2m3: 0-1 2m4-2m7: 0-1 3m+: 0-1
Track: LH: 0-1 RH: 0-1 Tight: 0-0 Gall: 0-1
Aids: Bl: 0-0 Vi: 0-0 Tstrap: 0-0
Best Rating: 61 5/00 Bang 2m1f good NHF

Kauroa Mail (NZ)

101 **77**

8-y-o b g First Norman (USA)-Penny Letter (NZ) (One Pound Sterling)
B P J Baugh (A King 5/5) Mrs C Norlander

Placings:54F/0-U03053000400 **(2316)**
2001/02: 26^{U}G, 17^{0}GF, 20^{3}GS, 22^{0}GF, 20^{5}G, 20^{3}GF, 20^{0}GF, 20^{0}G, 20^{0}GF, 20^{4}S, 16^{0}S, 20^{0}GS

	Starts	1st	2nd	3rd	Win & Pl
Hurdles	12	0	0	2	958
Career Total	**16**	**0**	**0**	**2**	**1249**

Going: Sf: 0-2 GS: 0-2 Gd: 0-3 GF: - Fm: 0-5
Distance: 2m/2m3: 0-2 2m4-2m7: 0-9 3m+: 0-1
Track: LH: 0-9 RH: 0-3 Tight: 0-5 Gall: 0-1
Aids: Bl: 0-0 Vi: 0-0 Tstrap: 0-0
Best Rating: 105 12/99 Uttx 2m soft Hdl

Keaneo (IRE)

90(92h) (97h)**88**

7-y-o b g Aristocracy-Nessa-Pride (IRE) (Balboa)
N A Twiston-Davies H R Mould

Placings:4F00-1P02003 **(4566)**
2001/02: 20^{1}G, 21^{P}G, 20^{0}G, 21^{2}GS, 20^{0}G, 20^{0}S, 16^{3}G

	Starts	1st	2nd	3rd	Win & Pl
Hurdles	5	1	1	0	4540
Chases	2	0	0	1	647
Career Total	**11**	**1**	**1**	**1**	**5187**

97	9/01	Prth	2m4f110y	F(0-100)HHdl	GD	£3484

Total win prize-money £3484

Going: Sf: 0-1 GS: 0-1 Gd: 1-5 GF: - Fm: 0-0
Distance: 2m/2m3: 0-1 **2m4-2m7: 1-6** 3m+: 0-0
Track: LH: 0-2 **RH: 1-5** Tight: 0-1 Gall: 0-2
Aids: Bl: 0-0 Vi: 0-0 Tstrap: 0-0
Best Rating: 100 9/00 Chep 2m110y good NHF

Modest novice chaser, won a moderate two and a half mile handicap hurdle at Perth in September 2001. Suited by good ground, two and a half miles and front running tactics. Has broken blood-vessels

Kedge Anchor Man

105 **106**

11-y-o b g Bustino-Jenny Mere (Brigadier Gerard)
N A Gaselee Anthony M Green

Placings:3/F/2265/**6U2F4/02115** **(4136)**
2001/02: 20^{0}S, 17^{2}G, 20^{1}GS, 20^{1}HY, 22^{5}GS

	Starts	1st	2nd	3rd	Win & Pl
Hurdles	5	2	1	0	7190
Career Total	**16**	**2**	**4**	**1**	**10474**

106	2/02	Sand	2m4f110y	D(0-110)HHdl	HVY	£4446
100	1/02	Hntg	2m4f110y	F(0-95)HHdl	G-S	£2024

Total win prize-money £6470

Going: Sf: 1-2 GS: 1-2 Gd: 0-1 GF: - Fm: 0-0
Distance: 2m/2m3: 0-1 **2m4-2m7: 2-4** 3m+: 0-0
Track: LH: 0-1 **RH: 2-4** Tight: 0-0 **Gall: 1-1**
Aids: Bl: 0-0 Vi: 0-0 Tstrap: 0-0
Best Rating: 119 12/99 Extr 2m7f110y gd-sft Ch

Landed two weak novices' handicap hurdles early in 2002. Stays two and a half miles, effective on testing ground.

Keen Leader (IRE)

113 **154**

6-y-o b g Supreme Leader-Keen Gale (IRE) (Strong Gale)
J J O'Neill Mrs Stewart Catherwood

Placings:1-111F **(4229)**
2001/02: 21^{1}HY, 20^{1}S, 20^{1}HY, 21^{F}GS

	Starts	1st	2nd	3rd	Win & Pl
Hurdles	4	3	0	0	19245
Career Total	**5**	**4**	**0**	**0**	**22087**

154	2/02	Uttx	2m4f110y	A Hdl	HVY	£12000
126	1/02	Leic	2m4f110y	E Hdl	SFT	£3052
114	12/01	Towc	2m5f	D Hdl	HVY	£4192
124	4/01	Prth	2m110y	H NHF	HVY	£2842

Total win prize-money £22087

Going: Sf: 3-3 GS: 0-1 Gd: 0-0 GF: - Fm: 0-0
Distance: 2m/2m3: 0-0 **2m4-2m7: 3-4** 3m+: 0-0
Track: LH: 1-2 **RH: 2-2** Tight: 0-0 Gall: 0-1
Aids: Bl: 0-0 Vi: 0-0 Tstrap: 0-0
Best Rating: 154 3/02 Chel 2m5f gd-sft Hdl

Promising potential chaser, scored on his first four starts over hurdles before falling when in front in the Royal & SunAlliance Hurdle. Handles soft conditions well, but unproven on faster. Stays two and a half miles.

Keen To The Last (FR)

109(103h) (102h)**119**

10-y-o ch g Keen-Derniere Danse (Gay Mecene (USA))
Mrs S J Smith D E Allen & Mr S Balmer

Placings:03223/13442/**2122/P44514/22-12F22641P** **(4596)**
2001/02: 20^{1}G, 20^{2}S, 25^{F}G, 22^{2}S, 20^{2}S, 20^{6}S, 19^{4}S, 21^{1}S, 20^{P}G

	Starts	1st	2nd	3rd	Win & Pl
Hurdles	1	1	0	0	2562
Chases	8	1	3	0	8494
Career Total	**31**	**5**	**11**	**3**	**32036**

116	3/02	Sedg	2m5f	D(0-115)HCh	SFT	£4284
102	10/01	Sthl	2m4f110y	E(0-115)HHdl	GD	£2562
117	3/00	MRas	2m4f	F(0-110)HCh	G-F	£3581
119	3/99	Newc	2m4f	E Ch	SFT	£4195
95	10/96	Weth	2m4f110y	E Hdl	GD	£2075

Total win prize-money £16698

Going: Sf: 1-6 GS: 0-0 Gd: 1-3 GF: - Fm: 0-0
Distance: 2m/2m3: 0-1 **2m4-2m7: 2-7** 3m+: 0-1
Track: **LH: 2-7** RH: 0-2 **Tight: 2-6** Gall: 0-0
Aids: Bl: 0-0 Vi: 0-0 Tstrap: 0-0
Best Rating: 119 6/00 MRas 2m6f110y gd-sft Ch

Modest chaser, effective at around two and a half miles. Needs the top of the ground to stay three miles but handles all types of going.

Keen Waters

99 **89**

8-y-o b m Keen-Miss Oasis (Green Desert (USA))
R J Price Mrs K Oseman

Placings:5/1121/02F1FF530/12006S56-002366P **(1405)**
2001/02: 17^{0}G, 17^{0}F, 16^{2}G, 16^{3}G, 16^{6}GF, 16^{6}GF, 16^{P}GF

	Starts	1st	2nd	3rd	Win & Pl
Hurdles	7	0	1	1	1084
Career Total	**29**	**5**	**4**	**2**	**16207**

97	7/00	Wolv	2m	G Hdl	G-S	£1484
94	6/99	NAbb	2m110y	D Ch	G-F	£3718
105	8/98	MRas	2m1f110y	E(0-100)HHdl	GD	£2234
103	6/98	NAbb	2m1f	D Hdl	GD	£2872
94	6/98	MRas	2m1f110y	E Hdl	GD	£2460

Total win prize-money £12769

Going: Sf: 0-0 GS: 0-0 Gd: 0-3 GF: - Fm: 0-4
Distance: 2m/2m3: 0-7 2m4-2m7: 0-0 3m+: 0-0
Track: LH: 0-4 RH: 0-3 Tight: 0-1 Gall: 0-1

Aids: Bl: 0-0 Vi: 0-6 Tstrap: 0-7
Best Rating: 105 8/00 Worc 2m2f gd-fm Hdl

Keep Forgetting

78f 81f

5-y-o b g Grand Lodge (USA)-Ice Chocolate (USA) (Icecapade (USA))
D E Cantillon Mrs Catherine Reed

Placings:*0* **(0064)**
2001/02: 17^{0}GS

	Starts	1st	2nd	3rd	Win & Pl
NH Flat	1	0	0	0	
Career Total	**1**	**0**	**0**	**0**	

Going: Sf: 0-0 GS: 0-1 Gd: 0-0 GF: - Fm: 0-0
Distance: 2m/2m3: 0-1 2m4-2m7: 0-0 3m+: 0-0
Track: LH: 0-0 RH: 0-0 Tight: 0-1 Gall: 0-0
Aids: Bl: 0-0 Vi: 0-0 Tstrap: 0-0
Best Rating: 81 5/01 Folk 2m1f110y gd-sft NHF

Keep Me In Mind (IRE)

85 64

13-y-o b g Don't Forget Me-Gold Trinket (Golden Fleece (USA))
N R Mitchell Mrs E Mitchell

Placings:300/322252110/0203220651/03502401P05/544550/0**15F34FPP**/**P**5036422PP2/45256253**40**005**P**/100-06 **(0562)**
2001/02: 19^{0}G, 22^{6}GF

	Starts	1st	2nd	3rd	Win & Pl
Hurdles	2	0	0	0	0
Career Total	**78**	**6**	**13**	**7**	**43888**

86	10/00	Winc	2m6f	F(0-105)HHdl	G-S	£2795
106	10/97	Extr	2m1f110y	E(0-105)HCh	GD	£3127
116	1/96	Winc	2m	D(0-125)HHdl	G-S	£2862
116	4/95	Chep	2m4f110y	D(0-125)HHdl	FRM	£7887
120	4/94	Winc	2m	Hdl	SFT	£2495
112	3/94	Winc	2m	Hdl	G-S	£2337

Total win prize-money £21507

Going: Sf: 0-0 GS: 0-0 Gd: 0-1 GF: - Fm: 0-1
Distance: 2m/2m3: 0-1 2m4-2m7: 0-1 3m+: 0-0
Track: LH: 0-1 RH: 0-1 Tight: 0-1 Gall: 0-0
Aids: Bl: 0-0 Vi: 0-0 Tstrap: 0-2
Best Rating: 120 4/94 Winc 2m soft Hdl

Keep Smiling (IRE)

92 85

6-y-o b g Broken Hearted-Laugh Away (Furry Glen)
Miss H C Knight Mrs R A Humphries

Placings:64P **(2541)**
2001/02: 17^{6}S, 21^{4}G, 17^{P}GS

	Starts	1st	2nd	3rd	Win & Pl
Hurdles	3	0	0	0	274
Career Total	**3**	**0**	**0**	**0**	**274**

Going: Sf: 0-1 GS: 0-1 Gd: 0-1 GF: - Fm: 0-0
Distance: 2m/2m3: 0-2 2m4-2m7: 0-1 3m+: 0-0
Track: LH: 0-0 RH: 0-3 Tight: 0-0 Gall: 0-0
Aids: Bl: 0-0 Vi: 0-0 Tstrap: 0-0
Best Rating: 85 11/01 Kemp 2m5f good Hdl

Keeper's Call (IRE)

10-y-o b g Mandalus-Thistletopper (Le Bavard (FR))
R G Makin R G Makin

Placings:12/4/P-56 **(0427)**
2001/02: 25^{5}G, 33^{6}G

	Starts	1st	2nd	3rd	Win & Pl
Chases	2	0	0	0	0
Career Total	**6**	**1**	**1**	**0**	**2433**

108	4/99	Carl	3m2f	H Ch	GD	£1155

Total win prize-money £1155

Going: Sf: 0-0 GS: 0-0 Gd: 0-2 GF: - Fm: 0-0
Distance: 2m/2m3: 0-0 2m4-2m7: 0-0 3m+: 0-2
Track: LH: 0-1 RH: 0-0 Tight: 0-0 Gall: 0-0
Aids: Bl: 0-0 Vi: 0-0 Tstrap: 0-0
Best Rating: 113 4/99 Chel 3m1f110y gd-sft Ch

Keeps Going

7-y-o b g Teenoso (USA)-Celtic Slave (Celtic Cone)
T J Etherington Mrs J E Todd

Placings:*3P*/P-PPP **(4788)**
2001/02: 20^{P}HY, 19^{P}GF, 20^{P}F

	Starts	1st	2nd	3rd	Win & Pl
Hurdles	3	0	0	0	
Career Total	**6**	**0**	**0**	**1**	**244**

Going: Sf: 0-1 GS: 0-0 Gd: 0-0 GF: - Fm: 0-2
Distance: 2m/2m3: 0-0 2m4-2m7: 0-3 3m+: 0-0
Track: LH: 0-2 RH: 0-1 Tight: 0-2 Gall: 0-1
Aids: Bl: 0-1 Vi: 0-0 Tstrap: 0-0
Best Rating: 98 3/00 Carl 2m1f heavy NHF

Keiran (IRE)

107 101

8-y-o b g Be My Native (USA)-Myra Gaye (Buckskin (FR))
D M Forster D M Forster

Placings:60-241400 **(4896)**
2001/02: 20^{2}G, 21^{4}G, 16^{1}GF, 20^{4}G, 24^{0}G, 20^{0}G

	Starts	1st	2nd	3rd	Win & Pl
Hurdles	6	1	1	0	3754
Career Total	**8**	**1**	**1**	**0**	**3754**

101	11/01	Catt	2m	F(0-100)HHdl	G-F	£2607

Total win prize-money £2608

Going: Sf: 0-0 GS: 0-0 Gd: 0-5 GF: - Fm: 1-1
Distance: **2m/2m3: 1-1** 2m4-2m7: 0-4 3m+: 0-1
Track: **LH: 1-5** RH: 0-1 **Tight: 1-3** Gall: 0-1
Aids: Bl: 0-0 Vi: 0-0 Tstrap: 0-0
Best Rating: 101 11/01 Catt 2m gd-fm Hdl

A fair novice hurdler from a small yard. Stays two and a half miles, has won over two. Acts on a sound surface.

Kelami (FR)

101 120

4-y-o b g Lute Antique (FR)-Voltige De Nievre (FR) (Laniste)
F Doumen Queen Elizabeth

Placings:22P **(4250)**
2001/02: 16^{2}GS, 16^{2}S, 17^{P}G

	Starts	1st	2nd	3rd	Win & Pl
Hurdles	3	0	2	0	2700
Career Total	**3**	**0**	**2**	**0**	**2700**

Going: Sf: 0-1 GS: 0-1 Gd: 0-1 GF: - Fm: 0-0
Distance: 2m/2m3: 0-3 2m4-2m7: 0-0 3m+: 0-0
Track: LH: 0-2 RH: 0-1 Tight: 0-0 Gall: 0-2
Aids: Bl: 0-1 Vi: 0-0 Tstrap: 0-1
Best Rating: 120 2/02 Sand 2m110y soft Hdl

A lightly-raced maiden on the Flat, made a good start over hurdles when runner-up at Newbury in December and filled the same position in a similar event at Sandown in February.

Keldan Star (IRE)

8-y-o b g Top Of The World-Kylemore Abbess (Monksfield)
D Burchell B A Hall

Placings:P-FP **(0496)**
2001/02: 26^{F}GF, 16^{P}G

	Starts	1st	2nd	3rd	Win & Pl
Chases	2	0	0	0	
Career Total	**3**	**0**	**0**	**0**	

Going: Sf: 0-0 GS: 0-0 Gd: 0-1 GF: - Fm: 0-1
Distance: 2m/2m3: 0-1 2m4-2m7: 0-0 3m+: 0-1
Track: LH: 0-1 RH: 0-1 Tight: 0-1 Gall: 0-0
Aids: Bl: 0-0 Vi: 0-0 Tstrap: 0-0
Best Rating:

Kelly Canyon

10-y-o ch g Good Thyne (USA)-Kitty Castle (Rubor)
A M Thomson A M Thomson

Placings:P-0 **(4690)**
2001/02: 25^{0}GF

	Starts	1st	2nd	3rd	Win & Pl
Chases	1	0	0	0	
Career Total	**2**	**0**	**0**	**0**	

Going: Sf: 0-0 GS: 0-0 Gd: 0-0 GF: - Fm: 0-1
Distance: 2m/2m3: 0-0 2m4-2m7: 0-0 3m+: 0-1
Track: LH: 0-1 RH: 0-0 Tight: 0-1 Gall: 0-0
Aids: Bl: 0-0 Vi: 0-0 Tstrap: 0-1
Best Rating: 54 4/02 Kels 3m1f gd-fm Ch

Kelly Pride

80 72

5-y-o b g Alflora (IRE)-Pearly-B (IRE) (Gunner B)
J Howard Johnson Group Captain J A Prideaux

Placings:000 **(4040)**
2001/02: 16^{0}G, 16^{0}S, 17^{0}GS

	Starts	1st	2nd	3rd	Win & Pl
Hurdles	3	0	0	0	
Career Total	**3**	**0**	**0**	**0**	

Going: Sf: 0-1 GS: 0-1 Gd: 0-1 GF: - Fm: 0-0
Distance: 2m/2m3: 0-3 2m4-2m7: 0-0 3m+: 0-0
Track: LH: 0-0 RH: 0-3 Tight: 0-3 Gall: 0-0
Aids: Bl: 0-0 Vi: 0-0 Tstrap: 0-0
Best Rating: 72 1/02 Muss 2m good Hdl

Kellys Conquest

87 75

9-y-o b m El Conquistador-Kellys Special (Netherkelly)
J W Mullins F G Matthews

Placings:6F2214/**6135301/333-6PPP** **(3341)**
2001/02: 26^{6}G, 25^{P}G, 25^{P}G, 27^{P}S

	Starts	1st	2nd	3rd	Win & Pl
Chases	4	0	0	0	0
Career Total	**20**	**3**	**2**	**5**	**21239**

137	4/00	Chel	3m1f110y	C Ch	SFT	£8190
131	12/99	Extr	2m3f	D Ch	G-S	£4077
111	4/99	Extr	2m3f110y	E Hdl	G-S	£2329

Total win prize-money £14597

Going: Sf: 0-1 GS: 0-0 Gd: 0-3 GF: - Fm: 0-0
Distance: 2m/2m3: 0-0 2m4-2m7: 0-0 3m+: 0-4
Track: LH: 0-1 RH: 0-2 Tight: 0-2 Gall: 0-0
Aids: Bl: 0-0 Vi: 0-2 Tstrap: 0-0
Best Rating: **137** 12/00 Winc 2m5f gd-sft Ch

Relatively lightly-raced mare. Suited by soft ground, she may be best at distances short of three miles and has a good record at Exeter.

Kellystown Hero (IRE)

4-y-o ch f Shalford (IRE)-Maggies Pride (IRE) (Nashamaa)
T Wall T Wall

Placings:PFP **(4737)**
2001/02: 16^{P}GS, 17^{F}G, 16^{P}GF

	Starts	1st	2nd	3rd	Win & Pl
Hurdles	3	0	0	0	
Career Total	**3**	**0**	**0**	**0**	

Going: Sf: 0-0 GS: 0-1 Gd: 0-1 GF: - Fm: 0-1
Distance: 2m/2m3: 0-3 2m4-2m7: 0-0 3m+: 0-0
Track: LH: 0-0 RH: 0-3 Tight: 0-0 Gall: 0-0
Aids: Bl: 0-0 Vi: 0-0 Tstrap: 0-1
Best Rating:

Kelnik Glory

75

6-y-o b g Nalchik (USA)-Areal (IRE) (Roselier (FR))
B J Llewellyn G Button

Placings:*000*062-P **(0495)**
2001/02: 19^{P}G

	Starts	1st	2nd	3rd	Win & Pl
Hurdles	1	0	0	0	
Career Total	**7**	**0**	**1**	**0**	**623**

Going: Sf: 0-0 GS: 0-0 Gd: 0-1 GF: - Fm: 0-0
Distance: 2m/2m3: 0-0 2m4-2m7: 0-1 3m+: 0-0
Track: LH: 0-0 RH: 0-1 Tight: 0-0 Gall: 0-0
Aids: Bl: 0-1 Vi: 0-0 Tstrap: 0-0
Best Rating: **75** 4/01 Plum 2m5f heavy Hdl

Keltic Bard

104 108

5-y-o b g Emperor Jones (USA)-Broughton Singer (IRE) (Common Grounds)
C J Mann Roger Maggs

Placings:4-63245 **(4404)**
2001/02: 16^{6}G, 16^{3}GS, 16^{2}S, 16^{4}S, 17^{5}S

	Starts	1st	2nd	3rd	Win & Pl
Hurdles	5	0	1	1	1596
Career Total	**6**	**0**	**1**	**1**	**1899**

Going: Sf: 0-3 GS: 0-1 Gd: 0-1 GF: - Fm: 0-0
Distance: 2m/2m3: 0-5 2m4-2m7: 0-0 3m+: 0-0
Track: LH: 0-2 RH: 0-3 Tight: 0-2 Gall: 0-1
Aids: Bl: 0-0 Vi: 0-0 Tstrap: 0-0
Best Rating: **108** 2/02 Ludl 2m soft Hdl

Promising efforts in novice hurdles, looking likely to stay two and a half miles.

Keltic Heritage (IRE)

104 97

8-y-o gr g Roselier (FR)-Peek-A-Step (IRE) (Step Together (USA))
L A Dace Danny O'Sullivan

Placings:*5P0*/06P-32311202 **(4885)**
2001/02: 21^{3}GS, 22^{2}GF, 25^{3}S, 21^{1}GS, 22^{1}S, 17^{2}S, 22^{0}G, 27^{2}GF

	Starts	1st	2nd	3rd	Win & Pl
Hurdles	8	2	3	2	7606
Career Total	**14**	**2**	**3**	**2**	**7606**

91	1/02	Font	2m6f110y	F(0-90)HHdl	SFT	£2324
83	1/02	Hntg	2m5f110y	F(0-95)HHdl	G-S	£2058

Total win prize-money £4382

Going: Sf: 1-3 GS: 1-2 Gd: 0-1 GF: - Fm: 0-2
Distance: 2m/2m3: 0-1 **2m4-2m7: 2-5** 3m+: 0-2
Track: LH: 1-2 RH: 1-3 Tight: 1-4 Gall: 1-1
Aids: Bl: 0-0 Vi: 0-0 **Tstrap: 2-8**
Best Rating: **92** 4/02 Font 3m3f gd-fm Hdl

A winning ex-Irish pointer, he had been encountering unsuitable conditions and got off the mark in a moderate event over two miles five at Huntingdon in January 2002. Followed up at Fontwell, and ran well subsequently. Suited by any ground except very soft and stays two miles-six plus.

Keltic Lord

72 43

6-y-o b g Arctic Lord-Scarlet Dymond (Rymer)
R J Hodges Miss L Crossman

Placings:*00*/0-00 **(0912)**
2001/02: 16^{0}GF, 16^{0}GF

	Starts	1st	2nd	3rd	Win & Pl
Hurdles	2	0	0	0	
Career Total	**5**	**0**	**0**	**0**	

Going: Sf: 0-0 GS: 0-0 Gd: 0-0 GF: - Fm: 0-2
Distance: 2m/2m3: 0-2 2m4-2m7: 0-0 3m+: 0-0
Track: LH: 0-2 RH: 0-0 Tight: 0-1 Gall: 0-0
Aids: Bl: 0-0 Vi: 0-0 Tstrap: 0-0
Best Rating: **60** 2/00 Winc 2m good NHF

Kemal's Council (IRE)

102 113

6-y-o gr g Leading Counsel (USA)-Kemal's Princess (Kemal (FR))
J J O'Neill Bateman, Gilruth, Milward & Singleton

Placings:*403*-1222P **(4267)**
2001/02: 24^{1}S, 23^{2}GS, 20^{2}HY, 24^{2}G, 24^{P}S

	Starts	1st	2nd	3rd	Win & Pl
Hurdles	5	1	3	0	5686
Career Total	**8**	**1**	**3**	**1**	**6171**

113	5/01	Hexm	3m	E Hdl	SFT	£2688

Total win prize-money £2688

Going: Sf: 1-3 GS: 0-1 Gd: 0-1 GF: - Fm: 0-0
Distance: 2m/2m3: 0-0 2m4-2m7: 0-2 **3m+: 1-3**
Track: **LH: 1-3** RH: 0-2 Tight: 0-0 Gall: 0-0
Aids: Bl: 0-0 Vi: 0-0 Tstrap: 0-0
Best Rating: **113** 3/02 Extr 3m110y good Hdl

Fair handicap hurdler, stays three miles and acts well in soft ground.

Ken Risk (FR)

99 106

10-y-o gr g Kendor (FR)-Swiss Risk (FR) (Last Tycoon)
M C Pipe Jim Weeden

Placings:15231210/6/P43P-100 **(0836)**
2001/02: 17^{1}GF, 17^{0}G, 22^{0}GF

	Starts	1st	2nd	3rd	Win & Pl
Hurdles	3	1	0	0	2296
Career Total	**16**	**4**	**2**	**2**	**14403**

106	5/01	NAbb	2m1f	F(0-105)HHdl	G-F	£2296
117	3/98	Newb	2m110y	D(0-110)HHdl	HVY	£3680
119	2/98	Newb	2m110y	D(0-115)HHdl	GD	£3288
95	9/97	Extr	2m3f	E Hdl	G-F	£2358

Total win prize-money £11622

Going: Sf: 0-0 GS: 0-0 Gd: 0-1 GF: - Fm: 1-2
Distance: **2m/2m3: 1-2** 2m4-2m7: 0-1 3m+: 0-0
Track: **LH: 1-3** RH: 0-0 **Tight: 1-3** Gall: 0-0
Aids: Bl: 0-0 **Vi: 1-3** Tstrap: 0-0
Best Rating: **119** 2/98 Newb 2m110y good Hdl

Kendal Cavalier

73

12-y-o gr g Roselier (FR)-Kenda (Bargello)
W S Kittow Michael Wingfield Digby

Placings:2455/215**2404F0/13311P1/215P0/46560/00 60-P** **(3789)**
2001/02: 33^{P}S

	Starts	1st	2nd	3rd	Win & Pl
Chases	1	0	0	0	
Career Total	**35**	**6**	**4**	**2**	**80096**

154	12/98	Chep	3m5f110y	A HCh	HVY	£34935
143	4/98	Chel	3m2f110y	C(0-135)HCh	HVY	£7197
128	2/98	Uttx	3m2f	C HCh	SFT	£14395
128	1/98	Chel	4m1f	B HCh	G-S	£8286
106	10/97	Chep	3m	D Ch	GD	£3510
116	11/96	NAbb	3m3f	E Hdl	HVY	£2284

Total win prize-money £70610

Going: Sf: 0-1 GS: 0-0 Gd: 0-0 GF: - Fm: 0-0
Distance: 2m/2m3: 0-0 2m4-2m7: 0-0 3m+: 0-1
Track: LH: 0-1 RH: 0-0 Tight: 0-0 Gall: 0-1
Aids: Bl: 0-0 Vi: 0-0 Tstrap: 0-0
Best Rating: **154** 12/98 Chep 3m5f110y heavy Ch

He won the '98 Welsh National from out of the handicap but has lost his way badly since and has not shown any worthwhile form since November '98. A thorough stayer, he is not one to rely on.

Kennythorpe Boppy (IRE)

4-y-o ch g Aragon-Spark (IRE) (Flash Of Steel)
J S Wainwright R C Bond

Placings:U **(1718)**
2001/02: 16^{U}G

	Starts	1st	2nd	3rd	Win & Pl
Hurdles	1	0	0	0	

	Starts	1st	2nd	3rd
Career Total	1	0	0	0

Going: Sf: 0-0 GS: 0-0 Gd: 0-1 GF: - Fm: 0-0
Distance: 2m/2m3: 0-1 2m4-2m7: 0-0 3m+: 0-0
Track: LH: 0-1 RH: 0-0 Tight: 0-0 Gall: 0-0
Aids: Bl: 0-0 Vi: 0-0 Tstrap: 0-0
Best Rating:

Kentford Fern

100(103h) (95h)115

7-y-o b m El Conquistador-Busy Mittens (Nearly A Hand)
J W Mullins Kentford Racing

Placings:662P/1044-64 (2216)
2001/02: 22^{6}GS, 26^{4}G

	Starts	1st	2nd	3rd	Win & Pl
Hurdles	1	0	0	0	0
Chases	1	0	0	0	259
Career Total	10	1	1	0	4744

114 1/01 Font 2m6f110y E Hdl SFT £2534
Total win prize-money £2534

Going: Sf: 0-0 GS: 0-1 Gd: 0-1 GF: - Fm: 0-0
Distance: 2m/2m3: 0-0 2m4-2m7: 0-1 3m+: 0-1
Track: LH: 0-1 RH: 0-0 Tight: 0-1 Gall: 0-0
Aids: Bl: 0-0 Vi: 0-0 Tstrap: 0-0
Best Rating: 115 11/01 NAbb 3m2f110y good Ch

Out of a winning point to pointer, has abundant stamina. and is suited by plenty of give in the ground.

Kentish Bard (IRE)

10-y-o b g Phardante (FR)-Polly Ringling (Pollerton)
N A Gaselee Mrs Angus Watson

Placings:153/F24301/23/43-P (0364)
2001/02: 20^{P}GF

	Starts	1st	2nd	3rd	Win & Pl
Chases	1	0	0	0	
Career Total	14	2	2	4	8079

108 4/99 Extr 2m3f110y E Hdl G-S £2329
103 11/97 Chep 2m110y H NHF SFT £1618
Total win prize-money £3947

Going: Sf: 0-0 GS: 0-0 Gd: 0-0 GF: - Fm: 0-1
Distance: 2m/2m3: 0-0 2m4-2m7: 0-1 3m+: 0-0
Track: LH: 0-1 RH: 0-0 Tight: 0-1 Gall: 0-0
Aids: Bl: 0-0 Vi: 0-0 Tstrap: 0-0
Best Rating: 121 10/99 Extr 2m3f good Hdl

Kentish Lad (IRE)

6-y-o ch g Caerleon (USA)-Jaljuli (Jalmood (USA))
A Streeter Manor Racing Club

Placings:500000/0 (0877)
2001/02: 21^{0}G

	Starts	1st	2nd	3rd	Win & Pl
Hurdles	1	0	0	0	
Career Total	7	0	0	0	0

Going: Sf: 0-0 GS: 0-0 Gd: 0-1 GF: - Fm: 0-0
Distance: 2m/2m3: 0-0 2m4-2m7: 0-1 3m+: 0-0
Track: LH: 0-0 RH: 0-1 Tight: 0-1 Gall: 0-0
Aids: Bl: 0-0 Vi: 0-0 Tstrap: 0-0
Best Rating: 75 1/00 Catt 2m good Hdl

Kentish Rock

77 27

7-y-o b g Rock Hopper-Capel Lass (The Brianstan)
Mrs L C Jewell The Lively Lads

Placings:0P/0PP0 (3765)
2001/02: 16^{0}GS, 16^{P}G, 18^{P}G, 16^{0}GS

	Starts	1st	2nd	3rd	Win & Pl
Hurdles	4	0	0	0	
Career Total	6	0	0	0	

Going: Sf: 0-0 GS: 0-2 Gd: 0-2 GF: - Fm: 0-0
Distance: 2m/2m3: 0-4 2m4-2m7: 0-0 3m+: 0-0
Track: LH: 0-4 RH: 0-0 Tight: 0-4 Gall: 0-0
Aids: Bl: 0-1 Vi: 0-0 Tstrap: 0-0
Best Rating: 44 11/99 Worc 2m gd-sft NHF

Kerry Dancer

6-y-o ch m Ballet Royal (USA)-Muskerry Miss (IRE) (Bishop Of Orange)
H J Manners H J Manners

Placings:00P (4850)
2001/02: 17^{0}GF, 16^{0}G, 22^{P}G

	Starts	1st	2nd	3rd	Win & Pl
NH Flat	2	0	0	0	0
Hurdles	1	0	0	0	0
Career Total	3	0	0	0	

Going: Sf: 0-0 GS: 0-0 Gd: 0-2 GF: - Fm: 0-1
Distance: 2m/2m3: 0-2 2m4-2m7: 0-1 3m+: 0-0
Track: LH: 0-1 RH: 0-2 Tight: 0-1 Gall: 0-0
Aids: Bl: 0-0 Vi: 0-0 Tstrap: 0-0
Best Rating: 36 9/01 Hrfd 2m1f gd-fm NHF

Kerry Lads (IRE)

105(106h) (106h)132

7-y-o ch g Mister Lord (USA)-Minstrel Top (Black Minstrel)
Miss Lucinda V Russell Mrs C G Greig

Placings:340-30F3312132 (4835)
2001/02: 24^{3}S, 20^{0}GS, 24^{F}S, 24^{3}S, 24^{3}GS, 26^{1}HY, 20^{2}HY, 25^{1}HY, 26^{3}HY, 25^{2}G

	Starts	1st	2nd	3rd	Win & Pl
Hurdles	4	0	0	2	830
Chases	6	2	2	2	22484
Career Total	13	2	2	5	23803

124 3/02 Ayr 3m1f D Ch HVY £4452
111 1/02 Carl 3m2f D Ch HVY £4959
Total win prize-money £9412

Going: Sf: 2-7 GS: 0-2 Gd: 0-1 GF: - Fm: 0-0
Distance: 2m/2m3: 0-0 2m4-2m7: 0-2 3m+: 2-8
Track: LH: 1-5 RH: 1-4 Tight: 0-0 Gall: 0-1
Aids: Bl: 0-0 Vi: 0-0 Tstrap: 0-0
Best Rating: 132 4/02 Ayr 3m1f good Ch

A maiden over hurdles, he likes a test of stamina in the mud over fences. An improving individual.

Kerry Soldier Blue

13-y-o gr g Fine Blue-Kerry Maid (Maestoso)
R W A Price (R J Price 23/6) R W A Price

Placings:P3/P2/24P-62430F (4727)
2001/02: 24^{6}GF, 21^{2}G, 24^{4}GF, 19^{3}F, 22^{0}GF, 24^{F}GF

	Starts	1st	2nd	3rd	Win & Pl
Chases	6	0	1	1	1612
Career Total	13	0	3	2	3922

Going: Sf: 0-0 GS: 0-0 Gd: 0-1 GF: - Fm: 0-5
Distance: 2m/2m3: 0-1 2m4-2m7: 0-2 3m+: 0-3
Track: LH: 0-2 RH: 0-3 Tight: 0-2 Gall: 0-1
Aids: Bl: 0-0 Vi: 0-0 Tstrap: 0-0
Best Rating: 110 4/00 Chep 3m soft Ch

Key Debate

104(94h) 128

10-y-o b g Gildoran-Key To Heaven (Lucifer (USA))
T D Walford Mrs M Cooper

Placings:110563-20433U (1743)
2001/02: 28^{2}G, 30^{0}G, 21^{4}GF, 24^{3}GF, 25^{3}G, 25^{U}GS

	Starts	1st	2nd	3rd	Win & Pl
Chases	6	0	1	2	5054
Career Total	12	2	1	3	9353

136 5/00 Hexm 3m1f H Ch G-F £2408
136 5/00 Hntg 3m H Ch GD £1605
Total win prize-money £4014

Going: Sf: 0-0 GS: 0-1 Gd: 0-3 GF: - Fm: 0-2
Distance: 2m/2m3: 0-0 2m4-2m7: 0-1 3m+: 0-5
Track: LH: 0-6 RH: 0-0 Tight: 0-6 Gall: 0-0
Aids: Bl: 0-0 Vi: 0-0 Tstrap: 0-0
Best Rating: 136 5/00 Hexm 3m1f gd-fm Ch

Key Grip (IRE)

(71h) (29h)

11-y-o br g Black Minstrel-Estrella (Virginia Boy)
Mrs D Thomas Mrs D Thomas

Placings:U00/2441104020/14225440/1U2300460/04P OPP-6P (4734)
2001/02: 16^{6}S, 19^{P}F

	Starts	1st	2nd	3rd	Win & Pl
Hurdles	1	0	0	0	0
Chases	1	0	0	0	0
Career Total	38	4	5	1	15779

112 8/99 Ctml 2m1f110y F(0-100)HCh GD £2801
106 11/98 Hayd 2m4f E(0-125)HHdl SFT £2141
106 1/98 Catt 2m F(0-95)HHdl G-S £1730
108 12/97 Weth 2m D(0-110)HHdl SFT £2897
Total win prize-money £9570

Going: Sf: 0-1 GS: 0-0 Gd: 0-0 GF: - Fm: 0-1
Distance: 2m/2m3: 0-1 2m4-2m7: 0-1 3m+: 0-0
Track: LH: 0-0 RH: 0-2 Tight: 0-0 Gall: 0-0
Aids: Bl: 0-0 Vi: 0-0 Tstrap: 0-1
Best Rating: 116 9/99 Worc 2m soft Ch

Key To The City (IRE)

101 104

8-y-o b g Shalford (IRE)-Green Wings (General Assembly (USA))
C P Morlock (D G Bridgwater 29/7) West Lancs Antiques Export Racing

Placings:0/52/2200463 (2882)
2001/02: 16^{2}GS, 16^{2}GF, 17^{0}G, 16^{0}G, 16^{4}GF, 16^{6}G, 16^{3}G

	Starts	1st	2nd	3rd	Win & Pl
Hurdles	7	0	2	1	1690
Career Total	10	0	3	1	2432

Going: Sf: 0-0 GS: 0-1 Gd: 0-4 GF: - Fm: 0-2

Distance: 2m/2m3: 0-7 2m4-2m7: 0-0 3m+: 0-0
Track: LH: 0-4 RH: 0-3 Tight: 0-3 Gall: 0-0
Aids: Bl: 0-1 Vi: 0-0 Tstrap: 0-0
Best Rating: 104 7/01 Wolv 2m gd-fm Hdl

Has shown only moderate form in novice hurdles. Best suited by two miles and a sound surface.

Key To The Ebit (IRE)

65f

5-y-o b g Montelimar (USA)-Girseach (Furry Glen)
Miss K Marks Nick Shutts

Placings: *00* (4180)
2001/02: 17^{0}GS, 16^{0}GS

	Starts	1st	2nd	3rd	Win & Pl
NH Flat	2	0	0	0	
Career Total	**2**	**0**	**0**	**0**	

Going: Sf: 0-0 GS: 0-2 Gd: 0-0 GF: - Fm: 0-0
Distance: 2m/2m3: 0-2 2m4-2m7: 0-0 3m+: 0-0
Track: LH: 0-1 RH: 0-0 Tight: 0-1 Gall: 0-0
Aids: Bl: 0-0 Vi: 0-0 Tstrap: 0-1
Best Rating: 65 3/02 Strf 2m110y gd-sft NHF

Keynote (IRE)

90 80

10-y-o ch g Orchestra-St Moritz (Linacre)
R Rowe The Reality Partnership

Placings: *0/604/51FU/0-43* (3813)
2001/02: 16^{4}S, 21^{3}S

	Starts	1st	2nd	3rd	Win & Pl
Chases	2	0	0	1	489
Career Total	**11**	**1**	**0**	**1**	**2985**

118	2/00	Folk	2m5f	F(0-90)HCh	GD	£2496

Total win prize-money £2496

Going: Sf: 0-2 GS: 0-0 Gd: 0-0 GF: - Fm: 0-0
Distance: 2m/2m3: 0-1 2m4-2m7: 0-1 3m+: 0-0
Track: LH: 0-0 RH: 0-2 Tight: 0-2 Gall: 0-0
Aids: Bl: 0-0 Vi: 0-0 Tstrap: 0-0
Best Rating: 118 2/00 Folk 2m5f good Ch

Lightly-raced dual-purpose handicapper, best at around two and a half miles on good to soft. Not the most reliable jumper.

Keyssac (FR)

70 28

4-y-o b g Beyssac (FR)-Dhop La (FR) (Son Of Silver)
A M Hales Andrew L Cohen

Placings: *0U* (3285)
2001/02: 18^{0}G, 17^{U}S

	Starts	1st	2nd	3rd	Win & Pl
Hurdles	2	0	0	0	
Career Total	**2**	**0**	**0**	**0**	

Going: Sf: 0-1 GS: 0-0 Gd: 0-1 GF: - Fm: 0-0
Distance: 2m/2m3: 0-2 2m4-2m7: 0-0 3m+: 0-0
Track: LH: 0-1 RH: 0-1 Tight: 0-2 Gall: 0-0
Aids: Bl: 0-0 Vi: 0-0 Tstrap: 0-0
Best Rating: 28 12/01 Font 2m2f110y good Hdl

Khaladjistan (IRE)

84 67

4-y-o br c Tirol-Khaladja (IRE) (Akarad (FR))
N J Henderson Million In Mind Partnership (11)

Placings: *4535* (4873)
2001/02: 16^{4}S, 16^{5}S, 16^{3}GS, 16^{5}GF

	Starts	1st	2nd	3rd	Win & Pl
NH Flat	4	0	0	1	443
Career Total	**4**	**0**	**0**	**1**	**443**

Going: Sf: 0-2 GS: 0-1 Gd: 0-0 GF: - Fm: 0-1
Distance: 2m/2m3: 0-4 2m4-2m7: 0-0 3m+: 0-0
Track: LH: 0-2 RH: 0-1 Tight: 0-0 Gall: 0-0
Aids: Bl: 0-0 Vi: 0-0 Tstrap: 0-0
Best Rating: 102 1/02 Hayd 2m soft NHF

Some ability in bumpers and is going to need a test of stamina over hurdles.

Khaled (IRE)

90 83

7-y-o b g Petorius-Felin Special (Lyphard's Special (USA))
T Keddy P Harper

Placings: *U06* (2328)
2001/02: 16^{U}G, 16^{0}GS, 16^{6}G

	Starts	1st	2nd	3rd	Win & Pl
Hurdles	3	0	0	0	0
Career Total	**3**	**0**	**0**	**0**	**0**

Going: Sf: 0-0 GS: 0-1 Gd: 0-2 GF: - Fm: 0-0
Distance: 2m/2m3: 0-3 2m4-2m7: 0-0 3m+: 0-0
Track: LH: 0-1 RH: 0-2 Tight: 0-1 Gall: 0-1
Aids: Bl: 0-0 Vi: 0-0 Tstrap: 0-0
Best Rating: 83 11/01 Plum 2m good Hdl

Khan Kicker (IRE)

108 132

6-y-o b g Husyan (USA)-Orient Conquest (Dual)
Ferdy Murphy E H Birbeck,A Stewart,Sir David Landale

Placings: *422-0F21412* (4828)
2001/02: 16^{0}S, 20^{F}S, 17^{2}HY, 16^{1}S, 20^{4}HY, 16^{1}GF, 16^{2}G

	Starts	1st	2nd	3rd	Win & Pl
Hurdles	7	2	2	0	9270
Career Total	**10**	**2**	**4**	**0**	**11979**

116	4/02	Kels	2m110y	E Hdl	G-F	£3010
120	1/02	Muss	2m	E Hdl	SFT	£2814

Total win prize-money £5824

Going: Sf: 1-5 GS: 0-0 Gd: 0-1 GF: - Fm: 1-1
Distance: **2m/2m3: 2-5** 2m4-2m7: 0-2 3m+: 0-0
Track: LH: 1-5 RH: 1-2 **Tight: 2-2** Gall: 0-0
Aids: Bl: 0-0 Vi: 0-0 Tstrap: 0-0
Best Rating: 132 4/02 Ayr 2m good Hdl

Decent hurdler. Effective at two miles and acts on most types of ground.

Khatani (IRE)

113(90h) (100h)139

7-y-o b g Kahyasi-Khanata (USA) (Riverman (USA))
D R Gandolfo R E Brinkworth

Placings: *35351/111144-13235* (4851)
2001/02: 19^{1}G, 17^{3}GS, 21^{2}GF, 20^{3}G, 20^{5}G

	Starts	1st	2nd	3rd	Win & Pl
Chases	5	1	1	2	9326
Career Total	**16**	**6**	**1**	**4**	**31541**

124	5/01	Hrfd	2m3f	D Ch	GD	£4875
126	7/00	Worc	2m4f	C(0-135)HHdl	GD	£5395
123	6/00	Worc	2m4f	C(0-135)HHdl	GD	£4875
120	5/00	Worc	2m	D(0-120)HHdl	GD	£3497
119	5/00	Bang	2m1f	D(0-120)HHdl	GD	£4348
115	4/00	Font	2m2f110y	E Hdl	GD	£2240

Total win prize-money £25231

Going: Sf: 0-0 GS: 0-1 Gd: 1-3 GF: - Fm: 0-1
Distance: **2m/2m3: 1-2** 2m4-2m7: 0-3 3m+: 0-0
Track: LH: 0-3 **RH: 1-2** Tight: 0-3 Gall: 0-1
Aids: Bl: 0-0 Vi: 0-0 Tstrap: 0-0
Best Rating: 139 6/01 Strf 2m5f110y gd-fm Ch

Fair handicap chaser when the ground rides fast but has looked quirky on occasion. Back to winning form at Bangor in May over an extended two and a half miles.

Khayal (USA)

95(91h) (77h)80

8-y-o b g Green Dancer (USA)-Look Who's Dancing (USA) (Affirmed (USA))
P J Hobbs (C J Gray 23/10) Gordon James Cossey

Placings: 2P430/05/4403 (4729)
2001/02: 24^{4}GF, 22^{4}GF, 22^{0}G, 24^{3}GF

	Starts	1st	2nd	3rd	Win & Pl
Hurdles	3	0	0	0	0
Chases	1	0	0	1	556
Career Total	**11**	**0**	**1**	**2**	**1434**

Going: Sf: 0-0 GS: 0-0 Gd: 0-1 GF: - Fm: 0-3
Distance: 2m/2m3: 0-0 2m4-2m7: 0-2 3m+: 0-2
Track: LH: 0-2 RH: 0-0 Tight: 0-0 Gall: 0-0
Aids: Bl: 0-0 Vi: 0-0 Tstrap: 0-0
Best Rating: 84 8/97 NAbb 2m1f gd-fm Hdl

One-time decent pointer, his jumping lacks fluency under Rules.

Khayali (IRE)

99(88h) (77h)89

8-y-o b g Unfuwain (USA)-Coven (Sassafras (FR))
A R Dicken Mr & Mrs Raymond Anderson Green

Placings: 005P554264 (4521)
2001/02: 20^{0}G, 17^{0}GS, 16^{5}G, 21^{P}G, 16^{5}GF, 16^{5}G, 24^{4}S, 21^{2}S, 20^{6}HY, 20^{4}GS

	Starts	1st	2nd	3rd	Win & Pl
Hurdles	3	0	0	0	0
Chases	7	0	1	0	1507
Career Total	**10**	**0**	**1**	**0**	**1507**

Going: Sf: 0-3 GS: 0-2 Gd: 0-4 GF: - Fm: 0-1
Distance: 2m/2m3: 0-4 2m4-2m7: 0-5 3m+: 0-1
Track: LH: 0-5 RH: 0-5 Tight: 0-4 Gall: 0-1
Aids: Bl: 0-0 Vi: 0-0 Tstrap: 0-0
Best Rating: 89 11/01 Ayr 2m5f110y good Ch

A winner on the Flat, he is still a maiden over both hurdles and fences. Handles any ground.

Khayrawani (IRE)

118

10-y-o b/br g Caerleon (USA)-Khaiyla (Mill Reef (USA))
C Roche J P McManus

Placings: 045510/141616/213/6112/5/00-0PP0 (3265)
2001/02: 22^{0}G, 22^{P}GF, 24^{P}G, 25^{0}S

	Starts	1st	2nd	3rd	Win & Pl
Hurdles	4	0	0	0	
Career Total	**26**	**7**	**2**	**1**	**138452**

159	4/99	Aint	2m4f	B HHdl	GD	£14746
156	3/99	Chel	2m5f	A HHdl	G-S	£38600
144	4/98	Aint	2m4f	B HHdl	SFT	£14200

137	4/97	Fair	2m	HHdl	G-F	£12871
133	9/96	List	2m	HHdl	G-F	£16752
127	7/96	Klny	2m1f	HHdl	G-F	£13298
113	4/96	Thur	2m	Hdl	G-Y	£2824

Total win prize-money £113294

Going: Sf: 0-1 GS: 0-0 Gd: 0-2 GF: - Fm: 0-1
Distance: 2m/2m3: 0-0 2m4-2m7: 0-2 3m+: 0-2
Track: LH: 0-0 RH: 0-1 Tight: 0-0 Gall: 0-0
Aids: Bl: 0-0 Vi: 0-0 Tstrap: 0-0
Best Rating: 159 4/99 Aint 2m4f good Hdl

A useful Irish staying hurdler, he won competitive handicaps at Cheltenham and Aintree in the spring of 1999 but has been lightly raced since. Disappointing last season, he looks a shadow of his former self but is always worth noting when the money is down.

Khaysar (IRE)

99 **106**

4-y-o br g Pennekamp (USA)-Khaytada (IRE) (Doyoun)
Mrs L Wadham (R Curtis 27/12) Dingley Dell Racing Ltd

Placings:2FP033214 **(4906)**
2001/02: 17^{2}G, 17^{F}S, 16^{P}GS, 16^{0}S, 17^{3}GS, 16^{3}G, 16^{2}G, 17^{1}G, 19^{4}G

	Starts	1st	2nd	3rd	Win & Pl
Hurdles	9	1	2	2	7998
Career Total	**9**	**1**	**2**	**2**	**7998**

106	4/02	MRas	2m1f110y	D(0-115)Hdl	GD	£3302

Total win prize-money £5363

Going: Sf: 0-2 GS: 0-2 Gd: 1-5 GF: - Fm: 0-0
Distance: **2m/2m3: 1-8** 2m4-2m7: 0-1 3m+: 0-0
Track: LH: 0-3 **RH: 1-6 Tight: 1-5** Gall: 0-0
Aids: Bl: 0-0 Vi: 0-0 Tstrap: 0-0
Best Rating: 106 4/02 MRas 2m1f110y good Hdl

Ex-Irish, has shown promise so far over hurdles and won a small handicap at Market Rasen in April 2002.

Ki Chi Saga (USA)

10-y-o ch g Miswaki (USA)-Codilla (USA) (Caro)
Jean-Rene Auvray Lambourn Racing Limited

Placings:0P/P **(0191)**
2001/02: 23^{P}GF

	Starts	1st	2nd	3rd	Win & Pl
Hurdles	1	0	0	0	
Career Total	**3**	**0**	**0**	**0**	

Going: Sf: 0-0 GS: 0-0 Gd: 0-0 GF: - Fm: 0-1
Distance: 2m/2m3: 0-0 2m4-2m7: 0-0 3m+: 0-1
Track: LH: 0-1 RH: 0-0 Tight: 0-1 Gall: 0-0
Aids: Bl: 0-0 Vi: 0-0 Tstrap: 0-1
Best Rating:

Kick For Touch (IRE)

92 **93**

5-y-o ch g Insan (USA)-Anns Run (Deep Run)
Miss H C Knight Trevor Hemmings

Placings:64 **(4548)**
2001/02: 22^{6}GS, 21^{4}GF

	Starts	1st	2nd	3rd	Win & Pl
Hurdles	2	0	0	0	0
Career Total	**2**	**0**	**0**	**0**	**0**

Going: Sf: 0-0 GS: 0-1 Gd: 0-0 GF: - Fm: 0-1
Distance: 2m/2m3: 0-0 2m4-2m7: 0-2 3m+: 0-0
Track: LH: 0-1 RH: 0-1 Tight: 0-1 Gall: 0-1
Aids: Bl: 0-0 Vi: 0-0 Tstrap: 0-0
Best Rating: 93 4/02 Hntg 2m5f110y gd-fm Hdl

Kickham (IRE)

102f **139f**

6-y-o b g Supreme Leader-Knocknagow (Buckskin (FR))
E J O'Grady J P McManus

Placings:1-121 **(4679)**
2001/02: 16^{1}Y, 16^{2}Y, 17^{1}G

	Starts	1st	2nd	3rd	Win & Pl
NH Flat	3	2	1	0	24573
Career Total	**4**	**3**	**1**	**0**	**30093**

139	4/02	Aint	2m1f	A NHF	GD	£18000
125	12/01	Fair	2m	NHF	YLD	£5008
130	5/00	Punc	2m	NHF	YLD	£5520

Total win prize-money £28528

Going: Sf: 0-0 GS: 0-0 Gd: 1-1 GF: - Fm: 0-0
Distance: **2m/2m3: 2-3** 2m4-2m7: 0-0 3m+: 0-0
Track: LH: 0-0 **RH: 1-1** Tight: 0-0 Gall: 0-0
Aids: Bl: 0-0 Vi: 0-0 Tstrap: 0-0
Best Rating: 139 4/02 Aint 2m1f good NHF

Smart form in Irish bumpers and took the champion bumper at Aintree. Should make a decent novice hurdler next season.

Kidology (IRE)

100 **83**

6-y-o b g Petardia-Loveville (USA) (Assert)
R Johnson (W Storey 29/5) Foster Watson

Placings:0-000 **(2903)**
2001/02: 19^{0}GF, 16^{0}GS, 16^{0}GS

	Starts	1st	2nd	3rd	Win & Pl
Hurdles	3	0	0	0	
Career Total	**4**	**0**	**0**	**0**	

Going: Sf: 0-0 GS: 0-2 Gd: 0-0 GF: - Fm: 0-1
Distance: 2m/2m3: 0-2 2m4-2m7: 0-1 3m+: 0-0
Track: LH: 0-2 RH: 0-1 Tight: 0-1 Gall: 0-1
Aids: Bl: 0-0 Vi: 0-0 Tstrap: 0-1
Best Rating: 83 11/01 Newc 2m gd-sft Hdl

Kif D'Estruval (FR)

2

4-y-o b g Epervier Bleu-Vocation (FR) (Toujours Pret (USA))
Mrs H Dalton J Hales

Placings:0 **(3272)**
2001/02: 16^{0}S

	Starts	1st	2nd	3rd	Win & Pl
Hurdles	1	0	0	0	
Career Total	**1**	**0**	**0**	**0**	

Going: Sf: 0-1 GS: 0-0 Gd: 0-0 GF: - Fm: 0-0
Distance: 2m/2m3: 0-1 2m4-2m7: 0-0 3m+: 0-0
Track: LH: 0-1 RH: 0-0 Tight: 0-1 Gall: 0-0
Aids: Bl: 0-0 Vi: 0-0 Tstrap: 0-0
Best Rating:

Kilbragh Khan

61f **84f**

6-y-o br g Rakaposhi King-Kilbragh Dreamer (IRE) (Decent Fellow)
A J Wilson Mrs Elizabeth Allsop

Placings:*0* **(4499)**
2001/02: 16^{0}G

	Starts	1st	2nd	3rd	Win & Pl
NH Flat	0	0	0		
Career Total	**1**	**0**	**0**	**0**	

Going: Sf: 0-0 GS: 0-0 Gd: 0-1 GF: - Fm: 0-0
Distance: 2m/2m3: 0-1 2m4-2m7: 0-0 3m+: 0-0
Track: LH: 0-1 RH: 0-0 Tight: 0-0 Gall: 0-0
Aids: Bl: 0-0 Vi: 0-0 Tstrap: 0-0
Best Rating: 84 3/02 Hayd 2m good NHF

Kilbready Boy (IRE)

114

7-y-o ch g Beau Sher-Ginger Dee (Le Moss)
L Wells L Wells

Placings:2U3 **(3471)**
2001/02: 16^{2}GS, 20^{U}S, 21^{3}S

	Starts	1st	2nd	3rd	Win & Pl
NH Flat	1	0	1	0	3450
Chases	2	0	0	1	644
Career Total	**3**	**0**	**1**	**1**	**4094**

Going: Sf: 0-2 GS: 0-1 Gd: 0-0 GF: - Fm: 0-0
Distance: 2m/2m3: 0-1 2m4-2m7: 0-2 3m+: 0-0
Track: LH: 0-2 RH: 0-1 Tight: 0-2 Gall: 0-0
Aids: Bl: 0-0 Vi: 0-0 Tstrap: 0-0
Best Rating: 124 12/01 Chep 2m110y gd-sft NHF

Runner-up in a hot Chepstow bumper on his debut, he unseated in his first two starts over fences and may well have won the second of them. Still has plenty of scope and will win chases.

Kilcaroon (IRE)

87 **103**

7-y-o b g Jurado (USA)-Alfuraat (Auction Ring (USA))
J Howard Johnson W M G Black

Placings:*50/00*-63P **(4856)**
2001/02: 21^{6}S, 25^{3}GF, 25^{P}G

	Starts	1st	2nd	3rd	Win & Pl
Chases	3	0	0	1	641
Career Total	**7**	**0**	**0**	**1**	**641**

Going: Sf: 0-1 GS: 0-0 Gd: 0-1 GF: - Fm: 0-1
Distance: 2m/2m3: 0-0 2m4-2m7: 0-1 3m+: 0-2
Track: LH: 0-3 RH: 0-0 Tight: 0-2 Gall: 0-0
Aids: Bl: 0-0 Vi: 0-0 Tstrap: 0-0
Best Rating: 103 4/02 Kels 3m1f gd-fm Ch

Irish point winner but yet to show much here.

Kilcreggan

99 **95**

8-y-o b g Landyap (USA)-Lehmans Lot (Oats)
Mrs Barbara Waring (Mrs M Reveley 13/10) D Charlesworth

Placings:*463*/6-6304106 **(2649)**
2001/02: 22^{6}GF, 16^{3}GF, 21^{0}G, 17^{4}GS, 16^{1}G, 16^{0}S, 16^{6}G

	Starts	1st	2nd	3rd	Win & Pl
Hurdles	7	1	0	1	2163
Career Total	**11**	**1**	**0**	**2**	**2333**

95	10/01	Sthl	2m	G(0-95)HHdl	GD	£1939

Total win prize-money £1939

Going: Sf: 0-1 GS: 0-1 Gd: 1-3 GF: - Fm: 0-2
Distance: **2m/2m3: 1-5** 2m4-2m7: 0-2 3m+: 0-0
Track: **LH: 1-6** RH: 0-1 **Tight: 1-4** Gall: 0-0
Aids: Bl: 0-0 Vi: 0-0 Tstrap: 0-0
Best Rating: 100 10/98 Hntg 2m110y good NHF

Kildare Chiller (IRE)

109 **117**

8-y-o ch g Shahrastani (USA)-Ballycuirke (Taufan (USA))
P R Hedger P R Hedger

Placings:0500/101000/210F55-65222361 **(4413)**
2001/02: 18^{6}GS, 19^{5}G, 18^{2}G, 21^{2}S, 16^{2}HY, 22^{3}HY, 18^{6}S, 18^{1}S

	Starts	1st	2nd	3rd	Win & Pl
Hurdles	8	1	3	1	8470
Career Total	**24**	**4**	**4**	**1**	**17530**

109	3/02	Font	2m2f110y	D(0-115)HHdl	SFT	£5382
117	10/00	Font	2m2f110y	D(0-120)HHdl	G-S	£3168
106	11/98	Thur	2m2f	(0-102)HHdl	SFT	£2301
	5/98	Dpat	2m1f172y	Hdl	G-F	£1489

Total win prize-money £12342

Going: Sf: 1-5 GS: 0-1 Gd: 0-2 GF: - Fm: 0-0
Distance: **2m/2m3: 1-6** 2m4-2m7: 0-2 3m+: 0-0
Track: **LH: 1-8** RH: 0-0 **Tight: 1-7** Gall: 0-1
Aids: Bl: 0-0 Vi: 0-0 Tstrap: 0-0
Best Rating: 117 1/02 Plum 2m5f soft Hdl

Modest handicap hurdler who ended a long losing run at Fontwell in March 2002. Best at around two and a quarter miles on easy ground.

Kildorragh (IRE)

113 **133**

8-y-o b g Glacial Storm (USA)-Take A Dare (Pragmatic)
L Wells Jmd Racing

Placings:*0002045*/12-3PU1U1 **(2561)**
2001/02: 28^{3}GF, 26^{P}GS, 24^{U}G, 26^{1}GS, 27^{U}S, 26^{1}S

	Starts	1st	2nd	3rd	Win & Pl
Chases	6	2	0	1	16655
Career Total	**15**	**3**	**2**	**1**	**28042**

133	12/01	Chep	3m2f110y	C(0-130)HCh	SFT	£10166
133	11/01	Font	3m2f110y	D(0-125)HCh	G-S	£3818
131	2/01	Font	3m2f110y	H Ch	G-S	£7345

Total win prize-money £21330

Going: Sf: 1-2 GS: 1-2 Gd: 0-1 GF: - Fm: 0-1
Distance: 2m/2m3: 0-0 2m4-2m7: 0-0 **3m+: 2-6**
Track: **LH: 1-4** RH: 0-0 **Tight: 1-3** Gall: 0-1
Aids: Bl: 0-0 Vi: 0-0 Tstrap: 0-0
Best Rating: 133 12/01 Chep 3m2f110y soft Ch

An ex-Irish chaser, he ran in some decent hunter chases last term. Won back at Fontwell in November and won with a bit in hand at Chepstow the following month, once again proving his stamina. Stays three and a quarter miles. Acts on soft ground, handles a fast surface.

Kildrummy Castle

96 **96+**

10-y-o b g Komaite (USA)-Khadine (Astec)
Ferdy Murphy Major P H K Steveney

Placings:2/0000125/45122/2445/F/2-P06 **(4602)**
2001/02: 20^{P}GS, 20^{0}S, 20^{6}GF

	Starts	1st	2nd	3rd	Win & Pl
Chases	3	0	0	0	0
Career Total	**22**	**2**	**6**	**0**	**10608**

96	2/98	Sedg	2m110y	E(0-110)HCh	GD	£3254
79	3/97	Uttx	2m	E(0-100)HHdl	G-F	£2316

Total win prize-money £5570

Going: Sf: 0-1 GS: 0-1 Gd: 0-0 GF: - Fm: 0-1
Distance: 2m/2m3: 0-0 2m4-2m7: 0-3 3m+: 0-0
Track: LH: 0-1 RH: 0-2 Tight: 0-1 Gall: 0-1
Aids: Bl: 0-0 Vi: 0-0 Tstrap: 0-0
Best Rating: 100 3/98 Newc 2m110y good Ch

Kildysart Lady (IRE)

75 **58**

6-y-o b m King Of Shannon-Raj Kumari (Vitiges (FR))
C L Popham (Michael Hourigan 27/7) C L Popham

Placings:*000/00406004-0000*FP06P **(2926)**
2001/02: 16^{0}F, 16^{0}S, 16^{0}G, 16^{0}GS, 19^{F}F, 17^{P}S, 16^{0}GF, 19^{6}GS, 24^{P}GS

	Starts	1st	2nd	3rd	Win & Pl
NH Flat	1	0	0	0	0
Hurdles	7	0	0	0	0
Chases	1	0	0	0	0
Career Total	**20**	**0**	**0**	**0**	**384**

Going: Sf: 0-2 GS: 0-3 Gd: 0-1 GF: - Fm: 0-3
Distance: 2m/2m3: 0-7 2m4-2m7: 0-1 3m+: 0-1
Track: LH: 0-2 RH: 0-4 Tight: 0-5 Gall: 0-0
Aids: Bl: 0-1 Vi: 0-0 Tstrap: 0-0
Best Rating: 99 9/00 Baln 2m gd-yld Hdl

Kilgal

(100h) (113h)

9-y-o b g Jupiter Island-The Mount (Le Moss)
A Hollingsworth Perry Adams Kombined Motor Services Ltd

Placings:*660*PO/2322025/210040163-13PPU3 **(4528)**
2001/02: 27^{1}G, 27^{3}GF, 24^{P}GS, 24^{P}S, 20^{U}GS, 20^{3}GS

	Starts	1st	2nd	3rd	Win & Pl
Hurdles	3	1	0	2	4216
Chases	3	0	0	0	0
Career Total	**27**	**3**	**5**	**4**	**15732**

113	5/01	Strf	3m3f	E(0-115)HHdl	GD	£3157
108	3/01	MRas	2m5f110y	F(0-95)HHdl	G-S	£2719
106	6/00	Strf	2m6f110y	D Hdl	GD	£3363

Total win prize-money £9241

Going: Sf: 0-1 GS: 0-3 Gd: 1-1 GF: - Fm: 0-1
Distance: 2m/2m3: 0-0 2m4-2m7: 0-2 **3m+: 1-4**
Track: **LH: 1-6** RH: 0-0 **Tight: 1-5** Gall: 0-0
Aids: Bl: 0-0 Vi: 0-0 Tstrap: 0-0
Best Rating: 113 6/01 Strf 3m3f gd-fm Hdl

Ideally suited by good ground and trips between two miles six and three miles three over hurdles. Yet to complete over fences.

Killalongford (IRE)

103 **100**

5-y-o b g Tenby-Queen Crab (Private Walk)
Mrs S M Johnson (A Powell 16/1) Mrs M E Mason

Placings:00630 **(4052)**
2001/02: 22^{0}G, 16^{0}YS, 16^{6}YS, 20^{3}S, 19^{0}G

	Starts	1st	2nd	3rd	Win & Pl
Hurdles	5	0	0	1	387
Career Total	**5**	**0**	**0**	**1**	**387**

Going: Sf: 0-1 GS: 0-0 Gd: 0-2 GF: - Fm: 0-0
Distance: 2m/2m3: 0-3 2m4-2m7: 0-2 3m+: 0-0
Track: LH: 0-1 RH: 0-2 Tight: 0-0 Gall: 0-0
Aids: Bl: 0-0 Vi: 0-0 Tstrap: 0-0
Best Rating: 100 12/01 Navn 2m yld-sft Hdl

Killarney

100 **72**

4-y-o gr f Pursuit Of Love-Laune (AUS) (Kenmare (FR))
Miss Kate Milligan (R Hannon 14/9) E Whalley

Placings:0P0 **(4284)**
2001/02: 16^{0}S, 16^{P}S, 17^{0}GS

	Starts	1st	2nd	3rd	Win & Pl
Hurdles	3	0	0	0	
Career Total	**3**	**0**	**0**	**0**	

Going: Sf: 0-2 GS: 0-1 Gd: 0-0 GF: - Fm: 0-0
Distance: 2m/2m3: 0-3 2m4-2m7: 0-0 3m+: 0-0
Track: LH: 0-2 RH: 0-1 Tight: 0-2 Gall: 0-1
Aids: Bl: 0-0 Vi: 0-0 Tstrap: 0-0
Best Rating: 72 3/02 MRas 2m1f110y gd-sft Hdl

Killerine (FR)

112(111h) (114h)**126**

7-y-o b g Leading Counsel (USA)-Rose Petal (FR) (Pharly (FR))
Ian Williams Mr & Mrs John Poynton

Placings:3/212343/000P/432110P5-030116 **(4775)**
2001/02: 25^{0}G, 25^{3}S, 25^{0}G, 24^{1}GS, 26^{1}G, 22^{6}G

	Starts	1st	2nd	3rd	Win & Pl
Hurdles	1	0	0	0	0
Chases	5	2	0	1	13664
Career Total	**25**	**5**	**3**	**5**	**66984**

126	3/02	NAbb	3m2f110y	D(0-115)HCh	GD	£5538
118	3/02	Strf	3m	D(0-120)HCh	G-S	£7046
131	1/01	Catt	2m3f	E Ch	G-S	£3237
129	12/00	Hntg	2m4f110y	E Ch	HVY	£3611
	10/98	Autl	1m7f	HHdl	SFT	£15152

Total win prize-money £34584

Going: Sf: 0-1 GS: 1-1 Gd: 1-4 GF: - Fm: 0-0
Distance: 2m/2m3: 0-0 2m4-2m7: 0-1 **3m+: 2-5**
Track: **LH: 2-4** RH: 0-2 **Tight: 2-3** Gall: 0-1
Aids: Bl: 2-4 Vi: 0-0 Tstrap: 2-5
Best Rating: 131 1/01 Catt 2m3f gd-sft Ch

Ex-French, he made an encouraging start over fences and won twice in the winter of 2000 but lost his way and reverted to hurdles in the spring of 2001 to get his confidence back. Proved he stays well when winning chases at Stratford and Newton Abbot in March 2002. Likes to get his toe in.

Killing Time

11-y-o b g Good Times (ITY)-Kelly's Bid (Pitskelly)
Simon T Lewis Simon T Lewis

Placings:0032000P54/15P01U051/0P0306/6533010/3P/006350-006 **(1085)**
2001/02: 27^{0}GF, 25^{0}GF, 20^{6}G

	Starts	1st	2nd	3rd	Win & Pl
Hurdles	3	0	0	0	0
Career Total	**43**	**4**	**1**	**6**	**9335**

76	11/98	Tntn	2m1f	G(0-90)HHdl	GD	£1658
88	4/97	Extr	2m2f	G Hdl	G-F	£1767
78	2/97	Folk	2m1f110y	G(0-90)HHdl	HVY	£1639
88	9/96	Extr	2m3f	E Hdl	FRM	£2347

Total win prize-money £7414

Going: Sf: 0-0 GS: 0-0 Gd: 0-1 GF: - Fm: 0-2
Distance: 2m/2m3: 0-0 2m4-2m7: 0-1 3m+: 0-2
Track: LH: 0-3 RH: 0-0 Tight: 0-3 Gall: 0-0
Aids: Bl: 0-0 Vi: 0-0 Tstrap: 0-0
Best Rating: **88** 4/97 Extr 2m2f gd-fm Hdl

Killough Hill (IRE)

79f **66f**

5-y-o b g Fourstars Allstar (USA)-Bristol Fairy (Smartset)
C J Bennett C J Bennett

Placings:*0* **(4910)**
2001/02: 17^{0}G

	Starts	1st	2nd	3rd	Win & Pl
NH Flat	1	0	0	0	
Career Total	**1**	**0**	**0**	**0**	

Going: Sf: 0-0 GS: 0-0 Gd: 0-1 GF: - Fm: 0-0
Distance: 2m/2m3: 0-1 2m4-2m7: 0-0 3m+: 0-0
Track: LH: 0-0 RH: 0-1 Tight: 0-1 Gall: 0-0
Aids: Bl: 0-0 Vi: 0-0 Tstrap: 0-0
Best Rating: **66** 4/02 MRas 2m1f110y good NHF

Killultagh Storm (IRE)

117 **152**

8-y-o b g Mandalus-Rostrevor Lady (Kemal (FR))
W P Mullins Mrs Rose Boyd

Placings:*00*/60*33*301332211/133320124-**2U130536622** **(4938a)**
2001/02: 20^{2}YS, 20^{U}G, 18^{1}YS, 16^{3}Y, 17^{0}Y, 16^{5}G, 20^{3}HY, 16^{6}HY, 16^{6}G, 16^{2}GY, 16^{2}YS

	Starts	1st	2nd	3rd	Win & Pl
Chases	11	1	3	2	44289
Career Total	**35**	**6**	**7**	**10**	**120068**

152	11/01	DRoy	2m2f	Ch	Y-S	£20967
134	2/01	Naas	2m	Ch	SH	£6120
135	5/00	Punc	2m	(0-135)HHdl	GD	£8320
130	4/00	Fair	2m	HHdl	SFT	£39000
123	3/00	Leop	2m	(0-116)HHdl	GD	£5520
106	11/99	Fair	2m	(0-109)HHdl	SFT	£5236

Total win prize-money £85166

Going: Sf: 0-2 GS: 0-0 Gd: 0-3 GF: - Fm: 0-0
Distance: **2m/2m3: 1-8** 2m4-2m7: 0-3 3m+: 0-0
Track: LH: 0-4 RH: 0-3 Tight: 0-0 Gall: 0-1
Aids: Bl: 0-0 Vi: 0-0 Tstrap: 0-0
Best Rating: **152** 4/02 Fair 2m100y gd-yld Ch

A winner over hurdles and fences, he acts on good and soft ground and is effective at around two miles.

Killy Beach

81f **59f**

4-y-o b g Kuwait Beach (USA)-Spiritual Lily (Brianston Zipper)
J W Mullins J A G Meaden

Placings:*000* **(4887)**
2001/02: 16^{0}S, 17^{0}G, 18^{0}GF

	Starts	1st	2nd	3rd	Win & Pl
NH Flat	3	0	0	0	
Career Total	**3**	**0**	**0**	**0**	

Going: Sf: 0-1 GS: 0-0 Gd: 0-1 GF: - Fm: 0-1
Distance: 2m/2m3: 0-3 2m4-2m7: 0-0 3m+: 0-0
Track: LH: 0-2 RH: 0-1 Tight: 0-2 Gall: 0-0
Aids: Bl: 0-0 Vi: 0-0 Tstrap: 0-0
Best Rating: **59** 4/02 Font 2m2f110y gd-fm NHF

Kilt (FR)

68 **45**

4-y-o ch g Luchiroverte (IRE)-Unite Ii (FR) (Toujours Pret (USA))
Mrs L Williamson Halewood International Ltd

Placings:0P0 **(2002)**
2001/02: 16^{0}G, 17^{P}GS, 16^{0}S

	Starts	1st	2nd	3rd	Win & Pl
Hurdles	3	0	0	0	
Career Total	**3**	**0**	**0**	**0**	

Going: Sf: 0-1 GS: 0-1 Gd: 0-1 GF: - Fm: 0-0
Distance: 2m/2m3: 0-3 2m4-2m7: 0-0 3m+: 0-0
Track: LH: 0-2 RH: 0-1 Tight: 0-1 Gall: 0-0
Aids: Bl: 0-0 Vi: 0-0 Tstrap: 0-1
Best Rating: **45** 10/01 Kels 2m110y good Hdl

Kiltulaa Lad (IRE)

103 **124**

9-y-o ch g Phardante (FR)-Galway Shawl (Cure The Blues (USA))
D L Williams (P J Hobbs 24/8) N F Dawe

Placings:*4314*/2321/**PF45-2O13U5U** **(2410)**
2001/02: 20^{0}GF, 18^{0}GF, 16^{1}G, 17^{0}G, 16^{U}S, 16^{0}G, 19^{U}GS

	Starts	1st	2nd	3rd	Win & Pl
Hurdles	1	0	0	0	0
Chases	6	1	1	1	5657
Career Total	**19**	**3**	**3**	**3**	**11916**

124	10/01	Towc	2m110y	E Ch	GD	£3851
112	3/00	Chep	2m110y	D(0-125)HHdl	HVY	£2918
100	11/98	Ludl	2m	H NHF	GD	£1276

Total win prize-money £8047

Going: Sf: 0-1 GS: 0-1 Gd: 1-3 GF: - Fm: 0-2
Distance: **2m/2m3: 1-6** 2m4-2m7: 0-1 3m+: 0-0
Track: LH: 0-2 **RH: 1-5** Tight: 0-2 Gall: 0-0
Aids: Bl: 0-0 Vi: 0-0 Tstrap: 0-0
Best Rating: **124** 10/01 Towc 2m110y soft Ch

A bumper and hurdling winner in his early career, made a winning debut for Williams in a novice chase at Towcester in October, despite one almighty blunder, then ran well in a better race at Exeter. Favours front-running tactics.

Kilverts Cash

9-y-o b g Sula Bula-Tom's Comedy (Comedy Star (USA))
Mrs S M Johnson Colin Thomson

Placings:P **(3336)**
2001/02: 20^{P}G

	Starts	1st	2nd	3rd	Win & Pl
Chases	1	0	0	0	
Career Total	**1**	**0**	**0**	**0**	

Going: Sf: 0-0 GS: 0-0 Gd: 0-1 GF: - Fm: 0-0
Distance: 2m/2m3: 0-0 2m4-2m7: 0-1 3m+: 0-0
Track: LH: 0-0 RH: 0-1 Tight: 0-1 Gall: 0-0
Aids: Bl: 0-0 Vi: 0-0 Tstrap: 0-0
Best Rating:

Kimdaloo (IRE)

103(86h) (56h)**96**

10-y-o b g Mandalus-Kimin (Kibenka)
M A Barnes J G Graham

Placings:*0*/560/5P/4560**F10/U25-33P22223566** **(4872)**
2001/02: 16^{3}GF, 20^{3}F, 16^{P}GF, 17^{2}G, 17^{2}GS, 16^{2}GF, 20^{2}G, 16^{3}G, 16^{5}GS, 17^{6}G, 16^{6}GF

	Starts	1st	2nd	3rd	Win & Pl
Chases	11	0	4	3	6559
Career Total	**27**	**1**	**5**	**3**	**10784**

78	2/00	Newc	2m110y	E(0-105)HCh	SFT	£3143

Total win prize-money £3143

Going: Sf: 0-0 GS: 0-2 Gd: 0-4 GF: - Fm: 0-5
Distance: 2m/2m3: 0-9 2m4-2m7: 0-2 3m+: 0-0
Track: LH: 0-6 RH: 0-4 Tight: 0-4 Gall: 0-0
Aids: Bl: 0-0 Vi: 0-0 Tstrap: 0-9
Best Rating: **96** 9/01 Prth 2m good Ch

One-paced moderate chaser, suited by two miles and cut in the ground.

Kimoe Warrior

97 **73**

4-y-o ch g Royal Abjar (USA)-Thewaari (USA) (Eskimo (USA))
M Mullineaux Michael Mullineaux

Placings:F004354PP6 **(4324)**
2001/02: 17^{F}GS, 16^{0}GF, 16^{0}S, 17^{4}GS, 19^{3}GS, 16^{5}S, 16^{4}S, 20^{P}S, 20^{P}S, 17^{6}S

	Starts	1st	2nd	3rd	Win & Pl
Hurdles	10	0	0	1	687
Career Total	**10**	**0**	**0**	**1**	**687**

Going: Sf: 0-6 GS: 0-3 Gd: 0-0 GF: - Fm: 0-1
Distance: 2m/2m3: 0-7 2m4-2m7: 0-3 3m+: 0-0
Track: LH: 0-5 RH: 0-5 Tight: 0-4 Gall: 0-2
Aids: Bl: 0-0 Vi: 0-0 Tstrap: 0-1
Best Rating: **73** 12/01 Tntn 2m3f110y gd-sft Hdl

Kimothy

9-y-o br g Primitive Rising (USA)-Kimberley Rose (Monksfield)
Miss R Brewis Miss Rhona Brewis

Placings:P00P0/PPP/P **(1575)**
2001/02: 25^{P}G

	Starts	1st	2nd	3rd	Win & Pl
Chases	1	0	0	0	
Career Total	**9**	**0**	**0**	**0**	

Going: Sf: 0-0 GS: 0-0 Gd: 0-1 GF: - Fm: 0-0
Distance: 2m/2m3: 0-0 2m4-2m7: 0-0 3m+: 0-1
Track: LH: 0-1 RH: 0-0 Tight: 0-1 Gall: 0-0
Aids: Bl: 0-0 Vi: 0-0 Tstrap: 0-0
Best Rating: **37** 10/98 Sedg 2m1f gd-sft Hdl

Kincora (IRE)

11-y-o b g King Persian-Miss Noora (Ahonoora)
Ms Lisa Stock Mrs L Stock

Placings:*000000*/454/454P-U66 **(0579)**
2001/02: 26^{U}G, 24^{6}GF, 24^{6}GF

	Starts	1st	2nd	3rd	Win & Pl
Chases	3	0	0	0	0

Career Total	**16**	**0**	**0**	**0**	**562**

Going: Sf: 0-0 GS: 0-0 Gd: 0-1 GF: - Fm: 0-2
Distance: 2m/2m3: 0-0 2m4-2m7: 0-0 3m+: 0-3
Track: LH: 0-2 RH: 0-1 Tight: 0-3 Gall: 0-0
Aids: Bl: 0-0 Vi: 0-0 Tstrap: 0-0
Best Rating: 98 5/01 Strf 3m gd-fm Ch

Kind Of Blue

6-y-o gr m Terimon-Welsh Lustre (IRE) (Mandalus)
C J Mann Mrs L R Lovell

Placings:_00_-P5P **(2950)**
2001/02: 16^{P}S, 21^{5}G, 22^{P}S

	Starts	1st	2nd	3rd	Win & Pl
Hurdles	3	0	0	0	0
Career Total	**5**	**0**	**0**	**0**	**0**

Going: Sf: 0-2 GS: 0-0 Gd: 0-1 GF: - Fm: 0-0
Distance: 2m/2m3: 0-1 2m4-2m7: 0-2 3m+: 0-0
Track: LH: 0-1 RH: 0-1 Tight: 0-1 Gall: 0-0
Aids: Bl: 0-0 Vi: 0-0 Tstrap: 0-0
Best Rating: 74 12/00 Ludl 2m soft NHF

Kind Sir

96(97h) (96h)**101**
6-y-o b g Generous (IRE)-Noble Conquest (USA) (Vaguely Noble)
R Dickin Exors Of The Late B K Smith

Placings:23206/60P204-**0023P**3 **(0977)**
2001/02: 17^{0}GS, 16^{0}F, 16^{2}GF, 20^{3}G, 16^{P}G, 24^{3}GF

	Starts	1st	2nd	3rd	Win & Pl
Hurdles	1	0	0	1	328
Chases	5	0	1	1	1752
Career Total	**17**	**0**	**4**	**3**	**4865**

Going: Sf: 0-0 GS: 0-1 Gd: 0-2 GF: - Fm: 0-3
Distance: 2m/2m3: 0-4 2m4-2m7: 0-1 3m+: 0-1
Track: LH: 0-6 RH: 0-0 Tight: 0-4 Gall: 0-0
Aids: Bl: 0-0 Vi: 0-0 Tstrap: 0-0
Best Rating: 101 6/01 Worc 2m4f110y good Ch

Kinda Groovy

105 **81**
13-y-o b g Beveled (USA)-Tory Blues (Final Straw)
I Park Ian Park

Placings:0053/026605416/311120/660/165114625/250F60**P/P**401/641224**PP**6-060043P **(1234)**
2001/02: 20^{0}S, 24^{6}GF, 24^{0}F, 20^{0}G, 27^{4}GF, 27^{3}GF, 22^{P}GS

	Starts	1st	2nd	3rd	Win & Pl
Hurdles	7	0	0	1	382
Career Total	**58**	**9**	**6**	**3**	**26224**

94	5/00	Hexm	3m	F(0-105)HHdl	GD	£2531
88	3/00	Sedg	2m5f110y	G(0-90)HHdl	G-F	£1662
104	12/97	Sedg	3m3f110y	E(0-115)HHdl	GD	£2775
94	10/97	Carl	3m110y	E(0-115)HHdl	FRM	£2234
93	5/97	Hexm	2m4f110y	E(0-115)HHdl	G-F	£2404
	5/94	Hexm	2m4f110y	(0-100)HHdl	HRD	£2733
91	5/94	Sedg	2m5f110y	(0-110)HHdl	GD	£1900
96	5/94	Sedg	2m5f110y	Hdl	FRM	£2921
89	3/94	Sedg	2m5f110y	Hdl	G-F	£2110

Total win prize-money £21272

Going: Sf: 0-1 GS: 0-1 Gd: 0-1 GF: - Fm: 0-4
Distance: 2m/2m3: 0-0 2m4-2m7: 0-3 3m+: 0-4
Track: LH: 0-7 RH: 0-0 Tight: 0-3 Gall: 0-0
Aids: Bl: 0-6 Vi: 0-0 Tstrap: 0-0
Best Rating: 104 12/97 Sedg 3m3f110y good Hdl

Kindle A Flame

98 **98**
6-y-o b g Nomadic Way (USA)-Tees Gazette Girl (Kalaglow)
Mrs M Reveley Mrs M B Thwaites

Placings:_554_-00262 **(1903)**
2001/02: 21^{0}G, 17^{0}G, 21^{2}G, 22^{6}GS, 21^{2}G

	Starts	1st	2nd	3rd	Win & Pl
Hurdles	5	0	2	0	1472
Career Total	**8**	**0**	**2**	**0**	**1472**

Going: Sf: 0-0 GS: 0-1 Gd: 0-4 GF: - Fm: 0-0
Distance: 2m/2m3: 0-1 2m4-2m7: 0-4 3m+: 0-0
Track: LH: 0-5 RH: 0-0 Tight: 0-5 Gall: 0-0
Aids: Bl: 0-0 Vi: 0-0 Tstrap: 0-0
Best Rating: 98 10/01 Sedg 2m5f110y good Hdl

Staying novice hurdler, runner-up at Sedgefield in October over two miles five, looks likely to stay further.

Kinfauns Lady (IRE)

97 **83**
7-y-o b m King's Ride-Dalkey Sound (Crash Course)
D W Whillans E J Jamieson

Placings:_20_/P60-344F3P **(4491)**
2001/02: 18^{3}GS, 16^{4}S, 21^{4}HY, 24^{F}S, 24^{3}HY, 20^{P}GS

	Starts	1st	2nd	3rd	Win & Pl
Hurdles	6	0	0	2	1004
Career Total	**11**	**0**	**1**	**2**	**1431**

Going: Sf: 0-4 GS: 0-2 Gd: 0-0 GF: - Fm: 0-0
Distance: 2m/2m3: 0-2 2m4-2m7: 0-2 3m+: 0-2
Track: LH: 0-4 RH: 0-1 Tight: 0-3 Gall: 0-1
Aids: Bl: 0-0 Vi: 0-0 Tstrap: 0-0
Best Rating: 89 2/00 Ayr 2m heavy NHF

Modest hurdler, daughter of the useful chaser Dalkey Sound. Stays two and a quarter miles, suited by cut in the ground. May have found three miles to much of a stamina stretch.

King Bavard (IRE)

100(88h) **93**
8-y-o b g Jurado (USA)-Discerning Lady (Le Bavard (FR))
J I A Charlton Mr & Mrs Raymond Anderson Green

Placings:_0223/1_U04-**6F425** **(4521)**
2001/02: 20^{6}S, 24^{F}G, 24^{4}S, 24^{2}GS, 20^{5}GS

	Starts	1st	2nd	3rd	Win & Pl
Chases	5	0	1	0	1568
Career Total	**13**	**1**	**3**	**1**	**6719**

103	5/00	Dpat	2m4f110y	NHF	GD	£2760

Total win prize-money £2760

Going: Sf: 0-2 GS: 0-2 Gd: 0-1 GF: - Fm: 0-0
Distance: 2m/2m3: 0-0 2m4-2m7: 0-2 3m+: 0-3
Track: LH: 0-0 RH: 0-5 Tight: 0-3 Gall: 0-0
Aids: Bl: 0-0 Vi: 0-0 Tstrap: 0-0
Best Rating: 111 4/00 Ayr 2m good NHF

Modest chaser, stays three miles, does not want the ground too soft.

King Bee (IRE)

95 **89**
5-y-o b g Supreme Leader-Honey Come Back (Master Owen)
H D Daly Trevor Hemmings

Placings:305 **(3892)**
2001/02: 16^{3}S, 19^{0}S, 21^{5}HY

	Starts	1st	2nd	3rd	Win & Pl
Hurdles	3	0	0	1	394
Career Total	**3**	**0**	**0**	**1**	**394**

Going: Sf: 0-3 GS: 0-0 Gd: 0-0 GF: - Fm: 0-0
Distance: 2m/2m3: 0-1 2m4-2m7: 0-2 3m+: 0-0
Track: LH: 0-1 RH: 0-1 Tight: 0-1 Gall: 0-0
Aids: Bl: 0-0 Vi: 0-0 Tstrap: 0-0
Best Rating: 89 11/01 Uttx 2m soft Hdl

King Claudius (IRE)

96f **119f**
6-y-o b g King's Ride-Lepida (Royal Match)
P R Webber M C Banks

Placings:_13_ **(4032)**
2001/02: 16^{1}S, 16^{3}GS

	Starts	1st	2nd	3rd	Win & Pl
NH Flat	2	1	0	1	2398
Career Total	**2**	**1**	**0**	**1**	**2398**

108	1/02	Kemp	2m	H NHF	SFT	£2002

Total win prize-money £2002

Going: Sf: 1-1 GS: 0-1 Gd: 0-0 GF: - Fm: 0-0
Distance: **2m/2m3: 1-2** 2m4-2m7: 0-0 3m+: 0-0
Track: LH: 0-1 **RH: 1-1** Tight: 0-0 Gall: 0-1
Aids: Bl: 0-0 Vi: 0-0 Tstrap: 0-0
Best Rating: 119 3/02 Newb 2m110y gd-sft NHF

A half-brother to useful chaser Killusty, he made a winning debut in a Kempton bumper and ran well under a penalty next time.

King Cool (IRE)

96(99h) **88**
11-y-o b g Supreme Leader-Sno-Sleigh (Bargello)
John A Harris (J L Harris 10/5) Mrs Joan Martin

Placings:_6/0/0_345P5F-**60** **(1933)**
2001/02: 20^{6}G, 20^{0}G

	Starts	1st	2nd	3rd	Win & Pl
Chases	2	0	0	0	0
Career Total	**11**	**0**	**0**	**1**	**498**

Going: Sf: 0-0 GS: 0-0 Gd: 0-2 GF: - Fm: 0-0
Distance: 2m/2m3: 0-0 2m4-2m7: 0-2 3m+: 0-0
Track: LH: 0-1 RH: 0-1 Tight: 0-0 Gall: 0-1
Aids: Bl: 0-0 Vi: 0-0 Tstrap: 0-0
Best Rating: 104 12/00 Donc 2m4f heavy Hdl

King Cup (IRE)

9-y-o ch g Yashgan-Madness In Motion (IRE) (Le Johnstan)
B I Case Dudley C Moore

Placings:_0_P60250F/0-PPP **(3868)**
2001/02: 24^{P}S, 26^{P}S, 26^{P}GS

	Starts	1st	2nd	3rd	Win & Pl
Hurdles	1	0	0	0	0
Chases	2	0	0	0	0
Career Total	**12**	**0**	**1**	**0**	**701**

Going: Sf: 0-2 GS: 0-1 Gd: 0-0 GF: - Fm: 0-0
Distance: 2m/2m3: 0-0 2m4-2m7: 0-0 3m+: 0-3
Track: LH: 0-1 RH: 0-1 Tight: 0-2 Gall: 0-0

Aids: Bl: 0-1 Vi: 0-0 Tstrap: 0-3
Best Rating: 112 4/00 Chel 3m1f110y soft Ch

Modest staying chaser. Best on an easy surface.

King Curan (USA)

11-y-o b g Lear Fan (USA)-Runaway Lady (USA) (Caucasus (USA))
C J Hemsley R J A Willis

Placings:0/P0015/PP00/0F/00 **(3334)**
2001/02: 16^{0}S, 16^{0}G

	Starts	1st	2nd	3rd	Win & Pl
Hurdles	2	0	0	0	
Career Total	**14**	**1**	**0**	**0**	**1881**

68	10/97	Font	2m2f110y	G(0-95)HHdl	GD	£1881

Total win prize-money £1881

Going: Sf: 0-1 GS: 0-0 Gd: 0-1 GF: - Fm: 0-0
Distance: 2m/2m3: 0-2 2m4-2m7: 0-0 3m+: 0-0
Track: LH: 0-0 RH: 0-2 Tight: 0-0 Gall: 0-0
Aids: Bl: 0-1 Vi: 0-0 Tstrap: 0-0
Best Rating: 68 10/97 Font 2m2f110y good Hdl

King For A Day

98 90

6-y-o b g Machiavellian (USA)-Dizzy Heights (USA) (Danzig (USA))
Bob Jones Mrs Joan Marioni

Placings:465064/02033000 **(4236)**
2001/02: 26^{0}G, 19^{2}GS, 20^{0}HY, 20^{3}G, 21^{3}GS, 16^{0}S, 20^{0}HY, 21^{0}GF

	Starts	1st	2nd	3rd	Win & Pl
Hurdles	8	0	1	2	1131
Career Total	**14**	**0**	**1**	**2**	**1342**

Going: Sf: 0-3 GS: 0-2 Gd: 0-2 GF: - Fm: 0-1
Distance: 2m/2m3: 0-1 2m4-2m7: 0-6 3m+: 0-1
Track: LH: 0-2 RH: 0-6 Tight: 0-1 Gall: 0-4
Aids: Bl: 0-0 Vi: 0-0 Tstrap: 0-0
Best Rating: 90 1/02 Hntg 2m5f110y gd-sft Hdl

Is becoming expensive to follow.

King Georges (FR)

66 38

4-y-o b g Kadalko (FR)-Djoumi (FR) (Brezzo (FR))
J C Tuck The Try-Line Partnership

Placings:F0 **(4114)**
2001/02: 16^{F}S, 16^{0}G

	Starts	1st	2nd	3rd	Win & Pl
Hurdles	2	0	0	0	
Career Total	**2**	**0**	**0**	**0**	

Going: Sf: 0-1 GS: 0-0 Gd: 0-1 GF: - Fm: 0-0
Distance: 2m/2m3: 0-2 2m4-2m7: 0-0 3m+: 0-0
Track: LH: 0-0 RH: 0-2 Tight: 0-0 Gall: 0-0
Aids: Bl: 0-0 Vi: 0-0 Tstrap: 0-0
Best Rating: 38 3/02 Winc 2m good Hdl

King James

48 24

5-y-o b g Homo Sapien-Bowling Fort (Bowling Pin)
J Mackie A J Wall

Placings:0600B **(4684)**
2001/02: 16^{0}GF, 16^{6}G, 17^{0}G, 20^{0}S, 19^{B}GF

	Starts	1st	2nd	3rd	Win & Pl
NH Flat	3	0	0	0	0
Hurdles	2	0	0	0	0
Career Total	**5**	**0**	**0**	**0**	**0**

Going: Sf: 0-1 GS: 0-0 Gd: 0-2 GF: - Fm: 0-2
Distance: 2m/2m3: 0-3 2m4-2m7: 0-2 3m+: 0-0
Track: LH: 0-2 RH: 0-3 Tight: 0-1 Gall: 0-2
Aids: Bl: 0-0 Vi: 0-0 Tstrap: 0-4
Best Rating: 68 10/01 Hntg 2m110y good NHF

King Of Babylon (IRE)

10-y-o b g Persian Heights-My My Marie (Artaius (USA))
F L Matthews Mrs L Danton

Placings:56360R4/0343261F00/P056/00PR/P **(0258)**
2001/02: 24^{P}GF

	Starts	1st	2nd	3rd	Win & Pl
Chases	1	0	0	0	
Career Total	**26**	**1**	**1**	**3**	**3445**

67	10/96	Ludl	2m5f110y	G(0-90)HHdl	FRM	£1968

Total win prize-money £1968

Going: Sf: 0-0 GS: 0-0 Gd: 0-0 GF: - Fm: 0-1
Distance: 2m/2m3: 0-0 2m4-2m7: 0-0 3m+: 0-1
Track: LH: 0-1 RH: 0-0 Tight: 0-1 Gall: 0-0
Aids: Bl: 0-0 Vi: 0-0 Tstrap: 0-0
Best Rating: 93 1/96 Kemp 2m good Hdl

King Of Barbury (IRE)

101f 99f

5-y-o b g Moscow Society (USA)-Aine's Alice (IRE) (Drumalis)
A King Miss J M Bodycote

Placings:*42* **(4180)**
2001/02: 18^{4}S, 16^{2}GS

	Starts	1st	2nd	3rd	Win & Pl
NH Flat	2	0	1	0	886
Career Total	**2**	**0**	**1**	**0**	**886**

Going: Sf: 0-1 GS: 0-1 Gd: 0-0 GF: - Fm: 0-0
Distance: 2m/2m3: 0-2 2m4-2m7: 0-0 3m+: 0-0
Track: LH: 0-1 RH: 0-0 Tight: 0-1 Gall: 0-0
Aids: Bl: 0-0 Vi: 0-0 Tstrap: 0-0
Best Rating: 99 3/02 Strf 2m110y gd-sft NHF

He has shown ability in bumpers and should find races over hurdles.

King Of Mommur (IRE)

100(93h) (98h)119

7-y-o b g Fairy King (USA)-Monoglow (Kalaglow)
B G Powell The Three Bears Racing

Placings:6135/0P0-1155 **(1441)**
2001/02: 16^{1}GF, 20^{1}GF, 21^{5}G, 20^{5}GF

	Starts	1st	2nd	3rd	Win & Pl
Chases	4	2	0	0	5942
Career Total	**11**	**3**	**0**	**1**	**8999**

115	5/01	Font	2m4f	F Ch	G-F	£2973
119	5/01	Sthl	2m	F(0-110)HCh	G-F	£2968
115	3/00	Extr	2m3f110y	E Hdl	G-S	£2556

Total win prize-money £8498

Going: Sf: 0-0 GS: 0-0 Gd: 0-1 GF: - Fm: 2-3
Distance: 2m/2m3: 1-1 2m4-2m7: 1-3 3m+: 0-0
Track: LH: 1-2 RH: 0-0 Tight: 2-4 Gall: 0-0
Aids: Bl: 0-0 Vi: 0-0 Tstrap: 0-0
Best Rating: 119 5/01 Sthl 2m gd-fm Ch

King Of Sparta

109 131

9-y-o b g Kefaah (USA)-Khaizaraan (CAN) (Sham (USA))
J G Portman Mrs Richard Tice

Placings:P12/21102/**112133111134324/41024/3252U 0P-2023** **(2428)**
2001/02: 21^{2}GS, 20^{0}G, 20^{2}G, 22^{3}G

	Starts	1st	2nd	3rd	Win & Pl
Chases	4	0	2	1	5224
Career Total	**39**	**11**	**10**	**6**	**100193**

143	2/00	Winc	2m5f	D(0-125)HCh	GD	£6955
143	12/98	Chel	2m5f	C Ch	GD	£6909
135	12/98	Winc	2m5f	D(0-120)HCh	G-S	£4201
133	11/98	Winc	2m5f	E(0-105)HCh	GD	£7392
143	11/98	Tntn	2m3f	E(0-105)HCh	GD	£7392
113	7/98	NAbb	2m5f110y	E(0-120)Ch	G-F	£2762
110	6/98	Uttx	2m5f	C Ch	GD	£5340
119	5/98	Uttx	2m5f	D Ch	G-F	£3485
114	10/97	Plum	2m4f	D(0-120)HHdl	GD	£3159
114	9/97	Extr	2m2f	D(0-120)HHdl	G-F	£2007
89	4/97	Uttx	2m	E Hdl	G-F	£2432

Total win prize-money £52730

Going: Sf: 0-0 GS: 0-1 Gd: 0-3 GF: - Fm: 0-0
Distance: 2m/2m3: 0-0 2m4-2m7: 0-4 3m+: 0-0
Track: LH: 0-4 RH: 0-0 Tight: 0-1 Gall: 0-3
Aids: Bl: 0-0 Vi: 0-0 Tstrap: 0-0
Best Rating: 143 3/00 Newb 3m gd-fm Ch

He has lost his way slightly, but has been generally racing on ground softer than ideal. Well handicapped on the pick of his form, trips of around two and a half miles are the limit of his stamina.

King Of The Blues

89 65

10-y-o b g Rakaposhi King-Colonial Princess (Roscoe Blake)
Graeme Roe Mrs Alayne O'Connor

Placings:*325/06*402P/0/P00P02P0PP **(4513)**
2001/02: 19^{P}G, 16^{0}G, 20^{0}GF, 24^{P}GF, 26^{0}G, 20^{2}GS, 20^{P}S, 17^{0}G, 21^{P}G, 24^{P}GS

	Starts	1st	2nd	3rd	Win & Pl
Hurdles	10	0	1	0	657
Career Total	**20**	**0**	**3**	**1**	**1812**

Going: Sf: 0-1 GS: 0-2 Gd: 0-5 GF: - Fm: 0-2
Distance: 2m/2m3: 0-3 2m4-2m7: 0-4 3m+: 0-3
Track: LH: 0-5 RH: 0-4 Tight: 0-2 Gall: 0-1
Aids: Bl: 0-0 Vi: 0-0 Tstrap: 0-0
Best Rating: 88 1/97 Ludl 2m gd-fm NHF

Plating-class maiden hurdler.

King Of The Castle (IRE)

101 109

7-y-o b g Cataldi-Monashuna (Boreen (FR))
J J O'Neill (R J Hodges 30/6) Exors Of The Late

Robert Hitchins

Placings: *1/*F0PP1-2023100 **(2850)**
2001/02: 17^{2}G, 17^{0}GF, 17^{2}F, 17^{3}GF, 19^{1}GS, 16^{0}G, 21^{0}G

	Starts	1st	2nd	3rd	Win & Pl
Hurdles	7	1	2	1	5512
Career Total	**14**	**4**	**2**	**1**	**22704**

109	10/01	Extr	2m3f	E(0-115)HHdl	G-S	£3290
103	4/01	Tntn	2m1f	F(0-95)HHdl	GD	£2415
128	4/99	Aint	2m110y	A NHF	GD	£13200
109	3/99	Folk	2m1f110y	H NHF	G-S	£1577

Total win prize-money £20483

Going: Sf: 0-0 GS: 1-1 Gd: 0-3 GF: - Fm: 0-3
Distance: **2m/2m3: 1-6** 2m4-2m7: 0-1 3m+: 0-0
Track: LH: 0-2 **RH: 1-5** Tight: 0-2 Gall: 0-0
Aids: Bl: 0-0 Vi: 0-0 Tstrap: 0-0
Best Rating: 128 4/99 Aint 2m110y good NHF

He was a useful bumper horse, but has been very disappointing over hurdles and has had problems including breathing problems. Given considerate handling when scoring in modest handicap hurdle at Exeter in October, but disappointing since. Does not want to be put under too much pressure. Has won from two miles to two miles three. Seems to handle most surfaces.

King Of The Dawn

102 **118**

11-y-o b/br g Rakaposhi King-Dawn Encounter (Rymer)
Mark Campion Mrs J Howell

Placings: *14/*11206/03/03424P/32P03-U6321360P0 **(4751)**
2001/02: 17^{U}GS, 21^{6}GF, 20^{3}GF, 20^{2}G, 22^{1}S, 18^{3}GS, 20^{6}G, 20^{0}S, 20^{P}G, 20^{0}GF

	Starts	1st	2nd	3rd	Win & Pl
Chases	10	1	1	2	5173
Career Total	**30**	**4**	**4**	**6**	**20135**

113	10/01	Font	2m6f	F(0-95)HCh	SFT	£2899
116	11/97	Extr	2m1f110y	E Hdl	G-S	£2679
109	8/97	Tram	2m	Hdl	GD	£2712
98	9/96	Clon	2m	NHF	GD	£2471

Total win prize-money £10763

Going: Sf: 1-2 GS: 0-2 Gd: 0-3 GF: - Fm: 0-3
Distance: 2m/2m3: 0-2 **2m4-2m7: 1-8** 3m+: 0-0
Track: LH: 0-6 RH: 0-1 **Tight: 1-7** Gall: 0-0
Aids: Bl: 0-0 Vi: 0-0 Tstrap: 0-0
Best Rating: 118 4/01 Font 2m6f good Ch

Handles most types of ground. Suited by trips at around two and a half miles.

King Of The Forest (IRE)

86f **72f**

7-y-o b g Good Thyne (USA)-Coolbawn Lady (Laurence O)
R J Hodges Robert Hitchins

Placings: *5-0* **(0506)**
2001/02: 16^{0}GF

	Starts	1st	2nd	3rd	Win & Pl
NH Flat	1	0	0	0	
Career Total	**2**	**0**	**0**	**0**	**0**

Going: Sf: 0-0 GS: 0-0 Gd: 0-0 GF: - Fm: 0-1
Distance: 2m/2m3: 0-1 2m4-2m7: 0-0 3m+: 0-0
Track: LH: 0-0 RH: 0-1 Tight: 0-0 Gall: 0-1
Aids: Bl: 0-0 Vi: 0-0 Tstrap: 0-0
Best Rating: 88 10/00 Chep 2m110y gd-sft NHF

King Of The Light

98 **105**

8-y-o b g Rakaposhi King-Dawn Encounter (Rymer)
O Brennan Lady Anne Bentinck

Placings: *10/*043 **(3994)**
2001/02: 20^{0}G, 16^{4}GS, 20^{3}S

	Starts	1st	2nd	3rd	Win & Pl
Hurdles	3	0	0	1	446
Career Total	**5**	**1**	**0**	**1**	**2077**

115	2/00	Catt	2m	H NHF	GD	£1631

Total win prize-money £1631

Going: Sf: 0-1 GS: 0-1 Gd: 0-1 GF: - Fm: 0-0
Distance: 2m/2m3: 0-1 2m4-2m7: 0-2 3m+: 0-0
Track: LH: 0-3 RH: 0-0 Tight: 0-0 Gall: 0-1
Aids: Bl: 0-0 Vi: 0-0 Tstrap: 0-0
Best Rating: 115 4/00 Newc 2m gd-sft NHF

Lightly-raced, from the family of Dawn Run, he won his bumper debut, but is a tail swisher. However, there should be better to come from him over hurdles. Likes good to soft ground.

King On The Run (IRE)

114 **151**

9-y-o b g King's Ride-Fly Run (Deep Run)
Miss Venetia Williams Lady Harris

Placings: 31166/1U3/113-1 **(3381)**
2001/02: 20^{1}G

	Starts	1st	2nd	3rd	Win & Pl
Chases	1	1	0	0	13910
Career Total	**12**	**6**	**0**	**3**	**43817**

151	1/02	Kemp	2m4f110y	B(0-140)HCh	GD	£13910
137	11/00	Kemp	2m4f110y	B(0-140)HCh	SFT	£9178
142	11/00	Newb	2m4f	D(0-125)HCh	SFT	£5642
129	11/98	Wwck	2m4f110y	D Ch	GD	£3834
131	1/98	Kemp	2m5f	D Hdl	G-S	£3074
131	12/97	Strf	2m6f110y	E Hdl	SFT	£2500

Total win prize-money £38138

Going: Sf: 0-0 GS: 0-0 Gd: 1-1 GF: - Fm: 0-0
Distance: 2m/2m3: 0-0 **2m4-2m7: 1-1** 3m+: 0-0
Track: LH: 0-0 **RH: 1-1** Tight: 0-0 Gall: 0-0
Aids: Bl: 0-0 Vi: 0-0 Tstrap: 0-0
Best Rating: 151 1/02 Kemp 2m4f110y good Ch

A progressive chaser, he returned after a year's absence to win at Kempton in January 2002. Stays three miles and goes well fresh. Has won on good and soft ground.

King Paddy (IRE)

10-y-o b g King's Ride-Nebechal (Native Bazaar)
R C Bevan R C Bevan

Placings: 004203P/0PP/0/P **(2327)**
2001/02: 16^{P}S

	Starts	1st	2nd	3rd	Win & Pl
Hurdles	1	0	0	0	
Career Total	**12**	**0**	**1**	**1**	**1408**

Going: Sf: 0-1 GS: 0-0 Gd: 0-0 GF: - Fm: 0-0
Distance: 2m/2m3: 0-1 2m4-2m7: 0-0 3m+: 0-0
Track: LH: 0-1 RH: 0-0 Tight: 0-1 Gall: 0-0
Aids: Bl: 0-0 Vi: 0-0 Tstrap: 0-1

Best Rating: 102 1/98 Weth 2m4f110y soft Hdl

King Plato (IRE)

96 **93+**

5-y-o b g King's Ride-You Are A Lady (IRE) (Lord Americo)
A Crook Jay Dee Bloodstock Limited

Placings: *640* **(4771)**
2001/02: 16^{6}GS, 16^{4}HY, 16^{0}GF

	Starts	1st	2nd	3rd	Win & Pl
NH Flat	3	0	0	0	0
Career Total	**3**	**0**	**0**	**0**	**0**

Going: Sf: 0-1 GS: 0-1 Gd: 0-0 GF: - Fm: 0-1
Distance: 2m/2m3: 0-3 2m4-2m7: 0-0 3m+: 0-0
Track: LH: 0-2 RH: 0-0 Tight: 0-1 Gall: 0-1
Aids: Bl: 0-0 Vi: 0-0 Tstrap: 0-0
Best Rating: 87 3/02 Sthl 2m heavy NHF

Improved form when winning three mile conditional jockeys' handicap hurdle on soft ground at Bangor August 2002. Looks well handicapped if that performance was not a flash in the pan.

King Rooster

87 **82**

7-y-o b g Riverwise (USA)-Came Cottage (Nearly A Hand)
J G Portman Mrs Richard Tice

Placings: *00-*4FP **(3212)**
2001/02: 16^{4}GS, 17^{F}G, 19^{P}GS

	Starts	1st	2nd	3rd	Win & Pl
Hurdles	3	0	0	0	0
Career Total	**5**	**0**	**0**	**0**	**0**

Going: Sf: 0-0 GS: 0-2 Gd: 0-1 GF: - Fm: 0-0
Distance: 2m/2m3: 0-3 2m4-2m7: 0-0 3m+: 0-0
Track: LH: 0-3 RH: 0-0 Tight: 0-2 Gall: 0-1
Aids: Bl: 0-0 Vi: 0-0 Tstrap: 0-0
Best Rating: 82 9/01 Plum 2m gd-sft Hdl

King Torus (IRE)

109 **100**

12-y-o b g Torus-Kam A Dusk (Kambalda)
V R A Dartnall Nick Viney

Placings: 00/1110/1630233/351/61233100-20166P **(4865)**
2001/02: 21^{2}GF, 23^{0}G, 22^{1}GF, 24^{6}GF, 22^{6}GS, 23^{P}F

	Starts	1st	2nd	3rd	Win & Pl
Chases	6	1	1	0	6595
Career Total	**30**	**8**	**3**	**6**	**25831**

119	8/01	Font	2m6f	F(0-110)HCh	G-F	£3428
119	8/00	Font	2m6f	F(0-110)HCh	G-F	£3692
116	5/00	Winc	2m5f	H Ch	FRM	£1991
111	3/00	Font	2m4f	H Ch	G-F	£2212
98	5/98	Winc	2m5f	H Ch	GD	£2024
115	3/98	Tntn	3m	H Ch	G-S	£1068
112	5/97	Uttx	2m5f	H Ch	G-F	£1127
101	5/97	NAbb	2m5f110y	H Ch	GD	£1030

Total win prize-money £16576

Going: Sf: 0-0 GS: 0-1 Gd: 0-1 GF: - Fm: 1-4
Distance: 2m/2m3: 0-0 **2m4-2m7: 1-3** 3m+: 0-3
Track: LH: 0-3 RH: 0-1 **Tight: 1-4** Gall: 0-0
Aids: **Bl: 1-5** Vi: 0-0 Tstrap: 0-0
Best Rating: 119 8/01 Font 2m6f gd-fm Ch

One time useful hunter but is on the decline now.

King Triton (IRE)

92 84

5-y-o br g Mister Lord (USA)-Deepwater Woman (The Parson)

L Wells L Wells

Placings:3352 (4425)

2001/02: 17^{3}S, 18^{3}S, 25^{5}GS, 24^{2}HY

	Starts	1st	2nd	3rd	Win & Pl
NH Flat	2	0	0	2	457
Hurdles	2	0	1	0	772
Career Total	**4**	**0**	**1**	**2**	**1229**

Going: Sf: 0-3 GS: 0-1 Gd: 0-0 GF: - Fm: 0-0
Distance: 2m/2m3: 0-2 2m4-2m7: 0-0 3m+: 0-2
Track: LH: 0-1 RH: 0-0 Tight: 0-1 Gall: 0-0
Aids: Bl: 0-0 Vi: 0-0 Tstrap: 0-0
Best Rating: 85 12/01 Plum 2m2f soft NHF

Third in two bumpers. Well beaten over hurdles.

King Tut

80 70

6-y-o ch g Anshan-Fahrenheit (Mount Hagen (FR))

J G Given A Clarke

Placings:0P (1564)

2001/02: 17^{0}GS, 16^{P}GS

	Starts	1st	2nd	3rd	Win & Pl
Hurdles	2	0	0	0	
Career Total	**2**	**0**	**0**	**0**	

Going: Sf: 0-0 GS: 0-2 Gd: 0-0 GF: - Fm: 0-0
Distance: 2m/2m3: 0-2 2m4-2m7: 0-0 3m+: 0-0
Track: LH: 0-1 RH: 0-0 Tight: 0-0 Gall: 0-0
Aids: Bl: 0-0 Vi: 0-0 Tstrap: 0-0
Best Rating: 70 7/01 MRas 2m1f110y gd-sft Hdl

King Wizard (IRE)

8-y-o b/br g Supreme Leader-Magic User (Deep Run)

K Robson (P J Hobbs 2/5) Mrs M Armstrong

Placings:0335/552/000-0F (3749)

2001/02: 22^{0}GS, 24^{F}S

	Starts	1st	2nd	3rd	Win & Pl
Hurdles	1	0	0	0	0
Chases	1	0	0	0	0
Career Total	**12**	**0**	**1**	**2**	**1394**

Going: Sf: 0-1 GS: 0-1 Gd: 0-0 GF: - Fm: 0-0
Distance: 2m/2m3: 0-0 2m4-2m7: 0-1 3m+: 0-1
Track: LH: 0-0 RH: 0-1 Tight: 0-1 Gall: 0-0
Aids: Bl: 0-0 Vi: 0-0 Tstrap: 0-0
Best Rating: 120 4/99 Aint 2m110y good NHF

King's Banker (IRE)

108 138

11-y-o b g King's Ride-Wren's Princess (Wrens Hill)

N J Henderson J E H Collins

Placings:32F2/215/3P-1 (0344)

2001/02: 25^{1}G

	Starts	1st	2nd	3rd	Win & Pl
Chases	1	1	0	0	5616
Career Total	**10**	**2**	**3**	**2**	**15543**

138 5/01 Aint 3m1f D(0-120)HCh GD £5616
138 2/99 Kemp 3m D Ch GD £4182
Total win prize-money £9798

Going: Sf: 0-0 GS: 0-0 Gd: 1-1 GF: - Fm: 0-0
Distance: 2m/2m3: 0-0 2m4-2m7: 0-0 3m+: 1-1
Track: LH: 1-1 RH: 0-0 Tight: 1-1 Gall: 0-0
Aids: Bl: 0-0 Vi: 0-0 Tstrap: 0-0
Best Rating: 138 5/01 Aint 3m1f good Ch

King's Bounty

108 112

6-y-o b g Le Moss-Fit For A King (Royalty)

T D Easterby C H Stevens

Placings:003-542123 (4259)

2001/02: 16^{5}G, 20^{4}G, 25^{2}GS, 20^{1}S, 20^{2}S, 24^{3}HY

	Starts	1st	2nd	3rd	Win & Pl
Hurdles	6	1	2	1	4614
Career Total	**9**	**1**	**2**	**2**	**4841**

109 2/02 Newc 2m4f E Hdl SFT £2555
Total win prize-money £2555

Going: Sf: 1-3 GS: 0-1 Gd: 0-2 GF: - Fm: 0-0
Distance: 2m/2m3: 0-1 2m4-2m7: 1-3 3m+: 0-2
Track: LH: 1-6 RH: 0-0 Tight: 0-1 Gall: 1-3
Aids: Bl: 0-0 Vi: 0-0 Tstrap: 0-0
Best Rating: 112 3/02 Donc 2m4f soft Hdl

Creditable form in novice hurdles, staying on well to win at Newcastle in February 2002. Gets three miles.

King's Chambers

98 91

6-y-o ch g Sabrehill (USA)-Flower Girl (Pharly (FR))

J Parkes P J Cronin

Placings:F/0011F3-220P (3553)

2001/02: 17^{2}GF, 19^{2}GF, 19^{0}S, 19^{P}S

	Starts	1st	2nd	3rd	Win & Pl
Hurdles	4	0	2	0	1462
Career Total	**11**	**2**	**2**	**1**	**4731**

84 12/00 MRas 2m1f110y G(0-95)HHdl G-S £1505
76 11/00 MRas 2m3f110y G(0-95)HHdl SFT £1477
Total win prize-money £2982

Going: Sf: 0-2 GS: 0-0 Gd: 0-0 GF: - Fm: 0-2
Distance: 2m/2m3: 0-2 2m4-2m7: 0-2 3m+: 0-0
Track: LH: 0-1 RH: 0-3 Tight: 0-4 Gall: 0-0
Aids: Bl: 0-0 Vi: 0-0 Tstrap: 0-4
Best Rating: 91 9/01 MRas 2m3f110y gd-fm Hdl

King's Champion (IRE)

79f 74f

6-y-o b g King's Ride-Decent Slave (Decent Fellow)

Mrs Merrita Jones Speed 2911 Ltd

Placings:0 (2041)

2001/02: 16^{0}GS

	Starts	1st	2nd	3rd	Win & Pl
NH Flat	1	0	0	0	
Career Total	**1**	**0**	**0**	**0**	

Going: Sf: 0-0 GS: 0-1 Gd: 0-0 GF: - Fm: 0-0
Distance: 2m/2m3: 0-1 2m4-2m7: 0-0 3m+: 0-0
Track: LH: 0-0 RH: 0-1 Tight: 0-0 Gall: 0-0
Aids: Bl: 0-0 Vi: 0-0 Tstrap: 0-0
Best Rating: 74 11/01 Sand 2m110y gd-sft NHF

King's Country (IRE)

99 (46c)92

10-y-o b g King's Ride-Tatlock (Paico)

N B Mason N B Mason

Placings:005/4P2F5FP4/221-2001 (2901)

2001/02: 21^{2}G, 20^{0}G, 25^{0}S, 20^{1}S

	Starts	1st	2nd	3rd	Win & Pl
Hurdles	3	1	1	0	4569
Chases	1	0	0	0	0
Career Total	**18**	**2**	**4**	**0**	**9973**

92 12/01 Leic 2m4f110y F(0-105)HHdl SFT £3705
92 4/01 Prth 2m4f110y G(0-90)HHdl HVY £3465
Total win prize-money £7170

Going: Sf: 1-2 GS: 0-0 Gd: 0-2 GF: - Fm: 0-0
Distance: 2m/2m3: 0-0 2m4-2m7: 1-3 3m+: 0-1
Track: LH: 0-2 RH: 1-2 Tight: 0-1 Gall: 0-1
Aids: Bl: 0-0 Vi: 0-0 Tstrap: 1-3
Best Rating: 99 10/98 Kels 2m2f gd-sft Hdl

Stays two miles six, acts with cut in the ground.

King's Hero (IRE)

94(76h) (59h)86

7-y-o b g King's Ride-Dis Fiove (Le Bavard (FR))

A Ennis A T A Wates

Placings:0P-05204 (4510)

2001/02: 16^{0}G, 25^{5}G, 22^{2}G, 20^{0}S, 26^{4}G

	Starts	1st	2nd	3rd	Win & Pl
Hurdles	1	0	0	0	0
Chases	4	0	1	0	1113
Career Total	**7**	**0**	**1**	**0**	**1113**

Going: Sf: 0-1 GS: 0-0 Gd: 0-4 GF: - Fm: 0-0
Distance: 2m/2m3: 0-1 2m4-2m7: 0-2 3m+: 0-2
Track: LH: 0-1 RH: 0-2 Tight: 0-2 Gall: 0-0
Aids: Bl: 0-0 Vi: 0-0 Tstrap: 0-0
Best Rating: 86 1/02 Font 2m6f good Ch

Has shown ability in a couple of chases. Looks best suited to around two miles six on a sound surface.

King's Hussar

91(88h) (55h)66

7-y-o b g Be My Chief (USA)-Croire (IRE) (Lomond (USA))

J R Cornwall J R Cornwall

Placings:420501/542215F1066/0432F04-00P003U (4592)

2001/02: 16^{0}S, 26^{0}G, 20^{P}G, 26^{0}S, 26^{0}S, 26^{3}HY, 26^{U}G

	Starts	1st	2nd	3rd	Win & Pl
Hurdles	3	0	0	0	0
Chases	4	0	0	1	630
Career Total	**31**	**3**	**4**	**2**	**12295**

98 1/00 Sedg 3m3f110y F(0-105)HHdl SFT £2765
98 11/99 Sedg 3m3f110y G(0-95)HHdl GD £1490
91 4/99 Sedg 2m5f110y F(0-100)HHdl G-S £3715
Total win prize-money £7971

Going: Sf: 0-4 GS: 0-0 Gd: 0-3 GF: - Fm: 0-0
Distance: 2m/2m3: 0-1 2m4-2m7: 0-1 3m+: 0-5
Track: LH: 0-4 RH: 0-3 Tight: 0-1 Gall: 0-2
Aids: Bl: 0-1 Vi: 0-0 Tstrap: 0-1
Best Rating: 98 1/00 Sedg 3m3f110y soft Hdl

Winner three times over hurdles but little impact over fences. A lazy sort, he needs plenty of driving.

King's Reign (IRE)

6-y-o b g King's Ride-Lena's Reign (Quayside)
N A Twiston-Davies Mrs Lorna Berryman

Placings:*00P* **(4518)**
2001/02: 16^{0}GS, 16^{0}S, 21^{P}GS

	Starts	1st	2nd	3rd	Win & Pl
NH Flat	2	0	0	0	0
Hurdles	1	0	0	0	0
Career Total	**3**	**0**	**0**	**0**	

Going: Sf: 0-1 GS: 0-2 Gd: 0-0 GF: - Fm: 0-0
Distance: 2m/2m3: 0-2 2m4-2m7: 0-1 3m+: 0-0
Track: LH: 0-1 RH: 0-2 Tight: 0-0 Gall: 0-1
Aids: Bl: 0-0 Vi: 0-0 Tstrap: 0-0
Best Rating: 70 11/01 Sand 2m110y gd-sft NHF

King's Stride (IRE)

106(79h) (53h) 111

10-y-o b g King's Ride-Anavore (Darantus)
P Monteith Mrs Maud Monteith

Placings:0/3/4/12040U0-1P054104P0PPUP (4855)
2001/02: 16^{1}S, 20^{P}GF, 20^{0}GS, 21^{5}GF, 20^{4}GF, 17^{1}GS, 16^{0}G, 21^{4}G, 16^{P}S, 21^{0}G, 20^{P}G, 19^{P}S, 24^{U}S, 20^{P}G

	Starts	1st	2nd	3rd	Win & Pl
Chases	14	2	0	0	6707
Career Total	**24**	**3**	**1**	**1**	**11250**

111	8/01	Ctml	2m1f110y	F(0-100)HCh	G-S	£2769
110	5/01	Hexm	2m110y	F(0-105)HCh	SFT	£3346
96	9/00	Prth	2m4f110y	E Hdl	HVY	£2795

Total win prize-money £8910

Going: Sf: 1-4 GS: 1-2 Gd: 0-5 GF: - Fm: 0-3
Distance: **2m/2m3: 2-5** 2m4-2m7: 0-8 3m+: 0-1
Track: **LH: 2-9** RH: 0-5 **Tight: 1-6** Gall: 0-0
Aids: Bl: 0-0 Vi: 0-1 Tstrap: 0-0
Best Rating: 111 8/01 Ctml 2m1f110y gd-sft Ch

King's Travel (FR)

76 50

6-y-o gr g Balleroy (USA)-Travel Free (Be My Guest (USA))
G M McCourt P Ince

Placings:P-0 **(0341)**
2001/02: 16^{0}G

	Starts	1st	2nd	3rd	Win & Pl
Hurdles	1	0	0	0	
Career Total	**2**	**0**	**0**	**0**	

Going: Sf: 0-0 GS: 0-0 Gd: 0-1 GF: - Fm: 0-0
Distance: 2m/2m3: 0-1 2m4-2m7: 0-0 3m+: 0-0
Track: LH: 0-1 RH: 0-0 Tight: 0-1 Gall: 0-0
Aids: Bl: 0-0 Vi: 0-0 Tstrap: 0-0
Best Rating: 50 5/01 Aint 2m110y good Hdl

Kingchip Boy

13-y-o b g Petong-Silk St James (Pas De Seul)
M J Ryan M J Ryan

Placings:4/0/P-P **(0189)**
2001/02: 16^{P}GF

	Starts	1st	2nd	3rd	Win & Pl
Hurdles	1	0	0	0	
Career Total	**4**	**0**	**0**	**0**	

Going: Sf: 0-0 GS: 0-0 Gd: 0-0 GF: - Fm: 0-1
Distance: 2m/2m3: 0-1 2m4-2m7: 0-0 3m+: 0-0
Track: LH: 0-1 RH: 0-0 Tight: 0-1 Gall: 0-0
Aids: Bl: 0-0 Vi: 0-0 Tstrap: 0-0
Best Rating: 70 7/95 MRas 2m1f110y gd-fm Hdl

Kingdom Emperor

106 92

8-y-o b g Forzando-Wrangbrook (Shirley Heights)
W Clay F E And Mrs J J Brindley

Placings:21221320/4034230032/52U3032320**F3**/P20P0-065564334 **(1541)**
2001/02: 17^{0}G, 19^{6}G, 17^{5}G, 17^{5}F, 19^{6}GF, 16^{4}GF, 16^{3}GF, 19^{3}GF, 19^{4}G

	Starts	1st	2nd	3rd	Win & Pl
Hurdles	9	0	0	2	693
Career Total	**44**	**2**	**10**	**10**	**25005**

120	1/98	Chel	2m1f	C Hdl	G-S	£4622
97	10/97	Ludl	2m	E Hdl	G-F	£2360

Total win prize-money £6982

Going: Sf: 0-0 GS: 0-0 Gd: 0-4 GF: - Fm: 0-5
Distance: 2m/2m3: 0-5 2m4-2m7: 0-4 3m+: 0-0
Track: LH: 0-2 RH: 0-7 Tight: 0-3 Gall: 0-1
Aids: Bl: 0-0 Vi: 0-6 Tstrap: 0-0
Best Rating: 120 5/99 Hrfd 2m3f110y gd-sft Hdl

Kingdom Of Shades (USA)

80

12-y-o ch g Risen Star (USA)-Dancers Countess (USA) (Northern Dancer)
Miss Venetia Williams M J Fenn

Placings:5/2311/262320/**31221P**/**1215U0/PP** **(3793)**
2001/02: 28^{P}S, 26^{P}S

	Starts	1st	2nd	3rd	Win & Pl
Chases	2	0	0	0	
Career Total	**25**	**6**	**7**	**3**	**41553**

148	1/00	Chel	4m1f	B(0-150)HCh	SFT	£12181
145	12/99	Towc	3m1f	F(0-110)HCh	GD	£5225
135	3/99	Plum	2m5f	E Ch	SFT	£2992
128	1/99	Ling	3m	E Ch	HVY	£2948
125	2/96	Asct	2m110y	D Hdl	SFT	£3956
115	1/96	Ling	2m110y	E Hdl	HVY	£2739

Total win prize-money £30041

Going: Sf: 0-2 GS: 0-0 Gd: 0-0 GF: - Fm: 0-0
Distance: 2m/2m3: 0-0 2m4-2m7: 0-0 3m+: 0-2
Track: LH: 0-1 RH: 0-0 Tight: 0-0 Gall: 0-0
Aids: Bl: 0-0 Vi: 0-0 Tstrap: 0-0
Best Rating: 148 1/00 Chel 4m1f soft Ch

Largely consistent, he landed the Cheltenham four-miler at the New Year 2000 meeting in impressive fashion, but failed to cope with a 10lb rise when a disappointing favourite for the Warwick National 12 days later. Down the field in the 2000 Grand National, and absent for a long time subsequently.

Kingennie

71 83

9-y-o b m Dunbeath (USA)-Loch Brandy (Harwell)
Mrs D M Ewart Mrs J A Niven

Placings:*0143P6/PP-P***4P5PP** **(3508)**
2001/02: 22^{P}G, 16^{4}G, 22^{P}GS, 16^{5}S, 16^{P}G, 24^{P}S

	Starts	1st	2nd	3rd	Win & Pl
Hurdles	1	0	0	0	0
Chases	5	0	0	0	318
Career Total	**14**	**1**	**0**	**1**	**2984**

98	12/98	Newc	2m4f	E Hdl	SFT	£2284

Total win prize-money £2285

Going: Sf: 0-2 GS: 0-1 Gd: 0-3 GF: - Fm: 0-0
Distance: 2m/2m3: 0-3 2m4-2m7: 0-2 3m+: 0-1
Track: LH: 0-4 RH: 0-2 Tight: 0-4 Gall: 0-0
Aids: Bl: 0-0 Vi: 0-0 Tstrap: 0-1
Best Rating: 98 12/98 Newc 2m4f soft Hdl

Kingfisher Dawn

94 79

6-y-o ch m Alflora (IRE)-Legata (IRE) (Orchestra)
C Grant C E Whiteley

Placings:*5-06* **(2348)**
2001/02: 17^{0}GS, 21^{6}GS

	Starts	1st	2nd	3rd	Win & Pl
Hurdles	2	0	0	0	0
Career Total	**3**	**0**	**0**	**0**	**0**

Going: Sf: 0-0 GS: 0-2 Gd: 0-0 GF: - Fm: 0-0
Distance: 2m/2m3: 0-1 2m4-2m7: 0-1 3m+: 0-0
Track: LH: 0-0 RH: 0-2 Tight: 0-1 Gall: 0-0
Aids: Bl: 0-0 Vi: 0-0 Tstrap: 0-0
Best Rating: 79 10/01 Carl 2m1f gd-sft Hdl

Kingfishers Bonnet

86 58

6-y-o b m Hamas (IRE)-Mainmast (Bustino)
J M Bradley E R Griffiths

Placings:000P-500 **(2137)**
2001/02: 17^{5}S, 18^{0}GS, 17^{0}G

	Starts	1st	2nd	3rd	Win & Pl
Hurdles	3	0	0	0	0
Career Total	**7**	**0**	**0**	**0**	**0**

Going: Sf: 0-1 GS: 0-1 Gd: 0-1 GF: - Fm: 0-0
Distance: 2m/2m3: 0-3 2m4-2m7: 0-0 3m+: 0-0
Track: LH: 0-2 RH: 0-1 Tight: 0-3 Gall: 0-0
Aids: Bl: 0-1 Vi: 0-0 Tstrap: 0-0
Best Rating: 58 11/01 NAbb 2m1f soft Hdl

Winner on the flat in April 2000, although has shown very little since then.

Kingley Vale

92 100

8-y-o br g Neltino-Altaghaderry Run (Deep Run)
Mrs L Richards B Seal

Placings:*0/0/***3F2-1432** **(3288)**
2001/02: 25^{1}G, 25^{4}G, 22^{3}G, 25^{2}S

	Starts	1st	2nd	3rd	Win & Pl
Chases	4	1	1	1	6694
Career Total	**9**	**1**	**2**	**2**	**8810**

97	11/01	Folk	3m1f	E Ch	GD	£3666

Total win prize-money £3666

Going: Sf: 0-1 GS: 0-0 Gd: 1-3 GF: - Fm: 0-0
Distance: 2m/2m3: 0-0 2m4-2m7: 0-1 **3m+: 1-3**
Track: LH: 0-1 **RH: 1-3 Tight: 1-3** Gall: 0-1
Aids: Bl: 0-0 Vi: 0-0 Tstrap: 0-0
Best Rating: 100 1/02 Folk 3m1f soft Ch

Stays three miles plus and acts on good ground.

Kings Avenue

74f 72f

5-y-o b g Gran Alba (USA)-G W Supermare (Rymer)

G B Balding Mr & Mrs Tony Geake

Placings:*0* **(3777)**

2001/02: 16^{0}S

	Starts	1st	2nd	3rd	Win & Pl
NH Flat	1	0	0	0	
Career Total	**1**	**0**	**0**	**0**	

Going: Sf: 0-1 GS: 0-0 Gd: 0-0 GF: - Fm: 0-0
Distance: 2m/2m3: 0-1 2m4-2m7: 0-0 3m+: 0-0
Track: LH: 0-0 RH: 0-1 Tight: 0-0 Gall: 0-0
Aids: Bl: 0-0 Vi: 0-0 Tstrap: 0-0
Best Rating: 72 2/02 Sand 2m110y soft NHF

Kings Barador

7-y-o ch g Librate-Seasoned Ember (Royal Smoke)

Miss S Jakeway Miss S Jakeway

Placings:P **(4132)**

2001/02: 25^{P}G

	Starts	1st	2nd	3rd	Win & Pl
Chases	1	0	0	0	
Career Total	**1**	**0**	**0**	**0**	

Going: Sf: 0-0 GS: 0-0 Gd: 0-1 GF: - Fm: 0-0
Distance: 2m/2m3: 0-0 2m4-2m7: 0-0 3m+: 0-1
Track: LH: 0-0 RH: 0-1 Tight: 0-0 Gall: 0-0
Aids: Bl: 0-0 Vi: 0-0 Tstrap: 0-0
Best Rating:

Kings Boy (IRE)

(103h)

8-y-o ch g Be My Native (USA)-Love-In-A-Mist (Paddy's Stream)

N J Henderson Colin Frewin

Placings:311/6P/4P-P **(1954)**

2001/02: 20^{P}G

	Starts	1st	2nd	3rd	Win & Pl
Chases	1	0	0	0	
Career Total	**8**	**2**	**0**	**1**	**6880**

115	4/99	Asct	2m4f	D Hdl	G-F	£3728
130	1/99	Donc	2m4f	E Hdl	G-S	£2477

Total win prize-money £6207

Going: Sf: 0-0 GS: 0-0 Gd: 0-1 GF: - Fm: 0-0
Distance: 2m/2m3: 0-0 2m4-2m7: 0-1 3m+: 0-0
Track: LH: 0-1 RH: 0-0 Tight: 0-0 Gall: 0-0
Aids: Bl: 0-0 Vi: 0-0 Tstrap: 0-0
Best Rating: 130 1/99 Donc 2m4f gd-sft Hdl

Kings Castle (IRE)

109 143

7-y-o b g King's Ride-Kilmana (IRE) (Castle Keep)

R J Hodges Fieldspring Racing

Placings:*112/4116100* **(4231)**

2001/02: 20^{4}S, 22^{1}G, 20^{1}GS, 20^{6}S, 25^{1}S, 22^{0}S, 21^{0}GS

	Starts	1st	2nd	3rd	Win & Pl
Hurdles	7	3	0	0	24322
Career Total	**10**	**5**	**1**	**0**	**29323**

143	1/02	Wwck	3m1f	B HHdl	SFT	£8892
138	11/01	Aint	2m4f	C(0-130)HHdl	G-S	£10822
122	11/01	Winc	2m6f	E(0-115)HHdl	GD	£4212
113	2/00	Font	2m6f110y	E Hdl	G-S	£2590
122	2/00	Font	2m2f110y	H NHF	SFT	£1704

Total win prize-money £28222

Going: Sf: 1-4 GS: 1-2 Gd: 1-1 GF: - Fm: 0-0
Distance: 2m/2m3: 0-0 **2m4-2m7: 2-6** 3m+: 1-1
Track: LH: 1-4 RH: 1-2 **Tight: 1-1** Gall: 0-1
Aids: Bl: 0-0 Vi: 0-0 Tstrap: 0-0
Best Rating: 143 1/02 Wwck 3m1f soft Hdl

He is developing into a useful handicap hurdler and made it three wins out of four when bolting up at Warwick in January 2002. Disappointed next time. Very much suited by soft ground, he stays three miles.

Kings Cherry (IRE)

97 100

14-y-o b g King's Ride-Another Cherry (Le Bavard (FR))

J A B Old Martin Lovatt

Placings:*0/5O00/***04051416/3UP1PF/502215F/5244/0P242/06PFF-300P** **(4664)**

2001/02: 21^{3}GS, 25^{0}G, 20^{0}G, 21^{P}G

	Starts	1st	2nd	3rd	Win & Pl
Chases	4	0	0	1	750
Career Total	**44**	**4**	**5**	**2**	**32736**

118	2/97	Newb	2m1f	C(0-135)HCh	G-S	£4429
112	2/96	Chep	2m3f110y	B Ch	SFT	£6890
102	4/95	Tipp	2m4f	(0-123)HCh	SFT	£2712
102	3/95	Limk	2m6f	Ch	HVY	£2712

Total win prize-money £16745

Going: Sf: 0-0 GS: 0-1 Gd: 0-3 GF: - Fm: 0-0
Distance: 2m/2m3: 0-0 2m4-2m7: 0-3 3m+: 0-1
Track: LH: 0-4 RH: 0-0 Tight: 0-2 Gall: 0-1
Aids: Bl: 0-0 Vi: 0-0 Tstrap: 0-0
Best Rating: 133 4/00 Aint 2m6f good Ch

Getting a bit long in the tooth now and ran his best race for some time when runner-up in the John Hughes Chase at Aintree in 2000. Has shown little since.

Kings Court (IRE)

85 75

8-y-o b g Spanish Place (USA)-Charming Whisper (Deep Run)

J I A Charlton Steven Parlett

Placings:*06/6*0P-00P00 **(3911)**

2001/02: 16^{0}F, 22^{0}GS, 16^{P}GF, 16^{0}GS, 24^{0}GS

	Starts	1st	2nd	3rd	Win & Pl
Hurdles	5	0	0	0	
Career Total	**10**	**0**	**0**	**0**	**0**

Going: Sf: 0-0 GS: 0-3 Gd: 0-0 GF: - Fm: 0-2
Distance: 2m/2m3: 0-3 2m4-2m7: 0-1 3m+: 0-1
Track: LH: 0-4 RH: 0-1 Tight: 0-4 Gall: 0-0
Aids: Bl: 0-1 Vi: 0-0 Tstrap: 0-1
Best Rating: 97 6/00 Hexm 2m gd-fm NHF

Kings Delite (IRE)

87f 73f

4-y-o b f Rakaposhi King-Bella Delite (Uncle Pokey)

N A Twiston-Davies The Sauce Boys

Placings:*00* **(4552)**

2001/02: 16^{0}S, 16^{0}GF

	Starts	1st	2nd	3rd	Win & Pl
NH Flat	2	0	0	0	
Career Total	**2**	**0**	**0**	**0**	

Going: Sf: 0-1 GS: 0-0 Gd: 0-0 GF: - Fm: 0-1
Distance: 2m/2m3: 0-2 2m4-2m7: 0-0 3m+: 0-0
Track: LH: 0-0 RH: 0-2 Tight: 0-0 Gall: 0-1
Aids: Bl: 0-0 Vi: 0-0 Tstrap: 0-0
Best Rating: 73 3/02 Towc 2m soft NHF

Kings Inch

8-y-o b g Silver Season-Verona Queen (Majestic Streak)

J M Dun Mrs G R Dun

Placings:F0P/PP06P **(4898)**

2001/02: 16^{P}GS, 16^{P}GS, 16^{0}S, 16^{6}S, 16^{P}G

	Starts	1st	2nd	3rd	Win & Pl
Hurdles	4	0	0	0	0
Chases	1	0	0	0	0
Career Total	**8**	**0**	**0**	**0**	**0**

Going: Sf: 0-2 GS: 0-2 Gd: 0-1 GF: - Fm: 0-0
Distance: 2m/2m3: 0-5 2m4-2m7: 0-0 3m+: 0-0
Track: LH: 0-3 RH: 0-2 Tight: 0-2 Gall: 0-0
Aids: Bl: 0-0 Vi: 0-0 Tstrap: 0-1
Best Rating: 10 2/99 Kels 2m110y soft Hdl

Kings Linen (IRE)

75f 71f

6-y-o b g Persian Mews-Kings Princess (King's Ride)

B I Case Dudley C Moore

Placings:*0-0* **(0377)**

2001/02: 16^{0}GF

	Starts	1st	2nd	3rd	Win & Pl
NH Flat	1	0	0	0	
Career Total	**2**	**0**	**0**	**0**	

Going: Sf: 0-0 GS: 0-0 Gd: 0-0 GF: - Fm: 0-1
Distance: 2m/2m3: 0-1 2m4-2m7: 0-0 3m+: 0-0
Track: LH: 0-0 RH: 0-1 Tight: 0-0 Gall: 0-1
Aids: Bl: 0-0 Vi: 0-0 Tstrap: 0-0
Best Rating: 71 5/01 Hntg 2m110y gd-fm NHF

Kings Minstral (IRE)

102 92

12-y-o ch g Andretti-Tara Minstral Vii (Damsire Unregistered)

D A Lamb D A Lamb

Placings:000/4000P/2130P065/**5LU2214P2/F230/P4P/4P041** **(4769)**

2001/02: 21^{4}G, 27^{P}G, 27^{0}G, 24^{4}G, 25^{1}GF

	Starts	1st	2nd	3rd	Win & Pl
Chases	5	1	0	0	3295
Career Total	**37**	**3**	**5**	**2**	**14853**

92	4/02	Hexm	3m1f	G(0-90)HCh	G-F	£2534
92	11/97	Kels	3m1f	E Ch	G-F	£3452
76	11/96	Hexm	2m4f110y	E(0-100)HHdl	GD	£2595

Total win prize-money £8581

Going: Sf: 0-0 GS: 0-0 Gd: 0-4 GF: - Fm: 1-1
Distance: 2m/2m3: 0-0 2m4-2m7: 0-1 **3m+: 1-4**
Track: **LH: 1-4** RH: 0-1 Tight: 0-4 Gall: 0-0
Aids: Bl: 0-0 Vi: 0-0 Tstrap: 0-0
Best Rating: 102 7/99 Sedg 2m5f gd-fm Ch

Moderate handicap chaser. Stays beyond three miles and acts on a sound surface.

Kings Mistral (IRE)

104 122

9-y-o b g Strong Gale-Mrs Simpson (Kinglet)

P R Chamings R V Shaw

Placings:*024/02/00/12-*3P160 (4419)

2001/02: 24^{3}GS, 25^{P}S, 24^{1}S, 24^{6}G, 24^{0}GS

	Starts	1st	2nd	3rd	Win & Pl
Chases	5	1	0	1	6664
Career Total	**14**	**2**	**3**	**1**	**16317**

122	2/02	Sand	3m110y	E Ch	SFT	£5564
122	3/01	Sand	3m110y	E Ch	SFT	£7117

Total win prize-money £12682

Going: Sf: 1-2 GS: 0-2 Gd: 0-1 GF: - Fm: 0-0
Distance: 2m/2m3: 0-0 2m4-2m7: 0-0 **3m+: 1-5**
Track: LH: 0-1 **RH: 1-4** Tight: 0-1 Gall: 0-1
Aids: Bl: 0-0 Vi: 0-0 Tstrap: 0-0
Best Rating: 122 2/02 Sand 3m110y soft Ch

He sprang a surprise in the 2001 Grand Military Gold Cup at Sandown, and landed the Royal Artillery Gold Cup over the same course a year later. Jumps and stays well, and acts on soft ground.

Kings Own

9-y-o ch g Rymer-Deity (Red God)

Miss L V Davis Miss Louise Davis

Placings:*0/0/*F-P (4553)

2001/02: 17^{P}GF

	Starts	1st	2nd	3rd	Win & Pl
Hurdles	1	0	0	0	
Career Total	**4**	**0**	**0**	**0**	

Going: Sf: 0-0 GS: 0-0 Gd: 0-0 GF: - Fm: 0-1
Distance: 2m/2m3: 0-1 2m4-2m7: 0-0 3m+: 0-0
Track: LH: 0-0 RH: 0-1 Tight: 0-1 Gall: 0-0
Aids: Bl: 0-0 Vi: 0-0 Tstrap: 0-0
Best Rating: 52 7/98 Worc 2m gd-fm NHF

Kings Rapid (IRE)

83(102h) 112

8-y-o b g King's Ride-Smokey River (Over The River (FR))

N J Henderson Trevor Hemmings

Placings:*23/1-*3PP (3873)

2001/02: 20^{3}GF, 24^{P}S, 20^{P}GS

	Starts	1st	2nd	3rd	Win & Pl
Chases	3	0	0	1	502
Career Total	**6**	**1**	**1**	**2**	**3732**

121	11/00	Wwck	2m	E Hdl	HVY	£2380

Total win prize-money £2380

Going: Sf: 0-1 GS: 0-1 Gd: 0-0 GF: - Fm: 0-1
Distance: 2m/2m3: 0-0 2m4-2m7: 0-2 3m+: 0-1
Track: LH: 0-0 RH: 0-3 Tight: 0-0 Gall: 0-1
Aids: Bl: 0-0 Vi: 0-0 Tstrap: 0-0
Best Rating: 121 11/00 Wwck 2m heavy Hdl

Winner over hurdles, he was well held in a small field on his chase debut and faded quickly in next two outings. Acts on heavy ground, he is effective over two miles.

Kings Response (IRE)

10-y-o br g King's Ride-Kiltannon (Dalsaan)

D Brace David Brace

Placings:U (0831)

2001/02: 21^{U}GF

	Starts	1st	2nd	3rd	Win & Pl
Chases	1	0	0	0	
Career Total	**1**	**0**	**0**	**0**	

Going: Sf: 0-0 GS: 0-0 Gd: 0-0 GF: - Fm: 0-1
Distance: 2m/2m3: 0-0 2m4-2m7: 0-1 3m+: 0-0
Track: LH: 0-1 RH: 0-0 Tight: 0-1 Gall: 0-0
Aids: Bl: 0-0 Vi: 0-0 Tstrap: 0-0
Best Rating:

Kings Symphony (IRE)

55 21

8-y-o b g King's Ride-Quelliney (High Line)

Keith Thomas Keith Thomas

Placings:*5/0P60/P*500P (3369)

2001/02: 25^{P}S, 20^{5}GF, 23^{0}S, 20^{0}S, 20^{P}S

	Starts	1st	2nd	3rd	Win & Pl
Hurdles	3	0	0	0	0
Chases	2	0	0	0	0
Career Total	**10**	**0**	**0**	**0**	**0**

Going: Sf: 0-4 GS: 0-0 Gd: 0-0 GF: - Fm: 0-1
Distance: 2m/2m3: 0-0 2m4-2m7: 0-4 3m+: 0-1
Track: LH: 0-5 RH: 0-0 Tight: 0-0 Gall: 0-0
Aids: Bl: 0-0 Vi: 0-0 Tstrap: 0-0
Best Rating: 69 10/99 MRas 1m5f110y good NHF

Kings To Open

100 89

5-y-o b g First Trump-Shadiyama (Nishapour (FR))

P W Hiatt P Burton

Placings:025 (2274)

2001/02: 16^{0}S, 16^{2}GF, 16^{5}G

	Starts	1st	2nd	3rd	Win & Pl
Hurdles	3	0	1	0	599
Career Total	**3**	**0**	**1**	**0**	**599**

Going: Sf: 0-1 GS: 0-0 Gd: 0-1 GF: - Fm: 0-1
Distance: 2m/2m3: 0-3 2m4-2m7: 0-0 3m+: 0-0
Track: LH: 0-2 RH: 0-1 Tight: 0-1 Gall: 0-0
Aids: Bl: 0-0 Vi: 0-0 Tstrap: 0-3
Best Rating: 89 11/01 Wwck 2m good Hdl

Kingsbridge (IRE)

96(85h) (68h)92

8-y-o b g Cataldi-Rockport Rosa (IRE) (Roselier (FR))

M C Pipe M C Pipe

Placings:*0/P*06304 (1045)

2001/02: 18^{P}GF, 17^{0}F, 17^{6}GF, 16^{3}G, 22^{0}GF, 26^{4}GF

	Starts	1st	2nd	3rd	Win & Pl
Hurdles	3	0	0	0	0
Chases	3	0	0	1	701
Career Total	**7**	**0**	**0**	**1**	**701**

Going: Sf: 0-0 GS: 0-0 Gd: 0-1 GF: - Fm: 0-5
Distance: 2m/2m3: 0-4 2m4-2m7: 0-1 3m+: 0-1
Track: LH: 0-3 RH: 0-2 Tight: 0-4 Gall: 0-0
Aids: Bl: 0-0 Vi: 0-1 Tstrap: 0-0
Best Rating: 89 6/01 NAbb 2m110y good Ch

The winner of four points. Not inconvenienced by drop back to two miles when third at Newton Abbot July 2002. Acts on fast ground.

Kingscote Thunder (IRE)

88f 81f

5-y-o b g Montelimar (USA)-Sweet Thunder (Le Bavard (FR))

Noel T Chance Pulse Racing & Rowley-Williams

Placings:*0* (4423)

2001/02: 16^{0}GS

	Starts	1st	2nd	3rd	Win & Pl
NH Flat	1	0	0	0	
Career Total	**1**	**0**	**0**	**0**	

Going: Sf: 0-0 GS: 0-1 Gd: 0-0 GF: - Fm: 0-0
Distance: 2m/2m3: 0-1 2m4-2m7: 0-0 3m+: 0-0
Track: LH: 0-1 RH: 0-0 Tight: 0-0 Gall: 0-1
Aids: Bl: 0-0 Vi: 0-0 Tstrap: 0-0
Best Rating: 81 3/02 Newb 2m110y gd-sft NHF

Kingsdon (IRE)

75 68

5-y-o b g Brief Truce (USA)-Richly Deserved (IRE) (King's Lake (USA))

J G Fitzgerald (D Nicholls 20/10) Mike Browne

Placings:00 (4404)

2001/02: 16^{0}GS, 17^{0}S

	Starts	1st	2nd	3rd	Win & Pl
Hurdles	2	0	0	0	
Career Total	**2**	**0**	**0**	**0**	

Going: Sf: 0-1 GS: 0-1 Gd: 0-0 GF: - Fm: 0-0
Distance: 2m/2m3: 0-2 2m4-2m7: 0-0 3m+: 0-0
Track: LH: 0-2 RH: 0-0 Tight: 0-2 Gall: 0-0
Aids: Bl: 0-0 Vi: 0-0 Tstrap: 0-2
Best Rating: 71 3/02 Catt 2m gd-sft Hdl

Kingsdown Trix (IRE)

81(105h) (104h)55

8-y-o b g Contract Law (USA)-Three Of Trumps (Tyrnavos)

R J Smith The Kingsdowners

Placings:*0414P000/545115/056/316-*03020 (4869)

2001/02: 27^{0}G, 20^{3}GF, 22^{0}GF, 20^{2}GS, 20^{0}GF

	Starts	1st	2nd	3rd	Win & Pl
Hurdles	5	0	1	1	1356
Career Total	**25**	**4**	**1**	**2**	**14372**

104	4/01	Fknm	2m4f	F(0-105)HHdl	G-S	£3108
97	4/99	Fknm	2m4f	F(0-110)HHdl	GD	£3310
98	3/99	Font	2m6f110y	E(0-115)HHdl	G-F	£2477
93	12/97	Font	2m2f110y	E Hdl	SFT	£2532

Total win prize-money £11428

Going: Sf: 0-0 GS: 0-1 Gd: 0-1 GF: - Fm: 0-3
Distance: 2m/2m3: 0-0 2m4-2m7: 0-4 3m+: 0-1
Track: LH: 0-5 RH: 0-0 Tight: 0-2 Gall: 0-0
Aids: Bl: 0-0 Vi: 0-0 Tstrap: 0-0
Best Rating: 104 4/02 Chep 2m4f gd-sft Hdl

His hurdles wins have all come on tracks favouring those who race prominently. Stays two miles six and is suited by good ground.

Kingsmark (IRE)

115 **170**

9-y-o gr g Roselier (FR)-Gaye Le Moss (Le Moss)
M Todhunter Sir Robert Ogden

Placings:3/111120/51F1322/11160310-124 **(4677)**
2001/02: 24^{1}G, 24^{2}S, 36^{4}G

	Starts	1st	2nd	3rd	Win & Pl
Chases	3	1	1	0	61900
Career Total	**25**	**11**	**4**	**3**	**164640**

170	11/01	Hayd	3m	A HCh	GD	£27000
168	4/01	Aint	3m1f	B HCh	SFT	£26000
168	11/00	Hayd	3m	A HCh	SFT	£25200
150	10/00	MRas	3m1f	C(0-130)HCh	GD	£9178
151	10/00	Kels	3m1f	D(0-125)HCh	GD	£3887
141	1/00	Folk	3m2f	E Ch	SFT	£3510
147	11/99	Bang	3m110y	D Ch	SFT	£4842
137	1/99	Kemp	2m5f	D Hdl	HVY	£3793
121	12/98	Folk	2m6f110y	E Hdl	SFT	£2650
131	11/98	Folk	2m6f110y	F Hdl	SFT	£2008
116	10/98	Strf	2m6f110y	E Hdl	G-S	£2075

Total win prize-money £110146

Going: Sf: 0-1 GS: 0-0 Gd: 1-2 GF: - Fm: 0-0
Distance: 2m/2m3: 0-0 2m4-2m7: 0-0 **3m+: 1-3**
Track: **LH: 1-3** RH: 0-0 Tight: 0-1 Gall: 0-0
Aids: Bl: 0-0 Vi: 0-0 Tstrap: 0-0
Best Rating: 170 11/01 Hayd 3m good Ch

A high-class chaser, he was in good form in the autumn of 2000, being well placed to score a hat-trick culminating in the Edward Hanmer at Haydock. He failed to live up to that form afterwards over various trips, until relishing the desperate ground when scoring at Aintree in April 2001. His jumping let him down in the Whitbread, but he returned to win the Edward Hanmer for the second time, and finished runner-up in the Tommy Whittle. Suffered an over-reach when a distant fourth in the Grand National. He goes on good ground but is better with give.

Kingsmoor

92 **88**

6-y-o b g Regal Embers (IRE)-Cupids Bower (Owen Dudley)
K Bishop R D Cox

Placings:0-6 **(0214)**
2001/02: 22^{6}GF

	Starts	1st	2nd	3rd	Win & Pl
Hurdles	1	0	0	0	0
Career Total	**2**	**0**	**0**	**0**	**0**

Going: Sf: 0-0 GS: 0-0 Gd: 0-0 GF: - Fm: 0-1
Distance: 2m/2m3: 0-0 2m4-2m7: 0-1 3m+: 0-0
Track: LH: 0-0 RH: 0-1 Tight: 0-0 Gall: 0-0
Aids: Bl: 0-0 Vi: 0-0 Tstrap: 0-0
Best Rating: 88 5/01 Winc 2m6f gd-fm Hdl

Kingsthorpe

14-y-o ch g Brotherly (USA)-Miss Kewmill (Billion (USA))
M R Daniell Mervyn Jones

Placings:P/F00PF/0P/10/3 **(0227)**
2001/02: 24^{3}GF

	Starts	1st	2nd	3rd	Win & Pl
Chases	1	0	0	1	260
Career Total	**11**	**1**	**0**	**1**	**3158**

96	5/98	Strf	3m	H Ch	GD	£2898

Total win prize-money £2898

Going: Sf: 0-0 GS: 0-0 Gd: 0-0 GF: - Fm: 0-1
Distance: 2m/2m3: 0-0 2m4-2m7: 0-0 3m+: 0-1
Track: LH: 0-0 RH: 0-1 Tight: 0-0 Gall: 0-1
Aids: Bl: 0-0 Vi: 0-0 Tstrap: 0-0
Best Rating: 96 5/01 Hntg 3m gd-fm Ch

Kingston Venture

88 **80**

6-y-o b g Interrex (CAN)-Tricata (Electric)
W G M Turner Miss Corinne J Overton

Placings:23312/513-PP4 **(4389)**
2001/02: 19^{P}S, 21^{P}HY, 16^{4}S

	Starts	1st	2nd	3rd	Win & Pl
Hurdles	3	0	0	0	270
Career Total	**11**	**2**	**2**	**3**	**12357**

118	6/00	Strf	2m110y	C(0-135)HHdl	GD	£5239
91	11/99	Hrfd	2m1f	D Hdl	GD	£2885

Total win prize-money £8124

Going: Sf: 0-3 GS: 0-0 Gd: 0-0 GF: - Fm: 0-0
Distance: 2m/2m3: 0-1 2m4-2m7: 0-2 3m+: 0-0
Track: LH: 0-0 RH: 0-2 Tight: 0-1 Gall: 0-0
Aids: Bl: 0-1 Vi: 0-0 Tstrap: 0-0
Best Rating: 118 7/00 Wolv 2m4f110y good Hdl

Kingston-Banker

102 **115**

6-y-o b g Teamster-Happy Manda (Mandamus)
R H Alner H Wellstead

Placings:60-332 **(4729)**
2001/02: 23^{3}G, 20^{3}S, 24^{2}GF

	Starts	1st	2nd	3rd	Win & Pl
Chases	3	0	1	2	2463
Career Total	**5**	**0**	**1**	**2**	**2463**

Going: Sf: 0-1 GS: 0-0 Gd: 0-1 GF: - Fm: 0-1
Distance: 2m/2m3: 0-0 2m4-2m7: 0-1 3m+: 0-2
Track: LH: 0-2 RH: 0-1 Tight: 0-1 Gall: 0-0
Aids: Bl: 0-0 Vi: 0-0 Tstrap: 0-0
Best Rating: 115 4/02 Chep 3m gd-fm Ch

Modest chaser, who appears to need further than two miles seven.

Kingswood Manor

104(98h) (83h)**93**

10-y-o b g Exodal (USA)-Angelic Appeal (Star Appeal)
R J O'Sullivan Robert Allen

Placings:3/532/0/04031U32UP10P5 **(4510)**
2001/02: 19^{0}GF, 26^{4}GF, 22^{0}GF, 22^{3}GF, 23^{1}GF, 26^{U}GF, 22^{3}S, 26^{2}S, 26^{U}GS, 25^{P}G, 26^{1}S, 21^{0}S, 26^{P}S, 26^{5}G

	Starts	1st	2nd	3rd	Win & Pl
Hurdles	4	0	0	1	564
Chases	10	2	1	1	8213
Career Total	**19**	**2**	**2**	**4**	**10066**

93	1/02	Font	3m2f110y	E(0-100)HCh	SFT	£3061
93	8/01	Worc	2m7f110y	E Ch	G-F	£3445

Total win prize-money £6507

Going: Sf: 1-5 GS: 0-1 Gd: 0-2 GF: - Fm: 1-6
Distance: 2m/2m3: 0-0 2m4-2m7: 0-5 **3m+: 2-9**
Track: **LH: 1-4** RH: 0-3 **Tight: 1-9** Gall: 0-1
Aids: Bl: 2-7 Vi: 0-4 Tstrap: 0-0
Best Rating: 93 1/02 Font 3m2f110y soft Ch

Winner of a fast ground maiden chase in the summer but also handles soft. Failed to complete twice before scoring at Fontwell in January 2002. Stays three and a quarter miles.

Kinnahalla (IRE)

106 **122**

10-y-o b m Lancastrian-Eadestown (Kinglet)
G B Balding Roger J Spencer

Placings:44361232/42640112252216/022413/6-P1530 **(4049)**
2001/02: 28^{P}S, 30^{1}GS, 32^{5}GS, 30^{3}S, 30^{0}G

	Starts	1st	2nd	3rd	Win & Pl
Chases	5	1	0	1	8802
Career Total	**34**	**6**	**9**	**4**	**55045**

122	11/01	Hntg	3m6f110y	D(0-120)HCh	G-S	£8170
122	12/99	Extr	3m7f110y	D(0-120)HCh	G-S	£7181
119	4/99	Towc	3m1f	E(0-115)HCh	GD	£3406
106	12/98	Winc	3m1f110y	E(0-115)HCh	G-S	£3126
117	11/98	Ludl	3m3f110y	E(0-115)HCh	GD	£4143
83	2/98	Sand	2m6f	D(0-110)HHdl	GD	£3048

Total win prize-money £29076

Going: Sf: 0-2 GS: 1-2 Gd: 0-1 GF: - Fm: 0-0
Distance: 2m/2m3: 0-0 2m4-2m7: 0-0 **3m+: 1-5**
Track: LH: 0-2 **RH: 1-1** Tight: 0-1 **Gall: 1-2**
Aids: Bl: 0-0 Vi: 0-0 Tstrap: 0-0
Best Rating: 122 11/01 Hntg 3m6f110y gd-sft Ch

A fair staying mare who appreciates marathon trips, handles any ground but her wins have been mostly on good to soft ground.

Kinnescash (IRE)

9-y-o ch g Persian Heights-Gayla Orchestra (Lord Gayle (USA))
P Bowen D R James

Placings:302211/4131125P3/P0212030143310/64000/0222-P **(4667)**
2001/02: 20^{P}G

	Starts	1st	2nd	3rd	Win & Pl
Hurdles	1	0	0	0	
Career Total	**39**	**8**	**8**	**6**	**80564**

141	4/99	Aint	2m110y	B HHdl	GD	£19350
141	11/98	Aint	2m110y	C(0-135)HHdl	G-S	£10406
128	9/98	Hntg	2m4f110y	D(0-125)HHdl	G-F	£6840
117	6/97	MRas	2m1f110y	C(0-130)HHdl	GD	£8637
113	5/97	Hrfd	2m3f110y	D(0-120)HHdl	GD	£2864
123	5/97	Worc	2m	E Hdl	G-S	£2302
103	4/97	Chep	2m110y	E Hdl	FRM	£2808
103	3/97	Plum	2m1f	E Hdl	G-F	£2490

Total win prize-money £55698

Going: Sf: 0-0 GS: 0-0 Gd: 0-1 GF: - Fm: 0-0
Distance: 2m/2m3: 0-0 2m4-2m7: 0-1 3m+: 0-0
Track: LH: 0-1 RH: 0-0 Tight: 0-1 Gall: 0-0
Aids: Bl: 0-0 Vi: 0-0 Tstrap: 0-0
Best Rating: 141 4/99 Aint 2m110y good Hdl

Bought for just 1,500 guineas in September 1996, he has been a wonderful servant to his connections, winning a hatful of races including a valuable handicap at Aintree on Grand National Day in 1999. Best when forcing the pace, he stays beyond two miles and is particularly hard to beat in a tight finish. Ran well in the summer of 2000 without winning, but was off the track until reappearing on the Flat in March 2002.

Kinnino

92 **76**

8-y-o b g Polish Precedent (USA)-On Tiptoes (Shareef Dancer (USA))
G L Moore Exors Of The Late Mr A Moore

Placings:55-F0 **(2262)**
2001/02: 16^{F}S, 16^{0}G

	Starts	1st	2nd	3rd	Win & Pl
Hurdles	2	0	0	0	
Career Total	**4**	**0**	**0**	**0**	**0**

Going: Sf: 0-1 GS: 0-0 Gd: 0-1 GF: - Fm: 0-0
Distance: 2m/2m3: 0-2 2m4-2m7: 0-0 3m+: 0-0
Track: LH: 0-1 RH: 0-1 Tight: 0-1 Gall: 0-0
Aids: Bl: 0-0 Vi: 0-0 Tstrap: 0-0
Best Rating: 57 11/01 Kemp 2m good Hdl

Kino's Cross

106 **80**

13-y-o b g Relkino-Coral Delight (Idiots Delight)
A J Wilson N V Harvey

Placings:*6*004012/B320100/**4PPF**606331/4500/00321 2143/3262/0-F00002260 **(4589)**
2001/02: 17^{F}G, 17^{0}GS, 19^{0}GF, 16^{0}G, 16^{0}S, 16^{2}S, 17^{2}S, 22^{6}G, 16^{0}G

	Starts	1st	2nd	3rd	Win & Pl
Hurdles	9	0	2	0	1582
Career Total	**51**	**5**	**8**	**6**	**35859**

121	3/99	Winc	2m	D(0-125)HHdl	G-S	£5277
121	1/99	Winc	2m	D(0-125)HHdl	SFT	£5550
102	4/97	Worc	2m	D(0-125)HHdl	SFT	£3092
111	2/96	Weth	2m	B(0-140)HHdl	G-S	£7100
95	2/95	Winc	2m	F(0-105)HHdl	SFT	£2574

Total win prize-money £23593

Going: Sf: 0-3 GS: 0-1 Gd: 0-4 GF: - Fm: 0-1
Distance: 2m/2m3: 0-8 2m4-2m7: 0-1 3m+: 0-0
Track: LH: 0-5 RH: 0-4 Tight: 0-4 Gall: 0-1
Aids: Bl: 0-0 Vi: 0-0 Tstrap: 0-0
Best Rating: 121 11/99 Worc 2m gd-sft Hdl

Fair hurdler now at the veteran stage, he has never won beyond two miles and looks best with some cut.

Kippanour (USA)

103(91c) (68c)**101**

10-y-o b g Alleged (USA)-Innsbruck (General Assembly (USA))
A G Hobbs Furnish With Abbey

Placings:12323/33020005/P6**543365**P/P6/**16310P**214 406-56123016000 **(4568)**
2001/02: 24^{5}GF, 24^{6}GF, 26^{1}G, 26^{2}G, 22^{3}GS, 24^{0}G, 26^{1}S, 26^{6}S, 26^{0}S, 24^{0}S, 24^{0}G

	Starts	1st	2nd	3rd	Win & Pl
Hurdles	10	2	1	1	5904
Chases	1	0	0	0	0
Career Total	**47**	**6**	**5**	**8**	**22270**

101	1/02	Hrfd	3m2f	F(0-90)Hdl	SFT	£2765
93	9/01	Hntg	3m2f	F(0-90)HHdl	GD	£2044
89	11/00	Hntg	3m2f	G(0-95)HHdl	GD	£1951
102	7/00	Worc	2m7f110y	F(0-100)HCh	G-F	£2970
102	5/00	Uttx	3m2f	F(0-90)HCh	GD	£2960
89	9/95	Slig	2m	Hdl	GD	£2204

Total win prize-money £14897

Going: Sf: 1-4 GS: 0-1 Gd: 1-4 GF: - Fm: 0-2
Distance: 2m/2m3: 0-0 2m4-2m7: 0-1 **3m+: 2-10**
Track: LH: 0-3 **RH: 2-8** Tight: 0-0 **Gall: 1-4**
Aids: Bl: 1-5 Vi: 1-6 Tstrap: 0-0
Best Rating: 116 12/95 Chel 2m1f good Hdl

Mixes hurdling and chasing and stays very well. Finds soft ground bringing his stamina into play over marathon trips.

Kippour (FR)

67f **90f**

4-y-o b g Luchiroverte (IRE)-Obole Iii (FR) (Signani (FR))
H D Daly Trevor Hemmings

Placings:2 **(4603)**
2001/02: 16^{2}GF

	Starts	1st	2nd	3rd	Win & Pl
NH Flat	1	0	1	0	615
Career Total	**1**	**0**	**1**	**0**	**615**

Going: Sf: 0-0 GS: 0-0 Gd: 0-0 GF: - Fm: 0-1
Distance: 2m/2m3: 0-1 2m4-2m7: 0-0 3m+: 0-0
Track: LH: 0-1 RH: 0-0 Tight: 0-0 Gall: 0-0
Aids: Bl: 0-0 Vi: 0-0 Tstrap: 0-0
Best Rating: 90 4/02 Wwck 2m gd-fm NHF

Runner-up in a fast-ground Warwick bumper on his debut.

Kirat

116 **125**

4-y-o b g Darshaan-Kafsa (IRE) (Vayrann)
G L Moore (R Charlton 13/6) Brighthelm Racing

Placings:145 **(4651)**
2001/02: 16^{1}HY, 16^{4}S, 16^{5}G

	Starts	1st	2nd	3rd	Win & Pl
Hurdles	3	1	0	0	7255
Career Total	**3**	**1**	**0**	**0**	**7255**

109	2/02	Sand	2m110y	D Hdl	HVY	£4407

Total win prize-money £4407

Going: Sf: 1-2 GS: 0-0 Gd: 0-1 GF: - Fm: 0-0
Distance: 2m/2m3: 1-3 2m4-2m7: 0-0 3m+: 0-0
Track: LH: 0-2 **RH: 1-1** Tight: 0-1 Gall: 0-1
Aids: Bl: 0-0 Vi: 0-0 **Tstrap: 1-3**
Best Rating: 125 4/02 Aint 2m110y good Hdl

Beat a hotpot at Sandown on his hurdles debut and faced a stiff task next time.

Kirdford (IRE)

95 **83**

8-y-o b/br g Miners Lamp-Somelli (Candy Cane)
R H Buckler The Eight Optimists

Placings:056014/2-56 **(2045)**
2001/02: 20^{5}S, 22^{6}G

	Starts	1st	2nd	3rd	Win & Pl
Hurdles	2	0	0	0	0
Career Total	**9**	**1**	**1**	**0**	**4050**

83	4/00	Ludl	2m5f	E(0-105)HHdl	GD	£3250

Total win prize-money £3250

Going: Sf: 0-1 GS: 0-0 Gd: 0-1 GF: - Fm: 0-0
Distance: 2m/2m3: 0-0 2m4-2m7: 0-2 3m+: 0-0
Track: LH: 0-1 RH: 0-1 Tight: 0-0 Gall: 0-0
Aids: Bl: 0-0 Vi: 0-0 Tstrap: 0-0
Best Rating: 83 10/01 Chep 2m4f soft Hdl

Kirikou

80 **73**

4-y-o b g Mtoto-Nevis (Connaught)
D J Wintle (R F Johnson Houghton 27/6) R K Davies Engineering Ltd

Placings:00P **(3890)**
2001/02: 16^{0}HY, 16^{0}S, 16^{P}HY

	Starts	1st	2nd	3rd	Win & Pl
Hurdles	3	0	0	0	
Career Total	**3**	**0**	**0**	**0**	

Going: Sf: 0-3 GS: 0-0 Gd: 0-0 GF: - Fm: 0-0
Distance: 2m/2m3: 0-3 2m4-2m7: 0-0 3m+: 0-0
Track: LH: 0-2 RH: 0-1 Tight: 0-0 Gall: 0-1
Aids: Bl: 0-0 Vi: 0-0 Tstrap: 0-0
Best Rating: 73 2/02 Hntg 2m110y soft Hdl

Kirisnippa

7-y-o b g Beveled (USA)-Kiri Te (Liboi (USA))
A P Jones (R Curtis 28/6) D A Drake

Placings:P/P **(4422)**
2001/02: 16^{P}GS

	Starts	1st	2nd	3rd	Win & Pl
Hurdles	1	0	0	0	
Career Total	**2**	**0**	**0**	**0**	

Going: Sf: 0-0 GS: 0-1 Gd: 0-0 GF: - Fm: 0-0
Distance: 2m/2m3: 0-1 2m4-2m7: 0-0 3m+: 0-0
Track: LH: 0-1 RH: 0-0 Tight: 0-0 Gall: 0-1
Aids: Bl: 0-0 Vi: 0-0 Tstrap: 0-0
Best Rating:

Kirkfield (IRE)

7-y-o b m Commanche Run-Another Grange (Buckskin (FR))
J L Needham J L Needham

Placings:*0*-0P **(4544)**
2001/02: 19^{0}G, 26^{P}G

	Starts	1st	2nd	3rd	Win & Pl
Hurdles	2	0	0	0	
Career Total	**3**	**0**	**0**	**0**	

Going: Sf: 0-0 GS: 0-0 Gd: 0-2 GF: - Fm: 0-0
Distance: 2m/2m3: 0-0 2m4-2m7: 0-1 3m+: 0-1
Track: LH: 0-0 RH: 0-2 Tight: 0-0 Gall: 0-0
Aids: Bl: 0-0 Vi: 0-0 Tstrap: 0-0
Best Rating:

Kirkharle (IRE)

8-y-o b g Commanche Run-Dardy Daughter (Side Track)
Mrs A Hamilton Ian Hamilton

Placings:0P-342 **(4859)**
2001/02: 25^{3}S, 25^{4}GF, 25^{2}G

	Starts	1st	2nd	3rd	Win & Pl
Chases	3	0	1	1	1204
Career Total	**5**	**0**	**1**	**1**	**1204**

Going: Sf: 0-1 GS: 0-0 Gd: 0-1 GF: - Fm: 0-1
Distance: 2m/2m3: 0-0 2m4-2m7: 0-0 3m+: 0-3
Track: LH: 0-3 RH: 0-0 Tight: 0-1 Gall: 0-0
Aids: Bl: 0-0 Vi: 0-0 Tstrap: 0-0
Best Rating: 76 4/02 Hexm 3m1f good Ch

Modest pointer/hunter chaser, handles any ground.

Kit Smartie (IRE)

111 **142**

10-y-o b g Be My Native (USA)-Smart Cookie (Lord Gayle (USA))

D M Forster D M Forster

Placings:*63*/30513111/**12-0302PP** **(4394)**

2001/02: 20^{0}G, 25^{3}GS, 24^{0}G, 24^{2}S, 24^{P}GS, 32^{P}HY

	Starts	1st	2nd	3rd	Win & Pl
Chases	6	0	1	1	13308
Career Total	**18**	**5**	**2**	**4**	**38029**

136	11/00	Sedg	2m5f	C Ch	SFT	£6968
132	4/98	Prth	3m110y	B Hdl	G-S	£6193
126	4/98	Ayr	2m6f	C Hdl	GD	£4510
120	3/98	Sedg	2m5f110y	E Hdl	G-S	£2530
101	1/98	Hntg	2m5f110y	F(0-105)HHdl	G-S	£1982

Total win prize-money £22183

Going: Sf: 0-2 GS: 0-2 Gd: 0-2 GF: - Fm: 0-0
Distance: 2m/2m3: 0-0 2m4-2m7: 0-1 3m+: 0-5
Track: LH: 0-5 RH: 0-1 Tight: 0-3 Gall: 0-2
Aids: Bl: 0-0 Vi: 0-0 Tstrap: 0-5
Best Rating: **142** 1/02 Donc 3m soft Ch

Stays three miles. Acts on soft ground.

Kitimat

69 **89**

5-y-o b g Then Again-Quago (New Member)

R H Buckler Mrs Timothy Lewis

Placings:*06* **(2521)**

2001/02: 16^{0}G, 18^{6}S

	Starts	1st	2nd	3rd	Win & Pl
NH Flat	2	0	0	0	0
Career Total	**2**	**0**	**0**	**0**	**0**

Going: Sf: 0-1 GS: 0-0 Gd: 0-1 GF: - Fm: 0-0
Distance: 2m/2m3: 0-2 2m4-2m7: 0-0 3m+: 0-0
Track: LH: 0-1 RH: 0-0 Tight: 0-0 Gall: 0-0
Aids: Bl: 0-0 Vi: 0-0 Tstrap: 0-0
Best Rating: 81 10/01 Chel 2m110y good NHF

Kitley Creek

97 **85**

7-y-o b g Michelozzo (USA)-May Reef (IRE) (Simply Great (FR))

R G Frost Mrs J R Bastard

Placings:*105*-55 **(1617)**

2001/02: 17^{5}GF, 17^{5}GF

	Starts	1st	2nd	3rd	Win & Pl
Hurdles	2	0	0	0	0
Career Total	**5**	**1**	**0**	**0**	**1540**

91	6/00	NAbb	2m1f	H NHF	G-F	£1540

Total win prize-money £1540

Going: Sf: 0-0 GS: 0-0 Gd: 0-0 GF: - Fm: 0-2
Distance: 2m/2m3: 0-2 2m4-2m7: 0-0 3m+: 0-0
Track: LH: 0-1 RH: 0-1 Tight: 0-1 Gall: 0-0
Aids: Bl: 0-0 Vi: 0-0 Tstrap: 0-0
Best Rating: 91 6/00 NAbb 2m1f gd-fm NHF

Kittenkat

81(112h) (123h)**101**

8-y-o b m Riverwise (USA)-Cut Above The Rest (Indiaro)

N R Mitchell Piers Butler

Placings:*60*/02033P3P1/462411003P3P-34450460 **(4480)**

2001/02: 24^{3}GS, 24^{4}S, 20^{4}S, 20^{5}S, 22^{0}S, 24^{4}S, 22^{6}GS, 22^{0}G

	Starts	1st	2nd	3rd	Win & Pl
Hurdles	8	0	0	1	3648
Career Total	**31**	**3**	**2**	**6**	**26867**

123	12/00	Winc	2m6f	B HHdl	G-S	£8424
106	12/00	Folk	2m4f110y	C(0-130)HHdl	HVY	£6773
95	4/00	Extr	2m7f	E Hdl	HVY	£2254

Total win prize-money £17452

Going: Sf: 0-5 GS: 0-2 Gd: 0-1 GF: - Fm: 0-0
Distance: 2m/2m3: 0-0 2m4-2m7: 0-5 3m+: 0-3
Track: LH: 0-5 RH: 0-2 Tight: 0-0 Gall: 0-1
Aids: Bl: 0-0 Vi: 0-0 Tstrap: 0-0
Best Rating: **123** 4/01 Extr 2m6f110y gd-sft Hdl

A useful staying handicap hurdler, she loves the mud and runs well at Wincanton, but has tended to lose her place at a crucial stage before staying on again. Has won at up to two miles six and likes a right-handed track. Sophie Mitchell gets on well with her.

Klondike Charger (USA)

106 **121+**

8-y-o b g Crafty Prospector (USA)-Forever Waving (USA) (Hoist The Flag (USA))

P F Nicholls Mrs Jan Smith

Placings:0333/1P26/1212-5PP **(2776)**

2001/02: 26^{5}S, 24^{P}GS, 25^{P}G

	Starts	1st	2nd	3rd	Win & Pl
Chases	3	0	0	0	0
Career Total	**15**	**3**	**3**	**3**	**14649**

124	9/00	NAbb	3m2f110y	E Ch	G-F	£3234
124	5/00	Font	3m2f110y	E Ch	GD	£3580
100	10/99	Weth	3m1f	E(0-105)HHdl	G-F	£2304

Total win prize-money £9118

Going: Sf: 0-1 GS: 0-1 Gd: 0-1 GF: - Fm: 0-0
Distance: 2m/2m3: 0-0 2m4-2m7: 0-0 3m+: 0-3
Track: LH: 0-1 RH: 0-1 Tight: 0-1 Gall: 0-0
Aids: Bl: 0-1 Vi: 0-0 Tstrap: 0-0
Best Rating: **124** 9/00 NAbb 3m2f110y gd-fm Ch

Has won once over hurdles and twice over fences, although he has been lightly raced since winning a three-runner event at Newton Abbot in September 2000. Best on fast ground, not one to trust.

Knayton Knight (IRE)

9-y-o gr g Satco (FR)-No Slow (King's Ride)

J M Jefferson Mr & Mrs J M Davenport

Placings:*56*005P352/44P/R6P **(2630)**

2001/02: 20^{R}G, 22^{6}GS, 24^{P}S

	Starts	1st	2nd	3rd	Win & Pl
Hurdles	1	0	0	0	0
Chases	2	0	0	0	0
Career Total	**15**	**0**	**1**	**1**	**1130**

Going: Sf: 0-1 GS: 0-1 Gd: 0-1 GF: - Fm: 0-0
Distance: 2m/2m3: 0-0 2m4-2m7: 0-2 3m+: 0-1
Track: LH: 0-3 RH: 0-0 Tight: 0-1 Gall: 0-1
Aids: Bl: 0-0 Vi: 0-0 Tstrap: 0-0
Best Rating: 87 7/99 Strf 2m6f110y good Hdl

Knife Edge (USA)

113 **168**

7-y-o b h Kris S (USA)-My Turbulent Miss (USA) (My Dad George (USA))

M J P O'Brien J P McManus

Placings:111100/5536/**1112-311116F** **(4938a)**

2001/02: 18^{3}YS, 16^{1}Y, 16^{1}YS, 17^{1}Y, 16^{1}HY, 16^{6}GS, 16^{F}YS

	Starts	1st	2nd	3rd	Win & Pl
Chases	7	4	0	1	72065
Career Total	**21**	**11**	**1**	**2**	**185196**

160	2/02	Naas	2m	Ch	HVY	£23926
160	12/01	Leop	2m1f	Ch	YLD	£15725
151	12/01	Cork	2m	Ch	Y-S	£15725
140	11/01	Naas	2m	Ch	YLD	£10483
162	12/00	Leop	2m1f	Ch	SH	£33120
140	11/00	Naas	2m	Ch	Y-S	£5520
150	10/00	Cork	2m	Hdl	YLD	£31200
133	2/99	Leop	2m	Hdl	SH	£8671
130	1/99	Punc	2m	Hdl	HVY	£8671
129	12/98	Leop	2m	Hdl	SFT	£11260
127	12/98	Clon	2m	Hdl	SH	£2391

Total win prize-money £166698

Going: Sf: 1-1 GS: 0-1 Gd: 0-0 GF: - Fm: 0-0
Distance: **2m/2m3: 4-7** 2m4-2m7: 0-0 3m+: 0-0
Track: **LH: 3-4** RH: 0-1 Tight: 0-0 Gall: 0-1
Aids: Bl: 0-0 Vi: 0-0 Tstrap: 0-0
Best Rating: **168** 3/02 Chel 2m gd-sft Ch

Very useful over hurdles, he took well to fences in 2000/01, and landed the Denny Gold Medal at Leopardstown on his first run in J. P. McManus's colours. He has looked the best two-mile chaser in Ireland this season, winning four times, but never figured in the Queen Mother Champion Chase. Acts on soft ground.

Knight Nite (IRE)

6-y-o b g King's Ride-Ardfallon (IRE) (Supreme Leader)

J J O'Neill Mrs Jonjo O'Neill

Placings:F **(4107)**

2001/02: 22^{F}S

	Starts	1st	2nd	3rd	Win & Pl
Chases	1	0	0	0	
Career Total	**1**	**0**	**0**	**0**	

Going: Sf: 0-1 GS: 0-0 Gd: 0-0 GF: - Fm: 0-0
Distance: 2m/2m3: 0-0 2m4-2m7: 0-1 3m+: 0-0
Track: LH: 0-0 RH: 0-1 Tight: 0-0 Gall: 0-0
Aids: Bl: 0-0 Vi: 0-0 Tstrap: 0-0
Best Rating:

Knight Of Passion

(99h) (106h)**97**

10-y-o b g Arctic Lord-Lovelek (Golden Love)

C Tizzard R K Crabb

Placings:13/F20/02055 **(4049)**

2001/02: 24^{0}G, 22^{2}G, 22^{0}GS, 24^{5}HY, 30^{5}G

	Starts	1st	2nd	3rd	Win & Pl
Hurdles	4	0	1	0	780
Chases	1	0	0	0	0
Career Total	**10**	**1**	**2**	**1**	**6621**

133	4/99	Towc	3m1f	H Ch	SFT	£4123

Total win prize-money £4124

Going: Sf: 0-1 GS: 0-1 Gd: 0-3 GF: - Fm: 0-0
Distance: 2m/2m3: 0-0 2m4-2m7: 0-2 3m+: 0-3

Track: LH: 0-3 RH: 0-1 Tight: 0-1 Gall: 0-1
Aids: Bl: 0-0 Vi: 0-0 Tstrap: 0-0
Best Rating: 139 3/00 Chel 3m2f110y gd-fm Ch

Successful in point-to-points. He has placed form in hunters chases. Acts on good and soft ground. Stays three miles over fences.

Knight Of Silver

101 **69**

5-y-o gr g Presidium-Misty Rocket (Roan Rocket)
S Mellor The Knight Of Silver Partnership

Placings:P00P-U (0081)
2001/02: 17^{U}G

	Starts	1st	2nd	3rd	Win & Pl
Hurdles	1	0	0	0	
Career Total	**5**	**0**	**0**	**0**	

Going: Sf: 0-0 GS: 0-0 Gd: 0-1 GF: - Fm: 0-0
Distance: 2m/2m3: 0-1 2m4-2m7: 0-0 3m+: 0-0
Track: LH: 0-0 RH: 0-1 Tight: 0-0 Gall: 0-0
Aids: Bl: 0-0 Vi: 0-0 Tstrap: 0-0
Best Rating: 69 2/01 Wwck 2m soft Hdl

Knight Templar (IRE)

9-y-o b g Roselier (FR)-Rathsallagh Tartan (Strong Gale)
C P Dennis (M Todhunter 20/1) M J Harland

Placings:013/121P1/2F341/23P0-PP4315 (4892)
2001/02: 28^{P}G, 24^{P}GF, 25^{4}GF, 27^{3}S, 27^{1}GF, 31^{5}G

	Starts	1st	2nd	3rd	Win & Pl
Chases	6	1	0	1	2037
Career Total	**23**	**6**	**3**	**4**	**31631**

111	4/02	Sedg	3m3f	H Ch	G-F	£1512
132	3/00	Donc	3m2f	B(0-145)HCh	GD	£10481
132	4/99	Winc	3m1f110y	E Ch	GD	£3498
132	12/98	Font	3m2f110y	E Ch	G-S	£3037
129	10/98	Font	3m2f110y	E Ch	G-S	£2770
91	4/98	Font	3m3f	E Hdl	G-S	£2469

Total win prize-money £23768

Going: Sf: 0-1 GS: 0-0 Gd: 0-2 GF: - Fm: 1-3
Distance: 2m/2m3: 0-0 2m4-2m7: 0-0 **3m+: 1-6**
Track: **LH: 1-4** RH: 0-1 **Tight: 1-4** Gall: 0-0
Aids: Bl: 0-0 Vi: 0-1 Tstrap: 0-0
Best Rating: 132 5/00 Uttx 3m2f good Ch

A modest pointer and hunter chaser these days. Suited by three miles-two plus, handles cut in the ground but well suited by a sound surface

Knight's Crest (IRE)

101 **109**

12-y-o ch g The Parson-Sno-Cat (Arctic Slave)
R Dickin G Hutsby

Placings:040/042FP2/131P22/P-524645 (4600)
2001/02: 26^{5}G, 24^{2}G, 26^{4}S, 23^{6}GF, 24^{4}GS, 24^{5}GF

	Starts	1st	2nd	3rd	Win & Pl
Chases	6	0	1	0	1062
Career Total	**22**	**2**	**5**	**1**	**14953**

122	12/98	Wwck	3m2f	D Ch	G-S	£3964
114	11/98	Ludl	3m	E(0-115)HCh	GD	£3322

Total win prize-money £7287

Going: Sf: 0-1 GS: 0-1 Gd: 0-2 GF: - Fm: 0-2
Distance: 2m/2m3: 0-0 2m4-2m7: 0-0 3m+: 0-6
Track: LH: 0-3 RH: 0-1 Tight: 0-1 Gall: 0-0

Aids: Bl: 0-0 Vi: 0-0 Tstrap: 0-0
Best Rating: 125 3/99 Sand 3m110y gd-sft Ch

Lightly-raced, modest staying chaser who has won on good to soft. Has gone well at Warwick.

Knight's Emperor (IRE)

104 (109c)**103**

5-y-o b g Grand Lodge (USA)-So Kind (Kind Of Hush)
J L Spearing M Olden

Placings:F6-F12140 (2653)
2001/02: 16^{F}GF, 16^{1}GF, 17^{2}F, 16^{1}G, 16^{4}G, 16^{0}G

	Starts	1st	2nd	3rd	Win & Pl
Hurdles	5	2	1	0	5808
Chases	1	0	0	0	520
Career Total	**8**	**2**	**1**	**0**	**6328**

102	11/01	Hntg	2m110y	E Hdl	GD	£2429
101	9/01	Worc	2m	E Hdl	G-F	£2443

Total win prize-money £4872

Going: Sf: 0-0 GS: 0-0 Gd: 1-3 GF: - Fm: 1-3
Distance: **2m/2m3: 2-6** 2m4-2m7: 0-0 3m+: 0-0
Track: LH: 1-1 RH: 1-4 Tight: 0-1 **Gall: 1-2**
Aids: Bl: 0-0 Vi: 0-0 Tstrap: 0-0
Best Rating: 109 11/01 Wwck 2m110y good Ch

Fair novice hurdler, successful at Worcester in September and Huntingdon in November 2001. Suited by a sound surface.

Knighted

109 **122**

6-y-o b g Bigstone (IRE)-Missed Again (High Top)
T D Easterby Elite Racing Club

Placings:433234354/56313421225-F530205 (4301)
2001/02: 24^{F}G, 21^{5}GS, 24^{3}G, 24^{0}S, 22^{2}HY, 25^{0}S, 22^{5}HY

	Starts	1st	2nd	3rd	Win & Pl
Hurdles	7	0	1	1	4290
Career Total	**27**	**2**	**5**	**7**	**22035**

125	1/01	Weth	2m4f110y	E(0-115)HHdl	HVY	£2597
113	11/00	Aint	2m4f	F(0-100)HHdl	G-S	£4465

Total win prize-money £7063

Going: Sf: 0-4 GS: 0-1 Gd: 0-2 GF: - Fm: 0-0
Distance: 2m/2m3: 0-0 2m4-2m7: 0-3 3m+: 0-4
Track: LH: 0-5 RH: 0-1 Tight: 0-3 Gall: 0-1
Aids: Bl: 0-3 Vi: 0-0 Tstrap: 0-0
Best Rating: 125 2/01 Weth 3m1f soft Hdl

A fairly useful handicap hurdler, suited by two and a half miles on soft ground but stays three miles.

Knighton Star

73 **96+**

6-y-o b m Gildoran-Barrica (Main Reef)
R T Phillips R Argles

Placings:0-0 (2648)
2001/02: 16^{0}GS

	Starts	1st	2nd	3rd	Win & Pl
NH Flat	1	0	0	0	
Career Total	**2**	**0**	**0**	**0**	

Going: Sf: 0-0 GS: 0-1 Gd: 0-0 GF: - Fm: 0-0
Distance: 2m/2m3: 0-1 2m4-2m7: 0-0 3m+: 0-0
Track: LH: 0-0 RH: 0-1 Tight: 0-0 Gall: 0-1
Aids: Bl: 0-0 Vi: 0-0 Tstrap: 0-0
Best Rating: 88 4/01 Font 2m2f110y good NHF

Knightsbridge King

88 **71**

6-y-o ch g Michelozzo (USA)-Shahdjat (IRE) (Vayrann)
A King Knightsbridge Bc

Placings:20040 (4586)
2001/02: 16^{2}GS, 16^{0}GS, 21^{0}S, 20^{4}HY, 22^{0}G

	Starts	1st	2nd	3rd	Win & Pl
NH Flat	2	0	1	0	500
Hurdles	3	0	0	0	0
Career Total	**5**	**0**	**1**	**0**	**500**

Going: Sf: 0-2 GS: 0-2 Gd: 0-1 GF: - Fm: 0-0
Distance: 2m/2m3: 0-2 2m4-2m7: 0-3 3m+: 0-0
Track: LH: 0-1 RH: 0-4 Tight: 0-1 Gall: 0-2
Aids: Bl: 0-0 Vi: 0-0 Tstrap: 0-0
Best Rating: 94 12/01 Hntg 2m110y gd-sft NHF

Knock Leader (IRE)

110 **132**

10-y-o b g Supreme Leader-Julie Mack (Strong Gale)
P F Nicholls Antony Sofroniou

Placings:120211/U24214/B242P25-411 (2412)
2001/02: 25^{4}GS, 26^{1}G, 27^{1}GS

	Starts	1st	2nd	3rd	Win & Pl
Chases	3	2	0	0	6684
Career Total	**22**	**6**	**7**	**0**	**26053**

132	11/01	Tntn	3m3f	E(0-115)HCh	G-S	£4153
130	11/01	Wwck	3m2f	F(0-105)HCh	GD	£2530
126	3/99	Fknm	3m110y	D Ch	GD	£3456
116	2/98	Fknm	2m4f	D Hdl	G-F	£2653
111	1/98	Ling	2m110y	F Hdl	G-S	£1894
114	11/97	Wwck	2m	H NHF	GD	£1360

Total win prize-money £16051

Going: Sf: 0-0 GS: 1-2 Gd: 1-1 GF: - Fm: 0-0
Distance: 2m/2m3: 0-0 2m4-2m7: 0-0 **3m+: 2-3**
Track: LH: 1-1 RH: 1-1 **Tight: 1-1** Gall: 0-0
Aids: **Bl: 2-2** Vi: 0-0 Tstrap: 0-0
Best Rating: 132 11/01 Tntn 3m3f gd-sft Ch

A useful hurdler and novice chaser, he kept on finding one or two too good for himin 2000/01, but came back into form with a double over around three miles three furlongs in November 2001. Suited by three miles and a sound surface.

Knockaun Wood (IRE)

80 **80**

8-y-o ch g Be My Native (USA)-Misty Venture (Foggy Bell)
M Pitman Mrs Toni S Tipper

Placings:0/P-0 (3150)
2001/02: 18^{0}G

	Starts	1st	2nd	3rd	Win & Pl
Hurdles	1	0	0	0	
Career Total	**3**	**0**	**0**	**0**	

Going: Sf: 0-0 GS: 0-0 Gd: 0-1 GF: - Fm: 0-0
Distance: 2m/2m3: 0-1 2m4-2m7: 0-0 3m+: 0-0
Track: LH: 0-1 RH: 0-0 Tight: 0-1 Gall: 0-0
Aids: Bl: 0-0 Vi: 0-0 Tstrap: 0-0
Best Rating: 109 4/99 Chel 2m1f good Hdl

Knockdoo (IRE)

108(96c) (94c)**115**

9-y-o ch g Be My Native (USA)-Ashken (Artaius (USA))

J J O'Neill Strathayr Publishing Ltd

Placings:00/0000/241562/00515/3031016023-352U54 **(3693)**
2001/02: 27^{3}G, 20^{5}GS, 24^{2}G, 24^{U}S, 20^{5}HY, 20^{4}HY

	Starts	1st	2nd	3rd	Win & Pl
Hurdles	3	0	0	1	451
Chases	3	0	1	0	969
Career Total	**33**	**4**	**4**	**4**	**19842**

116	11/00	Carl	2m1f	F(0-110)HHdl	HVY	£2588
98	9/00	Gway	2m	(0-102)HHdl	YLD	£4416
81	9/99	Gway	2m	(0-102)HHdl	HVY	£3696
80	9/98	List	2m	(0-102)HHdl	Y-S	£4184

Total win prize-money £14886

Going: Sf: 0-3 GS: 0-1 Gd: 0-2 GF: - Fm: 0-0
Distance: 2m/2m3: 0-0 2m4-2m7: 0-3 3m+: 0-3
Track: LH: 0-5 RH: 0-0 Tight: 0-2 Gall: 0-0
Aids: Bl: 0-0 Vi: 0-1 Tstrap: 0-0
Best Rating: 116 11/00 Carl 2m1f heavy Hdl

A fair Handicapper hurdler in Ireland for Francis Flood, he joined Jonjo O'Neill and kicked off in good style over here, winning at Carlisle in November 2000. Stepped up in trip since, he has failed to build on that first success but was reported to have had breathing problems.

Knockholt

103 **100+**

6-y-o b g Be My Chief (USA)-Saffron Crocus (Shareef Dancer (USA))
S P C Woods S P C Woods

Placings:0 **(1260)**
2001/02: 16^{0}GF

	Starts	1st	2nd	3rd	Win & Pl
Hurdles	1	0	0	0	
Career Total	**1**	**0**	**0**	**0**	

Going: Sf: 0-0 GS: 0-0 Gd: 0-0 GF: - Fm: 0-1
Distance: 2m/2m3: 0-1 2m4-2m7: 0-0 3m+: 0-0
Track: LH: 0-0 RH: 0-1 Tight: 0-0 Gall: 0-1
Aids: Bl: 0-0 Vi: 0-0 Tstrap: 0-0
Best Rating: 58 8/01 Hntg 2m110y gd-fm Hdl

Fair handicapper on the Flat, placed in novice hurdles in the North in the summer.

Knockrigg (IRE)

97(107c) (108c)**81**

8-y-o ch g Commanche Run-Gaiety Lass (Le Moss)
G M McCourt Calypso Racing

Placings:000/0632201/254342136-4223F5200 **(4602)**
2001/02: 16^{4}G, 16^{2}GF, 20^{2}GS, 20^{3}S, 16^{F}GF, 17^{5}G, 20^{2}S, 17^{0}G, 20^{0}GF

	Starts	1st	2nd	3rd	Win & Pl
Hurdles	1	0	0	0	0
Chases	8	0	3	1	3972
Career Total	**28**	**2**	**7**	**4**	**17090**

106	2/01	Leic	2m	F(0-110)HCh	SFT	£3370
85	4/00	Cork	2m	(0-102)HHdl	G-Y	£4140

Total win prize-money £7511

Going: Sf: 0-2 GS: 0-1 Gd: 0-3 GF: - Fm: 0-3
Distance: 2m/2m3: 0-5 2m4-2m7: 0-4 3m+: 0-0
Track: LH: 0-6 RH: 0-3 Tight: 0-4 Gall: 0-0
Aids: Bl: 0-1 Vi: 0-0 Tstrap: 0-0
Best Rating: 108 7/01 Worc 2m4f110y soft Ch

Ordinary chaser, decent effort in January 2002 on his return from five months off.

Knocktopher Abbey

97 **105**

5-y-o ch g Pursuit Of Love-Kukri (Kris)
B R Millman Seasons Holidays

Placings:3 **(2139)**
2001/02: 17^{3}G

	Starts	1st	2nd	3rd	Win & Pl
Hurdles	1	0	0	1	452
Career Total	**1**	**0**	**0**	**1**	**452**

Going: Sf: 0-0 GS: 0-0 Gd: 0-1 GF: - Fm: 0-0
Distance: 2m/2m3: 0-1 2m4-2m7: 0-0 3m+: 0-0
Track: LH: 0-0 RH: 0-1 Tight: 0-1 Gall: 0-0
Aids: Bl: 0-0 Vi: 0-0 Tstrap: 0-0
Best Rating: 105 11/01 Tntn 2m1f good Hdl

Know Thyne (IRE)

60 **19**

8-y-o ch g Good Thyne (USA)-Bail Out (Quayside)
H D Daly (Mrs Jonah Wragg 25/5) Mrs R Gabb & The Hon Mrs A H Todd

Placings:1P **(3262)**
2001/02: 20^{1}GF, 21^{P}S

	Starts	1st	2nd	3rd	Win & Pl
NH Flat	1	1	0	0	3895
Hurdles	1	0	0	0	0
Career Total	**2**	**1**	**0**	**0**	**3895**

122	5/01	Tipp	2m4f	NHF	G-F	£3895

Total win prize-money £3895

Going: Sf: 0-1 GS: 0-0 Gd: 0-0 GF: - Fm: 1-1
Distance: 2m/2m3: 0-0 **2m4-2m7: 1-2** 3m+: 0-0
Track: LH: 0-0 RH: 0-0 Tight: 0-0 Gall: 0-0
Aids: Bl: 0-0 Vi: 0-0 Tstrap: 0-0
Best Rating: 122 5/01 Tipp 2m4f gd-fm NHF

Got off the mark at the first attempt in an Irish bumper over two miles four furlongs on good to firm.

Know-No-No (IRE)

(9h)**90**

13-y-o ch g Balboa-Simply Marvellous (Mon Capitaine)
A R Dicken A R Dicken

Placings:36/42/4532521/6F223/F63/1113211134P/5P3P/P-PB0 **(2723)**
2001/02: 16^{P}GF, 16^{B}GF, 17^{0}GF

	Starts	1st	2nd	3rd	Win & Pl
Hurdles	1	0	0	0	0
Chases	2	0	0	0	0
Career Total	**38**	**7**	**6**	**7**	**30509**

125	11/97	Kels	2m1f	D(0-120)HCh	G-F	£4006
119	9/97	Prth	2m	E(0-115)HCh	G-F	£3387
118	8/97	Prth	2m	F(0-100)HCh	GD	£3355
109	6/97	Prth	2m	E(0-115)HCh	G-F	£3017
103	5/97	Hexm	2m110y	E Ch	G-F	£2193
98	5/97	Prth	2m	E Ch	G-S	£3111
83	4/95	Prth	2m110y	D Hdl	GD	£2682

Total win prize-money £21753

Going: Sf: 0-0 GS: 0-0 Gd: 0-0 GF: - Fm: 0-3
Distance: 2m/2m3: 0-3 2m4-2m7: 0-0 3m+: 0-0
Track: LH: 0-2 RH: 0-0 Tight: 0-1 Gall: 0-0
Aids: Bl: 0-0 Vi: 0-0 Tstrap: 0-0
Best Rating: 125 11/97 Kels 2m1f gd-fm Ch

Knowhow (IRE)

89f **104f**

5-y-o br g Mister Lord (USA)-Mossy Mistress (IRE) (Le Moss)
M Pitman Malcolm C Denmark

Placings:3 **(3910)**
2001/02: 16^{3}G

	Starts	1st	2nd	3rd	Win & Pl
NH Flat	1	0	0	1	366
Career Total	**1**	**0**	**0**	**1**	**366**

Going: Sf: 0-0 GS: 0-0 Gd: 0-1 GF: - Fm: 0-0
Distance: 2m/2m3: 0-1 2m4-2m7: 0-0 3m+: 0-0
Track: LH: 0-0 RH: 0-1 Tight: 0-0 Gall: 0-0
Aids: Bl: 0-0 Vi: 0-0 Tstrap: 0-0
Best Rating: 104 2/02 Kemp 2m good NHF

Kolpatcheva (FR)

73

5-y-o b m Cricket Ball (USA)-Tosca De Bellouet (FR) (Olmeto)
G Brown Tom Segrue

Placings:325-5P **(3739)**
2001/02: 20^{5}G, 16^{P}S

	Starts	1st	2nd	3rd	Win & Pl
Chases	2	0	0	0	0
Career Total	**5**	**0**	**1**	**1**	**3143**

Going: Sf: 0-1 GS: 0-0 Gd: 0-1 GF: - Fm: 0-0
Distance: 2m/2m3: 0-1 2m4-2m7: 0-1 3m+: 0-0
Track: LH: 0-0 RH: 0-2 Tight: 0-0 Gall: 0-0
Aids: Bl: 0-0 Vi: 0-0 Tstrap: 0-0
Best Rating: 73 1/02 Leic 2m4f110y good Ch

Komasta

76 **34**

8-y-o b g Komaite (USA)-Sky Fighter (Hard Fought)
Mrs D A Butler Mrs D Butler

Placings:00004/0/0-0 **(0665)**
2001/02: 20^{0}G

	Starts	1st	2nd	3rd	Win & Pl
Hurdles	1	0	0	0	
Career Total	**8**	**0**	**0**	**0**	**0**

Going: Sf: 0-0 GS: 0-0 Gd: 0-1 GF: - Fm: 0-0
Distance: 2m/2m3: 0-0 2m4-2m7: 0-1 3m+: 0-0
Track: LH: 0-1 RH: 0-0 Tight: 0-0 Gall: 0-0
Aids: Bl: 0-0 Vi: 0-0 Tstrap: 0-0
Best Rating: 96 4/99 Hntg 2m110y good Hdl

Komori (IRE)

102 **103**

12-y-o b/br g Rising-Pandos Pet (Dusky Boy)
A M Crow Mrs H G Peplinski

Placings:B-0023P33 **(4856)**
2001/02: 25^{0}S, 24^{0}GF, 20^{2}HY, 25^{3}S, 20^{P}GS, 20^{3}GF, 25^{3}G

	Starts	1st	2nd	3rd	Win & Pl
Chases	7	0	1	3	3224
Career Total	**8**	**0**	**1**	**3**	**3224**

Going: Sf: 0-3 GS: 0-1 Gd: 0-1 GF: - Fm: 0-2
Distance: 2m/2m3: 0-0 2m4-2m7: 0-3 3m+: 0-4
Track: LH: 0-4 RH: 0-3 Tight: 0-0 Gall: 0-0
Aids: Bl: 0-0 Vi: 0-0 Tstrap: 0-0
Best Rating: 103 4/02 Carl 2m4f gd-fm Ch

Lightly-raced maiden pointer/hunter chaser jumped clumsily on his novice chase debut.

Konker

104 **130**

7-y-o ch g Selkirk (USA)-Helens Dreamgirl (Caerleon (USA))
Mrs M Reveley J & M Leisure / Unos Restaurant

Placings:5040/11315-66405004 **(4524)**
2001/02: 16^{6}G, 20^{6}GS, 16^{4}S, 16^{0}GS, 17^{5}HY, 16^{0}S, 16^{0}GS, 17^{4}G

	Starts	1st	2nd	3rd	Win & Pl
Hurdles	8	0	0	0	411
Career Total	**17**	**3**	**0**	**1**	**11816**

133	1/01	Weth	2m	C(0-130)HHdl	G-S	£5382
122	11/00	Newc	2m	E(0-115)HHdl	SFT	£2541
122	11/00	Weth	2m	E(0-105)HHdl	HVY	£2925

Total win prize-money £10848

Going: Sf: 0-3 GS: 0-3 Gd: 0-2 GF: - Fm: 0-0
Distance: 2m/2m3: 0-7 2m4-2m7: 0-1 3m+: 0-0
Track: LH: 0-6 RH: 0-2 Tight: 0-1 Gall: 0-3
Aids: Bl: 0-0 Vi: 0-0 Tstrap: 0-0
Best Rating: 133 1/01 Weth 2m gd-sft Hdl

Developed into a decent novice hurdler in the 2000/2001 season, winning three times on soft ground. Disappointed this term, but has dropped to a reasonable mark as a result. Suited by two miles and soft ground.

Kopeck (IRE)

92f **88f**

4-y-o ch g Moscow Society (USA)-Cashla (IRE) (Duky)
J T Gifford P H Betts

Placings:2 **(4639)**
2001/02: 16^{2}GF

	Starts	1st	2nd	3rd	Win & Pl
NH Flat	1	0	1	0	774
Career Total	**1**	**0**	**1**	**0**	**774**

Going: Sf: 0-0 GS: 0-0 Gd: 0-0 GF: - Fm: 0-1
Distance: 2m/2m3: 0-1 2m4-2m7: 0-0 3m+: 0-0
Track: LH: 0-0 RH: 0-1 Tight: 0-0 Gall: 0-0
Aids: Bl: 0-0 Vi: 0-0 Tstrap: 0-0
Best Rating: 88 4/02 Asct 2m110y gd-fm NHF

Korakor (FR)

111 **153**

8-y-o ch g Nikos-Aniflore (FR) (Satingo)
Ian Williams Mr And Mrs J D Cotton

Placings:1/31/331P/516434/PP4P1-051232 **(4831)**
2001/02: 20^{0}G, 20^{5}G, 19^{1}G, 20^{2}G, 21^{3}G, 20^{2}G

	Starts	1st	2nd	3rd	Win & Pl
Chases	6	1	2	1	22110
Career Total	**24**	**6**	**2**	**5**	**122693**

149	12/01	Donc	2m3f110y	C(0-135)HCh	GD	£7130
151	4/01	Ayr	2m4f	B HCh	GD	£10787
	11/99	Autl	2m4f110y	Ch	HVY	£21529
	11/98	Autl	2m4f110y	Ch	VS	£12121
	9/97	Autl	2m2f	Hdl	SFT	£22447
	4/97	Autl	1m7f	Hdl	VS	£13468

Total win prize-money £87483

Going: Sf: 0-0 GS: 0-0 Gd: 1-6 GF: - Fm: 0-0
Distance: 2m/2m3: 0-0 **2m4-2m7: 1-6** 3m+: 0-0
Track: **LH: 1-5** RH: 0-1 Tight: 0-1 **Gall: 1-3**
Aids: Bl: 0-0 Vi: 0-0 Tstrap: 0-0
Best Rating: 153 4/02 Ayr 2m4f good Ch

Handicap chaser. Stays two miles four furlongs and is effective on good ground.

Kosamet (IRE)

92 **62+**

5-y-o b g Jurado (USA)-Liffey's Choice (Little Buskins)
G M McCourt Mrs Susan McCarthy

Placings:0 **(0064)**
2001/02: 17^{0}GS

	Starts	1st	2nd	3rd	Win & Pl
NH Flat	1	0	0	0	
Career Total	**1**	**0**	**0**	**0**	

Going: Sf: 0-0 GS: 0-1 Gd: 0-0 GF: - Fm: 0-0
Distance: 2m/2m3: 0-1 2m4-2m7: 0-0 3m+: 0-0
Track: LH: 0-0 RH: 0-0 Tight: 0-1 Gall: 0-0
Aids: Bl: 0-0 Vi: 0-0 Tstrap: 0-0
Best Rating: 60 5/01 Folk 2m1f110y gd-sft NHF

Kosmic Lady

81 **53**

5-y-o b m Cosmonaut-Ktolo (Tolomeo)
P W Hiatt P J Morgan

Placings:040 **(2649)**
2001/02: 16^{0}G, 17^{4}S, 16^{0}G

	Starts	1st	2nd	3rd	Win & Pl
Hurdles	3	0	0	0	0
Career Total	**3**	**0**	**0**	**0**	**0**

Going: Sf: 0-1 GS: 0-0 Gd: 0-2 GF: - Fm: 0-0
Distance: 2m/2m3: 0-3 2m4-2m7: 0-0 3m+: 0-0
Track: LH: 0-1 RH: 0-2 Tight: 0-0 Gall: 0-0
Aids: Bl: 0-0 Vi: 0-0 Tstrap: 0-0
Best Rating: 55 12/01 Ludl 2m good Hdl

Krabloonik (FR)

109(116h) (92h)**143**

8-y-o b g Bering-Key Role (Be My Guest (USA))
J W Mullins Mrs Deborah Potter

Placings:550/33212U33/1P32342341/53650424-523P4440 **(4818)**
2001/02: 16^{5}GS, 16^{2}GF, 16^{3}GS, 19^{P}G, 18^{4}G, 16^{4}GS, 21^{4}G, 21^{0}GF

	Starts	1st	2nd	3rd	Win & Pl
Hurdles	1	0	0	0	0
Chases	7	0	1	1	5974
Career Total	**37**	**3**	**6**	**9**	**38162**

131	3/00	Newb	2m110y	C(0-130)HHdl	G-F	£5761
100	5/99	Weth	2m	D Hdl	GD	£2867
115	1/99	Winc	2m	F(0-110)HHdl	G-S	£2374

Total win prize-money £11004

Going: Sf: 0-0 GS: 0-3 Gd: 0-3 GF: - Fm: 0-2
Distance: 2m/2m3: 0-5 2m4-2m7: 0-3 3m+: 0-0
Track: LH: 0-2 RH: 0-6 Tight: 0-0 Gall: 0-2
Aids: Bl: 0-0 Vi: 0-1 Tstrap: 0-0
Best Rating: 143 12/01 Sand 2m gd-sft Ch

Useful hurdler and novice chaser at two miles. Acts on most types of ground.

Krack De L'Isle (FR)

90f **92f**

4-y-o b g Kadalko (FR)-Ceres De L'Isle (FR) (Bad Conduct (USA))
A C Whillans John J Elliot

Placings:44 **(4309)**
2001/02: 16^{4}HY, 16^{4}S

	Starts	1st	2nd	3rd	Win & Pl
NH Flat	2	0	0	0	0
Career Total	**2**	**0**	**0**	**0**	**0**

Going: Sf: 0-2 GS: 0-0 Gd: 0-0 GF: - Fm: 0-0
Distance: 2m/2m3: 0-2 2m4-2m7: 0-0 3m+: 0-0
Track: LH: 0-2 RH: 0-0 Tight: 0-0 Gall: 0-0
Aids: Bl: 0-0 Vi: 0-0 Tstrap: 0-0
Best Rating: 92 3/02 Ayr 2m soft NHF

Kumakawa

90 **84**

4-y-o ch g Dancing Spree (USA)-Maria Cappuccini (Siberian Express (USA))
D K Ivory (M J Polglase 14/3) R D Hartshorn

Placings:505 **(3495)**
2001/02: 16^{5}G, 16^{0}GS, 16^{5}S

	Starts	1st	2nd	3rd	Win & Pl
Hurdles	3	0	0	0	0
Career Total	**3**	**0**	**0**	**0**	**0**

Going: Sf: 0-1 GS: 0-1 Gd: 0-1 GF: - Fm: 0-0
Distance: 2m/2m3: 0-3 2m4-2m7: 0-0 3m+: 0-0
Track: LH: 0-2 RH: 0-1 Tight: 0-0 Gall: 0-3
Aids: Bl: 0-0 Vi: 0-0 Tstrap: 0-0
Best Rating: 84 11/01 Hntg 2m110y good Hdl

Decent effort on hurdles debut in November 2001, but well held in two subsequent efforts.

Kung Hei Fat Choi (IRE)

97 **108**

7-y-o b g Roselier (FR)-Gallant Blade (Fine Blade (USA))
J S Goldie (J M Brown 6/4) J M Brown

Placings:0506-34140 **(4678)**
2001/02: 24^{3}G, 18^{4}GY, 21^{1}HY, 25^{4}HY, 25^{0}G

	Starts	1st	2nd	3rd	Win & Pl
Chases	5	1	0	1	2404
Career Total	**9**	**1**	**0**	**1**	**2404**

108	3/02	Ayr	2m5f110y	H Ch	HVY	£1589

Total win prize-money £1589

Going: Sf: 1-2 GS: 0-0 Gd: 0-2 GF: - Fm: 0-0
Distance: 2m/2m3: 0-1 **2m4-2m7: 1-1** 3m+: 0-3
Track: **LH: 1-3** RH: 0-1 Tight: 0-2 Gall: 0-0
Aids: Bl: 0-0 Vi: 0-0 Tstrap: 0-0
Best Rating: 108 3/02 Ayr 2m5f110y heavy Ch

Staying chaser, acts well in soft ground.

Kurakka (IRE)

103(105h) (100h)**119**

9-y-o b g Florida Son-Helens Birthday (Quisling)
Noel T Chance Mrs M C Sweeney

Placings:2533/111F2/254P-23F **(3381)**
2001/02: 16^{2}HY, 19^{3}GS, 20^{F}G

	Starts	1st	2nd	3rd	Win & Pl
Hurdles	1	0	1	0	878
Chases	2	0	0	1	1580
Career Total	**16**	**3**	**4**	**3**	**30984**

145	1/99	Sand	2m4f110y	D Ch	G-S	£4569
143	12/98	Asct	2m3f110y	A Ch	G-S	£12260
135	11/98	Towc	2m110y	E Ch	SFT	£3042

Total win prize-money £19872

Going: Sf: 0-1 GS: 0-1 Gd: 0-1 GF: - Fm: 0-0
Distance: 2m/2m3: 0-1 2m4-2m7: 0-2 3m+: 0-0
Track: LH: 0-1 RH: 0-2 Tight: 0-0 Gall: 0-0
Aids: Bl: 0-0 Vi: 0-0 Tstrap: 0-0
Best Rating: 145 1/99 Sand 2m4f110y gd-sft Ch

A promising novice chaser in 1998-99, he was off for almost two years prior to an encouraging reappearance over hurdles at Fontwell in January 2001. Slightly disappointing over fences afterwards, he pulled up lame at Kempton in February and is obviously difficult to keep sound. Unlikely to stay beyond two and a half miles, he may be best when able to dominate and goes well fresh as on his Towcester reappearance this term over hurdles. He returned to fences at Chepstow after that, but was beaten a fair way.

Kustom Kit Grizzly (IRE)

97 77

7-y-o br g Be My Native (USA)-Bridgetown Girl (Al Sirat (USA))
S R Bowring Charterhouse Holdings Plc

Placings:3/06-0040P (0977)
2001/02: 20⁰G, 17⁰G, 24⁴GF, 22⁰GF, 24ᴾGF

	Starts	1st	2nd	3rd	Win & Pl
Hurdles	5	0	0	0	0
Career Total	8	0	0	1	236

Going: Sf: 0-0 GS: 0-0 Gd: 0-2 GF: - Fm: 0-3
Distance: 2m/2m3: 0-1 2m4-2m7: 0-2 3m+: 0-2
Track: LH: 0-3 RH: 0-2 Tight: 0-4 Gall: 0-0
Aids: Bl: 0-1 Vi: 0-0 Tstrap: 0-0
Best Rating: 77 6/01 MRas 3m gd-fm Hdl

Kustom Kit Kevin

6-y-o b g Local Suitor (USA)-Sweet Revival (Claude Monet (USA))
S R Bowring Charterhouse Holdings Plc

Placings:P (0065)
2001/02: 21ᴾG

	Starts	1st	2nd	3rd	Win & Pl
Hurdles	1	0	0	0	
Career Total	1	0	0	0	

Going: Sf: 0-0 GS: 0-0 Gd: 0-1 GF: - Fm: 0-0
Distance: 2m/2m3: 0-0 2m4-2m7: 0-1 3m+: 0-0
Track: LH: 0-1 RH: 0-0 Tight: 0-1 Gall: 0-0
Aids: Bl: 0-0 Vi: 0-0 Tstrap: 0-0
Best Rating:

Kut O Island (USA)

4-y-o br g Woodman (USA)-Cherry Jubilee (USA) (Coastal (USA))
D W P Arbuthnot Miss Helena Halling

Placings:P (4263)
2001/02: 16ᴾS

	Starts	1st	2nd	3rd	Win & Pl
Hurdles	1	0	0	0	
Career Total	1	0	0	0	

Going: Sf: 0-1 GS: 0-0 Gd: 0-0 GF: - Fm: 0-0
Distance: 2m/2m3: 0-1 2m4-2m7: 0-0 3m+: 0-0
Track: LH: 0-1 RH: 0-0 Tight: 0-0 Gall: 0-0
Aids: Bl: 0-0 Vi: 0-0 Tstrap: 0-1
Best Rating:

Kuuipo

89 65

5-y-o b m Puissance-Yankee Special (Bold Lad (IRE))
B S Rothwell S P Hudson

Placings:0-6 (1755)
2001/02: 16⁶GS

	Starts	1st	2nd	3rd	Win & Pl
Hurdles	1	0	0	0	0
Career Total	2	0	0	0	0

Going: Sf: 0-0 GS: 0-1 Gd: 0-0 GF: - Fm: 0-0
Distance: 2m/2m3: 0-1 2m4-2m7: 0-0 3m+: 0-0
Track: LH: 0-1 RH: 0-0 Tight: 0-1 Gall: 0-0
Aids: Bl: 0-0 Vi: 0-0 Tstrap: 0-1
Best Rating: 65 10/01 Strf 2m110y gd-sft Hdl

Still a maiden on both the flat and over hurdles, including in a seller at Stratford in October.

Kuwait Millennium

102 104

5-y-o b g Salse (USA)-Lypharitissima (FR) (Lightning (FR))
J Neville (M C Pipe 8/12) Miss Derien Edwards

Placings:2-342352512002 (4728)
2001/02: 18³GF, 22⁴GF, 19²GF, 16³GF, 16⁵S, 20²S, 19⁵GS, 17¹S, 19²S, 19⁰S, 19⁰S, 16²GF

	Starts	1st	2nd	3rd	Win & Pl
Hurdles	12	1	4	2	7193
Career Total	13	1	5	2	8013

95 1/02 Hrfd 2m1f F Hdl SFT £2586

Total win prize-money £2587

Going: Sf: 1-6 GS: 0-1 Gd: 0-0 GF: - Fm: 0-5
Distance: **2m/2m3: 1-6** 2m4-2m7: 0-6 3m+: 0-0
Track: LH: 0-7 **RH: 1-5** Tight: 0-8 Gall: 0-0
Aids: Bl: 0-1 Vi: 0-3 Tstrap: 0-2
Best Rating: 104 5/01 Font 2m2f110y gd-fm Hdl

Novice hurdler. Acts on soft and fast ground and is effective at around two miles.

Kuwait Rose

85 86

6-y-o b g Inchinor-Black Ivor (USA) (Sir Ivor)
Ferdy Murphy (K A Ryan 21/9) Mrs N L Spence

Placings:0F (1931)
2001/02: 17⁰G, 16ᶠG

	Starts	1st	2nd	3rd	Win & Pl
Hurdles	2	0	0	0	
Career Total	2	0	0	0	

Going: Sf: 0-0 GS: 0-0 Gd: 0-2 GF: - Fm: 0-0
Distance: 2m/2m3: 0-2 2m4-2m7: 0-0 3m+: 0-0
Track: LH: 0-2 RH: 0-0 Tight: 0-2 Gall: 0-0
Aids: Bl: 0-0 Vi: 0-0 Tstrap: 0-0
Best Rating: 86 11/01 Kels 2m110y good Hdl

Kylestone River

7-y-o b m Warcraft (USA)-Gypsy Promise (Balinger)
N Wilson H Barrons

Placings:0F (2307)
2001/02: 16⁰G, 19ᶠGF

	Starts	1st	2nd	3rd	Win & Pl
NH Flat	1	0	0	0	0
Hurdles	1	0	0	0	0
Career Total	2	0	0	0	

Going: Sf: 0-0 GS: 0-0 Gd: 0-1 GF: - Fm: 0-1
Distance: 2m/2m3: 0-2 2m4-2m7: 0-0 3m+: 0-0
Track: LH: 0-2 RH: 0-0 Tight: 0-2 Gall: 0-0
Aids: Bl: 0-0 Vi: 0-0 Tstrap: 0-0
Best Rating:

Kymani Prince (IRE)

108f 102f

6-y-o b g Shernazar-Best Of British (Young Generation)
L Lungo D Stronach & R Buck

Placings:3 (4019)
2001/02: 16³GS

	Starts	1st	2nd	3rd	Win & Pl
NH Flat	1	0	0	1	312
Career Total	1	0	0	1	312

Going: Sf: 0-0 GS: 0-1 Gd: 0-0 GF: - Fm: 0-0
Distance: 2m/2m3: 0-1 2m4-2m7: 0-0 3m+: 0-0
Track: LH: 0-1 RH: 0-0 Tight: 0-0 Gall: 0-1
Aids: Bl: 0-0 Vi: 0-0 Tstrap: 0-0
Best Rating: 102 3/02 Donc 2m110y gd-sft NHF

A narrow individual, seemed to flounder badly in the soft ground when a beaten favourite on his Doncaster debut in March.

Kyper Disco (FR)

95f 106f

4-y-o b g Epervier Bleu-Disconea (FR) (Bayolidaan (FR))
N J Henderson Newbury Racehorse Owners Group

Placings:25 (4423)
2001/02: 16²GS, 16⁵GS

	Starts	1st	2nd	3rd	Win & Pl
NH Flat	2	0	1	0	792
Career Total	2	0	1	0	792

Going: Sf: 0-0 GS: 0-2 Gd: 0-0 GF: - Fm: 0-0
Distance: 2m/2m3: 0-2 2m4-2m7: 0-0 3m+: 0-0
Track: LH: 0-2 RH: 0-0 Tight: 0-0 Gall: 0-2
Aids: Bl: 0-0 Vi: 0-0 Tstrap: 0-0
Best Rating: 106 3/02 Newb 2m110y gd-sft NHF

A French-bred, he is out of a middle-distance winner. Showed promise when runner-up on his debut in a Newbury bumper, held next time.

L S Lowry (USA)

102(71h) 120

6-y-o b g Thorn Dance (USA)-Queluz (USA) (Saratoga Six (USA))
Miss K M George Stableline

Placings:5426P/222113200-**PP3222243FU** (2130)
2001/02: 21ᴾGF, 20ᴾG, 16³G, 17²G, 20²GF, 20²GF, 21²GF, 19⁴G, 19³F, 24ᶠG, 20ᵁGF

	Starts	1st	2nd	3rd	Win & Pl
Chases	11	0	4	2	5929
Career Total	25	2	9	3	15643

95 6/00 Hexm 2m4f110y E Hdl G-F £2275
101 6/00 Hrfd 2m1f E Hdl G-F £2744

Total win prize-money £5019

Going: Sf: 0-0 GS: 0-0 Gd: 0-5 GF: - Fm: 0-6
Distance: 2m/2m3: 0-3 2m4-2m7: 0-7 3m+: 0-1
Track: LH: 0-8 RH: 0-2 Tight: 0-6 Gall: 0-1
Aids: Bl: 0-0 Vi: 0-0 Tstrap: 0-0
Best Rating: 120 7/01 Worc 2m good Ch

Winner of several modest events over hurdles. He has taken well to fences but keeps on finding one or two too good.

L'Ancress Princess

5-y-o b m Rock City-Premier Princess (Hard Fought)
Mrs A M Naughton D M Drury

Placings:P **(1838)**
2001/02: 16^{P}G

	Starts	1st	2nd	3rd	Win & Pl
Hurdles	1	0	0	0	
Career Total	**1**	**0**	**0**	**0**	

Going: Sf: 0-0 GS: 0-0 Gd: 0-1 GF: - Fm: 0-0
Distance: 2m/2m3: 0-1 2m4-2m7: 0-0 3m+: 0-0
Track: LH: 0-1 RH: 0-0 Tight: 0-1 Gall: 0-0
Aids: Bl: 0-0 Vi: 0-0 Tstrap: 0-0
Best Rating:

L'Epicurien (FR)

109(107h) (142h)**141**

6-y-o ch g Chef De Clan Ii (FR)-L'Epicurienne (FR) (Rex Magna (FR))
M C Pipe David L'Estrange

Placings:11314/463214-**12321F6** **(4652)**
2001/02: 17^{1}GS, 20^{2}G, 16^{3}GF, 19^{2}GF, 20^{1}G, 20^{F}GS, 20^{6}G

	Starts	1st	2nd	3rd	Win & Pl
Chases	7	2	2	1	21495
Career Total	**18**	**6**	**3**	**3**	**47224**

140 12/01 Kemp 2m4f110y C(0-130)HCh GD £14625
122 5/01 Extr 2m1f110y E Ch G-S £3428
142 4/01 Asct 2m4f C(0-130)HHdl HVY £6353
128 2/00 Kemp 2m D Hdl GD £3688
8/99 Vich 2m110y Hdl VS £4306
7/99 Pomp 1m2f110y Hdl GD £3229
Total win prize-money £35632

Going: Sf: 0-0 GS: 1-2 Gd: 1-3 GF: - Fm: 0-2
Distance: 2m/2m3: 1-2 2m4-2m7: 1-5 3m+: 0-0
Track: LH: 0-4 **RH: 2-3** Tight: 0-2 Gall: 0-1
Aids: **Bl: 2-7** Vi: 0-0 Tstrap: 0-0
Best Rating: 142 4/01 Hayd 2m soft Hdl

A French import, he was a decent hurdler and made a winning chasing debut at Exeter in May 2001 and scored again at Kempton in December. Fell early on in the Mildmay of Flete at this year's Festival. Took advantage of a drop in class when winning over an extended two miles at Bangor May 2002. Followed up under top weight in better company at Newton Abbot. Suited by a right-handed track, he acts on any ground and usually wears blinkers. Stays two and a half miles.

L'Etang Bleu (FR)

96 **93**

4-y-o gr g Graveron (FR)-Strawberry Jam (FR) (Fill My Hopes (FR))
M C Pipe (Y Fouin 22/6) The Dionysius Partnership

Placings:P4-6322222332 **(1725)**
2001/02: 15^{6}G, 15^{3}VS, 15^{2}VS, 17^{2}GS, 16^{2}G, 18^{2}GF, 17^{3}GF, 16^{3}GS, 17^{2}F

	Starts	1st	2nd	3rd	Win & Pl
Hurdles	9	0	5	3	9392
Career Total	**11**	**0**	**5**	**3**	**10653**

Going: Sf: 0-0 GS: 0-2 Gd: 0-2 GF: - Fm: 0-3
Distance: 2m/2m3: 0-6 2m4-2m7: 0-0 3m+: 0-0
Track: LH: 0-4 RH: 0-1 Tight: 0-5 Gall: 0-0
Aids: Bl: 0-2 Vi: 0-6 Tstrap: 0-0
Best Rating: 93 10/01 Tntn 2m1f firm Hdl

French import, has finished placed on numerous occasions in juvenile hurdles but has yet to win. Handles any ground.

L'Opera (FR)

106 **98**

9-y-o ch g Old Vic-Ma Pavlova (USA) (Irish River (FR))
Mrs L Richards W Smith

Placings:14F/5P240F/533214441/**F2P** **(0849)**
2001/02: 16^{F}GF, 21^{2}GS, 21^{P}GF

	Starts	1st	2nd	3rd	Win & Pl
Chases	3	0	1	0	1293
Career Total	**21**	**3**	**3**	**2**	**38304**

145 4/99 Chel 2m5f110y B HHdl GD £6814
144 11/98 Wwck 2m3f B(0-140)HHdl SFT £5400
129 2/97 Kemp 2m A Hdl GD £8750
Total win prize-money £20964

Going: Sf: 0-0 GS: 0-1 Gd: 0-0 GF: - Fm: 0-2
Distance: 2m/2m3: 0-1 2m4-2m7: 0-2 3m+: 0-0
Track: LH: 0-3 RH: 0-0 Tight: 0-3 Gall: 0-0
Aids: Bl: 0-0 Vi: 0-0 Tstrap: 0-0
Best Rating: 145 4/99 Chel 2m5f110y good Hdl

La Belle

71f **32f**

5-y-o b m Ezzoud (IRE)-Sit Elnaas (USA) (Sir Ivor)
W McKeown I Fox

Placings:0 **(1471)**
2001/02: 16^{0}G

	Starts	1st	2nd	3rd	Win & Pl
NH Flat	1	0	0	0	
Career Total	**1**	**0**	**0**	**0**	

Going: Sf: 0-0 GS: 0-0 Gd: 0-1 GF: - Fm: 0-0
Distance: 2m/2m3: 0-1 2m4-2m7: 0-0 3m+: 0-0
Track: LH: 0-0 RH: 0-1 Tight: 0-0 Gall: 0-0
Aids: Bl: 0-0 Vi: 0-0 Tstrap: 0-0
Best Rating: 32 9/01 Prth 2m110y good NHF

La Boheme (IRE)

(89h) (57h)

10-y-o b m Cardinal Flower-Annies Pet (Normandy)
J C Fox Mrs H F Prendergast

Placings:00-00664 **(0980)**
2001/02: 20^{0}G, 17^{0}GF, 16^{6}GF, 20^{6}G, 21^{4}G

	Starts	1st	2nd	3rd	Win & Pl
Hurdles	4	0	0	0	0
Chases	1	0	0	0	285
Career Total	**7**	**0**	**0**	**0**	**285**

Going: Sf: 0-0 GS: 0-0 Gd: 0-3 GF: - Fm: 0-2
Distance: 2m/2m3: 0-2 2m4-2m7: 0-3 3m+: 0-0
Track: LH: 0-4 RH: 0-1 Tight: 0-2 Gall: 0-1
Aids: Bl: 0-0 Vi: 0-0 Tstrap: 0-0
Best Rating: 57 7/01 Worc 2m4f good Hdl

La Colina (IRE)

87 **76**

7-y-o ch g Be My Native (USA)-Deep Stream (Deep Run)
C J Mann J E Brown

Placings:*0/004/00*55031500**F-0** **(1752)**
2001/02: 22^{0}G

	Starts	1st	2nd	3rd	Win & Pl
Chases	1	0	0	0	
Career Total	**16**	**1**	**0**	**1**	**3883**

89 9/00 Baln 2m4f Hdl G-Y £3312
Total win prize-money £3312

Going: Sf: 0-0 GS: 0-0 Gd: 0-1 GF: - Fm: 0-0
Distance: 2m/2m3: 0-0 2m4-2m7: 0-1 3m+: 0-0
Track: LH: 0-0 RH: 0-1 Tight: 0-1 Gall: 0-0
Aids: Bl: 0-0 Vi: 0-0 Tstrap: 0-0
Best Rating: 96 9/00 Baln 2m4f soft Hdl

La Landiere (FR)

104(105h) (122h)**114+**

7-y-o b/br m Synefos (USA)-As You Are (FR) (Saint Estephe (FR))
R T Phillips Mrs R J Skan

Placings:42112104/0200-5400 **(4879)**
2001/02: 16^{5}S, 16^{4}GS, 16^{0}GS, 16^{0}G

	Starts	1st	2nd	3rd	Win & Pl
Hurdles	4	0	0	0	530
Career Total	**16**	**3**	**3**	**0**	**17447**

120 2/00 Sand 2m110y D Hdl SFT £3753
129 12/99 Uttx 2m E Hdl SFT £2473
126 12/99 Tntn 2m1f C Hdl G-S £5158
Total win prize-money £11387

Going: Sf: 0-1 GS: 0-2 Gd: 0-1 GF: - Fm: 0-0
Distance: 2m/2m3: 0-4 2m4-2m7: 0-0 3m+: 0-0
Track: LH: 0-2 RH: 0-2 Tight: 0-0 Gall: 0-1
Aids: Bl: 0-0 Vi: 0-0 Tstrap: 0-0
Best Rating: 135 1/01 Chel 2m1f soft Hdl

A useful novice hurdler, she won three times in 1999/2000 over trips of around two miles, but has been held in decent company since then. Yet to prove she stays more than two miles one furlong. Suited by soft ground.

La Luna (IRE)

39f **73f**

5-y-o b m Gothland (FR)-Diane's Glen (Furry Glen)
Noel T Chance Mrs S Rowley-Williams

Placings:*0*-6 **(3290)**
2001/02: 17^{6}S

	Starts	1st	2nd	3rd	Win & Pl
NH Flat	1	0	0	0	0
Career Total	**2**	**0**	**0**	**0**	**0**

Going: Sf: 0-1 GS: 0-0 Gd: 0-0 GF: - Fm: 0-0
Distance: 2m/2m3: 0-1 2m4-2m7: 0-0 3m+: 0-0
Track: LH: 0-0 RH: 0-0 Tight: 0-1 Gall: 0-0
Aids: Bl: 0-0 Vi: 0-0 Tstrap: 0-0
Best Rating: 73 1/02 Folk 2m1f110y soft NHF

La Maestra (FR)

104 **88**

4-y-o b f Zayyani-Ginestra (USA) (L'Emigrant (USA))
Miss S J Wilton (M C Pipe 19/11) John Pointon And Sons

Placings:664-0231100 **(2671)**
2001/02: 17^{0}GS, 15^{2}VS, 18^{3}GF, 17^{1}F, 16^{1}GS, 16^{0}S, 16^{0}G

	Starts	1st	2nd	3rd	Win & Pl
Hurdles	7	2	1	1	8116
Career Total	**10**	**2**	**1**	**1**	**9377**

86	11/01	Leic	2m	G Hdl	G-S	£1981
79	10/01	Tntn	2m1f	F Hdl	FRM	£2639

Total win prize-money £4620

Going: Sf: 0-1 GS: 1-2 Gd: 0-1 GF: - Fm: 1-2
Distance: **2m/2m3: 2-6** 2m4-2m7: 0-0 3m+: 0-0
Track: LH: 0-3 **RH: 2-2 Tight: 1-2** Gall: 0-1
Aids: Bl: 0-0 Vi: 0-0 Tstrap: 0-0
Best Rating: 88 9/01 Font 2m2f110y gd-fm Hdl

A French import, she was dropped in class to land a modest claimer at Taunton and followed up in a seller at Leicester.

La Marette

87f 72f

4-y-o ch f Karinga Bay-Persistent Gunner (Gunner B)
R J Hodges Miss R Dobson

Placings:0006 **(4391)**
2001/02: 17^{0}S, 16^{0}GS, 16^{0}G, 16^{6}S

	Starts	1st	2nd	3rd	Win & Pl
NH Flat	4	0	0	0	0
Career Total	**4**	**0**	**0**	**0**	**0**

Going: Sf: 0-2 GS: 0-1 Gd: 0-1 GF: - Fm: 0-0
Distance: 2m/2m3: 0-4 2m4-2m7: 0-0 3m+: 0-0
Track: LH: 0-0 RH: 0-3 Tight: 0-1 Gall: 0-0
Aids: Bl: 0-0 Vi: 0-0 Tstrap: 0-0
Best Rating: 72 2/02 Ludl 2m good NHF

La Minera

74f 61f

4-y-o b f Miners Lamp-Bignor Girl (Torus)
R J Armson R J Armson

Placings:0 **(4410)**
2001/02: 17^{0}S

	Starts	1st	2nd	3rd	Win & Pl
NH Flat	1	0	0	0	
Career Total	**1**	**0**	**0**	**0**	

Going: Sf: 0-1 GS: 0-0 Gd: 0-0 GF: - Fm: 0-0
Distance: 2m/2m3: 0-1 2m4-2m7: 0-0 3m+: 0-0
Track: LH: 0-1 RH: 0-0 Tight: 0-1 Gall: 0-0
Aids: Bl: 0-0 Vi: 0-0 Tstrap: 0-0
Best Rating:

La Mioche (IRE)

92f 89f

5-y-o b m Bob's Return (IRE)-Canta Lair (The Parson)
L Wells L Wells

Placings:3 **(3606)**
2001/02: 18^{3}HY

	Starts	1st	2nd	3rd	Win & Pl
NH Flat	1	0	0	1	222
Career Total	**1**	**0**	**0**	**1**	**222**

Going: Sf: 0-1 GS: 0-0 Gd: 0-0 GF: - Fm: 0-0
Distance: 2m/2m3: 0-1 2m4-2m7: 0-0 3m+: 0-0
Track: LH: 0-1 RH: 0-0 Tight: 0-1 Gall: 0-0
Aids: Bl: 0-0 Vi: 0-0 Tstrap: 0-0
Best Rating: 89 2/02 Font 2m2f110y heavy NHF

La Tormenta (IRE)

86 60

9-y-o b m Glacial Storm (USA)-Green Gale (Strong Gale)
Miss D Cole Mrs Marilyn Cook

Placings:P6FPPP/004 **(1191)**
2001/02: 17^{0}GF, 20^{0}G, 20^{4}G

	Starts	1st	2nd	3rd	Win & Pl
Hurdles	3	0	0	0	0
Career Total	**9**	**0**	**0**	**0**	**0**

Going: Sf: 0-0 GS: 0-0 Gd: 0-2 GF: - Fm: 0-1
Distance: 2m/2m3: 0-1 2m4-2m7: 0-2 3m+: 0-0
Track: LH: 0-3 RH: 0-0 Tight: 0-2 Gall: 0-0
Aids: Bl: 0-0 Vi: 0-0 Tstrap: 0-0
Best Rating: 60 8/01 Bang 2m4f good Hdl

La Yolam

101 99

4-y-o ch f Unfuwain (USA)-Massorah (FR) (Habitat)
N J Henderson (B Hanbury 21/9) Roa Dawn Run Partnership

Placings:64 **(4559)**
2001/02: 16^{6}G, 16^{4}GF

	Starts	1st	2nd	3rd	Win & Pl
Hurdles	2	0	0	0	0
Career Total	**2**	**0**	**0**	**0**	**0**

Going: Sf: 0-0 GS: 0-0 Gd: 0-1 GF: - Fm: 0-1
Distance: 2m/2m3: 0-2 2m4-2m7: 0-0 3m+: 0-0
Track: LH: 0-1 RH: 0-1 Tight: 0-1 Gall: 0-0
Aids: Bl: 0-0 Vi: 0-0 Tstrap: 0-0
Best Rating: 89 4/02 Plum 2m gd-fm Hdl

Bought for 30,000gns off the Flat, has shown modest form over hurdles so far.

Laal Yan

97(102h) (82h)93

6-y-o b m Anshan-Cromarty (Shareef Dancer (USA))
J J O'Neill Dr Linda Barber

Placings:0402P323/50004-000032PP **(3457)**
2001/02: 20^{0}GS, 20^{0}S, 20^{0}G, 22^{0}GS, 16^{3}S, 25^{2}G, 26^{P}S, 26^{P}S

	Starts	1st	2nd	3rd	Win & Pl
Hurdles	5	0	0	1	436
Chases	3	0	1	0	2175
Career Total	**21**	**0**	**3**	**3**	**5483**

Going: Sf: 0-4 GS: 0-2 Gd: 0-2 GF: - Fm: 0-0
Distance: 2m/2m3: 0-1 2m4-2m7: 0-4 3m+: 0-3
Track: LH: 0-2 RH: 0-3 Tight: 0-0 Gall: 0-0
Aids: Bl: 0-3 Vi: 0-0 Tstrap: 0-1
Best Rating: 95 4/00 Ayr 2m4f good Hdl

Modest hurdler. Put in a better effort on her chasing debut without the blinkers. Stays three miles. Acts on a sound surface.

Laazim Afooz

105(80h) (103h)115

9-y-o b g Mtoto-Balwa (USA) (Danzig (USA))
R T Phillips Nut Club Partnership

Placings:023/0003121/002/**01112F4P-4333433564** **(4729)**
2001/02: 26^{4}G, 23^{3}G, 26^{3}GF, 24^{3}G, 24^{4}G, 24^{3}G, 24^{3}G, 24^{5}GS, 25^{6}S, 24^{4}GF

	Starts	1st	2nd	3rd	Win & Pl
Hurdles	1	0	0	1	535
Chases	9	0	0	4	3430
Career Total	**31**	**5**	**4**	**7**	**21261**

125	8/00	Strf	3m	F(0-105)HCh	G-F	£2941
120	6/00	Worc	2m7f110y	E Ch	G-F	£2938
130	6/00	Folk	3m2f	F(0-95)HCh	GD	£2486
104	9/98	NAbb	2m6f	E Hdl	G-F	£2088
99	8/98	NAbb	2m6f	D Hdl	G-F	£2805

Total win prize-money £13260

Going: Sf: 0-1 GS: 0-1 Gd: 0-6 GF: - Fm: 0-2
Distance: 2m/2m3: 0-0 2m4-2m7: 0-0 3m+: 0-10
Track: LH: 0-8 RH: 0-2 Tight: 0-6 Gall: 0-1
Aids: Bl: 0-0 Vi: 0-0 Tstrap: 0-10
Best Rating: 130 6/00 Folk 3m2f good Ch

Fairly consistent chaser at a low level. Suited by three miles and fast ground.

Labula Bay

8-y-o b g Sula Bula-Lady Barunbe (Deep Run)
Miss C F Elliott (C L Popham 17/2) H R Cook

Placings:*00*PP0/**16** **(4678)**
2001/02: 21^{1}G, 25^{6}G

	Starts	1st	2nd	3rd	Win & Pl
Chases	2	1	0	0	2023
Career Total	**7**	**1**	**0**	**0**	**2023**

122	3/02	Fknm	2m5f110y	H Ch	GD	£2022

Total win prize-money £2022

Going: Sf: 0-0 GS: 0-0 Gd: 1-2 GF: - Fm: 0-0
Distance: 2m/2m3: 0-0 **2m4-2m7: 1-1** 3m+: 0-1
Track: **LH: 1-2** RH: 0-0 **Tight: 1-2** Gall: 0-0
Aids: Bl: 0-0 Vi: 0-0 Tstrap: 0-0
Best Rating: 122 3/02 Fknm 2m5f110y good Ch

Laburnum Gold (IRE)

101 101

11-y-o b g Ragapan-Clashdermot Lady (Shackleton)
Ian Williams Terry Sanders

Placings:5/F404/F/0400/114/356-021P **(1463)**
2001/02: 16^{0}G, 17^{2}GF, 16^{1}G, 16^{P}G

	Starts	1st	2nd	3rd	Win & Pl
Hurdles	4	1	1	0	2630
Career Total	**20**	**3**	**1**	**1**	**7419**

101	9/01	Uttx	2m	G Hdl	GD	£1974
100	6/99	NAbb	2m1f	E Hdl	GD	£2392
97	5/99	Hntg	2m110y	G(0-95)HHdl	G-F	£1898

Total win prize-money £6264

Going: Sf: 0-0 GS: 0-0 Gd: 1-3 GF: - Fm: 0-1
Distance: **2m/2m3: 1-4** 2m4-2m7: 0-0 3m+: 0-0
Track: **LH: 1-3** RH: 0-1 Tight: 0-2 Gall: 0-0
Aids: Bl: 0-0 Vi: 0-0 Tstrap: 0-0
Best Rating: 105 6/00 NAbb 2m1f gd-fm Hdl

Lady B Warned (IRE)

84 56

5-y-o b m Zaffaran (USA)-Frostbite (Prince Tenderfoot (USA))
N A Twiston-Davies The 'Yes' - 'No' - Wait'....Sorries

Placings:40P20 **(4385)**
2001/02: 17^{4}S, 16^{0}G, 19^{P}HY, 17^{2}S, 22^{0}S

	Starts	1st	2nd	3rd	Win & Pl
NH Flat	2	0	0	0	0
Hurdles	3	0	1	0	892
Career Total	**5**	**0**	**1**	**0**	**892**

Going: Sf: 0-4 GS: 0-0 Gd: 0-1 GF: - Fm: 0-0
Distance: 2m/2m3: 0-3 2m4-2m7: 0-2 3m+: 0-0
Track: LH: 0-1 RH: 0-4 Tight: 0-1 Gall: 0-0
Aids: Bl: 0-0 Vi: 0-0 Tstrap: 0-0
Best Rating: 76 12/01 Hrfd 2m1f soft NHF

Very modest form in novice hurdles.

Lady Base

4-y-o b f Blushing Flame (USA)-Lady Marguerrite (Blakeney)
W S Kittow Midd Shire Racing

Placings:PP (3332)
2001/02: 16^{P}G, 21^{P}G

	Starts	1st	2nd	3rd	Win & Pl
Hurdles	2	0	0	0	
Career Total	**2**	**0**	**0**	**0**	

Going: Sf: 0-0 GS: 0-0 Gd: 0-2 GF: - Fm: 0-0
Distance: 2m/2m3: 0-1 2m4-2m7: 0-1 3m+: 0-0
Track: LH: 0-0 RH: 0-2 Tight: 0-0 Gall: 0-0
Aids: Bl: 0-0 Vi: 0-0 Tstrap: 0-0
Best Rating:

Lady Bob Back

94 70

5-y-o br m Bob Back (USA)-Whimbrel (Dara Monarch)
Mrs M Reveley John Wills

Placings:*60540* (4441)
2001/02: 16^{G}G, 16^{0}S, 17^{5}S, 16^{4}S, 22^{0}S

	Starts	1st	2nd	3rd	Win & Pl
NH Flat	4	0	0	0	0
Hurdles	1	0	0	0	0
Career Total	**5**	**0**	**0**	**0**	**0**

Going: Sf: 0-4 GS: 0-0 Gd: 0-1 GF: - Fm: 0-0
Distance: 2m/2m3: 0-4 2m4-2m7: 0-1 3m+: 0-0
Track: LH: 0-4 RH: 0-0 Tight: 0-2 Gall: 0-1
Aids: Bl: 0-0 Vi: 0-0 Tstrap: 0-0
Best Rating: 87 3/02 Donc 2m110y soft NHF

Had shown a modicum of ability in bumpers, but has shown no real promise so far over hurdles.

Lady Boston (FR)

5-y-o ch m Mansonnien (FR)-Boston Girl (FR) (Williamston Kid (USA))
N J Henderson David J Jackson

Placings:121F1P**F25U0**-FPP (4581)
2001/02: 16^{F}S, 16^{P}GS, 20^{P}G

	Starts	1st	2nd	3rd	Win & Pl		
Hurdles	3	0	0	0			
Career Total	**14**	**3**	**2**	**0**	**51929**		
9/00	Autl	2m2f	Hdl			VS	£19212
7/00	Autl	2m1f110y	Hdl			HVY	£11527
5/00	Engh	1m7f	Hdl			VS	£9606

Total win prize-money £40345

Going: Sf: 0-1 GS: 0-1 Gd: 0-1 GF: - Fm: 0-0
Distance: 2m/2m3: 0-2 2m4-2m7: 0-1 3m+: 0-0
Track: LH: 0-2 RH: 0-1 Tight: 0-0 Gall: 0-1
Aids: Bl: 0-0 Vi: 0-0 Tstrap: 0-0
Best Rating:

An ex-French recruit, she has won over hurdles and has been placed once over fences in France. Has failed to complete over hurdles in this country so far. Suited by testing ground and distances around two and a quarter miles.

Lady Buckland

9-y-o b m Gildoran-Four M'S (Majestic Maharaj)
P Haskins N B Jones

Placings:BP (0427)
2001/02: 28^{B}GF, 33^{P}G

	Starts	1st	2nd	3rd	Win & Pl
Chases	2	0	0	0	
Career Total	**2**	**0**	**0**	**0**	

Going: Sf: 0-0 GS: 0-0 Gd: 0-1 GF: - Fm: 0-1
Distance: 2m/2m3: 0-0 2m4-2m7: 0-0 3m+: 0-2
Track: LH: 0-1 RH: 0-0 Tight: 0-1 Gall: 0-0
Aids: Bl: 0-0 Vi: 0-0 Tstrap: 0-0
Best Rating:

Lady Cricket (FR)

122 176

8-y-o ch m Cricket Ball (USA)-Lady Mariza (Dunbeath (USA))
M C Pipe D A Johnson

Placings:1/110651/11044/**12120**/1402-212 (4234)
2001/02: 21^{2}HY, 17^{1}S, 20^{2}GS

	Starts	1st	2nd	3rd	Win & Pl		
Chases	3	1	2	0	44880		
Career Total	**24**	**10**	**5**	**0**	**252156**		
176	2/02	Newb	2m1f	A Ch		SFT	£20880
172	11/00	Chel	2m4f110y	A HCh		G-S	£46400
165	12/99	Chel	2m5f	B Ch		G-S	£9940
142	11/99	Chep	2m3f110y	A Ch		SFT	£14310
146	2/99	Font	2m2f110y	B Hdl		GD	£7265
157	2/99	Newb	2m5f	B HHdl		G-S	£5965
	4/98	Autl	2m3f110y	Hdl		VS	£35354
	11/97	Autl	2m2f	HHdl		HLD	£24691
	11/97	Autl	1m7f	Hdl		SFT	£13468
	4/97	Autl	1m7f	Hdl		SFT	£13468

Total win prize-money £191741

Going: Sf: 1-2 GS: 0-1 Gd: 0-0 GF: - Fm: 0-0
Distance: **2m/2m3: 1-1** 2m4-2m7: 0-2 3m+: 0-0
Track: **LH: 1-3** RH: 0-0 Tight: 0-0 **Gall: 1-3**
Aids: **Bl: 1-3** Vi: 0-0 Tstrap: 0-0
Best Rating: 176 3/02 Chel 2m4f110y gd-sft Ch

She put up a cracking performance to win the 2000 Thomas Pink (formerly Murphy's) Gold Cup on her seasonal reappearance, which shows how well she goes fresh. She did not seem to stay when tried over at least three miles in her next two starts and ran a bit better when runner-up in the Mumm Melling Chase at Aintree back over two and a half miles. Good effort on her belated return at Cheltenham in January 2002, and was a revelation in the Game Spirit Chase at Newbury over two miles next time before just being outstayed over two and a half by a stable companion at the Festival. Suited by soft ground, she has a tendency to make mistakes and is not the easiest of rides. Often blinkered.

Lady Cyrano

5-y-o b m Cyrano De Bergerac-Hazy Kay (IRE) (Treasure Kay)
B De Haan Brian A Lewendon & Mrs Carol Lewendon

Placings:0 (2274)
2001/02: 16^{0}G

	Starts	1st	2nd	3rd	Win & Pl
Hurdles	1	0	0	0	
Career Total	**1**	**0**	**0**	**0**	

Going: Sf: 0-0 GS: 0-0 Gd: 0-1 GF: - Fm: 0-0
Distance: 2m/2m3: 0-1 2m4-2m7: 0-0 3m+: 0-0
Track: LH: 0-1 RH: 0-0 Tight: 0-0 Gall: 0-0
Aids: Bl: 0-0 Vi: 0-0 Tstrap: 0-0
Best Rating:

Lady Elegance

6-y-o b m Lancastrian-Busy Girl (Bustiki)
F P Murtagh Bob Slee & Toby Noble

Placings:P (1927)
2001/02: 22^{P}G

	Starts	1st	2nd	3rd	Win & Pl
Hurdles	1	0	0	0	
Career Total	**1**	**0**	**0**	**0**	

Going: Sf: 0-0 GS: 0-0 Gd: 0-1 GF: - Fm: 0-0
Distance: 2m/2m3: 0-0 2m4-2m7: 0-1 3m+: 0-0
Track: LH: 0-1 RH: 0-0 Tight: 0-1 Gall: 0-0
Aids: Bl: 0-0 Vi: 0-0 Tstrap: 0-0
Best Rating:

Lady Faustus

100f 98f

5-y-o b m Faustus (USA)-Princess Lucy (Local Suitor (USA))
J J O'Neill D J Deer

Placings:*10* (4948a)
2001/02: 16^{1}HY, 16^{0}G

	Starts	1st	2nd	3rd	Win & Pl		
NH Flat	2	1	0	0	1561		
Career Total	**2**	**1**	**0**	**0**	**1561**		
98	3/02	Uttx	2m	H NHF		HVY	£1561

Total win prize-money £1561

Going: Sf: 1-1 GS: 0-0 Gd: 0-1 GF: - Fm: 0-0
Distance: **2m/2m3: 1-2** 2m4-2m7: 0-0 3m+: 0-0
Track: **LH: 1-1** RH: 0-1 Tight: 0-0 Gall: 0-0
Aids: Bl: 0-0 Vi: 0-0 Tstrap: 0-0
Best Rating: 98 3/02 Uttx 2m heavy NHF

Big mare. Won a bumper in bad ground at Uttoxeter in March on her debut.

Lady Fearless

5-y-o b m Cosmonaut-Lady Broker (Petorius)
M Mullineaux Esprit De Corps Racing

Placings:P (4326)
2001/02: 17^{P}S

	Starts	1st	2nd	3rd	Win & Pl
Hurdles	1	0	0	0	
Career Total	**1**	**0**	**0**	**0**	

Going: Sf: 0-1 GS: 0-0 Gd: 0-0 GF: - Fm: 0-0
Distance: 2m/2m3: 0-1 2m4-2m7: 0-0 3m+: 0-0
Track: LH: 0-0 RH: 0-1 Tight: 0-0 Gall: 0-0
Aids: Bl: 0-0 Vi: 0-0 Tstrap: 0-0
Best Rating:

Lady Inch

66 **37**

4-y-o b f Inchinor-Head Turner (My Dad Tom (USA))
Mrs L Wadham The Dyball Partnership

Placings:60 **(1141)**
2001/02: 16^{6}G, 16^{0}G

	Starts	1st	2nd	3rd	Win & Pl
Hurdles	2	0	0	0	0
Career Total	**2**	**0**	**0**	**0**	**0**

Going: Sf: 0-0 GS: 0-0 Gd: 0-2 GF: - Fm: 0-0
Distance: 2m/2m3: 0-2 2m4-2m7: 0-0 3m+: 0-0
Track: LH: 0-2 RH: 0-0 Tight: 0-2 Gall: 0-0
Aids: Bl: 0-0 Vi: 0-0 Tstrap: 0-0
Best Rating: 37 8/01 Strf 2m110y good Hdl

Lady Irene (IRE)

87 **77**

6-y-o br m Tirol-Felsen (IRE) (Ballad Rock)
T J Naughton Mrs L Archer

Placings:323/56P-4 **(0348)**
2001/02: 16^{4}G

	Starts	1st	2nd	3rd	Win & Pl
Hurdles	1	0	0	0	0
Career Total	**7**	**0**	**1**	**2**	**1572**

Going: Sf: 0-0 GS: 0-0 Gd: 0-1 GF: - Fm: 0-0
Distance: 2m/2m3: 0-1 2m4-2m7: 0-0 3m+: 0-0
Track: LH: 0-1 RH: 0-0 Tight: 0-1 Gall: 0-0
Aids: Bl: 0-0 Vi: 0-0 Tstrap: 0-0
Best Rating: 80 4/00 NAbb 2m1f heavy Hdl

Lady Jones

105 **92**

5-y-o b/br m Emperor Jones (USA)-So Beguiling (USA) (Woodman (USA))
P L Gilligan Mrs Jean Routledge

Placings:055 **(4519)**
2001/02: 16^{0}S, 16^{5}GF, 21^{5}GS

	Starts	1st	2nd	3rd	Win & Pl
Hurdles	3	0	0	0	0
Career Total	**3**	**0**	**0**	**0**	**0**

Going: Sf: 0-1 GS: 0-1 Gd: 0-0 GF: - Fm: 0-1
Distance: 2m/2m3: 0-2 2m4-2m7: 0-1 3m+: 0-0
Track: LH: 0-0 RH: 0-3 Tight: 0-0 Gall: 0-2
Aids: Bl: 0-0 Vi: 0-0 Tstrap: 0-0
Best Rating: 92 2/02 Hntg 2m110y soft Hdl

Just modest form in a couple of two mile maiden hurdles so far. Should stay farther and is likely to be suited by plenty of give underfoot.

Lady Laureate

116 **120**

4-y-o b f Sir Harry Lewis (USA)-Cyrillic (Rock City)
G C Bravery Blackfoot Bloodstock

Placings:64 **(4651)**
2001/02: 16^{6}G, 16^{4}G

	Starts	1st	2nd	3rd	Win & Pl
Hurdles	2	0	0	0	5000
Career Total	**2**	**0**	**0**	**0**	**5000**

Going: Sf: 0-0 GS: 0-0 Gd: 0-2 GF: - Fm: 0-0
Distance: 2m/2m3: 0-2 2m4-2m7: 0-0 3m+: 0-0
Track: LH: 0-1 RH: 0-1 Tight: 0-1 Gall: 0-0
Aids: Bl: 0-0 Vi: 0-0 Tstrap: 0-0
Best Rating: 120 4/02 Aint 2m110y good Hdl

Four times a winner on the level, she ran a promising race when highly tried on her hurdling debut and again was far from disgraced in top juvenile company at Aintree.

Lady Lewis

97f **84f**

6-y-o b m Sir Harry Lewis (USA)-Gaygo Lady (Gay Fandango (USA))
L G Cottrell Mike Rowe

Placings:3 **(1245)**
2001/02: 16^{3}GF

	Starts	1st	2nd	3rd	Win & Pl
NH Flat	1	0	0	1	214
Career Total	**1**	**0**	**0**	**1**	**214**

Going: Sf: 0-0 GS: 0-0 Gd: 0-0 GF: - Fm: 0-1
Distance: 2m/2m3: 0-1 2m4-2m7: 0-0 3m+: 0-0
Track: LH: 0-1 RH: 0-0 Tight: 0-0 Gall: 0-0
Aids: Bl: 0-0 Vi: 0-0 Tstrap: 0-0
Best Rating: 84 8/01 Worc 2m gd-fm NHF

Lady Llancillo (IRE)

101f **101f**

5-y-o ch m Alflora (IRE)-Minora (IRE) (Cataldi)
C R Egerton R F Bailey

Placings:3 **(4595)**
2001/02: 16^{3}G

	Starts	1st	2nd	3rd	Win & Pl
NH Flat	1	0	0	1	253
Career Total	**1**	**0**	**0**	**1**	**253**

Going: Sf: 0-0 GS: 0-0 Gd: 0-1 GF: - Fm: 0-0
Distance: 2m/2m3: 0-1 2m4-2m7: 0-0 3m+: 0-0
Track: LH: 0-1 RH: 0-0 Tight: 0-0 Gall: 0-0
Aids: Bl: 0-0 Vi: 0-0 Tstrap: 0-0
Best Rating: 101 4/02 Uttx 2m good NHF

Promising bumper debut.

Lady Manilla (IRE)

100 **94**

7-y-o b m Lord Americo-Pacific Ocean (Optimistic Pirate)
M E Sowersby (R T Phillips 30/4) M E Sowersby

Placings:0/600-203 **(2179)**
2001/02: 16^{2}S, 16^{0}S, 23^{3}G

	Starts	1st	2nd	3rd	Win & Pl
Hurdles	3	0	1	1	1334
Career Total	**7**	**0**	**1**	**1**	**1334**

Going: Sf: 0-2 GS: 0-0 Gd: 0-1 GF: - Fm: 0-0
Distance: 2m/2m3: 0-2 2m4-2m7: 0-1 3m+: 0-0
Track: LH: 0-3 RH: 0-0 Tight: 0-1 Gall: 0-0
Aids: Bl: 0-0 Vi: 0-0 Tstrap: 0-0
Best Rating: 94 4/01 Plum 2m soft Hdl

Lady Mantilla

74 **38**

6-y-o b m Michelozzo (USA)-Chelworth Countess (Noalto)
Dr P Pritchard (R Curtis 8/5) B S Hicks

Placings:4/500-00P004P **(4854)**
2001/02: 24^{0}F, 17^{0}S, 17^{P}HY, 21^{0}HY, 16^{0}GS, 20^{4}HY, 22^{P}G

	Starts	1st	2nd	3rd	Win & Pl
Hurdles	7	0	0	0	268
Career Total	**11**	**0**	**0**	**0**	**268**

Going: Sf: 0-4 GS: 0-1 Gd: 0-1 GF: - Fm: 0-1
Distance: 2m/2m3: 0-3 2m4-2m7: 0-3 3m+: 0-1
Track: LH: 0-4 RH: 0-3 Tight: 0-4 Gall: 0-0
Aids: Bl: 0-0 Vi: 0-0 Tstrap: 0-0
Best Rating: 85 1/01 Folk 2m1f110y heavy NHF

Has shown little resolution at the business end over hurdles.

Lady Molly

7-y-o br m Our Jock-Bonne Fille (Bonne Noel)
R T Phillips Ryefield Racing

Placings:2-4P **(4126)**
2001/02: 16^{4}HY, 19^{P}G

	Starts	1st	2nd	3rd	Win & Pl
Hurdles	2	0	0	0	0
Career Total	**3**	**0**	**1**	**0**	**504**

Going: Sf: 0-1 GS: 0-0 Gd: 0-1 GF: - Fm: 0-0
Distance: 2m/2m3: 0-1 2m4-2m7: 0-1 3m+: 0-0
Track: LH: 0-1 RH: 0-1 Tight: 0-1 Gall: 0-0
Aids: Bl: 0-0 Vi: 0-0 Tstrap: 0-0
Best Rating: 87 4/01 MRas 2m1f110y heavy NHF

Lady Normandie

62

5-y-o b m Emperor Fountain-Scawsby Lees (Stanford)
W G M Turner Hawks And Doves Racing Syndicate

Placings:P-P0 **(4021)**
2001/02: 17^{P}S, 16^{0}S

	Starts	1st	2nd	3rd	Win & Pl
Hurdles	2	0	0	0	
Career Total	**3**	**0**	**0**	**0**	

Going: Sf: 0-2 GS: 0-0 Gd: 0-0 GF: - Fm: 0-0
Distance: 2m/2m3: 0-2 2m4-2m7: 0-0 3m+: 0-0
Track: LH: 0-0 RH: 0-2 Tight: 0-1 Gall: 0-1
Aids: Bl: 0-0 Vi: 0-0 Tstrap: 0-0
Best Rating:

Lady Noso

11-y-o b m Teenoso (USA)-Canford Abbas (Hasty Word)
R J King Mrs S King

Placings:053/PP/P **(2778)**
2001/02: 22^{P}G

	Starts	1st	2nd	3rd	Win & Pl
Hurdles	1	0	0	0	
Career Total	**6**	**0**	**0**	**1**	**453**

Going: Sf: 0-0 GS: 0-0 Gd: 0-1 GF: - Fm: 0-0
Distance: 2m/2m3: 0-0 2m4-2m7: 0-1 3m+: 0-0
Track: LH: 0-0 RH: 0-0 Tight: 0-0 Gall: 0-0
Aids: Bl: 0-0 Vi: 0-0 Tstrap: 0-0
Best Rating: 85 3/96 Towc 2m5f soft Hdl

Lady Of Gortmerron (IRE)

103(71h) (82h)122

10-y-o gr m Orchestra-Tara Grey (General Ironside)
N A Twiston-Davies Cheltenham Racing Ltd

Placings:14224102/166432P4U2/1221U6P-445P0 **(4821)**
2001/02: 26^{4}GS, 24^{4}GS, 28^{5}S, 29^{P}HY, 24^{0}G

	Starts	1st	2nd	3rd	Win & Pl
Hurdles	1	0	0	0	0
Chases	4	0	0	0	937
Career Total	**30**	**5**	**7**	**1**	**42324**

140	11/00	Hayd	3m4f110y	C(0-135)HCh	HVY	£13198
128	10/00	Carl	3m2f	E(0-115)HCh	GD	£4173
101	10/99	Ludl	3m	D Ch	G-F	£4565
116	3/99	Extr	3m2f	E Hdl	SFT	£2406
110	10/98	Chel	3m1f110y	C Hdl	GD	£4531

Total win prize-money £28875

Going: Sf: 0-2 GS: 0-2 Gd: 0-1 GF: - Fm: 0-0
Distance: 2m/2m3: 0-0 2m4-2m7: 0-0 3m+: 0-5
Track: LH: 0-2 RH: 0-2 Tight: 0-0 Gall: 0-0
Aids: Bl: 0-3 Vi: 0-0 Tstrap: 0-0
Best Rating: 140 11/00 Hayd 3m4f110y heavy Ch

A dogged stayer, she appreciated forcing tactics when winning on heavy ground at Haydock in November 2000. Still fairly treated, but has shown little in 2001/2002. Has run well fresh in the past. Stays three and a half miles and acts on soft/heavy ground.

Lady Of Jazz

80 27

5-y-o b m Alhijaz-Fairy Ballerina (Fairy King (USA))
N J Hawke Gordon C Fox

Placings:00P-0P **(0793)**
2001/02: 22^{0}G, 22^{P}GF

	Starts	1st	2nd	3rd	Win & Pl
Hurdles	2	0	0	0	
Career Total	**5**	**0**	**0**	**0**	

Going: Sf: 0-0 GS: 0-0 Gd: 0-1 GF: - Fm: 0-1
Distance: 2m/2m3: 0-0 2m4-2m7: 0-2 3m+: 0-0
Track: LH: 0-2 RH: 0-0 Tight: 0-2 Gall: 0-0
Aids: Bl: 0-0 Vi: 0-0 Tstrap: 0-0
Best Rating: 27 6/01 NAbb 2m6f good Hdl

Lady Of The Lamp

104 92

7-y-o b m Miners Lamp-Lady Westgate (Welsh Chanter)
P J Jones P J Jones

Placings:0004/P00036/122P1P0-P6143P0 **(3763)**
2001/02: 24^{P}F, 24^{6}GF, 23^{1}G, 24^{4}HY, 23^{3}HY, 22^{P}HY, 24^{0}S

	Starts	1st	2nd	3rd	Win & Pl
Hurdles	6	1	0	1	4711
Chases	1	0	0	0	0
Career Total	**24**	**3**	**2**	**2**	**11347**

92	11/01	Hayd	2m7f110y	E(0-115)HHdl	GD	£3737
87	2/01	Tntn	3m110y	F(0-100)HHdl	HVY	£3003
78	5/00	Towc	3m	F(0-100)HHdl	SFT	£1856

Total win prize-money £8597

Going: Sf: 0-4 GS: 0-0 Gd: 1-1 GF: - Fm: 0-2
Distance: 2m/2m3: 0-0 2m4-2m7: 0-1 **3m+: 1-6**
Track: **LH: 1-3** RH: 0-4 Tight: 0-2 Gall: 0-0
Aids: Bl: 0-0 Vi: 0-0 Tstrap: 0-0
Best Rating: 92 11/01 Hayd 2m7f110y good Hdl

Fair staying hurdler, suited by three miles and soft ground, although has won on faster.

Lady Peta (IRE)

109 122

12-y-o b g The Parson-Smooth Run (Deep Run)
N J Henderson B M Collins

Placings:1442/211526/32121P **(1487)**
2001/02: 16^{3}G, 20^{2}F, 21^{1}GF, 20^{2}GS, 23^{1}G, 24^{P}GF

	Starts	1st	2nd	3rd	Win & Pl
Chases	6	2	2	1	9841
Career Total	**16**	**5**	**5**	**1**	**21256**

109	7/01	Worc	2m7f110y	E Ch	GD	£3376
122	6/01	NAbb	2m5f110y	E(0-115)HCh	G-F	£3528
96	11/96	Wind	2m4f	D Hdl	GD	£2602
94	11/96	Ludl	2m	E Hdl	G-F	£2262
99	5/95	Hrfd	2m1f	H NHF	GD	£1618

Total win prize-money £13388

Going: Sf: 0-0 GS: 0-1 Gd: 1-2 GF: - Fm: 1-3
Distance: 2m/2m3: 0-1 2m4-2m7: 1-3 3m+: 1-2
Track: **LH: 2-3** RH: 0-2 **Tight: 1-1** Gall: 0-2
Aids: Bl: 0-0 Vi: 0-0 Tstrap: 0-0
Best Rating: 123 2/97 Winc 2m6f gd-fm Hdl

An inappropriately-named gelding, he came back from a long absence to win over fences at Newton Abbot andt Worcester in the summer of 2001. Broke down at Huntingdon. (DEAD)

Lady Qc (IRE)

98 90

6-y-o b m Leading Counsel (USA)-Tuesdaynightmare (Celtic Cone)
L Lungo Mrs Sheila Macleod

Placings:43-2400 **(4896)**
2001/02: 19^{2}GF, 20^{4}G, 16^{0}S, 20^{0}G

	Starts	1st	2nd	3rd	Win & Pl
Hurdles	4	0	1	0	545
Career Total	**6**	**0**	**1**	**1**	**883**

Going: Sf: 0-1 GS: 0-0 Gd: 0-2 GF: - Fm: 0-1
Distance: 2m/2m3: 0-2 2m4-2m7: 0-2 3m+: 0-0
Track: LH: 0-2 RH: 0-2 Tight: 0-2 Gall: 0-1
Aids: Bl: 0-0 Vi: 0-0 Tstrap: 0-0
Best Rating: 90 11/01 Catt 2m3f gd-fm Hdl

Showed promise when runner-up on her hurdles debut in November but disappointed when odds on subsequently.

Lady Sage (IRE)

66f 26f

4-y-o b f Kahyasi-Prussian Storm (IRE) (Strong Gale)
C Grant The Hon Mrs M Faulkner

Placings:00 **(4595)**
2001/02: 16^{0}S, 16^{0}G

	Starts	1st	2nd	3rd	Win & Pl
NH Flat	2	0	0	0	
Career Total	**2**	**0**	**0**	**0**	

Going: Sf: 0-1 GS: 0-0 Gd: 0-1 GF: - Fm: 0-0
Distance: 2m/2m3: 0-2 2m4-2m7: 0-0 3m+: 0-0
Track: LH: 0-2 RH: 0-0 Tight: 0-0 Gall: 0-1
Aids: Bl: 0-0 Vi: 0-0 Tstrap: 0-0
Best Rating: 26 4/02 Uttx 2m good NHF

Lady Santana (IRE)

5-y-o b m Doyoun-Santana Lady (IRE) (Blakeney)
R S Brookhouse Mrs S J Brookhouse

Placings:P **(3510)**
2001/02: 17^{P}S

	Starts	1st	2nd	3rd	Win & Pl
Hurdles	1	0	0	0	
Career Total	**1**	**0**	**0**	**0**	

Going: Sf: 0-1 GS: 0-0 Gd: 0-0 GF: - Fm: 0-0
Distance: 2m/2m3: 0-1 2m4-2m7: 0-0 3m+: 0-0
Track: LH: 0-0 RH: 0-1 Tight: 0-1 Gall: 0-0
Aids: Bl: 0-0 Vi: 0-0 Tstrap: 0-0
Best Rating:

Lady Solrski

19

5-y-o b m Petoski-Flaxen Tina (Beau Tudor)
M A Barnes Solway Racing Syndicate

Placings:600 **(4768)**
2001/02: 16^{6}HY, 16^{0}S, 16^{0}GF

	Starts	1st	2nd	3rd	Win & Pl
NH Flat	2	0	0	0	0
Hurdles	1	0	0	0	0
Career Total	**3**	**0**	**0**	**0**	**0**

Going: Sf: 0-2 GS: 0-0 Gd: 0-0 GF: - Fm: 0-1
Distance: 2m/2m3: 0-3 2m4-2m7: 0-0 3m+: 0-0
Track: LH: 0-2 RH: 0-0 Tight: 0-0 Gall: 0-0
Aids: Bl: 0-0 Vi: 0-0 Tstrap: 0-0
Best Rating: 88 3/02 Ayr 2m heavy NHF

Showed ability on this racecourse debut.

Lady Speckles (IRE)

6-y-o b m Husyan (USA)-Sunalina (Sunyboy)
K Bishop Mrs E M Charlton

Placings:6-0 **(4181)**
2001/02: 19^{0}S

	Starts	1st	2nd	3rd	Win & Pl
Hurdles	1	0	0	0	
Career Total	**2**	**0**	**0**	**0**	**0**

Going: Sf: 0-1 GS: 0-0 Gd: 0-0 GF: - Fm: 0-0
Distance: 2m/2m3: 0-0 2m4-2m7: 0-1 3m+: 0-0
Track: LH: 0-0 RH: 0-1 Tight: 0-1 Gall: 0-0
Aids: Bl: 0-0 Vi: 0-0 Tstrap: 0-0
Best Rating: 74 4/01 Winc 2m soft NHF

Lady Turk (FR)

106 125

5-y-o b m Baby Turk-Alyda (FR) (Dalal (FR))
C Tizzard (M C Pipe 14/2) R G Tizzard

Placings:44/P540P0P0P20-P541132P11P **(4136)**
2001/02: 18^{P}HO, 17^{5}GS, 17^{4}VS, 20^{1}G, 18^{1}GF, 19^{3}G, 22^{2}GS, 22^{P}G, 22^{1}HY, 17^{1}S, 22^{P}GS

	Starts	1st	2nd	3rd	Win & Pl
Hurdles	8	4	1	1	9859
Chases	3	0	0	0	1649
Career Total	**24**	**4**	**2**	**1**	**24437**

112	2/02	Tntn	2m1f	G Hdl	SFT	£1775
125	2/02	Font	2m6f110y	G Hdl	HVY	£1932
107	8/01	Font	2m2f110y	E Hdl	G-F	£2408
102	7/01	Worc	2m4f	E Hdl	GD	£2436

Total win prize-money £8551

Going: Sf: 2-2 GS: 0-3 Gd: 1-3 GF: - Fm: 1-1
Distance: 2m/2m3: 2-5 2m4-2m7: 2-6 3m+: 0-0
Track: **LH: 3-4** RH: 1-3 **Tight: 3-3** Gall: 0-1
Aids: Bl: 0-2 Vi: 2-4 Tstrap: 2-4
Best Rating: 125 2/02 Font 2m6f110y heavy Hdl

Fair hurdler, stays two miles-six and acts on a sound surface.

Lady Vienna

86 **69**

5-y-o ch m Weldnaas (USA)-Fresh Lady (IRE) (Fresh Breeze (USA))
W G M Turner D & J Racing

Placings:U2034-003 **(2288)**
2001/02: 16^{0}GS, 17^{0}G, 17^{3}GF

	Starts	1st	2nd	3rd	Win & Pl
Hurdles	3	0	0	1	258
Career Total	**8**	**0**	**1**	**2**	**1304**

Going: Sf: 0-0 GS: 0-1 Gd: 0-1 GF: - Fm: 0-1
Distance: 2m/2m3: 0-3 2m4-2m7: 0-0 3m+: 0-0
Track: LH: 0-1 RH: 0-2 Tight: 0-2 Gall: 0-0
Aids: Bl: 0-1 Vi: 0-1 Tstrap: 0-0
Best Rating: 78 10/00 Winc 2m gd-sft Hdl

Lady Ward (IRE)

100 **78**

4-y-o b f Mujadil (USA)-Sans Ceriph (IRE) (Thatching)
Ms A E Embiricos (M H Tompkins 9/1) Ms A E Embiricos

Placings:51 **(4682)**
2001/02: 16^{5}S, 17^{1}GF

	Starts	1st	2nd	3rd	Win & Pl
Hurdles	2	1	0	0	2107
Career Total	**2**	**1**	**0**	**0**	**2107**

71	4/02	Hrfd	2m1f	G Hdl	G-F	£2107

Total win prize-money £2107

Going: Sf: 0-1 GS: 0-0 Gd: 0-0 GF: - Fm: 1-1
Distance: **2m/2m3: 1-2** 2m4-2m7: 0-0 3m+: 0-0
Track: LH: 0-1 **RH: 1-1** Tight: 0-1 Gall: 0-0
Aids: Bl: 0-0 Vi: 0-0 Tstrap: 0-0
Best Rating: 71 4/02 Hrfd 2m1f gd-fm Hdl

Selling class hurdler. Acts on a sound surface and is best at around two miles.

Lady Widd (IRE)

60f **65f**

4-y-o ch f Commanche Run-Lady Geeno (IRE) (Cheval)
S J Marshall S J Marshall

Placings:000 **(3999)**
2001/02: 16^{0}S, 16^{0}S, 16^{0}S

	Starts	1st	2nd	3rd	Win & Pl
NH Flat	3	0	0	0	
Career Total	**3**	**0**	**0**	**0**	

Going: Sf: 0-3 GS: 0-0 Gd: 0-0 GF: - Fm: 0-0
Distance: 2m/2m3: 0-3 2m4-2m7: 0-0 3m+: 0-0
Track: LH: 0-1 RH: 0-1 Tight: 0-1 Gall: 0-1
Aids: Bl: 0-0 Vi: 0-0 Tstrap: 0-0
Best Rating: 65 2/02 Muss 2m soft NHF

Ladyrosaro (IRE)

83f

5-y-o b m Roselier (FR)-Leadaro (IRE) (Supreme Leader)
Mrs M Reveley Meter Syndicate

Placings:5 **(3331)**
2001/02: 16^{5}S

	Starts	1st	2nd	3rd	Win & Pl
NH Flat	1	0	0	0	0
Career Total	**1**	**0**	**0**	**0**	**0**

Going: Sf: 0-1 GS: 0-0 Gd: 0-0 GF: - Fm: 0-0
Distance: 2m/2m3: 0-1 2m4-2m7: 0-0 3m+: 0-0
Track: LH: 0-0 RH: 0-0 Tight: 0-0 Gall: 0-0
Aids: Bl: 0-0 Vi: 0-0 Tstrap: 0-0
Best Rating: 83 1/02 Newc 2m soft NHF

Laffah (USA)

97 **94**

7-y-o b g Silver Hawk (USA)-Sakiyah (USA) (Secretariat (USA))
G L Moore Richard Green (fine Paintings)

Placings:6260114/P56/031-00 **(4633)**
2001/02: 17^{0}GS, 20^{0}GF

	Starts	1st	2nd	3rd	Win & Pl
Hurdles	2	0	0	0	
Career Total	**15**	**3**	**1**	**1**	**8775**

102	0/00	Folk	2m0f110y	E(0-115)HHdl	GD	[illegible]
102	3/99	Extr	2m1f110y	E(0-115)HHdl	GD	£2827
102	3/99	Tntn	2m1f	F(0-95)HHdl	SFT	£2661

Total win prize-money £7872

Going: Sf: 0-0 GS: 0-1 Gd: 0-0 GF: - Fm: 0-1
Distance: 2m/2m3: 0-1 2m4-2m7: 0-1 3m+: 0-0
Track: LH: 0-0 RH: 0-2 Tight: 0-1 Gall: 0-0
Aids: Bl: 0-0 Vi: 0-0 Tstrap: 0-2
Best Rating: 102 6/00 Folk 2m6f110y good Hdl

Moderate staying hurdler, suited by a right-handed track.

Laganside (IRE)

108 **130**

9-y-o b g Montelimar (USA)-Ruby Girl (Crash Course)
L Lungo Mrs Jacqueline Conroy

Placings:106313/1P4-266451P **(3353)**
2001/02: 20^{2}GS, 16^{6}GS, 22^{6}G, 16^{4}G, 19^{5}GF, 24^{1}G, 20^{P}G

	Starts	1st	2nd	3rd	Win & Pl
Chases	7	1	1	0	7838
Career Total	**16**	**4**	**1**	**2**	**20090**

122	12/01	Muss	3m	D(0-120)HCh	GD	£6126
130	5/00	Prth	2m4f110y	E(0-115)HCh	GD	£4940
119	12/99	Muss	2m4f	E Ch	G-S	£4221
82	5/99	Dpat	2m1f172y	Hdl	G-F	£1994

Total win prize-money £17282

Going: Sf: 0-0 GS: 0-2 Gd: 1-4 GF: - Fm: 0-1
Distance: 2m/2m3: 0-3 2m4-2m7: 0-3 **3m+: 1-1**
Track: LH: 0-3 **RH: 1-4 Tight: 1-4** Gall: 0-1
Aids: Bl: 0-0 Vi: 0-1 **Tstrap: 1-2**
Best Rating: 130 5/01 Prth 2m4f110y gd-sft Ch

Fair chaser, seems to handle most ground. Stays three miles and is suited by a sharp, right-handed track.

Lago

101 **91**

4-y-o b g Maelstrom Lake-Jugendliebe (IRE) (Persian Bold)
M W Easterby B Bargh T Swain J Walsh & P Bown

Placings:6B0603 **(4330)**
2001/02: 16^{6}G, 17^{B}S, 16^{0}GS, 16^{6}S, 16^{0}GS, 17^{3}S

	Starts	1st	2nd	3rd	Win & Pl
Hurdles	6	0	0	1	471
Career Total	**6**	**0**	**0**	**1**	**471**

Going: Sf: 0-3 GS: 0-2 Gd: 0-1 GF: - Fm: 0-0
Distance: 2m/2m3: 0-6 2m4-2m7: 0-0 3m+: 0-0
Track: LH: 0-5 RH: 0-1 Tight: 0-2 Gall: 0-2
Aids: Bl: 0-0 Vi: 0-0 Tstrap: 0-0
Best Rating: 91 12/01 MRas 2m1f110y soft Hdl

Lago Di Levico

84 **59**

5-y-o ch g Pelder (IRE)-Langton Herring (Nearly A Hand)
H S Howe M R Lavis

Placings:FUP-0R00 **(1493)**
2001/02: 17^{0}G, 17^{R}GF, 17^{0}GF, 17^{0}GF

	Starts	1st	2nd	3rd	Win & Pl
Hurdles	4	0	0	0	
Career Total	**7**	**0**	**0**	**0**	

Going: Sf: 0-0 GS: 0-0 Gd: 0-1 GF: - Fm: 0-3
Distance: 2m/2m3: 0-4 2m4-2m7: 0-0 3m+: 0-0
Track: LH: 0-3 RH: 0-1 Tight: 0-3 Gall: 0-0
Aids: Bl: 0-0 Vi: 0-0 Tstrap: 0-0
Best Rating: 87 9/00 Hntg 2m110y gd-fm Hdl

Laird O'Rhynie

56 **25**

10-y-o gr g Scallywag-Kinsham Dene (Kampala)
K G Wingrove J H Bache

Placings:4/P00 **(2335)**
2001/02: 22^{P}S, 16^{0}S, 16^{0}GF

	Starts	1st	2nd	3rd	Win & Pl
Hurdles	3	0	0	0	
Career Total	**4**	**0**	**0**	**0**	**0**

Going: Sf: 0-2 GS: 0-0 Gd: 0-0 GF: - Fm: 0-1
Distance: 2m/2m3: 0-2 2m4-2m7: 0-1 3m+: 0-0
Track: LH: 0-2 RH: 0-1 Tight: 0-0 Gall: 0-0
Aids: Bl: 0-0 Vi: 0-0 Tstrap: 0-0
Best Rating: 73 11/96 Wwck 2m gd-fm NHF

Lakefield Leader (IRE)

101(103c) (91c)**112**

11-y-o b g Supreme Leader-Debonair Dolly (Cidrax (FR))
C Tizzard (N J Henderson 27/1) I R Snowden

Placings:0/425/12/51320/216P-P3 **(4517)**
2001/02: 25^{P}G, 22^{3}GS

	Starts	1st	2nd	3rd	Win & Pl
Chases	2	0	0	1	318
Career Total	**17**	**3**	**4**	**2**	**17234**

119	11/00	Towc	2m6f	E Ch	SFT	£2925
134	3/00	Newb	2m5f	D(0-125)HHdl	SFT	£5297
113	5/98	Uttx	3m110y	E Hdl	GD	£2400

Total win prize-money £10623

Going: Sf: 0-0 GS: 0-1 Gd: 0-1 GF: - Fm: 0-0
Distance: 2m/2m3: 0-0 2m4-2m7: 0-1 3m+: 0-1
Track: LH: 0-0 RH: 0-2 Tight: 0-0 Gall: 0-0

Aids: Bl: 0-0 Vi: 0-0 Tstrap: 0-0
Best Rating: **134** 4/00 Asct 3m soft Hdl

A one-time useful staying hurdler, he lost his way when put over fences. Handles soft and fast ground.

Lakefield Rambler (IRE)

107 **137**

10-y-o b g Lafontaine (USA)-Debonair Dolly (Cidrax (FR))
P F Nicholls A J Powell F A Bonsal J Schlesinger

Placings:U00/00/41/1315-4P (3889)
2001/02: 26^{4}S, 24^{P}GS

	Starts	1st	2nd	3rd	Win & Pl
Chases	2	0	0	0	540
Career Total	**13**	**3**	**0**	**1**	**19810**

143	12/00	Folk	3m2f	D Ch	SFT	£4095
130	5/00	Chel	3m1f110y	H Ch	GD	£3484
138	4/00	Aint	3m1f	B Ch	GD	£9051

Total win prize-money £16630

Going: Sf: 0-1 GS: 0-1 Gd: 0-0 GF: - Fm: 0-0
Distance: 2m/2m3: 0-0 2m4-2m7: 0-0 3m+: 0-2
Track: LH: 0-1 RH: 0-1 Tight: 0-0 Gall: 0-0
Aids: Bl: 0-0 Vi: 0-0 Tstrap: 0-0
Best Rating: **143** 12/00 Folk 3m2f soft Ch

A cracking hunter chaser, he has a future in handicaps judged on a promising fifth to Browjoshy at Warwick in January 2001. Likely to stay long distances, he may be best on decent ground.

Lakeland Pride (IRE)

94(48c) **89**

7-y-o gr g Pips Pride-Divine Apsara (Godswalk (USA))
M A Barnes M Barnes

Placings:5335/06/344351244P-65P0 (0805)
2001/02: 16^{6}GF, 23^{5}F, 20^{P}GF, 16^{0}GF

	Starts	1st	2nd	3rd	Win & Pl
Hurdles	3	0	0	0	0
Chases	1	0	0	0	0
Career Total	**20**	**1**	**1**	**4**	**6898**

95	7/00	Uttx	2m4f110y	D Hdl	G-F	£3591

Total win prize-money £3591

Going: Sf: 0-0 GS: 0-0 Gd: 0-0 GF: - Fm: 0-4
Distance: 2m/2m3: 0-2 2m4-2m7: 0-1 3m+: 0-1
Track: LH: 0-1 RH: 0-2 Tight: 0-0 Gall: 0-0
Aids: Bl: 0-0 Vi: 0-0 Tstrap: 0-2
Best Rating: **101** 7/00 Sedg 2m110y firm Ch

Lakeside Lad

105 **108**

10-y-o b g St Columbus-Beyond The Trimm (Trimmingham)
R Wilman (T Wall 31/7) Mrs Joanna Hughes

Placings:*0L*/PB24/UU322PUF33/U4P-5F400P2 (4916)
2001/02: 20^{5}G, 25^{F}F, 23^{4}G, 24^{0}GF, 23^{0}G, 26^{P}GF, 27^{2}GF

	Starts	1st	2nd	3rd	Win & Pl
Chases	7	0	1	0	1592
Career Total	**26**	**0**	**4**	**3**	**5734**

Going: Sf: 0-0 GS: 0-0 Gd: 0-3 GF: - Fm: 0-4
Distance: 2m/2m3: 0-0 2m4-2m7: 0-1 3m+: 0-6
Track: LH: 0-7 RH: 0-0 Tight: 0-3 Gall: 0-0

Aids: Bl: 0-0 Vi: 0-0 Tstrap: 0-0
Best Rating: **108** 4/00 Ludl 3m good Ch

Modest novice chaser, stays three miles plus. Acts on a sound surface.

Lambadora

103 **86**

4-y-o ch f Suave Dancer (USA)-Lust (Pursuit Of Love)
J G M O'Shea (Miss J A Camacho 4/3) Gary Roberts

Placings:400 (4044)
2001/02: 16^{4}S, 17^{0}S, 17^{0}GS

	Starts	1st	2nd	3rd	Win & Pl
Hurdles	3	0	0	0	0
Career Total	**3**	**0**	**0**	**0**	**0**

Going: Sf: 0-2 GS: 0-1 Gd: 0-0 GF: - Fm: 0-0
Distance: 2m/2m3: 0-3 2m4-2m7: 0-0 3m+: 0-0
Track: LH: 0-2 RH: 0-1 Tight: 0-3 Gall: 0-0
Aids: Bl: 0-0 Vi: 0-0 Tstrap: 0-1
Best Rating: **86** 1/02 Catt 2m soft Hdl

Winning plater over hurdles, acts on fast ground.

Lambhill Stakes (IRE)

84f **91f**

4-y-o gr g King's Ride-Summerhill Express (IRE) (Roselier (FR))
J M Jefferson Ashleybank Investments Limited

Placings:*0* (4841)
2001/02: 16^{0}G

	Starts	1st	2nd	3rd	Win & Pl
NH Flat	1	0	0	0	
Career Total	**1**	**0**	**0**	**0**	

Going: Sf: 0-0 GS: 0-0 Gd: 0-1 GF: - Fm: 0-0
Distance: 2m/2m3: 0-1 2m4-2m7: 0-0 3m+: 0-0
Track: LH: 0-1 RH: 0-0 Tight: 0-0 Gall: 0-0
Aids: Bl: 0-0 Vi: 0-0 Tstrap: 0-0
Best Rating: **91** 4/02 Ayr 2m good NHF

Lambrini Bianco (IRE)

97f **89f**

4-y-o br g Roselier (FR)-Darjoy (Darantus)
Mrs L Williamson Halewood International Ltd

Placings:*10* (4679)
2001/02: 17^{1}S, 17^{0}G

	Starts	1st	2nd	3rd	Win & Pl
NH Flat	2	1	0	0	1729
Career Total	**2**	**1**	**0**	**0**	**1729**

89	3/02	Bang	2m1f	H NHF	SFT	£1729

Total win prize-money £1729

Going: Sf: 1-1 GS: 0-0 Gd: 0-1 GF: - Fm: 0-0
Distance: **2m/2m3: 1-2** 2m4-2m7: 0-0 3m+: 0-0
Track: **LH: 1-1** RH: 0-0 **Tight: 1-1** Gall: 0-0
Aids: Bl: 0-0 Vi: 0-0 Tstrap: 0-0
Best Rating: **89** 3/02 Bang 2m1f soft NHF

Half-brother to some smart staying chasers, including 1995 Grand National winner Royal Athlete. Made the perfect start to his career when winning a soft ground bumper at Bangor in March.

Lambrini Knight (IRE)

76 **34**

9-y-o b g John French-Annalough Rose (Mugatpura)
Mrs L Williamson Halewood International Ltd

Placings:*01*/PP/0P0P0 (4025)
2001/02: 16^{0}G, 16^{P}S, 17^{0}HY, 17^{P}S, 16^{0}S

	Starts	1st	2nd	3rd	Win & Pl
Hurdles	5	0	0	0	
Career Total	**9**	**1**	**0**	**0**	**1392**

110	12/98	Hrfd	2m1f	H NHF	SFT	£1392

Total win prize-money £1392

Going: Sf: 0-4 GS: 0-0 Gd: 0-1 GF: - Fm: 0-0
Distance: 2m/2m3: 0-5 2m4-2m7: 0-0 3m+: 0-0
Track: LH: 0-2 RH: 0-3 Tight: 0-2 Gall: 0-1
Aids: Bl: 0-0 Vi: 0-0 Tstrap: 0-0
Best Rating: **110** 12/98 Hrfd 2m1f soft NHF

Lambrini Mist

69f

4-y-o gr g Terimon-Miss Fern (Cruise Missile)
Mrs L Williamson Halewood International Ltd

Placings:*3* (4784)
2001/02: 18^{3}GF

	Starts	1st	2nd	3rd	Win & Pl
NH Flat	1	0	0	1	245
Career Total	**1**	**0**	**0**	**1**	**245**

Going: Sf: 0-0 GS: 0-0 Gd: 0-0 GF: 0-0 Fm: 0-1
Distance: 2m/2m3: 0-1 2m4-2m7: 0-0 3m+: 0-0
Track: LH: 0-0 RH: 0-0 Tight: 0-0 Gall: 0-0
Aids: Bl: 0-0 Vi: 0-0 Tstrap: 0-0
Best Rating: **69** 4/02 Plum 2m2f gd-fm NHF

Shaped with promise on his bumper debut.

Lambrini Prince

103 **104**

8-y-o b g Derrylin-Flying Faith (Rymer)
Mrs L Williamson Halewood International Ltd

Placings:000/P-23F22U323 (4409)
2001/02: 26^{2}GS, 22^{3}G, 24^{F}GS, 22^{2}S, 24^{2}HY, 26^{U}HY, 26^{3}HY, 24^{2}S, 24^{3}S

	Starts	1st	2nd	3rd	Win & Pl
Chases	9	0	4	3	7929
Career Total	**13**	**0**	**4**	**3**	**7929**

Going: Sf: 0-6 GS: 0-2 Gd: 0-1 GF: - Fm: 0-0
Distance: 2m/2m3: 0-0 2m4-2m7: 0-2 3m+: 0-7
Track: LH: 0-5 RH: 0-0 Tight: 0-3 Gall: 0-0
Aids: Bl: 0-0 Vi: 0-0 Tstrap: 0-0
Best Rating: **104** 3/02 Bang 3m110y soft Ch

Modest novice chaser at around three miles on soft/heavy ground.

Lammoski (IRE)

78 **42**

5-y-o ch g Hamas (IRE)-Penny In My Shoe (USA) (Sir Ivor)
M C Chapman G C R Pryke

Placings:0300-00 (1501)
2001/02: 17^{0}GF, 17^{0}G

	Starts	1st	2nd	3rd	Win & Pl
Hurdles	2	0	0	0	

Career Total	6	0	0	1	223

Going: Sf: 0-0 GS: 0-0 Gd: 0-1 GF: - Fm: 0-1
Distance: 2m/2m3: 0-2 2m4-2m7: 0-0 3m+: 0-0
Track: LH: 0-1 RH: 0-1 Tight: 0-2 Gall: 0-0
Aids: Bl: 0-0 Vi: 0-0 Tstrap: 0-0
Best Rating: 65 10/00 Ludl 2m gd-fm Hdl

Lancashire Lass

82 **59**

6-y-o b m Lancastrian-Chanelle (The Parson)
J S King P A Deal

Placings:00600-6 **(0045)**
2001/02: 17^{6}GS

	Starts	1st	2nd	3rd	Win & Pl
Hurdles	1	0	0	0	0
Career Total	6	0	0	0	0

Going: Sf: 0-0 GS: 0-1 Gd: 0-0 GF: - Fm: 0-0
Distance: 2m/2m3: 0-1 2m4-2m7: 0-0 3m+: 0-0
Track: LH: 0-0 RH: 0-1 Tight: 0-0 Gall: 0-0
Aids: Bl: 0-0 Vi: 0-0 Tstrap: 0-0
Best Rating: 70 11/00 Tntn 2m1f good NHF

Lancastrian Jet (IRE)

105 **138**

11-y-o b g Lancastrian-Kilmurray Jet (Le Bavard (FR))
H D Daly The Hon Mrs A E Heber-Percy

Placings:0/P2211/41252/121U5P/5535P-2133 **(3740)**
2001/02: 26^{2}S, 32^{1}GS, 28^{3}S, 23^{3}S

	Starts	1st	2nd	3rd	Win & Pl
Chases	4	1	1	2	11755
Career Total	26	6	6	3	55561

137	12/01	Extr	4m	D(0-125)HCh	G-S	£8255
141	1/00	Sand	3m5f110y	B HCh	SFT	£20800
141	10/99	Towc	3m1f	E(0-115)HCh	GD	£3142
136	12/98	Towc	3m1f	C(0-130)HCh	SFT	£4926
129	4/98	Uttx	3m2f	E Ch	SFT	£3801
126	3/98	Tntn	3m	E Ch	G-S	£2918

Total win prize-money £43842

Going: Sf: 0-3 GS: 1-1 Gd: 0-0 GF: - Fm: 0-0
Distance: 2m/2m3: 0-0 2m4-2m7: 0-0 **3m+: 1-4**
Track: LH: 0-0 RH: 0-2 Tight: 0-0 Gall: 0-0
Aids: Bl: 0-0 Vi: 0-0 Tstrap: 0-0
Best Rating: 141 1/00 Sand 3m5f110y soft Ch

Veteran staying chaser, best going right-handed on soft ground and likes stiff tracks like Towcester. Stays four miles.

Lance Armstrong (IRE)

112 **140**

12-y-o ch g Lancastrian-Wolver Rose (Wolver Hollow)
R H Alner G L Porter

Placings:0F116/123116/341/444210/04F1413P-032320 **(4419)**
2001/02: 23^{0}GS, 24^{3}G, 24^{2}G, 24^{3}S, 26^{2}GS, 24^{0}GS

	Starts	1st	2nd	3rd	Win & Pl
Chases	6	0	2	2	8842
Career Total	34	9	4	5	60502

140	1/01	Kemp	3m	C(0-135)HCh	SFT	£7312
140	11/00	Chep	2m3f110y	C(0-130)HCh	HVY	£5671
140	3/00	Winc	2m5f	C(0-135)HCh	G-S	£6825
131	3/98	Newb	2m4f	C(0-135)HCh	G-S	£5020
126	3/97	Extr	2m3f110y	E(0-115)HCh	G-S	£2835
113	2/97	Leic	2m4f110y	E(0-110)HCh	GD	£2906
86	12/96	Sthl	2m4f110y	E Hdl	GD	£2301
101	3/96	Plum	2m5f	E Ch	G-S	£3015
113	2/96	Wind	2m5f	E Ch	GD	£3559

Total win prize-money £39447

Going: Sf: 0-1 GS: 0-3 Gd: 0-2 GF: - Fm: 0-0
Distance: 2m/2m3: 0-0 2m4-2m7: 0-0 3m+: 0-6
Track: LH: 0-2 RH: 0-4 Tight: 0-0 Gall: 0-1
Aids: Bl: 0-0 Vi: 0-0 Tstrap: 0-0
Best Rating: 140 3/02 Chep 3m2f110y gd-sft Ch

He is effective over a variety of trips but probably best around three miles nowadays. Suited by easy ground, he jumps soundly.

Land Girl

99 **65**

4-y-o b f General Monash (USA)-Charming Madam (General Holme (USA))
J G M O'Shea (Miss S E Hall 7/10) Bill Tyler

Placings:0 **(1574)**
2001/02: 16^{0}G

	Starts	1st	2nd	3rd	Win & Pl
Hurdles	1	0	0	0	
Career Total	1	0	0	0	

Going: Sf: 0-0 GS: 0-0 Gd: 0-1 GF: - Fm: 0-0
Distance: 2m/2m3: 0-1 2m4-2m7: 0-0 3m+: 0-0
Track: LH: 0-1 RH: 0-0 Tight: 0-1 Gall: 0-0
Aids: Bl: 0-0 Vi: 0-0 Tstrap: 0-0
Best Rating: 58 10/01 Kels 2m110y good Hdl

Landenstown (IRE)

104 **97**

14-y-o br g Furry Glen-Divine Drapes (Divine Gift)
Mrs P Ford Hon J Borwick

Placings:610/66605006/312/14/4PP1U2 **(1664)**
2001/02: 24^{4}F, 22^{P}GF, 21^{P}GF, 24^{1}G, 24^{U}GF, 24^{2}G

	Starts	1st	2nd	3rd	Win & Pl
Chases	6	1	1	0	4273
Career Total	22	4	2	1	10478

97	8/01	Strf	3m	F(0-105)HCh	GD	£3052
105	3/98	Ludl	3m	H Ch	GD	£1584
108	5/95	Dund	2m153y	Hdl	FRM	£2204
	9/93	DRoy	2m	NHF	GD	£1483

Total win prize-money £8325

Going: Sf: 0-0 GS: 0-0 Gd: 1-2 GF: - Fm: 0-4
Distance: 2m/2m3: 0-0 2m4-2m7: 0-2 **3m+: 1-4**
Track: **LH: 1-4** RH: 0-2 **Tight: 1-5** Gall: 0-0
Aids: Bl: 0-0 Vi: 0-0 Tstrap: 0-0
Best Rating: 108 6/95 Dund 2m4f153y firm Hdl

Landican Lad

5-y-o b g Petong-Dancing Daughter (Dance In Time (CAN))
Miss C J E Caroe Miss C J E Caroe

Placings:P0-4PPP **(2642)**
2001/02: 16^{4}GF, 19^{P}G, 17^{P}G, 21^{P}GS

	Starts	1st	2nd	3rd	Win & Pl
Hurdles	4	0	0	0	0
Career Total	6	0	0	0	0

Going: Sf: 0-0 GS: 0-1 Gd: 0-2 GF: - Fm: 0-1
Distance: 2m/2m3: 0-2 2m4-2m7: 0-2 3m+: 0-0
Track: LH: 0-0 RH: 0-4 Tight: 0-2 Gall: 0-2
Aids: Bl: 0-0 Vi: 0-0 Tstrap: 0-2
Best Rating: 32 1/01 Muss 2m good Hdl

Landing Light (IRE)

119 **170**

7-y-o b g In The Wings-Gay Hellene (Ela-Mana-Mou)
N J Henderson Mr & Mrs John Poynton

Placings:1/311P1-1156 **(4959a)**
2001/02: 16^{1}GS, 16^{1}G, 16^{5}GS, 16^{6}GY

	Starts	1st	2nd	3rd	Win & Pl
Hurdles	4	2	0	0	59528
Career Total	10	6	0	1	182792

164	12/01	Kemp	2m	A Hdl	GD	£29750
161	12/01	Newc	2m	A Hdl	G-S	£22200
170	4/01	Sand	2m110y	A Hdl	SFT	£49300
154	2/01	Newb	2m110y	A HHdl	SFT	£58000
147	1/01	Chel	2m1f	B(0-145)HHdl	SFT	£11095
134	2/00	Winc	2m	D Hdl	GD	£3623

Total win prize-money £173970

Going: Sf: 0-0 GS: 1-2 Gd: 1-1 GF: - Fm: 0-0
Distance: **2m/2m3: 2-4** 2m4-2m7: 0-0 3m+: 0-0
Track: LH: 1-2 RH: 1-2 Tight: 0-0 **Gall: 1-1**
Aids: Bl: 0-0 Vi: 0-0 Tstrap: 0-0
Best Rating: 170 4/01 Sand 2m110y soft Hdl

A high-class hurdler who won five times from six starts during 2001 including the Tote Gold Trophy, the Coral Eurobet Championship Hurdle, the Fighting Fifth and the Christmas Hurdle. He needs plenty of stoking and usually responds to his rider's urgings, but they went too quick for him in the 2002 Champion Hurdle and he never got competitive. Genuine and possesses a useful turn of foot. Best over a stiff two miles with the ground good or softer, but not heavy.

Landing Slot (USA)

95 **71**

7-y-o b g Personal Hope (USA)-Durability (USA) (Affirmed (USA))
E W Tuer E Tuer

Placings:P/04000-PP50 **(2723)**
2001/02: 16^{P}G, 17^{P}S, 16^{5}S, 17^{0}GF

	Starts	1st	2nd	3rd	Win & Pl
Hurdles	4	0	0	0	0
Career Total	10	0	0	0	0

Going: Sf: 0-2 GS: 0-0 Gd: 0-1 GF: - Fm: 0-1
Distance: 2m/2m3: 0-4 2m4-2m7: 0-0 3m+: 0-0
Track: LH: 0-3 RH: 0-0 Tight: 0-2 Gall: 0-0
Aids: Bl: 0-1 Vi: 0-0 Tstrap: 0-0
Best Rating: 89 10/00 Carl 2m1f gd-sft Hdl

Langton Green

(100h) (93h) **101**

7-y-o b g Green Adventure (USA)-Langton Lass (Nearly A Hand)
H D Daly Major And Mrs C A R Lockhart

Placings:3002U-5FR **(2654)**
2001/02: 20^{5}GS, 16^{F}G, 20^{R}G

	Starts	1st	2nd	3rd	Win & Pl
Hurdles	1	0	0	0	0
Chases	2	0	0	0	0
Career Total	8	0	1	1	872

Going: Sf: 0-0 GS: 0-1 Gd: 0-2 GF: - Fm: 0-0
Distance: 2m/2m3: 0-1 2m4-2m7: 0-2 3m+: 0-0

Track: LH: 0-1 RH: 0-2 Tight: 0-2 Gall: 0-0
Aids: Bl: 0-0 Vi: 0-0 Tstrap: 0-0
Best Rating: 101 11/01 Hrfd 2m good Ch

Lanmire Leader (IRE)

88(95h) (92h)92
7-y-o b g Supreme Leader-Dark Fluff (Mandalus)
A Ennis Equine America Uk

Placings: *06*-2P5225 (4056)
2001/02: 22^{2}HY, 21^{P}G, 20^{5}G, 21^{2}S, 20^{2}S, 20^{5}S

	Starts	1st	2nd	3rd	Win & Pl
Hurdles	2	0	1	0	670
Chases	4	0	2	0	2239
Career Total	**8**	**0**	**3**	**0**	**2909**

Going: Sf: 0-4 GS: 0-0 Gd: 0-2 GF: - Fm: 0-0
Distance: 2m/2m3: 0-0 2m4-2m7: 0-6 3m+: 0-0
Track: LH: 0-1 RH: 0-4 Tight: 0-4 Gall: 0-0
Aids: Bl: 0-0 Vi: 0-0 Tstrap: 0-0
Best Rating: 92 2/02 Leic 2m4f110y soft Ch

He is a modest sort over hurdles and fences at around two and a half miles, although he has recently been tried over further. Acts on soft ground.

Lanmire Tower (IRE)

109(109h) 139
8-y-o b g Celio Rufo-Lanigans Tower (The Parson)
J J O'Neill Rowfield Racing

Placings: *00*/F050R/501134/2035-**12P1F13** (4903)
2001/02: 24^{1}G, 22^{2}G, 24^{P}G, 24^{1}G, 32^{F}GS, 25^{1}G, 24^{3}G

	Starts	1st	2nd	3rd	Win & Pl
Chases	7	3	1	1	26766
Career Total	**24**	**5**	**2**	**3**	**34453**

139	4/02	Chel	3m1f110y	B Ch	GD	£15008
139	2/02	Ludl	3m	E Ch	GD	£3425
95	10/01	Hntg	3m	E Ch	GD	£3626
107	10/99	Weth	3m1f	F(0-100)HHdl	GD	£1835
100	10/99	Carl	2m4f110y	E(0-105)HHdl	GD	£2332

Total win prize-money £26227

Going: Sf: 0-0 GS: 0-1 Gd: 3-6 GF: - Fm: 0-0
Distance: 2m/2m3: 0-0 2m4-2m7: 0-1 **3m+: 3-6**
Track: LH: 1-4 **RH: 2-3** Tight: 1-1 **Gall: 2-5**
Aids: **Bl: 2-4** Vi: 0-0 Tstrap: 0-0
Best Rating: 139 4/02 Chel 3m1f110y good Ch

A fair novice chaser, he stays three miles and seems best on a right-handed track. Rather a quirky sort, he likes good ground and won under those conditions at Huntingdon and Ludlow, but was fortunate to win his third novice chase of the season at Cheltenham in April 2002.

Lannkar (IRE)

101 125
6-y-o b g Bob Back (USA)-Lankarana (Auction Ring (USA))
M C Pipe D A Johnson

Placings: *15*/3231-13 (0346)
2001/02: 20^{1}F, 20^{3}G

	Starts	1st	2nd	3rd	Win & Pl
Hurdles	2	1	0	1	2745
Career Total	**8**	**3**	**1**	**3**	**11083**

125	5/01	Sthl	2m4f110y	E Hdl	FRM	£2233
112	4/01	MRas	2m3f110y	D Hdl	G-S	£4228
115	1/00	Ludl	2m	H NHF	G-S	£1725

Total win prize-money £8187

Going: Sf: 0-0 GS: 0-0 Gd: 0-1 GF: - Fm: 1-1
Distance: 2m/2m3: 0-0 **2m4-2m7: 1-2** 3m+: 0-0
Track: **LH: 1-2** RH: 0-0 **Tight: 1-2** Gall: 0-0
Aids: Bl: 0-0 Vi: 0-0 Tstrap: 0-0
Best Rating: 125 5/01 Aint 2m4f good Hdl

Lannkaran (IRE)

111 135
9-y-o b g Shardari-Lankarana (Auction Ring (USA))
H D Daly The Hon Mr Simon Sainsbury

Placings: 0211/05/**313411**/643P1-P3FP0214 (4845)
2001/02: 20^{P}GS, 21^{3}S, 22^{F}HY, 20^{P}S, 24^{0}G, 20^{2}S, 22^{1}G, 24^{4}G

	Starts	1st	2nd	3rd	Win & Pl
Hurdles	1	0	0	0	0
Chases	7	1	1	1	7326
Career Total	**25**	**7**	**2**	**4**	**34359**

135	4/02	Towc	2m6f	D(0-125)HCh	GD	£5252
127	4/01	Hntg	3m	D(0-120)HCh	SFT	£4855
144	4/00	Strf	3m	D Ch	GD	£4374
134	3/00	Towc	2m6f	E Ch	SFT	£3198
125	12/99	Towc	2m6f	D Ch	SFT	£4574
131	4/98	Chel	2m1f	D Hdl	HVY	£3680
124	3/98	Chep	2m110y	E Hdl	GD	£2444

Total win prize-money £28380

Going: Sf: 0-4 GS: 0-1 Gd: 1-3 GF: - Fm: 0-0
Distance: 2m/2m3: 0-0 **2m4-2m7: 1-6** 3m+: 0-2
Track: LH: 0-5 **RH: 1-3** Tight: 0-4 Gall: 0-0
Aids: Bl: 0-1 Vi: 0-0 Tstrap: 0-0
Best Rating: 144 4/00 Strf 3m good Ch

A smart hurdler, he did well when switched to fences in the 1999/2000 season and is an effective sort in handicap chases at around three miles. His best form of late has come at around two and a half miles. Best on soft ground and appreciates prominent tactics.

Lanos (POL)

90 89
4-y-o ch g Special Power-Lubeka (POL) (Milione (FR))
T R George Mrs S Nelson,Allan Stennett,Terry Warner

Placings: 03 (4284)
2001/02: 16^{0}G, 17^{3}GS

	Starts	1st	2nd	3rd	Win & Pl
Hurdles	2	0	0	1	565
Career Total	**2**	**0**	**0**	**1**	**565**

Going: Sf: 0-0 GS: 0-1 Gd: 0-1 GF: - Fm: 0-0
Distance: 2m/2m3: 0-2 2m4-2m7: 0-0 3m+: 0-0
Track: LH: 0-0 RH: 0-2 Tight: 0-1 Gall: 0-0
Aids: Bl: 0-0 Vi: 0-0 Tstrap: 0-0
Best Rating: 89 3/02 MRas 2m1f110y gd-sft Hdl

Prolific winner on the Flat in his native Poland but struggling to make his mark over hurdles here.

Lanoso (IRE)

4-y-o b g Charnwood Forest (IRE)-Silver Spark (USA) (Silver Hawk (USA))
H M Kavanagh (C R Egerton 27/6) Mrs S Kavanagh

Placings: P (2162)
2001/02: 16^{P}G

	Starts	1st	2nd	3rd	Win & Pl
Hurdles	1	0	0	0	
Career Total	**1**	**0**	**0**	**0**	

Going: Sf: 0-0 GS: 0-0 Gd: 0-1 GF: - Fm: 0-0
Distance: 2m/2m3: 0-1 2m4-2m7: 0-0 3m+: 0-0
Track: LH: 0-1 RH: 0-0 Tight: 0-0 Gall: 0-0
Aids: Bl: 0-0 Vi: 0-0 Tstrap: 0-1
Best Rating:

Lantaur Lad (IRE)

102 113
8-y-o b g Brush Aside (USA)-Gleann Oge (Proverb)
A King Lady Harris

Placings: 2 (3996)
2001/02: 24^{2}S

	Starts	1st	2nd	3rd	Win & Pl
Chases	1	0	1	0	1016
Career Total	**1**	**0**	**1**	**0**	**1016**

Going: Sf: 0-1 GS: 0-0 Gd: 0-0 GF: - Fm: 0-0
Distance: 2m/2m3: 0-0 2m4-2m7: 0-0 3m+: 0-1
Track: LH: 0-1 RH: 0-0 Tight: 0-0 Gall: 0-1
Aids: Bl: 0-0 Vi: 0-0 Tstrap: 0-0
Best Rating: 113 3/02 Donc 3m soft Ch

A grand, big type, he won two Irish points and ran a fine first race here when runner up in a novices' chase at Doncaster in March.

Lantic Bay

90 63
5-y-o b m Afzal-Silent Dancer (Quiet Fling (USA))
J C Tuck J C Tuck

Placings: P-4P0 (2137)
2001/02: 18^{4}GF, 16^{P}S, 17^{0}G

	Starts	1st	2nd	3rd	Win & Pl
Hurdles	3	0	0	0	0
Career Total	**4**	**0**	**0**	**0**	**0**

Going: Sf: 0-1 GS: 0-0 Gd: 0-1 GF: - Fm: 0-1
Distance: 2m/2m3: 0-3 2m4-2m7: 0-0 3m+: 0-0
Track: LH: 0-2 RH: 0-1 Tight: 0-3 Gall: 0-0
Aids: Bl: 0-0 Vi: 0-0 Tstrap: 0-0
Best Rating: 63 11/01 Tntn 2m1f good Hdl

Lanzerac

108 148
5-y-o b g Lycius (USA)-Watership (USA) (Foolish Pleasure (USA))
John A Harris (J L Harris 28/5) Cleartherm Ltd

Placings: *46-42*2213230 (4665)
2001/02: 16^{4}GF, 16^{2}GF, 16^{2}G, 16^{2}G, 20^{1}S, 21^{3}S, 21^{2}S, 21^{3}GS, 24^{0}G

	Starts	1st	2nd	3rd	Win & Pl
NH Flat	2	0	1	0	482
Hurdles	7	1	3	2	20721
Career Total	**11**	**1**	**4**	**2**	**21203**

96	12/01	Leic	2m4f110y	D Hdl	SFT	£3562

Total win prize-money £3562

Going: Sf: 1-3 GS: 0-1 Gd: 0-3 GF: - Fm: 0-2
Distance: 2m/2m3: 0-4 **2m4-2m7: 1-4** 3m+: 0-1
Track: LH: 0-4 **RH: 1-3** Tight: 0-1 Gall: 0-4
Aids: Bl: 0-0 Vi: 0-0 Tstrap: 0-0
Best Rating: 148 3/02 Chel 2m5f gd-sft Hdl

A decent front-running hurdler, he acts on good and soft ground and is effective from two miles to two miles five furlongs. Ran really well to be third in the Royal &

SunAlliance Hurdle at the 2002 Festival.

Lanzlo (FR)

110 **115**

5-y-o b/br g Le Balafre (FR)-L'Eternite (FR) (Cariellor (FR))

P J Hobbs Winton Bloodstock Ltd

Placings:120F23-115500 **(4853)**

2001/02: 16^{1}G, 16^{1}GF, 20^{5}GF, 16^{5}G, 16^{0}GF, 16^{0}G

	Starts	1st	2nd	3rd	Win & Pl
Hurdles	6	2	0	0	6479
Career Total	**12**	**3**	**2**	**1**	**11970**

113	9/01	Strf	2m110y	D(0-125)HHdl	G-F	£3458
115	7/01	Strf	2m110y	F(0-110)HHdl	GD	£3020
115	9/00	Chep	2m110y	D Hdl	GD	£3347

Total win prize-money £9827

Going: Sf: 0-0 GS: 0-0 Gd: 1-3 GF: - Fm: 1-3
Distance: **2m/2m3: 2-5** 2m4-2m7: 0-1 3m+: 0-0
Track: **LH: 2-5** RH: 0-1 **Tight: 2-3** Gall: 0-0
Aids: Bl: 0-0 Vi: 0-0 Tstrap: 0-0
Best Rating: 115 7/01 Strf 2m110y good Hdl

Modest handicap hurdler, effective on a sound surface.

Laouen (FR)

103f **129f**

4-y-o br g Funny Baby (FR)-Olive Noire (FR) (Cadoudal (FR))

L Lungo Ashley Bank Investments & Dr K Fraser

Placings:*12* **(4841)**

2001/02: 16^{1}HY, 16^{2}G

	Starts	1st	2nd	3rd	Win & Pl
NH Flat	2	1	1	0	2744
Career Total	**2**	**1**	**1**	**0**	**2744**

106	3/02	Ayr	2m	H NHF	HVY	£1788

Total win prize-money £1780

Going: Sf: 1-1 GS: 0-0 Gd: 0-1 GF: - Fm: 0-0
Distance: **2m/2m3: 1-2** 2m4-2m7: 0-0 3m+: 0-0
Track: **LH: 1-2** RH: 0-0 Tight: 0-0 Gall: 0-0
Aids: Bl: 0-0 Vi: 0-0 Tstrap: 0-0
Best Rating: 129 4/02 Ayr 2m good NHF

Winning bumper performer. Effective over two miles.

Lapland (IRE)

72 **84**

5-y-o b g Arctic Lord-Ride Of Honour (King's Ride)

N A Callaghan G C Hartigan

Placings:P25 **(3142)**

2001/02: 16^{P}S, 20^{2}S, 23^{5}S

	Starts	1st	2nd	3rd	Win & Pl
Hurdles	3	0	1	0	1096
Career Total	**3**	**0**	**1**	**0**	**1096**

Going: Sf: 0-3 GS: 0-0 Gd: 0-0 GF: - Fm: 0-0
Distance: 2m/2m3: 0-1 2m4-2m7: 0-1 3m+: 0-1
Track: LH: 0-2 RH: 0-1 Tight: 0-2 Gall: 0-0
Aids: Bl: 0-0 Vi: 0-0 Tstrap: 0-0
Best Rating: 84 12/01 Leic 2m4f110y soft Hdl

Acts on soft ground and is effective at two miles four furlongs.

Last Option

10-y-o br g Primitive Rising (USA)-Saint Motunde (Tyrant (USA))

R Tate R Tate

Placings:12/21O3231/121F2/33P4-431U6 **(4839)**

2001/02: 26^{4}G, 24^{3}S, 26^{1}G, 21^{U}G, 33^{6}G

	Starts	1st	2nd	3rd	Win & Pl
Chases	5	1	0	1	26949
Career Total	**23**	**6**	**5**	**5**	**61550**

139	3/02	Chel	3m2f110y	B Ch	GD	£26000
118	4/00	Towc	2m6f	H Ch	GD	£1610
132	5/99	Strf	3m	H Ch	G-S	£2136
135	4/99	Chel	3m2f110y	H Ch	GD	£3598
114	5/98	Strf	3m4f	H Ch	GD	£5507
106	4/98	Weth	3m1f	H Ch	G-S	£1067

Total win prize-money £39920

Going: Sf: 0-1 GS: 0-0 Gd: 1-4 GF: - Fm: 0-0
Distance: 2m/2m3: 0-0 2m4-2m7: 0-1 **3m+: 1-4**
Track: **LH: 1-4** RH: 0-0 Tight: 0-1 **Gall: 1-2**
Aids: Bl: 0-0 Vi: 0-0 Tstrap: 0-0
Best Rating: 139 3/02 Chel 3m2f110y good Ch

A leading hunter chaser, he was fourth in the Scottish Grand National in 2001 and landed the Cheltenham Foxhunters' in 2002. He clearly stays marathon distances and appreciates decent ground.

Last Symphony

5-y-o b g Last Tycoon-Dancing Heights (IRE) (High Estate)

Denys Smith (J A Moore 20/2) Mrs J M Moore

Placings:FP **(3856)**

2001/02: 16^{F}HY, 16^{P}S

	Starts	1st	2nd	3rd	Win & Pl
Hurdles	2	0	0	0	
Career Total	**2**	**0**	**0**	**0**	

Going: Sf: 0-2 GS: 0-0 Gd: 0-0 GF: - Fm: 0-0
Distance: 2m/2m3: 0-2 2m4-2m7: 0-0 3m+: 0-0
Track: LH: 0-2 RH: 0-0 Tight: 0-0 Gall: 0-1
Aids: Bl: 0-0 Vi: 0-0 Tstrap: 0-0
Best Rating:

Last Try (IRE)

104 **114**

11-y-o ch g Try My Best (USA)-Alpenwind (Tumble Wind (USA))

B S Rothwell H J Harenberg

Placings:*555*/60611430/**42631/4412522446/3133221 21236/302U42223-04356000** **(4872)**

2001/02: 16^{0}G, 16^{4}GF, 16^{3}GS, 16^{5}S, 19^{6}GF, 16^{0}S, 17^{0}GF, 16^{0}GF

	Starts	1st	2nd	3rd	Win & Pl
Chases	8	0	0	1	1213
Career Total	**55**	**7**	**12**	**9**	**51836**

119	10/99	Bang	2m4f110y	D(0-125)HCh	SFT	£6175
116	9/99	Sedg	2m5f	E(0-115)HCh	GD	£4146
118	6/99	Uttx	2m	D(0-120)HCh	GD	£3712
103	6/98	Uttx	2m	D(0-120)HCh	GD	£4084
112	3/98	Sedg	2m110y	C Ch	G-S	£5670
99	12/96	Catt	2m	F(0-95)HHdl	GD	£2138
94	11/96	Catt	2m	E(0-100)HHdl	G-F	£1830

Total win prize-money £27758

Going: Sf: 0-2 GS: 0-1 Gd: 0-1 GF: - Fm: 0-4
Distance: 2m/2m3: 0-8 2m4-2m7: 0-0 3m+: 0-0
Track: LH: 0-8 RH: 0-0 Tight: 0-4 Gall: 0-1
Aids: Bl: 0-0 Vi: 0-0 Tstrap: 0-8
Best Rating: 121 2/01 Sedg 2m110y soft Ch

Fair handicap chaser. Best suited by two/two and a half miles. Has run well at Sedgefield. Last won back in 1999. Acts on soft ground.

Lastman (USA)

101(109c) (124c)**108**

7-y-o b/br g Fabulous Dancer (USA)-Rivala (USA) (Riverman (USA))

J G Portman (J J O'Neill 12/10) Two Generations Partnership

Placings:0532/PPP16022/**2F2**F**2345-251351P**3U002 **(4550)**

2001/02: 20^{2}GS, 20^{5}GS, 16^{1}F, 16^{3}F, 16^{5}GF, 20^{1}G, 20^{P}GS, 19^{3}GS, 19^{U}G, 18^{0}HY, 16^{0}S, 21^{2}GF

	Starts	1st	2nd	3rd	Win & Pl
Hurdles	5	0	1	1	1599
Chases	7	2	1	1	8596
Career Total	**32**	**3**	**8**	**4**	**20659**

124	10/01	Hntg	2m4f110y	E(0-105)HCh	GD	£3090
89	5/01	Hexm	2m110y	E Ch	FRM	£3013
109	2/00	Muss	2m	E Hdl	G-S	£2296

Total win prize-money £8400

Going: Sf: 0-2 GS: 0-4 Gd: 1-2 GF: - Fm: 1-4
Distance: 2m/2m3: 1-7 2m4-2m7: 1-5 3m+: 0-0
Track: LH: 1-6 RH: 1-6 Tight: 0-3 **Gall: 1-5**
Aids: Bl: 0-0 Vi: 0-0 Tstrap: 0-0
Best Rating: 128 9/00 Uttx 3m gd-sft Ch

Goes well over two miles and acts on most types of ground, but is most effective on a sound surface. Has switched back to hurdles in late 2001/early 2002.

Lastofthecash

6-y-o b g Ballacashtal (CAN)-Blue Empress (Blue Cashmere)

Dr P Pritchard Three Of A Kind Racing

Placings:00 **(2657)**

2001/02: 16^{0}S, 19^{0}GS

	Starts	1st	2nd	3rd	Win & Pl
Hurdles	2	0	0	0	
Career Total	**2**	**0**	**0**	**0**	

Going: Sf: 0-1 GS: 0-1 Gd: 0-0 GF: - Fm: 0-0
Distance: 2m/2m3: 0-1 2m4-2m7: 0-1 3m+: 0-0
Track: LH: 0-1 RH: 0-1 Tight: 0-1 Gall: 0-0
Aids: Bl: 0-0 Vi: 0-0 Tstrap: 0-0
Best Rating:

Latalomne (USA)

116(113h) **176**

8-y-o ch g Zilzal (USA)-Sanctuary (Welsh Pageant)

B Ellison Alderclad Roofing/k M Everitt

Placings:13/0111-15F6 **(4663)**

2001/02: 16^{1}G, 16^{5}GS, 16^{F}GS, 20^{6}G

	Starts	1st	2nd	3rd	Win & Pl
Chases	4	1	0	0	18019
Career Total	**10**	**5**	**0**	**1**	**35915**

168	11/01	Chel	2m	B(0-145)HCh	GD	£14218
143	2/01	Sedg	2m5f	E Ch	G-S	£3103
135	1/01	Muss	2m	E Ch	G-S	£3393
134	1/01	Muss	2m	D Ch	GD	£4270
119	2/00	Catt	2m	E Hdl	GD	£3103

Total win prize-money £28091

Going: Sf: 0-0 GS: 0-2 Gd: 1-2 GF: - Fm: 0-0
Distance: **2m/2m3: 1-3** 2m4-2m7: 0-1 3m+: 0-0
Track: **LH: 1-3** RH: 0-1 Tight: 0-1 **Gall: 1-2**

Aids: Bl: 0-0 Vi: 0-0 Tstrap: 0-0
Best Rating: 176 3/02 Chel 2m gd-sft Ch

He won a competitive handicap at the Thomas Pink meeting at Cheltenham, but found the easy ground against him when taking on the top two-milers in the Tingle Creek. He was in front when crashing out two out in the Queen Mother Champion Chase but flopped at Aintree over two and a half. Still has time to vindicate his trainer's high opinion of him. Still unexposed, he usually jumps well and remains a decent prospect for better-class two-mile chases.

Latchford (IRE)

92(95h) **108**

10-y-o ch g Carlingford Castle-Comeragh Princess (Le Moss)
Ian Williams Ten Strong Racing

Placings:00241/11PFF/21P4/0F0P-3F **(0662)**
2001/02: 24^{3}GF, 24^{F}F

	Starts	1st	2nd	3rd	Win & Pl
Chases	2	0	0	1	542
Career Total	**20**	**4**	**2**	**1**	**16380**

117	5/99	Uttx	3m110y	B(0-140)HHdl	G-F	£6123
119	5/98	Prth	3m110y	D(0-120)HHdl	G-F	£2818
110	5/98	Font	2m6f110y	E(0-110)HHdl	GD	£2553
116	4/98	Worc	3m	E(0-100)HHdl	G-S	£2110

Total win prize-money £13606

Going: Sf: 0-0 GS: 0-0 Gd: 0-0 GF: - Fm: 0-2
Distance: 2m/2m3: 0-0 2m4-2m7: 0-0 3m+: 0-2
Track: LH: 0-0 RH: 0-2 Tight: 0-0 Gall: 0-1
Aids: Bl: 0-0 Vi: 0-0 Tstrap: 0-0
Best Rating: 119 5/98 Prth 3m110y gd-fm Hdl

Late Arrival

49

5-y-o b g Emperor Jones (USA)-Try Vickers (USA) (Fuzzbuster (USA))
A Crook (D Morris 25/5) The Adbrokes Partnership

Placings:0F **(1676)**
2001/02: 16^{0}G, 17^{F}G

	Starts	1st	2nd	3rd	Win & Pl
Hurdles	2	0	0	0	
Career Total	**2**	**0**	**0**	**0**	

Going: Sf: 0-0 GS: 0-0 Gd: 0-2 GF: - Fm: 0-0
Distance: 2m/2m3: 0-2 2m4-2m7: 0-0 3m+: 0-0
Track: LH: 0-1 RH: 0-1 Tight: 0-1 Gall: 0-0
Aids: Bl: 0-0 Vi: 0-0 Tstrap: 0-0
Best Rating: 49 10/01 Sedg 2m1f good Hdl

Late Harvest (NZ)

90(95h) (83h)**84**

10-y-o b g Tarrago (ITY)-Pamira (AUS) (Nassau (AUS))
A J Deakin (B P J Baugh 31/7) A J Deakin

Placings:5/P05/203233FP**05-65063FP0** **(4757)**
2001/02: 16^{6}F, 16^{5}F, 22^{0}GF, 16^{6}G, 16^{3}S, 20^{F}GF, 20^{P}GF, 16^{0}GF

	Starts	1st	2nd	3rd	Win & Pl
Hurdles	3	0	0	0	0
Chases	5	0	0	1	424
Career Total	**22**	**0**	**2**	**4**	**3091**

Going: Sf: 0-1 GS: 0-0 Gd: 0-1 GF: - Fm: 0-6
Distance: 2m/2m3: 0-5 2m4-2m7: 0-3 3m+: 0-0
Track: LH: 0-7 RH: 0-1 Tight: 0-3 Gall: 0-0
Aids: Bl: 0-0 Vi: 0-3 Tstrap: 0-0
Best Rating: 91 9/00 Hrfd 2m3f110y gd-sft Hdl

Modest dual-purpose handicapper over the minimum trip.

Lateagain

79 **49**

7-y-o b g Be My Native (USA)-Ruckinge Girl (Eborneezer)
A Parker R A Bartlett

Placings:0PP-0 **(1467)**
2001/02: 20^{0}G

	Starts	1st	2nd	3rd	Win & Pl
Hurdles	1	0	0	0	
Career Total	**4**	**0**	**0**	**0**	

Going: Sf: 0-0 GS: 0-0 Gd: 0-1 GF: - Fm: 0-0
Distance: 2m/2m3: 0-0 2m4-2m7: 0-1 3m+: 0-0
Track: LH: 0-0 RH: 0-1 Tight: 0-0 Gall: 0-0
Aids: Bl: 0-0 Vi: 0-0 Tstrap: 0-0
Best Rating: 49 4/01 Muss 2m1f gd-fm Hdl

Lateen

81 **27**

7-y-o b m Midyan (USA)-Sail Loft (Shirley Heights)
J E Collinson Mrs E M Collinson

Placings:0 **(0914)**
2001/02: 22^{0}GF

	Starts	1st	2nd	3rd	Win & Pl
Hurdles	1	0	0	0	
Career Total	**1**	**0**	**0**	**0**	

Going: Sf: 0-0 GS: 0-0 Gd: 0-0 GF: - Fm: 0-1
Distance: 2m/2m3: 0-0 2m4-2m7: 0-1 3m+: 0-0
Track: LH: 0-1 RH: 0-0 Tight: 0-1 Gall: 0-0
Aids: Bl: 0-0 Vi: 0-0 Tstrap: 0-0
Best Rating: 27 7/01 Strf 2m6f110y gd-fm Hdl

Latimer's Place

113 **110**

6-y-o b g Teenoso (USA)-Pennethorne Place (Deep Run)
G B Balding Sir Christopher Wates

Placings:01641 **(4154)**
2001/02: 17^{0}G, 17^{1}GS, 16^{6}GS, 20^{4}HY, 20^{1}GS

	Starts	1st	2nd	3rd	Win & Pl
NH Flat	1	0	0	0	0
Hurdles	4	2	0	0	24987
Career Total	**5**	**2**	**0**	**0**	**24987**

110	3/02	Sand	2m4f110y	A HHdl	G-S	£21460
103	12/01	Extr	2m1f	E Hdl	G-S	£3185

Total win prize-money £24645

Going: Sf: 0-1 GS: 2-3 Gd: 0-1 GF: - Fm: 0-0
Distance: 2m/2m3: 1-3 2m4-2m7: 1-2 3m+: 0-0
Track: LH: 0-0 **RH: 2-5** Tight: 0-0 Gall: 0-1
Aids: Bl: 0-0 Vi: 0-0 Tstrap: 0-0
Best Rating: 110 3/02 Sand 2m4f110y gd-sft Hdl

Surprise winner of a novices' hurdle at Exeter in December 2001, he went on to land the EBF Final at Sandown in March 2002. Stays two and a half miles and looks best on good ground.

Latin Bay

(79h) (28h)

7-y-o b g Superlative-Hugging (Beveled (USA))
A E Jones Mrs Susan Pullin

Placings:500/050-0P **(4560)**
2001/02: 17^{0}GF, 17^{P}GF

	Starts	1st	2nd	3rd	Win & Pl
Hurdles	1	0	0	0	0
Chases	1	0	0	0	0
Career Total	**8**	**0**	**0**	**0**	**0**

Going: Sf: 0-0 GS: 0-0 Gd: 0-0 GF: - Fm: 0-2
Distance: 2m/2m3: 0-2 2m4-2m7: 0-0 3m+: 0-0
Track: LH: 0-2 RH: 0-0 Tight: 0-2 Gall: 0-0
Aids: Bl: 0-0 Vi: 0-0 Tstrap: 0-0
Best Rating: 67 7/00 Worc 2m4f gd-fm Hdl

Latour

5-y-o b/br m Sri Pekan (USA)-Fenny Rough (Home Guard (USA))
A M Hales Andrew L Cohen

Placings:PP **(2064)**
2001/02: 16^{P}GS, 16^{P}G

	Starts	1st	2nd	3rd	Win & Pl
Hurdles	2	0	0	0	
Career Total	**2**	**0**	**0**	**0**	

Going: Sf: 0-0 GS: 0-1 Gd: 0-1 GF: - Fm: 0-0
Distance: 2m/2m3: 0-2 2m4-2m7: 0-0 3m+: 0-0
Track: LH: 0-1 RH: 0-1 Tight: 0-1 Gall: 0-1
Aids: Bl: 0-0 Vi: 0-1 Tstrap: 0-0
Best Rating:

Latterly (USA)

(105h) (81h)

7-y-o b g Cryptoclearance (USA)-Latest Scandal (USA) (Two Davids (USA))
F Jordan F Jordan

Placings:00/P-P403304**PU** **(1804)**
2001/02: 19^{P}G, 17^{4}F, 16^{0}GF, 20^{3}GF, 19^{3}GF, 24^{0}GF, 22^{4}GF, 25^{P}S, 24^{U}GF

	Starts	1st	2nd	3rd	Win & Pl
Hurdles	7	0	0	2	487
Chases	2	0	0	0	0
Career Total	**12**	**0**	**0**	**2**	**487**

Going: Sf: 0-1 GS: 0-0 Gd: 0-1 GF: - Fm: 0-7
Distance: 2m/2m3: 0-3 2m4-2m7: 0-3 3m+: 0-3
Track: LH: 0-5 RH: 0-4 Tight: 0-4 Gall: 0-0
Aids: Bl: 0-1 Vi: 0-0 Tstrap: 0-7
Best Rating: 81 6/01 Hrfd 2m1f firm Hdl

Laudation (IRE)

10-y-o ch g Bold Arrangement-Hooray Lady (Ahonoora)
Mrs D A Hamer C J Hamer

Placings:6/P0P **(3987)**
2001/02: 17^{P}S, 17^{0}S, 19^{P}S

	Starts	1st	2nd	3rd	Win & Pl
Hurdles	3	0	0	0	
Career Total	**4**	**0**	**0**	**0**	

Going: Sf: 0-3 GS: 0-0 Gd: 0-0 GF: - Fm: 0-0
Distance: 2m/2m3: 0-2 2m4-2m7: 0-1 3m+: 0-0
Track: LH: 0-0 RH: 0-3 Tight: 0-2 Gall: 0-0
Aids: Bl: 0-0 Vi: 0-1 Tstrap: 0-0

Best Rating:

Lauderdale

105(99h) (81h)101

6-y-o b g Sula Bula-Miss Tullulah (Hubble Bubble)
Miss Lucinda V Russell Kelso Members Lowflyers Club

Placings:*206P5P*-550001P60 **(4687)**
2001/02: 16^{5}S, 16^{5}G, 20^{0}S, 16^{0}G, 22^{0}GS, 24^{1}HY, 24^{P}HY, 27^{6}S, 25^{0}GF

	Starts	1st	2nd	3rd	Win & Pl
Hurdles	8	1	0	0	3080
Chases	1	0	0	0	0
Career Total	**15**	**1**	**1**	**0**	**3714**

81 2/02 Ayr 3m110y E Hdl HVY £3080
Total win prize-money £3080

Going: Sf: 1-5 GS: 0-1 Gd: 0-2 GF: - Fm: 0-1
Distance: 2m/2m3: 0-3 2m4-2m7: 0-2 **3m+: 1-4**
Track: **LH: 1-6** RH: 0-2 Tight: 0-4 Gall: 0-0
Aids: Bl: 0-0 Vi: 0-0 Tstrap: 0-0
Best Rating: 91 4/02 Kels 3m1f gd-fm Ch

Shock winner of a novice hurdle at Ayr in February 2002, stamina is his forte.

Laugharne Park (IRE)

74 40

5-y-o b g Fourstars Allstar (USA)-Frantesa (Red Sunset)
Miss Venetia Williams Seasons Holidays

Placings:6-4P **(1406)**
2001/02: 22^{4}G, 16^{P}GF

	Starts	1st	2nd	3rd	Win & Pl
Hurdles	2	0	0	0	0
Career Total	3	0	0	0	0

Going: Sf: 0-0 GS: 0-0 Gd: 0-1 GF: - Fm: 0-1
Distance: 2m/2m3: 0-1 2m4-2m7: 0-1 3m+: 0-0
Track: LH: 0-2 RH: 0-0 Tight: 0-1 Gall: 0-0
Aids: Bl: 0-1 Vi: 0-0 Tstrap: 0-0
Best Rating: 48 3/01 Plum 2m heavy Hdl

Laundmower

96f 96f

6-y-o br g Perpendicular-Sound Work (Workboy)
Mrs S J Smith John Endersby

Placings:*3* **(4098)**
2001/02: 16^{3}GS

	Starts	1st	2nd	3rd	Win & Pl
NH Flat	1	0	0	1	246
Career Total	1	0	0	1	246

Going: Sf: 0-0 GS: 0-1 Gd: 0-0 GF: - Fm: 0-0
Distance: 2m/2m3: 0-1 2m4-2m7: 0-0 3m+: 0-0
Track: LH: 0-1 RH: 0-0 Tight: 0-1 Gall: 0-0
Aids: Bl: 0-0 Vi: 0-0 Tstrap: 0-0
Best Rating: 96 3/02 Catt 2m gd-sft NHF

Third on his debut in a modest bumper at Catterick in March.

Laurel Prince

108 98

6-y-o b g Reprimand-Laurel Queen (IRE) (Viking (USA))
W Clay (F Lloyd 1/3) F Lloyd

Placings:456342/0433624120-640033F06U5P55 **(4847)**
2001/02: 20^{6}G, 16^{4}G, 19^{0}G, 19^{0}G, 16^{3}GF, 16^{3}GF, 20^{F}G, 20^{0}S, 16^{6}S, 17^{U}G, 17^{5}HY, 16^{P}S, 17^{5}G, 20^{5}G

	Starts	1st	2nd	3rd	Win & Pl
Hurdles	14	0	0	2	1003
Career Total	**30**	**1**	**3**	**5**	**8018**

98 1/01 Donc 2m110y F(0-100)HHdl GD £2159
Total win prize-money £2160

Going: Sf: 0-4 GS: 0-0 Gd: 0-8 GF: - Fm: 0-2
Distance: 2m/2m3: 0-9 2m4-2m7: 0-5 3m+: 0-0
Track: LH: 0-9 RH: 0-5 Tight: 0-5 Gall: 0-2
Aids: Bl: 0-0 Vi: 0-6 Tstrap: 0-0
Best Rating: 98 5/01 Weth 2m good Hdl

Moderate handicap hurdler at around two miles on a sound surface.

Laurieston Flo (IRE)

4-y-o b f Nicolotte-Brown Foam (Horage)
J W Mullins (B J Meehan 3/5) Mrs Caroline Taylor

Placings:5 **(1481)**
2001/02: 16^{5}GS

	Starts	1st	2nd	3rd	Win & Pl
Hurdles	1	0	0	0	0
Career Total	1	0	0	0	0

Going: Sf: 0-0 GS: 0-1 Gd: 0-0 GF: - Fm: 0-0
Distance: 2m/2m3: 0-1 2m4-2m7: 0-0 3m+: 0-0
Track: LH: 0-1 RH: 0-0 Tight: 0-1 Gall: 0-0
Aids: Bl: 0-0 Vi: 0-0 Tstrap: 0-0
Best Rating:

Lava

81 69

6-y-o b m Tragic Role (USA)-Dishcloth (Fury Royal)
G B Balding Mrs Geoffrey Reeve

Placings:*0-0P60* **(3383)**
2001/02: 16^{0}G, 21^{P}S, 16^{6}G, 16^{0}GS

	Starts	1st	2nd	3rd	Win & Pl
NH Flat	1	0	0	0	0
Hurdles	3	0	0	0	0
Career Total	5	0	0	0	0

Going: Sf: 0-1 GS: 0-1 Gd: 0-2 GF: - Fm: 0-0
Distance: 2m/2m3: 0-3 2m4-2m7: 0-1 3m+: 0-0
Track: LH: 0-1 RH: 0-3 Tight: 0-0 Gall: 0-0
Aids: Bl: 0-0 Vi: 0-0 Tstrap: 0-0
Best Rating: 79 11/00 Extr 2m1f gd-sft NHF

Lavender Lady (IRE)

98 85

6-y-o b/br m Lord Americo-Polarogan (Tarqogan)
G M Moore A J Racehorses

Placings:*0-044P* **(4304)**
2001/02: 17^{0}G, 16^{4}S, 17^{4}GS, 16^{P}S

	Starts	1st	2nd	3rd	Win & Pl
NH Flat	3	0	0	0	0
Hurdles	1	0	0	0	0
Career Total	5	0	0	0	0

Going: Sf: 0-2 GS: 0-1 Gd: 0-1 GF: - Fm: 0-0
Distance: 2m/2m3: 0-4 2m4-2m7: 0-0 3m+: 0-0
Track: LH: 0-2 RH: 0-1 Tight: 0-2 Gall: 0-0
Aids: Bl: 0-0 Vi: 0-0 Tstrap: 0-0
Best Rating: 88 3/02 MRas 2m1f110y gd-sft NHF

Laveron

106 136

7-y-o b/br h Konigsstuhl (GER)-La Virginia (GER) (Surumu (GER))
F Doumen D Grauert

Placings:323411
2001/02: 19^{3}HY, 24^{2}G, 22^{3}S, 21^{4}G, 18^{1}VS, 20^{1}VS

	Starts	1st	2nd	3rd	Win & Pl
Hurdles	5	1	1	2	19629
Chases	1	1	0	0	42791
Career Total	**6**	**2**	**1**	**2**	**62420**

4/02 Autl 2m4f110y HCh VS £42791
4/02 Autl 2m2f Hdl VS £11779
Total win prize-money £54570

Going: Sf: 0-2 GS: 0-0 Gd: 0-2 GF: - Fm: 0-0
Distance: 2m/2m3: 1-1 2m4-2m7: 1-4 3m+: 0-1
Track: LH: 0-1 RH: 0-3 Tight: 0-0 Gall: 0-0
Aids: Bl: 0-0 Vi: 0-0 Tstrap: 0-0
Best Rating: 123 2/02 Kemp 2m5f good Hdl

Fair French-trained novice staying hurdler, he pulls hard and does not always jump well. Acts on good to soft.

Law Unto Himself

4-y-o b g Contract Law (USA)-Malacanang (Riboboy (USA))
N J Hawke The Fairway Boys

Placings:*50* **(4506)**
2001/02: 16^{5}S, 17^{0}G

	Starts	1st	2nd	3rd	Win & Pl
NH Flat	2	0	0	0	0
Career Total	2	0	0	0	0

Going: Sf: 0-1 GS: 0-0 Gd: 0-1 GF: - Fm: 0-0
Distance: 2m/2m3: 0-2 2m4-2m7: 0-0 3m+: 0-0
Track: LH: 0-1 RH: 0-1 Tight: 0-1 Gall: 0-0
Aids: Bl: 0-0 Vi: 0-0 Tstrap: 0-0
Best Rating: 77 3/02 Winc 2m soft NHF

Lawful Contract (IRE)

7-y-o br g Contract Law (USA)-Lucciola (FR) (Auction Ring (USA))
Graeme Roe G B Perry & Roe Racing

Placings:PP/P/PP **(0773)**
2001/02: 19^{P}G, 16^{P}GF

	Starts	1st	2nd	3rd	Win & Pl
Hurdles	2	0	0	0	
Career Total	5	0	0	0	

Going: Sf: 0-0 GS: 0-0 Gd: 0-1 GF: - Fm: 0-1
Distance: 2m/2m3: 0-1 2m4-2m7: 0-1 3m+: 0-0
Track: LH: 0-1 RH: 0-1 Tight: 0-0 Gall: 0-0
Aids: Bl: 0-0 Vi: 0-0 Tstrap: 0-0
Best Rating:

Lazy But Lively (IRE)

105 110

6-y-o br g Supreme Leader-Oriel Dream (Oats)

R F Fisher S P Marsh

Placings:00662-53FF10115 **(4488)**
2001/02: 21^{5}G, 17^{3}G, 20^{F}S, 20^{F}S, 20^{1}HY, 20^{0}S, 24^{1}HY, 24^{1}HY, 20^{5}GS

	Starts	1st	2nd	3rd	Win & Pl
Hurdles	9	3	0	1	9597
Career Total	**14**	**3**	**1**	**1**	**10158**

110 3/02 Hexm 3m E Hdl HVY £2551
110 3/02 Ayr 3m110y D(0-115)HHdl HVY £3601
103 11/01 Carl 2m4f E Hdl HVY £3094
Total win prize-money £9247

Going: Sf: 3-6 GS: 0-1 Gd: 0-2 GF: - Fm: 0-0
Distance: 2m/2m3: 0-1 2m4-2m7: 1-6 **3m+: 2-2**
Track: **LH: 2-5** RH: 0-0 Tight: 0-2 Gall: 0-1
Aids: Bl: 0-0 Vi: 0-0 Tstrap: 0-0
Best Rating: 110 3/02 Hexm 3m heavy Hdl

Had looked pretty exposed prior to scoring in good style at Carlisle in November 2001. Landed a double over three miles at Ayr and Hexham in March 2002, but was well held at Carlisle after that. Goes well in heavy ground.

Lazzaz

90 **89**

4-y-o b g Muhtarram (USA)-Astern (USA) (Polish Navy (USA))
P W Hiatt (Miss H M Irving 22/6) Phil Kelly

Placings:4 **(2209)**
2001/02: 17^{4}G

	Starts	1st	2nd	3rd	Win & Pl
Hurdles	1	0	0	0	0
Career Total	**1**	**0**	**0**	**0**	**0**

Going: Sf: 0-0 GS: 0-0 Gd: 0-1 GF: - Fm: 0-0
Distance: 2m/2m3: 0-1 2m4-2m7: 0-0 3m+: 0-0
Track: LH: 0-0 RH: 0-1 Tight: 0-0 Gall: 0-0
Aids: Bl: 0-0 Vi: 0-0 Tstrap: 0-0
Best Rating: 89 11/01 Hrfd 2m1f good Hdl

Le Cabro D'Or

103 **141**

8-y-o b g Gildoran-Deirdre's Choice (Golden Love)
John R Upson Ramsay Donald Brown

Placings:12U2P3 **(4878)**
2001/02: 24^{1}S, 24^{2}GS, 26^{U}HY, 26^{2}HY, 32^{P}GS, 24^{3}G

	Starts	1st	2nd	3rd	Win & Pl
Chases	6	1	2	1	8650
Career Total	**6**	**1**	**2**	**1**	**8650**

141 11/01 Uttx 3m D Ch SFT £4483
Total win prize-money £4484

Going: Sf: 1-3 GS: 0-2 Gd: 0-1 GF: - Fm: 0-0
Distance: 2m/2m3: 0-0 2m4-2m7: 0-0 **3m+: 1-6**
Track: **LH: 1-4** RH: 0-2 Tight: 0-0 Gall: 0-2
Aids: Bl: 0-0 Vi: 0-0 Tstrap: 0-0
Best Rating: 141 1/02 Uttx 3m2f heavy Ch

He has developed into an effective front-running staying chaser suited by soft ground. Stamina is his strong suit.

Le Cavalier (USA)

86 **73**

5-y-o b g Mister Baileys-Secret Deed (USA) (Shadeed (USA))
A Bailey Ms Jayne Morton

Placings:60 **(2274)**
2001/02: 16^{6}S, 16^{0}G

	Starts	1st	2nd	3rd	Win & Pl
Hurdles	2	0	0	0	0
Career Total	**2**	**0**	**0**	**0**	**0**

Going: Sf: 0-1 GS: 0-0 Gd: 0-1 GF: - Fm: 0-0
Distance: 2m/2m3: 0-2 2m4-2m7: 0-0 3m+: 0-0
Track: LH: 0-2 RH: 0-0 Tight: 0-0 Gall: 0-0
Aids: Bl: 0-0 Vi: 0-0 Tstrap: 0-0
Best Rating: 73 11/01 Uttx 2m soft Hdl

Le Prince

(102h) (85h)**110**

7-y-o ch g Le Moss-Yuan Princess (Tender King)
H D Daly N F Williams

Placings:6363/10-2 **(0367)**
2001/02: 24^{2}G

	Starts	1st	2nd	3rd	Win & Pl
Chases	1	0	1	0	1004
Career Total	**7**	**1**	**1**	**2**	**4688**

92 11/00 Ludl 2m5f E Hdl GD £2834
Total win prize-money £2834

Going: Sf: 0-0 GS: 0-0 Gd: 0-1 GF: - Fm: 0-0
Distance: 2m/2m3: 0-0 2m4-2m7: 0-0 3m+: 0-1
Track: LH: 0-0 RH: 0-0 Tight: 0-0 Gall: 0-0
Aids: Bl: 0-0 Vi: 0-0 Tstrap: 0-0
Best Rating: 110 5/01 Wwck 3m110y good Ch

Le Roi Miguel (FR)

100 **121**

4-y-o b g Point Of No Return (FR)-Loumir (USA) (Bob's Dusty (USA))
P F Nicholls (B Dutruel 10/10) Mrs J Stewart

Placings:6212 **(3263)**
2001/02: 18^{6}VS, 18^{2}VS, 16^{1}G, 16^{2}S

	Starts	1st	2nd	3rd	Win & Pl
Hurdles	4	1	2	0	16900
Career Total	**4**	**1**	**2**	**0**	**16900**

116 11/01 Newb 2m110y C Hdl GD £5447
Total win prize-money £5447

Going: Sf: 0-1 GS: 0-0 Gd: 1-1 GF: - Fm: 0-0
Distance: **2m/2m3: 1-4** 2m4-2m7: 0-0 3m+: 0-0
Track: **LH: 1-2** RH: 0-0 Tight: 0-0 **Gall: 1-1**
Aids: Bl: 0-0 Vi: 0-0 Tstrap: 0-0
Best Rating: 121 1/02 Wwck 2m soft Hdl

Placed over hurdles in France, he beat a poor field with ease on his British debut at Newbury and ran well against older horses at Warwick. Seen as a long-term chasing prospect. Has won on good to soft ground.

Le Sauvage (IRE)

96 **85**

7-y-o b g Tirol-Cistus (Sun Prince)
D W Barker The Ebor Partnership

Placings:00/5534/1126-0P0 **(4747)**
2001/02: 20^{0}GS, 22^{P}HY, 20^{0}G

	Starts	1st	2nd	3rd	Win & Pl
Hurdles	3	0	0	0	
Career Total	**13**	**2**	**1**	**1**	**5976**

105 10/00 Carl 2m4f110y E(0-105)HHdl SFT £2497
102 10/00 Carl 2m4f110y F(0-100)HHdl G-S £2289
Total win prize-money £4787

Going: Sf: 0-1 GS: 0-1 Gd: 0-1 GF: - Fm: 0-0
Distance: 2m/2m3: 0-0 2m4-2m7: 0-3 3m+: 0-0
Track: LH: 0-1 RH: 0-1 Tight: 0-1 Gall: 0-0
Aids: Bl: 0-0 Vi: 0-0 Tstrap: 0-0
Best Rating: 110 11/00 Carl 2m4f110y heavy Hdl

Hit form, albeit belatedly, over hurdles in October 2000, but had just the one run in 2001 and has yet to find his feet in 2002. Best with cut over two and a half miles. Goes well at Carlisle.

Le Siffleur

4-y-o b g Kris-Tinashaan (IRE) (Darshaan)
J Howard Johnson Hertford Offset Limited

Placings:0 **(4750)**
2001/02: 17^{0}G

	Starts	1st	2nd	3rd	Win & Pl
NH Flat	1	0	0	0	
Career Total	**1**	**0**	**0**	**0**	

Going: Sf: 0-0 GS: 0-0 Gd: 0-1 GF: - Fm: 0-0
Distance: 2m/2m3: 0-1 2m4-2m7: 0-0 3m+: 0-0
Track: LH: 0-0 RH: 0-1 Tight: 0-0 Gall: 0-0
Aids: Bl: 0-0 Vi: 0-0 Tstrap: 0-0
Best Rating:

Le Ski D'Or

87f **75f**

6-y-o b g Petoski-Page Of Gold (Goldhill)
D R Gandolfo A W F Clapperton

Placings:60 **(2173)**
2001/02: 17^{6}S, 16^{0}S

	Starts	1st	2nd	3rd	Win & Pl
NH Flat	2	0	0	0	0
Career Total	**2**	**0**	**0**	**0**	**0**

Going: Sf: 0-2 GS: 0-0 Gd: 0-0 GF: - Fm: 0-0
Distance: 2m/2m3: 0-2 2m4-2m7: 0-0 3m+: 0-0
Track: LH: 0-2 RH: 0-0 Tight: 0-1 Gall: 0-0
Aids: Bl: 0-0 Vi: 0-0 Tstrap: 0-0
Best Rating: 75 10/01 Bang 2m1f soft NHF

Le Touquet (FR)

89 **91**

6-y-o b g Petit Loup (USA)-Vertevoie (FR) (Tip Moss (FR))
R Dickin Double Eight Ltd

Placings:6P0 **(2662)**
2001/02: 16^{6}G, 21^{P}S, 17^{0}G

	Starts	1st	2nd	3rd	Win & Pl
Hurdles	3	0	0	0	0
Career Total	**3**	**0**	**0**	**0**	**0**

Going: Sf: 0-1 GS: 0-0 Gd: 0-2 GF: - Fm: 0-0
Distance: 2m/2m3: 0-2 2m4-2m7: 0-1 3m+: 0-0
Track: LH: 0-1 RH: 0-1 Tight: 0-0 Gall: 0-1
Aids: Bl: 0-0 Vi: 0-0 Tstrap: 0-0
Best Rating: 91 12/01 Chel 2m1f good Hdl

No form of note as yet.

Leaburn (IRE)

109(96h) **138**

9-y-o b g Tremblant-Conderlea (Scorpio (FR))

P J Hobbs The Guiburn Set

Placings:2U20/1**F41124/21346-416562** **(4495)**
2001/02: 17^{4}G, 17^{1}GS, 20^{6}G, 17^{5}S, 19^{6}G, 16^{2}G

	Starts	1st	2nd	3rd	Win & Pl
Chases	6	1	1	0	7036
Career Total	**22**	**5**	**5**	**1**	**36158**

138	10/01	Strf	2m1f110y	D(0-120)HCh	G-S	£4095
140	11/00	Newb	2m1f	(0-135)Ch	HVY	£9374
135	2/00	Winc	2m	C Ch	GD	£5817
140	1/00	Tntn	2m110y	D Ch	G-S	£4192
109	12/99	Wwck	2m2f110y	E Hdl	SFT	£3095

Total win prize-money £26577

Going: Sf: 0-1 GS: 1-1 Gd: 0-4 GF: - Fm: 0-0
Distance: **2m/2m3: 1-4** 2m4-2m7: 0-2 3m+: 0-0
Track: **LH: 1-4** RH: 0-2 **Tight: 1-1** Gall: 0-2
Aids: Bl: 0-0 Vi: 0-0 **Tstrap: 1-5**
Best Rating: 140 11/00 Newb 2m1f heavy Ch

He was disappointing after winning gamely at Newbury in November and is not particularly consistent, although he did manage to get back to winning ways at Stratford in October 2001. Best in a tongue tie, he goes well on soft ground and is suited by two miles.

Lead Story (IRE)

110

9-y-o br g Lead On Time (USA)-Mashmoon (USA) (Habitat)
G Chambers Mrs M Trueman

Placings:P000/P/**21P50-6106** **(4659)**
2001/02: 21^{6}GF, 26^{1}GF, 19^{0}G, 24^{6}G

	Starts	1st	2nd	3rd	Win & Pl
Chases	4	1	0	0	2177
Career Total	**14**	**2**	**1**	**0**	**4811**

110	5/01	NAbb	3m2f110y	H Ch	G-F	£2177
122	6/00	NAbb	3m2f110y	H Ch	GD	£2177

Total win prize-money £4354

Going: Sf: 0-0 GS: 0-0 Gd: 0-2 GF: - Fm: 1-2
Distance: 2m/2m3: 0-0 2m4-2m7: 0-2 **3m+: 1-2**
Track: **LH: 1-1** RH: 0-3 **Tight: 1-2** Gall: 0-0
Aids: Bl: 0-0 Vi: 0-0 Tstrap: 0-0
Best Rating: 122 6/00 NAbb 3m2f110y good Ch

Fair staying hunter chaser, suited by three miles plus and fast ground. Has gained his two wins at newton Abbot.

Lead Vocalist (IRE)

13-y-o ch g Orchestra-Eternal Youth (Continuation)
Miss Lucy Brack Miss Lucky Brack

Placings:*1200*/13350100/3143311/3/0**62460/2/P** **(4777)**
2001/02: 25^{P}G

	Starts	1st	2nd	3rd	Win & Pl
Chases	1	0	0	0	
Career Total	**28**	**6**	**3**	**6**	**24459**

115	4/96	Chep	2m4f110y	D(0-125)HHdl	G-F	£3090
112	3/96	Sand	2m6f	D(0-125)HHdl	G-S	£3629
104	10/95	Worc	2m4f	B(0-140)HHdl	GD	£4987
98	2/95	Fknm	2m4f	D Hdl	G-S	£2650
108	11/94	Leic	2m	Hdl	SFT	£2105
105	12/93	Hntg	2m110y	NHF	G-S	£1951

Total win prize-money £18415

Going: Sf: 0-0 GS: 0-0 Gd: 0-1 GF: - Fm: 0-0
Distance: 2m/2m3: 0-0 2m4-2m7: 0-0 3m+: 0-1
Track: LH: 0-0 RH: 0-1 Tight: 0-1 Gall: 0-0
Aids: Bl: 0-0 Vi: 0-0 Tstrap: 0-0

Best Rating: 120 1/99 Donc 3m gd-sft Ch

Leader Supreme (IRE)

90 90

7-y-o b m Supreme Leader-Country Daisy Vii (Damsire Unregistered)
J R Jenkins Humphrey Solomons

Placings:*0*-F6 **(1013)**
2001/02: 20^{F}GF, 20^{6}G

	Starts	1st	2nd	3rd	Win & Pl
Hurdles	2	0	0	0	0
Career Total	**3**	**0**	**0**	**0**	**0**

Going: Sf: 0-0 GS: 0-0 Gd: 0-1 GF: - Fm: 0-1
Distance: 2m/2m3: 0-0 2m4-2m7: 0-2 3m+: 0-0
Track: LH: 0-2 RH: 0-0 Tight: 0-1 Gall: 0-0
Aids: Bl: 0-0 Vi: 0-0 Tstrap: 0-0
Best Rating: 92 4/01 Kemp 2m good NHF

Leading Optimist

99 116

7-y-o b g Henbit (USA)-Leading Line (Leading Man)
M C Pipe M C Pipe

Placings:*2/0*50-311321123 **(2602)**
2001/02: 24^{3}F, 27^{1}GF, 26^{1}F, 22^{3}GF, 24^{2}G, 27^{1}GF, 26^{1}GF, 22^{2}GF, 22^{3}G

	Starts	1st	2nd	3rd	Win & Pl
Hurdles	9	4	2	3	14483
Career Total	**13**	**4**	**3**	**3**	**14952**

116	9/01	Hrfd	3m2f	F(0-110)HHdl	G-F	£3444
93	7/01	NAbb	3m3f	E Hdl	G-F	£2884
93	6/01	Hrfd	3m2f	E Hdl	FRM	£3178
101	5/01	Font	3m3f	E Hdl	G-F	£2418

Total win prize-money £11925

Going: Sf: 0-0 GS: 0-0 Gd: 0-2 GF: - Fm: 4-7
Distance: 2m/2m3: 0-0 2m4-2m7: 0-3 **3m+: 4-6**
Track: LH: 1-5 **RH: 2-3 Tight: 2-6** Gall: 0-0
Aids: Bl: 0-0 Vi: 0-0 Tstrap: 0-0
Best Rating: 116 9/01 Hrfd 3m2f gd-fm Hdl

Moderate staying hurdler, best at extreme trips, he likes a lively surface.

Leading Spirit (IRE)

103 91

10-y-o b g Fairy King (USA)-Shopping (FR) (Sheshoon)
A G Newcombe Lavis Medical Systems

Placings:53/5RR/014PP-4104120 **(2338)**
2001/02: 17^{4}GS, 22^{1}GF, 22^{0}GF, 20^{4}GF, 22^{1}GF, 21^{2}GS, 24^{0}GF

	Starts	1st	2nd	3rd	Win & Pl
Hurdles	7	2	1	0	5472
Career Total	**17**	**3**	**1**	**1**	**7751**

88	8/01	NAbb	2m6f	G(0-95)HHdl	G-F	£2331
91	5/01	NAbb	2m6f	G(0-95)HHdl	G-F	£2457
91	7/00	MRas	2m5f110y	G(0-90)HHdl	G-F	£1554

Total win prize-money £6342

Going: Sf: 0-0 GS: 0-2 Gd: 0-0 GF: - Fm: 2-5
Distance: 2m/2m3: 0-1 **2m4-2m7: 2-5** 3m+: 0-1
Track: **LH: 2-5** RH: 0-2 **Tight: 2-5** Gall: 0-0
Aids: Bl: 0-0 Vi: 0-0 Tstrap: 0-0
Best Rating: 108 2/97 Asct 2m110y gd-fm Hdl

Effective at around two miles six furlongs, he acts on a sound surface.

Leagues (NZ)

101 96

7-y-o b g Kenfair (NZ)-Hidden Depths (NZ) (Beaufort Sea (USA))
Mrs L C Taylor Mrs W Morrell

Placings:5000 **(4848)**
2001/02: 16^{5}G, 20^{0}HY, 16^{0}GS, 16^{0}G

	Starts	1st	2nd	3rd	Win & Pl
Hurdles	4	0	0	0	0
Career Total	**4**	**0**	**0**	**0**	**0**

Going: Sf: 0-1 GS: 0-1 Gd: 0-2 GF: - Fm: 0-0
Distance: 2m/2m3: 0-3 2m4-2m7: 0-1 3m+: 0-0
Track: LH: 0-3 RH: 0-1 Tight: 0-1 Gall: 0-2
Aids: Bl: 0-0 Vi: 0-0 Tstrap: 0-0
Best Rating: 96 12/01 Donc 2m110y good Hdl

Leamlara Rose (IRE)

81 63

11-y-o b m Le Moss-Clash Boreen (Arapaho)
Mrs S M Johnson Mrs P A Wallis

Placings:30P **(0670)**
2001/02: 25^{3}G, 26^{0}G, 00^{P}G

	Starts	1st	2nd	3rd	Win & Pl
Chases	3	0	0	1	339
Career Total	**3**	**0**	**0**	**1**	**339**

Going: Sf: 0-0 GS: 0-0 Gd: 0-3 GF: - Fm: 0-0
Distance: 2m/2m3: 0-0 2m4-2m7: 0-0 3m+: 0-3
Track: LH: 0-1 RH: 0-2 Tight: 0-0 Gall: 0-0
Aids: Bl: 0-0 Vi: 0-0 Tstrap: 0-0
Best Rating: 63 5/01 Hrfd 3m1f110y good Ch

Leanadis Rose

81 46

4-y-o b f Namaqualand (USA)-Fiorini (Formidable (USA))
Miss A Stokell (M F Barraclough 30/9) Mrs M McMahon

Placings:0P500U **(2512)**
2001/02: 17^{0}G, 17^{P}G, 18^{5}GF, 17^{0}GF, 16^{0}GF, 16^{U}S

	Starts	1st	2nd	3rd	Win & Pl
Hurdles	6	0	0	0	0
Career Total	**6**	**0**	**0**	**0**	**0**

Going: Sf: 0-1 GS: 0-0 Gd: 0-2 GF: - Fm: 0-3
Distance: 2m/2m3: 0-6 2m4-2m7: 0-0 3m+: 0-0
Track: LH: 0-4 RH: 0-2 Tight: 0-4 Gall: 0-1
Aids: Bl: 0-1 Vi: 0-0 Tstrap: 0-0
Best Rating: 47 8/01 Font 2m2f110y gd-fm Hdl

Leap In The Dark (IRE)

76 36

13-y-o br g Shadeed (USA)-Star Guide (FR) (Targowice (USA))
Miss L C Siddall Mrs D J Morris

Placings:00000/P05663333203354/33112231435365 55520/46025**P4U**4020/0/506-P00 **(0966)**

2001/02: 20^{P}F, 20^{0}G, 21^{0}GS

	Starts	1st	2nd	3rd	Win & Pl
Hurdles	3	0	0	0	
Career Total	**58**	**3**	**6**	**11**	**14877**

95	10/97	Carl	2m4f110y	E(0-100)HHdl	G-F	£2262
95	9/97	Hexm	2m4f110y	E(0-100)HHdl	G-F	£2343
87	8/97	Sthl	2m4f110y	F Hdl	GD	£1939

Total win prize-money £6545

Going: Sf: 0-0 GS: 0-1 Gd: 0-1 GF: - Fm: 0-1
Distance: 2m/2m3: 0-0 2m4-2m7: 0-3 3m+: 0-0
Track: LH: 0-2 RH: 0-0 Tight: 0-0 Gall: 0-0
Aids: Bl: 0-0 Vi: 0-0 Tstrap: 0-0
Best Rating: 95 2/98 Muss 2m4f good Hdl

Leaping Lady (IRE)

75 **55**

7-y-o b m Phardante (FR)-Narcone (Kambalda)
Miss Tina Jackson H L Thompson

Placings:*00*/440PPP **(4871)**
2001/02: 19^{4}GF, 19^{4}G, 20^{0}G, 23^{P}GS, 20^{P}GF, 25^{P}GF

	Starts	1st	2nd	3rd	Win & Pl
Hurdles	5	0	0	0	0
Chases	1	0	0	0	0
Career Total	**8**	**0**	**0**	**0**	**0**

Going: Sf: 0-0 GS: 0-1 Gd: 0-2 GF: - Fm: 0-3
Distance: 2m/2m3: 0-2 2m4-2m7: 0-3 3m+: 0-1
Track: LH: 0-5 RH: 0-1 Tight: 0-2 Gall: 0-1
Aids: Bl: 0-0 Vi: 0-0 Tstrap: 0-1
Best Rating: 55 12/01 Catt 2m3f good Hdl

Learn The Lingo

89f **87f**

6-y-o b g Teenoso (USA)-Charlotte Gray (Rolfe (USA))
Mrs H Dalton David M Hughes

Placings:*40* **(4242)**
2001/02: 16^{4}G, 16^{0}GF

	Starts	1st	2nd	3rd	Win & Pl
NH Flat	2	0	0	0	0
Career Total	**2**	**0**	**0**	**0**	**0**

Going: Sf: 0-0 GS: 0-0 Gd: 0-1 GF: - Fm: 0-1
Distance: 2m/2m3: 0-2 2m4-2m7: 0-0 3m+: 0-0
Track: LH: 0-0 RH: 0-2 Tight: 0-0 Gall: 0-1
Aids: Bl: 0-0 Vi: 0-0 Tstrap: 0-0
Best Rating: 87 12/01 Ludl 2m good NHF

Showed ability on first start in bumper company but disappointing favourite next time.

Leatherback (IRE)

107 **112**

4-y-o b g Turtle Island (IRE)-Phyllode (Pharly (FR))
N A Callaghan M Tabor

Placings:3361 **(4275)**
2001/02: 16^{3}G, 16^{3}G, 16^{6}S, 16^{1}G

	Starts	1st	2nd	3rd	Win & Pl
Hurdles	4	1	0	2	4263
Career Total	**4**	**1**	**0**	**2**	**4263**

109	3/02	Fknm	2m	E Hdl	GD	£2618

Total win prize-money £2618

Going: Sf: 0-1 GS: 0-0 Gd: 1-3 GF: - Fm: 0-0
Distance: **2m/2m3: 1-4** 2m4-2m7: 0-0 3m+: 0-0
Track: **LH: 1-3** RH: 0-1 **Tight: 1-1** Gall: 0-1
Aids: Bl: 0-0 Vi: 0-0 Tstrap: 0-0
Best Rating: 112 12/01 Kemp 2m good Hdl

Ran in decent company over hurdles before winning a small race at Fakenha. Needed soft ground on the Flat.

Leckampton

92f **74f**

6-y-o b m Bedford (USA)-I'm Unforgettable (Dublin Taxi)
D G Bridgwater I W Thompson

Placings:*0* **(1245)**
2001/02: 16^{0}GF

	Starts	1st	2nd	3rd	Win & Pl
NH Flat	1	0	0	0	
Career Total	**1**	**0**	**0**	**0**	

Going: Sf: 0-0 GS: 0-0 Gd: 0-0 GF: - Fm: 0-1
Distance: 2m/2m3: 0-1 2m4-2m7: 0-0 3m+: 0-0
Track: LH: 0-1 RH: 0-0 Tight: 0-0 Gall: 0-0
Aids: Bl: 0-0 Vi: 0-0 Tstrap: 0-0
Best Rating: 74 8/01 Worc 2m gd-fm NHF

Ledgendry Line

110(114h) **141**

9-y-o b g Mtoto-Eider (Niniski (USA))
Mrs M Reveley The Home & Away Partnership

Placings:21134/**21212**/143-**55F5** **(4914)**
2001/02: 24^{5}G, 25^{5}GS, 25^{F}GS, 20^{5}G

	Starts	1st	2nd	3rd	Win & Pl
Chases	4	0	0	0	750
Career Total	**17**	**5**	**4**	**2**	**30453**

143	11/00	Newc	2m4f	D(0-125)HHdl	G-S	£5109
122	1/00	Sedg	2m5f	E Ch	SFT	£3003
113	10/99	Kels	3m1f	E Ch	GD	£3566
127	1/98	Newc	2m	B Hdl	G-S	£6356
110	12/97	Kels	2m110y	D Hdl	G-S	£2829

Total win prize-money £20863

Going: Sf: 0-0 GS: 0-2 Gd: 0-2 GF: - Fm: 0-0
Distance: 2m/2m3: 0-0 2m4-2m7: 0-1 3m+: 0-3
Track: LH: 0-2 RH: 0-2 Tight: 0-2 Gall: 0-0
Aids: Bl: 0-0 Vi: 0-0 Tstrap: 0-0
Best Rating: 147 2/00 Kels 3m1f gd-sft Ch

A useful chaser, lightly raced over jumps recently. Stays three miles. Loves the mud but has shown ability on faster.

Ledham (USA)

87 **101**

6-y-o ch g Diesis-First Tracks (USA) (Alleged (USA))
C J Mann Macajack

Placings:2320/2231F-040 **(0790)**
2001/02: 17^{0}F, 18^{4}GF, 19^{0}GF

	Starts	1st	2nd	3rd	Win & Pl
Hurdles	3	0	0	0	0
Career Total	**12**	**1**	**4**	**2**	**6344**

103	8/00	Hntg	2m110y	F Hdl	G-F	£2074

Total win prize-money £2075

Going: Sf: 0-0 GS: 0-2 Gd: 0-0 GF: - Fm: 0-3
Distance: 2m/2m3: 0-2 2m4-2m7: 0-1 3m+: 0-0
Track: LH: 0-1 RH: 0-2 Tight: 0-3 Gall: 0-0
Aids: Bl: 0-0 Vi: 0-0 Tstrap: 0-3
Best Rating: 124 3/00 Chel 2m1f gd-fm Hdl

Lee's Rosie (IRE)

84 **46**

7-y-o b m Zaffaran (USA)-Muse Of Fire (Laurence O)
N A Twiston-Davies Mrs Lee Payne

Placings:*05*-0PP **(2949)**
2001/02: 16^{0}S, 21^{P}S, 22^{P}S

	Starts	1st	2nd	3rd	Win & Pl
Hurdles	3	0	0	0	
Career Total	**5**	**0**	**0**	**0**	**0**

Going: Sf: 0-3 GS: 0-0 Gd: 0-0 GF: - Fm: 0-0
Distance: 2m/2m3: 0-1 2m4-2m7: 0-2 3m+: 0-0
Track: LH: 0-1 RH: 0-2 Tight: 0-1 Gall: 0-0
Aids: Bl: 0-0 Vi: 0-0 Tstrap: 0-0
Best Rating: 79 1/01 Ludl 2m soft NHF

Left Bank (IRE)

101(100h) (77h)**85**

6-y-o ch g Over The River (FR)-My Friend Fashion (Laurence O)
Mrs M Reveley C C Buckley

Placings:*00*-400260**633** **(4751)**
2001/02: 22^{4}G, 20^{0}G, 24^{0}S, 20^{2}G, 22^{6}GS, 25^{0}GS, 24^{6}S, 25^{3}GS, 20^{3}GF

	Starts	1st	2nd	3rd	Win & Pl
Hurdles	6	0	1	0	574
Chases	3	0	0	2	998
Career Total	**11**	**0**	**1**	**2**	**1572**

Going: Sf: 0-2 GS: 0-3 Gd: 0-3 GF: - Fm: 0-1
Distance: 2m/2m3: 0-0 2m4-2m7: 0-5 3m+: 0-4
Track: LH: 0-7 RH: 0-2 Tight: 0-4 Gall: 0-1
Aids: Bl: 0-0 Vi: 0-0 Tstrap: 0-0
Best Rating: 85 4/02 Uttx 2m4f gd-fm Ch

Has achieved little so far over both hurdles and fences and blinkers had little effect.

Legal Coup

4-y-o gr f Contract Law (USA)-What A Coup (Malicious)
B A Pearce The Lawbreakers

Placings:PP05 **(4507)**
2001/02: 16^{P}GS, 17^{P}S, 16^{0}G, 21^{5}G

	Starts	1st	2nd	3rd	Win & Pl
Hurdles	4	0	0	0	0
Career Total	**4**	**0**	**0**	**0**	**0**

Going: Sf: 0-1 GS: 0-1 Gd: 0-2 GF: - Fm: 0-0
Distance: 2m/2m3: 0-3 2m4-2m7: 0-1 3m+: 0-0
Track: LH: 0-2 RH: 0-2 Tight: 0-3 Gall: 0-0
Aids: Bl: 0-0 Vi: 0-1 Tstrap: 0-0
Best Rating:

Legal Lunch (USA)

113 **132**

7-y-o b g Alleged (USA)-Dinner Surprise (USA) (Lyphard (USA))
R M Stronge Berkshire Commercial Components Ltd

Placings:02120-124 **(2664)**
2001/02: 20^{1}G, 20^{2}GS, 24^{4}G

	Starts	1st	2nd	3rd	Win & Pl
Hurdles	3	1	1	0	14549
Career Total	**8**	**2**	**3**	**0**	**22617**

132	10/01	Sthl	2m4f110y	C(0-130)HHdl	GD	£6890
126	2/01	Font	2m6f110y	E Hdl	G-S	£3167

Total win prize-money £10058

Going: Sf: 0-0 GS: 0-1 Gd: 1-2 GF: - Fm: 0-0
Distance: 2m/2m3: 0-0 **2m4-2m7: 1-2** 3m+: 0-1
Track: **LH: 1-2** RH: 0-0 **Tight: 1-1** Gall: 0-0
Aids: Bl: 0-0 Vi: 0-0 Tstrap: 0-0
Best Rating: 132 12/01 Chel 3m good Hdl

A useful recruit over hurdles, he has been branded ungenuine in the past, but made an impressive return to the winter game at Southwell in October and did nothing wrong at Chepstow. Will make a chaser in time. He travels well in his races and stays two and a half miles.

Legal Native (IRE)

87f 71f

6-y-o br m Be My Native (USA)-Tullahought (Jaazeiro (USA))
R J Price E G Bevan

Placings:_00-02_ (1384)
2001/02: 16^{0}GF, 17^{2}GF

	Starts	1st	2nd	3rd	Win & Pl
NH Flat	2	0	1	0	448
Career Total	**4**	**0**	**1**	**0**	**448**

Going: Sf: 0-0 GS: 0-0 Gd: 0-0 GF: - Fm: 0-2
Distance: 2m/2m3: 0-2 2m4-2m7: 0-0 3m+: 0-0
Track: LH: 0-1 RH: 0-1 Tight: 0-0 Gall: 0-0
Aids: Bl: 0-0 Vi: 0-0 Tstrap: 0-0
Best Rating: 71 9/01 Hrfd 2m1f gd-fm NHF

Legal Perk (IRE)

8-y-o b m Executive Perk-Running Valley (Buckskin (FR))
J L Needham J L Needham

Placings:0-06 (1655)
2001/02: 21^{0}GF, 17^{6}G

	Starts	1st	2nd	3rd	Win & Pl
Hurdles	2	0	0	0	0
Career Total	**3**	**0**	**0**	**0**	**0**

Going: Sf: 0-0 GS: 0-0 Gd: 0-1 GF: - Fm: 0-1
Distance: 2m/2m3: 0-1 2m4-2m7: 0-1 3m+: 0-0
Track: LH: 0-1 RH: 0-0 Tight: 0-1 Gall: 0-0
Aids: Bl: 0-0 Vi: 0-0 Tstrap: 0-0
Best Rating: 51 2/01 Ludl 2m gd-sft Hdl

Legal Petition

8-y-o b m Petoski-Legal Aid (Legal Eagle)
L G Cottrell P R Hill

Placings:_00/P_-2 (0319)
2001/02: 19^{2}F

	Starts	1st	2nd	3rd	Win & Pl
Chases	1	0	1	0	511
Career Total	**4**	**0**	**1**	**0**	**511**

Going: Sf: 0-0 GS: 0-0 Gd: 0-0 GF: - Fm: 0-1
Distance: 2m/2m3: 0-0 2m4-2m7: 0-1 3m+: 0-0
Track: LH: 0-0 RH: 0-1 Tight: 0-0 Gall: 0-0
Aids: Bl: 0-0 Vi: 0-0 Tstrap: 0-0
Best Rating: 91 5/01 Extr 2m3f110y firm Ch

Legal Right (USA)

114 170

9-y-o b g Alleged (USA)-Rose Red (USA) (Northern Dancer)
J J O'Neill Russell McAllister

Placings:231101/**4P121**/**P111**/13-41542 (3486)
2001/02: 25^{4}G, 24^{1}S, 24^{5}G, 26^{4}S, 25^{2}HY

	Starts	1st	2nd	3rd	Win & Pl
Chases	5	1	1	0	52939
Career Total	**22**	**10**	**3**	**2**	**184144**

157	12/01	Hayd	3m	A Ch	SFT	£26100
177	12/00	Asct	3m110y	B HCh	SFT	£29250
176	12/99	Chel	2m5f	A HCh	G-S	£46100
160	11/99	Newb	2m4f	B(0-145)HCh	GD	£12900
151	11/99	Chel	2m4f110y	D(0-125)HCh	GD	£10601
127	3/99	Kels	3m1f	D Ch	GD	£4952
133	1/99	Ludl	2m4f	E Ch	G-S	£2853
132	4/98	Weth	2m	D(0-125)HHdl	G-S	£2950
126	2/98	Newc	2m	E Hdl	GD	£2547
120	1/98	Ludl	2m	F Hdl	G-S	£2190

Total win prize-money £140443

Going: Sf: 1-3 GS: 0-0 Gd: 0-2 GF: - Fm: 0-0
Distance: 2m/2m3: 0-0 2m4-2m7: 0-0 **3m+: 1-5**
Track: **LH: 1-4** RH: 0-1 Tight: 0-0 Gall: 0-1
Aids: Bl: 0-0 Vi: 0-0 **Tstrap: 1-4**
Best Rating: 177 12/00 Asct 3m110y soft Ch

He is highly talented, but has been a nightmare to train as he is intermittently lame. Winner of the Tripleprint Gold Cup in December 1999, he was off for a year before making a winning return to action in Ascot's Tote Silver Trophy. On his only subsequent start of that season, he travelled well for a long way when third to First Gold in the Martell Cup at Aintree. A disappointing favourite in the Charlie Hall Chase at Wetherby on his return in 2001/02, he bounced back with a defeat of Kingsmark in the Tommy Whittle Chase before being well beaten in the King George. Decent effort in a warm handicap at Warwick before chasing home Rince Ri at Cheltenham. Suited by give in the ground, he subsequently had to retire due to recurrent lameness.

Legal Treaty

85 75

7-y-o b g Dutch Treat-Bronze Eagle (Legal Eagle)
C T Pogson C T Pogson

Placings:_0/0500P/P5000_**PPP** (2899)
2001/02: 20^{PS}, 27^{5}G, 20^{0}G, 20^{0}G, 21^{0}GS, 24^{PS}, 16^{PG}, 16^{PG}

	Starts	1st	2nd	3rd	Win & Pl
Hurdles	6	0	0	0	0
Chases	2	0	0	0	0
Career Total	**14**	**0**	**0**	**0**	**0**

Going: Sf: 0-2 GS: 0-1 Gd: 0-5 GF: - Fm: 0-0
Distance: 2m/2m3: 0-2 2m4-2m7: 0-4 3m+: 0-2
Track: LH: 0-6 RH: 0-2 Tight: 0-3 Gall: 0-2
Aids: Bl: 0-1 Vi: 0-0 Tstrap: 0-0
Best Rating: 75 11/01 Hayd 2m4f good Hdl

Legendary Lover (IRE)

90 84

8-y-o b g Fairy King (USA)-Broken Romance (IRE) (Ela-Mana-Mou)
J R Jenkins S C Finance Limited

Placings:42P/62100/5-5P4P (4037)
2001/02: 16^{5}S, 21^{P}GS, 16^{4}GS, 18^{P}S

	Starts	1st	2nd	3rd	Win & Pl
Hurdles	4	0	0	0	0
Career Total	**13**	**1**	**2**	**0**	**4315**

106	11/99	Font	2m4f	E Hdl	GD	£2495

Total win prize-money £2495

Going: Sf: 0-2 GS: 0-2 Gd: 0-0 GF: - Fm: 0-0
Distance: 2m/2m3: 0-3 2m4-2m7: 0-1 3m+: 0-0
Track: LH: 0-3 RH: 0-1 Tight: 0-3 Gall: 0-1
Aids: Bl: 0-0 Vi: 0-4 Tstrap: 0-0
Best Rating: 106 11/99 Font 2m4f good Hdl

A moderate recruit from the Flat, he has yet to make his mark over hurdles, but looks capable of better.

Leggies Legacy

103 97

11-y-o b g Jupiter Island-Hit The Line (Saulingo)
L Wells A Russell & P B Davis Insurance

Placings:_0/P/U_14-3205 (4885)
2001/02: 21^{3}S, 21^{2}HY, 21^{0}GS, 27^{5}GF

	Starts	1st	2nd	3rd	Win & Pl
Hurdles	4	0	1	1	1984
Career Total	**9**	**1**	**1**	**1**	**4602**

86	3/01	Plum	2m5f	E Hdl	HVY	£2618

Total win prize-money £2618

Going: Sf: 0-2 GS: 0-1 Gd: 0-0 GF: - Fm: 0-1
Distance: 2m/2m3: 0-0 2m4-2m7: 0-3 3m+: 0-1
Track: LH: 0-2 RH: 0-1 Tight: 0-4 Gall: 0-0
Aids: Bl: 0-1 Vi: 0-0 Tstrap: 0-0
Best Rating: 97 2/02 Plum 2m5f heavy Hdl

Modest point to pointer. Fair novice hurdler. Stays two miles five. Acts on soft/heavy ground.

Leggy Lady

77 53

6-y-o b m Sir Harry Lewis (USA)-Lady Minstrel (Tudor Music)
B J Llewellyn Thomas Leonard

Placings:0 (0267)
2001/02: 17^{0}G

	Starts	1st	2nd	3rd	Win & Pl
Hurdles	1	0	0	0	
Career Total	**1**	**0**	**0**	**0**	

Going: Sf: 0-0 GS: 0-0 Gd: 0-1 GF: - Fm: 0-0
Distance: 2m/2m3: 0-1 2m4-2m7: 0-0 3m+: 0-0
Track: LH: 0-0 RH: 0-1 Tight: 0-0 Gall: 0-0
Aids: Bl: 0-0 Vi: 0-0 Tstrap: 0-0
Best Rating: 58 5/01 Hrfd 2m1f good Hdl

Leila

99 80

7-y-o b m Aragon-Carpe Diem (Good Times (ITY))
Miss E C Lavelle D F Jordan

Placings:_0/000FP/P60-_**PP042P** (1944)
2001/02: 24^{P}G, 26^{P}GF, 21^{0}GF, 26^{4}GF, 22^{2}S, 26^{P}GS

	Starts	1st	2nd	3rd	Win & Pl
Hurdles	1	0	0	0	0
Chases	5	0	1	0	1136
Career Total	**15**	**0**	**1**	**0**	**1136**

Going: Sf: 0-1 GS: 0-1 Gd: 0-1 GF: - Fm: 0-3
Distance: 2m/2m3: 0-0 2m4-2m7: 0-2 3m+: 0-4
Track: LH: 0-3 RH: 0-0 Tight: 0-4 Gall: 0-0
Aids: Bl: 0-0 Vi: 0-0 Tstrap: 0-0
Best Rating: 80 10/01 Font 2m6f soft Ch

Leith Hill Star

96 79

6-y-o ch m Comme L'Etoile-Sunnyday (Sunley Builds)
R Rowe Mrs N F Maltby

Placings:*40*-0404 **(3763)**
2001/02: 21^{0}G, 21^{4}G, 22^{0}G, 24^{4}S

	Starts	1st	2nd	3rd	Win & Pl
Hurdles	4	0	0	0	0
Career Total	6	0	0	0	0

Going: Sf: 0-1 GS: 0-0 Gd: 0-3 GF: - Fm: 0-0
Distance: 2m/2m3: 0-0 2m4-2m7: 0-3 3m+: 0-1
Track: LH: 0-3 RH: 0-1 Tight: 0-4 Gall: 0-0
Aids: Bl: 0-0 Vi: 0-0 Tstrap: 0-0
Best Rating: 91 1/01 Folk 2m1f110y heavy NHF

Leith Lynx

96 48
5-y-o ch m Minster Son-Pinkie Hill (Le Coq D'Or)
P Monteith P Monteith

Placings:*0*-00P **(3326)**
2001/02: 17^{0}GF, 16^{0}G, 16^{P}S

	Starts	1st	2nd	3rd	Win & Pl
NH Flat	2	0	0	0	0
Hurdles	1	0	0	0	0
Career Total	4	0	0	0	

Going: Sf: 0-1 GS: 0-0 Gd: 0-1 GF: - Fm: 0-1
Distance: 2m/2m3: 0-3 2m4-2m7: 0-0 3m+: 0-0
Track: LH: 0-1 RH: 0-1 Tight: 0-1 Gall: 0-1
Aids: Bl: 0-0 Vi: 0-0 Tstrap: 0-0
Best Rating: 82 4/01 Ayr 2m gd-fm NHF

Leitrim Cottage (IRE)

101(88h) (78h)109
11-y-o b g Yashgan-New Talent (The Parson)
T P McGovern B & M McHugh Ltd Civil Engineering

Placings:*0*/P/06F5U12/11FU30/3221-0453PP0404 **(4563)**
2001/02: 25^{0}S, 24^{4}S, 29^{5}G, 25^{3}S, 25^{P}HY, 29^{P}HY, 26^{0}S, 25^{4}GS, 28^{0}S, 26^{4}GF

	Starts	1st	2nd	3rd	Win & Pl
Hurdles	3	0	0	0	0
Chases	7	0	0	1	1628
Career Total	**29**	**4**	**3**	**3**	**16918**

115 11/00 MRas 3m4f110y F(0-110)HCh SFT £3347
94 11/99 MRas 3m1f E(0-115)HCh G-S £3276
84 11/99 Towc 3m E(0-100)HHdl GD £2232
88 4/99 Plum 2m5f G(0-90)HCh GD £2617
Total win prize-money £11476

Going: Sf: 0-7 GS: 0-1 Gd: 0-1 GF: - Fm: 0-1
Distance: 2m/2m3: 0-0 2m4-2m7: 0-0 3m+: 0-10
Track: LH: 0-1 RH: 0-3 Tight: 0-2 Gall: 0-0
Aids: Bl: 0-8 Vi: 0-0 Tstrap: 0-0
Best Rating: 115 11/00 MRas 3m4f110y soft Ch

He has been lightly raced since winning a handicap chase in November 2000. Acts on good and soft ground and stays three miles four furlongs.

Lenny The Lion

91 71
5-y-o b g Bin Ajwaad (IRE)-Patriotic (Hotfoot)
Mrs M Reveley A D Simmons

Placings:60R-0 **(0640)**
2001/02: 19^{0}GF

	Starts	1st	2nd	3rd	Win & Pl
Hurdles	1	0	0	0	
Career Total	4	0	0	0	0

Going: Sf: 0-0 GS: 0-0 Gd: 0-0 GF: - Fm: 0-1
Distance: 2m/2m3: 0-0 2m4-2m7: 0-1 3m+: 0-0
Track: LH: 0-0 RH: 0-1 Tight: 0-1 Gall: 0-0
Aids: Bl: 0-0 Vi: 0-0 Tstrap: 0-0
Best Rating: 83 11/00 Newc 2m soft Hdl

Leonato (FR)

86 81
10-y-o b g Law Society (USA)-Gala Parade (Alydar (USA))
J G Given Colin G R Booth

Placings:0P0 **(4161)**
2001/02: 20^{0}G, 20^{P}G, 25^{0}GS

	Starts	1st	2nd	3rd	Win & Pl
Hurdles	3	0	0	0	
Career Total	3	0	0	0	

Going: Sf: 0-0 GS: 0-1 Gd: 0-2 GF: - Fm: 0-0
Distance: 2m/2m3: 0-0 2m4-2m7: 0-2 3m+: 0-1
Track: LH: 0-2 RH: 0-0 Tight: 0-0 Gall: 0-2
Aids: Bl: 0-0 Vi: 0-0 Tstrap: 0-0
Best Rating: 81 3/02 Wwck 3m1f gd-sft Hdl

Leopard Rock (IRE)

99 105
7-y-o b g Be My Native (USA)-Fight For It (Strong Gale)
B De Haan Mrs Hilary Jackson

Placings:*154*/140165020000-40U50P **(4844)**
2001/02: 20^{4}GF, 20^{0}GF, 16^{U}S, 19^{5}G, 22^{0}G, 24^{P}G

	Starts	1st	2nd	3rd	Win & Pl
Hurdles	6	0	0	0	0
Career Total	**21**	**3**	**1**	**0**	**12006**

102 7/00 Klny 2m1f Hdl GD £4416
99 5/00 Klny 2m1f Hdl G-F £3864
81 5/99 Gowr 2m NHF GD £2148
Total win prize-money £10428

Going: Sf: 0-1 GS: 0-0 Gd: 0-3 GF: - Fm: 0-2
Distance: 2m/2m3: 0-2 2m4-2m7: 0-3 3m+: 0-1
Track: LH: 0-3 RH: 0-3 Tight: 0-1 Gall: 0-0
Aids: Bl: 0-1 Vi: 0-0 Tstrap: 0-0
Best Rating: 116 1/01 Thur 2m4f heavy Hdl

Leopard Spot (IRE)

94 98
4-y-o b g Sadler's Wells (USA)-Savoureuse Lady (Caerleon (USA))
J J O'Neill (A P O'Brien 1/11) Mrs Jonjo O'Neill

Placings:0563 **(4493)**
2001/02: 16^{0}G, 17^{5}GS, 16^{6}S, 16^{3}G

	Starts	1st	2nd	3rd	Win & Pl
Hurdles	4	0	0	1	748
Career Total	**4**	**0**	**0**	**1**	**748**

Going: Sf: 0-1 GS: 0-1 Gd: 0-2 GF: - Fm: 0-0
Distance: 2m/2m3: 0-4 2m4-2m7: 0-0 3m+: 0-0
Track: LH: 0-2 RH: 0-2 Tight: 0-1 Gall: 0-0
Aids: Bl: 0-0 Vi: 0-0 Tstrap: 0-0
Best Rating: 99 3/02 Hayd 2m good Hdl

Formerly with Aidan O'Brien, best effort when third at Haydock in March.

Lescer's Lad

79f 83f
5-y-o b g Perpendicular-Grange Gracie (Oats)
B Ellison L Turnbull

Placings:*0* **(4771)**
2001/02: 16^{0}GF

	Starts	1st	2nd	3rd	Win & Pl
NH Flat	1	0	0	0	
Career Total	1	0	0	0	

Going: Sf: 0-0 GS: 0-0 Gd: 0-0 GF: - Fm: 0-1
Distance: 2m/2m3: 0-1 2m4-2m7: 0-0 3m+: 0-0
Track: LH: 0-0 RH: 0-0 Tight: 0-0 Gall: 0-0
Aids: Bl: 0-0 Vi: 0-0 Tstrap: 0-0
Best Rating: 83 4/02 Hexm 2m110y gd-fm NHF

Lesdream

5-y-o b g Morpeth-Lesbet (Hotfoot)
R G Frost Mrs L W Carlson

Placings:*4*-0P **(3758)**
2001/02: 16^{0}S, 17^{P}S

	Starts	1st	2nd	3rd	Win & Pl
NH Flat	1	0	0	0	
Hurdles	1	0	0	0	
Career Total	3	0	0	0	0

Going: Sf: 0-2 GS: 0-0 Gd: 0-0 GF: - Fm: 0-0
Distance: 2m/2m3: 0-2 2m4-2m7: 0-0 3m+: 0-0
Track: LH: 0-0 RH: 0-2 Tight: 0-1 Gall: 0-0
Aids: Bl: 0-0 Vi: 0-0 Tstrap: 0-0
Best Rating: 94 4/01 Tntn 2m1f gd-fm NHF

Lesmacadam (IRE)

11-y-o b m Digamist (USA)-Fiodoir (Weavers Hall)
D A Nolan Mrs J McFadyen-Murray

Placings:00/00-PU **(0800)**
2001/02: 16^{P}GF, 16^{U}GF

	Starts	1st	2nd	3rd	Win & Pl
Hurdles	2	0	0	0	
Career Total	6	0	0	0	

Going: Sf: 0-0 GS: 0-0 Gd: 0-0 GF: - Fm: 0-2
Distance: 2m/2m3: 0-2 2m4-2m7: 0-0 3m+: 0-0
Track: LH: 0-0 RH: 0-2 Tight: 0-0 Gall: 0-0
Aids: Bl: 0-0 Vi: 0-0 Tstrap: 0-1
Best Rating: 6 6/00 Baln 2m good Hdl

Lester Longfellow

74f 59f
6-y-o b/br g Riverwise (USA)-Cut Above The Rest (Indiaro)
N R Mitchell N R Mitchell

Placings:*0* **(3883)**
2001/02: 16^{0}GS

	Starts	1st	2nd	3rd	Win & Pl
NH Flat	1	0	0	0	
Career Total	1	0	0	0	

Going: Sf: 0-0 GS: 0-1 Gd: 0-0 GF: - Fm: 0-0
Distance: 2m/2m3: 0-1 2m4-2m7: 0-0 3m+: 0-0
Track: LH: 0-0 RH: 0-1 Tight: 0-0 Gall: 0-0
Aids: Bl: 0-0 Vi: 0-0 Tstrap: 0-0
Best Rating: 59 2/02 Winc 2m gd-sft NHF

Let Rip

8-y-o b g Nalchik (USA)-Delbounty (Bounteous)
Mrs A Price Mrs B Brown

Placings: *00/F*-P (4126)
2001/02: 19^{P}G

	Starts	1st	2nd	3rd	Win & Pl
Hurdles	1	0	0	0	
Career Total	4	0	0	0	

Going: Sf: 0-0 GS: 0-0 Gd: 0-1 GF: - Fm: 0-0
Distance: 2m/2m3: 0-0 2m4-2m7: 0-1 3m+: 0-0
Track: LH: 0-0 RH: 0-1 Tight: 0-0 Gall: 0-0
Aids: Bl: 0-0 Vi: 0-1 Tstrap: 0-0
Best Rating: 71 12/99 Ludl 2m good NHF

Let's Fly (FR)

97(100h) (110h)93
7-y-o b g Rose Laurel-Harpyes (FR) (Quart De Vin (FR))
Mrs M Reveley Sir Robert Ogden

Placings: *110*-1P2 (4303)
2001/02: 16^{1}GS, 16^{P}S, 16^{2}HY

	Starts	1st	2nd	3rd	Win & Pl
Hurdles	3	1	1	0	4343
Career Total	**6**	**3**	**1**	**0**	**8428**

103	10/01	Uttx	2m	E Hdl	G-S	£3250
112	12/00	Hntg	2m110y	H NHF	HVY	£1554
114	11/00	Weth	2m	H NHF	HVY	£2530

Total win prize-money £7335

Going: Sf: 0-2 GS: 1-1 Gd: 0-0 GF: - Fm: 0-0
Distance: **2m/2m3: 1-3** 2m4-2m7: 0-0 3m+: 0-0
Track: **LH: 1-3** RH: 0-0 Tight: 0-0 Gall: 0-0
Aids: Bl: 0-0 Vi: 0-0 Tstrap: 0-0
Best Rating: 114 11/00 Weth 2m heavy NHF

A dual heavy ground bumper winner at the end of 2000, he has been lightly raced since, but did manage to win over hurdles at Uttoxeter in October 2001 and at Southwell in May 2002. Disappointing on his chasing debut. Very much suited by soft ground.

Lets Be Frank

91(83c) 69
11-y-o b g Malaspina-Letitica (Deep Run)
E L James Mrs M M Stobart

Placings: *40/00000*/22111512/**3P**112/**31PF**/**133P0**/330 040-P0 (1408)
2001/02: 19^{P}G, 20^{0}GF

	Starts	1st	2nd	3rd	Win & Pl
Hurdles	2	0	0	0	
Career Total	**37**	**8**	**4**	**6**	**35491**

134	11/99	Uttx	2m4f	D(0-125)HCh	G-S	£4097
134	12/98	Leic	2m4f110y	E Ch	GD	£3340
124	1/98	Donc	2m4f	C(0-135)HHdl	GD	£4185
125	12/97	MRas	2m3f110y	D(0-125)HHdl	HVY	£4653
120	2/97	Wwck	2m4f110y	E(0-115)HHdl	GD	£2433
102	12/96	Wwck	2m3f	D(0-105)HHdl	G-F	£2999
110	12/96	Wind	2m4f	F(0-105)HHdl	GD	£2101
102	11/96	Hrfd	2m3f110y	E(0-100)HHdl	G-S	£2388

Total win prize-money £26198

Going: Sf: 0-0 GS: 0-0 Gd: 0-1 GF: - Fm: 0-1
Distance: 2m/2m3: 0-0 2m4-2m7: 0-2 3m+: 0-0
Track: LH: 0-1 RH: 0-1 Tight: 0-0 Gall: 0-0
Aids: Bl: 0-0 Vi: 0-0 Tstrap: 0-0
Best Rating: 134 12/99 Leic 2m4f110y good Ch

Lets Go Dutch

105 100
6-y-o b m Nicholas Bill-Dutch Majesty (Homing)
K Bishop Mrs E K Ellis

Placings: U2-4351F (4420)
2001/02: 17^{4}GS, 17^{3}S, 22^{5}S, 19^{1}S, 21^{F}GS

	Starts	1st	2nd	3rd	Win & Pl
Hurdles	5	1	0	1	4025
Career Total	**7**	**1**	**1**	**1**	**4640**

100	3/02	Tntn	2m3f110y	D Hdl	SFT	£3649

Total win prize-money £3649

Going: Sf: 1-3 GS: 0-2 Gd: 0-0 GF: - Fm: 0-0
Distance: 2m/2m3: 0-2 **2m4-2m7: 1-3** 3m+: 0-0
Track: LH: 0-1 **RH: 1-4 Tight: 1-2** Gall: 0-1
Aids: Bl: 0-0 Vi: 0-0 Tstrap: 0-0
Best Rating: 100 3/02 Tntn 2m3f110y soft Hdl

Modest hurdler, promises to stay beyond two and a half miles and acts in soft ground. Won a Taunton maiden hurdles under strong driving in March 2002.

Lettherebelight

8-y-o b g Prince Of Darkness (IRE)-Duvessa (Glen Quaich)
I G Cottrell C J Down

Placings: 0-0 (0214)
2001/02: 22^{0}GF

	Starts	1st	2nd	3rd	Win & Pl
Hurdles	1	0	0	0	
Career Total	2	0	0	0	

Going: Sf: 0-0 GS: 0-0 Gd: 0-0 GF: - Fm: 0-1
Distance: 2m/2m3: 0-0 2m4-2m7: 0-1 3m+: 0-0
Track: LH: 0-0 RH: 0-1 Tight: 0-0 Gall: 0-0
Aids: Bl: 0-0 Vi: 0-0 Tstrap: 0-0
Best Rating:

Liam's River (IRE)

92(91h) (77h)95
10-y-o b g Over The River (FR)-Just A Maid (Rarity)
J Wade John Wade

Placings: 0/5/4/0-4P2 (4195)
2001/02: 20^{4}S, 25^{P}GS, 21^{2}S

	Starts	1st	2nd	3rd	Win & Pl
Hurdles	2	0	0	0	0
Chases	1	0	1	0	939
Career Total	7	0	1	0	939

Going: Sf: 0-2 GS: 0-1 Gd: 0-0 GF: - Fm: 0-0
Distance: 2m/2m3: 0-0 2m4-2m7: 0-2 3m+: 0-1
Track: LH: 0-3 RH: 0-0 Tight: 0-1 Gall: 0-0
Aids: Bl: 0-0 Vi: 0-0 Tstrap: 0-0
Best Rating: 95 3/02 Sedg 2m5f soft Ch

Has switched to fences late in life. Runner-up on his chasing bow at Sedgefield in March.

Liberty Bell

71 54
7-y-o b/br g Ardkinglass-Melaura Belle (Meldrum)
R T Phillips Something For The Weekend

Placings: *366*-00P (4588)
2001/02: 20^{0}S, 21^{0}S, 22^{P}G

	Starts	1st	2nd	3rd	Win & Pl
Hurdles	3	0	0	0	
Career Total	**6**	**0**	**0**	**1**	**240**

Going: Sf: 0-2 GS: 0-0 Gd: 0-1 GF: - Fm: 0-0
Distance: 2m/2m3: 0-0 2m4-2m7: 0-3 3m+: 0-0
Track: LH: 0-1 RH: 0-2 Tight: 0-0 Gall: 0-1
Aids: Bl: 0-0 Vi: 0-0 Tstrap: 0-0
Best Rating: 105 1/01 Ludl 2m soft NHF

Liberty Hill

7-y-o b g Golden Heights-Free Credit (Deep Run)
John R Upson T B Brown

Placings: 6PP (3357)
2001/02: 24^{6}S, 27^{P}S, 24^{P}HY

	Starts	1st	2nd	3rd	Win & Pl
Hurdles	3	0	0	0	0
Career Total	**3**	**0**	**0**	**0**	**0**

Going: Sf: 0-3 GS: 0-0 Gd: 0-0 GF: - Fm: 0-0
Distance: 2m/2m3: 0-0 2m4-2m7: 0-0 3m+: 0-3
Track: LH: 0-2 RH: 0-1 Tight: 0-1 Gall: 0-0
Aids: Bl: 0-0 Vi: 0-0 Tstrap: 0-0
Best Rating:

Liberty Taker

6-y-o b m Green Adventure (USA)-Blazing Affair Vii (Damsire Unregistered)
H A McWilliams Mrs M A Taylor

Placings: *0*P (1025)
2001/02: 17^{0}GF, 17^{P}GF

	Starts	1st	2nd	3rd	Win & Pl
NH Flat	2	0	0	0	
Career Total	2	0	0	0	

Going: Sf: 0-0 GS: 0-0 Gd: 0-0 GF: - Fm: 0-2
Distance: 2m/2m3: 0-2 2m4-2m7: 0-0 3m+: 0-0
Track: LH: 0-1 RH: 0-1 Tight: 0-2 Gall: 0-0
Aids: Bl: 0-0 Vi: 0-0 Tstrap: 0-0
Best Rating:

Libido

104(103h) 124
7-y-o b g Good Thyne (USA)-Country Mistress (Town And Country)
H D Daly The Hopeful Partnership

Placings: 3024-25U (1954)
2001/02: 20^{2}G, 25^{5}G, 20^{U}G

	Starts	1st	2nd	3rd	Win & Pl
Chases	3	0	1	0	1326
Career Total	7	**0**	**2**	**1**	**4312**

Going: Sf: 0-0 GS: 0-0 Gd: 0-3 GF: 0-0 Fm: 0-0
Distance: 2m/2m3: 0-0 2m4-2m7: 0-2 3m+: 0-1
Track: LH: 0-2 RH: 0-1 Tight: 0-1 Gall: 0-0
Aids: Bl: 0-0 Vi: 0-0 Tstrap: 0-0
Best Rating: 124 9/01 Bang 2m4f110y good Ch

Lieutenant Fancy

6-y-o ch g Kris-Noirmant (Dominion)
R Ford Richard Ford

Placings:P **(1842)**
2001/02: 24^{P}S

	Starts	1st	2nd	3rd	Win & Pl
Hurdles	1	0	0	0	
Career Total	**1**	**0**	**0**	**0**	

Going: Sf: 0-1 GS: 0-0 Gd: 0-0 GF: - Fm: 0-0
Distance: 2m/2m3: 0-0 2m4-2m7: 0-0 3m+: 0-1
Track: LH: 0-0 RH: 0-1 Tight: 0-0 Gall: 0-0
Aids: Bl: 0-0 Vi: 0-0 Tstrap: 0-0
Best Rating:

Life Companion

9-y-o ch g Weld-Broadlands (Swing Easy (USA))
R T Phillips G Lansbury

Placings:0PP/P **(1013)**
2001/02: 20^{P}G

	Starts	1st	2nd	3rd	Win & Pl
Hurdles	1	0	0	0	
Career Total	**4**	**0**	**0**	**0**	

Going: Sf: 0-0 GS: 0-0 Gd: 0-1 GF: - Fm: 0-0
Distance: 2m/2m3: 0-0 2m4-2m7: 0-1 3m+: 0-0
Track: LH: 0-1 RH: 0-0 Tight: 0-0 Gall: 0-0
Aids: Bl: 0-0 Vi: 0-0 Tstrap: 0-0
Best Rating: **10** 5/99 Chep 2m110y good NHF

Life's Work

10-y-o b g Lyphento (USA)-Travail Girl (Forties Field (FR))
Mrs C M Gorman (Nick Gifford 16/5) M Gorman

Placings:340/2101/321PF02P204/1P0-1FF **(3755)**
2001/02: 26^{1}G, 25^{F}G, 20^{F}S

	Starts	1st	2nd	3rd	Win & Pl
Chases	3	1	0	0	1313
Career Total	**24**	**5**	**4**	**2**	**20353**

118	5/01	Folk	3m2f	H Ch	GD	£1313
125	2/01	Sand	2m4f110y	H Ch	SFT	£2768
133	10/99	Asct	2m3f110y	D Ch	GD	£4730
110	1/99	Tntn	2m3f110y	F(0-110)HHdl	SFT	£2326
106	11/98	Extr	2m6f	E(0-105)HHdl	SFT	£2921

Total win prize-money £14059

Going: Sf: 0-1 GS: 0-0 Gd: 1-2 GF: - Fm: 0-0
Distance: 2m/2m3: 0-0 2m4-2m7: 0-1 **3m+: 1-2**
Track: LH: 0-0 **RH: 1-3 Tight: 1-2** Gall: 0-0
Aids: Bl: 0-0 Vi: 0-0 Tstrap: 0-0
Best Rating: **133** 12/99 Wwck 2m4f soft Ch

Light Programme

98 **76**
8-y-o b g El Gran Senor (USA)-Nashmeel (USA) (Blushing Groom (FR))
A L Forbes Tony Forbes

Placings:5/0-5P0 **(2349)**
2001/02: 24^{5}GS, 20^{P}S, 19^{0}GS

	Starts	1st	2nd	3rd	Win & Pl
Hurdles	3	0	0	0	0
Career Total	**5**	**0**	**0**	**0**	**0**

Going: Sf: 0-1 GS: 0-2 Gd: 0-0 GF: - Fm: 0-0
Distance: 2m/2m3: 0-0 2m4-2m7: 0-2 3m+: 0-1
Track: LH: 0-1 RH: 0-2 Tight: 0-2 Gall: 0-0
Aids: Bl: 0-0 Vi: 0-0 Tstrap: 0-1
Best Rating: **72** 1/00 Leic 2m soft Hdl

A disappointing performer, he hinted at some ability over hurdles in 2001, but improved a lot to win a moderate novices' handicap at Wolverhampton in July 2002.

Light Reflections

114(79h) (47h)**98**
9-y-o b g Rainbow Quest (USA)-Tajfah (USA) (Shadeed (USA))
P G Murphy Miss J Collison

Placings:000/0F3F461/26PPP-5352P453 **(4882)**
2001/02: 22^{5}HY, 29^{3}G, 25^{5}G, 26^{2}G, 26^{P}S, 26^{4}S, 28^{5}S, 26^{3}GF

	Starts	1st	2nd	3rd	Win & Pl
Hurdles	1	0	0	0	0
Chases	7	0	1	2	3872
Career Total	**23**	**1**	**2**	**3**	**7795**

98	4/00	Plum	3m2f	F(0-95)HCh	SFT	£2678

Total win prize-money £2678

Going: Sf: 0-4 GS: 0-0 Gd: 0-3 GF: - Fm: 0-1
Distance: 2m/2m3: 0-0 2m4-2m7: 0-1 3m+: 0-7
Track: LH: 0-0 RH: 0-2 Tight: 0-5 Gall: 0-0
Aids: Bl: 0-0 Vi: 0-0 Tstrap: 0-0
Best Rating: **98** 4/02 Font 3m2f110y gd-fm Ch

Moderate staying chaser, a regular at the south coast tracks. Has won on soft, acts on good.

Light The Fuse (IRE)

91 **105**
10-y-o b g Electric-Celtic Bombshell (Celtic Cone)
Miss H C Knight A F Lousada

Placings:21/0/6O4446422/2-023F **(2026)**
2001/02: 20^{0}G, 21^{2}GF, 20^{3}G, 20^{F}S

	Starts	1st	2nd	3rd	Win & Pl
Hurdles	3	0	1	1	1287
Chases	1	0	0	0	0
Career Total	**17**	**1**	**5**	**1**	**7601**

110	4/97	Prth	2m110y	H NHF	GD	£2052

Total win prize-money £2052

Going: Sf: 0-1 GS: 0-0 Gd: 0-2 GF: - Fm: 0-1
Distance: 2m/2m3: 0-0 2m4-2m7: 0-4 3m+: 0-0
Track: LH: 0-2 RH: 0-1 Tight: 0-1 Gall: 0-1
Aids: Bl: 0-0 Vi: 0-0 Tstrap: 0-0
Best Rating: **110** 4/97 Prth 2m110y good NHF

Light The River (IRE)

95 **93**
8-y-o b/br g Over The River (FR)-Mysterious Light (Strong Gale)
N B Mason (Andrew Turnell 10/5) N B Mason

Placings:P50344/PP-PP661305 **(3625)**
2001/02: 25^{P}S, 24^{P}F, 20^{6}S, 27^{6}S, 25^{1}S, 21^{3}S, 25^{0}GS, 22^{5}S

	Starts	1st	2nd	3rd	Win & Pl
Chases	8	1	0	1	4048
Career Total	**16**	**1**	**0**	**2**	**5526**

93	12/01	Hexm	3m1f	E(0-105)HCh	SFT	£3591

Total win prize-money £3591

Going: Sf: 1-6 GS: 0-1 Gd: 0-0 GF: - Fm: 0-1
Distance: 2m/2m3: 0-0 2m4-2m7: 0-3 **3m+: 1-5**
Track: **LH: 1-6** RH: 0-2 Tight: 0-5 Gall: 0-0
Aids: Bl: 1-4 Vi: 0-0 Tstrap: 1-6
Best Rating: **98** 12/99 Leic 2m good Ch

Modest staying chaser. Showed improved for to win a moderate Hexham novice handicap in December 2001 when blinkers were applied.

Light The Sky

9-y-o b g Lighter-Saleander (Leander)
Mrs L Pomfret (N J Pomfret 24/2) Lt-Col Brian Abraham

Placings:0-4P4 **(4137)**
2001/02: 20^{4}GF, 21^{P}G, 24^{4}G

	Starts	1st	2nd	3rd	Win & Pl
Chases	3	0	0	0	85
Career Total	**4**	**0**	**0**	**0**	**85**

Going: Sf: 0-0 GS: 0-0 Gd: 0-2 GF: - Fm: 0-1
Distance: 2m/2m3: 0-0 2m4-2m7: 0-2 3m+: 0-1
Track: LH: 0-0 RH: 0-2 Tight: 0-0 Gall: 0-1
Aids: Bl: 0-0 Vi: 0-0 Tstrap: 0-1
Best Rating: **79** 5/01 Hntg 2m4f110y gd-fm Ch

Lightning Ridge

4-y-o b f Lightning Dealer-Amazing News (Mazilier (USA))
D R C Elsworth Quakers Yard Racing Club

Placings:0 **(1821)**
2001/02: 16^{0}GS

	Starts	1st	2nd	3rd	Win & Pl
Hurdles	1	0	0	0	
Career Total	**1**	**0**	**0**	**0**	

Going: Sf: 0-0 GS: 0-1 Gd: 0-0 GF: - Fm: 0-0
Distance: 2m/2m3: 0-1 2m4-2m7: 0-0 3m+: 0-0
Track: LH: 0-0 RH: 0-1 Tight: 0-0 Gall: 0-0
Aids: Bl: 0-0 Vi: 0-0 Tstrap: 0-0
Best Rating:

Lightning Star (USA)

(111h)
7-y-o b g El Gran Senor (USA)-Cuz's Star (USA) (Galaxy Libra)
T P McGovern Ashley Carr Racing (5)

Placings:535/02303121233/403321310-P **(0967)**
2001/02: 20^{P}GS

	Starts	1st	2nd	3rd	Win & Pl
Chases	1	0	0	0	
Career Total	**24**	**4**	**4**	**8**	**14144**

112	2/01	Towc	2m	F(0-110)HHdl	HVY	£1876
114	1/01	Folk	2m1f110y	G Hdl	HVY	£1554
101	1/00	Folk	2m1f110y	G Hdl	SFT	£1519
100	12/99	Chep	2m4f	G Hdl	G-S	£1679

Total win prize-money £6628

Going: Sf: 0-0 GS: 0-1 Gd: 0-0 GF: - Fm: 0-0
Distance: 2m/2m3: 0-0 2m4-2m7: 0-1 3m+: 0-0
Track: LH: 0-0 RH: 0-0 Tight: 0-0 Gall: 0-0
Aids: Bl: 0-1 Vi: 0-0 Tstrap: 0-0
Best Rating: **114** 1/01 Folk 2m1f110y heavy Hdl

Lightning Strikes (IRE)

8-y-o b g Zaffaran (USA)-Nimbi (Orchestra)
O Sherwood R B Holt

Placings: *231/1/P* **(2027)**
2001/02: 20^{PS}

	Starts	1st	2nd	3rd	Win & Pl
Hurdles	1	0	0	0	
Career Total	**5**	**2**	**1**	**1**	**4847**

110	10/99	Bang	2m1f	E Hdl	G-S	£2305
100	5/99	Uttx	2m	H NHF	GD	£1899

Total win prize-money £4206

Going: Sf: 0-1 GS: 0-0 Gd: 0-0 GF: - Fm: 0-0
Distance: 2m/2m3: 0-0 2m4-2m7: 0-1 3m+: 0-0
Track: LH: 0-1 RH: 0-0 Tight: 0-0 Gall: 0-0
Aids: Bl: 0-0 Vi: 0-0 Tstrap: 0-0
Best Rating: 110 10/99 Bang 2m1f gd-sft Hdl

Won a bumper in May 1999 and followed up at Bangor over hurdles, he then had over two years off before pulling up on his return in November. Acts with cut in the ground.

Like-A-Butterfly (IRE)

118 156

6-y-o b m Montelimar (USA)-Swifts Butterfly (Furry Glen)
C Roche J P McManus

Placings: *111*-111113 **(4944a)**
2001/02: $16^{1}YS$, $16^{1}Y$, $20^{1}Y$, $18^{1}HY$, $16^{1}GS$, $20^{3}G$

	Starts	1st	2nd	3rd	Win & Pl
Hurdles	6	5	0	1	124680
Career Total	**9**	**8**	**0**	**1**	**149866**

147	3/02	Chel	2m110y	A Hdl	G-S	£52200
156	2/02	Leop	2m2f	Hdl	HVY	£23926
139	12/01	Leop	2m4f	Hdl	YLD	£8911
142	12/01	Fair	2m	Hdl	YLD	£28830
110	11/01	Navn	2m	Hdl	Y-S	£5842
142	4/01	Leop	2m	NHF	SH	£15725
141	1/01	Leop	2m2f	NHF	SFT	£5564
133	1/01	Naas	2m	NHF	SFT	£3895

Total win prize-money £144897

Going: Sf: 1-1 GS: 1-1 Gd: 0-1 GF: - Fm: 0-0
Distance: **2m/2m3: 4-4** 2m4-2m7: 1-2 3m+: 0-0
Track: **LH: 4-4** RH: 1-2 Tight: 0-0 Gall: 0-0
Aids: Bl: 0-0 Vi: 0-0 Tstrap: 0-0
Best Rating: 156 2/02 Leop 2m2f heavy Hdl

Top flight bumper horse, she went on to maintain her unbeaten record in her first four hurdle starts and gained her fifth when taking the Supreme Novices at the Cheltenham Festival. Stays two and a half miles and acts in the mud. Has won over two on good ground. Has the build of a chaser.

Lilardo

100 73

5-y-o b/br m Son Pardo-Jimlil (Nicholas Bill)
B Palling Mrs M M Palling

Placings: 3554-0P0 **(4176)**
2001/02: $17^{0}G$, $19^{P}F$, $19^{0}GS$

	Starts	1st	2nd	3rd	Win & Pl
Hurdles	3	0	0	0	
Career Total	**7**	**0**	**0**	**1**	**439**

Going: Sf: 0-0 GS: 0-1 Gd: 0-1 GF: - Fm: 0-1
Distance: 2m/2m3: 0-2 2m4-2m7: 0-1 3m+: 0-0
Track: LH: 0-1 RH: 0-2 Tight: 0-2 Gall: 0-0
Aids: Bl: 0-0 Vi: 0-0 Tstrap: 0-0
Best Rating: 73 5/01 Hrfd 2m1f good Hdl

Lill's Star Lad

4-y-o ch g Kasakov-Lady Khadija (Nicholas Bill)
Mrs S Lamyman Alan Malcolmson

Placings: *0* **(4317)**
2001/02: $16^{0}HY$

	Starts	1st	2nd	3rd	Win & Pl
NH Flat	1	0	0	0	
Career Total	**1**	**0**	**0**	**0**	

Going: Sf: 0-1 GS: 0-0 Gd: 0-0 GF: - Fm: 0-0
Distance: 2m/2m3: 0-1 2m4-2m7: 0-0 3m+: 0-0
Track: LH: 0-1 RH: 0-0 Tight: 0-1 Gall: 0-0
Aids: Bl: 0-0 Vi: 0-0 Tstrap: 0-0
Best Rating:

Lillieplant (IRE)

10-y-o b m Aristocracy-Canute Princess (Torenaga)
B J Llewellyn (E J Ford 17/3) A J Plant

Placings: 6040-000 **(0846)**
2001/02: $17^{0}G$, $16^{0}GF$, $22^{0}GF$

	Starts	1st	2nd	3rd	Win & Pl
Hurdles	3	0	0	0	
Career Total	**7**	**0**	**0**	**0**	**0**

Going: Sf: 0-0 GS: 0-0 Gd: 0-1 GF: - Fm: 0-2
Distance: 2m/2m3: 0-2 2m4-2m7: 0-1 3m+: 0-0
Track: LH: 0-2 RH: 0-1 Tight: 0-1 Gall: 0-0
Aids: Bl: 0-0 Vi: 0-0 Tstrap: 0-0
Best Rating: 69 4/01 Hntg 2m110y soft Hdl

Lincoln Cross (IRE)

105f 100f

7-y-o b g Lord Americo-Keen Cross (IRE) (Black Minstrel)
O Sherwood O M C Sherwood

Placings: *02* **(1649)**
2001/02: $17^{0}G$, $16^{2}G$

	Starts	1st	2nd	3rd	Win & Pl
NH Flat	2	0	1	0	415
Career Total	**2**	**0**	**1**	**0**	**415**

Going: Sf: 0-0 GS: 0-0 Gd: 0-2 GF: - Fm: 0-0
Distance: 2m/2m3: 0-2 2m4-2m7: 0-0 3m+: 0-0
Track: LH: 0-1 RH: 0-1 Tight: 0-1 Gall: 0-1
Aids: Bl: 0-0 Vi: 0-0 Tstrap: 0-0
Best Rating: 100 10/01 Hntg 2m110y good NHF

Lincoln Dean

6-y-o b g Mtoto-Play With Me (IRE) (Alzao (USA))
F P Murtagh (J S Goldie 16/10) Clayton Bigley Partnership Ltd

Placings: P0 **(3349)**
2001/02: $16^{P}S$, $16^{0}G$

	Starts	1st	2nd	3rd	Win & Pl
Hurdles	2	0	0	0	
Career Total	**2**	**0**	**0**	**0**	

Going: Sf: 0-1 GS: 0-0 Gd: 0-1 GF: - Fm: 0-0
Distance: 2m/2m3: 0-2 2m4-2m7: 0-0 3m+: 0-0
Track: LH: 0-1 RH: 0-1 Tight: 0-1 Gall: 0-0
Aids: Bl: 0-0 Vi: 0-0 Tstrap: 0-1
Best Rating:

Lincoln Star

4-y-o b g Lugana Beach-Esilam (Frimley Park)
A G Hobbs J Parfitt

Placings: *00* **(4743)**
2001/02: $17^{0}S$, $16^{0}GF$

	Starts	1st	2nd	3rd	Win & Pl
NH Flat	2	0	0	0	
Career Total	**2**	**0**	**0**	**0**	

Going: Sf: 0-1 GS: 0-0 Gd: 0-0 GF: - Fm: 0-1
Distance: 2m/2m3: 0-2 2m4-2m7: 0-0 3m+: 0-0
Track: LH: 0-0 RH: 0-2 Tight: 0-0 Gall: 0-0
Aids: Bl: 0-0 Vi: 0-0 Tstrap: 0-0
Best Rating: 60 4/02 Ludl 2m gd-fm NHF

Line Of Conquest

12-y-o b g El Conquistador-High Finesse (High Line)
J W Mullins Miss C A James

Placings: *S10/0/0/P121610/45/FP* **(2543)**
2001/02: $16^{F}S$, $17^{P}GS$

	Starts	1st	2nd	3rd	Win & Pl
Chases	2	0	0	0	
Career Total	**16**	**4**	**1**	**0**	**13557**

114	2/98	Wwck	2m	C(0-135)HHdl	GD	£4045
108	12/97	Wwck	2m	C(0-130)HHdl	SFT	£3606
111	11/97	Bang	2m1f	E Hdl	G-S	£2724
108	3/95	Sand	2m110y	H NHF	SFT	£1940

Total win prize-money £12316

Going: Sf: 0-1 GS: 0-1 Gd: 0-0 GF: - Fm: 0-0
Distance: 2m/2m3: 0-2 2m4-2m7: 0-0 3m+: 0-0
Track: LH: 0-1 RH: 0-1 Tight: 0-0 Gall: 0-0
Aids: Bl: 0-0 Vi: 0-0 Tstrap: 0-0
Best Rating: 125 11/98 Newb 2m110y good Hdl

Linens Girl

6-y-o br m Thowra (FR)-Stocktina (Tina's Pet)
B G Powell D & J Newell

Placings: 0P-P **(0499)**
2001/02: $17^{P}G$

	Starts	1st	2nd	3rd	Win & Pl
Hurdles	1	0	0	0	
Career Total	**3**	**0**	**0**	**0**	

Going: Sf: 0-0 GS: 0-0 Gd: 0-1 GF: - Fm: 0-0
Distance: 2m/2m3: 0-1 2m4-2m7: 0-0 3m+: 0-0
Track: LH: 0-0 RH: 0-1 Tight: 0-0 Gall: 0-0
Aids: Bl: 0-1 Vi: 0-0 Tstrap: 0-0
Best Rating: 45 2/01 Hntg 2m110y gd-sft Hdl

Lingham Bridesmaid

97 **70**

6-y-o b m Minster Son-Lingham Bride (Deep Run)
Mrs D Thomson (J R Turner 8/6) Tillyrie Racing Club

Placings:*6-6*30003P6PP3 **(4898)**
2001/02: 16^{6}GF, 20^{3}F, 22^{0}G, 16^{0}G, 22^{0}GS, 20^{3}G, 16^{P}S, 20^{6}S, 24^{P}S, 22^{P}HY, 16^{3}G

	Starts	1st	2nd	3rd	Win & Pl
NH Flat	1	0	0	0	0
Hurdles	10	0	0	3	1427
Career Total	**12**	**0**	**0**	**3**	**1427**

Going: Sf: 0-4 GS: 0-1 Gd: 0-4 GF: - Fm: 0-2
Distance: 2m/2m3: 0-4 2m4-2m7: 0-6 3m+: 0-1
Track: LH: 0-6 RH: 0-5 Tight: 0-8 Gall: 0-1
Aids: Bl: 0-0 Vi: 0-0 Tstrap: 0-0
Best Rating: 70 12/01 Muss 2m4f good Hdl

Modest hurdler, has been well beaten in ordinary company. Seems best on a sound surface.

Liniyan (IRE)

105 **120**

7-y-o b g Kahyasi-Linnga (IRE) (Shardari)
Miss Venetia Williams Mrs P A H Hartley

Placings:*210*/13P/UF-P61P **(3400)**
2001/02: 26^{P}GS, 22^{6}S, 26^{1}G, 26^{P}S

	Starts	1st	2nd	3rd	Win & Pl
Chases	4	1	0	0	3776
Career Total	**12**	**3**	**1**	**1**	**9033**

105	12/01	Font	3m2f110y	E Ch	GD	£3776
113	10/99	Strf	2m6f110y	E Hdl	G-S	£2040
98	3/99	Strf	2m110y	H NHF	HVY	£2305

Total win prize-money £8122

Going: Sf: 0-2 GS: 0-1 Gd: 1-1 GF: - Fm: 0-0
Distance: 2m/2m3: 0-0 2m4-2m7: 0-1 **3m+: 1-3**
Track: LH: 0-0 RH: 0-1 **Tight: 1-2** Gall: 0-0
Aids: Bl: 0-0 Vi: 0-0 **Tstrap: 1-2**
Best Rating: 120 4/01 Hntg 3m soft Ch

Has won a bumper and a novices' hurdle back in 1999, but had real trouble completing in his early starts over fences and the race he won in a tongue tie at Fontwell in December 2001 was a non-event. Has had breathing problems. Stays three and a quarter miles. Acts on soft ground.

Link Copper

13-y-o ch g Whistlefield-Letitica (Deep Run)
Mrs E J Taplin Mrs E J Taplin

Placings:5P/PP/2P/4 **(4735)**
2001/02: 23^{4}F

	Starts	1st	2nd	3rd	Win & Pl
Chases	1	0	0	0	136
Career Total	**7**	**0**	**1**	**0**	**646**

Going: Sf: 0-0 GS: 0-0 Gd: 0-0 GF: - Fm: 0-1
Distance: 2m/2m3: 0-0 2m4-2m7: 0-0 3m+: 0-1
Track: LH: 0-0 RH: 0-1 Tight: 0-0 Gall: 0-0
Aids: Bl: 0-0 Vi: 0-0 Tstrap: 0-0
Best Rating: 91 5/97 Winc 2m5f firm Ch

Linlathen

12-y-o ch g Move Off-Loch Brandy (Harwell)
P Hutchinson Mrs P J Hutchinson

Placings:465/2F511/124/141U233234243/252B/UF/F 344-4UU **(0556)**
2001/02: 21^{4}GF, 22^{U}G, 24^{U}GF

	Starts	1st	2nd	3rd	Win & Pl
Chases	3	0	0	0	0
Career Total	**37**	**5**	**7**	**5**	**23349**

106	6/97	Prth	3m	E Ch	G-F	£3061
118	5/97	Prth	2m4f110y	D(0-120)HHdl	G-S	£2818
103	5/96	Weth	2m	D Hdl	GD	£2810
105	5/96	Kels	2m6f110y	D(0-125)HHdl	SFT	£2941
100	1/96	Muss	2m4f	E(0-100)HHdl	GD	£3346

Total win prize-money £14977

Going: Sf: 0-0 GS: 0-0 Gd: 0-1 GF: - Fm: 0-2
Distance: 2m/2m3: 0-0 2m4-2m7: 0-2 3m+: 0-1
Track: LH: 0-1 RH: 0-2 Tight: 0-2 Gall: 0-1
Aids: Bl: 0-0 Vi: 0-0 Tstrap: 0-0
Best Rating: 118 11/97 Ayr 2m4f gd-sft Hdl

Linning Wine (IRE)

80 **70**

6-y-o b g Scenic-Zallaka (IRE) (Shardari)
B G Powell The Winning Line

Placings:*103*-0 **(1847)**
2001/02: 16^{0}G

	Starts	1st	2nd	3rd	Win & Pl
Hurdles	1	0	0	0	
Career Total	**4**	**1**	**0**	**1**	**1940**

107	1/01	Kemp	2m	H NHF	SFT	£1673

Total win prize-money £1673

Going: Sf: 0-0 GS: 0-0 Gd: 0-1 GF: - Fm: 0-0
Distance: 2m/2m3: 0-1 2m4-2m7: 0-0 3m+: 0-0
Track: LH: 0-0 RH: 0-1 Tight: 0-0 Gall: 0-0
Aids: Bl: 0-0 Vi: 0-0 Tstrap: 0-0
Best Rating: 107 4/01 MRas 1m5f110y gd-sft NHF

Lipica (IRE)

4-y-o b f Night Shift (USA)-Top Knot (High Top)
K R Burke Paul Green

Placings:P **(3621)**
2001/02: 17^{P}GS

	Starts	1st	2nd	3rd	Win & Pl
Hurdles	1	0	0	0	
Career Total	**1**	**0**	**0**	**0**	

Going: Sf: 0-0 GS: 0-1 Gd: 0-0 GF: - Fm: 0-0
Distance: 2m/2m3: 0-1 2m4-2m7: 0-0 3m+: 0-0
Track: LH: 0-0 RH: 0-1 Tight: 0-1 Gall: 0-0
Aids: Bl: 0-0 Vi: 0-0 Tstrap: 0-1
Best Rating: mfy

Lirkimalong

88 **64**

9-y-o ch g Lir-Kimberley Ann (St Columbus)
Miss S Young B R J Young

Placings:U0 **(3511)**
2001/02: 16^{U}S, 17^{0}S

	Starts	1st	2nd	3rd	Win & Pl
Hurdles	2	0	0	0	
Career Total	**2**	**0**	**0**	**0**	

Going: Sf: 0-2 GS: 0-0 Gd: 0-0 GF: - Fm: 0-0
Distance: 2m/2m3: 0-2 2m4-2m7: 0-0 3m+: 0-0
Track: LH: 0-1 RH: 0-1 Tight: 0-1 Gall: 0-0
Aids: Bl: 0-0 Vi: 0-0 Tstrap: 0-0
Best Rating: 64 1/02 Tntn 2m1f soft Hdl

Lirsleftover

96 **90**

10-y-o ch g Lir-Full Tan (Dairialatan)
Miss S Young B R J Young

Placings:605F56 **(4184)**
2001/02: 19^{6}F, 21^{0}G, 26^{5}GF, 19^{F}S, 23^{5}G, 24^{6}S

	Starts	1st	2nd	3rd	Win & Pl
Chases	6	0	0	0	0
Career Total	**6**	**0**	**0**	**0**	**0**

Going: Sf: 0-2 GS: 0-0 Gd: 0-2 GF: - Fm: 0-2
Distance: 2m/2m3: 0-0 2m4-2m7: 0-3 3m+: 0-3
Track: LH: 0-2 RH: 0-3 Tight: 0-2 Gall: 0-0
Aids: Bl: 0-0 Vi: 0-0 Tstrap: 0-0
Best Rating: 90 5/01 Chel 2m5f good Ch

Lisa-B (IRE)

97 **76**

5-y-o b m Case Law-Nishiki (USA) (Brogan (USA))
D L Williams Wentworths Racing Group

Placings:55060 **(4752)**
2001/02: 16^{5}G, 16^{5}HY, 16^{0}S, 21^{6}GS, 16^{0}GF

	Starts	1st	2nd	3rd	Win & Pl
Hurdles	5	0	0	0	0
Career Total	**5**	**0**	**0**	**0**	**0**

Going: Sf: 0-2 GS: 0-1 Gd: 0-1 GF: - Fm: 0-1
Distance: 2m/2m3: 0-4 2m4-2m7: 0-1 3m+: 0-0
Track: LH: 0-2 RH: 0-3 Tight: 0-0 Gall: 0-0
Aids: Bl: 0-0 Vi: 0-0 Tstrap: 0-1
Best Rating: 74 12/01 Ludl 2m good Hdl

Selling hurdler.

Lisaan (IRE)

107 **132**

5-y-o ch g Bigstone (IRE)-Linnga (IRE) (Shardari)
William Durkan Mrs Beatrice Durkan

Placings:00116-50B4031200 **(4674)**
2001/02: 16^{5}G, 16^{0}S, 20^{B}YS, 20^{4}YS, 20^{0}S, 18^{3}Y, 16^{1}S, 16^{2}GS, 16^{0}HY, 16^{0}G

	Starts	1st	2nd	3rd	Win & Pl
Hurdles	10	1	1	1	15097
Career Total	**15**	**3**	**1**	**1**	**39009**

129	1/02	Cork	2m	(0-123)HHdl	SFT	£9969
134	2/01	Leop	2m	Hdl	HVY	£18346
119	1/01	Gowr	2m	Hdl	SFT	£5564

Total win prize-money £33881

Going: Sf: 1-4 GS: 0-1 Gd: 0-2 GF: - Fm: 0-0
Distance: **2m/2m3: 1-7** 2m4-2m7: 0-3 3m+: 0-0
Track: LH: 0-3 RH: 0-3 Tight: 0-1 Gall: 0-0
Aids: **Bl: 1-7** Vi: 0-0 Tstrap: 0-0
Best Rating: 134 2/01 Leop 2m heavy Hdl

A fair Irish hurdler, he acts very well with cut in the ground and goes well over two miles. Comes to hand January/February time.

Lisdante (IRE)

103 127

9-y-o b g Phardante (FR)-Shuil Eile (Deep Run)

Mrs S J Smith Keith Nicholson

Placings:004F3F4/200042P23P231/1P15P-52 **(4870)**

2001/02: 20⁵GS, 23²GF

	Starts	1st	2nd	3rd	Win & Pl
Chases	2	0	1	0	1690
Career Total	**27**	**3**	**5**	**3**	**26636**

114	11/00	Weth	3m1f	D(0-120)HCh	HVY	£6608
115	6/00	MRas	2m6f110y	E(0-105)HCh	G-F	£4290
109	4/00	Weth	3m5f	C HCh	SFT	£5980

Total win prize-money £16878

Going: Sf: 0-0 GS: 0-1 Gd: 0-0 GF: - Fm: 0-1
Distance: 2m/2m3: 0-0 2m4-2m7: 0-1 3m+: 0-1
Track: LH: 0-0 RH: 0-1 Tight: 0-0 Gall: 0-0
Aids: Bl: 0-0 Vi: 0-0 Tstrap: 0-0
Best Rating: **115** 6/00 MRas 2m6f110y gd-fm Ch

Fair chaser, stays well and handles most types of ground. In good form in the early summer of 2002.

Lislaughtin Abbey

106 118

10-y-o ch g Nicholas Bill-Kates Fling (USA) (Quiet Fling (USA))

O Brennan T W R Bayley

Placings:0/P00P/211U53221311/1FF212410121/U225 P-P244P316 **(4920)**

2001/02: 24ᴾS, 16²S, 19⁴GF, 19⁴G, 19ᴾS, 21³G, 21¹GF, 21⁶GF

	Starts	1st	2nd	3rd	Win & Pl
Chases	8	1	1	1	6150
Career Total	**41**	**6**	**8**	**5**	**33746**

109	4/02	Sedg	2m5f	D(0-115)HCh	G-F	£3874
126	4/00	Fknm	2m5f110y	F(0-110)HCh	GD	£4621
126	3/00	Fknm	2m5f110y	D(0-120)HCh	GD	£3974
119	12/99	Fknm	2m110y	F(0-100)HCh	GD	£2263
98	5/99	Fknm	2m5f110y	F(0-110)HCh	G-F	£3989
92	10/98	Sthl	2m4f110y	E(0-110)HCh	GD	£2997

Total win prize-money £21721

Going: Sf: 0-3 GS: 0-0 Gd: 0-2 GF: - Fm: 1-3
Distance: 2m/2m3: 0-2 **2m4-2m7: 1-5** 3m+: 0-1
Track: **LH: 1-8** RH: 0-0 **Tight: 1-6** Gall: 0-2
Aids: Bl: 0-0 Vi: 0-0 Tstrap: 0-0
Best Rating: **126** 12/00 Fknm 3m110y gd-sft Ch

A Fakenham specialist, he has won four times at the Norfolk track. Best on good ground or faster, he stays three miles, but is probably better over shorter.

Lislaughtin Cross (IRE)

7-y-o ch g Bustomi-Petham Belle (Red Alert)

O Brennan Mrs Pat Brennan

Placings:0P **(4519)**

2001/02: 17⁰S, 21ᴾGS

	Starts	1st	2nd	3rd	Win & Pl
NH Flat	1	0	0	0	0
Hurdles	1	0	0	0	0
Career Total	**2**	**0**	**0**	**0**	

Going: Sf: 0-1 GS: 0-1 Gd: 0-0 GF: - Fm: 0-0
Distance: 2m/2m3: 0-1 2m4-2m7: 0-1 3m+: 0-0
Track: LH: 0-0 RH: 0-2 Tight: 0-1 Gall: 0-0
Aids: Bl: 0-0 Vi: 0-0 Tstrap: 0-0
Best Rating:

Lismeenan (IRE)

103 94

8-y-o ch g Be My Native (USA)-Sakanda (IRE) (Vayrann)

C P Morlock Mrs Z S Clark

Placings:63405/315F25414/P003 **(4853)**

2001/02: 19ᴾGS, 16⁰GF, 16⁰G, 16³G

	Starts	1st	2nd	3rd	Win & Pl
Hurdles	4	0	0	1	566
Career Total	**18**	**2**	**1**	**3**	**10248**

109	11/99	Naas	2m	(0-132)HHdl	Y-S	£5236
99	6/99	Rosc	2m	Hdl	G-F	£2516

Total win prize-money £7754

Going: Sf: 0-0 GS: 0-1 Gd: 0-2 GF: - Fm: 0-1
Distance: 2m/2m3: 0-4 2m4-2m7: 0-0 3m+: 0-0
Track: LH: 0-1 RH: 0-3 Tight: 0-1 Gall: 0-0
Aids: Bl: 0-0 Vi: 0-0 Tstrap: 0-0
Best Rating: **109** 11/99 Fair 2m yld-sft Hdl

Won a maiden hurdle in Ireland before winning a handicap hurdle in 1999. Returned from nearly two years off when making his British debut at Exeter in November 2001, but was pulled up. Looks suited by two miles and most types of ground, bar extremes of going. Showed definite signs of a return to form when running well from out of the handicap at Stratford April 2002.

Liss A Paoraigh (IRE)

118 160

7-y-o b m Husyan (USA)-Shuil Liss (Deep Run)

John E Kiely Mrs N Flynn

Placings:31/11112-312F20 **(4190)**

2001/02: 16³S, 20¹Y, 20²Y, 16FY, 16²HY, 16⁰GS

	Starts	1st	2nd	3rd	Win & Pl
Hurdles	6	1	2	1	48722
Career Total	**13**	**6**	**3**	**2**	**104463**

160	11/01	Navn	2m4f	Hdl	YLD	£19657
137	12/00	Fair	2m	Hdl	Y-S	£23400
116	11/00	Naas	2m3f	Hdl	Y-S	£4692
128	10/00	Gowr	2m1f	Hdl	SFT	£4416
123	5/00	Punc	2m	NHF	GD	£13000
99	3/00	Clon	2m2f	NHF	G-Y	£3036

Total win prize-money £68201

Going: Sf: 0-2 GS: 0-1 Gd: 0-0 GF: - Fm: 0-0
Distance: 2m/2m3: 0-4 **2m4-2m7: 1-2** 3m+: 0-0
Track: **LH: 1-4** RH: 0-1 Tight: 0-0 Gall: 0-0
Aids: Bl: 0-0 Vi: 0-0 Tstrap: 0-0
Best Rating: **160** 12/01 Fair 2m4f yield Hdl

She ran up a sequence of five wins in bumpers and hurdles in Ireland before meeting the very smart Colonel Braxton at Leopardstown on her final start of 2000/01 and coming off second-best. Ran consistently against the top hurdlers in 2001/02. Effective at two miles but at her best over two and a half miles on ground with give. She is a very tough, game mare.

Listen To Us (IRE)

89f 82f

6-y-o b g Mandalus-Lady Laburnum (Carlingford Castle)

N J Henderson Mrs Brenda Russell

Placings:5 **(0684)**

2001/02: 17⁵G

	Starts	1st	2nd	3rd	Win & Pl
NH Flat	1	0	0	0	0
Career Total	**1**	**0**	**0**	**0**	**0**

Going: Sf: 0-0 GS: 0-0 Gd: 0-1 GF: - Fm: 0-0
Distance: 2m/2m3: 0-1 2m4-2m7: 0-0 3m+: 0-0
Track: LH: 0-1 RH: 0-0 Tight: 0-1 Gall: 0-0
Aids: Bl: 0-0 Vi: 0-0 Tstrap: 0-0
Best Rating: **82** 6/01 NAbb 2m1f good NHF

Listen Up

102 99

7-y-o b m Good Thyne (USA)-Inbisat (Beldale Flutter (USA))

R T Phillips The Listeners

Placings:110-032P **(4420)**

2001/02: 16⁰GS, 20³S, 19²HY, 21ᴾGS

	Starts	1st	2nd	3rd	Win & Pl
Hurdles	4	0	1	1	1556
Career Total	**7**	**2**	**1**	**1**	**4790**

102	3/01	MRas	2m1f110y	H NHF	GD	£1736
110	1/01	Folk	2m1f110y	H NHF	HVY	£1498

Total win prize-money £3234

Going: Sf: 0-2 GS: 0-2 Gd: 0-0 GF: - Fm: 0-0
Distance: 2m/2m3: 0-1 2m4-2m7: 0-3 3m+: 0-0
Track: LH: 0-1 RH: 0-2 Tight: 0-1 Gall: 0-1
Aids: Bl: 0-0 Vi: 0-0 Tstrap: 0-0
Best Rating: **110** 1/01 Folk 2m1f110y heavy NHF

Twice a winner in bumpers, she has been placed in novice hurdles at around two and a half miles. Suited by soft ground.

Litchanine (FR)

9-y-o gr g Linamix (FR)-Margello (Bargello)

M C Pipe P A D Scouller

Placings:12/0522P304/F4P/P5-121 **(0577)**

2001/02: 20¹GF, 21²G, 21¹GF

	Starts	1st	2nd	3rd	Win & Pl
Chases	3	2	1	0	5283
Career Total	**18**	**3**	**4**	**1**	**49450**

122	6/01	Strf	2m5f110y	H Ch	G-F	£3188
115	5/01	Hntg	2m4f110y	H Ch	G-F	£1098
	3/98	Autl	2m1f110y	Hdl	SFT	£14141

Total win prize-money £18429

Going: Sf: 0-0 GS: 0-0 Gd: 0-1 GF: - Fm: 2-2
Distance: 2m/2m3: 0-0 **2m4-2m7: 2-3** 3m+: 0-0
Track: LH: 1-1 RH: 1-1 Tight: 1-1 Gall: 1-1
Aids: Bl: 0-0 Vi: 0-0 Tstrap: 0-0
Best Rating: **122** 6/01 Strf 2m5f110y gd-fm Ch

Little Alfie (IRE)

81 76

5-y-o b g Shahanndeh-Debbies Scud (IRE) (Roselier (FR))

B S Rothwell Brian Rothwell

Placings:00 **(4873)**

2001/02: 16⁰HY, 16⁰GF

	Starts	1st	2nd	3rd	Win & Pl
NH Flat	2	0	0	0	
Career Total	**2**	**0**	**0**	**0**	

Going: Sf: 0-1 GS: 0-0 Gd: 0-0 GF: - Fm: 0-1
Distance: 2m/2m3: 0-2 2m4-2m7: 0-0 3m+: 0-0

Track: LH: 0-2 RH: 0-0 Tight: 0-1 Gall: 0-0
Aids: Bl: 0-0 Vi: 0-0 Tstrap: 0-0
Best Rating: 61 3/02 Sthl 2m heavy NHF

Little Big Horse (IRE)

103 **85+**

6-y-o b g Little Bighorn-Little Gort (Roselier (FR))
Mrs S J Smith Paul J Dixon

Placings:2660P **(4857)**
2001/02: 16^{2}G, 16^{6}G, 16^{6}G, 19^{0}GS, 20^{P}G

	Starts	1st	2nd	3rd	Win & Pl
NH Flat	2	0	1	0	674
Hurdles	3	0	0	0	
Career Total	**5**	**0**	**1**	**0**	**674**

Going: Sf: 0-0 GS: 0-1 Gd: 0-4 GF: - Fm: 0-0
Distance: 2m/2m3: 0-3 2m4-2m7: 0-2 3m+: 0-0
Track: LH: 0-4 RH: 0-1 Tight: 0-1 Gall: 0-2
Aids: Bl: 0-0 Vi: 0-0 Tstrap: 0-0
Best Rating: 103 11/01 Weth 2m good NHF

Is only small and cheaply bought and after showing some ability in bumpers is only very moderate so far over hurdles.

Little Brockwell (IRE)

9-y-o ch m Nestor-Tacovaon (Avocat)
A Parker W E Philipson

Placings:PU5P **(4859)**
2001/02: 21^{P}S, 25^{U}GS, 27^{5}S, 25^{P}G

	Starts	1st	2nd	3rd	Win & Pl
Chases	4	0	0	0	0
Career Total	**4**	**0**	**0**	**0**	**0**

Going: Sf: 0-2 GS: 0-1 Gd: 0-1 GF: - Fm: 0-0
Distance: 2m/2m3: 0-0 2m4-2m7: 0-1 3m+: 0-3
Track: LH: 0-3 RH: 0-0 Tight: 0-2 Gall: 0-0
Aids: Bl: 0-0 Vi: 0-0 Tstrap: 0-0
Best Rating: mfy

Useful staying pointer but has yet to make any impact under Rules.

Little Brown Bear (IRE)

8-y-o br g Strong Gale-Gladtogetit (Green Shoon)
R Ford G B Barlow

Placings:P-3F3142 **(4846)**
2001/02: 25^{3}GF, 24^{F}GF, 24^{3}S, 24^{1}GS, 26^{4}GS, 24^{2}G

	Starts	1st	2nd	3rd	Win & Pl
Chases	6	1	1	2	6944
Career Total	**7**	**1**	**1**	**2**	**6944**
100 2/02 Muss 3m	E(0-105)HCh			G-S	£5096

Total win prize-money £5096

Going: Sf: 0-1 GS: 1-2 Gd: 0-1 GF: - Fm: 0-2
Distance: 2m/2m3: 0-0 2m4-2m7: 0-0 **3m+: 1-6**
Track: LH: 0-3 **RH: 1-3 Tight: 1-3** Gall: 0-1
Aids: Bl: 0-0 Vi: 0-0 Tstrap: 0-0
Best Rating: 111 4/02 Bang 3m110y good Ch

A modest pointer and a plodder under Rules, is suited by positive tactics and won two modest handicaps on a sound surface in the first half of 2002. Acts on a sound surface, stays three miles plus.

Little Bud

103 **100**

8-y-o br m Lord Bud-Sindur (Rolfe (USA))
Miss A M Newton-Smith Mrs John Grist

Placings:6/0660P/6020/P030144-154011FP54 **(4782)**
2001/02: 17^{1}GS, 17^{5}GF, 16^{4}GF, 21^{0}GS, 21^{1}GS, 16^{1}G, 16^{F}G, 16^{P}GF, 21^{5}GF, 16^{4}GF

	Starts	1st	2nd	3rd	Win & Pl
Hurdles	10	3	0	0	7196
Career Total	**27**	**4**	**1**	**1**	**10934**
95 11/01 Plum 2m	F(0-110)HHdl			GD	£3178
95 11/01 Plum 2m5f	F(0-90)HHdl			G-S	£2352
89 5/01 Folk 2m1f110y	G(0-95)HHdl			G-S	£1666
80 11/00 Plum 2m	F Hdl			HVY	£2278

Total win prize-money £9475

Going: Sf: 0-0 GS: 2-3 Gd: 1-2 GF: - Fm: 0-5
Distance: **2m/2m3: 2-7** 2m4-2m7: 1-3 3m+: 0-0
Track: **LH: 2-7** RH: 1-3 **Tight: 3-9** Gall: 0-1
Aids: Bl: 0-0 Vi: 0-0 Tstrap: 0-0
Best Rating: 100 12/01 Plum 2m good Hdl

A selling-class hurdler, she stays two miles five furlongs and likes the ground to be "either fast or sloppy" according to her trainer. Not the most consistent, she goes particularly well at Plumpton where she has won three times.

Little Chapel (IRE)

6-y-o b m College Chapel-Istaraka (IRE) (Darshaan)
G H Yardley Philip Jones

Placings:P **(1797)**
2001/02: 16^{P}S

	Starts	1st	2nd	3rd	Win & Pl
Hurdles	1	0	0	0	
Career Total	**1**	**0**	**0**	**0**	

Going: Sf: 0-1 GS: 0-0 Gd: 0-0 GF: - Fm: 0-0
Distance: 2m/2m3: 0-1 2m4-2m7: 0-0 3m+: 0-0
Track: LH: 0-1 RH: 0-0 Tight: 0-0 Gall: 0-0
Aids: Bl: 0-0 Vi: 0-0 Tstrap: 0-0
Best Rating:

Little Docker (IRE)

105 **106**

5-y-o b g Vettori (IRE)-Fair Maid Of Kent (USA) (Diesis)
T D Easterby C H Stevens

Placings:421 **(2767)**
2001/02: 20^{4}G, 16^{2}G, 19^{1}G

	Starts	1st	2nd	3rd	Win & Pl
Hurdles	3	1	1	0	3694
Career Total	**3**	**1**	**1**	**0**	**3694**
106 12/01 Catt 2m3f	E Hdl			GD	£2565

Total win prize-money £2566

Going: Sf: 0-0 GS: 0-0 Gd: 1-3 GF: - Fm: 0-0
Distance: **2m/2m3: 1-2** 2m4-2m7: 0-1 3m+: 0-0
Track: **LH: 1-3** RH: 0-0 **Tight: 1-1** Gall: 0-0
Aids: Bl: 0-0 Vi: 0-0 Tstrap: 0-0
Best Rating: 106 12/01 Catt 2m3f good Hdl

Promising efforts in novice hurdles in the autumn, looking a stayer.

Little Dragon

75(55h) (20h)**36**

7-y-o b m Teenoso (USA)-Boreen's Glory (Boreen (FR))
R H Alner Club Ten

Placings:06/PP-05 **(4780)**
2001/02: 16^{0}G, 17^{5}GF

	Starts	1st	2nd	3rd	Win & Pl
Hurdles	1	0	0	0	0
Chases	1	0	0	0	0
Career Total	**6**	**0**	**0**	**0**	**0**

Going: Sf: 0-0 GS: 0-0 Gd: 0-1 GF: - Fm: 0-1
Distance: 2m/2m3: 0-2 2m4-2m7: 0-0 3m+: 0-0
Track: LH: 0-1 RH: 0-1 Tight: 0-1 Gall: 0-0
Aids: Bl: 0-0 Vi: 0-0 Tstrap: 0-0
Best Rating: 55 11/99 Tntn 2m1f good NHF

Little Elle

97 **87**

8-y-o ch m Minster Son-Eillie On (Spur On)
J L Goulding M W Shirvinton

Placings:0/0060/032-43104650 **(3362)**
2001/02: 16^{4}GF, 20^{3}GF, 20^{1}GF, 22^{0}GS, 17^{4}S, 16^{6}GF, 19^{5}G, 25^{0}GS

	Starts	1st	2nd	3rd	Win & Pl
Hurdles	8	1	0	1	3678
Career Total	**16**	**1**	**1**	**2**	**4726**
81 6/01 Prth 2m4f110y	D Hdl			G-F	£3406

Total win prize-money £3406

Going: Sf: 0-1 GS: 0-2 Gd: 0-1 GF: - Fm: 1-4
Distance: 2m/2m3: 0-4 **2m4-2m7: 1-3** 3m+: 0-1
Track: LH: 0-6 **RH: 1-2** Tight: 0-4 Gall: 0-0
Aids: Bl: 0-0 Vi: 0-0 Tstrap: 0-0
Best Rating: 87 5/01 Hexm 2m4f110y gd-fm Hdl

Little Farmer

97 **95**

8-y-o b g Little Wolf-Sea Farmer (Cantab)
D M Grissell Christopher Hall

Placings:P-43 **(0431)**
2001/02: 20^{4}G, 17^{3}GF

	Starts	1st	2nd	3rd	Win & Pl
Hurdles	2	0	0	1	364
Career Total	**3**	**0**	**0**	**1**	**364**

Going: Sf: 0-0 GS: 0-0 Gd: 0-1 GF: - Fm: 0-1
Distance: 2m/2m3: 0-1 2m4-2m7: 0-1 3m+: 0-0
Track: LH: 0-0 RH: 0-2 Tight: 0-1 Gall: 0-1
Aids: Bl: 0-0 Vi: 0-0 Tstrap: 0-0
Best Rating: 95 5/01 Folk 2m1f110y gd-fm Hdl

Little Feat

102f **92f**

7-y-o b m Terimon-Run On Stirling (Celtic Cone)
Ian Williams J L Rowsell

Placings:10-1 **(1263)**
2001/02: 16^{1}GF

	Starts	1st	2nd	3rd	Win & Pl
NH Flat	1	1	0	0	1467
Career Total	**3**	**2**	**0**	**0**	**2923**
92 8/01 Hntg 2m110y	H NHF			G-F	£1466
103 7/00 Worc 2m	H NHF			GD	£1456

Total win prize-money £2923

Going: Sf: 0-0 GS: 0-0 Gd: 0-0 GF: - Fm: 1-1
Distance: 2m/2m3: 1-1 2m4-2m7: 0-0 3m+: 0-0
Track: LH: 0-0 **RH: 1-1** Tight: 0-0 **Gall: 1-1**
Aids: Bl: 0-0 Vi: 0-0 Tstrap: 0-0
Best Rating: 103 7/00 Worc 2m good NHF

Little Flirt (IRE)

5-y-o ch m Roselier (FR)-Powleyvale (Roi Guillaume (FR))
B S Rothwell Mrs Liz Hunt

Placings:*0* **(4860)**
2001/02: 16^{0}G

	Starts	1st	2nd	3rd	Win & Pl
NH Flat	1	0	0	0	
Career Total	**1**	**0**	**0**	**0**	

Going: Sf: 0-0 GS: 0-0 Gd: 0-1 GF: - Fm: 0-0
Distance: 2m/2m3: 0-1 2m4-2m7: 0-0 3m+: 0-0
Track: LH: 0-0 RH: 0-0 Tight: 0-0 Gall: 0-0
Aids: Bl: 0-0 Vi: 0-0 Tstrap: 0-0
Best Rating:

Little Flora

106 103
6-y-o ch m Alflora (IRE)-Sister's Choice (Lepanto (GER))
A Scott Mrs A Scott

Placings:0/00P35003-02334312355046101 **(4919)**
2001/02: 21^{0}G, 20^{2}GF, 20^{3}GF, 20^{3}GS, 20^{4}G, 19^{3}G, 21^{1}GF, 19^{2}GF, 20^{3}G, 22^{5}GS, 21^{5}GF, 20^{0}G, 16^{4}S, 20^{6}G, 16^{1}GF, 20^{0}G, 21^{1}GF

	Starts	1st	2nd	3rd	Win & Pl
Hurdles	17	3	2	4	11103
Career Total	**26**	**3**	**2**	**6**	**11992**

103	4/02	Sedg	2m5f110y	E(0-105)HHdl	G-F	£2618
90	4/02	Hexm	2m110y	E Hdl	G-F	£2835
91	7/01	Sedg	2m5f110y	E Hdl	G-F	£2471

Total win prize-money £7924

Going: Sf: 0-1 GS: 0-2 Gd: 0-7 GF: - Fm: 3-7
Distance: 2m/2m3: 1-2 **2m4-2m7: 2-15** 3m+: 0-0
Track: **LH: 2-12** RH: 0-4 **Tight: 2-7** Gall: 0-1
Aids: Bl: 0-0 Vi: 0-0 Tstrap: 0-0
Best Rating: 103 4/02 Sedg 2m5f110y gd-fm Hdl

Moderate hurdler, best on a sound surface and sharp tracks. Was winning for the third time when successful at Sedgefield in April. Appreciates fast ground.

Little Herman (IRE)

79 90
6-y-o b g Mandalus-Kilbricken Bay (Salluceva)
J A B Old W E Sturt

Placings:*060* **(3892)**
2001/02: 16^{0}G, 20^{6}GS, 21^{0}HY

	Starts	1st	2nd	3rd	Win & Pl
NH Flat	1	0	0	0	0
Hurdles	2	0	0	0	0
Career Total	**3**	**0**	**0**	**0**	**0**

Going: Sf: 0-1 GS: 0-1 Gd: 0-1 GF: - Fm: 0-0
Distance: 2m/2m3: 0-1 2m4-2m7: 0-2 3m+: 0-0
Track: LH: 0-0 RH: 0-2 Tight: 0-0 Gall: 0-0
Aids: Bl: 0-0 Vi: 0-0 Tstrap: 0-0
Best Rating: 90 1/02 Asct 2m4f gd-sft Hdl

Little Hooligan

85 40
11-y-o b/br g Rabdan-Nutwood Emma (Henbit (USA))
J S Smith G W Hackling

Placings:1540P12023200/6532345140500/64434521/P40P03/451502256/6006*6-0* **(0983)**
2001/02: 19^{0}G

	Starts	1st	2nd	3rd	Win & Pl
Hurdles	1	0	0	0	
Career Total	**55**	**5**	**7**	**5**	**15762**

74	10/99	Extr	2m3f	G(0-95)HHdl	GD	£1672
69	11/97	Tntn	2m1f	G(0-90)HHdl	GD	£1889
83	11/96	Tntn	2m1f	G(0-90)HHdl	G-F	£2004
74	10/95	Extr	2m1f110y	G(0-95)HHdl	G-F	£1861
65	8/95	Extr	2m1f110y	E Hdl	HRD	£2211

Total win prize-money £9638

Going: Sf: 0-0 GS: 0-0 Gd: 0-1 GF: - Fm: 0-0
Distance: 2m/2m3: 0-1 2m4-2m7: 0-0 3m+: 0-0
Track: LH: 0-1 RH: 0-0 Tight: 0-1 Gall: 0-0
Aids: Bl: 0-1 Vi: 0-0 Tstrap: 0-0
Best Rating: 89 12/95 Extr 2m2f good Hdl

Little Les

95 83
6-y-o b g Jumbo Hirt (USA)-Hand On Heart (IRE) (Taufan (USA))
F P Murtagh (J L Eyre 1/8) L Irving

Placings:*P-50P05SP* **(3553)**
2001/02: 17^{5}G, 17^{0}GF, 17^{P}GS, 16^{0}S, 17^{5}GF, 16^{S}GS, 19^{P}S

	Starts	1st	2nd	3rd	Win & Pl
Hurdles	7	0	0	0	0
Career Total	**8**	**0**	**0**	**0**	**0**

Going: Sf: 0-2 GS: 0-2 Gd: 0-1 GF: - Fm: 0-2
Distance: 2m/2m3: 0-7 2m4-2m7: 0-0 3m+: 0-0
Track: LH: 0-6 RH: 0-0 Tight: 0-6 Gall: 0-0
Aids: Bl: 0-0 Vi: 0-0 Tstrap: 0-0
Best Rating: 71 8/01 Ctml 2m1f110y good Hdl

Selling hurdler.

Little Miss Prim

91 91
6-y-o b m Gildoran-Laced Up (IRE) (The Parson)
J G O'Neill J G O'Neill

Placings:*4-00P5* **(2662)**
2001/02: 16^{0}GF, 16^{0}G, 21^{P}S, 17^{5}G

	Starts	1st	2nd	3rd	Win & Pl
NH Flat	2	0	0	0	0
Hurdles	2	0	0	0	0
Career Total	**5**	**0**	**0**	**0**	**0**

Going: Sf: 0-1 GS: 0-0 Gd: 0-2 GF: - Fm: 0-1
Distance: 2m/2m3: 0-3 2m4-2m7: 0-1 3m+: 0-0
Track: LH: 0-3 RH: 0-1 Tight: 0-0 Gall: 0-1
Aids: Bl: 0-0 Vi: 0-0 Tstrap: 0-0
Best Rating: 91 12/01 Chel 2m1f good Hdl

Little Mister

48 4
6-y-o ch g Gran Alba (USA)-Chrissytino (Baron Blakeney)
N R Mitchell N J Powell

Placings:*00* **(1846)**
2001/02: 17^{0}GF, 22^{0}G

	Starts	1st	2nd	3rd	Win & Pl
NH Flat	1	0	0	0	0
Hurdles	1	0	0	0	0
Career Total	**2**	**0**	**0**	**0**	

Going: Sf: 0-0 GS: 0-0 Gd: 0-1 GF: - Fm: 0-1
Distance: 2m/2m3: 0-1 2m4-2m7: 0-1 3m+: 0-0
Track: LH: 0-0 RH: 0-1 Tight: 0-1 Gall: 0-0
Aids: Bl: 0-0 Vi: 0-0 Tstrap: 0-0
Best Rating: 4 10/01 Winc 2m6f good Hdl

Little Native (IRE)

7-y-o b/br g Be My Native (USA)-Royal Character (Reformed Character)
R Kelvin-Hughes R Kelvin-Hughes

Placings:P **(0218)**
2001/02: 21^{P}GF

	Starts	1st	2nd	3rd	Win & Pl
Chases	1	0	0	0	
Career Total	**1**	**0**	**0**	**0**	

Going: Sf: 0-0 GS: 0-0 Gd: 0-0 GF: - Fm: 0-1
Distance: 2m/2m3: 0-0 2m4-2m7: 0-1 3m+: 0-0
Track: LH: 0-0 RH: 0-1 Tight: 0-0 Gall: 0-0
Aids: Bl: 0-0 Vi: 0-0 Tstrap: 0-0
Best Rating:

Little Notice (IRE)

95 100
11-y-o b g Cheval-A Weeks Notice (IRE) (Ovac (ITY))
H D Daly Miss S M Carpenter

Placings:40F/6/3/1421F5P0/20-2F **(0671)**
2001/02: 24^{2}F, 24^{F}G

	Starts	1st	2nd	3rd	Win & Pl
Hurdles	2	0	1	0	712
Career Total	**17**	**2**	**3**	**1**	**11116**

110	11/99	Ludl	3m	E(0-105)HCh	GD	£3891
100	5/99	Hrfd	3m1f110y	E(0-115)HCh	G-S	£3590

Total win prize-money £7482

Going: Sf: 0-0 GS: 0-0 Gd: 0-1 GF: - Fm: 0-1
Distance: 2m/2m3: 0-0 2m4-2m7: 0-0 3m+: 0-2
Track: LH: 0-2 RH: 0-0 Tight: 0-1 Gall: 0-0
Aids: Bl: 0-2 Vi: 0-0 Tstrap: 0-0
Best Rating: 110 11/99 Ludl 3m good Ch

Little Petoski

83 65
7-y-o b g Petoski-Littledrunkgirl (Carlingford Castle)
M J Gingell (Michael Hourigan 27/5) The Good Craic Club

Placings:*50005-5*P550P **(2952)**
2001/02: 20^{5}GF, 18^{P}S, 20^{5}S, 20^{5}S, 16^{0}GS, 16^{P}S

	Starts	1st	2nd	3rd	Win & Pl
NH Flat	1	0	0	0	0
Hurdles	5	0	0	0	0
Career Total	**11**	**0**	**0**	**0**	**0**

Going: Sf: 0-4 GS: 0-1 Gd: 0-0 GF: - Fm: 0-1
Distance: 2m/2m3: 0-3 2m4-2m7: 0-3 3m+: 0-0
Track: LH: 0-4 RH: 0-1 Tight: 0-4 Gall: 0-0
Aids: Bl: 0-0 Vi: 0-0 Tstrap: 0-0
Best Rating: 87 5/01 Tipp 2m4f gd-fm NHF

Little Pippin

108 **120**

6-y-o ch m Rudimentary (USA)-Accuracy (Gunner B)
G B Balding Miss B Swire

Placings:63-313124F **(3399)**
2001/02: 18^{3}GS, 18^{1}GS, 19^{3}G, 19^{1}S, 20^{2}S, 20^{4}G, 18^{F}S

	Starts	1st	2nd	3rd	Win & Pl
Hurdles	7	2	1	2	10734
Career Total	**9**	**2**	**1**	**3**	**11123**

115	12/01	Wwck	2m3f	D Hdl	SFT	£3668
112	10/01	Font	2m2f110y	D(0-120)HHdl	G-S	£3465

Total win prize-money £7133

Going: Sf: 1-3 GS: 1-2 Gd: 0-2 GF: - Fm: 0-0
Distance: **2m/2m3: 2-5** 2m4-2m7: 0-2 3m+: 0-0
Track: **LH: 2-5** RH: 0-1 **Tight: 1-5** Gall: 0-1
Aids: Bl: 0-0 Vi: 0-0 Tstrap: 0-0
Best Rating: **120** 1/02 Font 2m2f110y soft Hdl

Fair handicap hurdler, she acted on a soft surface and stayed two miles three furlongs. Killed in a fall at Fontwell in January. (DEAD)

Little River (IRE)

9-y-o ch g Over The River (FR)-Genevretta (Tall Noble (USA))
Miss Maria D Myco (J Wade 20/1) Miss Maria D Myco

Placings:*60/*S **(0473)**
2001/02: 20^{S}GF

	Starts	1st	2nd	3rd	Win & Pl
Chases	1	0	0	0	
Career Total	**3**	**0**	**0**	**0**	**0**

Going: Sf: 0-0 GS: 0-0 Gd: 0-0 GF: - Fm: 0-1
Distance: 2m/2m3: 0-0 2m4-2m7: 0-1 3m+: 0-0
Track: LH: 0-1 RH: 0-0 Tight: 0-0 Gall: 0-0
Aids: Bl: 0-0 Vi: 0-0 Tstrap: 0-0
Best Rating: **53** 10/98 Sedg 2m1f good NHF

Little Ross

96 **89**

7-y-o b g St Ninian-Little Katrina (Little Buskins)
D M Grissell Mr Barry & Dame Sheila Noakes

Placings:*0/5*-06 **(4411)**
2001/02: 22^{0}S, 18^{6}S

	Starts	1st	2nd	3rd	Win & Pl
Hurdles	2	0	0	0	0
Career Total	**4**	**0**	**0**	**0**	**0**

Going: Sf: 0-2 GS: 0-0 Gd: 0-0 GF: - Fm: 0-0
Distance: 2m/2m3: 0-1 2m4-2m7: 0-1 3m+: 0-0
Track: LH: 0-2 RH: 0-0 Tight: 0-2 Gall: 0-0
Aids: Bl: 0-0 Vi: 0-0 Tstrap: 0-0
Best Rating: **96** 4/00 Hntg 2m110y good NHF

Little Sky

5-y-o gr m Terimon-Brown Coast (Oats)
D Mullarkey Dune Racing

Placings:*0* **(2466)**
2001/02: 17^{0}HY

	Starts	1st	2nd	3rd	Win & Pl
NH Flat	1	0	0	0	
Career Total	**1**	**0**	**0**	**0**	

Going: Sf: 0-1 GS: 0-0 Gd: 0-0 GF: - Fm: 0-0
Distance: 2m/2m3: 0-1 2m4-2m7: 0-0 3m+: 0-0
Track: LH: 0-0 RH: 0-0 Tight: 0-1 Gall: 0-0
Aids: Bl: 0-0 Vi: 0-0 Tstrap: 0-0
Best Rating:

Little Sport (IRE)

86f **109f**

5-y-o ch g Moscow Society (USA)-Ath Dara (Duky)
A Scott Andy Scott

Placings:*206* **(4900)**
2001/02: 16^{2}HY, 17^{0}G, 16^{6}G

	Starts	1st	2nd	3rd	Win & Pl
NH Flat	3	0	1	0	519
Career Total	**3**	**0**	**1**	**0**	**519**

Going: Sf: 0-1 GS: 0-0 Gd: 0-2 GF: - Fm: 0-0
Distance: 2m/2m3: 0-3 2m4-2m7: 0-0 3m+: 0-0
Track: LH: 0-0 RH: 0-1 Tight: 0-0 Gall: 0-0
Aids: Bl: 0-0 Vi: 0-0 Tstrap: 0-0
Best Rating: **109** 3/02 Newc 2m heavy NHF

Runner-up in a bumper on his debut.

Little Starlight

74 **34**

6-y-o gr m Gunner B-Moon Charter (Runnymede)
T Wall D Pugh

Placings:*0*64400P0-00P **(0927)**
2001/02: 20^{0}GF, 20^{0}G, 25^{P}GF

	Starts	1st	2nd	3rd	Win & Pl
Hurdles	3	0	0	0	
Career Total	**11**	**0**	**0**	**0**	**449**

Going: Sf: 0-0 GS: 0-0 Gd: 0-1 GF: - Fm: 0-2
Distance: 2m/2m3: 0-0 2m4-2m7: 0-2 3m+: 0-1
Track: LH: 0-3 RH: 0-0 Tight: 0-2 Gall: 0-1
Aids: Bl: 0-2 Vi: 0-0 Tstrap: 0-0
Best Rating: **66** 6/00 Worc 2m good NHF

Little Task

101 **92**

4-y-o b g Environment Friend-Lucky Thing (Green Desert (USA))
J S Wainwright (H A McWilliams 27/7) Keith Jackson

Placings:14340 **(4757)**
2001/02: 16^{1}GF, 17^{4}G, 16^{3}GF, 16^{4}G, 16^{0}GF

	Starts	1st	2nd	3rd	Win & Pl
Hurdles	5	1	0	1	3387
Career Total	**5**	**1**	**0**	**1**	**3387**

83	9/01	Strf	2m110y	E Hdl	G-F	£3041

Total win prize-money £3042

Going: Sf: 0-0 GS: 0-0 Gd: 0-2 GF: - Fm: 1-3
Distance: **2m/2m3: 1-5** 2m4-2m7: 0-0 3m+: 0-0
Track: **LH: 1-4** RH: 0-1 **Tight: 1-2** Gall: 0-1
Aids: Bl: 0-0 Vi: 0-0 Tstrap: 0-0
Best Rating: **92** 9/01 Hntg 2m110y gd-fm Hdl

Modest hurdler over the minimum trip, winning twice at Wetherby. Suited by fast ground.

Little Tuska (IRE)

108(89h) (82h)**92**

12-y-o gr g Step Together (USA)-Peek-A-Boo (Bustino)
N B Mason N B Mason

Placings:06/**P041/6P651/231130630230F0F5**55**/2421 2-PP43F026353** **(4855)**
2001/02: 17^{P}G, 16^{P}S, 16^{4}S, 16^{3}S, 16^{F}GF, 20^{0}GS, 16^{2}HY, 20^{6}S, 21^{3}S, 20^{5}HY, 20^{3}G

	Starts	1st	2nd	3rd	Win & Pl
Chases	11	0	1	3	2554
Career Total	**45**	**5**	**6**	**7**	**28887**

95	9/00	Plum	2m1f	F(0-110)HCh	G-F	£2908
108	6/99	Hrfd	2m3f	E(0-115)HCh	GD	£4201
112	6/99	Prth	2m	E(0-115)HCh	SFT	£3387
90	5/99	Hexm	2m110y	F(0-100)HCh	GD	£2945
104	4/98	Prth	2m	D Ch	G-S	£4500

Total win prize-money £17945

Going: Sf: 0-7 GS: 0-1 Gd: 0-2 GF: - Fm: 0-1
Distance: 2m/2m3: 0-6 2m4-2m7: 0-5 3m+: 0-0
Track: LH: 0-7 RH: 0-4 Tight: 0-6 Gall: 0-2
Aids: Bl: 0-9 Vi: 0-0 Tstrap: 0-10
Best Rating: **112** 6/99 Prth 2m soft Ch

Modest chaser who has had just the one win since the summer of 1999, he is getting on now and is best at around two miles one these days. Acts on most surfaces.

Little Vera

7-y-o b m Carlingford Castle-Bonnyhill Lass (Royal Fountain)
N Wilson G Griffin

Placings:*0/0*UP-P **(0233)**
2001/02: 24^{P}GF

	Starts	1st	2nd	3rd	Win & Pl
Chases	1	0	0	0	
Career Total	**5**	**0**	**0**	**0**	

Going: Sf: 0-0 GS: 0-0 Gd: 0-0 GF: - Fm: 0-1
Distance: 2m/2m3: 0-0 2m4-2m7: 0-0 3m+: 0-1
Track: LH: 0-1 RH: 0-0 Tight: 0-1 Gall: 0-0
Aids: Bl: 0-0 Vi: 0-0 Tstrap: 0-0
Best Rating: **55** 6/99 Hexm 2m soft NHF

Little Veralyn

103 **97**

7-y-o b m Good Thyne (USA)-The Little Bag (True Song)
M C Pipe Dr D B A Silk

Placings:130 **(0682)**
2001/02: 17^{1}GS, 22^{3}GF, 22^{0}G

	Starts	1st	2nd	3rd	Win & Pl
Hurdles	3	1	0	1	2689
Career Total	**3**	**1**	**0**	**1**	**2689**

97	5/01	Extr	2m1f	E Hdl	G-S	£2254

Total win prize-money £2254

Going: Sf: 0-0 GS: 1-1 Gd: 0-1 GF: - Fm: 0-1
Distance: **2m/2m3: 1-1** 2m4-2m7: 0-2 3m+: 0-0
Track: LH: 0-2 **RH: 1-1** Tight: 0-2 Gall: 0-0
Aids: Bl: 0-0 Vi: 0-0 **Tstrap: 1-3**
Best Rating: **97** 5/01 Extr 2m1f gd-sft Hdl

Little Worsall (IRE)

101(100c) **72**

9-y-o ch g Broadsword (USA)-In My View (King's Ride)
A Crook (Mrs K J Tutty 7/4) P Swift, I Bennett, Mrs G Lovell

Placings:*40*P/6P/P**32U0-PF**330P **(1463)**
2001/02: 16^{P}GF, 17^{F}G, 17^{3}GF, 16^{3}GF, 16^{0}GF, 16^{P}G

	Starts	1st	2nd	3rd	Win & Pl
Hurdles	4	0	0	2	570
Chases	2	0	0	0	0
Career Total	**16**	**0**	**1**	**3**	**2318**

Going: Sf: 0-0 GS: 0-0 Gd: 0-2 GF: - Fm: 0-4
Distance: 2m/2m3: 0-6 2m4-2m7: 0-0 3m+: 0-0
Track: LH: 0-3 RH: 0-3 Tight: 0-2 Gall: 0-1
Aids: Bl: 0-0 Vi: 0-0 Tstrap: 0-0
Best Rating: 89 3/99 Muss 2m good NHF

Live In Lover (IRE)

4-y-o b g Up And At 'Em-Inesse (Simply Great (FR))
P C Haslam Mrs B Hawkins

Placings:P **(2301)**
2001/02: 16^{P}GF

	Starts	1st	2nd	3rd	Win & Pl
Hurdles	1	0	0	0	
Career Total	**1**	**0**	**0**	**0**	

Going: Sf: 0-0 GS: 0-0 Gd: 0-0 GF: - Fm: 0-1
Distance: 2m/2m3: 0-1 2m4-2m7: 0-0 3m+: 0-0
Track: LH: 0-1 RH: 0-0 Tight: 0-1 Gall: 0-0
Aids: Bl: 0-0 Vi: 0-0 Tstrap: 0-0
Best Rating:

Live The Dream

112 **127**
4-y-o b f Exit To Nowhere (USA)-Inveraven (Alias Smith (USA))
M C Pipe (J Hetherton 22/9) The Reims Partnership

Placings:1122060 **(4813)**
2001/02: 16^{1}G, 16^{1}G, 16^{2}GS, 16^{2}S, 17^{0}G, 20^{6}G, 17^{0}GF

	Starts	1st	2nd	3rd	Win & Pl
Hurdles	7	2	2	0	21671
Career Total	**7**	**2**	**2**	**0**	**21671**

127	11/01	Asct	2m110y	B Hdl	GD	£8209
97	11/01	Wwck	2m	D Hdl	GD	£3423

Total win prize money £11630

Going: Sf: 0-1 GS: 0-1 Gd: 2-4 GF: - Fm: 0-1
Distance: **2m/2m3: 2-6** 2m4-2m7: 0-1 3m+: 0-0
Track: LH: 1-6 RH: 1-1 Tight: 0-1 Gall: 0-2
Aids: Bl: 0-0 Vi: 0-4 Tstrap: 0-0
Best Rating: 127 12/01 Chep 2m110y gd-sft Hdl

A winning plater on the Flat, she made a successful debut over hurdles with an all-the-way win at Warwick in November 2001 and followed up in better grade at Ascot. Runner-up in a Grade One event at Chepstow and another decent event at Warwick, she likes to dominate and could never do that in the Triumph. A tough sort, suited by two miles and a sound surface.

Live'N'Learnlass

104 **96**
6-y-o ch m Hatim (USA)-Hazel Leaf (Le Moss)
A Scott Miss Victoria Scott Jnr

Placings:*604*-402314452 **(3913)**
2001/02: 17^{4}GS, 16^{0}F, 17^{2}G, 17^{3}GS, 17^{1}G, 16^{4}G, 21^{4}S, 19^{5}S, 20^{2}GS

	Starts	1st	2nd	3rd	Win & Pl
NH Flat	1	0	0	0	0
Hurdles	8	1	2	1	4768
Career Total	**12**	**1**	**2**	**1**	**4768**

94	10/01	Sedg	2m1f	E Hdl	GD	£2450

Total win prize-money £2450

Going: Sf: 0-2 GS: 0-3 Gd: 1-3 GF: - Fm: 0-1
Distance: **2m/2m3: 1-7** 2m4-2m7: 0-2 3m+: 0-0
Track: **LH: 1-8** RH: 0-1 **Tight: 1-8** Gall: 0-0
Aids: Bl: 0-0 Vi: 0-0 Tstrap: 0-0
Best Rating: 96 2/02 Muss 2m4f gd-sft Hdl

Modest hurdler, stays two and a half miles, does not want the ground too soft.

Lively Dessert (IRE)

108 **129d**
9-y-o b g Be My Native (USA)-Liffey Travel (Le Bavard (FR))
F P Murtagh (J J O'Neill 15/1) W Four Times

Placings:000/000025632/0F*0*0000**4P06/01131201-PPP33** **(4394)**
2001/02: 26^{P}S, 28^{P}S, 28^{P}S, 25^{3}HY, 32^{3}HY

	Starts	1st	2nd	3rd	Win & Pl
Chases	5	0	0	2	5383
Career Total	**36**	**4**	**3**	**4**	**33969**

129	4/01	Prth	3m	C Ch	HVY	£7702
129	12/00	Ayr	3m1f	D(0-125)HCh	SFT	£7231
113	10/00	Aint	3m1f	F(0-105)HCh	GD	£5213
118	10/00	Sthl	3m110y	F(0-100)HCh	HVY	£2723

Total win prize-money £22871

Going: Sf: 0-5 GS: 0-0 Gd: 0-0 GF: - Fm: 0-0
Distance: 2m/2m3: 0-0 2m4-2m7: 0-0 3m+: 0-5
Track: LH: 0-3 RH: 0-1 Tight: 0-1 Gall: 0-0
Aids: Bl: 0-0 Vi: 0-1 Tstrap: 0-0
Best Rating: 129 4/01 Prth 3m heavy Ch

Fair handicap chaser. Acts on soft ground, goes well for Tony McCoy.

Lively Felix

86 **58**
5-y-o b g Presidium-Full Of Life (Wolverlife)
W Clay M D H Racing

Placings:6P30-000P000 **(4904)**
2001/02: 16^{0}G, 17^{0}S, 16^{0}HY, 16^{P}HY, 17^{0}GS, 16^{0}GF, 17^{0}G

	Starts	1st	2nd	3rd	Win & Pl
Hurdles	7	0	0	0	
Career Total	**11**	**0**	**0**	**1**	**359**

Going: Sf: 0-3 GS: 0-1 Gd: 0-2 GF: - Fm: 0-1
Distance: 2m/2m3: 0-7 2m4-2m7: 0-0 3m+: 0-0
Track: LH: 0-5 RH: 0-2 Tight: 0-3 Gall: 0-0
Aids: Bl: 0-0 Vi: 0-3 Tstrap: 0-1
Best Rating: 74 12/00 Folk 2m1f110y heavy Hdl

Poor hurdling form, best with cut in the ground.

Livin It Up (IRE)

94 **63**
12-y-o br g Roselier (FR)-Its Good Ere (Import)
Mrs J B Ross (N G Richards 13/10) H R C Catherwood

Placings:14P/U3241F0/43/P1/3214U25/P-P00 **(4608a)**
2001/02: 24^{P}G, 20^{0}S, 24^{0}S

	Starts	1st	2nd	3rd	Win & Pl
Hurdles	1	0	0	0	0
Chases	2	0	0	0	0
Career Total	**25**	**4**	**3**	**3**	**19506**

124	12/99	Extr	2m1f110y	E(0-115)HCh	G-S	£4229
113	3/99	Naas	2m40y	(0-102)HCh	Y-S	£3498
117	3/97	Navn	2m1f	Ch	SFT	£3051
105	2/96	Navn	2m2f	Hdl	HVY	£3177

Total win prize-money £13958

Going: Sf: 0-2 GS: 0-0 Gd: 0-1 GF: - Fm: 0-0
Distance: 2m/2m3: 0-0 2m4-2m7: 0-1 3m+: 0-2
Track: LH: 0-1 RH: 0-0 Tight: 0-1 Gall: 0-0
Aids: Bl: 0-0 Vi: 0-0 Tstrap: 0-0
Best Rating: 124 12/99 Extr 2m1f110y gd-sft Ch

Formerly trained in Ireland, he has been a fair staying chaser on his day but has been lightly raced in recent seasons. Suited by two miles and soft ground.

Lizzy Gecko

14-y-o b m Majestic Maharaj-Daring Liz (Dairialatan)
W W Dennis Mrs Jill Dennis

Placings:6-2 **(0252)**
2001/02: 26^{2}GF

	Starts	1st	2nd	3rd	Win & Pl
Chases	1	0	1	0	1096
Career Total	**2**	**0**	**1**	**0**	**1096**

Going: Sf: 0-0 GS: 0-0 Gd: 0-0 GF: - Fm: 0-1
Distance: 2m/2m3: 0-0 2m4-2m7: 0-0 3m+: 0-1
Track: LH: 0-1 RH: 0-0 Tight: 0-1 Gall: 0-0
Aids: Bl: 0-0 Vi: 0-0 Tstrap: 0-0
Best Rating:

Lizzys First

92 **84**
10-y-o b g Town And Country-Lizzy Longstocking (Jimsun)
B R Millman Stephen Goss

Placings:0P/FU21311455/55264/0**UFPP0P0-030** **(3987)**
2001/02: 19^{0}G, 16^{3}HY, 19^{0}S

	Starts	1st	2nd	3rd	Win & Pl
Hurdles	3	0	0	1	279
Career Total	**28**	**3**	**2**	**2**	**10211**

107	2/99	Tntn	2m3f110y	E(0-115)HHdl	G-S	£2775
107	2/99	Tntn	2m3f110y	E(0-105)HHdl	G-S	£2309
92	12/98	Extr	2m1f110y	E(0-100)HHdl	SFT	£2532

Total win prize-money £7616

Going: Sf: 0-2 GS: 0-0 Gd: 0-1 GF: - Fm: 0-0
Distance: 2m/2m3: 0-2 2m4-2m7: 0-1 3m+: 0-0
Track: LH: 0-1 RH: 0-2 Tight: 0-2 Gall: 0-0
Aids: Bl: 0-0 Vi: 0-0 Tstrap: 0-0
Best Rating: 119 11/00 NAbb 2m5f110y heavy Ch

Moderate hurdler, on the downgrade. Stays two and a half miles and suited by soft ground.

Lobuche (IRE)

102(105h) (97h)**103**
7-y-o b g Petardia-Lhotse (IRE) (Shernazar)
M C Chapman K D Blanch

Placings:21/360366540240055/16233230-04100521200P**0354P** **(4557)**
2001/02: 16^{0}F, 17^{4}G, 19^{1}GF, 22^{0}GF, 16^{0}GF, 20^{5}GF, 17^{2}G, 19^{1}GF, 24^{2}GF, 19^{0}S, 24^{0}GS, 21^{P}G, 16^{0}GS, 24^{3}GS, 25^{5}S, 20^{4}GS, 25^{P}G

	Starts	1st	2nd	3rd	Win & Pl
Hurdles	12	2	2	0	8138
Chases	5	0	0	1	596
Career Total	**42**	**4**	**6**	**6**	**20508**

97	9/01	MRas	2m3f110y	E(0-115)HHdl	G-F	£3332
97	6/01	MRas	2m3f110y	F(0-105)HHdl	G-F	£2949
91	5/00	Ctml	2m1f110y	G(0-90)HHdl	GD	£3582
99	3/99	MRas	2m1f110y	D Hdl	G-S	£3367

Total win prize-money £13233

Going: Sf: 0-2 GS: 0-4 Gd: 0-4 GF: - Fm: 2-7
Distance: 2m/2m3: 0-5 **2m4-2m7: 2-7** 3m+: 0-5
Track: LH: 0-9 **RH: 2-8 Tight: 2-16** Gall: 0-0
Aids: Bl: 0-0 Vi: 0-0 **Tstrap: 2-16**
Best Rating: 104 3/00 Chel 2m1f gd-fm Hdl

Likes Market Rasen and won his third race there in September 2001 from just four career victories over hurdles. Stays well and must have fast ground. Wears a tongue tie.

Loc A Lua (IRE)

87(95h) 88

10-y-o b g Rising-Alchymya (Cosmo)
A King A J Davies

Placings:0/06-3P (0494)
2001/02: 26^{3}G, 25^{P}G

	Starts	1st	2nd	3rd	Win & Pl
Chases	2	0	0	1	564
Career Total	**5**	**0**	**0**	**1**	**564**

Going: Sf: 0-0 GS: 0-0 Gd: 0-2 GF: - Fm: 0-0
Distance: 2m/2m3: 0-0 2m4-2m7: 0-0 3m+: 0-2
Track: LH: 0-0 RH: 0-2 Tight: 0-1 Gall: 0-0
Aids: Bl: 0-1 Vi: 0-0 Tstrap: 0-0
Best Rating: 88 5/01 Folk 3m2f good Ch

Loch Sound

(80h) (90h)

6-y-o b g Primitive Rising (USA)-Lochcross (Lochnager)
C W Thornton Mrs Jill Murphy

Placings:0F0-00 (0642)
2001/02: 16^{0}F, 20^{0}GF

	Starts	1st	2nd	3rd	Win & Pl
Hurdles	1	0	0	0	0
Chases	1	0	0	0	0
Career Total	**5**	**0**	**0**	**0**	

Going: Sf: 0-0 GS: 0-0 Gd: 0-0 GF: - Fm: 0-2
Distance: 2m/2m3: 0-1 2m4-2m7: 0-1 3m+: 0-0
Track: LH: 0-1 RH: 0-1 Tight: 0-2 Gall: 0-0
Aids: Bl: 0-0 Vi: 0-0 Tstrap: 0-0
Best Rating: 90 4/01 Ayr 2m good Ch

Lochbuy Junior (FR)

103 113

7-y-o b g Saumarez-Chalabiah (Akarad (FR))
T D Easterby The G-Guck Group

Placings:F2/4415P2P5-2PP (2345)
2001/02: 21^{2}G, 16^{P}G, 20^{P}GS

	Starts	1st	2nd	3rd	Win & Pl
Hurdles	3	0	1	0	1844
Career Total	**13**	**1**	**3**	**0**	**6682**

115	11/00	Catt	2m3f	F(0-110)HHdl	G-S	£1911

Total win prize-money £1911

Going: Sf: 0-0 GS: 0-1 Gd: 0-2 GF: - Fm: 0-0
Distance: 2m/2m3: 0-1 2m4-2m7: 0-2 3m+: 0-0
Track: LH: 0-2 RH: 0-1 Tight: 0-1 Gall: 0-1
Aids: Bl: 0-0 Vi: 0-0 Tstrap: 0-0
Best Rating: 115 11/00 Catt 2m3f gd-sft Hdl

A fair novice hurdler for Micky Hammond last term. Had his first run for new connections and his first outing since April when runner-up at Market Rasen in October 2001, pulled up as though something was amiss in two subsequent starts. Best at around two miles and a half on an easy surface.

Lochiedubs

99 89

7-y-o br g Cragador-Linn Falls (Royal Fountain)
Mrs L B Normile Mrs D J Bell

Placings:3-535034 (4880)
2001/02: 16^{5}GF, 17^{3}GS, 20^{5}G, 20^{0}G, 16^{3}GF, 20^{4}G

	Starts	1st	2nd	3rd	Win & Pl
NH Flat	2	0	0	1	241
Hurdles	4	0	0	1	716
Career Total	**7**	**0**	**0**	**3**	**1363**

Going: Sf: 0-0 GS: 0-1 Gd: 0-3 GF: - Fm: 0-2
Distance: 2m/2m3: 0-3 2m4-2m7: 0-3 3m+: 0-0
Track: LH: 0-4 RH: 0-2 Tight: 0-2 Gall: 0-1
Aids: Bl: 0-0 Vi: 0-0 Tstrap: 0-0
Best Rating: 100 10/01 Carl 2m1f gd-sft NHF

Lochinvar Lady

35f

5-y-o b m Mandalus-Lady Budd (IRE) (Strong Gale)
C N Kellett D H & Mrs R E Muir

Placings:0-0 (0359)
2001/02: 17^{0}GS

	Starts	1st	2nd	3rd	Win & Pl
NH Flat	1	0	0	0	
Career Total	**2**	**0**	**0**	**0**	

Going: Sf: 0-0 GS: 0-1 Gd: 0-0 GF: - Fm: 0-0
Distance: 2m/2m3: 0-1 2m4-2m7: 0-0 3m+: 0-0
Track: LH: 0-1 RH: 0-0 Tight: 0-1 Gall: 0-0
Aids: Bl: 0-0 Vi: 0-0 Tstrap: 0-0
Best Rating: 35 4/01 MRas 2m1f110y heavy NHF

Lochlass (IRE)

47

8-y-o b m Distinctly North (USA)-Littleton Song (Song)
R J Price My Left Foot Racing Syndicate

Placings:4/0/060P245/06550PP000-00 (1088)
2001/02: 19^{0}G, 16^{0}GF

	Starts	1st	2nd	3rd	Win & Pl
Hurdles	2	0	0	0	
Career Total	**21**	**0**	**1**	**0**	**533**

Going: Sf: 0-0 GS: 0-0 Gd: 0-1 GF: - Fm: 0-1
Distance: 2m/2m3: 0-2 2m4-2m7: 0-0 3m+: 0-0
Track: LH: 0-2 RH: 0-0 Tight: 0-1 Gall: 0-0
Aids: Bl: 0-1 Vi: 0-0 Tstrap: 0-0
Best Rating: 72 5/00 Ctml 2m1f110y gd-fm Hdl

Lochnomore

9-y-o br g Lochnager-Chocolate Ripple (Hasty Word)
Mrs Jane Thornton (J D Downes 20/1) Mrs Jane Thornton

Placings:F/4-P (3653)
2001/02: 24^{P}S

	Starts	1st	2nd	3rd	Win & Pl
Chases	1	0	0	0	
Career Total	**3**	**0**	**0**	**0**	**174**

Going: Sf: 0-1 GS: 0-0 Gd: 0-0 GF: - Fm: 0-0
Distance: 2m/2m3: 0-0 2m4-2m7: 0-0 3m+: 0-1
Track: LH: 0-0 RH: 0-1 Tight: 0-0 Gall: 0-1
Aids: Bl: 0-0 Vi: 0-0 Tstrap: 0-0
Best Rating: 108 5/00 Chel 2m5f good Ch

Multiple winning pointer, not always the most fluent over his fences. Acts on most surfaces bar extremes of ground.

Lockington

95 89

6-y-o ch g Carlingford Castle-Race To The Rhythm (Deep Run)
Ian Williams Run For Fun

Placings:003 (3222)
2001/02: 16^{0}S, 19^{0}G, 22^{3}G

	Starts	1st	2nd	3rd	Win & Pl
NH Flat	1	0	0	0	0
Hurdles	2	0	0	1	409
Career Total	**3**	**0**	**0**	**1**	**409**

Going: Sf: 0-1 GS: 0-0 Gd: 0-2 GF: - Fm: 0-0
Distance: 2m/2m3: 0-1 2m4-2m7: 0-2 3m+: 0-0
Track: LH: 0-1 RH: 0-2 Tight: 0-0 Gall: 0-0
Aids: Bl: 0-0 Vi: 0-0 Tstrap: 0-0
Best Rating: 89 1/02 Winc 2m6f good Hdl

Lodestar (IRE)

80f 82f

5-y-o br g Good Thyne (USA)-Lets Compromise (No Argument)
Ian Williams Sir Robert Ogden

Placings:0 (4841)
2001/02: 16^{0}G

	Starts	1st	2nd	3rd	Win & Pl
NH Flat	1	0	0	0	
Career Total	**1**	**0**	**0**	**0**	

Going: Sf: 0-0 GS: 0-0 Gd: 0-1 GF: - Fm: 0-0
Distance: 2m/2m3: 0-1 2m4-2m7: 0-0 3m+: 0-0
Track: LH: 0-1 RH: 0-0 Tight: 0-0 Gall: 0-0
Aids: Bl: 0-0 Vi: 0-0 Tstrap: 0-0
Best Rating: 82 4/02 Ayr 2m good NHF

Log On Intersky (IRE)

111 93

6-y-o ch g Insan (USA)-Arctic Mo (IRE) (Mandalus)
J Howard Johnson (N A Twiston-Davies 27/10) Interskyracing.Com

Placings:00-030FP32 (4896)
2001/02: 20^{0}G, 20^{3}G, 24^{0}S, 20^{F}GF, 20^{P}S, 20^{3}GF, 20^{2}G

	Starts	1st	2nd	3rd	Win & Pl
Hurdles	6	0	1	2	2284
Chases	1	0	0	0	0
Career Total	**9**	**0**	**1**	**2**	**2284**

Going: Sf: 0-2 GS: 0-0 Gd: 0-3 GF: - Fm: 0-2
Distance: 2m/2m3: 0-0 2m4-2m7: 0-6 3m+: 0-1
Track: LH: 0-2 RH: 0-5 Tight: 0-3 Gall: 0-0

Aids: Bl: 0-0 Vi: 0-0 Tstrap: 0-4
Best Rating: 93 4/02 Prth 2m4f110y good Hdl

Novice hurdler. Stays two miles four furlongs and is effective on good ground.

Logician (NZ)

116 **159**

11-y-o b g Lord Ballina (AUS)-Thornton Lady (NZ) (Sound Reason (CAN))
I A Balding R Roulston

Placings:3/2/1021143-140F64B2 **(4901)**
2001/02: 17^{1}GS, 19^{4}G, 19^{0}G, 26^{F}S, 21^{6}HY, 16^{4}G, 36^{B}G, 16^{2}G

	Starts	1st	2nd	3rd	Win & Pl
Chases	8	1	1	0	15958
Career Total	**17**	**4**	**3**	**2**	**63622**

154	5/01	Bang	2m1f110y	E Ch	G-S	£3607
	9/00	Moon	2m	Ch	FRM	£5743
	7/00	Moon	2m2f110y	Ch	SFT	£26807
	6/00	Sann	1m6f	Hdl	SFT	£5743

Total win prize-money £41901

Going: Sf: 0-2 GS: 1-1 Gd: 0-5 GF: - Fm: 0-0
Distance: **2m/2m3: 1-3** 2m4-2m7: 0-3 3m+: 0-2
Track: **LH: 1-5** RH: 0-3 **Tight: 1-2** Gall: 0-2
Aids: Bl: 0-0 Vi: 0-0 **Tstrap: 1-5**
Best Rating: 159 11/01 Asct 2m3f110y good Ch

A former Australian-trained novice chaser, he has failed to reach the heights that connections would have hoped for since arriving in this country, though he has run well against some decent rivals. Best suited to a sound surface, he is effective at two miles but has been tried over further with little success.

Lokomotiv

96 **67**

6-y-o b g Salse (USA)-Rainbow's End (My Swallow)
M Madgwick (J M Bradley 24/8) M Madgwick

Placings:P06P0 **(4509)**
2001/02: 20^{P}GF, 16^{0}GS, 18^{6}GS, 21^{P}S, 16^{0}G

	Starts	1st	2nd	3rd	Win & Pl
Hurdles	5	0	0	0	0
Career Total	**5**	**0**	**0**	**0**	**0**

Going: Sf: 0-1 GS: 0-2 Gd: 0-1 GF: - Fm: 0-1
Distance: 2m/2m3: 0-3 2m4-2m7: 0-2 3m+: 0-0
Track: LH: 0-5 RH: 0-0 Tight: 0-4 Gall: 0-0
Aids: Bl: 0-0 Vi: 0-0 Tstrap: 0-0
Best Rating: 67 11/01 Plum 2m gd-sft Hdl

Lolanita

49f **67f**

4-y-o b f Anita's Prince-Jimlil (Nicholas Bill)
B Palling Mrs M M Palling

Placings:*000* **(4180)**
2001/02: 17^{0}S, 16^{0}HY, 16^{0}GS

	Starts	1st	2nd	3rd	Win & Pl
NH Flat	3	0	0	0	
Career Total	**3**	**0**	**0**	**0**	

Going: Sf: 0-2 GS: 0-1 Gd: 0-0 GF: - Fm: 0-0
Distance: 2m/2m3: 0-3 2m4-2m7: 0-0 3m+: 0-0
Track: LH: 0-1 RH: 0-0 Tight: 0-0 Gall: 0-0
Aids: Bl: 0-0 Vi: 0-0 Tstrap: 0-0
Best Rating: 67 3/02 Strf 2m110y gd-sft NHF

London Lights

94 **95**

8-y-o b g Slip Anchor-Pageantry (Welsh Pageant)
Lady Connell Lady Connell

Placings:2/P0P12-4 **(0587)**
2001/02: 16^{4}GF

	Starts	1st	2nd	3rd	Win & Pl
Hurdles	1	0	0	0	0
Career Total	**7**	**1**	**2**	**0**	**3378**

95	4/01	Hntg	2m110y	G(0-90)HHdl	SFT	£1911

Total win prize-money £1911

Going: Sf: 0-0 GS: 0-0 Gd: 0-0 GF: - Fm: 0-1
Distance: 2m/2m3: 0-1 2m4-2m7: 0-0 3m+: 0-0
Track: LH: 0-1 RH: 0-0 Tight: 0-1 Gall: 0-0
Aids: Bl: 0-0 Vi: 0-0 Tstrap: 0-0
Best Rating: 95 4/01 Extr 2m1f soft Hdl

Londoner (USA)

109 **116**

4-y-o ch g Sky Classic (CAN)-Love And Affection (USA) (Exclusive Era (USA))
M C Pipe (H R A Cecil 12/7) D A Johnson

Placings:U1P00 **(4840)**
2001/02: 16^{U}GS, 17^{1}S, 17^{P}G, 16^{0}G, 16^{0}G

	Starts	1st	2nd	3rd	Win & Pl
Hurdles	5	1	0	0	3833
Career Total	**5**	**1**	**0**	**0**	**3833**

116	2/02	Tntn	2m1f	D Hdl	SFT	£3832

Total win prize-money £3833

Going: Sf: 1-1 GS: 0-1 Gd: 0-3 GF: - Fm: 0-0
Distance: **2m/2m3: 1-5** 2m4-2m7: 0-0 3m+: 0-0
Track: LH: 0-3 **RH: 1-2 Tight: 1-2** Gall: 0-1
Aids: Bl: 0-0 Vi: 0-0 Tstrap: 0-0
Best Rating: 116 2/02 Tntn 2m1f soft Hdl

Sold out of Henry Cecil's yard for 100,000gns, he was ante-post favourite for the Triumph Hurdle, but cocked his jaw and unshipped his rider on his debut at Kempton. Redeemed himself at Taunton next time, even if it was a rather lacklustre performance, but was pulled up in the Triumph and has since disappointed at both Aintree and Ayr. Wears a net muzzle and is suited by a bit of give in the ground.

Lone Soldier (FR)

93(100c) (118c)**103**

6-y-o ch g Songlines (FR)-Caring Society (Caerleon (USA))
P J Hobbs The Quintet

Placings:22P431/54020-401440 **(1142)**
2001/02: 17^{4}F, 17^{0}GF, 16^{1}GF, 16^{4}G, 17^{4}G, 16^{0}G

	Starts	1st	2nd	3rd	Win & Pl
Hurdles	3	0	0	0	0
Chases	3	1	0	0	3726
Career Total	**17**	**2**	**3**	**1**	**9805**

118	6/01	Worc	2m	E Ch	G-F	£3260
102	3/00	Tntn	2m1f	F(0-100)HHdl	GD	£2107

Total win prize-money £5367

Going: Sf: 0-0 GS: 0-0 Gd: 0-3 GF: - Fm: 1-3
Distance: **2m/2m3: 1-6** 2m4-2m7: 0-0 3m+: 0-0
Track: **LH: 1-5** RH: 0-1 Tight: 0-4 Gall: 0-0
Aids: Bl: 0-0 Vi: 0-0 **Tstrap: 1-6**
Best Rating: 118 6/01 Worc 2m gd-fm Ch

Winning hurdler/chaser, suited by fast ground.

Long Lunch (IRE)

97(97h) (97h)**111**

10-y-o b g Executive Perk-Bell Walks Rose (Decent Fellow)
N J Henderson Ian Agnew

Placings:1/02-4PB26P **(4399)**
2001/02: 16^{4}G, 20^{P}G, 24^{B}GF, 23^{2}G, 22^{6}G, 22^{P}GS

	Starts	1st	2nd	3rd	Win & Pl
Hurdles	1	0	0	0	0
Chases	5	0	1	0	968
Career Total	**9**	**1**	**2**	**0**	**2890**

104	10/98	Hntg	2m110y	H NHF	GD	£1213

Total win prize-money £1214

Going: Sf: 0-0 GS: 0-1 Gd: 0-4 GF: - Fm: 0-1
Distance: 2m/2m3: 0-1 2m4-2m7: 0-3 3m+: 0-2
Track: LH: 0-3 RH: 0-3 Tight: 0-0 Gall: 0-2
Aids: Bl: 0-0 Vi: 0-0 Tstrap: 0-0
Best Rating: 111 12/01 Leic 2m7f110y good Ch

Acts on good ground and is effective from two miles to three miles.

Long Shot

97f **98f**

5-y-o b m Sir Harry Lewis (USA)-Kovalevskia (Ardross)
N J Henderson W H Ponsonby

Placings:*4210* **(4823)**
2001/02: 10^{4}G, 17^{2}G, 10^{1}G, 17^{0}G

	Starts	1st	2nd	3rd	Win & Pl
NH Flat	4	1	1	0	2144
Career Total	**4**	**1**	**1**	**0**	**2144**

93	4/02	Fknm	2m	H NHF	GD	£1540

Total win prize-money £1540

Going: Sf: 0-1 GS: 0-0 Gd: 1-3 GF: - Fm: 0-0
Distance: **2m/2m3: 1-4** 2m4-2m7: 0-0 3m+: 0-0
Track: **LH: 1-2** RH: 0-1 **Tight: 1-1** Gall: 0-1
Aids: Bl: 0-0 Vi: 0-0 Tstrap: 0-0
Best Rating: 98 1/02 Tntn 2m1f soft NHF

Progressed to win her third bumper. Acts on good and soft ground.

Long Walk (IRE)

102 **109**

5-y-o b g King's Ride-Seanaphobal Lady (Kambalda)
H D Daly The Earl Cadogan

Placings:32252 **(4880)**
2001/02: 17^{3}GS, 20^{2}S, 16^{2}HY, 19^{5}S, 20^{2}G

	Starts	1st	2nd	3rd	Win & Pl
NH Flat	1	0	0	1	307
Hurdles	4	0	3	0	3344
Career Total	**5**	**0**	**3**	**1**	**3651**

Going: Sf: 0-3 GS: 0-1 Gd: 0-1 GF: - Fm: 0-0
Distance: 2m/2m3: 0-3 2m4-2m7: 0-2 3m+: 0-0
Track: LH: 0-2 RH: 0-2 Tight: 0-0 Gall: 0-1
Aids: Bl: 0-0 Vi: 0-0 Tstrap: 0-0
Best Rating: 109 2/02 Sand 2m110y heavy Hdl

A half-brother to winning chaser Cornish Gale, he has been placed in novice hurdles. Looks a stayer.

Look In The Mirror

11-y-o b g Rakaposhi King-Moaning Jenny (Privy Seal)
Fergal O'Brien Miss E M Shirley-Beavan

Placings:*00*06P/42P025/21PPP/**2/1241-4105** **(4826)**
2001/02: 25^{4}G, 28^{1}GF, 26^{0}G, 26^{5}G

	Starts	1st	2nd	3rd	Win & Pl
Chases	4	1	0	0	17355
Career Total	**25**	**4**	**5**	**0**	**26574**

133	6/01	Strf	3m4f	B Ch	G-F	£17355
118	4/01	Extr	2m7f110y	H Ch	SFT	£2282
118	5/00	Hrfd	3m1f110y	H Ch	GD	£2100
93	5/98	Hrfd	3m2f	G(0-95)HHdl	GD	£1593

Total win prize-money £23330

Going: Sf: 0-0 GS: 0-0 Gd: 0-3 GF: - Fm: 1-1
Distance: 2m/2m3: 0-0 2m4-2m7: 0-0 **3m+: 1-4**
Track: **LH: 1-3** RH: 0-1 **Tight: 1-1** Gall: 0-2
Aids: Bl: 0-0 Vi: 0-0 Tstrap: 0-0
Best Rating: 133 6/01 Strf 3m4f gd-fm Ch

Useful point-to-pointer/hunter chaser. Stays three and a half miles. Has won on most types of ground but does not want it too sticky.

Look Sharpe

11-y-o b g Looking Glass-Washburn Flyer (Owen Dudley)
N Wilson T S Sharpe

Placings:*20*/P-U5 **(0569)**
2001/02: 23^{U}F, 20^{5}F

	Starts	1st	2nd	3rd	Win & Pl
Chases	2	0	0	0	0
Career Total	**5**	**0**	**1**	**0**	**456**

Going: Sf: 0-0 GS: 0-0 Gd: 0-0 GF: - Fm: 0-2
Distance: 2m/2m3: 0-0 2m4-2m7: 0-1 3m+: 0-1
Track: LH: 0-1 RH: 0-0 Tight: 0-0 Gall: 0-0
Aids: Bl: 0-0 Vi: 0-0 Tstrap: 0-0
Best Rating: 86 5/01 Weth 2m4f110y firm Ch

Looking Deadly

78(102h) (72h)**51**
8-y-o b m Neltino-Princess Constanza (Relkino)
F P Murtagh Teddy Bears & Big Bear Syndicate

Placings:*00000*/2P-**0500PP** **(3442)**
2001/02: 17^{0}G, 17^{5}S, 17^{0}HY, 16^{0}S, 19^{P}G, 16^{P}HY

	Starts	1st	2nd	3rd	Win & Pl
Hurdles	3	0	0	0	0
Chases	3	0	0	0	0
Career Total	**13**	**0**	**1**	**0**	**676**

Going: Sf: 0-4 GS: 0-0 Gd: 0-2 GF: - Fm: 0-0
Distance: 2m/2m3: 0-6 2m4-2m7: 0-0 3m+: 0-0
Track: LH: 0-4 RH: 0-2 Tight: 0-3 Gall: 0-0
Aids: Bl: 0-0 Vi: 0-0 Tstrap: 0-0
Best Rating: 85 5/00 Kels 2m110y good Hdl

Looking Forward

77 **92**
6-y-o b g Primitive Rising (USA)-Gilzie Bank (New Brig)
Ferdy Murphy (S E Kettlewell 28/12) Mrs G Handley

Placings:P53 **(4580)**
2001/02: 19^{P}G, 20^{5}HY, 16^{3}G

	Starts	1st	2nd	3rd	Win & Pl
Chases	3	0	0	1	473
Career Total	**3**	**0**	**0**	**1**	**473**

Going: Sf: 0-1 GS: 0-0 Gd: 0-2 GF: - Fm: 0-0
Distance: 2m/2m3: 0-2 2m4-2m7: 0-1 3m+: 0-0
Track: LH: 0-3 RH: 0-0 Tight: 0-1 Gall: 0-0
Aids: Bl: 0-0 Vi: 0-0 Tstrap: 0-0
Best Rating: 92 4/02 Weth 2m good Ch

Looks Like Reign

8-y-o b g Royal Vulcan-Spy The Ark (Arkan)
N Wilson H Barrons

Placings:P **(1584)**
2001/02: 19^{P}GS

	Starts	1st	2nd	3rd	Win & Pl
Hurdles	1	0	0	0	
Career Total	**1**	**0**	**0**	**0**	

Going: Sf: 0-0 GS: 0-1 Gd: 0-0 GF: - Fm: 0-0
Distance: 2m/2m3: 0-0 2m4-2m7: 0-1 3m+: 0-0
Track: LH: 0-0 RH: 0-1 Tight: 0-1 Gall: 0-0
Aids: Bl: 0-0 Vi: 0-0 Tstrap: 0-0
Best Rating:

Looks Like Trouble (IRE)

113 **170**
10-y-o b g Zaffaran (USA)-Lavengaddy (Balgaddy)
Noel T Chance T Collins

Placings:523/**U25111/31P11/1-10** **(4252)**
2001/02: 21^{1}GS, 26^{0}G

	Starts	1st	2nd	3rd	Win & Pl
Chases	2	1	0	0	13585
Career Total	**17**	**8**	**2**	**2**	**343251**

170	1/02	Winc	2m5f	B Ch	G-S	£13585
183	11/00	DRoy	3m	Ch	G-Y	£55000
183	3/00	Chel	3m2f110y	A Ch	G-F	£162400
183	1/00	Chel	3m1f110y	A Ch	G-S	£30000
175	12/99	Sand	3m110y	B Ch	GD	£7405
176	3/99	Chel	3m110y	A Ch	G-S	£59000
148	2/99	Sand	3m110y	D(0-115)HCh	GD	£3987
133	1/99	Donc	3m	D Ch	G-S	£4640

Total win prize-money £336017

Going: Sf: 0-0 **GS: 1-1** Gd: 0-1 GF: - Fm: 0-0
Distance: 2m/2m3: 0-0 **2m4-2m7: 1-1** 3m+: 0-1
Track: LH: 0-1 **RH: 1-1** Tight: 0-0 Gall: 0-1
Aids: Bl: 0-0 Vi: 0-0 Tstrap: 0-0
Best Rating: 183 11/00 DRoy 3m gd-yld Ch

He developed into a top-class chaser in 1999/2000, culminating in his Cheltenham Gold Cup victory in which he slammed Florida Pearl by five lengths, breaking the course record in the process. He returned to the fray at Down Royal in November for the second running of the James Nicholson Wine Merchant Champion Chase, jumping superbly to win unchallenged, but injured his near-fore tendon during the race and his career was in some doubt. He responded well to a firing operation and made a successful return to action in the John Bull Chase at Wincanton in January 2002, jumping well throughout. Jumped to the right when well beaten in the Gold Cup and was found subsequently to have a recurrence of his previous tendon injury. He was subsequently retired. Stayed three and a quarter miles and was best on a sound surface.

Loop The Loup

106 **132**
6-y-o b g Petit Loup (USA)-Mithi Al Gamar (USA) (Blushing Groom (FR))
Mrs M Reveley Mr And Mrs J D Cotton

Placings:0/102-3 **(4834)**
2001/02: 22^{3}G

	Starts	1st	2nd	3rd	Win & Pl
Hurdles	1	0	0	1	1075
Career Total	**5**	**1**	**1**	**1**	**6108**

130	12/00	Muss	2m4f	E Hdl	GD	£2840

Total win prize-money £2841

Going: Sf: 0-0 GS: 0-0 Gd: 0-1 GF: - Fm: 0-0
Distance: 2m/2m3: 0-0 2m4-2m7: 0-1 3m+: 0-0
Track: LH: 0-1 RH: 0-0 Tight: 0-0 Gall: 0-0
Aids: Bl: 0-0 Vi: 0-0 Tstrap: 0-0
Best Rating: 130 12/00 Muss 2m4f good Hdl

Mixes hurdling with racing on the Flat. Best over two and a half miles and fast ground, but needs a strong pace and a galloping track.

Loose Chippins (IRE)

47 **22**
4-y-o b f Bigstone (IRE)-Fortune Teller (Troy)
G L Moore Mrs J Moore

Placings:0 **(3751)**
2001/02: 16^{0}HY

	Starts	1st	2nd	3rd	Win & Pl
Hurdles	1	0	0	0	
Career Total	**1**	**0**	**0**	**0**	

Going: Sf: 0-1 GS: 0-0 Gd: 0-0 GF: - Fm: 0-0
Distance: 2m/2m3: 0-1 2m4-2m7: 0-0 3m+: 0-0
Track: LH: 0-0 RH: 0-1 Tight: 0-0 Gall: 0-0
Aids: Bl: 0-0 Vi: 0-0 Tstrap: 0-0
Best Rating: 22 2/02 Sand 2m110y heavy Hdl

Lord 'N' Master (IRE)

100 **97**
6-y-o b g Lord Americo-Miss Good Night (Buckskin (FR))
R Rowe Dr B Alexander

Placings:565 **(4411)**
2001/02: 22^{5}S, 20^{6}S, 18^{5}S

	Starts	1st	2nd	3rd	Win & Pl
Hurdles	3	0	0	0	0
Career Total	**3**	**0**	**0**	**0**	**0**

Going: Sf: 0-3 GS: 0-0 Gd: 0-0 GF: - Fm: 0-0
Distance: 2m/2m3: 0-1 2m4-2m7: 0-2 3m+: 0-0
Track: LH: 0-2 RH: 0-0 Tight: 0-3 Gall: 0-0
Aids: Bl: 0-0 Vi: 0-0 Tstrap: 0-0
Best Rating: 97 2/02 Font 2m6f110y soft Hdl

Lord Alexander (IRE)

(48h)
9-y-o b g Lord Americo-Polly Ringling (Pollerton)
B N Doran A F Heselton

Placings:*06*P/1F-**00P** **(0973)**
2001/02: 16^{0}GF, 16^{0}GF, 16^{P}GF

	Starts	1st	2nd	3rd	Win & Pl
Hurdles	2	0	0	0	0
Chases	1	0	0	0	0
Career Total	**8**	**1**	**0**	**0**	**3744**

85	8/00	NAbb	2m110y	E Ch	G-F	£3744

Total win prize-money £3744

Going: Sf: 0-0 GS: 0-0 Gd: 0-0 GF: - Fm: 0-3
Distance: 2m/2m3: 0-3 2m4-2m7: 0-0 3m+: 0-0
Track: LH: 0-3 RH: 0-0 Tight: 0-2 Gall: 0-0
Aids: Bl: 0-0 Vi: 0-0 Tstrap: 0-0
Best Rating: 85 8/00 NAbb 2m110y gd-fm Ch

Lord Alvinru (IRE)

90 87

5-y-o b g Lord Americo-Alvinru (Sandalay)
G A Swinbank Arnie Flower

Placings:04032 (4768)
2001/02: 16^{0}GF, 17^{4}S, 17^{0}GS, 19^{3}GF, 16^{2}GF

	Starts	1st	2nd	3rd	Win & Pl
NH Flat	1	0	0	0	0
Hurdles	4	0	1	1	1350
Career Total	**5**	**0**	**1**	**1**	**1350**

Going: Sf: 0-1 GS: 0-1 Gd: 0-0 GF: - Fm: 0-3
Distance: 2m/2m3: 0-4 2m4-2m7: 0-1 3m+: 0-0
Track: LH: 0-2 RH: 0-2 Tight: 0-3 Gall: 0-0
Aids: Bl: 0-0 Vi: 0-0 Tstrap: 0-0
Best Rating: 87 4/02 Hexm 2m110y gd-fm Hdl

Improving slowly over hurdles in the spring of 2002.

Lord Angus

94 84

6-y-o ch g Rock Hopper-Mystic Memory (Ela-Mana-Mou)
Mrs D M Ewart Mrs J A Niven

Placings:00P030 (4689)
2001/02: 16^{0}G, 17^{0}G, 22^{P}GS, 20^{0}GF, 20^{3}G, 16^{0}GF

	Starts	1st	2nd	3rd	Win & Pl
NH Flat	2	0	0	0	0
Hurdles	4	0	0	1	436
Career Total	**6**	**0**	**0**	**1**	**436**

Going: Sf: 0-0 GS: 0-1 Gd: 0-3 GF: - Fm: 0-2
Distance: 2m/2m3: 0-3 2m4-2m7: 0-3 3m+: 0-0
Track: LH: 0-3 RH: 0-3 Tight: 0-4 Gall: 0-0
Aids: Bl: 0-0 Vi: 0-0 Tstrap: 0-0
Best Rating: 84 12/01 Muss 2m4f good Hdl

Modest hurdler, stays two miles-four.

Lord Brex (FR)

100 129

6-y-o gr h Saint Estephe (FR)-Light Moon (FR) (Mendez (FR))
P J Hobbs Terry Warner

Placings:31451/2-000P (4667)
2001/02: 16^{0}G, 16^{0}S, 20^{0}S, 20^{P}G

	Starts	1st	2nd	3rd	Win & Pl
Hurdles	4	0	0	0	
Career Total	**10**	**2**	**1**	**1**	**45291**

136	4/00	Aint	2m110y	A Hdl	GD	£24000
126	1/00	Sand	2m110y	D Hdl	SFT	£4400

Total win prize-money £28401

Going: Sf: 0-2 GS: 0-0 Gd: 0-2 GF: - Fm: 0-0
Distance: 2m/2m3: 0-2 2m4-2m7: 0-2 3m+: 0-0
Track: LH: 0-2 RH: 0-2 Tight: 0-1 Gall: 0-1
Aids: Bl: 0-4 Vi: 0-0 Tstrap: 0-0
Best Rating: 137 5/00 Punc 2m good Hdl

After a smart juvenile hurdling campaign in 1999/2000, he was gelded and operated on for a breathing problem. He was well held on his reappearance at Christmas 2001 and has given limited encouragement since. Connections believe he will stay three miles. Acts on good to soft/soft ground.

Lord Broadway (IRE)

100(95h) (91h)90

6-y-o b g Shardari-Country Course (IRE) (Crash Course)
N M Babbage D G & D J Robinson

Placings:50-0PP25 (4107)
2001/02: 20^{0}G, 21^{P}GS, 24^{P}GS, 20^{2}S, 22^{5}S

	Starts	1st	2nd	3rd	Win & Pl
Hurdles	1	0	0	0	0
Chases	4	0	1	0	1116
Career Total	**7**	**0**	**1**	**0**	**1116**

Going: Sf: 0-2 GS: 0-2 Gd: 0-1 GF: - Fm: 0-0
Distance: 2m/2m3: 0-0 2m4-2m7: 0-4 3m+: 0-1
Track: LH: 0-1 RH: 0-4 Tight: 0-1 Gall: 0-0
Aids: Bl: 0-0 Vi: 0-0 Tstrap: 0-0
Best Rating: 97 3/01 Strf 2m110y soft NHF

Fair handicap chaser. Goes well over two miles four furlongs, he acts on a soft surface.

Lord Capitaine (IRE)

101 123

8-y-o b/br g Mister Lord (USA)-Salvation Sue (Mon Capitaine)
J Howard Johnson The Scottish Steeplechasing Partnership

Placings:P311P/645635P-U511 (2072)
2001/02: 26^{U}GF, 25^{5}GF, 27^{1}G, 27^{1}S

	Starts	1st	2nd	3rd	Win & Pl
Chases	4	2	0	0	5474
Career Total	**16**	**4**	**0**	**2**	**13943**

123	11/01	Sedg	3m3f	F(0-100)HCh	SFT	£2569
115	10/01	Sedg	3m3f	F(0-100)HCh	GD	£2905
126	2/00	Sedg	3m3f	D Ch	G-S	£3575
116	1/00	Muss	2m4f	E Ch	SFT	£3282

Total win prize-money £12332

Going: Sf: 1-1 GS: 0-0 Gd: 1-1 GF: - Fm: 0-2
Distance: 2m/2m3: 0-0 2m4-2m7: 0-0 **3m+: 2-4**
Track: **LH: 2-3** RH: 0-0 **Tight: 2-2** Gall: 0-0
Aids: Bl: 0-0 Vi: 0-0 Tstrap: 0-2
Best Rating: 126 2/00 Sedg 3m3f gd-sft Ch

Steadily improving, he looks very much an out-and-out stayer. He is unbeaten over fences in three starts over the three mile three furlong trip at Sedgefield.

Lord Dal (FR)

9-y-o b g Cadoudal (FR)-Lady Corteira (FR) (Carvin)
R Waley-Cohen Robert Waley-Cohen

Placings:1235/140124/2624/4-UP (3895)
2001/02: 25^{U}S, 26^{P}HY

	Starts	1st	2nd	3rd	Win & Pl
Chases	2	0	0	0	
Career Total	**17**	**3**	**4**	**1**	**28461**

126	1/99	Tram	2m4f	Ch	SH	£3376
124	11/98	Naas	2m4f	HHdl	YLD	£8445
103	12/97	Leop	2m	Hdl	HVY	£4069

Total win prize-money £15891

Going: Sf: 0-2 GS: 0-0 Gd: 0-0 GF: - Fm: 0-0
Distance: 2m/2m3: 0-0 2m4-2m7: 0-0 3m+: 0-2
Track: LH: 0-1 RH: 0-1 Tight: 0-0 Gall: 0-0
Aids: Bl: 0-0 Vi: 0-0 Tstrap: 0-0
Best Rating: 129 11/99 Naas 2m4f yld-sft Hdl

Lord Dixon (IRE)

86 51

6-y-o b/br g Lord Americo-Dixons Dutchess (IRE) (Over The River (FR))
M C Pipe David Manning Associates

Placings:2-300 (1793)
2001/02: 17^{3}F, 22^{0}G, 20^{0}S

	Starts	1st	2nd	3rd	Win & Pl
NH Flat	1	0	0	1	313
Hurdles	2	0	0	0	0
Career Total	**4**	**0**	**1**	**1**	**313**

Going: Sf: 0-1 GS: 0-0 Gd: 0-1 GF: - Fm: 0-1
Distance: 2m/2m3: 0-1 2m4-2m7: 0-2 3m+: 0-0
Track: LH: 0-2 RH: 0-1 Tight: 0-1 Gall: 0-0
Aids: Bl: 0-0 Vi: 0-0 Tstrap: 0-0
Best Rating: 109 4/01 Tntn 2m1f gd-fm NHF

Lord Edwards Army (IRE)

108 120

7-y-o b g Warcraft (USA)-Celtic Bombshell (Celtic Cone)
P Mullins P M Brady

Placings:630/000-4116541022O5 (4923a)
2001/02: 16^{4}Y, 19^{1}G, 17^{1}GF, 16^{6}YS, 17^{5}GY, 16^{4}G, 20^{1}GF, 24^{0}G, 16^{2}Y, 19^{2}YS, 24^{0}G, 20^{5}Y

	Starts	1st	2nd	3rd	Win & Pl
NH Flat	4	2	0	0	7444
Hurdles	8	1	2	0	13710
Career Total	**18**	**3**	**2**	**1**	**21489**

115	9/01	List	2m4f	Hdl	G-F	£7862
107	7/01	Bell	2m1f	NHF	G-F	£3895
97	6/01	Kbgn	2m3f	NHF	GD	£3338

Total win prize-money £15097

Going: Sf: 0-0 GS: 0-0 Gd: 1-4 GF: - Fm: 2-2
Distance: **2m/2m3: 2-8** 2m4-2m7: 1-2 3m+: 0-2
Track: **LH: 1-4** RH: 0-2 Tight: 0-1 Gall: 0-0
Aids: Bl: 0-0 Vi: 0-0 Tstrap: 0-0
Best Rating: 120 11/01 Navn 2m yield Hdl

Novice hurdler. Stays two and a half miles. Acts on a sound surface.

Lord Efisio

4-y-o b g Efisio-Vax Lady (Millfontaine)
M F Harris M Harris

Placings:P (3890)
2001/02: 16^{P}HY

	Starts	1st	2nd	3rd	Win & Pl
Hurdles	1	0	0	0	
Career Total	**1**	**0**	**0**	**0**	

Going: Sf: 0-1 GS: 0-0 Gd: 0-0 GF: - Fm: 0-0
Distance: 2m/2m3: 0-1 2m4-2m7: 0-0 3m+: 0-0
Track: LH: 0-1 RH: 0-0 Tight: 0-0 Gall: 0-0
Aids: Bl: 0-0 Vi: 0-0 Tstrap: 0-0
Best Rating:

Lord Esker (IRE)

100 120

10-y-o b g Glacial Storm (USA)-April Rhapsody (Main Reef)

R J Hodges Major A W C Pearn

Placings: *0/*12F264F/151/153212631/45164PPP-025P13P6 **(1153)**

2001/02: 20^{0}GF, 16^{2}GF, 16^{5}GS, 16^{P}GF, 16^{1}GF, 16^{3}G, 17^{P}GF, 26^{6}GF

	Starts	1st	2nd	3rd	Win & Pl
Chases	8	1	1	1	4296
Career Total	**36**	**8**	**5**	**3**	**34301**

120	7/01	NAbb	2m110y	F(0-100)HCh	G-F	£2891
130	7/00	Uttx	2m4f	C(0-135)HCh	G-F	£6646
130	4/00	Font	2m2f	E(0-115)HCh	GD	£2957
130	11/99	Font	2m2f	D(0-125)HCh	GD	£3701
124	5/99	Aint	2m4f	E Ch	G-S	£2908
125	5/99	Uttx	2m	E Ch	GD	£3087
124	7/98	Worc	2m	E(0-100)HCh	G-F	£3276
83	5/97	DRoy	2m	Hdl	G-F	£1695

Total win prize-money £27164

Going: Sf: 0-0 GS: 0-1 Gd: 0-1 GF: - Fm: 1-6
Distance: **2m/2m3: 1-6** 2m4-2m7: 0-1 3m+: 0-1
Track: **LH: 1-6** RH: 0-1 **Tight: 1-7** Gall: 0-1
Aids: Bl: 0-0 Vi: 0-0 Tstrap: 0-0
Best Rating: 130 7/00 Uttx 2m4f gd-fm Ch

Best on decent ground, he is an ordinary two-mile handicap chaser and should pick up another race around the smaller tracks when conditions are favourable.

Lord Fleet (IRE)

100 (103h)96

8-y-o b g Aristocracy-Sweet And Fleet (Whistling Deer)

J R Cornwall (A J Martin 23/7) J R Cornwall

Placings: *P*-P1F4PP **(2309)**

2001/02: 20^{P}F, 17^{1}F, 17^{F}YS, 21^{4}GF, 22^{P}S, 20^{P}GS

	Starts	1st	2nd	3rd	Win & Pl
Hurdles	2	1	0	0	3478
Chases	4	0	0	0	324
Career Total	**7**	**1**	**0**	**0**	**3802**

103	6/01	Dpat	2m1f172y	Hdl	FRM	£3477

Total win prize-money £3478

Going: Sf: 0-1 GS: 0-1 Gd: 0-0 GF: - Fm: 1-3
Distance: **2m/2m3: 1-2** 2m4-2m7: 0-4 3m+: 0-0
Track: LH: 0-1 RH: 0-2 Tight: 0-2 Gall: 0-1
Aids: Bl: 0-0 Vi: 0-0 **Tstrap: 1-5**
Best Rating: 103 6/01 Dpat 2m1f172y firm Hdl

Lord Harry (IRE)

10-y-o b g Mister Lord (USA)-Vickies Gold (Golden Love)

Mrs Edward Crow M J Parr

Placings: 2/3/1126-1PF **(3875)**

2001/02: 24^{1}GS, 28^{P}GF, 24^{F}GS

	Starts	1st	2nd	3rd	Win & Pl
Chases	3	1	0	0	2940
Career Total	**9**	**3**	**2**	**1**	**15265**

117	5/01	Bang	3m110y	H Ch	G-S	£2940
131	6/00	Strf	3m4f	H Ch	GD	£7410
116	5/00	Bang	3m110y	H Ch	GD	£3461

Total win prize-money £13811

Going: Sf: 0-0 GS: 1-2 Gd: 0-0 GF: - Fm: 0-1
Distance: 2m/2m3: 0-0 2m4-2m7: 0-0 **3m+: 1-3**
Track: **LH: 1-2** RH: 0-1 **Tight: 1-2** Gall: 0-1
Aids: Bl: 0-1 Vi: 0-0 Tstrap: 0-0
Best Rating: 131 6/00 Strf 3m4f good Ch

A smart hunter chaser/point-to-pointer, he stays long distances and goes well on decent ground. Basically a sound jumper.

Lord Jack (IRE)

103 107

6-y-o ch g Mister Lord (USA)-Gentle Gill (Pollerton)

N G Richards Trevor Hemmings

Placings: 0561120 **(4491)**

2001/02: 22^{0}GS, 22^{5}G, 20^{6}GS, 20^{1}S, 24^{1}S, 22^{2}HY, 20^{0}GS

	Starts	1st	2nd	3rd	Win & Pl
Hurdles	7	2	1	0	7045
Career Total	**7**	**2**	**1**	**0**	**7045**

107	2/02	Muss	3m	D(0-110)HHdl	SFT	£3526
107	1/02	Muss	2m4f	E(0-100)HHdl	SFT	£2744

Total win prize-money £6270

Going: Sf: 2-3 GS: 0-3 Gd: 0-1 GF: - Fm: 0-0
Distance: 2m/2m3: 0-0 2m4-2m7: 1-6 3m+: 1-1
Track: LH: 0-4 **RH: 2-2 Tight: 2-4** Gall: 0-1
Aids: Bl: 0-0 Vi: 0-0 **Tstrap: 2-4**
Best Rating: 107 2/02 Muss 3m soft Hdl

Progressed to win a hurdle over two and a half miles on his debut in handicap company. Followed up over three miles, and clearly stays well.

Lord Jim (IRE)

96 108

10-y-o b g Kahyasi-Sarah Georgina (Persian Bold)

R J Hodges (G A Butler 20/6) Mrs S Y Thomas

Placings: 111/P0P2/245 **(3778)**

2001/02: 21^{2}GS, 25^{4}S, 24^{5}GS

	Starts	1st	2nd	3rd	Win & Pl
Chases	3	0	1	0	2561
Career Total	**10**	**3**	**2**	**0**	**32529**

143	1/98	Sand	2m6f	B Hdl	SFT	£10162
145	12/97	Chel	3m	A Hdl	GD	£9555
112	12/97	Chep	2m110y	D Hdl	SFT	£3155

Total win prize-money £22873

Going: Sf: 0-1 GS: 2-2 Gd: 0-0 GF: - Fm: 0-0
Distance: 2m/2m3: 0-0 2m4-2m7: 0-1 3m+: 0-2
Track: LH: 0-0 RH: 0-3 Tight: 0-0 Gall: 0-0
Aids: Bl: 0-0 Vi: 0-0 Tstrap: 0-0
Best Rating: 145 4/99 Asct 3m gd-fm Hdl

Quite a useful stayer on the Flat, he was unbeaten in three starts as a novice hurdler, beating a good field at Cheltenham and franking the form at Sandown. A genuine sort, he disappointed for much of last season, however he salvaged a little consolation on his final start when second to Galant Moss at Ascot, showing his liking staying distances and good ground. Well held in three runs over fences in 2001/02.

Lord Joshua (IRE)

108 118

4-y-o b c King's Theatre (IRE)-Lady Joshua (IRE) (Royal Academy (USA))

N J Henderson (G A Butler 25/10) Mrs William S Farish

Placings: 31P **(4250)**

2001/02: 16^{3}S, 16^{1}S, 17^{P}G

	Starts	1st	2nd	3rd	Win & Pl
Hurdles	3	1	0	1	5208
Career Total	**3**	**1**	**0**	**1**	**5208**

118	3/02	Newb	2m110y	D Hdl	SFT	£4524

Total win prize-money £4524

Going: Sf: 1-2 GS: 0-0 Gd: 0-1 GF: - Fm: 0-0
Distance: **2m/2m3: 1-3** 2m4-2m7: 0-0 3m+: 0-0
Track: **LH: 1-2** RH: 0-1 Tight: 0-0 **Gall: 1-2**
Aids: Bl: 0-0 Vi: 0-0 Tstrap: 0-0
Best Rating: 118 3/02 Newb 2m110y soft Hdl

Expensive purchase off the Flat who finished a good third on his hurdle debut at Kempton in February on soft. Jumped better when successful next time. Looks best suited by two miles on a sound surface.

Lord Khalice (IRE)

111 123

11-y-o b g King's Ride-Khalice (Khalkis)

Ferdy Murphy Exors Of The Late Mr G A Hubbard

Placings: 24022/1/1P**56FUP**/P2423203134/3-34113 **(3928)**

2001/02: 26^{3}G, 26^{4}G, 26^{1}S, 24^{1}GS, 26^{3}HY

	Starts	1st	2nd	3rd	Win & Pl
Chases	5	2	0	2	8672
Career Total	**30**	**5**	**6**	**6**	**27913**

120	2/02	Fknm	3m110y	F(0-100)HCh	G-S	£4143
123	1/02	Folk	3m2f	F(0-100)HCh	SFT	£3318
111	3/00	Hntg	3m	E(0-115)HCh	SFT	£3061
113	10/98	MRas	3m	D(0-125)HHdl	SFT	£3096
96	10/97	Uttx	2m6f110y	C Hdl	GD	£4086

Total win prize-money £17707

Going: Sf: 1-2 GS: 1-1 Gd: 0-2 GF: - Fm: 0-0
Distance: 2m/2m3: 0-0 2m4-2m7: 0-0 **3m+: 2-5**
Track: LH: 1-1 RH: 1-1 **Tight: 2-3** Gall: 0-0
Aids: Bl: 0-0 Vi: 0-0 Tstrap: 0-0
Best Rating: 123 1/02 Folk 3m2f soft Ch

Fair chaser. Acts on a soft surface, he goes well from two miles six plus. Goes well at Huntingdon.

Lord Knox (IRE)

12-y-o ch g Tale Quale-Lady Knox (Dalsaan)

Mrs K Clark Ms K Clark

Placings: P/6/2-3 **(4534)**

2001/02: 21^{3}G

	Starts	1st	2nd	3rd	Win & Pl
Chases	1	0	0	1	316
Career Total	**4**	**0**	**1**	**1**	**764**

Going: Sf: 0-0 GS: 0-0 Gd: 0-1 GF: - Fm: 0-0
Distance: 2m/2m3: 0-0 2m4-2m7: 0-1 3m+: 0-0
Track: LH: 0-1 RH: 0-0 Tight: 0-1 Gall: 0-0
Aids: Bl: 0-0 Vi: 0-0 Tstrap: 0-0
Best Rating: 95 5/00 Folk 2m5f good Ch

Moderate pointer/hunter chaser.

Lord Lamb

104(102h) 132

10-y-o gr g Dunbeath (USA)-Caroline Lamb (Hotfoot)

Mrs M Reveley A Sharratt & J Renton

Placings: *10/114/*11120/511/23413F-16 **(0803)**

2001/02: 25^{1}GF, 24^{6}GF

	Starts	1st	2nd	3rd	Win & Pl
Chases	2	1	0	0	3626
Career Total	**21**	**10**	**2**	**2**	**40296**

132	5/01	Ayr	3m1f	E Ch	G-F	£3626
126	1/01	Leic	2m4f110y	D Ch	SFT	£4371

150	12/99	Hayd	2m4f	C(0-135)HHdl	SFT	£5264
140	12/99	Donc	2m110y	B(0-140)HHdl	G-S	£6989
127	12/98	Weth	2m	D Hdl	SFT	£3197
121	12/98	Newc	2m	E Hdl	SFT	£2421
131	12/98	Newc	2m	E Hdl	SFT	£2379
113	3/97	Hntg	2m110y	H NHF	G-F	£1329
105	12/96	Muss	2m	H NHF	G-F	£1138
107	3/96	Ayr	2m	H NHF	GD	£1544

Total win prize-money £32259

Going: Sf: 0-0 GS: 0-0 Gd: 0-0 GF: - Fm: 1-2
Distance: 2m/2m3: 0-0 2m4-2m7: 0-0 **3m+: 1-2**
Track: **LH: 1-1** RH: 0-1 Tight: 0-0 Gall: 0-0
Aids: Bl: 0-0 Vi: 0-0 Tstrap: 0-0
Best Rating: 150 12/99 Hayd 2m4f soft Hdl

Talented but quirky, he did not look a natural in novice chases, tending to hurdle the obstacles and throwing away more than one winning opportunity. However, he is with the right stable and will be well handicapped if getting his act together next season.

Lord Lane

94 **63**

9-y-o bl g Lord Bud-Gala Lane (Gala Performance (USA))
J M Dun J M Dun

Placings:00/0P0P-P40PP (2471)
2001/02: 16^{P}GS, 20^{4}GF, 22^{0}G, 21^{P}G, 18^{P}GS

	Starts	1st	2nd	3rd	Win & Pl
Hurdles	4	0	0	0	261
Chases	1	0	0	0	0
Career Total	**11**	**0**	**0**	**0**	**261**

Going: Sf: 0-0 GS: 0-2 Gd: 0-2 GF: - Fm: 0-1
Distance: 2m/2m3: 0-2 2m4-2m7: 0-3 3m+: 0-0
Track: LH: 0-3 RH: 0-2 Tight: 0-2 Gall: 0-0
Aids: Bl: 0-0 Vi: 0-0 Tstrap: 0-0
Best Rating: 82 4/00 Carl 2m1f gd-sft Hdl

Lord Lard (IRE)

8-y-o b g Lord Americo-Shuil Ard (Quayside)
S Flook S Flook

Placings:P (4179)
2001/02: 24^{P}GS

	Starts	1st	2nd	3rd	Win & Pl
Chases	1	0	0	0	
Career Total	**1**	**0**	**0**	**0**	

Going: Sf: 0-0 GS: 0-1 Gd: 0-0 GF: - Fm: 0-0
Distance: 2m/2m3: 0-0 2m4-2m7: 0-0 3m+: 0-1
Track: LH: 0-1 RH: 0-0 Tight: 0-1 Gall: 0-0
Aids: Bl: 0-0 Vi: 0-0 Tstrap: 0-0
Best Rating:

Lord Luker (IRE)

92f **91f**

6-y-o b g Lord Americo-Canon's Dream (Le Bavard (FR))
Miss H C Knight Luker Bros (removals & Storage) Ltd

Placings:*6* (0272)
2001/02: 17^{6}G

	Starts	1st	2nd	3rd	Win & Pl
NH Flat	1	0	0	0	0
Career Total	**1**	**0**	**0**	**0**	**0**

Going: Sf: 0-0 GS: 0-0 Gd: 0-1 GF: - Fm: 0-0
Distance: 2m/2m3: 0-1 2m4-2m7: 0-0 3m+: 0-0
Track: LH: 0-0 RH: 0-1 Tight: 0-0 Gall: 0-0
Aids: Bl: 0-0 Vi: 0-0 Tstrap: 0-0
Best Rating: 91 5/01 Hrfd 2m1f good NHF

Lord Lupin (IRE)

84f **84f**

6-y-o b g Sadler's Wells (USA)-Penza (Soviet Star (USA))
T H Caldwell T H Caldwell

Placings:*2-00* (3503)
2001/02: 17^{0}GS, 16^{0}S

	Starts	1st	2nd	3rd	Win & Pl
NH Flat	2	0	0	0	
Career Total	**3**	**0**	**1**	**0**	**726**

Going: Sf: 0-1 GS: 0-1 Gd: 0-0 GF: - Fm: 0-0
Distance: 2m/2m3: 0-2 2m4-2m7: 0-0 3m+: 0-0
Track: LH: 0-0 RH: 0-1 Tight: 0-0 Gall: 0-0
Aids: Bl: 0-0 Vi: 0-0 Tstrap: 0-0
Best Rating: 116 2/01 Kemp 2m gd-sft NHF

Lord Max

79 **49**

10-y-o br g Arctic Lord-Thames Air (Crash Course)
Mrs S Richardson Mrs S L Richardson

Placings:*50*/P063/3/F-P0 (0378)
2001/02: 25^{P}G, 24^{0}GF

	Starts	1st	2nd	3rd	Win & Pl
Chases	2	0	0	0	
Career Total	**10**	**0**	**0**	**2**	**1121**

Going: Sf: 0-0 GS: 0-0 Gd: 0-1 GF: - Fm: 0-1
Distance: 2m/2m3: 0-0 2m4-2m7: 0-0 3m+: 0-2
Track: LH: 0-0 RH: 0-2 Tight: 0-0 Gall: 0-1
Aids: Bl: 0-0 Vi: 0-0 Tstrap: 0-0
Best Rating: 103 5/99 Ludl 3m gd-fm Ch

Lord Moose (IRE)

86 **129**

8-y-o b g Mister Lord (USA)-Moose (IRE) (Royal Fountain)
H D Daly The Hon Mr Simon Sainsbury

Placings:PF1/P01 (4009)
2001/02: 20^{P}GS, 20^{0}S, 22^{1}S

	Starts	1st	2nd	3rd	Win & Pl
Chases	3	1	0	0	9009
Career Total	**6**	**2**	**0**	**0**	**14144**

129	3/02	Newb	2m6f110y	D(0-120)HCh	SFT	£9009
116	4/00	Asct	2m4f	C Hdl	SFT	£5135

Total win prize-money £14144

Going: Sf: 1-2 GS: 0-1 Gd: 0-0 GF: - Fm: 0-0
Distance: 2m/2m3: 0-0 **2m4-2m7: 1-3** 3m+: 0-0
Track: **LH: 1-2** RH: 0-1 Tight: 0-0 **Gall: 1-1**
Aids: Bl: 0-0 Vi: 0-0 Tstrap: 0-0
Best Rating: 129 3/02 Newb 2m6f110y soft Ch

Did not complete either of his first two runs over fences, but won his hurdles debut in the spring of 2000 in soft ground. Returned to fences, he put a couple of poor performances behind him when scoring at Newbury in March 2002. A staying chaser in the making.

Lord Native (IRE)

101 **96**

7-y-o b g Be My Native (USA)-Whakapohane (Kampala)
N J Henderson Carlton Burns Ltd

Placings:106/02-1 (0644)
2001/02: 17^{1}GF

	Starts	1st	2nd	3rd	Win & Pl
Hurdles	1	1	0	0	2510
Career Total	**6**	**2**	**1**	**0**	**5950**

96	6/01	MRas	2m1f110y	E Hdl	G-F	£2509
92	7/99	Klny	2m1f	NHF	G-F	£2915

Total win prize-money £5426

Going: Sf: 0-0 GS: 0-0 Gd: 0-0 GF: - Fm: 1-1
Distance: **2m/2m3: 1-1** 2m4-2m7: 0-0 3m+: 0-0
Track: LH: 0-0 **RH: 1-1 Tight: 1-1** Gall: 0-0
Aids: Bl: 0-0 Vi: 0-0 Tstrap: 0-0
Best Rating: 110 1/01 Fknm 2m soft Hdl

Lord Nellsson

102 **98**

6-y-o b g Arctic Lord-Miss Petronella (Petoski)
J S King Dajam Ltd

Placings:3600 (4484)
2001/02: 16^{3}G, 17^{6}S, 16^{0}GS, 17^{0}G

	Starts	1st	2nd	3rd	Win & Pl
Hurdles	4	0	0	1	525
Career Total	**4**	**0**	**0**	**1**	**525**

Going: Sf: 0-1 GS: 0-1 Gd: 0-2 GF: - Fm: 0-0
Distance: 2m/2m3: 0-4 2m4-2m7: 0-0 3m+: 0-0
Track: LH: 0-0 RH: 0-4 Tight: 0-1 Gall: 0-0
Aids: Bl: 0-0 Vi: 0-0 Tstrap: 0-0
Best Rating: 98 11/01 Kemp 2m good Hdl

Lord Noelie (IRE)

115 **180**

9-y-o b g Lord Americo-Leallen (Le Bavard (FR))
Miss H C Knight Executive Racing

Placings:4/16F14/2121/4U2-F4503 (4648)
2001/02: 25^{F}G, 26^{4}S, 25^{5}HY, 26^{0}G, 25^{3}G

	Starts	1st	2nd	3rd	Win & Pl
Chases	5	0	0	1	18200
Career Total	**18**	**4**	**3**	**1**	**139095**

164	3/00	Chel	3m110y	A Ch	GD	£66700
152	11/99	Newb	3m	C Ch	GD	£6440
130	2/99	Winc	2m6f	B Hdl	G-S	£10755
112	10/98	Strf	2m6f110y	D Hdl	GD	£3183

Total win prize-money £87078

Going: Sf: 0-2 GS: 0-0 Gd: 0-3 GF: - Fm: 0-0
Distance: 2m/2m3: 0-0 2m4-2m7: 0-0 3m+: 0-5
Track: LH: 0-5 RH: 0-0 Tight: 0-1 Gall: 0-3
Aids: Bl: 0-0 Vi: 0-0 Tstrap: 0-0
Best Rating: 180 12/01 Newb 3m2f110y soft Ch

He landed Cheltenham's Royal & SunAlliance Chase in 2000, albeit not a vintage edition, and it is likely that the best has yet to be seen of him over the larger obstacles. Fourth at Wincanton on his reappearance last season, he was an early casualty next time. He missed a number of engagements because of unsuitably soft ground, but ran well on a soft surface at Aintree when runner-up to First Gold. He has looked close to a return to form in 2001/2002 and faded to finish tenth after racing prominently in the 2002 Gold Cup (saddle slipped). Burst a blood vessel when third behind Florida Pearl at Aintree. Stays three miles.

Lord North (IRE)

107 **127**

7-y-o b g Mister Lord (USA)-Mrs Hegarty (Decent Fellow)

P R Webber Jerry Wright

Placings:*4P*-3150 **(4824)**

2001/02: 16^{3}G, 16^{1}GF, 19^{5}G, 16^{0}G

	Starts	1st	2nd	3rd	Win & Pl
Chases	4	1	0	1	3859
Career Total	**6**	**1**	**0**	**1**	**3859**

105	11/01	Leic	2m	E Ch	G-F	£3307

Total win prize-money £3308

Going: Sf: 0-0 GS: 0-0 Gd: 0-3 GF: - Fm: 1-1
Distance: **2m/2m3: 1-3** 2m4-2m7: 0-1 3m+: 0-0
Track: LH: 0-3 **RH: 1-1** Tight: 0-0 Gall: 0-2
Aids: Bl: 0-0 Vi: 0-0 Tstrap: 0-0
Best Rating: 127 12/01 Donc 2m3f110y good Ch

A grand big sort who was third to Barton and October Mist on his chasing debut. Game winner of a Leicester novice chase in November 2001. Benefited from a rival's last fence fall when winning two and a half mile handicap on soft ground at Bangor May 2002.

Lord O'All Seasons (IRE)

106 **130**

9-y-o b/br g Mister Lord (USA)-Autumn News (Giolla Mear)

N J Henderson S Keeling

Placings:01-P223 **(4428)**

2001/02: 24^{P}G, 23^{2}S, 24^{2}GS, 23^{3}HY

	Starts	1st	2nd	3rd	Win & Pl
Chases	4	0	2	1	6060
Career Total	**6**	**1**	**2**	**1**	**10526**

110	2/01	Leic	2m7f110y	D Ch	SFT	£4466

Total win prize-money £4466

Going: Sf: 0-2 GS: 0-1 Gd: 0-1 GF: - Fm: 0-0
Distance: 2m/2m3: 0-0 2m4-2m7: 0-1 3m+: 0-3
Track: LH: 0-1 RH: 0-3 Tight: 0-1 Gall: 0-0
Aids: Bl: 0-0 Vi: 0-0 Tstrap: 0-0
Best Rating: 130 2/02 Ludl 3m gd-sft Ch

Lightly raced, fair chaser, he is effective at three miles and acts on soft ground.

Lord Of Love

105 **109**

7-y-o b g Noble Patriarch-Gymcrak Lovebird (Taufan (USA))

D Burchell Mouse Racing

Placings:2360410221246/64052130F423F06255/216 005P00-322000 **(4853)**

2001/02: 17^{3}S, 22^{2}GS, 20^{2}GS, 16^{0}GS, 20^{0}HY, 16^{0}G

	Starts	1st	2nd	3rd	Win & Pl
Hurdles	6	0	2	1	4463
Career Total	**46**	**4**	**10**	**4**	**26854**

122	5/00	Strf	3m3f	E(0-115)HHdl	G-F	£2898
112	12/99	Hrfd	2m3f110y	F(0-105)HHdl	HVY	£3137
120	2/99	Ling	2m3f110y	E Hdl	SFT	£2108
107	12/98	Font	2m2f110y	E Hdl	G-S	£1935

Total win prize-money £10078

Going: Sf: 0-2 GS: 0-3 Gd: 0-1 GF: - Fm: 0-0
Distance: 2m/2m3: 0-3 2m4-2m7: 0-3 3m+: 0-0
Track: LH: 0-4 RH: 0-2 Tight: 0-3 Gall: 0-0
Aids: Bl: 0-0 Vi: 0-0 Tstrap: 0-0
Best Rating: 124 2/99 Font 2m2f110y good Hdl

Appreciates give in the ground, and stays two miles six, but does not seem to stay three miles plus unless the ground rides fast.

Lord Of The Flies (IRE)

(100c) (120c)**65**

9-y-o b/br g Lord Americo-Beau's Trout (Beau Charmeur (FR))

Miss H C Knight Winter Madness

Placings:*10/4*220F301/1421F22F/060-60 **(0242)**

2001/02: 17^{6}G, 21^{0}GF

	Starts	1st	2nd	3rd	Win & Pl
Hurdles	1	0	0	0	0
Chases	1	0	0	0	0
Career Total	**23**	**4**	**5**	**1**	**18171**

125	11/99	Uttx	2m	D Ch	G-S	£3826
115	5/99	Extr	2m1f110y	E(0-115)HHdl	G-F	£3241
112	4/99	Extr	2m1f110y	E(0-105)HHdl	G-S	£2826
104	1/98	Donc	2m110y	H NHF	GD	£1413

Total win prize-money £11306

Going: Sf: 0-0 GS: 0-0 Gd: 0-1 GF: - Fm: 0-1
Distance: 2m/2m3: 0-1 2m4-2m7: 0-1 3m+: 0-0
Track: LH: 0-0 RH: 0-1 Tight: 0-0 Gall: 0-0
Aids: Bl: 0-0 Vi: 0-0 Tstrap: 0-0
Best Rating: 136 3/00 Strf 2m4f good Ch

Fair 2m-2m4f hurdler/chaser who goes well at Exeter. Below form recently.

Lord Of The Land

104(92h) **104**

9-y-o b g Lord Bud-Saint Motunde (Tyrant (USA))

Mrs E Slack A Slack

Placings:*650/000/61110431130/044***UFP**0-621 **(0471)**

2001/02: 21^{6}G, 20^{2}GF, 25^{1}GF

	Starts	1st	2nd	3rd	Win & Pl
Chases	3	1	1	0	3792
Career Total	**27**	**6**	**1**	**2**	**17037**

104	5/01	Hexm	3m1f	F(0-95)HCh	G-F	£2716
119	9/99	Sedg	2m5f110y	D(0-125)HHdl	GD	£2914
107	9/99	Kels	2m6f110y	F(0-105)HHdl	G-F	£2276
119	6/99	Hexm	2m4f110y	F(0-105)HHdl	G-F	£2607
104	5/99	Hexm	2m4f110y	E Hdl	G-F	£1716
96	5/99	Kels	2m2f	E Hdl	G-F	£1955

Total win prize-money £14186

Going: Sf: 0-0 GS: 0-0 Gd: 0-1 GF: - Fm: 1-2
Distance: 2m/2m3: 0-0 2m4-2m7: 0-2 **3m+: 1-1**
Track: **LH: 1-3** RH: 0-0 Tight: 0-1 Gall: 0-0
Aids: Bl: 0-0 Vi: 0-0 Tstrap: 0-0
Best Rating: 119 9/99 Sedg 2m5f110y good Hdl

Modest staying chaser, suited by fast ground.

Lord Of The Loch (IRE)

106 **112**

11-y-o b/br g Lord Americo-Loughamaire (Brave Invader (USA))

W G Young (M Todhunter 15/1) W G Young

Placings:*U243/4*/1333/1-5401536320 **(4893)**

2001/02: 20^{5}S, 16^{4}S, 20^{0}S, 20^{1}S, 20^{5}S, 20^{3}GS, 22^{6}HY, 22^{3}GF, 20^{2}GF, 20^{0}G

	Starts	1st	2nd	3rd	Win & Pl
Hurdles	10	1	1	2	5731
Career Total	**20**	**3**	**2**	**6**	**12331**

112	2/02	Muss	2m4f	F(0-100)HHdl	SFT	£3038
107	2/01	Carl	2m1f	F(0-105)HHdl	HVY	£2702
101	5/99	Prth	2m4f110y	E Hdl	SFT	£2409

Total win prize-money £8150

Going: Sf: 1-6 GS: 0-1 Gd: 0-1 GF: - Fm: 0-2
Distance: 2m/2m3: 0-1 **2m4-2m7: 1-9** 3m+: 0-0
Track: LH: 0-6 **RH: 1-3 Tight: 1-3** Gall: 0-1
Aids: Bl: 0-0 Vi: 0-0 Tstrap: 0-0
Best Rating: 112 2/02 Muss 2m4f soft Hdl

Fair hurdler, lightly raced due to leg trouble, he likes the mud and stays two and a half miles.

Lord Of The Manor (SWE)

(95h) (70 h)

5-y-o b g Spectacular Tide (USA)-Sobhiato (AUS) (Motavato (USA))

D W P Arbuthnot Eastwind Racing Ltd

Placings:0606 **(1240)**

2001/02: 20^{0}GF, 24^{6}S, 22^{0}GF, 24^{6}GF

	Starts	1st	2nd	3rd	Win & Pl
Hurdles	4	0	0	0	0
Career Total	**4**	**0**	**0**	**0**	**0**

Going: Sf: 0-1 GS: 0-0 Gd: 0-0 GF: - Fm: 0-3
Distance: 2m/2m3: 0-0 2m4-2m7: 0-2 3m+: 0-2
Track: LH: 0-4 RH: 0-0 Tight: 0-1 Gall: 0-0
Aids: Bl: 0-0 Vi: 0-0 Tstrap: 0-2
Best Rating: 60 8/01 Strf 2m6f110y gd-fm Hdl

Lord Of The North (IRE)

66f **43f**

5-y-o br g Arctic Lord-Ballyfin Maid (IRE) (Boreen (FR))

M R Ewer-Hoad Mrs J E Taylor

Placings:*0* **(2041)**

2001/02: 16^{0}GS

	Starts	1st	2nd	3rd	Win & Pl
NH Flat	1	0	0	0	
Career Total	**1**	**0**	**0**	**0**	

Going: Sf: 0-0 GS: 0-1 Gd: 0-0 GF: - Fm: 0-0
Distance: 2m/2m3: 0-1 2m4-2m7: 0-0 3m+: 0-0
Track: LH: 0-0 RH: 0-1 Tight: 0-0 Gall: 0-0
Aids: Bl: 0-0 Vi: 0-0 Tstrap: 0-0
Best Rating: 43 11/01 Sand 2m110y gd-sft NHF

Lord Of The Park (IRE)

67f **33f**

5-y-o b g Lord Americo-Wind Chimes (The Parson)

John R Upson Middleham Park Racing V

Placings:*0* **(1905)**

2001/02: 17^{0}G

	Starts	1st	2nd	3rd	Win & Pl
NH Flat	1	0	0	0	
Career Total	**1**	**0**	**0**	**0**	

Going: Sf: 0-0 GS: 0-0 Gd: 0-1 GF: - Fm: 0-0
Distance: 2m/2m3: 0-1 2m4-2m7: 0-0 3m+: 0-0
Track: LH: 0-1 RH: 0-0 Tight: 0-1 Gall: 0-0
Aids: Bl: 0-0 Vi: 0-0 Tstrap: 0-0
Best Rating: 33 11/01 Sedg 2m1f good NHF

Lord Of The River (IRE)

114 **142**

10-y-o br g Lord Americo-Well Over (Over The River (FR))

N J Henderson B T Stewart-Brown

Placings:5/11415/1F2112/5U2 **(4955a)**

2001/02: 24^{5}G, 25^{U}G, 25^{2}G

	Starts	1st	2nd	3rd	Win & Pl
Chases	3	0	1	0	7495
Career Total	**15**	**6**	**3**	**0**	**89122**

160	2/99	Asct	3m110y	A Ch	GD	£19050
160	12/98	Kemp	3m	A Ch	G-S	£22715
129	11/98	Extr	2m3f	C Ch	SFT	£5433
123	3/98	Newb	2m5f	D Hdl	HVY	£3038
120	12/97	Uttx	2m4f110y	E Hdl	G-S	£1945
107	11/97	Wind	2m4f	D Hdl	GD	£2810

Total win prize-money £54992

Going: Sf: 0-0 GS: 0-0 Gd: 0-3 GF: - Fm: 0-0
Distance: 2m/2m3: 0-0 2m4-2m7: 0-0 3m+: 0-3
Track: LH: 0-1 RH: 0-2 Tight: 0-1 Gall: 0-0
Aids: Bl: 0-0 Vi: 0-0 Tstrap: 0-0
Best Rating: 160 2/99 Asct 3m110y good Ch

He looked a smart prospect when completing the Feltham-Reynoldstown novices' chase double in the build-up toward Cheltenham's Royal & SunAlliance Chase in 1998/1999. Unfortunately luck deserted him when second to Looks Like Trouble at the Festival - he suffered an over reach and twisted a plate and was absent for nearly three years before returning at Kempton in February 2002. Stays three miles, acts on soft ground.

Lord Of The Sky

(105h) (132h)

9-y-o b g Lord Bud-Fardella (ITY) (Molvedo)

L Lungo S E Constable

Placings:*11*/621F234/11111P-51 **(2469)**

2001/02: 20^{5}GS, 22^{1}GS

	Starts	1st	2nd	3rd	Win & Pl
Hurdles	2	1	0	0	3526
Career Total	**17**	**9**	**2**	**1**	**35226**

132	12/01	Kels	2m6f110y	D(0-125)HHdl	G-S	£3526
141	2/01	Kels	3m1f	C Ch	SFT	£7280
141	12/00	Newc	2m4f	E Ch	SFT	£3350
139	11/00	Carl	2m4f110y	D Ch	SFT	£4329
141	11/00	Ayr	2m4f	D Ch	G-S	£3887
126	10/00	Carl	2m4f110y	E Ch	G-S	£3253
111	12/99	Ayr	2m4f	E Hdl	HVY	£2850
121	11/98	Hexm	2m	H NHF	HVY	£1332
106	11/98	Ayr	2m	H NHF	G-S	£1287

Total win prize-money £31097

Going: Sf: 0-0 GS: 1-2 Gd: 0-0 GF: - Fm: 0-0
Distance: 2m/2m3: 0-0 **2m4-2m7: 1-2** 3m+: 0-0
Track: **LH: 1-2** RH: 0-0 **Tight: 1-1** Gall: 0-0
Aids: Bl: 0-0 Vi: 0-0 Tstrap: 0-0
Best Rating: 141 2/01 Kels 3m1f soft Ch

He looked very smart when winning his first five novice chases in 2000.01, the only negative being a habit of jumping out to the right. Beaten on appalling ground at Perth in April 2001, he will stay long distances but has broken blood-vessels in the past. Won over hurdles at Kelso in December 2001.

Lord Of The West (IRE)

99 **93**

13-y-o b g Mister Lord (USA)-Caroline's Girl (Roman Warrior)

J J O'Neill Anne Duchess Of Westminster

Placings:P/6UP10P0/1113P2F/1124F2515/122P1/P3 P30F/PRU50 **(2146)**

2001/02: 23^{P}GF, 26^{R}GS, 24^{U}G, 25^{5}G, 31^{0}G

	Starts	1st	2nd	3rd	Win & Pl
Chases	5	0	0	0	0
Career Total	**40**	**9**	**5**	**3**	**55463**

150	12/98	Donc	3m2f	B(0-140)HCh	GD	£7757
145	5/98	Uttx	3m	B HCh	G-S	£7191
141	3/98	Wwck	3m2f	D(0-125)HCh	G-S	£3525
128	11/97	Carl	3m	C(0-130)HCh	FRM	£5404
128	10/97	Carl	3m	C(0-135)HCh	FRM	£4557
120	12/96	Leic	3m	D(0-125)HCh	G-F	£4449
112	12/96	Worc	2m7f110y	F(0-100)HCh	G-S	£2910
113	11/96	Ludl	3m	E(0-115)HCh	G-F	£3501
104	3/96	Uttx	2m6f110y	E(0-115)HHdl	GD	£2274

Total win prize-money £41571

Going: Sf: 0-0 GS: 0-1 Gd: 0-3 GF: - Fm: 0-1
Distance: 2m/2m3: 0-0 2m4-2m7: 0-0 3m+: 0-5
Track: LH: 0-3 RH: 0-1 Tight: 0-1 Gall: 0-0
Aids: Bl: 0-1 Vi: 0-0 Tstrap: 0-0
Best Rating: 150 12/98 Donc 3m2f good Ch

He has been a useful staying chaser in his time, but has been on the sidelines and has become a thoroughly moody customer in recent seasons. Ran better until unseating his rider at Bangor in October, although he was disappointing next time at Wincanton.

Lord Omni (USA)

96 **77**

5-y-o ch g El Prado (IRE)-Muskoka Ice (USA) (It's Freezing (USA))

R H Buckler (T D Barron 28/7) Mrs Liz Jones

Placings:060P0P **(2517)**

2001/02: 17^{0}GF, 16^{6}GF, 17^{0}F, 16^{P}G, 16^{0}GF, 21^{P}S

	Starts	1st	2nd	3rd	Win & Pl
Hurdles	6	0	0	0	0
Career Total	**6**	**0**	**0**	**0**	**0**

Going: Sf: 0-1 GS: 0-0 Gd: 0-1 GF: - Fm: 0-4
Distance: 2m/2m3: 0-5 2m4-2m7: 0-1 3m+: 0-0
Track: LH: 0-1 RH: 0-5 Tight: 0-2 Gall: 0-0
Aids: Bl: 0-0 Vi: 0-0 Tstrap: 0-1
Best Rating: 77 10/01 Tntn 2m1f firm Hdl

Lord Pat (IRE)

104 **90**

11-y-o ch g Mister Lord (USA)-Arianrhod (L'Homme Arme)

Miss Kate Milligan The L P Club

Placings:05/05000/321P1033P/62P00/432-0124666 **(4432)**

2001/02: 18^{0}G, 20^{1}G, 20^{2}G, 20^{4}GS, 20^{6}S, 17^{6}S, 20^{6}HY

	Starts	1st	2nd	3rd	Win & Pl
Hurdles	7	1	1	0	2717
Career Total	**31**	**3**	**4**	**4**	**12260**

90	11/01	Newc	2m4f	F(0-90)HHdl	GD	£2009
91	1/99	Muss	2m4f	F(0-100)HHdl	SFT	£4533
81	11/98	Sedg	2m1f	G(0-95)HHdl	G-S	£1626

Total win prize-money £8169

Going: Sf: 0-3 GS: 0-1 Gd: 1-3 GF: - Fm: 0-0
Distance: 2m/2m3: 0-2 **2m4-2m7: 1-5** 3m+: 0-0
Track: **LH: 1-6** RH: 0-1 Tight: 0-3 **Gall: 1-2**
Aids: Bl: 0-0 Vi: 0-0 Tstrap: 0-0
Best Rating: 91 11/99 Kels 2m110y good Hdl

A low-grade handicapper, he appears in better shape than ever judged on his recent consistent efforts. Best hurdles form is at two and a half miles on good ground.

Lord Perseus (IRE)

100f **102f**

5-y-o ch g Mister Lord (USA)-Greek Empress (Royal Buck)

M Pitman J F Garrett

Placings:*30* **(4679)**

2001/02: 16^{3}S, 17^{0}G

	Starts	1st	2nd	3rd	Win & Pl
NH Flat	2	0	0	1	288
Career Total	**2**	**0**	**0**	**1**	**288**

Going: Sf: 0-1 GS: 0-0 Gd: 0-1 GF: - Fm: 0-0
Distance: 2m/2m3: 0-2 2m4-2m7: 0-0 3m+: 0-0
Track: LH: 0-0 RH: 0-1 Tight: 0-0 Gall: 0-0
Aids: Bl: 0-0 Vi: 0-0 Tstrap: 0-0
Best Rating: 102 1/02 Kemp 2m soft NHF

Promising third in a Kempton bumper on his debut.

Lord Pierce

79 **80**

4-y-o b g Tragic Role (USA)-Mirkan Honey (Ballymore)

J Howard Johnson (M Johnston 5/1) Hertford Offset Limited

Placings:24 **(4139)**

2001/02: 16^{2}S, 16^{4}HY

	Starts	1st	2nd	3rd	Win & Pl
Hurdles	2	0	1	0	1115
Career Total	**2**	**0**	**1**	**0**	**1115**

Going: Sf: 0-2 GS: 0-0 Gd: 0-0 GF: - Fm: 0-0
Distance: 2m/2m3: 0-2 2m4-2m7: 0-0 3m+: 0-0
Track: LH: 0-1 RH: 0-1 Tight: 0-1 Gall: 0-0
Aids: Bl: 0-0 Vi: 0-0 Tstrap: 0-0
Best Rating: 80 2/02 Muss 2m soft Hdl

A winner on heaavy ground on the Flat, he was runner-up on his hurdling bow.

Lord Podgski (IRE)

108(89h) (93h)**124**

11-y-o b g Lord Americo-Linoski (Malinowski (USA))

P Monteith Mrs G Smyth

Placings:*3/131*/15/255242/F/0U-212561P **(1198)**

2001/02: 16^{2}GF, 16^{1}S, 20^{2}G, 20^{5}G, 16^{6}GF, 23^{1}GF, 20^{P}G

	Starts	1st	2nd	3rd	Win & Pl
Chases	7	2	2	0	11944
Career Total	**22**	**5**	**5**	**2**	**21214**

120	7/01	Uttx	2m7f	D Ch	G-F	£4497
124	5/01	Prth	2m	D Ch	SFT	£4810
100	11/97	Newc	2m	E Hdl	G-F	£2263
108	4/97	Prth	2m110y	H NHF	GD	£2052
111	1/97	Ayr	2m	H NHF	GD	£1329

Total win prize-money £14953

Going: Sf: 1-1 GS: 0-0 Gd: 0-3 GF: - Fm: 1-3
Distance: 2m/2m3: 1-3 2m4-2m7: 1-4 3m+: 0-0
Track: LH: 1-3 RH: 1-4 Tight: 0-3 Gall: 0-0
Aids: Bl: 0-0 Vi: 0-0 Tstrap: 0-0
Best Rating: 124 5/01 Prth 2m soft Ch

Lord Powerstown (IRE)

(64h) (10h)

7-y-o b g Lord Americo-Smashed Free (IRE) (Carlingford Castle)

Mrs L B Normile John Findlay

Placings:00-P0SPPF **(1250)**

2001/02: 16^{P}G, 20^{0}GS, 24^{S}GF, 20^{P}GF, 21^{P}GF, 26^{F}G

	Starts	1st	2nd	3rd	Win & Pl
Hurdles	5	0	0	0	0
Chases	1	0	0	0	0
Career Total	**8**	**0**	**0**	**0**	

Going: Sf: 0-0 GS: 0-1 Gd: 0-2 GF: - Fm: 0-3
Distance: 2m/2m3: 0-1 2m4-2m7: 0-3 3m+: 0-2
Track: LH: 0-3 RH: 0-3 Tight: 0-2 Gall: 0-0
Aids: Bl: 0-0 Vi: 0-0 Tstrap: 0-0
Best Rating: 10 5/01 Prth 2m4f110y gd-sft Hdl

Lord Rapier

86 121

9-y-o b g Broadsword (USA)-Doddycross (Deep Run)

D J Caro Ms S Elliott

Placings:322/61-1 **(0054)**

2001/02: 24^{1}G

	Starts	1st	2nd	3rd	Win & Pl
Hurdles	1	1	0	0	3416
Career Total	**6**	**2**	**2**	**1**	**7211**

121	5/01	Bang	3m	E Hdl	GD	£3416
104	4/01	Hntg	2m5f110y	E Hdl	SFT	£2478

Total win prize-money £5894

Going: Sf: 0-0 GS: 0-0 Gd: 1-1 GF: - Fm: 0-0
Distance: 2m/2m3: 0-0 2m4-2m7: 0-0 **3m+: 1-1**
Track: **LH: 1-1** RH: 0-0 **Tight: 1-1** Gall: 0-0
Aids: Bl: 0-0 Vi: 0-0 Tstrap: 0-0
Best Rating: 121 5/01 Bang 3m good Hdl

Lord Richfield (NZ)

92(97c) (111c)90

11-y-o b g Kirmann-Lady Grange (NZ) (Sir Bart (NZ))

B P J Baugh (S A Brookshaw 4/5) Dave Arrowsmith

Placings:22502/21513144353/**P5F02U4UPP**/**22002P 5-30360** **(4847)**

2001/02: 17^{3}GS, 20^{0}S, 17^{3}GS, 21^{6}HY, 20^{0}G

	Starts	1st	2nd	3rd	Win & Pl
Hurdles	4	0	0	1	548
Chases	1	0	0	1	690
Career Total	**38**	**3**	**8**	**5**	**23477**

115	12/98	Uttx	2m	C(0-130)HHdl	G-S	£5225
114	11/98	Uttx	2m	D(0-125)HHdl	SFT	£2843
102	10/98	Strf	2m6f110y	E Hdl	G-S	£2075

Total win prize-money £10143

Going: Sf: 0-2 GS: 0-2 Gd: 0-1 GF: - Fm: 0-0
Distance: 2m/2m3: 0-2 2m4-2m7: 0-3 3m+: 0-0
Track: LH: 0-4 RH: 0-1 Tight: 0-3 Gall: 0-0
Aids: Bl: 0-0 Vi: 0-1 Tstrap: 0-0
Best Rating: 115 11/00 Hayd 2m heavy Hdl

Lord Rochester

96(109h) (124h)104+

6-y-o b g Distant Relative-Kentfield (Busted)

C J Mann London Central Portfolio Limited

Placings:523/12132314-03F053114 **(1862)**

2001/02: 16^{0}GF, 17^{3}F, 16^{F}GF, 16^{0}GF, 16^{5}GF, 18^{3}GF, 21^{1}GF, 20^{1}G, 21^{4}G

	Starts	1st	2nd	3rd	Win & Pl
Hurdles	9	2	0	2	8418
Career Total	**20**	**5**	**3**	**5**	**19327**

121	10/01	Chep	2m4f	D(0-125)HHdl	GD	£3474
117	9/01	Plum	2m5f	D(0-125)HHdl	G-F	£3342
123	10/00	Folk	2m1f110y	F(0-110)HHdl	G-F	£1757
110	5/00	Font	2m2f110y	E Hdl	GD	£2285
104	5/00	Folk	2m1f110y	E Hdl	GD	£2432

Total win prize-money £13293

Going: Sf: 0-0 GS: 0-0 Gd: 1-2 GF: - Fm: 1-7
Distance: 2m/2m3: 0-6 **2m4-2m7: 2-3** 3m+: 0-0
Track: **LH: 2-7** RH: 0-2 **Tight: 1-5** Gall: 0-1
Aids: **Bl: 2-9** Vi: 0-0 Tstrap: 0-0
Best Rating: 124 10/01 Chel 2m5f good Hdl

Fair hurdler. Effective over two and a half miles, he is suited by good to firm ground. Usually wears blinkers.

Lord Sam (IRE)

104f 123f

6-y-o b/br g Supreme Leader-Russian Gale (IRE) (Strong Gale)

V R A Dartnall Plain Peeps

Placings:11 **(4423)**

2001/02: 16^{1}S, 16^{1}GS

	Starts	1st	2nd	3rd	Win & Pl
NH Flat	2	2	0	0	4851
Career Total	**2**	**2**	**0**	**0**	**4851**

123	3/02	Newb	2m110y	H NHF	G-S	£2576
121	2/02	Sand	2m110y	H NHF	SFT	£2275

Total win prize-money £4851

Going: Sf: 1-1 GS: 1-1 Gd: 0-0 GF: - Fm: 0-0
Distance: **2m/2m3: 2-2** 2m4-2m7: 0-0 3m+: 0-0
Track: LH: 1-1 RH: 1-1 Tight: 0-0 **Gall: 1-1**
Aids: Bl: 0-0 Vi: 0-0 Tstrap: 0-0
Best Rating: 123 3/02 Newb 2m110y gd-sft NHF

Promising winner of his first two bumpers.

Lord Sandrovitch (IRE)

105 124

7-y-o b g Be My Native (USA)-Killiney Side (General Ironside)

M W Easterby Harold Winton & Gordon Winton

Placings:20/35211/P-21FUP **(4439)**

2001/02: 16^{2}S, 20^{1}S, 20^{F}S, 24^{U}HY, 17^{P}S

	Starts	1st	2nd	3rd	Win & Pl
Chases	5	1	1	0	4028
Career Total	**13**	**3**	**3**	**1**	**13046**

124	1/02	Newc	2m4f	E Ch	SFT	£3071
125	1/00	Asct	2m4f	C Hdl	G-S	£5096
114	1/00	Font	2m2f110y	E Hdl	G-S	£2607

Total win prize-money £10775

Going: Sf: 1-5 GS: 0-0 Gd: 0-0 GF: - Fm: 0-0
Distance: 2m/2m3: 0-2 **2m4-2m7: 1-2** 3m+: 0-1
Track: **LH: 1-4** RH: 0-1 Tight: 0-3 **Gall: 1-2**
Aids: Bl: 0-0 Vi: 0-0 Tstrap: 0-0
Best Rating: 125 1/00 Asct 2m4f gd-sft Hdl

Fair novice hurdler in 2000. Lightly raced over fences since, but has shown ability. Suited by soft ground.

Lord Scroop (IRE)

108(97h) 101

8-y-o br g Supreme Leader-Henry Woman (IRE) (Mandalus)

Mrs K Walton (M J Wilkinson 19/5) The White Liners

Placings:0/54432/PU03P-**P5U34P2PP4** **(4746)**

2001/02: 20^{P}GS, 22^{5}G, 24^{U}G, 23^{3}GF, 24^{4}GS, 23^{P}G, 24^{2}S, 24^{P}S, 26^{P}GS, 20^{4}GF

	Starts	1st	2nd	3rd	Win & Pl
Hurdles	1	0	0	0	0
Chases	9	0	1	1	2253
Career Total	**21**	**0**	**2**	**3**	**3975**

Going: Sf: 0-2 GS: 0-3 Gd: 0-3 GF: - Fm: 0-2
Distance: 2m/2m3: 0-0 2m4-2m7: 0-3 3m+: 0-7
Track: LH: 0-1 RH: 0-9 Tight: 0-4 Gall: 0-2
Aids: Bl: 0-2 Vi: 0-0 Tstrap: 0-1
Best Rating: 106 11/99 Chel 2m110y good NHF

Maiden over flights. Stays three miles.

Lord Seamus

113(96h) (88h)145

7-y-o b g Arctic Lord-Erica Superba (Langton Heath)

K C Bailey I F W Buchan

Placings:0/40-0434F231 **(4634)**

2001/02: 22^{0}GF, 23^{4}F, 21^{3}G, 25^{4}G, 23^{F}G, 24^{2}G, 24^{3}G, 24^{1}GF

	Starts	1st	2nd	3rd	Win & Pl
Hurdles	2	0	0	0	0
Chases	6	1	1	2	13943
Career Total	**11**	**1**	**1**	**2**	**13943**

145	4/02	Asct	3m110y	B Ch	G-F	£10998

Total win prize-money £10998

Going: Sf: 0-0 GS: 0-0 Gd: 0-5 GF: - Fm: 1-3
Distance: 2m/2m3: 0-0 2m4-2m7: 0-3 **3m+: 1-5**
Track: LH: 0-1 **RH: 1-7** Tight: 0-3 Gall: 0-0
Aids: Bl: 0-0 Vi: 0-0 Tstrap: 0-0
Best Rating: 145 4/02 Asct 3m110y gd-fm Ch

Moderate form in novice chases until bolting up over three miles on fast ground at Ascot in April 2002. Still has some scope.

Lord Strickland

111(106h) (111h)127

9-y-o b g Strong Gale-Lady Rag (Ragapan)

P J Hobbs Miss H L Cope

Placings:0660/41450306/1113214-401321454 **(1729)**

2001/02: 22^{4}GF, 22^{0}GF, 22^{1}GF, 22^{3}G, 22^{2}GF, 21^{1}GF, 24^{4}GF, 23^{5}GF, 24^{4}F

	Starts	1st	2nd	3rd	Win & Pl
Hurdles	6	1	1	1	4053
Chases	3	1	0	0	4191
Career Total	**28**	**7**	**2**	**3**	**25577**

127	8/01	NAbb	2m5f110y	F(0-105)HCh	G-F	£3654
110	7/01	Strf	2m6f110y	F(0-110)HHdl	G-F	£2572
118	8/00	Hntg	2m4f110y	E Ch	G-F	£3445
119	6/00	NAbb	2m6f	F(0-105)HHdl	G-F	£2988
116	5/00	Font	2m6f110y	E(0-115)HHdl	GD	£2411
115	5/00	Winc	2m6f	F(0-100)HHdl	FRM	£3133
85	5/99	Kbgn	2m3f	Hdl	GD	£2455

Total win prize-money £20662

Going: Sf: 0-0 GS: 0-0 Gd: 0-1 GF: - Fm: 2-8
Distance: 2m/2m3: 0-0 **2m4-2m7: 2-6** 3m+: 0-3
Track: **LH: 2-7** RH: 0-2 **Tight: 2-8** Gall: 0-0
Aids: Bl: 0-0 Vi: 0-0 Tstrap: 0-0
Best Rating: 127 8/01 NAbb 2m5f110y gd-fm Ch

Fair staying hurdler/chaser, suited by fast ground. Has front run but suited by a sharp track and waiting tactics.

Lord Tennyson (IRE)

6-y-o br g Good Thyne (USA)-Emma's Way (IRE) (Le Bavard (FR))
S Gollings R L Houlton

Placings:050 (1957)
2001/02: 17^{0}S, 16^{5}S, 25^{0}G

	Starts	1st	2nd	3rd	Win & Pl
NH Flat	2	0	0	0	0
Hurdles	1	0	0	0	0
Career Total	**3**	**0**	**0**	**0**	**0**

Going: Sf: 0-2 GS: 0-0 Gd: 0-1 GF: - Fm: 0-0
Distance: 2m/2m3: 0-2 2m4-2m7: 0-0 3m+: 0-1
Track: LH: 0-1 RH: 0-1 Tight: 0-2 Gall: 0-0
Aids: Bl: 0-1 Vi: 0-0 Tstrap: 0-0
Best Rating: 74 10/01 Fknm 2m soft NHF

Lord Token

78 **28**
8-y-o b g Lighter-Lady Token (Roscoe Blake)
Mrs S J Smith Mrs S Smith

Placings:P0PP (4785)
2001/02: 16^{P}GS, 20^{0}G, 19^{P}S, 16^{P}F

	Starts	1st	2nd	3rd	Win & Pl
Hurdles	4	0	0	0	
Career Total	**4**	**0**	**0**	**0**	

Going: Sf: 0-1 GS: 0-1 Gd: 0-1 GF: - Fm: 0-1
Distance: 2m/2m3: 0-3 2m4-2m7: 0-1 3m+: 0-0
Track: LH: 0-4 RH: 0-0 Tight: 0-1 Gall: 0-1
Aids: Bl: 0-0 Vi: 0-0 Tstrap: 0-0
Best Rating: 28 10/01 Weth 2m4f110y good Hdl

Lord Transcend (IRE)

103 **93**
5-y-o gr g Aristocracy-Capincur Lady (Over The River (FR))
J Howard Johnson Transcend

Placings:1 (4431)
2001/02: 16^{1}HY

	Starts	1st	2nd	3rd	Win & Pl
Hurdles	1	1	0	0	2660
Career Total	**1**	**1**	**0**	**0**	**2660**

93	3/02	Newc	2m	E Hdl	HVY	£2660

Total win prize-money £2660

Going: Sf: 1-1 GS: 0-0 Gd: 0-0 GF: - Fm: 0-0
Distance: **2m/2m3: 1-1** 2m4-2m7: 0-0 3m+: 0-0
Track: **LH: 1-1** RH: 0-0 Tight: 0-0 **Gall: 1-1**
Aids: Bl: 0-0 Vi: 0-0 Tstrap: 0-0
Best Rating: 93 3/02 Newc 2m heavy Hdl

Landed a novices' hurdle on his debut. That was over two miles, but he is likely to stay further.

Lord Warford

86(98h) (90h)**97+**
7-y-o b g Bustino-Jupiter's Message (Jupiter Island)
Miss Venetia Williams Peter Richardson

Placings:03/0432/160-605 (4535)
2001/02: 20^{6}S, 22^{0}S, 20^{5}G

	Starts	1st	2nd	3rd	Win & Pl
Hurdles	3	0	0	0	0
Career Total	**12**	**1**	**1**	**2**	**6412**

114	5/00	NAbb	2m6f	C Hdl	G-F	£4810

Total win prize-money £4810

Going: Sf: 0-2 GS: 0-0 Gd: 0-1 GF: - Fm: 0-0
Distance: 2m/2m3: 0-0 2m4-2m7: 0-3 3m+: 0-0
Track: LH: 0-3 RH: 0-0 Tight: 0-2 Gall: 0-0
Aids: Bl: 0-0 Vi: 0-0 Tstrap: 0-1
Best Rating: 114 5/00 NAbb 2m6f gd-fm Hdl

Lord York (IRE)

116(102h) (115h)**151**
10-y-o b g Strong Gale-Bunkilla (Arctic Slave)
Ian Williams Sir Robert Ogden

Placings:2013/4560/1411222101 1/2060-113133323 (4838)
2001/02: 17^{1}G, 16^{1}GF, 20^{3}G, 16^{1}G, 16^{3}GF, 16^{3}G, 16^{3}G, 16^{2}G, 16^{3}G

	Starts	1st	2nd	3rd	Win & Pl
Hurdles	1	0	0	1	850
Chases	8	3	1	4	50003
Career Total	**32**	**10**	**6**	**6**	**100379**

148	11/01	Asct	2m	A(0-150)HCh	GD	£18119
140	[illegible]	[illegible]	2m110y	C(0-135)HCh	G-F	[illegible]
148	5/01	Extr	2m1f110y	D(0-125)HCh	GD	£4826
148	4/00	Ayr	2m	B HCh	GD	£13312
132	4/00	Ayr	2m	C Ch	GD	£5752
148	3/00	Newb	2m2f110y	D(0-125)HCh	G-F	£7247
143	10/99	Towc	2m110y	E(0-115)HCh	GD	£3142
132	10/99	Extr	2m1f	D(0-110)HCh	GD	£3837
117	9/99	MRas	2m6f110y	E Ch	G-F	£3286
110	3/98	Donc	2m4f	E Hdl	GD	£2658

Total win prize-money £68851

Going: Sf: 0-0 GS: 0-0 Gd: 2-7 GF: - Fm: 1-2
Distance: **2m/2m3: 3-8** 2m4-2m7: 0-1 3m+: 0-0
Track: LH: 0-5 **RH: 3-4** Tight: 0-2 **Gall: 1-2**
Aids: **Bl: 3-9** Vi: 0-0 Tstrap: 0-0
Best Rating: 151 4/02 Aint 2m good Ch

A useful two-mile handicap chaser on his day, he is consistent but has kept finding one or two too good since winning at Ascot in November 2001. Wears blinkers nowadays and benefits from forcing tactics on good or fast ground.

Lord Youky (FR)

105(107h) (106h)**127**
8-y-o b g Cadoudal (FR)-Lady Corteira (FR) (Carvin)
Ian Williams Sir Robert Ogden

Placings:2/43-11FFP25 (4634)
2001/02: 19^{1}G, 20^{1}G, 24^{F}GF, 20^{F}G, 24^{P}G, 24^{2}G, 24^{5}GF

	Starts	1st	2nd	3rd	Win & Pl
Hurdles	2	2	0	0	5313
Chases	5	0	1	0	1524
Career Total	**10**	**2**	**2**	**1**	**8169**

106	10/01	Sthl	2m4f110y	E Hdl	GD	£2569
103	10/01	Hrfd	2m3f110y	E Hdl	GD	£2744

Total win prize-money £5313

Going: Sf: 0-0 GS: 0-0 Gd: 2-5 GF: - Fm: 0-2
Distance: 2m/2m3: 0-0 **2m4-2m7: 2-3** 3m+: 0-4
Track: LH: 1-2 RH: 1-5 **Tight: 1-4** Gall: 0-0
Aids: Bl: 0-0 Vi: 0-0 Tstrap: 0-0
Best Rating: 127 2/02 Ludl 3m good Ch

Won two novice hurdles in a row in October 2001, but an unlucky faller on his first two starts over fences. Acts on good ground and is effective at three miles.

Lordberniebouffant (IRE)

112 **131**
9-y-o b g Denel (FR)-Noon Hunting (Green Shoon)
J T Gifford The Marvellous Partnership

Placings:*53*24212/**33F004/413124-3051F0** (4913)
2001/02: 25^{3}G, 27^{0}S, 24^{5}S, 24^{1}GS, 32^{F}HY, 29^{0}G

	Starts	1st	2nd	3rd	Win & Pl
Chases	6	1	0	1	13553
Career Total	**25**	**4**	**4**	**5**	**60025**

131	3/02	Newb	3m	C(0-130)HCh	G-S	£9552
131	1/01	Font	3m4f	D(0-125)HCh	SFT	£13650
117	9/00	Hntg	3m	E Ch	G-F	£3607
125	3/99	Sand	2m4f110y	A HHdl	SFT	£16299

Total win prize-money £43111

Going: Sf: 0-3 GS: 1-1 Gd: 0-2 GF: - Fm: 0-0
Distance: 2m/2m3: 0-0 2m4-2m7: 0-0 **3m+: 1-6**
Track: **LH: 1-2** RH: 0-4 Tight: 0-2 **Gall: 1-1**
Aids: Bl: 0-0 Vi: 0-0 Tstrap: 0-0
Best Rating: 131 3/02 Newb 3m gd-sft Ch

A decent staying handicap chaser, he acts on most types of ground, but does not like it heavy. Stays three and a half miles.

Lords Best (IRE)

105 **114**
6-y-o b g Mister Lord (USA)-Ballinlonig Star (Black Minstrel)
A King Jerry Wright, Peter Smith & Jules Sigler

Placings:34224 (4816)
2001/02: 17^{3}G, 19^{4}GS, 21^{2}S, 19^{2}G, 21^{4}GF

	Starts	1st	2nd	3rd	Win & Pl
Hurdles	5	0	2	1	4854
Career Total	**5**	**0**	**2**	**1**	**4854**

Going: Sf: 0-1 GS: 0-1 Gd: 0-2 GF: - Fm: 0-1
Distance: 2m/2m3: 0-3 2m4-2m7: 0-2 3m+: 0-0
Track: LH: 0-3 RH: 0-2 Tight: 0-0 Gall: 0-3
Aids: Bl: 0-0 Vi: 0-0 Tstrap: 0-0
Best Rating: 114 3/02 Extr 2m3f good Hdl

Fairly useful form when placed in novice hurdles, he stays two miles-five, acts on good and soft ground. Has hung right-handed.

Lordston (IRE)

98 **68**
6-y-o b g Mister Lord (USA)-Dawstown (Golden Love)
J T Gifford John Plackett

Placings:*6*-0 (0372)
2001/02: 16^{0}GF

	Starts	1st	2nd	3rd	Win & Pl
Hurdles	1	0	0	0	
Career Total	**2**	**0**	**0**	**0**	**0**

Going: Sf: 0-0 GS: 0-0 Gd: 0-0 GF: - Fm: 0-1
Distance: 2m/2m3: 0-1 2m4-2m7: 0-0 3m+: 0-0
Track: LH: 0-0 RH: 0-1 Tight: 0-0 Gall: 0-1
Aids: Bl: 0-0 Vi: 0-0 Tstrap: 0-0
Best Rating: 95 4/01 Asct 2m110y heavy NHF

Lordus (IRE)

6-y-o b g Lord Americo-Deep Statement (IRE) (Strong Statement (USA))
M Bradstock Ms L A Durcan

Placings: *6*-R (0320)
2001/02: 17^{R}F

	Starts	1st	2nd	3rd	Win & Pl
NH Flat	1	0	0	0	
Career Total	**2**	**0**	**0**	**0**	

Going: Sf: 0-0 GS: 0-0 Gd: 0-0 GF: - Fm: 0-1
Distance: 2m/2m3: 0-1 2m4-2m7: 0-0 3m+: 0-0
Track: LH: 0-0 RH: 0-1 Tight: 0-0 Gall: 0-0
Aids: Bl: 0-0 Vi: 0-0 Tstrap: 0-0
Best Rating: 96 11/00 Ludl 2m good NHF

Lorenzino (IRE)

109 **132**

5-y-o ch g Thunder Gulch (USA)-Russian Ballet (USA) (Nijinsky (CAN))
J J O'Neill P Piller

Placings: 12-152110 (4647)
2001/02: 17^{1}GS, 20^{5}GS, 19^{2}GS, 20^{1}G, 21^{1}G, 24^{0}G

	Starts	1st	2nd	3rd	Win & Pl
Hurdles	6	3	1	0	27144
Career Total	**8**	**4**	**2**	**0**	**30816**

130	2/02	Kemp	2m5f	C(0-130)HHdl	GD	£13942
125	11/01	Weth	2m4f110y	C(0-130)HHdl	GD	£7020
120	5/01	Bang	2m1f	D(0-120)HHdl	G-S	£4485
120	2/01	Weth	2m	E Hdl	SFT	£2628

Total win prize-money £28077

Going: Sf: 0-0 GS: 1-3 Gd: 2-3 GF: - Fm: 0-0
Distance: 2m/2m3: 1-2 **2m4-2m7: 2-3** 3m+: 0-1
Track: **LH: 2-5** RH: 1-1 **Tight: 1-3** Gall: 0-0
Aids: Bl: 0-0 Vi: 0-0 Tstrap: 0-0
Best Rating: 130 2/02 Kemp 2m5f good Hdl

He won one of his two starts over hurdles in the 2000/01 season and won again on his handicap debut at Bangor in May, but was below that form until winning at Wetherby in November, before following up Kempton three months later. Suited by cut in the ground and around two miles, to two miles four furlongs. Did not stay three miles on fast ground at Aintree.

Lorgnette

106 **108**

8-y-o b m Emperor Fountain-Speckyfoureyes (Blue Cashmere)
R H Alner Alvin Trowbridge

Placings: *316*453-513514 (4385)
2001/02: 22^{5}GF, 22^{1}GF, 22^{3}G, 22^{5}G, 21^{1}G, 22^{4}S

	Starts	1st	2nd	3rd	Win & Pl
Hurdles	6	2	0	1	5838
Career Total	**12**	**3**	**0**	**3**	**8318**

108	11/01	Plum	2m5f	E Hdl	GD	£2460
96	10/01	Winc	2m6f	F(0-105)HHdl	G-F	£3052
95	10/00	Tntn	2m1f	H NHF	GD	£1536

Total win prize-money £7050

Going: Sf: 0-1 GS: 0-0 Gd: 1-3 GF: - Fm: 1-2
Distance: 2m/2m3: 0-0 **2m4-2m7: 2-6** 3m+: 0-0
Track: LH: 1-1 RH: 1-5 **Tight: 1-1** Gall: 0-0
Aids: Bl: 0-0 Vi: 0-0 Tstrap: 0-0
Best Rating: 108 11/01 Plum 2m5f good Hdl

Loss Adjuster

83 **42**

5-y-o gr g Mazaad-Overdraft (Bustino)
C N Kellett R P Kernohan

Placings: *00*-50P (1581)
2001/02: 20^{5}GS, 19^{0}GF, 24^{P}GS

	Starts	1st	2nd	3rd	Win & Pl
Hurdles	3	0	0	0	0
Career Total	**5**	**0**	**0**	**0**	**0**

Going: Sf: 0-0 GS: 0-2 Gd: 0-0 GF: - Fm: 0-1
Distance: 2m/2m3: 0-0 2m4-2m7: 0-2 3m+: 0-1
Track: LH: 0-1 RH: 0-2 Tight: 0-2 Gall: 0-0
Aids: Bl: 0-0 Vi: 0-1 Tstrap: 0-0
Best Rating: 54 2/01 Towc 2m heavy NHF

Lost Keys (IRE)

112 **105**

8-y-o b m Phardante (FR)-Eadestown (Kinglet)
K C Bailey Stan Miller,Max Aitken,Bill & John Craig

Placings: 030P-23FP (0791)
2001/02: 25^{2}G, 24^{3}GF, 21^{F}GF, 22^{P}GF

	Starts	1st	2nd	3rd	Win & Pl
Chases	4	0	1	1	1636
Career Total	**8**	**0**	**1**	**2**	**1972**

Going: Sf: 0-0 GS: 0-0 Gd: 0-1 GF: - Fm: 0-3
Distance: 2m/2m3: 0-0 2m4-2m7: 0-2 3m+: 0-2
Track: LH: 0-1 RH: 0-3 Tight: 0-2 Gall: 0-1
Aids: Bl: 0-0 Vi: 0-0 Tstrap: 0-0
Best Rating: 105 6/01 Strf 2m5f110y gd-fm Ch

Lost The Plot

104 **96**

7-y-o b m Lyphento (USA)-La Comedienne (Comedy Star (USA))
D W P Arbuthnot The Kennet Partnership

Placings: *11*/3000/226-430542 (2784)
2001/02: 17^{4}GF, 16^{3}GF, 16^{0}GF, 16^{5}G, 16^{4}G, 16^{2}G

	Starts	1st	2nd	3rd	Win & Pl
Hurdles	6	0	1	1	1861
Career Total	**15**	**2**	**3**	**2**	**18973**

107	4/99	Chel	2m1f	H NHF	GD	£14070
97	2/99	Font	2m2f110y	H NHF	GD	£1556

Total win prize-money £15627

Going: Sf: 0-0 GS: 0-0 Gd: 0-3 GF: - Fm: 0-3
Distance: 2m/2m3: 0-6 2m4-2m7: 0-0 3m+: 0-0
Track: LH: 0-3 RH: 0-3 Tight: 0-1 Gall: 0-0
Aids: Bl: 0-0 Vi: 0-0 Tstrap: 0-0
Best Rating: 107 4/99 Chel 2m1f good NHF

A winner of her two bumpers in the spring of 1999, she seems to have lived up to her name after a promising start over timber.

Lost Your Marbles (IRE)

9-y-o b m Mandalus-Greenstead Lady (Great Nephew)
J W Mullins J H Mead

Placings: *00*P/U-P (1848)
2001/02: 25^{P}G

	Starts	1st	2nd	3rd	Win & Pl
Chases	1	0	0	0	
Career Total	**5**	**0**	**0**	**0**	

Going: Sf: 0-0 GS: 0-0 Gd: 0-1 GF: - Fm: 0-0
Distance: 2m/2m3: 0-0 2m4-2m7: 0-0 3m+: 0-1
Track: LH: 0-0 RH: 0-1 Tight: 0-0 Gall: 0-0
Aids: Bl: 0-0 Vi: 0-0 Tstrap: 0-0
Best Rating: 54 9/98 Worc 2m gd-fm NHF

Lotschen Princess

56f

5-y-o b m Henbit (USA)-Princess Semele (Imperial Fling (USA))
D R Gandolfo A W F Clapperton

Placings: *0* (3154)
2001/02: 18^{0}G

	Starts	1st	2nd	3rd	Win & Pl
NH Flat	1	0	0	0	
Career Total	**1**	**0**	**0**	**0**	

Going: Sf: 0-0 GS: 0-0 Gd: 0-1 GF: - Fm: 0-0
Distance: 2m/2m3: 0-1 2m4-2m7: 0-0 3m+: 0-0
Track: LH: 0-1 RH: 0-0 Tight: 0-1 Gall: 0-0
Aids: Bl: 0-0 Vi: 0-0 Tstrap: 0-0
Best Rating:

Lottery Ticket (IRE)

13-y-o b g The Parson-Beauty Run (Deep Run)
S J Robinson S J Robinson

Placings: *2021*/3220PB/**2UP5**/324FFP125/P4PP/U-56 (4199)
2001/02: 24^{5}GF, 27^{6}S

	Starts	1st	2nd	3rd	Win & Pl
Chases	2	0	0	0	0
Career Total	**30**	**2**	**7**	**2**	**10664**

112	3/98	Uttx	3m2f	E(0-110)HCh	GD	£2934
105	4/95	Hexm	2m	H NHF	SFT	£1465

Total win prize-money £4400

Going: Sf: 0-1 GS: 0-0 Gd: 0-0 GF: - Fm: 0-1
Distance: 2m/2m3: 0-0 2m4-2m7: 0-0 3m+: 0-2
Track: LH: 0-2 RH: 0-0 Tight: 0-2 Gall: 0-0
Aids: Bl: 0-0 Vi: 0-0 Tstrap: 0-0
Best Rating: 118 3/96 Chel 2m5f gd-sft Hdl

A long time loser now a veteran who is usually given a very untidy ride. Best torn up.

Lou's Wish

87 **66**

5-y-o b g Thatching-Shamaka (Kris)
M J Polglase Brian Androlia

Placings: 06P (2006)
2001/02: 16^{0}F, 16^{6}GF, 16^{P}S

	Starts	1st	2nd	3rd	Win & Pl
Hurdles	3	0	0	0	0
Career Total	**3**	**0**	**0**	**0**	**0**

Going: Sf: 0-1 GS: 0-0 Gd: 0-0 GF: - Fm: 0-2
Distance: 2m/2m3: 0-3 2m4-2m7: 0-0 3m+: 0-0
Track: LH: 0-3 RH: 0-0 Tight: 0-2 Gall: 0-0
Aids: Bl: 0-2 Vi: 0-0 Tstrap: 0-0
Best Rating: 66 8/01 Sthl 2m gd-fm Hdl

Louder Please

6-y-o b g Petoski-Lynemore (Nearly A Hand)

H D Daly Sir P Payne-Gallwey & Mrs M P Wiggin

Placings: *00-F* (0267)
2001/02: 17^{F}G

	Starts	1st	2nd	3rd	Win & Pl
Hurdles	1	0	0	0	
Career Total	3	0	0	0	

Going: Sf: 0-0 GS: 0-0 Gd: 0-1 GF: - Fm: 0-0
Distance: 2m/2m3: 0-1 2m4-2m7: 0-0 3m+: 0-0
Track: LH: 0-0 RH: 0-1 Tight: 0-0 Gall: 0-0
Aids: Bl: 0-0 Vi: 0-0 Tstrap: 0-0
Best Rating: 82 12/00 Ludl 2m soft NHF

Loudy Rowdy (IRE)

101 78
11-y-o br g Strong Gale-Express Film (Ashmore (FR))
Mrs J K M Oliver The British Beef Partnership

Placings: *14/F0/***P0/044P5P** (4856)
2001/02: 16^{0}G, 21^{4}S, 24^{4}GS, 27^{P}HY, 20^{5}GF, 25^{P}G

	Starts	1st	2nd	3rd	Win & Pl
Chases	6	0	0	0	238
Career Total	12	1	0	0	3615
108 10/97 Wxfd 2m	NHF			G-F	£3221

Total win prize-money £3222

Going: Sf: 0-2 GS: 0-1 Gd: 0-2 GF: - Fm: 0-1
Distance: 2m/2m3: 0-1 2m4-2m7: 0-2 3m+: 0-3
Track: LH: 0-5 RH: 0-1 Tight: 0-3 Gall: 0-1
Aids: Bl: 0-0 Vi: 0-0 Tstrap: 0-0
Best Rating: 108 10/97 Wxfd 2m gd-fm NHF

Lough Lein Lady (IRE)

(73h) (22h)
7-y-o ch m Alphabatim (USA)-Cap Reform (IRE) (Phardante (FR))
A W Carroll Roger Clarke And Adam Simpson

Placings: *0*-**U0PP** (4590)
2001/02: 24^{U}S, 21^{0}G, 22^{P}S, 24^{P}G

	Starts	1st	2nd	3rd	Win & Pl
Hurdles	1	0	0	0	0
Chases	3	0	0	0	0
Career Total	5	0	0	0	

Going: Sf: 0-2 GS: 0-0 Gd: 0-2 GF: - Fm: 0-0
Distance: 2m/2m3: 0-0 2m4-2m7: 0-2 3m+: 0-2
Track: LH: 0-2 RH: 0-2 Tight: 0-1 Gall: 0-0
Aids: Bl: 0-0 Vi: 0-0 Tstrap: 0-0
Best Rating: 48 5/00 Tipp 2m2f gd-fm NHF

Lovable Outlaw (IRE)

11-y-o br g Henbit (USA)-Sweet Tulip (Beau Chapeau)
Miss M E Rowland Miss G Devey

Placings: **1P1P/43/PBP** (4238)
2001/02: 30^{P}S, 25^{B}S, 24^{P}GF

	Starts	1st	2nd	3rd	Win & Pl
Chases	3	0	0	0	
Career Total	9	2	0	1	8253
110 12/97 Sthl 3m110y	E(0-100)HCh			GD	£3234
104 11/97 Uttx 3m	D Ch			SFT	£4260

Total win prize-money £7494

Going: Sf: 0-2 GS: 0-0 Gd: 0-0 GF: - Fm: 0-1
Distance: 2m/2m3: 0-0 2m4-2m7: 0-0 3m+: 0-3
Track: LH: 0-1 RH: 0-2 Tight: 0-0 Gall: 0-2
Aids: Bl: 0-0 Vi: 0-2 Tstrap: 0-3
Best Rating: 110 12/97 Sthl 3m110y good Ch

A lightly-raced ex-Irish pointer, has gurgled. Acts on good and soft ground and is suited by staying trips.

Love Diamonds (IRE)

92 81
6-y-o b g Royal Academy (USA)-Baby Diamonds (Habitat)
Miss C Dyson (R Dickin 17/7) Miss C Dyson

Placings: **004454P** (4820)
2001/02: 17^{0}GS, 17^{0}G, 17^{4}G, 17^{4}G, 16^{5}GF, 16^{4}GF, 17^{P}G

	Starts	1st	2nd	3rd	Win & Pl
Hurdles	7	0	0	0	521
Career Total	7	0	0	0	521

Going: Sf: 0-0 GS: 0-1 Gd: 0-4 GF: - Fm: 0-2
Distance: 2m/2m3: 0-7 2m4-2m7: 0-0 3m+: 0-0
Track: LH: 0-5 RH: 0-2 Tight: 0-3 Gall: 0-1
Aids: Bl: 0-0 Vi: 0-0 Tstrap: 0-5
Best Rating: 81 9/01 Worc 2m gd-fm Hdl

Love Kiss (IRE)

95 89
7-y-o b g Brief Truce (USA)-Pendulina (Prince Tenderfoot (USA))
W Storey K Knox

Placings: **256501P** (4096)
2001/02: 17^{2}GS, 17^{5}G, 16^{6}G, 20^{5}S, 19^{0}S, 16^{1}S, 19^{P}GS

	Starts	1st	2nd	3rd	Win & Pl
Hurdles	7	1	1	0	3382
Career Total	7	1	1	0	3382
89 1/02 Newc 2m	E(0-105)HHdl			SFT	£2646

Total win prize-money £2646

Going: Sf: 1-3 GS: 0-2 Gd: 0-2 GF: - Fm: 0-0
Distance: **2m/2m3: 1-6** 2m4-2m7: 0-1 3m+: 0-0
Track: **LH: 1-6** RH: 0-0 Tight: 0-5 **Gall: 1-1**
Aids: Bl: 0-0 Vi: 0-0 **Tstrap: 1-4**
Best Rating: 89 1/02 Newc 2m soft Hdl

Modest hurdler, best a two miles on very soft ground although acts on faster. Has broken blood-vessels. Suited by hold-up tactics.

Love Mail

85f 88f
4-y-o b f Pursuit Of Love-Wizardry (Shirley Heights)
Mrs S C Bradburne C Lysaght, J Wall, M Pougatch

Placings: *105* (4499)
2001/02: 16^{1}G, 16^{0}GS, 16^{5}G

	Starts	1st	2nd	3rd	Win & Pl
NH Flat	3	1	0	0	1589
Career Total	3	1	0	0	1589
85 1/02 Muss 2m	H NHF			GD	£1589

Total win prize-money £1589

Going: Sf: 0-0 GS: 0-1 Gd: 1-2 GF: - Fm: 0-0
Distance: **2m/2m3: 1-3** 2m4-2m7: 0-0 3m+: 0-0
Track: LH: 0-2 **RH: 1-1 Tight: 1-1** Gall: 0-0
Aids: Bl: 0-0 Vi: 0-0 Tstrap: 0-0
Best Rating: 88 3/02 Hayd 2m good NHF

Flat-bred, she made a winning debut in a Musselburgh bumper.

Love Potion

97 94
7-y-o br m Neltino-Celtic Honey (Celtic Cone)
E L James Mrs J N Humphreys

Placings: *2/030*-**005** (4048)
2001/02: 16^{0}GS, 16^{0}S, 19^{5}G

	Starts	1st	2nd	3rd	Win & Pl
Hurdles	3	0	0	0	0
Career Total	7	0	1	1	727

Going: Sf: 0-1 GS: 0-1 Gd: 0-1 GF: - Fm: 0-0
Distance: 2m/2m3: 0-3 2m4-2m7: 0-0 3m+: 0-0
Track: LH: 0-1 RH: 0-2 Tight: 0-0 Gall: 0-2
Aids: Bl: 0-0 Vi: 0-0 Tstrap: 0-0
Best Rating: 94 2/02 Newb 2m110y soft Hdl

Lovelock (FR)

92(99h) 79
7-y-o b g Tel Quel (FR)-Luvvy Duvvy (FR) (Pampabird)
A Crook Cornelius Lysaght

Placings: *4/0004/42/0005*-**0P00P** (1089)
2001/02: 20^{0}G, 17^{P}G, 20^{0}GF, 16^{0}GF, 23^{P}GF

	Starts	1st	2nd	3rd	Win & Pl
Chases	5	0	0	0	
Career Total	16	0	1	0	740

Going: Sf: 0-0 GS: 0-0 Gd: 0-2 GF: - Fm: 0-3
Distance: 2m/2m3: 0-2 2m4-2m7: 0-2 3m+: 0-1
Track: LH: 0-3 RH: 0-2 Tight: 0-2 Gall: 0-0
Aids: Bl: 0-2 Vi: 0-1 Tstrap: 0-0
Best Rating: 94 11/00 Newc 2m gd-sft Hdl

Lovely Hurling (IRE)

10-y-o ch g Orchestra-Madonna Pica (Salluceva)
G A Ham Mrs C M Budd

Placings: **P** (4411)
2001/02: 18^{P}S

	Starts	1st	2nd	3rd	Win & Pl
Hurdles	1	0	0	0	
Career Total	1	0	0	0	

Going: Sf: 0-1 GS: 0-0 Gd: 0-0 GF: - Fm: 0-0
Distance: 2m/2m3: 0-1 2m4-2m7: 0-0 3m+: 0-0
Track: LH: 0-1 RH: 0-0 Tight: 0-1 Gall: 0-0
Aids: Bl: 0-0 Vi: 0-0 Tstrap: 0-0
Best Rating:

Lovers Tale

70f 36f
4-y-o b g Pursuit Of Love-Kintail (Kris)
H M Kavanagh Mrs S Kavanagh

Placings: *0* (4423)
2001/02: 16^{0}GS

	Starts	1st	2nd	3rd	Win & Pl
NH Flat	1	0	0	0	
Career Total	1	0	0	0	

Going: Sf: 0-0 GS: 0-1 Gd: 0-0 GF: - Fm: 0-0
Distance: 2m/2m3: 0-1 2m4-2m7: 0-0 3m+: 0-0
Track: LH: 0-1 RH: 0-0 Tight: 0-0 Gall: 0-1
Aids: Bl: 0-0 Vi: 0-0 Tstrap: 0-0
Best Rating: 36 3/02 Newb 2m110y gd-sft NHF

Lovingandkissing

90f **69f**

5-y-o ch m Rudimentary (USA)-Elusive (Little Current (USA))
M J Roberts Mike Roberts

Placings:*60* **(3154)**
2001/02: 17^{6}S, 18^{0}G

	Starts	1st	2nd	3rd	Win & Pl
NH Flat	2	0	0	0	0
Career Total	**2**	**0**	**0**	**0**	**0**

Going: Sf: 0-1 GS: 0-0 Gd: 0-1 GF: - Fm: 0-0
Distance: 2m/2m3: 0-2 2m4-2m7: 0-0 3m+: 0-0
Track: LH: 0-1 RH: 0-0 Tight: 0-2 Gall: 0-0
Aids: Bl: 0-0 Vi: 0-0 Tstrap: 0-0
Best Rating: 69 1/02 Font 2m2f110y good NHF

Loxley-Lad

83(86c) (43c)**62**

10-y-o gr g Zambrano-Loxley Air (Romany Air)
C J Gray A C Heal

Placings:P-P006P **(0794)**
2001/02: 22^{P}GS, 16^{0}GF, 18^{0}GF, 17^{6}G, 22^{P}GF

	Starts	1st	2nd	3rd	Win & Pl
Hurdles	4	0	0	0	0
Chases	1	0	0	0	0
Career Total	**6**	**0**	**0**	**0**	**0**

Going: Sf: 0-0 GS: 0-1 Gd: 0-1 GF: - Fm: 0-3
Distance: 2m/2m3: 0-3 2m4-2m7: 0-2 3m+: 0-0
Track: LH: 0-2 RH: 0-1 Tight: 0-3 Gall: 0-1
Aids: Bl: 0-0 Vi: 0-2 Tstrap: 0-0
Best Rating: 62 6/01 NAbb 2m1f good Hdl

Lubo's Liability (IRE)

78 **52**

6-y-o b/br g Wood Chanter-Tuftarney (Mandalus)
L Wells David Gower

Placings:0-0P **(0797)**
2001/02: 16^{0}GF, 17^{P}GF

	Starts	1st	2nd	3rd	Win & Pl
Hurdles	2	0	0	0	0
Career Total	**3**	**0**	**0**	**0**	**0**

Going: Sf: 0-0 GS: 0-0 Gd: 0-0 GF: - Fm: 0-2
Distance: 2m/2m3: 0-2 2m4-2m7: 0-0 3m+: 0-0
Track: LH: 0-1 RH: 0-1 Tight: 0-1 Gall: 0-1
Aids: Bl: 0-0 Vi: 0-0 Tstrap: 0-0
Best Rating: 53 3/01 Plum 2m heavy Hdl

Lucerne (IRE)

94 **77**

6-y-o ch m Insan (USA)-Old Clover (Over The River (FR))
C P Morlock Pell-Mell Partners

Placings:0006 **(4588)**
2001/02: 17^{0}GS, 16^{0}GS, 19^{0}G, 22^{6}G

	Starts	1st	2nd	3rd	Win & Pl
Hurdles	4	0	0	0	0
Career Total	**4**	**0**	**0**	**0**	**0**

Going: Sf: 0-0 GS: 0-2 Gd: 0-2 GF: - Fm: 0-0
Distance: 2m/2m3: 0-3 2m4-2m7: 0-1 3m+: 0-0
Track: LH: 0-0 RH: 0-4 Tight: 0-1 Gall: 0-0
Aids: Bl: 0-0 Vi: 0-0 Tstrap: 0-0
Best Rating: 77 3/02 Extr 2m3f good Hdl

Lucien (IRE)

90f **85f**

4-y-o ch g Catrail (USA)-What A Candy (USA) (Key To The Mint (USA))
N J Henderson B T Stewart-Brown

Placings:*00* **(4423)**
2001/02: 16^{0}GS, 16^{0}GS

	Starts	1st	2nd	3rd	Win & Pl
NH Flat	2	0	0	0	
Career Total	**2**	**0**	**0**	**0**	

Going: Sf: 0-0 GS: 0-2 Gd: 0-0 GF: - Fm: 0-0
Distance: 2m/2m3: 0-2 2m4-2m7: 0-0 3m+: 0-0
Track: LH: 0-2 RH: 0-0 Tight: 0-0 Gall: 0-2
Aids: Bl: 0-0 Vi: 0-0 Tstrap: 0-0
Best Rating: 85 3/02 Newb 2m110y gd-sft NHF

Well beaten in soft ground bumpers, but did better on faster ground at Perth in May.

Luck In Run'In

81 **65**

9-y-o b g Lapierre-Lady Run (Deep Run)
R N Bevis R J Bevis

Placings:*6000/0060* **(3457)**
2001/02: 20^{0}G, 22^{0}S, 23^{6}G, 26^{0}S

	Starts	1st	2nd	3rd	Win & Pl
Hurdles	2	0	0	0	0
Chases	2	0	0	0	0
Career Total	**8**	**0**	**0**	**0**	**0**

Going: Sf: 0-2 GS: 0-0 Gd: 0-2 GF: - Fm: 0-0
Distance: 2m/2m3: 0-0 2m4-2m7: 0-2 3m+: 0-2
Track: LH: 0-3 RH: 0-1 Tight: 0-1 Gall: 0-0
Aids: Bl: 0-0 Vi: 0-0 Tstrap: 0-0
Best Rating: 82 11/98 Hayd 2m soft NHF

Lucky Archer

95 **87**

9-y-o b g North Briton-Preobrajenska (Double Form)
Ian Williams James Burley, Andrew Wyer, Philippa Wyer

Placings:43/U60/20 **(1988)**
2001/02: 16^{2}GF, 16^{0}G

	Starts	1st	2nd	3rd	Win & Pl
Hurdles	2	0	1	0	710
Career Total	**7**	**0**	**1**	**1**	**1014**

Going: Sf: 0-0 GS: 0-0 Gd: 0-1 GF: - Fm: 0-1
Distance: 2m/2m3: 0-2 2m4-2m7: 0-0 3m+: 0-0
Track: LH: 0-0 RH: 0-2 Tight: 0-0 Gall: 0-0
Aids: Bl: 0-0 Vi: 0-0 Tstrap: 0-0
Best Rating: 87 10/01 Winc 2m gd-fm Hdl

Lucky Bay (IRE)

(102h) (119h)**124+**

6-y-o b g Convinced-Current Liability (Caribo)
Miss H C Knight Executive Racing

Placings:*6*-512P **(4665)**
2001/02: 22^{5}S, 22^{1}GF, 22^{2}G, 24^{P}G

	Starts	1st	2nd	3rd	Win & Pl
Hurdles	4	1	1	0	6160
Career Total	**5**	**1**	**1**	**0**	**6160**
114 11/01 Winc 2m6f C Hdl				G-F	£5343

Total win prize-money £5343

Going: Sf: 0-1 GS: 0-0 Gd: 0-2 GF: - Fm: 1-1
Distance: 2m/2m3: 0-0 **2m4-2m7: 1-3** 3m+: 0-1
Track: LH: 0-2 **RH: 1-2** Tight: 0-2 Gall: 0-0
Aids: Bl: 0-0 Vi: 0-0 Tstrap: 0-0
Best Rating: 114 1/02 Winc 2m6f good Hdl

Got off the mark over hurdles at Wincanton in November 2001 on fast ground, over two miles six furlongs, before a good second in a similar race back at Wincanton in January 2002. Should stay further.

Lucky Brush (IRE)

8-y-o b g Brush Aside (USA)-Luck Daughter (Lucky Brief)
J Barclay (Miss Caroline Barclay 21/4) Jamie Alexander

Placings:3 **(0338)**
2001/02: 20^{3}S

	Starts	1st	2nd	3rd	Win & Pl
Chases	1	0	0	1	331
Career Total	**1**	**0**	**0**	**1**	**331**

Going: Sf: 0-1 GS: 0-0 Gd: 0-0 GF: - Fm: 0-0
Distance: 2m/2m3: 0-0 2m4-2m7: 0-1 3m+: 0-0
Track: LH: 0-0 RH: 0-1 Tight: 0-0 Gall: 0-0
Aids: Bl: 0-0 Vi: 0-0 Tstrap: 0-0
Best Rating: 69 5/01 Prth 2m4f110y soft Ch

Lucky Clover

109(85h) **137**

10-y-o ch g Push On-Winning Clover (Winden)
C Tizzard Mrs P O Perry

Placings:F0P0P-1P2211221P **(2665)**
2001/02: 23^{1}F, 23^{P}G, 26^{2}G, 21^{2}GF, 26^{1}G, 26^{1}GF, 23^{2}GF, 24^{2}G, 31^{1}G, 31^{P}GS

	Starts	1st	2nd	3rd	Win & Pl
Chases	10	4	4	0	38322
Career Total	**15**	**4**	**4**	**0**	**38322**
137 11/01 Chel 3m7f B Ch				GD	£21157
126 8/01 NAbb 3m2f110y E(0-105)HCh				G-F	£3410
130 8/01 NAbb 3m2f110y E Ch				GD	£3376
100 5/01 Extr 2m7f110y E Ch				FRM	£4166

Total win prize-money £32113

Going: Sf: 0-0 GS: 0-1 Gd: 2-5 GF: - Fm: 2-4
Distance: 2m/2m3: 0-0 2m4-2m7: 0-1 **3m+: 4-9**
Track: **LH: 3-8** RH: 1-2 **Tight: 2-4** Gall: 0-1
Aids: **Bl: 1-3** Vi: 0-0 Tstrap: 0-0
Best Rating: 137 11/01 Chel 3m7f good Ch

Fair staying chaser on fast ground. In good form in the summer of 2001, but put in his place by Southern Star at Cheltenham in October 2001. Put in a brave performance to win the Sporting Index Cross Country Chase at Cheltenham in November.

Lucky Do (IRE)

87f **85f**

5-y-o b g Camden Town-Lane Baloo (Lucky Brief)
G M McCourt D A N Ross

Placings:*60* **(4887)**
2001/02: 16^{6}GF, 18^{0}GF

	Starts	1st	2nd	3rd	Win & Pl
NH Flat	2	0	0	0	0
Career Total	**2**	**0**	**0**	**0**	**0**

Going: Sf: 0-0 GS: 0-0 Gd: 0-0 GF: - Fm: 0-2
Distance: 2m/2m3: 0-2 2m4-2m7: 0-0 3m+: 0-0
Track: LH: 0-1 RH: 0-1 Tight: 0-1 Gall: 0-0
Aids: Bl: 0-0 Vi: 0-0 Tstrap: 0-0
Best Rating: 85 4/02 Asct 2m110y gd-fm NHF

Lucky Duck

49f

5-y-o ch g Minster Son-Petroc Concert (Tina's Pet)
J Howard Johnson J Howard Johnson

Placings:*0* (4771)
2001/02: 16^{0}GF

	Starts	1st	2nd	3rd	Win & Pl
NH Flat	1	0	0	0	
Career Total	**1**	**0**	**0**	**0**	

Going: Sf: 0-0 GS: 0-0 Gd: 0-0 GF: - Fm: 0-1
Distance: 2m/2m3: 0-1 2m4-2m7: 0-0 3m+: 0-0
Track: LH: 0-0 RH: 0-0 Tight: 0-0 Gall: 0-0
Aids: Bl: 0-0 Vi: 0-0 Tstrap: 0-0
Best Rating: 49 4/02 Hexm 2m110y gd-fm NHF

Lucky Gipsy

99f 91f

6-y-o b m Minster Son-Go Gipsy (Move Off)
C Grant A Dawson

Placings:22 (1025)
2001/02: 16^{2}GS, 17^{2}GF

	Starts	1st	2nd	3rd	Win & Pl
NH Flat	2	0	2	0	899
Career Total	**2**	**0**	**2**	**0**	**899**

Going: Sf: 0-0 GS: 0-1 Gd: 0-0 GF: - Fm: 0-1
Distance: 2m/2m3: 0-2 2m4-2m7: 0-0 3m+: 0-0
Track: LH: 0-2 RH: 0-0 Tight: 0-1 Gall: 0-0
Aids: Bl: 0-0 Vi: 0-0 Tstrap: 0-0
Best Rating: 91 6/01 Hexm 2m gd-sft NHF

Lucky Heather (IRE)

93 82

5-y-o b m Soviet Lad (USA)-Idrak (Young Generation)
R J Baker Graham Brown

Placings:650P (2952)
2001/02: 16^{6}GS, 16^{5}GF, 16^{0}G, 16^{P}S

	Starts	1st	2nd	3rd	Win & Pl
Hurdles	4	0	0	0	0
Career Total	**4**	**0**	**0**	**0**	**0**

Going: Sf: 0-1 GS: 0-1 Gd: 0-1 GF: - Fm: 0-1
Distance: 2m/2m3: 0-4 2m4-2m7: 0-0 3m+: 0-0
Track: LH: 0-2 RH: 0-2 Tight: 0-1 Gall: 0-0
Aids: Bl: 0-0 Vi: 0-0 Tstrap: 0-0
Best Rating: 82 11/01 Ludl 2m gd-fm Hdl

Moderate maiden over hurdles.

Lucky Jim

10-y-o b g Faustus (USA)-Lola Black (FR) (Relkino)
Miss K Lovelace Miss K Lovelace

Placings:P (0428)
2001/02: 21^{P}G

	Starts	1st	2nd	3rd	Win & Pl
Chases	1	0	0	0	
Career Total	**1**	**0**	**0**	**0**	

Going: Sf: 0-0 GS: 0-0 Gd: 0-1 GF: - Fm: 0-0
Distance: 2m/2m3: 0-0 2m4-2m7: 0-1 3m+: 0-0
Track: LH: 0-0 RH: 0-0 Tight: 0-0 Gall: 0-0
Aids: Bl: 0-0 Vi: 0-0 Tstrap: 0-0
Best Rating:

Lucky Joe (IRE)

103(83c) (83c)73

9-y-o br g Denel (FR)-Breezy Dawn (Kemal (FR))
J White Nick Quesnel

Placings:P-PP4 (4686)
2001/02: 18^{P}G, 22^{P}S, 26^{4}GF

	Starts	1st	2nd	3rd	Win & Pl
Hurdles	3	0	0	0	0
Career Total	**4**	**0**	**0**	**0**	**0**

Going: Sf: 0-1 GS: 0-0 Gd: 0-1 GF: - Fm: 0-1
Distance: 2m/2m3: 0-1 2m4-2m7: 0-1 3m+: 0-1
Track: LH: 0-1 RH: 0-2 Tight: 0-2 Gall: 0-0
Aids: Bl: 0-0 Vi: 0-0 Tstrap: 0-0
Best Rating: 73 4/02 Hrfd 3m2f gd-fm Hdl

Won twice between the flags in 2001. Modest form under Rules in 2002.

Lucky Judge

101 110

5-y-o b g Saddlers' Hall (IRE)-Lady Lydia (Ela-Mana-Mou)
G A Swinbank Mrs I Gibson

Placings:514 (3362)
2001/02: 16^{5}G, 20^{1}GF, 25^{4}GS

	Starts	1st	2nd	3rd	Win & Pl
Hurdles	3	1	0	0	2828
Career Total	**3**	**1**	**0**	**0**	**2828**
110 12/01 Muss 2m4f E Hdl G-F					£2828
					Total win prize-money £2828

Going: Sf: 0-0 GS: 0-1 Gd: 0-1 GF: - Fm: 1-1
Distance: 2m/2m3: 0-1 **2m4-2m7: 1-1** 3m+: 0-1
Track: LH: 0-2 **RH: 1-1 Tight: 1-2** Gall: 0-0
Aids: Bl: 0-0 Vi: 0-0 Tstrap: 0-0
Best Rating: 110 12/01 Muss 2m4f gd-fm Hdl

A stayer on the Flat, made a promising start to his hurdling career, winning at Musselburgh in December 2001.

Lucky Lucky Bob (USA)

71f 55f

5-y-o b g Alleged (USA)-Alloy (FR) (Pharly (FR))
E A Wheeler (N E Berry 26/2) The Square Milers

Placings:*00* (2341)
2001/02: 16^{0}GS, 16^{0}GF

	Starts	1st	2nd	3rd	Win & Pl
NH Flat	2	0	0	0	
Career Total	**2**	**0**	**0**	**0**	

Going: Sf: 0-0 GS: 0-1 Gd: 0-0 GF: - Fm: 0-1
Distance: 2m/2m3: 0-2 2m4-2m7: 0-0 3m+: 0-0
Track: LH: 0-0 RH: 0-2 Tight: 0-0 Gall: 0-0
Aids: Bl: 0-0 Vi: 0-0 Tstrap: 0-0
Best Rating: 55 11/01 Sand 2m110y gd-sft NHF

Lucky Master (IRE)

101(99c) (116c)100

10-y-o b g Roselier (FR)-Golden Chestnut (Green Shoon)
John R Upson Mrs Ann Key

Placings:*005*/26426421/**22013363**/5-46PP240 (4877)
2001/02: 28^{4}G, 24^{6}GF, 24^{P}GF, 32^{P}GF, 21^{2}GS, 24^{4}G, 24^{0}G

	Starts	1st	2nd	3rd	Win & Pl
Hurdles	3	0	1	0	1020
Chases	4	0	0	0	859
Career Total	**27**	**2**	**6**	**3**	**18300**
128 11/99 Uttx 3m E Ch G-S					£3501
91 4/99 Sedg 2m5f110y E Hdl G-F					£2582
					Total win prize-money £6084

Going: Sf: 0-0 GS: 0-1 Gd: 0-3 GF: - Fm: 0-3
Distance: 2m/2m3: 0-0 2m4-2m7: 0-1 3m+: 0-6
Track: LH: 0-2 RH: 0-3 Tight: 0-2 Gall: 0-0
Aids: Bl: 0-0 Vi: 0-0 Tstrap: 0-0
Best Rating: 128 1/00 Folk 3m2f soft Ch

Out of sorts over fences but returned to form when reverting to hurdling. Stays very well and likes fast ground.

Lucky Mick (IRE)

103 103

7-y-o b g Husyan (USA)-Kindly Go (IRE) (Buckley)
J I A Charlton H Proud

Placings:*02*/*00*-32451 (4788)
2001/02: 17^{3}HY, 20^{2}S, 20^{4}S, 24^{5}S, 20^{1}F

	Starts	1st	2nd	3rd	Win & Pl
Hurdles	5	1	1	1	4084
Career Total	**9**	**1**	**2**	**1**	**4556**
93 4/02 Newc 2m4f E Hdl FRM					£2779
					Total win prize-money £2779

Going: Sf: 0-4 GS: 0-0 Gd: 0-0 GF: - Fm: 1-1
Distance: 2m/2m3: 0-1 **2m4-2m7: 1-3** 3m+: 0-1
Track: **LH: 1-4** RH: 0-1 Tight: 0-0 **Gall: 1-3**
Aids: Bl: 0-0 Vi: 0-0 **Tstrap: 1-5**
Best Rating: 110 4/00 Carl 2m1f gd-sft NHF

Novice hurdler, handles firm ground and stays two and a half miles. Has worn a tongue-strap.

Lucky Penny

98f 95f

6-y-o ch m Karinga Bay-Redgrave Rose (Tug Of War)
K Bishop D J Bridger & D M Bell

Placings:*450* (4823)
2001/02: 16^{4}GF, 16^{5}G, 17^{0}G

	Starts	1st	2nd	3rd	Win & Pl
NH Flat	3	0	0	0	0
Career Total	**3**	**0**	**0**	**0**	**0**

Going: Sf: 0-0 GS: 0-0 Gd: 0-2 GF: - Fm: 0-1
Distance: 2m/2m3: 0-3 2m4-2m7: 0-0 3m+: 0-0
Track: LH: 0-3 RH: 0-0 Tight: 0-0 Gall: 0-1
Aids: Bl: 0-0 Vi: 0-0 Tstrap: 0-0
Best Rating: 95 4/02 Uttx 2m good NHF

Glimmer of promise in bumpers.

Lucky Ross (IRE)

11-y-o gr g Roselier (FR)-Hope You'Re Lucky (Quayside)
Alan Armstrong (H D Daly 10/2) Belle Vue Stables Racing

Placings:050/436231/20/**4142P-UP** **(3984)**
2001/02: 25^{U}G, 31^{P}GS

	Starts	1st	2nd	3rd	Win & Pl
Chases	2	0	0	0	
Career Total	**18**	**2**	**3**	**2**	**11361**

109	12/00	Hrfd	3m1f110y	E Ch	HVY	£3513
86	4/99	Hrfd	3m2f	E Hdl	G-F	£3116

Total win prize-money £6629

Going: Sf: 0-0 GS: 0-1 Gd: 0-1 GF: - Fm: 0-0
Distance: 2m/2m3: 0-0 2m4-2m7: 0-0 3m+: 0-2
Track: LH: 0-1 RH: 0-0 Tight: 0-1 Gall: 0-0
Aids: Bl: 0-0 Vi: 0-0 Tstrap: 0-0
Best Rating: 114 3/00 Bang 3m good Hdl

Lucky Sinna (IRE)

102 **119**

6-y-o b/br g Insan (USA)-Bit Of A Chance (Lord Ha Ha)
J T Gifford John Plackett

Placings:3/444-2343F **(4854)**
2001/02: 21^{2}S, 21^{3}G, 21^{4}GS, 22^{3}G, 22^{F}G

	Starts	1st	2nd	3rd	Win & Pl
Hurdles	5	0	1	2	2879
Career Total	**9**	**0**	**1**	**3**	**5879**

Going: Sf: 0-1 GS: 0-1 Gd: 0-3 GF: - Fm: 0-0
Distance: 2m/2m3: 0-0 2m4-2m7: 0-5 3m+: 0-0
Track: LH: 0-3 RH: 0-2 Tight: 0-2 Gall: 0-1
Aids: Bl: 0-0 Vi: 0-0 Tstrap: 0-1
Best Rating: 126 4/00 Asct 2m110y soft NHF

Lightly-raced novice hurdler, appears not to find much off the bridle and has become rather disappointing. Does not want heavy ground.

Lucky Teeny (IRE)

5-y-o ch m Phardante (FR)-Rusty Iron (General Ironside)
D G Bridgwater Mrs C Kelly

Placings:346 **(4112)**
2001/02: 17^{3}S, 16^{4}HY, 16^{6}S

	Starts	1st	2nd	3rd	Win & Pl
NH Flat	3	0	0	1	228
Career Total	**3**	**0**	**0**	**1**	**228**

Going: Sf: 0-3 GS: 0-0 Gd: 0-0 GF: - Fm: 0-0
Distance: 2m/2m3: 0-3 2m4-2m7: 0-0 3m+: 0-0
Track: LH: 0-1 RH: 0-2 Tight: 0-0 Gall: 0-0
Aids: Bl: 0-0 Vi: 0-0 Tstrap: 0-0
Best Rating: 81 3/02 Towc 2m soft NHF

has shown some ability in bumpers.

Lucky Time (IRE)

102 **109**

10-y-o b g Phardante (FR)-Rock Ellie (Random Shot)
Ferdy Murphy K Lee

Placings:5/224-0 **(4490)**
2001/02: 20^{0}GS

	Starts	1st	2nd	3rd	Win & Pl
Chases	1	0	0	0	
Career Total	**5**	**0**	**2**	**0**	**2250**

Going: Sf: 0-0 GS: 0-1 Gd: 0-0 GF: - Fm: 0-0
Distance: 2m/2m3: 0-0 2m4-2m7: 0-1 3m+: 0-0
Track: LH: 0-0 RH: 0-1 Tight: 0-0 Gall: 0-0
Aids: Bl: 0-0 Vi: 0-0 Tstrap: 0-0
Best Rating: 94 5/00 Ctml 2m5f110y good Ch

Novice chaser, stays two miles three furlongs and acts on good and fast ground.

Lucky Uno

6-y-o b g Rock City-Free Skip (Free State)
R Wilman H G Norman

Placings:PP **(4752)**
2001/02: 19^{P}GF, 16^{P}GF

	Starts	1st	2nd	3rd	Win & Pl
Hurdles	2	0	0	0	
Career Total	**2**	**0**	**0**	**0**	

Going: Sf: 0-0 GS: 0-0 Gd: 0-0 GF: - Fm: 0-2
Distance: 2m/2m3: 0-1 2m4-2m7: 0-1 3m+: 0-0
Track: LH: 0-1 RH: 0-1 Tight: 0-0 Gall: 0-1
Aids: Bl: 0-0 Vi: 0-0 Tstrap: 0-0
Best Rating:

Pulled up on first two starts over hurdles.

Lucys Lad

101 (84h) (14h) **103**

8-y-o b g Le Moss-Lucy Lastic (Tycoon Ii)
Miss Venetia Williams Ali Bar Bar

Placings:03P4P/021P6-0P **(4847)**
2001/02: 24^{0}G, 20^{P}G

	Starts	1st	2nd	3rd	Win & Pl
Hurdles	2	0	0	0	
Career Total	**12**	**1**	**1**	**1**	**6220**

103	12/00	Ludl	3m	F(0-100)HCh	G-S	£4745

Total win prize-money £4745

Going: Sf: 0-0 GS: 0-0 Gd: 0-2 GF: - Fm: 0-0
Distance: 2m/2m3: 0-0 2m4-2m7: 0-1 3m+: 0-1
Track: LH: 0-1 RH: 0-1 Tight: 0-1 Gall: 0-0
Aids: Bl: 0-0 Vi: 0-0 Tstrap: 0-0
Best Rating: 103 12/00 Ludl 3m gd-sft Ch

A fair staying handicap chaser who is prone to mistakes. Has won on good and easier ground.

Ludere (IRE)

100 **98**

7-y-o ch g Desse Zenny (USA)-White Jasmin (Jalmood (USA))
B J Llewellyn The Trade Import Agency Ltd

Placings:65/16406/430132-2143 **(3167)**
2001/02: 16^{2}G, 19^{1}GS, 16^{4}GS, 16^{3}S

	Starts	1st	2nd	3rd	Win & Pl
Hurdles	4	1	1	1	3164
Career Total	**17**	**3**	**2**	**3**	**8104**

93	12/01	Tntn	2m3f110y	G Hdl	G-S	£1596
97	12/00	Tntn	2m3f110y	G Hdl	SFT	£1533
89	7/99	Sedg	2m1f	E Hdl	G-F	£2302

Total win prize-money £5432

Going: Sf: 0-1 GS: 1-2 Gd: 0-1 GF: - Fm: 0-0
Distance: 2m/2m3: 0-3 **2m4-2m7: 1-1** 3m+: 0-0
Track: LH: 0-2 **RH: 1-2 Tight: 1-2** Gall: 0-0
Aids: Bl: 0-0 Vi: 0-0 Tstrap: 0-0
Best Rating: 98 1/02 Leic 2m soft Hdl

Plating class hurdler, stays two and a half. Won the same selling hurdle at Taunton in December for two years running.

Luke Warm

105 **123**

12-y-o ch g Nearly A Hand-Hot 'n Scopey (Hot Brandy)
D R Gandolfo Nigel Stafford

Placings:4660/52433/2131P2/12100/0F32646/214421 35-33415F56 **(4414)**
2001/02: 22^{3}GS, 20^{3}S, 20^{4}G, 22^{1}HY, 22^{5}G, 24^{F}S, 24^{5}GS, 28^{6}S

	Starts	1st	2nd	3rd	Win & Pl
Chases	8	1	0	2	19417
Career Total	**43**	**7**	**7**	**7**	**61168**

123	12/01	Towc	2m6f	C(0-130)HCh	HVY	£16680
121	12/00	Towc	2m6f	C(0-130)HCh	HVY	£10374
120	10/00	Font	2m6f	D(0-120)HCh	GD	£4231
115	2/99	MRas	2m4f	C(0-135)HCh	SFT	£6872
105	1/99	Wwck	2m4f110y	E(0-115)HCh	SFT	£3301
95	12/97	Tntn	2m3f	F(0-95)HCh	GD	£2836
105	11/97	NAbb	2m5f110y	E(0-100)HCh	SFT	£2818

Total win prize-money £47115

Going: Sf: 1-4 GS: 0-2 Gd: 0-2 GF: - Fm: 0-0
Distance: 2m/2m3: 0-0 **2m4-2m7: 1-5** 3m+: 0-3
Track: LH: 0-3 **RH: 1-3** Tight: 0-2 Gall: 0-3
Aids: Bl: 0-0 Vi: 0-0 Tstrap: 0-0
Best Rating: 123 2/02 Kemp 3m soft Ch

He is a multiple winner of modest events over fences at the minor tracks, but is not as effective at the big venues. Suited by soft ground and trips between two and a half and two and three-quarter miles.

Lumaca (IRE)

103 **88**

7-y-o b g Riberetto-Broken Mirror (Push On)
J Neville C G Bolton

Placings:046/5602-15P0 **(4568)**
2001/02: 24^{1}S, 26^{5}S, 24^{P}HY, 24^{0}G

	Starts	1st	2nd	3rd	Win & Pl
Hurdles	4	1	0	0	2594
Career Total	**11**	**1**	**1**	**0**	**3583**

88	1/02	Tntn	3m110y	E(0-110)HHdl	SFT	£2593

Total win prize-money £2594

Going: Sf: 1-3 GS: 0-0 Gd: 0-1 GF: - Fm: 0-0
Distance: 2m/2m3: 0-0 2m4-2m7: 0-0 **3m+: 1-4**
Track: LH: 0-1 **RH: 1-3 Tight: 1-2** Gall: 0-1
Aids: Bl: 0-0 Vi: 0-0 Tstrap: 0-0
Best Rating: 103 2/00 Kemp 2m soft NHF

He defied a 297-day absence when successful at Taunton in January and is clearly at home in the mud.

Luna Nova

92 **53**

4-y-o b g Aragon-Lucidity (Vision (USA))
D Moffatt (C W Thornton 15/8) The Sheroot Partnership

Placings:0PP **(4397)**
2001/02: 16^{0}S, 16^{P}S, 18^{P}HY

	Starts	1st	2nd	3rd	Win & Pl
Hurdles	3	0	0	0	
Career Total	**3**	**0**	**0**	**0**	

Going: Sf: 0-3 GS: 0-0 Gd: 0-0 GF: - Fm: 0-0
Distance: 2m/2m3: 0-3 2m4-2m7: 0-0 3m+: 0-0
Track: LH: 0-3 RH: 0-0 Tight: 0-2 Gall: 0-1
Aids: Bl: 0-0 Vi: 0-0 Tstrap: 0-1
Best Rating: 37 1/02 Newc 2m soft Hdl

Lunajaz

5-y-o ch g Alhijaz-Lunagraphe (USA) (Time For A Change (USA))
T M Jones Robert Le Blanc

Placings:5-P (0007)
2001/02: 16^{PS}

	Starts	1st	2nd	3rd	Win & Pl
Hurdles	1	0	0	0	
Career Total	2	0	0	0	0

Going: Sf: 0-1 GS: 0-0 Gd: 0-0 GF: - Fm: 0-0
Distance: 2m/2m3: 0-1 2m4-2m7: 0-0 3m+: 0-0
Track: LH: 0-1 RH: 0-0 Tight: 0-1 Gall: 0-0
Aids: Bl: 0-0 Vi: 0-0 Tstrap: 0-0
Best Rating: 78 9/00 Plum 2m gd-fm Hdl

Lunar Crystal (IRE)

110 123+

4-y-o b g Shirley Heights-Solar Crystal (IRE) (Alzao (USA))
M C Pipe (D R C Elsworth 29/7) Teddington Racing Club

Placings:25 (4006)
2001/02: 16^{2}GS, 16^{5}S

	Starts	1st	2nd	3rd	Win & Pl
Hurdles	2	0	1	0	1140
Career Total	2	0	1	0	1140

Going: Sf: 0-1 GS: 0-1 Gd: 0-0 GF: - Fm: 0-0
Distance: 2m/2m3: 0-2 2m4-2m7: 0-0 3m+: 0-0
Track: LH: 0-1 RH: 0-1 Tight: 0-0 Gall: 0-1
Aids: Bl: 0-0 Vi: 0-0 Tstrap: 0-0
Best Rating: 99 3/02 Newb 2m110y soft Hdl

A fair performer on the Flat, he developed into a promising novice hurdler in the summer of 2002. Seems to handle most types of ground and is suited by forcing tactics.

Lunar Lord

104 101

6-y-o b g Elmaamul (USA)-Cache (Bustino)
D Burchell Brian Williams

Placings:2515-54 (2220)
2001/02: 16^{5}G, 17^{4}G

	Starts	1st	2nd	3rd	Win & Pl
Hurdles	2	0	0	0	0
Career Total	6	1	1	0	3118

105 1/01 Chep 2m110y E Hdl G-S £2555
Total win prize-money £2555

Going: Sf: 0-0 GS: 0-0 Gd: 0-2 GF: - Fm: 0-0
Distance: 2m/2m3: 0-2 2m4-2m7: 0-0 3m+: 0-0
Track: LH: 0-2 RH: 0-0 Tight: 0-1 Gall: 0-0
Aids: Bl: 0-0 Vi: 0-0 Tstrap: 0-0
Best Rating: 105 1/01 Chep 2m110y gd-sft Hdl

Lunar Maxwell

106 99

7-y-o b g Dancing High-Pauper Moon (Pauper)
J I A Charlton J W Robson

Placings:*4443*/62400-62132 (4240)
2001/02: 16^{6}F, 25^{2}G, 23^{1}G, 25^{3}GS, 26^{2}GF

	Starts	1st	2nd	3rd	Win & Pl
Hurdles	5	1	2	1	4331
Career Total	14	1	3	2	5343

93 11/01 Weth 2m7f F(0-100)HHdl GD £2506
Total win prize-money £2506

Going: Sf: 0-0 GS: 0-1 Gd: 1-2 GF: - Fm: 0-2
Distance: 2m/2m3: 0-1 **2m4-2m7: 1-1** 3m+: 0-3
Track: **LH: 1-4** RH: 0-1 Tight: 0-1 Gall: 0-1
Aids: Bl: 0-0 Vi: 0-0 Tstrap: 0-0
Best Rating: 102 4/00 Carl 2m1f gd-sft NHF

Staying novice, appreciated the step up to three miles in the autumn of 2001. Suited by good ground.

Lunardi (IRE)

101 102

4-y-o b g Indian Ridge-Gold Tear (USA) (Tejano (USA))
D L Williams (D K Weld 20/10) N F Dawe

Placings:5421565046 (4813)
2001/02: 16^{5}G, 16^{4}HY, 16^{2}G, 17^{1}G, 16^{5}G, 16^{6}GS, 16^{5}S, 18^{0}S, 16^{4}GF, 17^{6}GF

	Starts	1st	2nd	3rd	Win & Pl
Hurdles	10	1	1	0	4364
Career Total	10	1	1	0	4364

102 11/01 Hrfd 2m1f E Hdl GD £2471
Total win prize-money £2471

Going: Sf: 0-3 GS: 0-1 Gd: 1-4 GF: - Fm: 0-2
Distance: **2m/2m3: 1-10** 2m4-2m7: 0-0 3m+: 0-0
Track: LH: 0-5 **RH: 1-4** Tight: 0-1 Gall: 0-3
Aids: Bl: 0-0 Vi: 0-2 Tstrap: 0-0
Best Rating: 102 11/01 Hrfd 2m1f good Hdl

Ex-Irish, winner of a good ground Hereford novices' hurdle over two miles one furlong on his second start in this country. Found wanting in better class since. Has won on good to soft ground.

Lunevision (FR)

81 62

4-y-o b f Solid Illusion (USA)-Lumiere Celeste (FR) (Always Fair (USA))
H J Collingridge The Headquarters Partnership Iv

Placings:60 (1821)
2001/02: 16^{6}GF, 16^{0}GS

	Starts	1st	2nd	3rd	Win & Pl
Hurdles	2	0	0	0	0
Career Total	2	0	0	0	0

Going: Sf: 0-0 GS: 0-1 Gd: 0-0 GF: - Fm: 0-1
Distance: 2m/2m3: 0-2 2m4-2m7: 0-0 3m+: 0-0
Track: LH: 0-1 RH: 0-1 Tight: 0-1 Gall: 0-0
Aids: Bl: 0-0 Vi: 0-0 Tstrap: 0-0
Best Rating: 62 10/01 Kemp 2m gd-sft Hdl

Lurgoe (IRE)

(78h)

9-y-o ch g Camden Town-Knockananig (Pitpan)
J J O'Neill Euan & Bernardine Roger

Placings:0/3322332/1F345232023-P (0068)
2001/02: 27^{P}G

	Starts	1st	2nd	3rd	Win & Pl
Chases	1	0	0	0	
Career Total	20	1	6	7	14166

120 5/00 Sedg 2m5f E Ch G-F £3315
Total win prize-money £3315

Going: Sf: 0-0 GS: 0-0 Gd: 0-1 GF: - Fm: 0-0
Distance: 2m/2m3: 0-0 2m4-2m7: 0-0 3m+: 0-1
Track: LH: 0-1 RH: 0-0 Tight: 0-1 Gall: 0-0
Aids: Bl: 0-0 Vi: 0-1 Tstrap: 0-0
Best Rating: 120 11/00 Ayr 2m5f110y soft Ch

Lurpak Legend (IRE)

99(102h) (92h)85

8-y-o br g Castle Keep-Welsh Tan (Welsh Saint)
Mrs M Reveley The Mary Reveley Racing Club

Placings:000000/352152U013/22F060406-601450 (3747)
2001/02: 17^{6}GS, 21^{0}G, 16^{1}S, 16^{4}G, 16^{5}GS, 16^{0}S

	Starts	1st	2nd	3rd	Win & Pl
Hurdles	3	1	0	0	1932
Chases	3	0	0	0	0
Career Total	31	3	4	2	10686

92 12/01 Catt 2m G(0-95)HHdl SFT £1932
93 3/00 Catt 2m3f F(0-100)HHdl G-F £1918
76 10/99 Carl 2m4f110y F(0-100)HHdl GD £2290
Total win prize-money £6140

Going: Sf: 1-2 GS: 0-2 Gd: 0-2 GF: - Fm: 0-0
Distance: **2m/2m3: 1-5** 2m4-2m7: 0-1 3m+: 0-0
Track: **LH: 1-5** RH: 0-1 **Tight: 1-6** Gall: 0-0
Aids: Bl: 0-0 Vi: 0-0 Tstrap: 0-0
Best Rating: 103 5/00 MRas 2m4f gd-sft Ch

Mixes hurdles and chases, and returned to form when winning a seller over the smaller obstacles at Catterick in December 2001.

Luscombe

9-y-o b g Tirol-Slipalong (Slippered)
P J Jones P J Jones

Placings:0P/03010/**UP006P**/031PPPP-P (4650)
2001/02: 21^{P}G

	Starts	1st	2nd	3rd	Win & Pl
Chases	1	0	0	0	
Career Total	21	2	0	2	5416

87 11/00 Plum 3m2f F(0-100)HCh HVY £2717
77 1/99 Extr 2m1f110y F(0-100)HHdl HVY £1942
Total win prize-money £4659

Going: Sf: 0-0 GS: 0-0 Gd: 0-1 GF: - Fm: 0-0
Distance: 2m/2m3: 0-0 2m4-2m7: 0-1 3m+: 0-0
Track: LH: 0-1 RH: 0-0 Tight: 0-1 Gall: 0-0
Aids: Bl: 0-0 Vi: 0-0 Tstrap: 0-0
Best Rating: 87 11/00 Plum 3m2f heavy Ch

His only victory over fences was a weak amateurs' handicap in November 2000 in heavy ground. He has since failed to finish six times from his last seven starts. Has worn blinkers and a tongue-strap.

Lussino (FR)

110 122

6-y-o b g Esprit Du Nord (USA)-Lumiere Du Feu (FR) (Zino)

K C Bailey G P D Milne

Placings:06-511521 (4644)
2001/02: 16^{5}HY, 16^{1}GS, 17^{1}S, 17^{5}HY, 16^{2}GS, 16^{1}G

	Starts	1st	2nd	3rd	Win & Pl
Hurdles	6	3	1	0	16177
Career Total	**8**	**3**	**1**	**0**	**16177**

122	4/02	Ludl	2m	D(0-120)HHdl	GD	£5200
110	1/02	Tntn	2m1f	D(0-120)HHdl	SFT	£3526
118	1/02	Hntg	2m110y	E(0-100)HHdl	G-S	£2590

Total win prize-money £11316

Going: Sf: 1-3 GS: 1-2 Gd: 1-1 GF: - Fm: 0-0
Distance: **2m/2m3: 3-6** 2m4-2m7: 0-0 3m+: 0-0
Track: LH: 0-3 **RH: 3-3** Tight: 1-1 Gall: 1-3
Aids: Bl: 0-0 Vi: 0-0 Tstrap: 0-0
Best Rating: 122 4/02 Ludl 2m good Hdl

A useful stayer on the Flat, who has gradually got his act together over hurdles and won easily at Huntingdon in January 2002 before following up under a penalty at Taunton, he again showed a liking for a sound surface when winning at Ludlow in April 2002. However, he does act on soft ground and is well suited by two miles.

Luthrie Lass

7-y-o ch m Rakaposhi King-Lillie's Brig (New Brig)
J Barclay Alexander Family

Placings:UPP - (4875)
2001/02: 16^{U}HY, 16^{P}S, 24^{P}G

	Starts	1st	2nd	3rd	Win & Pl
Hurdles	3	0	0	0	
Career Total	**3**	**0**	**0**	**0**	

Going: Sf: 0-2 GS: 0-0 Gd: 0-1 GF: - Fm: 0-0
Distance: 2m/2m3: 0-2 2m4-2m7: 0-0 3m+: 0-1
Track: LH: 0-2 RH: 0-1 Tight: 0-0 Gall: 0-0
Aids: Bl: 0-0 Vi: 0-0 Tstrap: 0-0
Best Rating:

Jumped poorly to unseat rider on hurdles debut.

Lutine Bell

99 **76**
7-y-o b g Fairy King (USA)-Bell Toll (High Line)
H J Collingridge D T Thom

Placings:P04/5F-1F (0850)
2001/02: 16^{1}GF, 16^{F}GF

	Starts	1st	2nd	3rd	Win & Pl
Hurdles	2	1	0	0	2001
Career Total	**7**	**1**	**0**	**0**	**2001**

76	6/01	Fknm	2m	G(0-90)HHdl	G-F	£2001

Total win prize-money £2001

Going: Sf: 0-0 GS: 0-0 Gd: 0-0 GF: - Fm: 1-2
Distance: **2m/2m3: 1-2** 2m4-2m7: 0-0 3m+: 0-0
Track: **LH: 1-2** RH: 0-0 **Tight: 1-2** Gall: 0-0
Aids: Bl: 0-0 Vi: 0-0 **Tstrap: 1-1**
Best Rating: 76 6/01 Fknm 2m gd-fm Hdl

Luzcadou (FR)

108(112h) **144**
9-y-o b g Cadoudal (FR)-Luzenia (FR) (Armos)
Ferdy Murphy A G Chappell

Placings:FF461P40123/36531/F5110P/066P1P-0042UF00 (4664)
2001/02: 25^{0}GS, 24^{0}S, 20^{4}S, 20^{2}S, 24^{U}G, 29^{F}G, 24^{0}GS, 21^{0}G

	Starts	1st	2nd	3rd	Win & Pl
Chases	8	0	1	0	3277
Career Total	**36**	**6**	**2**	**3**	**150826**

119	12/00	Newc	2m4f	C(0-135)HHdl	SFT	£5187
158	2/00	Ayr	2m4f	B(0-145)HCh	HVY	£13065
151	1/00	Ayr	2m4f	B(0-140)HCh	SFT	£9197
111	12/97	Carl	2m4f110y	E Hdl	SFT	£2038
	3/97	Autl	1m7f110y	Ch		£35671

Total win prize-money £80969

Going: Sf: 0-3 GS: 0-2 Gd: 0-3 GF: - Fm: 0-0
Distance: 2m/2m3: 0-0 2m4-2m7: 0-3 3m+: 0-5
Track: LH: 0-6 RH: 0-2 Tight: 0-1 Gall: 0-2
Aids: Bl: 0-1 Vi: 0-4 Tstrap: 0-0
Best Rating: 158 2/00 Ayr 2m4f heavy Ch

A winner over hurdles and fences, he is suited by soft ground and two and a half miles, but has yet to prove he stays three miles. Well beaten in useful company this term, but just touched off on his fourth start.

Lydia's Echo

6-y-o b m Backchat (USA)-Lydia's Well (Current Magic)
J W Mullins Richard Bailey

Placings:0 (3883)
2001/02: 16^{0}GS

	Starts	1st	2nd	3rd	Win & Pl
NH Flat	1	0	0	0	
Career Total	**1**	**0**	**0**	**0**	

Going: Sf: 0-0 GS: 0-1 Gd: 0-0 GF: - Fm: 0-0
Distance: 2m/2m3: 0-1 2m4-2m7: 0-0 3m+: 0-0
Track: LH: 0-0 RH: 0-1 Tight: 0-0 Gall: 0-0
Aids: Bl: 0-0 Vi: 0-0 Tstrap: 0-0
Best Rating: 72 2/02 Winc 2m gd-sft NHF

Lynton Lad

91 **72**
10-y-o b g Superpower-House Maid (Habitat)
M J Gingell Gentlemen Don't Work On Mondays

Placings:0P/653P (1305)
2001/02: 16^{6}GF, 16^{5}GF, 18^{3}GF, 19^{P}GF

	Starts	1st	2nd	3rd	Win & Pl
Hurdles	4	0	0	1	335
Career Total	**6**	**0**	**0**	**1**	**335**

Going: Sf: 0-0 GS: 0-0 Gd: 0-0 GF: - Fm: 0-4
Distance: 2m/2m3: 0-3 2m4-2m7: 0-1 3m+: 0-0
Track: LH: 0-3 RH: 0-1 Tight: 0-3 Gall: 0-0
Aids: Bl: 0-0 Vi: 0-2 Tstrap: 0-0
Best Rating: 72 8/01 Sthl 2m gd-fm Hdl

Lyphard's Fable (USA)

11-y-o b g Al Nasr (FR)-Affirmative Fable (USA) (Affirmed (USA))
T R George O D Plunkett

Placings:0P04/40004233F6F/F064/2FF126263/24233 25/5050/0-6 (0258)
2001/02: 24^{6}GF

	Starts	1st	2nd	3rd	Win & Pl
Chases	1	0	0	0	0
Career Total	**41**	**1**	**7**	**5**	**9500**

74	12/97	Chep	2m4f110y	G Hdl	SFT	£1898

Total win prize-money £1898

Going: Sf: 0-0 GS: 0-0 Gd: 0-0 GF: - Fm: 0-1
Distance: 2m/2m3: 0-0 2m4-2m7: 0-0 3m+: 0-1
Track: LH: 0-1 RH: 0-0 Tight: 0-1 Gall: 0-0
Aids: Bl: 0-0 Vi: 0-0 Tstrap: 0-0
Best Rating: 89 11/98 Plum 2m4f soft Hdl

Lypharita's Risk (FR)

104(99h) (99h)**109**
7-y-o b g Take Risks (FR)-Patissima (FR) (Lightning (FR))
P F Nicholls Derek Millard

Placings:P6/2423344-352P (1804)
2001/02: 18^{3}GF, 16^{5}GF, 24^{2}GF, 24^{P}GF

	Starts	1st	2nd	3rd	Win & Pl
Chases	4	0	1	1	1640
Career Total	**13**	**0**	**3**	**3**	**4647**

Going: Sf: 0-0 GS: 0-0 Gd: 0-0 GF: - Fm: 0-4
Distance: 2m/2m3: 0-2 2m4-2m7: 0-0 3m+: 0-2
Track: LH: 0-1 RH: 0-2 Tight: 0-3 Gall: 0-0
Aids: Bl: 0-0 Vi: 0-0 Tstrap: 0-2
Best Rating: 109 10/01 Ludl 3m gd-fm Ch

Lyreen Wonder

117(109h) (140h)**157**
9-y-o ch g Derrylin-Coole Pilate (Celtic Cone)
A L T Moore Lyreen Syndicate

Placings:41B2/**F22F11UF1/1F02-1213U** (4677)
2001/02: 24^{1}YS, 24^{2}Y, 24^{1}YS, 24^{3}S, 36^{U}G

	Starts	1st	2nd	3rd	Win & Pl
Hurdles	1	0	1	0	3524
Chases	4	2	0	1	67743
Career Total	**22**	**7**	**5**	**1**	**149998**

157	1/02	Leop	3m	HCh	Y-S	£39877
157	11/01	Navn	3m	HCh	Y-S	£26209
151	11/00	Navn	3m	HCh	SFT	£26000
126	4/00	Cork	3m	Ch	G-Y	£10400
134	2/00	Navn	2m4f	Ch	SH	£4968
126	2/00	Naas	2m	Ch	SFT	£5544
126	12/98	Chep	2m110y	B Hdl	HVY	£18120

Total win prize-money £131119

Going: Sf: 0-1 GS: 0-0 Gd: 0-1 GF: - Fm: 0-0
Distance: 2m/2m3: 0-0 2m4-2m7: 0-0 **3m+: 2-5**
Track: **LH: 2-4** RH: 0-1 Tight: 0-1 Gall: 0-0
Aids: Bl: 0-0 Vi: 0-0 Tstrap: 0-0
Best Rating: 157 1/02 Leop 3m yld-sft Ch

A useful if somewhat clumsy chaser, he may be best over three miles where the slower pace places less stress on his jumping. He has hung left and may be unsuited by right-handed tracks. Untested beyond three miles.

Lyrical Seal

12-y-o b m Dubassoff (USA)-Sea-Rosemary (Seaepic (USA))
Miss S Waugh Mrs J Dening

Placings:*00*/6P66P/43PP43/1-6 (4132)
2001/02: 25^{6}G

	Starts	1st	2nd	3rd	Win & Pl
Chases	1	0	0	0	0
Career Total	**15**	**1**	**0**	**2**	**2894**

95	5/00	Hrfd	3m1f110y	H Ch	G-S	£1540

Total win prize-money £1541

Going: Sf: 0-0 GS: 0-0 Gd: 0-1 GF: - Fm: 0-0
Distance: 2m/2m3: 0-0 2m4-2m7: 0-0 3m+: 0-1
Track: LH: 0-0 RH: 0-1 Tight: 0-0 Gall: 0-0
Aids: Bl: 0-1 Vi: 0-0 Tstrap: 0-0
Best Rating: 95 5/00 Hrfd 3m1f110y gd-sft Ch

Lyringo

79 64

8-y-o b m Rustingo-Lyricist (Averof)
P D Evans S R Brown

Placings: *05/54*P41-00 (0495)
2001/02: 21^{0}G, 19^{0}G

	Starts	1st	2nd	3rd	Win & Pl
Hurdles	2	0	0	0	
Career Total	**9**	**1**	**0**	**0**	**2016**

82 10/00 Strf 2m110y G Hdl SFT £2016
Total win prize-money £2016

Going: Sf: 0-0 GS: 0-0 Gd: 0-2 GF: - Fm: 0-0
Distance: 2m/2m3: 0-0 2m4-2m7: 0-2 3m+: 0-0
Track: LH: 0-0 RH: 0-1 Tight: 0-0 Gall: 0-0
Aids: Bl: 0-0 Vi: 0-0 Tstrap: 0-0
Best Rating: 88 8/00 Worc 2m gd-fm NHF

Lysandros (IRE)

83(106h) (100h)86

8-y-o b g Lycius (USA)-Trojan Relation (Trojan Fen)
Noel T Chance Premier Chance Racing

Placings: 0030/430216 (3160)
2001/02: 16^{4}G, 18^{3}GS, 20^{0}S, 19^{2}GS, 19^{1}GS, 19^{6}S

	Starts	1st	2nd	3rd	Win & Pl
Hurdles	5	1	1	1	5319
Chases	1	0	0	0	0
Career Total	**10**	**1**	**1**	**2**	**5589**

100 12/01 Tntn 2m3f110y D(0-120)HHdl G-S £3786
Total win prize-money £3786

Going: Sf: 0-2 GS: 1-3 Gd: 0-1 GF: - Fm: 0-0
Distance: 2m/2m3: 0-3 **2m4-2m7: 1-3** 3m+: 0-0
Track: LH: 0-2 **RH: 1-4 Tight: 1-3** Gall: 0-0
Aids: Bl: 0-0 Vi: 0-0 Tstrap: 0-0
Best Rating: 100 12/01 Tntn 2m3f110y gd-sft Hdl

Modest handicap hurdler, suited by a sharp track and easy ground.

M-Reg

13-y-o b g Politico (USA)-Heckley Surprise (Foggy Bell)
Giles Smyly Miss S Smyly

Placings: P/2P/F (0229)
2001/02: 30^{F}GF

	Starts	1st	2nd	3rd	Win & Pl
Chases	1	0	0	0	
Career Total	**4**	**0**	**1**	**0**	**624**

Going: Sf: 0-0 GS: 0-0 Gd: 0-0 GF: - Fm: 0-1
Distance: 2m/2m3: 0-0 2m4-2m7: 0-0 3m+: 0-1
Track: LH: 0-0 RH: 0-1 Tight: 0-0 Gall: 0-1
Aids: Bl: 0-0 Vi: 0-0 Tstrap: 0-0
Best Rating: 87 5/98 Fknm 3m110y good Ch

Ma Barnicle (IRE)

95 94

9-y-o ch m Al Hareb (USA)-Soltina (Sun Prince)
T D McCarthy Mrs D H McCarthy

Placings: 0P0/520220000/12231225/04P-4 (4638)
2001/02: 19^{4}GF

	Starts	1st	2nd	3rd	Win & Pl
Chases	1	0	0	0	0
Career Total	**24**	**2**	**7**	**1**	**11089**

108 10/99 Worc 2m F(0-100)HCh GD £2350
98 6/99 NAbb 2m1f F(0-100)HHdl GD £2759
Total win prize-money £5110

Going: Sf: 0-0 GS: 0-0 Gd: 0-0 GF: - Fm: 0-1
Distance: 2m/2m3: 0-0 2m4-2m7: 0-1 3m+: 0-0
Track: LH: 0-0 RH: 0-1 Tight: 0-0 Gall: 0-0
Aids: Bl: 0-0 Vi: 0-0 Tstrap: 0-0
Best Rating: 108 11/99 Worc 2m good Ch

Maas (IRE)

102 82

7-y-o br h Elbio-Payne's Grey (Godswalk (USA))
N B Mason N B Mason

Placings: P036P (4898)
2001/02: 16^{P}GS, 16^{0}GS, 16^{3}GS, 16^{6}S, 16^{P}G

	Starts	1st	2nd	3rd	Win & Pl
Hurdles	5	0	0	1	269
Career Total	**5**	**0**	**0**	**1**	**269**

Going: Sf: 0-1 GS: 0-3 Gd: 0-1 GF: - Fm: 0-0
Distance: 2m/2m3: 0-5 2m4-2m7: 0-0 3m+: 0-0
Track: LH: 0-2 RH: 0-3 Tight: 0-1 Gall: 0-1
Aids: Bl: 0-0 Vi: 0-0 Tstrap: 0-2
Best Rating: 82 12/01 Leic 2m gd-sft Hdl

Mabel's Memory (IRE)

106 100

9-y-o b m Over The River (FR)-Polar Mistress (IRE) (Strong Gale)
C Tizzard (R H Alner 29/7) Alvin Trowbridge

Placings: P3/66P0-64412P2P5P (4882)
2001/02: 16^{0}G, 21^{4}GF, 21^{4}G, 26^{1}GF, 25^{2}G, 22^{P}G, 16^{2}G, 21^{P}HY, 16^{5}G, 26^{P}GF

	Starts	1st	2nd	3rd	Win & Pl
Chases	10	1	2	0	7093
Career Total	**16**	**1**	**2**	**1**	**7723**

87 9/01 Font 3m2f110y E(0-105)HCh G-F £3168
Total win prize-money £3169

Going: Sf: 0-1 GS: 0-0 Gd: 0-6 GF: - Fm: 1-3
Distance: 2m/2m3: 0-3 2m4-2m7: 0-4 **3m+: 1-3**
Track: LH: 0-5 RH: 0-3 **Tight: 1-4** Gall: 0-1
Aids: Bl: 0-0 Vi: 0-0 Tstrap: 0-0
Best Rating: 100 12/01 Winc 2m good Ch

She appeared suited by the step up in trip when winning over three and a quarter miles at Fontwell in September 2001. Acts on a sound surface.

Mac Five (IRE)

73

7-y-o gr g Sharp Victor (USA)-Fine Flame (Le Prince)
C L Popham Mrs S J Popham

Placings: *0*-PP (0681)
2001/02: 21^{P}GF, 26^{P}G

	Starts	1st	2nd	3rd	Win & Pl
Chases	2	0	0	0	
Career Total	**3**	**0**	**0**	**0**	

Going: Sf: 0-0 GS: 0-0 Gd: 0-1 GF: - Fm: 0-1
Distance: 2m/2m3: 0-0 2m4-2m7: 0-1 3m+: 0-1
Track: LH: 0-2 RH: 0-0 Tight: 0-2 Gall: 0-0
Aids: Bl: 0-0 Vi: 0-0 Tstrap: 0-0
Best Rating:

Macalan (FR)

87 78

6-y-o ch g Saint Cyrien (FR)-Lady Darling (Darshaan)
M Todhunter Sir Robert Ogden

Placings: 14/P0P-5 (0664)
2001/02: 16^{5}F

	Starts	1st	2nd	3rd	Win & Pl
Hurdles	1	0	0	0	0
Career Total	**6**	**1**	**0**	**0**	**4844**

5/99 Roya 1m7f Hdl GD £2691
Total win prize-money £2691

Going: Sf: 0-0 GS: 0-0 Gd: 0-0 GF: - Fm: 0-1
Distance: 2m/2m3: 0-1 2m4-2m7: 0-0 3m+: 0-0
Track: LH: 0-0 RH: 0-1 Tight: 0-0 Gall: 0-0
Aids: Bl: 0-0 Vi: 0-0 Tstrap: 0-0
Best Rating: 78 6/01 Prth 2m110y firm Hdl

Macaw-Bay (IRE)

100(104h) (98h)112

8-y-o b m Strong Gale-Billys Pet (Le Moss)
A W Carroll Gary J Roberts

Placings: *2344*/615F61P3/15-6F2PP04 (4822)
2001/02: 19^{0}G, 16^{F}G, 20^{2}GS, 20^{P}G, 20^{P}GS, 20^{0}GF, 21^{4}G

	Starts	1st	2nd	3rd	Win & Pl
Hurdles	3	0	0	0	1508
Chases	4	0	1	0	1227
Career Total	**21**	**3**	**2**	**2**	**20278**

112 5/00 Fknm 2m4f F(0-95)HHdl FRM £1764
112 2/00 Newb 2m3f C HHdl G-S £10530
101 10/99 Winc 2m E Hdl G-F £2080
Total win prize-money £14374

Going: Sf: 0-0 GS: 0-2 Gd: 0-4 GF: - Fm: 0-1
Distance: 2m/2m3: 0-2 2m4-2m7: 0-5 3m+: 0-0
Track: LH: 0-2 RH: 0-5 Tight: 0-1 Gall: 0-3
Aids: Bl: 0-0 Vi: 0-0 Tstrap: 0-0
Best Rating: 112 12/01 Hntg 2m4f110y gd-sft Ch

A fair hurdler, she has shown ability over fences although tends to make mistakes. Best at around two and a half miles on a sound surface. Runs well fresh.

Maceo (GER)

102 112

8-y-o ch g Acatenango (GER)-Metropolitan Star (USA) (Lyphard (USA))
Mrs M Reveley Les De La Haye

Placings: 030/4-02241F (4393)
2001/02: 17^{0}GF, 16^{2}G, 20^{2}GS, 22^{4}GS, 16^{1}GS, 18^{F}HY

	Starts	1st	2nd	3rd	Win & Pl
Hurdles	6	1	2	0	7142
Career Total	**10**	**1**	**2**	**1**	**7521**

112 3/02 Newb 2m110y D(0-110)HHdl G-S £4582
Total win prize-money £4583

Going: Sf: 0-1 GS: 1-3 Gd: 0-1 GF: - Fm: 0-1
Distance: **2m/2m3: 1-4** 2m4-2m7: 0-2 3m+: 0-0
Track: **LH: 1-5** RH: 0-1 Tight: 0-4 **Gall: 1-1**
Aids: Bl: 0-0 Vi: 0-0 Tstrap: 0-0
Best Rating: 112 3/02 Newb 2m110y gd-sft Hdl

High-class performer on the Flat in his native Germany. Now with Mary Reveley, he proved suited by the drop back in trip and drying ground when winning easily at Newbury in March, but he fell next time in heavy ground at Kelso.

Macfin (IRE)

9-y-o b g Brevet-Lough Sholin (Kemal (FR))
Miss Louise Allan T M Fowler

Placings:P (0323)
2001/02: 25^{P}G

	Starts	1st	2nd	3rd	Win & Pl
Chases	1	0	0	0	
Career Total	**1**	**0**	**0**	**0**	

Going: Sf: 0-0 GS: 0-0 Gd: 0-1 GF: - Fm: 0-0
Distance: 2m/2m3: 0-0 2m4-2m7: 0-0 3m+: 0-1
Track: LH: 0-0 RH: 0-1 Tight: 0-1 Gall: 0-0
Aids: Bl: 0-0 Vi: 0-0 Tstrap: 0-0
Best Rating:

Macgeorge (IRE)

111 **151**
12-y-o b g Mandalus-Colleen Donn (Le Moss)
R Lee Mr & Mrs J H Watson

Placings:*443*/3215/**U5F1122/1U44111/126441/4PU2F/4-435163** (4661)
2001/02: 26^{4}G, 22^{3}G, 24^{5}S, 26^{1}S, 29^{6}G, 25^{3}G

	Starts	1st	2nd	3rd	Win & Pl
Chases	6	1	0	2	13646
Career Total	**39**	**10**	**5**	**4**	**126507**

151	2/02	Wwck	3m2f	C(0-130)HCh	SFT	£7020
170	4/99	Aint	3m1f	A Ch	G-S	£38275
157	11/98	Wwck	3m2f	B(0-140)HCh	GD	£7236
147	3/98	Newb	3m	B HCh	G-S	£7726
145	3/98	Newb	3m	C(0-135)HCh	HVY	£7600
138	2/98	Leic	2m7f110y	C(0-130)HCh	GD	£5390
125	5/97	Worc	2m7f110y	E Ch	G-S	£3455
133	2/97	Leic	2m4f110y	E(0-115)HCh	G-F	£3179
128	1/97	Weth	2m4f110y	D(0-110)HCh	GD	£3480
116	2/96	Hayd	2m6f	D Hdl	HVY	£3263

Total win prize-money £86627

Going: Sf: 1-2 GS: 0-0 Gd: 0-4 GF: - Fm: 0-0
Distance: 2m/2m3: 0-0 2m4-2m7: 0-1 **3m+: 1-5**
Track: **LH: 1-6** RH: 0-0 Tight: 0-2 Gall: 0-1
Aids: Bl: 0-0 Vi: 0-0 Tstrap: 0-0
Best Rating: 170 4/99 Aint 3m1f gd-sft Ch

A useful chaser at his best, his greatest day came at Aintree in 1999 when he won the Martell Cup. He was off the track for 18 months and has run with credit since returning, including a win at Warwick in February 2002. Often let down by his jumping, he does not like being crowded and is consequently at his best in a small field. Stays three miles and acts on soft ground.

Machalini

109(88h) (103h)**119**
9-y-o b g Machiavellian (USA)-Trescalini (IRE) (Sadler's Wells (USA))
T R George Mr & Mrs D A Gamble

Placings:02F54/5**0232432411/15/6PP2P5315-3423336531** (1804)
2001/02: 27^{3}G, 26^{4}GF, 25^{2}G, 25^{3}GF, 23^{3}G, 25^{3}GF, 24^{6}G, 28^{5}GS, 25^{3}GF, 24^{1}GF

	Starts	1st	2nd	3rd	Win & Pl
Hurdles	1	0	0	0	0
Chases	9	1	1	5	7585
Career Total	**37**	**5**	**6**	**8**	**29344**

119	10/01	Ludl	3m	F(0-100)HCh	G-F	£3062
119	2/01	Muss	3m	F(0-95)HCh	GD	£3122
128	5/99	Ludl	3m	E(0-105)HCh	G-F	£4344
123	4/99	Ludl	2m4f	D(0-120)HCh	GD	£3850
110	4/99	Plum	2m2f	F Ch	GD	£2558

Total win prize-money £16939

Going: Sf: 0-0 GS: 0-1 Gd: 0-4 GF: - Fm: 1-5
Distance: 2m/2m3: 0-0 2m4-2m7: 0-0 **3m+: 1-10**
Track: LH: 0-4 **RH: 1-6 Tight: 1-6** Gall: 0-1
Aids: Bl: 0-0 Vi: 0-1 Tstrap: 0-0
Best Rating: 128 5/99 Ludl 3m gd-fm Ch

Effective handicap chaser over three miles on fast ground, suited by a sharp track.

Machete Man

7-y-o b g Broadsword (USA)-Ribo Melody (Riboboy (USA))
P R Webber J G Phillips

Placings:*45*-F (1914)
2001/02: 16^{F}G

	Starts	1st	2nd	3rd	Win & Pl
Chases	1	0	0	0	
Career Total	**3**	**0**	**0**	**0**	**0**

Going: Sf: 0-0 GS: 0-0 Gd: 0-1 GF: - Fm: 0-0
Distance: 2m/2m3: 0-1 2m4-2m7: 0-0 3m+: 0-0
Track: LH: 0-1 RH: 0-0 Tight: 0-0 Gall: 0-0
Aids: Bl: 0-0 Vi: 0-0 Tstrap: 0-0
Best Rating: 93 11/00 Towc 2m soft NHF

Half-brother to the staying hurdler, Melody Maid.

Machrie Bay

95 **104**
5-y-o b g Emarati (USA)-Fleeting Rainbow (Rainbow Quest (USA))
Miss E C Lavelle Mrs R J Lavelle

Placings:023-24 (1029)
2001/02: 16^{2}GF, 19^{4}G

	Starts	1st	2nd	3rd	Win & Pl
Hurdles	2	0	1	0	694
Career Total	**5**	**0**	**2**	**1**	**1808**

Going: Sf: 0-0 GS: 0-0 Gd: 0-1 GF: - Fm: 0-1
Distance: 2m/2m3: 0-2 2m4-2m7: 0-0 3m+: 0-0
Track: LH: 0-1 RH: 0-1 Tight: 0-1 Gall: 0-1
Aids: Bl: 0-0 Vi: 0-0 Tstrap: 0-0
Best Rating: 105 3/01 Hntg 2m110y soft Hdl

Macintosh (NZ)

82 **53**
10-y-o gr g Straight Strike (USA)-Arctic Frost (Arctic Tern (USA))
N B Mason N B Mason

Placings:00/P4261600-000 (1347)
2001/02: 16^{0}GF, 17^{0}G, 17^{0}GF

	Starts	1st	2nd	3rd	Win & Pl
Hurdles	3	0	0	0	
Career Total	**13**	**1**	**1**	**0**	**2147**

79	10/00	Sedg	2m1f	G(0-90)HHdl	G-S	£1704

Total win prize-money £1705

Going: Sf: 0-0 GS: 0-0 Gd: 0-1 GF: - Fm: 0-2
Distance: 2m/2m3: 0-3 2m4-2m7: 0-0 3m+: 0-0
Track: LH: 0-3 RH: 0-0 Tight: 0-2 Gall: 0-0
Aids: Bl: 0-3 Vi: 0-0 Tstrap: 0-3
Best Rating: 88 3/00 Bang 2m1f good Hdl

Mackenzie (IRE)

90 **82**
6-y-o b g Mandalus-Crinkle Lady (Buckskin (FR))
Miss Lucinda V Russell Mrs C J Kerr

Placings:*4435* (4522)
2001/02: 16^{4}GS, 20^{4}HY, 16^{3}HY, 17^{5}G

	Starts	1st	2nd	3rd	Win & Pl
NH Flat	1	0	0	0	0
Hurdles	3	0	0	1	354
Career Total	**4**	**0**	**0**	**1**	**354**

Going: Sf: 0-2 GS: 0-1 Gd: 0-1 GF: - Fm: 0-0
Distance: 2m/2m3: 0-3 2m4-2m7: 0-1 3m+: 0-0
Track: LH: 0-3 RH: 0-1 Tight: 0-0 Gall: 0-0
Aids: Bl: 0-0 Vi: 0-0 Tstrap: 0-0
Best Rating: 96 11/01 Ayr 2m gd-sft NHF

Needs to learn to settle over hurdles. He looks like a staying chaser type.

Macnance (IRE)

106 **101**
6-y-o b m Mandalus-Colleen Donn (Le Moss)
R Lee Mrs Keith Lowry

Placings:26 (3874)
2001/02: 16^{2}S, 16^{6}S

	Starts	1st	2nd	3rd	Win & Pl
Hurdles	2	0	1	0	908
Career Total	**2**	**0**	**1**	**0**	**908**

Going: Sf: 0-2 GS: 0-0 Gd: 0-0 GF: - Fm: 0-0
Distance: 2m/2m3: 0-2 2m4-2m7: 0-0 3m+: 0-0
Track: LH: 0-0 RH: 0-2 Tight: 0-0 Gall: 0-1
Aids: Bl: 0-0 Vi: 0-0 Tstrap: 0-0
Best Rating: 95 2/02 Hntg 2m110y soft Hdl

Acts on soft ground and is effective over two miles.

Maconnor (IRE)

92f **75f**
5-y-o b g Religiously (USA)-Door Belle (Fidel)
H D Daly Daniel O'Connor

Placings:0 (4166)
2001/02: 16^{0}GS

	Starts	1st	2nd	3rd	Win & Pl
NH Flat	1	0	0	0	
Career Total	**1**	**0**	**0**	**0**	

Going: Sf: 0-0 GS: 0-1 Gd: 0-0 GF: - Fm: 0-0
Distance: 2m/2m3: 0-1 2m4-2m7: 0-0 3m+: 0-0
Track: LH: 0-1 RH: 0-0 Tight: 0-0 Gall: 0-0
Aids: Bl: 0-0 Vi: 0-0 Tstrap: 0-0
Best Rating: 75 3/02 Wwck 2m gd-sft NHF

Macrobert's Reply (IRE)

6-y-o ch g Phardante (FR)-Koshear (Hardgreen (USA))
P F Nicholls Old Moss Farm

Placings: *0-0* (4586)
2001/02: 22^{0}G

	Starts	1st	2nd	3rd	Win & Pl
Hurdles	1	0	0	0	
Career Total	2	0	0	0	

Going: Sf: 0-0 GS: 0-0 Gd: 0-1 GF: - Fm: 0-0
Distance: 2m/2m3: 0-0 2m4-2m7: 0-1 3m+: 0-0
Track: LH: 0-0 RH: 0-1 Tight: 0-0 Gall: 0-0
Aids: Bl: 0-0 Vi: 0-0 Tstrap: 0-0
Best Rating: 5 4/01 Fair 2m yld-sft NHF

Macy (IRE)

93 79
9-y-o ch g Sharp Charter-Lumax (Maximilian)
R Dickin Mrs M Payne

Placings: *1440/23416P/4P5F4046P/FF3040/3536-60* (0828)
2001/02: 20^{6}GF, 24^{0}GF

	Starts	1st	2nd	3rd	Win & Pl		
Chases	2	0	0	0	0		
Career Total	31	2	1	4	6341		
99	12/97	Wwck	2m3f	E(0-105)HHdl	SFT	£2713	
69	2/97	Font	2m2f	H NHF	G-F	£1213	

Total win prize-money £3927

Going: Sf: 0-0 GS: 0-0 Gd: 0-0 GF: - Fm: 0-2
Distance: 2m/2m3: 0-0 2m4-2m7: 0-1 3m+: 0-1
Track: LH: 0-2 RH: 0-0 Tight: 0-0 Gall: 0-0
Aids: Bl: 0-0 Vi: 0-0 Tstrap: 0-0
Best Rating: 105 11/00 Wwck 2m soft Ch

Mad Jack

7-y-o b g Mazaad-Glazepta Final (Final Straw)
Ronald Thompson Haggswood Partnerships

Placings: *00/P* (0451)
2001/02: 23^{P}F

	Starts	1st	2nd	3rd	Win & Pl
Hurdles	1	0	0	0	
Career Total	3	0	0	0	

Going: Sf: 0-0 GS: 0-0 Gd: 0-0 GF: - Fm: 0-1
Distance: 2m/2m3: 0-0 2m4-2m7: 0-1 3m+: 0-0
Track: LH: 0-1 RH: 0-0 Tight: 0-0 Gall: 0-0
Aids: Bl: 0-0 Vi: 0-0 Tstrap: 0-0
Best Rating: 65 1/00 Donc 2m110y gd-fm NHF

Madam Flora

102 92
5-y-o b m Alflora (IRE)-Madam's Choice (New Member)
M J Weeden T J Swaffield

Placings: *30-36230* (4420)
2001/02: 17^{3}GF, 20^{6}GS, 16^{2}GS, 19^{3}HY, 21^{0}GS

	Starts	1st	2nd	3rd	Win & Pl
NH Flat	1	0	0	1	253
Hurdles	4	0	1	1	1441
Career Total	7	0	1	3	1941

Going: Sf: 0-1 GS: 0-3 Gd: 0-0 GF: - Fm: 0-1
Distance: 2m/2m3: 0-2 2m4-2m7: 0-3 3m+: 0-0
Track: LH: 0-2 RH: 0-3 Tight: 0-0 Gall: 0-1
Aids: Bl: 0-0 Vi: 0-0 Tstrap: 0-0
Best Rating: 99 11/01 Extr 2m1f gd-fm NHF

Modest novice, placed in bumpers and over hurdles. Acts on soft.

Madam Gunner

70f 21f
7-y-o ch m Gunner B-Head Lass (Funny Man)
R N Bevis J E Stockton

Placings: *00* (1858)
2001/02: 17^{0}G, 17^{0}S

	Starts	1st	2nd	3rd	Win & Pl
NH Flat	2	0	0	0	
Career Total	2	0	0	0	

Going: Sf: 0-1 GS: 0-0 Gd: 0-1 GF: - Fm: 0-0
Distance: 2m/2m3: 0-2 2m4-2m7: 0-0 3m+: 0-0
Track: LH: 0-2 RH: 0-0 Tight: 0-2 Gall: 0-0
Aids: Bl: 0-0 Vi: 0-0 Tstrap: 0-0
Best Rating: 21 10/01 Bang 2m1f good NHF

Madam Karinga

75f 44f
4-y-o ch f Karinga Bay-Last Shower (Town And Country)
J Gallagher Mrs D P Williams & Mr G H Williams

Placings: *00* (4539)
2001/02: 16^{0}S, 16^{0}G

	Starts	1st	2nd	3rd	Win & Pl
NH Flat	2	0	0	0	
Career Total	2	0	0	0	

Going: Sf: 0-1 GS: 0-0 Gd: 0-1 GF: - Fm: 0-0
Distance: 2m/2m3: 0-2 2m4-2m7: 0-0 3m+: 0-0
Track: LH: 0-1 RH: 0-1 Tight: 0-1 Gall: 0-0
Aids: Bl: 0-0 Vi: 0-0 Tstrap: 0-0
Best Rating: 44 4/02 Fknm 2m good NHF

Madam Mosso

105 95+
6-y-o b m Le Moss-Rochestown Lass (Deep Run)
Mrs A M Thorpe Mrs A M Thorpe

Placings: *0* (3811)
2001/02: 18^{0}S

	Starts	1st	2nd	3rd	Win & Pl
NH Flat	1	0	0	0	
Career Total	1	0	0	0	

Going: Sf: 0-1 GS: 0-0 Gd: 0-0 GF: - Fm: 0-0
Distance: 2m/2m3: 0-1 2m4-2m7: 0-0 3m+: 0-0
Track: LH: 0-1 RH: 0-0 Tight: 0-1 Gall: 0-0
Aids: Bl: 0-0 Vi: 0-0 Tstrap: 0-0
Best Rating: 44 2/02 Font 2m2f110y soft NHF

Won poor 3 mile maiden hurdle at Uttoxeter in heavy ground June 2002. Appears suited by some give underfoot.

Madam's Man

111 106
6-y-o b g Sir Harry Lewis (USA)-Madam-M (Tina's Pet)
N A Twiston-Davies H R Mould

Placings: *000223* (4874)
2001/02: 16^{0}G, 16^{0}G, 16^{0}S, 25^{2}GS, 24^{2}GS, 20^{3}G

	Starts	1st	2nd	3rd	Win & Pl
NH Flat	2	0	0	0	0
Hurdles	4	0	2	1	2318
Career Total	6	0	2	1	2318

Going: Sf: 0-1 GS: 0-2 Gd: 0-3 GF: - Fm: 0-0
Distance: 2m/2m3: 0-3 2m4-2m7: 0-1 3m+: 0-2
Track: LH: 0-2 RH: 0-3 Tight: 0-0 Gall: 0-0
Aids: Bl: 0-0 Vi: 0-0 Tstrap: 0-0
Best Rating: 106 3/02 Wwck 3m1f gd-sft Hdl

Defied top weight to win a three mile novices handicap hurdle at Worcester June 2002.

Madame Derry

10-y-o ch m Derrylin-Teletex (Pollerton)
Mrs K Lundberg-Young Mrs Kin Lundberg-Young

Placings: *0* (2411)
2001/02: 19^{0}GS

	Starts	1st	2nd	3rd	Win & Pl
Hurdles	1	0	0	0	
Career Total	1	0	0	0	

Going: Sf: 0-0 GS: 0-1 Gd: 0-0 GF: - Fm: 0-0
Distance: 2m/2m3: 0-0 2m4-2m7: 0-1 3m+: 0-0
Track: LH: 0-0 RH: 0-1 Tight: 0-1 Gall: 0-0
Aids: Bl: 0-0 Vi: 0-0 Tstrap: 0-0
Best Rating:

Madame La Claire

(75h) (36h)
9-y-o ch m Superlativo-Tyrian Princess (Comedy Star (USA))
H Alexander (J Parkes 19/5) Miss A M Rees

Placings: *00P* (2554)
2001/02: 21^{0}G, 25^{0}G, 24^{P}S

	Starts	1st	2nd	3rd	Win & Pl
Hurdles	2	0	0	0	0
Chases	1	0	0	0	0
Career Total	3	0	0	0	

Going: Sf: 0-1 GS: 0-0 Gd: 0-2 GF: - Fm: 0-0
Distance: 2m/2m3: 0-0 2m4-2m7: 0-1 3m+: 0-2
Track: LH: 0-2 RH: 0-0 Tight: 0-2 Gall: 0-0
Aids: Bl: 0-0 Vi: 0-0 Tstrap: 0-0
Best Rating: 36 5/01 Sedg 2m5f110y good Hdl

Madame Poulet

84f 70f
6-y-o gr m Gold Dust-Came Cottage (Nearly A Hand)
N R Mitchell Mrs E Mitchell

Placings: *0* (0078)
2001/02: 17^{0}G

	Starts	1st	2nd	3rd	Win & Pl
NH Flat	1	0	0	0	
Career Total	1	0	0	0	

Going: Sf: 0-0 GS: 0-0 Gd: 0-1 GF: - Fm: 0-0
Distance: 2m/2m3: 0-1 2m4-2m7: 0-0 3m+: 0-0
Track: LH: 0-0 RH: 0-1 Tight: 0-0 Gall: 0-0
Aids: Bl: 0-0 Vi: 0-0 Tstrap: 0-0
Best Rating: 70 5/01 Extr 2m1f good NHF

Maddy's Supreme (IRE)

100 92
6-y-o b m Supreme Leader-Shannon Lough (IRE) (Deep Run)
T D Easterby J Henderson (co Durham)

Placings: *05223* (4520)

2001/02: 16^{0}G, 16^{5}S, 17^{2}S, 21^{2}S, 20^{3}G

	Starts	1st	2nd	3rd	Win & Pl
NH Flat	1	0	0	0	0
Hurdles	4	0	2	1	1935
Career Total	**5**	**0**	**2**	**1**	**1935**

Going: Sf: 0-3 GS: 0-0 Gd: 0-2 GF: - Fm: 0-0
Distance: 2m/2m3: 0-3 2m4-2m7: 0-2 3m+: 0-0
Track: LH: 0-4 RH: 0-0 Tight: 0-2 Gall: 0-1
Aids: Bl: 0-0 Vi: 0-0 Tstrap: 0-0
Best Rating: 92 3/02 Sedg 2m5f110y soft Hdl

Placed in modest company in novice hurdles. Stays two and a half miles plus, handles good and soft ground.

Made To Measure (IRE)

66 19

8-y-o b g Macmillion-Bethena Blue (Blue Rullah)
J C Fox Shirley M & Peter G Palmer

Placings:P00 **(2429)**
2001/02: 22^{P}S, 19^{0}G, 24^{0}G

	Starts	1st	2nd	3rd	Win & Pl
Hurdles	3	0	0	0	
Career Total	**3**	**0**	**0**	**0**	

Going: Sf: 0-1 GS: 0-0 Gd: 0-2 GF: - Fm: 0-0
Distance: 2m/2m3: 0-1 2m4-2m7: 0-1 3m+: 0-1
Track: LH: 0-3 RH: 0-0 Tight: 0-1 Gall: 0-2
Aids: Bl: 0-0 Vi: 0-0 Tstrap: 0-0
Best Rating: 19 11/01 Newb 2m3f good Hdl

Moderate ability shown so far.

Madforit

4-y-o b g Prince Sabo-Elusive (Little Current (USA))
M J Roberts Mike Roberts

Placings:4 **(4784)**
2001/02: 18^{4}GF

	Starts	1st	2nd	3rd	Win & Pl
NH Flat	1	0	0	0	0
Career Total	**1**	**0**	**0**	**0**	**0**

Going: Sf: 0-0 GS: 0-0 Gd: 0-0 GF: - Fm: 0-1
Distance: 2m/2m3: 0-1 2m4-2m7: 0-0 3m+: 0-0
Track: LH: 0-0 RH: 0-0 Tight: 0-0 Gall: 0-0
Aids: Bl: 0-0 Vi: 0-0 Tstrap: 0-0
Best Rating:

Madhaze (IRE)

96 88

11-y-o ch g Zaffaran (USA)-Canhaar (Sparkler)
A E Jones Mrs L P Green

Placings:2/0P4P **(4886)**
2001/02: 24^{0}G, 22^{P}S, 20^{4}GF, 18^{P}GF

	Starts	1st	2nd	3rd	Win & Pl
Hurdles	1	0	0	0	0
Chases	3	0	0	0	197
Career Total	**5**	**0**	**1**	**0**	**582**

Going: Sf: 0-1 GS: 0-0 Gd: 0-1 GF: - Fm: 0-2
Distance: 2m/2m3: 0-1 2m4-2m7: 0-2 3m+: 0-1
Track: LH: 0-2 RH: 0-0 Tight: 0-3 Gall: 0-1
Aids: Bl: 0-0 Vi: 0-0 Tstrap: 0-0
Best Rating: 100 9/96 Worc 2m gd-fm NHF

Very lightly raced, seems best on fast ground.

Madmidge

57f 33f

7-y-o b/br g Jendali (USA)-No Rejection (Mummy's Pet)
Mrs S Lamyman Exors Of The Late A Snipe

Placings:*0-0* **(0239)**
2001/02: 16^{0}GF

	Starts	1st	2nd	3rd	Win & Pl
NH Flat	1	0	0	0	
Career Total	**2**	**0**	**0**	**0**	

Going: Sf: 0-0 GS: 0-0 Gd: 0-0 GF: - Fm: 0-1
Distance: 2m/2m3: 0-1 2m4-2m7: 0-0 3m+: 0-0
Track: LH: 0-1 RH: 0-0 Tight: 0-1 Gall: 0-0
Aids: Bl: 0-0 Vi: 0-0 Tstrap: 0-0
Best Rating: 33 4/01 MRas 2m1f110y heavy NHF

Maenad

11-y-o gr m Sharrood (USA)-Now In Session (USA) (Diesis)
K A Nelmes K A Nelmes

Placings:*02300/P/0/0P* **(4483)**
2001/02: 21^{0}G, 19^{P}G

	Starts	1st	2nd	3rd	Win & Pl
Chases	2	0	0	0	
Career Total	**9**	**0**	**1**	**1**	**516**

Going: Sf: 0-0 GS: 0-0 Gd: 0-2 GF: - Fm: 0-0
Distance: 2m/2m3: 0-0 2m4-2m7: 0-2 3m+: 0-0
Track: LH: 0-0 RH: 0-2 Tight: 0-1 Gall: 0-0
Aids: Bl: 0-0 Vi: 0-0 Tstrap: 0-0
Best Rating: 84 11/95 Folk 2m1f110y gd-fm NHF

Magenko (IRE)

96 88

5-y-o ch g Forest Wind (USA)-Bebe Auction (IRE) (Auction Ring (USA))
F P Murtagh R & J Wharton

Placings:604440-3030340401 **(4917)**
2001/02: 21^{3}G, 20^{0}S, 17^{3}S, 18^{0}GS, 17^{3}HY, 17^{4}S, 17^{0}S, 20^{4}HY, 16^{0}F, 21^{1}GF

	Starts	1st	2nd	3rd	Win & Pl
Hurdles	10	1	0	3	9768
Career Total	**16**	**1**	**0**	**3**	**10006**

88 4/02 Sedg 2m5f110y G HHdl G-F £8209
Total win prize-money £8210

Going: Sf: 0-6 GS: 0-1 Gd: 0-1 GF: - Fm: 1-2
Distance: 2m/2m3: 0-6 **2m4-2m7: 1-4** 3m+: 0-0
Track: **LH: 1-9** RH: 0-0 **Tight: 1-7** Gall: 0-2
Aids: Bl: 0-2 Vi: 0-0 Tstrap: 0-0
Best Rating: 88 4/02 Sedg 2m5f110y gd-fm Hdl

Broke his duck at the 16th attempt when landing a valuable selling handicap hurdle at Sedgefield in April.

Maggie's Pet

78 63

5-y-o b m Minshaanshu Amad (USA)-Run Fast For Gold (Deep Run)
G M McCourt Len Purdy

Placings:*500P* **(3234)**
2001/02: 17^{5}S, 17^{0}GF, 16^{0}G, 16^{P}GS

	Starts	1st	2nd	3rd	Win & Pl
NH Flat	2	0	0	0	0
Hurdles	2	0	0	0	0
Career Total	**4**	**0**	**0**	**0**	**0**

Going: Sf: 0-1 GS: 0-1 Gd: 0-1 GF: - Fm: 0-1
Distance: 2m/2m3: 0-4 2m4-2m7: 0-0 3m+: 0-0
Track: LH: 0-0 RH: 0-4 Tight: 0-1 Gall: 0-1
Aids: Bl: 0-0 Vi: 0-0 Tstrap: 0-0
Best Rating: 84 11/01 Extr 2m1f gd-fm NHF

Maggies Brother

9-y-o b g Brotherly (USA)-Sallisses (Pamroy)
Mrs G M Shail (R Shail 3/2) Mrs G M Shail

Placings:PF-52 **(4755)**
2001/02: 24^{5}GF, 23^{2}GF

	Starts	1st	2nd	3rd	Win & Pl
Chases	2	0	1	0	466
Career Total	**4**	**0**	**1**	**0**	**466**

Going: Sf: 0-0 GS: 0-0 Gd: 0-0 GF: - Fm: 0-2
Distance: 2m/2m3: 0-0 2m4-2m7: 0-1 3m+: 0-1
Track: LH: 0-1 RH: 0-1 Tight: 0-0 Gall: 0-1
Aids: Bl: 0-0 Vi: 0-0 Tstrap: 0-0
Best Rating: 84 4/02 Uttx 2m7f gd-fm Ch

Winning pointer/hunter chaser over three miles, acts on most types of ground.

Magic Amour

4-y-o ch g Sanglamore (USA)-Rakli (Warning)
Ian Williams Mrs Maggie Bull

Placings:*00* **(4032)**
2001/02: 16^{0}GS, 16^{0}GS

	Starts	1st	2nd	3rd	Win & Pl
NH Flat	2	0	0	0	
Career Total	**2**	**0**	**0**	**0**	

Going: Sf: 0-0 GS: 0-2 Gd: 0-0 GF: - Fm: 0-0
Distance: 2m/2m3: 0-2 2m4-2m7: 0-0 3m+: 0-0
Track: LH: 0-1 RH: 0-1 Tight: 0-0 Gall: 0-2
Aids: Bl: 0-0 Vi: 0-0 Tstrap: 0-0
Best Rating:

Magic Box

95 88+

4-y-o b g Magic Ring (IRE)-Princess Poquito (Hard Fought)
Miss Kate Milligan (A P Jarvis 2/9) R A W Racing

Placings:4030 **(3352)**
2001/02: 16^{4}G, 16^{0}S, 16^{3}G, 20^{0}G

	Starts	1st	2nd	3rd	Win & Pl
Hurdles	4	0	0	1	333
Career Total	**4**	**0**	**0**	**1**	**333**

Going: Sf: 0-1 GS: 0-0 Gd: 0-3 GF: - Fm: 0-0
Distance: 2m/2m3: 0-3 2m4-2m7: 0-1 3m+: 0-0
Track: LH: 0-3 RH: 0-1 Tight: 0-2 Gall: 0-1
Aids: Bl: 0-0 Vi: 0-0 Tstrap: 0-0
Best Rating: 73 12/01 Donc 2m110y good Hdl

A keen sort over hurdles, he had been previously beaten in selling company before taking a conditional jockeys' event at Sedgefield in July 2002. Suited by trips around two miles on fast ground.

Magic Circle (FR)

91 83

10-y-o b g Bering-Lucky Round (Auction Ring (USA))

P W Hiatt Sovereign Racing

Placings:5/5/1/524/P-P5P (0667)

2001/02: 17^{P}GS, 20^{5}G, 20^{P}G

	Starts	1st	2nd	3rd	Win & Pl
Chases	3	0	0	0	0
Career Total	**10**	**1**	**1**	**0**	**4203**

5/97	Navn	2m	NHF	Y-S	£3051

Total win prize-money £3052

Going: Sf: 0-0 GS: 0-1 Gd: 0-2 GF: - Fm: 0-0
Distance: 2m/2m3: 0-1 2m4-2m7: 0-2 3m+: 0-0
Track: LH: 0-2 RH: 0-1 Tight: 0-2 Gall: 0-0
Aids: Bl: 0-0 Vi: 0-0 Tstrap: 0-0
Best Rating: 118 12/98 Kemp 2m gd-sft Hdl

Magic Combination (IRE)

115 138

9-y-o b g Scenic-Etage (Ile De Bourbon (USA))

L Lungo Sw Transport (swindon) Ltd & R J Gilbert

Placings:630/P/1U1/P10/0500-01102005 (4393)

2001/02: 16^{0}G, 19^{1}G, 17^{1}GS, 16^{0}G, 16^{2}S, 20^{0}S, 23^{0}HY, 18^{5}HY

	Starts	1st	2nd	3rd	Win & Pl
Hurdles	8	2	1	0	33499
Career Total	**22**	**5**	**1**	**1**	**61631**

138	7/01	MRas	2m1f110y	B(0-140)HHdl	G-S	£20065
135	5/01	MRas	2m3f110y	C(0-130)HHdl	GD	£5772
129	3/00	Sand	2m110y	B HHdl	GD	£21450
130	2/99	Asct	2m4f	E(0-120)HHdl	G-S	£3550
113	1/99	Kemp	2m5f	E(0-110)HHdl	SFT	£2766

Total win prize money £53604

Going: Sf: 0-4 GS: 1-1 Gd: 1-3 GF: - Fm: 0-0
Distance: 2m/2m3: 1-5 2m4-2m7: 1-2 3m+: 0-1
Track: LH: 0-5 **RH: 1-1 Tight: 1-2** Gall: 0-0
Aids: Bl: 0-0 Vi: 0-0 Tstrap: 0-0
Best Rating: 138 11/01 DRoy 2m soft Hdl

A smart hurdler and winner of the Imperial Cup in the 1999/2000 season, he is nothing like as good as he was, but does pop up from time to time.

Magic Dancer (IRE)

107 122

9-y-o b g Carefree Dancer (USA)-Giveushope (Whistling Deer)

Capt J A George (P J Hobbs 29/11) Captain & Mrs J A George

Placings:20206046/66/62110621/222P60-4B5345 (4532)

2001/02: 25^{4}F, 25^{B}GF, 23^{5}GF, 27^{3}GS, 25^{4}S, 26^{5}GS

	Starts	1st	2nd	3rd	Win & Pl
Chases	6	0	0	1	1413
Career Total	**30**	**3**	**7**	**1**	**27664**

128	4/00	Asct	3m110y	B Ch	SFT	£10946
119	1/00	Hntg	2m5f110y	D(0-120)HHdl	G-S	£3178
118	12/99	Extr	2m3f110y	D(0-110)HHdl	G-S	£3168

Total win prize-money £17293

Going: Sf: 0-1 GS: 0-2 Gd: 0-0 GF: - Fm: 0-3
Distance: 2m/2m3: 0-0 2m4-2m7: 0-0 3m+: 0-6
Track: LH: 0-1 RH: 0-3 Tight: 0-1 Gall: 0-0
Aids: Bl: 0-3 Vi: 0-1 Tstrap: 0-0
Best Rating: 137 11/00 Kemp 3m soft Ch

He is difficult to win with and a rather quirky sort. He stays three miles but is not one to place much faith in.

Magic Feathers

92 62

4-y-o b g Anabaa (USA)-Plume Magique (Kenmare (FR))

M E Sowersby A Milner

Placings:U0PPP0P (4871)

2001/02: 17^{U}GS, 16^{0}S, 20^{P}S, 17^{P}GS, 24^{P}HY, 23^{0}G, 25^{P}GF

	Starts	1st	2nd	3rd	Win & Pl
Hurdles	7	0	0	0	
Career Total	**7**	**0**	**0**	**0**	

Going: Sf: 0-3 GS: 0-2 Gd: 0-1 GF: - Fm: 0-1
Distance: 2m/2m3: 0-3 2m4-2m7: 0-2 3m+: 0-2
Track: LH: 0-4 RH: 0-3 Tight: 0-3 Gall: 0-1
Aids: Bl: 0-0 Vi: 0-0 Tstrap: 0-0
Best Rating: 62 2/02 Muss 2m soft Hdl

Magic Of Sydney (IRE)

6-y-o b g Broken Hearted-Chat Her Up (Proverb)

R Rowe Ann & John Symes

Placings:06 (0000)

2001/02: 22^{0}G, 18^{6}HY

	Starts	1st	2nd	3rd	Win & Pl
Hurdles	2	0	0	0	0
Career Total	**2**	**0**	**0**	**0**	**0**

Going: Sf: 0-1 GS: 0-0 Gd: 0-1 GF: - Fm: 0-0
Distance: 2m/2m3: 0-1 2m4-2m7: 0-1 3m+: 0-0
Track: LH: 0-2 RH: 0-0 Tight: 0-2 Gall: 0-0
Aids: Bl: 0-0 Vi: 0-0 Tstrap: 0-0
Best Rating:

No sign of ability in two novice hurdles.

Magic Route (IRE)

5-y-o b g Mr Confusion (IRE)-Another Chapter (Respect)

J Howard Johnson Michael Thompson

Placings:0P (2117)

2001/02: 17^{0}G, 16^{P}GS

	Starts	1st	2nd	3rd	Win & Pl
NH Flat	1	0	0	0	0
Hurdles	1	0	0	0	0
Career Total	**2**	**0**	**0**	**0**	

Going: Sf: 0-0 GS: 0-1 Gd: 0-1 GF: - Fm: 0-0
Distance: 2m/2m3: 0-2 2m4-2m7: 0-0 3m+: 0-0
Track: LH: 0-2 RH: 0-0 Tight: 0-2 Gall: 0-0
Aids: Bl: 0-0 Vi: 0-0 Tstrap: 0-0
Best Rating:

Magic To Do (IRE)

102 87

4-y-o b g Spectrum (IRE)-Smouldering (IRE) (Caerleon (USA))

O Sherwood (R F Johnson Houghton 25/10) Antony Sofroniou

Placings:0040 (4417)

2001/02: 16^{0}GS, 16^{0}S, 20^{4}S, 16^{0}GS

	Starts	1st	2nd	3rd	Win & Pl
Hurdles	4	0	0	0	0
Career Total	**4**	**0**	**0**	**0**	**0**

Going: Sf: 0-2 GS: 0-2 Gd: 0-0 GF: - Fm: 0-0
Distance: 2m/2m3: 0-3 2m4-2m7: 0-1 3m+: 0-0
Track: LH: 0-2 RH: 0-1 Tight: 0-1 Gall: 0-2
Aids: Bl: 0-3 Vi: 0-0 Tstrap: 0-0
Best Rating: 76 3/02 Newb 2m110y gd-sft Hdl

Won a selling hurdle at Folkestone in May 2002.

Magic Waters

109 104

4-y-o b g Ezzoud (IRE)-Paradise Waters (Celestial Storm (USA))

T D Easterby D F Sills

Placings:251224P (3393)

2001/02: 16^{2}G, 16^{5}G, 16^{1}G, 16^{2}G, 16^{2}S, 16^{4}GS, 20^{P}GS

	Starts	1st	2nd	3rd	Win & Pl
Hurdles	7	1	3	0	6023
Career Total	**7**	**1**	**3**	**0**	**6023**

102	11/01	Newc	2m	E Hdl	GD	£2639

Total win prize-money £2639

Going: Sf: 0-1 GS: 0-2 Gd: 1-4 GF: - Fm: 0-0
Distance: **2m/2m3: 1-6** 2m4-2m7: 0-1 3m+: 0-0
Track: **LH: 1-7** RH: 0-0 Tight: 0-1 **Gall: 1-1**
Aids: **Bl: 1-5** Vi: 0-0 Tstrap: 0-0
Best Rating: 104 11/01 Weth 2m good Hdl

Second at Wetherby on his hurdling debut, he was a little disappointing stepped up to Listed class next time. He did redeem himself, however, when a winner at Newcastle in November on good ground. He will get further than two miles and can handle soft ground.

Magical Approach (IRE)

76 52

12-y-o ch g Callernish-Farm Approach (Tug Of War)

Giles Smyly Capt B D A Ridge

Placings:2FFB/F3231135/303023/03P010-0 (4135)

2001/02: 24^{0}G

	Starts	1st	2nd	3rd	Win & Pl
Chases	1	0	0	0	
Career Total	**25**	**3**	**3**	**7**	**30329**

124	2/01	Fair	2m4f	(0-116)HCh	HVY	£5564
124	2/99	Punc	3m2f	HCh	HVY	£8671
121	1/99	Gowr	2m4f	(0-116)HCh	SFT	£3683

Total win prize-money £17920

Going: Sf: 0-0 GS: 0-0 Gd: 0-1 GF: - Fm: 0-0
Distance: 2m/2m3: 0-0 2m4-2m7: 0-0 3m+: 0-1
Track: LH: 0-0 RH: 0-1 Tight: 0-0 Gall: 0-0
Aids: Bl: 0-0 Vi: 0-0 Tstrap: 0-0
Best Rating: 127 2/00 Punc 3m2f soft Ch

Magical Bailiwick (IRE)

109 105

6-y-o ch g Magical Wonder (USA)-Alpine Dance (USA) (Apalachee (USA))

R J Baker Islands Racing Connection

Placings:0530P-15P362505 (4500)

2001/02: 17^{1}S, 17^{5}G, 17^{P}GS, 17^{3}G, 20^{6}S, 17^{2}HY, 19^{5}S, 16^{0}GS, 17^{5}G

	Starts	1st	2nd	3rd	Win & Pl
Hurdles	9	1	1	1	4294
Career Total	**14**	**1**	**1**	**2**	**4778**

93	11/01	NAbb	2m1f	E Hdl	SFT	£2968

Total win prize-money £2968

Going: Sf: 1-4 GS: 0-2 Gd: 0-3 GF: - Fm: 0-0
Distance: 2m/2m3: 1-7 2m4-2m7: 0-2 3m+: 0-0
Track: LH: 1-4 RH: 0-5 Tight: 1-5 Gall: 0-1
Aids: Bl: 0-0 Vi: 0-0 Tstrap: 0-0
Best Rating: 108 1/01 Leic 2m heavy Hdl

Moderate hurdler. Effective over 17 furlongs. Acts on soft ground.

Magical Knight

79 **71**

4-y-o b g Sir Harry Lewis (USA)-Formal Affair (Rousillon (USA))
R T Phillips The Old Foresters Partnership

Placings:0 **(3460)**
2001/02: 16^{0}HY

	Starts	1st	2nd	3rd	Win & Pl
Hurdles	1	0	0	0	
Career Total	**1**	**0**	**0**	**0**	

Going: Sf: 0-1 GS: 0-0 Gd: 0-0 GF: - Fm: 0-0
Distance: 2m/2m3: 0-1 2m4-2m7: 0-0 3m+: 0-0
Track: LH: 0-1 RH: 0-0 Tight: 0-0 Gall: 0-0
Aids: Bl: 0-0 Vi: 0-0 Tstrap: 0-0
Best Rating: 71 1/02 Wwck 2m heavy Hdl

Magique Etoile (IRE)

(98h) (72h)

6-y-o b m Magical Wonder (USA)-She's A Dancer (IRE) (Alzao (USA))
Dr J R J Naylor Gallery Racing

Placings:05/30-500 **(4601)**
2001/02: 17^{5}G, 16^{0}S, 16^{0}GF

	Starts	1st	2nd	3rd	Win & Pl
Hurdles	3	0	0	0	0
Career Total	**7**	**0**	**0**	**1**	**344**

Going: Sf: 0-1 GS: 0-0 Gd: 0-1 GF: - Fm: 0-1
Distance: 2m/2m3: 0-3 2m4-2m7: 0-0 3m+: 0-0
Track: LH: 0-1 RH: 0-2 Tight: 0-0 Gall: 0-0
Aids: Bl: 0-0 Vi: 0-0 Tstrap: 0-0
Best Rating: 77 9/00 Plum 2m gd-fm Hdl

Magnetic Storm (IRE)

101 **88**

9-y-o b g Glacial Storm (USA)-Glittering Moon (Proverb)
M Todhunter Mrs Carole Stephenson

Placings:0P050/P54-33UUP **(4905)**
2001/02: 16^{3}GS, 16^{3}S, 16^{U}S, 19^{U}G, 17^{P}GF

	Starts	1st	2nd	3rd	Win & Pl
Chases	5	0	0	2	890
Career Total	**13**	**0**	**0**	**2**	**1208**

Going: Sf: 0-2 GS: 0-1 Gd: 0-1 GF: - Fm: 0-1
Distance: 2m/2m3: 0-5 2m4-2m7: 0-0 3m+: 0-0
Track: LH: 0-4 RH: 0-1 Tight: 0-5 Gall: 0-0
Aids: Bl: 0-0 Vi: 0-0 Tstrap: 0-0
Best Rating: 88 11/01 Sedg 2m110y soft Ch

He produced his best piece of form when third in a two-mile chase at Sedgefield in November. He was running from a stone out of the handicap that day.

Magni Momenti

97 **72**

7-y-o b m King's Signet (USA)-Halka (Daring March)
B G Powell Ms J Kaye

Placings:46/06R0-P0R3R **(0773)**
2001/02: 22^{P}F, 17^{0}GF, 17^{R}G, 17^{3}G, 16^{R}GF

	Starts	1st	2nd	3rd	Win & Pl
Hurdles	5	0	0	1	340
Career Total	**11**	**0**	**0**	**1**	**340**

Going: Sf: 0-0 GS: 0-0 Gd: 0-2 GF: - Fm: 0-3
Distance: 2m/2m3: 0-4 2m4-2m7: 0-1 3m+: 0-0
Track: LH: 0-3 RH: 0-1 Tight: 0-3 Gall: 0-0
Aids: Bl: 0-0 Vi: 0-1 Tstrap: 0-0
Best Rating: 72 6/01 NAbb 2m1f good Hdl

Magnus (FR)

89 **101**

6-y-o b g Roakarad-Volcania (FR) (Neustrien (FR))
M C Pipe (J Ortet 1/11) D A Johnson

Placings:F11336-111150 **(4231)**
2001/02: 18^{1}VS, 20^{1}VS, 24^{1}VS, 20^{1}HO, 21^{5}GS, 21^{0}GS

	Starts	1st	2nd	3rd	Win & Pl
Hurdles	6	4	0	0	173618
Career Total	**12**	**6**	**0**	**2**	**199660**

11/01	Autl	2m4f110y	Hdl	HLD	£48497
11/01	Autl	3m	Hdl	VS	£67895
10/01	Autl	2m4f110y	Hdl	VS	£31038
9/01	Autl	2m2f	HHdl	VS	£26188
2/01	Pau	2m3f	Hdl	SFT	£8729
1/01	Pau	2m3f	Hdl	HVY	£5820

Total win prize-money £188167

Going: Sf: 0-0 GS: 0-2 Gd: 0-0 GF: - Fm: 0-0
Distance: 2m/2m3: 1-1 2m4-2m7: 2-4 3m+: 1-1
Track: LH: 2-4 RH: 0-0 Tight: 0-0 Gall: 0-2
Aids: Bl: 0-0 Vi: 0-0 Tstrap: 0-0
Best Rating: 101 3/02 Chel 2m5f gd-sft Hdl

A French import bought by David Johnson for FF3,500,000, he was a multiple Graded race winner in France and was bidding for a five-timer over hurdles when disappointing on his British debut at Newbury. He was subsequently found to have burst a blood-vessel.

Magslad

88 **48**

12-y-o ch g Jumbo Hirt (USA)-Welsh Diamond (High Top)
Ms Liz Harrison David Alan Harrison

Placings:0/111161P3/3/54/25/5/0 **(1640)**
2001/02: 26^{0}GS

	Starts	1st	2nd	3rd	Win & Pl
Chases	1	0	0	0	
Career Total	**16**	**5**	**1**	**2**	**12284**

114	12/95	Sedg	2m5f110y	E Hdl	GD	£2382
94	11/95	Sedg	2m5f110y	E Hdl	G-F	£2122
97	10/95	Sedg	2m1f110y	H NHF	G-F	£1611
102	10/95	Carl	2m1f	H NHF	G-F	£1203
94	10/95	Ludl	2m	H NHF	FRM	£1339

Total win prize-money £8659

Going: Sf: 0-0 GS: 0-1 Gd: 0-0 GF: - Fm: 0-0
Distance: 2m/2m3: 0-0 2m4-2m7: 0-0 3m+: 0-1
Track: LH: 0-0 RH: 0-1 Tight: 0-0 Gall: 0-0
Aids: Bl: 0-0 Vi: 0-0 Tstrap: 0-0
Best Rating: 117 11/97 Hayd 2m6f soft Hdl

Mahout (IRE)

79 **48**

6-y-o b g Teamster-Stripe (Bustino)
G M McCourt Mrs Kathy Stuart

Placings:60P-5 **(1359)**
2001/02: 16^{5}GF

	Starts	1st	2nd	3rd	Win & Pl
Hurdles	1	0	0	0	
Career Total	**4**	**0**	**0**	**0**	

Going: Sf: 0-0 GS: 0-0 Gd: 0-0 GF: - Fm: 0-1
Distance: 2m/2m3: 0-1 2m4-2m7: 0-0 3m+: 0-0
Track: LH: 0-1 RH: 0-0 Tight: 0-1 Gall: 0-0
Aids: Bl: 0-0 Vi: 0-0 Tstrap: 0-0
Best Rating: 89 9/00 Worc 2m gd-fm NHF

Maid To Love (IRE)

92 **84**

5-y-o ch m Petardia-Lomond Heights (IRE) (Lomond (USA))
M C Pipe (I A Wood 19/5) Sandicroft Stud Syndicate

Placings:2P0203P **(1728)**
2001/02: 17^{2}G, 16^{P}GF, 16^{0}G, 17^{2}GF, 18^{0}GF, 20^{3}GS, 19^{P}F

	Starts	1st	2nd	3rd	Win & Pl
Hurdles	7	0	2	1	1549
Career Total	**7**	**0**	**2**	**1**	**1549**

Going: Sf: 0-0 GS: 0-1 Gd: 0-2 GF: - Fm: 0-4
Distance: 2m/2m3: 0-5 2m4-2m7: 0-2 3m+: 0-0
Track: LH: 0-4 RH: 0-2 Tight: 0-4 Gall: 0-0
Aids: Bl: 0-0 Vi: 0-5 Tstrap: 0-0
Best Rating: 84 6/01 NAbb 2m1f good Hdl

Maid To Talk

91(96h) (62h)**73**

8-y-o b m Arctic Lord-Chatty Lass (Le Bavard (FR))
W S Coltherd S Coltherd

Placings:*00/*0P0-0P600P **(3350)**
2001/02: 22^{0}G, 22^{P}GS, 22^{6}GS, 22^{0}GS, 16^{0}GS, 20^{P}G

	Starts	1st	2nd	3rd	Win & Pl
Hurdles	6	0	0	0	0
Career Total	**11**	**0**	**0**	**0**	**0**

Going: Sf: 0-0 GS: 0-4 Gd: 0-2 GF: - Fm: 0-0
Distance: 2m/2m3: 0-1 2m4-2m7: 0-5 3m+: 0-0
Track: LH: 0-5 RH: 0-1 Tight: 0-5 Gall: 0-0
Aids: Bl: 0-0 Vi: 0-0 Tstrap: 0-6
Best Rating: 62 10/01 Kels 2m6f110y good Hdl

Maiden Flight (IRE)

97 **88**

6-y-o b m Jurado (USA)-Dream Of Money (IRE) (Good Thyne (USA))
P R Webber W S Watt

Placings:6-04 **(4881)**
2001/02: 17^{0}GS, 18^{4}GF

	Starts	1st	2nd	3rd	Win & Pl
NH Flat	1	0	0	0	0
Hurdles	1	0	0	0	0

	Starts	1st	2nd	3rd	Win & Pl
Career Total	3	0	0	0	0

Going: Sf: 0-0 GS: 0-1 Gd: 0-0 GF: - Fm: 0-1
Distance: 2m/2m3: 0-2 2m4-2m7: 0-0 3m+: 0-0
Track: LH: 0-2 RH: 0-0 Tight: 0-2 Gall: 0-0
Aids: Bl: 0-0 Vi: 0-0 Tstrap: 0-0
Best Rating: 93 4/01 Font 2m2f110y good NHF

Maidstone Magic (IRE)

96 66

7-y-o b g Balinger-Anyone's Fancy (Callernish)
J R Best F G Wilson

Placings:U5U (1673)
2001/02: 24^{U}GF, 16^{5}G, 16^{U}G

	Starts	1st	2nd	3rd	Win & Pl
Chases	3	0	0	0	0
Career Total	3	0	0	0	0

Going: Sf: 0-0 GS: 0-0 Gd: 0-2 GF: - Fm: 0-1
Distance: 2m/2m3: 0-2 2m4-2m7: 0-0 3m+: 0-1
Track: LH: 0-0 RH: 0-3 Tight: 0-1 Gall: 0-1
Aids: Bl: 0-0 Vi: 0-0 Tstrap: 0-0
Best Rating:

Maidstone Magnet (IRE)

82 42

8-y-o br g Distinctly North (USA)-Douriya (Brave Invader (USA))
J R Best F G Wilson

Placings:0P/PP5/P-P60 (1670)
2001/02: 24^{P}GF, 16^{6}G, 21^{0}G

	Starts	1st	2nd	3rd	Win & Pl
Chases	3	0	0	0	0
Career Total	9	0	0	0	0

Going: Sf: 0-0 GS: 0-0 Gd: 0-2 GF: - Fm: 0-1
Distance: 2m/2m3: 0-1 2m4-2m7: 0-1 3m+: 0-1
Track: LH: 0-0 RH: 0-3 Tight: 0-1 Gall: 0-1
Aids: Bl: 0-0 Vi: 0-0 Tstrap: 0-0
Best Rating: 67 6/99 NAbb 2m5f110y good Ch

Little sign of ability.

Maidstone Mighty

102 95

6-y-o b g Sir Harry Lewis (USA)-Letterewe (Alias Smith (USA))
D M Grissell F G Wilson

Placings:0332 (3816)
2001/02: 18^{0}GS, 17^{3}S, 22^{3}HY, 22^{2}S

	Starts	1st	2nd	3rd	Win & Pl
NH Flat	1	0	0	0	0
Hurdles	3	0	1	2	1502
Career Total	4	0	1	2	1502

Going: Sf: 0-3 GS: 0-1 Gd: 0-0 GF: - Fm: 0-0
Distance: 2m/2m3: 0-2 2m4-2m7: 0-2 3m+: 0-0
Track: LH: 0-0 RH: 0-3 Tight: 0-3 Gall: 0-0
Aids: Bl: 0-0 Vi: 0-0 Tstrap: 0-0
Best Rating: 95 2/02 Folk 2m6f110y soft Hdl

Shaped with promise over hurdles on third start in the mud. Looked as if further than this extended two miles six would suit.

Maidstone Monarch (IRE)

98 72

9-y-o b/br g King's Ride-Curragh Breeze (Furry Glen)
J R Best F G Wilson

Placings:3/00P6/P30455P3-0P (0362)
2001/02: 16^{0}G, 24^{P}GF

	Starts	1st	2nd	3rd	Win & Pl
Chases	2	0	0	0	
Career Total	15	0	0	3	2173

Going: Sf: 0-0 GS: 0-0 Gd: 0-1 GF: - Fm: 0-1
Distance: 2m/2m3: 0-1 2m4-2m7: 0-0 3m+: 0-1
Track: LH: 0-1 RH: 0-1 Tight: 0-2 Gall: 0-0
Aids: Bl: 0-0 Vi: 0-0 Tstrap: 0-0
Best Rating: 94 1/98 Font 2m2f soft NHF

Maidstone Monument (IRE)

109(86h) (53h)111

7-y-o b g Jurado (USA)-Loreto Lady (Brave Invader (USA))
Mrs A M Thorpe (J R Best 7/5) Don Jenkins

Placings:50/P24153PP0-P06053432P (1403)
2001/02: 16^{P}S, 17^{0}GS, 21^{6}GS, 16^{0}GF, 20^{5}GF, 21^{3}G, 24^{4}GF, 21^{3}GF, 26^{2}GF, 24^{P}G

	Starts	1st	2nd	3rd	Win & Pl
Hurdles	3	0	0	0	0
Chases	7	0	1	2	2170
Career Total	21	1	2	3	6779

85 6/00 Hexm 2m D Hdl G-F £3143
Total win prize-money £3143

Going: Sf: 0-1 GS: 0-2 Gd: 0-2 GF: - Fm: 0-5
Distance: 2m/2m3: 0-3 2m4-2m7: 0-4 3m+: 0-3
Track: LH: 0-9 RH: 0-1 Tight: 0-10 Gall: 0-0
Aids: Bl: 0-1 Vi: 0-0 Tstrap: 0-0
Best Rating: 101 9/01 NAbb 3m2f110y gd-fm Ch

Modest chaser, stays well but lacks a turn of foot.

Maidwell

6-y-o b m Broadsword (USA)-Blakeney Sound (Blakeney)
Graham Smith Run For Fun

Placings:0 (1832)
2001/02: 16^{0}G

	Starts	1st	2nd	3rd	Win & Pl
NH Flat	1	0	0	0	
Career Total	1	0	0	0	

Going: Sf: 0-0 GS: 0-0 Gd: 0-1 GF: - Fm: 0-0
Distance: 2m/2m3: 0-1 2m4-2m7: 0-0 3m+: 0-0
Track: LH: 0-1 RH: 0-0 Tight: 0-1 Gall: 0-0
Aids: Bl: 0-0 Vi: 0-0 Tstrap: 0-0
Best Rating:

Mail Shot (IRE)

75 33

7-y-o b g Maledetto (IRE)-Pallachine (FR) (Lichine (USA))
Mrs E H Heath Mrs E H Heath

Placings:P/0P (1581)
2001/02: 19^{0}GF, 24^{P}GS

	Starts	1st	2nd	3rd	Win & Pl
Hurdles	2	0	0	0	
Career Total	3	0	0	0	

Going: Sf: 0-0 GS: 0-1 Gd: 0-0 GF: - Fm: 0-1
Distance: 2m/2m3: 0-0 2m4-2m7: 0-1 3m+: 0-1
Track: LH: 0-0 RH: 0-2 Tight: 0-2 Gall: 0-0
Aids: Bl: 0-0 Vi: 0-0 Tstrap: 0-0
Best Rating: 33 9/01 MRas 2m3f110y gd-fm Hdl

Mair Cariad

56f 48f

6-y-o b m Homo Sapien-Vitry (Vitiges (FR))
H W Lavis G Lavis

Placings:0 (1093)
2001/02: 16^{0}GF

	Starts	1st	2nd	3rd	Win & Pl
NH Flat	1	0	0	0	
Career Total	1	0	0	0	

Going: Sf: 0-0 GS: 0-0 Gd: 0-0 GF: - Fm: 0-1
Distance: 2m/2m3: 0-1 2m4-2m7: 0-0 3m+: 0-0
Track: LH: 0-1 RH: 0-0 Tight: 0-0 Gall: 0-0
Aids: Bl: 0-0 Vi: 0-0 Tstrap: 0-0
Best Rating: 48 8/01 Worc 2m gd-fm NHF

Maitre De Musique (FR)

11-y-o ch g Quai Voltaire (USA)-Mativa (FR) (Satingo)
Mrs G B Walford Dr M P Tate

Placings:10/003430/55420/1/422P23/P13P664/53-63 (4833)
2001/02: 25^{6}G, 27^{3}G

	Starts	1st	2nd	3rd	Win & Pl
Chases	2	0	0	1	434
Career Total	31	3	4	6	22834

133 11/99 Newc 2m4f D(0-125)HCh GD £3793
122 12/97 Weth 2m4f110y D Ch GD £3756
109 2/95 Kemp 2m H NHF HVY £1996
Total win prize-money £9546

Going: Sf: 0-0 GS: 0-0 Gd: 0-2 GF: - Fm: 0-0
Distance: 2m/2m3: 0-0 2m4-2m7: 0-0 3m+: 0-2
Track: LH: 0-2 RH: 0-0 Tight: 0-0 Gall: 0-0
Aids: Bl: 0-0 Vi: 0-0 Tstrap: 0-1
Best Rating: 133 12/99 Weth 2m4f110y gd-sft Ch

Majadou (FR)

102 130

8-y-o b g Cadoudal (FR)-Majathen (FR) (Carmarthen (FR))
M C Pipe C M , B J & R F Batterham li

Placings:13/0011115/014334/55P-0 (4234)
2001/02: 20^{0}GS

	Starts	1st	2nd	3rd	Win & Pl
Chases	1	0	0	0	
Career Total	19	6	0	3	98718

166 12/99 Chel 2m110y B HCh G-S £9918
166 3/99 Chel 2m4f110y B HCh G-S £35400
135 2/99 Ling 2m D Ch SFT £4298
150 1/99 Ling 2m E Ch HVY £3276
153 1/99 Chel 2m5f C Ch G-S £7002
3/98 Autl 2m1f110y Hdl VS £10101
Total win prize-money £69998

Going: Sf: 0-0 GS: 0-1 Gd: 0-0 GF: - Fm: 0-0
Distance: 2m/2m3: 0-0 2m4-2m7: 0-1 3m+: 0-0
Track: LH: 0-1 RH: 0-0 Tight: 0-0 Gall: 0-1
Aids: Bl: 0-0 Vi: 0-0 Tstrap: 0-0
Best Rating: 166 12/99 Chel 2m110y gd-sft Ch

A ready winner of the 1999 Mildmay of Flete Chase, he was punished by the Handicapper for that, and his only win since was over two miles at Cheltenham in December 1999. He has run only respectably since over a variety of trips, although three miles appears too far for him. Appreciates an easy surface.

Majed (FR)

92(116h) (150h) **116**

6-y-o b g Fijar Tango (FR)-Full Of Passion (USA) (Blushing Groom (FR))
M C Pipe Sandicroft Stud Syndicate Ii

Placings:46PP05**0/62042**321111-1210**F0** **(4913)**
2001/02: 20^{1}GS, 20^{2}S, 22^{1}G, 25^{0}GS, 36^{F}G, 29^{0}G

	Starts	1st	2nd	3rd	Win & Pl
Hurdles	4	2	1	0	36983
Chases	2	0	0	0	0
Career Total	**24**	**6**	**4**	**1**	**66092**

150	12/01	Winc	2m6f	B HHdl	GD	£8430
145	11/01	Chep	2m4f	B HHdl	G-S	£22750
128	4/01	Ayr	3m110y	B HHdl	GD	£7228
127	4/01	Extr	2m1f	E Hdl	G-S	£2153
133	3/01	Strf	2m6f110y	D Hdl	SFT	£3965
115	2/01	Plum	2m	E Hdl	SFT	£2075

Total win prize-money £46603

Going: Sf: 0-1 GS: 1-2 Gd: 1-3 GF: - Fm: 0-0
Distance: 2m/2m3: 0-0 **2m4-2m7: 2-3** 3m+: 0-3
Track: LH: 1-4 RH: 1-2 Tight: 0-1 Gall: 0-1
Aids: Bl: 0-0 **Vi: 2-6** Tstrap: 0-0
Best Rating: 150 12/01 Winc 2m6f good Hdl

Ex-French, he completed a four-timer over hurdles in April 2001 and made a winning reappearance in the Tote Silver Trophy at Chepstow in November of that year. Won a qualifier for the Pertemps Hurdle at Wincanton but disappointed in the final at Cheltenham and was running over fences for the first time in this country when falling in the Grand National. Seems to cope with all types of ground. Stays three miles and usually wears headgear.

Majestic (IRE)

113(104c) (137c) **138**

7-y-o b g Belmez (USA)-Noble Lily (USA) (Vaguely Noble)
Ian Williams Patrick Kelly

Placings:111P/112-6F555 **(4818)**
2001/02: 23^{6}G, 20^{F}F, 22^{5}GS, 21^{5}GS, 21^{5}GF

	Starts	1st	2nd	3rd	Win & Pl
Hurdles	4	0	0	0	0
Chases	1	0	0	0	0
Career Total	**12**	**5**	**1**	**0**	**21988**

136	1/01	Fknm	3m110y	D Ch	SFT	£4067
124	11/00	Newc	2m4f	E Ch	G-S	£2918
138	11/99	Chel	2m5f	B Hdl	GD	£7370
138	10/99	Chel	2m5f	D Hdl	GD	£3876
119	10/99	Plum	2m5f	E Hdl	G-F	£2600

Total win prize-money £20833

Going: Sf: 0-0 GS: 0-2 Gd: 0-1 GF: - Fm: 0-2
Distance: 2m/2m3: 0-0 2m4-2m7: 0-4 3m+: 0-1
Track: LH: 0-4 RH: 0-1 Tight: 0-0 Gall: 0-2
Aids: Bl: 0-5 Vi: 0-0 Tstrap: 0-5
Best Rating: 143 1/01 Fknm 3m110y soft Ch

Successful over fences twice in the 2000/2001 season, he is also effective over hurdles, having notched up a hat-trick in 1999. Off the track for ten months before reappearing in February 2002 and went on to run a blinder in the Coral Cup at the Festival. He stays three miles and handles any ground. Usually wears blinkers and a tongue tie.

Majestic Approach (IRE)

94 **118**

8-y-o br g Mandalus-Approach The Dawn (IRE) (Orchestra)
P R Webber J Dean & K Smith-Bingham

Placings:1P0PP5 **(4909)**
2001/02: 20^{1}GF, 20^{P}G, 21^{0}G, 32^{P}GS, 24^{P}GF, 20^{5}GF

	Starts	1st	2nd	3rd	Win & Pl
Chases	6	1	0	0	3263
Career Total	**6**	**1**	**0**	**0**	**3263**

118	12/01	Leic	2m4f110y	E Ch	G-F	£3263

Total win prize-money £3263

Going: Sf: 0-0 GS: 0-1 Gd: 0-2 GF: - Fm: 1-3
Distance: 2m/2m3: 0-0 **2m4-2m7: 1-4** 3m+: 0-2
Track: LH: 0-1 **RH: 1-5** Tight: 0-2 Gall: 0-1
Aids: Bl: 0-0 Vi: 0-0 Tstrap: 0-0
Best Rating: 118 12/01 Leic 2m4f110y gd-fm Ch

Landed a novice chase at Leicester on his debut under Rules, but has shown little since.

Majestic Bay (IRE)

95 **110**

6-y-o b g Unfuwain (USA)-That'Ll Be The Day (IRE) (Thatching)
J A B Old (P W Harris 29/9) W J Smith And M D Dudley

Placings:0654 **(4400)**
2001/02: 16^{0}G, 16^{6}GS, 20^{5}GS, 21^{4}S

	Starts	1st	2nd	3rd	Win & Pl
Hurdles	4	0	0	0	486
Career Total	**4**	**0**	**0**	**0**	**486**

Going: Sf: 0-1 GS: 0-2 Gd: 0-1 GF: - Fm: 0-0
Distance: 2m/2m3: 0-2 2m4-2m7: 0-2 3m+: 0-0
Track: LH: 0-3 RH: 0-1 Tight: 0-0 Gall: 0-4
Aids: Bl: 0-0 Vi: 0-0 Tstrap: 0-0
Best Rating: 110 3/02 Donc 2m4f gd-sft Hdl

A useful winner on the Flat for Peter Harris, he is now with Jim Old. Has been well beaten over hurdles so far at up to two miles four. Should stay further. Acts on any ground

Majestic Storm (IRE)

85 **53**

9-y-o b/br g Glacial Storm (USA)-Grin And Bear It (Deep Run)
Mrs L B Normile Mrs L Maben

Placings:F3RP0/P0/UPU **(4877)**
2001/02: 20^{U}GF, 24^{P}S, 24^{U}G

	Starts	1st	2nd	3rd	Win & Pl
Hurdles	1	0	0	0	0
Chases	2	0	0	0	0
Career Total	**10**	**0**	**0**	**1**	**404**

Going: Sf: 0-1 GS: 0-0 Gd: 0-1 GF: - Fm: 0-1
Distance: 2m/2m3: 0-0 2m4-2m7: 0-1 3m+: 0-2
Track: LH: 0-0 RH: 0-3 Tight: 0-2 Gall: 0-0
Aids: Bl: 0-0 Vi: 0-0 Tstrap: 0-0
Best Rating: 84 12/98 Wwck 3m2f gd-sft Ch

Very moderate form shown over fences so far.

Majlis (IRE)

110 **128**

5-y-o b g Caerleon (USA)-Ploy (Posse (USA))
T R George Terry Warner

Placings:623P-2041110P **(4662)**
2001/02: 16^{2}G, 16^{0}G, 16^{4}GS, 17^{1}GS, 16^{1}G, 16^{1}GS, 16^{0}GS, 16^{P}G

	Starts	1st	2nd	3rd	Win & Pl
Hurdles	8	3	1	0	30951
Career Total	**12**	**3**	**2**	**1**	**34631**

128	1/02	Kemp	2m	B(0-145)HHdl	G-S	£23200
122	1/02	Winc	2m	E Hdl	GD	£2940
120	12/01	Tntn	2m1f	E(0-115)HHdl	G-S	£3948

Total win prize-money £30089

Going: Sf: 0-0 GS: 2-4 Gd: 1-4 GF: - Fm: 0-0
Distance: 2m/2m3: 3-8 2m4-2m7: 0-0 3m+: 0-0
Track: LH: 0-2 **RH: 3-6 Tight: 1-2** Gall: 0-0
Aids: Bl: 3-5 Vi: 0-0 Tstrap: 0-0
Best Rating: 128 1/02 Kemp 2m gd-sft Hdl

He has shown a good level of ability over hurdles and completed a hat-trick in the Lanzarote at Kempton in January 2002 before running unplaced in the Imperial Cup. Acts on good/ good to soft ground and is effective over two miles.

Major Adams

95 **94**

7-y-o b g Roscoe Blake-Celtic View (Celtic Cone)
Mrs H Dalton G S Williams

Placings:*033*-0400 **(4387)**
2001/02: 20^{0}S, 16^{4}HY, 16^{0}GS, 16^{0}S

	Starts	1st	2nd	3rd	Win & Pl
Hurdles	4	0	0	0	0
Career Total	**7**	**0**	**0**	**2**	**489**

Going: Sf: 0-3 GS: 0-1 Gd: 0-0 GF: - Fm: 0-0
Distance: 2m/2m3: 0-3 2m4-2m7: 0-1 3m+: 0-0
Track: LH: 0-2 RH: 0-2 Tight: 0-0 Gall: 0-0
Aids: Bl: 0-0 Vi: 0-0 Tstrap: 0-0
Best Rating: 94 2/02 Winc 2m gd-sft Hdl

Has shown placed form in bumpers. Has raced keenly.

Major Adventure (IRE)

111 **118**

9-y-o b g Glacial Storm (USA)-Dual Adventure (Deep Run)
Ian Williams A Stennett

Placings:1410/**2PP-553U3U** **(4775)**
2001/02: 22^{5}S, 25^{5}G, 20^{3}S, 24^{U}S, 25^{3}G, 22^{U}G

	Starts	1st	2nd	3rd	Win & Pl
Chases	6	0	0	2	1066
Career Total	**13**	**2**	**1**	**2**	**17531**

116	2/00	Uttx	2m6f110y	C(0-135)HHdl	SFT	£12866
107	11/99	Worc	2m4f	E Hdl	G-S	£2687

Total win prize-money £15555

Going: Sf: 0-3 GS: 0-0 Gd: 0-3 GF: - Fm: 0-0
Distance: 2m/2m3: 0-0 2m4-2m7: 0-3 3m+: 0-3

Track: LH: 0-0 RH: 0-6 Tight: 0-3 Gall: 0-0
Aids: Bl: 0-0 Vi: 0-1 Tstrap: 0-0
Best Rating: 118 1/01 Chep 3m gd-sft Ch

An Irish point-to-point winner, he was a useful hurdler but he has yet to reach that level of form over fences. Effective in soft ground.

Major Ballaby (IRE)

89(96c) (21c)89

7-y-o b g Balla Cove-Surreal (Bustino)
Mrs S A Bramall Winning Post Racing Syndicate

Placings:5P0210/00/6-00F0 **(3956a)**
2001/02: 16^{0}Y, 16^{0}YS, 16^{F}G, 18^{0}S

	Starts	1st	2nd	3rd	Win & Pl
Hurdles	2	0	0	0	0
Chases	2	0	0	0	0
Career Total	**13**	**1**	**1**	**0**	**2941**

114	3/99	Ayr	2m	E Hdl	SFT	£2238

Total win prize-money £2238

Going: Sf: 0-1 GS: 0-0 Gd: 0-1 GF: - Fm: 0-0
Distance: 2m/2m3: 0-4 2m4-2m7: 0-0 3m+: 0-0
Track: LH: 0-1 RH: 0-2 Tight: 0-1 Gall: 0-0
Aids: Bl: 0-0 Vi: 0-0 Tstrap: 0-0
Best Rating: 114 3/99 Ayr 2m soft Hdl

A winner over hurlded, he acts well on a soft surface and goes well over two miles.

Major Barbara

92 64

7-y-o b m Infantry-Veritate (Roman Warrior)
M J Wilkinson Mark Wilkinson

Placings:0/0P-060 **(2948)**
2001/02: 19^{0}GF, 20^{6}GS, 20^{0}G

	Starts	1st	2nd	3rd	Win & Pl
Hurdles	3	0	0	0	0
Career Total	**6**	**0**	**0**	**0**	**0**

Going: Sf: 0-0 GS: 0-1 Gd: 0-1 GF: - Fm: 0-1
Distance: 2m/2m3: 0-1 2m4-2m7: 0-2 3m+: 0-0
Track: LH: 0-2 RH: 0-1 Tight: 0-2 Gall: 0-0
Aids: Bl: 0-0 Vi: 0-0 Tstrap: 0-0
Best Rating: 69 3/00 Uttx 2m good NHF

Major Bell

86 96

14-y-o br g Silly Prices-Melaura Belle (Meldrum)
A C Whillans A C Whillans

Placings:453545/412130521/016324/21111/12332/04 2F320/303541UU10/P4043U/0-25P **(0803)**
2001/02: 25^{2}G, 24^{5}F, 24^{P}GF

	Starts	1st	2nd	3rd	Win & Pl
Chases	3	0	1	0	1728
Career Total	**58**	**11**	**9**	**9**	**132079**

143	4/99	Weth	3m1f	B(0-145)HCh	GD	£8309
138	1/99	Donc	3m	B(0-145)HCh	GD	£24478
131	11/96	Bang	2m4f110y	D(0-125)HCh	G-S	£4667
138	4/96	Ayr	2m4f	B HCh	G-S	£7107
122	3/96	Chep	3m	C HCh	G-S	£13615
117	2/96	Ayr	2m4f	D(0-120)HCh	GD	£4620
111	1/96	Kels	3m1f	D Ch	G-S	£3983
125	11/94	Kels	2m6f110y	(0-130)HHdl	GD	£3501
116	4/94	Ayr	2m4f	Hdl	GD	£5680
93	1/94	Catt	2m3f	Hdl	G-S	£2364
100	12/93	Muss	3m	Hdl	G-F	£1955

Total win prize-money £80284

Going: Sf: 0-0 GS: 0-0 Gd: 0-1 GF: - Fm: 0-2
Distance: 2m/2m3: 0-0 2m4-2m7: 0-0 3m+: 0-3
Track: LH: 0-1 RH: 0-2 Tight: 0-1 Gall: 0-0
Aids: Bl: 0-0 Vi: 0-0 Tstrap: 0-0
Best Rating: 146 3/97 Chel 2m5f good Ch

Major Bit

92(77h) (79h)78

6-y-o b g Henbit (USA)-Cute Pam (Pamroy)
S A Brookshaw Steven Brookshaw Racing Partnership I

Placings:00-206PP05 **(4849)**
2001/02: 16^{2}GF, 20^{0}G, 20^{6}S, 20^{P}GS, 21^{P}S, 22^{0}G, 24^{5}G

	Starts	1st	2nd	3rd	Win & Pl
NH Flat	1	0	1	0	500
Hurdles	5	0	0	0	0
Chases	1	0	0	0	0
Career Total	**9**	**0**	**1**	**0**	**500**

Going: Sf: 0-2 GS: 0-1 Gd: 0-3 GF: - Fm: 0-1
Distance: 2m/2m3: 0-1 2m4-2m7: 0-5 3m+: 0-1
Track: LH: 0-4 RH: 0-3 Tight: 0-2 Gall: 0-0
Aids: Bl: 0-0 Vi: 0-0 Tstrap: 0-7
Best Rating: 81 10/01 Ludl 2m gd-fm NHF

Major Blaze

89 67

10-y-o b g Royal Vulcan-Loughnavalley (Candy Cane)
A J Chamberlain F J Brennan

Placings:000F/50 **(4565)**
2001/02: 20^{5}S, 16^{0}G

	Starts	1st	2nd	3rd	Win & Pl
Hurdles	2	0	0	0	0
Career Total	**6**	**0**	**0**	**0**	**0**

Going: Sf: 0-1 GS: 0-0 Gd: 0-1 GF: - Fm: 0-0
Distance: 2m/2m3: 0-1 2m4-2m7: 0-1 3m+: 0-0
Track: LH: 0-1 RH: 0-1 Tight: 0-0 Gall: 0-0
Aids: Bl: 0-0 Vi: 0-0 Tstrap: 0-0
Best Rating: 67 4/02 Towc 2m good Hdl

Major Blue

97f 97f

7-y-o ch g Scallywag-Town Blues (Charlottown)
J G M O'Shea H G Llewellyn

Placings:34 **(2173)**
2001/02: 17^{3}S, 16^{4}S

	Starts	1st	2nd	3rd	Win & Pl
NH Flat	2	0	0	1	247
Career Total	**2**	**0**	**0**	**1**	**247**

Going: Sf: 0-2 GS: 0-0 Gd: 0-0 GF: - Fm: 0-0
Distance: 2m/2m3: 0-2 2m4-2m7: 0-0 3m+: 0-0
Track: LH: 0-2 RH: 0-0 Tight: 0-1 Gall: 0-0
Aids: Bl: 0-0 Vi: 0-0 Tstrap: 0-0
Best Rating: 97 10/01 Bang 2m1f soft NHF

Went down fighting on his debut in a bumper.

Major Drive (IRE)

89 64

4-y-o b g Sadler's Wells (USA)-Puck's Castle (Shirley Heights)
J Howard Johnson (J H M Gosden 27/9) Peter Gormley

Placings:0650 **(4915)**
2001/02: 16^{0}S, 17^{6}HY, 17^{5}S, 17^{0}GF

	Starts	1st	2nd	3rd	Win & Pl
Hurdles	4	0	0	0	0
Career Total	**4**	**0**	**0**	**0**	**0**

Going: Sf: 0-3 GS: 0-0 Gd: 0-0 GF: - Fm: 0-1
Distance: 2m/2m3: 0-4 2m4-2m7: 0-0 3m+: 0-0
Track: LH: 0-4 RH: 0-0 Tight: 0-3 Gall: 0-1
Aids: Bl: 0-0 Vi: 0-0 Tstrap: 0-0
Best Rating: 64 2/02 Sedg 2m1f soft Hdl

Well held in novice hurdle company.

Major Lando (GER)

113 124

5-y-o b/br g Lando (GER)-Majoritat (GER) (Konigsstuhl (GER))
M C Pipe The Macca & Growler Partnership

Placings:1214132 **(1554)**
2001/02: 16^{1}G, 17^{2}G, 16^{1}GF, 17^{4}GS, 17^{1}G, 17^{3}GF, 16^{2}G

	Starts	1st	2nd	3rd	Win & Pl
Hurdles	7	3	2	1	17183
Career Total	**7**	**3**	**2**	**1**	**17183**

124	8/01	NAbb	2m1f	D Hdl	GD	£3393
111	6/01	Strf	2m110y	E Hdl	G-F	£3272
118	5/01	Aint	2m110y	D Hdl	GD	£3598

Total win prize-money £10265

Going: Sf: 0-0 GS: 0-1 Gd: 2-4 GF: - Fm: 1-2
Distance: 2m/2m3: 3-7 2m4-2m7: 0-0 3m+: 0-0
Track: LH: 3-6 RH: 0-0 Tight: 3-5 Gall: 0-0
Aids: Bl: 0-0 Vi: 0-1 Tstrap: 0-0
Best Rating: 124 10/01 Chep 2m110y good Hdl

He won three modest events over hurdles during the summer of 2001, but broke a leg at Chepstow in October. (DEAD).

Major Sharpe (IRE)

104(98h) (102h)115+

10-y-o b g Phardante (FR)-Winsome Doe (Buckskin (FR))
B J M Ryall B J M Ryall

Placings:2/32/F-2PPPP **(4686)**
2001/02: 24^{2}F, 27^{P}G, 22^{P}G, 21^{P}GF, 26^{P}GF

	Starts	1st	2nd	3rd	Win & Pl
Hurdles	4	0	1	0	882
Chases	1	0	0	0	0
Career Total	**9**	**0**	**3**	**1**	**3637**

Going: Sf: 0-0 GS: 0-0 Gd: 0-2 GF: - Fm: 0-3
Distance: 2m/2m3: 0-0 2m4-2m7: 0-2 3m+: 0-3
Track: LH: 0-3 RH: 0-2 Tight: 0-4 Gall: 0-0
Aids: Bl: 0-0 Vi: 0-0 Tstrap: 0-0
Best Rating: 115 3/00 Folk 3m2f gd-fm Ch

A maiden over jumps until making all in a handicap chase in June 2002. Stays three miles plus, effective on good ground.

Major Sponsor (IRE)

105 141

10-y-o b g Strong Gale-Hue 'N' Cry (IRE) (Denel (FR))
G M Moore S P Graham Ltd

Placings:0/0356113/121123/32132355/1122P-4F3440 **(2144)**
2001/02: 20^{4}GF, 20^{F}GS, 16^{3}GF, 20^{4}G, 16^{4}G, 16^{0}G

Starts	1st	2nd	3rd	Win & Pl	
Chases	6	0	0	1	4093
Career Total	**33**	**8**	**6**	**7**	**48919**

152	8/00	Sedg	2m5f	D(0-125)HCh	GD	£4212
152	7/00	Sedg	2m110y	E(0-115)HCh	G-F	£3432
127	11/99	Newc	2m110y	D Ch	GD	£4143
138	1/99	Newc	2m	B Hdl	SFT	£7555
131	1/99	Catt	2m3f	E Hdl	GD	£2500
121	10/98	Sthl	2m	E Hdl	GD	£2290
130	3/98	Dpat	2m1f172y	NHF	YLD	£2978
116	3/98	DRoy	2m	NHF	GD	£1489

Total win prize-money £28599

Going: Sf: 0-0 GS: 0-1 Gd: 0-3 GF: - Fm: 0-2
Distance: 2m/2m3: 0-3 2m4-2m7: 0-3 3m+: 0-0
Track: LH: 0-3 RH: 0-2 Tight: 0-1 Gall: 0-1
Aids: Bl: 0-0 Vi: 0-0 Tstrap: 0-0
Best Rating: 152 8/00 Sedg 2m5f good Ch

A free-running individual, who was a decent hurdler, he has not quite lived up to expectations over fences and his only two wins to date were at Sedgefield during the summer of 2000. He is best on good or fast ground, although he has won on softer and is probably best around two and a half miles has something to prove these days.

Major West

9-y-o ch g Gunner B-Little Ginger (Cawston's Clown)
R H Goldie P Baillie

Placings: *00*/PP (4746)
2001/02: 16^{P}S, 20^{P}GF

	Starts	1st	2nd	3rd	Win & Pl
Chases	2	0	0	0	
Career Total	**4**	**0**	**0**	**0**	

Going: Sf: 0-1 GS: 0-0 Gd: 0-0 GF: - Fm: 0-1
Distance: 2m/2m3: 0-1 2m4-2m7: 0-1 3m+: 0-0
Track: LH: 0-1 RH: 0-1 Tight: 0-0 Gall: 0-1
Aids: Bl: 0-0 Vi: 0-0 Tstrap: 0-0
Best Rating: 77 11/99 Hexm 2m good NHF

Lightly-raced and little form so far.

Major's Law (IRE)

98 85

13-y-o b g Law Society (USA)-Maryinsky (USA) (Northern Dancer)
H H G Owen H H G Owen

Placings: 3523215/2PP23/12145/36045/2503111P/56/16P/PP-PP4 (4560)
2001/02: 22^{P}S, 20^{P}HY, 17^{4}GF

	Starts	1st	2nd	3rd	Win & Pl
Hurdles	1	0	0	0	0
Chases	2	0	0	0	0
Career Total	**40**	**7**	**6**	**5**	**22225**

80	3/00	Leic	2m	H Ch	G-S	£2338
108	1/98	Leic	2m4f110y	D(0-125)HHdl	HVY	£3835
95	9/97	Strf	2m6f110y	D(0-120)HHdl	GD	£2696
89	9/97	Bang	2m4f	E(0-110)HHdl	GD	£3517
91	2/95	Hntg	2m110y	E(0-115)HHdl	SFT	£2302
84	12/94	Sthl	2m	Hdl	SFT	£1847
101	4/93	Plum	2m1f	Hdl	GD	£1636

Total win prize-money £18173

Going: Sf: 0-2 GS: 0-0 Gd: 0-0 GF: - Fm: 0-1
Distance: 2m/2m3: 0-1 2m4-2m7: 0-2 3m+: 0-0
Track: LH: 0-3 RH: 0-0 Tight: 0-3 Gall: 0-0
Aids: Bl: 0-1 Vi: 0-0 Tstrap: 0-0
Best Rating: 108 1/98 Leic 2m4f110y heavy Hdl

Majority Verdict

103 119

6-y-o b g Leading Counsel (USA)-Culm Valley (Port Corsair)
H D Daly Gibson, Goddard & Hamer

Placings: *21*-2 (2315)
2001/02: 16^{2}GS

	Starts	1st	2nd	3rd	Win & Pl
Hurdles	1	0	1	0	1296
Career Total	**3**	**1**	**2**	**0**	**4987**

124	3/01	Strf	2m110y	H NHF	SFT	£3241

Total win prize-money £3241

Going: Sf: 0-0 GS: 0-1 Gd: 0-0 GF: - Fm: 0-0
Distance: 2m/2m3: 0-1 2m4-2m7: 0-0 3m+: 0-0
Track: LH: 0-1 RH: 0-0 Tight: 0-1 Gall: 0-0
Aids: Bl: 0-0 Vi: 0-0 Tstrap: 0-0
Best Rating: 124 3/01 Strf 2m110y soft NHF

Make My Day (FR)

110 122

8-y-o b m Akarad (FR)-Masada (SWE) (Jimmy Reppin)
T M Walsh Edward Cawley

Placings: 0002431123/010432033-402064620 (4704a)
2001/02: 24^{4}YS, 20^{0}S, 24^{2}Y, 24^{0}YS, 19^{6}SH, 24^{4}S, 20^{6}S, 22^{2}HY, 22^{0}GY

	Starts	1st	2nd	3rd	Win & Pl
Hurdles	9	0	2	0	8309
Career Total	**29**	**3**	**5**	**5**	**34124**

116	11/00	Tram	2m4f	(0-95)Hdl	HVY	£3312
116	4/00	Fair	2m6f	(0-123)HHdl	Y-S	£3864
94	3/00	Naas	2m3f	HHdl	Y-S	£5520

Total win prize-money £12696

Going: Sf: 0-4 GS: 0-0 Gd: 0-0 GF: - Fm: 0-0
Distance: 2m/2m3: 0-1 2m4-2m7: 0-4 3m+: 0-4
Track: LH: 0-6 RH: 0-3 Tight: 0-0 Gall: 0-0
Aids: Bl: 0-0 Vi: 0-0 Tstrap: 0-0
Best Rating: 122 3/02 Uttx 2m6f110y heavy Hdl

Irish trained, he had a successful time in 2000, but has struggled with the Handicapper since. Stays two miles six and enjoys cut in the ground.

Make The Call

88 47

5-y-o b m Syrtos-Dawn Call (Rymer)
B N Doran T D Galer

Placings: *000* (4724)
2001/02: 16^{0}GF, 21^{0}G, 16^{0}GF

	Starts	1st	2nd	3rd	Win & Pl
NH Flat	1	0	0	0	0
Hurdles	2	0	0	0	0
Career Total	**3**	**0**	**0**	**0**	

Going: Sf: 0-0 GS: 0-0 Gd: 0-1 GF: - Fm: 0-2
Distance: 2m/2m3: 0-2 2m4-2m7: 0-1 3m+: 0-0
Track: LH: 0-2 RH: 0-1 Tight: 0-0 Gall: 0-0
Aids: Bl: 0-0 Vi: 0-0 Tstrap: 0-0
Best Rating: 48 6/01 Worc 2m gd-fm NHF

Makhpiya Patahn (IRE)

10-y-o gr g Nestor-Our Mare Mick (Choral Society)
J H Young (J W Mullins 17/2) J H Young

Placings: 0P0/55/4425P5/4 (4763)
2001/02: 24^{4}GF

	Starts	1st	2nd	3rd	Win & Pl
Chases	1	0	0	0	212
Career Total	**12**	**0**	**1**	**0**	**2739**

Going: Sf: 0-0 GS: 0-0 Gd: 0-0 GF: - Fm: 0-1
Distance: 2m/2m3: 0-0 2m4-2m7: 0-0 3m+: 0-1
Track: LH: 0-0 RH: 0-1 Tight: 0-0 Gall: 0-0
Aids: Bl: 0-0 Vi: 0-0 Tstrap: 0-0
Best Rating: 98 11/99 Winc 3m1f110y good Ch

Makin' Doo (IRE)

12-y-o ch g Black Minstrel-Ariannrun (Deep Run)
Mrs V J Makin (R G Makin 20/1) R G Makin

Placings: 0P50/33P4/5P44-0P53P (4871)
2001/02: 21^{0}G, 24^{P}S, 27^{5}S, 20^{3}HY, 25^{P}GF

	Starts	1st	2nd	3rd	Win & Pl
Hurdles	3	0	0	1	381
Chases	2	0	0	0	0
Career Total	**17**	**0**	**0**	**3**	**1849**

Going: Sf: 0-3 GS: 0-0 Gd: 0-1 GF: - Fm: 0-1
Distance: 2m/2m3: 0-0 2m4-2m7: 0-2 3m+: 0-3
Track: LH: 0-3 RH: 0-1 Tight: 0-3 Gall: 0-0
Aids: Bl: 0-0 Vi: 0-0 Tstrap: 0-0
Best Rating: 99 3/01 MRas 3m1f gd-sft Ch

Modest pointer/hurdler, stays three miles.

Malakal (IRE)

92 76

6-y-o b g Shernazar-Malmada (USA) (Fappiano (USA))
B J Curley Mrs B J Curley

Placings: PP-64PP (2901)
2001/02: 17^{6}GS, 20^{4}G, 20^{P}S, 20^{P}S

	Starts	1st	2nd	3rd	Win & Pl
Hurdles	4	0	0	0	0
Career Total	**6**	**0**	**0**	**0**	**0**

Going: Sf: 0-2 GS: 0-1 Gd: 0-1 GF: - Fm: 0-0
Distance: 2m/2m3: 0-1 2m4-2m7: 0-3 3m+: 0-0
Track: LH: 0-1 RH: 0-3 Tight: 0-1 Gall: 0-1
Aids: Bl: 0-0 Vi: 0-0 Tstrap: 0-0
Best Rating: 76 5/01 Folk 2m1f110y gd-sft Hdl

Malakand (IRE)

86f 53f

4-y-o b g Dolphin Street (FR)-Malmada (USA) (Fappiano (USA))
A Crook The Mushroom Club

Placings: *00* (4750)
2001/02: 16^{0}GS, 17^{0}G

	Starts	1st	2nd	3rd	Win & Pl
NH Flat	2	0	0	0	
Career Total	**2**	**0**	**0**	**0**	

Going: Sf: 0-0 GS: 0-1 Gd: 0-1 GF: - Fm: 0-0
Distance: 2m/2m3: 0-2 2m4-2m7: 0-0 3m+: 0-0
Track: LH: 0-1 RH: 0-1 Tight: 0-1 Gall: 0-0
Aids: Bl: 0-0 Vi: 0-0 Tstrap: 0-0
Best Rating: 53 1/02 Catt 2m gd-sft NHF

Malandrin (FR)

106 138

7-y-o ch g Albert Du Berlais (FR)-Maieta (FR) (Fast (FR))

G Macaire J-M Reillier

Placings:0F5500/4P4B2O11-516211115 **(2665)**

2001/02: 21^{5}S, 21^{1}G, 29^{6}, 21^{2}, 22^{1}S, 25^{1}G, 18^{1}G, 20^{1}VS, 31^{5}GS

	Starts	1st	2nd	3rd	Win & Pl
Chases	9	5	1	0	27604
Career Total	**23**	**7**	**2**	**0**	**36934**

10/01	Autl	2m4f110y	Ch	VS	£11639
9/01	Pomp	2m2f	Ch	GD	£3395
8/01	Pomp	3m1f	Ch	GD	£3395
8/01	Pomp	2m6f110y	Ch	SFT	£3395
6/01	Vich	2m5f110y	Ch	GD	£3492
11/00	Toul	2m1f110y	Ch	SFT	£2882
11/00	Agen	2m	Hdl	VS	£2882

Total win prize-money £31080

Going: Sf: 1-2 GS: 0-1 Gd: 3-3 GF: - Fm: 0-0
Distance: 2m/2m3: 1-1 **2m4-2m7: 3-5** 3m+: 1-3
Track: LH: 0-1 RH: 0-0 Tight: 0-0 Gall: 0-0
Aids: Bl: 0-0 Vi: 0-0 Tstrap: 0-0
Best Rating: 138 12/01 Chel 3m7f gd-sft Ch

Very useful in France, but failed to stay three miles seven in a cross-country chase on his British debut at Cheltenham. He acts well with cut in the ground, and is effective around two to three miles.

Malarkey

102 99

5-y-o b g Mukaddamah (USA)-Malwiya (USA) (Shahrastani (USA))

P R Hedger (J A Osborne 20/10) Jay Dee Bloodstock Limited

Placings:0435 **(4031)**

2001/02: 16^{0}G, 16^{4}G, 16^{3}S, 16^{5}GS

	Starts	1st	2nd	3rd	Win & Pl
Hurdles	4	0	0	1	384
Career Total	**4**	**0**	**0**	**1**	**384**

Going: Sf: 0-1 GS: 0-1 Gd: 0-2 GF: - Fm: 0-0
Distance: 2m/2m3: 0-4 2m4-2m7: 0-0 3m+: 0-0
Track: LH: 0-4 RH: 0-0 Tight: 0-2 Gall: 0-2
Aids: Bl: 0-0 Vi: 0-0 Tstrap: 0-0
Best Rating: 99 3/02 Newb 2m110y gd-sft Hdl

Going the right way over hurdles.

Malawi

95 71

12-y-o ch g Northern State (USA)-Nyeri (Saint Crespin Iii)

W A Bethell W A Bethell

Placings:56P/6232331P/32113/5434/12F1/P-4P **(1859)**

2001/02: 28^{4}GS, 24^{P}S

	Starts	1st	2nd	3rd	Win & Pl
Chases	2	0	0	0	266
Career Total	**27**	**5**	**4**	**6**	**25863**

107	1/99	Hntg	3m	D(0-120)HCh	SFT	£4370
110	10/98	Bang	3m110y	D(0-120)HCh	GD	£4947
110	1/96	Newc	3m	E Ch	GD	£3246
101	11/95	Weth	3m110y	D Ch	GD	£3470
97	2/95	Newc	3m	E(0-115)HHdl	G-S	£2337

Total win prize-money £18370

Going: Sf: 0-1 GS: 0-1 Gd: 0-0 GF: - Fm: 0-0
Distance: 2m/2m3: 0-0 2m4-2m7: 0-0 3m+: 0-2
Track: LH: 0-1 RH: 0-1 Tight: 0-2 Gall: 0-0
Aids: Bl: 0-2 Vi: 0-0 Tstrap: 0-0
Best Rating: 115 2/96 Nott 3m110y good Ch

Malbaum (GER)

79

8-y-o b g King's Lake (USA)-Maxi's Dream (Coquelin (USA))

D G Bridgwater D G Bridgwater

Placings:040P/1260/0-P **(2899)**

2001/02: 16^{P}G

	Starts	1st	2nd	3rd	Win & Pl
Hurdles	1	0	0	0	
Career Total	**10**	**1**	**1**	**0**	**2991**

96	5/99	Worc	2m4f	F(0-100)HHdl	G-F	£2325

Total win prize-money £2325

Going: Sf: 0-0 GS: 0-0 Gd: 0-1 GF: - Fm: 0-0
Distance: 2m/2m3: 0-1 2m4-2m7: 0-0 3m+: 0-0
Track: LH: 0-0 RH: 0-1 Tight: 0-0 Gall: 0-0
Aids: Bl: 0-1 Vi: 0-0 Tstrap: 0-0
Best Rating: 103 6/99 Uttx 2m4f110y good Hdl

Malbec (IRE)

5-y-o b g Lord Americo-Key Door (IRE) (Beau Charmeur (FR))

Miss A M Newton-Smith Julian Smith

Placings:P **(4854)**

2001/02: 22^{P}G

	Starts	1st	2nd	3rd	Win & Pl
Hurdles	1	0	0	0	
Career Total	**1**	**0**	**0**	**0**	

Going: Sf: 0-0 GS: 0-0 Gd: 0-1 GF: - Fm: 0-0
Distance: 2m/2m3: 0-0 2m4-2m7: 0-1 3m+: 0-0
Track: LH: 0-1 RH: 0-0 Tight: 0-1 Gall: 0-0
Aids: Bl: 0-0 Vi: 0-0 Tstrap: 0-0
Best Rating:

Male Order (IRE)

97 84

8-y-o b g Mandalus-Deep Lass (Deep Run)

L Lungo R A Bartlett

Placings:060P **(2909)**

2001/02: 17^{0}GS, 16^{6}G, 16^{0}G, 25^{P}GS

	Starts	1st	2nd	3rd	Win & Pl
Hurdles	4	0	0	0	0
Career Total	**4**	**0**	**0**	**0**	**0**

Going: Sf: 0-0 GS: 0-2 Gd: 0-2 GF: - Fm: 0-0
Distance: 2m/2m3: 0-3 2m4-2m7: 0-0 3m+: 0-1
Track: LH: 0-3 RH: 0-1 Tight: 0-1 Gall: 0-0
Aids: Bl: 0-0 Vi: 0-0 Tstrap: 0-0
Best Rating: 84 10/01 Aint 2m110y good Hdl

Male-Ana-Mou (IRE)

89 94

9-y-o ch g Ela-Mana-Mou-Glasson Lady (GER) (Priamos (GER))

Jamie Poulton Oh So Bright Syndicate

Placings:32110/1-P00 **(4633)**

2001/02: 20^{P}S, 16^{0}GS, 20^{0}GF

	Starts	1st	2nd	3rd	Win & Pl
Hurdles	3	0	0	0	
Career Total	**9**	**3**	**1**	**1**	**32733**

142	11/00	Newb	2m110y	A(0-145)HHdl	HVY	£13800
145	2/00	Font	2m4f	B Hdl	G-S	£13715
106	1/00	Plum	2m	E Hdl	SFT	£2520

Total win prize-money £30035

Going: Sf: 0-1 GS: 0-1 Gd: 0-0 GF: - Fm: 0-1
Distance: 2m/2m3: 0-1 2m4-2m7: 0-2 3m+: 0-0
Track: LH: 0-0 RH: 0-2 Tight: 0-1 Gall: 0-0
Aids: Bl: 0-0 Vi: 0-0 Tstrap: 0-0
Best Rating: 145 2/00 Font 2m4f gd-sft Hdl

A decent middle-distance handicapper on the Flat, he caused something of a surprise when beating three high-class established hurdlers in a valuable event at Fontwell in February 2000. Reappeared at Fontwell in February 2002, but was pulled up after colliding with the running rail and failed to shine on his second start.

Malek (IRE)

106 110

6-y-o b g Tremblant-Any Offers (Paddy's Stream)

Mrs M Reveley Mrs J W Furness

Placings:3U1 **(4311)**

2001/02: 16^{3}HY, 25^{U}GS, 24^{1}HY

	Starts	1st	2nd	3rd	Win & Pl
NH Flat	1	0	0	1	249
Chases	2	1	0	0	3159
Career Total	**3**	**1**	**0**	**1**	**3408**

110	3/02	Sthl	3m110y	E Ch	HVY	£3159

Total win prize-money £3159

Going: Sf: 1-2 GS: 0-1 Gd: 0-0 GF: - Fm: 0-0
Distance: 2m/2m3: 0-1 2m4-2m7: 0-0 **3m+: 1-2**
Track: **LH: 1-2** RH: 0-0 **Tight: 1-1** Gall: 0-0
Aids: Bl: 0-0 Vi: 0-0 Tstrap: 0-0
Best Rating: 110 3/02 Sthl 3m110y heavy Ch

Promising debut in an ordinary Ayr bumper but hopelessly let down by his jumping when tried in a hunter chase. Landed a novice chase in terrible ground at Southwell.

Malian (IRE)

87 80

6-y-o b/br g Arcane (USA)-Rhein Valley (IRE) (King's Lake (USA))

Mrs P N Dutfield Edwin Phillips

Placings:00-U50 **(0795)**

2001/02: 21^{U}GF, 22^{5}G, 22^{0}GF

	Starts	1st	2nd	3rd	Win & Pl
Hurdles	2	0	0	0	0
Chases	1	0	0	0	0
Career Total	**5**	**0**	**0**	**0**	**0**

Going: Sf: 0-0 GS: 0-0 Gd: 0-1 GF: - Fm: 0-2
Distance: 2m/2m3: 0-0 2m4-2m7: 0-3 3m+: 0-0
Track: LH: 0-3 RH: 0-0 Tight: 0-3 Gall: 0-0
Aids: Bl: 0-2 Vi: 0-0 Tstrap: 0-3
Best Rating: 80 6/01 NAbb 2m6f good Hdl

Malihabad (IRE)

87 80

13-y-o ch g Shahrastani (USA)-Mill River (FR) (Mill Reef (USA))

C J Gray A C Heal

Placings: *04/14146P/0400/06/003456/60***F425340/0P/ 3P44P** (1379)

2001/02: 21^{3}GF, 21^{P}GF, 26^{4}G, 21^{4}G, 25^{P}GF

	Starts	1st	2nd	3rd	Win & Pl
Chases	5	0	0	1	1137
Career Total	**36**	**2**	**1**	**3**	**10127**

110	12/93	Fair	2m	Hdl	Y-S	£3338
	5/93	Dund	2m135y	NHF	GD	£2413

Total win prize-money £5753

Going: Sf: 0-0 GS: 0-0 Gd: 0-2 GF: - Fm: 0-3
Distance: 2m/2m3: 0-0 2m4-2m7: 0-3 3m+: 0-2
Track: LH: 0-4 RH: 0-1 Tight: 0-4 Gall: 0-0
Aids: Bl: 0-0 Vi: 0-0 Tstrap: 0-0
Best Rating: 110 12/93 Fair 2m yld-sft Hdl

Mallory

106 **85**

8-y-o b g North Col-Veritate (Roman Warrior)
M J Wilkinson D J Price

Placings: *120/*0P-4P32 (4160)

2001/02: 17^{4}S, 20^{P}S, 16^{3}GS, 16^{2}GS

	Starts	1st	2nd	3rd	Win & Pl
Hurdles	4	0	1	1	987
Career Total	**9**	**1**	**2**	**1**	**3244**

115	12/99	Hntg	2m110y	H NHF	GD	£1800

Total win prize-money £1800

Going: Sf: 0-2 GS: 0-2 Gd: 0-0 GF: - Fm: 0-0
Distance: 2m/2m3: 0-3 2m4-2m7: 0-1 3m+: 0-0
Track: LH: 0-1 RH: 0-3 Tight: 0-1 Gall: 0-1
Aids: Bl: 0-0 Vi: 0-0 Tstrap: 0-0
Best Rating: 115 2/00 Folk 2m1f110y soft NHF

A decent bumper winner, he has taken time to get his act together over hurdles.

Maltese Cross (IRE)

13-y-o br g Supreme Leader-Nevada Lady (Trimmingham)
R Hirons Mrs John Cardwell

Placings: *00/P/P-PP* (0358)

2001/02: 25^{P}G, 24^{P}GS

	Starts	1st	2nd	3rd	Win & Pl
Chases	2	0	0	0	
Career Total	**6**	**0**	**0**	**0**	

Going: Sf: 0-0 GS: 0-1 Gd: 0-1 GF: - Fm: 0-0
Distance: 2m/2m3: 0-0 2m4-2m7: 0-0 3m+: 0-2
Track: LH: 0-2 RH: 0-0 Tight: 0-1 Gall: 0-0
Aids: Bl: 0-0 Vi: 0-0 Tstrap: 0-0
Best Rating:

Malvolio

59f **37f**

6-y-o b g Theatrical Charmer-Sancilia (Dalsaan)
Dr J D Scargill Mrs Maureen Coppitters

Placings: *0* (0377)

2001/02: 16^{0}GF

	Starts	1st	2nd	3rd	Win & Pl
NH Flat	1	0	0	0	
Career Total	**1**	**0**	**0**	**0**	

Going: Sf: 0-0 GS: 0-0 Gd: 0-0 GF: - Fm: 0-1
Distance: 2m/2m3: 0-1 2m4-2m7: 0-0 3m+: 0-0
Track: LH: 0-0 RH: 0-1 Tight: 0-0 Gall: 0-1
Aids: Bl: 0-0 Vi: 0-0 Tstrap: 0-0
Best Rating: 37 5/01 Hntg 2m110y gd-fm NHF

Mambo (IRE)

100 **98**

4-y-o b g Ashkalani (IRE)-Bold Tango (FR) (In Fijar (USA))
N J Henderson Mrs Belinda Harvey

Placings: 2-22 (1956)

2001/02: 15^{2}HY, 16^{2}G

	Starts	1st	2nd	3rd	Win & Pl
Hurdles	2	0	2	0	5828
Career Total	**3**	**0**	**3**	**0**	**10678**

Going: Sf: 0-1 GS: 0-0 Gd: 0-1 GF: - Fm: 0-0
Distance: 2m/2m3: 0-1 2m4-2m7: 0-0 3m+: 0-0
Track: LH: 0-1 RH: 0-0 Tight: 0-0 Gall: 0-0
Aids: Bl: 0-0 Vi: 0-0 Tstrap: 0-0
Best Rating: 98 11/01 Wwck 2m good Hdl

Ex-French, he showed ability on his British hurdling debut at Warwick and should win races.

Mamboesque (USA)

95 **85**

4-y-o b g Miesque's Son (USA)-Brawl (USA) (Fit To Fight (USA))
W Clay (T D Barron 15/10) F E And Mrs J J Brindley

Placings: 333 (4424)

2001/02: 16^{3}HY, 16^{3}S, 16^{3}HY

	Starts	1st	2nd	3rd	Win & Pl
Hurdles	3	0	0	3	1965
Career Total	**3**	**0**	**0**	**3**	**1965**

Going: Sf: 0-3 GS: 0-0 Gd: 0-0 GF: - Fm: 0-0
Distance: 2m/2m3: 0-3 2m4-2m7: 0-0 3m+: 0-0
Track: LH: 0-2 RH: 0-1 Tight: 0-0 Gall: 0-1
Aids: Bl: 0-0 Vi: 0-0 Tstrap: 0-0
Best Rating: 85 1/02 Donc 2m110y soft Hdl

Soft-ground selling-class novice hurdler.

Mamica

98 **71**

12-y-o b g Idiots Delight-Fishermans Lass (Articulate)
G Prodromou Alan Macalister

Placings: *0402P/***2F4PP0/F2344U510/413PU/435PP0/ 465C5306** (4043)

2001/02: 21^{4}S, 27^{6}S, 29^{5}S, 22^{C}S, 16^{5}S, 24^{3}GS, 20^{0}S, 25^{6}S

	Starts	1st	2nd	3rd	Win & Pl
Chases	8	0	0	1	640
Career Total	**39**	**2**	**3**	**4**	**12296**

107	11/98	Hexm	2m4f110y	F(0-105)HCh	HVY	£3002
93	3/98	Newc	3m	E Ch	G-F	£2892

Total win prize-money £5894

Going: Sf: 0-7 GS: 0-1 Gd: 0-0 GF: - Fm: 0-0
Distance: 2m/2m3: 0-1 2m4-2m7: 0-3 3m+: 0-4
Track: LH: 0-4 RH: 0-3 Tight: 0-6 Gall: 0-1
Aids: Bl: 0-0 Vi: 0-7 Tstrap: 0-0
Best Rating: 108 11/98 Hexm 2m4f110y heavy Ch

Modest form in 2001/2 after returning from an absence.

Mamideos (IRE)

95f **110f**

5-y-o br g Good Thyne (USA)-Heavenly Artist (IRE) (Heavenly Manna)
T R George Silkword Racing Partnership

Placings: *41* (4269)

2001/02: 16^{4}G, 16^{1}S

	Starts	1st	2nd	3rd	Win & Pl
NH Flat	2	1	0	0	1641
Career Total	**2**	**1**	**0**	**0**	**1641**

110	3/02	Chep	2m110y	H NHF	SFT	£1640

Total win prize-money £1641

Going: Sf: 1-1 GS: 0-0 Gd: 0-1 GF: - Fm: 0-0
Distance: **2m/2m3: 1-2** 2m4-2m7: 0-0 3m+: 0-0
Track: **LH: 1-1** RH: 0-1 Tight: 0-0 Gall: 0-0
Aids: Bl: 0-0 Vi: 0-0 Tstrap: 0-0
Best Rating: 110 3/02 Chep 2m110y soft NHF

Showed ability on his Kempton bumper debut, but probably found that track too sharp, scored next time at Chepstow. Stayer in the making. Acts on heavy ground.

Man Murphy (IRE)

110 **121**

6-y-o b g Euphemism-Been About (IRE) (Remainder Man)
Mrs M Reveley W Manners

Placings: *1-3*311165P (4816)

2001/02: 17^{3}G, 16^{3}G, 16^{1}GS, 17^{1}HY, 19^{1}S, 16^{6}S, 20^{5}GS, 21^{P}GF

	Starts	1st	2nd	3rd	Win & Pl
NH Flat	1	0	0	1	225
Hurdles	7	3	0	1	12266
Career Total	**9**	**4**	**0**	**2**	**14150**

121	1/02	Catt	2m3f	D Hdl	SFT	£3377
121	1/02	Carl	2m1f	D Hdl	HVY	£3526
102	11/01	Newc	2m	D Hdl	G-S	£3570
106	1/01	Catt	2m	H NHF	G-S	£1659

Total win prize-money £12133

Going: Sf: 2-3 GS: 1-2 Gd: 0-2 GF: - Fm: 0-1
Distance: **2m/2m3: 3-6** 2m4-2m7: 0-2 3m+: 0-0
Track: **LH: 2-6** RH: 1-2 Tight: 1-2 Gall: 1-3
Aids: Bl: 0-0 Vi: 0-0 Tstrap: 0-0
Best Rating: 121 3/02 Sand 2m4f110y gd-sft Hdl

A winner of a Catterick bumper on his debut, he then landed a hat-trick over hurdles at Newcastle, Carlisle and Catterick. He likes the mud and has a mischievous streak in him. Effective at up to two miles three furlongs.

Man Of Steele (IRE)

9-y-o b g Ala Hounak-Church Brae (The Parson)
Miss L Alner The Hon Miss D Harding

Placings: 263/3-3 (4755)

2001/02: 23^{3}GF

	Starts	1st	2nd	3rd	Win & Pl
Chases	1	0	0	1	233
Career Total	**5**	**0**	**1**	**3**	**1460**

Going: Sf: 0-0 GS: 0-0 Gd: 0-0 GF: - Fm: 0-1
Distance: 2m/2m3: 0-0 2m4-2m7: 0-1 3m+: 0-0
Track: LH: 0-1 RH: 0-0 Tight: 0-0 Gall: 0-0
Aids: Bl: 0-0 Vi: 0-0 Tstrap: 0-0
Best Rating: 96 4/00 Asct 3m110y good Ch

Former winning pointer.

Man Of The Match

100 **98**

12-y-o b g Vital Season-Kate The Shrew (Comedy Star (USA))

M Pitman Mrs Elizabeth Pearce

Placings:003/0F3326325/5/P432 **(0974)**
2001/02: 20^{P}G, 26^{4}GF, 21^{3}G, 24^{2}GF

	Starts	1st	2nd	3rd	Win & Pl
Chases	4	0	1	1	1557
Career Total	**17**	**0**	**3**	**5**	**5235**

Going: Sf: 0-0 GS: 0-0 Gd: 0-2 GF: - Fm: 0-2
Distance: 2m/2m3: 0-0 2m4-2m7: 0-2 3m+: 0-2
Track: LH: 0-4 RH: 0-0 Tight: 0-3 Gall: 0-0
Aids: Bl: 0-0 Vi: 0-0 Tstrap: 0-0
Best Rating: 98 7/01 Strf 2m5f110y good Ch

Man On The Hill (IRE)

112 **153**

8-y-o b g Mandalus-Gipsey Jo (Furry Glen)
Ferdy Murphy D A Johnson

Placings:*4/01/*21130/34P-1111U43P2 **(4836)**
2001/02: 21^{1}G, 21^{1}G, 21^{1}S, 20^{1}S, 22^{U}HY, 24^{4}G, 24^{3}S, 24^{P}GS, 20^{2}G

	Starts	1st	2nd	3rd	Win & Pl
Chases	9	4	1	1	35535
Career Total	**20**	**7**	**2**	**3**	**49302**

151	12/01	Hayd	2m4f	B Ch	SFT	£12480
153	11/01	Sedg	2m5f	C Ch	SFT	£6776
130	11/01	Sedg	2m5f	E Ch	GD	£3168
136	5/01	Sedg	2m5f	E Ch	GD	£3529
148	1/00	Hayd	2m4f	F Hdl	SFT	£2730
138	12/99	Hayd	2m	D Hdl	SFT	£3338
102	12/98	Navn	2m	NHF	HVY	£2391

Total win prize-money £34415

Going: Sf: 2-4 GS: 0-1 Gd: 2-4 GF: - Fm: 0-0
Distance: 2m/2m3: 0-0 **2m4-2m7: 4-6** 3m+: 0-3
Track: LH: 4-7 RH: 0-2 **Tight: 3-3** Gall: 0-2
Aids: Bl: 0-0 Vi: 0-0 Tstrap: 0-0
Best Rating: 153 4/02 Ayr 2m4f good Ch

He made an impressive start to his career with Martin Pipe, but having disappointed after this he was moved to Ferdy Murphy's stable and notched up four wins on the trot over fences. Held in better company since. Acts well on easy ground and enjoys front-running. Has room for improvement over fences. Has won at up to two miles five over fences.

Manacota

5-y-o ch m Cotation-Nice Mana (FR) (Nice Havrais (USA))
R D E Woodhouse & Mrs I Reynolds

Placings:*0P* **(3443)**
2001/02: 17^{0}GS, 17^{P}S

	Starts	1st	2nd	3rd	Win & Pl
NH Flat	2	0	0	0	
Career Total	**2**	**0**	**0**	**0**	

Going: Sf: 0-1 GS: 0-1 Gd: 0-0 GF: - Fm: 0-0
Distance: 2m/2m3: 0-2 2m4-2m7: 0-0 3m+: 0-0
Track: LH: 0-2 RH: 0-0 Tight: 0-2 Gall: 0-0
Aids: Bl: 0-0 Vi: 0-0 Tstrap: 0-0
Best Rating:

Manasis (NZ)

91 **82**

11-y-o b g Tom's Shu (USA)-Ruakiwi Nymph (NZ) (Sea Anchor)
S A Brookshaw M L Davison

Placings:301/FP2/FP4P21P3/P4P2331/1-604066 **(3335)**
2001/02: 17^{6}G, 20^{0}G, 24^{4}GF, 20^{0}G, 24^{6}G, 20^{6}G

	Starts	1st	2nd	3rd	Win & Pl
Chases	6	0	0	0	370
Career Total	**28**	**4**	**3**	**4**	**20101**

114	2/01	Donc	2m3f110y	H Ch	GD	£1225
127	2/00	Donc	2m3f110y	E(0-115)HCh	GD	£2973
116	2/99	Donc	2m3f110y	E(0-105)HCh	G-F	£3252
106	3/97	Wwck	2m4f110y	E Hdl	GD	£2197

Total win prize-money £9650

Going: Sf: 0-0 GS: 0-0 Gd: 0-5 GF: - Fm: 0-1
Distance: 2m/2m3: 0-1 2m4-2m7: 0-3 3m+: 0-2
Track: LH: 0-2 RH: 0-4 Tight: 0-5 Gall: 0-0
Aids: Bl: 0-3 Vi: 0-0 Tstrap: 0-0
Best Rating: 127 2/00 Donc 2m3f110y good Ch

Often makes the frame, but does not win as often as he should. He goes well at Doncaster and was very impressive when winning there in February 2000. He was then off the track for a year before winning a hunter chase over the exact same course and distance. Suited by two and a half miles and fast ground.

Mancini

92(93c) (74c)**56**

9-y-o b/br g Nomination-Roman Blue (Charlottown)
J A B Old Mrs Anne Yearley

Placings:000352/500/0-60P4046 **(4267)**
2001/02: 22^{6}HY, 26^{0}G, 26^{P}HY, 24^{4}S, 26^{0}S, 22^{4}S, 24^{6}S

	Starts	1st	2nd	3rd	Win & Pl
Hurdles	4	0	0	0	0
Chases	3	0	0	0	243
Career Total	**17**	**0**	**1**	**1**	**1362**

Going: Sf: 0-6 GS: 0-0 Gd: 0-1 GF: - Fm: 0-0
Distance: 2m/2m3: 0-0 2m4-2m7: 0-2 3m+: 0-5
Track: LH: 0-4 RH: 0-3 Tight: 0-4 Gall: 0-1
Aids: Bl: 0-5 Vi: 0-0 Tstrap: 0-0
Best Rating: 101 4/99 Worc 3m gd-sft Hdl

Mandalay Man (IRE)

9-y-o br g Mandalus-Nice Little Earner (Warpath)
Mrs S C Bradburne Mrs C J Kerr

Placings:*0*/000PP-0 **(0176)**
2001/02: 16^{0}GF

	Starts	1st	2nd	3rd	Win & Pl
Chases	1	0	0	0	
Career Total	**7**	**0**	**0**	**0**	

Going: Sf: 0-0 GS: 0-0 Gd: 0-0 GF: - Fm: 0-1
Distance: 2m/2m3: 0-1 2m4-2m7: 0-0 3m+: 0-0
Track: LH: 0-1 RH: 0-0 Tight: 0-0 Gall: 0-0
Aids: Bl: 0-0 Vi: 0-0 Tstrap: 0-0
Best Rating: 57 10/00 Carl 3m110y soft Hdl

Mandicat (IRE)

109

12-y-o b g Mandalus-Apicat (Buckskin (FR))
J G Fitzgerald Mrs Elizabeth Shouler

Placings:*3345*/342/1223U0/P **(2309)**
2001/02: 20^{P}GS

	Starts	1st	2nd	3rd	Win & Pl
Chases	1	0	0	0	
Career Total	**14**	**1**	**3**	**4**	**8295**

107	11/99	Weth	2m4f110y	D Hdl	GD	£2705

Total win prize-money £2705

Going: Sf: 0-0 GS: 0-1 Gd: 0-0 GF: - Fm: 0-0
Distance: 2m/2m3: 0-0 2m4-2m7: 0-1 3m+: 0-0
Track: LH: 0-0 RH: 0-1 Tight: 0-0 Gall: 0-1
Aids: Bl: 0-0 Vi: 0-0 Tstrap: 0-0
Best Rating: 125 1/00 Weth 2m4f110y soft Ch

Mandoob

93 **105**

5-y-o b g Zafonic (USA)-Thaidah (CAN) (Vice Regent (CAN))
B R Johnson Kevin Nolan

Placings:63 **(2515)**
2001/02: 16^{6}G, 16^{3}S

	Starts	1st	2nd	3rd	Win & Pl
Hurdles	2	0	0	1	356
Career Total	**2**	**0**	**0**	**1**	**356**

Going: Sf: 0-1 GS: 0-0 Gd: 0-1 GF: - Fm: 0-0
Distance: 2m/2m3: 0-2 2m4-2m7: 0-0 3m+: 0-0
Track: LH: 0-1 RH: 0-1 Tight: 0-1 Gall: 0-0
Aids: Bl: 0-0 Vi: 0-0 Tstrap: 0-1
Best Rating: 105 12/01 Plum 2m soft Hdl

A modest winner on the Flat, he has shown a little ability over hurdles. Handles soft ground.

Mandy Chat (IRE)

92(72h) (55h)**78**

9-y-o b m Mandalus-Double Talk (Dublin Taxi)
P T Dalton Mrs Julie Martin

Placings:*50*/P-P600P44PP2 **(4685)**
2001/02: 19^{P}G, 16^{6}GF, 20^{0}GF, 16^{0}GF, 23^{P}GF, 17^{4}GS, 16^{4}GF, 16^{P}GS, 16^{P}G, 16^{2}GF

	Starts	1st	2nd	3rd	Win & Pl
Hurdles	2	0	0	0	0
Chases	8	0	1	0	1017
Career Total	**13**	**0**	**1**	**0**	**1017**

Going: Sf: 0-0 GS: 0-2 Gd: 0-2 GF: - Fm: 0-6
Distance: 2m/2m3: 0-8 2m4-2m7: 0-1 3m+: 0-1
Track: LH: 0-7 RH: 0-2 Tight: 0-3 Gall: 0-0
Aids: Bl: 0-0 Vi: 0-0 Tstrap: 0-0
Best Rating: 85 5/99 Clon 2m soft NHF

Runner-up in two mile hunters' chase in April 2002.

Mane Frame

106 **110**

7-y-o b g Unfuwain (USA)-Moviegoer (Pharly (FR))
H Morrison Zycko Ltd

Placings:233-1PP **(4633)**
2001/02: 21^{1}GS, 22^{P}HY, 20^{P}GF

	Starts	1st	2nd	3rd	Win & Pl
Hurdles	3	1	0	0	5720
Career Total	**6**	**1**	**1**	**2**	**7644**

110	3/02	Newb	2m5f	D(0-125)HHdl	G-S	£5720

Total win prize-money £5720

Going: Sf: 0-1 GS: 1-1 Gd: 0-0 GF: - Fm: 0-1
Distance: 2m/2m3: 0-0 **2m4-2m7: 1-3** 3m+: 0-0
Track: LH: 1-2 RH: 0-1 Tight: 0-0 **Gall: 1-1**
Aids: Bl: 0-0 Vi: 0-0 Tstrap: 0-0
Best Rating: 113 2/01 Ludl 2m gd-sft Hdl

A useful stayer on the Flat, but is lightly raced over hurdles. Fair form so far, good winner on his handicap debut at Newbury in March. Looks best suited by two and a half miles on soft ground.

Manhattan Castle (IRE)

13-y-o br g Strong Gale-Allamanda (FR) (Versailles Ii)
Miss S E Cook (G M McCourt 15/7) Ms Barbara Ashby-Jones

Placings:5*43*/1221311P3/**1F41U44/01P13/2015135/4 4P23/3232/413506UPF-3U3PP** (4852)
2001/02: 21^{3}GF, 20^{U}G, 20^{3}G, 24^{P}G, 24^{P}G

	Starts	1st	2nd	3rd	Win & Pl
Chases	5	0	0	2	1059
Career Total	**54**	**11**	**6**	**11**	**113142**

142	7/00	Strf	2m4f	D(0-125)HCh	G-F	£6987
112	2/98	Thur	2m4f	Ch	SFT	£11217
146	1/98	Naas	2m3f	HCh	HVY	£4765
144	4/97	Fair	2m4f	HCh	G-F	£9579
137	1/97	Leop	2m3f	HCh	G-Y	£5425
141	1/96	Leop	2m1f	Ch	SFT	£9974
126	11/95	Tipp	2m	Ch	GD	£5425
132	2/95	Leop	2m	HHdl	SH	£6782
118	1/95	Punc	2m4f	Hdl	HVY	£3730
125	12/94	Leop	2m2f	(0-120)HHdl	SFT	£6523
104	10/94	Tipp	2m	Hdl	SFT	£3261

Total win prize-money £73673

Going: Sf: 0-0 GS: 0-0 Gd: 0-4 GF: - Fm: 0-1
Distance: 2m/2m3: 0-0 2m4-2m7: 0-3 3m+: 0-2
Track: LH: 0-3 RH: 0-2 Tight: 0-4 Gall: 0-0
Aids: Bl: 0-0 Vi: 0-0 Tstrap: 0-0
Best Rating: 146 11/99 Fair 2m soft Ch

A smart chaser in his prime, he has deteriorated and tends to make mistakes nowadays.

Manhattan Island

7-y-o b g Suave Dancer (USA)-Rostova (Blakeney)
D L Williams N F Dawe

Placings:60P/P (1842)
2001/02: 24^{P}S

	Starts	1st	2nd	3rd	Win & Pl
Hurdles	1	0	0	0	
Career Total	**4**	**0**	**0**	**0**	

Going: Sf: 0-1 GS: 0-0 Gd: 0-0 GF: - Fm: 0-0
Distance: 2m/2m3: 0-0 2m4-2m7: 0-0 3m+: 0-1
Track: LH: 0-0 RH: 0-1 Tight: 0-0 Gall: 0-0
Aids: Bl: 0-0 Vi: 0-0 Tstrap: 0-0
Best Rating: 77 9/98 List 2m gd-yld Hdl

Manhattan Rainbow (IRE)

86

11-y-o b g Mandalus-Clara Girl (Fine Blade (USA))
Miss Lucinda V Russell Mrs C J Kerr

Placings:*0*/P/3S23P32405/P1201/1PP0-P (1462)
2001/02: 24^{P}G

	Starts	1st	2nd	3rd	Win & Pl
Chases	1	0	0	0	
Career Total	**22**	**3**	**3**	**3**	**11098**

117	5/00	Kels	3m1f	H Ch	G-S	£1918
120	4/00	Kels	3m1f	H Ch	SFT	£2247
96	2/00	Kels	3m1f	H Ch	G-S	£2352

Total win prize-money £6517

Going: Sf: 0-0 GS: 0-0 Gd: 0-1 GF: - Fm: 0-0
Distance: 2m/2m3: 0-0 2m4-2m7: 0-0 3m+: 0-1
Track: LH: 0-0 RH: 0-1 Tight: 0-0 Gall: 0-0
Aids: Bl: 0-0 Vi: 0-0 Tstrap: 0-0
Best Rating: 120 4/00 Kels 3m1f soft Ch

Manhunter (IRE)

6-y-o b g Mandalus-Pinata (Deep Run)
D R C Elsworth W V M W & Mrs E S Robins

Placings:*6-0*P (4398)
2001/02: 16^{0}G, 24^{P}S

	Starts	1st	2nd	3rd	Win & Pl
NH Flat	1	0	0	0	0
Hurdles	1	0	0	0	0
Career Total	**3**	**0**	**0**	**0**	**0**

Going: Sf: 0-1 GS: 0-0 Gd: 0-1 GF: - Fm: 0-0
Distance: 2m/2m3: 0-1 2m4-2m7: 0-0 3m+: 0-1
Track: LH: 0-1 RH: 0-1 Tight: 0-0 Gall: 0-1
Aids: Bl: 0-0 Vi: 0-0 Tstrap: 0-0
Best Rating: 96 1/01 Kemp 2m soft NHF

Manikato (USA)

92 **70**

8-y-o b g Clever Trick (USA)-Pasampsi (USA) (Crow (FR))
R Curtis Mrs K M Curtis

Placings:P/P5-6 (1544)
2001/02: 17^{6}G

	Starts	1st	2nd	3rd	Win & Pl
Hurdles	1	0	0	0	0
Career Total	**4**	**0**	**0**	**0**	**0**

Going: Sf: 0-0 GS: 0-0 Gd: 0-1 GF: - Fm: 0-0
Distance: 2m/2m3: 0-1 2m4-2m7: 0-0 3m+: 0-0
Track: LH: 0-0 RH: 0-1 Tight: 0-0 Gall: 0-0
Aids: Bl: 0-0 Vi: 0-0 Tstrap: 0-0
Best Rating: 74 9/00 Worc 2m gd-fm Hdl

Maninga

104 **116**

6-y-o ch m Karinga Bay-Amberush (No Rush)
Mrs L Richards The Maninga Partnership

Placings:*5-0*4411P (4420)
2001/02: 18^{0}GS, 20^{4}GS, 20^{4}GS, 22^{1}S, 21^{1}S, 21^{P}GS

	Starts	1st	2nd	3rd	Win & Pl
NH Flat	1	0	0	0	0
Hurdles	5	2	0	0	7473
Career Total	**7**	**2**	**0**	**0**	**7473**

116	3/02	Towc	2m5f	E Hdl	SFT	£3136
108	2/02	Winc	2m6f	D Hdl	SFT	£3640

Total win prize-money £6776

Going: Sf: 2-2 GS: 0-4 Gd: 0-0 GF: - Fm: 0-0
Distance: 2m/2m3: 0-1 **2m4-2m7: 2-5** 3m+: 0-0
Track: LH: 0-2 **RH: 2-3** Tight: 0-0 Gall: 0-1
Aids: Bl: 0-0 Vi: 0-0 Tstrap: 0-0
Best Rating: 116 3/02 Towc 2m5f soft Hdl

A useful and improving novice, she got off the mark over hurdles at Wincanton in February 2002 and followed up in good style at Towcester. Stays two miles six and acts on soft ground.

Manitou Springs

88f **87f**

5-y-o br g Mandalus-Swift Conveyance (IRE) (Strong Gale)
P Winkworth P Winkworth

Placings:*0* (3883)
2001/02: 16^{0}GS

	Starts	1st	2nd	3rd	Win & Pl
NH Flat	1	0	0	0	
Career Total	**1**	**0**	**0**	**0**	

Going: Sf: 0-0 GS: 0-1 Gd: 0-0 GF: - Fm: 0-0
Distance: 2m/2m3: 0-1 2m4-2m7: 0-0 3m+: 0-0
Track: LH: 0-0 RH: 0-1 Tight: 0-0 Gall: 0-0
Aids: Bl: 0-0 Vi: 0-0 Tstrap: 0-0
Best Rating: 87 2/02 Winc 2m gd-sft NHF

Mankind

107 **98**

11-y-o b g Rakaposhi King-Mandarling (Mandalus)
J A T De Giles J A T De Giles

Placings:*00*/1/P6PP0/3P0230/10P/1 (0795)
2001/02: 22^{1}GF

	Starts	1st	2nd	3rd	Win & Pl
Hurdles	1	1	0	0	2415
Career Total	**18**	**3**	**1**	**2**	**7371**

98	6/01	NAbb	2m6f	G(0-95)HHdl	G-F	£2415
98	5/99	Hrfd	2m3f110y	G Hdl	GD	£1857
98	4/97	Strf	2m5f110y	H Ch	GD	£2038

Total win prize-money £6311

Going: Sf: 0-0 GS: 0-0 Gd: 0-0 GF: - Fm: 1-1
Distance: 2m/2m3: 0-0 **2m4-2m7: 1-1** 3m+: 0-0
Track: **LH: 1-1** RH: 0-0 **Tight: 1-1** Gall: 0-0
Aids: Bl: 0-0 Vi: 0-0 Tstrap: 0-0
Best Rating: 98 6/01 NAbb 2m6f gd-fm Hdl

Mansa Musa (IRE)

103 **121**

7-y-o br g Hamas (IRE)-Marton Maid (Silly Season)
N J Henderson W H Ponsonby

Placings:0202-120 (1442)
2001/02: 16^{1}GF, 17^{2}GF, 18^{0}GF

	Starts	1st	2nd	3rd	Win & Pl
Hurdles	3	1	1	0	3405
Career Total	**7**	**1**	**3**	**0**	**4849**

104	5/01	Hntg	2m110y	E Hdl	G-F	£2676

Total win prize-money £2677

Going: Sf: 0-0 GS: 0-0 Gd: 0-0 GF: - Fm: 1-3
Distance: **2m/2m3: 1-3** 2m4-2m7: 0-0 3m+: 0-0
Track: LH: 0-1 **RH: 1-2** Tight: 0-2 **Gall: 1-1**
Aids: Bl: 0-0 Vi: 0-0 Tstrap: 0-0
Best Rating: 121 4/01 Fknm 2m gd-sft Hdl

Mantastic (IRE)

12-y-o b g Mandalus-Fifi L'Amour (Fair Turn)
J Cullinan S M Atkins

Placings:*000L5005/24/04F/3/U-P* (0009)
2001/02: 26^{P}GS

	Starts	1st	2nd	3rd	Win & Pl
Chases	1	0	0	0	
Career Total	**16**	**0**	**1**	**1**	**1094**

Going: Sf: 0-0 GS: 0-1 Gd: 0-0 GF: - Fm: 0-0
Distance: 2m/2m3: 0-0 2m4-2m7: 0-0 3m+: 0-1
Track: LH: 0-0 RH: 0-0 Tight: 0-0 Gall: 0-0
Aids: Bl: 0-0 Vi: 0-0 Tstrap: 0-0
Best Rating: 101 5/95 Tram 2m good Hdl

Manteeno

67(95h) (78h)63

8-y-o b g Teenoso (USA)-Manenda (Mandalus)
Mrs D Thomson Mrs Dorothy Thomson

Placings:*040*/P/0PPP05-5P66 **(2183)**
2001/02: 16^5GF, 20^PG, 16^6S, 16^6G

	Starts	1st	2nd	3rd	Win & Pl
Hurdles	1	0	0	0	0
Chases	3	0	0	0	0
Career Total	**14**	**0**	**0**	**0**	**0**

Going: Sf: 0-1 GS: 0-0 Gd: 0-2 GF: - Fm: 0-1
Distance: 2m/2m3: 0-3 2m4-2m7: 0-1 3m+: 0-0
Track: LH: 0-2 RH: 0-2 Tight: 0-0 Gall: 0-0
Aids: Bl: 0-0 Vi: 0-0 Tstrap: 0-0
Best Rating: 99 1/99 Ludl 2m soft NHF

Mantilla

93 96

5-y-o b m Son Pardo-Well Tried (IRE) (Thatching)
J D Frost (R G Frost 14/2) R G Frost

Placings:2F6 **(4504)**
2001/02: 16^2GF, 17^FS, 17^6G

	Starts	1st	2nd	3rd	Win & Pl
Hurdles	3	0	1	0	602
Career Total	**3**	**0**	**1**	**0**	**602**

Going: Sf: 0-1 GS: 0-0 Gd: 0-1 GF: - Fm: 0-1
Distance: 2m/2m3: 0-3 2m4-2m7: 0-0 3m+: 0-0
Track: LH: 0-1 RH: 0-2 Tight: 0-2 Gall: 0-0
Aids: Bl: 0-0 Vi: 0-0 Tstrap: 0-0
Best Rating: 96 11/01 Ludl 2m gd-fm Hdl

Maiden on the flat, he acts on good to firm ground and goes well over two miles.

Mantusis (IRE)

108 133

7-y-o ch g Pursuit Of Love-Mana (GER) (Windwurf (GER))
P J Hobbs R J B Partners

Placings:0-31111112 **(1442)**
2001/02: 17^3F, 17^1G, 17^1GF, 17^1GF, 17^1G, 17^1G, 17^1GF, 18^2GF

	Starts	1st	2nd	3rd	Win & Pl
Hurdles	8	6	1	1	27173
Career Total	**9**	**6**	**1**	**1**	**27173**

133	8/01	NAbb	2m1f	B HHdl	G-F	£8248
117	8/01	Bang	2m1f	D Hdl	GD	£3656
115	7/01	NAbb	2m1f	D Hdl	GD	£3376
120	7/01	NAbb	2m1f	D Hdl	G-F	£3478
109	6/01	NAbb	2m1f	D Hdl	G-F	£3554
117	6/01	NAbb	2m1f	D Hdl	GD	£3511

Total win prize-money £25826

Going: Sf: 0-0 GS: 0-0 Gd: 3-3 GF: - Fm: 3-5
Distance: **2m/2m3: 6-8** 2m4-2m7: 0-0 3m+: 0-0
Track: **LH: 6-7** RH: 0-1 **Tight: 6-7** Gall: 0-0
Aids: Bl: 0-0 Vi: 0-0 Tstrap: 0-0
Best Rating: 133 8/01 NAbb 2m1f gd-fm Hdl

He ran up a six-timer in novice hurdles at the start of the season, five of them at Newton Abbot. His run came to an end at Fontwell and life is unlikely to get any easier.

Manx Magic (USA)

108(107h) (147h)154

9-y-o b g Imperial Falcon (CAN)-Spirited Away (USA) (Vaguely Noble)
M C Pipe J P Kennedy

Placings:*0323/003*11210/53014-211156F **(4677)**
2001/02: 23^2G, 24^1G, 26^1G, 24^1G, 24^5G, 32^6GS, 36^FG

	Starts	1st	2nd	3rd	Win & Pl
Hurdles	1	0	1	0	3150
Chases	6	3	0	0	22782
Career Total	**24**	**7**	**3**	**4**	**49280**

154	11/01	Chel	3m110y	B Ch	GD	£14576
150	6/01	NAbb	3m2f110y	D Ch	GD	£4192
140	5/01	Wwck	3m110y	E Ch	GD	£3263
144	2/01	Winc	2m6f	C(0-135)HHdl	GD	£8658
128	3/00	Extr	3m1f110y	E Hdl	G-S	£3050
125	1/00	Weth	2m7f	E Hdl	SFT	£2537
125	1/00	Wwck	2m4f110y	E Hdl	SFT	£3143

Total win prize-money £39422

Going: Sf: 0-0 GS: 0-1 Gd: 3-6 GF: - Fm: 0-0
Distance: 2m/2m3: 0-0 2m4-2m7: 0-0 **3m+: 3-7**
Track: **LH: 2-6** RH: 0-0 Tight: 1-2 Gall: 1-3
Aids: Bl: 0-0 Vi: 0-3 Tstrap: 0-0
Best Rating: 154 11/01 Chel 3m110y good Ch

Successful over hurdles and fences, he was fatally injured in the Grand National. (DEAD)

Manx Shadow

5-y-o b/br m Contract Law (USA)-Inbisat (Beldale Flutter (USA))
K W Hogg K W Hogg

Placings:PP **(1637)**
2001/02: 17^PG, 17^PGS

	Starts	1st	2nd	3rd	Win & Pl
Hurdles	2	0	0	0	
Career Total	**2**	**0**	**0**	**0**	

Going: Sf: 0-0 GS: 0-1 Gd: 0-1 GF: - Fm: 0-0
Distance: 2m/2m3: 0-2 2m4-2m7: 0-0 3m+: 0-0
Track: LH: 0-1 RH: 0-1 Tight: 0-1 Gall: 0-0
Aids: Bl: 0-0 Vi: 0-0 Tstrap: 0-0
Best Rating:

Maori Chief (IRE)

8-y-o br g Jolly Jake (NZ)-Monatrim (Le Moss)
Dr P Pritchard Steven R Hanney

Placings:00P/PPPF-P **(0252)**
2001/02: 26^PGF

	Starts	1st	2nd	3rd	Win & Pl
Chases	1	0	0	0	
Career Total	**8**	**0**	**0**	**0**	

Going: Sf: 0-0 GS: 0-0 Gd: 0-0 GF: - Fm: 0-1
Distance: 2m/2m3: 0-0 2m4-2m7: 0-0 3m+: 0-1
Track: LH: 0-1 RH: 0-0 Tight: 0-1 Gall: 0-0
Aids: Bl: 0-0 Vi: 0-0 Tstrap: 0-0
Best Rating: 67 1/00 Wwck 2m4f110y soft Hdl

Maousse Honor (FR)

107(98h) (116h)127+

7-y-o b m Hero's Honor (USA)-Maousse (FR) (Labus (FR))
M C Pipe Sean Lucey

Placings:22/111/5PP **(3884)**
2001/02: 19^5GS, 16^PGS, 16^PGS

	Starts	1st	2nd	3rd	Win & Pl
Hurdles	3	0	0	0	0
Career Total	**8**	**3**	**2**	**0**	**33596**

114	8/99	NAbb	2m1f	E Hdl	GD	£2459
130	7/99	Worc	2m	D Hdl	G-F	£3150
	5/99	Autl	2m2f	Hdl	VS	£16146

Total win prize-money £21755

Going: Sf: 0-0 GS: 0-3 Gd: 0-0 GF: - Fm: 0-0
Distance: 2m/2m3: 0-3 2m4-2m7: 0-0 3m+: 0-0
Track: LH: 0-1 RH: 0-2 Tight: 0-0 Gall: 0-1
Aids: Bl: 0-0 Vi: 0-0 Tstrap: 0-0
Best Rating: 130 7/99 Worc 2m gd-fm Hdl

Ex-French mare, won three times in the summer of 1999 before sustaining an injury. Promising comeback late in 2001, but has run badly since. Won first two starts over fences in the summer of 2002. Acts on fast ground, suited by trips around two miles, likes to front-run.

Map Boy

4-y-o b g Chaddleworth (IRE)-Chaconia Girl (Bay Express)
Jamie Poulton (B R Johnson 24/6) M C Trevena

Placings:FP **(1821)**
2001/02: 16^FGS, 16^PGS

	Starts	1st	2nd	3rd	Win & Pl
Hurdles	2	0	0	0	
Career Total	**2**	**0**	**0**	**0**	

Going: Sf: 0-0 GS: 0-2 Gd: 0-0 GF: - Fm: 0-0
Distance: 2m/2m3: 0-2 2m4-2m7: 0-0 3m+: 0-0
Track: LH: 0-1 RH: 0-1 Tight: 0-1 Gall: 0-0
Aids: Bl: 0-0 Vi: 0-0 Tstrap: 0-0
Best Rating:

Mapleton

108(81h) (66h)118+

9-y-o br g Skyliner-Maple Syrup (Charlottown)
Mrs S J Smith Keith Middleton

Placings:606605P/23420/503340323/2221P-422402PP5 **(4855)**
2001/02: 16^4G, 20^2G, 24^2G, 25^4GS, 16^0G, 20^2GS, 22^PS, 20^PHY, 20^5G

	Starts	1st	2nd	3rd	Win & Pl
Hurdles	1	0	0	0	0
Chases	8	0	3	0	3181
Career Total	**35**	**1**	**9**	**5**	**14322**

100	7/00	Sthl	3m110y	E Ch	G-F	£2921

Total win prize-money £2922

Going: Sf: 0-2 GS: 0-2 Gd: 0-5 GF: - Fm: 0-0
Distance: 2m/2m3: 0-2 2m4-2m7: 0-5 3m+: 0-2
Track: LH: 0-6 RH: 0-3 Tight: 0-7 Gall: 0-1
Aids: Bl: 0-0 Vi: 0-0 Tstrap: 0-0
Best Rating: 117 10/01 Sthl 2m4f110y good Ch

Consistent chaser at a low level, he seems to handle all types of ground and stays three miles.

Maragun (GER)

107 (110c)131

6-y-o b g General Assembly (USA)-Marcelia (GER) (Priamos (GER))

M C Pipe Emlyn Hughes & Stuart Mercer

Placings:3P-311261304 **(4828)**

2001/02: 22^{3}GS, 17^{1}GF, 16^{1}GF, 18^{2}GS, 16^{6}G, 16^{1}G, 16^{3}G, 16^{0}G, 16^{4}G

	Starts	1st	2nd	3rd	Win & Pl
Hurdles	9	3	1	2	10947
Career Total	**11**	**3**	**1**	**3**	**11333**

120	11/01	Hntg	2m110y	E Hdl	GD	£2429
119	8/01	Uttx	2m	D Hdl	G-F	£3360
123	6/01	MRas	2m1f110y	F(0-100)HHdl	G-F	£2902

Total win prize-money £8691

Going: Sf: 0-0 GS: 0-2 Gd: 1-5 GF: - Fm: 2-2
Distance: **2m/2m3: 3-8** 2m4-2m7: 0-1 3m+: 0-0
Track: LH: 1-5 **RH: 2-3** Tight: 1-3 Gall: 1-1
Aids: Bl: 0-0 Vi: 0-1 Tstrap: 0-0
Best Rating: 131 11/01 Asct 2m110y good Hdl

A decent winner on the Flat in Germany, he has taken well to hurdles, winning ordinary novice events in the Midlands in 2001. Held in better company. Suited by fast ground and two miles.

Maraud

103 92+

8-y-o ch g Midyan (USA)-Peak Squaw (USA) (Icecapade (USA))

M E Sowersby David Dyer

Placings:1313/0560060/513/33F56 **(4908)**

2001/02: 25^{3}GF, 25^{3}S, 27^{F}S, 27^{5}S, 21^{6}G

	Starts	1st	2nd	3rd	Win & Pl
Hurdles	5	0	0	2	1178
Career Total	**19**	**3**	**0**	**5**	**10014**

97	7/99	Sedg	3m3f110y	E(0-115)HHdl	G-F	£2745
110	2/98	Muss	2m	E Hdl	G-F	£2735
98	12/97	Catt	2m	E Hdl	GD	£1912

Total win prize-money £7393

Going: Sf: 0-3 GS: 0-0 Gd: 0-1 GF: - Fm: 0-1
Distance: 2m/2m3: 0-0 2m4-2m7: 0-1 3m+: 0-4
Track: LH: 0-4 RH: 0-1 Tight: 0-5 Gall: 0-0
Aids: Bl: 0-0 Vi: 0-0 Tstrap: 0-0
Best Rating: 110 3/98 Kels 2m110y good Hdl

A winner on the Flat, he has been successful over hurdles at around two miles, but appears more effective at around three miles.

Marauder (IRE)

(69h) (44h)

9-y-o b g Yashgan-Sweet Slievenamon (Arctic Slave)

Mrs A Price Mrs A Price

Placings:0/P04P/0-00PPP **(1625)**

2001/02: 16^{0}GF, 17^{0}F, 25^{P}GF, 25^{P}G, 24^{P}GF

	Starts	1st	2nd	3rd	Win & Pl
Hurdles	2	0	0	0	0
Chases	3	0	0	0	0
Career Total	**11**	**0**	**0**	**0**	**204**

Going: Sf: 0-0 GS: 0-0 Gd: 0-1 GF: - Fm: 0-4
Distance: 2m/2m3: 0-2 2m4-2m7: 0-0 3m+: 0-3
Track: LH: 0-1 RH: 0-4 Tight: 0-1 Gall: 0-0
Aids: Bl: 0-0 Vi: 0-0 Tstrap: 0-0
Best Rating: 49 10/99 Hrfd 2m1f gd-fm Hdl

Marble Arch

114 162

6-y-o b g Rock Hopper-Mayfair Minx (St Columbus)

H Morrison M S Wilson, R Sweet, Mrs Mary Wilson

Placings:*653*/534223411-011P2 **(4190)**

2001/02: 16^{0}G, 16^{1}GS, 16^{1}G, 16^{P}S, 16^{2}GS

	Starts	1st	2nd	3rd	Win & Pl
Hurdles	5	2	1	0	127150
Career Total	**17**	**4**	**3**	**3**	**141219**

158	12/01	Asct	2m110y	B(0-155)HHdl	GD	£58000
141	11/01	Newb	2m110y	C(0-130)HHdl	G-S	£9750
118	4/01	Ayr	2m	C Hdl	GD	£5443
118	3/01	Asct	2m110y	D(0-120)HHdl	HVY	£5213

Total win prize-money £78407

Going: Sf: 0-1 GS: 1-2 Gd: 1-2 GF: - Fm: 0-0
Distance: **2m/2m3: 2-5** 2m4-2m7: 0-0 3m+: 0-0
Track: LH: 1-4 RH: 1-1 Tight: 0-0 **Gall: 1-2**
Aids: Bl: 0-0 Vi: 0-0 Tstrap: 0-0
Best Rating: 162 3/02 Chel 2m110y gd-sft Hdl

He is very talented, but is a difficult ride who does not always find as much off the bridle as looks likely. Ruby Walsh rode him to perfection at Newbury in November and Williamson continued his success in the Ladbroke Handicap Hurdle at Ascot at Christmas. Pulled up on heavy ground in the Tote Gold Trophy, for which he started favourite. Ran a blinder to finish runner-up in the 2002 Champion Hurdle back on a sounder surface. Suited by two miles. Has won on good ground and heavy.

Marble City (IRE)

9-y-o br g Young Man (FR)-Marble Bash (IRE) (Aristocracy)

M Pitman Malcolm C Denmark

Placings:*0P4040*/**P43623P/522/6FU1222-F** **(1664)**

2001/02: 24^{F}G

	Starts	1st	2nd	3rd	Win & Pl
Chases	1	0	0	0	0
Career Total	**24**	**1**	**6**	**2**	**14086**

110	1/01	Font	2m6f	F(0-90)HCh	SFT	£3010

Total win prize-money £3010

Going: Sf: 0-0 GS: 0-0 Gd: 0-1 GF: - Fm: 0-0
Distance: 2m/2m3: 0-0 2m4-2m7: 0-0 3m+: 0-1
Track: LH: 0-1 RH: 0-0 Tight: 0-1 Gall: 0-0
Aids: Bl: 0-0 Vi: 0-1 Tstrap: 0-0
Best Rating: 110 3/01 Wwck 2m4f110y soft Ch

Marble Man (IRE)

86 87

12-y-o ch g Henbit (USA)-Flameing Run (Deep Run)

B W Murray (R H R Tierney 26/5) R H R Tierney

Placings:4P62/4123213/2134151242/45541F30/PP/P 0-46 **(0740)**

2001/02: 22^{4}G, 16^{6}GS

	Starts	1st	2nd	3rd	Win & Pl
Chases	2	0	0	0	0
Career Total	**35**	**6**	**6**	**4**	**30724**

111	12/98	Muss	2m	F(0-95)HCh	G-F	£2823
111	2/98	Carl	2m	D(0-125)HCh	SFT	£3387
109	12/97	Sedg	2m110y	E(0-110)HCh	SFT	£3488
102	10/97	Carl	2m	D(0-125)HCh	G-F	£3355
97	2/97	Carl	2m	D(0-125)HCh	G-S	£3747
78	10/96	Kels	2m110y	E Hdl	FRM	£2402

Total win prize-money £19204

Going: Sf: 0-0 GS: 0-1 Gd: 0-1 GF: - Fm: 0-0
Distance: 2m/2m3: 0-1 2m4-2m7: 0-1 3m+: 0-0
Track: LH: 0-1 RH: 0-1 Tight: 0-1 Gall: 0-0
Aids: Bl: 0-0 Vi: 0-0 Tstrap: 0-0
Best Rating: 111 1/99 Muss 2m gd-sft Ch

March North

107 113

7-y-o b g Petoski-Coral Delight (Idiots Delight)

Mrs P Robeson Ron Collins

Placings:*435*/5631-56164F6 **(3775)**

2001/02: 16^{5}GF, 16^{6}G, 16^{1}G, 17^{6}G, 21^{4}GS, 18^{F}HY, 20^{6}S

	Starts	1st	2nd	3rd	Win & Pl
Hurdles	7	1	0	0	6874
Career Total	**14**	**2**	**0**	**2**	**9375**

113	11/01	Hntg	2m110y	D(0-120)HHdl	GD	£6873
106	1/01	Fknm	2m	F(0-110)HHdl	SFT	£1838

Total win prize-money £8712

Going: Sf: 0-2 GS: 0-1 Gd: 1-3 GF: - Fm: 0-1
Distance: **2m/2m3: 1-5** 2m4-2m7: 0-2 3m+: 0-0
Track: LH: 0-3 **RH: 1-4** Tight: 0-1 **Gall: 1-3**
Aids: Bl: 0-0 Vi: 0-0 Tstrap: 0-0
Best Rating: 113 11/01 Hntg 2m110y good Hdl

A fair handicapper over hurdles, barely stays two miles and is best on a sharp track. Handles good ground or softer.

Marchaway (IRE)

9-y-o b g Magical Strike (USA)-Milly Whiteway (Great Whiteway (USA))

N M Babbage Ten Away Partnership

Placings:0F0/00051160/B0061506F0U/**355303/PFP** **(2148)**

2001/02: 25^{P}S, 20^{F}S, 21^{P}G

	Starts	1st	2nd	3rd	Win & Pl
Hurdles	3	0	0	0	
Career Total	**31**	**3**	**0**	**3**	**12164**

106	12/98	Punc	2m4f	(0-127)HHdl	SH	£5380
97	3/98	Naas	2m	(0-102)HHdl	Y-S	£2680
104	2/98	Naas	2m3f	(0-102)HHdl	SFT	£2978

Total win prize-money £11038

Going: Sf: 0-2 GS: 0-0 Gd: 0-1 GF: - Fm: 0-0
Distance: 2m/2m3: 0-0 2m4-2m7: 0-2 3m+: 0-1
Track: LH: 0-2 RH: 0-0 Tight: 0-0 Gall: 0-1
Aids: Bl: 0-2 Vi: 0-0 Tstrap: 0-0
Best Rating: 108 3/00 Plum 3m1f110y good Hdl

Marche Militaire (IRE)

101 86

4-y-o b g Corrouge (USA)-Rose Deer (Whistling Deer)

L Lungo Mrs Ann Fortune

Placings:0112 **(4139)**

2001/02: 16^{0}G, 16^{1}G, 16^{1}S, 16^{2}HY

	Starts	1st	2nd	3rd	Win & Pl
Hurdles	4	2	1	0	7680
Career Total	**4**	**2**	**1**	**0**	**7680**

86	2/02	Muss	2m	D Hdl	SFT	£3623
85	12/01	Muss	2m	E Hdl	GD	£3192

Total win prize-money £6816

Going: Sf: 1-2 GS: 0-0 Gd: 1-2 GF: - Fm: 0-0
Distance: **2m/2m3: 2-4** 2m4-2m7: 0-0 3m+: 0-0

Track: LH: 0-2 **RH: 2-2 Tight: 2-2** Gall: 0-0
Aids: Bl: 0-0 Vi: 0-0 Tstrap: 0-0
Best Rating: 86 3/02 Ayr 2m heavy Hdl

Improved from his debut to win a juvenile event at Musselburgh in December. Landed a similar event there in February.

Marching Marquis (IRE)

11-y-o b g Aristocracy-Lady Go Marching (USA) (Go Marching (USA))
John R Upson Ramsay Donald Brown

Placings: *21*/UU2130/**32P11/12/3P-P** **(4567)**
2001/02: 22^{P}G

	Starts	1st	2nd	3rd	Win & Pl
Chases	1	0	0	0	
Career Total	**18**	**5**	**4**	**3**	**22652**

120	2/00	Newb	3m	H Ch	G-S	£2100
118	4/99	Hntg	2m4f110y	H Ch	GD	£1451
106	3/99	Sand	2m4f110y	H Ch	G-F	£1940
116	2/97	Wwck	2m4f110y	D Hdl	G-F	£3377
111	3/96	Sand	2m110y	H NHF	SFT	£1416

Total win prize-money £10287

Going: Sf: 0-0 GS: 0-0 Gd: 0-1 GF: - Fm: 0-0
Distance: 2m/2m3: 0-0 2m4-2m7: 0-1 3m+: 0-0
Track: LH: 0-0 RH: 0-1 Tight: 0-0 Gall: 0-0
Aids: Bl: 0-0 Vi: 0-0 Tstrap: 0-0
Best Rating: 135 3/00 Chel 3m110y good Ch

A useful hunter chaser in his prime, second in the 2000 Kim Muir at Cheltenham. Suited by front-running tactics. Off the track for over 18 months before reappearing in spring 2002. Stays three miles. Has won on good and soft ground.

Marching Orders (IRE)

114 **113**
6-y-o b g Nashwan (USA)-Minstrels Folly (USA) (The Minstrel (CAN))
R Ford D W Watson

Placings: 1P405 **(4157)**
2001/02: 16^{1}G, 16^{P}S, 16^{4}S, 16^{0}GS, 16^{5}GS

	Starts	1st	2nd	3rd	Win & Pl
Hurdles	5	1	0	0	3234
Career Total	**5**	**1**	**0**	**0**	**3234**

113	10/01	Aint	2m110y	E Hdl	GD	£3234

Total win prize-money £3234

Going: Sf: 0-2 GS: 0-2 Gd: 1-1 GF: - Fm: 0-0
Distance: **2m/2m3: 1-5** 2m4-2m7: 0-0 3m+: 0-0
Track: **LH: 1-3** RH: 0-2 **Tight: 1-1** Gall: 0-1
Aids: Bl: 0-0 Vi: 0-0 Tstrap: 0-0
Best Rating: 113 10/01 Aint 2m110y good Hdl

Good form on the Flat in Ireland in 1999, he made a successful start to hurdling at Aintree in October of 2001, but has not gone on from there. Best over two miles on good ground.

Marciano

80 **42**
6-y-o b g Rock Hopper-Raintree Venture (Good Times (ITY))
Mrs P Sly F Allan

Placings: 66205/443P-00 **(0877)**
2001/02: 20^{0}G, 21^{0}G

	Starts	1st	2nd	3rd	Win & Pl
Hurdles	2	0	0	0	
Career Total	**11**	**0**	**1**	**1**	**1138**

Going: Sf: 0-0 GS: 0-0 Gd: 0-2 GF: - Fm: 0-0
Distance: 2m/2m3: 0-0 2m4-2m7: 0-2 3m+: 0-0
Track: LH: 0-1 RH: 0-1 Tight: 0-1 Gall: 0-0
Aids: Bl: 0-0 Vi: 0-0 Tstrap: 0-0
Best Rating: 78 5/00 Fknm 2m7f110y firm Hdl

Marcovina (IRE)

86 **53**
4-y-o ch g Erin's Isle-Irish Call (USA) (Irish River (FR))
M Todhunter (J S Bolger 19/5) Ugm Racing Club

Placings: 0 **(4486)**
2001/02: 17^{0}GS

	Starts	1st	2nd	3rd	Win & Pl
Hurdles	1	0	0	0	
Career Total	**1**	**0**	**0**	**0**	

Going: Sf: 0-0 GS: 0-1 Gd: 0-0 GF: - Fm: 0-0
Distance: 2m/2m3: 0-1 2m4-2m7: 0-0 3m+: 0-0
Track: LH: 0-0 RH: 0-1 Tight: 0-0 Gall: 0-0
Aids: Bl: 0-0 Vi: 0-0 Tstrap: 0-0
Best Rating: 53 3/02 Carl 2m1f gd-sft Hdl

Marcus Maximus (USA)

104 **118**
7-y-o ch g Woodman (USA)-Star Pastures (Northfields (USA))
H D Daly (N A Callaghan 13/12) Ludlow Racing Partnership

Placings: 3-1210PP1 **(4640)**
2001/02: 16^{1}S, 16^{2}G, 16^{1}G, 16^{0}S, 16^{P}GS, 21^{P}S, 16^{1}G

	Starts	1st	2nd	3rd	Win & Pl
Hurdles	7	3	1	0	8914
Career Total	**8**	**3**	**1**	**1**	**9166**

98	4/02	Ludl	2m	G Hdl	GD	£3250
106	11/01	Kemp	2m	F(0-100)HHdl	GD	£2926
103	11/01	Strf	2m110y	G Hdl	SFT	£2044

Total win prize-money £8220

Going: Sf: 1-3 GS: 0-1 Gd: 2-3 GF: - Fm: 0-0
Distance: **2m/2m3: 3-6** 2m4-2m7: 0-1 3m+: 0-0
Track: LH: 1-1 **RH: 2-6 Tight: 1-1** Gall: 0-2
Aids: Bl: 0-0 Vi: 0-0 Tstrap: 0-0
Best Rating: 111 11/01 Hntg 2m110y good Hdl

A decent performer on the Flat at one time, he likes fast ground and won twice at Ludlow in the spring of 2002, the first of them a seller.

Marcus William (IRE)

89f **94f**
5-y-o ch g Roselier (FR)-River Swell (IRE) (Over The River (FR))
B G Powell P H Betts

Placings: *6U* **(4552)**
2001/02: 16^{6}S, 16^{U}GF

	Starts	1st	2nd	3rd	Win & Pl
NH Flat	2	0	0	0	0
Career Total	**2**	**0**	**0**	**0**	**0**

Going: Sf: 0-1 GS: 0-0 Gd: 0-0 GF: - Fm: 0-1
Distance: 2m/2m3: 0-2 2m4-2m7: 0-0 3m+: 0-0
Track: LH: 0-0 RH: 0-2 Tight: 0-0 Gall: 0-1
Aids: Bl: 0-0 Vi: 0-0 Tstrap: 0-0
Best Rating: 94 1/02 Kemp 2m soft NHF

Mardani (IRE)

103 **122**
7-y-o b g Fairy King (USA)-Marmana (USA) (Blushing Groom (FR))
R S Brookhouse R S Brookhouse

Placings: 2-3121P46 **(4818)**
2001/02: 19^{3}G, 17^{1}F, 17^{2}GF, 20^{1}G, 21^{P}GS, 19^{4}GF, 21^{6}GF

	Starts	1st	2nd	3rd	Win & Pl
Hurdles	7	2	1	1	7088
Career Total	**8**	**2**	**2**	**1**	**7866**

103	7/01	Worc	2m4f	E Hdl	GD	£2464
111	5/01	Extr	2m1f	E Hdl	FRM	£3130

Total win prize-money £5594

Going: Sf: 0-0 GS: 0-1 Gd: 1-2 GF: - Fm: 1-4
Distance: 2m/2m3: 1-2 2m4-2m7: 1-5 3m+: 0-0
Track: LH: 1-4 RH: 1-3 Tight: 0-2 Gall: 0-2
Aids: Bl: 0-0 Vi: 0-0 Tstrap: 0-0
Best Rating: 113 4/02 MRas 2m3f110y gd-fm Hdl

A staying Handicapper on the Flat, he did well over hurdles on a sound surface in the summer of 2001 and returned to form when upped to three miles and fitted with a visor in May 2002.

Marigliano (USA)

107(91h) (98h)**119**
9-y-o b g Riverman (USA)-Mount Holyoke (Golden Fleece (USA))
K A Morgan T Pryke,B Jones,S Alcock,K Morgan

Placings: P0/L034/F2113313/1104**2312/31022U-P0563P** **(4554)**
2001/02: 16^{P}GF, 17^{0}GS, 16^{5}G, 16^{6}S, 16^{3}GS, 17^{P}G

	Starts	1st	2nd	3rd	Win & Pl
Hurdles	1	0	0	0	0
Chases	5	0	0	1	595
Career Total	**34**	**7**	**5**	**7**	**42791**

124	1/01	Fknm	2m110y	F(0-110)HCh	SFT	£2525
121	3/00	MRas	2m1f110y	D Ch	G-F	£5124
128	11/99	Hntg	2m110y	C(0-130)HHdl	G-F	£10365
116	11/99	Worc	2m	C(0-130)HHdl	G-S	£4744
111	2/99	Catt	2m	C(0-130)HHdl	GD	£4770
109	1/99	Catt	2m	D(0-120)HHdl	GD	£2775
119	12/98	Hayd	2m	E(0-120)HHdl	SFT	£2232

Total win prize-money £32536

Going: Sf: 0-1 GS: 0-2 Gd: 0-2 GF: - Fm: 0-1
Distance: 2m/2m3: 0-6 2m4-2m7: 0-0 3m+: 0-0
Track: LH: 0-1 RH: 0-5 Tight: 0-4 Gall: 0-2
Aids: Bl: 0-0 Vi: 0-0 Tstrap: 0-0
Best Rating: 128 11/99 Hntg 2m110y gd-fm Hdl

Versatile gelding who has won under all codes and goes particularly well on a tight track. Handles anything but extremes of ground. Mostly out of form this term.

Marino West (IRE)

(97h) (104h)
7-y-o ch g Phardante (FR)-Seanaphobal Lady (Kambalda)
N M Babbage Provex Products Ltd

Placings: 61P **(4817)**
2001/02: 19^{6}G, 20^{1}GF, 24^{P}GF

	Starts	1st	2nd	3rd	Win & Pl

	Starts	1st	2nd	3rd	Win & Pl
Hurdles	3	1	0	0	5369
Career Total	**3**	**1**	**0**	**0**	**5369**

104 4/02 Asct 2m4f C Hdl G-F £5369
Total win prize-money £5369

Going: Sf: 0-0 GS: 0-0 Gd: 0-1 GF: - Fm: 1-2
Distance: 2m/2m3: 0-1 **2m4-2m7: 1-1** 3m+: 0-1
Track: LH: 0-0 **RH: 1-2** Tight: 0-0 Gall: 0-0
Aids: Bl: 0-0 Vi: 0-0 Tstrap: 0-0
Best Rating: 104 4/02 Asct 2m4f gd-fm Hdl

He showed nothing on his hurdling debut, but won a weak novice event at Ascot on his second start. Suited by two and a half miles and fast ground.

Marisol (IRE)

96(79h) (53h)101
9-y-o b m Mujtahid (USA)-Stanerra's Star (Shadeed (USA))
A G Hobbs (Miss L Day 23/5) J Parfitt

Placings:*0/4204/0/*P0-FP021P **(1403)**
2001/02: 21^{F}GF, 21^{P}G, 24^{0}GF, 21^{2}G, 23^{1}GF, 24^{P}G

	Starts	1st	2nd	3rd	Win & Pl
Hurdles	1	0	0	0	0
Chases	5	1	1	0	4632
Career Total	**14**	**1**	**2**	**0**	**5476**

101 8/01 Worc 2m7f110y E(0-105)HCh G-F £3571
Total win prize-money £3572

Going: Sf: 0-0 GS: 0-0 Gd: 0-3 GF: - Fm: 1-3
Distance: 2m/2m3: 0-0 2m4-2m7: 0-3 **3m+: 1-3**
Track: **LH: 1-4** RH: 0-1 Tight: 0-3 Gall: 0-0
Aids: Bl: 0-0 Vi: 0-0 **Tstrap: 1-3**
Best Rating: 101 8/01 Worc 2m7f110y gd-fm Ch

Marjeune

95 76
5-y-o b m Marju (IRE)-Ann Veronica (IRE) (Sadler's Wells (USA))
J G Portman (J G Smyth-Osbourne 1/10) The Breakaways

Placings:030 **(2204)**
2001/02: 20^{0}G, 16^{3}S, 16^{0}GS

	Starts	1st	2nd	3rd	Win & Pl
Hurdles	3	0	0	1	278
Career Total	**3**	**0**	**0**	**1**	**278**

Going: Sf: 0-1 GS: 0-1 Gd: 0-1 GF: - Fm: 0-0
Distance: 2m/2m3: 0-2 2m4-2m7: 0-1 3m+: 0-0
Track: LH: 0-1 RH: 0-2 Tight: 0-1 Gall: 0-0
Aids: Bl: 0-0 Vi: 0-0 Tstrap: 0-0
Best Rating: 76 11/01 Leic 2m gd-sft Hdl

Mark Equal

106 110
6-y-o b g Nicholas Bill-Dissolution (Henbit (USA))
M C Pipe Heeru Kirpalani Racing

Placings:*5-*3104 **(4764)**
2001/02: 17^{3}G, 19^{1}S, 16^{0}GS, 16^{4}GF

	Starts	1st	2nd	3rd	Win & Pl
NH Flat	1	0	0	1	327
Hurdles	3	1	0	0	4470
Career Total	**5**	**1**	**0**	**1**	**4797**

110 1/02 Tntn 2m3f110y D Hdl SFT £4130
Total win prize-money £4130

Going: Sf: 1-1 GS: 0-1 Gd: 0-1 GF: - Fm: 0-1
Distance: 2m/2m3: 0-3 **2m4-2m7: 1-1** 3m+: 0-0
Track: LH: 0-2 **RH: 1-2 Tight: 1-3** Gall: 0-0
Aids: Bl: 0-0 Vi: 0-0 Tstrap: 0-0
Best Rating: 110 1/02 Tntn 2m3f110y soft Hdl

Showed ability in bumpers before getting off the mark on his hurdling debut. Acts on soft ground and is effective over two miles three.

Mark-Antony (IRE)

(75c) (93c)
8-y-o ch g Phardante (FR)-Judysway (Deep Run)
Miss Venetia Williams (G B Balding 23/6) David M Williams

Placings:0-F0FP **(3515)**
2001/02: 19^{F}G, 16^{0}GF, 25^{F}G, 19^{P}S

	Starts	1st	2nd	3rd	Win & Pl
Hurdles	1	0	0	0	
Chases	3	0	0	0	
Career Total	**5**	**0**	**0**	**0**	

Going: Sf: 0-1 GS: 0-0 Gd: 0-2 GF: - Fm: 0-1
Distance: 2m/2m3: 0-2 2m4-2m7: 0-1 3m+: 0-1
Track: LH: 0-1 RH: 0-3 Tight: 0-2 Gall: 0-0
Aids: Bl: 0-0 Vi: 0-0 Tstrap: 0-0
Best Rating: 93 5/01 Hrfd 2m3f good Ch

Market Scan (IRE)

96 108
9-y-o b g King's Ride-Cothill Lady (IRE) (Orchestra)
J J O'Neill Mr Richard Seed & Mrs Maralyn Seed

Placings:*2/1/*5432-4 **(1844)**
2001/02: 25^{4}S

	Starts	1st	2nd	3rd	Win & Pl
Chases	1	0	0	0	649
Career Total	**7**	**1**	**2**	**1**	**6112**

112 10/98 Carl 2m4f110y E Hdl HVY £2500
Total win prize-money £2500

Going: Sf: 0-1 GS: 0-0 Gd: 0-0 GF: - Fm: 0-0
Distance: 2m/2m3: 0-0 2m4-2m7: 0-0 3m+: 0-1
Track: LH: 0-0 RH: 0-1 Tight: 0-0 Gall: 0-0
Aids: Bl: 0-0 Vi: 0-0 Tstrap: 0-0
Best Rating: 129 1/01 Weth 3m1f heavy Ch

Returned from two years' absence with leg trouble last season, and ran well without winning. Still a novice, he is on a fair mark and should be able to find a race or two at around three miles on soft ground.

Marlborough (IRE)

116 175
10-y-o br g Strong Gale-Wrekenogan (Tarqogan)
N J Henderson Sir Robert Ogden

Placings:5213/U111FF/PU1216/111-34F0 **(4839)**
2001/02: 24^{3}S, 26^{4}G, 36^{F}G, 33^{0}G

	Starts	1st	2nd	3rd	Win & Pl
Chases	4	0	0	1	21600
Career Total	**23**	**9**	**2**	**2**	**204884**

175 4/01 Sand 3m110y A Ch G-S £58000
175 2/01 Winc 3m1f110y B Ch GD £16932
176 12/00 Chel 3m1f110y B HCh SFT £28678
168 3/00 Chel 3m110y B HCh GD £39000
161 1/00 Kemp 3m C(0-135)HCh GD £6955
141 1/99 Kemp 3m D Ch SFT £4924
138 12/98 Ling 3m E Ch SFT £3326
141 11/98 Worc 2m4f110y E Ch HVY £3600
126 3/98 Newb 2m5f D Hdl G-S £3793
Total win prize-money £165211

Going: Sf: 0-1 GS: 0-0 Gd: 0-3 GF: - Fm: 0-0
Distance: 2m/2m3: 0-0 2m4-2m7: 0-0 3m+: 0-4
Track: LH: 0-4 RH: 0-0 Tight: 0-1 Gall: 0-2
Aids: Bl: 0-0 Vi: 0-0 Tstrap: 0-0
Best Rating: 176 12/00 Chel 3m1f110y soft Ch

He took a while to realise his potential but, ran out a fluent winner of the William Hill Handicap Chase at the Festival in 2000. He won three out of three in the 2000/01 season. Including a success in Sandown's 'substitute Gold Cup', the Tote Gold Trophy Chase. Good effort on his belated return at Newbury in February 2002, before finishing fourth in the Gold Cup. Fell at the first in the Grand National and well beaten the Scottish version. Stays three miles. Acts on good/good to soft ground.

Marmaduke (IRE)

111 116
6-y-o ch g Perugino (USA)-Sympathy (Precocious)
M Pitman Martin Butler

Placings:201220-341646 **(2314)**
2001/02: 16^{3}GF, 16^{4}GF, 16^{1}G, 19^{6}GS, 19^{4}G, 16^{6}G

	Starts	1st	2nd	3rd	Win & Pl
Hurdles	6	1	0	1	7072
Career Total	**12**	**2**	**3**	**1**	**11229**

116 10/01 Hntg 2m110y C(0-130)HHdl GD £5432
116 12/00 Ludl 2m F Hdl SFT £2436
Total win prize-money £7868

Going: Sf: 0-0 GS: 0-1 Gd: 1-3 GF: - Fm: 0-2
Distance: **2m/2m3: 1-6** 2m4-2m7: 0-0 3m+: 0-0
Track: LH: 0-4 **RH: 1-2** Tight: 0-3 **Gall: 1-3**
Aids: Bl: 0-0 Vi: 0-0 Tstrap: 0-0
Best Rating: 116 10/01 Hntg 2m110y good Hdl

Winner of a claiming hurdle at Ludlow in December 2000, he picked up a handicap at Huntingdon in October though his cause was helped by the misfortune of others.

Marmaduke Jinks

(90h) (107h)
8-y-o b g Primitive Rising (USA)-Keldholme (Derek H)
Mrs M Reveley Minster Commercials

Placings: *1/*316F-F **(1741)**
2001/02: 17^{F}G

	Starts	1st	2nd	3rd	Win & Pl
Chases	1	0	0	0	
Career Total	**6**	**2**	**0**	**1**	**5756**

108 2/01 Hayd 2m D Hdl HVY £3640
111 1/00 Newc 2m H NHF SFT £1736
Total win prize-money £5376

Going: Sf: 0-0 GS: 0-0 Gd: 0-1 GF: - Fm: 0-0
Distance: 2m/2m3: 0-1 2m4-2m7: 0-0 3m+: 0-0
Track: LH: 0-1 RH: 0-0 Tight: 0-1 Gall: 0-0
Aids: Bl: 0-0 Vi: 0-0 Tstrap: 0-0
Best Rating: 111 1/00 Newc 2m soft NHF

Marquis Of Bedford

8-y-o ch g Bedford (USA)-Marque De Soleil (Sunyboy)
Giles Smyly Miss S Smyly

Placings:0 **(0070)**
2001/02: 21^{0}G

	Starts	1st	2nd	3rd	Win & Pl
Chases	1	0	0	0	
Career Total	**1**	**0**	**0**	**0**	

Going: Sf: 0-0 GS: 0-0 Gd: 0-1 GF: - Fm: 0-0
Distance: 2m/2m3: 0-0 2m4-2m7: 0-1 3m+: 0-0
Track: LH: 0-1 RH: 0-0 Tight: 0-1 Gall: 0-0
Aids: Bl: 0-0 Vi: 0-1 Tstrap: 0-0
Best Rating: 25 5/01 Sedg 2m5f good Ch

Marrowfat Lady (IRE)

11-y-o b m Astronef-Lady Topknot (High Top)
Miss L V Davis Miss Louise Davis

Placings:00P62/P6/F00/0P/**PPP/F** (1802)
2001/02: 16^{F}GF

	Starts	1st	2nd	3rd	Win & Pl
Chases	1	0	0	0	
Career Total	16	0	1	0	689

Going: Sf: 0-0 GS: 0-0 Gd: 0-0 GF: - Fm: 0-1
Distance: 2m/2m3: 0-1 2m4-2m7: 0-0 3m+: 0-0
Track: LH: 0-0 RH: 0-1 Tight: 0-1 Gall: 0-0
Aids: Bl: 0-0 Vi: 0-0 Tstrap: 0-1
Best Rating: 80 4/95 Plum 2m1f firm Hdl

Marsh Marigold

90 66
8-y-o br m Tina's Pet-Pulga (Blakeney)
G Fierro G Fierro

Placings:0/0031440054635/25003300000/111356164 43601055P-00P (0672)
2001/02: 16^{0}G, 17^{0}G, 20^{P}GF

	Starts	1st	2nd	3rd	Win & Pl
Hurdles	3	0	0	0	
Career Total	46	6	1	6	18508

99	11/00	Chep	2m110y	F(0-90)Hdl	HVY	£1883
99	7/00	Worc	2m2f	E(0-115)HHdl	G-F	£4160
97	5/00	Hexm	2m	E(0-115)HHdl	GD	£1831
90	5/00	Worc	2m	F(0-105)HHdl	G-F	£2604
99	5/00	Towc	2m	F(0-105)HHdl	G-F	£2007
85	11/98	Leic	2m	G Hdl	SFT	£2616

Total win prize-money £15102

Going: Sf: 0-0 GS: 0-0 Gd: 0-2 GF: - Fm: 0-1
Distance: 2m/2m3: 0-2 2m4-2m7: 0-1 3m+: 0-0
Track: LH: 0-2 RH: 0-1 Tight: 0-1 Gall: 0-1
Aids: Bl: 0-0 Vi: 0-0 Tstrap: 0-0
Best Rating: 99 11/00 Chep 2m110y heavy Hdl

Marsh Mellow

(81h)
7-y-o b g High Kicker (USA)-Snugfit Annie (Midyan (USA))
R J Hodges P E Axon

Placings:06/00/0P-**F0** (0496)
2001/02: 18^{F}GF, 16^{0}G

	Starts	1st	2nd	3rd	Win & Pl
Chases	2	0	0	0	
Career Total	8	0	0	0	0

Going: Sf: 0-0 GS: 0-0 Gd: 0-1 GF: - Fm: 0-1
Distance: 2m/2m3: 0-2 2m4-2m7: 0-0 3m+: 0-0
Track: LH: 0-0 RH: 0-1 Tight: 0-1 Gall: 0-0
Aids: Bl: 0-0 Vi: 0-0 Tstrap: 0-0
Best Rating: 84 4/99 Plum 2m1f gd-sft Hdl

Marsham (IRE)

(79h)
9-y-o b g King's Ride-Inagh's Image (Menelek)
G F H Charles-Jones S P Tindall

Placings:*0000*/00/PP050-PU (0796)
2001/02: 17^{P}G, 16^{U}GF

	Starts	1st	2nd	3rd	Win & Pl
Hurdles	1	0	0	0	0
Chases	1	0	0	0	0
Career Total	13	0	0	0	0

Going: Sf: 0-0 GS: 0-0 Gd: 0-1 GF: - Fm: 0-1
Distance: 2m/2m3: 0-2 2m4-2m7: 0-0 3m+: 0-0
Track: LH: 0-2 RH: 0-0 Tight: 0-2 Gall: 0-0
Aids: Bl: 0-1 Vi: 0-0 Tstrap: 0-0
Best Rating: 90 10/99 Navn 2m gd-yld Hdl

Marteeny

7-y-o b m Teenoso (USA)-Marejo (Creetown)
J B Walton F T Walton

Placings:*0000*/046500-0 (0222)
2001/02: 20^{0}GF

	Starts	1st	2nd	3rd	Win & Pl
Hurdles	1	0	0	0	
Career Total	11	0	0	0	0

Going: Sf: 0-0 GS: 0-0 Gd: 0-0 GF: - Fm: 0-1
Distance: 2m/2m3: 0-0 2m4-2m7: 0-1 3m+: 0-0
Track: LH: 0-1 RH: 0-0 Tight: 0-0 Gall: 0-0
Aids: Bl: 0-0 Vi: 0-0 Tstrap: 0-0
Best Rating: 76 10/00 Kels 2m6f110y good Hdl

Martha Leader (IRE)

(76h)
10-y-o b g Supreme Leader-Madame Martha (Carlingford Castle)
D C Robinson D C Robinson

Placings:P00-P (1992)
2001/02: 24^{P}G

	Starts	1st	2nd	3rd	Win & Pl
Chases	2	0	0	0	
Career Total	4	0	0	0	

Going: Sf: 0-0 GS: 0-0 Gd: 0-1 GF: - Fm: 0-0
Distance: 2m/2m3: 0-0 2m4-2m7: 0-0 3m+: 0-1
Track: LH: 0-0 RH: 0-1 Tight: 0-0 Gall: 0-0
Aids: Bl: 0-0 Vi: 0-0 Tstrap: 0-0
Best Rating: 54 1/01 Kemp 2m soft Hdl

Martha Reilly (IRE)

106 89
6-y-o ch m Rainbows For Life (CAN)-Debach Delight (Great Nephew)
Mrs Barbara Waring
Charlsworth,Shapter,Haggerty,Mcdonnell

Placings:522215 (2202)
2001/02: 22^{5}GF, 22^{2}G, 24^{2}GF, 24^{2}G, 22^{1}S, 20^{5}GS

	Starts	1st	2nd	3rd	Win & Pl
Hurdles	6	1	3	0	5271
Career Total	6	1	3	0	**5271**

89	11/01	Strf	2m6f110y	E Hdl	SFT	£2628

Total win prize-money £2629

Going: Sf: 1-1 GS: 0-1 Gd: 0-2 GF: - Fm: 0-2
Distance: 2m/2m3: 0-0 **2m4-2m7: 1-4** 3m+: 0-2
Track: **LH: 1-5** RH: 0-1 **Tight: 1-4** Gall: 0-0
Aids: Bl: 0-0 Vi: 0-0 Tstrap: 0-0
Best Rating: 89 11/01 Strf 2m6f110y soft Hdl

Put a run of seconds to an end with a win in a Stratford hurdle over an extended two miles six furlongs on soft ground in November 2001.

Martha's Boy (IRE)

11-y-o b g Supreme Leader-Madame Martha (Carlingford Castle)
D C Robinson Mrs Marion Robinson

Placings:111/P/P-PP (3808)
2001/02: 24^{P}G, 26^{P}S

	Starts	1st	2nd	3rd	Win & Pl
Chases	2	0	0	0	
Career Total	7	3	0	0	10771

112	4/98	Hntg	3m	H Ch	G-S	£1236
134	4/98	Aint	3m1f	C Ch	G-S	£7253
123	3/98	Strf	3m	H Ch	GD	£2281

Total win prize-money £10771

Going: Sf: 0-1 GS: 0-0 Gd: 0-1 GF: - Fm: 0-0
Distance: 2m/2m3: 0-0 2m4-2m7: 0-0 3m+: 0-2
Track: LH: 0-0 RH: 0-1 Tight: 0-1 Gall: 0-0
Aids: Bl: 0-0 Vi: 0-0 Tstrap: 0-0
Best Rating: 134 4/98 Aint 3m1f gd-sft Ch

A former very promising hunter chaser, he broke down at Folkestone in May 1998 and has not been the same in limited appearances since.

Martinez (IRE)

82 69
6-y-o b g Tirol-Elka (USA) (Val De L'Orne (FR))
K F Clutterbuck (C W Thornton 21/5) K F Clutterbuck

Placings:030-0P (2322)
2001/02: 16^{0}GF, 20^{P}S

	Starts	1st	2nd	3rd	Win & Pl
Hurdles	2	0	0	0	
Career Total	5	0	0	1	294

Going: Sf: 0-1 GS: 0-0 Gd: 0-0 GF: - Fm: 0-1
Distance: 2m/2m3: 0-1 2m4-2m7: 0-1 3m+: 0-0
Track: LH: 0-2 RH: 0-0 Tight: 0-1 Gall: 0-0
Aids: Bl: 0-0 Vi: 0-0 Tstrap: 0-0
Best Rating: 83 2/01 Sedg 2m1f gd-sft Hdl

Martley Road (IRE)

75 36
7-y-o b g Sharifabad (IRE)-On The Road (On Your Mark)
N A Twiston-Davies Mrs S Tainton

Placings:*00*/5P-0 (0058)
2001/02: 17^{0}GS

	Starts	1st	2nd	3rd	Win & Pl
Hurdles	1	0	0	0	
Career Total	5	0	0	0	0

Going: Sf: 0-0 GS: 0-1 Gd: 0-0 GF: - Fm: 0-0
Distance: 2m/2m3: 0-1 2m4-2m7: 0-0 3m+: 0-0
Track: LH: 0-0 RH: 0-1 Tight: 0-1 Gall: 0-0
Aids: Bl: 0-0 Vi: 0-0 Tstrap: 0-0
Best Rating: 69 11/99 Chep 2m110y gd-sft NHF

Mary Farrell

84 **56**

8-y-o ch m Henbit (USA)-Don't Be Late (Pollerton)

M C Pipe Tim Kilroe

Placings: *U4/0/P-00P* **(0979)**

2001/02: 17^{0}GS, 16^{0}G, 27^{P}G

	Starts	1st	2nd	3rd	Win & Pl
Hurdles	3	0	0	0	
Career Total	**7**	**0**	**0**	**0**	**0**

Going: Sf: 0-0 GS: 0-1 Gd: 0-2 GF: - Fm: 0-0
Distance: 2m/2m3: 0-2 2m4-2m7: 0-0 3m+: 0-1
Track: LH: 0-2 RH: 0-1 Tight: 0-1 Gall: 0-0
Aids: Bl: 0-0 Vi: 0-0 Tstrap: 0-0
Best Rating: **86** 4/98 Hexm 2m heavy NHF

Mary Lane

60 **6**

6-y-o ch m Nomadic Way (USA)-Scotch Imp (Imperial Fling (USA))

N Wilson James Ritchie

Placings: *00-0* **(0475)**

2001/02: 17^{0}G

	Starts	1st	2nd	3rd	Win & Pl
Hurdles	1	0	0	0	
Career Total	**3**	**0**	**0**	**0**	

Going: Sf: 0-0 GS: 0-0 Gd: 0-1 GF: - Fm: 0-0
Distance: 2m/2m3: 0-1 2m4-2m7: 0-0 3m+: 0-0
Track: LH: 0-0 RH: 0-1 Tight: 0-1 Gall: 0-0
Aids: Bl: 0-0 Vi: 0-0 Tstrap: 0-0
Best Rating: **15** 1/01 Weth 2m heavy NHF

Mary-B

6-y-o b m Thowra (FR)-Charmonix (Scottish Reel)

J White Mrs P A White

Placings: *0* **(1154)**

2001/02: 17^{0}GF

	Starts	1st	2nd	3rd	Win & Pl
NH Flat	1	0	0	0	
Career Total	**1**	**0**	**0**	**0**	

Going: Sf: 0-0 GS: 0-0 Gd: 0-0 GF: - Fm: 0-1
Distance: 2m/2m3: 0-1 2m4-2m7: 0-0 3m+: 0-0
Track: LH: 0-1 RH: 0-0 Tight: 0-1 Gall: 0-0
Aids: Bl: 0-0 Vi: 0-0 Tstrap: 0-0
Best Rating:

Marymine (IRE)

6-y-o gr m Scallywag-Designer (Celtic Cone)

T Wall Derek & Mrs Marie Dean

Placings: *0P-0U* **(3865)**

2001/02: 16^{0}G, 16^{U}GS

	Starts	1st	2nd	3rd	Win & Pl
NH Flat	1	0	0	0	0
Hurdles	1	0	0	0	0
Career Total	**4**	**0**	**0**	**0**	

Going: Sf: 0-0 GS: 0-1 Gd: 0-1 GF: - Fm: 0-0
Distance: 2m/2m3: 0-2 2m4-2m7: 0-0 3m+: 0-0
Track: LH: 0-1 RH: 0-1 Tight: 0-0 Gall: 0-0
Aids: Bl: 0-0 Vi: 0-0 Tstrap: 0-0
Best Rating: **57** 12/00 Ludl 2m soft NHF

Mashhoor (USA)

83 **59**

4-y-o b g Thunder Gulch (USA)-Memorive (USA) (Riverman (USA))

B J Llewellyn (C E Brittain 13/9) B W Parren

Placings: 600 **(4006)**

2001/02: 16^{6}HY, 16^{0}HY, 16^{0}S

	Starts	1st	2nd	3rd	Win & Pl
Hurdles	3	0	0	0	0
Career Total	**3**	**0**	**0**	**0**	**0**

Going: Sf: 0-3 GS: 0-0 Gd: 0-0 GF: - Fm: 0-0
Distance: 2m/2m3: 0-3 2m4-2m7: 0-0 3m+: 0-0
Track: LH: 0-3 RH: 0-0 Tight: 0-1 Gall: 0-1
Aids: Bl: 0-2 Vi: 0-0 Tstrap: 0-0
Best Rating: **59** 2/02 Wwck 2m heavy Hdl

Massenet (IRE)

84 **91**

7-y-o b g Caerleon (USA)-Massawippi (Be My Native (USA))

D J Wintle Hugh M Duffy

Placings: 3030/1 **(0052)**

2001/02: 20^{1}G

	Starts	1st	2nd	3rd	Win & Pl
Hurdles	1	1	0	0	2604
Career Total	**5**	**1**	**0**	**2**	**3582**

91	5/01	Bang	2m4f	G(0-95)HHdl	GD	£2604

Total win prize-money £2604

Going: Sf: 0-0 GS: 0-0 Gd: 1-1 GF: - Fm: 0-0
Distance: 2m/2m3: 0-0 **2m4-2m7: 1-1** 3m+: 0-0
Track: **LH: 1-1** RH: 0-0 **Tight: 1-1** Gall: 0-0
Aids: Bl: 0-0 Vi: 0-0 Tstrap: 0-0
Best Rating: **91** 5/01 Bang 2m4f good Hdl

Massimo (CAN)

98 **85**

4-y-o b g Numerous (USA)-Qui Bid (USA) (Spectacular Bid (USA))

J J O'Neill (Charles O'Brien 24/10) Mrs Jonjo O'Neill

Placings: PF20 **(4579)**

2001/02: 16^{P}S, 17^{F}GS, 16^{2}HY, 16^{0}G

	Starts	1st	2nd	3rd	Win & Pl
Hurdles	4	0	1	0	1060
Career Total	**4**	**0**	**1**	**0**	**1060**

Going: Sf: 0-2 GS: 0-1 Gd: 0-1 GF: - Fm: 0-0
Distance: 2m/2m3: 0-4 2m4-2m7: 0-0 3m+: 0-0
Track: LH: 0-2 RH: 0-2 Tight: 0-1 Gall: 0-0
Aids: Bl: 0-0 Vi: 0-0 Tstrap: 0-1
Best Rating: **85** 3/02 Uttx 2m heavy Hdl

Signs of ability on the Flat in Ireland but poor form here over hurdles.

Master Beveled

101(104h) **112**

12-y-o b g Beveled (USA)-Miss Anniversary (Tachypous)

P D Evans Mrs E J Williams

Placings: 5/112206/2200/053122/2321230/23430332U 4/1545504-316P **(1823)**

2001/02: 16^{3}GF, 20^{1}GF, 16^{6}GF, 16^{P}GS

	Starts	1st	2nd	3rd	Win & Pl
Hurdles	1	0	0	0	0
Chases	3	1	0	1	3634
Career Total	**45**	**6**	**11**	**8**	**122540**

112	8/01	Font	2m4f	E Ch	G-F	£3120
137	10/00	Kemp	2m	B Hdl	G-S	£6792
159	1/99	Hayd	2m	A Hdl	SFT	£15475
153	2/98	Sand	2m110y	B Hdl	GD	£10113
109	11/95	Wind	2m	E Hdl	G-S	£2302
111	11/95	Ayr	2m	E Hdl	GD	£2400

Total win prize-money £40205

Going: Sf: 0-0 GS: 0-1 Gd: 0-0 GF: - Fm: 1-3
Distance: 2m/2m3: 0-3 **2m4-2m7: 1-1** 3m+: 0-0
Track: LH: 0-2 RH: 0-1 **Tight: 1-2** Gall: 0-0
Aids: Bl: 0-0 Vi: 0-2 Tstrap: 0-0
Best Rating: **159** 2/99 Sand 2m110y gd-sft Hdl

A very useful hurdler in his time, he is now retired.

Master Billyboy (IRE)

81f **76f**

4-y-o b g Old Vic-Clonodfoy (Strong Gale)

Mrs S D Williams William Peto

Placings: *0* **(4032)**

2001/02: 16^{0}GS

	Starts	1st	2nd	3rd	Win & Pl
NH Flat	1	0	0	0	
Career Total	**1**	**0**	**0**	**0**	

Going: Sf: 0-0 GS: 0-1 Gd: 0-0 GF: - Fm: 0-0
Distance: 2m/2m3: 0-1 2m4-2m7: 0-0 3m+: 0-0
Track: LH: 0-1 RH: 0-0 Tight: 0-0 Gall: 0-1
Aids: Bl: 0-0 Vi: 0-0 Tstrap: 0-0
Best Rating: **76** 3/02 Newb 2m110y gd-sft NHF

Master Boston (IRE)

14-y-o gr g Soughaan (USA)-Ballinoe Lass (Captain James)

R D E Woodhouse R D E Woodhouse

Placings: 006/02033540413361U50/5412311F3022/4 21111B50U/PP4U/543425260/5326F56P/61/150-4 **(4262)**

2001/02: 20^{4}HY

	Starts	1st	2nd	3rd	Win & Pl
Chases	1	0	0	0	0
Career Total	**69**	**11**	**8**	**8**	**58145**

114	2/01	Bang	2m4f110y	H Ch	HVY	£1498
106	2/00	Fknm	2m5f110y	H Ch	GD	£2180
129	1/96	Kemp	2m4f110y	B(0-145)HCh	GD	£8169
129	1/96	Weth	2m4f110y	D(0-125)HCh	SFT	£3947
129	12/95	Hayd	2m4f	C(0-135)HCh	GD	£5083
127	12/95	Weth	2m4f110y	B(0-140)HCh	GD	£4459
121	1/95	Chel	2m5f	C Ch	G-S	£4879
103	12/94	Sedg	2m5f	Ch	G-S	£2732
109	11/94	Wwck	2m4f110y	(0-140)HHdl	G-S	£3678
100	3/94	Sedg	2m5f110y	Hdl	GD	£2061
94	11/93	Newc	2m4f	Hdl	G-S	£2057

Total win prize-money £40748

Going: Sf: 0-1 GS: 0-0 Gd: 0-0 GF: - Fm: 0-0
Distance: 2m/2m3: 0-0 2m4-2m7: 0-1 3m+: 0-0
Track: LH: 0-1 RH: 0-0 Tight: 0-0 Gall: 0-0
Aids: Bl: 0-0 Vi: 0-0 Tstrap: 0-0
Best Rating: **129** 3/96 Chel 2m5f good Ch

Moderate two and a half-mile chaser. He is deteriorating and has been hunter chasing.

Master Chet (IRE)

88(94c) (86c)81

12-y-o b g Callernish-C C Meade (Paddy's Stream)
Miss Z C Davison Barry Ward

Placings:1P/12/PU/FPP-33F0U4PP0U40 **(4885)**
2001/02: 27^{3}GF, 24^{3}G, 32^{F}GF, 23^{0}GF, 25^{U}GS, 23^{4}GF, 33^{P}S, 26^{P}G, 23^{0}G, 25^{U}GS, 20^{4}GF, 27^{0}GF

	Starts	1st	2nd	3rd	Win & Pl
Hurdles	4	0	0	2	1050
Chases	8	0	0	0	0
Career Total	**21**	**2**	**1**	**2**	**8704**

119 10/98 Towc 3m1f E(0-115)HCh G-S £2804
115 12/97 Wwck 3m2f E Ch G-S £3362
Total win prize-money £6167

Going: Sf: 0-1 GS: 0-2 Gd: 0-3 GF: - Fm: 0-6
Distance: 2m/2m3: 0-0 2m4-2m7: 0-1 3m+: 0-11
Track: LH: 0-2 RH: 0-5 Tight: 0-4 Gall: 0-0
Aids: Bl: 0-9 Vi: 0-0 Tstrap: 0-5
Best Rating: 119 12/98 Towc 3m1f soft Ch

Master Club Royal

107(47h) 101

7-y-o b g Teenoso (USA)-Miss Club Royal (Avocat)
D McCain Halewood International Ltd

Placings:*6*P/53**F4335-303P32244** **(4088)**
2001/02: 20^{3}G, 26^{0}S, 24^{3}S, 25^{P}GS, 22^{3}S, 27^{2}HY, 24^{2}S, 27^{1}S, 24^{1}S

	Starts	1st	2nd	3rd	Win & Pl
Chases	9	0	2	3	5586
Career Total	**18**	**0**	**2**	**6**	**7547**

Going: Sf: 0-7 GS: 0-1 Gd: 0-1 GF: - Fm: 0-0
Distance: 2m/2m3: 0-0 2m4-2m7: 0-2 3m+: 0-7
Track: LH: 0-6 RH: 0-1 Tight: 0-6 Gall: 0-0
Aids: Bl: 0-4 Vi: 0-1 Tstrap: 0-0
Best Rating: 101 1/02 Sedg 3m3f heavy Ch

Ordinary placed form over fences and is not difficult to beat.

Master Cool

4-y-o br g Cool Jazz-Karen's Lady Luck (Primitive Rising (USA))
G M Moore Geoffrey Clarkson

Placings:F **(0965)**
2001/02: 17^{F}GS

	Starts	1st	2nd	3rd	Win & Pl
Hurdles	1	0	0	0	
Career Total	**1**	**0**	**0**	**0**	

Going: Sf: 0-0 GS: 0-1 Gd: 0-0 GF: - Fm: 0-0
Distance: 2m/2m3: 0-1 2m4-2m7: 0-0 3m+: 0-0
Track: LH: 0-0 RH: 0-0 Tight: 0-0 Gall: 0-0
Aids: Bl: 0-0 Vi: 0-0 Tstrap: 0-0
Best Rating:

Master Cooper (IRE)

91 97

8-y-o b g Kahyasi-Arabian Princess (Taufan (USA))
D R C Elsworth D S Dunne

Placings:F420/16/0340-00 **(4116)**
2001/02: 16^{0}GS, 16^{0}G

	Starts	1st	2nd	3rd	Win & Pl
Hurdles	2	0	0	0	

	Starts	1st	2nd	3rd	Win & Pl
Career Total	**12**	**1**	**1**	**1**	**3990**

102 9/98 Clon 2m Hdl G-F £2241
Total win prize-money £2242

Going: Sf: 0-0 GS: 0-1 Gd: 0-1 GF: - Fm: 0-0
Distance: 2m/2m3: 0-2 2m4-2m7: 0-0 3m+: 0-0
Track: LH: 0-0 RH: 0-2 Tight: 0-0 Gall: 0-0
Aids: Bl: 0-0 Vi: 0-0 Tstrap: 0-0
Best Rating: 120 2/01 Newb 2m110y soft Hdl

Fair two-mile handicap hurdler, best on a sound surface.

Master Flash (IRE)

9-y-o ch g The Bart (USA)-Continuity Lass (Continuation)
Miss V J Parvin Andrew Nicholls

Placings:*0*00P-PU **(4777)**
2001/02: 25^{P}GS, 25^{U}G

	Starts	1st	2nd	3rd	Win & Pl
Chases	2	0	0	0	
Career Total	**7**	**0**	**0**	**0**	

Going: Sf: 0-0 GS: 0-1 Gd: 0-1 GF: - Fm: 0-0
Distance: 2m/2m3: 0-0 2m4-2m7: 0-0 3m+: 0-2
Track: LH: 0-0 RH: 0-2 Tight: 0-2 Gall: 0-0
Aids: Bl: 0-0 Vi: 0-0 Tstrap: 0-0
Best Rating: 72 6/00 Naas 2m3f yield NHF

Master George

107 126

5-y-o b g Mtoto-Topwinder (USA) (Topsider (USA))
I A Balding David R Watson & Duncan Lofts

Placings:02P **(4229)**
2001/02: 16^{0}S, 21^{2}G, 21^{P}GS

	Starts	1st	2nd	3rd	Win & Pl
Hurdles	3	0	1	0	2360
Career Total	**3**	**0**	**1**	**0**	**2360**

Going: Sf: 0-1 GS: 0-1 Gd: 0-1 GF: - Fm: 0-0
Distance: 2m/2m3: 0-1 2m4-2m7: 0-2 3m+: 0-0
Track: LH: 0-2 RH: 0-1 Tight: 0-0 Gall: 0-2
Aids: Bl: 0-0 Vi: 0-0 Tstrap: 0-0
Best Rating: 126 2/02 Kemp 2m5f good Hdl

A decent middle-distance handicapper on the level, he has shown ability over hurdles in decent company.

Master Ginger Pop

77 85

6-y-o b g Supreme Leader-Ruckinge Girl (Eborneezer)
Mrs S D Williams William Peto

Placings:*0*-FP005P **(4544)**
2001/02: 22^{F}G, 24^{P}G, 19^{0}G, 22^{0}G, 24^{5}G, 26^{P}G

	Starts	1st	2nd	3rd	Win & Pl
Hurdles	6	0	0	0	0
Career Total	**7**	**0**	**0**	**0**	**0**

Going: Sf: 0-0 GS: 0-0 Gd: 0-6 GF: - Fm: 0-0
Distance: 2m/2m3: 0-1 2m4-2m7: 0-2 3m+: 0-3
Track: LH: 0-0 RH: 0-6 Tight: 0-1 Gall: 0-0
Aids: Bl: 0-0 Vi: 0-0 Tstrap: 0-0
Best Rating: 85 3/02 Extr 3m110y good Hdl

Master Henry (GER)

102(56h) 108

8-y-o b g Mille Balles (FR)-Maribelle (GER) (Windwurf (GER))
Ian Williams Thurlestone Hotel Racing Club

Placings:6/261206-2322P** **(0871)**
2001/02: 16^{2}F, 16^{3}GF, 16^{2}GF, 17^{2}GF, 16^{P}GS

	Starts	1st	2nd	3rd	Win & Pl
Chases	5	0	3	1	4031
Career Total	**12**	**1**	**5**	**1**	**7567**

98 8/00 Ctml 2m1f110y E(0-105)HHdl GD £2338
Total win prize-money £2338

Going: Sf: 0-0 GS: 0-1 Gd: 0-0 GF: - Fm: 0-4
Distance: 2m/2m3: 0-5 2m4-2m7: 0-0 3m+: 0-0
Track: LH: 0-4 RH: 0-1 Tight: 0-5 Gall: 0-0
Aids: Bl: 0-0 Vi: 0-0 Tstrap: 0-0
Best Rating: 108 6/01 MRas 2m1f110y gd-fm Ch

Master Jones

69 34

5-y-o b g Emperor Jones (USA)-Tight Spin (High Top)
Mrs H L Walton R Rayner

Placings:0 **(4906)**
2001/02: 19^{0}G

	Starts	1st	2nd	3rd	Win & Pl
Hurdles	1	0	0	0	
Career Total	**1**	**0**	**0**	**0**	

Going: Sf: 0-0 GS: 0-0 Gd: 0-1 GF: - Fm: 0-0
Distance: 2m/2m3: 0-0 2m4-2m7: 0-1 3m+: 0-0
Track: LH: 0-0 RH: 0-1 Tight: 0-1 Gall: 0-0
Aids: Bl: 0-0 Vi: 0-0 Tstrap: 0-0
Best Rating: 34 4/02 MRas 2m3f110y good Hdl

Master Laughter

80 35

11-y-o b g Sulaafah (USA)-Miss Comedy (Comedy Star (USA))
B G Powell (J Scott 16/5) Mrs C C Scott

Placings:R00 **(0781)**
2001/02: 19^{RF}, 22^{0}G, 20^{0}G

	Starts	1st	2nd	3rd	Win & Pl
Hurdles	2	0	0	0	0
Chases	1	0	0	0	0
Career Total	**3**	**0**	**0**	**0**	

Going: Sf: 0-0 GS: 0-0 Gd: 0-2 GF: - Fm: 0-1
Distance: 2m/2m3: 0-0 2m4-2m7: 0-3 3m+: 0-0
Track: LH: 0-2 RH: 0-1 Tight: 0-1 Gall: 0-0
Aids: Bl: 0-1 Vi: 0-0 Tstrap: 0-0
Best Rating: 35 6/01 NAbb 2m6f good Hdl

Master Millfield (IRE)

10-y-o b g Prince Rupert (FR)-Calash (Indian King (USA))
R J Baker David Heath

Placings:444P/463123114/P60/103-P **(2660)**
2001/02: 19^{P}GS

	Starts	1st	2nd	3rd	Win & Pl
Chases	1	0	0	0	
Career Total	**20**	**4**	**1**	**3**	**12793**

114 8/00 NAbb 2m1f E(0-115)HHdl G-F £2555
125 8/98 Worc 2m D(0-125)HHdl G-F £2859
113 8/98 NAbb 2m1f E(0-100)HHdl G-F £2911

107	6/98	NAbb	2m1f	E(0-100)HHdl	FRM	£2183

Total win prize-money £10510

Going: Sf: 0-0 GS: 0-1 Gd: 0-0 GF: - Fm: 0-0
Distance: 2m/2m3: 0-1 2m4-2m7: 0-0 3m+: 0-0
Track: LH: 0-0 RH: 0-1 Tight: 0-1 Gall: 0-0
Aids: Bl: 0-0 Vi: 0-0 Tstrap: 0-0
Best Rating: **125** 8/98 Worc 2m gd-fm Hdl

Master Nova

12-y-o b g Ra Nova-Maid Of The Manor (Hotfoot)
H Alexander N Baillie

Placings: 114/221/F/314P/132P63/3-PP **(0878)**
2001/02: 25^{P}GF, 22^{P}G

	Starts	1st	2nd	3rd	Win & Pl
Chases	2	0	0	0	
Career Total	**20**	**5**	**3**	**4**	**23517**

121	5/99	Weth	3m1f	D Ch	GD	£3915
127	11/98	Newc	3m	E Ch	GD	£2892
89	3/96	Kels	2m6f110y	D Hdl	GD	£2541
109	12/94	Leop	2m	NHF	HVY	£3914
	12/94	Punc	2m	NHF	SFT	£2935

Total win prize-money £16199

Going: Sf: 0-0 GS: 0-0 Gd: 0-1 GF: - Fm: 0-1
Distance: 2m/2m3: 0-0 2m4-2m7: 0-1 3m+: 0-1
Track: LH: 0-1 RH: 0-1 Tight: 0-1 Gall: 0-0
Aids: Bl: 0-1 Vi: 0-0 Tstrap: 0-0
Best Rating: **127** 11/98 Newc 3m good Ch

Master Of Illusion (IRE)

103 **125**

9-y-o ch g Castle Keep-Galloping Gold Vii (Damsire Unregistered)
R Lee Mrs G Goddard,Ben Hinchcliff & Des Murray

Placings: 40/03P210320P20P/23524102/2433211-63PP3P **(4503)**
2001/02: 26^{6}S, 24^{3}S, 24^{P}G, 25^{P}HY, 24^{3}GS, 26^{P}G

	Starts	1st	2nd	3rd	Win & Pl
Hurdles	1	0	0	0	0
Chases	5	0	0	2	2154
Career Total	**36**	**4**	**8**	**7**	**32563**

125	4/01	NAbb	3m2f110y	E(0-115)HCh	SFT	£5538
125	3/01	Strf	3m	D(0-120)HCh	SFT	£7150
125	3/00	Folk	3m2f	E Ch	G-F	£3645
99	11/98	Clon	3m	Hdl	SFT	£3288

Total win prize-money £19622

Going: Sf: 0-3 GS: 0-1 Gd: 0-2 GF: - Fm: 0-0
Distance: 2m/2m3: 0-0 2m4-2m7: 0-0 3m+: 0-6
Track: LH: 0-5 RH: 0-0 Tight: 0-4 Gall: 0-1
Aids: Bl: 0-0 Vi: 0-5 Tstrap: 0-0
Best Rating: **125** 3/02 Strf 3m gd-sft Ch

Fair staying chaser, suited by soft ground and a sharp track and stays in excess of three miles, but looks high in the handicap just now. Regularly fitted with a visor.

Master Pilgrim

114 **136**

10-y-o b g Supreme Leader-Patterdon (Precipice Wood)
Miss Venetia Williams The Winning Line

Placings: 352/46242/2110/1F-4154 **(2849)**
2001/02: 20^{4}GS, 20^{1}GS, 20^{5}S, 20^{4}G

	Starts	1st	2nd	3rd	Win & Pl
Chases	4	1	0	0	8439
Career Total	**18**	**4**	**4**	**1**	**26744**

136	11/01	Aint	2m4f	D(0-125)HCh	G-S	£6987
134	1/01	Winc	2m5f	D Ch	SFT	£5280
132	2/99	Font	2m6f110y	D(0-120)HHdl	GD	£5277
131	2/99	Font	2m2f110y	E Hdl	SFT	£2565

Total win prize-money £20110

Going: Sf: 0-1 GS: 1-2 Gd: 0-1 GF: - Fm: 0-0
Distance: 2m/2m3: 0-0 **2m4-2m7: 1-4** 3m+: 0-0
Track: **LH: 1-2** RH: 0-2 **Tight: 1-1** Gall: 0-0
Aids: Bl: 0-0 Vi: 0-0 Tstrap: 0-0
Best Rating: **136** 11/01 Aint 2m4f gd-sft Ch

Lightly raced, he managed just two runs in the 2000/01 season, winning a two-finisher novice chase in January before falling when in with every chance at Market Rasen three months later. Regained the winning thread by the minimum margin at Aintree in November, but beaten in decent company subsequently. Probably best around two and a half miles, he goes well on easy ground.

Master Rex

115 **130**

7-y-o ch g Interrex (CAN)-Whose Lady (USA) (Master Willie)
B De Haan Miss Louise Challis

Placings: 20-2113511 **(2287)**
2001/02: 17^{2}G, 17^{1}GF, 17^{1}GS, 16^{3}GF, 17^{5}S, 16^{1}G, 16^{1}G

	Starts	1st	2nd	3rd	Win & Pl
Hurdles	7	4	1	1	18723
Career Total	**9**	**4**	**2**	**1**	**19417**

130	11/01	Asct	2m110y	C(0-135)HHdl	GD	£8170
127	11/01	Kemp	2m	F(0-110)HHdl	GD	£3125
110	6/01	NAbb	2m1f	E Hdl	G-S	£3031
110	5/01	Folk	2m1f110y	E Hdl	G-F	£2548

Total win prize-money £16876

Going: Sf: 0-1 GS: 1-1 Gd: 2-3 GF: - Fm: 1-2
Distance: **2m/2m3: 4-7** 2m4-2m7: 0-0 3m+: 0-0
Track: LH: 1-2 **RH: 3-5 Tight: 2-3** Gall: 0-0
Aids: Bl: 0-0 Vi: 0-0 Tstrap: 0-0
Best Rating: **130** 11/01 Asct 2m110y good Hdl

Fair hurdler. A winner in novice and handicap company. Best trip around two miles on a sound surface but has won on soft. Needs a strong pace in his races.

Master Ride (IRE)

83 **114**

7-y-o b g King's Ride-Cahore (Quayside)
E Stanners Doubleprint

Placings: 4/1P-0 **(1795)**
2001/02: 20^{0}S

	Starts	1st	2nd	3rd	Win & Pl
Hurdles	1	0	0	0	
Career Total	**4**	**1**	**0**	**0**	**2996**

114	3/01	Font	2m2f110y	D Hdl	HVY	£2996

Total win prize-money £2996

Going: Sf: 0-1 GS: 0-0 Gd: 0-0 GF: - Fm: 0-0
Distance: 2m/2m3: 0-0 2m4-2m7: 0-1 3m+: 0-0
Track: LH: 0-1 RH: 0-0 Tight: 0-0 Gall: 0-0
Aids: Bl: 0-0 Vi: 0-0 Tstrap: 0-0
Best Rating: **114** 3/01 Font 2m2f110y heavy Hdl

Master Rocky

10-y-o b g Jumbo Hirt (USA)-Dunlean (Leander)
W T Reed P J McDonald

Placings: F/F **(0205)**
2001/02: 25^{F}G

	Starts	1st	2nd	3rd	Win & Pl
Chases	1	0	0	0	
Career Total	**2**	**0**	**0**	**0**	

Going: Sf: 0-0 GS: 0-0 Gd: 0-1 GF: - Fm: 0-0
Distance: 2m/2m3: 0-0 2m4-2m7: 0-0 3m+: 0-1
Track: LH: 0-1 RH: 0-0 Tight: 0-0 Gall: 0-0
Aids: Bl: 0-0 Vi: 0-0 Tstrap: 0-0
Best Rating:

Master Russell (IRE)

99 **93**

8-y-o b g Supreme Leader-Quality Suite (Prince Hansel)
Mrs A L M King (C R Barwell 14/5) Aiden Murphy

Placings: 400/05540/FU250-030 **(4772)**
2001/02: 19^{0}G, 17^{3}GF, 21^{0}G

	Starts	1st	2nd	3rd	Win & Pl
Hurdles	3	0	0	1	397
Career Total	**16**	**0**	**1**	**1**	**1430**

Going: Sf: 0-0 GS: 0-0 Gd: 0-2 GF: - Fm: 0-1
Distance: 2m/2m3: 0-2 2m4-2m7: 0-1 3m+: 0-0
Track: LH: 0-1 RH: 0-2 Tight: 0-2 Gall: 0-0
Aids: Bl: 0-0 Vi: 0-1 Tstrap: 0-0
Best Rating: **105** 1/00 Font 2m2f110y gd-sft Hdl

Master Satchmo (IRE)

96(99h) (62h)**84**

12-y-o b g Orchestra-Precious Petra (Bing Ii)
Mrs L C Jewell Mrs A Emanuel

Placings: 543/22/000/53/0233101012P230P-6106 **(1644)**
2001/02: 20^{6}GS, 24^{1}GF, 20^{0}GF, 26^{6}G

	Starts	1st	2nd	3rd	Win & Pl
Hurdles	1	0	0	0	0
Chases	3	1	0	0	2974
Career Total	**29**	**4**	**5**	**5**	**15205**

84	5/01	Fknm	3m110y	E Ch	G-F	£2973
101	11/00	Plum	2m5f	F Hdl	HVY	£2769
101	10/00	Font	2m4f	G(0-95)HHdl	G-S	£1928
97	5/00	Ctml	2m1f110y	D Hdl	G-F	£3168

Total win prize-money £10841

Going: Sf: 0-0 GS: 0-1 Gd: 0-1 GF: - Fm: 1-2
Distance: 2m/2m3: 0-0 2m4-2m7: 0-2 **3m+: 1-2**
Track: **LH: 1-3** RH: 0-1 **Tight: 1-3** Gall: 0-1
Aids: Bl: 0-0 Vi: 0-0 Tstrap: 0-0
Best Rating: **101** 11/00 Plum 2m5f heavy Hdl

Master Tern (USA)

104(114h) (144h)**137**

7-y-o ch g Generous (IRE)-Young Hostess (FR) (Arctic Tern (USA))
J J O'Neill J P McManus

Placings:232/040111/260-3F113 (4231)
2001/02: 17^{3}S, 16^{F}HY, 16^{1}G, 16^{1}S, 21^{3}GS

	Starts	1st	2nd	3rd	Win & Pl
Hurdles	1	0	0	1	8050
Chases	4	2	0	1	7165
Career Total	**17**	**5**	**3**	**3**	**73320**

118	3/02	Hntg	2m110y	E Ch	SFT	£2992
137	1/02	Leic	2m	E Ch	GD	£3536
140	3/00	Chel	2m1f	A HHdl	G-F	£30000
143	3/00	Kels	2m2f	B Hdl	G-S	£14365
134	1/00	Chel	2m1f	D(0-120)HHdl	G-S	£7442

Total win prize-money £58337

Going: Sf: 1-3 GS: 0-1 Gd: 1-1 GF: - Fm: 0-0
Distance: **2m/2m3: 2-4** 2m4-2m7: 0-1 3m+: 0-0
Track: LH: 0-3 **RH: 2-2** Tight: 0-2 **Gall: 1-2**
Aids: Bl: 0-0 Vi: 0-0 Tstrap: 0-0
Best Rating: 149 12/00 Hayd 2m4f heavy Hdl

Winner of the Vincent O'Brien County Hurdle at Cheltenham in March 2000, he has not looked an absolute natural over fences but got off the mark at the third time of asking at Leicester and followed up at Huntingdon. Returned to hurdles to run a blinder in the Coral Cup at the 2002 Festival. Has a bright turn of foot.

Master Toby

12-y-o b g War Hero-Great Destiny (Deep Run)
Mrs S Gardner D V Gardner

Placings:00/1223362/5/**U14U/P/00P/P**-0 (0121)
2001/02: 19^{0}F

	Starts	1st	2nd	3rd	Win & Pl
Hurdles	1	0	0	0	
Career Total	**20**	**2**	**3**	**2**	**9283**

120	2/97	Leic	3m	D Ch	GD	£4207
79	9/94	Sthl	2m4f110y	Hdl	GD	£1831

Total win prize-money £6039

Going: Sf: 0-0 GS: 0-0 Gd: 0-0 GF: - Fm: 0-1
Distance: 2m/2m3: 0-0 2m4-2m7: 0-1 3m+: 0-0
Track: LH: 0-0 RH: 0-1 Tight: 0-1 Gall: 0-0
Aids: Bl: 0-0 Vi: 0-0 Tstrap: 0-0
Best Rating: 120 2/97 Leic 3m good Ch

Master Trix (IRE)

110f 118f
5-y-o b g Lord Americo-Bannow Drive (IRE) (Miners Lamp)
M Pitman Patrick Bancroft

Placings:16 (4423)
2001/02: 18^{1}S, 16^{6}GS

	Starts	1st	2nd	3rd	Win & Pl
NH Flat	2	1	0	0	1638
Career Total	**2**	**1**	**0**	**0**	**1638**

118	2/02	Font	2m2f110y	H NHF	SFT	£1638

Total win prize-money £1638

Going: Sf: 1-1 GS: 0-1 Gd: 0-0 GF: - Fm: 0-0
Distance: **2m/2m3: 1-2** 2m4-2m7: 0-0 3m+: 0-0
Track: **LH: 1-2** RH: 0-0 **Tight: 1-1** Gall: 0-1
Aids: Bl: 0-0 Vi: 0-0 Tstrap: 0-0
Best Rating: 118 2/02 Font 2m2f110y soft NHF

A full-brother to Flying Trix, he made a winning debut in a Fontwell bumper. Looks a stayer.

Master Trump

65 28
4-y-o b g First Trump-Anhaar (Ela-Mana-Mou)
J J O'Neill Mrs Jonjo O'Neill

Placings:0 (1718)
2001/02: 16^{0}G

	Starts	1st	2nd	3rd	Win & Pl
Hurdles	1	0	0	0	
Career Total	**1**	**0**	**0**	**0**	

Going: Sf: 0-0 GS: 0-0 Gd: 0-1 GF: - Fm: 0-0
Distance: 2m/2m3: 0-1 2m4-2m7: 0-0 3m+: 0-0
Track: LH: 0-1 RH: 0-0 Tight: 0-0 Gall: 0-0
Aids: Bl: 0-0 Vi: 0-0 Tstrap: 0-0
Best Rating: 28 10/01 Weth 2m good Hdl

Master Wood

102 109
11-y-o b g Wonderful Surprise-Miss Wood (Precipice Wood)
C Grant Roy Robinson

Placings:5600/**PP4111FFPP326/P1P15104/1F31-PPP** (4442)
2001/02: 20^{P}S, 22^{P}S, 25^{P}S

	Starts	1st	2nd	3rd	Win & Pl
Chases	3	0	0	0	
Career Total	**31**	**8**	**1**	**2**	**51160**

142	12/00	Weth	2m4f110y	B HCh	SFT	£15008
141	10/00	Kels	2m6f110y	D(0-120)HCh	SFT	£4654
140	3/00	Weth	2m4f110y	C(0-135)HCh	G-S	£7182
121	1/00	Weth	2m4f110y	D(0-125)HCh	SFT	£4177
117	11/99	Weth	3m1f	D(0-125)HCh	GD	£4090
124	11/98	Weth	3m1f	D Ch	GD	£4248
113	10/98	Weth	2m4f110y	C HCh	GD	£4739
124	10/98	Carl	2m4f110y	E Ch	HVY	£2918

Total win prize-money £47017

Going: Sf: 0-3 GS: 0-0 Gd: 0-0 GF: - Fm: 0-0
Distance: 2m/2m3: 0-0 2m4-2m7: 0-2 3m+: 0-1
Track: LH: 0-2 RH: 0-1 Tight: 0-2 Gall: 0-1
Aids: Bl: 0-0 Vi: 0-0 Tstrap: 0-0
Best Rating: 142 12/00 Weth 2m4f110y soft Ch

A Wetherby specialist, he often front runs and is quite useful when allowed to bully the opposition. Best short of three miles, he goes well on soft or heavy ground but has been bang out of form for some time.

Match Maker (GER)

87 87
5-y-o b/br g Winged Love (IRE)-Musette (GER) (Limbo (GER))
T D Easterby D F Sills

Placings:P363P-0PP3 (4772)
2001/02: 20^{0}S, 16^{P}G, 20^{P}GS, 21^{3}G

	Starts	1st	2nd	3rd	Win & Pl
Hurdles	4	0	0	1	343
Career Total	**9**	**0**	**0**	**3**	**1340**

Going: Sf: 0-1 GS: 0-1 Gd: 0-2 GF: - Fm: 0-0
Distance: 2m/2m3: 0-1 2m4-2m7: 0-3 3m+: 0-0
Track: LH: 0-2 RH: 0-1 Tight: 0-2 Gall: 0-0
Aids: Bl: 0-1 Vi: 0-0 Tstrap: 0-0
Best Rating: 96 2/01 Catt 2m soft Hdl

Matrix (AUS)

86f 98f
5-y-o b g Centaine (AUS)-Iced Lass (NZ) (Half Iced (USA))
K C Bailey Mrs M C Sweeney

Placings:00 (4423)
2001/02: 16^{0}G, 16^{0}GS

	Starts	1st	2nd	3rd	Win & Pl
NH Flat	2	0	0	0	
Career Total	**2**	**0**	**0**	**0**	

Going: Sf: 0-0 GS: 0-1 Gd: 0-1 GF: - Fm: 0-0
Distance: 2m/2m3: 0-2 2m4-2m7: 0-0 3m+: 0-0
Track: LH: 0-1 RH: 0-1 Tight: 0-0 Gall: 0-1
Aids: Bl: 0-0 Vi: 0-0 Tstrap: 0-0
Best Rating: 98 2/02 Kemp 2m good NHF

Matt Holland

100 104
9-y-o b g Makbul-Shirley Grove (Vulgan Slave)
Mrs L Wadham Waterhall Racing

Placings:10/342-3 (0352)
2001/02: 22^{3}G

	Starts	1st	2nd	3rd	Win & Pl
Hurdles	1	0	0	1	600
Career Total	**6**	**1**	**1**	**2**	**3382**

122	11/98	Worc	2m	H NHF	HVY	£1329

Total win prize-money £1329

Going: Sf: 0-0 GS: 0-0 Gd: 0-1 GF: - Fm: 0-0
Distance: 2m/2m3: 0-0 2m4-2m7: 0-1 3m+: 0-0
Track: LH: 0-1 RH: 0-0 Tight: 0-1 Gall: 0-0
Aids: Bl: 0-0 Vi: 0-0 Tstrap: 0-0
Best Rating: 122 11/98 Worc 2m heavy NHF

Mattan

104(107h) (98h)117
6-y-o b g Chaddleworth (IRE)-Gilded Omen (Faustus (USA))
P F Nicholls (B J Llewellyn 10/5) Mel Fordham

Placings:504P1P/PP60411-151 (2216)
2001/02: 24^{1}F, 27^{5}GF, 26^{1}G

	Starts	1st	2nd	3rd	Win & Pl
Hurdles	2	1	0	0	2492
Chases	1	1	0	0	3368
Career Total	**16**	**5**	**0**	**0**	**11390**

117	11/01	NAbb	3m2f110y	E(0-105)HCh	GD	£3368
98	5/01	Sthl	3m110y	F(0-105)HHdl	FRM	£2492
97	3/01	Plum	3m1f110y	F(0-95)HHdl	HVY	£2341
79	12/00	Tntn	3m110y	G(0-90)HHdl	SFT	£1673
79	3/00	MRas	2m1f110y	G(0-95)HHdl	G-F	£1515

Total win prize-money £11391

Going: Sf: 0-0 GS: 0-0 Gd: 1-1 GF: - Fm: 1-2
Distance: 2m/2m3: 0-0 2m4-2m7: 0-0 **3m+: 2-3**
Track: **LH: 2-3** RH: 0-0 **Tight: 2-3** Gall: 0-0
Aids: **Bl: 1-1** Vi: 0-0 Tstrap: 0-0
Best Rating: 117 11/01 NAbb 3m2f110y good Ch

Has won on firm and soft ground in plating-class hurdles and made a pleasing start to his chasing career with victory at Newton Abbot in a three mile two furlong novices event.

Maurangi

92 71
11-y-o b g Warning-Spin Dry (High Top)
B W Murray M E Foxton

Placings:014/P0P53/5 (0224)
2001/02: 16^{5}GF

	Starts	1st	2nd	3rd	Win & Pl
Hurdles	1	0	0	0	0
Career Total	**9**	**1**	**0**	**1**	**2716**

91	4/98	Uttx	2m	E Hdl	G-S	£2494

Total win prize-money £2495

Going: Sf: 0-0 GS: 0-0 Gd: 0-0 GF: - Fm: 0-1
Distance: 2m/2m3: 0-1 2m4-2m7: 0-0 3m+: 0-0
Track: LH: 0-1 RH: 0-0 Tight: 0-0 Gall: 0-0
Aids: Bl: 0-0 Vi: 0-0 Tstrap: 0-0
Best Rating: **91** 4/98 Hntg 2m110y gd-sft Hdl

Mavourneen (IRE)

(84h)

9-y-o b m Strong Gale-Coliemore (Coliseum)
E Stanners James Thorburn-Muirhead&john Kevin Lomax

Placings:*60006/50-0* **(0719)**
2001/02: 16^{0}F

	Starts	1st	2nd	3rd	Win & Pl
Chases	1	0	0	0	
Career Total	**8**	**0**	**0**	**0**	**0**

Going: Sf: 0-0 GS: 0-0 Gd: 0-0 GF: - Fm: 0-1
Distance: 2m/2m3: 0-1 2m4-2m7: 0-0 3m+: 0-0
Track: LH: 0-0 RH: 0-1 Tight: 0-0 Gall: 0-0
Aids: Bl: 0-0 Vi: 0-0 Tstrap: 0-0
Best Rating: **82** 3/00 Winc 2m6f good Hdl

Mawthook (USA)

10f

4-y-o ch g Silver Hawk (USA)-Zakiyya (USA) (Dayjur (USA))
J R Turner Oliver J Turner

Placings:*0* **(4771)**
2001/02: 16^{0}GF

	Starts	1st	2nd	3rd	Win & Pl
NH Flat	1	0	0	0	
Career Total	**1**	**0**	**0**	**0**	

Going: Sf: 0-0 GS: 0-0 Gd: 0-0 GF: - Fm: 0-1
Distance: 2m/2m3: 0-1 2m4-2m7: 0-0 3m+: 0-0
Track: LH: 0-0 RH: 0-0 Tight: 0-0 Gall: 0-0
Aids: Bl: 0-0 Vi: 0-0 Tstrap: 0-0
Best Rating: **10** 4/02 Hexm 2m110y gd-fm NHF

Max Bee Jay

4-y-o b g Imp Society (USA)-Dulzura (Daring March)
I W McInnes (A P Jarvis 8/8) I W McInnes

Placings:UF **(3856)**
2001/02: 16^{U}S, 16^{F}S

	Starts	1st	2nd	3rd	Win & Pl
Hurdles	2	0	0	0	
Career Total	**2**	**0**	**0**	**0**	

Going: Sf: 0-2 GS: 0-0 Gd: 0-0 GF: - Fm: 0-0
Distance: 2m/2m3: 0-2 2m4-2m7: 0-0 3m+: 0-0
Track: LH: 0-2 RH: 0-0 Tight: 0-1 Gall: 0-1
Aids: Bl: 0-0 Vi: 0-0 Tstrap: 0-0
Best Rating:

Max Pride

108(102h) (83h)**122**

7-y-o br g Good Thyne (USA)-An Bothar Dubh (Strong Gale)
R Dickin Mrs J Cumiskey, M Doocey & K Doocey

Placings:05P/**241UP**-**211F344P** **(4753)**
2001/02: 21^{2}G, 25^{1}S, 22^{1}G, 22^{F}HY, 25^{3}HY, 30^{4}G, 26^{4}GS, 26^{P}GF

	Starts	1st	2nd	3rd	Win & Pl
Hurdles	1	0	1	0	872
Chases	7	2	0	1	16539
Career Total	**16**	**3**	**2**	**1**	**21505**

122	11/01	Newb	2m6f110y	E(0-115)HCh	GD	£5850
105	10/01	Towc	3m1f	D(0-120)HCh	SFT	£8437
110	2/01	Leic	2m4f110y	F(0-95)HCh	SFT	£2931

Total win prize-money £17219

Going: Sf: 1-3 GS: 0-1 Gd: 1-3 GF: - Fm: 0-1
Distance: 2m/2m3: 0-0 2m4-2m7: 1-3 3m+: 1-5
Track: LH: 1-3 RH: 1-4 Tight: 0-0 **Gall: 1-1**
Aids: Bl: 0-0 Vi: 0-0 Tstrap: 0-0
Best Rating: **122** 12/01 Towc 2m6f heavy Ch

Fair handicap chaser, he stays three miles one furlong and acts on a soft surface.

Maxie McDonald (IRE)

107 **120**

9-y-o b g Homo Sapien-Lovely Sanara (Proverb)
N A Twiston-Davies Mrs J E Meek

Placings:*000*/4P-**B122121F** **(2668)**
2001/02: 21^{B}GF, 20^{1}G, 24^{2}GF, 20^{2}GF, 23^{1}G, 20^{2}G, 24^{1}GF, 21^{F}G

	Starts	1st	2nd	3rd	Win & Pl
Chases	8	3	3	0	19863
Career Total	**13**	**3**	**3**	**0**	**20195**

118	11/01	Asct	3m110y	C(0-130)HCh	G-F	£8180
107	7/01	Worc	2m7f110y	F(0-110)HCh	GD	£2429
106	5/01	Bang	2m4f110y	F(0-105)HCh	GD	£3626

Total win prize-money £14235

Going: Sf: 0-0 GS: 0-0 Gd: 2-4 GF: - Fm: 1-4
Distance: 2m/2m3: 0-0 2m4-2m7: 1-5 **3m+: 2-3**
Track: **LH: 2-4** RH: 1-4 **Tight: 1-1** Gall: 0-3
Aids: Bl: 0-0 Vi: 0-0 Tstrap: 0-0
Best Rating: **120** 10/01 Chel 2m4f110y good Ch

He has taken well to chasing, winning three times in 2001, and continues to improve. Suited by good ground and stays three miles.

Maximize (IRE)

114(81h) (88h)**151**

8-y-o b g Mandalus-Lone Run (Kemal (FR))
Miss H C Knight Lady Vestey

Placings:322446-**2121162** **(4903)**
2001/02: 25^{2}G, 25^{1}G, 24^{2}S, 24^{1}G, 24^{1}G, 24^{6}GS, 24^{2}G

	Starts	1st	2nd	3rd	Win & Pl
Chases	7	3	3	0	47968
Career Total	**13**	**3**	**5**	**1**	**51561**

151	12/01	Kemp	3m	A Ch	GD	£29750
134	11/01	Kemp	3m	D Ch	GD	£4153
131	10/01	Winc	3m1f110y	D Ch	GD	£4407

Total win prize-money £38311

Going: Sf: 0-1 GS: 0-1 Gd: 3-5 GF: - Fm: 0-0
Distance: 2m/2m3: 0-0 2m4-2m7: 0-0 **3m+: 3-7**
Track: LH: 0-3 **RH: 3-4** Tight: 0-0 Gall: 0-1
Aids: Bl: 0-0 Vi: 0-0 Tstrap: 0-0
Best Rating: **151** 4/02 Sand 3m110y good Ch

Successful in point to points, he developed into a very useful novice chaser in 2001/2002, including a success in the Feltham at Kempton over Christmas. Jumps well and stays three miles on good ground, but that looks as much as his stamina will allow.

Maximum Makeup (IRE)

62 **24**

5-y-o b g Mujadil (USA)-Oileann Carrig (Pitcairn)
A C Whillans C Bird

Placings:00 **(3349)**
2001/02: 16^{0}S, 16^{0}G

	Starts	1st	2nd	3rd	Win & Pl
Hurdles	2	0	0	0	
Career Total	**2**	**0**	**0**	**0**	

Going: Sf: 0-1 GS: 0-0 Gd: 0-1 GF: - Fm: 0-0
Distance: 2m/2m3: 0-2 2m4-2m7: 0-0 3m+: 0-0
Track: LH: 0-1 RH: 0-1 Tight: 0-1 Gall: 0-0
Aids: Bl: 0-0 Vi: 0-0 Tstrap: 0-0
Best Rating: **24** 12/01 Ayr 2m soft Hdl

Little show over hurdles to date.

Maximus (IRE)

103 **123**

7-y-o br g Un Desperado (FR)-Fais Vite (USA) (Sharpen Up)
D M Grissell Cockerell Cowing Racing

Placings:110-4U000 **(4633)**
2001/02: 19^{4}GS, 20^{U}G, 16^{0}GS, 19^{0}GS, 20^{0}GF

	Starts	1st	2nd	3rd	Win & Pl
Hurdles	4	0	0	0	424
Chases	1	0	0	0	0
Career Total	**8**	**2**	**0**	**0**	**8387**

123	2/01	Newb	2m110y	C Hdl	SFT	£6045
116	1/01	Plum	2m	E Hdl	SFT	£1918

Total win prize-money £7963

Going: Sf: 0-0 GS: 0-3 Gd: 0-1 GF: - Fm: 0-1
Distance: 2m/2m3: 0-3 2m4-2m7: 0-2 3m+: 0-0
Track: LH: 0-3 RH: 0-2 Tight: 0-1 Gall: 0-2
Aids: Bl: 0-1 Vi: 0-0 Tstrap: 0-0
Best Rating: **123** 10/01 Strf 2m3f gd-sft Hdl

A winner of a point-to-point. he won his first two starts over hurdles at the start of 2001, but has been well beaten since. Best on soft ground and is effective at around two miles.

Mayb-Mayb

84 **78**

12-y-o ch g Gunner B-Mayotte (Little Buskins)
J Neville Ian Muir

Placings:*03*/040/51F111/P2P310223P/4501P0P-000PP **(4035)**
2001/02: 22^{0}GS, 27^{0}G, 25^{0}HY, 26^{P}GS, 22^{P}S

	Starts	1st	2nd	3rd	Win & Pl
Hurdles	5	0	0	0	
Career Total	**33**	**6**	**3**	**3**	**21605**

115	1/01	Winc	2m6f	E(0-115)HHdl	SFT	£3332
115	1/00	Plum	2m5f	D(0-125)HHdl	SFT	£3136
108	4/97	Worc	3m	E(0-100)HHdl	SFT	£2775
97	3/97	Plum	2m4f	F(0-100)HHdl	G-S	£2012
89	2/97	Plum	2m4f	F(0-100)HHdl	SFT	£1941
77	2/97	Plum	2m4f	F(0-105)HHdl	G-S	£2194

Total win prize-money £15391

Going: Sf: 0-2 GS: 0-2 Gd: 0-1 GF: - Fm: 0-0
Distance: 2m/2m3: 0-0 2m4-2m7: 0-2 3m+: 0-3
Track: LH: 0-2 RH: 0-1 Tight: 0-2 Gall: 0-0
Aids: Bl: 0-5 Vi: 0-0 Tstrap: 0-5
Best Rating: **115** 1/01 Winc 2m6f soft Hdl

Maybe Just Maybe (IRE)

5-y-o b g Tirol-Templemore (IRE) (Alzao (USA))
Mrs A M Thorpe Just Maybe Club

Placings:*0-0* **(3338)**
2001/02: 16^{0}G

	Starts	1st	2nd	3rd	Win & Pl
NH Flat	1	0	0	0	
Career Total	**2**	**0**	**0**	**0**	

Going: Sf: 0-0 GS: 0-0 Gd: 0-1 GF: - Fm: 0-0
Distance: 2m/2m3: 0-1 2m4-2m7: 0-0 3m+: 0-0
Track: LH: 0-0 RH: 0-1 Tight: 0-0 Gall: 0-0
Aids: Bl: 0-0 Vi: 0-0 Tstrap: 0-0
Best Rating: 41 1/02 Ludl 2m good NHF

Maybe The Business

104f **136f**
6-y-o ch g Karinga Bay-Music Interpreter (Kampala)
P F Nicholls R G Williams

Placings:*11* **(4841)**
2001/02: 16^{1}S, 16^{1}G

	Starts	1st	2nd	3rd	Win & Pl
NH Flat	2	2	0	0	5292
Career Total	**2**	**2**	**0**	**0**	**5292**

136	4/02	Ayr	2m	H NHF	GD	£3342
118	3/02	Winc	2m	H NHF	SFT	£1949

Total win prize-money £5293

Going: Sf: 1-1 GS: 0-0 Gd: 1-1 GF: - Fm: 0-0
Distance: **2m/2m3: 2-2** 2m4-2m7: 0-0 3m+: 0-0
Track: LH: 1-1 RH: 1-1 Tight: 0-0 Gall: 0-0
Aids: Bl: 0-0 Vi: 0-0 Tstrap: 0-0
Best Rating: 136 4/02 Ayr 2m good NHF

Winning bumper performer. Effective over two miles and acts on good ground.

Maybe'N

5-y-o ch g Deploy-Travel Mystery (Godswalk (USA))
M Ranger (Mrs P Sly 24/2) P J Turner

Placings:4P60-P **(4735)**
2001/02: 23^{P}F

	Starts	1st	2nd	3rd	Win & Pl
Chases	1	0	0	0	
Career Total	**5**	**0**	**0**	**0**	0

Going: Sf: 0-0 GS: 0-0 Gd: 0-0 GF: - Fm: 0-1
Distance: 2m/2m3: 0-0 2m4-2m7: 0-0 3m+: 0-1
Track: LH: 0-0 RH: 0-1 Tight: 0-0 Gall: 0-0
Aids: Bl: 0-0 Vi: 0-0 Tstrap: 0-0
Best Rating: 88 1/01 Folk 2m1f110y heavy Hdl

Maybelle

75 **50**
7-y-o b m Royal Vulcan-Full Of Love (Full Of Hope)
J S King W J Lee

Placings:*00-0* **(4640)**
2001/02: 16^{0}G

	Starts	1st	2nd	3rd	Win & Pl
Hurdles	1	0	0	0	
Career Total	**3**	**0**	**0**	**0**	

Going: Sf: 0-0 GS: 0-0 Gd: 0-1 GF: - Fm: 0-0
Distance: 2m/2m3: 0-1 2m4-2m7: 0-0 3m+: 0-0
Track: LH: 0-0 RH: 0-1 Tight: 0-0 Gall: 0-0
Aids: Bl: 0-0 Vi: 0-0 Tstrap: 0-0
Best Rating: 50 4/02 Ludl 2m good Hdl

Maybeseven

103(91h) **98**
8-y-o gr g Baron Blakeney-Ninth Of May (Comedy Star (USA))
M J Wilkinson The Diamond Seven Partnership

Placings:00/44613/P04P-**P13P6PPP** **(4514)**
2001/02: 26^{P}G, 25^{1}G, 26^{3}GS, 24^{P}G, 24^{6}GS, 24^{P}G, 25^{P}S, 25^{P}GS

	Starts	1st	2nd	3rd	Win & Pl
Chases	8	1	0	1	3935
Career Total	**19**	**2**	**0**	**2**	**6866**

98	10/01	Folk	3m1f	F(0-100)HCh	GD	£3347
96	2/00	Hntg	3m2f	F(0-110)HHdl	SFT	£2296

Total win prize-money £5644

Going: Sf: 0-1 GS: 0-3 Gd: 1-4 GF: - Fm: 0-0
Distance: 2m/2m3: 0-0 2m4-2m7: 0-0 **3m+: 1-8**
Track: LH: 0-1 **RH: 1-6 Tight: 1-3** Gall: 0-2
Aids: Bl: 0-0 Vi: 0-0 Tstrap: 0-0
Best Rating: [illegible] 11/01 Plum 3m2f gd-sft Ch

A selling-class stayer, has been succesful in modest races over hurdles and fences. Won a weak contest on his second start over fences at Folkestone in October 2001. Suited by cut in the ground and goes well on a right-handed track.

Mayerling

70f **63f**
5-y-o b m Old Vic-Manon Lescaut (Then Again)
Miss E C Lavelle Mrs R J Lavelle

Placings:*0* **(4112)**
2001/02: 16^{0}S

	Starts	1st	2nd	3rd	Win & Pl
NH Flat	1	0	0	0	
Career Total	**1**	**0**	**0**	**0**	

Going: Sf: 0-1 GS: 0-0 Gd: 0-0 GF: - Fm: 0-0
Distance: 2m/2m3: 0-1 2m4-2m7: 0-0 3m+: 0-0
Track: LH: 0-0 RH: 0-1 Tight: 0-0 Gall: 0-0
Aids: Bl: 0-0 Vi: 0-0 Tstrap: 0-0
Best Rating: 63 3/02 Towc 2m soft NHF

Mayo Minor

7-y-o b m Jumbo Hirt (USA)-Miss Mayo (Rubor)
M Todhunter Mrs R C Carr

Placings:*0P* **(1927)**
2001/02: 17^{0}G, 22^{P}G

	Starts	1st	2nd	3rd	Win & Pl
NH Flat	1	0	0	0	0
Hurdles	1	0	0	0	0
Career Total	**2**	**0**	**0**	**0**	

Going: Sf: 0-0 GS: 0-0 Gd: 0-2 GF: - Fm: 0-0
Distance: 2m/2m3: 0-1 2m4-2m7: 0-1 3m+: 0-0
Track: LH: 0-2 RH: 0-0 Tight: 0-2 Gall: 0-0
Aids: Bl: 0-0 Vi: 0-0 Tstrap: 0-0
Best Rating:

Mazamet (USA)

95(99c) (98c)**79**
9-y-o b g Elmaamul (USA)-Miss Mazepah (USA) (Nijinsky (CAN))
O O'Neill Merry Fellows

Placings:442/2250/45002/60625634 **(3161)**
2001/02: 17^{6}GS, 21^{0}GS, 23^{6}GF, 20^{2}G, 21^{5}GF, 24^{6}G, 21^{3}GF, 26^{4}S

	Starts	1st	2nd	3rd	Win & Pl
Hurdles	3	0	0	1	388
Chases	5	0	1	0	1338
Career Total	**20**	**0**	**5**	**1**	**5723**

Going: Sf: 0-1 GS: 0-2 Gd: 0-2 GF: - Fm: 0-3
Distance: 2m/2m3: 0-1 2m4-2m7: 0-4 3m+: 0-3
Track: LH: 0-6 RH: 0-2 Tight: 0-5 Gall: 0-0
Aids: Bl: 0-3 Vi: 0-0 Tstrap: 0-0
Best Rating: 107 1/97 Chel 2m1f gd-fm Hdl

Not a straightforward customer. Thoroughly exposed over hurdles and has shown only moderate ability over fences.

Mazeed (IRE)

101 **84**
9-y-o ch g Lycius (USA)-Maraatib (IRE) (Green Desert (USA))
Miss K M George Stableline

Placings:P0P3250/6261330400-032155000 **(4731)**
2001/02: 19^{0}G, 19^{3}GF, 20^{2}G, 19^{1}G, 22^{5}G, 22^{5}GF, 21^{0}GF, 19^{0}GF, 17^{0}F

	Starts	1st	2nd	3rd	Win & Pl
Hurdles	9	1	1	1	3593
Career Total	**26**	**2**	**3**	**4**	**8927**

84	7/01	Strf	2m3f	F(0-95)HHdl	GD	£2744
86	7/00	Sedg	2m5f110y	E Hdl	FRM	£2296

Total win prize-money £5040

Going: Sf: 0-0 GS: 0-0 Gd: 1-4 GF: - Fm: 0-5
Distance: **2m/2m3: 1-3** 2m4-2m7: 0-0 3m+: 0-0
Track: **LH: 1-5** RH: 0-4 **Tight: 1-5** Gall: 0-0
Aids: Bl: 0-0 **Vi: 1-9** Tstrap: 0-0
Best Rating: 86 7/00 Sedg 2m5f110y firm Hdl

Mazileo

104(103h) (91h)**131**
9-y-o b g Mazilier (USA)-Embroglio (USA) (Empery (USA))
Ian Williams T J And Mrs H Parrott

Placings:*41/5*P052/1101621/**31U31F15F**/400-06033F414P **(4918)**
2001/02: 20^{0}GF, 20^{6}G, 19^{0}G, 25^{3}G, 21^{3}G, 24^{F}G, 24^{4}G, 25^{1}GF, 26^{4}GF, 28^{P}GF

	Starts	1st	2nd	3rd	Win & Pl
Hurdles	2	0	0	0	0
Chases	8	1	0	2	11234
Career Total	**36**	**9**	**2**	**4**	**46955**

131	4/02	Hrfd	3m1f110y	E(0-110)HCh	G-F	£7577
133	11/99	Hayd	2m4f	B Ch	G-S	£11265
131	11/99	Ludl	2m4f	E Ch	GD	£3533
132	9/99	Hntg	2m110y	E Ch	G-F	£3441
124	4/99	Towc	2m	D(0-125)HHdl	GD	£3829
110	11/98	Ludl	2m	E Hdl	GD	£2948
122	10/98	Hrfd	2m1f	E Hdl	G-F	£2829
116	10/98	NAbb	2m1f	E Hdl	GD	£2583

90	3/97	NAbb	2m1f	H NHF	G-F	£1299

Total win prize-money £39306

Going: Sf: 0-0 GS: 0-0 Gd: 0-6 GF: - Fm: 1-4
Distance: 2m/2m3: 0-1 2m4-2m7: 0-3 **3m+: 1-6**
Track: LH: 0-8 **RH: 1-2** Tight: 0-2 Gall: 0-4
Aids: Bl: 0-0 Vi: 0-0 Tstrap: 0-0
Best Rating: 133 11/99 Hayd 2m4f gd-sft Ch

He was absent for a year after falling at Ascot in February 2000, then made his comeback with an eye-catching run over a trip short of his best over hurdles in January 2001. He is best at two and a half miles but does stay three. Acts on a sound surface and may have been a shade fortunate when winning at Hereford in April 2002.

Mccaslin

6-y-o gr g Grey Desire-Chapel Haven (IRE) (King Persian)
J R Norton Elsa Crankshaw & G Allan

Placings:*0-000P* **(2343)**
2001/02: 17^{0}G, 16^{0}GS, 17^{0}S, 20^{P}GS

	Starts	1st	2nd	3rd	Win & Pl
NH Flat	3	0	0	0	0
Hurdles	1	0	0	0	0
Career Total	**5**	**0**	**0**	**0**	

Going: Sf: 0-1 GS: 0-2 Gd: 0-1 GF: - Fm: 0-0
Distance: 2m/2m3: 0-3 2m4-2m7: 0-1 3m+: 0-0
Track: LH: 0-3 RH: 0-1 Tight: 0-1 Gall: 0-1
Aids: Bl: 0-0 Vi: 0-0 Tstrap: 0-0
Best Rating: 54 5/01 Bang 2m1f good NHF

McGregor The Third

88(101h) (74h)**85**
16-y-o ch g Nearly A Hand-Arctic Dawn (Arctic Slave)
Mrs L B Normile Mrs D A Whitaker

Placings:111266L/1121253/1123/5F/P2115/415-430 **(0803)**
2001/02: 24^{4}GF, 24^{3}F, 24^{0}GF

	Starts	1st	2nd	3rd	Win & Pl
Hurdles	1	0	0	1	422
Chases	2	0	0	0	0
Career Total	**31**	**11**	**5**	**3**	**77009**

104	5/00	Ctml	3m2f	D Hdl	G-F	£3103
140	10/99	Kels	3m1f	D(0-125)HCh	GD	£3857
134	9/99	Kels	3m1f	D(0-125)HCh	G-F	£3740
130	1/98	Chel	3m1f	B Ch	G-S	£8609
140	9/97	Strf	3m	C(0-130)HCh	GD	£4890
129	11/96	Chel	3m7f	B Ch	GD	£8488
132	10/96	Uttx	3m2f	D(0-120)HCh	G-F	£7002
132	9/96	Sedg	2m5f	E(0-115)HCh	G-F	£3254
122	11/95	Chel	3m	B Ch	GD	£7002
111	10/95	Newc	3m	E Ch	FRM	£2684
130	10/95	Carl	2m4f110y	D Ch	G-F	£3436

Total win prize-money £56069

Going: Sf: 0-0 GS: 0-0 Gd: 0-0 GF: - Fm: 0-3
Distance: 2m/2m3: 0-0 2m4-2m7: 0-0 3m+: 0-3
Track: LH: 0-0 RH: 0-3 Tight: 0-0 Gall: 0-0
Aids: Bl: 0-0 Vi: 0-0 Tstrap: 0-0
Best Rating: 140 10/99 Kels 3m1f good Ch

This ex-eventer was a standing dish around Cheltenham's cross-country circuit. Came back from an absence in the summer of 2001. (DEAD)

Mcsnappy

94 **95**
5-y-o ch g Risk Me (FR)-Nannie Annie (Persian Bold)
J W Mullins Seamus Mullins

Placings:*22-3403* **(4637)**
2001/02: 16^{3}HY, 16^{4}GS, 16^{0}GS, 20^{3}GF

	Starts	1st	2nd	3rd	Win & Pl
NH Flat	3	0	0	1	331
Hurdles	1	0	0	1	826
Career Total	**6**	**0**	**2**	**2**	**3024**

Going: Sf: 0-1 GS: 0-2 Gd: 0-0 GF: - Fm: 0-1
Distance: 2m/2m3: 0-3 2m4-2m7: 0-1 3m+: 0-0
Track: LH: 0-1 RH: 0-3 Tight: 0-0 Gall: 0-0
Aids: Bl: 0-0 Vi: 0-0 Tstrap: 0-0
Best Rating: 104 3/01 Wwck 2m heavy NHF

Ran with promise in bumpers and looks best with cut in the ground.

Mead (IRE)

109f **106f**
5-y-o b g Mujadil (USA)-Sweetest Thing (IRE) (Prince Rupert (FR))
J Mackie Lyonshall Racing

Placings:*22* **(4019)**
2001/02: 16^{2}GS, 16^{2}GS

	Starts	1st	2nd	3rd	Win & Pl
NH Flat	2	0	2	0	1119
Career Total	**2**	**0**	**2**	**0**	**1119**

Going: Sf: 0-0 GS: 0-2 Gd: 0-0 GF: - Fm: 0-0
Distance: 2m/2m3: 0-2 2m4-2m7: 0-0 3m+: 0-0
Track: LH: 0-2 RH: 0-0 Tight: 0-1 Gall: 0-1
Aids: Bl: 0-0 Vi: 0-0 Tstrap: 0-0
Best Rating: 106 3/02 Donc 2m110y gd-sft NHF

Has finished runner-up on both his bumper starts on soft ground.

Meadowbank

113(95h) (102h)**135**
8-y-o b g Meadowbrook-Polypodium (Politico (USA))
M W Easterby Lord Manton

Placings:4U5/**2211FP-P1F3503** **(4582)**
2001/02: 26^{P}S, 25^{1}G, 27^{F}S, 20^{3}GS, 26^{5}GS, 24^{0}G, 25^{3}G

	Starts	1st	2nd	3rd	Win & Pl
Hurdles	1	0	0	1	500
Chases	6	1	0	1	6812
Career Total	**16**	**3**	**2**	**2**	**17397**

135	11/01	Weth	3m1f	D(0-120)HCh	GD	£5245
134	2/01	Weth	3m1f	D Ch	SFT	£3757
135	1/01	Weth	3m1f	D Ch	G-S	£3978

Total win prize-money £12981

Going: Sf: 0-2 GS: 0-2 Gd: 1-3 GF: - Fm: 0-0
Distance: 2m/2m3: 0-0 2m4-2m7: 0-1 **3m+: 1-6**
Track: **LH: 1-5** RH: 0-2 Tight: 0-1 Gall: 0-1
Aids: Bl: 0-0 Vi: 0-0 Tstrap: 0-0
Best Rating: 139 11/00 Weth 3m1f soft Ch

Useful staying chaser. A grand, big type, he acts on good ground and soft. His trainer considers him a potential Grand National horse.

Meadowleck

13-y-o b m Meadowbrook-Leckywil (Menelek)
W G Young W G Young

Placings:*0/0R0*P0663SP0/404000060000P/00F00040 0F0B500/PP00P446330U60F6665P/00P0**PF**5PP650/ P/**PPP**-P **(0780)**
2001/02: 20^{P}G

	Starts	1st	2nd	3rd	Win & Pl
Hurdles	1	0	0	0	
Career Total	**77**	**0**	**0**	**3**	**1121**

Going: Sf: 0-0 GS: 0-0 Gd: 0-1 GF: - Fm: 0-0
Distance: 2m/2m3: 0-0 2m4-2m7: 0-1 3m+: 0-0
Track: LH: 0-1 RH: 0-0 Tight: 0-0 Gall: 0-0
Aids: Bl: 0-0 Vi: 0-0 Tstrap: 0-1
Best Rating: 64 1/97 Ayr 3m110y good Hdl

Meadows Boy

96 **113**
10-y-o gr g Derrylin-What A Coup (Malicious)
R Lee (B Palling 13/12) Richard Edwards

Placings:*0040*540/**36RU**00/53UP0F-R4RR104R **(4164)**
2001/02: 22^{R}GF, 22^{4}F, 22^{R}G, 21^{R}G, 21^{1}HY, 17^{0}HY, 16^{4}GS, 21^{R}GS

	Starts	1st	2nd	3rd	Win & Pl
Hurdles	8	1	0	0	2525
Career Total	**27**	**1**	**0**	**2**	**3437**

100	1/02	Wwck	2m5f	F(0-90)Hdl	HVY	£2212

Total win prize-money £2212

Going: Sf: 1-2 GS: 0-2 Gd: 0-2 GF: - Fm: 0-2
Distance: 2m/2m3: 0-2 **2m4-2m7: 1-6** 3m+: 0-0
Track: LH: 0-1 RH: 0-4 Tight: 0-0 Gall: 0-1
Aids: Bl: 0-0 Vi: 0-0 Tstrap: 0-2
Best Rating: 116 11/00 Winc 2m6f soft Hdl

He had become unreliable, often refusing to start, before beating a big field at Warwick in January. Stays well.

Meander (IRE)

102(96h) **113**
7-y-o br g Mandalus-Lady Rerico (Pamroy)
Miss H C Knight M E R Allsopp

Placings:*46*/40-2210 **(3230)**
2001/02: 20^{2}GF, 21^{2}GF, 24^{1}G, 24^{0}GS

	Starts	1st	2nd	3rd	Win & Pl
Chases	4	1	2	0	6209
Career Total	**8**	**1**	**2**	**0**	**6438**

108	12/01	Sthl	3m110y	E Ch	GD	£3846

Total win prize-money £3847

Going: Sf: 0-0 GS: 0-1 Gd: 1-1 GF: - Fm: 0-2
Distance: 2m/2m3: 0-0 2m4-2m7: 0-2 **3m+: 1-2**
Track: **LH: 1-1** RH: 0-3 **Tight: 1-2** Gall: 0-1
Aids: Bl: 0-0 Vi: 0-0 Tstrap: 0-0
Best Rating: 113 11/01 Winc 2m5f gd-fm Ch

Showed little over hurdles, but has the build to do better over fences and has shown promise. Looks to need three miles and acts on soft and good.

Mears First

6-y-o gr g Wing Park-Siberian Swing (Siberian Express (USA))
C L Popham Mears Group Plc

Placings:*0*-PPP **(4736)**
2001/02: 17^{P}S, 17^{P}HY, 17^{P}F

	Starts	1st	2nd	3rd	Win & Pl
Hurdles	3	0	0	0	
Career Total	**4**	**0**	**0**	**0**	

Going: Sf: 0-2 GS: 0-0 Gd: 0-0 GF: - Fm: 0-1
Distance: 2m/2m3: 0-3 2m4-2m7: 0-0 3m+: 0-0
Track: LH: 0-2 RH: 0-1 Tight: 0-2 Gall: 0-0
Aids: Bl: 0-1 Vi: 0-0 Tstrap: 0-1
Best Rating:

Medelai

100 **63**
6-y-o b m Marju (IRE)-No Islands (Lomond (USA))
A G Juckes (Ms A E Embiricos 16/8) A C W Price

Placings:UUP **(2560)**
2001/02: 16^{U}S, 16^{U}G, 20^{P}S

	Starts	1st	2nd	3rd	Win & Pl
Hurdles	3	0	0	0	
Career Total	**3**	**0**	**0**	**0**	

Going: Sf: 0-2 GS: 0-0 Gd: 0-1 GF: - Fm: 0-0
Distance: 2m/2m3: 0-2 2m4-2m7: 0-1 3m+: 0-0
Track: LH: 0-3 RH: 0-0 Tight: 0-2 Gall: 0-0
Aids: Bl: 0-1 Vi: 0-0 Tstrap: 0-0
Best Rating:

Medium Wave

105(96h) (77h)**112**
10-y-o b g Domynsky-Alumia (Great Nephew)
S E H Sherwood The Perseverance Mob

Placings:33/354P4/0133U3/226P3541-442350P **(3983)**
2001/02: 19^{4}GS, 16^{4}GS, 19^{2}G, 19^{3}S, 20^{5}G, 17^{0}HY, 24^{P}G

	Starts	1st	2nd	3rd	Win & Pl
Hurdles	2	0	0	0	0
Chases	5	0	1	1	1599
Career Total	**28**	**2**	**3**	**8**	**13928**

112	4/01	Hrfd	2m	F(0-110)HCh	GD	£4202
108	12/99	Ludl	2m	F(0-110)HHdl	GD	£2775

Total win prize-money £6977

Going: Sf: 0-2 GS: 0-2 Gd: 0-3 GF: - Fm: 0-0
Distance: 2m/2m3: 0-4 2m4-2m7: 0-2 3m+: 0-1
Track: LH: 0-0 RH: 0-7 Tight: 0-1 Gall: 0-0
Aids: Bl: 0-6 Vi: 0-1 Tstrap: 0-5
Best Rating: 112 11/01 Hrfd 2m3f good Ch

Won over hurdles in December 1999, but had to wait nearly two years too follow up and he did that at Hereford in April 2001, although he has looked held since. Does not find much under pressure.

Meg's Memory (IRE)

98 **100**
9-y-o b m Superlative-Meanz Beanz (High Top)
A Streeter Centaur Racing Ltd

Placings:514/5456451/254/5104-02P000 **(4578)**
2001/02: 20^{0}G, 21^{2}G, 20^{P}S, 21^{0}GS, 20^{0}S, 23^{0}G

	Starts	1st	2nd	3rd	Win & Pl
Hurdles	6	0	1	0	742
Career Total	**23**	**3**	**2**	**0**	**7457**

99	3/01	Hntg	2m5f110y	G(0-90)HHdl	SFT	£1855
95	4/98	MRas	2m1f110y	G(0-95)HHdl	SFT	£1576
85	2/97	Catt	2m	E Hdl	GD	£2458

Total win prize-money £5889

Going: Sf: 0-2 GS: 0-1 Gd: 0-3 GF: - Fm: 0-0
Distance: 2m/2m3: 0-0 2m4-2m7: 0-6 3m+: 0-0
Track: LH: 0-2 RH: 0-3 Tight: 0-2 Gall: 0-1
Aids: Bl: 0-0 Vi: 0-0 Tstrap: 0-0
Best Rating: 100 5/01 Wwck 2m5f good Hdl

Mega (IRE)

86 **83**
6-y-o b m Petardia-Gobolino (Don)
M H Tompkins Mystic Meg Limited

Placings:0/55 **(4548)**
2001/02: 16^{5}GS, 21^{5}GF

	Starts	1st	2nd	3rd	Win & Pl
Hurdles	2	0	0	0	0
Career Total	**3**	**0**	**0**	**0**	**0**

Going: Sf: 0-0 GS: 0-1 Gd: 0-0 GF: - Fm: 0-1
Distance: 2m/2m3: 0-1 2m4-2m7: 0-1 3m+: 0-0
Track: LH: 0-0 RH: 0-2 Tight: 0-0 Gall: 0-2
Aids: Bl: 0-0 Vi: 0-0 Tstrap: 0-0
Best Rating: 83 1/02 Hntg 2m110y gd-sft Hdl

Megaera

97(90h) (73h)**106**
8-y-o b g Petoski-Notinhand (Nearly A Hand)
N B Mason N B Mason

Placings:360/45-4 **(2184)**
2001/02: 21^{4}G

	Starts	1st	2nd	3rd	Win & Pl
Chases	1	0	0	0	327
Career Total	**6**	**0**	**0**	**1**	**901**

Going: Sf: 0-0 GS: 0-0 Gd: 0-1 GF: - Fm: 0-0
Distance: 2m/2m3: 0-0 2m4-2m7: 0-1 3m+: 0-0
Track: LH: 0-1 RH: 0-0 Tight: 0-0 Gall: 0-0
Aids: Bl: 0-0 Vi: 0-0 Tstrap: 0-0
Best Rating: 106 4/01 Weth 2m gd-sft Ch

Megans Mystery (IRE)

62
12-y-o b g Corvaro (USA)-Megans Choice (Furry Glen)
Miss S E Forster C Storey

Placings:5/0PPP/0P **(1467)**
2001/02: 20^{0}G, 20^{P}G

	Starts	1st	2nd	3rd	Win & Pl
Hurdles	2	0	0	0	
Career Total	**7**	**0**	**0**	**0**	**0**

Going: Sf: 0-0 GS: 0-0 Gd: 0-2 GF: - Fm: 0-0
Distance: 2m/2m3: 0-0 2m4-2m7: 0-2 3m+: 0-0
Track: LH: 0-0 RH: 0-2 Tight: 0-0 Gall: 0-0
Aids: Bl: 0-0 Vi: 0-0 Tstrap: 0-2
Best Rating: 80 6/99 Hexm 2m soft Hdl

Megazine

97 **83**
8-y-o b g Shaab-Sherzine (Gorytus (USA))
M Hill Martin Hill

Placings:*0/00*05053/4-0P0 **(4011)**
2001/02: 19^{0}S, 16^{P}HY, 21^{0}S

	Starts	1st	2nd	3rd	Win & Pl
Hurdles	2	0	0	0	0
Chases	1	0	0	0	0
Career Total	**12**	**0**	**0**	**1**	**418**

Going: Sf: 0-3 GS: 0-0 Gd: 0-0 GF: - Fm: 0-0
Distance: 2m/2m3: 0-1 2m4-2m7: 0-2 3m+: 0-0
Track: LH: 0-1 RH: 0-2 Tight: 0-1 Gall: 0-1
Aids: Bl: 0-0 Vi: 0-0 Tstrap: 0-0
Best Rating: 83 4/00 Extr 2m1f110y heavy Hdl

Moderate hurdler, likes soft ground, stays 22 furlongs.

Mel In Blue (FR)

96f **106f**
4-y-o b g Pistolet Bleu (IRE)-Calligraphie (FR) (Rb Chesne)
N J Henderson Robert Waley-Cohen

Placings:*1* **(4032)**
2001/02: 16^{1}GS

	Starts	1st	2nd	3rd	Win & Pl
NH Flat	1	1	0	0	2772
Career Total	**1**	**1**	**0**	**0**	**2772**

106	3/02	Newb	2m110y	H NHF	G-S	£2772

Total win prize-money £2772

Going: Sf: 0-0 GS: 1-1 Gd: 0-0 GF: - Fm: 0-0
Distance: 2m/2m3: 1-1 2m4-2m7: 0-0 3m+: 0-0
Track: LH: 1-1 RH: 0-0 Tight: 0-0 **Gall: 1-1**
Aids: Bl: 0-0 Vi: 0-0 Tstrap: 0-0
Best Rating: 106 3/02 Newb 2m110y gd-sft NHF

A French-bred, he just edged out one of his stable-mates in a Newbury bumper in March. Seemed suited by the drying ground that day.

Melledgan (IRE)

104 **104**
5-y-o b m Catrail (USA)-Dark Hyacinth (IRE) (Darshaan)
Miss S J Wilton (R Guest 17/9) John Pointon And Sons

Placings:1336P **(4662)**
2001/02: 17^{1}G, 16^{3}G, 16^{3}S, 16^{6}GS, 16^{P}G

	Starts	1st	2nd	3rd	Win & Pl
Hurdles	5	1	0	2	4128
Career Total	**5**	**1**	**0**	**2**	**4128**

104	11/01	Tntn	2m1f	E Hdl	GD	£3164

Total win prize-money £3164

Going: Sf: 0-1 GS: 0-1 Gd: 1-3 GF: - Fm: 0-0
Distance: 2m/2m3: 1-5 2m4-2m7: 0-0 3m+: 0-0
Track: LH: 0-4 **RH: 1-1 Tight: 1-3** Gall: 0-2
Aids: Bl: 0-0 Vi: 0-0 Tstrap: 0-0
Best Rating: 104 1/02 Donc 2m110y soft Hdl

A winner on her hurdling debut at Taunton in November 2001, she continued to run well subsequently, with a couple of good efforts at Doncaster. Acts on most types of ground.

Melling

11-y-o b g Thowra (FR)-Miss Melmore (Nishapour (FR))
R J Hodges Miss R Dobson

Placings:*00*/4330U2203223/3414323516/6653355-0 **(0125)**
2001/02: 24^{0}F

	Starts	1st	2nd	3rd	Win & Pl
Chases	1	0	0	0	
Career Total	**32**	**2**	**5**	**9**	**20680**

109	3/00	Chep	2m3f110y	D(0-110)HCh	GD	£3997
109	12/99	Tntn	3m	D(0-110)HCh	G-S	£4279

Total win prize-money £8278

Going: Sf: 0-0 GS: 0-0 Gd: 0-0 GF: - Fm: 0-1
Distance: 2m/2m3: 0-0 2m4-2m7: 0-0 3m+: 0-1
Track: LH: 0-0 RH: 0-1 Tight: 0-1 Gall: 0-0
Aids: Bl: 0-0 Vi: 0-0 Tstrap: 0-0
Best Rating: **109** 3/00 Chep 2m3f110y good Ch

Melodie D'Avril (FR)

83 76

5-y-o b m Varese (FR)-Miss Geralde (FR) (Carmarthen (FR))
M C Pipe C R Fleet

Placings:0301434-500 **(0846)**
2001/02: 19^{5}G, 20^{0}GF, 22^{0}GF

	Starts	1st	2nd	3rd	Win & Pl
Hurdles	3	0	0	0	0
Career Total	**10**	**1**	**0**	**2**	**8798**

10/00 Autl 2m2f Hdl HVY £6244
Total win prize-money £6244

Going: Sf: 0-0 GS: 0-0 Gd: 0-1 GF: - Fm: 0-2
Distance: 2m/2m3: 0-1 2m4-2m7: 0-2 3m+: 0-0
Track: LH: 0-3 RH: 0-0 Tight: 0-1 Gall: 0-0
Aids: Bl: 0-0 Vi: 0-0 Tstrap: 0-0
Best Rating: **101** 11/00 Newb 2m110y gd-sft Hdl

Mels Baby (IRE)

9-y-o br g Contract Law (USA)-Launch The Raft (Home Guard (USA))
J L Eyre Ms Melanie Jayne Eyre

Placings:P **(2117)**
2001/02: 16^{P}GS

	Starts	1st	2nd	3rd	Win & Pl
Hurdles	1	0	0	0	
Career Total	**1**	**0**	**0**	**0**	

Going: Sf: 0-0 GS: 0-1 Gd: 0-0 GF: - Fm: 0-0
Distance: 2m/2m3: 0-1 2m4-2m7: 0-0 3m+: 0-0
Track: LH: 0-1 RH: 0-0 Tight: 0-1 Gall: 0-0
Aids: Bl: 0-0 Vi: 0-0 Tstrap: 0-0
Best Rating:

Melstair

93 73

7-y-o b g Terimon-Kevins Lady (Alzao (USA))
A R Dicken Got To Be In It To Win It Partnership

Placings:*00U00*/055F53403-PP004P0 **(4898)**
2001/02: 16^{P}S, 20^{P}GS, 20^{0}G, 18^{0}GS, 20^{4}G, 20^{P}S, 16^{0}G

	Starts	1st	2nd	3rd	Win & Pl
Hurdles	7	0	0	0	0
Career Total	**21**	**0**	**0**	**2**	**843**

Going: Sf: 0-2 GS: 0-2 Gd: 0-3 GF: - Fm: 0-0
Distance: 2m/2m3: 0-3 2m4-2m7: 0-4 3m+: 0-0
Track: LH: 0-4 RH: 0-3 Tight: 0-2 Gall: 0-2
Aids: Bl: 0-0 Vi: 0-0 Tstrap: 0-0
Best Rating: **79** 1/01 Muss 2m4f gd-sft Hdl

Moderate hurdler, does not want the ground too soft.

Melton Made (IRE)

95(66h) (40h)92

9-y-o br g Strong Gale-Pamela's Princess (Black Minstrel)
Ferdy Murphy Exors Of The Late Mr G A Hubbard

Placings:*040/203030/315652440330*/**U5B555-50P** **(3444)**
2001/02: 21^{5}G, 26^{0}G, 24^{P}GS

	Starts	1st	2nd	3rd	Win & Pl
Hurdles	1	0	0	0	0
Chases	2	0	0	0	0
Career Total	**30**	**1**	**2**	**5**	**7376**

106 9/99 MRas 2m3f110y D(0-120)HHdl G-F £3185
Total win prize-money £3186

Going: Sf: 0-0 GS: 0-1 Gd: 0-2 GF: - Fm: 0-0
Distance: 2m/2m3: 0-0 2m4-2m7: 0-1 3m+: 0-2
Track: LH: 0-1 RH: 0-2 Tight: 0-2 Gall: 0-1
Aids: Bl: 0-0 Vi: 0-0 Tstrap: 0-3
Best Rating: **119** 12/99 Folk 2m5f good Ch

Meltonian

91 84

5-y-o ch g Past Glories-Meltonby (Sayf El Arab (USA))
K C Bailey (J Hetherton 17/5) Have Fun Racing Partnership

Placings:*4O4P* **(4816)**
2001/02: 16^{4}GF, 16°S, 16^{4}GF, 21^{P}GF

	Starts	1st	2nd	3rd	Win & Pl
NH Flat	3	0	0	0	0
Hurdles	1	0	0	0	0
Career Total	**4**	**0**	**0**	**0**	**0**

Going: Sf: 0-1 GS: 0-0 Gd: 0-0 GF: - Fm: 0-3
Distance: 2m/2m3: 0-3 2m4-2m7: 0-1 3m+: 0-0
Track: LH: 0-2 RH: 0-2 Tight: 0-0 Gall: 0-2
Aids: Bl: 0-0 Vi: 0-0 Tstrap: 0-0
Best Rating: **97** 4/02 Hntg 2m110y gd-fm NHF

Mely Moss (FR)

108 118

11-y-o ch g Tip Moss (FR)-The Exception (FR) (Melyno)
C R Egerton Darren C Mercer

Placings:226F146/**1F20/132/21/2/B-60** **(4677)**
2001/02: 24^{6}G, 36^{0}G

	Starts	1st	2nd	3rd	Win & Pl
Chases	2	0	0	0	0
Career Total	**20**	**4**	**6**	**1**	**209590**

125 4/99 Chel 3m2f110y H Ch G-S £4143
142 1/97 Uttx 2m5f C(0-130)HCh GD £4435
5/95 Autl 2m4f110y Ch HLD £17964
3/95 Autl 2m2f Hdl HLD £17964
Total win prize-money £44507

Going: Sf: 0-0 GS: 0-0 Gd: 0-2 GF: - Fm: 0-0
Distance: 2m/2m3: 0-0 2m4-2m7: 0-0 3m+: 0-2
Track: LH: 0-1 RH: 0-1 Tight: 0-1 Gall: 0-0
Aids: Bl: 0-0 Vi: 0-0 Tstrap: 0-0
Best Rating: **153** 4/00 Aint 4m4f good Ch

Very lightly raced, he was returning from a two-year break when finishing an excellent second in the 1999 Martell Fox Hunters' Chase at Aintree. He followed that with a cosy win at Cheltenham on his only other start that season and returned to Aintree in 2000 to finish second in the National on his only start of the year. Reappeared in the 2001 National, after having undergone a wind operation but was brought down at the eighth. He jumps with pin-point accuracy but has clearly been difficult to train, and is therefore probably best caught fresh. Had a nice run round and was not knocked about at Sandown in March but was out of contention when falling two out on a repeat bid in the 'National. Acts on a sound surface, handles soft.

Memphis Dancer

7-y-o b m Shareef Dancer (USA)-Wollow Maid (Wollow)
M W Easterby Peter Armitage

Placings:000/40/0 **(0201)**
2001/02: 16^{0}G

	Starts	1st	2nd	3rd	Win & Pl
Hurdles	1	0	0	0	
Career Total	**6**	**0**	**0**	**0**	**0**

Going: Sf: 0-0 GS: 0-0 Gd: 0-1 GF: - Fm: 0-0
Distance: 2m/2m3: 0-1 2m4-2m7: 0-0 3m+: 0-0
Track: LH: 0-1 RH: 0-0 Tight: 0-0 Gall: 0-0
Aids: Bl: 0-0 Vi: 0-0 Tstrap: 0-0
Best Rating: **61** 12/98 Muss 2m good Hdl

Memsahib Ofesteem

110 114

11-y-o gr m Neltino-Occatillo (Maris Piper)
S Gollings Tony French & Robert Jones

Placings:*130/302024/2P45215124/001/65P62435*-03424165336 **(4822)**
2001/02: 19^{0}GF, 20^{3}GS, 20^{4}G, 24^{2}G, 20^{4}G, 20^{1}S, 24^{6}S, 21^{5}G, 22^{3}HY, 24^{3}GF, 21^{6}G

	Starts	1st	2nd	3rd	Win & Pl
Hurdles	11	1	1	3	11856
Career Total	**41**	**5**	**7**	**6**	**29531**

114 1/02 Donc 2m4f C(0-135)HHdl SFT £5616
120 3/00 Chep 2m4f D(0-125)HHdl GD £3575
114 2/99 Fknm 2m E(0-115)HHdl G-S £2978
106 1/99 Donc 2m4f E(0-115)HHdl G-S £3055
100 2/97 Donc 2m110y H NHF GD £1035
Total win prize-money £16260

Going: Sf: 1-3 GS: 0-1 Gd: 0-5 GF: - Fm: 0-2
Distance: 2m/2m3: 0-0 **2m4-2m7: 1-8** 3m+: 0-3
Track: **LH: 1-8** RH: 0-3 Tight: 0-3 **Gall: 1-4**
Aids: Bl: 0-0 Vi: 0-0 Tstrap: 0-0
Best Rating: **120** 3/00 Chep 2m4f good Hdl

Fair hurdler, best over two and a half miles and appreciates good ground or easy ground, but has won on heavy.

Mendip Son

12-y-o b g Hallgate-Silver Surprise (Son Of Silver)
Mrs H E Rees Mrs H E Rees

Placings:*0/5P202/0*/**35-3** **(0255)**
2001/02: 20^{3}GF

	Starts	1st	2nd	3rd	Win & Pl
Chases	1	0	0	1	255
Career Total	**10**	**0**	**2**	**2**	**1801**

Going: Sf: 0-0 GS: 0-0 Gd: 0-0 GF: - Fm: 0-1
Distance: 2m/2m3: 0-0 2m4-2m7: 0-1 3m+: 0-0
Track: LH: 0-1 RH: 0-0 Tight: 0-1 Gall: 0-0
Aids: Bl: 0-1 Vi: 0-0 Tstrap: 0-0
Best Rating: **89** 3/95 Plum 2m1f heavy Hdl

Menelek Lord (IRE)

97(50h) 112

8-y-o b g Yashgan-Higcham (Le Moss)

A Streeter Dantom Production Solutions Ltd

Placings:44625F64/03214FU2-P44 (4313)
2001/02: 24^{P}GS, 28^{4}S, 24^{4}HY

	Starts	1st	2nd	3rd	Win & Pl
Hurdles	1	0	0	0	0
Chases	2	0	0	0	636
Career Total	**19**	**1**	**3**	**1**	**8360**

112	12/00	MRas	3m1f	E(0-105)HCh	SFT	£3607

Total win prize-money £3608

Going: Sf: 0-2 GS: 0-1 Gd: 0-0 GF: - Fm: 0-0
Distance: 2m/2m3: 0-0 2m4-2m7: 0-0 3m+: 0-3
Track: LH: 0-2 RH: 0-1 Tight: 0-3 Gall: 0-0
Aids: Bl: 0-0 Vi: 0-3 Tstrap: 0-0
Best Rating: 112 4/01 Hayd 3m soft Ch

Menesonic (IRE)

104 **138**

12-y-o b g Meneval (USA)-Kandy Kate (Pry)
R H Alner Mrs W H Walter

Placings:*20402525*/3423513/**1F15532/122223/61332 30/P135-1446** (4819)
2001/02: 24^{1}GS, 25^{4}G, 25^{4}GS, 26^{6}GF

	Starts	1st	2nd	3rd	Win & Pl
Chases	4	1	0	0	9895
Career Total	**43**	**7**	**10**	**9**	**70566**

138	11/01	Sand	3m110y	C(0-135)HCh	G-S	£8697
138	11/00	Winc	3m1f110y	C(0-135)HCh	SFT	£8417
138	11/99	Font	3m2f110y	D(0-125)HCh	GD	£4634
140	10/98	Winc	3m1f110y	E(0-110)HCh	G-S	£4240
119	11/97	Kemp	3m	D Ch	G-S	£3371
105	10/97	Winc	3m1f110y	D Ch	GD	£3743
109	3/97	Extr	3m2f	E Hdl	G-S	£2452

Total win prize-money £35557

Going: Sf: 0-0 GS: 1-2 Gd: 0-1 GF: - Fm: 0-1
Distance: 2m/2m3: 0-0 2m4-2m7: 0-0 **3m+: 1-4**
Track: LH: 0-1 **RH: 1-2** Tight: 0-0 Gall: 0-1
Aids: Bl: 0-0 Vi: 0-0 Tstrap: 0-0
Best Rating: 140 10/98 Winc 3m1f110y gd-sft Ch

He is devoid of pace, but stays forever and tries hard. He goes best when fresh and did so again when winning a weak event at Sandown on his reappearance in November 2001

Mensch (IRE)

88 **75**

6-y-o ch g Husyan (USA)-Floating Dollar (Master Owen)
A M Hales Andrew L Cohen

Placings:U0-600 (4601)
2001/02: 20^{6}GS, 17^{0}GS, 16^{0}GF

	Starts	1st	2nd	3rd	Win & Pl
Hurdles	3	0	0	0	0
Career Total	**5**	**0**	**0**	**0**	**0**

Going: Sf: 0-0 GS: 0-2 Gd: 0-0 GF: - Fm: 0-1
Distance: 2m/2m3: 0-2 2m4-2m7: 0-1 3m+: 0-0
Track: LH: 0-2 RH: 0-1 Tight: 0-2 Gall: 0-0
Aids: Bl: 0-1 Vi: 0-0 Tstrap: 0-0
Best Rating: 75 3/02 MRas 2m1f110y gd-sft Hdl

Lightly-raced individual with modest form to date. Has only raced with give underfoot.

Mental Pressure

85 **62**

9-y-o ch g Polar Falcon (USA)-Hysterical (High Top)
Mrs M Reveley The Mary Reveley Racing Club

Placings:0 (2684)
2001/02: 16^{0}G

	Starts	1st	2nd	3rd	Win & Pl
Hurdles	1	0	0	0	
Career Total	**1**	**0**	**0**	**0**	

Going: Sf: 0-0 GS: 0-0 Gd: 0-1 GF: - Fm: 0-0
Distance: 2m/2m3: 0-1 2m4-2m7: 0-0 3m+: 0-0
Track: LH: 0-1 RH: 0-0 Tight: 0-0 Gall: 0-1
Aids: Bl: 0-0 Vi: 0-0 Tstrap: 0-0
Best Rating: 62 12/01 Donc 2m110y good Hdl

Mercato (FR)

104 **117**

6-y-o b g Mansonnien (FR)-Royal Lie (FR) (Garde Royale)
J R Best Mercato 1

Placings:*43/21*525611F-0P056 (2788)
2001/02: 17^{0}GS, 19^{P}GS, 21^{0}GS, 20^{5}G, 20^{6}G

	Starts	1st	2nd	3rd	Win & Pl
Hurdles	5	0	0	0	0
Career Total	**16**	**3**	**2**	**1**	**10968**

117	3/01	MRas	2m1f110y	F(0-105)HHdl	G-S	£5356
113	3/01	Font	2m2f110y	E(0-115)HHdl	SFT	£2628
100	10/00	Hntg	2m110y	H NHF	G-F	£1561

Total win prize-money £9546

Going: Sf: 0-0 GS: 0-3 Gd: 0-2 GF: - Fm: 0-0
Distance: 2m/2m3: 0-2 2m4-2m7: 0-3 3m+: 0-0
Track: LH: 0-2 RH: 0-3 Tight: 0-2 Gall: 0-0
Aids: Bl: 0-0 Vi: 0-0 Tstrap: 0-3
Best Rating: 117 4/01 MRas 2m3f110y gd-sft Hdl

Fair handicap hurdler, stays two miles-five, acts on any ground but suited by some cut.

Mercede (IRE)

104 **75**

5-y-o b m Perugino (USA)-Miss Busybody (IRE) (Phardante (FR))
N Wilson (J Balding 19/11) Josef Fusenich

Placings:0560 (4904)
2001/02: 17^{0}HY, 16^{5}HY, 16^{F}F, 17^{0}G

	Starts	1st	2nd	3rd	Win & Pl
Hurdles	4	0	0	0	0
Career Total	**4**	**0**	**0**	**0**	**0**

Going: Sf: 0-2 GS: 0-0 Gd: 0-1 GF: - Fm: 0-1
Distance: 2m/2m3: 0-4 2m4-2m7: 0-0 3m+: 0-0
Track: LH: 0-3 RH: 0-1 Tight: 0-3 Gall: 0-1
Aids: Bl: 0-0 Vi: 0-0 Tstrap: 0-1
Best Rating: 75 4/02 Newc 2m firm Hdl

Winning plater over hurdles.

Merchant Prince

82 **37**

6-y-o b g Flying Tyke-Bellinote (FR) (Noir Et Or)
A Smith Alfred Smith

Placings:0 (1505)
2001/02: 17^{0}G

	Starts	1st	2nd	3rd	Win & Pl
Hurdles	1	0	0	0	
Career Total	**1**	**0**	**0**	**0**	

Going: Sf: 0-0 GS: 0-0 Gd: 0-1 GF: - Fm: 0-0
Distance: 2m/2m3: 0-1 2m4-2m7: 0-0 3m+: 0-0
Track: LH: 0-1 RH: 0-0 Tight: 0-1 Gall: 0-0
Aids: Bl: 0-0 Vi: 0-0 Tstrap: 0-0
Best Rating: 49 10/01 Sedg 2m1f good Hdl

Meriel's Mistake (IRE)

106 **104**

7-y-o b m Commanche Run-Cathedral Street (Boreen Beag)
R Rowe W Packham & S Packham

Placings:*030*/1FPP-01P32P4 (4885)
2001/02: 19^{0}GS, 22^{1}GS, 24^{P}HY, 24^{3}GS, 24^{2}S, 22^{P}GS, 27^{4}GF

	Starts	1st	2nd	3rd	Win & Pl
Hurdles	7	1	1	1	4860
Career Total	**14**	**2**	**1**	**2**	**8823**

99	11/01	Font	2m6f110y	F(0-110)HHdl	G-S	£2310
96	12/00	Hntg	2m4f110y	D Hdl	SFT	£3737

Total win prize-money £6048

Going: Sf: 0-2 GS: 1-4 Gd: 0-0 GF: - Fm: 0-1
Distance: 2m/2m3: 0-1 **2m4-2m7: 1-2** 3m+: 0-4
Track: **LH: 1-3** RH: 0-3 **Tight: 1-2** Gall: 0-2
Aids: Bl: 0-0 Vi: 0-0 Tstrap: 0-0
Best Rating: 104 1/02 Newb 3m110y gd-sft Hdl

An inconsistent handicap hurdler, she stays three miles and likes to get her toe in.

Merlo (IRE)

86

7-y-o b g Supreme Leader-Playwright (Furry Glen)
Mrs L B Normile (Miss F M Crowley 25/6) The Friar Tuck Racing Club

Placings:*0* 0056P (4874)
2001/02: 16^{0}HY, 16^{0}G, 20^{5}GF, 24^{6}GS, 20^{P}G

	Starts	1st	2nd	3rd	Win & Pl
NH Flat	3	0	0	0	0
Hurdles	2	0	0	0	0
Career Total	**6**	**0**	**0**	**0**	**0**

Going: Sf: 0-1 GS: 0-1 Gd: 0-2 GF: - Fm: 0-1
Distance: 2m/2m3: 0-2 2m4-2m7: 0-2 3m+: 0-1
Track: LH: 0-0 RH: 0-2 Tight: 0-1 Gall: 0-0
Aids: Bl: 0-0 Vi: 0-0 Tstrap: 0-1
Best Rating: 113 2/01 Fair 2m heavy NHF

Merry Chieftain (IRE)

13-y-o b g Supreme Leader-Merry Memories (Anthony)
P Haskins N B Jones

Placings:*0/0/P3/035*P/BP04 (4727)
2001/02: 25^{P}G, 25^{P}G, 24^{0}GF, 24^{4}GF

	Starts	1st	2nd	3rd	Win & Pl
Chases	4	0	0	0	270
Career Total	**12**	**0**	**0**	**2**	**817**

Going: Sf: 0-0 GS: 0-0 Gd: 0-2 GF: - Fm: 0-2
Distance: 2m/2m3: 0-0 2m4-2m7: 0-0 3m+: 0-4
Track: LH: 0-2 RH: 0-1 Tight: 0-1 Gall: 0-0
Aids: Bl: 0-0 Vi: 0-0 Tstrap: 0-0
Best Rating: 90 5/95 Klny 2m1f gd-fm NHF

Merry Display (IRE)

7-y-o b m Air Display (USA)-Alienta (IRE) (Tumble Wind (USA))
Simon T Lewis Simon T Lewis

Placings:*0-0P*P (3332)
2001/02: 17^{0}G, 17^{P}GF, 21^{P}G

	Starts	1st	2nd	3rd	Win & Pl
NH Flat	2	0	0	0	0
Hurdles	1	0	0	0	0
Career Total	**4**	**0**	**0**	**0**	

Going: Sf: 0-0 GS: 0-0 Gd: 0-2 GF: - Fm: 0-1
Distance: 2m/2m3: 0-2 2m4-2m7: 0-1 3m+: 0-0
Track: LH: 0-0 RH: 0-2 Tight: 0-0 Gall: 0-0
Aids: Bl: 0-0 Vi: 0-0 Tstrap: 0-0
Best Rating: 46 10/00 Chel 2m110y good NHF

Merry Masquerade (IRE)

101(115h) (131h)**121**

11-y-o b g King's Ride-Merry Madness (Raise You Ten)
Mrs M Reveley G S Brown

Placings:*341*/02111/31010/1212/00135-6**425FP02** (4442)
2001/02: 25^{6}G, 24^{4}S, 25^{2}G, 20^{5}S, 30^{F}S, 25^{P}GS, 24^{0}GS, 25^{2}S

	Starts	1st	2nd	3rd	Win & Pl
Hurdles	2	0	0	0	0
Chases	6	0	2	0	3696
Career Total	**30**	**9**	**5**	**3**	**79161**

155	2/01	Kemp	3m110y	A HHdl	G-S	£13200
158	2/00	Hayd	2m7f110y	B HHdl	HVY	£7498
157	1/00	Uttx	3m110y	C(0-135)HHdl	SFT	£14495
132	4/99	Ayr	2m6f	B(0-145)HHdl	HVY	£5936
129	3/99	Newc	3m	C(0-130)HHdl	SFT	£6937
128	4/98	Uttx	3m110y	E(0-100)HHdl	SFT	£2431
120	3/98	Ayr	3m110y	D(0-115)HHdl	G-S	£3652
96	2/98	Ayr	2m6f	E Hdl	HVY	£2374
105	2/97	Ayr	2m	H NHF	SFT	£1380

Total win prize-money £57906

Going: Sf: 0-4 GS: 0-2 Gd: 0-2 GF: - Fm: 0-0
Distance: 2m/2m3: 0-0 2m4-2m7: 0-1 3m+: 0-7
Track: LH: 0-7 RH: 0-1 Tight: 0-1 Gall: 0-1
Aids: Bl: 0-1 Vi: 0-0 Tstrap: 0-0
Best Rating: 159 2/00 Kemp 3m110y soft Hdl

An out-and-out stayer, he relishes testing conditions. Successful over hurdles, he now runs over fences, but has proved nowhere near as good over the larger obstacles so far. Stays three miles plus.

Merry Minstrel (IRE)

103 **103**

9-y-o b g Black Minstrel-Merry Lesa (Dalesa)
C J Mann (Miss Louise Wood 14/7) Hugh Villiers

Placings:060/266F-U01311 (1483)
2001/02: 20^{U}G, 20^{0}GF, 18^{1}F, 20^{3}GY, 16^{1}GY, 17^{1}GS

	Starts	1st	2nd	3rd	Win & Pl
Chases	6	3	0	1	13648
Career Total	**13**	**3**	**1**	**1**	**14352**

103	9/01	Plum	2m1f	E(0-105)HCh	G-S	£3136
88	7/01	Wxfd	2m	(0-95)HCh	G-Y	£5564
90	6/01	Dpat	2m2f	(0-95)HCh	FRM	£4326

Total win prize-money £13028

Going: Sf: 0-0 GS: 1-1 Gd: 0-1 GF: - Fm: 1-2
Distance: **2m/2m3: 3-3** 2m4-2m7: 0-3 3m+: 0-0
Track: **LH: 1-1** RH: 0-0 **Tight: 1-1** Gall: 0-0
Aids: Bl: 0-0 Vi: 0-0 Tstrap: 0-0
Best Rating: 103 9/01 Plum 2m1f gd-sft Ch

A half-brother to Merry Gale, won two races in Ireland before coming to Britain. Got off the mark at the first attempt at Plumpton and looks progressive.

Merry Mole (IRE)

8-y-o b g Good Thyne (USA)-Merry Miss (Deep Run)
J A B Old R P Fry

Placings:*0*P-P (4513)
2001/02: 24^{P}GS

	Starts	1st	2nd	3rd	Win & Pl
Hurdles	1	0	0	0	
Career Total	**3**	**0**	**0**	**0**	

Going: Sf: 0-0 GS: 0-1 Gd: 0-0 GF: - Fm: 0-0
Distance: 2m/2m3: 0-0 2m4-2m7: 0-0 3m+: 0-1
Track: LH: 0-0 RH: 0-1 Tight: 0-0 Gall: 0-0
Aids: Bl: 0-0 Vi: 0-0 Tstrap: 0-0
Best Rating:

Merry Path (IRE)

106 **133**

8-y-o br g Alphabatim (USA)-Smokey Path (IRE) (Scallywag)
T P Tate (O Sherwood 11/6) B T Stewart-Brown

Placings:43413/**2321F122F/1-P02552PU** (4664)
2001/02: 28^{P}G, 24^{0}GF, 26^{2}G, 25^{5}G, 24^{5}G, 19^{2}G, 19^{P}S, 21^{U}G

	Starts	1st	2nd	3rd	Win & Pl
Chases	8	0	2	0	3463
Career Total	**23**	**4**	**6**	**3**	**31791**

137	10/00	Extr	3m1f110y	D(0-120)HCh	GD	£4095
126	2/00	Ludl	3m	E Ch	G-F	£3640
130	12/99	Donc	3m	D Ch	G-F	£4992
119	3/99	Newb	2m5f	D Hdl	G-F	£3322

Total win prize-money £16051

Going: Sf: 0-1 GS: 0-0 Gd: 0-6 GF: - Fm: 0-1
Distance: 2m/2m3: 0-0 2m4-2m7: 0-3 3m+: 0-5
Track: LH: 0-8 RH: 0-0 Tight: 0-5 Gall: 0-3
Aids: Bl: 0-0 Vi: 0-1 Tstrap: 0-0
Best Rating: 137 10/00 Extr 3m1f110y good Ch

A fair handicap chaser when the ground rides good or faster, he has been lightly raced of late.

Merry People (IRE)

14-y-o b g Lafontaine (USA)-Merry Madness (Raise You Ten)
Mrs P N Dutfield K Casey, K McHugh, Mrs M Dowling

Placings:4055151241200/311**1203P625F/1420102P**0/01**422161P0/51451150330/P266202**4**P60/P6**66**U/P1 U-PP** (0829)
2001/02: 21^{P}GF, 24^{P}GF

	Starts	1st	2nd	3rd	Win & Pl
Chases	2	0	0	0	
Career Total	**76**	**15**	**11**	**4**	**82927**

132	8/00	Tral	2m4f	HCh	Y-S	£12480
132	8/97	Tral	2m4f	HCh	HVY	£12772
137	8/97	Tram	2m6f	Ch	GD	£2712
125	6/97	Tral	2m4f	(0-116)HCh	FRM	£3391
122	9/96	Kbgn	3m1f	(0-109)HCh	GD	£3530
118	8/96	Kbgn	3m1f	(0-109)HCh	GD	£2824
111	5/96	Klny	2m4f	Ch	GD	£4201
107	7/95	Klny	2m1f	HCh	YLD	£3391
106	5/95	Klny	2m	(0-102)HCh	G-F	£3391
103	7/94	Kbgn	2m5f	Ch	GD	£2448
120	7/94	Bell	3m	(0-116)HHdl	GD	£2611
119	6/94	Naas	2m	(0-116)HHdl	FRM	£2937
114	10/93	Tral	2m2f	HHdl	GD	£3709
105	9/93	Kbgn	2m3f	HHdl	G-F	£2411
98	8/93	Tram	2m4f	Hdl	GD	£2413

Total win prize-money £65228

Going: Sf: 0-0 GS: 0-0 Gd: 0-0 GF: - Fm: 0-2
Distance: 2m/2m3: 0-0 2m4-2m7: 0-1 3m+: 0-1
Track: LH: 0-2 RH: 0-0 Tight: 0-2 Gall: 0-0
Aids: Bl: 0-1 Vi: 0-0 Tstrap: 0-0
Best Rating: 145 4/99 Aint 4m4f good Ch

Ran a remarkable race as a 200-1 no-hoper in the 1999 Grand National, holding every chance when unseating at the penultimate fence. Well past his best now.

Mersey Beat

108(112h) (115h)**123**

8-y-o ch g Rock Hopper-Handy Dancer (Green God)
G L Moore Straight Forward Racing

Placings:U26/124112/0025/010**242-6P**0**P5U** (4551)
2001/02: 16^{6}G, 17^{P}S, 16^{0}G, 20^{P}G, 16^{5}G, 16^{U}GF

	Starts	1st	2nd	3rd	Win & Pl
Hurdles	1	0	0	0	0
Chases	5	0	0	0	0
Career Total	**25**	**4**	**6**	**0**	**20955**

127	5/00	Towc	2m	D(0-120)HHdl	G-F	£2996
138	11/98	Tntn	2m1f	C HHdl	GD	£3940
126	11/98	Wind	2m	E Hdl	G-S	£2530
104	8/98	Strf	2m110y	E Hdl	G-F	£2010

Total win prize-money £11477

Going: Sf: 0-1 GS: 0-0 Gd: 0-4 GF: - Fm: 0-1
Distance: 2m/2m3: 0-5 2m4-2m7: 0-1 3m+: 0-0
Track: LH: 0-1 RH: 0-4 Tight: 0-2 Gall: 0-1
Aids: Bl: 0-2 Vi: 0-0 Tstrap: 0-0
Best Rating: 138 11/98 Tntn 2m1f good Hdl

A fair two-mile handicap hurdler. Suited by fast ground.

Mershiginer (IRE)

100 **88**

9-y-o b g King's Ride-Shelleys Rocky Gem (Kemal (FR))
G B Balding The Whisperers

Placings:*6*/522F302/**4BR**/B00F4-3U0 (0672)
2001/02: 17^{3}G, 16^{U}GF, 20^{0}GF

	Starts	1st	2nd	3rd	Win & Pl
Hurdles	3	0	0	1	300
Career Total	**19**	**0**	**3**	**2**	**2980**

Going: Sf: 0-0 GS: 0-0 Gd: 0-1 GF: - Fm: 0-2
Distance: 2m/2m3: 0-2 2m4-2m7: 0-1 3m+: 0-0
Track: LH: 0-1 RH: 0-2 Tight: 0-0 Gall: 0-1
Aids: Bl: 0-0 Vi: 0-0 Tstrap: 0-0
Best Rating: 109 10/99 Extr 2m1f good Ch

Merv's Magic

7-y-o gr g Daily Sport Soon-Judy's Dowry (Dragonara

Palace (USA))
R J Baker Mrs Sue Rowe

Placings:*6U* **(4479)**
2001/02: 17^{6}GF, 19^{U}G

	Starts	1st	2nd	3rd	Win & Pl
NH Flat	1	0	0	0	0
Hurdles	1	0	0	0	0
Career Total	**2**	**0**	**0**	**0**	**0**

Going: Sf: 0-0 GS: 0-0 Gd: 0-1 GF: - Fm: 0-1
Distance: 2m/2m3: 0-2 2m4-2m7: 0-0 3m+: 0-0
Track: LH: 0-1 RH: 0-1 Tight: 0-1 Gall: 0-0
Aids: Bl: 0-0 Vi: 0-0 Tstrap: 0-0
Best Rating: 67 8/01 NAbb 2m1f gd-fm NHF

Mervs Bin Boy

7-y-o b g Desert Dirham (USA)-Tees Wheelie Bin (Balliol)
A G Juckes M P Tokley

Placings:*OP* **(4174)**
2001/02: 16°HY, 22^{P}GS

	Starts	1st	2nd	3rd	Win & Pl
NH Flat	1	0	0	0	0
Hurdles	1	0	0	0	0
Career Total	**2**	**0**	**0**	**0**	

Going: Sf: 0-1 GS: 0-1 Gd: 0-0 GF: - Fm: 0-0
Distance: 2m/2m3: 0-1 2m4-2m7: 0-1 3m+: 0-0
Track: LH: 0-1 RH: 0-1 Tight: 0-1 Gall: 0-0
Aids: Bl: 0-0 Vi: 0-0 Tstrap: 0-0
Best Rating:

Mervsintrouble

5-y-o b g Primitive Rising (USA)-Bodfari (Lighter)
Mrs L Williamson P H Morris

Placings:*0* **(1858)**
2001/02: 17^{0}S

	Starts	1st	2nd	3rd	Win & Pl
NH Flat	1	0	0	0	
Career Total	**1**	**0**	**0**	**0**	

Going: Sf: 0-1 GS: 0-0 Gd: 0-0 GF: - Fm: 0-0
Distance: 2m/2m3: 0-1 2m4-2m7: 0-0 3m+: 0-0
Track: LH: 0-1 RH: 0-0 Tight: 0-1 Gall: 0-0
Aids: Bl: 0-0 Vi: 0-0 Tstrap: 0-0
Best Rating: mfy

Mestre Sala (FR)

106(95h) (100h)131
7-y-o b g Al Nasr (FR)-Light Lida (USA) (Alleged (USA))
H D Daly Mrs Strachan, Mrs Gabb & Mrs Graham

Placings:*10/1152/041* **(1909)**
2001/02: 16^{0}G, 16^{4}GF, 20^{1}S

	Starts	1st	2nd	3rd	Win & Pl
Hurdles	1	0	0	0	
Chases	2	1	0	0	4216
Career Total	**9**	**4**	**1**	**0**	**12083**

131	11/01	Strf	2m4f	D Ch	SFT	£3965
117	12/99	Extr	2m1f110y	E Hdl	G-S	£3248
115	11/99	Uttx	2m	E Hdl	SFT	£2337
105	2/99	Winc	2m	H NHF	G-S	£1474

Total win prize-money £11024

Going: Sf: 1-1 GS: 0-0 Gd: 0-1 GF: - Fm: 0-1
Distance: 2m/2m3: 0-2 **2m4-2m7: 1-1** 3m+: 0-0
Track: **LH: 1-3** RH: 0-0 **Tight: 1-1** Gall: 0-0
Aids: Bl: 0-0 Vi: 0-0 Tstrap: 0-0
Best Rating: 131 11/01 Strf 2m4f soft Ch

Winner of a Wincanton bumper last term, he was down the field in the Festival bumper. He won his first two starts over hurdles, scoring very easily at Uttoxeter but having to work much harder at Exeter, before a fair run under topweight in a novice handicap. He put into practice what he learnt on his chasing debut when winning a novice chase at Stratford in November. Sadly, he finished badly lame, but trainer Henry Daly hopes the horse is young enough to come back from this injury. He is best when held up on easy ground.

Metal Detector (IRE)

97 106
5-y-o b g Treasure Hunter-Las-Cancellas (Monksfield)
K C Bailey (Cathal McCarthy 19/6) Mrs Ann Allen

Placings:0230 **(2418)**
2001/02: 16^{0}G, 20^{2}F, 16^{3}GF, 16^{0}HY

	Starts	1st	2nd	3rd	Win & Pl
NH Flat	1	0	1	0	774
Hurdles	3	0	0	1	544
Career Total	**4**	**0**	**1**	**1**	**1319**

Going: Sf: 0-1 GS: 0-0 Gd: 0-1 GF: - Fm: 0-2
Distance: 2m/2m3: 0-3 2m4-2m7: 0-1 3m+: 0-0
Track: LH: 0-1 RH: 0-0 Tight: 0-0 Gall: 0-0
Aids: Bl: 0-0 Vi: 0-0 Tstrap: 0-0
Best Rating: 97 6/01 Navn 2m gd-fm Hdl

Meteorite (IRE)

100 91
6-y-o b g Bigstone (IRE)-Winning Appeal (FR) (Law Society (USA))
J M P Eustace Mrs T S Matthews

Placings:3/62 **(1392)**
2001/02: 16^{6}GF, 20^{2}GF

	Starts	1st	2nd	3rd	Win & Pl
Hurdles	2	0	1	0	736
Career Total	**3**	**0**	**1**	**1**	**1076**

Going: Sf: 0-0 GS: 0-0 Gd: 0-0 GF: - Fm: 0-2
Distance: 2m/2m3: 0-1 2m4-2m7: 0-1 3m+: 0-0
Track: LH: 0-1 RH: 0-1 Tight: 0-0 Gall: 0-1
Aids: Bl: 0-0 Vi: 0-0 Tstrap: 0-0
Best Rating: 101 2/00 Donc 2m4f good Hdl

Metro Fashion (IRE)

11-y-o ch g Carlingford Castle-Good Resemblance (Kemal (FR))
O O'Neill James A Atkin

Placings:*0/0/00-PPP* **(1543)**
2001/02: 20^{P}G, 24^{P}GF, 19^{P}G

	Starts	1st	2nd	3rd	Win & Pl
Hurdles	2	0	0	0	0
Chases	1	0	0	0	0
Career Total	**7**	**0**	**0**	**0**	

Going: Sf: 0-0 GS: 0-0 Gd: 0-2 GF: - Fm: 0-1
Distance: 2m/2m3: 0-1 2m4-2m7: 0-1 3m+: 0-1
Track: LH: 0-2 RH: 0-1 Tight: 0-1 Gall: 0-0
Aids: Bl: 0-0 Vi: 0-0 Tstrap: 0-0
Best Rating: 64 8/97 Worc 2m good Hdl

Mezzo Princess

10-y-o b m Remezzo-Kam Tsin Princess (Prince Regent (FR))
Miss Katie Thory (K Goldsworthy 15/3) Mike Lurcock

Placings:P0/PP4PF **(4777)**
2001/02: 20^{P}GF, 24^{P}GF, 26^{4}G, 21^{P}G, 25^{F}G

	Starts	1st	2nd	3rd	Win & Pl
Chases	5	0	0	0	0
Career Total	**7**	**0**	**0**	**0**	**0**

Going: Sf: 0-0 GS: 0-0 Gd: 0-3 GF: - Fm: 0-2
Distance: 2m/2m3: 0-0 2m4-2m7: 0-2 3m+: 0-3
Track: LH: 0-4 RH: 0-1 Tight: 0-4 Gall: 0-0
Aids: Bl: 0-0 Vi: 0-0 Tstrap: 0-0
Best Rating: 80 4/02 MRas 3m1f good Ch

Poor pointer and bad hunter chaser.

Mi Odds

96 89+
6-y-o b g Sure Blade (USA)-Vado Via (Ardross)
Ian Williams (Mrs N Macauley 7/7) G Wiltshire

Placings:10 **(4601)**
2001/02: 17^{1}G, 16^{0}GF

	Starts	1st	2nd	3rd	Win & Pl
Hurdles	2	1	0	0	2086
Career Total	**2**	**1**	**0**	**0**	**2086**

89	3/02	Hrfd	2m1f	G Hdl	GD	£2086

Total win prize-money £2086

Going: Sf: 0-0 GS: 0-0 Gd: 1-1 GF: - Fm: 0-1
Distance: **2m/2m3: 1-2** 2m4-2m7: 0-0 3m+: 0-0
Track: LH: 0-1 **RH: 1-1** Tight: 0-0 Gall: 0-0
Aids: Bl: 0-0 Vi: 0-0 Tstrap: 0-0
Best Rating: 89 3/02 Hrfd 2m1f good Hdl

A useful performer on the All-Weather, he won a seller on his hurdling debut.

Mia Fort

9-y-o ch m Bold Fort-Mia Xandra (Nearly A Hand)
P D Evans E A McGuinness

Placings:P **(0720)**
2001/02: 26^{P}F

	Starts	1st	2nd	3rd	Win & Pl
Hurdles	1	0	0	0	
Career Total	**1**	**0**	**0**	**0**	

Going: Sf: 0-0 GS: 0-0 Gd: 0-0 GF: - Fm: 0-1
Distance: 2m/2m3: 0-0 2m4-2m7: 0-0 3m+: 0-1
Track: LH: 0-0 RH: 0-1 Tight: 0-0 Gall: 0-0
Aids: Bl: 0-0 Vi: 0-0 Tstrap: 0-1
Best Rating:

Miaheyyun

94 66
6-y-o b g Bonny Scot (IRE)-Daunt Not (Kalaglow)
B J Llewellyn B Finneral

Placings:*3/6-00050* **(1142)**
2001/02: 16^{0}GF, 22^{0}G, 17^{0}GF, 19^{5}G, 16^{0}G

	Starts	1st	2nd	3rd	Win & Pl
Hurdles	5	0	0	0	0
Career Total	**7**	**0**	**0**	**1**	**219**

Going: Sf: 0-0 GS: 0-0 Gd: 0-3 GF: - Fm: 0-2
Distance: 2m/2m3: 0-4 2m4-2m7: 0-1 3m+: 0-0
Track: LH: 0-5 RH: 0-0 Tight: 0-4 Gall: 0-0
Aids: Bl: 0-2 Vi: 0-0 Tstrap: 0-1
Best Rating: 85 5/00 Chep 2m110y firm NHF

Mice Design (IRE)

98 **100**

5-y-o b g Presidium-Diplomatist (Dominion)
K C Bailey (N P Littmoden 12/10) Mice Group Plc

Placings:51320 **(3464)**
2001/02: 16^5GS, 20^1G, 17^3S, 17^2S, 16^0S

	Starts	1st	2nd	3rd	Win & Pl
Hurdles	5	1	1	1	3675
Career Total	**5**	**1**	**1**	**1**	**3675**
86 10/01 Hntg	2m4f110y E Hdl			GD	£2590

Total win prize-money £2590

Going: Sf: 0-3 GS: 0-1 Gd: 1-1 GF: - Fm: 0-0
Distance: 2m/2m3: 0-4 **2m4-2m7: 1-1** 3m+: 0-0
Track: LH: 0-2 **RH: 1-3** Tight: 0-1 **Gall: 1-2**
Aids: Bl: 0-0 Vi: 0-0 Tstrap: 0-0
Best Rating: 100 1/02 Hrfd 2m1f soft Hdl

Moderate hurdler, he acts on good ground and is effective over two miles four.

Mice Ideas (IRE)

6-y-o ch g Fayruz-Tender Encounter (Prince Tenderfoot (USA))
O O'Neill (N P Littmoden 1/10) J A Danahar

Placings:5/PP **(2899)**
2001/02: 20^PS, 16^PG

	Starts	1st	2nd	3rd	Win & Pl
Hurdles	2	0	0	0	
Career Total	**3**	**0**	**0**	**0**	**0**

Going: Sf: 0-1 GS: 0-0 Gd: 0-1 GF: - Fm: 0-0
Distance: 2m/2m3: 0-1 2m4-2m7: 0-1 3m+: 0-0
Track: LH: 0-1 RH: 0-1 Tight: 0-0 Gall: 0-0
Aids: Bl: 0-0 Vi: 0-0 Tstrap: 0-0
Best Rating: 72 11/99 Aint 2m110y good Hdl

Mice World (IRE)

102 **83**

5-y-o b g River Falls-Naglaa (USA) (State Dinner (USA))
K C Bailey (N P Littmoden 2/6) Mice Group Plc

Placings:0050 **(4540)**
2001/02: 16^0GF, 22^0GF, 16^5S, 19^0G

	Starts	1st	2nd	3rd	Win & Pl
Hurdles	4	0	0	0	0
Career Total	**4**	**0**	**0**	**0**	**0**

Going: Sf: 0-1 GS: 0-0 Gd: 0-1 GF: - Fm: 0-2
Distance: 2m/2m3: 0-2 2m4-2m7: 0-2 3m+: 0-0
Track: LH: 0-2 RH: 0-2 Tight: 0-1 Gall: 0-2
Aids: Bl: 0-0 Vi: 0-0 Tstrap: 0-0
Best Rating: 83 1/02 Donc 2m110y soft Hdl

Poor maiden on the flat, he shaped with a little promise over hurdles at Doncaster in January 2002.

Michael Finnegan (IRE)

109 **104**

9-y-o b/br g Phardante (FR)-Decent Slave (Decent Fellow)
Miss L C Siddall Mrs D J Morris

Placings:040/0360F2140/4313P6663-P056124 **(2902)**
2001/02: 16^PF, 16^0S, 16^5S, 16^6S, 16^1HY, 16^2S, 16^4S

	Starts	1st	2nd	3rd	Win & Pl
Hurdles	7	1	1	0	3033
Career Total	**28**	**3**	**2**	**4**	**11220**
101 12/01 Leic	2m	F(0-110)HHdl		HVY	£2261
107 12/00 Hayd	2m	F(0-110)HHdl		HVY	£2576
85 2/00 Muss	2m	E(0-105)HHdl		GD	£2769

Total win prize-money £7606

Going: Sf: 1-6 GS: 0-0 Gd: 0-0 GF: - Fm: 0-1
Distance: **2m/2m3: 1-7** 2m4-2m7: 0-0 3m+: 0-0
Track: LH: 0-5 **RH: 1-2** Tight: 0-1 Gall: 0-0
Aids: Bl: 0-0 Vi: 0-0 Tstrap: 0-0
Best Rating: 107 12/00 Newc 2m soft Hdl

Goes well over two miles and is effective on good and heavy ground.

Michael's Princess

96 **88**

7-y-o b m King's Ride-Kathy Cook (Glenstal (USA))
M J Gingell (N A Twiston-Davies 22/1) Gentlemen Don't Work On Mondays

Placings:645530-U62605F0 **(4535)**
2001/02: 27^UG, 23^6G, 24^2HY, 22^6S, 26^0S, 21^5S, 24^FHY, 20^0G

	Starts	1st	2nd	3rd	Win & Pl
Hurdles	8	0	1	0	1615
Career Total	**14**	**0**	**1**	**1**	**2155**

Going: Sf: 0-5 GS: 0-0 Gd: 0-3 GF: - Fm: 0-0
Distance: 2m/2m3: 0-0 2m4-2m7: 0-3 3m+: 0-5
Track: LH: 0-5 RH: 0-3 Tight: 0-4 Gall: 0-1
Aids: Bl: 0-0 Vi: 0-0 Tstrap: 0-0
Best Rating: 88 12/01 Towc 3m heavy Hdl

Moderate maiden hurdler.

Michaelmas Daizy

90 **78**

7-y-o b m Michelozzo (USA)-Hals Lass (Halsall)
A G Hobbs Netherley Racing

Placings:53004/300-5 **(1240)**
2001/02: 24^5GF

	Starts	1st	2nd	3rd	Win & Pl
Hurdles	1	0	0	0	0
Career Total	**9**	**0**	**0**	**2**	**891**

Going: Sf: 0-0 GS: 0-0 Gd: 0-0 GF: - Fm: 0-1
Distance: 2m/2m3: 0-0 2m4-2m7: 0-0 3m+: 0-1
Track: LH: 0-1 RH: 0-0 Tight: 0-0 Gall: 0-0
Aids: Bl: 0-0 Vi: 0-0 Tstrap: 0-0
Best Rating: 85 11/99 Wwck 2m good NHF

Michel De Moeurs (FR)

104(106h) (113h)**129**

7-y-o ch g Northern Fashion (USA)-See That Girl (FR) (Dancer's Image (USA))
P F Nicholls Derek Millard

Placings:0225/3145361232-42 **(0349)**
2001/02: 17^4GS, 17^2GS

	Starts	1st	2nd	3rd	Win & Pl
Chases	2	0	1	0	1619
Career Total	**16**	**2**	**5**	**3**	**16453**
103 1/01 Tntn	2m1f	E Hdl		HVY	£2046
113 10/00 Strf	2m110y	E Hdl		SFT	£2985

Total win prize-money £5032

Going: Sf: 0-0 GS: 0-2 Gd: 0-0 GF: - Fm: 0-0
Distance: 2m/2m3: 0-2 2m4-2m7: 0-0 3m+: 0-0
Track: LH: 0-1 RH: 0-1 Tight: 0-1 Gall: 0-0
Aids: Bl: 0-0 Vi: 0-0 Tstrap: 0-0
Best Rating: 129 5/01 Strf 2m1f110y gd-sft Ch

He has had quite a busy season and has won two small races at Stratford and Taunton, but he has also looked a bit quirky on occasions and needs plenty of rousting along.

Michigan Blue

108 **130**

10-y-o b g Rakaposhi King-Starquin (IRE) (Strong Gale)
M J M Evans Mrs J Z Munday

Placings:0/040622/PU/5304562/056-F11112P **(3589)**
2001/02: 17^FG, 19^1G, 16^1GS, 16^1G, 16^1S, 16^2G, 16^PHY

	Starts	1st	2nd	3rd	Win & Pl
Hurdles	1	0	0	0	0
Chases	6	4	1	0	15928
Career Total	**26**	**4**	**4**	**1**	**18807**
130 12/01 Hrfd	2m	E(0-105)HCh		SFT	£3251
124 11/01 Hrfd	2m	E(0-105)HCh		GD	£3178
109 10/01 Hrfd	2m	F(0-110)HCh		G-S	£3307
109 10/01 Hrfd	2m3f	G(0-95)HCh		GD	£3062

Total win prize-money £12801

Going: Sf: 1-2 GS: 1-1 Gd: 2-4 GF: - Fm: 0-0
Distance: **2m/2m3: 4-7** 2m4-2m7: 0-0 3m+: 0-0
Track: LH: 0-1 **RH: 4-6** Tight: 0-0 Gall: 0-0
Aids: Bl: 0-0 Vi: 0-0 Tstrap: 0-0
Best Rating: 130 12/01 Asct 2m good Ch

Improving chaser who likes to get his toe in but handles good ground. He stays 2m3f, jumps well, and excels at Hereford.

Mick Mackie (IRE)

9-y-o b g Glacial Storm (USA)-Telamonia (Ballymoss)
Miss A Nolan Mrs R Mackness & Mrs Vanessa Ramm

Placings:36U3/P03 **(3861)**
2001/02: 25^PS, 21^0G, 19^3S

	Starts	1st	2nd	3rd	Win & Pl
Chases	3	0	0	1	228
Career Total	**7**	**0**	**0**	**3**	**983**

Going: Sf: 0-2 GS: 0-0 Gd: 0-1 GF: - Fm: 0-0
Distance: 2m/2m3: 0-0 2m4-2m7: 0-2 3m+: 0-1
Track: LH: 0-2 RH: 0-0 Tight: 0-0 Gall: 0-1
Aids: Bl: 0-0 Vi: 0-0 Tstrap: 0-0
Best Rating: 94 2/02 Donc 2m3f110y soft Ch

Mick Murphy (IRE)

38

5-y-o b g Jurado (USA)-Lee Ford Lady (Kemal (FR))
Mrs E Slack A Slack

Placings:*00* **(4750)**
2001/02: 17^{0}G, 17^{0}G

	Starts	1st	2nd	3rd	Win & Pl
NH Flat	2	0	0	0	
Career Total	**2**	**0**	**0**	**0**	

Going: Sf: 0-0 GS: 0-0 Gd: 0-2 GF: - Fm: 0-0
Distance: 2m/2m3: 0-2 2m4-2m7: 0-0 3m+: 0-0
Track: LH: 0-0 RH: 0-2 Tight: 0-0 Gall: 0-0
Aids: Bl: 0-0 Vi: 0-0 Tstrap: 0-0
Best Rating: 57 4/02 Carl 2m1f good NHF

Micklow Minster

103(80c) **105**
8-y-o ch g Minster Son-Scotto's Regret (Celtic Cone)
C Grant W Raw

Placings:*00*/0624163150/53P0-5 **(0958)**
2001/02: 27^{5}GF

	Starts	1st	2nd	3rd	Win & Pl
Hurdles	1	0	0	0	0
Career Total	**17**	**2**	**1**	**2**	**7871**
112 1/00	Catt	3m1f110y	E Hdl	GD	£2786
108 11/99	Newc	2m4f	D Hdl	G-S	£2944

Total win prize-money £5730

Going: Sf: 0-0 GS: 0-0 Gd: 0-0 GF: - Fm: 0-1
Distance: 2m/2m3: 0-0 2m4-2m7: 0-0 3m+: 0-1
Track: LH: 0-1 RH: 0-0 Tight: 0-1 Gall: 0-0
Aids: Bl: 0-0 Vi: 0-0 Tstrap: 0-0
Best Rating: 112 1/00 Catt 3m1f110y good Hdl

Mickthecutaway (IRE)

115 **136**
10-y-o b g Rontino-Le-Mu-Co (Varano)
Mrs H Dalton J N Dalton

Placings:U/3260/3/1/**UU1120-212611** **(4407)**
2001/02: 24^{2}S, 25^{1}HY, 24^{2}S, 23^{6}S, 24^{1}S, 20^{1}S

	Starts	1st	2nd	3rd	Win & Pl
Chases	6	3	2	0	17910
Career Total	**19**	**6**	**4**	**2**	**30741**

136 3/02	Bang	2m4f110y	C(0-135)HCh	SFT	£6955
136 3/02	Bang	3m110y	D(0-120)HCh	SFT	£5169
128 12/01	Towc	3m1f	E(0-115)HCh	HVY	£3445
122 2/01	Sand	3m110y	D(0-115)HCh	SFT	£5164
117 1/01	Leic	2m7f110y	F(0-95)HCh	SFT	£3251
111 3/00	Leic	2m7f110y	H Ch	G-S	£2249

Total win prize-money £26235

Going: Sf: 3-6 GS: 0-0 Gd: 0-0 GF: - Fm: 0-0
Distance: 2m/2m3: 0-0 2m4-2m7: 1-1 **3m+: 2-5**
Track: **LH: 2-4** RH: 1-2 **Tight: 2-2** Gall: 0-1
Aids: Bl: 0-0 Vi: 0-0 Tstrap: 0-0
Best Rating: 136 3/02 Bang 2m4f110y soft Ch

Front-running chaser who stays particularly well but is effective over two and a half miles as he showed at Bangor in March 2002. In great heart this term, jumps for fun and loves testing ground.

Mickthetrick

74f **46f**
6-y-o b g Henbit (USA)-Catherine Tudor (Tudor Wood)
I Emmerson Ian Emmerson

Placings:*00* **(2772)**
2001/02: 16^{0}G, 16^{0}GF

	Starts	1st	2nd	3rd	Win & Pl
NH Flat	2	0	0	0	
Career Total	**2**	**0**	**0**	**0**	

Going: Sf: 0-0 GS: 0-0 Gd: 0-2 GF: - Fm: 0-0
Distance: 2m/2m3: 0-2 2m4-2m7: 0-0 3m+: 0-0
Track: LH: 0-2 RH: 0-0 Tight: 0-1 Gall: 0-1
Aids: Bl: 0-0 Vi: 0-0 Tstrap: 0-0
Best Rating: 46 12/01 Catt 2m good NHF

Middlehamparkflyer

4-y-o b f Missed Flight-Ma Rivale (Last Tycoon)
P C Haslam D Frame & Middleham Park Racing

Placings:PU **(2301)**
2001/02: 16^{P}G, 16^{U}GF

	Starts	1st	2nd	3rd	Win & Pl
Hurdles	2	0	0	0	
Career Total	**2**	**0**	**0**	**0**	

Going: Sf: 0-0 GS: 0-0 Gd: 0-1 GF: - Fm: 0-1
Distance: 2m/2m3: 0-2 2m4-2m7: 0-0 3m+: 0-0
Track: LH: 0-2 RH: 0-0 Tight: 0-1 Gall: 0-0
Aids: Bl: 0-0 Vi: 0-0 Tstrap: 0-0
Best Rating:

Middleway

38
6-y-o b g Milieu-Galway Gal (Proverb)
Miss Kate Milligan Mrs J M L Milligan

Placings:*0*0P0 **(4768)**
2001/02: 17^{0}G, 19^{0}G, 16^{P}HY, 16^{0}GF

	Starts	1st	2nd	3rd	Win & Pl
NH Flat	1	0	0	0	0
Hurdles	3	0	0	0	0
Career Total	**4**	**0**	**0**	**0**	

Going: Sf: 0-1 GS: 0-0 Gd: 0-2 GF: - Fm: 0-1
Distance: 2m/2m3: 0-4 2m4-2m7: 0-0 3m+: 0-0
Track: LH: 0-3 RH: 0-0 Tight: 0-2 Gall: 0-1
Aids: Bl: 0-0 Vi: 0-0 Tstrap: 0-0
Best Rating: 62 10/01 Sedg 2m1f good NHF

Midland Flame (IRE)

102(105h) (118h)**117**
7-y-o b g Un Desperado (FR)-Lathanona (Reformed Character)
Miss H C Knight Trevor Hemmings

Placings:*23*-1123P43 **(4816)**
2001/02: 17^{1}G, 16^{1}G, 16^{2}G, 16^{3}GS, 21^{P}S, 20^{4}G, 21^{3}GF

	Starts	1st	2nd	3rd	Win & Pl
Hurdles	7	2	1	2	19011
Career Total	**9**	**2**	**2**	**3**	**19880**
109 10/01	Winc	2m	D Hdl	GD	£3250
116 10/01	Bang	2m1f	E Hdl	GD	£3136

Total win prize-money £6386

Going: Sf: 0-1 GS: 0-1 Gd: 2-4 GF: - Fm: 0-1
Distance: **2m/2m3: 2-4** 2m4-2m7: 0-3 3m+: 0-0
Track: LH: 1-5 RH: 1-1 **Tight: 1-2** Gall: 0-2
Aids: Bl: 0-0 Vi: 0-0 Tstrap: 0-0
Best Rating: 118 4/02 Chel 2m5f110y gd-fm Hdl

Useful novice hurdler, winner of two small races last autumn. Reasonable efforts in better company subsequently. Made a promising start to his chasing career when a narrowly beaten favourite at Exeter May 2002. Best suited by good ground, a strong pace and trips in excess of two miles.

Midlem Melody

82 **63**
6-y-o b m Syrtos-Singing Hills (Crash Course)
W S Coltherd S Coltherd

Placings:*060*U64 **(4065)**
2001/02: 17^{0}GS, 17^{6}G, 16^{0}GS, 16^{U}GS, 17^{6}S, 21^{4}S

	Starts	1st	2nd	3rd	Win & Pl
NH Flat	3	0	0	0	0
Hurdles	3	0	0	0	0
Career Total	**6**	**0**	**0**	**0**	**0**

Going: Sf: 0-2 GS: 0-3 Gd: 0-1 GF: - Fm: 0-0
Distance: 2m/2m3: 0-5 2m4-2m7: 0-1 3m+: 0-0
Track: LH: 0-5 RH: 0-1 Tight: 0-4 Gall: 0-0
Aids: Bl: 0-0 Vi: 0-0 Tstrap: 0-0
Best Rating: 80 11/01 Ayr 2m gd-sft NHF

Moderate novice hurdler. Acts with cut.

Midnight Coup

90(93h) (79h)**84**
6-y-o br g First Trump-Anhaar (Ela-Mana-Mou)
B G Powell (G T Hourigan 8/6) Mark Barrett Racing

Placings:400/0P0-006 **(1224)**
2001/02: 21^{0}GF, 22^{0}G, 20^{6}GF

	Starts	1st	2nd	3rd	Win & Pl
Hurdles	3	0	0	0	0
Career Total	**9**	**0**	**0**	**0**	**129**

Going: Sf: 0-0 GS: 0-0 Gd: 0-1 GF: - Fm: 0-2
Distance: 2m/2m3: 0-0 2m4-2m7: 0-2 3m+: 0-1
Track: LH: 0-0 RH: 0-0 Tight: 0-1 Gall: 0-0
Aids: Bl: 0-1 Vi: 0-0 Tstrap: 0-0
Best Rating: 84 1/01 Cork 2m4f soft Hdl

Midnight Emperor (IRE)

92(106h) (109h)**99**
7-y-o b g Supreme Leader-Calfstown Night (Bargello)
R J Hodges Unity Farm Holiday Centre Ltd

Placings:*4/2/023*-530**55FPF** **(2929)**
2001/02: 16^{5}G, 17^{3}GS, 20^{0}G, 19^{5}G, 16^{5}S, 20^{F}G, 20^{P}G, 24^{F}GS

	Starts	1st	2nd	3rd	Win & Pl
Hurdles	3	0	0	1	433
Chases	5	0	0	0	0
Career Total	**13**	**0**	**2**	**2**	**2129**

Going: Sf: 0-1 GS: 0-2 Gd: 0-5 GF: - Fm: 0-0
Distance: 2m/2m3: 0-4 2m4-2m7: 0-3 3m+: 0-1
Track: LH: 0-4 RH: 0-4 Tight: 0-5 Gall: 0-0
Aids: Bl: 0-0 Vi: 0-0 Tstrap: 0-0
Best Rating: 109 4/01 Winc 2m soft Hdl

Midnight Gunner

102(110h) (94h)**105**
8-y-o b g Gunner B-Light Tonight (Lighter)
C J Price M G Racing

Placings:000P06/226C363-41P2612P (4568)
2001/02: 19^{4}G, 19^{1}G, 21^{P}GF, 19^{2}G, 19^{6}HY, 24^{1}G, 24^{2}HY, 24^{P}G

	Starts	1st	2nd	3rd	Win & Pl
Hurdles	4	1	2	0	6233
Chases	4	1	0	0	3365
Career Total	**21**	**2**	**4**	**2**	**12059**

93	2/02	Ludl	3m	E(0-105)HHdl	GD	£4576
102	5/01	Hrfd	2m3f	F Ch	GD	£2990

Total win prize-money £7566

Going: Sf: 0-2 GS: 0-0 Gd: 2-5 GF: - Fm: 0-1
Distance: 2m/2m3: 1-3 2m4-2m7: 0-2 3m+: 1-3
Track: LH: 0-2 **RH: 2-6** Tight: 0-2 Gall: 0-0
Aids: Bl: 0-0 Vi: 0-0 Tstrap: 0-0
Best Rating: 105 5/01 Hrfd 2m3f good Ch

Effective over hurdles and fences, he stays three miles and likes good ground.

Midnight Jazz (IRE)

101 85

12-y-o b g Shardari-Round Midnight (Star Appeal)
J Harriman John Harriman

Placings:030/000051306**P2**/P5/0U22/0P-0P626 (4527)
2001/02: 17^{0}G, 16^{P}S, 16^{6}G, 16^{2}GS, 16^{6}GS

	Starts	1st	2nd	3rd	Win & Pl
Hurdles	5	0	1	0	757
Career Total	**27**	**1**	**4**	**2**	**5720**

109	1/97	Tram	2m	Hdl	Y-S	£2204

Total win prize-money £2204

Going: Sf: 0-1 GS: 0-2 Gd: 0-2 GF: - Fm: 0-0
Distance: 2m/2m3: 0-5 2m4-2m7: 0-0 3m+: 0-0
Track: LH: 0-2 RH: 0-3 Tight: 0-1 Gall: 0-0
Aids: Bl: 0-0 Vi: 0-0 Tstrap: 0-0
Best Rating: 109 1/97 Tram 2m yld-sft Hdl

Midnight Marshman

6-y-o b g Witham Lad-Midnight Mischief (Bairn (USA))
Mrs E Slack A Slack

Placings:P (0470)
2001/02: 20^{P}GF

	Starts	1st	2nd	3rd	Win & Pl
Hurdles	1	0	0	0	
Career Total	**1**	**0**	**0**	**0**	

Going: Sf: 0-0 GS: 0-0 Gd: 0-0 GF: - Fm: 0-1
Distance: 2m/2m3: 0-0 2m4-2m7: 0-1 3m+: 0-0
Track: LH: 0-1 RH: 0-0 Tight: 0-0 Gall: 0-0
Aids: Bl: 0-0 Vi: 0-0 Tstrap: 0-0
Best Rating:

Midnight Missile

5-y-o b g Arms And The Man-Rewbell (Andy Rew)
Mrs D A Hamer D J Phillips

Placings:00 (1384)
2001/02: 16^{0}GF, 17^{0}GF

	Starts	1st	2nd	3rd	Win & Pl
NH Flat	2	0	0	0	
Career Total	**2**	**0**	**0**	**0**	

Going: Sf: 0-0 GS: 0-0 Gd: 0-0 GF: - Fm: 0-2
Distance: 2m/2m3: 0-2 2m4-2m7: 0-0 3m+: 0-0
Track: LH: 0-1 RH: 0-1 Tight: 0-0 Gall: 0-0
Aids: Bl: 0-0 Vi: 0-0 Tstrap: 0-0
Best Rating: 33 9/01 Hrfd 2m1f gd-fm NHF

Midnight Moon

96 73

7-y-o b g Jupiter Island-Nunswalk (The Parson)
B D Leavy Mrs Alurie O'Sullivan

Placings:0000-4P (4443)
2001/02: 24^{4}HY, 27^{P}S

	Starts	1st	2nd	3rd	Win & Pl
Hurdles	2	0	0	0	0
Career Total	**6**	**0**	**0**	**0**	**0**

Going: Sf: 0-2 GS: 0-0 Gd: 0-0 GF: - Fm: 0-0
Distance: 2m/2m3: 0-0 2m4-2m7: 0-0 3m+: 0-2
Track: LH: 0-2 RH: 0-0 Tight: 0-1 Gall: 0-0
Aids: Bl: 0-0 Vi: 0-0 Tstrap: 0-1
Best Rating: 73 3/02 Hexm 3m heavy Hdl

Modest hurdler, stays three miles.

Midnight Rose (IRE)

57 25

6-y-o b m Torus-Night Rose (Sovereign Gleam)
J S King J E Garrett

Placings:00-0P (1769)
2001/02: 16^{0}GF, 17^{P}G

	Starts	1st	2nd	3rd	Win & Pl
Hurdles	2	0	0	0	
Career Total	**4**	**0**	**0**	**0**	

Going: Sf: 0-0 GS: 0-0 Gd: 0-1 GF: - Fm: 0-1
Distance: 2m/2m3: 0-2 2m4-2m7: 0-0 3m+: 0-0
Track: LH: 0-0 RH: 0-2 Tight: 0-0 Gall: 0-0
Aids: Bl: 0-0 Vi: 0-0 Tstrap: 0-0
Best Rating: 74 1/01 Kemp 2m soft NHF

Midnight Service (IRE)

13-y-o b g The Parson-Stringfellows (Laurence O)
Mrs J A Saunders T Newton

Placings:P/P/3/5-P (0231)
2001/02: 24^{P}GF

	Starts	1st	2nd	3rd	Win & Pl
Chases	1	0	0	0	
Career Total	**5**	**0**	**0**	**1**	**136**

Going: Sf: 0-0 GS: 0-0 Gd: 0-0 GF: - Fm: 0-1
Distance: 2m/2m3: 0-0 2m4-2m7: 0-0 3m+: 0-1
Track: LH: 0-0 RH: 0-1 Tight: 0-0 Gall: 0-1
Aids: Bl: 0-1 Vi: 0-0 Tstrap: 0-0
Best Rating: 87 5/00 Towc 3m1f gd-fm Ch

Midy's Risk (FR)

103 113

5-y-o gr g Take Risks (FR)-Martine Midy (FR) (Lashkari)
Mrs N Smith Tony Hayward And Barry Fulton

Placings:00-23513 (4389)
2001/02: 17^{2}GS, 16^{3}G, 18^{5}S, 16^{1}HY, 16^{3}S

	Starts	1st	2nd	3rd	Win & Pl
Hurdles	5	1	1	2	6193
Career Total	**7**	**1**	**1**	**2**	**6193**

113	2/02	Plum	2m	E Hdl	HVY	£2761

Total win prize-money £2762

Going: Sf: 1-3 GS: 0-1 Gd: 0-1 GF: - Fm: 0-0
Distance: **2m/2m3: 1-5** 2m4-2m7: 0-0 3m+: 0-0
Track: **LH: 1-2** RH: 0-3 **Tight: 1-3** Gall: 0-0
Aids: Bl: 0-0 Vi: 0-0 Tstrap: 0-0
Best Rating: 113 2/02 Plum 2m heavy Hdl

Ex-French, he showed his first sign of ability over hurdles at Taunton in December 2001 and continued to run well before getting off the mark in a maiden hurdle in very testing ground at Plumpton in February. Suited by two miles and easy ground.

Mighty Fine

49

8-y-o gr g Arzanni-Kate Kimberley (Sparkler)
Mrs E Slack A Slack

Placings:0/2S40/0-0 (1639)
2001/02: 20^{0}GS

	Starts	1st	2nd	3rd	Win & Pl
Hurdles	1	0	0	0	
Career Total	**7**	**0**	**1**	**0**	**460**

Going: Sf: 0-0 GS: 0-1 Gd: 0-0 GF: - Fm: 0-0
Distance: 2m/2m3: 0-0 2m4-2m7: 0-1 3m+: 0-0
Track: LH: 0-0 RH: 0-0 Tight: 0-0 Gall: 0-0
Aids: Bl: 0-0 Vi: 0-0 Tstrap: 0-0
Best Rating: 98 3/00 Newc 2m good Hdl

Mighty Magic

72 42

7-y-o b m Magic Ring (IRE)-Mighty Flash (Rolfe (USA))
N R Mitchell Mrs V A Tory

Placings:5/0-0 (0598)
2001/02: 17^{0}G

	Starts	1st	2nd	3rd	Win & Pl
Hurdles	1	0	0	0	
Career Total	**3**	**0**	**0**	**0**	**0**

Going: Sf: 0-0 GS: 0-0 Gd: 0-1 GF: - Fm: 0-0
Distance: 2m/2m3: 0-1 2m4-2m7: 0-0 3m+: 0-0
Track: LH: 0-1 RH: 0-0 Tight: 0-1 Gall: 0-0
Aids: Bl: 0-0 Vi: 0-0 Tstrap: 0-0
Best Rating: 86 12/98 Sand 2m110y good Hdl

Mighty Man (IRE)

7-y-o b g Mandalus-Mossy Mistress (IRE) (Le Moss)
O Brennan Lady Anne Bentinck

Placings:0-PP (2579)
2001/02: 20^{P}G, 20^{P}S

	Starts	1st	2nd	3rd	Win & Pl
Hurdles	1	0	0	0	0
Chases	1	0	0	0	0
Career Total	**3**	**0**	**0**	**0**	

Going: Sf: 0-1 GS: 0-0 Gd: 0-1 GF: - Fm: 0-0
Distance: 2m/2m3: 0-0 2m4-2m7: 0-2 3m+: 0-0
Track: LH: 0-2 RH: 0-0 Tight: 0-0 Gall: 0-0
Aids: Bl: 0-0 Vi: 0-0 Tstrap: 0-0
Best Rating:

Mighty Mini

84 73

6-y-o b m Buckley-Here Comes Tibby (Royal Fountain)
M A Barnes (O Brennan 23/1) Miss J Robinson

Placings: *605*000 **(4198)**
2001/02: 16[6]S, 16[0]S, 20[5]GS, 21[0]HY, 16[0]HY, 21[0]S

	Starts	1st	2nd	3rd	Win & Pl
NH Flat	2	0	0	0	0
Hurdles	4	0	0	0	0
Career Total	**6**	**0**	**0**	**0**	**0**

Going: Sf: 0-5 GS: 0-1 Gd: 0-0 GF: - Fm: 0-0
Distance: 2m/2m3: 0-3 2m4-2m7: 0-3 3m+: 0-0
Track: LH: 0-5 RH: 0-1 Tight: 0-3 Gall: 0-1
Aids: Bl: 0-0 Vi: 0-0 Tstrap: 0-0
Best Rating: 73 12/01 Hntg 2m4f110y gd-sft Hdl

Modest hurdler. Stamina does not look her forte.

Mighty Mist (IRE)

105 113

4-y-o gr g Paris House-Morgiana (Godswalk (USA))
G M Lyons P M Dowling

Placings:206301044 **(4840)**
2001/02: 16[2]YS, 16[0]SH, 16[6]Y, 16[3]Y, 16[0]Y, 16[1]HY, 20[0]S, 16[4]GY, 16[4]G

	Starts	1st	2nd	3rd	Win & Pl
Hurdles	9	1	1	1	7600
Career Total	**9**	**1**	**1**	**1**	**7600**
110 2/02 Naas 2m Hdl				HVY	£4656

Total win prize-money £4656

Going: Sf: 1-2 GS: 0-0 Gd: 0-1 GF: - Fm: 0-0
Distance: **2m/2m3: 1-8** 2m4-2m7: 0-1 3m+: 0-0
Track: **LH: 1-3** RH: 0-4 Tight: 0-0 Gall: 0-0
Aids: Bl: 0-0 Vi: 0-0 Tstrap: 0-0
Best Rating: 113 4/02 Fair 2m gd-yld Hdl

Mighty Montefalco

105 116

6-y-o b g Mtoto-Glendera (Glenstal (USA))
J J O'Neill Mrs Peter S Thompson

Placings: *3*661 **(4850)**
2001/02: 16[3]G, 25[6]G, 21[6]S, 22[1]G

	Starts	1st	2nd	3rd	Win & Pl
NH Flat	1	0	0	1	208
Hurdles	3	1	0	0	3231
Career Total	**4**	**1**	**0**	**1**	**3438**
116 4/02 Strf 2m6f110y E Hdl				GD	£3230

Total win prize-money £3231

Going: Sf: 0-1 GS: 0-0 Gd: 1-3 GF: - Fm: 0-0
Distance: 2m/2m3: 0-1 **2m4-2m7: 1-2** 3m+: 0-1
Track: **LH: 1-2** RH: 0-2 **Tight: 1-1** Gall: 0-2
Aids: Bl: 0-0 Vi: 0-0 Tstrap: 0-0
Best Rating: 116 4/02 Strf 2m6f110y good Hdl

Novice hurdler. Stays two miles six furlongs and acts on a sound surface.

Mighty Moss (IRE)

11-y-o b g Moscow Society (USA)-Derry Girl (Rarity)
F A Hutsby (R T Phillips 20/1) K Hutsby

Placings: *11233*/112222/2134/1151/4P-U225 **(4186)**
2001/02: 26[U]G, 22[2]HY, 24[2]GS, 24[5]S

	Starts	1st	2nd	3rd	Win & Pl
Chases	4	0	2	0	2459
Career Total	**25**	**8**	**8**	**3**	**65744**
140 4/00 Ayr 3m3f110y H Ch				GD	£2795
133 2/00 Hntg 3m H Ch				SFT	£1260
120 2/00 Hntg 3m H Ch				SFT	£1144
149 1/98 Chel 3m B Hdl				G-S	£6156
133 11/96 Chep 2m4f110y C Hdl				SFT	£3965
117 11/96 Worc 2m4f E Hdl				GD	£2722
118 1/96 Nott 2m H NHF				G-S	£1721
108 12/95 Hntg 2m110y H NHF				G-S	£1722

Total win prize-money £21487

Going: Sf: 0-2 GS: 0-1 Gd: 0-1 GF: - Fm: 0-0
Distance: 2m/2m3: 0-0 2m4-2m7: 0-1 3m+: 0-3
Track: LH: 0-0 RH: 0-2 Tight: 0-1 Gall: 0-1
Aids: Bl: 0-0 Vi: 0-0 Tstrap: 0-0
Best Rating: 155 3/98 Chel 3m good Hdl

Once a top class staying hurdler (placed twice at the Cheltenham Festival), he took well to hunter chasing in the spring of 2000 but proved a touch disappointing in handicaps last term. Still lightly-raced over fences.

Mighty Rising

7-y-o b g Primitive Rising (USA)-Mighty Miss (Doc Marten)
M E Sowersby Paul Clifton

Placings:P-P **(0088)**
2001/02: 25[P]S

	Starts	1st	2nd	3rd	Win & Pl
Chases	1	0	0	0	
Career Total	**2**	**0**	**0**	**0**	

Going: Sf: 0-1 GS: 0-0 Gd: 0-0 GF: - Fm: 0-0
Distance: 2m/2m3: 0-0 2m4-2m7: 0-0 3m+: 0-1
Track: LH: 0-1 RH: 0-0 Tight: 0-0 Gall: 0-0
Aids: Bl: 0-0 Vi: 0-0 Tstrap: 0-0
Best Rating:

Mighty Strong

103 121

8-y-o b g Strong Gale-Muffet's Spider (Rymer)
N J Henderson Mrs Johnny Reed

Placings:44/510-PP102 **(4537)**
2001/02: 17[P]G, 20[P]G, 17[1]G, 17[0]S, 21[2]G

	Starts	1st	2nd	3rd	Win & Pl
Chases	5	1	1	0	6856
Career Total	**10**	**2**	**1**	**0**	**11424**
121 1/02 Newb 2m1f D(0-120)HCh				GD	£5590
118 12/00 Donc 2m110y D Ch				HVY	£3867

Total win prize-money £9458

Going: Sf: 0-1 GS: 0-0 Gd: 1-4 GF: - Fm: 0-0
Distance: **2m/2m3: 1-3** 2m4-2m7: 0-2 3m+: 0-0
Track: **LH: 1-4** RH: 0-1 Tight: 0-2 **Gall: 1-2**
Aids: Bl: 0-0 Vi: 0-0 Tstrap: 0-0
Best Rating: 121 1/02 Newb 2m1f good Ch

Front-running handicap chaser, he is effective at two miles on ground ranging from good to heavy.

Mighty Surprise

94 88

6-y-o b m Sure Blade (USA)-Flash-By (Ilium)
P J Hobbs Mrs Anona Taylor

Placings: *0*/344155-3 **(1226)**
2001/02: 22[3]GF

	Starts	1st	2nd	3rd	Win & Pl
Hurdles	1	0	0	1	327
Career Total	**8**	**1**	**0**	**2**	**3319**
92 8/00 NAbb 2m6f E Hdl				G-F	£2697

Total win prize-money £2698

Going: Sf: 0-0 GS: 0-0 Gd: 0-0 GF: - Fm: 0-1
Distance: 2m/2m3: 0-0 2m4-2m7: 0-1 3m+: 0-0
Track: LH: 0-1 RH: 0-0 Tight: 0-1 Gall: 0-0
Aids: Bl: 0-0 Vi: 0-0 Tstrap: 0-0
Best Rating: 92 8/00 NAbb 2m6f gd-fm Hdl

Migration

110 118

6-y-o b g Rainbow Quest (USA)-Armeria (USA) (Northern Dancer)
M Pitman Just Good Fun Club

Placings:600 **(3886)**
2001/02: 16[6]G, 16[0]S, 16[0]GS

	Starts	1st	2nd	3rd	Win & Pl
Hurdles	3	0	0	0	0
Career Total	**3**	**0**	**0**	**0**	**0**

Going: Sf: 0-1 GS: 0-1 Gd: 0-1 GF: - Fm: 0-0
Distance: 2m/2m3: 0-3 2m4-2m7: 0-0 3m+: 0-0
Track: LH: 0-2 RH: 0-1 Tight: 0-0 Gall: 0-1
Aids: Bl: 0-0 Vi: 0-0 Tstrap: 0-0
Best Rating: 118 2/02 Kemp 2m gd-sft Hdl

A winner on the Flat and runner-up in listed company, he has yet to show that same level of form over hurdles.

Migwar

88 62

9-y-o b g Unfuwain (USA)-Pick Of The Pops (High Top)
R Craggs Ray Craggs

Placings:P/0-4 **(0644)**
2001/02: 17[4]GF

	Starts	1st	2nd	3rd	Win & Pl
Hurdles	1	0	0	0	0
Career Total	**3**	**0**	**0**	**0**	**0**

Going: Sf: 0-0 GS: 0-0 Gd: 0-0 GF: - Fm: 0-1
Distance: 2m/2m3: 0-1 2m4-2m7: 0-0 3m+: 0-0
Track: LH: 0-0 RH: 0-1 Tight: 0-1 Gall: 0-0
Aids: Bl: 0-0 Vi: 0-0 Tstrap: 0-0
Best Rating: 62 6/01 MRas 2m1f110y gd-fm Hdl

Mijico (IRE)

94f 112f

6-y-o b g Lord Americo-Mijette (Pauper)
Ferdy Murphy Mrs R D Cairns

Placings: *265* **(4552)**
2001/02: 17[2]S, 16[6]HY, 16[5]GF

	Starts	1st	2nd	3rd	Win & Pl
NH Flat	3	0	1	0	460
Career Total	**3**	**0**	**1**	**0**	**460**

Going: Sf: 0-2 GS: 0-0 Gd: 0-0 GF: - Fm: 0-1
Distance: 2m/2m3: 0-3 2m4-2m7: 0-0 3m+: 0-0
Track: LH: 0-0 RH: 0-3 Tight: 0-0 Gall: 0-1
Aids: Bl: 0-0 Vi: 0-0 Tstrap: 0-0
Best Rating: 112 11/01 Carl 2m1f soft NHF

Closely related to the useful Coolaw, he finished runner-up on his bumper debut at Carlisle in November and needs further.

Mike Simmons

82 **104**

6-y-o b g Ballacashtal (CAN)-Lady Crusty (Golden Dipper)

L P Grassick L P Grassick

Placings:0014/033531-006 **(4150)**

2001/02: 16^{0}GF, 25^{0}HY, 24^{6}GS

	Starts	1st	2nd	3rd	Win & Pl
Hurdles	3	0	0	0	0
Career Total	**13**	**2**	**0**	**3**	**7482**

104	4/01	Font	2m4f	F(0-100)HHdl	GD	£2761
83	2/00	Tntn	2m1f	E Hdl	SFT	£2472

Total win prize-money £5234

Going: Sf: 0-1 GS: 0-1 Gd: 0-0 GF: - Fm: 0-1
Distance: 2m/2m3: 0-1 2m4-2m7: 0-0 3m+: 0-2
Track: LH: 0-2 RH: 0-0 Tight: 0-0 Gall: 0-0
Aids: Bl: 0-0 Vi: 0-0 Tstrap: 0-0
Best Rating: 104 4/01 Font 2m4f good Hdl

A fair handicap hurdler. Best at around two and a half miles. Has won on good and soft ground.

Mike Stan (IRE)

94

11-y-o b g Rontino-Fair Pirouette (Fair Turn)

L Lungo J M Crichton

Placings:540/14110U2/4223111/62F11/33F0-P **(0344)**

2001/02: 25^{P}G

	Starts	1st	2nd	3rd	Win & Pl
Chases	1	0	0	0	
Career Total	**27**	**8**	**4**	**3**	**58473**

149	4/00	Carl	3m2f	D(0-125)HCh	SFT	£4426
134	2/00	Muss	2m4f	D(0-120)HCh	G-S	£4891
149	4/99	Ayr	3m1f	C HCh	SFT	£25532
128	3/99	Ayr	3m1f	D Ch	SFT	£4570
134	2/99	Muss	3m	E(0-105)HCh	FRM	£3192
116	1/98	Ayr	2m4f	D Hdl	G-S	£3345
107	12/97	Uttx	3m110y	E(0-100)HHdl	G-S	£2515
96	11/97	Carl	2m4f110y	E(0-100)HHdl	FRM	£2388

Total win prize-money £50863

Going: Sf: 0-0 GS: 0-0 Gd: 0-1 GF: - Fm: 0-0
Distance: 2m/2m3: 0-0 2m4-2m7: 0-0 3m+: 0-1
Track: LH: 0-1 RH: 0-0 Tight: 0-1 Gall: 0-0
Aids: Bl: 0-0 Vi: 0-0 Tstrap: 0-0
Best Rating: 149 4/00 Carl 3m2f soft Ch

He was given some weak tactical rides last season, being held up off the pace when he lacks a decisive turn of foot. Stays three miles plus. He handles most types of ground.

Mike's Dream

69 **47**

10-y-o b g Motivate-Carreg Goch (Kala Shikari)

G F Edwards (C L Popham 9/5) G F Edwards

Placings:*0*/P-F600 **(1612)**

2001/02: 24^{F}GF, 22^{6}GF, 16^{0}GS, 22^{0}GF

	Starts	1st	2nd	3rd	Win & Pl
Hurdles	3	0	0	0	0
Chases	1	0	0	0	0
Career Total	**6**	**0**	**0**	**0**	**0**

Going: Sf: 0-0 GS: 0-1 Gd: 0-0 GF: - Fm: 0-3
Distance: 2m/2m3: 0-1 2m4-2m7: 0-2 3m+: 0-1
Track: LH: 0-3 RH: 0-0 Tight: 0-3 Gall: 0-0
Aids: Bl: 0-0 Vi: 0-0 Tstrap: 0-0
Best Rating: 47 10/01 Extr 2m6f110y gd-fm Hdl

Mikes Melody (IRE)

94 **90**

6-y-o b g Accordion-Dalana's Pet Vii (Damsire Unregistered)

C Weedon Bob Keen

Placings:*05*-4P **(3766)**

2001/02: 16^{4}G, 20^{P}GS

	Starts	1st	2nd	3rd	Win & Pl
Hurdles	2	0	0	0	250
Career Total	**4**	**0**	**0**	**0**	**250**

Going: Sf: 0-0 GS: 0-1 Gd: 0-1 GF: - Fm: 0-0
Distance: 2m/2m3: 0-1 2m4-2m7: 0-1 3m+: 0-0
Track: LH: 0-1 RH: 0-1 Tight: 0-1 Gall: 0-0
Aids: Bl: 0-0 Vi: 0-0 Tstrap: 0-0
Best Rating: 90 10/01 Winc 2m good Hdl

Mikhail (USA)

73 **64**

5-y-o ch g Nureyev (USA)-Rythmical (USA) (Fappiano (USA))

N J Hawke R J & Mrs J A Peake

Placings:*0000* **(3882)**

2001/02: 17^{0}G, 16^{0}G, 16^{0}GS, 16^{0}GS

	Starts	1st	2nd	3rd	Win & Pl
NH Flat	2	0	0	0	0
Hurdles	2	0	0	0	0
Career Total	**4**	**0**	**0**	**0**	

Going: Sf: 0-0 GS: 0-2 Gd: 0-2 GF: - Fm: 0-0
Distance: 2m/2m3: 0-4 2m4-2m7: 0-0 3m+: 0-0
Track: LH: 0-2 RH: 0-2 Tight: 0-1 Gall: 0-0
Aids: Bl: 0-0 Vi: 0-0 Tstrap: 0-0
Best Rating: 64 1/02 Winc 2m gd-sft Hdl

Milan King (IRE)

95(89c) (90c)**94**

9-y-o b g King's Ride-Milan Moss (Le Moss)

A J Lockwood Chester Bosomworth

Placings:5P00F00*0*/P040F05F/041051P6P2/2011000 0-030P40 **(1347)**

2001/02: 16^{0}F, 16^{3}GS, 16^{0}GF, 17^{P}GF, 17^{4}GF, 17^{0}GF

	Starts	1st	2nd	3rd	Win & Pl
Hurdles	5	0	0	1	294
Chases	1	0	0	0	0
Career Total	**40**	**4**	**2**	**1**	**8708**

101	9/00	Sedg	2m1f	F(0-105)HHdl	GD	£1855
101	7/00	Sedg	2m1f	F(0-105)HHdl	G-F	£1918
83	2/00	Sedg	2m1f	F(0-100)HHdl	G-S	£1991
77	12/99	MRas	2m1f110y	G(0-95)HHdl	GD	£1584

Total win prize-money £7350

Going: Sf: 0-0 GS: 0-1 Gd: 0-0 GF: - Fm: 0-5
Distance: 2m/2m3: 0-6 2m4-2m7: 0-0 3m+: 0-0
Track: LH: 0-5 RH: 0-1 Tight: 0-5 Gall: 0-0
Aids: Bl: 0-0 Vi: 0-0 Tstrap: 0-0
Best Rating: 101 9/00 Sedg 2m1f good Hdl

Mildan Grace

6-y-o b m Afzal-An Bothar Dubh (Strong Gale)

A Hollingsworth A Hollingsworth

Placings:*0-0P* **(0580)**

2001/02: 17^{0}GS, 22^{P}GF

	Starts	1st	2nd	3rd	Win & Pl
NH Flat	1	0	0	0	0
Hurdles	1	0	0	0	0
Career Total	**3**	**0**	**0**	**0**	

Going: Sf: 0-0 GS: 0-1 Gd: 0-0 GF: - Fm: 0-1
Distance: 2m/2m3: 0-1 2m4-2m7: 0-1 3m+: 0-0
Track: LH: 0-2 RH: 0-0 Tight: 0-2 Gall: 0-0
Aids: Bl: 0-0 Vi: 0-0 Tstrap: 0-0
Best Rating:

Mildon (IRE)

74 **35**

6-y-o ch g Dolphin Street (FR)-Lycia (Targowice (USA))

J R Weymes Don Raper

Placings:050-0P **(4096)**

2001/02: 17^{0}S, 19^{P}GS

	Starts	1st	2nd	3rd	Win & Pl
Hurdles	2	0	0	0	
Career Total	**5**	**0**	**0**	**0**	**0**

Going: Sf: 0-1 GS: 0-1 Gd: 0-0 GF: - Fm: 0-0
Distance: 2m/2m3: 0-2 2m4-2m7: 0-0 3m+: 0-0
Track: LH: 0-2 RH: 0-0 Tight: 0-2 Gall: 0-0
Aids: Bl: 0-0 Vi: 0-0 Tstrap: 0-1
Best Rating: 79 2/01 Sedg 2m5f110y soft Hdl

Well held in modest company over hurdles. Suited to an easy surface. Has worn blinkers and a visor.

Military Miss

82f **63f**

6-y-o b m Infantry-Stone Madness (Yukon Eric (CAN))

J E Long Paul Stamp

Placings:*060* **(4112)**

2001/02: 17^{0}HY, 16^{6}HY, 16^{0}S

	Starts	1st	2nd	3rd	Win & Pl
NH Flat	3	0	0	0	0
Career Total	**3**	**0**	**0**	**0**	**0**

Going: Sf: 0-3 GS: 0-0 Gd: 0-0 GF: - Fm: 0-0
Distance: 2m/2m3: 0-3 2m4-2m7: 0-0 3m+: 0-0
Track: LH: 0-0 RH: 0-2 Tight: 0-1 Gall: 0-0
Aids: Bl: 0-0 Vi: 0-0 Tstrap: 0-0
Best Rating: 63 1/02 Towc 2m heavy NHF

Mill Afrique

98 **93**

6-y-o b m Mtoto-Milinetta (Milford)

Mrs M Reveley R Meredith

Placings:60/206602-5121P **(1629)**

2001/02: 21^{5}G, 21^{1}GF, 21^{2}G, 20^{1}GF, 21^{P}GF

	Starts	1st	2nd	3rd	Win & Pl
Hurdles	5	2	1	0	4501
Career Total	**13**	**2**	**3**	**0**	**5825**

93	9/01	Hntg	2m4f110y	F(0-90)HHdl	G-F	£2107
83	5/01	Hntg	2m5f110y	G(0-95)HHdl	G-F	£1890

Total win prize-money £3997

Going: Sf: 0-0 GS: 0-0 Gd: 0-2 GF: - Fm: 2-3
Distance: 2m/2m3: 0-0 **2m4-2m7: 2-5** 3m+: 0-0
Track: LH: 0-1 **RH: 2-3** Tight: 0-2 **Gall: 2-2**
Aids: Bl: 0-0 Vi: 0-0 Tstrap: 0-0
Best Rating: 93 10/01 Ludl 2m5f gd-fm Hdl

Finnaly got off the mark at Huntingdon over two miles

four furlongs after some good place efforts.

Mill Emerald

108 **108+**

5-y-o b m Old Vic-Milinetta (Milford)

Mrs M Reveley (A King 12/11) R Meredith

Placings:04001503 **(4786)**

2001/02: 16^0G, 20^4GS, 16^0G, 21^0GS, 20^1S, 24^5S, 21^0S, 20^3F

	Starts	1st	2nd	3rd	Win & Pl
Hurdles	8	1	0	1	2188
Career Total	**8**	**1**	**0**	**1**	**2188**

79	1/02	Newc	2m4f	G(0-95)HHdl	SFT	£1932

Total win prize-money £1932

Going: Sf: 1-3 GS: 0-2 Gd: 0-2 GF: - Fm: 0-1
Distance: 2m/2m3: 0-2 **2m4-2m7: 1-5** 3m+: 0-1
Track: **LH: 1-6** RH: 0-1 Tight: 0-2 **Gall: 1-6**
Aids: Bl: 0-0 Vi: 0-0 Tstrap: 0-0
Best Rating: 79 1/02 Newc 2m4f soft Hdl

Plating-class hurdler, clear winner of a Newcastle seller in January 2002 and seemed to show much improved form when taking a claimer at Wetherby in May. Suited by two and a half miles and soft ground and followwed up despite a stiff weight rise in a valuable seller at Uttoxeter in June.

Mill End Venture (IRE)

61

6-y-o b g Namaqualand (USA)-Risk All (Run The Gantlet (USA))

D Shaw J C Fretwell

Placings:30/6-0 **(0421)**

2001/02: 24^0G

	Starts	1st	2nd	3rd	Win & Pl
Hurdles	1	0	0	0	
Career Total	**4**	**0**	**0**	**1**	**400**

Going: Sf: 0-0 GS: 0-0 Gd: 0-1 GF: - Fm: 0-0
Distance: 2m/2m3: 0-0 2m4-2m7: 0-0 3m+: 0-1
Track: LH: 0-1 RH: 0-0 Tight: 0-1 Gall: 0-0
Aids: Bl: 0-0 Vi: 0-0 Tstrap: 0-0
Best Rating: 64 7/99 MRas 2m1f110y gd-fm Hdl

Mill Lord (IRE)

100 **86**

9-y-o b g Aristocracy-Millflower (Millfontaine)

C J Drewe W P Long

Placings:000/04/05PFPP-P3434500 **(4734)**

2001/02: 19^PG, 20^3GF, 19^4G, 16^3GF, 19^4GF, 21^5G, 16^0G, 19^0F

	Starts	1st	2nd	3rd	Win & Pl
Chases	8	0	0	2	1045
Career Total	**19**	**0**	**0**	**2**	**1045**

Going: Sf: 0-0 GS: 0-0 Gd: 0-4 GF: - Fm: 0-4
Distance: 2m/2m3: 0-4 2m4-2m7: 0-4 3m+: 0-0
Track: LH: 0-1 RH: 0-7 Tight: 0-3 Gall: 0-0
Aids: Bl: 0-6 Vi: 0-0 Tstrap: 0-0
Best Rating: 86 11/01 Extr 2m3f110y gd-fm Ch

Moderate chaser, best at two miles on a sound surface.

Mill O'The Rags (IRE)

13-y-o b g Strong Gale-Lady Rag (Ragapan)

Neil King Mrs E M Clarke

Placings:065P5/1514/144121152/22PP4P2/21P5P/43 P/463 **(0556)**

2001/02: 24^4GF, 21^6G, 24^3GF

	Starts	1st	2nd	3rd	Win & Pl
Chases	3	0	0	1	192
Career Total	**36**	**7**	**6**	**2**	**24341**

103	5/98	Weth	2m4f110y	H Ch	G-F	£1308
107	10/96	Hntg	2m4f110y	F(0-95)HCh	GD	£2940
101	10/96	Towc	2m110y	E Ch	G-F	£2877
95	9/96	Plum	2m5f	E Ch	G-F	£2976
88	5/96	Hrfd	2m1f	E(0-100)HHdl	FRM	£2070
80	11/95	Towc	2m	F(0-100)HHdl	FRM	£2180
73	5/95	Towc	2m	D Hdl	G-F	£2903

Total win prize-money £17255

Going: Sf: 0-0 GS: 0-0 Gd: 0-1 GF: - Fm: 0-2
Distance: 2m/2m3: 0-0 2m4-2m7: 0-1 3m+: 0-2
Track: LH: 0-0 RH: 0-3 Tight: 0-1 Gall: 0-2
Aids: Bl: 0-0 Vi: 0-0 Tstrap: 0-0
Best Rating: 110 5/97 Hntg 2m4f110y gd-fm Ch

Mill Orchid

108(00h) (09h)**104**

8-y-o b m Henbit (USA)-Milinetta (Milford)

Mrs M Reveley (A King 14/11) R Meredith

Placings:56001/54P0P453/522023504-5661U424P **(4909)**

2001/02: 21^5GF, 18^6GF, 19^6GF, 22^1G, 21^UG, 16^4GS, 20^2GS, 24^4GF, 20^PGF

	Starts	1st	2nd	3rd	Win & Pl
Hurdles	2	0	0	0	0
Chases	7	1	1	0	4298
Career Total	**31**	**2**	**4**	**2**	**10887**

98	10/01	MRas	2m6f110y	E(0-105)HCh	GD	£3510
82	4/99	MRas	2m1f110y	G(0-95)HHdl	SFT	£1576

Total win prize-money £5086

Going: Sf: 0-0 GS: 0-2 Gd: 1-2 GF: - Fm: 0-5
Distance: 2m/2m3: 0-3 **2m4-2m7: 1-5** 3m+: 0-1
Track: LH: 0-2 **RH: 1-7 Tight: 1-5** Gall: 0-3
Aids: Bl: 0-0 Vi: 0-0 Tstrap: 0-0
Best Rating: 104 1/02 Hntg 2m4f110y gd-sft Ch

Selling class over hurdles. Looked to need a longer trip when competing at around two miles over fences and duly scored on chasing bow in the 2001 season over two mile- six at Market Rasen in October. Acts on an easy surface.

Mill Tower

50f

5-y-o b g Milieu-Tringa (GER) (Kaiseradler)

R Nixon G R S Nixon

Placings:0 **(2729)**

2001/02: 17^0GF

	Starts	1st	2nd	3rd	Win & Pl
NH Flat	1	0	0	0	
Career Total	**1**	**0**	**0**	**0**	

Going: Sf: 0-0 GS: 0-0 Gd: 0-0 GF: - Fm: 0-1
Distance: 2m/2m3: 0-1 2m4-2m7: 0-0 3m+: 0-0
Track: LH: 0-0 RH: 0-0 Tight: 0-0 Gall: 0-0
Aids: Bl: 0-0 Vi: 0-0 Tstrap: 0-0

Best Rating: 50 12/01 Muss 2m1f gd-fm NHF

Milla's Man (IRE)

76

10-y-o b g Satco (FR)-Rullahola (Blue Rullah)

W W Dennis W W Dennis

Placings:0/02255/2/FF **(4184)**

2001/02: 25^FS, 24^FS

	Starts	1st	2nd	3rd	Win & Pl
Chases	2	0	0	0	
Career Total	**9**	**0**	**3**	**0**	**2558**

Going: Sf: 0-2 GS: 0-0 Gd: 0-0 GF: - Fm: 0-0
Distance: 2m/2m3: 0-0 2m4-2m7: 0-0 3m+: 0-2
Track: LH: 0-0 RH: 0-2 Tight: 0-1 Gall: 0-0
Aids: Bl: 0-0 Vi: 0-0 Tstrap: 0-0
Best Rating: 118 6/99 NAbb 2m5f110y good Ch

Millcroft Riviera (IRE)

101 **128**

11-y-o b g Henbit (USA)-Rathtrim (Strong Gale)

R H Alner John Carter

Placings:36/53410/1U31U3/1243P/1P42/52305-161253P **(1356)**

2001/02: 21^1GF, 21^6G, 20^1GF, 20^2G, 21^5G, 22^3GF, 24^PGF

	Starts	1st	2nd	3rd	Win & Pl
Chases	7	2	1	1	9839
Career Total	**34**	**7**	**4**	**7**	**37606**

128	6/01	Strf	2m4f	E(0-115)HCh	G-F	£3500
128	5/01	NAbb	2m5f110y	F(0-110)HCh	G-F	£3731
118	10/99	Chep	2m3f110y	C(0-130)HCh	G-F	£5912
119	9/98	Hntg	2m4f110y	D(0-125)HCh	G-F	£3510
128	2/98	Kemp	2m4f110y	D(0-125)HCh	GD	£4182
96	9/97	Extr	2m1f110y	D Ch	G-F	£3612
85	1/97	Tntn	2m3f110y	E Hdl	GD	£1934

Total win prize-money £26384

Going: Sf: 0-0 GS: 0-0 Gd: 0-3 GF: - Fm: 2-4
Distance: 2m/2m3: 0-0 **2m4-2m7: 2-6** 3m+: 0-1
Track: **LH: 2-6** RH: 0-0 **Tight: 2-7** Gall: 0-0
Aids: Bl: 0-0 Vi: 0-0 Tstrap: 0-0
Best Rating: 128 6/01 Strf 2m4f gd-fm Ch

He is rather inconsistent. Best on a sound surface at around two and a half miles, and goes well fresh.

Millcroft Seaspray (IRE)

105 **118**

6-y-o br g Good Thyne (USA)-Bucks Gift (IRE) (Buckley)

R H Alner John Carter

Placings:40-3122 **(4480)**

2001/02: 21^3S, 24^1S, 24^2S, 22^2G

	Starts	1st	2nd	3rd	Win & Pl
Hurdles	4	1	2	1	6551
Career Total	**6**	**1**	**2**	**1**	**6551**

110	1/02	Tntn	3m110y	D Hdl	SFT	£4139

Total win prize-money £4139

Going: Sf: 1-3 GS: 0-0 Gd: 0-1 GF: - Fm: 0-0
Distance: 2m/2m3: 0-0 2m4-2m7: 0-2 **3m+: 1-2**
Track: LH: 0-1 **RH: 1-2 Tight: 1-3** Gall: 0-0
Aids: Bl: 0-0 Vi: 0-0 Tstrap: 0-0
Best Rating: 118 3/02 Extr 2m6f110y good Hdl

A first foal of an unraced sister to the chaser Granville Girl, he is lightly-raced and showed ability on his second start over hurdles. Stepped up to three miles to get off the mark at Taunton in January 2002, and ran well subsequently.

Millenium Way (IRE)

112

8-y-o ch g Ikdam-Fine Drapes (Le Bavard (FR))
O Sherwood The Chamberlain Addiscott Partnership

Placings:2242330/**33P33-PP** **(0681)**
2001/02: 25^{P}G, 26^{P}G

	Starts	1st	2nd	3rd	Win & Pl
Chases	2	0	0	0	
Career Total	**14**	**0**	**3**	**6**	**6782**

Going: Sf: 0-0 GS: 0-0 Gd: 0-2 GF: - Fm: 0-0
Distance: 2m/2m3: 0-0 2m4-2m7: 0-0 3m+: 0-2
Track: LH: 0-1 RH: 0-1 Tight: 0-1 Gall: 0-0
Aids: Bl: 0-0 Vi: 0-0 Tstrap: 0-0
Best Rating: 112 4/01 Tntn 3m gd-fm Ch

Millennium Minx

5-y-o b m Red Rainbow-Lassitter (Damister (USA))
B G Powell D Tye

Placings:P **(1034)**
2001/02: 17^{P}G

	Starts	1st	2nd	3rd	Win & Pl
Hurdles	1	0	0	0	
Career Total	**1**	**0**	**0**	**0**	

Going: Sf: 0-0 GS: 0-0 Gd: 0-1 GF: - Fm: 0-0
Distance: 2m/2m3: 0-1 2m4-2m7: 0-0 3m+: 0-0
Track: LH: 0-1 RH: 0-0 Tight: 0-1 Gall: 0-0
Aids: Bl: 0-0 Vi: 0-0 Tstrap: 0-0
Best Rating:

Millennium Pearl

92 **63**

7-y-o b g Aragon-Little Egret (Carwhite)
W Storey The Pearl Divers

Placings:00/046-000P **(1678)**
2001/02: 20^{0}F, 20^{0}GS, 22^{0}G, 21^{P}G

	Starts	1st	2nd	3rd	Win & Pl
Hurdles	4	0	0	0	
Career Total	**9**	**0**	**0**	**0**	**243**

Going: Sf: 0-0 GS: 0-1 Gd: 0-2 GF: - Fm: 0-1
Distance: 2m/2m3: 0-0 2m4-2m7: 0-4 3m+: 0-0
Track: LH: 0-4 RH: 0-0 Tight: 0-2 Gall: 0-0
Aids: Bl: 0-0 Vi: 0-0 Tstrap: 0-0
Best Rating: 73 2/00 Weth 2m soft NHF

Millersford

107 **114**

11-y-o b g Meadowbrook-My Seer (Menelek)
N A Gaselee Mrs Derek Fletcher

Placings:0240/14552/**33235U/3531F2345/PF503/611 P4P3-20605** **(4184)**
2001/02: 24^{2}F, 24^{0}GF, 26^{6}G, 24^{0}S, 24^{5}S

	Starts	1st	2nd	3rd	Win & Pl
Chases	5	0	1	0	1524
Career Total	**41**	**4**	**5**	**8**	**24704**
119	6/00	Uttx	3m	D(0-120)HCh	G-F	£4176
119	5/00	Towc	2m6f	F(0-90)Ch	SFT	£2415
110	11/98	Wind	3m	E Ch	G-S	£3549
99	11/96	Kemp	2m5f	E Hdl	GD	£2360

Total win prize-money £12501

Going: Sf: 0-2 GS: 0-0 Gd: 0-1 GF: - Fm: 0-2
Distance: 2m/2m3: 0-0 2m4-2m7: 0-0 3m+: 0-5
Track: LH: 0-2 RH: 0-3 Tight: 0-5 Gall: 0-0
Aids: Bl: 0-0 Vi: 0-0 Tstrap: 0-0
Best Rating: 119 6/00 Uttx 3m gd-fm Ch

Modest chaser these days, acts on good ground, stays three miles.

Milligan (FR)

115 **156**

7-y-o b g Exit To Nowhere (USA)-Madigan Mill (Mill Reef (USA))
Miss Venetia Williams G H Leatham

Placings:01/3103360-12044031 **(4837)**
2001/02: 16^{1}G, 16^{2}G, 16^{0}G, 16^{4}G, 16^{4}HY, 16^{0}GS, 16^{3}G, 16^{1}G

	Starts	1st	2nd	3rd	Win & Pl
Hurdles	8	2	1	1	57643
Career Total	**17**	**4**	**1**	**4**	**82101**
146	4/02	Ayr	2m	A HHdl	GD	£15600
156	5/01	Hayd	2m	A HHdl	GD	£27000
133	10/00	Weth	2m	C(0-135)HHdl	G-S	£4888
119	3/00	Catt	2m	E Hdl	G-F	£3152

Total win prize-money £50641

Going: Sf: 0-1 GS: 0-1 Gd: 2-6 GF: - Fm: 0-0
Distance: **2m/2m3: 2-8** 2m4-2m7: 0-0 3m+: 0-0
Track: **LH: 2-5** RH: 0-3 Tight: 0-1 Gall: 0-0
Aids: Bl: 0-0 Vi: 0-0 Tstrap: 0-0
Best Rating: 156 12/01 Kemp 2m good Hdl

Good handicap hurdler, who landed the Scottish Champion Hurdle in April 2002. Suited by two miles, decent ground and a flat track, he jumps soundly and is sure to make a chaser in time.

Millionformerthyr

60 **22**

6-y-o b m Mon Tresor-Regal Salute (Dara Monarch)
Mrs L C Jewell (A G Hobbs 31/10) Mrs A Greengrow

Placings:0000 **(2598)**
2001/02: 16^{0}GS, 22^{0}GS, 16^{0}GF, 18^{0}G

	Starts	1st	2nd	3rd	Win & Pl
Hurdles	4	0	0	0	
Career Total	**4**	**0**	**0**	**0**	

Going: Sf: 0-0 GS: 0-2 Gd: 0-1 GF: - Fm: 0-1
Distance: 2m/2m3: 0-3 2m4-2m7: 0-1 3m+: 0-0
Track: LH: 0-3 RH: 0-1 Tight: 0-3 Gall: 0-0
Aids: Bl: 0-0 Vi: 0-1 Tstrap: 0-0
Best Rating: 22 11/01 Ludl 2m gd-fm Hdl

Millions

105 **86**

5-y-o b g Bering-Miznah (IRE) (Sadler's Wells (USA))
Ferdy Murphy (K A Ryan 21/5) Platinum Racing Club Limited

Placings:U04150 **(1618)**
2001/02: 16^{U}GF, 17^{0}GF, 16^{4}G, 21^{1}GF, 24^{5}G, 21^{0}G

	Starts	1st	2nd	3rd	Win & Pl
Hurdles	6	1	0	0	2772
Career Total	**6**	**1**	**0**	**0**	**2772**
86	9/01	Sedg	2m5f110y	E Hdl	G-F	£2772

Total win prize-money £2772

Going: Sf: 0-0 GS: 0-0 Gd: 0-3 GF: - Fm: 1-3
Distance: 2m/2m3: 0-3 **2m4-2m7: 1-2** 3m+: 0-1
Track: **LH: 1-3** RH: 0-3 **Tight: 1-3** Gall: 0-0
Aids: Bl: 0-0 Vi: 0-0 Tstrap: 0-0
Best Rating: 86 9/01 Sedg 2m5f110y gd-fm Hdl

Millsofballysodare (IRE)

11-y-o b g Supreme Leader-Regency View (Royal Highway)
O O'Neill R S Lanchbury

Placings:00500/0-URU **(0849)**
2001/02: 24^{U}GF, 21^{R}GS, 21^{U}GF

	Starts	1st	2nd	3rd	Win & Pl
Chases	3	0	0	0	
Career Total	**9**	**0**	**0**	**0**	**0**

Going: Sf: 0-0 GS: 0-1 Gd: 0-0 GF: - Fm: 0-2
Distance: 2m/2m3: 0-0 2m4-2m7: 0-2 3m+: 0-1
Track: LH: 0-3 RH: 0-0 Tight: 0-3 Gall: 0-0
Aids: Bl: 0-0 Vi: 0-0 Tstrap: 0-0
Best Rating: 81 10/96 Gway 2m soft Hdl

Millstock

12-y-o b m Interrex (CAN)-Millingdale (Tumble Wind (USA))
Miss Natasha J Stallard Miss Natasha J Stallard

Placings:0500FP/U **(0070)**
2001/02: 21^{U}G

	Starts	1st	2nd	3rd	Win & Pl
Chases	1	0	0	0	
Career Total	**7**	**0**	**0**	**0**	

Going: Sf: 0-0 GS: 0-0 Gd: 0-1 GF: - Fm: 0-0
Distance: 2m/2m3: 0-0 2m4-2m7: 0-1 3m+: 0-0
Track: LH: 0-1 RH: 0-0 Tight: 0-1 Gall: 0-0
Aids: Bl: 0-0 Vi: 0-0 Tstrap: 0-0
Best Rating: 62 11/94 Hntg 2m110y good Hdl

Millyhenry

109 **117**

11-y-o b g White Prince (USA)-Milly's Chance (Mljet)
C Tizzard L G Tizzard

Placings:P/4061323034-323P641P2 **(4658)**
2001/02: 24^{3}G, 27^{2}GS, 26^{3}S, 25^{P}G, 24^{6}S, 26^{4}S, 26^{1}HY, 26^{P}G, 24^{2}G

	Starts	1st	2nd	3rd	Win & Pl
Chases	9	1	2	2	9085
Career Total	**20**	**2**	**3**	**5**	**17992**
117	2/02	Plum	3m2f	D(0-115)Ch	HVY	£4252
123	12/00	Tntn	3m	D Ch	SFT	£4348

Total win prize-money £8602

Going: Sf: 1-4 GS: 0-1 Gd: 0-4 GF: - Fm: 0-0
Distance: 2m/2m3: 0-0 2m4-2m7: 0-0 **3m+: 1-9**
Track: LH: 0-1 RH: 0-5 Tight: 0-6 Gall: 0-0
Aids: Bl: 0-1 Vi: 0-0 Tstrap: 0-0
Best Rating: 123 12/00 Tntn 3m soft Ch

Multiple point winner in 2000, he has shown his best form under Rules at Taunton. He won a marathon in the mud at Plumpton in February 2002. An out-and-out stayer, he won on fast ground in his younger days but tends to race on good to soft or softer these days.

Milnstorm (IRE)

(91h) (86h)

6-y-o b g Glacial Storm (USA)-Miss Performance (IRE) (Lancastrian)

Miss H C Knight H R Siegle

Placings:*0-3000* **(4656)**

2001/02: 16^{3}G, 20^{0}S, 16^{0}GS, 19^{0}GS

	Starts	1st	2nd	3rd	Win & Pl
Hurdles	3	0	0	1	371
Chases	1	0	0	0	0
Career Total	**5**	**0**	**0**	**1**	**371**

Going: Sf: 0-1 GS: 0-2 Gd: 0-1 GF: - Fm: 0-0
Distance: 2m/2m3: 0-3 2m4-2m7: 0-1 3m+: 0-0
Track: LH: 0-1 RH: 0-3 Tight: 0-1 Gall: 0-1
Aids: Bl: 0-0 Vi: 0-0 Tstrap: 0-0
Best Rating: 86 11/01 Winc 2m good Hdl

Milton Heights

75f 48f

7-y-o b m Golden Heights-Solnager (Lochnager)

B I Case D W Lloyd Thomas

Placings:*6* **(1753)**

2001/02: 17^{6}G

	Starts	1st	2nd	3rd	Win & Pl
NH Flat	1	0	0	0	0
Career Total	**1**	**0**	**0**	**0**	**0**

Going: Sf: 0-0 GS: 0-0 Gd: 0-1 GF: - Fm: 0-0
Distance: 2m/2m3: 0-1 2m4-2m7: 0-0 3m+: 0-0
Track: LH: 0-0 RH: 0-1 Tight: 0-1 Gall: 0-0
Aids: Bl: 0-0 Vi: 0-0 Tstrap: 0-0
Best Rating: 48 10/01 MRas 2m1f110y good NHF

Minalco

66 22

6-y-o ch m Minster Son-La Millie (Nonoalco (USA))

Miss Lucinda V Russell Mrs M J Schoenberg

Placings:*6* **(0659)**

2001/02: 20^{6}F

	Starts	1st	2nd	3rd	Win & Pl
Hurdles	1	0	0	0	0
Career Total	**1**	**0**	**0**	**0**	**0**

Going: Sf: 0-0 GS: 0-0 Gd: 0-0 GF: - Fm: 0-1
Distance: 2m/2m3: 0-0 2m4-2m7: 0-1 3m+: 0-0
Track: LH: 0-0 RH: 0-1 Tight: 0-0 Gall: 0-0
Aids: Bl: 0-0 Vi: 0-0 Tstrap: 0-0
Best Rating: 22 6/01 Prth 2m4f110y firm Hdl

Mincarlo

90f 105f

6-y-o ch m Karinga Bay-Atlantic View (Crash Course)

G B Balding G B Balding And Tony Geake

Placings:*010* **(4823)**

2001/02: 16^{0}GS, 16^{1}S, 17^{0}G

	Starts	1st	2nd	3rd	Win & Pl
NH Flat	3	1	0	0	2300
Career Total	**3**	**1**	**0**	**0**	**2300**

105 3/02 Towc 2m H NHF SFT £2299

Total win prize-money £2300

Going: Sf: 1-1 GS: 0-1 Gd: 0-1 GF: - Fm: 0-0
Distance: **2m/2m3: 1-3** 2m4-2m7: 0-0 3m+: 0-0
Track: LH: 0-1 **RH: 1-2** Tight: 0-0 Gall: 0-1
Aids: Bl: 0-0 Vi: 0-0 **Tstrap: 1-3**
Best Rating: 105 3/02 Towc 2m soft NHF

Got off the mark at the second attempt in a Towcester bumper. Handles easy ground and has worn a tongue tie.

Mind Bender

6-y-o b g Homo Sapien-Rare Deal (Pitpan)

C C Bealby North Lodge Racing

Placings:*0F* **(1957)**

2001/02: 17^{0}GS, 25^{F}G

	Starts	1st	2nd	3rd	Win & Pl
NH Flat	1	0	0	0	0
Hurdles	1	0	0	0	0
Career Total	**2**	**0**	**0**	**0**	

Going: Sf: 0-0 GS: 0-1 Gd: 0-1 GF: - Fm: 0-0
Distance: 2m/2m3: 0-1 2m4-2m7: 0-0 3m+: 0-1
Track: LH: 0-0 RH: 0-1 Tight: 0-1 Gall: 0-0
Aids: Bl: 0-0 Vi: 0-0 Tstrap: 0-0
Best Rating: 6 10/01 MRas 2m1f110y gd-sft NHF

Mind How You Go (FR)

106f 108f

4-y-o b g Hernando (FR)-Cos I Do (IRE) (Double Schwartz)

J R Best A Fiver In Mind Partnership

Placings:*110* **(4679)**

2001/02: 16^{1}GS, 16^{1}S, 17^{0}G

	Starts	1st	2nd	3rd	Win & Pl
NH Flat	3	2	0	0	10036
Career Total	**3**	**2**	**0**	**0**	**10036**

108 2/02 Wwck 2m A NHF SFT £8307
92 1/02 Catt 2m H NHF G-S £1729

Total win prize-money £10036

Going: Sf: 1-1 GS: 1-1 Gd: 0-1 GF: - Fm: 0-0
Distance: **2m/2m3: 2-3** 2m4-2m7: 0-0 3m+: 0-0
Track: **LH: 2-2** RH: 0-0 **Tight: 1-1** Gall: 0-0
Aids: Bl: 0-0 Vi: 0-0 Tstrap: 0-0
Best Rating: 108 2/02 Wwck 2m soft NHF

Won a bumper on his racecourse debut on easy ground.

Mindanao

109 111

6-y-o b m Most Welcome-Salala (Connaught)

F P Murtagh (Miss J A Camacho 19/10) Bob Slee Toby Noble & J B

Placings:10F023 **(4875)**

2001/02: 16^{1}S, 17^{0}S, 16^{F}GS, 16^{0}HY, 17^{2}GS, 24^{3}G

	Starts	1st	2nd	3rd	Win & Pl
Hurdles	6	1	1	1	4510
Career Total	**6**	**1**	**1**	**1**	**4510**

111 1/02 Newc 2m E Hdl SFT £3052

Total win prize-money £3052

Going: Sf: 1-3 GS: 0-2 Gd: 0-1 GF: - Fm: 0-0
Distance: **2m/2m3: 1-5** 2m4-2m7: 0-0 3m+: 0-1
Track: **LH: 1-4** RH: 0-2 Tight: 0-2 **Gall: 1-1**
Aids: Bl: 0-0 Vi: 0-0 Tstrap: 0-0
Best Rating: 111 1/02 Newc 2m soft Hdl

A middle distance handicapper on the Flat, made a successful winning debut over hurdles at Newcastle in January 2002. Suited by soft ground.

Minden Rose

9-y-o b m Lord Bud-Two Travellers (Deep Run)

Peter Maddison Peter Maddison

Placings:FP **(3653)**

2001/02: 20^{F}GF, 24^{P}S

	Starts	1st	2nd	3rd	Win & Pl
Chases	2	0	0	0	
Career Total	**2**	**0**	**0**	**0**	

Going: Sf: 0-1 GS: 0-0 Gd: 0-0 GF: - Fm: 0-1
Distance: 2m/2m3: 0-0 2m4-2m7: 0-1 3m+: 0-1
Track: LH: 0-1 RH: 0-1 Tight: 0-1 Gall: 0-1
Aids: Bl: 0-0 Vi: 0-0 Tstrap: 0-0
Best Rating:

Mine's A Gin (IRE)

11-y-o gr g Roselier (FR)-Cathedral Street (Boreen Beag)

K Cumings (R J Baker 27/1) R Dunsford

Placings:4-3P **(0425)**

2001/02: 23^{3}G, 21^{P}G

	Starts	1st	2nd	3rd	Win & Pl
Chases	2	0	0	1	245
Career Total	**3**	**0**	**0**	**1**	**383**

Going: Sf: 0-0 GS: 0-0 Gd: 0-2 GF: - Fm: 0-0
Distance: 2m/2m3: 0-0 2m4-2m7: 0-1 3m+: 0-1
Track: LH: 0-0 RH: 0-1 Tight: 0-0 Gall: 0-0
Aids: Bl: 0-0 Vi: 0-0 Tstrap: 0-0
Best Rating: 105 5/01 Extr 2m7f110y good Ch

Winning pointer who holds form well once in the groove. Versatile as regards ground, capable of winning under Rules.

Mine's A Murphys

98f 98f

6-y-o b g Broadsword (USA)-Sparkling Time (USA) (Olden Times)

Miss Venetia Williams M Horton, R Horton, A Good

Placings:*10* **(2887)**

2001/02: 17^{1}S, 16^{0}GS

	Starts	1st	2nd	3rd	Win & Pl
NH Flat	2	1	0	0	1726
Career Total	**2**	**1**	**0**	**0**	**1726**

98 10/01 Bang 2m1f H NHF SFT £1725

Total win prize-money £1726

Going: Sf: 1-1 GS: 0-1 Gd: 0-0 GF: - Fm: 0-0
Distance: **2m/2m3: 1-2** 2m4-2m7: 0-0 3m+: 0-0
Track: **LH: 1-2** RH: 0-0 **Tight: 1-1** Gall: 0-0
Aids: Bl: 0-0 Vi: 0-0 Tstrap: 0-0
Best Rating: 98 10/01 Bang 2m1f soft NHF

A half-brother to Sparkling Cone, he made a winning debut in a bumper at Bangor-on-Dee.

Minella Gold (IRE)

13-y-o b g The Parson-Slieveglagh Queen (Proverb)
Alistair M Brown Mrs June Brown

Placings:312/2U1131203/3F/F556UP/66P2336/34/0U6 **(4892)**
2001/02: 25^{0}GS, 25^{U}HY, 31^{6}G

	Starts	1st	2nd	3rd	Win & Pl
Chases	3	0	0	0	0
Career Total	**32**	**4**	**4**	**7**	**28486**

137	1/96	Navn	2m4f	Hdl	HVY	£3177
129	12/95	Fair	3m	Hdl	G-Y	£6782
119	11/95	Tipp	2m4f	Hdl	GD	£2712
115	4/95	Fair	2m	NHF	GD	£4747

Total win prize-money £17421

Going: Sf: 0-1 GS: 0-1 Gd: 0-1 GF: - Fm: 0-0
Distance: 2m/2m3: 0-0 2m4-2m7: 0-0 3m+: 0-3
Track: LH: 0-1 RH: 0-0 Tight: 0-1 Gall: 0-0
Aids: Bl: 0-0 Vi: 0-0 Tstrap: 0-1
Best Rating: 139 4/96 Punc 3m soft Hdl

Minella Silver (IRE)

9-y-o gr g Roselier (FR)-Mrs Minella (Deep Run)
Mrs Jane Thornton (J D Downes 4/5) Miss Hannah Hinckley

Placings:0/1-1P **(4253)**
2001/02: 24^{1}GS, 26^{P}G

	Starts	1st	2nd	3rd	Win & Pl
Chases	2	1	0	0	1528
Career Total	**4**	**2**	**0**	**0**	**4550**

107	5/01	Bang	3m110y	H Ch	G-S	£1527
124	3/01	Asct	3m110y	H Ch	SFT	£3022

Total win prize-money £4551

Going: Sf: 0-0 GS: 1-1 Gd: 0-1 GF: - Fm: 0-0
Distance: 2m/2m3: 0-0 2m4-2m7: 0-0 **3m+: 1-2**
Track: **LH: 1-2** RH: 0-0 **Tight: 1-1** Gall: 0-1
Aids: Bl: 0-0 Vi: 0-0 Tstrap: 0-0
Best Rating: 124 3/01 Asct 3m110y soft Ch

A multiple winner in hunter chases and points, he is suited by three miles and soft ground.

Minella Storm (IRE)

103(34h) 111

10-y-o b g Strong Gale-Maul-More (Deep Run)
D J Wintle Mrs B Grainger, Mr L Nash & Mr D Bishop

Placings:12462120/F60/20263/243**444-0241** **(1230)**
2001/02: 24^{0}GF, 23^{2}GF, 20^{4}GF, 24^{1}GF

	Starts	1st	2nd	3rd	Win & Pl
Chases	4	1	1	0	5165
Career Total	**26**	**3**	**7**	**2**	**22947**

105	8/01	Uttx	3m	E Ch	G-F	£3584
121	2/98	Navn	2m2f	Hdl	SFT	£2680
113	5/97	Klny	2m1f	NHF	Y-S	£3391

Total win prize-money £9655

Going: Sf: 0-0 GS: 0-0 Gd: 0-0 GF: - Fm: 1-4
Distance: 2m/2m3: 0-0 2m4-2m7: 0-2 **3m+: 1-2**
Track: **LH: 1-4** RH: 0-0 Tight: 0-1 Gall: 0-0
Aids: **Bl: 1-1** Vi: 0-0 Tstrap: 0-0
Best Rating: 124 1/00 Leic 2m4f110y soft Hdl

Ex-Irish, he has shown ability over hurdles and fences in this country.

Miner's Gamble

74 79

5-y-o b g Miners Lamp-Just Rosie (Sula Bula)
A P Jones Aldbourne Racing Group

Placings:0-3PPP **(2936)**
2001/02: 16^{3}G, 16^{P}G, 17^{P}HY, 16^{P}G

	Starts	1st	2nd	3rd	Win & Pl
Hurdles	4	0	0	1	321
Career Total	**5**	**0**	**0**	**1**	**321**

Going: Sf: 0-1 GS: 0-0 Gd: 0-3 GF: - Fm: 0-0
Distance: 2m/2m3: 0-4 2m4-2m7: 0-0 3m+: 0-0
Track: LH: 0-2 RH: 0-2 Tight: 0-2 Gall: 0-1
Aids: Bl: 0-0 Vi: 0-0 Tstrap: 0-1
Best Rating: 79 10/01 Sthl 2m good Hdl

Miners Daughter

5-y-o b m Miners Lamp-Roxie Corina (Impecunious)
R H Alner Miss E A Tucker

Placings:00 **(2596)**
2001/02: 16^{0}S, 17^{0}S

	Starts	1st	2nd	3rd	Win & Pl
NH Flat	2	0	0	0	
Career Total	**2**	**0**	**0**	**0**	

Going: Sf: 0-2 GS: 0-0 Gd: 0-0 GF: - Fm: 0-0
Distance: 2m/2m3: 0-2 2m4-2m7: 0-0 3m+: 0-0
Track: LH: 0-1 RH: 0-0 Tight: 0-1 Gall: 0-0
Aids: Bl: 0-0 Vi: 0-0 Tstrap: 0-0
Best Rating:

Mingling

92 110

5-y-o b g Wolfhound (USA)-On The Tide (Slip Anchor)
C J Mann (M H Tompkins 22/9) A Ball D Bellamy W Harrison-Allan

Placings:04 **(3244)**
2001/02: 16^{0}G, 16^{4}GS

	Starts	1st	2nd	3rd	Win & Pl
Hurdles	2	0	0	0	400
Career Total	**2**	**0**	**0**	**0**	**400**

Going: Sf: 0-0 GS: 0-1 Gd: 0-1 GF: - Fm: 0-0
Distance: 2m/2m3: 0-2 2m4-2m7: 0-0 3m+: 0-0
Track: LH: 0-1 RH: 0-1 Tight: 0-0 Gall: 0-1
Aids: Bl: 0-0 Vi: 0-0 Tstrap: 0-0
Best Rating: 110 1/02 Asct 2m110y gd-sft Hdl

Mini Dare

78f 88f

5-y-o b g Derrylin-Minim (Rymer)
O Sherwood Furrows Ltd

Placings:6 **(4377)**
2001/02: 16^{6}S

	Starts	1st	2nd	3rd	Win & Pl
NH Flat	1	0	0	0	0
Career Total	**1**	**0**	**0**	**0**	**0**

Going: Sf: 0-1 GS: 0-0 Gd: 0-0 GF: - Fm: 0-0
Distance: 2m/2m3: 0-1 2m4-2m7: 0-0 3m+: 0-0
Track: LH: 0-0 RH: 0-1 Tight: 0-0 Gall: 0-0
Aids: Bl: 0-0 Vi: 0-0 Tstrap: 0-0
Best Rating: 80 3/02 Ludl 2m soft NHF

Mini Mandy

97f 116f

6-y-o b m Petoski-Cindie Girl (Orchestra)
R H Buckler R H Buckler

Placings:4-13 **(4823)**
2001/02: 17^{1}GF, 17^{3}G

	Starts	1st	2nd	3rd	Win & Pl
NH Flat	2	1	0	1	4555
Career Total	**3**	**1**	**0**	**1**	**4555**

105	11/01	Extr	2m1f	H NHF	G-F	£1767

Total win prize-money £1768

Going: Sf: 0-0 GS: 0-0 Gd: 0-1 GF: - Fm: 1-1
Distance: **2m/2m3: 1-2** 2m4-2m7: 0-0 3m+: 0-0
Track: LH: 0-1 **RH: 1-1** Tight: 0-0 Gall: 0-1
Aids: Bl: 0-0 Vi: 0-0 Tstrap: 0-0
Best Rating: 116 4/02 Chel 2m1f good NHF

Confirmed the promise of her bumper debut, winning next time out on a sound surface.

Mini Sensation (IRE)

109(61h) 150

9-y-o b g Be My Native (USA)-Minorettes Girl (Strong Gale)
J J O'Neill J P McManus

Placings:361P/0210/11-11203P2 **(4299)**
2001/02: 25^{1}G, 24^{1}GS, 24^{2}G, 20^{0}S, 20^{3}GS, 24^{P}GS, 34^{2}HY

	Starts	1st	2nd	3rd	Win & Pl
Chases	7	2	2	1	31776
Career Total	**17**	**6**	**3**	**2**	**59732**

150	11/01	Bang	3m110y	D Ch	G-S	£5537
123	11/01	Weth	3m1f	D Ch	GD	£4134
140	11/00	Hayd	2m4f	B(0-140)HHdl	SFT	£10257
140	10/00	Weth	2m4f110y	C(0-130)HHdl	SFT	£7085
116	2/00	Gowr	2m4f	(0-130)HHdl	Y-S	£5520
105	2/99	Gowr	2m	Hdl	SH	£3683

Total win prize-money £36216

Going: Sf: 0-2 GS: 1-3 Gd: 1-2 GF: - Fm: 0-0
Distance: 2m/2m3: 0-0 2m4-2m7: 0-2 **3m+: 2-5**
Track: **LH: 2-4** RH: 0-3 **Tight: 1-1** Gall: 0-1
Aids: Bl: 0-0 Vi: 0-0 Tstrap: 0-0
Best Rating: 150 11/01 Bang 3m110y gd-sft Ch

Won two hurdles races in Ireland. Now with Jonjo O'Neill and won twice over hurdles and twice over fences in the winter of 2001. Finished second in the Midlands National at Uttoxeter. Stays well. Suited by soft ground.

Miniatura (IRE)

106 108

7-y-o ch g Accordion-Dalana's Pet Vii (Damsire Unregistered)
C J Mann J E Brown, N Edgley & R Lucas

Placings:40/34322-331P3 **(4240)**
2001/02: 21^{3}G, 19^{3}G, 25^{1}G, 24^{P}G, 26^{3}GF

	Starts	1st	2nd	3rd	Win & Pl
Hurdles	5	1	0	3	4639
Career Total	**12**	**1**	**2**	**5**	**7818**

108	11/01	Wwck	3m1f	D Hdl	GD	£3423

Total win prize-money £3423

Going: Sf: 0-0 GS: 0-0 Gd: 1-4 GF: - Fm: 0-1
Distance: 2m/2m3: 0-0 2m4-2m7: 0-2 **3m+: 1-3**
Track: LH: 0-1 RH: 0-3 Tight: 0-2 Gall: 0-1
Aids: Bl: 0-0 Vi: 0-0 Tstrap: 0-0
Best Rating: 108 3/02 Hntg 3m2f gd-fm Hdl

He relished the extended three miles when getting off the mark over hurdles at Warwick in November and should find further success over that sort of trip.

Minibelle

98 92

10-y-o br m Macmillion-Pokey's Belle (Uncle Pokey)
D L Williams Miss B W Palmer

Placings:*566P0/604P46/***43514UP5** **(1379)**
2001/02: 20^{4}GF, 24^{3}GF, 21^{5}G, 27^{1}GF, 26^{4}G, 26^{U}GF, 27^{P}GF, 25^{5}GF

	Starts	1st	2nd	3rd	Win & Pl
Chases	8	1	0	1	4543
Career Total	**19**	**1**	**0**	**1**	**4543**

92	7/01	Sedg	3m3f	D Ch	G-F	£3802

Total win prize-money £3803

Going: Sf: 0-0 GS: 0-0 Gd: 0-2 GF: - Fm: 1-6
Distance: 2m/2m3: 0-0 2m4-2m7: 0-2 **3m+: 1-6**
Track: **LH: 1-5** RH: 0-1 **Tight: 1-7** Gall: 0-0
Aids: Bl: 0-0 Vi: 0-0 Tstrap: 0-0
Best Rating: 92 7/01 Sedg 3m3f gd-fm Ch

Minioso

88(96h) 115

8-y-o b m Teenoso (USA)-Four M'S (Majestic Maharaj)
Mrs S J Smith T And B Benson

Placings:*044341/152F1-5F* **(1928)**
2001/02: 20^{5}G, 22^{F}G

	Starts	1st	2nd	3rd	Win & Pl
Chases	2	0	0	0	0
Career Total	**13**	**3**	**1**	**1**	**13110**

115	4/01	MRas	2m4f	D Ch	HVY	£5824
108	5/00	Kels	2m6f110y	D(0-125)HHdl	GD	£3152
102	3/00	Kels	2m6f110y	E Hdl	G-S	£2044

Total win prize-money £11021

Going: Sf: 0-0 GS: 0-0 Gd: 0-2 GF: - Fm: 0-0
Distance: 2m/2m3: 0-0 2m4-2m7: 0-2 3m+: 0-0
Track: LH: 0-2 RH: 0-0 Tight: 0-1 Gall: 0-0
Aids: Bl: 0-0 Vi: 0-0 Tstrap: 0-0
Best Rating: 120 2/01 Catt 2m3f soft Ch

Minister For Fun (IRE)

14-y-o b g The Parson-Little Credit (Little Buskins)
M Sheppard R G Jenkins

Placings:36/04161F/22221P4F/20P/14/50U/05 (0474)
2001/02: 25^{0}G, 22^{5}G

	Starts	1st	2nd	3rd	Win & Pl
Chases	2	0	0	0	0
Career Total	**26**	**4**	**5**	**1**	**26918**

108	3/98	Sand	2m4f110y	H Ch	G-S	£2788
112	8/94	Rosc	2m4f	Hdl	GD	£2609
115	4/94	Fair	2m4f	HCh	SFT	£3942
101	12/93	Thur	3m	(0-120)Ch	SFT	£2411

Total win prize-money £11753

Going: Sf: 0-0 GS: 0-0 Gd: 0-2 GF: - Fm: 0-0
Distance: 2m/2m3: 0-0 2m4-2m7: 0-1 3m+: 0-1
Track: LH: 0-1 RH: 0-1 Tight: 0-1 Gall: 0-0
Aids: Bl: 0-0 Vi: 0-0 Tstrap: 0-0
Best Rating: 127 5/96 Wxfd 2m4f good Ch

Minivet

(112h) (117h)111

7-y-o b g Midyan (USA)-Bronzewing (Beldale Flutter (USA))
T D Easterby The Pertemps Professionals

Placings:21211101/PC0-P56F3 **(1582)**
2001/02: 20^{P}S, 17^{5}GS, 16^{6}GF, 21^{F}GF, 22^{3}GS

	Starts	1st	2nd	3rd	Win & Pl
Hurdles	3	0	0	0	0
Chases	2	0	0	1	578
Career Total	**16**	**5**	**2**	**1**	**21153**

132	4/00	Ayr	2m	C Hdl	GD	£5135
134	1/00	Donc	2m110y	C(0-135)HHdl	GD	£5850
118	1/00	Kels	2m110y	D Hdl	GD	£3201
118	1/00	Muss	2m	E Hdl	GD	£2415
123	12/99	Donc	2m110y	E Hdl	G-S	£1976

Total win prize-money £18578

Going: Sf: 0-1 GS: 0-2 Gd: 0-0 GF: - Fm: 0-2
Distance: 2m/2m3: 0-2 2m4-2m7: 0-3 3m+: 0-0
Track: LH: 0-3 RH: 0-1 Tight: 0-3 Gall: 0-0
Aids: Bl: 0-0 Vi: 0-0 Tstrap: 0-0
Best Rating: 134 1/00 Donc 2m110y good Hdl

Formerly decent hurdler, he lacks the size required for fences.

Minsgill Glen

83f 79f

6-y-o b m Minster Son-Gilmanscleuch (IRE) (Mandalus)
Mrs J K M Oliver Miss J S Peat

Placings:*000* **(4860)**
2001/02: 17^{0}G, 17^{0}G, 16^{0}G

	Starts	1st	2nd	3rd	Win & Pl
NH Flat	3	0	0	0	
Career Total	**3**	**0**	**0**	**0**	

Going: Sf: 0-0 GS: 0-0 Gd: 0-3 GF: - Fm: 0-0
Distance: 2m/2m3: 0-3 2m4-2m7: 0-0 3m+: 0-0
Track: LH: 0-0 RH: 0-2 Tight: 0-0 Gall: 0-0
Aids: Bl: 0-0 Vi: 0-0 Tstrap: 0-0
Best Rating: 79 4/02 Carl 2m1f good NHF

Minster Fair

58f 88f

4-y-o b f Minster Son-Fair Echo (Quality Fair)
A C Whillans E Waugh

Placings:*04* **(4145)**
2001/02: 16^{0}S, 16^{4}HY

	Starts	1st	2nd	3rd	Win & Pl
NH Flat	2	0	0	0	0
Career Total	**2**	**0**	**0**	**0**	**0**

Going: Sf: 0-2 GS: 0-0 Gd: 0-0 GF: - Fm: 0-0
Distance: 2m/2m3: 0-2 2m4-2m7: 0-0 3m+: 0-0
Track: LH: 0-1 RH: 0-1 Tight: 0-1 Gall: 0-0
Aids: Bl: 0-0 Vi: 0-0 Tstrap: 0-0
Best Rating: 88 3/02 Ayr 2m heavy NHF

Lacked a turn of foot on first two bumper starts.

Minster Glory

109 149

11-y-o b g Minster Son-Rapid Glory (Hittite Glory)
M W Easterby Mrs P A H Hartley

Placings:002F/1/331U554/12223232/311F211/20106-42112 (2905)
2001/02: 16^{4}G, 16^{2}GS, 17^{1}G, 17^{1}GS, 16^{2}GS

	Starts	1st	2nd	3rd	Win & Pl
Chases	5	2	2	0	14643
Career Total	**37**	**10**	**10**	**5**	**49675**

145	11/01	MRas	2m1f110y	D(0-120)HCh	G-S	£4498
131	11/01	Kels	2m1f	E(0-115)HCh	GD	£3770
135	12/00	Muss	2m	E(0-115)HCh	GD	£2866
129	3/00	Newc	2m110y	E(0-115)HCh	GD	£3074
125	2/00	Catt	2m	E(0-115)HCh	GD	£3503
122	1/00	Newc	2m110y	E(0-115)HCh	SFT	£2983
121	12/99	Catt	2m	F(0-105)HCh	G-F	£2862
105	11/98	Newc	2m110y	E(0-115)HCh	GD	£2762
97	12/97	Catt	2m	E Ch	GD	£3113
83	5/95	Weth	2m	E Hdl	G-F	£2635

Total win prize-money £32071

Going: Sf: 0-0 GS: 1-3 Gd: 1-2 GF: - Fm: 0-0
Distance: **2m/2m3: 2-5** 2m4-2m7: 0-0 3m+: 0-0
Track: LH: 1-3 RH: 1-2 **Tight: 2-2** Gall: 0-0
Aids: Bl: 0-0 Vi: 0-0 Tstrap: 0-0
Best Rating: 149 12/01 Weth 2m gd-sft Ch

Progressive handicap chaser, he won consecutive races at Kelso and Market Rasen in November 2001 before running a good second in the Grade Two Castleford Chase at Wetherby. Best around two miles on good or slightly easier ground, he races prominently.

Minster Madam

86 43

8-y-o ch m Minster Son-Spring Garden (Silly Prices)
J Wade John Wade

Placings:*00-006P* **(2349)**
2001/02: 17^{0}GF, 17^{0}GF, 17^{6}G, 19^{P}GS

	Starts	1st	2nd	3rd	Win & Pl
Hurdles	4	0	0	0	0
Career Total	**6**	**0**	**0**	**0**	**0**

Going: Sf: 0-0 GS: 0-1 Gd: 0-1 GF: - Fm: 0-2
Distance: 2m/2m3: 0-3 2m4-2m7: 0-1 3m+: 0-0
Track: LH: 0-3 RH: 0-1 Tight: 0-4 Gall: 0-0
Aids: Bl: 0-0 Vi: 0-0 Tstrap: 0-0
Best Rating: 77 12/00 Muss 2m good NHF

Minster Sunshine

110 116

8-y-o ch g Minster Son-Own Free Will (Nicholas Bill)
K C Bailey J H King & Mrs S C Renshaw

Placings:*35/0-63542* **(4311)**
2001/02: 20^{6}G, 21^{3}G, 24^{5}GS, 20^{4}GS, 24^{2}HY

	Starts	1st	2nd	3rd	Win & Pl
Chases	5	0	1	1	1977
Career Total	**8**	**0**	**1**	**2**	**2255**

Going: Sf: 0-1 GS: 0-2 Gd: 0-2 GF: - Fm: 0-0
Distance: 2m/2m3: 0-0 2m4-2m7: 0-3 3m+: 0-2
Track: LH: 0-1 RH: 0-4 Tight: 0-2 Gall: 0-3
Aids: Bl: 0-0 Vi: 0-0 Tstrap: 0-0
Best Rating: 116 12/01 Folk 2m5f good Ch

Modest placed form in novice chases. Possibly best at short of three miles.

Minster York

107(93h) (82h)125+

8-y-o ch g Minster Son-Another Treat (Derring Do)
A Crook The Adbrokes Partnership

Placings:0035000P/45PP-32614343043 **(4895)**
2001/02: 16^{3}GF, 16^{2}GF, 17^{6}G, 16^{1}G, 16^{4}G, 16^{3}G, 16^{4}GS, 16^{3}S, 16^{0}HY, 17^{4}GF, 20^{3}G

	Starts	1st	2nd	3rd	Win & Pl
Hurdles	3	0	0	1	228
Chases	8	1	1	3	6916
Career Total	**23**	**1**	**1**	**5**	**7532**

100	9/01	Sedg	2m110y	E Ch	GD	£3435

Total win prize-money £3435

Going: Sf: 0-2 GS: 0-1 Gd: 1-5 GF: - Fm: 0-3
Distance: **2m/2m3: 1-10** 2m4-2m7: 0-1 3m+: 0-0
Track: **LH: 1-8** RH: 0-3 **Tight: 1-8** Gall: 0-1
Aids: Bl: 0-0 Vi: 0-0 Tstrap: 0-0
Best Rating: **105** 4/02 Kels 2m1f gd-fm Ch

Suited by two miles and a sound surface, he likes to dominate.

Minstrel Fair (IRE)

87f 87f

5-y-o b g Roselier (FR)-Minstrel Park (Black Minstrel)
Mrs S J Smith Trevor Hemmings

Placings:065 **(4750)**
2001/02: 17^{0}GS, 16^{6}GS, 17^{5}G

	Starts	1st	2nd	3rd	Win & Pl
NH Flat	3	0	0	0	0
Career Total	**3**	**0**	**0**	**0**	**0**

Going: Sf: 0-0 GS: 0-2 Gd: 0-1 GF: - Fm: 0-0
Distance: 2m/2m3: 0-3 2m4-2m7: 0-0 3m+: 0-0
Track: LH: 0-1 RH: 0-1 Tight: 0-1 Gall: 0-0
Aids: Bl: 0-0 Vi: 0-0 Tstrap: 0-0
Best Rating: **87** 4/02 Carl 2m1f good NHF

Minstrel Gem

58 22

5-y-o b g Mon Tresor-My Serenade (USA) (Sensitive Prince (USA))
B D Leavy D B Holmes

Placings:0 **(0777)**
2001/02: 16^{0}GF

	Starts	1st	2nd	3rd	Win & Pl
Hurdles	1	0	0	0	
Career Total	**1**	**0**	**0**	**0**	

Going: Sf: 0-0 GS: 0-0 Gd: 0-0 GF: - Fm: 0-1
Distance: 2m/2m3: 0-1 2m4-2m7: 0-0 3m+: 0-0
Track: LH: 0-1 RH: 0-0 Tight: 0-0 Gall: 0-0
Aids: Bl: 0-0 Vi: 0-0 Tstrap: 0-0
Best Rating: **22** 6/01 Worc 2m gd-fm Hdl

Minus Four (IRE)

4-y-o b c Standiford (USA)-Minibar (Dominion)
L A Dace Noel Monaghan

Placings:FF **(1956)**
2001/02: 17^{F}F, 16^{F}G

	Starts	1st	2nd	3rd	Win & Pl
Hurdles	2	0	0	0	
Career Total	**2**	**0**	**0**	**0**	

Going: Sf: 0-0 GS: 0-0 Gd: 0-1 GF: - Fm: 0-1
Distance: 2m/2m3: 0-2 2m4-2m7: 0-0 3m+: 0-0
Track: LH: 0-1 RH: 0-1 Tight: 0-1 Gall: 0-0
Aids: Bl: 0-0 Vi: 0-0 Tstrap: 0-0
Best Rating:

Minusla

97 68

8-y-o ch m Minster Son-Macusla (Lighter)
Mrs J O Barr J O Barr

Placings:50/601/P660 **(1351)**
2001/02: 19^{P}GF, 27^{6}GF, 27^{6}GF, 21^{0}GF

	Starts	1st	2nd	3rd	Win & Pl
Hurdles	4	0	0	0	0
Career Total	**9**	**1**	**0**	**0**	**1945**

84	3/00	Sedg	3m3f110y	F Hdl	G-F	£1944

Total win prize-money £1945

Going: Sf: 0-0 GS: 0-0 Gd: 0-0 GF: - Fm: 0-4
Distance: 2m/2m3: 0-0 2m4-2m7: 0-2 3m+: 0-2
Track: LH: 0-3 RH: 0-1 Tight: 0-4 Gall: 0-0
Aids: Bl: 0-0 Vi: 0-0 Tstrap: 0-0
Best Rating: **84** 3/00 Sedg 3m3f110y gd-fm Hdl

Miracle Island

100 122

7-y-o b g Jupiter Island-Running Game (Run The Gantlet (USA))
K R Burke Champagne Racing

Placings:F3116F312414P0/00PP-41135 **(1501)**
2001/02: 17^{4}GS, 18^{1}GF, 16^{1}GF, 17^{3}S, 17^{5}G

	Starts	1st	2nd	3rd	Win & Pl
Hurdles	5	2	0	1	8117
Career Total	**23**	**6**	**1**	**3**	**22087**

122	5/01	Newc	2m	D(0-120)HHdl	G-F	£3978
116	5/01	Font	2m2f110y	F Hdl	G-F	£2572
124	2/00	Font	2m2f110y	E(0-115)HHdl	SFT	£5395
124	12/99	Folk	2m1f110y	F(0-110)HHdl	SFT	£1759
109	9/99	NAbb	2m1f	E Hdl	G-F	£2305
106	8/99	Worc	2m	F Hdl	SFT	£2087

Total win prize-money £18098

Going: Sf: 0-1 GS: 0-1 Gd: 0-1 GF: - Fm: 2-2
Distance: **2m/2m3: 2-5** 2m4-2m7: 0-0 3m+: 0-0
Track: **LH: 2-3** RH: 0-1 Tight: 1-3 Gall: 1-1
Aids: Bl: 0-0 Vi: 0-0 **Tstrap: 2-4**
Best Rating: **124** 2/00 Font 2m2f110y soft Hdl

Miracle Kid (USA)

108 111

8-y-o b g Red Ransom (USA)-Fan Mail (USA) (Zen (USA))
N J Henderson Elite Racing Club

Placings:333/234-04P21310 **(2167)**
2001/02: 17^{0}G, 19^{4}G, 17^{P}GS, 16^{2}GF, 17^{1}GF, 17^{3}F, 16^{1}G, 16^{0}G

	Starts	1st	2nd	3rd	Win & Pl
Hurdles	8	2	1	1	7544
Career Total	**14**	**2**	**2**	**5**	**11041**

111	11/01	Wwck	2m	D(0-125)HHdl	GD	£3339
102	10/01	Extr	2m1f	E Hdl	G-F	£2765

Total win prize-money £6104

Going: Sf: 0-0 GS: 0-1 Gd: 1-4 GF: - Fm: 1-3
Distance: **2m/2m3: 2-7** 2m4-2m7: 0-1 3m+: 0-0
Track: LH: 1-4 RH: 1-4 Tight: 0-3 Gall: 0-0
Aids: Bl: 0-0 Vi: 0-0 Tstrap: 0-0
Best Rating: **111** 11/01 Wwck 2m good Hdl

He has had his problems, but returned to form in the autumn of 2001 on fast ground with wins at Exeter and Warwick. Suited by positive tactics.

Miraggio

24

6-y-o b g Alhijaz-Doppio (Dublin Taxi)
M J Wilkinson C O King

Placings:0P/0-P **(0010)**
2001/02: 25^{P}S

	Starts	1st	2nd	3rd	Win & Pl
Hurdles	1	0	0	0	
Career Total	**4**	**0**	**0**	**0**	

Going: Sf: 0-1 GS: 0-0 Gd: 0-0 GF: - Fm: 0-0
Distance: 2m/2m3: 0-0 2m4-2m7: 0-0 3m+: 0-1
Track: LH: 0-0 RH: 0-0 Tight: 0-0 Gall: 0-0
Aids: Bl: 0-0 Vi: 0-0 Tstrap: 0-0
Best Rating: **24** 4/01 Hrfd 2m1f good Hdl

Mirjan (IRE)

111 135

6-y-o b g Tenby-Mirana (IRE) (Ela-Mana-Mou)
L Lungo Mrs Barbara Lungo

Placings:63101/1406500-03100102 **(4834)**
2001/02: 16^{0}G, 24^{3}GS, 20^{1}F, 20^{0}G, 20^{0}G, 20^{1}GS, 16^{0}S, 22^{2}G

	Starts	1st	2nd	3rd	Win & Pl
Hurdles	8	2	1	1	11317
Career Total	**20**	**5**	**1**	**2**	**45904**

135	11/01	Newc	2m4f	D(0-125)HHdl	G-S	£5018
131	5/01	Weth	2m4f110y	D(0-120)HHdl	FRM	£3620
133	5/00	Hayd	2m	A HHdl	GD	£24000
128	4/00	Chel	2m1f	B Hdl	SFT	£6760
109	3/00	Kels	2m110y	E Hdl	G-S	£2478

Total win prize-money £41877

Going: Sf: 0-1 GS: 1-2 Gd: 0-4 GF: - Fm: 1-1
Distance: 2m/2m3: 0-2 **2m4-2m7: 2-5** 3m+: 0-1
Track: **LH: 2-6** RH: 0-2 Tight: 0-1 **Gall: 1-1**
Aids: **Bl: 2-4** Vi: 0-1 Tstrap: 0-0
Best Rating: **135** 4/02 Ayr 2m6f good Hdl

Handicap hurdler. He is best around two and a half miles nowadays. Has won on fast ground and soft.

Mirmillon (FR)

7-y-o b g Cadoudal (FR)-Princesse Lane (FR) (Tip Moss (FR))
M C Pipe (B Secly 29/9) P A Deal

Placings:06/1P10F/P0021/1205005-F0RRPP **(3265)**
2001/02: 21^{F}HY, 22^{0}S, 21^{R}VS, 16^{R}GS, 19^{P}GS, 25^{P}S

	Starts	1st	2nd	3rd	Win & Pl
Hurdles	2	0	0	0	0
Chases	4	0	0	0	0
Career Total	**25**	**4**	**2**	**0**	**122417**

5/00	Autl	2m1f110y	Ch	VS	£10567
4/00	Autl	2m4f110y	HHdl	HVY	£43228
6/98	Autl	2m1f110y	Hdl	SFT	£30303
5/98	Autl	2m1f110y	Hdl	VS	£10101

Total win prize-money £94199

Going: Sf: 0-3 GS: 0-2 Gd: 0-0 GF: - Fm: 0-0
Distance: 2m/2m3: 0-2 2m4-2m7: 0-3 3m+: 0-1
Track: LH: 0-1 RH: 0-1 Tight: 0-0 Gall: 0-1
Aids: Bl: 0-1 Vi: 0-0 Tstrap: 0-0
Best Rating: mfy

A French import, suited by soft ground. Refused on his last run in France and on his British debut.

Miros (GER)

106 **151**

5-y-o ch g Kamiros Ii-Miss Page (Gorytus (USA))
J J O'Neill P Byrne

Placings:P111 **(3263)**
2001/02: 16^{P}GS, 16^{1}S, 16^{1}S, 16^{1}S

	Starts	1st	2nd	3rd	Win & Pl
Hurdles	4	3	0	0	23258
Career Total	**4**	**3**	**0**	**0**	**23258**

151	1/02	Wwck	2m	A Hdl	SFT	£15960
120	12/01	Hayd	2m	D Hdl	SFT	£3657
100	11/01	Hayd	2m	D Hdl	SFT	£3640

Total win prize-money £23258

Going: Sf: 3-3 GS: 0-1 Gd: 0-0 GF: - Fm: 0-0
Distance: **2m/2m3: 3-4** 2m4-2m7: 0-0 3m+: 0-0
Track: **LH: 3-4** RH: 0-0 Tight: 0-1 Gall: 0-0
Aids: Bl: 0-0 Vi: 0-0 Tstrap: 0-0
Best Rating: 151 1/02 Wwck 2m soft Hdl

A winner on the Flat in Germany, he scored a double over hurdles at Haydock towards the end of 2001 and followed up impressively in a Grade One at Warwick. Sadly, he suffered a fatal heart attack on the gallops in February 2002.

Misalliance

98 **71**

7-y-o ch m Elmaamul (USA)-Cabaret Artiste (Shareef Dancer (USA))
M E Sowersby T J Stubbins

Placings:00P36035005/55P064-10P0005 **(4257)**
2001/02: 16^{1}S, 19^{0}GF, 21^{P}S, 17^{0}S, 16^{0}S, 17^{0}S, 16^{5}HY

	Starts	1st	2nd	3rd	Win & Pl
Hurdles	7	1	0	0	1894
Career Total	**24**	**1**	**0**	**2**	**2405**

71	5/01	Hexm	2m	G Hdl	SFT	£1893

Total win prize-money £1894

Going: Sf: 1-6 GS: 0-0 Gd: 0-0 GF: - Fm: 0-1
Distance: **2m/2m3: 1-5** 2m4-2m7: 0-2 3m+: 0-0
Track: **LH: 1-6** RH: 0-1 Tight: 0-4 Gall: 0-0
Aids: Bl: 0-0 Vi: 0-0 **Tstrap: 1-7**
Best Rating: 80 2/00 Sedg 2m1f gd-sft Hdl

Misconduct

108 **119**

8-y-o gr m Risk Me (FR)-Grey Cree (Creetown)
J G Portman The Playmates

Placings:0061110/2164/00512354P164-43155 **(2666)**
2001/02: 17^{4}S, 16^{3}G, 16^{1}GS, 16^{5}G, 17^{5}G

	Starts	1st	2nd	3rd	Win & Pl
Hurdles	5	1	0	1	9568
Career Total	**28**	**7**	**2**	**2**	**35709**

117	11/01	Sand	2m110y	C(0-130)HHdl	G-S	£8463
117	2/01	Asct	2m110y	D(0-120)HHdl	HVY	£4212
112	11/00	Kemp	2m	F(0-110)HHdl	SFT	£2863
116	2/00	Asct	2m110y	D(0-120)HHdl	SFT	£3386
110	3/99	Fknm	2m	D(0-120)HHdl	GD	£5279
106	3/99	Catt	2m	F(0-95)HHdl	SFT	£2374
103	2/99	Folk	2m1f110y	F(0-95)HHdl	G-S	£2107

Total win prize-money £28686

Going: Sf: 0-1 GS: 1-1 Gd: 0-3 GF: - Fm: 0-0
Distance: **2m/2m3: 1-5** 2m4-2m7: 0-0 3m+: 0-0
Track: LH: 0-2 **RH: 1-3** Tight: 0-0 Gall: 0-1
Aids: Bl: 0-0 Vi: 0-0 Tstrap: 0-0
Best Rating: 119 12/01 Chel 2m1f good Hdl

Suited by two miles and cut in the ground, she has been successful on the flat and over hurdles.

Mishead

100 **87**

4-y-o ch g Unfuwain (USA)-Green Jannat (USA) (Alydar (USA))
M C Chapman N Malbon

Placings:30446 **(4330)**
2001/02: 17^{3}S, 17^{0}GS, 17^{4}GS, 17^{4}GS, 17^{6}S

	Starts	1st	2nd	3rd	Win & Pl
Hurdles	5	0	0	1	662
Career Total	**5**	**0**	**0**	**1**	**662**

Going: Sf: 0-2 GS: 0-3 Gd: 0-0 GF: - Fm: 0-0
Distance: 2m/2m3: 0-5 2m4-2m7: 0-0 3m+: 0-0
Track: LH: 0-1 RH: 0-4 Tight: 0-5 Gall: 0-0
Aids: Bl: 0-0 Vi: 0-0 Tstrap: 0-0
Best Rating: 86 3/02 MRas 2m1f110y gd-sft Hdl

Plating-class juvenile hurdler.

Miss Alicia (IRE)

74 **54**

5-y-o br m Un Desperado (FR)-Theme Music (Tudor Music)
N A Twiston-Davies The Lawnmower Gang

Placings:0-0P **(0431)**
2001/02: 16^{0}GF, 17^{P}GF

	Starts	1st	2nd	3rd	Win & Pl
Hurdles	2	0	0	0	
Career Total	**3**	**0**	**0**	**0**	

Going: Sf: 0-0 GS: 0-0 Gd: 0-0 GF: - Fm: 0-2
Distance: 2m/2m3: 0-2 2m4-2m7: 0-0 3m+: 0-0
Track: LH: 0-0 RH: 0-2 Tight: 0-1 Gall: 0-0
Aids: Bl: 0-0 Vi: 0-0 Tstrap: 0-0
Best Rating: 84 4/01 Tntn 2m1f gd-fm NHF

Miss All Alone

88 **67**

7-y-o ch m Crofthall-Uninvited (De My Guest (USA))
Mrs P Sly (J A Glover 21/5) Countrywide Classics Limited

Placings:3/1465-0P50 **(4853)**
2001/02: 16^{0}GF, 16^{P}GF, 16^{5}S, 16^{0}G

	Starts	1st	2nd	3rd	Win & Pl
Hurdles	4	0	0	0	0
Career Total	**9**	**1**	**0**	**1**	**3322**

100	12/00	Leic	2m	E Hdl	HVY	£2863

Total win prize-money £2863

Going: Sf: 0-1 GS: 0-0 Gd: 0-1 GF: - Fm: 0-2
Distance: 2m/2m3: 0-4 2m4-2m7: 0-0 3m+: 0-0
Track: LH: 0-2 RH: 0-2 Tight: 0-2 Gall: 0-1
Aids: Bl: 0-1 Vi: 0-0 Tstrap: 0-0
Best Rating: 106 1/01 Leic 2m heavy Hdl

Moderate hurdler, best at two miles, suited by testing ground.

Miss Arzanni

96 **90**

7-y-o b m Arzanni-Mangro (Mandamus)
V R A Dartnall J G K Borrett

Placings:6054-624 **(0906)**
2001/02: 16^{6}GF, 22^{2}GF, 20^{4}G

	Starts	1st	2nd	3rd	Win & Pl
Hurdles	3	0	1	0	870
Career Total	**7**	**0**	**1**	**0**	**870**

Going: Sf: 0-0 GS: 0-0 Gd: 0-1 GF: - Fm: 0-2
Distance: 2m/2m3: 0-1 2m4-2m7: 0-2 3m+: 0-0
Track: LH: 0-2 RH: 0-1 Tight: 0-1 Gall: 0-0
Aids: Bl: 0-0 Vi: 0-0 Tstrap: 0-0
Best Rating: 90 5/01 NAbb 2m6f gd-fm Hdl

Miss B Bennett (IRE)

85(62c) **41**

8-y-o b m Denel (FR)-Miss Bobby Bennett (King's Lake (USA))
Miss K M George P J Soward

Placings:0/541/P22005/4051312**FF**-05**P**00 **(1806)**
2001/02: 27^{0}GF, 22^{5}G, 20^{P}GS, 24^{0}GS, 24^{0}GF

	Starts	1st	2nd	3rd	Win & Pl
Hurdles	4	0	0	0	0
Chases	1	0	0	0	0
Career Total	**24**	**3**	**3**	**1**	**10200**

91	8/00	NAbb	2m6f	G Hdl	G-F	£1806
108	8/00	NAbb	2m6f	F(0-105)HHdl	G-F	£2730
114	4/99	Tntn	3m110y	E Hdl	G-S	£2504

Total win prize-money £7040

Going: Sf: 0-0 GS: 0-2 Gd: 0-1 GF: - Fm: 0-2
Distance: 2m/2m3: 0-0 2m4-2m7: 0-2 3m+: 0-3
Track: LH: 0-3 RH: 0-2 Tight: 0-4 Gall: 0-0
Aids: Bl: 0-0 Vi: 0-1 Tstrap: 0-1
Best Rating: 114 4/99 Tntn 3m110y gd-sft Hdl

Miss Blue Ice

4-y-o b f Michelozzo (USA)-Miss Vaigly Blue (Vaigly Great)
P Wegmann Mrs P J Campbell

Placings:P **(4910)**
2001/02: 17^{P}G

	Starts	1st	2nd	3rd	Win & Pl
NH Flat	1	0	0	0	
Career Total	**1**	**0**	**0**	**0**	

Going: Sf: 0-0 GS: 0-0 Gd: 0-1 GF: - Fm: 0-0
Distance: 2m/2m3: 0-1 2m4-2m7: 0-0 3m+: 0-0
Track: LH: 0-0 RH: 0-1 Tight: 0-1 Gall: 0-0
Aids: Bl: 0-0 Vi: 0-0 Tstrap: 0-0
Best Rating:

Miss Bubbles (IRE)

8-y-o b m Conquering Hero (USA)-Alitos Choice (Baptism)
F P Murtagh Peter Diggle

Placings:P **(3822)**
2001/02: 21^{P}S

	Starts	1st	2nd	3rd	Win & Pl
Chases	1	0	0	0	
Career Total	**1**	**0**	**0**	**0**	

Going: Sf: 0-1 GS: 0-0 Gd: 0-0 GF: - Fm: 0-0
Distance: 2m/2m3: 0-0 2m4-2m7: 0-1 3m+: 0-0
Track: LH: 0-1 RH: 0-0 Tight: 0-1 Gall: 0-0
Aids: Bl: 0-0 Vi: 0-0 Tstrap: 0-0

Best Rating:

Modest pointer.

Miss Cash

86 **24**

5-y-o b m Rock Hopper-Miss Cashtal (IRE) (Ballacashtal (CAN))
M E Sowersby R D Seldon

Placings:4PP-PP (1724)
2001/02: 17PG, 25PG

	Starts	1st	2nd	3rd	Win & Pl
Hurdles	2	0	0	0	
Career Total	**5**	**0**	**0**	**0**	**244**

Going: Sf: 0-0 GS: 0-0 Gd: 0-2 GF: - Fm: 0-0
Distance: 2m/2m3: 0-1 2m4-2m7: 0-0 3m+: 0-1
Track: LH: 0-2 RH: 0-0 Tight: 0-1 Gall: 0-0
Aids: Bl: 0-0 Vi: 0-0 Tstrap: 0-0
Best Rating: 70 9/00 Bang 2m1f gd-fm Hdl

Miss Chloe (IRE)

7-y-o b m King's Ride-Audley Lady (Deep Run)
C J Drewe Trip Syndicate

Placings:*0/0*P-P (0124)
2001/02: 24PF

	Starts	1st	2nd	3rd	Win & Pl
Hurdles	1	0	0	0	
Career Total	**4**	**0**	**0**	**0**	

Going: Sf: 0-0 GS: 0-0 Gd: 0-0 GF: - Fm: 0-1
Distance: 2m/2m3: 0-0 2m4-2m7: 0-0 3m+: 0-1
Track: LH: 0-0 RH: 0-1 Tight: 0-1 Gall: 0-0
Aids: Bl: 0-0 Vi: 0-0 Tstrap: 0-0
Best Rating: 51 4/99 Towc 2m good NHF

Miss Cool

109 **127**

6-y-o b m Jupiter Island-Laurel Diver (Celtic Cone)
M C Pipe N G Mills

Placings:*103*-13 (4485)
2001/02: 161GS, 193G

	Starts	1st	2nd	3rd	Win & Pl
Hurdles	2	1	0	1	3092
Career Total	**5**	**2**	**0**	**2**	**6919**
127 2/02 Ludl	2m	E Hdl	G-S		£2688
107 9/00 Chep	2m110y	H NHF	GD		£1617

Total win prize-money £4305

Going: Sf: 0-0 GS: 1-1 Gd: 0-1 GF: - Fm: 0-0
Distance: **2m/2m3: 1-2** 2m4-2m7: 0-0 3m+: 0-0
Track: LH: 0-0 **RH: 1-2** Tight: 0-0 Gall: 0-0
Aids: Bl: 0-0 Vi: 0-0 Tstrap: 0-0
Best Rating: 127 2/02 Ludl 2m gd-sft Hdl

A sister to Mr Cool, she showed useful form in bumpers and made a winning debut over hurdles in February 2002. Probably does not want the ground too fast.

Miss Egypt (IRE)

56f

6-y-o br m Alphabatim (USA)-Enchanted Queen (Tender King)
Lindsay Woods Miss Maria McKinney

Placings:*0-0F00* (2473)
2001/02: 160F, 16FGF, 160F, 170GY, 160GS

	Starts	1st	2nd	3rd	Win & Pl
NH Flat	2	0	0	0	0
Hurdles	3	0	0	0	0
Career Total	**6**	**0**	**0**	**0**	

Going: Sf: 0-0 GS: 0-1 Gd: 0-0 GF: - Fm: 0-3
Distance: 2m/2m3: 0-5 2m4-2m7: 0-0 3m+: 0-0
Track: LH: 0-1 RH: 0-0 Tight: 0-1 Gall: 0-0
Aids: Bl: 0-1 Vi: 0-0 Tstrap: 0-0
Best Rating: 56 2/01 Muss 2m good NHF

Miss Ellie

105 **98**

6-y-o b m Elmaamul (USA)-Jussoli (Don)
Mrs S C Bradburne Mrs C J Kerr

Placings:*560*/3P511PU-45P603 (2727)
2001/02: 224GF, 205S, 22PGS, 216G, 160GS, 243GF

	Starts	1st	2nd	3rd	Win & Pl
Hurdles	6	0	0	1	753
Career Total	**16**	**2**	**0**	**2**	**8149**
105 1/01 Muss	2m4f	F(0-100)HHdl	G-S		£3164
95 1/01 Muss	2m4f	F(0-100)HHdl	GD		£3780

Total win prize-money £6944

Going: Sf: 0-1 GS: 0-2 Gd: 0-1 GF: - Fm: 0-2
Distance: 2m/2m3: 0-1 2m4-2m7: 0-4 3m+: 0-1
Track: LH: 0-4 RH: 0-2 Tight: 0-4 Gall: 0-0
Aids: Bl: 0-0 Vi: 0-0 Tstrap: 0-0
Best Rating: 105 1/01 Muss 2m4f gd-sft Hdl

Moderate handicapper over hurdles, best at around two and a half miles with cut in the ground.

Miss Fara (FR)

110 **142**

7-y-o ch m Galetto (FR)-Faracha (FR) (Kenmare (FR))
M C Pipe Mrs Christine Painting

Placings:200U/11211300F/4P-413P5060 (4231)
2001/02: 164GF, 191GS, 213G, 16PG, 225G, 200G, 206S, 210GS

	Starts	1st	2nd	3rd	Win & Pl
Hurdles	7	1	0	1	7386
Chases	1	0	0	0	0
Career Total	**23**	**5**	**2**	**2**	**31542**
142 10/01 Strf	2m3f	C(0-135)HHdl	G-S		£5512
135 12/99 Chel	2m1f	C(0-135)HHdl	GD		£6905
133 11/99 Tntn	2m1f	C HHdl	GD		£4765
113 10/99 Towc	2m	D Hdl	GD		£3129
100 9/99 Tntn	2m3f110y	D Hdl	G-F		£2640

Total win prize-money £22951

Going: Sf: 0-1 GS: 1-2 Gd: 0-4 GF: - Fm: 0-1
Distance: **2m/2m3: 1-3** 2m4-2m7: 0-5 3m+: 0-0
Track: **LH: 1-5** RH: 0-2 **Tight: 1-3** Gall: 0-3
Aids: Bl: 0-0 Vi: 0-0 Tstrap: 0-0
Best Rating: 142 10/01 Chel 2m5f good Hdl

Miss Fencote

101 **80**

6-y-o b m Phardante (FR)-Jack's The Girl (IRE) (Supreme Leader)
P Beaumont Mrs H M Richardson

Placings:*06*-0B6535 (4745)
2001/02: 200G, 16BGS, 206S, 215S, 203GS, 245G

	Starts	1st	2nd	3rd	Win & Pl
Hurdles	6	0	0	1	498
Career Total	**8**	**0**	**0**	**1**	**498**

Going: Sf: 0-2 GS: 0-2 Gd: 0-2 GF: - Fm: 0-0
Distance: 2m/2m3: 0-1 2m4-2m7: 0-4 3m+: 0-1
Track: LH: 0-4 RH: 0-1 Tight: 0-2 Gall: 0-2
Aids: Bl: 0-0 Vi: 0-0 Tstrap: 0-0
Best Rating: 80 3/02 Carl 2m4f gd-sft Hdl

Glimmer of ability in novices' hurdles. Best effort came over two and a half miles on good to soft ground.

Miss Flinders

5-y-o b m Sula Bula-Pollys Owen (Master Owen)
J W Mullins Mrs M I Barton

Placings:*06* (2782)
2001/02: 170HY, 216G

	Starts	1st	2nd	3rd	Win & Pl
NH Flat	1	0	0	0	0
Hurdles	1	0	0	0	0
Career Total	**2**	**0**	**0**	**0**	**0**

Going: Sf: 0-1 GS: 0-0 Gd: 0-1 GF: - Fm: 0-0
Distance: 2m/2m3: 0-1 2m4-2m7: 0-1 3m+: 0-0
Track: LH: 0-1 RH: 0-1 Tight: 0-1 Gall: 0-0
Aids: Bl: 0-0 Vi: 0-0 Tstrap: 0-0
Best Rating: 60 12/01 NAbb 2m1f heavy NHF

Miss Flora

6-y-o b m Alflora (IRE)-Immodest Miss (Daring Display (USA))
J K Cresswell J K S Cresswell

Placings:*0-P* (0423)
2001/02: 17PG

	Starts	1st	2nd	3rd	Win & Pl
NH Flat	1	0	0	0	
Career Total	**2**	**0**	**0**	**0**	

Going: Sf: 0-0 GS: 0-0 Gd: 0-1 GF: - Fm: 0-0
Distance: 2m/2m3: 0-1 2m4-2m7: 0-0 3m+: 0-0
Track: LH: 0-1 RH: 0-0 Tight: 0-1 Gall: 0-0
Aids: Bl: 0-0 Vi: 0-0 Tstrap: 0-0
Best Rating:

Miss Foley

86(84c) (26c)**82**

9-y-o b m Thethingaboutitis (USA)-Rue De Remarque (The Noble Player (USA))
D McCain Mrs S K Maan

Placings:*0/00*6330/45P5-02P3PP0P (1194)
2001/02: 200GF, 202G, 24PG, 203GF, 25PGS, 27PGF, 170G, 20PGS

	Starts	1st	2nd	3rd	Win & Pl
Hurdles	6	0	1	1	1411
Chases	2	0	0	0	0
Career Total	**19**	**0**	**1**	**3**	**2806**

Going: Sf: 0-0 GS: 0-2 Gd: 0-3 GF: - Fm: 0-3
Distance: 2m/2m3: 0-1 2m4-2m7: 0-4 3m+: 0-3
Track: LH: 0-7 RH: 0-1 Tight: 0-5 Gall: 0-0
Aids: Bl: 0-3 Vi: 0-1 Tstrap: 0-0
Best Rating: 82 5/01 Bang 2m4f good Hdl

Miss Green

7-y-o b m Greensmith-Miss Comedy (Comedy Star (USA))
Miss L Bower Miss J Wilkinson

Placings:P (4655)
2001/02: 17^{P}GS

	Starts	1st	2nd	3rd	Win & Pl
Hurdles	1	0	0	0	
Career Total	**1**	**0**	**0**	**0**	

Going: Sf: 0-0 GS: 0-1 Gd: 0-0 GF: - Fm: 0-0
Distance: 2m/2m3: 0-1 2m4-2m7: 0-0 3m+: 0-0
Track: LH: 0-0 RH: 0-1 Tight: 0-1 Gall: 0-0
Aids: Bl: 0-0 Vi: 0-0 Tstrap: 0-0
Best Rating:

Miss Greenacres

7-y-o ch m Seymour Hicks (FR)-Greenacres Girl (Tycoon Ii)
T Wall Harton Manor Racing Club

Placings:0PU0PP-P (1624)
2001/02: 16^{P}GF

	Starts	1st	2nd	3rd	Win & Pl
Hurdles	1	0	0	0	
Career Total	**7**	**0**	**0**	**0**	

Going: Sf: 0-0 GS: 0-0 Gd: 0-0 GF: - Fm: 0-1
Distance: 2m/2m3: 0-1 2m4-2m7: 0-0 3m+: 0-0
Track: LH: 0-0 RH: 0-1 Tight: 0-0 Gall: 0-0
Aids: Bl: 0-0 Vi: 0-0 Tstrap: 0-0
Best Rating: 52 8/00 Worc 2m gd-fm Hdl

Miss Janica

100 **72**

4-y-o b f Sir Harry Lewis (USA)-Supreme Wonder (IRE) (Supreme Leader)
Miss Venetia Williams Lady Harris

Placings:6 (4595)
2001/02: 16^{6}G

	Starts	1st	2nd	3rd	Win & Pl
NH Flat	1	0	0	0	0
Career Total	**1**	**0**	**0**	**0**	**0**

Going: Sf: 0-0 GS: 0-0 Gd: 0-1 GF: - Fm: 0-0
Distance: 2m/2m3: 0-1 2m4-2m7: 0-0 3m+: 0-0
Track: LH: 0-1 RH: 0-0 Tight: 0-0 Gall: 0-0
Aids: Bl: 0-0 Vi: 0-0 Tstrap: 0-0
Best Rating: 88 4/02 Uttx 2m good NHF

Unseated her rider at the start after being unruly in the paddock on her hurdling debut. Also looked a tricky customer next time. Is one to be wary of.

Miss Jeff (FR)

90 **87+**

4-y-o ch f Mansonnien (FR)-Miss Jefferson (FR) (Jefferson)
M C Pipe (A Hosselet 22/6) Matt Archer & Miss Jean Broadhurst

Placings:60130 (1925)
2001/02: 15^{6}HY, 15^{0}VS, 15^{1}VS, 16^{3}G, 16^{0}G

	Starts	1st	2nd	3rd	Win & Pl
Hurdles	5	1	0	1	6731
Career Total	**5**	**1**	**0**	**1**	**6731**

	6/01	Autl	1m7f	Hdl	VS	£6305

Total win prize-money £6305

Going: Sf: 0-1 GS: 0-0 Gd: 0-2 GF: - Fm: 0-0
Distance: 2m/2m3: 0-2 2m4-2m7: 0-0 3m+: 0-0
Track: LH: 0-1 RH: 0-1 Tight: 0-1 Gall: 0-0
Aids: Bl: 0-0 Vi: 0-0 Tstrap: 0-0
Best Rating: 70 7/01 Strf 2m110y good Hdl

Winner over hurdles in France but has cut little ice here so far.

Miss K C

6-y-o b m Roviris-Miss Gaylord (Cavo Doro)
P M Rich B Meadmore

Placings:P (2392)
2001/02: 20^{P}S

	Starts	1st	2nd	3rd	Win & Pl
Hurdles	1	0	0	0	
Career Total	**1**	**0**	**0**	**0**	

Going: Sf: 0-1 GS: 0-0 Gd: 0-0 GF: - Fm: 0-0
Distance: 2m/2m3: 0-0 2m4-2m7: 0-1 3m+: 0-0
Track: LH: 0-1 RH: 0-0 Tight: 0-0 Gall: 0-0
Aids: Bl: 0-0 Vi: 0-0 Tstrap: 0-0
Best Rating:

Miss Kitz

66 **26**

6-y-o b m Cruise Missile-Frau Kitz (Master Buck)
C Tizzard The Villagers

Placings:00000 (3759)
2001/02: 17^{0}GF, 17^{0}G, 16^{0}GS, 17^{0}S, 17^{0}S

	Starts	1st	2nd	3rd	Win & Pl
NH Flat	2	0	0	0	0
Hurdles	3	0	0	0	0
Career Total	**5**	**0**	**0**	**0**	

Going: Sf: 0-2 GS: 0-1 Gd: 0-1 GF: - Fm: 0-1
Distance: 2m/2m3: 0-5 2m4-2m7: 0-0 3m+: 0-0
Track: LH: 0-1 RH: 0-3 Tight: 0-4 Gall: 0-0
Aids: Bl: 0-1 Vi: 0-0 Tstrap: 0-0
Best Rating: 60 6/01 NAbb 2m1f good NHF

Miss Lacroix

105 **84**

7-y-o b m Picea-Smartie Lee (Dominion)
R Hollinshead Mrs Norma Harris

Placings:0656/6001/5010041336-02263U04630 (4847)
2001/02: 17^{0}F, 16^{2}GF, 19^{2}GF, 19^{6}S, 17^{3}G, 22^{U}GS, 16^{0}S, 16^{4}G, 16^{6}S, 16^{3}GF, 20^{0}G

	Starts	1st	2nd	3rd	Win & Pl
Hurdles	11	0	2	2	3351
Career Total	**29**	**3**	**2**	**4**	**12714**

87	12/00	Ludl	2m	F(0-110)HHdl	SFT	£3178
84	5/00	MRas	2m1f110y	F(0-105)HHdl	G-S	£2074
71	8/99	Bang	2m1f	E(0-105)HHdl	GD	£2931

Total win prize-money £8185

Going: Sf: 0-3 GS: 0-1 Gd: 0-3 GF: - Fm: 0-4
Distance: 2m/2m3: 0-7 2m4-2m7: 0-4 3m+: 0-0
Track: LH: 0-4 RH: 0-7 Tight: 0-4 Gall: 0-1
Aids: Bl: 0-0 Vi: 0-0 Tstrap: 0-0
Best Rating: 87 2/01 Ludl 2m gd-sft Hdl

Handicap hurdler, at her best when able to dominate. She has run well on fast ground, but is better suited by cut. Stays two and a half miles.

Miss Lippy

71 **34**

5-y-o b m Emperor Jones (USA)-Anatroccolo (Ile De Bourbon (USA))
P J Hobbs Colin Brown Racing Ii

Placings:00 (0724)
2001/02: 17^{0}GS, 17^{0}F

	Starts	1st	2nd	3rd	Win & Pl
NH Flat	1	0	0	0	0
Hurdles	1	0	0	0	0
Career Total	**2**	**0**	**0**	**0**	

Going: Sf: 0-0 GS: 0-1 Gd: 0-0 GF: - Fm: 0-1
Distance: 2m/2m3: 0-2 2m4-2m7: 0-0 3m+: 0-0
Track: LH: 0-1 RH: 0-1 Tight: 0-1 Gall: 0-0
Aids: Bl: 0-0 Vi: 0-0 Tstrap: 0-0
Best Rating: 34 6/01 Hrfd 2m1f firm Hdl

Miss Man

8-y-o ch m Man Among Men (IRE)-Rustys Special (Rustingo)
R L Brown R L Brown

Placings:00/0P-P (2129)
2001/02: 16^{P}GF

	Starts	1st	2nd	3rd	Win & Pl
Hurdles	1	0	0	0	
Career Total	**5**	**0**	**0**	**0**	

Going: Sf: 0-0 GS: 0-0 Gd: 0-0 GF: - Fm: 0-1
Distance: 2m/2m3: 0-1 2m4-2m7: 0-0 3m+: 0-0
Track: LH: 0-0 RH: 0-1 Tight: 0-0 Gall: 0-0
Aids: Bl: 0-0 Vi: 0-0 Tstrap: 0-0
Best Rating: 87 10/99 Tntn 2m1f gd-fm NHF

Miss Mattie Ross

91 **75**

6-y-o b m Milieu-Mother Machree (Bing Ii)
S J Marshall S J Marshall

Placings:PP (4689)
2001/02: 16^{P}HY, 16^{P}GF

	Starts	1st	2nd	3rd	Win & Pl
Hurdles	2	0	0	0	
Career Total	**2**	**0**	**0**	**0**	

Going: Sf: 0-1 GS: 0-0 Gd: 0-0 GF: - Fm: 0-1
Distance: 2m/2m3: 0-2 2m4-2m7: 0-0 3m+: 0-0
Track: LH: 0-2 RH: 0-0 Tight: 0-1 Gall: 0-1
Aids: Bl: 0-0 Vi: 0-0 Tstrap: 0-0
Best Rating:

Miss Melrose

85 **51**

5-y-o ch m Bob Back (USA)-Whatagale (Strong Gale)
L Lungo Mrs C Coxen

Placings:06 (2729)
2001/02: 16^{0}G, 17^{6}GF

	Starts	1st	2nd	3rd	Win & Pl
NH Flat	2	0	0	0	0
Career Total	**2**	**0**	**0**	**0**	**0**

Going: Sf: 0-0 GS: 0-0 Gd: 0-1 GF: - Fm: 0-1
Distance: 2m/2m3: 0-2 2m4-2m7: 0-0 3m+: 0-0
Track: LH: 0-1 RH: 0-0 Tight: 0-0 Gall: 0-0
Aids: Bl: 0-0 Vi: 0-0 Tstrap: 0-0
Best Rating: 70 12/01 Muss 2m1f gd-fm NHF

Miss Nel

65 **23**

7-y-o b m Denel (FR)-Ice Lass (Heroic Air)
R H Goldie Robert H Goldie

Placings:P0 **(4894)**
2001/02: 16^{P}HY, 16^{0}G

	Starts	1st	2nd	3rd	Win & Pl
Hurdles	2	0	0	0	
Career Total	**2**	**0**	**0**	**0**	

Going: Sf: 0-1 GS: 0-0 Gd: 0-1 GF: - Fm: 0-0
Distance: 2m/2m3: 0-2 2m4-2m7: 0-0 3m+: 0-0
Track: LH: 0-1 RH: 0-1 Tight: 0-0 Gall: 0-0
Aids: Bl: 0-0 Vi: 0-0 Tstrap: 0-0
Best Rating: 23 4/02 Prth 2m110y good Hdl

Showed little enthusiasm, pulling up on her hurdles debut.

Miss O'Grady (IRE)

10-y-o ch m Over The River (FR)-Polar Mistress (IRE) (Strong Gale)
Miss L Alner (R H Alner 11/5) Mrs J M Miller

Placings:1/U/PP2U **(4118)**
2001/02: 20^{P}GS, 21^{P}GF, 24^{2}S, 25^{U}G

	Starts	1st	2nd	3rd	Win & Pl
Chases	4	0	1	0	884
Career Total	**6**	**1**	**1**	**0**	**2962**
107 4/99 Chel	2m5f	H Ch		G-S	£2078

Total win prize-money £2078

Going: Sf: 0-1 GS: 0-1 Gd: 0-1 GF: - Fm: 0-1
Distance: 2m/2m3: 0-0 2m4-2m7: 0-2 3m+: 0-2
Track: LH: 0-1 RH: 0-3 Tight: 0-2 Gall: 0-0
Aids: Bl: 0-0 Vi: 0-0 Tstrap: 0-0
Best Rating: 107 4/99 Chel 2m5f gd-sft Ch

Useful pointer/hunter chaser. Has been held in the past couple of seasons.

Miss Pennyhill (IRE)

94 **104**

9-y-o b m Conquering Hero (USA)-Teodosia (Ashmore (FR))
A Sadik A Sadik

Placings:0244510U0/4320505645/341FF322420/4PU 554PF/5131P-PF2 **(2477)**
2001/02: 25^{P}G, 25^{F}G, 19^{2}S

	Starts	1st	2nd	3rd	Win & Pl
Chases	3	0	1	0	1084
Career Total	**46**	**4**	**6**	**4**	**24636**
113 5/00 Hrfd	3m1f110y	E(0-115)HCh		G-S	£4147
113 5/00 Hrfd	3m1f110y	F(0-105)HCh		GD	£3900
103 12/98 Hrfd	2m3f	D(0-110)HCh		SFT	£4492
98 1/97 Thur	2m	Hdl		GD	£2204

Total win prize-money £14744

Going: Sf: 0-1 GS: 0-0 Gd: 0-2 GF: - Fm: 0-0
Distance: 2m/2m3: 0-1 2m4-2m7: 0-0 3m+: 0-2
Track: LH: 0-0 RH: 0-3 Tight: 0-0 Gall: 0-0
Aids: Bl: 0-0 Vi: 0-0 Tstrap: 0-0
Best Rating: 113 5/00 Hrfd 3m1f110y gd-sft Ch

Modest chaser, stays an extended three miles, goes well in soft ground and likes Hereford.

Miss Portcello

9-y-o b m Bybicello-Port Mallaig (Royal Fountain)
Mrs J M Hollands (Trainer Unknown 24/2) W F Jeffrey

Placings:3U **(4690)**
2001/02: 25^{3}GS, 25^{U}GF

	Starts	1st	2nd	3rd	Win & Pl
Chases	2	0	0	1	227
Career Total	**2**	**0**	**0**	**1**	**227**

Going: Sf: 0-0 GS: 0-1 Gd: 0-0 GF: - Fm: 0-1
Distance: 2m/2m3: 0-0 2m4-2m7: 0-0 3m+: 0-2
Track: LH: 0-1 RH: 0-0 Tight: 0-1 Gall: 0-0
Aids: Bl: 0-0 Vi: 0-0 Tstrap: 0-0
Best Rating: 99 3/02 Catt 3m1f110y gd-sft Ch

Modest form in ladies' points and hunter chases.

Miss Rennenski

96 **73**

6-y-o b m Petoski-Miss Wrensborough (Buckskin (FR))
D R Gandolfo D R Gandolfo Ltd

Placings:0-063P **(4565)**
2001/02: 18^{0}HY, 19^{6}HY, 21^{3}GS, 16^{P}G

	Starts	1st	2nd	3rd	Win & Pl
Hurdles	4	0	0	1	284
Career Total	**5**	**0**	**0**	**1**	**284**

Going: Sf: 0-2 GS: 0-1 Gd: 0-1 GF: - Fm: 0-0
Distance: 2m/2m3: 0-2 2m4-2m7: 0-2 3m+: 0-0
Track: LH: 0-1 RH: 0-3 Tight: 0-1 Gall: 0-0
Aids: Bl: 0-0 Vi: 0-0 Tstrap: 0-0
Best Rating: 92 4/01 Font 2m2f110y good NHF

Miss Samantha

79 **43**

4-y-o b f Emarati (USA)-Puella Bona (Handsome Sailor)
M D I Usher Mrs J Black

Placings:00 **(4408)**
2001/02: 17^{0}G, 17^{0}S

	Starts	1st	2nd	3rd	Win & Pl
Hurdles	2	0	0	0	
Career Total	**2**	**0**	**0**	**0**	

Going: Sf: 0-1 GS: 0-0 Gd: 0-1 GF: - Fm: 0-0
Distance: 2m/2m3: 0-2 2m4-2m7: 0-0 3m+: 0-0
Track: LH: 0-1 RH: 0-1 Tight: 0-1 Gall: 0-0
Aids: Bl: 0-0 Vi: 0-0 Tstrap: 0-0
Best Rating: 45 3/02 Hrfd 2m1f good Hdl

Miss Soprano

87f

6-y-o ch m Opera Ghost-Miss Levantine (Levanter)
S G Knight Mrs P M Underhill

Placings:P0-6 **(1154)**
2001/02: 17^{6}GF

	Starts	1st	2nd	3rd	Win & Pl
NH Flat	1	0	0	0	0
Career Total	**3**	**0**	**0**	**0**	**0**

Going: Sf: 0-0 GS: 0-0 Gd: 0-0 GF: - Fm: 0-1
Distance: 2m/2m3: 0-1 2m4-2m7: 0-0 3m+: 0-0
Track: LH: 0-1 RH: 0-0 Tight: 0-1 Gall: 0-0
Aids: Bl: 0-0 Vi: 0-0 Tstrap: 0-0
Best Rating: 87 4/01 Tntn 2m1f gd-fm NHF

Miss Talbot (IRE)

6-y-o b m Good Thyne (USA)-South Ofthe Border (Mandalus)
H D Daly (Ian Williams 11/7) D Mills

Placings:0PP **(4048)**
2001/02: 16^{0}G, 21^{P}G, 19^{P}G

	Starts	1st	2nd	3rd	Win & Pl
NH Flat	1	0	0	0	0
Hurdles	2	0	0	0	0
Career Total	**3**	**0**	**0**	**0**	

Going: Sf: 0-0 GS: 0-0 Gd: 0-3 GF: - Fm: 0-0
Distance: 2m/2m3: 0-2 2m4-2m7: 0-1 3m+: 0-0
Track: LH: 0-1 RH: 0-2 Tight: 0-0 Gall: 0-0
Aids: Bl: 0-0 Vi: 0-0 Tstrap: 0-0
Best Rating: 56 7/01 Worc 2m good NHF

Miss Tango

105 **119**

5-y-o b m Batshoof-Spring Flyer (IRE) (Waajib)
M C Pipe Codan Trust Company Limited

Placings:21252-231P1 **(1729)**
2001/02: 16^{2}G, 20^{3}G, 22^{1}GF, 24^{P}S, 24^{1}F

	Starts	1st	2nd	3rd	Win & Pl
Hurdles	5	2	1	1	6755
Career Total	**10**	**3**	**4**	**1**	**12219**
119 10/01 Tntn	3m110y	F(0-110)HHdl		FRM	£3455
117 9/01 NAbb	2m6f	G Hdl		G-F	£2198
100 10/00 Ludl	2m	E Hdl		G-F	£2569

Total win prize-money £8223

Going: Sf: 0-1 GS: 0-0 Gd: 0-2 GF: - Fm: 2-2
Distance: 2m/2m3: 0-1 2m4-2m7: 1-2 3m+: 1-2
Track: LH: 1-3 RH: 1-2 **Tight: 2-4** Gall: 0-0
Aids: Bl: 0-0 Vi: 0-0 Tstrap: 0-0
Best Rating: 119 10/01 Tntn 3m110y firm Hdl

She has run her best races with McCoy aboard and has shown a marked preference for top of the ground. Successfuly stepped up to three miles at Taunton in October.

Miss Tippins

5-y-o br m Regal Embers (IRE)-Winter Gem (Hasty Word)
T Wall A Wright

Placings:0 **(3862)**
2001/02: 16^{0}S

	Starts	1st	2nd	3rd	Win & Pl
NH Flat	1	0	0	0	
Career Total	**1**	**0**	**0**	**0**	

Going: Sf: 0-1 GS: 0-0 Gd: 0-0 GF: - Fm: 0-0
Distance: 2m/2m3: 0-1 2m4-2m7: 0-0 3m+: 0-0
Track: LH: 0-1 RH: 0-0 Tight: 0-0 Gall: 0-1
Aids: Bl: 0-0 Vi: 0-0 Tstrap: 0-0
Best Rating:

Miss Urtica

5-y-o b m Henbit (USA)-Mistress Boreen (Boreen (FR))
P R Hedger J D Sells

Placings:F (2877)
2001/02: 16^{F}G

	Starts	1st	2nd	3rd	Win & Pl
Hurdles	1	0	0	0	
Career Total	1	0	0	0	

Going: Sf: 0-0 GS: 0-0 Gd: 0-1 GF: - Fm: 0-0
Distance: 2m/2m3: 0-1 2m4-2m7: 0-0 3m+: 0-0
Track: LH: 0-0 RH: 0-1 Tight: 0-0 Gall: 0-0
Aids: Bl: 0-0 Vi: 0-0 Tstrap: 0-0
Best Rating:

Miss Wizadora

95(56h) 101

7-y-o ch m Gildoran-Lizzie The Twig (Precipice Wood)
Simon Earle W S Grant

Placings:5/5500/3P0-3601 (1997)
2001/02: 21^{3}GF, 25^{6}G, 20^{0}GF, 21^{1}S

	Starts	1st	2nd	3rd	Win & Pl
Hurdles	1	0	0	0	0
Chases	3	1	0	1	3925
Career Total	12	1	0	2	4261

101 11/01 NAbb 2m5f110y E(0-105)HCh SFT £3376
Total win prize-money £3377

Going: Sf: 1-1 GS: 0-0 Gd: 0-1 GF: - Fm: 0-2
Distance: 2m/2m3: 0-0 **2m4-2m7: 1-3** 3m+: 0-1
Track: **LH: 1-4** RH: 0-0 **Tight: 1-3** Gall: 0-0
Aids: Bl: 0-0 Vi: 0-0 Tstrap: 0-0
Best Rating: 101 11/01 NAbb 2m5f110y soft Ch

Had shown little until winning at Newton Abbot in November 2001 from 11lb out of the handicap.

Miss Woodpigeon

95 77

6-y-o b m Landyap (USA)-Pigeon Loft (IRE) (Bellypha)
R G Frost Christine And Aubrey Loze

Placings:00-41400 (3757)
2001/02: 17^{4}G, 17^{1}GF, 19^{4}GS, 16^{0}G, 17^{0}S

	Starts	1st	2nd	3rd	Win & Pl
NH Flat	2	1	0	0	2177
Hurdles	3	0	0	0	415
Career Total	7	1	0	0	2592

101 8/01 NAbb 2m1f H NHF G-F £2177
Total win prize-money £2177

Going: Sf: 0-1 GS: 0-1 Gd: 0-2 GF: - Fm: 1-1
Distance: **2m/2m3: 1-4** 2m4-2m7: 0-1 3m+: 0-0
Track: **LH: 1-2** RH: 0-3 **Tight: 1-4** Gall: 0-0
Aids: Bl: 0-0 Vi: 0-0 Tstrap: 0-0
Best Rating: 101 8/01 NAbb 2m1f gd-fm NHF

Bumper winner on firm ground in the summer.

Miss Woodstick

(103h) (97h)97

6-y-o b m Teenoso (USA)-Born Bossy (Eborneezer)
J L Spearing Dougle & Celia Clapham & Harold Porter

Placings:0/300032-25UPP1 (4544)
2001/02: 26^{2}G, 25^{5}G, 24^{U}GF, 25^{P}G, 24^{P}G, 26^{1}G

	Starts	1st	2nd	3rd	Win & Pl
Hurdles	3	1	1	0	3712
Chases	3	0	0	0	0
Career Total	13	1	2	2	4897

97 4/02 Hrfd 3m2f E Hdl GD £2912
Total win prize-money £2912

Going: Sf: 0-0 GS: 0-0 Gd: 1-5 GF: - Fm: 0-1
Distance: 2m/2m3: 0-0 2m4-2m7: 0-0 **3m+: 1-6**
Track: LH: 0-0 **RH: 1-5** Tight: 0-2 Gall: 0-0
Aids: Bl: 0-0 Vi: 0-1 Tstrap: 0-0
Best Rating: 97 4/02 Hrfd 3m2f good Hdl

Moderate novice hurdler, acts on a sound surface and has plenty of stamina.

Miss World (IRE)

5-y-o b m Mujadil (USA)-Great Land (USA) (Friend's Choice (USA))
P S McEntee Mrs B A McEntee

Placings:P-P (1258)
2001/02: 20^{P}GF

	Starts	1st	2nd	3rd	Win & Pl
Hurdles	1	0	0	0	
Career Total	2	0	0	0	

Going: Sf: 0-0 GS: 0-0 Gd: 0-0 GF: - Fm: 0-1
Distance: 2m/2m3: 0-0 2m4-2m7: 0-1 3m+: 0-0
Track: LH: 0-0 RH: 0-1 Tight: 0-0 Gall: 0-1
Aids: Bl: 0-0 Vi: 0-0 Tstrap: 0-1
Best Rating:

Missed Call (IRE)

95 75

10-y-o b g Phardante (FR)-Una's Run (Deep Run)
M Wellings The 1471 Racing Partnership

Placings:026P3/354303/6P/PP460 (4011)
2001/02: 21^{P}GF, 22^{P}G, 22^{4}GF, 19^{6}G, 21^{0}S

	Starts	1st	2nd	3rd	Win & Pl
Hurdles	5	0	0	0	0
Career Total	18	0	1	4	1841

Going: Sf: 0-1 GS: 0-0 Gd: 0-2 GF: - Fm: 0-2
Distance: 2m/2m3: 0-1 2m4-2m7: 0-4 3m+: 0-0
Track: LH: 0-4 RH: 0-0 Tight: 0-3 Gall: 0-1
Aids: Bl: 0-0 Vi: 0-0 Tstrap: 0-0
Best Rating: 97 5/98 Sthl 2m2f good Hdl

Missed Edition

4-y-o ch f Missed Flight-Exclusive Edition (IRE) (Bob Back (USA))
M J Gingell Mrs C Foster

Placings:0 (3236)
2001/02: 16^{0}GS

	Starts	1st	2nd	3rd	Win & Pl
NH Flat	1	0	0	0	
Career Total	1	0	0	0	

Going: Sf: 0-0 GS: 0-1 Gd: 0-0 GF: - Fm: 0-0
Distance: 2m/2m3: 0-1 2m4-2m7: 0-0 3m+: 0-0
Track: LH: 0-0 RH: 0-1 Tight: 0-0 Gall: 0-1
Aids: Bl: 0-0 Vi: 0-0 Tstrap: 0-0
Best Rating:

Mission Hills

76 49

7-y-o b m Faustus (USA)-Hot Case (Upper Case (USA))
B G Powell P M T Partnership

Placings:5 (0724)
2001/02: 17^{5}F

	Starts	1st	2nd	3rd	Win & Pl
Hurdles	1	0	0	0	0
Career Total	1	0	0	0	0

Going: Sf: 0-0 GS: 0-0 Gd: 0-0 GF: - Fm: 0-1
Distance: 2m/2m3: 0-1 2m4-2m7: 0-0 3m+: 0-0
Track: LH: 0-0 RH: 0-1 Tight: 0-0 Gall: 0-0
Aids: Bl: 0-0 Vi: 0-0 Tstrap: 0-0
Best Rating: 49 6/01 Hrfd 2m1f firm Hdl

Mission Lord (IRE)

8-y-o b g Mac's Imp (USA)-Amber Giotto (Wolverlife)
M J Spuffard (Mrs F Goldsworthy 1/6) Miss F Goldsworthy

Placings:PP (4165)
2001/02: 21^{P}GF, 26^{P}G

	Starts	1st	2nd	3rd	Win & Pl
Chases	2	0	0	0	
Career Total	2	0	0	0	

Going: Sf: 0-0 GS: 0-0 Gd: 0-1 GF: - Fm: 0-1
Distance: 2m/2m3: 0-0 2m4-2m7: 0-1 3m+: 0-1
Track: LH: 0-2 RH: 0-0 Tight: 0-1 Gall: 0-0
Aids: Bl: 0-0 Vi: 0-0 Tstrap: 0-0
Best Rating:

Maiden pointer, pulled up on his only three starts since May 2000. Likes a sound surface.

Mismass

83(93h) (62h)62

9-y-o b m Then Again-Massawa (FR) (Tennyson (FR))
D J Wintle P J R Gardner

Placings:00/0/04062/600P (1092)
2001/02: 16^{6}GF, 16^{0}GF, 16^{0}S, 20^{P}GF

	Starts	1st	2nd	3rd	Win & Pl
Hurdles	2	0	0	0	0
Chases	2	0	0	0	0
Career Total	12	0	1	0	1244

Going: Sf: 0-1 GS: 0-0 Gd: 0-0 GF: - Fm: 0-3
Distance: 2m/2m3: 0-3 2m4-2m7: 0-1 3m+: 0-0
Track: LH: 0-3 RH: 0-1 Tight: 0-1 Gall: 0-1
Aids: Bl: 0-0 Vi: 0-0 Tstrap: 0-0
Best Rating: 75 9/99 Worc 2m gd-fm Ch

Missy-Moo

90 52

6-y-o gr m Gran Alba (USA)-Lady Gwenmore (Town And Country)
Dr J R J Naylor Howard Smith

Placings:00P-00500 (4731)
2001/02: 16^{0}G, 22^{0}G, 21^{5}GS, 22^{0}S, 17^{0}F

	Starts	1st	2nd	3rd	Win & Pl
Hurdles	5	0	0	0	0
Career Total	8	0	0	0	0

Going: Sf: 0-1 GS: 0-1 Gd: 0-2 GF: - Fm: 0-1

Distance: 2m/2m3: 0-2 2m4-2m7: 0-3 3m+: 0-0
Track: LH: 0-1 RH: 0-4 Tight: 0-1 Gall: 0-0
Aids: Bl: 0-0 Vi: 0-0 Tstrap: 0-0
Best Rating: 58 6/00 NAbb 2m1f gd-fm NHF

Mist Of Silver

7-y-o gr g Henbit (USA)-Linen Thread (Broxted)
Mrs H Dalton J R Salter

Placings:000/P (0449)
2001/02: 20^{P}F

	Starts	1st	2nd	3rd	Win & Pl
Hurdles	1	0	0	0	
Career Total	**4**	**0**	**0**	**0**	

Going: Sf: 0-0 GS: 0-0 Gd: 0-0 GF: - Fm: 0-1
Distance: 2m/2m3: 0-0 2m4-2m7: 0-1 3m+: 0-0
Track: LH: 0-1 RH: 0-0 Tight: 0-0 Gall: 0-0
Aids: Bl: 0-0 Vi: 0-0 Tstrap: 0-0
Best Rating: 92 4/00 Ayr 2m good NHF

Mister Benjamin (IRE)

100(107h) (112h)**138**
7-y-o b g Polish Patriot (USA)-Frau Ahuyentante (ARG) (Frari (ARG))
P F Nicholls Terry Green

Placings:31P303/215122-1F64 (4527)
2001/02: 19^{1}F, 21^{F}GS, 20^{6}G, 16^{4}GS

	Starts	1st	2nd	3rd	Win & Pl
Hurdles	2	0	0	0	0
Chases	2	1	0	0	5051
Career Total	**16**	**4**	**3**	**3**	**18897**

138	5/01	Tntn	2m3f	D Ch	FRM	£5050
133	1/01	Donc	2m3f110y	D Ch	GD	£4446
128	11/00	Tntn	2m3f110y	D(0-120)HHdl	G-S	£2977
128	12/99	Ling	2m3f110y	E Hdl	G-S	£2505

Total win prize-money £14979

Going: Sf: 0-0 GS: 0-2 Gd: 0-1 GF: - Fm: 1-1
Distance: **2m/2m3: 1-2** 2m4-2m7: 0-2 3m+: 0-0
Track: LH: 0-3 **RH: 1-1 Tight: 1-2** Gall: 0-0
Aids: Bl: 0-0 Vi: 0-0 Tstrap: 0-0
Best Rating: 138 5/01 Tntn 2m3f firm Ch

Decent hurdler/chaser, seems best at around two and ahalf miles on a sound surface, although handles a little cut.

Mister Bigtime (IRE)

107(108h) **131**
8-y-o br g Roselier (FR)-Cnoc An Oir (Goldhill)
R Rowe Mrs Jean R Bishop

Placings:452320-33220 (4233)
2001/02: 19^{3}G, 24^{3}G, 22^{2}HY, 24^{2}G, 32^{0}GS

	Starts	1st	2nd	3rd	Win & Pl
Chases	5	0	2	2	5843
Career Total	**11**	**0**	**4**	**3**	**10481**

Going: Sf: 0-1 GS: 0-1 Gd: 0-3 GF: - Fm: 0-0
Distance: 2m/2m3: 0-0 2m4-2m7: 0-2 3m+: 0-3
Track: LH: 0-2 RH: 0-3 Tight: 0-0 Gall: 0-2
Aids: Bl: 0-0 Vi: 0-0 Tstrap: 0-0
Best Rating: 131 1/02 Newb 3m good Ch

Placed over hurdles and over fences, he acts on good ground but handles softer. Stays three miles.

Mister Bromley

51f **87f**
5-y-o ch g Minster Son-Little Bromley (Riberetto)
M A Barnes A Eubank

Placings:00 (4526)
2001/02: 16^{0}HY, 17^{0}G

	Starts	1st	2nd	3rd	Win & Pl
NH Flat	2	0	0	0	
Career Total	**2**	**0**	**0**	**0**	

Going: Sf: 0-1 GS: 0-0 Gd: 0-1 GF: - Fm: 0-0
Distance: 2m/2m3: 0-2 2m4-2m7: 0-0 3m+: 0-0
Track: LH: 0-1 RH: 0-1 Tight: 0-0 Gall: 0-0
Aids: Bl: 0-0 Vi: 0-0 Tstrap: 0-0
Best Rating: 87 3/02 Ayr 2m heavy NHF

Modest bumper debut.

Mister Club Royal

85(82h) (63h)**73**
6-y-o b g Alflora (IRE)-Miss Club Royal (Avocat)
D McCain Halewood International Ltd

Placings:0003F (4574)
2001/02: 17^{0}S, 20^{0}HY, 17^{0}HY, 19^{3}S, 21^{F}GS

	Starts	1st	2nd	3rd	Win & Pl
NH Flat	1	0	0	0	0
Hurdles	2	0	0	0	0
Chases	2	0	0	1	735
Career Total	**5**	**0**	**0**	**1**	**735**

Going: Sf: 0-4 GS: 0-1 Gd: 0-0 GF: - Fm: 0-0
Distance: 2m/2m3: 0-3 2m4-2m7: 0-2 3m+: 0-0
Track: LH: 0-2 RH: 0-2 Tight: 0-2 Gall: 0-0
Aids: Bl: 0-0 Vi: 0-0 Tstrap: 0-0
Best Rating: 73 3/02 Tntn 2m3f soft Ch

Signs of ability over fences.

Mister Dave'S (IRE)

101 **94**
7-y-o ch g Bluffer-Tacovaon (Avocat)
Mrs S J Smith David Campbell

Placings:0605P01 (4871)
2001/02: 17^{0}S, 20^{6}S, 20^{0}HY, 20^{5}S, 22^{P}HY, 20^{0}GS, 25^{1}GF

	Starts	1st	2nd	3rd	Win & Pl
NH Flat	1	0	0	0	0
Hurdles	6	1	0	0	2443
Career Total	**7**	**1**	**0**	**0**	**2443**

94	4/02	Weth	3m1f	F(0-95)HHdl	G-F	£2443

Total win prize-money £2443

Going: Sf: 0-5 GS: 0-1 Gd: 0-0 GF: - Fm: 1-1
Distance: 2m/2m3: 0-1 2m4-2m7: 0-5 **3m+: 1-1**
Track: **LH: 1-5** RH: 0-1 Tight: 0-1 Gall: 0-1
Aids: Bl: 0-0 Vi: 0-0 Tstrap: 0-0
Best Rating: 94 4/02 Weth 3m1f gd-fm Hdl

Well beaten until opening his account in a modest novices' handicap at Wetherby in April.

Mister Deep (IRE)

24
8-y-o b g Mister Lord (USA)-Deep Pond (IRE) (Long Pond)
R H Alner J C Browne

Placings:6-P (0087)
2001/02: 26^{P}G

	Starts	1st	2nd	3rd	Win & Pl
Hurdles	1	0	0	0	
Career Total	**2**	**0**	**0**	**0**	**0**

Going: Sf: 0-0 GS: 0-0 Gd: 0-1 GF: - Fm: 0-0
Distance: 2m/2m3: 0-0 2m4-2m7: 0-0 3m+: 0-1
Track: LH: 0-0 RH: 0-1 Tight: 0-0 Gall: 0-0
Aids: Bl: 0-0 Vi: 0-0 Tstrap: 0-0
Best Rating: 24 4/01 Tntn 3m110y good Hdl

Mister Demolition

7-y-o b g Broadsword (USA)-Faint Praise (Lepanto (GER))
P F Nicholls R M Penny

Placings:P (0104)
2001/02: 18^{P}GF

	Starts	1st	2nd	3rd	Win & Pl
Hurdles	1	0	0	0	
Career Total	**1**	**0**	**0**	**0**	

Going: Sf: 0-0 GS: 0-0 Gd: 0-0 GF: - Fm: 0-1
Distance: 2m/2m3: 0-1 2m4-2m7: 0-0 3m+: 0-0
Track: LH: 0-1 RH: 0-0 Tight: 0-1 Gall: 0-0
Aids: Bl: 0-0 Vi: 0-0 Tstrap: 0-0
Best Rating:

Mister Doc

4-y-o ch g Most Welcome-Red Poppy (IRE) (Coquelin (USA))
D W Barker L H Gilmurray & T J Docherty

Placings:P (4044)
2001/02: 17^{P}GS

	Starts	1st	2nd	3rd	Win & Pl
Hurdles	1	0	0	0	
Career Total	**1**	**0**	**0**	**0**	

Going: Sf: 0-0 GS: 0-1 Gd: 0-0 GF: - Fm: 0-0
Distance: 2m/2m3: 0-1 2m4-2m7: 0-0 3m+: 0-0
Track: LH: 0-0 RH: 0-1 Tight: 0-1 Gall: 0-0
Aids: Bl: 0-0 Vi: 0-0 Tstrap: 0-0
Best Rating:

Mister Doon (IRE)

103 **117**
9-y-o b g Mister Lord (USA)-Knockadoon (Golden Love)
Miss S Edwards Maurice E Pinto

Placings:02/0102/615P0-U4P2036 (4885)
2001/02: 20^{U}GS, 24^{4}G, 22^{P}S, 22^{2}S, 22^{0}G, 24^{3}GF, 27^{6}GF

	Starts	1st	2nd	3rd	Win & Pl
Hurdles	6	0	1	1	2704
Chases	1	0	0	0	0
Career Total	**18**	**2**	**3**	**1**	**10103**

125	12/00	Font	2m6f110y	F(0-110)HHdl	SFT	£2373
112	2/00	Kemp	2m5f	D Hdl	GD	£3802

Total win prize-money £6176

Going: Sf: 0-2 GS: 0-1 Gd: 0-2 GF: - Fm: 0-2
Distance: 2m/2m3: 0-0 2m4-2m7: 0-4 3m+: 0-3
Track: LH: 0-2 RH: 0-2 Tight: 0-3 Gall: 0-0
Aids: Bl: 0-2 Vi: 0-0 Tstrap: 0-0
Best Rating: 125 12/00 Font 2m6f110y soft Hdl

Fair staying hurdler, most effective on soft ground although handles a sound surface, has worn blinkers.

Mister Ermyn

9-y-o ch g Minster Son-Rosana Park (Music Boy)
L Montague Hall J Daniels

Placings:*310*/625/P/O60/1011PUS2UPP-P5 **(1675)**
2001/02: 22^{P}GF, 17^{5}HY

	Starts	1st	2nd	3rd	Win & Pl
Hurdles	2	0	0	0	0
Career Total	**23**	**4**	**2**	**1**	**11953**

100	8/00	Worc	2m4f	F(0-100)HHdl	G-F	£1904
92	7/00	Strf	2m3f	E(0-105)HHdl	G-F	£2744
83	5/00	Folk	2m1f110y	G(0-95)HHdl	GD	£1645
95	2/97	Asct	2m110y	H NHF	G-F	£2274

Total win prize-money £8567

Going: Sf: 0-1 GS: 0-0 Gd: 0-0 GF: - Fm: 0-1
Distance: 2m/2m3: 0-1 2m4-2m7: 0-1 3m+: 0-0
Track: LH: 0-1 RH: 0-1 Tight: 0-2 Gall: 0-0
Aids: Bl: 0-2 Vi: 0-0 Tstrap: 0-0
Best Rating: 101 11/00 Chel 2m110y gd-sft Hdl

Mister Falcon (FR)

102 **106**

5-y-o b g Passing Sale (FR)-Falcon Crest (FR) (Cadoudal (FR))
M C Pipe Telefocus Limited

Placings:363-122113655P **(4119)**
2001/02: 22^{1}F, 16^{2}GF, 22^{2}GS, 22^{1}GF, 22^{1}GF, 27^{3}G, 24^{6}GF, 22^{5}GF, 24^{5}GF, 22^{P}G

	Starts	1st	2nd	3rd	Win & Pl
Hurdles	10	3	2	1	11217
Career Total	**13**	**3**	**2**	**3**	**11935**

99	7/01	Strf	2m6f110y	D Hdl	G-F	£3666
101	6/01	NAbb	2m6f	D Hdl	G-F	£3241
103	5/01	Sthl	2m4f110y	E Hdl	FRM	£2233

Total win prize-money £9141

Going: Sf: 0-0 GS: 0-1 Gd: 0-2 GF: - Fm: 3-7
Distance: 2m/2m3: 0-1 **2m4-2m7: 3-6** 3m+: 0-3
Track: **LH: 3-7** RH: 0-3 **Tight: 3-6** Gall: 0-0
Aids: Bl: 0-0 **Vi: 3-10** Tstrap: 0-0
Best Rating: 106 6/01 NAbb 2m6f gd-sft Hdl

Mister Generosity (IRE)

84 **91**

11-y-o b g King's Ride-Brownstown Lady (Charlottesvilles Flyer)
C Weedon Mrs J M Jeyes

Placings:*0/040P/F012PP/03210/F/*P55-0P **(1893)**
2001/02: 22^{0}GF, 20^{P}GS

	Starts	1st	2nd	3rd	Win & Pl
Hurdles	2	0	0	0	
Career Total	**22**	**2**	**2**	**1**	**7425**

98	2/99	Ludl	3m2f110y	E(0-115)HHdl	GD	£3501
74	3/98	Winc	2m6f	F(0-100)HHdl	GD	£2248

Total win prize-money £5749

Going: Sf: 0-0 GS: 0-1 Gd: 0-0 GF: - Fm: 0-1
Distance: 2m/2m3: 0-0 2m4-2m7: 0-2 3m+: 0-0
Track: LH: 0-1 RH: 0-0 Tight: 0-2 Gall: 0-0
Aids: Bl: 0-1 Vi: 0-0 Tstrap: 0-0
Best Rating: 98 2/99 Ludl 3m2f110y good Hdl

Mister Graham

96(101c) (106c)**69**

7-y-o b g Rock Hopper-Celestial Air (Rheingold)
Mrs S J Smith Keith Nicholson

Placings:*203*/650050/3325-3005P650 **(1488)**
2001/02: 20^{3}G, 20^{0}G, 22^{0}GF, 21^{5}GF, 24^{P}GF, 20^{6}GF, 17^{5}GS, 20^{0}GF

	Starts	1st	2nd	3rd	Win & Pl
Hurdles	3	0	0	0	0
Chases	5	0	0	1	784
Career Total	**21**	**0**	**2**	**4**	**3327**

Going: Sf: 0-0 GS: 0-1 Gd: 0-2 GF: - Fm: 0-5
Distance: 2m/2m3: 0-1 2m4-2m7: 0-6 3m+: 0-1
Track: LH: 0-5 RH: 0-3 Tight: 0-5 Gall: 0-1
Aids: Bl: 0-0 Vi: 0-0 Tstrap: 0-0
Best Rating: 106 5/01 MRas 2m4f good Ch

Mister H

90f **80f**

5-y-o b g Thowra (FR)-Sicilian Vespers (Mummy's Game)
J Cullinan Turf 2000 Limited

Placings:*545* **(1019)**
2001/02: 17^{5}GF, 16^{4}G, 16^{5}G

	Starts	1st	2nd	3rd	Win & Pl
NH Flat	3	0	0	0	0
Career Total	**0**	**0**	**0**	**0**	**0**

Going: Sf: 0-0 GS: 0-0 Gd: 0-2 GF: - Fm: 0-1
Distance: 2m/2m3: 0-3 2m4-2m7: 0-0 3m+: 0-0
Track: LH: 0-2 RH: 0-0 Tight: 0-1 Gall: 0-0
Aids: Bl: 0-0 Vi: 0-0 Tstrap: 0-0
Best Rating: 80 7/01 Worc 2m good NHF

Mister Havana

68 **40**

5-y-o br g Pelder (IRE)-Cee Beat (Bairn (USA))
E A Wheeler E A Wheeler

Placings:0 **(2328)**
2001/02: 16^{0}G

	Starts	1st	2nd	3rd	Win & Pl
Hurdles	1	0	0	0	
Career Total	**1**	**0**	**0**	**0**	

Going: Sf: 0-0 GS: 0-0 Gd: 0-1 GF: - Fm: 0-0
Distance: 2m/2m3: 0-1 2m4-2m7: 0-0 3m+: 0-0
Track: LH: 0-1 RH: 0-0 Tight: 0-1 Gall: 0-0
Aids: Bl: 0-0 Vi: 0-0 Tstrap: 0-0
Best Rating: 40 11/01 Plum 2m good Hdl

Mister Horatio

94 **108**

12-y-o b g Derring Rose-Miss Horatio (Spartan General)
P Bowen W D Lewis

Placings:*6/1/24U/54022/24223/F003*-36300P **(1826)**
2001/02: 19^{3}GS, 24^{6}GF, 22^{3}GF, 21^{0}GF, 23^{0}G, 20^{P}G

	Starts	1st	2nd	3rd	Win & Pl
Chases	6	0	0	2	1002
Career Total	**25**	**1**	**6**	**4**	**7282**

96	4/97	Sthl	3m110y	H Ch	GD	£1084

Total win prize-money £1084

Going: Sf: 0-0 GS: 0-1 Gd: 0-2 GF: - Fm: 0-3

Distance: 2m/2m3: 0-0 2m4-2m7: 0-4 3m+: 0-2
Track: LH: 0-3 RH: 0-3 Tight: 0-3 Gall: 0-1
Aids: Bl: 0-5 Vi: 0-0 Tstrap: 0-2
Best Rating: 111 3/00 Newb 2m6f110y gd-fm Ch

Mister Kingston

107 **85**

11-y-o ch g Kinglet-Flaxen Tina (Beau Tudor)
R Dickin Mrs C M Dickin

Placings:53642/UP-6BPP33300 **(2273)**
2001/02: 25^{6}G, 24^{B}GF, 21^{P}G, 23^{P}G, 23^{3}GF, 26^{3}GF, 25^{3}G, 26^{0}G, 24^{0}G

	Starts	1st	2nd	3rd	Win & Pl
Chases	9	0	0	3	1603
Career Total	**16**	**0**	**1**	**4**	**3497**

Going: Sf: 0-0 GS: 0-0 Gd: 0-6 GF: - Fm: 0-3
Distance: 2m/2m3: 0-0 2m4-2m7: 0-1 3m+: 0-8
Track: LH: 0-5 RH: 0-2 Tight: 0-2 Gall: 0-0
Aids: Bl: 0-0 Vi: 0-4 Tstrap: 0-0
Best Rating: 107 4/00 Towc 3m1f good Ch

Modest staying chaser.

Mister Magpie

96 **95**

6-y-o gr g Neltino-Magic (Sweet Revenge)
T R George Timothy N Chick

Placings:*035*001 **(4894)**
2001/02: 16^{0}G, 16^{3}GS, 16^{5}GS, 22^{0}G, 20^{0}G, 16^{1}G

	Starts	1st	2nd	3rd	Win & Pl
NH Flat	3	0	0	1	229
Hurdles	3	1	0	0	3744
Career Total	**6**	**1**	**0**	**1**	**3973**

95	4/02	Prth	2m110y	D Hdl	GD	£3744

Total win prize-money £3744

Going: Sf: 0-0 GS: 0-2 Gd: 1-4 GF: - Fm: 0-0
Distance: **2m/2m3: 1-4** 2m4-2m7: 0-2 3m+: 0-0
Track: LH: 0-1 **RH: 1-5** Tight: 0-0 Gall: 0-2
Aids: Bl: 0-0 Vi: 0-0 Tstrap: 0-0
Best Rating: 100 2/02 Winc 2m gd-sft NHF

A chaser in the making, he has shown ability in bumpers over two miles. Will stay further.

Mister McGoldrick

108 **115**

5-y-o b g Sabrehill (USA)-Anchor Inn (Be My Guest (USA))
Mrs S J Smith (J G Given 11/1) Richard Longley

Placings:00-6001104 **(4879)**
2001/02: 16^{6}HY, 16^{0}S, 16^{0}GS, 16^{1}GS, 17^{1}S, 20^{0}G, 16^{4}G

	Starts	1st	2nd	3rd	Win & Pl
Hurdles	7	2	0	0	7767
Career Total	**9**	**2**	**0**	**0**	**7767**

115	3/02	Bang	2m1f	E Hdl	SFT	£3262
112	3/02	Donc	2m110y	E(0-105)HHdl	G-S	£4062

Total win prize-money £7325

Going: Sf: 1-3 GS: 1-2 Gd: 0-2 GF: - Fm: 0-0
Distance: **2m/2m3: 2-6** 2m4-2m7: 0-1 3m+: 0-0
Track: **LH: 2-4** RH: 0-3 Tight: 1-2 Gall: 1-2
Aids: Bl: 0-0 Vi: 0-0 Tstrap: 0-0
Best Rating: 115 3/02 Bang 2m1f soft Hdl

Fair two-mile novice hurdler on the upgrade. Landed a gamble at Doncaster in March 2002 on debut for Sue Smith before following up in style at Bangor. Well suited by soft ground and has the scope to make a chaser.

Mister Morose (IRE)

113 141

12-y-o b g King's Ride-Girseach (Furry Glen)
N A Twiston-Davies H R Mould

Placings:211F3/106/11UU443/1F5111/61556-300 **(4676)**
2001/02: 21^{3}HY, 16^{0}GS, 20^{0}G

	Starts	1st	2nd	3rd	Win & Pl
Hurdles	3	0	0	1	5750
Career Total	**29**	**10**	**1**	**3**	**185324**

170	11/00	Winc	2m	A HHdl	G-S	£15000
170	4/00	Chep	2m110y	B HHdl	HVY	£13305
153	4/00	Ayr	2m	A HHdl	GD	£17030
167	4/00	Aint	2m4f	A Hdl	GD	£60000
151	10/99	Bang	2m1f110y	C(0-130)HCh	SFT	£5795
151	11/98	Chel	2m	A Ch	G-S	£12440
157	11/98	Chep	2m4f110y	B HHdl	G-S	£22821
137	11/96	Newb	2m110y	B(0-140)HHdl	G-S	£4900
125	1/96	Winc	2m	E Hdl	G-S	£2757
112	12/95	Ling	2m110y	H NHF	HVY	£1371

Total win prize-money £155421

Going: Sf: 0-1 GS: 0-1 Gd: 0-1 GF: - Fm: 0-0
Distance: 2m/2m3: 0-1 2m4-2m7: 0-2 3m+: 0-0
Track: LH: 0-3 RH: 0-0 Tight: 0-1 Gall: 0-1
Aids: Bl: 0-1 Vi: 0-0 Tstrap: 0-0
Best Rating: 170 11/00 Winc 2m gd-sft Hdl

He made all at Wincanton in November 2000 but was held in the Bula and Christmas hurdles thereafter. Missed the rest of the season with a leg injury. Fair effort at Cheltenham on his reappearance in 2002. He remains relatively unexposed over fences, but is not a natural jumper. Suited by two miles. Has won on good ground and heavy.

Mister Muddypaws

64 125

12-y-o b g Celtic Cone-Jane's Daughter (Pitpan)
Mrs A M Naughton (J Howard Johnson 4/5) T W Ellwood

Placings:2346/4121/**P4P4**/**U3452231**/**FF433P1P**/105 **P-P1P** **(4918)**
2001/02: 28^{P}G, 24^{1}F, 28^{P}GF

	Starts	1st	2nd	3rd	Win & Pl
Chases	3	1	0	0	5872
Career Total	**35**	**6**	**4**	**5**	**48025**

125	4/02	Newc	3m	D(0-120)HCh	FRM	£5872
131	5/00	Sedg	3m4f	D(0-125)HCh	G-F	£10822
126	3/00	Sedg	3m4f	D(0-120)HCh	G-F	£4212
131	4/99	Sedg	3m4f	C(0-130)HCh	G-S	£11422
100	11/95	Carl	3m110y	E Hdl	G-F	£2136
89	5/95	Hexm	2m4f110y	Hdl	G-F	£2469

Total win prize-money £36935

Going: Sf: 0-0 GS: 0-0 Gd: 0-1 GF: - Fm: 1-2
Distance: 2m/2m3: 0-0 2m4-2m7: 0-0 **3m+: 1-3**
Track: **LH: 1-3** RH: 0-0 Tight: 0-2 **Gall: 1-1**
Aids: Bl: 0-1 Vi: 0-0 Tstrap: 0-0
Best Rating: 131 5/00 Sedg 3m4f gd-fm Ch

A dour stayer, suited by fast ground, he beat his sole opponent at Newcastle in April.

Mister One

111 148

11-y-o b/br g Buckley-Miss Redlands (Dubassoff (USA))
C Tizzard C L Tizzard

Placings:4/113FP33/35012U0-10512 **(4819)**
2001/02: 25^{1}G, 24^{0}GS, 24^{5}S, 30^{1}G, 26^{2}GF

	Starts	1st	2nd	3rd	Win & Pl
Chases	5	2	1	0	18020
Career Total	**20**	**5**	**2**	**4**	**53316**

148	3/02	Extr	3m6f110y	D(0-125)HCh	GD	£8417
143	1/02	Winc	3m1f110y	D(0-125)HCh	GD	£5580
129	2/01	Sand	3m110y	E Ch	SFT	£5486
143	12/99	Chel	3m1f110y	C Ch	GD	£6905
142	11/99	Chel	3m110y	B Ch	GD	£9530

Total win prize-money £35920

Going: Sf: 0-1 GS: 0-1 Gd: 2-2 GF: - Fm: 0-1
Distance: 2m/2m3: 0-0 2m4-2m7: 0-0 **3m+: 2-5**
Track: LH: 0-1 **RH: 1-3** Tight: 0-0 Gall: 0-1
Aids: Bl: 0-0 Vi: 0-0 Tstrap: 0-0
Best Rating: 148 4/02 Chel 3m2f110y gd-fm Ch

A thorough stayer, he was slightly inconsistent in 2000/2001 and did not always impress with his attitude, but he has been in good heart in 2002. Best on decent ground and when fresh.

Mister Party

7-y-o b g Henbit (USA)-Sally's Dove (Celtic Cone)
H D Daly Louise Daly's Partnership

Placings:00/PF **(2949)**
2001/02: 19^{P}S, 22^{F}S

	Starts	1st	2nd	3rd	Win & Pl
Hurdles	2	0	0	0	
Career Total	**4**	**0**	**0**	**0**	

Going: Sf: 0-2 GS: 0-0 Gd: 0-0 GF: - Fm: 0-0
Distance: 2m/2m3: 0-0 2m4-2m7: 0-2 3m+: 0-0
Track: LH: 0-1 RH: 0-1 Tight: 0-1 Gall: 0-0
Aids: Bl: 0-0 Vi: 0-0 Tstrap: 0-0
Best Rating: 71 2/00 Towc 2m heavy NHF

Mister Pepper (IRE)

84

6-y-o br g Leading Counsel (USA)-Bold Strike (FR) (Bold Lad (USA))
K F O'Brien Denis J Reddan

Placings:6/P-435P **(4678)**
2001/02: 25^{4}SH, 24^{3}S, 24^{5}S, 25^{P}G

	Starts	1st	2nd	3rd	Win & Pl
Chases	4	0	0	1	598
Career Total	**6**	**0**	**0**	**1**	**598**

Going: Sf: 0-2 GS: 0-0 Gd: 0-1 GF: - Fm: 0-0
Distance: 2m/2m3: 0-0 2m4-2m7: 0-0 3m+: 0-4
Track: LH: 0-1 RH: 0-1 Tight: 0-1 Gall: 0-0
Aids: Bl: 0-1 Vi: 0-0 Tstrap: 0-0
Best Rating: 84 3/02 Dpat 3m soft Ch

Mister Pickwick (IRE)

99(102c) (88c)88

7-y-o b g Commanche Run-Buckfast Lass (Buckskin (FR))
G L Moore (M Pitman 5/6) Barry Prichard & Wayne Russell

Placings:3036001F/4P02FPP-P46P0304 **(4882)**
2001/02: 27^{P}G, 27^{4}G, 21^{6}GS, 22^{P}HY, 16^{0}S, 17^{3}G, 21^{0}GF, 26^{4}GF

	Starts	1st	2nd	3rd	Win & Pl
Hurdles	7	0	0	1	304
Chases	1	0	0	0	0
Career Total	**23**	**1**	**1**	**3**	**4252**

102	4/00	Plum	3m1f110y	E(0-105)HHdl	G-S	£2660

Total win prize-money £2660

Going: Sf: 0-2 GS: 0-1 Gd: 0-3 GF: - Fm: 0-2
Distance: 2m/2m3: 0-2 2m4-2m7: 0-3 3m+: 0-3
Track: LH: 0-3 RH: 0-4 Tight: 0-5 Gall: 0-1
Aids: Bl: 0-6 Vi: 0-1 Tstrap: 0-0
Best Rating: 102 4/00 Plum 3m1f110y gd-sft Hdl

Moderate hurdler/chaser, stays well and seems to handle any ground.

Mister Pq

89 76

6-y-o ch g Ardkinglass-Well Off (Welsh Pageant)
J G Smyth-Osbourne Pq International/euromedia

Placings:F05-405F **(1137)**
2001/02: 19^{4}F, 21^{0}GF, 20^{5}G, 22^{F}G

	Starts	1st	2nd	3rd	Win & Pl
Hurdles	4	0	0	0	0
Career Total	**7**	**0**	**0**	**0**	**0**

Going: Sf: 0-0 GS: 0-0 Gd: 0-2 GF: - Fm: 0-2
Distance: 2m/2m3: 0-0 2m4-2m7: 0-4 3m+: 0-0
Track: LH: 0-2 RH: 0-2 Tight: 0-2 Gall: 0-1
Aids: Bl: 0-0 Vi: 0-0 Tstrap: 0-0
Best Rating: 81 12/00 Hntg 2m5f110y soft Hdl

Mister Putt (USA)

100 100

4-y-o b/br g Mister Baileys-Theresita (GER) (Surumu (GER))
Mrs N Smith (J A Osborne 7/7) Tony Hayward And Barry Fulton

Placings:0432P **(4417)**
2001/02: 16^{0}G, 18^{4}G, 18^{3}S, 16^{2}GS, 16^{P}GS

	Starts	1st	2nd	3rd	Win & Pl
Hurdles	5	0	1	1	1789
Career Total	**5**	**0**	**1**	**1**	**1789**

Going: Sf: 0-1 GS: 0-2 Gd: 0-2 GF: - Fm: 0-0
Distance: 2m/2m3: 0-5 2m4-2m7: 0-0 3m+: 0-0
Track: LH: 0-4 RH: 0-1 Tight: 0-2 Gall: 0-2
Aids: Bl: 0-0 Vi: 0-0 Tstrap: 0-0
Best Rating: 100 3/02 Newb 2m110y gd-sft Hdl

Placed form over hurdles so far in novice events and in handicap company. Suited by good ground.

Mister Rm

82 61

10-y-o b g Dominion-La Cabrilla (Carwhite)
N A Twiston-Davies Mr F J Mills & Mr W Mills

Placings:1154142F24/26433/533200626/01115F3/P-000 **(3643)**
2001/02: 24^{0}G, 20^{0}HY, 16^{0}S

	Starts	1st	2nd	3rd	Win & Pl
Hurdles	3	0	0	0	
Career Total	**35**	**6**	**5**	**5**	**48887**

138	10/99	Hntg	2m4f110y	E Ch	G-F	£3129
138	9/99	Prth	2m	D Ch	SFT	£5524
125	9/99	Bang	2m4f110y	D Ch	G-F	£4260
111	12/96	Uttx	2m	E Hdl	G-S	£2631
113	10/96	Chel	2m110y	E(0-135)HHdl	G-F	£2220
112	10/96	MRas	2m1f110y	E Hdl	GD	£2388

Total win prize-money £20152

Going: Sf: 0-2 GS: 0-0 Gd: 0-1 GF: - Fm: 0-0
Distance: 2m/2m3: 0-1 2m4-2m7: 0-1 3m+: 0-1
Track: LH: 0-1 RH: 0-1 Tight: 0-0 Gall: 0-0
Aids: Bl: 0-0 Vi: 0-0 Tstrap: 0-0
Best Rating: 138 10/99 Hntg 2m4f110y gd-fm Ch

A winner of three novice chases in 1999, he has been lightly raced since then and was off the track for 14 months before pulling up on his return at Kempton in February 2001.

Mister Sandrovitch (IRE)

76 **29**

9-y-o b g Be My Native (USA)-Salufair (Salluceva)
A R Dicken Tony Curson

Placings: *10*/053060/P4/P0 (1817)
2001/02: 22PG, 17OS

	Starts	1st	2nd	3rd	Win & Pl
Hurdles	2	0	0	0	
Career Total	**12**	**1**	**0**	**1**	**2085**

102 12/97 NAbb 2m1f H NHF HVY £1131
Total win prize-money £1131

Going: Sf: 0-1 GS: 0-0 Gd: 0-1 GF: - Fm: 0-0
Distance: 2m/2m3: 0-1 2m4-2m7: 0-1 3m+: 0-0
Track: LH: 0-1 RH: 0-1 Tight: 0-1 Gall: 0-0
Aids: Bl: 0-0 Vi: 0-0 Tstrap: 0-0
Best Rating: 102 12/97 NAbb 2m1f heavy NHF

Mister Webb

96 **91**

5-y-o b g Whittingham (IRE)-Ruda (FR) (Free Round (USA))
Dr J R J Naylor Norman E Webb

Placings: 34 (2274)
2001/02: 173S, 164G

	Starts	1st	2nd	3rd	Win & Pl
Hurdles	2	0	0	1	423
Career Total	**2**	**0**	**0**	**1**	**423**

Going: Sf: 0-1 GS: 0-0 Gd: 0-1 GF: - Fm: 0-0
Distance: 2m/2m3: 0-2 2m4-2m7: 0-0 3m+: 0-0
Track: LH: 0-2 RH: 0-0 Tight: 0-1 Gall: 0-0
Aids: Bl: 0-0 Vi: 0-0 Tstrap: 0-0
Best Rating: 91 11/01 Wwck 2m good Hdl

A maiden stayer on the Flat, shaped as though he is going to need a stiffer test of stamina when third over two miles one on his Newton Abbot hurdles bow.

Mister Wellard

97f **124f**

5-y-o b g Sir Harry Lewis (USA)-Cream By Post (Torus)
P F Nicholls T C Frost

Placings: *1* (4900)
2001/02: 161G

	Starts	1st	2nd	3rd	Win & Pl
NH Flat	1	1	0	0	3556
Career Total	**1**	**1**	**0**	**0**	**3556**

124 4/02 Prth 2m110y H NHF GD £3556
Total win prize-money £3556

Going: Sf: 0-0 GS: 0-0 Gd: 1-1 GF: - Fm: 0-0
Distance: **2m/2m3: 1-1** 2m4-2m7: 0-0 3m+: 0-0
Track: LH: 0-0 **RH: 1-1** Tight: 0-0 Gall: 0-0
Aids: Bl: 0-0 Vi: 0-0 Tstrap: 0-0
Best Rating: 124 4/02 Prth 2m110y good NHF

Misti Hunter (IRE)

86 **87**

13-y-o gr g Roselier (FR)-Lovely Stranger (Le Bavard (FR))
Miss L C Siddall Mrs D Ibbotson

Placings: *6*00P0000/0323**2314**1/P/240-030 (0643)
2001/02: 250S, 223G, 220GF

	Starts	1st	2nd	3rd	Win & Pl
Chases	3	0	0	1	352
Career Total	**24**	**2**	**3**	**4**	**9554**

88 4/96 MRas 3m1f E(0-100)HCh G-F £2999
85 11/95 Hexm 3m1f F Ch G-F £2707
Total win prize-money £5706

Going: Sf: 0-1 GS: 0-0 Gd: 0-1 GF: - Fm: 0-1
Distance: 2m/2m3: 0-0 2m4-2m7: 0-2 3m+: 0-1
Track: LH: 0-1 RH: 0-2 Tight: 0-2 Gall: 0-0
Aids: Bl: 0-0 Vi: 0-0 Tstrap: 0-0
Best Rating: 105 5/00 MRas 2m6f110y gd-sft Ch

Mistletoe (IRE)

111(98h) **148**

8-y-o gr m Montelimar (USA)-Nancy's Sister (The Parson)
K C Bailey (N J Henderson 17/1) Mrs John Loudon

Placings: 2235/252-23211 (4297)
2001/02: 162S, 203GS, 202G, 201GS, 211HY

	Starts	1st	2nd	3rd	Win & Pl
Chases	5	2	2	1	26186
Career Total	**12**	**2**	**6**	**2**	**29514**

148 3/02 Uttx 2m5f A HCh HVY £18760
132 2/02 Ludl 2m4f D Ch G-S £4680
Total win prize-money £23440

Going: Sf: 1-2 GS: 1-2 Gd: 0-1 GF: - Fm: 0-0
Distance: 2m/2m3: 0-1 **2m4-2m7: 2-4** 3m+: 0-0
Track: LH: 1-2 RH: 1-3 **Tight: 1-2** Gall: 0-1
Aids: Bl: 0-0 Vi: 0-0 Tstrap: 0-0
Best Rating: 148 3/02 Uttx 2m5f heavy Ch

Decent placed efforts in novice chases for Nicky Henderson before winning at Ludlow on her first start for Kim Bailey and followed up with a fine victory in the Tattersalls Mares' Final at Uttoxeter. Jumps well and stays two and a half miles. Acts on good to soft/soft ground.

Mistress Millie (IRE)

82 **69**

6-y-o ch m St Ninian-Nearly Married (Nearly A Hand)
A W Carroll Miss E J Marley

Placings: *5* (4743)
2001/02: 165GF

	Starts	1st	2nd	3rd	Win & Pl
NH Flat	1	0	0	0	0
Career Total	**1**	**0**	**0**	**0**	**0**

Going: Sf: 0-0 GS: 0-0 Gd: 0-0 GF: - Fm: 0-1
Distance: 2m/2m3: 0-1 2m4-2m7: 0-0 3m+: 0-0
Track: LH: 0-0 RH: 0-1 Tight: 0-0 Gall: 0-0
Aids: Bl: 0-0 Vi: 0-0 Tstrap: 0-0
Best Rating: 90 4/02 Ludl 2m gd-fm NHF

Misty Blues

95 **82**

6-y-o b m Pontevecchio Notte-Bay Blues (Cure The Blues (USA))
R G Frost D C And Mrs T M Fisher

Placings: *00*/3PP-002 (0832)
2001/02: 170GF, 170G, 172GF

	Starts	1st	2nd	3rd	Win & Pl
Hurdles	3	0	1	0	1094
Career Total	**8**	**0**	**1**	**1**	**1431**

Going: Sf: 0-0 GS: 0-0 Gd: 0-1 GF: - Fm: 0-2
Distance: 2m/2m3: 0-3 2m4-2m7: 0-0 3m+: 0-0
Track: LH: 0-3 RH: 0-0 Tight: 0-3 Gall: 0-0
Aids: Bl: 0-0 Vi: 0-0 Tstrap: 0-0
Best Rating: 82 6/01 NAbb 2m1f gd-fm Hdl

Misty Class (IRE)

106(106h) (137h)**136**

10-y-o gr g Roselier (FR)-Toevarro (Raga Navarro (ITY))
Mrs S J Smith Widdop Wanderers

Placings: *4*/205600/6143**25261**/14**52F23F31U**/2C113 P04P-14020 (2686)
2001/02: 241GF, 254F, 250G, 252GS, 260G

	Starts	1st	2nd	3rd	Win & Pl
Hurdles	2	1	0	0	5733
Chases	3	0	1	0	2779
Career Total	**41**	**7**	**7**	**4**	**57230**

137 5/01 Sthl 3m110y C(0-130)HHdl G-F £5733
147 12/00 Donc 3m2f B(0-140)HCh G-S £10773
147 12/00 Weth 3m1f C(0-130)HCh SFT £5915
125 3/00 Kels 3m1f D Ch G-S £5200
103 5/99 Weth 2m4f110y D Hdl G-F £3078
124 4/99 Ayr 2m6f C HHdl HVY £7327
98 10/98 Towc 2m5f E(0-100)HHdl G-S £2402
Total win prize-money £40431

Going: Sf: 0-0 GS: 0-1 Gd: 0-2 GF: - Fm: 1-2
Distance: 2m/2m3: 0-0 2m4-2m7: 0-0 **3m+: 1-5**
Track: **LH: 1-5** RH: 0-0 **Tight: 1-2** Gall: 0-1
Aids: Bl: 0-0 Vi: 0-0 Tstrap: 0-0
Best Rating: 147 12/00 Donc 3m2f gd-sft Ch

He jumps and stays and was well ridden by Dominic Elsworth when winning two handicap chases in December 2000. Below par afterwards until winning over hurdles at Southwell in May 2001. Returned over hurdles at Wetherby in November 2001, but ran better when put back over fences. Has won on soft and good ground. Stays three miles.

Misty Dawn

102f **108f**

6-y-o gr g King's Ride-Dawn Spinner (Arctic Lord)
P Winkworth D Turnbull, R Robinson, R Scott

Placings: *1* (0108)
2001/02: 181GF

	Starts	1st	2nd	3rd	Win & Pl
NH Flat	1	1	0	0	1967
Career Total	**1**	**1**	**0**	**0**	**1967**

108 5/01 Font 2m2f110y H NHF G-F £1967
Total win prize-money £1967

Going: Sf: 0-0 GS: 0-0 Gd: 0-0 GF: - Fm: 1-1
Distance: **2m/2m3: 1-1** 2m4-2m7: 0-0 3m+: 0-0
Track: **LH: 1-1** RH: 0-0 **Tight: 1-1** Gall: 0-0
Aids: Bl: 0-0 Vi: 0-0 Tstrap: 0-0
Best Rating: 108 5/01 Font 2m2f110y gd-fm NHF

Misty Path (IRE)

6-y-o gr m Buckskin (FR)-Party Cloak (New Member)
D McCain B Dunn

Placings:*P* **(3985)**
2001/02: 16^{P}G

	Starts	1st	2nd	3rd	Win & Pl
NH Flat	1	0	0	0	
Career Total	**1**	**0**	**0**	**0**	

Going: Sf: 0-0 GS: 0-0 Gd: 0-1 GF: - Fm: 0-0
Distance: 2m/2m3: 0-1 2m4-2m7: 0-0 3m+: 0-0
Track: LH: 0-0 RH: 0-1 Tight: 0-0 Gall: 0-0
Aids: Bl: 0-0 Vi: 0-0 Tstrap: 0-0
Best Rating:

Misty Ramble (IRE)

100(101h) **112**
7-y-o b g Roselier (FR)-Ramble Bramble (Random Shot)
Ferdy Murphy Frickley Holdings Ltd

Placings:*0/0*420-34352 **(4395)**
2001/02: 25^{3}GS, 28^{4}S, 24^{3}HY, 21^{5}S, 25^{2}HY

	Starts	1st	2nd	3rd	Win & Pl
Chases	5	0	1	2	2978
Career Total	**10**	**0**	**2**	**2**	**3981**

Going: Sf: 0-4 GS: 0-1 Gd: 0-0 GF: - Fm: 0-0
Distance: 2m/2m3: 0-0 2m4-2m7: 0-1 3m+: 0-4
Track: LH: 0-4 RH: 0-1 Tight: 0-4 Gall: 0-0
Aids: Bl: 0-0 Vi: 0-0 Tstrap: 0-0
Best Rating: 112 11/01 Kels 3m1f gd-sft Ch

Moderate form shown over both hurdles and fences.

Misty Ridge (IRE)

101(82c) (68c)**96+**
7-y-o b g Moscow Society (USA)-Abigail's Dream (Kalaglow)
Mrs S J Smith Widdop Wanderers

Placings:*0/05*-030265U **(1502)**
2001/02: 16^{0}G, 20^{3}F, 20^{0}G, 16^{2}G, 17^{6}GF, 20^{5}GF, 21^{U}G

	Starts	1st	2nd	3rd	Win & Pl
Hurdles	5	0	1	1	1465
Chases	2	0	0	0	0
Career Total	**10**	**0**	**1**	**1**	**1465**

Going: Sf: 0-0 GS: 0-0 Gd: 0-4 GF: - Fm: 0-3
Distance: 2m/2m3: 0-3 2m4-2m7: 0-4 3m+: 0-0
Track: LH: 0-6 RH: 0-1 Tight: 0-2 Gall: 0-1
Aids: Bl: 0-0 Vi: 0-0 Tstrap: 0-0
Best Rating: 93 4/01 Ayr 2m gd-fm NHF

Improved form since wearing blinkers and won Class D handicap over just short of two and a half miles at Market Rasen in June 2002. Acts on good to firm.

Mitcheldean (IRE)

105(105h) (119h)**138**
6-y-o b g Be My Native (USA)-Pil Eagle (FR) (Piling (USA))
M Pitman Ray Pascoe

Placings:*35*/P3112-**3132U3** **(4849)**
2001/02: 24^{3}GS, 22^{1}HY, 24^{3}G, 20^{2}S, 19^{U}GS, 24^{3}G

	Starts	1st	2nd	3rd	Win & Pl
Chases	6	1	1	3	9850
Career Total	**13**	**3**	**2**	**5**	**19321**

138	12/01	Towc	2m6f	D Ch	HVY	£5798
119	4/01	Asct	2m4f	D Hdl	HVY	£5096
106	2/01	Fknm	2m4f	D Hdl	SFT	£3214

Total win prize-money £14108

Going: Sf: 1-2 GS: 0-2 Gd: 0-2 GF: - Fm: 0-0
Distance: 2m/2m3: 0-0 **2m4-2m7: 1-3** 3m+: 0-3
Track: LH: 0-4 **RH: 1-2** Tight: 0-2 Gall: 0-0
Aids: Bl: 0-0 Vi: 0-0 Tstrap: 0-0
Best Rating: 138 12/01 Towc 2m6f heavy Ch

Made a lot of mistakes on his chasing debut at Stratford in October of 2001, but won at Towcester next time. Held since, not jumping fluently. Acts well with cut in the ground, and stays two and three-quarter miles.

Mithak (USA)

90 **117**
8-y-o b g Silver Hawk (USA)-Kapalua Butterfly (USA) (Stagedoor Johnny)
R T Phillips T Milson C Merson P Nichols R Stokes

Placings:3133/12/065-P40U03 **(4173)**
2001/02: 20^{P}S, 24^{4}GS, 24^{0}GS, 20^{U}S, 20^{0}S, 25^{3}GS

	Starts	1st	2nd	3rd	Win & Pl
Hurdles	6	0	0	1	859
Career Total	**15**	**2**	**1**	**4**	**8579**

124	5/99	Strf	2m6f110y	E Hdl	G-S	£2738
114	1/99	Ludl	2m5f110y	F Hdl	SFT	£2255

Total win prize-money £4993

Going: Sf: 0-3 GS: 0-3 Gd: 0-0 GF: - Fm: 0-0
Distance: 2m/2m3: 0-0 2m4-2m7: 0-3 3m+: 0-3
Track: LH: 0-3 RH: 0-2 Tight: 0-2 Gall: 0-2
Aids: Bl: 0-0 Vi: 0-0 Tstrap: 0-0
Best Rating: 131 10/99 Chep 2m4f soft Hdl

Useful handicap hurdler. Not the best of jumpers. Best at around two miles on good to soft ground.

Mithraic (IRE)

98 **96**
10-y-o b g Kefaah (USA)-Persian's Glory (Prince Tenderfoot (USA))
W S Cunningham Mrs Vicky Cunningham

Placings:5000/1233034/233P1P/124P00/313F/S-24 **(1667)**
2001/02: 17^{2}GF, 16^{4}G

	Starts	1st	2nd	3rd	Win & Pl
Hurdles	2	0	1	0	478
Career Total	**30**	**4**	**4**	**7**	**12995**

106	8/99	Sthl	2m	G Hdl	G-F	£1537
87	5/98	Sthl	2m	G Hdl	GD	£1758
115	2/98	Newc	2m	G(0-95)HHdl	GD	£1700
102	9/96	Prth	2m110y	E Hdl	G-F	£2780

Total win prize-money £7775

Going: Sf: 0-0 GS: 0-0 Gd: 0-1 GF: - Fm: 0-1
Distance: 2m/2m3: 0-2 2m4-2m7: 0-0 3m+: 0-0
Track: LH: 0-1 RH: 0-1 Tight: 0-2 Gall: 0-0
Aids: Bl: 0-0 Vi: 0-0 Tstrap: 0-0
Best Rating: 115 2/98 Newc 2m good Hdl

Mizyan (IRE)

102 **112**
14-y-o b g Melyno-Maid Of Erin (USA) (Irish River (FR))
P F Nicholls P Maltby

Placings:110/23144/02322F0P/31P/3420/3/3/**330** **(0723)**
2001/02: 24^{3}F, 24^{3}GF, 25^{0}F

	Starts	1st	2nd	3rd	Win & Pl
Chases	3	0	0	2	1332
Career Total	**28**	**4**	**5**	**8**	**19250**

123	12/94	Fknm	2m4f	(0-115)HHdl	GD	£2772
117	2/93	Sthl	2m2f	(0-110)HHdl	STD	£1844
85	3/92	Sthl	2m	Hdl	STD	£1327
96	1/92	Sthl	2m	Hdl	STD	£1446

Total win prize-money £7392

Going: Sf: 0-0 GS: 0-0 Gd: 0-0 GF: - Fm: 0-3
Distance: 2m/2m3: 0-0 2m4-2m7: 0-0 3m+: 0-3
Track: LH: 0-1 RH: 0-2 Tight: 0-2 Gall: 0-0
Aids: Bl: 0-1 Vi: 0-0 Tstrap: 0-0
Best Rating: 128 11/92 Chep 2m110y soft Hdl

Mo's Boy

98 **101**
11-y-o b g Sulaafah (USA)-Ridans Girl (Ridan)
Mrs S J Smith Leigh Musketeer Racing Club

Placings:*0/6*03/26U3413/0**352/34U0351U-5F06443** **(1270)**
2001/02: 16^{5}G, 20^{F}F, 17^{0}G, 21^{6}GF, 16^{4}GF, 20^{4}G, 20^{3}GF

	Starts	1st	2nd	3rd	Win & Pl
Chases	7	0	0	1	789
Career Total	**30**	**2**	**2**	**7**	**10579**

101	8/00	Ctml	2m1f110y	F(0-100)HCh	GD	£2704
102	8/98	Bang	2m1f	E(0-100)HHdl	GD	£2850

Total win prize-money £5554

Going: Sf: 0-0 GS: 0-0 Gd: 0-3 GF: - Fm: 0-4
Distance: 2m/2m3: 0-3 2m4-2m7: 0-4 3m+: 0-0
Track: LH: 0-6 RH: 0-1 Tight: 0-5 Gall: 0-0
Aids: Bl: 0-0 Vi: 0-0 Tstrap: 0-0
Best Rating: 109 10/99 Hexm 2m110y good Ch

Mo's Keliro

10-y-o b m Lir-Bossy Cleo (Proud Challenge)
Mrs J Marsh Clive Fowlie

Placings:6/5/F **(4727)**
2001/02: 24^{F}GF

	Starts	1st	2nd	3rd	Win & Pl
Chases	1	0	0	0	
Career Total	**3**	**0**	**0**	**0**	**0**

Going: Sf: 0-0 GS: 0-0 Gd: 0-0 GF: - Fm: 0-1
Distance: 2m/2m3: 0-0 2m4-2m7: 0-0 3m+: 0-1
Track: LH: 0-1 RH: 0-0 Tight: 0-0 Gall: 0-0
Aids: Bl: 0-0 Vi: 0-0 Tstrap: 0-0
Best Rating: 67 5/99 Chep 3m good Ch

Mobaye (FR)

8-y-o ch g Le Nain Jaune (FR)-Sainte Etoile (FR) (Saint Cyrien (FR))
J Neville J Neville

Placings:*0/0*PP/0PP6FP/P **(0556)**
2001/02: 24^{P}GF

	Starts	1st	2nd	3rd	Win & Pl
Chases	1	0	0	0	
Career Total	**11**	**0**	**0**	**0**	**0**

Going: Sf: 0-0 GS: 0-0 Gd: 0-0 GF: - Fm: 0-1
Distance: 2m/2m3: 0-0 2m4-2m7: 0-0 3m+: 0-1
Track: LH: 0-0 RH: 0-1 Tight: 0-0 Gall: 0-1
Aids: Bl: 0-0 Vi: 0-0 Tstrap: 0-0

Best Rating: 81 2/00 Font 2m2f soft Ch

Modajjaj

10-y-o ch g Polish Precedent (USA)-Upend (Main Reef)
Miss L Bower M V Kirby

Placings:00/P060/P (3814)
2001/02: 17^{PS}

	Starts	1st	2nd	3rd	Win & Pl
Hurdles	1	0	0	0	
Career Total	**7**	**0**	**0**	**0**	

Going: Sf: 0-1 GS: 0-0 Gd: 0-0 GF: - Fm: 0-0
Distance: 2m/2m3: 0-1 2m4-2m7: 0-0 3m+: 0-0
Track: LH: 0-0 RH: 0-1 Tight: 0-1 Gall: 0-0
Aids: Bl: 0-1 Vi: 0-0 Tstrap: 0-0
Best Rating: 77 2/00 Hntg 2m110y soft Hdl

Modem (NZ)

109 **133**
8-y-o br g Omnicorp (NZ)-Replica (NZ) (Creag-An-Sgor)
S E H Sherwood T N Siviter

Placings:121-115 (0676)
2001/02: 17^{1}G, 16^{1}G, 16^{5}GF

	Starts	1st	2nd	3rd	Win & Pl
Hurdles	3	2	0	0	11531
Career Total	**6**	**4**	**1**	**0**	**17638**

133	5/01	Aint	2m110y	B(0-145)HHdl	GD	£6929
125	5/01	Bang	2m1f	E(0-115)HHdl	GD	£4602
114	10/00	Chel	2m110y	E(0-135)HHdl	GD	£3445
107	9/00	Worc	2m	E Hdl	G-F	£1897

Total win prize-money £16873

Going: Sf: 0-0 GS: 0-0 Gd: 2-2 GF: - Fm: 0-1
Distance: **2m/2m3: 2-3** 2m4-2m7: 0-0 3m+: 0-0
Track: **LH: 2-3** RH: 0-0 **Tight: 2-2** Gall: 0-0
Aids: Bl: 0-0 Vi: 0-0 Tstrap: 0-0
Best Rating: **133** 5/01 Aint 2m110y good Hdl

Mogul

95 **92**
8-y-o b g Formidable (USA)-Madiyla (Darshaan)
R J Baker R J Baker

Placings:U/0P/246-0640 (0795)
2001/02: 17^{0}GF, 19^{6}G, 17^{4}G, 22^{0}GF

	Starts	1st	2nd	3rd	Win & Pl
Hurdles	4	0	0	0	0
Career Total	**10**	**0**	**1**	**0**	**644**

Going: Sf: 0-0 GS: 0-0 Gd: 0-2 GF: - Fm: 0-2
Distance: 2m/2m3: 0-2 2m4-2m7: 0-2 3m+: 0-0
Track: LH: 0-3 RH: 0-1 Tight: 0-3 Gall: 0-0
Aids: Bl: 0-1 Vi: 0-0 Tstrap: 0-0
Best Rating: **96** 8/00 NAbb 2m1f good Hdl

Mojo

69 **52**
6-y-o gr g Mtoto-Pepper Star (IRE) (Salt Dome (USA))
Miss A Stokell (G M Moore 11/1) Mrs S E Cooper

Placings:00-0U00 (4546)
2001/02: 16^{0}G, 16^{U}GF, 16^{0}G, 16^{0}GF

	Starts	1st	2nd	3rd	Win & Pl
Hurdles	4	0	0	0	
Career Total	**6**	**0**	**0**	**0**	

Going: Sf: 0-0 GS: 0-0 Gd: 0-2 GF: - Fm: 0-2
Distance: 2m/2m3: 0-4 2m4-2m7: 0-0 3m+: 0-0
Track: LH: 0-2 RH: 0-2 Tight: 0-2 Gall: 0-2
Aids: Bl: 0-0 Vi: 0-0 Tstrap: 0-0
Best Rating: **52** 3/02 Fknm 2m good Hdl

Has shown modest form to date over hurdles.

Moll Kettle (IRE)

105
7-y-o b m Supreme Leader-Axxon Choice (Tarqogan)
Denis P Murphy Road House Syndicate

Placings:0/200011-0505420PP (4932a)
2001/02: 22^{0}G, 16^{5}YS, 22^{0}Y, 16^{5}YS, 20^{4}HY, 20^{2}HY, 16^{0}S, 21^{P}HY, 20^{P}YS

	Starts	1st	2nd	3rd	Win & Pl
Hurdles	1	0	0	0	0
Chases	8	0	1	0	2751
Career Total	**16**	**2**	**2**	**0**	**20857**

97	11/00	Navn	2m2f	Hdl	HVY	£11880
85	10/00	Dpat	2m1f172y	Hdl	YLD	£2345

Total win prize-money £14226

Going: Sf: 0-4 GS: 0-0 Gd: 0-1 GF: - Fm: 0-0
Distance: 2m/2m3: 0-3 2m4-2m7: 0-6 3m+: 0-0
Track: LH: 0-1 RH: 0-2 Tight: 0-0 Gall: 0-0
Aids: Bl: 0-0 Vi: 0-0 Tstrap: 0-0
Best Rating: **108** 5/00 Cork 2m gd-yld NHF

A winner twice over hurdles. Fair handicap chaser at around two and a half miles. Acts on soft/heavy ground.

Molly Irwin (IRE)

4-y-o b f General Monash (USA)-Bunny Run (Dowsing (USA))
B J Llewellyn T G B Racing Club

Placings:P (1626)
2001/02: 16^{P}GF

	Starts	1st	2nd	3rd	Win & Pl
Hurdles	1	0	0	0	
Career Total	**1**	**0**	**0**	**0**	

Going: Sf: 0-0 GS: 0-0 Gd: 0-0 GF: - Fm: 0-1
Distance: 2m/2m3: 0-1 2m4-2m7: 0-0 3m+: 0-0
Track: LH: 0-0 RH: 0-1 Tight: 0-0 Gall: 0-0
Aids: Bl: 0-0 Vi: 0-0 Tstrap: 0-0
Best Rating:

Molly Smith (IRE)

7-y-o b m Be My Native (USA)-Yukon Law (Goldhill)
T Wall Mrs B Smith

Placings:0P (2474)
2001/02: 16^{0}S, 19^{P}S

	Starts	1st	2nd	3rd	Win & Pl
NH Flat	1	0	0	0	0
Hurdles	1	0	0	0	0
Career Total	**2**	**0**	**0**	**0**	

Going: Sf: 0-2 GS: 0-0 Gd: 0-0 GF: - Fm: 0-0
Distance: 2m/2m3: 0-1 2m4-2m7: 0-1 3m+: 0-0
Track: LH: 0-1 RH: 0-1 Tight: 0-0 Gall: 0-0
Aids: Bl: 0-0 Vi: 0-0 Tstrap: 0-0
Best Rating: **69** 11/01 Hayd 2m soft NHF

Momentous Jones

101 **110**
5-y-o b g Emperor Jones (USA)-Ivory Moment (USA) (Sir Ivor)
M Madgwick Peter Taplin

Placings:35F515105-F5454P6 (4413)
2001/02: 18^{F}GS, 16^{5}GS, 18^{4}G, 20^{5}G, 18^{4}HY, 21^{P}GS, 18^{6}S

	Starts	1st	2nd	3rd	Win & Pl
Hurdles	7	0	0	0	944
Career Total	**16**	**2**	**0**	**1**	**6099**

110	1/01	Font	2m2f110y	E Hdl	SFT	£2502
110	12/00	Font	2m2f110y	E Hdl	SFT	£2317

Total win prize-money £4820

Going: Sf: 0-2 GS: 0-3 Gd: 0-2 GF: - Fm: 0-0
Distance: 2m/2m3: 0-5 2m4-2m7: 0-2 3m+: 0-0
Track: LH: 0-5 RH: 0-1 Tight: 0-5 Gall: 0-1
Aids: Bl: 0-0 Vi: 0-1 Tstrap: 0-0
Best Rating: **110** 12/01 Font 2m2f110y good Hdl

Moments In Time

88 **57**
4-y-o b f Emperor Jones (USA)-Dame Helene (USA) (Sir Ivor)
M J Ryan Four Jays Racing Partnership

Placings:600 (2301)
2001/02: 16^{6}G, 16^{0}GS, 16^{0}GF

	Starts	1st	2nd	3rd	Win & Pl
Hurdles	3	0	0	0	0
Career Total	**3**	**0**	**0**	**0**	**0**

Going: Sf: 0-0 GS: 0-1 Gd: 0-1 GF: - Fm: 0-1
Distance: 2m/2m3: 0-3 2m4-2m7: 0-0 3m+: 0-0
Track: LH: 0-1 RH: 0-2 Tight: 0-1 Gall: 0-1
Aids: Bl: 0-1 Vi: 0-0 Tstrap: 0-0
Best Rating: **57** 11/01 Hntg 2m110y good Hdl

Mon Arc En Ciel (FR)

68 **20**
7-y-o b/br g Silver Rainbow-La Bonne Etoile (FR) (Margouillat (FR))
R Mathew Mrs Robin Mathew

Placings:0500/0PPPP (4842)
2001/02: 16^{0}S, 16^{P}S, 17^{P}HY, 19^{P}G, 20^{P}G

	Starts	1st	2nd	3rd	Win & Pl
Hurdles	5	0	0	0	
Career Total	**9**	**0**	**0**	**0**	**0**

Going: Sf: 0-3 GS: 0-0 Gd: 0-2 GF: - Fm: 0-0
Distance: 2m/2m3: 0-4 2m4-2m7: 0-1 3m+: 0-0
Track: LH: 0-3 RH: 0-2 Tight: 0-2 Gall: 0-1
Aids: Bl: 0-0 Vi: 0-0 Tstrap: 0-0
Best Rating: **85** 2/00 Newb 2m110y gd-sft Hdl

Monacle

99 **91**
8-y-o b g Saddlers' Hall (IRE)-Endless Joy (Law Society (USA))
John Berry Chris Benest

Placings:511P-30 (4568)

2001/02: 18^{3}S, 24^{0}G

	Starts	1st	2nd	3rd	Win & Pl
Hurdles	2	0	0	1	378
Career Total	**6**	**2**	**0**	**1**	**5131**

113	10/00	Plum	2m5f	E Hdl	SFT	£2411
101	10/00	Font	2m4f	F Hdl	GD	£2341

Total win prize-money £4754

Going: Sf: 0-1 GS: 0-0 Gd: 0-1 GF: - Fm: 0-0
Distance: 2m/2m3: 0-1 2m4-2m7: 0-0 3m+: 0-1
Track: LH: 0-1 RH: 0-1 Tight: 0-1 Gall: 0-0
Aids: Bl: 0-0 Vi: 0-0 Tstrap: 0-0
Best Rating: **113** 10/00 Plum 2m5f soft Hdl

Winning novice hurdler in 2001/2, also a decent performer on the All-Weather.

Monarch's Pursuit

112 **136**

8-y-o b g Pursuit Of Love-Last Detail (Dara Monarch)
T D Easterby Mrs Jean P Connew

Placings:115/0/F/3253U162-2201F504 **(4495)**
2001/02: 16^{2}G, 17^{2}GS, 20^{0}S, 16^{1}S, 16^{F}G, 16^{5}HY, 19^{0}GS, 16^{4}G

	Starts	1st	2nd	3rd	Win & Pl
Chases	8	1	2	0	10834
Career Total	**21**	**4**	**4**	**2**	**29966**

136	12/01	Uttx	2m	C(0-135)HCh	SFT	£6727
127	2/01	Catt	2m3f	D Ch	SFT	£4212
120	11/97	Weth	2m	A Hdl	G-F	£8955
108	10/97	Weth	2m	D Hdl	G-F	£2810

Total win prize-money £22705

Going: Sf: 1-3 GS: 0-2 Gd: 0-3 GF: - Fm: 0-0
Distance: **2m/2m3: 1-6** 2m4-2m7: 0-2 3m+: 0-0
Track: **LH: 1-7** RH: 0-1 Tight: 0-2 Gall: 0-1
Aids: Bl: 0-3 Vi: 0-0 **Tstrap: 1-6**
Best Rating: **136** 12/01 Uttx 2m soft Ch

He is an effective sort in modest handicap chases. Stays two and a half miles, but better suited by shorter. Acts on soft ground.

Monash Freeway (IRE)

103 **95**

4-y-o ch c General Monash (USA)-Pennine Pearl (IRE) (Pennine Walk)
Miss Jacqueline S Doyle A W Regan

Placings:23 **(1956)**
2001/02: 16^{2}GF, 16^{3}G

	Starts	1st	2nd	3rd	Win & Pl
Hurdles	2	0	1	1	1179
Career Total	**2**	**0**	**1**	**1**	**1179**

Going: Sf: 0-0 GS: 0-0 Gd: 0-1 GF: - Fm: 0-1
Distance: 2m/2m3: 0-2 2m4-2m7: 0-0 3m+: 0-0
Track: LH: 0-1 RH: 0-1 Tight: 0-0 Gall: 0-1
Aids: Bl: 0-0 Vi: 0-0 Tstrap: 0-0
Best Rating: **95** 11/01 Wwck 2m good Hdl

Little sign of ability on all starts on the Flat, but he has shown ability over hurdles and looks sure to find a race.

Monger Lane

112 **120**

6-y-o b m Karinga Bay-Grace Moore (Deep Run)
K Bishop Slabs And Lucan

Placings:*03/4-0*503011 **(4822)**

2001/02: 17^{0}G, 21^{5}HY, 24^{0}HY, 22^{3}S, 21^{0}S, 21^{1}GS, 21^{1}G

	Starts	1st	2nd	3rd	Win & Pl
NH Flat	1	0	0	0	0
Hurdles	6	2	0	1	43364
Career Total	**10**	**2**	**0**	**2**	**45499**

120	4/02	Chel	2m5f110y	A HHdl	GD	£19604
109	3/02	Newb	2m5f	A HHdl	G-S	£23200

Total win prize-money £42804

Going: Sf: 0-4 GS: 1-1 Gd: 1-2 GF: - Fm: 0-0
Distance: 2m/2m3: 0-1 **2m4-2m7: 2-5** 3m+: 0-1
Track: **LH: 2-3** RH: 0-4 Tight: 0-0 **Gall: 2-2**
Aids: Bl: 0-0 Vi: 0-0 Tstrap: 0-0
Best Rating: **120** 4/02 Chel 2m5f110y good Hdl

Placed in bumpers and over hurdles before causing a surprise by winning the valuable mares' final at Newbury in March 2002. Followed up in similar event at Cheltenham next time. Stays well and acts in soft ground.

Monicasman (IRE)

12-y-o br g Callernish-Sengirrefcha (Reformed Character)
Miss Caroline Barclay (J Barclay 15/5) Jamie Alexander

Placings:*115*/121O6/066233/21F125/3F23/3F3PP-605 **(4124)**
2001/02: 24^{6}GF, 24^{0}S, 21^{5}HY

	Starts	1st	2nd	3rd	Win & Pl
Chases	3	0	0	0	0
Career Total	**32**	**6**	**5**	**6**	**27580**

124	2/99	Fknm	3m110y	F(0-100)HCh	G-S	£4005
120	12/98	MRas	3m1f	E(0-105)HCh	HVY	£3860
116	3/96	Newb	2m110y	C Hdl	G-S	£4302
97	10/95	Chel	2m110y	D Hdl	G-F	£2850
115	3/95	Donc	2m110y	H NHF	GD	£1444
110	2/95	Nott	2m	H NHF	G-S	£1560

Total win prize-money £18023

Going: Sf: 0-2 GS: 0-0 Gd: 0-0 GF: - Fm: 0-1
Distance: 2m/2m3: 0-0 2m4-2m7: 0-1 3m+: 0-2
Track: LH: 0-1 RH: 0-2 Tight: 0-1 Gall: 0-0
Aids: Bl: 0-0 Vi: 0-0 Tstrap: 0-0
Best Rating: **124** 12/99 MRas 2m6f110y gd-sft Ch

Monifeth Man (IRE)

110(103c) (113c)**129**

7-y-o b g Be My Native (USA)-Outdoor Ivy (Deep Run)
M F Morris David Lloyd

Placings:061/P4PF-PP0450 **(4231)**
2001/02: 21^{P}S, 24^{P}G, 16^{0}YS, 17^{4}YS, 16^{5}S, 21^{0}GS

	Starts	1st	2nd	3rd	Win & Pl
Hurdles	3	0	0	0	0
Chases	3	0	0	0	393
Career Total	**13**	**1**	**0**	**0**	**6233**

118	1/00	Leop	2m4f	Hdl	YLD	£5520

Total win prize-money £5520

Going: Sf: 0-2 GS: 0-1 Gd: 0-1 GF: - Fm: 0-0
Distance: 2m/2m3: 0-3 2m4-2m7: 0-2 3m+: 0-1
Track: LH: 0-2 RH: 0-1 Tight: 0-0 Gall: 0-1
Aids: Bl: 0-0 Vi: 0-0 Tstrap: 0-6
Best Rating: **129** 3/02 Chel 2m5f gd-sft Hdl

Irish hurdler/chaser, generally well held in 2001/2.

Monitor

92 (104h)**128+**

8-y-o ch g Machiavellian (USA)-Instant Desire (USA) (Northern Dancer)
G M Lyons Trio Syndicate

Placings:0/42P0/011300-0344P **(4836)**
2001/02: 16^{0}G, 18^{3}GY, 16^{4}Y, 16^{4}G, 20^{P}G

	Starts	1st	2nd	3rd	Win & Pl
Hurdles	1	0	0	0	0
Chases	4	0	0	1	2860
Career Total	**16**	**2**	**1**	**2**	**15060**

120	8/00	Kbgn	2m3f	(0-116)HHdl	G-F	£6072
120	8/00	Cork	2m4f	Hdl	Y-S	£4416

Total win prize-money £10488

Going: Sf: 0-0 GS: 0-0 Gd: 0-3 GF: - Fm: 0-0
Distance: 2m/2m3: 0-4 2m4-2m7: 0-1 3m+: 0-0
Track: LH: 0-2 RH: 0-2 Tight: 0-0 Gall: 0-1
Aids: Bl: 0-0 Vi: 0-0 Tstrap: 0-5
Best Rating: **122** 11/01 Chel 2m good Ch

Three time winner on the Flat, he has scored over hurdles and fences. Acts on most types of ground, and is effective by two and a half miles.

Monkerhostin (FR)

113(110c) (137c)**134**

5-y-o b g Shining Steel-Ladoun (FR) (Kaldoun (FR))
O Sherwood (J F Bernard 23/6) M G St Quinton

Placings:3-1235221501 **(4853)**
2001/02: 17^{1}GS, 17^{2}GS, 16^{3}S, 16^{5}G, 16^{2}G, 16^{2}G, 17^{1}S, 16^{5}GS, 16^{0}G, 16^{1}G

	Starts	1st	2nd	3rd	Win & Pl
Hurdles	6	3	1	0	12237
Chases	4	0	2	1	9313
Career Total	**11**	**3**	**3**	**2**	**24460**

132	4/02	Strf	2m110y	D(0-120)HHdl	GD	£3679
122	2/02	Sedg	2m1f	E Hdl	SFT	£2583
	5/01	Pari	2m1f	Hdl	G-S	£4850

Total win prize-money £11112

Going: Sf: 1-2 GS: 1-3 Gd: 1-5 GF: - Fm: 0-0
Distance: **2m/2m3: 3-10** 2m4-2m7: 0-0 3m+: 0-0
Track: **LH: 2-3** RH: 0-4 **Tight: 2-3** Gall: 0-0
Aids: Bl: 0-0 Vi: 0-0 Tstrap: 0-0
Best Rating: **137** 12/01 Kemp 2m good Ch

Winning ex-French hurdler, had shown ability over fences before taking a Sedgefield novice hurdle and finishing fifth in the Imperial Cup. Appreciated drop in class when defying top weight at Stratford in April. Acts on good but suited by cut in the ground. All his wins have come at two miles one furlong.

Monkey Island

103(99h) **115**

7-y-o b g Jupiter Island-Mikey's Monkey (Monksfield)
Ferdy Murphy The Monkey Island Partnership

Placings:*00*/554-30PFP340 **(4855)**
2001/02: 20^{3}GS, 20^{0}G, 19^{P}G, 24^{F}G, 24^{P}G, 24^{3}S, 25^{4}G, 20^{0}G

	Starts	1st	2nd	3rd	Win & Pl
Chases	8	0	0	2	1161
Career Total	**13**	**0**	**0**	**2**	**1161**

Going: Sf: 0-1 GS: 0-1 Gd: 0-6 GF: - Fm: 0-0
Distance: 2m/2m3: 0-0 2m4-2m7: 0-4 3m+: 0-4
Track: LH: 0-3 RH: 0-4 Tight: 0-4 Gall: 0-1
Aids: Bl: 0-3 Vi: 0-0 Tstrap: 0-0
Best Rating: **115** 12/01 Muss 3m good Ch

Front-running chaser, improved for the application of blinkers.

Monks Jay (IRE)

97 **103**

13-y-o br g Monksfield-Boro Penny (Normandy)
A J Wilson J A Cover

Placings:00P004P/04F4651223/134154PP13/F0P46/41554/P31504626-10PU6 **(1229)**
2001/02: 24^{1}F, 28^{0}GF, 32^{P}GF, 25^{U}GF, 20^{6}GF

	Starts	1st	2nd	3rd	Win & Pl
Chases	5	1	0	0	4953
Career Total	**51**	**7**	**3**	**4**	**32471**

103	5/01	Tntn	3m	F(0-105)HCh	FRM	£4953
103	6/00	Fknm	2m5f110y	F(0-100)HCh	GD	£3324
96	1/00	Hntg	2m4f110y	F(0-100)HCh	G-S	£2671
96	4/97	Extr	2m2f	D(0-125)HCh	FRM	£3798
96	11/96	Winc	2m5f	E(0-115)HCh	GD	£4328
91	5/96	Towc	2m110y	E(0-115)HCh	G-F	£3013
91	2/96	Ludl	2m	G(0-95)HCh	GD	£2814

Total win prize-money £24904

Going: Sf: 0-0 GS: 0-0 Gd: 0-0 GF: - Fm: 1-5
Distance: 2m/2m3: 0-0 2m4-2m7: 0-1 **3m+: 1-4**
Track: LH: 0-2 **RH: 1-2 Tight: 1-3** Gall: 0-0
Aids: Bl: 0-0 Vi: 0-0 Tstrap: 0-0
Best Rating: 103 5/01 Tntn 3m firm Ch

Monnaie Forte (IRE)

112 **135**

12-y-o b g Strong Gale-Money Run (Deep Run)
J R Adam James R Adam

Placings:10/1P1FFF111/P12112312/P56/06042F224/232PP2-3304P2P **(4831)**
2001/02: 20^{3}GF, 24^{3}GF, 22^{0}GY, 20^{4}G, 20^{P}GS, 19^{2}GF, 20^{P}G

	Starts	1st	2nd	3rd	Win & Pl
Chases	7	0	1	2	9135
Career Total	**45**	**10**	**10**	**4**	**93460**

128	4/98	Asct	2m110y	C(0-135)HHdl	GD	£5015
135	1/98	Ayr	2m4f	B(0-145)HCh	G-S	£12475
139	1/98	Sand	2m	B HCh	G-S	£7139
110	11/97	Ayr	2m	B(0-140)HCh	G-S	£6317
116	4/97	Asct	2m110y	B(0-140)HHdl	G-F	£5622
103	3/97	Carl	2m1f	E(0-115)HHdl	GD	£2213
103	3/97	Kels	2m2f	D(0-120)HHdl	GD	£2827
86	11/96	Ayr	2m4f	D(0-105)HCh	GD	£3616
89	3/95	Hntg	2m110y	E Hdl	SFT	£2635

Total win prize-money £47863

Going: Sf: 0-0 GS: 0-1 Gd: 0-2 GF: - Fm: 0-3
Distance: 2m/2m3: 0-0 2m4-2m7: 0-6 3m+: 0-1
Track: LH: 0-3 RH: 0-3 Tight: 0-2 Gall: 0-0
Aids: Bl: 0-0 Vi: 0-0 Tstrap: 0-0
Best Rating: 143 4/99 Asct 2m3f110y gd-fm Ch

He has not won since April 1998 but ran a decent race when second in a competitive two and a half mile handicap at Ayr in April 2001 and did the same thing at Ascot a year later, but pulled up next time. Suited by good ground, he is getting long in the tooth, but can win another handicap.

Monotony (IRE)

9-y-o b g Over The River (FR)-Alamo Bay (Torenaga)
N Waggott Mrs J Waggott

Placings:P626P062/050/**PP** **(2634)**
2001/02: 20^{P}S, 25^{P}S

	Starts	1st	2nd	3rd	Win & Pl
Chases	2	0	0	0	0
Career Total	**13**	**0**	**2**	**0**	**1208**

Going: Sf: 0-2 GS: 0-0 Gd: 0-0 GF: - Fm: 0-0
Distance: 2m/2m3: 0-0 2m4-2m7: 0-1 3m+: 0-1
Track: LH: 0-2 RH: 0-0 Tight: 0-0 Gall: 0-0
Aids: Bl: 0-0 Vi: 0-0 Tstrap: 0-0
Best Rating: 97 12/97 Kels 2m6f110y gd-sft Hdl

Monsieur De Rien (FR)

82(96h) (78h)**84**

7-y-o b/br g Vorias (USA)-Inmemoriam (IRE) (Buckskin (FR))
W Jenks Mrs C S Wilson

Placings:06/0045-0000P4 **(3867)**
2001/02: 20^{0}G, 17^{0}G, 21^{0}G, 19^{0}S, 24^{P}G, 24^{4}G

	Starts	1st	2nd	3rd	Win & Pl
Hurdles	3	0	0	0	0
Chases	3	0	0	0	264
Career Total	**12**	**0**	**0**	**0**	**264**

Going: Sf: 0-1 GS: 0-0 Gd: 0-5 GF: - Fm: 0-0
Distance: 2m/2m3: 0-2 2m4-2m7: 0-2 3m+: 0-2
Track: LH: 0-2 RH: 0-4 Tight: 0-4 Gall: 0-0
Aids: Bl: 0-0 Vi: 0-0 Tstrap: 0-0
Best Rating: 100 2/00 Asct 2m110y soft NHF

Monsieur Poirot (IRE)

84f **98f**

5-y-o b g Lapierre-Mallia Miss (IRE) (Executive Perk)
Mrs S C Bradburne J G Bradburne

Placings:0 **(4900)**
2001/02: 16^{0}G

	Starts	1st	2nd	3rd	Win & Pl
NH Flat	1	0	0	0	
Career Total	**1**	**0**	**0**	**0**	

Going: Sf: 0-0 GS: 0-0 Gd: 0-1 GF: - Fm: 0-0
Distance: 2m/2m3: 0-1 2m4-2m7: 0-0 3m+: 0-0
Track: LH: 0-0 RH: 0-1 Tight: 0-0 Gall: 0-0
Aids: Bl: 0-0 Vi: 0-0 Tstrap: 0-0
Best Rating: 98 4/02 Prth 2m110y good NHF

Monsieur Tagel (FR)

98(104h) (66h)**121**

6-y-o b g Tagel (USA)-Miss Zonissa (FR) (Zino)
Ian Williams J Cullen Thermals Ltd

Placings:10442622/511F134F0-501033UF **(4585)**
2001/02: 24^{5}S, 20^{0}G, 20^{1}GF, 19^{0}GS, 20^{3}G, 24^{3}G, 24^{U}G, 25^{F}G

	Starts	1st	2nd	3rd	Win & Pl
Hurdles	2	0	0	0	0
Chases	6	1	0	2	4838
Career Total	**25**	**5**	**3**	**3**	**21745**

121	11/01	Ludl	2m4f	E Ch	G-F	£3770
127	10/00	Strf	2m6f110y	D(0-120)HHdl	G-S	£3068
123	9/00	Chep	2m4f	D(0-125)HHdl	GD	£3415
124	9/00	Hntg	2m4f110y	D(0-120)HHdl	G-F	£4348
97	10/99	Worc	2m	E Hdl	GD	£2215

Total win prize-money £16818

Going: Sf: 0-1 GS: 0-1 Gd: 0-5 GF: - Fm: 1-1
Distance: 2m/2m3: 0-1 **2m4-2m7: 1-3** 3m+: 0-4
Track: LH: 0-2 **RH: 1-6 Tight: 1-7** Gall: 0-0
Aids: Bl: 0-0 Vi: 0-0 Tstrap: 0-0
Best Rating: 127 12/00 MRas 2m3f110y gd-sft Hdl

A winning hurdler, he jumped well when successful at Ludlow on his chasing debut. Has won on good and soft. Best at trips around two and a half miles.

Mont Aca (FR)

(98h) (106h)**128**

7-y-o b g Phantom Breeze-Azuzuama (FR) (Cadoudal (FR))
P J Hobbs Major And Mrs P I C Payne

Placings:1242004/213P1-3FF **(2200)**
2001/02: 20^{3}G, 20^{F}G, 22^{F}G

	Starts	1st	2nd	3rd	Win & Pl
Hurdles	1	0	0	1	535
Chases	2	0	0	0	0
Career Total	**15**	**3**	**3**	**2**	**15071**

128	4/01	Extr	2m3f110y	E Ch	SFT	£3952
128	12/00	Tntn	2m3f	F(0-110)HCh	SFT	£3198
111	10/99	Extr	2m1f	E Hdl	GD	£2514

Total win prize-money £9664

Going: Sf: 0-0 GS: 0-0 Gd: 0-3 GF: - Fm: 0-0
Distance: 2m/2m3: 0-0 2m4-2m7: 0-3 3m+: 0-0
Track: LH: 0-2 RH: 0-0 Tight: 0-0 Gall: 0-1
Aids: Bl: 0-0 Vi: 0-0 Tstrap: 0-0
Best Rating: 128 4/01 Extr 2m3f110y soft Ch

He stepped up on his hurdles form when sent chasing and has the makings of a fair handicapper around two and a half miles.

Mont Misere (FR)

99 **120**

6-y-o b g Mont Basile (FR)-Pique Flamme (FR) (Lou Piguet (FR))
G Macaire A M Chiche

Placings:22/11114-1316P
2001/02: 21^{1}G, 21^{3}G, 21^{1}S, 20^{6}S, 18^{P}HY

	Starts	1st	2nd	3rd	Win & Pl
Chases	5	2	0	1	10373
Career Total	**12**	**6**	**2**	**1**	**52065**

120	1/02	Folk	2m5f	D Ch	SFT	£4504
	6/01	Diep	2m5f	Ch	GD	£3686
	9/00	Stra	2m3f	Hdl	VS	£10567
	9/00	Chol	2m1f	Hdl	G-S	£10567
	8/00	Vich	2m3f110y	Hdl	GD	£5764
	7/00	Vich	2m110y	Hdl	GD	£3362

Total win prize-money £38451

Going: Sf: 1-3 GS: 0-0 Gd: 1-2 GF: - Fm: 0-0
Distance: 2m/2m3: 0-1 **2m4-2m7: 2-4** 3m+: 0-0
Track: LH: 0-0 **RH: 1-1 Tight: 1-2** Gall: 0-0
Aids: Bl: 0-0 Vi: 0-0 Tstrap: 0-0
Best Rating: 120 1/02 Folk 2m5f soft Ch

A winner over hurdles and fences in France, he made a successful British debut in a modest novice chase at Folkestone in January 2002, but may have been a little fortunate. Suited by trips around two and a half miles. Has won on good and soft ground.

Montagnette

96 **76**

8-y-o ch m Gildoran-Deep Crevasse (Rolfe (USA))
M R Bosley Girls On Top Racing 2000

Placings:4000/454220/205PF126-06 **(3763)**
2001/02: 24^{0}HY, 24^{6}S

	Starts	1st	2nd	3rd	Win & Pl
Hurdles	2	0	0	0	0
Career Total	**20**	**1**	**4**	**0**	**4133**

74 2/01 Towc 2m5f G(0-90)HHdl HVY £1694
Total win prize-money £1694

Going: Sf: 0-2 GS: 0-0 Gd: 0-0 GF: - Fm: 0-0
Distance: 2m/2m3: 0-0 2m4-2m7: 0-0 3m+: 0-2
Track: LH: 0-0 RH: 0-2 Tight: 0-1 Gall: 0-0
Aids: Bl: 0-0 Vi: 0-0 Tstrap: 0-0
Best Rating: 85 11/98 Wwck 2m soft NHF

Montalcino (IRE)

120 **156**

6-y-o b g Robellino (USA)-Only Gossip (USA) (Trempolino (USA))
Miss Venetia Williams The Winning Line

Placings:11P-3522400 **(4954a)**
2001/02: 20^{3}G, 16^{5}GS, 21^{2}GS, 21^{2}HY, 20^{4}S, 24^{0}G, 24^{0}G

	Starts	1st	2nd	3rd	Win & Pl
Hurdles	7	0	2	1	18880
Career Total	**10**	**2**	**2**	**1**	**50603**

145 4/01 Aint 2m4f A Hdl SFT £29000
126 3/01 Hntg 2m110y E Hdl SFT £2723
Total win prize-money £31723

Going: Sf: 0-2 GS: 0-2 Gd: 0-3 GF: - Fm: 0-0
Distance: 2m/2m3: 0-1 2m4-2m7: 0-4 3m+: 0-2
Track: LH: 0-3 RH: 0-2 Tight: 0-1 Gall: 0-3
Aids: Bl: 0-1 Vi: 0-0 Tstrap: 0-0
Best Rating: 156 1/02 Chel 2m5f110y heavy Hdl

A useful middle-distance performer on the Flat, he was impressive on his hurdling debut and slaughtered a fair field on testing ground in the Martell Mersey Novices' Hurdle at Aintree. Held in useful company last term, he produced a better effort at Cheltenham in January. Has won over two and two and a half miles. He needs soft ground to perform at his best but he is not a fluent hurdler.

Montasareen (USA)

97 **100**

5-y-o b/br h Rainbow Quest (USA)-Oshima (USA) (Mr Prospector (USA))
P Bowen G Morris

Placings:2325534P-33P0P6P **(3761)**
2001/02: 16^{3}GF, 20^{3}GF, 20^{P}G, 16^{0}G, 19^{P}GS, 19^{6}S, 19^{P}S

	Starts	1st	2nd	3rd	Win & Pl
Hurdles	7	0	0	2	743
Career Total	**15**	**0**	**2**	**4**	**5115**

Going: Sf: 0-2 GS: 0-1 Gd: 0-2 GF: - Fm: 0-2
Distance: 2m/2m3: 0-2 2m4-2m7: 0-5 3m+: 0-0
Track: LH: 0-2 RH: 0-5 Tight: 0-4 Gall: 0-1
Aids: Bl: 0-0 Vi: 0-0 Tstrap: 0-0
Best Rating: 100 5/01 Sthl 2m gd-fm Hdl

Montayral (FR)

110 **141**

5-y-o b g Lesotho (USA)-Demi Lune De Mars (FR) (Fast (FR))
P F Nicholls (F Rohaut 10/10) Million In Mind Partnership (11)

Placings:2233-4341231211FU **(4878)**
2001/02: 17^{4}GS, 17^{3}VS, 17^{4}VS, 20^{1}S, 20^{2}S, 16^{3}HY, 20^{1}HY, 19^{2}G, 26^{1}GS, 26^{1}G, 25^{F}G, 24^{U}G

	Starts	1st	2nd	3rd	Win & Pl
Chases	12	4	2	2	28678
Career Total	**16**	**4**	**4**	**4**	**40849**

134 4/02 Uttx 3m2f E Ch GD £3445
135 3/02 Plum 3m2f E Ch G-S £3022
115 2/02 Plum 2m4f E Ch HVY £3728
128 12/01 Bang 2m4f110y D Ch SFT £4095
Total win prize-money £14291

Going: Sf: 2-4 GS: 1-2 Gd: 1-4 GF: - Fm: 0-0
Distance: 2m/2m3: 0-4 2m4-2m7: 2-4 3m+: 2-4
Track: **LH: 3-5** RH: 0-3 **Tight: 2-2** Gall: 0-1
Aids: Bl: 0-0 Vi: 0-0 Tstrap: 0-0
Best Rating: 141 4/02 Chel 3m1f110y good Ch

Placed over hurdles and fences in France, he won over two and a half miles on his chasing debut in this country at Bangor in December 2001, but did not jump well when slammed by Seebald next time. A drop in class saw him hit winning form after that at Plumpton and Uttoxeter and he would have completed the hat trick at Cheltenham had he not fallen two out and did something similar at Perth in April. Stays three and a quarter miles.

Monte Carlo (IRE)

95 **106**

5-y-o b g Rainbows For Life (CAN)-Roberts Pride (Roberto (USA))
L Montague Hall J Daniels

Placings:0 **(3909)**
2001/02: 21^{0}G

	Starts	1st	2nd	3rd	Win & Pl
Hurdles	1	0	0	0	
Career Total	**1**	**0**	**0**	**0**	

Going: Sf: 0-0 GS: 0-0 Gd: 0-1 GF: - Fm: 0-0
Distance: 2m/2m3: 0-0 2m4-2m7: 0-1 3m+: 0-0
Track: LH: 0-0 RH: 0-1 Tight: 0-0 Gall: 0-0
Aids: Bl: 0-0 Vi: 0-0 Tstrap: 0-0
Best Rating: 106 2/02 Kemp 2m5f good Hdl

Monte Cresta (IRE)

105(93h) (76h)**113**

9-y-o b/br m Montelimar (USA)-Winter Run (Deep Run)
Mrs S C Bradburne Mrs John Etherton

Placings:0412F/24P/F03F64514F/45254P44-1P342P3 **(3678)**
2001/02: 24^{1}S, 26^{P}GS, 22^{3}G, 25^{4}GS, 29^{2}S, 24^{P}S, 25^{3}HY

	Starts	1st	2nd	3rd	Win & Pl
Chases	7	1	1	2	9020
Career Total	**33**	**3**	**4**	**3**	**22131**

113 5/01 Prth 3m E(0-115)HCh SFT £5720
121 3/00 Ayr 3m1f D Ch HVY £4484
102 1/98 Kels 2m2f E Hdl HVY £2472
Total win prize-money £12677

Going: Sf: 1-4 GS: 0-2 Gd: 0-1 GF: - Fm: 0-0
Distance: 2m/2m3: 0-0 2m4-2m7: 0-1 **3m+: 1-6**
Track: LH: 0-6 **RH: 1-1** Tight: 0-2 Gall: 0-1
Aids: Bl: 0-0 Vi: 0-0 Tstrap: 0-0
Best Rating: 121 3/00 Uttx 2m5f good Ch

Not noted for her consistency, she stays three miles and acts in heavy ground..

Monte Cristo (FR)

94 **105**

4-y-o ch g Bigstone (IRE)-El Quahirah (FR) (Cadoudal (FR))
Mrs L C Taylor (S Kalley 2/12) Mrs L C Taylor

Placings:435531P **(4840)**
2001/02: 15^{4}VS, 18^{3}HY, 18^{5}HY, 16^{5}HY, 16^{3}G, 16^{1}G, 16^{P}G

	Starts	1st	2nd	3rd	Win & Pl
Hurdles	7	1	0	2	12143
Career Total	**7**	**1**	**0**	**2**	**12143**

106 3/02 Hayd 2m D Hdl GD £4862
Total win prize-money £4862

Going: Sf: 0-3 GS: 0-0 Gd: 1-3 GF: - Fm: 0-0
Distance: **2m/2m3: 1-6** 2m4-2m7: 0-0 3m+: 0-0
Track: **LH: 1-3** RH: 0-1 Tight: 0-0 Gall: 0-0
Aids: Bl: 0-4 Vi: 0-0 Tstrap: 0-0
Best Rating: 106 3/02 Hayd 2m good Hdl

Placed three times in the mud over hurdles in France where he was a winner on the Flat. Progressive and opened his account at Haydock in March.

Monte Rouge (IRE)

92f **110f**

5-y-o ch g Montelimar (USA)-Drumdeels Star (IRE) (Le Bavard (FR))
Miss L C Siddall The Full Monte Partnership

Placings:2-55 **(3701)**
2001/02: 16^{5}S, 16^{5}S

	Starts	1st	2nd	3rd	Win & Pl
NH Flat	2	0	0	0	0
Career Total	**3**	**0**	**1**	**0**	**560**

Going: Sf: 0-2 GS: 0-0 Gd: 0-0 GF: - Fm: 0-0
Distance: 2m/2m3: 0-2 2m4-2m7: 0-0 3m+: 0-0
Track: LH: 0-2 RH: 0-0 Tight: 0-0 Gall: 0-1
Aids: Bl: 0-0 Vi: 0-0 Tstrap: 0-0
Best Rating: 110 1/02 Hayd 2m soft NHF

Monteba (IRE)

101 **107**

10-y-o br g Montelimar (USA)-Sheeba Queen (Crozier)
Mrs P Sly The Ring Partnership

Placings:22/3/501/233/PPF3-22042 **(2115)**
2001/02: 21^{2}GF, 24^{2}GF, 25^{0}G, 21^{4}S, 21^{2}G

	Starts	1st	2nd	3rd	Win & Pl
Chases	5	0	3	0	4221
Career Total	**18**	**1**	**6**	**4**	**12064**

94 8/98 Cork 2m1f Hdl YLD £3288
Total win prize-money £3288

Going: Sf: 0-1 GS: 0-0 Gd: 0-2 GF: - Fm: 0-2
Distance: 2m/2m3: 0-0 2m4-2m7: 0-3 3m+: 0-2
Track: LH: 0-4 RH: 0-1 Tight: 0-4 Gall: 0-0
Aids: Bl: 0-0 Vi: 0-0 Tstrap: 0-0
Best Rating: 107 11/01 Folk 2m5f good Ch

Monteri

6-y-o gr g Terimon-Absolutely Blue (Absalom)
T Wall T Wall

Placings:00P **(1842)**
2001/02: 17^{0}GS, 17^{0}G, 24^{P}S

	Starts	1st	2nd	3rd	Win & Pl
NH Flat	2	0	0	0	0
Hurdles	1	0	0	0	0
Career Total	**3**	**0**	**0**	**0**	

Going: Sf: 0-1 GS: 0-1 Gd: 0-1 GF: - Fm: 0-0
Distance: 2m/2m3: 0-2 2m4-2m7: 0-0 3m+: 0-1
Track: LH: 0-0 RH: 0-3 Tight: 0-2 Gall: 0-0
Aids: Bl: 0-0 Vi: 0-0 Tstrap: 0-0
Best Rating: 43 10/01 MRas 2m1f110y gd-sft NHF

Monticello (IRE)

(96h) (76h)
10-y-o ch g Accordion-Erck (Sun Prince)
J S Moore Brian A Lewendon & Mrs Carol Lewendon

Placings:002/524/P3115F0-30 **(0596)**
2001/02: 16^{3}GF, 17^{0}G

	Starts	1st	2nd	3rd	Win & Pl
Hurdles	2	0	0	1	248
Career Total	**15**	**2**	**2**	**2**	**4789**

76	10/00	Extr	2m1f	G(0-95)HHdl	GD	£1696
76	10/00	Extr	2m3f	G(0-95)HHdl	GD	£1687

Total win prize-money £3384

Going: Sf: 0-0 GS: 0-0 Gd: 0-1 GF: - Fm: 0-1
Distance: 2m/2m3: 0-2 2m4-2m7: 0-0 3m+: 0-0
Track: LH: 0-1 RH: 0-1 Tight: 0-1 Gall: 0-1
Aids: Bl: 0-0 Vi: 0-0 Tstrap: 0-0
Best Rating: 82 4/98 Extr 2m2f soft Hdl

Montifault (FR)

114 162
7-y-o ch g Morespeed-Tarde (FR) (Kashtan (FR))
P F Nicholls Mrs A E Fulton

Placings:056/1P13/**233121-1P1P** **(4913)**
2001/02: 25^{1}G, 26^{P}S, 21^{1}G, 29^{P}G

	Starts	1st	2nd	3rd	Win & Pl
Chases	4	2	0	0	37060
Career Total	**17**	**6**	**2**	**3**	**73042**

144	12/01	Winc	2m5f	B Ch	GD	£11060
162	11/01	Winc	3m1f110y	A(0-150)HCh	GD	£26000
137	4/01	Font	2m6f	C Ch	GD	£7410
147	4/01	Asct	3m110y	B Ch	SFT	£10764
115	4/00	Plum	2m5f	E Hdl	HVY	£2674
127	11/99	Worc	2m4f	E Hdl	GD	£2495

Total win prize-money £60403

Going: Sf: 0-1 GS: 0-0 Gd: 2-3 GF: - Fm: 0-0
Distance: 2m/2m3: 0-0 2m4-2m7: 1-1 3m+: 1-3
Track: LH: 0-1 **RH: 2-3** Tight: 0-0 Gall: 0-1
Aids: Bl: 0-0 Vi: 0-0 Tstrap: 0-0
Best Rating: 162 11/01 Winc 3m1f110y good Ch

He did not look back after having a soft palate operation and was in fine form over fences during the spring of 2001. Impressive winning return in the Badger Beer at Wincanton in 2001, but pulled up in the Hennessy in December. Fortunate winner back at Wincanton on Boxing Day, but was pulled up early in the Attheraces Gold Cup. Acts on any ground and stays three miles.

Montpelier (IRE)

108 142
9-y-o b g Montelimar (USA)-Liscarton (Le Bavard (FR))
N J Henderson The 2020 Droxford Partnership

Placings:40/2F5003/**11P0-3112** **(2849)**
2001/02: 16^{3}G, 19^{1}S, 21^{1}G, 20^{2}G

	Starts	1st	2nd	3rd	Win & Pl
Chases	4	2	1	1	15781
Career Total	**16**	**4**	**2**	**2**	**25629**

140	12/01	Chel	2m5f	E(0-125)HCh	GD	£8502
140	12/01	Hrfd	2m3f	E(0-115)HCh	SFT	£3523
134	10/00	Chel	2m4f110y	D(0-110)HCh	GD	£5642
121	10/00	Hrfd	2m3f	E(0-105)HCh	GD	£3435

Total win prize-money £21102

Going: Sf: 1-1 GS: 0-0 Gd: 1-3 GF: - Fm: 0-0
Distance: 2m/2m3: 1-2 2m4-2m7: 1-2 3m+: 0-0
Track: LH: 1-1 RH: 1-3 Tight: 0-0 **Gall: 1-1**
Aids: Bl: 0-0 Vi: 0-0 Tstrap: 0-0

Best Rating: 142 12/01 Kemp 2m4f110y good Ch

Winner at Hereford and Cheltenham as a novice in October 2000, he returned to winning ways at Hereford in December 2001 and followed up in really good style at Cheltenham. He was just beaten at Kempton over Christmas off a higher mark. Suited by around two and a half miles and looks progressive.

Montrave

82(56h) 66
13-y-o ch g Netherkelly-Streakella (Firestreak)
Miss Lucinda V Russell D St Clair

Placings:0035/04350/61554220/**3202132/541F154/34 141214/364343/0260P660/0-4P00** **(3611)**
2001/02: 16^{4}G, 25^{P}S, 20^{0}G, 20^{0}S

	Starts	1st	2nd	3rd	Win & Pl
Hurdles	1	0	0	0	0
Chases	3	0	0	0	465
Career Total	**58**	**7**	**7**	**8**	**36360**

121	3/98	Ayr	2m	D(0-125)HCh	G-S	£4175
121	1/98	Ayr	2m	E(0-115)HCh	G-S	£3072
113	12/97	Muss	2m4f	D(0-120)HCh	GD	£3468
117	1/97	Ayr	2m4f	E(0-115)HCh	GD	£3090
108	12/96	Muss	2m4f	D(0-120)HCh	FRM	£3485
110	3/96	Ayr	2m	E Ch	GD	£3223
92	10/94	Ayr	2m4f	Hdl	GD	£1976

Total win prize-money £22491

Going: Sf: 0-2 GS: 0-0 Gd: 0-2 GF: - Fm: 0-0
Distance: 2m/2m3: 0-1 2m4-2m7: 0-2 3m+: 0-1
Track: LH: 0-2 RH: 0-2 Tight: 0-2 Gall: 0-0
Aids: Bl: 0-0 Vi: 0-0 Tstrap: 0-0
Best Rating: 121 3/98 Ayr 2m gd-sft Ch

Montreal (FR)

109 140
5-y-o b/br g Chamberlin (FR)-Massada (FR) (Kashtan (FR))
M C Pipe D A Johnson

Placings:3/2123P-611035 **(4647)**
2001/02: 16^{6}G, 24^{1}G, 22^{1}S, 25^{0}S, 25^{3}GS, 24^{5}G

	Starts	1st	2nd	3rd	Win & Pl
Hurdles	6	2	0	1	22224
Career Total	**12**	**3**	**2**	**3**	**39263**

134	12/01	Sand	2m6f	C(0-130)HHdl	SFT	£7410
128	11/01	Asct	3m	B(0-150)HHdl	GD	£8814
115	11/00	Chel	2m110y	B Hdl	G-S	£7052

Total win prize-money £23277

Going: Sf: 1-2 GS: 0-1 Gd: 1-3 GF: - Fm: 0-0
Distance: 2m/2m3: 0-1 2m4-2m7: 1-1 3m+: 1-4
Track: LH: 0-2 **RH: 2-3** Tight: 0-1 Gall: 0-1
Aids: Bl: 0-0 Vi: 0-0 Tstrap: 0-0
Best Rating: 140 3/02 Chel 3m1f110y gd-sft Hdl

Formerly trained in France, he benefited from the step up to three miles when scoring at Ascot in November 2001, and added to that at Sandown. Ran well when third in a competitive handicap at Cheltenham in March and was in the process of running a big race when losing his action at Aintree. Stays three miles. Acts on good to soft/soft ground.

Montroe (IRE)

111 138
10-y-o gr g Roselier (FR)-Cathedral Street (Boreen Beag)
R Rowe The Montroe Partnership

Placings:56/65431111/50620210/114250/5030PF-40PP04 **(4951a)**
2001/02: 24^{4}GS, 27^{0}G, 32^{P}GS, 24^{P}GS, 21^{0}G, 31^{4}G

	Starts	1st	2nd	3rd	Win & Pl
Chases	6	0	0	0	1942
Career Total	**36**	**7**	**3**	**2**	**70750**

138	1/00	Asct	3m110y	B(0-145)HCh	GD	£11252
126	12/99	Chel	2m5f	E(0-125)HCh	GD	£7002
114	3/99	Folk	3m2f	D Ch	GD	£3947
140	4/98	Chel	2m5f110y	C HHdl	HVY	£11332
129	3/98	Sand	2m4f110y	A HHdl	SFT	£17775
131	2/98	Sand	2m4f110y	D(0-120)HHdl	GD	£3517
119	1/98	Wind	2m4f	E Hdl	GD	£2022

Total win prize-money £56853

Going: Sf: 0-0 GS: 0-3 Gd: 0-3 GF: - Fm: 0-0
Distance: 2m/2m3: 0-0 2m4-2m7: 0-1 3m+: 0-5
Track: LH: 0-3 RH: 0-2 Tight: 0-1 Gall: 0-2
Aids: Bl: 0-4 Vi: 0-0 Tstrap: 0-0
Best Rating: 142 12/00 Chel 3m1f110y soft Ch

Useful on his day, he is sometimes mulish at the start and is one to treat with caution. Ran with credit on his first outing for six months at Kempton in October 2001, but has been disappointing since then. Three miles looks an insufficient test for him these days. Seems to act on any ground.

Montu

73f 53f
5-y-o ch g Gunner B-Promitto (Roaring Riva)
Miss K M George Exterior Profiles Ltd

Placings:0 **(3661)**
2001/02: 16^{0}S

	Starts	1st	2nd	3rd	Win & Pl
NH Flat	1	0	0	0	
Career Total	**1**	**0**	**0**	**0**	

Going: Sf: 0-1 GS: 0-0 Gd: 0-0 GF: - Fm: 0-0
Distance: 2m/2m3: 0-1 2m4-2m7: 0-0 3m+: 0-0
Track: LH: 0-0 RH: 0-1 Tight: 0-0 Gall: 0-0
Aids: Bl: 0-0 Vi: 0-0 Tstrap: 0-0
Best Rating: 53 2/02 Winc 2m soft NHF

Monty Be Quick

92f 87f
6-y-o ch g Mon Tresor-Spartiquick (Spartan General)
J M Castle J M Castle

Placings:600 **(4552)**
2001/02: 16^{6}GS, 16^{0}S, 16^{0}GF

	Starts	1st	2nd	3rd	Win & Pl
NH Flat	3	0	0	0	0
Career Total	**3**	**0**	**0**	**0**	**0**

Going: Sf: 0-1 GS: 0-1 Gd: 0-0 GF: 0-1 Fm: 0-1
Distance: 2m/2m3: 0-3 2m4-2m7: 0-0 3m+: 0-0
Track: LH: 0-0 RH: 0-3 Tight: 0-0 Gall: 0-2
Aids: Bl: 0-0 Vi: 0-0 Tstrap: 0-0
Best Rating: 87 4/02 Hntg 2m110y gd-fm NHF

Monty's Double (IRE)

92 92
5-y-o b g Montelimar (USA)-Macamore Rose (Torus)
O Sherwood W S Watt

Placings:5 (4906)

2001/02: 19^{5}G

	Starts	1st	2nd	3rd	Win & Pl
Hurdles	1	0	0	0	0
Career Total	**1**	**0**	**0**	**0**	**0**

Going: Sf: 0-0 GS: 0-0 Gd: 0-1 GF: - Fm: 0-0
Distance: 2m/2m3: 0-0 2m4-2m7: 0-1 3m+: 0-0
Track: LH: 0-0 RH: 0-1 Tight: 0-1 Gall: 0-0
Aids: Bl: 0-0 Vi: 0-0 Tstrap: 0-0
Best Rating: 92 4/02 MRas 2m3f110y good Hdl

Monty's Pass (IRE)

113 (112h) **152**

9-y-o b g Montelimar (USA)-Friars Pass (Monksfield)
James Joseph Mangan Dee Racing Syndicate

Placings:21/22460212421/4531323PF03-1326212336552 (4664)

2001/02: 20^{1}GF, 21^{3}F, 20^{2}G, 22^{6}GY, 22^{2}G, 20^{1}G, 24^{2}GF, 24^{3}Y, 20^{3}G, 24^{6}YS, 16^{5}HY, 20^{5}GS, 21^{2}G

	Starts	1st	2nd	3rd	Win & Pl
Hurdles	1	0	0	0	0
Chases	12	2	4	3	64325
Career Total	**37**	**6**	**11**	**7**	**103108**

143	8/01	Tral	2m4f	HCh	GD	£18346
132	5/01	Tipp	2m4f	(0-130)HCh	G-F	£7233
118	6/00	Gowr	2m4f	(0-102)HCh	G-Y	£3588
112	4/00	List	2m4f	(0-95)HCh	SH	£4416
107	12/99	DRoy	2m4f	(0-102)HCh	HVY	£2464
107	4/99	Cork	3m	Ch	SH	£3069

Total win prize-money £39118

Going: Sf: 0-1 GS: 0-1 Gd: 1-5 GF: - Fm: 1-3
Distance: 2m/2m3: 0-1 **2m4-2m7: 2-9** 3m+: 0-3
Track: LH: 0-4 RH: 0-2 Tight: 0-1 Gall: 0-2
Aids: Bl: 0-0 Vi: 0-0 Tstrap: 0-0
Best Rating: 152 4/02 Aint 2m5f110y good Ch

A useful Irish chaser, suited by two and a half miles and good ground or faster, although stays three miles. Finished third to Shooting Light at Cheltenham in October 2001, and ran another good race at the 2002 Festival. Third in the Topham over the big Aintree fences.

Monty's Quest (IRE)

99 **82**

7-y-o b g Montelimar (USA)-A Bit Of Luck (IRE) (Good Thyne (USA))
J L Eyre Williams Frankland

Placings:_06/_232-0 (0203)

2001/02: 20^{0}G

	Starts	1st	2nd	3rd	Win & Pl
Hurdles	1	0	0	0	
Career Total	**6**	**0**	**2**	**1**	**1714**

Going: Sf: 0-0 GS: 0-0 Gd: 0-1 GF: - Fm: 0-0
Distance: 2m/2m3: 0-0 2m4-2m7: 0-1 3m+: 0-0
Track: LH: 0-1 RH: 0-0 Tight: 0-0 Gall: 0-0
Aids: Bl: 0-0 Vi: 0-0 Tstrap: 0-0
Best Rating: 98 9/00 Uttx 2m6f110y gd-sft Hdl

Monty's Theme (IRE)

96 **116**

8-y-o b/br g Montelimar (USA)-Theme Music (Tudor Music)
P Wegmann (P F Nicholls 27/8) P Wegmann

Placings:3-3F1145P (2954)

2001/02: 26^{3}G, 24^{F}GF, 21^{1}G, 22^{1}GF, 20^{4}GF, 21^{5}GF, 21^{P}S

	Starts	1st	2nd	3rd	Win & Pl
Chases	7	2	0	1	7550
Career Total	**8**	**2**	**0**	**2**	**8219**

116	8/01	Font	2m6f	E(0-105)HCh	G-F	£3201
111	7/01	NAbb	2m5f110y	E Ch	GD	£3444

Total win prize-money £6645

Going: Sf: 0-1 GS: 0-0 Gd: 1-2 GF: - Fm: 1-4
Distance: 2m/2m3: 0-0 **2m4-2m7: 2-5** 3m+: 0-2
Track: **LH: 1-4** RH: 0-2 **Tight: 2-6** Gall: 0-0
Aids: Bl: 0-0 Vi: 0-1 Tstrap: 0-0
Best Rating: 116 8/01 Font 2m6f gd-fm Ch

Won his first three starts in point to points. Acts on a sound surface. Won a maiden chase and a novice event when with Paul Nicholls. Stays three miles.

Montys Tag (IRE)

9-y-o b g Montelimar (USA)-Herbal Lady (Good Thyne (USA))
S R Andrews R Andrews

Placings:_3/_132 (4517)

2001/02: 21^{1}S, 26^{3}GS, 22^{2}GS

	Starts	1st	2nd	3rd	Win & Pl
Chases	3	1	1	1	1879
Career Total	**4**	**1**	**1**	**2**	**2114**

114	2/02	Folk	2m5f	H Ch	SFT	£1079

Total win prize-money £1079

Going: Sf: 1-1 GS: 0-2 Gd: 0-0 GF: - Fm: 0-0
Distance: 2m/2m3: 0-0 **2m4-2m7: 1-2** 3m+: 0-1
Track: LH: 0-0 **RH: 1-2 Tight: 1-1** Gall: 0-0
Aids: Bl: 0-0 Vi: 0-0 Tstrap: 0-0
Best Rating: 117 3/02 Towc 2m6f gd-sft Ch

Able hunter chaser, effective on good ground and stays well. Landed the prestigious John Corbet Cup at Stratford in May 2002.

Monyman (IRE)

12-y-o b g Mandalus-Superdora (Super Slip)
J M Turner J M Turner

Placings:_01/_433262/51211314/323/5610/554/P0-PP2 (0326)

2001/02: 24^{P}GF, 24^{P}GF, 21^{2}G

	Starts	1st	2nd	3rd	Win & Pl
Chases	3	0	1	0	546
Career Total	**31**	**6**	**5**	**5**	**28348**

127	3/99	Newc	2m110y	E(0-115)HCh	SFT	£3436
127	4/97	Ayr	2m	C(0-135)HCh	GD	£5182
105	1/97	Muss	2m	E Ch	G-F	£3097
105	12/96	Catt	2m	E Ch	GD	£3042
105	11/96	Kels	2m1f	E(0-100)HCh	GD	£3048
99	4/95	Carl	2m1f	H NHF	FRM	£1339

Total win prize-money £19148

Going: Sf: 0-0 GS: 0-0 Gd: 0-1 GF: - Fm: 0-2
Distance: 2m/2m3: 0-0 2m4-2m7: 0-1 3m+: 0-2
Track: LH: 0-1 RH: 0-2 Tight: 0-2 Gall: 0-1
Aids: Bl: 0-1 Vi: 0-0 Tstrap: 0-0
Best Rating: 127 3/99 Newc 2m110y soft Ch

Moody Blues (IRE)

108 **115**

8-y-o ch g Orchestra-Blue Rainbow (Balinger)
A M Hales Andrew L Cohen

Placings:3PF (3857)

2001/02: 24^{3}GS, 26^{P}HY, 24^{F}S

	Starts	1st	2nd	3rd	Win & Pl
Chases	3	0	0	1	487
Career Total	**3**	**0**	**0**	**1**	**487**

Going: Sf: 0-2 GS: 0-1 Gd: 0-0 GF: - Fm: 0-0
Distance: 2m/2m3: 0-0 2m4-2m7: 0-0 3m+: 0-3
Track: LH: 0-1 RH: 0-1 Tight: 0-0 Gall: 0-2
Aids: Bl: 0-0 Vi: 0-0 Tstrap: 0-0
Best Rating: 115 1/02 Hntg 3m gd-sft Ch

A winning pointer in Ireland.

Moon Colony

100 **93**

9-y-o b g Top Ville-Honeymooning (USA) (Blushing Groom (FR))
A L Forbes Tony Forbes

Placings:0/00235-235 (1831)

2001/02: 16^{2}G, 17^{3}GS, 16^{5}G

	Starts	1st	2nd	3rd	Win & Pl
Hurdles	3	0	1	1	1418
Career Total	**9**	**0**	**2**	**2**	**2266**

Going: Sf: 0-0 GS: 0-1 Gd: 0-2 GF: - Fm: 0-0
Distance: 2m/2m3: 0-3 2m4-2m7: 0-0 3m+: 0-0
Track: LH: 0-2 RH: 0-1 Tight: 0-2 Gall: 0-0
Aids: Bl: 0-0 Vi: 0-0 Tstrap: 0-0
Best Rating: 93 9/01 Uttx 2m good Hdl

Moon Devil (IRE)

98 **97**

12-y-o br g Strong Gale-Moynalvey Lass (Tower Walk)
Mark Campion Sir Colin Southgate

Placings:_2/_043/3202124/14P40/P20P560/2-35 (0839)

2001/02: 20^{3}G, 23^{5}G

	Starts	1st	2nd	3rd	Win & Pl
Chases	2	0	0	1	1058
Career Total	**26**	**2**	**6**	**3**	**24421**

146	11/98	Newb	2m4f	B(0-140)HCh	G-S	£7062
134	2/98	Newb	2m1f	D Ch	GD	£3707

Total win prize-money £10770

Going: Sf: 0-0 GS: 0-0 Gd: 0-2 GF: - Fm: 0-0
Distance: 2m/2m3: 0-0 2m4-2m7: 0-1 3m+: 0-1
Track: LH: 0-2 RH: 0-0 Tight: 0-0 Gall: 0-0
Aids: Bl: 0-0 Vi: 0-0 Tstrap: 0-0
Best Rating: 146 11/98 Newb 2m4f gd-sft Ch

Moon Glow (IRE)

99(100h) (100h) **110**

6-y-o b g Fayruz-Jarmar Moon (Unfuwain (USA))
J Gallagher Mrs V W Jones

Placings:150/4P-0543FP620500 (1988)

2001/02: 17^{0}G, 16^{5}F, 17^{4}G, 16^{3}G, 17^{F}G, 16^{P}G, 16^{6}GF, 16^{2}GF, 19^{0}G, 17^{5}G, 16^{0}G, 16^{0}G

	Starts	1st	2nd	3rd	Win & Pl
Hurdles	12	0	1	1	1098
Career Total	**17**	**1**	**1**	**1**	**4502**

94	10/99	Weth	2m	D Hdl	G-F	£3129

Total win prize-money £3129

Going: Sf: 0-0 GS: 0-0 Gd: 0-9 GF: - Fm: 0-3
Distance: 2m/2m3: 0-11 2m4-2m7: 0-1 3m+: 0-0
Track: LH: 0-9 RH: 0-3 Tight: 0-8 Gall: 0-0
Aids: Bl: 0-5 Vi: 0-0 Tstrap: 0-0
Best Rating: 100 9/01 Plum 2m gd-fm Hdl

He looked a decent prospect when winning on his hurdling debut at Wetherby a couple of seasons ago, but he has been on the decline since and has changed stables. Some promise over fences in May 2002.

Moon Island

89 **48**

8-y-o b m Jupiter Island-Wild Moon (Belfalas)
S J Gilmore Mrs Vera Steggles

Placings:*00*/0P00 **(4724)**
2001/02: 19^{0}S, 22^{P}GS, 19^{0}GF, 16^{0}GF

	Starts	1st	2nd	3rd	Win & Pl
Hurdles	4	0	0	0	
Career Total	**6**	**0**	**0**	**0**	

Going: Sf: 0-1 GS: 0-1 Gd: 0-0 GF: - Fm: 0-2
Distance: 2m/2m3: 0-2 2m4-2m7: 0-2 3m+: 0-0
Track: LH: 0-3 RH: 0-1 Tight: 0-2 Gall: 0-0
Aids: Bl: 0-1 Vi: 0-2 Tstrap: 0-0
Best Rating: 36 4/02 Chep 2m110y gd-fm Hdl

Moon Royale

82 **59**

4-y-o ch f Royal Abjar (USA)-Ragged Moon (Raga Navarro (ITY))
Denys Smith B Batey

Placings:0 **(1418)**
2001/02: 17^{0}G

	Starts	1st	2nd	3rd	Win & Pl
Hurdles	1	0	0	0	
Career Total	**1**	**0**	**0**	**0**	

Going: Sf: 0-0 GS: 0-0 Gd: 0-1 GF: - Fm: 0-0
Distance: 2m/2m3: 0-1 2m4-2m7: 0-0 3m+: 0-0
Track: LH: 0-1 RH: 0-0 Tight: 0-1 Gall: 0-0
Aids: Bl: 0-0 Vi: 0-0 Tstrap: 0-0
Best Rating: 59 9/01 Sedg 2m1f good Hdl

Moon Spinner

107 **96**

5-y-o b m Elmaamul (USA)-Lunabelle (Idiots Delight)
N J Henderson Queen Elizabeth

Placings:*51*224 **(3874)**
2001/02: 16^{5}G, 16^{1}G, 21^{2}G, 21^{2}G, 16^{4}S

	Starts	1st	2nd	3rd	Win & Pl
NH Flat	2	1	0	0	1477
Hurdles	3	0	2	0	1944
Career Total	**5**	**1**	**2**	**0**	**3421**

90	7/01	Worc	2m	H NHF	GD	£1477

Total win prize-money £1477

Going: Sf: 0-1 GS: 0-0 Gd: 1-4 GF: - Fm: 0-0
Distance: **2m/2m3: 1-3** 2m4-2m7: 0-2 3m+: 0-0
Track: **LH: 1-2** RH: 0-3 Tight: 0-0 Gall: 0-1
Aids: Bl: 0-0 Vi: 0-0 Tstrap: 0-0
Best Rating: 96 2/02 Hntg 2m110y soft Hdl

A winner of a Worcester bumper in July 2001, she has shown ability over hurdles. Stays two and a half miles.

Moondigua (IRE)

101 **123**

10-y-o b g Beau Sher-Donna Chimene (Royal Gunner (USA))
P A Fahy (M C Pipe 29/6) Gone West Racing Syndicate

Placings:*112*F*1*P14/1PP/**1F3110P/0PU-6PP** **(2105a)**
2001/02: 24^{6}GS, 24^{P}GF, 28^{P}Y

	Starts	1st	2nd	3rd	Win & Pl
Chases	3	0	0	0	0
Career Total	**24**	**8**	**1**	**1**	**48331**

148	2/00	Wwck	3m1f110y	C Ch	SFT	£7840
148	1/00	Chel	2m5f	C HCh	G-S	£10676
140	11/99	Chel	2m4f110y	B Ch	GD	£10171
145	1/99	Wwck	2m4f110y	D(0-125)HHdl	SFT	£2997
121	2/98	Thur	2m6f	Hdl	SFT	£3276
122	12/97	Leop	2m	NHF	HVY	£4069
111	10/97	Gway	2m	NHF	YLD	£4069
103	6/97	Navn	2m	NHF	YLD	£2712

Total win prize-money £45811

Going: Sf: 0-0 GS: 0-1 Gd: 0-0 GF: - Fm: 0-1
Distance: 2m/2m3: 0-0 2m4-2m7: 0-0 3m+: 0-3
Track: LH: 0-2 RH: 0-0 Tight: 0-2 Gall: 0-0
Aids: Bl: 0-0 Vi: 0-0 Tstrap: 0-0
Best Rating: 148 2/00 Wwck 3m1f110y soft Ch

His form tailed off toward the end of the 1999-2000 campaign and did not recover last term. A moderate jumper.

Moonlake (IRE)

109 **108**

7-y-o b g Durgam (USA)-Joyful Prospect (Hello Gorgeous (USA))
Ferdy Murphy Mr And Mrs Neil Iveson

Placings:*002601*-230100 **(4939a)**
2001/02: 16^{2}GS, 19^{3}S, 16^{0}S, 16^{1}S, 16^{0}G, 20^{0}Y

	Starts	1st	2nd	3rd	Win & Pl
Hurdles	6	1	1	1	5101
Career Total	**12**	**2**	**2**	**1**	**8307**

108	3/02	Ludl	2m	E(0-105)HHdl	SFT	£4104
108	10/00	Aint	2m110y	E Hdl	GD	£2470

Total win prize-money £6575

Going: Sf: 1-3 GS: 0-1 Gd: 0-1 GF: - Fm: 0-0
Distance: **2m/2m3: 1-5** 2m4-2m7: 0-1 3m+: 0-0
Track: LH: 0-2 **RH: 1-4** Tight: 0-2 Gall: 0-1
Aids: Bl: 0-0 Vi: 0-0 Tstrap: 0-0
Best Rating: 108 3/02 Ludl 2m soft Hdl

Handicap hurdler, effective at two miles in soft ground.

Moonlight Invader (IRE)

8-y-o br g Darshaan-Mashmoon (USA) (Habitat)
J G Portman A S B Portman

Placings:404/P-F **(1645)**
2001/02: 20^{F}G

	Starts	1st	2nd	3rd	Win & Pl
Chases	1	0	0	0	
Career Total	**5**	**0**	**0**	**0**	0

Going: Sf: 0-0 GS: 0-0 Gd: 0-1 GF: - Fm: 0-0
Distance: 2m/2m3: 0-0 2m4-2m7: 0-1 3m+: 0-0
Track: LH: 0-0 RH: 0-1 Tight: 0-0 Gall: 0-1
Aids: Bl: 0-0 Vi: 0-0 Tstrap: 0-0
Best Rating: 89 11/98 Ludl 2m5f110y good Hdl

Moonlight Monty

95 **99**

6-y-o ch g Elmaamul (USA)-Lovers Light (Grundy)
Rodger Sweeney (B Ellison 22/6) Mrs J B Sweeney

Placings:P4-213P **(1532a)**
2001/02: 21^{2}G, 20^{1}GF, 20^{3}G, 20^{P}GF

	Starts	1st	2nd	3rd	Win & Pl
Hurdles	4	1	1	1	3460
Career Total	**6**	**1**	**1**	**1**	**3460**

99	5/01	Hexm	2m4f110y	F Hdl	G-F	£2321

Total win prize-money £2321

Going: Sf: 0-0 GS: 0-0 Gd: 0-2 GF: - Fm: 1-2
Distance: 2m/2m3: 0-0 **2m4-2m7: 1-4** 3m+: 0-0
Track: **LH: 1-4** RH: 0-0 Tight: 0-1 Gall: 0-0
Aids: Bl: 0-0 Vi: 0-0 Tstrap: 0-0
Best Rating: 99 5/01 Hexm 2m4f110y gd-fm Hdl

Moonlight Seas

6-y-o b m Sabrehill (USA)-Fair Seas (General Assembly (USA))
D R Wellicome D R Wellicome

Placings:12PP6/PP **(1269)**
2001/02: 16^{P}GF, 17^{P}GF

	Starts	1st	2nd	3rd	Win & Pl
Hurdles	2	0	0	0	
Career Total	**7**	**1**	**1**	**0**	**3991**

88	9/99	Hrfd	2m1f	E Hdl	GD	£2542

Total win prize-money £2542

Going: Sf: 0-0 GS: 0-0 Gd: 0-0 GF: - Fm: 0-2
Distance: 2m/2m3: 0-2 2m4-2m7: 0-0 3m+: 0-0
Track: LH: 0-2 RH: 0-0 Tight: 0-1 Gall: 0-0
Aids: Bl: 0-1 Vi: 0-0 Tstrap: 0-0
Best Rating: 88 10/99 Asct 2m110y good Hdl

Moonlight Venture

106 **87**

10-y-o b g Jupiter Island-Moonlight Bay (Palm Track)
M Todhunter R Smalley

Placings:*00*/P50463440**062F**0/2F**P0**/134216214F0/04P0-45220 **(1234)**
2001/02: 20^{4}G, 21^{5}G, 27^{2}GF, 27^{2}GF, 22^{0}GS

	Starts	1st	2nd	3rd	Win & Pl
Hurdles	5	0	2	0	1568
Career Total	**40**	**3**	**6**	**2**	**11825**

85	9/99	Sedg	2m1f	F(0-105)HHdl	G-F	£2024
87	7/99	Sedg	2m5f110y	F(0-100)HHdl	G-F	£2267
75	6/99	Hexm	2m	F(0-95)HHdl	G-F	£2170

Total win prize-money £6463

Going: Sf: 0-0 GS: 0-1 Gd: 0-2 GF: - Fm: 0-2
Distance: 2m/2m3: 0-0 2m4-2m7: 0-3 3m+: 0-2
Track: LH: 0-4 RH: 0-1 Tight: 0-4 Gall: 0-0
Aids: Bl: 0-0 Vi: 0-0 Tstrap: 0-0
Best Rating: 89 2/98 Muss 3m good Ch

Moonlighter

12-y-o b m Lighter-Skidmore (Paddy's Stream)
C F C Jackson Miss Sarah Jackson

Placings:*500*/6P32P/P065/50**P222/PP23/5F-1554** **(4569)**
2001/02: 24^{1}S, 23^{5}S, 25^{5}S, 22^{4}G

	Starts	1st	2nd	3rd	Win & Pl
Chases	4	1	0	0	1233
Career Total	**28**	**1**	**5**	**2**	**6076**

94 2/02 Hntg 3m H Ch SFT £1072
Total win prize-money £1073

Going: Sf: 1-3 GS: 0-0 Gd: 0-1 GF: - Fm: 0-0
Distance: 2m/2m3: 0-0 2m4-2m7: 0-1 **3m+: 1-3**
Track: LH: 0-0 **RH: 1-4** Tight: 0-0 **Gall: 1-1**
Aids: Bl: 0-0 **Vi: 1-4** Tstrap: 0-0
Best Rating: 101 3/02 Leic 2m7f110y soft Ch

Modest staying maiden under Rules. Acts with cut in the ground.

Moonlighting

(80c)
5-y-o b m Lugana Beach-White Flash (Sure Blade (USA))
B R Johnson (D R C Elsworth 27/7) Kevin Nolan

Placings:6U (4780)
2001/02: 17^{6}S, 17^{U}GF

	Starts	1st	2nd	3rd	Win & Pl
Hurdles	1	0	0	0	0
Chases	1	0	0	0	0
Career Total	**2**	**0**	**0**	**0**	**0**

Going: Sf: 0-1 GS: 0-0 Gd: 0-0 GF: - Fm: 0-1
Distance: 2m/2m3: 0-2 2m4-2m7: 0-0 3m+: 0-0
Track: LH: 0-1 RH: 0-1 Tight: 0-2 Gall: 0-0
Aids: Bl: 0-1 Vi: 0-0 Tstrap: 0-0
Best Rating: 80 4/02 Plum 2m1f gd-fm Ch

Moonlite Magic (IRE)

101 **96**
8-y-o br g Phardante (FR)-Lucey Allen (Strong Gale)
Ferdy Murphy John Duddy

Placings:3500-F02251U04 (4196)
2001/02: 26^{F}GF, 23^{0}GF, 20^{2}GS, 24^{2}S, 23^{5}G, 27^{1}S, 21^{U}HY, 24^{0}S, 27^{4}S

	Starts	1st	2nd	3rd	Win & Pl
Hurdles	9	1	2	0	2882
Career Total	**13**	**1**	**2**	**1**	**3097**

93 11/01 Sedg 3m3f110y G(0-90)HHdl SFT £1547
Total win prize-money £1547

Going: Sf: 1-5 GS: 0-1 Gd: 0-1 GF: - Fm: 0-2
Distance: 2m/2m3: 0-0 2m4-2m7: 0-3 **3m+: 1-6**
Track: **LH: 1-6** RH: 0-2 **Tight: 1-4** Gall: 0-2
Aids: **Bl: 1-4** Vi: 0-1 Tstrap: 0-0
Best Rating: 97 10/00 Sthl 2m soft NHF

He is suited by marathon trips and soft ground. Has run well in blinkers.

Moonraking

90 **88**
9-y-o gr g Rusticaro (FR)-Lunaire (Try My Best (USA))
W Clay Lee Heath

Placings:0P/422113056/661-0P000000 (4573)
2001/02: 19^{0}G, 16^{P}G, 17^{0}G, 16^{0}GF, 16^{0}GF, 17^{0}G, 21^{0}GS, 20^{0}G

	Starts	1st	2nd	3rd	Win & Pl
Hurdles	8	0	0	0	
Career Total	**22**	**3**	**2**	**1**	**7514**

101 11/00 Ludl 2m G Hdl GD £1991
98 11/99 Hrfd 2m1f G(0-95)HHdl GD £2070
97 11/99 Ludl 2m G(0-95)HHdl GD £2038
Total win prize-money £6100

Going: Sf: 0-0 GS: 0-1 Gd: 0-5 GF: - Fm: 0-2
Distance: 2m/2m3: 0-5 2m4-2m7: 0-3 3m+: 0-0
Track: LH: 0-4 RH: 0-4 Tight: 0-2 Gall: 0-0
Aids: Bl: 0-1 Vi: 0-6 Tstrap: 0-0
Best Rating: 102 12/99 Ludl 2m good Hdl

Effective at around two miles and acts on good ground.

Moonshine Bay (IRE)

106(109h) (118h)**141**
8-y-o b g Executive Perk-Sister Of Slane (The Parson)
J T Gifford Mrs Timothy Pilkington

Placings:*06*/30114/125040-3R23113F (4851)
2001/02: 20^{3}G, 16^{R}S, 16^{2}G, 16^{3}G, 20^{1}G, 20^{1}S, 18^{3}HY, 20^{F}G

	Starts	1st	2nd	3rd	Win & Pl
Hurdles	2	0	0	2	2370
Chases	6	2	1	1	10159
Career Total	**21**	**5**	**2**	**4**	**26746**

141 3/02 Font 2m4f D Ch SFT £4010
141 1/02 Font 2m4f E Ch GD £3276
122 11/00 Winc 2m D(0-120)HHdl SFT £5265
114 3/99 Sand 2m110y D Hdl G-S £2905
100 11/98 Folk 2m1f110y E Hdl SFT £2264
Total win prize-money £17722

Going: Sf: 1-3 GS: 0-0 Gd: 1-5 GF: - Fm: 0-0
Distance: 2m/2m3: 0-4 **2m4-2m7: 2-4** 3m+: 0-0
Track: LH: 0-3 RH: 0-3 **Tight: 2-5** Gall: 0-0
Aids: Bl: 0-0 Vi: 0-0 Tstrap: 0-0
Best Rating: 141 3/02 Font 2m4f soft Ch

Suited by two and a half miles on good/good to soft ground. He has been successful over both hurdles and fences.

Moor Hall Lady

98 **88**
11-y-o gr m Rambo Dancer (CAN)-Forgiving (Jellaby)
R S Brookhouse R S Brookhouse

Placings:*00*/452604/6/3F/F61F4150/6533050-236P560 (1383)
2001/02: 22^{2}GF, 19^{3}GF, 20^{6}GF, 20^{P}GS, 19^{5}G, 22^{6}GF, 26^{0}GF

	Starts	1st	2nd	3rd	Win & Pl
Hurdles	7	0	1	1	1490
Career Total	**33**	**2**	**2**	**4**	**9707**

106 9/99 Bang 2m1f D Hdl G-F £3095
98 7/99 Strf 2m110y E Hdl GD £2999
Total win prize-money £6094

Going: Sf: 0-0 GS: 0-1 Gd: 0-1 GF: - Fm: 0-5
Distance: 2m/2m3: 0-2 2m4-2m7: 0-4 3m+: 0-1
Track: LH: 0-5 RH: 0-2 Tight: 0-3 Gall: 0-0
Aids: Bl: 0-0 Vi: 0-0 Tstrap: 0-0
Best Rating: 106 9/99 Bang 2m1f gd-fm Hdl

Moor Hall Rock

101(75c) (60c)**85**
7-y-o b g Rock Hopper-Forgiving (Jellaby)
R S Brookhouse R S Brookhouse

Placings:*P/0*000-34060 (3336)
2001/02: 17^{3}G, 20^{4}G, 17^{0}GF, 16^{6}G, 20^{0}G

	Starts	1st	2nd	3rd	Win & Pl
Hurdles	4	0	0	1	450
Chases	1	0	0	0	0
Career Total	**10**	**0**	**0**	**1**	**450**

Going: Sf: 0-0 GS: 0-0 Gd: 0-4 GF: - Fm: 0-1
Distance: 2m/2m3: 0-3 2m4-2m7: 0-2 3m+: 0-0
Track: LH: 0-2 RH: 0-3 Tight: 0-3 Gall: 0-1
Aids: Bl: 0-0 Vi: 0-0 Tstrap: 0-0
Best Rating: 91 10/00 Chel 2m110y good NHF

Modest maiden hurdler, has shown a little ability on good ground.

Moor Lane

113 **148**
10-y-o b g Primitive Rising (USA)-Navos (Tyrnavos)
I A Balding R P B Michaelson

Placings:2/311F/12/51120 (4664)
2001/02: 20^{5}G, 24^{1}G, 24^{1}S, 24^{2}GS, 21^{0}G

	Starts	1st	2nd	3rd	Win & Pl
Chases	5	2	1	0	52425
Career Total	**12**	**5**	**3**	**1**	**75234**

148 1/02 Donc 3m A(0-145)HCh SFT £39871
132 1/02 Newb 3m C(0-135)HCh GD £8931
144 9/99 Extr 2m6f110y E(0-115)HCh G-S £4279
130 1/99 Donc 2m3f110y D Ch GD £4211
133 11/98 Newb 2m4f C Ch SFT £7108
Total win prize-money £64401

Going: Sf: 1-1 GS: 0-1 Gd: 1-3 GF: - Fm: 0-0
Distance: 2m/2m3: 0-0 2m4-2m7: 0-2 **3m+: 2-3**
Track: **LH: 2-4** RH: 0-1 Tight: 0-1 **Gall: 2-3**
Aids: Bl: 0-0 Vi: 0-0 Tstrap: 0-0
Best Rating: 148 3/02 Newb 3m gd-sft Ch

An ex-pointer, he is a lightly-raced handicap chaser, effective at two and a half miles, but showed improved form when stepped up to three miles, winning the Great Yorkshire at the start of the year. A leading ante-post fancy for the Grand National, he was forced to go for the Topham instead after missing the cut but ran no sort of race. He jumps well and acts on good ground and softer.

Moore Appeal

5-y-o b m Homo Sapien-Star Leader (Kafu)
W M Brisbourne C W Moore

Placings:*0* (2321)
2001/02: 17^{0}GS

	Starts	1st	2nd	3rd	Win & Pl
NH Flat	1	0	0	0	
Career Total	**1**	**0**	**0**	**0**	

Going: Sf: 0-0 GS: 0-1 Gd: 0-0 GF: - Fm: 0-0
Distance: 2m/2m3: 0-1 2m4-2m7: 0-0 3m+: 0-0
Track: LH: 0-0 RH: 0-0 Tight: 0-0 Gall: 0-0
Aids: Bl: 0-0 Vi: 0-0 Tstrap: 0-0
Best Rating:

Moore's Melodies (IRE)

96(81c) (50c)**87**
11-y-o br g Orchestra-Markree Castle (Pitpan)
M J Gingell Dr Tom Alexander

Placings:0050/00010/P/P/55-260 (0720)

2001/02: 23^{2}F, 20^{6}GF, 26^{0}F

	Starts	1st	2nd	3rd	Win & Pl
Hurdles	3	0	1	0	1014
Career Total	**16**	**1**	**1**	**0**	**3992**

106	2/98	Naas	2m4f	(0-109)HCh	SFT	£2978

Total win prize-money £2978

Going: Sf: 0-0 GS: 0-0 Gd: 0-0 GF: - Fm: 0-3
Distance: 2m/2m3: 0-0 2m4-2m7: 0-2 3m+: 0-1
Track: LH: 0-2 RH: 0-1 Tight: 0-1 Gall: 0-0
Aids: Bl: 0-0 Vi: 0-1 Tstrap: 0-0
Best Rating: 106 2/98 Naas 2m4f soft Ch

Moorland Highflyer

11-y-o b/br g Karlinsky (USA)-Moorland Heath Vii (Damsire Unregistered)
T Long (A G Hobbs 10/3) Unity Farm Holiday Centre Ltd

Placings:F4U/U241F43122125/PUPP/U3F5P2PP3-0P0 **(4659)**
2001/02: 24^{0}G, 25^{P}F, 24^{0}G

	Starts	1st	2nd	3rd	Win & Pl
Chases	3	0	0	0	
Career Total	**32**	**3**	**5**	**3**	**19762**

114	4/99	Chep	3m2f110y	D(0-120)HCh	SFT	£4162
108	1/99	Ludl	3m	E(0-115)HCh	G-S	£3582
102	6/98	NAbb	3m2f110y	E(0-110)HCh	GD	£3550

Total win prize-money £11296

Going: Sf: 0-0 GS: 0-0 Gd: 0-2 GF: - Fm: 0-1
Distance: 2m/2m3: 0-0 2m4-2m7: 0-0 3m+: 0-3
Track: LH: 0-0 RH: 0-2 Tight: 0-1 Gall: 0-1
Aids: Bl: 0-1 Vi: 0-0 Tstrap: 0-1
Best Rating: 121 4/99 Chel 3m2f110y good Ch

Moorlands Again

60 40

7-y-o b g Then Again-Sandford Springs (USA) (Robellino (USA))
J M Bradley Mrs Lynda M Williams

Placings:55/0 **(2000)**
2001/02: 17^{0}S

	Starts	1st	2nd	3rd	Win & Pl
Hurdles	1	0	0	0	
Career Total	**3**	**0**	**0**	**0**	**0**

Going: Sf: 0-1 GS: 0-0 Gd: 0-0 GF: - Fm: 0-0
Distance: 2m/2m3: 0-1 2m4-2m7: 0-0 3m+: 0-0
Track: LH: 0-1 RH: 0-0 Tight: 0-1 Gall: 0-0
Aids: Bl: 0-0 Vi: 0-0 Tstrap: 0-0
Best Rating: 95 10/99 Worc 2m gd-fm NHF

Moorlands Spring

101 106

8-y-o b g Then Again-Sandford Springs (USA) (Robellino (USA))
J G Given R W L Bowden

Placings:00625636P/64524P-12 **(0275)**
2001/02: 20^{1}G, 20^{2}GF

	Starts	1st	2nd	3rd	Win & Pl
Chases	2	1	1	0	7267
Career Total	**17**	**1**	**3**	**1**	**9097**

106	5/01	Weth	2m4f110y	D(0-110)HCh	GD	£4147

Total win prize-money £4147

Going: Sf: 0-0 GS: 0-0 Gd: 1-1 GF: - Fm: 0-1
Distance: 2m/2m3: 0-0 **2m4-2m7: 1-2** 3m+: 0-0
Track: **LH: 1-1** RH: 0-1 Tight: 0-0 Gall: 0-0
Aids: Bl: 0-0 Vi: 0-0 Tstrap: 0-0
Best Rating: 106 5/01 Prth 2m4f110y gd-fm Ch

Moose Malloy

98 66

5-y-o ch g Formidable (USA)-Jolimo (Fortissimo)
M J Ryan Extraman Ltd

Placings:40-603P **(1139)**
2001/02: 16^{6}GF, 17^{0}G, 16^{3}GF, 22^{P}G

	Starts	1st	2nd	3rd	Win & Pl
Hurdles	4	0	0	1	438
Career Total	**6**	**0**	**0**	**1**	**438**

Going: Sf: 0-0 GS: 0-0 Gd: 0-2 GF: - Fm: 0-2
Distance: 2m/2m3: 0-3 2m4-2m7: 0-1 3m+: 0-0
Track: LH: 0-2 RH: 0-2 Tight: 0-3 Gall: 0-1
Aids: Bl: 0-3 Vi: 0-0 Tstrap: 0-0
Best Rating: 86 9/00 Hntg 2m110y gd-fm Hdl

Moral Justice (IRE)

107 (114h) 121

9-y-o b g Lafontaine (USA)-Proven Right (IRE) (Kemal (FR))
S J Gilmore (J A Berry 13/10) Miss Jumbo Frost

Placings:0/52122PP **(4817)**
2001/02: 16^{0}GY, 16^{1}G, 24^{5}G, 20^{2}GF, 20^{1}F, 24^{2}G, 22^{2}G, 24^{P}S, 24^{P}GF

	Starts	1st	2nd	3rd	Win & Pl
NH Flat	2	1	0	0	3617
Hurdles	4	1	1	0	6468
Chases	3	0	2	0	2968
Career Total	**9**	**2**	**3**	**0**	**13052**

109	9/01	Fair	2m4f	Hdl	FRM	£5564
105	8/01	Kbgn	2m	NHF	GD	£3616

Total win prize-money £9182

Going: Sf: 0-1 GS: 0-0 Gd: 1-4 GF: - Fm: 1-3
Distance: 2m/2m3: 1-2 2m4-2m7: 1-3 3m+: 0-4
Track: LH: 0-1 **RH: 1-2** Tight: 0-0 Gall: 0-1
Aids: Bl: 0-0 Vi: 0-0 Tstrap: 0-0
Best Rating: 132 10/01 Gowr 2m6f good Ch

Managed to win a couple of moderate chases in June 2002. Looks best on fast ground and over distances short of three miles. Suited by forcing tactics.

Moral Support (IRE)

99(99h) (118h) 142

10-y-o ch g Zaffaran (USA)-Marians Pride (Pry)
C J Mann Tom & Evelyn Yates

Placings:4010/42F/345150P6/1111236B-23PP (3587)
2001/02: 24^{2}S, 24^{3}S, 29^{P}GS, 28^{P}HY

	Starts	1st	2nd	3rd	Win & Pl
Hurdles	1	0	1	0	1650
Chases	3	0	0	1	3850
Career Total	**27**	**6**	**3**	**3**	**70961**

153	12/00	Chep	3m	A HCh	HVY	£21000
135	11/00	Hntg	3m6f110y	C(0-130)HCh	G-S	£6955
139	11/00	Newb	3m	D(0-110)HCh	SFT	£4368
135	11/00	Kemp	3m	D(0-110)HCh	SFT	£4777
104	2/00	Thur	3m	(0-95)HHdl	HVY	£3588
100	3/97	Tipp	2m4f	Hdl	G-Y	£3391

Total win prize-money £44080

Going: Sf: 0-3 GS: 0-1 Gd: 0-0 GF: - Fm: 0-0
Distance: 2m/2m3: 0-0 2m4-2m7: 0-0 3m+: 0-4
Track: LH: 0-3 RH: 0-1 Tight: 0-0 Gall: 0-0
Aids: Bl: 0-0 Vi: 0-0 Tstrap: 0-0
Best Rating: 153 2/01 Hayd 3m heavy Ch

A half-brother to Dorans Pride, he ran over both hurdles and fences for Mouse Morris when trained in Ireland, but really hit form when joining Charlie Mann in the winter of 2000. He notched up four wins in handicaps on the bounce over fences, including one over a marathon three miles six furlongs, and was a creditable second in the Welsh National. Ran a bit flat in the spring of 2001 and ended the season when brought down at the eighth in the Grand National. Failed to find his form last season. He has won from three miles to three miles six over fences. Acts on soft ground. has reportedly joined Stan Moore.

Mordon Boy (IRE)

108 119

10-y-o ch g Persian Mews-Kindly (Tarqogan)
J J O'Neill J P McManus

Placings:50/40/2265064/013U-P1P04 **(4918)**
2001/02: 24^{P}S, 25^{1}F, 26^{P}GS, 25^{0}G, 28^{4}GF

	Starts	1st	2nd	3rd	Win & Pl
Chases	5	1	0	0	4253
Career Total	**20**	**2**	**2**	**1**	**10615**

119	5/01	Weth	3m1f	F(0-110)HCh	FRM	£3167
116	9/00	Bang	3m110y	F(0-100)HCh	G-F	£4290

Total win prize-money £7458

Going: Sf: 0-1 GS: 0-1 Gd: 0-1 GF: - Fm: 1-2
Distance: 2m/2m3: 0-0 2m4-2m7: 0-0 **3m+: 1-5**
Track: **LH: 1-4** RH: 0-1 Tight: 0-2 Gall: 0-0
Aids: Bl: 0-1 Vi: 0-0 Tstrap: 0-0
Best Rating: 123 1/01 Catt 3m1f110y gd-sft Ch

He must have fast ground and scored under those conditions at Bangor in September 2000 and at Wetherby. Suited by three miles, he tends to struggle when the going gets soft.

Mordros

12-y-o b g Interrex (CAN)-Jay Jays Dream (Shaab)
Mrs J Scrivens Mrs J Scrivens

Placings:0/4/0/PUP-P **(4505)**
2001/02: 21^{P}G

	Starts	1st	2nd	3rd	Win & Pl
Chases	1	0	0	0	
Career Total	**7**	**0**	**0**	**0**	**0**

Going: Sf: 0-0 GS: 0-0 Gd: 0-1 GF: - Fm: 0-0
Distance: 2m/2m3: 0-0 2m4-2m7: 0-1 3m+: 0-0
Track: LH: 0-1 RH: 0-0 Tight: 0-1 Gall: 0-0
Aids: Bl: 0-0 Vi: 0-0 Tstrap: 0-0
Best Rating: 68 4/97 Worc 2m gd-fm Hdl

More Flair

51f 44f

5-y-o ch m Alflora (IRE)-Marejo (Creetown)
J B Walton F T Walton

Placings:00 **(3443)**
2001/02: 16^{0}S, 17^{0}S

	Starts	1st	2nd	3rd	Win & Pl
NH Flat	2	0	0	0	
Career Total	**2**	**0**	**0**	**0**	

Going: Sf: 0-2 GS: 0-0 Gd: 0-0 GF: - Fm: 0-0
Distance: 2m/2m3: 0-2 2m4-2m7: 0-0 3m+: 0-0

Track: LH: 0-1 RH: 0-0 Tight: 0-1 Gall: 0-0
Aids: Bl: 0-0 Vi: 0-0 Tstrap: 0-0
Best Rating: 44 1/02 Sedg 2m1f soft NHF

More Rush (IRE)

101 **105**

10-y-o b g Lancastrian-Roselle (Derring Rose)
J J O'Neill Ian G M Dalgleish

Placings:6/20P6/13 **(4514)**
2001/02: 25^{1}S, 25^{3}GS

	Starts	1st	2nd	3rd	Win & Pl
Chases	2	1	0	1	3603
Career Total	**7**	**1**	**1**	**1**	**4683**

105 3/02 Hrfd 3m1f110y F(0-90)HCh SFT £3094
Total win prize-money £3094

Going: Sf: 1-1 GS: 0-1 Gd: 0-0 GF: - Fm: 0-0
Distance: 2m/2m3: 0-0 2m4-2m7: 0-0 **3m+: 1-2**
Track: LH: 0-0 **RH: 1-2** Tight: 0-0 Gall: 0-0
Aids: Bl: 0-0 Vi: 0-0 Tstrap: 0-0
Best Rating: 105 3/02 Hrfd 3m1f110y soft Ch

He made the most of a lenient handicap mark when winning on his return from a two-year absence on his first start for his new stable at Hereford in March. Stays three miles. Acts on good to soft/soft ground.

More Sirens (IRE)

93 **83**

4-y-o ch f Night Shift (USA)-Lower The Tone (IRE) (Phone Trick (USA))
P R Webber (Mrs J R Ramsden 1/7) The Huntingdon Hopefuls

Placings:F0 **(2891)**
2001/02: 16^{F}G, 16^{0}G

	Starts	1st	2nd	3rd	Win & Pl
Hurdles	2	0	0	0	
Career Total	**2**	**0**	**0**	**0**	

Going: Sf: 0-0 GS: 0-0 Gd: 0-2 GF: - Fm: 0-0
Distance: 2m/2m3: 0-2 2m4-2m7: 0-0 3m+: 0-0
Track: LH: 0-0 RH: 0-2 Tight: 0-0 Gall: 0-1
Aids: Bl: 0-0 Vi: 0-0 Tstrap: 0-0
Best Rating: 83 11/01 Hntg 2m110y good Hdl

A miler on the Flat, she fell on her hurdles bow but had jumped well up until then. Well held next time.

More Tears (IRE)

94 **61**

6-y-o b g Witness Box (USA)-Anyone's Fancy (Callernish)
N J Hawke M J Disney

Placings:FF0-PF35 **(3401)**
2001/02: 22^{P}GF, 22^{F}GF, 19^{3}GS, 22^{5}S

	Starts	1st	2nd	3rd	Win & Pl
Hurdles	4	0	0	1	352
Career Total	**7**	**0**	**0**	**1**	**352**

Going: Sf: 0-1 GS: 0-1 Gd: 0-0 GF: - Fm: 0-2
Distance: 2m/2m3: 0-1 2m4-2m7: 0-3 3m+: 0-0
Track: LH: 0-1 RH: 0-1 Tight: 0-1 Gall: 0-0
Aids: Bl: 0-0 Vi: 0-0 Tstrap: 0-0
Best Rating: 71 2/01 Tntn 2m1f heavy Hdl

Moreover (IRE)

106 **93**

4-y-o b f Caerleon (USA)-Overcall (Bustino)
M W Easterby (Sir Mark Prescott 20/10) J T Stimpson

Placings:34 **(3408)**
2001/02: 16^{3}S, 16^{4}S

	Starts	1st	2nd	3rd	Win & Pl
Hurdles	2	0	0	1	436
Career Total	**2**	**0**	**0**	**1**	**436**

Going: Sf: 0-2 GS: 0-0 Gd: 0-0 GF: - Fm: 0-0
Distance: 2m/2m3: 0-2 2m4-2m7: 0-0 3m+: 0-0
Track: LH: 0-1 RH: 0-1 Tight: 0-0 Gall: 0-1
Aids: Bl: 0-0 Vi: 0-0 Tstrap: 0-0
Best Rating: 93 1/02 Newc 2m soft Hdl

Fair stayer on the Flat, still a maiden over hurdles.

Moreton Wood Moss

84 **81**

7-y-o ch g Le Moss-Moreton Wood Petal (Rakaposhi King)
R Ford P C & S E Handley

Placings:FP0 **(4591)**
2001/02: 24^{F}GS, 20^{P}HY, 16^{0}G

	Starts	1st	2nd	3rd	Win & Pl
Hurdles	3	0	0	0	
Career Total	**3**	**0**	**0**	**0**	

Going: Sf: 0-1 GS: 0-1 Gd: 0-1 GF: - Fm: 0-0
Distance: 2m/2m3: 0-1 2m4-2m7: 0-1 3m+: 0-1
Track: LH: 0-2 RH: 0-1 Tight: 0-2 Gall: 0-0
Aids: Bl: 0-0 Vi: 0-0 Tstrap: 0-0
Best Rating: 83 4/02 Uttx 2m good Hdl

Morimont (FR)

105 **116**

7-y-o b g Cyborg (FR)-Fond Froide (Bellman (FR))
J J O'Neill Mrs B J Lockhart

Placings:P0P/F2F31/550-060 **(2571)**
2001/02: 20^{0}G, 21^{6}G, 22^{0}S

	Starts	1st	2nd	3rd	Win & Pl
Hurdles	3	0	0	0	0
Career Total	**14**	**1**	**1**	**1**	**18885**

1/00 Pau 2m2f HHdl GD £13449
Total win prize-money £13449

Going: Sf: 0-1 GS: 0-0 Gd: 0-2 GF: - Fm: 0-0
Distance: 2m/2m3: 0-0 2m4-2m7: 0-3 3m+: 0-0
Track: LH: 0-2 RH: 0-1 Tight: 0-0 Gall: 0-1
Aids: Bl: 0-1 Vi: 0-0 Tstrap: 0-0
Best Rating: 120 12/00 Newb 2m3f soft Hdl

Lightly-raced ex-French, he has looked held in decent company since arriving in this country.

Morning Alf

97(77c) **88**

9-y-o gr g Scallywag-Rose Window (Artaius (USA))
R S Brookhouse (Miss H M Irving 23/5) R S Brookhouse

Placings:*00/04/040***U2P**04-21P **(3868)**
2001/02: 25^{2}S, 24^{1}G, 26^{P}GS

	Starts	1st	2nd	3rd	Win & Pl
Hurdles	3	1	1	0	3710
Career Total	**15**	**1**	**2**	**0**	**4857**

88 5/01 Bang 3m E Hdl GD £2989
Total win prize-money £2989

Going: Sf: 0-1 GS: 0-1 Gd: 1-1 GF: - Fm: 0-0
Distance: 2m/2m3: 0-0 2m4-2m7: 0-0 **3m+: 1-3**
Track: **LH: 1-1** RH: 0-1 **Tight: 1-1** Gall: 0-0
Aids: **Bl: 1-2** Vi: 0-1 Tstrap: 0-0
Best Rating: 88 5/01 Bang 3m good Hdl

Morning Flight (IRE)

81 **76**

6-y-o b m Supreme Leader-Morning Jane (IRE) (Over The River (FR))
Noel T Chance Top Flight Racing 2

Placings:0P **(3397)**
2001/02: 18^{0}G, 20^{P}S

	Starts	1st	2nd	3rd	Win & Pl
Hurdles	2	0	0	0	
Career Total	**2**	**0**	**0**	**0**	

Going: Sf: 0-1 GS: 0-0 Gd: 0-1 GF: - Fm: 0-0
Distance: 2m/2m3: 0-1 2m4-2m7: 0-1 3m+: 0-0
Track: LH: 0-1 RH: 0-0 Tight: 0-2 Gall: 0-0
Aids: Bl: 0-0 Vi: 0-0 Tstrap: 0-0
Best Rating: 76 1/02 Font 2m2f110y good Hdl

Morning Glory

58

6-y-o b m Polar Falcon (USA)-Round Midnight (Star Appeal)
Miss C J E Caroe Miss C J E Caroe

Placings:*05/*0P-0 **(0060)**
2001/02: 17^{0}GS

	Starts	1st	2nd	3rd	Win & Pl
Hurdles	1	0	0	0	
Career Total	**5**	**0**	**0**	**0**	**0**

Going: Sf: 0-0 GS: 0-1 Gd: 0-0 GF: - Fm: 0-0
Distance: 2m/2m3: 0-1 2m4-2m7: 0-0 3m+: 0-0
Track: LH: 0-0 RH: 0-1 Tight: 0-1 Gall: 0-0
Aids: Bl: 0-0 Vi: 0-1 Tstrap: 0-0
Best Rating: 45 5/00 Towc 2m gd-fm Hdl

Morning Mist (IRE)

80 **88**

10-y-o b g Supreme Leader-Luton Flyer (Condorcet (FR))
Mrs H Dalton Kevin Glastonbury

Placings:*0262/00215/***F000/**U-50 **(0371)**
2001/02: 20^{5}G, 21^{0}G

	Starts	1st	2nd	3rd	Win & Pl
Hurdles	2	0	0	0	0
Career Total	**16**	**1**	**3**	**0**	**2710**

94 9/98 Dpat 2m1f172y Hdl SFT £1494
Total win prize-money £1495

Going: Sf: 0-0 GS: 0-0 Gd: 0-2 GF: - Fm: 0-0
Distance: 2m/2m3: 0-0 2m4-2m7: 0-2 3m+: 0-0
Track: LH: 0-1 RH: 0-0 Tight: 0-1 Gall: 0-0
Aids: Bl: 0-0 Vi: 0-0 Tstrap: 0-0
Best Rating: 100 9/98 Baln 2m4f gd-yld NHF

Morning Suit

75 **24**

8-y-o b g Reprimand-Morica (Moorestyle)
A J Chamberlain A J Chamberlain

Placings: *600600*/44360-000 (0914)
2001/02: 19^{0}G, 20^{0}G, 22^{0}GF

	Starts	1st	2nd	3rd	Win & Pl
Hurdles	3	0	0	0	
Career Total	**14**	**0**	**0**	**1**	**292**

Going: Sf: 0-0 GS: 0-0 Gd: 0-2 GF: - Fm: 0-1
Distance: 2m/2m3: 0-0 2m4-2m7: 0-3 3m+: 0-0
Track: LH: 0-2 RH: 0-1 Tight: 0-1 Gall: 0-0
Aids: Bl: 0-0 Vi: 0-0 Tstrap: 0-0
Best Rating: 83 11/99 Wwck 2m good NHF

Mornington

7-y-o b g Shirley Heights-Habibay (Habitat)
G Prodromou Michael Odysseas

Placings: *00/0*-P (0594)
2001/02: 20^{P}GF

	Starts	1st	2nd	3rd	Win & Pl
Hurdles	1	0	0	0	
Career Total	**4**	**0**	**0**	**0**	

Going: Sf: 0-0 GS: 0-0 Gd: 0-0 GF: - Fm: 0-1
Distance: 2m/2m3: 0-0 2m4-2m7: 0-1 3m+: 0-0
Track: LH: 0-1 RH: 0-0 Tight: 0-1 Gall: 0-0
Aids: Bl: 0-0 Vi: 0-0 Tstrap: 0-0
Best Rating: 61 11/99 Chep 2m110y gd-sft NHF

Morph

65 14
8-y-o gr g Baron Blakeney-Amber Marsh (Arctic Kanda)
R H York R H York

Placings: *P0/00* (0559)
2001/02: 17^{0}GS, 22^{0}GF

	Starts	1st	2nd	3rd	Win & Pl
Hurdles	2	0	0	0	
Career Total	**4**	**0**	**0**	**0**	

Going: Sf: 0-0 GS: 0-1 Gd: 0-0 GF: - Fm: 0-1
Distance: 2m/2m3: 0-1 2m4-2m7: 0-1 3m+: 0-0
Track: LH: 0-1 RH: 0-1 Tight: 0-2 Gall: 0-0
Aids: Bl: 0-0 Vi: 0-0 Tstrap: 0-0
Best Rating: 14 5/01 Folk 2m1f110y gd-sft Hdl

Morris Piper

9-y-o b g Long Leave-Miss Cone (Celtic Cone)
Mrs Monique Pike I W Farley

Placings: 3/P-0P0P (0561)
2001/02: 21^{0}GF, 19^{P}F, 21^{0}G, 21^{P}GF

	Starts	1st	2nd	3rd	Win & Pl
Chases	4	0	0	0	
Career Total	**6**	**0**	**0**	**1**	**172**

Going: Sf: 0-0 GS: 0-0 Gd: 0-1 GF: - Fm: 0-3
Distance: 2m/2m3: 0-0 2m4-2m7: 0-4 3m+: 0-0
Track: LH: 0-1 RH: 0-2 Tight: 0-1 Gall: 0-0
Aids: Bl: 0-0 Vi: 0-0 Tstrap: 0-0
Best Rating: 104 3/00 Winc 2m5f gd-sft Ch

Morstock

111 113
12-y-o gr g Beveled (USA)-Miss Melmore (Nishapour (FR))
R J Hodges Mrs M Fairbairn

Placings: 04335411446/2230340/4U221232636/32214 6343U/33F223/45210634003/633F0441-23540603544U (4886)
2001/02: 16^{2}G, 16^{3}GF, 19^{5}F, 16^{4}GF, 21^{0}G, 16^{6}G, 20^{0}G, 18^{3}HY, 16^{5}S, 16^{4}S, 16^{4}G, 18^{U}GF

	Starts	1st	2nd	3rd	Win & Pl
Chases	12	0	1	2	2390
Career Total	**76**	**6**	**12**	**18**	**51892**

120	4/01	Font	2m2f	E(0-115)HCh	GD	£3797
128	12/99	Winc	2m	D(0-120)HCh	SFT	£4143
120	1/98	Kemp	2m	C(0-135)HCh	SFT	£4765
115	11/96	Winc	2m	C(0-135)HHdl	GD	£3470
103	1/95	Winc	2m	E(0-110)HHdl	GD	£2574
94	12/94	Winc	2m	(0-100)HHdl	GD	£2267

Total win prize-money £21018

Going: Sf: 0-3 GS: 0-0 Gd: 0-5 GF: - Fm: 0-4
Distance: 2m/2m3: 0-10 2m4-2m7: 0-2 3m+: 0-0
Track: LH: 0-2 RH: 0-8 Tight: 0-6 Gall: 0-0
Aids: Bl: 0-0 Vi: 0-0 Tstrap: 0-0
Best Rating: 128 12/99 Winc 2m soft Ch

He has always been best around two miles and acts on all types of ground. Took advantage of being dropped in the ratings with back-to-back victories at Exeter and Newton Abbot in May 2002.

Morticia

4-y-o b f Rudimentary (USA)-Valkyrie (Bold Lad (IRE))
M A Barnes M Barnes

Placings: *0* (4860)
2001/02: 16^{0}G

	Starts	1st	2nd	3rd	Win & Pl
NH Flat	1	0	0	0	
Career Total	**1**	**0**	**0**	**0**	

Going: Sf: 0-0 GS: 0-0 Gd: 0-1 GF: - Fm: 0-0
Distance: 2m/2m3: 0-1 2m4-2m7: 0-0 3m+: 0-0
Track: LH: 0-0 RH: 0-0 Tight: 0-0 Gall: 0-0
Aids: Bl: 0-0 Vi: 0-0 Tstrap: 0-1
Best Rating:

Moscow Dancer (IRE)

73 58
5-y-o ch g Moscow Society (USA)-Cromhill Lady (Miners Lamp)
K Bishop J Stephenson

Placings: *000* (4485)
2001/02: 16^{0}S, 19^{0}S, 19^{0}G

	Starts	1st	2nd	3rd	Win & Pl
NH Flat	1	0	0	0	0
Hurdles	2	0	0	0	0
Career Total	**3**	**0**	**0**	**0**	**0**

Going: Sf: 0-2 GS: 0-0 Gd: 0-1 GF: - Fm: 0-0
Distance: 2m/2m3: 0-2 2m4-2m7: 0-1 3m+: 0-0
Track: LH: 0-1 RH: 0-2 Tight: 0-1 Gall: 0-0
Aids: Bl: 0-0 Vi: 0-0 Tstrap: 0-0
Best Rating: 79 1/02 Hayd 2m soft NHF

Moscow Express (IRE)

117 170
10-y-o ch g Moscow Society (USA)-Corrielek (Menelek)
Miss F M Crowley John Corr

Placings: *1/21*21111/1433322/0161111425F0U5/1111 3FF/2151F433141-3102512P1014 (4945a)
2001/02: 16^{3}GY, 20^{1}G, 22^{0}GY, 20^{2}GY, 24^{5}YS, 20^{1}S, 16^{2}YS, 24^{P}Y, 24^{1}S, 26^{0}G, 20^{1}SH, 25^{4}G

	Starts	1st	2nd	3rd	Win & Pl
Chases	12	4	2	1	68999
Career Total	**59**	**24**	**8**	**7**	**296586**

150	3/02	Navn	2m4f	Ch	SH	£8889
165	2/02	Gowr	3m	Ch	SFT	£11963
170	11/01	Clon	2m4f	Ch	SFT	£23588
162	7/01	Klny	2m4f	Ch	GD	£8911
170	4/01	Fair	3m1f	Ch	SFT	£65524
162	2/01	Naas	2m	Ch	Y-S	£23588
163	10/00	Thur	2m1f	Ch	G-Y	£4968
140	7/00	Klny	2m4f	Ch	G-F	£5520
152	7/99	Gway	2m6f	HCh	G-F	£35859
154	7/99	Tipp	2m4f	HCh	G-Y	£7366
120	5/99	Cork	2m5f	Ch	G-Y	£4603
126	5/99	Tipp	2m4f	Ch	GD	£3683
142	9/98	List	2m	Ch	G-Y	£4184
139	8/98	Tram	2m6f	HCh	G-F	£5978
139	7/98	Gway	2m6f	Ch	YLD	£5679
117	7/98	Klny	2m4f	Ch	GD	£2989
119	6/98	Cork	2m1f	Ch	GD	£3276
144	10/97	Towc	2m	C(0-135)HHdl	G-F	£3387
131	4/97	Fair	2m4f	Hdl	G-F	£6782
120	3/97	Leop	2m4f	Hdl	GD	£3051
120	2/97	Fair	2m4f	Hdl	G-Y	£4069
106	11/96	Punc	2m	Hdl	YLD	£3177
105	10/96	Navn	2m	NHF	GD	£2177
100	4/96	List	2m	NHF	SFT	£3530

Total win prize-money £253751

Going: Sf: 2-2 GS: 0-0 Gd: 1-3 GF: - Fm: 0-0
Distance: 2m/2m3: 0-2 **2m4-2m7: 3-5** 3m+: 1-5
Track: LH: 1-3 **RH: 2-4** Tight: 0-0 Gall: 0-1
Aids: Bl: 0-0 Vi: 0-0 **Tstrap: 2-5**
Best Rating: 170 11/01 Clon 2m4f soft Ch

He is a very useful performer when conditions are right, as he proved with a defeat of Florida Pearl in the Powers Gold Label Tote Gold Cup at Fairyhouse in April 2001. He might have been flattered by that result, as the balance of his form does not read anything like as well, but he picked up place money in good company over both hurdles and fences. Has continued to run well last season, scoring in valuable events at Clonmel and Gowran. He likes decent ground, and two and half to three miles is his trip.

Moscow Flyer (IRE)

120 (170h) 175
8-y-o b g Moscow Society (USA)-Meelick Lady (IRE) (Duky)
Mrs John Harrington Brian Kearney

Placings: *6343*/1110/13121F21-F111F11 (4953a)
2001/02: 18^{F}GY, 16^{1}Y, 16^{1}S, 17^{1}Y, 17^{F}HY, 16^{1}GS, 16^{1}G

	Starts	1st	2nd	3rd	Win & Pl
Chases	7	5	0	0	164485
Career Total	**23**	**12**	**2**	**3**	**324195**

165	4/02	Punc	2m	Ch	GD	£32331
175	3/02	Chel	2m	A Ch	G-S	£72500
161	12/01	Leop	2m1f	Ch	YLD	£39314
161	11/01	Punc	2m	Ch	SFT	£13104
133	11/01	DRoy	2m	Ch	YLD	£7233
170	4/01	Leop	2m	Hdl	SH	£55645
165	12/00	Leop	2m	Hdl	HVY	£15600
151	11/00	Punc	2m	Hdl	SFT	£10400
150	5/00	Punc	2m	Hdl	YLD	£24800
133	11/99	Fair	2m	Hdl	SFT	£26116
121	11/99	DRoy	2m	Hdl	SFT	£8705

117	10/99	Punc	2m	Hdl	YLD	£3696

Total win prize-money £309447

Going: Sf: 1-2 GS: 1-1 Gd: 1-1 GF: - Fm: 0-0
Distance: **2m/2m3: 5-7** 2m4-2m7: 0-0 3m+: 0-0
Track: LH: 2-3 RH: 2-3 Tight: 0-0 **Gall: 1-1**
Aids: Bl: 0-0 Vi: 0-0 Tstrap: 0-0
Best Rating: 175 3/02 Chel 2m gd-sft Ch

A high-class chaser, he switched to fences in October 2001 but was a faller on his debut. Learnt plenty from that and won his next three starts, improving with every run. Fell at Leopardstown in January 2002 but the ground was bottomless and he bounced back to top form when successful in the 2002 Arkle Chase at Cheltenham. Completed a fine season with an easy win at Punchestown. Best at around two miles on yielding, soft ground.

Moscow Gold (IRE)

76 **54**

5-y-o ch g Moscow Society (USA)-Vesper Time (The Parson)
R J Smith Janet Baker, David Smyth, Barry Hughes

Placings:*00* **(4873)**
2001/02: 16^{0}GF, 16^{0}GF

	Starts	1st	2nd	3rd	Win & Pl
NH Flat	2	0	0	0	
Career Total	**2**	**0**	**0**	**0**	

Going: Sf: 0-0 GS: 0-0 Gd: 0-0 GF: - Fm: 0-2
Distance: 2m/2m3: 0-2 2m4-2m7: 0-0 3m+: 0-0
Track: LH: 0-1 RH: 0-1 Tight: 0-0 Gall: 0-0
Aids: Bl: 0-0 Vi: 0-0 Tstrap: 0-1
Best Rating: 77 4/02 Weth 2m gd-fm NHF

Moss Deeping

71 **65**

10-y-o ch g Le Moss-Lady Run (Deep Run)
R N Bevis Mrs Ina Clutton

Placings:P50P **(3702)**
2001/02: 20^{P}G, 17^{5}GS, 16^{0}HY, 19^{P}HY

	Starts	1st	2nd	3rd	Win & Pl
Hurdles	4	0	0	0	0
Career Total	**4**	**0**	**0**	**0**	**0**

Going: Sf: 0-2 GS: 0-1 Gd: 0-1 GF: - Fm: 0-0
Distance: 2m/2m3: 0-2 2m4-2m7: 0-2 3m+: 0-0
Track: LH: 0-3 RH: 0-1 Tight: 0-2 Gall: 0-0
Aids: Bl: 0-0 Vi: 0-0 Tstrap: 0-2
Best Rating: 65 12/01 Bang 2m1f gd-sft Hdl

Moss Harvey

108 **140**

7-y-o ch g Le Moss-Wings Ground (Murrayfield)
J M Jefferson J R Salter

Placings:53-1111226P **(4665)**
2001/02: 22^{1}GS, 22^{1}G, 24^{1}GS, 24^{1}GS, 24^{2}S, 23^{2}HY, 21^{6}GS, 24^{P}G

	Starts	1st	2nd	3rd	Win & Pl
Hurdles	8	4	2	0	22252
Career Total	**10**	**4**	**2**	**1**	**22532**

140	12/01	Bang	3m	C(0-135)HHdl	G-S	£6929
131	12/01	Newc	3m	D Hdl	G-S	£3454
108	11/01	Kels	2m6f110y	E Hdl	GD	£3136
97	10/01	Kels	2m6f110y	E Hdl	G-S	£2544

Total win prize-money £16065

Going: Sf: 0-2 GS: 3-4 Gd: 1-2 GF: - Fm: 0-0
Distance: 2m/2m3: 0-0 2m4-2m7: 2-3 3m+: 2-5
Track: **LH: 4-8** RH: 0-0 **Tight: 3-4** Gall: 1-3
Aids: Bl: 0-0 Vi: 0-0 Tstrap: 0-0
Best Rating: 140 2/02 Hayd 2m7f110y heavy Hdl

A winning pointer, he scored a four-timer over hurdles towards the end of 2001, before a couple of good seconds in tough novice and handicap company. However, he was a well beaten sixth in the Royal & SunAlliance novice hurdle at Cheltenham in March 2002. Stays three miles and handles soft, although may prefer better ground.

Moss Pageant

100 **90**

12-y-o b g Then Again-Water Pageant (Welsh Pageant)
J B Walton F T Walton

Placings:PP0/0/**PF224/54P324312/433P41F333P/04 452PP0P/2-5063** **(3442)**
2001/02: 16^{5}G, 16^{0}S, 16^{6}S, 16^{3}HY

	Starts	1st	2nd	3rd	Win & Pl
Chases	4	0	0	1	357
Career Total	**43**	**2**	**6**	**8**	**17588**

104	12/98	Newc	2m110y	D(0-125)HCh	SFT	£3468
98	3/98	Newc	2m110y	E(0-115)HCh	GD	£2710

Total win prize-money £6179

Going: Sf: 0-3 GS: 0-0 Gd: 0-1 GF: - Fm: 0-0
Distance: 2m/2m3: 0-4 2m4-2m7: 0-0 3m+: 0-0
Track: LH: 0-4 RH: 0-0 Tight: 0-2 Gall: 0-2
Aids: Bl: 0-0 Vi: 0-0 Tstrap: 0-4
Best Rating: 104 1/99 Catt 2m good Ch

A modest chaser with a liking for Newcastle where he has won twice in the last two seasons. He has done little of note besides those successes. Likes give in the ground.

Moss Run (IRE)

82

8-y-o b g Commanche Run-Glenreigh Moss (Le Moss)
Miss F M Crowley (A E Jessop 10/5) Allan Jessop

Placings:*0/50P/000U-P2* **(2493a)**
2001/02: 20^{P}F, 18^{2}YS

	Starts	1st	2nd	3rd	Win & Pl
Hurdles	2	0	1	0	903
Career Total	**10**	**0**	**1**	**0**	**903**

Going: Sf: 0-0 GS: 0-0 Gd: 0-0 GF: - Fm: 0-1
Distance: 2m/2m3: 0-1 2m4-2m7: 0-1 3m+: 0-0
Track: LH: 0-1 RH: 0-0 Tight: 0-1 Gall: 0-0
Aids: Bl: 0-0 Vi: 0-0 Tstrap: 0-0
Best Rating: 85 2/00 Wwck 2m soft NHF

Most Stylish

95 **81**

5-y-o ch m Most Welcome-Corman-Style (Ahonoora)
L Lungo Elite Racing Club

Placings:21P606 **(1724)**
2001/02: 16^{2}GS, 16^{1}F, 16^{P}GF, 16^{6}GF, 21^{0}GS, 25^{6}G

	Starts	1st	2nd	3rd	Win & Pl
Hurdles	6	1	1	0	3397
Career Total	**6**	**1**	**1**	**0**	**3397**

77	5/01	Hexm	2m	E Hdl	FRM	£2545

Total win prize-money £2546

Going: Sf: 0-0 GS: 0-2 Gd: 0-1 GF: - Fm: 1-3
Distance: **2m/2m3: 1-4** 2m4-2m7: 0-1 3m+: 0-1
Track: **LH: 1-2** RH: 0-3 Tight: 0-0 Gall: 0-0
Aids: Bl: 0-0 Vi: 0-0 Tstrap: 0-0
Best Rating: 81 10/01 Weth 3m1f good Hdl

Winner of a maiden hurdle on fast ground in the spring of 2001, and subsequently successful on the Flat. Seems to handle any ground.

Mostarsil (USA)

96 **87**

4-y-o ch g Kingmambo (USA)-Naazeq (Nashwan (USA))
Jedd O'Keeffe (A C Stewart 18/8) Andrew Clarke

Placings:403 **(3856)**
2001/02: 16^{4}G, 16^{0}S, 16^{3}S

	Starts	1st	2nd	3rd	Win & Pl
Hurdles	3	0	0	1	344
Career Total	**3**	**0**	**0**	**1**	**344**

Going: Sf: 0-2 GS: 0-0 Gd: 0-1 GF: - Fm: 0-0
Distance: 2m/2m3: 0-3 2m4-2m7: 0-0 3m+: 0-0
Track: LH: 0-2 RH: 0-1 Tight: 0-2 Gall: 0-1
Aids: Bl: 0-0 Vi: 0-0 Tstrap: 0-0
Best Rating: 87 1/02 Catt 2m soft Hdl

Maiden selling hurdler.

Mostyn

11-y-o ch g Astral Master-Temple Rock (Melody Rock)
John Tuck R Weaver

Placings:6P/0-P1 **(0319)**
2001/02: 25^{P}G, 19^{1}F

	Starts	1st	2nd	3rd	Win & Pl
Chases	2	1	0	0	1661
Career Total	**5**	**1**	**0**	**0**	**1661**

96	5/01	Extr	2m3f110y	H Ch	FRM	£1660

Total win prize-money £1661

Going: Sf: 0-0 GS: 0-0 Gd: 0-1 GF: - Fm: 1-1
Distance: 2m/2m3: 0-0 **2m4-2m7: 1-1** 3m+: 0-1
Track: LH: 0-0 **RH: 1-2** Tight: 0-0 Gall: 0-0
Aids: Bl: 0-0 Vi: 0-0 Tstrap: 0-0
Best Rating: 96 5/01 Extr 2m3f110y firm Ch

Motafayel

96f **94f**

4-y-o b g Unfuwain (USA)-Hamaya (USA) (Mr Prospector (USA))
K A Morgan Euroteam Ltd T/a National Window System

Placings:*520* **(4046)**
2001/02: 16^{5}GS, 16^{2}S, 17^{0}GS

	Starts	1st	2nd	3rd	Win & Pl
NH Flat	3	0	1	0	533
Career Total	**3**	**0**	**1**	**0**	**533**

Going: Sf: 0-1 GS: 0-2 Gd: 0-0 GF: - Fm: 0-0
Distance: 2m/2m3: 0-3 2m4-2m7: 0-0 3m+: 0-0
Track: LH: 0-1 RH: 0-2 Tight: 0-3 Gall: 0-0
Aids: Bl: 0-0 Vi: 0-0 Tstrap: 0-0
Best Rating: 94 2/02 Muss 2m soft NHF

Hamdan-Al-Maktoum cast-off. Ran well enough on his debut in a Musselburgh bumper.

Motcomb Jam (IRE)

91f **90f**

5-y-o b g Frimaire-Flying Flo Jo (USA) (Aloma's Ruler (USA))

C J Mann Bix Racers

Placings:*40* **(4639)**

2001/02: 16^{4}G, 16^{0}GF

	Starts	1st	2nd	3rd	Win & Pl
NH Flat	2	0	0	0	0
Career Total	**2**	**0**	**0**	**0**	**0**

Going: Sf: 0-0 GS: 0-0 Gd: 0-1 GF: - Fm: 0-1
Distance: 2m/2m3: 0-2 2m4-2m7: 0-0 3m+: 0-0
Track: LH: 0-1 RH: 0-1 Tight: 0-0 Gall: 0-1
Aids: Bl: 0-0 Vi: 0-0 Tstrap: 0-0
Best Rating: 90 4/02 Asct 2m110y gd-fm NHF

Motellino (IRE)

93 **84**

8-y-o ch g Montelimar (USA)-Macamore Rose (Torus)

K C Bailey Mrs Sharon C Nelson

Placings:P-4P5P **(4889)**

2001/02: 24^{4}S, 20^{P}GS, 24^{5}G, 26^{P}G

	Starts	1st	2nd	3rd	Win & Pl
Chases	4	0	0	0	271
Career Total	**5**	**0**	**0**	**0**	**271**

Going: Sf: 0-1 GS: 0-1 Gd: 0-2 GF: - Fm: 0-0
Distance: 2m/2m3: 0-0 2m4-2m7: 0-1 3m+: 0-3
Track: LH: 0-2 RH: 0-1 Tight: 0-0 Gall: 0-1
Aids: Bl: 0-1 Vi: 0-0 Tstrap: 0-0
Best Rating: 84 11/01 Uttx 3m soft Ch

Pulled-up on his chase debut at Huntingdon. Better effort when reappearing in November 2001. Stays three miles. Acts on soft ground.

Motet

84 **84**

8-y-o b g Mtoto-Guest Artiste (Be My Guest (USA))

J R Best H J Jarvis

Placings:50613/3P041F/0R5-03PP **(1940)**

2001/02: 22^{0}G, 20^{3}GF, 22^{P}HY, 21^{P}GS

	Starts	1st	2nd	3rd	Win & Pl
Hurdles	4	0	0	1	221
Career Total	**18**	**2**	**0**	**3**	**7606**

112	4/00	Plum	2m5f	E(0-115)HHdl	G-S	£2618
100	3/99	Newb	2m5f	D Hdl	G-F	£3338

Total win prize-money £5957

Going: Sf: 0-1 GS: 0-1 Gd: 0-1 GF: - Fm: 0-1
Distance: 2m/2m3: 0-0 2m4-2m7: 0-4 3m+: 0-0
Track: LH: 0-2 RH: 0-2 Tight: 0-3 Gall: 0-1
Aids: Bl: 0-0 Vi: 0-0 Tstrap: 0-1
Best Rating: 112 4/00 Plum 2m5f gd-sft Hdl

Mother Goose

6-y-o ch m Alflora (IRE)-Country Seat (Paddy's Stream)

S A Brookshaw Mr John G Cox

Placings:*5-00*0PU **(4494)**

2001/02: 17^{0}GS, 16^{0}S, 21^{0}G, 24^{P}HY, 22^{U}G

	Starts	1st	2nd	3rd	Win & Pl
NH Flat	2	0	0	0	0
Hurdles	3	0	0	0	0

Career Total	**6**	**0**	**0**	**0**	**0**

Going: Sf: 0-2 GS: 0-1 Gd: 0-2 GF: - Fm: 0-0
Distance: 2m/2m3: 0-2 2m4-2m7: 0-2 3m+: 0-1
Track: LH: 0-4 RH: 0-1 Tight: 0-1 Gall: 0-0
Aids: Bl: 0-0 Vi: 0-0 Tstrap: 0-0
Best Rating: 92 2/01 Hayd 2m soft NHF

Mothers Help

96 **116**

7-y-o b m Relief Pitcher-Laundry Maid (Forzando)

D L Williams Berkshire Commercial Components Ltd

Placings:13362442/32433425546/111530F-PPP **(2754)**

2001/02: 20^{P}G, 27^{P}G, 33^{P}S

	Starts	1st	2nd	3rd	Win & Pl
Chases	3	0	0	0	
Career Total	**29**	**4**	**4**	**6**	**23659**

133	6/00	MRas	2m6f110y	E(0-115)HCh	G-S	£3543
133	5/00	Hntg	2m4f110y	E Ch	G-S	£2921
107	5/00	MRas	2m4f	D Ch	G-S	£4729
109	11/98	Wind	2m	E Hdl	G-S	£2460

Total win prize-money £13653

Going: Sf: 0-1 GS: 0-0 Gd: 0-2 GF: - Fm: 0-0
Distance: 2m/2m3: 0-0 2m4-2m7: 0-1 3m+: 0-2
Track: LH: 0-1 RH: 0-2 Tight: 0-2 Gall: 0-1
Aids: Bl: 0-0 Vi: 0-0 Tstrap: 0-2
Best Rating: 133 6/00 MRas 2m6f110y gd-sft Ch

Fair low-grade staying handicap chaser on fast ground.

Moulouya (FR)

(98h) (95h)**111**

7-y-o gr m Turgeon (USA)-Charabia (FR) (Bazin)

J R Best Mercato 1

Placings:2220/1301-03555F **(4884)**

2001/02: 16^{0}G, 20^{3}S, 21^{5}G, 20^{5}GS, 18^{5}GS, 22^{F}GF

	Starts	1st	2nd	3rd	Win & Pl
Hurdles	3	0	0	1	792
Chases	3	0	0	0	0
Career Total	**14**	**2**	**3**	**2**	**8289**

114	10/00	Hntg	2m4f110y	E Hdl	G-F	£2481
112	5/00	Folk	2m1f110y	E(0-115)HHdl	GD	£2453

Total win prize-money £4936

Going: Sf: 0-1 GS: 0-2 Gd: 0-2 GF: - Fm: 0-1
Distance: 2m/2m3: 0-2 2m4-2m7: 0-4 3m+: 0-0
Track: LH: 0-2 RH: 0-3 Tight: 0-3 Gall: 0-1
Aids: Bl: 0-0 Vi: 0-0 Tstrap: 0-0
Best Rating: 114 10/00 Hntg 2m4f110y gd-fm Hdl

A winner on the Flat in France, she is effective in moderate company over hurdles. She stays an extended two miles four furlongs, appreciates positive tactics and seems to act on any ground, although best served by a fast surface. Showed ability over fences in the spring of 2002.

Mounsey Castle

96f **100f**

5-y-o ch g Carlingford Castle-Gay Ticket (New Member)

P J Hobbs Alan Peterson

Placings:*46* **(4269)**

2001/02: 16^{4}S, 16^{6}S

	Starts	1st	2nd	3rd	Win & Pl
NH Flat	2	0	0	0	0
Career Total	**2**	**0**	**0**	**0**	**0**

Going: Sf: 0-2 GS: 0-0 Gd: 0-0 GF: - Fm: 0-0
Distance: 2m/2m3: 0-2 2m4-2m7: 0-0 3m+: 0-0
Track: LH: 0-1 RH: 0-1 Tight: 0-0 Gall: 0-0
Aids: Bl: 0-0 Vi: 0-0 Tstrap: 0-0
Best Rating: 96 3/02 Chep 2m110y soft NHF

Landed a bumper at Chepstow in May 2002. Likes fast ground.

Mount Prague (IRE)

114 **138**

8-y-o br g Lord Americo-Celtic Duchess (Ya Zaman (USA))

K C Bailey W J Ives

Placings:*4/1305461/0F31F23-13453P* **(4775)**

2001/02: 20^{1}G, 20^{3}GS, 24^{4}GS, 20^{5}S, 20^{3}G, 22^{P}G

	Starts	1st	2nd	3rd	Win & Pl
Chases	6	1	0	2	6898
Career Total	**21**	**4**	**1**	**5**	**19571**

138	1/02	Ludl	2m4f	D(0-115)HCh	GD	£4537
133	12/00	Hntg	2m110y	F(0-105)HCh	HVY	£2699
112	3/00	DRoy	2m	Hdl	G-Y	£2760
111	10/99	Gway	2m	NHF	SFT	£4004

Total win prize-money £14001

Going: Sf: 0-1 GS: 0-2 Gd: 1-3 GF: - Fm: 0-0
Distance: 2m/2m3: 0-0 **2m4-2m7: 1-5** 3m+: 0-1
Track: LH: 0-0 **RH: 1-6 Tight: 1-5** Gall: 0-1
Aids: Bl: 0-0 Vi: 0-0 Tstrap: 0-0
Best Rating: 138 1/02 Ludl 2m4f good Ch

Suited by soft ground and two miles, all his wins have been on right-handed tracks. He came back to win at Ludlow on the back of a ten-month lay-off having fractured a pastern. He goes to post early.

Mount Vernon (IRE)

92 **72**

6-y-o b g Darshaan-Chellita (Habitat)

P Wegmann P Wegmann

Placings:*6P/0-5* **(0355)**

2001/02: 17^{5}GS

	Starts	1st	2nd	3rd	Win & Pl
Hurdles	1	0	0	0	0
Career Total	**4**	**0**	**0**	**0**	**0**

Going: Sf: 0-0 GS: 0-1 Gd: 0-0 GF: - Fm: 0-0
Distance: 2m/2m3: 0-1 2m4-2m7: 0-0 3m+: 0-0
Track: LH: 0-1 RH: 0-0 Tight: 0-1 Gall: 0-0
Aids: Bl: 0-0 Vi: 0-0 Tstrap: 0-0
Best Rating: 72 5/01 Bang 2m1f gd-sft Hdl

Mountain Flyer

98 **107**

7-y-o b g North Col-Emma Wright (Skyliner)

J W Mullins B R Edgeley

Placings:*0200*/P364F-54FFF **(1483)**

2001/02: 17^{5}GS, 16^{4}GF, 21^{F}GF, 21^{F}GF, 17^{F}GS

	Starts	1st	2nd	3rd	Win & Pl
Chases	5	0	0	0	273
Career Total	**14**	**0**	**1**	**1**	**1929**

Going: Sf: 0-0 GS: 0-2 Gd: 0-0 GF: - Fm: 0-3
Distance: 2m/2m3: 0-3 2m4-2m7: 0-2 3m+: 0-0
Track: LH: 0-4 RH: 0-1 Tight: 0-4 Gall: 0-0
Aids: Bl: 0-0 Vi: 0-0 Tstrap: 0-0
Best Rating: 107 6/01 NAbb 2m5f110y gd-fm Ch

Mountain Man (FR)

4-y-o b g Cadoudal (FR)-Montagne Bleue (Legend Of France (USA))
S E H Sherwood The Hon Mrs S Sherwood

Placings:*0* **(4410)**
2001/02: 17^{0}S

	Starts	1st	2nd	3rd	Win & Pl
NH Flat	1	0	0	0	
Career Total	**1**	**0**	**0**	**0**	

Going: Sf: 0-1 GS: 0-0 Gd: 0-0 GF: - Fm: 0-0
Distance: 2m/2m3: 0-1 2m4-2m7: 0-0 3m+: 0-0
Track: LH: 0-1 RH: 0-0 Tight: 0-1 Gall: 0-0
Aids: Bl: 0-0 Vi: 0-0 Tstrap: 0-0
Best Rating: mfy

Mountain Native (IRE)

6-y-o ch g Be My Native (USA)-Mountain Beauty (IRE) (Executive Perk)
P J Hobbs Ellway Racing & P A Deal

Placings:*0* **(4032)**
2001/02: 16^{0}GS

	Starts	1st	2nd	3rd	Win & Pl
NH Flat	1	0	0	0	
Career Total	**1**	**0**	**0**	**0**	

Going: Sf: 0-0 GS: 0-1 Gd: 0-0 GF: - Fm: 0-0
Distance: 2m/2m3: 0-1 2m4-2m7: 0-0 3m+: 0-0
Track: LH: 0-1 RH: 0-0 Tight: 0-0 Gall: 0-1
Aids: Bl: 0-0 Vi: 0-0 Tstrap: 0-0
Best Rating: 97 3/02 Newb 2m110y gd-sft NHF

Showed promise in a decent bumper on racecourse debut.

Mountain Path

12-y-o b g Rakaposhi King-Donna Farina (Little Buskins)
T H Caldwell Mrs Pat Wharfe

Placings:312/52151P/123/31P6/P **(1837)**
2001/02: 25^{P}G

	Starts	1st	2nd	3rd	Win & Pl
Chases	1	0	0	0	
Career Total	**17**	**5**	**3**	**3**	**27599**

134	1/00	Hntg	3m	D(0-120)HCh	G-S	£4306
136	11/98	Worc	2m7f110y	D(0-120)HCh	HVY	£7262
125	3/98	Sand	3m110y	D(0-110)HCh	G-S	£3533
126	1/98	Wind	3m	E(0-105)HCh	G-S	£4261
77	2/97	Tntn	3m110y	E Hdl	G-S	£2638

Total win prize-money £22003

Going: Sf: 0-0 GS: 0-0 Gd: 0-1 GF: - Fm: 0-0
Distance: 2m/2m3: 0-0 2m4-2m7: 0-0 3m+: 0-1
Track: LH: 0-1 RH: 0-0 Tight: 0-1 Gall: 0-0
Aids: Bl: 0-0 Vi: 0-0 Tstrap: 0-0
Best Rating: 136 11/98 Worc 2m7f110y heavy Ch

Mountain Thyne (IRE)

9-y-o br g Good Thyne (USA)-Vanhalensdarling (Green Shoon)
Mrs R L Elliot (Trainer Unknown 10/2) J P Elliot

Placings:32 **(4690)**
2001/02: 25^{3}HY, 25^{2}GF

	Starts	1st	2nd	3rd	Win & Pl
Chases	2	0	1	1	1181
Career Total	**2**	**0**	**1**	**1**	**1181**

Going: Sf: 0-1 GS: 0-0 Gd: 0-0 GF: - Fm: 0-1
Distance: 2m/2m3: 0-0 2m4-2m7: 0-0 3m+: 0-2
Track: LH: 0-2 RH: 0-0 Tight: 0-2 Gall: 0-0
Aids: Bl: 0-0 Vi: 0-0 Tstrap: 0-0
Best Rating: 104 4/02 Kels 3m1f gd-fm Ch

Mounthooley

101 **103**

6-y-o ch g Karinga Bay-Gladys Emmanuel (Idiots Delight)
B Mactaggart Ashleybank Investments Limited

Placings:*0042* **(4832)**
2001/02: 17^{0}GS, 16^{0}GS, 16^{4}GF, 20^{2}G

	Starts	1st	2nd	3rd	Win & Pl
NH Flat	2	0	0	0	0
Hurdles	2	0	1	0	1714
Career Total	**4**	**0**	**1**	**0**	**1714**

Going: Sf: 0-0 GS: 0-2 Gd: 0-1 GF: - Fm: 0-1
Distance: 2m/2m3: 0-3 2m4-2m7: 0-1 3m+: 0-0
Track: LH: 0-3 RH: 0-1 Tight: 0-1 Gall: 0-0
Aids: Bl: 0-0 Vi: 0-0 Tstrap: 0-0
Best Rating: 103 4/02 Ayr 2m4f good Hdl

Mountrath Rock

95 **83**

5-y-o b m Rock Hopper-Point Of Law (Law Society (USA))
Miss B Sanders J M Quinn

Placings:4-3 **(4781)**
2001/02: 16^{3}GF

	Starts	1st	2nd	3rd	Win & Pl
Hurdles	1	0	0	1	453
Career Total	**2**	**0**	**0**	**1**	**453**

Going: Sf: 0-0 GS: 0-0 Gd: 0-0 GF: - Fm: 0-1
Distance: 2m/2m3: 0-1 2m4-2m7: 0-0 3m+: 0-0
Track: LH: 0-1 RH: 0-0 Tight: 0-1 Gall: 0-0
Aids: Bl: 0-1 Vi: 0-0 Tstrap: 0-1
Best Rating: 83 4/02 Plum 2m gd-fm Hdl

Raced keenly on her second start over hurdles, but showed some promise.

Mouse Bird (IRE)

98 **93**

12-y-o b g Glow (USA)-Irish Bird (USA) (Sea-Bird Ii)
D R Gandolfo Osbert Pierce

Placings:4/230/122423/12**F5**/**343134223**/**122241**/**025 2P**/**2P11P-PP65430P** **(4266)**
2001/02: 20^{P}GS, 20^{P}GS, 20^{6}S, 20^{5}S, 21^{4}S, 20^{3}S, 26^{0}S, 29^{P}S

	Starts	1st	2nd	3rd	Win & Pl
Chases	8	0	0	1	753
Career Total	**47**	**7**	**13**	**7**	**57345**

126	3/01	Wwck	2m4f110y	D(0-125)HCh	HVY	£4462
126	3/01	Plum	2m4f	F(0-110)HCh	HVY	£2982
124	2/99	Hayd	2m4f	B(0-145)HCh	SFT	£13758
121	10/98	Strf	2m1f110y	C(0-135)HCh	G-S	£4792
110	1/98	Ling	2m	E Ch	G-S	£2736
124	11/96	NAbb	2m1f	C(0-130)HHdl	HVY	£3420
103	11/95	NAbb	2m1f	D Hdl	SFT	£2948

Total win prize-money £35100

Going: Sf: 0-6 GS: 0-2 Gd: 0-0 GF: - Fm: 0-0
Distance: 2m/2m3: 0-0 2m4-2m7: 0-6 3m+: 0-2
Track: LH: 0-7 RH: 0-0 Tight: 0-7 Gall: 0-0
Aids: Bl: 0-2 Vi: 0-5 Tstrap: 0-0
Best Rating: 126 3/01 Wwck 2m4f110y heavy Ch

A bit of a character, he has to be in the right mood to apply his best and loved the mud when winning at both Plumpton and Warwick in March 2001.

Mouseski

103(95c) (102c)**100**

8-y-o b g Petoski-Worth Matravers (National Trust)
R J Hodges M H Dare

Placings:*020/5*-**4P3F**613 **(4736)**
2001/02: 17^{4}G, 17^{P}GS, 16^{3}G, 19^{F}S, 16^{6}S, 17^{1}G, 17^{3}F

	Starts	1st	2nd	3rd	Win & Pl
Hurdles	3	1	0	1	3322
Chases	4	0	0	1	604
Career Total	**11**	**1**	**1**	**2**	**4407**

100	3/02	Extr	2m1f	E(0-100)HHdl	GD	£2884

Total win prize-money £2884

Going: Sf: 0-2 GS: 0-1 Gd: 1-3 GF: - Fm: 0-1
Distance: **2m/2m3: 1-7** 2m4-2m7: 0-0 3m+: 0-0
Track: LH: 0-1 **RH: 1-6** Tight: 0-2 Gall: 0-0
Aids: Bl: 0-0 Vi: 0-0 Tstrap: 0-0
Best Rating: 102 11/01 Plum 2m1f good Ch

Appreciated the return to hurdles after struggling over fences, winning at Exeter in March 2002. Appreciates good ground.

Movie Man

10-y-o ch g Move Off-Malmo (Free State)
P Beaumont Mrs E Dixon

Placings:00046/24600/424P21/PF12P-R **(0208)**
2001/02: 24^{R}F

	Starts	1st	2nd	3rd	Win & Pl
Chases	1	0	0	0	
Career Total	**22**	**2**	**4**	**0**	**9753**

105	1/01	Catt	3m1f110y	F(0-100)HCh	G-S	£3486
74	8/97	Ctml	3m2f	E Hdl	G-F	£2145

Total win prize-money £5631

Going: Sf: 0-0 GS: 0-0 Gd: 0-0 GF: - Fm: 0-1
Distance: 2m/2m3: 0-0 2m4-2m7: 0-0 3m+: 0-1
Track: LH: 0-1 RH: 0-0 Tight: 0-1 Gall: 0-0
Aids: Bl: 0-0 Vi: 0-0 Tstrap: 0-0
Best Rating: 105 2/01 Sedg 3m3f soft Ch

Moving Earth (IRE)

113 **140**

9-y-o b g Brush Aside (USA)-Park Breeze (IRE) (Strong Gale)
P F Nicholls R M Penny

Placings:2/F/F1-31L6351 **(4914)**
2001/02: 20^{3}G, 21^{1}G, 21^{L}GS, 20^{6}GS, 21^{3}G, 24^{5}G, 20^{1}G

	Starts	1st	2nd	3rd	Win & Pl
Chases	7	2	0	2	25371
Career Total	**11**	**3**	**1**	**2**	**28873**

140	4/02	Sand	2m4f110y	B(0-145)HCh	GD	£17400

138	1/02	Winc	2m5f	D(0-120)HCh	GD	£5027
125	3/01	Font	2m2f	F Ch	SFT	£2873

Total win prize-money £25301

Going: Sf: 0-0 GS: 0-2 Gd: 2-5 GF: - Fm: 0-0
Distance: 2m/2m3: 0-0 **2m4-2m7: 2-6** 3m+: 0-1
Track: LH: 0-1 **RH: 2-6** Tight: 0-1 Gall: 0-1
Aids: Bl: 0-0 Vi: 0-0 **Tstrap: 1-4**
Best Rating: 140 4/02 Sand 2m4f110y good Ch

A multiple winner in point to points, he had trouble completing in his early starts under Rules but got it right over two and a quarter miles at Fontwell in March 2001. He has scored over two miles five since and gets three miles, but ran his best race when taking a valuable handicap at Sandown's end of season meeting. He has tended to start very slowly and once refused to start at all early in 2002 which makes him a dodgy betting proposition.

Moving On Up

111 **132**

8-y-o b g Salse (USA)-Thundercloud (Electric)
C J Mann (D K Weld 21/10) Hugh Villiers

Placings:134/1500/0210-0P35F0305P **(4939a)**
2001/02: 16^{0}G, 16^{P}GY, 17^{3}GF, 16^{5}GS, 16^{F}GS, 16^{0}S, 16^{3}S, 17^{0}G, 16^{5}G, 20^{P}Y

	Starts	1st	2nd	3rd	Win & Pl
Hurdles	10	0	0	2	3663
Career Total	**21**	**3**	**1**	**3**	**27679**

134	12/00	Leop	2m	HHdl	HVY	£7176
127	0/99	Tral	2m1f	HHdl	YLD	£8705
111	12/98	Leop	2m	Hdl	HVY	£4184

Total win prize-money £20066

Going: Sf: 0-2 GS: 0-2 Gd: 0-3 GF: - Fm: 0-1
Distance: 2m/2m3: 0-9 2m4-2m7: 0-1 3m+: 0-0
Track: LH: 0-4 RH: 0-3 Tight: 0-1 Gall: 0-3
Aids: Bl: 0-9 Vi: 0-0 Tstrap: 0-0
Best Rating: 134 12/00 Leop 2m heavy Hdl

Prolific winner of Flat and hurdle races in Ireland. Bought for 15,000gns at Newmarket Autumn Sales. Now with Charlie Mann, but was well held at Ascot in January 2002 and has been let down by his jumping since. Suited by two miles and soft ground

Mowbray (USA)

101 **109**

7-y-o b/br g Opening Verse (USA)-Peppy Raja (USA) (Raja Baba (USA))
G L Moore Graham Parker

Placings:430-223 **(0837)**
2001/02: 20^{2}G, 20^{2}GF, 20^{3}G

	Starts	1st	2nd	3rd	Win & Pl
Hurdles	3	0	2	1	1818
Career Total	**6**	**0**	**2**	**2**	**4023**

Going: Sf: 0-0 GS: 0-0 Gd: 0-2 GF: - Fm: 0-1
Distance: 2m/2m3: 0-0 2m4-2m7: 0-3 3m+: 0-0
Track: LH: 0-3 RH: 0-0 Tight: 0-0 Gall: 0-0
Aids: Bl: 0-0 Vi: 0-0 Tstrap: 0-0
Best Rating: 110 1/01 Kemp 2m soft Hdl

Moykon (IRE)

66 **14**

5-y-o b g Gothland (FR)-Yawa Prince (IRE) (Yawa)

Miss H C Knight Mrs J K Peutherer

Placings:*60* **(4506)**
2001/02: 16^{6}G, 17^{0}G

	Starts	1st	2nd	3rd	Win & Pl
NH Flat	2	0	0	0	0
Career Total	**2**	**0**	**0**	**0**	**0**

Going: Sf: 0-0 GS: 0-0 Gd: 0-2 GF: - Fm: 0-0
Distance: 2m/2m3: 0-2 2m4-2m7: 0-0 3m+: 0-0
Track: LH: 0-1 RH: 0-1 Tight: 0-1 Gall: 0-0
Aids: Bl: 0-0 Vi: 0-0 Tstrap: 0-0
Best Rating: 82 12/01 Ludl 2m good NHF

Mploy (IRE)

5-y-o ch g Deploy-Sweet Quest (Rainbow Quest (USA))
Ferdy Murphy Mrs Marlene Kynaston

Placings:*00* **(1833)**
2001/02: 16^{0}GF, 20^{0}G

	Starts	1st	2nd	3rd	Win & Pl
NH Flat	1	0	0	0	0
Hurdles	1	0	0	0	0
Career Total	**2**	**0**	**0**	**0**	

Going: Sf: 0-0 GS: 0-0 Gd: 0-1 GF: - Fm: 0-1
Distance: 2m/2m3: 0-1 2m4-2m7: 0-1 3m+: 0-0
Track: LH: 0-1 RH: 0-1 Tight: 0-1 Gall: 0-1
Aids; Bl: 0-0 Vi: 0-0 Tstrap: 0-0
Best Rating: 77 5/01 Hntg 2m110y gd-fm NHF

Mr Baxter Basics

120 **148**

11-y-o b g Lighter-Phyll-Tarquin (Tarqogan)
Miss Venetia Williams (T J Taaffe 4/5) P Ryan

Placings:*0*/*66*1242/**F512F21U/111/P041431/U0364-253P** **(4234)**
2001/02: 16^{2}GY, 21^{5}HY, 24^{3}G, 20^{P}GS

	Starts	1st	2nd	3rd	Win & Pl
Chases	4	0	1	1	14497
Career Total	**34**	**8**	**5**	**3**	**62631**

151	4/00	Fair	2m100y	HCh	G-Y	£10400
147	1/00	Fair	2m100y	Ch	SFT	£6624
142	7/98	Klny	2m4f	Ch	G-Y	£8445
122	5/98	Cork	2m5f	Ch	GD	£0
138	5/98	Navn	2m2f	HCh	Y-S	£5956
132	3/98	Leop	2m2f	(0-130)HCh	G-Y	£2978
	12/97	Cork	2m	Ch	HVY	£3391

Total win prize-money £37796

Going: Sf: 0-1 GS: 0-1 Gd: 0-1 GF: - Fm: 0-0
Distance: 2m/2m3: 0-1 2m4-2m7: 0-2 3m+: 0-1
Track: LH: 0-2 RH: 0-1 Tight: 0-0 Gall: 0-2
Aids: Bl: 0-0 Vi: 0-0 Tstrap: 0-0
Best Rating: 151 4/00 Fair 2m100y gd-yld Ch

A decent handicap chaser when trained in Ireland, he was set some stiff tasks in 2001/2. Has joined Venetia Williams. Best at around two/two and a half miles on soft ground.

Mr Bean

98(97h) (61h)**93**

12-y-o b g Salse (USA)-Goody Blake (Blakeney)
Mrs S M Johnson (S Flook 14/5) S Flook

Placings:45/115245/3/**20U02/024F5/2001336361234 460/256243513055/0041504P0P-0062004PP (1804)**
2001/02: 25^{0}G, 28^{0}GF, 25^{6}GF, 26^{2}GF, 22^{0}GF, 26^{0}G, 25^{4}GF, 19^{P}S, 24^{P}GF

	Starts	1st	2nd	3rd	Win & Pl
Hurdles	3	0	0	0	0
Chases	6	0	1	0	1365
Career Total	**66**	**6**	**9**	**7**	**27462**

93	8/00	NAbb	3m2f110y	F(0-100)HCh	GD	£2691
91	8/99	Uttx	3m110y	D(0-120)HHdl	G-F	£2911
103	10/98	Chep	2m3f110y	G(0-95)HCh	GD	£1870
103	6/98	NAbb	2m110y	D(0-120)HCh	FRM	£3403
97	8/94	Hrfd	2m1f	Hdl	FRM	£1630
91	8/94	Uttx	2m	Hdl	G-F	£2253

Total win prize-money £14760

Going: Sf: 0-1 GS: 0-0 Gd: 0-2 GF: - Fm: 0-6
Distance: 2m/2m3: 0-0 2m4-2m7: 0-2 3m+: 0-7
Track: LH: 0-5 RH: 0-4 Tight: 0-4 Gall: 0-1
Aids: Bl: 0-0 Vi: 0-0 Tstrap: 0-0
Best Rating: 103 10/98 Chep 2m3f110y good Ch

Mr Ben Gunn

99(100h) (99h)**98**

10-y-o ch g Newski (USA)-Long John Silvia (Celtic Cone)
J D Frost (R G Frost 7/11) P A Tylor

Placings:64-5003F0 **(4047)**
2001/02: 17^{5}G, 22^{0}F, 22^{0}GF, 23^{3}GS, 21^{F}S, 17^{0}G

	Starts	1st	2nd	3rd	Win & Pl
Hurdles	4	0	0	0	0
Chases	2	0	0	1	645
Career Total	**8**	**0**	**0**	**1**	**645**

Going: Sf: 0-1 GS: 0-1 Gd: 0-2 GF: - Fm: 0-2
Distance: 2m/2m3: 0-2 2m4-2m7: 0-3 3m+: 0-1
Track: LH: 0-1 RH: 0-3 Tight: 0-1 Gall: 0-0
Aids: Bl: 0-0 Vi: 0-0 Tstrap: 0-0
Best Rating: 99 5/01 Extr 2m1f good Hdl

Looked a bit quirky in points but did win a maiden (good). Has shown limited promise over hurdles and seems to need a sound surface. Won a weak novice chase at Market Rasen in August 2002.

Mr Bombastique (IRE)

105 **98**

8-y-o b g Classic Music (USA)-Duende (High Top)
P Bowen G Morris

Placings:305/P/31145506U/0-0020321U **(1152)**
2001/02: 22^{0}GS, 21^{0}G, 20^{2}GF, 19^{0}GF, 22^{3}GF, 22^{2}G, 22^{1}GF, 22^{U}GF

	Starts	1st	2nd	3rd	Win & Pl
Hurdles	8	1	2	1	4174
Career Total	**22**	**3**	**2**	**3**	**11878**

98	7/01	Uttx	2m6f110y	F(0-100)HHdl	G-F	£2702
98	7/99	Bang	2m4f	E(0-115)HHdl	G-F	£4299
98	7/99	Strf	2m6f110y	F(0-110)HHdl	GD	£2463

Total win prize-money £9464

Going: Sf: 0-0 GS: 0-1 Gd: 0-2 GF: - Fm: 1-5
Distance: 2m/2m3: 0-0 **2m4-2m7: 1-8** 3m+: 0-0
Track: **LH: 1-5** RH: 0-1 Tight: 0-4 Gall: 0-0
Aids: Bl: 0-0 Vi: 0-0 Tstrap: 0-0
Best Rating: 98 7/01 Uttx 2m6f110y gd-fm Hdl

Mr Bossman (IRE)

109 **130**

9-y-o b g Jolly Jake (NZ)-Imperial Greeting (Be My

Guest (USA))
N B Mason N B Mason

Placings:0/0/0000/1PP5-52211133 **(4652)**
2001/02: 16^{5}S, 16^{2}G, 20^{2}GS, 20^{1}G, 16^{1}S, 21^{1}G, 22^{3}GS, 20^{3}G

	Starts	1st	2nd	3rd	Win & Pl
Chases	8	3	2	2	21834
Career Total	**18**	**4**	**2**	**2**	**23378**

130	3/02	Fknm	2m5f110y	D(0-120)HCh	GD	£4347
115	2/02	Muss	2m	D(0-110)HCh	SFT	£7150
125	1/02	Muss	2m4f	E(0-110)HCh	GD	£3640
113	2/01	Sedg	2m5f	H Ch	G-S	£1543

Total win prize-money £16681

Going: Sf: 1-2 GS: 0-2 Gd: 2-4 GF: - Fm: 0-0
Distance: 2m/2m3: 1-3 **2m4-2m7: 2-5** 3m+: 0-0
Track: LH: 1-6 **RH: 2-2 Tight: 3-5** Gall: 0-1
Aids: Bl: 0-0 Vi: 0-0 **Tstrap: 3-7**
Best Rating: 130 4/02 Aint 2m4f good Ch

A progressive point-to-pointer in 2000, he won a maiden hunter chase at the start of 2001, but did not repeat that level of form and was prone to jumping errors. The fitting of a tongue tie appears to have done him some good this season and he bounced back to form with a double at Musselburgh and a win at Fakenham at the start of 2002. Acts on good and good to soft, stays two miles five.

Mr Bruno

(100h) (55h)
9-y-o ch g Primitive Rising (USA)-Thelmas Secret (Secret Ace)
M A Barnes S C Brown

Placings:34U5003/0UF0/60/55156-0PP **(1199)**
2001/02: 24^{0}F, 21^{P}GF, 24^{P}G

	Starts	1st	2nd	3rd	Win & Pl
Hurdles	2	0	0	0	0
Chases	1	0	0	0	0
Career Total	**21**	**1**	**0**	**2**	**3538**

82	5/00	Hexm	3m1f	F(0-95)HCh	GD	£2727

Total win prize-money £2727

Going: Sf: 0-0 GS: 0-0 Gd: 0-1 GF: - Fm: 0-2
Distance: 2m/2m3: 0-0 2m4-2m7: 0-1 3m+: 0-2
Track: LH: 0-2 RH: 0-1 Tight: 0-1 Gall: 0-0
Aids: Bl: 0-0 Vi: 0-0 Tstrap: 0-2
Best Rating: 82 5/00 Hexm 3m1f good Ch

Mr Bureaucrat (NZ)

13-y-o b/br g Markella (FR)-Katex (NZ) (Ex Officio (AUS))
I R Bennett I R Bennett

Placings:14P/4540PU4/5/P **(0338)**
2001/02: 20^{P}S

	Starts	1st	2nd	3rd	Win & Pl
Chases	1	0	0	0	
Career Total	**12**	**1**	**0**	**0**	**3311**

97	11/95	Uttx	2m	E Hdl	G-F	£2484

Total win prize-money £2484

Going: Sf: 0-1 GS: 0-0 Gd: 0-0 GF: - Fm: 0-0
Distance: 2m/2m3: 0-0 2m4-2m7: 0-1 3m+: 0-0
Track: LH: 0-0 RH: 0-1 Tight: 0-0 Gall: 0-0
Aids: Bl: 0-0 Vi: 0-0 Tstrap: 0-0
Best Rating: 120 11/95 Leic 2m gd-sft Hdl

Mr Busby

108(87c) **96**
9-y-o b g La Grange Music-Top-Anna (IRE) (Ela-Mana-Mou)
John A Harris D Wilcox & Mrs A Sedgwick

Placings:100/21242130/4F/60P666P-023633403 **(4553)**
2001/02: 16^{0}S, 16^{2}S, 16^{3}S, 20^{6}G, 16^{3}S, 16^{3}HY, 16^{4}S, 20^{0}S, 17^{3}GF

	Starts	1st	2nd	3rd	Win & Pl
Hurdles	9	0	1	4	2290
Career Total	**29**	**3**	**4**	**5**	**13190**

110	2/99	Hayd	2m	C HHdl	SFT	£4485
97	11/98	MRas	2m1f110y	E Hdl	HVY	£2477
111	1/98	Newc	2m	H NHF	G-S	£1392

Total win prize-money £8356

Going: Sf: 0-7 GS: 0-0 Gd: 0-1 GF: - Fm: 0-1
Distance: 2m/2m3: 0-7 2m4-2m7: 0-2 3m+: 0-0
Track: LH: 0-5 RH: 0-4 Tight: 0-1 Gall: 0-2
Aids: Bl: 0-0 Vi: 0-0 Tstrap: 0-0
Best Rating: 119 12/99 Uttx 2m soft Ch

He has not won a race for almost three years. Best at two miles on soft ground.

Mr Carrigann (IRE)

9-y-o b g Commanche Run-Madam's Well (Pitpan)
Mrs A C Tate (M Tate 1/7) P J Kennedy

Placings:4/34121/P **(3997)**
2001/02: 16^{P}S

	Starts	1st	2nd	3rd	Win & Pl
Hurdles	1	0	0	0	
Career Total	**7**	**2**	**1**	**1**	**7449**

106	4/00	Hrfd	2m3f110y	F Hdl	GD	£3068
106	11/99	Tram	2m	NHF	YLD	£2772

Total win prize-money £5840

Going: Sf: 0-1 GS: 0-0 Gd: 0-0 GF: - Fm: 0-0
Distance: 2m/2m3: 0-1 2m4-2m7: 0-0 3m+: 0-0
Track: LH: 0-1 RH: 0-0 Tight: 0-0 Gall: 0-1
Aids: Bl: 0-0 Vi: 0-0 Tstrap: 0-0
Best Rating: 106 4/00 Hrfd 2m3f110y good Hdl

Ex-Irish, he won over hurdles at Hereford in April 2000 and was well held in two outings on the Flat the following year.

Mr Cavallo (IRE)

101(103c) (93c)**100**
10-y-o b g The Bart (USA)-Mrs Guru (Le Bavard (FR))
Miss Lucinda V Russell Peter J S Russell

Placings:000S/22230/P121141614036445 0/0333132 04023540/00324125006-023PS2140 **(1383)**
2001/02: 20^{0}GF, 20^{2}F, 20^{3}GF, 20^{P}GS, 27^{S}GF, 27^{2}G, 27^{1}GF, 20^{4}G, 26^{0}GF

	Starts	1st	2nd	3rd	Win & Pl
Hurdles	6	1	1	0	3804
Chases	3	0	1	1	1640
Career Total	**61**	**8**	**10**	**9**	**36301**

100	8/01	Sedg	3m3f110y	F(0-110)HHdl	G-F	£2674
105	8/00	Prth	2m4f110y	E(0-115)HHdl	GD	£3351
102	7/99	Wolv	2m4f110y	F(0-110)HHdl	G-S	£2686
107	10/98	Carl	2m4f110y	E(0-100)HHdl	GD	£2388
105	8/98	Ctml	2m6f	E(0-100)HHdl	GD	£2215
100	8/98	Bang	2m4f110y	E(0-100)HCh	GD	£3631
99	7/98	Sedg	2m5f110y	E(0-110)HHdl	G-S	£2250
86	7/98	Sedg	2m5f110y	F Hdl	G-F	£1954

Total win prize-money £21149

Going: Sf: 0-0 GS: 0-1 Gd: 0-2 GF: - Fm: 1-6
Distance: 2m/2m3: 0-0 2m4-2m7: 0-5 **3m+: 1-4**
Track: **LH: 1-6** RH: 0-3 **Tight: 1-4** Gall: 0-0
Aids: Bl: 0-0 Vi: 0-0 Tstrap: 0-0
Best Rating: 107 10/98 Carl 2m4f110y good Hdl

He is a modest out-and-out stayer these days.

Mr Chataway (IRE)

11-y-o b g Le Bavard (FR)-Swift Invader (Brave Invader (USA))
D M Grissell Mrs Eric Boucher

Placings:0/00/22452/342P/456/0U **(0321)**
2001/02: 20^{0}GF, 26^{U}G

	Starts	1st	2nd	3rd	Win & Pl
Chases	2	0	0	0	
Career Total	**17**	**0**	**4**	**1**	**4102**

Going: Sf: 0-0 GS: 0-0 Gd: 0-1 GF: - Fm: 0-1
Distance: 2m/2m3: 0-0 2m4-2m7: 0-1 3m+: 0-1
Track: LH: 0-0 RH: 0-1 Tight: 0-2 Gall: 0-0
Aids: Bl: 0-0 Vi: 0-0 Tstrap: 0-0
Best Rating: 104 4/98 Font 2m6f110y gd-sft Hdl

Mr Christie

100 **92**
10-y-o b g Doulab (USA)-Hi There (High Top)
Miss L C Siddall Lynn Siddall Racing

Placings:000/3P0455325146502/124060501005/4P5 06PU00305424/3020023354/026051131000-6361001062 **(4261)**
2001/02: 22^{6}GS, 24^{3}S, 24^{6}HY, 23^{1}HY, 24^{0}GS, 27^{0}HY, 24^{1}S, 26^{0}S, 24^{6}S, 24^{2}HY

	Starts	1st	2nd	3rd	Win & Pl
Hurdles	10	2	1	1	7326
Career Total	**77**	**8**	**8**	**8**	**30386**

92	1/02	Newc	3m	F(0-100)HHdl	SFT	£2212
92	12/01	Hayd	2m7f110y	F(0-110)HHdl	HVY	£3705
92	12/00	Hrfd	3m2f	F(0-100)HHdl	HVY	£3227
88	10/00	Sedg	3m3f110y	F(0-100)HHdl	G-S	£2289
82	10/00	Hexm	3m	F(0-100)HHdl	HVY	£2107
103	3/98	Hntg	3m2f	E(0-110)HHdl	SFT	£2495
103	5/97	Uttx	3m110y	E Hdl	G-S	£2410
93	2/97	Muss	3m	E(0-100)HHdl	G-S	£2807

Total win prize-money £21253

Going: Sf: 2-8 GS: 0-2 Gd: 0-0 GF: - Fm: 0-0
Distance: 2m/2m3: 0-0 2m4-2m7: 0-1 **3m+: 2-9**
Track: **LH: 2-6** RH: 0-4 Tight: 0-1 **Gall: 1-4**
Aids: Bl: 0-0 Vi: 0-0 **Tstrap: 2-10**
Best Rating: 103 5/98 Uttx 3m110y gd-sft Hdl

Moderate staying hurdler, well suited by soft ground. Usually tongue tied.

Mr Collins

97 **96**
8-y-o b g Brush Aside (USA)-Music Interpreter (Kampala)
R Tate (N J Henderson 10/2) R Tate

Placings:1P2/P-5 **(4097)**
2001/02: 25^{5}GS

	Starts	1st	2nd	3rd	Win & Pl
Chases	1	0	0	0	0
Career Total	**5**	**1**	**1**	**0**	**3413**

114	10/99	Chel	2m110y	H NHF	GD	£2710

Total win prize-money £2710

Going: Sf: 0-0 GS: 0-1 Gd: 0-0 GF: - Fm: 0-0
Distance: 2m/2m3: 0-0 2m4-2m7: 0-0 3m+: 0-1
Track: LH: 0-0 RH: 0-0 Tight: 0-0 Gall: 0-0
Aids: Bl: 0-0 Vi: 0-0 Tstrap: 0-1
Best Rating: 114 3/00 Tntn 3m110y good Hdl

Hunter chaser/pointer. Stays three miles but effective at shorter. Appreciates a sound surface.

Mr Cool

112(114h) (153h)**148**

8-y-o b g Jupiter Island-Laurel Diver (Celtic Cone)
M C Pipe N G Mills

Placings: *10/111*111/121023-**120114** **(4836)**
2001/02: 16^{1}S, 20^{2}S, 16^{0}GS, 19^{1}GS, 16^{1}GF, 20^{4}G

	Starts	1st	2nd	3rd	Win & Pl
Hurdles	1	0	0	0	0
Chases	5	3	1	0	17711
Career Total	**20**	**12**	**3**	**1**	**76190**

146	4/02	Chep	2m110y	E Ch	G-F	£4204
143	4/02	Tntn	2m3f	D Ch	G-S	£4702
148	11/01	NAbb	2m110y	D Ch	SFT	£3812
160	12/00	Newb	2m110y	B Hdl	SFT	£7020
155	11/00	Newb	2m3f	C(0-135)HHdl	SFT	£5954
136	3/00	Uttx	2m	D Hdl	GD	£3688
119	2/00	Sand	2m110y	D Hdl	SFT	£3770
127	2/00	Folk	2m1f110y	F Hdl	G-S	£2068
136	12/99	Chep	2m110y	A NHF	HVY	£7450
126	11/99	Aint	2m110y	H NHF	GD	£2008
119	11/99	Winc	2m	H NHF	GD	£1601
104	6/98	Sthl	2m	H NHF	GD	£1208

Total win prize-money £47509

Going: Sf: 1-2 GS: 1-2 Gd: 0-1 GF: - Fm: 1-1
Distance: **2m/2m3: 3-4** 2m4-2m7: 0-2 3m+: 0-0
Track: **LH: 2-5** RH: 1-1 **Tight: 2-2** Gall: 0-1
Aids: Bl: 0-0 Vi: 0-0 Tstrap: 0-0
Best Rating: 160 12/00 Newb 2m110y soft Hdl

A very useful hurdler, he won over fences at Newton Abbot in November 2001. Held in Listed company next time, a drop back down in class saw him complete a double at Taunton and Chepstow, but was again outclassed at Ayr. Has won on good and soft, but would not want it too testing.

Mr Cospector

105 **124**

5-y-o b g Cosmonaut-L'Ancressaan (Dalsaan)
T H Caldwell R Cabrera-Vargas

Placings: 653F22143 **(4174)**
2001/02: 16^{6}S, 17^{5}HY, 20^{3}S, 20^{F}HY, 20^{2}S, 20^{2}GS, 20^{1}HY, 20^{4}GS, 22^{3}GS

	Starts	1st	2nd	3rd	Win & Pl
Hurdles	9	1	2	2	12542
Career Total	**9**	**1**	**2**	**2**	**12542**

124	2/02	Hayd	2m4f	B HHdl	HVY	£8885

Total win prize-money £8886

Going: Sf: 1-6 GS: 0-3 Gd: 0-0 GF: - Fm: 0-0
Distance: 2m/2m3: 0-2 **2m4-2m7: 1-7** 3m+: 0-0
Track: **LH: 1-8** RH: 0-1 Tight: 0-1 Gall: 0-1
Aids: Bl: 0-0 Vi: 0-0 Tstrap: 0-0
Best Rating: 124 2/02 Hayd 2m4f heavy Hdl

Useful novice hurdler. Stays two and a half miles, but looks as though he needs three. Acts on soft ground and broke his duck in February 2002 in the mud.

Mr Custard

10-y-o b g Newski (USA)-May Owen (Master Owen)
Miss L J C Sweeting Miss L J C Sweeting

Placings: 332P-50003 **(4852)**
2001/02: 21^{5}GF, 24^{0}GF, 24^{0}GF, 21^{0}G, 24^{3}G

	Starts	1st	2nd	3rd	Win & Pl
Chases	5	0	0	1	432
Career Total	**9**	**0**	**1**	**3**	**1895**

Going: Sf: 0-0 GS: 0-0 Gd: 0-2 GF: - Fm: 0-3
Distance: 2m/2m3: 0-0 2m4-2m7: 0-2 3m+: 0-3
Track: LH: 0-4 RH: 0-1 Tight: 0-4 Gall: 0-0
Aids: Bl: 0-0 Vi: 0-0 Tstrap: 0-0
Best Rating: 108 5/00 Strf 3m gd-fm Ch

Held under Rules, he is a three-mile Ladies Open specialist, landing a hat-trick from his only runs this season. Has not run on extremes of ground and recent wins have come on the easy side of good ground.

Mr Dennehy (IRE)

13-y-o ch g Callernish-Down By The River (Over The River (FR))
John Allen N Walker

Placings: P/U-P **(0580)**
2001/02: 22^{P}GF

	Starts	1st	2nd	3rd	Win & Pl
Hurdles	1	0	0	0	
Career Total	**3**	**0**	**0**	**0**	

Going: Sf: 0-0 GS: 0-0 Gd: 0-0 GF: - Fm: 0-1
Distance: 2m/2m3: 0-0 2m4-2m7: 0-1 3m+: 0-0
Track: LH: 0-1 RH: 0-0 Tight: 0-1 Gall: 0-0
Aids: Bl: 0-0 Vi: 0-0 Tstrap: 0-0
Best Rating:

Mr Dow Jones (IRE)

10-y-o b g The Bart (USA)-Roseowen (Derring Rose)
K Goldsworthy Mrs L Goldsworthy

Placings: *0*F1/2P30/331U310-330011431 **(4826)**
2001/02: 25^{3}G, 24^{3}GS, 21^{0}G, 28^{0}GF, 25^{1}HY, 25^{1}G, 20^{4}S, 24^{3}G, 26^{1}G

	Starts	1st	2nd	3rd	Win & Pl
Chases	9	3	0	3	10834
Career Total	**23**	**6**	**1**	**7**	**23095**

130	4/02	Chel	3m2f110y	H Ch	GD	£5798
130	3/02	Hrfd	3m1f110y	H Ch	GD	£1928
121	2/02	Hrfd	3m1f110y	H Ch	HVY	£1865
114	4/01	Hrfd	2m3f	H Ch	GD	£2719
114	2/01	Ludl	3m	H Ch	G-S	£2628
114	4/99	Chep	3m	H Ch	HVY	£3598

Total win prize-money £18541

Going: Sf: 1-2 GS: 0-1 Gd: 2-5 GF: - Fm: 0-1
Distance: 2m/2m3: 0-0 2m4-2m7: 0-2 **3m+: 3-7**
Track: LH: 1-3 **RH: 2-5** Tight: 0-4 **Gall: 1-1**
Aids: Bl: 0-0 Vi: 0-0 Tstrap: 0-0
Best Rating: 130 4/02 Chel 3m2f110y good Ch

Useful hunter chaser, pays his way each season. Likes cut in the ground.

Mr Evans

100f **99f**

7-y-o ch g Current Edition (IRE)-Manor Park Crumpet (True Song)
P Bowen John Jones

Placings: *100* **(2394)**
2001/02: 16^{1}G, 16^{0}S, 16^{0}S

	Starts	1st	2nd	3rd	Win & Pl
NH Flat	3	1	0	0	1579
Career Total	**3**	**1**	**0**	**0**	**1579**

99	10/01	Sthl	2m	H NHF	GD	£1578

Total win prize-money £1579

Going: Sf: 0-2 GS: 0-0 Gd: 1-1 GF: - Fm: 0-0
Distance: **2m/2m3: 1-3** 2m4-2m7: 0-0 3m+: 0-0
Track: **LH: 1-3** RH: 0-0 **Tight: 1-1** Gall: 0-0
Aids: Bl: 0-0 Vi: 0-0 Tstrap: 0-0
Best Rating: 99 10/01 Sthl 2m good NHF

Mr Fitz (IRE)

80

9-y-o b g Andretti-Lisalway Lass (Wolverlife)
L Wells Mrs J Gadd

Placings: *P0000/0*-6 **(0010)**
2001/02: 25^{6}S

	Starts	1st	2nd	3rd	Win & Pl
Hurdles	1	0	0	0	0
Career Total	**7**	**0**	**0**	**0**	**0**

Going: Sf: 0-1 GS: 0-0 Gd: 0-0 GF: - Fm: 0-0
Distance: 2m/2m3: 0-0 2m4-2m7: 0-0 3m+: 0-1
Track: LH: 0-0 RH: 0-0 Tight: 0-0 Gall: 0-0
Aids: Bl: 0-0 Vi: 0-0 Tstrap: 0-0
Best Rating: 80 4/01 Hntg 2m5f110y soft Hdl

Mr Fluffy

107 **120+**

5-y-o br g Charmer-Hinton Bairn (Balinger)
P J Hobbs (W McKeown 17/5) The Cockpit Crew

Placings: *25*-3504 **(4422)**
2001/02: 16^{3}GS, 19^{5}S, 16^{0}GS, 16^{4}GS

	Starts	1st	2nd	3rd	Win & Pl
NH Flat	1	0	0	1	347
Hurdles	3	0	0	0	347
Career Total	**6**	**0**	**1**	**1**	**1147**

Going: Sf: 0-1 GS: 0-3 Gd: 0-0 GF: - Fm: 0-0
Distance: 2m/2m3: 0-4 2m4-2m7: 0-0 3m+: 0-0
Track: LH: 0-2 RH: 0-2 Tight: 0-0 Gall: 0-1
Aids: Bl: 0-0 Vi: 0-0 Tstrap: 0-0
Best Rating: 103 11/01 Sand 2m110y gd-sft NHF

He has shown some ability in bumpers. Won back-to-back two and a half mile novice hurdles in the summer of 2002. Considered a chaser in the making.

Mr Foxy

7-y-o ch g Bold Fox-Mac's Sister (Krayyan)
J S Haldane Gordon E Davidson

Placings: *P/0* **(0181)**
2001/02: 16^{0}GF

	Starts	1st	2nd	3rd	Win & Pl
NH Flat	1	0	0	0	
Career Total	**2**	**0**	**0**	**0**	

Going: Sf: 0-0 GS: 0-0 Gd: 0-0 GF: - Fm: 0-1
Distance: 2m/2m3: 0-1 2m4-2m7: 0-0 3m+: 0-0
Track: LH: 0-1 RH: 0-0 Tight: 0-0 Gall: 0-0
Aids: Bl: 0-0 Vi: 0-0 Tstrap: 0-0

Best Rating:

Mr Frangipani (IRE)

112 | 139

11-y-o ch g Phardante (FR)-Croom Cross (Menelek)
N G Richards Ashleybank Investments Limited

Placings:*20/000*/F34/**F2413FU1/5/11** (2400)
2001/02: 20^{1}GS, 25^{1}G

	Starts	1st	2nd	3rd	Win & Pl
Chases	2	2	0	0	11694
Career Total	**19**	**4**	**2**	**2**	**22263**

139 11/01 Weth 3m1f D(0-125)HCh GD £3991
133 5/01 Bang 2m4f110y D(0-120)HCh G-S £7702
133 5/99 Hexm 2m4f110y E(0-105)HCh GD £3414
121 2/99 Ayr 2m5f110y E Ch SFT £3908
Total win prize-money £19017

Going: Sf: 0-0 GS: 1-1 Gd: 1-1 GF: - Fm: 0-0
Distance: 2m/2m3: 0-0 2m4-2m7: 1-1 3m+: 1-1
Track: **LH: 2-2** RH: 0-0 **Tight: 1-1** Gall: 0-0
Aids: Bl: 0-0 Vi: 0-0 Tstrap: 0-0
Best Rating: 139 11/01 Weth 3m1f good Ch

Fair novice chaser who needs a left-handed track, he came back to win after an 18-month lay-off at Bangor in May 2001. Added a win at Wetherby in November, although he did not jump fluently. Stays three miles. Best with give underfoot.

Mr Freebie (DEN)

12-y-o b g Viking (USA)-Sirenivo (USA) (Sir Ivor)
D E Ingle Mrs M C Banks

Placings:31/2P0U-5 (0229)
2001/02: 30^{5}GF

	Starts	1st	2nd	3rd	Win & Pl
Chases	1	0	0	0	0
Career Total	**7**	**1**	**1**	**1**	**3004**

115 3/00 Towc 3m1f H Ch SFT £1288
Total win prize-money £1288

Going: Sf: 0-0 GS: 0-0 Gd: 0-0 GF: - Fm: 0-1
Distance: 2m/2m3: 0-0 2m4-2m7: 0-0 3m+: 0-1
Track: LH: 0-0 RH: 0-1 Tight: 0-0 Gall: 0-1
Aids: Bl: 0-0 Vi: 0-0 Tstrap: 0-1
Best Rating: 115 5/00 Chel 4m1f good Ch

Mr Gisby (USA)

104 | 109

4-y-o b g Chief's Crown (USA)-Double Lock (Home Guard (USA))
D R C Elsworth Nightmare Partnership

Placings:3P55 (3285)
2001/02: 16^{3}GS, 16^{P}G, 16^{5}G, 17^{5}S

	Starts	1st	2nd	3rd	Win & Pl
Hurdles	4	0	0	1	553
Career Total	**4**	**0**	**0**	**1**	**553**

Going: Sf: 0-1 GS: 0-1 Gd: 0-2 GF: - Fm: 0-0
Distance: 2m/2m3: 0-4 2m4-2m7: 0-0 3m+: 0-0
Track: LH: 0-0 RH: 0-4 Tight: 0-1 Gall: 0-0
Aids: Bl: 0-0 Vi: 0-0 Tstrap: 0-0
Best Rating: 109 12/01 Kemp 2m good Hdl

Very modest on the Flat, he has shown ability over hurdles at a fair level.

Mr Greensmit

7-y-o ch g Greensmith-Bedelia (Mr Fluorocarbon)
A J Chamberlain I M Ledbury

Placings:*600*/P-P (0580)
2001/02: 22^{P}GF

	Starts	1st	2nd	3rd	Win & Pl
Hurdles	1	0	0	0	
Career Total	**5**	**0**	**0**	**0**	**0**

Going: Sf: 0-0 GS: 0-0 Gd: 0-0 GF: - Fm: 0-1
Distance: 2m/2m3: 0-0 2m4-2m7: 0-1 3m+: 0-0
Track: LH: 0-1 RH: 0-0 Tight: 0-1 Gall: 0-0
Aids: Bl: 0-0 Vi: 0-0 Tstrap: 0-0
Best Rating: 96 2/00 Sedg 2m1f gd-sft NHF

Mr Grimsdale (IRE)

100 | 84

10-y-o ch g Grimesgill (USA)-Lady Rose Walk (Sir Herbert)
Mrs A C Tate A J Chambers

Placings:*0*/U21/0-P65 (4543)
2001/02: 20^{P}S, 24^{6}GF, 19^{5}G

	Starts	1st	2nd	3rd	Win & Pl
Hurdles	1	0	0	0	0
Chases	2	0	0	0	0
Career Total	**8**	**1**	**1**	**0**	**2115**

108 4/00 Uttx 2m7f H Ch HVY £1540
Total win prize-money £1540

Going: Sf: 0-1 GS: 0-0 Gd: 0-1 GF: - Fm: 0-1
Distance: 2m/2m3: 0-1 2m4-2m7: 0-1 3m+: 0-1
Track: LH: 0-1 RH: 0-2 Tight: 0-0 Gall: 0-2
Aids: Bl: 0-0 Vi: 0-0 Tstrap: 0-0
Best Rating: 108 4/00 Uttx 2m7f heavy Ch

Mr Half Sharp

9-y-o ch g Mr Fluorocarbon-Star Shell (Queens Hussar)
Sidney J Smith (B S Rothwell 10/2) Sidney J Smith

Placings:0P/4F050/13 (4763)
2001/02: 22^{1}G, 24^{3}GF

	Starts	1st	2nd	3rd	Win & Pl
Chases	2	1	0	1	2510
Career Total	**9**	**1**	**0**	**1**	**2790**

105 4/02 Towc 2m6f D Ch GD £2086
Total win prize-money £2087

Going: Sf: 0-0 GS: 0-0 Gd: 1-1 GF: - Fm: 0-1
Distance: 2m/2m3: 0-0 **2m4-2m7: 1-1** 3m+: 0-1
Track: LH: 0-0 **RH: 1-2** Tight: 0-0 Gall: 0-0
Aids: Bl: 0-0 Vi: 0-0 Tstrap: 0-0
Best Rating: 105 4/02 Towc 2m6f good Ch

Improving hunter chaser. Won easily at Towcester in April 2002 over two miles six furlongs. Suited by good to soft ground or faster.

Mr Illuminator

62 | 10

6-y-o ch g Gildoran-Voolin (Jimmy Reppin)
C J Price Dextra Lighting Systems

Placings:0P (2949)
2001/02: 19^{0}G, 22^{P}S

	Starts	1st	2nd	3rd	Win & Pl
Hurdles	2	0	0	0	
Career Total	**2**	**0**	**0**	**0**	

Going: Sf: 0-1 GS: 0-0 Gd: 0-1 GF: - Fm: 0-0
Distance: 2m/2m3: 0-1 2m4-2m7: 0-1 3m+: 0-0
Track: LH: 0-2 RH: 0-0 Tight: 0-1 Gall: 0-1
Aids: Bl: 0-0 Vi: 0-0 Tstrap: 0-0
Best Rating: 10 11/01 Newb 2m3f good Hdl

Mr Jake

108(96h) | (72h)102

9-y-o b g Safawan-Miss Tealeaf (USA) (Lear Fan (USA))
H E Haynes Mrs H E Haynes

Placings:*200/0*/06612/00314 (3797)
2001/02: 16^{0}G, 19^{0}G, 20^{3}GS, 24^{1}GF, 26^{4}S

	Starts	1st	2nd	3rd	Win & Pl
Hurdles	2	0	0	0	0
Chases	3	1	0	1	4562
Career Total	**14**	**2**	**2**	**1**	**8507**

98 8/01 Strf 3m E(0-105)HCh G-F £3510
78 7/99 Strf 2m3f E(0-105)HHdl GD £2840
Total win prize-money £6350

Going: Sf: 0-1 GS: 0-1 Gd: 0-2 GF: - Fm: 1-1
Distance: 2m/2m3: 0-1 2m4-2m7: 0-2 **3m+: 1-2**
Track: **LH: 1-2** RH: 0-2 **Tight: 1-1** Gall: 0-1
Aids: Bl: 0-0 Vi: 0-0 Tstrap: 0-0
Best Rating: 102 7/01 MRas 2m4f gd-sft Ch

Lightly raced. Scored once over hurdles but showed his forte to be the chasing game when scoring comfortably on only his second start over fences at Stratford in August 2001. Stays three miles. Jumps well. Acts on fast ground.

Mr Jeeves (IRE)

9-y-o ch g Denel (FR)-Lonely Wind (Tumble Wind (USA))
J Howard Johnson J Howard Johnson

Placings:000/0*3*1005133430/05504065/F-U (2122)
2001/02: 28^{U}GS

	Starts	1st	2nd	3rd	Win & Pl
Chases	1	0	0	0	
Career Total	**25**	**2**	**0**	**4**	**8960**

111 10/98 Gway 2m6f Ch HVY £3885
90 9/98 Kbgn 2m3f Hdl SFT £1942
Total win prize-money £5829

Going: Sf: 0-0 GS: 0-1 Gd: 0-0 GF: - Fm: 0-0
Distance: 2m/2m3: 0-0 2m4-2m7: 0-0 3m+: 0-1
Track: LH: 0-1 RH: 0-0 Tight: 0-1 Gall: 0-0
Aids: Bl: 0-0 Vi: 0-0 Tstrap: 0-0
Best Rating: 111 10/98 Gway 2m6f heavy Ch

Mr Laggan

102(95h) | (74h)90

7-y-o b g Tina's Pet-Galway Gal (Proverb)
Miss Kate Milligan Mrs J M L Milligan

Placings:*56*P4-30600P (4855)
2001/02: 24^{3}G, 22^{0}G, 16^{8}S, 20^{0}GS, 20^{0}GS, 20^{P}G

	Starts	1st	2nd	3rd	Win & Pl
Hurdles	3	0	0	1	426
Chases	3	0	0	0	0
Career Total	**10**	**0**	**0**	**1**	**426**

Going: Sf: 0-1 GS: 0-2 Gd: 0-3 GF: - Fm: 0-0
Distance: 2m/2m3: 0-1 2m4-2m7: 0-4 3m+: 0-1
Track: LH: 0-5 RH: 0-1 Tight: 0-3 Gall: 0-0
Aids: Bl: 0-0 Vi: 0-0 Tstrap: 0-0
Best Rating: 96 9/00 MRas 1m5f110y gd-fm NHF

In the frame over hurdles and fences, but yet to win and looks modest

Mr Lamb

82 **80**

7-y-o gr g Deploy-Caroline Lamb (Hotfoot)
M C Pipe D A Johnson

Placings: 1/1F2F/F0005-00 (3908)
2001/02: 23^{0}HY, 21^{0}G

	Starts	1st	2nd	3rd	Win & Pl
Hurdles	2	0	0	0	
Career Total	12	2	1	0	9775

119	10/99	Chel	2m110y	D Hdl		GD	£4071
99	1/99	Muss	2m	H NHF		G-S	£1563

Total win prize-money £5636

Going: Sf: 0-1 GS: 0-0 Gd: 0-1 GF: - Fm: 0-0
Distance: 2m/2m3: 0-0 2m4-2m7: 0-1 3m+: 0-1
Track: LH: 0-1 RH: 0-1 Tight: 0-0 Gall: 0-0
Aids: Bl: 0-0 Vi: 0-0 Tstrap: 0-0
Best Rating: 137 3/00 Chel 2m110y good Hdl

Sold for big money after winning a bumper, he started off promisingly over hurdles in 1999 but has disappointed and thus dropped down the handicap since. Not the best of jumpers.

Mr Magget (IRE)

88 **81**

10-y-o gr g Salluceva-Linda Dudley (Owen Dudley)
Miss H M Irving Noel Warner

Placings: 0/0002054/04652/P00/F3F0 (0555)
2001/02: 26^{F}GS, 24^{3}GF, 20^{F}G, 20^{0}GF

	Starts	1st	2nd	3rd	Win & Pl
Chases	4	0	0	1	265
Career Total	20	0	2	1	1326

Going: Sf: 0-0 GS: 0-1 Gd: 0-1 GF: - Fm: 0-2
Distance: 2m/2m3: 0-0 2m4-2m7: 0-2 3m+: 0-2
Track: LH: 0-1 RH: 0-2 Tight: 0-2 Gall: 0-1
Aids: Bl: 0-0 Vi: 0-0 Tstrap: 0-0
Best Rating: 101 1/98 Tram 2m4f heavy Ch

Mr Magnetic (IRE)

11-y-o b g Point North-Miss Ironside (General Ironside)
Dominic Harvey (H D Daly 3/2) Dominic Harvey

Placings: 505/041235F1/3FP340/0/1 (4659)
2001/02: 24^{1}G

	Starts	1st	2nd	3rd	Win & Pl
Chases	1	1	0	0	2664
Career Total	19	3	1	3	11050

113	4/02	Tntn	3m	H Ch		GD	£2664
116	4/98	Hrfd	3m1f110y	E Ch		G-S	£3130
104	6/97	Gowr	2m4f		NHF	G-Y	£2712

Total win prize-money £8507

Going: Sf: 0-0 GS: 0-0 Gd: 1-1 GF: - Fm: 0-0
Distance: 2m/2m3: 0-0 2m4-2m7: 0-0 **3m+: 1-1**
Track: LH: 0-0 **RH: 1-1 Tight: 1-1** Gall: 0-0
Aids: Bl: 0-0 Vi: 0-0 Tstrap: 0-0
Best Rating: 116 2/99 Bang 3m6f gd-sft Ch

Ex-Irish, he stays three miles and handles testing ground well but is not a natural jumper of fences.

Mr Mahdlo

111 **113+**

8-y-o b g Rakaposhi King-Fedelm (Celtic Cone)
R D E Woodhouse M K Oldham

Placings: 000/335F25212PP/42P21PPP/P4P22PP-PPP (4576)
2001/02: 24^{P}S, 32^{P}HY, 26^{P}GS

	Starts	1st	2nd	3rd	Win & Pl
Chases	3	0	0	0	
Career Total	32	2	7	2	15224

127	1/00	Weth	3m1f	D(0-125)HCh	SFT	£3825
96	1/99	Ayr	3m110y	F(0-110)HHdl	HVY	£2851

Total win prize-money £6676

Going: Sf: 0-2 GS: 0-1 Gd: 0-0 GF: - Fm: 0-0
Distance: 2m/2m3: 0-0 2m4-2m7: 0-0 3m+: 0-3
Track: LH: 0-3 RH: 0-0 Tight: 0-1 Gall: 0-1
Aids: Bl: 0-0 Vi: 0-0 Tstrap: 0-1
Best Rating: 127 1/00 Weth 3m1f soft Ch

He looked an improving young chaser when winning back in 2000, but has also been pulled up a worrying number of times since. Dropped right down the handicap as a result and has run better from May 2002 onwards. Acts on good an easier ground.

Mr Mann (IRE)

100 **102**

9-y-o ch g Duky-Slan Abhaile (Trimmingham)
Noel T Chance Mrs J M Porter

Placings: F2-3F4P2 (4562)
2001/02: 24^{3}GF, 21^{F}G, 19^{4}GS, 21^{P}S, 20^{2}GF

	Starts	1st	2nd	3rd	Win & Pl
Chases	5	0	1	1	1325
Career Total	7	0	2	1	2142

Going: Sf: 0-1 GS: 0-1 Gd: 0-1 GF: - Fm: 0-2
Distance: 2m/2m3: 0-1 2m4-2m7: 0-3 3m+: 0-1
Track: LH: 0-3 RH: 0-1 Tight: 0-4 Gall: 0-0
Aids: Bl: 0-0 Vi: 0-0 Tstrap: 0-0
Best Rating: 102 5/01 Strf 3m gd-fm Ch

Moderate chaser, stays three miles, acts on any ground.

Mr Markham (IRE)

105(113h) (145h)**124**

10-y-o b g Naheez (USA)-Brighter Gail (Bustineto)
J T Gifford Felix Rosenstiel's Widow & Son

Placings: 115/221303/13441P210/400F-305015500 (4914)
2001/02: 18^{3}S, 21^{0}G, 16^{5}G, 24^{0}G, 21^{1}GS, 22^{5}S, 20^{5}S, 20^{0}GS, 20^{0}G

	Starts	1st	2nd	3rd	Win & Pl
Hurdles	7	1	0	1	11813
Chases	2	0	0	0	0
Career Total	31	7	3	4	57199

145	1/02	Kemp	2m5f	C(0-130)HHdl	G-S	£7442
134	3/00	Font	2m4f	D Ch	G-S	£3753
140	1/00	Plum	2m1f	E Ch	SFT	£3006
140	10/99	Asct	2m110y	B(0-150)HHdl	GD	£6097
143	12/97	Asct	2m110y	B Hdl	G-S	£8091
117	2/97	Newb	2m110y	H NHF	GD	£7006
105	11/96	Sand	2m110y	H NHF	GD	£1997

Total win prize-money £37396

Going: Sf: 0-3 GS: 1-2 Gd: 0-4 GF: - Fm: 0-0
Distance: 2m/2m3: 0-2 **2m4-2m7: 1-6** 3m+: 0-1
Track: LH: 0-3 **RH: 1-5** Tight: 0-1 Gall: 0-2
Aids: **Bl: 1-4** Vi: 0-0 Tstrap: 0-0
Best Rating: 151 2/00 Asct 2m3f110y gd-sft Ch

A winner of bumpers, hurdle races and a winner over fences. He acts on good to soft ground and is effective at two to two and a half miles, but yet to prove he stays three. Bounced back to form when blinkered in a Kempton handicap hurdle in January 2002 but their effect seems to have worn off lately.

Mr Match

9-y-o b g Lighter-Penny's Colours (Hornet)
M J Gingell M J Gingell

Placings: PP5P-PP (0589)
2001/02: 16^{P}GF, 16^{P}GF

	Starts	1st	2nd	3rd	Win & Pl
Hurdles	1	0	0	0	0
Chases	1	0	0	0	0
Career Total	6	0	0	0	0

Going: Sf: 0-0 GS: 0-0 Gd: 0-0 GF: - Fm: 0-2
Distance: 2m/2m3: 0-2 2m4-2m7: 0-0 3m+: 0-0
Track: LH: 0-2 RH: 0-0 Tight: 0-2 Gall: 0-0
Aids: Bl: 0-0 Vi: 0-1 Tstrap: 0-0
Best Rating:

Mr McDuff (IRE)

94 (77c)**90**

6-y-o b g Mandalus-Le Glen (Le Bavard (FR))
R H Alner P M De Wilde

Placings: 5-P55U36 (4586)
2001/02: 22^{P}GF, 22^{5}G, 24^{5}GS, 20^{U}S, 20^{3}S, 22^{6}G

	Starts	1st	2nd	3rd	Win & Pl
Hurdles	4	0	0	0	0
Chases	2	0	0	1	476
Career Total	7	0	0	1	476

Going: Sf: 0-2 GS: 0-1 Gd: 0-2 GF: - Fm: 0-1
Distance: 2m/2m3: 0-0 2m4-2m7: 0-5 3m+: 0-1
Track: LH: 0-1 RH: 0-5 Tight: 0-0 Gall: 0-0
Aids: Bl: 0-0 Vi: 0-0 Tstrap: 0-0
Best Rating: 90 10/01 Winc 2m6f good Hdl

Mr Micky (IRE)

99 **81**

4-y-o b g Rudimentary (USA)-Top Berry (High Top)
T D Easterby David & Steven Dudley

Placings: 00 (2150)
2001/02: 16^{0}S, 16^{0}G

	Starts	1st	2nd	3rd	Win & Pl
Hurdles	2	0	0	0	
Career Total	2	0	0	0	

Going: Sf: 0-1 GS: 0-0 Gd: 0-1 GF: - Fm: 0-0
Distance: 2m/2m3: 0-2 2m4-2m7: 0-0 3m+: 0-0
Track: LH: 0-2 RH: 0-0 Tight: 0-0 Gall: 0-1
Aids: Bl: 0-0 Vi: 0-0 Tstrap: 0-0
Best Rating: 81 11/01 Newc 2m good Hdl

Mr Miller (IRE)

10-y-o b g The Bart (USA)-Celtic Connection (Martinmas)
Mrs Heather Silk Peter Flaherty

Placings:P243/PPB434P64/P (4253)
2001/02: 26^{P}G

	Starts	1st	2nd	3rd	Win & Pl
Chases	1	0	0	0	
Career Total	**14**	**0**	**1**	**2**	**2093**

Going: Sf: 0-0 GS: 0-0 Gd: 0-1 GF: - Fm: 0-0
Distance: 2m/2m3: 0-0 2m4-2m7: 0-0 3m+: 0-1
Track: LH: 0-1 RH: 0-0 Tight: 0-0 Gall: 0-1
Aids: Bl: 0-0 Vi: 0-0 Tstrap: 0-0
Best Rating: 92 2/99 Plum 3m1f110y soft Ch

Modest chaser who had to drop to points to score after 14 attempts. Stays three miles on good to soft.

Mr Montague (IRE)

105 113

10-y-o b g Pennine Walk-Ballyewry (Prince Tenderfoot (USA))
C N Kellett C I P Racing

Placings:40/3432233/2123F/531425006/00131240-640F12311P6PF (4844)
2001/02: 21^{6}GF, 19^{4}GF, 20^{0}GF, 20^{F}GF, 21^{1}G, 22^{2}GF, 22^{3}G, 24^{1}GF, 24^{1}G, 24^{P}GF, 19^{6}GF, 24^{P}F, 24^{F}G

	Starts	1st	2nd	3rd	Win & Pl
Hurdles	12	3	1	1	8022
Chases	1	0	0	0	0
Career Total	**44**	**7**	**7**	**8**	**26406**

113	9/01	Uttx	3m110y	D(0-125)HHdl	GD	£3328
89	8/01	Sthl	3m110y	F Hdl	G-F	£1827
109	7/01	MRas	2m5f110y	G(0-95)HHdl	GD	£1764
113	8/00	Bang	2m4f	F(0-105)HHdl	GD	£3688
99	6/00	Uttx	2m	G(0-95)HHdl	G-F	£1757
100	7/99	Strf	2m1f110y	E Ch	GD	£3145
93	6/98	Sthl	2m	E Hdl	GD	£2358

Total win prize-money £17870

Going: Sf: 0-0 GS: 0-0 Gd: 2-4 GF: - Fm: 1-9
Distance: 2m/2m3: 0-1 2m4-2m7: 1-7 **3m+: 2-5**
Track: **LH: 2-8** RH: 1-3 **Tight: 2-7** Gall: 0-0
Aids: **Bl: 2-4** Vi: 1-5 Tstrap: 0-0
Best Rating: 113 9/01 Uttx 3m110y good Hdl

Mr Moonbeam (IRE)

10-y-o b g Satco (FR)-Rosy Moon (FR) (Sheshoon)
P H Morris (Mrs John Harrington 24/3) P H Morris

Placings:P0/06/P (4846)
2001/02: 24^{P}G

	Starts	1st	2nd	3rd	Win & Pl
Chases	1	0	0	0	
Career Total	**5**	**0**	**0**	**0**	

Going: Sf: 0-0 GS: 0-0 Gd: 0-1 GF: - Fm: 0-0
Distance: 2m/2m3: 0-0 2m4-2m7: 0-0 3m+: 0-1
Track: LH: 0-1 RH: 0-0 Tight: 0-1 Gall: 0-0
Aids: Bl: 0-0 Vi: 0-0 Tstrap: 0-0
Best Rating: 44 4/99 Fair 2m6f gd-yld Hdl

Mr No Man

95 91

6-y-o b g Cosmonaut-Christmas Show (Petorius)
J G Fitzgerald The No Man Partnership

Placings:5233/4-1 (0201)
2001/02: 16^{1}G

	Starts	1st	2nd	3rd	Win & Pl
Hurdles	1	1	0	0	2856
Career Total	**6**	**1**	**1**	**2**	**3787**

91	5/01	Weth	2m	E Hdl	GD	£2856

Total win prize-money £2856

Going: Sf: 0-0 GS: 0-0 Gd: 1-1 GF: - Fm: 0-0
Distance: **2m/2m3: 1-1** 2m4-2m7: 0-0 3m+: 0-0
Track: **LH: 1-1** RH: 0-0 Tight: 0-0 Gall: 0-0
Aids: Bl: 0-0 Vi: 0-0 Tstrap: 0-0
Best Rating: 97 3/01 MRas 2m1f110y gd-sft Hdl

Mr Nomanners

75f 74f

6-y-o ch g Then Again-Walnut Way (Gambling Debt)
G A Ham Corey M Gardner

Placings:00 (1799)
2001/02: 16^{0}G, 16^{0}S

	Starts	1st	2nd	3rd	Win & Pl
NH Flat	2	0	0	0	
Career Total	**2**	**0**	**0**	**0**	

Going: Sf: 0-1 GS: 0-0 Gd: 0-1 GF: - Fm: 0-0
Distance: 2m/2m3: 0-2 2m4-2m7: 0-0 3m+: 0-0
Track: LH: 0-2 RH: 0-0 Tight: 0-0 Gall: 0-0
Aids: Bl: 0-0 Vi: 0-0 Tstrap: 0-0
Best Rating: 74 10/01 Chep 2m110y good NHF

Mr Pendleberry

94(91c) (89c)93

8-y-o ch g Symbolic-Antonoua (Anton Lad)
A Dickman Mike Smallman

Placings:000/1P5/4264 (4093)
2001/02: 20^{4}G, 20^{2}GS, 21^{6}S, 25^{4}GS

	Starts	1st	2nd	3rd	Win & Pl
Hurdles	2	0	1	0	828
Chases	2	0	0	0	240
Career Total	**10**	**1**	**1**	**0**	**3477**

104	5/99	Prth	2m4f110y	E Hdl	SFT	£2409

Total win prize-money £2410

Going: Sf: 0-1 GS: 0-2 Gd: 0-1 GF: - Fm: 0-0
Distance: 2m/2m3: 0-0 2m4-2m7: 0-3 3m+: 0-1
Track: LH: 0-4 RH: 0-0 Tight: 0-2 Gall: 0-1
Aids: Bl: 0-0 Vi: 0-0 Tstrap: 0-0
Best Rating: 104 5/99 Prth 2m4f110y soft Hdl

Modest hurdler, has shown fair form in modest company since returning from in excess of two years off in late 2001. Has achieved little over fences so far.

Mr Percy (IRE)

106(109h) (146h)148

11-y-o ch g John French-Rathvilly Flier (Peacock (FR))
J T Gifford Felix Rosenstiel's Widow & Son

Placings:0/335/11F320/21100/16F/3240/3122-0252 (4818)
2001/02: 16^{0}G, 17^{2}S, 21^{5}G, 21^{2}GF

	Starts	1st	2nd	3rd	Win & Pl
Hurdles	2	0	1	0	3216
Chases	2	0	1	0	2544
Career Total	**30**	**6**	**7**	**5**	**79138**

136	1/01	Leic	2m	E Ch	SFT	£3627
157	10/98	Asct	2m110y	B HHdl	HVY	£5090
143	1/98	Chel	2m1f	B(0-145)HHdl	G-S	£6126
142	11/97	Chel	2m110y	B HHdl	GD	£29271
114	11/96	Hntg	2m110y	E Hdl	GD	£2722
119	9/96	Hntg	2m110y	E Hdl	FRM	£2722

Total win prize-money £49561

Going: Sf: 0-1 GS: 0-0 Gd: 0-2 GF: - Fm: 0-1
Distance: 2m/2m3: 0-2 2m4-2m7: 0-2 3m+: 0-0
Track: LH: 0-3 RH: 0-1 Tight: 0-0 Gall: 0-3
Aids: Bl: 0-0 Vi: 0-0 Tstrap: 0-0
Best Rating: 157 12/00 Chel 2m1f soft Hdl

A useful hurdler, he acts on most types of ground and stays two and a half miles.

Mr Perry (IRE)

103(95c) (83c)89

6-y-o br g Perugino (USA)-Elegant Tune (USA) (Alysheba (USA))
R M Stronge (A Crook 16/5) Peter J Douglas Engineering

Placings:F33/P4F00-PP3343201 (1564)
2001/02: 16^{P}F, 16^{P}GS, 16^{3}GF, 16^{3}GS, 16^{4}GF, 16^{3}G, 16^{2}GF, 16^{0}GF, 16^{1}GS

	Starts	1st	2nd	3rd	Win & Pl
Hurdles	8	1	1	3	3353
Chases	1	0	0	0	0
Career Total	**17**	**1**	**1**	**5**	**4325**

89	10/01	Uttx	2m	G Hdl	G-S	£1750

Total win prize-money £1750

Going: Sf: 0-0 GS: 1-3 Gd: 0-1 GF: - Fm: 0-5
Distance: **2m/2m3: 1-9** 2m4-2m7: 0-0 3m+: 0-0
Track: **LH: 1-7** RH: 0-2 Tight: 0-4 Gall: 0-1
Aids: Bl: 0-0 Vi: 0-1 Tstrap: 0-0
Best Rating: 91 1/01 Catt 2m gd-sft Hdl

Mr Pistachio (IRE)

(94c) (96c)

7-y-o b g Royal Fountain-Knockananig (Pitpan)
Miss K Marks Nick Shutts

Placings:P-22P (2754)
2001/02: 24^{2}GS, 25^{2}G, 33^{P}S

	Starts	1st	2nd	3rd	Win & Pl
Chases	3	0	2	0	1051
Career Total	**4**	**0**	**2**	**0**	**1051**

Going: Sf: 0-1 GS: 0-1 Gd: 0-1 GF: - Fm: 0-0
Distance: 2m/2m3: 0-0 2m4-2m7: 0-0 3m+: 0-3
Track: LH: 0-3 RH: 0-0 Tight: 0-3 Gall: 0-0
Aids: Bl: 0-0 Vi: 0-0 Tstrap: 0-0
Best Rating: 96 5/01 Aint 3m1f good Ch

A winner of a couple of point to points, he showed ability in a couple of novice hunter chases in the spring of 2001, but pulled up when running over four miles in December 2001. Does not want the ground too soft.

Mr Playfull

12-y-o br g Teamwork-Blue Nursery (Blue Rullah)
Mrs L C Jewell Mrs Linda Jewell

Placings:0403/202432331/2241422U3/21F1FP13/2P425F343/13F455440015/F0P1-PPP (4511)
2001/02: 20^{P}GS, 24^{P}HY, 20^{P}G

	Starts	1st	2nd	3rd	Win & Pl
Chases	3	0	0	0	
Career Total	**58**	**8**	**10**	**9**	**45113**

120	9/00	NAbb	2m5f110y	D(0-125)HCh	G-F	£4036

120	3/00	NAbb	2m5f110y	E(0-115)HCh	GD	£3057
123	5/99	Extr	2m7f110y	D(0-120)HCh	G-F	£4684
121	4/98	Tntn	3m	D(0-120)Ch	SFT	£3615
109	9/97	NAbb	2m5f110y	D(0-120)HCh	GD	£3441
107	5/97	Extr	2m3f110y	F(0-105)HCh	GD	£3249
97	10/96	Extr	2m6f110y	D Ch	G-F	£4140
89	4/96	NAbb	2m1f	E(0-100)HHdl	G-S	£2410

Total win prize-money £28636

Going: Sf: 0-1 GS: 0-1 Gd: 0-1 GF: - Fm: 0-0
Distance: 2m/2m3: 0-0 2m4-2m7: 0-2 3m+: 0-1
Track: LH: 0-3 RH: 0-0 Tight: 0-3 Gall: 0-0
Aids: Bl: 0-0 Vi: 0-0 Tstrap: 0-0
Best Rating: 123 5/99 Extr 2m7f110y gd-fm Ch

Fair handicap chaser. Has won up to three miles over fences but not for a couple of years and looks better suited by two miles-five these days. Acts on a sound surface, handles softer.

Mr Poppleton

13-y-o ch g Ballacashtal (CAN)-Greenstead Lady (Great Nephew)
A Philips Miss Jane Williams

Placings:P/0042P/0003003/065232323/30**B455**/1PP4 56/0/P **(0227)**
2001/02: 24^{P}GF

	Starts	1st	2nd	3rd	Win & Pl
Chases	1	0	0	0	
Career Total	**36**	**1**	**4**	**6**	**8298**

110	5/98	Towc	2m110y	E(0-100)HCh	G-F	£3315

Total win prize-money £3316

Going: Sf: 0-0 GS: 0-0 Gd: 0-0 GF: - Fm: 0-1
Distance: 2m/2m3: 0-0 2m4-2m7: 0-0 3m+: 0-1
Track: LH: 0-0 RH: 0-1 Tight: 0-0 Gall: 0-1
Aids: Bl: 0-0 Vi: 0-0 Tstrap: 0-0
Best Rating: 110 5/98 Towc 2m110y gd-fm Ch

Mr Rathmore (IRE)

100 **84**
8-y-o gr g Valville (FR)-Lady Grasp (Ballad Rock)
N A Twiston-Davies Geoffrey And Donna Keeys

Placings:*00*/4353P6-5 **(0085)**
2001/02: 17^{5}G

	Starts	1st	2nd	3rd	Win & Pl
Hurdles	1	0	0	0	0
Career Total	**9**	**0**	**0**	**2**	**1099**

Going: Sf: 0-0 GS: 0-0 Gd: 0-1 GF: - Fm: 0-0
Distance: 2m/2m3: 0-1 2m4-2m7: 0-0 3m+: 0-0
Track: LH: 0-0 RH: 0-1 Tight: 0-0 Gall: 0-0
Aids: Bl: 0-0 Vi: 0-0 Tstrap: 0-0
Best Rating: 89 1/01 Ludl 2m soft Hdl

Mr Smudge

10-y-o ch g Fearless Action (USA)-Amerian County (Amerian (USA))
Mrs F J Marriott C Marriott

Placings:3PPP-P1 **(0429)**
2001/02: 30^{P}GF, 25^{1}G

	Starts	1st	2nd	3rd	Win & Pl
Chases	2	1	0	0	3689
Career Total	**6**	**1**	**0**	**1**	**4337**

102	5/01	Chel	3m1f110y	H Ch	GD	£3688

Total win prize-money £3689

Going: Sf: 0-0 GS: 0-0 Gd: 1-1 GF: - Fm: 0-1
Distance: 2m/2m3: 0-0 2m4-2m7: 0-0 **3m+: 1-2**
Track: LH: 0-0 RH: 0-1 Tight: 0-0 Gall: 0-1
Aids: Bl: 0-0 Vi: 0-0 Tstrap: 0-0
Best Rating: 102 5/01 Chel 3m1f110y good Ch

Mr Snaggle (IRE)

96(108h) (80h)**80**
13-y-o ch g Pollerton-Truly Deep (Deep Run)
Simon Earle A Galvin

Placings:*0543164/04P1000/56033300/35*23303**F111** 1/2330512/34446P2/303025-400053P **(2356)**
2001/02: 17^{4}G, 20^{0}GF, 18^{0}GF, 16^{0}G, 16^{5}S, 16^{3}G, 16^{P}S

	Starts	1st	2nd	3rd	Win & Pl
Hurdles	4	0	0	0	0
Chases	3	0	0	1	363
Career Total	**62**	**7**	**5**	**14**	**34330**

98	3/99	Tntn	2m3f110y	E(0-115)HHdl	SFT	£2775
107	4/97	Towc	2m110y	E(0-115)HCh	G-F	£3000
93	4/97	Extr	2m3f110y	D(0-120)HHdl	FRM	£2862
106	3/97	Towc	2m110y	D(0-125)HCh	G-F	£3435
94	3/97	Ludl	2m4f	D Ch	G-F	£3371
104	12/94	Thur	2m2f	(0-116)HHdl	G-Y	£2609
99	12/93	Limk	2m	Hdl	HVY	£3709

Total win prize-money £21766

Going: Sf: 0-2 GS: 0-0 Gd: 0-3 GF: - Fm: 0-2
Distance: 2m/2m3: 0-6 2m4-2m7: 0-1 3m+: 0-0
Track: LH: 0-2 RH: 0-4 Tight: 0-2 Gall: 0-0
Aids: Bl: 0-0 Vi: 0-0 Tstrap: 0-0
Best Rating: 109 11/99 Catt 2m3f gd-fm Ch

Mr Snowman

10-y-o b g Lightning Dealer-Eventime (Hot Brandy)
Mrs T J Hill S N Wilshire

Placings:122/11B-0 **(0063)**
2001/02: 26^{0}G

	Starts	1st	2nd	3rd	Win & Pl
Chases	1	0	0	0	
Career Total	**7**	**3**	**2**	**0**	**6414**

130	3/01	Wwck	3m2f	H Ch	SFT	£1295
122	5/00	Towc	2m6f	H Ch	G-F	£1482
122	3/00	Leic	2m4f110y	H Ch	G-S	£2171

Total win prize-money £4948

Going: Sf: 0-0 GS: 0-0 Gd: 0-1 GF: - Fm: 0-0
Distance: 2m/2m3: 0-0 2m4-2m7: 0-0 3m+: 0-1
Track: LH: 0-0 RH: 0-1 Tight: 0-1 Gall: 0-0
Aids: Bl: 0-0 Vi: 0-0 Tstrap: 0-0
Best Rating: 130 3/01 Wwck 3m2f soft Ch

Smart hunter chaser who enjoys an easy surface.

Mr Speculator

91 **68**
9-y-o ch g Kefaah (USA)-Humanity (Ahonoora)
J L Spearing Kinnersley Racing Club

Placings:0344/543111150/065543P015/42066-0000 **(1228)**
2001/02: 17^{0}G, 17^{0}GF, 16^{0}GF, 16^{0}GF

	Starts	1st	2nd	3rd	Win & Pl
Hurdles	4	0	0	0	
Career Total	**32**	**5**	**1**	**3**	**17377**

101	4/00	MRas	2m1f110y	F(0-105)HHdl	G-F	£4836
107	10/98	Tntn	2m1f	E(0-115)HHdl	FRM	£3387
104	9/98	MRas	2m1f110y	E(0-100)HHdl	GD	£2416
98	9/98	Uttx	2m	E Hdl	G-F	£2232
107	8/98	Strf	2m110y	E Hdl	G-F	£1996

Total win prize-money £14868

Going: Sf: 0-0 GS: 0-0 Gd: 0-1 GF: - Fm: 0-3
Distance: 2m/2m3: 0-4 2m4-2m7: 0-0 3m+: 0-0
Track: LH: 0-3 RH: 0-1 Tight: 0-3 Gall: 0-0
Aids: Bl: 0-2 Vi: 0-0 Tstrap: 0-0
Best Rating: 107 6/00 Hrfd 2m1f gd-fm Hdl

Mr Splodge

41
8-y-o b g Gildoran-Ethels Course (Crash Course)
P Winkworth Patrick Evans

Placings:*040*/235P-0 **(0242)**
2001/02: 21^{0}GF

	Starts	1st	2nd	3rd	Win & Pl
Hurdles	1	0	0	0	
Career Total	**8**	**0**	**1**	**1**	**1129**

Going: Sf: 0-0 GS: 0-0 Gd: 0-0 GF: - Fm: 0-1
Distance: 2m/2m3: 0-0 2m4-2m7: 0-1 3m+: 0-0
Track: LH: 0-0 RH: 0-0 Tight: 0-0 Gall: 0-0
Aids: Bl: 0-0 Vi: 0-0 Tstrap: 0-0
Best Rating: 90 11/00 Plum 2m5f heavy Hdl

Mr Squiggle (IRE)

4-y-o b g Persian Bold-Soul Fire (IRE) (Exactly Sharp (USA))
A Dickman Mike Smallman

Placings:R **(1718)**
2001/02: 16^{R}G

	Starts	1st	2nd	3rd	Win & Pl
Hurdles	1	0	0	0	
Career Total	**1**	**0**	**0**	**0**	

Going: Sf: 0-0 GS: 0-0 Gd: 0-1 GF: - Fm: 0-0
Distance: 2m/2m3: 0-1 2m4-2m7: 0-0 3m+: 0-0
Track: LH: 0-1 RH: 0-0 Tight: 0-0 Gall: 0-0
Aids: Bl: 0-0 Vi: 0-0 Tstrap: 0-0
Best Rating:

Mr Tees Components

(64h)
10-y-o br g Strong Gale-Culinary (Tower Walk)
Mrs L Williamson Miss Denise Foode

Placings:*2/53*602035/5/0P-P **(0367)**
2001/02: 24^{P}G

	Starts	1st	2nd	3rd	Win & Pl
Chases	1	0	0	0	
Career Total	**13**	**0**	**2**	**2**	**1779**

Going: Sf: 0-0 GS: 0-0 Gd: 0-1 GF: - Fm: 0-0
Distance: 2m/2m3: 0-0 2m4-2m7: 0-0 3m+: 0-1
Track: LH: 0-0 RH: 0-0 Tight: 0-0 Gall: 0-0
Aids: Bl: 0-0 Vi: 0-0 Tstrap: 0-0
Best Rating: 97 11/97 Weth 2m good NHF

Mr Thurlstone

9-y-o b g Landyap (USA)-Maywell (Harwell)

Mrs H O Graham (R G Frost 10/2) Mrs H O Graham

Placings:0/0/PP **(4690)**
2001/02: 25^{P}GS, 25^{P}GF

	Starts	1st	2nd	3rd	Win & Pl
Chases	2	0	0	0	
Career Total	4	0	0	0	

Going: Sf: 0-0 GS: 0-1 Gd: 0-0 GF: - Fm: 0-1
Distance: 2m/2m3: 0-0 2m4-2m7: 0-0 3m+: 0-2
Track: LH: 0-1 RH: 0-0 Tight: 0-1 Gall: 0-0
Aids: Bl: 0-0 Vi: 0-0 Tstrap: 0-0
Best Rating: 63 5/99 Extr 2m1f110y gd-fm NHF

Mr Timbrology (IRE)

95 **110**

8-y-o b g Insan (USA)-Mary Kate (Callernish)
R H Alner P M De Wilde

Placings:0/2415/33-P41 **(4729)**
2001/02: 20^{P}G, 19^{4}GS, 24^{1}GF

	Starts	1st	2nd	3rd	Win & Pl
Chases	3	1	0	0	3918
Career Total	10	2	1	2	8302

110 4/02 Chep 3m E(0-110)HCh G-F £3610
102 1/00 Towc 2m E Hdl HVY £2695
Total win prize-money £6306

Going: Sf: 0-0 GS: 0-1 Gd: 0-1 GF: - Fm: 1-1
Distance: 2m/2m3: 0-0 2m4-2m7: 0-2 **3m+: 1-1**
Track: **LH: 1-2** RH: 0-1 Tight: 0-0 Gall: 0-0
Aids: Bl: 0-0 Vi: 0-0 Tstrap: 0-0
Best Rating: 118 11/00 Leic 2m gd-sft Ch

Modest chaser, stays three miles and acts on fast ground.

Mr Windsor

7-y-o gr g Cruise Missile-Crossing Star Vii (Damsire Unregistered)
S J Marshall S J Marshall

Placings:P0 **(3785)**
2001/02: 24^{P}S, 20^{0}S

	Starts	1st	2nd	3rd	Win & Pl
Hurdles	2	0	0	0	
Career Total	2	0	0	0	

Going: Sf: 0-2 GS: 0-0 Gd: 0-0 GF: - Fm: 0-0
Distance: 2m/2m3: 0-0 2m4-2m7: 0-1 3m+: 0-1
Track: LH: 0-2 RH: 0-0 Tight: 0-0 Gall: 0-2
Aids: Bl: 0-0 Vi: 0-0 Tstrap: 0-0
Best Rating:

Mr Woodentop (IRE)

106 **122**

6-y-o b g Roselier (FR)-Una's Polly (Pollerton)
L Lungo Ashleybank Investments Limited

Placings:4-211S1 **(4830)**
2001/02: 16^{2}GS, 20^{1}S, 20^{1}S, 21^{S}S, 24^{1}G

	Starts	1st	2nd	3rd	Win & Pl
NH Flat	1	0	1	0	511
Hurdles	4	3	0	0	13383
Career Total	6	3	1	0	13894

122 4/02 Ayr 3m110y B HHdl GD £7250
122 12/01 Ayr 2m4f E Hdl SFT £2492
114 12/01 Hayd 2m4f D Hdl SFT £3640
Total win prize-money £13383

Going: Sf: 2-3 GS: 0-1 Gd: 1-1 GF: - Fm: 0-0
Distance: 2m/2m3: 0-1 **2m4-2m7: 2-3** 3m+: 1-1
Track: **LH: 3-5** RH: 0-0 Tight: 0-1 Gall: 0-0
Aids: Bl: 0-0 Vi: 0-0 Tstrap: 0-0
Best Rating: 122 4/02 Ayr 3m110y good Hdl

A brother to a winning point-to-pointer, he confirmed the ability of his two bumper runs with a win over hurdles on soft ground. Followed up at Ayr. He fell next time, but bounced right back to his best at Ayr in April 2002.

Mr Woodland

96(103h) (116h)**120+**

8-y-o br g Landyap (USA)-Wood Corner (Sit In The Corner (USA))
J D Frost (R G Frost 7/2) P A Tylor

Placings:4322150F3 **(4861)**
2001/02: 17^{4}G, 17^{3}GF, 17^{2}G, 16^{2}S, 22^{1}G, 22^{5}S, 19^{0}S, 19^{F}G, 22^{3}F

	Starts	1st	2nd	3rd	Win & Pl
Hurdles	9	1	2	2	6131
Career Total	9	1	2	2	6131

116 1/02 Winc 2m6f E Hdl GD £2859
Total win prize-money £2860

Going: Sf: 0-3 GS: 0-0 Gd: 1-4 GF: - Fm: 0-2
Distance: 2m/2m3: 0-6 **2m4-2m7: 1-3** 3m+: 0-0
Track: LH: 0-5 **RH: 1-3** Tight: 0-3 Gall: 0-1
Aids: Bl: 0-0 Vi: 0-0 Tstrap: 0-0
Best Rating: 116 2/02 Winc 2m6f soft Hdl

Gradually improved over hurdles and got off the mark at Wincanton in January 2002. Made a successful chasing debut at Newton Abbot in July. Stays two miles six. Acts on ground good and faster.

Mrs Be (IRE)

99f **97f**

6-y-o ch m Be My Native (USA)-Kilbrack (Perspex)
W S Kittow J H Burbidge

Placings:4 **(0108)**
2001/02: 18^{4}GF

	Starts	1st	2nd	3rd	Win & Pl
NH Flat	1	0	0	0	0
Career Total	1	0	0	0	0

Going: Sf: 0-0 GS: 0-0 Gd: 0-0 GF: - Fm: 0-1
Distance: 2m/2m3: 0-1 2m4-2m7: 0-0 3m+: 0-0
Track: LH: 0-1 RH: 0-0 Tight: 0-1 Gall: 0-0
Aids: Bl: 0-0 Vi: 0-0 Tstrap: 0-0
Best Rating: 97 5/01 Font 2m2f110y gd-fm NHF

Mrs Dangle

(101h) (85h)**56**

7-y-o b m Broadsword (USA)-Witches Run (Deep Run)
P J Hobbs Miss H L Cope

Placings:45-00P30 **(4600)**
2001/02: 17^{0}S, 19^{0}G, 22^{P}S, 24^{3}S, 24^{0}GF

	Starts	1st	2nd	3rd	Win & Pl
Hurdles	4	0	0	1	431
Chases	1	0	0	0	0
Career Total	7	0	0	1	431

Going: Sf: 0-3 GS: 0-0 Gd: 0-1 GF: - Fm: 0-1
Distance: 2m/2m3: 0-2 2m4-2m7: 0-1 3m+: 0-2
Track: LH: 0-2 RH: 0-2 Tight: 0-3 Gall: 0-0
Aids: Bl: 0-0 Vi: 0-0 Tstrap: 0-0
Best Rating: 91 1/01 Chep 2m110y gd-sft NHF

Modest handicap hurdler, she favours soft ground. Stays three miles.

Mrs Duf

104 **98**

8-y-o b m Teenoso (USA)-Hatherley (Deep Run)
R H Alner R Alner

Placings:2350-12 **(4048)**
2001/02: 21^{1}G, 19^{2}G

	Starts	1st	2nd	3rd	Win & Pl
Hurdles	2	1	1	0	3624
Career Total	6	1	2	1	4333

98 11/01 Plum 2m5f E Hdl GD £2450
Total win prize-money £2450

Going: Sf: 0-0 GS: 0-0 Gd: 1-2 GF: - Fm: 0-0
Distance: 2m/2m3: 0-1 **2m4-2m7: 1-1** 3m+: 0-0
Track: **LH: 1-1** RH: 0-1 **Tight: 1-1** Gall: 0-0
Aids: Bl: 0-0 Vi: 0-0 Tstrap: 0-0
Best Rating: 102 12/00 Tntn 2m1f soft NHF

She showed some ability in bumpers before making a successful hurdling debut at Plumpton. Stays well.

Mrs Jodi

103 **116**

6-y-o b m Yaheeb (USA)-Knayton Lass (Presidium)
J M Jefferson Mr & Mrs J M Davenport

Placings:231161/0500-4256F1032P **(4879)**
2001/02: 16^{4}G, 16^{2}G, 16^{5}G, 20^{6}GS, 16^{F}S, 17^{1}S, 16^{0}GS, 20^{3}GS, 16^{2}GF, 16^{P}G

	Starts	1st	2nd	3rd	Win & Pl
Hurdles	10	1	2	1	7364
Career Total	20	4	3	2	18774

116 1/02 Carl 2m1f D(0-120)HHdl SFT £3510
109 2/00 Hayd 2m C HHdl SFT £5408
98 12/99 MRas 2m1f110y E Hdl G-S £2495
86 11/99 Newc 2m E Hdl GD £2316
Total win prize-money £13729

Going: Sf: 1-2 GS: 0-3 Gd: 0-4 GF: - Fm: 0-1
Distance: **2m/2m3: 1-8** 2m4-2m7: 0-2 3m+: 0-0
Track: LH: 0-6 **RH: 1-3** Tight: 0-2 Gall: 0-0
Aids: Bl: 0-0 Vi: 0-0 Tstrap: 0-0
Best Rating: 116 4/02 Kels 2m110y gd-fm Hdl

A useful handicap hurdler, she acts on good and soft ground and she seems suited by a test of stamina. Best at around two miles.

Mrs Pickles

103 **89**

7-y-o gr m Northern Park (USA)-Able Mabel (Absalom)
M D I Usher Midweek Racing

Placings:060/000P5/4-F22215F **(4577)**
2001/02: 21^{F}GS, 24^{2}GS, 16^{2}S, 24^{2}S, 21^{1}HY, 21^{5}S, 24^{F}G

	Starts	1st	2nd	3rd	Win & Pl
Hurdles	7	1	3	0	4365
Career Total	16	1	3	0	4365

89 2/02 Plum 2m5f E(0-105)HHdl HVY £2457
Total win prize-money £2457

Going: Sf: 1-4 GS: 0-2 Gd: 0-1 GF: - Fm: 0-0
Distance: 2m/2m3: 0-1 **2m4-2m7: 1-3** 3m+: 0-3
Track: **LH: 1-4** RH: 0-3 **Tight: 1-3** Gall: 0-2
Aids: Bl: 0-0 Vi: 0-0 Tstrap: 0-0
Best Rating: 89 2/02 Plum 2m5f heavy Hdl

Moderate hurdler, suited by soft ground.

Mrs Quigley (IRE)

8-y-o b m Mandalus-Arumah (Arapaho)
G M McCourt R O Addis

Placings:00-0 **(0054)**
2001/02: 24^{0}G

	Starts	1st	2nd	3rd	Win & Pl
Hurdles	1	0	0	0	
Career Total	**3**	**0**	**0**	**0**	

Going: Sf: 0-0 GS: 0-0 Gd: 0-1 GF: - Fm: 0-0
Distance: 2m/2m3: 0-0 2m4-2m7: 0-0 3m+: 0-1
Track: LH: 0-1 RH: 0-0 Tight: 0-1 Gall: 0-0
Aids: Bl: 0-0 Vi: 0-0 Tstrap: 0-0
Best Rating: 66 8/00 NAbb 2m1f good NHF

Mrs Ritchie

91f 86f
5-y-o b m Teenoso (USA)-Material Girl (Busted)
M Pitman Just Good Fun Club

Placings:5 **(4539)**
2001/02: 16^{5}G

	Starts	1st	2nd	3rd	Win & Pl
NH Flat	1	0	0	0	0
Career Total	**1**	**0**	**0**	**0**	**0**

Going: Sf: 0-0 GS: 0-0 Gd: 0-1 GF: - Fm: 0-0
Distance: 2m/2m3: 0-1 2m4-2m7: 0-0 3m+: 0-0
Track: LH: 0-1 RH: 0-0 Tight: 0-1 Gall: 0-0
Aids: Bl: 0-0 Vi: 0-0 Tstrap: 0-0
Best Rating: 81 4/02 Fknm 2m good NHF

Mrs Sherman

99(90h) (59h)69
7-y-o b m Derrylin-Temporary Affair (Mandalus)
Mrs L Williamson M Williamson

Placings:3064060-603U46345 **(4769)**
2001/02: 17^{6}S, 16^{0}G, 16^{3}S, 20^{U}G, 21^{4}S, 20^{6}HY, 17^{3}S, 24^{4}HY, 25^{5}GF

	Starts	1st	2nd	3rd	Win & Pl
Hurdles	2	0	0	0	0
Chases	7	0	0	2	1572
Career Total	**16**	**0**	**0**	**3**	**1816**

Going: Sf: 0-6 GS: 0-0 Gd: 0-2 GF: - Fm: 0-1
Distance: 2m/2m3: 0-4 2m4-2m7: 0-3 3m+: 0-2
Track: LH: 0-8 RH: 0-1 Tight: 0-6 Gall: 0-0
Aids: Bl: 0-6 Vi: 0-0 Tstrap: 0-0
Best Rating: 98 10/00 Bang 2m1f soft NHF

Ms Trude (IRE)

94f 101f
5-y-o b m Montelimar (USA)-Pencil (Crash Course)
A W Carroll Gary J Roberts

Placings:200 **(4823)**
2001/02: 16^{2}S, 16^{0}G, 17^{0}G

	Starts	1st	2nd	3rd	Win & Pl
NH Flat	3	0	1	0	657
Career Total	**3**	**0**	**1**	**0**	**657**

Going: Sf: 0-1 GS: 0-0 Gd: 0-2 GF: - Fm: 0-0
Distance: 2m/2m3: 0-3 2m4-2m7: 0-0 3m+: 0-0
Track: LH: 0-2 RH: 0-1 Tight: 0-0 Gall: 0-1
Aids: Bl: 0-0 Vi: 0-0 Tstrap: 0-0
Best Rating: 101 4/02 Chel 2m1f good NHF

A half-sister to Manus The Man, she made an encouraging debut in a Towcester bumper in March 2002. Not disgraced next time.

Muallaf (IRE)

10-y-o b g Unfuwain (USA)-Honourable Sheba (USA) (Roberto (USA))
Mrs A M Woodrow Mrs Ann Woodrow

Placings:002/0P0P0/PS **(0375)**
2001/02: 17^{P}GS, 16^{S}GF

	Starts	1st	2nd	3rd	Win & Pl
Hurdles	2	0	0	0	0
Career Total	**10**	**0**	**1**	**0**	**471**

Going: Sf: 0-0 GS: 0-1 Gd: 0-0 GF: - Fm: 0-1
Distance: 2m/2m3: 0-2 2m4-2m7: 0-0 3m+: 0-0
Track: LH: 0-0 RH: 0-2 Tight: 0-1 Gall: 0-1
Aids: Bl: 0-0 Vi: 0-0 Tstrap: 0-0
Best Rating: 77 4/97 Chep 2m110y firm NHF

Muckle Mavis

98 85
6-y-o b m Nomadic Way (USA)-The Muckle Quine (Hubbly Bubbly (USA))
Miss Lucinda V Russell Miss G Joughin

Placings:00-505P2P **(4876)**
2001/02: 16^{5}GS, 16^{0}GS, 20^{5}GF, 20^{P}G, 24^{2}S, 24^{P}G

	Starts	1st	2nd	3rd	Win & Pl
Hurdles	6	0	1	0	775
Career Total	**8**	**0**	**1**	**0**	**775**

Going: Sf: 0-1 GS: 0-2 Gd: 0-2 GF: - Fm: 0-1
Distance: 2m/2m3: 0-2 2m4-2m7: 0-2 3m+: 0-2
Track: LH: 0-3 RH: 0-3 Tight: 0-3 Gall: 0-1
Aids: Bl: 0-0 Vi: 0-0 Tstrap: 0-0
Best Rating: 85 3/02 Ayr 3m110y soft Hdl

Mucky Jim

106 84
7-y-o b g Teenoso (USA)-Miss Muck (Balinger)
N A Twiston-Davies The 'Yes' - 'No' - Wait'....Sorries

Placings:2150P-13U00 **(3983)**
2001/02: 20^{1}GF, 24^{3}GF, 22^{U}GS, 24^{0}S, 24^{0}G

	Starts	1st	2nd	3rd	Win & Pl
Hurdles	5	1	0	1	2490
Career Total	**10**	**2**	**1**	**1**	**4397**

84	8/01	Worc	2m4f	F(0-100)HHdl	G-F	£1995
110	7/00	Worc	2m	H NHF	G-F	£1491

Total win prize-money £3486

Going: Sf: 0-1 GS: 0-1 Gd: 0-1 GF: - Fm: 1-2
Distance: 2m/2m3: 0-0 **2m4-2m7: 1-2** 3m+: 0-3
Track: **LH: 1-2** RH: 0-2 Tight: 0-1 Gall: 0-0
Aids: Bl: 0-0 Vi: 0-0 Tstrap: 0-0
Best Rating: 111 7/00 Worc 2m good NHF

Mudlark

94(84c) (82c)42
10-y-o b g Salse (USA)-Mortal Sin (USA) (Green Forest (USA))
J R Norton J Norton

Placings:00460/23/3F/420646/050-0F6P6P **(4573)**
2001/02: 21^{0}G, 20^{F}GS, 19^{6}G, 21^{P}S, 21^{6}S, 20^{P}G

	Starts	1st	2nd	3rd	Win & Pl
Hurdles	2	0	0	0	0
Chases	4	0	0	0	0
Career Total	**24**	**0**	**2**	**2**	**1742**

Going: Sf: 0-2 GS: 0-1 Gd: 0-3 GF: - Fm: 0-0
Distance: 2m/2m3: 0-1 2m4-2m7: 0-5 3m+: 0-0
Track: LH: 0-5 RH: 0-1 Tight: 0-5 Gall: 0-0
Aids: Bl: 0-0 Vi: 0-6 Tstrap: 0-0
Best Rating: 88 10/98 Weth 3m1f good Hdl

Maiden selling hurdler. Well held in similar company over fences.

Muhami (IRE)

98 86
5-y-o b g Phardante (FR)-The Vicarette (IRE) (The Parson)
Ferdy Murphy The Poppet Partnership

Placings:05066 **(4880)**
2001/02: 17^{0}GS, 19^{5}S, 20^{0}S, 20^{6}G, 20^{6}G

	Starts	1st	2nd	3rd	Win & Pl
NH Flat	1	0	0	0	0
Hurdles	4	0	0	0	0
Career Total	**5**	**0**	**0**	**0**	**0**

Going: Sf: 0-2 GS: 0-1 Gd: 0-2 GF: - Fm: 0-0
Distance: 2m/2m3: 0-2 2m4-2m7: 0-3 3m+: 0-0
Track: LH: 0-2 RH: 0-2 Tight: 0-1 Gall: 0-1
Aids: Bl: 0-0 Vi: 0-0 Tstrap: 0-0
Best Rating: 91 10/01 Carl 2m1f gd-sft NHF

Muharib Lady (IRE)

102 79
7-y-o b m Muharib (USA)-Brickhill Lady (Le Bavard (FR))
P G Murphy P G Murphy

Placings:0/0030-30342303556 **(4686)**
2001/02: 20^{3}GF, 23^{0}GF, 25^{3}GS, 24^{4}G, 24^{2}GF, 26^{3}G, 25^{0}G, 21^{3}G, 24^{5}S, 26^{5}G, 26^{6}GF

	Starts	1st	2nd	3rd	Win & Pl
Hurdles	11	0	1	4	1865
Career Total	**16**	**0**	**1**	**5**	**2244**

Going: Sf: 0-1 GS: 0-1 Gd: 0-5 GF: - Fm: 0-4
Distance: 2m/2m3: 0-0 2m4-2m7: 0-2 3m+: 0-9
Track: LH: 0-5 RH: 0-6 Tight: 0-4 Gall: 0-1
Aids: Bl: 0-0 Vi: 0-0 Tstrap: 0-0
Best Rating: 79 3/02 Hrfd 3m2f good Hdl

She is exposed as moderate but does stay well.

Muhtadi (IRE)

106 83
9-y-o br g Marju (IRE)-Moon Parade (Welsh Pageant)
S B Clark S B Clark

Placings:0156/001/0000350/00/10P0-10 **(4579)**
2001/02: 17^{1}S, 16^{0}G

	Starts	1st	2nd	3rd	Win & Pl
Hurdles	2	1	0	0	1946
Career Total	**22**	**4**	**0**	**1**	**8698**

83	3/02	Sedg	2m1f	G(0-90)HHdl	SFT	£1946
79	1/01	Catt	2m	G(0-90)HHdl	G-S	£1666
87	3/98	Plum	2m	E Ch	SFT	£2956
90	3/97	Winc	2m	F Hdl	GD	£1900

Total win prize-money £8468

Going: Sf: 1-1 GS: 0-0 Gd: 0-1 GF: - Fm: 0-0
Distance: **2m/2m3: 1-2** 2m4-2m7: 0-0 3m+: 0-0
Track: **LH: 1-2** RH: 0-0 **Tight: 1-1** Gall: 0-0
Aids: **Bl: 1-2** Vi: 0-0 Tstrap: 0-0
Best Rating: 90 3/97 Bang 2m1f good Hdl

A winner on the Flat, he is effective at around two miles on a soft surface over hurdles.

Mujalina (IRE)

99 **111**

4-y-o b g Mujadil (USA)-Talina's Law (IRE) (Law Society (USA))
M C Pipe (G Macaire 7/9) Mr & Mrs M Bovingdon & C Langley

Placings:41115 **(2162)**
2001/02: 17^{4}, 17^{1}S, 15^{1}G, 16^{1}GF, 16^{5}G

	Starts	1st	2nd	3rd	Win & Pl
Hurdles	5	3	0	0	13446
Career Total	**5**	**3**	**0**	**0**	**13446**

111	10/01	Ludl	2m	E Hdl	G-F	£2681
	9/01	Autl	1m7f	Hdl	GD	£6305
	8/01	Diep	2m1f	Hdl	SFT	£3685

Total win prize-money £12671

Going: Sf: 1-1 GS: 0-0 Gd: 1-2 GF: - Fm: 1-1
Distance: **2m/2m3: 2-4** 2m4-2m7: 0-0 3m+: 0-0
Track: LH: 0-1 **RH: 1-1** Tight: 0-0 Gall: 0-0
Aids: Bl: 0-0 Vi: 0-0 Tstrap: 0-0
Best Rating: 111 10/01 Ludl 2m gd-fm Hdl

A winner twice in France before winning a weak race easily on his British debut at Ludlow. finished lame next time.

Mukdar (USA)

85 **73**

8-y-o b/br g Gulch (USA)-Give Thanks (Relko)
K C Bailey A & A Cutler And S Wood

Placings:6331142U155150/100/PP0P-0 **(0210)**
2001/02: 16^{0}F

	Starts	1st	2nd	3rd	Win & Pl
Hurdles	1	0	0	0	
Career Total	**22**	**5**	**1**	**2**	**16867**

124	5/99	Ludl	2m	D(0-120)HHdl	G-F	£2801
130	12/98	Hntg	2m110y	D(0-125)HHdl	SFT	£5407
116	11/98	Kemp	2m	E(0-110)HHdl	G-S	£2263
110	9/98	Hntg	2m110y	E Hdl	G-F	£2652
105	8/98	NAbb	2m1f	E Hdl	G-F	£2414

Total win prize-money £15539

Going: Sf: 0-0 GS: 0-0 Gd: 0-0 GF: - Fm: 0-1
Distance: 2m/2m3: 0-1 2m4-2m7: 0-0 3m+: 0-0
Track: LH: 0-1 RH: 0-0 Tight: 0-1 Gall: 0-0
Aids: Bl: 0-0 Vi: 0-0 Tstrap: 0-0
Best Rating: 130 12/98 Hntg 2m110y soft Hdl

Mulkev Prince (IRE)

101(77h) (73h)**120**

11-y-o b g Lancastrian-Waltzing Shoon (Green Shoon)
David Pearson (J Howard Johnson 12/10) David Pearson

Placings:*6/30*O1O2/33**OFP**24P/6**122102/F545P2/6**25
304/**5411U3F**-0**5F126** **(4650)**
2001/02: 17^{0}GS, 16^{5}GS, 19^{F}S, 20^{1}S, 20^{2}S, 21^{6}G

	Starts	1st	2nd	3rd	Win & Pl
Hurdles	1	0	0	0	0
Chases	5	1	1	0	3015
Career Total	**47**	**6**	**8**	**5**	**46770**

120	3/02	Leic	2m4f110y	H Ch	SFT	£2219
141	10/00	Carl	2m	D(0-125)HCh	GD	£4095
141	9/00	Prth	2m	E(0-115)HCh	HVY	£5408
141	2/98	Fair	2m	Ch	Y-S	£11217
117	11/97	Thur	2m	Ch	Y-S	£2204
108	2/96	Fair	2m2f	Hdl	G-Y	£3177

Total win prize-money £28321

Going: Sf: 1-3 GS: 0-2 Gd: 0-1 GF: - Fm: 0-0
Distance: 2m/2m3: 0-2 **2m4-2m7: 1-4** 3m+: 0-0
Track: LH: 0-2 **RH: 1-4** Tight: 0-3 Gall: 0-1
Aids: Bl: 0-0 Vi: 0-0 Tstrap: 0-0
Best Rating: 141 11/00 Weth 2m soft Ch

A one-time decent handicapper, he is still an effective sort in hunter chases. Probably best around two miles, although has won over two and a half, he has form on a variety of ground.

Mullaghmore (IRE)

81 **66**

6-y-o b g Petardia-Comfrey Glen (Glenstal (USA))
M Kettle Greenacres

Placings:0 **(1759)**
2001/02: 16^{0}GS

	Starts	1st	2nd	3rd	Win & Pl
Hurdles	1	0	0	0	
Career Total	**1**	**0**	**0**	**0**	

Going: Sf: 0-0 GS: 0-1 Gd: 0-0 GF: - Fm: 0-0
Distance: 2m/2m3: 0-1 2m4-2m7: 0-0 3m+: 0-0
Track: LH: 0-1 RH: 0-0 Tight: 0-1 Gall: 0-0
Aids: Bl: 0-0 Vi: 0-0 Tstrap: 0-0
Best Rating: 66 10/01 Strf 2m110y gd-sft Hdl

Won three times on the flat, but has yet to show that form over hurdles.

Mullensgrove

8-y-o b g Derrylin-Wedding Song (True Song)
D Lowe (J A Pickering 10/2) D J Lowe

Placings:*00*/PP-2 **(4288)**
2001/02: 25^{2}GS

	Starts	1st	2nd	3rd	Win & Pl
Chases	1	0	1	0	382
Career Total	**5**	**0**	**1**	**0**	**382**

Going: Sf: 0-0 GS: 0-1 Gd: 0-0 GF: - Fm: 0-0
Distance: 2m/2m3: 0-0 2m4-2m7: 0-0 3m+: 0-1
Track: LH: 0-0 RH: 0-1 Tight: 0-1 Gall: 0-0
Aids: Bl: 0-0 Vi: 0-0 Tstrap: 0-0
Best Rating: 98 3/02 MRas 3m1f gd-sft Ch

Progressive hunter at a modest level, in great heart between the flags in 2002 and duly landed his first hunter chase at Bangor in May. Well suited by a sound surface.

Mulligan Express

(94h) **105**

8-y-o ch g Phardante (FR)-Tsarella (Mummy's Pet)
Ferdy Murphy Peter Mulligan

Placings:*0*/511-3 **(1814)**
2001/02: 20^{3}S

	Starts	1st	2nd	3rd	Win & Pl
Chases	1	0	0	1	702
Career Total	**5**	**2**	**0**	**1**	**5468**

117	2/01	Carl	2m4f110y	E Hdl	SFT	£1975
100	2/01	Carl	2m4f110y	E Hdl	HVY	£2790

Total win prize-money £4765

Going: Sf: 0-1 GS: 0-0 Gd: 0-0 GF: - Fm: 0-0
Distance: 2m/2m3: 0-0 2m4-2m7: 0-1 3m+: 0-0
Track: LH: 0-0 RH: 0-1 Tight: 0-0 Gall: 0-0
Aids: Bl: 0-0 Vi: 0-0 Tstrap: 0-0
Best Rating: 117 2/01 Carl 2m4f110y soft Hdl

Mulsanne

51 **10**

4-y-o b g Clantime-Prim Lass (Reprimand)
P A Pritchard P A Pritchard

Placings:00P **(1800)**
2001/02: 16^{0}G, 16^{0}GF, 16^{P}GF

	Starts	1st	2nd	3rd	Win & Pl
Hurdles	3	0	0	0	
Career Total	**3**	**0**	**0**	**0**	

Going: Sf: 0-0 GS: 0-0 Gd: 0-1 GF: - Fm: 0-2
Distance: 2m/2m3: 0-3 2m4-2m7: 0-0 3m+: 0-0
Track: LH: 0-2 RH: 0-1 Tight: 0-2 Gall: 0-0
Aids: Bl: 0-1 Vi: 0-0 Tstrap: 0-0
Best Rating: 10 8/01 Strf 2m110y good Hdl

Multi Franchise

103(87h) (77h)**97**

9-y-o ch g Gabitat-Gabibti (IRE) (Dara Monarch)
D L Williams (R M Stronge 6/7) Miss B W Palmer

Placings:4/4F50213505506/62452000**5P04**056/6**F**02
214-30005**3P441UP4F** **(2138)**
2001/02: 17^{3}F, 16^{0}GF, 20^{0}GF, 16^{0}GF, 16^{5}GS, 20^{3}GF, 24^{P}GF, 22^{4}GF, 21^{4}GF, 25^{1}GF, 28^{U}GS, 25^{P}G, 18^{4}GS, 19^{F}G

	Starts	1st	2nd	3rd	Win & Pl
Hurdles	5	0	0	1	444
Chases	9	1	0	1	4795
Career Total	**50**	**3**	**5**	**3**	**12925**

95	9/01	Hrfd	3m1f110y	E(0-105)HCh	G-F	£3532
87	8/00	Bang	2m1f	G(0-95)HHdl	GD	£2268
81	11/98	Plum	2m1f	F Hdl	SFT	£2390

Total win prize-money £8191

Going: Sf: 0-0 GS: 0-3 Gd: 0-2 GF: - Fm: 1-9
Distance: 2m/2m3: 0-6 2m4-2m7: 0-4 **3m+: 1-4**
Track: LH: 0-5 **RH: 1-7** Tight: 0-8 Gall: 0-1
Aids: Bl: 0-0 Vi: 0-1 Tstrap: 0-0
Best Rating: 97 8/01 MRas 2m4f gd-fm Ch

Multigirl

5-y-o br m Ballet Royal (USA)-Last Colours (Afzal)
H J Manners H J Manners

Placings:00U-PP **(1728)**
2001/02: 18^{P}GS, 19^{P}F

	Starts	1st	2nd	3rd	Win & Pl
Hurdles	2	0	0	0	
Career Total	**5**	**0**	**0**	**0**	

Going: Sf: 0-0 GS: 0-1 Gd: 0-0 GF: - Fm: 0-1
Distance: 2m/2m3: 0-1 2m4-2m7: 0-1 3m+: 0-0
Track: LH: 0-1 RH: 0-1 Tight: 0-2 Gall: 0-0
Aids: Bl: 0-0 Vi: 0-0 Tstrap: 0-0
Best Rating: 41 10/00 Winc 2m gd-sft Hdl

Mumaris (USA)

106(108h) (126h)119

8-y-o b/br g Capote (USA)-Barakat (Bustino)

Mark Campion (P Hughes 18/3) Faulkner West

Placings:31613/04043400-44405F520223 **(4598)**

2001/02: 16^{4}SH, 18^{4}S, 22^{4}HY, 16^{0}YS, 20^{5}Y, 17^{F}YS, 16^{5}YS, 20^{2}HY, 16^{0}HY, 16^{2}S, 16^{2}S, 16^{3}GF

	Starts	1st	2nd	3rd	Win & Pl
Hurdles	4	0	0	0	1573
Chases	8	0	3	1	3084
Career Total	**25**	**2**	**3**	**4**	**13879**

107	8/98	Cork	2m	Hdl	FRM	£3586
119	7/98	Bell	2m1f	Hdl	G-F	£2391

Total win prize-money £5978

Going: Sf: 0-6 GS: 0-0 Gd: 0-0 GF: - Fm: 0-1
Distance: 2m/2m3: 0-9 2m4-2m7: 0-3 3m+: 0-0
Track: LH: 0-2 RH: 0-4 Tight: 0-0 Gall: 0-0
Aids: Bl: 0-0 Vi: 0-0 Tstrap: 0-0
Best Rating: 126 10/01 Gway 2m sft-hvy Hdl

Mumbai

107(87h) (67h)96

6-y-o b g Theatrical Charmer-Lehzen (Posse (USA))

M A Barnes The Purple Patch Racing Club

Placings:05PFP05U2-UB052U24U30 **(4895)**

2001/02: 16^{U}S, 20^{B}GF, 16^{0}F, 16^{5}S, 16^{2}S, 16^{U}GS, 16^{2}HY, 16^{4}S, 25^{U}GF, 16^{3}F, 20^{0}G

	Starts	1st	2nd	3rd	Win & Pl
Hurdles	1	0	0	0	0
Chases	10	0	2	1	3991
Career Total	**20**	**0**	**3**	**1**	**5135**

Going: Sf: 0-5 GS: 0-1 Gd: 0-1 GF: - Fm: 0-4
Distance: 2m/2m3: 0-8 2m4-2m7: 0-2 3m+: 0-1
Track: LH: 0-8 RH: 0-3 Tight: 0-3 Gall: 0-2
Aids: Bl: 0-0 Vi: 0-0 Tstrap: 0-0
Best Rating: 96 4/02 Newc 2m110y firm Ch

A strong-travelling type, he has been placed a number of times in minor chase company.

Mumuqa (IRE)

104(94h) (89h)123

10-y-o ch g Noalto-Princess Isabella (Divine Gift)

B S Rothwell (C R Egerton 6/7) J T Brown

Placings:42/11/F-03245P34P604 **(4872)**

2001/02: 16^{0}G, 16^{3}GS, 16^{2}GF, 17^{4}GF, 16^{5}G, 21^{P}GS, 16^{3}G, 17^{4}GS, 16^{P}G, 16^{6}G, 19^{0}S, 16^{4}GF

	Starts	1st	2nd	3rd	Win & Pl
Hurdles	4	0	1	1	977
Chases	8	0	0	1	1558
Career Total	**17**	**2**	**2**	**2**	**10118**

123	9/99	Sedg	2m110y	E Ch	G-F	£3650
116	9/99	NAbb	2m110y	E Ch	G-F	£2766

Total win prize-money £6418

Going: Sf: 0-1 GS: 0-3 Gd: 0-5 GF: - Fm: 0-3
Distance: 2m/2m3: 0-11 2m4-2m7: 0-1 3m+: 0-0
Track: LH: 0-12 RH: 0-0 Tight: 0-8 Gall: 0-0
Aids: Bl: 0-1 Vi: 0-0 Tstrap: 0-0
Best Rating: 123 7/01 Wolv 2m gd-sft Ch

Muntafi

11-y-o b g Unfuwain (USA)-Princess Sucree (USA) (Roberto (USA))

Simon T Lewis Simon T Lewis

Placings:44251144/5030P5/0/P/1P1/P/6PP4P-0PPP **(1622)**

2001/02: 19^{0}GS, 25^{P}G, 25^{P}F, 25^{P}G

	Starts	1st	2nd	3rd	Win & Pl
Chases	4	0	0	0	
Career Total	**29**	**4**	**1**	**1**	**16790**

99	4/99	Chel	3m1f110y	H Ch	G-S	£2232
92	3/99	Tntn	3m	H Ch	SFT	£2038
104	2/95	Hayd	2m	B HHdl	HVY	£7064
96	2/95	Newb	2m110y	F(0-105)HHdl	HVY	£3418

Total win prize-money £14752

Going: Sf: 0-0 GS: 0-1 Gd: 0-2 GF: - Fm: 0-1
Distance: 2m/2m3: 0-0 2m4-2m7: 0-1 3m+: 0-3
Track: LH: 0-0 RH: 0-3 Tight: 0-0 Gall: 0-0
Aids: Bl: 0-0 Vi: 0-0 Tstrap: 0-0
Best Rating: 105 12/95 Hayd 2m good Hdl

Murchan Benwood (IRE)

94 70

5-y-o b m Ridgewood Ben-Ardnamurchan (Ardross)

A Streeter The Mwm Racing Syndicate

Placings:006-506544F **(4540)**

2001/02: 17^{5}F, 16^{0}G, 16^{6}G, 17^{5}S, 19^{4}S, 17^{4}HY, 19^{F}G

	Starts	1st	2nd	3rd	Win & Pl
NH Flat	1	0	0	0	0
Hurdles	6	0	0	0	0
Career Total	**10**	**0**	**0**	**0**	**0**

Going: Sf: 0-3 GS: 0-0 Gd: 0-3 GF: - Fm: 0-1
Distance: 2m/2m3: 0-5 2m4-2m7: 0-2 3m+: 0-0
Track: LH: 0-2 RH: 0-5 Tight: 0-2 Gall: 0-0
Aids: Bl: 0-0 Vi: 0-1 Tstrap: 0-0
Best Rating: 80 5/01 Extr 2m1f firm NHF

Murder Moss (IRE)

99(77h) 99

12-y-o ch g Doulab (USA)-Northern Wind (Northfields (USA))

W S Coltherd S Coltherd

Placings:P/PP/2/4/4PPU041/23/0-20 **(4856)**

2001/02: 25^{2}GF, 25^{0}G

	Starts	1st	2nd	3rd	Win & Pl
Chases	2	0	1	0	724
Career Total	**17**	**1**	**3**	**1**	**5278**

100	5/99	Hexm	3m1f	H Ch	GD	£2641

Total win prize-money £2642

Going: Sf: 0-0 GS: 0-0 Gd: 0-1 GF: - Fm: 0-1
Distance: 2m/2m3: 0-0 2m4-2m7: 0-0 3m+: 0-2
Track: LH: 0-2 RH: 0-0 Tight: 0-0 Gall: 0-0
Aids: Bl: 0-0 Vi: 0-0 Tstrap: 0-0
Best Rating: 100 5/99 Hexm 3m1f good Ch

Moderate chaser. Stays three miles and acts on a sound surface.

Murfs Dilemma (IRE)

88 86

7-y-o ch g Broken Hearted-Lock The Bar (Kambalda)

P Winkworth P Winkworth

Placings:4 **(4684)**

2001/02: 19^{4}GF

	Starts	1st	2nd	3rd	Win & Pl
Hurdles	1	0	0	0	0
Career Total	**1**	**0**	**0**	**0**	**0**

Going: Sf: 0-0 GS: 0-0 Gd: 0-0 GF: - Fm: 0-1
Distance: 2m/2m3: 0-0 2m4-2m7: 0-1 3m+: 0-0
Track: LH: 0-0 RH: 0-1 Tight: 0-0 Gall: 0-0
Aids: Bl: 0-0 Vi: 0-0 Tstrap: 0-0
Best Rating: 86 4/02 Hrfd 2m3f110y gd-fm Hdl

A half-brother to dual Irish bumper winner Hunters Bar. Finished fourth in maiden hurdle at 20/1 on debut.

Murray's Million

102 120

10-y-o b g Macmillion-Random Select (Random Shot)

J S Smith Cotswold Connection

Placings:*000*/P0332220/34**300**231/62**U63P1511**/6334123421-5664 **(2953)**

2001/02: 20^{5}GS, 20^{6}S, 20^{6}GS, 17^{4}S

	Starts	1st	2nd	3rd	Win & Pl
Chases	4	0	0	0	660
Career Total	**43**	**6**	**7**	**9**	**44881**

120	4/01	Winc	2m5f	D(0-120)HCh	SFT	£5213
114	12/00	Donc	2m3f110y	C(0-135)HCh	G-S	£7505
120	4/00	Extr	2m1f110y	D(0-115)HCh	HVY	£4582
117	3/00	Uttx	2m4f	F(0-100)HCh	GD	£3363
106	2/00	Bang	2m1f110y	D(0-110)HCh	G-S	£4121
99	4/99	Wwck	2m4f110y	E(0-100)HHdl	SFT	£2934

Total win prize-money £27722

Going: Sf: 0-2 GS: 0-2 Gd: 0-0 GF: - Fm: 0-0
Distance: 2m/2m3: 0-1 2m4-2m7: 0-3 3m+: 0-0
Track: LH: 0-3 RH: 0-1 Tight: 0-3 Gall: 0-0
Aids: Bl: 0-0 Vi: 0-0 Tstrap: 0-0
Best Rating: 120 4/01 Winc 2m5f soft Ch

Decent handicap chaser at around two and a half miles in minor company.

Murrendi (IRE)

96 90

4-y-o b g Ashkalani (IRE)-Formaestre (IRE) (Formidable (USA))

R J O'Sullivan (M R Channon 15/10) Jack Joseph

Placings:F5 **(3709)**

2001/02: 16^{F}G, 16^{5}HY

	Starts	1st	2nd	3rd	Win & Pl
Hurdles	2	0	0	0	0
Career Total	**2**	**0**	**0**	**0**	**0**

Going: Sf: 0-1 GS: 0-0 Gd: 0-1 GF: - Fm: 0-0
Distance: 2m/2m3: 0-2 2m4-2m7: 0-0 3m+: 0-0
Track: LH: 0-2 RH: 0-0 Tight: 0-2 Gall: 0-0
Aids: Bl: 0-0 Vi: 0-0 Tstrap: 0-0
Best Rating: 90 12/01 Plum 2m good Hdl

Murt's Man (IRE)

112 155

8-y-o b g Be My Native (USA)-Autumn Queen (Menelek)

P F Nicholls Derek Millard

Placings:3F1B/2F21PU-262P21PP **(4913)**

2001/02: 25^{2}G, 24^{6}G, 26^{2}S, 25^{P}GS, 24^{2}S, 26^{1}GS, 36^{P}G, 29^{P}G

	Starts	1st	2nd	3rd	Win & Pl
Chases	8	1	3	0	20336
Career Total	**18**	**3**	**5**	**1**	**36918**

155	3/02	Chep	3m2f110y	B(0-145)HCh	G-S	£10773

145	1/01	Winc	3m1f110y	C(0-135)HCh	SFT	£8307
121	3/00	Donc	3m	E Ch	G-S	£3006

Total win prize-money £22086

Going: Sf: 0-2 GS: 1-2 Gd: 0-4 GF: - Fm: 0-0
Distance: 2m/2m3: 0-0 2m4-2m7: 0-0 **3m+: 1-8**
Track: **LH: 1-4** RH: 0-4 Tight: 0-2 Gall: 0-0
Aids: Bl: 0-1 Vi: 0-0 Tstrap: 0-0
Best Rating: 155 3/02 Chep 3m2f110y gd-sft Ch

A fair staying chaser, although not the most fluent of jumpers. Best at around three miles on soft/heavy ground.

Musally

95 75

5-y-o ch g Muhtarram (USA)-Flourishing (IRE) (Trojan Fen)
W Jenks The Glazeley Partnership

Placings:P0-06F0 **(4847)**
2001/02: 16^{0}GS, 17^{6}S, 16^{F}GF, 20^{0}G

	Starts	1st	2nd	3rd	Win & Pl
Hurdles	4	0	0	0	0
Career Total	**6**	**0**	**0**	**0**	**0**

Going: Sf: 0-1 GS: 0-1 Gd: 0-1 GF: - Fm: 0-1
Distance: 2m/2m3: 0-3 2m4-2m7: 0-1 3m+: 0-0
Track: LH: 0-3 RH: 0-1 Tight: 0-2 Gall: 0-0
Aids: Bl: 0-0 Vi: 0-0 Tstrap: 0-0
Best Rating: 75 3/02 Tntn 2m1f soft Hdl

Musalse

102 94

7-y-o b g Salse (USA)-Musical Sally (USA) (The Minstrel (CAN))
John R Upson K Hancock & P M Haslam

Placings:42/2-2 **(0641)**
2001/02: 24^{2}GF

	Starts	1st	2nd	3rd	Win & Pl
Hurdles	1	0	1	0	747
Career Total	**4**	**0**	**3**	**0**	**2501**

Going: Sf: 0-0 GS: 0-0 Gd: 0-0 GF: - Fm: 0-1
Distance: 2m/2m3: 0-0 2m4-2m7: 0-0 3m+: 0-1
Track: LH: 0-0 RH: 0-1 Tight: 0-1 Gall: 0-0
Aids: Bl: 0-0 Vi: 0-0 Tstrap: 0-0
Best Rating: 95 8/99 Ctml 2m6f good Hdl

Musardo (FR)

(110c) (135c)137

7-y-o b g Grand Tresor (FR)-La Musardiere (FR) (Cadoudal (FR))
J Bertran De Balanda (Miss Venetia Williams 19/5)
J P Raymond

Placings:32/042131P1/2041142/45606-35
2001/02: 20^{3}G, 19^{5}HY

	Starts	1st	2nd	3rd	Win & Pl
Hurdles	1	0	0	0	3725
Chases	1	0	0	1	1336
Career Total	**24**	**5**	**4**	**3**	**166088**

11/99	Engh	2m3f	Hdl	HLD	£32293
10/99	Engh	2m1f110y	Hdl	VS	£23681
4/99	Engh	2m1f	Ch	VS	£12917
12/98	Engh	2m1f110y	Hdl	HLD	£30303
10/98	Engh	1m7f110y	Ch	VS	£12121

Total win prize-money £111315

Going: Sf: 0-1 GS: 0-0 Gd: 0-1 GF: - Fm: 0-0
Distance: 2m/2m3: 0-1 2m4-2m7: 0-1 3m+: 0-0
Track: LH: 0-1 RH: 0-0 Tight: 0-0 Gall: 0-0
Aids: Bl: 0-1 Vi: 0-0 Tstrap: 0-0
Best Rating: 137 11/01 Engh 2m3f heavy Hdl

Muscadin

4-y-o br g Shaamit (IRE)-As Mustard (Keen)
N G Richards James Callow

Placings:*P* **(3613)**
2001/02: 16^{PS}

	Starts	1st	2nd	3rd	Win & Pl
NH Flat	1	0	0	0	
Career Total	**1**	**0**	**0**	**0**	

Going: Sf: 0-1 GS: 0-0 Gd: 0-0 GF: - Fm: 0-0
Distance: 2m/2m3: 0-1 2m4-2m7: 0-0 3m+: 0-0
Track: LH: 0-0 RH: 0-1 Tight: 0-1 Gall: 0-0
Aids: Bl: 0-0 Vi: 0-0 Tstrap: 0-0
Best Rating:

Music Therapy (IRE)

12-y-o b g Roselier (FR)-Suny Salome (Sunyboy)
Ms Polly Stockton C J Stockton

Placings:*0/003/2111/1-U54* **(4055)**
2001/02: 25^{U}HY, 26^{5}S, 23^{4}S

	Starts	1st	2nd	3rd	Win & Pl
Chases	3	0	0	0	390
Career Total	**12**	**4**	**1**	**1**	**12409**

133	3/01	Plum	3m2f	H Ch	HVY	£1302
135	3/98	Newb	3m	D Ch	G-S	£3574
124	3/98	Ling	3m	E Ch	G-S	£3184
124	12/97	Hntg	2m4f110y	E Ch	G-S	£2698

Total win prize-money £10758

Going: Sf: 0-3 GS: 0-0 Gd: 0-0 GF: - Fm: 0-0
Distance: 2m/2m3: 0-0 2m4-2m7: 0-0 3m+: 0-3
Track: LH: 0-0 RH: 0-2 Tight: 0-1 Gall: 0-0
Aids: Bl: 0-0 Vi: 0-0 Tstrap: 0-1
Best Rating: 135 3/98 Newb 3m gd-sft Ch

Musical Mayhem (IRE)

106 115

9-y-o b g Shernazar-Minstrels Folly (USA) (The Minstrel (CAN))
D J Wintle A A Wintle

Placings:*10/122/142/01/1* **(1137)**
2001/02: 22^{1}G

	Starts	1st	2nd	3rd	Win & Pl
Hurdles	1	1	0	0	2310
Career Total	**11**	**5**	**3**	**0**	**19230**

115	8/01	Strf	2m6f110y	F Hdl	GD	£2310
115	9/99	List	2m	Hdl	Y-S	£4312
119	7/98	Gway	2m4f	Hdl	YLD	£3586
113	7/97	Tipp	2m	NHF	GD	£2882
100	2/97	Fair	2m	NHF	G-Y	£3051

Total win prize-money £16144

Going: Sf: 0-0 GS: 0-0 Gd: 1-1 GF: - Fm: 0-0
Distance: 2m/2m3: 0-0 **2m4-2m7: 1-1** 3m+: 0-0
Track: **LH: 1-1** RH: 0-0 **Tight: 1-1** Gall: 0-0
Aids: Bl: 0-0 Vi: 0-0 Tstrap: 0-0
Best Rating: 119 7/98 Gway 2m4f yield Hdl

An effective hurdler at a modest level, he stays well and likes fast ground.

Musical Sling (IRE)

83 64

9-y-o b g Orchestra-Coctail Bid (Mandalus)
P J Hobbs Terry Warner

Placings:311330/**P31PP1/PPP** **(4388)**
2001/02: 27^{PS}, 29^{P}HY, 25^{PS}

	Starts	1st	2nd	3rd	Win & Pl
Chases	3	0	0	0	
Career Total	**15**	**4**	**0**	**4**	**15096**

131	4/00	Winc	3m1f110y	E Ch	G-S	£3815
137	1/00	Towc	3m1f	E Ch	HVY	£3380
105	12/98	Extr	2m1f110y	D Hdl	GD	£3676
112	11/98	Worc	2m4f	E Hdl	HVY	£2547

Total win prize-money £13420

Going: Sf: 0-3 GS: 0-0 Gd: 0-0 GF: - Fm: 0-0
Distance: 2m/2m3: 0-0 2m4-2m7: 0-0 3m+: 0-3
Track: LH: 0-1 RH: 0-2 Tight: 0-1 Gall: 0-0
Aids: Bl: 0-0 Vi: 0-0 Tstrap: 0-0
Best Rating: 137 1/00 Towc 3m1f heavy Ch

Handicap chaser, he acts on a soft surface and stays three miles.

Musical Tassel (IRE)

84 82

8-y-o ch m Orchestra-Tassel Tip (Linacre)
B J Eckley M Jones

Placings:40P/2-0300 **(1042)**
2001/02: 22^{0}G, 17^{3}G, 22^{0}G, 16^{0}GF

	Starts	1st	2nd	3rd	Win & Pl
Hurdles	4	0	0	1	395
Career Total	**8**	**0**	**1**	**1**	**1307**

Going: Sf: 0-0 GS: 0-0 Gd: 0-3 GF: - Fm: 0-1
Distance: 2m/2m3: 0-2 2m4-2m7: 0-2 3m+: 0-0
Track: LH: 0-3 RH: 0-1 Tight: 0-2 Gall: 0-0
Aids: Bl: 0-1 Vi: 0-0 Tstrap: 0-0
Best Rating: 82 4/01 NAbb 2m1f soft Hdl

Musketry

87 79

6-y-o b g Terimon-Mousquetade (Moulton)
N A Graham R E S Greenwood

Placings:F-5 **(0589)**
2001/02: 16^{5}GF

	Starts	1st	2nd	3rd	Win & Pl
Chases	1	0	0	0	0
Career Total	**2**	**0**	**0**	**0**	**0**

Going: Sf: 0-0 GS: 0-0 Gd: 0-0 GF: - Fm: 0-1
Distance: 2m/2m3: 0-1 2m4-2m7: 0-0 3m+: 0-0
Track: LH: 0-1 RH: 0-0 Tight: 0-1 Gall: 0-0
Aids: Bl: 0-0 Vi: 0-0 Tstrap: 0-0
Best Rating: 79 6/01 Fknm 2m110y gd-fm Ch

Mustang Molly

96 100

10-y-o br m Soldier Rose-Little 'N' Game (Convolvulus)
Andrew J Martin (P W Hiatt 6/1) A J Martin

Placings:P5/2P0P (4638)
2001/02: 16^{2}G, 21^{P}GF, 16^{0}S, 19^{P}GF

	Starts	1st	2nd	3rd	Win & Pl
Chases	4	0	1	0	908
Career Total	**6**	**0**	**1**	**0**	**908**

Going: Sf: 0-1 GS: 0-0 Gd: 0-1 GF: - Fm: 0-2
Distance: 2m/2m3: 0-2 2m4-2m7: 0-2 3m+: 0-0
Track: LH: 0-1 RH: 0-2 Tight: 0-1 Gall: 0-0
Aids: Bl: 0-0 Vi: 0-0 Tstrap: 0-0
Best Rating: 100 5/01 Chel 2m110y good Ch

Mutadarra (IRE)

102(93c) (84c)96
9-y-o ch g Mujtahid (USA)-Silver Echo (Caerleon (USA))
J W Mullins (G M McCourt 25/10) M S Green

Placings:014/634-310454300P (3605)
2001/02: 16^{3}GS, 16^{1}GF, 16^{0}GF, 16^{4}G, 16^{5}GF, 16^{4}GF, 19^{3}G, 22^{0}G, 16^{0}S, 22^{P}HY

	Starts	1st	2nd	3rd	Win & Pl
Hurdles	8	1	0	2	2572
Chases	2	0	0	0	264
Career Total	**16**	**2**	**0**	**3**	**5987**

86 8/01 Worc 2m G Hdl G-F £1591
97 3/00 Hntg 2m110y E Hdl G-F £2870
Total win prize-money £4462

Going: Sf: 0-2 GS: 0-1 Gd: 0-3 GF: - Fm: 1-4
Distance: 2m/2m3: 1-7 2m4-2m7: 0-3 3m+: 0-0
Track: LH: 1-4 RH: 0-4 Tight: 0-4 Gall: 0-0
Aids: Bl: 0-0 Vi: 0-0 Tstrap: 0-0
Best Rating: 97 10/00 Hrfd 2m3f110y good Hdl

Plating class over hurdles. Stays 22 furlongs on fast ground.

Mutakarrim

95 128
5-y-o ch g Mujtahid (USA)-Alyakkh (IRE) (Sadler's Wells (USA))
D K Weld Dr Michael Smurfit

Placings:030 (4188)
2001/02: 16^{0}S, 16^{3}HY, 16^{0}GS

	Starts	1st	2nd	3rd	Win & Pl
Hurdles	3	0	0	1	752
Career Total	**3**	**0**	**0**	**1**	**752**

Going: Sf: 0-2 GS: 0-1 Gd: 0-0 GF: - Fm: 0-0
Distance: 2m/2m3: 0-3 2m4-2m7: 0-0 3m+: 0-0
Track: LH: 0-2 RH: 0-0 Tight: 0-0 Gall: 0-0
Aids: Bl: 0-1 Vi: 0-0 Tstrap: 0-0
Best Rating: 117 2/02 Gowr 2m soft Hdl

Listed class middle-distance horse on the Flat. Showed promise in a Grade Two on hurdles debut. A little disappointing when favourite next time. Acts on any ground.

Mutasarrif (IRE)

88(92c) (95c)63
9-y-o b g Polish Patriot (USA)-Bouffant (High Top)
G F White F V White

Placings:550/130015F0/3400F43F/53PF60 (4872)
2001/02: 16^{5}G, 16^{3}G, 17^{P}G, 16^{F}GF, 16^{6}G, 16^{0}GF

	Starts	1st	2nd	3rd	Win & Pl
Chases	6	0	0	1	517
Career Total	**25**	**2**	**0**	**4**	**8233**

107 2/99 Sedg 2m1f F(0-100)HHdl GD £2635
103 5/98 Ctml 2m1f110y D Hdl G-F £2944
Total win prize-money £5579

Going: Sf: 0-0 GS: 0-0 Gd: 0-4 GF: - Fm: 0-2
Distance: 2m/2m3: 0-6 2m4-2m7: 0-0 3m+: 0-0
Track: LH: 0-5 RH: 0-1 Tight: 0-4 Gall: 0-0
Aids: Bl: 0-0 Vi: 0-0 Tstrap: 0-5
Best Rating: 107 2/99 Sedg 2m1f good Hdl

Muted Gift

75 32
4-y-o ch f King's Signet (USA)-Ballet On Ice (FR) (Fijar Tango (FR))
W G M Turner Darren Coombes

Placings:0600 (4021)
2001/02: 16^{0}HY, 16^{6}HY, 16^{0}HY, 16^{0}S

	Starts	1st	2nd	3rd	Win & Pl
Hurdles	4	0	0	0	0
Career Total	**4**	**0**	**0**	**0**	**0**

Going: Sf: 0-4 GS: 0-0 Gd: 0-0 GF: - Fm: 0-0
Distance: 2m/2m3: 0-4 2m4-2m7: 0-0 3m+: 0-0
Track: LH: 0-3 RH: 0-1 Tight: 0-1 Gall: 0-1
Aids: Bl: 0-0 Vi: 0-0 Tstrap: 0-0
Best Rating: 32 2/02 Plum 2m heavy Hdl

My Ace

106f 93f
4-y-o b f Definite Article-Miss Springtime (Bluebird (USA))
Mrs H Dalton R L Burrows

Placings:3 (4873)
2001/02: 16^{3}GF

	Starts	1st	2nd	3rd	Win & Pl
NH Flat	1	0	0	1	277
Career Total	**1**	**0**	**0**	**1**	**277**

Going: Sf: 0-0 GS: 0-0 Gd: 0-0 GF: - Fm: 0-1
Distance: 2m/2m3: 0-1 2m4-2m7: 0-0 3m+: 0-0
Track: LH: 0-1 RH: 0-0 Tight: 0-0 Gall: 0-0
Aids: Bl: 0-0 Vi: 0-0 Tstrap: 0-0
Best Rating: 93 4/02 Weth 2m gd-fm NHF

Has shown form in bumpers.

My Baron

6-y-o gr g Baron Blakeney-Redfields Swallow (Cragador)
B G Powell Mrs S E Watts

Placings:5PP (3148)
2001/02: 21^{5}G, 21^{P}G, 22^{P}G

	Starts	1st	2nd	3rd	Win & Pl
Hurdles	3	0	0	0	0
Career Total	**3**	**0**	**0**	**0**	**0**

Going: Sf: 0-0 GS: 0-0 Gd: 0-3 GF: - Fm: 0-0
Distance: 2m/2m3: 0-0 2m4-2m7: 0-3 3m+: 0-0
Track: LH: 0-3 RH: 0-0 Tight: 0-3 Gall: 0-0
Aids: Bl: 0-0 Vi: 0-0 Tstrap: 0-0
Best Rating:

My Baton

105(102h) 116
7-y-o ch g Orchestra-Laurello (Bargello)
P Beaumont Trevor Hemmings

Placings:2102/1362P6-P42222 (4878)
2001/02: 22^{P}GS, 24^{4}GS, 23^{2}GS, 20^{2}S, 26^{2}GF, 24^{2}G

	Starts	1st	2nd	3rd	Win & Pl
Chases	6	0	4	0	6713
Career Total	**16**	**2**	**7**	**1**	**15193**

102 11/00 Hayd 2m4f D Hdl SFT £3510
116 2/00 Hayd 2m H NHF SFT £2102
Total win prize-money £5613

Going: Sf: 0-1 GS: 0-3 Gd: 0-1 GF: - Fm: 0-1
Distance: 2m/2m3: 0-0 2m4-2m7: 0-2 3m+: 0-4
Track: LH: 0-1 RH: 0-4 Tight: 0-2 Gall: 0-1
Aids: Bl: 0-0 Vi: 0-0 Tstrap: 0-0
Best Rating: 138 4/00 Ayr 2m good NHF

Fair chaser, stays three miles plus, acts on any ground

My Best Man

15-y-o br g True Song-Eventime (Hot Brandy)
Mrs T J Hill Alan Hill

Placings:0/22/43643 (4111)
2001/02: 20^{4}GF, 21^{3}G, 25^{6}G, 31^{4}GS, 25^{3}S

	Starts	1st	2nd	3rd	Win & Pl
Chases	5	0	0	2	540
Career Total	**8**	**0**	**2**	**2**	**1137**

Going: Sf: 0-1 GS: 0-1 Gd: 0-2 GF: - Fm: 0-1
Distance: 2m/2m3: 0-0 2m4-2m7: 0-2 3m+: 0-3
Track: LH: 0-1 RH: 0-0 Tight: 0-1 Gall: 0-0
Aids: Bl: 0-5 Vi: 0-0 Tstrap: 0-0
Best Rating: 93 3/02 Towc 3m1f soft Ch

Modest veteran pointer/hunter chaser, suited by cut in the ground.

My Bold Boyo

102 93
7-y-o b g Never So Bold-My Rosie (Forzando)
K Bishop E T Roberts

Placings:3006P511 (4866)
2001/02: 17^{3}GF, 17^{0}G, 16^{0}S, 16^{6}GF, 19^{P}GS, 16^{5}G, 17^{1}F, 17^{1}F

	Starts	1st	2nd	3rd	Win & Pl
Hurdles	8	2	0	1	6219
Career Total	**8**	**2**	**0**	**1**	**6219**

93 4/02 Extr 2m1f E(0-105)HHdl FRM £2954
82 4/02 Extr 2m1f F(0-100)HHdl FRM £2870
Total win prize-money £5824

Going: Sf: 0-1 GS: 0-1 Gd: 0-2 GF: - Fm: 2-4
Distance: 2m/2m3: 2-8 2m4-2m7: 0-0 3m+: 0-0
Track: LH: 0-1 RH: 2-7 Tight: 0-0 Gall: 0-0
Aids: Bl: 0-0 Vi: 0-0 Tstrap: 0-0
Best Rating: 93 4/02 Extr 2m1f firm Hdl

A winner on the Flat, had shown promise over hurdles before scoring back to back victories at Exeter in April 2002. Suited by fast ground.

My Brighteye Deer

43
7-y-o b m Presidium-Brig's Gazelle (Lord Nelson (FR))
I Park Mrs C Park

Placings:0/PP06P (4857)
2001/02: 21^{P}HY, 20^{P}GS, 16^{0}HY, 17^{6}GF, 20^{P}G

	Starts	1st	2nd	3rd	Win & Pl
Hurdles	5	0	0	0	0
Career Total	**6**	**0**	**0**	**0**	**0**

Going: Sf: 0-2 GS: 0-1 Gd: 0-1 GF: - Fm: 0-1
Distance: 2m/2m3: 0-2 2m4-2m7: 0-3 3m+: 0-0
Track: LH: 0-5 RH: 0-0 Tight: 0-2 Gall: 0-2
Aids: Bl: 0-0 Vi: 0-0 Tstrap: 0-0
Best Rating: 43 4/02 Sedg 2m1f gd-fm Hdl

My Buster

87 **78**

10-y-o ch g Move Off-Young Lamb (Sea Hawk II)
Miss Kate Milligan Mrs J M L Milligan

Placings:244/0/400/636/PP2P-2 **(0551)**
2001/02: 24^{2}GF

	Starts	1st	2nd	3rd	Win & Pl
Chases	1	0	1	0	884
Career Total	**15**	**0**	**3**	**1**	**2404**

Going: Sf: 0-0 GS: 0-0 Gd: 0-0 GF: - Fm: 0-1
Distance: 2m/2m3: 0-0 2m4-2m7: 0-0 3m+: 0-1
Track: LH: 0-1 RH: 0-0 Tight: 0-0 Gall: 0-1
Aids: Bl: 0-0 Vi: 0-1 Tstrap: 0-0
Best Rating: 104 3/96 Donc 2m110y good NHF

My Cheeky Man

11-y-o ch g Cisto (FR)-Regal Flutter (Henry The Seventh)
A King Mrs A A Shutes

Placings:360/111/U0/300305P/000-P **(0269)**
2001/02: 19^{P}G

	Starts	1st	2nd	3rd	Win & Pl
Hurdles	1	0	0	0	
Career Total	**19**	**3**	**0**	**3**	**11077**

121 3/97 MRas 2m3f110y D(0-120)HHdl G-F £3043
125 2/97 MRas 2m1f110y D Hdl GD £3300
99 2/97 Towc 2m E Hdl SFT £1976
Total win prize-money £8320

Going: Sf: 0-0 GS: 0-0 Gd: 0-1 GF: - Fm: 0-0
Distance: 2m/2m3: 0-0 2m4-2m7: 0-1 3m+: 0-0
Track: LH: 0-0 RH: 0-1 Tight: 0-0 Gall: 0-0
Aids: Bl: 0-1 Vi: 0-0 Tstrap: 0-0
Best Rating: 125 2/97 MRas 2m1f110y good Hdl

My Dilemma

90 **80**

6-y-o b m Pursuit Of Love-Butosky (Busted)
J A Gilbert C L Jennison, M D Bromley, N S A Dragone

Placings:032PP0/0/5UP **(1666)**
2001/02: 16^{5}GF, 16^{U}GS, 16^{P}G

	Starts	1st	2nd	3rd	Win & Pl
Chases	3	0	0	0	0
Career Total	**9**	**0**	**1**	**1**	**935**

Going: Sf: 0-0 GS: 0-1 Gd: 0-1 GF: - Fm: 0-1
Distance: 2m/2m3: 0-3 2m4-2m7: 0-0 3m+: 0-0
Track: LH: 0-2 RH: 0-1 Tight: 0-1 Gall: 0-1
Aids: Bl: 0-0 Vi: 0-0 Tstrap: 0-0
Best Rating: 80 8/01 Hntg 2m110y gd-fm Ch

My Flyer (IRE)

66(62c) (22c)

8-y-o b g Castle Keep-Pampered Finch Vii (Damsire Unregistered)
J S King Mrs P M King

Placings:0/0U45F-00 **(2211)**
2001/02: 17^{0}GS, 19^{0}G

	Starts	1st	2nd	3rd	Win & Pl
Hurdles	1	0	0	0	0
Chases	1	0	0	0	0
Career Total	**8**	**0**	**0**	**0**	**0**

Going: Sf: 0-0 GS: 0-1 Gd: 0-1 GF: - Fm: 0-0
Distance: 2m/2m3: 0-1 2m4-2m7: 0-1 3m+: 0-0
Track: LH: 0-0 RH: 0-2 Tight: 0-0 Gall: 0-0
Aids: Bl: 0-0 Vi: 0-0 Tstrap: 0-0
Best Rating: 65 12/00 Extr 2m1f heavy Hdl

My Friend Billy (IRE)

10-y-o ch g Yashgan-Super Boreen (Boreen (FR))
Mrs N S Sharpe B Owen

Placings:0PP0FP/P **(3642)**
2001/02: 24^{P}GS

	Starts	1st	2nd	3rd	Win & Pl
Chases	1	0	0	0	
Career Total	**7**	**0**	**0**	**0**	

Going: Sf: 0-0 GS: 0-1 Gd: 0-0 GF: - Fm: 0-0
Distance: 2m/2m3: 0-0 2m4-2m7: 0-0 3m+: 0-1
Track: LH: 0-0 RH: 0-1 Tight: 0-1 Gall: 0-0
Aids: Bl: 0-0 Vi: 0-0 Tstrap: 0-0
Best Rating: 47 5/97 Wwck 2m good NHF

My Galliano (IRE)

97(107h) (98h)**104**

6-y-o b g Muharib (USA)-Hogan Stand (Buckskin (FR))
B G Powell L Gilbert

Placings:00/0452125-U60FP31425 **(4660)**
2001/02: 17^{U}GF, 16^{6}G, 16^{0}GF, 16^{F}G, 16^{P}GS, 16^{3}G, 16^{1}GF, 16^{4}G, 16^{2}G, 17^{5}G

	Starts	1st	2nd	3rd	Win & Pl
Hurdles	8	1	1	1	5589
Chases	2	0	0	0	0
Career Total	**19**	**2**	**3**	**1**	**10532**

98 11/01 Winc 2m E(0-115)HHdl G-F £3523
94 11/00 Kemp 2m F(0-100)HHdl SFT £2756
Total win prize-money £6279

Going: Sf: 0-0 GS: 0-1 Gd: 0-6 GF: - Fm: 1-3
Distance: **2m/2m3: 1-10** 2m4-2m7: 0-0 3m+: 0-0
Track: LH: 0-2 **RH: 1-8** Tight: 0-2 Gall: 0-1
Aids: Bl: 0-0 Vi: 0-0 Tstrap: 0-0
Best Rating: 104 10/01 Hrfd 2m good Ch

A fair handicapper at around two miles, he is effective on any ground. Fell on his chasing debut, but should be given another chance.

My Godson

52

12-y-o br g Valiyar-Blessit (So Blessed)
F Watson F Watson

Placings:0006/0/B-0P **(4898)**
2001/02: 17^{0}G, 16^{P}G

	Starts	1st	2nd	3rd	Win & Pl
Hurdles	2	0	0	0	
Career Total	**8**	**0**	**0**	**0**	**0**

Going: Sf: 0-0 GS: 0-0 Gd: 0-2 GF: - Fm: 0-0
Distance: 2m/2m3: 0-2 2m4-2m7: 0-0 3m+: 0-0
Track: LH: 0-0 RH: 0-2 Tight: 0-1 Gall: 0-0
Aids: Bl: 0-0 Vi: 0-0 Tstrap: 0-0
Best Rating: 60 11/97 Catt 2m good Hdl

My Good Son (NZ)

109(104c) (110c)**91**

7-y-o b g The Son (NZ)-Meadow Hall (NZ) (Pikehall (USA))
Ian Williams (S A Brookshaw 5/8) Men Behaving Sadly Partnership

Placings:4003210/010P-U0P650P1F1 **(4920)**
2001/02: 24^{U}GF, 20^{0}G, 20^{P}G, 17^{6}YS, 22^{5}GY, 25^{0}S, 24^{P}GS, 26^{1}GF, 24^{F}GF, 21^{1}GF

	Starts	1st	2nd	3rd	Win & Pl
Hurdles	2	0	0	0	0
Chases	8	2	0	0	6904
Career Total	**21**	**4**	**1**	**1**	**15553**

110 4/02 Sedg 2m5f D(0-120)HCh G-F £4075
110 4/02 Plum 3m2f F(0-90)HCh G-F £2828
103 2/01 Hayd 2m4f D(0-120)HHdl HVY £3552
99 3/00 Ludl 2m5f E Hdl GD £2899
Total win prize-money £13356

Going: Sf: 0-1 GS: 0-1 Gd: 0-2 GF: - Fm: 2-4
Distance: 2m/2m3: 0-1 2m4-2m7: 1-4 3m+: 1-5
Track: **LH: 1-3** RH: 0-3 **Tight: 1-5** Gall: 0-0
Aids: **Bl: 2-6** Vi: 0-0 Tstrap: 0-1
Best Rating: 110 4/02 Sedg 2m5f gd-fm Ch

Moderate hurdler/chaser, handles heavy ground but prefers faster. Stays two and a half miles.

My Legal Eagle (IRE)

106 **103**

8-y-o b g Law Society (USA)-Majestic Nurse (On Your Mark)
R J Price E G Bevan

Placings:420/6/5P06 **(2653)**
2001/02: 16^{5}G, 16^{P}G, 20^{0}GS, 16^{6}G

	Starts	1st	2nd	3rd	Win & Pl
Hurdles	4	0	0	0	0
Career Total	**8**	**0**	**1**	**0**	**719**

Going: Sf: 0-0 GS: 0-1 Gd: 0-3 GF: - Fm: 0-0
Distance: 2m/2m3: 0-3 2m4-2m7: 0-1 3m+: 0-0
Track: LH: 0-2 RH: 0-2 Tight: 0-1 Gall: 0-0
Aids: Bl: 0-0 Vi: 0-0 Tstrap: 0-0
Best Rating: 97 10/98 Chep 2m110y good Hdl

Handicap hurdler. Effective at around two miles and acts on most types of ground.

My Line

97 **89**

5-y-o b g Perpendicular-My Desire (Grey Desire)
Mrs M Reveley J And A Spensley

Placings:0 **(2399)**
2001/02: 16^{0}G

	Starts	1st	2nd	3rd	Win & Pl
Hurdles	1	0	0	0	

	Starts	1st	2nd	3rd	Win & Pl
Career Total	1	0	0	0	

Going: Sf: 0-0 GS: 0-0 Gd: 0-1 GF: - Fm: 0-0
Distance: 2m/2m3: 0-1 2m4-2m7: 0-0 3m+: 0-0
Track: LH: 0-1 RH: 0-0 Tight: 0-0 Gall: 0-0
Aids: Bl: 0-0 Vi: 0-0 Tstrap: 0-0
Best Rating: 89 11/01 Weth 2m good Hdl

My Man Dan (IRE)

98 **110**

9-y-o b g Phardante (FR)-Arctic Tartan (Deep Run)
B De Haan Flora Charlie Limited

Placings:*4021/166/02* **(3891)**
2001/02: 22^{0}G, 20^{2}HY

	Starts	1st	2nd	3rd	Win & Pl
Chases	2	0	1	0	1252
Career Total	**9**	**2**	**2**	**0**	**6838**

105	5/99	Weth	2m	E Hdl	G-F	£2460
111	4/99	Winc	2m	E Hdl	GD	£2542

Total win prize-money £5002

Going: Sf: 0-1 GS: 0-0 Gd: 0-1 GF: - Fm: 0-0
Distance: 2m/2m3: 0-0 2m4-2m7: 0-2 3m+: 0-0
Track: LH: 0-2 RH: 0-0 Tight: 0-0 Gall: 0-1
Aids: Bl: 0-0 Vi: 0-0 Tstrap: 0-0
Best Rating: 111 4/99 Winc 2m good Hdl

He returned from over two years off the track in December 2001 at Newbury, but was well beaten. Decent effort next time. Acts on a sound surface and is effective over two miles.

My Native Land (IRE)

98 **101**

7-y-o b g Be My Native (USA)-Papukeena (Simbir)
Miss T M Ide (F Flood 21/11) Miss Tracey Ide

Placings:60-*6523000204* **(3459)**
2001/02: 16^{6}GF, 17^{5}F, 16^{2}S, 20^{3}SH, 20^{0}F, 16^{0}Y, 16^{0}YS, 22^{2}S, 22^{0}G, 21^{4}HY

	Starts	1st	2nd	3rd	Win & Pl
NH Flat	3	0	0	0	0
Hurdles	7	0	2	1	2363
Career Total	**12**	**0**	**2**	**1**	**2363**

Going: Sf: 0-3 GS: 0-0 Gd: 0-1 GF: - Fm: 0-3
Distance: 2m/2m3: 0-5 2m4-2m7: 0-5 3m+: 0-0
Track: LH: 0-1 RH: 0-2 Tight: 0-0 Gall: 0-0
Aids: Bl: 0-0 Vi: 0-0 Tstrap: 0-0
Best Rating: 101 8/01 Slig 2m4f sft-hvy Hdl

My Shenandoah (IRE)

112 **123**

11-y-o br g Derrylin-Edwina's Dawn (Space King)
J Howard Johnson Gordon Brown/bert Watson

Placings:*60060U/O311216/35U2653/660115-5553012* **(4893)**
2001/02: 16^{5}G, 17^{5}HY, 24^{5}G, 20^{3}S, 16^{0}S, 21^{1}GS, 20^{2}G

	Starts	1st	2nd	3rd	Win & Pl
Hurdles	7	1	1	1	6177
Career Total	**33**	**6**	**3**	**4**	**25297**

116	3/02	MRas	2m5f110y	D(0-115)HHdl	G-S	£3445
113	4/01	Muss	2m4f	D(0-120)HHdl	G-F	£4355
104	3/01	MRas	2m5f110y	E(0-115)HHdl	GD	£2604
108	2/98	Muss	2m4f	E(0-115)HHdl	GD	£2895
104	1/98	Muss	2m4f	E(0-100)HHdl	G-S	£2696
93	12/97	Muss	2m4f	E(0-100)HHdl	GD	£2724

Total win prize-money £18719

Going: Sf: 0-3 GS: 1-1 Gd: 0-3 GF: - Fm: 0-0
Distance: 2m/2m3: 0-3 **2m4-2m7: 1-3** 3m+: 0-1
Track: LH: 0-1 **RH: 1-5 Tight: 1-4** Gall: 0-0
Aids: Bl: 0-0 Vi: 0-0 Tstrap: 0-0
Best Rating: 123 4/02 Prth 2m4f110y good Hdl

Decent handicap hurdler, he is best at around two and a half miles on a sound surface. He has shown good form at Musselburgh and won the same race at Market Rasen in consecutive seasons. Much best on a right-handed track and needs decent ground.

My Shout

10-y-o b g Nicholas Bill-Ruth's River (Young Man (FR))
Mrs Caroline Bailey Mrs D P G Flory

Placings:22P/2-2 **(0254)**
2001/02: 24^{2}GF

	Starts	1st	2nd	3rd	Win & Pl
Chases	1	0	1	0	586
Career Total	**5**	**0**	**4**	**0**	**2251**

Going: Sf: 0-0 GS: 0-0 Gd: 0-0 GF: - Fm: 0-1
Distance: 2m/2m3: 0-0 2m4-2m7: 0-0 3m+: 0-1
Track: LH: 0-1 RH: 0-0 Tight: 0-1 Gall: 0-0
Aids: Bl: 0-0 Vi: 0-0 Tstrap: 0-0
Best Rating: 103 3/00 Leic 2m4f110y gd-sft Ch

My Sweet Lord (IRE)

74(82h) (4h)**61**

8-y-o b g Bustomi-The Red Mare (Sagaro)
Mrs M Reveley Jemm Partnership

Placings:*4000000-00* **(0204)**
2001/02: 21^{0}G, 20^{0}G

	Starts	1st	2nd	3rd	Win & Pl
Chases	2	0	0	0	
Career Total	**9**	**0**	**0**	**0**	**0**

Going: Sf: 0-0 GS: 0-0 Gd: 0-2 GF: - Fm: 0-0
Distance: 2m/2m3: 0-0 2m4-2m7: 0-2 3m+: 0-0
Track: LH: 0-2 RH: 0-0 Tight: 0-1 Gall: 0-0
Aids: Bl: 0-0 Vi: 0-0 Tstrap: 0-0
Best Rating: 97 10/00 Sedg 2m1f gd-sft NHF

My Tern (IRE)

95 **100**

8-y-o b m Glacial Storm (USA)-My Duchess (Duky)
L Wells P Dutton, F Ford, D Sillwood

Placings:*25/F610010/430-P4* **(2464)**
2001/02: 25^{P}S, 22^{4}HY

	Starts	1st	2nd	3rd	Win & Pl
Hurdles	2	0	0	0	0
Career Total	**14**	**2**	**1**	**1**	**5781**

100	3/99	Plum	2m4f	F(0-105)HHdl	HVY	£2372
95	12/98	Winc	2m	E Hdl	SFT	£2346

Total win prize-money £4719

Going: Sf: 0-2 GS: 0-0 Gd: 0-0 GF: - Fm: 0-0
Distance: 2m/2m3: 0-0 2m4-2m7: 0-1 3m+: 0-1
Track: LH: 0-0 RH: 0-1 Tight: 0-1 Gall: 0-0
Aids: Bl: 0-0 Vi: 0-0 Tstrap: 0-0
Best Rating: 100 4/01 Newb 2m3f soft Hdl

She has managed to win small races at Wincanton and Plumpton this term, but has been found out in better company. Suited by soft ground.

My Very Own (IRE)

89 **88**

4-y-o ch g Persian Bold-Cossack Princess (IRE) (Lomond (USA))
K C Bailey (N P Littmoden 5/11) Mrs Gillian Curley

Placings:0 **(3882)**
2001/02: 16^{0}GS

	Starts	1st	2nd	3rd	Win & Pl
Hurdles	1	0	0	0	
Career Total	**1**	**0**	**0**	**0**	

Going: Sf: 0-0 GS: 0-1 Gd: 0-0 GF: - Fm: 0-0
Distance: 2m/2m3: 0-1 2m4-2m7: 0-0 3m+: 0-0
Track: LH: 0-0 RH: 0-1 Tight: 0-0 Gall: 0-0
Aids: Bl: 0-0 Vi: 0-0 Tstrap: 0-0
Best Rating: 45 2/02 Winc 2m gd-sft Hdl

Mydante (IRE)

110 **116**

7-y-o b m Phardante (FR)-Carminda (Proverb)
J S Moore Ernie Houghton

Placings:*340/310366433/505142-1260243354310* **(4822)**
2001/02: 24^{1}G, 27^{2}G, 22^{6}GF, 21^{0}YS, 24^{2}G, 24^{4}S, 24^{3}GF, 22^{4}GS, 24^{5}S, 21^{4}HY, 24^{3}GS, 24^{1}GF, 21^{0}G

	Starts	1st	2nd	3rd	Win & Pl
Hurdles	13	2	2	3	13921
Career Total	**31**	**4**	**3**	**8**	**37218**

116	4/02	Uttx	3m110y	D(0-125)HHdl	G-F	£4329
111	5/01	Extr	3m110y	C(0-135)HHdl	GD	£5664
99	4/01	Newb	3m110y	F(0-100)HHdl	SFT	£3461
91	10/99	Navn	2m2f	Hdl	Y-S	£13258

Total win prize-money £26714

Going: Sf: 0-3 GS: 0-2 Gd: 1-4 GF: - Fm: 1-3
Distance: 2m/2m3: 0-0 2m4-2m7: 0-5 **3m+: 2-8**
Track: LH: 1-8 RH: 1-4 Tight: 0-5 Gall: 0-1
Aids: Bl: 0-0 Vi: 0-1 Tstrap: 0-0
Best Rating: 116 4/02 Uttx 3m110y gd-fm Hdl

Took advantage of the Handicapper's leniency when easy winner of uncompetitive fast-ground three-mile handicap hurdle at Uttoxeter in April 2002. Stays well.

Mylo

102 **91**

4-y-o gr g Faustus (USA)-Bellifontaine (FR) (Bellypha)
J J O'Neill D J Deer

Placings:2 **(3883)**
2001/02: 16^{2}GS

	Starts	1st	2nd	3rd	Win & Pl
NH Flat	1	0	1	0	488
Career Total	**1**	**0**	**1**	**0**	**488**

Going: Sf: 0-0 GS: 0-1 Gd: 0-0 GF: - Fm: 0-0
Distance: 2m/2m3: 0-1 2m4-2m7: 0-0 3m+: 0-0
Track: LH: 0-0 RH: 0-1 Tight: 0-0 Gall: 0-0
Aids: Bl: 0-0 Vi: 0-0 Tstrap: 0-0
Best Rating: 95 2/02 Winc 2m gd-sft NHF

Runner-up in all three starts in bumpers.

Mystere (IRE)

92 **141**

9-y-o b m Montelimar (USA)-Fine Gale (Strong Gale)
Miss Venetia Williams Mrs Christine Davies

Placings:_05_/14/**3413/0-1** **(3288)**
2001/02: 25^{1}S

	Starts	1st	2nd	3rd	Win & Pl
Chases	1	1	0	0	6841
Career Total	**10**	**3**	**0**	**2**	**15287**

141 1/02 Folk 3m1f E(0-110)HCh SFT £6841
125 2/00 Towc 2m6f D Ch SFT £4069
120 11/98 Uttx 2m6f110y E Hdl SFT £2536
Total win prize-money £13447

Going: Sf: 1-1 GS: 0-0 Gd: 0-0 GF: - Fm: 0-0
Distance: 2m/2m3: 0-0 2m4-2m7: 0-0 **3m+: 1-1**
Track: LH: 0-0 **RH: 1-1 Tight: 1-1** Gall: 0-0
Aids: Bl: 0-0 Vi: 0-0 Tstrap: 0-0
Best Rating: 141 1/02 Folk 3m1f soft Ch

Suited by soft ground. Won her first start for Venetia Williams at Folkestone in January 2002. Stays at least three miles. Acts on an easy surface. Has had problems.

Mystic Hill

93 **71**

11-y-o b g Shirley Heights-Nuryana (Nureyev (USA))
J Joseph Jack Joseph

Placings:044121/4363031/212240/6/0-P06000 **(4035)**
2001/02: 22^{P}S, 20^{0}S, 22^{6}GS, 19^{0}G, 21^{0}GS, 22^{0}S

	Starts	1st	2nd	3rd	Win & Pl
Hurdles	6	0	0	0	0
Career Total	**27**	**4**	**4**	**3**	**14282**

114 6/98 NAbb 2m6f D(0-120)HHdl GD £2775
94 3/98 NAbb 2m1f F(0-100)HHdl SFT £1827
94 4/97 Extr 2m3f110y E(0-110)HHdl G-F £2528
77 4/97 Tntn 2m1f F Hdl FRM £2039
Total win prize-money £9171

Going: Sf: 0-3 GS: 0-2 Gd: 0-1 GF: - Fm: 0-0
Distance: 2m/2m3: 0-1 2m4-2m7: 0-5 3m+: 0-0
Track: LH: 0-5 RH: 0-1 Tight: 0-3 Gall: 0-1
Aids: Bl: 0-0 Vi: 0-0 Tstrap: 0-0
Best Rating: 114 6/98 NAbb 2m6f good Hdl

Mystic Major

10-y-o b g Wace (USA)-Mystic Mintet (King Log)
Mrs I Hughes E R Hughes

Placings:F **(4645)**
2001/02: 24^{F}G

	Starts	1st	2nd	3rd	Win & Pl
Chases	1	0	0	0	
Career Total	**1**	**0**	**0**	**0**	

Going: Sf: 0-0 GS: 0-0 Gd: 0-1 GF: - Fm: 0-0
Distance: 2m/2m3: 0-0 2m4-2m7: 0-0 3m+: 0-1
Track: LH: 0-0 RH: 0-1 Tight: 0-1 Gall: 0-0
Aids: Bl: 0-0 Vi: 0-0 Tstrap: 0-0
Best Rating:

Mystic Ridge

97(83h) **95**

8-y-o ch g Mystiko (USA)-Vallauris (Faustus (USA))
R Lee Osborne House Limited

Placings:P000/0-63 **(0420)**
2001/02: 17^{6}GS, 17^{3}G

	Starts	1st	2nd	3rd	Win & Pl
Chases	2	0	0	1	498
Career Total	**7**	**0**	**0**	**1**	**498**

Going: Sf: 0-0 GS: 0-1 Gd: 0-1 GF: - Fm: 0-0
Distance: 2m/2m3: 0-2 2m4-2m7: 0-0 3m+: 0-0
Track: LH: 0-2 RH: 0-0 Tight: 0-2 Gall: 0-0
Aids: Bl: 0-0 Vi: 0-0 Tstrap: 0-0
Best Rating: 95 5/01 Bang 2m1f110y good Ch

Mystic-Gem

6-y-o ch g Mystiko (USA)-Ela-Yianni-Mou (Anfield)
Jedd O'Keeffe Mrs H E Aitkin

Placings:_0_/P **(4774)**
2001/02: 17^{P}G

	Starts	1st	2nd	3rd	Win & Pl
Hurdles	1	0	0	0	
Career Total	**2**	**0**	**0**	**0**	

Going: Sf: 0-0 GS: 0-0 Gd: 0-1 GF: - Fm: 0-0
Distance: 2m/2m3: 0-1 2m4-2m7: 0-0 3m+: 0-0
Track: LH: 0-0 RH: 0-1 Tight: 0-1 Gall: 0-0
Aids: Bl: 0-0 Vi: 0-0 Tstrap: 0-0
Best Rating:

Mytimie (IRE)

104 **111**

7-y-o b g Be My Native (USA)-Snoqualmie (Warpath)
J M Jefferson Mr & Mrs Raymond Anderson Green

Placings:_134_/260-P13222P **(4689)**
2001/02: 16^{P}G, 16^{1}GS, 16^{3}G, 22^{2}GS, 20^{2}S, 18^{2}HY, 16^{P}GF

	Starts	1st	2nd	3rd	Win & Pl
Hurdles	7	1	3	1	9639
Career Total	**13**	**2**	**4**	**2**	**12995**

104 10/01 Kels 2m110y E Hdl G-S £2439
114 11/99 Carl 2m1f H NHF SFT £1658
Total win prize-money £4098

Going: Sf: 0-2 GS: 1-2 Gd: 0-2 GF: - Fm: 0-1
Distance: **2m/2m3: 1-5** 2m4-2m7: 0-2 3m+: 0-0
Track: **LH: 1-7** RH: 0-0 **Tight: 1-4** Gall: 0-1
Aids: Bl: 0-0 Vi: 0-0 Tstrap: 0-0
Best Rating: 114 11/99 Carl 2m1f soft NHF

Novice hurdler, appreciates cut in the ground and is probably best at up to two and a half miles.

Mytton's Moment (IRE)

73 **36**

6-y-o b g Waajib-Late Swallow (My Swallow)
A Bailey Gordon Mytton

Placings:3122104/5-0 **(0419)**
2001/02: 20^{0}G

	Starts	1st	2nd	3rd	Win & Pl
Hurdles	1	0	0	0	
Career Total	**9**	**2**	**2**	**1**	**7413**

102 11/99 Uttx 2m E Hdl G-S £2603
83 9/99 Kels 2m110y E Hdl G-F £2192
Total win prize-money £4795

Going: Sf: 0-0 GS: 0-0 Gd: 0-1 GF: - Fm: 0-0
Distance: 2m/2m3: 0-0 2m4-2m7: 0-1 3m+: 0-0
Track: LH: 0-1 RH: 0-0 Tight: 0-1 Gall: 0-0
Aids: Bl: 0-1 Vi: 0-0 Tstrap: 0-0
Best Rating: 102 1/00 Donc 2m110y good Hdl

Myttons Mistake

9-y-o b g Rambo Dancer (CAN)-Hi-Hunsley (Swing Easy (USA))
R J Baker P Slade

Placings:0/P **(2335)**
2001/02: 16^{P}GF

	Starts	1st	2nd	3rd	Win & Pl
Hurdles	1	0	0	0	
Career Total	**2**	**0**	**0**	**0**	

Going: Sf: 0-0 GS: 0-0 Gd: 0-0 GF: - Fm: 0-1
Distance: 2m/2m3: 0-1 2m4-2m7: 0-0 3m+: 0-0
Track: LH: 0-0 RH: 0-1 Tight: 0-0 Gall: 0-0
Aids: Bl: 0-0 Vi: 0-0 Tstrap: 0-0
Best Rating: 69 11/99 Tntn 2m1f good Hdl

Nadderwater

10-y-o br g Arctic Lord-Flying Cherub (Osiris)
Mrs J G Retter Mrs J G Retter

Placings:P/PP **(4051)**
2001/02: 16^{P}S, 24^{P}G

	Starts	1st	2nd	3rd	Win & Pl
Hurdles	2	0	0	0	
Career Total	**3**	**0**	**0**	**0**	

Going: Sf: 0-1 GS: 0-0 Gd: 0-1 GF: - Fm: 0-0
Distance: 2m/2m3: 0-1 2m4-2m7: 0-0 3m+: 0-1
Track: LH: 0-1 RH: 0-1 Tight: 0-0 Gall: 0-1
Aids: Bl: 0-0 Vi: 0-0 Tstrap: 0-0
Best Rating:

Nadjati (USA)

13-y-o ch g Assert-Najidiya (USA) (Riverman (USA))
D M Grissell Christopher Hall

Placings:33/F340/1122**U**33/4114440/U33**P16/5**0454/**4/11/32-34F** **(0556)**
2001/02: 26^{3}G, 25^{4}G, 24^{F}GF

	Starts	1st	2nd	3rd	Win & Pl
Chases	3	0	0	1	188
Career Total	**39**	**7**	**3**	**9**	**29427**

120 5/99 Font 3m2f110y H Ch G-F £1213
112 5/99 Folk 3m2f H Ch G-F £1913
93 6/96 Strf 2m4f E Ch G-F £3324
106 9/95 Worc 2m D(0-120)HHdl G-F £2745
106 8/95 Worc 2m C(0-135)HHdl G-F £3397
106 10/94 Winc 2m (0-125)HHdl FRM £2635
104 9/94 Chel 2m110y Hdl G-F £2389
Total win prize-money £17621

Going: Sf: 0-0 GS: 0-0 Gd: 0-2 GF: - Fm: 0-1
Distance: 2m/2m3: 0-0 2m4-2m7: 0-0 3m+: 0-3
Track: LH: 0-0 RH: 0-3 Tight: 0-2 Gall: 0-1
Aids: Bl: 0-0 Vi: 0-0 Tstrap: 0-0
Best Rating: 126 4/93 Aint 2m110y gd-fm Hdl

Nafith

6-y-o ch g Elmaamul (USA)-Wanisa (USA) (Topsider (USA))
L R James Mrs Carol Lloyd James

Placings:35O0/15000-0 (0877)
2001/02: 21^{0}G

	Starts	1st	2nd	3rd	Win & Pl
Hurdles	1	0	0	0	
Career Total	10	1	0	1	3311

98 6/00 Strf 2m110y E(0-105)HHdl GD £3016
Total win prize-money £3016

Going: Sf: 0-0 GS: 0-0 Gd: 0-1 GF: - Fm: 0-0
Distance: 2m/2m3: 0-0 2m4-2m7: 0-1 3m+: 0-0
Track: LH: 0-0 RH: 0-1 Tight: 0-1 Gall: 0-0
Aids: Bl: 0-0 Vi: 0-0 Tstrap: 0-0
Best Rating: 98 6/00 Strf 2m110y good Hdl

Nahthen Lad (IRE)

13-y-o b g Good Thyne (USA)-Current Call (Electrify)
Mrs V J Danahar J A Danahar

Placings:4/1P311606/121121/6P2P0/33P6F4/52P30P/13/P320 (4650)
2001/02: 25^{P}S, 31^{3}GS, 26^{2}G, 21^{0}G

	Starts	1st	2nd	3rd	Win & Pl
Chases	4	0	1	1	710
Career Total	38	8	5	6	122505

149 10/99 Asct 3m110y B HCh GD £8486
155 3/96 Chel 3m110y A Ch G-S £54672
137 1/96 Hayd 2m4f D Ch SFT £3779
125 1/96 Wwck 2m4f110y D Ch G-S £4074
120 11/95 Chel 2m5f C(0-130)HHdl GD £2837
109 2/95 Hntg 2m5f110y C Hdl G-S £7230
109 1/95 Hayd 2m4f E Hdl HVY £2472
99 10/94 Towc 2m Hdl GD £2075
Total win prize-money £85617

Going: Sf: 0-1 GS: 0-1 Gd: 0-2 GF: - Fm: 0-0
Distance: 2m/2m3: 0-0 2m4-2m7: 0-1 3m+: 0-3
Track: LH: 0-2 RH: 0-1 Tight: 0-1 Gall: 0-0
Aids: Bl: 0-3 Vi: 0-1 Tstrap: 0-0
Best Rating: 155 3/96 Chel 3m110y gd-sft Ch

A former high-class chaser but a modest hunter drawing his pension now.

Naj-De

82 83+
4-y-o ch g Zafonic (USA)-River Jig (USA) (Irish River (FR))
S Dow (P F I Cole 8/10) Mrs A M Upsdell

Placings:0 (3210)
2001/02: 16^{0}GS

	Starts	1st	2nd	3rd	Win & Pl
Hurdles	1	0	0	0	
Career Total	1	0	0	0	

Going: Sf: 0-0 GS: 0-1 Gd: 0-0 GF: - Fm: 0-0
Distance: 2m/2m3: 0-1 2m4-2m7: 0-0 3m+: 0-0
Track: LH: 0-1 RH: 0-0 Tight: 0-0 Gall: 0-1
Aids: Bl: 0-0 Vi: 0-0 Tstrap: 0-0
Best Rating:

Najjm (USA)

107 135
5-y-o br g Dynaformer (USA)-Azusa (USA) (Flying Paster (USA))
N J Henderson Raymond Tooth

Placings:511-1 (0361)
2001/02: 16^{1}GF

	Starts	1st	2nd	3rd	Win & Pl
Hurdles	1	1	0	0	5135
Career Total	4	3	0	0	13548

135 5/01 Ling 2m110y C Hdl G-F £5135
135 4/01 Ayr 2m4f C(0-130)HHdl G-F £4836
126 4/01 Newb 2m110y D Hdl SFT £3577
Total win prize-money £13548

Going: Sf: 0-0 GS: 0-0 Gd: 0-0 GF: - Fm: 1-1
Distance: 2m/2m3: 1-1 2m4-2m7: 0-0 3m+: 0-0
Track: LH: 1-1 RH: 0-0 Tight: 1-1 Gall: 0-0
Aids: Bl: 0-0 Vi: 0-0 Tstrap: 0-0
Best Rating: 135 5/01 Ling 2m110y gd-fm Hdl

Scored at Newbury on his second start over hurdles and looks progressive, going on to complete the hat-trick in the spring of 2001.

Naked Oat

67
7-y-o b g Imp Society (USA)-Bajina (Dancing Brave (USA))
B Smart The Dyball Partnership

Placings:0 (3319)
2001/02: 16^{0}GS

	Starts	1st	2nd	3rd	Win & Pl
Hurdles	1	0	0	0	
Career Total	1	0	0	0	

Going: Sf: 0-0 GS: 0-1 Gd: 0-0 GF: - Fm: 0-0
Distance: 2m/2m3: 0-1 2m4-2m7: 0-0 3m+: 0-0
Track: LH: 0-0 RH: 0-1 Tight: 0-0 Gall: 0-1
Aids: Bl: 0-0 Vi: 0-0 Tstrap: 0-0
Best Rating: 67 1/02 Hntg 2m110y gd-sft Hdl

Nakhal

92 57
9-y-o b g Puissance-Rambadale (Vaigly Great)
A G Newcombe Derek Walker

Placings:2000P0/00P50662/400-004 (0979)
2001/02: 17^{0}GS, 20^{0}G, 27^{4}G

	Starts	1st	2nd	3rd	Win & Pl
Hurdles	3	0	0	0	0
Career Total	20	0	2	0	1172

Going: Sf: 0-0 GS: 0-1 Gd: 0-2 GF: - Fm: 0-0
Distance: 2m/2m3: 0-1 2m4-2m7: 0-1 3m+: 0-1
Track: LH: 0-2 RH: 0-1 Tight: 0-2 Gall: 0-0
Aids: Bl: 0-0 Vi: 0-0 Tstrap: 0-0
Best Rating: 83 12/98 Tntn 2m1f good Hdl

Name Of Our Father (USA)

9-y-o b g Northern Baby (CAN)-Ten Hail Marys (USA) (Halo (USA))
W J Bryan W J Bryan

Placings:13622/F21301122221115/2324254134/35/P P (0474)
2001/02: 24^{P}GS, 22^{P}G

	Starts	1st	2nd	3rd	Win & Pl
Chases	2	0	0	0	
Career Total	34	8	10	5	38026

120 12/98 Ludl 3m E(0-115)HCh G-S £2736
125 11/97 Chep 3m C(0-130)HHdl SFT £3420
130 11/97 Asct 3m B HHdl G-S £5342
121 11/97 Winc 2m6f C(0-130)HHdl GD £4045
124 9/97 Extr 2m6f F(0-105)HHdl G-F £2682
104 8/97 Ctml 2m6f D(0-120)HHdl G-F £2182
100 5/97 Hrfd 2m3f110y E Hdl G-F £2472
90 12/96 Wwck 2m E Hdl G-F £3036
Total win prize-money £25918

Going: Sf: 0-0 GS: 0-1 Gd: 0-1 GF: - Fm: 0-0
Distance: 2m/2m3: 0-0 2m4-2m7: 0-1 3m+: 0-1
Track: LH: 0-1 RH: 0-1 Tight: 0-2 Gall: 0-0
Aids: Bl: 0-0 Vi: 0-0 Tstrap: 0-0
Best Rating: 130 11/97 Asct 3m gd-sft Hdl

Nameless Wonder (IRE)

90 102
6-y-o b g Supreme Leader-Miss Kylogue (IRE) (Lancastrian)
N J Henderson Major Christopher Hanbury

Placings:600 (4400)
2001/02: 16^{6}S, 20^{0}GS, 21^{0}S

	Starts	1st	2nd	3rd	Win & Pl
NH Flat	1	0	0	0	0
Hurdles	2	0	0	0	0
Career Total	3	0	0	0	0

Going: Sf: 0-2 GS: 0-1 Gd: 0-0 GF: - Fm: 0-0
Distance: 2m/2m3: 0-1 2m4-2m7: 0-2 3m+: 0-0
Track: LH: 0-3 RH: 0-0 Tight: 0-0 Gall: 0-1
Aids: Bl: 0-0 Vi: 0-0 Tstrap: 0-0
Best Rating: 102 3/02 Newb 2m5f soft Hdl

Fair debut effort when sixth in a soft ground Chepstow bumper but showed little on hurdling bow over two and a half miles.

Nampara Cove

7-y-o b/br g Roscoe Blake-Lothian Lily (Alias Smith (USA))
R G Russ R G Russ

Placings:P (4859)
2001/02: 25^{P}G

	Starts	1st	2nd	3rd	Win & Pl
Chases	1	0	0	0	
Career Total	1	0	0	0	

Going: Sf: 0-0 GS: 0-0 Gd: 0-1 GF: - Fm: 0-0
Distance: 2m/2m3: 0-0 2m4-2m7: 0-0 3m+: 0-1
Track: LH: 0-1 RH: 0-0 Tight: 0-0 Gall: 0-0
Aids: Bl: 0-0 Vi: 0-0 Tstrap: 0-0
Best Rating:

Napoleon Bonaparte (IRE)

87f 100f
5-y-o b g Insan (USA)-Chiminee Fly (Proverb)
M Pitman H Spooner,I Weaver,E Benson,T Fearey

Placings:00 (4269)
2001/02: 16^{0}G, 16^{0}S

	Starts	1st	2nd	3rd	Win & Pl
NH Flat	2	0	0	0	
Career Total	2	0	0	0	

Going: Sf: 0-1 GS: 0-0 Gd: 0-1 GF: - Fm: 0-0
Distance: 2m/2m3: 0-2 2m4-2m7: 0-0 3m+: 0-0
Track: LH: 0-1 RH: 0-1 Tight: 0-0 Gall: 0-0

Aids: Bl: 0-0 Vi: 0-0 Tstrap: 0-0
Best Rating: 100 2/02 Kemp 2m good NHF

Narrogin (USA)

74(97h) (79h)69

7-y-o ch g Strike The Gold (USA)-Best Regalia (Sharpen Up)
D J Wintle D J Wintle

Placings:33/5/5-0010355 (3344)
2001/02: 16^{0}S, 16^{0}GS, 19^{1}GS, 20^{0}S, 16^{3}HY, 16^{5}S, 19^{5}S

	Starts	1st	2nd	3rd	Win & Pl
Hurdles	6	1	0	1	1868
Chases	1	0	0	0	0
Career Total	**11**	**1**	**0**	**3**	**2572**

70	11/01	MRas	2m3f110y	G(0-90)HHdl	G-S	£1631

Total win prize-money £1631

Going: Sf: 0-5 GS: 1-2 Gd: 0-0 GF: - Fm: 0-0
Distance: 2m/2m3: 0-5 **2m4-2m7: 1-2** 3m+: 0-0
Track: LH: 0-2 **RH: 1-5 Tight: 1-3** Gall: 0-0
Aids: **Bl: 1-4** Vi: 0-0 Tstrap: 0-0
Best Rating: 96 10/98 Ludl 2m gd-fm Hdl

Selling-class hurdler, has won over two and a half miles with cut in the ground and first time blinkers.

Narrow Water (IRE)

98 118

9-y-o b g Mazaad-Miss Doogles (Beau Charmeur (FR))
Ferdy Murphy Getjar Limited

Placings:21211-PPPF6P (4299)
2001/02: 27^{P}S, 24^{P}S, 26^{P}S, 33^{F}S, 26^{6}GS, 34^{P}HY

	Starts	1st	2nd	3rd	Win & Pl
Chases	6	0	0	0	0
Career Total	**11**	**3**	**2**	**0**	**45570**

152	2/01	Newc	4m1f	B(0-150)HCh	HVY	£34800
149	2/01	Carl	3m2f	D Ch	HVY	£4114
151	11/00	Weth	3m1f	D Ch	SFT	£4123

Total win prize-money £43038

Going: Sf: 0-5 GS: 0-1 Gd: 0-0 GF: - Fm: 0-0
Distance: 2m/2m3: 0-0 2m4-2m7: 0-0 3m+: 0-6
Track: LH: 0-6 RH: 0-0 Tight: 0-1 Gall: 0-2
Aids: Bl: 0-0 Vi: 0-0 Tstrap: 0-4
Best Rating: 152 2/01 Newc 4m1f heavy Ch

A winning pointer in Northern Ireland, he enjoyed a superb first season under Rules and put up a game effort to win the Tote Northern National at Newcastle in February 2001. Pulled up on first three starts this season but showed signs of a revival before falling next time. Often wears a tongue strap. Stays all day and acts on soft/heavy ground.

Narwhal (IRE)

102f 103f

4-y-o b/br g Naheez (USA)-Well Why (IRE) (The Parson)
J T Gifford Mrs S N J Embiricos

Placings:2 (4423)
2001/02: 16^{2}GS

	Starts	1st	2nd	3rd	Win & Pl
NH Flat	1	0	1	0	736
Career Total	**1**	**0**	**1**	**0**	**736**

Going: Sf: 0-0 GS: 0-1 Gd: 0-0 GF: - Fm: 0-0
Distance: 2m/2m3: 0-1 2m4-2m7: 0-0 3m+: 0-0
Track: LH: 0-1 RH: 0-0 Tight: 0-0 Gall: 0-1
Aids: Bl: 0-0 Vi: 0-0 Tstrap: 0-0
Best Rating: 103 3/02 Newb 2m110y gd-sft NHF

Runner-up on his bumper debut.

Nashkapour (IRE)

93 85

9-y-o b g Caerleon (USA)-Nashkara (Shirley Heights)
P J Hobbs Seamus Carroll

Placings:026245/646-3 (0495)
2001/02: 19^{3}G

	Starts	1st	2nd	3rd	Win & Pl
Hurdles	1	0	0	1	340
Career Total	**10**	**0**	**2**	**1**	**1436**

Going: Sf: 0-0 GS: 0-0 Gd: 0-1 GF: - Fm: 0-0
Distance: 2m/2m3: 0-0 2m4-2m7: 0-1 3m+: 0-0
Track: LH: 0-0 RH: 0-1 Tight: 0-0 Gall: 0-0
Aids: Bl: 0-0 Vi: 0-0 Tstrap: 0-0
Best Rating: 109 11/98 Punc 2m soft Hdl

Nashville Star (USA)

11-y-o ch g Star De Naskra (USA)-Mary Davies (Tyrnavos)
R Mathew Robin Mathew

Placings:211340P10/6P5/4054010660/34331424363/5023045/P00/0P6-650 (4886)
2001/02: 21^{6}GF, 16^{5}GF, 18^{0}GF

	Starts	1st	2nd	3rd	Win & Pl
Chases	3	0	0	0	0
Career Total	**49**	**5**	**3**	**7**	**28585**

97	12/97	Wind	2m	D(0-125)HCh	GD	£4232
100	2/97	Bang	2m1f	E(0-110)HHdl	GD	£3517
100	3/95	Newb	2m110y	B HHdl	GD	£5994
87	10/94	Newc	2m110y	Hdl	FRM	£2232
86	10/94	Carl	2m1f	Hdl	GD	£1927

Total win prize-money £17905

Going: Sf: 0-0 GS: 0-0 Gd: 0-0 GF: - Fm: 0-3
Distance: 2m/2m3: 0-2 2m4-2m7: 0-1 3m+: 0-0
Track: LH: 0-1 RH: 0-1 Tight: 0-2 Gall: 0-1
Aids: Bl: 0-0 Vi: 0-3 Tstrap: 0-0
Best Rating: 124 12/98 Chel 2m110y good Ch

Naskeag Point (IRE)

72 84

8-y-o gr g Roselier (FR)-Madam Beau (Le Tricolore)
C P Morlock Pell-Mell Partners

Placings:5P6/FPP-P4 (2113)
2001/02: 25^{P}S, 25^{4}G

	Starts	1st	2nd	3rd	Win & Pl
Chases	2	0	0	0	282
Career Total	**8**	**0**	**0**	**0**	**282**

Going: Sf: 0-1 GS: 0-0 Gd: 0-1 GF: - Fm: 0-0
Distance: 2m/2m3: 0-0 2m4-2m7: 0-0 3m+: 0-2
Track: LH: 0-0 RH: 0-2 Tight: 0-1 Gall: 0-0
Aids: Bl: 0-1 Vi: 0-0 Tstrap: 0-0
Best Rating: 84 11/01 Folk 3m1f good Ch

Nasone (IRE)

96 90

11-y-o b g Nearly A Nose (USA)-Skateaway (Condorcet (FR))
Miss M Bryant Miss M Bryant

Placings:10/42500/2/0/03252352/035-2P (0425)
2001/02: 21^{2}G, 21^{P}G

	Starts	1st	2nd	3rd	Win & Pl
Chases	2	0	1	0	458
Career Total	**22**	**1**	**6**	**3**	**11968**

99	3/96	Newb	2m110y	H NHF	G-S	£1521

Total win prize-money £1522

Going: Sf: 0-0 GS: 0-0 Gd: 0-2 GF: - Fm: 0-0
Distance: 2m/2m3: 0-0 2m4-2m7: 0-2 3m+: 0-0
Track: LH: 0-0 RH: 0-1 Tight: 0-1 Gall: 0-0
Aids: Bl: 0-1 Vi: 0-0 Tstrap: 0-0
Best Rating: 123 11/97 Winc 2m5f good Ch

Nathan's Boy

102 84

6-y-o gr g Tragic Role (USA)-Gold Belt (IRE) (Bellypha)
A Streeter (R Hollinshead 26/6) Mrs J Hughes

Placings:04UP (4178)
2001/02: 16^{0}S, 16^{4}S, 16^{U}HY, 16^{P}GS

	Starts	1st	2nd	3rd	Win & Pl
Hurdles	4	0	0	0	0
Career Total	**4**	**0**	**0**	**0**	**0**

Going: Sf: 0-3 GS: 0-1 Gd: 0-0 GF: - Fm: 0-0
Distance: 2m/2m3: 0-4 2m4-2m7: 0-0 3m+: 0-0
Track: LH: 0-3 RH: 0-1 Tight: 0-1 Gall: 0-1
Aids: Bl: 0-0 Vi: 0-0 Tstrap: 0-0
Best Rating: 84 1/02 Donc 2m110y soft Hdl

Successful on the Flat, he is still a maiden over hurdles. Acts on good and soft ground.

Nativa Negra (IRE)

5-y-o br m Be My Native (USA)-Jayells Dream (Space King)
A King All The King's Men

Placings:20 (3345)
2001/02: 17^{2}S, 17^{0}S

	Starts	1st	2nd	3rd	Win & Pl
NH Flat	2	0	1	0	456
Career Total	**2**	**0**	**1**	**0**	**456**

Going: Sf: 0-2 GS: 0-0 Gd: 0-0 GF: - Fm: 0-0
Distance: 2m/2m3: 0-2 2m4-2m7: 0-0 3m+: 0-0
Track: LH: 0-0 RH: 0-1 Tight: 0-0 Gall: 0-0
Aids: Bl: 0-0 Vi: 0-0 Tstrap: 0-0
Best Rating: 82 12/01 Hrfd 2m1f soft NHF

Native Affair (IRE)

106 107

8-y-o ch g Be My Native (USA)-Queens Romance (Imperial Fling (USA))
L Lungo Strathayr Publishing Ltd

Placings:03110/UP00/503-23220 (3349)
2001/02: 20^{2}GF, 16^{3}G, 16^{2}GF, 19^{2}S, 16^{0}G

	Starts	1st	2nd	3rd	Win & Pl
Hurdles	5	0	3	1	2739
Career Total	**17**	**2**	**3**	**3**	**6118**

116	12/98	Muss	2m	H NHF	GD	£1521
111	12/98	Catt	2m	H NHF	GD	£1276

Total win prize-money £2799

Going: Sf: 0-1 GS: 0-0 Gd: 0-2 GF: - Fm: 0-2
Distance: 2m/2m3: 0-4 2m4-2m7: 0-1 3m+: 0-0

Track: LH: 0-3 RH: 0-2 Tight: 0-4 Gall: 0-0
Aids: Bl: 0-0 Vi: 0-0 Tstrap: 0-1
Best Rating: 118 4/99 Aint 2m110y good NHF

Fair form in novice hurdles before breaking a leg at Perth in May 2002. (DEAD)

Native Bid (IRE)

101 **114**

7-y-o b m Be My Native (USA)-Coctail Bid (Mandalus)
N J Henderson J Hanson

Placings:*11*-1 **(2877)**
2001/02: 16^{1}G

	Starts	1st	2nd	3rd	Win & Pl
Hurdles	1	1	0	0	2751
Career Total	**3**	**3**	**0**	**0**	**18551**

114	12/01	Winc	2m	E Hdl	GD	£2751
119	4/01	Kemp	2m	A NHF	GD	£14365
113	1/01	Fknm	2m	H NHF	SFT	£1435

Total win prize-money £18551

Going: Sf: 0-0 GS: 0-0 Gd: 1-1 GF: - Fm: 0-0
Distance: **2m/2m3: 1-1** 2m4-2m7: 0-0 3m+: 0-0
Track: LH: 0-0 **RH: 1-1** Tight: 0-0 Gall: 0-0
Aids: Bl: 0-0 Vi: 0-0 Tstrap: 0-0
Best Rating: 119 4/01 Kemp 2m good NHF

Won both her bumpers, one of which was Listed, and confirmed this form with a well-schooled win on her hurdles debut.

Native Buck (IRE)

101 **130**

9-y-o ch g Be My Native (USA)-Buckskins Chat (Buckskin (FR))
T R George The One Over Par Partnership

Placings:00/063212/**22P**/**1411P** **(4233)**
2001/02: 21^{1}S, 24^{4}S, 24^{1}HY, 26^{1}HY, 32^{P}GS

	Starts	1st	2nd	3rd	Win & Pl
Chases	5	3	0	0	18897
Career Total	**16**	**4**	**4**	**1**	**25429**

130	2/02	Uttx	3m2f	B HCh	HVY	£10976
126	12/01	Hayd	3m	D(0-110)HCh	HVY	£4114
119	11/01	Uttx	2m5f	F(0-110)HCh	SFT	£3532
91	12/98	Uttx	3m110y	E(0-100)HHdl	SFT	£2431

Total win prize-money £21056

Going: Sf: 3-4 GS: 0-1 Gd: 0-0 GF: - Fm: 0-0
Distance: 2m/2m3: 0-0 2m4-2m7: 1-1 **3m+: 2-4**
Track: **LH: 3-5** RH: 0-0 Tight: 0-0 Gall: 0-1
Aids: Bl: 0-0 Vi: 0-0 Tstrap: 0-0
Best Rating: 130 2/02 Uttx 3m2f heavy Ch

Progressed over hurdles to become a fair staying chasing prospect, but has had a variety of injuries since 1998. Stays three miles. Acts on an easy surface. Has been in fine form this term in testing conditions.

Native Cannon (IRE)

71 **69**

9-y-o b g Be My Native (USA)-Plamas (Tumble Wind (USA))
C R Barwell The Hole In The Wall Gang

Placings:0000P/P0/000/0P0-00P **(0671)**
2001/02: 22^{0}GS, 22^{0}GF, 24^{P}G

	Starts	1st	2nd	3rd	Win & Pl
Hurdles	3	0	0	0	
Career Total	**16**	**0**	**0**	**0**	

Going: Sf: 0-0 GS: 0-1 Gd: 0-1 GF: - Fm: 0-1

Distance: 2m/2m3: 0-0 2m4-2m7: 0-2 3m+: 0-1
Track: LH: 0-1 RH: 0-1 Tight: 0-0 Gall: 0-0
Aids: Bl: 0-0 Vi: 0-0 Tstrap: 0-1
Best Rating: 69 4/01 Kemp 2m5f good Hdl

Native Cloth

8-y-o b g Be My Native (USA)-Dishcloth (Fury Royal)
F Jordan D Pugh

Placings:0 **(1404)**
2001/02: 17^{0}G

	Starts	1st	2nd	3rd	Win & Pl
Hurdles	1	0	0	0	
Career Total	**1**	**0**	**0**	**0**	

Going: Sf: 0-0 GS: 0-0 Gd: 0-1 GF: - Fm: 0-0
Distance: 2m/2m3: 0-1 2m4-2m7: 0-0 3m+: 0-0
Track: LH: 0-1 RH: 0-0 Tight: 0-1 Gall: 0-0
Aids: Bl: 0-0 Vi: 0-0 Tstrap: 0-0
Best Rating:

Native Commander (IRE)

113(65h) (66h)**120**

7-y-o b g Be My Native (USA)-The Better Half (IRE) (Deep Run)
Patrick Morris (R H Alner 0/3) O P Dyme

Placings:*0*/004*000*-0102640 **(4926a)**
2001/02: 16^{0}GF, 16^{1}Y, 16^{0}YS, 16^{2}YS, 16^{6}SH, 16^{4}Y, 20^{0}Y

	Starts	1st	2nd	3rd	Win & Pl
Hurdles	1	0	0	0	0
Chases	6	1	1	0	9140
Career Total	**14**	**1**	**1**	**0**	**9430**

115	11/01	Naas	2m	Ch	YLD	£6955

Total win prize-money £6956

Going: Sf: 0-0 GS: 0-0 Gd: 0-0 GF: - Fm: 0-1
Distance: **2m/2m3: 1-6** 2m4-2m7: 0-1 3m+: 0-0
Track: **LH: 1-2** RH: 0-2 Tight: 0-1 Gall: 0-0
Aids: Bl: 0-0 Vi: 0-0 Tstrap: 0-0
Best Rating: 120 1/02 Thur 2m yld-sft Ch

Native Cove (IRE)

10-y-o b g Be My Native (USA)-Down All The Coves (Athenius)
E Haddock E Haddock

Placings:P/2/F0PP-P3025 **(4585)**
2001/02: 25^{P}G, 24^{3}GF, 26^{0}G, 31^{2}GS, 25^{5}G

	Starts	1st	2nd	3rd	Win & Pl
Chases	5	0	1	1	1059
Career Total	**11**	**0**	**2**	**1**	**1698**

Going: Sf: 0-0 GS: 0-1 Gd: 0-3 GF: - Fm: 0-1
Distance: 2m/2m3: 0-0 2m4-2m7: 0-0 3m+: 0-5
Track: LH: 0-0 RH: 0-3 Tight: 0-0 Gall: 0-1
Aids: Bl: 0-0 Vi: 0-1 Tstrap: 0-0
Best Rating: 111 4/00 Ludl 3m good Ch

Modest hunter chaser, stays well.

Native Eire (IRE)

78(95h) (98h)**76**

8-y-o b g Be My Native (USA)-Ballyline Dancer (Giolla Mear)

N Wilson Mrs N C Wilson

Placings:*0*/065B-0F5051 **(4065)**
2001/02: 23^{0}G, 20^{F}G, 21^{5}S, 16^{0}GF, 23^{5}GS, 21^{1}S

	Starts	1st	2nd	3rd	Win & Pl
Hurdles	2	1	0	0	2569
Chases	4	0	0	0	0
Career Total	**11**	**1**	**0**	**0**	**2569**

98	3/02	Sedg	2m5f110y	E Hdl	SFT	£2569

Total win prize-money £2569

Going: Sf: 1-2 GS: 0-1 Gd: 0-2 GF: - Fm: 0-1
Distance: 2m/2m3: 0-1 **2m4-2m7: 1-4** 3m+: 0-1
Track: **LH: 1-4** RH: 0-1 **Tight: 1-2** Gall: 0-0
Aids: Bl: 0-0 Vi: 0-0 Tstrap: 0-0
Best Rating: 108 2/01 Catt 2m3f soft Ch

Maiden novice chaser. Got off the mark at the third time of asking over hurdles in a Sedgefield amateur event. Handles soft.

Native Emperor

111 **139**

6-y-o br g Be My Native (USA)-Fiona's Blue (Crash Course)
J J O'Neill Exors Of The Late Robert Hitchins

Placings:*55*/13145P-012114 **(4193)**
2001/02: 21^{0}G, 22^{1}HY, 24^{2}GS, 25^{1}HY, 22^{1}HY, 25^{4}GS

	Starts	1st	2nd	3rd	Win & Pl
Hurdles	6	3	1	0	24207
Career Total	**14**	**5**	**1**	**1**	**33310**

139	2/02	Uttx	2m6f110y	C(0-135)HHdl	HVY	£10504
132	1/02	Wwck	3m1f	D(0-125)HHdl	HVY	£3688
114	12/01	NAbb	2m6f	D(0-125)HHdl	HVY	£5382
123	11/00	Asct	2m4f	C Hdl	SFT	£4862
100	10/00	Strf	2m6f110y	D Hdl	SFT	£3289

Total win prize-money £27726

Going: Sf: 3-3 GS: 0-2 Gd: 0-1 GF: - Fm: 0-0
Distance: 2m/2m3: 0-0 **2m4-2m7: 2-3** 3m+: 1-3
Track: **LH: 2-5** RH: 0-0 **Tight: 1-2** Gall: 0-2
Aids: Bl: 0-0 Vi: 0-0 Tstrap: 0-0
Best Rating: 139 3/02 Chel 3m1f110y gd-sft Hdl

Fair hurdler who is best between two and a half miles and three miles when there is plenty of cut in the ground.

Native Estates (IRE)

109 **134**

10-y-o b g Be My Native (USA)-Sesetta (Lucky Brief)
Noel Meade Mrs B M McKinney

Placings:*32*/*4*11210F/**2215**/**32310FP**/4304234-40403 **(4963a)**
2001/02: 24^{4}Y, 24^{0}YS, 20^{4}S, 25^{0}GS, 24^{3}GY

	Starts	1st	2nd	3rd	Win & Pl
Hurdles	5	0	0	1	2305
Career Total	**33**	**6**	**6**	**6**	**75560**

122	1/00	Thur	2m6f	Ch	SH	£4140
135	1/99	Leop	2m5f	Ch	HVY	£7366
142	2/98	Leop	2m2f	Hdl	Y-S	£11217
134	12/97	Navn	2m	Hdl	HVY	£4069
130	12/97	Fair	2m	Hdl	GD	£3730
108	11/97	Navn	2m	NHF	G-Y	£3051

Total win prize-money £33574

Going: Sf: 0-1 GS: 0-1 Gd: 0-0 GF: - Fm: 0-0
Distance: 2m/2m3: 0-0 2m4-2m7: 0-1 3m+: 0-4
Track: LH: 0-3 RH: 0-2 Tight: 0-0 Gall: 0-1
Aids: Bl: 0-0 Vi: 0-0 Tstrap: 0-0
Best Rating: 145 12/98 Leop 2m1f soft Ch

He was a good novice chaser in 1998/9 and won in heavy ground at Thurles and finishing third in the Paddy Power in 1999/2000. Campaigned over hurdles since then, as he is rated much lower over the smaller obstacles.

Native Field (IRE)

97 **91**

13-y-o b g Be My Native (USA)-Broomfield Ceili (Northfields (USA))

D J Wintle John W Egan

Placings: *111*/0013/2022300/6116/1105/132056/3301 1000-030245 **(4657)**

2001/02: 16^{0}S, 21^{3}HY, 20^{0}S, 21^{2}HY, 22^{4}S, 24^{5}G

	Starts	1st	2nd	3rd	Win & Pl
Hurdles	6	0	1	1	1008
Career Total	**42**	**11**	**5**	**6**	**38415**

104	1/01	Leic	2m4f110y	F Hdl	HVY	£2723
113	1/01	Folk	2m6f110y	G(0-90)HHdl	HVY	£1568
113	11/99	Hayd	2m4f	F Hdl	G-S	£1987
125	12/98	Hayd	2m7f110y	C(0-130)HHdl	SFT	£3896
116	11/98	NAbb	2m6f	D(0-125)HHdl	SFT	£2739
122	12/97	Towc	2m5f	F Hdl	SFT	£2104
111	11/97	Hayd	2m4f	F Hdl	SFT	£2120
90	3/94	Strf	2m110y	Hdl	G-S	£2070
	4/93	Aint	2m110y	NHF	G-F	£7400
	3/93	Donc	2m110y	NHF	FRM	£1772
	2/93	Donc	2m110y	NHF	FRM	£1574

Total win prize-money £29954

Going: Sf: 0-5 GS: 0-0 Gd: 0-1 GF: - Fm: 0-0
Distance: 2m/2m3: 0-1 2m4-2m7: 0-4 3m+: 0-1
Track: LH: 0-3 RH: 0-3 Tight: 0-3 Gall: 0-0
Aids: Bl: 0-0 Vi: 0-0 Tstrap: 0-0
Best Rating: 125 12/98 Hayd 2m7f110y soft Hdl

Veteran hurdler, suited by two and a half miles.

Native Fling (IRE)

105(50h) **138**

10-y-o b g Be My Native (USA)-Queens Romance (Imperial Fling (USA))

P J Hobbs Christine And Aubrey Loze

Placings: *30*/100635/5/131122221/11/4050-1P2543 **(4891)**

2001/02: 17^{1}S, 20^{P}G, 16^{2}HY, 16^{5}S, 17^{4}S, 16^{3}G

	Starts	1st	2nd	3rd	Win & Pl
Hurdles	1	0	0	0	0
Chases	5	1	1	1	9904
Career Total	**30**	**8**	**5**	**4**	**41401**

138	11/01	Strf	2m1f110y	D(0-125)HCh	SFT	£6077
131	10/99	Strf	2m1f110y	C(0-135)HCh	G-S	£6419
120	10/99	Extr	2m1f	D(0-125)HHdl	GD	£3436
126	4/99	Punc	2m2f	Ch	YLD	£6138
120	1/99	Extr	2m1f110y	F(0-100)HCh	HVY	£2377
134	12/98	Hrfd	2m	E(0-100)HCh	G-S	£2801
109	11/98	NAbb	2m1f	E Hdl	SFT	£2200
98	10/96	Dpat	2m1f172y	NHF	G-Y	£1412

Total win prize-money £30862

Going: Sf: 1-4 GS: 0-0 Gd: 0-2 GF: - Fm: 0-0
Distance: **2m/2m3: 1-5** 2m4-2m7: 0-1 3m+: 0-0
Track: **LH: 1-3** RH: 0-2 **Tight: 1-2** Gall: 0-1
Aids: Bl: 0-0 Vi: 0-1 Tstrap: 0-0
Best Rating: 138 1/02 Uttx 2m heavy Ch

A progressive chaser in 1999, he missed a year and was out of form until winning on his seasonal debut in a fair handicap at Stratford in November 2001. He has tended to do too much too soon in some of his subsequent efforts and needs to settle better. Effective up to two and a quarter miles, he likes to get his toe in and remains relatively unexposed over fences.

Native Fox

105 **101**

7-y-o br m Be My Native (USA)-Leinthall Fox (Deep Run)

J L Needham Miss Joanna Needham

Placings: *01242*-2P4 **(0794)**

2001/02: 19^{2}G, 22^{P}G, 22^{4}GF

	Starts	1st	2nd	3rd	Win & Pl
Hurdles	3	0	1	0	800
Career Total	**8**	**1**	**3**	**0**	**3574**

113	6/00	Uttx	2m	H NHF	GD	£1575

Total win prize-money £1575

Going: Sf: 0-0 GS: 0-0 Gd: 0-2 GF: - Fm: 0-1
Distance: 2m/2m3: 0-0 2m4-2m7: 0-3 3m+: 0-0
Track: LH: 0-2 RH: 0-1 Tight: 0-2 Gall: 0-0
Aids: Bl: 0-0 Vi: 0-0 Tstrap: 0-0
Best Rating: 113 6/00 Uttx 2m good NHF

Modest hurdler, stays two and three-quarter miles.

Native Glen (IRE)

(88h) (67h)

8-y-o b g Be My Native (USA)-The Gargle Monster (Furry Glen)

D J Wintle (Gerard Farrell 25/11) J Huckle

Placings: *000550/0140P/000P*-00PP **(4129)**

2001/02: 16^{0}Y, 20^{0}GS, 19^{P}HY, 16^{P}G

	Starts	1st	2nd	3rd	Win & Pl
Hurdles	1	0	0	0	0
Chases	3	0	0	0	0
Career Total	**19**	**1**	**0**	**0**	**3295**

90	9/99	Gowr	2m	Hdl	Y-S	£3080

Total win prize-money £3080

Going: Sf: 0-1 GS: 0-1 Gd: 0-1 GF: - Fm: 0-0
Distance: 2m/2m3: 0-3 2m4-2m7: 0-1 3m+: 0-0
Track: LH: 0-1 RH: 0-2 Tight: 0-1 Gall: 0-0
Aids: Bl: 0-0 Vi: 0-0 Tstrap: 0-4
Best Rating: 90 9/99 Gowr 2m yld-sft Hdl

A winner of a maiden hurdle at Gowran Park in 1999, he has shown little form in Ireland in the last two years.

Native Hunter (IRE)

6-y-o br g Be My Native (USA)-Huntstown Gale (IRE) (Strong Gale)

C R Egerton Mrs Evelyn Hankinson

Placings: P **(2284)**

2001/02: 24^{P}G

	Starts	1st	2nd	3rd	Win & Pl
Hurdles	1	0	0	0	
Career Total	**1**	**0**	**0**	**0**	

Going: Sf: 0-0 GS: 0-0 Gd: 0-1 GF: - Fm: 0-0
Distance: 2m/2m3: 0-0 2m4-2m7: 0-0 3m+: 0-1
Track: LH: 0-0 RH: 0-1 Tight: 0-0 Gall: 0-0
Aids: Bl: 0-0 Vi: 0-0 Tstrap: 0-0
Best Rating:

Native Isle (IRE)

88 **77**

10-y-o ch g Be My Native (USA)-Shuil Ard (Quayside)

D J Caro D J Caro

Placings: PPP-5P5PP **(4590)**

2001/02: 23^{5}G, 25^{P}S, 21^{5}S, 25^{P}S, 24^{P}G

	Starts	1st	2nd	3rd	Win & Pl
Chases	5	0	0	0	0
Career Total	**8**	**0**	**0**	**0**	**0**

Going: Sf: 0-3 GS: 0-0 Gd: 0-2 GF: - Fm: 0-0
Distance: 2m/2m3: 0-0 2m4-2m7: 0-1 3m+: 0-4
Track: LH: 0-1 RH: 0-4 Tight: 0-1 Gall: 0-0
Aids: Bl: 0-0 Vi: 0-0 Tstrap: 0-0
Best Rating: 77 12/01 Leic 2m7f110y good Ch

Native King (IRE)

108 **134**

10-y-o b g Be My Native (USA)-Outdoor Ivy (Deep Run)

A J Lidderdale (E Stanners 14/12) Doubleprint

Placings: *3133/11P4/5020-2262004P* **(4266)**

2001/02: 23^{2}GS, 24^{2}GS, 20^{6}G, 26^{2}S, 27^{0}S, 31^{0}GS, 22^{4}S, 29^{P}S

	Starts	1st	2nd	3rd	Win & Pl
Chases	8	0	3	0	5684
Career Total	**20**	**3**	**4**	**3**	**23419**

139	1/00	Wwck	2m4f	C Ch	SFT	£7046
131	11/99	Worc	2m4f110y	E Ch	G-S	£3332
112	12/98	Sand	2m110y	D Hdl	GD	£2996

Total win prize-money £13374

Going: Sf: 0-4 GS: 0-3 Gd: 0-1 GF: - Fm: 0-0
Distance: 2m/2m3: 0-0 2m4-2m7: 0-2 3m+: 0-6
Track: LH: 0-6 RH: 0-2 Tight: 0-4 Gall: 0-0
Aids: Bl: 0-1 Vi: 0-1 Tstrap: 0-1
Best Rating: 139 1/00 Wwck 2m4f soft Ch

He has been bitterly disappointing since winning his first two starts over fences in 1999-2000, often finding one or two too good. Effective over three miles, he lacks finishing pace but should win an ordinary handicap. Suited by cut.

Native Man (IRE)

108 **136**

8-y-o b g Be My Native (USA)-Try Your Case (Proverb)

J J O'Neill Anne Duchess Of Westminster

Placings: 5*143*/1213050/220124-4PPU41211P **(4582)**

2001/02: 21^{4}GS, 20^{P}G, 16^{P}GS, 21^{U}G, 20^{4}S, 20^{1}GS, 20^{2}G, 24^{1}G, 24^{1}GS, 25^{P}G

	Starts	1st	2nd	3rd	Win & Pl
Chases	10	3	1	0	20106
Career Total	**27**	**7**	**5**	**2**	**39129**

136	2/02	Ludl	3m	D(0-125)HCh	G-S	£10192
127	2/02	Ludl	3m	E(0-105)HCh	GD	£4953
116	1/02	Hntg	2m4f110y	F(0-100)HCh	G-S	£2758
126	8/00	Bang	2m4f110y	D Ch	GD	£3786
111	7/99	Tipp	2m4f	Hdl	G-Y	£3683
97	5/99	Tipp	2m	Hdl	G-F	£3069
104	12/98	Thur	2m	NHF	HVY	£2391

Total win prize-money £30832

Going: Sf: 0-1 GS: 2-4 Gd: 1-5 GF: - Fm: 0-0
Distance: 2m/2m3: 0-1 2m4-2m7: 1-6 **3m+: 2-3**
Track: LH: 0-5 **RH: 3-5 Tight: 2-6** Gall: 1-1
Aids: Bl: 0-0 Vi: 0-0 **Tstrap: 2-2**
Best Rating: 136 2/02 Ludl 3m gd-sft Ch

Bounced back to form early in 2002, and has shown improvement for the fitting of a tongue tie and the step up to three miles, winning twice at Ludlow. Not the most fluent of jumpers, however.

Native New Yorker (IRE)

103 **117+**

7-y-o b g Be My Native (USA)-Sunbath (Krayyan)

R Rowe Ann & John Symes

Placings: *1*200-1 **(1571)**

2001/02: 18^{1}S

	Starts	1st	2nd	3rd	Win & Pl
Hurdles	1	1	0	0	2461
Career Total	**5**	**2**	**1**	**0**	**3383**

112	10/01	Font	2m2f110y	E Hdl	SFT	£2460

Total win prize-money £2461

Going: Sf: 1-1 GS: 0-0 Gd: 0-0 GF: - Fm: 0-0
Distance: **2m/2m3: 1-1** 2m4-2m7: 0-0 3m+: 0-0
Track: **LH: 1-1** RH: 0-0 **Tight: 1-1** Gall: 0-0
Aids: Bl: 0-0 Vi: 0-0 Tstrap: 0-0
Best Rating: 112 10/01 Font 2m2f110y soft Hdl

Landed an ordinary novice hurdle in testing conditions at Fontwell.

Native Peach (IRE)

115 **117**

7-y-o ch g Be My Native (USA)-Larry's Peach (Laurence O)

J A B Old W E Sturt

Placings: *0*-1366 **(4161)**

2001/02: 25^{1}G, 26^{3}G, 24^{6}G, [illegible]

	Starts	1st	2nd	3rd	Win & Pl
Hurdles	4	1	0	1	3920
Career Total	**5**	**1**	**0**	**1**	**3920**

96	5/01	Wwck	3m1f	E Hdl	GD	£2824

Total win prize-money £2825

Going: Sf: 0-0 GS: 0-1 Gd: 1-3 GF: - Fm: 0-0
Distance: 2m/2m3: 0-0 2m4-2m7: 0-0 **3m+: 1-4**
Track: LH: 0-2 RH: 0-0 Tight: 0-0 Gall: 0-2
Aids: Bl: 0-0 Vi: 0-0 Tstrap: 0-0
Best Rating: 117 10/01 Chel 3m1f110y good Hdl

Out of a mare who won over three miles over hurdles and two and a half miles over fences. Winner over hurdles. Suited by a sound surface.

Native Recruit (IRE)

102 **117**

9-y-o ch g Be My Native (USA)-Castle Stream (Paddy's Stream)

P G Murphy Mrs Dianne Abel

Placings: *35/311541/F3F/11P33*-4P **(2849)**

2001/02: 20^{4}G, 20^{P}G

	Starts	1st	2nd	3rd	Win & Pl
Chases	2	0	0	0	339
Career Total	**18**	**5**	**0**	**5**	**22861**

125	7/00	Uttx	2m5f	C Ch	G-F	£6938
127	6/00	Uttx	2m5f	D Ch	GD	£3770
124	3/99	Asct	2m4f	D Hdl	G-F	£3647
125	11/98	Ludl	2m5f110y	E Hdl	GD	£2563
127	11/98	Ludl	2m5f110y	F Hdl	GD	£2626

Total win prize-money £19546

Going: Sf: 0-0 GS: 0-0 Gd: 0-2 GF: - Fm: 0-0
Distance: 2m/2m3: 0-0 2m4-2m7: 0-2 3m+: 0-0
Track: LH: 0-0 RH: 0-2 Tight: 0-0 Gall: 0-0
Aids: Bl: 0-0 Vi: 0-0 Tstrap: 0-0
Best Rating: 128 7/00 MRas 2m4f gd-fm Ch

A winner over hurdles and fences, he was off the track for 14 months after October 2000. Suited by trips of around two and a half miles.

Native Ritual (IRE)

72 **43**

5-y-o ch g Be My Native (USA)-Hibiscus (Green Shoon)

H D Daly Trevor Hemmings

Placings: 00 **(3280)**

2001/02: 20^{0}G, 17^{0}HY

	Starts	1st	2nd	3rd	Win & Pl
Hurdles	2	0	0	0	
Career Total	**2**	**0**	**0**	**0**	

Going: Sf: 0-1 GS: 0-0 Gd: 0-1 GF: - Fm: 0-0
Distance: 2m/2m3: 0-1 2m4-2m7: 0-1 3m+: 0-0
Track: LH: 0-1 RH: 0-1 Tight: 0-0 Gall: 0-0
Aids: Bl: 0-0 Vi: 0-0 Tstrap: 0-0
Best Rating: 43 11/01 Hayd 2m4f good Hdl

Native Runner (IRE)

78 **46**

6-y-o ch g Be My Native (USA)-Deep Devotion (Deep Run)

J Howard Johnson Group Captain J A Prideaux

Placings: P06P-0 **(0224)**

2001/02: 16^{0}GF

	Starts	1st	2nd	3rd	Win & Pl
Hurdles	1	0	0	0	
Career Total	**5**	**0**	**0**	**0**	**0**

Going: Sf: 0-0 GS: 0-0 Gd: 0-0 GF: - Fm: 0-1
Distance: 2m/2m3: 0-1 2m4-2m7: 0-0 3m+: 0-0
Track: LH: 0-1 RH: 0-0 Tight: 0-0 Gall: 0-0
Aids: Bl: 0-0 Vi: 0-0 Tstrap: 0-1
Best Rating: 77 1/01 Muss 2m good Hdl

Native Scout (IRE)

120 **146**

6-y-o b g Be My Native (USA)-Carmels Castle (Deep Run)

Donal Hassett Mark F Sheasby

Placings: *32002-1*301121264 **(4940a)**

2001/02: 17^{1}G, 16^{3}G, 18^{0}S, 16^{1}SH, 16^{1}Y, 18^{2}Y, 16^{1}S, 16^{2}YS, 16^{6}GS, 16^{4}Y

	Starts	1st	2nd	3rd	Win & Pl
NH Flat	1	1	0	0	4173
Hurdles	9	3	2	1	40448
Career Total	**15**	**4**	**4**	**2**	**46950**

130	12/01	Limk	2m	Hdl	SFT	£8346
120	11/01	Clon	2m	Hdl	YLD	£6120
120	10/01	Gway	2m	Hdl	SH	£5286
113	5/01	Klny	2m1f	NHF	GD	£4173

Total win prize-money £23927

Going: Sf: 1-2 GS: 0-1 Gd: 1-2 GF: - Fm: 0-0
Distance: **2m/2m3: 4-10** 2m4-2m7: 0-0 3m+: 0-0
Track: LH: 0-2 **RH: 1-3** Tight: 0-0 Gall: 0-0
Aids: Bl: 0-0 Vi: 0-0 Tstrap: 0-3
Best Rating: 146 3/02 Chel 2m110y gd-sft Hdl

Decent Irish novice hurdler. Acts on soft ground.

Native Society (IRE)

99 **119**

9-y-o b g Be My Native (USA)-Society News (Law Society (USA))

N J Henderson Nicholas Cooper

Placings: *1422/2/FP*-1 **(1992)**

2001/02: 24^{1}G

	Starts	1st	2nd	3rd	Win & Pl
Chases	1	1	0	0	4960
Career Total	**8**	**2**	**3**	**0**	**10084**

119	11/01	Kemp	3m	D(0-110)HCh	GD	£4959
109	5/98	Wxfd	2m	NHF	GD	£2382

Total win prize-money £7343

Going: Sf: 0-0 GS: 0-0 Gd: 1-1 GF: - Fm: 0-0
Distance: 2m/2m3: 0-0 2m4-2m7: 0-0 **3m+: 1-1**
Track: LH: 0-0 **RH: 1-1** Tight: 0-0 Gall: 0-0
Aids: Bl: 0-0 Vi: 0-0 Tstrap: 0-0
Best Rating: 119 11/01 Kemp 3m good Ch

Won a Wexford bumper in May '98 and showed ability over hurdles in Ireland. Finished second to Canasta on his first run in this country. Fell on his chasing debut at Fontwell after an absence of over a year due to problems. Was a rather fortunate winner on his reappearance at Kempton in November over three miles, only his second run over fences.

Native Speaker (IRE)

100 **134**

9-y-o ch g Be My Native (USA)-My Wonder (Deep Run)

P R Webber J Dougall

Placings: *13/35/13P53/1PP* **(4635)**

2001/02: 21^{1}GS, 20^{P}S, 19^{P}GF

	Starts	1st	2nd	3rd	Win & Pl
Chases	3	1	0	0	7215
Career Total	**12**	**3**	**0**	**4**	**14916**

134	2/02	Winc	2m5f	D(0-120)HCh	G-S	£7215
136	11/99	MRas	2m4f	D Ch	G-S	£4221
109	3/98	Newb	2m110y	H NHF	G-S	£1411

Total win prize-money £12847

Going: Sf: 0-1 GS: 1-1 Gd: 0-0 GF: - Fm: 0-1
Distance: 2m/2m3: 0-0 **2m4-2m7: 1-3** 3m+: 0-0
Track: LH: 0-0 **RH: 1-3** Tight: 0-1 Gall: 0-0
Aids: Bl: 0-0 Vi: 0-0 Tstrap: 0-0
Best Rating: 136 12/00 Sand 2m4f110y good Ch

From the family of the Champion Hurdler For Auction, he made a successful chasing debut at Market Rasen in November 1999, but has been lightly raced since and had been off the track for two years before winning a Wincanton handicap at the start of 2002. Best over two and a half miles on an good or a slightly easy surface.

Native Sun (IRE)

7-y-o ch g Be My Native (USA)-Koshear (Hardgreen (USA))

P R Chamings Peter Oldfield

Placings: *0*P **(3754)**

2001/02: 16^{0}S, 16^{P}HY

	Starts	1st	2nd	3rd	Win & Pl
NH Flat	1	0	0	0	0
Hurdles	1	0	0	0	0
Career Total	**2**	**0**	**0**	**0**	

Going: Sf: 0-2 GS: 0-0 Gd: 0-0 GF: - Fm: 0-0
Distance: 2m/2m3: 0-2 2m4-2m7: 0-0 3m+: 0-0
Track: LH: 0-1 RH: 0-1 Tight: 0-0 Gall: 0-0
Aids: Bl: 0-0 Vi: 0-0 Tstrap: 0-0
Best Rating: 48 12/01 Wwck 2m soft NHF

Native Thunder (IRE)

94 **91**

7-y-o b g Be My Native (USA)-Huntstown Gale (IRE) (Strong Gale)

C R Egerton Mrs Sandra A Roe

Placings:5/645 **(4494)**

2001/02: 24^{6}S, 16^{4}GS, 22^{5}G

	Starts	1st	2nd	3rd	Win & Pl
Hurdles	3	0	0	0	348
Career Total	**4**	**0**	**0**	**0**	**348**

Going: Sf: 0-1 GS: 0-1 Gd: 0-1 GF: - Fm: 0-0
Distance: 2m/2m3: 0-1 2m4-2m7: 0-1 3m+: 0-1
Track: LH: 0-1 RH: 0-2 Tight: 0-0 Gall: 0-0
Aids: Bl: 0-0 Vi: 0-0 Tstrap: 0-0
Best Rating: 119 2/00 Kemp 2m soft NHF

Has shown limited ability in bumpers and novices' hurdles.

Native Trump (IRE)

75 **91**

8-y-o b g Be My Native (USA)-Rural Ramble (IRE) (Camden Town)

C P Morlock Mr P J & Mrs T Woods

Placings:04/03/06-0P **(0374)**

2001/02: 22^{0}GF, 26^{P}GF

	Starts	1st	2nd	3rd	Win & Pl
Hurdles	2	0	0	0	
Career Total	**8**	**0**	**0**	**1**	**538**

Going: Sf: 0-0 GS: 0-0 Gd: 0-0 GF: - Fm: 0-2
Distance: 2m/2m3: 0-0 2m4-2m7: 0-1 3m+: 0-1
Track: LH: 0-0 RH: 0-2 Tight: 0-0 Gall: 0-1
Aids: Bl: 0-0 Vi: 0-0 Tstrap: 0-0
Best Rating: 98 10/99 Strf 2m6f110y gd-fm Hdl

Native Upmanship (IRE)

118 **176**

9-y-o ch g Be My Native (USA)-Hi' Upham (Deep Run)

A L T Moore Mrs John Magnier

Placings:31/4012221/11141/114P4-2221212 **(4945a)**

2001/02: 16^{2}GY, 20^{2}S, 24^{2}Y, 20^{1}HY, 16^{2}GS, 20^{1}G, 25^{2}G

	Starts	1st	2nd	3rd	Win & Pl
Chases	7	2	5	0	188766
Career Total	**26**	**11**	**8**	**1**	**377736**

174	4/02	Aint	2m4f	A Ch	GD	£69600
176	1/02	Thur	2m4f	Ch	HVY	£19938
176	12/00	Punc	2m4f	Ch	SH	£26000
160	11/00	Navn	2m	Ch	HVY	£10880
170	4/00	Fair	2m4f	Ch	SFT	£31880
152	2/00	Leop	2m5f	Ch	YLD	£26000
160	12/99	Leop	2m1f	Ch	SH	£29017
137	11/99	Navn	2m4f	Ch	YLD	£4312
138	4/99	Punc	2m4f	Hdl	YLD	£27678
114	12/98	Leop	2m2f	Hdl	SFT	£4184
114	4/98	Punc	2m	NHF	HVY	£5956

Total win prize-money £255451

Going: Sf: 1-2 GS: 0-1 Gd: 1-2 GF: - Fm: 0-0
Distance: 2m/2m3: 0-2 **2m4-2m7: 2-3** 3m+: 0-2
Track: LH: 1-4 RH: 1-3 **Tight: 1-1** Gall: 0-1
Aids: Bl: 0-0 Vi: 0-0 Tstrap: 0-0
Best Rating: 176 4/02 Punc 3m1f good Ch

A leading novice in the 1999/2000 season, he is very able on his day and has been tried over a variety of trips since showing useful form over two to three miles. Ran a blinder to finish runner-up in the 2002 Queen Mother Champion Chase and appreciated the step up to two and a half miles when taking the Martell Chase at Aintree. Suited by soft ground.

Native Wit (IRE)

109 **134**

9-y-o b m Be My Native (USA)-Joca (Rarity)

Miss Venetia Williams (Ferdy Murphy 12/5) Mrs Toni S Tipper

Placings:45261020/555133511221/404-005P **(3880)**

2001/02: 20^{0}GF, 20^{0}G, 24^{5}S, 21^{P}GS

	Starts	1st	2nd	3rd	Win & Pl
Chases	4	0	0	0	0
Career Total	**27**	**5**	**4**	**2**	**42329**

143	3/00	Uttx	2m5f	C HCh	GD	£17810
131	12/99	Hntg	2m4f110y	D Ch	GD	£3972
135	11/99	Carl	2m4f110y	D Ch	G-S	£4435
96	6/99	Tral	2m4f	(0-109)HHdl	GD	£3314
95	11/98	Thur	2m6f110y	Hdl	HVY	£2839

Total win prize-money £32373

Going: Sf: 0-1 GS: 0-1 Gd: 0-1 GF: - Fm: 0-1
Distance: 2m/2m3: 0-0 2m4-2m7: 0-3 3m+: 0-1
Track: LH: 0-3 RH: 0-1 Tight: 0-1 Gall: 0-2
Aids: Bl: 0-0 Vi: 0-0 Tstrap: 0-0
Best Rating: 143 3/00 Uttx 2m5f good Ch

A useful novice chaser in 1999/2000, she was lightly raced in 2001, showing her only real form when fourth in a hot handicap at Sandown in April 2001. Moved to Venetia Williams since then, although has been well held. Best at around two and a half miles. Acts on good/good to soft ground.

Natsamreb

88 **65**

7-y-o b m Greensmith-Learctic (Lepanto (GER))

C Tizzard C Raymond

Placings:60-6 **(0124)**

2001/02: 24^{6}F

	Starts	1st	2nd	3rd	Win & Pl
Hurdles	1	0	0	0	0
Career Total	**3**	**0**	**0**	**0**	**0**

Going: Sf: 0-0 GS: 0-0 Gd: 0-0 GF: - Fm: 0-1
Distance: 2m/2m3: 0-0 2m4-2m7: 0-0 3m+: 0-1
Track: LH: 0-0 RH: 0-1 Tight: 0-1 Gall: 0-0
Aids: Bl: 0-0 Vi: 0-0 Tstrap: 0-0
Best Rating: 65 5/01 Tntn 3m110y firm Hdl

Natural (IRE)

97 **86**

5-y-o b g Bigstone (IRE)-You Make Me Real (USA) (Give Me Strength (USA))

F P Murtagh (John Berry 5/11) G & P Barker Ltd/globe Engineering

Placings:450P2P **(4874)**

2001/02: 16^{4}GS, 17^{5}HY, 16^{0}HY, 16^{P}GS, 16^{2}S, 20^{P}G

	Starts	1st	2nd	3rd	Win & Pl
Hurdles	6	0	1	0	875
Career Total	**6**	**0**	**1**	**0**	**875**

Going: Sf: 0-3 GS: 0-2 Gd: 0-1 GF: - Fm: 0-0
Distance: 2m/2m3: 0-5 2m4-2m7: 0-1 3m+: 0-0
Track: LH: 0-4 RH: 0-2 Tight: 0-2 Gall: 0-1
Aids: Bl: 0-0 Vi: 0-1 Tstrap: 0-0
Best Rating: 86 3/02 Kels 2m110y soft Hdl

Natural Talent

93 **94**

10-y-o ch g Kris-Tropicaro (FR) (Caro)

R J Baker Churchgoers Anonymous

Placings:20/0023/P/3P0P/0-00440P **(1101)**

2001/02: 17^{0}GS, 20^{0}GF, 25^{4}G, 25^{4}F, 21^{0}GF, 22^{P}G

	Starts	1st	2nd	3rd	Win & Pl
Hurdles	1	0	0	0	0
Chases	5	0	0	0	334
Career Total	**18**	**0**	**2**	**2**	**2025**

Going: Sf: 0-0 GS: 0-1 Gd: 0-2 GF: - Fm: 0-3
Distance: 2m/2m3: 0-1 2m4-2m7: 0-3 3m+: 0-2
Track: LH: 0-4 RH: 0-2 Tight: 0-4 Gall: 0-0
Aids: Bl: 0-4 Vi: 0-0 Tstrap: 0-0
Best Rating: 94 5/01 Hrfd 3m1f110y good Ch

Naughty Dandy (IRE)

96(86h) (65h)**83**

9-y-o gr g Celio Rufo-Annie Will Run (Deep Run)

N A Twiston-Davies N A Twiston-Davies

Placings:006P/666PF4 **(4505)**

2001/02: 24^{6}G, 19^{6}G, 24^{6}GF, 26^{P}HY, 24^{F}G, 21^{4}G

	Starts	1st	2nd	3rd	Win & Pl
Hurdles	1	0	0	0	0
Chases	5	0	0	0	0
Career Total	**10**	**0**	**0**	**0**	**0**

Going: Sf: 0-1 GS: 0-0 Gd: 0-4 GF: - Fm: 0-1
Distance: 2m/2m3: 0-1 2m4-2m7: 0-1 3m+: 0-4
Track: LH: 0-3 RH: 0-3 Tight: 0-3 Gall: 0-0
Aids: Bl: 0-0 Vi: 0-0 Tstrap: 0-0
Best Rating: 93 3/00 Chep 2m4f gd-sft Hdl

Naunton Downs

78 **48**

8-y-o b g Teenoso (USA)-Kitty Come Home (Monsanto (FR))

R J Smith Dick Hibberd

Placings:0/065/P **(4726)**

2001/02: 20^{P}GF

	Starts	1st	2nd	3rd	Win & Pl
Hurdles	1	0	0	0	
Career Total	**5**	**0**	**0**	**0**	**0**

Going: Sf: 0-0 GS: 0-0 Gd: 0-0 GF: - Fm: 0-1
Distance: 2m/2m3: 0-0 2m4-2m7: 0-1 3m+: 0-0
Track: LH: 0-1 RH: 0-0 Tight: 0-0 Gall: 0-0
Aids: Bl: 0-0 Vi: 0-0 Tstrap: 0-0
Best Rating: 89 12/99 Wwck 2m soft NHF

Nautical Star

99 **81**

7-y-o b g Slip Anchor-Comic Talent (Pharly (FR))

A C Whillans (J W Hills 6/9) Mrs Helen Greggan

Placings:005P41 **(4898)**

2001/02: 16^{0}G, 16^{0}G, 16^{5}S, 25^{P}GS, 20^{4}S, 16^{1}G

	Starts	1st	2nd	3rd	Win & Pl
Hurdles	6	1	0	0	3692
Career Total	**6**	**1**	**0**	**0**	**3692**

81	4/02	Prth	2m110y	G(0-90)HHdl	GD	£3692

Total win prize-money £3692

Going: Sf: 0-2 GS: 0-1 Gd: 1-3 GF: - Fm: 0-0
Distance: **2m/2m3: 1-4** 2m4-2m7: 0-1 3m+: 0-1
Track: LH: 0-5 **RH: 1-1** Tight: 0-2 Gall: 0-1
Aids: Bl: 0-0 Vi: 0-0 Tstrap: 0-0
Best Rating: 81 4/02 Prth 2m110y good Hdl

Got off the mark at the fifth attempt over hurdles at Perth in April. Acts well on decent ground.

Navarone

103 **125**

8-y-o b g Gunner B-Anamasi (Idiots Delight)
N A Twiston-Davies A J Cresser

Placings:*554*/4224315/**33PP110** **(4895)**
2001/02: 25^{3}G, 24^{3}S, 20^{P}G, 22^{P}G, 20^{1}GF, 20^{1}GF, 20^{0}G

	Starts	1st	2nd	3rd	Win & Pl
Chases	7	2	0	2	8172
Career Total	**17**	**3**	**2**	**3**	**14291**

125	4/02	Uttx	2m4f	E(0-100)HCh	G-F	£3373
119	4/02	Wwck	2m4f110y	F(0-90)HCh	G-F	£3220
104	3/00	Ling	2m7f	D Hdl	GD	£3373

Total win prize-money £9968

Going: Sf: 0-1 GS: 0-0 Gd: 0-4 GF: - Fm: 2-2
Distance: 2m/2m3: 0-0 **2m4-2m7: 2-5** 3m+: 0-2
Track: **LH: 2-5** RH: 0-2 Tight: 0-2 Gall: 0-1
Aids: Bl: 0-0 Vi: 0-0 **Tstrap: 2-5**
Best Rating: 125 4/02 Uttx 2m4f gd-fm Ch

A hurdle winner over two miles-seven, scored over fences at Warwick and Uttoxeter in April 2002. Suited by positive tactics and a sound surface. Wears a tongue tie.

Navarre Samson (FR)

103 **114**

7-y-o b/br g Ganges (USA)-L'Eternite (FR) (Cariellor (FR))
P J Hobbs Winton Bloodstock Ltd

Placings:1111122360/204012/1-22 **(1340)**
2001/02: 20^{2}GF, 22^{2}GF

	Starts	1st	2nd	3rd	Win & Pl
Hurdles	2	0	2	0	1282
Career Total	**19**	**7**	**6**	**1**	**30659**

125	8/00	Strf	2m6f110y	F Hdl	G-F	£2492
120	7/99	Strf	2m6f110y	D(0-125)HHdl	GD	£3231
118	11/98	Sand	2m110y	D Hdl	GD	£2736
120	10/98	Weth	2m	A Hdl	GD	£8819
120	9/98	Extr	2m1f	E Hdl	GD	£2242
120	8/98	Worc	2m	E Hdl	GD	£2285
111	8/98	Worc	2m	E Hdl	G-F	£2355

Total win prize-money £24162

Going: Sf: 0-0 GS: 0-0 Gd: 0-0 GF: - Fm: 0-2
Distance: 2m/2m3: 0-0 2m4-2m7: 0-2 3m+: 0-0
Track: LH: 0-1 RH: 0-0 Tight: 0-2 Gall: 0-0
Aids: Bl: 0-0 Vi: 0-0 Tstrap: 0-2
Best Rating: 125 8/00 Strf 2m6f110y gd-fm Hdl

Modest hurdler, suited by fast ground.

Naviasky (IRE)

86 **84**

7-y-o b/br g Scenic-Black Molly (IRE) (High Top)
D Nicholls (Miss Venetia Williams 28/11) D Nicholls

Placings:34/40P **(2389)**

2001/02: 17^{4}S, 16^{0}G, 16^{P}S

	Starts	1st	2nd	3rd	Win & Pl
Hurdles	3	0	0	0	0
Career Total	**5**	**0**	**0**	**1**	**404**

Going: Sf: 0-2 GS: 0-0 Gd: 0-1 GF: - Fm: 0-0
Distance: 2m/2m3: 0-3 2m4-2m7: 0-0 3m+: 0-0
Track: LH: 0-3 RH: 0-0 Tight: 0-1 Gall: 0-0
Aids: Bl: 0-0 Vi: 0-0 Tstrap: 0-0
Best Rating: 107 11/98 Sand 2m110y good Hdl

A useful Flat handicapper, he has looked a non-stayer in a few runs over hurdles.

Nazzaro

95 **79**

13-y-o b g Town And Country-Groundsel (Reform)
W G M Turner Mrs Tracy Turner

Placings:326/231P222/**2U12134/11F114/F0PP4/PUP/ 26231P6/5**5304110/5642O65-0640 **(4035)**
2001/02: 22^{0}S, 21^{6}HY, 22^{4}HY, 22^{0}S

	Starts	1st	2nd	3rd	Win & Pl
Hurdles	4	0	0	0	0
Career Total	**57**	**10**	**10**	**5**	**46027**

109	2/00	Folk	2m6f110y	F(0-95)HHdl	SFT	£1974
109	2/00	Font	2m6f110y	G(0-95)HHdl	SFT	£2310
116	3/99	Font	3m2f110y	D(0-125)HCh	SFT	£3834
123	2/96	Font	3m2f110y	D(0-120)HCh	SFT	£3827
112	1/96	Font	3m2f110y	D(0-125)HCh	SFT	£4386
118	12/95	Bang	4m1f	E(0-115)HCh	G-S	£4318
114	11/95	NAbb	3m2f110y	D(0-120)HCh	SFT	£5168
94	12/94	Sthl	3m110y	Ch	SFT	£2455
88	11/94	Sthl	3m110y	HCh	SFT	£2858
104	1/94	Folk	2m6f110y	Hdl	HVY	£1543

Total win prize-money £32665

Going: Sf: 0-4 GS: 0-0 Gd: 0-0 GF: - Fm: 0-0
Distance: 2m/2m3: 0-0 2m4-2m7: 0-4 3m+: 0-0
Track: LH: 0-3 RH: 0-1 Tight: 0-4 Gall: 0-0
Aids: Bl: 0-4 Vi: 0-0 Tstrap: 0-0
Best Rating: 123 2/96 Font 3m2f110y soft Ch

Ndr's Cash For Fun

109 **77**

9-y-o b g Ballacashtal (CAN)-Basic Fun (Teenoso (USA))
A W Carroll Group 1 Racing (1994) Ltd

Placings:*00/0*/P-0P1P1430 **(4917)**
2001/02: 22^{0}G, 22^{P}S, 16^{1}S, 16^{P}HY, 19^{1}S, 21^{4}S, 24^{3}G, 21^{0}GF

	Starts	1st	2nd	3rd	Win & Pl
Hurdles	8	2	0	1	3939
Career Total	**12**	**2**	**0**	**1**	**3939**

73	2/02	Tntn	2m3f110y	G(0-95)HHdl	SFT	£1750
73	1/02	Leic	2m	G(0-90)HHdl	SFT	£1939

Total win prize-money £3689

Going: Sf: 2-5 GS: 0-0 Gd: 0-2 GF: - Fm: 0-1
Distance: 2m/2m3: 1-2 2m4-2m7: 1-5 3m+: 0-1
Track: LH: 0-5 **RH: 2-3 Tight: 1-7** Gall: 0-0
Aids: Bl: 0-0 Vi: 0-0 Tstrap: 0-0
Best Rating: 82 4/98 Asct 2m110y good NHF

Lightly raced selling-class hurdler, who had a habit of pulling up early in his career. Needs humouring.

Ne M'Oublie Pas (FR)

108 **105**

6-y-o b/br g Shining Steel-Irish Lullaby (FR) (Prince Tenderfoot (USA))
P J Hobbs Triple Two

Placings:10436/P**23003P4-0404021** **(1104)**
2001/02: 19^{0}GS, 21^{4}GF, 24^{0}GF, 23^{4}G, 23^{0}G, 26^{2}G, 26^{1}G

	Starts	1st	2nd	3rd	Win & Pl
Chases	7	1	1	0	4205
Career Total	**20**	**2**	**2**	**3**	**13235**

105	8/01	NAbb	3m2f110y	F(0-90)HCh	GD	£2513
	8/99	Claf	2m	Hdl	HLD	£4306

Total win prize-money £6819

Going: Sf: 0-0 GS: 0-1 Gd: 1-4 GF: - Fm: 0-2
Distance: 2m/2m3: 0-0 2m4-2m7: 0-2 **3m+: 1-5**
Track: **LH: 1-5** RH: 0-2 **Tight: 1-3** Gall: 0-1
Aids: Bl: 0-1 Vi: 0-0 Tstrap: 0-0
Best Rating: 105 8/01 NAbb 3m2f110y good Ch

Nearly A Score

95(89h) (73h)**114**

10-y-o b m Nearly A Hand-Boherash (Boreen (FR))
J D Frost (R G Frost 28/2) T R Watts

Placings:*00*/5/**2354F4**5/**252035-U3F543** **(4405)**
2001/02: 21^{U}GF, 19^{3}GS, 10^{F}S, 20^{5}S, 20^{4}GS, 17^{3}G

	Starts	1st	2nd	3rd	Win & Pl
Chases	6	0	0	2	3855
Career Total	**22**	**0**	**3**	**4**	**14203**

Going: Sf: 0-3 GS: 0-2 Gd: 0-0 GF: - Fm: 0-1
Distance: 2m/2m3: 0-1 2m4-2m7: 0-5 3m+: 0-0
Track: LH: 0-5 RH: 0-1 Tight: 0-4 Gall: 0-0
Aids: Bl: 0-0 Vi: 0-0 Tstrap: 0-0
Best Rating: 114 11/01 Chep 2m3f110y gd-sft Ch

A winning pointer, is somewhat inconsistent and has yet to get her head in front under Rules, often jumping less than fluently. Looks best at around two and a half miles. Acts on soft ground.

Nearlymissed Daisy

82 **66**

8-y-o b m Presidium-Nearly Married (Nearly A Hand)
M C Pipe Mrs Pam Pengelly

Placings:0-50 **(0124)**
2001/02: 17^{5}GS, 24^{0}F

	Starts	1st	2nd	3rd	Win & Pl
Hurdles	2	0	0	0	0
Career Total	**3**	**0**	**0**	**0**	**0**

Going: Sf: 0-0 GS: 0-1 Gd: 0-0 GF: - Fm: 0-1
Distance: 2m/2m3: 0-1 2m4-2m7: 0-0 3m+: 0-1
Track: LH: 0-0 RH: 0-2 Tight: 0-1 Gall: 0-0
Aids: Bl: 0-0 Vi: 0-0 Tstrap: 0-0
Best Rating: 66 5/01 Extr 2m1f gd-sft Hdl

Needsmoretime (IRE)

10-y-o b g Strong Gale-Sue's A Lady (Le Moss)
S J Robinson S J Robinson

Placings:*05*R52P00400/53600P2FP0RP/3 **(4335)**

2001/02: 27^{3}S

	Starts	1st	2nd	3rd	Win & Pl
Chases	1	0	0	1	214
Career Total	**24**	**0**	**2**	**2**	**3319**

Going: Sf: 0-1 GS: 0-0 Gd: 0-0 GF: - Fm: 0-0
Distance: 2m/2m3: 0-0 2m4-2m7: 0-0 3m+: 0-1
Track: LH: 0-1 RH: 0-0 Tight: 0-1 Gall: 0-0
Aids: Bl: 0-0 Vi: 0-0 Tstrap: 0-0
Best Rating: 105 12/98 Leop 2m4f heavy Hdl

Dual point winner, very limited ability under Rules.

Needwood Brave

100 **93**

4-y-o b g Lion Cavern (USA)-Woodcrest (Niniski (USA))
J G Fitzgerald Tim Kilroe

Placings:*S30FP* **(3356)**
2001/02: 16^{S}GF, 16^{3}G, 16^{0}S, 16^{F}G, 16^{P}HY

	Starts	1st	2nd	3rd	Win & Pl
Hurdles	5	0	0	1	549
Career Total	**5**	**0**	**0**	**1**	**549**

Going: Sf: 0-2 GS: 0-0 Gd: 0-2 GF: - Fm: 0-1
Distance: 2m/2m3: 0-5 2m4-2m7: 0-0 3m+: 0-0
Track: LH: 0-5 RH: 0-0 Tight: 0-1 Gall: 0-0
Aids: Bl: 0-0 Vi: 0-3 Tstrap: 0-0
Best Rating: 93 10/01 Weth 2m good Hdl

Needwood Legend

(73h) (60h)

9-y-o b/br g Rolfe (USA)-Enchanting Kate (Enchantment)
A J Wilson Mrs M J Wilson

Placings:*2000/00P424004/06053505-PP* **(2882)**
2001/02: 16^{P}GF, 16^{P}G

	Starts	1st	2nd	3rd	Win & Pl
Hurdles	1	0	0	0	0
Chases	1	0	0	0	0
Career Total	**23**	**0**	**2**	**1**	**1881**

Going: Sf: 0-0 GS: 0-0 Gd: 0-1 GF: - Fm: 0-1
Distance: 2m/2m3: 0-2 2m4-2m7: 0-0 3m+: 0-0
Track: LH: 0-0 RH: 0-2 Tight: 0-0 Gall: 0-1
Aids: Bl: 0-0 Vi: 0-0 Tstrap: 0-0
Best Rating: 90 9/98 Worc 2m gd-fm Hdl

Needwood Lion

109(102h) (107h)**124**

9-y-o b g Rolfe (USA)-Arctic Lion (Arctic Slave)
H D Daly The Earl Cadogan

Placings:*26/606511/021FF46-305352* **(4876)**
2001/02: 16^{3}S, 20^{0}GS, 16^{5}S, 16^{3}HY, 16^{5}S, 20^{2}G

	Starts	1st	2nd	3rd	Win & Pl
Hurdles	1	0	0	1	373
Chases	5	0	1	1	3454
Career Total	**21**	**3**	**3**	**2**	**15218**

140	1/01	Uttx	2m	D Ch	HVY	£4143
104	4/00	Hrfd	2m3f110y	E(0-105)HHdl	SFT	£2970
96	3/00	Tntn	2m1f	F(0-105)HHdl	SFT	£2524

Total win prize-money £9639

Going: Sf: 0-4 GS: 0-1 Gd: 0-1 GF: - Fm: 0-0
Distance: 2m/2m3: 0-4 2m4-2m7: 0-2 3m+: 0-0
Track: LH: 0-3 RH: 0-3 Tight: 0-1 Gall: 0-1
Aids: Bl: 0-0 Vi: 0-0 Tstrap: 0-0
Best Rating: 140 1/01 Winc 2m5f soft Ch

A headstrong individual, he made all on heavy ground in a novice chase at Uttoxeter in January 2001 and was travelling best when falling on his next two starts. Given a few confidence boosters over hurdles thereafter, he showed return to form when second over two and a half miles at Perth in April 2002.

Needwood Missile

85f **86f**

6-y-o b g Sizzling Melody-Sea Dart (Air Trooper)
J L Spearing Bryan Mathieson

Placings:*0/5* **(0239)**
2001/02: 16^{5}GF

	Starts	1st	2nd	3rd	Win & Pl
NH Flat	1	0	0	0	0
Career Total	**2**	**0**	**0**	**0**	**0**

Going: Sf: 0-0 GS: 0-0 Gd: 0-0 GF: - Fm: 0-1
Distance: 2m/2m3: 0-1 2m4-2m7: 0-0 3m+: 0-0
Track: LH: 0-1 RH: 0-0 Tight: 0-1 Gall: 0-0
Aids: Bl: 0-0 Vi: 0-0 Tstrap: 0-0
Best Rating: 86 5/01 Sthl 2m gd-fm NHF

Needwood Mystic

84 **86**

7-y-o b m Rolfe (USA)-Enchanting Kate (Enchantment)
Mrs A J Perrett Mrs G Harwood

Placings:3 **(2061)**
2001/02: 20^{3}GS

	Starts	1st	2nd	3rd	Win & Pl
Hurdles	1	0	0	1	341
Career Total	**1**	**0**	**0**	**1**	**341**

Going: Sf: 0-0 GS: 0-1 Gd: 0-0 GF: - Fm: 0-0
Distance: 2m/2m3: 0-0 2m4-2m7: 0-1 3m+: 0-0
Track: LH: 0-0 RH: 0-0 Tight: 0-1 Gall: 0-0
Aids: Bl: 0-0 Vi: 0-0 Tstrap: 0-0
Best Rating: 86 11/01 Font 2m4f gd-sft Hdl

A game front-running mare, she made a promising debut over hurdles and is suited by a sound surface.

Needwood Spirit

105 **110**

7-y-o b g Rolfe (USA)-Needwood Nymph (Bold Owl)
Mrs A M Naughton (H Alexander 16/5) Famous Five Racing

Placings:*45/00P01-5611146* **(3282)**
2001/02: 16^{5}GF, 16^{6}GS, 17^{1}S, 20^{1}HY, 16^{1}S, 24^{4}G, 20^{6}S

	Starts	1st	2nd	3rd	Win & Pl
Hurdles	7	3	0	0	12713
Career Total	**14**	**4**	**0**	**0**	**14640**

95	12/01	Hexm	2m	D(0-125)HHdl	SFT	£7020
110	11/01	Carl	2m4f	F(0-105)HHdl	HVY	£2299
110	11/01	Carl	2m1f	F(0-110)HHdl	SFT	£2664
87	4/01	Fknm	2m	G(0-90)HHdl	G-S	£1926

Total win prize-money £13910

Going: Sf: 3-4 GS: 0-1 Gd: 0-1 GF: - Fm: 0-1
Distance: **2m/2m3: 2-4** 2m4-2m7: 1-2 3m+: 0-1
Track: LH: 1-2 RH: 1-3 Tight: 0-2 Gall: 0-0
Aids: Bl: 0-0 Vi: 0-0 Tstrap: 0-0
Best Rating: 110 11/01 Carl 2m4f heavy Hdl

Runs under both codes. A staying handicapper on the level, he won three times over hurdles in the autumn of 2001. Stays two and a half miles. Acts on an easy surface.

Neilstoneside (IRE)

4-y-o b f General Monash (USA)-Lady Counsel (IRE) (Law Society (USA))
M J Ryan Charles Alan McKechnie

Placings:*00UPP* **(4881)**
2001/02: 16^{0}GS, 16^{0}GF, 20^{U}GF, 22^{P}G, 18^{P}GF

	Starts	1st	2nd	3rd	Win & Pl
NH Flat	2	0	0	0	0
Hurdles	3	0	0	0	0
Career Total	**5**	**0**	**0**	**0**	

Going: Sf: 0-0 GS: 0-1 Gd: 0-1 GF: - Fm: 0-3
Distance: 2m/2m3: 0-3 2m4-2m7: 0-2 3m+: 0-0
Track: LH: 0-3 RH: 0-2 Tight: 0-3 Gall: 0-1
Aids: Bl: 0-0 Vi: 0-1 Tstrap: 0-0
Best Rating: 69 3/02 Hntg 2m110y gd-fm NHF

Neily Joe (IRE)

10-y-o b g Balinger-Merry Mirth (Menelek)
A J Chamberlain Mrs A T Lodge

Placings:*0/PF* **(4264)**
2001/02: 24^{P}S, 19^{F}S

	Starts	1st	2nd	3rd	Win & Pl
Chases	2	0	0	0	
Career Total	**3**	**0**	**0**	**0**	

Going: Sf: 0-2 GS: 0-0 Gd: 0-0 GF: - Fm: 0-0
Distance: 2m/2m3: 0-0 2m4-2m7: 0-1 3m+: 0-1
Track: LH: 0-1 RH: 0-1 Tight: 0-1 Gall: 0-0
Aids: Bl: 0-0 Vi: 0-0 Tstrap: 0-0
Best Rating: 59 10/98 Chel 2m110y gd-sft NHF

Nelly Moser

95f **89f**

5-y-o gr m Neltino-Boreen's Glory (Boreen (FR))
Mrs D Haine Mrs Diana Haine

Placings:*0* **(4595)**
2001/02: 16^{0}G

	Starts	1st	2nd	3rd	Win & Pl
NH Flat	1	0	0	0	
Career Total	**1**	**0**	**0**	**0**	

Going: Sf: 0-0 GS: 0-0 Gd: 0-1 GF: - Fm: 0-0
Distance: 2m/2m3: 0-1 2m4-2m7: 0-0 3m+: 0-0
Track: LH: 0-1 RH: 0-0 Tight: 0-0 Gall: 0-0
Aids: Bl: 0-0 Vi: 0-0 Tstrap: 0-0
Best Rating: 89 4/02 Uttx 2m good NHF

Modest form in bumpers.

Nelsons Flagship

49 **13**

4-y-o b g Petong-Marie's Crusader (IRE) (Last Tycoon)
Miss E C Lavelle (J Akehurst 26/5) Fraser Miller

Placings:0 **(3210)**
2001/02: 16^{0}GS

	Starts	1st	2nd	3rd	Win & Pl
Hurdles	1	0	0	0	
Career Total	**1**	**0**	**0**	**0**	

Going: Sf: 0-0 GS: 0-1 Gd: 0-0 GF: - Fm: 0-0
Distance: 2m/2m3: 0-1 2m4-2m7: 0-0 3m+: 0-0
Track: LH: 0-1 RH: 0-0 Tight: 0-0 Gall: 0-1
Aids: Bl: 0-0 Vi: 0-0 Tstrap: 0-0

Best Rating: 13 1/02 Newb 2m110y gd-sft Hdl

Nemisto

104(103h) (77h)119

8-y-o gr g Mystiko (USA)-Nemesia (Mill Reef (USA))

R Lee Will Roseff

Placings:62P/5330201/51252201/0056F-33355PP **(4543)**

2001/02: 17^{3}GS, 21^{3}GF, 21^{3}S, 20^{5}S, 18^{5}HY, 16^{P}GS, 19^{P}G

	Starts	1st	2nd	3rd	Win & Pl
Hurdles	2	0	0	0	0
Chases	5	0	0	3	1757
Career Total	**30**	**3**	**5**	**5**	**19281**

128	3/00	Chep	2m110y	D Hdl	GD	£3256
124	12/99	Hrfd	2m1f	E(0-115)HHdl	SFT	£2762
114	5/99	Hrfd	2m1f	D(0-110)HHdl	GD	£2560

Total win prize-money £8579

Going: Sf: 0-3 GS: 0-2 Gd: 0-1 GF: - Fm: 0-1
Distance: 2m/2m3: 0-4 2m4-2m7: 0-3 3m+: 0-0
Track: LH: 0-5 RH: 0-2 Tight: 0-5 Gall: 0-0
Aids: Bl: 0-0 Vi: 0-0 Tstrap: 0-7
Best Rating: 128 3/00 Chep 2m110y good Hdl

Won a novice hurdle over two miles in March 2000. More encouraging efforts over fences. Acts on soft, handles a sound surface. Stays two and a half miles.

Nephite (NZ)

113(95h) (84h)108

8-y-o b g Star Way-Te Akau Charmer (NZ) (Sir Tristram)

N B Mason N B Mason

Placings:56633233005-441365131231P **(4891)**

2001/02: 17^{4}GS, 16^{4}GF, 16^{1}S, 20^{3}S, 17^{6}S, 16^{5}G, 16^{1}S, 16^{3}GS, 16^{1}S, 16^{2}S, 17^{3}G, 17^{1}G, 16^{P}G

	Starts	1st	2nd	3rd	Win & Pl
Hurdles	1	0	0	0	0
Chases	12	4	1	3	17299
Career Total	**24**	**4**	**2**	**7**	**19535**

108	4/02	MRas	2m1f110y	E(0-105)HCh	GD	£3570
108	1/02	Newc	2m110y	E(0-105)HCh	SFT	£3032
97	1/02	Fknm	2m110y	F(0-100)HCh	SFT	£4342
92	10/01	Carl	2m	F(0-100)HCh	SFT	£2038

Total win prize-money £13882

Going: Sf: 3-6 GS: 0-2 Gd: 1-4 GF: - Fm: 0-1
Distance: **2m/2m3: 4-12** 2m4-2m7: 0-1 3m+: 0-0
Track: LH: 2-8 RH: 2-5 **Tight: 2-6** Gall: 1-2
Aids: Bl: 0-0 Vi: 0-0 **Tstrap: 1-2**
Best Rating: 108 4/02 MRas 2m1f110y good Ch

Suited by two miles on both soft and good ground, he is a consistent handicap chaser.

Neptune's Orbit (NZ)

87(99h) (85h)55

8-y-o ch g Crested Wave (USA)-Constellation (NZ) (Zamazaan (FR))

T R George Terry Warner & Partners

Placings:653P-40U0 **(1045)**

2001/02: 21^{4}G, 21^{0}G, 24^{U}GF, 26^{0}GF

	Starts	1st	2nd	3rd	Win & Pl
Hurdles	2	0	0	0	0
Chases	2	0	0	0	0
Career Total	**8**	**0**	**0**	**1**	**332**

Going: Sf: 0-0 GS: 0-0 Gd: 0-2 GF: - Fm: 0-2
Distance: 2m/2m3: 0-0 2m4-2m7: 0-2 3m+: 0-2
Track: LH: 0-3 RH: 0-0 Tight: 0-2 Gall: 0-0
Aids: Bl: 0-0 Vi: 0-0 Tstrap: 0-0
Best Rating: 88 11/00 Towc 2m soft Hdl

Nero's Palace

95 77

5-y-o b g Emperor Jones (USA)-Sayulita (Habitat)

M Todhunter (C Grant 27/9) Peter Boddy

Placings:456 **(4906)**

2001/02: 16^{4}GF, 16^{5}G, 19^{6}G

	Starts	1st	2nd	3rd	Win & Pl
NH Flat	2	0	0	0	0
Hurdles	1	0	0	0	0
Career Total	**3**	**0**	**0**	**0**	**0**

Going: Sf: 0-0 GS: 0-0 Gd: 0-2 GF: - Fm: 0-1
Distance: 2m/2m3: 0-2 2m4-2m7: 0-1 3m+: 0-0
Track: LH: 0-0 RH: 0-3 Tight: 0-1 Gall: 0-1
Aids: Bl: 0-0 Vi: 0-0 Tstrap: 0-0
Best Rating: 77 4/02 MRas 2m3f110y good Hdl

Nether Another

5-y-o b m Another Sam-Poppy Kelly (Netherkelly)

M J Gingell Miss S Wilson

Placings:0 **(3290)**

2001/02: 17^{0}S

	Starts	1st	2nd	3rd	Win & Pl
NH Flat	1	0	0	0	
Career Total	**1**	**0**	**0**	**0**	

Going: Sf: 0-1 GS: 0-0 Gd: 0-0 GF: - Fm: 0-0
Distance: 2m/2m3: 0-1 2m4-2m7: 0-0 3m+: 0-0
Track: LH: 0-0 RH: 0-0 Tight: 0-1 Gall: 0-0
Aids: Bl: 0-0 Vi: 0-0 Tstrap: 0-0
Best Rating:

Nettles

47

4-y-o br g Cyrano De Bergerac-Sylvandra (Mazilier (USA))

R Williams R Williams

Placings:0 **(1355)**

2001/02: 16^{0}GF

	Starts	1st	2nd	3rd	Win & Pl
Hurdles	1	0	0	0	
Career Total	**1**	**0**	**0**	**0**	

Going: Sf: 0-0 GS: 0-0 Gd: 0-0 GF: - Fm: 0-1
Distance: 2m/2m3: 0-1 2m4-2m7: 0-0 3m+: 0-0
Track: LH: 0-1 RH: 0-0 Tight: 0-1 Gall: 0-0
Aids: Bl: 0-0 Vi: 0-0 Tstrap: 0-0
Best Rating:

Neutron (IRE)

93 113

5-y-o ch g Nucleon (USA)-Balistic Princess (Lomond (USA))

M C Pipe Matt Archer & Miss Jean Broadhurst

Placings:2212200-4600 **(1026)**

2001/02: 17^{4}GF, 20^{6}G, 20^{0}GF, 22^{0}G

	Starts	1st	2nd	3rd	Win & Pl
Hurdles	4	0	0	0	318
Career Total	**11**	**1**	**4**	**0**	**8214**

110	9/00	Cork	2m	Hdl	GD	£3864

Total win prize-money £3864

Going: Sf: 0-0 GS: 0-0 Gd: 0-2 GF: - Fm: 0-2
Distance: 2m/2m3: 0-1 2m4-2m7: 0-3 3m+: 0-0
Track: LH: 0-4 RH: 0-0 Tight: 0-3 Gall: 0-0
Aids: Bl: 0-0 Vi: 0-1 Tstrap: 0-0
Best Rating: 113 5/01 NAbb 2m1f gd-fm Hdl

Neva-Agree

99 77

10-y-o ch g St Columbus-Nee-Argee (Rymer)

R J Armson R J Armson

Placings:2/P43P-P33P02 **(2944)**

2001/02: 26^{P}GF, 24^{3}GF, 24^{3}GF, 25^{P}G, 27^{0}G, 24^{2}G

	Starts	1st	2nd	3rd	Win & Pl
Chases	6	0	1	2	2257
Career Total	**11**	**0**	**2**	**3**	**3373**

Going: Sf: 0-0 GS: 0-0 Gd: 0-3 GF: - Fm: 0-3
Distance: 2m/2m3: 0-0 2m4-2m7: 0-0 3m+: 0-6
Track: LH: 0-4 RH: 0-2 Tight: 0-4 Gall: 0-1
Aids: Bl: 0-4 Vi: 0-0 Tstrap: 0-0
Best Rating: 81 4/00 MRas 3m1f gd-fm Ch

A winner of two point-to-points, has shown bits of form under rules. Acts on good ground.

Never (FR)

110 138

5-y-o b g Vettori (IRE)-Neraida (USA) (Glboulee (CAN))

F Doumen (E Danel 30/11) Sir Peter O'Sullevan

Placings:411000 **(4674)**

2001/02: 18^{4}HY, 17^{1}HY, 16^{1}G, 16^{0}GS, 16^{0}GS, 16^{0}G

	Starts	1st	2nd	3rd	Win & Pl
Hurdles	6	2	0	0	22799
Career Total	**6**	**2**	**0**	**0**	**22799**

138	12/01	Asct	2m110y	A Hdl	GD	£13100
	11/01	Engh	2m1f110y	Hdl	HVY	£9699

Total win prize-money £22799

Going: Sf: 1-2 GS: 0-2 Gd: 1-2 GF: - Fm: 0-0
Distance: **2m/2m3: 2-6** 2m4-2m7: 0-0 3m+: 0-0
Track: LH: 0-2 **RH: 1-2** Tight: 0-1 Gall: 0-0
Aids: Bl: 0-0 Vi: 0-0 Tstrap: 0-0
Best Rating: 138 12/01 Asct 2m110y good Hdl

French-trained hurdler, won nicely on his British debut at Ascot in December 2001, ahead of Image de Marque II, but well held since. Suited by two miles, acts on a good and easy surface.

Never Can Tell

107 92

6-y-o ch g Emarati (USA)-Farmer's Pet (Sharrood (USA))

M Mullineaux Mrs Renee Farrington-Kirkham

Placings:P22050024F0/0020514-402644403 **(3704)**

2001/02: 16^{4}F, 17^{0}F, 19^{2}GF, 20^{6}GS, 17^{4}G, 17^{4}GS, 16^{4}S, 21^{0}GS, 17^{3}HY

	Starts	1st	2nd	3rd	Win & Pl
Hurdles	9	0	1	1	1630
Career Total	**27**	**1**	**5**	**1**	**6864**

92	1/01	Winc	2m	F Hdl	G-S	£1949

Total win prize-money £1950

Going: Sf: 0-2 GS: 0-3 Gd: 0-1 GF: - Fm: 0-3
Distance: 2m/2m3: 0-6 2m4-2m7: 0-3 3m+: 0-0
Track: LH: 0-2 RH: 0-7 Tight: 0-3 Gall: 0-1
Aids: Bl: 0-0 Vi: 0-0 Tstrap: 0-0
Best Rating: 94 2/00 MRas 2m1f110y gd-sft Hdl

Modest handicap hurdler with a poor win- to-runs ratio.

Never Ending Story

84 **70**

4-y-o b f Deploy-Bold Gem (Never So Bold)
O Sherwood (E J Alston 31/8) Ledwidge Best Dellal Forde

Placings:6 **(2209)**
2001/02: 17^{6}G

	Starts	1st	2nd	3rd	Win & Pl
Hurdles	1	0	0	0	0
Career Total	**1**	**0**	**0**	**0**	**0**

Going: Sf: 0-0 GS: 0-0 Gd: 0-1 GF: - Fm: 0-0
Distance: 2m/2m3: 0-1 2m4-2m7: 0-0 3m+: 0-0
Track: LH: 0-0 RH: 0-1 Tight: 0-0 Gall: 0-0
Aids: Bl: 0-0 Vi: 0-0 Tstrap: 0-0
Best Rating: 70 11/01 Hrfd 2m1f good Hdl

Never Forget Bowie

84 **62**

6-y-o b g Superpower-Heldigvis (Hot Grove)
R Allan Robert Miller-Bakewell

Placings:*0/000*00 **(4689)**
2001/02: 16^{0}G, 17^{0}GF, 16^{0}G, 16^{0}S, 16^{0}GF

	Starts	1st	2nd	3rd	Win & Pl
NH Flat	3	0	0	0	0
Hurdles	2	0	0	0	0
Career Total	**6**	**0**	**0**	**0**	

Going: Sf: 0-1 GS: 0-0 Gd: 0-2 GF: - Fm: 0-2
Distance: 2m/2m3: 0-5 2m4-2m7: 0-0 3m+: 0-0
Track: LH: 0-3 RH: 0-1 Tight: 0-3 Gall: 0-0
Aids: Bl: 0-0 Vi: 0-0 Tstrap: 0-3
Best Rating: 65 12/01 Muss 2m good NHF

Never In Debt

85(110c) **53**

10-y-o ch g Nicholas Bill-Deep In Debt (Deep Run)
E R Clough (A G Hobbs 14/5) E R Clough

Placings:*120/341104/2P/*P524F425/4P-FPP **(4091)**
2001/02: 20^{F}GS, 21^{P}G, 24^{P}S

	Starts	1st	2nd	3rd	Win & Pl
Chases	3	0	0	0	
Career Total	**24**	**3**	**4**	**1**	**13020**

110	2/98	Tntn	2m3f110y	D(0-120)HHdl	G-F	£2814
108	1/98	Tntn	2m3f110y	D Hdl	SFT	£2913
99	9/96	Worc	2m	H NHF	G-F	£1385

Total win prize-money £7112

Going: Sf: 0-1 GS: 0-1 Gd: 0-1 GF: - Fm: 0-0
Distance: 2m/2m3: 0-0 2m4-2m7: 0-2 3m+: 0-1
Track: LH: 0-1 RH: 0-0 Tight: 0-1 Gall: 0-0
Aids: Bl: 0-0 Vi: 0-0 Tstrap: 0-0
Best Rating: 115 11/98 Chel 2m5f gd-sft Hdl

Never Promise (FR)

77 **38**

4-y-o b f Cadeaux Genereux-Yazeanhaa (USA) (Zilzal (USA))
J Neville (B W Hills 14/9) Mrs Theresa O'Toole

Placings:00 **(4737)**
2001/02: 17^{0}GS, 16^{0}GF

	Starts	1st	2nd	3rd	Win & Pl
Hurdles	2	0	0	0	
Career Total	**2**	**0**	**0**	**0**	

Going: Sf: 0-0 GS: 0-1 Gd: 0-0 GF: - Fm: 0-1
Distance: 2m/2m3: 0-2 2m4-2m7: 0-0 3m+: 0-0
Track: LH: 0-0 RH: 0-2 Tight: 0-1 Gall: 0-0
Aids: Bl: 0-0 Vi: 0-1 Tstrap: 0-0
Best Rating: 38 4/02 Ludl 2m gd-fm Hdl

Never Think Twice

9-y-o b g Never So Bold-Hope And Glory (USA) (Well Decorated (USA))
Brian Hurst Brian Hurst

Placings:P **(1615)**
2001/02: 17^{P}GF

	Starts	1st	2nd	3rd	Win & Pl
Hurdles	1	0	0	0	
Career Total	**1**	**0**	**0**	**0**	

Going: Sf: 0-0 GS: 0-0 Gd: 0-0 GF: - Fm: 0-1
Distance: 2m/2m3: 0-1 2m4-2m7: 0-0 3m+: 0-0
Track: LH: 0-0 RH: 0-1 Tight: 0-0 Gall: 0-0
Aids: Bl: 0-0 Vi: 0-0 Tstrap: 0-0
Best Rating:

Never Wonder (IRE)

106(82h) (112h)**117**

7-y-o b g John French-Mistress Anna (Arapaho)
M Bradstock Ever The Optimists

Placings:01-4123 **(4372)**
2001/02: 24^{4}G, 24^{1}G, 26^{2}GS, 24^{3}GS

	Starts	1st	2nd	3rd	Win & Pl
Chases	4	1	1	1	7070
Career Total	**6**	**2**	**1**	**1**	**9374**

117	12/01	Donc	3m	D Ch	GD	£5267
112	4/01	Extr	2m6f110y	E Hdl	SFT	£2304

Total win prize-money £7572

Going: Sf: 0-0 GS: 0-2 Gd: 1-2 GF: - Fm: 0-0
Distance: 2m/2m3: 0-0 2m4-2m7: 0-0 **3m+: 1-4**
Track: **LH: 1-1** RH: 0-1 Tight: 0-1 **Gall: 1-1**
Aids: Bl: 0-0 Vi: 0-0 Tstrap: 0-0
Best Rating: 117 3/02 Plum 3m2f gd-sft Ch

A winning pointer, he won at Doncaster on his second start over fences. Likes to make the running.

New Bird (GER)

109 **136**

7-y-o b g Bluebird (USA)-Nouvelle Amour (GER) (Esclavo (FR))
Mrs H Dalton David M Hughes

Placings:3124012/3060/31-216F302 **(4824)**
2001/02: 19^{2}G, 16^{1}G, 16^{6}GS, 16^{F}S, 16^{3}S, 17^{0}G, 16^{2}G

	Starts	1st	2nd	3rd	Win & Pl
Chases	7	1	2	1	11933
Career Total	**20**	**4**	**4**	**4**	**28144**

135	5/01	Aint	2m	D(0-125)HCh	GD	£5502
127	4/01	Weth	2m	E Ch	G-S	£3233
122	4/99	Hrfd	2m1f	D Hdl	G-F	£3009
117	12/98	Kemp	2m	C Hdl	SFT	£5083

Total win prize-money £16829

Going: Sf: 0-2 GS: 0-1 Gd: 1-4 GF: - Fm: 0-0
Distance: **2m/2m3: 1-7** 2m4-2m7: 0-0 3m+: 0-0
Track: **LH: 1-5** RH: 0-2 **Tight: 1-1** Gall: 0-2
Aids: Bl: 0-0 Vi: 0-0 Tstrap: 0-0
Best Rating: 136 4/02 Chel 2m110y good Ch

Handicap chaser, best at two miles and likes to make the running. Does not want the ground too soft.

New Development

77 **55**

6-y-o b g Sizzling Melody-Silver's Girl (Sweet Monday)
N B Mason (T Wall 26/7) N B Mason

Placings:*U00*-00000F **(2510)**
2001/02: 19^{0}G, 16^{0}GF, 16^{0}G, 22^{0}GS, 17^{0}S, 16^{F}S

	Starts	1st	2nd	3rd	Win & Pl
Hurdles	6	0	0	0	
Career Total	**9**	**0**	**0**	**0**	

Going: Sf: 0-2 GS: 0-1 Gd: 0-2 GF: - Fm: 0-1
Distance: 2m/2m3: 0-4 2m4-2m7: 0-2 3m+: 0-0
Track: LH: 0-5 RH: 0-1 Tight: 0-6 Gall: 0-0
Aids: Bl: 0-0 Vi: 0-0 Tstrap: 0-0
Best Rating: 55 11/01 Kels 2m110y good Hdl

New Horizon (IRE)

80 **75**

4-y-o b g General Monash (USA)-Gulf Craft (IRE) (Petorius)
D Brace (J A Osborne 12/8) David Brace

Placings:06 **(1558)**
2001/02: 16^{0}GF, 16^{6}G

	Starts	1st	2nd	3rd	Win & Pl
Hurdles	2	0	0	0	0
Career Total	**2**	**0**	**0**	**0**	**0**

Going: Sf: 0-0 GS: 0-0 Gd: 0-1 GF: - Fm: 0-1
Distance: 2m/2m3: 0-2 2m4-2m7: 0-0 3m+: 0-0
Track: LH: 0-2 RH: 0-0 Tight: 0-1 Gall: 0-0
Aids: Bl: 0-0 Vi: 0-0 Tstrap: 0-0
Best Rating: 75 10/01 Chep 2m110y good Hdl

New Leaf (IRE)

(85h) (76h)

10-y-o b g Brush Aside (USA)-Page Of Gold (Goldhill)
D R Gandolfo Mrs D J Hues

Placings:*0261/254504/332313/2/3300-*0 **(0107)**
2001/02: 22^{0}GF

	Starts	1st	2nd	3rd	Win & Pl
Hurdles	1	0	0	0	
Career Total	**22**	**2**	**4**	**6**	**16276**

107	11/98	Asct	3m110y	C HCh	GD	£6807
95	3/97	Carl	2m1f	E Hdl	G-S	£2122

Total win prize-money £8930

Going: Sf: 0-0 GS: 0-0 Gd: 0-0 GF: - Fm: 0-1
Distance: 2m/2m3: 0-0 2m4-2m7: 0-1 3m+: 0-0
Track: LH: 0-1 RH: 0-0 Tight: 0-1 Gall: 0-0
Aids: Bl: 0-0 Vi: 0-0 Tstrap: 0-0
Best Rating: 107 11/00 Leic 2m7f110y gd-sft Ch

New Rising

104 **111**

10-y-o b g Primitive Rising (USA)-Saucy (Saucy Kit)
P Winkworth Bill Naylor

Placings:5F43/0F/433254454/42412-FPP04P **(4819)**
2001/02: 23^{F}GF, 29^{P}G, 32^{P}GS, 24^{0}GS, 28^{4}S, 26^{P}GF

	Starts	1st	2nd	3rd	Win & Pl
Chases	6	0	0	0	1355
Career Total	**26**	**1**	**3**	**3**	**18753**

126	1/01	Fknm	3m5f110y	C(0-130)HCh	SFT	£6630

Total win prize-money £6630

Going: Sf: 0-1 GS: 0-2 Gd: 0-1 GF: - Fm: 0-2
Distance: 2m/2m3: 0-0 2m4-2m7: 0-0 3m+: 0-6
Track: LH: 0-1 RH: 0-2 Tight: 0-0 Gall: 0-2
Aids: Bl: 0-0 Vi: 0-5 Tstrap: 0-0
Best Rating: 126 3/01 Ling 3m4f110y heavy Ch

Rather slow, he requires a real test of stamina. Usually visored.

Newgate Wells (IRE)

104 **100**

8-y-o b g Accordion-Newgate Fairy (Flair Path)
Noel T Chance Newgate Syndicate

Placings:2/02542524 **(4530)**
2001/02: 20^{0}S, 16^{2}S, 20^{5}GS, 24^{4}S, 22^{2}HY, 22^{5}S, 20^{2}S, [illegible]

	Starts	1st	2nd	3rd	Win & Pl
Hurdles	8	0	3	0	2847
Career Total	**9**	**0**	**4**	**0**	**3525**

Going: Sf: 0-6 GS: 0-2 Gd: 0-0 GF: - Fm: 0-0
Distance: 2m/2m3: 0-1 2m4-2m7: 0-6 3m+: 0-1
Track: LH: 0-6 RH: 0-2 Tight: 0-2 Gall: 0-1
Aids: Bl: 0-0 Vi: 0-0 Tstrap: 0-0
Best Rating: 111 2/00 Asct 2m110y soft NHF

A brother to Dato Star, he made a very promising bumper debut at Ascot, but has been held over hurdles since.

Newhall (IRE)

118 **135**

4-y-o b f Shernazar-Graffogue (IRE) (Red Sunset)
F Flood Mrs H McParland

Placings:3121232 **(4952a)**
2001/02: 16^{3}YS, 16^{1}Y, 16^{2}SH, 16^{1}HY, 17^{2}G, 16^{3}G, 16^{2}G

	Starts	1st	2nd	3rd	Win & Pl
Hurdles	7	2	3	2	85525
Career Total	**7**	**2**	**3**	**2**	**85525**

135	2/02	Leop	2m	Hdl	HVY	£16748
117	12/01	Leop	2m	Hdl	YLD	£20967

Total win prize-money £37716

Going: Sf: 1-1 GS: 0-0 Gd: 0-3 GF: - Fm: 0-0
Distance: **2m/2m3: 2-7** 2m4-2m7: 0-0 3m+: 0-0
Track: **LH: 2-4** RH: 0-3 Tight: 0-1 Gall: 0-1
Aids: Bl: 0-0 Vi: 0-0 Tstrap: 0-0
Best Rating: 135 2/02 Leop 2m heavy Hdl

Put up a smart performance to score at the 2001 Leopardstown Christmas meeting and was given a Grade Three event in the Stewards' room on her return to Leopardstown in February. Runner-up in the Triumph Hurdle, but no match for Scolardy, and ran another good race at Punchestown. Acts on good and soft ground.

Newhaven Lad (IRE)

7-y-o b g Erdelistan (FR)-Gaye Design (Carlingford Castle)
I W McInnes (M F Morris 15/11) Ian McInnes

Placings:02/0000-PPPP **(3450)**
2001/02: 24^{P}GF, 16^{P}Y, 20^{P}G, 20^{P}GS

	Starts	1st	2nd	3rd	Win & Pl
NH Flat	1	0	0	0	0
Hurdles	3	0	0	0	0
Career Total	**10**	**0**	**1**	**0**	**896**

Going: Sf: 0-0 GS: 0-1 Gd: 0-1 GF: - Fm: 0-1
Distance: 2m/2m3: 0-1 2m4-2m7: 0-2 3m+: 0-1
Track: LH: 0-2 RH: 0-0 Tight: 0-1 Gall: 0-1
Aids: Bl: 0-1 Vi: 0-0 Tstrap: 0-0
Best Rating: 93 2/01 Clon 2m heavy Hdl

Newick Park

100(107h) **120**

7-y-o gr g Chilibang-Quilpee Mai (Pee Mai)
D M Grissell Newick Park Partnership

Placings:151P-1616P **(4168)**
2001/02: 16^{1}G, 16^{6}GS, 20^{1}GS, 20^{6}G, 20^{P}GS

	Starts	1st	2nd	3rd	Win & Pl
Chases	5	2	0	0	9100
Career Total	**9**	**4**	**0**	**0**	**13439**

120	12/01	Sand	2m4f110y	D(0-115)HCh	G-S	£5694
105	10/01	Folk	2m	E Ch	GD	£3406
100	11/00	Folk	2m1f110y	E Hdl	HVY	£2390
105	6/00	Folk	2m1f110y	F Hdl	GD	£1948

Total win prize-money £13440

Going: Sf: 0-0 GS: 1-3 Gd: 1-2 GF: - Fm: 0-0
Distance: 2m/2m3: 1-2 2m4-2m7: 1-3 3m+: 0-0
Track: LH: 0-1 **RH: 2-4 Tight: 1-2** Gall: 0-0
Aids: Bl: 0-0 Vi: 0-0 Tstrap: 0-0
Best Rating: 120 12/01 Sand 2m4f110y gd-sft Ch

An improving sort, he likes Folkestone and won two hurdles and a chase there between June 2000 and October 2001. Showed he could do it elsewhere when winning at Sandown in December. Suited by two to two and a half miles and cut in the ground.

Newkidontheblock (IRE)

94 **80**

7-y-o b g Be My Native (USA)-Jenny's Child (Crash Course)
J R Jenkins R M Ellis

Placings:106/65-5 **(4637)**
2001/02: 20^{5}GF

	Starts	1st	2nd	3rd	Win & Pl
Hurdles	1	0	0	0	0
Career Total	**6**	**1**	**0**	**0**	**1694**

99	3/00	Hntg	2m110y	H NHF	G-F	£1694

Total win prize-money £1694

Going: Sf: 0-0 GS: 0-0 Gd: 0-0 GF: - Fm: 0-1
Distance: 2m/2m3: 0-0 2m4-2m7: 0-1 3m+: 0-0
Track: LH: 0-0 RH: 0-1 Tight: 0-0 Gall: 0-0
Aids: Bl: 0-0 Vi: 0-0 Tstrap: 0-0
Best Rating: 107 4/00 Font 2m2f110y good NHF

Newryman

91 **57**

7-y-o ch g Statoblest-With Love (Be My Guest (USA))
G P Kelly A M McArdle

Placings:0/000P/0P-000 **(2669)**
2001/02: 16^{0}GF, 16^{0}G, 16^{0}G

	Starts	1st	2nd	3rd	Win & Pl
Hurdles	3	0	0	0	
Career Total	**10**	**0**	**0**	**0**	

Going: Sf: 0-0 GS: 0-0 Gd: 0-2 GF: - Fm: 0-1
Distance: 2m/2m3: 0-3 2m4-2m7: 0-0 3m+: 0-0
Track: LH: 0-3 RH: 0-0 Tight: 0-1 Gall: 0-1
Aids: Bl: 0-0 Vi: 0-0 Tstrap: 0-0
Best Rating: 64 11/99 Weth 2m good NHF

Completely useless under every code.

News Maker (IRE)

105 **107**

6-y-o b g Good Thyne (USA)-Announcement (Laurence O)
Mrs H Dalton Mrs Caroline Shaw

Placings:301334 **(4023)**
2001/02: 16^{3}G, 16^{0}S, 20^{1}S, 19^{3}S, 26^{3}S, 26^{4}S

	Starts	1st	2nd	3rd	Win & Pl
NH Flat	2	0	0	1	226
Hurdles	4	1	0	2	3455
Career Total	**6**	**1**	**0**	**0**	**0000**

100	12/01	Uttx	2m4f110y	E Hdl	SFT	£2681

Total win prize-money £2681

Going: Sf: 1-5 GS: 0-0 Gd: 0-1 GF: - Fm: 0-0
Distance: 2m/2m3: 0-2 **2m4-2m7: 1-2** 3m+: 0-2
Track: **LH: 1-3** RH: 0-3 Tight: 0-1 Gall: 0-2
Aids: Bl: 0-0 Vi: 0-0 Tstrap: 0-0
Best Rating: 107 2/02 Hntg 3m2f soft Hdl

A half-brother to Gentle Buck. Modest staying hurdler. Acts with cut. Has won over two and a half miles but ran well over three and a quarter miles at Huntingdon.

Newsplayer (IRE)

90f **102f**

6-y-o br g Alphabatim (USA)-Another Tycoon (IRE) (Phardante (FR))
R T Phillips The News Player Partnership

Placings:0-30 **(4841)**
2001/02: 16^{3}S, 16^{0}G

	Starts	1st	2nd	3rd	Win & Pl
NH Flat	2	0	0	1	292
Career Total	**3**	**0**	**0**	**1**	**292**

Going: Sf: 0-1 GS: 0-0 Gd: 0-1 GF: - Fm: 0-0
Distance: 2m/2m3: 0-2 2m4-2m7: 0-0 3m+: 0-0
Track: LH: 0-1 RH: 0-1 Tight: 0-0 Gall: 0-0
Aids: Bl: 0-0 Vi: 0-0 Tstrap: 0-0
Best Rating: 102 3/02 Ludl 2m soft NHF

Newton Commanche (IRE)

96f **91f**

5-y-o b m Commanche Run-Ravens Way (IRE) (Niels)
K C Bailey J H And N J Foxon

Placings:6630 **(4823)**
2001/02: 16^{6}GS, 16^{6}G, 16^{3}G, 17^{0}G

	Starts	1st	2nd	3rd	Win & Pl
NH Flat	4	0	0	1	220
Career Total	**4**	**0**	**0**	**1**	**220**

Going: Sf: 0-0 GS: 0-1 Gd: 0-3 GF: - Fm: 0-0
Distance: 2m/2m3: 0-4 2m4-2m7: 0-0 3m+: 0-0
Track: LH: 0-3 RH: 0-1 Tight: 0-2 Gall: 0-1
Aids: Bl: 0-0 Vi: 0-0 Tstrap: 0-0
Best Rating: 91 4/02 Fknm 2m good NHF

Progressive form in bumpers.

Newton Venture

91f 82f

6-y-o b m Petoski-Handy Venture (Nearly A Hand)
K C Bailey J H And N J Foxon

Placings:*54* **(0684)**
2001/02: 17^{5}GS, 17^{4}G

	Starts	1st	2nd	3rd	Win & Pl
NH Flat	2	0	0	0	0
Career Total	**2**	**0**	**0**	**0**	**0**

Going: Sf: 0-0 GS: 0-1 Gd: 0-1 GF: - Fm: 0-0
Distance: 2m/2m3: 0-2 2m4-2m7: 0-0 3m+: 0-0
Track: LH: 0-2 RH: 0-0 Tight: 0-2 Gall: 0-0
Aids: Bl: 0-0 Vi: 0-0 Tstrap: 0-0
Best Rating: 82 5/01 Bang 2m1f gd-sft NHF

Newtown Breeze (IRE)

83 94

5-y-o ch m Forest Wind (USA)-Calm Waters (IRE) (M Double M (USA))
T Hogan Mrs Josephine Hogan

Placings:P6550P00 **(4606a)**
2001/02: 20^{P}GF, 16^{6}G, 16^{5}YS, 16^{5}SH, 16^{0}S, 18^{P}YS, 19^{0}GS, 17^{0}S

	Starts	1st	2nd	3rd	Win & Pl
Hurdles	8	0	0	0	
Career Total	**8**	**0**	**0**	**0**	

Going: Sf: 0-2 GS: 0-1 Gd: 0-1 GF: - Fm: 0-1
Distance: 2m/2m3: 0-7 2m4-2m7: 0-1 3m+: 0-0
Track: LH: 0-1 RH: 0-1 Tight: 0-1 Gall: 0-0
Aids: Bl: 0-7 Vi: 0-0 Tstrap: 0-8
Best Rating: 94 7/01 Baln 2m yld-sft Hdl

Newtownhen (IRE)

7-y-o b m Peacock (FR)-Cutty Sark (Strong Gale)
A C Whillans Stephen Gilchrist

Placings:PPP **(4878)**
2001/02: 20^{P}HY, 26^{P}GS, 24^{P}G

	Starts	1st	2nd	3rd	Win & Pl
Chases	3	0	0	0	
Career Total	**3**	**0**	**0**	**0**	

Going: Sf: 0-1 GS: 0-1 Gd: 0-1 GF: - Fm: 0-0
Distance: 2m/2m3: 0-0 2m4-2m7: 0-1 3m+: 0-2
Track: LH: 0-0 RH: 0-3 Tight: 0-0 Gall: 0-0
Aids: Bl: 0-0 Vi: 0-0 Tstrap: 0-0
Best Rating:

Next Chapter (IRE)

92 64

4-y-o b/br f Cois Na Tine (IRE)-Book Choice (North Summit)
G M McCourt (A P Jarvis 27/8) Christopher Shankland

Placings:06 **(2671)**
2001/02: 17^{0}GS, 16^{6}G

	Starts	1st	2nd	3rd	Win & Pl
Hurdles	2	0	0	0	0
Career Total	**2**	**0**	**0**	**0**	**0**

Going: Sf: 0-0 GS: 0-1 Gd: 0-1 GF: - Fm: 0-0
Distance: 2m/2m3: 0-2 2m4-2m7: 0-0 3m+: 0-0
Track: LH: 0-1 RH: 0-1 Tight: 0-1 Gall: 0-1
Aids: Bl: 0-0 Vi: 0-0 Tstrap: 0-0
Best Rating: 64 12/01 Donc 2m110y good Hdl

Niagara (IRE)

106 100+

5-y-o b g Rainbows For Life (CAN)-Highbrook (USA) (Alphabatim (USA))
M H Tompkins Pollards Stables

Placings:2 **(4724)**
2001/02: 16^{2}GF

	Starts	1st	2nd	3rd	Win & Pl
Hurdles	1	0	1	0	816
Career Total	**1**	**0**	**1**	**0**	**816**

Going: Sf: 0-0 GS: 0-0 Gd: 0-0 GF: - Fm: 0-1
Distance: 2m/2m3: 0-1 2m4-2m7: 0-0 3m+: 0-0
Track: LH: 0-1 RH: 0-0 Tight: 0-0 Gall: 0-0
Aids: Bl: 0-0 Vi: 0-0 Tstrap: 0-0
Best Rating: 91 4/02 Chep 2m110y gd-fm Hdl

A decent handicapper on the Flat. Runner-up on both starts over hurdles. Likes fast ground.

Nibble

75 44

14-y-o b g Nicholas Bill-Sigh (Highland Melody)
M J Gingell G I Cooper

Placings:50 **(0720)**
2001/02: 20^{5}GF, 26^{0}F

	Starts	1st	2nd	3rd	Win & Pl
Hurdles	2	0	0	0	0
Career Total	**2**	**0**	**0**	**0**	**0**

Going: Sf: 0-0 GS: 0-0 Gd: 0-0 GF: - Fm: 0-2
Distance: 2m/2m3: 0-0 2m4-2m7: 0-1 3m+: 0-1
Track: LH: 0-1 RH: 0-1 Tight: 0-1 Gall: 0-0
Aids: Bl: 0-0 Vi: 0-0 Tstrap: 0-0
Best Rating: 44 6/01 Fknm 2m4f gd-fm Hdl

Nice Approach (IRE)

9-y-o ch g Over The River (FR)-Gayles Approach (Strong Gale)
J W Dufosee Nice Approach Partnership

Placings:2P0/3U5P3P0/50205P00P/40P-P2P **(0497)**
2001/02: 26^{P}G, 21^{2}G, 25^{P}G

	Starts	1st	2nd	3rd	Win & Pl
Chases	3	0	1	0	672
Career Total	**25**	**0**	**3**	**2**	**3391**

Going: Sf: 0-0 GS: 0-0 Gd: 0-3 GF: - Fm: 0-0
Distance: 2m/2m3: 0-0 2m4-2m7: 0-1 3m+: 0-2
Track: LH: 0-0 RH: 0-3 Tight: 0-2 Gall: 0-0
Aids: Bl: 0-1 Vi: 0-0 Tstrap: 0-0
Best Rating: 92 5/01 Folk 2m5f good Ch

Nice Balance (USA)

77 52

7-y-o b g Shadeed (USA)-Fellwaati (USA) (Alydar (USA))
M C Chapman Paul Stead

Placings:*0050*/P05/F6F-P00 **(4553)**
2001/02: 19^{P}G, 17^{0}GS, 17^{0}GF

	Starts	1st	2nd	3rd	Win & Pl
Hurdles	3	0	0	0	
Career Total	**13**	**0**	**0**	**0**	**0**

Going: Sf: 0-0 GS: 0-1 Gd: 0-1 GF: - Fm: 0-1
Distance: 2m/2m3: 0-2 2m4-2m7: 0-1 3m+: 0-0
Track: LH: 0-0 RH: 0-3 Tight: 0-3 Gall: 0-0
Aids: Bl: 0-1 Vi: 0-0 Tstrap: 0-0
Best Rating: 84 4/99 MRas 1m5f110y good NHF

Nichol Fifty

8-y-o b g Old Vic-Jawaher (IRE) (Dancing Brave (USA))
D Nicholls (M H Tompkins 12/6) A A Bloodstock Ltd

Placings:41P/00/P **(2903)**
2001/02: 16^{P}GS

	Starts	1st	2nd	3rd	Win & Pl		
Hurdles	1	0	0	0			
Career Total	**6**	**1**	**0**	**0**	**3192**		
114 3/98	MRas	2m1f110y	D Hdl			G-S	£2979

Total win prize-money £2980

Going: Sf: 0-0 GS: 0-1 Gd: 0-0 GF: - Fm: 0-0
Distance: 2m/2m3: 0-1 2m4-2m7: 0-0 3m+: 0-0
Track: LH: 0-1 RH: 0-0 Tight: 0-0 Gall: 0-0
Aids: Bl: 0-0 Vi: 0-0 Tstrap: 0-0
Best Rating: 114 3/98 MRas 2m1f110y gd-sft Hdl

Well held on his return to hurdles since missing a season, although he hinted at better to come in a warm race at Kempton.

Nicholas Plant

102(100h) (64h)94

13-y-o ch g Nicholas Bill-Bustilly (Busted)
J S Goldie Mrs M F Paterson

Placings:*30*/6P400/644141001/3000U05563/012613355**U122222/13UFF**21**U5U**/053/**PP**0**PF**/P340**P**0P-6PP524**U6** **(4855)**
2001/02: 20^{6}S, 20^{P}GS, 20^{P}HY, 22^{5}HY, 20^{2}HY, 23^{4}G, 25^{U}GF, 20^{6}G

	Starts	1st	2nd	3rd	Win & Pl
Hurdles	5	0	0	0	0
Chases	3	0	1	0	876
Career Total	**75**	**8**	**8**	**8**	**36397**

119	3/98	Ayr	2m4f	D(0-120)HCh	SFT	£3880
110	5/97	Weth	2m4f110y	C(0-130)HCh	G-S	£4532
107	2/97	Ayr	2m4f	D(0-125)HCh	SFT	£3522
98	10/96	Kels	2m6f110y	D(0-120)HHdl	FRM	£2528
100	5/96	Hexm	2m4f110y	E(0-110)HHdl	G-F	£2005
104	5/95	Hexm	2m4f110y	D(0-120)HHdl	G-S	£3027
85	2/95	Ayr	2m	F(0-105)HHdl	HVY	£2696
70	1/95	Ayr	2m4f	G(0-90)HHdl	SFT	£2379

Total win prize-money £24571

Going: Sf: 0-4 GS: 0-1 Gd: 0-2 GF: - Fm: 0-1
Distance: 2m/2m3: 0-0 2m4-2m7: 0-7 3m+: 0-1
Track: LH: 0-8 RH: 0-0 Tight: 0-0 Gall: 0-0

Aids: Bl: 0-0 Vi: 0-0 Tstrap: 0-0
Best Rating: **119** 3/98 Ayr 2m4f soft Ch

Veteran handicap chaser who is on the downgrade. All his wins have been gained on left-handed tracks and he is indifferent to the state of the ground.

Niciara (IRE)

98 **92**

5-y-o b g Soviet Lad (USA)-Verusa (IRE) (Petorius)
M C Chapman W P Gaff

Placings:11-45 **(4558)**
2001/02: 17^{4}S, 19^{5}GF

	Starts	1st	2nd	3rd	Win & Pl
Hurdles	2	0	0	0	0
Career Total	**4**	**2**	**0**	**0**	**5121**

111	9/00	Sedg	2m1f	E Hdl	GD	£2408
102	8/00	Ctml	2m1f110y	E Hdl	G-S	£2712

Total win prize-money £5121

Going: Sf: 0-1 GS: 0-0 Gd: 0-0 GF: - Fm: 0-1
Distance: 2m/2m3: 0-1 2m4-2m7: 0-1 3m+: 0-0
Track: LH: 0-1 RH: 0-1 Tight: 0-2 Gall: 0-0
Aids: Bl: 0-0 Vi: 0-0 Tstrap: 0-0
Best Rating: **111** 9/00 Sedg 2m1f good Hdl

Nick Ross

95 **67**

11-y-o b g Ardross-Nicolini (Nicholas Bill)
Miss R Brewis R Brewis

Placings:0/00/330023/4/06/P-0 **(1579)**
2001/02: 22^{0}G

	Starts	1st	2nd	3rd	Win & Pl
Hurdles	1	0	0	0	
Career Total	**14**	**0**	**1**	**3**	**2261**

Going: Sf: 0-0 GS: 0-0 Gd: 0-1 GF: - Fm: 0-0
Distance: 2m/2m3: 0-0 2m4-2m7: 0-1 3m+: 0-0
Track: LH: 0-1 RH: 0-0 Tight: 0-1 Gall: 0-0
Aids: Bl: 0-0 Vi: 0-0 Tstrap: 0-0
Best Rating: **100** 10/97 Hexm 2m good Hdl

Nick The Jewel

(66h) (36h) **92**

7-y-o b g Nicholas Bill-Bijou Georgie (Rhodomantade)
J S King Marlborough Racing Partnership

Placings:*0*F004 **(4598)**
2001/02: 16^{0}G, 17^{F}GS, 22^{0}G, 19^{0}S, 16^{4}GF

	Starts	1st	2nd	3rd	Win & Pl
NH Flat	1	0	0	0	0
Hurdles	3	0	0	0	0
Chases	1	0	0	0	266
Career Total	**5**	**0**	**0**	**0**	**266**

Going: Sf: 0-1 GS: 0-1 Gd: 0-2 GF: - Fm: 0-1
Distance: 2m/2m3: 0-3 2m4-2m7: 0-2 3m+: 0-0
Track: LH: 0-0 RH: 0-4 Tight: 0-1 Gall: 0-0
Aids: Bl: 0-0 Vi: 0-0 Tstrap: 0-0
Best Rating: **92** 4/02 Wwck 2m110y gd-fm Ch

Nick The Third

6-y-o b g Royal Vulcan-No Grandad (Strong Gale)
John R Upson Sir Nicholas Wilson

Placings:*0*0P **(2949)**
2001/02: 16^{0}G, 20^{0}S, 22^{P}S

	Starts	1st	2nd	3rd	Win & Pl
NH Flat	1	0	0	0	0
Hurdles	2	0	0	0	0
Career Total	**3**	**0**	**0**	**0**	

Going: Sf: 0-2 GS: 0-0 Gd: 0-1 GF: - Fm: 0-0
Distance: 2m/2m3: 0-1 2m4-2m7: 0-2 3m+: 0-0
Track: LH: 0-2 RH: 0-1 Tight: 0-2 Gall: 0-0
Aids: Bl: 0-0 Vi: 0-0 Tstrap: 0-0
Best Rating: **50** 10/01 Sthl 2m good NHF

Nick's Choice

103 **110**

6-y-o b g Sula Bula-Clare's Choice (Pragmatic)
D Burchell (R J Price 29/12) Don Gould

Placings:343005263/P0134-421P00611F **(4500)**
2001/02: 17^{4}G, 21^{2}GF, 20^{1}G, 20^{P}G, 16^{0}S, 19^{0}G, 19^{6}S, 17^{1}S, 19^{1}S, 17^{F}G

	Starts	1st	2nd	3rd	Win & Pl
Hurdles	10	3	1	0	10121
Career Total	**24**	**4**	**2**	**4**	**14942**

110	3/02	Hrfd	2m3f110y	F(0-100)HHdl	SFT	£3653
94	2/02	Tntn	2m1f	E(0-105)HHdl	SFT	£2782
101	5/01	Bang	2m4f	F(0-100)HHdl	GD	£2530
92	3/01	Extr	2m1f	F(0-100)HHdl	HVY	£2506

Total win prize-money £11473

Going: Sf: 2-4 GS: 0-0 Gd: 1-5 GF: - Fm: 0-1
Distance: 2m/2m3: 1-5 **2m4-2m7: 2-5** 3m+: 0-0
Track: LH: 1-6 **RH: 2-3 Tight: 2-6** Gall: 0-1
Aids: Bl: 0-1 Vi: 0-0 Tstrap: 0-0
Best Rating: **110** 3/02 NAbb 2m1f good Hdl

Stays two and a half miles and acts on good and heavy ground. Comes good in the spring.

Nickel Sun (IRE)

109 **119+**

6-y-o b g Phardante (FR)-Deep Green (Deep Run)
Mrs S J Smith Keith Nicholson

Placings:*22153*512 **(4867)**
2001/02: 16^{2}GF, 16^{2}GF, 17^{1}S, 16^{5}G, 19^{3}G, 16^{5}G, 17^{1}G, 16^{2}GF

	Starts	1st	2nd	3rd	Win & Pl
NH Flat	4	1	2	0	2437
Hurdles	4	1	1	1	4262
Career Total	**8**	**2**	**3**	**1**	**6699**

101	4/02	Carl	2m1f	E Hdl	GD	£2975
96	9/01	MRas	2m1f110y	H NHF	SFT	£1596

Total win prize-money £4571

Going: Sf: 1-1 GS: 0-0 Gd: 1-4 GF: - Fm: 0-3
Distance: **2m/2m3: 2-8** 2m4-2m7: 0-0 3m+: 0-0
Track: LH: 0-6 **RH: 2-2 Tight: 1-2** Gall: 0-1
Aids: Bl: 0-0 Vi: 0-0 Tstrap: 0-0
Best Rating: **106** 11/01 Chel 2m110y good NHF

Progressive hurdles form in the spring of 2002. Stays two and a half miles.

Nickel Sundancer

98 **84**

6-y-o b g Alflora (IRE)-Gunna Be Precious (Gunner B)
Mrs S J Smith Keith Nicholson

Placings:03P **(2631)**
2001/02: 19^{0}GF, 17^{3}GS, 16^{P}S

	Starts	1st	2nd	3rd	Win & Pl
Hurdles	3	0	0	1	428
Career Total	**3**	**0**	**0**	**1**	**428**

Going: Sf: 0-1 GS: 0-1 Gd: 0-0 GF: - Fm: 0-1
Distance: 2m/2m3: 0-2 2m4-2m7: 0-1 3m+: 0-0
Track: LH: 0-1 RH: 0-2 Tight: 0-2 Gall: 0-0
Aids: Bl: 0-0 Vi: 0-0 Tstrap: 0-0
Best Rating: **84** 11/01 MRas 2m1f110y gd-sft Hdl

Nickit (IRE)

71 **64**

6-y-o gr g Roselier (FR)-Run Trix (Deep Run)
M J Wilkinson John Nicholls (banbury) Ltd

Placings:4060 **(4173)**
2001/02: 16^{4}S, 20^{0}G, 20^{6}S, 25^{0}GS

	Starts	1st	2nd	3rd	Win & Pl
Hurdles	4	0	0	0	0
Career Total	**4**	**0**	**0**	**0**	**0**

Going: Sf: 0-2 GS: 0-1 Gd: 0-1 GF: - Fm: 0-0
Distance: 2m/2m3: 0-1 2m4-2m7: 0-2 3m+: 0-1
Track: LH: 0-3 RH: 0-0 Tight: 0-0 Gall: 0-2
Aids: Bl: 0-0 Vi: 0-0 Tstrap: 0-0
Best Rating: **64** 1/02 Donc 2m4f soft Hdl

Nigel's Lad (IRE)

106 (100c) (140c) **144**

10-y-o b g Dominion Royale-Back To Earth (FR) (Vayrann)
P C Haslam N C Dunnington & Mark Watson

Placings:2115/12214113/125/**1P311/U**025-**2**555P1 **(4636)**
2001/02: 20^{2}GF, 24^{5}GF, 25^{5}G, 24^{5}GS, 21^{P}GS, 24^{1}GF

	Starts	1st	2nd	3rd	Win & Pl
Hurdles	4	1	0	0	6273
Chases	2	0	1	0	3224
Career Total	**30**	**11**	**6**	**2**	**68107**

143	4/02	Asct	3m	C(0-135)HHdl	G-F	£6272
139	3/00	Weth	2m	C HCh	G-S	£5811
135	1/00	Newc	2m110y	E Ch	SFT	£2866
131	11/99	Carl	2m	D Ch	SFT	£4162
155	5/98	Hayd	2m7f110y	B Hdl	GD	£8693
154	3/98	Uttx	2m6f110y	C(0-135)HHdl	GD	£8689
138	2/98	MRas	2m5f110y	B HHdl	GD	£5422
140	12/97	Muss	3m	D(0-125)HHdl	GD	£3002
136	5/97	Aint	2m4f	D Hdl	GD	£2788
128	3/97	Donc	2m4f	E Hdl	GD	£2547
117	2/97	Newc	2m	E Hdl	GD	£2494

Total win prize-money £52754

Going: Sf: 0-0 GS: 0-2 Gd: 0-1 GF: - Fm: 1-3
Distance: 2m/2m3: 0-0 2m4-2m7: 0-2 **3m+: 1-4**
Track: LH: 0-3 **RH: 1-3** Tight: 0-3 Gall: 0-0
Aids: Bl: 0-0 Vi: 0-0 Tstrap: 0-0
Best Rating: **155** 10/98 Weth 3m1f good Hdl

Formerly a decent dual-purpose horse, he became disappointing during 2001, but bounced back to win a three-mile hurdle at Ascot in April 2002 when able to dominate from the front. Acts on any ground, but best on an easy surface.

Nigello

107 **125**

10-y-o b g El Conquistador-Saffron Poser (Sagaro)
R H Alner Mrs J R Webber

Placings:*505P*/21312P3/2P1P-42F3F0400 **(3866)**

2001/02: 20^{4}GS, 21^{2}GF, 24^{F}F, 24^{3}GF, 24^{F}GF, 19^{0}GS, 20^{4}G, 24^{0}S, 20^{0}G

	Starts	1st	2nd	3rd	Win & Pl
Chases	9	0	1	1	2355
Career Total	**24**	**3**	**4**	**3**	**19348**

125	11/00	Ludl	3m	E(0-115)HCh	GD	£4114
118	12/99	Ludl	2m4f	D(0-115)HCh	GD	£4357
121	10/99	Hrfd	2m3f	E(0-105)HCh	G-F	£3615

Total win prize-money £12088

Going: Sf: 0-1 GS: 0-2 Gd: 0-2 GF: - Fm: 0-4
Distance: 2m/2m3: 0-1 2m4-2m7: 0-4 3m+: 0-4
Track: LH: 0-1 RH: 0-8 Tight: 0-9 Gall: 0-0
Aids: Bl: 0-1 Vi: 0-0 Tstrap: 0-0
Best Rating: 125 11/01 Ludl 3m gd-fm Ch

Fair chaser, best at three miles on good ground.

Night Fever (IRE)

95 **73**

9-y-o b m Zaffaran (USA)-Kasperova (He Loves Me)
R H Alner Mrs M A T Potter

Placings:*0*P30PPP/30-36F3P **(4882)**
2001/02: 25^{3}G, 26^{6}G, 26^{F}S, 25^{3}G, 26^{P}GF

	Starts	1st	2nd	3rd	Win & Pl
Chases	5	0	0	2	1593
Career Total	**14**	**0**	**0**	**4**	**3004**

Going: Sf: 0-1 GS: 0-0 Gd: 0-3 GF: - Fm: 0-1
Distance: 2m/2m3: 0-0 2m4-2m7: 0-0 3m+: 0-5
Track: LH: 0-1 RH: 0-2 Tight: 0-2 Gall: 0-0
Aids: Bl: 0-0 Vi: 0-0 Tstrap: 0-0
Best Rating: 96 11/00 Winc 3m1f110y gd-sft Ch

Novice chaser, stays three miles but is only of modest ability.

Night Fighter (GER)

104 **106**

7-y-o b g Dashing Blade-Nouvelle (GER) (Nandino (GER))
N B Mason N B Mason

Placings:060/2240056/P-121F44305 **(2722)**
2001/02: 16^{1}GF, 17^{2}G, 16^{1}G, 17^{F}GS, 16^{4}G, 16^{4}GS, 16^{3}GS, 16^{0}GS, 17^{5}G

	Starts	1st	2nd	3rd	Win & Pl
Hurdles	9	2	1	1	5472
Career Total	**20**	**2**	**3**	**1**	**6782**

106	10/01	Towc	2m	F(0-100)HHdl	GD	£2723
98	9/01	Worc	2m	G(0-90)HHdl	G-F	£1671

Total win prize-money £4395

Going: Sf: 0-0 GS: 0-4 Gd: 1-4 GF: - Fm: 1-1
Distance: **2m/2m3: 2-9** 2m4-2m7: 0-0 3m+: 0-0
Track: LH: 1-5 RH: 1-4 Tight: 0-1 Gall: 0-2
Aids: Bl: 0-0 Vi: 0-0 **Tstrap: 2-9**
Best Rating: 106 11/01 Newc 2m gd-sft Hdl

A come-from-behind hurdler who does not stay beyond two miles, he acts on good and good to firm ground.

Night In A Million

87(80h) (31h)**85**

11-y-o br g Night Shift (USA)-Ridalia (Ridan)
Mrs L Williamson David Manning Associates

Placings:3303/600402056644/3455404132/5P324/05 34/10230410-000P004 **(1388)**
2001/02: 17^{0}GS, 20^{0}GF, 17^{0}G, 20^{P}G, 22^{0}GS, 17^{0}G, 26^{4}GF

	Starts	1st	2nd	3rd	Win & Pl
Hurdles	3	0	0	0	0
Chases	4	0	0	0	232
Career Total	**50**	**3**	**4**	**8**	**12387**

98	8/00	NAbb	2m6f	G(0-95)HHdl	GD	£1883
99	5/00	Bang	2m4f	G(0-95)HHdl	G-S	£2499
85	3/97	Plum	2m4f	E(0-110)HHdl	G-F	£2637

Total win prize-money £7019

Going: Sf: 0-0 GS: 0-2 Gd: 0-3 GF: - Fm: 0-2
Distance: 2m/2m3: 0-3 2m4-2m7: 0-3 3m+: 0-1
Track: LH: 0-7 RH: 0-0 Tight: 0-4 Gall: 0-0
Aids: Bl: 0-0 Vi: 0-2 Tstrap: 0-1
Best Rating: 99 5/00 Bang 2m4f gd-sft Hdl

Night Music

84 **70**

5-y-o b/br m Piccolo-Oribi (Top Ville)
G F Edwards G F Edwards

Placings:00F4 **(2657)**
2001/02: 22^{0}G, 17^{0}S, 16^{F}S, 19^{4}GS

	Starts	1st	2nd	3rd	Win & Pl
Hurdles	4	0	0	0	0
Career Total	**4**	**0**	**0**	**0**	**0**

Going: Sf: 0-2 GS: 0-1 Gd: 0-1 GF: - Fm: 0-0
Distance: 2m/2m3: 0-2 2m4-2m7: 0-2 3m+: 0-0
Track: LH: 0-1 RH: 0-3 Tight: 0-2 Gall: 0-0
Aids: Bl: 0-0 Vi: 0-0 Tstrap: 0-0
Best Rating: 70 11/01 Towc 2m soft Hdl

Night Riot (IRE)

10-y-o b g Riot Helmet-Evening Bun (Baragoi)
R Johnson The Oak Inn Syndicate

Placings:6 **(2403)**
2001/02: 20^{6}HY

	Starts	1st	2nd	3rd	Win & Pl
Chases	1	0	0	0	0
Career Total	**1**	**0**	**0**	**0**	**0**

Going: Sf: 0-1 GS: 0-0 Gd: 0-0 GF: - Fm: 0-0
Distance: 2m/2m3: 0-0 2m4-2m7: 0-1 3m+: 0-0
Track: LH: 0-0 RH: 0-1 Tight: 0-0 Gall: 0-0
Aids: Bl: 0-0 Vi: 0-0 Tstrap: 0-0
Best Rating:

Night Run (IRE)

67f **78f**

5-y-o b m Supreme Leader-Rugged Run (Deep Run)
G M Moore A J Coupland

Placings:*300* **(4526)**
2001/02: 17^{3}S, 16^{0}S, 17^{0}G

	Starts	1st	2nd	3rd	Win & Pl
NH Flat	3	0	0	1	223
Career Total	**3**	**0**	**0**	**1**	**223**

Going: Sf: 0-2 GS: 0-0 Gd: 0-1 GF: - Fm: 0-0
Distance: 2m/2m3: 0-3 2m4-2m7: 0-0 3m+: 0-0
Track: LH: 0-1 RH: 0-2 Tight: 0-2 Gall: 0-0
Aids: Bl: 0-0 Vi: 0-0 Tstrap: 0-0
Best Rating: 78 1/02 Sedg 2m1f soft NHF

Showed a glimmer of promise in bumper on heavy ground on racecourse debut.

Night Sight (USA)

75 **40**

5-y-o b g Eagle Eyed (USA)-El Hamo (USA) (Search For Gold (USA))
M C Chapman David Fravigar-Alan Mann

Placings:0-0 **(0475)**
2001/02: 17^{0}G

	Starts	1st	2nd	3rd	Win & Pl
Hurdles	1	0	0	0	
Career Total	**2**	**0**	**0**	**0**	

Going: Sf: 0-0 GS: 0-0 Gd: 0-1 GF: - Fm: 0-0
Distance: 2m/2m3: 0-1 2m4-2m7: 0-0 3m+: 0-0
Track: LH: 0-0 RH: 0-1 Tight: 0-1 Gall: 0-0
Aids: Bl: 0-0 Vi: 0-0 Tstrap: 0-0
Best Rating: 80 1/01 Donc 2m110y good Hdl

Nijway

87 **74**

12-y-o b g Nijin (USA)-Runaway Girl (FR) (Homeric)
M A Barnes M Barnes

Placings:00P40/P2R044241/33F06U4FU31U12P1/31 24052/P13P/PUP44/1400P-S00P6060 **(4855)**
2001/02: 25^{S}GF, 21^{0}G, 25^{0}G, 27^{P}G, 25^{6}S, 25^{0}GS, 20^{6}GF, 20^{0}G

	Starts	1st	2nd	3rd	Win & Pl
Hurdles	1	0	0	0	0
Chases	7	0	0	0	0
Career Total	**59**	**7**	**5**	**5**	**32509**

110	5/00	Sedg	3m3f	F(0-110)HCh	G-F	£3955
110	3/99	Ayr	2m4f	D(0-120)HCh	SFT	£3736
93	5/97	Hexm	3m1f	E(0-115)HCh	G-F	£2406
96	4/97	Kels	3m1f	D(0-120)HCh	G-F	£3986
88	3/97	Carl	3m	F(0-105)HCh	GD	£3355
88	3/97	Sedg	2m5f	E Ch	GD	£3023
82	4/96	Prth	2m110y	D(0-110)HHdl	SFT	£3941

Total win prize-money £24405

Going: Sf: 0-1 GS: 0-1 Gd: 0-4 GF: - Fm: 0-2
Distance: 2m/2m3: 0-0 2m4-2m7: 0-3 3m+: 0-5
Track: LH: 0-7 RH: 0-1 Tight: 0-5 Gall: 0-0
Aids: Bl: 0-0 Vi: 0-0 Tstrap: 0-8
Best Rating: 110 5/00 Sedg 3m3f gd-fm Ch

Niki Dee (IRE)

12-y-o b g Phardante (FR)-Curragh Breeze (Furry Glen)
P Beaumont George Dilger

Placings:4032/1/F2/21P112/1P2222P3/P-FP **(4897)**
2001/02: 36^{F}G, 24^{P}G

	Starts	1st	2nd	3rd	Win & Pl
Chases	2	0	0	0	
Career Total	**24**	**5**	**8**	**2**	**127741**

163	11/99	Uttx	2m5f	C(0-135)HCh	SFT	£5918
129	2/99	Weth	2m4f110y	D Ch	GD	£3806
113	2/99	Muss	3m	E Ch	GD	£3550
132	12/98	Weth	2m4f110y	D Ch	GD	£3782
106	10/95	Bang	2m4f	E(0-110)HHdl	GD	£2708

Total win prize-money £19765

Going: Sf: 0-0 GS: 0-0 Gd: 0-2 GF: - Fm: 0-0
Distance: 2m/2m3: 0-0 2m4-2m7: 0-0 3m+: 0-2
Track: LH: 0-1 RH: 0-1 Tight: 0-1 Gall: 0-0
Aids: Bl: 0-0 Vi: 0-0 Tstrap: 0-0
Best Rating: 163 1/00 Donc 3m good Ch

A useful chaser around three miles during the 1999-

2000 season and suited by good ground, he has been lightly-raced of late.

Nile Princess

5-y-o b m Riverwise (USA)-Royal Buskins (White Prince (USA))
N R Mitchell M Andrew

Placings:P00P-P0SFP (2288)
2001/02: 17^{P}F, 22^{0}GF, 19^{S}F, 20^{F}GS, 17^{P}GF

	Starts	1st	2nd	3rd	Win & Pl
Hurdles	5	0	0	0	
Career Total	**9**	**0**	**0**	**0**	

Going: Sf: 0-0 GS: 0-1 Gd: 0-0 GF: - Fm: 0-4
Distance: 2m/2m3: 0-2 2m4-2m7: 0-3 3m+: 0-0
Track: LH: 0-1 RH: 0-3 Tight: 0-3 Gall: 0-0
Aids: Bl: 0-0 Vi: 0-0 Tstrap: 0-0
Best Rating: 71 2/01 Kemp 2m gd-sft NHF

Nimbus Stratus

81 29

9-y-o br g Welsh Captain-Touching Clouds (Touching Wood (USA))
R G Frost Mrs J F Bury

Placings:53436P/06-0 (0562)
2001/02: 22^{0}GF

	Starts	1st	2nd	3rd	Win & Pl
Hurdles	1	0	0	0	
Career Total	**9**	**0**	**0**	**2**	**821**

Going: Sf: 0-0 GS: 0-0 Gd: 0-0 GF: - Fm: 0-1
Distance: 2m/2m3: 0-0 2m4-2m7: 0-1 3m+: 0-0
Track: LH: 0-1 RH: 0-0 Tight: 0-1 Gall: 0-0
Aids: Bl: 0-0 Vi: 0-0 Tstrap: 0-0
Best Rating: 86 10/99 Chep 2m110y soft Hdl

Nine O Three (IRE)

111 122

13-y-o b g Supreme Leader-Grenache (Menelek)
Mrs S D Williams Bideford Tool Ltd

Placings:0/630000133040/3F2005343/350001/61226/1006/405/03F1114/2000-6143F (1993)
2001/02: 27^{6}GF, 27^{1}GF, 22^{4}G, 24^{3}S, 24^{F}G

	Starts	1st	2nd	3rd	Win & Pl
Hurdles	5	1	0	1	6842
Career Total	**56**	**8**	**4**	**9**	**41284**

122	6/01	NAbb	3m3f	C(0-130)HHdl	G-F	£4867
117	10/99	Worc	2m4f	C(0-130)HHdl	GD	£6840
110	9/99	NAbb	3m3f	D(0-125)HHdl	G-F	£2859
99	7/99	Worc	3m	C(0-135)HHdl	G-F	£4796
115	12/97	Tntn	2m1f	D(0-125)HHdl	GD	£2794
104	6/96	Worc	2m4f	D(0-120)HHdl	G-F	£3965
103	2/96	Tntn	2m1f	F(0-105)HHdl	G-S	£2284
	2/94	Thur	2m	NHF	SFT	£2628

Total win prize-money £31036

Going: Sf: 0-1 GS: 0-0 Gd: 0-2 GF: - Fm: 1-2
Distance: 2m/2m3: 0-0 2m4-2m7: 0-1 **3m+: 1-4**
Track: **LH: 1-3** RH: 0-2 **Tight: 1-4** Gall: 0-0
Aids: Bl: 0-0 Vi: 0-0 Tstrap: 0-0
Best Rating: 124 9/00 MRas 3m gd-fm Hdl

Veteran fast-ground staying hurdler.

Ninnolo (IRE)

84 82

5-y-o b g Perugino (USA)-Primo Stampari (Primo Dominie)
C N Allen newmarketconnections.com

Placings:FSP6U4 (1807)
2001/02: 16^{F}G, 16^{S}GF, 16^{P}G, 18^{6}GF, 16^{U}G, 16^{4}S

	Starts	1st	2nd	3rd	Win & Pl
Hurdles	6	0	0	0	0
Career Total	**6**	**0**	**0**	**0**	**0**

Going: Sf: 0-1 GS: 0-0 Gd: 0-3 GF: - Fm: 0-2
Distance: 2m/2m3: 0-6 2m4-2m7: 0-0 3m+: 0-0
Track: LH: 0-4 RH: 0-2 Tight: 0-3 Gall: 0-1
Aids: Bl: 0-0 Vi: 0-0 Tstrap: 0-2
Best Rating: 82 9/01 Font 2m2f110y gd-fm Hdl

Nip On

99(63c) 98

8-y-o b g Dunbeath (USA)-Popping On (Sonnen Gold)
J R Turner Robin Ellerbeck

Placings:0001/053P53F10/0-20 (4747)
2001/02: 17^{2}G, 20^{0}G

	Starts	1st	2nd	3rd	Win & Pl
Hurdles	2	0	1	0	996
Career Total	**16**	**2**	**1**	**2**	**7338**

102	3/00	Sedg	3m3f110y	D(0-120)HHdl	G-F	£2938
95	4/99	Hexm	2m4f110y	E Hdl	GD	£2106

Total win prize-money £5134

Going: Sf: 0-0 GS: 0-0 Gd: 0-2 GF: - Fm: 0-0
Distance: 2m/2m3: 0-1 2m4-2m7: 0-1 3m+: 0-0
Track: LH: 0-0 RH: 0-1 Tight: 0-0 Gall: 0-0
Aids: Bl: 0-0 Vi: 0-0 Tstrap: 0-0
Best Rating: 102 3/00 Sedg 3m3f110y gd-fm Hdl

Modest hurdler, stays three miles plus but effective over much shorter, Appreciates good ground or faster.

Nite Owler

8-y-o b g Saddlers' Hall (IRE)-Lorne Lady (Local Suitor (USA))
N Waggott Mrs J Waggott

Placings:P (1506)
2001/02: 17^{P}G

	Starts	1st	2nd	3rd	Win & Pl
Hurdles	1	0	0	0	
Career Total	**1**	**0**	**0**	**0**	

Going: Sf: 0-0 GS: 0-0 Gd: 0-1 GF: - Fm: 0-0
Distance: 2m/2m3: 0-1 2m4-2m7: 0-0 3m+: 0-0
Track: LH: 0-1 RH: 0-0 Tight: 0-1 Gall: 0-0
Aids: Bl: 0-0 Vi: 0-0 Tstrap: 0-0
Best Rating:

Nizaal (USA)

89 95

11-y-o ch g Diesis-Shicklah (USA) (The Minstrel (CAN))
T A K Cuthbert J J H Walker

Placings:03/03/P/043/0-PP5 (4829)
2001/02: 16^{P}S, 16^{P}S, 16^{5}G

	Starts	1st	2nd	3rd	Win & Pl
Chases	3	0	0	0	0
Career Total	**12**	**0**	**0**	**3**	**1888**

Going: Sf: 0-2 GS: 0-0 Gd: 0-1 GF: - Fm: 0-0
Distance: 2m/2m3: 0-3 2m4-2m7: 0-0 3m+: 0-0
Track: LH: 0-3 RH: 0-0 Tight: 0-0 Gall: 0-2
Aids: Bl: 0-0 Vi: 0-0 Tstrap: 0-0
Best Rating: 100 4/00 Ayr 2m good Ch

Lightly-raced dual-purpose maiden. Likes cut in the ground.

No Case To Answer (IRE)

93(100c) 91

8-y-o br g Good Thyne (USA)-One Way Only (Le Bavard (FR))
Mrs S C Bradburne Timothy Hardie

Placings:03/003P362-35P (3745)
2001/02: 22^{3}GF, 24^{5}G, 24^{P}S

	Starts	1st	2nd	3rd	Win & Pl
Hurdles	3	0	0	1	424
Career Total	**12**	**0**	**1**	**4**	**3297**

Going: Sf: 0-1 GS: 0-0 Gd: 0-1 GF: - Fm: 0-1
Distance: 2m/2m3: 0-0 2m4-2m7: 0-1 3m+: 0-2
Track: LH: 0-1 RH: 0-2 Tight: 0-2 Gall: 0-0
Aids: Bl: 0-0 Vi: 0-0 Tstrap: 0-0
Best Rating: 101 1/01 Muss 3m gd-sft Ch

No Chanco

7-y-o ch m St Ninian-Wellwotdouthink (Rymer)
Mrs M Reveley A Flannigan

Placings:01-5P (3911)
2001/02: 16^{5}G, 24^{P}GS

	Starts	1st	2nd	3rd	Win & Pl
NH Flat	1	0	0	0	0
Hurdles	1	0	0	0	0
Career Total	**4**	**1**	**0**	**0**	**1554**

109	12/00	Muss	2m	H NHF	GD	£1554

Total win prize-money £1554

Going: Sf: 0-0 GS: 0-1 Gd: 0-1 GF: - Fm: 0-0
Distance: 2m/2m3: 0-1 2m4-2m7: 0-0 3m+: 0-1
Track: LH: 0-0 RH: 0-2 Tight: 0-2 Gall: 0-0
Aids: Bl: 0-0 Vi: 0-0 Tstrap: 0-0
Best Rating: 109 12/00 Muss 2m good NHF

A Musselburgh bumper winner in 2000, returned from a year's absence at the same track.

No Collusion (IRE)

102f 117f

6-y-o b g Buckskin (FR)-Miss Ironside (General Ironside)
Noel T Chance T Collins

Placings:10 (4235)
2001/02: 16^{1}G, 16^{0}GS

	Starts	1st	2nd	3rd	Win & Pl
NH Flat	2	1	0	0	2678
Career Total	**2**	**1**	**0**	**0**	**2678**

117	12/01	Newb	2m110y	H NHF	GD	£2677

Total win prize-money £2678

Going: Sf: 0-0 GS: 0-1 Gd: 1-1 GF: - Fm: 0-0
Distance: **2m/2m3: 1-2** 2m4-2m7: 0-0 3m+: 0-0
Track: **LH: 1-2** RH: 0-0 Tight: 0-0 **Gall: 1-1**
Aids: Bl: 0-0 Vi: 0-0 Tstrap: 0-0
Best Rating: 117 12/01 Newb 2m110y good NHF

Decent bumper performer. Acts on good ground and is suited by two miles.

No Discount (IRE)

109 130

8-y-o b g Be My Native (USA)-Flameing Run (Deep Run)
T M Walsh Seamus Ross

Placings:*0452321*/3121122/P-**P462B413FF** **(4704a)**
2001/02: 25^{P}Y, 20^{4}YS, 19^{6}Y, 21^{2}YS, 21^{B}SH, 24^{4}HY, 24^{1}S, 21^{3}HY, 24^{F}GS, 22^{F}GY

	Starts	1st	2nd	3rd	Win & Pl
Hurdles	1	0	0	0	0
Chases	9	1	1	1	12090
Career Total	**25**	**5**	**6**	**3**	**67910**

130 2/02 Navn 3m Ch SFT £7831
137 2/00 Naas 2m4f Hdl YLD £10400
127 1/00 Naas 2m3f Hdl SFT £4416
126 12/99 Punc 2m4f Hdl SFT £4312
103 3/99 Dpat 2m1f172y NHF YLD £3069
Total win prize-money £30029

Going: Sf: 1-3 GS: 0-1 Gd: 0-0 GF: - Fm: 0-0
Distance: 2m/2m3: 0-1 2m4-2m7: 0-5 **3m+: 1-4**
Track: **LH: 1-5** RH: 0-5 Tight: 0-0 Gall: 0-1
Aids: Bl: 0-0 Vi: 0-0 Tstrap: 0-0
Best Rating: 154 4/00 Aint 3m110y good Hdl

A very good novice hurdler in 1999/2000, he has only won once over fences, in February 2002, without reaching the heights once predicted for him. Stays three miles. Acts on soft ground.

No Dramas (IRE)

95 85

9-y-o br g Be My Native (USA)-Madam Owen (Master Owen)
C J Mann Mrs C J Mann

Placings:0/3P3P53 **(1397)**
2001/02: 22^{3}G, 25^{P}GS, 27^{3}GF, 27^{P}G, 24^{5}GF, 24^{3}GF

	Starts	1st	2nd	3rd	Win & Pl
Hurdles	6	0	0	3	1124
Career Total	**7**	**0**	**0**	**3**	**1124**

Going: Sf: 0-0 GS: 0-1 Gd: 0-2 GF: - Fm: 0-3
Distance: 2m/2m3: 0-0 2m4-2m7: 0-1 3m+: 0-5
Track: LH: 0-6 RH: 0-0 Tight: 0-4 Gall: 0-0
Aids: Bl: 0-0 Vi: 0-0 Tstrap: 0-1
Best Rating: 85 7/01 NAbb 3m3f gd-fm Hdl

No Fear (IRE)

89f 98f

6-y-o b g Warcraft (USA)-Mandalaw (IRE) (Mandalus)
Mrs S J Smith Mrs S Smith

Placings:*2* **(4750)**
2001/02: 17^{2}G

	Starts	1st	2nd	3rd	Win & Pl
NH Flat	1	0	1	0	714
Career Total	**1**	**0**	**1**	**0**	**714**

Going: Sf: 0-0 GS: 0-0 Gd: 0-1 GF: - Fm: 0-0
Distance: 2m/2m3: 0-1 2m4-2m7: 0-0 3m+: 0-0
Track: LH: 0-0 RH: 0-1 Tight: 0-0 Gall: 0-0
Aids: Bl: 0-0 Vi: 0-0 Tstrap: 0-0
Best Rating: 98 4/02 Carl 2m1f good NHF

No Finer Man (IRE)

11-y-o b g Lord Americo-Ballaroe Bar (Bargello)
Ferdy Murphy W J Gott

Placings:*055/425*/**54P2-PP** **(0839)**
2001/02: 22^{P}GF, 23^{P}G

	Starts	1st	2nd	3rd	Win & Pl
Chases	2	0	0	0	
Career Total	**12**	**0**	**2**	**0**	**2066**

Going: Sf: 0-0 GS: 0-0 Gd: 0-1 GF: - Fm: 0-1
Distance: 2m/2m3: 0-0 2m4-2m7: 0-1 3m+: 0-1
Track: LH: 0-1 RH: 0-1 Tight: 0-1 Gall: 0-0
Aids: Bl: 0-0 Vi: 0-0 Tstrap: 0-0
Best Rating: 116 2/01 Carl 2m4f110y soft Ch

No Forecast (IRE)

131

8-y-o b g Executive Perk-Guess Twice (Deep Run)
A M Hales Andrew L Cohen

Placings:*5120*/0F6/4-1 **(2940)**
2001/02: 22^{1}G

	Starts	1st	2nd	3rd	Win & Pl
Chases	1	1	0	0	5996
Career Total	**9**	**2**	**1**	**0**	**8462**

131 12/01 Newb 2m6f110y D(0-110)HCh GD £5996
108 12/98 Folk 2m1f110y H NHF SFT £1234
Total win prize-money £7231

Going: Sf: 0-0 GS: 0-0 Gd: 1-1 GF: - Fm: 0-0
Distance: 2m/2m3: 0-0 **2m4-2m7: 1-1** 3m+: 0-0
Track: **LH: 1-1** RH: 0-0 Tight: 0-0 **Gall: 1-1**
Aids: Bl: 0-0 Vi: 0-0 Tstrap: 0-0
Best Rating: 131 12/01 Newb 2m6f110y good Ch

Stays two miles-six, and handles cut in the ground. Made most in a novices' handicap chase at Newbury in December 2001.

No Gimmicks (IRE)

106 94

10-y-o b g Lord Americo-Catspaw (Laurence O)
J G Fitzgerald J G Fitzgerald

Placings:*33*/12565/P**3FF**/0-01420**U**2230 **(4877)**
2001/02: 19^{0}S, 25^{1}G, 27^{4}HY, 24^{2}S, 24^{0}S, 25^{U}GS, 27^{2}S, 21^{2}S, 23^{3}G, 24^{0}G

	Starts	1st	2nd	3rd	Win & Pl
Hurdles	9	1	3	1	4443
Chases	1	0	0	0	0
Career Total	**22**	**2**	**4**	**4**	**9111**

94 12/01 Catt 3m1f110y E(0-115)HHdl GD £2450
100 11/97 MRas 2m5f110y E Hdl G-S £2705
Total win prize-money £5155

Going: Sf: 0-6 GS: 0-1 Gd: 1-3 GF: - Fm: 0-0
Distance: 2m/2m3: 0-1 2m4-2m7: 0-2 **3m+: 1-7**
Track: **LH: 1-9** RH: 0-1 **Tight: 1-6** Gall: 0-2
Aids: Bl: 0-1 Vi: 0-1 Tstrap: 0-0
Best Rating: 108 12/97 Weth 2m7f good Hdl

Plating-class hurdler who has already tried his hand over fences.

No Kidding

104(88h) (98h)108

8-y-o b g Teenoso (USA)-Vaigly Fine (Vaigly Great)
J I A Charlton Miss J Palmer

Placings:*0200*P/214F5020-**42561F403452** **(4789)**
2001/02: 16^{4}F, 16^{2}GF, 16^{5}GF, 17^{6}G, 16^{1}GF, 20^{F}GF, 16^{4}GS, 16^{0}GS, 16^{3}S, 16^{4}S, 16^{5}G, 16^{2}F

	Starts	1st	2nd	3rd	Win & Pl
Chases	12	1	2	1	7795
Career Total	**25**	**2**	**5**	**1**	**13172**

108 11/01 Catt 2m D Ch G-F £4153
84 5/00 Kels 2m2f D Hdl G-F £3035
Total win prize-money £7190

Going: Sf: 0-2 GS: 0-2 Gd: 0-2 GF: - Fm: 1-6
Distance: **2m/2m3: 1-11** 2m4-2m7: 0-1 3m+: 0-0
Track: **LH: 1-8** RH: 0-4 **Tight: 1-6** Gall: 0-2
Aids: Bl: 0-0 Vi: 0-0 Tstrap: 0-0
Best Rating: 108 2/02 Muss 2m soft Ch

Winner of a novices' chase at Catterick in November, he is suited by a left-handed track and good to firm ground.

No Language Please (IRE)

95 74

8-y-o ch g Arapahos (FR)-Strong Language (Formidable (USA))
R Curtis Mrs G Fletcher

Placings:2PP3/PP64P-36PP **(2645)**
2001/02: 19^{3}F, 22^{6}GF, 24^{P}GF, 24^{P}GS

	Starts	1st	2nd	3rd	Win & Pl
Hurdles	2	0	0	1	255
Chases	2	0	0	0	0
Career Total	**13**	**0**	**1**	**2**	**1776**

Going: Sf: 0-0 GS: 0-1 Gd: 0-0 GF: - Fm: 0-3
Distance: 2m/2m3: 0-0 2m4-2m7: 0-2 3m+: 0-2
Track: LH: 0-1 RH: 0-3 Tight: 0-3 Gall: 0-1
Aids: Bl: 0-0 Vi: 0-0 Tstrap: 0-0
Best Rating: 90 4/00 Plum 2m4f gd-sft Ch

No Loss

8-y-o b g Ardross-Lady Geneva (Royalty)
S Pike Stewart Pike

Placings:P **(2290)**
2001/02: 23^{P}GF

	Starts	1st	2nd	3rd	Win & Pl
Chases	1	0	0	0	
Career Total	**1**	**0**	**0**	**0**	

Going: Sf: 0-0 GS: 0-0 Gd: 0-0 GF: - Fm: 0-1
Distance: 2m/2m3: 0-0 2m4-2m7: 0-0 3m+: 0-1
Track: LH: 0-0 RH: 0-1 Tight: 0-0 Gall: 0-0
Aids: Bl: 0-0 Vi: 0-0 Tstrap: 0-0
Best Rating:

No Mercy

84 83

6-y-o ch g Faustus (USA)-Nashville Blues (IRE) (Try My Best (USA))
B A Pearce Richard J Gray

Placings:6550-P0P **(1763)**
2001/02: 16^{P}G, 16^{0}GF, 16^{P}S

	Starts	1st	2nd	3rd	Win & Pl
Hurdles	3	0	0	0	
Career Total	**7**	**0**	**0**	**0**	**0**

Going: Sf: 0-1 GS: 0-0 Gd: 0-1 GF: - Fm: 0-1
Distance: 2m/2m3: 0-3 2m4-2m7: 0-0 3m+: 0-0

Track: LH: 0-3 RH: 0-0 Tight: 0-3 Gall: 0-0
Aids: Bl: 0-1 Vi: 0-0 Tstrap: 0-0
Best Rating: 86 9/00 Worc 2m gd-fm Hdl

No Moore Bills

96 **81**

7-y-o b m Nicholas Bill-Grace Moore (Deep Run)
K Bishop Slabs And Lucan

Placings:4/4000/20P6-40PP **(1611)**
2001/02: 17^{4}GS, 20^{0}G, 22^{P}GF, 19^{P}GF

	Starts	1st	2nd	3rd	Win & Pl
Hurdles	4	0	0	0	0
Career Total	**13**	**0**	**1**	**0**	**588**

Going: Sf: 0-0 GS: 0-1 Gd: 0-1 GF: - Fm: 0-2
Distance: 2m/2m3: 0-2 2m4-2m7: 0-2 3m+: 0-0
Track: LH: 0-2 RH: 0-2 Tight: 0-2 Gall: 0-0
Aids: Bl: 0-0 Vi: 0-0 Tstrap: 0-3
Best Rating: 86 10/99 Bang 2m1f soft NHF

No Morals

82 **59**

11-y-o b g Royal Vulcan-Osmium (Petong)
R J Baker W M Comerford

Placings:0P630/P/2/P0/P-4 **(0720)**
2001/02: 26^{4}F

	Starts	1st	2nd	3rd	Win & Pl
Hurdles	1	0	0	0	0
Career Total	**11**	**0**	**1**	**1**	**967**

Going: Sf: 0-0 GS: 0-0 Gd: 0-0 GF: - Fm: 0-1
Distance: 2m/2m3: 0-0 2m4-2m7: 0-0 3m+: 0-1
Track: LH: 0-0 RH: 0-1 Tight: 0-0 Gall: 0-0
Aids: Bl: 0-0 Vi: 0-0 Tstrap: 0-0
Best Rating: 76 7/98 Worc 3m gd-fm Hdl

No More Hassle (IRE)

110 **135**

9-y-o ch g Magical Wonder (USA)-Friendly Ann (Artaius (USA))
J Akehurst The No Hassle Partnership

Placings:01110/3303535/22212F22/1201U3201/P50-01445P2 **(3324)**
2001/02: 24^{0}GF, 23^{1}GF, 24^{4}GF, 25^{4}G, 26^{5}S, 24^{P}G, 24^{2}GS

	Starts	1st	2nd	3rd	Win & Pl
Chases	7	1	1	0	9470
Career Total	**39**	**8**	**9**	**5**	**47145**

127	6/01	Worc	2m7f110y	C(0-135)HCh	G-F	£7117
142	4/00	Hntg	3m	D(0-120)HCh	GD	£4189
136	12/99	MRas	2m6f110y	D(0-120)HCh	G-S	£3821
113	5/99	MRas	2m4f	D Ch	G-F	£3977
109	11/98	Hntg	2m4f110y	E Ch	GD	£3311
120	2/97	Hayd	2m	C HHdl	GD	£5015
90	1/97	Towc	2m	E(0-110)HHdl	G-S	£2477
98	12/96	MRas	2m1f110y	E Hdl	GD	£2758

Total win prize-money £32668

Going: Sf: 0-1 GS: 0-1 Gd: 0-2 GF: - Fm: 1-3
Distance: 2m/2m3: 0-0 2m4-2m7: 0-0 **3m+: 1-7**
Track: **LH: 1-5** RH: 0-2 Tight: 0-3 Gall: 0-2
Aids: Bl: 0-0 Vi: 0-0 Tstrap: 0-0
Best Rating: 142 4/00 Hntg 3m good Ch

He often seems to be holding something back, but is a capable sort in handicap chases. Better on right-handed tracks. Acts on a sound surface. Stays three miles.

No More Nice Guy (IRE)

13-y-o b g Remainder Man-Vaguely Decent (Decent Fellow)
D C Turner Mrs M E Turner

Placings:00/P/04/3-654P **(3991)**
2001/02: 21^{6}GF, 26^{5}G, 26^{4}GF, 24^{P}S

	Starts	1st	2nd	3rd	Win & Pl
Chases	4	0	0	0	262
Career Total	**10**	**0**	**0**	**1**	**786**

Going: Sf: 0-1 GS: 0-0 Gd: 0-1 GF: - Fm: 0-2
Distance: 2m/2m3: 0-0 2m4-2m7: 0-1 3m+: 0-3
Track: LH: 0-3 RH: 0-1 Tight: 0-4 Gall: 0-0
Aids: Bl: 0-0 Vi: 0-0 Tstrap: 0-0
Best Rating: 92 6/00 NAbb 3m2f110y good Ch

No Nay Never (IRE)

72 **67**

7-y-o b g Tremblant-Monread (Le Tricolore)
J W Mullins Ian McGready, Rob McGready, Adam Day

Placings:034/6-60B0 **(3229)**
2001/02: 22^{6}S, 19^{0}S, 16^{B}G, 21^{0}GS

	Starts	1st	2nd	3rd	Win & Pl
Hurdles	4	0	0	0	0
Career Total	**8**	**0**	**0**	**1**	**232**

Going: Sf: 0-2 GS: 0-1 Gd: 0-1 GF: - Fm: 0-0
Distance: 2m/2m3: 0-1 2m4-2m7: 0-3 3m+: 0-0
Track: LH: 0-0 RH: 0-4 Tight: 0-1 Gall: 0-1
Aids: Bl: 0-0 Vi: 0-0 Tstrap: 0-0
Best Rating: 83 3/00 Ludl 2m good NHF

No Need For Alarm

117 **131**

7-y-o ch m Romany Rye-Sunley Words (Sunley Builds)
P F Nicholls Mr Tony Fear & Mr Patrick Quinn

Placings:22U1110 **(4822)**
2001/02: 18^{2}GF, 16^{2}HY, 16^{U}HY, 17^{1}S, 16^{1}HY, 16^{1}G, 21^{0}G

	Starts	1st	2nd	3rd	Win & Pl
NH Flat	1	0	1	0	562
Hurdles	6	3	1	0	11950
Career Total	**7**	**3**	**2**	**0**	**12512**

131	4/02	Uttx	2m	C(0-135)HHdl	GD	£5486
125	3/02	Sthl	2m	E Hdl	HVY	£2604
120	3/02	Bang	2m1f	E Hdl	SFT	£3122

Total win prize-money £11212

Going: Sf: 2-4 GS: 0-0 Gd: 1-2 GF: - Fm: 0-1
Distance: **2m/2m3: 3-6** 2m4-2m7: 0-1 3m+: 0-0
Track: **LH: 3-7** RH: 0-0 **Tight: 2-5** Gall: 0-1
Aids: Bl: 0-0 Vi: 0-0 Tstrap: 0-0
Best Rating: 131 4/02 Uttx 2m good Hdl

Fair front-running hurdler and ex-pointer. Unlucky not to score at Plumpton in February 2002, easy winner of her next three runs. Handles any ground.

No Quarter (IRE)

98 **103**

9-y-o ch g Persian Mews-Back To Bahrain (Mandalus)
K C Bailey Mrs C A Waters

Placings:31P0/43341 **(4519)**
2001/02: 20^{4}HY, 22^{3}S, 20^{3}S, 21^{4}S, 21^{1}GS

	Starts	1st	2nd	3rd	Win & Pl
Hurdles	5	1	0	2	2834
Career Total	**9**	**2**	**0**	**3**	**4341**

103	3/02	Towc	2m5f	F Hdl	G-S	£1953
107	12/98	Towc	2m	H NHF	SFT	£1287

Total win prize-money £3240

Going: Sf: 0-4 GS: 1-1 Gd: 0-0 GF: - Fm: 0-0
Distance: 2m/2m3: 0-0 **2m4-2m7: 1-5** 3m+: 0-0
Track: LH: 0-3 **RH: 1-2** Tight: 0-1 Gall: 0-1
Aids: Bl: 0-0 Vi: 0-0 Tstrap: 0-0
Best Rating: 110 4/99 Ayr 2m soft NHF

No Retreat (NZ)

115 **130**

9-y-o b g Exattic (USA)-Lerwick (NZ) (Thoreau (FR))
B P J Baugh M W & A N Harris

Placings:3/11322/1/5PPPP-5503400P **(4839)**
2001/02: 27^{5}S, 24^{5}G, 24^{0}S, 24^{3}GS, 26^{4}GS, 24^{0}GS, 21^{0}G, 33^{P}G

	Starts	1st	2nd	3rd	Win & Pl
Chases	8	0	0	1	3908
Career Total	**20**	**3**	**2**	**3**	**54260**

149	10/99	Winc	2m5f	A HCh	G-F	£19350
141	11/98	Hayd	2m4f	B Ch	HVY	£11160
132	11/98	Newb	2m4f	D(0-120)Ch	G-S	£4286

Total win prize-money £34796

Going: Sf: 0-2 GS: 0-3 Gd: 0-3 GF: - Fm: 0-0
Distance: 2m/2m3: 0-0 2m4-2m7: 0-1 3m+: 0-7
Track: LH: 0-7 RH: 0-1 Tight: 0-2 Gall: 0-4
Aids: Bl: 0-0 Vi: 0-0 Tstrap: 0-0
Best Rating: 149 10/99 Winc 2m5f gd-fm Ch

Once a smart front-running chaser, he has had injury problems and pulled up four times in 2001. Has changed stables since and put in some decent efforts last term. Acts on most types of ground. Best at three miles plus.

No Sam No

98 **81**

4-y-o b f Reprimand-Samjamallfran (Blakeney)
Mrs K Walton (J A Osborne 1/9) Mrs K Walton

Placings:40006 **(4670)**
2001/02: 16^{4}G, 16^{0}G, 16^{0}G, 17^{0}GS, 21^{6}GF

	Starts	1st	2nd	3rd	Win & Pl
Hurdles	5	0	0	0	0
Career Total	**5**	**0**	**0**	**0**	**0**

Going: Sf: 0-0 GS: 0-1 Gd: 0-3 GF: - Fm: 0-1
Distance: 2m/2m3: 0-4 2m4-2m7: 0-1 3m+: 0-0
Track: LH: 0-3 RH: 0-2 Tight: 0-3 Gall: 0-0
Aids: Bl: 0-0 Vi: 0-0 Tstrap: 0-0
Best Rating: 64 9/01 Prth 2m110y good Hdl

No Shenanigans (IRE)

95f **134f**

5-y-o b g King's Ride-Melarka (Dara Monarch)
N J Henderson Mrs Christopher Hanbury

Placings:14 **(4679)**
2001/02: 16^{1}GS, 17^{4}G

	Starts	1st	2nd	3rd	Win & Pl
NH Flat	2	1	0	0	4202

Career Total	2	1	0	0	4202

116 3/02 Sand 2m110y H NHF G-S £2551

Total win prize-money £2552

Going: Sf: 0-0 GS: 1-1 Gd: 0-1 GF: - Fm: 0-0

Distance: **2m/2m3: 1-2** 2m4-2m7: 0-0 3m+: 0-0

Track: LH: 0-0 **RH: 1-1** Tight: 0-0 Gall: 0-0

Aids: Bl: 0-0 Vi: 0-0 Tstrap: 0-0

Best Rating: 134 4/02 Aint 2m1f good NHF

Well backed to make a winning debut in a Sandown bumper and did so, but only just. That may have been a decent event and he ran with plenty of credit when fourth in the champion bumper at Aintree. A fine-long term prospect.

No Tale To Tell (IRE)

(97c) **64**

8-y-o b g Be My Native (USA)-Amberley (Deep Run)

M Wellings Mrs M A Powis

Placings:*433/331220/***34F***P0-000P* **(4844)**

2001/02: 20^{0}S, 24^{0}S, 22^{0}GS, 24^{P}G

	Starts	1st	2nd	3rd	Win & Pl
Hurdles	4	0	0	0	
Career Total	**18**	**1**	**2**	**5**	**13288**

121 11/99 Ludl 2m5f E Hdl GD £2346

Total win prize-money £2346

Going: Sf: 0-2 GS: 0-1 Gd: 0-1 GF: - Fm: 0-0

Distance: 2m/2m3: 0-0 2m4-2m7: 0-2 3m+: 0-2

Track: LH: 0-3 RH: 0-1 Tight: 0-1 Gall: 0-1

Aids: Bl: 0-0 Vi: 0-0 Tstrap: 0-0

Best Rating: 141 2/00 Winc 2m6f gd-sft Hdl

So named because he has no tail, was a useful novice hurdler in 1999/2000. Did not take to fences in 2000/2001 and has reverted to hurdles. Stays three miles. Has won at up to two miles five. Has won on a sound surface, acts on heavy.

No Visibility (IRE)

101 **101**

7-y-o b g Glacial Storm (USA)-Duhallow Lady (IRE) (Torus)

R H Alner (Henry De Bromhead 22/7) David O Moon

Placings:*60/*43000P-0005U **(4684)**

2001/02: 16^{0}YS, 16^{0}G, 16^{0}G, 16^{5}G, 19^{U}GF

	Starts	1st	2nd	3rd	Win & Pl
Hurdles	5	0	0	0	0
Career Total	**13**	**0**	**0**	**1**	**748**

Going: Sf: 0-0 GS: 0-0 Gd: 0-3 GF: - Fm: 0-1

Distance: 2m/2m3: 0-4 2m4-2m7: 0-1 3m+: 0-0

Track: LH: 0-0 RH: 0-2 Tight: 0-0 Gall: 0-0

Aids: Bl: 0-0 Vi: 0-0 Tstrap: 0-0

Best Rating: 104 3/02 Winc 2m good Hdl

Noble Baron

102f **104f**

6-y-o gr g Karinga Bay-Grey Baroness (Baron Blakeney)

C G Cox T Y Bissett

Placings:*01* **(3502)**

2001/02: 16^{0}S, 16^{1}S

	Starts	1st	2nd	3rd	Win & Pl
NH Flat	2	1	0	0	2013
Career Total	**2**	**1**	**0**	**0**	**2013**

104 1/02 Kemp 2m H NHF SFT £2012

Total win prize-money £2013

Going: Sf: 1-2 GS: 0-0 Gd: 0-0 GF: - Fm: 0-0

Distance: **2m/2m3: 1-2** 2m4-2m7: 0-0 3m+: 0-0

Track: LH: 0-1 **RH: 1-1** Tight: 0-0 Gall: 0-0

Aids: Bl: 0-0 Vi: 0-0 Tstrap: 0-0

Best Rating: 104 1/02 Kemp 2m soft NHF

Surprise winner of a Kempton bumper in January 2002, having finished last on his debut.

Noble Calling (FR)

74 **66**

5-y-o b h Caller I.D. (USA)-Specificity (USA) (Alleged (USA))

R J Hodges R J Hodges

Placings:0 **(1994)**

2001/02: 17^{0}S

	Starts	1st	2nd	3rd	Win & Pl
Hurdles	1	0	0	0	
Career Total	**1**	**0**	**0**	**0**	

Going: Sf: 0-1 GS: 0-0 Gd: 0-0 GF: - Fm: 0-0

Distance: 2m/2m3: 0-1 2m4-2m7: 0-0 3m+: 0-0

Track: LH: 0-1 RH: 0-0 Tight: 0-1 Gall: 0-0

Aids: Bl: 0-0 Vi: 0-0 Tstrap: 0-0

Best Rating: 66 11/01 NAbb 2m1f soft Hdl

Well beaten on hurdling debut.

Noble Challenge

6-y-o ch g Formidable (USA)-What A Challenge (Sallust)

C J Drewe Mrs M R Taylor

Placings:*0*PU **(4684)**

2001/02: 17^{0}GF, 16^{P}S, 19^{U}GF

	Starts	1st	2nd	3rd	Win & Pl
NH Flat	1	0	0	0	0
Hurdles	2	0	0	0	0
Career Total	**3**	**0**	**0**	**0**	

Going: Sf: 0-1 GS: 0-0 Gd: 0-0 GF: - Fm: 0-2

Distance: 2m/2m3: 0-2 2m4-2m7: 0-1 3m+: 0-0

Track: LH: 0-1 RH: 0-1 Tight: 0-2 Gall: 0-0

Aids: Bl: 0-0 Vi: 0-0 Tstrap: 0-0

Best Rating:

Noble Comic

108 **119**

11-y-o b g Silly Prices-Barony (Ribston)

C Tizzard R E Dimond

Placings:*0P/6FP/*413152P5-0211504 **(1730)**

2001/02: 16^{0}GF, 16^{2}GF, 21^{1}G, 16^{1}G, 21^{5}GF, 20^{0}GF, 24^{4}F

	Starts	1st	2nd	3rd	Win & Pl
Chases	7	2	1	0	9344
Career Total	**20**	**4**	**2**	**1**	**18840**

111 8/01 NAbb 2m110y F(0-110)HCh GD £4315

114 7/01 NAbb 2m5f110y D(0-120)HCh GD £3776

119 6/00 NAbb 2m110y D Ch G-F £3711

115 6/00 NAbb 2m5f110y D Ch GD £3779

Total win prize-money £15585

Going: Sf: 0-0 GS: 0-0 Gd: 2-2 GF: - Fm: 0-5

Distance: 2m/2m3: 1-3 2m4-2m7: 1-3 3m+: 0-1

Track: **LH: 2-5** RH: 0-1 **Tight: 2-7** Gall: 0-0

Aids: Bl: 0-0 Vi: 0-0 Tstrap: 0-0

Best Rating: 119 6/00 NAbb 2m110y gd-fm Ch

Fair handicap chaser, successful four times at Newton Abbot. Likes good ground, effective at up to 21 furlongs.

Noble Cyrano

92 **87**

7-y-o ch g Generous (IRE)-Miss Bergerac (Bold Lad (IRE))

Jedd O'Keeffe Wetherby Racing Bureau 38

Placings:36F **(3266)**

2001/02: 16^{3}GS, 16^{6}S, 20^{F}G

	Starts	1st	2nd	3rd	Win & Pl
Hurdles	3	0	0	1	371
Career Total	**3**	**0**	**0**	**1**	**371**

Going: Sf: 0-1 GS: 0-1 Gd: 0-1 GF: - Fm: 0-0

Distance: 2m/2m3: 0-2 2m4-2m7: 0-1 3m+: 0-0

Track: LH: 0-3 RH: 0-0 Tight: 0-0 Gall: 0-1

Aids: Bl: 0-0 Vi: 0-0 Tstrap: 0-0

Best Rating: 87 11/01 Ayr 2m gd-sft Hdl

Noble Deed (IRE)

85f **74f**

5-y-o b g Lord Americo-Legal Statement (IRE) (Strong Statement (USA))

Miss H C Knight Winter Madness

Placings:*0* **(4423)**

2001/02: 16^{0}GS

	Starts	1st	2nd	3rd	Win & Pl
NH Flat	1	0	0	0	
Career Total	**1**	**0**	**0**	**0**	

Going: Sf: 0-0 GS: 0-1 Gd: 0-0 GF: - Fm: 0-0

Distance: 2m/2m3: 0-1 2m4-2m7: 0-0 3m+: 0-0

Track: LH: 0-1 RH: 0-0 Tight: 0-0 Gall: 0-1

Aids: Bl: 0-0 Vi: 0-0 Tstrap: 0-0

Best Rating: 74 3/02 Newb 2m110y gd-sft NHF

Noble Demand (USA)

104 **107**

7-y-o b g Red Ransom (USA)-Noble Nordic (USA) (Vaguely Noble)

M J Weeden Mrs E A Haycock

Placings:3443234/4PP-4453 **(4028)**

2001/02: 19^{4}GS, 22^{4}GS, 20^{5}S, 21^{3}GS

	Starts	1st	2nd	3rd	Win & Pl
Hurdles	4	0	0	1	1294
Career Total	**14**	**0**	**1**	**4**	**6798**

Going: Sf: 0-1 GS: 0-3 Gd: 0-0 GF: - Fm: 0-0

Distance: 2m/2m3: 0-1 2m4-2m7: 0-3 3m+: 0-0

Track: LH: 0-2 RH: 0-2 Tight: 0-0 Gall: 0-2

Aids: Bl: 0-0 Vi: 0-0 Tstrap: 0-0

Best Rating: 130 1/99 Chel 2m1f soft Hdl

Decent juvenile hurdler in 1999/2000, has had his problems since but is gradually slipping in the weights. Goes well fresh, best on an easy surface.

Noble Hymn

9-y-o br g Arctic Lord-Soraway (Choral Society)

Mrs C M Mulhall Mrs C M Mulhall

Placings:3000/5P/F (4097)
2001/02: 25^F GS

	Starts	1st	2nd	3rd	Win & Pl
Chases	1	0	0	0	
Career Total	**7**	**0**	**0**	**1**	**153**

Going: Sf: 0-0 GS: 0-1 Gd: 0-0 GF: - Fm: 0-0
Distance: 2m/2m3: 0-0 2m4-2m7: 0-0 3m+: 0-1
Track: LH: 0-0 RH: 0-0 Tight: 0-0 Gall: 0-0
Aids: Bl: 0-0 Vi: 0-0 Tstrap: 0-1
Best Rating: 80 10/98 Sedg 2m1f good NHF

Noble Justice (IRE)

103(93h) (97h)116
6-y-o b g Jurado (USA)-Furry Hope (Furry Glen)
R J Hodges (P F Cashman 6/5) Fieldspring Racing

Placings:03212 (2879)
2001/02: 18^0 G, 22^3 GF, 22^2 G, 21^1 GF, 21^2 G

	Starts	1st	2nd	3rd	Win & Pl
NH Flat	1	0	0	0	0
Hurdles	2	0	1	1	1004
Chases	2	1	1	0	7055
Career Total	**5**	**1**	**2**	**1**	**8059**

116 11/01 Winc 2m5f D Ch G-F £4290
Total win prize-money £4290

Going: Sf: 0-0 GS: 0-0 Gd: 0-3 GF: - Fm: 1-2
Distance: 2m/2m3: 0-1 **2m4-2m7: 1-4** 3m+: 0-0
Track: LH: 0-0 **RH: 1-4** Tight: 0-0 Gall: 0-0
Aids: Bl: 0-0 Vi: 0-0 Tstrap: 0-1
Best Rating: 116 12/01 Winc 2m5f good Ch

Lightly-raced hurdler, made a successful chasing debut at Wincanton in November 2001, Suited by a sound surface.

Noble Pasao (IRE)

110 108
5-y-o b g Alzao (USA)-Belle Passe (Be My Guest (USA))
Andrew Turnell Mrs Claire Hollowood

Placings:2531-6235 (4688)
2001/02: 16^6 GF, 16^2 G, 16^3 GS, 16^5 GF

	Starts	1st	2nd	3rd	Win & Pl
Hurdles	4	0	1	1	1598
Career Total	**8**	**1**	**2**	**2**	**6015**

104 4/01 Extr 2m1f E(0-105)HHdl SFT £2895
Total win prize-money £2895

Going: Sf: 0-0 GS: 0-1 Gd: 0-1 GF: 0-2
Distance: 2m/2m3: 0-4 2m4-2m7: 0-0 3m+: 0-0
Track: LH: 0-3 RH: 0-1 Tight: 0-2 Gall: 0-0
Aids: Bl: 0-0 Vi: 0-0 Tstrap: 0-0
Best Rating: 108 11/01 Leic 2m gd-sft Hdl

A moderate handicapper over hurdles, suited to around two miles with cut in the ground.

Noble Spy (IRE)

103 105
8-y-o b g Lord Americo-Flashey Blond (Buckskin (FR))
Mrs D A Hamer J.M.B Pugh

Placings:405/F00-1334F232 (3792)
2001/02: 20^1 GF, 20^3 GF, 20^3 S, 21^4 GF, 20^F GS, 25^2 HY, 24^3 S, 25^2 S

	Starts	1st	2nd	3rd	Win & Pl
Hurdles	8	1	2	3	6386
Career Total	**14**	**1**	**2**	**3**	**6386**

84 8/01 Worc 2m4f F Hdl G-F £1981
Total win prize-money £1981

Going: Sf: 0-4 GS: 0-1 Gd: 0-0 GF: - Fm: 1-3
Distance: 2m/2m3: 0-0 **2m4-2m7: 1-5** 3m+: 0-3
Track: **LH: 1-5** RH: 0-1 Tight: 0-0 Gall: 0-1
Aids: Bl: 0-0 Vi: 0-0 Tstrap: 0-0
Best Rating: 105 2/02 Wwck 3m1f soft Hdl

Modest handicap hurdler, has won on a sound surface over two and a half miles but is effective in heavy ground too.

Noble Star

10-y-o b g Jester-Mickley Spacetrail (Space King)
Mrs J M Bush Mrs J M Bush

Placings:0 (0228)
2001/02: 20^0 GF

	Starts	1st	2nd	3rd	Win & Pl
Chases	1	0	0	0	
Career Total	**1**	**0**	**0**	**0**	

Going: Sf: 0-0 GS: 0-0 Gd: 0-0 GF: - Fm: 0-1
Distance: 2m/2m3: 0-0 2m4-2m7: 0-1 3m+: 0-0
Track: LH: 0-0 RH: 0-1 Tight: 0-0 Gall: 0-1
Aids: Bl: 0-0 Vi: 0-0 Tstrap: 0-0
Best Rating:

Nocksky (IRE)

91 55
9-y-o b g Niniski (USA)-Olivana (GER) (Sparkler)
M C Pipe Terry Neill

Placings:211F0P/P103/111/PP0 (4661)
2001/02: 24^P GS, 23^P G, 25^0 G

	Starts	1st	2nd	3rd	Win & Pl
Chases	3	0	0	0	
Career Total	**16**	**6**	**1**	**1**	**24349**

135 7/99 Worc 2m7f110y E Ch G-F £3195
131 7/99 Wolv 2m4f110y E Ch G-F £3329
126 7/99 NAbb 3m2f110y E Ch G-S £3176
131 2/99 Hayd 2m4f D(0-120)HHdl SFT £2840
132 12/97 Leop 3m Hdl HVY £6782
82 9/97 Dund 3m Hdl Y-S £2204
Total win prize-money £21528

Going: Sf: 0-0 GS: 0-1 Gd: 0-2 GF: - Fm: 0-0
Distance: 2m/2m3: 0-0 2m4-2m7: 0-0 3m+: 0-3
Track: LH: 0-2 RH: 0-1 Tight: 0-1 Gall: 0-1
Aids: Bl: 0-0 Vi: 0-0 Tstrap: 0-0
Best Rating: 135 7/99 Worc 2m7f110y gd-fm Ch

He was given an enterprising ride when finishing third at Aintree in April 1999 and made a successful switch to fences with a hat-trick in the summer of that year. Was off the track for nearly three and a half years before making his reappearance in the Kim Muir at the Cheltenham Festival but was pulled up there and has shown nothing since. He stays at least three miles and acts on any ground.

Noel's Pride

108(100c) (109c)110
6-y-o b g Good Thyne (USA)-Kavali (Blakeney)
J M Jefferson Pride Of Yorkshire Racing Club

Placings:032/24-121211352 (2074)
2001/02: 16^1 GF, 16^2 GF, 16^1 GS, 22^2 GF, 21^1 GF, 24^1 GF, 24^3 G, 22^5 G, 21^2 S

	Starts	1st	2nd	3rd	Win & Pl
Hurdles	9	4	3	1	16792
Career Total	**14**	**4**	**5**	**2**	**18037**

110 8/01 Uttx 3m110y E(0-115)HHdl G-F £3465
105 7/01 Sedg 2m5f110y D(0-125)HHdl G-F £3276
95 6/01 Hexm 2m E Hdl G-S £2534
90 5/01 Hexm 2m E Hdl G-F £2716
Total win prize-money £11991

Going: Sf: 0-1 GS: 1-1 Gd: 0-2 GF: - Fm: 3-5
Distance: **2m/2m3: 2-3** 2m4-2m7: 1-4 3m+: 1-2
Track: **LH: 4-8** RH: 0-1 **Tight: 1-4** Gall: 0-1
Aids: Bl: 0-0 Vi: 0-0 Tstrap: 0-0
Best Rating: 110 11/01 Sedg 2m5f110y soft Hdl

He showed the benefit of a soft-palate operation when winning four times in the summer of 2001. Suited by fast ground, although he has won on easier. He stays three miles and has tried his hand unsuccessfully so far over fences.

Noisetine (FR)

102 105
4-y-o ch f Mansonnien (FR)-Notabilite (FR) (No Pass No Sale)
Miss Venetia Williams Mrs Jean F P Yeomans

Placings:303-1511 (4575)
2001/02: 15^1 G, 16^5 GS, 22^1 S, 20^1 G

	Starts	1st	2nd	3rd	Win & Pl
Hurdles	4	3	0	0	9669
Career Total	**7**	**3**	**0**	**2**	**14033**

99 4/02 Uttx 2m4f110y E Hdl GD £3045
105 3/02 Winc 2m6f E Hdl SFT £2744
5/01 Fntb 1m7f Hdl GD £3880
Total win prize-money £9669

Going: Sf: 1-1 GS: 0-1 Gd: 2-2 GF: - Fm: 0-0
Distance: 2m/2m3: 0-1 **2m4-2m7: 2-2** 3m+: 0-0
Track: LH: 1-1 RH: 1-2 Tight: 0-0 Gall: 0-1
Aids: Bl: 0-0 Vi: 0-0 Tstrap: 0-0
Best Rating: 105 3/02 Winc 2m6f soft Hdl

Got off the mark in Britain with a novice hurdle double in the spring, having already been successful in over France. Acts on soft ground and is effective over two miles six furlongs.

Noisy Miner (IRE)

87 66
10-y-o b g Kambalda-Furry Lady (Furry Glen)
R T Phillips Mrs R J Skan

Placings:11/11PP000/P22F5111P/6P/5F0U-06P (4889)
2001/02: 24^0 G, 21^6 S, 26^P G

	Starts	1st	2nd	3rd	Win & Pl
Chases	3	0	0	0	0
Career Total	**27**	**7**	**2**	**0**	**25268**

140 2/99 Leic 2m7f110y C(0-130)HCh G-S £7165
128 1/99 Ludl 3m E(0-115)HCh G-S £2970
124 12/98 Ludl 3m D(0-125)HCh GD £3810
116 11/97 Aint 2m4f C Hdl G-S £3629
116 11/97 Chep 2m4f110y D Hdl G-S £2615
103 3/97 Winc 2m H NHF G-F £1490
111 2/97 Winc 2m H NHF GD £1264
Total win prize-money £22945

Going: Sf: 0-1 GS: 0-0 Gd: 0-2 GF: - Fm: 0-0
Distance: 2m/2m3: 0-0 2m4-2m7: 0-1 3m+: 0-2
Track: LH: 0-0 RH: 0-2 Tight: 0-2 Gall: 0-0
Aids: Bl: 0-0 Vi: 0-0 Tstrap: 0-0
Best Rating: 140 2/99 Leic 2m7f110y gd-sft Ch

Noix D'Acajou

95f 71f

5-y-o ch g Deploy-Our Aisling (Blakeney)
Miss K Marks Nick Shutts

Placings: *00-4P* (1753)
2001/02: 16^{4}GF, 17^{P}G

	Starts	1st	2nd	3rd	Win & Pl
NH Flat	2	0	0	0	0
Career Total	4	0	0	0	0

Going: Sf: 0-0 GS: 0-0 Gd: 0-1 GF: - Fm: 0-1
Distance: 2m/2m3: 0-2 2m4-2m7: 0-0 3m+: 0-0
Track: LH: 0-0 RH: 0-2 Tight: 0-1 Gall: 0-0
Aids: Bl: 0-0 Vi: 0-0 Tstrap: 0-2
Best Rating: 71 10/01 Ludl 2m gd-fm NHF

Nokimover

103(102h) (108h)118

8-y-o ch g Scallywag-Town Blues (Charlottown)
J G M O'Shea H G Llewellyn

Placings: 400/113551-05 (4683)
2001/02: 17^{0}HY, 19^{5}GF

	Starts	1st	2nd	3rd	Win & Pl
Hurdles	1	0	0	0	0
Chases	1	0	0	0	0
Career Total	11	3	0	1	7874

108	4/01	Hrfd	3m2f	E Hdl	GD	£2296
101	12/00	Hrfd	2m3f110y	E Hdl	HVY	£2954
101	11/00	Aint	2m1f	H NHF	G-S	£2275

Total win prize-money £7525

Going: Sf: 0-1 GS: 0-0 Gd: 0-0 GF: - Fm: 0-1
Distance: 2m/2m3: 0-2 2m4-2m7: 0-0 3m+: 0-0
Track: LH: 0-0 RH: 0-2 Tight: 0-0 Gall: 0-0
Aids: Bl: 0-0 Vi: 0-0 Tstrap: 0-0
Best Rating: 108 4/01 Hrfd 3m2f good Hdl

Able but quirky hurdler, was getting round for the first time over fences when successful at Uttoxeter in June 2002.

Nolt (FR)

4-y-o b g Nikos-L'Eternite (FR) (Cariellor (FR))
J Lesbordes A Brakha

Placings: 6540
2001/02: 17^{6}VS, 17^{5}HY, 18^{4}VS, 18^{0}VS

	Starts	1st	2nd	3rd	Win & Pl
Hurdles	4	0	0	0	2331
Career Total	4	0	0	0	2331

Going: Sf: 0-1 GS: 0-0 Gd: 0-0 GF: - Fm: 0-0
Distance: 2m/2m3: 0-4 2m4-2m7: 0-0 3m+: 0-0
Track: LH: 0-1 RH: 0-0 Tight: 0-0 Gall: 0-1
Aids: Bl: 0-0 Vi: 0-0 Tstrap: 0-0
Best Rating:

Decent ten-furlong winner on the Flat in France, acts in heavy ground. He was held over hurdles on his British debut.

Nomiret (IRE)

74 44

5-y-o b g Terimon-Country Carnival (Town And Country)
J Howard Johnson Michael Thompson

Placings: 0000 (4553)
2001/02: 16^{0}G, 16^{0}S, 17^{0}GS, 17^{0}GF

	Starts	1st	2nd	3rd	Win & Pl
NH Flat	1	0	0	0	0
Hurdles	3	0	0	0	0
Career Total	4	0	0	0	

Going: Sf: 0-1 GS: 0-1 Gd: 0-1 GF: - Fm: 0-1
Distance: 2m/2m3: 0-4 2m4-2m7: 0-0 3m+: 0-0
Track: LH: 0-1 RH: 0-3 Tight: 0-4 Gall: 0-0
Aids: Bl: 0-0 Vi: 0-0 Tstrap: 0-0
Best Rating: 44 4/02 MRas 2m1f110y gd-fm Hdl

Non So (FR)

112 120

4-y-o b g Definite Article-Irish Woman (FR) (Assert)
N J Henderson (C Boutin 8/7) Roa Dawn Run Partnership

Placings: 0211P (4250)
2001/02: 16^{0}G, 16^{2}G, 17^{1}S, 18^{1}S, 17^{P}G

	Starts	1st	2nd	3rd	Win & Pl
Hurdles	5	2	1	0	5982
Career Total	5	2	1	0	5982

107	1/02	Font	2m2f110y	E Hdl	SFT	£2653
115	1/02	Folk	2m1f110y	E Hdl	SFT	£2632

Total win prize-money £5285

Going: Sf: 2-2 GS: 0-0 Gd: 0-3 GF: - Fm: 0-0
Distance: **2m/2m3: 2-5** 2m4-2m7: 0-0 3m+: 0-0
Track: LH: 1-4 RH: 1-1 **Tight: 2-3** Gall: 0-2
Aids: Bl: 0-0 Vi: 0-0 Tstrap: 0-0
Best Rating: 120 12/01 Plum 2m good Hdl

Improved on her debut effort when second at Plumpton in December 2001. Scored a double on soft ground at the start of 2002, the second of which saw him finish very tired and his jockey dismount immediately after crossing the winning line. Acts on a sound surface, but won on the level in France on an easier surface.

Non Vintage (IRE)

100(102h) (68h)86

11-y-o ch g Shy Groom (USA)-Great Alexandra (Runnett)
M C Chapman Rasen Goes Racing

Placings: 34231/21300364356/024144FO6650010/45330405243P2003/34635432133436230405/55053065/65400-041 (1045)
2001/02: 17^{0}G, 21^{4}GS, 26^{1}GF

	Starts	1st	2nd	3rd	Win & Pl
Hurdles	1	0	0	0	0
Chases	2	1	0	0	3575
Career Total	83	6	7	17	65770

86	7/01	Uttx	3m2f	F(0-90)HCh	G-F	£3575
113	8/98	Ctml	2m1f110y	D(0-120)HCh	G-S	£3418
128	2/97	MRas	2m1f110y	D(0-120)HHdl	GD	£2796
130	10/96	MRas	2m1f110y	C(0-135)HHdl	GD	£3355
119	11/95	Asct	2m110y	B(0-145)HHdl	GD	£6691
90	3/95	Ludl	2m	E Hdl	G-S	£2528

Total win prize-money £22364

Going: Sf: 0-0 GS: 0-1 Gd: 0-1 GF: - Fm: 1-1
Distance: 2m/2m3: 0-1 2m4-2m7: 0-1 **3m+: 1-1**
Track: **LH: 1-1** RH: 0-1 Tight: 0-1 Gall: 0-0
Aids: Bl: 0-0 Vi: 0-0 Tstrap: 0-0
Best Rating: 133 11/95 Newc 2m good Hdl

His strike rate is very moderate despite several placings. He tends to drop himself out and has become unreliable.

Nona's Lass

67f 14f

5-y-o b m Clantime-Festive Lassie (North Briton)
A Streeter Green Card Golfers

Placings: *0* (1657)
2001/02: 17^{0}G

	Starts	1st	2nd	3rd	Win & Pl
NH Flat	1	0	0	0	0
Career Total	1	0	0	0	

Going: Sf: 0-0 GS: 0-0 Gd: 0-1 GF: - Fm: 0-0
Distance: 2m/2m3: 0-1 2m4-2m7: 0-0 3m+: 0-0
Track: LH: 0-1 RH: 0-0 Tight: 0-1 Gall: 0-0
Aids: Bl: 0-0 Vi: 0-0 Tstrap: 0-0
Best Rating: 14 10/01 Bang 2m1f good NHF

None Stirred (IRE)

103(78h) 128

12-y-o b g Supreme Leader-Double Wrapped (Double U Jay)
J T Gifford Colin Frewin

Placings: 32/31/2126/4R303/21313-14P4F54F4P (4882)
2001/02: 20^{1}GS, 22^{4}GS, 20^{P}G, 25^{4}G, 26^{F}G, 25^{5}S, 20^{4}HY, 20^{F}S, 20^{4}GS, 26^{P}GF

	Starts	1st	2nd	3rd	Win & Pl
Chases	10	1	0	0	4855
Career Total	28	5	4	6	24134

128	4/01	Plum	2m4f	E(0-115)HCh	G-S	£3622
128	11/00	Folk	2m	F(0-95)HCh	SFT	£2717
120	10/00	Chep	2m4f	D(0-120)HHdl	G-S	£2918
114	12/97	Font	2m6f110y	E(0-110)HHdl	SFT	£2406
103	1/97	Ling	2m110y	E(0-105)HHdl	SFT	£2407

Total win prize-money £14073

Going: Sf: 0-3 GS: 1-3 Gd: 0-3 GF: - Fm: 0-1
Distance: 2m/2m3: 0-0 **2m4-2m7: 1-6** 3m+: 0-4
Track: **LH: 1-3** RH: 0-4 **Tight: 1-6** Gall: 0-1
Aids: Bl: 0-0 Vi: 0-0 Tstrap: 0-0
Best Rating: 128 4/01 Plum 2m4f gd-sft Ch

A winner over hurdles and fences, he acts on a soft surface and goes well from two miles to two miles six furlongs.

Nordance Prince (IRE)

112 154

11-y-o b g Nordance (USA)-Shirleys Princess (Sandhurst Prince)
Miss Venetia Williams Pinks Gym & Leisure Wear Ltd

Placings: 3/335534/112211001/11/1211FFF4/053 (4914)
2001/02: 16^{0}GS, 16^{5}G, 20^{3}G

	Starts	1st	2nd	3rd	Win & Pl
Chases	3	0	0	1	4800
Career Total	29	10	3	5	131245

161	1/00	Asct	2m	A HCh	G-S	£30000
161	12/99	Weth	2m	A HCh	G-S	£19300
161	11/99	Asct	2m3f110y	A HCh	GD	£29775
146	10/98	Chel	2m	C Ch	GD	£4719
137	10/98	Towc	2m110y	E(0-120)Ch	GD	£2815
128	4/98	Prth	2m110y	D Hdl	GD	£3499
128	2/98	Donc	2m110y	B(0-140)HHdl	G-F	£5234
130	2/98	Sand	2m110y	E(0-115)HHdl	GD	£2840
99	5/97	Hntg	2m110y	E Hdl	G-F	£2355
113	5/97	NAbb	2m1f	E Hdl	G-F	£2505

Total win prize-money £103045

Going: Sf: 0-0 GS: 0-1 Gd: 0-2 GF: - Fm: 0-0
Distance: 2m/2m3: 0-2 2m4-2m7: 0-1 3m+: 0-0
Track: LH: 0-2 RH: 0-1 Tight: 0-1 Gall: 0-1
Aids: Bl: 0-0 Vi: 0-0 Tstrap: 0-0
Best Rating: 161 1/00 Asct 2m gd-sft Ch

Formerly a high-class handicap chaser a few seasons ago, including when beating Flagship Uberalles in the 2000 Victor Chandler, he then fell in three consecutive races and was off the track for almost two years. Slowly returning to form, he acts on good or easier ground.

Nordic Breeze (IRE)

95 **86**

10-y-o b/br g Nordico (USA)-Baby Clair (Gulf Pearl)
M C Pipe Malcolm B Jones

Placings:453/132U30/F1123442400/043144/4230P/0 00 **(3515)**
2001/02: 20^{0}S, 20^{0}GS, 19^{0}S

	Starts	1st	2nd	3rd	Win & Pl
Hurdles	3	0	0	0	
Career Total	**34**	**4**	**4**	**6**	**27413**

121	3/99	Winc	2m5f	E Ch	GD	£3844
120	5/97	Uttx	2m	E Hdl	GD	£2389
110	5/97	NAbb	2m1f	D Hdl	G-S	£2855
90	10/96	Uttx	2m	E Hdl	G-F	£2410

Total win prize-money £11500

Going: Sf: 0-2 GS: 0-1 Gd: 0-0 GF: - Fm: 0-0
Distance: 2m/2m3: 0-0 2m4-2m7: 0-3 3m+: 0-0
Track: LH: 0-2 RH: 0-1 Tight: 0-1 Gall: 0-0
Aids: Bl: 0-0 Vi: 0-3 Tstrap: 0-0
Best Rating: 133 3/97 Chel 2m110y good Hdl

Nordic Crest (IRE)

101 **128**

8-y-o b g Danehill (USA)-Feather Glen (Glenstal (USA))
P R Webber The Silver Cod Partnership

Placings:04251/3/14P3-P22 **(0829)**
2001/02: 20^{P}GF, 24^{2}F, 24^{2}GF

	Starts	1st	2nd	3rd	Win & Pl
Chases	3	0	2	0	2887
Career Total	**13**	**2**	**3**	**2**	**16593**

112	10/00	Towc	2m110y	E Ch	G-F	£3504
102	4/98	Ayr	2m	C HHdl	GD	£3817

Total win prize-money £7322

Going: Sf: 0-0 GS: 0-0 Gd: 0-0 GF: - Fm: 0-3
Distance: 2m/2m3: 0-0 2m4-2m7: 0-1 3m+: 0-2
Track: LH: 0-2 RH: 0-1 Tight: 0-2 Gall: 0-0
Aids: Bl: 0-0 Vi: 0-0 Tstrap: 0-0
Best Rating: 128 6/01 Strf 3m gd-fm Ch

Likely to be best around two and a half miles, he is nothing out the ordinary but should win a handicap on decent ground.

Nordic Prince (IRE)

100(66h) **128**

11-y-o b g Nordance (USA)-Royal Desire (Royal Match)
J G M O'Shea Blue Shirts

Placings: *11*/03/133123P/1P/**R3440/423231111231PP230-46264** **(2561)**
2001/02: 24^{4}G, 28^{6}S, 21^{2}S, 28^{6}S, 26^{4}S

	Starts	1st	2nd	3rd	Win & Pl
Chases	5	0	1	0	2394
Career Total	**40**	**10**	**6**	**9**	**50022**

128	11/00	Wwck	3m2f	D(0-120)HCh	HVY	£4020
125	10/00	Strf	3m	D(0-125)HCh	G-S	£3757
118	10/00	Bang	3m110y	D(0-120)HCh	SFT	£6857
92	8/00	Sthl	3m110y	E Ch	GD	£2815
92	8/00	Sthl	3m110y	G Hdl	G-F	£1501
126	10/98	Worc	2m4f	C(0-130)HHdl	GD	£3769
108	2/98	Font	2m6f110y	E Hdl	GD	£2553
101	8/97	Uttx	2m4f110y	D Hdl	GD	£2773
	11/95	Hexm	2m	H NHF	GD	£1371
	11/95	Worc	2m	H NHF	G-F	£2052

Total win prize-money £31471

Going: Sf: 0-4 GS: 0-0 Gd: 0-1 GF: - Fm: 0-0
Distance: 2m/2m3: 0-0 2m4-2m7: 0-1 3m+: 0-4
Track: LH: 0-5 RH: 0-0 Tight: 0-2 Gall: 0-0
Aids: Bl: 0-0 Vi: 0-0 Tstrap: 0-0
Best Rating: 128 11/01 Uttx 2m5f soft Ch

He was in fine form in the second half of 2000, winning a selling hurdle before scoring four times over fences. A rise in the handicap appeared to find him out afterwards, but he has hinted at a return to form. Acts on all ground and stays further than three miles.

Nordisk Legend

91 **88**

10-y-o b g Colmore Row-Nordic Rose (DEN) (Drumhead)
Mrs D Thomson Mrs Dorothy Thomson

Placings:666/5340P00/0/626050U/5454-35P **(0804)**
2001/02: 20^{3}GF, 16^{5}F, 20^{P}GF

	Starts	1st	2nd	3rd	Win & Pl
Chases	3	0	0	1	1560
Career Total	**25**	**0**	**1**	**2**	**3648**

Going: Sf: 0-0 GS: 0-0 Gd: 0-0 GF: - Fm: 0-3
Distance: 2m/2m3: 0-1 2m4-2m7: 0-2 3m+: 0-0
Track: LH: 0-0 RH: 0-3 Tight: 0-0 Gall: 0-0
Aids: Bl: 0-0 Vi: 0-0 Tstrap: 0-0
Best Rating: 92 1/01 Muss 2m gd-sft Ch

Norlandic (NZ)

109 **130**

10-y-o ch g First Norman (USA)-April Snow (NZ) (Icelandic)
P J Hobbs The Till House Partnership

Placings:06/3/5521511/2122/154UP3-33 **(2310)**
2001/02: 23^{3}GF, 30^{3}GS

	Starts	1st	2nd	3rd	Win & Pl
Chases	2	0	0	2	2034
Career Total	**22**	**5**	**4**	**4**	**31764**

139	10/00	Extr	2m7f110y	D(0-125)HCh	SFT	£5096
139	12/99	Winc	3m1f110y	D(0-120)HCh	GD	£4143
130	4/99	Extr	2m7f110y	E(0-105)HCh	G-S	£4079
121	3/99	Extr	2m7f110y	E(0-105)HCh	GD	£5054
103	2/99	Tntn	3m110y	F(0-110)HHdl	G-S	£2246

Total win prize-money £20619

Going: Sf: 0-0 GS: 0-1 Gd: 0-0 GF: - Fm: 0-1
Distance: 2m/2m3: 0-0 2m4-2m7: 0-0 3m+: 0-2
Track: LH: 0-0 RH: 0-2 Tight: 0-0 Gall: 0-1
Aids: Bl: 0-0 Vi: 0-0 Tstrap: 0-0
Best Rating: 139 10/00 Extr 2m7f110y soft Ch

Fair staying chaser on good ground or softer.He has won all his races on right-handed courses and goes well at Exeter, but has been hindered by a tendency to make mistakes.

Norman Conquest (USA)

8-y-o ch g Miswaki (USA)-Grand Luxe (CAN) (Sir Ivor)
A Crook B & K Associates

Placings:2064/024602000/5124P/FPP **(2771)**
2001/02: 16^{P}G, 24^{P}G, 16^{P}G

	Starts	1st	2nd	3rd	Win & Pl
Chases	3	0	0	0	
Career Total	**21**	**1**	**4**	**0**	**6920**

94	12/99	Catt	2m	D Ch	GD	£4030

Total win prize-money £4030

Going: Sf: 0-0 GS: 0-0 Gd: 0-3 GF: - Fm: 0-0
Distance: 2m/2m3: 0-2 2m4-2m7: 0-0 3m+: 0-1
Track: LH: 0-2 RH: 0-1 Tight: 0-2 Gall: 0-0
Aids: Bl: 0-1 Vi: 0-1 Tstrap: 0-0
Best Rating: 101 1/00 Folk 2m5f gd-sft Ch

Normanby Road (NZ)

84(59c) **63**

11-y-o br g First Norman (USA)-Gladstone Lass (NZ) (Silver Blaze (USA))
G M McCourt N H Oliver

Placings:5505/1141134B3400/3533604P-P0 **(0375)**
2001/02: 16^{P}F, 16^{0}GF

	Starts	1st	2nd	3rd	Win & Pl
Hurdles	2	0	0	0	
Career Total	**26**	**4**	**0**	**5**	**15303**

113	7/99	NAbb	2m1f	D(0-120)HHdl	G-F	£2723
104	7/99	Worc	2m	E(0-115)HHdl	G-F	£2582
108	5/99	Strf	2m110y	E(0-105)HHdl	GD	£3272
95	5/99	Hrfd	2m1f	E(0-105)HHdl	G-S	£2598

Total win prize-money £11176

Going: Sf: 0-0 GS: 0-0 Gd: 0-0 GF: - Fm: 0-2
Distance: 2m/2m3: 0-2 2m4-2m7: 0-0 3m+: 0-0
Track: LH: 0-1 RH: 0-1 Tight: 0-1 Gall: 0-1
Aids: Bl: 0-0 Vi: 0-0 Tstrap: 0-0
Best Rating: 114 12/99 Ludl 2m good Ch

Normania (NZ)

10-y-o b g First Norman (USA)-Brigania (NZ) (Brigand (USA))
Miss Sarah West (Miss S Edwards 10/2) Pete Frayne

Placings:*20*/0430214/**3P3F/FP3/FF-5** **(4865)**
2001/02: 23^{5}F

	Starts	1st	2nd	3rd	Win & Pl
Chases	1	0	0	0	0
Career Total	**19**	**1**	**2**	**4**	**5841**

89	2/98	Hntg	2m4f110y	E(0-105)HHdl	GD	£2897

Total win prize-money £2898

Going: Sf: 0-0 GS: 0-0 Gd: 0-0 GF: - Fm: 0-1
Distance: 2m/2m3: 0-0 2m4-2m7: 0-0 3m+: 0-1
Track: LH: 0-0 RH: 0-1 Tight: 0-0 Gall: 0-0
Aids: Bl: 0-0 Vi: 0-0 Tstrap: 0-0
Best Rating: 100 4/00 Hntg 2m4f110y good Ch

A progressive hurdler, some promise in hunter chases in the spring of 2002

Normarange (IRE)

107 108+

12-y-o ch g Lancastrian-Perdeal (Perspex)

P R Rodford Mrs B Curtis

Placings:3/3221U/211/4431/05446/424-00543 (4600)

2001/02: 21^{0}G, 24^{0}S, 24^{5}S, 24^{4}S, 24^{3}GF

	Starts	1st	2nd	3rd	Win & Pl
Chases	5	0	0	1	628
Career Total	**26**	**4**	**4**	**4**	**23013**

115	4/99	Extr	2m3f	D(0-125)HCh	G-S	£4562
103	11/97	Wind	2m5f	D(0-120)HCh	G-F	£4150
100	11/97	Plum	2m5f	D(0-120)HCh	G-F	£3460
86	3/97	Plum	2m2f	F Ch	G-F	£2678

Total win prize-money £14851

Going: Sf: 0-3 GS: 0-0 Gd: 0-1 GF: - Fm: 0-1
Distance: 2m/2m3: 0-0 2m4-2m7: 0-1 3m+: 0-4
Track: LH: 0-0 RH: 0-4 Tight: 0-3 Gall: 0-0
Aids: Bl: 0-0 Vi: 0-0 Tstrap: 0-0
Best Rating: 115 4/99 Extr 2m3f gd-sft Ch

Veteran chaser, best suited by a sound surface, stays three miles. Has gone well at Plumpton in the past.

Norse

81 62

9-y-o ch g Risk Me (FR)-Absent Lover (Nearly A Hand)

S E H Sherwood Jack Moody Limited

Placings:P (4405)

2001/02: 17^{P}S

	Starts	1st	2nd	3rd	Win & Pl
Chases	1	0	0	0	
Career Total	**1**	**0**	**0**	**0**	

Going: Sf: 0-1 GS: 0-0 Gd: 0-0 GF: - Fm: 0-0
Distance: 2m/2m3: 0-1 2m4-2m7: 0-0 3m+: 0-0
Track: LH: 0-1 RH: 0-0 Tight: 0-1 Gall: 0-0
Aids: Bl: 0-0 Vi: 0-0 Tstrap: 0-0
Best Rating:

Third foal of a multiple winner on the Flat at up to ten furlongs, showed little promise in a weak maiden chase on debut.

Norski Lad

78(90h) (91h)157

7-y-o b g Niniski (USA)-Lady Norcliffe (USA) (Norcliffe (CAN))

P F Nicholls Derek Millard

Placings:11011/51P33/10PP1-U02 (4501)

2001/02: 24^{U}S, 19^{0}GS, 27^{2}G

	Starts	1st	2nd	3rd	Win & Pl
Hurdles	1	0	1	0	644
Chases	2	0	0	0	0
Career Total	**18**	**7**	**1**	**2**	**38443**

157	4/01	Prth	3m	B HCh	HVY	£10549
145	10/00	Chep	2m3f110y	C(0-130)HCh	G-S	£5703
138	1/00	Kemp	3m	C Ch	GD	£7117
154	4/99	Ayr	2m4f	C HHdl	SFT	£4500
126	4/99	Chep	2m4f110y	E Hdl	SFT	£2220
139	1/99	Sand	2m110y	D Hdl	SFT	£3550
129	1/99	Extr	2m1f110y	E Hdl	HVY	£2394

Total win prize-money £36036

Going: Sf: 0-1 GS: 0-1 Gd: 0-1 GF: - Fm: 0-0
Distance: 2m/2m3: 0-0 2m4-2m7: 0-1 3m+: 0-2
Track: LH: 0-3 RH: 0-0 Tight: 0-1 Gall: 0-0
Aids: Bl: 0-0 Vi: 0-0 Tstrap: 0-0
Best Rating: 157 4/01 Prth 3m heavy Ch

He has never quite fulfilled the promise of his early hurdling career and struggles when asked to tackle smart opposition over fences. Possibly best when fresh as when winning at Chepstow in October 2000 and at Perth in April 2001. Stays three miles and acts on soft ground.

North City

95 81

11-y-o b g Scorpio (FR)-Lady Solstice (Vital Season)

Mrs H L Walton David Seed

Placings:00/04PPP-2P (0433)

2001/02: 24^{2}GF, 25^{P}GF

	Starts	1st	2nd	3rd	Win & Pl
Chases	2	0	1	0	915
Career Total	**9**	**0**	**1**	**0**	**1000**

Going: Sf: 0-0 GS: 0-0 Gd: 0-0 GF: - Fm: 0-2
Distance: 2m/2m3: 0-0 2m4-2m7: 0-0 3m+: 0-2
Track: LH: 0-1 RH: 0-1 Tight: 0-2 Gall: 0-0
Aids: Bl: 0-2 Vi: 0-0 Tstrap: 0-0
Best Rating: 81 5/01 Fknm 3m110y gd-fm Ch

North Croft

6-y-o b g North Street-Sock Jinks (New Member)

C J Gray Mrs T Frampton

Placings:00 (1799)

2001/02: 17^{0}GF, 16^{0}S

	Starts	1st	2nd	3rd	Win & Pl
NH Flat	2	0	0	0	
Career Total	**2**	**0**	**0**	**0**	

Going: Sf: 0-1 GS: 0-0 Gd: 0-0 GF: - Fm: 0-1
Distance: 2m/2m3: 0-2 2m4-2m7: 0-0 3m+: 0-0
Track: LH: 0-1 RH: 0-1 Tight: 0-0 Gall: 0-0
Aids: Bl: 0-0 Vi: 0-0 Tstrap: 0-0
Best Rating: 51 9/01 Hrfd 2m1f gd-fm NHF

North Face

76(99h) (80h)59

5-y-o ch g Factual (USA)-Northgate Dancer (Ile De Bourbon (USA))

Miss Lucinda V Russell Mrs L R Joughin

Placings:060-41F2P (3464)

2001/02: 16^{4}GF, 16^{1}GF, 16^{F}GF, 16^{2}G, 16^{P}S

	Starts	1st	2nd	3rd	Win & Pl
Hurdles	5	1	1	0	3960
Career Total	**8**	**1**	**1**	**0**	**3960**

80	6/01	Prth	2m110y	E Hdl	G-F	£3003

Total win prize-money £3003

Going: Sf: 0-1 GS: 0-0 Gd: 0-1 GF: - Fm: 1-3
Distance: **2m/2m3: 1-5** 2m4-2m7: 0-0 3m+: 0-0
Track: LH: 0-2 **RH: 1-3** Tight: 0-0 Gall: 0-2
Aids: Bl: 0-0 Vi: 0-0 Tstrap: 0-0
Best Rating: 80 12/01 Donc 2m110y good Hdl

North Kilkenny (IRE)

105(67c) 106

11-y-o ch g Ragapan-Princess Geeno (Cheval)

R H Alner Col S R Allen

Placings:3F514R0/1U42F5/4F1406-6255F0F (4588)

2001/02: 16^{6}G, 17^{2}HY, 20^{5}S, 16^{5}GF, 16^{F}G, 22^{0}G, 22^{F}G

	Starts	1st	2nd	3rd	Win & Pl
Hurdles	7	0	1	0	834
Career Total	**26**	**3**	**2**	**1**	**13372**

106	11/00	Winc	2m	F(0-100)HHdl	SFT	£2723
122	9/99	Plum	2m1f	F(0-110)HCh	G-F	£2721
122	2/99	Tntn	2m3f	D Ch	G-S	£3736

Total win prize-money £9181

Going: Sf: 0-2 GS: 0-0 Gd: 0-4 GF: - Fm: 0-1
Distance: 2m/2m3: 0-4 2m4-2m7: 0-3 3m+: 0-0
Track: LH: 0-2 RH: 0-5 Tight: 0-1 Gall: 0-0
Aids: Bl: 0-0 Vi: 0-0 Tstrap: 0-0
Best Rating: 122 12/99 Plum 2m4f good Ch

North Moss

80 28

9-y-o b g Scorpio (FR)-Bint Al Arab (Ahonoora)

F P Murtagh Denis Tumelty

Placings:0/00/3230P/535-005 (0518)

2001/02: 24^{0}S, 20^{0}GF, 20^{5}F

	Starts	1st	2nd	3rd	Win & Pl
Hurdles	3	0	0	0	0
Career Total	**14**	**0**	**1**	**3**	**1587**

Going: Sf: 0-1 GS: 0-0 Gd: 0-0 GF: - Fm: 0-2
Distance: 2m/2m3: 0-0 2m4-2m7: 0-2 3m+: 0-1
Track: LH: 0-2 RH: 0-1 Tight: 0-0 Gall: 0-0
Aids: Bl: 0-0 Vi: 0-0 Tstrap: 0-0
Best Rating: 79 10/99 Hexm 3m good Hdl

North Of Kala (IRE)

103(106h) (114h)115

9-y-o b g Distinctly North (USA)-Hi Kala (Kampala)

G L Moore B Lennard

Placings:00/00S440/200U0F/24410/2113-3P122 (1253)

2001/02: 16^{3}GF, 16^{P}GF, 16^{1}GF, 16^{2}GF, 18^{2}GF

	Starts	1st	2nd	3rd	Win & Pl
Hurdles	1	0	0	1	375
Chases	4	1	2	0	5055
Career Total	**28**	**4**	**5**	**2**	**16060**

115	6/01	Fknm	2m110y	E Ch	G-F	£2902
114	8/00	Font	2m2f110y	E(0-115)HHdl	G-F	£2576
112	5/00	Font	2m2f110y	F(0-105)HHdl	GD	£2369
114	11/99	Winc	2m	F(0-100)HHdl	GD	£2374

Total win prize-money £10222

Going: Sf: 0-0 GS: 0-0 Gd: 0-0 GF: - Fm: 1-5
Distance: **2m/2m3: 1-5** 2m4-2m7: 0-0 3m+: 0-0
Track: **LH: 1-4** RH: 0-0 **Tight: 1-4** Gall: 0-0
Aids: Bl: 0-0 Vi: 0-0 Tstrap: 0-0
Best Rating: 115 8/01 Font 2m2f gd-fm Ch

Northern Accord

96 93

8-y-o b g Akarad (FR)-Sioux City (Simply Great (FR))

M Dods Mrs R Olivier

Placings:5/F52/54P/224330-415 (0449)

2001/02: 16^{4}S, 16^{1}GF, 20^{5}F

	Starts	1st	2nd	3rd	Win & Pl
Hurdles	3	1	0	0	2115
Career Total	**16**	**1**	**3**	**2**	**5445**

90	5/01	Hexm	2m	G(0-95)HHdl	G-F	£2114

Total win prize-money £2115

Going: Sf: 0-1 GS: 0-0 Gd: 0-0 GF: - Fm: 1-2

Distance: **2m/2m3: 1-2** 2m4-2m7: 0-1 3m+: 0-0
Track: **LH: 1-3** RH: 0-0 Tight: 0-0 Gall: 0-0
Aids: Bl: 0-1 Vi: 0-0 Tstrap: 0-0
Best Rating: 106 3/99 Donc 2m110y gd-sft Hdl

Northern Castle (IRE)

95 **85**

4-y-o b g Distinctly North (USA)-Dunbally (Dunphy)
P C Haslam Kary-On Racing Partnership

Placings:0000 **(4772)**
2001/02: 16^{0}G, 16^{0}G, 16^{0}S, 21^{0}G

	Starts	1st	2nd	3rd	Win & Pl
Hurdles	4	0	0	0	
Career Total	**4**	**0**	**0**	**0**	

Going: Sf: 0-1 GS: 0-0 Gd: 0-3 GF: - Fm: 0-0
Distance: 2m/2m3: 0-3 2m4-2m7: 0-1 3m+: 0-0
Track: LH: 0-3 RH: 0-1 Tight: 0-2 Gall: 0-0
Aids: Bl: 0-0 Vi: 0-0 Tstrap: 0-0
Best Rating: 85 1/02 Catt 2m soft Hdl

Northern Echo

97 **79**

5-y-o b g Pursuit Of Love-Stop Press (USA) (Sharpen Up)
M Dods M J K Dods

Placings:643FP2P0R **(3363)**
2001/02: 17^{6}GF, 17^{4}G, 17^{3}GF, 16^{F}G, 17^{P}G, 17^{2}G, 20^{P}S, 16^{0}G, 16^{R}GS

	Starts	1st	2nd	3rd	Win & Pl
Hurdles	9	0	1	1	754
Career Total	**9**	**0**	**1**	**1**	**754**

Going: Sf: 0-1 GS: 0-1 Gd: 0-5 GF: - Fm: 0-2
Distance: 2m/2m3: 0-8 2m4-2m7: 0-1 3m+: 0-0
Track: LH: 0-7 RH: 0-2 Tight: 0-7 Gall: 0-1
Aids: Bl: 0-1 Vi: 0-5 Tstrap: 0-6
Best Rating: 79 9/01 Hrfd 2m1f gd-fm Hdl

A poor performer on the level and over hurdles.

Northern Fleet

101(98h) (84h)**91**

9-y-o b g Slip Anchor-Kamkova (USA) (Northern Dancer)
Mark Campion Mrs J Howell

Placings:24244/212/0/0502460/35-0446PPP **(3333)**
2001/02: 20^{0}GS, 20^{4}GS, 20^{4}GF, 25^{6}G, 19^{P}G, 24^{P}G, 24^{P}G

	Starts	1st	2nd	3rd	Win & Pl
Hurdles	1	0	0	0	0
Chases	6	0	0	0	499
Career Total	**25**	**1**	**5**	**1**	**8004**

103 8/97 Hntg 2m4f110y E Hdl GD £2232
Total win prize-money £2233

Going: Sf: 0-0 GS: 0-2 Gd: 0-4 GF: - Fm: 0-1
Distance: 2m/2m3: 0-0 2m4-2m7: 0-4 3m+: 0-3
Track: LH: 0-1 RH: 0-5 Tight: 0-2 Gall: 0-1
Aids: Bl: 0-1 Vi: 0-0 Tstrap: 0-0
Best Rating: 110 10/97 Hntg 2m4f110y good Hdl

Formerly a useful stayer on the Flat, but now a plating class performer over hurdles following several poor efforts over fences.

Northern Motto

94 **76**

9-y-o b g Mtoto-Soulful (FR) (Zino)
J S Goldie Alf Chadwick

Placings:U/025U3/2543/30/55343-00P4F0 **(3915)**
2001/02: 22^{0}GS, 20^{0}GS, 20^{P}G, 24^{4}S, 24^{F}S, 20^{0}GS

	Starts	1st	2nd	3rd	Win & Pl
Hurdles	6	0	0	0	0
Career Total	**23**	**0**	**2**	**5**	**4282**

Going: Sf: 0-2 GS: 0-3 Gd: 0-1 GF: - Fm: 0-0
Distance: 2m/2m3: 0-0 2m4-2m7: 0-4 3m+: 0-2
Track: LH: 0-2 RH: 0-4 Tight: 0-6 Gall: 0-0
Aids: Bl: 0-0 Vi: 0-0 Tstrap: 0-0
Best Rating: 104 10/99 Weth 3m1f gd-fm Hdl

A winning middle-distance handicapper on the Flat, he has not shown much over hurdles of late.

Northern Native (IRE)

96f **103f**

6-y-o br m Be My Native (USA)-Charming Mo (IRE) (Callernish)
Mrs M Reveley W J Smith M D Dudley C Raines M J Hutton

Placings:*2-12* **(3770)**
2001/02: 17^{1}G, 16^{2}GS

	Starts	1st	2nd	3rd	Win & Pl
NH Flat	2	1	1	0	2010
Career Total	**3**	**1**	**2**	**0**	**2442**

92 11/01 Sedg 2m1f H NHF GD £1568
Total win prize-money £1568

Going: Sf: 0-0 GS: 0-1 Gd: 1-1 GF: - Fm: 0-0
Distance: **2m/2m3: 1-2** 2m4-2m7: 0-0 3m+: 0-0
Track: **LH: 1-2** RH: 0-0 **Tight: 1-2** Gall: 0-0
Aids: Bl: 0-0 Vi: 0-0 Tstrap: 0-0
Best Rating: 113 11/00 Hrfd 2m1f soft NHF

Related to Supreme Novices' Hurdle winner Tourist Attraction, she was runner-up to a decent sort on her debut at Hereford on soft ground. Won on her next start nearly a year later in a Sedgefield bumper. She is not very big but is certainly tough.

Northern Prospect (IRE)

97f **99f**

5-y-o ch g Be My Native (USA)-Lucky House (Pollerton)
A Scott A & J Scott Ltd

Placings:*023* **(4309)**
2001/02: 17^{0}S, 16^{2}GS, 16^{3}S

	Starts	1st	2nd	3rd	Win & Pl
NH Flat	3	0	1	1	731
Career Total	**3**	**0**	**1**	**1**	**731**

Going: Sf: 0-2 GS: 0-1 Gd: 0-0 GF: - Fm: 0-0
Distance: 2m/2m3: 0-3 2m4-2m7: 0-0 3m+: 0-0
Track: LH: 0-2 RH: 0-1 Tight: 0-1 Gall: 0-0
Aids: Bl: 0-0 Vi: 0-0 Tstrap: 0-0
Best Rating: 99 3/02 Ayr 2m soft NHF

Modest form when runner-up in a bumper at Catterick in March on only his second-ever start.

Northern Raider (IRE)

76 **57**

4-y-o b g College Chapel-Pepper And Salt (IRE) (Double Schwartz)
N Wilson (Andrew Turnell 24/9) Chris Johnson

Placings:0100P **(4330)**
2001/02: 16^{0}G, 16^{1}S, 16^{0}S, 17^{0}S, 17^{P}S

	Starts	1st	2nd	3rd	Win & Pl
Hurdles	5	1	0	0	1897
Career Total	**5**	**1**	**0**	**0**	**1897**

57 12/01 Uttx 2m G Hdl SFT £1897
Total win prize-money £1897

Going: Sf: 1-4 GS: 0-0 Gd: 0-1 GF: - Fm: 0-0
Distance: **2m/2m3: 1-5** 2m4-2m7: 0-0 3m+: 0-0
Track: **LH: 1-5** RH: 0-0 Tight: 0-2 Gall: 0-1
Aids: Bl: 0-1 Vi: 0-0 Tstrap: 0-0
Best Rating: 57 12/01 Uttx 2m soft Hdl

Northern Singer

12-y-o ch g Norwick (USA)-Be Lyrical (Song)
R J Hodges Joe Panes

Placings:*000*/060/0002416/**331UP1FP1/2/PU550/P6/66-00** **(0737)**
2001/02: 10^{0}G, 10^{0}GS

	Starts	1st	2nd	3rd	Win & Pl
Chases	2	0	0	0	
Career Total	**34**	**4**	**2**	**2**	**14139**

95 4/97 Tntn 2m110y E Ch FRM £3317
100 2/97 Tntn 2m110y E(0-100)HCh G-S £2913
93 1/97 Ludl 2m E(0-105)HCh G-F £2948
83 3/96 Uttx 2m E(0-100)HHdl GD £2379
Total win prize-money £11560

Going: Sf: 0-0 GS: 0-1 Gd: 0-1 GF: - Fm: 0-0
Distance: 2m/2m3: 0-2 2m4-2m7: 0-0 3m+: 0-0
Track: LH: 0-1 RH: 0-1 Tight: 0-2 Gall: 0-0
Aids: Bl: 0-0 Vi: 0-0 Tstrap: 0-1
Best Rating: 100 2/97 Tntn 2m110y gd-sft Ch

Northern Sound (IRE)

110 **147**

9-y-o b m Montelimar (USA)-Castle Felda (Le Moss)
Paul A Roche James Treacy

Placings:R/R/15032452115/P051610-PPPP45U2403P **(4955a)**
2001/02: 29^{P}G, 25^{P}G, 24^{P}YS, 28^{P}Y, 25^{4}GY, 24^{5}YS, 24^{U}SH, 24^{2}S, 25^{4}S, 24^{0}GS, 29^{3}GY, 25^{P}G

	Starts	1st	2nd	3rd	Win & Pl
Chases	12	0	1	1	14209
Career Total	**32**	**5**	**3**	**2**	**58002**

137 2/01 Fair 3m1f HCh HVY £13104
139 1/01 Fair 3m1f (0-116)HCh HVY £5564
118 4/00 Cork 3m HCh YLD £7800
120 3/00 Gowr 3m HCh YLD £10400
85 5/99 Dund 3m Ch GD £2148
Total win prize-money £39018

Going: Sf: 0-2 GS: 0-1 Gd: 0-3 GF: - Fm: 0-0
Distance: 2m/2m3: 0-0 2m4-2m7: 0-0 3m+: 0-12
Track: LH: 0-3 RH: 0-7 Tight: 0-0 Gall: 0-1
Aids: Bl: 0-1 Vi: 0-0 Tstrap: 0-0
Best Rating: 147 4/02 Fair 3m5f gd-yld Ch

A fair soft-ground staying handicap chaser, she seems

to go well at Fairyhouse. Finished eighth in the Kim Muir at the 2002 Festival.

Northern Starlight

95 134

11-y-o b g Northern State (USA)-Ganadora (Good Times (ITY))

M C Pipe Arthur Souch

Placings:623023/411214/11111/F121112122/31U022/4534011/UP-0U (4664)

2001/02: 23^{0}GS, 21^{U}G

	Starts	1st	2nd	3rd	Win & Pl
Chases	2	0	0	0	
Career Total	**44**	**16**	**9**	**4**	**170861**

153	4/00	Aint	2m6f	B(0-150)HCh	GD	£26000
154	4/00	Asct	2m3f110y	B HCh	GD	£10072
150	12/98	Chel	2m5f	A HCh	GD	£47144
150	12/97	Chel	2m5f	B Ch	GD	£7335
145	11/97	Chep	2m3f110y	A Ch	G-S	£12800
140	10/97	Worc	2m4f110y	D Ch	GD	£3782
119	10/97	Ludl	2m4f	E Ch	G-F	£2827
132	5/97	Uttx	2m	C(0-135)HHdl	GD	£3436
136	4/97	Extr	2m3f110y	C(0-130)HHdl	FRM	£4448
121	3/97	NAbb	2m1f	D(0-125)Hdl	G-F	£2849
135	3/97	Winc	2m	D(0-120)HHdl	G-F	£2805
119	3/97	Winc	2m	C(0-130)HHdl	GD	£3415
117	2/97	Winc	2m	D(0-125)Hdl	G-F	£2826
104	11/95	Tntn	2m1f	B HHdl	GD	£4719
96	10/95	Tntn	2m1f	G(0-90)HHdl	G-F	£2176
83	9/95	Tntn	2m1f	G Hdl	G-F	£1886

Total win prize-money £138522

Going: Sf: 0-0 GS: 0-1 Gd: 0-1 GF: - Fm: 0-0
Distance: 2m/2m3: 0-0 2m4-2m7: 0-1 3m+: 0-1
Track: LH: 0-1 RH: 0-1 Tight: 0-1 Gall: 0-0
Aids: Bl: 0-0 Vi: 0-0 Tstrap: 0-0
Best Rating: 156 4/99 Sand 2m4f110y good Ch

Only small but a tough, genuine performer who is best at two miles-four on a quick surface.

Northern Tennessee (IRE)

98 110

7-y-o ch g Muharib (USA)-Corun Girl (Apollo Eight)

B G Powell Tony Head

Placings:6/3-10251 (4906)

2001/02: 16^{1}G, 20^{0}S, 20^{2}GS, 16^{5}S, 19^{1}G

	Starts	1st	2nd	3rd	Win & Pl
NH Flat	1	1	0	0	1799
Hurdles	4	1	1	0	4728
Career Total	**7**	**2**	**1**	**1**	**6983**

110	4/02	MRas	2m3f110y	D Hdl	GD	£4046
103	5/01	Hntg	2m110y	H NHF	GD	£1799

Total win prize-money £5845

Going: Sf: 0-2 GS: 0-1 Gd: 2-2 GF: - Fm: 0-0
Distance: 2m/2m3: 1-2 2m4-2m7: 1-3 3m+: 0-0
Track: LH: 0-1 **RH: 2-3** Tight: 1-2 Gall: 1-1
Aids: Bl: 0-0 Vi: 0-0 Tstrap: 0-0
Best Rating: 110 4/02 MRas 2m3f110y good Hdl

Showed plenty of ability in bumpers, winning at Huntingdon. Won novice hurdle over just short of two and a half miles at Market Rasen April 2002. Appears to prefer a sound surface.

Northern Trio (FR)

69 21

5-y-o b g Aragon-Northern Notion (USA) (Northern Baby (CAN))

Mrs Barbara Waring E S Chivers

Placings:P0P (4326)

2001/02: 19^{P}S, 19^{0}GS, 17^{P}S

	Starts	1st	2nd	3rd	Win & Pl
Hurdles	3	0	0	0	
Career Total	**3**	**0**	**0**	**0**	

Going: Sf: 0-2 GS: 0-1 Gd: 0-0 GF: - Fm: 0-0
Distance: 2m/2m3: 0-2 2m4-2m7: 0-1 3m+: 0-0
Track: LH: 0-1 RH: 0-2 Tight: 0-1 Gall: 0-0
Aids: Bl: 0-0 Vi: 0-1 Tstrap: 0-0
Best Rating: 21 3/02 Strf 2m3f gd-sft Hdl

Northern Union (CAN)

95(108c) 120

11-y-o b g Alwasmi (USA)-Loving Cup (USA) (Big Spruce (USA))

A Parker Mr & Mrs Raymond Anderson Green

Placings:0/23/22525/2511213/24-1 (0449)

2001/02: 20^{1}F

	Starts	1st	2nd	3rd	Win & Pl
Hurdles	1	1	0	0	2604
Career Total	**18**	**4**	**7**	**2**	**18411**

105	5/01	Weth	2m4f110y	F Hdl	FRM	£2604
117	2/00	Muss	2m4f	E(0-115)HHdl	GD	£3900
117	11/99	Kels	2m6f110y	D(0-125)HHdl	GD	£2867
113	11/99	Kels	2m6f110y	F(0-100)HHdl	GD	£2234

Total win prize-money £11606

Going: Sf: 0-0 GS: 0-0 Gd: 0-0 GF: - Fm: 1-1
Distance: 2m/2m3: 0-0 **2m4-2m7: 1-1** 3m+: 0-0
Track: **LH: 1-1** RH: 0-0 Tight: 0-0 Gall: 0-0
Aids: Bl: 0-0 Vi: 0-0 Tstrap: 0-0
Best Rating: 120 4/01 Ayr 2m6f good Hdl

Northern Yarn (IRE)

69 72

9-y-o b g Le Bavard (FR)-Northern Push (Push On)

A P Jones (Ms J Dawes 12/5) Mrs L Bedford

Placings:0P/P/6034PPP6 (4510)

2001/02: 20^{6}GF, 24^{0}GF, 24^{3}S, 26^{4}G, 26^{P}S, 24^{P}GS, 24^{P}S, 26^{6}G

	Starts	1st	2nd	3rd	Win & Pl
Chases	8	0	0	1	893
Career Total	**11**	**0**	**0**	**1**	**893**

Going: Sf: 0-3 GS: 0-1 Gd: 0-2 GF: - Fm: 0-2
Distance: 2m/2m3: 0-0 2m4-2m7: 0-1 3m+: 0-7
Track: LH: 0-4 RH: 0-1 Tight: 0-2 Gall: 0-1
Aids: Bl: 0-2 Vi: 0-1 Tstrap: 0-5
Best Rating: 72 12/01 Plum 3m2f good Ch

A winner in point-to-points but has shown only ordinary form over regulation fences. Does not want the ground too soft.

Northwing

(86h) (47h)

6-y-o b g Minshaanshu Amad (USA)-Kicking Bird (Bold Owl)

G B Balding Mrs D Claessen-Brierton

Placings:000/0R-000P (1035)

2001/02: 17^{0}GF, 21^{0}GF, 20^{0}G, 21^{P}G

	Starts	1st	2nd	3rd	Win & Pl
Hurdles	3	0	0	0	0
Chases	3	0	0	0	0
Career Total	**9**	**0**	**0**	**0**	

Going: Sf: 0-0 GS: 0-0 Gd: 0-2 GF: - Fm: 0-2
Distance: 2m/2m3: 0-1 2m4-2m7: 0-3 3m+: 0-0
Track: LH: 0-3 RH: 0-1 Tight: 0-2 Gall: 0-1
Aids: Bl: 0-0 Vi: 0-3 Tstrap: 0-0
Best Rating: 62 3/00 Chep 2m110y good Hdl

Norwood Park (NZ)

75f 47f

5-y-o b g Centaine (AUS)-Janine (NZ) (Wharf (USA))

Mrs M Reveley David J Jackson

Placings:0 (2772)

2001/02: 16^{0}G

	Starts	1st	2nd	3rd	Win & Pl
NH Flat	1	0	0	0	
Career Total	**1**	**0**	**0**	**0**	

Going: Sf: 0-0 GS: 0-0 Gd: 0-1 GF: - Fm: 0-0
Distance: 2m/2m3: 0-1 2m4-2m7: 0-0 3m+: 0-0
Track: LH: 0-1 RH: 0-0 Tight: 0-1 Gall: 0-0
Aids: Bl: 0-0 Vi: 0-0 Tstrap: 0-0
Best Rating: 47 12/01 Catt 2m good NHF

Nosam

106 132

12-y-o b g Idiots Delight-Socher (Anax)

N B Mason N B Mason

Placings:0/6/1120/406U5113313423P3/23343114112200/06254622F1-3120352105 (4876)

2001/02: 24^{3}GF, 19^{1}GF, 21^{2}GS, 20^{0}G, 20^{3}GS, 19^{5}S, 20^{2}GS, 19^{1}S, 19^{0}GF, 20^{5}G

	Starts	1st	2nd	3rd	Win & Pl
Chases	10	2	2	2	18031
Career Total	**56**	**12**	**10**	**10**	**88922**

129	3/02	Donc	2m3f110y	E(0-110)HCh	SFT	£3514
132	9/01	List	2m3f	(0-123)HCh	G-F	£7862
125	4/01	Prth	2m4f110y	D(0-125)HCh	HVY	£7962
135	1/00	Donc	2m3f110y	C(0-130)HCh	GD	£7020
134	1/00	Leic	2m4f110y	D(0-120)HCh	GD	£5785
128	11/99	Catt	2m3f	E(0-115)HCh	G-F	£5572
124	11/99	Ayr	2m4f	D(0-120)HCh	GD	£3821
117	1/99	Donc	2m3f110y	C(0-130)HCh	G-S	£5930
107	11/98	Sedg	2m5f	E Ch	G-S	£2940
103	10/98	Sedg	2m5f	E Ch	G-S	£3065
103	8/97	Ctml	2m6f	E Hdl	G-F	£2250
103	5/97	Ctml	2m6f	E Hdl	G-F	£2447

Total win prize-money £58174

Going: Sf: 1-2 GS: 0-3 Gd: 0-2 GF: - Fm: 1-3
Distance: 2m/2m3: 1-1 2m4-2m7: 1-8 3m+: 0-1
Track: **LH: 1-6** RH: 0-3 Tight: 0-2 **Gall: 1-2**
Aids: Bl: 0-0 Vi: 0-0 **Tstrap: 2-10**
Best Rating: 135 9/00 Uttx 2m5f gd-sft Ch

Successful over hurdles and fences. He is as tough as old boots and is effective on any ground, he is best around two and a half miles and races with his tongue tied.

Noshinannikin

110(111h) (129h)139

8-y-o ch g Anshan-Preziosa (Homing)

M W Easterby Stephen J Curtis

Placings:202/41045/14F1UR2/PP3P-P4412241P0C (4891)

2001/02: 17^{P}GS, 16^{4}G, 20^{4}GS, 16^{1}GS, 16^{2}S, 16^{2}S, 20^{4}S, 16^{1}GS, 19^{P}GS, 16^{0}GS, 16^{C}G

	Starts	1st	2nd	3rd	Win & Pl
Hurdles	6	1	2	0	7818
Chases	5	1	0	0	4545
Career Total	**30**	**5**	**5**	**1**	**26328**

139	2/02	Hntg	2m110y	D(0-120)HCh	G-S	£3864
128	12/01	Newc	2m	E(0-115)HHdl	G-S	£3396
139	1/00	Weth	2m	E Ch	SFT	£3003
108	11/99	Hexm	2m110y	E Ch	GD	£3152
107	11/98	Newc	2m4f	E Hdl	G-S	£2410

Total win prize-money £15826

Going: Sf: 0-3 GS: 2-6 Gd: 0-2 GF: - Fm: 0-0
Distance: 2m/2m3: 2-8 2m4-2m7: 0-3 3m+: 0-0
Track: LH: 1-9 RH: 1-2 Tight: 0-2 Gall: 2-6
Aids: Bl: 0-0 Vi: 0-0 Tstrap: 1-7
Best Rating: 143 4/00 Aint 2m4f good Ch

A winner over hurdles and fences, he acts on good and soft ground and is effective at around two miles to two miles four furlongs.

Not Fade Away

87 66

4-y-o b g Ezzoud (IRE)-Green Flower (USA) (Fappiano (USA))
Miss E C Lavelle (R M Beckett 16/10) Mr & Mrs J R Lavelle

Placings:600 (4034)
2001/02: 18^{6}S, 22^{0}S, 20^{0}S

	Starts	1st	2nd	3rd	Win & Pl
Hurdles	3	0	0	0	0
Career Total	**3**	**0**	**0**	**0**	**0**

Going: Sf: 0-3 GS: 0-0 Gd: 0-0 GF: - Fm: 0-0
Distance: 2m/2m3: 0-1 2m4-2m7: 0-2 3m+: 0-0
Track: LH: 0-2 RH: 0-0 Tight: 0-3 Gall: 0-0
Aids: Bl: 0-0 Vi: 0-1 Tstrap: 0-1
Best Rating: 66 1/02 Font 2m2f110y soft Hdl

Not For Parrot (IRE)

96(99c) (82c)74

10-y-o ch g Be My Native (USA)-Sugar Quay (Quayside)
T R George T R George

Placings:0/234/21642/65506/3-P56004P (1306)
2001/02: 16^{P}F, 17^{5}G, 18^{6}GF, 16^{0}S, 19^{0}G, 17^{4}G, 17^{P}GF

	Starts	1st	2nd	3rd	Win & Pl
Hurdles	3	0	0	0	0
Chases	4	0	0	0	0
Career Total	**22**	**1**	**3**	**2**	**5823**

98	11/98	Winc	2m	E Hdl	G-S	£2430

Total win prize-money £2430

Going: Sf: 0-1 GS: 0-0 Gd: 0-3 GF: - Fm: 0-3
Distance: 2m/2m3: 0-7 2m4-2m7: 0-0 3m+: 0-0
Track: LH: 0-5 RH: 0-1 Tight: 0-6 Gall: 0-0
Aids: Bl: 0-2 Vi: 0-0 Tstrap: 0-0
Best Rating: 104 4/99 Worc 2m gd-sft Hdl

Not Forgotten (USA)

94 67

8-y-o b g St Jovite (USA)-Past Remembered (USA) (Solford (USA))
M R Ewer-Hoad Jay Byrds Partnership

Placings:3333/302012/05P5-0P53 (4507)
2001/02: 22^{0}GF, 21^{P}GS, 22^{5}HY, 21^{3}G

	Starts	1st	2nd	3rd	Win & Pl
Hurdles	4	0	0	1	301
Career Total	**18**	**1**	**2**	**6**	**5259**

77	11/98	Hntg	3m2f	G(0-95)HHdl	GD	£2430

Total win prize-money £2430

Going: Sf: 0-1 GS: 0-1 Gd: 0-1 GF: - Fm: 0-1
Distance: 2m/2m3: 0-0 2m4-2m7: 0-4 3m+: 0-0
Track: LH: 0-3 RH: 0-1 Tight: 0-4 Gall: 0-0
Aids: Bl: 0-2 Vi: 0-0 Tstrap: 0-0
Best Rating: 77 12/98 Towc 2m5f soft Hdl

Not Really (IRE)

76 35

11-y-o ch g Buckskin (FR)-Corrib Colleen (Little Buskins)
Lady Eliza Mays-Smith Lady Eliza Mays-Smith

Placings:013/5/5P-0 (2537)
2001/02: 21^{0}G

	Starts	1st	2nd	3rd	Win & Pl
Chases	1	0	0	0	
Career Total	**7**	**1**	**0**	**1**	**3078**

100	3/98	Extr	2m3f110y	E Hdl	SFT	£2742

Total win prize-money £2742

Going: Sf: 0-0 GS: 0-0 Gd: 0-1 GF: - Fm: 0-0
Distance: 2m/2m3: 0-0 2m4-2m7: 0-1 3m+: 0-0
Track: LH: 0-0 RH: 0-1 Tight: 0-0 Gall: 0-0
Aids: Bl: 0-0 Vi: 0-0 Tstrap: 0-0
Best Rating: 100 3/98 Extr 2m3f110y soft Hdl

Not The Ritz (IRE)

93 95

6-y-o b g Petoski-Glengarra Princess (Cardinal Flower)
Ferdy Murphy (W P Mullins 2/8) Kbro Racing Group

Placings:40U42 (4548)
2001/02: 16^{4}GY, 18^{0}GY, 20^{U}S, 20^{4}S, 21^{2}GF

	Starts	1st	2nd	3rd	Win & Pl
NH Flat	2	0	0	0	226
Hurdles	3	0	1	0	810
Career Total	**5**	**0**	**1**	**0**	**1036**

Going: Sf: 0-2 GS: 0-0 Gd: 0-0 GF: - Fm: 0-1
Distance: 2m/2m3: 0-2 2m4-2m7: 0-3 3m+: 0-0
Track: LH: 0-1 RH: 0-2 Tight: 0-0 Gall: 0-2
Aids: Bl: 0-0 Vi: 0-0 Tstrap: 0-0
Best Rating: 101 6/01 Naas 2m gd-yld NHF

Not Too Late

7-y-o b g Sula Bula-Princess Eleigh (New Member)
B G Powell Tim Pickup

Placings:0 (1245)
2001/02: 16^{0}GF

	Starts	1st	2nd	3rd	Win & Pl
NH Flat	1	0	0	0	
Career Total	**1**	**0**	**0**	**0**	

Going: Sf: 0-0 GS: 0-0 Gd: 0-0 GF: - Fm: 0-1
Distance: 2m/2m3: 0-1 2m4-2m7: 0-0 3m+: 0-0
Track: LH: 0-1 RH: 0-0 Tight: 0-0 Gall: 0-0
Aids: Bl: 0-0 Vi: 0-0 Tstrap: 0-0
Best Rating:

Not Too Shabby

84f 73f

5-y-o b g Contract Law (USA)-Lady Be Brave (Laurence O)
W Storey The Wayward Lads

Placings:500 (2729)
2001/02: 17^{5}GS, 16^{0}G, 17^{0}GF

	Starts	1st	2nd	3rd	Win & Pl
NH Flat	3	0	0	0	0
Career Total	**3**	**0**	**0**	**0**	**0**

Going: Sf: 0-0 GS: 0-1 Gd: 0-1 GF: - Fm: 0-1
Distance: 2m/2m3: 0-3 2m4-2m7: 0-0 3m+: 0-0
Track: LH: 0-2 RH: 0-0 Tight: 0-1 Gall: 0-0
Aids: Bl: 0-0 Vi: 0-0 Tstrap: 0-0
Best Rating: 73 10/01 Sedg 2m1f gd-sft NHF

Notagainthen

6-y-o b m Then Again-Fairy Ballerina (Fairy King (USA))
S G Knight Malcolm Enticott

Placings:54/65006-0 (0499)
2001/02: 17^{0}G

	Starts	1st	2nd	3rd	Win & Pl
Hurdles	1	0	0	0	
Career Total	**8**	**0**	**0**	**0**	**232**

Going: Sf: 0-0 GS: 0-0 Gd: 0-1 GF: - Fm: 0-0
Distance: 2m/2m3: 0-1 2m4-2m7: 0-0 3m+: 0-0
Track: LH: 0-0 RH: 0-1 Tight: 0-0 Gall: 0-0
Aids: Bl: 0-0 Vi: 0-0 Tstrap: 0-0
Best Rating: 59 11/99 Newb 2m110y gd-fm Hdl

Nothingtotellme (IRE)

11-y-o gr g Roselier (FR)-Tower Road (Polaroid)
I R Ferguson R A Bartlett

Placings:4/345 (4833)
2001/02: 24^{3}S, 24^{4}GY, 27^{5}G

	Starts	1st	2nd	3rd	Win & Pl
Chases	3	0	0	0	607
Career Total	**4**	**0**	**0**	**1**	**607**

Going: Sf: 0-1 GS: 0-0 Gd: 0-1 GF: - Fm: 0-0
Distance: 2m/2m3: 0-0 2m4-2m7: 0-0 3m+: 0-3
Track: LH: 0-1 RH: 0-0 Tight: 0-0 Gall: 0-0
Aids: Bl: 0-0 Vi: 0-1 Tstrap: 0-0
Best Rating: 98 3/02 DRoy 3m soft Ch

Notional (IRE)

95 71

6-y-o b m Lucky Guest-Sportin' Notion (USA) (Sportin' Life (USA))
J L Spearing (A Sadik 15/9) A Sadik

Placings:060/06000500P (1406)
2001/02: 17^{0}GF, 16^{6}G, 16^{0}GF, 17^{0}G, 20^{0}G, 16^{5}G, 16^{0}GF, 17^{0}GF, 16^{P}GF

	Starts	1st	2nd	3rd	Win & Pl
Hurdles	9	0	0	0	0
Career Total	**12**	**0**	**0**	**0**	**0**

Going: Sf: 0-0 GS: 0-0 Gd: 0-4 GF: - Fm: 0-5
Distance: 2m/2m3: 0-8 2m4-2m7: 0-1 3m+: 0-0
Track: LH: 0-9 RH: 0-0 Tight: 0-6 Gall: 0-0
Aids: Bl: 0-1 Vi: 0-0 Tstrap: 0-5
Best Rating: **71** 6/01 Fknm 2m gd-fm Hdl

Notty

90 **65**

7-y-o ch m Nicholas Bill-Silver Empress (Octavo (USA))
P Hayward P Hayward

Placings:6/0P/P-PPP (2716)
2001/02: 20^{P}S, 21^{P}S, 19^{P}G

	Starts	1st	2nd	3rd	Win & Pl
Hurdles	3	0	0	0	
Career Total	**7**	**0**	**0**	**0**	**0**

Going: Sf: 0-2 GS: 0-0 Gd: 0-1 GF: - Fm: 0-0
Distance: 2m/2m3: 0-0 2m4-2m7: 0-3 3m+: 0-0
Track: LH: 0-0 RH: 0-2 Tight: 0-1 Gall: 0-0
Aids: Bl: 0-0 Vi: 0-0 Tstrap: 0-1
Best Rating: **46** 10/99 Font 2m2f110y good Hdl

Nouf

113 **114**

6-y-o b m Efisio-Miss Witch (High Line)
K C Bailey (K A Ryan 21/9) Mrs N L Spence

Placings:02314 (4178)
2001/02: 16^{0}GS, 16^{2}GS, 16^{3}S, 16^{1}S, 16^{4}GS

	Starts	1st	2nd	3rd	Win & Pl
Hurdles	5	1	1	1	4322
Career Total	**5**	**1**	**1**	**1**	**4322**

110	2/02	Hntg	2m110y	E Hdl	SFT	£2583

Total win prize-money £2583

Going: Sf: 1-2 GS: 0-3 Gd: 0-0 GF: - Fm: 0-0
Distance: **2m/2m3: 1-5** 2m4-2m7: 0-0 3m+: 0-0
Track: LH: 0-1 **RH: 1-4** Tight: 0-1 **Gall: 1-2**
Aids: Bl: 0-0 Vi: 0-0 Tstrap: 0-0
Best Rating: **113** 3/02 Strf 2m110y gd-sft Hdl

A winner on the Flat, she made the frame in ordinary novice hurdles before winning at Huntingdon in February 2002. Suited by two miles and soft ground, used to handle good to firm on the Flat.

Nought To Ninety

31f

4-y-o b g Mazaad-Bonnyhill Lass (Royal Fountain)
C Grant Chris Grant

Placings:*0* (4860)
2001/02: 16^{0}G

	Starts	1st	2nd	3rd	Win & Pl
NH Flat	1	0	0	0	
Career Total	**1**	**0**	**0**	**0**	

Going: Sf: 0-0 GS: 0-0 Gd: 0-1 GF: - Fm: 0-0
Distance: 2m/2m3: 0-1 2m4-2m7: 0-0 3m+: 0-0
Track: LH: 0-0 RH: 0-0 Tight: 0-0 Gall: 0-0
Aids: Bl: 0-0 Vi: 0-0 Tstrap: 0-0
Best Rating: **31** 4/02 Hexm 2m110y good NHF

Noughtynova

91f **102f**

5-y-o b m Petoski-Nova Spirit (Electric)
M S Saunders M S Saunders

Placings:*25* (4506)
2001/02: 16^{2}S, 17^{5}G

	Starts	1st	2nd	3rd	Win & Pl
NH Flat	2	0	1	0	557
Career Total	**2**	**0**	**1**	**0**	**557**

Going: Sf: 0-1 GS: 0-0 Gd: 0-1 GF: - Fm: 0-0
Distance: 2m/2m3: 0-2 2m4-2m7: 0-0 3m+: 0-0
Track: LH: 0-1 RH: 0-1 Tight: 0-1 Gall: 0-0
Aids: Bl: 0-0 Vi: 0-0 Tstrap: 0-0
Best Rating: **102** 3/02 Winc 2m soft NHF

Nousayri (IRE)

105 **96**

7-y-o b g Slip Anchor-Noufiyla (Top Ville)
R Hollinshead Ed Weetman

Placings:*6/132/*232666-320 (3450)
2001/02: 24^{3}S, 23^{2}HY, 20^{0}GS

	Starts	1st	2nd	3rd	Win & Pl
Hurdles	3	0	1	1	1488
Career Total	**13**	**1**	**4**	**3**	**5970**

103	5/99	Prth	2m110y	H NHF	HVY	£1987

Total win prize-money £1987

Going: Sf: 0-2 GS: 0-1 Gd: 0-0 GF: - Fm: 0-0
Distance: 2m/2m3: 0-0 2m4-2m7: 0-1 3m+: 0-2
Track: LH: 0-3 RH: 0-0 Tight: 0-2 Gall: 0-0
Aids: Bl: 0-0 Vi: 0-0 Tstrap: 0-0
Best Rating: **122** 12/99 Hntg 2m110y good NHF

Nouveau Cheval

107 **119**

7-y-o b m Picea-Freeracer (Free State)
M C Pipe Sandicroft Stud Syndicate Ii

Placings:541015/1/3111U2 (4408)
2001/02: 21^{3}HY, 16^{1}S, 17^{1}S, 20^{1}S, 16^{U}GS, 17^{2}S

	Starts	1st	2nd	3rd	Win & Pl
Hurdles	6	3	1	1	7743
Career Total	**13**	**6**	**1**	**1**	**16043**

119	3/02	Donc	2m4f	F Hdl	SFT	£2415
110	2/02	Folk	2m1f110y	G Hdl	SFT	£2282
94	2/02	Ludl	2m	G Hdl	SFT	£2061
115	6/99	Worc	2m4f	D(0-120)HHdl	G-F	£3116
109	4/99	Plum	2m4f	E Hdl	G-S	£2460
104	2/99	Hntg	2m110y	E Hdl	G-S	£2724

Total win prize-money £15059

Going: Sf: 3-5 GS: 0-1 Gd: 0-0 GF: - Fm: 0-0
Distance: **2m/2m3: 2-4** 2m4-2m7: 1-2 3m+: 0-0
Track: LH: 1-3 **RH: 2-3** Tight: 1-3 Gall: 1-1
Aids: Bl: 0-0 Vi: 0-0 **Tstrap: 3-6**
Best Rating: **119** 3/02 Donc 2m4f soft Hdl

Has come back better than ever after a year and a half absence and has made hay in sellers and claimers over hurdles. Stays two miles four furlongs. Well suited by plenty of give under foot.

Nova Champ

104 **116**

14-y-o ch g Nearly A Hand-Laval (Cheval)
Mrs S J Smith Mrs C E Van Praagh

Placings:3660/**2U323F52341/154/1P331321P/211433 40355/31461B5-2212P0F** (2400)
2001/02: 24^{2}G, 26^{2}GS, 26^{1}GS, 24^{2}G, 26^{P}S, 31^{0}G, 25^{F}G

	Starts	1st	2nd	3rd	Win & Pl
Chases	7	1	3	0	8907
Career Total	**52**	**10**	**8**	**11**	**58414**

116	9/01	Plum	3m2f	D(0-125)HCh	G-S	£3854
116	9/00	Sedg	3m3f	E(0-115)HCh	GD	£3668
114	5/00	Uttx	3m2f	D(0-120)HCh	GD	£5056
120	7/99	Strf	3m	D(0-120)HCh	GD	£4987
120	7/99	MRas	3m1f	F(0-110)HCh	G-F	£3109
120	10/98	Uttx	3m2f	D(0-120)HCh	GD	£6905
113	7/98	Strf	3m	E(0-110)HCh	G-F	£2823
110	5/98	Worc	2m7f110y	F(0-105)HCh	GD	£3002
98	5/97	Hrfd	3m1f110y	F(0-105)HCh	GD	£2560
86	3/96	Catt	3m1f110y	E(0-100)HCh	GD	£3051

Total win prize-money £39020

Going: Sf: 0-1 GS: 1-2 Gd: 0-4 GF: - Fm: 0-0
Distance: 2m/2m3: 0-0 2m4-2m7: 0-0 **3m+: 1-7**
Track: LH: 0-5 RH: 0-1 Tight: 0-3 Gall: 0-0
Aids: Bl: 0-0 Vi: 0-0 Tstrap: 0-0
Best Rating: **120** 9/99 Kels 3m1f gd-fm Ch

A genuine veteran staying chaser, he was back to his best when gamely winning at Plumpton in September and ran well next time. Suited by three miles plus and good ground.

Nova Girl

99 **81**

7-y-o b m Vital Season-Sols Joker (Comedy Star (USA))
P R Rodford P R Rodford

Placings:P-4504 (1952)
2001/02: 18^{4}GF, 22^{5}GF, 20^{0}G, 22^{4}GF

	Starts	1st	2nd	3rd	Win & Pl
Hurdles	4	0	0	0	0
Career Total	**5**	**0**	**0**	**0**	**0**

Going: Sf: 0-0 GS: 0-0 Gd: 0-1 GF: 0-3
Distance: 2m/2m3: 0-1 2m4-2m7: 0-3 3m+: 0-0
Track: LH: 0-1 RH: 0-2 Tight: 0-1 Gall: 0-0
Aids: Bl: 0-0 Vi: 0-0 Tstrap: 0-0
Best Rating: **81** 9/01 Font 2m2f110y gd-fm Hdl

Novatara

10-y-o ch g Ra Nova-Asphaltara (Scallywag)
R W Gardiner A Ayers

Placings:32/0-P11 (4137)
2001/02: 24^{P}GF, 21^{1}G, 24^{1}G

	Starts	1st	2nd	3rd	Win & Pl
Chases	3	2	0	0	5096
Career Total	**6**	**2**	**1**	**1**	**6087**

98	3/02	Sand	3m110y	H Ch	GD	£2912
98	5/01	Folk	2m5f	H Ch	GD	£2184

Total win prize-money £5096

Going: Sf: 0-0 GS: 0-0 Gd: 2-2 GF: - Fm: 0-1
Distance: 2m/2m3: 0-0 2m4-2m7: 1-1 3m+: 1-2
Track: LH: 0-1 **RH: 2-2 Tight: 1-2** Gall: 0-0
Aids: **Bl: 2-2** Vi: 0-0 Tstrap: 0-0
Best Rating: **98** 3/02 Sand 3m110y good Ch

A useful hunter/pointer, he stays three miles and is suited by decent ground. Has a useful turn of foot.

Novi Sad (IRE)

93f 97f

4-y-o b g Norwich-Shuil Na Gale (Strong Gale)
L Wells Mrs Carrie Zetter-Wells

Placings: *02* **(4887)**
2001/02: 16^{0}GS, 18^{2}GF

	Starts	1st	2nd	3rd	Win & Pl
NH Flat	2	0	1	0	590
Career Total	**2**	**0**	**1**	**0**	**590**

Going: Sf: 0-0 GS: 0-1 Gd: 0-0 GF: - Fm: 0-1
Distance: 2m/2m3: 0-2 2m4-2m7: 0-0 3m+: 0-0
Track: LH: 0-1 RH: 0-1 Tight: 0-1 Gall: 0-0
Aids: Bl: 0-0 Vi: 0-0 Tstrap: 0-0
Best Rating: 97 4/02 Font 2m2f110y gd-fm NHF

A brother to El Viejo, ran well in a Fontwell bumper in April 2002.

Now Young Man (IRE)

101(66c) 96

13-y-o br g Callernish-Claddagh Pride (Bargello)
L Lungo Mrs Barbara Lungo

Placings: *60/0411P00/435/14/6052/42031/F40/0214P-23* **(1678)**
2001/02: 22^{2}G, 21^{3}G

	Starts	1st	2nd	3rd	Win & Pl
Hurdles	2	0	1	1	1082
Career Total	**33**	**5**	**4**	**3**	**20402**

94	10/00	Kels	2m6f110y	F(0-110)HHdl	G-S	£2716
113	9/98	Carl	3m2f	E(0-115)HCh	GD	£3485
108	4/97	Kels	3m1f	H Ch	G-F	£2736
101	11/94	Kels	2m6f110y	Hdl	GD	£2981
87	11/94	Kels	2m6f110y	Hdl	G-F	£2477

Total win prize-money £14396

Going: Sf: 0-0 GS: 0-0 Gd: 0-2 GF: - Fm: 0-0
Distance: 2m/2m3: 0-0 2m4-2m7: 0-2 3m+: 0-0
Track: LH: 0-2 RH: 0-0 Tight: 0-2 Gall: 0-0
Aids: Bl: 0-1 Vi: 0-0 Tstrap: 0-0
Best Rating: 113 9/98 Carl 3m2f good Ch

Nowell House

103 102

6-y-o ch g Polar Falcon (USA)-Langtry Lady (Pas De Seul)
M W Easterby Bernard Bargh & John Walsh

Placings: 214-406 **(3858)**
2001/02: 16^{4}GS, 16^{0}GS, 16^{6}S

	Starts	1st	2nd	3rd	Win & Pl
Hurdles	3	0	0	0	638
Career Total	**6**	**1**	**1**	**0**	**3414**

101	2/01	Sedg	2m1f	E Hdl	G-S	£2044

Total win prize-money £2044

Going: Sf: 0-1 GS: 0-2 Gd: 0-0 GF: - Fm: 0-0
Distance: 2m/2m3: 0-3 2m4-2m7: 0-0 3m+: 0-0
Track: LH: 0-2 RH: 0-1 Tight: 0-0 Gall: 0-2
Aids: Bl: 0-0 Vi: 0-0 Tstrap: 0-0
Best Rating: 102 12/01 Hntg 2m110y gd-sft Hdl

Noyan

12-y-o ch g Northern Baby (CAN)-Istiska (FR) (Irish River (FR))
D L Williams (Miss C F Elliott 17/2) Miss B W Palmer

Placings: 50121212F25/302000/**1F12141**/5065PP/**P21 1/21060-21P651** **(4865)**
2001/02: 25^{2}G, 24^{1}GF, 24^{P}GS, 25^{6}G, 22^{5}G, 23^{1}F

	Starts	1st	2nd	3rd	Win & Pl
Chases	6	2	1	0	6230
Career Total	**45**	**12**	**9**	**1**	**81925**

126	4/02	Extr	2m7f110y	H Ch	FRM	£2250
118	5/01	Fknm	3m110y	H Ch	G-F	£1579
126	5/00	Folk	3m2f	H Ch	GD	£1859
119	3/00	Sand	3m110y	E Ch	G-F	£4212
112	3/00	Extr	3m1f	H Ch	G-F	£2052
144	4/97	Punc	3m1f	Ch	GD	£36831
133	2/97	Donc	2m3f110y	D(0-115)HCh	GD	£3600
118	1/97	Catt	2m	E Ch	GD	£3336
111	12/96	Muss	2m4f	E Ch	G-F	£2953
114	12/94	Newc	2m4f	Hdl	GD	£3243
120	12/94	Muss	2m4f	(0-100)HHdl	G-F	£2253
96	11/94	Ayr	2m	Hdl	GD	£1924

Total win prize-money £66096

Going: Sf: 0-0 GS: 0-1 Gd: 0-3 GF: - Fm: 2-2
Distance: 2m/2m3: 0-0 2m4-2m7: 0-1 **3m+: 2-5**
Track: LH: 1-3 RH: 1-3 **Tight: 1-4** Gall: 0-0
Aids: Bl: 0-0 Vi: 0-0 Tstrap: 0-0
Best Rating: 144 4/97 Punc 3m1f good Ch

A cracking novice chaser in the 1997/1998 campaign, he had his fair share of training problems and did not return to winning form until 2000/2001 when dropped in class to hunter chases and points. Needs a sound surface and three miles plus. Won a point and hunter chases on a sound surface in 2002. Often front runs.

Nuclear Beach

69 1

7-y-o b g Henbit (USA)-Rose Orchard (Rouser)
M J Ryan The Beach Boys

Placings: P-P0 **(0192)**
2001/02: 24^{P}G, 24^{0}GF

	Starts	1st	2nd	3rd	Win & Pl
Chases	2	0	0	0	
Career Total	**3**	**0**	**0**	**0**	

Going: Sf: 0-0 GS: 0-0 Gd: 0-1 GF: - Fm: 0-1
Distance: 2m/2m3: 0-0 2m4-2m7: 0-0 3m+: 0-2
Track: LH: 0-1 RH: 0-1 Tight: 0-1 Gall: 0-1
Aids: Bl: 0-0 Vi: 0-0 Tstrap: 0-0
Best Rating: 1 5/01 Fknm 3m110y gd-fm Ch

Nun So Good

6-y-o ch m Beau Sher-She's No Nun (The Parson)
C P Morlock Mrs Z S Clark

Placings: *P* **(0911)**
2001/02: 16^{P}G

	Starts	1st	2nd	3rd	Win & Pl
NH Flat	1	0	0	0	
Career Total	**1**	**0**	**0**	**0**	

Going: Sf: 0-0 GS: 0-0 Gd: 0-1 GF: - Fm: 0-0
Distance: 2m/2m3: 0-1 2m4-2m7: 0-0 3m+: 0-0
Track: LH: 0-1 RH: 0-0 Tight: 0-0 Gall: 0-0
Aids: Bl: 0-0 Vi: 0-0 Tstrap: 0-0
Best Rating:

Nunnety (IRE)

44

9-y-o br m Supreme Leader-Henry Woman (IRE) (Mandalus)
C P Morlock The Sporting Connection

Placings: *0/4PP0/04543200-P* **(0682)**
2001/02: 22^{P}G

	Starts	1st	2nd	3rd	Win & Pl
Hurdles	1	0	0	0	
Career Total	**14**	**0**	**1**	**1**	**990**

Going: Sf: 0-0 GS: 0-0 Gd: 0-1 GF: - Fm: 0-0
Distance: 2m/2m3: 0-0 2m4-2m7: 0-1 3m+: 0-0
Track: LH: 0-1 RH: 0-0 Tight: 0-1 Gall: 0-0
Aids: Bl: 0-0 Vi: 0-0 Tstrap: 0-0
Best Rating: 74 3/01 Plum 3m1f110y heavy Hdl

Nuvellino

7-y-o b g Robellino (USA)-Furry Dance (USA) (Nureyev (USA))
P J Hobbs The Cockpit Crew

Placings: 240/0/5-F **(0085)**
2001/02: 17^{F}G

	Starts	1st	2nd	3rd	Win & Pl
Hurdles	1	0	0	0	
Career Total	**6**	**0**	**1**	**0**	**1668**

Going: Sf: 0-0 GS: 0-0 Gd: 0-1 GF: - Fm: 0-0
Distance: 2m/2m3: 0-1 2m4-2m7: 0-0 3m+: 0-0
Track: LH: 0-0 RH: 0-1 Tight: 0-0 Gall: 0-0
Aids: Bl: 0-0 Vi: 0-0 Tstrap: 0-0
Best Rating: 133 3/99 Chel 2m1f gd-sft Hdl

O J Selym (IRE)

102(94h) (92h)113

8-y-o b g Be My Native (USA)-Myle Avenue (Push On)
H D Daly Mrs R Stachan,J Nesbitt,A Clay,D Graham

Placings: *00*/5405-46P **(2645)**
2001/02: 16^{4}S, 22^{6}G, 24^{P}GS

	Starts	1st	2nd	3rd	Win & Pl
Chases	3	0	0	0	472
Career Total	**9**	**0**	**0**	**0**	**472**

Going: Sf: 0-1 GS: 0-1 Gd: 0-1 GF: - Fm: 0-0
Distance: 2m/2m3: 0-1 2m4-2m7: 0-1 3m+: 0-1
Track: LH: 0-1 RH: 0-2 Tight: 0-0 Gall: 0-2
Aids: Bl: 0-0 Vi: 0-0 Tstrap: 0-0
Best Rating: 103 2/01 Towc 2m heavy Hdl

O So Bossy

12-y-o ch g Sousa-Bubbling Spirit (Hubble Bubble)
A W Congdon A W Congdon

Placings: F/4-U **(3991)**
2001/02: 24^{U}S

	Starts	1st	2nd	3rd	Win & Pl
Chases	1	0	0	0	
Career Total	**3**	**0**	**0**	**0**	**0**

Going: Sf: 0-1 GS: 0-0 Gd: 0-0 GF: - Fm: 0-0

Distance: 2m/2m3: 0-0 2m4-2m7: 0-0 3m+: 0-1
Track: LH: 0-0 RH: 0-1 Tight: 0-1 Gall: 0-0
Aids: Bl: 0-0 Vi: 0-0 Tstrap: 0-0
Best Rating: 97 2/02 Tntn 3m soft Ch

O'Fiaich's Hope (IRE)

12-y-o b g Convinced-Harry's Hope (Master Buck)
P Hutchinson Mrs P J Hutchinson

Placings:0/40*0*0006/0/30306**U44/0-U** **(3817)**
2001/02: 21^{U}S

	Starts	1st	2nd	3rd	Win & Pl
Chases	1	0	0	0	
Career Total	**19**	**0**	**0**	**2**	**1069**

Going: Sf: 0-1 GS: 0-0 Gd: 0-0 GF: - Fm: 0-0
Distance: 2m/2m3: 0-0 2m4-2m7: 0-1 3m+: 0-0
Track: LH: 0-0 RH: 0-1 Tight: 0-1 Gall: 0-0
Aids: Bl: 0-0 Vi: 0-0 Tstrap: 0-0
Best Rating: 89 11/97 Navn 2m4f yield Hdl

Oa Baldixe (FR)

102 **142**

8-y-o gr g Linamix (FR)-Bal D'Oa (FR) (Noir Et Or)
Noel Meade The High Street Racing Synd

Placings:0/112120/00-**2F21F41464** **(4937a)**
2001/02: 22^{2}GY, 22^{F}Y, 20^{2}YS, 21^{1}GY, 24^{F}SH, 21^{4}HY, 21^{1}HY, 32^{4}GS, 29^{6}GY, 20^{4}YS

	Starts	1st	2nd	3rd	Win & Pl
Chases	10	2	2	0	25388
Career Total	**19**	**5**	**4**	**0**	**52066**

142	3/02	Leop	2m5f	Ch	HVY	£8972
139	1/02	Fair	2m5f120y	Ch	G-Y	£6773
148	12/99	Leop	2m4f	Hdl	SFT	£6160
139	11/99	Navn	2m4f	Hdl	Y-S	£10156
134	11/99	Fair	2m4f	Hdl	G-Y	£3080

Total win prize-money £35142

Going: Sf: 1-2 GS: 0-1 Gd: 0-0 GF: - Fm: 0-0
Distance: 2m/2m3: 0-0 **2m4-2m7: 2-7** 3m+: 0-3
Track: **LH: 1-4** RH: 0-2 Tight: 0-0 Gall: 0-1
Aids: Bl: 0-0 Vi: 0-0 Tstrap: 0-0
Best Rating: 148 12/99 Leop 2m4f soft Hdl

A one-time very smart hurdler, he has taken quite well to fences last season. Found out by the four-mile trip in Cheltenham's National Hunt Chase.

Oaklands Millie (IRE)

93 **65**

9-y-o b m Millfontaine-Milpe (Milan)
I Park Ian Park

Placings:065PP **(3362)**
2001/02: 16^{0}GF, 16^{6}F, 19^{5}G, 21^{P}GF, 25^{P}GS

	Starts	1st	2nd	3rd	Win & Pl
Hurdles	5	0	0	0	0
Career Total	**5**	**0**	**0**	**0**	**0**

Going: Sf: 0-0 GS: 0-1 Gd: 0-1 GF: - Fm: 0-3
Distance: 2m/2m3: 0-2 2m4-2m7: 0-2 3m+: 0-1
Track: LH: 0-4 RH: 0-1 Tight: 0-3 Gall: 0-0
Aids: Bl: 0-0 Vi: 0-0 Tstrap: 0-0
Best Rating: 65 5/01 Hexm 2m firm Hdl

Oath Of Allegiance (IRE)

108 **103**

7-y-o b m Supreme Leader-Kasam (General Ironside)
Mrs M Reveley Mrs Susan McDonald

Placings:*2120*/425335-3503 **(4420)**
2001/02: 21^{3}G, 17^{5}G, 16^{0}GS, 21^{3}GS

	Starts	1st	2nd	3rd	Win & Pl
Hurdles	4	0	0	2	4832
Career Total	**14**	**1**	**3**	**4**	**10939**

102	1/00	Catt	2m	H NHF	GD	£1904

Total win prize-money £1904

Going: Sf: 0-0 GS: 0-2 Gd: 0-2 GF: - Fm: 0-0
Distance: 2m/2m3: 0-2 2m4-2m7: 0-2 3m+: 0-0
Track: LH: 0-4 RH: 0-0 Tight: 0-2 Gall: 0-2
Aids: Bl: 0-0 Vi: 0-0 Tstrap: 0-0
Best Rating: 110 2/00 Fknm 2m good NHF

A bumper winner at Catterick in January 2000. Has proved expensive to follow since. Has a tendency to race keenly. Needs a strong pace and easy ground at trips around two miles, stays further.

Oboedire (IRE)

102 **111**

9-y-o br g Royal Fountain-Another Pride (Golden Love)
Sir John Barlow Bt T D B Barlow

Placings:21P3P **(4233)**
2001/02: 25^{2}G, 24^{1}S, 24^{P}S, 26^{3}HY, 32^{P}GS

	Starts	1st	2nd	3rd	Win & Pl
Chases	5	1	1	1	13238
Career Total	**5**	**1**	**1**	**1**	**13238**

111	11/01	Hayd	3m	B Ch	SFT	£9597

Total win prize-money £9598

Going: Sf: 1-3 GS: 0-1 Gd: 0-1 GF: - Fm: 0-0
Distance: 2m/2m3: 0-0 2m4-2m7: 0-0 **3m+: 1-5**
Track: **LH: 1-5** RH: 0-0 Tight: 0-1 Gall: 0-1
Aids: Bl: 0-0 Vi: 0-0 Tstrap: 0-0
Best Rating: 111 11/01 Hayd 3m soft Ch

A winning point to pointer, he landed a novice chase at Haydock in November 2001. Likes soft ground. Stays three miles plus.

Occam (IRE)

93 **77**

8-y-o ch g Sharp Victor (USA)-Monterana (Sallust)
A Bailey Sandybrow Stables Ltd

Placings:00/0-0 **(4404)**
2001/02: 17^{0}S

	Starts	1st	2nd	3rd	Win & Pl
Hurdles	1	0	0	0	
Career Total	**4**	**0**	**0**	**0**	

Going: Sf: 0-1 GS: 0-0 Gd: 0-0 GF: - Fm: 0-0
Distance: 2m/2m3: 0-1 2m4-2m7: 0-0 3m+: 0-0
Track: LH: 0-1 RH: 0-0 Tight: 0-1 Gall: 0-0
Aids: Bl: 0-0 Vi: 0-0 Tstrap: 0-0
Best Rating: 63 3/02 Bang 2m1f soft Hdl

Occold (IRE)

113 **149**

11-y-o b g Over The River (FR)-My Puttens (David Jack)
Ferdy Murphy Exors Of The Late Mr G A Hubbard

Placings:3/12311F2/3P1P12 **(4897)**
2001/02: 26^{3}HY, 25^{P}S, 25^{1}HY, 24^{P}G, 26^{1}GS, 24^{2}G

	Starts	1st	2nd	3rd	Win & Pl
Chases	6	2	1	1	19592
Career Total	**14**	**5**	**3**	**3**	**41848**

149	3/02	Carl	3m2f	D(0-125)HCh	G-S	£5538
136	1/02	Towc	3m1f	C(0-130)HCh	HVY	£8365
145	1/98	Kemp	3m	D Ch	G-S	£4375
139	12/97	Hntg	2m4f110y	E Ch	G-S	£2675
99	10/97	Strf	2m6f110y	D Hdl	GD	£3213

Total win prize-money £24169

Going: Sf: 1-3 GS: 1-1 Gd: 0-2 GF: - Fm: 0-0
Distance: 2m/2m3: 0-0 2m4-2m7: 0-0 **3m+: 2-6**
Track: LH: 0-1 **RH: 2-5** Tight: 0-0 Gall: 0-0
Aids: Bl: 0-0 Vi: 0-0 Tstrap: 0-0
Best Rating: 153 4/98 Aint 3m1f soft Ch

He was a good novice in the 1997/1998 season but picked up an injury and was sidelined for a long time. Won long-distance chases on soft ground early in 2002.

Ocean Line (IRE)

104 **110**

7-y-o b g Kefaah (USA)-Tropic Sea (IRE) (Sure Blade (USA))
J J O'Neill The Cartmel Syndicate

Placings:3003P11-10540213 **(1918)**
2001/02: 16^{1}GF, 19^{0}GF, 16^{5}GF, 24^{4}G, 17^{0}GS, 16^{2}G, 16^{1}GF, 16^{3}G

	Starts	1st	2nd	3rd	Win & Pl
Hurdles	8	2	1	1	12602
Career Total	**15**	**4**	**1**	**3**	**20453**

108	10/01	Ludl	2m	D(0-120)HHdl	G-F	£5057
110	5/01	Ayr	2m	D(0-125)HHdl	G-F	£5183
109	10/00	Ludl	2m	D(0-120)HHdl	G-F	£5057
99	10/00	Ludl	2m	G Hdl	G-F	£1960

Total win prize-money £17258

Going: Sf: 0-0 GS: 0-1 Gd: 0-3 GF: - Fm: 2-4
Distance: **2m/2m3: 2-6** 2m4-2m7: 0-1 3m+: 0-1
Track: LH: 1-5 RH: 1-3 Tight: 0-3 Gall: 0-0
Aids: Bl: 0-0 Vi: 0-0 Tstrap: 0-0
Best Rating: 110 11/01 Weth 2m good Hdl

He is an effective sort in minor handicap hurdles, best on fast ground.

Ocean Love (IRE)

79 **66**

4-y-o b f Dolphin Street (FR)-Scuba Diver (King's Lake (USA))
C Weedon (M L W Bell 15/8) Alf Chadwick

Placings:0560P **(4417)**
2001/02: 16^{0}G, 16^{5}S, 16^{6}GS, 16^{0}GS, 16^{P}GS

	Starts	1st	2nd	3rd	Win & Pl
Hurdles	5	0	0	0	0
Career Total	**5**	**0**	**0**	**0**	**0**

Going: Sf: 0-1 GS: 0-3 Gd: 0-1 GF: - Fm: 0-0
Distance: 2m/2m3: 0-5 2m4-2m7: 0-0 3m+: 0-0
Track: LH: 0-2 RH: 0-3 Tight: 0-1 Gall: 0-1
Aids: Bl: 0-0 Vi: 0-0 Tstrap: 0-0
Best Rating: 66 1/02 Kemp 2m gd-sft Hdl

Ocean Peak (NZ)

84(118c) **78**

9-y-o b g Gay Apollo-Red Sea (NZ) (Noble Bijou (USA))
B P J Baugh (S A Brookshaw 23/5) M N Dennis

Placings:1/**P1U**00-00P0 (2004)
2001/02: 17^{0}G, 19^{0}G, 20^{P}G, 16^{0}S

	Starts	1st	2nd	3rd	Win & Pl
Hurdles	4	0	0	0	
Career Total	**10**	**2**	**0**	**0**	**5764**

124	12/00	Ludl	2m	D Ch	G-S	£3779
	5/99	Trap	1m4f	Hdl	G-S	£1984

Total win prize-money £5764

Going: Sf: 0-1 GS: 0-0 Gd: 0-3 GF: - Fm: 0-0
Distance: 2m/2m3: 0-2 2m4-2m7: 0-2 3m+: 0-0
Track: LH: 0-3 RH: 0-1 Tight: 0-2 Gall: 0-0
Aids: Bl: 0-0 Vi: 0-0 Tstrap: 0-0
Best Rating: 124 12/00 Ludl 2m gd-sft Ch

Ocean Prince (FR)

91 **93**

6-y-o b g Dolphin Street (FR)-Dumayla (Shernazar)
D G Bridgwater The Losers

Placings:2204/54F (0873)
2001/02: 22^{5}GF, 20^{4}GF, 25^{F}GS

	Starts	1st	2nd	3rd	Win & Pl
Hurdles	3	0	0	0	0
Career Total	**7**	**0**	**2**	**0**	**1393**

Going: Sf: 0-0 GS: 0-1 Gd: 0-0 GF: - Fm: 0-2
Distance: 2m/2m3: 0-0 2m4-2m7: 0-2 3m+: 0-1
Track: LH: 0-3 RH: 0-0 Tight: 0-2 Gall: 0-0
Aids: Bl: 0-0 Vi: 0-0 Tstrap: 0-2
Best Rating: 101 11/99 Uttx 2m gd-sft Hdl

Ocean Tide

107 **110**

5-y-o b g Deploy-Dancing Tide (Pharly (FR))
R Ford (J G Given 21/8) A Eyres & D F Price

Placings:5030-2133 (4844)
2001/02: 20^{2}S, 20^{1}GS, 22^{3}G, 24^{3}G

	Starts	1st	2nd	3rd	Win & Pl
Hurdles	4	1	1	2	6739
Career Total	**8**	**1**	**1**	**3**	**7115**

105	2/02	Muss	2m4f	D(0-115)HHdl	G-S	£4212

Total win prize-money £4212

Going: Sf: 0-1 GS: 1-1 Gd: 0-2 GF: - Fm: 0-0
Distance: 2m/2m3: 0-0 **2m4-2m7: 1-3** 3m+: 0-1
Track: LH: 0-2 **RH: 1-2 Tight: 1-3** Gall: 0-0
Aids: Bl: 0-0 **Vi: 1-4** Tstrap: 0-0
Best Rating: 110 4/02 Bang 3m good Hdl

Better known as a stayer on the Flat, he had shown ability over hurdles before scoring at Musselburgh in February 2002 and run with credit subsequently.

Ocean Trout

6-y-o b m Sea Raven (IRE)-Rosa Trout (Goldhill)
R D E Woodhouse R D E Woodhouse

Placings:30-0 (4198)
2001/02: 21^{0}S

	Starts	1st	2nd	3rd	Win & Pl
Hurdles	1	0	0	0	
Career Total	**3**	**0**	**0**	**1**	**280**

Going: Sf: 0-1 GS: 0-0 Gd: 0-0 GF: - Fm: 0-0
Distance: 2m/2m3: 0-0 2m4-2m7: 0-1 3m+: 0-0
Track: LH: 0-1 RH: 0-0 Tight: 0-1 Gall: 0-0
Aids: Bl: 0-0 Vi: 0-0 Tstrap: 0-0
Best Rating: 15 2/01 Weth 2m soft NHF

Ocseola Boy (IRE)

8-y-o b g Zaffaran (USA)-Mcbrides Reject (Avocat)
R J Smith S McConville

Placings:PP-P (1137)
2001/02: 22^{P}G

	Starts	1st	2nd	3rd	Win & Pl
Hurdles	1	0	0	0	
Career Total	**3**	**0**	**0**	**0**	

Going: Sf: 0-0 GS: 0-0 Gd: 0-1 GF: - Fm: 0-0
Distance: 2m/2m3: 0-0 2m4-2m7: 0-1 3m+: 0-0
Track: LH: 0-1 RH: 0-0 Tight: 0-1 Gall: 0-0
Aids: Bl: 0-0 Vi: 0-0 Tstrap: 0-0
Best Rating:

October Mist (IRE)

103(109h) **144**

8-y-o gr g Roselier (FR)-Bonny Joe (Derring Rose)
Mrs M Reveley Mrs E A Murray

Placings:*2/3*311116/1163-**121FP5** (4836)
2001/02: 16^{1}G, 16^{2}G, 20^{1}S, 16^{F}GS, 16^{P}G, 20^{5}G

	Starts	1st	2nd	3rd	Win & Pl
Chases	6	2	1	0	9703
Career Total	**10**	**8**	**2**	**3**	**39517**

133	12/01	Weth	2m4f110y	D Ch	SFT	£4576
144	11/01	Weth	2m	E Ch	GD	£3857
159	11/00	Hayd	2m6f	B(0-140)HHdl	HVY	£6683
150	11/00	Ayr	2m4f	C(0-130)HHdl	SFT	£5018
148	2/00	Hayd	2m	C HHdl	HVY	£4914
122	1/00	Kels	2m2f	E Hdl	GD	£2394
119	12/99	Weth	2m4f110y	D(0-110)HHdl	G-S	£3577
96	12/99	MRas	2m1f110y	D Hdl	G-S	£3051

Total win prize-money £34073

Going: Sf: 1-1 GS: 0-1 Gd: 1-4 GF: - Fm: 0-0
Distance: 2m/2m3: 1-4 2m4-2m7: 1-2 3m+: 0-0
Track: **LH: 2-5** RH: 0-1 Tight: 0-0 Gall: 0-0
Aids: Bl: 0-0 Vi: 0-0 Tstrap: 0-0
Best Rating: 159 11/00 Hayd 2m6f heavy Hdl

A handsome individual, he made a good start over fences in the autumn of 2001, including beating Barton on his debut. Despite winning again at that track the following month, he has not achieved as much as looked likely. Suited by a flat, left-handed track, he is best on easy ground.

Odagh Odyssey (IRE)

113 **147**

8-y-o ch g Ikdam-Riverside Willow (Callernish)
Miss E C Lavelle R J Lavelle

Placings:*4*0004/**F111-3P11** (2791)
2001/02: 20^{3}GS, 19^{P}S, 20^{1}G, 19^{1}G

	Starts	1st	2nd	3rd	Win & Pl
Chases	4	2	0	1	22670
Career Total	**13**	**5**	**0**	**1**	**34079**

147	12/01	Asct	2m3f110y	B(0-145)HCh	GD	£17342
144	12/01	Leic	2m4f110y	E(0-115)HCh	GD	£4403
144	4/01	Hntg	2m4f110y	E Ch	SFT	£3777
130	1/01	Tntn	2m3f	D(0-110)HCh	SFT	£4407
126	12/00	Tntn	2m3f	F(0-95)HCh	SFT	£3224

Total win prize-money £33155

Going: Sf: 0-1 GS: 0-1 Gd: 2-2 GF: - Fm: 0-0
Distance: 2m/2m3: 0-0 **2m4-2m7: 2-4** 3m+: 0-0
Track: LH: 0-2 **RH: 2-2** Tight: 0-1 Gall: 0-0
Aids: Bl: 0-0 Vi: 0-0 Tstrap: 0-0
Best Rating: 147 12/01 Asct 2m3f110y good Ch

Progressive handicap chaser, suited by two and a half miles and good ground or softer. Needs to race right-handed.

Oddlydodd (IRE)

91 **101**

6-y-o b g Tremblant-Poor Times (IRE) (Roselier (FR))
T Keddy (J White 17/12) Ady Boughen

Placings:*00*PP410 (4415)
2001/02: 16^{0}G, 17^{0}S, 17^{P}HY, 21^{P}G, 21^{4}HY, 21^{1}GS, 22^{0}S

	Starts	1st	2nd	3rd	Win & Pl
NH Flat	2	0	0	0	0
Hurdles	5	1	0	0	3570
Career Total	**7**	**1**	**0**	**0**	**3570**

101	3/02	Wwck	2m5f	D(0-115)HHdl	G-S	£3570

Total win prize-money £3570

Going: Sf: 0-4 GS: 1-1 Gd: 0-2 GF: - Fm: 0-0
Distance: 2m/2m3: 0-3 **2m4-2m7: 1-4** 3m+: 0-0
Track: LH: 0-3 RH: 0-1 Tight: 0-4 Gall: 0-0
Aids: Bl: 0-0 Vi: 0-0 Tstrap: 0-0
Best Rating: 101 3/02 Wwck 2m5f gd-sft Hdl

In good form for his new trainer overcoming a dental problem which resulted in some wayward behaviour. Attacked his hurdles when off the mark at Warwick in March 2002.

Odyssey

92(96h) (100h)**110**

6-y-o b g Slip Anchor-Circo (Main Reef)
P J Hobbs R N Scott & A W Pearson

Placings:0250-1646 (1255)
2001/02: 22^{1}GF, 22^{6}G, 21^{4}G, 22^{6}GF

	Starts	1st	2nd	3rd	Win & Pl
Hurdles	2	1	0	0	2499
Chases	2	0	0	0	256
Career Total	**8**	**1**	**1**	**0**	**3492**

100	5/01	Font	2m6f110y	F(0-110)HHdl	G-F	£2499

Total win prize-money £2499

Going: Sf: 0-0 GS: 0-0 Gd: 0-2 GF: - Fm: 1-2
Distance: 2m/2m3: 0-0 **2m4-2m7: 1-4** 3m+: 0-0
Track: **LH: 1-3** RH: 0-0 **Tight: 1-4** Gall: 0-0
Aids: Bl: 0-1 Vi: 0-0 Tstrap: 0-0
Best Rating: 110 7/01 Strf 2m5f110y good Ch

Off Limits (NZ)

75 **57**

6-y-o ch g Hula Town (NZ)-Offrande (NZ) (Decies)
N J Henderson Michael Buckley

Placings:*5*-0 (0673)
2001/02: 16^{0}GF

	Starts	1st	2nd	3rd	Win & Pl
Hurdles	1	0	0	0	
Career Total	**2**	**0**	**0**	**0**	**0**

Going: Sf: 0-0 GS: 0-0 Gd: 0-0 GF: - Fm: 0-1
Distance: 2m/2m3: 0-1 2m4-2m7: 0-0 3m+: 0-0
Track: LH: 0-1 RH: 0-0 Tight: 0-0 Gall: 0-0
Aids: Bl: 0-0 Vi: 0-0 Tstrap: 0-0
Best Rating: 82 8/00 NAbb 2m1f good NHF

Off The Hook (IRE)

91 79

6-y-o b g Montelimar (USA)-Hook's Close (Kemal (FR))

C Grant Akv Cladding Fabrications Ltd

Placings: *00305P*-400 (2306)

2001/02: 16^{4}G, 20^{0}S, 16^{0}GF

	Starts	1st	2nd	3rd	Win & Pl
Hurdles	3	0	0	0	0
Career Total	9	0	0	1	247

Going: Sf: 0-1 GS: 0-0 Gd: 0-1 GF: - Fm: 0-1
Distance: 2m/2m3: 0-2 2m4-2m7: 0-1 3m+: 0-0
Track: LH: 0-2 RH: 0-0 Tight: 0-2 Gall: 0-0
Aids: Bl: 0-0 Vi: 0-0 Tstrap: 0-0
Best Rating: 109 12/00 Folk 2m1f110y heavy NHF

Off The Wood

67 25

6-y-o gr m Baron Blakeney-Rocquelle (Coquelin (USA))

Mrs Barbara Waring (John Allen 12/5) J Thow Wood

Placings: *00*P (3403)

2001/02: 16^{0}GF, 16^{0}G, 20^{P}S

	Starts	1st	2nd	3rd	Win & Pl
NH Flat	2	0	0	0	0
Hurdles	1	0	0	0	0
Career Total	3	0	0	0	

Going: Sf: 0-1 GS: 0-0 Gd: 0-1 GF: - Fm: 0-1
Distance: 2m/2m3: 0-2 2m4-2m7: 0-1 3m+: 0-0
Track: LH: 0-1 RH: 0-2 Tight: 0-1 Gall: 0-0
Aids: Bl: 0-0 Vi: 0-0 Tstrap: 0-0
Best Rating: 46 12/01 Ludl 2m good NHF

Offshore (IRE)

9-y-o b g Over The River (FR)-Parsons Princess (The Parson)

S Breen F R Jackson

Placings: *344*/P (3810)

2001/02: 26^{P}S

	Starts	1st	2nd	3rd	Win & Pl
Chases	1	0	0	0	
Career Total	4	0	0	1	193

Going: Sf: 0-1 GS: 0-0 Gd: 0-0 GF: - Fm: 0-0
Distance: 2m/2m3: 0-0 2m4-2m7: 0-0 3m+: 0-1
Track: LH: 0-0 RH: 0-0 Tight: 0-1 Gall: 0-0
Aids: Bl: 0-0 Vi: 0-0 Tstrap: 0-0
Best Rating: 103 4/98 Chel 2m1f heavy NHF

Oh Jamila

83 48

4-y-o b f Ezzoud (IRE)-True Bird (IRE) (In The Wings)

W R Muir Wooburn Racing

Placings: P5 (1472)

2001/02: 17^{P}GF, 17^{5}S

	Starts	1st	2nd	3rd	Win & Pl
Hurdles	2	0	0	0	0
Career Total	2	0	0	0	0

Going: Sf: 0-1 GS: 0-0 Gd: 0-0 GF: - Fm: 0-1
Distance: 2m/2m3: 0-2 2m4-2m7: 0-0 3m+: 0-0
Track: LH: 0-0 RH: 0-2 Tight: 0-1 Gall: 0-0
Aids: Bl: 0-0 Vi: 0-0 Tstrap: 0-0
Best Rating: 48 9/01 MRas 2m1f110y soft Hdl

Oh No Whiskey

7-y-o br g Backchat (USA)-Wood Heath (Heres)

J G Portman Miss R Wakeford

Placings: *60P0*/FPP (4170)

2001/02: 24^{F}GS, 24^{P}G, 26^{P}GS

	Starts	1st	2nd	3rd	Win & Pl
Chases	3	0	0	0	
Career Total	7	0	0	0	0

Going: Sf: 0-0 GS: 0-2 Gd: 0-1 GF: - Fm: 0-0
Distance: 2m/2m3: 0-0 2m4-2m7: 0-0 3m+: 0-3
Track: LH: 0-1 RH: 0-1 Tight: 0-2 Gall: 0-0
Aids: Bl: 0-0 Vi: 0-1 Tstrap: 0-0
Best Rating: 85 11/99 Wwck 2m good NHF

Oh Olla (IRE)

74 48

8-y-o b m Homo Sapien-Giolla's Bone (Pitpan)

A E Jones Graham Brown

Placings: *0/0PP/P*-000 (1268)

2001/02: 16^{0}GF, 17^{0}GF, 17^{0}GF

	Starts	1st	2nd	3rd	Win & Pl
Hurdles	3	0	0	0	
Career Total	8	0	0	0	

Going: Sf: 0-0 GS: 0-0 Gd: 0-0 GF: - Fm: 0-3
Distance: 2m/2m3: 0-3 2m4-2m7: 0-0 3m+: 0-0
Track: LH: 0-3 RH: 0-0 Tight: 0-2 Gall: 0-0
Aids: Bl: 0-0 Vi: 0-0 Tstrap: 0-0
Best Rating: 88 10/99 Tntn 2m1f gd-fm NHF

Oh So Cosy (IRE)

(97h)

9-y-o br g Mandalus-Milan Pride (Northern Guest (USA))

Miss S E Forster (A R Dicken 9/5) C Storey

Placings: *0/50/502301F/024F4/40500*-FP0 (0802)

2001/02: 20^{F}G, 25^{P}G, 16^{0}GF

	Starts	1st	2nd	3rd	Win & Pl
Chases	3	0	0	0	
Career Total	23	1	2	1	4941

98	3/99	Kels	2m6f110y	E Hdl	GD	£1982

Total win prize-money £1982

Going: Sf: 0-0 GS: 0-0 Gd: 0-2 GF: - Fm: 0-1
Distance: 2m/2m3: 0-1 2m4-2m7: 0-1 3m+: 0-1
Track: LH: 0-2 RH: 0-1 Tight: 0-0 Gall: 0-0
Aids: Bl: 0-0 Vi: 0-0 Tstrap: 0-0
Best Rating: 105 10/00 Kels 2m6f110y gd-sft Hdl

Oh So Different

90 74

7-y-o b g Teenoso (USA)-Coole Pilate (Celtic Cone)

O Sherwood B T Stewart-Brown

Placings: P-5 (0352)

2001/02: 22^{5}G

	Starts	1st	2nd	3rd	Win & Pl
Hurdles	1	0	0	0	0
Career Total	2	0	0	0	0

Going: Sf: 0-0 GS: 0-0 Gd: 0-1 GF: - Fm: 0-0
Distance: 2m/2m3: 0-0 2m4-2m7: 0-1 3m+: 0-0
Track: LH: 0-1 RH: 0-0 Tight: 0-1 Gall: 0-0
Aids: Bl: 0-0 Vi: 0-0 Tstrap: 0-0
Best Rating: 74 5/01 Strf 2m6f110y good Hdl

Oh So Quiet

10-y-o ch g Kind Of Hush-Clear As Crystal (Whitstead)

K Cumings Mrs P A Tory

Placings: F (0254)

2001/02: 24^{F}GF

	Starts	1st	2nd	3rd	Win & Pl
Chases	1	0	0	0	
Career Total	1	0	0	0	

Going: Sf: 0-0 GS: 0-0 Gd: 0-0 GF: - Fm: 0-1
Distance: 2m/2m3: 0-0 2m4-2m7: 0-0 3m+: 0-1
Track: LH: 0-1 RH: 0-0 Tight: 0-1 Gall: 0-0
Aids: Bl: 0-0 Vi: 0-0 Tstrap: 0-0
Best Rating: 87 5/01 Strf 3m gd-fm Ch

Oh So Wisley

103 103

7-y-o b g Teenoso (USA)-Easy Horse (FR) (Carmarthen (FR))

N A Twiston-Davies The Wisley Golf Partnership

Placings: *0006/3213164*-1 (1395)

2001/02: 24^{1}GF

	Starts	1st	2nd	3rd	Win & Pl
Hurdles	1	1	0	0	2839
Career Total	12	3	1	2	9476

103	9/01	Worc	3m	F(0-100)HHdl	G-F	£2838
105	1/01	Tntn	3m110y	F(0-110)HHdl	HVY	£2271
98	11/00	Wwck	2m5f	D(0-110)HHdl	HVY	£2850

Total win prize-money £7961

Going: Sf: 0-0 GS: 0-0 Gd: 0-0 GF: - Fm: 1-1
Distance: 2m/2m3: 0-0 2m4-2m7: 0-0 3m+: 1-1
Track: LH: 1-1 RH: 0-0 Tight: 0-0 Gall: 0-0
Aids: Bl: 0-0 Vi: 0-0 Tstrap: 0-0
Best Rating: 105 1/01 Tntn 3m110y heavy Hdl

Ohmyword

6-y-o b m Henbit (USA)-Bell Cord (Beldale Flutter (USA))

R Lee Dan Jones Partnership

Placings: *0*-P (0045)

2001/02: 17^{P}GS

	Starts	1st	2nd	3rd	Win & Pl
Hurdles	1	0	0	0	
Career Total	2	0	0	0	

Going: Sf: 0-0 GS: 0-1 Gd: 0-0 GF: - Fm: 0-0
Distance: 2m/2m3: 0-1 2m4-2m7: 0-0 3m+: 0-0
Track: LH: 0-0 RH: 0-1 Tight: 0-0 Gall: 0-0
Aids: Bl: 0-0 Vi: 0-0 Tstrap: 0-0
Best Rating: 37 1/01 Donc 2m110y good NHF

Oisin Dubh (IRE)

13-y-o b/br g Supreme Leader-Gaoth Na Bride (Strong

Gale)
K Tork K Tork

Placings:0600/PP/PP (0325)
2001/02: 20PGF, 21PG

	Starts	1st	2nd	3rd	Win & Pl
Chases	2	0	0	0	
Career Total	8	0	0	0	

Going: Sf: 0-0 GS: 0-0 Gd: 0-1 GF: - Fm: 0-1
Distance: 2m/2m3: 0-0 2m4-2m7: 0-2 3m+: 0-0
Track: LH: 0-0 RH: 0-2 Tight: 0-1 Gall: 0-1
Aids: Bl: 0-0 Vi: 0-0 Tstrap: 0-0
Best Rating: 89 11/95 Clon 2m gd-yld Hdl

Ok So (IRE)

9-y-o ch g Naheez (USA)-Flowering Moss (IRE) (Le Moss)
K A Nelmes K A Nelmes

Placings:600/0F0P/3-62335 (4735)
2001/02: 266G, 252G, 243GF, 243S, 235F

	Starts	1st	2nd	3rd	Win & Pl
Chases	5	0	1	2	1178
Career Total	13	0	1	3	1830

Going: Sf: 0-1 GS: 0-0 Gd: 0-2 GF: - Fm: 0-2
Distance: 2m/2m3: 0-0 2m4-2m7: 0-0 3m+: 0-5
Track: LH: 0-1 RH: 0-4 Tight: 0-4 Gall: 0-0
Aids: Bl: 0-0 Vi: 0-0 Tstrap: 0-0
Best Rating: 107 3/02 Tntn 3m soft Ch

Point winner and maiden hunter chaser, jumps well.

Okeedokee (FR)

12-y-o gr g Kaldoun (FR)-Multitude (USA) (Lyphard (USA))
A W Carroll Michael Gates

Placings:F0/2/442414/5 (1761)
2001/02: 165S

	Starts	1st	2nd	3rd	Win & Pl
Hurdles	1	0	0	0	0
Career Total	10	1	2	0	8284

111	2/00	Leic	2m4f110y	D(0-120)HHdl	G-S	£5167

Total win prize-money £5168

Going: Sf: 0-1 GS: 0-0 Gd: 0-0 GF: - Fm: 0-0
Distance: 2m/2m3: 0-1 2m4-2m7: 0-0 3m+: 0-0
Track: LH: 0-1 RH: 0-0 Tight: 0-1 Gall: 0-0
Aids: Bl: 0-0 Vi: 0-0 Tstrap: 0-0
Best Rating: 111 2/00 Leic 2m4f110y gd-sft Hdl

Olabud

96 96
10-y-o ch g Lord Bud-Nugola (Derrylin)
J T Gifford Bill Naylor

Placings:P0P054/113/**F6-53** (0489)
2001/02: 165GF, 203GF

	Starts	1st	2nd	3rd	Win & Pl
Chases	2	0	0	1	458
Career Total	13	2	0	2	6161

113	10/99	Font	2m2f110y	D(0-120)HHdl	GD	£3109
108	10/99	Font	2m2f110y	E Hdl	GD	£1987

Total win prize-money £5098

Going: Sf: 0-0 GS: 0-0 Gd: 0-0 GF: - Fm: 0-2
Distance: 2m/2m3: 0-1 2m4-2m7: 0-1 3m+: 0-0
Track: LH: 0-1 RH: 0-0 Tight: 0-2 Gall: 0-0
Aids: Bl: 0-0 Vi: 0-0 Tstrap: 0-0
Best Rating: 113 10/99 Font 2m2f110y good Hdl

Old Archives (IRE)

89 68
13-y-o b g Rousillon (USA)-Museum Ball (USA) (Danzig (USA))
L Wells Mrs Carrie Zetter-Wells

Placings:34/21250/0554656464/546/5/35/2516F400/P-600P (2778)
2001/02: 216GF, 220G, 190G, 22PG

	Starts	1st	2nd	3rd	Win & Pl
Hurdles	4	0	0	0	0
Career Total	36	2	3	2	10338

94	12/99	Font	2m4f	F(0-100)HCh	GD	£3355
	7/94	Naas	2m	NHF	G-F	£2935

Total win prize-money £6291

Going: Sf: 0-0 GS: 0-0 Gd: 0-3 GF: - Fm: 0-1
Distance: 2m/2m3: 0-0 2m4-2m7: 0-4 3m+: 0-0
Track: LH: 0-0 RH: 0-2 Tight: 0-1 Gall: 0-1
Aids: Bl: 0-3 Vi: 0-0 Tstrap: 0-0
Best Rating: 104 6/95 Navn 2m gd-fm NHF

Old Bean (IRE)

97f 114f
6-y-o b g Eurobus-Princess Petara (IRE) (Petorius)
N J Henderson Wrestlers Racing

Placings:151 (4377)
2001/02: 161G, 165S, 161S

	Starts	1st	2nd	3rd	Win & Pl
NH Flat	3	2	0	0	4256
Career Total	3	2	0	0	4256

104	3/02	Ludl	2m	H NHF	SFT	£2044
114	1/02	Ludl	2m	H NHF	GD	£2212

Total win prize-money £4256

Going: Sf: 1-2 GS: 0-0 Gd: 1-1 GF: - Fm: 0-0
Distance: **2m/2m3: 2-3** 2m4-2m7: 0-0 3m+: 0-0
Track: LH: 0-0 **RH: 2-3** Tight: 0-0 Gall: 0-0
Aids: Bl: 0-0 Vi: 0-0 Tstrap: 0-0
Best Rating: 114 1/02 Ludl 2m good NHF

Won bumper convincingly on racecourse debut on good ground, and added a second win at Ludlow in softer conditions.

Old Hush Wing (IRE)

102 112
9-y-o b g Tirol-Saneena (Kris)
Mrs S J Smith (S E Kettlewell 22/6) Mrs B Ramsden

Placings:4/10521/5223136/13334/11005-6U454B6 (4869)
2001/02: 206F, 20UG, 204HY, 205S, 214GS, 24BGS, 206GF

	Starts	1st	2nd	3rd	Win & Pl
Hurdles	6	0	0	0	411
Chases	1	0	0	0	0
Career Total	30	6	3	5	28843

112	12/00	Hntg	2m5f110y	F Hdl	SFT	£1789
122	11/00	Hayd	2m4f	F Hdl	HVY	£2019
128	11/99	Sedg	2m5f110y	B HHdl	GD	£6273
125	11/98	Sedg	2m5f110y	B HHdl	G-S	£6677
106	5/98	Sedg	2m5f110y	E Hdl	GD	£2425
115	11/97	Sedg	2m5f110y	E Hdl	GD	£2705

Total win prize-money £21890

Going: Sf: 0-2 GS: 0-2 Gd: 0-1 GF: - Fm: 0-2
Distance: 2m/2m3: 0-0 2m4-2m7: 0-6 3m+: 0-1
Track: LH: 0-5 RH: 0-1 Tight: 0-1 Gall: 0-1
Aids: Bl: 0-0 Vi: 0-0 Tstrap: 0-0
Best Rating: 130 1/00 Wwck 2m4f110y soft Hdl

Fair hurdler over two and a half miles. Acts on soft/heavy ground but is getting a bit long in the tooth now.

Old Marsh (IRE)

110 120+
6-y-o b g Grand Lodge (USA)-Lolly Dolly (Alleged (USA))
Miss Venetia Williams Seasons And Paradise

Placings:4-4020 (4662)
2001/02: 164G, 160S, 162G, 160G

	Starts	1st	2nd	3rd	Win & Pl
Hurdles	4	0	1	0	788
Career Total	5	0	1	0	3288

Going: Sf: 0-1 GS: 0-0 Gd: 0-3 GF: - Fm: 0-0
Distance: 2m/2m3: 0-4 2m4-2m7: 0-0 3m+: 0-0
Track: LH: 0-3 RH: 0-1 Tight: 0-2 Gall: 0-0
Aids: Bl: 0-0 Vi: 0-0 Tstrap: 0-1
Best Rating: 120 3/02 Winc 2m good Hdl

A winner on the Flat in France, he was a good fourth in a valuable event at Aintree on his British debut over hurdles but did not step up on that in subsequent outings until winning three small races in the summer of 2002. Acts on good and soft ground.

Old Red (IRE)

104 104
12-y-o ch g Ela-Mana-Mou-Sea Port (Averof)
Mrs M Reveley A Flannigan

Placings:1303 (4788)
2001/02: 221G, 243GS, 250S, 203F

	Starts	1st	2nd	3rd	Win & Pl
Hurdles	4	1	0	2	4135
Career Total	4	1	0	2	4135

104	10/01	Kels	2m6f110y	E Hdl	GD	£3206

Total win prize-money £3206

Going: Sf: 0-1 GS: 0-1 Gd: 1-1 GF: - Fm: 0-1
Distance: 2m/2m3: 0-0 **2m4-2m7: 1-2** 3m+: 0-2
Track: **LH: 1-4** RH: 0-0 **Tight: 1-2** Gall: 0-2
Aids: Bl: 0-0 Vi: 0-0 Tstrap: 0-0
Best Rating: 104 10/01 Kels 2m6f110y good Hdl

The 1995 Cesarewitch winner, he made a late start over hurdles. Stays at least two miles-six and is suited by good ground or faster.

Old Rouvel (USA)

107 133
11-y-o b g Riverman (USA)-Marie De Russy (FR) (Sassafras (FR))
A King Mrs R D Cowell

Placings:2421P/2P20/5134-61514 (4647)
2001/02: 246G, 241GS, 245S, 241G, 244G

	Starts	1st	2nd	3rd	Win & Pl
Hurdles	5	2	0	0	16010
Career Total	18	4	4	1	30364

133	12/01	Kemp	3m110y	C(0-135)HHdl	GD	£7182
126	11/01	Chep	3m	B(0-150)HHdl	G-S	£6827
128	1/01	Kemp	3m110y	D(0-120)HHdl	SFT	£5164
113	3/98	Hntg	2m5f110y	E Hdl	GD	£2565

Total win prize-money £21740

Going: Sf: 0-1 GS: 1-1 Gd: 1-3 GF: - Fm: 0-0
Distance: 2m/2m3: 0-0 2m4-2m7: 0-0 **3m+: 2-5**
Track: LH: 1-3 RH: 1-2 Tight: 0-1 Gall: 0-0
Aids: Bl: 0-0 Vi: 0-0 Tstrap: 0-0
Best Rating: 133 4/02 Aint 3m110y good Hdl

A decent staying hurdler. He scored on his first outing for Alan King in what looked a moderate heat over three miles at Kempton in January 2001, but lost his way until returning to winning form ten months later and scored again at the end of the year. Not the most consistent sort, he seems well suited by a flat, right-handed track. Handles good ground or easier and best when fresh. Stays three miles.

Olde Oak

93(95h) (76h)**62**

8-y-o ch g Precocious-Quisissanno (Be My Guest (USA))
B Ellison (J S Wainwright 22/7) Mrs Jean Stapleton

Placings:0/4U5506P **(4905)**
2001/02: 16^{4}GF, 16^{U}G, 17^{5}GS, 17^{5}G, 17^{0}GS, 16^{6}G, 17^{P}GF

	Starts	1st	2nd	3rd	Win & Pl
Hurdles	6	0	0	0	0
Chases	1	0	0	0	0
Career Total	**8**	**0**	**0**	**0**	**0**

Going: Sf: 0-0 GS: 0-2 Gd: 0-3 GF: - Fm: 0-2
Distance: 2m/2m3: 0-7 2m4-2m7: 0-0 3m+: 0-0
Track: LH: 0-4 RH: 0-3 Tight: 0-6 Gall: 0-0
Aids: Bl: 0-0 Vi: 0-0 Tstrap: 0-7
Best Rating: 76 8/01 Sthl 2m gd-fm Hdl

Ole Gunnar (IRE)

93 **73**

10-y-o b g Le Bavard (FR)-Rareitess (Rarity)
M S Wilesmith M S Wilesmith

Placings:P **(0246)**
2001/02: 21^{P}GF

	Starts	1st	2nd	3rd	Win & Pl
Hurdles	1	0	0	0	
Career Total	**1**	**0**	**0**	**0**	

Going: Sf: 0-0 GS: 0-0 Gd: 0-0 GF: - Fm: 0-1
Distance: 2m/2m3: 0-0 2m4-2m7: 0-1 3m+: 0-0
Track: LH: 0-0 RH: 0-0 Tight: 0-0 Gall: 0-0
Aids: Bl: 0-0 Vi: 0-0 Tstrap: 0-0
Best Rating:

Oliberi

5

6-y-o b g First Trump-Rhiannon (Welsh Pageant)
Mrs J K M Oliver Miss J S Peat

Placings:50FP/0-0 **(1639)**
2001/02: 20^{0}GS

	Starts	1st	2nd	3rd	Win & Pl
Hurdles	1	0	0	0	
Career Total	**6**	**0**	**0**	**0**	**0**

Going: Sf: 0-0 GS: 0-1 Gd: 0-0 GF: - Fm: 0-0
Distance: 2m/2m3: 0-0 2m4-2m7: 0-1 3m+: 0-0
Track: LH: 0-0 RH: 0-0 Tight: 0-0 Gall: 0-0
Aids: Bl: 0-0 Vi: 0-0 Tstrap: 0-0
Best Rating: 39 1/01 Muss 2m good Hdl

Oliranar

(82h) (49h)

6-y-o gr g Gran Alba (USA)-April Rain (Lepanto (GER))
J R Best R Blake, N Webberley, A Paine, R Sackett

Placings:0PPU-P0000P **(4882)**
2001/02: 22^{P}HY, 17^{0}S, 16^{0}S, 16^{0}GS, 16^{0}G, 26^{P}GF

	Starts	1st	2nd	3rd	Win & Pl
Hurdles	5	0	0	0	0
Chases	1	0	0	0	0
Career Total	**10**	**0**	**0**	**0**	

Going: Sf: 0-3 GS: 0-1 Gd: 0-1 GF: - Fm: 0-1
Distance: 2m/2m3: 0-4 2m4-2m7: 0-1 3m+: 0-1
Track: LH: 0-2 RH: 0-3 Tight: 0-4 Gall: 0-1
Aids: Bl: 0-0 Vi: 0-0 Tstrap: 0-0
Best Rating: 49 3/02 Hntg 2m110y soft Hdl

Olitheaga

93 **96**

7-y-o ch g Safawan-Lyaaric (Privy Seal)
C J Mann The Property Racing Partnership

Placings: f2 **(1655)**
2001/02: 16^{1}GF, 17^{2}G

	Starts	1st	2nd	3rd	Win & Pl
NH Flat	1	1	0	0	1729
Hurdles	1	0	1	0	896
Career Total	**2**	**1**	**1**	**0**	**2625**

96 5/01 Hntg 2m110y H NHF G-F £1729
Total win prize-money £1729

Going: Sf: 0-0 GS: 0-0 Gd: 0-1 GF: - Fm: 1-1
Distance: **2m/2m3: 1-2** 2m4-2m7: 0-0 3m+: 0-0
Track: LH: 0-1 **RH: 1-1** Tight: 0-1 **Gall: 1-1**
Aids: Bl: 0-0 Vi: 0-0 Tstrap: 0-0
Best Rating: 96 10/01 Bang 2m1f good Hdl

Won a bumper at Huntingdon in May 2001 and was runner-up on his hurdling debut five months later.

Oliver Cromwell (IRE)

90(110h) (131h)**105?**

7-y-o br g Mandalus-Gemini Gale (Strong Gale)
P R Hedger Howard Spooner

Placings:556U513/221P1-P223301 **(4821)**
2001/02: 22^{P}S, 21^{2}G, 21^{2}GS, 24^{3}S, 20^{3}S, 25^{0}GS, 24^{1}G

	Starts	1st	2nd	3rd	Win & Pl
Hurdles	7	1	2	2	19649
Career Total	**19**	**4**	**4**	**3**	**41759**

131	4/02	Chel	3m	B(0-145)HHdl	GD	£10871
122	2/01	Kemp	2m5f	C(0-130)HHdl	G-S	£14072
129	1/01	Extr	2m3f	E(0-115)HHdl	HVY	£3136
98	3/00	Towc	2m	E(0-105)HHdl	GD	£2562

Total win prize-money £30642

Going: Sf: 0-3 GS: 0-2 Gd: 1-2 GF: - Fm: 0-0
Distance: 2m/2m3: 0-0 2m4-2m7: 0-4 **3m+: 1-3**
Track: LH: 0-1 RH: 0-5 Tight: 0-0 Gall: 0-1
Aids: Bl: 0-0 Vi: 0-0 Tstrap: 0-0
Best Rating: 131 4/02 Chel 3m good Hdl

A fair handicap hurdler, he ran his best race to date when winning a decent handicap hurdle at Kempton in February 2001, but was off the track for a long time afterwards. Running well without reward in 2001/02 before taking a good handicap hurdle at Cheltenham in April. Stays three miles and is suited by cut in the ground.

Olivety

99 **92**

7-y-o b g Lighter-Star Of Tycoon (Tycoon Ii)
J M Jefferson & Mrs K Hughes

Placings:5/02-3P **(4307)**
2001/02: 20^{3}G, 24^{P}S

	Starts	1st	2nd	3rd	Win & Pl
Hurdles	2	0	0	1	374
Career Total	**5**	**0**	**1**	**1**	**878**

Going: Sf: 0-1 GS: 0-0 Gd: 0-1 GF: - Fm: 0-0
Distance: 2m/2m3: 0-0 2m4-2m7: 0-1 3m+: 0-1
Track: LH: 0-2 RH: 0-0 Tight: 0-0 Gall: 0-1
Aids: Bl: 0-0 Vi: 0-0 Tstrap: 0-0
Best Rating: 101 11/99 Weth 2m good NHF

Olivier (USA)

96f **118f**

4-y-o ch g Theatrical-Izara (USA) (Blushing John (USA))
Miss Venetia Williams You Can Be Sure

Placings:2 **(4900)**
2001/02: 16^{2}G

	Starts	1st	2nd	3rd	Win & Pl
NH Flat	1	0	1	0	1016
Career Total	**1**	**0**	**1**	**0**	**1016**

Going: Sf: 0-0 GS: 0-0 Gd: 0-1 GF: - Fm: 0-0
Distance: 2m/2m3: 0-1 2m4-2m7: 0-0 3m+: 0-0
Track: LH: 0-0 RH: 0-1 Tight: 0-0 Gall: 0-0
Aids: Bl: 0-0 Vi: 0-0 Tstrap: 0-0
Best Rating: 118 4/02 Prth 2m110y good NHF

Olivo (IRE)

8-y-o ch g Priolo (USA)-Honourable Sheba (USA) (Roberto (USA))
C A Horgan J L Harrison

Placings:P **(3223)**
2001/02: 16^{P}G

	Starts	1st	2nd	3rd	Win & Pl
Hurdles	1	0	0	0	
Career Total	**1**	**0**	**0**	**0**	

Going: Sf: 0-0 GS: 0-0 Gd: 0-1 GF: - Fm: 0-0
Distance: 2m/2m3: 0-1 2m4-2m7: 0-0 3m+: 0-0
Track: LH: 0-0 RH: 0-1 Tight: 0-0 Gall: 0-0
Aids: Bl: 0-0 Vi: 0-0 Tstrap: 0-0
Best Rating:

Ollar House (IRE)

75 **41**

11-y-o b g Zaffaran (USA)-Lavengaddy (Balgaddy)
J Barclay J Barclay

Placings:0/PP-P **(4899)**
2001/02: 16^{P}G

	Starts	1st	2nd	3rd	Win & Pl
Chases	1	0	0	0	
Career Total	**4**	**0**	**0**	**0**	

Going: Sf: 0-0 GS: 0-0 Gd: 0-1 GF: - Fm: 0-0
Distance: 2m/2m3: 0-1 2m4-2m7: 0-0 3m+: 0-0
Track: LH: 0-0 RH: 0-1 Tight: 0-0 Gall: 0-0
Aids: Bl: 0-0 Vi: 0-0 Tstrap: 0-0
Best Rating: 82 12/98 Punc 2m soft NHF

Ollar Rose

102 (111h)127

7-y-o gr m Roselier (FR)-Shiona Anne (Royal Fountain)

James Devereux James Devereux

Placings:005100P26F4442-05301452304U (4297)

2001/02: 16^{0}G, 16^{5}Y, 18^{3}S, 16^{0}Y, 20^{1}S, 20^{4}Y, 20^{5}S, 20^{2}S, 18^{3}HY, 20^{0}S, 21^{4}HY, 21^{U}HY

				Starts	1st	2nd	3rd	Win & Pl
Hurdles				5	0	0	1	677
Chases				7	1	1	1	8962
Career Total				**26**	**2**	**3**	**2**	**17574**
127	11/01	Clon	2m4f	Ch		SFT		£6120
101	9/00	List	2m	Hdl		SH		£4456

Total win prize-money £10577

Going: Sf: 1-8 GS: 0-0 Gd: 0-1 GF: - Fm: 0-0
Distance: 2m/2m3: 0-5 **2m4-2m7: 1-7** 3m+: 0-0
Track: LH: 0-3 **RH: 1-4** Tight: 0-0 Gall: 0-0
Aids: Bl: 0-0 Vi: 0-0 Tstrap: 0-0
Best Rating: 127 11/01 Clon 2m4f soft Ch

Fair handicap hurdler/novice chaser. Stays two and a half miles. Acts on soft ground.

Ollejess

68 50

7-y-o ch m Scallywag-City's Sister (Maystreak)

N G Richards Sandicroft Stud 3

Placings:0 (4828)

2001/02: 16^{0}G

	Starts	1st	2nd	3rd	Win & Pl
Hurdles	1	0	0	0	
Career Total	**1**	**0**	**0**	**0**	

Going: Sf: 0-0 GS: 0-0 Gd: 0-1 GF: - Fm: 0-0
Distance: 2m/2m3: 0-1 2m4-2m7: 0-0 3m+: 0-0
Track: LH: 0-1 RH: 0-0 Tight: 0-0 Gall: 0-0
Aids: Bl: 0-0 Vi: 0-0 Tstrap: 0-0
Best Rating: 50 4/02 Ayr 2m good Hdl

Ollies Boy (IRE)

11-y-o br g Electric-Kilcor Rose (Pitpan)

J Barclay (Miss Caroline Barclay 21/4) Kinneston Racing

Placings:5/PPU3P55/PU0302F544P/0P002-2000P (1818)

2001/02: 16^{2}GS, 16^{0}F, 20^{0}G, 17^{0}G, 16^{P}S

	Starts	1st	2nd	3rd	Win & Pl
Hurdles	3	0	1	0	848
Chases	2	0	0	0	0
Career Total	**29**	**0**	**3**	**2**	**4881**

Going: Sf: 0-1 GS: 0-1 Gd: 0-2 GF: - Fm: 0-1
Distance: 2m/2m3: 0-4 2m4-2m7: 0-1 3m+: 0-0
Track: LH: 0-2 RH: 0-3 Tight: 0-1 Gall: 0-0
Aids: Bl: 0-0 Vi: 0-0 Tstrap: 0-0
Best Rating: 96 3/00 Kels 2m1f gd-sft Ch

Oloroso

68 55

5-y-o b g Piccolo-Saunders Lass (Hillandale)

J Neville Charles Saunders Ltd

Placings:0-6P (4275)

2001/02: 16^{6}S, 16^{P}G

	Starts	1st	2nd	3rd	Win & Pl
Hurdles	2	0	0	0	0
Career Total	**3**	**0**	**0**	**0**	**0**

Going: Sf: 0-1 GS: 0-0 Gd: 0-1 GF: - Fm: 0-0
Distance: 2m/2m3: 0-2 2m4-2m7: 0-0 3m+: 0-0
Track: LH: 0-2 RH: 0-0 Tight: 0-1 Gall: 0-0
Aids: Bl: 0-0 Vi: 0-0 Tstrap: 0-0
Best Rating: 55 7/01 Worc 2m soft Hdl

Omar's Odyssey (IRE)

7-y-o ch g Sharifabad (IRE)-Tales Of Homer (Home Guard (USA))

Mrs F Goldsworthy Mrs F Goldsworthy

Placings:0/PP (0428)

2001/02: 21^{P}GF, 21^{P}G

	Starts	1st	2nd	3rd	Win & Pl
Chases	2	0	0	0	
Career Total	**3**	**0**	**0**	**0**	

Going: Sf: 0-0 GS: 0-0 Gd: 0-1 GF: - Fm: 0-1
Distance: 2m/2m3: 0-0 2m4-2m7: 0-2 3m+: 0-0
Track: LH: 0-0 RH: 0-1 Tight: 0-0 Gall: 0-0
Aids: Bl: 0-0 Vi: 0-0 Tstrap: 0-0
Best Rating: 22 4/99 Folk 2m1f110y gd-fm Hdl

Omni Cosmo Touch (USA)

107(97c) (109c)120

6-y-o b g Trempolino (USA)-Wooden Pudden (USA) (Top Ville)

O Sherwood It Wasn't Us

Placings:221122-51412RR (1628)

2001/02: 21^{5}GF, 19^{1}GF, 19^{4}G, 20^{1}G, 20^{2}GF, 16^{R}GF, 20^{R}GF

				Starts	1st	2nd	3rd	Win & Pl
Hurdles				4	2	0	0	13220
Chases				3	0	1	0	942
Career Total				**13**	**4**	**5**	**0**	**22369**
120	6/01	Worc	2m4f	C(0-135)HHdl		GD		£5525
120	5/01	Ling	2m3f110y	D(0-125)HHdl		G-F		£7250
111	10/00	Tntn	2m1f	E Hdl		GD		£2891
98	9/00	Worc	2m	E Hdl		G-F		£1904

Total win prize-money £17571

Going: Sf: 0-0 GS: 0-0 Gd: 1-2 GF: - Fm: 1-5
Distance: 2m/2m3: 0-1 **2m4-2m7: 2-6** 3m+: 0-0
Track: **LH: 2-3** RH: 0-3 **Tight: 1-3** Gall: 0-1
Aids: Bl: 0-1 Vi: 0-0 Tstrap: 0-0
Best Rating: 120 6/01 Worc 2m4f good Hdl

Showed progressive form over hurdles but has become most reluctant to race and cannot be trusted. Effective on a sound surface. Stays an extended two miles three furlongs.

Omniheat

97 95

5-y-o b m Ezzoud (IRE)-Lady Bequick (Sharpen Up)

M J Ryan Mrs E Delaney

Placings:206 (4275)

2001/02: 16^{2}GS, 16^{0}S, 16^{6}G

	Starts	1st	2nd	3rd	Win & Pl
Hurdles	3	0	1	0	941
Career Total	**3**	**0**	**1**	**0**	**941**

Going: Sf: 0-1 GS: 0-1 Gd: 0-1 GF: - Fm: 0-0
Distance: 2m/2m3: 0-3 2m4-2m7: 0-0 3m+: 0-0
Track: LH: 0-2 RH: 0-1 Tight: 0-2 Gall: 0-1
Aids: Bl: 0-0 Vi: 0-0 Tstrap: 0-0
Best Rating: 95 10/01 Strf 2m110y gd-sft Hdl

On Air (GER)

6-y-o b h Goofalik (USA)-Ordinate (GER) (Surumu (GER))

Ian Williams Mrs V Griffiths

Placings:F (4597)

2001/02: 19^{F}GF

	Starts	1st	2nd	3rd	Win & Pl
Hurdles	1	0	0	0	
Career Total	**1**	**0**	**0**	**0**	

Going: Sf: 0-0 GS: 0-0 Gd: 0-0 GF: - Fm: 0-1
Distance: 2m/2m3: 0-1 2m4-2m7: 0-0 3m+: 0-0
Track: LH: 0-1 RH: 0-0 Tight: 0-0 Gall: 0-0
Aids: Bl: 0-0 Vi: 0-0 Tstrap: 0-0
Best Rating:

On Appeal (IRE)

84f 100f

6-y-o b g Buckskin (FR)-Little Quince (Laurence O)

D M Grissell Pps Racing

Placings:6 (0064)

2001/02: 17^{6}GS

	Starts	1st	2nd	3rd	Win & Pl
NH Flat	1	0	0	0	0
Career Total	**1**	**0**	**0**	**0**	**0**

Going: Sf: 0-0 GS: 0-1 Gd: 0-0 GF: - Fm: 0-0
Distance: 2m/2m3: 0-1 2m4-2m7: 0-0 3m+: 0-0
Track: LH: 0-0 RH: 0-0 Tight: 0-1 Gall: 0-0
Aids: Bl: 0-0 Vi: 0-0 Tstrap: 0-0
Best Rating: 100 5/01 Folk 2m1f110y gd-sft NHF

On Ice (IRE)

6-y-o ch g Pursuit Of Love-Ice Chocolate (USA) (Icecapade (USA))

F P Murtagh Mrs Anna Kenny

Placings:PP/0P (2402)

2001/02: 16^{0}S, 17^{P}HY

	Starts	1st	2nd	3rd	Win & Pl
NH Flat	1	0	0	0	0
Hurdles	1	0	0	0	0
Career Total	**4**	**0**	**0**	**0**	

Going: Sf: 0-2 GS: 0-0 Gd: 0-0 GF: - Fm: 0-0
Distance: 2m/2m3: 0-2 2m4-2m7: 0-0 3m+: 0-0
Track: LH: 0-1 RH: 0-1 Tight: 0-0 Gall: 0-0
Aids: Bl: 0-0 Vi: 0-0 Tstrap: 0-1
Best Rating:

On The Bone

10-y-o b m Lyphento (USA)-Lydia Languish (Hotfoot)

R Harvey K & A K Smith

Placings:6S (0577)

2001/02: 20^{6}GF, 21^{S}GF

	Starts	1st	2nd	3rd	Win & Pl
Chases	2	0	0	0	0
Career Total	**2**	**0**	**0**	**0**	**0**

Going: Sf: 0-0 GS: 0-0 Gd: 0-0 GF: - Fm: 0-2
Distance: 2m/2m3: 0-0 2m4-2m7: 0-2 3m+: 0-0
Track: LH: 0-1 RH: 0-1 Tight: 0-1 Gall: 0-1
Aids: Bl: 0-0 Vi: 0-0 Tstrap: 0-0
Best Rating:

On The Day (IRE)

79 90

5-y-o ch g Roselier (FR)-Solar Jet (Mandalus)
L Lungo R A Bartlett

Placings:3 (4441)
2001/02: 22^{3}S

	Starts	1st	2nd	3rd	Win & Pl
Hurdles	1	0	0	1	389
Career Total	**1**	**0**	**0**	**1**	**389**

Going: Sf: 0-1 GS: 0-0 Gd: 0-0 GF: - Fm: 0-0
Distance: 2m/2m3: 0-0 2m4-2m7: 0-1 3m+: 0-0
Track: LH: 0-1 RH: 0-0 Tight: 0-1 Gall: 0-0
Aids: Bl: 0-0 Vi: 0-0 Tstrap: 0-0
Best Rating: 90 3/02 Kels 2m6f110y soft Hdl

On The Game

7-y-o b m Unfuwain (USA)-All Glorious (Crowned Prince (USA))
D C O'Brien D C O'Brien

Placings:0/0P (4171)
2001/02: 16^{0}HY, 16^{P}GS

	Starts	1st	2nd	3rd	Win & Pl
Hurdles	2	0	0	0	
Career Total	**3**	**0**	**0**	**0**	

Going: Sf: 0-1 GS: 0-1 Gd: 0-0 GF: - Fm: 0-0
Distance: 2m/2m3: 0-2 2m4-2m7: 0-0 3m+: 0-0
Track: LH: 0-2 RH: 0-0 Tight: 0-2 Gall: 0-0
Aids: Bl: 0-0 Vi: 0-0 Tstrap: 0-0
Best Rating:

On The Luce

5-y-o b g Karinga Bay-Lirchur (Lir)
L Lungo S H C Racing

Placings:60 (3680)
2001/02: 16^{6}S, 16^{0}HY

	Starts	1st	2nd	3rd	Win & Pl
NH Flat	2	0	0	0	0
Career Total	**2**	**0**	**0**	**0**	**0**

Going: Sf: 0-2 GS: 0-0 Gd: 0-0 GF: - Fm: 0-0
Distance: 2m/2m3: 0-2 2m4-2m7: 0-0 3m+: 0-0
Track: LH: 0-1 RH: 0-0 Tight: 0-0 Gall: 0-0
Aids: Bl: 0-0 Vi: 0-0 Tstrap: 0-0
Best Rating: 85 1/02 Newc 2m soft NHF

On The Right Side

102 107

7-y-o b g Pursuit Of Love-La Masse (High Top)
Mrs S D Williams S A Douch

Placings:4/03200-1 (1853)
2001/02: 17^{1}S

	Starts	1st	2nd	3rd	Win & Pl
Hurdles	1	1	0	0	2618
Career Total	**7**	**1**	**1**	**1**	**4224**

107 10/01 Bang 2m1f E(0-105)HHdl SFT £2618
Total win prize-money £2618

Going: Sf: 1-1 GS: 0-0 Gd: 0-0 GF: - Fm: 0-0
Distance: 2m/2m3: 1-1 2m4-2m7: 0-0 3m+: 0-0
Track: LH: 1-1 RH: 0-0 **Tight: 1-1** Gall: 0-0
Aids: Bl: 0-0 Vi: 0-0 Tstrap: 0-0
Best Rating: 107 10/01 Bang 2m1f soft Hdl

Comfortable winner of a modest novices' handicap hurdle at Bangor in October 2001. Acts on soft ground.

On The Run (IRE)

102 90

8-y-o ch m Don't Forget Me-Chepstow House (USA) (Northern Baby (CAN))
D J Wintle D A Thorpe

Placings:00/206/632000/023F20-34061000 (1733)
2001/02: 19^{3}G, 17^{4}F, 21^{0}G, 16^{6}GF, 16^{1}GF, 16^{0}GF, 20^{0}GF, 19^{0}GS

	Starts	1st	2nd	3rd	Win & Pl
Hurdles	8	1	0	1	2223
Career Total	**25**	**1**	**4**	**3**	**5551**

85 8/01 Sthl 2m G Hdl G-F £1570
Total win prize-money £1571

Going: Sf: 0-0 GS: 0-1 Gd: 0-2 GF: - Fm: 1-5
Distance: 2m/2m3: 1-5 2m4-2m7: 0-3 3m+: 0-0
Track: LH: 1-4 RH: 0-4 **Tight: 1-2** Gall: 0-1
Aids: Bl: 0-0 Vi: 0-0 Tstrap: 0-1
Best Rating: 97 7/00 Worc 2m gd-fm Hdl

Plating class, she is effective on a flat left-handed track and is best over two miles on fast ground. Has shown improvement since racing with her tongue tied.

On The Take (IRE)

5-y-o b g Kahyasi-Malmada (USA) (Fappiano (USA))
B J Curley Mrs B J Curley

Placings:P-PPP (2897)
2001/02: 16^{P}F, 16^{P}HY, 20^{P}S

	Starts	1st	2nd	3rd	Win & Pl
Hurdles	3	0	0	0	
Career Total	**4**	**0**	**0**	**0**	

Going: Sf: 0-2 GS: 0-0 Gd: 0-0 GF: - Fm: 0-1
Distance: 2m/2m3: 0-2 2m4-2m7: 0-1 3m+: 0-0
Track: LH: 0-1 RH: 0-2 Tight: 0-1 Gall: 0-0
Aids: Bl: 0-0 Vi: 0-0 Tstrap: 0-0
Best Rating:

One Domino

107 98

5-y-o ch g Efisio-Dom One (Dominion)
M Dods North Briton Racing

Placings:3340-40421 (3350)
2001/02: 16^{4}G, 16^{0}G, 16^{4}G, 20^{2}G, 20^{1}G

	Starts	1st	2nd	3rd	Win & Pl
Hurdles	5	1	1	0	3214
Career Total	**9**	**1**	**1**	**2**	**3960**

98 1/02 Muss 2m4f G Hdl GD £2341
Total win prize-money £2342

Going: Sf: 0-0 GS: 0-0 Gd: 1-5 GF: - Fm: 0-0
Distance: 2m/2m3: 0-3 **2m4-2m7: 1-2** 3m+: 0-0
Track: LH: 0-2 **RH: 1-3 Tight: 1-4** Gall: 0-0
Aids: Bl: 1-1 Vi: 0-1 Tstrap: 0-0
Best Rating: 98 1/02 Muss 2m4f good Hdl

One paced hurdler, suited by a decent surface, stays two and a half miles. Easy winner of a seller in January in first-time blinkers.

One Knight (IRE)

111 134

6-y-o ch g Roselier (FR)-Midnights Daughter (IRE) (Long Pond)
P J Hobbs R Gibbs

Placings:*131*-1136 (3262)
2001/02: 20^{1}S, 20^{1}GS, 20^{3}S, 21^{6}S

	Starts	1st	2nd	3rd	Win & Pl
Hurdles	4	2	0	1	15369
Career Total	**7**	**4**	**0**	**2**	**20934**

134 11/01 Chep 2m4f A Hdl G-S £10500
119 10/01 Chep 2m4f E Hdl SFT £2569
119 3/01 Newb 2m110y H NHF HVY £2660
116 11/00 Winc 2m H NHF G-S £1645
Total win prize-money £17374

Going: Sf: 1-3 GS: 1-1 Gd: 0-0 GF: - Fm: 0-0
Distance: 2m/2m3: 0-0 **2m4-2m7: 2-4** 3m+: 0-0
Track: LH: 2-2 RH: 0-1 Tight: 0-0 Gall: 0-0
Aids: Bl: 0-0 Vi: 0-0 Tstrap: 0-0
Best Rating: 134 11/01 Chep 2m4f gd-sft Hdl

A winner of two bumpers in 2000/1, before winning his first two starts over hurdles, both of which at Chepstow over two miles four furlongs, although has failed to run up to his best since then. Stays well and acts in soft ground.

One Life To Live (IRE)

80 58

9-y-o gr g Classic Music (USA)-Fine Flame (Le Prince)
J S Wainwright Philip E Clark

Placings:6400-0P (1273)
2001/02: 16^{0}F, 24^{P}GF

	Starts	1st	2nd	3rd	Win & Pl
Hurdles	2	0	0	0	
Career Total	**6**	**0**	**0**	**0**	**0**

Going: Sf: 0-0 GS: 0-0 Gd: 0-0 GF: - Fm: 0-2
Distance: 2m/2m3: 0-1 2m4-2m7: 0-0 3m+: 0-1
Track: LH: 0-2 RH: 0-0 Tight: 0-1 Gall: 0-0
Aids: Bl: 0-0 Vi: 0-0 Tstrap: 0-0
Best Rating: 69 1/01 Muss 2m4f good Hdl

One Mans Legacy

9-y-o b m One Man Band-Storm Foot (Import)
Mrs Caroline Chadney Mrs Caroline Chadney

Placings:P (4685)
2001/02: 16^{P}GF

	Starts	1st	2nd	3rd	Win & Pl
Chases	1	0	0	0	
Career Total	**1**	**0**	**0**	**0**	

Going: Sf: 0-0 GS: 0-0 Gd: 0-0 GF: - Fm: 0-1
Distance: 2m/2m3: 0-1 2m4-2m7: 0-0 3m+: 0-0

Track: LH: 0-0 RH: 0-1 Tight: 0-0 Gall: 0-0
Aids: Bl: 0-0 Vi: 0-0 Tstrap: 0-0
Best Rating:

One More (IRE)

101(93h) **112**

6-y-o b g Roselier (FR)-Bea Marie (IRE) (King's Ride)
C Grant The Hon Mrs M Faulkner

Placings:365001-F13FF **(3392)**
2001/02: 20^{F}S, 25^{1}GS, 28^{3}S, 24^{F}HY, 25^{F}GS

	Starts	1st	2nd	3rd	Win & Pl
Chases	5	1	0	1	5717
Career Total	**11**	**2**	**0**	**2**	**7854**

112	11/01	Kels	3m1f	D Ch	G-S	£5284
90	2/01	Newc	3m	F(0-100)HHdl	HVY	£1855

Total win prize-money £7140

Going: Sf: 0-3 GS: 1-2 Gd: 0-0 GF: - Fm: 0-0
Distance: 2m/2m3: 0-0 2m4-2m7: 0-1 **3m+: 1-4**
Track: **LH: 1-3** RH: 0-2 **Tight: 1-2** Gall: 0-0
Aids: Bl: 0-0 Vi: 0-0 Tstrap: 0-0
Best Rating: 112 11/01 Kels 3m1f gd-sft Ch

A winner over three miles in heavy ground over hurdles and likes soft ground, but scored at Kelso in November. He looks a real stayer.

One More Dime (IRE)

61 **25**

12-y-o b m Mandalus-Deep Dollar (Deep Run)
J L Needham J L Needham

Placings:0500F0/034334P30/1300F/00PF00P01/3P3 40405/P-0 **(0052)**
2001/02: 20^{0}G

	Starts	1st	2nd	3rd	Win & Pl
Hurdles	1	0	0	0	
Career Total	**39**	**2**	**0**	**7**	**8115**

93	4/99	Ludl	2m5f110y	E(0-115)HHdl	G-S	£3200
72	5/97	Ludl	2m5f110y	E(0-100)HHdl	G-F	£2075

Total win prize-money £5275

Going: Sf: 0-0 GS: 0-0 Gd: 0-1 GF: - Fm: 0-0
Distance: 2m/2m3: 0-0 2m4-2m7: 0-1 3m+: 0-0
Track: LH: 0-1 RH: 0-0 Tight: 0-1 Gall: 0-0
Aids: Bl: 0-0 Vi: 0-0 Tstrap: 0-0
Best Rating: 93 4/99 Ludl 2m5f110y gd-sft Hdl

One Nation (IRE)

104(113h) **120**

7-y-o br g Be My Native (USA)-Diklers Run (Deep Run)
Miss H C Knight The Earl Cadogan

Placings:3/24F211/144134-23 **(2068)**
2001/02: 17^{2}G, 20^{3}G

	Starts	1st	2nd	3rd	Win & Pl
Chases	2	0	1	1	1991
Career Total	**15**	**4**	**3**	**3**	**24293**

129	1/01	Winc	2m	D(0-125)HHdl	SFT	£5187
121	10/00	Hrfd	2m1f	D(0-120)HHdl	GD	£2977
115	4/00	Winc	2m	E Hdl	G-S	£2604
112	3/00	Hntg	2m110y	E Hdl	SFT	£2440

Total win prize-money £13208

Going: Sf: 0-0 GS: 0-0 Gd: 0-2 GF: - Fm: 0-0
Distance: 2m/2m3: 0-1 2m4-2m7: 0-1 3m+: 0-0
Track: LH: 0-0 RH: 0-2 Tight: 0-0 Gall: 0-1
Aids: Bl: 0-0 Vi: 0-0 Tstrap: 0-0
Best Rating: 131 2/01 Asct 2m4f heavy Hdl

An imposing sort who did really well over hurdles, he ran a decent race to finish behind St Pirran on his chasing debut, but looked to need further. However, when stepped up in trip at Huntingdon next time, his jumping lacked fluency. All his wins so far have been on right-handed tracks.

One Of The Natives (IRE)

100 **100d**

8-y-o b g Be My Native (USA)-Take Me Home (Amoristic (USA))
Miss H C Knight (P F Nicholls 11/5) Miss Judy Pimblett

Placings:50/P-P34F **(4545)**
2001/02: 21^{P}GF, 24^{3}S, 20^{4}S, 19^{F}G

	Starts	1st	2nd	3rd	Win & Pl
Chases	4	0	0	1	976
Career Total	**7**	**0**	**0**	**1**	**976**

Going: Sf: 0-2 GS: 0-0 Gd: 0-1 GF: - Fm: 0-1
Distance: 2m/2m3: 0-1 2m4-2m7: 0-2 3m+: 0-1
Track: LH: 0-0 RH: 0-4 Tight: 0-1 Gall: 0-0
Aids: Bl: 0-0 Vi: 0-0 Tstrap: 0-0
Best Rating: 105 2/02 Tntn 3m soft Ch

One Stop

104 **89**

9-y-o b m Silly Prices-Allerdale (Cheb's Lad)
M A Barnes Michael Brennan

Placings:20F0/002223P66P/0560404160/34201300/0 012-42634P **(4524)**
2001/02: 17^{4}HY, 16^{2}S, 17^{6}S, 17^{3}S, 16^{4}HY, 17^{P}G

	Starts	1st	2nd	3rd	Win & Pl
Hurdles	6	0	1	1	2581
Career Total	**42**	**3**	**7**	**4**	**14477**

89	2/01	Carl	2m1f	D(0-120)HHdl	SFT	£3311
89	2/00	Newc	2m	G(0-95)HHdl	SFT	£1554
71	3/99	Newc	2m	F Hdl	SFT	£2305

Total win prize-money £7171

Going: Sf: 0-5 GS: 0-0 Gd: 0-1 GF: - Fm: 0-0
Distance: 2m/2m3: 0-6 2m4-2m7: 0-0 3m+: 0-0
Track: LH: 0-3 RH: 0-3 Tight: 0-1 Gall: 0-0
Aids: Bl: 0-0 Vi: 0-0 Tstrap: 0-0
Best Rating: 89 12/01 Hexm 2m soft Hdl

A fair handicap hurdler on easy ground, and goes well at Newcastle.

Oneanthreequarters (IRE)

87 **104**

10-y-o ch g King Luthier-Khaki Kate (Brigadier Gerard)
G Brown Tom Segrue

Placings:61F1333P6/P46031/P0P223P422-000 **(0723)**
2001/02: 19^{0}GS, 18^{0}GF, 25^{0}F

	Starts	1st	2nd	3rd	Win & Pl
Chases	3	0	0	0	
Career Total	**28**	**3**	**4**	**5**	**15604**

102	4/00	Sedg	2m5f	E(0-115)HCh	GD	£3523
117	10/98	Hrfd	3m1f110y	E(0-120)Ch	G-F	£2736
96	8/98	Ctml	2m5f110y	E Ch	GD	£2929

Total win prize-money £9188

Going: Sf: 0-0 GS: 0-1 Gd: 0-0 GF: - Fm: 0-2
Distance: 2m/2m3: 0-1 2m4-2m7: 0-1 3m+: 0-1
Track: LH: 0-0 RH: 0-2 Tight: 0-1 Gall: 0-0
Aids: Bl: 0-1 Vi: 0-0 Tstrap: 0-0
Best Rating: 117 10/98 Hrfd 3m1f110y gd-fm Ch

Onefourseven

104 **85**

9-y-o b g Jumbo Hirt (USA)-Dominance (Dominion)
F S Storey F S Storey

Placings:2224500 **(2342)**
2001/02: 19^{2}G, 21^{2}GF, 21^{2}GF, 24^{4}G, 20^{5}S, 20^{0}G, 16^{0}GS

	Starts	1st	2nd	3rd	Win & Pl
Hurdles	7	0	3	0	2588
Career Total	**7**	**0**	**3**	**0**	**2588**

Going: Sf: 0-1 GS: 0-1 Gd: 0-3 GF: - Fm: 0-2
Distance: 2m/2m3: 0-1 2m4-2m7: 0-5 3m+: 0-1
Track: LH: 0-4 RH: 0-2 Tight: 0-3 Gall: 0-2
Aids: Bl: 0-0 Vi: 0-0 Tstrap: 0-0
Best Rating: 85 11/01 Newc 2m4f good Hdl

Ones Enough

6-y-o b g Reprimand-Sea Fairy (Wollow)
T P McGovern Heart Of The South Racing

Placings:P **(0875)**
2001/02: 16^{P}GS

	Starts	1st	2nd	3rd	Win & Pl
Hurdles	1	0	0	0	
Career Total	**1**	**0**	**0**	**0**	

Going: Sf: 0-0 GS: 0-1 Gd: 0-0 GF: - Fm: 0-0
Distance: 2m/2m3: 0-1 2m4-2m7: 0-0 3m+: 0-0
Track: LH: 0-1 RH: 0-0 Tight: 0-1 Gall: 0-0
Aids: Bl: 0-0 Vi: 0-0 Tstrap: 0-0
Best Rating:

Only When Provoked (IRE)

102 **75**

4-y-o b g General Monash (USA)-Lyzia (IRE) (Lycius (USA))
A Streeter The Saturday Lunchtime Syndicate

Placings:6340033 **(4904)**
2001/02: 17^{6}G, 17^{3}G, 17^{4}G, 16^{0}GF, 17^{0}GS, 17^{3}G, 17^{3}G

	Starts	1st	2nd	3rd	Win & Pl
Hurdles	7	0	0	3	952
Career Total	**7**	**0**	**0**	**3**	**952**

Going: Sf: 0-0 GS: 0-1 Gd: 0-5 GF: - Fm: 0-1
Distance: 2m/2m3: 0-7 2m4-2m7: 0-0 3m+: 0-0
Track: LH: 0-4 RH: 0-3 Tight: 0-5 Gall: 0-0
Aids: Bl: 0-1 Vi: 0-2 Tstrap: 0-0
Best Rating: 75 4/02 MRas 2m1f110y good Hdl

Only Words (USA)

99 **82**

5-y-o ch g Shuailaan (USA)-Conversation Piece (USA) (Seeking The Gold (USA))
A J Lockwood Mrs Lynne Lumley

Placings:500356 **(4904)**

2001/02: 16^{5}S, 19^{0}G, 16^{0}GS, 17^{3}GS, 16^{5}GF, 17^{6}G

Starts		1st	2nd	3rd	Win & Pl
Hurdles	6	0	0	1	246
Career Total	**6**	**0**	**0**	**1**	**246**

Going: Sf: 0-1 GS: 0-2 Gd: 0-2 GF: - Fm: 0-1
Distance: 2m/2m3: 0-6 2m4-2m7: 0-0 3m+: 0-0
Track: LH: 0-3 RH: 0-3 Tight: 0-3 Gall: 0-1
Aids: Bl: 0-0 Vi: 0-0 Tstrap: 0-0
Best Rating: 82 3/02 MRas 2m1f110y gd-sft Hdl

Plating-class maiden hurdler.

Only You

100 **76**

6-y-o b g Gildoran-Outfield (Monksfield)
N A Twiston-Davies Roger Nicholls

Placings:*0*FP-5U00554PU4326 **(4898)**
2001/02: 20^{5}GF, 20^{U}GF, 20^{0}G, 19^{0}GF, 19^{5}GF, 26^{5}G, 20^{4}HY, 16^{P}HY, 20^{U}GS, 17^{4}G, 21^{3}GF, 20^{2}G, 16^{6}G

Starts		1st	2nd	3rd	Win & Pl
Hurdles	13	0	1	1	810
Career Total	**16**	**0**	**1**	**1**	**810**

Going: Sf: 0-2 GS: 0-1 Gd: 0-5 GF: - Fm: 0-5
Distance: 2m/2m3: 0-5 2m4-2m7: 0-7 3m+: 0-1
Track: LH: 0-3 RH: 0-9 Tight: 0-2 Gall: 0-3
Aids: Bl: 0-0 Vi: 0-0 Tstrap: 0-0
Best Rating: 76 4/02 Uttx 2m4f110y good Hdl

Plating-class hurdler. Suited by two and a half miles and fast ground.

Oo Ee Be

95 **79**

6-y-o b g Whittingham (IRE)-Miss Derby (USA) (Master Derby (USA))
M J M Evans Mrs J Z Munday

Placings:050304/5-00204 **(4542)**
2001/02: 16^{0}S, 16^{0}S, 17^{2}S, 17^{0}S, 17^{4}G

Starts		1st	2nd	3rd	Win & Pl
Hurdles	5	0	1	0	507
Career Total	**12**	**0**	**1**	**1**	**1105**

Going: Sf: 0-4 GS: 0-0 Gd: 0-1 GF: - Fm: 0-0
Distance: 2m/2m3: 0-5 2m4-2m7: 0-0 3m+: 0-0
Track: LH: 0-2 RH: 0-3 Tight: 0-3 Gall: 0-0
Aids: Bl: 0-0 Vi: 0-0 Tstrap: 0-0
Best Rating: 81 3/00 Extr 2m1f110y gd-fm Hdl

Modest maiden hurdler who appreciates patient tactics.

Oorain Elsie

7-y-o ch m Destroyer-Oorain Lass (Lord Nelson (FR))
Mrs D Thomson Mrs Dorothy Thomson

Placings:PPP **(4875)**
2001/02: 16^{P}S, 24^{P}HY, 24^{P}G

Starts		1st	2nd	3rd	Win & Pl
Hurdles	3	0	0	0	
Career Total	**3**	**0**	**0**	**0**	

Going: Sf: 0-2 GS: 0-0 Gd: 0-1 GF: - Fm: 0-0
Distance: 2m/2m3: 0-1 2m4-2m7: 0-0 3m+: 0-2
Track: LH: 0-2 RH: 0-1 Tight: 0-0 Gall: 0-1
Aids: Bl: 0-0 Vi: 0-0 Tstrap: 0-0
Best Rating:

Opal'Lou (FR)

101 **109**

6-y-o b m Garde Royale-Calligraphie (FR) (Rb Chesne)
P F Nicholls (E Sotteau 2/7) Formpave Ltd

Placings:5060/250040F-32363636 **(2410)**
2001/02: 17^{3}, 19^{2}, 16^{3}G, 16^{6}G, 16^{3}F, 16^{6}S, 21^{3}GF, 19^{6}GS

Starts		1st	2nd	3rd	Win & Pl
Hurdles	5	0	1	3	4160
Chases	3	0	0	1	660
Career Total	**19**	**0**	**2**	**4**	**7875**

Going: Sf: 0-1 GS: 0-1 Gd: 0-2 GF: - Fm: 0-2
Distance: 2m/2m3: 0-7 2m4-2m7: 0-1 3m+: 0-0
Track: LH: 0-1 RH: 0-2 Tight: 0-2 Gall: 0-0
Aids: Bl: 0-0 Vi: 0-0 Tstrap: 0-0
Best Rating: 109 11/01 Winc 2m5f gd-fm Ch

Well beaten behind Mr Cool at Newton Abbot on her debut.

Open Arms

97 **96**

6-y-o ch g Most Welcome-Amber Fizz (USA) (Effervescing (USA))
Mrs A L M King (J J O'Neill 25/1) Aiden Murphy

Placings:600 **(3469)**
2001/02: 16^{6}G, 16^{0}GS, 16^{0}S

Starts		1st	2nd	3rd	Win & Pl
Hurdles	3	0	0	0	0
Career Total	**3**	**0**	**0**	**0**	**0**

Going: Sf: 0-1 GS: 0-1 Gd: 0-1 GF: - Fm: 0-0
Distance: 2m/2m3: 0-3 2m4-2m7: 0-0 3m+: 0-0
Track: LH: 0-1 RH: 0-2 Tight: 0-0 Gall: 0-2
Aids: Bl: 0-0 Vi: 0-0 Tstrap: 0-0
Best Rating: 96 1/02 Winc 2m good Hdl

Open Ground (IRE)

110 **116**

5-y-o ch g Common Grounds-Poplina (USA) (Roberto (USA))
Ian Williams The Net Partnership

Placings:61161405-055110 **(4178)**
2001/02: 20^{0}GS, 16^{5}GS, 16^{5}S, 16^{1}S, 16^{1}S, 16^{0}GS

Starts		1st	2nd	3rd	Win & Pl
Hurdles	6	2	0	0	5512
Career Total	**14**	**5**	**0**	**0**	**16020**

116	3/02	Newb	2m110y	C(0-130)HHdl	SFT	£5512
118	1/01	Wwck	2m	D Hdl	SFT	£4777
110	11/00	MRas	2m1f110y	E Hdl	SFT	£2534
89	11/00	Wwck	2m	E Hdl	HVY	£2261

Total win prize-money £15085

Going: Sf: 2-3 GS: 0-3 Gd: 0-0 GF: - Fm: 0-0
Distance: **2m/2m3: 2-5** 2m4-2m7: 0-1 3m+: 0-0
Track: **LH: 2-6** RH: 0-0 Tight: 0-2 **Gall: 1-2**
Aids: Bl: 0-0 **Vi: 2-3** Tstrap: 0-0
Best Rating: 118 1/01 Donc 2m110y good Hdl

A confirmed mudlark, who has won on the Flat and over hurdles. Effective at around two miles over hurdles. Has been successful in a visor.

Open Invitation (IRE)

53(63c) (36c)**15**

8-y-o b g Hollow Hand-Nohoval Jane (Amoristic (USA))
P J Millington P J Millington

Placings:PP0 **(0430)**
2001/02: 25^{P}G, 20^{P}GF, 16^{0}G

Starts		1st	2nd	3rd	Win & Pl
Chases	3	0	0	0	
Career Total	**3**	**0**	**0**	**0**	

Going: Sf: 0-0 GS: 0-0 Gd: 0-2 GF: - Fm: 0-1
Distance: 2m/2m3: 0-1 2m4-2m7: 0-1 3m+: 0-1
Track: LH: 0-2 RH: 0-0 Tight: 0-1 Gall: 0-0
Aids: Bl: 0-0 Vi: 0-0 Tstrap: 0-0
Best Rating: 36 5/01 Chel 2m110y good Ch

Open The Box

6-y-o b m Teenoso (USA)-School Run (Deep Run)
Mrs H Dalton Mrs Jane Thornton

Placings:*00*P-P **(0844)**
2001/02: 19^{P}GF

Starts		1st	2nd	3rd	Win & Pl
Hurdles	1	0	0	0	
Career Total	**4**	**0**	**0**	**0**	

Going: Sf: 0-0 GS: 0-0 Gd: 0-0 GF: - Fm: 0-1
Distance: 2m/2m3: 0-1 2m4-2m7: 0-0 3m+: 0-0
Track: LH: 0-1 RH: 0-0 Tight: 0-1 Gall: 0-0
Aids: Bl: 0-0 Vi: 0-0 Tstrap: 0-0
Best Rating: 76 10/00 Chel 2m110y good NHF

Opening Bat

6-y-o b g Batshoof-Absalantra (Absalom)
Miss Z C Davison Mrs Gail Davison

Placings:*000* **(3154)**
2001/02: 17^{0}S, 17^{0}S, 18^{0}G

Starts		1st	2nd	3rd	Win & Pl
NH Flat	3	0	0	0	
Career Total	**3**	**0**	**0**	**0**	

Going: Sf: 0-2 GS: 0-0 Gd: 0-1 GF: - Fm: 0-0
Distance: 2m/2m3: 0-3 2m4-2m7: 0-0 3m+: 0-0
Track: LH: 0-1 RH: 0-0 Tight: 0-3 Gall: 0-0
Aids: Bl: 0-0 Vi: 0-0 Tstrap: 0-0
Best Rating: 54 12/01 Folk 2m1f110y soft NHF

Opening Range

11-y-o b m Nordico (USA)-Waveguide (Double Form)
R Williams R Williams

Placings:P/P **(4265)**
2001/02: 20^{P}S

Starts		1st	2nd	3rd	Win & Pl
Hurdles	1	0	0	0	
Career Total	**2**	**0**	**0**	**0**	

Going: Sf: 0-1 GS: 0-0 Gd: 0-0 GF: - Fm: 0-0
Distance: 2m/2m3: 0-0 2m4-2m7: 0-1 3m+: 0-0
Track: LH: 0-1 RH: 0-0 Tight: 0-0 Gall: 0-0
Aids: Bl: 0-0 Vi: 0-0 Tstrap: 0-0
Best Rating:

Optimistic Chris

97(104h) (109h)119

7-y-o b g Pharly (FR)-Gay Twenties (Lord Gayle (USA))

A Streeter Optimistic Racing

Placings:1416/235P36/004523-15101 **(4843)**

2001/02: 19^{1}S, 19^{5}GS, 20^{1}G, 20^{0}HY, 17^{1}G

	Starts	1st	2nd	3rd	Win & Pl
Hurdles	3	1	0	0	3178
Chases	2	2	0	0	8723
Career Total	**21**	**5**	**2**	**3**	**23839**

119	4/02	Bang	2m1f110y	D Ch	GD	£4485
110	12/01	Ludl	2m4f	D(0-115)HCh	GD	£4238
109	9/01	MRas	2m3f110y	E(0-115)HHdl	SFT	£3178
112	2/99	Kels	2m110y	C Hdl	SFT	£5359
96	12/98	Uttx	2m	G Hdl	SFT	£1658

Total win prize-money £18919

Going: Sf: 1-2 GS: 0-1 Gd: 2-2 GF: - Fm: 0-0
Distance: 2m/2m3: 1-2 **2m4-2m7: 2-3** 3m+: 0-0
Track: LH: 1-3 **RH: 2-2 Tight: 3-4** Gall: 0-0
Aids: Bl: 0-0 Vi: 0-1 Tstrap: 0-0
Best Rating: 119 4/02 Bang 2m1f110y good Ch

Fair chaser, won three races over fencesin 2001/02 and turned in a career best effort at Bangor in April. Acts on good ground or softer.

Optimistic Thinker

94(104h) (102h)125

8-y-o ch g Beveled (USA)-Racemosa (Town Crier)

T R George M R C Opperman

Placings:102P61P/2223/412P1UP6-P234014P **(4587)**

2001/02: 16^{P}G, 17^{2}S, 16^{3}G, 16^{4}S, 16^{0}G, 16^{1}GS, 17^{4}S, 16^{P}G

	Starts	1st	2nd	3rd	Win & Pl
Hurdles	5	0	1	1	1423
Chases	3	1	0	0	4212
Career Total	**27**	**5**	**6**	**2**	**21409**

125	1/02	Hntg	2m110y	D(0-115)HCh	G-S	£3893
128	11/00	Uttx	2m	D Ch	HVY	£3944
123	10/00	Hntg	2m110y	E(0-105)HCh	G-F	£3052
103	3/99	NAbb	2m1f	F(0-100)HHdl	SFT	£1760
109	10/98	MRas	1m5f110y	H NHF	HVY	£1234

Total win prize-money £13886

Going: Sf: 0-3 GS: 1-1 Gd: 0-4 GF: - Fm: 0-0
Distance: **2m/2m3: 1-8** 2m4-2m7: 0-0 3m+: 0-0
Track: LH: 0-2 **RH: 1-6** Tight: 0-1 **Gall: 1-1**
Aids: Bl: 0-1 Vi: 0-0 Tstrap: 0-0
Best Rating: 128 11/00 Uttx 2m heavy Ch

A winner of a bumper, over hurdles and over fences. Made a winning return to fences in January 2002 after some moderate efforts over hurdles. Acts on most types of ground and is effective at around two miles.

Or Royal (FR)

11-y-o gr g Kendor (FR)-Pomme Royale (FR) (Shergar)

R Lee Mrs C Lee

Placings:1/111213/333220/336R30PR/53125RP/613PR60R-R **(0840)**

2001/02: 20^{R}G

	Starts	1st	2nd	3rd	Win & Pl
Hurdles	1	0	0	0	
Career Total	**37**	**7**	**4**	**9**	**166757**

129	5/00	Weth	2m4f110y	F Hdl	G-S	£1820
146	10/99	Weth	2m	C(0-135)HHdl	GD	£4792
157	3/97	Chel	2m	A Ch	GD	£53762
135	12/96	Chep	2m3f110y	D Ch	G-S	£3689
117	11/96	Chep	2m110y	E Ch	G-S	£3070

Total win prize-money £67136

Going: Sf: 0-0 GS: 0-0 Gd: 0-1 GF: - Fm: 0-0
Distance: 2m/2m3: 0-0 2m4-2m7: 0-1 3m+: 0-0
Track: LH: 0-1 RH: 0-0 Tight: 0-0 Gall: 0-0
Aids: Bl: 0-0 Vi: 0-1 Tstrap: 0-0
Best Rating: 171 3/98 Chel 2m good Ch

Once a top novice chaser (won the Arkle Chase in 1997), he now runs mostly on the Flat and has been successful in modest staying events.

Orange Alert

8-y-o b m Gildoran-Special Venture (Giolla Mear)

G B Balding Mrs J Greaves

Placings:000U **(4485)**

2001/02: 19^{U}G

	Starts	1st	2nd	3rd	Win & Pl
Hurdles	1	0	0	0	
Career Total	**4**	**0**	**0**	**0**	

Going: Sf: 0-0 GS: 0-0 Gd: 0-1 GF: - Fm: 0-0
Distance: 2m/2m3: 0-1 2m4-2m7: 0-0 3m+: 0-0
Track: LH: 0-0 RH: 0-1 Tight: 0-0 Gall: 0-0
Aids: Bl: 0-0 Vi: 0-0 Tstrap: 0-0
Best Rating: 85 11/99 Worc 2m gd-sft NHF

Orange Order (IRE)

110(85h) 125

9-y-o ch g Generous (IRE)-Fleur D'Oranger (Northfields (USA))

G M Moore Mrs A Roddis

Placings:6P/62106504/013502060L00/11615062/1135433150-**4214123F3** **(1350)**

2001/02: 21^{4}G, 16^{2}F, 20^{1}GF, 20^{4}G, 20^{1}GF, 21^{2}GF, 20^{3}G, 24^{F}GF, 21^{3}GF

	Starts	1st	2nd	3rd	Win & Pl
Chases	9	2	2	2	11098
Career Total	**49**	**10**	**5**	**6**	**34809**

111	7/01	Wolv	2m4f110y	E Ch	G-F	£3376
125	6/01	MRas	2m4f	E Ch	G-F	£3851
119	9/00	Sedg	2m5f110y	D(0-120)HHdl	GD	£3575
114	5/00	Weth	2m	E(0-115)HHdl	G-S	£2485
101	5/00	Sedg	2m1f	F(0-100)HHdl	G-F	£2492
102	9/99	Sedg	2m1f	G(0-95)HHdl	G-F	£2066
102	7/99	Sedg	2m1f	G(0-95)HHdl	G-F	£1884
100	7/99	Sedg	2m1f	F(0-100)HHdl	G-F	£2010
109	6/98	Tral	2m	(0-102)Hdl	GD	£2382
102	9/97	Clon	2m	Hdl	Y-S	£2543

Total win prize-money £26666

Going: Sf: 0-0 GS: 0-0 Gd: 0-3 GF: - Fm: 2-6
Distance: 2m/2m3: 0-1 **2m4-2m7: 2-7** 3m+: 0-1
Track: LH: 1-8 RH: 1-1 **Tight: 2-7** Gall: 0-0
Aids: Bl: 0-0 Vi: 0-0 Tstrap: 0-0
Best Rating: 125 6/01 MRas 2m4f gd-fm Ch

Sedgefield specialist over hurdles, has taken time to find his feet over fences. Suited by fast ground.

Orange Place (IRE)

107 94

11-y-o ch g Nordance (USA)-Little Red Hut (Habitat)

B J Llewellyn Lodge Cross Partnership

Placings:0/P/45422/063/00-2032 **(2711)**

2001/02: 17^{2}GS, 17^{0}G, 16^{3}S, 16^{2}HY

	Starts	1st	2nd	3rd	Win & Pl
Hurdles	4	0	2	1	1628
Career Total	**16**	**0**	**4**	**2**	**3167**

Going: Sf: 0-2 GS: 0-1 Gd: 0-1 GF: - Fm: 0-0
Distance: 2m/2m3: 0-4 2m4-2m7: 0-0 3m+: 0-0
Track: LH: 0-1 RH: 0-3 Tight: 0-2 Gall: 0-0
Aids: Bl: 0-0 Vi: 0-0 Tstrap: 0-0
Best Rating: 100 1/00 Leic 2m soft Hdl

Has proved difficult to win with.

Orangerie (IRE)

93 99

4-y-o b g Darshaan-Fleur D'Oranger (Northfields (USA))

P J Hobbs (Sir Mark Prescott 4/10) Richard Green (fine Paintings)

Placings:4 **(3584)**

2001/02: 16^{4}S

	Starts	1st	2nd	3rd	Win & Pl
Hurdles	1	0	0	0	335
Career Total	**1**	**0**	**0**	**0**	**335**

Going: Sf: 0-1 GS: 0-0 Gd: 0-0 GF: - Fm: 0-0
Distance: 2m/2m3: 0-1 2m4-2m7: 0-0 3m+: 0-0
Track: LH: 0-0 RH: 0-1 Tight: 0-0 Gall: 0-0
Aids: Bl: 0-0 Vi: 0-0 Tstrap: 0-0
Best Rating: 99 2/02 Sand 2m110y soft Hdl

Orbicularis (IRE)

6-y-o b g Supreme Leader-Liffey Travel (Le Bavard (FR))

R F Fisher Great Head House Estates Limited

Placings:000 **(2402)**

2001/02: 17^{0}GS, 17^{0}S, 17^{0}HY

	Starts	1st	2nd	3rd	Win & Pl
NH Flat	2	0	0	0	0
Hurdles	1	0	0	0	0
Career Total	**3**	**0**	**0**	**0**	

Going: Sf: 0-2 GS: 0-1 Gd: 0-0 GF: - Fm: 0-0
Distance: 2m/2m3: 0-3 2m4-2m7: 0-0 3m+: 0-0
Track: LH: 0-0 RH: 0-3 Tight: 0-0 Gall: 0-0
Aids: Bl: 0-0 Vi: 0-0 Tstrap: 0-0
Best Rating: 87 10/01 Carl 2m1f gd-sft NHF

Orchard Fields (IRE)

99f 100f

5-y-o b g Lord Americo-Art Lover (IRE) (Over The River (FR))

J G Fitzgerald J G Fitzgerald

Placings:06 **(2181)**

2001/02: 16^{0}S, 16^{6}G

	Starts	1st	2nd	3rd	Win & Pl
NH Flat	2	0	0	0	0
Career Total	**2**	**0**	**0**	**0**	**0**

Going: Sf: 0-1 GS: 0-0 Gd: 0-1 GF: - Fm: 0-0
Distance: 2m/2m3: 0-2 2m4-2m7: 0-0 3m+: 0-0
Track: LH: 0-2 RH: 0-0 Tight: 0-0 Gall: 0-0
Aids: Bl: 0-0 Vi: 0-0 Tstrap: 0-0
Best Rating: 100 11/01 Hayd 2m soft NHF

Orchard Wonder

5-y-o ch m Opera Ghost-Happy Wonder (Levanter)
Mrs A Duffield John E F Skelton

Placings:*0* **(4790)**
2001/02: 16^{0}F

	Starts	1st	2nd	3rd	Win & Pl
NH Flat	1	0	0	0	
Career Total	**1**	**0**	**0**	**0**	

Going: Sf: 0-0 GS: 0-0 Gd: 0-0 GF: - Fm: 0-1
Distance: 2m/2m3: 0-1 2m4-2m7: 0-0 3m+: 0-0
Track: LH: 0-0 RH: 0-0 Tight: 0-0 Gall: 0-0
Aids: Bl: 0-0 Vi: 0-0 Tstrap: 0-0
Best Rating:

Orchestra's Boy (IRE)

7-y-o b g Homo Sapien-Ballycurnane Lady (Orchestra)
Mrs A M Thorpe Mrs A M Thorpe

Placings:*0200* **(2456)**
2001/02: 16^{0}G, 16^{2}G, 16^{0}GS, 21^{0}S

	Starts	1st	2nd	3rd	Win & Pl
NH Flat	3	0	1	0	422
Hurdles	1	0	0	0	0
Career Total	**4**	**0**	**1**	**0**	**422**

Going: Sf: 0-1 GS: 0-1 Gd: 0-2 GF: - Fm: 0-0
Distance: 2m/2m3: 0-3 2m4-2m7: 0-1 3m+: 0-0
Track: LH: 0-2 RH: 0-1 Tight: 0-0 Gall: 0-0
Aids: Bl: 0-0 Vi: 0-0 Tstrap: 0-0
Best Rating: 93 7/01 Worc 2m good NHF

Order Of Malta

70 **26**

8-y-o ch m Baron Blakeney-Yuan Princess (Tender King)
J L Spearing N F Williams

Placings:*0-0U0* **(1075)**
2001/02: 17^{0}G, 17^{U}GF, 19^{0}GF

	Starts	1st	2nd	3rd	Win & Pl
Hurdles	3	0	0	0	
Career Total	**4**	**0**	**0**	**0**	

Going: Sf: 0-0 GS: 0-0 Gd: 0-1 GF: - Fm: 0-2
Distance: 2m/2m3: 0-3 2m4-2m7: 0-0 3m+: 0-0
Track: LH: 0-2 RH: 0-1 Tight: 0-2 Gall: 0-0
Aids: Bl: 0-0 Vi: 0-0 Tstrap: 0-0
Best Rating: 26 5/01 Hrfd 2m1f good Hdl

Orient Bay (IRE)

7-y-o b g Commanche Run-East Link (IRE) (Over The River (FR))
T P Tate Mrs M Dickinson

Placings:*4-U* **(0340)**
2001/02: 25^{U}G

	Starts	1st	2nd	3rd	Win & Pl
Chases	1	0	0	0	
Career Total	**2**	**0**	**0**	**0**	**0**

Going: Sf: 0-0 GS: 0-0 Gd: 0-1 GF: - Fm: 0-0
Distance: 2m/2m3: 0-0 2m4-2m7: 0-0 3m+: 0-1

Track: LH: 0-1 RH: 0-0 Tight: 0-1 Gall: 0-0
Aids: Bl: 0-0 Vi: 0-0 Tstrap: 0-0
Best Rating: 92 5/00 Prth 2m110y gd-sft NHF

Oriental Boy (IRE)

10-y-o b g Boreen (FR)-Arctic Sue (Arctic Slave)
P Monteith Oriental Boy Partnership

Placings:*00/P052/F12214/PFFP26/036-0* **(2121)**
2001/02: 22^{0}GS

	Starts	1st	2nd	3rd	Win & Pl
Hurdles	1	0	0	0	
Career Total	**22**	**2**	**4**	**1**	**14646**

116 3/99 Wwck 2m4f110y C HCh SFT £6840
116 11/98 NAbb 2m5f110y E(0-100)HCh SFT £3134
Total win prize-money £9974

Going: Sf: 0-0 GS: 0-1 Gd: 0-0 GF: - Fm: 0-0
Distance: 2m/2m3: 0-0 2m4-2m7: 0-1 3m+: 0-0
Track: LH: 0-1 RH: 0-0 Tight: 0-1 Gall: 0-0
Aids: Bl: 0-0 Vi: 0-0 Tstrap: 0-0
Best Rating: 116 1/00 Sthl 2m4f110y gd-sft Ch

Oriental Mist (IRE)

85 **54**

4-y-o gr g Balla Cove-Donna Katrina (King's Lake (USA))
Miss L A Perratt Oriental Mist Partnership

Placings:50P **(3504)**
2001/02: 16^{5}G, 16^{0}S, 16^{P}S

	Starts	1st	2nd	3rd	Win & Pl
Hurdles	3	0	0	0	
Career Total	**3**	**0**	**0**	**0**	**0**

Going: Sf: 0-2 GS: 0-0 Gd: 0-1 GF: - Fm: 0-0
Distance: 2m/2m3: 0-3 2m4-2m7: 0-0 3m+: 0-0
Track: LH: 0-1 RH: 0-2 Tight: 0-2 Gall: 0-1
Aids: Bl: 0-0 Vi: 0-0 Tstrap: 0-0
Best Rating: 54 12/01 Muss 2m good Hdl

Oriental Style (IRE)

111 **108**

8-y-o ro g Indian Ridge-Bazaar Promise (Native Bazaar)
P R Rodford (G B Balding 13/2) Les Trott

Placings:55033/55042U442123/54/651P4B3 **(4503)**
2001/02: 20^{6}G, 20^{5}S, 20^{1}S, 22^{P}HY, 20^{4}S, 25^{B}S, 26^{3}G

	Starts	1st	2nd	3rd	Win & Pl
Chases	7	1	0	1	3837
Career Total	**26**	**2**	**3**	**4**	**11299**

108 1/02 Wwck 2m4f110y F(0-90)HCh SFT £2705
98 3/99 NAbb 2m5f110y E(0-115)HCh SFT £2788
Total win prize-money £5494

Going: Sf: 1-5 GS: 0-0 Gd: 0-2 GF: - Fm: 0-0
Distance: 2m/2m3: 0-0 **2m4-2m7: 1-5** 3m+: 0-2
Track: **LH: 1-4** RH: 0-2 Tight: 0-4 Gall: 0-0
Aids: **Bl: 1-5** Vi: 0-2 Tstrap: 0-0
Best Rating: 108 3/02 NAbb 3m2f110y good Ch

Returned to form in blinkers in a handicap chase at Warwick in January 2002, but he was held next time at Leicester. Soft ground and two and a half miles suit.

Orinoco's Flight (IRE)

72 **37**

4-y-o ch g Spectrum (IRE)-Silk Route (USA) (Shahrastani (USA))
J J O'Neill (J G Given 5/11) C D Carr

Placings:0P **(3860)**
2001/02: 16^{0}S, 20^{P}S

	Starts	1st	2nd	3rd	Win & Pl
Hurdles	2	0	0	0	
Career Total	**2**	**0**	**0**	**0**	

Going: Sf: 0-2 GS: 0-0 Gd: 0-0 GF: - Fm: 0-0
Distance: 2m/2m3: 0-1 2m4-2m7: 0-1 3m+: 0-0
Track: LH: 0-2 RH: 0-0 Tight: 0-1 Gall: 0-1
Aids: Bl: 0-0 Vi: 0-0 Tstrap: 0-0
Best Rating: 37 1/02 Catt 2m soft Hdl

Orlando Sunrise (IRE)

96 **93**

5-y-o ch m Dolphin Street (FR)-Miss Belgravia (USA) (Smarten (USA))
Ian Williams Charles Eden

Placings:3060 **(3645)**
2001/02: 16^{3}GS, 17^{0}G, 16^{6}S, 16^{0}S

	Starts	1st	2nd	3rd	Win & Pl
Hurdles	4	0	0	1	471
Career Total	**4**	**0**	**0**	**1**	**471**

Going: Sf: 0-2 GS: 0-1 Gd: 0-1 GF: - Fm: 0-0
Distance: 2m/2m3: 0-4 2m4-2m7: 0-0 3m+: 0-0
Track: LH: 0-1 RH: 0-3 Tight: 0-2 Gall: 0-0
Aids: Bl: 0-0 Vi: 0-0 Tstrap: 0-0
Best Rating: 93 10/01 Strf 2m110y gd-sft Hdl

Still a maiden, although she has run some fair races.

Orleans (IRE)

94 **92**

7-y-o b g Scenic-Guest House (What A Guest)
G A Ham G A Ham

Placings:03/5-2O0 **(1131)**
2001/02: 16^{2}GF, 20^{0}S, 16^{0}GF

	Starts	1st	2nd	3rd	Win & Pl
Hurdles	3	0	1	0	580
Career Total	**6**	**0**	**1**	**1**	**910**

Going: Sf: 0-1 GS: 0-0 Gd: 0-0 GF: - Fm: 0-2
Distance: 2m/2m3: 0-2 2m4-2m7: 0-1 3m+: 0-0
Track: LH: 0-3 RH: 0-0 Tight: 0-0 Gall: 0-0
Aids: Bl: 0-0 Vi: 0-1 Tstrap: 0-0
Best Rating: 92 6/01 Worc 2m gd-fm Hdl

Oro Street (IRE)

98 **116**

6-y-o b g Dolphin Street (FR)-Love Unlimited (Dominion)
D G Bridgwater Led Astray Again Partnership

Placings:124/0520-30060 **(1395)**
2001/02: 17^{3}G, 19^{0}G, 20^{0}GF, 20^{6}GF, 24^{0}GF

	Starts	1st	2nd	3rd	Win & Pl
Hurdles	5	0	0	1	708
Career Total	**12**	**1**	**2**	**1**	**6996**

120	2/00	Wwck	2m	E Hdl	GD	£2913

Total win prize-money £2913

Going: Sf: 0-0 GS: 0-0 Gd: 0-2 GF: - Fm: 0-3
Distance: 2m/2m3: 0-1 2m4-2m7: 0-3 3m+: 0-1
Track: LH: 0-4 RH: 0-1 Tight: 0-2 Gall: 0-0
Aids: Bl: 0-0 Vi: 0-0 Tstrap: 0-2
Best Rating: 120 2/00 Wwck 2m good Hdl

Orsuno (GER)

103(57c) **124**

8-y-o b g Konigsstuhl (GER)-Orvida (FR) (Lichine (USA))
Miss Venetia Williams Knightsbridge Bc

Placings:321/5F6022033/314-1105P **(4496)**
2001/02: 16^{1}GS, 20^{1}G, 16^{0}GS, 16^{5}GS, 22^{P}G

	Starts	1st	2nd	3rd	Win & Pl
Hurdles	5	2	0	0	10829
Career Total	**20**	**4**	**3**	**4**	**23653**

124	1/02	Font	2m4f	C(0-135)HHdl	GD	£7345
118	12/01	Chep	2m110y	D(0-120)HHdl	G-S	£3484
121	5/00	Uttx	2m	D Ch	GD	£3705
121	4/99	Uttx	2m	E Hdl	G-S	£2820

Total win prize-money £17354

Going: Sf: 0-0 GS: 1-3 Gd: 1-2 GF: - Fm: 0-0
Distance: 2m/2m3: 1-3 2m4-2m7: 1-2 3m+: 0-0
Track: **LH: 1-2** RH: 0-2 **Tight: 1-1** Gall: 0-0
Aids: Bl: 0-0 Vi: 0-0 Tstrap: 0-0
Best Rating: 124 1/02 Font 2m4f good Hdl

Fair hurdler, who showed ability over fences in 2000 despite jumping problems. Absent after November 2000 until winning a Chepstow handicap hurdle easily in December 2001 and following up at Fontwell in a similar event. Acted on good and good to soft ground. (DEAD)

Orswell Crest

105(77h) **107**

8-y-o b g Crested Lark-Slave's Bangle (Prince Rheingold)
P J Hobbs The Mane Chance Partnership

Placings:0/063-0245U **(4889)**
2001/02: 20^{0}G, 26^{2}G, 23^{4}G, 26^{5}G, 26^{U}G

	Starts	1st	2nd	3rd	Win & Pl
Chases	5	0	1	0	1489
Career Total	**9**	**0**	**1**	**1**	**2101**

Going: Sf: 0-0 GS: 0-0 Gd: 0-5 GF: - Fm: 0-0
Distance: 2m/2m3: 0-0 2m4-2m7: 0-1 3m+: 0-4
Track: LH: 0-3 RH: 0-1 Tight: 0-2 Gall: 0-1
Aids: Bl: 0-0 Vi: 0-0 Tstrap: 0-0
Best Rating: 107 11/01 NAbb 3m2f110y good Ch

Fair staying novice chaser, does not want the ground too fast. Stays three and a quarter miles.

Orswell Lad

13-y-o b g Pragmatic-Craftsmans Made (Jimsun)
Miss C Wright R M E Wright

Placings:5453/1452/141P1/2542213402/33/3P/4P **(4165)**
2001/02: 24^{4}S, 26^{P}G

	Starts	1st	2nd	3rd	Win & Pl
Chases	2	0	0	0	0
Career Total	**29**	**5**	**5**	**5**	**34594**

128	2/98	Ling	3m	C(0-130)HCh	G-S	£4987
125	3/97	NAbb	2m5f110y	E(0-115)HCh	HVY	£2764
120	1/97	NAbb	2m5f110y	D(0-125)HCh	HVY	£3696
119	11/96	NAbb	2m5f110y	E(0-100)HCh	HVY	£2982
103	12/94	Wwck	2m4f110y	Hdl	HVY	£2565

Total win prize-money £16995

Going: Sf: 0-1 GS: 0-0 Gd: 0-1 GF: - Fm: 0-0
Distance: 2m/2m3: 0-0 2m4-2m7: 0-0 3m+: 0-2
Track: LH: 0-2 RH: 0-0 Tight: 0-0 Gall: 0-1
Aids: Bl: 0-2 Vi: 0-0 Tstrap: 0-0
Best Rating: 134 12/99 Extr 3m1f gd-sft Ch

A shadow of his former self, now competing in hunter chases without success.

Orswellthatenswell

76 **82**

11-y-o b g Ballacashtal (CAN)-A'Dhahirah (Beldale Flutter (USA))
R Tate R Tate

Placings:16505060/0R53/6/140-0645P **(0908)**
2001/02: 21^{0}G, 21^{6}GF, 20^{4}F, 20^{5}GF, 23^{P}G

	Starts	1st	2nd	3rd	Win & Pl
Chases	5	0	0	0	303
Career Total	**21**	**2**	**0**	**1**	**3664**

104	5/00	Weth	2m4f110y	H Ch	G-S	£1641
88	11/97	NAbb	2m1f	H NHF	G-F	£1213

Total win prize-money £2856

Going: Sf: 0-0 GS: 0-0 Gd: 0-2 GF: - Fm: 0-3
Distance: 2m/2m3: 0-0 2m4-2m7: 0-4 3m+: 0-1
Track: LH: 0-5 RH: 0-0 Tight: 0-3 Gall: 0-0
Aids: Bl: 0-0 Vi: 0-0 Tstrap: 0-0
Best Rating: 104 5/00 Weth 2m4f110y gd-sft Ch

Oscar Performance (IRE)

97(99h) (98+h)**106+**

7-y-o b g Roselier (FR)-Miss Iverk (Torus)
R H Buckler (P M J Doyle 25/5) Twentyman

Placings:P000 **(4398)**
2001/02: 18^{P}G, 20^{0}GF, 22^{0}S, 24^{0}S

	Starts	1st	2nd	3rd	Win & Pl
NH Flat	2	0	0	0	
Hurdles	2	0	0	0	
Career Total	**4**	**0**	**0**	**0**	

Going: Sf: 0-2 GS: 0-0 Gd: 0-1 GF: - Fm: 0-1
Distance: 2m/2m3: 0-1 2m4-2m7: 0-2 3m+: 0-1
Track: LH: 0-2 RH: 0-0 Tight: 0-1 Gall: 0-1
Aids: Bl: 0-0 Vi: 0-0 Tstrap: 0-0
Best Rating: 64 2/02 Font 2m6f110y soft Hdl

Ex-Irish, he put up improved form to win a Towcester novice hurdle in May 2002.

Oscar Wilde

98 **96**

10-y-o b g Arctic Lord-Topsy Bee (Be Friendly)
R H Alner Paul Green

Placings:50/422/F014F/0P2 **(4681)**
2001/02: 21^{0}G, 21^{P}GS, 25^{2}GF

	Starts	1st	2nd	3rd	Win & Pl
Chases	3	0	1	0	2165
Career Total	**13**	**1**	**3**	**0**	**10540**

118	11/99	Winc	2m5f	E(0-105)HCh	GD	£5381

Total win prize-money £5381

Going: Sf: 0-0 GS: 0-1 Gd: 0-1 GF: - Fm: 0-1
Distance: 2m/2m3: 0-0 2m4-2m7: 0-2 3m+: 0-1
Track: LH: 0-0 RH: 0-3 Tight: 0-0 Gall: 0-0
Aids: Bl: 0-0 Vi: 0-0 Tstrap: 0-0
Best Rating: 118 11/99 Winc 2m5f good Ch

Fair chaser at trips around two miles five on a sound surface. Disappointing since returning from a lengthy absence.

Oscarsexpress

5-y-o ch m Gunner B-Anchor Express (Carlingford Castle)
D Burchell D A Malam

Placings:600 **(4743)**
2001/02: 16^{6}HY, 16^{0}S, 16^{0}GF

	Starts	1st	2nd	3rd	Win & Pl
NH Flat	3	0	0	0	0
Career Total	**3**	**0**	**0**	**0**	**0**

Going: Sf: 0-2 GS: 0-0 Gd: 0-0 GF: - Fm: 0-1
Distance: 2m/2m3: 0-3 2m4-2m7: 0-0 3m+: 0-0
Track: LH: 0-1 RH: 0-2 Tight: 0-0 Gall: 0-0
Aids: Bl: 0-0 Vi: 0-0 Tstrap: 0-0
Best Rating: 77 2/02 Wwck 2m heavy NHF

Oscarvana

81 **71**

8-y-o b g Landyap (USA)-Allied Beaumel (Jimmy Reppin)
R G Frost P A Tylor

Placings:F0U **(2289)**
2001/02: 16^{F}S, 19^{0}GF, 17^{U}GF

	Starts	1st	2nd	3rd	Win & Pl
Hurdles	3	0	0	0	
Career Total	**3**	**0**	**0**	**0**	

Going: Sf: 0-1 GS: 0-0 Gd: 0-0 GF: - Fm: 0-2
Distance: 2m/2m3: 0-3 2m4-2m7: 0-0 3m+: 0-0
Track: LH: 0-1 RH: 0-2 Tight: 0-0 Gall: 0-0
Aids: Bl: 0-0 Vi: 0-0 Tstrap: 0-0
Best Rating: 71 11/01 Extr 2m3f gd-fm Hdl

Ososhot

104 **115**

9-y-o b g Teenoso (USA)-Duckdown (Blast)
A J Wilson (Ian Williams 12/5) The Winning Line

Placings:1/U/52564F5-060113 **(3877)**
2001/02: 21^{0}GF, 17^{6}S, 20^{0}G, 22^{1}G, 22^{1}GS, 22^{3}GS

	Starts	1st	2nd	3rd	Win & Pl
Hurdles	6	2	0	1	7567
Career Total	**15**	**3**	**1**	**1**	**9813**

114	1/02	Winc	2m6f	D(0-115)HHdl	G-S	£3556
104	12/01	Winc	2m6f	F(0-100)HHdl	GD	£2709
116	3/99	Ludl	2m	H NHF	SFT	£1493

Total win prize-money £7759

Going: Sf: 0-1 GS: 1-2 Gd: 1-2 GF: - Fm: 0-1
Distance: 2m/2m3: 0-1 **2m4-2m7: 2-5** 3m+: 0-0
Track: LH: 0-0 **RH: 2-5** Tight: 0-0 Gall: 0-0
Aids: Bl: 0-0 Vi: 0-0 Tstrap: 0-0
Best Rating: 116 11/00 MRas 2m1f110y gd-sft Hdl

Fair staying hurdler. He has had problems settling in his races in the past but was amenable to restraint when scoring in a handicap hurdle over two miles six at Wincanton in December 2001, before following up over the same course and distance in January 2002. Acts on good and soft ground and appears on the upgrade.

Ossie Dale (IRE)

9-y-o ch g Balinger-Brickey Shalow (Cheval)
Mrs A Price Mrs A Price

Placings:PP-P (0271)
2001/02: 25^{P}G

	Starts	1st	2nd	3rd	Win & Pl
Chases	1	0	0	0	
Career Total	**3**	**0**	**0**	**0**	

Going: Sf: 0-0 GS: 0-0 Gd: 0-1 GF: - Fm: 0-0
Distance: 2m/2m3: 0-0 2m4-2m7: 0-0 3m+: 0-1
Track: LH: 0-0 RH: 0-1 Tight: 0-0 Gall: 0-0
Aids: Bl: 0-0 Vi: 0-0 Tstrap: 0-0
Best Rating:

Other Club

88 91
8-y-o ch g Kris-Tura (Northfields (USA))
J G Portman The Other Clubbers

Placings:446251/0 (0107)
2001/02: 22^{0}GF

	Starts	1st	2nd	3rd	Win & Pl
Hurdles	1	0	0	0	
Career Total	**7**	**1**	**1**	**0**	**4706**

101 4/99 Hrfd 2m3f110y E(0-105)HHdl G-F £3438
Total win prize-money £3438

Going: Sf: 0-0 GS: 0-0 Gd: 0-0 GF: - Fm: 0-1
Distance: 2m/2m3: 0-0 2m4-2m7: 0-1 3m+: 0-0
Track: LH: 0-1 RH: 0-0 Tight: 0-1 Gall: 0-0
Aids: Bl: 0-0 Vi: 0-0 Tstrap: 0-0
Best Rating: 108 12/98 Tntn 2m1f good Hdl

Otter Valley

10-y-o b m Scallywag-Tom's Nap Hand (Some Hand)
O J Carter O J Carter

Placings:*0P/P/*PP (0793)
2001/02: 17^{P}GS, 22^{P}GF

	Starts	1st	2nd	3rd	Win & Pl
Hurdles	2	0	0	0	
Career Total	**5**	**0**	**0**	**0**	

Going: Sf: 0-0 GS: 0-1 Gd: 0-0 GF: - Fm: 0-1
Distance: 2m/2m3: 0-1 2m4-2m7: 0-1 3m+: 0-0
Track: LH: 0-2 RH: 0-0 Tight: 0-2 Gall: 0-0
Aids: Bl: 0-0 Vi: 0-0 Tstrap: 0-0
Best Rating: 32 5/98 Hrfd 2m1f good NHF

Otters Wick

8-y-o b m Java Tiger-Noss Head (New Brig)
John R Upson T L Brooks

Placings:PP (0724)
2001/02: 22^{P}GF, 17^{P}F

	Starts	1st	2nd	3rd	Win & Pl
Hurdles	2	0	0	0	
Career Total	**2**	**0**	**0**	**0**	

Going: Sf: 0-0 GS: 0-0 Gd: 0-0 GF: - Fm: 0-2
Distance: 2m/2m3: 0-1 2m4-2m7: 0-1 3m+: 0-0
Track: LH: 0-1 RH: 0-1 Tight: 0-1 Gall: 0-0
Aids: Bl: 0-1 Vi: 0-0 Tstrap: 0-0
Best Rating:

Oudalmuteena (IRE)

72(102h) (94h)48
7-y-o b g Lahib (USA)-Roxy Music (IRE) (Song)
C J Gray Riverdance Consortium

Placings:040/060123P400P-4P04400 (4480)
2001/02: 22^{4}GF, 21^{P}GS, 21^{0}HY, 16^{4}S, 20^{4}S, 17^{0}G, 22^{0}G

	Starts	1st	2nd	3rd	Win & Pl
Hurdles	7	0	0	0	0
Career Total	**21**	**1**	**1**	**1**	**4143**

88 12/00 Extr 2m3f F(0-100)HHdl HVY £2548
Total win prize-money £2548

Going: Sf: 0-3 GS: 0-1 Gd: 0-2 GF: - Fm: 0-1
Distance: 2m/2m3: 0-2 2m4-2m7: 0-5 3m+: 0-0
Track: LH: 0-1 RH: 0-4 Tight: 0-1 Gall: 0-1
Aids: Bl: 0-0 Vi: 0-0 Tstrap: 0-0
Best Rating: 94 2/02 Winc 2m soft Hdl

Oulton Broad

(105h) (101h)
6-y-o b g Midyan (USA)-Lady Quachita (USA) (Sovereign Dancer (USA))
M R Ewer-Hoad J A Ewer,G Brice,R Barnett,A Pullinger

Placings:55F31111P/000PP-003060P4P (4847)
2001/02: 17^{0}GS, 19^{0}G, 21^{3}GF, 22^{0}G, 16^{6}GS, 20^{0}G, 16^{P}GF, 16^{4}G, 20^{P}G

	Starts	1st	2nd	3rd	Win & Pl
Hurdles	9	0	0	1	492
Career Total	**23**	**4**	**0**	**2**	**15691**

122 4/00 Asct 2m4f C(0-130)HHdl SFT £6402
102 3/00 Hrfd 2m3f110y D(0-120)HHdl GD £3497
115 2/00 Folk 2m1f110y F(0-95)HHdl SFT £2366
106 2/00 Hrfd 2m3f110y F Hdl GD £2534
Total win prize-money £14800

Going: Sf: 0-0 GS: 0-2 Gd: 0-5 GF: - Fm: 0-2
Distance: 2m/2m3: 0-4 2m4-2m7: 0-5 3m+: 0-0
Track: LH: 0-3 RH: 0-6 Tight: 0-4 Gall: 0-3
Aids: Bl: 0-0 Vi: 0-0 Tstrap: 0-0
Best Rating: 122 4/00 Asct 2m4f soft Hdl

A fair handicap hurdler from two-two and a half miles, but became disappointing until running better in some modest events in the summer of 2002. Acts on soft, but handles good ground.

Our Bandbox

94 73
6-y-o ch g Risk Me (FR)-Treble Top (USA) (Miswaki (USA))
P J Hobbs Exe Valley Racing

Placings:54F/6-P05 (1269)
2001/02: 17^{P}G, 16^{0}GF, 17^{5}GF

	Starts	1st	2nd	3rd	Win & Pl
Hurdles	3	0	0	0	0
Career Total	**7**	**0**	**0**	**0**	**0**

Going: Sf: 0-0 GS: 0-0 Gd: 0-1 GF: - Fm: 0-2
Distance: 2m/2m3: 0-3 2m4-2m7: 0-0 3m+: 0-0
Track: LH: 0-3 RH: 0-0 Tight: 0-2 Gall: 0-0
Aids: Bl: 0-0 Vi: 0-0 Tstrap: 0-0
Best Rating: 78 10/99 Tntn 2m1f gd-fm Hdl

Our Boy (IRE)

7-y-o b g Convinced-Miss Polymer (Doulab (USA))
J G Cromwell (F Flood 28/5) Denis J Reddan

Placings:00/63-213P0F (4949a)
2001/02: 25^{2}G, 24^{1}G, 25^{3}G, 24^{P}S, 21^{0}G, 25^{F}G

	Starts	1st	2nd	3rd	Win & Pl
Chases	6	1	1	1	6117
Career Total	**10**	**1**	**1**	**2**	**6605**

110 5/01 Navn 3m Ch GD £4173
Total win prize-money £4173

Going: Sf: 0-1 GS: 0-0 Gd: 1-5 GF: - Fm: 0-0
Distance: 2m/2m3: 0-0 2m4-2m7: 0-1 **3m+: 1-5**
Track: LH: 0-1 RH: 0-2 Tight: 0-1 Gall: 0-0
Aids: Bl: 0-0 Vi: 0-0 **Tstrap: 1-6**
Best Rating: 116 5/01 Fair 3m1f good Ch

Irish hunter chase winner, does not want the ground too heavy.

Our Carol (IRE)

90 69
10-y-o br m Buckskin (FR)-Hampton Grange (Boreen (FR))
H J Collingridge Exors Of The Late V J Dolan

Placings:*00/4002/0000PF35P/4PF3134/*F3P-0000 (3654)
2001/02: 21^{0}G, 19^{0}G, 20^{0}G, 26^{0}S

	Starts	1st	2nd	3rd	Win & Pl
Hurdles	4	0	0	0	
Career Total	**29**	**1**	**1**	**4**	**5835**

103 2/00 Carl 3m110y E Hdl HVY £2506
Total win prize-money £2506

Going: Sf: 0-1 GS: 0-0 Gd: 0-3 GF: - Fm: 0-0
Distance: 2m/2m3: 0-1 2m4-2m7: 0-2 3m+: 0-1
Track: LH: 0-2 RH: 0-1 Tight: 0-0 Gall: 0-2
Aids: Bl: 0-0 Vi: 0-0 Tstrap: 0-0
Best Rating: 103 3/00 Carl 3m110y heavy Hdl

Our Dad Bob

73 48
6-y-o ch g Keen-Royal Shoe (Hotfoot)
M C Pipe Mrs Alison C Farrant

Placings:*361/*26 (3155)
2001/02: 17^{2}HY, 19^{6}S

	Starts	1st	2nd	3rd	Win & Pl
NH Flat	1	0	1	0	662
Hurdles	1	0	0	0	0
Career Total	**5**	**1**	**1**	**1**	**2610**

95 3/00 Wwck 2m H NHF SFT £1694
Total win prize-money £1694

Going: Sf: 0-2 GS: 0-0 Gd: 0-0 GF: - Fm: 0-0
Distance: 2m/2m3: 0-1 2m4-2m7: 0-1 3m+: 0-0
Track: LH: 0-1 RH: 0-1 Tight: 0-1 Gall: 0-0
Aids: Bl: 0-0 Vi: 0-0 Tstrap: 0-0
Best Rating: 114 12/01 NAbb 2m1f heavy NHF

Our Emily (IRE)

46
4-y-o b f Charnwood Forest (IRE)-Lacinia (Groom Dancer (USA))
T Keddy Mrs Julie Mitchell

Placings:0 (1355)

2001/02: 16^{0}GF

	Starts	1st	2nd	3rd	Win & Pl
Hurdles	1	0	0	0	
Career Total	**1**	**0**	**0**	**0**	

Going: Sf: 0-0 GS: 0-0 Gd: 0-0 GF: - Fm: 0-1
Distance: 2m/2m3: 0-1 2m4-2m7: 0-0 3m+: 0-0
Track: LH: 0-1 RH: 0-0 Tight: 0-1 Gall: 0-0
Aids: Bl: 0-0 Vi: 0-0 Tstrap: 0-0
Best Rating:

Our Emmanuel (IRE)

83 **68**

8-y-o br g Ashford (USA)-Most (Our Mirage)
P R Webber Paul Webber

Placings:00P (2064)
2001/02: 16^{0}GF, 17^{0}G, 16^{P}G

	Starts	1st	2nd	3rd	Win & Pl
Hurdles	3	0	0	0	
Career Total	**3**	**0**	**0**	**0**	

Going: Sf: 0-0 GS: 0-0 Gd: 0-2 GF: - Fm: 0-1
Distance: 2m/2m3: 0-3 2m4-2m7: 0-0 3m+: 0-0
Track: LH: 0-2 RH: 0-1 Tight: 0-1 Gall: 0-1
Aids: Bl: 0-0 Vi: 0-0 Tstrap: 0-0
Best Rating: 68 9/01 Bang 2m1f good Hdl

Our Ethel

70f **00f**

4-y-o ch f Be My Chief (USA)-Annes Gift (Ballymoss)
Mrs M Reveley Minster Commercials

Placings:*10* (4823)
2001/02: 16^{1}S, 17^{0}G

	Starts	1st	2nd	3rd	Win & Pl
NH Flat	2	1	0	0	2321
Career Total	**2**	**1**	**0**	**0**	**2321**

86	2/02	Muss	2m	H NHF	SFT	£2320

Total win prize-money £2321

Going: Sf: 1-1 GS: 0-0 Gd: 0-1 GF: - Fm: 0-0
Distance: **2m/2m3: 1-2** 2m4-2m7: 0-0 3m+: 0-0
Track: LH: 0-1 **RH: 1-1 Tight: 1-1** Gall: 0-1
Aids: Bl: 0-0 Vi: 0-0 Tstrap: 0-0
Best Rating: 86 2/02 Muss 2m soft NHF

From a good family, she made a winning debut in a Musselburgh bumper.

Our Fugley (NZ)

85 (47h)**96**

8-y-o gr g Sun And Shine-Pogue Arish (NZ) (Blarney Kiss (USA))
Mrs D Thomson The Coutts McGregor Clan

Placings:0V/0F10/0-4P (0802)
2001/02: 16^{4}F, 16^{P}GF

	Starts	1st	2nd	3rd	Win & Pl
Chases	2	0	0	0	322
Career Total	**9**	**1**	**0**	**0**	**2478**

86	1/00	Ludl	2m	G(0-95)HHdl	GD	£2156

Total win prize-money £2156

Going: Sf: 0-0 GS: 0-0 Gd: 0-0 GF: - Fm: 0-2
Distance: 2m/2m3: 0-2 2m4-2m7: 0-0 3m+: 0-0
Track: LH: 0-0 RH: 0-2 Tight: 0-0 Gall: 0-0
Aids: Bl: 0-0 Vi: 0-0 Tstrap: 0-0
Best Rating: 96 6/01 Prth 2m firm Ch

Our Ghillie

105 **95**

9-y-o ch g Gildoran-Lizzie The Twig (Precipice Wood)
P R Webber Mrs P L Aldersey

Placings:*440*/0P/**P3541/4P-U6F** (0576)
2001/02: 25^{U}G, 25^{6}G, 28^{F}GF

	Starts	1st	2nd	3rd	Win & Pl
Chases	3	0	0	0	0
Career Total	**15**	**1**	**0**	**1**	**6278**

110	4/00	Ludl	3m	D(0-110)HCh	GD	£5135

Total win prize-money £5135

Going: Sf: 0-0 GS: 0-0 Gd: 0-2 GF: - Fm: 0-1
Distance: 2m/2m3: 0-0 2m4-2m7: 0-0 3m+: 0-3
Track: LH: 0-1 RH: 0-2 Tight: 0-1 Gall: 0-0
Aids: Bl: 0-0 Vi: 0-0 Tstrap: 0-0
Best Rating: 110 4/00 Ludl 3m good Ch

Our Indulgence (IRE)

73 **54**

4-y-o ch g Prince Of Birds (USA)-Megan's Dream (IRE) (Fayruz)
T D Easterby Mrs Barabara Woodworth

Placings:0 (1355)
2001/02: 16^{0}GF

	Starts	1st	2nd	3rd	Win & Pl
Hurdles	1	0	0	0	
Career Total	**1**	**0**	**0**	**0**	

Going: Sf: 0-0 GS: 0-0 Gd: 0-0 GF: - Fm: 0-1
Distance: 2m/2m3: 0-1 2m4-2m7: 0-0 3m+: 0-0
Track: LH: 0-1 RH: 0-0 Tight: 0-1 Gall: 0-0
Aids: Bl: 0-0 Vi: 0-0 Tstrap: 0-0
Best Rating: 54 9/01 Strf 2m110y gd-fm Hdl

Our Jolly Swagman

107 **113**

7-y-o b g Thowra (FR)-Queens Dowry (Dominion)
J W Mullins F G Matthews

Placings:*5*0P6/**U0P121-54131PU26** (4503)
2001/02: 25^{5}G, 26^{4}S, 26^{1}G, 26^{3}G, 20^{1}HY, 23^{P}S, 26^{U}HY, 20^{2}GS, 26^{6}G

	Starts	1st	2nd	3rd	Win & Pl
Chases	9	2	1	1	9546
Career Total	**19**	**4**	**2**	**1**	**16474**

113	1/02	Plum	2m4f	D(0-125)HCh	HVY	£3916
103	12/01	Plum	3m2f	F(0-110)HCh	GD	£3916
97	4/01	Plum	3m2f	F(0-90)HCh	SFT	£3038
87	1/01	Plum	3m2f	F(0-90)HCh	G-S	£3094

Total win prize-money £13964

Going: Sf: 1-4 GS: 0-1 Gd: 1-4 GF: - Fm: 0-0
Distance: 2m/2m3: 0-0 2m4-2m7: 1-2 3m+: 1-7
Track: **LH: 1-3** RH: 0-2 **Tight: 1-4** Gall: 0-0
Aids: Bl: 0-0 Vi: 0-0 Tstrap: 0-0
Best Rating: 113 1/02 Plum 2m4f heavy Ch

Fair staying chaser. Acts on a soft surface. All his wins have come at Plumpton. Stays three and a quarter miles.

Our Kev (IRE)

97 **96**

6-y-o b g Be My Native (USA)-Sunbath (Krayyan)
R Rowe Mrs Jean R Bishop

Placings:06P0 (4398)
2001/02: 19^{0}GS, 21^{6}S, 22^{P}S, 24^{0}S

	Starts	1st	2nd	3rd	Win & Pl
Hurdles	4	0	0	0	0
Career Total	**4**	**0**	**0**	**0**	**0**

Going: Sf: 0-3 GS: 0-1 Gd: 0-0 GF: - Fm: 0-0
Distance: 2m/2m3: 0-1 2m4-2m7: 0-2 3m+: 0-1
Track: LH: 0-2 RH: 0-2 Tight: 0-1 Gall: 0-2
Aids: Bl: 0-0 Vi: 0-0 Tstrap: 0-0
Best Rating: 96 3/02 Newb 3m110y soft Hdl

Showed definite promise in a two mile five furlong novice hurdle at Kempton on second start and looks to have a future. Handles soft ground.

Our Krissie

99 **79**

4-y-o b f Kris-Shehana (USA) (The Minstrel (CAN))
C Grant (M Johnston 29/9) J Henderson (co Durham)

Placings:02003 (4139)
2001/02: 16^{0}G, 17^{2}S, 16^{0}GS, 20^{0}G, 16^{3}HY

	Starts	1st	2nd	3rd	Win & Pl
Hurdles	5	0	1	1	1190
Career Total	**5**	**0**	**1**	**1**	**1190**

Going: Sf: 0-2 GS: 0-1 Gd: 0-2 GF: - Fm: 0-0
Distance: 2m/2m3: 0-4 2m4-2m7: 0-1 3m+: 0-0
Track: LH: 0-3 RH: 0-2 Tight: 0-2 Gall: 0-1
Aids: Bl: 0-0 Vi: 0-0 Tstrap: 0-0
Best Rating: 79 12/01 MRas 2m1f110y soft Hdl

An edgy sort, held in handicap company over hurdles.

Our Man Dennis

8-y-o b g Arzanni-Pendocks Polly (Grey Steel)
Mrs P Ford Mrs S J Williams

Placings:*50/00/*43450-PP (2650)
2001/02: 24^{P}G, 16^{P}G

	Starts	1st	2nd	3rd	Win & Pl
Hurdles	1	0	0	0	0
Chases	1	0	0	0	0
Career Total	**11**	**0**	**0**	**1**	**736**

Going: Sf: 0-0 GS: 0-0 Gd: 0-2 GF: - Fm: 0-0
Distance: 2m/2m3: 0-1 2m4-2m7: 0-0 3m+: 0-1
Track: LH: 0-1 RH: 0-1 Tight: 0-2 Gall: 0-0
Aids: Bl: 0-0 Vi: 0-0 Tstrap: 0-0
Best Rating: 85 9/00 Chep 2m110y good Hdl

Our Man Flin (IRE)

9-y-o br g Mandalus-Flinging (Good Times (ITY))
Miss E C M Neyens (Ms A E Embiricos 24/3) The Flindicate

Placings:*0/43P0/606P3/0P/6* (4525)
2001/02: 26^{6}GS

	Starts	1st	2nd	3rd	Win & Pl
Chases	1	0	0	0	0
Career Total	**13**	**0**	**0**	**2**	**373**

Going: Sf: 0-0 GS: 0-1 Gd: 0-0 GF: - Fm: 0-0
Distance: 2m/2m3: 0-0 2m4-2m7: 0-0 3m+: 0-1
Track: LH: 0-0 RH: 0-1 Tight: 0-0 Gall: 0-0
Aids: Bl: 0-0 Vi: 0-0 Tstrap: 0-0
Best Rating: 89 12/98 Towc 2m soft Hdl

Our Man Friday (IRE)

96(97h) **108**

7-y-o br g Lord Americo-Brown Pearl (Tap On Wood)

R Rowe Mrs Jean R Bishop

Placings:05-55350 **(4600)**

2001/02: 20^{5}G, 22^{5}G, 25^{3}G, 22^{5}GS, 24^{0}GF

	Starts	1st	2nd	3rd	Win & Pl
Chases	5	0	0	1	421
Career Total	**7**	**0**	**0**	**1**	**421**

Going: Sf: 0-0 GS: 0-1 Gd: 0-3 GF: - Fm: 0-1
Distance: 2m/2m3: 0-0 2m4-2m7: 0-3 3m+: 0-2
Track: LH: 0-2 RH: 0-2 Tight: 0-1 Gall: 0-2
Aids: Bl: 0-0 Vi: 0-0 Tstrap: 0-0
Best Rating: 108 12/01 Folk 3m1f good Ch

Our Slimbridge

99 **102**

14-y-o b/br g Top Ville-Bird Point (USA) (Alleged (USA))

A W Carroll John McKenna

Placings:401430/11414/PP1064/1/012P/4/1/11/2142-424P **(3823)**

2001/02: 16^{4}S, 21^{2}HY, 21^{4}HY, 27^{P}S

	Starts	1st	2nd	3rd	Win & Pl
Hurdles	4	0	1	0	672
Career Total	**34**	**11**	**4**	**1**	**28929**

96	1/01	Plum	2m5f	G Hdl	HVY	£2268
111	1/00	Leic	2m4f110y	F Hdl	SFT	£2709
115	12/99	Towc	2m5f	F Hdl	SFT	£1940
110	2/99	Towc	2m5f	G(0-95)HHdl	SFT	£1884
104	1/96	Leic	2m4f110y	D(0-120)HHdl	SFT	£3444
114	5/94	Worc	2m2f	(0-120)HHdl	FRM	£2057
113	11/93	Wwck	2m4f110y	Hdl	G-S	£1751
115	1/93	Donc	2m110y	(0-125)HHdl	GD	£2831
109	11/92	MRas	2m1f110y	(0-125)HHdl	GD	£2808
103	10/92	Worc	2m	Hdl	GD	£1763
103	1/92	Wolv	2m	Hdl	GD	£1541

Total win prize-money £24998

Going: Sf: 0-4 GS: 0-0 Gd: 0-0 GF: - Fm: 0-0
Distance: 2m/2m3: 0-1 2m4-2m7: 0-2 3m+: 0-1
Track: LH: 0-3 RH: 0-1 Tight: 0-3 Gall: 0-0
Aids: Bl: 0-0 Vi: 0-0 Tstrap: 0-0
Best Rating: 115 12/99 Towc 2m5f soft Hdl

A veteran, he has a good record at Towcester, likes soft ground and a trip of two and a half miles plus.

Our Tommy

104 **102**

9-y-o ch g Ardross-Ina's Farewell (Random Shot)

C J Price Mrs H L Price

Placings:F/P501 **(4162)**

2001/02: 25^{P}S, 20^{5}G, 23^{0}S, 20^{1}G

	Starts	1st	2nd	3rd	Win & Pl
Chases	4	1	0	0	4046
Career Total	**5**	**1**	**0**	**0**	**4046**

102	3/02	Wwck	2m4f110y	E(0-105)HCh	GD	£4046

Total win prize-money £4046

Going: Sf: 0-2 GS: 0-0 Gd: 1-2 GF: - Fm: 0-0
Distance: 2m/2m3: 0-0 **2m4-2m7: 1-2** 3m+: 0-2
Track: **LH: 1-1** RH: 0-3 Tight: 0-1 Gall: 0-0
Aids: Bl: 0-0 Vi: 0-0 Tstrap: 0-0
Best Rating: 102 3/02 Wwck 2m4f110y good Ch

Winning pointer, a shock winner of a novices' handicap chase at Warwick in March 2002.

Ourman (IRE)

103(99h) **112**

6-y-o b g Good Thyne (USA)-Magic Minstrel (Pitpan)

T P Tate B T Stewart-Brown

Placings:*0633*-12C **(4409)**

2001/02: 27^{1}HY, 25^{2}HY, 24^{C}S

	Starts	1st	2nd	3rd	Win & Pl
Chases	3	1	1	0	4317
Career Total	**7**	**1**	**1**	**2**	**5076**

112	1/02	Sedg	3m3f	E Ch	HVY	£3045

Total win prize-money £3045

Going: Sf: 1-3 GS: 0-0 Gd: 0-0 GF: - Fm: 0-0
Distance: 2m/2m3: 0-0 2m4-2m7: 0-0 **3m+: 1-3**
Track: **LH: 1-3** RH: 0-0 **Tight: 1-2** Gall: 0-0
Aids: Bl: 0-0 Vi: 0-0 Tstrap: 0-2
Best Rating: 112 3/02 Ayr 3m1f heavy Ch

Got off the mark on his chasing debut at Sedgefield in January 2002. Stays three and a half miles. Acts on soft ground.

Out Of The Shadows

108 **112**

6-y-o gr m Rock Hopper-Shadows Of Silver (Carwhite)

Mrs M Reveley Mrs Linda Corbett

Placings:*0/03*-F1416 **(4138)**

2001/02: 16^{F}G, 16^{1}G, 16^{4}G, 16^{1}G, 16^{6}GS

	Starts	1st	2nd	3rd	Win & Pl
Hurdles	5	2	0	0	6825
Career Total	**8**	**2**	**0**	**1**	**7265**

112	1/02	Donc	2m110y	E Hdl	GD	£3290
107	11/01	Hayd	2m	D Hdl	GD	£3535

Total win prize-money £6825

Going: Sf: 0-0 GS: 0-1 Gd: 2-4 GF: - Fm: 0-0
Distance: **2m/2m3: 2-5** 2m4-2m7: 0-0 3m+: 0-0
Track: **LH: 2-4** RH: 0-1 Tight: 0-1 **Gall: 1-2**
Aids: Bl: 0-0 Vi: 0-0 Tstrap: 0-0
Best Rating: 112 1/02 Donc 2m110y good Hdl

Promise in novice events before taking a mares only race at Haydock in November. Has since scored at Doncaster. Open to improvement and looks a chasing type for the long term.

Outlaw Express (IRE)

89 **92**

6-y-o b g Un Desperado (FR)-Surprise Packet (Torus)

P R Webber Economic Security 2

Placings:*35006000*P **(4871)**

2001/02: 17^{3}GS, 16^{5}S, 16^{0}S, 17^{0}G, 22^{6}S, 17^{0}HY, 18^{0}S, 16^{0}GF, 25^{P}GF

	Starts	1st	2nd	3rd	Win & Pl
NH Flat	2	0	0	1	272
Hurdles	7	0	0	0	0
Career Total	**9**	**0**	**0**	**1**	**272**

Going: Sf: 0-5 GS: 0-1 Gd: 0-1 GF: - Fm: 0-2
Distance: 2m/2m3: 0-7 2m4-2m7: 0-1 3m+: 0-1
Track: LH: 0-7 RH: 0-1 Tight: 0-3 Gall: 0-2
Aids: Bl: 0-0 Vi: 0-1 Tstrap: 0-0
Best Rating: 106 5/01 Folk 2m1f110y gd-sft NHF

Outlook Good (IRE)

105 **125**

8-y-o br g Strong Gale-Dis Fiove (Le Bavard (FR))

J J O'Neill (A L T Moore 18/11) J P McManus

Placings:023/051/0*0032512*-6325020 **(2849)**

2001/02: 20^{6}GY, 19^{3}GF, 19^{2}GF, 18^{5}YS, 20^{0}G, 16^{2}S, 20^{0}G

	Starts	1st	2nd	3rd	Win & Pl
Chases	7	0	2	1	3719
Career Total	**21**	**2**	**5**	**3**	**19737**

130	2/01	Fair	2m2f	Ch	YLD	£6677
92	4/00	Cork	2m4f	Hdl	G-Y	£4140

Total win prize-money £10817

Going: Sf: 0-1 GS: 0-0 Gd: 0-2 GF: - Fm: 0-2
Distance: 2m/2m3: 0-4 2m4-2m7: 0-3 3m+: 0-0
Track: LH: 0-2 RH: 0-2 Tight: 0-1 Gall: 0-1
Aids: Bl: 0-4 Vi: 0-0 Tstrap: 0-0
Best Rating: 130 2/01 Fair 2m2f yield Ch

Fair ex-Irish chaser, was switched to Jonjo O'Neill in December 2001. Acts well with cut in the ground and is effective at up to two and a half miles.

Outrageouse

4-y-o b g Be My Chief (USA)-Pink Brief (IRE) (Ela-Mana-Mou)

Andrew Reid A S Reid

Placings:P **(2037)**

2001/02: 16^{P}GS

	Starts	1st	2nd	3rd	Win & Pl
Hurdles	1	0	0	0	
Career Total	**1**	**0**	**0**	**0**	

Going: Sf: 0-0 GS: 0-1 Gd: 0-0 GF: - Fm: 0-0
Distance: 2m/2m3: 0-1 2m4-2m7: 0-0 3m+: 0-0
Track: LH: 0-0 RH: 0-1 Tight: 0-0 Gall: 0-0
Aids: Bl: 0-0 Vi: 0-0 Tstrap: 0-0
Best Rating:

Outstanding Talent

97 **77**

5-y-o gr m Environment Friend-Chaleureuse (Final Straw)

A W Carroll Group 1 Racing (1994) Ltd

Placings:0-4060 **(2671)**

2001/02: 16^{4}GF, 16^{0}G, 17^{6}GS, 16^{0}G

	Starts	1st	2nd	3rd	Win & Pl
Hurdles	4	0	0	0	0
Career Total	**5**	**0**	**0**	**0**	**0**

Going: Sf: 0-0 GS: 0-1 Gd: 0-2 GF: - Fm: 0-1
Distance: 2m/2m3: 0-4 2m4-2m7: 0-0 3m+: 0-0
Track: LH: 0-1 RH: 0-3 Tight: 0-1 Gall: 0-2
Aids: Bl: 0-0 Vi: 0-0 Tstrap: 0-0
Best Rating: 77 10/01 Ludl 2m gd-fm Hdl

Over Anxious (IRE)

106 **117**

6-y-o ch g Over The River (FR)-Legal Statement (IRE) (Strong Statement (USA))

R H Alner Paul Green

Placings:06 **(4400)**

2001/02: 24^{0}GS, 21^{6}S

	Starts	1st	2nd	3rd	Win & Pl
Hurdles	2	0	0	0	0

	Starts	1st	2nd	3rd	Win & Pl
Career Total	**2**	**0**	**0**	**0**	**0**

Going: Sf: 0-1 GS: 0-1 Gd: 0-0 GF: - Fm: 0-0
Distance: 2m/2m3: 0-0 2m4-2m7: 0-1 3m+: 0-1
Track: LH: 0-2 RH: 0-0 Tight: 0-0 Gall: 0-2
Aids: Bl: 0-0 Vi: 0-0 Tstrap: 0-0
Best Rating: 117 3/02 Newb 3m110y gd-sft Hdl

A point-to-point winner in Ireland, he made a highly promising debut over three miles on his hurdles debut. His future lies over fences.

Over Charged (IRE)

86 **56**

5-y-o b g Over The River (FR)-Rookery Lady (IRE) (Callernish)
J M Jefferson Richard Collins

Placings: *3PP0* **(3785)**
2001/02: 16^{3}S, 20^{P}GS, 25^{P}GS, 20^{0}S

	Starts	1st	2nd	3rd	Win & Pl
NH Flat	1	0	0	1	327
Hurdles	3	0	0	0	0
Career Total	**4**	**0**	**0**	**1**	**327**

Going: Sf: 0-2 GS: 0-2 Gd: 0-0 GF: - Fm: 0-0
Distance: 2m/2m3: 0-1 2m4-2m7: 0-2 3m+: 0-1
Track: LH: 0-3 RH: 0-1 Tight: 0-1 Gall: 0-2
Aids: Bl: 0-0 Vi: 0-0 Tstrap: 0-0
Best Rating: 56 2/02 Newc 2m4f soft Hdl

Over The Bar (IRE)

108 **150**

6-y-o b/br g King's Ride-Merry Madness (Raise You Ten)
E J O'Grady J P McManus

Placings: *13-1132* **(4229)**
2001/02: 20^{1}YS, 20^{1}Y, 20^{3}Y, 21^{2}GS

	Starts	1st	2nd	3rd	Win & Pl
Hurdles	4	2	1	1	56357
Career Total	**6**	**3**	**1**	**2**	**60954**

142	12/01	Navn	2m4f	Hdl	YLD	£18346
130	11/01	Navn	2m4f	Hdl	Y-S	£15725
125	2/01	Fair	2m	NHF	Y-S	£4173

Total win prize-money £38246

Going: Sf: 0-0 GS: 0-1 Gd: 0-0 GF: - Fm: 0-0
Distance: 2m/2m3: 0-0 **2m4-2m7: 2-4** 3m+: 0-0
Track: **LH: 2-3** RH: 0-0 Tight: 0-0 Gall: 0-1
Aids: Bl: 0-0 Vi: 0-0 Tstrap: 0-0
Best Rating: 150 3/02 Chel 2m5f gd-sft Hdl

Useful Irish hurdler, scored twice on easy ground at Navan before running second in the Royal & SunAlliance Hurdle. Stays two and a half miles plus and is suited by cut.

Over The Beck (IRE)

(65h)

9-y-o b g Over The River (FR)-Echo Creek (IRE) (Strong Gale)
J M Jefferson Richard Collins

Placings: *61016113/600P/453/***U03P**-P3 **(0877)**
2001/02: 20^{P}G, 21^{3}G

	Starts	1st	2nd	3rd	Win & Pl
Hurdles	2	0	0	1	252
Career Total	**21**	**4**	**0**	**4**	**11708**

107	2/98	Muss	3m	D(0-110)HHdl	G-F	£3556
96	2/98	Newc	2m4f	F(0-105)HHdl	GD	£2071
83	12/97	Muss	2m4f	E Hdl	GD	£2305
95	11/97	Catt	2m	H NHF	GD	£1287

Total win prize-money £9220

Going: Sf: 0-0 GS: 0-0 Gd: 0-2 GF: - Fm: 0-0
Distance: 2m/2m3: 0-0 2m4-2m7: 0-2 3m+: 0-0
Track: LH: 0-1 RH: 0-1 Tight: 0-1 Gall: 0-0
Aids: Bl: 0-0 Vi: 0-1 Tstrap: 0-2
Best Rating: 107 2/98 Muss 3m gd-fm Hdl

Over The Burn

102(101h) **103**

10-y-o b g Over The River (FR)-Sharp Vixen (Laurence O)
B Mactaggart Boysaday Racing

Placings: P555/0/401P-PP **(4889)**
2001/02: 25^{P}GF, 26^{P}G

	Starts	1st	2nd	3rd	Win & Pl
Chases	2	0	0	0	
Career Total	**11**	**1**	**0**	**0**	**2749**

83	2/01	Carl	3m110y	E Hdl	SFT	£2521

Total win prize-money £2521

Going: Sf: 0-0 GS: 0-0 Gd: 0-1 GF: - Fm: 0-1
Distance: 2m/2m3: 0-0 2m4-2m7: 0-0 3m+: 0-2
Track: LH: 0-1 RH: 0-0 Tight: 0-1 Gall: 0-0
Aids: Bl: 0-0 Vi: 0-0 Tstrap: 0-0
Best Rating: 83 2/01 Carl 3m110y soft Hdl

Over The First (IRE)

112 **136**

7-y-o b/br g Orchestra-Ruby Lodge (Peacock (FR))
C F Swan Trotters Ind Trading Syndicate

Placings: *0030/13*5015016-031610PU5310 **(4652)**
2001/02: 17^{0}G, 17^{3}G, 16^{1}HY, 17^{6}SH, 16^{1}YS, 17^{0}Y, 16^{P}YS, 20^{U}HY, 20^{5}S, 16^{3}HY, 17^{1}SH, 20^{0}G

	Starts	1st	2nd	3rd	Win & Pl
Chases	12	3	0	2	22306
Career Total	**25**	**6**	**0**	**4**	**36171**

129	3/02	Navn	2m1f	(0-127)HCh	SH	£7975
136	11/01	Cork	2m	(0-109)HCh	Y-S	£6677
114	10/01	Tipp	2m	Ch	HVY	£5842
120	1/01	Thur	2m	Hdl	HVY	£6677
116	11/00	Thur	2m	Hdl	SFT	£2760
104	8/00	Tral	2m1f	NHF	SFT	£3588

Total win prize-money £33520

Going: Sf: 1-4 GS: 0-0 Gd: 0-3 GF: - Fm: 0-0
Distance: **2m/2m3: 3-9** 2m4-2m7: 0-3 3m+: 0-0
Track: **LH: 2-6** RH: 0-2 Tight: 0-1 Gall: 0-0
Aids: Bl: 0-0 Vi: 0-0 Tstrap: 0-0
Best Rating: 136 11/01 Cork 2m yld-sft Ch

Over The Furze (IRE)

115 **154**

9-y-o ch g Over The River (FR)-Furry Gran (Furry Glen)
J A Berry Mrs Maeve McMorrow

Placings: *0/320/1162/***4111F5-42FP2P** **(4299)**
2001/02: 16^{4}GY, 24^{2}YS, 25^{F}Y, 24^{P}Y, 16^{2}HY, 34^{P}HY

	Starts	1st	2nd	3rd	Win & Pl
Chases	6	0	2	0	15260
Career Total	**20**	**5**	**4**	**1**	**47581**

141	12/00	Leop	3m	Ch	HVY	£10400
136	12/00	Navn	2m6f	Ch	HVY	£5796
125	11/00	Clon	2m4f	Ch	HVY	£4416
115	12/99	Clon	2m2f	Hdl	SH	£3388
105	11/99	Clon	2m4f	Hdl	Y-S	£3141

Total win prize-money £27142

Going: Sf: 0-2 GS: 0-0 Gd: 0-0 GF: - Fm: 0-0
Distance: 2m/2m3: 0-2 2m4-2m7: 0-0 3m+: 0-4
Track: LH: 0-5 RH: 0-1 Tight: 0-0 Gall: 0-0
Aids: Bl: 0-0 Vi: 0-0 Tstrap: 0-0
Best Rating: 154 2/02 Naas 2m heavy Ch

Useful irish chaser, stays three miles, acts on heavy ground.

Over The Tweed

40f

5-y-o b m Presidium-Nicolini (Nicholas Bill)
J S Haldane J S Haldane

Placings: *0* **(1471)**
2001/02: 16^{0}G

	Starts	1st	2nd	3rd	Win & Pl
NH Flat	1	0	0	0	
Career Total	**1**	**0**	**0**	**0**	

Going: Sf: 0-0 GS: 0-0 Gd: 0-1 GF: - Fm: 0-0
Distance: 2m/2m3: 0-1 2m4-2m7: 0-0 3m+: 0-0
Track: LH: 0-0 RH: 0-1 Tight: 0-0 Gall: 0-0
Aids: Bl: 0-0 Vi: 0-0 Tstrap: 0-0
Best Rating:

Over The Water (IRE)

100 **121**

10-y-o gr g Over The River (FR)-Shanacloon Lass (General Ironside)
R H Alner The Droop Partners

Placings: P260/036/311/**R3561/513F-02PP50** **(4658)**
2001/02: 20^{0}GS, 21^{2}G, 22^{P}G, 20^{P}G, 23^{5}G, 24^{0}G

	Starts	1st	2nd	3rd	Win & Pl
Chases	6	0	1	0	1638
Career Total	**25**	**4**	**2**	**4**	**22565**

121	10/00	Winc	2m5f	F(0-110)HCh	G-S	£5135
120	4/00	Ludl	2m4f	E(0-115)HCh	GD	£5850
120	11/98	Winc	2m5f	E Ch	GD	£3192
129	11/98	Kemp	2m4f110y	D Ch	G-S	£3735

Total win prize-money £17913

Going: Sf: 0-0 GS: 0-1 Gd: 0-5 GF: - Fm: 0-0
Distance: 2m/2m3: 0-0 2m4-2m7: 0-4 3m+: 0-2
Track: LH: 0-2 RH: 0-4 Tight: 0-2 Gall: 0-1
Aids: Bl: 0-0 Vi: 0-0 Tstrap: 0-0
Best Rating: 129 11/98 Kemp 2m4f110y gd-sft Ch

Fair front-running chaser, best on good or softer at short of three miles.

Over Zealous (IRE)

101 (59h)**107**

10-y-o ch g Over The River (FR)-Chatty Di (Le Bavard (FR))
John R Upson Middleham Park Racing X

Placings: 0000/245/U11112/22P4RP-05361PP **(4514)**
2001/02: 20^{0}S, 22^{5}S, 30^{3}GS, 26^{6}S, 26^{1}S, 27^{P}S, 25^{P}GS

	Starts	1st	2nd	3rd	Win & Pl
Hurdles	1	0	0	0	0
Chases	6	1	0	1	3227
Career Total	**26**	**5**	**4**	**1**	**20350**

107	1/02	Wwck	3m2f	F(0-95)HCh	SFT	£2705
108	1/00	Newc	3m6f	D(0-125)HCh	SFT	£3753
103	12/99	Sedg	3m3f	F(0-110)HCh	G-S	£3579
105	11/99	Newc	3m	F(0-90)HCh	G-S	£2866
103	11/99	Sedg	3m3f	F(0-100)HCh	GD	£2670

Total win prize-money £15575

Going: Sf: 1-5 GS: 0-2 Gd: 0-0 GF: - Fm: 0-0
Distance: 2m/2m3: 0-0 2m4-2m7: 0-2 **3m+: 1-5**
Track: LH: **1-3** RH: 0-2 Tight: 0-1 Gall: 0-1
Aids: Bl: **1-3** Vi: 0-0 Tstrap: 0-0
Best Rating: 114 11/00 Newc 3m6f soft Ch

Fair handicap chaser, stays very well. Best on an easy surface. Goes well at Newcastle. Got back to winning ways in first-time blinkers at Warwick in January 2002.

Overflowing River (IRE)

13-y-o ch g Over The River (FR)-Side Wink (Quayside)
J Wade John Wade

Placings:F54/41/14P/512312P/P1/31/1-0 **(0427)**
2001/02: 33^{0}G

	Starts	1st	2nd	3rd	Win & Pl
Chases	1	0	0	0	
Career Total	**21**	**7**	**2**	**2**	**30695**

122	5/00	Chel	4m1f	H Ch	GD	£5005
122	3/00	Sedg	3m3f	H Ch	G-F	£1190
120	4/99	Chel	4m1f	H Ch	G-S	£4435
104	2/98	MRas	3m4f110y	D(0-120)HCh	GD	£3998
106	10/97	Sedg	3m3f	F(0-100)HCh	G-F	£2726
91	5/96	Sedg	3m3f	E(0-110)HCh	FRM	£3910
94	4/96	Hexm	3m1f	E Ch	GD	£3425

Total win prize-money £24690

Going: Sf: 0-0 GS: 0-0 Gd: 0-1 GF: - Fm: 0-0
Distance: 2m/2m3: 0-0 2m4-2m7: 0-0 3m+: 0-1
Track: LH: 0-0 RH: 0-0 Tight: 0-0 Gall: 0-0
Aids: Bl: 0-0 Vi: 0-0 Tstrap: 0-0
Best Rating: 122 5/00 Chel 4m1f good Ch

He stays all day (twice successful over four miles and a furlong at Cheltenham) and is a useful hunter at his best. Suited by aggressive tactics, he jumps economically and bounces off quick ground.

Oversman

97(74c) 89
9-y-o b g Keen-Jamaican Punch (IRE) (Shareef Dancer (USA))
M J M Evans (B J Llewellyn 29/9) Mrs J Z Munday

Placings:025/14033/2040421231/000122363/6P4P0P -554023P00 **(3334)**
2001/02: 17^{5}GS, 22^{5}GF, 22^{4}GF, 21^{0}GS, 22^{2}G, 20^{3}GF, 21^{P}GS, 16^{0}G, 16^{0}G

	Starts	1st	2nd	3rd	Win & Pl
Hurdles	9	0	1	1	969
Career Total	**42**	**4**	**7**	**6**	**14784**

102	1/00	Sedg	2m1f	G(0-95)HHdl	SFT	£1589
91	2/99	Donc	2m110y	G Hdl	G-F	£1646
91	1/99	Muss	2m	G Hdl	G-S	£2248
83	5/97	Weth	2m	E Hdl	G-S	£2232

Total win prize-money £7716

Going: Sf: 0-0 GS: 0-3 Gd: 0-3 GF: - Fm: 0-3
Distance: 2m/2m3: 0-3 2m4-2m7: 0-6 3m+: 0-0
Track: LH: 0-4 RH: 0-3 Tight: 0-6 Gall: 0-0
Aids: Bl: 0-7 Vi: 0-0 Tstrap: 0-9
Best Rating: 106 1/00 Muss 2m good Hdl

Plating-class hurdler/chaser.

Owen's Pet (IRE)

105(73h) (94h)109
8-y-o b g Alphabatim (USA)-Ballinlovane (Le Moss)
R T Phillips Archmold Ltd

Placings:63-P023 **(4889)**
2001/02: 20^{P}S, 19^{0}S, 26^{2}GS, 26^{3}G

	Starts	1st	2nd	3rd	Win & Pl
Hurdles	2	0	0	0	0
Chases	2	0	1	1	2050
Career Total	**6**	**0**	**1**	**2**	**2379**

Going: Sf: 0-2 GS: 0-1 Gd: 0-1 GF: - Fm: 0-0
Distance: 2m/2m3: 0-0 2m4-2m7: 0-2 3m+: 0-2
Track: LH: 0-0 RH: 0-3 Tight: 0-1 Gall: 0-0
Aids: Bl: 0-0 Vi: 0-0 Tstrap: 0-0
Best Rating: 109 4/02 Carl 3m2f gd-sft Ch

Former Irish point winner. Modest form over hurdles before running well on chasing debut at Carlisle in April 2002.

Owenbwee (IRE)

11-y-o b g Broussard (USA)-Cookstown Lady (Linacre)
Mrs Beverley Moore-Williams (R H Buckler 3/2) Mrs Richard Fuller

Placings:6/31431142500/00405/52251400P1/26P/44 036/4 **(3755)**
2001/02: 20^{4}S

	Starts	1st	2nd	3rd	Win & Pl
Chases	1	0	0	0	0
Career Total	**36**	**5**	**4**	**3**	**21981**

111	4/98	Chep	2m110y	E Ch	HVY	£2788
114	8/97	Slig	2m4f	Ch	Y-S	£2712
119	11/95	Clon	2m	Hdl	G-Y	£4069
118	10/95	Wxfd	2m2f100y	Hdl	G-Y	£3221
98	6/95	Wxfd	2m2f100y	NHF	GD	£2712

Total win prize-money £15505

Going: Sf: 0-1 GS: 0-0 Gd: 0-0 GF: - Fm: 0-0
Distance: 2m/2m3: 0-0 2m4-2m7: 0-1 3m+: 0-0
Track: LH: 0-0 RH: 0-1 Tight: 0-0 Gall: 0-0
Aids: Bl: 0-0 Vi: 0-0 Tstrap: 0-0
Best Rating: 120 12/95 Leop 2m2f yld-sft Hdl

Owthorpe Borders

97 95
9-y-o b g Rolfe (USA)-Star Route (Owen Dudley)
John A Harris Mrs Margaret Marston

Placings:6/05/000-1P **(1095)**
2001/02: 19^{1}G, 24^{P}GF

	Starts	1st	2nd	3rd	Win & Pl
Hurdles	2	1	0	0	3543
Career Total	**8**	**1**	**0**	**0**	**3543**

95	7/01	MRas	2m3f110y	D Hdl	GD	£3542

Total win prize-money £3543

Going: Sf: 0-0 GS: 0-0 Gd: 1-1 GF: - Fm: 0-1
Distance: 2m/2m3: 0-0 **2m4-2m7: 1-1** 3m+: 0-1
Track: LH: 0-0 **RH: 1-2 Tight: 1-2** Gall: 0-0
Aids: Bl: 0-0 Vi: 0-0 Tstrap: 0-0
Best Rating: 95 7/01 MRas 2m3f110y good Hdl

Owthorpe Hill

8-y-o br g Scorpio (FR)-Star Route (Owen Dudley)
John A Harris Mrs Margaret Marston

Placings:0/PP **(3994)**
2001/02: 21^{P}S, 20^{P}S

	Starts	1st	2nd	3rd	Win & Pl
Hurdles	2	0	0	0	
Career Total	**3**	**0**	**0**	**0**	

Going: Sf: 0-2 GS: 0-0 Gd: 0-0 GF: - Fm: 0-0
Distance: 2m/2m3: 0-0 2m4-2m7: 0-2 3m+: 0-0
Track: LH: 0-1 RH: 0-0 Tight: 0-0 Gall: 0-1
Aids: Bl: 0-0 Vi: 0-0 Tstrap: 0-0
Best Rating: 12 3/00 Donc 2m110y good NHF

Oxidor (IRE)

107 90
7-y-o br g Be My Native (USA)-Euroblend (IRE) (The Parson)
C P Morlock D And Mrs H Woodhall

Placings:6/000015-6360015 **(4599)**
2001/02: 24^{6}G, 24^{3}S, 22^{0}GS, 26^{0}S, 24^{0}S, 26^{1}GF, 25^{5}GF

	Starts	1st	2nd	3rd	Win & Pl
Hurdles	7	1	0	1	2830
Career Total	**14**	**2**	**0**	**1**	**5871**

90	3/02	Hntg	3m2f	E(0-110)HHdl	G-F	£2492
96	2/01	Uttx	2m6f110y	F(0-105)HHdl	SFT	£3041

Total win prize-money £5534

Going: Sf: 0-3 GS: 0-1 Gd: 0-1 GF: - Fm: 1-2
Distance: 2m/2m3: 0-0 2m4-2m7: 0-1 **3m+: 1-6**
Track: LH: 0-1 **RH: 1-4** Tight: 0-2 **Gall: 1-1**
Aids: Bl: 1-2 Vi: 0-0 Tstrap: 1-3
Best Rating: 100 11/99 Weth 2m good NHF

Shock winner in low-grade company at Huntingdon in March 2002. Likes fast ground.

Oyster Bay

97 85
6-y-o b m Mandalus-Holy Times (IRE) (The Parson)
A Streeter Martin Jump

Placings:0-510P6030 **(4573)**
2001/02: 17^{5}G, 16^{1}S, 20^{0}GS, 24^{P}HY, 16^{6}S, 16^{0}HY, 17^{3}S, 20^{0}G

	Starts	1st	2nd	3rd	Win & Pl
NH Flat	2	1	0	0	1953
Hurdles	6	0	0	1	324
Career Total	**9**	**1**	**0**	**1**	**2277**

97	11/01	Uttx	2m	H NHF	SFT	£1953

Total win prize-money £1953

Going: Sf: 1-5 GS: 0-1 Gd: 0-2 GF: - Fm: 0-0
Distance: **2m/2m3: 1-5** 2m4-2m7: 0-2 3m+: 0-1
Track: **LH: 1-6** RH: 0-2 Tight: 0-2 Gall: 0-2
Aids: Bl: 0-0 Vi: 0-2 Tstrap: 0-0
Best Rating: 97 11/01 Uttx 2m soft NHF

Plating class hurdler who handles soft ground.

Ozawa (IRE)

81 63
5-y-o gr g Brief Truce (USA)-Classy (Kalaglow)
M E Sowersby (J W Payne 2/7) Racing Ladies

Placings:5PP **(1581)**
2001/02: 16^{5}GF, 21^{P}G, 24^{P}GS

	Starts	1st	2nd	3rd	Win & Pl
Hurdles	3	0	0	0	1
Career Total	**3**	**0**	**0**	**0**	**1**

Going: Sf: 0-0 GS: 0-1 Gd: 0-1 GF: - Fm: 0-1

Distance: 2m/2m3: 0-1 2m4-2m7: 0-1 3m+: 0-1
Track: LH: 0-2 RH: 0-1 Tight: 0-3 Gall: 0-0
Aids: Bl: 0-1 Vi: 0-0 Tstrap: 0-0
Best Rating: 63 7/01 Sthl 2m gd-fm Hdl

Ozzie Jones

111 **133**

11-y-o b g Formidable (USA)-Distant Relation (Great Nephew)
K R Pearce Keith R Pearce

Placings:4516552P50F/4500/3453/**22021214/131432 114/126P16-46P31331** **(4852)**
2001/02: 28^{4}GF, 24^{6}GF, 25^{P}GF, 23^{3}GF, 24^{1}GF, 27^{3}GF, 26^{3}GS, 24^{1}G

	Starts	1st	2nd	3rd	Win & Pl
Chases	8	2	0	3	10900
Career Total	**50**	**11**	**7**	**7**	**53546**

130	4/02	Strf	3m	H Ch	GD	£3020
133	8/01	Sthl	3m110y	E(0-115)HCh	G-F	£4368
133	9/00	Plum	3m2f	D(0-125)HCh	GD	£3789
117	5/00	Ludl	3m	H Ch	GD	£2404
133	10/99	Plum	3m2f	C(0-130)HCh	G-F	£7215
110	10/99	Ludl	3m	E(0-115)HHdl	G-F	£3464
133	7/99	Wolv	3m1f	D(0-120)HCh	G-F	£3934
133	5/99	Hrfd	3m1f110y	E(0-115)HCh	GD	£3631
131	9/98	Hntg	3m	E(0-110)HCh	G-F	£2906
115	7/98	Bang	3m110y	E(0-115)HCh	GD	£4162
76	10/94	Ludl	2m	Hdl	FRM	£1987

Total win prize-money £40885

Going: Sf: 0-0 GS: 0-1 Gd: 1-1 GF: - Fm: 1-6
Distance: 2m/2m3: 0-0 2m4-2m7: 0-0 **3m+: 2-8**
Track: **LH: 2-7** RH: 0-0 **Tight: 2-6** Gall: 0-0
Aids: Bl: 0-1 Vi: 0-0 Tstrap: 0-0
Best Rating: 133 8/01 Sthl 3m110y gd-fm Ch

A fast ground staying handicap chaser, he is usually most effective in the first half of the season. Shows his form blinkered or not, and should continue to find winning opportunities. Clear cut winner of hunter chase at Stratford April 2002 and followed up at the same course in June.

Paarl Rock

106 **109**

7-y-o ch h Common Grounds-Markievicz (IRE) (Doyoun)
G Barnett J C Bradbury

Placings:3 **(0573)**
2001/02: 16^{3}GF

	Starts	1st	2nd	3rd	Win & Pl
Hurdles	1	0	0	1	592
Career Total	**1**	**0**	**0**	**1**	**592**

Going: Sf: 0-0 GS: 0-0 Gd: 0-0 GF: - Fm: 0-1
Distance: 2m/2m3: 0-1 2m4-2m7: 0-0 3m+: 0-0
Track: LH: 0-1 RH: 0-0 Tight: 0-1 Gall: 0-0
Aids: Bl: 0-0 Vi: 0-1 Tstrap: 0-0
Best Rating: 109 6/01 Strf 2m110y gd-fm Hdl

Pace Stalker (USA)

114(98h) (87h)**108**

6-y-o b g Lear Fan (USA)-In The Habit (USA) (Lyphard (USA))
G L Moore Phil Collins

Placings:4300/4U20204-**1U54F553U** **(3815)**
2001/02: 16^{1}G, 16^{U}F, 17^{5}GS, 16^{4}G, 16^{F}G, 21^{5}G, 16^{5}S, 16^{3}S, 16^{U}S

	Starts	1st	2nd	3rd	Win & Pl
Hurdles	2	0	0	0	0
Chases	7	1	0	1	3419
Career Total	**20**	**1**	**2**	**2**	**5945**

108	5/01	Folk	2m	F(0-90)Ch	GD	£2639

Total win prize-money £2639

Going: Sf: 0-3 GS: 0-1 Gd: 1-4 GF: - Fm: 0-1
Distance: **2m/2m3: 1-8** 2m4-2m7: 0-1 3m+: 0-0
Track: LH: 0-3 **RH: 1-6 Tight: 1-8** Gall: 0-0
Aids: **Bl: 1-7** Vi: 0-0 Tstrap: 0-6
Best Rating: 108 5/01 Folk 2m good Ch

Fair hurdler/chaser, seems suited by two miles and cut in the ground, wears blinkers and goes well at Folkestone.

Pacifyc (IRE)

102 **98**

7-y-o b g Brief Truce (USA)-Ocean Blue (IRE) (Bluebird (USA))
John A Harris (Exors Of The Late J L Harris 2/7) Mrs A E Harris

Placings:1P00 **(3268)**
2001/02: 17^{1}GF, 19^{P}S, 16^{0}S, 20^{0}G

	Starts	1st	2nd	3rd	Win & Pl
Hurdles	4	1	0	0	1673
Career Total	**4**	**1**	**0**	**0**	**1673**

98	9/01	MRas	2m1f110y	G Hdl	G-F	£1673

Total win prize-money £1673

Going: Sf: 0-2 GS: 0-0 Gd: 0-1 GF: - Fm: 1-1
Distance: **2m/2m3: 1-2** 2m4-2m7: 0-2 3m+: 0-0
Track: LH: 0-1 **RH: 1-3 Tight: 1-2** Gall: 0-1
Aids: Bl: 0-0 Vi: 0-0 **Tstrap: 1-4**
Best Rating: 98 9/01 MRas 2m1f110y gd-fm Hdl

Of little account on the Flat, but he has had wind problems and a tongue-strap may have been the key in helping him make a winning hurdling debut in a seller at Market Rasen in September 2001.

Pacon (GER)

95(99c) (109c)**120**

9-y-o br g Polar Falcon (USA)-Padang (GER) (Ile De Bourbon (USA))
Mrs S A Bramall M Stanners

Placings:4634/10034500/6434160200 **(4796a)**
2001/02: 16^{6}YS, 16^{4}F, 19^{3}G, 20^{4}G, 19^{1}G, 20^{6}GF, 18^{0}Y, 16^{2}S, 16^{0}S, 20^{0}Y

	Starts	1st	2nd	3rd	Win & Pl
Hurdles	9	1	0	1	6956
Chases	1	0	1	0	956
Career Total	**22**	**2**	**1**	**3**	**22813**

120	6/01	Naas	2m3f	(0-109)HHdl	GD	£4729
101	7/99	Klny	2m1f	HHdl	GD	£11562

Total win prize-money £16293

Going: Sf: 0-2 GS: 0-0 Gd: 1-3 GF: - Fm: 0-2
Distance: **2m/2m3: 1-7** 2m4-2m7: 0-3 3m+: 0-0
Track: LH: 0-2 RH: 0-1 Tight: 0-1 Gall: 0-1
Aids: Bl: 0-0 Vi: 0-0 Tstrap: 0-0
Best Rating: 120 6/01 Naas 2m3f good Hdl

Modest hurdler, best at around two miles three on good ground. Showed promise on his chasing debut in sloppy ground.

Paddington Jones (IRE)

99 **80**

9-y-o b g Camden Town-Bann River (Over The River (FR))
M E Sowersby M E Sowersby

Placings:400/4000/**54453332202/540-6650P4456** **(1420)**
2001/02: 16^{6}GF, 17^{6}G, 20^{5}GF, 21^{0}GF, 24^{P}GF, 27^{4}GF, 26^{4}G, 21^{5}GF, 16^{6}G

	Starts	1st	2nd	3rd	Win & Pl
Chases	9	0	0	0	556
Career Total	**30**	**0**	**3**	**3**	**7603**

Going: Sf: 0-0 GS: 0-0 Gd: 0-3 GF: - Fm: 0-6
Distance: 2m/2m3: 0-3 2m4-2m7: 0-3 3m+: 0-3
Track: LH: 0-7 RH: 0-2 Tight: 0-8 Gall: 0-0
Aids: Bl: 0-2 Vi: 0-0 Tstrap: 0-0
Best Rating: 104 11/99 Aint 2m good Ch

Paddy Mul

5-y-o ch h Democratic (USA)-My Pretty Niece (Great Nephew)
W Storey Gremlin Racing

Placings:0P **(2767)**
2001/02: 17^{0}G, 19^{P}G

	Starts	1st	2nd	3rd	Win & Pl
Hurdles	2	0	0	0	
Career Total	**2**	**0**	**0**	**0**	

Going: Sf: 0-0 GS: 0-0 Gd: 0-2 GF: - Fm: 0-0
Distance: 2m/2m3: 0-2 2m4-2m7: 0-0 3m+: 0-0
Track: LH: 0-2 RH: 0-0 Tight: 0-2 Gall: 0-0
Aids: Bl: 0-0 Vi: 0-0 Tstrap: 0-2
Best Rating:

Paddy The Driver (IRE)

99 **90**

6-y-o b g Grand Plaisir (IRE)-Jude's Hollow (IRE) (Hollow Hand)
R G Frost Torquay Boyz Racing Syndicate

Placings:40 64306P **(3384)**
2001/02: 22^{6}G, 17^{4}GF, 22^{3}GF, 17^{0}S, 16^{6}S, 16^{P}GS

	Starts	1st	2nd	3rd	Win & Pl
Hurdles	6	0	0	1	690
Career Total	**8**	**0**	**0**	**1**	**866**

Going: Sf: 0-2 GS: 0-1 Gd: 0-1 GF: - Fm: 0-2
Distance: 2m/2m3: 0-4 2m4-2m7: 0-2 3m+: 0-0
Track: LH: 0-5 RH: 0-1 Tight: 0-4 Gall: 0-0
Aids: Bl: 0-0 Vi: 0-0 Tstrap: 0-0
Best Rating: 90 7/01 NAbb 2m1f gd-fm Hdl

Paddy The Optimist (IRE)

83f **86f**

6-y-o b g Leading Counsel (USA)-Erne Duchess (IRE) (Duky)
T R George M R C Opperman

Placings:6 **(3338)**
2001/02: 16^{6}G

	Starts	1st	2nd	3rd	Win & Pl
NH Flat	1	0	0	0	0
Career Total	**1**	**0**	**0**	**0**	**0**

Going: Sf: 0-0 GS: 0-0 Gd: 0-1 GF: - Fm: 0-0
Distance: 2m/2m3: 0-1 2m4-2m7: 0-0 3m+: 0-0
Track: LH: 0-0 RH: 0-1 Tight: 0-0 Gall: 0-0
Aids: Bl: 0-0 Vi: 0-0 Tstrap: 0-0
Best Rating: 86 1/02 Ludl 2m good NHF

Paddy The Piper (IRE)

93f 118f

5-y-o b g Witness Box (USA)-Divine Dibs (Raise You Ten)
L Lungo Devey Group Limited

Placings:3 (4900)
2001/02: 16^{3}G

	Starts	1st	2nd	3rd	Win & Pl
NH Flat	1	0	0	1	508
Career Total	**1**	**0**	**0**	**1**	**508**

Going: Sf: 0-0 GS: 0-0 Gd: 0-1 GF: - Fm: 0-0
Distance: 2m/2m3: 0-1 2m4-2m7: 0-0 3m+: 0-0
Track: LH: 0-0 RH: 0-1 Tight: 0-0 Gall: 0-0
Aids: Bl: 0-0 Vi: 0-0 Tstrap: 0-0
Best Rating: 118 4/02 Prth 2m110y good NHF

Paddy's Profiles (IRE)

90 78

8-y-o b g Euphemism-Dame Niamh (IRE) (Buckskin (FR))
Miss K M George Exterior Profiles Ltd

Placings:0/004-65 (0318)
2001/02: 22^{6}GF, 22^{5}F

	Starts	1st	2nd	3rd	Win & Pl
Hurdles	2	0	0	0	0
Career Total	**6**	**0**	**0**	**0**	**0**

Going: Sf: 0-0 GS: 0-0 Gd: 0-0 GF: - Fm: 0-2
Distance: 2m/2m3: 0-0 2m4-2m7: 0-2 3m+: 0-0
Track: LH: 0-1 RH: 0-0 Tight: 0-1 Gall: 0-0
Aids: Bl: 0-0 Vi: 0-0 Tstrap: 0-0
Best Rating: 79 1/01 Tntn 2m3f110y soft Hdl

Paddy's Return (IRE)

108 138

10-y-o b g Kahyasi-Bayazida (Bustino)
Ferdy Murphy Paddy O'Donnell

Placings:11221/3F031/51253/2F4463/13234133/326UU-43U100R (4951a)
2001/02: 25^{4}GS, 31^{3}G, 27^{U}S, 31^{1}GS, 21^{0}G, 24^{0}GS, 31^{R}G

	Starts	1st	2nd	3rd	Win & Pl
Hurdles	1	0	0	0	0
Chases	6	1	0	1	17681
Career Total	**41**	**8**	**6**	**10**	**214760**

138	12/01	Chel	3m7f	C(0-135)HCh	G-S	£14105
	1/00	Cagn	2m5f110y	Hdl	GD	£21529
113	10/99	Kels	3m1f	E Ch	GD	£2835
171	12/97	Asct	3m1f110y	A Hdl	G-S	£27055
163	4/97	Punc	3m	Hdl	GD	£21485
140	3/96	Chel	2m1f	A Hdl	GD	£44608
121	11/95	Asct	2m110y	C Hdl	GD	£4299
103	11/95	Sedg	2m1f110y	E Hdl	G-F	£2206

Total win prize-money £138123

Going: Sf: 0-1 GS: 1-3 Gd: 0-3 GF: - Fm: 0-0
Distance: 2m/2m3: 0-0 2m4-2m7: 0-1 **3m+: 1-6**
Track: **LH: 1-5** RH: 0-1 Tight: 0-2 Gall: 0-1
Aids: Bl: 0-4 **Vi: 1-2** Tstrap: 0-0
Best Rating: 171 12/97 Asct 3m1f110y gd-sft Hdl

Former Triumph Hurdle winner but better known as a staying chaser these days. He caused chaos when running loose in the 2001 Grand National but had run well over the big fences when third in the Becher Chase earlier in the season, he won a croos-country chase at Cheltenham in December 2001. Goes well on good ground.

Paddy's Wolf

11-y-o b g Little Wolf-Paddy's Delight (Paddy's Birthday)
G L Moore (Grahame A Dedman 21/4) Grahame A Dedman

Placings:4PP/0P-UPP (0774)
2001/02: 20^{U}GF, 21^{P}GF, 23^{P}GF

	Starts	1st	2nd	3rd	Win & Pl
Chases	3	0	0	0	
Career Total	**8**	**0**	**0**	**0**	**251**

Going: Sf: 0-0 GS: 0-0 Gd: 0-0 GF: - Fm: 0-3
Distance: 2m/2m3: 0-0 2m4-2m7: 0-2 3m+: 0-1
Track: LH: 0-2 RH: 0-1 Tight: 0-1 Gall: 0-1
Aids: Bl: 0-0 Vi: 0-0 Tstrap: 0-0
Best Rating: 55 3/00 Font 2m2f110y gd-fm Hdl

Paddyspearl

42

8-y-o b g Henbit (USA)-La Furze (Winden)
A W Carroll A Bayman

Placings:00P-PP0PP (4095)
2001/02: 22^{P}GS, 16^{P}G, 16^{0}GF, 16^{P}GS, 16^{P}GS

	Starts	1st	2nd	3rd	Win & Pl
Hurdles	4	0	0	0	0
Chases	1	0	0	0	0
Career Total	**8**	**0**	**0**	**0**	

Going: Sf: 0-0 GS: 0-3 Gd: 0-1 GF: - Fm: 0-1
Distance: 2m/2m3: 0-4 2m4-2m7: 0-1 3m+: 0-0
Track: LH: 0-3 RH: 0-1 Tight: 0-1 Gall: 0-0
Aids: Bl: 0-0 Vi: 0-0 Tstrap: 0-1
Best Rating:

Pagan King (IRE)

107 118

6-y-o b g Unblest-Starinka (Risen Star (USA))
Mrs L Wadham R B Holt

Placings:046200-2314 (3380)
2001/02: 16^{2}G, 17^{3}G, 16^{1}G, 16^{4}GS

	Starts	1st	2nd	3rd	Win & Pl
Hurdles	4	1	1	1	13820
Career Total	**10**	**1**	**2**	**1**	**16110**

113	12/01	Kemp	2m	C(0-130)HHdl	GD	£6955

Total win prize-money £6955

Going: Sf: 0-0 GS: 0-1 Gd: 1-3 GF: - Fm: 0-0
Distance: **2m/2m3: 1-4** 2m4-2m7: 0-0 3m+: 0-0
Track: LH: 0-1 **RH: 1-3** Tight: 0-0 Gall: 0-2
Aids: Bl: 0-0 Vi: 0-0 Tstrap: 0-0
Best Rating: 118 1/02 Kemp 2m gd-sft Hdl

Fair handicap hurdler, he showed improved form in late 2001 winning a good race at Kempton over Christmas. Best at around two miles. Suited by soft ground but acts on good, often held up and has a turn of foot.

Pagan Upstart

6-y-o b g Primitive Rising (USA)-Bramcote Centenary (Alleging (USA))
N Wilson Mrs N C Wilson

Placings:0-0 (0239)
2001/02: 16^{0}GF

	Starts	1st	2nd	3rd	Win & Pl
NH Flat	1	0	0	0	
Career Total	**2**	**0**	**0**	**0**	

Going: Sf: 0-0 GS: 0-0 Gd: 0-0 GF: - Fm: 0-1
Distance: 2m/2m3: 0-1 2m4-2m7: 0-0 3m+: 0-0
Track: LH: 0-1 RH: 0-0 Tight: 0-1 Gall: 0-0
Aids: Bl: 0-0 Vi: 0-0 Tstrap: 0-0
Best Rating: 24 3/01 MRas 2m1f110y good NHF

Pailitas (GER)

107 80

5-y-o b g Lomitas-Pradera (GER) (Abary (GER))
Ian Williams C N Barnes

Placings:0P0P (4540)
2001/02: 16^{0}G, 16^{P}S, 16^{0}S, 19^{P}G

	Starts	1st	2nd	3rd	Win & Pl
Hurdles	4	0	0	0	
Career Total	**4**	**0**	**0**	**0**	

Going: Sf: 0-2 GS: 0-0 Gd: 0-2 GF: - Fm: 0-0
Distance: 2m/2m3: 0-3 2m4-2m7: 0-1 3m+: 0-0
Track: LH: 0-2 RH: 0-2 Tight: 0-0 Gall: 0-1
Aids: Bl: 0-0 Vi: 0-0 Tstrap: 0-0
Best Rating: 47 11/01 Wwck 2m good Hdl

Headstrong handicap hurdler, disqualified and placed second after passing the post first at Uttoxeter in June 2002.

Palace (FR)

6-y-o b g Rahotep (FR)-La Musardiere (FR) (Cadoudal (FR))
P F Nicholls B L Blinman

Placings:0/06P (2277)
2001/02: 17^{0}F, 16^{6}G, 22^{P}GF

	Starts	1st	2nd	3rd	Win & Pl
NH Flat	2	0	0	0	0
Hurdles	1	0	0	0	0
Career Total	**4**	**0**	**0**	**0**	**0**

Going: Sf: 0-0 GS: 0-0 Gd: 0-1 GF: - Fm: 0-2
Distance: 2m/2m3: 0-2 2m4-2m7: 0-1 3m+: 0-0
Track: LH: 0-0 RH: 0-3 Tight: 0-0 Gall: 0-0
Aids: Bl: 0-0 Vi: 0-0 Tstrap: 0-2
Best Rating: 83 11/01 Winc 2m good NHF

Palace Guard

10-y-o br g Daring March-Royal Brush (King Of Spain)
P Bowen Chris Wall

Placings:00/60F/0P-0P (4540)
2001/02: 16^{0}S, 19^{P}G

	Starts	1st	2nd	3rd	Win & Pl
Hurdles	2	0	0	0	
Career Total	9	0	0	0	0

Going: Sf: 0-1 GS: 0-0 Gd: 0-1 GF: - Fm: 0-0
Distance: 2m/2m3: 0-1 2m4-2m7: 0-1 3m+: 0-0
Track: LH: 0-1 RH: 0-1 Tight: 0-1 Gall: 0-0
Aids: Bl: 0-0 Vi: 0-0 Tstrap: 0-0
Best Rating: 71 8/99 Strf 2m110y good Hdl

Palace Parade (USA)

97 **85**

12-y-o ch g Cure The Blues (USA)-Parasail (USA) (In Reality)
Ms J Channon (G F H Charles-Jones 25/10) T D H Hughes

Placings:F6U6045/5P0/365UP2/UP0042/43P10U/05P P0/4/16-00P (3991)
2001/02: 23^{0}GF, 24^{0}GF, 24^{P}S

	Starts	1st	2nd	3rd	Win & Pl
Chases	3	0	0	0	
Career Total	39	2	2	2	5403

96	5/00	Font	3m2f110y	H Ch	GD	£1484
92	1/98	Wind	2m6f110y	G(0-95)HHdl	GD	£2132

Total win prize-money £3617

Going: Sf: 0-1 GS: 0-0 Gd: 0-0 GF: - Fm: 0-2
Distance: 2m/2m3: 0-0 2m4-2m7: 0-0 3m+: 0-3
Track: LH: 0-0 RH: 0-3 Tight: 0-2 Gall: 0-0
Aids: Bl: 0-0 Vi: 0-0 Tstrap: 0-0
Best Rating: 96 5/00 Font 3m2f110y good Ch

Palacegate King

55

13-y-o ch g King Among Kings-Market Blues (Porto Bello)
A C Whillans Chas N Whillans

Placings:12664025/3243611222/11001/001/0460303/2103632/62143446/304610230/20-P (0335)
2001/02: 20^{P}S

	Starts	1st	2nd	3rd	Win & Pl
Hurdles	1	0	0	0	
Career Total	60	10	11	9	61967

118	2/00	Carl	2m1f	E(0-115)HHdl	HVY	£2674
122	11/98	Kels	2m2f	D(0-125)HHdl	HVY	£2731
122	12/97	Ayr	2m4f	D(0-125)HHdl	SFT	£2784
120	2/96	Kels	2m110y	B HHdl	SFT	£6775
120	4/95	Hexm	2m	E(0-115)HHdl	SFT	£2402
120	1/95	Hayd	2m	B HHdl	SFT	£6947
110	11/94	Hexm	2m	(0-110)HHdl	HVY	£2128
103	3/94	Hexm	2m	(0-110)HHdl	HVY	£1676
102	3/94	Carl	2m1f	(0-110)HHdl	HVY	£2511
96	12/92	Newc	2m110y	Hdl	SFT	£1646

Total win prize-money £32275

Going: Sf: 0-1 GS: 0-0 Gd: 0-0 GF: - Fm: 0-0
Distance: 2m/2m3: 0-0 2m4-2m7: 0-1 3m+: 0-0
Track: LH: 0-0 RH: 0-1 Tight: 0-0 Gall: 0-0
Aids: Bl: 0-0 Vi: 0-0 Tstrap: 0-0
Best Rating: 122 11/98 Kels 2m2f heavy Hdl

Paladus (IRE)

10-y-o b g Mandalus-Lucy's Pal (Random Shot)
C W Thornton M Gleason

Placings:1653/0/3P-P (0208)
2001/02: 24^{P}F

	Starts	1st	2nd	3rd	Win & Pl
Chases	1	0	0	0	
Career Total	8	1	0	2	2459

91	9/97	DRoy	2m4f	Hdl	G-F	£1695

Total win prize-money £1696

Going: Sf: 0-0 GS: 0-0 Gd: 0-0 GF: - Fm: 0-1
Distance: 2m/2m3: 0-0 2m4-2m7: 0-0 3m+: 0-1
Track: LH: 0-1 RH: 0-0 Tight: 0-1 Gall: 0-0
Aids: Bl: 0-0 Vi: 0-0 Tstrap: 0-0
Best Rating: 97 4/98 Newc 3m soft Hdl

Palais (IRE)

85 **73**

7-y-o b g Darshaan-Dance Festival (Nureyev (USA))
J L Harris J South

Placings:46000/300-P6P (0553)
2001/02: 20^{P}F, 26^{6}GF, 26^{P}GF

	Starts	1st	2nd	3rd	Win & Pl
Hurdles	3	0	0	0	0
Career Total	11	0	0	1	419

Going: Sf: 0-0 GS: 0-0 Gd: 0-0 GF: - Fm: 0-3
Distance: 2m/2m3: 0-0 2m4-2m7: 0-1 3m+: 0-2
Track: LH: 0-1 RH: 0-2 Tight: 0-1 Gall: 0-2
Aids: Bl: 0-0 Vi: 0-0 Tstrap: 0-0
Best Rating: 93 10/99 Strf 2m110y gd-fm Hdl

Modest hurdler, effective over three miles on softish ground.

Palarshan (FR)

101 **133**

4-y-o b/br g Darshaan-Palavera (FR) (Bikala)
H D Daly (Mme P Vanova 1/2) Mrs A L Wood

Placings:131 (4813)
2001/02: 14^{1}G, 16^{3}VS, 17^{1}GF

	Starts	1st	2nd	3rd	Win & Pl
Hurdles	3	2	0	1	11187
Career Total	3	2	0	1	11187

133	4/02	Chel	2m1f	B Hdl	G-F	£8541
	8/01	Pard	1m6f	Hdl	GD	£542

Total win prize-money £9083

Going: Sf: 0-0 GS: 0-0 Gd: 1-1 GF: - Fm: 1-1
Distance: 2m/2m3: 1-2 2m4-2m7: 0-0 3m+: 0-0
Track: LH: 1-1 RH: 0-0 Tight: 0-0 **Gall: 1-1**
Aids: Bl: 0-0 Vi: 0-0 Tstrap: 0-0
Best Rating: 133 4/02 Chel 2m1f gd-fm Hdl

A winner on the Flat in France and over hurdles in the Czech Republic, he was an impressive winner on his British debut at Cheltenham but finished sore. A scopey sort, he should make a chaser in time.

Palisander (IRE)

104 **104**

8-y-o ch g Conquering Hero (USA)-Classic Choice (Patch)
R Ford Dave Teasdale & Keith Hesketh

Placings:46F036104/13313132P0/22132-52 (3473)
2001/02: 20^{5}S, 16^{2}S

	Starts	1st	2nd	3rd	Win & Pl
Chases	2	0	1	0	929
Career Total	26	5	5	6	18747

111	6/00	Prth	2m	E Ch	HVY	£3419
97	11/99	Towc	2m	G Hdl	GD	£1562
97	10/99	Worc	2m	F(0-105)HHdl	G-F	£1856
88	5/99	Hexm	2m	G Hdl	SFT	£2025
86	3/99	Bang	2m1f	G(0-95)HHdl	G-S	£2337

Total win prize-money £11200

Going: Sf: 0-2 GS: 0-0 Gd: 0-0 GF: - Fm: 0-0
Distance: 2m/2m3: 0-1 2m4-2m7: 0-1 3m+: 0-0
Track: LH: 0-0 RH: 0-2 Tight: 0-1 Gall: 0-0
Aids: Bl: 0-0 Vi: 0-0 Tstrap: 0-2
Best Rating: 111 6/00 Prth 2m4f110y good Ch

A fair sort in modest handicap chases, he is best suited by two miles and soft ground.

Palmason

8-y-o b m Minster Son-Palmahalm (Mandrake Major)
Mrs M Evans W J Evans

Placings:0P-P (0124)
2001/02: 24^{P}F

	Starts	1st	2nd	3rd	Win & Pl
Hurdles	1	0	0	0	
Career Total	3	0	0	0	

Going: Sf: 0-0 GS: 0-0 Gd: 0-0 GF: - Fm: 0-1
Distance: 2m/2m3: 0-0 2m4-2m7: 0-0 3m+: 0-1
Track: LH: 0-0 RH: 0-1 Tight: 0-1 Gall: 0-0
Aids: Bl: 0-0 Vi: 0-0 Tstrap: 0-0
Best Rating:

Palouse (IRE)

(96h) (139h) **130**

6-y-o b g Toulon-Hop Picker (USA) (Plugged Nickle (USA))
P J Rothwell G Kinch

Placings:60/020411244-3031134F0 (2499a)
2001/02: 16^{3}G, 16^{0}GY, 16^{3}G, 17^{1}G, 20^{1}G, 17^{3}GF, 21^{4}S, 16^{F}G, 16^{0}Y

	Starts	1st	2nd	3rd	Win & Pl
Hurdles	4	0	0	2	2242
Chases	5	2	0	1	10960
Career Total	20	4	2	3	32854

130	9/01	Tral	2m4f	Ch	GD	£7233
115	8/01	Baln	2m1f	Ch	GD	£7790
139	9/00	Kbgn	2m	Hdl	G-Y	£3312
122	8/00	Rosc	2m	Hdl	FRM	£2760

Total win prize-money £21096

Going: Sf: 0-1 GS: 0-0 Gd: 2-5 GF: - Fm: 0-1
Distance: 2m/2m3: 1-7 2m4-2m7: 1-2 3m+: 0-0
Track: LH: 0-1 RH: 0-2 Tight: 0-0 Gall: 0-1
Aids: Bl: 0-2 Vi: 0-0 Tstrap: 0-0
Best Rating: 139 5/01 Fair 2m good Hdl

A winning Irish hurdler over two miles, he made a winning switch to fences in the summer of 2001, with back to back wins at Ballinrobe and Tralee, but he has been disappointing since. Untried beyond two miles five. Acts on a sound surface.

Palua

100 **111**

5-y-o b g Sri Pekan (USA)-Reticent Bride (IRE) (Shy Groom (USA))
I A Balding Exors Of The Late Robert Hitchins

Placings:4 (3872)
2001/02: 20^{4}S

	Starts	1st	2nd	3rd	Win & Pl
Hurdles	1	0	0	0	808
Career Total	**1**	**0**	**0**	**0**	**808**

Going: Sf: 0-1 GS: 0-0 Gd: 0-0 GF: - Fm: 0-0
Distance: 2m/2m3: 0-0 2m4-2m7: 0-1 3m+: 0-0
Track: LH: 0-0 RH: 0-1 Tight: 0-0 Gall: 0-1
Aids: Bl: 0-0 Vi: 0-0 Tstrap: 0-0
Best Rating: 111 2/02 Hntg 2m4f110y soft Hdl

Second in the Cesarewitch on his final start of the 2001 turf season, he was fit from the Flat when running well on his hurdles debut. Looks a potentially useful recruit.

Pamela Anshan

94 **65**

5-y-o b m Anshan-Have Form (Haveroid)
P R Rodford Mrs Christine Priest

Placings:5555 **(1397)**
2001/02: 17^{5}GS, 17^{5}G, 16^{5}GF, 24^{5}GF

	Starts	1st	2nd	3rd	Win & Pl
Hurdles	4	0	0	0	0
Career Total	**4**	**0**	**0**	**0**	**0**

Going: Sf: 0-0 GS: 0-1 Gd: 0-1 GF: - Fm: 0-2
Distance: 2m/2m3: 0-3 2m4-2m7: 0-0 3m+: 0-1
Track: LH: 0-4 RH: 0-0 Tight: 0-2 Gall: 0-0
Aids: Bl: 0-0 Vi: 0-0 Tstrap: 0-0
Best Rating: 65 8/01 Worc 2m gd-fm Hdl

Pangeran (USA)

10-y-o ch g Forty Niner (USA)-Smart Heiress (USA) (Vaguely Noble)
Neil King Mrs Jill McVay

Placings:42622505/423U/3622/143UU/31P3-32460 **(4638)**
2001/02: 21^{3}G, 24^{2}GF, 21^{4}G, 16^{6}S, 19^{0}GF

	Starts	1st	2nd	3rd	Win & Pl
Chases	5	0	1	1	752
Career Total	**30**	**2**	**7**	**6**	**9507**

116	5/00	Uttx	2m5f	H Ch	GD	£1742
98	5/99	Folk	2m5f	H Ch	G-F	£1472

Total win prize-money £3214

Going: Sf: 0-1 GS: 0-0 Gd: 0-2 GF: - Fm: 0-2
Distance: 2m/2m3: 0-1 2m4-2m7: 0-3 3m+: 0-1
Track: LH: 0-1 RH: 0-4 Tight: 0-2 Gall: 0-1
Aids: Bl: 0-0 Vi: 0-0 Tstrap: 0-0
Best Rating: 116 5/00 Uttx 2m5f good Ch

Panhandle

97 **86**

8-y-o b m Riverwise (USA)-Pallanda (Pablond)
N R Mitchell N R Mitchell

Placings:*000*/PP5-36P2P000 **(4484)**
2001/02: 17^{3}GS, 21^{6}G, 22^{P}HY, 16^{2}S, 16^{P}S, 17^{0}S, 22^{0}S, 17^{0}G

	Starts	1st	2nd	3rd	Win & Pl
Hurdles	8	0	1	1	1914
Career Total	**14**	**0**	**1**	**1**	**1914**

Going: Sf: 0-5 GS: 0-1 Gd: 0-2 GF: - Fm: 0-0
Distance: 2m/2m3: 0-5 2m4-2m7: 0-3 3m+: 0-0
Track: LH: 0-3 RH: 0-5 Tight: 0-3 Gall: 0-0
Aids: Bl: 0-0 Vi: 0-0 Tstrap: 0-0
Best Rating: 86 5/01 Extr 2m1f gd-sft Hdl

Exposed as a very modest hurdler.

Panmure (IRE)

75 **67**

6-y-o b g Alphabatim (USA)-Serjitak (Saher)
N J Henderson Bartlett-Dennison-Niven

Placings:304 **(3766)**
2001/02: 16^{3}G, 21^{0}G, 20^{4}GS

	Starts	1st	2nd	3rd	Win & Pl
NH Flat	1	0	0	1	608
Hurdles	2	0	0	0	0
Career Total	**3**	**0**	**0**	**1**	**608**

Going: Sf: 0-0 GS: 0-1 Gd: 0-2 GF: - Fm: 0-0
Distance: 2m/2m3: 0-1 2m4-2m7: 0-2 3m+: 0-0
Track: LH: 0-3 RH: 0-0 Tight: 0-1 Gall: 0-1
Aids: Bl: 0-0 Vi: 0-0 Tstrap: 0-0
Best Rating: 104 10/01 Chel 2m110y good NHF

Well touted before his debut in a Cheltenham bumper. He looks the type to improve for a sterner test of stamina.

Panooras Lord (IRE)

94 **93**

8-y-o b g Topanoora-Ladyship (Windjammer (USA))
J S Wainwright J S Wainwright

Placings:6320/5P0200010/U0/1PP046-000 **(2509)**
2001/02: 16^{0}G, 20^{0}S, 19^{0}S

	Starts	1st	2nd	3rd	Win & Pl
Hurdles	3	0	0	0	
Career Total	**24**	**2**	**2**	**1**	**5118**

98	6/00	Fknm	2m	G(0-90)HHdl	GD	£1876
87	4/99	Hntg	2m110y	G(0-100)HHdl	G-F	£1926

Total win prize-money £3802

Going: Sf: 0-2 GS: 0-0 Gd: 0-1 GF: - Fm: 0-0
Distance: 2m/2m3: 0-2 2m4-2m7: 0-1 3m+: 0-0
Track: LH: 0-3 RH: 0-0 Tight: 0-2 Gall: 0-0
Aids: Bl: 0-0 Vi: 0-0 Tstrap: 0-0
Best Rating: 98 6/00 Fknm 2m good Hdl

Pantypwll Boy

64f **27f**

6-y-o b g Ajjaj-Narbeth Coin (Glasgow Central)
Mrs D A Hamer W Thomas

Placings:*0* **(1545)**
2001/02: 17^{0}G

	Starts	1st	2nd	3rd	Win & Pl
NH Flat	1	0	0	0	
Career Total	**1**	**0**	**0**	**0**	

Going: Sf: 0-0 GS: 0-0 Gd: 0-1 GF: - Fm: 0-0
Distance: 2m/2m3: 0-1 2m4-2m7: 0-0 3m+: 0-0
Track: LH: 0-0 RH: 0-1 Tight: 0-0 Gall: 0-0
Aids: Bl: 0-0 Vi: 0-0 Tstrap: 0-0
Best Rating: 27 10/01 Hrfd 2m1f good NHF

Papanui

80 **45**

5-y-o b m Nomination-Cutlass Princess (USA) (Cutlass (USA))
Miss C J E Caroe Miss C J E Caroe

Placings:U00-0000 **(1131)**
2001/02: 16^{0}GF, 16^{0}G, 19^{0}G, 16^{0}GF

	Starts	1st	2nd	3rd	Win & Pl
Hurdles	4	0	0	0	
Career Total	**7**	**0**	**0**	**0**	

Going: Sf: 0-0 GS: 0-0 Gd: 0-2 GF: - Fm: 0-2
Distance: 2m/2m3: 0-3 2m4-2m7: 0-1 3m+: 0-0
Track: LH: 0-3 RH: 0-1 Tight: 0-2 Gall: 0-0
Aids: Bl: 0-0 Vi: 0-0 Tstrap: 0-0
Best Rating: 55 12/00 Folk 2m1f110y heavy Hdl

Paperising

111(101h) (128h)**158**

10-y-o b g Primitive Rising (USA)-Eye Bee Aitch (Move Off)
N G Richards The Jockeys Whips

Placings:*1040*/2411215P/**51F111**/4F/5112P-01P14 **(4897)**
2001/02: 20^{0}S, 20^{1}HY, 24^{P}G, 20^{1}GS, 24^{4}G

	Starts	1st	2nd	3rd	Win & Pl
Hurdles	2	1	0	0	3575
Chases	3	1	0	0	13483
Career Total	**30**	**12**	**3**	**0**	**90673**

128	3/02	Carl	2m4f	D(0-125)HHdl	G-S	£3575
152	2/02	Ayr	2m4f	B(0-145)HCh	HVY	£12431
151	2/01	Uttx	3m	C(0-130)HCh	SFT	£6741
145	1/01	Ayr	2m4f	B(0-140)HCh	G-S	£9742
140	4/98	Ayr	3m1f	C HCh	GD	£25330
140	3/98	Bang	3m110y	D Ch	G-S	£4377
139	3/98	Ayr	3m1f	D Ch	G-S	£3626
123	2/98	Kels	3m1f	D Ch	G-S	£4021
117	2/97	Carl	2m4f110y	E Hdl	SFT	£2738
108	12/96	Hexm	3m	E Hdl	G-S	£2805
104	12/96	Sedg	2m5f110y	E Hdl	GD	£1935
90	3/96	Carl	2m1f	H NHF	GD	£1479

Total win prize-money £78803

Going: Sf: 1-2 GS: 1-1 Gd: 0-2 GF: - Fm: 0-0
Distance: 2m/2m3: 0-0 **2m4-2m7: 2-3** 3m+: 0-2
Track: **LH: 1-2** RH: 0-2 Tight: 0-0 Gall: 0-0
Aids: Bl: 0-0 Vi: 0-0 Tstrap: 0-0
Best Rating: 154 4/01 Aint 3m1f soft Ch

He has had something of an interrupted career through injury, but has a decent strike rate since 1998. Regained the winning threat at Kelso in May 2002 , he is best on soft ground at up to three miles and is suited by sharpish left-handed tracks.

Papua

93(111h) (134h)**130**

8-y-o ch g Green Dancer (USA)-Fairy Tern (Mill Reef (USA))
J White (I A Balding 7/10) Nick Quesnel

Placings:61P/242042/260613533 **(2789)**
2001/02: 16^{2}GF, 16^{6}GF, 16^{0}GF, 17^{6}GS, 17^{1}GS, 17^{3}G, 18^{5}S, 16^{3}S, 16^{3}G

	Starts	1st	2nd	3rd	Win & Pl
Hurdles	7	1	1	1	6834
Chases	2	0	0	2	2180
Career Total	**18**	**2**	**4**	**3**	**28257**

127	8/01	Ctml	2m1f110y	D(0-125)HHdl	G-S	£3464
126	2/98	Wind	2m	B Hdl	G-F	£7351

Total win prize-money £10816

Going: Sf: 0-2 GS: 1-2 Gd: 0-2 GF: - Fm: 0-3
Distance: **2m/2m3: 1-9** 2m4-2m7: 0-0 3m+: 0-0
Track: **LH: 1-6** RH: 0-1 **Tight: 1-5** Gall: 0-0
Aids: Bl: 0-2 **Vi: 1-3** Tstrap: 0-0
Best Rating: 134 6/01 Strf 2m110y gd-fm Hdl

He has been often placed over hurdles, but has only won twice and never really hit the heights that seemed possible. Did not set the world alight over fences for his new trainer in late 2001.

Par Three (IRE)

101 **113**

6-y-o b g King's Ride-Four Shares (The Parson)
J J O'Neill (E Bolger 21/5) J P McMcManus

Placings:032P (3772)
2001/02: 20^{0}GF, 24^{3}S, 25^{2}GS, 20^{P}S

	Starts	1st	2nd	3rd	Win & Pl
NH Flat	1	0	0	0	0
Chases	3	0	1	1	2135
Career Total	**4**	**0**	**1**	**1**	**2135**

Going: Sf: 0-2 GS: 0-1 Gd: 0-0 GF: - Fm: 0-1
Distance: 2m/2m3: 0-0 2m4-2m7: 0-2 3m+: 0-2
Track: LH: 0-2 RH: 0-1 Tight: 0-1 Gall: 0-0
Aids: Bl: 0-0 Vi: 0-0 Tstrap: 0-0
Best Rating: **113** 12/01 Strf 3m soft Ch

Winning pointer in Ireland, he has progressed steadily over fences until going wrong at Sandown in February. (DEAD)

Parade Racer

11-y-o b g Derring Rose-Dusky Damsel (Sahib)
Tim Butt Tim Butt

Placings:56/PP42F153/F/**PP43444P/3/3203** (4892)
2001/02: [illegible]^{3}HY, [illegible]^{2}G, [illegible]^{0}HY, [illegible]^{3}G

	Starts	1st	2nd	3rd	Win & Pl
Chases	4	0	1	2	3264
Career Total	**24**	**1**	**2**	**5**	**8147**

80 1/97 Towc 2m5f G(0-95)HHdl G-S £2232
Total win prize-money £2233

Going: Sf: 0-3 GS: 0-0 Gd: 0-1 GF: - Fm: 0-0
Distance: 2m/2m3: 0-0 2m4-2m7: 0-1 3m+: 0-3
Track: LH: 0-1 RH: 0-1 Tight: 0-1 Gall: 0-0
Aids: Bl: 0-0 Vi: 0-0 Tstrap: 0-0
Best Rating: **111** 3/02 Leic 2m7f110y soft Ch

Fair pointer/hunter chaser, stays three miles. Acts on any ground.

Paradise Garden (USA)

69 **58**

5-y-o b g Septieme Ciel (USA)-Water Course (USA) (Irish River (FR))
P L Clinton (Denys Smith 7/9) P L Clinton

Placings:0P (1346)
2001/02: 17^{0}G, 17^{P}GF

	Starts	1st	2nd	3rd	Win & Pl
Hurdles	2	0	0	0	
Career Total	**2**	**0**	**0**	**0**	

Going: Sf: 0-0 GS: 0-0 Gd: 0-1 GF: - Fm: 0-1
Distance: 2m/2m3: 0-2 2m4-2m7: 0-0 3m+: 0-0
Track: LH: 0-2 RH: 0-0 Tight: 0-2 Gall: 0-0
Aids: Bl: 0-0 Vi: 0-0 Tstrap: 0-0
Best Rating: **58** 8/01 Ctml 2m1f110y good Hdl

Parahandy (IRE)

12-y-o b g Lancastrian-Dishcloth (Fury Royal)
J W Mullins G E Heard

Placings:2246/UF11/4P345/1/224224-53 (0576)
2001/02: 23^{5}GS, 28^{3}GF

	Starts	1st	2nd	3rd	Win & Pl
Chases	2	0	0	1	678
Career Total	**22**	**3**	**6**	**2**	**29690**

135 11/99 NAbb 3m2f110y B(0-140)HCh G-S £8439
129 4/98 Winc 3m1f110y E Ch G-S £3226
135 4/98 Font 3m2f110y E(0-115)HCh G-S £3377
Total win prize-money £15043

Going: Sf: 0-0 GS: 0-1 Gd: 0-0 GF: - Fm: 0-1
Distance: 2m/2m3: 0-0 2m4-2m7: 0-0 3m+: 0-2
Track: LH: 0-1 RH: 0-1 Tight: 0-1 Gall: 0-0
Aids: Bl: 0-0 Vi: 0-0 Tstrap: 0-0
Best Rating: **135** 4/01 Newb 3m soft Ch

A thorough stayer, he is entering the veteran stage. Suited by cut in the ground.

Paraveredus (FR)

6-y-o br g Mansonnien (FR)-Parallele (GER) (Jolly Jinks S (HOL))
A Crook The Blue Devils Partnership

Placings:0/0P-PP (1622)
2001/02: 20^{P}G, 25^{P}G

	Starts	1st	2nd	3rd	Win & Pl
Chases	2	0	0	0	
Career Total	**5**	**0**	**0**	**0**	

Going: Sf: 0-0 GS: 0-0 Gd: 0-0 GF: - Fm: 0-0
Distance: 2m/2m3: 0-0 2m4-2m7: 0-1 3m+: 0-1
Track: LH: 0-0 RH: 0-2 Tight: 0-0 Gall: 0-0
Aids: Bl: 0-1 Vi: 0-0 Tstrap: 0-0
Best Rating: **79** 4/00 Carl 2m1f gd-sft NHF

Pardan

8-y-o b g Pharly (FR)-Silent Pool (Relkino)
B Palling Mrs M M Palling

Placings:43/0P46/43P142/P-U0 (2926)
2001/02: 19^{U}GS, 24^{0}GS

	Starts	1st	2nd	3rd	Win & Pl
Hurdles	2	0	0	0	
Career Total	**15**	**1**	**1**	**2**	**3003**

94 3/00 Tntn 2m3f110y G(0-90)HHdl GD £1526
Total win prize-money £1526

Going: Sf: 0-0 GS: 0-2 Gd: 0-0 GF: - Fm: 0-0
Distance: 2m/2m3: 0-0 2m4-2m7: 0-1 3m+: 0-1
Track: LH: 0-0 RH: 0-2 Tight: 0-2 Gall: 0-0
Aids: Bl: 0-0 Vi: 0-0 Tstrap: 0-0
Best Rating: **94** 4/00 Hrfd 2m3f110y soft Hdl

Pardishar (IRE)

104 **100**

4-y-o b c Kahyasi-Parapa (IRE) (Akarad (FR))
G L Moore (Sir Michael Stoute 18/8) Mike Charlton And Rodger Sargent

Placings:0 (4651)
2001/02: 16^{0}G

	Starts	1st	2nd	3rd	Win & Pl
Hurdles	1	0	0	0	
Career Total	**1**	**0**	**0**	**0**	

Going: Sf: 0-0 GS: 0-0 Gd: 0-1 GF: - Fm: 0-0
Distance: 2m/2m3: 0-1 2m4-2m7: 0-0 3m+: 0-0
Track: LH: 0-1 RH: 0-0 Tight: 0-1 Gall: 0-0
Aids: Bl: 0-0 Vi: 0-0 Tstrap: 0-0
Best Rating: **76** 4/02 Aint 2m110y good Hdl

Paris Knight (IRE)

4-y-o b g Paris House-Bykova (Petoski)
B J Llewellyn (A Berry 2/9) B J Llewellyn

Placings:P (2209)
2001/02: 17^{P}G

	Starts	1st	2nd	3rd	Win & Pl
Hurdles	1	0	0	0	
Career Total	**1**	**0**	**0**	**0**	

Going: Sf: 0-0 GS: 0-0 Gd: 0-1 GF: - Fm: 0-0
Distance: 2m/2m3: 0-1 2m4-2m7: 0-0 3m+: 0-0
Track: LH: 0-0 RH: 0-1 Tight: 0-0 Gall: 0-0
Aids: Bl: 0-0 Vi: 0-0 Tstrap: 0-0
Best Rating:

Paris Pike (IRE)

103 **157**

10-y-o b g Satco (FR)-Bouise (Royal Buck)
Ferdy Murphy Major & Mrs Ivan Straker

Placings:4104/434432212/1121111/2P66FP (4839)
2001/02: 25^{2}GS, 24^{P}Y, 25^{6}HY, 24^{6}S, 36^{F}G, 33^{P}G

	Starts	1st	2nd	3rd	Win & Pl
Chases	6	0	1	0	3959
Career Total	**26**	**8**	**5**	**2**	**103592**

168 4/00 Ayr 4m1f A HCh GD £42000
163 3/00 Uttx 3m2f C HCh GD £18395
150 3/00 Kels 3m1f B(0-150)HCh G-S £8513
148 2/00 Kels 3m1f C Ch G-S £7150
120 11/99 Kels 3m1f D Ch GD £4221
101 5/99 Prth 3m110y E Hdl HVY £2990
115 2/99 Clon 3m Hdl SFT £3069
106 10/97 Leop 2m4f NHF G Y £4069
Total win prize-money £90408

Going: Sf: 0-2 GS: 0-1 Gd: 0-2 GF: - Fm: 0-0
Distance: 2m/2m3: 0-0 2m4-2m7: 0-0 3m+: 0-6
Track: LH: 0-6 RH: 0-0 Tight: 0-2 Gall: 0-2
Aids: Bl: 0-0 Vi: 0-0 Tstrap: 0-0
Best Rating: **168** 4/00 Ayr 4m1f good Ch

He was most progressive in the spring of 2000, culminating in victory in the Scottish National. Sidelined with a leg injury the following season, he ran well on his return at Kelso in 2001 but was pulled up with a muscle problem next time. Not disgraced at Newbury in February. Well fancied for the Grand National, but came down at the first, before pulling up in the Scottish version. Stays well and likes decent ground.

Parish Oak

108 **80**

7-y-o b g Rakaposhi King-Poppy's Pride (Uncle Pokey)
Ian Williams Mrs M Mann

Placings:05P0-U00 (4187)
2001/02: 17^{U}GF, 16^{0}S, 19^{0}S

	Starts	1st	2nd	3rd	Win & Pl
Hurdles	3	0	0	0	
Career Total	**7**	**0**	**0**	**0**	**0**

Going: Sf: 0-2 GS: 0-0 Gd: 0-0 GF: - Fm: 0-1
Distance: 2m/2m3: 0-2 2m4-2m7: 0-1 3m+: 0-0
Track: LH: 0-0 RH: 0-3 Tight: 0-2 Gall: 0-1
Aids: Bl: 0-0 Vi: 0-0 Tstrap: 0-1
Best Rating: **89** 12/00 Hntg 2m110y heavy NHF

Modest hurdler, stays two miles plus and handles cut in the ground.

Parisian Inferno (IRE)

4-y-o b g Paris House-La Fille De Feu (Never So Bold)
N A Smith P E T Chandler

Placings:PP (3890)
2001/02: 16^{P}G, 16^{P}HY

	Starts	1st	2nd	3rd	Win & Pl
Hurdles	2	0	0	0	
Career Total	**2**	**0**	**0**	**0**	

Going: Sf: 0-1 GS: 0-0 Gd: 0-1 GF: - Fm: 0-0
Distance: 2m/2m3: 0-2 2m4-2m7: 0-0 3m+: 0-0
Track: LH: 0-2 RH: 0-0 Tight: 0-0 Gall: 0-1
Aids: Bl: 0-0 Vi: 0-0 Tstrap: 0-0
Best Rating:

Park Place (IRE)

103 **89**

7-y-o gr g Husyan (USA)-Iron Mermaid (General Ironside)
J I A Charlton W F Trueman

Placings:*105*-665 (2343)
2001/02: 16^{6}GF, 22^{6}G, 20^{5}GS

	Starts	1st	2nd	3rd	Win & Pl
NH Flat	1	0	0	0	0
Hurdles	2	0	0	0	0
Career Total	**6**	**1**	**0**	**0**	**1918**

112	5/00	Prth	2m110y	H NHF	G-S	£1918

Total win prize-money £1918

Going: Sf: 0-0 GS: 0-1 Gd: 0-1 GF: - Fm: 0-1
Distance: 2m/2m3: 0-1 2m4-2m7: 0-2 3m+: 0-0
Track: LH: 0-2 RH: 0-0 Tight: 0-1 Gall: 0-1
Aids: Bl: 0-0 Vi: 0-0 Tstrap: 0-0
Best Rating: 112 5/00 Prth 2m110y gd-sft NHF

Parliamentarian (IRE)

71

13-y-o br g Idiots Delight-Elect (New Member)
A Ennis J G M Wates

Placings:P04/P/**P5/240P152P/2112F24/21UU4540/55 34P/1500-006** (1945)
2001/02: 20^{0}GF, 21^{0}G, 17^{6}GS

	Starts	1st	2nd	3rd	Win & Pl
Chases	3	0	0	0	0
Career Total	**41**	**5**	**6**	**1**	**24129**

105	5/00	Font	2m4f	F(0-110)HCh	GD	£3087
110	5/98	Towc	2m110y	D(0-125)HCh	G-F	£3548
101	11/97	Font	2m2f	D(0-125)HCh	G-S	£3590
113	10/97	Towc	2m110y	E(0-115)HCh	G-F	£2864
91	3/97	Sand	3m110y	D(0-110)HCh	GD	£3517

Total win prize-money £16608

Going: Sf: 0-0 GS: 0-1 Gd: 0-1 GF: - Fm: 0-1
Distance: 2m/2m3: 0-1 2m4-2m7: 0-2 3m+: 0-0
Track: LH: 0-1 RH: 0-1 Tight: 0-3 Gall: 0-0
Aids: Bl: 0-3 Vi: 0-0 Tstrap: 0-0
Best Rating: 113 10/97 Towc 2m110y gd-fm Ch

Parlour Game

105 **112**

6-y-o br m Petoski-Henry's True Love (Random Shot)
H D Daly T F F Nixon

Placings:*31F0*-63P55 (4822)
2001/02: 16^{6}S, 20^{3}S, 21^{P}GS, 16^{5}GS, 21^{5}G

	Starts	1st	2nd	3rd	Win & Pl
Hurdles	5	0	0	1	533
Career Total	**9**	**1**	**0**	**2**	**3354**

117	1/01	Sthl	2m	E Hdl	HVY	£2590

Total win prize-money £2590

Going: Sf: 0-2 GS: 0-2 Gd: 0-1 GF: - Fm: 0-0
Distance: 2m/2m3: 0-2 2m4-2m7: 0-3 3m+: 0-0
Track: LH: 0-3 RH: 0-2 Tight: 0-1 Gall: 0-2
Aids: Bl: 0-0 Vi: 0-0 Tstrap: 0-0
Best Rating: 117 1/01 Sthl 2m heavy Hdl

She easily won a Southwell novice hurdle in January 2001, but things have not really gone her way since. Suited by soft ground.

Parman's Pride

45f **5f**

6-y-o b m Queen's Soldier (USA)-Free Sally (Daring March)
A G Hobbs Robin J Reip

Placings:*00* (3563)
2001/02: 16^{0}G, 16^{0}HY

	Starts	1st	2nd	3rd	Win & Pl
NH Flat	2	0	0	0	
Career Total	**2**	**0**	**0**	**0**	

Going: Sf: 0-1 GS: 0-0 Gd: 0-1 GF: - Fm: 0-0
Distance: 2m/2m3: 0-2 2m4-2m7: 0-0 3m+: 0-0
Track: LH: 0-0 RH: 0-2 Tight: 0-0 Gall: 0-0
Aids: Bl: 0-0 Vi: 0-0 Tstrap: 0-0
Best Rating: 5 1/02 Ludl 2m good NHF

Parsons Boy

104 **124**

13-y-o ch g The Parson-Kylogue Daisy (Little Buskins)
Mrs L Williamson P H Morris

Placings:*06*0660P/**26511113/1103/6PP1P13/3354233 P/P4064P/1-12P** (1816)
2001/02: 25^{1}S, 30^{2}G, 26^{P}S

	Starts	1st	2nd	3rd	Win & Pl
Chases	3	1	1	0	4396
Career Total	**44**	**10**	**3**	**7**	**52922**

94	5/01	Hexm	3m1f	H Ch	SFT	£2688
98	4/01	Hayd	3m	F(0-105)HCh	SFT	£3601
131	4/98	Bang	3m110y	D(0-125)HCh	SFT	£5015
128	3/98	Bang	3m110y	D(0-125)HCh	G-S	£4443
125	11/96	Hayd	3m4f110y	B(0-140)HCh	GD	£6729
122	11/96	Carl	3m	D(0-125)HCh	GD	£4535
106	3/96	Bang	3m110y	D Ch	HVY	£4071
114	3/96	Newc	3m	E Ch	SFT	£3165
100	2/96	Weth	3m110y	D Ch	G-S	£3821
101	2/96	Kels	3m1f	E Ch	SFT	£3050

Total win prize-money £41121

Going: Sf: 1-2 GS: 0-0 Gd: 0-1 GF: - Fm: 0-0
Distance: 2m/2m3: 0-0 2m4-2m7: 0-0 **3m+: 1-3**
Track: **LH: 1-2** RH: 0-1 Tight: 0-1 Gall: 0-0
Aids: Bl: 0-0 Vi: 0-0 Tstrap: 0-0
Best Rating: 131 4/98 Worc 2m7f110y gd-sft Ch

Party Animal (IRE)

104 **120**

10-y-o b g Buckskin (FR)-More Chat (Torenaga)
K C Bailey David G W Curtis

Placings:453/23/1U-3 (1958)
2001/02: 26^{3}G

	Starts	1st	2nd	3rd	Win & Pl
Chases	1	0	0	1	362
Career Total	**8**	**1**	**1**	**3**	**5155**

120	11/00	Hrfd	3m1f110y	F(0-90)HCh	G-S	£2710

Total win prize-money £2711

Going: Sf: 0-0 GS: 0-0 Gd: 0-1 GF: - Fm: 0-0
Distance: 2m/2m3: 0-0 2m4-2m7: 0-0 3m+: 0-1
Track: LH: 0-1 RH: 0-0 Tight: 0-0 Gall: 0-0
Aids: Bl: 0-0 Vi: 0-0 Tstrap: 0-0
Best Rating: 120 11/01 Wwck 3m2f good Ch

Lightly raced, he won an amateur handicap chase at Hereford in 2000, but was off the track for 11 months after falling next time. Ran a creditable race on his return at Warwick and should win more races over fences.

Party Lad (IRE)

98(96h) **104**

9-y-o b g King's Ride-Lantern Lass (Monksfield)
N A Twiston-Davies Mrs R Mackness

Placings:*03/P10/0624F2*-**1U4PP** (4814)
2001/02: 25^{1}S, 24^{U}GF, 20^{4}GS, 26^{P}S, 21^{P}GF

	Starts	1st	2nd	3rd	Win & Pl
Chases	5	1	0	0	3937
Career Total	**16**	**2**	**2**	**1**	**11046**

95	5/01	Hexm	3m1f	E Ch	SFT	£3399
98	1/00	Cork	2m	Hdl	SH	£3864

Total win prize-money £7264

Going: Sf: 1-2 GS: 0-1 Gd: 0-0 GF: - Fm: 0-2
Distance: 2m/2m3: 0-0 2m4-2m7: 0-2 **3m+: 1-3**
Track: **LH: 1-4** RH: 0-1 Tight: 0-2 Gall: 0-1
Aids: Bl: 0-0 Vi: 0-0 Tstrap: 0-0
Best Rating: 119 2/01 Tntn 3m heavy Ch

Modest novice chaser, stays three miles, acts on soft ground. Not the best of jumpers.

Party Spirit (IRE)

82f **44f**

4-y-o b g Good Thyne (USA)-Emmodee (Bowling Pin)
R D E Woodhouse Go Racing

Placings:*0* (3368)
2001/02: 16^{0}GS

	Starts	1st	2nd	3rd	Win & Pl
NH Flat	1	0	0	0	
Career Total	**1**	**0**	**0**	**0**	

Going: Sf: 0-0 GS: 0-1 Gd: 0-0 GF: - Fm: 0-0
Distance: 2m/2m3: 0-1 2m4-2m7: 0-0 3m+: 0-0
Track: LH: 0-1 RH: 0-0 Tight: 0-1 Gall: 0-0
Aids: Bl: 0-0 Vi: 0-0 Tstrap: 0-0
Best Rating: 44 1/02 Catt 2m gd-sft NHF

Pas De Probleme (IRE)

75 **39**

6-y-o ch g Ela-Mana-Mou-Torriglia (USA) (Nijinsky (CAN))
J G Portman Captain Francis Burne

Placings:P-0 (2129)
2001/02: 16^{0}GF

Starts	1st	2nd	3rd	Win & Pl
Hurdles	1	0	0	0	
Career Total	2	0	0	0	

Going: Sf: 0-0 GS: 0-0 Gd: 0-0 GF: - Fm: 0-1
Distance: 2m/2m3: 0-1 2m4-2m7: 0-0 3m+: 0-0
Track: LH: 0-0 RH: 0-1 Tight: 0-0 Gall: 0-0
Aids: Bl: 0-0 Vi: 0-0 Tstrap: 0-0
Best Rating: 39 11/01 Ludl 2m gd-fm Hdl

Pash Pronto

85 53

8-y-o ch g Roselier (FR)-Lidoma (IRE) (Dominion)
M C Pipe Mrs Angie Malde

Placings:PF6PU-600 (0834)
2001/02: 22^{6}F, 22^{0}GF, 27^{0}GF

	Starts	1st	2nd	3rd	Win & Pl
Hurdles	3	0	0	0	0
Career Total	8	0	0	0	0

Going: Sf: 0-0 GS: 0-0 Gd: 0-0 GF: - Fm: 0-3
Distance: 2m/2m3: 0-0 2m4-2m7: 0-2 3m+: 0-1
Track: LH: 0-2 RH: 0-0 Tight: 0-2 Gall: 0-0
Aids: Bl: 0-0 Vi: 0-1 Tstrap: 0-3
Best Rating: 53 5/01 Extr 2m6f110y firm Hdl

Passereau (FR)

104(89h) 114?

6-y-o b g Fijar Tango (FR)-Becebege (FR) (Iron Duke (FR))
C N Kellett Sean A Taylor

Placings:0412/06P354005U1644F-0P21322P5PP51 (4909)
2001/02: 20^{0}GF, 25^{P}G, 17^{2}G, 17^{1}GS, 16^{3}S, 16^{2}HY, 19^{2}G, 17^{P}S, 20^{5}S, 16^{P}S, 20^{P}GS, 16^{5}G, 20^{1}GF

	Starts	1st	2nd	3rd	Win & Pl
Chases	13	2	3	1	12317
Career Total	32	4	4	2	32053

107	4/02	MRas	2m4f	E(0-105)HCh	G-F	£3744
105	11/01	Plum	2m1f	F(0-110)HCh	G-S	£2912
109	2/01	Bang	2m1f110y	D(0-110)HCh	HVY	£4212
	1/00	Pau	2m2f	Hdl	HVY	£5764

Total win prize-money £16632

Going: Sf: 0-5 GS: 1-2 Gd: 0-4 GF: - Fm: 1-2
Distance: 2m/2m3: 1-7 2m4-2m7: 1-5 3m+: 0-1
Track: LH: 1-6 RH: 1-6 **Tight: 2-6** Gall: 0-3
Aids: Bl: 0-0 Vi: 0-2 Tstrap: 0-1
Best Rating: 109 2/01 Bang 2m1f110y heavy Ch

Fair handicap chaser. Suited by sharp left-handed tracks, two/two and a half miles and a sound surface.

Passing Danger (FR)

94 97

7-y-o b g Passing Sale (FR)-Destination Danger (FR) (Bois Mineau (FR))
G F White F V White

Placings:3162030/00000340/P-2506 (1023)
2001/02: 20^{2}F, 16^{5}G, 21^{0}GF, 21^{6}GF

	Starts	1st	2nd	3rd	Win & Pl
Hurdles	4	0	1	0	744
Career Total	20	1	2	3	5253

87	11/98	Clon	2m	Hdl	SFT	£2690

Total win prize-money £2690

Going: Sf: 0-0 GS: 0-0 Gd: 0-1 GF: - Fm: 0-3
Distance: 2m/2m3: 0-1 2m4-2m7: 0-3 3m+: 0-0
Track: LH: 0-4 RH: 0-0 Tight: 0-2 Gall: 0-0
Aids: Bl: 0-0 Vi: 0-0 Tstrap: 0-0
Best Rating: 106 1/99 Thur 2m heavy Hdl

Passing Shadow (IRE)

80 68

7-y-o br g Air Display (USA)-Here To-Day (King's Equity)
J Mackie N J Sessions

Placings:0-P56 (2034)
2001/02: 22^{P}GS, 24^{5}G, 24^{6}GS

	Starts	1st	2nd	3rd	Win & Pl
Hurdles	3	0	0	0	0
Career Total	4	0	0	0	0

Going: Sf: 0-0 GS: 0-2 Gd: 0-1 GF: - Fm: 0-0
Distance: 2m/2m3: 0-0 2m4-2m7: 0-1 3m+: 0-2
Track: LH: 0-3 RH: 0-0 Tight: 0-1 Gall: 0-0
Aids: Bl: 0-0 Vi: 0-0 Tstrap: 0-0
Best Rating: 68 11/01 Chep 3m gd-sft Hdl

Passing Wind (NZ)

105 96

8-y-o br g Beau Zephyr (AUS)-Miss Row (NZ) (Long Row)
S G Griffiths S G Griffiths

Placings:33F03FFP-1F22060P (4739)
2001/02: 17^{1}GS, 17^{F}G, 17^{2}S, 20^{2}S, 19^{0}GS, 21^{6}G, 24^{0}GS, 21^{P}GF

	Starts	1st	2nd	3rd	Win & Pl
Hurdles	8	1	2	0	4626
Career Total	16	1	2	3	5909

93	8/01	Bang	2m1f	E(0-105)HHdl	G-S	£3122

Total win prize-money £3122

Going: Sf: 0-2 GS: 1-3 Gd: 0-2 GF: - Fm: 0-1
Distance: **2m/2m3: 1-3** 2m4-2m7: 0-4 3m+: 0-1
Track: **LH: 1-5** RH: 0-3 **Tight: 1-4** Gall: 0-1
Aids: Bl: 0-0 Vi: 0-0 Tstrap: 0-0
Best Rating: 96 11/01 Uttx 2m4f110y soft Hdl

A New Zealand import, he has shown modest ability over hurdles. Appreciates a little cut in the ground.

Pastiche

63 37

8-y-o b m Kylian (USA)-Titian Beauty (Auction Ring (USA))
Mrs L C Jewell Mrs Val Morgan

Placings:0 (1417)
2001/02: 16^{0}GF

	Starts	1st	2nd	3rd	Win & Pl
Hurdles	1	0	0	0	
Career Total	1	0	0	0	

Going: Sf: 0-0 GS: 0-0 Gd: 0-0 GF: - Fm: 0-1
Distance: 2m/2m3: 0-1 2m4-2m7: 0-0 3m+: 0-0
Track: LH: 0-1 RH: 0-0 Tight: 0-1 Gall: 0-0
Aids: Bl: 0-0 Vi: 0-0 Tstrap: 0-0
Best Rating: 37 9/01 Plum 2m gd-fm Hdl

Pat's Gesture

8-y-o br g Orchestra-Arpal Magic (Master Owen)
Ferdy Murphy Geoff Adam

Placings:35246/000-PF (4064)
2001/02: 20^{P}G, 16^{F}S

	Starts	1st	2nd	3rd	Win & Pl
Hurdles	1	0	0	0	0
Chases	1	0	0	0	0
Career Total	10	0	1	1	647

Going: Sf: 0-1 GS: 0-0 Gd: 0-1 GF: - Fm: 0-0
Distance: 2m/2m3: 0-1 2m4-2m7: 0-1 3m+: 0-0
Track: LH: 0-2 RH: 0-0 Tight: 0-1 Gall: 0-0
Aids: Bl: 0-0 Vi: 0-0 Tstrap: 0-0
Best Rating: 97 2/00 Muss 2m gd-sft NHF

Pateley (IRE)

92(111c) (117c)75

8-y-o b g Cataldi-Suir Venture (Roselier (FR))
John R Upson (P J Hobbs 6/8) K Hancock & P M Haslam

Placings:64103/00B1023564/2253R60-62233PF04 (4754)
2001/02: 19^{6}G, 21^{2}GF, 21^{2}GF, 24^{3}G, 21^{3}G, 22^{P}G, 16^{F}GS, 16^{0}GS, 24^{4}GF

	Starts	1st	2nd	3rd	Win & Pl
Hurdles	4	0	0	0	333
Chases	5	0	2	2	3699
Career Total	31	2	5	5	14331

112	11/99	Thur	2m	Hdl	Y-S	£2217
102	1/99	Fair	2m	NHF	HVY	£2762

Total win prize-money £4980

Going: Sf: 0-0 GS: 0-2 Gd: 0-4 GF: - Fm: 0-3
Distance: 2m/2m3: 0-3 2m4-2m7: 0-4 3m+: 0-2
Track: LH: 0-7 RH: 0-2 Tight: 0-6 Gall: 0-0
Aids: Bl: 0-4 Vi: 0-0 Tstrap: 0-0
Best Rating: 124 12/00 Chep 2m3f110y heavy Ch

Not the most straightforward customer, he has shown ability over hurdles and fences since coming from Ireland. has worn blinkers.

Patriarch Express

92f

5-y-o b g Noble Patriarch-Jaydeeglen (Bay Express)
G A Harker M Muir

Placings:2 (4860)
2001/02: 16^{2}G

	Starts	1st	2nd	3rd	Win & Pl
NH Flat	1	0	1	0	486
Career Total	1	0	1	0	486

Going: Sf: 0-0 GS: 0-0 Gd: 0-1 GF: - Fm: 0-0
Distance: 2m/2m3: 0-1 2m4-2m7: 0-0 3m+: 0-0
Track: LH: 0-0 RH: 0-0 Tight: 0-0 Gall: 0-0
Aids: Bl: 0-0 Vi: 0-0 Tstrap: 0-0
Best Rating: 92 4/02 Hexm 2m110y good NHF

Patrono (IRE)

83 63

6-y-o b g Executive Perk-Mawbeg Holly (Golden Love)
M Pitman Malcolm C Denmark

Placings:60P **(3909)**
2001/02: 16^{6}GS, 20^{0}S, 21^{P}G

	Starts	1st	2nd	3rd	Win & Pl
Hurdles	3	0	0	0	0
Career Total	**3**	**0**	**0**	**0**	**0**

Going: Sf: 0-1 GS: 0-1 Gd: 0-1 GF: - Fm: 0-0
Distance: 2m/2m3: 0-1 2m4-2m7: 0-2 3m+: 0-0
Track: LH: 0-1 RH: 0-2 Tight: 0-0 Gall: 0-2
Aids: Bl: 0-0 Vi: 0-0 Tstrap: 0-0
Best Rating: 63 1/02 Donc 2m4f soft Hdl

Pats Castle

77f **29f**

5-y-o ch m Carlingford Castle-Penair (Good Times (ITY))
P R Johnson P Johnson

Placings:006 **(1044)**
2001/02: 16^{0}GF, 16^{0}G, 16^{6}GF

	Starts	1st	2nd	3rd	Win & Pl
NH Flat	3	0	0	0	0
Career Total	**3**	**0**	**0**	**0**	**0**

Going: Sf: 0-0 GS: 0-0 Gd: 0-1 GF: - Fm: 0-2
Distance: 2m/2m3: 0-3 2m4-2m7: 0-0 3m+: 0-0
Track: LH: 0-3 RH: 0-0 Tight: 0-0 Gall: 0-0
Aids: Bl: 0-0 Vi: 0-0 Tstrap: 0-0
Best Rating: 29 7/01 Uttx 2m gd-fm NHF

Pats Cross (IRE)

(94c)

13-y-o b g Abednego-No Hunting (No Time)
A Crook James Byrne

Placings:5205350040/20/P/214/1P2143/U21P33F-PP0 **(1395)**
2001/02: 25^{P}GF, 26^{P}GS, 24^{0}GF

	Starts	1st	2nd	3rd	Win & Pl
Hurdles	1	0	0	0	0
Chases	2	0	0	0	0
Career Total	**32**	**4**	**5**	**4**	**18533**

130	8/00	Ctml	3m2f	D(0-120)HCh	GD	£3783
127	1/00	Catt	3m1f110y	F(0-100)HCh	GD	£2873
108	5/99	Ctml	2m5f110y	E Ch	GD	£2965
99	4/99	Hexm	3m1f	H Ch	GD	£1109

Total win prize-money £10731

Going: Sf: 0-0 GS: 0-1 Gd: 0-0 GF: - Fm: 0-2
Distance: 2m/2m3: 0-0 2m4-2m7: 0-0 3m+: 0-3
Track: LH: 0-3 RH: 0-0 Tight: 0-2 Gall: 0-0
Aids: Bl: 0-0 Vi: 0-0 Tstrap: 0-0
Best Rating: 130 2/01 Hayd 3m heavy Ch

Patsy Veale (IRE)

110 **127**

7-y-o b g Accordion-Bermuda Castle (Carlingford Castle)
John Queally M A Ryan

Placings:20/21213-13403006 **(4256)**
2001/02: 20^{1}F, 20^{3}G, 16^{4}G, 21^{0}YS, 16^{3}YS, 21^{0}G, 16^{0}HY, 17^{6}G

	Starts	1st	2nd	3rd	Win & Pl
Hurdles	8	1	0	2	10266
Career Total	**15**	**3**	**3**	**3**	**20411**

120	5/01	Dund	2m4f153y	(0-123)HHdl	FRM	£6677
107	9/00	Gway	2m	Hdl	YLD	£4416
107	6/00	Dund	2m135y	NHF	FRM	£2760

Total win prize-money £13853

Going: Sf: 0-1 GS: 0-0 Gd: 0-4 GF: - Fm: 1-1
Distance: 2m/2m3: 0-4 **2m4-2m7: 1-4** 3m+: 0-0
Track: LH: 0-2 RH: 0-2 Tight: 0-0 Gall: 0-2
Aids: Bl: 0-0 Vi: 0-0 Tstrap: 0-0
Best Rating: 127 3/02 Chel 2m1f good Hdl

Winner of a bumper and has been successful over hurdles. Acts on a sound surface, and is effective at around two miles to two miles four furlongs.

Pauhutzanka (IRE)

95 **75**

8-y-o b g Lord Americo-Prudent Birdie (Lucifer (USA))
Lindsay Woods (D J Wintle 14/11) Hugh M Duffy

Placings:*0/30*FP540*5*F45/06055P00-66254P **(4202a)**
2001/02: 16^{6}GF, 17^{6}GF, 22^{2}HY, 20^{5}GS, 20^{4}S, 17^{P}S

	Starts	1st	2nd	3rd	Win & Pl
Hurdles	6	0	1	0	446
Career Total	**26**	**0**	**1**	**1**	**1275**

Going: Sf: 0-3 GS: 0-1 Gd: 0-0 GF: - Fm: 0-2
Distance: 2m/2m3: 0-3 2m4-2m7: 0-3 3m+: 0-0
Track: LH: 0-1 RH: 0-4 Tight: 0-4 Gall: 0-0
Aids: Bl: 0-0 Vi: 0-0 Tstrap: 0-0
Best Rating: 106 3/00 Leop 2m good Hdl

Pauls Dream (IRE)

7-y-o ch g Deep Society-Pampered Sally (Paddy's Stream)
Mrs S C Bradburne A Irvine

Placings:PP **(4880)**
2001/02: 16^{P}GF, 20^{P}G

	Starts	1st	2nd	3rd	Win & Pl
Hurdles	2	0	0	0	
Career Total	**2**	**0**	**0**	**0**	

Going: Sf: 0-0 GS: 0-0 Gd: 0-1 GF: - Fm: 0-1
Distance: 2m/2m3: 0-1 2m4-2m7: 0-1 3m+: 0-0
Track: LH: 0-1 RH: 0-1 Tight: 0-1 Gall: 0-0
Aids: Bl: 0-0 Vi: 0-0 Tstrap: 0-0
Best Rating:

Paulton

101 **89**

9-y-o b g Lugana Beach-Runcina (Runnett)
K Bishop Slabs And Lucan

Placings:P4630423/1322/2520P/000/6641-3264150 **(3342)**
2001/02: 20^{3}G, 22^{2}GF, 22^{6}GF, 21^{4}GS, 17^{1}GF, 22^{5}GS, 19^{0}S

	Starts	1st	2nd	3rd	Win & Pl
Hurdles	7	1	1	1	2877
Career Total	**31**	**3**	**6**	**4**	**10539**

89	11/01	Extr	2m1f	G(0-95)HHdl	G-F	£1802
78	4/01	Extr	2m1f	G(0-95)HHdl	G-S	£1932
73	5/97	Extr	2m2f	G Hdl	GD	£1818

Total win prize-money £5554

Going: Sf: 0-1 GS: 0-2 Gd: 0-1 GF: - Fm: 1-3
Distance: **2m/2m3: 1-1** 2m4-2m7: 0-6 3m+: 0-0
Track: LH: 0-4 **RH: 1-2** Tight: 0-5 Gall: 0-0
Aids: **Bl: 1-7** Vi: 0-0 Tstrap: 0-0
Best Rating: 92 11/98 Tntn 2m3f110y good Hdl

Handicap hurdler, acts on most types of ground and is effective over two miles.

Pauntley Gofa

102(108h) (112h)**123+**

6-y-o b g Afzal-Gotageton (Oats)
J L Spearing Clapham & Partners

Placings:*2/2*60-10P1**F**3 **(4644)**
2001/02: 17^{1}G, 16^{0}GF, 17^{P}S, 16^{1}GF, 16^{F}G, 16^{3}G

	Starts	1st	2nd	3rd	Win & Pl
Hurdles	5	2	0	1	7273
Chases	1	0	0	0	0
Career Total	**10**	**2**	**2**	**1**	**8262**

109	11/01	Ludl	2m	D Hdl	G-F	£3558
112	5/01	MRas	2m1f110y	E Hdl	GD	£2914

Total win prize-money £6473

Going: Sf: 0-1 GS: 0-0 Gd: 1-3 GF: - Fm: 1-2
Distance: **2m/2m3: 2-6** 2m4-2m7: 0-0 3m+: 0-0
Track: LH: 0-1 **RH: 2-5 Tight: 1-3** Gall: 0-0
Aids: Bl: 0-0 Vi: 0-0 Tstrap: 0-0
Best Rating: 116 12/01 Ludl 2m good Ch

A big backward sort, he took time to come to himself but got off the mark on his third outing over hurdles. Scored again at Ludlow in November 2001. Best suited by two miles and a sound surface. Successful over fences in June 2002.

Paxford Jack

106 **102**

6-y-o ch g Alflora (IRE)-Rakajack (Rakaposhi King)
M F Harris (M W Easterby 28/10) M Harris

Placings:*3*333U-40341P40 **(4896)**
2001/02: 16^{4}S, 16^{0}G, 20^{3}HY, 22^{4}S, 17^{1}HY, 25^{P}S, 21^{4}HY, 20^{0}G

	Starts	1st	2nd	3rd	Win & Pl
Hurdles	8	1	0	1	3890
Career Total	**13**	**1**	**0**	**5**	**5128**

98	1/02	Folk	2m1f110y	D(0-115)HHdl	HVY	£3286

Total win prize-money £3287

Going: Sf: 1-6 GS: 0-0 Gd: 0-2 GF: - Fm: 0-0
Distance: **2m/2m3: 1-3** 2m4-2m7: 0-4 3m+: 0-1
Track: LH: 0-1 **RH: 1-5 Tight: 1-3** Gall: 0-0
Aids: Bl: 0-0 Vi: 0-0 Tstrap: 0-0
Best Rating: 102 10/01 Towc 2m soft Hdl

He has made the frame on several occasions over hurdles, but did not get off the mark until winning a modest four-runner handicap at Folkestone in January 2002. Stays further than two miles and his best efforts have been on soft ground.

Paxford Lady

5-y-o b m Alflora (IRE)-Rakajack (Rakaposhi King)
M F Harris Warwick Racecourse Owners Club

Placings:500PP **(4875)**
2001/02: 17^{5}HY, 16^{0}G, 16^{0}HY, 19^{P}S, 24^{P}G

	Starts	1st	2nd	3rd	Win & Pl
NH Flat	3	0	0	0	
Hurdles	2	0	0	0	
Career Total	**5**	**0**	**0**	**0**	

Going: Sf: 0-3 GS: 0-0 Gd: 0-2 GF: - Fm: 0-0
Distance: 2m/2m3: 0-3 2m4-2m7: 0-1 3m+: 0-1
Track: LH: 0-1 RH: 0-3 Tight: 0-2 Gall: 0-0
Aids: Bl: 0-1 Vi: 0-0 Tstrap: 0-0
Best Rating: 70 12/01 Folk 2m1f110y heavy NHF

Paxford Trooper

8-y-o b g Gunner B-Say Shanaz (Tickled Pink)
M F Harris M Harris

Placings:5/P0 **(4152)**
2001/02: 22^{P}S, 20^{0}GS

	Starts	1st	2nd	3rd	Win & Pl
Hurdles	2	0	0	0	
Career Total	**3**	**0**	**0**	**0**	**0**

Going: Sf: 0-1 GS: 0-1 Gd: 0-0 GF: - Fm: 0-0
Distance: 2m/2m3: 0-0 2m4-2m7: 0-2 3m+: 0-0
Track: LH: 0-1 RH: 0-1 Tight: 0-1 Gall: 0-0
Aids: Bl: 0-0 Vi: 0-0 Tstrap: 0-0
Best Rating: 87 5/98 Worc 2m gd-fm NHF

Payford Bridge

65 **54**
9-y-o br g Lighter-Saucy Laura (Crozier)
Mrs P Ford Mrs Rosie Newman

Placings:P/P-0PP6 **(4756)**
2001/02: 19^{0}S, 24^{P}HY, 20^{P}GF, 20^{6}GF

	Starts	1st	2nd	3rd	Win & Pl
Hurdles	3	0	0	0	0
Chases	1	0	0	0	0
Career Total	**6**	**0**	**0**	**0**	**0**

Going: Sf: 0-2 GS: 0-0 Gd: 0-0 GF: - Fm: 0-2
Distance: 2m/2m3: 0-0 2m4-2m7: 0-3 3m+: 0-1
Track: LH: 0-2 RH: 0-2 Tight: 0-0 Gall: 0-1
Aids: Bl: 0-0 Vi: 0-0 Tstrap: 0-0
Best Rating: 54 4/02 Uttx 2m4f110y gd-fm Hdl

Paymaster (NZ)

102(100h) (103h)**113+**
7-y-o ch g Norman Pentaquad (USA)-Tivy (NZ) (Noble Bijou (USA))
Miss H C Knight A Auer J Collins And J Eddis

Placings:3155 **(4597)**
2001/02: 16^{3}G, 19^{1}GF, 21^{5}G, 19^{5}GF

	Starts	1st	2nd	3rd	Win & Pl
Hurdles	4	1	0	1	4636
Career Total	**4**	**1**	**0**	**1**	**4636**

103 11/01 Extr 2m3f D Hdl G-F £4075
Total win prize-money £4076

Going: Sf: 0-0 GS: 0-0 Gd: 0-2 GF: - Fm: 1-2
Distance: **2m/2m3: 1-3** 2m4-2m7: 0-1 3m+: 0-0
Track: LH: 0-1 **RH: 1-3** Tight: 0-0 Gall: 0-0
Aids: Bl: 0-0 Vi: 0-0 **Tstrap: 1-1**
Best Rating: 103 4/02 Wwck 2m3f gd-fm Hdl

A New Zealand import, he confirmed the promise shown on his hurdling debut in October 2001 with a win a month later in a novices' hurdle at Exeter. A sound jumper, he is suited to at least two miles three furlongs on a sound surface.

Pc's Eurocruiser (IRE)

98 **86**
6-y-o b g Fayruz-Kuwait Night (Morston (FR))
A Crook Jay Dee Bloodstock Limited

Placings:0OP/055261-P00033 **(3765)**
2001/02: 16^{P}G, 17^{0}G, 17^{0}S, 16^{0}S, 16^{3}GS, 16^{3}GS

	Starts	1st	2nd	3rd	Win & Pl
Hurdles	6	0	0	2	522
Career Total	**15**	**1**	**1**	**2**	**3724**

82 9/00 MRas 2m1f110y F(0-100)HHdl G-F £2747
Total win prize-money £2748

Going: Sf: 0-2 GS: 0-2 Gd: 0-2 GF: - Fm: 0-0
Distance: 2m/2m3: 0-6 2m4-2m7: 0-0 3m+: 0-0
Track: LH: 0-4 RH: 0-2 Tight: 0-5 Gall: 0-0
Aids: Bl: 0-0 Vi: 0-0 Tstrap: 0-0
Best Rating: 86 2/02 Fknm 2m gd-sft Hdl

Moderate hurdler. Acts on a sound surface and is effective over two miles.

Peace Frog (IRE)

6-y-o b g Commanche Run-Wayward Beauty (Tepukei)
Miss K Marks Nick Shutts

Placings:P-P **(0087)**
2001/02: 26^{P}G

	Starts	1st	2nd	3rd	Win & Pl
Hurdles	1	0	0	0	
Career Total	**2**	**0**	**0**	**0**	

Going: Sf: 0-0 GS: 0-0 Gd: 0-1 GF: - Fm: 0-0
Distance: 2m/2m3: 0-0 2m4-2m7: 0-0 3m+: 0-1
Track: LH: 0-0 RH: 0-1 Tight: 0-0 Gall: 0-0
Aids: Bl: 0-0 Vi: 0-0 Tstrap: 0-0
Best Rating:

Peace Of Amber

9-y-o ch m Prince Of Peace-Bay Augusta (Langton Heath)
V R A Dartnall (Miss D Cole 20/11) Mrs Katie Squire

Placings:0P/60PP **(4501)**
2001/02: 22^{6}GF, 22^{0}G, 26^{P}G, 27^{P}G

	Starts	1st	2nd	3rd	Win & Pl
Hurdles	3	0	0	0	0
Chases	1	0	0	0	0
Career Total	**6**	**0**	**0**	**0**	**0**

Going: Sf: 0-0 GS: 0-0 Gd: 0-3 GF: - Fm: 0-1
Distance: 2m/2m3: 0-0 2m4-2m7: 0-2 3m+: 0-2
Track: LH: 0-2 RH: 0-0 Tight: 0-2 Gall: 0-0
Aids: Bl: 0-0 Vi: 0-0 Tstrap: 0-0
Best Rating:

Peacemaker (IRE)

110 **108**
10-y-o br g Strong Gale-Gamonda (Gala Performance (USA))
J R Cornwall J R Cornwall

Placings:*00*P3/404/040P/P22035-121222F5F4 **(1991)**
2001/02: 21^{1}GF, 22^{2}G, 21^{1}G, 20^{2}GF, 25^{2}GF, 24^{2}GF, 20^{F}S, 20^{5}G, 24^{F}G, 24^{4}G

	Starts	1st	2nd	3rd	Win & Pl
Chases	10	2	4	0	13813
Career Total	**27**	**2**	**6**	**2**	**18222**

96 7/01 Strf 2m5f110y E(0-105)HCh GD £3328
96 6/01 Fknm 2m5f110y F(0-100)HCh G-F £3562
Total win prize-money £6891

Going: Sf: 0-1 GS: 0-0 Gd: 1-5 GF: - Fm: 1-4
Distance: 2m/2m3: 0-0 **2m4-2m7: 2-6** 3m+: 0-4
Track: **LH: 2-6** RH: 0-4 **Tight: 2-8** Gall: 0-1
Aids: Bl: 0-0 Vi: 0-0 Tstrap: 0-0
Best Rating: 108 9/01 Strf 3m gd-fm Ch

Peachy (IRE)

94 **104**
7-y-o b g Un Desperado (FR)-Little Peach (Ragapan)
R T Phillips Colin Pocock

Placings:*1*/F-3F **(4126)**
2001/02: 16^{3}GS, 19^{F}G

	Starts	1st	2nd	3rd	Win & Pl
Hurdles	2	0	0	1	384
Career Total	**4**	**1**	**0**	**1**	**2099**

104 3/00 Folk 2m1f110y H NHF G-F £1715
Total win prize-money £1715

Going: Sf: 0-0 GS: 0-1 Gd: 0-1 GF: - Fm: 0-0
Distance: 2m/2m3: 0-1 2m4-2m7: 0-1 3m+: 0-0
Track: LH: 0-0 RH: 0-2 Tight: 0-0 Gall: 0-0
Aids: Bl: 0-0 Vi: 0-0 Tstrap: 0-0
Best Rating: 104 3/02 Hrfd 2m3f110y good Hdl

Bumper winner with fair form in novice hurdles.

Peacock Theatre

102 **83**
4-y-o b g Red Rainbow-Fine Art (IRE) (Tate Gallery (USA))
A Streeter (J M Bradley 20/7) N Heath

Placings:0104050 **(4061)**
2001/02: 17^{0}GF, 17^{1}S, 16^{0}S, 16^{4}GS, 20^{0}S, 20^{5}S, 17^{0}S

	Starts	1st	2nd	3rd	Win & Pl
Hurdles	7	1	0	0	1561
Career Total	**7**	**1**	**0**	**0**	**1561**

83 9/01 MRas 2m1f110y G Hdl SFT £1561
Total win prize-money £1561

Going: Sf: 1-5 GS: 0-1 Gd: 0-0 GF: - Fm: 0-1
Distance: **2m/2m3: 1-5** 2m4-2m7: 0-2 3m+: 0-0
Track: LH: 0-3 **RH: 1-4 Tight: 1-2** Gall: 0-1
Aids: Bl: 0-2 **Vi: 1-4** Tstrap: 0-0
Best Rating: 83 9/01 MRas 2m1f110y soft Hdl

Peafield (IRE)

13-y-o b g Torus-La'Bavette (Le Bavard (FR))
P York A R Parrish

Placings:65203504P/20F4/00405/220 **(0497)**
2001/02: 24^{2}GF, 26^{2}G, 25^{0}G

	Starts	1st	2nd	3rd	Win & Pl
Chases	3	0	2	0	1072
Career Total	**21**	**0**	**4**	**1**	**3493**

Going: Sf: 0-0 GS: 0-0 Gd: 0-2 GF: - Fm: 0-1
Distance: 2m/2m3: 0-0 2m4-2m7: 0-0 3m+: 0-3
Track: LH: 0-0 RH: 0-3 Tight: 0-1 Gall: 0-1
Aids: Bl: 0-0 Vi: 0-0 Tstrap: 0-0
Best Rating: 107 5/01 Folk 3m2f good Ch

Pealings (IRE)

110(94h) **122**
10-y-o gr g Wood Chanter-Ten-Cents (Taste Of Honey)
Ferdy Murphy Exors Of The Late Mr G A Hubbard

Placings: *0U644/031135510/4P2122010/2R44025/006 5-2P1144024* (4748)

2001/02: 24^{2}G, 24^{P}GF, 24^{1}S, 26^{1}HY, 24^{4}S, 24^{4}G, 28^{0}S, 26^{2}G, 26^{4}GF

	Starts	1st	2nd	3rd	Win & Pl
Chases	9	2	2	0	11142
Career Total	**43**	**7**	**7**	**2**	**48008**

122	1/02	Plum	3m2f	E Ch	HVY	£3262
122	1/02	Fknm	3m110y	D Ch	SFT	£4161
125	3/99	Ling	2m3f110y	C(0-135)HHdl	G-S	£7262
126	12/98	Uttx	2m4f110y	B(0-145)HHdl	SFT	£5094
111	2/98	Asct	2m4f	E(0-120)HHdl	GD	£3680
106	10/97	Hntg	2m4f110y	E Hdl	G-F	£2530
104	10/97	Hntg	2m4f110y	E Hdl	GD	£2372

Total win prize-money £28365

Going: Sf: 2-4 GS: 0-0 Gd: 0-3 GF: - Fm: 0-2
Distance: 2m/2m3: 0-0 2m4-2m7: 0-0 **3m+: 2-9**
Track: **LH: 1-3** RH: 0-4 **Tight: 1-2** Gall: 0-2
Aids: Bl: 0-0 Vi: 0-0 Tstrap: 0-0
Best Rating: 129 2/00 Asct 2m4f soft Hdl

A one-time decent handicap hurdler, he won two ordinary novices' chases in January 2002. Stays three miles, acts in soft ground.

Pearl Harbor

5-y-o b g Distant Relative-Peace Dance (Bikala)
M W Easterby Guy Reed

Placings: *0* (1478)

2001/02: 17^{0}S

	Starts	1st	2nd	3rd	Win & Pl
NH Flat	1	0	0	0	
Career Total	**1**	**0**	**0**	**0**	

Going: Sf: 0-1 GS: 0-0 Gd: 0-0 GF: - Fm: 0-0
Distance: 2m/2m3: 0-1 2m4-2m7: 0-0 3m+: 0-0
Track: LH: 0-0 RH: 0-1 Tight: 0-1 Gall: 0-0
Aids: Bl: 0-0 Vi: 0-0 Tstrap: 0-1
Best Rating:

Pearlstone

98 **95**

6-y-o b m Teenoso (USA)-Pearly Dream (Rymer)
W Jenks Michael Stoddart

Placings: *06-6441U* (3645)

2001/02: 17^{6}G, 17^{4}S, 16^{4}G, 16^{1}GS, 16^{U}S

	Starts	1st	2nd	3rd	Win & Pl
NH Flat	2	0	0	0	0
Hurdles	3	1	0	0	2471
Career Total	**7**	**1**	**0**	**0**	**2471**

95	1/02	Sthl	2m	E Hdl	G-S	£2471

Total win prize-money £2471

Going: Sf: 0-2 GS: 1-1 Gd: 0-2 GF: - Fm: 0-0
Distance: **2m/2m3: 1-5** 2m4-2m7: 0-0 3m+: 0-0
Track: **LH: 1-4** RH: 0-1 **Tight: 1-3** Gall: 0-0
Aids: Bl: 0-0 Vi: 0-0 Tstrap: 0-0
Best Rating: 95 1/02 Sthl 2m gd-sft Hdl

Has shown some ability in bumpers and novice events, winning a poor affair at Southwell.

Peartree House (IRE)

103 **112**

8-y-o b g Simply Majestic (USA)-Fashion Front (Habitat)
Mrs M Reveley (D Nicholls 29/9) P D Savill

Placings: 3561 (4781)

2001/02: 16^{3}G, 16^{5}S, 17^{6}S, 16^{1}GF

	Starts	1st	2nd	3rd	Win & Pl
Hurdles	4	1	0	1	3560
Career Total	**4**	**1**	**0**	**1**	**3560**

112	4/02	Plum	2m	E Hdl	G-F	£3167

Total win prize-money £3168

Going: Sf: 0-2 GS: 0-0 Gd: 0-1 GF: - Fm: 1-1
Distance: **2m/2m3: 1-4** 2m4-2m7: 0-0 3m+: 0-0
Track: **LH: 1-2** RH: 0-2 **Tight: 1-4** Gall: 0-0
Aids: Bl: 0-0 Vi: 0-0 Tstrap: 0-0
Best Rating: 112 4/02 Plum 2m gd-fm Hdl

Confirmed ability he showed on hurdles debut when cruising home to take a modest novices' event in April 2002 on fast ground.

Pebble Moon

100(106h) (92h)**110**

6-y-o gr g Efisio-Jazz (Sharrood (USA))
Miss Lucinda V Russell (P J Hobbs 2/5) J D I Bell

Placings: 0411F3/0054-**2F0P40UF01P** (4308)

2001/02: 19^{2}GS, 20^{F}GS, 17^{0}G, 21^{P}G, 20^{4}S, 20^{0}S, 20^{U}GS, 20^{F}S, 24^{0}S, 20^{1}HY, 21^{P}S

	Starts	1st	2nd	3rd	Win & Pl
Hurdles	2	0	0	0	0
Chases	9	1	1	0	4768
Career Total	**21**	**3**	**1**	**1**	**11725**

84	3/02	Ayr	2m4f	E Ch	HVY	£3840
97	1/00	Font	2m6f110y	F(0-110)HHdl	GD	£2170
94	1/00	Plum	2m	D Hdl	HVY	£3545

Total win prize-money £9556

Going: Sf: 1-6 GS: 0-2 Gd: 0-3 GF: - Fm: 0-0
Distance: 2m/2m3: 0-1 **2m4-2m7: 1-9** 3m+: 0-1
Track: **LH: 1-6** RH: 0-4 Tight: 0-4 Gall: 0-0
Aids: Bl: 0-5 **Vi: 1-4** Tstrap: 0-0
Best Rating: 110 5/01 Extr 2m3f110y gd-sft Ch

Modest hrudler, suited by two and a half miles and soft ground.

Peccadillo (IRE)

119 **143**

8-y-o br g Un Desperado (FR)-First Mistake (Posse (USA))
R H Alner Dwight Makins

Placings: 60/63212/315-**2133143F** (4914)

2001/02: 17^{2}GF, 21^{1}GF, 20^{3}G, 17^{3}GS, 16^{1}G, 19^{4}G, 19^{3}GF, 20^{F}G

	Starts	1st	2nd	3rd	Win & Pl
Chases	8	2	1	3	14229
Career Total	**18**	**4**	**3**	**5**	**23734**

143	12/01	Winc	2m	E(0-115)HCh	GD	£4075
130	10/01	Winc	2m5f	F(0-110)HCh	G-F	£4173
125	12/00	Winc	2m	E(0-115)HCh	G-S	£4290
109	3/00	Folk	2m	F(0-100)HCh	G-F	£2422

Total win prize-money £14961

Going: Sf: 0-0 GS: 0-1 Gd: 1-4 GF: - Fm: 1-3
Distance: 2m/2m3: 1-3 2m4-2m7: 1-5 3m+: 0-0
Track: LH: 0-2 **RH: 2-6** Tight: 0-2 Gall: 0-1
Aids: Bl: 0-0 Vi: 0-0 Tstrap: 0-0
Best Rating: 143 12/01 Winc 2m good Ch

He is at his best when able to establish an uncontested lead. Jumps well, acts on fast ground and goes particularly well at Wincanton.

Peculiar Choice

61f **28f**

6-y-o b m Perpendicular-Robins Choice (Scallywag)
R Tate R Tate

Placings: *0* (0911)

2001/02: 16^{0}G

	Starts	1st	2nd	3rd	Win & Pl
NH Flat	1	0	0	0	
Career Total	**1**	**0**	**0**	**0**	

Going: Sf: 0-0 GS: 0-0 Gd: 0-1 GF: - Fm: 0-0
Distance: 2m/2m3: 0-1 2m4-2m7: 0-0 3m+: 0-0
Track: LH: 0-1 RH: 0-0 Tight: 0-0 Gall: 0-0
Aids: Bl: 0-0 Vi: 0-0 Tstrap: 0-0
Best Rating: 28 7/01 Worc 2m good NHF

Pedro Pete

113 **127**

5-y-o ch g Fraam-Stride Home (Absalom)
N J Henderson Thurloe Thoroughbreds Vii

Placings: 123P-60 (2802)

2001/02: 16^{6}S, 16^{0}G

	Starts	1st	2nd	3rd	Win & Pl
Hurdles	2	0	0	0	825
Career Total	**6**	**1**	**1**	**1**	**10329**

130	1/01	Kemp	2m	D Hdl	SFT	£4485

Total win prize-money £4485

Going: Sf: 0-1 GS: 0-0 Gd: 0-1 GF: - Fm: 0-0
Distance: 2m/2m3: 0-2 2m4-2m7: 0-0 3m+: 0-0
Track: LH: 0-0 RH: 0-2 Tight: 0-0 Gall: 0-0
Aids: Bl: 0-0 Vi: 0-0 Tstrap: 0-0
Best Rating: 130 1/01 Kemp 2m soft Hdl

Backed for the Triumph Hurdle prior to his debut victory at Kempton in January 2001 where he cruised round, he came up against Jair Du Cochet at Cheltenham and struggled in decent company subsequently. He may have to have a flat track to show his best.

Peejay Hobbs

104 **92+**

4-y-o ch g Alhijaz-Hicklam Millie (Absalom)
P G Murphy Harold Winton

Placings: 3430 (3515)

2001/02: 17^{3}GS, 16^{4}G, 17^{3}S, 19^{0}S

	Starts	1st	2nd	3rd	Win & Pl
Hurdles	4	0	0	2	608
Career Total	**4**	**0**	**0**	**2**	**608**

Going: Sf: 0-2 GS: 0-1 Gd: 0-1 GF: - Fm: 0-0
Distance: 2m/2m3: 0-3 2m4-2m7: 0-1 3m+: 0-0
Track: LH: 0-0 RH: 0-4 Tight: 0-2 Gall: 0-0
Aids: Bl: 0-0 Vi: 0-0 Tstrap: 0-0
Best Rating: 69 1/02 Tntn 2m3f110y soft Hdl

Modest hurdler, successful in selling and claiming company in the summer of 2002. Stays two and three-quarter miles.

Peerless

7-y-o b g Arctic Lord-Florence May (Grange Melody)
J S King D R Peppiatt

Placings: *00/500-***0FP** (0553)

2001/02: 19^{0}G, 24^{F}GF, 26^{P}GF

	Starts	1st	2nd	3rd	Win & Pl
Hurdles	1	0	0	0	0
Chases	2	0	0	0	0
Career Total	**8**	**0**	**0**	**0**	**0**

Going: Sf: 0-0 GS: 0-0 Gd: 0-1 GF: - Fm: 0-2
Distance: 2m/2m3: 0-1 2m4-2m7: 0-0 3m+: 0-2
Track: LH: 0-0 RH: 0-3 Tight: 0-0 Gall: 0-2
Aids: Bl: 0-1 Vi: 0-0 Tstrap: 0-0
Best Rating: 74 12/00 Newb 2m3f soft Hdl

Peerless Motion (IRE)

95 **111**

7-y-o b g Caerleon (USA)-Final Figure (USA) (Super Concorde (USA))
C J Mann The Icy Fire Partnership

Placings:*23/10/213-360* **(1890)**
2001/02: 17^{3}GF, 17^{6}G, 16^{0}G

	Starts	1st	2nd	3rd	Win & Pl
Hurdles	3	0	0	1	636
Career Total	**10**	**2**	**2**	**3**	**8682**
109 2/01 Tntn 2m1f E Hdl HVY					£2702
91 10/99 Punc 2m NHF G-Y					£3080
				Total win prize-money	£5782

Going: Sf: 0-0 GS: 0-0 Gd: 0-2 GF: - Fm: 0-1
Distance: 2m/2m3: 0-3 2m4-2m7: 0-0 3m+: 0-0
Track: LH: 0-3 RH: 0-0 Tight: 0-2 Gall: 0-0
Aids: Bl: 0-0 Vi: 0-0 Tstrap: 0-0
Best Rating: 111 5/01 NAbb 2m1f gd-fm Hdl

A bumper winner, he gained an easy win at Taunton last season and ran some other fine races. He acts on very soft ground, but his trainer believes he needs it faster.

Peeyoutwo

7-y-o b g Golden Heights-Nyika (Town And Country)
Mrs D A Hamer Power Units (1953) Ltd

Placings:*100P* **(2716)**
2001/02: 17^{1}GF, 16^{0}G, 16^{0}GF, 19^{P}G

	Starts	1st	2nd	3rd	Win & Pl
NH Flat	3	1	0	0	2170
Hurdles	1	0	0	0	0
Career Total	**4**	**1**	**0**	**0**	**2170**
91 8/01 NAbb 2m1f H NHF G-F					£2170
				Total win prize-money	£2170

Going: Sf: 0-0 GS: 0-0 Gd: 0-2 GF: - Fm: 1-2
Distance: **2m/2m3: 1-3** 2m4-2m7: 0-1 3m+: 0-0
Track: **LH: 1-2** RH: 0-2 **Tight: 1-1** Gall: 0-0
Aids: Bl: 0-0 Vi: 0-0 Tstrap: 0-0
Best Rating: 97 10/01 Chel 2m110y good NHF

Pegasus The Paddy (IRE)

88f **63f**

5-y-o b g Dolphin Street (FR)-Saintly Guest (What A Guest)
J J O'Neill Mrs Margaret Canty-Shepherd

Placings:*0-6* **(1649)**
2001/02: 16^{6}G

	Starts	1st	2nd	3rd	Win & Pl
NH Flat	1	0	0	0	0
Career Total	**2**	**0**	**0**	**0**	**0**

Going: Sf: 0-0 GS: 0-0 Gd: 0-1 GF: - Fm: 0-0
Distance: 2m/2m3: 0-1 2m4-2m7: 0-0 3m+: 0-0
Track: LH: 0-0 RH: 0-1 Tight: 0-0 Gall: 0-1
Aids: Bl: 0-0 Vi: 0-0 Tstrap: 0-1
Best Rating: 63 10/01 Hntg 2m110y good NHF

Peggy Sioux (IRE)

90f **93f**

5-y-o b m Little Bighorn-Gayable (Gay Fandango (USA))
J I A Charlton John Hogg

Placings:*300* **(4595)**
2001/02: 16^{3}S, 17^{0}GS, 16^{0}G

	Starts	1st	2nd	3rd	Win & Pl
NH Flat	3	0	0	1	332
Career Total	**3**	**0**	**0**	**1**	**332**

Going: Sf: 0-1 GS: 0-1 Gd: 0-1 GF: - Fm: 0-0
Distance: 2m/2m3: 0-3 2m4-2m7: 0-0 3m+: 0-0
Track: LH: 0-1 RH: 0-2 Tight: 0-2 Gall: 0-0
Aids: Bl: 0-0 Vi: 0-0 Tstrap: 0-0
Best Rating: 93 2/02 Muss 2m soft NHF

Peggy's Song

4-y-o b f Mind Games-Miss Whittingham (IRE) (Fayruz)
D L Williams D L Williams

Placings:*P* **(1412)**
2001/02: 16^{P}GF

	Starts	1st	2nd	3rd	Win & Pl
Hurdles	1	0	0	0	
Career Total	**1**	**0**	**0**	**0**	

Going: Sf: 0-0 GS: 0-0 Gd: 0-0 GF: - Fm: 0-1
Distance: 2m/2m3: 0-1 2m4-2m7: 0-0 3m+: 0-0
Track: LH: 0-1 RH: 0-0 Tight: 0-1 Gall: 0-0
Aids: Bl: 0-0 Vi: 0-0 Tstrap: 0-0
Best Rating:

Peggys Delight

96 **77**

7-y-o ch m Minster Son-Chasers' Bar (Oats)
J R Turner J E Swiers

Placings:*00/000P5-00* **(0663)**
2001/02: 21^{0}G, 16^{0}F

	Starts	1st	2nd	3rd	Win & Pl
Hurdles	2	0	0	0	
Career Total	**9**	**0**	**0**	**0**	**0**

Going: Sf: 0-0 GS: 0-0 Gd: 0-1 GF: - Fm: 0-1
Distance: 2m/2m3: 0-1 2m4-2m7: 0-1 3m+: 0-0
Track: LH: 0-1 RH: 0-1 Tight: 0-1 Gall: 0-0
Aids: Bl: 0-0 Vi: 0-0 Tstrap: 0-0
Best Rating: 77 1/01 Muss 2m4f good Hdl

Pego

57f **58f**

4-y-o b f Syrtos-Romantic Melody (Battle Hymn)
G F Bridgwater D Aymes

Placings:*00* **(4329)**
2001/02: 16^{0}HY, 17^{0}S

	Starts	1st	2nd	3rd	Win & Pl
NH Flat	2	0	0	0	
Career Total	**2**	**0**	**0**	**0**	

Going: Sf: 0-2 GS: 0-0 Gd: 0-0 GF: - Fm: 0-0
Distance: 2m/2m3: 0-2 2m4-2m7: 0-0 3m+: 0-0
Track: LH: 0-1 RH: 0-1 Tight: 0-0 Gall: 0-0
Aids: Bl: 0-0 Vi: 0-0 Tstrap: 0-0
Best Rating: 20 2/02 Wwck 2m heavy NHF

Pekan Heights (USA)

6-y-o br g Green Dancer (USA)-Battle Drum (USA) (Alydar (USA))
P D Evans Mrs Claire Massey

Placings:*3/431114-F* **(0581)**
2001/02: 16^{F}GF

	Starts	1st	2nd	3rd	Win & Pl
Hurdles	1	0	0	0	
Career Total	**8**	**3**	**0**	**2**	**8803**
113 8/00 Uttx 2m E Hdl G-F					£2597
113 8/00 Bang 2m1f E(0-105)HHdl GD					£2899
98 6/00 Worc 2m F Hdl G-F					£1995
				Total win prize-money	£7491

Going: Sf: 0-0 GS: 0-0 Gd: 0-0 GF: - Fm: 0-1
Distance: 2m/2m3: 0-1 2m4-2m7: 0-0 3m+: 0-0
Track: LH: 0-1 RH: 0-0 Tight: 0-1 Gall: 0-0
Aids: Bl: 0-0 Vi: 0-1 Tstrap: 0-0
Best Rating: 114 9/00 Bang 2m1f gd-fm Hdl

Pekanese (IRE)

74 **45**

5-y-o b g Sri Pekan (USA)-Tootle (Main Reef)
R T Phillips Dozen Dreamers Partnership

Placings:*660-00* **(1439)**
2001/02: 21^{0}G, 18^{0}GF

	Starts	1st	2nd	3rd	Win & Pl
Hurdles	2	0	0	0	
Career Total	**5**	**0**	**0**	**0**	**0**

Going: Sf: 0-0 GS: 0-0 Gd: 0-1 GF: - Fm: 0-1
Distance: 2m/2m3: 0-1 2m4-2m7: 0-1 3m+: 0-0
Track: LH: 0-1 RH: 0-0 Tight: 0-1 Gall: 0-0
Aids: Bl: 0-1 Vi: 0-0 Tstrap: 0-0
Best Rating: 77 2/01 Tntn 2m1f heavy Hdl

Pelagos (FR)

85 **119**

7-y-o gr g Exit To Nowhere (USA)-Southern Maid (USA) (Northern Dancer)
F Bruce Miller (R Charlton 19/5) Mr And Mrs Michael E Hoffman

Placings:*12340* **(4251)**
2001/02: 18^{1}F, 20^{2}F, 19^{3}F, 20^{4}F, 24^{0}G

	Starts	1st	2nd	3rd	Win & Pl
Hurdles	5	1	1	1	24685
Career Total	**5**	**1**	**1**	**1**	**24685**
5/01 Malv 2m2f Hdl FRM					£10000
				Total win prize-money	£10000

Going: Sf: 0-0 GS: 0-0 Gd: 0-1 GF: - Fm: 1-4
Distance: **2m/2m3: 1-2** 2m4-2m7: 0-2 3m+: 0-1
Track: LH: 0-0 RH: 0-0 Tight: 0-0 Gall: 0-0
Aids: Bl: 0-0 Vi: 0-0 Tstrap: 0-1
Best Rating: 119 3/02 Chel 3m good Hdl

Modest staying handicapper on the Flat. Has run over hurdles and fences in America. Has won on fast ground.

Pele Mele

6-y-o b/br g Milieu-Hiltie Skiltie (Liberated)
A M Crow Mrs H G Peplinski

Placings:*60* **(4900)**
2001/02: 17^{6}G, 16^{0}G

	Starts	1st	2nd	3rd	Win & Pl
NH Flat	2	0	0	0	0
Career Total	**2**	**0**	**0**	**0**	**0**

Going: Sf: 0-0 GS: 0-0 Gd: 0-2 GF: - Fm: 0-0
Distance: 2m/2m3: 0-2 2m4-2m7: 0-0 3m+: 0-0
Track: LH: 0-0 RH: 0-2 Tight: 0-0 Gall: 0-0
Aids: Bl: 0-0 Vi: 0-0 Tstrap: 0-0
Best Rating: 85 4/02 Carl 2m1f good NHF

Pele Mele (FR)

84 82
7-y-o b g Tel Quel (FR)-Star System (FR) (Northern Treat (USA))
Miss Venetia Williams Cheltenham Racing Ltd

Placings:00 **(4114)**
2001/02: 16^{0}S, 16^{0}G

	Starts	1st	2nd	3rd	Win & Pl
Hurdles	2	0	0	0	
Career Total	**2**	**0**	**0**	**0**	

Going: Sf: 0-1 GS: 0-0 Gd: 0-1 GF: - Fm: 0-0
Distance: 2m/2m3: 0-2 2m4-2m7: 0-0 3m+: 0-0
Track: LH: 0-1 RH: 0-1 Tight: 0-1 Gall: 0-0
Aids: Bl: 0-0 Vi: 0-0 Tstrap: 0-1
Best Rating: 82 3/02 Winc 2m good Hdl

Pembroke Square (IRE)

100(90h) 117
7-y-o b g Tenby-The Poachers Lady (IRE) (Salmon Leap (USA))
P C Ritchens Fraser Miller

Placings:*05325/13142/0P-***6432** **(3498)**
2001/02: 20^{6}S, 24^{4}G, 24^{3}G, 24^{2}S

	Starts	1st	2nd	3rd	Win & Pl
Chases	4	0	1	1	2861
Career Total	**16**	**2**	**3**	**3**	**14876**

130 11/99 Asct 3m C Hdl GD £4856
111 5/99 Towc 3m D Hdl G-F £3406
Total win prize-money £8263

Going: Sf: 0-2 GS: 0-0 Gd: 0-2 GF: - Fm: 0-0
Distance: 2m/2m3: 0-0 2m4-2m7: 0-1 3m+: 0-3
Track: LH: 0-2 RH: 0-2 Tight: 0-1 Gall: 0-1
Aids: Bl: 0-0 Vi: 0-2 Tstrap: 0-4
Best Rating: 137 2/00 Asct 3m soft Hdl

A decent handicap hurdler and fair novice chaser, he stays three miles.

Pendant

(103h) (76h)
7-y-o b g Warning-Emerald (USA) (El Gran Senor (USA))
K A Morgan Friends R Four

Placings:3P104/00-6PP **(2645)**
2001/02: 20^{6}GF, 19^{P}GF, 24^{P}GS

	Starts	1st	2nd	3rd	Win & Pl
Hurdles	2	0	0	0	0
Chases	1	0	0	0	0
Career Total	**10**	**1**	**0**	**1**	**2728**

96 1/00 Catt 2m3f E Hdl GD £2362
Total win prize-money £2363

Going: Sf: 0-0 GS: 0-1 Gd: 0-0 GF: - Fm: 0-2
Distance: 2m/2m3: 0-0 2m4-2m7: 0-2 3m+: 0-1
Track: LH: 0-1 RH: 0-2 Tight: 0-1 Gall: 0-1
Aids: Bl: 0-1 Vi: 0-2 Tstrap: 0-2
Best Rating: 96 4/00 MRas 2m5f110y gd-fm Hdl

Pendragon

10-y-o b g Bold Fox-Celtic Royale (Celtic Cone)
Mrs Sarah Faulks Mrs Sarah Faulks

Placings:26 **(4402)**
2001/02: 25^{2}S, 22^{6}GS

	Starts	1st	2nd	3rd	Win & Pl
Chases	2	0	1	0	621
Career Total	**2**	**0**	**1**	**0**	**621**

Going: Sf: 0-1 GS: 0-1 Gd: 0-0 GF: - Fm: 0-0
Distance: 2m/2m3: 0-0 2m4-2m7: 0-1 3m+: 0-1
Track: LH: 0-1 RH: 0-1 Tight: 0-0 Gall: 0-1
Aids: Bl: 0-0 Vi: 0-0 Tstrap: 0-0
Best Rating: 96 3/02 Towc 3m1f soft Ch

Modest pointer/hunter chaser, suited by good ground or softer.

Penguin Bay

91 (62c)84
6-y-o b g Rock Hopper-Corn Lily (Aragon)
Mrs M Reveley Mrs Susan McDonald

Placings:*330-3*030 **(2399)**
2001/02: 16^{3}GF, 20^{0}GS, 16^{3}S, 16^{0}G

	Starts	1st	2nd	3rd	Win & Pl
NH Flat	1	0	0	1	219
Hurdles	2	0	0	1	560
Chases	1	0	0	0	0
Career Total	**7**	**0**	**0**	**4**	**1232**

Going: Sf: 0-1 GS: 0-1 Gd: 0-1 GF: - Fm: 0-1
Distance: 2m/2m3: 0-3 2m4-2m7: 0-1 3m+: 0-0
Track: LH: 0-2 RH: 0-0 Tight: 0-0 Gall: 0-0
Aids: Bl: 0-0 Vi: 0-0 Tstrap: 0-0
Best Rating: 107 5/00 Hntg 2m110y gd-sft NHF

Placed form over hurdles but lacks a turn of foot.

Peninsula Boy

99 109
9-y-o br g Good Thyne (USA)-Solent Express (Undulate (USA))
P J Hobbs Poundffald Inn Racing Club

Placings:*0/40443121364P40/F21P/3-3*P2 **(4889)**
2001/02: 24^{3}S, 24^{P}G, 26^{2}G

	Starts	1st	2nd	3rd	Win & Pl
Chases	3	0	1	1	2200
Career Total	**23**	**3**	**3**	**4**	**14302**

120 6/99 Worc 2m7f110y E Ch G-F £3202
104 10/98 Towc 3m E(0-100)HHdl G-F £2145
98 9/98 Carl 2m4f110y E Hdl GD £2388
Total win prize-money £7735

Going: Sf: 0-1 GS: 0-0 Gd: 0-2 GF: - Fm: 0-0
Distance: 2m/2m3: 0-0 2m4-2m7: 0-0 3m+: 0-3
Track: LH: 0-0 RH: 0-2 Tight: 0-2 Gall: 0-0
Aids: Bl: 0-0 Vi: 0-0 Tstrap: 0-0
Best Rating: 120 6/99 Worc 2m7f110y gd-fm Ch

Fair hurdler at around three miles. Made a decent start to chasing in 1999 but was absent for nearly a year before returning in June 2000. Off the track for over 18 months subsequently due to injury but showed he still retains ability on his reappearance. Has only ever won on a sound surface.

Penncaler (IRE)

12-y-o ch g Callernish-Pennyland (Le Bavard (FR))
Mrs T J Hill Michael Emmanuel

Placings:*60/3036/F403P/2U5P2F46/U* **(4165)**
2001/02: 26^{U}G

	Starts	1st	2nd	3rd	Win & Pl
Chases	1	0	0	0	
Career Total	**20**	**0**	**2**	**3**	**4116**

Going: Sf: 0-0 GS: 0-0 Gd: 0-1 GF: - Fm: 0-0
Distance: 2m/2m3: 0-0 2m4-2m7: 0-0 3m+: 0-1
Track: LH: 0-1 RH: 0-0 Tight: 0-0 Gall: 0-0
Aids: Bl: 0-1 Vi: 0-0 Tstrap: 0-0
Best Rating: 107 3/96 Newb 2m5f gd-sft Hdl

Pennieflora

84f 57f
5-y-o b m Alflora (IRE)-Pennethorne Place (Deep Run)
G B Balding Sir Christopher Wates

Placings:*0* **(0108)**
2001/02: 18^{0}GF

	Starts	1st	2nd	3rd	Win & Pl
NH Flat	1	0	0	0	
Career Total	**1**	**0**	**0**	**0**	

Going: Sf: 0-0 GS: 0-0 Gd: 0-0 GF: - Fm: 0-1
Distance: 2m/2m3: 0-1 2m4-2m7: 0-0 3m+: 0-0
Track: LH: 0-1 RH: 0-0 Tight: 0-1 Gall: 0-0
Aids: Bl: 0-0 Vi: 0-0 Tstrap: 0-0
Best Rating: 57 5/01 Font 2m2f110y gd-fm NHF

Penninoir

(76h) (73h)
6-y-o br m Royal Fountain-The Pride Of Pokey (Uncle Pokey)
Mrs S C Bradburne R H Black

Placings:*00P0P50* **(4874)**
2001/02: 17^{0}GS, 17^{0}GF, 20^{P}HY, 16^{0}HY, 24^{P}S, 22^{5}S, 20^{0}G

	Starts	1st	2nd	3rd	Win & Pl
NH Flat	2	0	0	0	0
Hurdles	5	0	0	0	0
Career Total	**7**	**0**	**0**	**0**	**0**

Going: Sf: 0-4 GS: 0-1 Gd: 0-1 GF: - Fm: 0-1
Distance: 2m/2m3: 0-3 2m4-2m7: 0-3 3m+: 0-1
Track: LH: 0-4 RH: 0-1 Tight: 0-1 Gall: 0-0
Aids: Bl: 0-0 Vi: 0-0 Tstrap: 0-0
Best Rating: 73 3/02 Kels 2m6f110y soft Hdl

Modest hurdler yet to prove her stamina.

Penny Rich (IRE)

111 **140**

8-y-o br g Little Bighorn-Musical Puss (Orchestra)
T Hogan C P McGuinness

Placings:*232/210*0651610132020335-PF3PP **(4190)**
2001/02: 16^{P}S, 16^{F}Y, 16^{3}Y, 16^{P}HY, 16^{P}GS

	Starts	1st	2nd	3rd	Win & Pl
Hurdles	5	0	0	1	3629
Career Total	**27**	**4**	**5**	**5**	**59602**

126 9/00 List 2m HHdl HVY £13480
131 8/00 Tral 2m Hdl SFT £6424
118 8/00 Tram 2m (0-130)HHdl G-F £6560
101 5/00 Klny 2m1f NHF GD £3588
Total win prize-money £30052

Going: Sf: 0-2 GS: 0-1 Gd: 0-0 GF: - Fm: 0-0
Distance: 2m/2m3: 0-5 2m4-2m7: 0-0 3m+: 0-0
Track: LH: 0-3 RH: 0-1 Tight: 0-0 Gall: 0-0
Aids: Bl: 0-0 Vi: 0-0 Tstrap: 0-0
Best Rating: 159 1/01 Leop 2m soft Hdl

A useful Irish-trained handicapper, he produced a career-best effort when third in the 2001 Irish Champion Hurdle, despite being somewhat flattered. Mainly out of form last season. Suited by two miles on a soft surface, but acts on faster ground.

Pennyahei

(98c)

11-y-o b m Malaspina-Pennyazena (Pamroy)
S A Brookshaw Miss H Brookshaw

Placings:P/UO6P065P4/2203220530/**5P0F2041U/44 660260-P** **(0213)**
2001/02: 24^{P}F

	Starts	1st	2nd	3rd	Win & Pl
Hurdles	1	0	0	0	
Career Total	**38**	**1**	**6**	**2**	**10307**

102 3/00 Uttx 3m2f F(0-110)HCh GD £3835
Total win prize-money £3835

Going: Sf: 0-0 GS: 0-0 Gd: 0-0 GF: - Fm: 0-1
Distance: 2m/2m3: 0-0 2m4-2m7: 0-0 3m+: 0-1
Track: LH: 0-1 RH: 0-0 Tight: 0-1 Gall: 0-0
Aids: Bl: 0-0 Vi: 0-0 Tstrap: 0-0
Best Rating: 102 5/00 Hrfd 3m1f110y good Ch

Pennybridge (IRE)

97 **128**

13-y-o ch g Orchestra-Little Snob (Aristocracy)
A King Roland Stables Inc

Placings:*0/032042*4/0F1015F0500640/11O**F212F/224 630/16F011/P2/15F2/46-6** **(0452)**
2001/02: 25^{6}F

	Starts	1st	2nd	3rd	Win & Pl
Chases	1	0	0	0	0
Career Total	**51**	**9**	**8**	**2**	**39588**

146 10/99 Weth 2m4f110y B(0-150)HCh GD £8606
138 11/97 Aint 2m4f D(0-125)HCh GD £5303
126 9/97 Sedg 2m5f E(0-115)HCh G-F £2656
118 7/97 DRoy 2m4f (0-123)HCh FRM £3391
99 2/96 Dpat 2m2f Ch SFT £1412
114 10/95 DRoy 2m (0-116)HHdl G-F £1356
111 5/95 DRoy 2m4f (0-116)HHdl G-F £1356
101 9/94 Dpat 2m1f172y HHdl GD £1467
92 8/94 Dpat 2m1f172y Hdl GD £1467
Total win prize-money £27017

Going: Sf: 0-0 GS: 0-0 Gd: 0-0 GF: - Fm: 0-1
Distance: 2m/2m3: 0-0 2m4-2m7: 0-0 3m+: 0-1

Track: LH: 0-1 RH: 0-0 Tight: 0-0 Gall: 0-0
Aids: Bl: 0-0 Vi: 0-0 Tstrap: 0-0
Best Rating: 146 10/99 Weth 2m4f110y good Ch

A former winner of the Marlborough Cup over timber, he must have fast ground.

Pennys From Heaven

104 **89**

8-y-o gr g Generous (IRE)-Heavenly Cause (USA) (Grey Dawn Ii)
Miss T M Ide (D Nicholls 16/11) Miss Tracey Ide

Placings:05/040/023 **(4757)**
2001/02: 17^{0}G, 17^{2}GS, 16^{3}GF

	Starts	1st	2nd	3rd	Win & Pl
Hurdles	3	0	1	1	1181
Career Total	**8**	**0**	**1**	**1**	**1483**

Going: Sf: 0-0 GS: 0-1 Gd: 0-1 GF: - Fm: 0-1
Distance: 2m/2m3: 0-3 2m4-2m7: 0-0 3m+: 0-0
Track: LH: 0-1 RH: 0-2 Tight: 0-1 Gall: 0-0
Aids: Bl: 0-0 Vi: 0-0 Tstrap: 0-0
Best Rating: 95 3/98 Kels 2m110y good Hdl

Modest form in a sporadic hurdling career. Showed improved form when twice placed in novice hurdles in April 2002. Should be suited by two and a half miles.

Pension Fund

98 **84**

8-y-o b g Emperor Fountain-Navarino Bay (Averof)
M W Easterby Stephen J Curtis

Placings:P40-40 **(2903)**
2001/02: 16^{4}S, 16^{0}GS

	Starts	1st	2nd	3rd	Win & Pl
Hurdles	2	0	0	0	285
Career Total	**5**	**0**	**0**	**0**	**285**

Going: Sf: 0-1 GS: 0-1 Gd: 0-0 GF: - Fm: 0-0
Distance: 2m/2m3: 0-2 2m4-2m7: 0-0 3m+: 0-0
Track: LH: 0-2 RH: 0-0 Tight: 0-0 Gall: 0-0
Aids: Bl: 0-0 Vi: 0-0 Tstrap: 0-0
Best Rating: 100 12/00 Donc 2m110y gd-sft Hdl

A fair handicapper on the Flat at between a mile and ten furlongs. Not as good over flights.

Penthouse Minstrel

95 **96**

8-y-o b/br g Seven Hearts-Pentameron (Heres)
C J Gray A S Litston

Placings:542P **(2432)**
2001/02: 22^{5}GS, 22^{4}GF, 27^{2}GF, 21^{P}GS

	Starts	1st	2nd	3rd	Win & Pl
Hurdles	4	0	1	0	691
Career Total	**4**	**0**	**1**	**0**	**691**

Going: Sf: 0-0 GS: 0-2 Gd: 0-0 GF: - Fm: 0-2
Distance: 2m/2m3: 0-0 2m4-2m7: 0-3 3m+: 0-1
Track: LH: 0-1 RH: 0-1 Tight: 0-1 Gall: 0-1
Aids: Bl: 0-0 Vi: 0-0 Tstrap: 0-0
Best Rating: 96 5/01 Winc 2m6f gd-fm Hdl

Pentland Squire

101 **76**

11-y-o b g Belfort (FR)-Sparkler Superb (Grisaille)
Miss C J E Caroe Miss C J E Caroe

Placings:*00*/032355/12222122/05321/P304-F4 **(3648)**
2001/02: 16^{F}HY, 16^{4}S

	Starts	1st	2nd	3rd	Win & Pl
Hurdles	2	0	0	0	0
Career Total	**27**	**3**	**8**	**4**	**14164**

113 4/00 Hexm 2m E(0-115)HHdl GD £2688
106 12/97 Sedg 2m1f E(0-100)HHdl GD £2346
98 9/97 Carl 2m1f F(0-100)HHdl G-F £2276
Total win prize-money £7310

Going: Sf: 0-2 GS: 0-0 Gd: 0-0 GF: - Fm: 0-0
Distance: 2m/2m3: 0-2 2m4-2m7: 0-0 3m+: 0-0
Track: LH: 0-0 RH: 0-2 Tight: 0-0 Gall: 0-1
Aids: Bl: 0-0 Vi: 0-0 Tstrap: 0-0
Best Rating: 115 3/00 Weth 2m gd-sft Hdl

Peover Eye

7-y-o ch g Milieu-Gusty Brook (Meadowbrook)
M Mullineaux Mrs C M Brown

Placings:P-P **(0054)**
2001/02: 24^{P}G

	Starts	1st	2nd	3rd	Win & Pl
Hurdles	1	0	0	0	
Career Total	**2**	**0**	**0**	**0**	

Going: Sf: 0-0 GS: 0-0 Gd: 0-1 GF: - Fm: 0-0
Distance: 2m/2m3: 0-0 2m4-2m7: 0-0 3m+: 0-1
Track: LH: 0-1 RH: 0-0 Tight: 0-1 Gall: 0-0
Aids: Bl: 0-0 Vi: 0-0 Tstrap: 0-0
Best Rating:

Pepeta

88 **54**

5-y-o b m Presidium-Mighty Flash (Rolfe (USA))
D L Williams N F Dawe

Placings:0P00 **(3670)**
2001/02: 17^{0}F, 21^{P}G, 16^{0}GS, 21^{0}S

	Starts	1st	2nd	3rd	Win & Pl
Hurdles	4	0	0	0	
Career Total	**4**	**0**	**0**	**0**	

Going: Sf: 0-1 GS: 0-1 Gd: 0-1 GF: - Fm: 0-1
Distance: 2m/2m3: 0-2 2m4-2m7: 0-2 3m+: 0-0
Track: LH: 0-1 RH: 0-3 Tight: 0-1 Gall: 0-1
Aids: Bl: 0-0 Vi: 0-0 Tstrap: 0-2
Best Rating: 54 10/01 Tntn 2m1f firm Hdl

Per Amore (IRE)

110 **109**

4-y-o ch g General Monash (USA)-Danny's Miracle (Superlative)
P J Hobbs (Kevin Prendergast 21/10) R J B Partners

Placings:323311 **(4737)**
2001/02: 16^{3}Y, 17^{2}S, 16^{3}HY, 16^{3}G, 16^{1}G, 16^{1}GF

	Starts	1st	2nd	3rd	Win & Pl
Hurdles	6	2	1	3	8940
Career Total	**6**	**2**	**1**	**3**	**8940**

103 4/02 Ludl 2m E Hdl G-F £3020
109 4/02 Ludl 2m D Hdl GD £3900
Total win prize-money £6921

Going: Sf: 0-2 GS: 0-0 Gd: 1-2 GF: - Fm: 1-1
Distance: **2m/2m3: 2-6** 2m4-2m7: 0-0 3m+: 0-0
Track: LH: 0-1 **RH: 2-4** Tight: 0-1 Gall: 0-0

Aids: Bl: 2-2 Vi: 0-0 Tstrap: 0-0
Best Rating: 109 4/02 Ludl 2m good Hdl

Ex-Irish gelding with winning form on the Flat in Ireland at around a mile. Won two Ludlow novice hurdles in the spring of 2002. Goes well on fast ground, handles a softer surface.

Peradventure (IRE)

101 **95**

7-y-o b g Persian Bold-Missed Opportunity (IRE) (Exhibitioner)
A Crook David J Jackson

Placings:54121/000PF-P03 **(4670)**
2001/02: 16^{P}S, 16^{0}GS, 21^{3}GF

	Starts	1st	2nd	3rd	Win & Pl
Hurdles	3	0	0	1	279
Career Total	**13**	**2**	**1**	**1**	**7337**

119	4/00	Weth	2m	D Hdl	SFT	£3103
116	3/00	Weth	2m	E Hdl	G-S	£2870

Total win prize-money £5974

Going: Sf: 0-1 GS: 0-1 Gd: 0-0 GF: - Fm: 0-1
Distance: 2m/2m3: 0-2 2m4-2m7: 0-1 3m+: 0-0
Track: LH: 0-3 RH: 0-0 Tight: 0-1 Gall: 0-0
Aids: Bl: 0-0 Vi: 0-0 Tstrap: 0-0
Best Rating: 119 4/00 Weth 2m soft Hdl

A winner on the Flat and over hurdles, he acts on good and soft ground and is best over two miles. Out of form until dropped into selling company in the spring of 2002.

Perange (FR)

106 **138**

6-y-o ch g Perrault-La Mesange (FR) (Olmeto)
P F Nicholls (M Rolland 2/5) Mrs J Stewart

Placings:0060541-313321 **(3806)**
2001/02: 18^{3}HO, 16^{1}GS, 16^{3}GS, 21^{3}G, 17^{2}G, 20^{1}S

	Starts	1st	2nd	3rd	Win & Pl
Chases	6	2	1	3	17651
Career Total	**13**	**3**	**1**	**3**	**30251**

137	2/02	Font	2m4f	C Ch	SFT	£6230
122	10/01	Uttx	2m	D Ch	G-S	£4875
	3/01	Autl	2m3f110y	HHdl	HVY	£9699

Total win prize-money £20804

Going: Sf: 1-1 GS: 1-2 Gd: 0-2 GF: - Fm: 0-0
Distance: 2m/2m3: 1-4 2m4-2m7: 1-2 3m+: 0-0
Track: **LH: 1-3** RH: 0-1 **Tight: 1-3** Gall: 0-0
Aids: Bl: 0-0 Vi: 0-0 Tstrap: 0-0
Best Rating: 138 10/01 Kemp 2m gd-sft Ch

He went off the boil after a promising start over fences, but bounced back after a break to win at Fontwell in January. Stays two and a half miles.

Perchancer (IRE)

107 **118**

6-y-o ch g Perugino (USA)-Irish Hope (Nishapour (FR))
P C Haslam Middleham Park Racing & N P Green

Placings:3-1F24 **(4848)**
2001/02: 20^{1}G, 20^{F}HY, 16^{2}S, 16^{4}G

	Starts	1st	2nd	3rd	Win & Pl
Hurdles	4	1	1	0	4025
Career Total	**5**	**1**	**1**	**1**	**4432**

116	11/01	Weth	2m4f110y	E Hdl	GD	£2744

Total win prize-money £2744

Going: Sf: 0-2 GS: 0-0 Gd: 1-2 GF: - Fm: 0-0
Distance: 2m/2m3: 0-2 **2m4-2m7: 1-2** 3m+: 0-0
Track: **LH: 1-4** RH: 0-0 Tight: 0-1 Gall: 0-0
Aids: Bl: 0-0 Vi: 0-0 Tstrap: 0-0
Best Rating: **122** 4/02 Strf 2m110y good Hdl

Modest hurdler. Best around two and a half miles. Acts on a sound surface. Mixes hurdling with runs on the All-Weather.

Perching (IRE)

84 **76**

8-y-o b g Strong Gale-Fiona's Blue (Crash Course)
J T Gifford John Plackett

Placings:50/UF0412/P5 **(4729)**
2001/02: 24^{P}GF, 24^{5}GF

	Starts	1st	2nd	3rd	Win & Pl
Chases	2	0	0	0	0
Career Total	**10**	**1**	**1**	**0**	**6588**

118	3/00	Ling	3m	D Ch	GD	£4186

Total win prize-money £4186

Going: Sf: 0-0 GS: 0-0 Gd: 0-0 GF: - Fm: 0-2
Distance: 2m/2m3: 0-0 2m4-2m7: 0-0 3m+: 0-2
Track: LH: 0-1 RH: 0-1 Tight: 0-0 Gall: 0-1
Aids: Bl: 0-0 Vi: 0-0 Tstrap: 0-0
Best Rating: 123 4/00 Font 2m6f good Ch

Percolator (IRE)

81(96h) (111h)**121**

8-y-o b g Executive Perk-Cherry Jubilee (Le Bavard (FR))
P F Nicholls R G Eddy

Placings:63342/P5441-415P45P **(4882)**
2001/02: 22^{4}GF, 24^{1}S, 26^{5}GS, 24^{P}S, 22^{4}S, 21^{5}S, 26^{P}GF

	Starts	1st	2nd	3rd	Win & Pl
Hurdles	1	0	0	0	0
Chases	6	1	0	0	4538
Career Total	**17**	**2**	**1**	**2**	**9172**

121	10/01	Chep	3m	D Ch	SFT	£3844
111	4/01	Winc	2m6f	F(0-95)HHdl	SFT	£3080

Total win prize-money £6925

Going: Sf: 1-4 GS: 0-1 Gd: 0-0 GF: - Fm: 0-2
Distance: 2m/2m3: 0-0 2m4-2m7: 0-3 **3m+: 1-4**
Track: **LH: 1-2** RH: 0-3 Tight: 0-1 Gall: 0-1
Aids: Bl: 0-0 Vi: 0-0 **Tstrap: 1-6**
Best Rating: 121 10/01 Chep 3m soft Ch

Somewhat fortunate winner on his chase debut at Chepstow in October 2001.(DEAD)

Percy Beck

99 **87+**

6-y-o ch g Minster Son-Kate O'Kirkham (Le Bavard (FR))
P Needham P Needham

Placings:000/05UP **(4857)**
2001/02: 17^{0}S, 17^{5}GS, 16^{U}GF, 20^{P}G

	Starts	1st	2nd	3rd	Win & Pl
Hurdles	4	0	0	0	0
Career Total	**7**	**0**	**0**	**0**	**0**

Going: Sf: 0-1 GS: 0-1 Gd: 0-1 GF: - Fm: 0-1
Distance: 2m/2m3: 0-3 2m4-2m7: 0-1 3m+: 0-0
Track: LH: 0-2 RH: 0-1 Tight: 0-1 Gall: 0-0
Aids: Bl: 0-0 Vi: 0-0 Tstrap: 0-0
Best Rating: 71 3/02 Carl 2m1f gd-sft Hdl

Modest hurdler, turned in a much improved effort when breaking his duck in handicap company at Wetherby in May.

Percy Braithwaite (IRE)

100(100c) (100c)**90**

10-y-o b g Kahyasi-Nasseem (FR) (Zeddaan)
Mrs P Ford W E Donohue, A Fraser, K Marritt

Placings:41001U/22362530/**3P234/464411/23F46P-04445200** **(3161)**
2001/02: 17^{0}F, 16^{4}GF, 17^{4}G, 16^{4}GF, 17^{5}GF, 21^{2}GF, 16^{0}S, 26^{0}S

	Starts	1st	2nd	3rd	Win & Pl
Hurdles	4	0	1	0	763
Chases	4	0	0	0	596
Career Total	**39**	**4**	**6**	**5**	**22153**

111	4/00	Hntg	2m110y	D(0-115)HCh	GD	£4048
96	2/00	Ludl	2m	F(0-100)HCh	GD	£2873
105	4/97	Ludl	2m	E Hdl	FRM	£2248
100	1/97	Ludl	2m	E Hdl	G-F	£2682

Total win prize-money £11852

Going: Sf: 0-2 GS: 0-0 Gd: 0-1 GF: - Fm: 0-5
Distance: 2m/2m3: 0-6 2m4-2m7: 0-1 3m+: 0-1
Track: LH: 0-4 RH: 0-3 Tight: 0-4 Gall: 0-0
Aids: Bl: 0-0 Vi: 0-0 Tstrap: 0-0
Best Rating: 111 11/00 MRas 2m1f110y gd-sft Ch

Moderate hurdler at around two miles on fast ground.

Percy Parkeeper

110 **133**

9-y-o b g Teenoso (USA)-True Clown (True Song)
N A Twiston-Davies Mr & Mrs Peter Orton

Placings:*1224*/F40213F/**3454-0113450PP** **(4891)**
2001/02: 20^{0}GS, 16^{1}G, 16^{1}G, 16^{3}G, 17^{4}S, 19^{5}G, 16^{0}G, 21^{P}GF, 16^{P}G

	Starts	1st	2nd	3rd	Win & Pl
Chases	9	2	0	1	11732
Career Total	**24**	**4**	**3**	**3**	**21116**

133	10/01	Hrfd	2m	E(0-115)HCh	GD	£3376
125	9/01	Prth	2m	E(0-115)HCh	GD	£5369
124	2/99	Kemp	2m5f	D Hdl	GD	£3009
107	1/98	Hntg	2m110y	H NHF	G-S	£1402

Total win prize-money £13158

Going: Sf: 0-1 GS: 0-1 Gd: 2-6 GF: - Fm: 0-1
Distance: **2m/2m3: 2-6** 2m4-2m7: 0-3 3m+: 0-0
Track: LH: 0-6 **RH: 2-3** Tight: 0-1 Gall: 0-4
Aids: Bl: 0-2 Vi: 0-0 Tstrap: 0-0
Best Rating: 133 11/01 Chel 2m good Ch

A former decent novice hurdler who has had his problems, he gained his first chase win at Perth in September 2001 and followed up in good style at Hereford, but held subsequently. He is suited by two miles and good ground, but does stay further. Likes to dominate.

Percy-Verance (IRE)

99 **83**

4-y-o ch g Dolphin Street (FR)-Sinology (Rainbow Quest (USA))
A Dickman Mike Smallman

Placings:00 **(2301)**
2001/02: 16^{0}G, 16^{0}GF

	Starts	1st	2nd	3rd	Win & Pl
Hurdles	2	0	0	0	
Career Total	**2**	**0**	**0**	**0**	

Going: Sf: 0-0 GS: 0-0 Gd: 0-1 GF: - Fm: 0-1
Distance: 2m/2m3: 0-2 2m4-2m7: 0-0 3m+: 0-0
Track: LH: 0-2 RH: 0-0 Tight: 0-1 Gall: 0-1
Aids: Bl: 0-0 Vi: 0-0 Tstrap: 0-1
Best Rating: 83 11/01 Newc 2m good Hdl

Perfect Fellow

111 138

8-y-o b g Teamster-G W Supermare (Rymer)
Miss H C Knight The Unlucky For Some Partnership

Placings: *10/11/0/31-41* **(2849)**
2001/02: 20^{4}GS, 20^{1}G

	Starts	1st	2nd	3rd	Win & Pl
Chases	2	1	0	0	11211
Career Total	**9**	**5**	**0**	**1**	**21562**

138 12/01	Kemp	2m4f110y	D(0-120)HCh	GD	£10676
126 12/00	Folk	2m5f	D Ch	SFT	£3848
126 1/99	Folk	2m6f110y	E Hdl	HVY	£2427
108 12/98	Strf	2m6f110y	E Hdl	SFT	£2250
90 3/98	NAbb	2m1f	H NHF	SFT	£1236

Total win prize-money £20437

Going: Sf: 0-0 GS: 0-1 Gd: 1-1 GF: - Fm: 0-0
Distance: 2m/2m3: 0-0 **2m4-2m7: 1-2** 3m+: 0-0
Track: LH: 0-0 **RH: 1-2** Tight: 0-0 Gall: 0-0
Aids: Bl: 0-0 Vi: 0-0 Tstrap: 0-0
Best Rating: 138 12/01 Kemp 2m4f110y good Ch

Won two novice hurdle races in fine style in 1998/99 both times indicating a liking for soft ground and distances just short of three miles. Lightly raced over fences since and was off the track for a year after December 2000, but bounced back to score in game style at Kempton on Boxing Day 2001.

Perfect Light

13-y-o b g Salmon Leap (USA)-Sheer Gold (Yankee Gold)
M J Jackson Peter Nash

Placings: 0/0F/32/4/0PP/F **(3984)**
2001/02: 31^{F}GS

	Starts	1st	2nd	3rd	Win & Pl
Chases	1	0	0	0	
Career Total	**10**	**0**	**1**	**1**	**1177**

Going: Sf: 0-0 GS: 0-1 Gd: 0-0 GF: - Fm: 0-0
Distance: 2m/2m3: 0-0 2m4-2m7: 0-0 3m+: 0-1
Track: LH: 0-0 RH: 0-0 Tight: 0-0 Gall: 0-0
Aids: Bl: 0-0 Vi: 0-0 Tstrap: 0-0
Best Rating: 93 11/94 Hexm 2m good Hdl

Perfect Minstrel (IRE)

92 76

11-y-o b g Black Minstrel-Ashford Doll (Pitcairn)
N A Twiston-Davies Mrs Ian McKie

Placings: 0/P45P **(1244)**
2001/02: 21^{P}GF, 23^{4}G, 23^{5}GF, 23^{P}GF

	Starts	1st	2nd	3rd	Win & Pl
Chases	4	0	0	0	260
Career Total	**5**	**0**	**0**	**0**	**260**

Going: Sf: 0-0 GS: 0-0 Gd: 0-1 GF: - Fm: 0-3
Distance: 2m/2m3: 0-0 2m4-2m7: 0-1 3m+: 0-3
Track: LH: 0-4 RH: 0-0 Tight: 0-1 Gall: 0-0
Aids: Bl: 0-1 Vi: 0-0 Tstrap: 0-1
Best Rating: 76 7/01 Worc 2m7f110y good Ch

Perfect Native (IRE)

44f

4-y-o br f Be My Native (USA)-Perfect Excuse (Certingo)
F Lloyd F Lloyd

Placings: *0* **(3999)**
2001/02: 16^{0}S

	Starts	1st	2nd	3rd	Win & Pl
NH Flat	1	0	0	0	
Career Total	**1**	**0**	**0**	**0**	

Going: Sf: 0-1 GS: 0-0 Gd: 0-0 GF: - Fm: 0-0
Distance: 2m/2m3: 0-1 2m4-2m7: 0-0 3m+: 0-0
Track: LH: 0-1 RH: 0-0 Tight: 0-0 Gall: 0-1
Aids: Bl: 0-0 Vi: 0-0 Tstrap: 0-0
Best Rating:

Perfect Pal (IRE)

11-y-o ch g Mulhollande (USA)-Gone (Whistling Wind)
M J Coombe J Coombe

Placings: *110*/U00/62P0/PU/50042/PF **(3153)**
2001/02: 19^{P}GS, 20^{F}G

	Starts	1st	2nd	3rd	Win & Pl
Chases	2	0	0	0	
Career Total	**19**	**2**	**2**	**0**	**4761**

96 4/95	Asct	2m110y	H NHF	FRM	£2337
96 3/95	Ling	2m110y	H NHF	HVY	£1245

Total win prize-money £3582

Going: Sf: 0-0 GS: 0-1 Gd: 0-1 GF: - Fm: 0-0
Distance: 2m/2m3: 0-1 2m4-2m7: 0-1 3m+: 0-0
Track: LH: 0-0 RH: 0-1 Tight: 0-2 Gall: 0-0
Aids: Bl: 0-1 Vi: 0-0 Tstrap: 0-0
Best Rating: 96 4/95 Asct 2m110y firm NHF

Perfect Venue (IRE)

98 116

9-y-o b g Danehill (USA)-Welsh Fantasy (Welsh Pageant)
A J Wilson (N J Henderson 19/7) Mrs Barrie Gallop

Placings: 53/21132000/66006-4000F **(2653)**
2001/02: 19^{4}GF, 16^{0}GF, 19^{0}G, 19^{0}GS, 16^{F}G

	Starts	1st	2nd	3rd	Win & Pl
Hurdles	5	0	0	0	558
Career Total	**20**	**2**	**2**	**2**	**11018**

128 1/99	Tntn	2m1f	E Hdl	SFT	£2421
118 12/98	Tntn	2m1f	C Hdl	GD	£4197

Total win prize-money £6618

Going: Sf: 0-0 GS: 0-1 Gd: 0-2 GF: - Fm: 0-2
Distance: 2m/2m3: 0-3 2m4-2m7: 0-2 3m+: 0-0
Track: LH: 0-3 RH: 0-2 Tight: 0-3 Gall: 0-1
Aids: Bl: 0-2 Vi: 0-0 Tstrap: 0-1
Best Rating: 131 11/00 Newb 2m110y gd-sft Hdl

Perfectpeter (IRE)

8-y-o br g Decent Fellow-Naturally Enough (Aglojo)
Mrs Susan E Busby (N G Richards 10/2) Miss Susan E Busby

Placings: 4340-2P01P **(3895)**
2001/02: 25^{2}S, 24^{P}GS, 20^{0}GS, 25^{1}GS, 26^{P}HY

	Starts	1st	2nd	3rd	Win & Pl
Hurdles	1	1	0	0	2414
Chases	4	0	1	0	1046
Career Total	**9**	**1**	**1**	**1**	**4513**

77 7/01	Wolv	3m1f	E Hdl	G-S	£2413

Total win prize-money £2414

Going: Sf: 0-2 GS: 1-3 Gd: 0-0 GF: - Fm: 0-0
Distance: 2m/2m3: 0-0 2m4-2m7: 0-1 **3m+: 1-4**
Track: **LH: 1-4** RH: 0-1 **Tight: 1-1** Gall: 0-0
Aids: Bl: 0-3 Vi: 0-0 Tstrap: 0-0
Best Rating: 91 5/01 Hexm 3m1f soft Ch

Perky Brave (IRE)

9-y-o b g Executive Perk-The Potwalluper (Brave Invader (USA))
A Parker Mr & Mrs Raymond Anderson Green

Placings: *5/12*/P **(1745)**
2001/02: 22^{P}GS

	Starts	1st	2nd	3rd	Win & Pl
Hurdles	1	0	0	0	
Career Total	**4**	**1**	**1**	**0**	**2464**

97 5/99	Dpat	2m4f110y	NHF	G-F	£1994

Total win prize-money £1995

Going: Sf: 0-0 GS: 0-1 Gd: 0-0 GF: - Fm: 0-0
Distance: 2m/2m3: 0-0 2m4-2m7: 0-1 3m+: 0-0
Track: LH: 0-1 RH: 0-0 Tight: 0-1 Gall: 0-0
Aids: Bl: 0-0 Vi: 0-0 Tstrap: 0-0
Best Rating: 113 11/99 Ayr 2m good NHF

Perky Lad (IRE)

10-y-o b g Executive Perk-Radalgo (Ballad Rock)
R H York R H York

Placings: *0/004430*/0F3040F/0160 **(4650)**
2001/02: 16^{0}G, 21^{1}G, 28^{6}GF, 21^{0}G

	Starts	1st	2nd	3rd	Win & Pl
Chases	4	1	0	0	1489
Career Total	**18**	**1**	**0**	**2**	**2500**

100 5/01	Folk	2m5f	H Ch	GD	£1488

Total win prize-money £1489

Going: Sf: 0-0 GS: 0-0 Gd: 1-3 GF: - Fm: 0-1
Distance: 2m/2m3: 0-1 **2m4-2m7: 1-2** 3m+: 0-1
Track: LH: 0-2 **RH: 1-2 Tight: 1-4** Gall: 0-0
Aids: Bl: 0-0 Vi: 0-0 Tstrap: 0-0
Best Rating: 102 2/98 Clon 2m2f yld-sft NHF

Ex-Irish, won a hunter chase on good ground last year, otherwise well held.

Perouse

94f 112f

4-y-o ch g Alderbrook-Track Angel (Ardoon)
L Lungo J Dickson

Placings: *221* **(4860)**
2001/02: 16^{2}S, 17^{2}G, 16^{1}G

	Starts	1st	2nd	3rd	Win & Pl
NH Flat	3	1	2	0	2703
Career Total	**3**	**1**	**2**	**0**	**2703**

93 4/02	Hexm	2m110y	H NHF	GD	£1701

Total win prize-money £1701

Going: Sf: 0-1 GS: 0-0 Gd: 1-2 GF: - Fm: 0-0

Distance: 2m/2m3: 1-3 2m4-2m7: 0-0 3m+: 0-0
Track: LH: 0-1 RH: 0-1 Tight: 0-0 Gall: 0-0
Aids: Bl: 0-0 Vi: 0-0 Tstrap: 0-0
Best Rating: 112 4/02 Carl 2m1f good NHF

Runner-up in two bumpers in the spring of 2002 before winning at Hexham.

Perpetuity

77 48

4-y-o ch g Timeless Times (USA)-Boadicea's Chariot (Commanche Run)
Mrs H Dalton (A Bailey 24/8) Ray Bailey

Placings:40 (4044)
2001/02: 16^{4}GF, 17^{0}GS

	Starts	1st	2nd	3rd	Win & Pl
Hurdles	2	0	0	0	0
Career Total	**2**	**0**	**0**	**0**	**0**

Going: Sf: 0-0 GS: 0-1 Gd: 0-0 GF: - Fm: 0-1
Distance: 2m/2m3: 0-2 2m4-2m7: 0-0 3m+: 0-0
Track: LH: 0-1 RH: 0-1 Tight: 0-1 Gall: 0-0
Aids: Bl: 0-0 Vi: 0-0 Tstrap: 0-0
Best Rating: 48 8/01 Uttx 2m gd-fm Hdl

Perrianna

6-y-o b m Perpendicular-Scalby Anna (Sir Mago)
M E Sowersby Paul Clifton

Placings:*F*-0P (0451)
2001/02: 24^{0}S, 23^{P}F

	Starts	1st	2nd	3rd	Win & Pl
Hurdles	2	0	0	0	
Career Total	**3**	**0**	**0**	**0**	

Going: Sf: 0-1 GS: 0-0 Gd: 0-0 GF: - Fm: 0-1
Distance: 2m/2m3: 0-0 2m4-2m7: 0-1 3m+: 0-1
Track: LH: 0-2 RH: 0-0 Tight: 0-0 Gall: 0-0
Aids: Bl: 0-0 Vi: 0-0 Tstrap: 0-0
Best Rating:

Persian Bandit (IRE)

4-y-o b g Idris (IRE)-Ce Soir (Northern Baby (CAN))
J R Jenkins (Eddie Creighton 13/1) R M Ellis

Placings:0 (4559)
2001/02: 16^{0}GF

	Starts	1st	2nd	3rd	Win & Pl
Hurdles	1	0	0	0	
Career Total	**1**	**0**	**0**	**0**	

Going: Sf: 0-0 GS: 0-0 Gd: 0-0 GF: - Fm: 0-1
Distance: 2m/2m3: 0-1 2m4-2m7: 0-0 3m+: 0-0
Track: LH: 0-1 RH: 0-0 Tight: 0-1 Gall: 0-0
Aids: Bl: 0-0 Vi: 0-0 Tstrap: 0-0
Best Rating:

Persian Boy (IRE)

10-y-o b g Brush Aside (USA)-Bargara (Bargello)
J M Turner J M Turner

Placings:04PP/05**PP**/5/3P-6P (0325)
2001/02: 20^{6}GF, 21^{P}G

	Starts	1st	2nd	3rd	Win & Pl
Chases	2	0	0	0	0
Career Total	**13**	**0**	**0**	**1**	**326**

Going: Sf: 0-0 GS: 0-0 Gd: 0-1 GF: - Fm: 0-1
Distance: 2m/2m3: 0-0 2m4-2m7: 0-2 3m+: 0-0
Track: LH: 0-0 RH: 0-2 Tight: 0-1 Gall: 0-1
Aids: Bl: 0-1 Vi: 0-0 Tstrap: 0-0
Best Rating: 91 5/00 Folk 2m5f good Ch

Persian Butterfly

10-y-o b m Dancing Dissident (USA)-Butterfly Kiss (Beldale Flutter (USA))
C W Loggin Steven Astaire

Placings:P0P040/1P024422353P/0564400/5/4F6 (0585)
2001/02: 20^{4}GF, 24^{F}GS, 24^{6}GF

	Starts	1st	2nd	3rd	Win & Pl
Chases	3	0	0	0	128
Career Total	**29**	**1**	**3**	**2**	**5226**

76 5/97 Strf 2m110y G Hdl GD £2090
Total win prize-money £2091

Going: Sf: 0-0 GS: 0-1 Gd: 0-0 GF: - Fm: 0-2
Distance: 2m/2m3: 0-0 2m4-2m7: 0-1 3m+: 0-2
Track: LH: 0-3 RH: 0-0 Tight: 0-3 Gall: 0-0
Aids: Bl: 0-0 Vi: 0-0 Tstrap: 0-0
Best Rating: 95 1/98 Ling 2m4f110y gd-sft Ch

Persian Clover

98(100h) (91h)99

8-y-o b m Abutammam-Winning Clover (Winden)
B N Doran R W Mitchell

Placings:56-0204 (0796)
2001/02: 20^{0}G, 17^{2}G, 16^{0}GF, 16^{4}GF

	Starts	1st	2nd	3rd	Win & Pl
Hurdles	2	0	1	0	790
Chases	2	0	0	0	298
Career Total	**6**	**0**	**1**	**0**	**1088**

Going: Sf: 0-0 GS: 0-0 Gd: 0-2 GF: - Fm: 0-2
Distance: 2m/2m3: 0-3 2m4-2m7: 0-1 3m+: 0-0
Track: LH: 0-2 RH: 0-2 Tight: 0-1 Gall: 0-1
Aids: Bl: 0-0 Vi: 0-0 Tstrap: 0-0
Best Rating: 99 6/01 Worc 2m gd-fm Ch

Persian Dream (IRE)

90 90

9-y-o b m Mazaad-Irish Dream (Ovac (ITY))
N R Mitchell Mr And Mrs Andrew May

Placings:4410/52-3 (0434)
2001/02: 17^{3}GF

	Starts	1st	2nd	3rd	Win & Pl
Hurdles	1	0	0	1	426
Career Total	**7**	**1**	**1**	**1**	**4266**

94 3/97 Thur 2m Hdl GD £2712
Total win prize-money £2713

Going: Sf: 0-0 GS: 0-0 Gd: 0-0 GF: - Fm: 0-1
Distance: 2m/2m3: 0-1 2m4-2m7: 0-0 3m+: 0-0
Track: LH: 0-0 RH: 0-1 Tight: 0-1 Gall: 0-0
Aids: Bl: 0-0 Vi: 0-0 Tstrap: 0-0
Best Rating: 94 3/97 Thur 2m good Hdl

Persian King (IRE)

98 91

5-y-o ch g Persian Bold-Queen's Share (Main Reef)
J A B Old W E Sturt

Placings:5-66 (1556)
2001/02: 16^{6}GF, 16^{6}G

	Starts	1st	2nd	3rd	Win & Pl
Hurdles	2	0	0	0	0
Career Total	**3**	**0**	**0**	**0**	**0**

Going: Sf: 0-0 GS: 0-0 Gd: 0-1 GF: - Fm: 0-1
Distance: 2m/2m3: 0-2 2m4-2m7: 0-0 3m+: 0-0
Track: LH: 0-2 RH: 0-0 Tight: 0-0 Gall: 0-0
Aids: Bl: 0-0 Vi: 0-0 Tstrap: 0-0
Best Rating: 78 10/01 Chep 2m110y good Hdl

Persona Pride

8-y-o gr g St Enodoc-Le Jour Fortune (Twilight Alley)
Mrs B Brown (Mrs Billy Brown 15/5) Percy Priday

Placings:P64P (4741)
2001/02: 20^{P}GF, 25^{6}G, 25^{4}G, 24^{P}GF

	Starts	1st	2nd	3rd	Win & Pl
Chases	4	0	0	0	0
Career Total	**4**	**0**	**0**	**0**	**0**

Going: Sf: 0-0 GS: 0-0 Gd: 0-2 GF: - Fm: 0-2
Distance: 2m/2m3: 0-0 2m4-2m7: 0-1 3m+: 0-3
Track: LH: 0-1 RH: 0-3 Tight: 0-1 Gall: 0-0
Aids: Bl: 0-0 Vi: 0-0 Tstrap: 0-0
Best Rating: 90 3/02 Hrfd 3m1f110y good Ch

Persrolla

89(85h) (68h)85

8-y-o br m Persian Bold-Primrolla (Relko)
B D Leavy (R Lee 5/5) The Five Nations Partnership

Placings:*0*/04/0/16P-P4F06 (1354)
2001/02: 19^{P}G, 20^{4}S, 22^{F}GF, 16^{0}GF, 21^{6}GF

	Starts	1st	2nd	3rd	Win & Pl
Hurdles	3	0	0	0	270
Chases	2	0	0	0	0
Career Total	**12**	**1**	**0**	**0**	**2532**

85 5/00 Extr 2m1f E Hdl GD £2058
Total win prize-money £2058

Going: Sf: 0-1 GS: 0-0 Gd: 0-1 GF: - Fm: 0-3
Distance: 2m/2m3: 0-1 2m4-2m7: 0-4 3m+: 0-0
Track: LH: 0-4 RH: 0-1 Tight: 0-1 Gall: 0-0
Aids: Bl: 0-0 Vi: 0-0 Tstrap: 0-5
Best Rating: 88 2/99 Kemp 2m good Hdl

Pertemps (IRE)

98 101

9-y-o ch g Good Thyne (USA)-Julia's Pauper (Pauper)
A Streeter Pertemps Group Limited

Placings:*600*F5/3522224P6/1 (0723)
2001/02: 25^{1}F

	Starts	1st	2nd	3rd	Win & Pl
Chases	1	1	0	0	3283
Career Total	**15**	**1**	**4**	**1**	**6477**

101 6/01 Hrfd 3m1f110y G(0-90)HCh FRM £3283
Total win prize-money £3283

Going: Sf: 0-0 GS: 0-0 Gd: 0-0 GF: - Fm: 1-1
Distance: 2m/2m3: 0-0 2m4-2m7: 0-0 **3m+: 1-1**

Track: LH: 0-0 **RH: 1-1** Tight: 0-0 Gall: 0-0
Aids: Bl: 0-0 **Vi: 1-1** Tstrap: 0-0
Best Rating: 101 6/01 Hrfd 3m1f110y firm Ch

Pertemps Babe

57f **34f**

5-y-o b g Gildoran-Brilliant Future (Welsh Saint)
A D Smith Pertemps Group Limited

Placings:*00* **(2142)**
2001/02: 17^{0}GS, 17^{0}G

	Starts	1st	2nd	3rd	Win & Pl
NH Flat	2	0	0	0	
Career Total	**2**	**0**	**0**	**0**	

Going: Sf: 0-0 GS: 0-1 Gd: 0-1 GF: - Fm: 0-0
Distance: 2m/2m3: 0-2 2m4-2m7: 0-0 3m+: 0-0
Track: LH: 0-0 RH: 0-1 Tight: 0-0 Gall: 0-0
Aids: Bl: 0-0 Vi: 0-0 Tstrap: 0-0
Best Rating: 34 10/01 Extr 2m1f gd-sft NHF

Pertemps Boycott (IRE)

99 **71**

4-y-o b g Indian Ridge-Coupe D'Hebe (Ile De Bourbon (USA))
H Alexander (N Tinkler 12/9) Alastair Baillie

Placings:02P30P01 **(4904)**
2001/02: 17^{0}GF, 17^{3}S, 16^{P}G, 16^{3}GF, 16^{0}G, 16^{P}G, 16^{0}G, 17^{4}G

	Starts	1st	2nd	3rd	Win & Pl
Hurdles	8	0	0	2	492
Career Total	**8**	**0**	**0**	**2**	**492**

Going: Sf: 0-1 GS: 0-0 Gd: 0-5 GF: - Fm: 0-2
Distance: 2m/2m3: 0-8 2m4-2m7: 0-0 3m+: 0-0
Track: LH: 0-3 RH: 0-5 Tight: 0-5 Gall: 0-1
Aids: Bl: 0-0 Vi: 0-0 Tstrap: 0-0
Best Rating: 67 4/02 MRas 2m1f110y good Hdl

He had shown very little over hurdles before landing a seller at Hexham in June 2002.

Pertemps Cindrella

109 **82**

7-y-o ch m Almoojid-Cinderella Derek (Hittite Glory)
B D Leavy (A D Smith 29/11) J A Provan

Placings:*33060*/P030/0F522250-5F012200P4 **(4491)**
2001/02: 19^{5}F, 19^{F}F, 20^{0}GS, 16^{1}HY, 17^{2}GS, 16^{2}S, 16^{0}GS, 16^{0}HY, 16^{P}GS, 20^{4}GS

	Starts	1st	2nd	3rd	Win & Pl
Hurdles	10	1	2	0	3392
Career Total	**27**	**1**	**5**	**3**	**5688**

82	11/01	Uttx	2m	G(0-90)HHdl	HVY	£1897

Total win prize-money £1897

Going: Sf: 1-3 GS: 0-5 Gd: 0-0 GF: - Fm: 0-2
Distance: 2m/2m3: 1-6 2m4-2m7: 0-4 3m+: 0-0
Track: LH: 1-4 RH: 0-4 Tight: 0-4 Gall: 0-1
Aids: Bl: 0-0 Vi: 0-0 Tstrap: 0-0
Best Rating: 82 12/01 Bang 2m1f gd-sft Hdl

Suited by testing conditions, she won a poor seller at Uttoxeter in November 2001.

Pertemps Mission

91 **82**

8-y-o b g Safawan-Heresheis (Free State)
Mrs Lydia Pearce Michael C Whatley

Placings:3/35 **(1393)**
2001/02: 24^{3}GF, 24^{5}GF

	Starts	1st	2nd	3rd	Win & Pl
Hurdles	2	0	0	1	653
Career Total	**3**	**0**	**0**	**2**	**1059**

Going: Sf: 0-0 GS: 0-0 Gd: 0-0 GF: - Fm: 0-2
Distance: 2m/2m3: 0-0 2m4-2m7: 0-0 3m+: 0-2
Track: LH: 0-1 RH: 0-1 Tight: 0-1 Gall: 0-0
Aids: Bl: 0-0 Vi: 0-0 Tstrap: 0-0
Best Rating: 101 4/99 Hntg 2m5f110y gd-fm Hdl

Pertemps Peaches

76f **50f**

5-y-o b m Gildoran-Peristyle (Tolomeo)
A Streeter Pertemps Group Limited

Placings:*00* **(4289)**
2001/02: 16^{0}G, 17^{0}GS

	Starts	1st	2nd	3rd	Win & Pl
NH Flat	2	0	0	0	
Career Total	**2**	**0**	**0**	**0**	

Going: Sf: 0-0 GS: 0-1 Gd: 0-1 GF: - Fm: 0-0
Distance: 2m/2m3: 0-2 2m4-2m7: 0-0 3m+: 0-0
Track: LH: 0-0 RH: 0-2 Tight: 0-1 Gall: 0-0
Aids: Bl: 0-0 Vi: 0-0 Tstrap: 0-0
Best Rating: 54 3/02 MRas 2m1f110y gd-sft NHF

Pertemps Polo

5-y-o b g Petoski-Pertemps Partner (Bairn (USA))
A Streeter Pertemps Group Limited

Placings:P **(1624)**
2001/02: 16^{P}GF

	Starts	1st	2nd	3rd	Win & Pl
Hurdles	1	0	0	0	
Career Total	**1**	**0**	**0**	**0**	

Going: Sf: 0-0 GS: 0-0 Gd: 0-0 GF: - Fm: 0-1
Distance: 2m/2m3: 0-1 2m4-2m7: 0-0 3m+: 0-0
Track: LH: 0-0 RH: 0-1 Tight: 0-0 Gall: 0-0
Aids: Bl: 0-0 Vi: 0-0 Tstrap: 0-0
Best Rating:

Pertemps Profile

104 **103**

6-y-o b g Petoski-Peristyle (Tolomeo)
A Streeter Pertemps Group Limited

Placings:*165*/UP4-16P35020 **(4240)**
2001/02: 20^{1}GS, 21^{6}S, 21^{P}GS, 19^{3}S, 20^{5}S, 20^{0}G, 26^{2}S, 26^{0}GF

	Starts	1st	2nd	3rd	Win & Pl
Hurdles	8	1	1	1	4730
Career Total	**14**	**2**	**1**	**1**	**6550**

100	5/01	Bang	2m4f	D(0-110)HHdl	G-S	£3612
96	2/00	Towc	2m	H NHF	HVY	£1820

Total win prize-money £5432

Going: Sf: 0-4 GS: 1-2 Gd: 0-1 GF: - Fm: 0-1
Distance: 2m/2m3: 0-0 **2m4-2m7: 1-6** 3m+: 0-2
Track: LH: 1-2 RH: 0-6 **Tight: 1-2** Gall: 0-3

Aids: Bl: 0-2 Vi: 0-3 Tstrap: 0-0
Best Rating: 103 2/02 Hntg 3m2f soft Hdl

Ordinary novice hurdler, stays two and a half miles.

Pertemps Silenus

78f **69f**

4-y-o b g Silca Blanka (IRE)-Silvie (Kind Of Hush)
A D Smith Pertemps Group Limited

Placings:*00* **(4180)**
2001/02: 16^{0}S, 16^{0}GS

	Starts	1st	2nd	3rd	Win & Pl
NH Flat	2	0	0	0	
Career Total	**2**	**0**	**0**	**0**	

Going: Sf: 0-1 GS: 0-1 Gd: 0-0 GF: - Fm: 0-0
Distance: 2m/2m3: 0-2 2m4-2m7: 0-0 3m+: 0-0
Track: LH: 0-0 RH: 0-1 Tight: 0-0 Gall: 0-0
Aids: Bl: 0-0 Vi: 0-0 Tstrap: 0-0
Best Rating: 69 2/02 Sand 2m110y soft NHF

Pertemps Susie

95 **88**

6-y-o b m Gildoran-Brilliant Future (Welsh Saint)
A Streeter Pertemps Group Limited

Placings:*006*-164 **(1404)**
2001/02: 17^{1}F, 17^{6}F, 17^{4}G

	Starts	1st	2nd	3rd	Win & Pl
NH Flat	1	1	0	0	2188
Hurdles	2	0	0	0	0
Career Total	**6**	**1**	**0**	**0**	**2188**

95	5/01	Extr	2m1f	H NHF	FRM	£2187

Total win prize-money £2188

Going: Sf: 0-0 GS: 0-0 Gd: 0-1 GF: - Fm: 1-2
Distance: 2m/2m3: 1-3 2m4-2m7: 0-0 3m+: 0-0
Track: LH: 0-1 **RH: 1-2** Tight: 0-1 Gall: 0-0
Aids: Bl: 0-0 Vi: 0-0 Tstrap: 0-0
Best Rating: 95 5/01 Extr 2m1f firm NHF

Pertemps Timmy

83f **88f**

4-y-o b g Petoski-Brilliant Future (Welsh Saint)
A Streeter Pertemps Group Limited

Placings:3 **(4242)**
2001/02: 16^{3}GF

	Starts	1st	2nd	3rd	Win & Pl
NH Flat	1	0	0	1	227
Career Total	**1**	**0**	**0**	**1**	**227**

Going: Sf: 0-0 GS: 0-0 Gd: 0-0 GF: - Fm: 0-1
Distance: 2m/2m3: 0-1 2m4-2m7: 0-0 3m+: 0-0
Track: LH: 0-0 RH: 0-1 Tight: 0-0 Gall: 0-1
Aids: Bl: 0-0 Vi: 0-0 Tstrap: 0-0
Best Rating: 88 3/02 Hntg 2m110y gd-fm NHF

Third first time in a bumper at Huntingdon in March.

Pertino

103 **112**

6-y-o b g Terimon-Persian Fountain (IRE) (Persian Heights)
J M Jefferson W Fouracres, T Pryke & D Willis

Placings:5412153/P0056P-P0F12205212 **(4869)**
2001/02: 20^{P}S, 16^{0}G, 17^{F}GS, 16^{1}G, 16^{2}G, 20^{2}S, 16^{0}GS,

20^{5}GS, 16^{2}G, 17^{1}G, 20^{2}GF

	Starts	1st	2nd	3rd	Win & Pl
Hurdles	11	2	4	0	10715
Career Total	**24**	**4**	**5**	**1**	**18565**

112	4/02	Carl	2m1f	D(0-120)HHdl	GD	£3486
106	10/01	Kels	2m110y	E(0-115)HHdl	GD	£2821
120	2/00	Muss	2m	D Hdl	G-S	£3087
104	1/00	Newc	2m	E Hdl	SFT	£2558

Total win prize-money £11954

Going: Sf: 0-2 GS: 0-3 Gd: 2-5 GF: - Fm: 0-1
Distance: **2m/2m3: 2-7** 2m4-2m7: 0-4 3m+: 0-0
Track: LH: 1-7 RH: 1-4 **Tight: 1-3** Gall: 0-1
Aids: Bl: 0-0 Vi: 0-0 Tstrap: 0-0
Best Rating: 120 2/00 Muss 2m gd-sft Hdl

Ran well in handicap hurdles in the autumn of 2001 and returned to form in the spring of 2002.

Pessimistic Dick

103(85h) **102**

9-y-o b g Derrylin-Tycoon Moon (Tycoon Ii)
H Morrison (Mrs D Thomson 15/5) The Tam Pepper Racing Club

Placings:5505/262P4533/P**1036F30F52/PP0**P-**P534** **(2781)**
2001/02: 26^{P}GF, 24^{5}S, 21^{3}G, 24^{4}G

	Starts	1st	2nd	3rd	Win & Pl
Chases	4	0	0	1	902
Career Total	**31**	**1**	**3**	**5**	**9174**

85	9/99	Carl	2m4f110y	E Ch	G-F	£3096

Total win prize-money £3096

Going: Sf: 0-1 GS: 0-0 Gd: 0-2 GF: - Fm: 0-1
Distance: 2m/2m3: 0-0 2m4-2m7: 0-1 3m+: 0-3
Track: LH: 0-1 RH: 0-2 Tight: 0-2 Gall: 0-0
Aids: Bl: 0-0 Vi: 0-0 Tstrap: 0-0
Best Rating: 99 12/01 Winc 2m5f good Ch

Petale De Rose (IRE)

79f **74f**

6-y-o gr m Roselier (FR)-Fair Mark (On Your Mark)
M Pitman Mrs T Brown

Placings:*50* **(3862)**
2001/02: 17^{5}S, 16^{0}S

	Starts	1st	2nd	3rd	Win & Pl
NH Flat	2	0	0	0	0
Career Total	**2**	**0**	**0**	**0**	**0**

Going: Sf: 0-2 GS: 0-0 Gd: 0-0 GF: - Fm: 0-0
Distance: 2m/2m3: 0-2 2m4-2m7: 0-0 3m+: 0-0
Track: LH: 0-1 RH: 0-0 Tight: 0-1 Gall: 0-1
Aids: Bl: 0-0 Vi: 0-0 Tstrap: 0-0
Best Rating: 74 2/02 Donc 2m110y soft NHF

Petanque (IRE)

85f **105f**

6-y-o b g King's Ride-Phargara (IRE) (Phardante (FR))
N J Henderson P J D Pottinger

Placings:*1* **(2648)**
2001/02: 16^{1}GS

	Starts	1st	2nd	3rd	Win & Pl
NH Flat	1	1	0	0	1750
Career Total	**1**	**1**	**0**	**0**	**1750**

105	12/01	Hntg	2m110y	H NHF	G-S	£1750

Total win prize-money £1750

Going: Sf: 0-0 GS: 1-1 Gd: 0-0 GF: - Fm: 0-0
Distance: **2m/2m3: 1-1** 2m4-2m7: 0-0 3m+: 0-0
Track: LH: 0-0 **RH: 1-1** Tight: 0-0 **Gall: 1-1**
Aids: Bl: 0-0 Vi: 0-0 Tstrap: 0-0
Best Rating: 105 12/01 Hntg 2m110y gd-sft NHF

Convincing bumper winner on racecourse debut.

Pete The Parson (IRE)

102 **116**

13-y-o b g The Parson-Gemelek (Menelek)
J A B Old Pete The Parson Partnership

Placings:*23*/33/03**U1211**/**621123**/5360/5P63/5F6-36FP43 **(4529)**
2001/02: 16^{3}HY, 17^{6}G, 16^{F}HY, 19^{P}GS, 18^{4}GS, 19^{3}GS

	Starts	1st	2nd	3rd	Win & Pl
Chases	6	0	0	2	2025
Career Total	**34**	**5**	**4**	**9**	**38312**

140	1/98	Chel	2m5f	B HCh	G-S	£8184
142	12/97	Towc	2m110y	D(0-125)HCh	SFT	£3665
121	4/96	Extr	2m2f	D(0-125)HCh	GD	£3915
116	3/96	Chep	2m3f110y	E Ch	G-S	£2914
109	2/96	Chep	2m110y	E Ch	SFT	£3078

Total win prize-money £21759

Going: Sf: 0-2 GS: 0-3 Gd: 0-1 GF: - Fm: 0-0
Distance: 2m/2m3: 0-4 2m4-2m7: 0-2 3m+: 0-0
Track: LH: 0-4 RH: 0-2 Tight: 0-0 Gall: 0-2
Aids: Bl: 0-0 Vi: 0-0 Tstrap: 0-0
Best Rating: 146 11/98 Newb 2m1f soft Ch

Veteran handicap chaser, he is effective on good and soft ground, and stays two miles five furlongs. Not always the most reliable jumper.

Peter's Imp (IRE)

88 **79**

7-y-o b g Imp Society (USA)-Catherine Clare (Sallust)
A Berry Mr & Mrs Peter Foden

Placings:060 **(3688)**
2001/02: 16^{0}S, 17^{6}HY, 16^{0}HY

	Starts	1st	2nd	3rd	Win & Pl
Hurdles	3	0	0	0	0
Career Total	**3**	**0**	**0**	**0**	**0**

Going: Sf: 0-3 GS: 0-0 Gd: 0-0 GF: - Fm: 0-0
Distance: 2m/2m3: 0-3 2m4-2m7: 0-0 3m+: 0-0
Track: LH: 0-2 RH: 0-1 Tight: 0-0 Gall: 0-0
Aids: Bl: 0-0 Vi: 0-0 Tstrap: 0-0
Best Rating: 79 2/02 Hayd 2m heavy Hdl

Has shown limited ability over hurdles to date.

Peter's Two Fun (FR)

104 **99**

5-y-o b g Funambule (USA)-Spinner's Mate (FR) (Miller's Mate)
M C Pipe (C Aubert 26/10) P A Deal

Placings:F30P-25S543 **(4866)**
2001/02: 18^{2}VS, 17^{5}S, 16^{S}HY, 17^{5}GS, 17^{4}F, 17^{3}F

	Starts	1st	2nd	3rd	Win & Pl
Hurdles	6	0	1	1	3574
Career Total	**10**	**0**	**1**	**2**	**5447**

Going: Sf: 0-2 GS: 0-1 Gd: 0-0 GF: - Fm: 0-2
Distance: 2m/2m3: 0-6 2m4-2m7: 0-0 3m+: 0-0
Track: LH: 0-1 RH: 0-4 Tight: 0-3 Gall: 0-0
Aids: Bl: 0-0 Vi: 0-0 Tstrap: 0-0
Best Rating: 98 4/02 Extr 2m1f firm Hdl

Front-running hurdler. Ran the opposition ragged when winning a poor maiden hurdle over two and a half miles at Worcester June 2002.

Peterson's Cay (IRE)

95f **94f**

4-y-o b g Grand Lodge (USA)-Columbian Sand (IRE) (Salmon Leap (USA))
Mrs M Reveley Lucayan Stud

Placings:42 **(4790)**
2001/02: 16^{4}GS, 16^{2}F

	Starts	1st	2nd	3rd	Win & Pl
NH Flat	2	0	1	0	512
Career Total	**2**	**0**	**1**	**0**	**512**

Going: Sf: 0-0 GS: 0-1 Gd: 0-0 GF: - Fm: 0-1
Distance: 2m/2m3: 0-2 2m4-2m7: 0-0 3m+: 0-0
Track: LH: 0-1 RH: 0-0 Tight: 0-1 Gall: 0-0
Aids: Bl: 0-0 Vi: 0-0 Tstrap: 0-0
Best Rating: 94 4/02 Newc 2m firm NHF

Flat-bred but has looked short of speed in bumpers.

Peteuresque (USA)

91 **99**

5-y-o ch g Peteski (CAN)-Miss Ultimo (USA) (Screen King (USA))
R H Buckler Woodland Flowers

Placings:4-6 **(2139)**
2001/02: 17^{6}G

	Starts	1st	2nd	3rd	Win & Pl
Hurdles	1	0	0	0	0
Career Total	**2**	**0**	**0**	**0**	**0**

Going: Sf: 0-0 GS: 0-0 Gd: 0-1 GF: - Fm: 0-0
Distance: 2m/2m3: 0-1 2m4-2m7: 0-0 3m+: 0-0
Track: LH: 0-0 RH: 0-1 Tight: 0-1 Gall: 0-0
Aids: Bl: 0-0 Vi: 0-0 Tstrap: 0-0
Best Rating: 99 4/01 Winc 2m soft Hdl

Petite Dreams

78f **49f**

4-y-o b f Samim (USA)-Miss Cashtal (IRE) (Ballacashtal (CAN))
S Gollings R A Redmile

Placings:*00* **(4289)**
2001/02: 16^{0}S, 17^{0}GS

	Starts	1st	2nd	3rd	Win & Pl
NH Flat	2	0	0	0	
Career Total	**2**	**0**	**0**	**0**	

Going: Sf: 0-1 GS: 0-1 Gd: 0-0 GF: - Fm: 0-0
Distance: 2m/2m3: 0-2 2m4-2m7: 0-0 3m+: 0-0
Track: LH: 0-1 RH: 0-1 Tight: 0-1 Gall: 0-1
Aids: Bl: 0-0 Vi: 0-0 Tstrap: 0-0
Best Rating: 53 3/02 MRas 2m1f110y gd-sft NHF

Petite Risk

114 **99**

8-y-o ch m Risk Me (FR)-Technology (FR) (Top Ville)
D M Lloyd D M Lloyd

Placings:1213/03/F220042U2/32500-U2112113 (4527)
2001/02: 17US, $16^{2}GS$, $17^{1}G$, $16^{1}G$, $17^{2}S$, $16^{1}S$, $16^{1}GS$, $16^{3}GS$

	Starts	1st	2nd	3rd	Win & Pl
Hurdles	8	4	2	1	9646
Career Total	**28**	**6**	**8**	**4**	**22245**

90	3/02	Ludl	2m	F Hdl	G-S	£2649
99	3/02	Hntg	2m110y	G Hdl	SFT	£1657
95	12/01	Leic	2m	G Hdl	GD	£1981
89	12/01	Hrfd	2m1f	G Hdl	GD	£1897
112	3/98	Ludl	2m	E Hdl	G-S	£2684
116	3/98	Plum	2m1f	F Hdl	GD	£1935

Total win prize-money £12805

Going: Sf: 1-3 GS: 1-3 Gd: 2-2 GF: - Fm: 0-0
Distance: **2m/2m3: 4-8** 2m4-2m7: 0-0 3m+: 0-0
Track: LH: 0-1 **RH: 4-7** Tight: 0-1 **Gall: 1-1**
Aids: Bl: 0-0 Vi: 0-0 Tstrap: 0-0
Best Rating: **125** 3/99 Winc 2m good Hdl

In fine heart in lowly hurdles in 2001-02, effective on soft ground.

Petolinski

92f **86f**

4-y-o b g Petoski-Olnistar (FR) (Balsamo (FR))
J S King R B Denny

Placings:*60* (4423)
2001/02: $16^{6}GS$, $16^{0}GS$

	Starts	1st	2nd	3rd	Win & Pl
NH Flat	2	0	0	0	0
Career Total	**2**	**0**	**0**	**0**	**0**

Going: Sf: 0-0 GS: 0-2 Gd: 0-0 GF: - Fm: 0-0
Distance: 2m/2m3: 0-2 2m4-2m7: 0-0 3m+: 0-0
Track: LH: 0-1 RH: 0-1 Tight: 0-0 Gall: 0-1
Aids: Bl: 0-0 Vi: 0-0 Tstrap: 0-0
Best Rating: **86** 2/02 Winc 2m gd-sft NHF

Petrea

7-y-o b m St Ninian-Polypodium (Politico (USA))
T D Walford Mrs E C York

Placings:*50*-00PP (1678)
2001/02: $21^{0}GF$, $16^{0}GF$, $27^{P}GS$, $21^{P}G$

	Starts	1st	2nd	3rd	Win & Pl
Hurdles	4	0	0	0	
Career Total	**6**	**0**	**0**	**0**	**0**

Going: Sf: 0-0 GS: 0-1 Gd: 0-1 GF: - Fm: 0-2
Distance: 2m/2m3: 0-1 2m4-2m7: 0-2 3m+: 0-1
Track: LH: 0-3 RH: 0-0 Tight: 0-3 Gall: 0-0
Aids: Bl: 0-1 Vi: 0-0 Tstrap: 0-0
Best Rating: **78** 4/01 Muss 2m1f gd-fm NHF

Petriba

6-y-o gr h Tina's Pet-Sharriba (Sharrood (USA))
D Moffatt Greengate Lease Syndicate

Placings:*0* (4771)
2001/02: $16^{0}GF$

	Starts	1st	2nd	3rd	Win & Pl
NH Flat	1	0	0	0	
Career Total	**1**	**0**	**0**	**0**	

Going: Sf: 0-0 GS: 0-0 Gd: 0-0 GF: - Fm: 0-1
Distance: 2m/2m3: 0-1 2m4-2m7: 0-0 3m+: 0-0
Track: LH: 0-0 RH: 0-0 Tight: 0-0 Gall: 0-0
Aids: Bl: 0-0 Vi: 0-0 Tstrap: 0-0
Best Rating:

Petrie

5-y-o ch g Fraam-Canadian Capers (Ballacashtal (CAN))
B G Powell (D N Carey 13/11) D N Carey

Placings:PP (2063)
2001/02: $16^{P}GF$, $16^{P}G$

	Starts	1st	2nd	3rd	Win & Pl
Hurdles	2	0	0	0	
Career Total	**2**	**0**	**0**	**0**	

Going: Sf: 0-0 GS: 0-0 Gd: 0-1 GF: - Fm: 0-1
Distance: 2m/2m3: 0-2 2m4-2m7: 0-0 3m+: 0-0
Track: LH: 0-1 RH: 0-1 Tight: 0-1 Gall: 0-1
Aids: Bl: 0-0 Vi: 0-0 Tstrap: 0-0
Best Rating:

Petrouge

92 **86**

6-y-o b g Petoski-Red Spider (Red God)
Mrs C J Robinson Jeremy Beasley

Placings:*500*305P (4686)
2001/02: $16^{5}GF$, $17^{0}G$, $16^{0}G$, $19^{3}S$, $20^{0}S$, $19^{5}G$, $26^{P}GF$

	Starts	1st	2nd	3rd	Win & Pl
NH Flat	3	0	0	0	0
Hurdles	4	0	0	1	407
Career Total	**7**	**0**	**0**	**1**	**407**

Going: Sf: 0-2 GS: 0-0 Gd: 0-3 GF: - Fm: 0-2
Distance: 2m/2m3: 0-3 2m4-2m7: 0-3 3m+: 0-1
Track: LH: 0-3 RH: 0-4 Tight: 0-2 Gall: 0-1
Aids: Bl: 0-0 Vi: 0-0 Tstrap: 0-0
Best Rating: **86** 1/02 Hrfd 2m3f110y soft Hdl

Pettree (IRE)

99 **118**

8-y-o ch g King Persian-Whackers World (Whistling Deer)
N A Twiston-Davies Pettifer Ltd

Placings:*U02*/6623FP/1UU (4009)
2001/02: $20^{1}G$, 22US, 22US

	Starts	1st	2nd	3rd	Win & Pl
Chases	3	1	0	0	4154
Career Total	**12**	**1**	**2**	**1**	**6636**

118	11/01	Wwck	2m4f110y	D(0-125)HCh	GD	£4153

Total win prize-money £4154

Going: Sf: 0-2 GS: 0-0 Gd: 1-1 GF: - Fm: 0-0
Distance: 2m/2m3: 0-0 **2m4-2m7: 1-3** 3m+: 0-0
Track: **LH: 1-2** RH: 0-0 Tight: 0-0 Gall: 0-1
Aids: Bl: 0-0 Vi: 0-0 Tstrap: 0-0
Best Rating: **118** 11/01 Wwck 2m4f110y good Ch

Never hit the heights over hurdles despite some fine efforts, but came back from a season's absence to make a winning chasing debut at Warwick in November. Lost the rider on his next two starts. Stays three miles.

Petulance

72 **35**

7-y-o b m Young Senor (USA)-Silk Touch (Lochnager)
R Dickin Mrs Yvonne Allsop

Placings:*5*PP-0P (0348)
2001/02: $17^{0}G$, $16^{P}G$

	Starts	1st	2nd	3rd	Win & Pl
Hurdles	2	0	0	0	
Career Total	**5**	**0**	**0**	**0**	**0**

Going: Sf: 0-0 GS: 0-0 Gd: 0-2 GF: - Fm: 0-0
Distance: 2m/2m3: 0-2 2m4-2m7: 0-0 3m+: 0-0
Track: LH: 0-1 RH: 0-1 Tight: 0-1 Gall: 0-0
Aids: Bl: 0-0 Vi: 0-0 Tstrap: 0-0
Best Rating: **62** 5/00 Hrfd 2m1f good NHF

Petuntse

105 **114**

8-y-o b g Phountzi (USA)-Alipampa (IRE) (Glenstal (USA))
Mrs M Reveley Chicken Kiev Syndicate

Placings:U03/5UU4P/12120520-115331520 (4418)
2001/02: $16^{1}G$, $16^{1}S$, $16^{5}G$, $16^{3}GS$, $16^{3}GS$, $16^{1}S$, $16^{5}S$, $16^{2}S$, $16^{0}GS$

	Starts	1st	2nd	3rd	Win & Pl
Hurdles	9	3	1	2	12197
Career Total	**25**	**5**	**4**	**3**	**19290**

114	2/02	Muss	2m	D(0-120)HHdl	SFT	£4192
110	11/01	Hayd	2m	D(0-120)HHdl	SFT	£3447
104	11/01	Weth	2m	F(0-110)HHdl	GD	£2688
91	7/00	Strf	2m110y	G Hdl	G-F	£2044
86	5/00	Extr	2m1f	F(0-100)HHdl	G-F	£2408

Total win prize-money £14701

Going: Sf: 2-4 GS: 0-3 Gd: 1-2 GF: - Fm: 0-0
Distance: **2m/2m3: 3-9** 2m4-2m7: 0-0 3m+: 0-0
Track: **LH: 2-6** RH: 1-3 **Tight: 1-2** Gall: 0-4
Aids: Bl: 0-0 Vi: 0-0 Tstrap: 0-0
Best Rating: **114** 3/02 Donc 2m110y soft Hdl

Hold-up horse who acts on any ground. Suited by two miles, he had a fine seaso in 2001/02, winning three times but looks high enough in the weights now.

Peyton Jones

9-y-o b g Presidium-York Street (USA) (Diamond Shoal)
Mrs D M Grissell Peter Tipples

Placings:P00/P/P (0322)
2001/02: $21^{P}G$

	Starts	1st	2nd	3rd	Win & Pl
Chases	1	0	0	0	
Career Total	**5**	**0**	**0**	**0**	

Going: Sf: 0-0 GS: 0-0 Gd: 0-1 GF: - Fm: 0-0
Distance: 2m/2m3: 0-0 2m4-2m7: 0-1 3m+: 0-0
Track: LH: 0-0 RH: 0-1 Tight: 0-1 Gall: 0-0
Aids: Bl: 0-0 Vi: 0-0 Tstrap: 0-0
Best Rating:

Phaedair

12-y-o b g Strong Gale-Festive Season (Silly Season)
F E Sutherland Miss H P J Scheffers

Placings:P/05UP/3/055-P0P (0427)
2001/02: $24^{P}GF$, $24^{0}GF$, $33^{P}G$

	Starts	1st	2nd	3rd	Win & Pl
Chases	3	0	0	0	
Career Total	**12**	**0**	**0**	**1**	**750**

Going: Sf: 0-0 GS: 0-0 Gd: 0-1 GF: - Fm: 0-2
Distance: 2m/2m3: 0-0 2m4-2m7: 0-0 3m+: 0-3
Track: LH: 0-1 RH: 0-1 Tight: 0-1 Gall: 0-1
Aids: Bl: 0-0 Vi: 0-0 Tstrap: 0-0
Best Rating: 66 5/00 Towc 2m6f gd-fm Ch

Phal

91 **94**

8-y-o b g Derrylin-Royal Birthday (St Paddy)
T G Mills Glen Antill

Placings:5/110/66-3 **(1442)**
2001/02: 18^{3}GF

	Starts	1st	2nd	3rd	Win & Pl
Hurdles	1	0	0	1	450
Career Total	**7**	**2**	**0**	**1**	**3742**

106	9/99	Hntg	2m110y	H NHF	G-F	£1646
110	8/99	Worc	2m	H NHF	SFT	£1646

Total win prize-money £3292

Going: Sf: 0-0 GS: 0-0 Gd: 0-0 GF: - Fm: 0-1
Distance: 2m/2m3: 0-1 2m4-2m7: 0-0 3m+: 0-0
Track: LH: 0-1 RH: 0-0 Tight: 0-1 Gall: 0-0
Aids: Bl: 0-0 Vi: 0-0 Tstrap: 0-0
Best Rating: 110 8/99 Worc 2m soft NHF

Phantom Mist

6-y-o b m Opera Ghost-Titian Mist (Town And Country)
Jean-Rene Auvray Lambourn Racing Limited

Placings:0 **(1411)**
2001/02: 16^{0}GF

	Starts	1st	2nd	3rd	Win & Pl
NH Flat	1	0	0	0	
Career Total	**1**	**0**	**0**	**0**	

Going: Sf: 0-0 GS: 0-0 Gd: 0-0 GF: - Fm: 0-1
Distance: 2m/2m3: 0-1 2m4-2m7: 0-0 3m+: 0-0
Track: LH: 0-1 RH: 0-0 Tight: 0-0 Gall: 0-0
Aids: Bl: 0-0 Vi: 0-0 Tstrap: 0-0
Best Rating:

Phar Breeze (IRE)

91 **80**

7-y-o b m Phardante (FR)-Glamorous Gale (Strong Gale)
Mrs J M Mann Mrs J M E Mann

Placings:000-060R6F06 **(4854)**
2001/02: 17^{0}G, 16^{6}G, 16^{0}GS, 21^{R}G, 20^{6}S, 17^{F}S, 16^{0}GF, 22^{6}G

	Starts	1st	2nd	3rd	Win & Pl
NH Flat	1	0	0	0	0
Hurdles	7	0	0	0	0
Career Total	**11**	**0**	**0**	**0**	**0**

Going: Sf: 0-2 GS: 0-1 Gd: 0-4 GF: - Fm: 0-1
Distance: 2m/2m3: 0-5 2m4-2m7: 0-3 3m+: 0-0
Track: LH: 0-4 RH: 0-4 Tight: 0-3 Gall: 0-1
Aids: Bl: 0-0 Vi: 0-0 Tstrap: 0-0
Best Rating: 81 1/01 Kemp 2m soft NHF

Phar Echo (IRE)

101(46h) **93**

11-y-o b g Phardante (FR)-Borecca (Boreen (FR))
Mrs H O Graham Mrs H O Graham

Placings:04/3041310P/5232/12F0F015/420523505/0 04400-03156 **(4692)**
2001/02: 24^{0}GF, 25^{3}GF, 32^{1}HY, 32^{5}HY, 25^{6}GF

	Starts	1st	2nd	3rd	Win & Pl
Chases	5	1	0	1	5362
Career Total	**42**	**5**	**5**	**5**	**24566**

90	3/02	Hexm	4m	F(0-100)HCh	HVY	£3916
106	3/99	Ayr	2m6f	F(0-110)HHdl	SFT	£2815
101	10/98	Carl	3m110y	E(0-115)HHdl	HVY	£2388
97	3/97	Ayr	2m	D(0-110)HHdl	SFT	£2933
93	1/97	Ayr	2m4f	D(0-110)HHdl	GD	£3218

Total win prize-money £15270

Going: Sf: 1-2 GS: 0-0 Gd: 0-0 GF: - Fm: 0-3
Distance: 2m/2m3: 0-0 2m4-2m7: 0-0 **3m+: 1-5**
Track: **LH: 1-4** RH: 0-1 Tight: 0-2 Gall: 0-0
Aids: **Bl: 1-5** Vi: 0-0 Tstrap: 0-0
Best Rating: 106 3/99 Ayr 2m6f soft Hdl

Moderate staying chaser, suited by extreme distances. Acts on good and heavy ground. Usually blinkered.

Phar From A Fiddle (IRE)

107(103h) (107h)**140**

6-y-o b/br g Phardante (FR)-Lucycello (Monksfield)
P F Nicholls Mrs J Stewart

Placings:0U2-22114444 **(4666)**
2001/02: 22^{2}GF, 22^{2}GS, 20^{1}G, 25^{1}G, 20^{4}G, 20^{4}G, 24^{4}GS, 25^{4}G

	Starts	1st	2nd	3rd	Win & Pl
Hurdles	2	0	2	0	2214
Chases	6	2	0	0	23501
Career Total	**11**	**2**	**3**	**0**	**26567**

140	11/01	Winc	3m1f110y	D(0-110)HCh	GD	£6955
140	10/01	Chel	2m4f110y	D(0-110)HCh	GD	£8697

Total win prize-money £15652

Going: Sf: 0-0 GS: 0-2 Gd: 2-5 GF: - Fm: 0-1
Distance: 2m/2m3: 0-0 2m4-2m7: 1-5 3m+: 1-3
Track: LH: 1-6 RH: 1-2 Tight: 0-2 **Gall: 1-3**
Aids: Bl: 0-0 Vi: 0-0 Tstrap: 0-0
Best Rating: 140 11/01 Chel 2m4f110y good Ch

He showed ability over hurdles but was always going to come into his own when tackling fences. He jumped well when successful on his chasing debut at Cheltenham in October 2001, and followed up at Wincanton. Beaten in handicaps subsequently, he is thought not to want the ground too soft. Stays three miles plus.

Phar From Chance

97 **100**

7-y-o ch g Phardante (FR)-Chancer's Last (Foggy Bell)
P F Nicholls B C Marshall

Placings:5 **(1770)**
2001/02: 23^{5}GS

	Starts	1st	2nd	3rd	Win & Pl
Chases	1	0	0	0	0
Career Total	**1**	**0**	**0**	**0**	**0**

Going: Sf: 0-0 GS: 0-1 Gd: 0-0 GF: - Fm: 0-0
Distance: 2m/2m3: 0-0 2m4-2m7: 0-0 3m+: 0-1
Track: LH: 0-0 RH: 0-1 Tight: 0-0 Gall: 0-0
Aids: Bl: 0-0 Vi: 0-0 Tstrap: 0-0
Best Rating: 91 10/01 Extr 2m7f110y gd-sft Ch

The winner of three points. Did not appear to stay three and a quarter miles when third in poor maiden chase at Southwell July 2002.

Phar From Fair (IRE)

89f **88f**

5-y-o b g Phardante (FR)-Wintry Shower (Strong Gale)
L Wells Mrs Carrie Zetter-Wells

Placings:4 **(4639)**
2001/02: 16^{4}GF

	Starts	1st	2nd	3rd	Win & Pl
NH Flat	1	0	0	0	0
Career Total	**1**	**0**	**0**	**0**	**0**

Going: Sf: 0-0 GS: 0-0 Gd: 0-0 GF: - Fm: 0-1
Distance: 2m/2m3: 0-1 2m4-2m7: 0-0 3m+: 0-0
Track: LH: 0-0 RH: 0-1 Tight: 0-0 Gall: 0-0
Aids: Bl: 0-0 Vi: 0-0 Tstrap: 0-0
Best Rating: 88 4/02 Asct 2m110y gd-fm NHF

Phar Glory (IRE)

107 **93**

7-y-o b g Phardante (FR)-Prudent Rose (IRE) (Strong Gale)
A J Lidderdale George Ward

Placings:001 **(4730)**
2001/02: 22^{0}S, 24^{0}GS, 20^{1}GF

	Starts	1st	2nd	3rd	Win & Pl
Hurdles	3	1	0	0	2674
Career Total	**3**	**1**	**0**	**0**	**2674**

90	4/02	Chep	2m4f	E Hdl	G-F	£2674

Total win prize-money £2674

Going: Sf: 0-1 GS: 0-1 Gd: 0-0 GF: - Fm: 1-1
Distance: 2m/2m3: 0-0 **2m4-2m7: 1-2** 3m+: 0-1
Track: **LH: 1-3** RH: 0-0 Tight: 0-1 Gall: 0-1
Aids: Bl: 0-0 Vi: 0-0 Tstrap: 0-0
Best Rating: 90 4/02 Chep 2m4f gd-fm Hdl

Won a weak novice hurdle at Chepstow in April. Stays two and a half miles plus, should make a chaser.

Phar Jeffen (IRE)

107 **140**

7-y-o ch g Phardante (FR)-Clever Milly (Precipice Wood)
R J Hodges Fieldspring Racing

Placings:6056420/2113-64F213211 **(4516)**
2001/02: 19^{6}GS, 16^{4}S, 17^{F}G, 16^{2}G, 16^{1}G, 20^{3}S, 16^{2}GS, 16^{1}G, 16^{1}GS

	Starts	1st	2nd	3rd	Win & Pl
Hurdles	1	0	0	0	0
Chases	8	3	2	1	22641
Career Total	**20**	**5**	**4**	**2**	**30861**

140	3/02	Towc	2m110y	C Ch	G-S	£6126
138	3/02	Sand	2m	C Ch	GD	£6760
122	12/01	Ludl	2m	E(0-115)HCh	GD	£5782
97	6/00	Baln	2m	Hdl	G-Y	£3036
	5/00	DRoy	2m	NHF	GD	£2760

Total win prize-money £24464

Going: Sf: 0-2 GS: 1-3 Gd: 2-4 GF: - Fm: 0-0
Distance: **2m/2m3: 3-8** 2m4-2m7: 0-1 3m+: 0-0
Track: LH: 0-2 **RH: 3-7 Tight: 1-4** Gall: 0-0
Aids: Bl: 0-0 Vi: 0-0 Tstrap: 0-0
Best Rating: 140 3/02 Towc 2m110y gd-sft Ch

He won a bumper and a maiden hurdle in Ireland in 2000 and has developed into a decent novice chaser in 2001/02. Two miles is his ideal trip and he is best on a sound surface and going right-handed.

Phar Less Hassle (IRE)

101(110c) (96c) **102**

10-y-o b g Phardante (FR)-Little Hassle (Buckskin (FR))

T P McGovern Mark Holman

Placings:021211O20/UU43245/3213343U0-P22652 **(2952)**

2001/02: 24^{P}GS, 21^{2}G, 16^{2}S, 17^{6}S, 22^{5}G, 16^{2}S

	Starts	1st	2nd	3rd	Win & Pl
Hurdles	5	0	3	0	1802
Chases	1	0	0	0	0
Career Total	**31**	**4**	**8**	**5**	**22166**

124	11/00	Plum	2m4f	D(0-125)HCh	HVY	£4007
131	1/99	Plum	2m4f	E Hdl	HVY	£2792
122	12/98	Plum	2m4f	E Hdl	G-S	£2547
116	11/98	Plum	2m4f	E Hdl	SFT	£2547

Total win prize-money £11897

Going: Sf: 0-3 GS: 0-1 Gd: 0-2 GF: - Fm: 0-0
Distance: 2m/2m3: 0-3 2m4-2m7: 0-2 3m+: 0-1
Track: LH: 0-4 RH: 0-2 Tight: 0-5 Gall: 0-0
Aids: Bl: 0-0 Vi: 0-0 Tstrap: 0-0
Best Rating: 131 2/99 Wwck 2m4f110y gd-sft Hdl

Modest hurdler/chaser, he goes well at Plumpton and is particularly suited by soft ground.

Phar Too Gifted

101 **79**

7-y-o b m Phardante (FR)-Gaelic Charm (IRE) (Deep Run)

S Dow (R T Phillips 3/6) Whitgift Racing Limited

Placings:3/000P-P4325P **(1674)**

2001/02: 21^{P}G, 16^{4}GF, 19^{3}G, 20^{2}GF, 20^{5}GF, 22^{P}HY

	Starts	1st	2nd	3rd	Win & Pl
Hurdles	6	0	1	1	1087
Career Total	**11**	**0**	**1**	**2**	**1520**

Going: Sf: 0-1 GS: 0-0 Gd: 0-2 GF: - Fm: 0-3
Distance: 2m/2m3: 0-2 2m4-2m7: 0-4 3m+: 0-0
Track: LH: 0-2 RH: 0-2 Tight: 0-4 Gall: 0-1
Aids: Bl: 0-0 Vi: 0-0 Tstrap: 0-0
Best Rating: 79 8/01 Font 2m4f gd-fm Hdl

Pharanear (IRE)

94 **100**

12-y-o b g Camden Town-Monas River (River Beauty)

J J O'Neill A Stennett

Placings:2121006/4513111P30/31F11/45P31054/0P2/0550 **(3215)**

2001/02: 24^{0}GS, 22^{5}S, 24^{5}GS, 24^{0}GS

	Starts	1st	2nd	3rd	Win & Pl
Hurdles	4	0	0	0	0
Career Total	**37**	**10**	**3**	**4**	**95215**

146	2/99	Kemp	3m110y	A HHdl	SFT	£12512
152	3/97	Chel	3m1f110y	B HHdl	GD	£27910
144	2/97	Kemp	3m110y	A HHdl	GD	£12034
123	12/96	Worc	2m4f110y	E Ch	G-S	£3605
141	1/96	Wwck	2m4f110y	B HHdl	G-S	£7460
123	12/95	Bang	3m	B(0-140)HHdl	GD	£4851
130	11/95	Chep	2m4f110y	C Hdl	SFT	£3848
111	8/95	Tral	2m4f	Hdl	G-F	£3391
114	3/95	Navn	2m	NHF	SH	£3051
102	10/94	Punc	2m	NHF	GD	£2935

Total win prize-money £81602

Going: Sf: 0-1 GS: 0-3 Gd: 0-0 GF: - Fm: 0-0
Distance: 2m/2m3: 0-0 2m4-2m7: 0-1 3m+: 0-3
Track: LH: 0-4 RH: 0-0 Tight: 0-1 Gall: 0-1
Aids: Bl: 0-0 Vi: 0-0 Tstrap: 0-0
Best Rating: 152 12/99 Winc 2m6f soft Hdl

A former smart hurdler, he has been lightly raced of late. Stays three miles. Acts on soft ground.

Pharaway Citizen (IRE)

101 **100**

7-y-o ch g Phardante (FR)-Boreen Citizen (Boreen (FR))

T R George (Eugene M O'Sullivan 19/5) Pharaway Partnership

Placings:P32 **(4854)**

2001/02: 24^{P}G, 24^{3}S, 22^{2}G

	Starts	1st	2nd	3rd	Win & Pl
Hurdles	3	0	1	1	1361
Career Total	**3**	**0**	**1**	**1**	**1361**

Going: Sf: 0-1 GS: 0-0 Gd: 0-2 GF: - Fm: 0-0
Distance: 2m/2m3: 0-0 2m4-2m7: 0-1 3m+: 0-2
Track: LH: 0-1 RH: 0-1 Tight: 0-2 Gall: 0-0
Aids: Bl: 0-0 Vi: 0-0 Tstrap: 0-0
Best Rating: 100 4/02 Strf 2m6f110y good Hdl

A winner between the flags in Ireland. Will probably need fences to be seen at his best.

Pharbeitfrome (IRE)

109 **93+**

8-y-o b g Phardante (FR)-Asigh Glen (Furry Glen)

N Wilson (A L T Moore 13/5) G Griffin

Placings:0/00F310F/P04P-0UPF43 **(4872)**

2001/02: 20^{0}G, 25^{U}G, 22^{P}S, 17^{F}G, 20^{4}GF, 16^{3}GF

	Starts	1st	2nd	3rd	Win & Pl
Chases	6	0	0	1	771
Career Total	**18**	**1**	**0**	**2**	**3944**

109	3/00	Dpat	2m2f	Ch	SFT	£2345

Total win prize-money £2346

Going: Sf: 0-1 GS: 0-0 Gd: 0 3 GF: - Fm: 0-2
Distance: 2m/2m3: 0-2 2m4-2m7: 0-3 3m+: 0-1
Track: LH: 0-2 RH: 0-3 Tight: 0-2 Gall: 0-0
Aids: Bl: 0-0 Vi: 0-0 Tstrap: 0-5
Best Rating: 109 3/00 Dpat 2m2f soft Ch

Modest handicap chaser.

Phardante Flyer (IRE)

95(99h) **120**

8-y-o ch g Phardante (FR)-Shannon Lek (Menelek)

P J Hobbs Mrs Karola Vann

Placings:2/1141141/24-2P **(2937)**

2001/02: 16^{2}GF, 18^{P}G

	Starts	1st	2nd	3rd	Win & Pl
Chases	2	0	1	0	1208
Career Total	**12**	**5**	**3**	**0**	**38254**

144	4/00	Aint	2m110y	A Hdl	GD	£21000
123	2/00	Ludl	2m	E Hdl	GD	£2352
120	1/00	Winc	2m	E Hdl	G-S	£2205
114	11/99	Wwck	2m	H NHF	GD	£1856
113	11/99	Sand	2m110y	H NHF	GD	£1658

Total win prize-money £29071

Going: Sf: 0-0 GS: 0-0 Gd: 0-1 GF: - Fm: 0-1
Distance: 2m/2m3: 0-2 2m4-2m7: 0-0 3m+: 0-0
Track: LH: 0-2 RH: 0-0 Tight: 0-0 Gall: 0-1
Aids: Bl: 0-0 Vi: 0-0 Tstrap: 0-0
Best Rating: 144 4/00 Aint 2m110y good Hdl

A dual bumper winner during the 1999/2000 season, he subsequently landed a couple of ordinary novice hurdles, before finishing a fine fourth in the Supreme Novices' and landing the big two-mile novice hurdle at Aintree. He only ran twice last term and has clearly had his problems. Made a promising chasing debut in September 2001 but did not jump well in a better race. Best at two miles on a sound surface.

Phardor

74 **50**

7-y-o b m Phardante (FR)-Sister Of Gold (The Parson)

K C Bailey Mrs Jennifer Heaton

Placings:0005P0 **(0929)**

2001/02: 17^{0}G, 17^{0}G, 17^{0}G, 22^{5}GF, 25^{P}GS, 20^{0}GF

	Starts	1st	2nd	3rd	Win & Pl
NH Flat	3	0	0	0	0
Hurdles	3	0	0	0	0
Career Total	**6**	**0**	**0**	**0**	**0**

Going: Sf: 0-0 GS: 0-1 Gd: 0-3 GF: - Fm: 0-2
Distance: 2m/2m3: 0-3 2m4-2m7: 0-2 3m+: 0-1
Track: LH: 0-5 RH: 0-1 Tight: 0-5 Gall: 0-0
Aids: Bl: 0-3 Vi: 0-0 Tstrap: 0-0
Best Rating: 55 5/01 Bang 2m1f good NHF

Pharlen's Dream (IRE)

69f **37f**

6-y-o b m Phardante (FR)-Local Dream (Deep Run)

R H Buckler R H Buckler

Placings:0 **(4595)**

2001/02: 16^{0}G

	Starts	1st	2nd	3rd	Win & Pl
NH Flat	1	0	0	0	
Career Total	**1**	**0**	**0**	**0**	

Going: Sf: 0-0 GS: 0-0 Gd: 0-1 GF: - Fm: 0-0
Distance: 2m/2m3: 0-1 2m4-2m7: 0-0 3m+: 0-0
Track: LH: 0-1 RH: 0-0 Tight: 0-0 Gall: 0-0
Aids: Bl: 0-0 Vi: 0-0 Tstrap: 0-0
Best Rating: 37 4/02 Uttx 2m good NHF

Pharly Reef

105 **102**

10-y-o b g Pharly (FR)-Hay Reef (Mill Reef (USA))

D Burchell Vivian Guy

Placings:6020/00612/4U26621/1154/S35065 **(4853)**

2001/02: 17^{S}G, 17^{3}G, 17^{5}GS, 16^{0}G, 17^{6}GF, 16^{5}G

	Starts	1st	2nd	3rd	Win & Pl
Hurdles	6	0	0	1	367
Career Total	**26**	**4**	**4**	**1**	**18839**

113	11/99	Chep	2m110y	D(0-125)HHdl	SFT	£2845
109	7/99	Strf	2m110y	C(0-130)HHdl	GD	£4926
98	4/99	Bang	2m1f	F(0-100)HHdl	GD	£3858
80	12/96	Fknm	2m	G(0-95)HHdl	GD	£2733

Total win prize-money £14364

Going: Sf: 0-0 GS: 0-1 Gd: 0-4 GF: - Fm: 0-1
Distance: 2m/2m3: 0-6 2m4-2m7: 0-0 3m+: 0-0
Track: LH: 0-5 RH: 0-1 Tight: 0-5 Gall: 0-0
Aids: Bl: 0-0 Vi: 0-0 Tstrap: 0-0

Best Rating: 113 11/99 Chep 2m110y soft Hdl

Modest hurdler around two miles who is entering the veteran stage and has struggled to hold his form in recent years. Goes well on good and soft ground.

Pharmistice (IRE)

11-y-o b g Phardante (FR)-Lucylet (Kinglet)
Mrs P C Stirling Mrs P C Stirling

Placings:*006/10/2140*/0-4 (4692)
2001/02: 25^{4}GF

	Starts	1st	2nd	3rd	Win & Pl
Chases	1	0	0	0	0
Career Total	**11**	**2**	**1**	**0**	**5936**

83	11/97	Kels	2m6f110y	D(0-125)HHdl	G-F	£2738
80	12/96	Kels	2m6f110y	E Hdl	GD	£2346

Total win prize-money £5084

Going: Sf: 0-0 GS: 0-0 Gd: 0-0 GF: - Fm: 0-1
Distance: 2m/2m3: 0-0 2m4-2m7: 0-0 3m+: 0-1
Track: LH: 0-1 RH: 0-0 Tight: 0-1 Gall: 0-0
Aids: Bl: 0-0 Vi: 0-0 Tstrap: 0-0
Best Rating: 101 4/02 Kels 3m1f gd-fm Ch

Pharpen (IRE)

84 81
8-y-o b g Phardante (FR)-Penthouse Pearl (Green Shoon)
Mrs C J Robinson Mrs Caroline Robinson

Placings:2F-50 (2201)
2001/02: 20^{5}G, 20^{0}G

	Starts	1st	2nd	3rd	Win & Pl
Hurdles	2	0	0	0	0
Career Total	**4**	**0**	**1**	**0**	**440**

Going: Sf: 0-0 GS: 0-0 Gd: 0-2 GF: - Fm: 0-0
Distance: 2m/2m3: 0-0 2m4-2m7: 0-2 3m+: 0-0
Track: LH: 0-2 RH: 0-0 Tight: 0-1 Gall: 0-0
Aids: Bl: 0-0 Vi: 0-0 Tstrap: 0-0
Best Rating: 86 6/00 NAbb 2m1f gd-fm NHF

Pharpost (IRE)

97 100
7-y-o b g Phardante (FR)-Branstown Lady (Deep Run)
Miss Venetia Williams (N J Henderson 19/5) D E Harrison

Placings:*136*-41 (1912)
2001/02: 19^{4}GF, 22^{1}S

	Starts	1st	2nd	3rd	Win & Pl
Hurdles	2	1	0	0	2618
Career Total	**5**	**2**	**0**	**1**	**4518**

100	11/01	Strf	2m6f110y	E Hdl	SFT	£2618
114	11/00	Ludl	2m	H NHF	GD	£1652

Total win prize-money £4270

Going: Sf: 1-1 GS: 0-0 Gd: 0-0 GF: - Fm: 0-1
Distance: 2m/2m3: 0-0 **2m4-2m7: 1-2** 3m+: 0-0
Track: **LH: 1-2** RH: 0-0 **Tight: 1-2** Gall: 0-0
Aids: Bl: 0-0 Vi: 0-0 Tstrap: 0-0
Best Rating: 114 11/00 Ludl 2m good NHF

From a useful family, he won a good Ludlow bumper on his racecourse debut and progressed to win on his second attempt over hurdles over an extended two miles six furlongs at Stratford in November 2002.

Phase Eight Girl

103 77
6-y-o b m Warrshan (USA)-Bugsy's Sister (Aragon)
J Hetherton Peter Urquhart

Placings:363P0046-4124544 (4908)
2001/02: 20^{4}GF, 16^{1}GF, 16^{2}F, 17^{4}GF, 17^{5}S, 21^{4}G, 21^{4}G

	Starts	1st	2nd	3rd	Win & Pl
Hurdles	7	1	1	0	2893
Career Total	**15**	**1**	**1**	**2**	**3474**

77	5/01	Hntg	2m110y	G(0-95)HHdl	G-F	£1736

Total win prize-money £1736

Going: Sf: 0-1 GS: 0-0 Gd: 0-2 GF: - Fm: 1-4
Distance: **2m/2m3: 1-4** 2m4-2m7: 0-3 3m+: 0-0
Track: LH: 0-2 **RH: 1-5** Tight: 0-4 **Gall: 1-1**
Aids: Bl: 0-0 Vi: 0-0 Tstrap: 0-0
Best Rating: 77 6/01 MRas 2m1f110y gd-fm Hdl

Small mare, winning hurdler who needs good ground.

Phidelia (IRE)

62f 76f
4-y-o ch f Classic Memory-Feodora (Songedor)
N G Richards Greystoke Stables Ltd

Placings:0 (4499)
2001/02: 16^{0}G

	Starts	1st	2nd	3rd	Win & Pl
NH Flat	1	0	0	0	
Career Total	**1**	**0**	**0**	**0**	

Going: Sf: 0-0 GS: 0-0 Gd: 0-1 GF: - Fm: 0-0
Distance: 2m/2m3: 0-1 2m4-2m7: 0-0 3m+: 0-0
Track: LH: 0-1 RH: 0-0 Tight: 0-0 Gall: 0-0
Aids: Bl: 0-0 Vi: 0-0 Tstrap: 0-0
Best Rating: 76 3/02 Hayd 2m good NHF

Phil Sanders

(95h) (78h)
8-y-o br g Arctic Lord-Charossa (Ardross)
Miss B Sanders Mrs J M Laycock

Placings:*00/5PP/210*-5F (3379)
2001/02: 22^{5}GF, 24^{F}G

	Starts	1st	2nd	3rd	Win & Pl
Hurdles	1	0	0	0	0
Chases	1	0	0	0	0
Career Total	**10**	**1**	**1**	**0**	**2996**

99	10/00	Folk	2m6f110y	E Hdl	G-F	£2306

Total win prize-money £2307

Going: Sf: 0-0 GS: 0-0 Gd: 0-1 GF: - Fm: 0-1
Distance: 2m/2m3: 0-0 2m4-2m7: 0-1 3m+: 0-1
Track: LH: 0-1 RH: 0-1 Tight: 0-1 Gall: 0-0
Aids: Bl: 0-0 Vi: 0-0 Tstrap: 0-2
Best Rating: 100 1/00 Kemp 2m5f good Hdl

Useful hurdler at around two miles six. Acts on a sound surface. Slightly inconsistent.

Phil The Fencer

83 85
6-y-o gr g Neltino-Who's Free (Sit In The Corner (USA))
John Allen John Allen, Michael Gray, Vicki Jameson

Placings:*5*-50FP2 (3766)
2001/02: 16^{5}GF, 16^{0}S, 22^{F}S, 22^{P}HY, 20^{2}GS

	Starts	1st	2nd	3rd	Win & Pl
NH Flat	2	0	0	0	0
Hurdles	3	0	1	0	955
Career Total	**6**	**0**	**1**	**0**	**955**

Going: Sf: 0-3 GS: 0-1 Gd: 0-0 GF: - Fm: 0-1
Distance: 2m/2m3: 0-2 2m4-2m7: 0-3 3m+: 0-0
Track: LH: 0-4 RH: 0-1 Tight: 0-3 Gall: 0-1
Aids: Bl: 0-0 Vi: 0-0 Tstrap: 0-0
Best Rating: 85 2/02 Fknm 2m4f gd-sft Hdl

Phildari (IRE)

107 108
6-y-o b g Shardari-Philosophical (Welsh Chanter)
P R Webber Peter Garnett

Placings:*00*-022423 (4400)
2001/02: 18^{0}GS, 19^{2}G, 22^{2}G, 21^{4}S, 21^{2}G, 21^{3}S

	Starts	1st	2nd	3rd	Win & Pl
NH Flat	1	0	0	0	0
Hurdles	5	0	3	1	4408
Career Total	**8**	**0**	**3**	**1**	**4408**

Going: Sf: 0-2 GS: 0-1 Gd: 0-3 GF: - Fm: 0-0
Distance: 2m/2m3: 0-1 2m4-2m7: 0-5 3m+: 0-0
Track: LH: 0-1 RH: 0-4 Tight: 0-0 Gall: 0-1
Aids: Bl: 0-0 Vi: 0-0 Tstrap: 0-5
Best Rating: 108 3/02 Newb 2m5f soft Hdl

Little show in three bumpers. Showed improvement over hurdles since the fitting of a tongue tie. Looks best at around two and a half miles. Acts on good and soft ground. Should make a nice chaser.

Phillijo

6-y-o b m Teenoso (USA)-Phillimay (Scallywag)
R Lee Mr & Mrs J H Watson

Placings:*0*-66 (2131)
2001/02: 16^{6}S, 16^{6}GF

	Starts	1st	2nd	3rd	Win & Pl
Hurdles	2	0	0	0	0
Career Total	**3**	**0**	**0**	**0**	**0**

Going: Sf: 0-1 GS: 0-0 Gd: 0-0 GF: - Fm: 0-1
Distance: 2m/2m3: 0-2 2m4-2m7: 0-0 3m+: 0-0
Track: LH: 0-0 RH: 0-2 Tight: 0-0 Gall: 0-0
Aids: Bl: 0-0 Vi: 0-0 Tstrap: 0-0
Best Rating: 15 1/01 Weth 2m heavy NHF

Phillis Hill

84f 78f
5-y-o ch m Karinga Bay-Grace Moore (Deep Run)
K Bishop Slabs And Lucan

Placings:0 (2294)
2001/02: 17^{0}GF

	Starts	1st	2nd	3rd	Win & Pl
NH Flat	1	0	0	0	
Career Total	**1**	**0**	**0**	**0**	

Going: Sf: 0-0 GS: 0-0 Gd: 0-0 GF: - Fm: 0-1
Distance: 2m/2m3: 0-1 2m4-2m7: 0-0 3m+: 0-0
Track: LH: 0-0 RH: 0-1 Tight: 0-0 Gall: 0-0
Aids: Bl: 0-0 Vi: 0-0 Tstrap: 0-0
Best Rating: 78 11/01 Extr 2m1f gd-fm NHF

Philtre (IRE)

8-y-o b g Phardante (FR)-Forest Gale (Strong Gale)
Mrs H L Needham J D Callow

Placings:2P3U-1311046 **(4751)**
2001/02: 24^{1}G, 21^{3}G, 28^{1}GF, 23^{1}GF, 26^{0}G, 22^{4}GS, 20^{6}GF

	Starts	1st	2nd	3rd	Win & Pl
Chases	7	3	0	1	15707
Career Total	**11**	**3**	**1**	**2**	**16372**

120	6/01	Worc	2m7f110y	E Ch	G-F	£3190
120	6/01	Strf	3m4f	H Ch	G-F	£8287
120	5/01	Hntg	3m	E Ch	GD	£3731

Total win prize-money £15209

Going: Sf: 0-0 GS: 0-1 Gd: 1-3 GF: - Fm: 2-3
Distance: 2m/2m3: 0-0 2m4-2m7: 0-3 **3m+: 3-4**
Track: **LH: 2-4** RH: 1-2 Tight: 1-1 Gall: 1-2
Aids: Bl: 0-0 Vi: 0-0 Tstrap: 0-0
Best Rating: 120 6/01 Worc 2m7f110y gd-fm Ch

Useful hunter chase and point winner, he won three modest novice chases in the summer of 2001.Poor form in hunter chases in the spring of 2002. Needs a sound surface and stays three and a half miles.

Phoenix Phlyer

8-y-o b g Ardross-Brown Coast (Oats)
D Pipe (N A Twiston-Davies 10/3) Miss C C Stucley & J Duggan

Placings:500/005023/020P34312-00 **(4483)**
2001/02: 19^{0}F, 19^{0}G

	Starts	1st	2nd	3rd	Win & Pl
Hurdles	1	0	0	0	0
Chases	1	0	0	0	0
Career Total	**20**	**1**	**3**	**3**	**8586**

118	4/01	Extr	2m3f110y	F(0-95)HCh	G-S	£3447

Total win prize-money £3448

Going: Sf: 0-0 GS: 0-0 Gd: 0-1 GF: - Fm: 0-1
Distance: 2m/2m3: 0-0 2m4-2m7: 0-2 3m+: 0-0
Track: LH: 0-0 RH: 0-2 Tight: 0-1 Gall: 0-0
Aids: Bl: 0-1 Vi: 0-0 Tstrap: 0-0
Best Rating: 118 4/01 Extr 2m3f110y gd-sft Ch

Photographer (USA)

97 **101**

4-y-o b/br g Mountain Cat (USA)-Clickety Click (USA) (Sovereign Dancer (USA))
Mrs N Smith (Sir Michael Stoute 26/6) Tony Hayward, Barry Fulton, Jamie Bruce

Placings:404 **(4263)**
2001/02: 17^{4}S, 16^{0}G, 16^{4}S

	Starts	1st	2nd	3rd	Win & Pl
Hurdles	3	0	0	0	0
Career Total	**3**	**0**	**0**	**0**	**0**

Going: Sf: 0-2 GS: 0-0 Gd: 0-1 GF: - Fm: 0-0
Distance: 2m/2m3: 0-3 2m4-2m7: 0-0 3m+: 0-0
Track: LH: 0-1 RH: 0-2 Tight: 0-1 Gall: 0-0
Aids: Bl: 0-0 Vi: 0-0 Tstrap: 0-0
Best Rating: 101 2/02 Kemp 2m good Hdl

Modest ability over hurdles so far.

Phylozzo

6-y-o ch m Michelozzo (USA)-Phyllida Fox (Healaugh Fox)
C J Price Mrs C W Middleton

Placings:0 **(3157)**
2001/02: 17^{0}S

	Starts	1st	2nd	3rd	Win & Pl
Hurdles	1	0	0	0	
Career Total	**1**	**0**	**0**	**0**	

Going: Sf: 0-1 GS: 0-0 Gd: 0-0 GF: - Fm: 0-0
Distance: 2m/2m3: 0-1 2m4-2m7: 0-0 3m+: 0-0
Track: LH: 0-0 RH: 0-1 Tight: 0-0 Gall: 0-0
Aids: Bl: 0-0 Vi: 0-0 Tstrap: 0-0
Best Rating:

Physical Graffiti (USA)

105 **78**

5-y-o b g Mister Baileys-Gleaming Water (USA) (Pago Pago)
J A B Old Willie Robertson/nigel Dempster

Placings:04-40 **(2167)**
2001/02: 16^{4}G, 16^{0}G

	Starts	1st	2nd	3rd	Win & Pl
Hurdles	2	0	0	0	0
Career Total	**4**	**0**	**0**	**0**	**329**

Going: Sf: 0-0 GS: 0-0 Gd: 0-2 GF: - Fm: 0-0
Distance: 2m/2m3: 0-2 2m4-2m7: 0-0 3m+: 0-0
Track: LH: 0-2 RH: 0-0 Tight: 0-1 Gall: 0-0
Aids: Bl: 0-0 Vi: 0-0 Tstrap: 0-0
Best Rating: 78 10/01 Aint 2m110y good Hdl

Some signs of ability in all starts so far, but improvement needed to win a race.

Piccadilly

107(108h) (98 h)**93**

7-y-o ch m Belmez (USA)-Polly's Pear (USA) (Sassafras (FR))
Miss Kate Milligan S Ward

Placings:505234/5325-631U233 **(4919)**
2001/02: 21^{6}G, 21^{3}GS, 24^{1}GF, 22^{U}GF, 21^{2}G, 24^{3}G, 21^{3}GF

	Starts	1st	2nd	3rd	Win & Pl
Hurdles	4	1	0	2	2181
Chases	3	0	1	1	1311
Career Total	**17**	**1**	**3**	**5**	**5672**

87	8/01	Sthl	3m110y	G Hdl	G-F	£1575

Total win prize-money £1575

Going: Sf: 0-0 GS: 0-1 Gd: 0-3 GF: - Fm: 1-3
Distance: 2m/2m3: 0-0 2m4-2m7: 0-5 **3m+: 1-2**
Track: **LH: 1-4** RH: 0-2 **Tight: 1-6** Gall: 0-0
Aids: Bl: 0-0 Vi: 0-0 Tstrap: 0-0
Best Rating: 98 10/01 Sedg 2m5f good Ch

A fair hurdler, she was placed over fencesin the autumn of 2001. Jumping getting better with experience. Best on a sound surface.

Piccadilly Wood

8-y-o gr g Newski (USA)-Dark Acre (Peacock (FR))
P Wegmann J S Warner

Placings:PP **(1393)**
2001/02: 20^{P}GF, 24^{P}GF

	Starts	1st	2nd	3rd	Win & Pl
Hurdles	2	0	0	0	
Career Total	**2**	**0**	**0**	**0**	

Going: Sf: 0-0 GS: 0-0 Gd: 0-0 GF: - Fm: 0-2
Distance: 2m/2m3: 0-0 2m4-2m7: 0-1 3m+: 0-1
Track: LH: 0-2 RH: 0-0 Tight: 0-0 Gall: 0-0
Aids: Bl: 0-0 Vi: 0-0 Tstrap: 0-0
Best Rating:

Piccolitia

76 **64**

4-y-o ch f Piccolo-Miss Laetitia (IRE) (Entitled)
R H Alner (N A Graham 3/9) T H Chadney

Placings:0P **(2535)**
2001/02: 17^{0}G, 16^{P}G

	Starts	1st	2nd	3rd	Win & Pl
Hurdles	2	0	0	0	
Career Total	**2**	**0**	**0**	**0**	

Going: Sf: 0-0 GS: 0-0 Gd: 0-2 GF: - Fm: 0-0
Distance: 2m/2m3: 0-2 2m4-2m7: 0-0 3m+: 0-0
Track: LH: 0-0 RH: 0-2 Tight: 0-0 Gall: 0-0
Aids: Bl: 0-0 Vi: 0-0 Tstrap: 0-0
Best Rating: 64 11/01 Hrfd 2m1f good Hdl

Shown her best over a mile on the Flat.

Picket Piece

112(102h) **128**

11-y-o br g Shareef Dancer (USA)-Jouvencelle (Rusticaro (FR))
N A Twiston-Davies H R Mould

Placings:4/665111325/22130400/3F3220115-0P6B2 **(3691)**
2001/02: 24^{0}G, 26^{P}S, 19^{6}GS, 24^{B}HY, 24^{2}HY

	Starts	1st	2nd	3rd	Win & Pl
Chases	5	0	1	0	2970
Career Total	**32**	**6**	**6**	**4**	**62319**

134	3/01	Sand	3m110y	C(0-135)HCh	SFT	£7377
134	2/01	Leic	2m7f110y	E(0-115)HCh	SFT	£3836
138	11/99	Newb	2m3f	B(0-140)HHdl	G-S	£20832
116	2/99	Newb	2m110y	D(0-115)HHdl	G-S	£3028
120	1/99	Chel	2m1f	D(0-120)HHdl	SFT	£4758
94	1/99	Ludl	2m	E(0-105)HHdl	SFT	£2372

Total win prize-money £42205

Going: Sf: 0-3 GS: 0-1 Gd: 0-1 GF: - Fm: 0-0
Distance: 2m/2m3: 0-0 2m4-2m7: 0-1 3m+: 0-4
Track: LH: 0-5 RH: 0-0 Tight: 0-0 Gall: 0-1
Aids: Bl: 0-0 Vi: 0-0 Tstrap: 0-0
Best Rating: 138 11/00 MRas 2m5f110y gd-sft Hdl

He took some time to find his feet over fences but developed into a fair novice chaser in the spring of 2001. Suited by easy ground, he tries hard and stays three miles.

Pickett Point

4-y-o b g Magic Ring (IRE)-Bay Runner (Bay Express)
J J Bridger Mrs Julie I Lankshear

Placings:P **(1444)**
2001/02: 18^{P}GF

	Starts	1st	2nd	3rd	Win & Pl
Hurdles	1	0	0	0	
Career Total	**1**	**0**	**0**	**0**	

Going: Sf: 0-0 GS: 0-0 Gd: 0-0 GF: - Fm: 0-1
Distance: 2m/2m3: 0-1 2m4-2m7: 0-0 3m+: 0-0
Track: LH: 0-1 RH: 0-0 Tight: 0-1 Gall: 0-0
Aids: Bl: 0-0 Vi: 0-0 Tstrap: 0-0
Best Rating:

Picture Mee

67 **14**

4-y-o b f Aragon-Heemee (On Your Mark)
M A Barnes (B S Rothwell 16/1) J M Carlyle

Placings:0F **(4888)**
2001/02: 16^{0}S, 16^{F}G

	Starts	1st	2nd	3rd	Win & Pl
Hurdles	2	0	0	0	
Career Total	**2**	**0**	**0**	**0**	

Going: Sf: 0-1 GS: 0-0 Gd: 0-1 GF: - Fm: 0-0
Distance: 2m/2m3: 0-2 2m4-2m7: 0-0 3m+: 0-0
Track: LH: 0-1 RH: 0-1 Tight: 0-0 Gall: 0-1
Aids: Bl: 0-0 Vi: 0-0 Tstrap: 0-0
Best Rating: 14 1/02 Newc 2m soft Hdl

Picture Palace

101 **108**

4-y-o ch g Salse (USA)-Moviegoer (Pharly (FR))
T R George (Sir Mark Prescott 4/9) Mrs V Beeching,Alan Waller,James Layton

Placings:22220343 **(3860)**
2001/02: 17^{2}GS, 16^{2}G, 16^{2}GS, 16^{2}G, 21^{0}S, 16^{3}S, 16^{4}S, 20^{3}S

	Starts	1st	2nd	3rd	Win & Pl
Hurdles	8	0	4	2	8307
Career Total	**8**	**0**	**4**	**2**	**8307**

Going: Sf: 0-4 GS: 0-2 Gd: 0-2 GF: - Fm: 0-0
Distance: 2m/2m3: 0-6 2m4-2m7: 0-2 3m+: 0-0
Track: LH: 0-4 RH: 0-3 Tight: 0-1 Gall: 0-2
Aids: Bl: 0-6 Vi: 0-0 Tstrap: 0-0
Best Rating: 108 11/01 Chel 2m110y good Hdl

A winner on the Flat over two miles on fast ground, he has run some fair races over hurdles, but he has only the one pace and is proving hard to win with. Has raced mainly on soft ground over hurdles but won on fast ground on the level.

Pies Ar Us

62 **79**

5-y-o b g Perpendicular-Jendor (Condorcet (FR))
C W Fairhurst H Taylor & Sons

Placings:46 **(1197)**
2001/02: 17^{4}GF, 16^{6}G

	Starts	1st	2nd	3rd	Win & Pl
Hurdles	2	0	0	0	0
Career Total	**2**	**0**	**0**	**0**	**0**

Going: Sf: 0-0 GS: 0-0 Gd: 0-1 GF: - Fm: 0-1
Distance: 2m/2m3: 0-2 2m4-2m7: 0-0 3m+: 0-0
Track: LH: 0-1 RH: 0-1 Tight: 0-1 Gall: 0-0
Aids: Bl: 0-0 Vi: 0-0 Tstrap: 0-0
Best Rating: 79 7/01 Sedg 2m1f gd-fm Hdl

Pietro Bembo (IRE)

105(112h) **133**

8-y-o b g Midyan (USA)-Cut No Ice (Great Nephew)
Miss E C Lavelle (J Akehurst 27/7) Fraser Miller

Placings:0/42613125/F4100/0P5401-43 **(2036)**
2001/02: 16^{4}GS, 16^{3}GS

	Starts	1st	2nd	3rd	Win & Pl
Chases	2	0	0	1	1138
Career Total	**22**	**4**	**2**	**2**	**27949**

133	3/01	Asct	2m110y	B(0-140)HHdl	HVY	£7254
133	2/00	Kemp	2m	C(0-135)HHdl	SFT	£10481
130	3/99	Folk	2m1f110y	E Hdl	G-S	£2488
133	12/98	Winc	2m	E(0-100)HHdl	SFT	£2528

Total win prize-money £22751

Going: Sf: 0-0 GS: 0-2 Gd: 0-0 GF: - Fm: 0-0
Distance: 2m/2m3: 0-2 2m4-2m7: 0-0 3m+: 0-0
Track: LH: 0-0 RH: 0-2 Tight: 0-0 Gall: 0-0
Aids: Bl: 0-0 Vi: 0-0 Tstrap: 0-0
Best Rating: 133 11/01 Sand 2m gd-sft Ch

A decent front-running hurdler, he has yet to get off the mark over fences. Suited by soft ground.

Pigwigpeg

5-y-o br m Cut The Mustard (IRE)-Derwent River (Another River)
M A Barnes M Barnes

Placings:*P* **(0744)**
2001/02: 16^{P}GS

	Starts	1st	2nd	3rd	Win & Pl
NH Flat	1	0	0	0	
Career Total	**1**	**0**	**0**	**0**	

Going: Sf: 0-0 GS: 0-1 Gd: 0-0 GF: - Fm: 0-0
Distance: 2m/2m3: 0-1 2m4-2m7: 0-0 3m+: 0-0
Track: LH: 0-1 RH: 0-0 Tight: 0-0 Gall: 0-0
Aids: Bl: 0-0 Vi: 0-0 Tstrap: 0-0
Best Rating:

Pikachu Blue (IRE)

105(97h) (90h)**128**

6-y-o ch g Boyne Valley-Mary Glen (Glen Quaich)
Mrs S A Bramall Mrs S A Bramall

Placings:*000*-011**F0P** **(4961a)**
2001/02: 16^{0}YS, 24^{1}S, 21^{1}S, 24^{F}S, 24^{0}S, 25^{P}GY

	Starts	1st	2nd	3rd	Win & Pl
Hurdles	1	0	0	0	0
Chases	5	2	0	0	6250
Career Total	**9**	**2**	**0**	**0**	**6250**

124	2/02	Sedg	2m5f	E Ch	SFT	£3168
124	1/02	Muss	3m	E Ch	SFT	£3081

Total win prize-money £6250

Going: Sf: 2-4 GS: 0-0 Gd: 0-0 GF: - Fm: 0-0
Distance: 2m/2m3: 0-1 2m4-2m7: 1-1 3m+: 1-4
Track: LH: 1-3 RH: 1-3 **Tight: 2-2** Gall: 0-1
Aids: Bl: 0-0 Vi: 0-0 Tstrap: 0-0
Best Rating: 128 3/02 Limk 3m soft Ch

He showed ability over hurdles at around two miles in Ireland and appreciated the step up to three miles on his chasing debut, following up over a shorter trip next time. He clearly stays well and soft ground suits.

Pillager

77 **50**

5-y-o b g Reprimand-Emerald Ring (Auction Ring (USA))
Mrs A J Bowlby Mrs Amanda Bowlby

Placings:0 **(4527)**
2001/02: 16^{0}GS

	Starts	1st	2nd	3rd	Win & Pl
Hurdles	1	0	0	0	
Career Total	**1**	**0**	**0**	**0**	

Going: Sf: 0-0 GS: 0-1 Gd: 0-0 GF: - Fm: 0-0
Distance: 2m/2m3: 0-1 2m4-2m7: 0-0 3m+: 0-0
Track: LH: 0-1 RH: 0-0 Tight: 0-0 Gall: 0-0
Aids: Bl: 0-0 Vi: 0-0 Tstrap: 0-1
Best Rating: 50 4/02 Chep 2m110y gd-sft Hdl

Pillaging Pict

109 **115**

7-y-o ch g Primitive Rising (USA)-Carat Stick (Gold Rod)
J B Walton F T Walton

Placings:F63415F311 **(4895)**
2001/02: 25^{F}S, 17^{6}G, 20^{3}G, 24^{4}GS, 16^{1}GS, 16^{5}S, 16^{F}HY, 16^{3}HY, 20^{1}GS, 20^{1}G

	Starts	1st	2nd	3rd	Win & Pl
Chases	10	3	0	2	17524
Career Total	**10**	**3**	**0**	**2**	**17524**

115	4/02	Prth	2m4f110y	D(0-115)HCh	GD	£5863
110	4/02	Carl	2m4f	E(0-100)HCh	G-S	£3867
108	1/02	Catt	2m	E(0-105)HCh	G-S	£6071

Total win prize-money £15802

Going: Sf: 0-4 GS: 2-3 Gd: 1-3 GF: - Fm: 0-0
Distance: 2m/2m3: 1-5 **2m4-2m7: 2-3** 3m+: 0-2
Track: LH: 1-7 **RH: 2-3 Tight: 1-3** Gall: 0-3
Aids: Bl: 0-0 Vi: 0-0 Tstrap: 0-0
Best Rating: 115 4/02 Prth 2m4f110y good Ch

Modest chaser. Stays two and a half miles, appreciates cut, but does not want it too soft.

Pillar Of Fire (IRE)

101(105h) (103h)**103**

8-y-o gr g Roselier (FR)-Cousin Flo (True Song)
Ian Williams Paul Robson

Placings:*633*/40101-02**P4PF04P** **(4909)**
2001/02: 19^{0}G, 20^{2}GF, 20^{P}G, 20^{4}G, 24^{P}GS, 24^{F}G, 24^{0}G, 20^{4}G, 20^{P}GF

	Starts	1st	2nd	3rd	Win & Pl
Hurdles	1	0	0	0	0
Chases	8	0	1	0	1680
Career Total	**17**	**2**	**1**	**2**	**9153**

103	4/01	MRas	2m3f110y	D(0-120)HHdl	G-S	£3932
100	12/00	MRas	2m3f110y	F Hdl	G-S	£2562

Total win prize-money £6495

Going: Sf: 0-0 GS: 0-1 Gd: 0-6 GF: - Fm: 0-2
Distance: 2m/2m3: 0-0 2m4-2m7: 0-6 3m+: 0-3
Track: LH: 0-2 RH: 0-7 Tight: 0-4 Gall: 0-3
Aids: Bl: 0-0 Vi: 0-1 Tstrap: 0-0
Best Rating: 103 3/02 Wwck 2m4f110y good Ch

Dual hurdle race winner at Market Rasen in the past. Little impact over fences so far and has been known to run out over hurdles.

Pilot's Harbour

111 91

6-y-o b g Distant Relative-Lillemor (Connaught)
F P Murtagh Clayton Bigley Partnership Ltd

Placings:312342P0666-251P **(0958)**
2001/02: 24^{2}GF, 24^{5}GF, 24^{1}F, 27^{P}GF

	Starts	1st	2nd	3rd	Win & Pl
Hurdles	4	1	1	0	3123
Career Total	**15**	**2**	**3**	**2**	**8952**

92	5/01	Hexm	3m	F(0-100)HHdl	FRM	£2485
95	5/00	Ctml	2m1f110y	D Hdl	GD	£3152

Total win prize-money £5638

Going: Sf: 0-0 GS: 0-0 Gd: 0-0 GF: - Fm: 1-4
Distance: 2m/2m3: 0-0 2m4-2m7: 0-0 **3m+: 1-4**
Track: LH: 1-3 RH: 0-1 Tight: 0-1 Gall: 0-0
Aids: Bl: 0-0 Vi: 0-0 Tstrap: 0-0
Best Rating: 95 8/00 Ctml 2m6f good Hdl

Piltdown Chimes

7-y-o b m Arctic Lord-Houston Belle (Milford)
J R Best Mrs F A Veasey

Placings:*0*P-P **(3150)**
2001/02: 18^{P}G

	Starts	1st	2nd	3rd	Win & Pl
Hurdles	1	0	0	0	
Career Total	**3**	**0**	**0**	**0**	

Going: Sf: 0-0 GS: 0-0 Gd: 0-1 GF: - Fm: 0-0
Distance: 2m/2m3: 0-1 2m4-2m7: 0-0 3m+: 0-0
Track: LH: 0-1 RH: 0-0 Tight: 0-1 Gall: 0-0
Aids: Bl: 0-0 Vi: 0-0 Tstrap: 0-0
Best Rating: 52 11/00 Tntn 2m1f good NHF

Pine Hill (IRE)

12-y-o b m Yashgan-Trekking (Homing)
D J Wintle D J Renney

Placings:UP **(1406)**
2001/02: 22^{U}GS, 16^{P}GF

	Starts	1st	2nd	3rd	Win & Pl
Hurdles	2	0	0	0	
Career Total	**2**	**0**	**0**	**0**	

Going: Sf: 0-0 GS: 0-1 Gd: 0-0 GF: - Fm: 0-1
Distance: 2m/2m3: 0-1 2m4-2m7: 0-1 3m+: 0-0
Track: LH: 0-1 RH: 0-0 Tight: 0-0 Gall: 0-0
Aids: Bl: 0-0 Vi: 0-0 Tstrap: 0-0
Best Rating:

Pingo Hill (IRE)

96 78

10-y-o ch g Salt Dome (USA)-Andarta (Ballymore)
J Mackie R J Wright

Placings:*000*113FP0PF5/45435/112P5/6065-PP **(1618)**
2001/02: 19^{P}S, 21^{P}G

	Starts	1st	2nd	3rd	Win & Pl
Hurdles	2	0	0	0	
Career Total	**28**	**4**	**1**	**2**	**13445**

101	7/98	Bang	2m4f	E(0-115)HHdl	GD	£3582
96	5/98	Hntg	2m5f110y	G(0-95)HHdl	G-F	£1898
109	7/96	Wxfd	2m4f	Hdl	YLD	£2648
96	6/96	Limk	2m2f	Hdl	GD	£3530

Total win prize-money £11660

Going: Sf: 0-1 GS: 0-0 Gd: 0-1 GF: - Fm: 0-0
Distance: 2m/2m3: 0-0 2m4-2m7: 0-2 3m+: 0-0
Track: LH: 0-0 RH: 0-2 Tight: 0-1 Gall: 0-0
Aids: Bl: 0-0 Vi: 0-0 Tstrap: 0-0
Best Rating: 109 7/96 Wxfd 2m4f yield Hdl

Pinouli

8-y-o b m Jupiter Island-Poppy's Pride (Uncle Pokey)
D E Nicholls (Mrs D Haine 7/4) D E Nicholls

Placings:*00*/F **(4846)**
2001/02: 24^{F}G

	Starts	1st	2nd	3rd	Win & Pl
Chases	1	0	0	0	
Career Total	**3**	**0**	**0**	**0**	

Going: Sf: 0-0 GS: 0-0 Gd: 0-1 GF: - Fm: 0-0
Distance: 2m/2m3: 0-0 2m4-2m7: 0-0 3m+: 0-1
Track: LH: 0-1 RH: 0-0 Tight: 0-1 Gall: 0-0
Aids: Bl: 0-0 Vi: 0-0 Tstrap: 0-0
Best Rating: 77 12/98 Hntg 2m110y soft NHF

Pip Moss

7-y-o ch g Le Moss-My Aisling (John De Coombe)
J A B Old Mrs Jim Old

Placings:*0*-5F **(3558)**
2001/02: 17^{5}HY, 16^{F}HY

	Starts	1st	2nd	3rd	Win & Pl
NH Flat	1	0	0	0	0
Hurdles	1	0	0	0	0
Career Total	**3**	**0**	**0**	**0**	**0**

Going: Sf: 0-2 GS: 0-0 Gd: 0-0 GF: - Fm: 0-0
Distance: 2m/2m3: 0-2 2m4-2m7: 0-0 3m+: 0-0
Track: LH: 0-1 RH: 0-1 Tight: 0-1 Gall: 0-0
Aids: Bl: 0-0 Vi: 0-0 Tstrap: 0-0
Best Rating: 95 12/01 NAbb 2m1f heavy NHF

Moderate efforts in bumpers and fell on hurdles debut in January 2002.

Piper's Rock (IRE)

105(69h) 121

11-y-o ch g Zaffaran (USA)-Misclaire (Steeple Aston)
Miss E C Lavelle R J Lavelle

Placings:*000*P55413/2/21F2P0/3/1214P141F40-04P5PP (1729)
2001/02: 17^{0}G, 16^{4}GF, 19^{P}F, 24^{5}GF, 23^{P}GF, 24^{P}F

	Starts	1st	2nd	3rd	Win & Pl
Hurdles	1	0	0	0	0
Chases	5	0	0	0	262
Career Total	**34**	**6**	**4**	**2**	**30578**

112	10/00	Towc	2m	F(0-100)HHdl	G-F	£2289
124	8/00	NAbb	2m110y	D(0-125)HCh	G-S	£4007
124	6/00	NAbb	2m110y	E(0-115)HCh	GD	£3415
115	5/00	Bang	2m4f110y	D(0-120)HCh	G-S	£5577
114	10/98	Plum	2m5f	E(0-105)HCh	GD	£4901
88	4/97	Ludl	2m5f110y	E(0-100)HHdl	G-F	£2528

Total win prize-money £22719

Going: Sf: 0-0 GS: 0-0 Gd: 0-1 GF: - Fm: 0-5
Distance: 2m/2m3: 0-3 2m4-2m7: 0-0 3m+: 0-3
Track: LH: 0-3 RH: 0-3 Tight: 0-3 Gall: 0-0
Aids: Bl: 0-0 Vi: 0-5 Tstrap: 0-0
Best Rating: 124 8/00 NAbb 2m110y gd-sft Ch

Pipiji (IRE)

7-y-o gr m Pips Pride-Blue Alicia (Wolver Hollow)
M Wellings Mrs S E Jordan

Placings:P-P **(0216)**
2001/02: 16^{P}GF

	Starts	1st	2nd	3rd	Win & Pl
Hurdles	1	0	0	0	
Career Total	**2**	**0**	**0**	**0**	

Going: Sf: 0-0 GS: 0-0 Gd: 0-0 GF: - Fm: 0-1
Distance: 2m/2m3: 0-1 2m4-2m7: 0-0 3m+: 0-0
Track: LH: 0-0 RH: 0-1 Tight: 0-0 Gall: 0-0
Aids: Bl: 0-0 Vi: 0-0 Tstrap: 0-0
Best Rating:

Pipssalio (SPA)

100 103

5-y-o b h Pips Pride-Tesalia (SPA) (Finissimo (SPA))
Jamie Poulton Chris Steward & Christian Taylor

Placings:03 **(2328)**
2001/02: 16^{0}GS, 16^{3}G

	Starts	1st	2nd	3rd	Win & Pl
Hurdles	2	0	0	1	573
Career Total	**2**	**0**	**0**	**1**	**573**

Going: Sf: 0-0 GS: 0-1 Gd: 0-1 GF: - Fm: 0-0
Distance: 2m/2m3: 0-2 2m4-2m7: 0-0 3m+: 0-0
Track: LH: 0-1 RH: 0-1 Tight: 0-1 Gall: 0-0
Aids: Bl: 0-0 Vi: 0-0 Tstrap: 0-0
Best Rating: 103 11/01 Plum 2m good Hdl

Pirandello Due

74

8-y-o b g Teenoso (USA)-Bay Girl (Persian Bold)
B G Powell Richard & Carol Stainer

Placings:P0-4P **(0559)**
2001/02: 21^{4}GF, 22^{P}GF

	Starts	1st	2nd	3rd	Win & Pl
Hurdles	2	0	0	0	0
Career Total	**4**	**0**	**0**	**0**	**0**

Going: Sf: 0-0 GS: 0-0 Gd: 0-0 GF: - Fm: 0-2
Distance: 2m/2m3: 0-0 2m4-2m7: 0-2 3m+: 0-0
Track: LH: 0-1 RH: 0-0 Tight: 0-1 Gall: 0-0
Aids: Bl: 0-0 Vi: 0-0 Tstrap: 0-0
Best Rating: 74 4/01 Font 2m6f110y good Hdl

Pirate Minstrel (IRE)

10-y-o br g Black Minstrel-Ailwee Lady (USA) (Nikoli)
Pat Mitchell Mrs P S Hunt

Placings:*0*/003/P-P **(0569)**
2001/02: 20^{P}F

	Starts	1st	2nd	3rd	Win & Pl
Chases	1	0	0	0	
Career Total	**6**	**0**	**0**	**1**	**305**

Going: Sf: 0-0 GS: 0-0 Gd: 0-0 GF: - Fm: 0-1
Distance: 2m/2m3: 0-0 2m4-2m7: 0-1 3m+: 0-0
Track: LH: 0-1 RH: 0-0 Tight: 0-0 Gall: 0-0
Aids: Bl: 0-0 Vi: 0-0 Tstrap: 0-0
Best Rating: 84 3/99 Plum 2m4f soft Hdl

Pirro (IRE)

95 **68**

7-y-o ch g Persian Bold-Kindness Itself (IRE) (Ahonoora)

M H Tompkins P A & D G Sakal

Placings:P0/0-6 **(0241)**

2001/02: 16^{6}GF

	Starts	1st	2nd	3rd	Win & Pl
Hurdles	1	0	0	0	0
Career Total	**4**	**0**	**0**	**0**	**0**

Going: Sf: 0-0 GS: 0-0 Gd: 0-0 GF: - Fm: 0-1
Distance: 2m/2m3: 0-1 2m4-2m7: 0-0 3m+: 0-0
Track: LH: 0-1 RH: 0-0 Tight: 0-0 Gall: 0-0
Aids: Bl: 0-0 Vi: 0-0 Tstrap: 0-0
Best Rating: **78** 3/00 Catt 2m gd-fm Hdl

Pitchthedice

75 **39**

8-y-o b g Relief Pitcher-Rolling Dice (Balinger)

Mrs S C Bradburne The Five Square Partnership

Placings:P4P4U31/34PP5P-P0P **(1837)**

2001/02: 20^{P}GS, 16^{0}G, 25^{P}G

	Starts	1st	2nd	3rd	Win & Pl
Chases	3	0	0	0	
Career Total	**16**	**1**	**0**	**2**	**5383**

116	2/00	Newc	2m4f	D Ch		HVY	£3932

Total win prize-money £3933

Going: Sf: 0-0 GS: 0-1 Gd: 0-2 GF: - Fm: 0-0
Distance: 2m/2m3: 0-1 2m4-2m7: 0-1 3m+: 0-1
Track: LH: 0-1 RH: 0-2 Tight: 0-1 Gall: 0-0
Aids: Bl: 0-0 Vi: 0-0 Tstrap: 0-2
Best Rating: **116** 2/00 Newc 2m4f heavy Ch

Pizarro (IRE)

117f **152f**

5-y-o ch g Broken Hearted-Our Swan Lady (Swan's Rock)

E J O'Grady Edward Wallace

Placings:*1-11* **(4235)**

2001/02: 16^{1}HY, 16^{1}GS

	Starts	1st	2nd	3rd	Win & Pl
NH Flat	2	2	0	0	22445
Career Total	**3**	**3**	**0**	**0**	**29122**

152	3/02	Chel	2m110y	A NHF		G-S	£18000
127	2/02	Naas	2m		NHF	HVY	£4444
126	4/01	Fair	2m		NHF	SFT	£6677

Total win prize-money £29122

Going: Sf: 1-1 GS: 1-1 Gd: 0-0 GF: - Fm: 0-0
Distance: **2m/2m3: 2-2** 2m4-2m7: 0-0 3m+: 0-0
Track: **LH: 1-1** RH: 0-0 Tight: 0-0 Gall: 0-0
Aids: Bl: 0-0 Vi: 0-0 Tstrap: 0-0
Best Rating: **152** 3/02 Chel 2m110y gd-sft NHF

A tough Irish bumper horse, ran out a game winner of the 2002 Festival bumper, suited by soft ground.

Plaid Maid (IRE)

104 **145**

10-y-o b m Executive Perk-Tipperary Tartan (Rarity)

M Bradstock Lord Oaksey

Placings:3/0/0P4221/1313/1421P-23 **(4419)**

2001/02: 30^{2}G, 24^{3}GS

	Starts	1st	2nd	3rd	Win & Pl
Chases	2	0	1	1	5556
Career Total	**19**	**5**	**4**	**4**	**35043**

145	3/01	Extr	2m7f110y	D(0-125)HCh	HVY	£4839
142	1/01	Extr	2m7f110y	D(0-120)HCh	HVY	£4959
136	1/00	Extr	2m7f110y	D(0-120)HCh	HVY	£5421
117	12/99	Extr	2m7f110y	E(0-105)HCh	G-S	£4011
102	2/99	Tntn	3m110y	F(0-100)HHdl	G-S	£2822

Total win prize-money £22054

Going: Sf: 0-0 GS: 0-1 Gd: 0-1 GF: - Fm: 0-0
Distance: 2m/2m3: 0-0 2m4-2m7: 0-0 3m+: 0-2
Track: LH: 0-1 RH: 0-0 Tight: 0-0 Gall: 0-1
Aids: Bl: 0-0 Vi: 0-0 Tstrap: 0-0
Best Rating: **145** 3/02 Newb 3m gd-sft Ch

She has gained her last four wins over two miles seven and a half furlongs at Exeter and goes particularly well there. Suited by soft ground, she races prominently and is useful under the right conditions.

Plain Chant

80 **64**

5-y-o b g Doyoun-Sing Softly (Luthier)

B J Llewellyn (P W Harris 18/7) S Harrison

Placings:000P **(3449)**

2001/02: 16^{0}G, 17^{0}GS, 16^{0}S, 16^{P}GS

	Starts	1st	2nd	3rd	Win & Pl
Hurdles	4	0	0	0	
Career Total	**4**	**0**	**0**	**0**	

Going: Sf: 0-1 GS: 0-2 Gd: 0-1 GF: - Fm: 0-0
Distance: 2m/2m3: 0-4 2m4-2m7: 0-0 3m+: 0-0
Track: LH: 0-2 RH: 0-2 Tight: 0-3 Gall: 0-0
Aids: Bl: 0-0 Vi: 0-0 Tstrap: 0-0
Best Rating: **64** 11/01 Plum 2m good Hdl

Planet Ireland (IRE)

10-y-o b g Mandalus-Seapatrick (The Parson)

Mrs J M Hollands Mrs C J Kerr

Placings:PP/5040U/4PFP-PS0 **(4690)**

2001/02: 20^{P}S, 20^{S}GF, 25^{0}GF

	Starts	1st	2nd	3rd	Win & Pl
Chases	3	0	0	0	
Career Total	**14**	**0**	**0**	**0**	**460**

Going: Sf: 0-1 GS: 0-0 Gd: 0-0 GF: - Fm: 0-2
Distance: 2m/2m3: 0-0 2m4-2m7: 0-2 3m+: 0-1
Track: LH: 0-2 RH: 0-1 Tight: 0-1 Gall: 0-0
Aids: Bl: 0-0 Vi: 0-0 Tstrap: 0-0
Best Rating: **80** 5/01 Hexm 2m4f110y gd-fm Ch

Platonic-My-Eye (IRE)

105(102c) (126c)**115**

9-y-o ch g Over The River (FR)-Love-In-A-Mist (Paddy's Stream)

J J O'Neill J P McManus

Placings:0/1U30/F2500P/FP1F6-111P **(1476)**

2001/02: 24^{1}S, 25^{1}F, 24^{1}GF, 24^{P}S

	Starts	1st	2nd	3rd	Win & Pl
Hurdles	3	2	0	0	6486
Chases	1	1	0	0	6968
Career Total	**20**	**5**	**1**	**1**	**22521**

126	9/01	Strf	3m	D(0-125)HCh	G-F	£6968
111	5/01	Weth	3m1f	D Hdl	FRM	£3444
115	5/01	Prth	3m110y	E Hdl	SFT	£3041
126	2/01	Ludl	2m4f	F(0-100)HCh	GD	£4202
100	9/98	Gway	2m1f	Ch	HVY	£2989

Total win prize-money £20645

Going: Sf: 1-2 GS: 0-0 Gd: 0-0 GF: - Fm: 2-2
Distance: 2m/2m3: 0-0 2m4-2m7: 0-0 **3m+: 3-4**
Track: **LH: 2-2** RH: 1-2 **Tight: 1-2** Gall: 0-0
Aids: Bl: 0-0 Vi: 0-0 Tstrap: 0-0
Best Rating: **126** 9/01 Strf 3m gd-fm Ch

Play Games (USA)

95 **113**

14-y-o ch g Nijinsky (CAN)-Playful Queen (USA) (Majestic Prince (USA))

R Lee Exors Of The Late J O Beavan

Placings:0/51/P0/P1P3161/11511P5/323252123/412 P3534-P4 **(2553)**

2001/02: 16^{P}G, 16^{4}S

	Starts	1st	2nd	3rd	Win & Pl
Chases	2	0	0	0	0
Career Total	**38**	**10**	**5**	**6**	**42343**

115	10/00	Bang	2m1f110y	F(0-110)HCh	SFT	£4192
118	2/00	Hrfd	2m	F(0-100)HCh	GD	£3575
119	12/98	Strf	2m1f110y	E(0-120)HCh	SFT	£2804
119	11/98	Worc	2m	E(0-115)HCh	HVY	£3470
119	10/98	NAbb	2m110y	D(0-125)HCh	GD	£3322
104	9/98	NAbb	2m110y	F(0-100)HCh	G-S	£2436
108	5/98	Bang	2m1f110y	E(0-100)HCh	G-S	£3860
97	3/98	Leic	2m1f	E(0-115)HCh	GD	£3446
84	11/97	Hrfd	2m	F(0-95)HCh	G-S	£2866
93	11/94	Tntn	2m1f	Hdl	GD	£3712

Total win prize-money £33687

Going: Sf: 0-1 GS: 0-0 Gd: 0-1 GF: - Fm: 0-0
Distance: 2m/2m3: 0-2 2m4-2m7: 0-0 3m+: 0-0
Track: LH: 0-2 RH: 0-0 Tight: 0-2 Gall: 0-0
Aids: Bl: 0-0 Vi: 0-0 Tstrap: 0-2
Best Rating: **120** 10/00 Hrfd 2m good Ch

Prolific winner in his time, and still capable despite his years. Suited by a sharp, flat track.

Play It Cool

100 **78**

6-y-o ch g Almoojid-Pinston Cove (Shaab)

Mrs S D Williams Kernow Racing

Placings:F50 **(3383)**

2001/02: 19^{F}GF, 17^{5}G, 16^{0}GS

	Starts	1st	2nd	3rd	Win & Pl
Hurdles	3	0	0	0	0
Career Total	**3**	**0**	**0**	**0**	

Going: Sf: 0-0 GS: 0-1 Gd: 0-1 GF: - Fm: 0-1
Distance: 2m/2m3: 0-3 2m4-2m7: 0-0 3m+: 0-0
Track: LH: 0-1 RH: 0-2 Tight: 0-1 Gall: 0-0
Aids: Bl: 0-0 Vi: 0-0 Tstrap: 0-0
Best Rating: **78** 11/01 NAbb 2m1f good Hdl

Playaway (IRE)

95 **77**

8-y-o b g Black Minstrel-Actually Stell (Deep Run)

O Brennan Mrs Pat Brennan

Placings:*06*-0 **(0203)**

2001/02: 20^{0}G

	Starts	1st	2nd	3rd	Win & Pl
Hurdles	1	0	0	0	
Career Total	**3**	**0**	**0**	**0**	**0**

Going: Sf: 0-0 GS: 0-0 Gd: 0-1 GF: - Fm: 0-0
Distance: 2m/2m3: 0-0 2m4-2m7: 0-1 3m+: 0-0
Track: LH: 0-1 RH: 0-0 Tight: 0-0 Gall: 0-0
Aids: Bl: 0-0 Vi: 0-0 Tstrap: 0-0
Best Rating: 97 6/00 MRas 2m1f110y gd-fm NHF

Playful Dane (IRE)

5-y-o b g Dolphin Street (FR)-Omicida (IRE) (Danehill (USA))
W S Cunningham Mrs Ann Bell

Placings:*00* **(2729)**
2001/02: 17^{0}S, 17^{0}GF

	Starts	1st	2nd	3rd	Win & Pl
NH Flat	2	0	0	0	
Career Total	**2**	**0**	**0**	**0**	

Going: Sf: 0-1 GS: 0-0 Gd: 0-0 GF: - Fm: 0-1
Distance: 2m/2m3: 0-2 2m4-2m7: 0-0 3m+: 0-0
Track: LH: 0-0 RH: 0-1 Tight: 0-1 Gall: 0-0
Aids: Bl: 0-0 Vi: 0-0 Tstrap: 0-0
Best Rating:

Playinaround

87 **58**
5-y-o ch m Anshan-Karonga (Main Reef)
R H Alner Mrs A Hewitson

Placings:0050 **(1544)**
2001/02: 16^{0}GF, 16^{0}GF, 16^{5}GF, 17^{0}G

	Starts	1st	2nd	3rd	Win & Pl
Hurdles	4	0	0	0	0
Career Total	**4**	**0**	**0**	**0**	**0**

Going: Sf: 0-0 GS: 0-0 Gd: 0-1 GF: - Fm: 0-3
Distance: 2m/2m3: 0-4 2m4-2m7: 0-0 3m+: 0-0
Track: LH: 0-3 RH: 0-1 Tight: 0-0 Gall: 0-0
Aids: Bl: 0-0 Vi: 0-0 Tstrap: 0-0
Best Rating: 58 8/01 Worc 2m gd-fm Hdl

Playing Away

7-y-o ch m Northern Game-Ottery News (Pony Express)
O J Carter O J Carter

Placings:P/PP **(0794)**
2001/02: 17^{P}GS, 22^{P}GF

	Starts	1st	2nd	3rd	Win & Pl
Hurdles	2	0	0	0	
Career Total	**3**	**0**	**0**	**0**	

Going: Sf: 0-0 GS: 0-1 Gd: 0-0 GF: - Fm: 0-1
Distance: 2m/2m3: 0-1 2m4-2m7: 0-1 3m+: 0-0
Track: LH: 0-1 RH: 0-1 Tight: 0-1 Gall: 0-0
Aids: Bl: 0-0 Vi: 0-0 Tstrap: 0-0
Best Rating:

Playlord

9-y-o b g Arctic Lord-Show Rose (Coliseum)
J H Docker J H Docker

Placings:*3/0*5244P0/P/P **(3861)**
2001/02: 19^{P}S

	Starts	1st	2nd	3rd	Win & Pl
Chases	1	0	0	0	
Career Total	**10**	**0**	**1**	**1**	**1247**

Going: Sf: 0-1 GS: 0-0 Gd: 0-0 GF: - Fm: 0-0
Distance: 2m/2m3: 0-0 2m4-2m7: 0-1 3m+: 0-0
Track: LH: 0-1 RH: 0-0 Tight: 0-0 Gall: 0-1
Aids: Bl: 0-0 Vi: 0-0 Tstrap: 0-0
Best Rating: 107 4/98 Chel 2m1f heavy NHF

Playmaker

9-y-o b g Primo Dominie-Salacious (Sallust)
F P Murtagh Mrs Anna Kenny

Placings:0P400**P**/04FF000/6002BP/0P00-PPP **(0780)**
2001/02: 16^{P}F, 16^{P}GS, 20^{P}G

	Starts	1st	2nd	3rd	Win & Pl
Hurdles	2	0	0	0	0
Chases	1	0	0	0	0
Career Total	**26**	**0**	**1**	**0**	**888**

Going: Sf: 0-0 GS: 0-1 Gd: 0-1 GF: - Fm: 0-1
Distance: 2m/2m3: 0-2 2m4-2m7: 0-1 3m+: 0-0
Track: LH: 0-3 RH: 0-0 Tight: 0-0 Gall: 0-0
Aids: Bl: 0-1 Vi: 0-0 Tstrap: 0-0
Best Rating: 73 5/98 MRas 2m1f110y gd-fm Hdl

Playmore (IRE)

112 **109**
11-y-o ch g Ore-Playactress (Trimmingham)
Ian Williams O P J Meli

Placings:*00*/SP/10 **(0683)**
2001/02: 20^{1}GF, 26^{0}G

	Starts	1st	2nd	3rd	Win & Pl
Chases	2	1	0	0	2106
Career Total	**6**	**1**	**0**	**0**	**2106**

109	5/01	Hexm	2m4f110y	F Ch	G-F	£2106

Total win prize-money £2106

Going: Sf: 0-0 GS: 0-0 Gd: 0-1 GF: - Fm: 1-1
Distance: 2m/2m3: 0-0 **2m4-2m7: 1-1** 3m+: 0-1
Track: **LH: 1-2** RH: 0-0 Tight: 0-1 Gall: 0-0
Aids: Bl: 0-0 Vi: 0-0 Tstrap: 0-0
Best Rating: 109 5/01 Hexm 2m4f110y gd-fm Ch

Plazzotta (IRE)

5-y-o b g Sri Pekan (USA)-Porte Des Iles (IRE) (Kris)
M C Chapman Miss C T Hickford

Placings:P-U **(1099)**
2001/02: 19^{U}GF

	Starts	1st	2nd	3rd	Win & Pl
Hurdles	1	0	0	0	
Career Total	**2**	**0**	**0**	**0**	

Going: Sf: 0-0 GS: 0-0 Gd: 0-0 GF: - Fm: 0-1
Distance: 2m/2m3: 0-0 2m4-2m7: 0-1 3m+: 0-0
Track: LH: 0-0 RH: 0-1 Tight: 0-1 Gall: 0-0
Aids: Bl: 0-0 Vi: 0-0 Tstrap: 0-0
Best Rating:

Pleasant Dreams

70 **37**
7-y-o ch m Sabrehill (USA)-Tafila (Adonijah)
Denys Smith P & I Darling

Placings:F62/0 **(3819)**
2001/02: 17^{0}S

	Starts	1st	2nd	3rd	Win & Pl
Hurdles	1	0	0	0	
Career Total	**4**	**0**	**1**	**0**	**728**

Going: Sf: 0-1 GS: 0-0 Gd: 0-0 GF: - Fm: 0-0
Distance: 2m/2m3: 0-1 2m4-2m7: 0-0 3m+: 0-0
Track: LH: 0-1 RH: 0-0 Tight: 0-1 Gall: 0-0
Aids: Bl: 0-0 Vi: 0-0 Tstrap: 0-0
Best Rating: 91 12/99 Catt 2m good Hdl

Modest maiden hurdler. Favours prominent tactics.

Please Call (IRE)

13-y-o b g Flair Path-Javana (Levanter)
R R Collier R R Collier

Placings:*050/34000/02/4/***PP** **(3875)**
2001/02: 24^{P}S, 24^{P}GS

	Starts	1st	2nd	3rd	Win & Pl
Chases	2	0	0	0	
Career Total	**13**	**0**	**1**	**1**	**844**

Going: Sf: 0-1 GS: 0-1 Gd: 0-0 GF: - Fm: 0-0
Distance: 2m/2m3: 0-0 2m4-2m7: 0-0 3m+: 0-2
Track: LH: 0-0 RH: 0-2 Tight: 0-0 Gall: 0-2
Aids: Bl: 0-0 Vi: 0-0 Tstrap: 0-0
Best Rating: 74 10/00 Hntg [illegible] good Hdl

Plenty Courage

108(108h) (107h)**87**
8-y-o ch g Gildoran-Fastlass (Celtic Cone)
F S Storey F S Storey

Placings:*0351*11F/406P31/605F0-0255212510P**34** **(4868)**
2001/02: 20^{0}S, 20^{2}S, 20^{5}GF, 20^{5}GF, 21^{2}G, 21^{1}G, 17^{2}S, 21^{5}S, 20^{1}GS, 16^{0}S, 24^{P}G, 16^{3}HY, 20^{4}GF

	Starts	1st	2nd	3rd	Win & Pl
Hurdles	11	2	3	0	11261
Chases	2	0	0	1	748
Career Total	**31**	**6**	**3**	**3**	**22568**

107	11/01	Ayr	2m4f	C(0-130)HHdl	G-S	£5148
107	10/01	Sedg	2m5f110y	D(0-125)HHdl	GD	£3265
114	4/00	Carl	2m4f110y	D(0-125)HHdl	SFT	£3388
100	3/99	Hexm	2m	E Hdl	G-S	£2427
106	3/99	Ayr	2m	F Hdl	SFT	£2145
102	2/99	Muss	2m	H NHF	G-F	£1702

Total win prize-money £18076

Going: Sf: 0-6 GS: 1-1 Gd: 1-3 GF: - Fm: 0-3
Distance: 2m/2m3: 0-3 **2m4-2m7: 2-9** 3m+: 0-1
Track: **LH: 2-9** RH: 0-4 **Tight: 1-4** Gall: 0-0
Aids: Bl: 0-0 Vi: 0-0 Tstrap: 0-0
Best Rating: 114 4/00 Carl 2m4f110y soft Hdl

Moderate handicap hurdler, best at around two and a half miles on good to soft. He looked only modest over fences in the spring of 2002.

Plough Boy

103 **108**
4-y-o br g Komaite (USA)-Plough Hill (North Briton)
D E Cantillon J W Orbell

Placings:11 **(2324)**
2001/02: 16^{1}G, 16^{1}S

Starts	1st	2nd	3rd	Win & Pl
Hurdles	2	2	0	0	6751
Career Total	**2**	**2**	**0**	**0**	**6751**

108	11/01	Fknm	2m	D Hdl	SFT	£3237
106	11/01	Hntg	2m110y	D Hdl	GD	£3513

Total win prize-money £6751

Going: Sf: 1-1 GS: 0-0 Gd: 1-1 GF: - Fm: 0-0
Distance: **2m/2m3: 2-2** 2m4-2m7: 0-0 3m+: 0-0
Track: LH: 1-1 RH: 1-1 Tight: 1-1 Gall: 1-1
Aids: Bl: 0-0 Vi: 0-0 Tstrap: 0-0
Best Rating: 108 11/01 Fknm 2m soft Hdl

A plater on the Flat, has taken well to hurdles. Suited by cut in the ground.

Plumbob (IRE)

13-y-o br g Bob Back (USA)-Naujella (Malinowski (USA))
L Lungo Andrew W B Duncan

Placings:14200/6045503F53/00F043414204034/**2**/42 6/**21U4**/**F**1**625**/**3**0**5**00313122/4602**3-1** **(0743)**
2001/02: 20^{1}GS

	Starts	1st	2nd	3rd	Win & Pl
Chases	1	1	0	0	3493
Career Total	**60**	**7**	**9**	**8**	**33586**

95	6/01	Hexm	2m4f110y	E(0-115)HCh	G-S	£3493
105	2/00	Newc	3m	F(0-105)HHdl	HVY	£2033
104	1/00	Newc	2m4f	G(0-95)HHdl	SFT	£1557
123	11/98	Hexm	2m4f110y	G(0-90)HHdl	HVY	£2127
102	5/97	Uttx	2m5f	D Ch	G-S	£3468
102	12/94	Newc	2m4f	(0-125)HHdl	GD	£2738
	8/92	Tral	2m	Hdl	G-Y	£3548

Total win prize-money £18969

Going: Sf: 0-0 GS: 1-1 Gd: 0-0 GF: - Fm: 0-0
Distance: 2m/2m3: 0-0 **2m4-2m7: 1-1** 3m+: 0-0
Track: **LH: 1-1** RH: 0-0 Tight: 0-0 Gall: 0-0
Aids: Bl: 0-0 Vi: 0-0 Tstrap: 0-0
Best Rating: 123 11/98 Hexm 2m4f110y heavy Hdl

Pluralist (IRE)

100 **87**
6-y-o b g Mujadil (USA)-Encore Une Fois (IRE) (Shirley Heights)
Miss K M George Stableline

Placings:00-10332P **(1227)**
2001/02: 17^{1}GS, 17^{0}G, 16^{3}G, 21^{3}GF, 21^{2}GF, 20^{P}GF

	Starts	1st	2nd	3rd	Win & Pl
Hurdles	6	1	1	2	4194
Career Total	**8**	**1**	**1**	**2**	**4194**

87	5/01	Bang	2m1f	E Hdl	G-S	£2870

Total win prize-money £2870

Going: Sf: 0-0 GS: 1-1 Gd: 0-2 GF: - Fm: 0-3
Distance: **2m/2m3: 1-3** 2m4-2m7: 0-3 3m+: 0-0
Track: **LH: 1-6** RH: 0-0 **Tight: 1-4** Gall: 0-0
Aids: Bl: 0-0 Vi: 0-0 Tstrap: 0-0
Best Rating: 87 8/01 Sedg 2m5f110y gd-fm Hdl

Pluto

(78h) (63h)**63**
7-y-o b g Sharpo-No More Rosies (Warpath)
A Robson A Robson

Placings:_0_/03P/266P-**F0P**60 **(2185)**
2001/02: 20^{F}G, 20^{0}GS, 17^{P}G, 20^{6}S, 22^{0}GS

	Starts	1st	2nd	3rd	Win & Pl
Hurdles	2	0	0	0	0
Chases	3	0	0	0	0
Career Total	**13**	**0**	**1**	**1**	**1028**

Going: Sf: 0-1 GS: 0-2 Gd: 0-2 GF: - Fm: 0-0
Distance: 2m/2m3: 0-1 2m4-2m7: 0-4 3m+: 0-0
Track: LH: 0-2 RH: 0-1 Tight: 0-1 Gall: 0-0
Aids: Bl: 0-0 Vi: 0-0 Tstrap: 0-2
Best Rating: 74 11/00 Ayr 2m6f soft Hdl

Plutocrat

104 **127**
6-y-o b g Polar Falcon (USA)-Choire Mhor (Dominion)
L Lungo Miss S Blumberg

Placings:00P111/0P0P-6612P3 **(4770)**
2001/02: 17^{6}S, 16^{6}GS, 16^{1}GS, 24^{2}G, 22^{P}G, 20^{3}GF

	Starts	1st	2nd	3rd	Win & Pl
Hurdles	6	1	1	1	6257
Career Total	**16**	**4**	**1**	**1**	**14494**

115	11/01	Newc	2m	E(0-115)HHdl	G-S	£2541
106	2/00	Sand	2m110y	E(0-115)HHdl	SFT	£3575
94	1/00	Muss	2m	G(0-95)HHdl	GD	£2338
72	1/00	Muss	2m	G Hdl	SFT	£2324

Total win prize-money £10778

Going: Sf: 0-1 GS: 1-2 Gd: 0-2 GF: - Fm: 0-1
Distance: **2m/2m3: 1-3** 2m4-2m7: 0-2 3m+: 0-1
Track: **LH: 1-4** RH: 0-2 Tight: 0-2 **Gall: 1-1**
Aids: Bl: 0-0 Vi: 0-0 Tstrap: 0-0
Best Rating: 127 12/01 Muss 3m good Hdl

Effective over two miles. Suited by hold-up tactics off a strong pace. Acts on most types of ground.

Poacher's Pocket (IRE)

(89h)
8-y-o gr g Roselier (FR)-Sure Magic (Gleason (USA))
Noel T Chance A D Weller

Placings:44-PP **(2359)**
2001/02: 21^{P}GS, 22^{P}S

	Starts	1st	2nd	3rd	Win & Pl
Hurdles	1	0	0	0	0
Chases	1	0	0	0	0
Career Total	**4**	**0**	**0**	**0**	**0**

Going: Sf: 0-1 GS: 0-1 Gd: 0-0 GF: - Fm: 0-0
Distance: 2m/2m3: 0-0 2m4-2m7: 0-2 3m+: 0-0
Track: LH: 0-1 RH: 0-1 Tight: 0-1 Gall: 0-0
Aids: Bl: 0-0 Vi: 0-0 Tstrap: 0-0
Best Rating: 101 1/01 Hayd 2m6f soft Hdl

Poachers Run (IRE)

95(105h) (93h)**89**
7-y-o b m Executive Perk-Rugged Run (Deep Run)
G M Moore D J Bushell

Placings:_11_5110/2250P40-5**F045** **(4331)**
2001/02: 21^{5}S, 20^{F}GS, 16^{0}GS, 20^{4}S, 16^{5}S

	Starts	1st	2nd	3rd	Win & Pl
Hurdles	1	0	0	0	0
Chases	4	0	0	0	338
Career Total	**18**	**4**	**2**	**0**	**10869**

106	1/00	Sedg	2m5f110y	E Hdl	SFT	£2537
97	1/00	Sedg	2m5f110y	E Hdl	SFT	£2502
106	11/99	Hexm	2m	H NHF	GD	£1618
105	10/99	Carl	2m1f	H NHF	GD	£1710

Total win prize-money £8370

Going: Sf: 0-3 GS: 0-2 Gd: 0-0 GF: - Fm: 0-0
Distance: 2m/2m3: 0-2 2m4-2m7: 0-3 3m+: 0-0
Track: LH: 0-3 RH: 0-2 Tight: 0-5 Gall: 0-0
Aids: Bl: 0-3 Vi: 0-0 Tstrap: 0-0
Best Rating: 112 11/00 Hayd 2m7f110y soft Hdl

A winner twice over hurdles at Sedgefield, she has shown little aptitude for jumping fences.

Poetic Intrigue

106(87c) **96**
10-y-o b g Rymer-Deep Chat (Deep Run)
Miss Lucinda V Russell A R Trotter

Placings:F/UB5/6650664-0S35 **(0647)**
2001/02: 21^{0}G, 25^{S}GF, 24^{3}F, 24^{5}GF

	Starts	1st	2nd	3rd	Win & Pl
Hurdles	3	0	0	1	355
Chases	1	0	0	0	0
Career Total	**15**	**0**	**0**	**1**	**911**

Going: Sf: 0-0 GS: 0-0 Gd: 0-1 GF: - Fm: 0-3
Distance: 2m/2m3: 0-0 2m4-2m7: 0-1 3m+: 0-3
Track: LH: 0-3 RH: 0-1 Tight: 0-1 Gall: 0-0
Aids: Bl: 0-0 Vi: 0-0 Tstrap: 0-4
Best Rating: 96 4/01 Ayr 3m110y good Hdl

Point

77f **113f**
5-y-o b g Polish Precedent (USA)-Sixslip (USA) (Diesis)
W Jenks W Jenks

Placings:_140_ **(4679)**
2001/02: 16^{1}S, 16^{4}S, 17^{0}G

	Starts	1st	2nd	3rd	Win & Pl
NH Flat	3	1	0	0	2207
Career Total	**3**	**1**	**0**	**0**	**2207**

104	1/02	Newc	2m	H NHF	SFT	£1568

Total win prize-money £1568

Going: Sf: 1-2 GS: 0-0 Gd: 0-1 GF: - Fm: 0-0
Distance: **2m/2m3: 1-3** 2m4-2m7: 0-0 3m+: 0-0
Track: LH: 0-1 RH: 0-0 Tight: 0-0 Gall: 0-0
Aids: Bl: 0-0 Vi: 0-0 Tstrap: 0-0
Best Rating: 113 4/02 Aint 2m1f good NHF

Easy winner of his bumper debut, held in better company.

Polar Champ

111(107h) (130h)**137+**
9-y-o b g Polar Falcon (USA)-Ceramic (USA) (Raja Baba (USA))
M C Pipe The Reims Partnership

Placings:441200/54000/1111111430P-4101 **(4501)**
2001/02: 21^{4}HY, 20^{1}S, 21^{0}GS, 27^{1}G

	Starts	1st	2nd	3rd	Win & Pl
Hurdles	4	2	0	0	5380
Career Total	**26**	**10**	**1**	**1**	**38424**

116	3/02	NAbb	3m3f	F Hdl	GD	£2254
130	1/02	Leic	2m4f110y	F Hdl	SFT	£3125
155	10/00	Towc	3m	C(0-135)HHdl	G-S	£4745
141	8/00	Worc	3m	C(0-135)HHdl	G-F	£6710
154	7/00	NAbb	3m3f	C(0-130)HHdl	G-F	£4654
135	6/00	NAbb	2m6f	D(0-120)HHdl	G-F	£2887
134	6/00	Strf	3m3f	D(0-125)HHdl	GD	£3185
129	5/00	Uttx	3m110y	F(0-105)HHdl	G-F	£2051
113	5/00	Uttx	2m4f110y	G(0-100)HHdl	GD	£1715

115 12/98 Bang 2m1f E Hdl G-S £2358
Total win prize-money £33686

Going: Sf: 1-2 GS: 0-1 Gd: 1-1 GF: - Fm: 0-0
Distance: 2m/2m3: 0-0 2m4-2m7: 1-3 3m+: 1-1
Track: LH: 1-2 RH: 1-2 **Tight: 1-1** Gall: 0-1
Aids: Bl: 0-0 Vi: 0-0 Tstrap: 0-0
Best Rating: 155 10/00 Towc 3m gd-sft Hdl

Much improved after joining Martin Pipe, he won seven hurdle races on the bounce at up to three miles three furlongs between May and October 2000. Effective on any ground, he is not that well handicapped, and had to drop to a claimer to return to winning form in January 2002 before scoring over an extreme trip at Newton Abbot in March. Successful on his first three runs over fences in June and July.

Polar Party

8-y-o b m Arctic Lord-Festive Season (Silly Season)
R J Armson R J Armson

Placings:02/046F4-P **(0192)**
2001/02: 24^{P}GF

	Starts	1st	2nd	3rd	Win & Pl
Chases	1	0	0	0	
Career Total	**8**	**0**	**1**	**0**	**1922**

Going: Sf: 0-0 GS: 0-0 Gd: 0-0 GF: - Fm: 0-1
Distance: 2m/2m3: 0-0 2m4-2m7: 0-0 3m+: 0-1
Track: LH: 0-1 RH: 0-0 Tight: 0-1 Gall: 0-0
Aids: Bl: 0-0 Vi: 0-0 Tstrap: 0-0
Best Rating: 85 4/00 Tntn 2m3f gd-sft Ch

Polar Peer

(101h) (103h)
8-y-o b g Arctic Lord-Gilzie Bank (New Brig)
C J Mann Dodd Fox Hunter

Placings:0004/26-1P **(0505)**
2001/02: 22^{1}GF, 20^{P}GF

	Starts	1st	2nd	3rd	Win & Pl
Hurdles	1	1	0	0	2660
Chases	1	0	0	0	0
Career Total	**8**	**1**	**1**	**0**	**3670**

103 5/01 NAbb 2m6f E Hdl G-F £2660
Total win prize-money £2660

Going: Sf: 0-0 GS: 0-0 Gd: 0-0 GF: - Fm: 1-2
Distance: 2m/2m3: 0-0 **2m4-2m7: 1-2** 3m+: 0-0
Track: **LH: 1-1** RH: 0-1 **Tight: 1-1** Gall: 0-1
Aids: Bl: 0-0 Vi: 0-0 Tstrap: 0-0
Best Rating: 103 5/01 NAbb 2m6f gd-fm Hdl

Polar Prospect

112(107h) 145
9-y-o b g Polar Falcon (USA)-Littlemisstrouble (USA) (My Gallant (USA))
P J Hobbs Mr & Mrs Don Last And Bill Yates

Placings:1413021/222531252020/F530-**3212336312** **(4151)**
2001/02: 17^{3}GS, 20^{2}G, 16^{1}S, 16^{2}S, 16^{3}G, 19^{3}S, 20^{6}G, 16^{3}GS, 19^{1}G, 19^{2}GS

	Starts	1st	2nd	3rd	Win & Pl
Chases	10	2	3	4	16254
Career Total	**33**	**6**	**10**	**7**	**78076**

145 3/02 Extr 2m3f110y D Ch GD £4013
121 10/01 Towc 2m110y D Ch SFT £6129
141 12/98 Sand 2m110y B(0-150)HHdl GD £34562
125 4/98 Chep 2m110y E Hdl HVY £2374
119 1/98 Tntn 2m1f E Hdl SFT £2351
110 12/97 Uttx 2m E Hdl G-S £2557
Total win prize-money £51989

Going: Sf: 1-3 GS: 0-3 Gd: 1-4 GF: - Fm: 0-0
Distance: 2m/2m3: 1-5 2m4-2m7: 1-5 3m+: 0-0
Track: LH: 0-3 **RH: 2-7** Tight: 0-1 Gall: 0-0
Aids: **Bl: 1-5** Vi: 0-0 Tstrap: 0-0
Best Rating: 150 2/99 Asct 2m4f gd-sft Hdl

Formerly a solid performer over hurdles, he is a decent novice chaser effective at up to two and a half miles.

Polar Red

118 154
5-y-o ch g Polar Falcon (USA)-Sharp Top (Sharpo)
M C Pipe Stanley W Clarke

Placings:222110 **(4256)**
2001/02: 20^{2}GS, 20^{2}HY, 19^{2}G, 17^{1}HY, 16^{1}GS, 17^{0}G

	Starts	1st	2nd	3rd	Win & Pl
Hurdles	6	2	3	0	41424
Career Total	**6**	**2**	**3**	**0**	**41424**

154 3/02 Sand 2m110y B(0-150)HHdl G-S £26100
153 1/02 Chel 2m1f D(0-120)HHdl HVY £9360
Total win prize-money £35460

Going: Sf: 1-2 GS: 1-2 Gd: 0-2 GF: - Fm: 0-0
Distance: **2m/2m3: 2-4** 2m4-2m7: 0-2 3m+: 0-0
Track: LH: 1-3 RH: 1-3 Tight: 0-0 **Gall: 1-2**
Aids: Bl: 0-0 **Vi: 2-3** Tstrap: 0-0
Best Rating: 154 3/02 Sand 2m110y gd-sft Hdl

Novice hurdler, impressive winner of a handicap at Cheltenham in January in testing ground when dropped in trip and tried in a visor, and just landed a massive gamble in the Imperial Cup at Sandown. Failed to complete the hat-trick in the County Hurdle on faster ground. Suited by cut in the ground.

Polar Star

5-y-o b g Polar Falcon (USA)-Glowing With Pride (Ile De Bourbon (USA))
M C Pipe Mr & Mrs Malcolm B Jones

Placings:205-OF **(1803)**
2001/02: 17°F, 16^{F}GF

	Starts	1st	2nd	3rd	Win & Pl
Hurdles	2	0	0	0	
Career Total	**5**	**0**	**1**	**0**	**658**

Going: Sf: 0-0 GS: 0-0 Gd: 0-0 GF: - Fm: 0-2
Distance: 2m/2m3: 0-2 2m4-2m7: 0-0 3m+: 0-0
Track: LH: 0-0 RH: 0-2 Tight: 0-1 Gall: 0-0
Aids: Bl: 0-0 Vi: 0-0 Tstrap: 0-0
Best Rating: 100 1/01 Kemp 2m soft Hdl

Polar Summit (IRE)

96 84
6-y-o br g Top Of The World-Blackrath Beauty (Le Tricolore)
N A Twiston-Davies The Summit Partnership

Placings:50P-40 **(1865)**
2001/02: 24^{4}G, 25^{0}G

	Starts	1st	2nd	3rd	Win & Pl
Hurdles	2	0	0	0	0
Career Total	**5**	**0**	**0**	**0**	**0**

Going: Sf: 0-0 GS: 0-0 Gd: 0-2 GF: - Fm: 0-0
Distance: 2m/2m3: 0-0 2m4-2m7: 0-0 3m+: 0-2
Track: LH: 0-2 RH: 0-0 Tight: 0-1 Gall: 0-1
Aids: Bl: 0-0 Vi: 0-0 Tstrap: 0-0
Best Rating: 99 11/00 Chel 2m110y gd-sft NHF

Polden Pride

14-y-o b g Vital Season-Bybrook (Border Chief)
Mrs L Borradaile (G B Balding 17/2) Mrs L Borradaile

Placings:F000/50F515/122404311132UU1/11322214/ **310/F4441P4234F/6142323213/24212632P-0502434044** **(4852)**
2001/02: 22^{0}GF, 26^{5}G, 23^{0}G, 24^{2}G, 22^{4}GF, 23^{3}GF, 21^{4}GF, 24^{0}GF, 24^{4}G, 24^{4}G

	Starts	1st	2nd	3rd	Win & Pl
Chases	10	0	1	1	2756
Career Total	**76**	**14**	**15**	**10**	**75157**

116 6/00 Strf 3m D(0-125)HCh G-S £4095
118 12/99 Leic 2m4f110y D(0-125)HCh G-F £4467
118 8/99 Font 2m6f E(0-115)HCh G-F £3355
124 7/98 NAbb 2m5f110y D(0-120)HCh G-F £3387
117 5/97 NAbb 2m5f110y C(0-135)HCh G-S £4287
117 4/97 NAbb 2m5f110y D(0-125)HCh FRM £3533
110 5/96 NAbb 2m5f110y C(0-135)HCh GD £4765
104 5/96 Font 2m3f D(0-125)HCh G-F £3595
102 4/96 Font 2m2f E(0-120)HCh G-F £3206
102 10/95 Hrfd 2m3f F(0-100)HCh G-F £2690
99 9/95 Chel 3m1f110y E(0-110)HCh GD £3387
95 9/95 Worc 2m F(0-100)HCh G-F £2615
79 5/95 Hrfd 2m3f110y G(0-95)HHdl G-F £2070
70 4/95 NAbb 2m6f F(0-100)HHdl G-F £2712
Total win prize-money £48173

Going: Sf: 0-0 GS: 0-0 Gd: 0-5 GF: - Fm: 0-5
Distance: 2m/2m3: 0-0 2m4-2m7: 0-3 3m+: 0-7
Track: LH: 0-4 RH: 0-4 Tight: 0-7 Gall: 0-0
Aids: Bl: 0-0 Vi: 0-0 Tstrap: 0-0
Best Rating: 124 7/98 NAbb 2m5f110y gd-fm Ch

Game veteran chaser, suited by fast ground.

Poliantas (FR)

113 145
5-y-o b g Rasi Brasak-Popie D'Ecorcei (FR) (Balsamo (FR))
P F Nicholls Mark Tincknell

Placings:212P331-112121 **(4903)**
2001/02: 17^{1}GS, 20^{1}S, 19^{2}GS, 19^{1}S, 19^{2}GS, 24^{1}G

	Starts	1st	2nd	3rd	Win & Pl
Hurdles	1	1	0	0	10669
Chases	5	3	2	0	28751
Career Total	**13**	**6**	**4**	**2**	**56110**

145 4/02 Sand 3m110y B Ch GD £16337
105 3/02 Tntn 2m3f D Ch SFT £4777
132 2/02 Sand 2m4f110y D Ch SFT £4845
6/01 Pari 2m1f Hdl G-S £10669
4/01 Nanc 2m1f Hdl HLD £3880
10/00 Pari 2m1f Hdl HVY £4365
Total win prize-money £44875

Going: Sf: 2-2 GS: 1-3 Gd: 1-1 GF: - Fm: 0-0
Distance: **2m/2m3: 2-3** 2m4-2m7: 1-2 3m+: 1-1
Track: LH: 0-1 **RH: 3-4 Tight: 1-2** Gall: 0-1
Aids: Bl: 0-0 Vi: 0-0 Tstrap: 0-0
Best Rating: 145 4/02 Sand 3m110y good Ch

A narrow type, he is a winner over hurdles in France and has been very consistent since arriving in this country including two victories and Sandown and one at Taunton. He has won over three miles on fast ground, but that looked right on the limit of his stamina.

Polish Baron (IRE)

106 **113**

5-y-o b g Barathea (IRE)-Polish Mission (Polish Precedent (USA))

J White (P J Hobbs 24/8) Nick Quesnel

Placings:1156-121F41P0 **(4680)**

2001/02: 17^{1}GF, 20^{2}GF, 18^{1}G, 20^{F}G, 18^{4}S, 16^{1}S, 16^{P}HY, 17^{0}GF

	Starts	1st	2nd	3rd	Win & Pl
Hurdles	8	3	1	0	9982
Career Total	**12**	**5**	**1**	**0**	**18757**

103	2/02	Hntg	2m110y	F Hdl	SFT	£1895
110	12/01	Font	2m2f110y	G Hdl	GD	£3094
110	5/01	NAbb	2m1f	D(0-125)HHdl	G-F	£4134
107	1/01	Plum	2m	E Hdl	SFT	£1918
107	11/00	Hntg	2m110y	B Hdl	G-S	£6857

Total win prize-money £17900

Going: Sf: 1-3 GS: 0-0 Gd: 1-2 GF: - Fm: 1-3
Distance: **2m/2m3: 3-6** 2m4-2m7: 0-2 3m+: 0-0
Track: **LH: 2-5** RH: 1-2 **Tight: 2-5** Gall: 1-1
Aids: Bl: 0-0 Vi: 0-0 Tstrap: 0-0
Best Rating: 113 8/01 Worc 2m4f gd-fm Hdl

He has a good winning record over hurdles at a modest level at up to two and a quarter miles. Acts on fast ground, but is suited by softer.

Polish Flame

108 **131**

4-y-o b g Blushing Flame (USA)-Lady Emm (Emarati (USA))

Mrs M Reveley Falcon Assets

Placings:6114 **(2885)**

2001/02: 16^{6}G, 16^{1}GS, 16^{1}GS, 16^{4}GS

	Starts	1st	2nd	3rd	Win & Pl
Hurdles	4	2	0	0	7886
Career Total	**4**	**2**	**0**	**0**	**7886**

115	12/01	Newc	2m	D Hdl	G-S	£3386
110	11/01	Ayr	2m	E Hdl	G-S	£2999

Total win prize-money £6387

Going: Sf: 0-0 GS: 2-3 Gd: 0-1 GF: - Fm: 0-0
Distance: **2m/2m3: 2-4** 2m4-2m7: 0-0 3m+: 0-0
Track: **LH: 2-4** RH: 0-0 Tight: 0-0 **Gall: 1-1**
Aids: Bl: 0-0 Vi: 0-0 Tstrap: 0-0
Best Rating: 131 12/01 Chep 2m110y gd-sft Hdl

Decent hurdler suited by two miles and cut in the ground.

Polish Paddy (IRE)

99 **88+**

4-y-o b g Priolo (USA)-Polish Widow (Polish Precedent (USA))

J W Mullins (R Hannon 9/10) Denis Barry

Placings:05000601 **(4657)**

2001/02: 16^{0}G, 16^{5}G, 16^{0}GS, 18^{0}S, 19^{0}S, 26^{6}G, 19^{0}S, 24^{1}G

	Starts	1st	2nd	3rd	Win & Pl
Hurdles	8	1	0	0	1750
Career Total	**8**	**1**	**0**	**0**	**1750**

80	4/02	Tntn	3m110y	G(0-95)HHdl	GD	£1750

Total win prize-money £1750

Going: Sf: 0-3 GS: 0-1 Gd: 1-4 GF: - Fm: 0-0
Distance: 2m/2m3: 0-5 2m4-2m7: 0-1 **3m+: 1-2**
Track: LH: 0-4 **RH: 1-4 Tight: 1-3** Gall: 0-3
Aids: Bl: 0-0 **Vi: 1-1** Tstrap: 0-0
Best Rating: 87 12/01 Winc 2m good Hdl

Modest selling-class hurdler. Scored at Taunton and Huntingdon in the spring of 2002, both times in a visor. Looks to need trips of around three miles and fast ground.

Polish Pilot (IRE)

99(103h) (76h)**87**

7-y-o b g Polish Patriot (USA)-Va Toujours (Alzao (USA))

J R Cornwall J R Cornwall

Placings:3321602/43P0040-4P0P531543P4 **(4905)**

2001/02: 16^{4}GF, 16^{P}GF, 17^{0}GF, 20^{P}G, 20^{5}GF, 17^{3}S, 16^{1}GS, 16^{5}S, 16^{4}S, 17^{3}GS, 16^{P}HY, 17^{4}GF

	Starts	1st	2nd	3rd	Win & Pl
Hurdles	2	1	0	0	2352
Chases	10	0	0	2	2069
Career Total	**26**	**2**	**2**	**5**	**8435**

76	1/02	Sthl	2m	F(0-95)HHdl	G-S	£2352
105	11/99	Worc	2m	E(0-105)HHdl	GD	£2267

Total win prize-money £4620

Going: Sf: 0-4 GS: 1-2 Gd: 0-1 GF: - Fm: 0-5
Distance: **2m/2m3: 1-10** 2m4-2m7: 0-2 3m+: 0-0
Track: **LH: 1-4** RH: 0-8 **Tight: 1-8** Gall: 0-1
Aids: Bl: 0-1 Vi: 0-0 Tstrap: 0-5
Best Rating: 105 11/99 Worc 2m good Hdl

Very moderate hurdler/chaser, best at around two miles.

Polish Spirit

103(97h) (101h)**109**

7-y-o b g Emarati (USA)-Gentle Star (Comedy Star (USA))

P J Hobbs Peter Luff

Placings:44F00 **(4848)**

2001/02: 17^{4}S, 16^{4}G, 16^{F}GS, 16^{0}G, 16^{0}G

	Starts	1st	2nd	3rd	Win & Pl
Hurdles	5	0	0	0	286
Career Total	**5**	**0**	**0**	**0**	**286**

Going: Sf: 0-1 GS: 0-1 Gd: 0-3 GF: - Fm: 0-0
Distance: 2m/2m3: 0-5 2m4-2m7: 0-0 3m+: 0-0
Track: LH: 0-3 RH: 0-2 Tight: 0-3 Gall: 0-0
Aids: Bl: 0-0 Vi: 0-0 Tstrap: 0-0
Best Rating: 101 2/02 Winc 2m gd-sft Hdl

He has won over fences, but looks a quirky sort.

Politburo

103(94h) (74h)**107**

7-y-o b g Presidium-Kitty Come Home (Monsanto (FR))

J T Gifford Mrs J F Hall

Placings:*0/0*-005FP501 **(4780)**

2001/02: 17^{0}GS, 19^{0}GF, 18^{5}GF, 18^{F}S, 20^{P}S, 16^{5}GF, 16^{0}GS, 17^{1}GF

	Starts	1st	2nd	3rd	Win & Pl
Hurdles	6	0	0	0	0
Chases	2	1	0	0	3416
Career Total	**10**	**1**	**0**	**0**	**3416**

107	4/02	Plum	2m1f	E Ch	G-F	£3415

Total win prize-money £3416

Going: Sf: 0-2 GS: 0-2 Gd: 0-0 GF: - Fm: 1-4
Distance: **2m/2m3: 1-6** 2m4-2m7: 0-2 3m+: 0-0
Track: **LH: 1-4** RH: 0-4 **Tight: 1-6** Gall: 0-1
Aids: Bl: 0-0 Vi: 0-0 Tstrap: 0-0
Best Rating: 107 4/02 Plum 2m1f gd-fm Ch

Did not take to hurdling, but landed a weak novices' chase second time out on a sound surface.

Political Mandate

105 **88**

9-y-o br m Respect-Political Mill (Politico (USA))

R Nixon G R S Nixon

Placings:*0606/20000PP0002/PFP5P4F664P55/322P 0565P4/P00P0F3*-6043 **(0472)**

2001/02: 16^{6}S, 16^{0}GF, 16^{4}S, 20^{3}GF

	Starts	1st	2nd	3rd	Win & Pl
Chases	4	0	0	1	694
Career Total	**49**	**0**	**4**	**3**	**6365**

Going: Sf: 0-2 GS: 0-0 Gd: 0-0 GF: - Fm: 0-2
Distance: 2m/2m3: 0-3 2m4-2m7: 0-1 3m+: 0-0
Track: LH: 0-3 RH: 0-1 Tight: 0-0 Gall: 0-0
Aids: Bl: 0-0 Vi: 0-0 Tstrap: 0-0
Best Rating: 98 5/99 Prth 2m heavy Ch

Political Sox

100(105h) (77h)**87**

8-y-o br g Mirror Boy-Political Mill (Politico (USA))

R Nixon G R S Nixon

Placings:*640/466000425P340/605100*-05005230322340 **(4877)**

2001/02: 20^{0}GF, 20^{5}GF, 22^{0}G, 18^{0}G, 20^{5}G, 20^{2}HY, 20^{3}S, 24^{0}G, 24^{3}S, 20^{2}HY, 27^{2}S, 22^{3}HY, 27^{4}S, 24^{0}G

	Starts	1st	2nd	3rd	Win & Pl
Hurdles	14	0	3	3	4265
Career Total	**36**	**1**	**4**	**4**	**8662**

84	2/01	Kels	2m110y	F(0-100)HHdl	SFT	£2772

Total win prize-money £2772

Going: Sf: 0-7 GS: 0-0 Gd: 0-5 GF: - Fm: 0-2
Distance: 2m/2m3: 0-1 2m4-2m7: 0-8 3m+: 0-5
Track: LH: 0-10 RH: 0-3 Tight: 0-5 Gall: 0-3
Aids: Bl: 0-3 Vi: 0-0 Tstrap: 0-0
Best Rating: 95 4/99 Hexm 2m good NHF

Modest hurdler, stays three miles three, suited by soft ground.

Polka

89 **82**

7-y-o b g Slip Anchor-Peace Dance (Bikala)

V G Greenway V G Greenway

Placings:00060P **(4484)**

2001/02: 17^{0}G, 17^{0}HY, 17^{0}S, 17^{6}S, 24^{0}S, 17^{P}G

	Starts	1st	2nd	3rd	Win & Pl
Hurdles	6	0	0	0	0
Career Total	**6**	**0**	**0**	**0**	**0**

Going: Sf: 0-4 GS: 0-0 Gd: 0-2 GF: - Fm: 0-0
Distance: 2m/2m3: 0-5 2m4-2m7: 0-0 3m+: 0-1
Track: LH: 0-1 RH: 0-5 Tight: 0-5 Gall: 0-0
Aids: Bl: 0-0 Vi: 0-0 Tstrap: 0-0
Best Rating: 82 2/02 Tntn 2m1f soft Hdl

Polligana

95 **104**

6-y-o b g Lugana Beach-Pollibrig (Politico (USA))

V R A Dartnall (Miss D Cole 11/6) W Westacott

Placings:*00*023 **(4850)**

2001/02: 17^{0}G, 17^{0}S, 19^{0}S, 22^{2}G, 22^{3}G

Starts	1st	2nd	3rd	Win & Pl	
NH Flat	1	0	0	0	0
Hurdles	4	0	1	1	1334
Career Total	**5**	**0**	**1**	**1**	**1334**

Going: Sf: 0-2 GS: 0-0 Gd: 0-3 GF: - Fm: 0-0
Distance: 2m/2m3: 0-2 2m4-2m7: 0-3 3m+: 0-0
Track: LH: 0-2 RH: 0-3 Tight: 0-4 Gall: 0-0
Aids: Bl: 0-0 Vi: 0-0 Tstrap: 0-0
Best Rating: 104 4/02 Winc 2m6f good Hdl

Modest novice hurdler. Acts on good ground.

Polly Live Wire

8-y-o b m El Conquistador-Flash Wire (Flatbush)
P J Millington P J Millington

Placings:F0F0PPP-PPF4P (0427)
2001/02: 25^{P}S, 24^{P}GF, 31^{F}G, 25^{4}G, 33^{P}G

	Starts	1st	2nd	3rd	Win & Pl
Chases	5	0	0	0	145
Career Total	**12**	**0**	**0**	**0**	**145**

Going: Sf: 0-1 GS: 0-0 Gd: 0-3 GF: - Fm: 0-1
Distance: 2m/2m3: 0-0 2m4-2m7: 0-0 3m+: 0-5
Track: LH: 0-2 RH: 0-2 Tight: 0-2 Gall: 0-1
Aids: Bl: 0-0 Vi: 0-0 Tstrap: 0-0
Best Rating: 61 7/00 Strf 3m gd-fm Ch

Polly Pepperpot

84 58

5-y-o b m Phountzi (USA)-Mrs Pepperpot (Kinglet)
Dr P Pritchard A J Whiting

Placings:*00* (4881)
2001/02: 17^{0}G, 18^{0}GF

	Starts	1st	2nd	3rd	Win & Pl
NH Flat	1	0	0	0	0
Hurdles	1	0	0	0	0
Career Total	**2**	**0**	**0**	**0**	

Going: Sf: 0-0 GS: 0-0 Gd: 0-1 GF: - Fm: 0-1
Distance: 2m/2m3: 0-2 2m4-2m7: 0-0 3m+: 0-0
Track: LH: 0-2 RH: 0-0 Tight: 0-2 Gall: 0-0
Aids: Bl: 0-0 Vi: 0-0 Tstrap: 0-0
Best Rating: 58 4/02 Font 2m2f110y gd-fm Hdl

Polly Tino

73 40

6-y-o b m Neltino-Flying Mistress (Lear Jet)
R J Armson (Mrs P Sly 13/12) R J Armson

Placings:*00-0P00P* (4303)
2001/02: 16^{0}S, 20^{P}GS, 16^{0}S, 17^{0}GS, 16^{P}HY

	Starts	1st	2nd	3rd	Win & Pl
Hurdles	5	0	0	0	
Career Total	**7**	**0**	**0**	**0**	

Going: Sf: 0-3 GS: 0-2 Gd: 0-0 GF: - Fm: 0-0
Distance: 2m/2m3: 0-4 2m4-2m7: 0-1 3m+: 0-0
Track: LH: 0-2 RH: 0-3 Tight: 0-1 Gall: 0-1
Aids: Bl: 0-0 Vi: 0-0 Tstrap: 0-1
Best Rating: 60 3/01 MRas 2m1f110y good NHF

Polo Kit (IRE)

11-y-o b g Trempolino (USA)-Nikitina (Nijinsky (CAN))
Mrs N S Sharpe K Morgan

Placings:P5/PUP/P (1273)
2001/02: 24^{P}GF

	Starts	1st	2nd	3rd	Win & Pl
Hurdles	1	0	0	0	
Career Total	**6**	**0**	**0**	**0**	**0**

Going: Sf: 0-0 GS: 0-0 Gd: 0-0 GF: - Fm: 0-1
Distance: 2m/2m3: 0-0 2m4-2m7: 0-0 3m+: 0-1
Track: LH: 0-1 RH: 0-0 Tight: 0-1 Gall: 0-0
Aids: Bl: 0-0 Vi: 0-0 Tstrap: 0-0
Best Rating: 67 10/96 Plum 2m4f gd-fm Hdl

Poly Amanshaa (IRE)

99(105c) 100

10-y-o b/br g Nashamaa-Mombones (Lord Gayle (USA))
W Jarvis M C Banks

Placings:005143/22/3532/312/05**15414P/02U-24** (0502)
2001/02: 21^{2}GF, 21^{4}GF

	Starts	1st	2nd	3rd	Win & Pl
Hurdles	2	0	1	0	577
Career Total	**28**	**4**	**6**	**4**	**22399**

123	1/00	Donc	2m3f110y	D Ch	GD	£4134
121	12/99	Fknm	2m5f110y	D Ch	GD	£3635
97	5/98	Towc	2m	D(0-125)HHdl	G-F	£2805
87	4/96	Fknm	2m	E(0-100)HHdl	GD	£2885

Total win prize-money £13459

Going: Sf: 0-0 GS: 0-0 Gd: 0-0 GF: - Fm: 0-2
Distance: 2m/2m3: 0-0 2m4-2m7: 0-2 3m+: 0-0
Track: LH: 0-0 RH: 0-2 Tight: 0-0 Gall: 0-2
Aids: Bl: 0-0 Vi: 0-0 Tstrap: 0-0
Best Rating: 128 1/01 Donc 2m3f110y good Ch

Polydamas

82(96c) (119c)76

10-y-o b g Last Tycoon-Graecia Magna (USA) (Private Account (USA))
Dr P Pritchard David & Lesley Byrne

Placings:340/33131026/**11P1**/55030P0P (4853)
2001/02: 21^{5}GS, 21^{5}G, 20^{0}G, 24^{3}S, 19^{0}GS, 17^{P}S, 16^{0}GS, 16^{P}G

	Starts	1st	2nd	3rd	Win & Pl
Hurdles	2	0	0	0	0
Chases	6	0	0	1	667
Career Total	**23**	**5**	**1**	**5**	**23749**

140	1/00	Ludl	2m	E Ch	GD	£2873
142	12/99	Ludl	2m	E Ch	GD	£3192
142	11/99	Wwck	2m4f	D Ch	GD	£4085
108	3/98	Ludl	2m	E Hdl	GD	£2584
122	11/97	Newb	2m110y	C Hdl	SFT	£4240

Total win prize-money £16976

Going: Sf: 0-2 GS: 0-3 Gd: 0-3 GF: - Fm: 0-0
Distance: 2m/2m3: 0-4 2m4-2m7: 0-3 3m+: 0-1
Track: LH: 0-5 RH: 0-3 Tight: 0-5 Gall: 0-1
Aids: Bl: 0-1 Vi: 0-0 Tstrap: 0-0
Best Rating: 142 12/99 Ludl 2m good Ch

A useful novice hurdler in his day, he has been short of his best this term after missing a season. Suited by good ground.

Polyphony (USA)

(89h) (55h)

8-y-o b g Cox's Ridge (USA)-Populi (USA) (Star Envoy (USA))
D C O'Brien Mrs S Harris

Placings:5/32400/66/**36F6P-PP65** (3812)
2001/02: 26^{P}G, 17^{P}G, 20^{6}S, 17^{5}S

	Starts	1st	2nd	3rd	Win & Pl
Hurdles	2	0	0	0	0
Chases	2	0	0	0	0
Career Total	**17**	**0**	**1**	**2**	**1449**

Going: Sf: 0-2 GS: 0-0 Gd: 0-2 GF: - Fm: 0-0
Distance: 2m/2m3: 0-2 2m4-2m7: 0-1 3m+: 0-1
Track: LH: 0-1 RH: 0-3 Tight: 0-4 Gall: 0-0
Aids: Bl: 0-0 Vi: 0-1 Tstrap: 0-0
Best Rating: 90 1/99 Folk 2m6f110y heavy Hdl

Pontabula

12-y-o b g Sula Bula-Lady Penstone (Jimsun)
H J Manners H J Manners

Placings:*000325P*/1/21/3/3P3/3P (4517)
2001/02: 26^{3}G, 22^{P}GS

	Starts	1st	2nd	3rd	Win & Pl
Chases	2	0	0	1	168
Career Total	**16**	**2**	**2**	**5**	**5751**

107	3/00	Leic	2m4f110y	H Ch	GFT	£2010
86	5/96	Folk	2m5f	H Ch	GD	£1800

Total win prize-money £3810

Going: Sf: 0-0 GS: 0-1 Gd: 0-1 GF: - Fm: 0-0
Distance: 2m/2m3: 0-0 2m4-2m7: 0-1 3m+: 0-1
Track: LH: 0-1 RH: 0-1 Tight: 0-0 Gall: 0-0
Aids: Bl: 0-0 Vi: 0-0 Tstrap: 0-0
Best Rating: 109 3/99 Newb 3m soft Ch

A pointer who is too slow under Rules.

Pontius

98 92

5-y-o b g Terimon-Coole Pilate (Celtic Cone)
N A Twiston-Davies H R Mould

Placings:033 (4880)
2001/02: 22^{0}GS, 26^{3}G, 20^{3}G

	Starts	1st	2nd	3rd	Win & Pl
Hurdles	3	0	0	2	988
Career Total	**3**	**0**	**0**	**2**	**988**

Going: Sf: 0-0 GS: 0-1 Gd: 0-2 GF: - Fm: 0-0
Distance: 2m/2m3: 0-0 2m4-2m7: 0-2 3m+: 0-1
Track: LH: 0-1 RH: 0-2 Tight: 0-1 Gall: 0-0
Aids: Bl: 0-0 Vi: 0-0 Tstrap: 0-0
Best Rating: 92 4/02 Prth 2m4f110y good Hdl

Pooh Blair

31f 57f

5-y-o b m Contract Law (USA)-Saffron Delight (Idiots Delight)
J R Best Mrs C L Taylor

Placings:*00* (3606)
2001/02: 17^{0}S, 18^{0}HY

	Starts	1st	2nd	3rd	Win & Pl
NH Flat	2	0	0	0	
Career Total	**2**	**0**	**0**	**0**	

Going: Sf: 0-2 GS: 0-0 Gd: 0-0 GF: - Fm: 0-0
Distance: 2m/2m3: 0-2 2m4-2m7: 0-0 3m+: 0-0
Track: LH: 0-1 RH: 0-0 Tight: 0-2 Gall: 0-0
Aids: Bl: 0-0 Vi: 0-0 Tstrap: 0-0
Best Rating: **57** 1/02 Folk 2m1f110y soft NHF

Poon Hill (IRE)

99 **100**

6-y-o ch g Phardante (FR)-Pennyland (Le Bavard (FR))
R T Phillips Annapurna Partnership

Placings:4-32233 **(4513)**
2001/02: 17^{3}G, 16^{2}G, 20^{2}G, 24^{3}GS, 24^{3}GS

	Starts	1st	2nd	3rd	Win & Pl
NH Flat	2	0	1	1	987
Hurdles	3	0	1	2	1823
Career Total	**6**	**0**	**2**	**3**	**2810**

Going: Sf: 0-0 GS: 0-2 Gd: 0-3 GF: - Fm: 0-0
Distance: 2m/2m3: 0-2 2m4-2m7: 0-1 3m+: 0-2
Track: LH: 0-2 RH: 0-3 Tight: 0-1 Gall: 0-2
Aids: Bl: 0-0 Vi: 0-0 Tstrap: 0-0
Best Rating: **100** 3/02 Towc 3m gd-sft Hdl

Has shown definite promise in bumpers and novice hurdles, looking a stayer.

Poor Economics (IRE)

97 **66**

9-y-o b g Homo Sapien-Khalice (Khalkis)
Mrs H Dalton Mrs Heather Dalton

Placings:*00000P0/000P40-456* **(1045)**
2001/02: 25^{4}G, 24^{5}GF, 26^{6}GF

	Starts	1st	2nd	3rd	Win & Pl
Chases	3	0	0	0	247
Career Total	**16**	**0**	**0**	**0**	**558**

Going: Sf: 0-0 GS: 0-0 Gd: 0-1 GF: - Fm: 0-2
Distance: 2m/2m3: 0-0 2m4-2m7: 0-0 3m+: 0-3
Track: LH: 0-3 RH: 0-0 Tight: 0-1 Gall: 0-0
Aids: Bl: 0-0 Vi: 0-0 Tstrap: 0-0
Best Rating: **77** 2/01 Fknm 3m110y soft Ch

Popgoestheweasel

98 **84**

7-y-o b m Phardante (FR)-Poetic Light (Ardross)
Countess Goess-Saurau Countess Goess-Saurau

Placings:*1*-3F4 **(4726)**
2001/02: 20^{3}HY, 20^{F}S, 20^{4}GF

	Starts	1st	2nd	3rd	Win & Pl
Hurdles	3	0	0	1	381
Career Total	**4**	**1**	**0**	**1**	**1935**

101 12/00 Hntg 2m110y H NHF HVY £1554
Total win prize-money £1554

Going: Sf: 0-2 GS: 0-0 Gd: 0-0 GF: - Fm: 0-1
Distance: 2m/2m3: 0-0 2m4-2m7: 0-3 3m+: 0-0
Track: LH: 0-2 RH: 0-0 Tight: 0-1 Gall: 0-0
Aids: Bl: 0-0 Vi: 0-0 Tstrap: 0-0
Best Rating: **101** 12/00 Hntg 2m110y heavy NHF

Popsi's Cloggs

108 **108**

10-y-o ch g Joli Wasfi (USA)-Popsi's Poppet (Hill Clown (USA))
R Curtis The Popsi Partners

Placings:*3O/10*/PP**2P32/2U1P** **(4681)**
2001/02: 25^{2}G, 22^{U}G, 24^{1}G, 25^{P}GF

	Starts	1st	2nd	3rd	Win & Pl
Chases	4	1	1	0	6652
Career Total	**14**	**2**	**3**	**2**	**11774**

105 3/02 Sand 3m110y D(0-115)HCh GD £5772
95 5/98 Extr 2m2f H NHF GD £1486
Total win prize-money £7259

Going: Sf: 0-0 GS: 0-0 Gd: 1-3 GF: - Fm: 0-1
Distance: 2m/2m3: 0-0 2m4-2m7: 0-1 **3m+: 1-3**
Track: LH: 0-1 **RH: 1-3** Tight: 0-1 Gall: 0-1
Aids: Bl: 0-0 Vi: 0-0 Tstrap: 0-0
Best Rating: **108** 12/01 Folk 3m1f good Ch

Got off the mark at Sandown in March 2002. Suited by three miles and a sound surface.

Porak (IRE)

99 **114**

5-y-o ch g Perugino (USA)-Gayla Orchestra (Lord Gayle (USA))
G L Moore Allen, Manley, Pritchard, Russell

Placings:242 **(4171)**
2001/02: 16^{2}S, 16^{4}G, 16^{2}GS

	Starts	1st	2nd	3rd	Win & Pl
Hurdles	3	0	2	0	1959
Career Total	**3**	**0**	**2**	**0**	**1959**

Going: Sf: 0-1 GS: 0-1 Gd: 0-1 GF: - Fm: 0-0
Distance: 2m/2m3: 0-3 2m4-2m7: 0-0 3m+: 0-0
Track: LH: 0-2 RH: 0-1 Tight: 0-2 Gall: 0-0
Aids: Bl: 0-0 Vi: 0-0 Tstrap: 0-0
Best Rating: **114** 12/01 Plum 2m soft Hdl

A winner on the Flat, he showed promise over hurdles in 2001/02. Handles soft ground.

Porchester Close (IRE)

68f **37f**

4-y-o ch g Fourstars Allstar (USA)-Boardroom Belle (IRE) (Executive Perk)
M C Pipe D A Johnson

Placings:*0* **(4887)**
2001/02: 18^{0}GF

	Starts	1st	2nd	3rd	Win & Pl
NH Flat	1	0	0	0	
Career Total	**1**	**0**	**0**	**0**	

Going: Sf: 0-0 GS: 0-0 Gd: 0-0 GF: - Fm: 0-1
Distance: 2m/2m3: 0-1 2m4-2m7: 0-0 3m+: 0-0
Track: LH: 0-1 RH: 0-0 Tight: 0-1 Gall: 0-0
Aids: Bl: 0-0 Vi: 0-0 Tstrap: 0-0
Best Rating: **37** 4/02 Font 2m2f110y gd-fm NHF

Porlock Hill

8-y-o b g Petoski-Gay Ticket (New Member)
P J Hobbs Mrs S A Popham

Placings:P/FFP/**4RP** **(1244)**
2001/02: 16^{4}S, 26^{R}GF, 23^{P}GF

	Starts	1st	2nd	3rd	Win & Pl
Chases	3	0	0	0	212
Career Total	**7**	**0**	**0**	**0**	**212**

Going: Sf: 0-1 GS: 0-0 Gd: 0-0 GF: - Fm: 0-2
Distance: 2m/2m3: 0-1 2m4-2m7: 0-0 3m+: 0-2
Track: LH: 0-3 RH: 0-0 Tight: 0-0 Gall: 0-0
Aids: Bl: 0-0 Vi: 0-0 Tstrap: 0-0
Best Rating: **72** 7/01 Worc 2m soft Ch

Pornic (FR)

100(97h) (74h)**108**

8-y-o b g Shining Steel-Marie De Geneve (FR) (Nishapour (FR))
A Crook John Sinclair (haulage) Ltd

Placings:11436233/P5F053324223/110326431-50064033PPP **(4778)**
2001/02: 20^{5}GS, 16^{0}GF, 16^{0}GF, 16^{6}GF, 20^{4}G, 16^{0}GS, 17^{3}S, 16^{3}HY, 16^{P}S, 17^{P}G, 17^{P}G

	Starts	1st	2nd	3rd	Win & Pl
Hurdles	2	0	0	0	0
Chases	9	0	0	2	1662
Career Total	**40**	**5**	**5**	**10**	**36330**

108 4/01 MRas 2m1f110y E(0-115)HCh G-S £4078
118 6/00 Prth 2m E(0-115)HCh SFT £4095
120 5/00 MRas 2m1f110y D(0-120)HCh G-F £4192
5/98 Autl 2m2f Ch SFT £10101
Total win prize-money £22468

Going: Sf: 0-3 GS: 0-2 Gd: 0-3 GF: - Fm: 0-3
Distance: 2m/2m3: 0-9 2m4-2m7: 0-2 3m+: 0-0
Track: LH: 0-3 RH: 0-8 Tight: 0-4 Gall: 0-1
Aids: Bl: 0-0 Vi: 0-0 Tstrap: 0-0
Best Rating: **120** 5/00 MRas 2m1f110y gd-fm Ch

He is a real enigma who needs things to go his way over fences. Handles heavy.

Port Moresby (IRE)

81 **61**

4-y-o b g Tagula (IRE)-Santana Lady (IRE) (Blakeney)
N A Callaghan Martin Moore

Placings:04 **(2324)**
2001/02: 16^{0}G, 16^{4}S

	Starts	1st	2nd	3rd	Win & Pl
Hurdles	2	0	0	0	0
Career Total	**2**	**0**	**0**	**0**	**0**

Going: Sf: 0-1 GS: 0-0 Gd: 0-1 GF: - Fm: 0-0
Distance: 2m/2m3: 0-2 2m4-2m7: 0-0 3m+: 0-0
Track: LH: 0-1 RH: 0-1 Tight: 0-1 Gall: 0-1
Aids: Bl: 0-0 Vi: 0-0 Tstrap: 0-1
Best Rating: **61** 11/01 Fknm 2m soft Hdl

A useful Flat performer, has shown little over hurdles.

Port Valenska (IRE)

73 **42**

9-y-o b g Roi Danzig (USA)-Silvera (Ribero)
Dr P Pritchard Matthew Vick

Placings:0P00/50030000/0PP **(0641)**
2001/02: 17^{0}G, 22^{P}F, 24^{P}GF

	Starts	1st	2nd	3rd	Win & Pl
Hurdles	3	0	0	0	
Career Total	**15**	**0**	**0**	**1**	**246**

Going: Sf: 0-0 GS: 0-0 Gd: 0-1 GF: - Fm: 0-2
Distance: 2m/2m3: 0-1 2m4-2m7: 0-1 3m+: 0-1
Track: LH: 0-0 RH: 0-2 Tight: 0-1 Gall: 0-0
Aids: Bl: 0-0 Vi: 0-0 Tstrap: 0-0
Best Rating: **54** 9/97 MRas 2m1f110y good Hdl

Porters Lodge

9-y-o b g Balliol-Parabems (Swing Easy (USA))
R John Ronald & Lynn John

Placings:6PF-PP **(0563)**
2001/02: 19^{P}F, 26^{P}GF

	Starts	1st	2nd	3rd	Win & Pl
Chases	2	0	0	0	
Career Total	**5**	**0**	**0**	**0**	**0**

Going: Sf: 0-0 GS: 0-0 Gd: 0-0 GF: - Fm: 0-2
Distance: 2m/2m3: 0-0 2m4-2m7: 0-1 3m+: 0-1
Track: LH: 0-1 RH: 0-1 Tight: 0-1 Gall: 0-0
Aids: Bl: 0-0 Vi: 0-0 Tstrap: 0-0
Best Rating: 73 9/00 Extr 2m1f110y good Ch

Porterstown Dante (IRE)

92 90

10-y-o b g Phardante (FR)-Extra Chance (Pollerton)
G L Moore Grahame A Dedman

Placings:600/24UF/64P6-35P **(1594)**
2001/02: 20^{3}GF, 17^{5}GF, 16^{P}G

	Starts	1st	2nd	3rd	Win & Pl
Chases	3	0	0	1	471
Career Total	**14**	**0**	**1**	**1**	**1403**

Going: Sf: 0-0 GS: 0-0 Gd: 0-1 GF: - Fm: 0-2
Distance: 2m/2m3: 0-2 2m4-2m7: 0-1 3m+: 0-0
Track: LH: 0-2 RH: 0-1 Tight: 0-2 Gall: 0-1
Aids: Bl: 0-0 Vi: 0-0 Tstrap: 0-3
Best Rating: 99 1/99 Fair 2m heavy NHF

Portrack Junction (IRE)

79 57

5-y-o b g Common Grounds-Boldabsa (Persian Bold)
A B Mulholland Miss K Watson

Placings:50-00P **(1581)**
2001/02: 16^{0}GF, 17^{0}GF, 24^{P}GS

	Starts	1st	2nd	3rd	Win & Pl
Hurdles	3	0	0	0	
Career Total	**5**	**0**	**0**	**0**	**0**

Going: Sf: 0-0 GS: 0-1 Gd: 0-0 GF: - Fm: 0-2
Distance: 2m/2m3: 0-2 2m4-2m7: 0-0 3m+: 0-1
Track: LH: 0-0 RH: 0-3 Tight: 0-1 Gall: 0-1
Aids: Bl: 0-0 Vi: 0-0 Tstrap: 0-0
Best Rating: 71 11/00 Catt 2m good Hdl

Posh Spice (IRE)

11-y-o b m Neshad (USA)-Escalado (Homing)
Miss C F Elliott R Cook

Placings:35P611/2P-4 **(0321)**
2001/02: 26^{4}G

	Starts	1st	2nd	3rd	Win & Pl
Chases	1	0	0	0	113
Career Total	**9**	**2**	**1**	**1**	**5536**

93	3/98	Folk	2m6f110y	E(0-110)HHdl	GD	£2244
102	3/98	Plum	2m4f	F(0-105)HHdl	GD	£2176

Total win prize-money £4421

Going: Sf: 0-0 GS: 0-0 Gd: 0-1 GF: - Fm: 0-0
Distance: 2m/2m3: 0-0 2m4-2m7: 0-0 3m+: 0-1
Track: LH: 0-0 RH: 0-1 Tight: 0-1 Gall: 0-0
Aids: Bl: 0-0 Vi: 0-0 Tstrap: 0-0
Best Rating: 102 3/98 Plum 2m4f good Hdl

Posh Stick

53f 86f

5-y-o b m Rakaposhi King-Carat Stick (Gold Rod)
J B Walton F T Walton

Placings:000 **(4771)**
2001/02: 16^{0}S, 16^{0}HY, 16^{0}GF

	Starts	1st	2nd	3rd	Win & Pl
NH Flat	3	0	0	0	
Career Total	**3**	**0**	**0**	**0**	

Going: Sf: 0-2 GS: 0-0 Gd: 0-0 GF: - Fm: 0-1
Distance: 2m/2m3: 0-3 2m4-2m7: 0-0 3m+: 0-0
Track: LH: 0-1 RH: 0-0 Tight: 0-0 Gall: 0-0
Aids: Bl: 0-0 Vi: 0-0 Tstrap: 0-0
Best Rating: 86 3/02 Ayr 2m heavy NHF

Modest bumper form.

Poshgan (IRE)

77 56

8-y-o ch m Yashgan-Swanee Mistress (My Swanee)
R J Eckley Brian Eckley

Placings:000/646-00 **(1193)**
2001/02: 16^{0}G, 17^{0}GS

	Starts	1st	2nd	3rd	Win & Pl
Hurdles	2	0	0	0	
Career Total	**8**	**0**	**0**	**0**	**0**

Going: Sf: 0-0 GS: 0-1 Gd: 0-1 GF: - Fm: 0-0
Distance: 2m/2m3: 0-2 2m4-2m7: 0-0 3m+: 0-0
Track: LH: 0-2 RH: 0-0 Tight: 0-2 Gall: 0-0
Aids: Bl: 0-0 Vi: 0-0 Tstrap: 0-0
Best Rating: 83 5/99 Chep 2m110y good NHF

Possible Pardon (NZ)

115 123

8-y-o b g Iades (FR)-Wonderful Excuse (NZ) (Alibhai (NZ))
P J Hobbs B Pike

Placings:245-1144 **(4503)**
2001/02: 26^{1}GS, 26^{1}G, 25^{4}HY, 26^{4}G

	Starts	1st	2nd	3rd	Win & Pl
Chases	4	2	0	0	8192
Career Total	**7**	**2**	**1**	**0**	**8797**

123	1/02	Font	3m2f110y	E(0-110)HCh	GD	£3304
122	11/01	Plum	3m2f	D(0-110)HCh	G-S	£3818

Total win prize-money £7123

Going: Sf: 0-1 GS: 1-1 Gd: 1-2 GF: - Fm: 0-0
Distance: 2m/2m3: 0-0 2m4-2m7: 0-0 **3m+: 2-4**
Track: LH: 0-1 RH: 0-1 **Tight: 1-2** Gall: 0-0
Aids: **Bl: 2-4** Vi: 0-0 Tstrap: 0-0
Best Rating: 123 1/02 Font 3m2f110y good Ch

A winning point who had some reasonable form in a handful of hunter chases in the 2000/2001 season. Has looked to have a mind of his own in the past but had McCoy on board when scoring at Plumpton in November and Fontwell in January 2002, . Stays three and a quarter miles. Acts on an easy surface.

Posstick Mill

10-y-o b m Meadowbrook-Hope Of Oak (Leander)
I Emmerson Ian Emmerson

Placings:F06O0/PP **(2767)**
2001/02: 21^{P}G, 19^{P}G

	Starts	1st	2nd	3rd	Win & Pl
Hurdles	2	0	0	0	
Career Total	**7**	**0**	**0**	**0**	**0**

Going: Sf: 0-0 GS: 0-0 Gd: 0-2 GF: - Fm: 0-0
Distance: 2m/2m3: 0-1 2m4-2m7: 0-1 3m+: 0-0
Track: LH: 0-2 RH: 0-0 Tight: 0-2 Gall: 0-0
Aids: Bl: 0-0 Vi: 0-0 Tstrap: 0-0
Best Rating: 63 7/98 Sedg 2m110y gd-sft Ch

Potentate (USA)

103(111c) (84c)120

11-y-o b/br g Capote (USA)-Gay Fantastic (Ela-Mana-Mou)
M C Pipe Jim Weeden

Placings:1011/13011/30311/00**1121412/0310443/PU**
60P01P0-PP50525 **(4862)**
2001/02: 20^{P}GS, 22^{P}G, 20^{5}S, 25^{0}S, 20^{5}GS, 16^{2}GS, 19^{5}F

	Starts	1st	2nd	3rd	Win & Pl
Hurdles	5	0	1	0	1201
Chases	2	0	0	0	0
Career Total	**46**	**14**	**3**	**5**	**95393**

129	3/01	Ling	2m	D(0-120)HCh	HVY	£6792
147	12/99	Winc	2m5f	B Ch	SFT	£9725
161	4/99	Chep	2m110y	B Hdl	SFT	£6905
144	2/99	Hayd	2m	C Ch	SFT	£5868
148	12/98	Chep	2m3f110y	D Ch	HVY	£3805
124	12/98	Plum	2m	E Ch	SFT	£3387
158	4/98	Chep	2m110y	B Hdl	HVY	£7195
154	3/98	Newb	2m110y	B HHdl	G-S	£5195
141	3/97	Chep	2m110y	B Hdl	GD	£6947
139	3/97	Chep	2m4f110y	C(0-130)HHdl	G-S	£5637
123	11/96	Chep	2m110y	D(0-120)HHdl	G-S	£2784
110	4/96	Chep	2m110y	E Hdl	G-F	£2766
107	3/96	Chep	2m110y	E Hdl	SFT	£2472
116	12/95	Chep	2m110y	D Hdl	SFT	£3247

Total win prize-money £72731

Going: Sf: 0-2 GS: 0-3 Gd: 0-1 GF: - Fm: 0-1
Distance: 2m/2m3: 0-2 2m4-2m7: 0-4 3m+: 0-1
Track: LH: 0-5 RH: 0-1 Tight: 0-1 Gall: 0-1
Aids: Bl: 0-0 Vi: 0-0 Tstrap: 0-0
Best Rating: 161 4/99 Ayr 2m soft Hdl

Nothing like the force of old, he was given a superb attacking ride by Tony McCoy to win a weak handicap chase at Lingfield in March 2001. Effective on any ground, he has an excellent record at Chepstow.

Potoffairies (IRE)

108 106

7-y-o ch g Montelimar (USA)-Ladycastle (Pitpan)
Mrs S A Bramall Mrs S A Bramall

Placings:25246/11622-P420 **(4017)**
2001/02: 22^{P}S, 24^{4}HY, 24^{2}HY, 24^{0}GS

	Starts	1st	2nd	3rd	Win & Pl
Hurdles	4	0	1	0	3914
Career Total	**14**	**2**	**5**	**0**	**12912**

110	11/00	Ayr	2m4f	D(0-120)HHdl	G-S	£3042
109	11/00	Carl	2m4f110y	F(0-100)HHdl	HVY	£2324

Total win prize-money £5366

Going: Sf: 0-3 GS: 0-1 Gd: 0-0 GF: - Fm: 0-0
Distance: 2m/2m3: 0-0 2m4-2m7: 0-1 3m+: 0-3
Track: LH: 0-3 RH: 0-0 Tight: 0-0 Gall: 0-1
Aids: Bl: 0-3 Vi: 0-0 Tstrap: 0-0
Best Rating: 116 1/01 Ayr 3m110y gd-sft Hdl

Fair Irish handicap hurdler. Stays three miles. Acts on soft ground.

Potter's Bay (IRE)

108 **117**

13-y-o br g Strong Gale-Polly Puttens (Pollerton)
R Lee Mrs J E Potter

Placings:3/P342612/111132F/151P20/4U/046/5-54163U40 **(2526)**
2001/02: 23^{5}G, 21^{4}G, 20^{1}GF, 21^{6}GF, 20^{3}G, 16^{U}G, 20^{4}GF, 20^{0}G

	Starts	1st	2nd	3rd	Win & Pl
Chases	8	1	0	1	4357
Career Total	**35**	**8**	**4**	**4**	**44497**

117	8/01	Worc	2m4f110y	F(0-100)HCh	G-F	£3581
147	12/97	Donc	2m3f110y	B(0-145)HCh	GD	£4474
147	10/97	Chel	2m4f110y	C(0-135)HCh	G-F	£4372
131	12/96	Sand	2m4f110y	C Ch	GD	£4844
127	11/96	Chel	2m4f110y	C Ch	G-F	£4800
127	11/96	Weth	2m4f110y	C HCh	GD	£4589
108	5/96	Strf	2m6f110y	E Hdl	G-F	£2584
116	4/96	Weth	2m4f110y	D Hdl	GD	£2705

Total win prize-money £31951

Going: Sf: 0-0 GS: 0-0 Gd: 0-5 GF: - Fm: 1-3
Distance: 2m/2m3: 0-1 **2m4-2m7: 1-6** 3m+: 0-1
Track: **LH: 1-4** RH: 0-3 Tight: 0-2 Gall: 0-0
Aids: Bl: 0-0 Vi: 0-0 **Tstrap: 1-8**
Best Rating: 147 12/97 Donc 2m3f110y good Ch

He has enjoyed plenty of success over fences in the past, but, although winning at Worcester in August, is not too difficult to beat these days.

Powder Creek (IRE)

91f **108f**

5-y-o b g Little Bighorn-Our Dorcet (Condorcet (FR))
Mrs M Reveley T M McKain

Placings:*230* **(4032)**
2001/02: 17^{2}GF, 16^{3}GS, 16^{0}GS

	Starts	1st	2nd	3rd	Win & Pl
NH Flat	3	0	1	1	704
Career Total	**3**	**0**	**1**	**1**	**704**

Going: Sf: 0-0 GS: 0-2 Gd: 0-0 GF: - Fm: 0-1
Distance: 2m/2m3: 0-3 2m4-2m7: 0-0 3m+: 0-0
Track: LH: 0-1 RH: 0-2 Tight: 0-1 Gall: 0-2
Aids: Bl: 0-0 Vi: 0-0 Tstrap: 0-0
Best Rating: 102 6/01 MRas 2m1f110y gd-fm NHF

Appreciated the top of the ground when winning Worcester bumper May 2002, stepping up on previous form.

Power And Demand

89 **89**

5-y-o b g Formidable (USA)-Mazurkanova (Song)
Miss M Bragg Friends Of Rock Park

Placings:P0030 **(3992)**
2001/02: 17^{P}G, 17^{0}GS, 17^{0}S, 17^{3}S, 17^{0}S

	Starts	1st	2nd	3rd	Win & Pl
Hurdles	5	0	0	1	545
Career Total	**5**	**0**	**0**	**1**	**545**

Going: Sf: 0-3 GS: 0-1 Gd: 0-1 GF: - Fm: 0-0
Distance: 2m/2m3: 0-5 2m4-2m7: 0-0 3m+: 0-0
Track: LH: 0-0 RH: 0-5 Tight: 0-4 Gall: 0-0
Aids: Bl: 0-0 Vi: 0-0 Tstrap: 0-0
Best Rating: 89 2/02 Tntn 2m1f soft Hdl

Modest hurdler, he likes cut in the ground.

Power Unit

97 **91**

7-y-o ch g Risk Me (FR)-Hazel Bee (Starch Reduced)
Mrs D A Hamer Power Units (1953) Ltd

Placings:*2204* **(4174)**
2001/02: 17^{2}GF, 16^{2}S, 16^{0}G, 22^{4}GS

	Starts	1st	2nd	3rd	Win & Pl
NH Flat	3	0	2	0	1180
Hurdles	1	0	0	0	321
Career Total	**4**	**0**	**2**	**0**	**1501**

Going: Sf: 0-1 GS: 0-1 Gd: 0-1 GF: - Fm: 0-1
Distance: 2m/2m3: 0-3 2m4-2m7: 0-1 3m+: 0-0
Track: LH: 0-4 RH: 0-0 Tight: 0-2 Gall: 0-1
Aids: Bl: 0-0 Vi: 0-0 Tstrap: 0-0
Best Rating: 98 12/01 Newb 2m110y good NHF

Placed in bumpers and hurdles, seems to handle any ground.

Powerhouse

5-y-o ch g Superpower-Zealous (Hard Fought)
John R Upson Roger Langley

Placings:*P* **(1019)**
2001/02: 16^{P}G

	Starts	1st	2nd	3rd	Win & Pl
NH Flat	1	0	0	0	
Career Total	**1**	**0**	**0**	**0**	

Going: Sf: 0-0 GS: 0-0 Gd: 0-1 GF: - Fm: 0-0
Distance: 2m/2m3: 0-1 2m4-2m7: 0-0 3m+: 0-0
Track: LH: 0-1 RH: 0-0 Tight: 0-0 Gall: 0-0
Aids: Bl: 0-0 Vi: 0-0 Tstrap: 0-0
Best Rating:

Powernglory (IRE)

(88c) (88c)

11-y-o ch g Accordion-Fairfield Springs (Miami Springs)
John Moore J C Campbell

Placings:UPP*0*/P-P05 **(4727)**
2001/02: 21^{P}GF, 16^{0}G, 24^{5}GF

	Starts	1st	2nd	3rd	Win & Pl
Chases	3	0	0	0	0
Career Total	**8**	**0**	**0**	**0**	**0**

Going: Sf: 0-0 GS: 0-0 Gd: 0-1 GF: - Fm: 0-2
Distance: 2m/2m3: 0-1 2m4-2m7: 0-1 3m+: 0-1
Track: LH: 0-1 RH: 0-1 Tight: 0-0 Gall: 0-0
Aids: Bl: 0-0 Vi: 0-1 Tstrap: 0-3
Best Rating: 88 5/01 Chel 2m110y good Ch

Poynton Henry (IRE)

91

6-y-o b g Supreme Leader-Short Memories (Quisling)
R H Buckler The Desirables

Placings:*00*P-1P **(3215)**
2001/02: 22^{1}GF, 24^{P}GS

	Starts	1st	2nd	3rd	Win & Pl
Hurdles	2	1	0	0	2464
Career Total	**5**	**1**	**0**	**0**	**2464**

91	10/01	Extr	2m6f110y	E Hdl	G-F	£2464

Total win prize-money £2464

Going: Sf: 0-0 GS: 0-1 Gd: 0-0 GF: - Fm: 1-1
Distance: 2m/2m3: 0-0 **2m4-2m7: 1-1** 3m+: 0-1
Track: LH: 0-1 RH: 0-0 Tight: 0-0 Gall: 0-1
Aids: Bl: 0-0 Vi: 0-0 Tstrap: 0-0
Best Rating: 91 10/01 Extr 2m6f110y gd-fm Hdl

Caused a surprise on his first encounter with fast ground when winning a poor amateur event at Exeter in October 2001. Stays two miles six.

Prah Sands

97 **116**

9-y-o b g Henbit (USA)-Minor Furlong (Native Bazaar)
C Tizzard R P & S H Richards

Placings:0/4325P-2PPP42 **(4725)**
2001/02: 19^{2}F, 17^{P}GS, 16^{P}GS, 24^{P}S, 19^{4}GS, 16^{2}GF

	Starts	1st	2nd	3rd	Win & Pl
Chases	6	0	2	0	2967
Career Total	**12**	**0**	**3**	**1**	**5618**

Going: Sf: 0-1 GS: 0-3 Gd: 0-0 GF: - Fm: 0-2
Distance: 2m/2m3: 0-5 2m4-2m7: 0-0 3m+: 0-1
Track: LH: 0-2 RH: 0-4 Tight: 0-4 Gall: 0-0
Aids: Bl: 0-2 Vi: 0-0 Tstrap: 0-0
Best Rating: 117 11/00 Tntn 2m3f gd-sft Ch

Former winning pointer. Has become generally disappointing under Rules. Often wears headgear.

Prairie Minstrel (USA)

85 **48**

8-y-o b g Regal Intention (CAN)-Prairie Sky (USA) (Gone West (USA))
R Dickin E R C Beech & B Wilkinson

Placings:2223125P152/0025025622/21F111P/3 **(4543)**
2001/02: 19^{3}G

	Starts	1st	2nd	3rd	Win & Pl
Chases	1	0	0	1	651
Career Total	**29**	**6**	**10**	**2**	**27623**

116	8/99	Sthl	2m4f110y	E(0-105)HCh	G-F	£3125
107	8/99	MRas	2m4f	D Ch	G-F	£4413
114	7/99	MRas	2m4f	D Ch	G-F	£3795
115	5/99	Hntg	2m4f110y	E Ch	G-F	£2860
88	3/98	Wwck	2m	F(0-100)HHdl	SFT	£2244
92	11/97	Wind	2m	E Hdl	GD	£2407

Total win prize-money £18846

Going: Sf: 0-0 GS: 0-0 Gd: 0-1 GF: - Fm: 0-0
Distance: 2m/2m3: 0-1 2m4-2m7: 0-0 3m+: 0-0
Track: LH: 0-0 RH: 0-1 Tight: 0-0 Gall: 0-0
Aids: Bl: 0-0 Vi: 0-0 Tstrap: 0-0
Best Rating: 116 8/99 Sthl 2m4f110y gd-fm Ch

In fine form in fast-ground chases in the summer of '99 until breaking down. Satisfactory return after a long absence.

Prairie Run (IRE)

101 **85+**

6-y-o ch m Montelimar (USA)-Lady Leona (Leander)

L Lungo Riverstown Racing Syndicate

Placings:343 (4768)
2001/02: 16^{3}S, 16^{4}S, 16^{3}GF

	Starts	1st	2nd	3rd	Win & Pl
NH Flat	2	0	0	1	276
Hurdles	1	0	0	1	405
Career Total	**3**	**0**	**0**	**2**	**681**

Going: Sf: 0-2 GS: 0-0 Gd: 0-0 GF: - Fm: 0-1
Distance: 2m/2m3: 0-3 2m4-2m7: 0-0 3m+: 0-0
Track: LH: 0-0 RH: 0-1 Tight: 0-1 Gall: 0-0
Aids: Bl: 0-0 Vi: 0-0 Tstrap: 0-0
Best Rating: 93 1/02 Newc 2m soft NHF

She has shown modest ability on soft ground in bumpers and on fast ground over hurdles.

Prancing Blade

106 **125**

9-y-o b g Broadsword (USA)-Sparkling Cinders (Netherkelly)
N A Twiston-Davies Gavin Macechern

Placings:60/C4P0F6/222112F06/31115U4F-PP (4897)
2001/02: 25^{P}G, 24^{P}G

	Starts	1st	2nd	3rd	Win & Pl
Chases	2	0	0	0	
Career Total	**27**	**5**	**4**	**1**	**28137**

141	10/00	MRas	2m1f110y	C Ch	GD	£7215
138	9/00	Chep	2m3f110y	C Ch	GD	£6743
128	5/00	Bang	2m1f110y	E Ch	GD	£3510
116	10/99	Worc	2m2f	E Hdl	G-F	£2402
104	10/99	Hexm	2m	E Hdl	GD	£2364

Total win prize-money £22235

Going: Sf: 0-0 GS: 0-0 Gd: 0-2 GF: 0-0 Fm: 0-0
Distance: 2m/2m3: 0-0 2m4-2m7: 0-0 3m+: 0-2
Track: LH: 0-1 RH: 0-1 Tight: 0-1 Gall: 0-0
Aids: Bl: 0-0 Vi: 0-0 Tstrap: 0-0
Best Rating: 141 10/00 MRas 2m1f110y good Ch

Handicap chaser. Has been successful over hurdles. Stays three miles and acts on a sound surface.

Prate Box (IRE)

12-y-o b g Ela-Mana-Mou-Prattle On (Ballymore)
P R Chamings Mrs Peter Corbett

Placings:U/06033110/2602/0006441311F0/21F2/PPP-F (0190)
2001/02: 21^{F}GF

	Starts	1st	2nd	3rd	Win & Pl
Chases	1	0	0	0	
Career Total	**33**	**6**	**4**	**3**	**30410**

131	11/97	Chep	2m3f110y	C(0-135)HCh	G-S	£6905
121	3/97	Fair	2m4f	(0-109)HCh	GD	£4747
121	3/97	Naas	2m40y	(0-109)HCh	Y-S	£3051
111	1/97	Punc	2m	(0-109)HCh	Y-S	£3730
123	2/95	Clon	2m	Hdl	HVY	£3051
106	11/94	Clon	2m	Hdl	Y-S	£2446

Total win prize-money £23933

Going: Sf: 0-0 GS: 0-0 Gd: 0-0 GF: - Fm: 0-1
Distance: 2m/2m3: 0-0 2m4-2m7: 0-1 3m+: 0-0
Track: LH: 0-1 RH: 0-0 Tight: 0-1 Gall: 0-0
Aids: Bl: 0-0 Vi: 0-0 Tstrap: 0-0
Best Rating: 133 1/98 Kemp 2m4f110y gd-sft Ch

Precious Bane (IRE)

88f **87f**

4-y-o b g Bigstone (IRE)-Heavenward (USA) (Conquistador Cielo (USA))
B P J Baugh M W & A N Harris

Placings:6060 (4840)
2001/02: 16^{6}S, 16^{0}S, 16^{6}G, 16^{0}G

	Starts	1st	2nd	3rd	Win & Pl
NH Flat	1	0	0	0	0
Hurdles	3	0	0	0	0
Career Total	**4**	**0**	**0**	**0**	**0**

Going: Sf: 0-2 GS: 0-0 Gd: 0-2 GF: - Fm: 0-0
Distance: 2m/2m3: 0-4 2m4-2m7: 0-0 3m+: 0-0
Track: LH: 0-3 RH: 0-1 Tight: 0-0 Gall: 0-1
Aids: Bl: 0-0 Vi: 0-0 Tstrap: 0-0
Best Rating: 86 4/02 Ayr 2m good Hdl

Has shown little so far.

Precious Island

100(87h) (58h)**105**

9-y-o b m Jupiter Island-Burmese Ruby (Good Times (ITY))
C N Kellett J W & T J Ellis

Placings:5045/00500/00336626/P6522UF2553/3F212P032143P-2P6350506P3504 (4909)
2001/02: 20^{2}GS, 20^{P}G, 21^{6}GS, 20^{3}S, 20^{5}S, 20^{0}S, 20^{5}HY, 20^{0}GS, 23^{6}G, 23^{P}S, 20^{3}S, 24^{5}HY, 24^{0}GF, 20^{4}GF

	Starts	1st	2nd	3rd	Win & Pl
Hurdles	1	0	0	0	0
Chases	13	0	1	2	4430
Career Total	**55**	**2**	**8**	**8**	**20627**

105	1/01	Leic	2m4f110y	F(0-105)HCh	SFT	£3562
105	11/00	Wwck	2m4f110y	F(0-100)HCh	HVY	£2324

Total win prize-money £5886

Going: Sf: 0-6 GS: 0-3 Gd: 0-3 GF: - Fm: 0-2
Distance: 2m/2m3: 0-0 2m4-2m7: 0-6 3m+: 0-8
Track: LH: 0-4 RH: 0-9 Tight: 0-4 Gall: 0-1
Aids: Bl: 0-0 Vi: 0-0 Tstrap: 0-0
Best Rating: 105 5/01 Bang 2m4f110y gd-sft Ch

A staying chaser, he is a frustrating sort who is hard to win with.

Precious Moments

91f **88f**

6-y-o b m Polar Falcon (USA)-Brassy Nell (Dunbeath (USA))
J A Moore J A Moore

Placings:30 (3354)
2001/02: 16^{3}S, 16^{0}G

	Starts	1st	2nd	3rd	Win & Pl
NH Flat	2	0	0	1	208
Career Total	**2**	**0**	**0**	**1**	**208**

Going: Sf: 0-1 GS: 0-0 Gd: 0-1 GF: - Fm: 0-0
Distance: 2m/2m3: 0-2 2m4-2m7: 0-0 3m+: 0-0
Track: LH: 0-1 RH: 0-1 Tight: 0-2 Gall: 0-0
Aids: Bl: 0-0 Vi: 0-0 Tstrap: 0-0
Best Rating: 88 10/01 Fknm 2m soft NHF

Prelude To Fame (USA)

105 **107**

9-y-o b g Affirmed (USA)-Dance Call (USA) (Nijinsky (CAN))
Miss Kate Milligan Dr Roy Palmer

Placings:13602/2/1056F/23U4/060PP0-42 (3993)
2001/02: 20^{4}GS, 20^{2}S

	Starts	1st	2nd	3rd	Win & Pl
Hurdles	2	0	1	0	690
Career Total	**23**	**2**	**4**	**2**	**9256**

118	11/98	MRas	2m5f110y	E(0-115)HHdl	G-S	£2740
89	8/96	Ctml	2m1f110y	E Hdl	GD	£2215

Total win prize-money £4955

Going: Sf: 0-1 GS: 0-1 Gd: 0-0 GF: - Fm: 0-0
Distance: 2m/2m3: 0-0 2m4-2m7: 0-2 3m+: 0-0
Track: LH: 0-2 RH: 0-0 Tight: 0-0 Gall: 0-1
Aids: Bl: 0-0 Vi: 0-0 Tstrap: 0-0
Best Rating: 118 12/99 Weth 2m7f gd-sft Hdl

Modest hurdler. Claimed for just £3,000 after finishing runner-up at Doncaster in March.

Premier Bay

8-y-o b g Primo Dominie-Lydia Maria (Dancing Brave (USA))
R Barber (P J Hobbs 3/3) A M Mason

Placings:5415/564/PU53351/3 (4659)
2001/02: 24^{3}G

	Starts	1st	2nd	3rd	Win & Pl
Chases	1	0	0	1	381
Career Total	**15**	**2**	**0**	**3**	**5088**

103	9/99	NAbb	2m1f	G Hdl	G-F	£1919
113	3/98	Winc	2m	F Hdl	GD	£1800

Total win prize-money £3719

Going: Sf: 0-0 GS: 0-0 Gd: 0-1 GF: - Fm: 0-0
Distance: 2m/2m3: 0-0 2m4-2m7: 0-0 3m+: 0-1
Track: LH: 0-0 RH: 0-1 Tight: 0-1 Gall: 0-0
Aids: Bl: 0-0 Vi: 0-0 Tstrap: 0-0
Best Rating: 116 10/98 Chep 2m110y good Hdl

A modest dual-purpose preformer, best at around the minimum trip. Not always the cleanest jumper.

Premier Boy (IRE)

80 **71**

4-y-o b g Blues Traveller (IRE)-Little Min (Nebbiolo)
B S Rothwell Premier Protection Services Ltd

Placings:30P00 (2671)
2001/02: 16^{3}G, 16^{0}G, 16^{P}S, 16^{0}GF, 16^{0}G

	Starts	1st	2nd	3rd	Win & Pl
Hurdles	5	0	0	1	374
Career Total	**5**	**0**	**0**	**1**	**374**

Going: Sf: 0-1 GS: 0-0 Gd: 0-3 GF: - Fm: 0-1
Distance: 2m/2m3: 0-5 2m4-2m7: 0-0 3m+: 0-0
Track: LH: 0-5 RH: 0-0 Tight: 0-2 Gall: 0-1
Aids: Bl: 0-1 Vi: 0-0 Tstrap: 0-2
Best Rating: 71 10/01 Kels 2m110y good Hdl

Premier Drive (IRE)

109(110h) (121h)**132**

9-y-o ch g Black Minstrel-Ballyanihan (Le Moss)
G M Moore A W Sergeant

Placings:U6665/600315/21153P1-322F32111P (4878)
2001/02: 20^{3}S, 20^{2}GS, 20^{2}S, 25^{F}GS, 20^{3}HY, 16^{2}S, 20^{1}G, 20^{1}S, 16^{1}HY, 24^{P}G

Starts 1st 2nd 3rd Win & Pl

Hurdles	1	0	0	1	510
Chases	9	3	3	1	15105
Career Total	**28**	**7**	**4**	**4**	**29304**

132	3/02	Hexm	2m110y	E Ch	HVY	£3107
118	2/02	Leic	2m4f110y	E Ch	SFT	£3094
132	1/02	Leic	2m4f110y	D Ch	GD	£4403
121	4/01	Weth	2m4f110y	D Hdl	G-S	£3395
121	12/00	Weth	2m4f110y	E(0-105)HHdl	SFT	£2702
115	11/00	Weth	2m4f110y	D Hdl	HVY	£3250
99	1/00	Tram	2m	NHF	Y-S	£2760

Total win prize-money £22712

Going: Sf: 2-6 GS: 0-2 Gd: 1-2 GF: - Fm: 0-0
Distance: 2m/2m3: 1-2 **2m4-2m7: 2-6** 3m+: 0-2
Track: LH: 1-4 **RH: 2-5** Tight: 0-1 Gall: 0-0
Aids: Bl: 0-0 Vi: 0-0 Tstrap: 0-0
Best Rating: 132 3/02 Hexm 2m110y heavy Ch

He was a useful sort over hurdles and has also been successful over fences, scoring a treble at the start of 2002. Acts on good and soft ground and is effective up to two miles four.

Premier Estate (IRE)

101f **98f**

5-y-o b g Satco (FR)-Kettleby (IRE) (Tale Quale)
R Rowe Mrs Jacky Field

Placings:*6* **(3811)**
2001/02: 18^{6}S

	Starts	1st	2nd	3rd	Win & Pl
NH Flat	1	0	0	0	0
Career Total	**1**	**0**	**0**	**0**	**0**

Going: Sf: 0-1 GS: 0-0 Gd: 0-0 GF: - Fm: 0-0
Distance: 2m/2m3: 0-1 2m4-2m7: 0-0 3m+: 0-0
Track: LH: 0-1 RH: 0-0 Tight: 0-1 Gall: 0-0
Aids: Bl: 0-0 Vi: 0-0 Tstrap: 0-0
Best Rating: 98 2/02 Font 2m2f110y soft NHF

Premier First (IRE)

13-y-o br g Good Thyne (USA)-Bowerina (Daring Display (USA))
N J Pewter Major M S Edwards

Placings:*000000*/052045/0/040/6/6-O0U **(0579)**
2001/02: 20°GF, 21^{0}G, 24^{U}GF

	Starts	1st	2nd	3rd	Win & Pl
Chases	3	0	0	0	
Career Total	**21**	**0**	**1**	**0**	**1162**

Going: Sf: 0-0 GS: 0-0 Gd: 0-1 GF: - Fm: 0-2
Distance: 2m/2m3: 0-0 2m4-2m7: 0-2 3m+: 0-1
Track: LH: 0-1 RH: 0-2 Tight: 0-2 Gall: 0-1
Aids: Bl: 0-0 Vi: 0-0 Tstrap: 0-0
Best Rating: 84 1/96 Sedg 2m1f gd-fm Ch

Premier Generation (IRE)

98(111h) (113h)**115**

9-y-o b g Cadeaux Genereux-Bristle (Thatch (USA))
J Howard Johnson Gordon Brown/bert Watson

Placings:00/23/1211020/402/05001303-00550045 **(4891)**
2001/02: 16^{0}G, 16^{0}G, 16^{5}G, 16^{5}S, 16^{0}GS, 16^{0}S, 17^{4}GF, 16^{5}G

	Starts	1st	2nd	3rd	Win & Pl
Hurdles	7	0	0	0	0
Chases	1	0	0	0	0
Career Total	**30**	**4**	**4**	**3**	**31331**

130	12/00	Ludl	2m	E Ch	SFT	£3493
141	2/99	Kemp	2m	A Hdl	SFT	£9465
124	12/98	Wwck	2m	E Hdl	SFT	£3036
112	11/98	Chel	2m110y	D(0-110)HHdl	G-S	£7457

Total win prize-money £23453

Going: Sf: 0-2 GS: 0-1 Gd: 0-4 GF: - Fm: 0-1
Distance: 2m/2m3: 0-8 2m4-2m7: 0-0 3m+: 0-0
Track: LH: 0-5 RH: 0-3 Tight: 0-3 Gall: 0-0
Aids: Bl: 0-1 Vi: 0-0 Tstrap: 0-1
Best Rating: 141 2/99 Kemp 2m soft Hdl

He is able, but did not appear to enjoy chasing in 2001/02. Held over hurdles last term, he is dropping down the handicap as a result.

Premiere Alert (NOR)

6-y-o ch g Blue Alert-Premiere Balerina (SWE) (Bal Du Seigneur (USA))
R Williams R Williams

Placings:0 **(1406)**
2001/02: 16^{0}GF

	Starts	1st	2nd	3rd	Win & Pl
Hurdles	1	0	0	0	
Career Total	**1**	**0**	**0**	**0**	

Going: Sf: 0-0 GS: 0-0 Gd: 0-0 GF: - Fm: 0-1
Distance: 2m/2m3: 0-1 2m4-2m7: 0-0 3m+: 0-0
Track: LH: 0-1 RH: 0-0 Tight: 0-0 Gall: 0-0
Aids: Bl: 0-0 Vi: 0-0 Tstrap: 0-0
Best Rating:

Premiere Foulee (FR)

98 **73**

7-y-o ch m Sillery (USA)-Dee (Caerleon (USA))
F Jordan Warwick Davis

Placings:PP00P/P/004-223 **(1806)**
2001/02: 18^{2}GF, 19^{2}F, 24^{3}GF

	Starts	1st	2nd	3rd	Win & Pl
Hurdles	3	0	2	1	1638
Career Total	**12**	**0**	**2**	**1**	**1853**

Going: Sf: 0-0 GS: 0-0 Gd: 0-0 GF: - Fm: 0-3
Distance: 2m/2m3: 0-1 2m4-2m7: 0-1 3m+: 0-1
Track: LH: 0-1 RH: 0-2 Tight: 0-2 Gall: 0-0
Aids: Bl: 0-0 Vi: 0-0 Tstrap: 0-0
Best Rating: 73 10/01 Ludl 3m gd-fm Hdl

Running well in minor hurdles company in the autumn of 2001.

Present Bleu (FR)

110(98c) (134c)**138**

7-y-o b g Epervier Bleu-Lointaine (USA) (Lyphard's Wish (FR))
M C Pipe J-P Dubois

Placings:35222204/0401141205664/63101650P6-6015611112220 **(2666)**
2001/02: 19^{6}G, 20^{0}G, 16^{1}G, 16^{5}GF, 17^{6}G, 20^{1}GF, 16^{1}GF, 17^{1}GF, 19^{1}GF, 20^{2}G, 17^{2}S, 16^{2}GS, 17^{0}G

	Starts	1st	2nd	3rd	Win & Pl
Hurdles	10	5	1	0	16994
Chases	3	0	2	0	2815
Career Total	**44**	**10**	**8**	**2**	**73465**

138	10/01	Extr	2m3f	D(0-125)HHdl	G-F	£3380
133	10/01	Extr	2m1f	D(0-120)HHdl	G-F	£3419
121	9/01	Plum	2m	F Hdl	G-F	£2331
129	8/01	Font	2m4f	F Hdl	G-F	£2289
119	7/01	Worc	2m	E(0-115)HHdl	GD	£3454
	9/00	Autl	2m2f	Hdl	VS	£8646
	7/00	Claf	2m4f	HCh	SFT	£8621
	10/99	Sbri	2m3f	Hdl	SFT	£3229
	8/99	Claf	2m2f	Ch	VS	£9688
	8/99	Gran	2m2f	Ch	GD	£2691

Total win prize-money £47749

Going: Sf: 0-1 GS: 0-1 Gd: 1-6 GF: - Fm: 4-5
Distance: **2m/2m3: 4-9** 2m4-2m7: 1-4 3m+: 0-0
Track: LH: 2-9 RH: 2-3 **Tight: 2-7** Gall: 0-1
Aids: Bl: 0-0 **Vi: 4-8** Tstrap: 0-1
Best Rating: 138 10/01 Extr 2m3f gd-fm Hdl

Successful over hurdles and fences in France, he did not show much until fitted with a visor, then ran up a four-timer on fast ground over hurdles in the late summer/autumn of 2001. He stays two and a half miles.

Present Moment (IRE)

93f **73f**

4-y-o b g Presenting-Springphar (IRE) (Phardante (FR))
T P Tate T P Tate

Placings:*00* **(4873)**
2001/02: 16^{0}HY, 16^{0}GF

	Starts	1st	2nd	3rd	Win & Pl
NH Flat	2	0	0	0	
Career Total	**2**	**0**	**0**	**0**	

Going: Sf: 0-1 GS: 0-0 Gd: 0-0 GF: - Fm: 0-1
Distance: 2m/2m3: 0-2 2m4-2m7: 0-0 3m+: 0-0
Track: LH: 0-2 RH: 0-0 Tight: 0-0 Gall: 0-0
Aids: Bl: 0-0 Vi: 0-0 Tstrap: 0-0
Best Rating: 73 4/02 Weth 2m gd-fm NHF

Modest bumper form.

Presidio (GER)

99 **74**

7-y-o b g Konigsstuhl (GER)-Pradera (GER) (Abary (GER))
Ian Williams J Cullen Thermals Ltd

Placings:F0-0P063 **(4565)**
2001/02: 17^{0}G, 21^{P}GS, 16^{0}S, 16^{6}GS, 16^{3}G

	Starts	1st	2nd	3rd	Win & Pl
Hurdles	5	0	0	1	287
Career Total	**7**	**0**	**0**	**1**	**287**

Going: Sf: 0-1 GS: 0-2 Gd: 0-2 GF: - Fm: 0-0
Distance: 2m/2m3: 0-4 2m4-2m7: 0-1 3m+: 0-0
Track: LH: 0-2 RH: 0-3 Tight: 0-0 Gall: 0-1
Aids: Bl: 0-0 Vi: 0-0 Tstrap: 0-0
Best Rating: 81 2/01 Ludl 2m gd-sft Hdl

Multiple Flat winner in Germany but has achieved little over hurdles in Britain around two miles.

Press To Sting

104 **110**

13-y-o b g Scorpio (FR)-Olive Press (Ragapan)
A H Mactaggart Mrs A H Mactaggart

Placings:0/P/46FPP6/3UP-142P0 (4687)
2001/02: 20^{1}GS, 20^{4}S, 22^{2}G, 24^{P}GS, 25^{0}GF

	Starts	1st	2nd	3rd	Win & Pl
Chases	5	1	1	0	6401
Career Total	**16**	**1**	**1**	**1**	**7113**

110	10/01	Carl	2m4f	D Ch	G-S	£4465

Total win prize-money £4466

Going: Sf: 0-1 GS: 1-2 Gd: 0-1 GF: - Fm: 0-1
Distance: 2m/2m3: 0-0 **2m4-2m7: 1-3** 3m+: 0-2
Track: LH: 0-3 RH: 0-1 Tight: 0-2 Gall: 0-1
Aids: Bl: 0-0 Vi: 0-0 Tstrap: 0-0
Best Rating: 110 11/01 Kels 2m6f110y good Ch

Presto

95 **92**

5-y-o b g Namaqualand (USA)-Polish Dancer (USA) (Malinowski (USA))
Mrs Merrita Jones Speed 2911 Ltd

Placings:2-50020 (4654)
2001/02: 17^{5}GS, 16^{0}GS, 17^{0}S, 17^{2}S, 17^{0}GS

	Starts	1st	2nd	3rd	Win & Pl
Hurdles	5	0	1	0	838
Career Total	**6**	**0**	**2**	**0**	**1580**

Going: Sf: 0-2 GS: 0-3 Gd: 0-0 GF: - Fm: 0-0
Distance: 2m/2m3: 0-5 2m4-2m7: 0-0 3m+: 0-0
Track: LH: 0-0 RH: 0-5 Tight: 0-4 Gall: 0-1
Aids: Bl: 0-2 Vi: 0-0 Tstrap: 0-0
Best Rating: 92 3/02 Tntn 2m1f soft Hdl

Modest hurdler, probably stays beyond two miles.

Preston Brook

102 **103**

5-y-o b g Perpendicular-Tommys Dream (Le Bavard (FR))
M W Easterby Lord Daresbury

Placings:*20*-2322251P (4896)
2001/02: 17^{2}S, 17^{3}G, 20^{2}G, 20^{2}GS, 20^{2}GF, 25^{5}GS, 20^{1}HY, 20^{P}G

	Starts	1st	2nd	3rd	Win & Pl
NH Flat	2	0	1	1	676
Hurdles	6	1	3	0	5210
Career Total	**10**	**1**	**5**	**1**	**6344**

103	3/02	Sthl	2m4f110y	E Hdl	HVY	£2667

Total win prize-money £2667

Going: Sf: 1-2 GS: 0-2 Gd: 0-3 GF: - Fm: 0-1
Distance: 2m/2m3: 0-2 **2m4-2m7: 1-5** 3m+: 0-1
Track: **LH: 1-4** RH: 0-4 **Tight: 1-5** Gall: 0-1
Aids: Bl: 0-0 Vi: 0-0 Tstrap: 0-0
Best Rating: 103 3/02 Sthl 2m4f110y heavy Hdl

Placed in three bumpers on easy ground looking short of pace and in need of a longer trip. He has done much the same over hurdles, but did win in bad ground at Southwell in March 2002.

Presuming Ed (IRE)

9-y-o b g Nordico (USA)-Top Knot (High Top)
J R Tuck (Mrs J S Lewis 10/2) James R Tuck

Placings:3 (4483)
2001/02: 19^{3}G

	Starts	1st	2nd	3rd	Win & Pl
Chases	1	0	0	1	308
Career Total	**1**	**0**	**0**	**1**	**308**

Going: Sf: 0-0 GS: 0-0 Gd: 0-1 GF: - Fm: 0-0
Distance: 2m/2m3: 0-0 2m4-2m7: 0-1 3m+: 0-0
Track: LH: 0-0 RH: 0-1 Tight: 0-0 Gall: 0-0
Aids: Bl: 0-0 Vi: 0-0 Tstrap: 0-0
Best Rating: 105 3/02 Extr 2m3f110y good Ch

Fragile, lightly-raced hunter chaser/pointer. Stays three miles, acts on any ground.

Pretty Boy Blue

7-y-o gr g Portogon-Nicola Lisa (Dumbarnie)
Bill Davies Bill Davies

Placings:PP (4372)
2001/02: 19^{P}G, 24^{P}GS

	Starts	1st	2nd	3rd	Win & Pl
Hurdles	1	0	0	0	0
Chases	1	0	0	0	0
Career Total	**2**	**0**	**0**	**0**	

Going: Sf: 0-0 GS: 0-1 Gd: 0-1 GF: - Fm: 0-0
Distance: 2m/2m3: 0-0 2m4-2m7: 0-1 3m+: 0-1
Track: LH: 0-0 RH: 0-2 Tight: 0-1 Gall: 0-0
Aids: Bl: 0-0 Vi: 0-0 Tstrap: 0-0
Best Rating:

Prickly Paws

78f **75f**

7-y-o ch g Vital Season-Tinsel Rose (Porto Bello)
M Mullineaux S R Hope

Placings:*0* (0792)
2001/02: 17^{0}GF

	Starts	1st	2nd	3rd	Win & Pl
NH Flat	1	0	0	0	
Career Total	**1**	**0**	**0**	**0**	

Going: Sf: 0-0 GS: 0-0 Gd: 0-0 GF: - Fm: 0-1
Distance: 2m/2m3: 0-1 2m4-2m7: 0-0 3m+: 0-0
Track: LH: 0-0 RH: 0-1 Tight: 0-1 Gall: 0-0
Aids: Bl: 0-0 Vi: 0-0 Tstrap: 0-0
Best Rating: 75 6/01 MRas 2m1f110y gd-fm NHF

Priddy Fair

86 **84**

9-y-o b m North Briton-Rainbow Ring (Rainbow Quest (USA))
B Mactaggart Play Fair Partnership

Placings:10454/55P550/10430065/50542/1324-026 (1200)
2001/02: 16^{0}F, 16^{2}G, 20^{6}G

	Starts	1st	2nd	3rd	Win & Pl
Hurdles	3	0	1	0	676
Career Total	**31**	**3**	**3**	**2**	**10814**

98	5/00	Hexm	2m	G Hdl	G-F	£1883
83	5/98	Prth	2m110y	G(0-100)HHdl	G-F	£2808
83	12/96	Catt	2m	E Hdl	GD	£2364

Total win prize-money £7055

Going: Sf: 0-0 GS: 0-0 Gd: 0-2 GF: - Fm: 0-1
Distance: 2m/2m3: 0-2 2m4-2m7: 0-1 3m+: 0-0
Track: LH: 0-1 RH: 0-2 Tight: 0-0 Gall: 0-0
Aids: Bl: 0-0 Vi: 0-0 Tstrap: 0-0
Best Rating: 101 8/00 Prth 2m4f110y good Hdl

Pride Of India (IRE)

5-y-o b g Ezzoud (IRE)-Indian Queen (Electric)
K C Bailey (J L Dunlop 1/8) Sir Gordon Brunton

Placings:0 (2429)
2001/02: 24^{0}G

	Starts	1st	2nd	3rd	Win & Pl
Hurdles	1	0	0	0	
Career Total	**1**	**0**	**0**	**0**	

Going: Sf: 0-0 GS: 0-0 Gd: 0-1 GF: - Fm: 0-0
Distance: 2m/2m3: 0-0 2m4-2m7: 0-0 3m+: 0-1
Track: LH: 0-1 RH: 0-0 Tight: 0-0 Gall: 0-1
Aids: Bl: 0-1 Vi: 0-0 Tstrap: 0-0
Best Rating:

Pride Of The River (IRE)

93 **94**

7-y-o b g Executive Perk-Ardglass Pride (Golden Love)
N J Henderson Riverwood Racing

Placings:*3633* (4548)
2001/02: 16^{3}S, 19^{6}GS, 20^{3}HY, 21^{3}GF

	Starts	1st	2nd	3rd	Win & Pl
NH Flat	1	0	0	1	234
Hurdles	3	0	0	2	976
Career Total	**4**	**0**	**0**	**3**	**1210**

Going: Sf: 0-2 GS: 0-1 Gd: 0-0 GF: - Fm: 0-1
Distance: 2m/2m3: 0-2 2m4-2m7: 0-2 3m+: 0-0
Track: LH: 0-3 RH: 0-1 Tight: 0-0 Gall: 0-2
Aids: Bl: 0-0 Vi: 0-0 Tstrap: 0-0
Best Rating: 104 11/01 Chep 2m110y soft NHF

Showed promise on his bumper debut. Looks a potential stayer.

Prideway (IRE)

87 **58**

6-y-o b m Pips Pride-Up The Gates (Captain James)
W M Brisbourne B L Loador

Placings:0P (2899)
2001/02: 16^{0}G, 16^{P}G

	Starts	1st	2nd	3rd	Win & Pl
Hurdles	2	0	0	0	
Career Total	**2**	**0**	**0**	**0**	

Going: Sf: 0-0 GS: 0-0 Gd: 0-2 GF: - Fm: 0-0
Distance: 2m/2m3: 0-2 2m4-2m7: 0-0 3m+: 0-0
Track: LH: 0-0 RH: 0-2 Tight: 0-0 Gall: 0-0
Aids: Bl: 0-0 Vi: 0-0 Tstrap: 0-0
Best Rating: 60 12/01 Ludl 2m good Hdl

Pridewood Fuggle

106 **89**

12-y-o b g Little Wolf-Quick Reply (Tarqogan)
R J Price Mrs B Morris

Placings:*302/PP/0313045/361163540/FP20PP0-*40003616 (4847)
2001/02: 17^{4}G, 16^{0}S, 16^{0}S, 19^{0}S, 19^{3}S, 19^{6}S, 20^{1}G, 20^{6}G

	Starts	1st	2nd	3rd	Win & Pl
Hurdles	8	1	0	1	2231
Career Total	**36**	**4**	**2**	**6**	**14731**

84	4/02	Uttx	2m4f110y	G(0-90)HHdl	GD	£1981
99	2/00	Hrfd	2m1f	E(0-115)HHdl	GD	£2769

94	1/00	Tntn	2m3f110y	F(0-100)HHdl	G-S	£2678
88	3/99	Chep	2m110y	G(0-95)HHdl	HVY	£2248

Total win prize-money £9677

Going: Sf: 0-5 GS: 0-0 Gd: 1-3 GF: - Fm: 0-0
Distance: 2m/2m3: 0-3 **2m4-2m7: 1-5** 3m+: 0-0
Track: **LH: 1-2** RH: 0-6 Tight: 0-4 Gall: 0-0
Aids: Bl: 0-0 Vi: 0-0 Tstrap: 0-0
Best Rating: 99 2/00 Hrfd 2m1f good Hdl

Modest two-mile handicap hurdler, he is best with cut in the ground when given a patient ride. In good heart in 2002, stays two miles three.

Priestfield Boy (IRE)

5-y-o b g Un Desperado (FR)-Sandbank (IRE) (Kambalda)
C P Morlock The Shouting Men

Placings: *00* **(2942)**
2001/02: 16^{0}S, 16^{0}G

	Starts	1st	2nd	3rd	Win & Pl
NH Flat	2	0	0	0	
Career Total	**2**	**0**	**0**	**0**	

Going: Sf: 0-1 GS: 0-0 Gd: 0-1 GF: - Fm: 0-0
Distance: 2m/2m3: 0-2 2m4-2m7: 0-0 3m+: 0-0
Track: LH: 0-2 RH: 0-0 Tight: 0-0 Gall: 0-1
Aids: Bl: 0-0 Vi: 0-0 Tstrap: 0-0
Best Rating: 34 12/01 Wwck 2m soft NHF

Priestthorn (IRE)

95(103h) (68h)**84**

7-y-o b g Denel (FR)-Pollys Flake (Will Somers)
R H Alner C St V Fox

Placings: 06110-F4UP **(2880)**
2001/02: 25^{F}G, 23^{4}GF, 21^{U}G, 22^{P}G

	Starts	1st	2nd	3rd	Win & Pl
Hurdles	1	0	0	0	0
Chases	3	0	0	0	437
Career Total	**9**	**2**	**0**	**0**	**6068**

109	3/01	Extr	2m3f	E Hdl	HVY	£2287
109	3/01	Ling	2m7f	D Hdl	HVY	£3343

Total win prize-money £5631

Going: Sf: 0-0 GS: 0-0 Gd: 0-3 GF: - Fm: 0-1
Distance: 2m/2m3: 0-0 2m4-2m7: 0-2 3m+: 0-2
Track: LH: 0-0 RH: 0-4 Tight: 0-1 Gall: 0-0
Aids: Bl: 0-0 Vi: 0-0 Tstrap: 0-0
Best Rating: 109 3/01 Extr 2m3f heavy Hdl

Primaticcio (IRE)

7-y-o b g Priolo (USA)-Martinova (Martinmas)
V J Hughes V J Hughes

Placings: 04/2 **(4638)**
2001/02: 19^{2}GF

	Starts	1st	2nd	3rd	Win & Pl
Chases	1	0	1	0	842
Career Total	**3**	**0**	**1**	**0**	**1043**

Going: Sf: 0-0 GS: 0-0 Gd: 0-0 GF: - Fm: 0-1
Distance: 2m/2m3: 0-0 2m4-2m7: 0-1 3m+: 0-0
Track: LH: 0-0 RH: 0-1 Tight: 0-0 Gall: 0-0
Aids: Bl: 0-0 Vi: 0-0 Tstrap: 0-0
Best Rating: 114 4/02 Asct 2m3f110y gd-fm Ch

Progressive hunter chaser. Completed a four-timer when winning the Justitia Champion Hunters Chase at Stratford June 2002. Likes fast ground, wears headgear.

Prime Attraction

104f **103f**

5-y-o gr m Primitive Rising (USA)-My Friend Melody (Sizzling Melody)
W M Brisbourne Positive Partners

Placings: *100* **(1630)**
2001/02: 16^{1}GF, 16^{0}GF, 16^{0}GF

	Starts	1st	2nd	3rd	Win & Pl
NH Flat	3	1	0	0	1470
Career Total	**3**	**1**	**0**	**0**	**1470**

83	7/01	Uttx	2m	H NHF	G-F	£1470

Total win prize-money £1470

Going: Sf: 0-0 GS: 0-0 Gd: 0-0 GF: - Fm: 1-3
Distance: **2m/2m3: 1-3** 2m4-2m7: 0-0 3m+: 0-0
Track: **LH: 1-2** RH: 0-1 Tight: 0-0 Gall: 0-0
Aids: Bl: 0-0 Vi: 0-0 Tstrap: 0-0
Best Rating: 83 10/01 Ludl 2m gd-fm NHF

Winner twice in bumpers, acts on good ground.

Prime Course (IRE)

13-y-o b g Crash Course-Prime Mistress (Skymaster)
Mrs A Farrant (Miss A M Newton-Smith 3/3) E J Farrant

Placings: *00/0/P/4/U-P34* **(4172)**
2001/02: 26^{P}GS, 26^{3}G, 26^{4}GS

	Starts	1st	2nd	3rd	Win & Pl
Chases	3	0	0	1	225
Career Total	**9**	**0**	**0**	**1**	**306**

Going: Sf: 0-0 GS: 0-2 Gd: 0-1 GF: - Fm: 0-0
Distance: 2m/2m3: 0-0 2m4-2m7: 0-0 3m+: 0-3
Track: LH: 0-0 RH: 0-1 Tight: 0-1 Gall: 0-0
Aids: Bl: 0-0 Vi: 0-0 Tstrap: 0-1
Best Rating: 77 2/00 Folk 2m5f gd-sft Ch

Prime Minister

104 **77**

8-y-o ch g Be My Chief (USA)-Classic Design (Busted)
G E Jones G Elwyn Jones

Placings: P/6045 **(4326)**
2001/02: 17^{6}S, 16^{0}S, 17^{4}G, 17^{5}S

	Starts	1st	2nd	3rd	Win & Pl
Hurdles	4	0	0	0	0
Career Total	**5**	**0**	**0**	**0**	**0**

Going: Sf: 0-3 GS: 0-0 Gd: 0-1 GF: - Fm: 0-0
Distance: 2m/2m3: 0-4 2m4-2m7: 0-0 3m+: 0-0
Track: LH: 0-0 RH: 0-4 Tight: 0-0 Gall: 0-0
Aids: Bl: 0-0 Vi: 0-0 Tstrap: 0-0
Best Rating: 76 3/02 Hrfd 2m1f good Hdl

Prime Suspect

57

5-y-o b g Contract Law (USA)-Rodney's Sister (Leading Man)
R Williams R Williams

Placings: *0-000U* **(1013)**
2001/02: 16^{0}GF, 19^{0}G, 16^{0}GF, 20^{U}G

	Starts	1st	2nd	3rd	Win & Pl
NH Flat	1	0	0	0	0
Hurdles	3	0	0	0	0
Career Total	**5**	**0**	**0**	**0**	

Going: Sf: 0-0 GS: 0-0 Gd: 0-2 GF: - Fm: 0-2
Distance: 2m/2m3: 0-2 2m4-2m7: 0-2 3m+: 0-0
Track: LH: 0-2 RH: 0-2 Tight: 0-2 Gall: 0-1
Aids: Bl: 0-0 Vi: 0-0 Tstrap: 0-0
Best Rating: 52 5/01 Hntg 2m110y gd-fm NHF

Primero (IRE)

102 **108**

8-y-o b g Lycius (USA)-Pipitina (Bustino)
P F Nicholls Mrs Maureen Emery

Placings: PPP/U3P/133514F **(1443)**
2001/02: 21^{1}GF, 20^{3}GF, 21^{3}GF, 24^{5}GF, 26^{1}GF, 25^{4}GF, 26^{F}GF

	Starts	1st	2nd	3rd	Win & Pl
Chases	7	2	0	2	9843
Career Total	**13**	**2**	**0**	**3**	**10463**

108	8/01	Font	3m2f110y	F(0-90)HCh	G-F	£3542
108	6/01	Strf	2m5f110y	D(0-110)HCh	G-F	£4436

Total win prize-money £7979

Going: Sf: 0-0 GS: 0-0 Gd: 0-0 GF: - Fm: 2-7
Distance: 2m/2m3: 0-0 2m4-2m7: 1-3 3m+: 1-4
Track: **LH: 1-3** RH: 0-2 **Tight: 2-5** Gall: 0-0
Aids: Bl: 0-0 Vi: 0-0 **Tstrap: 2-7**
Best Rating: 108 8/01 Font 3m2f110y gd-fm Ch

moderate staying chaser, suited by fast ground, has had jumping problems.

Primitive Herb

102 **103**

6-y-o b g Primitive Rising (USA)-Mildame (Milford)
Mrs M Reveley M F Strawson

Placings: *061PPF* **(4554)**
2001/02: 16^{0}G, 20^{6}GS, 16^{1}G, 24^{P}S, 19^{P}S, 17^{F}G

	Starts	1st	2nd	3rd	Win & Pl
NH Flat	1	0	0	0	0
Chases	5	1	0	0	4251
Career Total	**6**	**1**	**0**	**0**	**4251**

103	12/01	Donc	2m110y	D Ch	GD	£4251

Total win prize-money £4251

Going: Sf: 0-2 GS: 0-1 Gd: 1-3 GF: - Fm: 0-0
Distance: **2m/2m3: 1-3** 2m4-2m7: 0-2 3m+: 0-1
Track: **LH: 1-5** RH: 0-1 Tight: 0-1 **Gall: 1-4**
Aids: Bl: 0-0 Vi: 0-0 Tstrap: 0-0
Best Rating: 103 12/01 Donc 2m110y good Ch

Successful over fences, he acts on good ground and is effective over two miles.

Primitive Satin

7-y-o ch g Primitive Rising (USA)-Satinanda (Leander)
R Tate R Tate

Placings: PU41 **(4859)**
2001/02: 25^{P}S, 24^{U}GF, 27^{4}S, 25^{1}G

	Starts	1st	2nd	3rd	Win & Pl
Chases	4	1	0	0	1567
Career Total	**4**	**1**	**0**	**0**	**1567**

90	4/02	Hexm	3m1f	H Ch	GD	£1566

Total win prize-money £1567

Going: Sf: 0-2 GS: 0-0 Gd: 1-1 GF: - Fm: 0-1
Distance: 2m/2m3: 0-0 2m4-2m7: 0-0 **3m+: 1-4**

Track: LH: 1-4 RH: 0-0 Tight: 0-2 Gall: 0-0
Aids: Bl: 1-1 Vi: 0-0 Tstrap: 0-0
Best Rating: 90 4/02 Hexm 3m1f good Ch

Fair pointer who got off the mark under Rules at Hexham in April. Stays three miles plus, acts on any ground, has worn blinkers.

Primitive Way

107 **114**

10-y-o b g Primitive Rising (USA)-Potterway (Velvet Prince)
Miss S E Forster The Hon Gerald Maitland-Carew

Placings:6213353P04P **(4878)**
2001/02: 21^{6}GF, 20^{2}G, 25^{1}G, 26^{3}S, 25^{3}GS, 22^{5}GS, 24^{3}G, 25^{P}HY, 25^{0}S, 25^{4}GF, 24^{P}G

	Starts	1st	2nd	3rd	Win & Pl
Chases	11	1	1	3	8672
Career Total	11	1	1	3	8672

100 10/01 Kels 3m1f E Ch GD £3201
Total win prize-money £3201

Going: Sf: 0-3 GS: 0-2 Gd: 1-4 GF: - Fm: 0-2
Distance: 2m/2m3: 0-0 2m4-2m7: 0-3 3m+: 1-8
Track: LH: 1-7 RH: 0-4 Tight: 1-7 Gall: 0-0
Aids: Bl: 0-3 Vi: 0-0 Tstrap: 0-0
Best Rating: 114 12/01 Muss 3m good Ch

Winning pointer, he got off the mark under Rules at Kelso in October 2001, but struggled in better company after that. Acts on good ground and is effective at three miles plus. Usually wears blinkers.

Primulas Daughter

8-y-o b m Say Primula-Niel's Crystal (Indiaro)
Mrs L C Jewell Mrs Vicky Palmer

Placings:P0 **(4547)**
2001/02: 21^{P}HY, 20^{0}GF

	Starts	1st	2nd	3rd	Win & Pl
Hurdles	1	0	0	0	0
Chases	1	0	0	0	0
Career Total	2	0	0	0	

Going: Sf: 0-1 GS: 0-0 Gd: 0-0 GF: - Fm: 0-1
Distance: 2m/2m3: 0-0 2m4-2m7: 0-2 3m+: 0-0
Track: LH: 0-1 RH: 0-1 Tight: 0-1 Gall: 0-1
Aids: Bl: 0-0 Vi: 0-0 Tstrap: 0-0
Best Rating:

Prince Albert

89 **72**

4-y-o ch g Rock City-Russell Creek (Sandy Creek)
J R Jenkins S A Barningham

Placings:2 **(2324)**
2001/02: 16^{2}S

	Starts	1st	2nd	3rd	Win & Pl
Hurdles	1	0	1	0	925
Career Total	1	0	1	0	925

Going: Sf: 0-1 GS: 0-0 Gd: 0-0 GF: - Fm: 0-0
Distance: 2m/2m3: 0-1 2m4-2m7: 0-0 3m+: 0-0
Track: LH: 0-1 RH: 0-0 Tight: 0-1 Gall: 0-0
Aids: Bl: 0-0 Vi: 0-0 Tstrap: 0-0
Best Rating: 72 11/01 Fknm 2m soft Hdl

Modest Flat performer, respectable effort on hurdling debut.

Prince Among Men

106 **111**

5-y-o b g Robellino (USA)-Forelino (USA) (Trempolino (USA))
M Todhunter Jim Ennis

Placings:1212-330 **(1803)**
2001/02: 17^{3}GS, 16^{3}G, 16^{0}GF

	Starts	1st	2nd	3rd	Win & Pl
Hurdles	3	0	0	2	1367
Career Total	7	2	2	2	8891

106 10/00 Ludl 2m E Hdl G-F £2807
106 8/00 Worc 2m E Hdl G-F £2775
Total win prize-money £5583

Going: Sf: 0-0 GS: 0-1 Gd: 0-1 GF: - Fm: 0-1
Distance: 2m/2m3: 0-3 2m4-2m7: 0-0 3m+: 0-0
Track: LH: 0-1 RH: 0-2 Tight: 0-1 Gall: 0-0
Aids: Bl: 0-0 Vi: 0-1 Tstrap: 0-0
Best Rating: 111 9/01 Prth 2m110y good Hdl

Prince Caspian

92 **88**

5-y-o ch g Mystiko (USA)-Real Princess (Aragon)
Miss E C Lavelle Lady Sieff

Placings:02 **(1032)**
2001/02: 17^{0}GF, 17^{2}G

	Starts	1st	2nd	3rd	Win & Pl
Hurdles	2	0	1	0	1039
Career Total	2	0	1	0	1039

Going: Sf: 0-0 GS: 0-0 Gd: 0-1 GF: - Fm: 0-1
Distance: 2m/2m3: 0-2 2m4-2m7: 0-0 3m+: 0-0
Track: LH: 0-2 RH: 0-0 Tight: 0-2 Gall: 0-0
Aids: Bl: 0-0 Vi: 0-0 Tstrap: 0-0
Best Rating: 88 7/01 NAbb 2m1f gd-fm Hdl

Prince Darkhan (IRE)

6-y-o br g Doyoun-Sovereign Dona (Sovereign Path)
M Smith Malcolm Smith

Placings:F **(0962)**
2001/02: 17^{F}GF

	Starts	1st	2nd	3rd	Win & Pl
Hurdles	1	0	0	0	
Career Total	1	0	0	0	

Going: Sf: 0-0 GS: 0-0 Gd: 0-0 GF: - Fm: 0-1
Distance: 2m/2m3: 0-1 2m4-2m7: 0-0 3m+: 0-0
Track: LH: 0-1 RH: 0-0 Tight: 0-1 Gall: 0-0
Aids: Bl: 0-0 Vi: 0-0 Tstrap: 0-0
Best Rating:

Prince De Berry

(94c) (57c)

11-y-o ch g Ballacashtal (CAN)-Hoonah (FR) (Luthier)
G A Ham (Mrs J L Le Brocq 23/9) N G Ahier

Placings:0464/U4/652P0F402/130/323/311046P-U062P320 **(4413)**
2001/02: 21^{U}GF, 18^{0}GF, 16^{6}G, 18^{2}G, 17^{P}G, 17^{3}GF, 20^{2}GF, 18^{0}S

	Starts	1st	2nd	3rd	Win & Pl
Hurdles	5	0	2	1	1335
Chases	3	0	0	0	0
Career Total	36	3	5	5	6837

8/00 LES 2m HHdl G-F £1050
8/00 LES 2m4f HHdl G-F £1050
7/98 LES 2m Hdl G-F £900
Total win prize-money £3000

Going: Sf: 0-1 GS: 0-0 Gd: 0-3 GF: - Fm: 0-4
Distance: 2m/2m3: 0-6 2m4-2m7: 0-2 3m+: 0-0
Track: LH: 0-5 RH: 0-1 Tight: 0-3 Gall: 0-0
Aids: Bl: 0-0 Vi: 0-0 Tstrap: 0-0
Best Rating: 79 1/95 Sand 2m110y soft Hdl

Prince De Galles

104 **95**

9-y-o b g Prince Des Coeurs (USA)-Royal Brush (King Of Spain)
P Bowen Chris Wall

Placings:0/2600221U30P-FFF04506 **(3983)**
2001/02: 26^{F}GF, 27^{F}G, 24^{F}GF, 24^{0}GF, 24^{4}GF, 24^{5}S, 26^{0}GS, 24^{6}G

	Starts	1st	2nd	3rd	Win & Pl
Hurdles	7	0	0	0	270
Chases	1	0	0	0	0
Career Total	20	1	3	1	6714

97 11/00 Ludl 3m F(0-105)HHdl GD £3493
Total win prize-money £3494

Going: Sf: 0-1 GS: 0-1 Gd: 0-2 GF: - Fm: 0-4
Distance: 2m/2m3: 0-0 2m4-2m7: 0-0 3m+: 0-8
Track: LH: 0-3 RH: 0-5 Tight: 0-3 Gall: 0-1
Aids: Bl: 0-0 Vi: 0-0 Tstrap: 0-0
Best Rating: 99 6/00 Uttx 2m4f110y good Hdl

Prince Du Soleil (FR)

89 **65**

6-y-o b g Cardoun (FR)-Revelry (FR) (Blakeney)
J R Jenkins R Bradbury

Placings:6 **(1484)**
2001/02: 16^{6}GS

	Starts	1st	2nd	3rd	Win & Pl
Hurdles	1	0	0	0	0
Career Total	1	0	0	0	0

Going: Sf: 0-0 GS: 0-1 Gd: 0-0 GF: - Fm: 0-0
Distance: 2m/2m3: 0-1 2m4-2m7: 0-0 3m+: 0-0
Track: LH: 0-1 RH: 0-0 Tight: 0-1 Gall: 0-0
Aids: Bl: 0-0 Vi: 0-0 Tstrap: 0-0
Best Rating: 65 9/01 Plum 2m gd-sft Hdl

Prince Dundee (FR)

98(98c) (108c) **107**

7-y-o ch g Ecossais (FR)-Princesse Normande (FR) (Belgio (FR))
J Neville Beacon Estates Ltd

Placings:26/2036/0315322-0P4U0UF0 **(4853)**
2001/02: 19^{0}G, 20^{P}GS, 16^{4}G, 19^{U}S, 20^{0}G, 16^{U}G, 20^{F}GF, 16^{0}G

	Starts	1st	2nd	3rd	Win & Pl
Hurdles	3	0	0	0	0
Chases	5	0	0	0	240
Career Total	21	1	4	3	7617

106 12/00 Folk 2m1f110y D(0-110)HHdl HVY £2957
Total win prize-money £2958

Going: Sf: 0-1 GS: 0-1 Gd: 0-5 GF: - Fm: 0-1

Distance: 2m/2m3: 0-4 2m4-2m7: 0-4 3m+: 0-0
Track: LH: 0-2 RH: 0-6 Tight: 0-4 Gall: 0-1
Aids: Bl: 0-2 Vi: 0-5 Tstrap: 0-0
Best Rating: 108 12/01 Ludl 2m good Ch

Fair handicap hurdler at around two and a half miles. Handles fast ground and soft. Yet to click over fences.

Prince Edmund

7-y-o b g Picea-Queens Pearl (Queens Hussar)
G Harris F Kitson

Placings:*00000*/6-P (4846)
2001/02: 24^{P}G

	Starts	1st	2nd	3rd	Win & Pl
Chases	1	0	0	0	
Career Total	**7**	**0**	**0**	**0**	**0**

Going: Sf: 0-0 GS: 0-0 Gd: 0-1 GF: - Fm: 0-0
Distance: 2m/2m3: 0-0 2m4-2m7: 0-0 3m+: 0-1
Track: LH: 0-1 RH: 0-0 Tight: 0-1 Gall: 0-0
Aids: Bl: 0-0 Vi: 0-0 Tstrap: 0-1
Best Rating: 87 2/00 Sand 2m110y soft NHF

Prince Highlight (IRE)

96(102h) (111h)**100+**
7-y-o b g Lord Americo-Madamme Highlights (Andretti)
Ferdy Murphy Mrs M B Scholey

Placings:*30*215-02553 (4496)
2001/02: 16^{0}G, 20^{2}G, 16^{5}G, 20^{5}S, 22^{3}G

	Starts	1st	2nd	3rd	Win & Pl
Hurdles	5	0	1	1	4218
Career Total	**10**	**1**	**2**	**2**	**9529**

107	4/01	Hayd	2m	D Hdl	SFT	£3945

Total win prize-money £3946

Going: Sf: 0-1 GS: 0-0 Gd: 0-4 GF: - Fm: 0-0
Distance: 2m/2m3: 0-2 2m4-2m7: 0-3 3m+: 0-0
Track: LH: 0-5 RH: 0-0 Tight: 0-0 Gall: 0-2
Aids: Bl: 0-0 Vi: 0-0 Tstrap: 0-0
Best Rating: 111 12/01 Donc 2m110y good Hdl

Got off the mark at Haydock in April 2001 on his second attempt over hurdles, but struggled afterwards until running very well back at Haydock in November 2001. Effective over two miles, but stays two and a half and acts on soft ground. Well beaten when runner-up on his chasing bow at Wetherby in May.

Prince Minata (IRE)

93 **85**
7-y-o b g Machiavellian (USA)-Aminata (Glenstal (USA))
P W Hiatt P W Hiatt

Placings:P0/P-30 (1473)
2001/02: 17^{3}G, 17^{0}S

	Starts	1st	2nd	3rd	Win & Pl
Hurdles	2	0	0	1	340
Career Total	**5**	**0**	**0**	**1**	**340**

Going: Sf: 0-1 GS: 0-0 Gd: 0-1 GF: - Fm: 0-0
Distance: 2m/2m3: 0-2 2m4-2m7: 0-0 3m+: 0-0
Track: LH: 0-1 RH: 0-1 Tight: 0-2 Gall: 0-0
Aids: Bl: 0-0 Vi: 0-0 Tstrap: 0-1
Best Rating: 85 9/01 Sedg 2m1f good Hdl

Prince Nicholas

101 **106**
7-y-o ch g Midyan (USA)-Its My Turn (Palm Track)
K W Hogg Auldyn Stud Ltd

Placings:244-2345 (4283)
2001/02: 17^{2}S, 17^{3}GS, 19^{4}G, 17^{5}GS

	Starts	1st	2nd	3rd	Win & Pl
Hurdles	4	0	1	1	1169
Career Total	**7**	**0**	**2**	**1**	**2106**

Going: Sf: 0-1 GS: 0-2 Gd: 0-1 GF: - Fm: 0-0
Distance: 2m/2m3: 0-3 2m4-2m7: 0-1 3m+: 0-0
Track: LH: 0-0 RH: 0-4 Tight: 0-3 Gall: 0-0
Aids: Bl: 0-0 Vi: 0-0 Tstrap: 0-0
Best Rating: 106 10/01 MRas 2m3f110y good Hdl

A 12-furlong winner on the Flat, has run well in novice hurdles without scoring. Appreciates cut in the ground, gets an extended two miles-one, but looked not to stay when tried over two and a half miles.

Prince Of Aragon

97 **82**
6-y-o b g Aragon-Queens Welcome (Northfields (USA))
D M Grissell Robin Smith

Placings:00/205 (4757)
2001/02: 20^{2}G, 20^{0}G, 16^{5}GF

	Starts	1st	2nd	3rd	Win & Pl
Hurdles	3	0	1	0	740
Career Total	**5**	**0**	**1**	**0**	**740**

Going: Sf: 0-0 GS: 0-0 Gd: 0-2 GF: - Fm: 0-1
Distance: 2m/2m3: 0-1 2m4-2m7: 0-2 3m+: 0-0
Track: LH: 0-1 RH: 0-2 Tight: 0-0 Gall: 0-1
Aids: Bl: 0-0 Vi: 0-0 Tstrap: 0-0
Best Rating: 82 4/02 Uttx 2m gd-fm Hdl

Poor hurdle form.

Prince Of Tara (IRE)

111 **147**
5-y-o b h Prince Of Birds (USA)-Fete Champetre (Welsh Pageant)
S J Mahon James J Swan

Placings:*222451*-14312F26 (4665)
2001/02: 17^{1}S, 20^{4}Y, 20^{3}Y, 24^{1}YS, 24^{2}S, 24^{F}S, 24^{2}S, 24^{6}G

	Starts	1st	2nd	3rd	Win & Pl
Hurdles	8	2	2	1	22026
Career Total	**14**	**3**	**5**	**1**	**29667**

137	1/02	Fair	3m	Hdl	Y-S	£7407
108	11/01	Dpat	2m1f172y	Hdl	SFT	£3477
113	4/01	Navn	2m	NHF	SH	£4173

Total win prize-money £15059

Going: Sf: 1-4 GS: 0-0 Gd: 0-1 GF: - Fm: 0-0
Distance: 2m/2m3: 1-1 2m4-2m7: 0-2 3m+: 1-5
Track: LH: 0-4 **RH: 2-4** Tight: 0-1 Gall: 0-0
Aids: Bl: 0-0 Vi: 0-0 Tstrap: 0-0
Best Rating: 147 2/02 Fair 3m soft Hdl

Very useful Irish novice hurdler, stays three miles.

Prince Of The Deep

5-y-o b g Prince Daniel (USA)-Sea Sand (Sousa)
P Monteith Mrs A F Tullie

Placings:PP (2917)
2001/02: 20^{P}GF, 20^{P}G

	Starts	1st	2nd	3rd	Win & Pl
Hurdles	2	0	0	0	
Career Total	**2**	**0**	**0**	**0**	

Going: Sf: 0-0 GS: 0-0 Gd: 0-1 GF: - Fm: 0-1
Distance: 2m/2m3: 0-0 2m4-2m7: 0-2 3m+: 0-0
Track: LH: 0-0 RH: 0-2 Tight: 0-2 Gall: 0-0
Aids: Bl: 0-0 Vi: 0-0 Tstrap: 0-0
Best Rating:

Prince On The Ter

88(87h) (93h)**69**
7-y-o b g Terimon-Princess Constanza (Relkino)
C L Popham (A King 29/11) C L Popham

Placings:50000-*030*PUP00P (3863)
2001/02: 18^{0}G, 25^{3}G, 20^{0}G, 22^{P}GS, 19^{U}GS, 19^{P}GS, 22^{0}S, 17^{0}S, 21^{P}GS

	Starts	1st	2nd	3rd	Win & Pl
NH Flat	1	0	0	0	0
Hurdles	6	0	0	1	356
Chases	2	0	0	0	0
Career Total	**14**	**0**	**0**	**1**	**356**

Going: Sf: 0-2 GS: 0-4 Gd: 0-3 GF: - Fm: 0-0
Distance: 2m/2m3: 0-4 2m4-2m7: 0-4 3m+: 0-1
Track: LH: 0-2 RH: 0-6 Tight: 0-5 Gall: 0-0
Aids: Bl: 0-0 Vi: 0-0 Tstrap: 0-3
Best Rating: 100 5/01 Fair 2m2f good NHF

Prince Skyburd

96 **83**
11-y-o b g Domynsky-Burntwood Lady (Royal Buck)
Mrs P M A Avison Mrs P M A Avison

Placings:45P00/**1113U3**/5P465/**66151524**/51F50-PP523PP (4333)
2001/02: 17^{P}G, 16^{P}GF, 20^{5}G, 16^{2}GS, 24^{3}G, 24^{P}GS, 21^{P}S

	Starts	1st	2nd	3rd	Win & Pl
Chases	7	0	1	1	1480
Career Total	**36**	**6**	**2**	**3**	**21921**

95	5/00	Hexm	2m110y	F(0-105)HCh	G-F	£3146
94	12/99	Muss	2m	F(0-95)HCh	G-S	£2762
87	11/99	Sedg	2m110y	F(0-100)HCh	GD	£2726
95	10/96	Bang	2m1f110y	E(0-115)HCh	G-F	£3818
98	9/96	Worc	2m	E(0-100)HCh	G-F	£3081
91	8/96	Sedg	2m110y	E Ch	G-F	£2905

Total win prize-money £18439

Going: Sf: 0-1 GS: 0-2 Gd: 0-3 GF: - Fm: 0-1
Distance: 2m/2m3: 0-3 2m4-2m7: 0-2 3m+: 0-2
Track: LH: 0-5 RH: 0-2 Tight: 0-5 Gall: 0-1
Aids: Bl: 0-0 Vi: 0-0 Tstrap: 0-5
Best Rating: 98 9/96 Worc 2m gd-fm Ch

Modest handicap chaser, best at two miles on decent ground.

Prince Slayer

92 **82**
6-y-o b g Batshoof-Top Sovereign (High Top)
T P McGovern Ahmed Abdel-Khaleq

Placings:2P3-6 (0475)
2001/02: 17^{6}G

	Starts	1st	2nd	3rd	Win & Pl
Hurdles	1	0	0	0	0
Career Total	**4**	**0**	**1**	**1**	**902**

Going: Sf: 0-0 GS: 0-0 Gd: 0-1 GF: - Fm: 0-0

Distance: 2m/2m3: 0-1 2m4-2m7: 0-0 3m+: 0-0
Track: LH: 0-0 RH: 0-1 Tight: 0-1 Gall: 0-0
Aids: Bl: 0-0 Vi: 0-0 Tstrap: 0-0
Best Rating: 103 2/01 Plum 2m soft Hdl

Prince Sorinieres (FR)

7-y-o br g Valanjou (FR)-Somewhat Better (Rheingold)
M C Pipe The Arthur White Partnership

Placings:11/111F422F30/P-P (0235)
2001/02: 20^{P}GF

	Starts	1st	2nd	3rd	Win & Pl
Chases	1	0	0	0	
Career Total	**14**	**5**	**2**	**1**	**39490**

8/99	Mesl	2m1f110y	Ch	SFT	£4306
6/99	Toul	2m1f110y	Ch	GD	£4844
5/99	Mesl	2m1f110y	Ch	SFT	£3767
3/99	Toul	2m1f110y	Hdl	VS	£11841
3/99	Chol	2m1f	Hdl	VS	£3229

Total win prize-money £27987

Going: Sf: 0-0 GS: 0-0 Gd: 0-0 GF: - Fm: 0-1
Distance: 2m/2m3: 0-0 2m4-2m7: 0-1 3m+: 0-0
Track: LH: 0-1 RH: 0-0 Tight: 0-1 Gall: 0-0
Aids: Bl: 0-0 Vi: 0-0 Tstrap: 0-0
Best Rating: 148 11/99 Towc 2m110y good Ch

Prince Tor

(82h) (68h)
9-y-o b g Roscoe Blake-Torus Queen (Torus)
B D Leavy K J Condliffe

Placings:652F6PPU/PUU55/PP0-000PF (4849)
2001/02: 20^{0}F, 16^{0}GF, 16^{0}G, 20^{P}GS, 24^{F}G

	Starts	1st	2nd	3rd	Win & Pl
Hurdles	3	0	0	0	0
Chases	2	0	0	0	0
Career Total	**21**	**0**	**1**	**0**	**351**

Going: Sf: 0-0 GS: 0-1 Gd: 0-2 GF: - Fm: 0-2
Distance: 2m/2m3: 0-2 2m4-2m7: 0-2 3m+: 0-1
Track: LH: 0-4 RH: 0-1 Tight: 0 1 Gall: 0-0
Aids: Bl: 0-2 Vi: 0-0 Tstrap: 0-2
Best Rating: 108 12/98 Bang 2m1f gd-sft NHF

Princeful (IRE)

128
11-y-o b g Electric-Iram (Proverb)
R J Hodges Exors Of The Late Robert Hitchins

Placings:11512P/241241/11B/6/P-6 (4911)
2001/02: 24^{6}G

	Starts	1st	2nd	3rd	Win & Pl
Hurdles	1	0	0	0	750
Career Total	**18**	**7**	**3**	**0**	**137924**

170	12/98	Asct	3m1f110y	A Hdl	SFT	£29573
160	11/98	Newb	3m110y	A Hdl	SFT	£12620
162	3/98	Chel	3m	A Hdl	GD	£57137
144	1/98	Chel	2m5f110y	B HHdl	G-S	£6085
109	2/97	Chep	2m110y	E Hdl	SFT	£2514
113	12/96	Towc	2m	H NHF	HVY	£1416
111	5/96	Worc	2m	H NHF	GD	£1332

Total win prize-money £110681

Going: Sf: 0-0 GS: 0-0 Gd: 0-1 GF: - Fm: 0-0
Distance: 2m/2m3: 0-0 2m4-2m7: 0-0 3m+: 0-1
Track: LH: 0-0 RH: 0-0 Tight: 0-0 Gall: 0-0
Aids: Bl: 0-0 Vi: 0-0 Tstrap: 0-0
Best Rating: 170 12/98 Asct 3m1f110y soft Hdl

Connections entertained the highest hopes for him over fences at one stage, but he was brought down on his chasing debut, suffering a career-threatening injury. The winner of the '98 Stayers' Hurdle, he had landed the Long Walk Hurdle in the gamest fashion later that year before disaster struck. Very lightly raced since, he is but a shadow of his former self.

Princess Emily (IRE)

59 22
4-y-o b f Dolphin Street (FR)-Partita (Polish Precedent (USA))
B S Rothwell Ms Denise S Doyle

Placings:0 (1141)
2001/02: 16^{0}G

	Starts	1st	2nd	3rd	Win & Pl
Hurdles	1	0	0	0	
Career Total	**1**	**0**	**0**	**0**	

Going: Sf: 0-0 GS: 0-0 Gd: 0-1 GF: - Fm: 0-0
Distance: 2m/2m3: 0-1 2m4-2m7: 0-0 3m+: 0-0
Track: LH: 0-1 RH: 0-0 Tight: 0-1 Gall: 0-0
Aids: Bl: 0-0 Vi: 0-0 Tstrap: 0-0
Best Rating: 22 8/01 Strf 2m110y good Hdl

Princess Londis

96(104h) (94h)83
7-y-o ch m Interrex (CAN)-Princess Lucianne (Stanford)
B De Haan C Richards

Placings:25/22232F-PP334006 (2333)
2001/02: 17^{P}G, 16^{P}GF, 16^{3}GF, 16^{3}GF, 16^{4}GF, 16^{0}G, 16^{0}GF, 17^{6}G

	Starts	1st	2nd	3rd	Win & Pl
Hurdles	6	0	0	2	682
Chases	2	0	0	0	0
Career Total	**16**	**0**	**5**	**3**	**5002**

Going: Sf: 0-0 GS: 0-0 Gd: 0-3 GF: - Fm: 0-5
Distance: 2m/2m3: 0-8 2m4-2m7: 0-0 3m+: 0-0
Track: LH: 0-3 RH: 0-5 Tight: 0-4 Gall: 0-1
Aids: Bl: 0-0 Vi: 0-0 Tstrap: 0-0
Best Rating: 101 8/00 Strf 2m110y gd-fm Hdl

Princess Of War

7-y-o b m Warrshan (USA)-Dutch Princess (Royalty)
J R Jenkins P W Piper

Placings:3143P44/50-PP (1014)
2001/02: 20^{P}GF, 16^{P}G

	Starts	1st	2nd	3rd	Win & Pl
Hurdles	2	0	0	0	
Career Total	**11**	**1**	**0**	**2**	**2418**

86	7/99	Worc	2m	H NHF	G-F	£1563

Total win prize-money £1564

Going: Sf: 0-0 GS: 0-0 Gd: 0-1 GF: - Fm: 0-1
Distance: 2m/2m3: 0-1 2m4-2m7: 0-1 3m+: 0-0
Track: LH: 0-1 RH: 0-1 Tight: 0-0 Gall: 0-1
Aids: Bl: 0-0 Vi: 0-0 Tstrap: 0-0
Best Rating: 97 10/99 Bang 2m1f gd-sft NHF

Princess Ria (IRE)

5-y-o b m Petong-Walking Saint (Godswalk (USA))
M E Sowersby (N P Littmoden 6/7) Racing Ladies

Placings:3 (1021)
2001/02: 21^{3}GF

	Starts	1st	2nd	3rd	Win & Pl
Hurdles	1	0	0	1	338
Career Total	**1**	**0**	**0**	**1**	**338**

Going: Sf: 0-0 GS: 0-0 Gd: 0-0 GF: - Fm: 0-1
Distance: 2m/2m3: 0-0 2m4-2m7: 0-1 3m+: 0-0
Track: LH: 0-1 RH: 0-0 Tight: 0-1 Gall: 0-0
Aids: Bl: 0-0 Vi: 0-0 Tstrap: 0-0
Best Rating:

Princess Sophie

100 73+
4-y-o b f Tragic Role (USA)-Octavia (Sallust)
K W Hogg Mrs Thelma White

Placings:0P (1718)
2001/02: 16^{0}G, 16^{P}G

	Starts	1st	2nd	3rd	Win & Pl
Hurdles	2	0	0	0	
Career Total	**2**	**0**	**0**	**0**	

Going: Sf: 0-0 GS: 0-0 Gd: 0-2 GF: - Fm: 0-0
Distance: 2m/2m3: 0-2 2m4-2m7: 0-0 3m+: 0-0
Track: LH: 0-2 RH: 0-0 Tight: 0-1 Gall: 0-0
Aids: Bl: 0-0 Vi: 0-0 Tstrap: 0-0
Best Rating: 62 10/01 Kels 2m110y good Hdl

Princess Tessa

104f 93f
6-y-o b m King's Ride-Kathy Cook (Glenstal (USA))
N A Twiston-Davies M P Wareing

Placings:240 (3236)
2001/02: 17^{2}G, 16^{4}HY, 16^{0}GS

	Starts	1st	2nd	3rd	Win & Pl
NH Flat	3	0	1	0	505
Career Total	**3**	**0**	**1**	**0**	**505**

Going: Sf: 0-1 GS: 0-1 Gd: 0-1 GF: - Fm: 0-0
Distance: 2m/2m3: 0-3 2m4-2m7: 0-0 3m+: 0-0
Track: LH: 0-1 RH: 0-2 Tight: 0-1 Gall: 0-1
Aids: Bl: 0-0 Vi: 0-0 Tstrap: 0-0
Best Rating: 93 12/01 Towc 2m heavy NHF

Runner-up in a Bangor bumper on her debut.

Princess Timon

5-y-o gr m Terimon-Royal Blaze (Scallywag)
L Wells Mrs Carrie Zetter-Wells

Placings:3-01P (1941)
2001/02: 17^{0}S, 17^{1}F, 21^{P}GS

	Starts	1st	2nd	3rd	Win & Pl
NH Flat	2	1	0	0	2300
Hurdles	1	0	0	0	0
Career Total	**4**	**1**	**0**	**1**	**2538**

89	10/01	Tntn	2m1f	H NHF	FRM	£2299

Total win prize-money £2300

Going: Sf: 0-1 GS: 0-1 Gd: 0-0 GF: - Fm: 1-1
Distance: **2m/2m3: 1-2** 2m4-2m7: 0-1 3m+: 0-0
Track: LH: 0-1 RH: 0-1 Tight: 0-2 Gall: 0-0

Aids: Bl: 0-0 Vi: 0-0 Tstrap: 0-0
Best Rating: 89 10/01 Tntn 2m1f firm NHF

Landed a moderate Taunton bumper on her third start.

Princesse Grec (FR)

98 66

4-y-o ch f Grand Tresor (FR)-Perimele (FR) (Mon Fils)
Dr P Pritchard The Honfleur Syndicate

Placings:00P0P00 **(4737)**
2001/02: 16^{0}G, 16^{0}G, 16^{P}G, 16^{0}GS, 20^{P}GS, 16^{0}S, 16^{0}GF

	Starts	1st	2nd	3rd	Win & Pl
Hurdles	7	0	0	0	
Career Total	**7**	**0**	**0**	**0**	

Going: Sf: 0-1 GS: 0-2 Gd: 0-3 GF: - Fm: 0-1
Distance: 2m/2m3: 0-6 2m4-2m7: 0-1 3m+: 0-0
Track: LH: 0-5 RH: 0-2 Tight: 0-0 Gall: 0-2
Aids: Bl: 0-0 Vi: 0-0 Tstrap: 0-0
Best Rating: 66 1/02 Newb 2m110y gd-sft Hdl

Ordinary form in decent novice hurdles to date over two miles on good/good to soft ground.

Principal Boy (IRE)

(104h) (83h)

9-y-o br g Cyrano De Bergerac-Shenley Lass (Prince Tenderfoot (USA))
G M Moore Mrs S E Cooper

Placings:P4040/P/0/2-1320345U **(1594)**
2001/02: 16^{1}GS, 16^{3}F, 16^{2}GS, 20^{0}G, 17^{3}GF, 17^{4}G, 21^{5}G, 16^{U}G

	Starts	1st	2nd	3rd	Win & Pl
Hurdles	7	1	1	2	4256
Chases	1	0	0	0	0
Career Total	**16**	**1**	**2**	**2**	**5184**

80 5/01 Prth 2m110y G(0-95)HHdl G-S £2968
Total win prize-money £2968

Going: Sf: 0-0 GS: 1-2 Gd: 0-4 GF: - Fm: 0-2
Distance: **2m/2m3: 1-6** 2m4-2m7: 0-2 3m+: 0-0
Track: LH: 0-7 **RH: 1-1** Tight: 0-4 Gall: 0-0
Aids: Bl: 0-0 Vi: 0-0 Tstrap: 0-0
Best Rating: 83 6/01 Hexm 2m gd-sft Hdl

Priory Rose (IRE)

60f 63f

5-y-o br m Roselier (FR)-Badsworth Madam (Over The River (FR))
G A Harker Geoff Bonson

Placings:6 **(3443)**
2001/02: 17^{6}S

	Starts	1st	2nd	3rd	Win & Pl
NH Flat	1	0	0	0	0
Career Total	**1**	**0**	**0**	**0**	**0**

Going: Sf: 0-1 GS: 0-0 Gd: 0-0 GF: - Fm: 0-0
Distance: 2m/2m3: 0-1 2m4-2m7: 0-0 3m+: 0-0
Track: LH: 0-1 RH: 0-0 Tight: 0-1 Gall: 0-0
Aids: Bl: 0-0 Vi: 0-0 Tstrap: 0-0
Best Rating: 63 1/02 Sedg 2m1f soft NHF

Priory Wood

81 41

6-y-o ch m Gunner B-Penlea Lady (Leading Man)
Mrs H Dalton Mrs S G Addinsell

Placings:*100* **(3874)**
2001/02: 17^{1}S, 17^{0}S, 16^{0}S

	Starts	1st	2nd	3rd	Win & Pl
NH Flat	2	1	0	0	1596
Hurdles	1	0	0	0	0
Career Total	**3**	**1**	**0**	**0**	**1596**

87 12/01 Hrfd 2m1f H NHF SFT £1596
Total win prize-money £1596

Going: Sf: 1-3 GS: 0-0 Gd: 0-0 GF: - Fm: 0-0
Distance: **2m/2m3: 1-3** 2m4-2m7: 0-0 3m+: 0-0
Track: LH: 0-0 **RH: 1-2** Tight: 0-1 Gall: 0-1
Aids: Bl: 0-0 Vi: 0-0 Tstrap: 0-0
Best Rating: 87 12/01 Hrfd 2m1f soft NHF

Made a winning debut in a Hereford bumper.

Private Jet (IRE)

13-y-o b g Dara Monarch-Torriglia (USA) (Nijinsky (CAN))
I A Brown P H Sanders

Placings:*400*/4F04262550/23/662/P15424P5/UPPPP/0B **(0473)**
2001/02: 21^{0}G, 20^{B}GF

	Starts	1st	2nd	3rd	Win & Pl
Chases	2	0	0	0	
Career Total	**33**	**1**	**5**	**1**	**4424**

90 5/98 Hexm 2m4f110y H Ch G-F £1283
Total win prize-money £1283

Going: Sf: 0-0 GS: 0-0 Gd: 0-1 GF: - Fm: 0-1
Distance: 2m/2m3: 0-0 2m4-2m7: 0-2 3m+: 0-0
Track: LH: 0-2 RH: 0-0 Tight: 0-1 Gall: 0-0
Aids: Bl: 0-0 Vi: 0-0 Tstrap: 0-0
Best Rating: 98 5/96 Sedg 2m5f firm Ch

Private Percival

9-y-o b g Arrasas (USA)-Romacina (Roman Warrior)
Jamie Poulton Jamie Poulton

Placings:0/464P4-0 **(0677)**
2001/02: 16^{0}GF

	Starts	1st	2nd	3rd	Win & Pl
Chases	1	0	0	0	
Career Total	**7**	**0**	**0**	**0**	**943**

Going: Sf: 0-0 GS: 0-0 Gd: 0-0 GF: - Fm: 0-1
Distance: 2m/2m3: 0-1 2m4-2m7: 0-0 3m+: 0-0
Track: LH: 0-1 RH: 0-0 Tight: 0-0 Gall: 0-0
Aids: Bl: 0-0 Vi: 0-0 Tstrap: 0-0
Best Rating: 97 3/01 Asct 2m3f110y soft Ch

Private Pete

9-y-o ch g Gunner B-Vedra (IRE) (Carlingford Castle)
Lady Connell Sir Michael Connell

Placings:P-1 **(4057)**
2001/02: 23^{1}S

	Starts	1st	2nd	3rd	Win & Pl
Chases	1	1	0	0	2139
Career Total	**2**	**1**	**0**	**0**	**2139**

101 3/02 Leic 2m7f110y H Ch SFT £2138
Total win prize-money £2139

Going: Sf: 1-1 GS: 0-0 Gd: 0-0 GF: - Fm: 0-0
Distance: 2m/2m3: 0-0 2m4-2m7: 0-0 **3m+: 1-1**
Track: LH: 0-0 **RH: 1-1** Tight: 0-0 Gall: 0-0
Aids: Bl: 0-0 Vi: 0-0 Tstrap: 0-0
Best Rating: 101 3/02 Leic 2m7f110y soft Ch

Full brother to Gunner Welburn, he won three of his first four starts over fences, including two points and looks a bright prospect. Acts with cut.

Prize Dancer (FR)

89 85

4-y-o ch g Suave Dancer (USA)-Spot Prize (USA) (Seattle Dancer (USA))
D R C Elsworth John Dwyer

Placings:60 **(3906)**
2001/02: 16^{6}HY, 16^{0}G

	Starts	1st	2nd	3rd	Win & Pl
Hurdles	2	0	0	0	0
Career Total	**2**	**0**	**0**	**0**	**0**

Going: Sf: 0-1 GS: 0-0 Gd: 0-1 GF: - Fm: 0-0
Distance: 2m/2m3: 0-2 2m4-2m7: 0-0 3m+: 0-0
Track: LH: 0-0 RH: 0-2 Tight: 0-0 Gall: 0-0
Aids: Bl: 0-0 Vi: 0-0 Tstrap: 0-0
Best Rating: 85 2/02 Kemp 2m good Hdl

A winner over 14 furlongs on the level, he has been disappointing so far over hurdles.

Pro Bono (IRE)

12-y-o ch g Tale Quale-Quality Suite (Prince Hansel)
M G Hazell W F Caudwell

Placings:*00030100*/4F3P2521/F3PU321/31U4P/3431 5U/P654/02F2P36-14 **(0429)**
2001/02: 24^{1}GF, 25^{4}G

	Starts	1st	2nd	3rd	Win & Pl
Chases	2	1	0	0	3658
Career Total	**47**	**6**	**5**	**8**	**20775**

106 5/01 Strf 3m H Ch G-F £3374
110 2/99 Fknm 2m5f110y H Ch G-S £2168
102 2/98 Fknm 2m5f110y H Ch GD £2158
98 4/97 Chel 2m110y H Ch G-F £2190
96 3/96 Fknm 2m5f110y H Ch G-F £2440
103 4/95 Thur 2m Hdl GD £2204
Total win prize-money £14536

Going: Sf: 0-0 GS: 0-0 Gd: 0-1 GF: - Fm: 1-1
Distance: 2m/2m3: 0-0 2m4-2m7: 0-0 **3m+: 1-2**
Track: **LH: 1-1** RH: 0-0 **Tight: 1-1** Gall: 0-0
Aids: Bl: 0-0 Vi: 0-0 Tstrap: 0-0
Best Rating: 112 5/98 Sthl 2m4f110y good Ch

Probus Lord

82 34

7-y-o b g Rough Stones-Decoyanne (Decoy Boy)
B R Millman Probus Farm Partnership

Placings:*05*/P **(3384)**
2001/02: 16^{P}GS

	Starts	1st	2nd	3rd	Win & Pl
Hurdles	1	0	0	0	
Career Total	**3**	**0**	**0**	**0**	**0**

Going: Sf: 0-0 GS: 0-1 Gd: 0-0 GF: - Fm: 0-0
Distance: 2m/2m3: 0-1 2m4-2m7: 0-0 3m+: 0-0
Track: LH: 0-0 RH: 0-1 Tight: 0-0 Gall: 0-0
Aids: Bl: 0-0 Vi: 0-0 Tstrap: 0-0
Best Rating: 77 12/99 Ludl 2m gd-sft NHF

Procedure (USA)

99 109

6-y-o b/br g Strolling Along (USA)-Bold Courtesan (USA) (Bold Bidder)

J A B Old W E Sturt

Placings:60206 **(4326)**

2001/02: 17^6S, 16^0GS, 17^2S, 16^0GS, 17^6S

	Starts	1st	2nd	3rd	Win & Pl
Hurdles	5	0	1	0	755
Career Total	**5**	**0**	**1**	**0**	**755**

Going: Sf: 0-3 GS: 0-2 Gd: 0-0 GF: - Fm: 0-0
Distance: 2m/2m3: 0-5 2m4-2m7: 0-0 3m+: 0-0
Track: LH: 0-2 RH: 0-3 Tight: 0-2 Gall: 0-1
Aids: Bl: 0-0 Vi: 0-0 Tstrap: 0-0
Best Rating: **109** 1/02 Tntn 2m1f soft Hdl

Successful twice on the Flat, his best effort was in January 2002 over two miles on soft ground when runner-up to Gone Far at Taunton.

Prodigal Son (IRE)

104 97

7-y-o b g Waajib-Nouveau Lady (IRE) (Taufan (USA))

Mrs V C Ward Prodigal Son Partnership

Placings:0/33200604-6P42151340 **(1865)**

2001/02: 21^6G, 20^PG, 20^4G, 22^2GF, 22^1G, 22^5G, 24^1GF, 24^3G, 21^4G, 25^0G

	Starts	1st	2nd	3rd	Win & Pl
Hurdles	10	2	1	1	7663
Career Total	**19**	**2**	**2**	**3**	**8997**

93	8/01	Uttx	3m110y	E Hdl	G-F	£2471
97	7/01	Strf	2m6f110y	E(0-115)HHdl	GD	£3588

Total win prize-money £6059

Going: Sf: 0-0 GS: 0-0 Gd: 1-8 GF: - Fm: 1-2
Distance: 2m/2m3: 0-0 2m4-2m7: 1-7 3m+: 1-3
Track: **LH: 2-10** RH: 0-0 **Tight: 1-6** Gall: 0-1
Aids: Bl: 0-0 **Vi: 2-7** Tstrap: 0-0
Best Rating: **97** 7/01 Strf 2m6f110y good Hdl

Profiler (USA)

103(97h) 108

7-y-o b g Capote (USA)-Magnificent Star (USA) (Silver Hawk (USA))

Mrs V C Ward Mrs J Morgan

Placings:55/2046444/0U1F1-PPPP3U **(3998)**

2001/02: 19^PG, 20^PF, 21^PG, 21^PS, 20^3G, 19US

	Starts	1st	2nd	3rd	Win & Pl
Hurdles	3	0	0	0	0
Chases	3	0	0	1	678
Career Total	**20**	**2**	**1**	**1**	**6777**

96	1/01	Donc	2m4f	E Hdl	GD	£2254
121	10/00	Folk	2m	E Ch	G-F	£2808

Total win prize-money £5062

Going: Sf: 0-2 GS: 0-0 Gd: 0-3 GF: - Fm: 0-1
Distance: 2m/2m3: 0-1 2m4-2m7: 0-5 3m+: 0-0
Track: LH: 0-5 RH: 0-1 Tight: 0-1 Gall: 0-1
Aids: Bl: 0-0 Vi: 0-1 Tstrap: 0-0
Best Rating: **121** 10/00 Folk 2m gd-fm Ch

A winner on the flat, over hurdles and fences. Needs a sound surface and goes well from two miles to two miles four.

Profluent (USA)

107(74c) 125

11-y-o ch g Sunshine Forever (USA)-Proflare (USA) (Mr Prospector (USA))

Mrs M Reveley Andy Peake & David Jackson

Placings:1/50634/1FPF/144106P/45550411450-26603 **(3373)**

2001/02: 20^2GS, 24^6GF, 24^6G, 24^0S, 20^3S

	Starts	1st	2nd	3rd	Win & Pl
Hurdles	5	0	1	1	2645
Career Total	**33**	**6**	**1**	**2**	**36043**

125	11/00	Catt	3m1f110y	E(0-115)HHdl	GD	£2800
119	11/00	Ayr	3m110y	D(0-125)HHdl	G-S	£3445
140	12/99	Kemp	3m	C(0-130)HCh	SFT	£10806
139	5/99	Weth	2m4f110y	C(0-135)HCh	G-F	£5995
140	10/98	Weth	2m4f110y	B HCh	GD	£7015

Total win prize-money £30062

Going: Sf: 0-2 GS: 0-1 Gd: 0-1 GF: - Fm: 0-1
Distance: 2m/2m3: 0-0 2m4-2m7: 0-2 3m+: 0-3
Track: LH: 0-3 RH: 0-2 Tight: 0-2 Gall: 0-1
Aids: Bl: 0-1 Vi: 0-2 Tstrap: 0-0
Best Rating: **140** 12/99 Kemp 3m soft Ch

Fair handicap hurdler, he has also been successful over fences. Acts on most types of ground and is effective at around three miles.

Prokofiev (USA)

104(102c) (122c)121

6-y-o br g Nureyev (USA)-Aviara (USA) (Cox's Ridge (USA))

J J O'Neill Mrs Sylvia Darlington

Placings:14/5520010-52350344 **(4301)**

2001/02: 20^5S, 24^2S, 22^3HY, 25^5S, 22^0HY, 25^3S, 21^4GS, 22^4HY

	Starts	1st	2nd	3rd	Win & Pl
Hurdles	5	0	0	1	2055
Chases	3	0	1	1	1976
Career Total	**17**	**2**	**2**	**2**	**20342**

134	2/01	Newc	2m4f	B(0-140)HHdl	HVY	£6366
109	12/99	Wwck	2m	C Hdl	SFT	£5912

Total win prize-money £12279

Going: Sf: 0-7 GS: 0-1 Gd: 0-0 GF: - Fm: 0-0
Distance: 2m/2m3: 0-0 2m4-2m7: 0-5 3m+: 0-3
Track: LH: 0-5 RH: 0-1 Tight: 0-1 Gall: 0-1
Aids: Bl: 0-4 Vi: 0-0 Tstrap: 0-4
Best Rating: **134** 2/01 Newc 2m4f heavy Hdl

Has plenty of ability, but a tendency to hang left and an awkward head-carriage indicate that he is not the most straightforward of rides. Modest form when tried over fences. Stays two and a half miles and is suited by soft ground.

Prominent

82(101h) (105h)115

8-y-o b g Primo Dominie-Mary Bankes (USA) (Northern Baby (CAN))

M W Easterby J W P Curtis

Placings:3/5FP304-063P **(4262)**

2001/02: 21^0G, 25^6F, 19^3GS, 20^PHY

	Starts	1st	2nd	3rd	Win & Pl
Hurdles	1	0	0	0	0
Chases	3	0	0	1	672
Career Total	**11**	**0**	**0**	**3**	**1333**

Going: Sf: 0-1 GS: 0-1 Gd: 0-1 GF: - Fm: 0-1
Distance: 2m/2m3: 0-0 2m4-2m7: 0-3 3m+: 0-1
Track: LH: 0-4 RH: 0-0 Tight: 0-1 Gall: 0-1
Aids: Bl: 0-0 Vi: 0-0 Tstrap: 0-0
Best Rating: **115** 3/02 Donc 2m3f110y gd-sft Ch

A successful pointer, he has struggled under Rules so far.

Prominent Profile (IRE)

95 106

9-y-o ch g Mazaad-Nakuru (IRE) (Mandalus)

N A Twiston-Davies The Son Partnership

Placings:10113034/13FU4/050U50 **(4029)**

2001/02: 20^0G, 22^5G, 24^0G, 20US, 19^5S, 20^0GS

	Starts	1st	2nd	3rd	Win & Pl
Chases	6	0	0	0	0
Career Total	**19**	**4**	**0**	**3**	**24393**

145	10/99	Chep	2m3f110y	D Ch	SFT	£4182
146	1/99	Weth	2m4f110y	D Hdl	SFT	£3038
132	12/98	Chep	2m110y	A NHF	HVY	£6280
115	10/98	Chel	2m110y	H NHF	G-S	£1940

Total win prize-money £15440

Going: Sf: 0-2 GS: 0-1 Gd: 0-3 GF: - Fm: 0-0
Distance: 2m/2m3: 0-1 2m4-2m7: 0-4 3m+: 0-1
Track: LH: 0-6 RH: 0-0 Tight: 0-3 Gall: 0-3
Aids: Bl: 0-3 Vi: 0-0 Tstrap: 0-0
Best Rating: **146** 1/99 Weth 2m4f110y soft Hdl

A former very useful novice hurdler, he has had his problems and is only ordinary over fences. Acts on soft ground.

Proper Primitive

101(76h) (52h)91

9-y-o gr m Primitive Rising (USA)-Nidd Bridges (Grey Ghost)

C J Drewe The Coskett Partnership

Placings:00/0P/002400365/P3P0101/05310P0-30F00600105 **(3289)**

2001/02: 20^3GF, 22^0GF, 16^FGF, 20^0GF, 20^0GS, 16^6S, 24^0G, 22^0G, 20^1G, 22^0G, 21^5S

	Starts	1st	2nd	3rd	Win & Pl
Hurdles	3	0	0	0	0
Chases	8	1	0	1	4339
Career Total	**38**	**4**	**1**	**4**	**15622**

87	12/01	Plum	2m4f	F(0-100)HCh	GD	£3818
100	10/00	Font	2m4f	F(0-105)HCh	G-S	£2730
94	3/00	Font	2m2f	F(0-100)HCh	G-F	£3440
82	11/99	Plum	2m1f	E Ch	G-F	£3282

Total win prize-money £13272

Going: Sf: 0-2 GS: 0-1 Gd: 1-4 GF: - Fm: 0-4
Distance: 2m/2m3: 0-2 **2m4-2m7: 1-8** 3m+: 0-1
Track: **LH: 1-2** RH: 0-4 **Tight: 1-9** Gall: 0-0
Aids: Bl: 0-0 Vi: 0-0 Tstrap: 0-0
Best Rating: **100** 10/00 Font 2m4f gd-sft Ch

Modest chaser at around two and ahalf miles.

Proper Squire (USA)

109 112+

5-y-o b g Bien Bien (USA)-La Cumbre (Sadler's Wells (USA))

C J Mann (B J Meehan 26/10) The Icy Fire Partnership

Placings:214P **(3809)**

2001/02: 20^2G, 22^1S, 24^4S, 22^PS

	Starts	1st	2nd	3rd	Win & Pl
Hurdles	4	1	1	0	5088
Career Total	**4**	**1**	**1**	**0**	**5088**

110	12/01	Strf	2m6f110y	E Hdl	SFT	£3125

Total win prize-money £3126

Going: Sf: 1-3 GS: 0-0 Gd: 0-1 GF: - Fm: 0-0
Distance: 2m/2m3: 0-0 **2m4-2m7: 1-3** 3m+: 0-1
Track: **LH: 1-4** RH: 0-0 **Tight: 1-2** Gall: 0-2
Aids: Bl: 0-0 Vi: 0-0 Tstrap: 0-0
Best Rating: 110 12/01 Strf 2m6f110y soft Hdl

Won a maiden hurdle on the soft on second start over an extended two miles six.

Property Zone

102 **85**

4-y-o b g Cool Jazz-Prime Property (IRE) (Tirol)
M W Easterby Alan Black & Co

Placings:60554 **(4867)**
2001/02: 16^{5}S, 16^{0}G, 16^{5}S, 17^{5}S, 16^{4}GF

	Starts	1st	2nd	3rd	Win & Pl
Hurdles	5	0	0	0	0
Career Total	**5**	**0**	**0**	**0**	**0**

Going: Sf: 0-3 GS: 0-0 Gd: 0-1 GF: - Fm: 0-1
Distance: 2m/2m3: 0-5 2m4-2m7: 0-0 3m+: 0-0
Track: LH: 0-5 RH: 0-0 Tight: 0-2 Gall: 0-0
Aids: Bl: 0-0 Vi: 0-0 Tstrap: 0-0
Best Rating: 85 3/02 Sedg 2m1f soft Hdl

Winner on the All-Weather but modest form over hurdles.

Propolis Power (IRE)

9-y-o ch g Simply Great (FR)-Now Then (Sandford Lad)
I Anderson Ian Anderson

Placings:050/P-P **(0418)**
2001/02: 20^{P}G

	Starts	1st	2nd	3rd	Win & Pl
Hurdles	1	0	0	0	
Career Total	**5**	**0**	**0**	**0**	**0**

Going: Sf: 0-0 GS: 0-0 Gd: 0-1 GF: - Fm: 0-0
Distance: 2m/2m3: 0-0 2m4-2m7: 0-1 3m+: 0-0
Track: LH: 0-1 RH: 0-0 Tight: 0-1 Gall: 0-0
Aids: Bl: 0-0 Vi: 0-0 Tstrap: 0-0
Best Rating: 66 11/96 Catt 2m gd-fm Hdl

Protagonist

92 **104**

4-y-o b/br g In The Wings-Fatah Flare (USA) (Alydar (USA))
P R Webber (M R Channon 15/5) Milbourne Lodge Partnership

Placings:0401 **(4417)**
2001/02: 16^{0}S, 16^{4}HY, 16^{0}G, 16^{1}GS

	Starts	1st	2nd	3rd	Win & Pl
Hurdles	4	1	0	0	4473
Career Total	**4**	**1**	**0**	**0**	**4473**

104 3/02 Newb 2m110y D(0-110)HHdl G-S £4134
Total win prize-money £4134

Going: Sf: 0-2 GS: 1-1 Gd: 0-1 GF: - Fm: 0-0
Distance: **2m/2m3: 1-4** 2m4-2m7: 0-0 3m+: 0-0
Track: **LH: 1-1** RH: 0-3 Tight: 0-0 **Gall: 1-1**
Aids: Bl: 0-0 Vi: 0-0 Tstrap: 0-0
Best Rating: 104 3/02 Newb 2m110y gd-sft Hdl

Stepped up on earlier efforts when successful on his handicap debut. Effective at two miles, may stay further.

Protaras Bay

8-y-o b g Superpower-Vivid Impression (Cure The Blues (USA))
H W Lavis (J Neville 27/11) H W Lavis

Placings:0/PP **(3702)**
2001/02: 21^{P}GS, 19^{P}HY

	Starts	1st	2nd	3rd	Win & Pl
Hurdles	2	0	0	0	
Career Total	**3**	**0**	**0**	**0**	

Going: Sf: 0-1 GS: 0-1 Gd: 0-0 GF: - Fm: 0-0
Distance: 2m/2m3: 0-0 2m4-2m7: 0-2 3m+: 0-0
Track: LH: 0-0 RH: 0-2 Tight: 0-1 Gall: 0-0
Aids: Bl: 0-0 Vi: 0-0 Tstrap: 0-0
Best Rating: 11 12/99 Leic 2m soft Hdl

Protector

106 **102**

5-y-o b g Be My Chief (USA)-Clicquot (Bold Lad (IRE))
C J Price (P J Hobbs 16/7) Dextra Lighting Systems

Placings:3125-4025205 **(3228)**
2001/02: 17^{4}GF, 20^{0}GF, 17^{2}GF, 16^{5}G, 17^{2}GF, 16^{0}GS, 16^{5}G

	Starts	1st	2nd	3rd	Win & Pl
Hurdles	7	0	2	0	1768
Career Total	**11**	**1**	**3**	**1**	**5503**

102 9/00 Font 2m2f110y E Hdl GD £2275
Total win prize-money £2275

Going: Sf: 0-0 GS: 0-1 Gd: 0-2 GF: - Fm: 0-4
Distance: 2m/2m3: 0-6 2m4-2m7: 0-1 3m+: 0-0
Track: LH: 0-6 RH: 0-1 Tight: 0-3 Gall: 0-0
Aids: Bl: 0-4 Vi: 0-0 Tstrap: 0-0
Best Rating: 109 9/00 Chep 2m110y good Hdl

Proud Fountain (IRE)

83 **80**

9-y-o br g Royal Fountain-Proud Polly (IRE) (Pollerton)
M J Wilkinson S N Wilshire

Placings:0/0-061P **(3161)**
2001/02: 21^{0}GF, 20^{6}GF, 26^{1}G, 26^{P}S

	Starts	1st	2nd	3rd	Win & Pl
Hurdles	4	1	0	0	1694
Career Total	**6**	**1**	**0**	**0**	**1694**

80 11/01 Hntg 3m2f G(0-95)HHdl GD £1694
Total win prize-money £1694

Going: Sf: 0-1 GS: 0-0 Gd: 1-1 GF: - Fm: 0-2
Distance: 2m/2m3: 0-0 2m4-2m7: 0-2 **3m+: 1-2**
Track: LH: 0-1 **RH: 1-2** Tight: 0-0 **Gall: 1-1**
Aids: Bl: 0-0 Vi: 0-0 Tstrap: 0-0
Best Rating: 80 11/01 Hntg 3m2f good Hdl

A winning pointer, showed plenty of stamina to winner a Huntingdon seller in November 2001. Suited by good ground.

Proud Western (USA)

70 **50**

4-y-o b/br c Gone West (USA)-Proud Lou (USA) (Proud Clarion)
B Ellison (A Fabre 3/6) Spring Cottage Syndicate

Placings:00 **(4275)**
2001/02: 16^{0}GS, 16^{0}G

	Starts	1st	2nd	3rd	Win & Pl
Hurdles	2	0	0	0	
Career Total	**2**	**0**	**0**	**0**	

Going: Sf: 0-0 GS: 0-1 Gd: 0-1 GF: - Fm: 0-0
Distance: 2m/2m3: 0-2 2m4-2m7: 0-0 3m+: 0-0
Track: LH: 0-2 RH: 0-0 Tight: 0-2 Gall: 0-0
Aids: Bl: 0-0 Vi: 0-0 Tstrap: 0-0
Best Rating: 53 3/02 Catt 2m gd-sft Hdl

Proverbial Gray

101 **65**

5-y-o ro m Norton Challenger-Clove Bud (Beau Charmeur (FR))
D R Gandolfo D R Gandolfo Ltd

Placings:*500* **(3290)**
2001/02: 17^{5}G, 16^{0}GS, 17^{0}S

	Starts	1st	2nd	3rd	Win & Pl
NH Flat	3	0	0	0	0
Career Total	**3**	**0**	**0**	**0**	**0**

Going: Sf: 0-1 GS: 0-1 Gd: 0-1 GF: - Fm: 0-0
Distance: 2m/2m3: 0-3 2m4-2m7: 0-0 3m+: 0-0
Track: LH: 0-0 RH: 0-2 Tight: 0-2 Gall: 0-1
Aids: Bl: 0-0 Vi: 0-0 Tstrap: 0-0
Best Rating: 65 10/01 MRas 2m1f110y good NHF

Prudent Miner (IRE)

11-y-o b g Miners Lamp-Prudent Birdie (Lucifer (USA))
Miss L Blackford R C Skinner

Placings:0/5/FP-F **(0077)**
2001/02: 23^{F}G

	Starts	1st	2nd	3rd	Win & Pl
Chases	1	0	0	0	
Career Total	**5**	**0**	**0**	**0**	**275**

Going: Sf: 0-0 GS: 0-0 Gd: 0-1 GF: - Fm: 0-0
Distance: 2m/2m3: 0-0 2m4-2m7: 0-0 3m+: 0-1
Track: LH: 0-0 RH: 0-1 Tight: 0-0 Gall: 0-0
Aids: Bl: 0-0 Vi: 0-0 Tstrap: 0-0
Best Rating: 52 10/98 DRoy 2m good NHF

Prussia

100 **91**

11-y-o b g Roi Danzig (USA)-Vagrant Maid (USA) (Honest Pleasure (USA))
W Clay N Brown & P Riley

Placings:65/22313300020/4F65333465**2**/**65152R**061 3121**U45**/060403**U**006/4124314144-0F000 **(2433)**
2001/02: 22^{0}GF, 22^{F}GF, 22^{0}GF, 19^{0}S, 20^{0}GS

	Starts	1st	2nd	3rd	Win & Pl
Hurdles	5	0	0	0	
Career Total	**65**	**8**	**7**	**9**	**26963**

102	9/00	Strf	2m6f110y	G(0-95)HHdl	GD	£1890
102	8/00	MRas	2m1f110y	G(0-95)HHdl	G-F	£1589
94	6/00	MRas	2m3f110y	G(0-90)HHdl	G-S	£1610
102	2/99	MRas	2m5f110y	F(0-115)HHdl	SFT	£2010
98	1/99	Uttx	2m	G Hdl	SFT	£1553
96	11/98	Bang	2m1f	G Hdl	GD	£2295
105	5/98	Uttx	3m2f	D Ch	G-F	£3485
96	7/96	Worc	2m4f	E Hdl	G-F	£2425

Total win prize-money £16857

Going: Sf: 0-1 GS: 0-1 Gd: 0-0 GF: - Fm: 0-3
Distance: 2m/2m3: 0-0 2m4-2m7: 0-5 3m+: 0-0
Track: LH: 0-4 RH: 0-1 Tight: 0-3 Gall: 0-0
Aids: Bl: 0-0 Vi: 0-0 Tstrap: 0-0
Best Rating: 105 7/98 Bang 3m110y good Ch

Psalmist

92 85

5-y-o ch m Mystiko (USA)-Son Et Lumiere (Rainbow Quest (USA))
Noel T Chance R W And J R Fidler

Placings:06P-25 **(0596)**
2001/02: 16^{2}G, 17^{5}G

	Starts	1st	2nd	3rd	Win & Pl
Hurdles	2	0	1	0	542
Career Total	**5**	**0**	**1**	**0**	**542**

Going: Sf: 0-0 GS: 0-0 Gd: 0-2 GF: - Fm: 0-0
Distance: 2m/2m3: 0-2 2m4-2m7: 0-0 3m+: 0-0
Track: LH: 0-2 RH: 0-0 Tight: 0-2 Gall: 0-0
Aids: Bl: 0-1 Vi: 0-0 Tstrap: 0-0
Best Rating: 98 12/00 Newb 2m110y soft Hdl

Ptah (IRE)

91 72

5-y-o b g Petardia-Davenport Goddess (IRE) (Classic Secret (USA))
J L Eyre Pinnacle Petardia Partnership

Placings:40-0P **(2909)**
2001/02: 16^{0}GS, 25^{P}GS

	Starts	1st	2nd	3rd	Win & Pl
Hurdles	2	0	0	0	
Career Total	**4**	**0**	**0**	**0**	**0**

Going: Sf: 0-0 GS: 0-2 Gd: 0-0 GF: - Fm: 0-0
Distance: 2m/2m3: 0-1 2m4-2m7: 0-0 3m+: 0-1
Track: LH: 0-2 RH: 0-0 Tight: 0-1 Gall: 0-0
Aids: Bl: 0-0 Vi: 0-0 Tstrap: 0-1
Best Rating: 93 2/01 Catt 2m soft Hdl

Ptarmigan

79f 45f

5-y-o ch g Rock Hopper-Tee Gee Jay (Northern Tempest (USA))
D E Cantillon Future Electrical Services Ltd

Placings:*0* **(1649)**
2001/02: 16^{0}G

	Starts	1st	2nd	3rd	Win & Pl
NH Flat	1	0	0	0	
Career Total	**1**	**0**	**0**	**0**	

Going: Sf: 0-0 GS: 0-0 Gd: 0-1 GF: - Fm: 0-0
Distance: 2m/2m3: 0-1 2m4-2m7: 0-0 3m+: 0-0
Track: LH: 0-0 RH: 0-1 Tight: 0-0 Gall: 0-1
Aids: Bl: 0-0 Vi: 0-0 Tstrap: 0-0
Best Rating: 45 10/01 Hntg 2m110y good NHF

Pull Off

83f 71f

7-y-o b g Push On-The Manson Flyer (Green Shoon)
Mrs M Evans W J Evans

Placings:5 **(1384)**
2001/02: 17^{5}GF

	Starts	1st	2nd	3rd	Win & Pl
NH Flat	1	0	0	0	0
Career Total	**1**	**0**	**0**	**0**	**0**

Going: Sf: 0-0 GS: 0-0 Gd: 0-0 GF: - Fm: 0-1
Distance: 2m/2m3: 0-1 2m4-2m7: 0-0 3m+: 0-0
Track: LH: 0-0 RH: 0-1 Tight: 0-0 Gall: 0-0
Aids: Bl: 0-0 Vi: 0-0 Tstrap: 0-0
Best Rating: 71 9/01 Hrfd 2m1f gd-fm NHF

Punchy (IRE)

110 114

6-y-o b/br g Freddie's Star-Baltimore Fox (IRE) (Arapahos (FR))
M Pitman G-Force Partnership

Placings:*1/20*-12212256 **(2259)**
2001/02: 21^{1}GF, 19^{2}GF, 22^{2}GF, 22^{1}GF, 20^{2}GF, 20^{2}G, 25^{5}G, 24^{6}G

	Starts	1st	2nd	3rd	Win & Pl
Hurdles	8	2	4	0	10823
Career Total	**11**	**3**	**5**	**0**	**13275**

108	9/01	NAbb	2m6f	E Hdl	G-F	£2912
107	5/01	Wwck	2m5f	E Hdl	G-F	£2950
112	4/00	Font	2m2f110y	H NHF	GD	£1998

Total win prize-money £7862

Going: Sf: 0-0 GS: 0-0 Gd: 0-3 GF: - Fm: 2-5
Distance: 2m/2m3: 0-0 **2m4-2m7: 2-6** 3m+: 0-2
Track: **LH: 1-5** RH: 0-2 **Tight: 1-3** Gall: 0-2
Aids: Bl: 0-0 Vi: 0-0 Tstrap: 0-0
Best Rating: 114 9/01 Worc 2m4f gd-fm Hdl

Decent novice hurdler, stays two and a half miles and seems to require a sound surface.

Puntal (FR)

114 153+

6-y-o b g Bering-Saveur (Ardross)
M C Pipe (F Belmont 1/11) Terry Neill

Placings:32P2224-05600 **(4665)**
2001/02: 21^{0}VS, 22^{5}S, 21^{6}VS, 21^{0}VS, 24^{0}G

	Starts	1st	2nd	3rd	Win & Pl
Hurdles	1	0	0	0	0
Chases	4	0	0	0	1212
Career Total	**12**	**0**	**4**	**1**	**35339**

Going: Sf: 0-1 GS: 0-0 Gd: 0-1 GF: - Fm: 0-0
Distance: 2m/2m3: 0-0 2m4-2m7: 0-4 3m+: 0-1
Track: LH: 0-1 RH: 0-0 Tight: 0-1 Gall: 0-0
Aids: Bl: 0-0 Vi: 0-0 Tstrap: 0-0
Best Rating: 131 4/02 Aint 3m110y good Hdl

A winner on the Flat in France, he ran with credit on his British debut at Aintree before completing a four-timer of front-running victories in novice hurdles in May 2002. Fell when sent back to contest a valuable handicap hurdle at Auteuil in June but maintained his improvement when winning a competitive Market Rasen handicap. Acts on fast and easy ground.

Punting Pete (IRE)

66(85c) (76c)27

12-y-o ch g Phardante (FR)-Silent Collection (Monksfield)
Miss K Marks Nick Shutts

Placings:*2/42113/F036000/66015032060/FPP0/P5P6 02/0506P-60* **(0773)**
2001/02: 16^{6}GF, 16^{0}GF

	Starts	1st	2nd	3rd	Win & Pl
Hurdles	1	0	0	0	0
Chases	1	0	0	0	0
Career Total	**41**	**3**	**4**	**3**	**22559**

134	10/97	Tipp	2m4f	Hdl	GD	£4747
128	12/95	Navn	2m	Hdl	Y-S	£4069
128	11/95	Leop	2m	Hdl	YLD	£4069

Total win prize-money £12886

Going: Sf: 0-0 GS: 0-0 Gd: 0-0 GF: - Fm: 0-2
Distance: 2m/2m3: 0-2 2m4-2m7: 0-0 3m+: 0-0
Track: LH: 0-2 RH: 0-0 Tight: 0-1 Gall: 0-0
Aids: Bl: 0-0 Vi: 0-0 Tstrap: 0-2
Best Rating: 136 12/95 Leop 2m yld-sft Hdl

Pur Tresor (FR)

105 103

5-y-o b g Tresorier (FR)-Ma Pure Folie (FR) (Maiymad)
G M Moore Mrs Mary And Miss Susan Hatfield

Placings:02334643622-20522F0PF **(4096)**
2001/02: 24^{2}S, 20^{0}GS, 20^{5}G, 20^{2}GS, 23^{2}S, 25^{F}G, 24^{0}S, 20^{P}S, 19^{F}GS

	Starts	1st	2nd	3rd	Win & Pl
Hurdles	9	0	3	0	3338
Career Total	**20**	**0**	**6**	**3**	**11136**

Going: Sf: 0-4 GS: 0-3 Gd: 0-2 GF: - Fm: 0-0
Distance: 2m/2m3: 0-1 2m4-2m7: 0-5 3m+: 0-3
Track: LH: 0-8 RH: 0-0 Tight: 0-2 Gall: 0-4
Aids: Bl: 0-0 Vi: 0-0 Tstrap: 0-9
Best Rating: 103 12/01 Catt 3m1f110y good Hdl

Ex-French, this keen individual has shown moderate ability over hurdles. He has raced in a tongue-tie and needs give in the ground.

Purbeck Wonder

6-y-o ro g Riverwise (USA)-Blue Wonder (Idiots Delight)
N R Mitchell N R Mitchell

Placings:*P* **(3811)**
2001/02: 18^{P}S

	Starts	1st	2nd	3rd	Win & Pl
NH Flat	1	0	0	0	
Career Total	**1**	**0**	**0**	**0**	

Going: Sf: 0-1 GS: 0-0 Gd: 0-0 GF: - Fm: 0-0
Distance: 2m/2m3: 0-1 2m4-2m7: 0-0 3m+: 0-0
Track: LH: 0-1 RH: 0-0 Tight: 0-1 Gall: 0-0
Aids: Bl: 0-0 Vi: 0-0 Tstrap: 0-0
Best Rating:

Pure Brief (IRE)

97 82

5-y-o b g Brief Truce (USA)-Epure (Bellypha)
A Streeter Mrs V D Gandola-Gray

Placings:U000 **(4646)**
2001/02: 16^{U}S, 16^{0}GS, 16^{0}S, 21^{0}G

	Starts	1st	2nd	3rd	Win & Pl
Hurdles	4	0	0	0	
Career Total	**4**	**0**	**0**	**0**	

Going: Sf: 0-2 GS: 0-1 Gd: 0-1 GF: - Fm: 0-0
Distance: 2m/2m3: 0-3 2m4-2m7: 0-1 3m+: 0-0
Track: LH: 0-1 RH: 0-3 Tight: 0-0 Gall: 0-2
Aids: Bl: 0-0 Vi: 0-0 Tstrap: 0-0
Best Rating: 79 1/02 Hntg 2m110y gd-sft Hdl

Pure Fun (IRE)

106 **95**

5-y-o b g Lord Americo-Rath Caola (Neltino)

P J Hobbs Miss I D Du Pre

Placings: *1*0055244 **(4896)**

2001/02: 16^{1}GF, 19^{0}GF, 19^{0}S, 16^{5}GS, 17^{5}G, 21^{2}GF, 20^{4}G, 20^{4}G

	Starts	1st	2nd	3rd	Win & Pl
NH Flat	1	1	0	0	1449
Hurdles	7	0	1	0	1879
Career Total	**8**	**1**	**1**	**0**	**3328**

95	8/01	Worc	2m	H NHF	G-F	£1449

Total win prize-money £1449

Going: Sf: 0-1 GS: 0-1 Gd: 0-3 GF: - Fm: 1-3
Distance: **2m/2m3: 1-4** 2m4-2m7: 0-4 3m+: 0-0
Track: **LH: 1-1** RH: 0-7 Tight: 0-0 Gall: 0-0
Aids: Bl: 0-0 Vi: 0-0 Tstrap: 0-0
Best Rating: 95 4/02 Ludl 2m5f gd-fm Hdl

Fast ground bumper winner, has shown modest form over hurdles.

Pure Steel (IRE)

99(96h) (75h)**106**

8-y-o b g Miners Lamp-Mary Deen (Avocat)

J I A Charlton (Miss S E Forster 24/6) M H Walton

Placings: *F*/P-434**U2F2** **(4868)**

2001/02: 20^{4}GF, 20^{3}GF, 19^{4}GS, 19^{U}S, 16^{2}S, 21^{F}S, 20^{2}GF

	Starts	1st	2nd	3rd	Win & Pl
Hurdles	2	0	0	1	523
Chases	5	0	2	0	2501
Career Total	**9**	**0**	**2**	**1**	**3024**

Going: Sf: 0-3 GS: 0-1 Gd: 0-0 GF: - Fm: 0-3
Distance: 2m/2m3: 0-3 2m4-2m7: 0-4 3m+: 0-0
Track: LH: 0-6 RH: 0-1 Tight: 0-2 Gall: 0-2
Aids: Bl: 0-0 Vi: 0-0 Tstrap: 0-0
Best Rating: 106 1/02 Catt 2m3f gd-sft Ch

Modest novice chaser, not the best of jumpers.

Purevalue (IRE)

(89h) (76h)

11-y-o b/br g Kefaah (USA)-Blaze Of Light (Blakeney)

M W Easterby Mrs Jean Turpin

Placings: *35*/0051231/34161/**U22113U/2P12P0/U1P1P/003P-6P** **(1757)**

2001/02: 17^{6}GS, 21^{P}GS

	Starts	1st	2nd	3rd	Win & Pl
Hurdles	1	0	0	0	0
Chases	1	0	0	0	0
Career Total	**38**	**9**	**5**	**5**	**40599**

138	2/00	Newc	3m	D(0-125)HCh	SFT	£3835
128	12/99	Newc	2m4f	D(0-125)HCh	SFT	£3972
122	11/98	Newc	3m	D(0-125)HCh	GD	£3501
120	3/98	Hexm	2m110y	E Ch	SFT	£3152
119	3/98	MRas	2m4f	D Ch	G-S	£4027
119	3/97	Newc	3m	C(0-130)HHdl	GD	£3403
109	2/97	Weth	2m7f	C(0-135)HHdl	GD	£2861
115	4/96	Weth	2m4f110y	D Hdl	GD	£2705
107	2/96	Hayd	2m	C HHdl	SFT	£3582

Total win prize-money £31041

Going: Sf: 0-0 GS: 0-2 Gd: 0-0 GF: - Fm: 0-0
Distance: 2m/2m3: 0-1 2m4-2m7: 0-1 3m+: 0-0
Track: LH: 0-1 RH: 0-1 Tight: 0-2 Gall: 0-0
Aids: Bl: 0-1 Vi: 0-0 Tstrap: 0-0
Best Rating: 138 2/00 Newc 3m soft Ch

Purple Jean

82 **62**

7-y-o gr m Perpendicular-Ask Jean (Ascertain (USA))

M E Sowersby M E Sowersby

Placings: *5*/0-PP0 **(4578)**

2001/02: 27^{P}S, 24^{P}HY, 23^{0}G

	Starts	1st	2nd	3rd	Win & Pl
Hurdles	3	0	0	0	
Career Total	**5**	**0**	**0**	**0**	**0**

Going: Sf: 0-2 GS: 0-0 Gd: 0-1 GF: - Fm: 0-0
Distance: 2m/2m3: 0-0 2m4-2m7: 0-1 3m+: 0-2
Track: LH: 0-3 RH: 0-0 Tight: 0-1 Gall: 0-0
Aids: Bl: 0-0 Vi: 0-0 Tstrap: 0-1
Best Rating: 62 4/01 Muss 3m gd-fm Hdl

Purple Lace

10-y-o b m Salse (USA)-Purple Prose (Rainbow Quest (USA))

H S Howe Kevin Daniel Crabb

Placings: *004/3*F6/F0P-P **(0562)**

2001/02: 22^{P}GF

	Starts	1st	2nd	3rd	Win & Pl
Hurdles	1	0	0	0	
Career Total	**10**	**0**	**0**	**1**	**180**

Going: Sf: 0-0 GS: 0-0 Gd: 0-0 GF: - Fm: 0-1
Distance: 2m/2m3: 0-0 2m4-2m7: 0-1 3m+: 0-0
Track: LH: 0-1 RH: 0-0 Tight: 0-1 Gall: 0-0
Aids: Bl: 0-0 Vi: 0-0 Tstrap: 0-0
Best Rating: 96 5/98 Hrfd 2m1f good NHF

Putup Or Shutup (IRE)

91 **103**

6-y-o br g Religiously (USA)-Nights Crack (Callernish)

K C Bailey Les McLaughlin

Placings: *0-1222*45 **(3929)**

2001/02: 16^{1}S, 17^{2}S, 18^{2}S, 20^{2}S, 24^{4}HY, 16^{5}HY

	Starts	1st	2nd	3rd	Win & Pl
NH Flat	3	1	2	0	2367
Hurdles	3	0	1	0	1096
Career Total	**7**	**1**	**3**	**0**	**3463**

103	10/01	Fknm	2m	H NHF	SFT	£1452

Total win prize-money £1453

Going: Sf: 1-6 GS: 0-0 Gd: 0-0 GF: - Fm: 0-0
Distance: **2m/2m3: 1-4** 2m4-2m7: 0-1 3m+: 0-1
Track: **LH: 1-3** RH: 0-1 **Tight: 1-3** Gall: 0-0
Aids: Bl: 0-0 Vi: 0-0 Tstrap: 0-0
Best Rating: 103 12/01 Leic 2m4f110y soft Hdl

Fair bumper performer, winner at Fakenham in October 2001, second on hurdling debut in December 2001 but failed to build on that.

Puzzle

65

4-y-o b g First Trump-Eldoret (High Top)

Lady Herries Lady Sarah Clutton

Placings: 4 **(4883)**

2001/02: 22^{4}GF

	Starts	1st	2nd	3rd	Win & Pl
Hurdles	1	0	0	0	0
Career Total	**1**	**0**	**0**	**0**	**0**

Going: Sf: 0-0 GS: 0-0 Gd: 0-0 GF: - Fm: 0-1
Distance: 2m/2m3: 0-0 2m4-2m7: 0-1 3m+: 0-0
Track: LH: 0-1 RH: 0-0 Tight: 0-1 Gall: 0-0
Aids: Bl: 0-0 Vi: 0-0 Tstrap: 0-0
Best Rating: 65 4/02 Font 2m6f110y gd-fm Hdl

Well-bred for Flat racing, showed little on his hurdling debut.

Puzzleman

86(92h) (67h)**69**

9-y-o ch g Henbit (USA)-Floreamus (Quayside)

D J Caro E McMichael & P Evans

Placings: *40*P/26/4-4P5P**00P** **(3444)**

2001/02: 22^{4}GF, 24^{P}GF, 21^{5}GF, 19^{P}G, 19^{0}GS, 22^{0}G, 24^{P}GS

	Starts	1st	2nd	3rd	Win & Pl
Hurdles	4	0	0	0	0
Chases	3	0	0	0	0
Career Total	**13**	**0**	**1**	**0**	**1082**

Going: Sf: 0-0 GS: 0-2 Gd: 0-2 GF: - Fm: 0-3
Distance: 2m/2m3: 0-1 2m4-2m7: 0-4 3m+: 0-2
Track: LH: 0-1 RH: 0-4 Tight: 0-3 Gall: 0-0
Aids: Bl: 0-1 Vi: 0-0 Tstrap: 0-0
Best Rating: 94 2/00 Ludl 2m5f gd-fm Hdl

Modest hurdler who likes to be held up.

Pyleigh

85f **76f**

7-y-o b g Gildoran-Miss Tullulah (Hubble Bubble)

Mrs H Pudd Mrs H Pudd

Placings: *0* **(1892)**

2001/02: 16^{0}G

	Starts	1st	2nd	3rd	Win & Pl
NH Flat	1	0	0	0	
Career Total	**1**	**0**	**0**	**0**	

Going: Sf: 0-0 GS: 0-0 Gd: 0-1 GF: - Fm: 0-0
Distance: 2m/2m3: 0-1 2m4-2m7: 0-0 3m+: 0-0
Track: LH: 0-1 RH: 0-0 Tight: 0-0 Gall: 0-0
Aids: Bl: 0-0 Vi: 0-0 Tstrap: 0-0
Best Rating: 76 10/01 Chel 2m110y good NHF

Pythagoras

101 **75**

5-y-o ch g Kris-Tricorne (Green Desert (USA))

M Sheppard (W R Muir 4/8) Mike Drake, Tim Doxsey, Ray Hitchin

Placings: 2306 **(1907)**

2001/02: 16^{2}GF, 16^{3}GF, 16^{0}GS, 16^{6}S

	Starts	1st	2nd	3rd	Win & Pl
Hurdles	4	0	1	1	909
Career Total	**4**	**0**	**1**	**1**	**909**

Going: Sf: 0-1 GS: 0-1 Gd: 0-0 GF: - Fm: 0-2
Distance: 2m/2m3: 0-4 2m4-2m7: 0-0 3m+: 0-0
Track: LH: 0-4 RH: 0-0 Tight: 0-1 Gall: 0-0
Aids: Bl: 0-0 Vi: 0-0 Tstrap: 0-0
Best Rating: 75 8/01 Worc 2m gd-fm Hdl

He has made no impression since being claimed after being runner-up in a Worcester seller.

Qu'Appelle

9-y-o ch g Teamster-Gay Rhythm (Quiet Fling (USA))
Mrs L A Syckelmoore R H Till

Placings:00/0 **(0228)**
2001/02: 20^{0}GF

	Starts	1st	2nd	3rd	Win & Pl
Chases	1	0	0	0	
Career Total	**3**	**0**	**0**	**0**	

Going: Sf: 0-0 GS: 0-0 Gd: 0-0 GF: - Fm: 0-1
Distance: 2m/2m3: 0-0 2m4-2m7: 0-1 3m+: 0-0
Track: LH: 0-0 RH: 0-1 Tight: 0-0 Gall: 0-1
Aids: Bl: 0-0 Vi: 0-0 Tstrap: 0-0
Best Rating: 46 2/97 Newb 2m110y good Hdl

Quabmatic

97 **98**

9-y-o b g Pragmatic-Good Skills (Bustino)
K Bishop Eric's Friends Racing Partnership

Placings:4/543533/540/426101/0-16P **(3389)**
2001/02: 20^{1}S, 19^{6}GS, 22^{P}GS

	Starts	1st	2nd	3rd	Win & Pl
Hurdles	3	1	0	0	2618
Career Total	**20**	**3**	**1**	**3**	**10465**

98	11/01	Uttx	2m4f110y	E(0-115)HHdl	SFT	£2618
104	4/00	Extr	2m1f110y	E(0-105)HHdl	HVY	£2928
104	3/00	Tntn	2m3f110y	F(0-115)HHdl	GD	£3209

Total win prize-money £8756

Going: Sf: 1-1 GS: 0-2 Gd: 0-0 GF: - Fm: 0-0
Distance: 2m/2m3: 0-1 **2m4-2m7: 1-2** 3m+: 0-0
Track: **LH: 1-2** RH: 0-1 Tight: 0-0 Gall: 0-1
Aids: Bl: 0-0 Vi: 0-0 Tstrap: 0-0
Best Rating: 104 4/00 Extr 2m1f110y heavy Hdl

A fair hurdler before a year-and-a-half lay-off, he came back from these leg problems to win first time out over two and a half miles at Uttoxeter in November. Disappointed subsequently.

Quainton Hills

99 **121**

8-y-o b g Gildoran-Spin Again (Royalty)
N A Gaselee D R Stoddart

Placings:203/**42F12U-4234** **(2939)**
2001/02: 20^{4}S, 23^{2}GF, 23^{3}GF, 24^{4}G

	Starts	1st	2nd	3rd	Win & Pl
Chases	4	0	1	1	2746
Career Total	**13**	**1**	**4**	**2**	**9670**

122	1/01	Leic	2m7f110y	F Ch	SFT	£2824

Total win prize-money £2824

Going: Sf: 0-1 GS: 0-0 Gd: 0-1 GF: - Fm: 0-2
Distance: 2m/2m3: 0-0 2m4-2m7: 0-1 3m+: 0-3
Track: LH: 0-2 RH: 0-2 Tight: 0-1 Gall: 0-1
Aids: Bl: 0-0 Vi: 0-0 Tstrap: 0-0
Best Rating: 122 1/01 Leic 2m7f110y soft Ch

A half-brother to Party Politics, he stays three miles but can be a sketchy jumper.

Quakers Field

107 **129**

9-y-o b h Anshan-Nosey (Nebbiolo)
G L Moore Bryan Pennick

Placings:215/10266341/**1UP1P** **(4666)**
2001/02: 20^{1}GS, 24^{U}G, 24^{P}GS, 22^{1}S, 25^{P}G

	Starts	1st	2nd	3rd	Win & Pl
Chases	5	2	0	0	8000
Career Total	**16**	**5**	**2**	**1**	**63213**

120	1/02	Font	2m6f	E Ch	SFT	£3710
129	11/01	Hntg	2m4f110y	D Ch	G-S	£4290
138	4/00	Aint	2m4f	B HHdl	GD	£14404
136	11/99	Asct	2m110y	C(0-135)HHdl	GD	£7002
135	4/97	Aint	2m110y	A Hdl	GD	£26234

Total win prize-money £55641

Going: Sf: 1-1 GS: 1-2 Gd: 0-2 GF: - Fm: 0-0
Distance: 2m/2m3: 0-0 **2m4-2m7: 2-2** 3m+: 0-3
Track: LH: 0-1 **RH: 1-3** Tight: 1-2 Gall: 1-2
Aids: Bl: 0-0 Vi: 0-0 Tstrap: 0-0
Best Rating: 138 4/00 Aint 2m4f good Hdl

A smart hurdler who has had injury problems. Likes Aintree and won a good handicap there in April 2000. Long absence afterwards, but returned to score on his chasing debut at Huntingdon in November 2001 and Fontwell. Stays two miles six furlongs and likes good ground.

Qualitair Survivor

7-y-o gr g Terimon-Comtec Princess (Gulf Pearl)
J Hetherton Qualitair Holdings Limited

Placings:256/2/36-PPP **(0500)**
2001/02: 16^{P}GF, 17^{P}GS, 16^{P}GF

	Starts	1st	2nd	3rd	Win & Pl
Hurdles	1	0	0	0	0
Chases	2	0	0	0	0
Career Total	**9**	**0**	**2**	**1**	**1183**

Going: Sf: 0-0 GS: 0-1 Gd: 0-0 GF: - Fm: 0-2
Distance: 2m/2m3: 0-3 2m4-2m7: 0-0 3m+: 0-0
Track: LH: 0-1 RH: 0-1 Tight: 0-1 Gall: 0-1
Aids: Bl: 0-0 Vi: 0-0 Tstrap: 0-0
Best Rating: 95 8/00 Hntg 2m110y gd-fm Hdl

Quarterstaff

97 **109**

8-y-o b g Charmer-Quaranta (Hotfoot)
C R Wilson (Mrs A Duffield 9/6) Mrs J Wilson (durham)

Placings:36P-2C33P2 **(2768)**
2001/02: 25^{2}S, 21^{C}G, 23^{3}G, 20^{3}GS, 19^{P}G, 19^{2}G

	Starts	1st	2nd	3rd	Win & Pl
Chases	6	0	2	2	2821
Career Total	**9**	**0**	**2**	**3**	**3169**

Going: Sf: 0-1 GS: 0-1 Gd: 0-4 GF: - Fm: 0-0
Distance: 2m/2m3: 0-1 2m4-2m7: 0-3 3m+: 0-2
Track: LH: 0-5 RH: 0-0 Tight: 0-1 Gall: 0-2
Aids: Bl: 0-0 Vi: 0-0 Tstrap: 0-0
Best Rating: 109 12/01 Catt 2m3f good Ch

Quatermass

6-y-o b g Karinga Bay-Panchellita (USA) (Pancho Villa (USA))
A Hollingsworth Kombined Motor Services Ltd

Placings:0-00P **(4530)**
2001/02: 16^{0}G, 16^{0}GS, 20^{P}GS

	Starts	1st	2nd	3rd	Win & Pl
NH Flat	2	0	0	0	0
Hurdles	1	0	0	0	0
Career Total	**4**	**0**	**0**	**0**	

Going: Sf: 0-0 GS: 0-2 Gd: 0-1 GF: - Fm: 0-0
Distance: 2m/2m3: 0-2 2m4-2m7: 0-1 3m+: 0-0
Track: LH: 0-2 RH: 0-0 Tight: 0-0 Gall: 0-0
Aids: Bl: 0-0 Vi: 0-0 Tstrap: 0-0
Best Rating: 50 6/01 Worc 2m good NHF

Quazar (IRE)

120 **137**

4-y-o b c Inzar (USA)-Evictress (IRE) (Sharp Victor (USA))
J J O'Neill C D Carr

Placings:1111P12011 **(4952a)**
2001/02: 17^{1}G, 17^{1}G, 16^{1}G, 16^{1}G, 16^{P}GS, 16^{1}S, 17^{2}HY, 17^{0}G, 16^{1}G, 16^{1}G

	Starts	1st	2nd	3rd	Win & Pl
Hurdles	10	7	1	0	138327
Career Total	**10**	**7**	**1**	**0**	**138327**

137	4/02	Punc	2m	Hdl	GD	£41901
137	4/02	Aint	2m110y	A Hdl	GD	£58000
132	1/02	Wwck	2m	B Hdl	SFT	£8736
117	11/01	Weth	2m	A Hdl	GD	£10627
114	10/01	Chel	2m110y	B Hdl	GD	£6857
106	9/01	Bang	2m1f	D Hdl	GD	£3402
87	8/01	Bang	2m1f	E Hdl	GD	£3052

Total win prize-money £132578

Going: Sf: 1-2 GS: 0-1 Gd: 6-7 GF: - Fm: 0-0
Distance: **2m/2m3: 7-10** 2m4-2m7: 0-0 3m+: 0-0
Track: **LH: 6-9** RH: 1-1 **Tight: 3-3** Gall: 0-2
Aids: Bl: 0-0 Vi: 0-0 **Tstrap: 6-9**
Best Rating: 137 4/02 Punc 2m good Hdl

A leading juvenile hurdler, he has won seven times over hurdles, and landed big-race successes at Aintree and Punchestown. Wears a tongue tie and promises to stay beyond two miles. Acts on good/good to soft ground.

Queen Of Araghty

5-y-o ch m Phardante (FR)-Queen's Darling (Le Moss)
M Todhunter Tim Kilroe

Placings:03 **(4750)**
2001/02: 16^{0}S, 17^{3}G

	Starts	1st	2nd	3rd	Win & Pl
NH Flat	2	0	0	1	357
Career Total	**2**	**0**	**0**	**1**	**357**

Going: Sf: 0-1 GS: 0-0 Gd: 0-1 GF: - Fm: 0-0
Distance: 2m/2m3: 0-2 2m4-2m7: 0-0 3m+: 0-0
Track: LH: 0-1 RH: 0-1 Tight: 0-0 Gall: 0-1
Aids: Bl: 0-0 Vi: 0-0 Tstrap: 0-0
Best Rating: 85 4/02 Carl 2m1f good NHF

Queen Uberalles (IRE)

90f **67f**

7-y-o ch m Accordion-Viking Splendor (Viking (USA))
M C Pipe A P Brady

Placings:0 **(0320)**
2001/02: 17^{0}F

	Starts	1st	2nd	3rd	Win & Pl
NH Flat	1	0	0	0	
Career Total	**1**	**0**	**0**	**0**	

Going: Sf: 0-0 GS: 0-0 Gd: 0-0 GF: - Fm: 0-1

Distance: 2m/2m3: 0-1 2m4-2m7: 0-0 3m+: 0-0
Track: LH: 0-0 RH: 0-1 Tight: 0-0 Gall: 0-0
Aids: Bl: 0-1 Vi: 0-0 Tstrap: 0-0
Best Rating: 67 5/01 Extr 2m1f firm NHF

Queen's Pageant

100 **95**

8-y-o ch m Risk Me (FR)-Mistral's Dancer (Shareef Dancer (USA))
J L Spearing Mrs Robert Heathcote

Placings:0431 **(4684)**
2001/02: 16^{0}GS, 16^{4}GF, 19^{3}GF, 19^{1}GF

	Starts	1st	2nd	3rd	Win & Pl
Hurdles	4	1	0	1	3498
Career Total	**4**	**1**	**0**	**1**	**3498**

95	4/02	Hrfd	2m3f110y	E Hdl	G-F	£3080

Total win prize-money £3080

Going: Sf: 0-0 GS: 0-1 Gd: 0-0 GF: - Fm: 1-3
Distance: 2m/2m3: 0-3 **2m4-2m7: 1-1** 3m+: 0-0
Track: LH: 0-1 **RH: 1-3** Tight: 0-0 Gall: 0-2
Aids: Bl: 0-0 Vi: 0-0 Tstrap: 0-0
Best Rating: 95 4/02 Hrfd 2m3f110y gd-fm Hdl

Appreciated sound surface when winning a maiden hurdle over 19 furlongs at Hereford in April 2002.

Queens Brigade

102(81h) (41h)**101**

10-y-o b g K-Battery-Queen Of Dara (Dara Monarch)
Miss V A Stephens (C J Mann 15/6) D G Stephens

Placings:*00*/566234/12U353B414P/1U00244U4/4U24 4F31305-0500 **(2926)**
2001/02: 16^{0}S, 16^{5}GF, 16^{0}GS, 24^{0}GS

	Starts	1st	2nd	3rd	Win & Pl
Hurdles	1	0	0	0	0
Chases	3	0	0	0	0
Career Total	**43**	**4**	**4**	**5**	**22507**

106	11/00	Catt	2m	F(0-105)HCh	G-S	£3802
105	5/99	Hexm	2m110y	E Ch	G-F	£2212
113	3/99	Hexm	2m110y	E Ch	G-S	£2946
92	5/98	Hexm	2m4f110y	F Hdl	G-S	£2390

Total win prize-money £11353

Going: Sf: 0-1 GS: 0-2 Gd: 0-0 GF: - Fm: 0-1
Distance: 2m/2m3: 0-3 2m4-2m7: 0-0 3m+: 0-1
Track: LH: 0-3 RH: 0-1 Tight: 0-2 Gall: 0-0
Aids: Bl: 0-0 Vi: 0-0 Tstrap: 0-0
Best Rating: 113 3/99 Hexm 2m110y gd-sft Ch

Queens House

53 **10**

7-y-o b m Arctic Lord-Courtlands Girl (Crimson Beau)
N R Mitchell Steve Lee

Placings:*0*P-0P **(0490)**
2001/02: 17^{0}F, 27^{P}GF

	Starts	1st	2nd	3rd	Win & Pl
Hurdles	2	0	0	0	
Career Total	**4**	**0**	**0**	**0**	

Going: Sf: 0-0 GS: 0-0 Gd: 0-0 GF: - Fm: 0-2
Distance: 2m/2m3: 0-1 2m4-2m7: 0-0 3m+: 0-1
Track: LH: 0-0 RH: 0-1 Tight: 0-1 Gall: 0-0
Aids: Bl: 0-0 Vi: 0-0 Tstrap: 0-0
Best Rating: 11 5/01 Extr 2m1f firm Hdl

Queens Stroller (IRE)

65 **32**

11-y-o b m Pennine Walk-Mount Isa (Miami Springs)
R E Peacock R E Peacock

Placings:4P/6/003-0 **(0673)**
2001/02: 16^{0}GF

	Starts	1st	2nd	3rd	Win & Pl
Hurdles	1	0	0	0	
Career Total	**7**	**0**	**0**	**1**	**692**

Going: Sf: 0-0 GS: 0-0 Gd: 0-0 GF: - Fm: 0-1
Distance: 2m/2m3: 0-1 2m4-2m7: 0-0 3m+: 0-0
Track: LH: 0-1 RH: 0-0 Tight: 0-0 Gall: 0-0
Aids: Bl: 0-0 Vi: 0-0 Tstrap: 0-0
Best Rating: 69 10/00 Towc 2m good Hdl

Queensway (IRE)

105 **113**

10-y-o b g Pennine Walk-Polaregina (FR) (Rex Magna (FR))
R M Carson (P J Hobbs 4/10) Mrs P Carson

Placings:*12*013/3445P21/1422/4FU100-561F35600 **(3815)**
2001/02: 16^{5}GF, 20^{6}GF, 17^{1}GF, 16^{F}G, 16^{3}GF, 19^{5}G, 20^{6}GS, 17^{0}G, 16^{0}S

	Starts	1st	2nd	3rd	Win & Pl
Chases	9	1	0	1	4540
Career Total	**31**	**6**	**4**	**3**	**23767**

113	8/01	Strf	2m1f110y	F(0-105)HCh	G-F	£4160
111	10/00	Ludl	2m	G(0-95)HCh	G-F	£2730
117	8/99	Prth	2m	F(0-100)HCh	G-F	£4182
93	4/99	Kels	2m1f	E Ch	G-F	£3582
100	4/98	Sedg	2m1f	E Hdl	SFT	£2582
109	5/97	Prth	2m110y	H NHF	G-S	£1020

Total win prize-money £18258

Going: Sf: 0-1 GS: 0-1 Gd: 0-3 GF: - Fm: 1-4
Distance: **2m/2m3: 1-7** 2m4-2m7: 0-2 3m+: 0-0
Track: **LH: 1-5** RH: 0-3 **Tight: 1-5** Gall: 0-2
Aids: Bl: 0-0 Vi: 0-0 **Tstrap: 1-9**
Best Rating: 117 8/99 Prth 2m gd-fm Ch

Quel Bon Choix (FR)

104 **110**

4-y-o b g Tel Quel (FR)-Special Marianna (FR) (Kaldoun (FR))
M C Pipe B A Kilpatrick

Placings:3232634212 **(4850)**
2001/02: 15^{3}, 16^{2}G, 17^{3}, 17^{2}S, 17^{6}G, 18^{3}G, 18^{4}S, 21^{2}S, 20^{1}GF, 22^{2}G

	Starts	1st	2nd	3rd	Win & Pl
Hurdles	9	1	4	2	12492
Chases	1	0	0	1	873
Career Total	**10**	**1**	**4**	**3**	**13365**

110	4/02	Uttx	2m4f110y	D Hdl	G-F	£4000

Total win prize-money £4001

Going: Sf: 0-3 GS: 0-0 Gd: 0-4 GF: - Fm: 1-1
Distance: 2m/2m3: 0-6 **2m4-2m7: 1-3** 3m+: 0-0
Track: **LH: 1-4** RH: 0-0 Tight: 0-2 Gall: 0-1
Aids: Bl: 0-2 Vi: 0-0 Tstrap: 0-0
Best Rating: 110 4/02 Strf 2m6f110y good Hdl

Has some useful juvenile hurdle form in France. Did not achieve much when easy winner of two and a half mile novice hurdle on faster ground at Uttoxeter in April 2002. Possibly a better effort when beaten odds on favourite at Stratford next time.

Quel Regal (FR)

77 **65**

4-y-o b g Comte Du Bourg (FR)-Rigala (FR) (Roi Dagobert)
A R Dicken Mr & Mrs Raymond Anderson Green

Placings:0030 **(3744)**
2001/02: 16^{0}G, 16^{0}S, 16^{3}S, 16^{0}S

	Starts	1st	2nd	3rd	Win & Pl
Hurdles	4	0	0	1	380
Career Total	**4**	**0**	**0**	**1**	**380**

Going: Sf: 0-3 GS: 0-0 Gd: 0-1 GF: - Fm: 0-0
Distance: 2m/2m3: 0-4 2m4-2m7: 0-0 3m+: 0-0
Track: LH: 0-1 RH: 0-3 Tight: 0-2 Gall: 0-1
Aids: Bl: 0-0 Vi: 0-0 Tstrap: 0-0
Best Rating: 65 2/02 Muss 2m soft Hdl

Little form over hurdles so far.

Questionaire

9-y-o b m Northern State (USA)-Broken Melody (Busted)
D O Stephens C C Morgan

Placings:1 **(4727)**
2001/02: 24^{1}GF

	Starts	1st	2nd	3rd	Win & Pl
Chases	1	1	0	0	3504
Career Total	**1**	**1**	**0**	**0**	**3504**

78	4/02	Chep	3m	H Ch	G-F	£3503

Total win prize-money £3504

Going: Sf: 0-0 GS: 0-0 Gd: 0-0 GF: - Fm: 1-1
Distance: 2m/2m3: 0-0 2m4-2m7: 0-0 **3m+: 1-1**
Track: **LH: 1-1** RH: 0-0 Tight: 0-0 Gall: 0-0
Aids: Bl: 0-0 Vi: 0-0 Tstrap: 0-0
Best Rating: 78 4/02 Chep 3m gd-fm Ch

Moderate hunter chaser, acts on fast ground.

Quetal (IRE)

9-y-o ch g Buckskin (FR)-Cantafleur (Cantab)
Mrs Laura J Young Miss K Kitching

Placings:2F44/F6P-11 **(4678)**
2001/02: 26^{1}G, 25^{1}G

	Starts	1st	2nd	3rd	Win & Pl
Chases	2	2	0	0	11999
Career Total	**9**	**2**	**1**	**0**	**13281**

119	4/02	Aint	3m1f	B Ch	GD	£10822
114	3/02	Wwck	3m2f	H Ch	GD	£1176

Total win prize-money £11999

Going: Sf: 0-0 GS: 0-0 Gd: 2-2 GF: - Fm: 0-0
Distance: 2m/2m3: 0-0 2m4-2m7: 0-0 **3m+: 2-2**
Track: **LH: 2-2** RH: 0-0 **Tight: 1-1** Gall: 0-0
Aids: Bl: 0-0 Vi: 0-0 Tstrap: 0-0
Best Rating: 119 4/02 Aint 3m1f good Ch

Winning pointer and hunter chaser, loves soft ground. Took the novices' hunter chase at Aintree on Grand National day.

Quick Response (IRE)

100 **102**

9-y-o gr g Roselier (FR)-Deceptive Response (Furry Glen)
M F Harris (M W Easterby 28/10) Warwick Racecourse Owners Club

Placings:F1PP-2P4P4PP **(4634)**
2001/02: 25^{2}S, 25^{P}G, 21^{4}G, 25^{P}HY, 25^{4}S, 23^{P}HY, 24^{P}GF

	Starts	1st	2nd	3rd	Win & Pl
Chases	7	0	1	0	2813
Career Total	**11**	**1**	**1**	**0**	**3911**

95 2/01 Folk 2m5f H Ch SFT £1098
Total win prize-money £1099

Going: Sf: 0-4 GS: 0-0 Gd: 0-2 GF: - Fm: 0-1
Distance: 2m/2m3: 0-0 2m4-2m7: 0-2 3m+: 0-5
Track: LH: 0-1 RH: 0-6 Tight: 0-1 Gall: 0-0
Aids: Bl: 0-0 Vi: 0-0 Tstrap: 0-0
Best Rating: 102 10/01 Towc 3m1f soft Ch

He has pulled up or fallen more times than he has completed a course, but when he does get round he is usually there or thereabouts. Likes to dominate. Stays three miles. Acts on soft ground.

Quickswood (IRE)

103 **105**

9-y-o b g Yashgan-Up To Trix (Over The River (FR))
C R Barwell Harvey Spack

Placings:*440*/4P056431/01**P**220202/**UF**P3100-0PP000500310 **(4480)**
2001/02: 24^{0}G, 27^{P}G, 27^{P}G, 24^{0}G, 24^{0}G, 24^{0}S, 24^{5}HY, 26^{0}S, 25^{0}HY, 20^{3}S, 21^{1}HY, 22^{0}G

	Starts	1st	2nd	3rd	Win & Pl
Hurdles	12	1	0	1	4285
Career Total	**39**	**4**	**4**	**3**	**21017**

105 2/02 Wwck 2m5f D(0-120)HHdl HVY £3598
113 2/01 Newb 3m110y C(0-130)HHdl SFT £5733
110 6/99 Worc 3m F(0-100)HHdl G-S £2111
101 5/99 Hrfd 3m2f E Hdl GD £2070
Total win prize-money £13513

Going: Sf: 1-6 GS: 0-0 Gd: 0-6 GF: - Fm: 0-0
Distance: 2m/2m3: 0-0 **2m4-2m7: 1-3** 3m+: 0-9
Track: LH: 0-3 RH: 0-6 Tight: 0-2 Gall: 0-0
Aids: Bl: 0-0 **Vi: 1-10** Tstrap: 0-0
Best Rating: 113 2/01 Newb 3m110y soft Hdl

Fair handicap hurdler. Suited by three miles and acts on most types of ground.

Quiet Leader (IRE)

92 **95**

6-y-o b m Supreme Leader-Quiet City (True Song)
R H Alner And Mrs M C Yeo

Placings:0F44P04 **(4861)**
2001/02: 17^{0}G, 22^{F}G, 22^{4}G, 22^{4}S, 26^{P}GS, 19^{0}S, 22^{4}F

	Starts	1st	2nd	3rd	Win & Pl
Hurdles	7	0	0	0	280
Career Total	**7**	**0**	**0**	**0**	**280**

Going: Sf: 0-2 GS: 0-1 Gd: 0-3 GF: - Fm: 0-1
Distance: 2m/2m3: 0-1 2m4-2m7: 0-5 3m+: 0-1
Track: LH: 0-0 RH: 0-5 Tight: 0-1 Gall: 0-0
Aids: Bl: 0-0 Vi: 0-0 Tstrap: 0-0
Best Rating: 95 2/02 Winc 2m6f soft Hdl

Quiet Sovereign

78f **81f**

5-y-o b m Supreme Leader-Quiet City (True Song)
Mrs D Haine Mrs Solna Thomson Jones

Placings:5 **(3770)**
2001/02: 16^{5}GS

	Starts	1st	2nd	3rd	Win & Pl
NH Flat	1	0	0	0	0
Career Total	**1**	**0**	**0**	**0**	**0**

Going: Sf: 0-0 GS: 0-1 Gd: 0-0 GF: - Fm: 0-0
Distance: 2m/2m3: 0-1 2m4-2m7: 0-0 3m+: 0-0
Track: LH: 0-1 RH: 0-0 Tight: 0-1 Gall: 0-0
Aids: Bl: 0-0 Vi: 0-0 Tstrap: 0-0
Best Rating: 81 2/02 Fknm 2m gd-sft NHF

Quiet Water (IRE)

98 **89+**

6-y-o br g Lord Americo-Sirana (Al Sirat (USA))
M J Wilkinson S N Wilshire

Placings:*040*-450 **(4113)**
2001/02: 16^{4}S, 16^{5}G, 16^{0}G

	Starts	1st	2nd	3rd	Win & Pl
Hurdles	3	0	0	0	330
Career Total	**6**	**0**	**0**	**0**	**330**

Going: Sf: 0-1 GS: 0-0 Gd: 0-2 GF: - Fm: 0-0
Distance: 2m/2m3: 0-0 2m4-2m7: 0-0 3m+: 0-0
Track: LH: 0-0 RH: 0-3 Tight: 0-0 Gall: 0-1
Aids: Bl: 0-0 Vi: 0-0 Tstrap: 0-0
Best Rating: 85 11/01 Hntg 2m110y good Hdl

Modest hurdler, suited by fast ground and step up in trip when scoring at Huntingdon in May 2002.

Quini Eagle (FR)

100 **112**

10-y-o gr g Dom Pasquini (FR)-Miss Eagle (FR) (Staunch Eagle (USA))
M C Pipe B A Kilpatrick

Placings:215431/05336/0-03 **(2659)**
2001/02: 22^{0}HY, 24^{3}GS

	Starts	1st	2nd	3rd	Win & Pl
Hurdles	2	0	0	1	540
Career Total	**14**	**2**	**1**	**4**	**8185**

110 3/97 Newb 2m5f D Hdl GD £4102
103 11/96 Kemp 2m H NHF G-S £1416
Total win prize-money £5520

Going: Sf: 0-1 GS: 0-1 Gd: 0-0 GF: - Fm: 0-0
Distance: 2m/2m3: 0-0 2m4-2m7: 0-1 3m+: 0-1
Track: LH: 0-1 RH: 0-1 Tight: 0-2 Gall: 0-0
Aids: Bl: 0-0 Vi: 0-2 Tstrap: 0-0
Best Rating: 123 3/00 Extr 2m7f gd-sft Hdl

Fair hurdler, lightly raced in recent years.

Quit The Pack (IRE)

88 **66**

4-y-o b/br g Grand Lodge (USA)-Treasure (IRE) (Treasure Kay)
R N Bevis (J S Bolger 6/7) Ewson Contractors And Steve Corbett

Placings:00P **(3860)**
2001/02: 16^{0}HY, 16^{0}S, 20^{P}S

	Starts	1st	2nd	3rd	Win & Pl
Hurdles	3	0	0	0	
Career Total	**3**	**0**	**0**	**0**	

Going: Sf: 0-3 GS: 0-0 Gd: 0-0 GF: - Fm: 0-0
Distance: 2m/2m3: 0-2 2m4-2m7: 0-1 3m+: 0-0
Track: LH: 0-2 RH: 0-1 Tight: 0-0 Gall: 0-1
Aids: Bl: 0-0 Vi: 0-0 Tstrap: 0-0
Best Rating: 66 2/02 Ludl 2m soft Hdl

Quixall Crossett

17-y-o b g Beverley Boy-Grange Classic (Stype Grange)
E M Caine Mrs Karen Woodhead

Placings:F/005445/U**P5063U/6PPFP**P0**3352**46**54440 F0U6FP6PU55/654U334405PPF**456P6/**66255046**BP5 **P65P05U0/50PP530P/4P-P6UU** (2184)
2001/02: 24^{P}GF, 25^{6}G, 25^{U}G, 21^{U}G

	Starts	1st	2nd	3rd	Win & Pl
Chases	4	0	0	0	0
Career Total	**103**	**0**	**2**	**6**	**8502**

Going: Sf: 0-0 GS: 0-0 Gd: 0-3 GF: - Fm: 0-1
Distance: 2m/2m3: 0-0 2m4-2m7: 0-1 3m+: 0-3
Track: LH: 0-4 RH: 0-0 Tight: 0-1 Gall: 0-0
Aids: Bl: 0-0 Vi: 0-0 Tstrap: 0-0
Best Rating: 72 5/97 MRas 2m4f gd-fm Ch

Ra Ra Rasputin

83 **52**

7-y-o b g Petong-Ra Ra Girl (Shack (USA))
B P J Baugh A J Deakin

Placings:00/00-00060 **(1306)**
2001/02: 16^{0}GF, 17^{0}GF, 19^{0}G, 16^{6}G, 17^{0}GF

	Starts	1st	2nd	3rd	Win & Pl
Hurdles	5	0	0	0	0
Career Total	**9**	**0**	**0**	**0**	**0**

Going: Sf: 0-0 GS: 0-0 Gd: 0-2 GF: - Fm: 0-3
Distance: 2m/2m3: 0-4 2m4-2m7: 0-1 3m+: 0-0
Track: LH: 0-2 RH: 0-3 Tight: 0-4 Gall: 0-0
Aids: Bl: 0-0 Vi: 0-0 Tstrap: 0-0
Best Rating: 53 3/00 Uttx 2m good Hdl

Racing Hawk (USA)

83 **51**

10-y-o ch g Silver Hawk (USA)-Lorn Lady (Lorenzaccio)
Miss J Wormall Mrs R Wormall

Placings:U/PP14P20435/32415011P/P/0 **(0232)**
2001/02: 21^{0}GF

	Starts	1st	2nd	3rd	Win & Pl
Hurdles	1	0	0	0	
Career Total	**22**	**4**	**2**	**2**	**8879**

101 8/98 MRas 2m5f110y G(0-95)HHdl GD £1632
101 7/98 MRas 2m5f110y G(0-90)HHdl G-F £1716
97 6/98 NAbb 2m6f G(0-95)HHdl FRM £1621
93 11/97 Uttx 2m4f110y G Hdl GD £1941
Total win prize-money £6911

Going: Sf: 0-0 GS: 0-0 Gd: 0-0 GF: - Fm: 0-1
Distance: 2m/2m3: 0-0 2m4-2m7: 0-1 3m+: 0-0
Track: LH: 0-0 RH: 0-1 Tight: 0-0 Gall: 0-1
Aids: Bl: 0-0 Vi: 0-0 Tstrap: 0-0
Best Rating: 101 8/98 MRas 2m5f110y good Hdl

Racingforyou Lass

85 **61**

4-y-o b f Moujeeb (USA)-Kentucky Mole Vii (Damsire Unregistered)

A Streeter Racing For You Limited

Placings:403 **(1231)**

2001/02: 16^{4}G, 16^{0}G, 16^{3}GF

	Starts	1st	2nd	3rd	Win & Pl
Hurdles	3	0	0	1	419
Career Total	**3**	**0**	**0**	**1**	**419**

Going: Sf: 0-0 GS: 0-0 Gd: 0-2 GF: - Fm: 0-1
Distance: 2m/2m3: 0-3 2m4-2m7: 0-0 3m+: 0-0
Track: LH: 0-3 RH: 0-0 Tight: 0-2 Gall: 0-0
Aids: Bl: 0-0 Vi: 0-0 Tstrap: 0-0
Best Rating: **61** 7/01 Strf 2m110y good Hdl

Radanpour (IRE)

102 **112**

10-y-o b g Kahyasi-Rajpoura (Kashmir Ii)

Mrs M Reveley The Mary Reveley Racing Club

Placings:*11*112FF350/0UP6P/425**20**P1/2250131/0**F4**5-034 **(1273)**

2001/02: 16^{0}G, 20^{3}F, 24^{4}GF

	Starts	1st	2nd	3rd	Win & Pl
Hurdles	3	0	0	1	372
Career Total	**36**	**7**	**5**	**3**	**31113**

118	3/00	MRas	2m5f110y	E(0-115)HHdl	G-F	£2671
108	1/00	Catt	2m3f	F(0-110)HHdl	GD	£2394
96	2/99	Catt	2m	G Hdl	GD	£2444
115	11/96	Navn	2m	Hdl	YLD	£7061
109	10/96	Punc	2m	Hdl	G-Y	£3177
119	9/96	List	2m	NHF	GD	£4237
105	5/96	Tram	2m4f	NHF	GD	£2295

Total win prize-money £24281

Going: Sf: 0-0 GS: 0-0 Gd: 0-1 GF: - Fm: 0-2
Distance: 2m/2m3: 0-1 2m4-2m7: 0-1 3m+: 0-1
Track: LH: 0-3 RH: 0-0 Tight: 0-1 Gall: 0-0
Aids: Bl: 0-1 Vi: 0-0 Tstrap: 0-0
Best Rating: **123** 11/96 Navn 2m4f yield Hdl

Radar (IRE)

108(61h) **122**

7-y-o b g Petardia-Soignee (Night Shift (USA))

Miss S E Forster C Storey

Placings:345/321-0112F4 **(4899)**

2001/02: 16^{0}S, 16^{1}S, 16^{1}S, 17^{2}S, 17^{F}GF, 16^{4}G

	Starts	1st	2nd	3rd	Win & Pl
Chases	6	2	1	0	11638
Career Total	**12**	**3**	**2**	**2**	**16043**

113	3/02	Sedg	2m110y	D Ch	SFT	£3844
115	3/02	Sedg	2m110y	C Ch	SFT	£6077
107	8/00	Worc	2m	E Hdl	G-F	£2756

Total win prize-money £12679

Going: Sf: 2-4 GS: 0-0 Gd: 0-1 GF: - Fm: 0-1
Distance: **2m/2m3: 2-6** 2m4-2m7: 0-0 3m+: 0-0
Track: **LH: 2-4** RH: 0-2 **Tight: 2-5** Gall: 0-0
Aids: Bl: 0-0 Vi: 0-0 Tstrap: 0-0
Best Rating: **122** 4/02 Kels 2m1f gd-fm Ch

A winner on the Flat, he has also been successful over hurdles and fences, effective over two miles. Acts on most types of ground.

Radiation (IRE)

108 **142**

9-y-o ch g Orchestra-Bernish Lass (Radical)

J J O'Neill Anne Duchess Of Westminster

Placings:*3*/113**41P14/32P1221/U44P2-R212** **(3789)**

2001/02: 24^{R}GS, 24^{2}HY, 24^{1}HY, 33^{2}S

	Starts	1st	2nd	3rd	Win & Pl
Chases	4	1	2	0	21533
Career Total	**25**	**7**	**6**	**3**	**75038**

140	1/02	Uttx	3m	D(0-125)HCh	HVY	£5244
134	4/00	Aint	3m1f	B HCh	GD	£14183
133	2/00	Carl	3m2f	D(0-125)HCh	HVY	£4114
133	4/99	Carl	3m2f	E Ch	G-S	£3186
119	2/99	Kels	3m1f	C Ch	SFT	£6776
110	11/98	Aint	3m110y	D(0-110)HHdl	G-S	£3687
108	10/98	Kels	2m6f110y	E Hdl	SFT	£2388

Total win prize-money £39581

Going: Sf: 1-3 GS: 0-1 Gd: 0-0 GF: - Fm: 0-0
Distance: 2m/2m3: 0-0 2m4-2m7: 0-0 **3m+: 1-4**
Track: **LH: 1-3** RH: 0-1 Tight: 0-0 Gall: 0-1
Aids: **Bl: 1-4** Vi: 0-0 Tstrap: 0-0
Best Rating: **142** 2/02 Newc 4m1f soft Ch

Harshly handicapped over fences last season, he stays well but has enough pace to be effective over shorter trips. Suited by soft ground, he can look a hard ride but is considered a Grand National prospect by connections. Enjoyed a slog in the mud at Uttoxeter in January, winning easily, and was caught close home in the Eider at Newcastle.

Radical Jack

73 **47**

5-y-o b g Presidium-Luckifosome (Smackover)

Denys Smith Lord Durham

Placings:00 **(1352)**

2001/02: 17^{0}GF, 17^{0}GF

	Starts	1st	2nd	3rd	Win & Pl
Hurdles	2	0	0	0	
Career Total	**2**	**0**	**0**	**0**	

Going: Sf: 0-0 GS: 0-0 Gd: 0-0 GF: - Fm: 0-2
Distance: 2m/2m3: 0-2 2m4-2m7: 0-0 3m+: 0-0
Track: LH: 0-2 RH: 0-0 Tight: 0-2 Gall: 0-0
Aids: Bl: 0-0 Vi: 0-0 Tstrap: 0-0
Best Rating: **47** 9/01 Sedg 2m1f gd-fm Hdl

Radical Stream (IRE)

10-y-o b g Radical-Knockeyon (Ragapan)

B R Johnson K Tork

Placings:4P/*00*000/0/**PP** **(0321)**

2001/02: 18^{P}GF, 26^{P}G

	Starts	1st	2nd	3rd	Win & Pl
Chases	2	0	0	0	
Career Total	**10**	**0**	**0**	**0**	**113**

Going: Sf: 0-0 GS: 0-0 Gd: 0-1 GF: - Fm: 0-1
Distance: 2m/2m3: 0-1 2m4-2m7: 0-0 3m+: 0-1
Track: LH: 0-0 RH: 0-1 Tight: 0-2 Gall: 0-0
Aids: Bl: 0-0 Vi: 0-0 Tstrap: 0-0
Best Rating: **74** 8/97 Slig 2m yield NHF

Radomsko

89 **60**

10-y-o ch g Polish Precedent (USA)-Mahabba (USA) (Elocutionist (USA))

S B Clark S B Clark

Placings:23/45/P-0 **(0067)**

2001/02: 17^{0}G

	Starts	1st	2nd	3rd	Win & Pl
Hurdles	1	0	0	0	
Career Total	**6**	**0**	**1**	**1**	**1162**

Going: Sf: 0-0 GS: 0-0 Gd: 0-1 GF: - Fm: 0-0
Distance: 2m/2m3: 0-1 2m4-2m7: 0-0 3m+: 0-0
Track: LH: 0-1 RH: 0-0 Tight: 0-1 Gall: 0-0
Aids: Bl: 0-0 Vi: 0-0 Tstrap: 0-0
Best Rating: **103** 1/99 Hntg 2m110y soft Hdl

Raffles Rooster

119 **139**

10-y-o ch g Galetto (FR)-Singapore Girl (FR) (Lyphard (USA))

Miss Venetia Williams Mark A Leatham

Placings:35/232/**142U1/251/51F01326-31524** **(4419)**

2001/02: 26^{3}G, 24^{1}GS, 24^{5}GS, 24^{2}G, 24^{4}GS

	Starts	1st	2nd	3rd	Win & Pl
Chases	5	1	1	1	12563
Career Total	**26**	**6**	**6**	**4**	**46454**

136	12/01	Sand	3m110y	D(0-120)HCh	G-S	£7150
135	2/01	Towc	3m1f	C(0-130)HCh	HVY	£5941
135	11/00	NAbb	3m2f110y	C(0-130)HCh	HVY	£7315
129	3/00	Tntn	3m	F(0-105)HCh	GD	£4777
114	2/99	Tntn	3m	E(0-115)HCh	G-S	£3875
121	11/98	Font	2m3f	E Ch	SFT	£2786

Total win prize-money £31845

Going: Sf: 0-0 GS: 1-3 Gd: 0-2 GF: - Fm: 0-0
Distance: 2m/2m3: 0-0 2m4-2m7: 0-0 **3m+: 1-5**
Track: LH: 0-2 **RH: 1-3** Tight: 0-1 Gall: 0-1
Aids: Bl: 0-0 Vi: 0-0 Tstrap: 0-0
Best Rating: **139** 3/02 Sand 3m110y good Ch

Once a useful Flat handicapper, he is a capable chaser. Suited by hold-up tactics and a test of stamina in heavy ground, although he does not find a great deal off the bit.

Ragamuff

1

11-y-o b g El Conquistador-Ragsi (Amerian (USA))

P J Hobbs R M E Wright

Placings:550/30**24214/P12231/411344**0**2/6CF1PFPP**-0 **(3512)**

2001/02: 24^{0}S

	Starts	1st	2nd	3rd	Win & Pl
Chases	1	0	0	0	
Career Total	**33**	**6**	**5**	**3**	**29077**

124	11/00	Chep	3m	F(0-110)HCh	SFT	£2597
120	11/99	NAbb	3m2f110y	F(0-110)HCh	SFT	£7545
114	11/99	Tntn	3m	F(0-105)HCh	GD	£2696
117	3/99	Hntg	3m	F(0-100)HCh	SFT	£2967
89	12/98	Hrfd	2m3f	F(0-105)HCh	G-S	£3191
94	1/98	Folk	2m5f	F(0-100)HCh	G-S	£2713

Total win prize-money £21711

Going: Sf: 0-1 GS: 0-0 Gd: 0-0 GF: - Fm: 0-0
Distance: 2m/2m3: 0-0 2m4-2m7: 0-0 3m+: 0-1
Track: LH: 0-0 RH: 0-1 Tight: 0-1 Gall: 0-0
Aids: Bl: 0-0 Vi: 0-0 Tstrap: 0-0
Best Rating: **124** 11/00 Chep 3m soft Ch

Ragdale Hall (USA)

101 105

5-y-o b g Bien Bien (USA)-Gift Of Dance (USA) (Trempolino (USA))

P J Hobbs (J H M Gosden 25/10) Jack Joseph

Placings:2 **(4114)**

2001/02: 16²G

	Starts	1st	2nd	3rd	Win & Pl
Hurdles	1	0	1	0	788
Career Total	**1**	**0**	**1**	**0**	**788**

Going: Sf: 0-0 GS: 0-0 Gd: 0-1 GF: - Fm: 0-0
Distance: 2m/2m3: 0-1 2m4-2m7: 0-0 3m+: 0-0
Track: LH: 0-0 RH: 0-1 Tight: 0-0 Gall: 0-0
Aids: Bl: 0-0 Vi: 0-0 Tstrap: 0-0
Best Rating: 105 3/02 Winc 2m good Hdl

Promising second on hurdling debut at Wincanton. A shade disappointing when beaten favourite at the same course next time but enjoyed a facile success in a weak event at Uttoxeter in June 2002. Reported by rider to have had a breathing problem at Worcester in August.

Ragu

96f 86f

4-y-o b f Contract Law (USA)-Marnworth (Funny Man)

Ferdy Murphy Raj Patel

Placings:0323 **(4771)**

2001/02: 16⁰S, 16³S, 16²G, 16³GF

	Starts	1st	2nd	3rd	Win & Pl
NH Flat	4	0	1	2	1075
Career Total	**4**	**0**	**1**	**2**	**1075**

Going: Sf: 0-2 GS: 0-0 Gd: 0-1 GF: - Fm: 0-1
Distance: 2m/2m3: 0-4 2m4-2m7: 0-0 3m+: 0-0
Track: LH: 0-2 RH: 0-0 Tight: 0-1 Gall: 0-1
Aids: Bl: 0-0 Vi: 0-0 Tstrap: 0-0
Best Rating: 86 4/02 Fknm 2m good NHF

Fair form in bumpers. Suited by cut in the ground.

Rain God

91 79

6-y-o b g Rainbow Quest (USA)-Mystic Goddess (USA) (Storm Bird (CAN))

N A Twiston-Davies Geoffrey And Donna Keeys

Placings:P0P/20-30 **(0564)**

2001/02: 17³F, 17⁰GF

	Starts	1st	2nd	3rd	Win & Pl
Hurdles	2	0	0	1	301
Career Total	**7**	**0**	**1**	**1**	**955**

Going: Sf: 0-0 GS: 0-0 Gd: 0-0 GF: - Fm: 0-2
Distance: 2m/2m3: 0-2 2m4-2m7: 0-0 3m+: 0-0
Track: LH: 0-1 RH: 0-1 Tight: 0-2 Gall: 0-0
Aids: Bl: 0-0 Vi: 0-0 Tstrap: 0-2
Best Rating: 79 5/01 Tntn 2m1f firm Hdl

Rainbow Chase (IRE)

93 91

4-y-o b g Rainbow Quest (USA)-Fayrooz (USA) (Gulch (USA))

S Magnier (J L Dunlop 25/6) Fergus Jones

Placings:0404 **(3611)**

2001/02: 16⁰G, 16⁴GS, 16⁰GS, 20⁴S

	Starts	1st	2nd	3rd	Win & Pl
Hurdles	4	0	0	0	261
Career Total	**4**	**0**	**0**	**0**	**261**

Going: Sf: 0-1 GS: 0-2 Gd: 0-1 GF: - Fm: 0-0
Distance: 2m/2m3: 0-3 2m4-2m7: 0-1 3m+: 0-0
Track: LH: 0-3 RH: 0-1 Tight: 0-1 Gall: 0-2
Aids: Bl: 0-0 Vi: 0-0 Tstrap: 0-0
Best Rating: 91 12/01 Newc 2m gd-sft Hdl

Rainbow Dance (IRE)

109 124+

6-y-o ch g Rainbows For Life (CAN)-Nishila (USA) (Green Dancer (USA))

J J O'Neill (Henry De Bromhead 22/7) Mrs G Smith

Placings:053254-0012656 **(4502)**

2001/02: 19⁰G, 16⁰G, 16¹G, 20²G, 22⁶GS, 25⁵S, 22⁶G

	Starts	1st	2nd	3rd	Win & Pl
NH Flat	1	1	0	0	3895
Hurdles	6	0	1	0	902
Career Total	**13**	**1**	**2**	**1**	**6431**

104	7/01	Tipp	2m	NHF	GD	£3895

Total win prize-money £3895

Going: Sf: 0-1 GS: 0-1 Gd: 1-5 GF: - Fm: 0-0
Distance: **2m/2m3: 1-3** 2m4-2m7: 0-3 3m+: 0-1
Track: LH: 0-3 RH: 0-1 Tight: 0-2 Gall: 0-0
Aids: Bl: 0-0 Vi: 0-0 Tstrap: 0-2
Best Rating: 112 5/00 Punc 2m yield NHF

Modest hurdler, who has reportedly suffered from breathing problems. Looked an improved performer in first-time blinkers when winning at Ludlow in May 2002, and a handicap at Worcester June. Effective on fast ground.

Rainbow Dust

6-y-o b m Sea Raven (IRE)-Ragroyal (Royal Palace)

Miss K M George Exterior Profiles Ltd

Placings:00 **(4126)**

2001/02: 10⁰G, 19⁰G

	Starts	1st	2nd	3rd	Win & Pl
NH Flat	1	0	0	0	0
Hurdles	1	0	0	0	0
Career Total	**2**	**0**	**0**	**0**	

Going: Sf: 0-1 GS: 0-0 Gd: 0-1 GF: - Fm: 0-0
Distance: 2m/2m3: 0-1 2m4-2m7: 0-1 3m+: 0-0
Track: LH: 0-0 RH: 0-2 Tight: 0-0 Gall: 0-0
Aids: Bl: 0-0 Vi: 0-0 Tstrap: 0-0
Best Rating: 25 2/02 Winc 2m soft NHF

Rainbow Frontier (IRE)

(47c)

8-y-o b g Law Society (USA)-Tatchers Mate (Thatching)

M C Pipe Clive D Smith

Placings:11111F2/1300005/3160/200-F **(0080)**

2001/02: 16ᶠG

	Starts	1st	2nd	3rd	Win & Pl
Hurdles	1	0	0	0	
Career Total	**22**	**7**	**2**	**2**	**75233**

151	1/00	Asct	2m110y	B HHdl	SFT	£10140
143	5/98	Hayd	2m	A HHdl	GD	£23365
140	12/97	Leop	2m	Hdl	HVY	£9579
134	11/97	Fair	2m	Hdl	Y-S	£6782
135	9/97	List	2m	Hdl	SFT	£3730
123	8/97	Tral	2m	Hdl		£3391

Total win prize-money £59362

Going: Sf: 0-0 GS: 0-0 Gd: 0-1 GF: - Fm: 0-0
Distance: 2m/2m3: 0-1 2m4-2m7: 0-0 3m+: 0-0
Track: LH: 0-1 RH: 0-0 Tight: 0-0 Gall: 0-0
Aids: Bl: 0-0 Vi: 0-0 Tstrap: 0-0
Best Rating: 151 2/00 Newb 2m110y gd-sft Hdl

Rainbow Hill

72 16

5-y-o b g Rainbow Quest (USA)-Hill Hopper (IRE) (Danehill (USA))

J J Quinn John Ward

Placings:0 **(1505)**

2001/02: 17⁰G

	Starts	1st	2nd	3rd	Win & Pl
Hurdles	1	0	0	0	
Career Total	**1**	**0**	**0**	**0**	

Going: Sf: 0-0 GS: 0-0 Gd: 0-1 GF: - Fm: 0-0
Distance: 2m/2m3: 0-1 2m4-2m7: 0-0 3m+: 0-0
Track: LH: 0-1 RH: 0-0 Tight: 0-1 Gall: 0-0
Aids: Bl: 0-0 Vi: 0-0 Tstrap: 0-0
Best Rating: 28 10/01 Sedg 2m1f good Hdl

Rainbow Raver (IRE)

98 79

6-y-o ch m Rainbows For Life (CAN)-Foolish Passion (USA) (Secretariat (USA))

J L Eyre Alma & Stewart Pinner

Placings:0F/30P **(1747)**

2001/02: 17³GF, 17⁰G, 17ᴾG

	Starts	1st	2nd	3rd	Win & Pl
Hurdles	3	0	0	1	239
Career Total	**5**	**0**	**0**	**1**	**239**

Going: Sf: 0-0 GS: 0-0 Gd: 0-2 GF: - Fm: 0-1
Distance: 2m/2m3: 0-3 2m4-2m7: 0-0 3m+: 0-0
Track: LH: 0-1 RH: 0-2 Tight: 0-3 Gall: 0-0
Aids: Bl: 0-0 Vi: 0-0 Tstrap: 0-0
Best Rating: 79 9/01 MRas 2m1f110y gd-fm Hdl

Rainbow Spirit (IRE)

102 100

5-y-o b g Rainbows For Life (CAN)-Merrie Moment (IRE) (Taufan (USA))

H Alexander (A P Jarvis 12/8) Mrs L J Bowers

Placings:515 **(4686)**

2001/02: 17⁵S, 24¹GS, 26⁵GF

	Starts	1st	2nd	3rd	Win & Pl
Hurdles	3	1	0	0	2814
Career Total	**3**	**1**	**0**	**0**	**2814**

100	2/02	Muss	3m	E Hdl	G-S	£2814

Total win prize-money £2814

Going: Sf: 0-1 GS: 1-1 Gd: 0-0 GF: - Fm: 0-1
Distance: 2m/2m3: 0-1 2m4-2m7: 0-0 **3m+: 1-2**
Track: LH: 0-1 **RH: 1-2 Tight: 1-2** Gall: 0-0
Aids: Bl: 0-0 Vi: 0-0 Tstrap: 0-0
Best Rating: 100 4/02 Hrfd 3m2f gd-fm Hdl

A stayer on the Flat, showed the benefit of the step up to three miles when scoring at Musselburgh in February. Seems to handle any ground.

Rainbow Star (FR)

94(75c) (58c)**66**

8-y-o b/br g Saumarez-In The Star (FR) (In Fijar (USA))

J S Smith W E Donohue

Placings:221P/214P**5/4P**11**F**/1P-P0**0**0P (4898)

2001/02: 19^{P}S, 17^{0}HY, 16^{0}S, 19^{0}S, 16^{P}G

	Starts	1st	2nd	3rd	Win & Pl
Hurdles	4	0	0	0	0
Chases	1	0	0	0	0
Career Total	**21**	**5**	**3**	**0**	**13123**

106	5/00	Hrfd	2m3f110y	G Hdl	GD	£1974
105	1/00	Plum	2m5f	G Hdl	SFT	£2292
99	1/00	Tntn	2m3f110y	G Hdl	SFT	£1519
116	5/98	NAbb	2m1f	D Hdl	G-F	£2832
99	3/98	NAbb	2m1f	F Hdl	SFT	£1962

Total win prize-money £10580

Going: Sf: 0-4 GS: 0-0 Gd: 0-1 GF: - Fm: 0-0
Distance: 2m/2m3: 0-3 2m4-2m7: 0-2 3m+: 0-0
Track: LH: 0-0 RH: 0-5 Tight: 0-3 Gall: 0-0
Aids: Bl: 0-5 Vi: 0-0 Tstrap: 0-0
Best Rating: 116 5/98 NAbb 2m1f gd-fm Hdl

Rainbow Sun

82 **55**

6-y-o ch g Minster Son-Rilin (Ribston)

N M Babbage John Cantrill

Placings:*40* (4887)

2001/02: 16^{4}GF, 18^{0}GF

	Starts	1st	2nd	3rd	Win & Pl
NH Flat	2	0	0	0	0
Career Total	**2**	**0**	**0**	**0**	**0**

Going: Sf: 0-0 GS: 0-0 Gd: 0-0 GF: - Fm: 0-2
Distance: 2m/2m3: 0-2 2m4-2m7: 0-0 3m+: 0-0
Track: LH: 0-2 RH: 0-0 Tight: 0-1 Gall: 0-0
Aids: Bl: 0-0 Vi: 0-0 Tstrap: 0-0
Best Rating: 91 4/02 Wwck 2m gd-fm NHF

Showed ability in a Warwick bumper on his debut.

Rainbow Times (IRE)

104 **129**

9-y-o b m Jareer (USA)-Princess The Great (USA) (Alleged (USA))

Ferdy Murphy Mrs J M Lancaster

Placings:060/0*66*/**25/4/1-230P221** (4541)

2001/02: 25^{2}GF, 25^{3}G, 28^{0}GS, 25^{P}GS, 20^{2}GS, 21^{2}HY, 25^{1}G

	Starts	1st	2nd	3rd	Win & Pl
Chases	7	1	3	1	12130
Career Total	**17**	**2**	**4**	**1**	**23479**

126	4/02	Hrfd	3m1f110y	E Ch	GD	£3657
129	4/01	Aint	3m1f	B Ch	HVY	£11017

Total win prize-money £14676

Going: Sf: 0-1 GS: 0-3 Gd: 1-2 GF: - Fm: 0-1
Distance: 2m/2m3: 0-0 2m4-2m7: 0-2 **3m+: 1-5**
Track: LH: 0-5 **RH: 1-2** Tight: 0-2 Gall: 0-0
Aids: **Bl: 1-3** Vi: 0-0 Tstrap: 0-0
Best Rating: 129 4/01 Aint 3m1f heavy Ch

Successful point to pointer. Fair novice chaser, stays three miles plus, acts on good and soft ground.

Rainbow Valley (GER)

79 **74**

7-y-o ch g Fabulous Dancer (USA)-Razoumova (Dominion)

D J Wintle R H L Barnes

Placings:PP-0 (0844)

2001/02: 19^{0}GF

	Starts	1st	2nd	3rd	Win & Pl
Hurdles	1	0	0	0	
Career Total	**3**	**0**	**0**	**0**	

Going: Sf: 0-0 GS: 0-0 Gd: 0-0 GF: - Fm: 0-1
Distance: 2m/2m3: 0-1 2m4-2m7: 0-0 3m+: 0-0
Track: LH: 0-1 RH: 0-0 Tight: 0-1 Gall: 0-0
Aids: Bl: 0-0 Vi: 0-0 Tstrap: 0-0
Best Rating: 74 7/01 Strf 2m3f gd-fm Hdl

Rainbows Aglitter

112 **114**

5-y-o ch g Rainbows For Life (CAN)-Chalet Waldegg (Monsanto (FR))

D R Gandolfo Nigel Stafford

Placings:*1*-12324P (4154)

2001/02: 16^{1}G, 16^{2}G, 16^{3}S, 16^{2}S, 16^{4}GS, 20^{P}GS

	Starts	1st	2nd	3rd	Win & Pl
Hurdles	6	1	2	1	6483
Career Total	**7**	**2**	**2**	**1**	**8167**

114	10/01	Sthl	2m	E Hdl	GD	£2247
105	1/01	Kemp	2m	H NHF	SFT	£1683

Total win prize-money £3931

Going: Sf: 0-2 GS: 0-2 Gd: 1-2 GF: - Fm: 0-0
Distance: **2m/2m3: 1-5** 2m4-2m7: 0-1 3m+: 0-0
Track: **LH: 1-2** RH: 0-4 **Tight: 1-2** Gall: 0-0
Aids: Bl: 0-0 Vi: 0-0 Tstrap: 0-0
Best Rating: 114 12/01 Sand 2m110y soft Hdl

He won a bumper in January 2001 on his racecourse debut and won as he liked on his hurdles bow at Southwell in October. He has continued to run well in some competitive events since then and looks ready for a step up beyond two miles. Apparently a highly-strung individual, he is suited by soft ground.

Rainha

91f **83f**

5-y-o b m Alflora (IRE)-Political Prospect (Politico (USA))

Ferdy Murphy J D Goodfellow

Placings:*03* (4289)

2001/02: 16^{0}S, 17^{3}GS

	Starts	1st	2nd	3rd	Win & Pl
NH Flat	2	0	0	1	231
Career Total	**2**	**0**	**0**	**1**	**231**

Going: Sf: 0-1 GS: 0-1 Gd: 0-0 GF: - Fm: 0-0
Distance: 2m/2m3: 0-2 2m4-2m7: 0-0 3m+: 0-0
Track: LH: 0-0 RH: 0-1 Tight: 0-1 Gall: 0-0
Aids: Bl: 0-0 Vi: 0-0 Tstrap: 0-0
Best Rating: 87 3/02 MRas 2m1f110y gd-sft NHF

Has looked on the slow side in bumpers.

Rainton

88 **64**

6-y-o gr g Kasakov-Strathleven (My Swanee)

J R Turner Yarm Racing Partnership

Placings:*0*/003P05**U**-00P (0329)

2001/02: 16^{0}S, 16^{0}GF, 16^{P}GS

	Starts	1st	2nd	3rd	Win & Pl
Hurdles	3	0	0	0	
Career Total	**11**	**0**	**0**	**1**	**500**

Going: Sf: 0-1 GS: 0-1 Gd: 0-0 GF: - Fm: 0-1
Distance: 2m/2m3: 0-3 2m4-2m7: 0-0 3m+: 0-0
Track: LH: 0-2 RH: 0-1 Tight: 0-0 Gall: 0-0
Aids: Bl: 0-2 Vi: 0-0 Tstrap: 0-0
Best Rating: 64 5/01 Hexm 2m gd-fm Hdl

Rainworth Lady

5-y-o b m Governor General-Monongelia (Welsh Pageant)

P W Hiatt George Patching

Placings:PP (2418)

2001/02: 16^{P}G, 16^{P}HY

	Starts	1st	2nd	3rd	Win & Pl
Hurdles	2	0	0	0	
Career Total	**2**	**0**	**0**	**0**	

Going: Sf: 0-1 GS: 0-0 Gd: 0-1 GF: - Fm: 0-0
Distance: 2m/2m3: 0-2 2m4-2m7: 0-0 3m+: 0-0
Track: LH: 0-1 RH: 0-1 Tight: 0-0 Gall: 0-0
Aids: Bl: 0-0 Vi: 0-0 Tstrap: 0-1
Best Rating:

Raisa's Gold (IRE)

4-y-o b f Goldmark (USA)-Princess Raisa (Indian King (USA))

B S Rothwell Brian Rothwell

Placings:F (1027)

2001/02: 16^{F}G

	Starts	1st	2nd	3rd	Win & Pl
Hurdles	1	0	0	0	
Career Total	**1**	**0**	**0**	**0**	

Going: Sf: 0-0 GS: 0-0 Gd: 0-1 GF: - Fm: 0-0
Distance: 2m/2m3: 0-1 2m4-2m7: 0-0 3m+: 0-0
Track: LH: 0-1 RH: 0-0 Tight: 0-1 Gall: 0-0
Aids: Bl: 0-0 Vi: 0-0 Tstrap: 0-0
Best Rating:

Raise A Glass

4-y-o ch c King's Signet (USA)-Anouska (Interrex (CAN))

C G Cox T Y Bissett

Placings:P (1027)

2001/02: 16^{P}G

	Starts	1st	2nd	3rd	Win & Pl
Hurdles	1	0	0	0	
Career Total	**1**	**0**	**0**	**0**	

Going: Sf: 0-0 GS: 0-0 Gd: 0-1 GF: - Fm: 0-0
Distance: 2m/2m3: 0-1 2m4-2m7: 0-0 3m+: 0-0
Track: LH: 0-1 RH: 0-0 Tight: 0-1 Gall: 0-0
Aids: Bl: 0-0 Vi: 0-0 Tstrap: 0-0

Best Rating:

Raise A McGregor

67 74

6-y-o br g Perpendicular-Gregory's Lady (Meldrum)
Mrs S J Smith Keith Nicholson

Placings:3*0*0-04 (4555)
2001/02: 16^{0}GS, 19^{4}GF

	Starts	1st	2nd	3rd	Win & Pl
NH Flat	1	0	0	0	0
Hurdles	1	0	0	0	0
Career Total	**5**	**0**	**0**	**1**	**213**

Going: Sf: 0-0 GS: 0-1 Gd: 0-0 GF: - Fm: 0-1
Distance: 2m/2m3: 0-1 2m4-2m7: 0-1 3m+: 0-0
Track: LH: 0-1 RH: 0-1 Tight: 0-1 Gall: 0-1
Aids: Bl: 0-0 Vi: 0-0 Tstrap: 0-0
Best Rating: 95 7/00 Worc 2m gd-fm NHF

Raise A Prince (FR)

9-y-o b g Machiavellian (USA)-Enfant D'Amour (USA) (Lyphard (USA))
S P C Woods Mrs L Woods

Placings:32PPU24-U (3319)
2001/02: 16^{U}GS

	Starts	1st	2nd	3rd	Win & Pl
Hurdles	1	0	0	0	
Career Total	**8**	**0**	**2**	**1**	**3321**

Going: Sf: 0-0 GS: 0-1 Gd: 0-0 GF: - Fm: 0-0
Distance: 2m/2m3: 0-1 2m4-2m7: 0-0 3m+: 0-0
Track: LH: 0-0 RH: 0-1 Tight: 0-0 Gall: 0-1
Aids: Bl: 0-0 Vi: 0-0 Tstrap: 0-1
Best Rating: 124 11/00 Asct 2m110y soft Hdl

Raise The Profile

6-y-o b m Sir Harry Lewis (USA)-Olnistar (FR) (Balsamo (FR))
Miss K M George Exterior Profiles Ltd

Placings:P (1912)
2001/02: 22^{P}S

	Starts	1st	2nd	3rd	Win & Pl
Hurdles	1	0	0	0	
Career Total	**1**	**0**	**0**	**0**	

Going: Sf: 0-1 GS: 0-0 Gd: 0-0 GF: - Fm: 0-0
Distance: 2m/2m3: 0-0 2m4-2m7: 0-1 3m+: 0-0
Track: LH: 0-1 RH: 0-0 Tight: 0-1 Gall: 0-0
Aids: Bl: 0-0 Vi: 0-0 Tstrap: 0-0
Best Rating:

Raka King

(78h) (36h)91

9-y-o b g Rakaposhi King-Spartan Native (Native Bazaar)
J A T De Giles J A T De Giles

Placings:*6*664/2FFF-6 (0087)
2001/02: 26^{6}G

	Starts	1st	2nd	3rd	Win & Pl
Hurdles	1	0	0	0	0
Career Total	**9**	**0**	**1**	**0**	**672**

Going: Sf: 0-0 GS: 0-0 Gd: 0-1 GF: - Fm: 0-0
Distance: 2m/2m3: 0-0 2m4-2m7: 0-0 3m+: 0-1
Track: LH: 0-0 RH: 0-1 Tight: 0-0 Gall: 0-0
Aids: Bl: 0-0 Vi: 0-0 Tstrap: 0-0
Best Rating: 95 12/99 Towc 2m good NHF

Rakaposhi Raid

82(102h) (76h)55

6-y-o b m Rakaposhi King-Minty Muncher (Idiots Delight)
N B Mason N B Mason

Placings:0005235045 (4871)
2001/02: 17^{0}G, 19^{0}S, 16^{0}GS, 20^{5}S, 20^{2}S, 19^{3}S, 24^{5}S, 17^{0}S, 24^{4}G, 25^{5}GF

	Starts	1st	2nd	3rd	Win & Pl
Hurdles	10	0	1	1	824
Career Total	**10**	**0**	**1**	**1**	**824**

Going: Sf: 0-6 GS: 0-1 Gd: 0-2 GF: - Fm: 0-1
Distance: 2m/2m3: 0-5 2m4-2m7: 0-2 3m+: 0-3
Track: LH: 0-7 RH: 0-3 Tight: 0-4 Gall: 0-2
Aids: Bl: 0-1 Vi: 0-0 Tstrap: 0-0
Best Rating: 76 2/02 Newc 3m soft Hdl

Plating-class hurdler, stays two miles-four, has been held over three miles to date. Suited by soft ground.

Rake Hey

100(34c) 93

8-y-o gr g Petong-Dancing Daughter (Dance In Time (CAN))
D G Bridgwater D G Bridgwater

Placings:652451112/500660/33F4P-2P45 (2638)
2001/02: 16^{2}GS, 16^{P}G, 17^{4}G, 16^{5}GS

	Starts	1st	2nd	3rd	Win & Pl
Hurdles	4	0	1	0	578
Career Total	**24**	**3**	**3**	**2**	**9407**

107	12/98	Hrfd	2m1f	E(0-105)HHdl	GD	£2318
108	11/98	Kemp	2m	E(0-100)HHdl	G-S	£2326
100	9/98	Hrfd	2m1f	G Hdl	G-F	£1595

Total win prize-money £6240

Going: Sf: 0-0 GS: 0-2 Gd: 0-2 GF: - Fm: 0-0
Distance: 2m/2m3: 0-4 2m4-2m7: 0-0 3m+: 0-0
Track: LH: 0-1 RH: 0-3 Tight: 0-1 Gall: 0-1
Aids: Bl: 0-0 Vi: 0-0 Tstrap: 0-1
Best Rating: 108 11/98 Kemp 2m gd-sft Hdl

Rakeeb (USA)

86(91h) 72

7-y-o ch g Irish River (FR)-Ice House (Northfields (USA))
M W Easterby Major M Watson

Placings:055/4504-0 (2632)
2001/02: 16^{0}S

	Starts	1st	2nd	3rd	Win & Pl
Chases	1	0	0	0	
Career Total	**8**	**0**	**0**	**0**	**0**

Going: Sf: 0-1 GS: 0-0 Gd: 0-0 GF: - Fm: 0-0
Distance: 2m/2m3: 0-1 2m4-2m7: 0-0 3m+: 0-0
Track: LH: 0-1 RH: 0-0 Tight: 0-0 Gall: 0-0
Aids: Bl: 0-0 Vi: 0-0 Tstrap: 0-0
Best Rating: 98 5/00 Hntg 2m110y good Hdl

Rakeira

10-y-o b m Rakaposhi King-Keira (Keren)
F P Murtagh R Paisley

Placings:P (0220)
2001/02: 16^{P}GF

	Starts	1st	2nd	3rd	Win & Pl
Hurdles	1	0	0	0	
Career Total	**1**	**0**	**0**	**0**	

Going: Sf: 0-0 GS: 0-0 Gd: 0-0 GF: - Fm: 0-1
Distance: 2m/2m3: 0-1 2m4-2m7: 0-0 3m+: 0-0
Track: LH: 0-1 RH: 0-0 Tight: 0-0 Gall: 0-0
Aids: Bl: 0-0 Vi: 0-0 Tstrap: 0-0
Best Rating:

Raleagh Native (IRE)

101(81h) (46h)126

9-y-o ch g Be My Native (USA)-Lagan Valley Rose (Avocat)
Miss A M Newton-Smith John Grist

Placings:1P/1F6/04/06F3P (4117)
2001/02: 19^{0}G, 25^{6}G, 21^{F}S, 21^{3}G, 21^{P}G

	Starts	1st	2nd	3rd	Win & Pl
Hurdles	1	0	0	0	0
Chases	4	0	0	1	774
Career Total	**12**	**2**	**0**	**1**	**7888**

126	10/98	Worc	2m2f	E Hdl	SFT	£2477
123	11/97	MRas	2m4f	D Ch	GD	£3834

Total win prize-money £6312

Going: Sf: 0-1 GS: 0-0 Gd: 0-4 GF: - Fm: 0-0
Distance: 2m/2m3: 0-1 2m4-2m7: 0-3 3m+: 0-1
Track: LH: 0-2 RH: 0-3 Tight: 0-1 Gall: 0-1
Aids: Bl: 0-0 Vi: 0-0 Tstrap: 0-0
Best Rating: 130 2/00 Winc 2m5f gd-sft Ch

Lightly-raced chaser, let down more than once by his jumping.

Ramallah

72 53

13-y-o b g Ra Nova-Anglophil (Philemon)
J Gallagher Miss Marie Steele

Placings:*2*/*3*1234/1606440/53031/2132/351211P/1PPF13/FP/P3PP-P06 (3287)
2001/02: 22^{P}HY, 22^{0}G, 22^{6}S

	Starts	1st	2nd	3rd	Win & Pl
Hurdles	2	0	0	0	0
Chases	1	0	0	0	0
Career Total	**44**	**9**	**5**	**8**	**39487**

136	2/99	Towc	3m1f	C(0-130)HCh	SFT	£6937
132	5/98	Extr	2m7f110y	D(0-120)HCh	GD	£3598
130	3/98	Towc	3m1f	D(0-125)HCh	G-S	£3783
120	3/98	Towc	2m6f	E Ch	SFT	£3236
125	2/98	Towc	2m6f	E Ch	GD	£3236
92	5/96	Hrfd	2m3f110y	D(0-120)HHdl	GD	£2905
94	5/96	Extr	2m3f110y	E(0-110)HHdl	G-S	£2428
92	10/94	Plum	2m4f	(0-105)HHdl	HVY	£3003
94	11/93	Hrfd	2m1f	Hdl	GD	£2029

Total win prize-money £31158

Going: Sf: 0-2 GS: 0-0 Gd: 0-1 GF: - Fm: 0-0
Distance: 2m/2m3: 0-0 2m4-2m7: 0-3 3m+: 0-0
Track: LH: 0-0 RH: 0-2 Tight: 0-1 Gall: 0-0
Aids: Bl: 0-0 Vi: 0-0 Tstrap: 0-0
Best Rating: 136 2/99 Towc 3m1f soft Ch

Ramanele (IRE)

7-y-o ch m Case Law-Casting Vote (USA) (Monteverdi)
J Howard Johnson J Howard Johnson

Placings: *00*/21F35/5020-PP0P **(1588)**
2001/02: 16^{P}GF, 20^{P}F, 16^{0}GS, 17^{P}GS

	Starts	1st	2nd	3rd	Win & Pl
Hurdles	4	0	0	0	
Career Total	**15**	**1**	**2**	**1**	**5729**

90	6/99	Cork	2m1f	Hdl	G-F	£3683

Total win prize-money £3683

Going: Sf: 0-0 GS: 0-2 Gd: 0-0 GF: - Fm: 0-2
Distance: 2m/2m3: 0-3 2m4-2m7: 0-1 3m+: 0-0
Track: LH: 0-4 RH: 0-0 Tight: 0-1 Gall: 0-0
Aids: Bl: 0-0 Vi: 0-0 Tstrap: 0-0
Best Rating: 93 7/00 Wxfd 2m4f gd-fm Hdl

Ramblees Holly

97f 83f
4-y-o ch g Alfie Dickins-Lucky Holly (General David)
R S Wood R S Wood

Placings: *30* **(4873)**
2001/02: 16^{3}F, 16^{0}GF

	Starts	1st	2nd	3rd	Win & Pl
NH Flat	2	0	0	1	256
Career Total	**2**	**0**	**0**	**1**	**256**

Going: Sf: 0-0 GS: 0-0 Gd: 0-0 GF: - Fm: 0-2
Distance: 2m/2m3: 0-2 2m4-2m7: 0-0 3m+: 0-0
Track: LH: 0-1 RH: 0-0 Tight: 0-0 Gall: 0-0
Aids: Bl: 0-0 Vi: 0-0 Tstrap: 0-0
Best Rating: 83 4/02 Newc 2m firm NHF

Ramblin' Man (IRE)

77 47
4-y-o b c Blues Traveller (IRE)-Saborinie (Prince Sabo)
P D Evans (M Blanshard 1/12) P Tarran

Placings: 60 **(1956)**
2001/02: 16^{6}GF, 16^{0}G

	Starts	1st	2nd	3rd	Win & Pl
Hurdles	2	0	0	0	0
Career Total	**2**	**0**	**0**	**0**	**0**

Going: Sf: 0-0 GS: 0-0 Gd: 0-1 GF: - Fm: 0-1
Distance: 2m/2m3: 0-2 2m4-2m7: 0-0 3m+: 0-0
Track: LH: 0-1 RH: 0-1 Tight: 0-0 Gall: 0-0
Aids: Bl: 0-0 Vi: 0-0 Tstrap: 0-0
Best Rating: 47 10/01 Ludl 2m gd-fm Hdl

Rambling Sam (IRE)

105 93
10-y-o b g Detroit Sam (FR)-Rambling Moss (Le Moss)
M J M Evans (G B Balding 7/10) M J M Evans

Placings: 405P003/02FPRF454/P462F55-25622024P **(3703)**
2001/02: 21^{2}GF, 24^{5}GF, 25^{6}F, 20^{2}GF, 20^{2}GF, 22^{0}S, 16^{2}S, 16^{4}G, 19^{P}HY

	Starts	1st	2nd	3rd	Win & Pl
Chases	9	0	4	0	4555
Career Total	**32**	**0**	**6**	**1**	**8374**

Going: Sf: 0-3 GS: 0-0 Gd: 0-1 GF: - Fm: 0-5
Distance: 2m/2m3: 0-3 2m4-2m7: 0-4 3m+: 0-2
Track: LH: 0-1 RH: 0-6 Tight: 0-3 Gall: 0-1
Aids: Bl: 0-0 Vi: 0-6 Tstrap: 0-9
Best Rating: 93 12/01 Hrfd 2m good Ch

A winner of a point-to-point, he showed moderate form over hurdles, but has done better over fences, although he often finds a few too good. Acts on soft ground.

Rambo Flyer

101 112
8-y-o b g Rambo Dancer (CAN)-Shiny Kay (Star Appeal)
Are Hyldmo Pegasus Racing

Placings: 111/111/1111F1P-11110 **(1920)**
2001/02: 17^{1}S, 16^{1}VS, 17^{1}S, 19^{1}VS, 16^{0}G

	Starts	1st	2nd	3rd	Win & Pl
Hurdles	5	4	0	0	18151
Career Total	**18**	**15**	**0**	**0**	**68180**

9/01	Ovrl	2m3f	Hdl	VS	£7629
9/01	Taby	2m1f	Hdl	SFT	£5365
8/01	Ovrl	2m	Hdl	VS	£5157
5/01	Ovrl	2m1f	Hdl	SFT	£0
10/00	Taby	2m3f	Hdl	GD	£2924
9/00	Taby	2m1f	Hdl	GD	£5482
8/00	Ovrl	2m	Hdl	SFT	£5012
7/00	Taby	2m1f	Hdl	HVY	£2924
5/00	Ovrl	2m	Hdl	SFT	£3662
9/99	Ovrl	2m3f	Hdl	HVY	£8502
9/99	Taby	2m1f	Hdl	GD	£5560
8/99	Taby	2m1f	Hdl	GD	£2224
9/98	Ovrl	2m1f165y	Hdl	HVY	£7381
9/98	Ovrl	2m	Hdl	HVY	£4294
7/98	Ovrl	2m	Hdl	VS	£2064

Total win prize-money £68180

Going: Sf: 2-2 GS: 0-0 Gd: 0-1 GF: - Fm: 0-0
Distance: **2m/2m3: 4-5** 2m4-2m7: 0-0 3m+: 0-0
Track: LH: 0-0 RH: 0-1 Tight: 0-0 Gall: 0-0
Aids: Bl: 0-0 Vi: 0-0 Tstrap: 0-1
Best Rating: 112 11/01 Asct 2m110y good Hdl

The best hurdler in Scandinavia, he is regularly partnered by Carl Llewellyn. Has never raced right-handed.

Rambo Nine

61 41
5-y-o b g Rambo Dancer (CAN)-Asmarina (Ascendant)
S R Bowring Mr J E Reed & Mr P M Sedgwick

Placings: 0 **(4092)**
2001/02: 16^{0}GS

	Starts	1st	2nd	3rd	Win & Pl
Hurdles	1	0	0	0	
Career Total	**1**	**0**	**0**	**0**	

Going: Sf: 0-0 GS: 0-1 Gd: 0-0 GF: - Fm: 0-0
Distance: 2m/2m3: 0-1 2m4-2m7: 0-0 3m+: 0-0
Track: LH: 0-1 RH: 0-0 Tight: 0-1 Gall: 0-0
Aids: Bl: 0-0 Vi: 0-0 Tstrap: 0-0
Best Rating: 44 3/02 Catt 2m gd-sft Hdl

Random Harvest (IRE)

111 148
13-y-o br g Strong Gale-Bavello (Le Bavard (FR))
Mrs M Reveley C C Buckley

Placings: 5/426/24120PU/B5324/U14121130/1/PP124 5PP-F321600F **(4582)**
2001/02: 25^{F}G, 25^{3}G, 25^{2}G, 25^{1}S, 25^{6}GS, 24^{0}G, 26^{0}GS, 25^{F}G

	Starts	1st	2nd	3rd	Win & Pl
Chases	8	1	1	1	10088
Career Total	**42**	**8**	**7**	**3**	**74212**

148	12/01	Weth	3m1f	C(0-130)HCh	SFT	£7560
146	11/00	Weth	3m1f	D(0-125)HCh	SFT	£3828
129	12/99	Weth	2m7f	D Hdl	G-S	£3207
156	12/98	Weth	3m1f	B HCh	SFT	£14732
156	12/98	Weth	3m1f	B(0-145)HCh	GD	£7100
143	10/98	MRas	3m1f	C(0-130)HCh	G-S	£6905
124	5/98	Weth	3m1f	C(0-135)HCh	G-F	£4719
116	1/97	Carl	2m4f110y	D(0-120)HCh	GD	£3566

Total win prize-money £51620

Going: Sf: 1-1 GS: 0-2 Gd: 0-5 GF: - Fm: 0-0
Distance: 2m/2m3: 0-0 2m4-2m7: 0-0 **3m+: 1-8**
Track: **LH: 1-8** RH: 0-0 Tight: 0-1 Gall: 0-2
Aids: Bl: 0-0 Vi: 0-0 Tstrap: 0-0
Best Rating: 159 1/99 Hayd 3m soft Ch

Formerly smart, he has been quite lightly raced in recent seasons and is not the force of old, although he has a good record at Wetherby. Best at around three miles on soft ground.

Random Native (IRE)

78f 55f
4-y-o br g Be My Native (USA)-Random Wind (Random Shot)
J G Fitzgerald Jim Ennis

Placings: 0 **(4410)**
2001/02: 17^{0}S

	Starts	1st	2nd	3rd	Win & Pl
NH Flat	1	0	0	0	
Career Total	**1**	**0**	**0**	**0**	

Going: Sf: 0-1 GS: 0-0 Gd: 0-0 GF: - Fm: 0-0
Distance: 2m/2m3: 0-1 2m4-2m7: 0-0 3m+: 0-0
Track: LH: 0-1 RH: 0-0 Tight: 0-1 Gall: 0-0
Aids: Bl: 0-0 Vi: 0-0 Tstrap: 0-0
Best Rating: 55 3/02 Bang 2m1f soft NHF

Randrich

5-y-o b m Alflora (IRE)-Randama (Akarad (FR))
P M Rich P M Rich

Placings: P **(1847)**
2001/02: 16^{P}G

	Starts	1st	2nd	3rd	Win & Pl
Hurdles	1	0	0	0	
Career Total	**1**	**0**	**0**	**0**	

Going: Sf: 0-0 GS: 0-0 Gd: 0-1 GF: - Fm: 0-0
Distance: 2m/2m3: 0-1 2m4-2m7: 0-0 3m+: 0-0
Track: LH: 0-0 RH: 0-1 Tight: 0-0 Gall: 0-0
Aids: Bl: 0-0 Vi: 0-0 Tstrap: 0-0
Best Rating:

Raneen Nashwan

99 94
6-y-o b g Nashwan (USA)-Raneen Alwatar (Sadler's Wells (USA))
R J Baker (M R Channon 1/12) M Channon

Placings: F0020 **(4731)**
2001/02: 22^{F}GF, 16^{0}S, 16^{0}G, 17^{2}GS, 17^{0}F

	Starts	1st	2nd	3rd	Win & Pl
Hurdles	5	0	1	0	800

	Starts	1st	2nd	3rd	Win & Pl
Career Total	**5**	**0**	**1**	**0**	**800**

Going: Sf: 0-1 GS: 0-1 Gd: 0-1 GF: - Fm: 0-2
Distance: 2m/2m3: 0-4 2m4-2m7: 0-1 3m+: 0-0
Track: LH: 0-1 RH: 0-4 Tight: 0-1 Gall: 0-1
Aids: Bl: 0-0 Vi: 0-0 Tstrap: 0-0
Best Rating: 94 4/02 Tntn 2m1f gd-sft Hdl

Moderate hurdler, suited by cut in the ground. Has a tendency to hinder himself by racing too keenly.

Ranfurly Castle

7-y-o b g Milieu-Milton Lass (Scallywag)
F P Murtagh William Armour

Placings:0P **(2635)**
2001/02: 17^{0}S, 24^{P}S

	Starts	1st	2nd	3rd	Win & Pl
NH Flat	1	0	0	0	0
Hurdles	1	0	0	0	0
Career Total	**2**	**0**	**0**	**0**	

Going: Sf: 0-2 GS: 0-0 Gd: 0-0 GF: - Fm: 0-0
Distance: 2m/2m3: 0-1 2m4-2m7: 0-0 3m+: 0-1
Track: LH: 0-1 RH: 0-1 Tight: 0-0 Gall: 0-0
Aids: Bl: 0-0 Vi: 0-0 Tstrap: 0-0
Best Rating: 21 11/01 Carl 2m1f soft NHF

Range Trader (NZ)

74 **44**

8-y-o gr g Truly Vain (AUS)-Respectful (NZ) (Standaan (FR))
P Beaumont (E J Alston 10/8) Trevor Hemmings

Placings:0-50P **(4774)**
2001/02: 16^{5}F, 17^{0}GS, 17^{P}G

	Starts	1st	2nd	3rd	Win & Pl
Hurdles	3	0	0	0	0
Career Total	**4**	**0**	**0**	**0**	**0**

Going: Sf: 0-0 GS: 0-1 Gd: 0-1 GF: - Fm: 0-1
Distance: 2m/2m3: 0-3 2m4-2m7: 0-0 3m+: 0-0
Track: LH: 0-1 RH: 0-2 Tight: 0-3 Gall: 0-0
Aids: Bl: 0-0 Vi: 0-0 Tstrap: 0-0
Best Rating: 60 2/01 Hayd 2m heavy Hdl

He won three times from 12 outings on the Flat in New Zealand and looks to need a sound surface over hurdles.

Rapid Liner

99 **81**

9-y-o b g Skyliner-Stellaris (Star Appeal)
J Gallagher Mrs V W Jones

Placings:00P6035/5P5/00006/P00P0-00PP **(3405)**
2001/02: 17^{0}GS, 18^{0}GF, 20^{P}G, 23^{P}G

	Starts	1st	2nd	3rd	Win & Pl
Chases	4	0	0	0	
Career Total	**24**	**0**	**0**	**1**	**297**

Going: Sf: 0-0 GS: 0-1 Gd: 0-2 GF: - Fm: 0-1
Distance: 2m/2m3: 0-2 2m4-2m7: 0-1 3m+: 0-1
Track: LH: 0-1 RH: 0-2 Tight: 0-3 Gall: 0-0
Aids: Bl: 0-0 Vi: 0-0 Tstrap: 0-1
Best Rating: 81 4/01 Font 2m2f good Ch

A modest individual. Mixes chasing with runs on the All-Weather.

Rapier

101 **98**

8-y-o b g Sharpo-Sahara Breeze (Ela-Mana-Mou)
A Streeter Green Card Golfers

Placings:10/356-2 **(4283)**
2001/02: 17^{2}GS

	Starts	1st	2nd	3rd	Win & Pl
Hurdles	1	0	1	0	492
Career Total	**6**	**1**	**1**	**1**	**3163**
106 12/98 Ayr 2m E Hdl				G-S	£2407

Total win prize-money £2408

Going: Sf: 0-0 GS: 0-1 Gd: 0-0 GF: - Fm: 0-0
Distance: 2m/2m3: 0-1 2m4-2m7: 0-0 3m+: 0-0
Track: LH: 0-0 RH: 0-1 Tight: 0-1 Gall: 0-0
Aids: Bl: 0-0 Vi: 0-0 Tstrap: 0-0
Best Rating: 106 12/98 Ayr 2m gd-sft Hdl

Selling hurdler these days.

Raqib

88 **72**

11-y-o b g Slip Anchor-Reine Maid (USA) (Mr Prospector (USA))
P C Ritchens P C Ritchens

Placings:13/2006351/20/44/**04131U1352/P5P4/0U-5** **(0043)**
2001/02: 19^{5}GS

	Starts	1st	2nd	3rd	Win & Pl
Chases	1	0	0	0	0
Career Total	**30**	**5**	**3**	**4**	**22005**

110	2/99	Ling	3m	D(0-120)HCh	SFT	£3538
117	12/98	Hrfd	3m1f110y	F(0-100)HCh	GD	£2801
108	11/98	Uttx	2m4f	E(0-105)HCh	SFT	£3282
107	4/96	Font	2m6f	E(0-110)HHdl	G-F	£2658
88	3/95	Newb	2m110y	D Hdl	GD	£3135

Total win prize-money £15416

Going: Sf: 0-0 GS: 0-1 Gd: 0-0 GF: - Fm: 0-0
Distance: 2m/2m3: 0-0 2m4-2m7: 0-1 3m+: 0-0
Track: LH: 0-0 RH: 0-1 Tight: 0-0 Gall: 0-0
Aids: Bl: 0-0 Vi: 0-0 Tstrap: 0-0
Best Rating: 117 12/98 Hrfd 3m1f110y good Ch

Rarchnamara (IRE)

108 **109**

7-y-o b g Commanche Run-Knollwood Court (Le Jean)
Ferdy Murphy John Duddy

Placings:400-42122322 **(2630)**
2001/02: 24^{4}S, 20^{2}GS, 20^{1}GS, 20^{2}G, 27^{2}GS, 27^{3}G, 27^{2}S, 24^{2}S

	Starts	1st	2nd	3rd	Win & Pl
Hurdles	8	1	5	1	6669
Career Total	**11**	**1**	**5**	**1**	**6669**
103 6/01 Hexm 2m4f110y E(0-105)HHdl				G-S	£2626

Total win prize-money £2626

Going: Sf: 0-3 GS: 1-3 Gd: 0-2 GF: - Fm: 0-0
Distance: 2m/2m3: 0-0 **2m4-2m7: 1-3** 3m+: 0-5
Track: **LH: 1-8** RH: 0-0 Tight: 0-4 Gall: 0-0
Aids: Bl: 0-3 Vi: 0-1 Tstrap: 0-0
Best Rating: 109 12/01 Hexm 3m soft Hdl

He has been stepped up in trip since his Hexham win over an extended two miles and a half in June 2001 and not disgraced subsequently. He has worn blinkers, and is suited by cut in the ground.

Rare Genius (USA)

86 **92**

6-y-o ch g Beau Genius (CAN)-Aunt Nola (USA) (Olden Times)
Ian Williams The Heyfleet Partnership

Placings:2 **(0844)**
2001/02: 19^{2}GF

	Starts	1st	2nd	3rd	Win & Pl
Hurdles	1	0	1	0	690
Career Total	**1**	**0**	**1**	**0**	**690**

Going: Sf: 0-0 GS: 0-0 Gd: 0-0 GF: - Fm: 0-1
Distance: 2m/2m3: 0-1 2m4-2m7: 0-0 3m+: 0-0
Track: LH: 0-1 RH: 0-0 Tight: 0-1 Gall: 0-0
Aids: Bl: 0-0 Vi: 0-0 Tstrap: 0-0
Best Rating: 92 7/01 Strf 2m3f gd-fm Hdl

Rare Talent

95 **86**

8-y-o b g Mtoto-Bold As Love (Lomond (USA))
S Gollings John King, Bill Hobson, Graham King

Placings:4/6 **(1305)**
2001/02: 19^{6}GF

	Starts	1st	2nd	3rd	Win & Pl
Hurdles	1	0	0	0	0
Career Total	**2**	**0**	**0**	**0**	**0**

Going: Sf: 0-0 GS: 0-0 Gd: 0-0 GF: - Fm: 0-1
Distance: 2m/2m3: 0-0 2m4-2m7: 0-1 3m+: 0-0
Track: LH: 0-0 RH: 0-1 Tight: 0-1 Gall: 0-0
Aids: Bl: 0-0 Vi: 0-0 Tstrap: 0-0
Best Rating: 86 9/01 MRas 2m3f110y gd-fm Hdl

Rascella

93f **87f**

7-y-o gr m Scallywag-Blue Gift (Hasty Word)
Mrs S J Smith J Townson

Placings:20 **(2772)**
2001/02: 17^{2}G, 16^{0}G

	Starts	1st	2nd	3rd	Win & Pl
NH Flat	2	0	1	0	440
Career Total	**2**	**0**	**1**	**0**	**440**

Going: Sf: 0-0 GS: 0-0 Gd: 0-2 GF: - Fm: 0-0
Distance: 2m/2m3: 0-2 2m4-2m7: 0-0 3m+: 0-0
Track: LH: 0-1 RH: 0-1 Tight: 0-2 Gall: 0-0
Aids: Bl: 0-0 Vi: 0-0 Tstrap: 0-0
Best Rating: 87 10/01 MRas 2m1f110y good NHF

A sister to fair hurdler Rascally, she ran well on her debut in a Market Rasen bumper.

Rash Decision (IRE)

106 **132**

7-y-o b g Rashar (USA)-Lady Nethertown (Windjammer (USA))
Anthony Mullins William D Day

Placings:060500/1410160-**P42211F640** **(2628a)**
2001/02: 16^{P}YS, 20^{4}GY, 17^{2}G, 16^{2}G, 16^{1}GF, 17^{1}GF, 18^{F}GF, 16^{6}G, 16^{4}G, 16^{0}S

	Starts	1st	2nd	3rd	Win & Pl
Chases	10	2	2	0	18416
Career Total	**23**	**5**	**2**	**0**	**27424**

132	9/01	Gway	2m1f	Ch	G-F	£7862
124	8/01	Tral	2m	Ch	G-F	£5564
96	9/00	Clon	2m	(0-102)HHdl	GD	£2760

90	6/00	Clon	2m	(0-95)HHdl	GD	£3312
86	5/00	Clon	2m	NHF	GD	£2760

Total win prize-money £22260

Going: Sf: 0-1 GS: 0-0 Gd: 0-4 GF: - Fm: 2-3
Distance: **2m/2m3: 2-9** 2m4-2m7: 0-1 3m+: 0-0
Track: LH: 0-1 **RH: 1-2** Tight: 0-0 Gall: 0-1
Aids: Bl: 0-0 Vi: 0-0 Tstrap: 0-0
Best Rating: 132 11/01 Chel 2m good Ch

An Irish-trained novice chaser, suited by two miles and fast ground.

Rash Reflection (IRE)

10-y-o b g Rashar (USA)-Mature Reflection (Broadsword (USA))
I McMath (T A K Cuthbert 10/2) Mrs A J McMath

Placings: *30/200020*/31P0UP4/1-050 **(4692)**
2001/02: 16^{0}G, 21^{5}S, 25^{0}GF

	Starts	1st	2nd	3rd	Win & Pl
Chases	3	0	0	0	0
Career Total	**19**	**2**	**2**	**2**	**6730**

101	4/01	Plum	2m	F(0-90)Hdl	HVY	£2744
101	6/98	Kbgn	2m3f	Hdl	GD	£1935

Total win prize-money £4680

Going: Sf: 0-1 GS: 0-0 Gd: 0-1 GF: - Fm: 0-1
Distance: 2m/2m3: 0-1 2m4-2m7: 0-1 3m+: 0-1
Track: LH: 0-2 RH: 0-1 Tight: 0-3 Gall: 0-0
Aids: Bl: 0-0 Vi: 0-0 Tstrap: 0-0
Best Rating: 111 3/99 Font 2m2f gd-fm Ch

Ex-Irish, former hurdle winner. Acts in the mud.

Rash Remark (IRE)

9-y-o ch g Rashar (USA)-Granig Rarity (Rarity)
M C Pipe D A Johnson

Placings: *02221101*/1FFF/PP **(4301)**
2001/02: 25^{P}S, 22^{P}HY

	Starts	1st	2nd	3rd	Win & Pl
Hurdles	2	0	0	0	
Career Total	**14**	**4**	**3**	**0**	**14054**

128	10/99	Chep	3m	D Ch	G-F	£3915
141	4/99	Chep	2m4f110y	E Hdl	SFT	£2206
150	3/99	Newb	2m5f	D Hdl	SFT	£3233
149	2/99	Hayd	2m6f	D Hdl	SFT	£3022

Total win prize-money £12377

Going: Sf: 0-2 GS: 0-0 Gd: 0-0 GF: - Fm: 0-0
Distance: 2m/2m3: 0-0 2m4-2m7: 0-1 3m+: 0-1
Track: LH: 0-1 RH: 0-0 Tight: 0-0 Gall: 0-0
Aids: Bl: 0-0 Vi: 0-0 Tstrap: 0-0
Best Rating: 150 3/99 Newb 2m5f soft Hdl

Rasta Man

14-y-o b g Ore-Bellino (Andrea Mantegna)
Mrs K Heard J Heard

Placings: *55/65234/3/3/0*/054 **(0563)**
2001/02: 21^{0}GF, 19^{5}F, 26^{4}GF

	Starts	1st	2nd	3rd	Win & Pl
Chases	3	0	0	0	0
Career Total	**13**	**0**	**1**	**3**	**1428**

Going: Sf: 0-0 GS: 0-0 Gd: 0-0 GF: - Fm: 0-3
Distance: 2m/2m3: 0-0 2m4-2m7: 0-2 3m+: 0-1
Track: LH: 0-1 RH: 0-2 Tight: 0-1 Gall: 0-0
Aids: Bl: 0-0 Vi: 0-0 Tstrap: 0-3
Best Rating: 94 3/99 NAbb 2m5f110y soft Ch

Rathbawn Prince (IRE)

110 (110h) 167

10-y-o ch g All Haste (USA)-Ellis Town (Camden Town)
D T Hughes T J Culhane

Placings: *141/55100/133200/0P2P3214U/21115U55P-2056F0* **(4913)**
2001/02: 29^{2}G, 22^{0}GY, 16^{5}HY, 20^{6}GS, 29^{F}GY, 29^{0}G

	Starts	1st	2nd	3rd	Win & Pl
Chases	6	0	1	0	20323
Career Total	**38**	**8**	**5**	**3**	**76995**

155	11/00	DRoy	2m2f	Ch	G-Y	£10400
132	10/00	Thur	2m6f	Ch	Y-S	£4416
121	10/00	Fair	2m2f	Hdl	G-Y	£3864
140	2/00	Fair	2m2f	Ch	HVY	£4692
105	10/98	Fair	2m	Hdl	YLD	£2989
120	3/98	Navn	2m	NHF	Y-S	£2680
117	4/97	Punc	2m	NHF	GD	£6782
105	10/96	Punc	2m	NHF	GD	£3177

Total win prize-money £39001

Going: Sf: 0-1 GS: 0-1 Gd: 0-2 GF: - Fm: 0-0
Distance: 2m/2m3: 0-1 2m4-2m7: 0-2 3m+: 0-3
Track: LH: 0-2 RH: 0-2 Tight: 0-0 Gall: 0-1
Aids: Bl: 0-0 Vi: 0-0 Tstrap: 0-0
Best Rating: 167 5/01 Fair 3m5f good Ch

A very useful staying chaser, runner-up in the 2001 Irish National, he has been lightly raced since. Has won on a sound surface but has run well on heavy.

Rathgibbon (IRE)

11-y-o b g Phardante (FR)-Harp Song (Auction Ring (USA))
R H Buckler Twentyman

Placings: *005222245/114413214350/0600015334/050 66P544431PU460/PU6532651222/5534416*-3 **(0011)**
2001/02: 20^{3}GS

	Starts	1st	2nd	3rd	Win & Pl
Chases	1	0	0	1	518
Career Total	**68**	**8**	**9**	**8**	**40083**

105	1/01	Plum	2m4f	F(0-105)HCh	G-S	£2996
105	3/00	Plum	2m4f	F(0-110)HCh	GD	£2762
110	12/98	Punc	2m	(0-123)HCh	SH	£4782
123	11/97	Naas	2m3f	Ch	SH	£4408
119	11/96	Tipp	2m4f	(0-123)HHdl	SFT	£2824
113	10/96	Tipp	2m4f	(0-130)HHdl	SFT	£2824
89	7/96	Wxfd	2m4f	Hdl	GD	£2841
103	7/96	Tipp	2m	NHF	G-F	£3001

Total win prize-money £26442

Going: Sf: 0-0 GS: 0-1 Gd: 0-0 GF: - Fm: 0-0
Distance: 2m/2m3: 0-0 2m4-2m7: 0-1 3m+: 0-0
Track: LH: 0-1 RH: 0-0 Tight: 0-1 Gall: 0-0
Aids: Bl: 0-0 Vi: 0-0 Tstrap: 0-0
Best Rating: 123 11/97 Naas 2m3f sft-hvy Ch

Ratified

101 (101h) (87h) 99

5-y-o b g Not In Doubt (USA)-Festival Of Magic (USA) (Clever Trick (USA))
M C Chapman Rasen Goes Racing

Placings: 0004024U54305 **(4907)**
2001/02: 19^{0}G, 20^{0}G, 16^{0}G, 16^{4}G, 16^{0}GS, 16^{2}GS, 16^{4}S, 16^{U}S, 16^{5}GS, 16^{4}S, 17^{3}G, 17^{0}G, 20^{5}GF

	Starts	1st	2nd	3rd	Win & Pl
Hurdles	6	0	1	0	672
Chases	7	0	0	1	2575
Career Total	**13**	**0**	**1**	**1**	**3247**

Going: Sf: 0-3 GS: 0-3 Gd: 0-6 GF: - Fm: 0-1
Distance: 2m/2m3: 0-10 2m4-2m7: 0-3 3m+: 0-0
Track: LH: 0-6 RH: 0-6 Tight: 0-8 Gall: 0-4
Aids: Bl: 0-0 Vi: 0-0 Tstrap: 0-0
Best Rating: 99 2/02 Wwck 2m110y soft Ch

Very modest placed form over hurdles and fences.

Rattle

80 57

9-y-o b g Mazilier (USA)-Snake Song (Mansingh (USA))
D A Nolan Mrs J McFadyen-Murray

Placings: 45000/2/0-4 **(0801)**
2001/02: 20^{4}GF

	Starts	1st	2nd	3rd	Win & Pl
Hurdles	1	0	0	0	262
Career Total	**8**	**0**	**1**	**0**	**877**

Going: Sf: 0-0 GS: 0-0 Gd: 0-0 GF: - Fm: 0-1
Distance: 2m/2m3: 0-0 2m4-2m7: 0-1 3m+: 0-0
Track: LH: 0-0 RH: 0-1 Tight: 0-0 Gall: 0-0
Aids: Bl: 0-0 Vi: 0-0 Tstrap: 0-0
Best Rating: 75 6/97 Prth 2m110y gd-fm Hdl

Ratty's Band

84 67

8-y-o ch g Gunner B-Arctic Ander (Leander)
Mrs L B Normile Mrs D A Whitaker

Placings: 0PP-50 **(4486)**
2001/02: 16^{5}S, 17^{0}GS

	Starts	1st	2nd	3rd	Win & Pl
Hurdles	2	0	0	0	0
Career Total	**5**	**0**	**0**	**0**	**0**

Going: Sf: 0-1 GS: 0-1 Gd: 0-0 GF: - Fm: 0-0
Distance: 2m/2m3: 0-2 2m4-2m7: 0-0 3m+: 0-0
Track: LH: 0-1 RH: 0-1 Tight: 0-0 Gall: 0-0
Aids: Bl: 0-0 Vi: 0-0 Tstrap: 0-0
Best Rating: 67 3/02 Ayr 2m soft Hdl

Raven Bay

6-y-o b g Sea Raven (IRE)-Star's Silver Face (Smokey Rockett)
Miss S E Forster A S Nelson

Placings: 0-PF **(1740)**
2001/02: 22^{P}G, 16^{F}G

	Starts	1st	2nd	3rd	Win & Pl
Hurdles	2	0	0	0	
Career Total	**3**	**0**	**0**	**0**	

Going: Sf: 0-0 GS: 0-0 Gd: 0-2 GF: - Fm: 0-0
Distance: 2m/2m3: 0-1 2m4-2m7: 0-1 3m+: 0-0
Track: LH: 0-2 RH: 0-0 Tight: 0-2 Gall: 0-0
Aids: Bl: 0-0 Vi: 0-0 Tstrap: 0-1
Best Rating:

Ravenswood (IRE)

111 139

5-y-o b g Warning-Green Lucia (Green Dancer (USA))

M C Pipe D A Johnson

Placings:236111 **(4834)**

2001/02: 17^{2}G, 16^{3}S, 19^{6}G, 16^{1}GS, 20^{1}G, 22^{1}G

	Starts	1st	2nd	3rd	Win & Pl
Hurdles	6	3	1	1	44394
Career Total	**6**	**3**	**1**	**1**	**44394**

139	4/02	Ayr	2m6f	B(0-150)HHdl	GD	£6988
134	4/02	Aint	2m4f	A HHdl	GD	£23200
124	3/02	Newb	2m110y	C(0-130)HHdl	G-S	£12815

Total win prize-money £43005

Going: Sf: 0-1 GS: 1-1 Gd: 2-4 GF: - Fm: 0-0
Distance: 2m/2m3: 1-4 **2m4-2m7: 2-2** 3m+: 0-0
Track: **LH: 3-4** RH: 0-2 Tight: 1-2 Gall: 1-1
Aids: Bl: 0-0 Vi: 0-0 **Tstrap: 3-6**
Best Rating: **139** 4/02 Ayr 2m6f good Hdl

Decent on the Flat, he disappointed over hurdles until landing a touch on his handicap debut and followed up from a much higher mark at Aintree, before completing the hat-trick at Ayr in April 2002. Effective at two miles but appreciates further, he acts on good to soft ground. Wears a tongue tie.

Raw Silk

101 94

4-y-o b g Rudimentary (USA)-Misty Silks (Scottish Heel)

J J O'Neill (M J Ryan 15/3) The Cartmel Syndicate

Placings:0420020111 **(4785)**

2001/02: 16^{0}GS, 16^{4}GF, 16^{2}HY, 16^{0}GS, 17^{0}GS, 16^{2}HY, 17^{0}S, 16^{1}G, 16^{1}G, 16^{1}F

	Starts	1st	2nd	3rd	Win & Pl
Hurdles	10	3	2	0	8861
Career Total	**10**	**3**	**2**	**0**	**8861**

94	4/02	Newc	2m	F Hdl	FRM	£2079
94	4/02	Fknm	2m	D(0-110)HHdl	GD	£3410
93	3/02	Fknm	2m	G(0-90)HHdl	GD	£1857

Total win prize-money £7347

Going: Sf: 0-3 GS: 0-3 Gd: 2-2 GF: - Fm: 1-2
Distance: **2m/2m3: 3-10** 2m4-2m7: 0-0 3m+: 0-0
Track: LH: 3-5 RH: 0-5 **Tight: 2-6** Gall: 1-2
Aids: **Bl: 3-6** Vi: 0-0 Tstrap: 0-0
Best Rating: **94** 4/02 Newc 2m firm Hdl

Modest hurdler, in good heart in the spring of 2002. Acts on good and firm ground. Best at around two miles.

Ray River

(97h) (66h)

10-y-o b g Waki River (FR)-Mrs Feathers (Pyjama Hunt)

K G Wingrove M M Foulger

Placings:5104401/55643406/31650/04/000 **(4573)**

2001/02: 21^{0}HY, 21^{0}GF, 20^{0}G

	Starts	1st	2nd	3rd	Win & Pl
Hurdles	3	0	0	0	
Career Total	**25**	**3**	**0**	**2**	**6884**

84	2/98	Font	2m6f110y	G(0-95)HHdl	GD	£2170
82	4/96	Uttx	2m4f110y	G(0-95)HHdl	G-F	£2141
77	10/95	Worc	2m	G Hdl	GD	£2038

Total win prize-money £6350

Going: Sf: 0-1 GS: 0-0 Gd: 0-1 GF: - Fm: 0-1
Distance: 2m/2m3: 0-0 2m4-2m7: 0-3 3m+: 0-0
Track: LH: 0-1 RH: 0-1 Tight: 0-0 Gall: 0-1
Aids: Bl: 0-2 Vi: 0-0 Tstrap: 0-0
Best Rating: **84** 2/98 Font 2m6f110y good Hdl

Ray Source (IRE)

111 105

7-y-o b g Lashkari-Salote (USA) (Forli (ARG))

Ian Williams John Poynton

Placings:*42/0*O6252/230-144 **(2581)**

2001/02: 24^{1}G, 25^{4}G, 23^{4}S

	Starts	1st	2nd	3rd	Win & Pl
Hurdles	3	1	0	0	3530
Career Total	**14**	**1**	**4**	**1**	**7687**

97	10/01	Sthl	3m110y	E Hdl	GD	£2982

Total win prize-money £2982

Going: Sf: 0-1 GS: 0-0 Gd: 1-2 GF: - Fm: 0-0
Distance: 2m/2m3: 0-0 2m4-2m7: 0-1 **3m+: 1-2**
Track: **LH: 1-3** RH: 0-0 **Tight: 1-1** Gall: 0-1
Aids: Bl: 0-0 Vi: 0-0 Tstrap: 0-0
Best Rating: **105** 10/01 Chel 3m1f110y good Hdl

Modest hurdler, two and half miles on good to soft are ideal conditions for him.

Raybrook (IRE)

7-y-o ch g Moscow Society (USA)-Vesper Time (The Parson)

Mrs L D Normile John Findlay

Placings:*2-05* **(2729)**

2001/02: 16^{0}GS, 17^{5}GF

	Starts	1st	2nd	3rd	Win & Pl
NH Flat	2	0	0	0	0
Career Total	**3**	**0**	**1**	**0**	**416**

Going: Sf: 0-0 GS: 0-1 Gd: 0-0 GF: - Fm: 0-1
Distance: 2m/2m3: 0-2 2m4-2m7: 0-0 3m+: 0-0
Track: LH: 0-1 RH: 0-0 Tight: 0-0 Gall: 0-0
Aids: Bl: 0-0 Vi: 0-0 Tstrap: 0-2
Best Rating: **96** 7/00 Worc 2m good NHF

Has shown ability in bumpers.

Raygale

92f 97f

5-y-o b g Superpower-Little Missile (Ile De Bourbon (USA))

D Eddy Mrs I Battla

Placings:*6-6420* **(4679)**

2001/02: 16^{6}G, 16^{4}GS, 16^{2}S, 17^{0}G

	Starts	1st	2nd	3rd	Win & Pl
NH Flat	4	0	1	0	448
Career Total	**5**	**0**	**1**	**0**	**448**

Going: Sf: 0-1 GS: 0-1 Gd: 0-2 GF: - Fm: 0-0
Distance: 2m/2m3: 0-4 2m4-2m7: 0-0 3m+: 0-0
Track: LH: 0-1 RH: 0-1 Tight: 0-0 Gall: 0-1
Aids: Bl: 0-0 Vi: 0-0 Tstrap: 0-0
Best Rating: **97** 1/02 Newc 2m soft NHF

Raymond's Lad

100 113

11-y-o b g Dubassoff (USA)-Flippit (Dairialatan)

P F Nicholls A G Fear

Placings:P-1U31 **(1144)**

2001/02: 26^{1}GF, 23^{U}F, 26^{3}G, 24^{1}GF

	Starts	1st	2nd	3rd	Win & Pl
Chases	4	2	0	1	6909
Career Total	**5**	**2**	**0**	**1**	**6909**

113	8/01	Sthl	3m110y	E Ch	G-F	£3188
113	5/01	Font	3m2f110y	E Ch	G-F	£3201

Total win prize-money £6390

Going: Sf: 0-0 GS: 0-0 Gd: 0-1 GF: - Fm: 2-3
Distance: 2m/2m3: 0-0 2m4-2m7: 0-0 **3m+: 2-4**
Track: **LH: 1-2** RH: 0-1 **Tight: 2-3** Gall: 0-0
Aids: Bl: 0-0 Vi: 0-0 Tstrap: 0-0
Best Rating: **113** 8/01 Sthl 3m110y gd-fm Ch

Rayware Boy (IRE)

109 92

6-y-o b g Scenic-Amata (USA) (Nodouble (USA))

D Shaw Rayton Racing

Placings:0256F0/05-1051U3 **(4013)**

2001/02: 17^{1}GS, 16^{0}GS, 16^{5}HY, 16^{1}S, 16^{U}HY, 16^{3}GS

	Starts	1st	2nd	3rd	Win & Pl
Hurdles	6	2	0	1	5466
Career Total	**14**	**2**	**1**	**1**	**6286**

92	1/02	Donc	2m110y	F(0-100)HHdl	SFT	£2754
82	12/01	Bang	2m1f	F(0-100)HHdl	G-S	£2086

Total win prize-money £4841

Going: Sf: 1-3 GS: 1-3 Gd: 0-0 GF: - Fm: 0-0
Distance: **2m/2m3: 2-6** 2m4-2m7: 0-0 3m+: 0-0
Track: **LH: 2-4** RH: 0-2 Tight: 1-1 Gall: 1-3
Aids: Bl: 0-0 Vi: 1-4 Tstrap: 0-0
Best Rating: **92** 3/02 Donc 2m110y gd-sft Hdl

He took advantage of a lenient handicap mark to score over hurdles in December 2001. He had looked held before returning to form at Doncaster in January 2002. Acts on soft ground.

Razer Blade

97(114h) (121h)117

7-y-o b g Teenoso (USA)-Sparkling Cinders (Netherkelly)

N J Henderson The Liars Poker Partnership

Placings:*1/12525-3* **(1989)**

2001/02: 20^{3}G

	Starts	1st	2nd	3rd	Win & Pl
Chases	1	0	0	1	760
Career Total	**7**	**2**	**2**	**1**	**11696**

129	11/00	Kemp	2m	D Hdl	SFT	£3737
135	4/00	Ayr	2m	H NHF	GD	£3071

Total win prize-money £6809

Going: Sf: 0-0 GS: 0-0 Gd: 0-1 GF: - Fm: 0-0
Distance: 2m/2m3: 0-0 2m4-2m7: 0-1 3m+: 0-0
Track: LH: 0-0 RH: 0-1 Tight: 0-0 Gall: 0-0
Aids: Bl: 0-0 Vi: 0-0 Tstrap: 0-0
Best Rating: **140** 2/01 Kemp 2m5f gd-sft Hdl

Winner of his only bumper, he made a winning debut over hurdles at Kempton and ran pretty well in defeat subsequently. Looks to need at least two and a half miles now. A shade disappointing on his chasing bow at Kempton in November.

Razor Ruddock (IRE)

85(64h) 84

8-y-o b g Brush Aside (USA)-Up An Octave (Octavo (USA))

J W Mullins Regal Racing

Placings:36P4/034/534P4U5-3 (0433)
2001/02: 25^{3}GF

	Starts	1st	2nd	3rd	Win & Pl
Chases	1	0	0	1	487
Career Total	**15**	**0**	**0**	**4**	**2911**

Going: Sf: 0-0 GS: 0-0 Gd: 0-0 GF: - Fm: 0-1
Distance: 2m/2m3: 0-0 2m4-2m7: 0-0 3m+: 0-1
Track: LH: 0-0 RH: 0-1 Tight: 0-1 Gall: 0-0
Aids: Bl: 0-0 Vi: 0-0 Tstrap: 0-0
Best Rating: **105** 10/98 Chel 2m110y gd-sft NHF

Razzamatazz

97 85
4-y-o b g Alhijaz-Salvezza (IRE) (Superpower)
R Dickin Mrs T Byrne-Mr J Cooper-Mrs M Cooper

Placings:6 (4597)
2001/02: 19^{6}GF

	Starts	1st	2nd	3rd	Win & Pl
Hurdles	1	0	0	0	0
Career Total	**1**	**0**	**0**	**0**	**0**

Going: Sf: 0-0 GS: 0-0 Gd: 0-0 GF: - Fm: 0-1
Distance: 2m/2m3: 0-1 2m4-2m7: 0-0 3m+: 0-0
Track: LH: 0-1 RH: 0-0 Tight: 0-0 Gall: 0-0
Aids: Bl: 0-0 Vi: 0-0 Tstrap: 0-0
Best Rating: **85** 4/02 Wwck 2m3f gd-fm Hdl

Reach The Clouds (IRE)

108(97h) (95h)128
10-y-o b g Lord Americo-Dusky Stream (Paddy's Stream)
John R Upson Middleham Park Racing Ix

Placings:0P0F63/1302325230/1325152/1323241/4F6 443220-522432F03 (4824)
2001/02: 16^{5}F, 16^{2}GF, 16^{2}G, 17^{4}S, 16^{3}S, 16^{2}S, 17^{F}S, 16^{0}G, 16^{3}G

	Starts	1st	2nd	3rd	Win & Pl
Hurdles	1	0	0	0	0
Chases	8	0	3	2	7506
Career Total	**48**	**5**	**12**	**10**	**47398**

128	4/00	Chel	2m110y	C(0-135)HCh	SFT	£10244
125	10/99	Bang	2m1f110y	F(0-110)HCh	G-S	£4045
115	4/99	Plum	2m2f	F(0-110)HCh	G-S	£2932
113	11/98	Folk	2m	E(0-100)HCh	G-S	£3436
82	10/97	Plum	2m1f	E(0-100)HHdl	GD	£2511

Total win prize-money £23170

Going: Sf: 0-4 GS: 0-0 Gd: 0-3 GF: - Fm: 0-2
Distance: 2m/2m3: 0-9 2m4-2m7: 0-0 3m+: 0-0
Track: LH: 0-8 RH: 0-0 Tight: 0-5 Gall: 0-1
Aids: Bl: 0-0 Vi: 0-0 Tstrap: 0-0
Best Rating: **128** 5/01 Sthl 2m gd-fm Ch

A consistent dual-purpose performer, he has notched up several wins over obstacles, but has tended to find one or two too good for himin recent seasons. He is suited by two miles or a bit further with some give in the ground.

Ready Money Creek (IRE)

74
11-y-o ch g Phardante (FR)-Chestnut Vale (Pollerton)
P F Nicholls The Bristol Based Barkers

Placings:2/14231/0250/4-5 (0215)
2001/02: 21^{5}GF

	Starts	1st	2nd	3rd	Win & Pl
Chases	1	0	0	0	0
Career Total	**12**	**2**	**3**	**1**	**9654**

118	3/97	Newb	3m110y	D Hdl	GD	£3176
102	11/96	Wind	2m	D Hdl	GD	£3078

Total win prize-money £6254

Going: Sf: 0-0 GS: 0-0 Gd: 0-0 GF: - Fm: 0-1
Distance: 2m/2m3: 0-0 2m4-2m7: 0-1 3m+: 0-0
Track: LH: 0-0 RH: 0-1 Tight: 0-0 Gall: 0-0
Aids: Bl: 0-1 Vi: 0-0 Tstrap: 0-0
Best Rating: **119** 4/96 Ayr 2m soft NHF

Real Estate

104(102h) (104h)102
8-y-o b g High Estate-Haitienne (FR) (Green Dancer (USA))
J S King Robert Skillen

Placings:4122130/451560040/04FP0-06F221300 (4643)
2001/02: 16^{0}GF, 16^{6}GF, 16^{F}G, 20^{2}G, 16^{2}S, 20^{1}G, 16^{3}S, 16^{0}S, 20^{0}G

	Starts	1st	2nd	3rd	Win & Pl
Hurdles	1	0	0	0	0
Chases	8	1	2	1	7264
Career Total	**30**	**4**	**4**	**2**	**28289**

102	2/02	Ludl	2m4f	E(0-110)HCh	GD	£4433
139	11/98	Asct	2m110y	B(0-145)HHdl	G-S	£6716
125	2/98	Uttx	2m	D Hdl	SFT	£3777
131	11/97	Asct	2m110y	B Hdl	G-S	£4901

Total win prize-money £19830

Going: Sf: 0-3 GS: 0-0 Gd: 1-4 GF: - Fm: 0-2
Distance: 2m/2m3: 0-6 **2m4-2m7: 1-3** 3m+: 0-0
Track: LH: 0-1 **RH: 1-7 Tight: 1-5** Gall: 0-1
Aids: Bl: 0-0 Vi: 0-0 Tstrap: 0-0
Best Rating: **139** 11/98 Asct 2m110y gd-sft Hdl

Formerly a decent hurdler, has been finding his feet over fences in 2002. Best over two and a half miles.

Real Fire (IRE)

98 73
8-y-o b g Astronef-Golden Arum (Home Guard (USA))
R Johnson Mrs H Gwin

Placings:331202P/4PPP040245P602400/0/0P-04051 (1678)
2001/02: 21^{0}GS, 17^{4}GF, 22^{0}GS, 22^{5}G, 21^{1}G

	Starts	1st	2nd	3rd	Win & Pl
Hurdles	5	1	0	0	1862
Career Total	**32**	**2**	**4**	**2**	**7606**

73	10/01	Sedg	2m5f110y	G(0-95)HHdl	GD	£1862
77	9/97	Prth	2m110y	E Hdl	G-F	£2558

Total win prize-money £4420

Going: Sf: 0-0 GS: 0-2 Gd: 1-2 GF: - Fm: 0-1
Distance: 2m/2m3: 0-1 **2m4-2m7: 1-4** 3m+: 0-0
Track: **LH: 1-4** RH: 0-0 **Tight: 1-4** Gall: 0-0
Aids: Bl: 0-0 Vi: 0-0 Tstrap: 0-0
Best Rating: **82** 10/97 Carl 2m1f gd-fm Hdl

Real Gent

12-y-o br g Mandalus-Gentle Madam (Camden Town)
S A Brookshaw J A Lee

Placings:0P (0427)
2001/02: 24^{0}G, 33^{P}G

	Starts	1st	2nd	3rd	Win & Pl
Chases	2	0	0	0	
Career Total	**2**	**0**	**0**	**0**	

Going: Sf: 0-0 GS: 0-0 Gd: 0-2 GF: - Fm: 0-0
Distance: 2m/2m3: 0-0 2m4-2m7: 0-0 3m+: 0-2
Track: LH: 0-0 RH: 0-0 Tight: 0-0 Gall: 0-0
Aids: Bl: 0-0 Vi: 0-0 Tstrap: 0-0
Best Rating: **10** 5/01 Wwck 3m110y good Ch

Real Progress (IRE)

14-y-o ch g Ashford (USA)-Dulcet Dido (Dike (USA))
D J Wintle D J Renney

Placings:4512220/S246516/2121431341/411344/432 5/43/3P/P-P (0776)
2001/02: 20^{P}GF

	Starts	1st	2nd	3rd	Win & Pl
Chases	1	0	0	0	
Career Total	**40**	**8**	**7**	**6**	**38436**

107	6/95	Strf	3m4f	D(0-125)HCh	GD	£3629
106	5/95	Uttx	3m2f	C(0-130)HCh	G-F	£4429
107	4/95	Uttx	3m2f	D(0-125)HCh	GD	£3647
102	12/94	Ludl	3m	(0-120)HCh	SFT	£3013
107	10/94	Hntg	3m	(0-120)HCh	GD	£2997
107	9/94	Hntg	3m	(0-110)HCh	G-F	£3020
99	4/94	Asct	2m3f110y	Ch	GD	£4104
97	11/92	Wind	2m	Hdl	SFT	£1305

Total win prize-money £26147

Going: Sf: 0-0 GS: 0-0 Gd: 0-0 GF: - Fm: 0-1
Distance: 2m/2m3: 0-0 2m4-2m7: 0-1 3m+: 0-0
Track: LH: 0-1 RH: 0-0 Tight: 0-0 Gall: 0-0
Aids: Bl: 0-0 Vi: 0-0 Tstrap: 0-0
Best Rating: **107** 6/96 Strf 3m4f gd-fm Ch

Real Shady

89f 107f
5-y-o b g Bob's Return (IRE)-Madam Margeaux (IRE) (Ardross)
M W Easterby Lord Daresbury

Placings:1-400 (3375)
2001/02: 16^{4}G, 17^{0}GS, 16^{0}S

	Starts	1st	2nd	3rd	Win & Pl
NH Flat	3	0	0	0	0
Career Total	**4**	**1**	**0**	**0**	**1589**

90	1/01	Newc	2m	H NHF	SFT	£1589

Total win prize-money £1589

Going: Sf: 0-1 GS: 0-1 Gd: 0-1 GF: - Fm: 0-0
Distance: 2m/2m3: 0-3 2m4-2m7: 0-0 3m+: 0-0
Track: LH: 0-2 RH: 0-0 Tight: 0-0 Gall: 0-0
Aids: Bl: 0-0 Vi: 0-0 Tstrap: 0-0
Best Rating: **107** 1/02 Hayd 2m soft NHF

Real Value (IRE)

11-y-o b g Matching Pair-Silent Verb (Proverb)
Mrs D M Grissell (D M Grissell 3/2) Cockerell Cowing Racing

Placings:12F2/P05513-F20P (4826)
2001/02: 23^{F}GS, 26^{2}S, 26^{0}G, 26^{P}G

	Starts	1st	2nd	3rd	Win & Pl
Chases	4	0	1	0	2130
Career Total	**14**	**2**	**3**	**1**	**22483**

141	2/01	Sand	3m110y	B(0-140)HCh	SFT	£9948

131	3/00	Newb	3m	H Ch	SFT	£1557

Total win prize-money £11506

Going: Sf: 0-1 GS: 0-1 Gd: 0-2 GF: - Fm: 0-0
Distance: 2m/2m3: 0-0 2m4-2m7: 0-0 3m+: 0-4
Track: LH: 0-2 RH: 0-1 Tight: 0-1 Gall: 0-2
Aids: Bl: 0-0 Vi: 0-0 Tstrap: 0-0
Best Rating: 146 3/00 Chel 3m2f110y gd-fm Ch

He developed into a top hunter chaser in 1999/2000, but found life tough in handicaps in 2001 and back in hunter chases in 2002. A thorough stayer, he seems to handle any ground but can make mistakes.

Realfoodattheffrwd

(92h) (77h)
8-y-o b g Golden Heights-Jolly Regal (Jolly Good)
M Todhunter The Bob Rixham Racing Club

Placings:02/0-P **(0450)**
2001/02: 23^{P}F

	Starts	1st	2nd	3rd	Win & Pl
Chases	1	0	0	0	
Career Total	**4**	**0**	**1**	**0**	**717**

Going: Sf: 0-0 GS: 0-0 Gd: 0-0 GF: - Fm: 0-1
Distance: 2m/2m3: 0-0 2m4-2m7: 0-0 3m+: 0-1
Track: LH: 0-0 RH: 0-0 Tight: 0-0 Gall: 0-0
Aids: Bl: 0-0 Vi: 0-0 Tstrap: 0-0
Best Rating: 82 3/00 Sedg 2m5f110y gd-fm Hdl

Rear Guard Action

6-y-o b g Almoojid-Belle Deirdrie (Mandamus)
P Butler G P Tresidder

Placings:P000 **(2334)**
2001/02: 18^{P}S, 16^{0}G, 20^{0}GS, 16^{0}G

	Starts	1st	2nd	3rd	Win & Pl
Hurdles	4	0	0	0	
Career Total	**4**	**0**	**0**	**0**	

Going: Sf: 0-1 GS: 0-1 Gd: 0-2 GF: - Fm: 0-0
Distance: 2m/2m3: 0-3 2m4-2m7: 0-1 3m+: 0-0
Track: LH: 0-2 RH: 0-1 Tight: 0-3 Gall: 0-0
Aids: Bl: 0-0 Vi: 0-1 Tstrap: 0-0
Best Rating:

Rear Window

99 80
8-y-o b g Night Shift (USA)-Last Clear Chance (USA) (Alleged (USA))
M J Ryan Dawn Build Ltd

Placings:5000/2P/0 **(2651)**
2001/02: 21^{0}G

	Starts	1st	2nd	3rd	Win & Pl
Hurdles	1	0	0	0	
Career Total	**7**	**0**	**1**	**0**	**600**

Going: Sf: 0-0 GS: 0-0 Gd: 0-1 GF: - Fm: 0-0
Distance: 2m/2m3: 0-0 2m4-2m7: 0-1 3m+: 0-0
Track: LH: 0-0 RH: 0-1 Tight: 0-0 Gall: 0-0
Aids: Bl: 0-0 Vi: 0-0 Tstrap: 0-0
Best Rating: 90 5/99 MRas 2m5f110y gd-fm Hdl

Rebel Son

107(65c) (89c)119
8-y-o b g Minster Son-Rebrona (Rebel Prince)
A Scott (J B Walton 17/5) Mrs J Yager

Placings:*00*P6400/6P-5522114124140 **(2689)**
2001/02: 19^{5}G, 17^{5}GF, 21^{2}GF, 24^{2}GF, 24^{1}G, 21^{1}GF, 24^{4}G, 21^{1}G, 21^{2}G, 22^{4}GS, 21^{1}G, 21^{4}S, 20^{0}G

	Starts	1st	2nd	3rd	Win & Pl
Hurdles	13	4	3	0	14435
Career Total	**22**	**4**	**3**	**0**	**14435**

119	11/01	Sedg	2m5f110y	F(0-105)HHdl	GD	£2597
107	10/01	Sedg	2m5f110y	E Hdl	GD	£2555
105	9/01	Sedg	2m5f110y	F(0-105)HHdl	G-F	£2023
112	8/01	Prth	3m110y	F(0-100)HHdl	GD	£3386

Total win prize-money £10562

Going: Sf: 0-1 GS: 0-1 Gd: 3-7 GF: - Fm: 1-4
Distance: 2m/2m3: 0-1 **2m4-2m7: 3-9** 3m+: 1-3
Track: **LH: 3-9** RH: 1-4 **Tight: 3-10** Gall: 0-1
Aids: Bl: 0-0 Vi: 0-0 Tstrap: 0-0
Best Rating: 119 11/01 Sedg 2m5f110y good Hdl

Stays well, and landed three novice hurdles in the north early in the season before scring in handicap company in November 2001. Loves Sedgefield. Needs a sound surface.

Rebel Yell (IRE)

11-y-o b m Noalto-Domestic Goddess (Roselier (FR))
N Jones Miss A J Morris

Placings:P **(0226)**
2001/02: 20^{P}GF

	Starts	1st	2nd	3rd	Win & Pl
Chases	1	0	0	0	
Career Total	**1**	**0**	**0**	**0**	

Going: Sf: 0-0 GS: 0-0 Gd: 0-0 GF: - Fm: 0-1
Distance: 2m/2m3: 0-0 2m4-2m7: 0-1 3m+: 0-0
Track: LH: 0-0 RH: 0-1 Tight: 0-0 Gall: 0-1
Aids: Bl: 0-0 Vi: 0-0 Tstrap: 0-0
Best Rating:

Rebel's Gift

103 78
9-y-o b g Genuine Gift (CAN)-Princess Veronica (Rebel Prince)
F P Murtagh S R Bainbridge & Mrs G Bainbridge

Placings:*0*P5/4FPP00104/6010F60-3303PP **(4196)**
2001/02: 22^{3}GS, 21^{3}G, 22^{0}G, 27^{3}S, 24^{P}G, 27^{P}S

	Starts	1st	2nd	3rd	Win & Pl
Hurdles	6	0	0	3	891
Career Total	**25**	**2**	**0**	**3**	**5294**

78	10/00	Kels	2m6f110y	F(0-105)HHdl	GD	£2786
78	2/00	Catt	2m3f	G(0-90)HHdl	GD	£1617

Total win prize-money £4403

Going: Sf: 0-2 GS: 0-1 Gd: 0-3 GF: - Fm: 0-0
Distance: 2m/2m3: 0-0 2m4-2m7: 0-3 3m+: 0-3
Track: LH: 0-5 RH: 0-1 Tight: 0-6 Gall: 0-0
Aids: Bl: 0-0 Vi: 0-0 Tstrap: 0-0
Best Rating: 78 9/01 Sedg 2m5f110y good Hdl

Twice a winner over hurdles on good ground, he also acts on an easier surface. Best form around two miles six furlongs but is out of form at present.

Reciprocity

6-y-o b m Thethingaboutitis (USA)-Koritsaki (Strong Gale)
B P J Baugh Andymark Racing

Placings:*00*P **(4126)**
2001/02: 16^{0}S, 16^{0}G, 19^{P}G

	Starts	1st	2nd	3rd	Win & Pl
NH Flat	2	0	0	0	0
Hurdles	1	0	0	0	0
Career Total	**3**	**0**	**0**	**0**	

Going: Sf: 0-1 GS: 0-0 Gd: 0-2 GF: - Fm: 0-0
Distance: 2m/2m3: 0-2 2m4-2m7: 0-1 3m+: 0-0
Track: LH: 0-0 RH: 0-2 Tight: 0-0 Gall: 0-0
Aids: Bl: 0-0 Vi: 0-0 Tstrap: 0-0
Best Rating:

Red Adhere

89(57c) (52c)42
7-y-o b g Insan (USA)-By The Lake (Tyrant (USA))
N B Mason Mrs D B Mason

Placings:P-000P **(4525)**
2001/02: 21^{0}G, 21^{0}S, 27^{0}S, 26^{P}GS

	Starts	1st	2nd	3rd	Win & Pl
Hurdles	2	0	0	0	0
Chases	2	0	0	0	0
Career Total	**5**	**0**	**0**	**0**	

Going: Sf: 0-2 GS: 0-1 Gd: 0-1 GF: - Fm: 0-0
Distance: 2m/2m3: 0-0 2m4-2m7: 0-2 3m+: 0-2
Track: LH: 0-3 RH: 0-1 Tight: 0-3 Gall: 0-0
Aids: Bl: 0-1 Vi: 0-0 Tstrap: 0-0
Best Rating: 52 2/02 Sedg 2m5f soft Ch

Modest dual-purpose performer.

Red Alert Man (IRE)

(79h) (77h)
6-y-o ch g Sharp Charter-Tukurua (Noalto)
Mrs L Williamson Halewood International Ltd

Placings:*00*6-F0F0P **(2944)**
2001/02: 16^{F}GS, 16^{0}S, 20^{F}GS, 20^{0}S, 24^{P}G

	Starts	1st	2nd	3rd	Win & Pl
Hurdles	3	0	0	0	0
Chases	2	0	0	0	0
Career Total	**8**	**0**	**0**	**0**	**0**

Going: Sf: 0-2 GS: 0-2 Gd: 0-1 GF: - Fm: 0-0
Distance: 2m/2m3: 0-2 2m4-2m7: 0-2 3m+: 0-1
Track: LH: 0-4 RH: 0-1 Tight: 0-2 Gall: 0-0
Aids: Bl: 0-0 Vi: 0-0 Tstrap: 0-0
Best Rating: 79 3/01 Hayd 2m heavy NHF

Moderate form in bumpers, over hurdles and over fences.

Red And Dangerous

7-y-o b g Afzal-Flori Wonder (Floriana)
Mrs D A Hamer Mrs J E Harries

Placings:*0*P **(3511)**
2001/02: 16^{0}GF, 17^{P}S

	Starts	1st	2nd	3rd	Win & Pl
NH Flat	1	0	0	0	0
Hurdles	1	0	0	0	0
Career Total	**2**	**0**	**0**	**0**	

Going: Sf: 0-1 GS: 0-0 Gd: 0-0 GF: - Fm: 0-1
Distance: 2m/2m3: 0-2 2m4-2m7: 0-0 3m+: 0-0
Track: LH: 0-0 RH: 0-2 Tight: 0-1 Gall: 0-0
Aids: Bl: 0-0 Vi: 0-0 Tstrap: 0-0
Best Rating:

Red Ark

109(100h) **153**

9-y-o ch g Gunner B-Minim (Rymer)

N B Mason Mrs D B Mason

Placings:*00*P/56064113211212 1B/12P14202F2-4P501100U **(4677)**

2001/02: 16^{4}GF, 24^{P}GF, 20^{5}G, 20^{0}S, 16^{1}S, 16^{1}S, 19^{0}GS, 16^{0}G, 36^{U}G

	Starts	1st	2nd	3rd	Win & Pl
Chases	9	2	0	0	20999
Career Total	**38**	**10**	**7**	**1**	**89184**

153	2/02	Sand	2m	C(0-135)HCh	SFT	£10140
144	1/02	Donc	2m110y	B(0-150)HCh	SFT	£10344
153	11/00	Newb	2m4f	B(0-145)HCh	SFT	£15648
115	9/00	MRas	2m3f110y	E(0-115)HHdl	G-F	£2808
150	4/00	Aint	2m4f	C HCh	GD	£11407
139	3/00	Sand	2m	C Ch	GD	£7403
129	1/00	Donc	2m110y	E(0-105)HCh	GD	£3282
125	1/00	Leic	2m7f110y	D(0-110)HCh	GD	£5980
109	11/99	Catt	2m	F(0-100)HHdl	G-F	£2705
104	11/99	Newc	2m4f	F(0-90)HHdl	GD	£2305

Total win prize-money £72026

Going: Sf: 2-3 GS: 0-1 Gd: 0-3 GF: - Fm: 0-2
Distance: **2m/2m3: 2-4** 2m4-2m7: 0-3 3m+: 0-2
Track: LH: 1-8 RH: 1-1 Tight: 0-1 **Gall: 1-4**
Aids: Bl: 0-0 Vi: 0-0 **Tstrap: 2-9**
Best Rating: **153** 2/02 Sand 2m soft Ch

A very useful handicap chaser, he is best suited to a sound surface. However, he has won on soft, and two and a half miles looks his best trip, although got off the mark in 2002 in heavy ground over two miles at Doncaster, where his stamina was a factor and he followed up over the same distance at Sandown. Reported to have gurgled when disappointing at Doncaster in March.

Red Blazer

110 **144**

11-y-o ch g Bustino-Klewraye (Lord Gayle (USA))

Miss H C Knight Miss H Knight

Placings:*120/3*/112/131P5/**2F52/F2-21R11** **(3873)**

2001/02: 20^{2}G, 16^{1}G, 16^{R}G, 16^{1}G, 20^{1}GS

	Starts	1st	2nd	3rd	Win & Pl
Chases	5	3	1	0	16648
Career Total	**23**	**8**	**6**	**2**	**56831**

144	2/02	Hntg	2m4f110y	D Ch	G-S	£4143
144	1/02	Kemp	2m	C Ch	GD	£6890
144	11/01	Kemp	2m	D Ch	GD	£4095
144	2/98	Hayd	2m	B Hdl	GD	£10211
145	12/97	Uttx	2m4f110y	B(0-145)HHdl	G-S	£4769
131	1/97	Leic	2m4f110y	Hdl	G-S	£3548
112	12/96	Towc	2m	E Hdl	HVY	£2897
111	2/95	Asct	2m110y	H NHF	HVY	£2620

Total win prize-money £39177

Going: Sf: 0-0 GS: 1-1 Gd: 2-4 GF: - Fm: 0-0
Distance: **2m/2m3: 2-3** 2m4-2m7: 1-2 3m+: 0-0
Track: LH: 0-0 **RH: 3-5** Tight: 0-0 **Gall: 1-1**
Aids: Bl: 0-0 Vi: 0-0 Tstrap: 0-0
Best Rating: **148** 4/98 Asct 3m gd-sft Hdl

Lightly-raced through recurrent leg problems. He got off the mark over fences at Kempton in November 2001, and scoredtwice early in the New Year. Stays two and a half miles and jumps well. Suited by a flat, right-handed track.

Red Blazer (NZ)

94 **101**

9-y-o ch g Omnicorp (NZ)-Gay Reef (Reform)

A W Carroll K Marshall

Placings:1235P/P6132P0-5 **(2259)**

2001/02: 24^{5}G

	Starts	1st	2nd	3rd	Win & Pl
Hurdles	1	0	0	0	0
Career Total	**13**	**2**	**2**	**2**	**6623**

109	12/00	Fknm	2m4f	F(0-100)HHdl	G-S	£1771
	8/99	Foxt	1m6f	Hdl	SFT	£2063

Total win prize-money £3834

Going: Sf: 0-0 GS: 0-0 Gd: 0-1 GF: - Fm: 0-0
Distance: 2m/2m3: 0-0 2m4-2m7: 0-0 3m+: 0-1
Track: LH: 0-0 RH: 0-1 Tight: 0-0 Gall: 0-0
Aids: Bl: 0-0 Vi: 0-0 Tstrap: 0-0
Best Rating: **109** 3/01 Hntg 2m5f110y soft Hdl

Red Bob

56 **14**

7-y-o b g Hatim (USA)-Mount St Mary'S (Lochnager)

A Parker A J Wight

Placings:0P **(4880)**

2001/02: 17^{0}GS, 20^{P}G

	Starts	1st	2nd	3rd	Win & Pl
Hurdles	2	0	0	0	
Career Total	**2**	**0**	**0**	**0**	

Going: Sf: 0-0 GS: 0-1 Gd: 0-1 GF: - Fm: 0-0
Distance: 2m/2m3: 0-1 2m4-2m7: 0-1 3m+: 0-0
Track: LH: 0-0 RH: 0-2 Tight: 0-0 Gall: 0-0
Aids: Bl: 0-0 Vi: 0-0 Tstrap: 0-0
Best Rating: **14** 3/02 Carl 2m1f gd-sft Hdl

Red Bordeaux

91 **49**

7-y-o b g Alzao (USA)-Marie De Flandre (FR) (Crystal Palace (FR))

J Akehurst A D Spence

Placings:4320/000350400/121336-P00 **(4035)**

2001/02: 16^{P}S, 20^{0}S, 22^{0}S

	Starts	1st	2nd	3rd	Win & Pl
Hurdles	3	0	0	0	
Career Total	**22**	**2**	**2**	**4**	**6036**

90	10/00	Folk	2m4f110y	G(0-95)HHdl	G-F	£1463
79	8/00	Worc	2m	G(0-90)HHdl	G-F	£1505

Total win prize-money £2968

Going: Sf: 0-3 GS: 0-0 Gd: 0-0 GF: - Fm: 0-0
Distance: 2m/2m3: 0-1 2m4-2m7: 0-2 3m+: 0-0
Track: LH: 0-1 RH: 0-2 Tight: 0-1 Gall: 0-1
Aids: Bl: 0-0 Vi: 0-0 Tstrap: 0-0
Best Rating: **91** 11/99 Wwck 2m good Hdl

Red Brae

90f **100f**

5-y-o b g Rakaposhi King-Sayshar (Sayfar)

J J O'Neill C D Carr

Placings:*5-04* **(4269)**

2001/02: 16^{0}GS, 16^{4}S

	Starts	1st	2nd	3rd	Win & Pl
NH Flat	2	0	0	0	0
Career Total	**3**	**0**	**0**	**0**	**0**

Going: Sf: 0-1 GS: 0-1 Gd: 0-0 GF: - Fm: 0-0
Distance: 2m/2m3: 0-2 2m4-2m7: 0-0 3m+: 0-0
Track: LH: 0-1 RH: 0-1 Tight: 0-0 Gall: 0-1
Aids: Bl: 0-0 Vi: 0-0 Tstrap: 0-0
Best Rating: **100** 3/02 Chep 2m110y soft NHF

Fair bumper performer. Has tended to race a bit keenly though.

Red Canyon (IRE)

112 **92+**

5-y-o b g Zieten (USA)-Bayazida (Bustino)

B I Case Lady Jane Grosvenor

Placings:0-04000435 **(4854)**

2001/02: 18^{0}GF, 16^{4}GF, 16^{0}GF, 17^{0}GF, 19^{0}G, 16^{4}G, 20^{3}G, 22^{5}G

	Starts	1st	2nd	3rd	Win & Pl
Hurdles	8	0	0	1	429
Career Total	**9**	**0**	**0**	**1**	**429**

Going: Sf: 0-0 GS: 0-0 Gd: 0-4 GF: - Fm: 0-4
Distance: 2m/2m3: 0-6 2m4-2m7: 0-2 3m+: 0-0
Track: LH: 0-6 RH: 0-2 Tight: 0-6 Gall: 0-1
Aids: Bl: 0-0 Vi: 0-0 Tstrap: 0-0
Best Rating: **89** 9/01 Uttx 2m good Hdl

Middle-distance Flat winner and moderate hurdler. Successful on first start for Andy Hobbs when winning a conditional novices handicap at Worcester June 2002 and has completed a hat-trick. Stays well. Acts on fast ground.

Red Card

7-y-o ch g Nearly A Hand-Ruby Celebration (New Member)

D R Gandolfo G C Hartigan

Placings:*0056*-P **(0010)**

2001/02: 25^{P}S

	Starts	1st	2nd	3rd	Win & Pl
Hurdles	1	0	0	0	
Career Total	**5**	**0**	**0**	**0**	**0**

Going: Sf: 0-1 GS: 0-0 Gd: 0-0 GF: - Fm: 0-0
Distance: 2m/2m3: 0-0 2m4-2m7: 0-0 3m+: 0-1
Track: LH: 0-0 RH: 0-0 Tight: 0-0 Gall: 0-0
Aids: Bl: 0-0 Vi: 0-0 Tstrap: 0-0
Best Rating: **79** 11/00 Winc 2m gd-sft NHF

Red Clover

6-y-o b m Rock City-Stupid Cupid (Idiots Delight)

R Rowe The Exclusive Partnership

Placings:*0*-FP **(4033)**

2001/02: 17^{F}HY, 20^{P}S

	Starts	1st	2nd	3rd	Win & Pl
Hurdles	2	0	0	0	
Career Total	**3**	**0**	**0**	**0**	

Going: Sf: 0-2 GS: 0-0 Gd: 0-0 GF: - Fm: 0-0
Distance: 2m/2m3: 0-1 2m4-2m7: 0-1 3m+: 0-0
Track: LH: 0-0 RH: 0-1 Tight: 0-2 Gall: 0-0
Aids: Bl: 0-0 Vi: 0-0 Tstrap: 0-0
Best Rating:

Red Emperor

108 108

8-y-o b g Emperor Fountain-Golden Curd (FR) (Nice Havrais (USA))

N B Mason N B Mason

Placings:304353565261152З/0060U1436U05-512632P15 **(4523)**

2001/02: 27^{5}S, 24^{1}GS, 30^{2}GS, 25^{6}G, 24^{3}S, 27^{2}S, 28^{P}S, 24^{1}HY, 26^{5}GS

	Starts	1st	2nd	3rd	Win & Pl
Chases	9	2	2	1	8070
Career Total	**37**	**5**	**4**	**6**	**21078**

108	3/02	Newc	3m	F(0-100)HCh	HVY	£2989
108	11/01	Newc	3m	F(0-90)HCh	G-S	£2597
104	11/00	Newc	3m	F(0-90)HCh	G-S	£2457
103	2/00	Carl	2m4f110y	F(0-110)HCh	HVY	£3526
91	1/00	Sthl	3m110y	F(0-90)HCh	G-S	£2643

Total win prize-money £14212

Going: Sf: 1-5 GS: 1-3 Gd: 0-1 GF: - Fm: 0-0
Distance: 2m/2m3: 0-0 2m4-2m7: 0-0 **3m+: 2-9**
Track: **LH: 2-8** RH: 0-1 Tight: 0-4 **Gall: 2-4**
Aids: **Bl: 2-8** Vi: 0-0 Tstrap: 0-0
Best Rating: 108 3/02 Newc 3m heavy Ch

Fair handicapper chaser at around three miles on an easy surface. Likes Newcastle, often wears blinkers.

Red Gold

85 100

8-y-o ch g Gula Dula Ruby Celebration (New Member)

Andrew Turnell Mrs C C Williams

Placings:0563PF-0F4 **(2555)**

2001/02: 24^{0}G, 22^{F}S, 24^{4}S

	Starts	1st	2nd	3rd	Win & Pl
Chases	3	0	0	0	0
Career Total	**9**	**0**	**0**	**1**	**673**

Going: Sf: 0-2 GS: 0-0 Gd: 0-1 GF: - Fm: 0-0
Distance: 2m/2m3: 0-0 2m4-2m7: 0-1 3m+: 0-2
Track: LH: 0-1 RH: 0-2 Tight: 0-1 Gall: 0-1
Aids: Bl: 0-0 Vi: 0-0 Tstrap: 0-0
Best Rating: 114 1/01 Leic 2m4f110y soft Ch

Red Guard

110(109h) 130

8-y-o ch g Soviet Star (USA)-Zinzara (USA) (Stagedoor Johnny)

J T Gifford L A Hooper

Placings:4552/062140/11/0410P-**622234F1** **(4884)**

2001/02: 16^{6}GS, 21^{2}G, 18^{2}G, 21^{2}G, 20^{3}S, 16^{4}G, 16^{F}GF, 22^{1}GF

	Starts	1st	2nd	3rd	Win & Pl
Chases	8	1	3	1	13216
Career Total	**25**	**5**	**5**	**1**	**41053**

119	4/02	Font	2m6f	C Ch	G-F	£7345
138	1/01	Asct	2m110y	B HHdl	SFT	£10185
133	10/99	Weth	2m	C(0-135)HHdl	G-F	£5018
120	10/99	Font	2m2f110y	C(0-135)HHdl	GD	£4719
124	12/98	Sand	2m110y	D(0-115)HHdl	GD	£4924

Total win prize-money £32195

Going: Sf: 0-1 GS: 0-1 Gd: 0-4 GF: - Fm: 1-2
Distance: 2m/2m3: 0-4 **2m4-2m7: 1-4** 3m+: 0-0
Track: LH: 0-2 RH: 0-5 **Tight: 1-2** Gall: 0-1
Aids: Bl: 0-0 Vi: 0-0 Tstrap: 0-0
Best Rating: 138 1/01 Asct 2m110y soft Hdl

Useful hurdler, and fair novice chaser if usually finding one or two too good. Acts on most types of ground and is effective at up to two miles-six, although that trip stretches his stamina. Has not always convinced in a finish and needs to come late.

Red Hare (NZ)

102(98h) (96h)106

8-y-o ch g Famous Star-Mutual Belle (NZ) (Western Bay (NZ))

N J Henderson Mrs T Styles

Placings:420-01PF6146 **(3215)**

2001/02: 16^{0}GF, 20^{1}GF, 24^{P}G, 22^{F}G, 20^{6}G, 24^{1}G, 22^{4}G, 24^{6}GS

	Starts	1st	2nd	3rd	Win & Pl
Hurdles	8	2	0	0	8244
Career Total	**11**	**2**	**1**	**0**	**9070**

96	11/01	Kemp	3m110y	D(0-120)HHdl	GD	£5352
95	6/01	Fknm	2m4f	E Hdl	G-F	£2891

Total win prize-money £8244

Going: Sf: 0-0 GS: 0-1 Gd: 1-5 GF: - Fm: 1-2
Distance: 2m/2m3: 0-1 2m4-2m7: 1-4 3m+: 1-3
Track: LH: 1-5 RH: 1-3 **Tight: 1-3** Gall: 0-1
Aids: Bl: 0-1 Vi: 0-0 Tstrap: 0-0
Best Rating: 105 11/00 Wwck 2m soft Hdl

A New Zealand import, is effective over three miles and acts on a sound surface. Potential staying chaser once he is more sure-footed over his jumps.

Red Heather

73 61

5-y-o b m Mistertopogigo (IRE)-That's Rich (Hot Spark)

D W Whillans Mrs H M Whillans

Placings:0 **(4438)**

2001/02: 16^{0}S

	Starts	1st	2nd	3rd	Win & Pl
Hurdles	1	0	0	0	
Career Total	**1**	**0**	**0**	**0**	

Going: Sf: 0-1 GS: 0-0 Gd: 0-0 GF: - Fm: 0-0
Distance: 2m/2m3: 0-1 2m4-2m7: 0-0 3m+: 0-0
Track: LH: 0-1 RH: 0-0 Tight: 0-1 Gall: 0-0
Aids: Bl: 0-0 Vi: 0-0 Tstrap: 0-0
Best Rating: 61 3/02 Kels 2m110y soft Hdl

Red Hot Indian (IRE)

94(99h) (100h)90

9-y-o b g Little Bighorn-Pepper Cannister (Lord Gayle (USA))

N B Mason Mrs D B Mason

Placings:1/43235/43213/P24-431 **(4553)**

2001/02: 21^{4}GS, 21^{3}G, 17^{1}GF

	Starts	1st	2nd	3rd	Win & Pl
Hurdles	1	1	0	0	1736
Chases	2	0	0	1	311
Career Total	**17**	**3**	**3**	**5**	**14161**

100	4/02	MRas	2m1f110y	G Hdl	G-F	£1736
111	2/00	Hntg	2m4f110y	D(0-120)HHdl	SFT	£5421
106	4/98	Prth	2m110y	H NHF	HVY	£2066

Total win prize-money £9223

Going: Sf: 0-0 GS: 0-1 Gd: 0-1 GF: - Fm: 1-1
Distance: **2m/2m3: 1-1** 2m4-2m7: 0-2 3m+: 0-0
Track: LH: 0-2 **RH: 1-1** **Tight: 1-3** Gall: 0-0
Aids: Bl: 0-0 Vi: 0-0 Tstrap: 0-1
Best Rating: 117 2/01 Plum 2m4f soft Ch

Modest hunter chase form, and successful in a selling hurdle at Easter 2002. Not a good jumper.

Red Hustler (IRE)

84 47

6-y-o ch g Husyan (USA)-Isoldes Tower (Balliol)

C Grant W Raw

Placings:056 **(4788)**

2001/02: 17^{0}GS, 20^{5}HY, 20^{6}F

	Starts	1st	2nd	3rd	Win & Pl
NH Flat	1	0	0	0	0
Hurdles	2	0	0	0	0
Career Total	**3**	**0**	**0**	**0**	**0**

Going: Sf: 0-1 GS: 0-1 Gd: 0-0 GF: - Fm: 0-1
Distance: 2m/2m3: 0-1 2m4-2m7: 0-2 3m+: 0-0
Track: LH: 0-2 RH: 0-1 Tight: 0-1 Gall: 0-2
Aids: Bl: 0-0 Vi: 0-0 Tstrap: 0-0
Best Rating: 82 3/02 MRas 2m1f110y gd-sft NHF

Red Imp

(107h) (120h)

6-y-o ch g Alflora (IRE)-Southend Scallywag (Tina's Pet)

N B Mason N B Mason

Placings:P00/51F11216222-0301F **(3622)**

2001/02: 16^{0}S, 16^{3}S, 20^{0}S, 16^{1}S, 17^{F}S

	Starts	1st	2nd	3rd	Win & Pl
Hurdles	4	1	0	1	6228
Chases	1	0	0	0	0
Career Total	**19**	**5**	**4**	**1**	**26985**

120	1/02	Donc	2m110y	C(0-130)HHdl	SFT	£5460
120	2/01	Catt	2m3f	D Hdl	SFT	£2887
97	12/00	Leic	2m4f110y	F(0-105)HHdl	HVY	£3614
97	12/00	Fknm	2m4f	E(0-105)HHdl	G-S	£3006
81	11/00	Newc	2m4f	F(0-90)HHdl	SFT	£2296

Total win prize-money £17264

Going: Sf: 1-5 GS: 0-0 Gd: 0-0 GF: - Fm: 0-0
Distance: **2m/2m3: 1-4** 2m4-2m7: 0-1 3m+: 0-0
Track: **LH: 1-3** RH: 0-1 Tight: 0-1 **Gall: 1-1**
Aids: Bl: 0-0 Vi: 0-0 **Tstrap: 1-3**
Best Rating: 120 1/02 Donc 2m110y soft Hdl

Improving hurdler in the 2000/2001 season. Back to form when winning a heavy-ground Doncaster handicap in January 2002. Stayed two and a half miles. Acted on soft ground. killed in a fall on his chasing debut. (DEAD)

Red Jupiter

5-y-o b g Jupiter Island-Glen Dancer (Furry Glen)

N B Mason N B Mason

Placings:0 **(4873)**

2001/02: 16^{0}GF

	Starts	1st	2nd	3rd	Win & Pl
NH Flat	1	0	0	0	
Career Total	**1**	**0**	**0**	**0**	

Going: Sf: 0-0 GS: 0-0 Gd: 0-0 GF: - Fm: 0-1
Distance: 2m/2m3: 0-1 2m4-2m7: 0-0 3m+: 0-0
Track: LH: 0-1 RH: 0-0 Tight: 0-0 Gall: 0-0
Aids: Bl: 0-0 Vi: 0-0 Tstrap: 0-0
Best Rating: 78 4/02 Weth 2m gd-fm NHF

Red Mail (USA)

57 21

4-y-o b g Red Ransom (USA)-Seattle Byline (USA) (Slew City Slew (USA))
T D McCarthy (M L W Bell 30/5) A D Spence

Placings:0 (1355)
2001/02: 16^{0}GF

	Starts	1st	2nd	3rd	Win & Pl
Hurdles	1	0	0	0	
Career Total	1	0	0	0	

Going: Sf: 0-0 GS: 0-0 Gd: 0-0 GF: - Fm: 0-1
Distance: 2m/2m3: 0-1 2m4-2m7: 0-0 3m+: 0-0
Track: LH: 0-1 RH: 0-0 Tight: 0-1 Gall: 0-0
Aids: Bl: 0-0 Vi: 0-0 Tstrap: 0-0
Best Rating: 21 9/01 Strf 2m110y gd-fm Hdl

Red Mimosa

6-y-o b m Gunner B-Super Gambler (Lighter)
N B Mason N B Mason

Placings:0 (1404)
2001/02: 17^{0}G

	Starts	1st	2nd	3rd	Win & Pl
Hurdles	1	0	0	0	
Career Total	1	0	0	0	

Going: Sf: 0-0 GS: 0-0 Gd: 0-1 GF: - Fm: 0-0
Distance: 2m/2m3: 0-1 2m4-2m7: 0-0 3m+: 0-0
Track: LH: 0-1 RH: 0-0 Tight: 0-1 Gall: 0-0
Aids: Bl: 0-0 Vi: 0-0 Tstrap: 0-0
Best Rating:

Red Minster

66 17
5-y-o b g Minster Son-Minty Muncher (Idiots Delight)
N B Mason N B Mason

Placings:000 (3766)
2001/02: 19^{0}S, 19^{0}GS, 20^{0}GS

	Starts	1st	2nd	3rd	Win & Pl
Hurdles	3	0	0	0	
Career Total	3	0	0	0	

Going: Sf: 0-1 GS: 0-2 Gd: 0-0 GF: - Fm: 0-0
Distance: 2m/2m3: 0-1 2m4-2m7: 0-2 3m+: 0-0
Track: LH: 0-2 RH: 0-1 Tight: 0-3 Gall: 0-0
Aids: Bl: 0-0 Vi: 0-0 Tstrap: 0-0
Best Rating: 17 2/02 MRas 2m3f110y gd-sft Hdl

Red Mist (IRE)

(39h)
8-y-o b g Asir-Shadowed Seas (IRE) (Le Bavard (FR))
M R Churches M R Churches

Placings:*P/P0/PP-PR* (1613)
2001/02: 20^{P}GF, 23^{R}GF

	Starts	1st	2nd	3rd	Win & Pl
Hurdles	1	0	0	0	0
Chases	1	0	0	0	0
Career Total	7	0	0	0	

Going: Sf: 0-0 GS: 0-0 Gd: 0-0 GF: - Fm: 0-2
Distance: 2m/2m3: 0-0 2m4-2m7: 0-1 3m+: 0-1
Track: LH: 0-0 RH: 0-1 Tight: 0-1 Gall: 0-0
Aids: Bl: 0-0 Vi: 0-0 Tstrap: 0-0
Best Rating:

Red Morocco (USA)

76 39
8-y-o gr g Seattle Dancer (USA)-Lady's Slipper (AUS) (Dancer's Image (USA))
Mrs P Townsley Jamie Butler & Paul Townsley

Placings:*6/40/*0U-0P (0341)
2001/02: 17^{0}GS, 16^{P}G

	Starts	1st	2nd	3rd	Win & Pl
Hurdles	2	0	0	0	
Career Total	7	0	0	0	176

Going: Sf: 0-0 GS: 0-1 Gd: 0-1 GF: - Fm: 0-0
Distance: 2m/2m3: 0-2 2m4-2m7: 0-0 3m+: 0-0
Track: LH: 0-1 RH: 0-1 Tight: 0-2 Gall: 0-0
Aids: Bl: 0-1 Vi: 0-0 Tstrap: 0-1
Best Rating: 90 3/98 Gowr 2m yld-sft NHF

Red Neck

11-y-o ch g Nishapour (FR)-Roda Haxan (Huntercombe)
John Moore Mrs C E Goldsworthy

Placings:3162P4/P/P/43-5 (0056)
2001/02: 24^{5}GS

	Starts	1st	2nd	3rd	Win & Pl
Chases	1	0	0	0	0
Career Total	10	1	1	2	4579

106 7/97 Worc 2m4f D Hdl G-F £2966
Total win prize-money £2966

Going: Sf: 0-0 GS: 0-1 Gd: 0-0 GF: - Fm: 0-0
Distance: 2m/2m3: 0-0 2m4-2m7: 0-0 3m+: 0-1
Track: LH: 0-1 RH: 0-0 Tight: 0-1 Gall: 0-0
Aids: Bl: 0-0 Vi: 0-0 Tstrap: 0-1
Best Rating: 106 7/97 Worc 2m4f gd-fm Hdl

Red Nose Lady

96f 97f
5-y-o b m Teenoso (USA)-Red Rambler (Rymer)
J M Jefferson Mrs M E Dixon

Placings:*225* (4860)
2001/02: 16^{2}S, 16^{2}HY, 16^{5}G

	Starts	1st	2nd	3rd	Win & Pl
NH Flat	3	0	2	0	1018
Career Total	3	0	2	0	1018

Going: Sf: 0-2 GS: 0-0 Gd: 0-1 GF: - Fm: 0-0
Distance: 2m/2m3: 0-3 2m4-2m7: 0-0 3m+: 0-0
Track: LH: 0-2 RH: 0-0 Tight: 0-0 Gall: 0-1
Aids: Bl: 0-0 Vi: 0-0 Tstrap: 0-0
Best Rating: 97 2/02 Donc 2m110y soft NHF

Runner-up in two mares' only bumpers.

Red Oassis

114(49h) (13h)96
11-y-o ch g Rymer-Heron's Mirage (Grey Mirage)
M J M Evans Mrs J Z Munday

Placings:*00F/4U10-P022* (4430)
2001/02: 16^{P}S, 20^{0}GS, 16^{2}S, 16^{2}HY

	Starts	1st	2nd	3rd	Win & Pl
Hurdles	1	0	0	0	0
Chases	3	0	2	0	1914
Career Total	11	1	2	0	4452

86 3/01 Wwck 2m110y F(0-90)HCh HVY £2538
Total win prize-money £2538

Going: Sf: 0-3 GS: 0-1 Gd: 0-0 GF: - Fm: 0-0
Distance: 2m/2m3: 0-3 2m4-2m7: 0-1 3m+: 0-0
Track: LH: 0-2 RH: 0-2 Tight: 0-0 Gall: 0-1
Aids: Bl: 0-0 Vi: 0-0 Tstrap: 0-0
Best Rating: 96 3/02 Uttx 2m heavy Ch

Winning point to pointer. Fair efforts under Rules over fences. Suited by two miles and good to soft ground but handles heavy. A careless jumper.

Red Perk (IRE)

5-y-o b g Executive Perk-Supreme View (Supreme Leader)
N B Mason N B Mason

Placings:*0* (4873)
2001/02: 16^{0}GF

	Starts	1st	2nd	3rd	Win & Pl
NH Flat	1	0	0	0	
Career Total	1	0	0	0	

Going: Sf: 0-0 GS: 0-0 Gd: 0-0 GF: - Fm: 0-1
Distance: 2m/2m3: 0-1 2m4-2m7: 0-0 3m+: 0-0
Track: LH: 0-1 RH: 0-0 Tight: 0-0 Gall: 0-0
Aids: Bl: 0-0 Vi: 0-0 Tstrap: 0-0
Best Rating: 56 4/02 Weth 2m gd-fm NHF

Red Radish

(44h)
7-y-o ch g Henbit (USA)-Miss Flossa (FR) (Big John (FR))
B I Case R P Brett

Placings:00P/PPPP-4PRP (3993)
2001/02: 20^{4}GF, 20^{P}G, 24^{R}GS, 20^{P}S

	Starts	1st	2nd	3rd	Win & Pl
Hurdles	1	0	0	0	0
Chases	3	0	0	0	251
Career Total	12	0	0	0	251

Going: Sf: 0-1 GS: 0-1 Gd: 0-1 GF: - Fm: 0-1
Distance: 2m/2m3: 0-0 2m4-2m7: 0-3 3m+: 0-1
Track: LH: 0-2 RH: 0-1 Tight: 0-2 Gall: 0-1
Aids: Bl: 0-0 Vi: 0-0 Tstrap: 0-3
Best Rating:

Red Raki

84 47
7-y-o b m Rakaposhi King-Lavenham's Last (Rymer)
N B Mason N B Mason

Placings:*66*04400P-0P0 (1387)
2001/02: 16^{0}GF, 22^{P}GS, 16^{0}G

	Starts	1st	2nd	3rd	Win & Pl
Hurdles	3	0	0	0	
Career Total	11	0	0	0	250

Going: Sf: 0-0 GS: 0-1 Gd: 0-1 GF: - Fm: 0-1
Distance: 2m/2m3: 0-2 2m4-2m7: 0-1 3m+: 0-0
Track: LH: 0-3 RH: 0-0 Tight: 0-1 Gall: 0-0
Aids: Bl: 0-0 Vi: 0-0 Tstrap: 0-3
Best Rating: 88 9/00 MRas 1m5f110y gd-fm NHF

Red Ramona

96 101
7-y-o b g Rudimentary (USA)-Apply (King's Lake (USA))

J Akehurst A D Spence

Placings:54FR (3402)

2001/02: 16^{5}G, 19^{4}G, 16^{F}G, 20^{R}S

	Starts	1st	2nd	3rd	Win & Pl
Hurdles	4	0	0	0	0
Career Total	**4**	**0**	**0**	**0**	**0**

Going: Sf: 0-1 GS: 0-0 Gd: 0-3 GF: - Fm: 0-0
Distance: 2m/2m3: 0-3 2m4-2m7: 0-1 3m+: 0-0
Track: LH: 0-1 RH: 0-3 Tight: 0-1 Gall: 0-0
Aids: Bl: 0-0 Vi: 0-0 Tstrap: 0-0
Best Rating: 101 12/01 Extr 2m3f good Hdl

Red Rampage

111(95h) (87h)**108**

7-y-o b g King's Ride-Mighty Fly (Comedy Star (USA))
N B Mason N B Mason

Placings:U40042464-5042031420P (4895)

2001/02: 20^{5}GF, 22^{0}GS, 19^{4}G, 25^{2}GS, 24^{0}G, 24^{3}S, 25^{1}GS, 25^{4}S, 25^{2}G, 20^{0}GF, 20^{P}G

	Starts	1st	2nd	3rd	Win & Pl
Hurdles	5	0	1	1	1311
Chases	6	1	1	0	4769
Career Total	**20**	**1**	**3**	**1**	**6984**

108 3/02 Catt 3m1f110y E(0-100)HCh G-S £3113
Total win prize-money £3114

Going: Sf: 0-2 GS: 1-3 Gd: 0-4 GF: - Fm: 0-2
Distance: 2m/2m3: 0-1 2m4-2m7: 0-4 **3m+: 1-6**
Track: **LH: 1-6** RH: 0-5 **Tight: 1-7** Gall: 0-0
Aids: **Bl: 1-6** Vi: 0-1 Tstrap: 0-0
Best Rating: 108 4/02 MRas 3m1f good Ch

A stayer over hurdles, he does not want the ground too soft. Successful in a three mile novices' chase at Catterick on only his second try over fences.

Red Rebel

10-y-o gr g Scallywag-Little Red Flower (Blakeney)
Mrs Caroline Bailey Mrs M E Moody

Placings:1FP/4UR/U (4058)

2001/02: 10^{U}G

	Starts	1st	2nd	3rd	Win & Pl
Chases	1	0	0	0	0
Career Total	**7**	**1**	**0**	**0**	**1532**

110 5/98 Uttx 3m2f H Ch GD £1433
Total win prize-money £1433

Going: Sf: 0-1 GS: 0-0 Gd: 0-0 GF: - Fm: 0-0
Distance: 2m/2m3: 0-1 2m4-2m7: 0-0 3m+: 0-0
Track: LH: 0-0 RH: 0-1 Tight: 0-0 Gall: 0-0
Aids: Bl: 0-0 Vi: 0-0 Tstrap: 0-0
Best Rating: 110 5/98 Uttx 3m2f good Ch

Fair pointer/hunter chaser, acts on any ground.

Red Revenge

97(83h) **97**

7-y-o b g Rakaposhi King-Just A Tipple (IRE) (Roselier (FR))
N B Mason N B Mason

Placings:260-PP022P3 (4521)

2001/02: 18^{P}GS, 19^{P}G, 20^{0}GS, 22^{2}S, 24^{2}S, 25^{P}S, 20^{3}GS

	Starts	1st	2nd	3rd	Win & Pl
Hurdles	1	0	0	0	0
Chases	6	0	2	1	2499
Career Total	**10**	**0**	**3**	**1**	**3031**

Going: Sf: 0-3 GS: 0-3 Gd: 0-1 GF: - Fm: 0-0
Distance: 2m/2m3: 0-2 2m4-2m7: 0-3 3m+: 0-2
Track: LH: 0-3 RH: 0-4 Tight: 0-5 Gall: 0-0
Aids: Bl: 0-0 Vi: 0-0 Tstrap: 0-5
Best Rating: 97 4/02 Carl 2m4f gd-sft Ch

Handicap chaser, suited by soft ground and three miles, but handles faster ground.

Red Rover

87 **65**

5-y-o ch m Infantry-M I Babe (Celtic Cone)
Mrs M Reveley J F Mernagh

Placings:PU00P (4122)

2001/02: 20^{P}GS, 23^{U}S, 16^{0}S, 19^{0}GS, 22^{P}HY

	Starts	1st	2nd	3rd	Win & Pl
Hurdles	5	0	0	0	
Career Total	**5**	**0**	**0**	**0**	

Going: Sf: 0-3 GS: 0-2 Gd: 0-0 GF: - Fm: 0-0
Distance: 2m/2m3: 0-1 2m4-2m7: 0-4 3m+: 0-0
Track: LH: 0-4 RH: 0-1 Tight: 0-1 Gall: 0-2
Aids: Bl: 0-0 Vi: 0-0 Tstrap: 0-0
Best Rating: 65 1/02 Newc 2m soft Hdl

Modest hurdler, she completed twice from her first five starts due to poor jumping.

Red September

92 **83**

5-y-o b g Presidium-Tangalooma (Hotfoot)
G M Moore Dr C I Emmerson

Placings:230-506 (1500)

2001/02: 20^{5}G, 16^{0}GF, 21^{6}G

	Starts	1st	2nd	3rd	Win & Pl
Hurdles	3	0	0	0	0
Career Total	**6**	**0**	**1**	**1**	**1119**

Going: Sf: 0-0 GS: 0-0 Gd: 0-2 GF: - Fm: 0-1
Distance: 2m/2m3: 0-1 2m4-2m7: 0-2 3m+: 0-0
Track: LH: 0-3 RH: 0-0 Tight: 0-2 Gall: 0-0
Aids: Bl: 0-0 Vi: 0-0 Tstrap: 0-0
Best Rating: 100 9/00 Sedg 2m1f good Hdl

Red Snapper (IRE)

83f **48f**

7-y-o b g Soviet Lad (USA)-Magic Picture (Deep Diver)
N A Twiston-Davies N A Twiston-Davies

Placings:05 (1044)

2001/02: 16^{0}G, 16^{5}GF

	Starts	1st	2nd	3rd	Win & Pl
NH Flat	2	0	0	0	0
Career Total	**2**	**0**	**0**	**0**	**0**

Going: Sf: 0-0 GS: 0-0 Gd: 0-1 GF: - Fm: 0-1
Distance: 2m/2m3: 0-2 2m4-2m7: 0-0 3m+: 0-0
Track: LH: 0-2 RH: 0-0 Tight: 0-0 Gall: 0-0
Aids: Bl: 0-0 Vi: 0-0 Tstrap: 0-0
Best Rating: 48 7/01 Uttx 2m gd-fm NHF

Red Socialite (IRE)

98f **88f**

5-y-o ch g Moscow Society (USA)-Dees Darling (IRE) (King Persian)
D R Gandolfo G C Hartigan

Placings:05 (4166)

2001/02: 16^{0}S, 16^{5}GS

	Starts	1st	2nd	3rd	Win & Pl
NH Flat	2	0	0	0	0
Career Total	**2**	**0**	**0**	**0**	**0**

Going: Sf: 0-1 GS: 0-1 Gd: 0-0 GF: - Fm: 0-0
Distance: 2m/2m3: 0-2 2m4-2m7: 0-0 3m+: 0-0
Track: LH: 0-2 RH: 0-0 Tight: 0-0 Gall: 0-0
Aids: Bl: 0-0 Vi: 0-0 Tstrap: 0-0
Best Rating: 88 3/02 Wwck 2m gd-sft NHF

Has shown some ability in bumpers.

Red Square Dawn

102 **73**

6-y-o b m Derrylin-Raise The Dawn (Rymer)
Mrs L Williamson Halewood International Ltd

Placings:02-0P0P642 (4779)

2001/02: 16^{0}S, 17^{P}GS, 16^{0}G, 21^{P}S, 19^{6}HY, 20^{4}G, 21^{2}GF

	Starts	1st	2nd	3rd	Win & Pl
Hurdles	7	0	1	0	799
Career Total	**9**	**0**	**2**	**0**	**1235**

Going: Sf: 0-3 GS: 0-1 Gd: 0-2 GF: - Fm: 0-1
Distance: 2m/2m3: 0-3 2m4-2m7: 0-4 3m+: 0-0
Track: LH: 0-5 RH: 0-2 Tight: 0-3 Gall: 0-0
Aids: Bl: 0-4 Vi: 0-0 Tstrap: 0-0
Best Rating: 73 4/02 Uttx 2m4f110y good Hdl

Poor form in novice hurdles.

Red Square Island

74 **70**

7-y-o ch g Jupiter Island-Queen Of The Nile (Hittite Glory)
Mrs L Williamson Miss Judy Eaton

Placings:P000 (4283)

2001/02: 16^{P}S, 16^{0}GS, 19^{0}S, 17^{0}GS

	Starts	1st	2nd	3rd	Win & Pl
Hurdles	4	0	0	0	
Career Total	**4**	**0**	**0**	**0**	

Going: Sf: 0-2 GS: 0-2 Gd: 0-0 GF: - Fm: 0-0
Distance: 2m/2m3: 0-3 2m4-2m7: 0-1 3m+: 0-0
Track: LH: 0-0 RH: 0-4 Tight: 0-2 Gall: 0-0
Aids: Bl: 0-0 Vi: 0-0 Tstrap: 0-0
Best Rating: 70 2/02 Ludl 2m gd-sft Hdl

Red Square King

79 **71+**

4-y-o ch g Sure Blade (USA)-Patscilla (Squill (USA))
Mrs L Williamson Halewood International Ltd

Placings:050 (3155)

2001/02: 17^{0}G, 17^{5}GS, 19^{0}S

	Starts	1st	2nd	3rd	Win & Pl
Hurdles	3	0	0	0	0
Career Total	**3**	**0**	**0**	**0**	**0**

Going: Sf: 0-1 GS: 0-1 Gd: 0-1 GF: - Fm: 0-0
Distance: 2m/2m3: 0-2 2m4-2m7: 0-1 3m+: 0-0
Track: LH: 0-1 RH: 0-2 Tight: 0-1 Gall: 0-0
Aids: Bl: 0-0 Vi: 0-0 Tstrap: 0-0
Best Rating: 50 11/01 Hrfd 2m1f good Hdl

Red Stranger (FR)

92 | 74

5-y-o b g Le Balafre (FR)-Abeille Royale (USA) (Turn To Mars (USA))

M C Pipe Terry Neill

Placings: *0-03*00524PP (3401)

2001/02: 17^{0}GF, 17^{3}G, 24^{0}G, 17^{0}GF, 16^{5}GF, 22^{2}GF, 24^{4}GF, 22^{P}G, 22^{P}S

	Starts	1st	2nd	3rd	Win & Pl
NH Flat	2	0	0	1	326
Hurdles	7	0	1	0	728
Career Total	**10**	**0**	**1**	**1**	**1054**

Going: Sf: 0-1 GS: 0-0 Gd: 0-3 GF: - Fm: 0-5
Distance: 2m/2m3: 0-4 2m4-2m7: 0-3 3m+: 0-2
Track: LH: 0-5 RH: 0-1 Tight: 0-5 Gall: 0-0
Aids: Bl: 0-0 Vi: 0-4 Tstrap: 0-1
Best Rating: 84 6/01 NAbb 2m1f good NHF

Has shown a little ability in bumpers and novice hurdles. Needs a distance of ground.

Red Striker

114(108h) | 157

8-y-o ch g Gunner B-Cover Your Money (Precipice Wood)

N B Mason N B Mason

Placings: *45/*2222211110/**2F1215141152-0P1PP** (4234)

2001/02: 20^{0}S, 25^{P}GS, 24^{1}S, 24^{P}G, 20^{P}GS

	Starts	1st	2nd	3rd	Win & Pl
Chases	5	1	0	0	26100
Career Total	**29**	**10**	**8**	**0**	**93162**

157	1/02	Hayd	3m	A HCh	SFT	£26100
151	4/01	Aint	2m4f	C HCh	SFT	£15925
133	3/01	Hntg	2m5f110y	D(0-125)HHdl	SFT	£3666
152	1/01	Newc	2m4f	A Ch	SFT	£14500
143	11/00	Carl	2m	D Ch	SFT	£4153
134	10/00	Kels	2m1f	E Ch	G-S	£2990
118	2/00	Bang	2m1f	E Hdl	G-S	£2828
118	2/00	Muss	2m4f	F(0-100)HHdl	G-S	£2743
115	1/00	Sthl	2m4f110y	E(0-105)HHdl	G-S	£2506
105	11/99	Kels	2m6f110y	E(0-105)HHdl	GD	£2815

Total win prize-money £78227

Going: Sf: 1-2 GS: 0-2 Gd: 0-1 GF: - Fm: 0-0
Distance: 2m/2m3: 0-0 2m4-2m7: 0-2 **3m+: 1-3**
Track: **LH: 1-4** RH: 0-1 Tight: 0-0 Gall: 0-1
Aids: Bl: 0-0 Vi: 0-0 **Tstrap: 1-5**
Best Rating: 157 1/02 Hayd 3m soft Ch

He enjoyed a cracking first season over fences, putting up an impressive display in a valuable novices' handicap at Aintree in April 2001. Began the New Year in encouraging style winning the Peter Marsh Chase. Effective over a variety of trips, he is probably best with some cut in the ground. Stays three miles.

Red Sun

108 | 110

5-y-o b g Foxhound (USA)-Superetta (Superlative)

A Streeter Bulls Head Racing Club

Placings: F6P-32FP662 (4848)

2001/02: 16^{3}GF, 17^{2}GS, 16^{F}G, 16^{P}HY, 16^{6}GS, 16^{6}G, 16^{2}G

	Starts	1st	2nd	3rd	Win & Pl
Hurdles	7	0	2	1	2368
Career Total	**10**	**0**	**2**	**1**	**2368**

Going: Sf: 0-1 GS: 0-2 Gd: 0-3 GF: - Fm: 0-1
Distance: 2m/2m3: 0-7 2m4-2m7: 0-0 3m+: 0-0
Track: LH: 0-6 RH: 0-1 Tight: 0-3 Gall: 0-0
Aids: Bl: 0-0 Vi: 0-0 Tstrap: 0-0
Best Rating: 110 4/02 Strf 2m110y good Hdl

Showed improved form when narrowly beaten in two mile novices' handicap hurdle at Stratford April 2002.

Red Supporter

81 | 82

5-y-o b m Priolo (USA)-Souveniers (Relko)

S Magnier M A Scaife

Placings: *002* (2307)

2001/02: 17^{0}GS, 16^{0}G, 19^{2}GF

	Starts	1st	2nd	3rd	Win & Pl
NH Flat	2	0	0	0	0
Hurdles	1	0	1	0	545
Career Total	**3**	**0**	**1**	**0**	**545**

Going: Sf: 0-0 GS: 0-1 Gd: 0-1 GF: - Fm: 0-1
Distance: 2m/2m3: 0-3 2m4-2m7: 0-0 3m+: 0-0
Track: LH: 0-3 RH: 0-0 Tight: 0-3 Gall: 0-0
Aids: Bl: 0-0 Vi: 0-1 Tstrap: 0-1
Best Rating: 82 11/01 Catt 2m3f gd-fm Hdl

Red Tower

60

7-y-o b g Damister (USA)-Tower Of Ivory (IRE) (Cyrano De Bergerac)

L Wells High As A Kite

Placings: *4/05/*06 (1222)

2001/02: 16^{0}GF, 18^{6}GF

	Starts	1st	2nd	3rd	Win & Pl
Hurdles	2	0	0	0	0
Career Total	**5**	**0**	**0**	**0**	**0**

Going: Sf: 0-0 GS: 0-0 Gd: 0-0 GF: - Fm: 0-2
Distance: 2m/2m3: 0-2 2m4-2m7: 0-0 3m+: 0-0
Track: LH: 0-2 RH: 0-0 Tight: 0-1 Gall: 0-0
Aids: Bl: 0-0 Vi: 0-0 Tstrap: 0-0
Best Rating: 97 4/99 MRas 1m5f110y soft NHF

Redde (IRE)

116 | 119

7-y-o ch g Classic Memory-Stoney Broke (Pauper)

R J Smith M Stock,D Jackson,R W Hibberd,C Harrison

Placings: *2110-*F51P21 (4149)

2001/02: 24^{F}GS, 20^{5}G, 17^{1}HY, 22^{P}HY, 16^{2}S, 20^{1}GS

	Starts	1st	2nd	3rd	Win & Pl
Hurdles	6	2	1	0	11156
Career Total	**10**	**4**	**2**	**0**	**21273**

119	3/02	Chep	2m4f	C(0-135)HHdl	G-S	£5018
116	1/02	Carl	2m1f	D Hdl	HVY	£3526
123	2/01	Newb	2m110y	B NHF	SFT	£8190
110	11/00	Chep	2m110y	H NHF	HVY	£1505

Total win prize-money £18239

Going: Sf: 1-3 GS: 1-2 Gd: 0-1 GF: - Fm: 0-0
Distance: 2m/2m3: 1-2 2m4-2m7: 1-3 3m+: 0-1
Track: LH: 1-4 RH: 1-2 Tight: 0-0 Gall: 0-1
Aids: Bl: 0-0 Vi: 0-0 Tstrap: 0-0
Best Rating: 123 2/01 Newb 2m110y soft NHF

A dual bumper winner, he relishes the mud and is a decent handicap hurdler from two to two and a half miles.

Redemption

116 | 159

7-y-o b g Sanglamore (USA)-Ypha (USA) (Lyphard (USA))

P R Webber Mr John Duggan & Mr Michael Purtill

Placings: 60460/31150F/**2FF116-12136P** (4255)

2001/02: 20^{1}G, 20^{2}G, 16^{1}GF, 16^{3}G, 16^{6}G, 21^{P}G

	Starts	1st	2nd	3rd	Win & Pl
Chases	6	2	1	1	29212
Career Total	**23**	**6**	**2**	**2**	**43102**

155	11/01	Asct	2m	B HCh	G-F	£13380
159	10/01	Weth	2m4f110y	B(0-145)HCh	GD	£9064
145	1/01	Weth	2m	E Ch	HVY	£3003
143	1/01	Plum	2m4f	E Ch	G-S	£2964
121	2/00	Ludl	2m	E Hdl	GD	£2352
118	12/99	Weth	2m	D Hdl	G-S	£3460

Total win prize-money £34224

Going: Sf: 0-0 GS: 0-0 Gd: 1-5 GF: - Fm: 1-1
Distance: 2m/2m3: 1-3 2m4-2m7: 1-3 3m+: 0-0
Track: LH: 1-3 RH: 1-3 Tight: 0-0 Gall: 0-1
Aids: Bl: 0-0 Vi: 0-0 Tstrap: 0-0
Best Rating: 159 1/02 Asct 2m good Ch

A talented individual, he took a couple of sloppy falls before winning two novice chases in the middle of the 2000/2001 season. He scored at Wetherby on his reappearance and at Ascot in November in the style of a progressive chaser, before running with credit at the same track subsequently. Stays two and a half miles but probably better over two miles in a strongly-run race. Acts on any ground, although arguably best on good or slightly softer.

Redgrave Wolf

99 | 83+

9-y-o ch m Little Wolf-Redgrave Rose (Tug Of War)

K Bishop Barford Park Racing

Placings: *3/000600/20255/12/*P0-0 (0074)

2001/02: 19^{0}G

	Starts	1st	2nd	3rd	Win & Pl
Chases	1	0	0	0	
Career Total	**17**	**1**	**3**	**1**	**4319**

85	5/99	Towc	3m	F(0-100)HHdl	G-F	£1807

Total win prize-money £1807

Going: Sf: 0-0 GS: 0-0 Gd: 0-1 GF: - Fm: 0-0
Distance: 2m/2m3: 0-0 2m4-2m7: 0-1 3m+: 0-0
Track: LH: 0-0 RH: 0-1 Tight: 0-0 Gall: 0-0
Aids: Bl: 0-1 Vi: 0-0 Tstrap: 0-0
Best Rating: 85 5/99 Extr 2m6f gd-fm Hdl

Redhanded

76 | 69

11-y-o ch m Scallywag-Hot Handed (Nearly A Hand)

D Brace David Brace

Placings: *30066/6P440/44/50* (1479)

2001/02: 23^{5}GF, 21^{0}GS

	Starts	1st	2nd	3rd	Win & Pl
Hurdles	2	0	0	0	0
Career Total	**14**	**0**	**0**	**1**	**374**

Going: Sf: 0-0 GS: 0-1 Gd: 0-0 GF: - Fm: 0-1
Distance: 2m/2m3: 0-0 2m4-2m7: 0-1 3m+: 0-1
Track: LH: 0-2 RH: 0-0 Tight: 0-2 Gall: 0-0
Aids: Bl: 0-0 Vi: 0-0 Tstrap: 0-0
Best Rating: 95 10/97 Bang 2m1f good NHF

Redmire

8-y-o b m Nomadic Way (USA)-Decent Sort (Decent Fellow)
Miss V J Parvin (Trainer Unknown 7/4) J H Hewitt

Placings:4 **(4777)**
2001/02: 25^{4}G

	Starts	1st	2nd	3rd	Win & Pl
Chases	1	0	0	0	84
Career Total	**1**	**0**	**0**	**0**	**84**

Going: Sf: 0-0 GS: 0-0 Gd: 0-1 GF: - Fm: 0-0
Distance: 2m/2m3: 0-0 2m4-2m7: 0-0 3m+: 0-1
Track: LH: 0-0 RH: 0-1 Tight: 0-1 Gall: 0-0
Aids: Bl: 0-0 Vi: 0-0 Tstrap: 0-0
Best Rating: 75 4/02 MRas 3m1f good Ch

Redouble

102 **90**
6-y-o b g First Trump-Sunflower Seed (Mummy's Pet)
B R Millman The Dragisic Partnership

Placings:0-0060202 **(4484)**
2001/02: 17^{0}F, 16^{0}GS, 17^{6}G, 21^{0}HY, 19^{2}HY, 17^{0}G, 17^{2}G

	Starts	1st	2nd	3rd	Win & Pl
Hurdles	7	0	2	0	1502
Career Total	**8**	**0**	**2**	**0**	**1502**

Going: Sf: 0-2 GS: 0-1 Gd: 0-3 GF: - Fm: 0-1
Distance: 2m/2m3: 0-5 2m4-2m7: 0-2 3m+: 0-0
Track: LH: 0-0 RH: 0-6 Tight: 0-1 Gall: 0-0
Aids: Bl: 0-1 Vi: 0-0 Tstrap: 0-0
Best Rating: 90 3/02 Extr 2m1f good Hdl

Modest hurdler, stays two and a half miles and acts on soft ground.

Redskin Raider (IRE)

98 **105**
6-y-o b g Commanche Run-Sheltered (IRE) (Strong Gale)
T R George Mrs Christine Davies

Placings:*00*-0033P20 **(4877)**
2001/02: 17^{0}S, 18^{0}G, 16^{3}GS, 19^{3}GS, 20^{P}GS, 22^{2}G, 24^{0}G

	Starts	1st	2nd	3rd	Win & Pl
NH Flat	1	0	0	0	0
Hurdles	6	0	1	2	1956
Career Total	**9**	**0**	**1**	**2**	**1956**

Going: Sf: 0-1 GS: 0-3 Gd: 0-3 GF: - Fm: 0-0
Distance: 2m/2m3: 0-3 2m4-2m7: 0-3 3m+: 0-1
Track: LH: 0-1 RH: 0-5 Tight: 0-3 Gall: 0-0
Aids: Bl: 0-0 Vi: 0-0 Tstrap: 0-0
Best Rating: 105 4/02 Winc 2m6f good Hdl

Fair two mile novice hurdler, he acts on an easy surface and stays two miles six.

Redwood Grove (USA)

100 **116**
6-y-o b g Woodman (USA)-Ikebana (IRE) (Sadler's Wells (USA))
N A Gaselee D R Stoddart

Placings:1435-06P50046 **(4550)**

2001/02: 17^{0}G, 17^{6}S, 16^{P}S, 16^{5}G, 24^{0}GS, 24^{0}S, 22^{4}GS, 21^{6}GF

	Starts	1st	2nd	3rd	Win & Pl
Hurdles	6	0	0	0	560
Chases	2	0	0	0	0
Career Total	**12**	**1**	**0**	**1**	**3849**

117	11/00	Wwck	2m	E Hdl	SFT	£2119

Total win prize-money £2120

Going: Sf: 0-3 GS: 0-2 Gd: 0-2 GF: - Fm: 0-1
Distance: 2m/2m3: 0-4 2m4-2m7: 0-2 3m+: 0-2
Track: LH: 0-2 RH: 0-6 Tight: 0-1 Gall: 0-2
Aids: Bl: 0-1 Vi: 0-0 Tstrap: 0-1
Best Rating: 119 3/01 Newb 2m110y heavy Hdl

Fair hurdler, but has failed to progress from a winning debut. Seems to handle most ground, but did not appear to take to chasing in autumn 2001.

Reeds Rains

4-y-o b f Mind Games-Me Spede (Valiyar)
T D Easterby Ron George

Placings:P **(1718)**
2001/02: 16^{P}G

	Starts	1st	2nd	3rd	Win & Pl
Hurdles	1	0	0	0	
Career Total	**1**	**0**	**0**	**0**	

Going: Sf: 0-0 GS: 0-0 Gd: 0-1 GF: - Fm: 0-0
Distance: 2m/2m3: 0-1 2m4-2m7: 0-0 3m+: 0-0
Track: LH: 0-1 RH: 0-0 Tight: 0-0 Gall: 0-0
Aids: Bl: 0-0 Vi: 0-0 Tstrap: 0-0
Best Rating: mfy

Reefer Dancer

89(94h) **45**
7-y-o ch g Keen-Silent Dancer (Quiet Fling (USA))
J C Tuck The Reefer Partnership

Placings:*60*P03/50060P-P0 **(0487)**
2001/02: 21^{P}GF, 18^{0}GF

	Starts	1st	2nd	3rd	Win & Pl
Chases	2	0	0	0	
Career Total	**13**	**0**	**0**	**1**	**356**

Going: Sf: 0-0 GS: 0-0 Gd: 0-0 GF: - Fm: 0-2
Distance: 2m/2m3: 0-1 2m4-2m7: 0-1 3m+: 0-0
Track: LH: 0-0 RH: 0-1 Tight: 0-1 Gall: 0-0
Aids: Bl: 0-0 Vi: 0-0 Tstrap: 0-0
Best Rating: 91 10/99 Chel 2m110y good NHF

Reel Dancer

101f **107f**
5-y-o b g Minshaanshu Amad (USA)-Sister Rosarii (USA) (Properantes (USA))
B De Haan The Play 4 Partnership

Placings:*632* **(4269)**
2001/02: 18^{6}G, 16^{3}S, 16^{2}S

	Starts	1st	2nd	3rd	Win & Pl
NH Flat	3	0	1	1	794
Career Total	**3**	**0**	**1**	**1**	**794**

Going: Sf: 0-2 GS: 0-0 Gd: 0-1 GF: - Fm: 0-0
Distance: 2m/2m3: 0-3 2m4-2m7: 0-0 3m+: 0-0
Track: LH: 0-2 RH: 0-1 Tight: 0-1 Gall: 0-0
Aids: Bl: 0-0 Vi: 0-0 Tstrap: 0-0
Best Rating: 107 2/02 Sand 2m110y soft NHF

Placed form in bumpers. Acts on soft/heavy ground.

Reel Handsome

101 **96**
10-y-o ch g Handsome Sailor-Reel Chance (Proverb)
C T Pogson C T Pogson

Placings:PPB360/3SP452-P4PU35F266400 **(4872)**
2001/02: 24^{P}F, 17^{4}GS, 22^{P}G, 24^{U}GF, 16^{3}GS, 16^{5}G, 20^{F}GS, 16^{2}S, 16^{6}S, 16^{6}HY, 17^{4}G, 17^{0}G, 16^{0}GF

	Starts	1st	2nd	3rd	Win & Pl
Chases	13	0	1	1	2007
Career Total	**25**	**0**	**2**	**3**	**5484**

Going: Sf: 0-3 GS: 0-3 Gd: 0-4 GF: - Fm: 0-3
Distance: 2m/2m3: 0-9 2m4-2m7: 0-2 3m+: 0-2
Track: LH: 0-5 RH: 0-8 Tight: 0-7 Gall: 0-2
Aids: Bl: 0-0 Vi: 0-0 Tstrap: 0-13
Best Rating: 96 4/02 MRas 2m1f110y good Ch

Moderate maiden, with his best recent effort coming over two miles on soft ground over fences.

Reeves (IRE)

83 **73**
10-y-o b g Caerleon (USA)-Kalkeen (Sheshoon)
F Jordan Mrs S J Le Gros

Placings:*211100*/000P/6P **(0552)**
2001/02: 17^{6}GF, 21^{P}GF

	Starts	1st	2nd	3rd	Win & Pl
Hurdles	2	0	0	0	0
Career Total	**12**	**3**	**1**	**0**	**14643**

105	8/96	Tral	2m	Hdl	G-Y	£7061
105	8/96	Gway	2m	NHF	G-F	£4237
105	7/96	Naas	2m3f	NHF	G-F	£2824

Total win prize-money £14124

Going: Sf: 0-0 GS: 0-0 Gd: 0-0 GF: - Fm: 0-2
Distance: 2m/2m3: 0-1 2m4-2m7: 0-1 3m+: 0-0
Track: LH: 0-1 RH: 0-1 Tight: 0-1 Gall: 0-1
Aids: Bl: 0-0 Vi: 0-0 Tstrap: 0-0
Best Rating: 105 8/96 Tral 2m gd-yld Hdl

Reflective Way

103 **102**
9-y-o ch m Mirror Boy-Craigie Way (Palm Track)
A C Whillans Duncan D Stewart

Placings:P0234 **(4889)**
2001/02: 24^{P}S, 21^{0}S, 25^{2}S, 26^{3}GS, 26^{4}G

	Starts	1st	2nd	3rd	Win & Pl
Hurdles	1	0	0	0	0
Chases	4	0	1	1	2407
Career Total	**5**	**0**	**1**	**1**	**2407**

Going: Sf: 0-3 GS: 0-1 Gd: 0-1 GF: - Fm: 0-0
Distance: 2m/2m3: 0-0 2m4-2m7: 0-1 3m+: 0-4
Track: LH: 0-2 RH: 0-2 Tight: 0-1 Gall: 0-0
Aids: Bl: 0-0 Vi: 0-0 Tstrap: 0-1
Best Rating: 93 3/02 Ayr 3m1f soft Ch

Improved over fences during the spring of 2002 and scored at Hexham in May. Suited by trips of around three miles and fast ground.

Reflex Blue

90 **81**
5-y-o b g Ezzoud (IRE)-Briggsmaid (Elegant Air)
R J Price (J W Hills 28/11) Fox And Cub Partnership

Placings:460006 **(4757)**
2001/02: 16^{4}GF, 19^{6}GF, 16^{0}G, 26^{0}GS, 26^{0}G, 16^{6}GF

	Starts	1st	2nd	3rd	Win & Pl
Hurdles	6	0	0	0	0
Career Total	**6**	**0**	**0**	**0**	**0**

Going: Sf: 0-0 GS: 0-1 Gd: 0-2 GF: - Fm: 0-3
Distance: 2m/2m3: 0-3 2m4-2m7: 0-1 3m+: 0-2
Track: LH: 0-3 RH: 0-3 Tight: 0-1 Gall: 0-1
Aids: Bl: 0-0 Vi: 0-0 Tstrap: 0-0
Best Rating: 81 8/01 Sthl 2m gd-fm Hdl

Held over hurdles.

Reflex Courier (IRE)

103 **109**

10-y-o b g Over The River (FR)-Thornpark Lady (Mandalus)
John R Upson Martin Tucker

Placings:425PBPF0/11PP23/314254-14PU36 (4497)
2001/02: 22^{1}G, 24^{4}GS, 24^{P}HY, 24^{U}S, 24^{3}S, 24^{6}G

	Starts	1st	2nd	3rd	Win & Pl
Chases	6	1	0	1	4890
Career Total	**26**	**4**	**3**	**3**	**19407**

106	11/01	Hayd	2m6f	F(0-110)HCh	GD	£3601
114	11/00	Leic	2m7f110y	F(0-110)HCh	G-S	£2678
114	11/99	MRas	3m1f	F(0-105)HCh	G-S	£3018
103	10/99	Bang	3m110y	F(0-105)HCh	SFT	£3875

Total win prize-money £13173

Going: Sf: 0-3 GS: 0-1 Gd: 1-2 GF: - Fm: 0-0
Distance: 2m/2m3: 0-0 **2m4-2m7: 1-1** 3m+: 0-5
Track: LH: 0-3 RH: 0-2 Tight: 0-2 Gall: 0-0
Aids: Bl: 0-0 Vi: 0-0 Tstrap: 0-0
Best Rating: 114 11/00 Leic 2m7f110y gd-sft Ch

Fair chaser, stays three miles, acts on good ground or softer.

Reflex Reaction (IRE)

96(86c) (39c)**62**

7-y-o b g Arapahos (FR)-Beswick Paper Lady (Giolla Mear)
John R Upson Mrs S Tucker

Placings:0/05P/2P-P440 **(3405)**
2001/02: 25^{P}GF, 21^{4}G, 24^{4}S, 23^{0}G

	Starts	1st	2nd	3rd	Win & Pl
Hurdles	2	0	0	0	316
Chases	2	0	0	0	0
Career Total	**10**	**0**	**1**	**0**	**999**

Going: Sf: 0-1 GS: 0-0 Gd: 0-2 GF: - Fm: 0-1
Distance: 2m/2m3: 0-0 2m4-2m7: 0-1 3m+: 0-3
Track: LH: 0-1 RH: 0-3 Tight: 0-0 Gall: 0-0
Aids: Bl: 0-0 Vi: 0-0 Tstrap: 0-0
Best Rating: 74 10/00 Towc 2m5f gd-fm Hdl

Regal Action (IRE)

(83h) (77h)

7-y-o b g King's Ride-Good Calx (Khalkis)
J J O'Neill A & G Oliver

Placings:0P0-P **(1276)**
2001/02: 24^{P}GF

	Starts	1st	2nd	3rd	Win & Pl
Chases	1	0	0	0	
Career Total	**4**	**0**	**0**	**0**	

Going: Sf: 0-0 GS: 0-0 Gd: 0-0 GF: - Fm: 0-1
Distance: 2m/2m3: 0-0 2m4-2m7: 0-0 3m+: 0-1
Track: LH: 0-1 RH: 0-0 Tight: 0-0 Gall: 0-0
Aids: Bl: 0-0 Vi: 0-0 Tstrap: 0-0
Best Rating: 77 4/01 Hayd 2m soft Hdl

Regal Air (IRE)

4-y-o b f Distinctly North (USA)-Dignified Air (FR) (Wolver Hollow)
L R James (B I Case 25/11) L R Lloyd-James

Placings:6 **(2324)**
2001/02: 16^{6}S

	Starts	1st	2nd	3rd	Win & Pl
Hurdles	1	0	0	0	0
Career Total	**1**	**0**	**0**	**0**	**0**

Going: Sf: 0-1 GS: 0-0 Gd: 0-0 GF: - Fm: 0-0
Distance: 2m/2m3: 0-1 2m4-2m7: 0-0 3m+: 0-0
Track: LH: 0-1 RH: 0-0 Tight: 0-1 Gall: 0-0
Aids: Bl: 0-0 Vi: 0-0 Tstrap: 0-0
Best Rating:

Regal Aura (IRE)

12-y-o ch g Glow (USA)-Dignified Air (FR) (Wolver Hollow)
D C O'Brien D C O'Brien

Placings:31131200/240006/**FP/6114/P214/3P14P/PP P-P (4172)**
2001/02: 26^{P}GS

	Starts	1st	2nd	3rd	Win & Pl
Chases	1	0	0	0	
Career Total	**33**	**7**	**3**	**3**	**24612**

100	2/99	Plum	2m5f	D(0-125)HCh	SFT	£3918
105	3/98	Plum	2m5f	E(0-110)HCh	SFT	£3210
90	3/97	Plum	2m5f	F(0-105)HCh	G-F	£2887
95	3/97	Plum	2m5f	E(0-110)HCh	G-S	£2837
93	12/93	Muss	2m	HHdl	GD	£2305
96	11/93	Kels	2m110y	Hdl	GD	£3420
91	10/93	Sedg	2m1f110y	Hdl	G-F	£1795

Total win prize-money £20373

Going: Sf: 0-0 GS: 0-1 Gd: 0-0 GF: - Fm: 0-0
Distance: 2m/2m3: 0-0 2m4-2m7: 0-0 3m+: 0-1
Track: LH: 0-0 RH: 0-0 Tight: 0-0 Gall: 0-0
Aids: Bl: 0-0 Vi: 0-0 Tstrap: 0-0
Best Rating: 105 3/98 Plum 2m5f soft Ch

Regal Bride

102 **75**

8-y-o b m Alhaatmi-Regal Ranee (Indian Ruler)
J R Cornwall Richard Chandler

Placings:PP30 **(3874)**
2001/02: 20^{P}G, 20^{P}G, 16^{3}S, 16^{0}S

	Starts	1st	2nd	3rd	Win & Pl
Hurdles	3	0	0	1	271
Chases	1	0	0	0	0
Career Total	**4**	**0**	**0**	**1**	**271**

Going: Sf: 0-2 GS: 0-0 Gd: 0-2 GF: - Fm: 0-0
Distance: 2m/2m3: 0-2 2m4-2m7: 0-2 3m+: 0-0
Track: LH: 0-1 RH: 0-3 Tight: 0-1 Gall: 0-2
Aids: Bl: 0-0 Vi: 0-0 Tstrap: 0-0
Best Rating: 75 2/02 Hntg 2m110y soft Hdl

Regal Exit (FR)

95 **124**

6-y-o ch g Exit To Nowhere (USA)-Regalante (Gairloch)
N J Henderson Brian Buckley

Placings:1312/6-000 **(4190)**
2001/02: 16^{0}GS, 16^{0}S, 16^{0}GS

	Starts	1st	2nd	3rd	Win & Pl
Hurdles	3	0	0	0	
Career Total	**8**	**2**	**1**	**1**	**29219**

134	3/00	Newb	2m110y	D Hdl	SFT	£3835
130	1/00	Chel	2m1f	B Hdl	SFT	£7020

Total win prize-money £10855

Going: Sf: 0-1 GS: 0-2 Gd: 0-0 GF: - Fm: 0-0
Distance: 2m/2m3: 0-3 2m4-2m7: 0-0 3m+: 0-0
Track: LH: 0-2 RH: 0-1 Tight: 0-0 Gall: 0-1
Aids: Bl: 0-0 Vi: 0-0 Tstrap: 0-0
Best Rating: 140 3/00 Chel 2m1f gd-fm Hdl

Beat all bar Snow Drop in the Triumph in 2000. He has had his problems and has been well held this term. Best at around two miles on soft ground.

Regal Holly

96 **118**

7-y-o b m Gildoran-Pusey Street (Native Bazaar)
C J Mann Dr David Harris & Mr Peter Simpson

Placings:*11*23/111135-034F00F5 **(3711)**
2001/02: 20^{0}GS, 24^{3}G, 20^{4}S, 21^{F}G, 20^{0}G, 21^{0}GS, 22^{F}HY, 21^{5}HY

	Starts	1st	2nd	3rd	Win & Pl
Hurdles	8	0	0	1	1655
Career Total	**18**	**6**	**1**	**3**	**43404**

130	2/01	Asct	2m4f	B(0-150)HHdl	HVY	£20923
123	1/01	Font	2m2f110y	D(0-125)HHdl	SFT	£4231
120	12/00	MRas	2m3f110y	D(0-125)HHdl	G-S	£7410
98	11/00	Catt	2m3f	F Hdl	GD	£1438
106	7/99	Worc	2m	H NHF	G-F	£1563
106	6/99	Worc	2m	H NHF	G-S	£1378

Total win prize-money £36947

Going: Sf: 0-3 GS: 0-2 Gd: 0-3 GF: - Fm: 0-0
Distance: 2m/2m3: 0-0 2m4-2m7: 0-7 3m+: 0-1
Track: LH: 0-3 RH: 0-4 Tight: 0-3 Gall: 0-0
Aids: Bl: 0-3 Vi: 0-0 Tstrap: 0-0
Best Rating: 130 2/01 Asct 2m4f heavy Hdl

A useful handicapper over hurdles in 2000/01 winning the William Hill Handicap Hurdle at Ascot. She has gone off the boil since then, however. Suited by ease in the ground, she is effective at around two miles to two miles four furlongs.

Regal Island

7-y-o b g Pharly (FR)-Regal Wonder (Stupendous)
N G Richards Mrs Linda Bott

Placings:*234*/05/4-0F **(3278)**
2001/02: 18^{0}GS, 17^{F}HY

	Starts	1st	2nd	3rd	Win & Pl
Hurdles	2	0	0	0	
Career Total	**8**	**0**	**1**	**1**	**717**

Going: Sf: 0-1 GS: 0-1 Gd: 0-0 GF: - Fm: 0-0
Distance: 2m/2m3: 0-2 2m4-2m7: 0-0 3m+: 0-0
Track: LH: 0-1 RH: 0-1 Tight: 0-1 Gall: 0-0
Aids: Bl: 0-0 Vi: 0-0 Tstrap: 0-0
Best Rating: 92 3/99 Catt 2m soft NHF

Regal River (IRE)

89 **83**

5-y-o b g Over The River (FR)-My Friend Fashion (Laurence O)

John R Upson Middleham Park Racing Xix

Placings:005P10 **(4415)**

2001/02: 20^{0}GF, 16^{0}S, 20^{5}G, 21^{P}GS, 24^{1}S, 22^{0}S

	Starts	1st	2nd	3rd	Win & Pl
Hurdles	6	1	0	0	2671
Career Total	**6**	**1**	**0**	**0**	**2671**

82 3/02 Towc 3m F(0-100)HHdl SFT £2670

Total win prize-money £2671

Going: Sf: 1-3 GS: 0-1 Gd: 0-1 GF: - Fm: 0-1
Distance: 2m/2m3: 0-1 2m4-2m7: 0-4 **3m+: 1-1**
Track: LH: 0-3 **RH: 1-3** Tight: 0-2 Gall: 0-1
Aids: Bl: 0-0 Vi: 0-0 Tstrap: 0-0
Best Rating: 83 11/01 Hayd 2m4f good Hdl

Fair handicap hurdler. Acts on a soft surface and is effective at three miles.

Regal Secret (IRE)

83 **2**

9-y-o b g Classic Secret (USA)-Majestic Nurse (On Your Mark)

H J Evans Mrs Jane Evans

Placings:000/05/P3P/0 **(1353)**

2001/02: 22^{0}GF

	Starts	1st	2nd	3rd	Win & Pl
Hurdles	1	0	0	0	
Career Total	**9**	**0**	**0**	**1**	**336**

Going: Sf: 0-0 GS: 0-0 Gd: 0-0 GF: - Fm: 0-1
Distance: 2m/2m3: 0-0 2m4-2m7: 0-1 3m+: 0-0
Track: LH: 0-1 RH: 0-0 Tight: 0-1 Gall: 0-0
Aids: Bl: 0-0 Vi: 0-0 Tstrap: 0-1
Best Rating: 70 5/99 Uttx 2m good Hdl

Regal Splendour (CAN)

82 **64**

9-y-o ch g Vice Regent (CAN)-Seattle Princess (USA) (Seattle Slew (USA))

I W McInnes (J W Mullins 21/5) Ian McInnes

Placings:60/0/0551PP-P000PP00 **(1580)**

2001/02: 17^{P}G, 16^{0}GF, 19^{0}GF, 21^{0}GS, 17^{P}GF, 17^{P}GF, 16^{0}G, 24^{0}GS

	Starts	1st	2nd	3rd	Win & Pl
Hurdles	8	0	0	0	
Career Total	**17**	**1**	**0**	**0**	**2698**

94 8/00 NAbb 2m1f F(0-100)HHdl G-F £2697

Total win prize-money £2698

Going: Sf: 0-0 GS: 0-2 Gd: 0-2 GF: - Fm: 0-4
Distance: 2m/2m3: 0-5 2m4-2m7: 0-2 3m+: 0-1
Track: LH: 0-2 RH: 0-5 Tight: 0-4 Gall: 0-1
Aids: Bl: 0-1 Vi: 0-0 Tstrap: 0-4
Best Rating: 94 8/00 NAbb 2m1f gd-fm Hdl

Regal Statesman (NZ)

(97h) (89h)**85**

9-y-o br g Vice Regal (NZ)-Hykit (NZ) (Swinging Junior)

O Brennan Lady Anne Bentinck

Placings:0/2PP-412PPP64 **(4871)**

2001/02: 16^{4}G, 23^{1}F, 20^{2}F, 20^{P}S, 25^{P}G, 19^{P}G, 24^{6}GS, 25^{4}GF

	Starts	1st	2nd	3rd	Win & Pl
Hurdles	6	1	1	0	4563
Chases	2	0	0	0	0
Career Total	**12**	**1**	**2**	**0**	**5335**

89 5/01 Weth 2m7f D Hdl FRM £3549

Total win prize-money £3549

Going: Sf: 0-1 GS: 0-1 Gd: 0-3 GF: - Fm: 1-3
Distance: 2m/2m3: 0-1 **2m4-2m7: 1-4** 3m+: 0-3
Track: **LH: 1-7** RH: 0-1 Tight: 0-0 Gall: 0-1
Aids: Bl: 0-0 Vi: 0-0 Tstrap: 0-0
Best Rating: 98 5/00 MRas 2m1f110y gd-fm Hdl

Novice hurdler, winner at Wetherby in 2001. Headstrong type.

Regal Vision (IRE)

101 **105**

5-y-o b g Emperor Jones (USA)-Shining Eyes (USA) (Mr Prospector (USA))

C G Cox The Lucky For Some Partnership

Placings:0-U124P34030 **(4817)**

2001/02: 16^{U}GF, 20^{1}G, 20^{2}G, 22^{4}G, 20^{P}HY, 21^{3}G, 22^{4}G, 24^{0}G, 21^{3}GF, 24^{0}GF

	Starts	1st	2nd	3rd	Win & Pl
Hurdles	10	1	1	2	3917
Career Total	**11**	**1**	**1**	**2**	**3917**

105 8/01 Bang 2m4f F Hdl GD £2268

Total win prize-money £2268

Going: Sf: 0-1 GS: 0-0 Gd: 1-6 GF: - Fm: 0-3
Distance: 2m/2m3: 0-1 **2m4-2m7: 1-7** 3m+: 0-2
Track: **LH: 1-5** RH: 0-4 **Tight: 1-4** Gall: 0-1
Aids: Bl: 0-3 Vi: 0-0 Tstrap: 0-0
Best Rating: 105 4/02 Hntg 2m5f110y gd-fm Hdl

Won a weak maiden hurdle at Bangor in 2001 and finished second in a better race there in October. Needs a test of stamina on a sound surface.

Reggae Rhythm (IRE)

75(77h) (113h)**98**

8-y-o b g Be My Native (USA)-Invery Lady (Sharpen Up)

Noel T Chance (Henry De Bromhead 14/11) Peter J Doyle

Placings:000*53*1*33*63/0020PF00/66231B465-025 **(3473)**

2001/02: 17^{0}G, 16^{2}Y, 16^{5}S

	Starts	1st	2nd	3rd	Win & Pl
Hurdles	1	0	1	0	1097
Chases	2	0	0	0	0
Career Total	**30**	**2**	**3**	**5**	**11607**

105 1/01 Tram 2m Hdl HVY £4451
102 11/98 Clon 2m NHF SFT £1942

Total win prize-money £6395

Going: Sf: 0-1 GS: 0-0 Gd: 0-1 GF: - Fm: 0-0
Distance: 2m/2m3: 0-3 2m4-2m7: 0-0 3m+: 0-0
Track: LH: 0-0 RH: 0-1 Tight: 0-1 Gall: 0-0
Aids: Bl: 0-0 Vi: 0-0 Tstrap: 0-0
Best Rating: 113 11/01 Tram 2m yield Hdl

An ex-Irish gelding who won over hurdles in his native country but failed to get off the mark over fences. Now with Noel Chance. Acts on soft/heavy ground.

Reggie Buck (USA)

110 **114**

8-y-o b/br g Alleged (USA)-Hello Memphis (USA) (Super Concorde (USA))

J Mackie Fools Who Dream

Placings:P0/25146/05121225/203UP2300-16U1215355 **(4593)**

2001/02: 16^{1}G, 16^{6}G, 17^{U}GS, 16^{1}G, 16^{2}G, 16^{1}G, 16^{5}GS, 16^{3}GS, 16^{5}S, 16^{5}G

	Starts	1st	2nd	3rd	Win & Pl
Hurdles	10	3	1	1	12765
Career Total	**34**	**6**	**7**	**3**	**31744**

114 11/01 Weth 2m D(0-125)HHdl GD £3445
114 10/01 Sthl 2m E(0-115)HHdl GD £2912
113 5/01 Hntg 2m110y F(0-105)HHdl GD £2922
113 1/00 Catt 2m D(0-120)HHdl GD £5547
100 12/99 Leic 2m F(0-110)HHdl GD £2332
99 1/99 Donc 2m110y F(0-110)HHdl GD £2066

Total win prize-money £19226

Going: Sf: 0-1 GS: 0-3 Gd: 3-6 GF: - Fm: 0-0
Distance: **2m/2m3: 3-10** 2m4-2m7: 0-0 3m+: 0-0
Track: **LH: 2-8** RH: 1-2 Tight: 1-2 Gall: 1-4
Aids: Bl: 0-0 Vi: 0-0 Tstrap: 0-0
Best Rating: 114 12/01 Hntg 2m110y gd-sft Hdl

A fair handicap hurdler, he acts well on good ground and is effective at around two miles.

Reggie Byrne

6-y-o b g Mon Tresor-Failand (Kala Shikari)

R Dickin Mrs Tessa Byrne

Placings:030/0 **(2269)**

2001/02: 19^{0}G

	Starts	1st	2nd	3rd	Win & Pl
Hurdles	1	0	0	0	
Career Total	**4**	**0**	**0**	**1**	**313**

Going: Sf: 0-0 GS: 0-0 Gd: 0-1 GF: - Fm: 0-0
Distance: 2m/2m3: 0-1 2m4-2m7: 0-0 3m+: 0-0
Track: LH: 0-1 RH: 0-0 Tight: 0-0 Gall: 0-0
Aids: Bl: 0-0 Vi: 0-0 Tstrap: 0-0
Best Rating: 74 12/99 Wwck 2m soft Hdl

Reginald Racquet (IRE)

85 **39**

6-y-o ch g Tremblant-Clonea Lady (IRE) (Lord Ha Ha)

Mrs A J Bowlby The Reg Partnership

Placings:*000*P6-050 **(1940)**

2001/02: 17^{0}GS, 19^{5}F, 21^{0}GS

	Starts	1st	2nd	3rd	Win & Pl
Hurdles	3	0	0	0	0
Career Total	**8**	**0**	**0**	**0**	**0**

Going: Sf: 0-0 GS: 0-2 Gd: 0-0 GF: - Fm: 0-1
Distance: 2m/2m3: 0-1 2m4-2m7: 0-2 3m+: 0-0
Track: LH: 0-1 RH: 0-2 Tight: 0-3 Gall: 0-0
Aids: Bl: 0-0 Vi: 0-0 Tstrap: 0-0
Best Rating: 71 5/00 Worc 2m gd-fm NHF

Reign Dance

11-y-o ch g Kinglet-Gay Criselle (Decoy Boy)

T D McCarthy Mrs D H McCarthy

Placings:13/44P/PP-P (0105)
2001/02: 20^{P}GF

	Starts	1st	2nd	3rd	Win & Pl
Chases	1	0	0	0	
Career Total	**8**	**1**	**0**	**1**	**2127**

102 3/98 Leic 2m4f110y H Ch SFT £1968
Total win prize-money £1968

Going: Sf: 0-0 GS: 0-0 Gd: 0-0 GF: - Fm: 0-1
Distance: 2m/2m3: 0-0 2m4-2m7: 0-1 3m+: 0-0
Track: LH: 0-0 RH: 0-0 Tight: 0-1 Gall: 0-0
Aids: Bl: 0-0 Vi: 0-0 Tstrap: 0-0
Best Rating: 102 3/98 Towc 2m6f gd-fm Ch

Reims (IRE)

83 77
4-y-o b g Topanoora-Fairy Folk (IRE) (Fairy King (USA))
T D Easterby Elite Racing Club

Placings:2 (1355)
2001/02: 16^{2}GF

	Starts	1st	2nd	3rd	Win & Pl
Hurdles	1	0	1	0	869
Career Total	**1**	**0**	**1**	**0**	**869**

Going: Sf: 0-0 GS: 0-0 Gd: 0-0 GF: - Fm: 0-1
Distance: 2m/2m3: 0-1 2m4-2m7: 0-0 3m+: 0-0
Track: LH: 0-1 RH: 0-0 Tight: 0-1 Gall: 0-0
Aids: Bl: 0-0 Vi: 0-0 Tstrap: 0-0
Best Rating: 77 9/01 Strf 2m110y gd-fm Hdl

Reiterate

99 83
9-y-o b m Then Again-Indubitable (Sharpo)
Mrs H M Bridges Mrs H M Bridges

Placings:P06/365 (4501)
2001/02: 20^{3}S, 21^{6}S, 27^{5}G

	Starts	1st	2nd	3rd	Win & Pl
Hurdles	3	0	0	1	362
Career Total	**6**	**0**	**0**	**1**	**362**

Going: Sf: 0-2 GS: 0-0 Gd: 0-1 GF: - Fm: 0-0
Distance: 2m/2m3: 0-0 2m4-2m7: 0-2 3m+: 0-1
Track: LH: 0-1 RH: 0-1 Tight: 0-2 Gall: 0-0
Aids: Bl: 0-0 Vi: 0-0 Tstrap: 0-0
Best Rating: 83 3/02 Ludl 2m5f soft Hdl

Winning pointer, modest novice hurdler.

Reiziger (FR)

103(115h) (138h)139
6-y-o gr g Balleroy (USA)-Dany Ohio (FR) (Script Ohio (USA))
P J Hobbs D Jones & B Thomas

Placings:121131133P-304141 (4026)
2001/02: 16^{3}G, 16^{0}G, 16^{4}HY, 16^{1}G, 19^{4}S, 18^{1}GS

	Starts	1st	2nd	3rd	Win & Pl
Hurdles	2	0	0	1	5175
Chases	4	2	0	0	10552
Career Total	**16**	**7**	**1**	**4**	**44295**

139 3/02 Newb 2m2f110y C Ch G-S £6890
117 12/01 Ludl 2m E Ch GD £3120
135 11/00 Chel 2m110y A Hdl G-S £12000
128 10/00 Extr 2m1f E Hdl GD £2710
115 6/00 NAbb 2m1f E Hdl GD £2492
115 5/00 Worc 2m E Hdl GD £2429
114 5/00 Ludl 2m E Hdl GD £2600
Total win prize-money £32241

Going: Sf: 0-2 GS: 1-1 Gd: 1-3 GF: - Fm: 0-0
Distance: **2m/2m3: 2-6** 2m4-2m7: 0-0 3m+: 0-0
Track: LH: 1-4 RH: 1-2 Tight: 1-2 Gall: 1-1
Aids: Bl: 0-0 Vi: 0-0 Tstrap: 0-0
Best Rating: 139 3/02 Newb 2m2f110y gd-sft Ch

Took to hurdling well in 2000/2001, winning several novice events and running well in better company. Switched to fences last term and got off the mark at Ludlow in December and also won at Newbury in March 2002. He is considered best when produced as late as possible, he acts well on good ground and is effective over two miles to two miles two.

Relative Delight

87 54
4-y-o b f Distant Relative-Pasja (IRE) (Posen (USA))
John A Harris (R Hollinshead 24/9) Ms S Queen

Placings:006F (4021)
2001/02: 16^{0}GF, 16^{0}G, 16^{6}HY, 16^{F}S

	Starts	1st	2nd	3rd	Win & Pl
Hurdles	4	0	0	0	0
Career Total	**4**	**0**	**0**	**0**	**0**

Going: Sf: 0-2 GS: 0-0 Gd: 0-1 GF: - Fm: 0-1
Distance: 2m/2m3: 0-4 2m4-2m7: 0-0 3m+: 0-0
Track: LH: 0-2 RH: 0-2 Tight: 0-0 Gall: 0-2
Aids: Bl: 0-0 Vi: 0-0 Tstrap: 0-0
Best Rating: 54 12/01 Donc 2m110y good Hdl

Relaxation (IRE)

108 139
10-y-o b g Orchestra-Lets Cruise (Deep Run)
H D Daly Mrs M P Wiggin & Sir P Payne-Gallwey

Placings:5/F24U21/0P00-1F (1864)
2001/02: 23^{1}GF, 24^{F}G

	Starts	1st	2nd	3rd	Win & Pl
Chases	2	1	0	0	4271
Career Total	**13**	**2**	**2**	**0**	**29737**

139 10/01 Extr 2m7f110y E(0-115)HCh G-F £4270
147 3/00 Chel 4m B Ch GD £21125
Total win prize-money £25396

Going: Sf: 0-0 GS: 0-0 Gd: 0-1 GF: - Fm: 1-1
Distance: 2m/2m3: 0-0 2m4-2m7: 0-0 **3m+: 1-2**
Track: LH: 0-1 **RH: 1-1** Tight: 0-0 Gall: 0-1
Aids: Bl: 0-0 Vi: 0-0 Tstrap: 0-0
Best Rating: 147 3/00 Chel 4m good Ch

A winning pointer, he gained his biggest moment when winning the four-mile National Hunt Chase at the 2000 Festival in clear-cut fashion. Stayed very well and relished fast ground. (DEAD)

Reliance Leader

6-y-o ch g Weld-Swift Messenger (Giolla Mear)
D L Williams Reliance Car Hire Services Ltd

Placings:00 (1845)
2001/02: 16^{0}G, 16^{0}S

	Starts	1st	2nd	3rd	Win & Pl
Hurdles	2	0	0	0	
Career Total	**2**	**0**	**0**	**0**	

Going: Sf: 0-1 GS: 0-0 Gd: 0-1 GF: - Fm: 0-0
Distance: 2m/2m3: 0-2 2m4-2m7: 0-0 3m+: 0-0
Track: LH: 0-0 RH: 0-2 Tight: 0-0 Gall: 0-0
Aids: Bl: 0-0 Vi: 0-0 Tstrap: 0-0
Best Rating:

Reluckino

12-y-o b g Buckley-Releta (Relkino)
Mrs D Mitchell The Bassett Partnership

Placings:00/30/002P/4/P02/0P1P/P0U (0427)
2001/02: 25^{P}G, 28^{0}GF, 33^{U}G

	Starts	1st	2nd	3rd	Win & Pl
Chases	3	0	0	0	
Career Total	**19**	**1**	**2**	**1**	**4745**

97 1/00 Plum 3m2f F(0-95)HCh SFT £2730
Total win prize-money £2730

Going: Sf: 0-0 GS: 0-0 Gd: 0-2 GF: - Fm: 0-1
Distance: 2m/2m3: 0-0 2m4-2m7: 0-0 3m+: 0-3
Track: LH: 0-1 RH: 0-1 Tight: 0-1 Gall: 0-0
Aids: Bl: 0-0 Vi: 0-0 Tstrap: 0-0
Best Rating: 97 1/00 Plum 3m2f soft Ch

Remanti

7-y-o b g Remezzo-Asti Spumante (FR) (Fireside Chat (USA))
B D Leavy J S Bickerton

Placings:P0/P/P-0 (0230)
2001/02: 16^{0}GF

	Starts	1st	2nd	3rd	Win & Pl
Hurdles	1	0	0	0	
Career Total	**5**	**0**	**0**	**0**	

Going: Sf: 0-0 GS: 0-0 Gd: 0-0 GF: - Fm: 0-1
Distance: 2m/2m3: 0-1 2m4-2m7: 0-0 3m+: 0-0
Track: LH: 0-0 RH: 0-1 Tight: 0-0 Gall: 0-1
Aids: Bl: 0-1 Vi: 0-0 Tstrap: 0-1
Best Rating: 57 4/99 MRas 1m5f110y good NHF

Remember Equiname

7-y-o gr m Belfort (FR)-Easby Mosella (Le Moss)
P Winkworth P Winkworth

Placings:0R0/P (1655)
2001/02: 17^{P}G

	Starts	1st	2nd	3rd	Win & Pl
Hurdles	1	0	0	0	
Career Total	**4**	**0**	**0**	**0**	

Going: Sf: 0-0 GS: 0-0 Gd: 0-1 GF: - Fm: 0-0
Distance: 2m/2m3: 0-1 2m4-2m7: 0-0 3m+: 0-0
Track: LH: 0-1 RH: 0-0 Tight: 0-1 Gall: 0-0
Aids: Bl: 0-0 Vi: 0-0 Tstrap: 0-0
Best Rating: 41 1/99 Hayd 2m soft NHF

Remember Star

102(95h) (80h)91
9-y-o ch m Don't Forget Me-Star Girl Gay (Lord Gayle (USA))
A D Smith Duckhaven Stud

Placings:60604P/000P304/404023344/260PP5110/10440-031601 (2291)
2001/02: 20^{0}G, 22^{3}GF, 17^{1}GF, 19^{6}S, 16^{0}G, 19^{1}GF

	Starts	1st	2nd	3rd	Win & Pl

Hurdles	4	1	0	1	2146
Chases	2	1	0	0	3693
Career Total	**42**	**5**	**2**	**4**	**13604**

91	11/01	Extr	2m3f110y	F(0-95)HCh	G-F	£3692
80	10/01	Extr	2m1f	G(0-95)HHdl	G-F	£1813
85	5/00	Extr	2m1f	G(0-95)HHdl	FRM	£1834
85	3/00	Extr	2m1f110y	G Hdl	G-F	£1939
72	3/00	Extr	2m1f110y	G(0-95)HHdl	G-S	£1599

Total win prize-money £10879

Going: Sf: 0-1 GS: 0-0 Gd: 0-2 GF: - Fm: 2-3
Distance: 2m/2m3: 1-3 2m4-2m7: 1-3 3m+: 0-0
Track: LH: 0-2 **RH: 2-4** Tight: 0-2 Gall: 0-0
Aids: Bl: 0-0 Vi: 0-0 **Tstrap: 1-3**
Best Rating: 91 11/01 Extr 2m3f110y gd-fm Ch

Plating-class hurdler/chaser, suited by fast ground and likes Exeter.

Remington (IRE)

87f 78f

4-y-o ch g Indian Ridge-Sea Harrier (Grundy)
Mrs S D Williams S A Douch

Placings:*0* (4639)
2001/02: 16^{0}GF

	Starts	1st	2nd	3rd	Win & Pl
NH Flat	1	0	0	0	
Career Total	**1**	**0**	**0**	**0**	

Going: Sf: 0-0 GS: 0-0 Gd: 0-0 GF: - Fm: 0-1
Distance: 2m/2m3: 0-1 2m4-2m7: 0-0 3m+: 0-0
Track: LH: 0-0 RH: 0-1 Tight: 0-0 Gall: 0-0
Aids: Bl: 0-0 Vi: 0-0 Tstrap: 0-0
Best Rating: 78 4/02 Asct 2m110y gd-fm NHF

Renaloo (IRE)

94(69h) 80

7-y-o gr g Tremblant-Rare Flower (Decent Fellow)
R Rowe Tim Clowes

Placings:*50046/006-056* (3815)
2001/02: 16^{0}G, 20^{5}GS, 16^{6}S

	Starts	1st	2nd	3rd	Win & Pl
Chases	3	0	0	0	0
Career Total	**11**	**0**	**0**	**0**	**0**

Going: Sf: 0-1 GS: 0-1 Gd: 0-1 GF: - Fm: 0-0
Distance: 2m/2m3: 0-2 2m4-2m7: 0-1 3m+: 0-0
Track: LH: 0-0 RH: 0-3 Tight: 0-2 Gall: 0-1
Aids: Bl: 0-0 Vi: 0-0 Tstrap: 0-0
Best Rating: 99 11/99 Wwck 2m good NHF

Renzo (IRE)

104 110

9-y-o b g Alzao (USA)-Watership (USA) (Foolish Pleasure (USA))
John A Harris (J L Harris 16/6) Cleartherm Ltd

Placings:1F2240/23220/U-60F24 (4010)
2001/02: 16^{6}G, 16^{0}GS, 16^{F}S, 16^{2}S, 16^{4}S

	Starts	1st	2nd	3rd	Win & Pl
Hurdles	5	0	1	0	2232
Career Total	**17**	**1**	**6**	**1**	**18195**

139	11/98	Asct	2m110y	C Hdl	G-S	£3940

Total win prize-money £3940

Going: Sf: 0-3 GS: 0-1 Gd: 0-1 GF: - Fm: 0-0
Distance: 2m/2m3: 0-5 2m4-2m7: 0-0 3m+: 0-0
Track: LH: 0-4 RH: 0-1 Tight: 0-0 Gall: 0-4
Aids: Bl: 0-0 Vi: 0-0 Tstrap: 0-0
Best Rating: 139 2/99 Asct 2m110y gd-sft Hdl

A stayer on the Flat, he won on his hurdling debut at Ascot in November 1998, but despite some creditable efforts in the meantime, failed to add to that over hurdles until winning at Market Rasen in June 2002. He has plenty of ability, but also a mind of his own. Acts on any ground and stays two and a half miles.

Repeat Performance (IRE)

4-y-o b g Mujadil (USA)-Encore Une Fois (IRE) (Shirley Heights)
W G M Turner P A N Bailey

Placings:P (1341)
2001/02: 17^{P}GF

	Starts	1st	2nd	3rd	Win & Pl
Hurdles	1	0	0	0	
Career Total	**1**	**0**	**0**	**0**	

Going: Sf: 0-0 GS: 0-0 Gd: 0-0 GF: - Fm: 0-1
Distance: 2m/2m3: 0-1 2m4-2m7: 0-0 3m+: 0-0
Track: LH: 0-1 RH: 0-0 Tight: 0-1 Gall: 0-0
Aids: Bl: 0-0 Vi: 0-0 Tstrap: 0-1
Best Rating:

Repulse Bay (IRE)

85 56

4-y-o b c Barathea (IRE)-Bourbon Topsy (Ile De Bourbon (USA))
J S Goldie (M R Channon 3/7) John Breslin

Placings:30P (2449)
2001/02: 16^{3}GS, 16^{0}GF, 16^{P}GS

	Starts	1st	2nd	3rd	Win & Pl
Hurdles	3	0	0	1	429
Career Total	**3**	**0**	**0**	**1**	**429**

Going: Sf: 0-0 GS: 0-2 Gd: 0-0 GF: - Fm: 0-1
Distance: 2m/2m3: 0-3 2m4-2m7: 0-0 3m+: 0-0
Track: LH: 0-3 RH: 0-0 Tight: 0-1 Gall: 0-1
Aids: Bl: 0-0 Vi: 0-0 Tstrap: 0-2
Best Rating: 56 11/01 Catt 2m gd-fm Hdl

Repunzel

105(103c) (88c)95

7-y-o b m Carlingford Castle-Hi-Rise Lady (Sunyboy)
N A Gaselee Michael Watt

Placings:*20*/0641/F05-64UP0P13 (3930)
2001/02: 16^{6}G, 16^{4}GF, 21^{U}GF, 20^{P}G, 19^{0}G, 22^{P}HY, 16^{1}HY, 16^{3}HY

	Starts	1st	2nd	3rd	Win & Pl
Hurdles	4	1	0	1	3794
Chases	4	0	0	0	243
Career Total	**17**	**2**	**1**	**1**	**7588**

95	1/02	Plum	2m	D(0-115)HHdl	HVY	£3304
98	4/00	Plum	2m	D Hdl	G-S	£2811

Total win prize-money £6115

Going: Sf: 1-3 GS: 0-0 Gd: 0-3 GF: - Fm: 0-2
Distance: **2m/2m3: 1-5** 2m4-2m7: 0-3 3m+: 0-0
Track: **LH: 1-5** RH: 0-2 **Tight: 1-5** Gall: 0-0
Aids: Bl: 0-0 Vi: 0-0 Tstrap: 0-0
Best Rating: 98 4/00 Plum 2m gd-sft Hdl

Modest handicap hurdler, suited by soft ground over two miles.

Resist The Force (USA)

12-y-o br g Shadeed (USA)-Countess Tully (Hotfoot)
M J Hogan Mrs Barbara Hogan

Placings:16P/P (0924)
2001/02: 17^{P}GF

	Starts	1st	2nd	3rd	Win & Pl
Hurdles	1	0	0	0	
Career Total	**4**	**1**	**0**	**0**	**3518**

109	11/96	Asct	2m110y	C Hdl	G-F	£3517

Total win prize-money £3518

Going: Sf: 0-0 GS: 0-0 Gd: 0-0 GF: - Fm: 0-1
Distance: 2m/2m3: 0-1 2m4-2m7: 0-0 3m+: 0-0
Track: LH: 0-1 RH: 0-0 Tight: 0-1 Gall: 0-0
Aids: Bl: 0-0 Vi: 0-0 Tstrap: 0-0
Best Rating: 110 12/96 Sand 2m110y good Hdl

Resistance (IRE)

63 29

5-y-o br g Phardante (FR)-Shean Hill (IRE) (Bar Dexter (USA))
G A Ham Corey M Gardner

Placings:*3-160* (1847)
2001/02: 17^{1}G, 16^{6}GF, 16^{0}G

	Starts	1st	2nd	3rd	Win & Pl
NH Flat	2	1	0	0	1785
Hurdles	1	0	0	0	0
Career Total	**4**	**1**	**0**	**1**	**2059**

99	5/01	Extr	2m1f	H NHF	GD	£1785

Total win prize-money £1785

Going: Sf: 0-0 GS: 0-0 Gd: 1-2 GF: - Fm: 0-1
Distance: **2m/2m3: 1-3** 2m4-2m7: 0-0 3m+: 0-0
Track: LH: 0-0 **RH: 1-3** Tight: 0-0 Gall: 0-1
Aids: Bl: 0-0 Vi: 0-0 Tstrap: 0-0
Best Rating: 106 5/01 Hntg 2m110y gd-fm NHF

Shaped well in above-average Fontwell bumper on debut and fulfilled that promise when winning at Exeter next time.

Restless Wind (IRE)

111 110

10-y-o b g Celio Rufo-Trulos (Three Dons)
G B Balding The Kingfisher Partnership

Placings:3UP/F5-340123 (4658)
2001/02: 24^{3}GS, 20^{4}S, 24^{0}G, 24^{1}S, 25^{2}S, 24^{3}G

	Starts	1st	2nd	3rd	Win & Pl
Chases	6	1	1	2	6746
Career Total	**11**	**1**	**1**	**3**	**7345**

106	3/02	Tntn	3m	F(0-90)Ch	SFT	£3150

Total win prize-money £3150

Going: Sf: 1-3 GS: 0-1 Gd: 0-2 GF: - Fm: 0-0
Distance: 2m/2m3: 0-0 2m4-2m7: 0-1 **3m+: 1-5**
Track: LH: 0-0 **RH: 1-6 Tight: 1-3** Gall: 0-1
Aids: Bl: 0-0 Vi: 0-0 Tstrap: 0-0
Best Rating: 110 3/02 Winc 3m1f110y soft Ch

Modest handicap chaser, stays three miles and acts in soft ground.

Ret Frem (IRE)

83(81h) (36h)89

9-y-o b g Posen (USA)-New Light (Reform)

A G Blackmore A G Blackmore

Placings:262/414/3/000/640645-0P056F6 (4547)
2001/02: 16^{0}G, 21^{P}G, 16^{0}GS, 21^{5}S, 24^{6}GS, 24^{F}G, 20^{6}GF

	Starts	1st	2nd	3rd	Win & Pl
Hurdles	1	0	0	0	0
Chases	6	0	0	0	0
Career Total	**23**	**1**	**2**	**1**	**4294**

82	9/97	Prth	2m4f110y	E Hdl	G-F	£2772

Total win prize-money £2772

Going: Sf: 0-1 GS: 0-2 Gd: 0-3 GF: - Fm: 0-1
Distance: 2m/2m3: 0-2 2m4-2m7: 0-3 3m+: 0-2
Track: LH: 0-2 RH: 0-5 Tight: 0-3 Gall: 0-3
Aids: Bl: 0-0 Vi: 0-1 Tstrap: 0-0
Best Rating: 89 3/02 Fknm 3m110y good Ch

Retribution

7-y-o b g Henbit (USA)-Snippet (Ragstone)
D McCain D McCain

Placings:*0/06*P-6PP (0800)
2001/02: 17^{6}GS, 16^{P}F, 16^{P}GF

	Starts	1st	2nd	3rd	Win & Pl
Hurdles	1	0	0	0	0
Chases	2	0	0	0	0
Career Total	**7**	**0**	**0**	**0**	**0**

Going: Sf: 0-0 GS: 0-1 Gd: 0-0 GF: - Fm: 0-2
Distance: 2m/2m3: 0-3 2m4-2m7: 0-0 3m+: 0-0
Track: LH: 0-1 RH: 0-2 Tight: 0-1 Gall: 0-0
Aids: Bl: 0-0 Vi: 0-0 Tstrap: 0-0
Best Rating: 88 4/00 Carl 2m1f gd-sft NHF

Retrospect

5-y-o ch g Sabrehill (USA)-Mysterious Maid (USA) (L'Emigrant (USA))
G Prodromou L Cohen

Placings:*00* (1586)
2001/02: 16^{0}GF, 17^{0}GS

	Starts	1st	2nd	3rd	Win & Pl
NH Flat	2	0	0	0	
Career Total	**2**	**0**	**0**	**0**	

Going: Sf: 0-0 GS: 0-1 Gd: 0-0 GF: - Fm: 0-1
Distance: 2m/2m3: 0-2 2m4-2m7: 0-0 3m+: 0-0
Track: LH: 0-1 RH: 0-1 Tight: 0-1 Gall: 0-0
Aids: Bl: 0-0 Vi: 0-0 Tstrap: 0-0
Best Rating:

Return The Call (IRE)

76f 65f
5-y-o b g Bob Back (USA)-Ring Four (IRE) (Supreme Leader)
Miss H C Knight H Stephen Smith & Harold Winton

Placings:*0* (2041)
2001/02: 16^{0}GS

	Starts	1st	2nd	3rd	Win & Pl
NH Flat	1	0	0	0	
Career Total	**1**	**0**	**0**	**0**	

Going: Sf: 0-0 GS: 0-1 Gd: 0-0 GF: - Fm: 0-0
Distance: 2m/2m3: 0-1 2m4-2m7: 0-0 3m+: 0-0
Track: LH: 0-0 RH: 0-1 Tight: 0-0 Gall: 0-0
Aids: Bl: 0-0 Vi: 0-0 Tstrap: 0-0
Best Rating: 65 11/01 Sand 2m110y gd-sft NHF

Returning

111(102h) 147
6-y-o b m Bob's Return (IRE)-Buck Comtess (USA) (Spend A Buck (USA))
Miss H C Knight Harold Winton

Placings:0001/4F3P511P23P-11112243F (4652)
2001/02: 17^{1}GF, 19^{1}F, 16^{1}GS, 19^{1}G, 16^{2}GS, 19^{2}G, 20^{4}GS, 19^{3}GS, 20^{F}G

	Starts	1st	2nd	3rd	Win & Pl
Chases	9	4	2	1	39859
Career Total	**24**	**7**	**3**	**3**	**51356**

145	11/01	Asct	2m3f110y	B Ch	GD	£9464
143	11/01	Sand	2m	D Ch	G-S	£4936
121	10/01	Tntn	2m3f	D Ch	FRM	£5538
121	10/01	Extr	2m1f110y	E Ch	G-F	£3526
110	12/00	Hrfd	2m3f110y	F(0-105)HHdl	HVY	£3344
104	12/00	Tntn	2m3f110y	D(0-120)HHdl	SFT	£2970
97	4/00	Carl	2m4f110y	E(0-105)HHdl	SFT	£2912

Total win prize-money £32692

Going: Sf: 0-0 GS: 1-4 Gd: 1-3 GF: - Fm: 2-2
Distance: **2m/2m3: 3-4** 2m4-2m7: 1-5 3m+: 0-0
Track: LH: 0-1 **RH: 4-8 Tight: 1-2** Gall: 0-0
Aids: Bl: 0-0 Vi: 0-0 Tstrap: 0-0
Best Rating: 147 12/01 Sand 2m gd-sft Ch

Ex-Irish mare, winner three times over hurdles in 2000/01. Took well to fences in the autumn of 2001, winning four times before finding the better novices too good, although not at all disgraced. She has won on fast ground, but looks ideally suited by cut. Stays two and a half miles.

Revamp (IRE)

64 17
5-y-o b g Shalford (IRE)-Golden Weaver (Reference Point)
D McCain D McCain

Placings:0P0 (4127)
2001/02: 17^{0}GS, 16^{P}HY, 17^{0}G

	Starts	1st	2nd	3rd	Win & Pl
Hurdles	3	0	0	0	
Career Total	**3**	**0**	**0**	**0**	

Going: Sf: 0-1 GS: 0-1 Gd: 0-1 GF: - Fm: 0-0
Distance: 2m/2m3: 0-3 2m4-2m7: 0-0 3m+: 0-0
Track: LH: 0-2 RH: 0-1 Tight: 0-1 Gall: 0-0
Aids: Bl: 0-1 Vi: 0-0 Tstrap: 0-0
Best Rating: 17 11/01 Bang 2m1f gd-sft Hdl

Revenge

101 96
6-y-o b g Saddlers' Hall (IRE)-Classic Heights (Shirley Heights)
C G Cox The Patient Dozen

Placings:3356/20300-0P52P (4502)
2001/02: 22^{0}S, 25^{P}S, 21^{5}HY, 20^{2}S, 22^{P}G

	Starts	1st	2nd	3rd	Win & Pl
Hurdles	5	0	1	0	1596
Career Total	**14**	**0**	**2**	**3**	**4181**

Going: Sf: 0-4 GS: 0-0 Gd: 0-1 GF: - Fm: 0-0
Distance: 2m/2m3: 0-0 2m4-2m7: 0-4 3m+: 0-1
Track: LH: 0-3 RH: 0-0 Tight: 0-2 Gall: 0-0
Aids: Bl: 0-4 Vi: 0-1 Tstrap: 0-0
Best Rating: 106 11/00 Wwck 2m5f heavy Hdl

Modest hurdler, stays two and a half miles.

Reverse Charge

95(109h) (121h)97
10-y-o b g Teenoso (USA)-Ebb And Flo (Forlorn River)
C Grant Ian W Glenton

Placings:0/31P20000/1211120/PP05OP-210062 (4487)
2001/02: 22^{2}G, 22^{1}S, 25^{0}S, 23^{0}HY, 24^{6}S, 26^{2}GS

	Starts	1st	2nd	3rd	Win & Pl
Hurdles	4	1	1	0	9184
Chases	2	0	1	0	1498
Career Total	**28**	**6**	**5**	**1**	**37481**

121	12/01	Hayd	2m6f	B(0-140)HHdl	SFT	£8238
128	1/00	Wwck	2m4f110y	B HHdl	SFT	£7264
130	12/99	Weth	2m7f	C(0-130)HHdl	G-S	£4857
116	12/99	Newc	2m4f	C(0-135)HHdl	SFT	£5272
105	11/99	MRas	2m1f110y	F(0-110)HHdl	G-S	£2290
92	7/98	MRas	2m1f110y	F Hdl	G-F	£1469

Total win prize-money £29392

Going: Sf: 1-4 GS: 0-1 Gd: 0-1 GF: - Fm: 0-0
Distance: 2m/2m3: 0-0 **2m4-2m7: 1-2** 3m+: 0-4
Track: **LH: 1-4** RH: 0-1 Tight: 0-1 Gall: 0-1
Aids: Bl: 0-0 Vi: 0-0 Tstrap: 0-0
Best Rating: 130 12/99 Weth 2m7f gd-sft Hdl

A tough staying hurdler, he won four times over hurdles in the 1999/2000 season over trips ranging from two miles one to two miles seven. Out of form the following season, he ran better on his reappearance in November 2001, and went on to win at Haydock a month later. Suited by soft ground. Showed little ability on his belated switch to fences.

Reverse Pace (IRE)

92f 99f
5-y-o b g Leading Counsel (USA)-Drumscap (IRE) (Remainder Man)
Mrs P Sly Terry O'Connor & Mark Ball

Placings:*06* (4552)
2001/02: 16^{0}GS, 16^{6}GF

	Starts	1st	2nd	3rd	Win & Pl
NH Flat	2	0	0	0	0
Career Total	**2**	**0**	**0**	**0**	**0**

Going: Sf: 0-0 GS: 0-1 Gd: 0-0 GF: - Fm: 0-1
Distance: 2m/2m3: 0-2 2m4-2m7: 0-0 3m+: 0-0
Track: LH: 0-0 RH: 0-2 Tight: 0-0 Gall: 0-1
Aids: Bl: 0-0 Vi: 0-0 Tstrap: 0-0
Best Rating: 99 3/02 Sand 2m110y gd-sft NHF

Reverse Swing

98 66
5-y-o b m Charmer-Milly Kelly (Murrayfield)
Mrs P Sly The Herons Partnership

Placings:060 (4025)
2001/02: 16^{0}G, 19^{6}GS, 16^{0}S

	Starts	1st	2nd	3rd	Win & Pl
Hurdles	3	0	0	0	0
Career Total	**3**	**0**	**0**	**0**	**0**

Going: Sf: 0-1 GS: 0-1 Gd: 0-1 GF: - Fm: 0-0
Distance: 2m/2m3: 0-2 2m4-2m7: 0-1 3m+: 0-0
Track: LH: 0-1 RH: 0-2 Tight: 0-1 Gall: 0-1
Aids: Bl: 0-0 Vi: 0-0 Tstrap: 0-0
Best Rating: 66 11/01 Wwck 2m good Hdl

Reviewer (IRE)

105 **122**

4-y-o b g Sadler's Wells (USA)-Clandestina (USA) (Secretariat (USA))

M C Pipe (M Meade 7/11) Martyn Meade

Placings:21P **(4250)**

2001/02: 16^{2}HY, 17^{1}GS, 17^{P}G

	Starts	1st	2nd	3rd	Win & Pl
Hurdles	3	1	1	0	4395
Career Total	**3**	**1**	**1**	**0**	**4395**

115 2/02 MRas 2m1f110y D Hdl G-S £3612

Total win prize-money £3612

Going: Sf: 0-1 GS: 1-1 Gd: 0-1 GF: - Fm: 0-0
Distance: **2m/2m3: 1-3** 2m4-2m7: 0-0 3m+: 0-0
Track: LH: 0-2 **RH: 1-1 Tight: 1-1** Gall: 0-1
Aids: Bl: 0-0 Vi: 0-0 Tstrap: 0-0
Best Rating: 122 1/02 Wwck 2m heavy Hdl

A winner on the Flat when trained by Martyn Meade, he found one too good on his hurdling debut but got off the mark next time. Suited to two miles and soft ground. A keen sort.

Reynolds House (IRE)

79 **45**

8-y-o br g Glacial Storm (USA)-Lucky House (Pollerton)

A E Jessop Mrs Gloria Jessop

Placings:*0P00/00-00* **(4160)**

2001/02: 16^{0}S, 16^{0}GS

	Starts	1st	2nd	3rd	Win & Pl
Hurdles	2	0	0	0	
Career Total	**8**	**0**	**0**	**0**	

Going: Sf: 0-1 GS: 0-1 Gd: 0-0 GF: - Fm: 0-0
Distance: 2m/2m3: 0-2 2m4-2m7: 0-0 3m+: 0-0
Track: LH: 0-1 RH: 0-1 Tight: 0-0 Gall: 0-1
Aids: Bl: 0-0 Vi: 0-0 Tstrap: 0-0
Best Rating: 73 10/00 Chep 2m4f gd-sft Hdl

Rhapsody In Blue (IRE)

106(99h) (78h)**83**

7-y-o b g Magical Strike (USA)-Palace Blue (IRE) (Dara Monarch)

R Ford Bricks, Bills & Beer

Placings:6300/00036/PP30F121420 **(4917)**

2001/02: 25^{P}S, 24^{P}G, 24^{3}GS, 25^{0}G, 22^{F}GS, 24^{1}GS, 21^{2}HY, 24^{1}S, 24^{4}S, 24^{2}G, 21^{0}GF

	Starts	1st	2nd	3rd	Win & Pl
Hurdles	8	2	1	1	2596
Chases	3	0	1	0	662
Career Total	**20**	**2**	**2**	**3**	**3964**

78 12/01 Tntn 3m110y G(0-90)HHdl G-S £1722

Total win prize-money £1722

Going: Sf: 1-4 GS: 1-3 Gd: 0-3 GF: - Fm: 0-1
Distance: 2m/2m3: 0-0 2m4-2m7: 0-3 **3m+: 2-8**
Track: LH: 0-6 **RH: 2-4 Tight: 2-7** Gall: 0-1
Aids: Bl: 0-0 Vi: 0-0 **Tstrap: 2-11**
Best Rating: 99 3/99 Newb 2m110y gd-fm Hdl

Landed a three-mile selling hurdle at Taunton over Christmas 2001 and dead-heated at Musselburgh in February 2002. Stays well and is suited by soft ground.

Rhapsody In White (IRE)

87 **60**

8-y-o b g Contract Law (USA)-Lux Aeterna (Sandhurst Prince)

A M Crow Einar G Poole

Placings:0/0/06 **(4857)**

2001/02: 16^{0}F, 20^{6}G

	Starts	1st	2nd	3rd	Win & Pl
Hurdles	2	0	0	0	0
Career Total	**4**	**0**	**0**	**0**	**0**

Going: Sf: 0-0 GS: 0-0 Gd: 0-1 GF: - Fm: 0-1
Distance: 2m/2m3: 0-1 2m4-2m7: 0-1 3m+: 0-0
Track: LH: 0-2 RH: 0-0 Tight: 0-0 Gall: 0-1
Aids: Bl: 0-0 Vi: 0-0 Tstrap: 0-0
Best Rating: 60 4/02 Hexm 2m4f110y good Hdl

Rhinestone Cowboy (IRE)

116f **151f**

6-y-o b g Be My Native (USA)-Monumental Gesture (Head For Heights)

J J O'Neill Mrs John Magnier

Placings:*12* **(4235)**

2001/02: 16^{1}S, 16^{2}GS

	Starts	1st	2nd	3rd	Win & Pl
NH Flat	2	1	1	0	9350
Career Total	**2**	**1**	**1**	**0**	**9350**

131 2/02 Asct 2m110y H NHF SFT £2450

Total win prize-money £2450

Going: Sf: 1-1 GS: 0-1 Gd: 0-0 GF: - Fm: 0-0
Distance: **2m/2m3: 1-2** 2m4-2m7: 0-0 3m+: 0-0
Track: LH: 0-1 **RH: 1-1** Tight: 0-0 Gall: 0-1
Aids: Bl: 0-0 Vi: 0-0 Tstrap: 0-0
Best Rating: 151 3/02 Chel 2m110y gd-sft NHF

High-class bumper performer, won well at Ascot before being narrowly beaten in the Festival bumper.

Rhythm King

96 **86**

7-y-o b g Rakaposhi King-Minim (Rymer)

J A B Old Mrs J A Fowler/the Kentish Men

Placings:*00-600* **(3511)**

2001/02: 19^{6}GS, 16^{0}GS, 17^{0}S

	Starts	1st	2nd	3rd	Win & Pl
Hurdles	3	0	0	0	0
Career Total	**5**	**0**	**0**	**0**	**0**

Going: Sf: 0-1 GS: 0-2 Gd: 0-0 GF: - Fm: 0-0
Distance: 2m/2m3: 0-3 2m4-2m7: 0-0 3m+: 0-0
Track: LH: 0-1 RH: 0-2 Tight: 0-1 Gall: 0-1
Aids: Bl: 0-0 Vi: 0-0 Tstrap: 0-0
Best Rating: 86 1/02 Tntn 2m1f soft Hdl

Lightly-raced gelding. Modest form so far over hurdles so far at trips around two miles.

Rhythmicall (IRE)

5-y-o b g In The Wings-Rhoman Ruby (IRE) (Rhoman Rule (USA))

B S Rothwell (Mrs A J Perrett 24/8) Ron Macdonald

Placings:0 **(2456)**

2001/02: 21^{0}S

	Starts	1st	2nd	3rd	Win & Pl
Hurdles	1	0	0	0	
Career Total	**1**	**0**	**0**	**0**	

Going: Sf: 0-1 GS: 0-0 Gd: 0-0 GF: - Fm: 0-0
Distance: 2m/2m3: 0-0 2m4-2m7: 0-1 3m+: 0-0
Track: LH: 0-0 RH: 0-0 Tight: 0-0 Gall: 0-0
Aids: Bl: 0-0 Vi: 0-0 Tstrap: 0-0
Best Rating:

Riapol

87 **58**

8-y-o ch g Ra Nova-Deep Love (Deep Run)

M J Wilkinson R G & R A Whitehead

Placings:00P060 **(1240)**

2001/02: 21^{0}GF, 20^{0}GF, 24^{P}G, 27^{0}G, 22^{6}G, 24^{0}GF

	Starts	1st	2nd	3rd	Win & Pl
Hurdles	6	0	0	0	0
Career Total	**7**	**0**	**0**	**0**	**0**

Going: Sf: 0-0 GS: 0-0 Gd: 0-3 GF: - Fm: 0-3
Distance: 2m/2m3: 0-0 2m4-2m7: 0-3 3m+: 0-3
Track: LH: 0-5 RH: 0-0 Tight: 0-2 Gall: 0-0
Aids: Bl: 0-0 Vi: 0-2 Tstrap: 0-0
Best Rating: 58 8/01 Strf 2m6f110y good Hdl

Ribble Assembly

93 **81**

7-y-o ch g Presidium-Spring Sparkle (Lord Gayle (USA))

H A McWilliams J K Brown & Partners

Placings:42500/3153P-0F4 **(2179)**

2001/02: 17^{0}G, 17^{F}GS, 23^{4}G

	Starts	1st	2nd	3rd	Win & Pl
Hurdles	3	0	0	0	0
Career Total	**13**	**1**	**1**	**2**	**4695**

93 9/00 Sedg 2m1f E Hdl SFT £2772

Total win prize-money £2772

Going: Sf: 0-0 GS: 0-1 Gd: 0-2 GF: - Fm: 0-0
Distance: 2m/2m3: 0-2 2m4-2m7: 0-1 3m+: 0-0
Track: LH: 0-2 RH: 0-1 Tight: 0-1 Gall: 0-0
Aids: Bl: 0-0 Vi: 0-0 Tstrap: 0-0
Best Rating: 96 12/99 Weth 2m gd-sft Hdl

Ribbon Of Light

41 **29**

4-y-o b g Spectrum (IRE)-Brush Away (Ahonoora)

Ian Williams (B W Hills 13/6) A L R Morton

Placings:0 **(2123)**

2001/02: 16^{0}G

	Starts	1st	2nd	3rd	Win & Pl
Hurdles	1	0	0	0	
Career Total	**1**	**0**	**0**	**0**	

Going: Sf: 0-0 GS: 0-0 Gd: 0-1 GF: - Fm: 0-0
Distance: 2m/2m3: 0-1 2m4-2m7: 0-0 3m+: 0-0
Track: LH: 0-1 RH: 0-0 Tight: 0-0 Gall: 0-1
Aids: Bl: 0-0 Vi: 0-0 Tstrap: 0-0
Best Rating: 29 11/01 Newb 2m110y good Hdl

Riccarton

93(100h) (83+h)95

9-y-o b g Nomination-Legendary Dancer (Shareef Dancer (USA))

D C Turner (J M Bradley 24/8) Mrs M E Turner

Placings:560/12603/06455P (2410)

2001/02: 16^{0}GF, 16^{6}GF, 17^{4}GF, 19^{5}F, 16^{5}S, 19^{P}GS

	Starts	1st	2nd	3rd	Win & Pl
Hurdles	2	0	0	0	0
Chases	4	0	0	0	271
Career Total	**14**	**1**	**1**	**1**	**4041**

89 9/99 Tntn 2m3f110y D Hdl G-F £2626

Total win prize-money £2626

Going: Sf: 0-1 GS: 0-1 Gd: 0-0 GF: - Fm: 0-4
Distance: 2m/2m3: 0-6 2m4-2m7: 0-0 3m+: 0-0
Track: LH: 0-3 RH: 0-3 Tight: 0-3 Gall: 0-0
Aids: Bl: 0-0 Vi: 0-0 Tstrap: 0-2
Best Rating: 99 11/99 Chel 2m110y good Hdl

Rice Point

9-y-o b g Gold Dust-My Kizzy (The Ditton)

John Squire John Squire

Placings:P (4735)

2001/02: 23^{P}F

	Starts	1st	2nd	3rd	Win & Pl
Chases	1	0	0	0	
Career Total	**1**	**0**	**0**	**0**	

Going: Sf: 0-0 GS: 0-0 Gd: 0-0 GF: - Fm: 0-1
Distance: 2m/2m3: 0-0 2m4-2m7: 0-0 3m+: 0-1
Track: LH: 0-0 RH: 0-1 Tight: 0-0 Gall: 0-0
Aids: Bl: 0-0 Vi: 0-0 Tstrap: 0-0
Best Rating:

Riches To Rags (IRE)

12-y-o ch g Castle Keep-Merry Buskins (Little Buskins)

R Williams R Williams

Placings:0/6/005/0422F55/53/P0 (4161)

2001/02: 21^{P}GS, 25^{0}GS

	Starts	1st	2nd	3rd	Win & Pl
Hurdles	2	0	0	0	
Career Total	**16**	**0**	**2**	**1**	**1657**

Going: Sf: 0-0 GS: 0-2 Gd: 0-0 GF: - Fm: 0-0
Distance: 2m/2m3: 0-0 2m4-2m7: 0-1 3m+: 0-1
Track: LH: 0-0 RH: 0-1 Tight: 0-0 Gall: 0-1
Aids: Bl: 0-1 Vi: 0-0 Tstrap: 0-0
Best Rating: 99 8/98 Worc 2m4f gd-fm Hdl

Not the most fluent, he is lightly raced and has shown nothing on his return from over a year and a half absence. Favours a sound surface.

Richie's Delight (IRE)

102(107c) (121c)99

9-y-o br g Phardante (FR)-Johnstown Love (IRE) (Golden Love)

Ferdy Murphy Exors Of The Late Mr G A Hubbard

Placings:S/405452P/351S42312F1/44P43364-4P022

(2309)

2001/02: 16^{4}GF, 20^{P}G, 20^{0}G, 17^{2}S, 20^{2}GS

	Starts	1st	2nd	3rd	Win & Pl
Hurdles	1	0	1	0	766
Chases	4	0	1	0	1371
Career Total	**32**	**3**	**5**	**4**	**19959**

109 4/00 Hntg 2m4f110y E Ch GD £3180
129 11/99 Hntg 2m4f110y D Ch G-F £4177
96 8/99 Hntg 2m4f110y E Hdl G-F £2835

Total win prize-money £10192

Going: Sf: 0-1 GS: 0-1 Gd: 0-2 GF: - Fm: 0-1
Distance: 2m/2m3: 0-2 2m4-2m7: 0-3 3m+: 0-0
Track: LH: 0-2 RH: 0-3 Tight: 0-3 Gall: 0-2
Aids: Bl: 0-0 Vi: 0-0 Tstrap: 0-0
Best Rating: 129 12/99 Leic 2m4f110y gd-fm Ch

Moderate chaser, acts on any ground, particularly suited by two and a half miles at Huntingdon.

Richter Scale (IRE)

85 99

8-y-o b/br g Strong Gale-Molten (Ore)

C R Egerton Decoupage Partnership

Placings:0/1P6 (4636)

2001/02: 22^{1}G, 22^{P}S, 24^{6}GF

	Starts	1st	2nd	3rd	Win & Pl
Hurdles	3	1	0	0	2275
Career Total	**4**	**1**	**0**	**0**	**2275**

99 10/01 Winc 2m6f E Hdl GD £2275

Total win prize-money £2275

Going: Sf: 0-1 GS: 0-0 Gd: 1-1 GF: - Fm: 0-1
Distance: 2m/2m3: 0-0 **2m4-2m7: 1-2** 3m+: 0-1
Track: LH: 0-0 **RH: 1-3** Tight: 0-0 Gall: 0-0
Aids: Bl: 0-0 Vi: 0-0 Tstrap: 0-0
Best Rating: 99 10/01 Winc 2m6f good Hdl

Lightly raced. He won a novice hurdle at Wincanton in October 2001, but then disappointed in higher grade on softer ground.

Ricko (NZ)

92 106

8-y-o b g Defensive Play (USA)-Native Hawk (NZ) (War Hawk)

B G Powell D & J Newell

Placings:42212F-0 (0581)

2001/02: 16^{0}GF

	Starts	1st	2nd	3rd	Win & Pl
Hurdles	1	0	0	0	
Career Total	**7**	**1**	**3**	**0**	**4497**

6/00 Trap 1m4f110y Hdl HVY £1393

Total win prize-money £1393

Going: Sf: 0-0 GS: 0-0 Gd: 0-0 GF: - Fm: 0-1
Distance: 2m/2m3: 0-1 2m4-2m7: 0-0 3m+: 0-0
Track: LH: 0-1 RH: 0-0 Tight: 0-1 Gall: 0-0
Aids: Bl: 0-0 Vi: 0-0 Tstrap: 0-0
Best Rating: 110 1/01 Plum 2m soft Hdl

Front-running novice chaser. Possibly unlucky when falling two out whilst still in the lead at Newton Abbot July 2002.

Ricky B

89 71

6-y-o b g Rakaposhi King-Fililode (Mossberry)

M Wellings The 1471 Racing Partnership

Placings:00-00PP5 (4573)

2001/02: 21^{0}GF, 24^{0}G, 20^{P}S, 19^{P}GS, 20^{5}G

	Starts	1st	2nd	3rd	Win & Pl
Hurdles	5	0	0	0	0
Career Total	**7**	**0**	**0**	**0**	**0**

Going: Sf: 0-1 GS: 0-1 Gd: 0-2 GF: - Fm: 0-1
Distance: 2m/2m3: 0-1 2m4-2m7: 0-3 3m+: 0-1
Track: LH: 0-3 RH: 0-1 Tight: 0-2 Gall: 0-0
Aids: Bl: 0-0 Vi: 0-0 Tstrap: 0-0
Best Rating: 51 4/02 Uttx 2m4f110y good Hdl

Rideaway Rose (IRE)

96f 90f

6-y-o b m King's Ride-Miss Rockaway (Le Moss)

D Brace David Brace

Placings:04 (1799)

2001/02: 16^{0}G, 16^{4}S

	Starts	1st	2nd	3rd	Win & Pl
NH Flat	2	0	0	0	0
Career Total	**2**	**0**	**0**	**0**	**0**

Going: Sf: 0-1 GS: 0-0 Gd: 0-1 GF: - Fm: 0-0
Distance: 2m/2m3: 0-2 2m4-2m7: 0-0 3m+: 0-0
Track: LH: 0-2 RH: 0-0 Tight: 0-0 Gall: 0-0
Aids: Bl: 0-0 Vi: 0-0 Tstrap: 0-0
Best Rating: 90 10/01 Chep 2m110y soft NHF

Ridgeway (IRE)

96 97

7-y-o b g Indian Ridge-Regal Promise (Pitskelly)

M W Easterby Mrs M E Curtis

Placings:32-55 (3347)

2001/02: 16^{5}S, 16^{5}G

	Starts	1st	2nd	3rd	Win & Pl
Hurdles	2	0	0	0	0
Career Total	**4**	**0**	**1**	**1**	**1637**

Going: Sf: 0-1 GS: 0-0 Gd: 0-1 GF: - Fm: 0-0
Distance: 2m/2m3: 0-2 2m4-2m7: 0-0 3m+: 0-0
Track: LH: 0-1 RH: 0-1 Tight: 0-1 Gall: 0-0
Aids: Bl: 0-0 Vi: 0-0 Tstrap: 0-0
Best Rating: 104 12/00 Donc 2m110y gd-sft Hdl

Ridgewood Bay (IRE)

5-y-o b m Ridgewood Ben-Another Baileys (Deploy)

J C Fox Lord Mutton Racing Partnership

Placings:600P-P (0841)

2001/02: 16^{P}G

	Starts	1st	2nd	3rd	Win & Pl
Hurdles	1	0	0	0	
Career Total	**5**	**0**	**0**	**0**	**0**

Going: Sf: 0-0 GS: 0-0 Gd: 0-1 GF: - Fm: 0-0
Distance: 2m/2m3: 0-1 2m4-2m7: 0-0 3m+: 0-0
Track: LH: 0-1 RH: 0-0 Tight: 0-0 Gall: 0-0
Aids: Bl: 0-0 Vi: 0-0 Tstrap: 0-0
Best Rating: 45 1/01 Wwck 2m soft Hdl

Rift Valley (IRE)

106 117

7-y-o b g Good Thyne (USA)-Necochea (Julio Mariner)

G M McCourt Mrs Kathy Stuart

Placings:*4210*/6446020-11111 **(1243)**
2001/02: 20^{1}G, 17^{1}G, 20^{1}GF, 24^{1}GF, 20^{1}GF

	Starts	1st	2nd	3rd	Win & Pl
Hurdles	5	5	0	0	22069
Career Total	**16**	**6**	**2**	**0**	**25043**

117	8/01	Worc	2m4f	D(0-120)HHdl	G-F	£4238
115	8/01	Worc	3m	C(0-135)HHdl	G-F	£5363
110	7/01	Wolv	2m4f110y	D(0-125)HHdl	G-F	£6727
117	7/01	MRas	2m1f110y	E(0-105)HHdl	GD	£3206
108	6/01	Worc	2m4f	E(0-105)HHdl	GD	£2534
98	12/99	Ludl	2m	H NHF	G-S	£1763

Total win prize-money £23833

Going: Sf: 0-0 GS: 0-0 Gd: 2-2 GF: - Fm: 3-3
Distance: 2m/2m3: 1-1 **2m4-2m7: 3-3** 3m+: 1-1
Track: **LH: 4-4** RH: 1-1 **Tight: 2-2** Gall: 0-0
Aids: Bl: 0-0 **Vi: 5-5** Tstrap: 0-0
Best Rating: 117 8/01 Worc 2m4f gd-fm Hdl

Rigadoon (IRE)

101(100h) (84h)107

6-y-o b g Be My Chief (USA)-Loucoum (FR) (Iron Duke (FR))
M W Easterby C Buckton, K Mercer & A Ford

Placings:1F0/6-55354 **(2908)**
2001/02: 24^{5}G, 20^{5}G, 16^{3}G, 25^{5}GS, 20^{4}GS

	Starts	1st	2nd	3rd	Win & Pl
Hurdles	1	0	0	0	0
Chases	1	0	0	1	301
Career Total	**9**	**1**	**0**	**1**	**3896**

102	11/99	Weth	2m	D Hdl	GD	£2914

Total win prize-money £2915

Going: Sf: 0-0 GS: 0-2 Gd: 0-3 GF: - Fm: 0-0
Distance: 2m/2m3: 0-1 2m4-2m7: 0-2 3m+: 0-2
Track: LH: 0-4 RH: 0-1 Tight: 0-1 Gall: 0-0
Aids: Bl: 0-1 Vi: 0-0 Tstrap: 0-0
Best Rating: 107 12/01 Weth 2m4f110y gd-sft Ch

Modest hurdler/chaser, suited by a sound surface.

Right

101 101

7-y-o b m Teenoso (USA)-Left (Remainder Man)
D McCain Clayton Bigley Partnership Ltd

Placings:*5*F1 **(4408)**
2001/02: 17^{5}GS, 17^{F}S, 17^{1}S

	Starts	1st	2nd	3rd	Win & Pl
NH Flat	1	0	0	0	0
Hurdles	2	1	0	0	2268
Career Total	**3**	**1**	**0**	**0**	**2268**

101	3/02	Bang	2m1f	F Hdl	SFT	£2268

Total win prize-money £2268

Going: Sf: 1-2 GS: 0-1 Gd: 0-0 GF: - Fm: 0-0
Distance: **2m/2m3: 1-3** 2m4-2m7: 0-0 3m+: 0-0
Track: **LH: 1-2** RH: 0-1 **Tight: 1-3** Gall: 0-0
Aids: Bl: 0-0 Vi: 0-0 Tstrap: 0-0
Best Rating: 101 3/02 Bang 2m1f soft Hdl

Off the mark in weak claiming hurdle at Bangor. Open to improvement, handles soft ground.

Right To Reply (IRE)

99(106h) (115h)127

8-y-o b/br g Executive Perk-Sesheta (Tumble Wind (USA))
Noel T Chance A D Weller

Placings:*2410*/12-1 **(1954)**
2001/02: 20^{1}G

	Starts	1st	2nd	3rd	Win & Pl
Chases	1	1	0	0	4030
Career Total	**7**	**3**	**2**	**0**	**12615**

127	11/01	Wwck	2m4f110y	D Ch	GD	£4030
141	3/01	Asct	2m4f	D Hdl	HVY	£5148
111	3/00	Folk	2m1f110y	H NHF	GD	£1683

Total win prize-money £10862

Going: Sf: 0-0 GS: 0-0 Gd: 1-1 GF: - Fm: 0-0
Distance: 2m/2m3: 0-0 **2m4-2m7: 1-1** 3m+: 0-0
Track: **LH: 1-1** RH: 0-0 Tight: 0-0 Gall: 0-0
Aids: Bl: 0-0 Vi: 0-0 Tstrap: 0-0
Best Rating: 141 3/01 Asct 2m4f heavy Hdl

A promising bumper horse, he won one of only two starts over hurdles and made a winning debut over fences at Warwick in November 2001. His jumping was patchy and he will need to improve it.

Rightsaidfred

14-y-o b g Lighter-Ladybank (Dear Gazelle)
S Gordon-Watson P A Bull

Placings:1/FF2/1112BF/132P0/P3126-12 **(4852)**
2001/02: 26^{1}GS, 24^{2}G

	Starts	1st	2nd	3rd	Win & Pl
Chases	2	1	1	0	2011
Career Total	**22**	**7**	**5**	**2**	**41747**

122	3/02	Plum	3m2f	H Ch	G-S	£1148
146	1/01	Winc	3m1f110y	D(0-125)HCh	G-S	£5343
142	12/99	Folk	3m2f	D(0-125)HCh	GD	£3710
142	1/99	Newb	3m2f110y	C(0-135)HCh	HVY	£10866
127	11/98	Folk	3m2f	E(0-110)HCh	G-S	£4260
119	11/98	Plum	3m1f110y	D(0-120)HCh	SFT	£4143
93	5/95	Folk	3m2f	H Ch	GD	£1774

Total win prize-money £31245

Going: Sf: 0-0 GS: 1-1 Gd: 0-1 GF: - Fm: 0-0
Distance: 2m/2m3: 0-0 2m4-2m7: 0-0 **3m+: 1-2**
Track: LH: 0-1 RH: 0-0 Tight: 0-1 Gall: 0-0
Aids: Bl: 0-0 Vi: 0-0 Tstrap: 0-0
Best Rating: 146 1/01 Winc 3m1f110y soft Ch

A sprightly veteran, he jumps well and stays. In good heart in point-to-points in the spring of 2002 before winning a hunter chase at Folkestone.

Rigmarole

111 122

4-y-o b g Fairy King (USA)-Cattermole (USA) (Roberto (USA))
P F Nicholls (P Bary 2/10) D J & F A Jackson

Placings:1463011 **(4915)**
2001/02: 16^{1}GS, 16^{4}GS, 16^{6}GS, 17^{3}S, 16^{0}G, 16^{1}GF, 17^{1}GF

	Starts	1st	2nd	3rd	Win & Pl
Hurdles	7	3	0	1	10437
Career Total	**7**	**3**	**0**	**1**	**10437**

122	4/02	Sedg	2m1f	E Hdl	G-F	£2576
97	4/02	Weth	2m	E Hdl	G-F	£3220
109	12/01	Weth	2m	D Hdl	G-S	£3759

Total win prize-money £9555

Going: Sf: 0-1 GS: 1-3 Gd: 0-1 GF: - Fm: 2-2
Distance: **2m/2m3: 3-7** 2m4-2m7: 0-0 3m+: 0-0
Track: **LH: 3-4** RH: 0-3 **Tight: 1-2** Gall: 0-0
Aids: Bl: 0-0 Vi: 0-0 **Tstrap: 2-5**
Best Rating: 122 4/02 Sedg 2m1f gd-fm Hdl

Ex-French, he looked a decent hurdling recruit when scoring in easy fashion at Wetherby in December 2001, but was then held in the face of stiffer tasks. Returned to form with wins on fast ground at Wetherby and Sedgefield in April 2002.

Rimfaxi

92 66

4-y-o ch g Risk Me (FR)-Legal Sound (Legal Eagle)
J M Jefferson J M Ranson

Placings:0026 **(2918)**
2001/02: 16^{0}G, 16^{0}S, 17^{2}GS, 16^{6}G

	Starts	1st	2nd	3rd	Win & Pl
Hurdles	4	0	1	0	769
Career Total	**4**	**0**	**1**	**0**	**769**

Going: Sf: 0-1 GS: 0-1 Gd: 0-2 GF: - Fm: 0-0
Distance: 2m/2m3: 0-4 2m4-2m7: 0-0 3m+: 0-0
Track: LH: 0-3 RH: 0-1 Tight: 0-3 Gall: 0-0
Aids: Bl: 0-0 Vi: 0-0 Tstrap: 0-0
Best Rating: 66 11/01 Bang 2m1f gd-sft Hdl

Rimosa

100 91

7-y-o b m Miners Lamp-Crosa (Crozier)
A P Jones A P Jones

Placings:*00*-PF035U **(4087)**
2001/02: 16^{P}GS, 16^{F}S, 16^{0}S, 16^{3}G, 16^{5}GS, 17^{U}S

	Starts	1st	2nd	3rd	Win & Pl
Hurdles	6	0	0	1	393
Career Total	**8**	**0**	**0**	**1**	**393**

Going: Sf: 0-3 GS: 0-2 Gd: 0-1 GF: - Fm: 0-0
Distance: 2m/2m3: 0-6 2m4-2m7: 0-0 3m+: 0-0
Track: LH: 0-3 RH: 0-3 Tight: 0-3 Gall: 0-0
Aids: Bl: 0-0 Vi: 0-0 Tstrap: 0-0
Best Rating: 91 10/01 Towc 2m soft Hdl

Rimpton Boy

63

7-y-o gr g Interrex (CAN)-Ardelle Grey (Ardross)
P F Nicholls Mrs Elaine Hutchinson

Placings:0-4 **(0249)**
2001/02: 22^{4}GF

	Starts	1st	2nd	3rd	Win & Pl
Hurdles	1	0	0	0	0
Career Total	**2**	**0**	**0**	**0**	**0**

Going: Sf: 0-0 GS: 0-0 Gd: 0-0 GF: - Fm: 0-1
Distance: 2m/2m3: 0-0 2m4-2m7: 0-1 3m+: 0-0
Track: LH: 0-1 RH: 0-0 Tight: 0-1 Gall: 0-0
Aids: Bl: 0-0 Vi: 0-0 Tstrap: 0-0
Best Rating: 63 4/01 Winc 2m6f soft Hdl

Rince Ri (IRE)

122 174

9-y-o ch g Orchestra-Mildred's Ball (Blue Refrain)
T M Walsh F M Moriarty

Placings:1114/11121/3213U/1-444213 **(3734a)**
2001/02: 16^{4}Y, 20^{4}S, 24^{4}Y, 24^{2}YS, 25^{1}HY, 24^{3}HY

	Starts	1st	2nd	3rd	Win & Pl
Chases	6	1	1	1	70512
Career Total	**21**	**10**	**3**	**3**	**259072**

174	1/02	Chel	3m1f110y	A Ch	HVY	£45000
167	12/00	Leop	3m	Ch	HVY	£52240

170	12/99	Leop	3m	Ch	SFT	£43750
157	4/99	Fair	2m4f	Ch	G-Y	£29017
131	2/99	Naas	2m4f	Ch	SH	£11562
113	1/99	Naas	3m	Ch	HVY	£8671
138	11/98	Navn	2m4f	Ch	SH	£4184
141	2/98	Navn	3m	Hdl	SFT	£8413
130	1/98	Navn	2m6f	Hdl	HVY	£3573
122	12/97	Navn	2m	Hdl	SFT	£3051

Total win prize-money £209467

Going: Sf: 1-3 GS: 0-0 Gd: 0-0 GF: - Fm: 0-0
Distance: 2m/2m3: 0-1 2m4-2m7: 0-1 **3m+: 1-4**
Track: **LH: 1-5** RH: 0-1 Tight: 0-0 **Gall: 1-1**
Aids: Bl: 0-0 Vi: 0-0 Tstrap: 0-0
Best Rating: 176 3/00 Chel 3m2f110y gd-fm Ch

Twice a winner of the Ericsson Chase at Leopardstown, he is a high-class three-mile chaser with not many miles on the clock. Would probably have finished third in the Gold Cup of 2000 but for unseating his rider, and landed the Pillar Property Chase at Cheltenham in January 2002 in bottomless ground before a good effort in the Hennessy at Leopardstown. Stays three and a quarter miles.

Ring De Sou (FR)

(79h) (69h)

5-y-o b g Ajdayt (USA)-Ring Ann (IRE) (Auction Ring (USA))
M C Pipe (F Danloux 1/6) Trevor Painting

Placings:000-4RR15P **(2752)**
2001/02: 20^{4}HO, 17^{R}HY, 17^{R}S, 17^{1}VS, 22^{5}GF, 20^{P}S

	Starts	1st	2nd	3rd	Win & Pl
Hurdles	1	0	0	0	0
Chases	5	1	0	0	9215
Career Total	**9**	**1**	**0**	**0**	**9215**

	6/01	Autl	2m1f110y	Ch	VS	£6305

Total win prize-money £6305

Going: Sf: 0-3 GS: 0-0 Gd: 0-0 GF: - Fm: 0-1
Distance: **2m/2m3: 1-3** 2m4-2m7: 0-3 3m+: 0-0
Track: LH: 0-2 RH: 0-0 Tight: 0-2 Gall: 0-0
Aids: **Bl: 1-1** Vi: 0-2 Tstrap: 0-0
Best Rating:

Ring The King

6-y-o b g Rakaposhi King-Dunsilly Bell (London Bells (CAN))
P Winkworth P Winkworth

Placings:P **(1947)**
2001/02: 19^{P}GF

	Starts	1st	2nd	3rd	Win & Pl
Hurdles	1	0	0	0	
Career Total	**1**	**0**	**0**	**0**	

Going: Sf: 0-0 GS: 0-0 Gd: 0-0 GF: - Fm: 0-1
Distance: 2m/2m3: 0-1 2m4-2m7: 0-0 3m+: 0-0
Track: LH: 0-0 RH: 0-1 Tight: 0-0 Gall: 0-0
Aids: Bl: 0-0 Vi: 0-0 Tstrap: 0-0
Best Rating:

Ringside View (IRE)

101 95

5-y-o b g Keen-Ringawoody (Auction Ring (USA))
C J Mann (Ferdy Murphy 30/6) Tom & Evelyn Yates

Placings:0200-631420 **(1135)**
2001/02: 16^{6}G, 18^{3}GF, 16^{1}G, 16^{4}G, 19^{2}G, 20^{0}GF

	Starts	1st	2nd	3rd	Win & Pl
Hurdles	6	1	1	1	3138
Career Total	**10**	**1**	**2**	**1**	**3828**

91	6/01	Worc	2m	G Hdl	GD	£1932

Total win prize-money £1932

Going: Sf: 0-0 GS: 0-0 Gd: 1-4 GF: - Fm: 0-2
Distance: **2m/2m3: 1-5** 2m4-2m7: 0-1 3m+: 0-0
Track: **LH: 1-6** RH: 0-0 Tight: 0-2 Gall: 0-0
Aids: Bl: 0-0 Vi: 0-0 Tstrap: 0-0
Best Rating: 95 7/01 Strf 2m3f good Hdl

Rio Grande (IRE)

77 74

8-y-o b g Un Desperado (FR)-Liffey's Choice (Little Buskins)
C R Barwell Tony Fiorillo

Placings:*10*/PP-0 **(4485)**
2001/02: 19^{0}G

	Starts	1st	2nd	3rd	Win & Pl
Hurdles	1	0	0	0	
Career Total	**5**	**1**	**0**	**0**	**3234**

90	9/99	Gway	2m	NHF	SFT	£3234

Total win prize-money £3234

Going: Sf: 0-0 GS: 0-0 Gd: 0-1 GF: - Fm: 0-0
Distance: 2m/2m3: 0-1 2m4-2m7: 0-0 3m+: 0-0
Track: LH: 0-0 RH: 0-1 Tight: 0-0 Gall: 0-0
Aids: Bl: 0-0 Vi: 0-0 Tstrap: 0-1
Best Rating: 90 9/99 Gway 2m soft NHF

Rio Santo (IRE)

7-y-o b g Alphabatim (USA)-Skimpan (Pitpan)
N J Pomfret W J Turcan

Placings:PPP **(1830)**
2001/02: 20^{P}G, 19^{P}G, 20^{P}G

	Starts	1st	2nd	3rd	Win & Pl
Hurdles	3	0	0	0	
Career Total	**3**	**0**	**0**	**0**	

Going: Sf: 0-0 GS: 0-0 Gd: 0-3 GF: - Fm: 0-0
Distance: 2m/2m3: 0-0 2m4-2m7: 0-3 3m+: 0-0
Track: LH: 0-2 RH: 0-1 Tight: 0-3 Gall: 0-0
Aids: Bl: 0-0 Vi: 0-0 Tstrap: 0-0
Best Rating:

Rio Tinto

101 94

7-y-o gr g Gran Alba (USA)-Hollow Creek (Tarqogan)
W Jenks Mrs Diane Snowden

Placings:*24/5*0F30-055115 **(4577)**
2001/02: 19^{0}S, 20^{5}S, 26^{5}GS, 26^{1}G, 24^{1}HY, 24^{5}G

	Starts	1st	2nd	3rd	Win & Pl
Hurdles	6	2	0	0	5671
Career Total	**13**	**2**	**1**	**1**	**6660**

94	3/02	Sthl	3m110y	F(0-100)HHdl	HVY	£3161
94	3/02	Hrfd	3m2f	F(0-95)HHdl	GD	£2509

Total win prize-money £5671

Going: Sf: 1-3 GS: 0-1 Gd: 1-2 GF: - Fm: 0-0
Distance: 2m/2m3: 0-0 2m4-2m7: 0-2 **3m+: 2-4**
Track: LH: 1-2 RH: 1-4 **Tight: 1-1** Gall: 0-0
Aids: **Bl: 2-3** Vi: 0-0 Tstrap: 0-0
Best Rating: 97 1/00 Ludl 2m gd-sft NHF

Modest hurdler, successfull in low-grade compan y at Southwell and Hereford. Stays three miles plus and effective on good ground.

Rio's Lord (IRE)

9-y-o b g Good Thyne (USA)-Rio Dulce (Rio Carmelo (FR))
P J Millington P J Millington

Placings:PUP0 **(0556)**
2001/02: 25^{P}G, 25^{U}G, 22^{P}G, 24^{0}GF

	Starts	1st	2nd	3rd	Win & Pl
Chases	4	0	0	0	
Career Total	**4**	**0**	**0**	**0**	

Going: Sf: 0-0 GS: 0-0 Gd: 0-3 GF: - Fm: 0-1
Distance: 2m/2m3: 0-0 2m4-2m7: 0-1 3m+: 0-3
Track: LH: 0-2 RH: 0-2 Tight: 0-2 Gall: 0-1
Aids: Bl: 0-0 Vi: 0-1 Tstrap: 0-0
Best Rating:

Rioja

7-y-o ch g Anshan-Executive Flare (Executive Man)
J K Price (M Wigham 27/2) J K Price

Placings:P **(4682)**
2001/02: 17^{P}GF

	Starts	1st	2nd	3rd	Win & Pl
Hurdles	1	0	0	0	
Career Total	**1**	**0**	**0**	**0**	

Going: Sf: 0-0 GS: 0-0 Gd: 0-0 GF: - Fm: 0-1
Distance: 2m/2m3: 0-1 2m4-2m7: 0-0 3m+: 0-0
Track: LH: 0-0 RH: 0-1 Tight: 0-0 Gall: 0-0
Aids: Bl: 0-0 Vi: 0-0 Tstrap: 0-0
Best Rating:

Rippling Surf

87 64

8-y-o br g Landyap (USA)-Fort Corner (Sit In The Corner (USA))
R G Frost P A Tylor

Placings:0P-0F0 **(1728)**
2001/02: 17^{0}GF, 17^{F}GF, 19^{0}F

	Starts	1st	2nd	3rd	Win & Pl
Hurdles	3	0	0	0	
Career Total	**5**	**0**	**0**	**0**	

Going: Sf: 0-0 GS: 0-0 Gd: 0-0 GF: - Fm: 0-3
Distance: 2m/2m3: 0-2 2m4-2m7: 0-1 3m+: 0-0
Track: LH: 0-1 RH: 0-2 Tight: 0-2 Gall: 0-0
Aids: Bl: 0-0 Vi: 0-0 Tstrap: 0-0
Best Rating: 64 7/01 NAbb 2m1f gd-fm Hdl

Rise Above (IRE)

8-y-o b m Simply Great (FR)-La Tanque (USA) (Last Raise (USA))
Miss K M George R J Matthews

Placings:4F0F/000330/4 **(0470)**
2001/02: 20^{4}GF

	Starts	1st	2nd	3rd	Win & Pl
Hurdles	1	0	0	0	0
Career Total	**11**	**0**	**0**	**2**	**466**

Going: Sf: 0-0 GS: 0-0 Gd: 0-0 GF: - Fm: 0-1
Distance: 2m/2m3: 0-0 2m4-2m7: 0-1 3m+: 0-0
Track: LH: 0-1 RH: 0-0 Tight: 0-0 Gall: 0-0
Aids: Bl: 0-0 Vi: 0-0 Tstrap: 0-0
Best Rating: 69 11/99 Sedg 2m5f110y good Hdl

Rising Dawn (IRE)

10-y-o ch g Rising-Bawnard Lady (Ragapan)
P J Millington P J Millington

Placings:0/0U (0258)
2001/02: 25^{0}G, 24^{U}GF

	Starts	1st	2nd	3rd	Win & Pl
Chases	2	0	0	0	
Career Total	**3**	**0**	**0**	**0**	

Going: Sf: 0-0 GS: 0-0 Gd: 0-1 GF: - Fm: 0-1
Distance: 2m/2m3: 0-0 2m4-2m7: 0-0 3m+: 0-2
Track: LH: 0-2 RH: 0-0 Tight: 0-1 Gall: 0-0
Aids: Bl: 0-0 Vi: 0-0 Tstrap: 0-0
Best Rating: 69 5/97 Prth 2m110y gd-sft NHF

Rising Generation (FR)

94(102c) (141c)**114**
5-y-o ch g Risen Star (USA)-Queen's Victory (FR) (Carmarthen (FR))
N G Richards Alistair Duff

Placings:43/2112F5-1131143P (4893)
2001/02: 18^{1}, 18^{1}S, 17^{3}G, 19^{1}VS, 19^{1}S, 16^{4}S, 17^{3}G, 20^{P}G

	Starts	1st	2nd	3rd	Win & Pl
Hurdles	3	1	0	1	4862
Chases	5	3	0	1	16973
Career Total	**16**	**6**	**2**	**3**	**33418**

141	1/02	Hrfd	2m3f	E Ch	SFT	£3302
	10/01	Nanc	2m3f	Hdl	VS	£4364
	9/01	Crao	2m2f110y	Ch	SFT	£5819

Total win prize-money £23151

Going: Sf: 2-3 GS: 0-0 Gd: 0-3 GF: - Fm: 0-0
Distance: **2m/2m3: 4-7** 2m4-2m7: 0-1 3m+: 0-0
Track: LH: 0-0 **RH: 1-4** Tight: 0-1 Gall: 0-0
Aids: Bl: 0-0 Vi: 0-0 Tstrap: 0-0
Best Rating: 141 1/02 Hrfd 2m3f soft Ch

A winner of two chases and three hurdles at around two and a quarter miles in the French Provinces. Thought to be best going right-handed. Scored in easy fashion on his British debut for Nicky Richards, stiff tasks subsequently. Suited by soft ground.

Rising On Up (IRE)

8-y-o b g Rising-Miss Mallard (Crash Course)
B J Eckley Brian Eckley

Placings:U/0 (0720)
2001/02: 26^{0}F

	Starts	1st	2nd	3rd	Win & Pl
Hurdles	1	0	0	0	
Career Total	**2**	**0**	**0**	**0**	

Going: Sf: 0-0 GS: 0-0 Gd: 0-0 GF: - Fm: 0-1
Distance: 2m/2m3: 0-0 2m4-2m7: 0-0 3m+: 0-1
Track: LH: 0-0 RH: 0-1 Tight: 0-0 Gall: 0-0
Aids: Bl: 0-0 Vi: 0-0 Tstrap: 0-0
Best Rating:

Rising Sap

12-y-o ch g Brotherly (USA)-Miss Kewmill (Billion (USA))
J D Downes J D Downes

Placings:PP0P/F (0226)
2001/02: 20^{F}GF

	Starts	1st	2nd	3rd	Win & Pl
Chases	1	0	0	0	
Career Total	**5**	**0**	**0**	**0**	

Going: Sf: 0-0 GS: 0-0 Gd: 0-0 GF: - Fm: 0-1
Distance: 2m/2m3: 0-0 2m4-2m7: 0-1 3m+: 0-0
Track: LH: 0-0 RH: 0-1 Tight: 0-0 Gall: 0-1
Aids: Bl: 0-1 Vi: 0-0 Tstrap: 0-0
Best Rating: 106 5/01 Hntg 2m4f110y gd-fm Ch

Rising Talisker

9-y-o ch m Primitive Rising (USA)-Dialect (Connaught)
J S Wainwright J S Wainwright

Placings:0036/5FU50/P-P (0079)
2001/02: 23^{P}G

	Starts	1st	2nd	3rd	Win & Pl
Hurdles	1	0	0	0	
Career Total	**11**	**0**	**0**	**1**	**460**

Going: Sf: 0-0 GS: 0-0 Gd: 0-1 GF: - Fm: 0-0
Distance: 2m/2m3: 0-0 2m4-2m7: 0-0 3m+: 0-1
Track: LH: 0-1 RH: 0-0 Tight: 0-0 Gall: 0-0
Aids: Bl: 0-0 Vi: 0-0 Tstrap: 0-0
Best Rating: 85 1/00 Sthl 2m4f110y gd-sft Hdl

Rising Trout

101 **97**
9-y-o ch g Primitive Rising (USA)-Rosa Trout (Goldhill)
R H Buckler Nick Elliott

Placings:*0520*/P/244130P42P/**6P2-PUPP1PP** (4751)
2001/02: 21^{P}GF, 25^{U}G, 24^{P}GF, 20^{P}G, 20^{1}G, 24^{P}GS, 20^{P}GF

	Starts	1st	2nd	3rd	Win & Pl
Chases	7	1	0	0	3198
Career Total	**25**	**2**	**4**	**1**	**10153**

97	12/01	Sthl	2m4f110y	E(0-105)HCh	GD	£3198
107	12/99	Sthl	2m4f110y	E(0-105)HHdl	SFT	£2337

Total win prize-money £5535

Going: Sf: 0-0 GS: 0-1 Gd: 1-3 GF: - Fm: 0-3
Distance: 2m/2m3: 0-0 **2m4-2m7: 1-4** 3m+: 0-3
Track: **LH: 1-4** RH: 0-3 **Tight: 1-5** Gall: 0-0
Aids: Bl: 0-0 Vi: 0-0 Tstrap: 0-0
Best Rating: 107 2/01 Ludl 2m4f good Ch

Completed once from seven starts in 2002, winning a modest handicap over two and half miles.

Risk Accessor (IRE)

113(76h) (148h)**148**
7-y-o b g Commanche Run-Bellatollah (Bellman (FR))
C Roche J P McManus

Placings:*22*/21251323-11F2331F2 (4623a)
2001/02: 20^{1}GY, 22^{1}Y, 20^{F}G, 20^{2}Y, 20^{3}S, 24^{3}SH, 16^{1}HY, 24^{F}GS, 24^{2}GY

	Starts	1st	2nd	3rd	Win & Pl
Hurdles	1	1	0	0	14677
Chases	8	2	2	2	32658
Career Total	**19**	**5**	**7**	**4**	**91209**

138	2/02	Thur	2m	Ch	HVY	£6349
140	10/01	Thur	2m6f	Ch	YLD	£7790
146	5/01	Fair	2m4f	Hdl	G-Y	£14677
130	1/01	Naas	2m4f	Hdl	SFT	£18346
135	10/00	Fair	2m4f	Hdl	G-Y	£4416

Total win prize-money £51580

Going: Sf: 1-2 GS: 0-1 Gd: 0-1 GF: - Fm: 0-0
Distance: 2m/2m3: 1-1 **2m4-2m7: 2-5** 3m+: 0-3
Track: LH: 0-3 **RH: 1-3** Tight: 0-0 Gall: 0-2
Aids: Bl: 0-0 Vi: 0-0 Tstrap: 0-0
Best Rating: 148 12/01 Fair 2m4f yield Ch

Winner twice over fences at Thurles, he races prominently and tends to make mistakes. Well beaten when falling in the Royal & SunAlliance at Cheltenham.

Risk Advisory (IRE)

(95h) (49h)
8-y-o b g Camden Town-Quick Romance (Lucky Brief)
Mrs S M Johnson (J W Mullins 30/6) Miss C E Manning

Placings:*4066*/0003P00B (3321)
2001/02: 24^{0}F, 22^{0}GF, 22^{0}GF, 22^{3}HY, 24^{P}S, 20^{0}S, 20^{0}HY, 24^{B}GS

	Starts	1st	2nd	3rd	Win & Pl
Hurdles	7	0	0	1	223
Chases	1	0	0	0	0
Career Total	**12**	**0**	**0**	**1**	**223**

Going: Sf: 0-4 GS: 0-1 Gd: 0-0 GF: - Fm: 0-0
Distance: 2m/2m3: 0-0 2m4-2m7: 0-5 3m+: 0-3
Track: LH: 0-3 RH: 0-5 Tight: 0-4 Gall: 0-1
Aids: Bl: 0-0 Vi: 0-0 Tstrap: 0-3
Best Rating: 95 12/99 Plum 2m5f heavy Hdl

Risky Dream

78 **55**
5-y-o ch m Risk Me (FR)-Jove's Voodoo (USA) (Northern Jove (CAN))
A W Carroll Dennis Deacon

Placings:0P (0493)
2001/02: 16^{0}G, 17^{P}G

	Starts	1st	2nd	3rd	Win & Pl
Hurdles	2	0	0	0	
Career Total	**2**	**0**	**0**	**0**	

Going: Sf: 0-0 GS: 0-0 Gd: 0-2 GF: - Fm: 0-0
Distance: 2m/2m3: 0-2 2m4-2m7: 0-0 3m+: 0-0
Track: LH: 0-1 RH: 0-1 Tight: 0-1 Gall: 0-0
Aids: Bl: 0-1 Vi: 0-0 Tstrap: 0-0
Best Rating: 55 5/01 Strf 2m110y good Hdl

Risky Flight

84 **50**
8-y-o ch g Risk Me (FR)-Stairway To Heaven (IRE) (Godswalk (USA))
A Smith Mrs Sheila Oakes

Placings:000/41/000 (1247)
2001/02: 19^{0}GF, 21^{0}G, 17^{0}G

	Starts	1st	2nd	3rd	Win & Pl
Hurdles	3	0	0	0	
Career Total	**8**	**1**	**0**	**0**	**1772**

79	10/98	Sedg	2m1f	G(0-90)HHdl	G-S	£1772

Total win prize-money £1772

Going: Sf: 0-0 GS: 0-0 Gd: 0-2 GF: - Fm: 0-1
Distance: 2m/2m3: 0-1 2m4-2m7: 0-2 3m+: 0-0

Track:	LH: 0-1 RH: 0-2 Tight: 0-3 Gall: 0-0
Aids:	Bl: 0-1 Vi: 0-0 Tstrap: 0-0
Best Rating:	**79** 10/98 Sedg 2m1f gd-sft Hdl

Risky Girl

66 **32**

7-y-o gr m Risk Me (FR)-Jove's Voodoo (USA) (Northern Jove (CAN))

H J Manners H J Manners

Placings:13/6 **(1490)**

2001/02: 20^{6}G

	Starts	1st	2nd	3rd	Win & Pl
Hurdles	1	0	0	0	0
Career Total	**3**	**1**	**0**	**1**	**2811**

88	11/98	Hrfd	2m1f	E Hdl	GD	£2556

Total win prize-money £2556

Going:	Sf: 0-0 GS: 0-0 Gd: 0-1 GF: - Fm: 0-0
Distance:	2m/2m3: 0-0 2m4-2m7: 0-1 3m+: 0-0
Track:	LH: 0-0 RH: 0-1 Tight: 0-0 Gall: 0-1
Aids:	Bl: 0-0 Vi: 0-0 Tstrap: 0-0
Best Rating:	**89** 12/98 Font 2m2f110y gd-sft Hdl

Risky Way

100 **109**

6-y-o b g Risk Me (FR)-Hot Sunday Sport (Star Appeal)

B S Rothwell Mike Gosse

Placings:104300/**2-32U42P** **(1192)**

2001/02: 16^{3}F, 20^{2}G, 17^{U}GF, 17^{4}GS, 20^{2}GF, 20^{P}G

	Starts	1st	2nd	3rd	Win & Pl
Chases	6	0	2	1	3146
Career Total	**15**	**1**	**3**	**2**	**6248**

85	9/99	MRas	2m1f110y	G Hdl	G-F	£1688

Total win prize-money £1688

Going:	Sf: 0-0 GS: 0-1 Gd: 0-2 GF: - Fm: 0-3
Distance:	2m/2m3: 0-3 2m4-2m7: 0-3 3m+: 0-0
Track:	LH: 0-4 RH: 0-1 Tight: 0-3 Gall: 0-0
Aids:	Bl: 0-0 Vi: 0-1 Tstrap: 0-0
Best Rating:	**109** 6/01 Worc 2m4f110y good Ch

Rith Ar Aghaidh (IRE)

88 **85**

7-y-o ch m Phardante (FR)-Shuil Ar Aghaidh (The Parson)

E Stanners George Ward

Placings:*00*/F1 **(1042)**

2001/02: 17^{F}GS, 16^{1}GF

	Starts	1st	2nd	3rd	Win & Pl
Hurdles	2	1	0	0	3402
Career Total	**4**	**1**	**0**	**0**	**3402**

85	7/01	Uttx	2m	D Hdl	G-F	£3402

Total win prize-money £3402

Going:	Sf: 0-0 GS: 0-1 Gd: 0-0 GF: - Fm: 1-1
Distance:	**2m/2m3: 1-2** 2m4-2m7: 0-0 3m+: 0-0
Track:	**LH: 1-1** RH: 0-1 Tight: 0-0 Gall: 0-0
Aids:	Bl: 0-0 Vi: 0-0 Tstrap: 0-0
Best Rating:	**90** 3/00 Uttx 2m good NHF

Rith Dubh (IRE)

112 **145**

10-y-o b g Black Minstrel-Deep Bonnie (Deep Run)

J J O'Neill J P McManus

Placings:1/52560/52420/11/236**6-23223221214** **(4961a)**

2001/02: 16^{2}S, 20^{3}G, 22^{2}GS, 22^{2}G, 20^{3}GS, 24^{2}GS, 20^{2}G, 24^{1}S, 24^{2}GS, 32^{1}GS, 25^{4}GY

	Starts	1st	2nd	3rd	Win & Pl
Chases	11	2	6	2	44410
Career Total	**28**	**5**	**10**	**3**	**57952**

145	3/02	Chel	4m	B Ch	G-S	£26000
131	2/02	Hntg	3m	C(0-125)HCh	SFT	£6857
127	6/99	Tipp	2m1f	Hdl	GD	£3376
105	6/99	Wxfd	2m	Hdl	G-F	£2639
110	3/97	Thur	2m2f	NHF	GD	£2712

Total win prize-money £41587

Going:	Sf: 1-2 GS: 1-5 Gd: 0-3 GF: - Fm: 0-0
Distance:	2m/2m3: 0-1 2m4-2m7: 0-5 **3m+: 2-5**
Track:	LH: 1-1 RH: 1-10 Tight: 0-2 **Gall: 2-3**
Aids:	**Bl: 2-9** Vi: 0-0 Tstrap: 0-0
Best Rating:	**145** 4/02 Punc 3m1f gd-yld Ch

Winner of bumpers and hurdle races in Ireland, he ended a series of frustrating runs with a useful win at Huntingdon at the start of 2002. He has a tendency to down tools when the pressure is applied, but was given a superb ride to win the National Hunt Chase at the Festival. Acts on everything but extremes of ground and stays really well.

Ritual

107(94h) (83h)**120**

7-y-o ch g Selkirk (USA)-Pure Formality (Forzando)

Miss Jacqueline S Doyle The Four 'X'

Placings:14F020/5-**21F2** **(3501)**

2001/02: 17^{2}S, 16^{1}GS, 16^{F}GS, 20^{2}S

	Starts	1st	2nd	3rd	Win & Pl
Hurdles	1	0	1	0	654
Chases	3	1	1	0	4137
Career Total	**11**	**2**	**3**	**0**	**8517**

112	12/01	Hntg	2m110y	F(0-105)HCh	G-S	£2569
104	10/99	Font	2m2f110y	E Hdl	GD	£1987

Total win prize-money £4557

Going:	Sf: 0-2 GS: 1-2 Gd: 0-0 GF: - Fm: 0-0
Distance:	**2m/2m3: 1-3** 2m4-2m7: 0-1 3m+: 0-0
Track:	LH: 0-1 **RH: 1-3** Tight: 0-1 **Gall: 1-2**
Aids:	Bl: 0-0 Vi: 0-0 Tstrap: 0-0
Best Rating:	**120** 1/02 Kemp 2m4f110y soft Ch

A winner on the flat and over hurdles for Simon Dow, he has made a decent start over fences for his current trainer. Stays two and a half miles.

Rival Bidder

5-y-o ch g Arzanni-Beltalong (Belfort (FR))

C P Morlock S Kimber

Placings:*0*-0 **(0102)**

2001/02: 18^{0}GF

	Starts	1st	2nd	3rd	Win & Pl
Hurdles	1	0	0	0	
Career Total	**2**	**0**	**0**	**0**	

Going:	Sf: 0-0 GS: 0-0 Gd: 0-0 GF: - Fm: 0-1
Distance:	2m/2m3: 0-1 2m4-2m7: 0-0 3m+: 0-0
Track:	LH: 0-1 RH: 0-0 Tight: 0-1 Gall: 0-0
Aids:	Bl: 0-0 Vi: 0-0 Tstrap: 0-0
Best Rating:	**15** 3/01 Hntg 2m110y soft NHF

River Amora (IRE)

101(89h) (86h)**98**

7-y-o b g Willie Joe (IRE)-That's Amora (Paddy's Stream)

P Butler (John J Walsh 27/7) Mrs P A Wood

Placings:055200034U66013 **(4780)**

2001/02: 17^{0}G, 16^{5}GF, 20^{5}GS, 16^{2}G, 16^{0}GS, 20^{0}G, 17^{0}G, 21^{3}G, 16^{4}S, 20^{U}HY, 21^{6}S, 16^{6}S, 21^{0}GF, 20^{1}GF, 17^{3}GF

	Starts	1st	2nd	3rd	Win & Pl
Hurdles	5	0	0	0	0
Chases	10	1	1	2	4823
Career Total	**15**	**1**	**1**	**2**	**4823**

98	4/02	Plum	2m4f	F Ch	G-F	£2557

Total win prize-money £2558

Going:	Sf: 0-4 GS: 0-2 Gd: 0-5 GF: - Fm: 1-4
Distance:	2m/2m3: 0-8 **2m4-2m7: 1-7** 3m+: 0-0
Track:	**LH: 1-6** RH: 0-8 **Tight: 1-10** Gall: 0-2
Aids:	Bl: 0-0 Vi: 0-0 Tstrap: 0-0
Best Rating:	**98** 4/02 Plum 2m4f gd-fm Ch

Moderate, lightly-raced hurdler/chaser. Suited by good/fast ground.

River Bay (IRE)

11-y-o b m Over The River (FR)-Derrynaflan (Karabas)

N J Henderson Riverwood Racing

Placings:*53/30213P3*/**1225523/4P25220P00/111/P-P** **(0590)**

2001/02: 24^{P}GF

	Starts	1st	2nd	3rd	Win & Pl
Chases		0	0	0	
Career Total	**31**	**5**	**7**	**5**	**32087**

120	11/99	Ludl	3m3f110y	E(0-115)HCh	GD	£4856
116	11/99	Kemp	3m	D(0-120)HCh	GD	£6905
110	10/99	Font	2m6f	D(0-120)HCh	GD	£3798
	11/97	MRas	2m4f	D Ch	G-S	£3795
	12/96	Extr	2m3f110y	Hdl	SFT	£3631

Total win prize-money £22987

Going:	Sf: 0-0 GS: 0-0 Gd: 0-0 GF: - Fm: 0-1
Distance:	2m/2m3: 0-0 2m4-2m7: 0-0 3m+: 0-1
Track:	LH: 0-1 RH: 0-0 Tight: 0-1 Gall: 0-0
Aids:	Bl: 0-1 Vi: 0-0 Tstrap: 0-0
Best Rating:	**120** 11/99 Ludl 3m3f110y good Ch

River Bug (IRE)

94 **116**

8-y-o ch g Over The River (FR)-Fiona's Wish (Wishing Star)

Jamie Poulton (John A Quinn 13/3) Ormonde Racing

Placings:050/**1P1** **(4414)**

2001/02: 25^{1}S, 32^{P}GS, 28^{1}S

	Starts	1st	2nd	3rd	Win & Pl
Chases	3	2	0	0	22120
Career Total	**6**	**2**	**0**	**0**	**22120**

116	3/02	Font	3m4f	D(0-125)HCh	SFT	£17615
96	3/02	Towc	3m1f	F(0-100)HCh	SFT	£4504

Total win prize-money £22120

Going:	Sf: 2-2 GS: 0-1 Gd: 0-0 GF: - Fm: 0-0
Distance:	2m/2m3: 0-0 2m4-2m7: 0-0 **3m+: 2-3**
Track:	LH: 0-1 **RH: 1-1** Tight: 0-0 Gall: 0-1
Aids:	Bl: 0-0 Vi: 0-0 Tstrap: 0-0
Best Rating:	**116** 3/02 Font 3m4f soft Ch

Irish trained and fit from pointing when winning a moderate Towcester chase in March 2002. Outclassed at

Cheltenham next time but bounced back to form when winning the Southern National at Fontwell. Stays well and suited by soft ground.

River Captain (USA)

109 **102**

9-y-o ch g Riverman (USA)-Katsura (USA) (Northern Dancer)

A Scott P Swift,I Bennett,H Harrison,Mrs L Lamb

Placings:40/210 **(2684)**

2001/02: 16^{2}GS, 16^{1}GS, 16^{0}G

	Starts	1st	2nd	3rd	Win & Pl
Hurdles	3	1	1	0	4366
Career Total	**5**	**1**	**1**	**0**	**4366**

100	12/01	Kels	2m110y	E Hdl	G-S	£3346

Total win prize-money £3346

Going: Sf: 0-0 GS: 1-2 Gd: 0-1 GF: - Fm: 0-0
Distance: 2m/2m3: 1-3 2m4-2m7: 0-0 3m+: 0-0
Track: **LH: 1-3** RH: 0-0 **Tight: 1-1** Gall: 0-2
Aids: Bl: 0-0 Vi: 0-0 Tstrap: 0-0
Best Rating: 102 11/01 Newc 2m gd-sft Hdl

Fair novice hurdler, comfortable winner at Kelso in December.

River City (IRE)

97 **95**

5-y-o b g Norwich-Shuil Na Lee (IRE) (Phardante (FR))

Noel T Chance Mrs S Rowley-Williams & Partners

Placings:*01* **(4639)**

2001/02: 17^{0}GS, 16^{1}GF

	Starts	1st	2nd	3rd	Win & Pl
NH Flat	2	1	0	0	2709
Career Total	**2**	**1**	**0**	**0**	**2709**

100	4/02	Asct	2m110y	H NHF	G-F	£2709

Total win prize-money £2709

Going: Sf: 0-0 GS: 0-1 Gd: 0-0 GF: - Fm: 1-1
Distance: **2m/2m3: 1-2** 2m4-2m7: 0-0 3m+: 0-0
Track: LH: 0-1 **RH: 1-1** Tight: 0-1 Gall: 0-0
Aids: Bl: 0-0 Vi: 0-0 Tstrap: 0-0
Best Rating: 100 4/02 Asct 2m110y gd-fm NHF

He ran away with a fast-ground Ascot bumper on his second start and was runner-up on his hurdling debut.

River Dawn (IRE)

99 **110**

10-y-o ch g Over The River (FR)-Morning Susan (Status Seeker)

T R George Mr L D Gamble & Miss K J Gamble

Placings:*60*/04P/2261P/23P/P2-6 **(1836)**

2001/02: 20^{6}GS

	Starts	1st	2nd	3rd	Win & Pl
Chases	1	0	0	0	326
Career Total	**16**	**1**	**4**	**1**	**12623**

127	3/99	Bang	2m4f110y	D Ch	SFT	£4233

Total win prize-money £4234

Going: Sf: 0-0 GS: 0-0 Gd: 0-1 GF: - Fm: 0-0
Distance: 2m/2m3: 0-0 2m4-2m7: 0-1 3m+: 0-0
Track: LH: 0-1 RH: 0-0 Tight: 0-1 Gall: 0-0
Aids: Bl: 0-0 Vi: 0-0 Tstrap: 0-0
Best Rating: 131 10/98 Chel 2m4f110y good Ch

He has shown some decent form over fences, but only has a victory in a maiden chase at Bangor in March 1999 to his name. Lightly raced of late.

River Don

93 **112**

10-y-o ch g Over The River (FR)-Jane's Daughter (Pitpan)

M W Easterby Mrs H Brown

Placings:6/321F/P/PP10-P4F **(2922)**

2001/02: 24^{P}G, 25^{4}S, 24^{F}G

	Starts	1st	2nd	3rd	Win & Pl
Chases	3	0	0	0	330
Career Total	**13**	**2**	**1**	**1**	**8385**

123	1/01	Catt	3m1f110y	F(0-105)HCh	G-S	£2744
116	12/98	Catt	3m1f110y	E Ch	GD	£3304

Total win prize-money £6049

Going: Sf: 0-1 GS: 0-0 Gd: 0-2 GF: - Fm: 0-0
Distance: 2m/2m3: 0-0 2m4-2m7: 0-0 3m+: 0-3
Track: LH: 0-2 RH: 0-1 Tight: 0-3 Gall: 0-0
Aids: Bl: 0-0 Vi: 0-0 Tstrap: 0-2
Best Rating: 123 1/01 Catt 3m1f110y gd-sft Ch

Lightly raced in recent seasons due to problems, he is able but not very consistent. Both of his wins over fences to date have come over the extended three miles one furlong at Catterick.

River Gold

8-y-o ch g River God (USA)-Lady St Clair (Young Generation)

J T Gifford Michael Opperman

Placings:*660*/53540/3PP-P **(0061)**

2001/02: 26^{P}G

	Starts	1st	2nd	3rd	Win & Pl
Chases	1	0	0	0	
Career Total	**12**	**0**	**0**	**2**	**1463**

Going: Sf: 0-0 GS: 0-0 Gd: 0-1 GF: - Fm: 0-0
Distance: 2m/2m3: 0-0 2m4-2m7: 0-0 3m+: 0-1
Track: LH: 0-0 RH: 0-1 Tight: 0-1 Gall: 0-0
Aids: Bl: 0-0 Vi: 0-0 Tstrap: 0-0
Best Rating: 105 2/99 Asct 2m110y gd-sft NHF

River Kwai

71f **25f**

5-y-o ch m Anshan-Brilliant (Never So Bold)

J J Bridger Mrs Julie Jenner

Placings:*0* **(0108)**

2001/02: 18^{0}GF

	Starts	1st	2nd	3rd	Win & Pl
NH Flat	1	0	0	0	
Career Total	**1**	**0**	**0**	**0**	

Going: Sf: 0-0 GS: 0-0 Gd: 0-0 GF: - Fm: 0-1
Distance: 2m/2m3: 0-1 2m4-2m7: 0-0 3m+: 0-0
Track: LH: 0-1 RH: 0-0 Tight: 0-1 Gall: 0-0
Aids: Bl: 0-0 Vi: 0-0 Tstrap: 0-0
Best Rating: 25 5/01 Font 2m2f110y gd-fm NHF

River Lossie

13-y-o b g Bustino-Forres (Thatch (USA))

Miss A Meakins Chris Brasher

Placings:*23*/11F10/321F1U/1135/0 **(4402)**

2001/02: 22^{0}GS

	Starts	1st	2nd	3rd	Win & Pl
Chases	1	0	0	0	
Career Total	**18**	**7**	**2**	**3**	**33085**

150	12/98	Ling	3m	C(0-135)HCh	SFT	£4935
149	11/98	Hayd	2m4f	C(0-135)HCh	G-S	£5159
130	4/96	Extr	2m3f110y	D Ch	GD	£3993
126	2/96	Newb	3m	C Ch	G-S	£5637
115	2/94	Leic	2m	Hdl	HVY	£4190
117	11/93	Kemp	2m	Hdl	GD	£2637
110	10/93	Font	2m2f	Hdl	G-S	£1987

Total win prize-money £28541

Going: Sf: 0-0 GS: 0-1 Gd: 0-0 GF: - Fm: 0-0
Distance: 2m/2m3: 0-0 2m4-2m7: 0-1 3m+: 0-0
Track: LH: 0-1 RH: 0-0 Tight: 0-0 Gall: 0-1
Aids: Bl: 0-0 Vi: 0-0 Tstrap: 0-0
Best Rating: 150 12/98 Ling 3m soft Ch

River Mere

73 **77**

8-y-o b g River God (USA)-Rupert's Daughter (Rupert Bear)

W M Brisbourne Mrs J E Webster

Placings:*502*-PP4P **(4847)**

2001/02: 16^{P}S, 16^{P}G, 20^{4}GF, 20^{P}G

	Starts	1st	2nd	3rd	Win & Pl
Hurdles	4	0	0	0	0
Career Total	**7**	**0**	**1**	**0**	**430**

Going: Sf: 0-1 GS: 0-0 Gd: 0-2 GF: - Fm: 0-1
Distance: 2m/2m3: 0-2 2m4-2m7: 0-2 3m+: 0-0
Track: LH: 0-2 RH: 0-2 Tight: 0-1 Gall: 0-0
Aids: Bl: 0-0 Vi: 0-0 Tstrap: 0-0
Best Rating: 91 10/00 Ludl 2m gd-fm NHF

River Ness

105 **100**

6-y-o br m Buckskin (FR)-Stubbin Moor (Kinglet)

N G Richards Dr Kenneth S Fraser

Placings:P-022011 **(4875)**

2001/02: 20^{0}GS, 22^{2}GS, 21^{2}S, 20^{0}G, 21^{1}S, 24^{1}G

	Starts	1st	2nd	3rd	Win & Pl
Hurdles	6	2	2	0	7598
Career Total	**7**	**2**	**2**	**0**	**7598**

100	4/02	Prth	3m110y	D Hdl	GD	£3731
100	3/02	Sedg	2m5f110y	E Hdl	SFT	£2618

Total win prize-money £6349

Going: Sf: 1-2 GS: 0-2 Gd: 1-2 GF: - Fm: 0-0
Distance: 2m/2m3: 0-0 2m4-2m7: 1-5 3m+: 1-1
Track: LH: 1-4 RH: 1-2 **Tight: 1-3** Gall: 0-0
Aids: Bl: 0-0 Vi: 0-0 Tstrap: 0-0
Best Rating: 100 4/02 Prth 3m110y good Hdl

Lightly raced over hurdles, she took two mares' only novices' hurdles in the spring of 2002. Stays three miles, handles good ground or softer.

River Of Gold (IRE)

(98h) (92h)

8-y-o b g Ikdam-Minnies River (IRE) (Over The River (FR))

B Mactaggart J McKinnon

Placings:3/P-32P **(2118)**

2001/02: 20^{3}GF, 20^{2}GF, 25^{P}GS

	Starts	1st	2nd	3rd	Win & Pl
Hurdles	2	0	1	1	1159
Chases	1	0	0	0	0
Career Total	**5**	**0**	**1**	**2**	**1525**

Going: Sf: 0-0 GS: 0-1 Gd: 0-0 GF: - Fm: 0-2
Distance: 2m/2m3: 0-0 2m4-2m7: 0-2 3m+: 0-1
Track: LH: 0-3 RH: 0-0 Tight: 0-1 Gall: 0-1
Aids: Bl: 0-0 Vi: 0-0 Tstrap: 0-0
Best Rating: **92** 5/01 Newc 2m4f gd-fm Hdl

River Paradise (IRE)

100 93

6-y-o ch g John French-Barbara Brook (Over The River (FR))
Ferdy Murphy Jobs Racing

Placings:F02 **(4583)**
2001/02: 22^{F}S, 20^{0}S, 20^{2}G

	Starts	1st	2nd	3rd	Win & Pl
Hurdles	3	0	1	0	898
Career Total	**3**	**0**	**1**	**0**	**898**

Going: Sf: 0-2 GS: 0-0 Gd: 0-1 GF: - Fm: 0-0
Distance: 2m/2m3: 0-0 2m4-2m7: 0-3 3m+: 0-0
Track: LH: 0-3 RH: 0-0 Tight: 0-1 Gall: 0-1
Aids: Bl: 0-0 Vi: 0-0 Tstrap: 0-0
Best Rating: **93** 4/02 Weth 2m4f110y good Hdl

River Rebel

8-y-o b g French Gondolier (USA)-Kidcello (Bybicello)
Mrs H O Graham Mrs H O Graham

Placings:0P6-P **(0094)**
2001/02: 25^{P}S

	Starts	1st	2nd	3rd	Win & Pl
Chases	1	0	0	0	
Career Total	**4**	**0**	**0**	**0**	0

Going: Sf: 0-1 GS: 0-0 Gd: 0-0 GF: - Fm: 0-0
Distance: 2m/2m3: 0-0 2m4-2m7: 0-0 3m+: 0-1
Track: LH: 0-1 RH: 0-0 Tight: 0-0 Gall: 0-0
Aids: Bl: 0-0 Vi: 0-0 Tstrap: 0-0
Best Rating: **59** 3/01 MRas 2m1f110y gd-sft Hdl

River Ride (IRE)

8-y-o b g King's Ride-Over The Village (IRE) (Over The River (FR))
E Stanners Doubleprint

Placings:P **(0968)**
2001/02: 17^{P}GS

	Starts	1st	2nd	3rd	Win & Pl
Hurdles	1	0	0	0	
Career Total	**1**	**0**	**0**	**0**	

Going: Sf: 0-0 GS: 0-1 Gd: 0-0 GF: - Fm: 0-0
Distance: 2m/2m3: 0-1 2m4-2m7: 0-0 3m+: 0-0
Track: LH: 0-0 RH: 0-0 Tight: 0-0 Gall: 0-0
Aids: Bl: 0-0 Vi: 0-0 Tstrap: 0-0
Best Rating:

River Rising

91 85

8-y-o br g Primitive Rising (USA)-Dragons Daughter (Mandrake Major)
Mrs A Duffield W R Wilson

Placings:P-430 **(0666)**
2001/02: 21^{4}G, 16^{3}GF, 20^{0}G

	Starts	1st	2nd	3rd	Win & Pl
Hurdles	3	0	0	1	424
Career Total	**4**	**0**	**0**	**1**	**424**

Going: Sf: 0-0 GS: 0-0 Gd: 0-2 GF: - Fm: 0-1
Distance: 2m/2m3: 0-1 2m4-2m7: 0-2 3m+: 0-0
Track: LH: 0-3 RH: 0-0 Tight: 0-1 Gall: 0-1
Aids: Bl: 0-0 Vi: 0-0 Tstrap: 0-0
Best Rating: **85** 5/01 Sedg 2m5f110y good Hdl

River Styx (IRE)

113(74h) 91

7-y-o ch g Over The River (FR)-Money For Honey (New Brig)
D McCain The Bankhouse Confederacy

Placings:*000*/2600-00442330 **(4751)**
2001/02: 17^{0}GS, 21^{0}G, 16^{4}GF, 16^{4}GF, 16^{2}G, 16^{3}G, 16^{3}GF, 20^{0}GF

	Starts	1st	2nd	3rd	Win & Pl
Chases	8	0	1	2	2918
Career Total	**15**	**0**	**2**	**2**	**3843**

Going: Sf: 0-0 GS: 0-1 Gd: 0-3 GF: - Fm: 0-4
Distance: 2m/2m3: 0-6 2m4-2m7: 0-2 3m+: 0-0
Track: LH: 0-4 RH: 0-4 Tight: 0-3 Gall: 0-2
Aids: Bl: 0-6 Vi: 0-0 Tstrap: 0-1
Best Rating: **106** 5/00 Aint 2m110y gd-fm Hdl

Modest maiden chaser, suited by two miles and usually blinkered.

River Trix (IRE)

(96h) (100h)

8-y-o b g Riverhead (USA)-Game Trix (Buckskin (FR))
N A Twiston-Davies The Viva Vialli Partnership

Placings:*0*/*0*P2-UPP20 **(3215)**
2001/02: 26^{U}G, 20^{P}G, 22^{P}G, 19^{2}G, 24^{0}GS

	Starts	1st	2nd	3rd	Win & Pl
Hurdles	2	0	1	0	936
Chases	3	0	0	0	0
Career Total	**9**	**0**	**2**	**0**	**1628**

Going: Sf: 0-0 GS: 0-1 Gd: 0-4 GF: - Fm: 0-0
Distance: 2m/2m3: 0-1 2m4-2m7: 0-2 3m+: 0-2
Track: LH: 0-3 RH: 0-2 Tight: 0-1 Gall: 0-4
Aids: Bl: 0-0 Vi: 0-0 Tstrap: 0-1
Best Rating: **100** 4/01 Winc 2m6f soft Hdl

Stays two miles six. Acts on good and soft ground.

River Unshion (IRE)

12-y-o ch g Aristocracy-Smurfette (Baptism)
P Hutchinson Mrs P J Hutchinson

Placings:*6040152521*/*32113*/2F2332UF5/13212210/0 3310P/2346-P0F **(4650)**
2001/02: 24^{P}GS, 21^{0}G, 21^{F}G

	Starts	1st	2nd	3rd	Win & Pl
Chases	3	0	0	0	
Career Total	**45**	**8**	**10**	**8**	**50320**

129	1/00	Ayr	2m4f	C(0-130)HCh	SFT	£5947
129	3/99	Sedg	2m5f	D(0-120)HCh	SFT	£4250
117	12/98	Newc	2m4f	D(0-125)HCh	SFT	£3436
116	9/98	Sedg	2m5f	E(0-115)HCh	GD	£4146
94	3/97	Sedg	2m5f	E Ch	G-F	£2753
95	2/97	Weth	2m4f110y	E Ch	HVY	£3317
114	4/96	Slig	3m	(0-109)HHdl	SFT	£2824
103	12/95	Limk	2m5f	Hdl	SFT	£3391

Total win prize-money £30068

Going: Sf: 0-0 GS: 0-1 Gd: 0-2 GF: - Fm: 0-0
Distance: 2m/2m3: 0-0 2m4-2m7: 0-2 3m+: 0-1
Track: LH: 0-2 RH: 0-0 Tight: 0-2 Gall: 0-0
Aids: Bl: 0-0 Vi: 0-0 Tstrap: 0-0
Best Rating: **129** 9/00 Sedg 2m5f soft Ch

He is not the force of old and proved disappointing for his new connections when tried in hunter chases.

River Wye (IRE)

108 126

10-y-o b g Jareer (USA)-Sun Gift (Guillaume Tell (USA))
G H Yardley Woodsfield Wanderers

Placings:64325/01P/241/2246**12U1F/32112/303-6064** **(4129)**
2001/02: 22^{6}G, 20^{0}S, 20^{6}GS, 16^{4}G

	Starts	1st	2nd	3rd	Win & Pl
Chases	4	0	0	0	348
Career Total	**32**	**6**	**7**	**4**	**42331**

143	3/00	Bang	2m4f110y	C(0-135)HCh	GD	£7247
143	2/00	Kemp	2m4f110y	C(0-130)HCh	SFT	£10481
141	2/99	Bang	2m1f110y	D(0-110)HCh	G-S	£3696
125	12/98	Ludl	2m	E Ch	G-S	£2775
117	5/98	Bang	2m1f	E(0-110)HHdl	GD	£2879
103	2/97	Strf	2m3f	(0-105)Hdl	GD	£2368

Total win prize-money £29448

Going: Sf: 0-1 GS: 0-1 Gd: 0-2 GF: - Fm: 0-0
Distance: 2m/2m3: 0-1 2m4-2m7: 0-3 3m+: 0-0
Track: LH: 0-2 RH: 0-2 Tight: 0-0 Gall: 0-1
Aids: Bl: 0-0 Vi: 0-0 Tstrap: 0-4
Best Rating: **143** 1/01 Donc 2m3f110y good Ch

A useful chaser a couple of seasons ago, he has failed to show much since. Suited by trips from two to two and a half miles and the ground good or softer.

Riverblue (IRE)

103 105

6-y-o b g Bluebird (USA)-La Riveraine (USA) (Riverman (USA))
D J Wintle Mrs Joan L Egan

Placings:2P **(3470)**
2001/02: 16^{2}GF, 17^{P}HY

	Starts	1st	2nd	3rd	Win & Pl
Hurdles	2	0	1	0	935
Career Total	**2**	**0**	**1**	**0**	**935**

Going: Sf: 0-1 GS: 0-0 Gd: 0-0 GF: - Fm: 0-1
Distance: 2m/2m3: 0-2 2m4-2m7: 0-0 3m+: 0-0
Track: LH: 0-1 RH: 0-1 Tight: 0-2 Gall: 0-0
Aids: Bl: 0-0 Vi: 0-0 Tstrap: 0-0
Best Rating: **105** 6/01 Strf 2m110y gd-fm Hdl

Useful handicapper on the Flat on a fast surface, he showed ability on his debut but was well beaten when pulled up on hurdles debut on heavy.

Riverlord

98(83h) (42h)88

8-y-o b g River God (USA)-Sultry (Sula Bula)
P R Rodford Miss S J Burgin

Placings:*00*/P6 **(4598)**
2001/02: 19^{P}G, 16^{6}GF

	Starts	1st	2nd	3rd	Win & Pl
Chases	2	0	0	0	0
Career Total	**4**	**0**	**0**	**0**	**0**

Going: Sf: 0-0 GS: 0-0 Gd: 0-1 GF: - Fm: 0-1
Distance: 2m/2m3: 0-1 2m4-2m7: 0-1 3m+: 0-0
Track: LH: 0-0 RH: 0-1 Tight: 0-0 Gall: 0-0
Aids: Bl: 0-0 Vi: 0-0 Tstrap: 0-0
Best Rating: 77 4/02 Wwck 2m110y gd-fm Ch

Riversdale (IRE)

105 **101**

6-y-o b g Elbio-Embustera (Sparkler)
J G Fitzgerald Mrs R A G Haggie

Placings:300-F3103 **(4094)**
2001/02: 17^{F}G, 16^{3}S, 17^{1}S, 16^{0}GS, 16^{3}GS

	Starts	1st	2nd	3rd	Win & Pl
Hurdles	5	1	0	2	2238
Career Total	**8**	**1**	**0**	**3**	**2494**

101 11/01 Sedg 2m1f G(0-95)HHdl SFT £1603
Total win prize-money £1603

Going: Sf: 1-2 GS: 0-2 Gd: 0-1 GF: - Fm: 0-0
Distance: **2m/2m3: 1-5** 2m4-2m7: 0-0 3m+: 0-0
Track: **LH: 1-4** RH: 0-1 **Tight: 1-4** Gall: 0-0
Aids: Bl: 0-0 Vi: 0-0 Tstrap: 0-1
Best Rating: 101 11/01 Sedg 2m1f soft Hdl

Modest hurdler, a winner of a seller at Sedgefield in the autumn of 2001.

Riverside Lodge (IRE)

98 **83**

8-y-o b g Riverhead (USA)-Huricane Dodo (Sexton Blake)
R D E Woodhouse R Priestley Developments Co Ltd

Placings:0PP/FP1PFPP/PP50-P3P **(4855)**
2001/02: 16^{P}S, 21^{3}GF, 20^{P}G

	Starts	1st	2nd	3rd	Win & Pl
Chases	3	0	0	1	596
Career Total	**17**	**1**	**0**	**1**	**5496**

90 12/99 Catt 2m3f F(0-100)HCh GD £4900
Total win prize-money £4900

Going: Sf: 0-1 GS: 0-0 Gd: 0-1 GF: - Fm: 0-1
Distance: 2m/2m3: 0-1 2m4-2m7: 0-2 3m+: 0-0
Track: LH: 0-3 RH: 0-0 Tight: 0-1 Gall: 0-0
Aids: Bl: 0-0 Vi: 0-0 Tstrap: 0-0
Best Rating: 90 12/99 Catt 2m3f good Ch

Riverside Run (IRE)

9-y-o b g Commanche Run-Annamoss (Le Moss)
Stephen Melrose Robert Miller-Bakewell

Placings:5/0P-P2PP **(3749)**
2001/02: 25^{P}S, 22^{2}G, 28^{P}GF, 24^{P}S

	Starts	1st	2nd	3rd	Win & Pl
Chases	4	0	1	0	703
Career Total	**7**	**0**	**1**	**0**	**703**

Going: Sf: 0-2 GS: 0-0 Gd: 0-1 GF: - Fm: 0-1
Distance: 2m/2m3: 0-0 2m4-2m7: 0-1 3m+: 0-3
Track: LH: 0-2 RH: 0-2 Tight: 0-3 Gall: 0-0
Aids: Bl: 0-0 Vi: 0-0 Tstrap: 0-1
Best Rating: 88 5/01 MRas 2m6f110y good Ch

Rivertown (NZ)

94 **91**

8-y-o b g Oak Ridge (FR)-Star Habit (NZ) (Habituate)
Mrs A J Perrett The Tuesday Syndicate

Placings:0-5 **(0230)**
2001/02: 16^{5}GF

	Starts	1st	2nd	3rd	Win & Pl
Hurdles	1	0	0	0	0
Career Total	**2**	**0**	**0**	**0**	**0**

Going: Sf: 0-0 GS: 0-0 Gd: 0-0 GF: - Fm: 0-1
Distance: 2m/2m3: 0-1 2m4-2m7: 0-0 3m+: 0-0
Track: LH: 0-0 RH: 0-1 Tight: 0-0 Gall: 0-1
Aids: Bl: 0-0 Vi: 0-0 Tstrap: 0-0
Best Rating: 91 5/01 Hntg 2m110y gd-fm Hdl

Riviere

93 **64**

7-y-o ch m Meadowbrook-Cimarron (Carnival Dancer)
Mrs M Reveley R G Fairs

Placings:*04/16/*0-0 **(0203)**
2001/02: 20^{0}G

	Starts	1st	2nd	3rd	Win & Pl
Hurdles	1	0	0	0	
Career Total	**6**	**1**	**0**	**0**	**1589**

111 1/00 Muss 2m H NHF SFT £1589
Total win prize-money £1589

Going: Sf: 0-0 GS: 0-0 Gd: 0-1 GF: - Fm: 0-0
Distance: 2m/2m3: 0-0 2m4-2m7: 0-1 3m+: 0-0
Track: LH: 0-1 RH: 0-0 Tight: 0-0 Gall: 0-0
Aids: Bl: 0-0 Vi: 0-0 Tstrap: 0-0
Best Rating: 111 1/00 Muss 2m soft NHF

Riyadh

96 **114**

4-y-o ch g Caerleon (USA)-Ausherra (USA) (Diesis)
M C Pipe (P F I Cole 6/10) A S Helaissi

Placings:32400 **(4653)**
2001/02: 16^{3}GS, 16^{2}GS, 20^{4}S, 17^{0}G, 20^{0}G

	Starts	1st	2nd	3rd	Win & Pl
Hurdles	5	0	1	1	1967
Career Total	**5**	**0**	**1**	**1**	**1967**

Going: Sf: 0-1 GS: 0-2 Gd: 0-2 GF: - Fm: 0-0
Distance: 2m/2m3: 0-3 2m4-2m7: 0-2 3m+: 0-0
Track: LH: 0-5 RH: 0-0 Tight: 0-1 Gall: 0-3
Aids: Bl: 0-0 Vi: 0-3 Tstrap: 0-0
Best Rating: 114 1/02 Newb 2m110y gd-sft Hdl

A useful stayer, but a difficult ride on the Flat, he made an encouraging start to hurdling with two promising efforts at Newbury. May have found the ground too soft at Haydock. He ran his best races on the level on good or faster ground. Has worn blinkers and a visor.

Road Racer (IRE)

101 **135**

9-y-o br g Scenic-Rally (Relko)
P R Webber Michael Coghlan

Placings:F11142/020P100/1/0531-22P3 **(4851)**
2001/02: 16^{2}GF, 17^{2}GF, 16^{P}G, 20^{3}G

	Starts	1st	2nd	3rd	Win & Pl
Chases	4	0	2	1	5260
Career Total	**22**	**6**	**4**	**2**	**39071**

133 4/01 Kemp 2m C(0-130)HCh GD £8153
123 10/99 Kemp 2m D Ch G-F £4135
135 3/99 Newb 2m110y B HHdl G-F £6905
131 1/98 Kemp 2m D Hdl SFT £2658
131 12/97 Ludl 2m E Hdl GD £2360
120 12/97 Hntg 2m110y E Hdl GD £2862
Total win prize-money £27075

Going: Sf: 0-0 GS: 0-0 Gd: 0-2 GF: - Fm: 0-2
Distance: 2m/2m3: 0-3 2m4-2m7: 0-1 3m+: 0-0
Track: LH: 0-3 RH: 0-1 Tight: 0-3 Gall: 0-1
Aids: Bl: 0-0 Vi: 0-4 Tstrap: 0-0
Best Rating: 135 6/01 Strf 2m1f110y gd-fm Ch

Useful chaser, he turned in some useful performances in two-mile handicaps during the spring of 2001, but was off the track for ten months until reappearing in April 2002. Suited by two miles on a flat track, and suited by good or faster ground.

Roaming Ronan (IRE)

80 **70**

4-y-o b g Sri Pekan (USA)-Maradata (IRE) (Shardari)
R W Thomson (J J O'Neill 19/10) R W Thomson

Placings:4503 **(4397)**
2001/02: 17^{4}G, 16^{5}GF, 17^{0}GS, 18^{3}HY

	Starts	1st	2nd	3rd	Win & Pl
Hurdles	4	0	0	1	398
Career Total	**4**	**0**	**0**	**1**	**398**

Going: Sf: 0-1 GS: 0-1 Gd: 0-1 GF: - Fm: 0-1
Distance: 2m/2m3: 0-4 2m4-2m7: 0-0 3m+: 0-0
Track: LH: 0-3 RH: 0-1 Tight: 0-3 Gall: 0-0
Aids: Bl: 0-1 Vi: 0-0 Tstrap: 0-0
Best Rating: 70 3/02 Kels 2m2f heavy Hdl

Rob Leach

121 **128**

5-y-o b g Robellino (USA)-Arc Empress Jane (IRE) (Rainbow Quest (USA))
G L Moore Richard Green (fine Paintings)

Placings:262-1431126 **(3380)**
2001/02: 16^{1}GS, 16^{4}G, 16^{3}S, 16^{1}G, 16^{1}S, 16^{2}GS, 16^{6}GS

	Starts	1st	2nd	3rd	Win & Pl
Hurdles	7	3	1	1	42741
Career Total	**10**	**3**	**3**	**1**	**44356**

128 12/01 Sand 2m110y A(0-150)HHdl SFT £31900
116 11/01 Plum 2m D Hdl GD £3721
108 9/01 Plum 2m E Hdl G-S £2520
Total win prize-money £38141

Going: Sf: 1-2 GS: 1-3 Gd: 1-2 GF: - Fm: 0-0
Distance: **2m/2m3: 3-7** 2m4-2m7: 0-0 3m+: 0-0
Track: **LH: 2-5** RH: 1-2 **Tight: 2-2** Gall: 0-1
Aids: **Bl: 1-3** Vi: 0-0 Tstrap: 0-0
Best Rating: 128 12/01 Newb 2m110y gd-sft Hdl

Improved with experience over hurdles last season, and got off the mark on his first run this term at Plumpton. Held in two runs at Chepstow after, but successfully returned to Plumpton and took a valuable handicap at Sandown when fitted with blinkers for the first time. Possibly a better effort when second in a conditions event at Newbury. Handles good ground or easier and obviously likes a sharp track.

Robber (IRE)

100f **92f**

5-y-o ch g Un Desperado (FR)-Christy's Girl (IRE) (Buckskin (FR))
P J Hobbs The Hedonists

Placings: *04* **(4166)**
2001/02: 16^{0}G, 16^{4}GS

	Starts	1st	2nd	3rd	Win & Pl
NH Flat	2	0	0	0	0
Career Total	**2**	**0**	**0**	**0**	**0**

Going: Sf: 0-0 GS: 0-1 Gd: 0-1 GF: - Fm: 0-0
Distance: 2m/2m3: 0-2 2m4-2m7: 0-0 3m+: 0-0
Track: LH: 0-1 RH: 0-1 Tight: 0-0 Gall: 0-0
Aids: Bl: 0-0 Vi: 0-0 Tstrap: 0-0
Best Rating: 92 3/02 Wwck 2m gd-sft NHF

In the frame in a bumper.

Robber Baron (IRE)

105 **122**

5-y-o ch g Un Desperado (FR)-N T Nad (Welsh Pageant)
Miss H C Knight The Radicals Partnership

Placings: *1-3226* **(4662)**
2001/02: 16^{3}G, 17^{2}G, 16^{2}GS, 16^{6}G

	Starts	1st	2nd	3rd	Win & Pl
NH Flat	1	0	0	1	1356
Hurdles	3	0	2	0	4194
Career Total	**5**	**1**	**2**	**1**	**7356**

110	3/01	Hntg	2m110y	H NHF	SFT	£1806

Total win prize-money £1806

Going: Sf: 0-0 GS: 0-1 Gd: 0-3 GF: - Fm: 0-0
Distance: 2m/2m3: 0-4 2m4-2m7: 0-0 3m+: 0-0
Track: LH: 0-3 RH: 0-1 Tight: 0-1 Gall: 0-1
Aids: Bl: 0-0 Vi: 0-0 Tstrap: 0-0
Best Rating: 122 2/02 Ludl 2m gd-sft Hdl

Got off the mark on his debut in a Huntingdon bumper in March 2001, before a fair third in a Listed event at Cheltenham. Runner-up to useful sorts twice over hurdles. Acts on good and soft ground. His future looks to lie over fences.

Robbie Jnr

6-y-o br g Weld-Owen Belle (Master Owen)
E McNamara Robert Butler

Placings: 001P **(4678)**
2001/02: 16^{0}YS, 17^{0}GF, 24^{1}S, 25^{P}G

	Starts	1st	2nd	3rd	Win & Pl
Hurdles	2	0	0	0	0
Chases	2	1	0	0	5926
Career Total	**4**	**1**	**0**	**0**	**5926**

86	3/02	Limk	3m	Ch	SFT	£5926

Total win prize-money £5926

Going: Sf: 1-1 GS: 0-0 Gd: 0-1 GF: - Fm: 0-1
Distance: 2m/2m3: 0-2 2m4-2m7: 0-0 **3m+: 1-2**
Track: LH: 0-1 **RH: 1-1** Tight: 0-1 Gall: 0-0
Aids: Bl: 0-0 Vi: 0-0 Tstrap: 0-0
Best Rating: 86 3/02 Limk 3m soft Ch

Robbie's Adventure

96 **90**

8-y-o ch g Le Coq D'Or-Mendick Adventure (Mandrake Major)
D L Williams Symbol Of Success Racing

Placings: 04/0P045103/**P3F134P-325** **(2707)**
2001/02: 26^{3}S, 26^{2}HY, 20^{5}G

	Starts	1st	2nd	3rd	Win & Pl
Chases	3	0	1	1	1285
Career Total	**20**	**2**	**1**	**4**	**7528**

96	1/01	Tntn	3m	F(0-95)HCh	HVY	£3139
86	2/00	Folk	2m1f110y	G(0-90)HHdl	SFT	£1547

Total win prize-money £4687

Going: Sf: 0-2 GS: 0-0 Gd: 0-1 GF: - Fm: 0-0
Distance: 2m/2m3: 0-0 2m4-2m7: 0-1 3m+: 0-2
Track: LH: 0-3 RH: 0-0 Tight: 0-1 Gall: 0-0
Aids: Bl: 0-0 Vi: 0-2 Tstrap: 0-0
Best Rating: 96 1/01 Tntn 3m heavy Ch

A fair staying chaser. Acts on an easy surface. Not the best of jumpers. Has run well in a visor.

Robbo

113 **153**

8-y-o b g Robellino (USA)-Basha (USA) (Chief's Crown (USA))
Mrs M Reveley The Scarth Racing Partnership

Placings: 1120/332221106/**U21123115/0124363-042P006** **(4831)**
2001/02: 20^{0}G, 25^{4}GS, 24^{2}S, 28^{P}HY, 24^{0}GS, 25^{0}G, 20^{6}G

	Starts	1st	2nd	3rd	Win & Pl
Chases	7	0	1	0	11543
Career Total	**36**	**9**	**8**	**5**	**102981**

159	11/00	Kels	3m1f	B(0-140)HCh	SFT	£8990
157	3/00	Carl	2m4f110y	C Ch	HVY	£7560
152	2/00	Newc	2m4f	B(0-140)HCh	HVY	£10432
118	11/99	Kels	2m6f110y	E Ch	GD	£3355
123	11/99	Ayr	2m4f	D Ch	GD	£3951
133	2/99	Newc	2m4f	B(0-140)HHdl	G-S	£6937
134	2/99	Ayr	2m4f	C(0-130)HHdl	SFT	£5790
118	1/98	Newc	2m	E Hdl	G-S	£2368
116	1/98	Ayr	2m	E Hdl	SFT	£2248

Total win prize-money £51635

Going: Sf: 0-2 GS: 0-2 Gd: 0-3 GF: - Fm: 0-0
Distance: 2m/2m3: 0-0 2m4-2m7: 0-2 3m+: 0-5
Track: LH: 0-7 RH: 0-0 Tight: 0-1 Gall: 0-2
Aids: Bl: 0-5 Vi: 0-2 Tstrap: 0-0
Best Rating: 159 12/00 Chel 2m5f soft Ch

Has plenty of ability, but sometimes appears a little quirky and tends to be best when coming off the pace. Suited by easy ground and a stiff track. Stays at least three miles over fences and wears blinkers.

Robella

99 **72**

6-y-o ch m Keen-Afrabela (African Sky)
K A Morgan Mrs Gilly Willett

Placings: *03-60034300* **(4765)**
2001/02: 16^{6}GF, 16^{0}GF, 17^{0}GF, 17^{3}G, 16^{4}GF, 16^{3}GS, 19^{0}GS, 16^{0}GF

	Starts	1st	2nd	3rd	Win & Pl
NH Flat	2	0	0	0	0
Hurdles	6	0	0	2	1058
Career Total	**10**	**0**	**0**	**3**	**1276**

Going: Sf: 0-0 GS: 0-2 Gd: 0-1 GF: - Fm: 0-5
Distance: 2m/2m3: 0-8 2m4-2m7: 0-0 3m+: 0-0
Track: LH: 0-5 RH: 0-2 Tight: 0-5 Gall: 0-1
Aids: Bl: 0-0 Vi: 0-0 Tstrap: 0-0
Best Rating: 72 1/02 Sthl 2m gd-sft Hdl

Weak form at around two miles over hurdles.

Robellando

95 **81**

5-y-o b g Robellino (USA)-Drama School (Young Generation)
B G Powell Ann Plummer & Partners

Placings: 43P-50P3P **(3459)**
2001/02: 19^{5}GF, 21^{0}G, 20^{P}S, 23^{3}S, 21^{P}HY

	Starts	1st	2nd	3rd	Win & Pl
Hurdles	5	0	0	1	346
Career Total	**8**	**0**	**0**	**2**	**736**

Going: Sf: 0-3 GS: 0-0 Gd: 0-1 GF: - Fm: 0-1
Distance: 2m/2m3: 0-1 2m4-2m7: 0-3 3m+: 0-1
Track: LH: 0-1 RH: 0-3 Tight: 0-1 Gall: 0-0
Aids: Bl: 0-2 Vi: 0-0 Tstrap: 0-0
Best Rating: 98 12/00 Folk 2m1f110y heavy Hdl

Modest novice hurdler, stays three miles.

Robellita

8-y-o b g Robellino (USA)-Miellita (King Emperor (USA))
P R Chamings (B G Powell 3/5) Angels Racing Syndicate

Placings: *04/0P/PP* **(3739)**
2001/02: 16^{P}G, 16^{P}S

	Starts	1st	2nd	3rd	Win & Pl
Chases	2	0	0	0	
Career Total	**6**	**0**	**0**	**0**	**0**

Going: Sf: 0-1 GS: 0-0 Gd: 0-1 GF: - Fm: 0-0
Distance: 2m/2m3: 0-2 2m4-2m7: 0-0 3m+: 0-0
Track: LH: 0-0 RH: 0-2 Tight: 0-0 Gall: 0-0
Aids: Bl: 0-0 Vi: 0-0 Tstrap: 0-0
Best Rating: 90 3/98 Hntg 2m110y good NHF

Robert The Bruce

93 **105**

7-y-o ch g Distinct Native-Kawarau Queen (Taufan (USA))
L Lungo G G Fraser

Placings: 333/31-2 **(1641)**
2001/02: 17^{2}GS

	Starts	1st	2nd	3rd	Win & Pl
Hurdles	1	0	1	0	698
Career Total	**6**	**1**	**1**	**4**	**4909**

96	5/00	Hexm	2m	E Hdl	GD	£2443

Total win prize-money £2444

Going: Sf: 0-0 GS: 0-1 Gd: 0-0 GF: - Fm: 0-0
Distance: 2m/2m3: 0-1 2m4-2m7: 0-0 3m+: 0-0
Track: LH: 0-0 RH: 0-1 Tight: 0-0 Gall: 0-0
Aids: Bl: 0-0 Vi: 0-0 Tstrap: 0-0
Best Rating: 105 10/01 Carl 2m1f gd-sft Hdl

Roberty Bob (IRE)

116 **143**

7-y-o ch g Bob Back (USA)-Inesdela (Wolver Hollow)
H D Daly P J H Wills

Placings: 43222/311 **(4298)**
2001/02: 21^{3}S, 22^{1}S, 26^{1}HY

	Starts	1st	2nd	3rd	Win & Pl
Chases	3	2	0	1	25280
Career Total	**8**	**2**	**3**	**2**	**28628**

143	3/02	Uttx	3m2f	B HCh	HVY	£19110
135	3/02	Towc	2m6f	D Ch	SFT	£5538

Total win prize-money £24648

Going: Sf: 2-3 GS: 0-0 Gd: 0-0 GF: - Fm: 0-0
Distance: 2m/2m3: 0-0 2m4-2m7: 1-2 3m+: 1-1
Track: LH: 1-2 RH: 1-1 Tight: 0-0 Gall: 0-0

Aids: Bl: 0-0 Vi: 0-0 Tstrap: 0-0
Best Rating: 143 3/02 Uttx 3m2f heavy Ch

Fair form over hurdles, he has shaped a lot better over fences, winning at Towcester and a valuable novices' handicap by a distance at Uttoxeter in March 2002. Stays beyond three miles and is suited by soft ground.

Robin Of Loxley (IRE)

11-y-o b g Lancastrian-Magic User (Deep Run)
Mrs G M Gladders P V M Egan

Placings:PP (0321)
2001/02: 26PG, 26PG

	Starts	1st	2nd	3rd	Win & Pl
Chases	2	0	0	0	
Career Total	2	0	0	0	

Going: Sf: 0-0 GS: 0-0 Gd: 0-2 GF: - Fm: 0-0
Distance: 2m/2m3: 0-0 2m4-2m7: 0-0 3m+: 0-2
Track: LH: 0-0 RH: 0-2 Tight: 0-2 Gall: 0-0
Aids: Bl: 0-0 Vi: 0-0 Tstrap: 0-0
Best Rating:

Robins Meg

101f 82f
6-y-o b m Skyliner-Home Dove (Homeboy)
J J Quinn Mrs Joan W Robinson

Placings:30 (1905)
2001/02: 17³S, 17⁰G

	Starts	1st	2nd	3rd	Win & Pl
NH Flat	2	0	0	1	228
Career Total	2	0	0	1	228

Going: Sf: 0-1 GS: 0-0 Gd: 0-1 GF: - Fm: 0-0
Distance: 2m/2m3: 0-2 2m4-2m7: 0-0 3m+: 0-0
Track: LH: 0-1 RH: 0-1 Tight: 0-2 Gall: 0-0
Aids: Bl: 0-0 Vi: 0-0 Tstrap: 0-0
Best Rating: 82 9/01 MRas 2m1f110y soft NHF

Robins Pride (IRE)

92 91
12-y-o b g Treasure Hunter-Barney's Sister (Abednego)
C L Popham Richard Weeks, P Littlejohns, A Staple

Placings:30/P0054/22F1521201/P22P3U2/P3312353 F/PU44142204F/053640624P1/655641U6U-00043 (3289)
2001/02: 16⁰G, 19⁰GF, 21⁰G, 25⁴G, 21³S

	Starts	1st	2nd	3rd	Win & Pl
Chases	5	0	0	1	1186
Career Total	69	7	11	8	39655

99	1/01	Tntn	3m	F(0-110)HCh	HVY	£3493
109	4/00	Winc	2m	E(0-115)HCh	G-S	£4270
111	12/98	Winc	2m	D(0-125)HCh	SFT	£3512
104	12/97	Winc	2m	D(0-125)HCh	G-S	£3626
106	3/96	NAbb	2m1f	F(0-100)HHdl	SFT	£2589
96	1/96	Winc	2m	F Hdl	G-S	£2617
80	5/95	Ctml	2m1f110y	E Hdl	GD	£2416

Total win prize-money £22528

Going: Sf: 0-1 GS: 0-0 Gd: 0-3 GF: - Fm: 0-1
Distance: 2m/2m3: 0-1 2m4-2m7: 0-3 3m+: 0-1
Track: LH: 0-0 RH: 0-4 Tight: 0-1 Gall: 0-0
Aids: Bl: 0-4 Vi: 0-0 Tstrap: 0-0
Best Rating: 116 2/99 Hntg 2m110y gd-sft Ch

Fair handicap chaser. Stays three miles. Loves the mud.

Roboastar (USA)

97 90
5-y-o b/br g Green Dancer (USA)-Sweet Alabastar (USA) (Gulch (USA))
P G Murphy Mrs John Spielman

Placings:404R0 (4502)
2001/02: 16⁴GS, 17⁰G, 19⁴S, 21ᴿHY, 22⁰G

	Starts	1st	2nd	3rd	Win & Pl
Hurdles	5	0	0	0	0
Career Total	5	0	0	0	0

Going: Sf: 0-2 GS: 0-1 Gd: 0-2 GF: - Fm: 0-0
Distance: 2m/2m3: 0-2 2m4-2m7: 0-3 3m+: 0-0
Track: LH: 0-2 RH: 0-2 Tight: 0-3 Gall: 0-0
Aids: Bl: 0-0 Vi: 0-0 Tstrap: 0-0
Best Rating: 90 10/01 Strf 2m110y gd-sft Hdl

Roborette (FR)

97 73
9-y-o b m Robore (FR)-Bentry (FR) (Ben Trovato (FR))
J Neville T A Wadsworth

Placings:0/311054/643P/P-03O00 (0907)
2001/02: 20⁰G, 22³GF, 22⁰G, 22⁰GF, 24⁰G

	Starts	1st	2nd	3rd	Win & Pl
Hurdles	5	0	0	1	351
Career Total	17	2	0	3	0704

99	11/98	Folk	2m1f110y	H NHF	SFT	£1203
100	11/98	Extr	2m1f	H NHF	SFT	£1287

Total win prize-money £2490

Going: Sf: 0-0 GS: 0-0 Gd: 0-3 GF: - Fm: 0-2
Distance: 2m/2m3: 0-0 2m4-2m7: 0-4 3m+: 0-1
Track: LH: 0-5 RH: 0-0 Tight: 0-4 Gall: 0-0
Aids: Bl: 0-0 Vi: 0-0 Tstrap: 0-5
Best Rating: 100 11/98 Extr 2m1f soft NHF

Robzelda

103 94
6-y-o b g Robellino (USA)-Zelda (USA) (Sharpen Up)
K A Ryan Tony Fawcett

Placings:463 (2631)
2001/02: 20⁴G, 16⁶G, 16³S

	Starts	1st	2nd	3rd	Win & Pl
Hurdles	3	0	0	1	570
Career Total	3	0	0	1	570

Going: Sf: 0-1 GS: 0-0 Gd: 0-2 GF: - Fm: 0-0
Distance: 2m/2m3: 0-2 2m4-2m7: 0-1 3m+: 0-0
Track: LH: 0-3 RH: 0-0 Tight: 0-0 Gall: 0-0
Aids: Bl: 0-0 Vi: 0-0 Tstrap: 0-0
Best Rating: 94 12/01 Hexm 2m soft Hdl

Rocastle Lad (IRE)

67f 40f
6-y-o gr g Roselier (FR)-Ivory Queen (Teenoso (USA))
N J Hawke N J McMullan

Placings:0 (2222)
2001/02: 17⁰G

	Starts	1st	2nd	3rd	Win & Pl
NH Flat	1	0	0	0	
Career Total	1	0	0	0	

Going: Sf: 0-0 GS: 0-0 Gd: 0-1 GF: - Fm: 0-0
Distance: 2m/2m3: 0-1 2m4-2m7: 0-0 3m+: 0-0
Track: LH: 0-1 RH: 0-0 Tight: 0-1 Gall: 0-0
Aids: Bl: 0-0 Vi: 0-0 Tstrap: 0-0
Best Rating: 40 11/01 NAbb 2m1f good NHF

Roccioso

86 72
5-y-o br g Pelder (IRE)-Priory Bay (Petong)
J C Fox Mrs J A Cleary

Placings:PP0-PP030 (4185)
2001/02: 16ᴾG, 16ᴾS, 16⁰G, 17³S, 17⁰S

	Starts	1st	2nd	3rd	Win & Pl
Hurdles	5	0	0	1	254
Career Total	8	0	0	1	254

Going: Sf: 0-3 GS: 0-0 Gd: 0-2 GF: - Fm: 0-0
Distance: 2m/2m3: 0-5 2m4-2m7: 0-0 3m+: 0-0
Track: LH: 0-1 RH: 0-4 Tight: 0-2 Gall: 0-2
Aids: Bl: 0-0 Vi: 0-0 Tstrap: 0-0
Best Rating: 73 12/00 Newb 2m110y soft Hdl

Very modest maiden hurdler.

Rochampbeau (IRE)

4-y-o ch f Rainbows For Life (CAN)-Brandywell (Skyliner)
N M Babbage Mrs Joan Nelson

Placings:0 (1231)
2001/02: 16⁰GF

	Starts	1st	2nd	3rd	Win & Pl
Hurdles	1	0	0	0	
Career Total	1	0	0	0	

Going: Sf: 0-0 GS: 0-0 Gd: 0-0 GF: - Fm: 0-1
Distance: 2m/2m3: 0-1 2m4-2m7: 0-0 3m+: 0-0
Track: LH: 0-1 RH: 0-0 Tight: 0-0 Gall: 0-0
Aids: Bl: 0-0 Vi: 0-0 Tstrap: 0-0
Best Rating:

Rock Falcon (IRE)

9-y-o ch g Polar Falcon (USA)-Rockfest (USA) (Stagedoor Johnny)
B Ellison (D Nicholls 31/5) Brian Ellison

Placings:61-LR (2903)
2001/02: 16ᴸF, 16ᴿGS

	Starts	1st	2nd	3rd	Win & Pl
Hurdles	2	0	0	0	
Career Total	4	1	0	0	2941

106	8/00	Strf	2m110y	E Hdl	G-F	£2941

Total win prize-money £2941

Going: Sf: 0-0 GS: 0-1 Gd: 0-0 GF: - Fm: 0-1
Distance: 2m/2m3: 0-2 2m4-2m7: 0-0 3m+: 0-0
Track: LH: 0-2 RH: 0-0 Tight: 0-0 Gall: 0-0
Aids: Bl: 0-0 Vi: 0-0 Tstrap: 0-2
Best Rating: 106 8/00 Strf 2m110y gd-fm Hdl

Rock Rose

104(104h) (87h)110
9-y-o b m Arctic Lord-Ovington Court (Prefairy)
C Tizzard (N R Mitchell 24/1) Mrs Angela Davis

Placings:5U5/P602O3-3B**U214P** (4516)
2001/02: 22^{3}GF, 22^{B}G, 19^{U}S, 20^{2}HY, 24^{1}S, 22^{4}GS, 16^{P}GS

	Starts	1st	2nd	3rd	Win & Pl
Hurdles	2	0	0	1	512
Chases	5	1	1	0	6718
Career Total	**16**	**1**	**2**	**2**	**8312**

110 2/02 Tntn 3m D Ch SFT £5284
Total win prize-money £5285

Going: Sf: 1-3 GS: 0-2 Gd: 0-1 GF: - Fm: 0-1
Distance: 2m/2m3: 0-2 2m4-2m7: 0-4 **3m+: 1-1**
Track: LH: 0-2 **RH: 1-5 Tight: 1-3** Gall: 0-1
Aids: Bl: 0-0 Vi: 0-0 Tstrap: 0-0
Best Rating: 110 2/02 Tntn 3m soft Ch

Has shown ability over both hurdles and fences in modest company. Won a decent chase over three miles in February 2002.

Rock Springs

4-y-o b g Rock City-Riva La Belle (Ron's Victory (USA))
J J Quinn Mrs B J Boocock

Placings:0 (3368)
2001/02: 16^{0}GS

	Starts	1st	2nd	3rd	Win & Pl
NH Flat	1	0	0	0	
Career Total	**1**	**0**	**0**	**0**	

Going: Sf: 0-0 GS: 0-1 Gd: 0-0 GF: - Fm: 0-0
Distance: 2m/2m3: 0-1 2m4-2m7: 0-0 3m+: 0-0
Track: LH: 0-1 RH: 0-0 Tight: 0-1 Gall: 0-0
Aids: Bl: 0-0 Vi: 0-0 Tstrap: 0-0
Best Rating:

Rock'n Cold (IRE)

107 **109**

4-y-o b g Bigstone (IRE)-Unalaska (IRE) (High Estate)
T R George (R M H Cowell 25/10) C Akers

Placings:5213 (4263)
2001/02: 17^{5}GS, 16^{2}HY, 17^{1}GS, 16^{3}S

	Starts	1st	2nd	3rd	Win & Pl
Hurdles	4	1	1	1	3990
Career Total	**4**	**1**	**1**	**1**	**3990**

109 3/02 MRas 2m1f110y E Hdl G-S £2765
Total win prize-money £2765

Going: Sf: 0-2 GS: 1-2 Gd: 0-0 GF: - Fm: 0-0
Distance: **2m/2m3: 1-4** 2m4-2m7: 0-0 3m+: 0-0
Track: LH: 0-2 **RH: 1-2 Tight: 1-2** Gall: 0-0
Aids: Bl: 0-0 Vi: 0-0 Tstrap: 0-0
Best Rating: 109 3/02 MRas 2m1f110y gd-sft Hdl

Modest form in juvenile hurdles., winning a moderate heat at Market Rasen. Has won on good to soft ground, handled softer.

Rockanroll

92 **101**

6-y-o b g Tragic Role (USA)-Last Note (Welsh Pageant)
Miss Jacqueline S Doyle The Rocknrollers

Placings:30/11-43 (4642)
2001/02: 16^{4}G, 16^{3}G

	Starts	1st	2nd	3rd	Win & Pl
Hurdles	2	0	0	1	600
Career Total	**6**	**2**	**0**	**2**	**3842**

99 6/00 Worc 2m H NHF GD £1466
93 5/00 Worc 2m H NHF G-F £1515
Total win prize-money £2983

Going: Sf: 0-0 GS: 0-0 Gd: 0-2 GF: - Fm: 0-0
Distance: 2m/2m3: 0-2 2m4-2m7: 0-0 3m+: 0-0
Track: LH: 0-0 RH: 0-2 Tight: 0-0 Gall: 0-0
Aids: Bl: 0-0 Vi: 0-0 Tstrap: 0-0
Best Rating: 101 3/02 Winc 2m good Hdl

Winner of two bumpers on good/good to firm ground. Has showed ability over hurdles at two miles on good ground.

Rockcliffe Gossip

109 **124**

10-y-o ch g Phardante (FR)-Clonmello (Le Bavard (FR))
N A Twiston-Davies Mrs Caroline Beresford-Wylie

Placings:322/222501/2**2152U335/U33P4-0322335P2** (4532)
2001/02: 25^{0}G, 26^{3}GS, 24^{2}G, 26^{2}G, 24^{3}GF, 33^{3}S, 27^{5}S, 29^{P}S, 26^{2}GS

	Starts	1st	2nd	3rd	Win & Pl
Chases	9	0	3	3	6429
Career Total	**32**	**2**	**11**	**8**	**22610**

104 10/99 Towc 2m6f E Ch GD £2739
118 4/99 Uttx 2m4f110y E(0-115)HHdl G-S £3225
Total win prize-money £5964

Going: Sf: 0-3 GS: 0-2 Gd: 0-3 GF: - Fm: 0-1
Distance: 2m/2m3: 0-0 2m4-2m7: 0-0 3m+: 0-9
Track: LH: 0-6 RH: 0-3 Tight: 0-3 Gall: 0-1
Aids: Bl: 0-1 Vi: 0-0 Tstrap: 0-0
Best Rating: 125 1/00 Wwck 2m4f soft Ch

Stays three mile plus and acts on good and good to soft ground. He often places but rarely wins.

Rockella

84f **43f**

5-y-o b m Primitive Rising (USA)-Little Ginger (Cawston's Clown)
T D Easterby P Baillie

Placings:60 (1657)
2001/02: 17^{6}S, 17^{0}G

	Starts	1st	2nd	3rd	Win & Pl
NH Flat	2	0	0	0	0
Career Total	**2**	**0**	**0**	**0**	**0**

Going: Sf: 0-1 GS: 0-0 Gd: 0-1 GF: - Fm: 0-0
Distance: 2m/2m3: 0-2 2m4-2m7: 0-0 3m+: 0-0
Track: LH: 0-1 RH: 0-1 Tight: 0-2 Gall: 0-0
Aids: Bl: 0-0 Vi: 0-0 Tstrap: 0-0
Best Rating: 43 9/01 MRas 2m1f110y soft NHF

Rockertree

3

7-y-o b g Rock Hopper-Snow Tree (Welsh Pageant)
R S Brookhouse R S Brookhouse

Placings:0/000-00 (1074)
2001/02: 16^{0}G, 16^{0}GF

	Starts	1st	2nd	3rd	Win & Pl
Hurdles	2	0	0	0	
Career Total	**6**	**0**	**0**	**0**	

Going: Sf: 0-0 GS: 0-0 Gd: 0-1 GF: - Fm: 0-1
Distance: 2m/2m3: 0-2 2m4-2m7: 0-0 3m+: 0-0
Track: LH: 0-2 RH: 0-0 Tight: 0-2 Gall: 0-0
Aids: Bl: 0-0 Vi: 0-0 Tstrap: 0-0
Best Rating: 83 10/00 Chel 2m110y good NHF

Rocket Man (IRE)

9-y-o b g Denel (FR)-Sofa River (FR) (Riverton (FR))
F Jordan Paul Wise

Placings:00/03/F0456P/6P (2926)
2001/02: 21^{6}S, 24^{P}GS

	Starts	1st	2nd	3rd	Win & Pl
Hurdles	2	0	0	0	0
Career Total	**12**	**0**	**0**	**1**	**163**

Going: Sf: 0-1 GS: 0-1 Gd: 0-0 GF: - Fm: 0-0
Distance: 2m/2m3: 0-0 2m4-2m7: 0-1 3m+: 0-1
Track: LH: 0-0 RH: 0-1 Tight: 0-1 Gall: 0-0
Aids: Bl: 0-0 Vi: 0-0 Tstrap: 0-0
Best Rating: 98 5/98 Hntg 2m110y gd-fm NHF

Rocket Radar

11-y-o b g Vouchsafe-Courtney Pennant (Angus)
Mrs J Hughes Mrs J Hughes

Placings:4/1/34/4P6-421 (4645)
2001/02: 23^{4}G, 25^{2}G, 24^{1}G

	Starts	1st	2nd	3rd	Win & Pl
Chases	3	1	1	0	3351
Career Total	**10**	**2**	**1**	**1**	**4834**

106 4/02 Ludl 3m H Ch GD £2800
106 4/99 Worc 2m7f110y H Ch G-S £1193
Total win prize-money £3993

Going: Sf: 0-0 GS: 0-0 Gd: 1-3 GF: - Fm: 0-0
Distance: 2m/2m3: 0-0 2m4-2m7: 0-0 **3m+: 1-3**
Track: LH: 0-0 **RH: 1-3 Tight: 1-1** Gall: 0-0
Aids: Bl: 0-0 Vi: 0-0 Tstrap: 0-1
Best Rating: 115 3/02 Hrfd 3m1f110y good Ch

Decent hunter chaser, likes yielding ground, but has also won on good to firm.

Rockforce

96 **140**

10-y-o ch g Rock City-Sleepline Princess (Royal Palace)
P F Nicholls G Z Mizel

Placings:40211F1/1111/5 (3697)
2001/02: 17^{5}S

	Starts	1st	2nd	3rd	Win & Pl
Chases	1	0	0	0	900
Career Total	**12**	**7**	**1**	**0**	**79923**

165 2/00 Asct 2m3f110y A Ch G-S £39000
161 2/00 Sand 2m B HCh GD £10237
154 1/00 Asct 2m C(0-130)HCh GD £6760
146 1/00 Kemp 2m D(0-125)HCh GD £4754
146 2/99 Asct 2m B Ch GD £11130
122 1/99 Ludl 2m E(0-105)HCh G-S £2762
122 1/99 Folk 2m E Ch SFT £3028
Total win prize-money £77673

Going: Sf: 0-1 GS: 0-0 Gd: 0-0 GF: - Fm: 0-0
Distance: 2m/2m3: 0-1 2m4-2m7: 0-0 3m+: 0-0
Track: LH: 0-1 RH: 0-0 Tight: 0-0 Gall: 0-1
Aids: Bl: 0-0 Vi: 0-0 Tstrap: 0-0
Best Rating: 165 2/00 Asct 2m3f110y gd-sft Ch

He developed into a smart performer early in 2000, completing a hat-trick in two-mile handicaps before landing the valuable Ascot Chase. Sadly he broke down in victory at Ascot, but ran a decent race after a two-year absence at Newbury in February 2002.

Rockland Park

102f 106f

7-y-o b g North Col-Snap Tin (Jimmy Reppin)
John R Upson Ramsay Donald Brown

Placings:*3* (0506)
2001/02: 16³GF

	Starts	1st	2nd	3rd	Win & Pl
NH Flat	1	0	0	1	241
Career Total	1	0	0	1	241

Going: Sf: 0-0 GS: 0-0 Gd: 0-0 GF: - Fm: 0-1
Distance: 2m/2m3: 0-1 2m4-2m7: 0-0 3m+: 0-0
Track: LH: 0-0 RH: 0-1 Tight: 0-0 Gall: 0-1
Aids: Bl: 0-0 Vi: 0-0 Tstrap: 0-0
Best Rating: 106 5/01 Hntg 2m110y gd-fm NHF

Rockview (IRE)

99(73h) (60h)81

7-y-o b g Mandalus-Saltee Star (Arapaho)
G M McCourt (Gerard Cully 31/5) Christopher Shankland

Placings:00/00/R-00P432R (4905)
2001/02: 18⁰GF, 16⁰GF, 20ᴾHY, 16⁴S, 16³S, 17²GF, 17ᴿGF

	Starts	1st	2nd	3rd	Win & Pl
Hurdles	2	0	0	0	0
Chases	5	0	1	1	1439
Career Total	12	0	1	1	1439

Going: Sf: 0-3 GS: 0-0 Gd: 0-0 GF: - Fm: 0-4
Distance: 2m/2m3: 0-6 2m4-2m7: 0-1 3m+: 0-0
Track: LH: 0-2 RH: 0-3 Tight: 0-4 Gall: 0-0
Aids: Bl: 0-0 Vi: 0-0 Tstrap: 0-0
Best Rating: 81 4/02 Plum 2m1f gd-fm Ch

Moderate ex-Irish chaser. Handles any ground.

Rockwelda

103(58h) 81

7-y-o b m Weld-Hill's Rocket (Hills Forecast)
M Sheppard R A Phillips

Placings:*0500/00U-B64* (0501)
2001/02: 19ᴮG, 24⁶GF, 24⁴GF

	Starts	1st	2nd	3rd	Win & Pl
Chases	3	0	0	0	0
Career Total	10	0	0	0	0

Going: Sf: 0-0 GS: 0-0 Gd: 0-1 GF: - Fm: 0-2
Distance: 2m/2m3: 0-1 2m4-2m7: 0-0 3m+: 0-2
Track: LH: 0-0 RH: 0-3 Tight: 0-0 Gall: 0-2
Aids: Bl: 0-3 Vi: 0-0 Tstrap: 0-0
Best Rating: 81 5/01 Hntg 3m gd-fm Ch

Rocky Island

110 110

5-y-o b g Rock Hopper-Queen's Eyot (Grundy)
J Mackie (Mrs M Reveley 2/2) Mrs Sue Adams

Placings:033030-60012311 (4572)
2001/02: 20⁶S, 17⁰S, 16⁰S, 16¹HY, 20²S, 20³S, 19¹S, 20¹G

	Starts	1st	2nd	3rd	Win & Pl
Hurdles	8	3	1	1	10302
Career Total	14	3	1	4	11531

110	4/02	Uttx	2m4f110y	E(0-110)HHdl	GD	£3570
102	3/02	Newb	2m3f	E(0-110)HHdl	SFT	£3342
93	2/02	Uttx	2m	G Hdl	HVY	£2002

Total win prize-money £8915

Going: Sf: 2-7 GS: 0-0 Gd: 1-1 GF: - Fm: 0-0
Distance: 2m/2m3: 2-4 2m4-2m7: 1-4 3m+: 0-0
Track: LH: 3-6 RH: 0-2 Tight: 0-1 Gall: 1-3
Aids: Bl: 0-0 Vi: 0-0 Tstrap: 0-0
Best Rating: 110 4/02 Uttx 2m4f110y good Hdl

A modest hurdler. Suited by two and a half miles and soft ground. Bought for 5,000gns after winning a seller at Uttoxeter and has proved a shrewd buy.

Rodalko (FR)

91f 97f

4-y-o b g Kadalko (FR)-Darling Rose (FR) (Rose Laurel)
O Sherwood J Palmer-Brown

Placings:*02* (4570)
2001/02: 16⁰GS, 16²G

	Starts	1st	2nd	3rd	Win & Pl
NH Flat	2	0	1	0	494
Career Total	2	0	1	0	494

Going: Sf: 0-0 GS: 0-1 Gd: 0-1 GF: - Fm: 0-0
Distance: 2m/2m3: 0-2 2m4-2m7: 0-0 3m+: 0-0
Track: LH: 0-1 RH: 0-1 Tight: 0-0 Gall: 0-1
Aids: Bl: 0-0 Vi: 0-0 Tstrap: 0-0
Best Rating: 97 3/02 Newb 2m110y gd-sft NHF

Has shown enough in two starts to suggest he can win a bumper.

Rodders

93 96

9-y-o b g Seymour Hicks (FR)-Supreme Issue (Bustiki)
J A Glover R W Metcalfe

Placings:*30*/40413/1/430-6045 (0882)
2001/02: 16⁶GF, 17⁰G, 19⁴F, 17⁵G

	Starts	1st	2nd	3rd	Win & Pl
Chases	4	0	0	0	273
Career Total	15	2	0	3	9197

116	5/99	MRas	2m1f110y	F(0-110)HCh	G-F	£3571
102	4/99	MRas	2m1f110y	D Ch	GD	£3977

Total win prize-money £7548

Going: Sf: 0-0 GS: 0-0 Gd: 0-2 GF: - Fm: 0-2
Distance: 2m/2m3: 0-4 2m4-2m7: 0-0 3m+: 0-0
Track: LH: 0-1 RH: 0-3 Tight: 0-3 Gall: 0-0
Aids: Bl: 0-0 Vi: 0-2 Tstrap: 0-1
Best Rating: 116 5/99 MRas 2m1f110y gd-fm Ch

Rodock (FR)

116(116c) 164

8-y-o b g Leading Counsel (USA)-High Light (FR) (Zino)
M C Pipe C M , B J & R F Batterham Ii

Placings:1112456/**121**F4-F12P4 (4902)
2001/02: 20ᶠG, 16¹S, 16²S, 20ᴾG, 16⁴G

	Starts	1st	2nd	3rd	Win & Pl
Hurdles	5	1	1	0	22780
Career Total	17	6	3	0	103054

164	1/02	Hayd	2m	A Hdl	SFT	£16660
137	3/01	Ling	2m4f110y	E Ch	HVY	£3088
150	1/01	Wwck	2m4f110y	D Ch	HVY	£4704
144	11/99	Chel	2m110y	B HHdl	GD	£31728
140	10/99	Extr	2m1f	E Hdl	GD	£2696
	9/99	Autl	2m2f	Hdl	SFT	£15070

Total win prize-money £73947

Going: Sf: 1-2 GS: 0-0 Gd: 0-3 GF: - Fm: 0-0
Distance: 2m/2m3: 1-3 2m4-2m7: 0-2 3m+: 0-0
Track: LH: 1-2 RH: 0-3 Tight: 0-1 Gall: 0-0
Aids: Bl: 0-0 Vi: 0-0 **Tstrap: 1-5**
Best Rating: 164 1/02 Hayd 2m soft Hdl

A French import, he looked a smart recruit to fences when winning hard held at Warwick in January 2001, but failed to convince with his jumping in subsequent efforts and successfully reverted to hurdling. Has won at up to two and a half miles over fences and is best with plenty of give in the ground. Usually tongue tied and can look temperamental at times.

Rodolfo

97f 104f

4-y-o b g Tragic Role (USA)-Be Discreet (Junius (USA))
O Sherwood Peter Davis

Placings:*1* (4910)
2001/02: 17¹G

	Starts	1st	2nd	3rd	Win & Pl
NH Flat	1	1	0	0	1799
Career Total	1	1	0	0	1799

104	4/02	MRas	2m1f110y	H NHF	GD	£1799

Total win prize-money £1799

Going: Sf: 0-0 GS: 0-0 Gd: 1-1 GF: - Fm: 0-0
Distance: 2m/2m3: 1-1 2m4-2m7: 0-0 3m+: 0-0
Track: LH: 0-0 **RH: 1-1 Tight: 1-1** Gall: 0-0
Aids: Bl: 0-0 Vi: 0-0 Tstrap: 0-0
Best Rating: 104 4/02 MRas 2m1f110y good NHF

Rodrigo (IRE)

(101h)

9-y-o b g Good Thyne (USA)-Magic Minstrel (Pitpan)
Ian Williams (H Rogers 20/10) Mark F Sheasby

Placings:*64*134212/4220650/1/**36**U65P6-0PP3 (4728)
2001/02: 16⁰G, 24ᴾGF, 24ᴾYS, 16³GF

	Starts	1st	2nd	3rd	Win & Pl
Hurdles	2	0	0	1	787
Chases	2	0	0	0	0
Career Total	27	3	4	3	13892

102	5/99	Clon	2m4f	Hdl	SFT	£3222
114	2/98	Clon	2m4f	Hdl	Y-S	£1935
102	10/97	Fair	2m	NHF	GD	£3051

Total win prize-money £8211

Going: Sf: 0-0 GS: 0-0 Gd: 0-1 GF: - Fm: 0-1
Distance: 2m/2m3: 0-2 2m4-2m7: 0-0 3m+: 0-2
Track: LH: 0-1 RH: 0-2 Tight: 0-0 Gall: 0-0
Aids: Bl: 0-1 Vi: 0-0 Tstrap: 0-0
Best Rating: 122 3/98 Fair 2m4f yield Hdl

Ex-Irish hurdler, does not look one to trust.

Rody (IRE)

77 51

5-y-o b/br g Foxhound (USA)-Capable Kate (IRE) (Alzao (USA))
F Jordan F Jordan

Placings:FPP (3979)
2001/02: 16ᶠS, 19ᴾS, 16ᴾG

	Starts	1st	2nd	3rd	Win & Pl
Hurdles	3	0	0	0	
Career Total	3	0	0	0	

Going: Sf: 0-2 GS: 0-0 Gd: 0-1 GF: - Fm: 0-0
Distance: 2m/2m3: 0-2 2m4-2m7: 0-1 3m+: 0-0
Track: LH: 0-1 RH: 0-2 Tight: 0-0 Gall: 0-0
Aids: Bl: 0-0 Vi: 0-0 Tstrap: 0-0
Best Rating:

Roger Ross

77 **69**

7-y-o b g Touch Of Grey-Foggy Dew (Smoggy)
R M Flower K & D Computers Ltd

Placings:00 **(1484)**
2001/02: 16^{0}GF, 16^{0}GS

	Starts	1st	2nd	3rd	Win & Pl
Hurdles	2	0	0	0	
Career Total	**2**	**0**	**0**	**0**	

Going: Sf: 0-0 GS: 0-1 Gd: 0-0 GF: - Fm: 0-1
Distance: 2m/2m3: 0-2 2m4-2m7: 0-0 3m+: 0-0
Track: LH: 0-2 RH: 0-0 Tight: 0-2 Gall: 0-0
Aids: Bl: 0-0 Vi: 0-0 Tstrap: 0-0
Best Rating: 69 9/01 Plum 2m gd-fm Hdl

Rogue Spirit

107 **102**

6-y-o b g Petong-Quick Profit (Formidable (USA))
R M Stronge (C J Mann 13/9) Mrs C C Regaldo-Gonzalez

Placings:35434B25F0 **(4848)**
2001/02: 17^{3}G, 20^{5}G, 16^{4}GF, 17^{3}GF, 17^{4}G, 16^{B}GF, 16^{2}GF, 16^{5}G, 16^{F}S, 16^{0}G

	Starts	1st	2nd	3rd	Win & Pl
Hurdles	10	0	1	2	1819
Career Total	**10**	**0**	**1**	**2**	**1819**

Going: Sf: 0-1 GS: 0-0 Gd: 0-5 GF: - Fm: 0-4
Distance: 2m/2m3: 0-9 2m4-2m7: 0-1 3m+: 0-0
Track: LH: 0-8 RH: 0-2 Tight: 0-6 Gall: 0-2
Aids: Bl: 0-7 Vi: 0-0 Tstrap: 0-0
Best Rating: 102 6/01 Strf 2m110y gd-fm Hdl

Rohan

91f **91f**

6-y-o gr g Norton Challenger-Acushla Macree (Mansingh (USA))
R F Johnson Houghton Mrs R F Johnson Houghton

Placings:*06-5* **(0685)**
2001/02: 17^{5}G

	Starts	1st	2nd	3rd	Win & Pl
NH Flat	1	0	0	0	0
Career Total	**3**	**0**	**0**	**0**	**0**

Going: Sf: 0-0 GS: 0-0 Gd: 0-1 GF: - Fm: 0-0
Distance: 2m/2m3: 0-1 2m4-2m7: 0-0 3m+: 0-0
Track: LH: 0-1 RH: 0-0 Tight: 0-1 Gall: 0-0
Aids: Bl: 0-0 Vi: 0-0 Tstrap: 0-0
Best Rating: 104 10/00 Extr 2m1f good NHF

Roi De Danse

54

7-y-o ch g Komaite (USA)-Princess Lucy (Local Suitor (USA))
Miss Z C Davison (M Quinn 20/7) The Avalon Restoration Partnership

Placings:0-0 **(4237)**
2001/02: 16^{0}GF

	Starts	1st	2nd	3rd	Win & Pl
Hurdles	1	0	0	0	
Career Total	**2**	**0**	**0**	**0**	

Going: Sf: 0-0 GS: 0-0 Gd: 0-0 GF: - Fm: 0-1
Distance: 2m/2m3: 0-1 2m4-2m7: 0-0 3m+: 0-0
Track: LH: 0-0 RH: 0-1 Tight: 0-0 Gall: 0-1
Aids: Bl: 0-0 Vi: 0-0 Tstrap: 0-0
Best Rating: 46 5/00 Worc 2m good Hdl

Roky Star (FR)

91 **94**

5-y-o b g Start Fast (FR)-Rosydolie (FR) (Dhausli (FR))
M R Bosley (J G Smyth-Osbourne 14/11) N Turner, D Kelly, D Merricks, R Jones

Placings:*33-0130* **(3696)**
2001/02: 16^{0}G, 17^{1}S, 16^{3}S, 16^{0}S

	Starts	1st	2nd	3rd	Win & Pl
NH Flat	2	1	0	0	1642
Hurdles	2	0	0	1	588
Career Total	**6**	**1**	**0**	**3**	**2962**

106	11/01	Folk	2m1f110y	H NHF		SFT	£1641

Total win prize-money £1642

Going: Sf: 1-3 GS: 0-0 Gd: 0-1 GF: - Fm: 0-0
Distance: **2m/2m3: 1-4** 2m4-2m7: 0-0 3m+: 0-0
Track: LH: 0-3 RH: 0-0 **Tight: 1-2** Gall: 0-1
Aids: Bl: 0-0 Vi: 0-0 Tstrap: 0-0
Best Rating: 106 11/01 Folk 2m1f110y soft NHF

He got off the mark in a bumper at Folkestone in November and should win a staying novice hurdle.

Rolfe (NZ)

104 **83**

12-y-o b g Tom's Shu (USA)-Tredia (NZ) (Mussorgsky)
Dr P Pritchard Mrs Grace Ann-Hanney

Placings:34502/31115**P3**/**P**/**P0P**011626/64324305P0/00013100-P62615U **(1308)**
2001/02: 17^{P}G, 17^{6}G, 17^{2}G, 16^{6}G, 20^{1}S, 20^{5}GF, 22^{U}GF

	Starts	1st	2nd	3rd	Win & Pl
Hurdles	6	1	1	0	2318
Chases	1	0	0	0	0
Career Total	**47**	**8**	**4**	**6**	**25910**

83	7/01	Worc	2m4f	G(0-90)HHdl	SFT	£1638
83	10/00	Sthl	2m	G(0-95)HHdl	HVY	£1515
83	8/00	NAbb	2m1f	F(0-100)HHdl	G-S	£2555
103	3/99	Ludl	2m	F Hdl	GD	£2339
108	3/99	Donc	2m4f	G Hdl	G-S	£1716
108	6/96	Uttx	2m4f110y	C Hdl	G-F	£4494
	5/96	Uttx	2m	E Hdl	GD	£2389
	5/96	Strf	2m110y	E(0-100)HHdl	G-F	£2598

Total win prize-money £19246

Going: Sf: 1-1 GS: 0-0 Gd: 0-4 GF: - Fm: 0-2
Distance: 2m/2m3: 0-4 **2m4-2m7: 1-3** 3m+: 0-0
Track: **LH: 1-5** RH: 0-2 Tight: 0-3 Gall: 0-0
Aids: Bl: 0-0 Vi: 0-0 Tstrap: 0-0
Best Rating: 116 4/99 Ludl 2m good Hdl

Rolfe's Belle

75 **12**

8-y-o b m Rolfe (USA)-Pokey's Belle (Uncle Pokey)
D L Williams Miss B W Palmer

Placings:*O0*-0P **(1221)**
2001/02: 22^{0}GF, 18^{P}GF

	Starts	1st	2nd	3rd	Win & Pl
Hurdles	2	0	0	0	
Career Total	**4**	**0**	**0**	**0**	

Going: Sf: 0-0 GS: 0-0 Gd: 0-0 GF: - Fm: 0-2
Distance: 2m/2m3: 0-1 2m4-2m7: 0-1 3m+: 0-0
Track: LH: 0-2 RH: 0-0 Tight: 0-2 Gall: 0-0
Aids: Bl: 0-0 Vi: 0-0 Tstrap: 0-0
Best Rating: 67 8/00 Hntg 2m110y gd-fm NHF

Rolfes Delight

93 **99+**

10-y-o b g Rolfe (USA)-Idiot's Run (Idiots Delight)
A E Jones Mrs J Whitburn

Placings:5/16-PP **(3273)**
2001/02: 22^{P}G, 26^{P}S

	Starts	1st	2nd	3rd	Win & Pl
Chases	2	0	0	0	
Career Total	**5**	**1**	**0**	**0**	**1463**

110	5/00	Bang	3m110y	H Ch	G-S	£1462

Total win prize-money £1463

Going: Sf: 0-1 GS: 0-0 Gd: 0-1 GF: - Fm: 0-0
Distance: 2m/2m3: 0-0 2m4-2m7: 0-1 3m+: 0-1
Track: LH: 0-1 RH: 0-0 Tight: 0-0 Gall: 0-1
Aids: Bl: 0-0 Vi: 0-0 Tstrap: 0-0
Best Rating: 110 5/00 Bang 3m110y gd-sft Ch

Won a three-mile novice hunter chase at Bangor in May 2000. Bounced back to form when landing a low-grade novices' handicap chase at Wincanton in May 2002.

Rollcall (IRE)

104 **124**

12-y-o br g Callernish-Coolbawn Lady (Laurence O)
R H Alner Pell-Mell Partners

Placings:0/P0/33110/12U46/5311-030 **(3341)**
2001/02: 26^{0}S, 26^{3}S, 27^{0}S

	Starts	1st	2nd	3rd	Win & Pl
Chases	3	0	0	1	605
Career Total	**20**	**5**	**1**	**4**	**21812**

124	2/01	Plum	3m2f	E(0-115)HCh	SFT	£3461
124	11/00	Tntn	3m3f	D(0-125)HCh	G-S	£3866
119	11/99	Winc	2m5f	E(0-115)HCh	GD	£4435
115	2/99	Plum	2m5f	F(0-100)HCh	SFT	£2802
112	12/98	Tntn	2m3f	F(0-95)HCh	G-S	£3283

Total win prize-money £17850

Going: Sf: 0-3 GS: 0-0 Gd: 0-0 GF: - Fm: 0-0
Distance: 2m/2m3: 0-0 2m4-2m7: 0-0 3m+: 0-3
Track: LH: 0-2 RH: 0-1 Tight: 0-2 Gall: 0-0
Aids: Bl: 0-0 Vi: 0-0 Tstrap: 0-0
Best Rating: 124 12/01 Wwck 3m2f soft Ch

A genuine staying chaser, although his wins have come in weak company.

Rolling Maul (IRE)

66 **11**

7-y-o b g Simply Great (FR)-Soyez Sage (FR) (Grundy)
Miss C J E Caroe (Michael Cunningham 5/8) Miss C J E Caroe

Placings:*30/040255/05410F00030*-200050364P **(3235)**
2001/02: 20^{2}G, 20^{0}GY, 25^{0}G, 24^{0}G, 17^{5}YS, 22^{0}GY, 21^{3}S, 21^{6}G, 22^{4}HY, 20^{P}GS

Starts **1st** **2nd** **3rd** **Win & Pl**

Chases	10	0	1	1	2778
Career Total	**29**	**1**	**2**	**3**	**8057**

82 7/00 Baln 2m4f (0-95)HHdl G-F £3312
Total win prize-money £3312

Going: Sf: 0-2 GS: 0-1 Gd: 0-4 GF: - Fm: 0-0
Distance: 2m/2m3: 0-1 2m4-2m7: 0-7 3m+: 0-2
Track: LH: 0-1 RH: 0-3 Tight: 0-2 Gall: 0-1
Aids: Bl: 0-4 Vi: 0-2 Tstrap: 0-0
Best Rating: **107** 11/00 Navn 2m4f soft Ch

Still a maiden over fences in Ireland, tends to run in snatches.

Rolling Tide (IRE)

93 **107**

6-y-o b g Alphabatim (USA)-St.Cristoph (The Parson)
N J Henderson B T Stewart-Brown

Placings:2-1 **(3869)**
2001/02: 16^{1}GS

	Starts	1st	2nd	3rd	Win & Pl
Hurdles	1	1	0	0	2678
Career Total	**2**	**1**	**1**	**0**	**3225**

107 2/02 Ludl 2m E Hdl G-S £2677
Total win prize-money £2678

Going: Sf: 0-0 GS: 1-1 Gd: 0-0 GF: - Fm: 0-0
Distance: **2m/2m3: 1-1** 2m4-2m7: 0-0 3m+: 0-0
Track: LH: 0-0 **RH: 1-1** Tight: 0-0 Gall: 0-0
Aids: Bl: 0-0 Vi: 0-0 Tstrap: 0-0
Best Rating: **107** 2/02 Ludl 2m gd-sft Hdl

Won an ordinary novice hurdle in February 2002 in good style.

Romacyn (IRE)

7-y-o ch m Commanche Run-Crazy Rose (FR) (Son Of Silver)
F P Murtagh Petroman Partnership

Placings:*0*PP **(3441)**
2001/02: 17^{0}G, 16^{P}G, 21^{P}HY

	Starts	1st	2nd	3rd	Win & Pl
NH Flat	1	0	0	0	0
Hurdles	2	0	0	0	0
Career Total	**3**	**0**	**0**	**0**	

Going: Sf: 0-1 GS: 0-0 Gd: 0-2 GF: - Fm: 0-0
Distance: 2m/2m3: 0-2 2m4-2m7: 0-1 3m+: 0-0
Track: LH: 0-3 RH: 0-0 Tight: 0-2 Gall: 0-0
Aids: Bl: 0-0 Vi: 0-0 Tstrap: 0-0
Best Rating: **43** 11/01 Sedg 2m1f good NHF

Romalito

69 **7**

12-y-o b g Robellino (USA)-Princess Zita (Manado)
Miss D Cole Mrs Marilyn Cook

Placings:4320/4640/2425000/F/323P0/0P **(0600)**
2001/02: 22^{0}GF, 27^{P}G

	Starts	1st	2nd	3rd	Win & Pl
Hurdles	2	0	0	0	
Career Total	**23**	**0**	**4**	**3**	**3926**

Going: Sf: 0-0 GS: 0-0 Gd: 0-1 GF: - Fm: 0-1
Distance: 2m/2m3: 0-0 2m4-2m7: 0-1 3m+: 0-1
Track: LH: 0-1 RH: 0-1 Tight: 0-1 Gall: 0-0
Aids: Bl: 0-0 Vi: 0-0 Tstrap: 0-0
Best Rating: **91** 4/94 Uttx 2m heavy Hdl

Roman Ark

105f

4-y-o br g Terimon-Larksmore (Royal Fountain)
J M Jefferson J M Jefferson

Placings:*1* **(4436)**
2001/02: 16^{1}HY

	Starts	1st	2nd	3rd	Win & Pl
NH Flat	1	1	0	0	1817
Career Total	**1**	**1**	**0**	**0**	**1817**

105 3/02 Newc 2m H NHF HVY £1816
Total win prize-money £1817

Going: Sf: 1-1 GS: 0-0 Gd: 0-0 GF: - Fm: 0-0
Distance: **2m/2m3: 1-1** 2m4-2m7: 0-0 3m+: 0-0
Track: LH: 0-0 RH: 0-0 Tight: 0-0 Gall: 0-0
Aids: Bl: 0-0 Vi: 0-0 Tstrap: 0-0
Best Rating: **105** 3/02 Newc 2m heavy NHF

Made a winning debut in a Newcastle bumper.

Roman Candle (IRE)

101 **72**

6-y-o b g Sabrehill (USA)-Penny Banger (IRE) (Pennine Walk)
Mrs Lucinda Featherstone (R Wilman 8/1) Largesse Racing

Placings:00F **(4867)**
2001/02: 21^{0}GS, 16^{0}G, 16^{F}GF

	Starts	1st	2nd	3rd	Win & Pl
Hurdles	3	0	0	0	
Career Total	**3**	**0**	**0**	**0**	

Going: Sf: 0-0 GS: 0-1 Gd: 0-1 GF: - Fm: 0-1
Distance: 2m/2m3: 0-2 2m4-2m7: 0-1 3m+: 0-0
Track: LH: 0-2 RH: 0-1 Tight: 0-0 Gall: 0-1
Aids: Bl: 0-0 Vi: 0-0 Tstrap: 0-0
Best Rating: **73** 4/02 Weth 2m gd-fm Hdl

Roman Governor (IRE)

60 **21**

8-y-o b g Rhoman Rule (USA)-Next Term (IRE) (Welsh Term)
H W Lavis H W Lavis

Placings:P-0UP **(0838)**
2001/02: 17^{0}G, 26^{U}F, 24^{P}G

	Starts	1st	2nd	3rd	Win & Pl
Hurdles	3	0	0	0	
Career Total	**4**	**0**	**0**	**0**	

Going: Sf: 0-0 GS: 0-0 Gd: 0-2 GF: - Fm: 0-1
Distance: 2m/2m3: 0-1 2m4-2m7: 0-0 3m+: 0-2
Track: LH: 0-1 RH: 0-2 Tight: 0-0 Gall: 0-0
Aids: Bl: 0-0 Vi: 0-0 Tstrap: 0-0
Best Rating: **26** 5/01 Hrfd 2m1f good Hdl

Roman Outlaw

107 **115**

10-y-o gr g Alias Smith (USA)-Roman Moor (Owen Anthony)
Mrs K Walton Mrs K Walton

Placings:*344/200441/4/0/*623P-4211PU55P **(4748)**
2001/02: 25^{4}G, 24^{2}GS, 30^{1}GS, 30^{1}S, 33^{P}S, 25^{U}HY, 25^{5}S, 26^{5}GS, 26^{P}GF

	Starts	1st	2nd	3rd	Win & Pl
Chases	9	2	1	0	8551
Career Total	**24**	**3**	**3**	**2**	**13607**

115 1/02 Newc 3m6f D(0-125)HCh SFT £4104
115 12/01 Newc 3m6f F(0-110)HCh G-S £3386
102 4/98 Hexm 2m4f110y E Hdl HVY £2789
Total win prize-money £10282

Going: Sf: 1-4 GS: 1-3 Gd: 0-1 GF: - Fm: 0-1
Distance: 2m/2m3: 0-0 2m4-2m7: 0-0 **3m+: 2-9**
Track: **LH: 2-7** RH: 0-2 Tight: 0-1 **Gall: 2-4**
Aids: Bl: 0-2 Vi: 0-0 Tstrap: 0-0
Best Rating: **115** 1/02 Newc 3m6f soft Ch

Fair handicap chaser. Scored a double over three miles six at Newcastle in 2001/02 and acts on a soft surface. Has worn sheepskin cheekpieces.

Roman Rampage

102 **112**

7-y-o b g Perpendicular-Roman Moor (Owen Anthony)
T D Easterby M P Burke

Placings:*221/34*-1 **(1833)**
2001/02: 20^{1}G

	Starts	1st	2nd	3rd	Win & Pl
Hurdles	1	1	0	0	3402
Career Total	**6**	**2**	**2**	**1**	**6706**

112 10/01 Aint 2m4f E Hdl GD £3402
112 1/00 Ayr 2m H NHF SFT £1662
Total win prize-money £5065

Going: Sf: 0-0 GS: 0-0 Gd: 1-1 GF: - Fm: 0-0
Distance: 2m/2m3: 0-0 **2m4-2m7: 1-1** 3m+: 0-0
Track: **LH: 1-1** RH: 0-0 **Tight: 1-1** Gall: 0-0
Aids: Bl: 0-0 Vi: 0-0 Tstrap: 0-0
Best Rating: **112** 10/01 Aint 2m4f good Hdl

A bumper winner, he overcame a break of ten months to get off the mark in good style at Aintree in October 2001 and will be even better over three miles.

Roman Star

7-y-o b g Teenoso (USA)-Mulloch Brae (Sunyboy)
A Crook Richard Berry

Placings:*400*-P **(1598)**
2001/02: 16^{P}G

	Starts	1st	2nd	3rd	Win & Pl
Hurdles	1	0	0	0	
Career Total	**4**	**0**	**0**	**0**	**0**

Going: Sf: 0-0 GS: 0-0 Gd: 0-1 GF: - Fm: 0-0
Distance: 2m/2m3: 0-1 2m4-2m7: 0-0 3m+: 0-0
Track: LH: 0-1 RH: 0-0 Tight: 0-1 Gall: 0-0
Aids: Bl: 0-0 Vi: 0-0 Tstrap: 0-0
Best Rating: **95** 11/00 Carl 2m1f heavy NHF

Roman Uproar

8-y-o ch m Primitive Rising (USA)-Roman Moor (Owen Anthony)
Mrs K Walton Mrs K Walton

Placings:*436/2436112/245431S*-0RP **(2946)**
2001/02: 20^{0}GS, 20^{R}GS, 24^{P}G

	Starts	1st	2nd	3rd	Win & Pl
Hurdles	3	0	0	0	
Career Total	**20**	**3**	**3**	**3**	**12504**

114 1/01 Newc 3m D(0-125)HHdl SFT £3360
111 4/00 Hexm 2m E Hdl GD £2604

92 3/00 Hexm 2m F(0-110)HHdl SFT £2436
Total win prize-money £8401

Going: Sf: 0-0 GS: 0-2 Gd: 0-1 GF: - Fm: 0-0
Distance: 2m/2m3: 0-0 2m4-2m7: 0-2 3m+: 0-1
Track: LH: 0-3 RH: 0-0 Tight: 0-1 Gall: 0-1
Aids: Bl: 0-0 Vi: 0-0 Tstrap: 0-0
Best Rating: 114 1/01 Newc 3m soft Hdl

Useful handicap hurdler. Acts on soft ground. Stays three miles.

Romantic Hero (IRE)

91 (78h) 110

6-y-o b g Supreme Leader-Right Love (Golden Love)
N A Gaselee Simon Harrap

Placings:43-F41 (4421)
2001/02: 19FS, 234S, 181GS

	Starts	1st	2nd	3rd	Win & Pl
Chases	3	1	0	0	5867
Career Total	**5**	**1**	**0**	**1**	**6196**

110 3/02 Newb 2m2f110y D(0-110)HCh G-S £5616
Total win prize-money £5616

Going: Sf: 0-2 GS: 1-1 Gd: 0-0 GF: - Fm: 0-0
Distance: **2m/2m3: 1-1** 2m4-2m7: 0-1 3m+: 0-1
Track: **LH: 1-2** RH: 0-1 Tight: 0-0 **Gall: 1-1**
Aids: Bl: 0-0 Vi: 0-0 Tstrap: 0-0
Best Rating: 110 3/02 Newb 2m2f110y gd-sft Ch

Lightly-raced novice chaser, suited by soft ground. Looks a progressive sort.

Romantic Native (IRE)

94 82

8-y-o b g Be My Native (USA)-Gay Seeker (Status Seeker)
R A Fahey The Killeen Partnership

Placings:400-4PP50 (4745)
2001/02: 204S, 17PS, 27PHY, 205GS, 240G

	Starts	1st	2nd	3rd	Win & Pl
Hurdles	3	0	0	0	0
Chases	2	0	0	0	0
Career Total	**8**	**0**	**0**	**0**	**0**

Going: Sf: 0-3 GS: 0-1 Gd: 0-1 GF: - Fm: 0-0
Distance: 2m/2m3: 0-1 2m4-2m7: 0-2 3m+: 0-2
Track: LH: 0-1 RH: 0-2 Tight: 0-2 Gall: 0-0
Aids: Bl: 0-2 Vi: 0-2 Tstrap: 0-0
Best Rating: 85 10/00 Carl 3m110y soft Hdl

Romany Chat

10-y-o b g Backchat (USA)-Ranee's Song (True Song)
Mrs Rosemary Gasson Mrs R Gasson

Placings:PP-0143P (4253)
2001/02: 240GS, 211G, 284GF, 243GS, 26PG

	Starts	1st	2nd	3rd	Win & Pl
Chases	5	1	0	1	3342
Career Total	**7**	**1**	**0**	**1**	**3342**

111 5/01 Chel 2m5f H Ch GD £2535
Total win prize-money £2535

Going: Sf: 0-0 GS: 0-2 Gd: 1-2 GF: - Fm: 0-1
Distance: 2m/2m3: 0-0 **2m4-2m7: 1-1** 3m+: 0-4
Track: LH: 0-3 RH: 0-1 Tight: 0-2 Gall: 0-2
Aids: Bl: 0-0 Vi: 0-0 Tstrap: 0-0
Best Rating: 111 2/02 Hntg 3m gd-sft Ch

Winning pointer, he goes on most ground.

Romany General

91 86

7-y-o b g Romany Rye-Furnace Lass Vii (Damsire Unregistered)
W Storey Reg Richardson

Placings:0P/0P03 (1352)
2001/02: 200F, 16PGS, 210GF, 173GF

	Starts	1st	2nd	3rd	Win & Pl
Hurdles	4	0	0	1	348
Career Total	**6**	**0**	**0**	**1**	**348**

Going: Sf: 0-0 GS: 0-1 Gd: 0-0 GF: - Fm: 0-3
Distance: 2m/2m3: 0-2 2m4-2m7: 0-2 3m+: 0-0
Track: LH: 0-4 RH: 0-0 Tight: 0-2 Gall: 0-0
Aids: Bl: 0-0 Vi: 0-0 Tstrap: 0-0
Best Rating: 86 9/01 Sedg 2m1f gd-fm Hdl

Romany Hill

95(67c) (24c)62

7-y-o b m Nomadic Way (USA)-Snarry Hill (Vitiges (FR))
C Grant Roy Robinson Partnership

Placings:00/P665405-0P0 (1667)
2001/02: 160G, 21PG, 160G

	Starts	1st	2nd	3rd	Win & Pl
Hurdles	1	0	0	0	0
Chases	2	0	0	0	0
Career Total	**12**	**0**	**0**	**0**	**0**

Going: Sf: 0-0 GS: 0-0 Gd: 0-3 GF: - Fm: 0-0
Distance: 2m/2m3: 0-2 2m4-2m7: 0-1 3m+: 0-0
Track: LH: 0-3 RH: 0-0 Tight: 0-3 Gall: 0-0
Aids: Bl: 0-0 Vi: 0-0 Tstrap: 0-0
Best Rating: 85 1/01 Muss 2m gd-sft Hdl

Romany Lass

78 58

6-y-o b m Romany Rye-Furnace Lass Vii (Damsire Unregistered)
W Storey Richardson Kelly O'Gara Partnership

Placings:0 (4860)
2001/02: 160G

	Starts	1st	2nd	3rd	Win & Pl
NH Flat	1	0	0	0	
Career Total	**1**	**0**	**0**	**0**	

Going: Sf: 0-0 GS: 0-0 Gd: 0-1 GF: - Fm: 0-0
Distance: 2m/2m3: 0-1 2m4-2m7: 0-0 3m+: 0-0
Track: LH: 0-0 RH: 0-0 Tight: 0-0 Gall: 0-0
Aids: Bl: 0-0 Vi: 0-0 Tstrap: 0-0
Best Rating: 43 4/02 Hexm 2m110y good NHF

Romany Move

97(89h) (62h)79

8-y-o b g Silly Prices-Go Gipsy (Move Off)
J Wade John Wade

Placings:50-00054P (4062)
2001/02: 210GF, 220G, 170G, 215S, 174S, 21PS

	Starts	1st	2nd	3rd	Win & Pl
Hurdles	3	0	0	0	0
Chases	3	0	0	0	238
Career Total	**8**	**0**	**0**	**0**	**238**

Going: Sf: 0-3 GS: 0-0 Gd: 0-2 GF: - Fm: 0-1
Distance: 2m/2m3: 0-2 2m4-2m7: 0-4 3m+: 0-0
Track: LH: 0-5 RH: 0-1 Tight: 0-6 Gall: 0-0
Aids: Bl: 0-0 Vi: 0-0 Tstrap: 0-0
Best Rating: 80 12/01 MRas 2m1f110y soft Ch

Rombalds (IRE)

90 81

7-y-o b g King's Ride-Deep Slaney (Deep Run)
M W Easterby Mrs E J Wright And Mr A D Bairstow

Placings:000-5 (0201)
2001/02: 165G

	Starts	1st	2nd	3rd	Win & Pl
Hurdles	1	0	0	0	
Career Total	**4**	**0**	**0**	**0**	**0**

Going: Sf: 0-0 GS: 0-0 Gd: 0-1 GF: - Fm: 0-0
Distance: 2m/2m3: 0-1 2m4-2m7: 0-0 3m+: 0-0
Track: LH: 0-1 RH: 0-0 Tight: 0-0 Gall: 0-0
Aids: Bl: 0-0 Vi: 0-0 Tstrap: 0-0
Best Rating: 87 11/00 Newc 2m gd-sft NHF

Romero

115(97c) (104+c)131

6-y-o b g Robellino (USA)-Casamurrae (Be My Guest (USA))
Miss E C Lavelle (J Akehurst 19/5) Fraser Miller Racing

Placings:1126201/234004-2124000042 (4758)
2001/02: 192GF, 161G, 162GS, 164G, 160G, 200G, 220S, 210G, 204GF, 162GF

	Starts	1st	2nd	3rd	Win & Pl
Hurdles	10	1	3	0	15281
Career Total	**23**	**4**	**6**	**1**	**42407**

131 11/01 Asct 2m110y B(0-150)HHdl GD £7121
123 4/00 Asct 2m110y C HHdl GD £4914
119 11/99 Asct 2m110y B Hdl GD £6742
109 10/99 Asct 2m110y C Hdl GD £4788
Total win prize-money £23566

Going: Sf: 0-1 GS: 0-1 Gd: 1-5 GF: - Fm: 0-3
Distance: **2m/2m3: 1-5** 2m4-2m7: 0-5 3m+: 0-0
Track: LH: 0-1 **RH: 1-8** Tight: 0-2 Gall: 0-0
Aids: Bl: 0-0 Vi: 0-2 Tstrap: 0-0
Best Rating: 131 11/01 Sand 2m110y gd-sft Hdl

He has won four times over hurdles at Ascot, but never anywhere else. Well held for the most part in 2001/2002, looking less than keen at times. Likes to make the running and seems best on good ground.

Romil Star (GER)

103 94

5-y-o b g Chief's Crown (USA)-Romelia (USA) (Woodman (USA))
R D Wylie M R Johnson

Placings:004 (4492)
2001/02: 160GS, 170S, 174GS

	Starts	1st	2nd	3rd	Win & Pl
Hurdles	3	0	0	0	0
Career Total	**3**	**0**	**0**	**0**	**0**

Going: Sf: 0-1 GS: 0-2 Gd: 0-0 GF: - Fm: 0-0

Distance: 2m/2m3: 0-3 2m4-2m7: 0-0 3m+: 0-0
Track: LH: 0-2 RH: 0-1 Tight: 0-2 Gall: 0-0
Aids: Bl: 0-0 Vi: 0-0 Tstrap: 0-1
Best Rating: 87 3/02 Carl 2m1f gd-sft Hdl

A Flat winner in Germany who progressed over hurdles to win on his handicap debut at Perth in May 2002. Races freely and handles any ground.

Rommel

73 **34**

5-y-o ch g Baron Blakeney-Sizzling Sun (Sunyboy)
B G Powell R B Felmingham

Placings:*4000* **(3647)**
2001/02: 17⁴S, 18⁰GS, 20⁰G, 21⁰S

	Starts	1st	2nd	3rd	Win & Pl
NH Flat	2	0	0	0	0
Hurdles	2	0	0	0	0
Career Total	**4**	**0**	**0**	**0**	**0**

Going: Sf: 0-2 GS: 0-1 Gd: 0-1 GF: - Fm: 0-0
Distance: 2m/2m3: 0-2 2m4-2m7: 0-2 3m+: 0-0
Track: LH: 0-0 RH: 0-3 Tight: 0-1 Gall: 0-0
Aids: Bl: 0-0 Vi: 0-0 Tstrap: 0-0
Best Rating: 81 9/01 MRas 2m1f110y soft NHF

Romney

103 **106**

5-y-o ch g Timeless Times (USA)-Ewe Lamb (Free State)
Mrs P Sly Thorney Racing Club

Placings:54233-215200 **(4550)**
2001/02: 20²F, 22¹S, 20⁵GS, 21²GS, 21⁰GS, 21⁰GF

	Starts	1st	2nd	3rd	Win & Pl
Hurdles	6	1	2	0	4637
Career Total	**11**	**1**	**3**	**2**	**6280**
106 11/01 Folk	2m6f110y E Hdl			SFT	£3003

Total win prize-money £3003

Going: Sf: 1-1 GS: 0-3 Gd: 0-0 GF: - Fm: 0-2
Distance: 2m/2m3: 0-0 **2m4-2m7: 1-6** 3m+: 0-0
Track: LH: 0-1 **RH: 1-5 Tight: 1-3** Gall: 0-2
Aids: Bl: 0-0 Vi: 0-0 Tstrap: 0-0
Best Rating: 108 1/01 Folk 2m1f110y heavy Hdl

He looked very inch a stayer when winning a two-mile-six novice hurdle in testing conditions at Folkestone in November. Appears to have his quirks.

Ron's Round

65 **23**

8-y-o ch g Ron's Victory (USA)-Magical Spirit (Top Ville)
A B Coogan (Miss K M George 18/7) A B Coogan

Placings:5/550202/213/0-0PP **(2011)**
2001/02: 16⁰G, 26ᴾG, 16ᴾS

	Starts	1st	2nd	3rd	Win & Pl
Hurdles	3	0	0	0	
Career Total	**14**	**1**	**3**	**1**	**4909**
105 5/99 MRas	2m1f110y E Hdl			G-F	£2626

Total win prize-money £2626

Going: Sf: 0-1 GS: 0-0 Gd: 0-2 GF: - Fm: 0-0
Distance: 2m/2m3: 0-2 2m4-2m7: 0-0 3m+: 0-1
Track: LH: 0-1 RH: 0-2 Tight: 0-0 Gall: 0-1
Aids: Bl: 0-0 Vi: 0-0 Tstrap: 0-0

Best Rating: 106 5/99 Uttx 2m gd-fm Hdl

Ronans Choice (IRE)

107 **97**

9-y-o b g Yashgan-Petite Port (IRE) (Decent Fellow)
G M McCourt Mrs Kathy Stuart

Placings:602PP-61 **(4882)**
2001/02: 19⁶F, 26¹GF

	Starts	1st	2nd	3rd	Win & Pl
Chases	2	1	0	0	2786
Career Total	**7**	**1**	**1**	**0**	**3698**
97 4/02 Font	3m2f110y F(0-100)HCh			G-F	£2786

Total win prize-money £2786

Going: Sf: 0-0 GS: 0-0 Gd: 0-0 GF: - Fm: 1-2
Distance: 2m/2m3: 0-0 2m4-2m7: 0-1 **3m+: 1-1**
Track: LH: 0-0 RH: 0-1 **Tight: 1-1** Gall: 0-0
Aids: **Bl: 1-1** Vi: 0-0 Tstrap: 0-0
Best Rating: 97 4/02 Font 3m2f110y gd-fm Ch

Lightly-raced ex-Irish pointer. Got off the mark when fitted with blinkers for the first time at Fontwell in April 2002. Stays well, seems to handles any ground.

Rookie

6-y-o b g Magic Ring (IRE)-Shot At Love (IRE) (Last Tycoon)
M J Gingell H G T Partnership

Placings:0-P **(0725)**
2001/02: 17ᴾF

	Starts	1st	2nd	3rd	Win & Pl
Hurdles	1	0	0	0	
Career Total	**2**	**0**	**0**	**0**	

Going: Sf: 0-0 GS: 0-0 Gd: 0-0 GF: - Fm: 0-1
Distance: 2m/2m3: 0-1 2m4-2m7: 0-0 3m+: 0-0
Track: LH: 0-0 RH: 0-1 Tight: 0-0 Gall: 0-0
Aids: Bl: 0-0 Vi: 0-0 Tstrap: 0-0
Best Rating: 16 6/00 Folk 2m1f110y good Hdl

Rooster

7-y-o b g Roi Danzig (USA)-Jussoli (Don)
D E Cantillon Mrs Edward Cantillon

Placings:35/4125/**F** **(0243)**
2001/02: 16ᶠGF

	Starts	1st	2nd	3rd	Win & Pl
Chases	1	0	0	0	
Career Total	**7**	**1**	**1**	**1**	**7012**
113 3/00 Donc	2m110y E(0-105)HHdl			GD	£5551

Total win prize-money £5551

Going: Sf: 0-0 GS: 0-0 Gd: 0-0 GF: - Fm: 0-1
Distance: 2m/2m3: 0-1 2m4-2m7: 0-0 3m+: 0-0
Track: LH: 0-0 RH: 0-0 Tight: 0-0 Gall: 0-0
Aids: Bl: 0-0 Vi: 0-0 Tstrap: 0-0
Best Rating: 113 3/00 Newc 2m good Hdl

Rooster Booster

117 **155**

8-y-o gr g Riverwise (USA)-Came Cottage (Nearly A Hand)
P J Hobbs Terry Warner

Placings:*0/23F1332/3PF2323P-5542214* **(4676)**
2001/02: 16⁵G, 16⁵S, 16⁴GS, 17²HY, 16²S, 17¹G, 20⁴G

	Starts	1st	2nd	3rd	Win & Pl
Hurdles	7	1	2	0	68514
Career Total	**23**	**2**	**6**	**6**	**116225**
155 3/02 Chel	2m1f A HHdl			GD	£33000
120 1/00 Tntn	2m1f D Hdl			SFT	£4284

Total win prize-money £37285

Going: Sf: 0-3 GS: 0-1 Gd: 1-3 GF: - Fm: 0-0
Distance: **2m/2m3: 1-6** 2m4-2m7: 0-1 3m+: 0-0
Track: **LH: 1-5** RH: 0-2 Tight: 0-1 **Gall: 1-3**
Aids: Bl: 0-0 Vi: 0-0 Tstrap: 0-0
Best Rating: 155 4/02 Aint 2m4f good Hdl

A top-class handicapper who is genuine, but is unlucky not to have won more decent prizes than he has. Made the frame in the Pierse Hurdle, Tote Gold Trophy and Imperial Cup in 2000/2001 and continued to run well the following season. Finished second in the Tote Gold Trophy before gaining a deserved win in the County Hurdle at Cheltenham and was a fine fourth in the Grade One Aintree Hurdle. He goes well on easy ground.

Rosalyons (IRE)

78(103h) (102h)**51**

8-y-o gr g Roselier (FR)-Coffee Shop (Bargello)
Mrs H O Graham Mrs H O Graham

Placings:5/06000-011U330PP4**F** **(4687)**
2001/02: 22⁰G, 22¹GS, 20¹S, 24ᵁGS, 20³GS, 22³GS, 24⁰G, 21ᴾG, 19ᴾGD, 20⁴HY, 25ᶠGF

	Starts	1st	2nd	3rd	Win & Pl
Hurdles	9	2	0	2	6640
Chases	2	0	0	0	263
Career Total	**17**	**2**	**0**	**2**	**6903**
102 10/01 Carl	2m4f E(0-105)HHdl			SFT	£2609
85 10/01 Kels	2m6f110y F(0-110)HHdl			G-S	£2716

Total win prize-money £5326

Going: Sf: 1-3 GS: 1-5 Gd: 0-2 GF: - Fm: 0-1
Distance: 2m/2m3: 0-1 **2m4-2m7: 2-6** 3m+: 0-4
Track: **LH: 1-9** RH: 0-1 **Tight: 1-6** Gall: 0-3
Aids: Bl: 0-1 Vi: 0-0 Tstrap: 0-0
Best Rating: 102 12/01 Kels 2m6f110y gd-sft Hdl

Had modest form to date but showed improved form in the autumn of 2001, winning twice in October at Kelso and Carlisle at up to two miles six. He has won on soft and good to soft.

Rosarian (IRE)

108f **123f**

5-y-o b g Fourstars Allstar (USA)-Only A Rose (Glint Of Gold)
V R A Dartnall A & D Enterprises (poole) Ltd

Placings:*4213* **(3784)**
2001/02: 17⁴G, 16²HY, 18¹G, 16³S

	Starts	1st	2nd	3rd	Win & Pl
NH Flat	4	1	1	1	2676
Career Total	**4**	**1**	**1**	**1**	**2676**
115 1/02 Font	2m2f110y H NHF			GD	£1680

Total win prize-money £1680

Going: Sf: 0-2 GS: 0-0 Gd: 1-2 GF: - Fm: 0-0
Distance: **2m/2m3: 1-4** 2m4-2m7: 0-0 3m+: 0-0
Track: **LH: 1-2** RH: 0-2 **Tight: 1-2** Gall: 0-0
Aids: Bl: 0-0 Vi: 0-0 Tstrap: 0-0
Best Rating: 123 2/02 Asct 2m110y soft NHF

Promise in bumpers, looking a staying type. Won a Fontwell bumper in January 2002 on good ground.

Rosco

(98h) (115h)

8-y-o b g Roscoe Blake-Silva Linda (Precipice Wood)

J T Gifford Miss J Semple

Placings:2/33223341/**43226-21** **(1762)**

2001/02: 20^{2}G, 25^{1}S

	Starts	1st	2nd	3rd	Win & Pl
Hurdles	2	1	1	0	4595
Career Total	**16**	**2**	**6**	**5**	**17137**

115	10/01	Plum	3m1f110y	D(0-120)HHdl	SFT	£3526
109	4/00	Strf	2m6f110y	E Hdl	GD	£2660

Total win prize-money £6186

Going: Sf: 1-1 GS: 0-0 Gd: 0-1 GF: - Fm: 0-0
Distance: 2m/2m3: 0-0 2m4-2m7: 0-1 **3m+: 1-1**
Track: LH: 0-1 RH: 0-0 Tight: 0-0 Gall: 0-0
Aids: Bl: 0-0 Vi: 0-0 Tstrap: 0-0
Best Rating: 121 3/00 Sand 2m4f110y good Hdl

Winner of a maiden hurdle in 2000, raced unsuccessfully over fences 2000/01 and lost his confidence. Has run well since returned to hurdles last term, winning at Plumpton. Suited by two and three-quarter to three miles and cut in the ground.

Rose D'April (FR)

100f 107f

5-y-o gr g April Night (FR)-Rose De Hoc (FR) (Rose Laurel)

L Lungo Ashleybank Investments Limited

Placings:0-120 **(4235)**

2001/02: 16^{1}G, 16^{2}G, 16^{0}GS

	Starts	1st	2nd	3rd	Win & Pl
NH Flat	3	1	1	0	2085
Career Total	**4**	**1**	**1**	**0**	**2085**

102	12/01	Catt	2m	H NHF	GD	£1631

Total win prize-money £1631

Going: Sf: 0-0 GS: 0-1 Gd: 1-2 GF: - Fm: 0-0
Distance: **2m/2m3: 1-3** 2m4-2m7: 0-0 3m+: 0-0
Track: **LH: 1-2** RH: 0-1 **Tight: 1-2** Gall: 0-0
Aids: Bl: 0-0 Vi: 0-0 Tstrap: 0-0
Best Rating: 107 1/02 Muss 2m good NHF

Decent bumper horse, a winner at Catterick and not disgraced under his penalty.

Rose Hill

89 67

6-y-o b m Sabrehill (USA)-Petite Rosanna (Ile De Bourbon (USA))

W Clay G A Greaves

Placings:2U/20-654 **(4752)**

2001/02: 20^{6}S, 16^{5}S, 16^{4}GF

	Starts	1st	2nd	3rd	Win & Pl
Hurdles	3	0	0	0	0
Career Total	**7**	**0**	**2**	**0**	**1817**

Going: Sf: 0-2 GS: 0-0 Gd: 0-0 GF: - Fm: 0-1
Distance: 2m/2m3: 0-2 2m4-2m7: 0-1 3m+: 0-0
Track: LH: 0-3 RH: 0-0 Tight: 0-0 Gall: 0-0
Aids: Bl: 0-0 Vi: 0-0 Tstrap: 0-0
Best Rating: 84 5/00 Hrfd 2m1f gd-sft Hdl

Selling hurdler.

Rose Of Tracarta (IRE)

102 110

7-y-o b m Husyan (USA)-Derravaragh Rose (IRE) (Strong Gale)

J W Mullins Mrs J M Bailey

Placings:112/4244-1412 **(2293)**

2001/02: 17^{1}GS, 17^{4}G, 16^{1}G, 19^{2}GF

	Starts	1st	2nd	3rd	Win & Pl
Hurdles	4	2	1	0	6240
Career Total	**11**	**4**	**3**	**0**	**14638**

109	11/01	Winc	2m	E Hdl	GD	£2597
101	5/01	Extr	2m1f	E Hdl	G-S	£2237
116	3/00	Winc	2m	H NHF	G-S	£1820
118	2/00	Wwck	2m	H NHF	GD	£1820

Total win prize-money £8474

Going: Sf: 0-0 GS: 1-1 Gd: 1-2 GF: - Fm: 0-1
Distance: **2m/2m3: 2-4** 2m4-2m7: 0-0 3m+: 0-0
Track: LH: 0-0 **RH: 2-4** Tight: 0-0 Gall: 0-0
Aids: Bl: 0-0 Vi: 0-0 Tstrap: 0-0
Best Rating: 124 4/00 Aint 2m110y good NHF

She has landed novice hurdles at Exeter and Wincanton. Likes to make the running and does not want the ground too soft.

Rose Tina

95 82

5-y-o b m Tina's Pet-Rosevear (IRE) (Contract Law (USA))

E A Wheeler Church Racing Partnership

Placings:U66-40450 **(3515)**

2001/02: 17^{4}GS, 16^{0}S, 20^{4}HY, 22^{5}S, 19^{0}S

	Starts	1st	2nd	3rd	Win & Pl
Hurdles	5	0	0	0	276
Career Total	**8**	**0**	**0**	**0**	**276**

Going: Sf: 0-4 GS: 0-1 Gd: 0-0 GF: - Fm: 0-0
Distance: 2m/2m3: 0-2 2m4-2m7: 0-3 3m+: 0-0
Track: LH: 0-2 RH: 0-3 Tight: 0-3 Gall: 0-0
Aids: Bl: 0-0 Vi: 0-0 Tstrap: 0-0
Best Rating: 82 12/01 Leic 2m4f110y heavy Hdl

Rosecharmer

88f 75f

5-y-o ch m Charmer-Rosie Cone (Celtic Cone)

Mrs P Sly Mrs P M Sly

Placings:000 **(4539)**

2001/02: 16^{0}GS, 16^{0}S, 16^{0}G

	Starts	1st	2nd	3rd	Win & Pl
NH Flat	3	0	0	0	
Career Total	**3**	**0**	**0**	**0**	

Going: Sf: 0-1 GS: 0-1 Gd: 0-1 GF: - Fm: 0-0
Distance: 2m/2m3: 0-3 2m4-2m7: 0-0 3m+: 0-0
Track: LH: 0-3 RH: 0-0 Tight: 0-2 Gall: 0-1
Aids: Bl: 0-0 Vi: 0-0 Tstrap: 0-0
Best Rating: 75 4/02 Fknm 2m good NHF

Rosegrove Rooster

80f 72f

5-y-o b g Henbit (USA)-Cornbelt (Oats)

C F C Jackson Joe Roper

Placings:00 **(4743)**

2001/02: 16^{0}S, 16^{0}GF

	Starts	1st	2nd	3rd	Win & Pl
NH Flat	2	0	0	0	
Career Total	**2**	**0**	**0**	**0**	

Going: Sf: 0-1 GS: 0-0 Gd: 0-0 GF: - Fm: 0-1
Distance: 2m/2m3: 0-2 2m4-2m7: 0-0 3m+: 0-0
Track: LH: 0-0 RH: 0-2 Tight: 0-0 Gall: 0-0
Aids: Bl: 0-0 Vi: 0-0 Tstrap: 0-0
Best Rating: 72 3/02 Ludl 2m soft NHF

Rosehill Doorbell

48

5-y-o b m Miners Lamp-Boherash (Boreen (FR))

G B Balding H M F McCall

Placings:00 **(1846)**

2001/02: 16^{0}GF, 22^{0}G

	Starts	1st	2nd	3rd	Win & Pl
NH Flat	1	0	0	0	0
Hurdles	1	0	0	0	0
Career Total	**2**	**0**	**0**	**0**	

Going: Sf: 0-0 GS: 0-0 Gd: 0-1 GF: - Fm: 0-1
Distance: 2m/2m3: 0-1 2m4-2m7: 0-1 3m+: 0-0
Track: LH: 0-1 RH: 0-1 Tight: 0-0 Gall: 0-0
Aids: Bl: 0-0 Vi: 0-0 Tstrap: 0-0
Best Rating: 26 6/01 Worc 2m gd-fm NHF

Roselier Bell (IRE)

62

9-y-o b g Roselier (FR)-Bell Walks Fancy (Entre Chat)

A Ennis Thomas J Farrell

Placings:0/033F30/34042F/**06005-0P** **(2112)**

2001/02: 20^{0}G, 20^{P}S

	Starts	1st	2nd	3rd	Win & Pl
Hurdles	2	0	0	0	
Career Total	**20**	**0**	**1**	**4**	**2663**

Going: Sf: 0-1 GS: 0-0 Gd: 0-1 GF: - Fm: 0-0
Distance: 2m/2m3: 0-0 2m4-2m7: 0-2 3m+: 0-0
Track: LH: 0-0 RH: 0-2 Tight: 0-1 Gall: 0-0
Aids: Bl: 0-0 Vi: 0-0 Tstrap: 0-0
Best Rating: 105 1/99 Punc 3m heavy Hdl

Rosencrantz (IRE)

112 125

10-y-o b g Sadler's Wells (USA)-Rosananti (Blushing Groom (FR))

Miss Venetia Williams M J Fenn

Placings:0/1112F3P10/**P43/5FU11/4P** **(4909)**

2001/02: 20^{4}GS, 20^{P}GF

	Starts	1st	2nd	3rd	Win & Pl
Chases	2	0	0	0	593
Career Total	**20**	**6**	**1**	**2**	**25305**

131	7/99	Wolv	2m	C(0-130)HCh	G-S	£6995
110	6/99	Strf	2m4f	E(0-115)HCh	G-F	£2960
122	3/97	Asct	2m110y	C(0-135)HHdl	GD	£4856
109	11/96	Tntn	2m1f	E Hdl	G-F	£2358
108	10/96	Winc	2m	E Hdl	G-F	£2635
90	5/96	Chep	2m110y	E Hdl	G-F	£2486

Total win prize-money £22291

Going: Sf: 0-0 GS: 0-1 Gd: 0-0 GF: - Fm: 0-1
Distance: 2m/2m3: 0-0 2m4-2m7: 0-2 3m+: 0-0
Track: LH: 0-1 RH: 0-1 Tight: 0-2 Gall: 0-0
Aids: Bl: 0-0 Vi: 0-0 Tstrap: 0-0
Best Rating: 131 7/99 Wolv 2m gd-sft Ch

Modest chaser, lightly raced recently. Possibly best at two miles.

Rosenkavalier (IRE)

87 81

8-y-o b g Classic Music (USA)-Top Bloom (Thatch (USA))

W S Kittow Mrs Judy Kittow

Placings:6300C6P (1728)

2001/02: 18^{6}GF, 17^{3}G, 16^{0}GF, 16^{0}G, 21^{C}G, 22^{6}G, 19^{P}F

	Starts	1st	2nd	3rd	Win & Pl
Hurdles	6	0	0	1	325
Chases	1	0	0	0	0
Career Total	**7**	**0**	**0**	**1**	**325**

Going: Sf: 0-0 GS: 0-0 Gd: 0-4 GF: - Fm: 0-3
Distance: 2m/2m3: 0-4 2m4-2m7: 0-3 3m+: 0-0
Track: LH: 0-6 RH: 0-1 Tight: 0-5 Gall: 0-0
Aids: Bl: 0-0 Vi: 0-0 Tstrap: 0-3
Best Rating: 81 6/01 NAbb 2m1f good Hdl

Roseta (IRE)

108(90h) (68h)105

10-y-o ch g Roselier (FR)-Urrin Valley Vii (Damsire Unregistered)

J J O'Neill P Piller

Placings:5/00/0PF/**1U4034-P013** (1153)

2001/02: 23^{P}G, 22^{0}GF, 22^{1}G, 26^{3}GF

	Starts	1st	2nd	3rd	Win & Pl
Hurdles	1	0	0	0	0
Chases	3	1	0	1	4256
Career Total	**16**	**2**	**0**	**2**	**8468**

99	7/01	MRas	2m6f110y	F(0-105)HCh	GD	£3835
105	5/00	Hexm	2m4f110y	E(0-105)HCh	GD	£3159

Total win prize-money £6994

Going: Sf: 0-0 GS: 0-0 Gd: 1-2 GF: - Fm: 0-2
Distance: 2m/2m3: 0-0 **2m4-2m7: 1-2** 3m+: 0-2
Track: LH: 0-2 **RH: 1-2 Tight: 1-3** Gall: 0-0
Aids: Bl: 0-0 Vi: 0-0 **Tstrap: 1-2**
Best Rating: 105 8/01 NAbb 3m2f110y gd-fm Ch

Rosetta

61 15

5-y-o b m Fraam-Starawak (Star Appeal)

R J Hodges Unity Farm Holiday Centre Ltd

Placings:U0 (2924)

2001/02: 16^{U}G, 17^{0}GS

	Starts	1st	2nd	3rd	Win & Pl
Hurdles	2	0	0	0	
Career Total	**2**	**0**	**0**	**0**	

Going: Sf: 0-0 GS: 0-1 Gd: 0-1 GF: - Fm: 0-0
Distance: 2m/2m3: 0-2 2m4-2m7: 0-0 3m+: 0-0
Track: LH: 0-0 RH: 0-2 Tight: 0-1 Gall: 0-0
Aids: Bl: 0-0 Vi: 0-0 Tstrap: 0-0
Best Rating: 15 12/01 Tntn 2m1f gd-sft Hdl

Rosewood Lady (IRE)

7-y-o b m Maledetto (IRE)-Thrill Seeker (IRE) (Treasure Kay)

W J Reed W J Reed

Placings:0P (2483)

2001/02: 17^{0}GF, 17^{P}HY

	Starts	1st	2nd	3rd	Win & Pl
Hurdles	2	0	0	0	
Career Total	**2**	**0**	**0**	**0**	

Going: Sf: 0-1 GS: 0-0 Gd: 0-0 GF: - Fm: 0-1
Distance: 2m/2m3: 0-2 2m4-2m7: 0-0 3m+: 0-0
Track: LH: 0-2 RH: 0-0 Tight: 0-2 Gall: 0-0
Aids: Bl: 0-0 Vi: 0-0 Tstrap: 0-0
Best Rating:

Rosie Redman (IRE)

95f 97f

5-y-o gr m Roselier (FR)-Carbia's Last (Palm Track)

J R Turner Miss S J Turner

Placings:3 (2401)

2001/02: 16^{3}G

	Starts	1st	2nd	3rd	Win & Pl
NH Flat	1	0	0	1	218
Career Total	**1**	**0**	**0**	**1**	**218**

Going: Sf: 0-0 GS: 0-0 Gd: 0-1 GF: - Fm: 0-0
Distance: 2m/2m3: 0-1 2m4-2m7: 0-0 3m+: 0-0
Track: LH: 0-1 RH: 0-0 Tight: 0-0 Gall: 0-0
Aids: Bl: 0-0 Vi: 0-0 Tstrap: 0-0
Best Rating: 97 11/01 Weth 2m good NHF

From a fair jumping family, she was third in a bumper on her debut.

Rospo

58f 21f

6-y-o b/br g Tromeros-East Gale (Oats)

Miss K B Roncoroni Miss K B Roncoroni

Placings:0 (4098)

2001/02: 16^{0}GS

	Starts	1st	2nd	3rd	Win & Pl
NH Flat	1	0	0	0	
Career Total	**1**	**0**	**0**	**0**	

Going: Sf: 0-0 GS: 0-1 Gd: 0-0 GF: - Fm: 0-0
Distance: 2m/2m3: 0-1 2m4-2m7: 0-0 3m+: 0-0
Track: LH: 0-1 RH: 0-0 Tight: 0-1 Gall: 0-0
Aids: Bl: 0-0 Vi: 0-0 Tstrap: 0-0
Best Rating: 21 3/02 Catt 2m gd-sft NHF

Ross Dancer (IRE)

103 86

10-y-o b g Ajraas (USA)-Crimson Crown (Lord Gayle (USA))

J S Moore Gerard P O'Loughlin

Placings:4530513/633**005**/1331325510/0042-05 (0517)

2001/02: 20^{0}G, 24^{5}F

	Starts	1st	2nd	3rd	Win & Pl
Hurdles	2	0	0	0	0
Career Total	**29**	**4**	**2**	**7**	**15773**

108	4/99	Towc	3m	F(0-105)HHdl	GD	£2011
105	7/98	Sedg	2m5f110y	D(0-120)HHdl	GD	£2765
100	5/98	Towc	2m5f	D(0-125)HHdl	GD	£2805
89	3/97	Towc	3m	F(0-105)HHdl	G-F	£2372

Total win prize-money £9955

Going: Sf: 0-0 GS: 0-0 Gd: 0-1 GF: - Fm: 0-1
Distance: 2m/2m3: 0-0 2m4-2m7: 0-1 3m+: 0-1
Track: LH: 0-2 RH: 0-0 Tight: 0-1 Gall: 0-0
Aids: Bl: 0-0 Vi: 0-0 Tstrap: 0-0
Best Rating: 108 4/99 Towc 3m good Hdl

Ross Minster (IRE)

110 138

8-y-o ro g Roselier (FR)-Face To Face (The Parson)

P J Hobbs The Country Side

Placings:*62*/150**121/53P1352-1235501** (4532)

2001/02: 26^{1}S, 26^{2}G, 26^{3}S, 25^{5}GS, 26^{5}S, 30^{0}G, 26^{1}GS

	Starts	1st	2nd	3rd	Win & Pl
Chases	7	2	1	1	11285
Career Total	**22**	**6**	**4**	**3**	**33487**

138	4/02	Chep	3m2f110y	D(0-120)HCh	G-S	£4124
134	11/01	NAbb	3m2f110y	D(0-120)HCh	SFT	£3767
131	1/01	Chep	3m2f110y	E(0-115)HCh	G-S	£3104
131	4/00	Uttx	3m2f	E Ch	HVY	£5540
130	2/00	Winc	3m1f110y	D Ch	G-S	£4348
115	11/99	Towc	3m	D Hdl	GD	£3051

Total win prize-money £23936

Going: Sf: 1-3 GS: 1-2 Gd: 0-2 GF: - Fm: 0-0
Distance: 2m/2m3: 0-0 2m4-2m7: 0-0 **3m+: 2-7**
Track: **LH: 2-5** RH: 0-1 **Tight: 1-2** Gall: 0-0
Aids: Bl: 0-1 Vi: 0-0 Tstrap: 0-0
Best Rating: 138 4/02 Chep 3m2f110y gd-sft Ch

Useful staying handicap chaser. Has won with and without blinkers. Needs strong handling. Acts on soft ground and good to soft. Stays three and a quarter miles.

Ross Park (IRE)

94 72

6-y-o b g Roselier (FR)-La Christyana (IRE) (The Parson)

J Howard Johnson J Howard Johnson

Placings:4 (4259)

2001/02: 24^{4}HY

	Starts	1st	2nd	3rd	Win & Pl
Hurdles	1	0	0	0	0
Career Total	**1**	**0**	**0**	**0**	**0**

Going: Sf: 0-1 GS: 0-0 Gd: 0-0 GF: - Fm: 0-0
Distance: 2m/2m3: 0-0 2m4-2m7: 0-0 3m+: 0-1
Track: LH: 0-1 RH: 0-0 Tight: 0-0 Gall: 0-0
Aids: Bl: 0-0 Vi: 0-0 Tstrap: 0-0
Best Rating: 72 3/02 Hexm 3m heavy Hdl

Ross Quay (IRE)

93 91

12-y-o b/br g Roselier (FR)-Cool Russ Quay (Quayside)

P Bowen P Bowen

Placings:2/12/**U1**/FPP-40P (1147)

2001/02: 24^{4}F, 22^{0}GF, 24^{P}GF

	Starts	1st	2nd	3rd	Win & Pl
Hurdles	3	0	0	0	0
Career Total	**11**	**2**	**2**	**0**	**7050**

105	8/99	Worc	2m4f110y	E Ch	G-F	£3013
113	10/98	Sthl	3m110y	E Hdl	GD	£2234

Total win prize-money £5248

Going: Sf: 0-0 GS: 0-0 Gd: 0-0 GF: - Fm: 0-3
Distance: 2m/2m3: 0-0 2m4-2m7: 0-1 3m+: 0-2
Track: LH: 0-3 RH: 0-0 Tight: 0-3 Gall: 0-0
Aids: Bl: 0-0 Vi: 0-0 Tstrap: 0-0
Best Rating: 113 10/98 Strf 2m6f110y good Hdl

Rossaleen

11-y-o b m Ardross-Tawny Silk (Little Buskins)
Mrs Peter Shaw Mrs Jilly Kelly

Placings:5/6-1 **(0324)**
2001/02: 31^{1}G

	Starts	1st	2nd	3rd	Win & Pl
Chases	1	1	0	0	3562
Career Total	**3**	**1**	**0**	**0**	**3562**

88	5/01	Folk	3m7f	H Ch	GD	£3562

Total win prize-money £3562

Going: Sf: 0-0 GS: 0-0 Gd: 1-1 GF: - Fm: 0-0
Distance: 2m/2m3: 0-0 2m4-2m7: 0-0 **3m+: 1-1**
Track: LH: 0-0 **RH: 1-1 Tight: 1-1** Gall: 0-0
Aids: Bl: 0-0 **Vi: 1-1** Tstrap: 0-0
Best Rating: 88 5/01 Folk 3m7f good Ch

Rossel (USA)

107 **102**

9-y-o b g Blushing John (USA)-Northern Aspen (USA) (Northern Dancer)
P Monteith Allan W Melville

Placings:141321105/3234655/11133**313342**/U**0211**/3 2540052 **(2264)**
2001/02: 16^{3}G, 17^{2}GS, 16^{5}G, 17^{4}G, 16^{0}G, 17^{0}S, 18^{5}G, 17^{2}S

	Starts	1st	2nd	3rd	Win & Pl
Hurdles	8	0	2	1	1939
Career Total	**40**	**10**	**6**	**9**	**37648**

135	1/00	Muss	2m	D(0-125)HCh	SFT	£4056
132	12/99	Sedg	2m110y	E(0-115)HCh	SFT	£3661
105	12/98	Ayr	2m	E Ch	HVY	£3187
139	10/98	Kels	2m110y	E(0-115)HHdl	SFT	£2276
133	10/98	Carl	2m1f	D(0-120)HHdl	HVY	£2654
135	10/98	Carl	2m1f	E(0-125)HHdl	GD	£2206
116	1/97	Kels	2m110y	C Hdl	GD	£3582
103	12/96	Muss	2m	E Hdl	G-F	£1815
108	11/96	Ayr	2m	E Hdl	GD	£2346
78	8/96	Prth	2m110y	E Hdl	G-F	£2190

Total win prize-money £27976

Going: Sf: 0-2 GS: 0-1 Gd: 0-5 GF: - Fm: 0-0
Distance: 2m/2m3: 0-8 2m4-2m7: 0-0 3m+: 0-0
Track: LH: 0-5 RH: 0-3 Tight: 0-5 Gall: 0-0
Aids: Bl: 0-0 Vi: 0-1 Tstrap: 0-0
Best Rating: 139 10/98 Kels 2m110y soft Hdl

Genuine dual-purpose gelding. (DEAD)

Rostropovich (IRE)

112 **137**

5-y-o gr g Sadler's Wells (USA)-Infamy (Shirley Heights)
M F Morris M A Kilduff

Placings:13316-14005 **(4954a)**
2001/02: 16^{1}G, 16^{4}Y, 16^{0}GS, 20^{0}G, 24^{5}G

	Starts	1st	2nd	3rd	Win & Pl
Hurdles	5	1	0	0	12675
Career Total	**10**	**3**	**0**	**2**	**28715**

137	5/01	Fair	2m	Hdl	GD	£10483
124	4/01	Cork	2m	Hdl	Y-S	£6120
109	1/01	Naas	2m	Hdl	SFT	£5564

Total win prize-money £22170

Going: Sf: 0-0 GS: 0-1 Gd: 1-3 GF: - Fm: 0-0
Distance: 2m/2m3: 1-3 2m4-2m7: 0-1 3m+: 0-1
Track: LH: 0-3 RH: 0-1 Tight: 0-1 Gall: 0-0
Aids: Bl: 0-0 Vi: 0-0 **Tstrap: 1-5**
Best Rating: 137 12/01 Leop 2m yield Hdl

Decent on the Flat, he he is best at two miles over hurdles. Acts on good and soft ground.

Rosy Light

8-y-o ch m Tigani-Pheasants Delight (K-Battery)
P Beaumont Geoff Pickering

Placings:0PP **(3271)**
2001/02: 17^{0}GS, 16^{P}S, 16^{P}G

	Starts	1st	2nd	3rd	Win & Pl
Hurdles	3	0	0	0	
Career Total	**3**	**0**	**0**	**0**	

Going: Sf: 0-1 GS: 0-1 Gd: 0-1 GF: - Fm: 0-0
Distance: 2m/2m3: 0-3 2m4-2m7: 0-0 3m+: 0-0
Track: LH: 0-2 RH: 0-1 Tight: 0-2 Gall: 0-1
Aids: Bl: 0-0 Vi: 0-0 Tstrap: 0-0
Best Rating:

Rouble (IRE)

115 **151**

6-y-o ch g Moscow Society (USA)-Cashla (IRE) (Duky)
J T Gifford P H Betts

Placings:1/422-4111S **(4229)**
2001/02: 20^{4}GS, 16^{1}G, 20^{1}S, 20^{1}S, 21^{S}GS

	Starts	1st	2nd	3rd	Win & Pl
Hurdles	5	3	0	0	36072
Career Total	**9**	**4**	**2**	**0**	**43164**

151	2/02	Font	2m4f	A Hdl	SFT	£17095
143	12/01	Sand	2m4f110y	A Hdl	SFT	£13100
135	11/01	Asct	2m110y	C Hdl	GD	£4914
127	4/00	Asct	2m110y	H NHF	SFT	£2646

Total win prize-money £37755

Going: Sf: 2-2 GS: 0-2 Gd: 1-1 GF: - Fm: 0-0
Distance: 2m/2m3: 1-1 **2m4-2m7: 2-4** 3m+: 0-0
Track: LH: 0-2 **RH: 2-2 Tight: 1-1** Gall: 0-1
Aids: Bl: 0-0 Vi: 0-0 Tstrap: 0-0
Best Rating: 151 2/02 Font 2m4f soft Hdl

A very useful novice hurdler who stayed two and a half miles but was dropped in trip to win at Ascot in November. Followed up at Sandown in good style and beat Jair du Cochet among others in a messy race at Fontwell. Tragically killed at the Cheltenham Festival. (DEAD)

Rough Gamble (IRE)

92(83h) (116h)**115**

8-y-o ch g Glacial Storm (USA)-Hope You'Re Lucky (Quayside)
A J Kennedy Fountain Syndicate

Placings:235024-4412202**0**02 **(3423a)**
2001/02: 20^{4}F, 16^{4}GF, 16^{1}YS, 20^{2}GF, 16^{2}GY, 20^{0}G, 16^{2}YS, 21^{0}G, 16^{0}YS, 21^{2}SH

	Starts	1st	2nd	3rd	Win & Pl
NH Flat	1	0	0	0	226
Hurdles	6	1	2	0	6895
Chases	3	0	2	0	3493
Career Total	**16**	**1**	**6**	**1**	**13409**

103	6/01	Rosc	2m	Hdl	Y-S	£3895

Total win prize-money £3895

Going: Sf: 0-0 GS: 0-0 Gd: 0-2 GF: - Fm: 0-3
Distance: 2m/2m3: 1-5 2m4-2m7: 0-5 3m+: 0-0
Track: LH: 0-1 RH: 0-2 Tight: 0-0 Gall: 0-1
Aids: Bl: 1-1 Vi: 0-0 Tstrap: 0-0
Best Rating: 116 8/01 Gway 2m gd-yld Hdl

He was a winner over hurdles in Ireland and ran fairly well on his chasing debut without setting the world alight.

Route Barree (FR)

88 **77**

4-y-o ch g Exit To Nowhere (USA)-Star Des Evees (FR) (Moulin)
S Dow Byerley Bloodstock

Placings:36 **(1412)**
2001/02: 16^{3}GF, 16^{6}GF

	Starts	1st	2nd	3rd	Win & Pl
Hurdles	2	0	0	1	435
Career Total	**2**	**0**	**0**	**1**	**435**

Going: Sf: 0-0 GS: 0-0 Gd: 0-0 GF: - Fm: 0-2
Distance: 2m/2m3: 0-2 2m4-2m7: 0-0 3m+: 0-0
Track: LH: 0-2 RH: 0-0 Tight: 0-2 Gall: 0-0
Aids: Bl: 0-0 Vi: 0-0 Tstrap: 0-0
Best Rating: 77 9/01 Plum 2m gd-fm Hdl

Route Sixty Six (IRE)

106 **110**

6-y-o b m Brief Truce (USA)-Lyphards Goddess (IRE) (Lyphard's Special (USA))
Jedd O'Keeffe Wetherby Racing Bureau 47

Placings:0F12-322PP **(3884)**
2001/02: 16^{3}G, 16^{2}GS, 16^{2}G, 16^{P}GS, 16^{P}GS

	Starts	1st	2nd	3rd	Win & Pl
Hurdles	5	0	2	1	5748
Career Total	**9**	**1**	**3**	**1**	**9854**

90	1/01	Muss	2m	E Hdl	GD	£2362

Total win prize-money £2363

Going: Sf: 0-0 GS: 0-3 Gd: 0-2 GF: - Fm: 0-0
Distance: 2m/2m3: 0-5 2m4-2m7: 0-0 3m+: 0-0
Track: LH: 0-0 RH: 0-5 Tight: 0-0 Gall: 0-2
Aids: Bl: 0-0 Vi: 0-0 Tstrap: 0-0
Best Rating: 110 12/01 Kemp 2m good Hdl

Successful over hurdles in January 2001, he has been held since. Suited by good ground, two miles, a sharp track and being held up.

Roveretto

109 **132**

7-y-o b g Robellino (USA)-Spring Flyer (IRE) (Waajib)
Mrs M Reveley Codan Trust Company Limited

Placings:222/5112/F013-40 **(4231)**
2001/02: 20^{4}S, 21^{0}GS

	Starts	1st	2nd	3rd	Win & Pl
Hurdles	2	0	0	0	799
Career Total	**13**	**3**	**4**	**1**	**17536**

142	12/00	Muss	3m	D(0-125)HHdl	GD	£5050
124	1/00	Catt	2m3f	E Hdl	GD	£2362
122	12/99	Muss	2m4f	E Hdl	G-S	£2905

Total win prize-money £10319

Going: Sf: 0-1 GS: 0-1 Gd: 0-0 GF: - Fm: 0-0
Distance: 2m/2m3: 0-0 2m4-2m7: 0-2 3m+: 0-0
Track: LH: 0-2 RH: 0-0 Tight: 0-0 Gall: 0-1
Aids: Bl: 0-0 Vi: 0-0 Tstrap: 0-0
Best Rating: 142 12/00 Muss 3m good Hdl

A lightly-raced but useful staying hurdler, he is best on good ground around a sharp track, goes well at Musselburgh. He is built to jump fences and will be very interesting when switched to that code.

Rovestar

108 **119**

11-y-o b g Le Solaret (FR)-Gilberts Choice (My Swanee)
C L Popham The Rovestar Partnership

Placings:*04*/453000/61003/**360R451412/4231310052/233205315336/11422P0FPU-0310413415** (4845)
2001/02: 17^{0}G, 16^{3}S, 16^{1}GS, 16^{0}GF, 16^{4}HY, 24^{1}S, 24^{3}S, 19^{4}GS, 24^{1}G, 24^{5}G

	Starts	1st	2nd	3rd	Win & Pl
Chases	10	3	0	2	16492
Career Total	**65**	**11**	**7**	**12**	**57532**

119	4/02	Tntn	3m	D(0-120)HCh	GD	£7020
115	1/02	Tntn	3m	E(0-110)HCh	SFT	£3640
110	11/01	Chep	2m110y	E(0-115)HCh	G-S	£3307
119	5/00	Towc	2m110y	D(0-125)HCh	SFT	£3848
119	5/00	Towc	2m110y	E(0-115)HCh	SFT	£3198
119	2/00	Towc	2m110y	D(0-120)HCh	SFT	£3861
119	2/99	Towc	2m110y	D(0-120)HCh	SFT	£3658
114	11/98	Wwck	2m	D(0-125)HCh	SFT	£3415
114	4/98	Winc	2m	E(0-115)HCh	G-S	£3550
114	3/98	NAbb	2m110y	F(0-100)HCh	SFT	£2448
92	11/96	Wwck	2m	E(0-100)HHdl	GD	£2692

Total win prize-money £40640

Going: Sf: 1-4 GS: 1-2 Gd: 1-3 GF: - Fm: 0-1
Distance: 2m/2m3: 1-5 2m4-2m7: 0-1 **3m+: 2-4**
Track: LH: 1-3 **RH: 2-7 Tight: 2-4** Gall: 0-0
Aids: **Bl: 3-10** Vi: 0-0 Tstrap: 0-0
Best Rating: 119 4/02 Bang 3m110y good Ch

Fair handicap chaser, goes really well at Towcester and excels in soft ground. Stays three miles, is effective over shorter.

Rowan Castle

79f **68f**

6-y-o ch g Broadsword (USA)-Brass Castle (IRE) (Carlingford Castle)
Sir John Barlow Bt Sir John Barlow

Placings:*00* (1858)
2001/02: 16^{0}GF, 17^{0}S

	Starts	1st	2nd	3rd	Win & Pl
NH Flat	2	0	0	0	
Career Total	**2**	**0**	**0**	**0**	

Going: Sf: 0-1 GS: 0-0 Gd: 0-0 GF: - Fm: 0-1
Distance: 2m/2m3: 0-2 2m4-2m7: 0-0 3m+: 0-0
Track: LH: 0-2 RH: 0-0 Tight: 0-1 Gall: 0-0
Aids: Bl: 0-0 Vi: 0-0 Tstrap: 0-0
Best Rating: 68 9/01 Worc 2m gd-fm NHF

Rowe's River (IRE)

(77h) (34h)

10-y-o ch g Roselier (FR)-Upton River (Over The River (FR))
K C Bailey K C Bailey

Placings:PF/PPF/0 (0232)
2001/02: 21^{0}GF

	Starts	1st	2nd	3rd	Win & Pl
Hurdles	1	0	0	0	
Career Total	**6**	**0**	**0**	**0**	

Going: Sf: 0-0 GS: 0-0 Gd: 0-0 GF: - Fm: 0-1
Distance: 2m/2m3: 0-0 2m4-2m7: 0-1 3m+: 0-0
Track: LH: 0-0 RH: 0-1 Tight: 0-0 Gall: 0-1
Aids: Bl: 0-0 Vi: 0-0 Tstrap: 0-0

Best Rating: 34 5/01 Hntg 2m5f110y gd-fm Hdl

Roxby Explorer

98 **93**

6-y-o b g Aragon-Super Blues (Welsh Captain)
O Sherwood (Mrs M Reveley 8/10) F. B. O. T. Racing

Placings:*133F* (4880)
2001/02: 17^{1}GS, 17^{3}S, 17^{3}GS, 20^{F}G

	Starts	1st	2nd	3rd	Win & Pl
NH Flat	1	1	0	0	1621
Hurdles	3	0	0	2	807
Career Total	**4**	**1**	**0**	**2**	**2428**

100	10/01	Sedg	2m1f	H NHF	G-S	£1620

Total win prize-money £1621

Going: Sf: 0-1 GS: 1-2 Gd: 0-1 GF: - Fm: 0-0
Distance: **2m/2m3: 1-3** 2m4-2m7: 0-1 3m+: 0-0
Track: **LH: 1-1** RH: 0-3 **Tight: 1-2** Gall: 0-0
Aids: Bl: 0-0 Vi: 0-0 Tstrap: 0-0
Best Rating: 100 10/01 Sedg 2m1f gd-sft NHF

Won a bumper for Mary Reveley before finishing third over hurdles on his debut for his new yard. Acts in soft ground.

Royal Allegiance

83 **77**

7-y-o ch g Kris-Wilayif (USA) (Danzig (USA))
P Wegmann P Wegmann

Placings:P0003006/4013005000-00P0 (1760)
2001/02: 17^{0}F, 17^{0}GF, 16^{P}GF, 16^{0}GS

	Starts	1st	2nd	3rd	Win & Pl
Hurdles	4	0	0	0	
Career Total	**23**	**1**	**0**	**2**	**3802**

85	10/00	Strf	2m110y	F(0-100)HHdl	G-S	£2828

Total win prize-money £2828

Going: Sf: 0-0 GS: 0-1 Gd: 0-0 GF: - Fm: 0-3
Distance: 2m/2m3: 0-4 2m4-2m7: 0-0 3m+: 0-0
Track: LH: 0-3 RH: 0-1 Tight: 0-3 Gall: 0-0
Aids: Bl: 0-0 Vi: 0-1 Tstrap: 0-0
Best Rating: 85 10/00 Strf 2m110y gd-sft Hdl

Royal Amaretto (IRE)

8-y-o b g Fairy King (USA)-Melbourne Miss (Chaparral (FR))
K A Morgan Euroteam Ltd T/a National Window System

Placings:1-P (1742)
2001/02: 16^{P}G

	Starts	1st	2nd	3rd	Win & Pl
Hurdles	1	0	0	0	
Career Total	**2**	**1**	**0**	**0**	**1799**

108	12/00	Muss	2m	E Hdl	GD	£1799

Total win prize-money £1799

Going: Sf: 0-0 GS: 0-0 Gd: 0-1 GF: - Fm: 0-0
Distance: 2m/2m3: 0-1 2m4-2m7: 0-0 3m+: 0-0
Track: LH: 0-1 RH: 0-0 Tight: 0-1 Gall: 0-0
Aids: Bl: 0-0 Vi: 0-0 Tstrap: 0-1
Best Rating: 108 12/00 Muss 2m good Hdl

Royal Arcane (IRE)

8-y-o ch g Arcane (USA)-Carbery Star (Kemal (FR))
H D Daly Paul Sandy

Placings:P (1842)
2001/02: 24^{P}S

	Starts	1st	2nd	3rd	Win & Pl
Hurdles	1	0	0	0	
Career Total	**1**	**0**	**0**	**0**	

Going: Sf: 0-1 GS: 0-0 Gd: 0-0 GF: - Fm: 0-0
Distance: 2m/2m3: 0-0 2m4-2m7: 0-0 3m+: 0-1
Track: LH: 0-0 RH: 0-1 Tight: 0-0 Gall: 0-0
Aids: Bl: 0-0 Vi: 0-0 Tstrap: 0-0
Best Rating:

Royal Arrow (USA)

98 **79**

6-y-o b g Dayjur (USA)-Buy The Firm (USA) (Affirmed (USA))
Ferdy Murphy Oak Wood Racing

Placings:4FF6-5553500 (4898)
2001/02: 16^{5}S, 16^{5}F, 16^{5}GS, 17^{3}S, 17^{5}G, 16^{0}GS, 16^{0}G

	Starts	1st	2nd	3rd	Win & Pl
Hurdles	7	0	0	1	229
Career Total	**11**	**0**	**0**	**1**	**229**

Going: Sf: 0-2 GS: 0-2 Gd: 0-2 GF: - Fm: 0-1
Distance: 2m/2m3: 0-7 2m4-2m7: 0-0 3m+: 0-0
Track: LH: 0-5 RH: 0-2 Tight: 0-2 Gall: 0-0
Aids: Bl: 0-0 Vi: 0-0 Tstrap: 0-0
Best Rating: 79 12/01 Hrfd 2m1f good Hdl

Royal Auclair (FR)

117(108h) (96h)**162**

5-y-o ch g Garde Royale-Carmonera (FR) (Carmont (FR))
M C Pipe Clive D Smith

Placings:531115-F111 (4255)
2001/02: 19^{F}GS, 17^{1}GS, 21^{1}HY, 21^{1}G

	Starts	1st	2nd	3rd	Win & Pl
Chases	4	3	0	0	63236
Career Total	**10**	**6**	**0**	**1**	**93155**

162	3/02	Chel	2m5f	A Ch	GD	£42000
149	1/02	Chel	2m5f	B HCh	HVY	£12720
129	12/01	Extr	2m1f110y	C Ch	G-S	£8515
143	2/01	Sand	2m110y	D Hdl	HVY	£4270
	12/00	Engh	2m1f110y	Hdl	HVY	£10567
	11/00	Engh	2m1f110y	Hdl	HVY	£9606

Total win prize-money £87680

Going: Sf: 1-1 GS: 1-2 Gd: 1-1 GF: - Fm: 0-0
Distance: 2m/2m3: 1-1 **2m4-2m7: 2-3** 3m+: 0-0
Track: **LH: 2-3** RH: 1-1 Tight: 0-0 **Gall: 2-2**
Aids: Bl: 0-0 Vi: 0-0 Tstrap: 0-0
Best Rating: 162 3/02 Chel 2m5f good Ch

A French import, he won over hurdles on very heavy ground at Sandown on his British debut in Februaru 2001, but ran poorly at Aintree. Fell at Chepstow on his chasing debut but made amends at Exeter in December 2001. Followed up at Cheltenham before making all in the Cathcart at the Festival. Stays two miles five furlongs, acts on soft ground.

Royal Barge

113

12-y-o b g Nearly A Hand-April Airs (Grey Mirage)
P Bowen P Bowen

Placings:3263/2311**113321**P/U20-P **(0069)**
2001/02: 28^{P}G

	Starts	1st	2nd	3rd	Win & Pl
Chases	1	0	0	0	
Career Total	**19**	**5**	**4**	**5**	**24534**

126	12/98	Extr	3m2f	D(0-125)HCh	SFT	£5034
115	7/98	Sedg	3m3f	D Ch	GD	£3533
120	7/98	Worc	2m7f110y	F(0-105)HCh	GD	£2798
117	6/98	Sthl	3m110y	E(0-110)HHdl	GD	£2305
93	5/98	Ctml	2m6f	D Hdl	G-F	£2992

Total win prize-money £16666

Going: Sf: 0-0 GS: 0-0 Gd: 0-1 GF: - Fm: 0-0
Distance: 2m/2m3: 0-0 2m4-2m7: 0-0 3m+: 0-1
Track: LH: 0-1 RH: 0-0 Tight: 0-1 Gall: 0-0
Aids: Bl: 0-0 Vi: 0-0 Tstrap: 0-0
Best Rating: **126** 12/98 Extr 3m2f soft Ch

Royal Beluga (USA)

107 **108**

5-y-o b g Rahy (USA)-Navratilovna (USA) (Nureyev (USA))
T R George M R C Opperman

Placings:24-5236 **(4178)**
2001/02: 17^{5}GS, 16^{2}GS, 16^{3}GS, 16^{6}GS

	Starts	1st	2nd	3rd	Win & Pl
Hurdles	4	0	1	1	1310
Career Total	**6**	**0**	**2**	**1**	**2243**

Going: Sf: 0-0 GS: 0-4 Gd: 0-0 GF: - Fm: 0-0
Distance: 2m/2m3: 0-4 2m4-2m7: 0-0 3m+: 0-0
Track: LH: 0-1 RH: 0-3 Tight: 0-2 Gall: 0-1
Aids: Bl: 0-0 Vi: 0-0 Tstrap: 0-3
Best Rating: **108** 1/02 Hntg 2m110y gd-sft Hdl

A winner on the Flat in France, has shown ability over hurdles. Suited by two miles and possibly best on soft ground.

Royal Boy

32f **9f**

5-y-o b g Rock City-Royal Girl (Kafu)
Miss S E Hall Miss S E Hall

Placings:*0* **(4526)**
2001/02: 17^{0}G

	Starts	1st	2nd	3rd	Win & Pl
NH Flat	1	0	0	0	
Career Total	**1**	**0**	**0**	**0**	

Going: Sf: 0-0 GS: 0-0 Gd: 0-1 GF: - Fm: 0-0
Distance: 2m/2m3: 0-1 2m4-2m7: 0-0 3m+: 0-0
Track: LH: 0-0 RH: 0-1 Tight: 0-0 Gall: 0-0
Aids: Bl: 0-0 Vi: 0-0 Tstrap: 0-0
Best Rating: **9** 4/02 Carl 2m1f good NHF

Royal Buckingham (IRE)

66

7-y-o b g Erdelistan (FR)-French Class (The Parson)
J A Moore J A Moore

Placings:*10/00*-P0P **(4898)**
2001/02: 16^{P}G, 16^{0}GF, 16^{P}G

	Starts	1st	2nd	3rd	Win & Pl
Hurdles	3	0	0	0	
Career Total	**7**	**1**	**0**	**0**	**1806**

107	1/00	Ludl	2m	H NHF	GD	£1806

Total win prize-money £1806

Going: Sf: 0-0 GS: 0-0 Gd: 0-2 GF: - Fm: 0-1
Distance: 2m/2m3: 0-3 2m4-2m7: 0-0 3m+: 0-0
Track: LH: 0-0 RH: 0-2 Tight: 0-1 Gall: 0-0
Aids: Bl: 0-0 Vi: 0-0 Tstrap: 0-0
Best Rating: **107** 1/00 Ludl 2m good NHF

Royal Castle (IRE)

8-y-o b g Caerleon (USA)-Sun Princess (English Prince)
M H Tompkins Mrs B Cross & Mr M Sakal

Placings:223/11500/1-P **(2600)**
2001/02: 18^{P}G

	Starts	1st	2nd	3rd	Win & Pl
Hurdles	1	0	0	0	
Career Total	**10**	**3**	**2**	**1**	**11773**

126	7/00	Strf	2m6f110y	E(0-115)HHdl	G-F	£3542
114	12/99	Donc	2m4f	E Hdl	G-F	£3113
109	11/99	Towc	2m5f	E Hdl	GD	£2775

Total win prize-money £9431

Going: Sf: 0-0 GS: 0-0 Gd: 0-1 GF: - Fm: 0-0
Distance: 2m/2m3: 0-1 2m4-2m7: 0-0 3m+: 0-0
Track: LH: 0-1 RH: 0-0 Tight: 0-1 Gall: 0-0
Aids: Bl: 0-0 Vi: 0-0 Tstrap: 0-0
Best Rating: **137** 3/00 Chel 2m5f good Hdl

Royal Cayras (FR)

94 **78**

4-y-o b g King's Theatre (IRE)-Paventia (USA) (Trempolino (USA))
M C Pipe (T Civel 6/6) M C Pipe

Placings:4426-212P4P60 **(4752)**
2001/02: 15^{2}VS, 17^{1}G, 17^{2}GF, 17^{P}S, 17^{4}GS, 16^{P}HY, 17^{6}S, 16^{0}GF

	Starts	1st	2nd	3rd	Win & Pl
Hurdles	8	1	2	0	6910
Career Total	**12**	**1**	**3**	**0**	**9432**

78	8/01	Bang	2m1f	E Hdl	GD	£2940

Total win prize-money £2940

Going: Sf: 0-3 GS: 0-1 Gd: 1-1 GF: - Fm: 0-2
Distance: **2m/2m3: 1-7** 2m4-2m7: 0-0 3m+: 0-0
Track: **LH: 1-4** RH: 0-3 **Tight: 1-6** Gall: 0-0
Aids: Bl: 0-0 Vi: 0-1 Tstrap: 0-3
Best Rating: **78** 9/01 NAbb 2m1f gd-fm Hdl

Modest hurdler, best at around the minimum trip on a sound surface.

Royal Charmer (NZ)

10-y-o ch g Palatable (USA)-Noble Charmer (NZ) (Noble Bijou (USA))
S B Clark S B Clark

Placings:0/23/14P-P **(0983)**
2001/02: 19^{P}G

	Starts	1st	2nd	3rd	Win & Pl
Hurdles	1	0	0	0	
Career Total	**7**	**1**	**1**	**1**	**4274**

113	10/00	Sthl	2m4f110y	E Ch	G-S	£2839

Total win prize-money £2839

Going: Sf: 0-0 GS: 0-0 Gd: 0-1 GF: - Fm: 0-0
Distance: 2m/2m3: 0-1 2m4-2m7: 0-0 3m+: 0-0
Track: LH: 0-1 RH: 0-0 Tight: 0-1 Gall: 0-0
Aids: Bl: 0-0 Vi: 0-0 Tstrap: 0-0
Best Rating: **113** 10/00 Sthl 2m4f110y gd-sft Ch

Royal Comic

7-y-o ch g Jester-Princess Wenllyan (White Prince (USA))
C R Barwell R L Black

Placings:U-P0F **(0680)**
2001/02: 22^{P}GS, 22^{0}GF, 22^{F}G

	Starts	1st	2nd	3rd	Win & Pl
Hurdles	3	0	0	0	
Career Total	**4**	**0**	**0**	**0**	

Going: Sf: 0-0 GS: 0-1 Gd: 0-1 GF: - Fm: 0-1
Distance: 2m/2m3: 0-0 2m4-2m7: 0-3 3m+: 0-0
Track: LH: 0-1 RH: 0-1 Tight: 0-1 Gall: 0-0
Aids: Bl: 0-0 Vi: 0-0 Tstrap: 0-0
Best Rating:

Royal Czarina

98 **84**

5-y-o ch m Czaravich (USA)-Sabrata (IRE) (Zino)
M Salaman M Salaman

Placings:2U5-00536U0 **(4601)**
2001/02: 16^{0}S, 19^{0}F, 16^{5}G, 19^{3}HY, 17^{6}G, 17^{U}S, 16^{0}GF

	Starts	1st	2nd	3rd	Win & Pl
Hurdles	7	0	0	1	339
Career Total	**10**	**0**	**1**	**1**	**999**

Going: Sf: 0-3 GS: 0-0 Gd: 0-2 GF: - Fm: 0-2
Distance: 2m/2m3: 0-5 2m4-2m7: 0-2 3m+: 0-0
Track: LH: 0-3 RH: 0-4 Tight: 0-3 Gall: 0-0
Aids: Bl: 0-0 Vi: 0-0 Tstrap: 0-0
Best Rating: **87** 10/00 Winc 2m gd-sft Hdl

Very modest hurdler, stays two and a half miles.

Royal Emperor (IRE)

96 **99**

6-y-o gr g Roselier (FR)-Boreen Bro (Boreen (FR))
J J O'Neill (R J Hodges 1/7) Exors Of The Late Robert Hitchins

Placings:*30/03*P-6F243 **(2051)**
2001/02: 19^{6}GF, 16^{F}GF, 17^{2}F, 19^{4}GF, 20^{3}S

	Starts	1st	2nd	3rd	Win & Pl
Hurdles	5	0	1	1	1178
Career Total	**10**	**0**	**1**	**3**	**2876**

Going: Sf: 0-1 GS: 0-0 Gd: 0-0 GF: - Fm: 0-4
Distance: 2m/2m3: 0-3 2m4-2m7: 0-2 3m+: 0-0
Track: LH: 0-3 RH: 0-1 Tight: 0-3 Gall: 0-0
Aids: Bl: 0-0 Vi: 0-0 Tstrap: 0-0
Best Rating: **112** 2/00 Newb 2m110y gd-sft NHF

Royal Enclosure (IRE)

86 **65**

4-y-o b g Royal Academy (USA)-Hi Bettina (Henbit (USA))

P D Evans Mike Nolan

Placings:500 **(4737)**
2001/02: 16^{5}GF, 16^{0}S, 16^{0}GF

	Starts	1st	2nd	3rd	Win & Pl
Hurdles	3	0	0	0	0
Career Total	**3**	**0**	**0**	**0**	**0**

Going: Sf: 0-1 GS: 0-0 Gd: 0-0 GF: - Fm: 0-2
Distance: 2m/2m3: 0-3 2m4-2m7: 0-0 3m+: 0-0
Track: LH: 0-1 RH: 0-2 Tight: 0-0 Gall: 0-0
Aids: Bl: 0-0 Vi: 0-3 Tstrap: 0-2
Best Rating: 65 10/01 Ludl 2m gd-fm Hdl

Royal Estate

101 **133**

9-y-o b g Rakaposhi King-Country Seat (Paddy's Stream)
N J Henderson Mrs T Stopford-Sackville

Placings:3-12 **(0670)**
2001/02: 25^{1}G, 23^{2}G

	Starts	1st	2nd	3rd	Win & Pl
Chases	2	1	1	0	3150
Career Total	**3**	**1**	**1**	**1**	**3687**
133 5/01	Hrfd	3m1f110y	H Ch	GD	£1787

Total win prize-money £1788

Going: Sf: 0-0 GS: 0-0 Gd: 1-2 GF: - Fm: 0-0
Distance: 2m/2m3: 0-0 2m4-2m7: 0-0 **3m+: 1-2**
Track: LH: 0-1 **RH: 1-1** Tight: 0-0 Gall: 0-0
Aids: Bl: 0-0 Vi: 0-0 Tstrap: 0-0
Best Rating: 133 5/01 Hrfd 3m1f110y good Ch

Won a hunter chaser before finishing runner-up in a novice event in the summer of 2001.

Royal Event

105 **115**

11-y-o ch g Rakaposhi King-Upham Reunion (Paridel)
D R Gandolfo A E Frost

Placings:013/223120/4212/21PP/P2/3140550-P33P216 **(4876)**
2001/02: 21^{P}GS, 20^{3}GS, 21^{3}G, 22^{P}G, 20^{2}GS, 21^{1}S, 20^{6}G

	Starts	1st	2nd	3rd	Win & Pl
Chases	7	1	1	2	9108
Career Total	**33**	**6**	**8**	**5**	**37682**

115 3/02	Winc	2m5f	E(0-110)HCh	SFT	£4251
119 11/00	Winc	2m5f	E(0-115)HCh	G-S	£5304
127 10/98	Strf	2m5f110y	C(0-135)HCh	GD	£5215
123 12/97	Sthl	2m	E Ch	GD	£3288
102 1/97	Wind	2m	D(0-120)HHdl	G-F	£2945
108 2/96	Nott	2m	H NHF	G-S	£1229

Total win prize-money £22233

Going: Sf: 1-1 GS: 0-3 Gd: 0-3 GF: - Fm: 0-0
Distance: 2m/2m3: 0-0 **2m4-2m7: 1-7** 3m+: 0-0
Track: LH: 0-3 **RH: 1-3** Tight: 0-1 Gall: 0-2
Aids: Bl: 0-0 Vi: 0-0 Tstrap: 0-0
Best Rating: 127 10/98 Strf 2m5f110y good Ch

A modest handicapper, he had rather lost his way until a better effort at Fontwell in October 2001. Successful at Wincanton in March. Best at around two and a half miles, a sound surface is essential.

Royal Expression

81 **37**

10-y-o b g Sylvan Express-Edwins' Princess (Owen Dudley)
G M Moore Mrs A Roddis

Placings:12242U1/11/233-0 **(3437)**
2001/02: 27^{0}HY

	Starts	1st	2nd	3rd	Win & Pl
Hurdles	1	0	0	0	
Career Total	**13**	**4**	**4**	**2**	**14446**

114 8/97	Uttx	2m4f110y	D(0-125)HHdl	GD	£2703
117 7/97	Strf	2m6f110y	E(0-110)HHdl	GD	£2304
115 4/96	Hexm	2m	E Hdl	GD	£2366
96 8/95	Prth	2m110y	E Hdl	G-F	£2179

Total win prize-money £9553

Going: Sf: 0-1 GS: 0-0 Gd: 0-0 GF: - Fm: 0-0
Distance: 2m/2m3: 0-0 2m4-2m7: 0-0 3m+: 0-1
Track: LH: 0-1 RH: 0-0 Tight: 0-1 Gall: 0-0
Aids: Bl: 0-0 Vi: 0-0 Tstrap: 0-0
Best Rating: 117 7/97 Strf 2m6f110y good Hdl

Royal Feelings

101(97h) (70h)**94**

8-y-o b g Feelings (FR)-Wedderburn (Royalty)
Mrs D Thomson The Good To Soft Firm

Placings:0600/5404-00 **(4766)**
2001/02: 22^{0}S, 20^{0}GF

	Starts	1st	2nd	3rd	Win & Pl
Hurdles	2	0	0	0	
Career Total	**10**	**0**	**0**	**0**	**239**

Going: Sf: 0-1 GS: 0-0 Gd: 0-0 GF: - Fm: 0-1
Distance: 2m/2m3: 0-0 2m4-2m7: 0-2 3m+: 0-0
Track: LH: 0-2 RH: 0-0 Tight: 0-1 Gall: 0-0
Aids: Bl: 0-0 Vi: 0-0 Tstrap: 0-0
Best Rating: 85 10/99 Kels 2m110y good Hdl

Maiden hurdler/ chaser.

Royal Gent

4-y-o b g Presidium-Harem Queen (Prince Regent (FR))
L R James Mrs M Lingwood

Placings:P **(1472)**
2001/02: 17^{P}S

	Starts	1st	2nd	3rd	Win & Pl
Hurdles	1	0	0	0	
Career Total	**1**	**0**	**0**	**0**	

Going: Sf: 0-1 GS: 0-0 Gd: 0-0 GF: - Fm: 0-0
Distance: 2m/2m3: 0-1 2m4-2m7: 0-0 3m+: 0-0
Track: LH: 0-0 RH: 0-1 Tight: 0-1 Gall: 0-0
Aids: Bl: 0-0 Vi: 0-0 Tstrap: 0-0
Best Rating:

Royal Glen (IRE)

73 **34**

4-y-o b f Royal Abjar (USA)-Sea Glen (IRE) (Glenstal (USA))
H A McWilliams James S Kennerley And Miss Jenny Hall

Placings:U0 **(2512)**
2001/02: 16^{U}G, 16^{0}S

	Starts	1st	2nd	3rd	Win & Pl
Hurdles	2	0	0	0	
Career Total	**2**	**0**	**0**	**0**	

Going: Sf: 0-1 GS: 0-0 Gd: 0-1 GF: - Fm: 0-0
Distance: 2m/2m3: 0-2 2m4-2m7: 0-0 3m+: 0-0
Track: LH: 0-2 RH: 0-0 Tight: 0-1 Gall: 0-1
Aids: Bl: 0-0 Vi: 0-0 Tstrap: 0-0
Best Rating: 34 12/01 Catt 2m soft Hdl

Royal Glint

78 **26**

13-y-o b m Glint Of Gold-Princess Matilda (Habitat)
H E Haynes Mrs H E Haynes

Placings:0/F02000/24F/0/6043P00060P/0/F00 **(1131)**
2001/02: 19^{F}G, 16^{0}GF, 16^{0}GF

	Starts	1st	2nd	3rd	Win & Pl
Hurdles	3	0	0	0	
Career Total	**26**	**0**	**2**	**1**	**1280**

Going: Sf: 0-0 GS: 0-0 Gd: 0-1 GF: - Fm: 0-2
Distance: 2m/2m3: 0-2 2m4-2m7: 0-1 3m+: 0-0
Track: LH: 0-2 RH: 0-1 Tight: 0-0 Gall: 0-0
Aids: Bl: 0-0 Vi: 0-0 Tstrap: 0-0
Best Rating: 79 5/94 Hrfd 2m1f gd-fm Hdl

Royal Minstrel (IRE)

100 **89**

5-y-o ch g Be My Guest (USA)-Shanntabariya (IRE) (Shernazar)
M H Tompkins P A & D G Sakal

Placings:00 **(2683)**
2001/02: 16^{0}G, 16^{0}G

	Starts	1st	2nd	3rd	Win & Pl
Hurdles	2	0	0	0	
Career Total	**2**	**0**	**0**	**0**	

Going: Sf: 0-0 GS: 0-0 Gd: 0-2 GF: - Fm: 0-0
Distance: 2m/2m3: 0-2 2m4-2m7: 0-0 3m+: 0-0
Track: LH: 0-2 RH: 0-0 Tight: 0-0 Gall: 0-1
Aids: Bl: 0-0 Vi: 0-0 Tstrap: 0-0
Best Rating: 89 11/01 Weth 2m good Hdl

Royal Mountbrowne

14-y-o b g Royal Vulcan-Star Shell (Queens Hussar)
A J Thomas A J Thomas

Placings:40/F2/1121360/FFP6213F60/311F012/06P1102156023/405P/33U034UF/6253/4002335U56PP-P **(0086)**
2001/02: 25^{P}G

	Starts	1st	2nd	3rd	Win & Pl
Chases	1	0	0	0	
Career Total	**70**	**10**	**8**	**10**	**173244**

152 12/96	Punc	2m4f	Ch	YLD	£23453
138 11/96	Clon	2m4f	Ch	Y-S	£13298
148 10/96	Leop	2m5f	Ch	YLD	£4943
142 4/96	Fair	2m4f	HCh	GD	£9974
144 1/96	Leop	3m	HCh	HVY	£16752
133 12/95	Limk	3m	(0-123)HCh	SFT	£3391
133 2/95	Fair	2m4f	Hdl	HVY	£4069
132 2/94	Navn	2m4f	Ch	HVY	£3614
123 12/93	Navn	2m4f	Ch	SFT	£4451
105 11/93	Clon	2m2f	Ch	SFT	£3895

Total win prize-money £87845

Going: Sf: 0-0 GS: 0-0 Gd: 0-1 GF: - Fm: 0-0
Distance: 2m/2m3: 0-0 2m4-2m7: 0-0 3m+: 0-1
Track: LH: 0-0 RH: 0-1 Tight: 0-0 Gall: 0-0
Aids: Bl: 0-1 Vi: 0-0 Tstrap: 0-0
Best Rating: 152 2/97 Naas 2m soft Ch

Royal Opal

50f **11f**

7-y-o b m Loretto Collection (USA)-Boxers Delight (Royal Boxer)
P M Rich Mrs M M Cook

Placings:*0* **(2215)**
2001/02: 17^{0}G

	Starts	1st	2nd	3rd	Win & Pl
NH Flat	1	0	0	0	
Career Total	**1**	**0**	**0**	**0**	

Going: Sf: 0-0 GS: 0-0 Gd: 0-1 GF: - Fm: 0-0
Distance: 2m/2m3: 0-1 2m4-2m7: 0-0 3m+: 0-0
Track: LH: 0-0 RH: 0-1 Tight: 0-0 Gall: 0-0
Aids: Bl: 0-0 Vi: 0-0 Tstrap: 0-0
Best Rating: 11 11/01 Hrfd 2m1f good NHF

Royal Origny (FR)

105

5-y-o b g Royal Charter (FR)-Force Nine (FR) (Luthier)
G Macaire R Fougedoire

Placings:434-313 **(3391)**
2001/02: 17^{3}VS, 18^{1}S, 23^{3}GS

	Starts	1st	2nd	3rd	Win & Pl
Hurdles	1	0	0	1	1309
Chases	2	1	0	1	3913
Career Total	**6**	**1**	**0**	**3**	**9393**

	10/01	Pina	2m2f110y	Ch	SFT	£3395

Total win prize-money £3395

Going: Sf: 1-1 GS: 0-1 Gd: 0-0 GF: - Fm: 0-0
Distance: **2m/2m3: 1-2** 2m4-2m7: 0-0 3m+: 0-1
Track: LH: 0-0 RH: 0-0 Tight: 0-0 Gall: 0-0
Aids: Bl: 0-0 Vi: 0-0 Tstrap: 0-0
Best Rating: 105 1/02 Weth 2m7f110y gd-sft Ch

Royal Partnership (IRE)

(98h) (83h)

6-y-o b g Royal Academy (USA)-Go Honey Go (General Assembly (USA))
D L Williams Reliance Car Hire Services Ltd

Placings:000P0-5P30 **(0977)**
2001/02: 17^{5}F, 17^{P}GF, 17^{3}G, 24^{0}GF

	Starts	1st	2nd	3rd	Win & Pl
Hurdles	4	0	0	1	458
Career Total	**9**	**0**	**0**	**1**	**458**

Going: Sf: 0-0 GS: 0-0 Gd: 0-1 GF: - Fm: 0-3
Distance: 2m/2m3: 0-3 2m4-2m7: 0-0 3m+: 0-1
Track: LH: 0-1 RH: 0-3 Tight: 0-3 Gall: 0-0
Aids: Bl: 0-0 Vi: 0-1 Tstrap: 0-1
Best Rating: 89 1/01 Tntn 2m1f heavy Hdl

Royal Pass

89 **80**

9-y-o ch g Royal Vulcan-Final Joy (Rapid Pass)
Miss S E Forster C Storey

Placings:2F0 **(1815)**
2001/02: 20^{2}GF, 26^{F}G, 24^{0}S

	Starts	1st	2nd	3rd	Win & Pl
Hurdles	2	0	1	0	1048
Chases	1	0	0	0	0
Career Total	**3**	**0**	**1**	**0**	**1048**

Going: Sf: 0-1 GS: 0-0 Gd: 0-1 GF: - Fm: 0-1
Distance: 2m/2m3: 0-0 2m4-2m7: 0-1 3m+: 0-2
Track: LH: 0-1 RH: 0-2 Tight: 0-1 Gall: 0-0
Aids: Bl: 0-0 Vi: 0-0 Tstrap: 0-0
Best Rating: 80 6/01 Prth 2m4f110y gd-fm Hdl

Royal Plum

106 **102**

6-y-o ch g Inchinor-Miss Plum (Ardross)
Mrs M Reveley Lucayan Stud

Placings:*6/210*-0501245 **(4817)**
2001/02: 20^{0}G, 21^{5}GF, 20^{0}G, 24^{1}G, 24^{2}S, 26^{4}GF, 24^{5}GF

	Starts	1st	2nd	3rd	Win & Pl
Hurdles	7	1	1	0	4482
Career Total	**11**	**2**	**2**	**0**	**6357**

102	1/02	Muss	3m	E(0-105)HHdl	GD	£3514
111	7/00	Worc	2m	H NHF	GD	£1456

Total win prize-money £4970

Going: Sf: 0-1 GS: 0-0 Gd: 1-3 GF: - Fm: 0-3
Distance: 2m/2m3: 0-0 2m4-2m7: 0-3 **3m+: 1-4**
Track: LH: 0-2 **RH: 1-4 Tight: 1-2** Gall: 0-3
Aids: **Bl: 1-2** Vi: 0-3 Tstrap: 0-0
Best Rating: 111 7/00 Worc 2m good NHF

Has failed to build on his good bumper form over obstacles, but won well upped to three miles and fitted with a visor at Musselburgh in January.

Royal Predica (FR)

115 **157**

8-y-o ch g Tip Moss (FR)-Girl Vamp (FR) (Kaldoun (FR))
M C Pipe P A Deal, J S Dale & A Stennett

Placings:1/344F2131P/4211FF/2PPP-2122P500 **(4913)**
2001/02: 20^{2}G, 21^{1}G, 20^{2}GS, 25^{2}G, 24^{P}S, 24^{5}GS, 36^{0}G, 29^{0}G

	Starts	1st	2nd	3rd	Win & Pl
Chases	8	1	3	0	27001
Career Total	**28**	**6**	**6**	**2**	**84516**

152	6/01	NAbb	2m5f110y	D(0-125)HCh	GD	£4085
157	2/00	Wwck	2m4f	B(0-140)HCh	SFT	£8784
139	1/00	Wwck	2m4f	C(0-135)HCh	SFT	£7117
142	4/99	Aint	2m4f	C HCh	G-S	£11235
104	1/99	Plum	2m	E Ch	HVY	£2915
	7/97	Diep	1m7f	Hdl	FRM	£3591

Total win prize-money £37728

Going: Sf: 0-1 GS: 0-2 Gd: 1-5 GF: - Fm: 0-0
Distance: 2m/2m3: 0-0 **2m4-2m7: 1-3** 3m+: 0-5
Track: **LH: 1-6** RH: 0-1 **Tight: 1-2** Gall: 0-2
Aids: Bl: 0-0 Vi: 0-0 **Tstrap: 1-8**
Best Rating: 157 12/01 Chel 3m1f110y good Ch

A very useful chaser when on song. Stays three miles, but looks better over shorter and is suited by good or softer ground.

Royal Presence (IRE)

60 **71**

7-y-o b m King's Ride-New Talent (The Parson)
P Winkworth (M Todhunter 9/5) D R Obank

Placings:*0050* **(2110)**
2001/02: 16^{0}GF, 17^{0}G, 16^{5}S, 22^{0}S

	Starts	1st	2nd	3rd	Win & Pl
NH Flat	2	0	0	0	0
Hurdles	2	0	0	0	0
Career Total	**4**	**0**	**0**	**0**	**0**

Going: Sf: 0-2 GS: 0-0 Gd: 0-1 GF: - Fm: 0-1
Distance: 2m/2m3: 0-3 2m4-2m7: 0-1 3m+: 0-0
Track: LH: 0-2 RH: 0-2 Tight: 0-2 Gall: 0-0
Aids: Bl: 0-0 Vi: 0-0 Tstrap: 0-0
Best Rating: 77 5/01 Ayr 2m gd-fm NHF

Royal Pretence

5-y-o b m Royal Fountain-Just Pretend (Sayyaf)
Miss Lucinda V Russell A R Trotter

Placings:*00* **(4771)**
2001/02: 17^{0}G, 16^{0}GF

	Starts	1st	2nd	3rd	Win & Pl
NH Flat	2	0	0	0	
Career Total	**2**	**0**	**0**	**0**	

Going: Sf: 0-0 GS: 0-0 Gd: 0-1 GF: - Fm: 0-1
Distance: 2m/2m3: 0-2 2m4-2m7: 0-0 3m+: 0-0
Track: LH: 0-0 RH: 0-1 Tight: 0-0 Gall: 0-0
Aids: Bl: 0-0 Vi: 0-0 Tstrap: 0-0
Best Rating: 54 4/02 Carl 2m1f good NHF

Royal Quest (IRE)

91 **82**

8-y-o b g Royal Fountain-Our Quest (Private Walk)
N J Henderson Nicholas Cooper

Placings:*00/04/6* **(4030)**
2001/02: 24^{6}GS

	Starts	1st	2nd	3rd	Win & Pl
Hurdles	1	0	0	0	0
Career Total	**5**	**0**	**0**	**0**	**385**

Going: Sf: 0-0 GS: 0-1 Gd: 0-0 GF: - Fm: 0-0
Distance: 2m/2m3: 0-0 2m4-2m7: 0-0 3m+: 0-1
Track: LH: 0-1 RH: 0-0 Tight: 0-0 Gall: 0-1
Aids: Bl: 0-0 Vi: 0-0 Tstrap: 0-0
Best Rating: 97 4/00 Asct 2m4f good Hdl

Posted fairly useful form in a two and a half mile Ascot novice hurdle in 2000 but off the track for a while after. Failed to show much over three miles on return to action. Well suited by good ground.

Royal Rapport

90 **94**

9-y-o ch g Rich Charlie-Miss Camellia (Sonnen Gold)
Mrs J A Wall T Wall

Placings:21/5005/P **(4645)**
2001/02: 24^{P}G

	Starts	1st	2nd	3rd	Win & Pl
Chases	1	0	0	0	
Career Total	**7**	**1**	**1**	**0**	**3006**

84	9/96	Hexm	2m	E Hdl	FRM	£2322

Total win prize-money £2322

Going: Sf: 0-0 GS: 0-0 Gd: 0-1 GF: - Fm: 0-0
Distance: 2m/2m3: 0-0 2m4-2m7: 0-0 3m+: 0-1
Track: LH: 0-0 RH: 0-1 Tight: 0-1 Gall: 0-0
Aids: Bl: 0-1 Vi: 0-0 Tstrap: 0-0
Best Rating: 84 9/96 Hexm 2m firm Hdl

Royal Reward (IRE)

100 75

8-y-o b g King's Ride-Fatima Rose (The Parson)
M Todhunter Mrs Kate Hall

Placings: *20*P04/UU0-5604 (3348)
2001/02: 22^{5}GF, 16^{6}G, 20^{0}G, 24^{4}G

	Starts	1st	2nd	3rd	Win & Pl
Hurdles	4	0	0	0	0
Career Total	12	0	1	0	444

Going: Sf: 0-0 GS: 0-0 Gd: 0-3 GF: - Fm: 0-1
Distance: 2m/2m3: 0-1 2m4-2m7: 0-2 3m+: 0-1
Track: LH: 0-3 RH: 0-1 Tight: 0-1 Gall: 0-0
Aids: Bl: 0-0 Vi: 0-0 Tstrap: 0-0
Best Rating: 106 11/99 Weth 2m good NHF

Royal Robbie

72 56

4-y-o b g Robellino (USA)-Moogie (Young Generation)
P Butler Mrs E Lucey-Butler

Placings: 000 (3377)
2001/02: 16^{0}GS, 16^{0}G, 16^{0}GS

	Starts	1st	2nd	3rd	Win & Pl
Hurdles	3	0	0	0	
Career Total	3	0	0	0	

Going: Sf: 0-0 GS: 0-2 Gd: 0-1 GF: - Fm: 0-0
Distance: 2m/2m3: 0-3 2m4-2m7: 0-0 3m+: 0-0
Track: LH: 0-0 RH: 0-3 Tight: 0-0 Gall: 0-0
Aids: Bl: 0-0 Vi: 0-0 Tstrap: 0-0
Best Rating: 56 1/02 Kemp 2m gd-sft Hdl

Royal Scandal

6-y-o br g Royal Fountain-Langton Lass (Nearly A Hand)
Mrs Susan Nock Gerard Nock

Placings: P (2716)
2001/02: 19^{P}G

	Starts	1st	2nd	3rd	Win & Pl
Hurdles	1	0	0	0	
Career Total	1	0	0	0	

Going: Sf: 0-0 GS: 0-0 Gd: 0-1 GF: - Fm: 0-0
Distance: 2m/2m3: 0-0 2m4-2m7: 0-1 3m+: 0-0
Track: LH: 0-0 RH: 0-1 Tight: 0-0 Gall: 0-0
Aids: Bl: 0-0 Vi: 0-0 Tstrap: 0-0
Best Rating:

Royal Signet

7-y-o ch m King's Signet (USA)-Ladiz (Persian Bold)
M J Weeden M J Weeden

Placings: 3-0 (0039)
2001/02: 22^{0}GS

	Starts	1st	2nd	3rd	Win & Pl
Hurdles	1	0	0	0	
Career Total	2	0	0	1	442

Going: Sf: 0-0 GS: 0-1 Gd: 0-0 GF: - Fm: 0-0
Distance: 2m/2m3: 0-0 2m4-2m7: 0-1 3m+: 0-0
Track: LH: 0-0 RH: 0-0 Tight: 0-0 Gall: 0-0
Aids: Bl: 0-0 Vi: 0-0 Tstrap: 0-0
Best Rating: 79 9/00 Worc 2m4f gd-fm Hdl

Royal Snoopy (IRE)

107(102h) (109h)132

9-y-o b/br g Royal Fountain-Lovely Snoopy (IRE) (Phardante (FR))
C J Mann The Dunnkirk Partnership

Placings: *1303*/50F43/034115511/62FU20-21323 (1822)
2001/02: 21^{2}G, 24^{1}GF, 24^{3}GF, 23^{2}GF, 24^{3}GS

	Starts	1st	2nd	3rd	Win & Pl
Chases	5	1	2	2	10059
Career Total	29	6	4	6	43985

116	5/01	Hntg	3m	E Ch	G-F	£3523
124	3/00	Sand	2m6f	D(0-120)HHdl	GD	£7345
124	2/00	Winc	2m6f	C(0-135)HHdl	GD	£8502
121	11/99	MRas	2m5f110y	F Hdl	G-S	£1975
116	11/99	Sand	2m6f	E(0-105)HHdl	GD	£3403
107	1/98	Fair	2m	NHF	SFT	£2680

Total win prize-money £27429

Going: Sf: 0-0 GS: 0-1 Gd: 0-1 GF: - Fm: 1-3
Distance: 2m/2m3: 0-0 2m4-2m7: 0-1 **3m+: 1-4**
Track: LH: 0-3 **RH: 1-2** Tight: 0-2 **Gall: 1-1**
Aids: **Bl: 1-5** Vi: 0-0 Tstrap: 0-0
Best Rating: 139 2/01 Ludl 2m4f gd-sft Ch

He is not entirely straightforward but is a useful handicap chaser. Possibly best when allowed to dominate, he seems to handle any ground. Finished third in the Charisma Gold Cup at Kempton in 2001. Usually wears blinkers and appreciates a sound surface.

Royal Temptation (USA)

(91h) (51h)

5-y-o b g Ghazi (USA)-Heirloom Majesty (USA) (His Majesty (USA))
Jedd O'Keeffe Only For Fun Partnership

Placings: 0P0-P00P (3351)
2001/02: 22^{P}G, 20^{0}G, 16^{0}S, 16^{P}G

	Starts	1st	2nd	3rd	Win & Pl
Hurdles	3	0	0	0	0
Chases	1	0	0	0	0
Career Total	7	0	0	0	

Going: Sf: 0-1 GS: 0-0 Gd: 0-3 GF: - Fm: 0-0
Distance: 2m/2m3: 0-2 2m4-2m7: 0-2 3m+: 0-0
Track: LH: 0-3 RH: 0-1 Tight: 0-3 Gall: 0-1
Aids: Bl: 0-0 Vi: 0-0 Tstrap: 0-3
Best Rating: 63 2/01 Muss 2m good Hdl

Royal Then (FR)

86

9-y-o ch g Garde Royale-Miss Then (FR) (Carmarthen (FR))
J Neville T A Wadsworth

Placings: F6P0/525010/2F6/1/FF (0582)
2001/02: 21^{F}G, 19^{F}GF

	Starts	1st	2nd	3rd	Win & Pl
Hurdles	2	0	0	0	
Career Total	16	2	2	0	5558

91	8/99	Font	2m2f110y	F(0-110)HHdl	G-F	£2267
84	2/98	Ludl	2m	G(0-95)HHdl	GD	£1721

Total win prize-money £3989

Going: Sf: 0-0 GS: 0-0 Gd: 0-1 GF: - Fm: 0-1
Distance: 2m/2m3: 0-1 2m4-2m7: 0-1 3m+: 0-0
Track: LH: 0-1 RH: 0-0 Tight: 0-1 Gall: 0-0
Aids: Bl: 0-0 Vi: 0-1 Tstrap: 0-0
Best Rating: 91 8/99 Font 2m2f110y gd-fm Hdl

Royal Toast (IRE)

10-y-o b g Supreme Leader-Hats Off (Manado)
N J Henderson Mrs Christopher Edwards

Placings: 414/1231P/3115/P (0369)
2001/02: 20^{P}G

	Starts	1st	2nd	3rd	Win & Pl
Chases	1	0	0	0	
Career Total	13	5	1	2	21660

143	1/00	Plum	2m4f	D(0-125)HCh	G-S	£6987
138	1/00	Plum	2m4f	D(0-125)HCh	SFT	£3809
127	3/99	Towc	2m110y	D Ch	GD	£3580
123	12/98	NAbb	2m110y	E Ch	SFT	£2736
110	12/97	Ling	2m110y	E Hdl	G-S	£2383

Total win prize-money £19498

Going: Sf: 0-0 GS: 0-0 Gd: 0-1 GF: - Fm: 0-0
Distance: 2m/2m3: 0-0 2m4-2m7: 0-1 3m+: 0-0
Track: LH: 0-1 RH: 0-0 Tight: 0-0 Gall: 0-0
Aids: Bl: 0-0 Vi: 0-0 Tstrap: 0-0
Best Rating: 143 1/00 Plum 2m4f gd-sft Ch

Royal Tommy (IRE)

105 135

10-y-o b g Royal Fountain-Cherry Token (Prince Hansel)
R H Buckler L G Kimber

Placings: PP2211/P211/P1B034-15P01 (4266)
2001/02: 28^{1}S, 26^{5}S, 28^{P}HY, 30^{0}G, 29^{1}S

	Starts	1st	2nd	3rd	Win & Pl
Chases	5	2	0	0	17199
Career Total	21	7	3	1	53513

135	3/02	Chep	3m5f110y	D(0-120)HCh	SFT	£4407
135	12/01	Hayd	3m4f110y	C(0-135)HCh	SFT	£12792
135	12/00	Chep	3m2f110y	C(0-130)HCh	HVY	£10348
135	2/00	Bang	3m6f	D(0-120)HCh	G-S	£5050
135	2/00	Towc	3m1f	C(0-130)HCh	SFT	£6910
112	4/99	Towc	2m6f	E Ch	SFT	£2819
94	4/99	Hrfd	3m1f110y	E Ch	G-F	£3485

Total win prize-money £45812

Going: **Sf: 2-4** GS: 0-0 Gd: 0-1 GF: - Fm: 0-0
Distance: 2m/2m3: 0-0 2m4-2m7: 0-0 **3m+: 2-5**
Track: **LH: 2-4** RH: 0-0 Tight: 0-0 Gall: 0-0
Aids: Bl: 0-1 Vi: 0-0 Tstrap: 0-0
Best Rating: 135 3/02 Chep 3m5f110y soft Ch

A dogged stayer, he took a decent chase over three and a half miles at Haydock in December 2001. Scored again when dropped in class at Chepstow in March. Suited by soft ground.

Royal Tradition (IRE)

82 71

9-y-o br g Royal Fountain-Just For Today (Proverb)
Mrs L C Jewell Leon Best

Placings: *0*/024P/0P (0738)
2001/02: 22^{0}GF, 22^{P}GS

	Starts	1st	2nd	3rd	Win & Pl
Hurdles	2	0	0	0	
Career Total	7	0	1	0	401

Going: Sf: 0-0 GS: 0-1 Gd: 0-0 GF: - Fm: 0-1
Distance: 2m/2m3: 0-0 2m4-2m7: 0-2 3m+: 0-0

Track: LH: 0-2 RH: 0-0 Tight: 0-2 Gall: 0-0
Aids: Bl: 0-0 Vi: 0-0 Tstrap: 0-0
Best Rating: 83 5/99 Hntg 2m110y gd-fm NHF

Royale De Vassy (FR)

109 **151**

8-y-o b m Royal Charter (FR)-Bayalika (FR) (Kashtan (FR))
Miss Venetia Williams Len Jakeman,J Davies,R Downes & J Lewis

Placings:61/3P33F02/12331230-613U (4192)
2001/02: 24^{6}G, 25^{1}G, 26^{3}S, 24^{U}GS

	Starts	1st	2nd	3rd	Win & Pl
Chases	4	1	0	1	35174
Career Total	**21**	**4**	**3**	**7**	**79192**

151	12/01	Chel	3m1f110y	B HCh	GD	£28496
146	11/00	Chel	3m110y	E(0-135)HCh	G-S	£7605
129	5/00	Uttx	3m	B HCh	GD	£10348
	5/99	LE L	2m1f	Ch	GD	£3767

Total win prize-money £50216

Going: Sf: 0-1 GS: 0-1 Gd: 1-2 GF: - Fm: 0-0
Distance: 2m/2m3: 0-0 2m4-2m7: 0-0 **3m+: 1-4**
Track: **LH: 1-4** RH: 0-0 Tight: 0-0 **Gall: 1-3**
Aids: Bl: 0-0 Vi: 0-0 Tstrap: 0-0
Best Rating: 151 12/01 Chel 3m1f110y good Ch

A useful handicap chaser, she is a sound jumper, stays beyond three miles but has enough pace to be effective over shorter distances. Acts on good and good to soft ground.

Roymillon (GER)

103 **85**

8-y-o b g Milesius (USA)-Royal Slope (USA) (His Majesty (USA))
D J Wintle John W Egan/graham Brown

Placings:005-06551403 (2292)
2001/02: 16^{0}G, 17^{6}GF, 20^{5}GF, 20^{5}G, 24^{1}G, 24^{4}GF, 24^{0}S, 22^{3}GF

	Starts	1st	2nd	3rd	Win & Pl
Hurdles	8	1	0	1	2336
Career Total	**11**	**1**	**0**	**1**	**2336**

85	7/01	Worc	3m	F(0-100)HHdl	GD	£1946

Total win prize-money £1946

Going: Sf: 0-1 GS: 0-0 Gd: 1-3 GF: - Fm: 0-4
Distance: 2m/2m3: 0-2 2m4-2m7: 0-3 **3m+: 1-3**
Track: **LH: 1-4** RH: 0-3 Tight: 0-3 Gall: 0-1
Aids: Bl: 0-1 Vi: 0-0 Tstrap: 0-0
Best Rating: 85 7/01 Worc 3m good Hdl

Royrace

88 **66**

10-y-o b g Wace (USA)-Royal Tycoon (Tycoon Ii)
W M Brisbourne Andrew Evans

Placings:0P5P5/54P/350P03P4U/FP02P0P04/3PP-0P (0677)
2001/02: 17^{0}G, 16^{P}GF

	Starts	1st	2nd	3rd	Win & Pl
Chases	2	0	0	0	
Career Total	**31**	**0**	**1**	**3**	**2501**

Going: Sf: 0-0 GS: 0-0 Gd: 0-1 GF: - Fm: 0-1
Distance: 2m/2m3: 0-2 2m4-2m7: 0-0 3m+: 0-0
Track: LH: 0-2 RH: 0-0 Tight: 0-1 Gall: 0-0
Aids: Bl: 0-0 Vi: 0-0 Tstrap: 0-0
Best Rating: 89 10/98 Bang 2m4f good Hdl

Rubihill

89 **66**

8-y-o b g Rubicund-Hill's Rocket (Hills Forecast)
Mrs S J Smith Eric Bentham & Craig Shields

Placings:*0/0*-004P (1724)
2001/02: 16^{0}GF, 17^{0}G, 19^{4}GS, 25^{P}G

	Starts	1st	2nd	3rd	Win & Pl
Hurdles	4	0	0	0	0
Career Total	**6**	**0**	**0**	**0**	**0**

Going: Sf: 0-0 GS: 0-1 Gd: 0-2 GF: - Fm: 0-1
Distance: 2m/2m3: 0-2 2m4-2m7: 0-1 3m+: 0-1
Track: LH: 0-3 RH: 0-1 Tight: 0-2 Gall: 0-0
Aids: Bl: 0-0 Vi: 0-0 Tstrap: 0-0
Best Rating: 66 8/01 Worc 2m gd-fm Hdl

Rubissimo (IRE)

9-y-o b g Phardante (FR)-Rubydora (Buckskin (FR))
F Doumen Henri De Pracomtal

Placings:4125023/205P3/2110FPP/30FPP0-434PP (2892)
2001/02: 20^{4}S, 21^{3}GS, 18^{4}HY, 25^{P}G, 24^{P}G

	Starts	1st	2nd	3rd	Win & Pl
Hurdles	1	0	0	0	1940
Chases	4	0	0	1	6693
Career Total	**30**	**3**	**4**	**4**	**180250**

6/99	Autl	2m6f	Ch	VS	£53821
5/99	Autl	2m5f110y	HCh	VS	£32293

Total win prize-money £97337

Going: Sf: 0-2 GS: 0-1 Gd: 0-2 GF: - Fm: 0-0
Distance: 2m/2m3: 0-1 2m4-2m7: 0-2 3m+: 0-2
Track: LH: 0-1 RH: 0-1 Tight: 0-0 Gall: 0-1
Aids: Bl: 0-5 Vi: 0-0 Tstrap: 0-0
Best Rating: 135 12/99 Ling 3m gd-sft Ch

Useful French chaser, obviously highly thought of by his stable as he was entered in the King George. Has failed to complete on his three runs over fences in Britain and has not won since June 1999.

Rubon Prince (IRE)

87 **47**

11-y-o ch g Kambalda-Oh Clare (Laurence O)
N B Mason N B Mason

Placings:*40U0*/63534302PU3/423503U24454240/P-U0 (1403)
2001/02: 26^{U}G, 24^{0}G

	Starts	1st	2nd	3rd	Win & Pl
Chases	2	0	0	0	
Career Total	**33**	**0**	**4**	**6**	**8009**

Going: Sf: 0-0 GS: 0-0 Gd: 0-2 GF: - Fm: 0-0
Distance: 2m/2m3: 0-0 2m4-2m7: 0-0 3m+: 0-2
Track: LH: 0-2 RH: 0-0 Tight: 0-2 Gall: 0-0
Aids: Bl: 0-0 Vi: 0-0 Tstrap: 0-0
Best Rating: 88 6/99 Prth 3m gd-sft Ch

Ruby Gale (IRE)

110 **128**

6-y-o b g Lord Americo-Well Over (Over The River (FR))
P F Nicholls Mrs Angela Tincknell

Placings:*0*-1210212 (4820)
2001/02: 17^{1}G, 17^{2}GS, 19^{1}G, 20^{0}GS, 16^{2}GS, 19^{1}G, 17^{2}G

	Starts	1st	2nd	3rd	Win & Pl
NH Flat	1	1	0	0	2289
Hurdles	6	2	3	0	11533
Career Total	**8**	**3**	**3**	**0**	**13822**

120	3/02	Extr	2m3f	E Hdl	GD	£2828
116	12/01	Extr	2m3f	E Hdl	GD	£2922
102	11/01	NAbb	2m1f	H NHF	GD	£2289

Total win prize-money £8040

Going: Sf: 0-0 GS: 0-3 Gd: 3-4 GF: - Fm: 0-0
Distance: **2m/2m3: 3-6** 2m4-2m7: 0-1 3m+: 0-0
Track: LH: 1-3 **RH: 2-4 Tight: 1-1** Gall: 0-1
Aids: Bl: 0-0 Vi: 0-0 Tstrap: 0-0
Best Rating: 128 4/02 Chel 2m1f good Hdl

Reproduced his winning bumper form in 2001/02, scoring twice over two miles-three at Exeter. Looks a future chaser. Travels well and is suited by good ground

Ruby Raven

88 **72**

5-y-o b m Sea Raven (IRE)-Give Us A Treat (Cree Song)
Mrs K Walton Mrs K Walton

Placings:006-04 (0332)
2001/02: 16^{0}G, 16^{4}GS

	Starts	1st	2nd	3rd	Win & Pl
Hurdles	2	0	0	0	0
Career Total	**5**	**0**	**0**	**0**	**0**

Going: Sf: 0-0 GS: 0-1 Gd: 0-1 GF: - Fm: 0-0
Distance: 2m/2m3: 0-2 2m4-2m7: 0-0 3m+: 0-0
Track: LH: 0-1 RH: 0-1 Tight: 0-0 Gall: 0-0
Aids: Bl: 0-0 Vi: 0-0 Tstrap: 0-2
Best Rating: 77 2/01 Muss 2m good Hdl

Ruby Ruby

4-y-o ch f Binary Star (USA)-Runabay (Run The Gantlet (USA))
W G M Turner Hawks And Doves Racing Syndicate

Placings:PO (2409)
2001/02: 17^{P}F, 17°GS

	Starts	1st	2nd	3rd	Win & Pl
Hurdles	2	0	0	0	
Career Total	**2**	**0**	**0**	**0**	

Going: Sf: 0-0 GS: 0-1 Gd: 0-0 GF: - Fm: 0-1
Distance: 2m/2m3: 0-2 2m4-2m7: 0-0 3m+: 0-0
Track: LH: 0-0 RH: 0-2 Tight: 0-2 Gall: 0-0
Aids: Bl: 0-0 Vi: 0-0 Tstrap: 0-0
Best Rating:

Ruby Star (IRE)

90f **76f**

6-y-o b m Grand Plaisir (IRE)-Running Stream (Paddy's Stream)
R H Alner A & D Enterprises (poole) Ltd

Placings:*03* (0436)
2001/02: 17^{0}G, 17^{3}GF

	Starts	1st	2nd	3rd	Win & Pl
NH Flat	2	0	0	1	225
Career Total	**2**	**0**	**0**	**1**	**225**

Going: Sf: 0-0 GS: 0-0 Gd: 0-1 GF: - Fm: 0-1
Distance: 2m/2m3: 0-2 2m4-2m7: 0-0 3m+: 0-0
Track: LH: 0-0 RH: 0-1 Tight: 0-1 Gall: 0-0
Aids: Bl: 0-0 Vi: 0-0 Tstrap: 0-0
Best Rating: 76 5/01 Folk 2m1f110y gd-fm NHF

Rudge Hill

6-y-o b g Almushmmir-Time After Time (High Award)
G A Ham Martin Smith (frome)

Placings:*00* **(4506)**
2001/02: 16^{0}S, 17^{0}G

	Starts	1st	2nd	3rd	Win & Pl
NH Flat	2	0	0	0	
Career Total	**2**	**0**	**0**	**0**	

Going: Sf: 0-1 GS: 0-0 Gd: 0-1 GF: - Fm: 0-0
Distance: 2m/2m3: 0-2 2m4-2m7: 0-0 3m+: 0-0
Track: LH: 0-1 RH: 0-1 Tight: 0-1 Gall: 0-0
Aids: Bl: 0-0 Vi: 0-0 Tstrap: 0-0
Best Rating:

Rudi Knight

105 **132**

7-y-o ch g Rudimentary (USA)-Fleeting Affair (Hotfoot)
Miss Venetia Williams Mr Derek D & Mrs Jean P Clee

Placings:413512362/3302122-0054 **(4531)**
2001/02: 16^{0}G, 20^{0}GS, 18^{5}G, 16^{4}GS

	Starts	1st	2nd	3rd	Win & Pl
Hurdles	4	0	0	0	783
Career Total	**20**	**3**	**5**	**4**	**32079**

130	2/01	Kemp	2m	C(0-135)HHdl	G-S	£10676
119	1/00	Font	2m2f110y	C(0-135)HHdl	G-S	£6142
107	7/99	NAbb	2m1f	E Hdl	G-F	£2671

Total win prize-money £19490

Going: Sf: 0-0 GS: 0-2 Gd: 0-2 GF: - Fm: 0-0
Distance: 2m/2m3: 0-3 2m4-2m7: 0-1 3m+: 0-0
Track: LH: 0-4 RH: 0-0 Tight: 0-1 Gall: 0-0
Aids: Bl: 0-0 Vi: 0-0 Tstrap: 0-0
Best Rating: 138 3/01 Newb 2m110y heavy Hdl

A winner on the Flat and over hurdles. Best at two miles, he seems to act on most types of ground. Often held up in his races.

Rudi's Girl

73 **12**

6-y-o b m Rudimentary (USA)-Charlton Athletic (Bustino)
C J Hemsley R J Barrett

Placings:0P-00 **(0552)**
2001/02: 16^{0}GF, 21^{0}GF

	Starts	1st	2nd	3rd	Win & Pl
Hurdles	2	0	0	0	
Career Total	**4**	**0**	**0**	**0**	

Going: Sf: 0-0 GS: 0-0 Gd: 0-0 GF: - Fm: 0-2
Distance: 2m/2m3: 0-1 2m4-2m7: 0-1 3m+: 0-0
Track: LH: 0-0 RH: 0-2 Tight: 0-0 Gall: 0-2
Aids: Bl: 0-0 Vi: 0-0 Tstrap: 0-0
Best Rating: 34 11/00 Wwck 2m soft Hdl

Rudi's Pleasure (IRE)

113 **111**

7-y-o ch g Buckskin (FR)-Kind Sir She Said (Decent Fellow)
E McNamara Robert Butler

Placings:0060/3160260335-46002321430 **(4704a)**
2001/02: 20^{4}GF, 19^{6}G, 20^{0}GF, 20^{0}YS, 20^{2}G, 24^{3}GF, 21^{2}G, 20^{1}S, 22^{4}HY, 24^{3}S, 22^{0}GY

	Starts	1st	2nd	3rd	Win & Pl
Hurdles	11	1	2	2	14592
Career Total	**25**	**2**	**3**	**5**	**22363**

106	12/01	Limk	2m4f	(0-116)HHdl	SFT	£8395
100	6/00	Tral	2m4f	(0-109)HHdl	SH	£3588

Total win prize-money £11983

Going: Sf: 1-3 GS: 0-0 Gd: 0-3 GF: - Fm: 0-3
Distance: 2m/2m3: 0-1 **2m4-2m7: 1-8** 3m+: 0-2
Track: LH: 0-2 **RH: 1-2** Tight: 0-0 Gall: 0-1
Aids: Bl: 0-0 Vi: 0-0 Tstrap: 0-0
Best Rating: 113 11/00 Chel 2m5f gd-sft Hdl

Fair Irish hurdler, suited by two and a half miles and soft ground.

Rudimental

8-y-o b g Rudimentary (USA)-Full Orchestra (Shirley Heights)
A King R Evans,G Mordaunt,M Kerr-Dineen,A King

Placings:P **(4326)**
2001/02: 17^{P}S

	Starts	1st	2nd	3rd	Win & Pl
Hurdles	1	0	0	0	
Career Total	**1**	**0**	**0**	**0**	

Going: Sf: 0-1 GS: 0-0 Gd: 0-0 GF: - Fm: 0-0
Distance: 2m/2m3: 0-1 2m4-2m7: 0-0 3m+: 0-0
Track: LH: 0-0 RH: 0-1 Tight: 0-0 Gall: 0-0
Aids: Bl: 0-0 Vi: 0-0 Tstrap: 0-0
Best Rating:

Rudolf Rassendyll (IRE)

85 **60**

7-y-o b g Supreme Leader-Chantel Rouge (Boreen (FR))
Miss Venetia Williams C R Nugent

Placings:*060* **(4880)**
2001/02: 16^{0}G, 17^{6}S, 20^{0}G

	Starts	1st	2nd	3rd	Win & Pl
NH Flat	1	0	0	0	0
Hurdles	2	0	0	0	0
Career Total	**3**	**0**	**0**	**0**	**0**

Going: Sf: 0-1 GS: 0-0 Gd: 0-2 GF: - Fm: 0-0
Distance: 2m/2m3: 0-2 2m4-2m7: 0-1 3m+: 0-0
Track: LH: 0-2 RH: 0-1 Tight: 0-1 Gall: 0-1
Aids: Bl: 0-0 Vi: 0-0 Tstrap: 0-0
Best Rating: 84 12/01 Newb 2m110y good NHF

Ruff Justice (IRE)

102f

6-y-o b/br g Cashel Court-Rugged View (Rugged Man)
P Mullins Mrs Helen Mullins

Placings:*00* **(4948a)**
2001/02: 17^{0}G, 16^{0}G

	Starts	1st	2nd	3rd	Win & Pl
NH Flat	2	0	0	0	
Career Total	**2**	**0**	**0**	**0**	

Going: Sf: 0-0 GS: 0-0 Gd: 0-2 GF: - Fm: 0-0
Distance: 2m/2m3: 0-2 2m4-2m7: 0-0 3m+: 0-0
Track: LH: 0-0 RH: 0-1 Tight: 0-0 Gall: 0-0
Aids: Bl: 0-0 Vi: 0-0 Tstrap: 0-0
Best Rating: 52 4/02 Aint 2m1f good NHF

Rufius (IRE)

107 **114**

9-y-o b g Celio Rufo-In View Lass (Tepukei)
P Kelsall Peter Kelsall

Placings:*4000/000P3/OP055F-55240* **(4634)**
2001/02: 20^{5}G, 20^{5}GS, 20^{2}G, 20^{4}G, 24^{0}GF

	Starts	1st	2nd	3rd	Win & Pl
Chases	5	0	1	0	1654
Career Total	**20**	**0**	**1**	**1**	**2346**

Going: Sf: 0-0 GS: 0-1 Gd: 0-3 GF: - Fm: 0-1
Distance: 2m/2m3: 0-0 2m4-2m7: 0-4 3m+: 0-1
Track: LH: 0-1 RH: 0-4 Tight: 0-2 Gall: 0-1
Aids: Bl: 0-0 Vi: 0-0 Tstrap: 0-0
Best Rating: 114 12/01 Leic 2m4f110y good Ch

Modest chaser. Best at trips around two and a half miles. Acts on a sound surface.

Rum Pointer (IRE)

6-y-o b g Turtle Island (IRE)-Osmunda (Mill Reef (USA))
R H Buckler K C B Mackenzie

Placings:432112-P **(2391)**
2001/02: 24^{P}S

	Starts	1st	2nd	3rd	Win & Pl
Hurdles	1	0	0	0	
Career Total	**7**	**2**	**2**	**1**	**17302**

130	1/01	Donc	2m4f	A Hdl	GD	£9600
119	1/01	Wwck	2m5f	D Hdl	SFT	£3874

Total win prize-money £13474

Going: Sf: 0-1 GS: 0-0 Gd: 0-0 GF: - Fm: 0-0
Distance: 2m/2m3: 0-0 2m4-2m7: 0-0 3m+: 0-1
Track: LH: 0-1 RH: 0-0 Tight: 0-0 Gall: 0-0
Aids: Bl: 0-0 Vi: 0-0 Tstrap: 0-0
Best Rating: 130 2/01 Newc 2m4f heavy Hdl

A useful handicapper on the Flat, this game individual took well to hurdles in 20000/01 and has notched up two wins and a string of placed efforts. Pulled up on his 2001/02 return and absent since. He is effective at around two and a half miles and has stamina in abundance. Best on an easy surface.

Rum Punch

91 **79**

5-y-o b h Shirley Heights-Gentle Persuasion (Bustino)
G M Moore Rum Bunch Syndicate

Placings:0P60-5 **(0739)**
2001/02: 20^{5}GS

	Starts	1st	2nd	3rd	Win & Pl
Hurdles	1	0	0	0	0
Career Total	**5**	**0**	**0**	**0**	**0**

Going: Sf: 0-0 GS: 0-1 Gd: 0-0 GF: - Fm: 0-0
Distance: 2m/2m3: 0-0 2m4-2m7: 0-1 3m+: 0-0
Track: LH: 0-1 RH: 0-0 Tight: 0-0 Gall: 0-0
Aids: Bl: 0-0 Vi: 0-0 Tstrap: 0-0
Best Rating: **82** 1/01 Newc 2m soft Hdl

Run For Paddy

104(111h) (146h)**150**
6-y-o b g Michelozzo (USA)-Deep Selection (IRE) (Deep Run)
Mrs H Dalton B Perkins

Placings:*230/*3111263-23411P1P **(4835)**
2001/02: 21^{2}G, 24^{3}G, 21^{4}HY, 24^{1}GS, 19^{1}GS, 21^{P}G, 25^{1}G, 25^{P}G

	Starts	1st	2nd	3rd	Win & Pl
Hurdles	3	0	1	1	6925
Chases	5	3	0	0	13149
Career Total	**18**	**6**	**3**	**4**	**45921**

150	4/02	MRas	3m1f	D Ch	GD	£4907
150	3/02	Donc	2m3f110y	D Ch	G-S	£4368
121	2/02	Fknm	3m110y	D Ch	G-S	£3874
132	10/00	Chel	2m5f	B(0-145)HHdl	GD	£8414
118	9/00	Uttx	2m6f110y	C Hdl	G-S	£4771
107	9/00	Font	2m2f110y	E Hdl	G-S	£2782

Total win prize-money £29116

Going: Sf: 0-1 GS: 2-2 Gd: 1-5 GF: - Fm: 0-0
Distance: 2m/2m3: 0-0 2m4-2m7: 1-4 **3m+: 2-4**
Track: **LH: 2-6** RH: 1-1 **Tight: 2-2** Gall: 1-4
Aids: Bl: 0-0 Vi: 0-0 Tstrap: 0-0
Best Rating: **156** 12/00 Chel 2m5f110y soft Hdl

Formerly a very useful novice hurdler when trained by Mark Pitman, he has run well in handicaps at Cheltenham this term for his new connections. Successful three times over fences but out of his depth in the Cathcart at Cheltenham. Stays three miles, and acts on good and good to soft ground.

Run For The Boys

80f **86f**
6-y-o ch g Michelozzo (USA)-Horns Lodge (High Line)
J S King E N Fry

Placings:*0* **(3910)**
2001/02: 16^{0}G

	Starts	1st	2nd	3rd	Win & Pl
NH Flat	1	0	0	0	
Career Total	**1**	**0**	**0**	**0**	

Going: Sf: 0-0 GS: 0-0 Gd: 0-1 GF: - Fm: 0-0
Distance: 2m/2m3: 0-1 2m4-2m7: 0-0 3m+: 0-0
Track: LH: 0-0 RH: 0-1 Tight: 0-0 Gall: 0-0
Aids: Bl: 0-0 Vi: 0-0 Tstrap: 0-0
Best Rating: **86** 2/02 Kemp 2m good NHF

Run Forrest (IRE)

90 **66**
5-y-o ch g Forest Wind (USA)-Katie's Delight (Relko)
Miss Sheena West Gerald West

Placings:5 **(1484)**
2001/02: 16^{5}GS

	Starts	1st	2nd	3rd	Win & Pl
Hurdles	1	0	0	0	0
Career Total	**1**	**0**	**0**	**0**	**0**

Going: Sf: 0-0 GS: 0-1 Gd: 0-0 GF: - Fm: 0-0
Distance: 2m/2m3: 0-1 2m4-2m7: 0-0 3m+: 0-0
Track: LH: 0-1 RH: 0-0 Tight: 0-1 Gall: 0-0
Aids: Bl: 0-0 Vi: 0-0 Tstrap: 0-0
Best Rating: **66** 9/01 Plum 2m gd-sft Hdl

Run River Run

95 **66**
8-y-o b m River God (USA)-Run Lady Run (General Ironside)
D R Gandolfo Mrs John Lee

Placings:*040*/5-5 **(1793)**
2001/02: 20^{5}S

	Starts	1st	2nd	3rd	Win & Pl
Hurdles	1	0	0	0	0
Career Total	**5**	**0**	**0**	**0**	**0**

Going: Sf: 0-1 GS: 0-0 Gd: 0-0 GF: - Fm: 0-0
Distance: 2m/2m3: 0-0 2m4-2m7: 0-1 3m+: 0-0
Track: LH: 0-1 RH: 0-0 Tight: 0-0 Gall: 0-0
Aids: Bl: 0-0 Vi: 0-0 Tstrap: 0-0
Best Rating: **83** 12/99 Hntg 2m110y good NHF

Run To The Glen

7-y-o b m Bold Fox-Glen Maye (Maystreak)
Mrs S M Johnson Miss S Troughton

Placings:*0*P **(1672)**
2001/02: 17^{0}G, 22^{P}HY

	Starts	1st	2nd	3rd	Win & Pl
NH Flat	1	0	0	0	0
Hurdles	1	0	0	0	0
Career Total	**2**	**0**	**0**	**0**	

Going: Sf: 0-1 GS: 0-0 Gd: 0-1 GF: - Fm: 0-0
Distance: 2m/2m3: 0-1 2m4-2m7: 0-1 3m+: 0-0
Track: LH: 0-0 RH: 0-2 Tight: 0-1 Gall: 0-0
Aids: Bl: 0-0 Vi: 0-0 Tstrap: 0-0
Best Rating: **38** 10/01 Hrfd 2m1f good NHF

Runaway Bishop (USA)

107 **94**
7-y-o b/br g Lear Fan (USA)-Valid Linda (USA) (Valid Appeal (USA))
Mrs A Duffield The Middleham Park Racing Club

Placings:*230/3*22342313/F-242 **(4786)**
2001/02: 25^{2}G, 24^{4}S, 20^{2}F

	Starts	1st	2nd	3rd	Win & Pl
Hurdles	3	0	2	0	1483
Career Total	**16**	**1**	**6**	**5**	**11215**

106	3/00	Folk	2m5f	D Ch	G-F	£4036

Total win prize-money £4037

Going: Sf: 0-1 GS: 0-0 Gd: 0-1 GF: - Fm: 0-1
Distance: 2m/2m3: 0-0 2m4-2m7: 0-1 3m+: 0-2
Track: LH: 0-2 RH: 0-1 Tight: 0-2 Gall: 0-1
Aids: Bl: 0-1 Vi: 0-0 Tstrap: 0-0
Best Rating: **119** 4/00 Font 2m6f good Ch

Fair chaser, plating class hurdler. Stays three miles over hurdles. Has won at up to two miles five over fences. Acts on a sound surface.

Runner Bean

97 **84**
8-y-o b/br g Henbit (USA)-Bean Alainn (Candy Cane)
B J Eckley Brian Eckley

Placings:*511*634P/403P **(1280)**
2001/02: 20^{4}G, 20^{0}G, 20^{3}GS, 24^{P}GF

	Starts	1st	2nd	3rd	Win & Pl
Hurdles	4	0	0	1	324
Career Total	**11**	**2**	**0**	**2**	**4401**

114	11/99	Ludl	2m	H NHF	GD	£1542
105	5/99	Uttx	2m	H NHF	G-F	£1763

Total win prize-money £3306

Going: Sf: 0-0 GS: 0-1 Gd: 0-2 GF: - Fm: 0-1
Distance: 2m/2m3: 0-0 2m4-2m7: 0-3 3m+: 0-1
Track: LH: 0-4 RH: 0-0 Tight: 0-1 Gall: 0-0
Aids: Bl: 0-1 Vi: 0-0 Tstrap: 0-0
Best Rating: **114** 11/99 Ludl 2m good NHF

Running Battle

6-y-o b m Lepanto (GER)-Running Cool (Record Run)
N J Hawke C G Newman

Placings:*0*P **(4385)**
2001/02: 17^{0}GF, 22^{P}S

	Starts	1st	2nd	3rd	Win & Pl
NH Flat	1	0	0	0	0
Hurdles	1	0	0	0	0
Career Total	**2**	**0**	**0**	**0**	

Going: Sf: 0-1 GS: 0-0 Gd: 0-0 GF: - Fm: 0-1
Distance: 2m/2m3: 0-1 2m4-2m7: 0-1 3m+: 0-0
Track: LH: 0-0 RH: 0-2 Tight: 0-0 Gall: 0-0
Aids: Bl: 0-0 Vi: 0-0 Tstrap: 0-0
Best Rating: **66** 11/01 Extr 2m1f gd-fm NHF

Running De Cerisy (FR)

107(107h) (114h)**113**
8-y-o ch g Lightning (FR)-Niloq (FR) (Nikos)
Miss S J Wilton (M C Pipe 26/11) John Pointon And Sons

Placings:1F1133P04/**041/FPP**-6511213**2**432403 **(4778)**
2001/02: 17^{6}GF, 19^{5}GF, 16^{1}GS, 17^{1}GS, 17^{2}G, 17^{1}GF, 17^{3}GF, 16^{2}G, 19^{4}G, 16^{3}GF, 17^{2}S, 16^{4}GS, 17^{0}G, 17^{3}G

	Starts	1st	2nd	3rd	Win & Pl
Hurdles	10	2	2	1	5567
Chases	4	1	1	2	5456
Career Total	**29**	**7**	**3**	**5**	**27009**

110	8/01	NAbb	2m1f	F Hdl	G-F	£2296
110	7/01	MRas	2m1f110y	F(0-105)HCh	G-S	£4251
114	7/01	Wolv	2m	G Hdl	G-S	£1621
116	11/98	Hrfd	2m	E(0-100)HCh	GD	£3126
114	9/97	NAbb	2m1f	E Hdl	SFT	£2148
108	8/97	Worc	2m	E Hdl	G-F	£2250
	6/97	Autl	1m7f	Hdl	SFT	£7295

Total win prize-money £22987

Going: Sf: 0-1 GS: 2-3 Gd: 0-5 GF: - Fm: 1-5
Distance: **2m/2m3: 3-12** 2m4-2m7: 0-2 3m+: 0-0
Track: **LH: 2-5** RH: 0-7 **Tight: 2-8** Gall: 0-0
Aids: Bl: 0-1 Vi: 0-0 Tstrap: 0-0
Best Rating: **116** 11/98 Hrfd 2m good Ch

Ex-French, he is best over two miles and acts on most types of ground.

Running Free (IRE)

75(78h) **62**
8-y-o b g Waajib-Selchis (Main Reef)

W S Cunningham C P M Racing

Placings:55P50/0-0P (0467)
2001/02: 21^0G, 20^PGF

	Starts	1st	2nd	3rd	Win & Pl
Chases	2	0	0	0	
Career Total	8	0	0	0	0

Going: Sf: 0-0 GS: 0-0 Gd: 0-1 GF: - Fm: 0-1
Distance: 2m/2m3: 0-0 2m4-2m7: 0-2 3m+: 0-0
Track: LH: 0-2 RH: 0-0 Tight: 0-1 Gall: 0-0
Aids: Bl: 0-0 Vi: 0-1 Tstrap: 0-0
Best Rating: 76 10/98 Ludl 2m5f110y gd-fm Hdl

Running Moss

117 **120**

10-y-o ch g Le Moss-Run'n Fly (Deep Run)
A H Mactaggart Mrs A H Mactaggart

Placings:P62/344412/P314-1321 (4394)
2001/02: 22^1G, 25^3GS, 25^2HY, 32^1HY

	Starts	1st	2nd	3rd	Win & Pl
Chases	4	2	1	1	32190
Career Total	17	4	3	3	42822

120	3/02	Kels	4m	C(0-135)HCh	HVY	£24534
119	11/01	Kels	2m6f110y	D(0-120)HCh	GD	£5148
119	11/00	Catt	3m1f110y	F(0-110)HCh	G-S	£4192
107	12/99	Sedg	3m3f	E Ch	SFT	£3299

Total win prize-money £37175

Going: Sf: 1-2 GS: 0-1 Gd: 1-1 GF: - Fm: 0-0
Distance: 2m/2m3: 0-0 2m4-2m7: 1-1 3m+: 1-3
Track: **LH: 2-4** RH: 0-0 **Tight: 2-2** Gall: 0-0
Aids: Bl: 0-0 Vi: 0-0 Tstrap: 0-0
Best Rating: 120 3/02 Kels 4m heavy Ch

Suited by a strongly-run race, he is a three-mile staying chaser who has been effective on a soft surface and good ground.

Running Times (USA)

104 **121**

5-y-o b g Brocco (USA)-Concert Peace (USA) (Hold Your Peace (USA))
M C Pipe (T D Easterby 12/5) Neil J Edwards

Placings:04-122401 (4265)
2001/02: 21^1G, 22^2G, 21^2G, 24^4G, 22^0GS, 20^1S

	Starts	1st	2nd	3rd	Win & Pl
Hurdles	6	2	2	0	8241
Career Total	8	2	2	0	8241

116	3/02	Chep	2m4f	F Hdl	SFT	£2016
102	5/01	Sedg	2m5f110y	E Hdl	GD	£2786

Total win prize-money £4802

Going: Sf: 1-1 GS: 0-1 Gd: 1-4 GF: - Fm: 0-0
Distance: 2m/2m3: 0-0 **2m4-2m7: 2-5** 3m+: 0-1
Track: **LH: 2-3** RH: 0-2 **Tight: 1-2** Gall: 0-1
Aids: Bl: 0-0 **Vi: 1-1** Tstrap: 0-0
Best Rating: 121 10/01 Chel 2m5f good Hdl

Suited by good ground, he is a useful plater over hurdles and was sold out of the Pipe yard after winning in May 2002.

Rush Off

63 **14**

7-y-o b g Robellino (USA)-Arusha (IRE) (Dance Of Life (USA))
G H Yardley Deblins Green Racing Partnership

Placings:0/063030-P0 (0587)
2001/02: 17^PG, 16^0GF

	Starts	1st	2nd	3rd	Win & Pl
Hurdles	2	0	0	0	
Career Total	9	0	0	2	847

Going: Sf: 0-0 GS: 0-0 Gd: 0-1 GF: - Fm: 0-1
Distance: 2m/2m3: 0-2 2m4-2m7: 0-0 3m+: 0-0
Track: LH: 0-1 RH: 0-1 Tight: 0-1 Gall: 0-0
Aids: Bl: 0-1 Vi: 0-0 Tstrap: 0-0
Best Rating: 86 1/01 Wwck 2m soft Hdl

Rushen Raider

104 **94**

10-y-o br g Reprimand-Travel Storm (Lord Gayle (USA))
P Needham P Needham

Placings:SP00/12/615/U22260/3P021050-40246306F0O (4917)
2001/02: 20^4GF, 20^0F, 21^2GF, 27^4GF, 21^6GF, 21^3G, 23^0G, 25^6S, 17^FS, 21^0S, 21^OGF

	Starts	1st	2nd	3rd	Win & Pl
Hurdles	11	0	1	1	1383
Career Total	34	3	6	2	14349

103	9/00	Sedg	2m5f110y	D(0-125)HHdl	SFT	£2892
112	9/98	Sedg	2m5f110y	D(0-120)HHdl	GD	£2726
102	5/97	MRas	2m1f110y	E Hdl	G-F	£2547

Total win prize-money £8167

Going: Sf: 0-3 GS: 0-0 Gd: 0-2 GF: - Fm: 0-6
Distance: 2m/2m3: 0-1 2m4-2m7: 0-7 3m+: 0-3
Track: LH: 0-11 RH: 0-0 Tight: 0-8 Gall: 0-0
Aids: Bl: 0-0 Vi: 0-0 Tstrap: 0-0
Best Rating: 115 9/99 Sedg 2m5f110y gd-fm Hdl

Modest staying hurdler, goes well at Sedgefield.

Rushing Again

76 **100**

7-y-o br g Rushmere-Saunders Grove (IRE) (Sunyboy)
P F Nicholls Hunt & Co (bournemouth) Ltd

Placings:20 (4586)
2001/02: 27^2S, 22^0G

	Starts	1st	2nd	3rd	Win & Pl
Hurdles	2	0	1	0	717
Career Total	2	0	1	0	717

Going: Sf: 0-1 GS: 0-0 Gd: 0-1 GF: - Fm: 0-0
Distance: 2m/2m3: 0-0 2m4-2m7: 0-1 3m+: 0-1
Track: LH: 0-0 RH: 0-1 Tight: 0-1 Gall: 0-0
Aids: Bl: 0-0 Vi: 0-0 Tstrap: 0-0
Best Rating: 100 3/02 Font 3m3f soft Hdl

Winning pointer, runner-up in a weak novice hurdle in March 2002. Stays well.

Rusk

82 **83**

9-y-o b g Pharly (FR)-Springwell (Miami Springs)
John Allen J Allen

Placings:0223/016P32F20/05542413F051220/05654 06P2-505 (1807)
2001/02: 20^5GF, 17^0GF, 16^5S

	Starts	1st	2nd	3rd	Win & Pl
Hurdles	3	0	0	0	0
Career Total	40	3	8	3	12194

94	3/00	Hntg	2m110y	G Hdl	SFT	£1641
89	10/99	Strf	2m110y	G Hdl	G-F	£1870
99	12/98	Hntg	2m110y	F Hdl	G-S	£2024

Total win prize-money £5536

Going: Sf: 0-1 GS: 0-0 Gd: 0-0 GF: - Fm: 0-2
Distance: 2m/2m3: 0-2 2m4-2m7: 0-1 3m+: 0-0
Track: LH: 0-1 RH: 0-2 Tight: 0-1 Gall: 0-1
Aids: Bl: 0-0 Vi: 0-0 Tstrap: 0-0
Best Rating: 99 4/00 Ludl 2m good Hdl

Rusnetto (IRE)

105 **98**

12-y-o b g Torus-Moynetto (Bustineto)
Mrs D A Hamer John Cole

Placings:53/P-34021P (1851)
2001/02: 20^3GF, 19^4F, 25^0G, 25^2G, 24^1GF, 25^PG

	Starts	1st	2nd	3rd	Win & Pl
Chases	6	1	1	1	5035
Career Total	9	1	1	2	5592

96	10/01	Ludl	3m	D(0-110)HCh	G-F	£3770

Total win prize-money £3770

Going: Sf: 0-0 GS: 0-0 Gd: 0-3 GF: - Fm: 1-3
Distance: 2m/2m3: 0-0 2m4-2m7: 0-2 **3m+: 1-4**
Track: LH: 0-1 **RH: 1-5 Tight: 1-1** Gall: 0-0
Aids: Bl: 0-0 **Vi: 1-6** Tstrap: 0-0
Best Rating: 98 10/01 Hrfd 3m1f110y good Ch

Russell House (IRE)

105 **103**

6-y-o b/br g Roselier (FR)-Salufair (Salluceva)
A King Mrs L Field

Placings:52-36200 (3672)
2001/02: 24^3G, 21^6G, 24^2G, 24^0GS, 24^0S

	Starts	1st	2nd	3rd	Win & Pl
Hurdles	5	0	1	1	2172
Career Total	7	0	2	1	2784

Going: Sf: 0-1 GS: 0-1 Gd: 0-3 GF: - Fm: 0-0
Distance: 2m/2m3: 0-0 2m4-2m7: 0-1 3m+: 0-4
Track: LH: 0-4 RH: 0-1 Tight: 0-1 Gall: 0-3
Aids: Bl: 0-0 Vi: 0-0 Tstrap: 0-0
Best Rating: 103 11/01 Newb 3m110y good Hdl

He looks an out and out stayer who appreciates a severe test of stamina.

Russian Court

104 **87**

6-y-o b g Soviet Lad (USA)-Court Town (Camden Town)
D R Gandolfo D R Gandolfo Ltd

Placings:4/06-3616540 (4601)
2001/02: 18^3GF, 16^6GF, 16^1S, 16^6G, 18^5S, 16^4S, 16^0GF

	Starts	1st	2nd	3rd	Win & Pl
Hurdles	7	1	0	1	3303
Career Total	10	1	0	1	3488

87	10/01	Plum	2m	F(0-100)HHdl	SFT	£2639

Total win prize-money £2639

Going: Sf: 1-3 GS: 0-0 Gd: 0-1 GF: - Fm: 0-3
Distance: **2m/2m3: 1-7** 2m4-2m7: 0-0 3m+: 0-0
Track: **LH: 1-5** RH: 0-2 **Tight: 1-3** Gall: 0-0
Aids: Bl: 0-0 Vi: 0-0 Tstrap: 0-0
Best Rating: 87 10/01 Plum 2m soft Hdl

Moderate handicap hurdler, got off the mark in a soft-ground Plumpton handicap. Does not find much off the bridle.

Russian Dancer

85

6-y-o b g Petoski-Merry Minuet (Trumpeter)
A Crook Paul Sellars

Placings:65-P (0203)
2001/02: 20PG

	Starts	1st	2nd	3rd	Win & Pl
Hurdles	1	0	0	0	
Career Total	**3**	**0**	**0**	**0**	**0**

Going: Sf: 0-0 GS: 0-0 Gd: 0-1 GF: - Fm: 0-0
Distance: 2m/2m3: 0-0 2m4-2m7: 0-1 3m+: 0-0
Track: LH: 0-1 RH: 0-0 Tight: 0-0 Gall: 0-0
Aids: Bl: 0-0 Vi: 0-0 Tstrap: 0-0
Best Rating: 85 4/01 Weth 2m4f110y gd-sft Hdl

Russian Friend

94f 91f

5-y-o b g Petoski-Courtlands Girl (Crimson Beau)
T P Tate T P Tate

Placings:453 (4410)
2001/02: 164S, 165GS, 173S

	Starts	1st	2nd	3rd	Win & Pl
NH Flat	3	0	0	1	247
Career Total	**3**	**0**	**0**	**1**	**247**

Going: Sf: 0-2 GS: 0-1 Gd: 0-0 GF: - Fm: 0-0
Distance: 2m/2m3: 0-3 2m4-2m7: 0-0 3m+: 0-0
Track: LH: 0-2 RH: 0-1 Tight: 0-3 Gall: 0-0
Aids: Bl: 0-0 Vi: 0-0 Tstrap: 0-0
Best Rating: 91 3/02 Catt 2m gd-sft NHF

Limited ability in three starts in bumpers.

Russian Gigolo (IRE)

105f 101f

5-y-o b g Toulon-Nanogan (Tarqogan)
N A Twiston-Davies Mrs Caroline Beresford-Wylie

Placings:4006 (4841)
2001/02: 164S, 160S, 160GS, 166G

	Starts	1st	2nd	3rd	Win & Pl
NH Flat	4	0	0	0	0
Career Total	**4**	**0**	**0**	**0**	**0**

Going: Sf: 0-2 GS: 0-1 Gd: 0-1 GF: - Fm: 0-0
Distance: 2m/2m3: 0-4 2m4-2m7: 0-0 3m+: 0-0
Track: LH: 0-4 RH: 0-0 Tight: 0-0 Gall: 0-0
Aids: Bl: 0-0 Vi: 0-0 Tstrap: 0-0
Best Rating: 101 4/02 Ayr 2m good NHF

Russian River

92 63

10-y-o b g Sulaafah (USA)-Ninotchka (Niniski (USA))
J J Bridger Michael Anthony O'Donnell

Placings:P0P/0PP500/04FP/156205P032/6P0-000 (0773)
2001/02: 160G, 160F, 160GF

	Starts	1st	2nd	3rd	Win & Pl
Hurdles	3	0	0	0	
Career Total	**29**	**1**	**2**	**1**	**3464**
86 9/99 Font	2m2f110y	G(0-95)HHdl		GD	£1865

Total win prize-money £1865

Going: Sf: 0-0 GS: 0-0 Gd: 0-1 GF: - Fm: 0-2
Distance: 2m/2m3: 0-3 2m4-2m7: 0-0 3m+: 0-0
Track: LH: 0-2 RH: 0-1 Tight: 0-1 Gall: 0-1
Aids: Bl: 0-0 Vi: 0-0 Tstrap: 0-0
Best Rating: 86 4/00 Winc 2m gd-sft Hdl

Rustic Revelry

105 109

9-y-o b g Afzal-Country Festival (Town And Country)
R H York R H York

Placings:00000/45/5F4/216-36O6005 (4638)
2001/02: 163G, 216GF, 23OGF, 246GF, 200G, 210G, 195GF

	Starts	1st	2nd	3rd	Win & Pl
Chases	7	0	0	1	454
Career Total	**20**	**1**	**1**	**1**	**2539**
99 5/00 Folk	2m5f	H Ch		GD	£1456

Total win prize-money £1456

Going: Sf: 0-0 GS: 0-0 Gd: 0-3 GF: - Fm: 0-4
Distance: 2m/2m3: 0-1 2m4-2m7: 0-4 3m+: 0-2
Track: LH: 0-4 RH: 0-2 Tight: 0-4 Gall: 0-0
Aids: Bl: 0-0 Vi: 0-0 Tstrap: 0-0
Best Rating: 110 5/00 Hntg 2m4f110y good Ch

Rusty Alntyne (IRE)

82f 75f

4-y-o ch g Rashar (USA)-Sky Rainbow (IRE) (Henbit (USA))
G M Moore Dr C I Emmerson

Placings:0 (4750)
2001/02: 170G

	Starts	1st	2nd	3rd	Win & Pl
NH Flat	1	0	0	0	
Career Total	**1**	**0**	**0**	**0**	

Going: Sf: 0-0 GS: 0-0 Gd: 0-1 GF: - Fm: 0-0
Distance: 2m/2m3: 0-1 2m4-2m7: 0-0 3m+: 0-0
Track: LH: 0-0 RH: 0-1 Tight: 0-0 Gall: 0-0
Aids: Bl: 0-0 Vi: 0-0 Tstrap: 0-0
Best Rating: 75 4/02 Carl 2m1f good NHF

Rusty Fellow

12-y-o b g Rustingo-Sallisses (Pamroy)
Mrs G M Shail (R Shail 1/6) Mrs G M Shail

Placings:32P3/23263/443P/54P5-610OPP (3984)
2001/02: 256G, 301GF, 330G, 28OGF, 24PGS, 31PGS

	Starts	1st	2nd	3rd	Win & Pl
Chases	6	1	0	0	1631
Career Total	**23**	**1**	**3**	**5**	**4590**
105 5/01 Hntg	3m6f110y	H Ch		G-F	£1631

Total win prize-money £1631

Going: Sf: 0-0 GS: 0-2 Gd: 0-2 GF: - Fm: 1-2
Distance: 2m/2m3: 0-0 2m4-2m7: 0-0 **3m+: 1-6**
Track: LH: 0-1 **RH: 1-3** Tight: 0-2 **Gall: 1-1**
Aids: Bl: 0-0 Vi: 0-0 Tstrap: 0-0
Best Rating: 105 5/01 Hntg 3m6f110y gd-fm Ch

Modest hunter chaser, stays very well, acts on any ground. Runs in snatches.

Rusty Flame

81 75

9-y-o ch g Rustingo-Amethea (True Song)
Mrs P Ford Mrs Patricia Collins

Placings:0/P/P/00PP (1400)
2001/02: 160G, 160F, 16PG, 20PG

	Starts	1st	2nd	3rd	Win & Pl
Chases	4	0	0	0	
Career Total	**7**	**0**	**0**	**0**	

Going: Sf: 0-0 GS: 0-0 Gd: 0-3 GF: - Fm: 0-1
Distance: 2m/2m3: 0-3 2m4-2m7: 0-1 3m+: 0-0
Track: LH: 0-2 RH: 0-2 Tight: 0-1 Gall: 0-0
Aids: Bl: 0-0 Vi: 0-0 Tstrap: 0-0
Best Rating: 75 6/01 Hrfd 2m firm Ch

Rusty Rob

8-y-o b g Rustingo-Marie Swift (Main Reef)
B J Llewellyn B J Llewellyn

Placings:00/006/P060-P (0677)
2001/02: 16PGF

	Starts	1st	2nd	3rd	Win & Pl
Chases	1	0	0	0	
Career Total	**10**	**0**	**0**	**0**	**0**

Going: Sf: 0-0 GS: 0-0 Gd: 0-0 GF: - Fm: 0-1
Distance: 2m/2m3: 0-1 2m4-2m7: 0-0 3m+: 0-0
Track: LH: 0-1 RH: 0-0 Tight: 0-0 Gall: 0-0
Aids: Bl: 0-0 Vi: 0-0 Tstrap: 0-1
Best Rating: 55 6/00 Uttx 2m gd-fm Hdl

Ruth's Boy (IRE)

101 94

13-y-o br g Lord Ha Ha-Club Belle (Al Sirat (USA))
Ms A E Embiricos Ms A E Embiricos

Placings:0/0/24/61224/2403621P5/34420F/2P-40P (1045)
2001/02: 244GF, 240GF, 26PGF

	Starts	1st	2nd	3rd	Win & Pl
Chases	3	0	0	0	0
Career Total	**29**	**2**	**7**	**2**	**14155**
94 10/98 Plum	3m1f110y	D(0-125)HCh		G-F	£3387
94 9/97 Plum	2m5f	E(0-100)HCh		G-F	£2943

Total win prize-money £6332

Going: Sf: 0-0 GS: 0-0 Gd: 0-0 GF: - Fm: 0-3
Distance: 2m/2m3: 0-0 2m4-2m7: 0-0 3m+: 0-3
Track: LH: 0-2 RH: 0-1 Tight: 0-1 Gall: 0-1
Aids: Bl: 0-0 Vi: 0-0 Tstrap: 0-0
Best Rating: 94 5/01 Fknm 3m110y gd-fm Ch

Rutledge Red (IRE)

107 107

6-y-o gr g Roselier (FR)-Katebeaujolais (Politico (USA))
J M Jefferson Ashleybank Investments Limited

Placings:0P2 (3551)
2001/02: 160S, 21PHY, 192S

	Starts	1st	2nd	3rd	Win & Pl
NH Flat	1	0	0	0	0
Hurdles	2	0	1	0	965
Career Total	**3**	**0**	**1**	**0**	**965**

Going: Sf: 0-3 GS: 0-0 Gd: 0-0 GF: - Fm: 0-0
Distance: 2m/2m3: 0-2 2m4-2m7: 0-1 3m+: 0-0
Track: LH: 0-2 RH: 0-1 Tight: 0-1 Gall: 0-0
Aids: Bl: 0-0 Vi: 0-0 Tstrap: 0-0
Best Rating: 107 1/02 Catt 2m3f soft Hdl

Has shown form on a soft surface over two miles three furlongs.

Ryalux (IRE)

116(104h) (119h)147

9-y-o b g Riverhead (USA)-Kings De Lema (IRE) (King's Ride)

A Crook William Lomax

Placings:221/12F111/3331P-22223F21 (4897)

2001/02: 20²G, 20²GS, 20²S, 19²S, 20³S, 20^FGS, 22²G, 24¹G

	Starts	1st	2nd	3rd	Win & Pl
Hurdles	1	0	1	0	2132
Chases	7	1	4	1	25663
Career Total	**22**	**7**	**8**	**4**	**53993**

142	4/02	Prth	3m	B HCh	GD	£12203
139	1/01	Weth	2m4f110y	D(0-125)HCh	G-S	£4160
135	3/00	Carl	2m	D Ch	G-S	£4368
119	3/00	Newc	2m4f	E Ch	GD	£3152
139	2/00	Newc	2m4f	E Ch	SFT	£3087
104	5/99	Hexm	2m	E Hdl	SFT	£2526
109	3/99	Newc	2m4f	E Hdl	GD	£2253

Total win prize-money £31750

Going: Sf: 0-3 GS: 0-2 Gd: 1-3 GF: - Fm: 0-0
Distance: 2m/2m3: 0-0 2m4-2m7: 0-7 **3m+: 1-1**
Track: LH: 0-7 **RH: 1-1** Tight: 0-2 Gall: 0-3
Aids: Bl: 0-0 Vi: 0-0 Tstrap: 0-0
Best Rating: 147 1/02 Donc 2m3f110y soft Ch

He has a consistent record over fences and ran well in the 2001/2002 season, being second five times before winning a decent Perth handicap. Stays two and a half miles. Acts on soft ground and was just denied when tried back over hurdles.

Ryans Star

9-y-o ch g North Col-Tapalong (True Song)

F A Hutsby H Hutsby

Placings:P (3817)

2001/02: 21^PS

	Starts	1st	2nd	3rd	Win & Pl
Chases	1	0	0	0	
Career Total	**1**	**0**	**0**	**0**	

Going: Sf: 0-1 GS: 0-0 Gd: 0-0 GF: - Fm: 0-0
Distance: 2m/2m3: 0-0 2m4-2m7: 0-1 3m+: 0-0
Track: LH: 0-0 RH: 0-1 Tight: 0-1 Gall: 0-0
Aids: Bl: 0-0 Vi: 0-0 Tstrap: 0-0
Best Rating:

Ryde On

104 94

6-y-o b m Petoski-Rydewells Daughter (Celtic Cone)

M Pitman Miss J E Hayward

Placings:54445 (4181)

2001/02: 16⁵G, 16⁴G, 16⁴GS, 21⁴G, 19⁵S

	Starts	1st	2nd	3rd	Win & Pl
NH Flat	2	0	0	0	0
Hurdles	3	0	0	0	286
Career Total	**5**	**0**	**0**	**0**	**286**

Going: Sf: 0-1 GS: 0-1 Gd: 0-3 GF: - Fm: 0-0
Distance: 2m/2m3: 0-3 2m4-2m7: 0-2 3m+: 0-0
Track: LH: 0-2 RH: 0-3 Tight: 0-1 Gall: 0-0
Aids: Bl: 0-0 Vi: 0-0 Tstrap: 0-0
Best Rating: 97 11/01 Wwck 2m good NHF

Ryde Regatta

90 73

7-y-o b m King's Ride-Paperchain (Articulate)

G B Balding Miss B Swire

Placings:00/06F-5300P000 (4657)

2001/02: 16⁵S, 20³GS, 19⁰GS, 20⁰S, 22^PS, 24⁰S, 22⁰S, 24⁰G

	Starts	1st	2nd	3rd	Win & Pl
Hurdles	8	0	0	1	427
Career Total	**13**	**0**	**0**	**1**	**427**

Going: Sf: 0-5 GS: 0-2 Gd: 0-1 GF: - Fm: 0-0
Distance: 2m/2m3: 0-2 2m4-2m7: 0-4 3m+: 0-2
Track: LH: 0-0 RH: 0-7 Tight: 0-3 Gall: 0-0
Aids: Bl: 0-0 Vi: 0-2 Tstrap: 0-0
Best Rating: 73 11/01 Leic 2m4f110y gd-sft Hdl

Rydon Lane (IRE)

96 95

6-y-o br g Toca Madera-Polocracy (IRE) (Aristocracy)

Mrs S D Williams D C Coard

Placings:0-004446 (4152)

2001/02: 16⁰S, 17⁰G, 17⁴GS, 16⁴GS, 17⁴S, 20⁶GS

	Starts	1st	2nd	3rd	Win & Pl
NH Flat	2	0	0	0	0
Hurdles	4	0	0	0	450
Career Total	**7**	**0**	**0**	**0**	**450**

Going: Sf: 0-2 GS: 0-3 Gd: 0-1 GF: - Fm: 0-0
Distance: 2m/2m3: 0-5 2m4-2m7: 0-1 3m+: 0-0
Track: LH: 0-3 RH: 0-3 Tight: 0-3 Gall: 0-0
Aids: Bl: 0-0 Vi: 0-0 Tstrap: 0-0
Best Rating: 95 1/02 Winc 2m gd-sft Hdl

Rye Brook

5-y-o b g Romany Rye-Nearly A Brook (Nearly A Hand)

R J Hodges Mrs S J Maltby

Placings:0P (4158)

2001/02: 16⁰S, 16^PGS

	Starts	1st	2nd	3rd	Win & Pl
NH Flat	2	0	0	0	
Career Total	**2**	**0**	**0**	**0**	

Going: Sf: 0-1 GS: 0-1 Gd: 0-0 GF: - Fm: 0-0
Distance: 2m/2m3: 0-2 2m4-2m7: 0-0 3m+: 0-0
Track: LH: 0-1 RH: 0-1 Tight: 0-0 Gall: 0-0
Aids: Bl: 0-0 Vi: 0-0 Tstrap: 0-0
Best Rating:

Rye Rum (IRE)

80 60

11-y-o br g Strong Gale-Eimers Pet (Paddy's Stream)

J W F Aynsley J W F Aynsley

Placings:0PP/PPP/P/PPP/P2/6035-P0LPP (0784)

2001/02: 25^PS, 20⁰GF, 20^LGF, 24^PGF, 25^PG

	Starts	1st	2nd	3rd	Win & Pl
Chases	5	0	0	0	
Career Total	**21**	**0**	**1**	**1**	**1253**

Going: Sf: 0-1 GS: 0-0 Gd: 0-1 GF: - Fm: 0-3
Distance: 2m/2m3: 0-0 2m4-2m7: 0-2 3m+: 0-3
Track: LH: 0-5 RH: 0-0 Tight: 0-0 Gall: 0-1
Aids: Bl: 0-4 Vi: 0-0 Tstrap: 0-0

Best Rating: 63 6/99 Hexm 2m4f110y gd-fm Ch

Ryeland

6-y-o b m Presidium-Ewe Lamb (Free State)

Mrs P Sly Thorney Racing Club

Placings:P (0646)

2001/02: 17^PGF

	Starts	1st	2nd	3rd	Win & Pl
Hurdles	1	0	0	0	
Career Total	**1**	**0**	**0**	**0**	

Going: Sf: 0-0 GS: 0-0 Gd: 0-0 GF: - Fm: 0-1
Distance: 2m/2m3: 0-1 2m4-2m7: 0-0 3m+: 0-0
Track: LH: 0-0 RH: 0-1 Tight: 0-1 Gall: 0-0
Aids: Bl: 0-0 Vi: 0-0 Tstrap: 0-0
Best Rating:

Ryka

77 49

7-y-o ch g Deploy-Velda (Thatch (USA))

W Clay S Taberner

Placings:00/P02-0 (0666)

2001/02: 20⁰G

	Starts	1st	2nd	3rd	Win & Pl
Hurdles	1	0	0	0	
Career Total	**6**	**0**	**1**	**0**	**814**

Going: Sf: 0-0 GS: 0-0 Gd: 0-1 GF: - Fm: 0-0
Distance: 2m/2m3: 0-0 2m4-2m7: 0-1 3m+: 0-0
Track: LH: 0-1 RH: 0-0 Tight: 0-0 Gall: 0-0
Aids: Bl: 0-0 Vi: 0-0 Tstrap: 0-0
Best Rating: 95 2/01 Uttx 2m soft Hdl

Rymin Thyne

13-y-o ch g Good Thyne (USA)-Mrs Popple (Deep Run)

Mrs S Y Farthing B W Farthing

Placings:P/P/0 (4727)

2001/02: 24⁰GF

	Starts	1st	2nd	3rd	Win & Pl
Chases	1	0	0	0	
Career Total	**3**	**0**	**0**	**0**	

Going: Sf: 0-0 GS: 0-0 Gd: 0-0 GF: - Fm: 0-1
Distance: 2m/2m3: 0-0 2m4-2m7: 0-0 3m+: 0-1
Track: LH: 0-1 RH: 0-0 Tight: 0-0 Gall: 0-0
Aids: Bl: 0-0 Vi: 0-0 Tstrap: 0-0
Best Rating: 40 4/02 Chep 3m gd-fm Ch

Rysanshyn

10-y-o b m Primitive Rising (USA)-Shining Bann (Bargello)

R Johnson Robert Johnson

Placings:6/50/P5-P (0804)

2001/02: 20^PGF

	Starts	1st	2nd	3rd	Win & Pl
Chases	1	0	0	0	
Career Total	**6**	**0**	**0**	**0**	**0**

Going: Sf: 0-0 GS: 0-0 Gd: 0-0 GF: - Fm: 0-1
Distance: 2m/2m3: 0-0 2m4-2m7: 0-1 3m+: 0-0
Track: LH: 0-0 RH: 0-1 Tight: 0-0 Gall: 0-0
Aids: Bl: 0-0 Vi: 0-0 Tstrap: 0-0

Best Rating: 43 10/96 Sedg 2m1f gd-fm Hdl

S'Assagir (FR)

87 (86h) **126**

6-y-o b g Shining Steel-Dalticia (FR) (Cadoudal (FR))
N J Henderson Sir Robert Ogden

Placings: *3/21*U0-**14P** **(3394)**
2001/02: 17^{1}S, 16^{4}G, 16^{P}GS, ^^

	Starts	1st	2nd	3rd	Win & Pl
Chases	3	1	0	0	3340
Career Total	**8**	**2**	**1**	**1**	**7537**

126	12/01	Plum	2m1f	E Ch	SFT	£3068
116	11/00	Ludl	2m	D Hdl	GD	£3435

Total win prize-money £6503

Going: Sf: 1-1 GS: 0-1 Gd: 0-1 GF: - Fm: 0-0
Distance: **2m/2m3: 1-3** 2m4-2m7: 0-0 3m+: 0-0
Track: **LH: 1-2** RH: 0-1 **Tight: 1-1** Gall: 0-0
Aids: Bl: 0-0 **Vi: 1-2** Tstrap: 0-0
Best Rating: 126 12/01 Plum 2m1f soft Ch

Made a winning chase debut at Plumpton in December. Looked reluctant subsequently.

Sabena Canyon

61 **35**

6-y-o b g Nalchik (USA)-Gay Saucy (Gay Meadow)
T Wall D P Constable

Placings: *00*-000 **(2649)**
2001/02: 17^{0}G, 16^{0}GF, 16^{0}G

	Starts	1st	2nd	3rd	Win & Pl
Hurdles	3	0	0	0	
Career Total	**5**	**0**	**0**	**0**	

Going: Sf: 0-0 GS: 0-0 Gd: 0-2 GF: - Fm: 0-1
Distance: 2m/2m3: 0-3 2m4-2m7: 0-0 3m+: 0-0
Track: LH: 0-1 RH: 0-2 Tight: 0-1 Gall: 0-0
Aids: Bl: 0-0 Vi: 0-0 Tstrap: 0-0
Best Rating: 62 10/00 Ludl 2m gd-fm NHF

Sabi Sand

94 **81**

6-y-o b m Minster Son-Radical Lady (Radical)
N B Mason N B Mason

Placings: 00006 **(3548)**
2001/02: 17^{0}G, 17^{0}GS, 16^{0}GS, 16^{0}S, 16^{6}S

	Starts	1st	2nd	3rd	Win & Pl
Hurdles	5	0	0	0	0
Career Total	**5**	**0**	**0**	**0**	**0**

Going: Sf: 0-2 GS: 0-2 Gd: 0-1 GF: - Fm: 0-0
Distance: 2m/2m3: 0-5 2m4-2m7: 0-0 3m+: 0-0
Track: LH: 0-3 RH: 0-2 Tight: 0-1 Gall: 0-2
Aids: Bl: 0-0 Vi: 0-0 Tstrap: 0-0
Best Rating: 81 12/01 Leic 2m gd-sft Hdl

Sabre King

14-y-o ch g Broadsword (USA)-King's Lavender (Kings Troop)
M F Loggin J Tredwell

Placings: 4PU **(0585)**
2001/02: 28^{4}GF, 33^{P}G, 24^{U}GF

	Starts	1st	2nd	3rd	Win & Pl
Chases	3	0	0	0	0
Career Total	**3**	**0**	**0**	**0**	**0**

Going: Sf: 0-0 GS: 0-0 Gd: 0-1 GF: - Fm: 0-2
Distance: 2m/2m3: 0-0 2m4-2m7: 0-0 3m+: 0-3
Track: LH: 0-2 RH: 0-0 Tight: 0-2 Gall: 0-0
Aids: Bl: 0-3 Vi: 0-0 Tstrap: 0-0
Best Rating: 102 5/01 Strf 3m4f gd-fm Ch

Sabresong

4-y-o ch f Sabrehill (USA)-Winsong Melody (Music Maestro)
P R Rodford (C A Dwyer 22/6) Les Trott

Placings: PFP **(2594)**
2001/02: 18^{P}GF, 16^{F}G, 17^{P}S

	Starts	1st	2nd	3rd	Win & Pl
Hurdles	3	0	0	0	
Career Total	**3**	**0**	**0**	**0**	

Going: Sf: 0-1 GS: 0-0 Gd: 0-1 GF: - Fm: 0-1
Distance: 2m/2m3: 0-3 2m4-2m7: 0-0 3m+: 0-0
Track: LH: 0-2 RH: 0-1 Tight: 0-2 Gall: 0-1
Aids: Bl: 0-1 Vi: 0-0 Tstrap: 0-1
Best Rating:

Sabrewing

69 **43**

6-y-o ch g Sir Harry Lewis (USA)-Lady Stock (Crofter (USA))
Mrs P Robeson Mrs P Robeson

Placings: *5/0*000 **(2011)**
2001/02: 17^{0}GS, 16^{0}G, 16^{0}S, 16^{0}S

	Starts	1st	2nd	3rd	Win & Pl
NH Flat	2	0	0	0	0
Hurdles	2	0	0	0	0
Career Total	**5**	**0**	**0**	**0**	**0**

Going: Sf: 0-2 GS: 0-1 Gd: 0-1 GF: - Fm: 0-0
Distance: 2m/2m3: 0-4 2m4-2m7: 0-0 3m+: 0-0
Track: LH: 0-1 RH: 0-3 Tight: 0-2 Gall: 0-1
Aids: Bl: 0-2 Vi: 0-0 Tstrap: 0-0
Best Rating: 78 3/00 Strf 2m110y good NHF

Sackville (IRE)

119 (130h) **172**

9-y-o b g Satco (FR)-Sackville Street (Ete Indien (USA))
Miss F M Crowley Seamus O'Farrell

Placings: 0*11*/13123111/5**221111111-131335FF** **(4945a)**
2001/02: 20^{1}G, 16^{3}Y, 25^{1}G, 20^{3}S, 24^{3}HY, 24^{5}HY, 26^{F}G, 25^{F}G

	Starts	1st	2nd	3rd	Win & Pl
Hurdles	1	0	0	1	730
Chases	7	2	0	2	71421
Career Total	**29**	**16**	**3**	**5**	**304299**

172	11/01	Weth	3m1f	A Ch	GD	£29000
155	5/01	Fair	2m4f	Ch	GD	£34354
172	4/01	Leop	3m	HCh	SH	£37500
167	4/01	Fair	2m4f	Ch	SFT	£19334
153	2/01	Naas	2m4f	Ch	Y-S	£15725
175	2/01	Leop	2m5f	Ch	HVY	£38951
159	1/01	Naas	3m	Ch	SFT	£18346
155	12/00	Fair	2m4f	Ch	Y-S	£23400
147	11/00	Chel	3m110y	B Ch	G-S	£10530
161	4/00	Aint	3m110y	A Hdl	GD	£27000
136	3/00	Navn	2m6f	Hdl	YLD	£4692
126	3/00	Gowr	2m	Hdl	YLD	£4416
140	1/00	Fair	2m4f	Hdl	SFT	£4416
111	9/99	List	2m6f	Hdl	Y-S	£6776
119	10/98	Gowr	2m4f	NHF	Y-S	£4782
101	8/98	Tral	2m1f	NHF	GD	£2989

Total win prize-money £282218

Going: Sf: 0-3 GS: 0-0 Gd: 2-4 GF: - Fm: 0-0
Distance: 2m/2m3: 0-1 2m4-2m7: 1-2 3m+: 1-5
Track: **LH: 1-3** RH: 0-3 Tight: 0-0 Gall: 0-1
Aids: Bl: 0-0 Vi: 0-0 Tstrap: 0-0
Best Rating: 175 2/01 Leop 2m5f heavy Ch

He had a wonderful 2000/2001 season, racking up seven wins including two in four days at Fairyhouse and Leopardstown in April. He won the Powers Gold Cup and the Charlie Hall Chase at Wetherby early last season. He then became very disappointing and appeared to lose his confidence completely. Now has much to prove. Seems to handle any ground.

Sacrifice

7-y-o b g Arctic Lord-Kellyann (Jellaby)
T Long Mike Cornish

Placings: 501 **(4545)**
2001/02: 20^{5}S, 19^{0}G, 19^{1}G

	Starts	1st	2nd	3rd	Win & Pl
Chases	3	1	0	0	2300
Career Total	**3**	**1**	**0**	**0**	**2300**

95	4/02	Hrfd	2m3f	H Ch	GD	£2299

Total win prize-money £2300

Going: Sf: 0-1 GS: 0-0 Gd: 1-2 GF: - Fm: 0-0
Distance: **2m/2m3: 1-1** 2m4-2m7: 0-2 3m+: 0-0
Track: LH: 0-0 **RH: 1-3** Tight: 0-0 Gall: 0-0
Aids: Bl: 0-0 Vi: 0-0 Tstrap: 0-0
Best Rating: 95 4/02 Hrfd 2m3f good Ch

Moderate hunter chaser at two to two and a half miles.

Sacundai (IRE)

118 **148**

5-y-o b g Hernando (FR)-Shahdiza (USA) (Blushing Groom (FR))
E J O'Grady Malm Syndicate

Placings: 15121255 **(4703a)**
2001/02: 16^{1}GF, 17^{5}G, 16^{1}HY, 16^{2}Y, 16^{1}Y, 18^{2}HY, 16^{5}GS, 16^{5}GY

	Starts	1st	2nd	3rd	Win & Pl
Hurdles	8	3	2	0	50954
Career Total	**8**	**3**	**2**	**0**	**50954**

136	12/01	Leop	2m	Hdl	YLD	£20967
105	10/01	Tipp	2m	Hdl	HVY	£7862
99	5/01	Tipp	2m	Hdl	G-F	£4451

Total win prize-money £33283

Going: Sf: 1-2 GS: 0-1 Gd: 0-1 GF: - Fm: 1-1
Distance: **2m/2m3: 3-8** 2m4-2m7: 0-0 3m+: 0-0
Track: **LH: 1-3** RH: 0-2 Tight: 0-0 Gall: 0-0
Aids: Bl: 0-0 Vi: 0-0 Tstrap: 0-0
Best Rating: 148 3/02 Chel 2m110y gd-sft Hdl

Decent novice hurdler, has won three times in Ireland and run well in good company besides. He loves soft ground, although he did break his duck on a sound surface. A staying-on fifth in the Supreme Novices' at the Cheltenham Festival.

Sad Mad Bad (USA)

111 **131**

8-y-o b g Sunny's Halo (CAN)-Quite Attractive (USA) (Well Decorated (USA))
Mrs M Reveley P D Savill

Placings:11410/**13111060/312P25/40062U32-311FP** **(4299)**
2001/02: 28^{3}G, 26^{1}GS, 29^{1}G, 33^{F}S, 34^{P}HY

	Starts	1st	2nd	3rd	Win & Pl
Chases	5	2	0	1	21558
Career Total	**32**	**10**	**4**	**4**	**86190**

131	11/01	Plum	3m5f	C(0-130)HCh	GD	£13340
131	10/01	Uttx	3m2f	E(0-115)HCh	G-S	£6500
138	1/00	Uttx	2m4f	B(0-140)HCh	SFT	£23200
118	3/99	Carl	2m4f110y	C Ch	SFT	£5472
130	2/99	MRas	2m4f	D Ch	SFT	£4027
137	12/98	Bang	2m4f110y	D Ch	G-S	£3582
110	11/98	MRas	2m4f	D Ch	G-S	£4608
125	2/98	Hayd	2m	C HHdl	GD	£5083
120	11/97	Newc	2m	D Hdl	GD	£2841
117	11/97	MRas	2m1f110y	D Hdl	GD	£2999

Total win prize-money £71654

Going: Sf: 0-2 GS: 1-1 Gd: 1-2 GF: - Fm: 0-0
Distance: 2m/2m3: 0-0 2m4-2m7: 0-0 **3m+: 2-5**
Track: **LH: 1-4** RH: 0-0 Tight: 0-1 Gall: 0-1
Aids: Bl: 1-2 Vi: 1-3 Tstrap: 0-0
Best Rating: 138 1/00 Uttx 2m4f soft Ch

An out-and-out stayer, he has a good record over fences, but is not the easiest of rides. Victorious at Uttoxeter and the Sussex National at Plumpton in 2001/02. Acts on soft ground. Has worn headgear.

Sadler's Realm

103 **138**

9-y-o b g Sadler's Wells (USA)-Rensaler (USA) (Stop The Music (USA))
P J Hobbs B D Racing

Placings:02/2012111220/1403043/**3321-P551** **(4529)**
2001/02: 20^{P}S, 20^{5}GS, 19^{5}GS, 19^{1}GS

	Starts	1st	2nd	3rd	Win & Pl
Chases	4	1	0	0	4495
Career Total	**27**	**7**	**6**	**4**	**55463**

138	4/02	Chep	2m3f110y	D(0-125)HCh	G-S	£4085
132	2/01	Sand	2m4f110y	D Ch	SFT	£4982
141	12/98	Chep	2m4f110y	B(0-140)HHdl	GD	£5319
111	1/98	Extr	2m3f110y	D(0-125)HHdl	HVY	£3340
115	12/97	Chep	2m110y	E(0-120)HHdl	HVY	£2320
108	12/97	Extr	2m2f	F(0-105)HHdl	SFT	£2176
114	11/97	Kemp	2m	F(0-100)HHdl	G-S	£1898

Total win prize-money £24120

Going: Sf: 0-1 GS: 1-3 Gd: 0-0 GF: - Fm: 0-0
Distance: 2m/2m3: 0-0 **2m4-2m7: 1-4** 3m+: 0-0
Track: **LH: 1-3** RH: 0-1 Tight: 0-0 Gall: 0-1
Aids: Bl: 0-0 Vi: 0-0 Tstrap: 0-0
Best Rating: 141 2/99 Newb 2m110y good Hdl

Effective up to two and a half miles over hurdles, he was highly tried over fences in 2000/2001, he got off the mark for the season at Chepstow in April.

Sadler's Rock (IRE)

100f **106f**

4-y-o b g Sadler's Wells (USA)-Triple Couronne (USA) (Riverman (USA))
G L Moore Regal Racing

Placings:*40* **(4679)**
2001/02: 16^{4}GS, 17^{0}G

	Starts	1st	2nd	3rd	Win & Pl
NH Flat	2	0	0	0	0
Career Total	**2**	**0**	**0**	**0**	**0**

Going: Sf: 0-0 GS: 0-1 Gd: 0-1 GF: - Fm: 0-0
Distance: 2m/2m3: 0-2 2m4-2m7: 0-0 3m+: 0-0
Track: LH: 0-1 RH: 0-0 Tight: 0-0 Gall: 0-1
Aids: Bl: 0-0 Vi: 0-0 Tstrap: 0-0
Best Rating: 106 4/02 Aint 2m1f good NHF

Sadler's Secret (IRE)

98(98c) **109**

7-y-o b g Sadler's Wells (USA)-Athyka (USA) (Secretariat (USA))
M C Pipe A S Helaissi

Placings:F42143350/013/4203**330PP**-0043P **(4754)**
2001/02: 23^{0}HY, 19^{0}G, 24^{4}S, 25^{3}GF, 24^{P}GF

	Starts	1st	2nd	3rd	Win & Pl
Hurdles	5	0	0	1	1064
Career Total	**26**	**2**	**2**	**7**	**12766**

118	4/00	Tntn	2m1f	F(0-110)HHdl	G-S	£2926
107	12/98	Plum	2m1f	E Hdl	SFT	£2512

Total win prize-money £5439

Going: Sf: 0-2 GS: 0-0 Gd: 0-1 GF: - Fm: 0-2
Distance: 2m/2m3: 0-1 2m4-2m7: 0-0 3m+: 0-4
Track: LH: 0-3 RH: 0-1 Tight: 0-1 Gall: 0-0
Aids: Bl: 0-2 Vi: 0-2 Tstrap: 0-0
Best Rating: 124 12/00 Tntn 3m110y soft Hdl

Frustrating staying handicap hurdler with a poor win-to-run ratio. Stays three miles, needs soft ground and is usually visored.

Sadr (NZ)

(100h) **132**

9-y-o b g Cache Of Gold (USA)-War Field (NZ) (War Hawk)
Mrs S A Bramall Mrs S A Bramall

Placings:63302/114344-**F3F** **(1834)**
2001/02: 22^{F}GY, 22^{3}G, 25^{F}G

	Starts	1st	2nd	3rd	Win & Pl
Chases	3	0	0	1	790
Career Total	**14**	**2**	**1**	**4**	**8540**

5/00	Elle	1m6f	Hdl	HVY	£1990
5/00	Trap	1m4f	Hdl	G-S	£1393

Total win prize-money £3383

Going: Sf: 0-0 GS: 0-0 Gd: 0-2 GF: - Fm: 0-0
Distance: 2m/2m3: 0-0 2m4-2m7: 0-2 3m+: 0-1
Track: LH: 0-1 RH: 0-0 Tight: 0-1 Gall: 0-0
Aids: Bl: 0-0 Vi: 0-0 Tstrap: 0-0
Best Rating: 134 12/00 Leop 2m heavy Hdl

A dual winner in New Zealand, he has had jumping problems over fences. Acts on an easy surface.

Safe Enough (IRE)

100 **85**

6-y-o ch g Safety Catch (USA)-Godfreys Cross (IRE) (Fine Blade (USA))
J T Gifford D S Norden & R S Norden

Placings:*00*/3-4 **(4724)**
2001/02: 16^{4}GF

	Starts	1st	2nd	3rd	Win & Pl
Hurdles	1	0	0	0	0
Career Total	**4**	**0**	**0**	**1**	**461**

Going: Sf: 0-0 GS: 0-0 Gd: 0-0 GF: - Fm: 0-1
Distance: 2m/2m3: 0-1 2m4-2m7: 0-0 3m+: 0-0
Track: LH: 0-1 RH: 0-0 Tight: 0-0 Gall: 0-0
Aids: Bl: 0-0 Vi: 0-0 Tstrap: 0-0
Best Rating: 101 10/00 Chep 2m110y gd-sft Hdl

Saffron Moss

12-y-o ch g Le Moss-Saffron's Daughter (Prince Hansel)
Mrs S M Farr Mrs S M Farr

Placings:*0/0*/1/FPP3U/FP/0P-P **(0077)**
2001/02: 23^{P}G

	Starts	1st	2nd	3rd	Win & Pl
Chases	1	0	0	0	
Career Total	**13**	**1**	**0**	**1**	**4066**

86	4/98	Chep	3m	H Ch	HVY	£3533

Total win prize-money £3534

Going: Sf: 0-0 GS: 0-0 Gd: 0-1 GF: - Fm: 0-0
Distance: 2m/2m3: 0-0 2m4-2m7: 0-0 3m+: 0-1
Track: LH: 0-0 RH: 0-1 Tight: 0-0 Gall: 0-0
Aids: Bl: 0-0 Vi: 0-0 Tstrap: 0-0
Best Rating: 86 4/98 Chep 3m heavy Ch

Saffron Sun

(104h) (106h)**77**

7-y-o b g Landyap (USA)-Saffron Bun (Sit In The Corner (USA))
J D Frost (R G Frost 2/10) Mrs J F Bury

Placings:*000*/3F005-01432613 **(4862)**
2001/02: 17^{0}GF, 17^{1}G, 20^{4}GS, 20^{3}GF, 22^{2}GF, 17^{6}GF, 17^{1}F, 19^{3}F

	Starts	1st	2nd	3rd	Win & Pl
Hurdles	8	2	1	2	7400
Career Total	**16**	**2**	**1**	**3**	**7782**

104	4/02	Extr	2m1f	E Hdl	FRM	£3066
92	6/01	NAbb	2m1f	F(0-100)HHdl	GD	£2667

Total win prize-money £5733

Going: Sf: 0-0 GS: 0-1 Gd: 1-1 GF: - Fm: 1-6
Distance: **2m/2m3: 2-5** 2m4-2m7: 0-3 3m+: 0-0
Track: LH: 1-5 RH: 1-3 **Tight: 1-4** Gall: 0-0
Aids: Bl: 0-0 Vi: 0-0 Tstrap: 0-0
Best Rating: 106 4/02 Extr 2m3f firm Hdl

Looks badly handicapped after being raised 13lb for winning poor novice hurdle at Exeter on comeback in April 2002. Likes fast ground.

Saffron Thyne

6-y-o ch m Good Thyne (USA)-Flash 'N' Run (Record Run)
M R Ewer-Hoad Southdowns Partnership

Placings:*0*P **(2461)**
2001/02: 17^{0}S, 20^{P}HY

	Starts	1st	2nd	3rd	Win & Pl
NH Flat	1	0	0	0	0
Hurdles	1	0	0	0	0
Career Total	**2**	**0**	**0**	**0**	

Going: Sf: 0-2 GS: 0-0 Gd: 0-0 GF: - Fm: 0-0
Distance: 2m/2m3: 0-1 2m4-2m7: 0-1 3m+: 0-0
Track: LH: 0-0 RH: 0-1 Tight: 0-2 Gall: 0-0
Aids: Bl: 0-0 Vi: 0-0 Tstrap: 0-0
Best Rating:

Safi

(67h) (37h)

7-y-o b g Generous (IRE)-Jasarah (IRE) (Green Desert (USA))
D McCain D McCain

Placings:PP/335003104/0204**524**U6-0 **(0841)**
2001/02: 16^{0}G

	Starts	1st	2nd	3rd	Win & Pl
Hurdles	1	0	0	0	
Career Total	**21**	**1**	**2**	**3**	**4720**

92 12/99 Donc 2m110y G Hdl G-F £1864
Total win prize-money £1864

Going: Sf: 0-0 GS: 0-0 Gd: 0-1 GF: - Fm: 0-0
Distance: 2m/2m3: 0-1 2m4-2m7: 0-0 3m+: 0-0
Track: LH: 0-1 RH: 0-0 Tight: 0-0 Gall: 0-0
Aids: Bl: 0-1 Vi: 0-0 Tstrap: 0-1
Best Rating: 94 7/00 Sedg 2m110y firm Ch

Saga Royale (FR)

92 **61**

6-y-o b m Garde Royale-Passionnante (FR) (Dike (USA))
D C O'Brien D C O'Brien

Placings:644/06-40004 **(4507)**
2001/02: 16^{4}G, 20^{0}GS, 17^{0}S, 21^{0}HY, 21^{4}G

	Starts	1st	2nd	3rd	Win & Pl
Hurdles	5	0	0	0	273
Career Total	**10**	**0**	**0**	**0**	**273**

Going: Sf: 0-2 GS: 0-1 Gd: 0-2 GF: - Fm: 0-0
Distance: 2m/2m3: 0-2 2m4-2m7: 0-3 3m+: 0-0
Track: LH: 0-3 RH: 0-2 Tight: 0-4 Gall: 0-1
Aids: Bl: 0-0 Vi: 0-1 Tstrap: 0-0
Best Rating: 77 2/00 Plum 2m soft Hdl

Sahara Reem (IRE)

90 **79**

8-y-o b m Don't Forget Me-River Reem (USA) (Irish River (FR))
J R Norton J Norton

Placings:*10/20*4060/P441U343/644-006 **(2076)**
2001/02: 24^{0}F, 21^{0}G, 21^{6}S

	Starts	1st	2nd	3rd	Win & Pl
Hurdles	3	0	0	0	0
Career Total	**22**	**2**	**1**	**2**	**4394**

98 12/99 Sedg 2m5f110y E Hdl SFT £1926
96 3/98 Donc 2m110y H NHF SFT £1276
Total win prize-money £3203

Going: Sf: 0-1 GS: 0-0 Gd: 0-1 GF: - Fm: 0-1
Distance: 2m/2m3: 0-0 2m4-2m7: 0-2 3m+: 0-1
Track: LH: 0-3 RH: 0-0 Tight: 0-3 Gall: 0-0
Aids: Bl: 0-0 Vi: 0-0 Tstrap: 0-0
Best Rating: 98 1/00 Sedg 2m5f110y soft Hdl

Sahhar

90 **91**

9-y-o ch g Sayf El Arab (USA)-Native Magic (Be My Native (USA))
B D Leavy Mrs Margaret Underwood

Placings:4/6F/0126340/6/510-03 **(0773)**
2001/02: 16^{0}GF, 16^{3}GF

	Starts	1st	2nd	3rd	Win & Pl
Hurdles	2	0	0	1	259
Career Total	**16**	**2**	**1**	**2**	**5056**

91 11/00 Ludl 2m G Hdl GD £1981
88 8/98 Worc 2m G(0-95)HHdl G-F £1744
Total win prize-money £3725

Going: Sf: 0-0 GS: 0-0 Gd: 0-0 GF: - Fm: 0-2
Distance: 2m/2m3: 0-2 2m4-2m7: 0-0 3m+: 0-0
Track: LH: 0-2 RH: 0-0 Tight: 0-1 Gall: 0-0
Aids: Bl: 0-0 Vi: 0-0 Tstrap: 0-0
Best Rating: 91 6/01 Worc 2m gd-fm Hdl

Saif Majrour

95 **76**

6-y-o b g Darshaan-Garconniere (Gay Mecene (USA))
M J Gingell (P R Webber 30/6) The Good Craic Club

Placings:*10-0*PP0040 **(4904)**
2001/02: 16^{0}G, 16^{P}S, 20^{P}GS, 16^{0}GS, 16^{0}G, 16^{4}G, 17^{0}G

	Starts	1st	2nd	3rd	Win & Pl
NH Flat	1	0	0	0	0
Hurdles	6	0	0	0	0
Career Total	**9**	**1**	**0**	**0**	**1463**

109 8/00 Worc 2m H NHF G-F £1463
Total win prize-money £1463

Going: Sf: 0-1 GS: 0-2 Gd: 0-4 GF: - Fm: 0-0
Distance: 2m/2m3: 0-6 2m4-2m7: 0-1 3m+: 0-0
Track: LH: 0-5 RH: 0-2 Tight: 0-4 Gall: 0-1
Aids: Bl: 0-0 Vi: 0-0 Tstrap: 0-0
Best Rating: 109 8/00 Worc 2m gd-fm NHF

Fast ground bumper winner, plating class over hurdles.

Sail On Sid

100 **89**

8-y-o b g Yachtsman (USA)-Greenhill's Girl (Radetzky)
Mrs A Duffield Mrs J Wilson (durham)

Placings:*3211/5FF50/P-006* **(0517)**
2001/02: 20^{0}S, 20^{0}F, 24^{6}F

	Starts	1st	2nd	3rd	Win & Pl
Hurdles	3	0	0	0	0
Career Total	**13**	**2**	**1**	**1**	**5240**

108 3/99 Kels 2m6f110y E Hdl GD £1982
107 3/99 Carl 2m4f110y E Hdl SFT £2430
Total win prize-money £4412

Going: Sf: 0-1 GS: 0-0 Gd: 0-0 GF: - Fm: 0-2
Distance: 2m/2m3: 0-0 2m4-2m7: 0-2 3m+: 0-1
Track: LH: 0-3 RH: 0-0 Tight: 0-0 Gall: 0-0
Aids: Bl: 0-0 Vi: 0-0 Tstrap: 0-3
Best Rating: 108 3/99 Kels 2m6f110y good Hdl

Sailep (FR)

88 **85**

10-y-o ch g Holst (USA)-Sweet Cashmere (FR) (Kashmir Ii)
R J Baker P Slade

Placings:P30006/312232/4030/**024P**/**205**06/01-0500 **(1439)**
2001/02: 17^{0}G, 17^{5}GF, 19^{0}GF, 18^{0}GF

	Starts	1st	2nd	3rd	Win & Pl
Hurdles	4	0	0	0	0
Career Total	**31**	**2**	**5**	**4**	**10389**

99 6/00 NAbb 2m1f F(0-105)HHdl GD £2296
94 11/96 Plum 2m1f E Hdl SFT £2574
Total win prize-money £4870

Going: Sf: 0-0 GS: 0-0 Gd: 0-1 GF: - Fm: 0-3
Distance: 2m/2m3: 0-3 2m4-2m7: 0-1 3m+: 0-0
Track: LH: 0-3 RH: 0-1 Tight: 0-3 Gall: 0-0
Aids: Bl: 0-0 Vi: 0-0 Tstrap: 0-0
Best Rating: 101 1/96 Wind 2m soft Hdl

Sailor A'Hoy

98 **95**

6-y-o b g Handsome Sailor-Eye Sight (Roscoe Blake)
M Mullineaux R Williamson

Placings:00-204 **(0881)**
2001/02: 16^{2}GF, 20^{0}GF, 17^{4}G

	Starts	1st	2nd	3rd	Win & Pl
Hurdles	3	0	1	0	765
Career Total	**5**	**0**	**1**	**0**	**765**

Going: Sf: 0-0 GS: 0-0 Gd: 0-1 GF: - Fm: 0-2
Distance: 2m/2m3: 0-2 2m4-2m7: 0-1 3m+: 0-0
Track: LH: 0-1 RH: 0-2 Tight: 0-1 Gall: 0-1
Aids: Bl: 0-0 Vi: 0-0 Tstrap: 0-0
Best Rating: 95 7/01 MRas 2m1f110y good Hdl

Sailor Jack (USA)

109 **96**

6-y-o b g Green Dancer (USA)-Chateaubrook (USA) (Alleged (USA))
D McCain Champ Chicken Co Ltd

Placings:66136/4056-122 **(0661)**
2001/02: 19^{1}F, 20^{2}GF, 24^{2}F

	Starts	1st	2nd	3rd	Win & Pl
Hurdles	3	1	2	0	3187
Career Total	**12**	**2**	**2**	**1**	**5122**

92 5/01 Tntn 2m3f110y G(0-100)HHdl FRM £1785
82 1/00 Catt 2m G Hdl GD £1708
Total win prize-money £3494

Going: Sf: 0-0 GS: 0-0 Gd: 0-0 GF: - Fm: 1-3
Distance: 2m/2m3: 0-0 **2m4-2m7: 1-2** 3m+: 0-1
Track: LH: 0-1 **RH: 1-2 Tight: 1-1** Gall: 0-0
Aids: **Bl: 1-3** Vi: 0-0 Tstrap: 0-0
Best Rating: 96 6/01 Prth 3m110y firm Hdl

Saint Albert

7-y-o ch g Keen-Thimbalina (Salmon Leap (USA))
Miss G Browne Mrs D C Samworth

Placings:0P **(2581)**
2001/02: 19^{0}GF, 23^{P}S

	Starts	1st	2nd	3rd	Win & Pl
Hurdles	2	0	0	0	
Career Total	**2**	**0**	**0**	**0**	

Going: Sf: 0-1 GS: 0-0 Gd: 0-0 GF: - Fm: 0-1
Distance: 2m/2m3: 0-1 2m4-2m7: 0-1 3m+: 0-0
Track: LH: 0-1 RH: 0-1 Tight: 0-0 Gall: 0-0
Aids: Bl: 0-0 Vi: 0-0 Tstrap: 0-0
Best Rating:

Saint Ciel (USA)

102 **78**

14-y-o b g Skywalker (USA)-Holy Tobin (USA) (J O Tobin (USA))
F Jordan Miss Laura Jordan

Placings:2000/360/2315216/1113F4/40562106/52160 0000/4532110250P4/6050110062P/0P2331322000/30 00426-0003024 **(2690)**
2001/02: 17^{0}G, 20^{0}G, 17^{0}G, 20^{3}S, 16^{0}S, 16^{2}HY, 16^{4}S

	Starts	1st	2nd	3rd	Win & Pl
Hurdles	7	0	1	1	936
Career Total	**86**	**12**	**13**	**9**	**50677**

112	12/99	Hayd	2m	F(0-110)HHdl	HVY	£2556
112	11/98	Hayd	2m4f	C(0-135)HHdl	G-S	£3701
111	11/98	Hayd	2m	D(0-120)HHdl	SFT	£2759
112	11/97	Uttx	2m	D(0-125)HHdl	G-S	£2830
112	11/97	Hayd	2m	D(0-120)HHdl	GD	£2717
109	11/96	Hayd	2m	D(0-120)HHdl	GD	£2759
106	2/96	Hayd	2m	D(0-120)HHdl	SFT	£2983
100	12/94	Uttx	2m	(0-130)HHdl	SFT	£2479
102	11/94	Hayd	2m	(0-125)HHdl	G-S	£3062
93	11/94	Hayd	2m	(0-125)HHdl	GD	£3111
87	2/94	Uttx	2m	HHdl	SFT	£1913
84	11/93	Worc	2m	HHdl	SFT	£2742

Total win prize-money £33615

Going: Sf: 0-4 GS: 0-0 Gd: 0-3 GF: - Fm: 0-0
Distance: 2m/2m3: 0-5 2m4-2m7: 0-2 3m+: 0-0
Track: LH: 0-7 RH: 0-0 Tight: 0-3 Gall: 0-0
Aids: Bl: 0-0 Vi: 0-0 Tstrap: 0-7
Best Rating: 126 11/91 Newb 2m100y good Hdl

He has been a very successful hurdler over the years and is a multiple scorer at both Haydock and Uttoxeter, but age caught up with him and he was honourably retired at haydock in Decmber 2001.

Saint Joseph

94 **111**

12-y-o ch g Lir-Kimberley Ann (St Columbus)
Miss S Young B R J Young

Placings:2/6432/05114/1B4-0634 **(4186)**
2001/02: 23^{0}G, 26^{6}G, 24^{3}S, 24^{4}S

	Starts	1st	2nd	3rd	Win & Pl
Chases	4	0	0	1	442
Career Total	**17**	**3**	**2**	**2**	**10866**
120 3/01	Extr	2m3f110y	H Ch	HVY	£2271
110 4/00	Tntn	3m	H Ch	G-S	£2891
104 3/00	Tntn	3m	H Ch	SFT	£3003

Total win prize-money £8166

Going: Sf: 0-2 GS: 0-0 Gd: 0-2 GF: - Fm: 0-0
Distance: 2m/2m3: 0-0 2m4-2m7: 0-0 3m+: 0-4
Track: LH: 0-0 RH: 0-3 Tight: 0-2 Gall: 0-0
Aids: Bl: 0-0 Vi: 0-0 Tstrap: 0-0
Best Rating: 120 3/01 Extr 2m3f110y heavy Ch

Saint Par (FR)

103 **118**

4-y-o gr g Saint Preuil (FR)-Paris Or (FR) (Noir Et Or)
P F Nicholls (A Chaille-Chaille 25/9) Prd Holdings Limited

Placings:454-233433111 **(4840)**
2001/02: 16^{2}, 17^{3}S, 17^{3}VS, 16^{4}S, 16^{3}S, 21^{3}S, 20^{1}GS, 16^{1}HY, 16^{1}G

	Starts	1st	2nd	3rd	Win & Pl
Hurdles	7	3	1	2	17170
Chases	2	0	0	2	7274
Career Total	**12**	**3**	**1**	**4**	**29777**
118 4/02	Ayr	2m	C Hdl	GD	£5180
111 3/02	Uttx	2m	D Hdl	HVY	£3445
96 3/02	Chep	2m4f	D Hdl	G-S	£3552

Total win prize-money £12178

Going: Sf: 1-5 GS: 1-1 Gd: 1-1 GF: - Fm: 0-0
Distance: **2m/2m3: 2-7** 2m4-2m7: 1-2 3m+: 0-0
Track: **LH: 3-4** RH: 0-1 Tight: 0-0 Gall: 0-0
Aids: Bl: 0-0 Vi: 0-0 Tstrap: 0-0
Best Rating: 118 4/02 Ayr 2m good Hdl

Useful hurdler. Stays two and a half miles and acts well in the mud, but is also effective on a faster surface.

Saint Romble (FR)

69 **94**

5-y-o b g Sassanian (USA)-Limatge (FR) (Trac)
P J Hobbs (T Trapenard 2/7) M G St Quinton

Placings:1-0064 **(3669)**
2001/02: 17^{0}GS, 19^{0}GS, 16^{6}G, 20^{4}S

	Starts	1st	2nd	3rd	Win & Pl
Hurdles	2	0	0	0	0
Chases	2	0	0	0	408
Career Total	**5**	**1**	**0**	**0**	**10107**
4/01	Engh	2m110y	Hdl	HVY	£9699

Total win prize-money £9699

Going: Sf: 0-1 GS: 0-2 Gd: 0-1 GF: - Fm: 0-0
Distance: 2m/2m3: 0-2 2m4-2m7: 0-2 3m+: 0-0
Track: LH: 0-0 RH: 0-2 Tight: 0-0 Gall: 0-0
Aids: Bl: 0-0 Vi: 0-0 Tstrap: 0-0
Best Rating: 94 2/02 Kemp 2m4f110y soft Ch

Lightly-raced French hurdler, suited by soft ground. Hinted at promise on chasing bow at Kempton in February.

Saintly Thoughts (USA)

7-y-o b/br g St Jovite (USA)-Free Thinker (USA) (Shadeed (USA))
K A Morgan Ian Guise

Placings:423/PPP **(4286)**
2001/02: 21^{P}GF, 25^{P}GF, 21^{P}GS

	Starts	1st	2nd	3rd	Win & Pl
Hurdles	3	0	0	0	
Career Total	**6**	**0**	**1**	**1**	**1130**

Going: Sf: 0-0 GS: 0-1 Gd: 0-0 GF: - Fm: 0-2
Distance: 2m/2m3: 0-0 2m4-2m7: 0-2 3m+: 0-1
Track: LH: 0-1 RH: 0-2 Tight: 0-2 Gall: 0-0
Aids: Bl: 0-0 Vi: 0-0 Tstrap: 0-0
Best Rating: 83 7/99 Klny 2m1f gd-fm Hdl

Sajomi Rona (IRE)

87 **77**

5-y-o ch g Riberetto-Mauma Lady (IRE) (Le Moss)
A Crook Jay Dee Bloodstock Limited

Placings:00050 **(4768)**
2001/02: 17^{0}G, 16^{0}GS, 20^{0}GF, 16^{5}HY, 16^{0}GF

	Starts	1st	2nd	3rd	Win & Pl
NH Flat	2	0	0	0	0
Hurdles	3	0	0	0	0
Career Total	**5**	**0**	**0**	**0**	**0**

Going: Sf: 0-1 GS: 0-1 Gd: 0-1 GF: - Fm: 0-2
Distance: 2m/2m3: 0-4 2m4-2m7: 0-1 3m+: 0-0
Track: LH: 0-3 RH: 0-1 Tight: 0-2 Gall: 0-0
Aids: Bl: 0-0 Vi: 0-0 Tstrap: 0-0
Best Rating: 77 3/02 Ayr 2m heavy Hdl

Modest hurdler.

Sakamoto

4-y-o b g Celtic Swing-Possessive Lady (Dara Monarch)
R C Spicer (I A Wood 10/9) John Purcell

Placings:P **(2523)**
2001/02: 16^{P}HY

	Starts	1st	2nd	3rd	Win & Pl
Hurdles	1	0	0	0	
Career Total	**1**	**0**	**0**	**0**	

Going: Sf: 0-1 GS: 0-0 Gd: 0-0 GF: - Fm: 0-0
Distance: 2m/2m3: 0-1 2m4-2m7: 0-0 3m+: 0-0
Track: LH: 0-0 RH: 0-1 Tight: 0-0 Gall: 0-0
Aids: Bl: 0-0 Vi: 0-0 Tstrap: 0-1
Best Rating:

Salaman (FR)

94 **66**

10-y-o b g Saumarez-Merry Sharp (Sharpen Up)
D C O'Brien D C O'Brien

Placings:03/60412P/P045/252004/404-05P500 **(4885)**
2001/02: 16^{0}G, 18^{5}GF, 21^{P}GS, 22^{5}GS, 22^{0}S, 27^{0}GF

	Starts	1st	2nd	3rd	Win & Pl
Hurdles	6	0	0	0	0
Career Total	**27**	**1**	**3**	**1**	**4794**
97 2/98	Folk	2m6f110y	E(0-115)HHdl	G-F	£2427

Total win prize-money £2427

Going: Sf: 0-1 GS: 0-2 Gd: 0-1 GF: - Fm: 0-2
Distance: 2m/2m3: 0-2 2m4-2m7: 0-3 3m+: 0-1
Track: LH: 0-5 RH: 0-0 Tight: 0-0 Gall: 0-0
Aids: Bl: 0-2 Vi: 0-0 Tstrap: 0-2
Best Rating: 97 3/99 Folk 2m6f110y gd-sft Hdl

Salami

6-y-o gr/ro g Desert Splendour-Crosby Place (Crooner)
G F H Charles-Jones Mrs L M Edwards

Placings:0P-P0P **(4479)**
2001/02: 24^{P}HY, 22^{0}S, 19^{P}G

	Starts	1st	2nd	3rd	Win & Pl
Hurdles	3	0	0	0	
Career Total	**5**	**0**	**0**	**0**	

Going: Sf: 0-2 GS: 0-0 Gd: 0-1 GF: - Fm: 0-0
Distance: 2m/2m3: 0-1 2m4-2m7: 0-1 3m+: 0-1
Track: LH: 0-2 RH: 0-1 Tight: 0-1 Gall: 0-0
Aids: Bl: 0-0 Vi: 0-0 Tstrap: 0-0
Best Rating: 57 12/00 Ludl 2m soft NHF

Salford

102(103h) **104**

7-y-o ch g Salse (USA)-Bustellina (Busted)
N J Hawke Mrs D A Wetherall

Placings:PP/02/51F1P030-P1PP **(1625)**
2001/02: 19^{P}GS, 21^{1}GF, 20^{P}S, 24^{P}GF

	Starts	1st	2nd	3rd	Win & Pl
Chases	4	1	0	0	4160
Career Total	**16**	**3**	**1**	**1**	**11302**
104 5/01	Winc	2m5f	F(0-100)HCh	G-F	£4160
99 12/00	Ludl	2m5f	F(0-105)HHdl	SFT	£2891
83 10/00	Extr	2m3f	E(0-115)HHdl	GD	£3198

Total win prize-money £10249

Going: Sf: 0-1 GS: 0-1 Gd: 0-0 GF: - Fm: 1-2
Distance: 2m/2m3: 0-0 **2m4-2m7: 1-3** 3m+: 0-1
Track: LH: 0-0 **RH: 1-4** Tight: 0-2 Gall: 0-0
Aids: Bl: 0-0 Vi: 0-0 Tstrap: 0-0

Best Rating: 104 10/01 Ludl 3m gd-fm Ch

Salierious (NZ)

107 70

7-y-o ch g Prince Salieri (AUS)-Analaw (NZ) (Diplomatic Agent (USA))

J C Tuck The Lammas Partnership

Placings:360/00P-062666 (1893)

2001/02: 17^{0}F, 21^{6}GF, 22^{2}GF, 19^{6}F, 24^{6}GF, 20^{6}GS

	Starts	1st	2nd	3rd	Win & Pl
Hurdles	6	0	1	0	556
Career Total	12	0	1	1	786

Going: Sf: 0-0 GS: 0-1 Gd: 0-0 GF: - Fm: 0-5
Distance: 2m/2m3: 0-1 2m4-2m7: 0-4 3m+: 0-1
Track: LH: 0-1 RH: 0-4 Tight: 0-4 Gall: 0-1
Aids: Bl: 0-2 Vi: 0-0 Tstrap: 0-0
Best Rating: 103 10/99 Tntn 2m1f gd-fm NHF

Salix Dancer

98 101

5-y-o b g Shareef Dancer (USA)-Willowbank (Gay Fandango (USA))

Pat Mitchell The Hamilton Partnership

Placings:03 (4237)

2001/02: 16^{0}S, 16^{3}GF

	Starts	1st	2nd	3rd	Win & Pl
Hurdles	2	0	0	1	394
Career Total	2	0	0	1	394

Going: Sf: 0-1 GS: 0-0 Gd: 0-0 GF: - Fm: 0-1
Distance: 2m/2m3: 0-2 2m4-2m7: 0-0 3m+: 0-0
Track: LH: 0-0 RH: 0-2 Tight: 0-0 Gall: 0-1
Aids: Bl: 0-0 Vi: 0-0 Tstrap: 0-0
Best Rating: 101 3/02 Hntg 2m110y gd-fm Hdl

Modest level of form over hurdles and an unlikely improver.

Sally Lightfoot

95 81

8-y-o ch m Derrylin-Vino Festa (Nebbiolo)

P T Dalton Miss Charlotte A I Perkins

Placings:*6/540*/03/P3530P (2416)

2001/02: 20^{P}GS, 20^{3}GF, 22^{5}GS, 17^{3}S, 20^{0}GS, 16^{P}HY

	Starts	1st	2nd	3rd	Win & Pl
Hurdles	6	0	0	2	675
Career Total	12	0	0	3	1213

Going: Sf: 0-2 GS: 0-3 Gd: 0-0 GF: - Fm: 0-1
Distance: 2m/2m3: 0-2 2m4-2m7: 0-4 3m+: 0-0
Track: LH: 0-4 RH: 0-2 Tight: 0-2 Gall: 0-1
Aids: Bl: 0-0 Vi: 0-0 Tstrap: 0-0
Best Rating: 90 3/99 Uttx 2m heavy NHF

No sign of ability until third at Huntingdon, although the form of the race does not look very strong. Stays two and a half miles.

Sally Scally

10-y-o ch m Scallywag-Petite Cone (Celtic Cone)

Miss Tina Jackson H L Thompson

Placings:3/*40666620P/6460*/PPP/6-2 (0070)

2001/02: 21^{2}G

	Starts	1st	2nd	3rd	Win & Pl
Chases	1	0	1	0	463
Career Total	19	0	2	1	1543

Going: Sf: 0-0 GS: 0-0 Gd: 0-1 GF: - Fm: 0-0
Distance: 2m/2m3: 0-0 2m4-2m7: 0-1 3m+: 0-0
Track: LH: 0-1 RH: 0-0 Tight: 0-1 Gall: 0-0
Aids: Bl: 0-0 Vi: 0-0 Tstrap: 0-0
Best Rating: 120 2/98 Winc 2m gd-fm Hdl

Modest hunter chaser, looks best at around two miles-five. Acts on a sound surface.

Sally's Twins

99(92h) (40h)74

9-y-o b m Dowsing (USA)-Bird Of Love (Ela-Mana-Mou)

A R Dicken D W Shaw

Placings:364/3660/P-644PP3 (4767)

2001/02: 20^{6}GF, 25^{4}GF, 24^{4}G, 27^{P}HY, 24^{P}S, 25^{3}GF

	Starts	1st	2nd	3rd	Win & Pl
Chases	6	0	0	1	821
Career Total	14	0	0	3	3059

Going: Sf: 0-2 GS: 0-0 Gd: 0-1 GF: - Fm: 0-3
Distance: 2m/2m3: 0-0 2m4-2m7: 0-1 3m+: 0-5
Track: LH: 0-4 RH: 0-2 Tight: 0-3 Gall: 0-0
Aids: Bl: 0-0 Vi: 0-0 Tstrap: 0-0
Best Rating: 99 12/96 Ling 2m110y gd-sft Hdl

Modest hurdler/chaser, suited by good to soft ground, has shown from on good to firm.

Salmon Cellar (IRE)

9-y-o ch g Roselier (FR)-Perfect Excuse (Certingo)

R Hollinshead George Graham (cumbria)

Placings:*50/40/0P60/03F004/5116PP*-PP (0870)

2001/02: 16^{P}GF, 20^{P}GS

	Starts	1st	2nd	3rd	Win & Pl
Chases	2	0	0	0	
Career Total	22	2	0	1	6881

109	6/00	Uttx	2m	E(0-105)HCh	GD	£3009
95	5/00	Hntg	2m4f110y	F(0-100)HCh	G-F	£3125

Total win prize-money £6136

Going: Sf: 0-0 GS: 0-1 Gd: 0-0 GF: - Fm: 0-1
Distance: 2m/2m3: 0-1 2m4-2m7: 0-1 3m+: 0-0
Track: LH: 0-2 RH: 0-0 Tight: 0-2 Gall: 0-0
Aids: Bl: 0-0 Vi: 0-0 Tstrap: 0-0
Best Rating: 109 6/00 Uttx 2m good Ch

Salmon Fly (IRE)

93 106

6-y-o b g Leading Counsel (USA)-Lola Sharp (Sharpen Up)

N J Henderson The Salmon Racing Partnership

Placings:*00*-4600 (4535)

2001/02: 17^{4}GS, 23^{6}S, 19^{0}S, 20^{0}G

	Starts	1st	2nd	3rd	Win & Pl
Hurdles	4	0	0	0	0
Career Total	6	0	0	0	0

Going: Sf: 0-2 GS: 0-1 Gd: 0-1 GF: - Fm: 0-0
Distance: 2m/2m3: 0-2 2m4-2m7: 0-1 3m+: 0-1
Track: LH: 0-4 RH: 0-0 Tight: 0-3 Gall: 0-1
Aids: Bl: 0-0 Vi: 0-0 Tstrap: 0-0
Best Rating: 106 3/02 Newb 2m3f soft Hdl

Modest, lightly raced hurdler. Seems suited by soft ground.

Saloup

101 87

4-y-o b f Wolfhound (USA)-Sarcita (Primo Dominie)

O Sherwood (M R Channon 11/7) Raymond Tooth

Placings:642 (4737)

2001/02: 16^{6}G, 16^{4}G, 16^{2}GF

	Starts	1st	2nd	3rd	Win & Pl
Hurdles	3	0	1	0	1163
Career Total	3	0	1	0	1163

Going: Sf: 0-0 GS: 0-0 Gd: 0-2 GF: - Fm: 0-1
Distance: 2m/2m3: 0-3 2m4-2m7: 0-0 3m+: 0-0
Track: LH: 0-0 RH: 0-3 Tight: 0-0 Gall: 0-0
Aids: Bl: 0-0 Vi: 0-0 Tstrap: 0-0
Best Rating: 87 4/02 Ludl 2m gd-fm Hdl

Stayed on quite nicely on her third run over hurdles.

Salt Hill King

70 37

5-y-o b g Rakaposhi King-Domtony (Martinmas)

N J Pomfret Peter Botham

Placings:0P (4594)

2001/02: 17^{0}GS, 16^{P}G

	Starts	1st	2nd	3rd	Win & Pl
Hurdles	2	0	0	0	
Career Total	2	0	0	0	

Going: Sf: 0-0 GS: 0-1 Gd: 0-1 GF: - Fm: 0-0
Distance: 2m/2m3: 0-2 2m4-2m7: 0-0 3m+: 0-0
Track: LH: 0-1 RH: 0-1 Tight: 0-1 Gall: 0-0
Aids: Bl: 0-0 Vi: 0-0 Tstrap: 0-0
Best Rating: 37 3/02 MRas 2m1f110y gd-sft Hdl

Saltis (IRE)

82(94c) (85c)37

10-y-o ch g Salt Dome (USA)-Mrs Tittlemouse (Nonoalco (USA))

Mrs Jane Galpin (A L Forbes 17/2) Mrs Jane Galpin

Placings:03320303/4354/0550F4/1 (4685)

2001/02: 16^{1}GF

	Starts	1st	2nd	3rd	Win & Pl
Chases	1	1	0	0	1908
Career Total	19	1	1	5	4584

85	4/02	Hrfd	2m	H Ch	G-F	£1907

Total win prize-money £1908

Going: Sf: 0-0 GS: 0-0 Gd: 0-0 GF: - Fm: 1-1
Distance: **2m/2m3: 1-1** 2m4-2m7: 0-0 3m+: 0-0
Track: LH: 0-0 **RH: 1-1** Tight: 0-0 Gall: 0-0
Aids: Bl: 0-0 Vi: 0-0 Tstrap: 0-0
Best Rating: 85 4/02 Hrfd 2m gd-fm Ch

Acts on the top of the ground and won a two-mile hunter chase in April 2002. Probably best at around two and a half miles.

Salvage

98(103h) (100h)110

7-y-o b g Kahyasi-Storm Weaver (USA) (Storm Bird (CAN))

Mrs D Thomson Bill Sneddon

Placings:031/33/254P23B4-344P535 (4879)

2001/02: 16^{3}GF, 20^{4}S, 20^{4}GF, 18^{P}HY, 17^{5}G, 16^{3}GF, 16^{5}G

	Starts	1st	2nd	3rd	Win & Pl
Hurdles	7	0	0	2	1885
Career Total	**20**	**1**	**2**	**6**	**9222**

93	4/99	Carl	2m1f	E Hdl	GD	£2612

Total win prize-money £2612

Going: Sf: 0-2 GS: 0-0 Gd: 0-2 GF: - Fm: 0-3
Distance: 2m/2m3: 0-5 2m4-2m7: 0-2 3m+: 0-0
Track: LH: 0-3 RH: 0-4 Tight: 0-2 Gall: 0-0
Aids: Bl: 0-0 Vi: 0-0 Tstrap: 0-0
Best Rating: 105 9/00 Prth 2m110y heavy Hdl

Modest hurdler/chaser, suited by fast ground.

Salvo

101(84h) (75h)108

11-y-o ch g K-Battery-Saleander (Leander)
Miss M Bragg W H Whitley

Placings:*000*/12352/**U**/**F5**/045613 **(2925)**
2001/02: 19^{0}GF, 19^{4}GS, 24^{5}GF, 19^{6}GF, 19^{1}GS, 19^{3}GS

	Starts	1st	2nd	3rd	Win & Pl
Hurdles	3	0	0	0	0
Chases	3	1	0	1	3933
Career Total	**17**	**2**	**2**	**2**	**7516**

108	12/01	Tntn	2m3f	F(0-110)HCh	G-S	£3444
	10/95	Hexm	2m	E Hdl	G-F	£2127

Total win prize-money £5572

Going: Sf: 0-0 GS: 1-3 Gd: 0-0 GF: - Fm: 0-3
Distance: **2m/2m3: 1-4** 2m4-2m7: 0-1 3m+: 0-1
Track: LH: 0-0 **RH: 1-6 Tight: 1-2** Gall: 0-0
Aids: Bl: 0-0 Vi: 0-0 Tstrap: 0-0
Best Rating: 108 12/01 Tntn 2m3f gd-sft Ch

Modest, lightly-raced hurdler/chaser. Showed his best form over fences when scoring at Taunton on December 2001. Seems to act on any ground.

Sam Quale (IRE)

101(95h) 133

10-y-o ch g Tale Quale-Samanthabrownthorn (Mandalus)
B Ellison E J Berry

Placings:0/1241UP-U1FF504 **(4775)**
2001/02: 21^{U}S, 22^{1}S, 21^{F}G, 24^{F}HY, 20^{5}GS, 25^{0}GF, 22^{4}G

	Starts	1st	2nd	3rd	Win & Pl
Chases	7	1	0	0	4739
Career Total	**14**	**3**	**1**	**0**	**13151**

133	12/01	MRas	2m6f110y	F(0-110)HCh	SFT	£4208
133	2/01	Newc	2m4f	E Ch	HVY	£3620
115	10/00	Sthl	3m110y	E Ch	SFT	£3612

Total win prize-money £11441

Going: Sf: 1-3 GS: 0-1 Gd: 0-2 GF: - Fm: 0-1
Distance: 2m/2m3: 0-0 **2m4-2m7: 1-5** 3m+: 0-2
Track: LH: 0-3 **RH: 1-4 Tight: 1-3** Gall: 0-1
Aids: Bl: 0-1 **Vi: 1-5** Tstrap: 0-0
Best Rating: 133 12/01 MRas 2m6f110y soft Ch

Soft-ground handicap chaser. Stays two and three-quarter miles.

Sam Rockett

101 92

9-y-o b g Petong-Art Deco (Artaius (USA))
P J Hobbs L G Kennard

Placings:600100/2114126/**3P**/**F**00040/605**4**552114-0040124 **(1152)**
2001/02: 27^{0}G, 22^{0}G, 22^{4}GF, 22^{0}GF, 27^{1}G, 22^{2}G, 22^{4}GF

	Starts	1st	2nd	3rd	Win & Pl
Hurdles	7	1	1	0	3795
Career Total	**38**	**7**	**4**	**1**	**20336**

92	8/01	NAbb	3m3f	F(0-105)HHdl	GD	£2961
91	9/00	Hrfd	3m2f	E(0-115)HHdl	G-F	£3090
90	8/00	Font	2m4f	F(0-100)HHdl	G-F	£2289
104	11/97	NAbb	2m1f	E(0-110)HHdl	G-F	£2253
91	9/97	NAbb	2m1f	G Hdl	GD	£1784
100	8/97	NAbb	2m1f	G(0-95)HHdl	G-F	£1860
80	1/97	Tntn	2m1f	G Hdl	G-F	£1857

Total win prize-money £16098

Going: Sf: 0-0 GS: 0-0 Gd: 1-4 GF: - Fm: 0-3
Distance: 2m/2m3: 0-0 2m4-2m7: 0-5 **3m+: 1-2**
Track: **LH: 1-7** RH: 0-0 **Tight: 1-7** Gall: 0-0
Aids: **Bl: 1-7** Vi: 0-0 Tstrap: 0-0
Best Rating: 104 11/97 NAbb 2m1f gd-fm Hdl

Low grade handicap hurdler. Needs marathon distances these days. Acts on ground good or faster.

Sam's Profiles

(89h) (65h)

8-y-o b g Infantry-Lady De-Lacy (Pitpan)
Miss K M George Exterior Profiles Ltd

Placings:6-55P **(4501)**
2001/02: 24^{5}HY, 21^{5}HY, 27^{P}G

	Starts	1st	2nd	3rd	Win & Pl
Hurdles	3	0	0	0	0
Career Total	**4**	**0**	**0**	**0**	**0**

Going: Sf: 0-2 GS: 0-0 Gd: 0-1 GF: - Fm: 0-0
Distance: 2m/2m3: 0-0 2m4-2m7: 0-1 3m+: 0-2
Track: LH: 0-3 RH: 0-0 Tight: 0-2 Gall: 0-0
Aids: Bl: 0-0 Vi: 0-0 Tstrap: 0-0
Best Rating: 87 1/01 Extr 2m1f heavy Hdl

Samakaan (IRE)

107 140

9-y-o b g Darshaan-Samarzana (USA) (Blushing Groom (FR))
Miss Venetia Williams Lady Harris

Placings:4/11U120/**11112**/**500-0P5336** **(4845)**
2001/02: 20^{0}G, 20^{P}S, 19^{5}G, 20^{3}S, 19^{3}S, 24^{6}G

	Starts	1st	2nd	3rd	Win & Pl
Chases	6	0	0	2	2106
Career Total	**21**	**7**	**2**	**2**	**71145**

157	3/00	Chel	2m110y	B HCh	G-F	£32500
153	3/00	Newb	2m2f110y	D Ch	SFT	£5978
145	2/00	Font	2m4f	D Ch	SFT	£4043
138	2/00	Folk	2m	D Ch	GD	£3926
127	4/99	Weth	2m	D Hdl	GD	£3127
127	2/99	Hayd	2m	D Hdl	SFT	£2970
124	1/99	Weth	2m	E Hdl	SFT	£2390

Total win prize-money £54935

Going: Sf: 0-3 GS: 0-0 Gd: 0-3 GF: - Fm: 0-0
Distance: 2m/2m3: 0-0 2m4-2m7: 0-5 3m+: 0-1
Track: LH: 0-5 RH: 0-1 Tight: 0-1 Gall: 0-3
Aids: Bl: 0-0 Vi: 0-0 Tstrap: 0-0
Best Rating: 160 4/00 Aint 2m good Ch

He stamped himself as a very promising performer when an easy winner of the Grand Annual at Cheltenham in the 1999/2000 season. Lightly raced in the 2000/2001 season due to breathing problems, his jumping was far from fluent and he failed to make the frame. He returned to action after a break in November 2001, but took a while to show anything and despite slipping down the ratings continues out of form.

Samarardo

99 84

5-y-o b g Son Pardo-Kinlet Vision (IRE) (Vision (USA))
L A Dace (N P Littmoden 5/1) Trojan Racing

Placings:0400 **(3987)**
2001/02: 16^{0}G, 16^{4}G, 22^{0}HY, 19^{0}S

	Starts	1st	2nd	3rd	Win & Pl
Hurdles	4	0	0	0	
Career Total	**4**	**0**	**0**	**0**	

Going: Sf: 0-2 GS: 0-0 Gd: 0-2 GF: - Fm: 0-0
Distance: 2m/2m3: 0-2 2m4-2m7: 0-2 3m+: 0-0
Track: LH: 0-2 RH: 0-2 Tight: 0-2 Gall: 0-1
Aids: Bl: 0-0 Vi: 0-0 Tstrap: 0-0
Best Rating: 84 12/01 Donc 2m110y good Hdl

Samata One (IRE)

7-y-o b g River Falls-Abadila (IRE) (Shernazar)
Jean-Rene Auvray Mrs N J G Green

Placings:PP **(0976)**
2001/02: 16^{P}GF, 16^{P}GF

	Starts	1st	2nd	3rd	Win & Pl
Hurdles	2	0	0	0	
Career Total	**2**	**0**	**0**	**0**	

Going: Sf: 0-0 GS: 0-0 Gd: 0-0 GF: - Fm: 0-2
Distance: 2m/2m3: 0-2 2m4-2m7: 0-0 3m+: 0-0
Track: LH: 0-2 RH: 0-0 Tight: 0-2 Gall: 0-0
Aids: Bl: 0-0 Vi: 0-0 Tstrap: 0-0
Best Rating:

Samba Sharply

99

11-y-o b g Rambo Dancer (CAN)-Sharper Still (Sharpen Up)
R M Flower Ian Clements

Placings:223/P2-UP **(1943)**
2001/02: 16^{U}G, 16^{P}GS

	Starts	1st	2nd	3rd	Win & Pl
Hurdles	2	0	0	0	
Career Total	**7**	**0**	**3**	**1**	**2600**

Going: Sf: 0-0 GS: 0-1 Gd: 0-1 GF: - Fm: 0-0
Distance: 2m/2m3: 0-2 2m4-2m7: 0-0 3m+: 0-0
Track: LH: 0-1 RH: 0-1 Tight: 0-1 Gall: 0-1
Aids: Bl: 0-0 Vi: 0-0 Tstrap: 0-2
Best Rating: 99 4/01 Plum 2m heavy Hdl

Sambolero (FR)

5-y-o gr g Round Sovereign (FR)-Havamira (FR) (Nice Havrais (USA))
P F Nicholls Allan Stennett & Terry Warner

Placings:0/56602624-0 **(3929)**
2001/02: 16^{0}HY

	Starts	1st	2nd	3rd	Win & Pl
Hurdles	1	0	0	0	
Career Total	**10**	**0**	**2**	**0**	**16818**

Going: Sf: 0-1 GS: 0-0 Gd: 0-0 GF: - Fm: 0-0
Distance: 2m/2m3: 0-1 2m4-2m7: 0-0 3m+: 0-0
Track: LH: 0-1 RH: 0-0 Tight: 0-1 Gall: 0-0
Aids: Bl: 0-0 Vi: 0-0 Tstrap: 0-0
Best Rating:

Sameeah (IRE)

52

6-y-o br m Perugino (USA)-Kayrava (Irish River (FR))
Miss J Feilden Hoofbeats Racing Club

Placings:0 **(1755)**
2001/02: 16^{0}GS

	Starts	1st	2nd	3rd	Win & Pl
Hurdles	1	0	0	0	
Career Total	**1**	**0**	**0**	**0**	

Going: Sf: 0-0 GS: 0-1 Gd: 0-0 GF: - Fm: 0-0
Distance: 2m/2m3: 0-1 2m4-2m7: 0-0 3m+: 0-0
Track: LH: 0-1 RH: 0-0 Tight: 0-1 Gall: 0-0
Aids: Bl: 0-0 Vi: 0-0 Tstrap: 0-0
Best Rating:

Sammorello (IRE)

(87h) (43h)

11-y-o b g Mandalus-Cherry Park (Netherkelly)
D G Bridgwater Mrs S A Macechern

Placings:*63*6001P215/P4**23511P/2/33PF/PF**-0P **(0839)**
2001/02: 22^{0}GF, 23^{P}G

	Starts	1st	2nd	3rd	Win & Pl
Hurdles	1	0	0	0	0
Chases	1	0	0	0	0
Career Total	**27**	**4**	**3**	**4**	**14431**

99	3/98	Hntg	3m	F(0-105)HCh	GD	£2665
97	2/98	Hntg	3m	E(0-110)HCh	GD	£3270
82	3/97	Ludl	3m2f110y	E(0-105)HHdl	G-F	£2190
72	2/97	Hrfd	3m2f	E Hdl	SFT	£1871

Total win prize-money £9997

Going: Sf: 0-0 GS: 0-0 Gd: 0-1 GF: - Fm: 0-1
Distance: 2m/2m3: 0-0 2m4-2m7: 0-1 3m+: 0-1
Track: LH: 0-2 RH: 0-0 Tight: 0-1 Gall: 0-0
Aids: Bl: 0-1 Vi: 0-1 Tstrap: 0-0
Best Rating: 105 2/00 Fknm 3m110y good Ch

Sammy Samba

4-y-o b g Be My Chief (USA)-Peggy Spencer (Formidable (USA))
C W Thornton Guy Reed

Placings:*3* **(3354)**
2001/02: 16^{3}G

	Starts	1st	2nd	3rd	Win & Pl
NH Flat	1	0	0	1	227
Career Total	**1**	**0**	**0**	**1**	**227**

Going: Sf: 0-0 GS: 0-0 Gd: 0-1 GF: - Fm: 0-0
Distance: 2m/2m3: 0-1 2m4-2m7: 0-0 3m+: 0-0
Track: LH: 0-0 RH: 0-1 Tight: 0-1 Gall: 0-0
Aids: Bl: 0-0 Vi: 0-0 Tstrap: 0-0
Best Rating: 88 1/02 Muss 2m good NHF

Third on his debut in a bumper for Chris Thornton. Successful on next start for Philip Hobbs at Newton Abbot July 2002 but pulled up on his hurdling debut.

Samon (GER)

119 **141**

5-y-o ch g Monsun (GER)-Savanna (GER) (Sassafras (FR))
M C Pipe The Macca & Growler Partnership

Placings:10 **(4229)**
2001/02: 17^{1}S, 21^{0}GS

	Starts	1st	2nd	3rd	Win & Pl
Hurdles	2	1	0	0	3033
Career Total	**2**	**1**	**0**	**0**	**3033**

141	1/02	Tntn	2m1f	E Hdl	SFT	£3033

Total win prize-money £3033

Going: Sf: 1-1 GS: 0-1 Gd: 0-0 GF: - Fm: 0-0
Distance: **2m/2m3: 1-1** 2m4-2m7: 0-1 3m+: 0-0
Track: LH: 0-1 **RH: 1-1 Tight: 1-1** Gall: 0-1
Aids: Bl: 0-0 Vi: 0-0 Tstrap: 0-0
Best Rating: 141 1/02 Tntn 2m1f soft Hdl

Winner on the Flat on Germany, he got off the mark over hurdles on his first attempt at Taunton beating subsequent winner Isio.Well beaten at the Festival in 2002. Acts on soft ground.

Samsaam (IRE)

96 **108**

5-y-o b g Sadler's Wells (USA)-Azyaa (Kris)
M C Pipe (J L Dunlop 28/9) Matt Archer & Miss Jean Broadhurst

Placings:41P **(4530)**
2001/02: 16^{4}GS, 16^{1}G, 20^{P}GS

	Starts	1st	2nd	3rd	Win & Pl
Hurdles	3	1	0	0	2758
Career Total	**3**	**1**	**0**	**0**	**2758**

108	3/02	Winc	2m	E Hdl	GD	£2758

Total win prize-money £2758

Going: Sf: 0-0 GS: 0-2 Gd: 1-1 GF: - Fm: 0-0
Distance: **2m/2m3: 1-2** 2m4-2m7: 0-1 3m+: 0-0
Track: LH: 0-1 **RH: 1-2** Tight: 0-0 Gall: 0-0
Aids: **Bl: 1-3** Vi: 0-0 Tstrap: 0-0
Best Rating: 108 3/02 Winc 2m good Hdl

A Group Three winner on the Flat for John Dunlop, he raced a shade too keenly when fourth on his hurdles bow but scored next time out when hold-up tactics were employed. Pulled up as if something was amiss next time. Has won over two miles but should stay further. Acts on good/good to soft ground.

Samuel Wilderspin

113 **150**

10-y-o b g Henbit (USA)-Littoral (Crash Course)
R Lee Stella Barnes And Steve Smith

Placings:*106*/321143/**6122P1/130/24P130-1512FP** **(4839)**
2001/02: 24^{1}G, 25^{5}G, 24^{1}HY, 26^{2}GS, 36^{F}G, 33^{P}G

	Starts	1st	2nd	3rd	Win & Pl
Chases	6	2	1	0	24741
Career Total	**30**	**9**	**5**	**4**	**73963**

150	2/02	Hayd	3m	B(0-140)HCh	HVY	£9653
150	11/01	Chel	3m110y	E(0-135)HCh	GD	£8736
146	2/01	Weth	3m1f	C(0-135)HCh	SFT	£6780
136	5/99	Towc	3m1f	E Ch	SFT	£3156
125	4/99	Wwck	3m2f	D Ch	SFT	£4465
122	1/99	Wwck	2m4f110y	D Ch	SFT	£4695
134	2/98	Wwck	2m4f110y	B Hdl	GD	£6807
111	1/98	Donc	2m4f	D Hdl	GD	£4136
116	2/97	Wwck	2m	H NHF	GD	£1028

Total win prize-money £49461

Going: Sf: 1-1 GS: 0-1 Gd: 1-4 GF: - Fm: 0-0
Distance: 2m/2m3: 0-0 2m4-2m7: 0-0 **3m+: 2-6**
Track: **LH: 2-6** RH: 0-0 Tight: 0-1 **Gall: 1-3**
Aids: Bl: 0-0 Vi: 0-0 **Tstrap: 2-6**
Best Rating: 150 3/02 Donc 3m2f gd-sft Ch

He has a history of breaking blood-vessels but did well for his new trainer in the 2000/2001 season. Probably best around three miles, he can carry his head awkwardly but is genuine. Won an amateur riders' chase at Cheltenham in November 2001 and a handicap chase at Haydock in February. Runner-up in Doncaster's Great Yorkshire Chase, but was an early faller in the Grand National and pulled up in the Scottish version. Stays well and acts on soft ground. Runs well fresh.

San Dimas (USA)

101 **88**

5-y-o gr g Distant View (USA)-Chrystophard (USA) (Lypheor)
R Allan (Andrew Turnell 8/9) Mrs R P Aggio

Placings:4-4P4026033 **(1745)**
2001/02: 16^{4}GF, 16^{P}GS, 17^{4}GF, 21^{0}G, 16^{2}GF, 17^{6}GF, 16^{0}GF, 22^{3}G, 22^{3}GS

	Starts	1st	2nd	3rd	Win & Pl
Hurdles	9	0	1	2	1228
Career Total	**10**	**0**	**1**	**2**	**1228**

Going: Sf: 0-0 GS: 0-2 Gd: 0-2 GF: - Fm: 0-5
Distance: 2m/2m3: 0-6 2m4-2m7: 0-3 3m+: 0-0
Track: LH: 0-7 RH: 0-2 Tight: 0-7 Gall: 0-0
Aids: Bl: 0-1 Vi: 0-3 Tstrap: 0-0
Best Rating: 88 10/01 Kels 2m6f110y gd-sft Hdl

San Francisco

107 **111**

8-y-o b g Aragon-Sirene Bleu Marine (USA) (Secreto (USA))
A C Whillans C Bird

Placings:32030/00213/2**5534/P04133U3052-3466110F3** **(4876)**
2001/02: 20^{3}GS, 20^{4}GF, 22^{6}HY, 19^{6}S, 16^{1}HY, 16^{1}S, 16^{0}HY, 21^{F}G, 20^{3}G

	Starts	1st	2nd	3rd	Win & Pl
Chases	9	2	0	2	9820
Career Total	**35**	**4**	**4**	**9**	**23755**

109	3/02	Ayr	2m	F(0-95)HCh	SFT	£2936
99	3/02	Ayr	2m	F(0-95)HCh	HVY	£4273
104	12/00	Newc	2m110y	F(0-90)Ch	SFT	£2380
99	3/99	Ayr	2m	D(0-110)HHdl	SFT	£2882

Total win prize-money £12473

Going: Sf: 2-5 GS: 0-1 Gd: 0-2 GF: - Fm: 0-1
Distance: **2m/2m3: 2-3** 2m4-2m7: 0-6 3m+: 0-0
Track: **LH: 2-5** RH: 0-3 Tight: 0-1 Gall: 0-2
Aids: Bl: 0-0 Vi: 0-0 **Tstrap: 2-8**
Best Rating: 113 2/01 Kels 2m1f soft Ch

Moderate handicap chaser, he handles testing ground and is best at around two miles.

San Giorgio

97 **87**

13-y-o b g Lighter-Gold Willow (Goldfella)
P Kelsall Peter Kelsall

Placings:*0*/P32P/1216**04U/4P**23/20/260/053045300-0003503 **(2574)**
2001/02: 21^{0}GF, 19^{0}G, 26^{0}G, 26^{3}G, 24^{5}S, 24^{0}GF, 24^{3}HY

	Starts	1st	2nd	3rd	Win & Pl
Hurdles	7	0	0	2	1074
Career Total	**37**	**2**	**5**	**6**	**14159**

90	11/95	Chel	3m1f110y	B HHdl	G-S	£4856
75	9/95	Worc	3m	F Hdl	G-F	£1996

Total win prize-money £6852

Going: Sf: 0-2 GS: 0-0 Gd: 0-3 GF: - Fm: 0-2

Distance: 2m/2m3: 0-0 2m4-2m7: 0-2 3m+: 0-5
Track: LH: 0-0 RH: 0-7 Tight: 0-0 Gall: 0-3
Aids: Bl: 0-2 Vi: 0-0 Tstrap: 0-0
Best Rating: 102 10/98 Hntg 3m2f good Hdl

San Marino (IRE)

87f 88f

6-y-o b g Torus-Lousion (Lucifer (USA))
Miss Venetia Williams P Ryan

Placings:4 (1813)
2001/02: 16^4S

	Starts	1st	2nd	3rd	Win & Pl
NH Flat	1	0	0	0	0
Career Total	**1**	**0**	**0**	**0**	**0**

Going: Sf: 0-1 GS: 0-0 Gd: 0-0 GF: - Fm: 0-0
Distance: 2m/2m3: 0-1 2m4-2m7: 0-0 3m+: 0-0
Track: LH: 0-1 RH: 0-0 Tight: 0-1 Gall: 0-0
Aids: Bl: 0-0 Vi: 0-0 Tstrap: 0-0
Best Rating: 88 10/01 Fknm 2m soft NHF

San Peire (FR)

87 83

5-y-o b g Cyborg (FR)-Shakapoura (FR) (Shakapour)
J Howard Johnson Comtake-Welding Engineering Specialists

Placings:0605 (4894)
2001/02: 17^0GF, 16^6G, 16^0GS, 16^5G

	Starts	1st	2nd	3rd	Win & Pl
NH Flat	1	0	0	0	0
Hurdles	3	0	0	0	0
Career Total	**4**	**0**	**0**	**0**	**0**

Going: Sf: 0-0 GS: 0-1 Gd: 0-2 GF: - Fm: 0-1
Distance: 2m/2m3: 0-4 2m4-2m7: 0-0 3m+: 0-0
Track: LH: 0-1 RH: 0-2 Tight: 0-2 Gall: 0-0
Aids: Bl: 0-0 Vi: 0-0 Tstrap: 0-0
Best Rating: 83 1/02 Muss 2m good Hdl

Sandabar

104 97

9-y-o b g Green Desert (USA)-Children's Corner (FR) (Top Ville)
N Waggott Mrs J Waggott

Placings:2600002/1223111/145/24-03362613000 (1461)
2001/02: 17^0G, 16^3F, 16^3GF, 16^6G, 16^2GF, 16^6GF, 17^1GF, 19^3GF, 16^0G, 16^0GF, 16^0G

	Starts	1st	2nd	3rd	Win & Pl
Hurdles	11	1	1	3	5046
Career Total	**30**	**6**	**6**	**4**	**21423**

97	7/01	Sedg	2m1f	F(0-105)HHdl	G-F	£1928
126	5/99	Weth	2m	D(0-120)HHdl	GD	£2786
116	9/98	Prth	2m110y	D Hdl	GD	£2788
113	9/98	Sedg	2m1f	F(0-105)HHdl	GD	£1954
104	8/98	Prth	2m110y	D Hdl	G-F	£2762
109	5/98	Kels	2m110y	E(0-105)HHdl	G-F	£1738

Total win prize-money £13958

Going: Sf: 0-0 GS: 0-0 Gd: 0-4 GF: - Fm: 1-7
Distance: **2m/2m3: 1-10** 2m4-2m7: 0-1 3m+: 0-0
Track: **LH: 1-6** RH: 0-5 **Tight: 1-6** Gall: 0-1
Aids: Bl: 0-0 Vi: 0-0 **Tstrap: 1-11**
Best Rating: 126 5/99 Weth 2m good Hdl

Sandbaggedagain

(99h) (79h)

8-y-o b g Prince Daniel (USA)-Paircullis (Tower Walk)
M W Easterby Mrs Joan Burnett & Steve Hull

Placings:66/60/6-5U (0917)
2001/02: 17^5GF, 21^UG

	Starts	1st	2nd	3rd	Win & Pl
Hurdles	1	0	0	0	0
Chases	1	0	0	0	0
Career Total	**7**	**0**	**0**	**0**	**0**

Going: Sf: 0-0 GS: 0-0 Gd: 0-1 GF: - Fm: 0-1
Distance: 2m/2m3: 0-1 2m4-2m7: 0-1 3m+: 0-0
Track: LH: 0-1 RH: 0-1 Tight: 0-2 Gall: 0-0
Aids: Bl: 0-0 Vi: 0-0 Tstrap: 0-0
Best Rating: 79 6/01 MRas 2m1f110y gd-fm Hdl

Sandholes (IRE)

111 104+

6-y-o gr m Tirol-Caroline Lady (JPN) (Caro)
Miss Lucinda V Russell Mrs Edith S Russell

Placings:662/2212-P40 (4879)
2001/02: 20^PS, 16^4GF, 16^0G

	Starts	1st	2nd	3rd	Win & Pl
Hurdles	3	0	0	0	276
Career Total	**10**	**1**	**4**	**0**	**6114**

90	8/00	Slig	2m	Hdl	YLD	£2760

Total win prize-money £2760

Going: Sf: 0-1 GS: 0-0 Gd: 0-1 GF: - Fm: 0-1
Distance: 2m/2m3: 0-2 2m4-2m7: 0-1 3m+: 0-0
Track: LH: 0-2 RH: 0-1 Tight: 0-1 Gall: 0-0
Aids: Bl: 0-0 Vi: 0-0 Tstrap: 0-0
Best Rating: 99 8/00 Uttx 2m gd-fm Hdl

Modest ex-Irish hurdler, won over the minimum trip on easy ground in August 2000 and went missing from then until spring 2002. Seems to handle any ground.

Sandles

92 74

4-y-o b g Komaite (USA)-Miss Calculate (Mummy's Game)
Miss K M George (K R Burke 5/12) Exterior Profiles Ltd

Placings:P00P6 (4866)
2001/02: 17^PS, 17^0S, 17^0S, 17^PS, 17^6F

	Starts	1st	2nd	3rd	Win & Pl
Hurdles	5	0	0	0	0
Career Total	**5**	**0**	**0**	**0**	**0**

Going: Sf: 0-4 GS: 0-0 Gd: 0-0 GF: - Fm: 0-1
Distance: 2m/2m3: 0-5 2m4-2m7: 0-0 3m+: 0-0
Track: LH: 0-0 RH: 0-5 Tight: 0-4 Gall: 0-0
Aids: Bl: 0-0 Vi: 0-0 Tstrap: 0-0
Best Rating: 74 1/02 Tntn 2m1f soft Hdl

Sandoran

103(101h) (99h)113

9-y-o b g Gildoran-Party Miss (West Partisan)
M Hill Double A Thoroughbreds

Placings:05400/F5PF4446F241/0P4151016/6526203-24023225 (3703)
2001/02: 21^2GF, 21^4G, 21^0G, 21^2HY, 19^3GS, 19^2S, 24^2S, 19^5HY

	Starts	1st	2nd	3rd	Win & Pl
Hurdles	1	0	1	0	741
Chases	7	0	3	1	4619
Career Total	**41**	**4**	**7**	**2**	**21469**

106	3/00	NAbb	2m6f	D(0-125)HHdl	GD	£2919
101	2/00	Tntn	2m3f110y	E(0-115)HHdl	SFT	£3073
96	1/00	Tntn	2m3f110y	F(0-105)HHdl	G-S	£2506
98	4/99	Extr	2m1f110y	E(0-105)HHdl	SFT	£2276

Total win prize-money £10775

Going: Sf: 0-4 GS: 0-1 Gd: 0-2 GF: - Fm: 0-1
Distance: 2m/2m3: 0-3 2m4-2m7: 0-4 3m+: 0-1
Track: LH: 0-4 RH: 0-4 Tight: 0-7 Gall: 0-0
Aids: Bl: 0-0 Vi: 0-2 Tstrap: 0-0
Best Rating: 113 1/02 Tntn 2m3f soft Ch

Fair chaser, stays two miles-six although effective at shorter. Handles any ground.

Sandros Boy

73 28

5-y-o b g Alhijaz-Bearnaise (IRE) (Cyrano De Bergerac)
Mrs N Macauley Mrs N Macauley

Placings:0-0 (1099)
2001/02: 19^0GF

	Starts	1st	2nd	3rd	Win & Pl
Hurdles	1	0	0	0	
Career Total	**2**	**0**	**0**	**0**	

Going: Sf: 0-0 GS: 0-0 Gd: 0-0 GF: - Fm: 0-1
Distance: 2m/2m3: 0-0 2m4-2m7: 0-1 3m+: 0-0
Track: LH: 0-0 RH: 0-1 Tight: 0-1 Gall: 0-0
Aids: Bl: 0-0 Vi: 0-0 Tstrap: 0-0
Best Rating: 28 8/01 MRas 2m3f110y gd-fm Hdl

Sands Rising

82f

5-y-o b g Primitive Rising (USA)-Celtic Sands (Celtic Cone)
R Johnson T L A Robson

Placings:00 (3550)
2001/02: 16^0S, 16^0S

	Starts	1st	2nd	3rd	Win & Pl
NH Flat	2	0	0	0	
Career Total	**2**	**0**	**0**	**0**	

Going: Sf: 0-2 GS: 0-0 Gd: 0-0 GF: - Fm: 0-0
Distance: 2m/2m3: 0-2 2m4-2m7: 0-0 3m+: 0-0
Track: LH: 0-0 RH: 0-0 Tight: 0-0 Gall: 0-0
Aids: Bl: 0-0 Vi: 0-0 Tstrap: 0-0
Best Rating: 82 1/02 Newc 2m soft NHF

Sandy Duff

104 137

8-y-o ch g Scottish Reel-Not Enough (Balinger)
P R Webber Michael H Watt

Placings:10/211P/2336P-113502 (4780)
2001/02: 16^1GF, 16^1G, 16^3G, 16^5GS, 16^0G, 17^2GF

	Starts	1st	2nd	3rd	Win & Pl
Chases	6	2	1	1	11407
Career Total	**17**	**5**	**3**	**3**	**24320**

137	10/01	Sthl	2m	E Ch	GD	£3357
121	5/01	Ling	2m	E Ch	G-F	£3549
121	1/00	Donc	2m110y	E Hdl	GD	£2814
121	12/99	Folk	2m1f110y	E Hdl	SFT	£2512
116	1/99	Ludl	2m	H NHF	SFT	£1546

Total win prize-money £13779

Going: Sf: 0-0 GS: 0-1 Gd: 1-3 GF: - Fm: 1-2
Distance: **2m/2m3: 2-6** 2m4-2m7: 0-0 3m+: 0-0
Track: **LH: 2-5** RH: 0-1 **Tight: 2-4** Gall: 0-1
Aids: Bl: 0-0 Vi: 0-1 Tstrap: 0-0
Best Rating: 143 12/00 Kemp 2m gd-sft Ch

A rangy type, he chased home Monsignor on his hurdling debut in 1999 before landing a couple of ordinary events. Switched to fences last season, he performed well without winning over the minimum trip. Got off the mark early in the 2001/2002 season on fast ground at Lingfield, before following up on good ground at Southwell. Held by the better novices. Suited by two miles and a sound surface.

Sandywell George

100 **76**

7-y-o ch g Zambrano-Farmcote Air (True Song)
L P Grassick David Lloyd & Mrs Carole Lloyd

Placings:*0/004*P-P603P **(4817)**
2001/02: 20^{P}F, 21^{6}S, 20^{0}GS, 24^{3}G, 24^{P}GF

	Starts	1st	2nd	3rd	Win & Pl
Hurdles	5	0	0	1	454
Career Total	**10**	**0**	**0**	**1**	**454**

Going: Sf: 0-1 GS: 0-1 Gd: 0-1 GF: - Fm: 0-2
Distance: 2m/2m3: 0-0 2m4-2m7: 0-3 3m+: 0-2
Track: LH: 0-3 RH: 0-0 Tight: 0-1 Gall: 0-0
Aids: Bl: 0-0 Vi: 0-0 Tstrap: 0-1
Best Rating: 87 1/01 Chep 2m110y gd-sft NHF

Poor form over hurdles.

Sankt Moritz (GER)

107 **132**

8-y-o b m Caerwent-Sunset Lady (GER) (Nebos (GER))
Josef Vana Ii Stal Helmut Schoch

Placings:11220/1542563 **(2665)**
2001/02: 21^{1}S, 25^{5}G, 25^{4}G, 29^{2}GF, 34^{5}GF, 31^{6}G, 31^{3}GS

	Starts	1st	2nd	3rd	Win & Pl
Chases	7	1	1	1	15134
Career Total	**12**	**3**	**3**	**1**	**17739**

5/01	Brem	2m5f	Ch		SFT	£6515
7/98	Aabe	2m1f	Hdl		GD	£1689
6/98	Hlub	2m1f	Ch		SFT	£174

Total win prize-money £8378

Going: Sf: 1-1 GS: 0-1 Gd: 0-3 GF: - Fm: 0-2
Distance: 2m/2m3: 0-0 **2m4-2m7: 1-1** 3m+: 0-6
Track: LH: 0-4 RH: 0-0 Tight: 0-0 Gall: 0-0
Aids: Bl: 0-0 Vi: 0-0 Tstrap: 0-0
Best Rating: 132 12/01 Chel 3m7f gd-sft Ch

Useful Czech-trained chaser, acts well with cut in the ground.

Santa Court

92(80h) **91**

7-y-o b g Be My Native (USA)-Christmas Show (Petorius)
R Dickin The Tenners Partnership

Placings:060/2206426/0134-0023 **(4773)**
2001/02: 16^{0}S, 16^{0}S, 19^{2}S, 25^{3}G

	Starts	1st	2nd	3rd	Win & Pl
Hurdles	1	0	0	0	0
Chases	3	0	1	1	2171
Career Total	**18**	**1**	**4**	**2**	**6579**

95	6/00	Worc	3m	F(0-100)HHdl	GD	£1939

Total win prize-money £1939

Going: Sf: 0-3 GS: 0-0 Gd: 0-1 GF: - Fm: 0-0
Distance: 2m/2m3: 0-3 2m4-2m7: 0-0 3m+: 0-1
Track: LH: 0-1 RH: 0-3 Tight: 0-2 Gall: 0-0
Aids: Bl: 0-0 Vi: 0-0 Tstrap: 0-0
Best Rating: 95 7/00 Worc 3m gd-fm Hdl

Winning hurdler/modest novice chaser, best on a sound surface. Stays three miles.

Santa Lucia

104 **96**

6-y-o b m Namaqualand (USA)-Villasanta (Corvaro (USA))
M Dods J A Wynn-Williams

Placings:F-60241 **(4874)**
2001/02: 17^{6}GS, 17^{0}GS, 20^{2}GS, 20^{4}GF, 20^{1}G

	Starts	1st	2nd	3rd	Win & Pl
Hurdles	5	1	1	0	4714
Career Total	**6**	**1**	**1**	**0**	**4714**

96	4/02	Prth	2m4f110y	D Hdl	GD	£3718

Total win prize-money £3718

Going: Sf: 0-0 GS: 0-3 Gd: 1-1 GF: - Fm: 0-1
Distance: 2m/2m3: 0-2 **2m4-2m7: 1-3** 3m+: 0-0
Track: LH: 0-1 **RH: 1-3** Tight: 0-1 Gall: 0-0
Aids: Bl: 0-0 Vi: 0-0 Tstrap: 0-0
Best Rating: 100 10/00 Hexm 2m heavy Hdl

Modest hurdler, suited by fast ground but handles softer. Stays two and a half miles.

Santa Nenita

8-y-o b m North Col-Betty Barlow (Sagaro)
A G Newcombe A G Newcombe

Placings:0-00F **(4590)**
2001/02: 20^{0}GS, 19^{0}GS, 24^{F}G

	Starts	1st	2nd	3rd	Win & Pl
Hurdles	2	0	0	0	0
Chases	1	0	0	0	0
Career Total	**4**	**0**	**0**	**0**	**0**

Going: Sf: 0-0 GS: 0-2 Gd: 0-1 GF: - Fm: 0-0
Distance: 2m/2m3: 0-0 2m4-2m7: 0-2 3m+: 0-1
Track: LH: 0-1 RH: 0-1 Tight: 0-2 Gall: 0-0
Aids: Bl: 0-0 Vi: 0-0 Tstrap: 0-0
Best Rating: 31 5/00 Hrfd 2m3f110y gd-sft Hdl

Santabless (IRE)

89 **115**

9-y-o b g Zaffaran (USA)-Nimbi (Orchestra)
Miss H C Knight Southern Brick & Tile Co Ltd

Placings:*30*/11513533/40/01F6 **(3498)**
2001/02: 22^{0}G, 24^{1}GS, 24^{F}GS, 24^{6}S

	Starts	1st	2nd	3rd	Win & Pl
Chases	4	1	0	0	5352
Career Total	**16**	**4**	**0**	**4**	**23714**

115	12/01	Tntn	3m	D Ch	G-S	£5352
125	1/99	Tntn	2m3f110y	D Hdl	SFT	£2931
117	12/98	Plum	2m4f	E Hdl	SFT	£2792
117	10/98	Chel	2m110y	D Hdl	GD	£3745

Total win prize-money £14821

Going: Sf: 0-1 GS: 1-2 Gd: 0-1 GF: - Fm: 0-0
Distance: 2m/2m3: 0-0 2m4-2m7: 0-1 **3m+: 1-3**
Track: LH: 0-1 **RH: 1-3 Tight: 1-1** Gall: 0-2
Aids: Bl: 0-0 Vi: 0-0 Tstrap: 0-0
Best Rating: 152 1/00 Chel 2m5f110y gd-sft Hdl

A one-time very useful novice hurdler for Mark Pitman, he did not disgrace himself on his chasing debut and first appearance in 634 days, and was handed his next race when his rivals all came a cropper. suited by easy ground.

Santella Boy (USA)

100(86h) (50h)**89**

10-y-o b g Turkoman (USA)-Dream Creek (USA) (The Minstrel (CAN))
Miss C Dyson Miss C Dyson

Placings:36/351321142F4/**112132/0PP4P**254/P0/004 23-04633 **(1276)**
2001/02: 22^{0}GF, 24^{4}GF, 27^{6}G, 26^{3}G, 24^{3}GF

	Starts	1st	2nd	3rd	Win & Pl
Hurdles	2	0	0	0	0
Chases	3	0	0	2	794
Career Total	**39**	**6**	**6**	**7**	**27926**

119	7/97	Sthl	3m110y	E Ch	G-F	£3593
119	6/97	Uttx	2m7f	D Ch	G-F	£3420
111	5/97	Extr	2m7f110y	D Ch	GD	£3550
95	9/96	Extr	2m6f	E(0-110)HHdl	FRM	£2611
101	8/96	Hntg	2m4f110y	E Hdl	G-F	£2192
92	6/96	MRas	3m	D Hdl	G-F	£2974

Total win prize-money £18343

Going: Sf: 0-0 GS: 0-0 Gd: 0-2 GF: - Fm: 0-3
Distance: 2m/2m3: 0-0 2m4-2m7: 0-1 3m+: 0-4
Track: LH: 0-3 RH: 0-2 Tight: 0-2 Gall: 0-1
Aids: Bl: 0-0 Vi: 0-0 Tstrap: 0-0
Best Rating: 119 7/97 Sthl 3m110y gd-fm Ch

Very modest chaser, stays well.

Santella Cape

70 **22**

9-y-o b g Alzao (USA)-Kijafa (USA) (Chief's Crown (USA))
N J Hawke N J Hawke

Placings:F3220P/0304**P32/0P1414450-P0** **(0723)**
2001/02: 22^{P}GF, 25^{0}F

	Starts	1st	2nd	3rd	Win & Pl
Chases	2	0	0	0	
Career Total	**24**	**2**	**3**	**3**	**10167**

102	8/00	Font	2m6f	E(0-105)HCh	G-F	£2876
100	7/00	Sthl	3m110y	E Ch	G-F	£2921

Total win prize-money £5798

Going: Sf: 0-0 GS: 0-0 Gd: 0-0 GF: - Fm: 0-2
Distance: 2m/2m3: 0-0 2m4-2m7: 0-1 3m+: 0-1
Track: LH: 0-0 RH: 0-1 Tight: 0-1 Gall: 0-0
Aids: Bl: 0-2 Vi: 0-0 Tstrap: 0-0
Best Rating: 102 10/00 Font 2m6f good Ch

Santenay (FR)

111 **117**

4-y-o b g Mister Mat (FR)-Guigone (FR) (Esprit Du Nord (USA))
P F Nicholls (J Bertran De Balanda 3/8) The Hon Mrs Townshend

Placings:522P14 **(4813)**
2001/02: 16^{5}HO, 17^{2}VS, 16^{2}G, 16^{P}GS, 16^{1}G, 17^{4}GF

	Starts	1st	2nd	3rd	Win & Pl
Hurdles	6	1	2	0	7544
Career Total	**6**	**1**	**2**	**0**	**7544**

116	3/02	Winc	2m	E Hdl	GD	£2758

Total win prize-money £2758

Going: Sf: 0-0 GS: 0-1 Gd: 1-2 GF: - Fm: 0-1
Distance: **2m/2m3: 1-6** 2m4-2m7: 0-0 3m+: 0-0
Track: LH: 0-2 **RH: 1-3** Tight: 0-0 Gall: 0-2
Aids: Bl: 0-0 Vi: 0-0 Tstrap: 0-0
Best Rating: 117 4/02 Chel 2m1f gd-fm Hdl

Ex-French, he eventually got off the mark over hurdles in this country at Wincanton in March 2002. Slightly disappointing next time.

Saone Et Loire (FR)

99 **84**

5-y-o b m Always Fair (USA)-Saone (USA) (Bering)
M C Pipe Yvonne Reynolds & Roger Stanley

Placings:23-4362401 **(4183)**
2001/02: 16^{4}S, 17^{3}S, 16^{6}GF, 19^{2}GS, 17^{4}S, 16^{0}G, 17^{1}S

	Starts	1st	2nd	3rd	Win & Pl
Hurdles	7	1	1	1	2477
Career Total	**9**	**1**	**2**	**2**	**3385**

84 3/02 Tntn 2m1f G Hdl SFT £1694
Total win prize-money £1694

Going: Sf: 1-4 GS: 0-1 Gd: 0-1 GF: - Fm: 0-1
Distance: **2m/2m3: 1-6** 2m4-2m7: 0-1 3m+: 0-0
Track: LH: 0-2 **RH: 1-5 Tight: 1-4** Gall: 0-0
Aids: Bl: 0-0 Vi: 1-2 Tstrap: 1-5
Best Rating: 85 2/01 Tntn 2m1f heavy Hdl

Plating-class hurdler, acts on soft ground.

Saorsie

101 **85+**

4-y-o b g Emperor Jones (USA)-Exclusive Lottery (Presidium)
J C Fox Lord Mutton Racing Partnership

Placings:0500 **(3356)**
2001/02: 16^{0}G, 16^{5}HY, 16^{0}GS, 16^{0}HY

	Starts	1st	2nd	3rd	Win & Pl
Hurdles	4	0	0	0	0
Career Total	**4**	**0**	**0**	**0**	**0**

Going: Sf: 0-2 GS: 0-1 Gd: 0-1 GF: - Fm: 0-0
Distance: 2m/2m3: 0-4 2m4-2m7: 0-0 3m+: 0-0
Track: LH: 0-3 RH: 0-1 Tight: 0-0 Gall: 0-2
Aids: Bl: 0-2 Vi: 0-0 Tstrap: 0-0
Best Rating: 71 11/01 Newb 2m110y good Hdl

Convincing winner of poor handicap hurdle over an extended two miles at Newton Abbot July 2002. May be on the upgrade.

Saragann (IRE)

(113h) (134h)

7-y-o b g Danehill (USA)-Sarliya (IRE) (Doyoun)
P J Hobbs Jay Dee Bloodstock Limited

Placings:235PPP6/4U44113-2131 **(1145)**
2001/02: 17^{2}GS, 16^{1}GF, 17^{3}GS, 16^{1}GF

	Starts	1st	2nd	3rd	Win & Pl
Hurdles	4	2	1	1	23662
Career Total	**18**	**4**	**2**	**3**	**57130**

134 8/01 Sthl 2m C(0-130)HHdl G-F £4810
130 6/01 Worc 2m B(0-140)HHdl G-F £14384
134 1/01 Kemp 2m4f110y E(0-115)HCh SFT £3737
125 11/00 Carl 2m E Ch SFT £3146
Total win prize-money £26079

Going: Sf: 0-0 GS: 0-2 Gd: 0-0 GF: - Fm: 2-2
Distance: **2m/2m3: 2-4** 2m4-2m7: 0-0 3m+: 0-0
Track: **LH: 2-3** RH: 0-0 **Tight: 1-2** Gall: 0-0
Aids: Bl: 0-0 Vi: 0-0 Tstrap: 0-0
Best Rating: 136 1/01 Tntn 2m3f soft Ch

He has proved adaptable since arriving from France, showing useful form over hurdles and fences on a variety of surfaces. Stays two and a half miles.

Sarah's Destiny

70 **46**

7-y-o gr m Riverwise (USA)-Tearful Sarah (Rugantino)
C W Mitchell C W Mitchell

Placings:*0/0*0PP-0 **(0314)**
2001/02: 17^{0}F

	Starts	1st	2nd	3rd	Win & Pl
Hurdles	1	0	0	0	
Career Total	**6**	**0**	**0**	**0**	

Going: Sf: 0-0 GS: 0-0 Gd: 0-0 GF: - Fm: 0-1
Distance: 2m/2m3: 0-1 2m4-2m7: 0-0 3m+: 0-0
Track: LH: 0-0 RH: 0-1 Tight: 0-0 Gall: 0-0
Aids: Bl: 0-0 Vi: 0-0 Tstrap: 0-0
Best Rating: 59 2/00 Winc 2m gd-sft NHF

Saras Delight

10-y-o b g Idiots Delight-Lady Bess (Straight Lad)
Major General C A Ramsay Major General C A Ramsay

Placings:*06*/03F3/3U1233/15/5-F **(4833)**
2001/02: 27^{F}G

	Starts	1st	2nd	3rd	Win & Pl
Chases	1	0	0	0	
Career Total	**16**	**2**	**1**	**5**	**8586**

110 4/00 Newc 3m F(0-105)HCh G-S £2902
107 12/98 Hrfd 3m1f110y F Ch G-S £2125
Total win prize-money £5027

Going: Sf: 0-0 GS: 0-0 Gd: 0-1 GF: - Fm: 0-0
Distance: 2m/2m3: 0-0 2m4-2m7: 0-0 3m+: 0-1
Track: LH: 0-1 RH: 0-0 Tight: 0-0 Gall: 0-0
Aids: Bl: 0-0 Vi: 0-0 Tstrap: 0-0
Best Rating: 110 4/00 Newc 3m gd-sft Ch

Sarasota (IRE)

100 **84**

7-y-o b g Lord Americo-Ceoltoir Dubh (Black Minstrel)
Mrs S D Williams F W & E P Ridge

Placings:060P-02P05 **(1544)**
2001/02: 17^{0}G, 17^{2}GF, 20^{P}G, 17^{0}G, 17^{5}G

	Starts	1st	2nd	3rd	Win & Pl
Hurdles	5	0	1	0	793
Career Total	**9**	**0**	**1**	**0**	**793**

Going: Sf: 0-0 GS: 0-0 Gd: 0-4 GF: - Fm: 0-1
Distance: 2m/2m3: 0-4 2m4-2m7: 0-1 3m+: 0-0
Track: LH: 0-3 RH: 0-2 Tight: 0-3 Gall: 0-0
Aids: Bl: 0-0 Vi: 0-0 Tstrap: 0-0
Best Rating: 84 5/01 NAbb 2m1f gd-fm Hdl

Sarasota Storm

105 **89**

10-y-o b g Petoski-Challanging (Mill Reef (USA))
R G Frost Miss H S Robarts

Placings:P2P0/P/UP/5341-221 **(1105)**
2001/02: 22^{2}G, 22^{2}GF, 22^{1}G

	Starts	1st	2nd	3rd	Win & Pl
Hurdles	3	1	2	0	4403
Career Total	**14**	**2**	**3**	**1**	**8034**

89 8/01 NAbb 2m6f F(0-110)HHdl GD £2919
80 10/00 Extr 2m6f110y F(0-100)HHdl GD £2450
Total win prize-money £5369

Going: Sf: 0-0 GS: 0-0 Gd: 1-2 GF: - Fm: 0-1
Distance: 2m/2m3: 0-0 **2m4-2m7: 1-3** 3m+: 0-0
Track: **LH: 1-3** RH: 0-0 **Tight: 1-3** Gall: 0-0
Aids: Bl: 0-0 Vi: 0-0 Tstrap: 0-0
Best Rating: 92 2/98 Tntn 2m1f gd-fm Hdl

Sarcoid (IRE)

12-y-o ch g Saronicos-Pretty Bonnet (Carlburg)
G C Evans (G D Hanmer 20/1) N Morgan

Placings:P **(4179)**
2001/02: 24^{P}GS

	Starts	1st	2nd	3rd	Win & Pl
Chases	1	0	0	0	
Career Total	**1**	**0**	**0**	**0**	

Going: Sf: 0-0 GS: 0-1 Gd: 0-0 GF: - Fm: 0-0
Distance: 2m/2m3: 0-0 2m4-2m7: 0-0 3m+: 0-1
Track: LH: 0-1 RH: 0-0 Tight: 0-1 Gall: 0-0
Aids: Bl: 0-0 Vi: 0-0 Tstrap: 0-0
Best Rating:

Sarena Pride (IRE)

92 **93**

5-y-o b m Persian Bold-Avidal Park (Horage)
R J O'Sullivan Sarena Mfg Ltd

Placings:465P **(3713)**
2001/02: 16^{4}GF, 18^{6}GS, 16^{5}S, 16^{P}HY

	Starts	1st	2nd	3rd	Win & Pl
Hurdles	4	0	0	0	0
Career Total	**4**	**0**	**0**	**0**	**0**

Going: Sf: 0-2 GS: 0-1 Gd: 0-0 GF: - Fm: 0-1
Distance: 2m/2m3: 0-4 2m4-2m7: 0-0 3m+: 0-0
Track: LH: 0-4 RH: 0-0 Tight: 0-4 Gall: 0-0
Aids: Bl: 0-2 Vi: 0-0 Tstrap: 0-0
Best Rating: 93 9/01 Plum 2m gd-fm Hdl

Sarena Special

5-y-o b g Lucky Guest-Lariston Gale (Pas De Seul)
J D Frost (R J O'Sullivan 18/7) Sarena Mfg Ltd

Placings:5-P **(4654)**
2001/02: 17^{P}GS

	Starts	1st	2nd	3rd	Win & Pl
Hurdles	1	0	0	0	
Career Total	**2**	**0**	**0**	**0**	**0**

Going: Sf: 0-0 GS: 0-1 Gd: 0-0 GF: - Fm: 0-0
Distance: 2m/2m3: 0-1 2m4-2m7: 0-0 3m+: 0-0
Track: LH: 0-0 RH: 0-1 Tight: 0-1 Gall: 0-0
Aids: Bl: 0-0 Vi: 0-0 Tstrap: 0-0
Best Rating: 75 10/00 Kemp 2m gd-sft Hdl

Sasha Star (IRE)

102 **60**

4-y-o b g Namaqualand (USA)-Trojan Relation (Trojan Fen)

G Brown T Curry

Placings:04605 (4271)
2001/02: 16^{0}G, 18^{4}GF, 16^{6}HY, 17^{0}S, 16^{5}G

	Starts	1st	2nd	3rd	Win & Pl
Hurdles	5	0	0	0	0
Career Total	5	**0**	**0**	**0**	**0**

Going: Sf: 0-2 GS: 0-0 Gd: 0-2 GF: - Fm: 0-1
Distance: 2m/2m3: 0-5 2m4-2m7: 0-0 3m+: 0-0
Track: LH: 0-3 RH: 0-2 Tight: 0-4 Gall: 0-0
Aids: Bl: 0-2 Vi: 0-0 Tstrap: 0-0
Best Rating: 60 12/01 Leic 2m heavy Hdl

Beaten in selling hurdles at up to 22 furlongs.

Saskia's Hero

108 **111**

15-y-o ch g Bairn (USA)-Comtec Princess (Gulf Pearl)
J Hetherton Qualitair Holdings Limited

Placings:*540*/601246/0253P50/*2*/FF011/P1121F/P/6P
41UP333P4/3P022650/314223-611PP (4855)
2001/02: 16^{6}GF, 20^{1}GF, 20^{1}GF, 20^{P}G, 20^{P}G

	Starts	1st	2nd	3rd	Win & Pl
Chases	5	2	0	0	6553
Career Total	59	**10**	**8**	**7**	**53828**

111	8/01	Sthl	2m4f110y	F(0-105)HCh	G-F	£3445
107	7/01	Sthl	2m4f110y	F(0-95)HCh	G-F	£3108
113	6/00	Hexm	2m4f110y	E(0-115)HCh	G-F	£3451
117	7/98	MRas	2m4f	C(0-135)HCh	G-F	£13470
101	6/96	Uttx	2m5f	(0-130)HCh	G-F	£4331
114	6/96	Sthl	2m	E(0-115)HCh	G-F	£4230
103	5/96	Hntg	2m110y	F(0-105)HCh	G-F	£2700
113	4/96	Hexm	2m110y	F(0-105)HCh	GD	£3038
98	4/96	Hexm	2m110y	E Ch	G-F	£3124
90	12/92	Catt	2m	Hdl	SFT	£1305

Total win prize-money £42205

Going: Sf: 0-0 GS: 0-0 Gd: 0-2 GF: - Fm: 2-3
Distance: 2m/2m3: 0-1 **2m4-2m7: 2-4** 3m+: 0-0
Track: **LH: 2-4** RH: 0-1 **Tight: 2-3** Gall: 0-1
Aids: Bl: 0-0 Vi: 0-0 Tstrap: 0-0
Best Rating: 118 7/96 Strf 2m4f gd-fm Ch

Saspys Lad

105 **108+**

5-y-o b g Faustus (USA)-Legendary Lady (Reprimand)
W M Brisbourne K J Oulton

Placings:0003-05133 (4536)
2001/02: 23^{0}HY, 19^{5}S, 16^{1}GS, 16^{3}GS, 16^{3}G

	Starts	1st	2nd	3rd	Win & Pl
Hurdles	5	1	0	2	2688
Career Total	9	**1**	**0**	**3**	**2948**

79	2/02	Fknm	2m	G(0-90)HHdl	G-S	£1892

Total win prize-money £1892

Going: Sf: 0-2 GS: 1-2 Gd: 0-1 GF: - Fm: 0-0
Distance: **2m/2m3: 1-4** 2m4-2m7: 0-0 3m+: 0-1
Track: **LH: 1-5** RH: 0-0 **Tight: 1-3** Gall: 0-0
Aids: Bl: 0-0 Vi: 0-0 Tstrap: 0-0
Best Rating: 83 4/02 Fknm 2m good Hdl

Regular in selling company, winning at Fakenham in February and at Newton Abbot in June 2002.

Sassy (IRE)

7-y-o b m Imp Society (USA)-Merrie Moment (IRE) (Taufan (USA))
P Bowen The Galloping Punters

Placings:6/63/P1143-P0 (2602)
2001/02: 21^{P}G, 22^{0}G

	Starts	1st	2nd	3rd	Win & Pl
Hurdles	2	0	0	0	
Career Total	**10**	**2**	**0**	**2**	**6405**

101	10/00	MRas	3m	E Hdl	GD	£3110
90	9/00	Plum	2m5f	E Hdl	GD	£2366

Total win prize-money £5477

Going: Sf: 0-0 GS: 0-0 Gd: 0-2 GF: - Fm: 0-0
Distance: 2m/2m3: 0-0 2m4-2m7: 0-2 3m+: 0-0
Track: LH: 0-2 RH: 0-0 Tight: 0-2 Gall: 0-0
Aids: Bl: 0-0 Vi: 0-0 Tstrap: 0-0
Best Rating: 101 12/00 Tntn 2m3f110y soft Hdl

Satanas (FR)

85f **88f**

4-y-o b g Dress Parade-Oiseau Noir (FR) (Rex Magna (FR))
O Sherwood M G St Quinton

Placings:*00* (4900)
2001/02: 16^{0}G, 16^{0}G

	Starts	1st	2nd	3rd	Win & Pl
NH Flat	2	0	0	0	
Career Total	2	**0**	**0**	**0**	

Going: Sf: 0-0 GS: 0-0 Gd: 0-2 GF: - Fm: 0-0
Distance: 2m/2m3: 0-2 2m4-2m7: 0-0 3m+: 0-0
Track: LH: 0-0 RH: 0-2 Tight: 0-0 Gall: 0-0
Aids: Bl: 0-0 Vi: 0-0 Tstrap: 0-0
Best Rating: 88 2/02 Kemp 2m good NHF

Satanta

88 **55**

5-y-o b g Cosmonaut-Expensive Gift (Record Token)
J W Mullins New Forest Racing Partnership

Placings:06 (1567)
2001/02: 17^{0}GF, 20^{6}GS

	Starts	1st	2nd	3rd	Win & Pl
NH Flat	1	0	0	0	0
Hurdles	1	0	0	0	0
Career Total	2	**0**	**0**	**0**	**0**

Going: Sf: 0-0 GS: 0-1 Gd: 0-0 GF: - Fm: 0-1
Distance: 2m/2m3: 0-1 2m4-2m7: 0-1 3m+: 0-0
Track: LH: 0-1 RH: 0-0 Tight: 0-2 Gall: 0-0
Aids: Bl: 0-0 Vi: 0-0 Tstrap: 0-0
Best Rating: 63 8/01 NAbb 2m1f gd-fm NHF

Satchmo (IRE)

106 **144**

10-y-o b g Satco (FR)-Taradale (Torus)
D M Grissell G J D Wragg

Placings:21U/24F211FP-066 (2443)
2001/02: 16^{0}G, 20^{6}G, 20^{6}S

	Starts	1st	2nd	3rd	Win & Pl
Chases	3	0	0	0	2025
Career Total	14	**3**	**3**	**0**	**31959**

157	3/01	Hntg	2m4f110y	B HCh	SFT	£10328
157	2/01	Kemp	2m4f110y	C(0-130)HCh	GD	£10871
146	3/00	Sand	2m4f110y	H Ch	G-F	£2436

Total win prize-money £23636

Going: Sf: 0-1 GS: 0-0 Gd: 0-2 GF: - Fm: 0-0
Distance: 2m/2m3: 0-1 2m4-2m7: 0-2 3m+: 0-0
Track: LH: 0-2 RH: 0-1 Tight: 0-0 Gall: 0-2
Aids: Bl: 0-0 Vi: 0-0 Tstrap: 0-0
Best Rating: 157 3/01 Hntg 2m4f110y soft Ch

A recruit from the hunter chase circuit, he improved steadily under Rules and won in fine style at Kempton and Huntingdon in the spring of 2001. Best over two and a half miles, he usually jumps well and appreciates a sounder surface, though he does act on soft. He was well beaten in good races before Christmas 2001.

Satshoon (IRE)

105 **137**

9-y-o b g Satco (FR)-Tudor Lady (Green Shoon)
P F Nicholls Paul K Barber

Placings:221U11-P1 (2539)
2001/02: 28^{P}S, 25^{1}G

	Starts	1st	2nd	3rd	Win & Pl
Chases	2	1	0	0	5187
Career Total	8	**4**	**2**	**0**	**19921**

135	12/01	Winc	3m1f110y	D(0-120)HCh	GD	£5187
137	4/01	Winc	3m1f110y	D Ch	SFT	£4988
133	4/01	Winc	3m1f110y	E Ch	SFT	£3757
129	1/01	Font	2m4f	E Ch	SFT	£3318

Total win prize-money £17251

Going: Sf: 0-1 GS: 0-0 Gd: 1-1 GF: - Fm: 0-0
Distance: 2m/2m3: 0-0 2m4-2m7: 0-0 **3m+: 1-2**
Track: LH: 0-1 **RH: 1-1** Tight: 0-1 Gall: 0-0
Aids: **Bl: 1-2** Vi: 0-0 Tstrap: 0-0
Best Rating: 137 4/01 Winc 3m1f110y soft Ch

Decent handicap chaser. He likes to get his toe in and stays three miles. Blinkers are needed to make him concentrate. Goes well at Wincanton.

Saucy Kirina

93 **58**

5-y-o b m Regal Embers (IRE)-Eleri (Rolfe (USA))
Mrs P Ford W E Donohue

Placings:0P-PP6P (4752)
2001/02: 19^{P}HY, 17^{P}S, 16^{6}G, 16^{P}GF

	Starts	1st	2nd	3rd	Win & Pl
Hurdles	4	0	0	0	0
Career Total	6	**0**	**0**	**0**	**0**

Going: Sf: 0-2 GS: 0-0 Gd: 0-1 GF: - Fm: 0-1
Distance: 2m/2m3: 0-3 2m4-2m7: 0-1 3m+: 0-0
Track: LH: 0-1 RH: 0-3 Tight: 0-0 Gall: 0-0
Aids: Bl: 0-0 Vi: 0-0 Tstrap: 0-0
Best Rating: 52 4/02 Ludl 2m good Hdl

Pulled up in four of first five starts over timber.

Saucy Night

83(78c) (54c)**61**

6-y-o ch g Anshan-Kiss In The Dark (Starry Night (USA))
C C Bealby R E N Gardiner

Placings:00P (3319)
2001/02: 16^{0}GS, 20^{0}G, 16^{P}GS

	Starts	1st	2nd	3rd	Win & Pl
Hurdles	3	0	0	0	
Career Total	3	**0**	**0**	**0**	

Going: Sf: 0-0 GS: 0-2 Gd: 0-1 GF: - Fm: 0-0
Distance: 2m/2m3: 0-2 2m4-2m7: 0-1 3m+: 0-0
Track: LH: 0-1 RH: 0-2 Tight: 0-0 Gall: 0-2
Aids: Bl: 0-0 Vi: 0-0 Tstrap: 0-0
Best Rating: 61 12/01 Donc 2m4f good Hdl

Sauvognie

88 **75**

6-y-o ch g Generous (IRE)-Radiant Bride (USA) (Blushing Groom (FR))
F Kirby Fred Kirby

Placings:_00633/0P_ **(2346)**
2001/02: 21^{0}G, 20^{P}GS

	Starts	1st	2nd	3rd	Win & Pl
Chases	2	0	0	0	
Career Total	**7**	**0**	**0**	**2**	**678**

Going: Sf: 0-0 GS: 0-1 Gd: 0-1 GF: - Fm: 0-0
Distance: 2m/2m3: 0-0 2m4-2m7: 0-2 3m+: 0-0
Track: LH: 0-2 RH: 0-0 Tight: 0-1 Gall: 0-1
Aids: Bl: 0-0 Vi: 0-0 Tstrap: 0-0
Best Rating: 79 3/00 Kels 2m2f gd-sft Hdl

Savanna Miss

73 **51**

4-y-o b f Son Pardo-Havana Miss (Cigar)
J W Mullins Ian M McGready

Placings:5 **(1141)**
2001/02: 16^{5}G

	Starts	1st	2nd	3rd	Win & Pl
Hurdles	1	0	0	0	0
Career Total	**1**	**0**	**0**	**0**	**0**

Going: Sf: 0-0 GS: 0-0 Gd: 0-1 GF: - Fm: 0-0
Distance: 2m/2m3: 0-1 2m4-2m7: 0-0 3m+: 0-0
Track: LH: 0-1 RH: 0-0 Tight: 0-1 Gall: 0-0
Aids: Bl: 0-0 Vi: 0-0 Tstrap: 0-0
Best Rating: 51 8/01 Strf 2m110y good Hdl

Savastar

6-y-o ch m Grey Desire-Star Leader (Kafu)
S A Brookshaw S A Brookshaw

Placings:_0P_ **(3590)**
2001/02: 16^{0}G, 16^{P}HY

	Starts	1st	2nd	3rd	Win & Pl
NH Flat	1	0	0	0	0
Hurdles	1	0	0	0	0
Career Total	**2**	**0**	**0**	**0**	

Going: Sf: 0-1 GS: 0-0 Gd: 0-1 GF: - Fm: 0-0
Distance: 2m/2m3: 0-2 2m4-2m7: 0-0 3m+: 0-0
Track: LH: 0-1 RH: 0-1 Tight: 0-0 Gall: 0-0
Aids: Bl: 0-0 Vi: 0-0 Tstrap: 0-0
Best Rating: 18 12/01 Ludl 2m good NHF

Save The Planet

97 **72**

5-y-o b m Environment Friend-Geoffreys Bird (Master Willie)
P Monteith Stan N Moffat

Placings:0-60P05 **(4785)**
2001/02: 20^{6}GF, 20^{0}G, 20^{P}S, 20^{0}G, 16^{5}F

	Starts	1st	2nd	3rd	Win & Pl
Hurdles	5	0	0	0	0
Career Total	**6**	**0**	**0**	**0**	**0**

Going: Sf: 0-1 GS: 0-0 Gd: 0-2 GF: - Fm: 0-2
Distance: 2m/2m3: 0-1 2m4-2m7: 0-4 3m+: 0-0
Track: LH: 0-2 RH: 0-3 Tight: 0-3 Gall: 0-2
Aids: Bl: 0-0 Vi: 0-3 Tstrap: 0-0

Best Rating: 72 12/01 Muss 2m4f gd-fm Hdl

Save The Pound (USA)

67 **33**

4-y-o br g Northern Flagship (USA)-Key Bid (USA) (Key To The Mint (USA))
T D Easterby C H Stevens

Placings:6 **(0965)**
2001/02: 17^{6}GS

	Starts	1st	2nd	3rd	Win & Pl
Hurdles	1	0	0	0	0
Career Total	**1**	**0**	**0**	**0**	**0**

Going: Sf: 0-0 GS: 0-1 Gd: 0-0 GF: - Fm: 0-0
Distance: 2m/2m3: 0-1 2m4-2m7: 0-0 3m+: 0-0
Track: LH: 0-0 RH: 0-0 Tight: 0-0 Gall: 0-0
Aids: Bl: 0-0 Vi: 0-0 Tstrap: 0-1
Best Rating: 33 7/01 MRas 2m1f110y gd-sft Hdl

Sawlajan (USA)

98 **87**

11-y-o ch g Woodman (USA)-Crafty Satin (USA) (Crimson Satan)
Mrs T J McInnes Skinner Mrs T J McInnes Skinner

Placings:0/2/230312B/0123011440P 60 **(10[illegible]0)**
2001/02: 20^{6}F, 22^{0}G

	Starts	1st	2nd	3rd	Win & Pl
Hurdles	2	0	0	0	0
Career Total	**22**	**4**	**4**	**3**	**24906**

120	9/00	Worc	2m4f	C(0-135)HHdl	G-F	£6862
120	8/00	Worc	2m4f	D(0-120)HHdl	G-F	£4121
115	6/00	Strf	2m110y	D(0-120)HHdl	G-S	£3562
102	8/99	Strf	2m6f110y	D Hdl	GD	£3148

Total win prize-money £17695

Going: Sf: 0-0 GS: 0-0 Gd: 0-1 GF: - Fm: 0-1
Distance: 2m/2m3: 0-0 2m4-2m7: 0-2 3m+: 0-0
Track: LH: 0-2 RH: 0-0 Tight: 0-1 Gall: 0-0
Aids: Bl: 0-0 Vi: 0-0 Tstrap: 0-0
Best Rating: 120 9/00 Worc 2m4f gd-fm Hdl

Saxon Duke

117 **133**

11-y-o b g Saxon Farm-Bucks Princess (Buckskin (FR))
P J Hobbs Saxon Duke Partnership

Placings:_610_/F32**12314**/22**F21/13234B/F1-F0302343** **(4266)**
2001/02: 25^{F}G, 24^{0}G, 32^{3}GS, 29^{0}GS, 27^{2}S, 26^{3}S, 29^{4}G, 29^{3}S

	Starts	1st	2nd	3rd	Win & Pl
Chases	8	0	1	3	5716
Career Total	**32**	**6**	**7**	**7**	**43306**

133	3/01	Wwck	3m5f	C(0-135)HCh	SFT	£6987
123	10/99	Chel	3m110y	E(0-125)HCh	GD	£4833
121	1/99	Extr	2m7f110y	E(0-115)HCh	HVY	£3038
108	4/98	Extr	2m7f110y	E(0-100)HCh	SFT	£3441
100	12/97	Tntn	3m	F(0-105)HCh	GD	£2822
107	2/96	Nott	2m	H NHF	G-S	£1236

Total win prize-money £22359

Going: Sf: 0-3 GS: 0-2 Gd: 0-3 GF: - Fm: 0-0
Distance: 2m/2m3: 0-0 2m4-2m7: 0-0 3m+: 0-8
Track: LH: 0-6 RH: 0-1 Tight: 0-2 Gall: 0-1
Aids: Bl: 0-0 Vi: 0-0 Tstrap: 0-0

Best Rating: 133 2/02 Wwck 3m2f soft Ch

A dour stayer, he goes well under testing conditions.

Saxon Mill

95 **97**

7-y-o ch g Saxon Farm-Djellaba (Decoy Boy)
Mrs Pippa Bickerton David Bickerton

Placings:_2602_/403-0P24P **(3450)**
2001/02: 20^{0}G, 19^{P}GF, 20^{2}S, 20^{4}S, 20^{P}GS

	Starts	1st	2nd	3rd	Win & Pl
Hurdles	5	0	1	0	1080
Career Total	**12**	**0**	**3**	**1**	**2854**

Going: Sf: 0-2 GS: 0-1 Gd: 0-1 GF: - Fm: 0-1
Distance: 2m/2m3: 0-0 2m4-2m7: 0-5 3m+: 0-0
Track: LH: 0-4 RH: 0-1 Tight: 0-3 Gall: 0-0
Aids: Bl: 0-0 Vi: 0-0 Tstrap: 0-0
Best Rating: 97 4/01 Hayd 2m soft Hdl

Handicap hurdler, effective over two and a half miles in soft ground.

Saxon Queen

99(86c) (63c)**90**

8-y-o b m Lord Bud-Saxon Slave (Be Friendly)
G Prodromou George Prodromou

Placings:44450-2S646**F**4241 **(4546)**
2001/02: 17^{2}G, 16^{S}S, 20^{6}S, 16^{4}S, 17^{6}S, 19^{F}G, 16^{4}GS, 17^{2}G, 16^{4}G, 16^{1}GF

	Starts	1st	2nd	3rd	Win & Pl
Hurdles	8	1	2	0	2809
Chases	2	0	0	0	0
Career Total	**15**	**1**	**2**	**0**	**2809**

81	4/02	Hntg	2m110y	G(0-90)HHdl	G-F	£1733

Total win prize-money £1733

Going: Sf: 0-4 GS: 0-1 Gd: 0-4 GF: - Fm: 1-1
Distance: **2m/2m3: 1-9** 2m4-2m7: 0-1 3m+: 0-0
Track: LH: 0-5 **RH: 1-5** Tight: 0-8 **Gall: 1-1**
Aids: Bl: 0-0 Vi: 0-0 Tstrap: 0-0
Best Rating: 86 10/01 MRas 2m1f110y good Hdl

Winner of a point-to point in May 2000, she has made the frame in selling hurdles.

Saxon Spirit

91f **75f**

6-y-o ch g Saxon Farm-Miss Date (Mandamus)
I R Brown I R Brown

Placings:_0_ **(4743)**
2001/02: 16^{0}GF

	Starts	1st	2nd	3rd	Win & Pl
NH Flat	1	0	0	0	
Career Total	**1**	**0**	**0**	**0**	

Going: Sf: 0-0 GS: 0-0 Gd: 0-0 GF: - Fm: 0-1
Distance: 2m/2m3: 0-1 2m4-2m7: 0-0 3m+: 0-0
Track: LH: 0-0 RH: 0-1 Tight: 0-0 Gall: 0-0
Aids: Bl: 0-0 Vi: 0-0 Tstrap: 0-0
Best Rating: 75 4/02 Ludl 2m gd-fm NHF

Saxon Victory (USA)

97(90h) (74h)**92**

7-y-o b g Nicholas (USA)-Saxon Shore (USA) (Halo (USA))

Mrs V C Ward Saxon Victory Partnership

Placings:3222023/40323500030/**F434502U6**00-6650046 (1276)
2001/02: 19^{6}G, 20^{6}G, 23^{5}G, 23^{0}G, 24^{0}G, 23^{4}GF, 24^{6}GF

	Starts	1st	2nd	3rd	Win & Pl
Chases	7	0	0	0	265
Career Total	**36**	**0**	**6**	**6**	**7280**

Going: Sf: 0-0 GS: 0-0 Gd: 0-5 GF: - Fm: 0-2
Distance: 2m/2m3: 0-1 2m4-2m7: 0-1 3m+: 0-5
Track: LH: 0-6 RH: 0-1 Tight: 0-2 Gall: 0-0
Aids: Bl: 0-0 Vi: 0-0 Tstrap: 0-5
Best Rating: 100 11/99 Hrfd 2m3f110y good Hdl

Sayeh (IRE)

91(107h) (128h)116

10-y-o b g Fool's Holme (USA)-Piffle (Shirley Heights)
P Bowen The Galloping Punters

Placings:14/11/1/0124**2PF6** (3153)
2001/02: 19^{0}G, 17^{1}F, 20^{2}GS, 20^{4}G, 16^{2}HY, 17^{P}G, 20^{F}S, 20^{6}G

	Starts	1st	2nd	3rd	Win & Pl
Hurdles	4	1	1	0	6331
Chases	4	0	1	0	1151
Career Total	**13**	**5**	**2**	**0**	**17861**
125 6/01 Hrfd	2m1f	F(0-110)HHdl	FRM	£3542	
128 8/99 Ctml	2m1f110y	D(0-125)HHdl	GD	£3532	
105 5/98 Hrfd	2m1f	E Hdl	GD	£2431	
113 5/98 Ludl	2m	E Hdl	G-F	£2425	
105 2/98 Tntn	2m1f	E Hdl	G-F	£1990	

Total win prize-money £13923

Going: Sf: 0-2 GS: 0-1 Gd: 0-4 GF: - Fm: 1-1
Distance: **2m/2m3: 1-3** 2m4-2m7: 0-5 3m+: 0-0
Track: LH: 0-5 **RH: 1-2** Tight: 0-5 Gall: 0-0
Aids: Bl: 0-0 Vi: 0-0 Tstrap: 0-0
Best Rating: 128 10/01 Uttx 2m4f110y gd-sft Hdl

He has been lightly raced in recent seasons and has obviously had his problems. He won a handicap hurdle in June 2001 and ran well subsequently, although he did try to refuse to race at Plumpton in December. Looks best on a sound surface.

Saywhen

101 90

10-y-o br g Say Primula-Practicality (Weavers Hall)
Mrs A Price Mrs A Price

Placings:05406P4U4 (4738)
2001/02: 20^{0}GF, 20^{5}GF, 25^{4}S, 25^{0}G, 24^{6}G, 24^{P}G, 24^{4}GS, 24^{U}G, 24^{4}GF

	Starts	1st	2nd	3rd	Win & Pl
Chases	9	0	0	0	901
Career Total	**9**	**0**	**0**	**0**	**901**

Going: Sf: 0-1 GS: 0-1 Gd: 0-4 GF: - Fm: 0-3
Distance: 2m/2m3: 0-0 2m4-2m7: 0-2 3m+: 0-7
Track: LH: 0-0 RH: 0-9 Tight: 0-7 Gall: 0-0
Aids: Bl: 0-0 Vi: 0-2 Tstrap: 0-3
Best Rating: 90 3/02 Ludl 3m gd-sft Ch

Winning pointer/maiden chaser.

Scabbard

66f 56f

6-y-o b g Broadsword (USA)-Rest (Dance In Time (CAN))
P R Webber Mr And Mrs R N Richmond-Watson

Placings:0 (2577)
2001/02: 16^{0}HY

	Starts	1st	2nd	3rd	Win & Pl
NH Flat	1	0	0	0	
Career Total	**1**	**0**	**0**	**0**	

Going: Sf: 0-1 GS: 0-0 Gd: 0-0 GF: - Fm: 0-0
Distance: 2m/2m3: 0-1 2m4-2m7: 0-0 3m+: 0-0
Track: LH: 0-0 RH: 0-1 Tight: 0-0 Gall: 0-0
Aids: Bl: 0-0 Vi: 0-0 Tstrap: 0-0
Best Rating: 56 12/01 Towc 2m heavy NHF

Scafell

5-y-o b g Puissance-One Half Silver (CAN) (Plugged Nickle (USA))
M A Barnes (C Smith 2/9) Miss J Robinson

Placings:PP (4673)
2001/02: 16^{P}S, 17^{P}GF

	Starts	1st	2nd	3rd	Win & Pl
Hurdles	2	0	0	0	
Career Total	**2**	**0**	**0**	**0**	

Going: Sf: 0-1 GS: 0-0 Gd: 0-0 GF: - Fm: 0-1
Distance: 2m/2m3: 0-2 2m4-2m7: 0-0 3m+: 0-0
Track: LH: 0-2 RH: 0-0 Tight: 0-1 Gall: 0-0
Aids: Bl: 0-0 Vi: 0-0 Tstrap: 0-2
Best Rating:

Scally Tag

9-y-o gr m Scallywag-Miss Mo Jo (Vaigly Great)
M Smith Malcolm Smith

Placings:0P/SP (4198)
2001/02: 21^{S}GF, 21^{P}S

	Starts	1st	2nd	3rd	Win & Pl
Hurdles	2	0	0	0	
Career Total	**4**	**0**	**0**	**0**	

Going: Sf: 0-1 GS: 0-0 Gd: 0-0 GF: - Fm: 0-1
Distance: 2m/2m3: 0-0 2m4-2m7: 0-2 3m+: 0-0
Track: LH: 0-2 RH: 0-0 Tight: 0-2 Gall: 0-0
Aids: Bl: 0-0 Vi: 0-0 Tstrap: 0-0
Best Rating: 7 11/98 Carl 2m1f soft NHF

Scalp (NZ)

38

10-y-o ch g Pre Catelan (AUS)-Bal In Flight (NZ) (Balmerino (NZ))
G M McCourt N H Oliver

Placings:P0/0 (0777)
2001/02: 16^{0}GF

	Starts	1st	2nd	3rd	Win & Pl
Hurdles	1	0	0	0	
Career Total	**3**	**0**	**0**	**0**	

Going: Sf: 0-0 GS: 0-0 Gd: 0-0 GF: - Fm: 0-1
Distance: 2m/2m3: 0-1 2m4-2m7: 0-0 3m+: 0-0
Track: LH: 0-1 RH: 0-0 Tight: 0-0 Gall: 0-0
Aids: Bl: 0-0 Vi: 0-0 Tstrap: 0-0
Best Rating:

Scarborough Fair (IRE)

86 57

5-y-o b g Synefos (USA)-Hue 'N' Cry (IRE) (Denel (FR))
J J O'Neill Sir Robert Ogden

Placings:0 (4030)
2001/02: 24^{0}GS

	Starts	1st	2nd	3rd	Win & Pl
Hurdles	1	0	0	0	
Career Total	**1**	**0**	**0**	**0**	

Going: Sf: 0-0 GS: 0-1 Gd: 0-0 GF: - Fm: 0-0
Distance: 2m/2m3: 0-0 2m4-2m7: 0-0 3m+: 0-1
Track: LH: 0-1 RH: 0-0 Tight: 0-0 Gall: 0-1
Aids: Bl: 0-0 Vi: 0-0 Tstrap: 0-0
Best Rating: 57 3/02 Newb 3m110y gd-sft Hdl

Scarlet Pimpernel

103(112h) 132

7-y-o b g Night Shift (USA)-Working Model (Ile De Bourbon (USA))
Mrs Mary Hambro Richard Hambro

Placings:1U26/0200-**F46135** (3881)
2001/02: 20^{F}S, 16^{4}GS, 16^{6}GS, 16^{1}GS, 20^{3}S, 16^{5}GS

	Starts	1st	2nd	3rd	Win & Pl
Chases	6	1	0	1	6170
Career Total	**14**	**2**	**2**	**1**	**15850**
132 1/02 Hntg	2m110y	D Ch	G-S	£5109	
132 1/99 Kemp	2m	D Hdl	SFT	£2814	

Total win prize-money £7923

Going: Sf: 0-2 GS: 1-4 Gd: 0-0 GF: - Fm: 0-0
Distance: **2m/2m3: 1-4** 2m4-2m7: 0-2 3m+: 0-0
Track: LH: 0-2 **RH: 1-4** Tight: 0-1 **Gall: 1-1**
Aids: Bl: 0-0 Vi: 0-0 **Tstrap: 1-3**
Best Rating: 144 12/00 Asct 2m110y heavy Hdl

A one-time decent hurdler, he had luck on his side when getting off the mark over fences in January. Best over two miles with cut in the ground.

Scarlet Poppy

81 53

7-y-o b m Petoski-Preachers Popsy (The Parson)
Miss Venetia Williams Mrs J M F Dibben

Placings:231/40 (3397)
2001/02: 16^{4}G, 20^{0}S

	Starts	1st	2nd	3rd	Win & Pl
NH Flat	1	0	0	0	802
Hurdles	1	0	0	0	0
Career Total	**5**	**1**	**1**	**1**	**15366**
117 4/00 Chel	2m1f	B NHF	SFT	£13877	

Total win prize-money £13878

Going: Sf: 0-1 GS: 0-0 Gd: 0-1 GF: - Fm: 0-0
Distance: 2m/2m3: 0-1 2m4-2m7: 0-1 3m+: 0-0
Track: LH: 0-0 RH: 0-1 Tight: 0-1 Gall: 0-0
Aids: Bl: 0-0 Vi: 0-0 Tstrap: 0-0
Best Rating: 117 4/00 Chel 2m1f soft NHF

Scavo (FR)

11-y-o b g Gay Minstrel (FR)-Passionnante (FR) (Dike (USA))
D C O'Brien D C O'Brien

Placings: 2/4/11326/P/P-PPP0 (4265)
2001/02: 20^{PS}, 21^{PS}, 21^{PS}, $20^{0}S$

	Starts	1st	2nd	3rd	Win & Pl
Hurdles	1	0	0	0	0
Chases	3	0	0	0	0
Career Total	**13**	**2**	**2**	**1**	**18639**
125 12/98 Plum 2m5f	C(0-135)HCh			G-S	£5868
118 11/98 Plum 2m5f	D Ch			SFT	£4182

Total win prize-money £10050

Going: Sf: 0-4 GS: 0-0 Gd: 0-0 GF: - Fm: 0-0
Distance: 2m/2m3: 0-0 2m4-2m7: 0-4 3m+: 0-0
Track: LH: 0-2 RH: 0-2 Tight: 0-3 Gall: 0-0
Aids: Bl: 0-1 Vi: 0-3 Tstrap: 0-0
Best Rating: 125 12/98 Ling 2m4f110y soft Ch

Scenic Storm (IRE)

99(97h) 94

7-y-o b g Scenic-Sit Elnaas (USA) (Sir Ivor)
Ferdy Murphy Leeds Plywood And Doors Ltd

Placings: 0/004-0P45P (4487)
2001/02: $21^{0}G$, $24^{P}GS$, $20^{4}G$, $24^{5}GS$, $26^{P}GS$

	Starts	1st	2nd	3rd	Win & Pl
Chases	5	0	0	0	339
Career Total	**9**	**0**	**0**	**0**	**339**

Going: Sf: 0-0 GS: 0-3 Gd: 0-2 GF: - Fm: 0-0
Distance: 2m/2m3: 0-0 2m4-2m7: 0-2 3m+: 0-3
Track: LH: 0-3 RH: 0-2 Tight: 0-2 Gall: 0-1
Aids: Bl: 0-0 Vi: 0-0 Tstrap: 0-0
Best Rating: 94 2/02 Fknm 3m110y gd-sft Ch

Very ordinary hurdling form in plating-class company to date.

Schemer (IRE)

66 80

7-y-o ch g Samhoi (USA)-Gambling Princess Vii (Damsire Unregistered)
Mrs S J Smith Mrs S Smith

Placings: 3-000 (3266)
2001/02: $16^{0}G$, $16^{0}G$, $20^{0}G$

	Starts	1st	2nd	3rd	Win & Pl
NH Flat	2	0	0	0	0
Hurdles	1	0	0	0	0
Career Total	**4**	**0**	**0**	**1**	**214**

Going: Sf: 0-0 GS: 0-0 Gd: 0-3 GF: - Fm: 0-0
Distance: 2m/2m3: 0-2 2m4-2m7: 0-1 3m+: 0-0
Track: LH: 0-3 RH: 0-0 Tight: 0-2 Gall: 0-1
Aids: Bl: 0-0 Vi: 0-0 Tstrap: 0-0
Best Rating: 95 9/00 Worc 2m gd-fm NHF

Runner-up in poor selling hurdle over an extended 21 furlongs at Southwell July 2002.

Schizo-Phonic

98 95

6-y-o ch m Gildoran-Trust To Luck (Mandamus)
B G Powell R J T 290 Limited

Placings: 403-2P34 (3397)
2001/02: $16^{2}S$, $21^{P}S$, $19^{3}GS$, $20^{4}S$

	Starts	1st	2nd	3rd	Win & Pl
NH Flat	1	0	1	0	492
Hurdles	3	0	0	1	705
Career Total	**7**	**0**	**1**	**2**	**1449**

Going: Sf: 0-3 GS: 0-1 Gd: 0-0 GF: - Fm: 0-0
Distance: 2m/2m3: 0-2 2m4-2m7: 0-2 3m+: 0-0
Track: LH: 0-2 RH: 0-1 Tight: 0-1 Gall: 0-1
Aids: Bl: 0-0 Vi: 0-0 Tstrap: 0-0
Best Rating: 99 2/01 Hayd 2m soft NHF

Schoodic Point (IRE)

7-y-o ch g Roselier (FR)-Madam Beau (Le Tricolore)
C P Morlock Pell-Mell Partners

Placings: 0-P (0352)
2001/02: $22^{P}G$

	Starts	1st	2nd	3rd	Win & Pl
Hurdles	1	0	0	0	
Career Total	**2**	**0**	**0**	**0**	

Going: Sf: 0-0 GS: 0-0 Gd: 0-1 GF: - Fm: 0-0
Distance: 2m/2m3: 0-0 2m4-2m7: 0-1 3m+: 0-0
Track: LH: 0-1 RH: 0-0 Tight: 0-1 Gall: 0-0
Aids: Bl: 0-0 Vi: 0-0 Tstrap: 0-0
Best Rating: 84 3/01 Hntg 2m110y soft NHF

Schuss

72f 78f

4-y-o b f Faustus (USA)-Scholastika (GER) (Alpenkonig (GER))
C W Thornton Mrs C Wilson

Placings: 25 (3750)
2001/02: $17^{2}S$, $16^{5}S$

	Starts	1st	2nd	3rd	Win & Pl
NH Flat	2	0	1	0	446
Career Total	**2**	**0**	**1**	**0**	**446**

Going: Sf: 0-2 GS: 0-0 Gd: 0-0 GF: - Fm: 0-0
Distance: 2m/2m3: 0-2 2m4-2m7: 0-0 3m+: 0-0
Track: LH: 0-1 RH: 0-1 Tight: 0-2 Gall: 0-0
Aids: Bl: 0-0 Vi: 0-0 Tstrap: 0-0
Best Rating: 78 1/02 Sedg 2m1f soft NHF

A well-bred filly, she showed promise in bumper on heavy ground on racecourse debut.

Scola Gravaca (IRE)

77f 80f

4-y-o ch g Petardia-Mystery Bid (Auction Ring (USA))
K A Morgan The Badlingham Syndicate

Placings: 00 (4771)
2001/02: $16^{0}GF$, $16^{0}GF$

	Starts	1st	2nd	3rd	Win & Pl
NH Flat	2	0	0	0	
Career Total	**2**	**0**	**0**	**0**	

Going: Sf: 0-0 GS: 0-0 Gd: 0-0 GF: - Fm: 0-2
Distance: 2m/2m3: 0-2 2m4-2m7: 0-0 3m+: 0-0
Track: LH: 0-0 RH: 0-1 Tight: 0-0 Gall: 0-1
Aids: Bl: 0-0 Vi: 0-0 Tstrap: 0-0
Best Rating: 80 3/02 Hntg 2m110y gd-fm NHF

Scolardy (IRE)

113 144

4-y-o b g Turtle Island (IRE)-Emerald Pendant (Nebos (GER))
W P Mullins David Flynn

Placings: 012121 (4250)
2001/02: $16^{0}SH$, $16^{1}YS$, $16^{2}Y$, $16^{1}YS$, $16^{2}HY$, $17^{1}G$

	Starts	1st	2nd	3rd	Win & Pl
Hurdles	6	3	2	0	69000
Career Total	**6**	**3**	**2**	**0**	**69000**
144 3/02 Chel 2m1f	A Hdl			GD	£52200
122 1/02 Thur 2m	Hdl			Y-S	£6138
110 11/01 Thur 2m	Hdl			Y-S	£3895

Total win prize-money £62233

Going: Sf: 0-1 GS: 0-0 Gd: 1-1 GF: - Fm: 0-0
Distance: **2m/2m3: 3-6** 2m4-2m7: 0-0 3m+: 0-0
Track: LH: 1-3 **RH: 2-3** Tight: 0-0 **Gall: 1-1**
Aids: Bl: 0-0 Vi: 0-0 Tstrap: 0-0
Best Rating: 144 3/02 Chel 2m1f good Hdl

Veru useful juvenile hurdler, consistent in Ireland before running away with the Triumph Hurdle. Goes well on good ground.

Sconced (USA)

7-y-o ch g Affirmed (USA)-Quaff (USA) (Raise A Cup (USA))
M J Polglase James S Kennerley And Miss Jenny Hall

Placings: 00/50 (3997)
2001/02: $24^{5}S$, $16^{0}S$

	Starts	1st	2nd	3rd	Win & Pl
Hurdles	2	0	0	0	0
Career Total	**4**	**0**	**0**	**0**	**0**

Going: Sf: 0-2 GS: 0-0 Gd: 0-0 GF: - Fm: 0-0
Distance: 2m/2m3: 0-1 2m4-2m7: 0-0 3m+: 0-1
Track: LH: 0-2 RH: 0-0 Tight: 0-0 Gall: 0-2
Aids: Bl: 0-2 Vi: 0-0 Tstrap: 0-0
Best Rating: 69 11/99 Carl 2m1f gd-sft Hdl

Scoop (IRE)

77(101h) (97h)85

6-y-o b m Scenic-Big Story (Cadeaux Genereux)
G M Moore Major E J Watt

Placings: 5633/P-21P32 (1072)
2001/02: $16^{2}F$, $16^{1}GF$, $16^{P}F$, $16^{3}G$, $17^{2}GF$

	Starts	1st	2nd	3rd	Win & Pl
Hurdles	5	1	2	1	3940
Career Total	**10**	**1**	**2**	**3**	**4743**
97 5/01 Hexm 2m	F(0-110)HHdl			G-F	£1848

Total win prize-money £1848

Going: Sf: 0-0 GS: 0-0 Gd: 0-1 GF: - Fm: 1-4
Distance: **2m/2m3: 1-5** 2m4-2m7: 0-0 3m+: 0-0
Track: **LH: 1-4** RH: 0-1 Tight: 0-2 Gall: 0-0
Aids: Bl: 0-0 Vi: 0-0 Tstrap: 0-0
Best Rating: 97 6/01 Prth 2m110y firm Hdl

Scoop Thirty Nine

80 22

4-y-o b f Petoski-Welsh Clover (Cruise Missile)
Mrs E Slack Mrs Evelyn Slack

Placings: P0 (2512)
2001/02: $16^{P}GS$, $16^{0}S$

	Starts	1st	2nd	3rd	Win & Pl
Hurdles	2	0	0	0	
Career Total	**2**	**0**	**0**	**0**	

Going: Sf: 0-1 GS: 0-1 Gd: 0-0 GF: - Fm: 0-0
Distance: 2m/2m3: 0-2 2m4-2m7: 0-0 3m+: 0-0
Track: LH: 0-2 RH: 0-0 Tight: 0-1 Gall: 0-0

Aids: Bl: 0-0 Vi: 0-0 Tstrap: 0-0
Best Rating:

Scoring Pedigree (IRE)

104 **119**

10-y-o b g King Luthier-Quick Romance (Lucky Brief)
J W Mullins Wilsford Racing Partnership

Placings:*01340*/1P/225/**3/3345-2345F12P23P2** **(4884)**
2001/02: 21^{2}GF, 21^{3}GF, 20^{4}GS, 20^{5}G, 20^{F}G, 21^{1}G, 19^{2}GF, 22^{P}G, 21^{2}G, 24^{3}GS, 21^{P}GF, 22^{2}GF

	Starts	1st	2nd	3rd	Win & Pl
Chases	12	1	4	2	11517
Career Total	**27**	**3**	**6**	**6**	**22883**

112	11/01	Folk	2m5f	F(0-90)Ch	GD	£3493
117	11/97	Kemp	2m5f	D Hdl	G-F	£2857
104	12/96	Bang	2m1f	H NHF	GD	£1658

Total win prize-money £8009

Going: Sf: 0-0 GS: 0-2 Gd: 1-5 GF: - Fm: 0-5
Distance: 2m/2m3: 0-0 **2m4-2m7: 1-11** 3m+: 0-1
Track: LH: 0-6 **RH: 1-5 Tight: 1-5** Gall: 0-4
Aids: Bl: 0-0 Vi: 0-1 Tstrap: 0-0
Best Rating: 126 2/99 Kemp 2m5f good Hdl

Useful hurdler, fair chaser who has had his share of problems. Finally got off the mark over fences in November 2001 when dropping in grade, and continued to run well subsequently without winning. Effective at up to two miles-six over fences. Does not want the ground too soft, has worn a visor.

Scorned (GER)

110 **111**

7-y-o b g Selkirk (USA)-Spurned (USA) (Robellino (USA))
I A Balding Kingsclere Stud

Placings:2 **(2683)**
2001/02: 16^{2}G

	Starts	1st	2nd	3rd	Win & Pl
Hurdles	1	0	1	0	940
Career Total	**1**	**0**	**1**	**0**	**940**

Going: Sf: 0-0 GS: 0-0 Gd: 0-1 GF: - Fm: 0-0
Distance: 2m/2m3: 0-1 2m4-2m7: 0-0 3m+: 0-0
Track: LH: 0-1 RH: 0-0 Tight: 0-0 Gall: 0-1
Aids: Bl: 0-0 Vi: 0-0 Tstrap: 0-0
Best Rating: 111 12/01 Donc 2m110y good Hdl

Listed class stayer on the Flat. Runner-up on his hurdles bow in winter of 2001. Suited by two miles. He has won on heavy and good ground on the level.

Scotmail Boy (IRE)

108 **130**

9-y-o b g Over The River (FR)-Princess Paula (Smoggy)
J Howard Johnson George Tobitt

Placings:05P/5000P/**2P13212/61P3-02P06P** **(4918)**
2001/02: 25^{0}G, 26^{2}HY, 28^{P}S, 33^{0}S, 21^{6}G, 28^{P}GF

	Starts	1st	2nd	3rd	Win & Pl
Chases	6	0	1	0	2120
Career Total	**25**	**3**	**4**	**2**	**23548**

116	11/00	Carl	3m2f	C(0-130)HCh	SFT	£6760
106	3/00	Sedg	2m5f	E Ch	G-F	£3342
103	1/00	Sedg	3m3f	E Ch	SFT	£2658

Total win prize-money £12762

Going: Sf: 0-3 GS: 0-0 Gd: 0-2 GF: - Fm: 0-1
Distance: 2m/2m3: 0-0 2m4-2m7: 0-1 3m+: 0-5
Track: LH: 0-4 RH: 0-1 Tight: 0-2 Gall: 0-1
Aids: Bl: 0-0 Vi: 0-0 Tstrap: 0-0
Best Rating: 130 11/01 Carl 3m2f heavy Ch

He set a personal best when third in the John Hughes Trophy Chase at Aintree on his final start of the 2000/2001, but suffered in the handicap as a result and was held last term. A sound jumper, he acts on any ground, stays well and is probably best without blinkers nowadays.

Scotmail Lad (IRE)

104 **130**

8-y-o b g Ilium-Nicholas Ferry (Floriferous)
G M Moore Gordon Brown/bert Watson

Placings:*041*/3134115135/52406/**222236322-P362245211PP** **(4876)**
2001/02: 25^{P}S, 21^{3}G, 20^{6}G, 21^{2}G, 21^{2}S, 20^{4}S, 22^{5}S, 20^{2}S, 20^{1}S, 20^{1}S, 25^{P}S, 20^{P}G

	Starts	1st	2nd	3rd	Win & Pl
Chases	12	2	3	1	12809
Career Total	**39**	**7**	**10**	**6**	**36076**

130	3/02	MRas	2m4f	E Ch	SFT	£3419
124	2/02	Leic	2m4f110y	E(0-105)HCh	SFT	£3627
122	3/99	Kels	2m6f110y	E(0-120)HHdl	SFT	£2892
125	1/99	Weth	2m4f110y	F(0-105)HHdl	HVY	£2066
123	12/98	Ayr	2m4f	E Hdl	HVY	£2794
100	10/98	Carl	2m1f	E Hdl	HVY	£2458
100	3/98	Hexm	2m	H NHF	GD	£1455

Total win prize-money £18711

Going: Sf: 2-8 GS: 0-0 Gd: 0-4 GF: - Fm: 0-0
Distance: 2m/2m3: 0-0 **2m4-2m7: 2-10** 3m+: 0-2
Track: LH: 0-8 **RH: 2-3 Tight: 1-3** Gall: 0-1
Aids: Bl: 0-3 **Vi: 2-5** Tstrap: 0-0
Best Rating: 130 3/02 MRas 2m4f soft Ch

Successful over hurdles, he got off the mark at the 18th attempt with a double over the larger obstacles. Acts on a very soft surface and has form on good ground. He is effective at up to two miles six.

Scots Grey

115 **131**

7-y-o gr g Terimon-Misowni (Niniski (USA))
N J Henderson W H Ponsonby

Placings:*2*165-445110320 **(4893)**
2001/02: 16^{4}GF, 19^{4}G, 20^{5}GF, 16^{1}G, 20^{1}G, 20^{0}G, 16^{3}GS, 20^{2}GF, 20^{0}G

	Starts	1st	2nd	3rd	Win & Pl
Hurdles	9	2	1	1	17387
Career Total	**13**	**3**	**2**	**1**	**20934**

125	12/01	Asct	2m4f	E(0-115)HHdl	GD	£6987
120	12/01	Ludl	2m	F(0-110)HHdl	GD	£3474
120	11/00	MRas	2m1f110y	E Hdl	G-S	£2634

Total win prize-money £13097

Going: Sf: 0-0 GS: 0-1 Gd: 2-5 GF: - Fm: 0-3
Distance: 2m/2m3: 1-3 2m4-2m7: 1-6 3m+: 0-0
Track: LH: 0-2 **RH: 2-6** Tight: 0-2 Gall: 0-0
Aids: Bl: 0-0 Vi: 0-0 Tstrap: 0-0
Best Rating: 131 4/02 Asct 2m4f gd-fm Hdl

Useful handicap hurdler, improved for the switch to front-running tactics, winning twice in a week in December 2001. Suited by decent ground, effective from two to two and a half miles.

Scottish Dance

96f **100f**

5-y-o ch m Bustino-Highland Lyric (Rymer)
N J Henderson Queen Elizabeth

Placings:*2122* **(3985)**
2001/02: 16^{2}G, 16^{1}GS, 18^{2}HY, 16^{2}G

	Starts	1st	2nd	3rd	Win & Pl
NH Flat	4	1	3	0	3194
Career Total	**4**	**1**	**3**	**0**	**3194**

98	1/02	Hntg	2m110y	H NHF	G-S	£1603

Total win prize-money £1603

Going: Sf: 0-1 GS: 1-1 Gd: 0-2 GF: - Fm: 0-0
Distance: **2m/2m3: 1-4** 2m4-2m7: 0-0 3m+: 0-0
Track: LH: 0-1 **RH: 1-3** Tight: 0-1 **Gall: 1-1**
Aids: Bl: 0-0 Vi: 0-0 Tstrap: 0-0
Best Rating: 100 2/02 Ludl 2m good NHF

Improved for her debut effort to get off the mark at Huntingdon over two miles on her second start. Held under a penalty. Acts on good to soft ground.

Scottish Memories (IRE)

121 **154**

6-y-o ch g Houmayoun (FR)-Interj (Salmon Leap (USA))
Noel Meade (J E Mulhern 31/7) Mrs Mary Halligan

Placings:20011 **(4940a)**
2001/02: 16^{2}Y, 18^{0}HY, 16^{0}GS, 16^{1}GY, 16^{1}Y

	Starts	1st	2nd	3rd	Win & Pl
Hurdles	5	2	1	0	56652
Career Total	**5**	**2**	**1**	**0**	**56652**

154	4/02	Punc	2m	Hdl	YLD	£32233
153	4/02	Fair	2m	Hdl	G-Y	£23128

Total win prize-money £55362

Going: Sf: 0-1 GS: 0-1 Gd: 0-0 GF: - Fm: 0-0
Distance: **2m/2m3: 2-5** 2m4-2m7: 0-0 3m+: 0-0
Track: LH: 0-2 **RH: 2-3** Tight: 0-0 Gall: 0-0
Aids: Bl: 0-0 Vi: 0-0 Tstrap: 0-2
Best Rating: 154 4/02 Punc 2m yield Hdl

Irish hurdler, improved to win top-class novice events at Fairyhouse and Punchestown in April 2002. Suited by soft ground.

Scottish Roots

7-y-o b g Roscoe Blake-Lothian Queen (Scorpio (FR))
C R Egerton Mrs C N Weatherby & Lady Daresbury

Placings:*350* **(4586)**
2001/02: 16^{3}G, 16^{5}G, 22^{0}G

	Starts	1st	2nd	3rd	Win & Pl
NH Flat	2	0	0	1	208
Hurdles	1	0	0	0	0
Career Total	**3**	**0**	**0**	**1**	**208**

Going: Sf: 0-0 GS: 0-0 Gd: 0-3 GF: - Fm: 0-0
Distance: 2m/2m3: 0-2 2m4-2m7: 0-1 3m+: 0-0
Track: LH: 0-1 RH: 0-2 Tight: 0-0 Gall: 0-1
Aids: Bl: 0-0 Vi: 0-0 Tstrap: 0-0
Best Rating: 102 10/01 Chel 2m110y good NHF

Scotton Green

103 **132**

11-y-o ch g Ardross-Grange Hill Girl (Workboy)

T D Easterby The I.B. & B.D.F. Partnership

Placings: *0P0/52/F31011/***220211226P/23P21130/2FP52253-PP225U30** **(4664)**
2001/02: 26^{P}S, 28^{P}S, 25^{2}G, 28^{2}S, 28^{5}HY, 33^{U}S, 34^{3}HY, 21^{0}G

	Starts	1st	2nd	3rd	Win & Pl
Chases	8	0	2	1	14243
Career Total	**45**	**7**	**13**	**5**	**121945**

132	2/00	Newc	4m1f	B(0-150)HCh	HVY	£29000
126	2/00	Catt	3m6f	C(0-130)HCh	GD	£7052
132	1/99	Catt	3m1f110y	E Ch	SFT	£4266
118	12/98	Hayd	3m	D(0-110)HCh	SFT	£3793
111	1/98	Ayr	3m110y	D(0-110)HHdl	G-S	£2897
97	1/98	Weth	2m4f110y	F(0-105)HHdl	SFT	£2150
94	11/97	Aint	2m4f	E(0-110)HHdl	GD	£2710

Total win prize-money £51871

Going: Sf: 0-6 GS: 0-0 Gd: 0-2 GF: - Fm: 0-0
Distance: 2m/2m3: 0-0 2m4-2m7: 0-1 3m+: 0-7
Track: LH: 0-6 RH: 0-1 Tight: 0-2 Gall: 0-1
Aids: Bl: 0-2 Vi: 0-0 Tstrap: 0-0
Best Rating: 132 3/02 Uttx 4m2f heavy Ch

A tough marathon runner, he ran his best race last term when third in the Midlands Grand National. Acts well on soft ground.

Scottstown

4-y-o b f Alhijaz-Cromarty (Shareef Dancer (USA))
M E Sowersby J Payne

Placings: *40*FPPP **(4772)**
2001/02: 17^{4}S, 16^{0}S, 20^{F}S, 17^{P}GS, 17^{P}GS, 21^{P}G

	Starts	1st	2nd	3rd	Win & Pl
NH Flat	2	0	0	0	0
Hurdles	4	0	0	0	0
Career Total	**6**	**0**	**0**	**0**	**0**

Going: Sf: 0-3 GS: 0-2 Gd: 0-1 GF: - Fm: 0-0
Distance: 2m/2m3: 0-4 2m4-2m7: 0-2 3m+: 0-0
Track: LH: 0-2 RH: 0-4 Tight: 0-5 Gall: 0-1
Aids: Bl: 0-1 Vi: 0-0 Tstrap: 0-0
Best Rating: 64 2/02 Muss 2m soft NHF

Scoundrel

84 **67**

11-y-o gr g Scallywag-Nicholcone (Celtic Cone)
A G Juckes Barry Hine

Placings: *23/111/PP/53-6U0* **(2926)**
2001/02: 26^{6}G, 16^{U}HY, 24^{0}GS

	Starts	1st	2nd	3rd	Win & Pl
Hurdles	3	0	0	0	0
Career Total	**12**	**3**	**1**	**2**	**6768**

98	1/97	Wind	2m4f	E Hdl	G-F	£2757
110	10/96	Ludl	2m	H NHF	FRM	£1316
93	10/96	Hntg	2m110y	H NHF	G-F	£1763

Total win prize-money £5838

Going: Sf: 0-1 GS: 0-1 Gd: 0-1 GF: - Fm: 0-0
Distance: 2m/2m3: 0-1 2m4-2m7: 0-0 3m+: 0-2
Track: LH: 0-0 RH: 0-3 Tight: 0-1 Gall: 0-1
Aids: Bl: 0-0 Vi: 0-0 Tstrap: 0-0
Best Rating: 110 10/96 Ludl 2m firm NHF

Scouser (IRE)

40 **33**

8-y-o b g King's Ride-Tony's Lass (Document)
Andrew Turnell Dr John Hollowood

Placings: *00/35300P/0-0* **(0089)**
2001/02: 16^{0}S

	Starts	1st	2nd	3rd	Win & Pl
Hurdles	1	0	0	0	0
Career Total	**10**	**0**	**0**	**2**	**717**

Going: Sf: 0-1 GS: 0-0 Gd: 0-0 GF: - Fm: 0-0
Distance: 2m/2m3: 0-1 2m4-2m7: 0-0 3m+: 0-0
Track: LH: 0-1 RH: 0-0 Tight: 0-0 Gall: 0-0
Aids: Bl: 0-0 Vi: 0-0 Tstrap: 0-0
Best Rating: 90 1/00 Muss 2m soft Hdl

Scowlin Brig

95 **61**

6-y-o ch g Minster Son-Gideonscleuch (Beverley Boy)
F P Murtagh D McLeod

Placings: *05*-P505 **(3507)**
2001/02: 20^{P}G, 16^{5}GS, 20^{0}G, 20^{5}S

	Starts	1st	2nd	3rd	Win & Pl
Hurdles	4	0	0	0	0
Career Total	**6**	**0**	**0**	**0**	**0**

Going: Sf: 0-1 GS: 0-1 Gd: 0-2 GF: - Fm: 0-0
Distance: 2m/2m3: 0-1 2m4-2m7: 0-3 3m+: 0-0
Track: LH: 0-1 RH: 0-3 Tight: 0-3 Gall: 0-0
Aids: Bl: 0-0 Vi: 0-0 Tstrap: 0-0
Best Rating: 76 2/01 Sedg 2m1f soft NHF

Scrahan Cross (IRE)

107 **148**

9-y-o b/br g Be My Native (USA)-Angolass (Al Sirat (USA))
J J O'Neill Russell McAllister

Placings: *30*0050522U32/42/111-1 **(1854)**
2001/02: 20^{1}S

	Starts	1st	2nd	3rd	Win & Pl
Chases	1	1	0	0	4800
Career Total	**18**	**4**	**4**	**2**	**28425**

148	10/01	Bang	2m4f110y	D(0-125)HCh	SFT	£4800
144	11/00	Carl	2m4f110y	E(0-115)HCh	SFT	£4046
126	5/00	Weth	3m1f	D Ch	G-S	£4214
136	5/00	Prth	3m	D Ch	GD	£4251

Total win prize-money £17311

Going: Sf: 1-1 GS: 0-0 Gd: 0-0 GF: - Fm: 0-0
Distance: 2m/2m3: 0-0 **2m4-2m7: 1-1** 3m+: 0-0
Track: **LH: 1-1** RH: 0-0 **Tight: 1-1** Gall: 0-0
Aids: Bl: 0-0 Vi: 0-0 Tstrap: 0-0
Best Rating: 148 10/01 Bang 2m4f110y soft Ch

He took a long time to get off the mark over fences, but then completed a hat-trick in the spring and autumn of 2000. Having his first run for almost a year when winning easily at Bangor in October 2001. Acts well in soft ground and stays three miles plus.

Scramble (USA)

4-y-o ch g Gulch (USA)-Syzygy (ARG) (Big Play (USA))
B Ellison (J H M Gosden 4/10) Keith Middleton

Placings: P **(2531)**
2001/02: 17^{P}S

	Starts	1st	2nd	3rd	Win & Pl
Hurdles	1	0	0	0	0
Career Total	**1**	**0**	**0**	**0**	**0**

Going: Sf: 0-1 GS: 0-0 Gd: 0-0 GF: - Fm: 0-0
Distance: 2m/2m3: 0-1 2m4-2m7: 0-0 3m+: 0-0
Track: LH: 0-0 RH: 0-1 Tight: 0-1 Gall: 0-0
Aids: Bl: 0-0 Vi: 0-0 Tstrap: 0-1
Best Rating:

Scratch The Dove

94 **80**

5-y-o b m Henbit (USA)-Coney Dove (Celtic Cone)
C J Price Cecil J Price

Placings: 400 **(3979)**
2001/02: 21^{4}G, 16^{0}S, 16^{0}G

	Starts	1st	2nd	3rd	Win & Pl
Hurdles	3	0	0	0	0
Career Total	**3**	**0**	**0**	**0**	**0**

Going: Sf: 0-1 GS: 0-0 Gd: 0-2 GF: - Fm: 0-0
Distance: 2m/2m3: 0-2 2m4-2m7: 0-1 3m+: 0-0
Track: LH: 0-0 RH: 0-3 Tight: 0-0 Gall: 0-0
Aids: Bl: 0-0 Vi: 0-0 Tstrap: 0-0
Best Rating: 80 2/02 Ludl 2m good Hdl

Maiden over hurdles. Has shown form over two and a half miles.

Scurry Dancer (FR)

88(105h) (88h)**109**

6-y-o b g Snurge-Fijar Dance (FR) (In Fiiar (USA))
O Sherwood The St Joseph Partnership

Placings: *1*-31PP3 **(4508)**
2001/02: 20^{3}S, 17^{1}G, 17^{P}HY, 22^{P}G, 17^{3}G

	Starts	1st	2nd	3rd	Win & Pl
Hurdles	4	1	0	1	3734
Chases	1	0	0	1	480
Career Total	**6**	**2**	**0**	**2**	**5789**

88	11/01	NAbb	2m1f	D Hdl	GD	£3259
103	12/00	Muss	2m	H NHF	GD	£1575

Total win prize-money £4834

Going: Sf: 0-2 GS: 0-0 Gd: 1-3 GF: - Fm: 0-0
Distance: **2m/2m3: 1-3** 2m4-2m7: 0-2 3m+: 0-0
Track: **LH: 1-3** RH: 0-2 **Tight: 1-4** Gall: 0-0
Aids: Bl: 0-0 Vi: 0-0 Tstrap: 0-0
Best Rating: 109 3/02 Plum 2m1f good Ch

He was reported to have made a noise on his hurdling debut at Fakenham in October 2001, but regained his winning ways the following month when he made all over two miles at Newton Abbot. Fair run on his chasing debut.

Sea Drifting

110 **123**

5-y-o b g Slip Anchor-Theme (IRE) (Sadler's Wells (USA))
Ferdy Murphy Mr & Mrs S Giles & Mr & Mrs J Taqvi

Placings: *110*-114P32 **(4816)**
2001/02: 20^{1}GS, 16^{1}S, 16^{4}S, 20^{P}HY, 20^{3}GS, 21^{2}GF

	Starts	1st	2nd	3rd	Win & Pl
Hurdles	6	2	1	1	17406
Career Total	**9**	**4**	**1**	**1**	**21172**

114	12/01	Ayr	2m	E Hdl	SFT	£2544
123	11/01	Newc	2m4f	D Hdl	G-S	£3328
112	2/01	Weth	2m	H NHF	SFT	£1701
108	1/01	Ludl	2m	H NHF	SFT	£2065

Total win prize-money £9640

Going: Sf: 1-3 GS: 1-2 Gd: 0-0 GF: - Fm: 0-1
Distance: 2m/2m3: 1-2 2m4-2m7: 1-4 3m+: 0-0

Track: LH: 2-5 RH: 0-1 Tight: 0-0 Gall: 1-2
Aids: Bl: 0-0 Vi: 0-0 Tstrap: 0-0
Best Rating: 123 4/02 Chel 2m5f110y gd-fm Hdl

A useful bumper horse, he made a winning debut over hurdles at Newcastle in November 2001. Followed up at Ayr and has run some fine races in defeat. Acts on soft ground and stays two and a half miles.

Sea Ferry (IRE)

112 **116**

6-y-o b g Ilium-Nicholas Ferry (Floriferous)
Noel T Chance A D Weller

Placings:121-21P (3255)
2001/02: 22^{2}S, 24^{1}S, 24^{P}S

	Starts	1st	2nd	3rd	Win & Pl
Hurdles	3	1	1	0	6917
Career Total	**6**	**3**	**2**	**0**	**13124**

116	11/01	Chep	3m	C(0-130)HHdl	SFT	£5434
111	2/01	Plum	2m5f	D Hdl	SFT	£3656
111	11/00	Folk	2m4f110y	F Hdl	HVY	£1827

Total win prize-money £10917

Going: Sf: 1-3 GS: 0-0 Gd: 0-0 GF: - Fm: 0-0
Distance: 2m/2m3: 0-0 2m4-2m7: 0-1 **3m+: 1-2**
Track: **LH: 1-3** RH: 0-0 Tight: 0-1 Gall: 0-1
Aids: Bl: 0-0 Vi: 0-0 Tstrap: 0-0
Best Rating: 116 11/01 Chep 3m soft Hdl

Lightly-raced staying hurdler. Gets three miles and acts on soft ground.

Sea Haitch Em

101 **58**

7-y-o ch g Norton Challenger-One Way Circuit (Windjammer (USA))
K A Morgan Mrs S J Storer

Placings:5000-045 (1678)
2001/02: 17^{0}GF, 21^{4}G, 21^{5}G

	Starts	1st	2nd	3rd	Win & Pl
Hurdles	3	0	0	0	0
Career Total	**7**	**0**	**0**	**0**	**0**

Going: Sf: 0-0 GS: 0-0 Gd: 0-2 GF: - Fm: 0-1
Distance: 2m/2m3: 0-1 2m4-2m7: 0-2 3m+: 0-0
Track: LH: 0-2 RH: 0-1 Tight: 0-3 Gall: 0-0
Aids: Bl: 0-0 Vi: 0-0 Tstrap: 0-0
Best Rating: 92 9/00 Worc 2m gd-fm NHF

Sea Isle

6-y-o ch m Selkirk (USA)-Miss Blitz (Formidable (USA))
H Alexander (J Parkes 13/6) Miss A M Rees

Placings:P (1931)
2001/02: 16^{P}G

	Starts	1st	2nd	3rd	Win & Pl
Hurdles	1	0	0	0	
Career Total	**1**	**0**	**0**	**0**	

Going: Sf: 0-0 GS: 0-0 Gd: 0-1 GF: - Fm: 0-0
Distance: 2m/2m3: 0-1 2m4-2m7: 0-0 3m+: 0-0
Track: LH: 0-1 RH: 0-0 Tight: 0-1 Gall: 0-0
Aids: Bl: 0-0 Vi: 0-0 Tstrap: 0-0
Best Rating:

Sea Knight (IRE)

78f **84f**

5-y-o b g Beau Sher-Meaney (Delamain (USA))
J I A Charlton J I A Charlton

Placings:0 (4900)
2001/02: 16^{0}G

	Starts	1st	2nd	3rd	Win & Pl
NH Flat	1	0	0	0	
Career Total	**1**	**0**	**0**	**0**	

Going: Sf: 0-0 GS: 0-0 Gd: 0-1 GF: - Fm: 0-0
Distance: 2m/2m3: 0-1 2m4-2m7: 0-0 3m+: 0-0
Track: LH: 0-0 RH: 0-1 Tight: 0-0 Gall: 0-0
Aids: Bl: 0-0 Vi: 0-0 Tstrap: 0-0
Best Rating: 84 4/02 Prth 2m110y good NHF

Sea Mark

108 **109+**

6-y-o ro g Warning-Mettlesome (Lomond (USA))
C Grant Akv Cladding Fabrications Ltd

Placings:40 (2683)
2001/02: 16^{4}G, 16^{0}G

	Starts	1st	2nd	3rd	Win & Pl
Hurdles	2	0	0	0	434
Career Total	**2**	**0**	**0**	**0**	**434**

Going: Sf: 0-0 GS: 0-0 Gd: 0-2 GF: - Fm: 0-0
Distance: 2m/2m3: 0-2 2m4-2m7: 0-0 3m+: 0-0
Track: LH: 0-2 RH: 0-0 Tight: 0-0 Gall: 0-1
Aids: Bl: 0-0 Vi: 0-0 Tstrap: 0-0
Best Rating: 105 11/01 Weth 2m good Hdl

A winner twice over seven furlongs on the Flat, he has won over hurdles but is largely disapointing. has worn blinkers.

Sea Minstrel

83 **44**

6-y-o b m Sea Raven (IRE)-Give Us A Treat (Cree Song)
J S Wainwright O R Dukes

Placings:6PP/0P0P (1421)
2001/02: 17^{0}GF, 17^{P}G, 17^{0}GF, 17^{P}G

	Starts	1st	2nd	3rd	Win & Pl
Hurdles	4	0	0	0	
Career Total	**7**	**0**	**0**	**0**	

Going: Sf: 0-0 GS: 0-0 Gd: 0-2 GF: - Fm: 0-2
Distance: 2m/2m3: 0-4 2m4-2m7: 0-0 3m+: 0-0
Track: LH: 0-1 RH: 0-3 Tight: 0-4 Gall: 0-0
Aids: Bl: 0-0 Vi: 0-0 Tstrap: 0-1
Best Rating: 44 6/01 MRas 2m1f110y gd-fm Hdl

Sea Pearl

100 **42**

8-y-o b m Derring Rose-Tillside Brig (New Brig)
Mrs S P Stretton Mr & Mrs Stretton

Placings:56P-P00 (4881)
2001/02: 19^{P}G, 20^{0}GF, 18^{0}GF

	Starts	1st	2nd	3rd	Win & Pl
Hurdles	3	0	0	0	
Career Total	**6**	**0**	**0**	**0**	

Going: Sf: 0-0 GS: 0-0 Gd: 0-1 GF: - Fm: 0-2
Distance: 2m/2m3: 0-2 2m4-2m7: 0-1 3m+: 0-0
Track: LH: 0-2 RH: 0-1 Tight: 0-1 Gall: 0-0
Aids: Bl: 0-0 Vi: 0-0 Tstrap: 0-0
Best Rating: 92 12/00 Tntn 2m1f soft NHF

Sea Princess

77f **41f**

5-y-o b m Sea Raven (IRE)-Mighty Miss (Doc Marten)
M E Sowersby M E Sowersby

Placings:0 (4873)
2001/02: 16^{0}GF

	Starts	1st	2nd	3rd	Win & Pl
NH Flat	1	0	0	0	
Career Total	**1**	**0**	**0**	**0**	

Going: Sf: 0-0 GS: 0-0 Gd: 0-0 GF: - Fm: 0-1
Distance: 2m/2m3: 0-1 2m4-2m7: 0-0 3m+: 0-0
Track: LH: 0-1 RH: 0-0 Tight: 0-0 Gall: 0-0
Aids: Bl: 0-0 Vi: 0-0 Tstrap: 0-0
Best Rating: 41 4/02 Weth 2m gd-fm NHF

Sea Tarth

80 **89**

11-y-o gr m Nicholas Bill-Seajan (Mandamus)
T R Kinsey Mrs T R Kinsey

Placings:122623400/440F340511/0U210/00P2-6 (0052)
2001/02: 20^{6}G

	Starts	1st	2nd	3rd	Win & Pl
Hurdles	1	0	0	0	0
Career Total	**29**	**4**	**5**	**2**	**13023**

87	8/99	Worc	2m7f110y	E Ch	SFT	£3036
91	4/99	Worc	3m	F(0-100)HHdl	G-S	£2409
86	4/99	Hrfd	3m2f	E(0-105)HHdl	G-F	£2431
106	5/97	Bang	2m1f	H NHF	GD	£1287

Total win prize-money £9164

Going: Sf: 0-0 GS: 0-0 Gd: 0-1 GF: - Fm: 0-0
Distance: 2m/2m3: 0-0 2m4-2m7: 0-1 3m+: 0-0
Track: LH: 0-1 RH: 0-0 Tight: 0-1 Gall: 0-0
Aids: Bl: 0-0 Vi: 0-0 Tstrap: 0-0
Best Rating: 106 6/97 Worc 2m good NHF

Seabrook Lad

11-y-o b g Derrylin-Moll (Rugantino)
C P Morlock (Mrs F Kehoe 14/4) Seabrook Partners

Placings:005/4F0214/634/**5U20115/23U2/PP-6P0** (1804)
2001/02: 24^{6}F, 25^{P}G, 24^{0}GF

	Starts	1st	2nd	3rd	Win & Pl
Chases	3	0	0	0	0
Career Total	**28**	**3**	**4**	**2**	**17196**

121	3/99	Ludl	3m	F(0-115)HCh	GD	£4758
120	2/99	Ludl	2m4f	F(0-100)HCh	GD	£2671
100	3/97	Hntg	2m5f110y	E Hdl	G-F	£2867

Total win prize-money £10298

Going: Sf: 0-0 GS: 0-0 Gd: 0-1 GF: - Fm: 0-2
Distance: 2m/2m3: 0-0 2m4-2m7: 0-0 3m+: 0-3
Track: LH: 0-1 RH: 0-2 Tight: 0-2 Gall: 0-0
Aids: Bl: 0-0 Vi: 0-0 Tstrap: 0-0
Best Rating: 125 12/99 Ludl 3m good Ch

Seahorse Boy (IRE)

5-y-o b g Petardia-Million At Dawn (IRE) (Fayruz)

Mrs A C Tate R C Smith

Placings:PP **(4591)**
2001/02: 19^{P}G, 16^{P}G

	Starts	1st	2nd	3rd	Win & Pl
Hurdles	2	0	0	0	
Career Total	**2**	**0**	**0**	**0**	

Going: Sf: 0-0 GS: 0-0 Gd: 0-2 GF: - Fm: 0-0
Distance: 2m/2m3: 0-1 2m4-2m7: 0-1 3m+: 0-0
Track: LH: 0-1 RH: 0-1 Tight: 0-0 Gall: 0-0
Aids: Bl: 0-0 Vi: 0-0 Tstrap: 0-0
Best Rating:

Search And Destroy (USA)

99 93
4-y-o b/br g Sky Classic (CAN)-Hunt The Thimble (USA) (Turn And Count (USA))
T R George (Sir Mark Prescott 4/8) Mrs R E R Rumboll

Placings:246 **(3641)**
2001/02: 16^{2}G, 17^{4}GS, 16^{6}S

	Starts	1st	2nd	3rd	Win & Pl
Hurdles	3	0	1	0	1066
Career Total	**3**	**0**	**1**	**0**	**1066**

Going: Sf: 0-1 GS: 0-1 Gd: 0-1 GF: - Fm: 0-0
Distance: 2m/2m3: 0-3 2m4-2m7: 0-0 3m+: 0-0
Track: LH: 0-1 RH: 0-2 Tight: 0-0 Gall: 0-0
Aids: Bl: 0-0 Vi: 0-0 Tstrap: 0-0
Best Rating: 93 10/01 Hrfd 2m1f gd-sft Hdl

Modest form over hurdles.

Search N' Destroy (NZ)

71f 66f
7-y-o b g Heroicity (AUS)-Nassa Charm (NZ) (Nassipour (USA))
Lady Connell Sir Michael Connell

Placings:0 **(2577)**
2001/02: 10^{0}HY

	Starts	1st	2nd	3rd	Win & Pl
NH Flat	1	0	0	0	
Career Total	**1**	**0**	**0**	**0**	

Going: Sf: 0-1 GS: 0-0 Gd: 0-0 GF: - Fm: 0-0
Distance: 2m/2m3: 0-1 2m4-2m7: 0-0 3m+: 0-0
Track: LH: 0-0 RH: 0-1 Tight: 0-0 Gall: 0-0
Aids: Bl: 0-0 Vi: 0-0 Tstrap: 0-0
Best Rating: 66 12/01 Towc 2m heavy NHF

Seasmith

101 97
7-y-o br/gr g Greensmith-Sea Spice (Precipice Wood)
L Lungo Miss S Blumberg

Placings:0-440 **(3688)**
2001/02: 16^{4}S, 17^{4}HY, 16^{0}HY

	Starts	1st	2nd	3rd	Win & Pl
Hurdles	3	0	0	0	271
Career Total	**4**	**0**	**0**	**0**	**271**

Going: Sf: 0-3 GS: 0-0 Gd: 0-0 GF: - Fm: 0-0
Distance: 2m/2m3: 0-3 2m4-2m7: 0-0 3m+: 0-0
Track: LH: 0-2 RH: 0-1 Tight: 0-0 Gall: 0-0
Aids: Bl: 0-0 Vi: 0-0 Tstrap: 0-0
Best Rating: 97 1/02 Carl 2m1f heavy Hdl

Has run with credit over hurdles in the mud.

Seattle Alley (USA)

101 94
9-y-o b g Seattle Dancer (USA)-Alyanaabi (USA) (Roberto (USA))
D J Wintle R Horne

Placings:6033012/1024/**PPF**PP4/4256/054441015P5 05-04414360500P **(4573)**
2001/02: 16^{0}S, 17^{4}G, 17^{4}S, 17^{1}G, 16^{4}S, 17^{3}G, 16^{6}S, 19^{0}S, 16^{5}S, 16^{0}GS, 22^{0}S, 20^{P}G

	Starts	1st	2nd	3rd	Win & Pl
Hurdles	11	1	0	1	424
Chases	1	0	0	0	0
Career Total	**46**	**5**	**3**	**3**	**19325**

98	11/00	Hrfd	2m1f	G Hdl	SFT	£1970
98	11/00	Hrfd	2m1f	G(0-95)HHdl	G-S	£1991
111	5/97	Hayd	2m	C HHdl	GD	£8862
89	3/97	Ling	2m110y	E Hdl	G-F	£2360

Total win prize-money £15187

Going: Sf: 0-7 GS: 0-1 Gd: 1-4 GF: - Fm: 0-0
Distance: **2m/2m3: 1-10** 2m4-2m7: 0-2 3m+: 0-0
Track: LH: 0-5 **RH: 1-7** Tight: 0-5 Gall: 0-1
Aids: Bl: 0-0 Vi: 0-0 Tstrap: 0-1
Best Rating: 121 3/97 Chel 2m1f good Hdl

Selling-class hurdler who likes soft ground and goes well at Hereford.

Seattle Art (USA)

106(90h) (63h)100
8-y-o b g Seattle Slew (USA)-Artiste (Artaius (USA))
P Monteith I Bell

Placings:0/0P/65553010F/63-52P00430FPP35U1 **(4855)**
2001/02: 20^{5}G, 16^{2}G, 16^{P}GS, 16^{0}G, 20^{0}S, 20^{4}GS, 16^{3}GF, 16^{0}S, 20^{F}G, 20^{P}S, 24^{P}S, 20^{3}GS, 16^{5}S, 17^{U}GF, 20^{1}G

	Starts	1st	2nd	3rd	Win & Pl
Hurdles	3	0	0	0	0
Chases	12	1	1	2	6472
Career Total	**29**	**2**	**1**	**4**	**10232**

93	4/02	Hexm	2m4f110y	F(0-95)HCh	GD	£3192
91	2/00	Muss	2m	E Ch	G-S	£3071

Total win prize-money £6263

Going: Sf: 0-5 GS: 0-3 Gd: 1-5 GF: - Fm: 0-2
Distance: 2m/2m3: 0-7 **2m4-2m7: 1-7** 3m+: 0-1
Track: **LH: 1-7** RH: 0-7 Tight: 0-8 Gall: 0-1
Aids: Bl: 0-0 Vi: 0-0 Tstrap: 0-0
Best Rating: 99 11/01 Ayr 2m4f gd-sft Ch

Moderate chaser, handles a left handed track but is suited by a right-handed track and good ground.

Seattle Lad (IRE)

10-y-o ch g Krayyan-Zedosa's Pet (Prince Bee)
M A Allen Mrs V J Davey

Placings:0PP **(4883)**
2001/02: 19^{0}G, 22^{P}G, 22^{P}GF

	Starts	1st	2nd	3rd	Win & Pl
Hurdles	3	0	0	0	
Career Total	**3**	**0**	**0**	**0**	

Going: Sf: 0-0 GS: 0-0 Gd: 0-2 GF: - Fm: 0-1
Distance: 2m/2m3: 0-1 2m4-2m7: 0-2 3m+: 0-0
Track: LH: 0-2 RH: 0-1 Tight: 0-2 Gall: 0-0
Aids: Bl: 0-0 Vi: 0-0 Tstrap: 0-0
Best Rating:

Seclude Fashions (IRE)

68 51
7-y-o b m Seclude (USA)-Grafton Fashions (Dikusa)
Cecil Mahon Clairmount Syndicate

Placings:000P **(4174)**
2001/02: 17^{0}YS, 16^{0}Y, 16^{0}GY, 22^{P}GS

	Starts	1st	2nd	3rd	Win & Pl
NH Flat	1	0	0	0	0
Hurdles	3	0	0	0	0
Career Total	**4**	**0**	**0**	**0**	

Going: Sf: 0-0 GS: 0-1 Gd: 0-0 GF: - Fm: 0-0
Distance: 2m/2m3: 0-3 2m4-2m7: 0-1 3m+: 0-0
Track: LH: 0-1 RH: 0-2 Tight: 0-1 Gall: 0-0
Aids: Bl: 0-0 Vi: 0-0 Tstrap: 0-0
Best Rating: 51 1/02 Fair 2m gd-yld Hdl

Second Helping

(56h)
8-y-o b g Emperor Fountain-April Rain (Lepanto (GER))
J R Best Second Helping Associated Group

Placings:00030050/2112511033/0003513**426-F** **(0478)**
2001/02: 17^{F}G

	Starts	1st	2nd	3rd	Win & Pl
Chases	1	0	0	0	
Career Total	**29**	**5**	**3**	**5**	**19563**

108	8/00	Hntg	2m110y	F(0-110)HHdl	G-F	£1920
110	10/99	Hntg	2m110y	C(0-130)HHdl	G-F	£4874
105	9/99	Plum	2m	E(0-105)HHdl	GD	£2818
94	6/99	Strf	2m110y	E Hdl	G-F	£2290
106	6/99	MRas	2m1f110y	F(0-100)HHdl	G-F	£3055

Total win prize-money £14958

Going: Sf: 0-0 GS: 0-0 Gd: 0-1 GF: - Fm: 0-0
Distance: 2m/2m3: 0-1 2m4-2m7: 0-0 3m+: 0-0
Track: LH: 0-0 RH: 0-1 Tight: 0-1 Gall: 0-0
Aids: Bl: 0-0 Vi: 0-0 Tstrap: 0-0
Best Rating: 110 11/99 Kemp 2m good Hdl

Second Pick (IRE)

6-y-o b g Doubletour (USA)-Wurli (Wolver Hollow)
R J Armson (C Weedon 28/1) R J Armson

Placings:000 **(4317)**
2001/02: 16^{0}S, 17^{0}GS, 16^{0}HY

	Starts	1st	2nd	3rd	Win & Pl
NH Flat	3	0	0	0	
Career Total	**3**	**0**	**0**	**0**	

Going: Sf: 0-2 GS: 0-1 Gd: 0-0 GF: - Fm: 0-0
Distance: 2m/2m3: 0-3 2m4-2m7: 0-0 3m+: 0-0
Track: LH: 0-1 RH: 0-2 Tight: 0-2 Gall: 0-0
Aids: Bl: 0-0 Vi: 0-0 Tstrap: 0-0
Best Rating: 34 1/02 Kemp 2m soft NHF

Second Time Around (IRE)

5-y-o b m Mukaddamah (USA)-Up The Gates (Captain James)
M C Chapman Eric Knowles

Placings:0-P **(0209)**
2001/02: 16^{PF}

	Starts	1st	2nd	3rd	Win & Pl
Hurdles	1	0	0	0	
Career Total	**2**	**0**	**0**	**0**	

Going: Sf: 0-0 GS: 0-0 Gd: 0-0 GF: - Fm: 0-1
Distance: 2m/2m3: 0-1 2m4-2m7: 0-0 3m+: 0-0
Track: LH: 0-1 RH: 0-0 Tight: 0-1 Gall: 0-0
Aids: Bl: 0-0 Vi: 0-0 Tstrap: 0-0
Best Rating:

Secret Alliance (IRE)

10-y-o b g Royal Fountain-Hardy Polly (Pollerton)
P C Handley P C Handley

Placings:5 **(4852)**
2001/02: 24^{5}G

	Starts	1st	2nd	3rd	Win & Pl
Chases	1	0	0	0	0
Career Total	**1**	**0**	**0**	**0**	**0**

Going: Sf: 0-0 GS: 0-0 Gd: 0-1 GF: - Fm: 0-0
Distance: 2m/2m3: 0-0 2m4-2m7: 0-0 3m+: 0-1
Track: LH: 0-1 RH: 0-0 Tight: 0-1 Gall: 0-0
Aids: Bl: 0-0 Vi: 0-0 Tstrap: 0-0
Best Rating: 67 4/02 Strf 3m good Ch

Secret Bay

95 **138**

13-y-o b g Zambrano-Secret Storm (Secret Ace)
Mrs Caroline Bailey Mrs J A Bowen

Placings:11/321/15/1112/12-261115 **(4650)**
2001/02: 25^{2}S, 28^{6}GF, 24^{1}GS, 24^{1}GS, 23^{1}S, 21^{5}G

	Starts	1st	2nd	3rd	Win & Pl
Chases	6	3	1	0	9653
Career Total	**19**	**11**	**4**	**1**	**35810**

122	3/02	Leic	2m7f110y	H Ch	SFT	£5070
138	2/02	Hntg	3m	H Ch	G-S	£1186
111	2/02	Ludl	3m	H Ch	G-S	£2628
129	3/01	MRas	3m1f	H Ch	G-S	£2262
138	3/00	Newb	2m6f110y	H Ch	G-F	£2216
125	3/00	Leic	2m4f110y	H Ch	G-S	£2310
128	2/00	Ludl	3m	H Ch	G-F	£2338
114	4/99	Uttx	2m7f	H Ch	G-S	£1593
118	4/98	Prth	3m	H Ch	G-S	£2318
114	4/97	Hntg	3m	H Ch	GD	£1220
114	4/97	Hexm	3m1f	H Ch	FRM	£1058

Total win prize-money £24202

Going: Sf: 1-2 GS: 2-2 Gd: 0-1 GF: - Fm: 0-1
Distance: 2m/2m3: 0-0 2m4-2m7: 0-1 **3m+: 3-5**
Track: LH: 0-3 **RH: 3-3** Tight: 1-3 Gall: 1-1
Aids: Bl: 0-0 Vi: 0-0 Tstrap: 0-0
Best Rating: 138 2/02 Hntg 3m gd-sft Ch

Veteran hunter chaser, prolific winner and twice runner-up in the Aintree Fox Hunters'. Stays three miles, acts on any ground.

Secret Bid (IRE)

12-y-o ch g Seclude (USA)-Trial Bid (Grundy)
R H Alner The Droop Partners

Placings:0500/1P5/**20UP**/4232213/2444316/0312444 0/P-5 **(0323)**
2001/02: 25^{5}G

	Starts	1st	2nd	3rd	Win & Pl
Chases	1	0	0	0	0
Career Total	**35**	**4**	**6**	**4**	**23289**

120	11/99	Folk	3m2f	F(0-110)HCh	G-F	£4279
119	3/99	Folk	3m2f	F(0-105)HCh	GD	£2469
115	1/98	Folk	3m2f	E(0-115)HCh	GD	£2849
93	10/95	Towc	3m	F(0-100)HHdl	G-F	£1996

Total win prize-money £11595

Going: Sf: 0-0 GS: 0-0 Gd: 0-1 GF: - Fm: 0-0
Distance: 2m/2m3: 0-0 2m4-2m7: 0-0 3m+: 0-1
Track: LH: 0-0 RH: 0-1 Tight: 0-1 Gall: 0-0
Aids: Bl: 0-0 Vi: 0-0 Tstrap: 0-0
Best Rating: 120 12/99 Folk 3m2f good Ch

Secret Can't Say (IRE)

8-y-o b m Jurado (USA)-Jims Cousin (Jimsun)
K Goldsworthy (P Bowen 14/8) Greenacre Racing Partnership Ltd

Placings:P-FP00U214656 **(4179)**
2001/02: 21^{F}GF, 25^{P}G, 16^{0}G, 21^{0}GF, 24^{U}GF, 25^{2}GS, 24^{1}GF, 24^{4}G, 22^{6}GF, 26^{5}GF, 24^{6}GS

	Starts	1st	2nd	3rd	Win & Pl
Hurdles	2	0	1	0	690
Chases	9	1	0	0	3775
Career Total	**12**	**1**	**1**	**0**	**4464**

98	7/01	Sthl	3m110y	E Ch	G-F	£3396

Total win prize-money £3396

Going: Sf: 0-0 GS: 0-2 Gd: 0-3 GF: - Fm: 1-6
Distance: 2m/2m3: 0-1 2m4-2m7: 0-3 **3m+: 1-7**
Track: **LH: 1-8** RH: 0-2 **Tight: 1-8** Gall: 0-0
Aids: Bl: 0-4 Vi: 0-0 **Tstrap: 1-9**
Best Rating: 98 7/01 Sthl 3m110y gd-fm Ch

Secret Drinker (IRE)

100 **78**

6-y-o b g Husyan (USA)-Try Le Reste (IRE) (Le Moss)
O Sherwood S Channing-Williams

Placings:*0*-005221 **(4173)**
2001/02: 22^{0}S, 24^{0}G, 22^{5}S, 22^{2}S, 22^{2}S, 25^{1}GS

	Starts	1st	2nd	3rd	Win & Pl
Hurdles	6	1	2	0	3673
Career Total	**7**	**1**	**2**	**0**	**3673**

78	3/02	Plum	3m1f110y	F(0-95)HHdl	G-S	£2278

Total win prize-money £2279

Going: Sf: 0-4 GS: 1-1 Gd: 0-1 GF: - Fm: 0-0
Distance: 2m/2m3: 0-0 2m4-2m7: 0-4 **3m+: 1-2**
Track: LH: 0-4 RH: 0-1 Tight: 0-3 Gall: 0-1
Aids: Bl: 0-0 Vi: 0-0 Tstrap: 0-0
Best Rating: 78 3/02 Plum 3m1f110y gd-sft Hdl

Progressed over hurdles to win a modest staying event in March.

Secret Native (IRE)

108 **134**

7-y-o b g Be My Native (USA)-Rivers Secret (Young Man (FR))
T J Taaffe Mrs Mary Ward

Placings:*5/6*0000/10**B020F**112-30362100 **(4647)**
2001/02: 20^{3}GF, 20^{0}YS, 20^{3}YS, 18^{6}Y, 20^{2}YS, 19^{1}SH, 21^{0}GS, 24^{0}G

	Starts	1st	2nd	3rd	Win & Pl
Hurdles	8	1	1	2	19038
Career Total	**24**	**4**	**3**	**2**	**39178**

134	1/02	Naas	2m3f	HHdl	SH	£10966
126	1/01	Leop	2m6f	(0-140)HHdl	SFT	£7862
122	12/00	Leop	2m2f	(0-120)HHdl	SH	£6624
94	7/00	Slig	2m	Hdl	G-F	£2760

Total win prize-money £28213

Going: Sf: 0-0 GS: 0-1 Gd: 0-1 GF: - Fm: 0-1
Distance: **2m/2m3: 1-2** 2m4-2m7: 0-5 3m+: 0-1
Track: **LH: 1-6** RH: 0-0 Tight: 0-1 Gall: 0-1
Aids: Bl: 0-0 Vi: 0-0 **Tstrap: 1-4**
Best Rating: 134 1/02 Naas 2m3f sft-hvy Hdl

Comfortable winner in testing ground at Naas in January 2002, but he was well beaten in the Coral Cup at Cheltenham in March 2002.

Secret Passion

65 **29**

4-y-o gr f Petong-Jamarj (Tyrnavos)
J M Bradley (P S McEntee 11/12) Marinos Ioannou

Placings:0 **(3979)**
2001/02: 16^{0}G

	Starts	1st	2nd	3rd	Win & Pl
Hurdles	1	0	0	0	
Career Total	**1**	**0**	**0**	**0**	

Going: Sf: 0-0 GS: 0-0 Gd: 0-1 GF: - Fm: 0-0
Distance: 2m/2m3: 0-1 2m4-2m7: 0-0 3m+: 0-0
Track: LH: 0-0 RH: 0-1 Tight: 0-0 Gall: 0-0
Aids: Bl: 0-0 Vi: 0-0 Tstrap: 0-0
Best Rating: 29 2/02 Ludl 2m good Hdl

Secret Progress (IRE)

80

6-y-o ch g Safety Catch (USA)-Lady Progress (Proverb)
I A Duncan Anthony McAlister

Placings:*0000* **(4449a)**
2001/02: 16^{0}S, 16^{0}HY, 22^{0}HY, 16^{0}S

	Starts	1st	2nd	3rd	Win & Pl
NH Flat	3	0	0	0	0
Hurdles	1	0	0	0	0
Career Total	**4**	**0**	**0**	**0**	

Going: Sf: 0-4 GS: 0-0 Gd: 0-0 GF: - Fm: 0-0
Distance: 2m/2m3: 0-3 2m4-2m7: 0-1 3m+: 0-0
Track: LH: 0-1 RH: 0-1 Tight: 0-0 Gall: 0-0
Aids: Bl: 0-0 Vi: 0-0 Tstrap: 0-0
Best Rating: 92 1/02 DRoy 2m soft NHF

Secret Sentiment

85 **77**

4-y-o b f Mark Of Esteem (IRE)-Sahara Baladee (USA) (Shadeed (USA))

A B Coogan (E A L Dunlop 21/9) A B Coogan

Placings:65P (3860)
2001/02: 16^{6}S, 16^{5}HY, 20^{P}S

	Starts	1st	2nd	3rd	Win & Pl
Hurdles	3	0	0	0	0
Career Total	**3**	**0**	**0**	**0**	**0**

Going: Sf: 0-3 GS: 0-0 Gd: 0-0 GF: - Fm: 0-0
Distance: 2m/2m3: 0-2 2m4-2m7: 0-1 3m+: 0-0
Track: LH: 0-1 RH: 0-2 Tight: 0-0 Gall: 0-2
Aids: Bl: 0-0 Vi: 0-0 Tstrap: 0-0
Best Rating: 77 2/02 Sand 2m110y heavy Hdl

Secret Streams (IRE)

8-y-o br g Over The River (FR)-Brigette's Secret (Good Thyne (USA))
C Sporborg Sir Chippendale Keswick

Placings:1P-20 (0428)
2001/02: 20^{2}GF, 21^{0}G

	Starts	1st	2nd	3rd	Win & Pl
Chases	2	0	1	0	338
Career Total	**4**	**1**	**1**	**0**	**3835**

108	3/01	Sand	2m4f110y	H Ch	SFT £3497

Total win prize-money £3497

Going: Sf: 0-0 GS: 0-0 Gd: 0-1 GF: - Fm: 0-1
Distance: 2m/2m3: 0-0 2m4-2m7: 0-2 3m+: 0-0
Track: LH: 0-0 RH: 0-1 Tight: 0-0 Gall: 0-1
Aids: Bl: 0-0 Vi: 0-0 Tstrap: 0-0
Best Rating: 108 3/01 Sand 2m4f110y soft Ch

Secret Truth

13-y-o ch m Nestor-Another Nitty (Country Retreat)
Andrew J Martin Andrew J Martin

Placings:PPPPPP/5/3P3P/4PPP-P152PP (4659)
2001/02: 25^{P}G, 21^{1}GF, 21^{5}G, 20^{2}S, 20^{P}S, 24^{P}G

	Starts	1st	2nd	3rd	Win & Pl
Chases	6	1	1	0	3195
Career Total	**20**	**1**	**1**	**2**	**3664**

96	5/01	Strf	2m5f110y	H Ch	G-F £2530

Total win prize-money £2531

Going: Sf: 0-2 GS: 0-0 Gd: 0-3 GF: - Fm: 1-1
Distance: 2m/2m3: 0-0 **2m4-2m7: 1-4** 3m+: 0-2
Track: **LH: 1-1** RH: 0-4 **Tight: 1-2** Gall: 0-0
Aids: Bl: 0-1 Vi: 0-0 Tstrap: 0-0
Best Rating: 100 2/02 Sand 2m4f110y soft Ch

Hunter chaser who has shown her best form on fast ground. Reportedly retired.

Secret Whisper

6-y-o ch m Infantry-Mossberry Fair (Mossberry)
M Wellings R P Dineen

Placings:006-P0 (0734)
2001/02: 19^{P}G, 22^{0}G

	Starts	1st	2nd	3rd	Win & Pl
Hurdles	2	0	0	0	
Career Total	**5**	**0**	**0**	**0**	**0**

Going: Sf: 0-0 GS: 0-0 Gd: 0-2 GF: - Fm: 0-0
Distance: 2m/2m3: 0-0 2m4-2m7: 0-2 3m+: 0-0
Track: LH: 0-1 RH: 0-1 Tight: 0-1 Gall: 0-0
Aids: Bl: 0-0 Vi: 0-0 Tstrap: 0-0
Best Rating: 76 11/00 Hrfd 2m1f gd-sft NHF

Secret's Out

106 91

6-y-o b g Polish Precedent (USA)-Secret Obsession (USA) (Secretariat (USA))
W Clay F Lloyd

Placings:0033/235-060542223030 (4774)
2001/02: 17^{0}G, 16^{6}GF, 17^{0}GF, 16^{5}GS, 16^{4}G, 16^{2}GF, 16^{2}G, 17^{2}GS, 16^{3}G, 17^{0}S, 17^{3}G, 17^{0}G

	Starts	1st	2nd	3rd	Win & Pl
Hurdles	12	0	3	2	3181
Career Total	**19**	**0**	**4**	**5**	**4907**

Going: Sf: 0-1 GS: 0-2 Gd: 0-6 GF: - Fm: 0-3
Distance: 2m/2m3: 0-12 2m4-2m7: 0-0 3m+: 0-0
Track: LH: 0-7 RH: 0-5 Tight: 0-10 Gall: 0-0
Aids: Bl: 0-0 Vi: 0-10 Tstrap: 0-0
Best Rating: 96 9/00 Uttx 2m gd-sft Hdl

Secrete Contract

81 74

4-y-o b g Contract Law (USA)-Secret Account (Blakeney)
Miss A M Newton-Smith (G L Moore 21/5) The Secrete Society Partnership

Placings:PP0 (4850)
2001/02: 16^{P}S, 22^{P}S, 22^{0}G

	Starts	1st	2nd	3rd	Win & Pl
Hurdles	3	0	0	0	
Career Total	**3**	**0**	**0**	**0**	

Going: Sf: 0-2 GS: 0-0 Gd: 0-1 GF: - Fm: 0-0
Distance: 2m/2m3: 0-1 2m4-2m7: 0-2 3m+: 0-0
Track: LH: 0-1 RH: 0-2 Tight: 0-2 Gall: 0-0
Aids: Bl: 0-1 Vi: 0-0 Tstrap: 0-0
Best Rating:

Securon Lady

11-y-o b m Derrylin-Thevicarsdaughter (The Parson)
M R Bosley Mrs Jean M O'Connor

Placings:0/06U (1144)
2001/02: 26^{6}G, 24^{U}GF

	Starts	1st	2nd	3rd	Win & Pl
Chases	2	0	0	0	0
Career Total	**4**	**0**	**0**	**0**	**0**

Going: Sf: 0-0 GS: 0-0 Gd: 0-1 GF: - Fm: 0-1
Distance: 2m/2m3: 0-0 2m4-2m7: 0-0 3m+: 0-2
Track: LH: 0-2 RH: 0-0 Tight: 0-2 Gall: 0-0
Aids: Bl: 0-1 Vi: 0-0 Tstrap: 0-0
Best Rating: 66 9/97 Worc 2m good NHF

Securon Rose (IRE)

96 72

6-y-o gr m Roselier (FR)-Hand Me Down (Cheval)
R Rowe Mrs R A Proctor

Placings:00-5605 (4415)
2001/02: 19^{5}GS, 20^{6}S, 26^{0}S, 22^{5}S

	Starts	1st	2nd	3rd	Win & Pl
Hurdles	4	0	0	0	0
Career Total	**6**	**0**	**0**	**0**	**0**

Going: Sf: 0-3 GS: 0-1 Gd: 0-0 GF: - Fm: 0-0
Distance: 2m/2m3: 0-0 2m4-2m7: 0-3 3m+: 0-1
Track: LH: 0-1 RH: 0-2 Tight: 0-3 Gall: 0-1
Aids: Bl: 0-0 Vi: 0-0 Tstrap: 0-0
Best Rating: 82 1/01 Kemp 2m soft NHF

Lightly raced hurdler. Raced mainly at trips around two and a half miles. Modest form to date.

See More Business (IRE)

118 181

12-y-o b g Seymour Hicks (FR)-Miss Redlands (Dubassoff (USA))
P F Nicholls Sir Robert Ogden

Placings:111/**122F/3111C/41P31/11141/1515-FP135** (4648)
2001/02: 24^{F}S, 29^{P}GS, 25^{1}GS, 26^{3}G, 25^{5}G

	Starts	1st	2nd	3rd	Win & Pl
Chases	5	1	0	1	52770
Career Total	**31**	**16**	**2**	**3**	**635803**

181	2/02	Winc	3m1f110y	A Ch	G-S	£16770
188	1/01	Chel	3m1f110y	A Ch	SFT	£49125
188	10/00	Weth	3m1f	A Ch	SFT	£27000
188	4/00	Aint	3m1f	A Ch	GD	£46900
188	2/00	Newb	3m	B Ch	G-S	£31000
188	12/99	Kemp	3m	A Ch	SFT	£65500
185	10/99	Weth	3m1f	A Ch	GD	£23800
178	3/99	Chel	3m2f110y	A Ch	G-S	£149600
178	12/98	Chep	3m	A HCh	GD	£20305
174	1/98	Chel	3m1f110y	B Ch	G-S	£16937
170	12/97	Kemp	3m	A Ch	SFT	£64374
160	12/97	Chep	3m	A HCh	SFT	£18606
131	11/96	Chep	2m3f110y	A Ch	G-S	£13786
144	12/95	Sand	2m6f	A Hdl	GD	£9555
126	11/95	Winc	2m6f	C Hdl	GD	£3727
130	11/95	Chep	2m4f110y	D Hdl	G-S	£2845

Total win prize-money £559833

Going: Sf: 0-1 GS: 1-2 Gd: 0-2 GF: - Fm: 0-0
Distance: 2m/2m3: 0-0 2m4-2m7: 0-0 **3m+: 1-5**
Track: LH: 0-4 **RH: 1-1** Tight: 0-1 Gall: 0-1
Aids: **Bl: 1-4** Vi: 0-0 Tstrap: 0-0
Best Rating: 188 1/01 Chel 3m1f110y soft Ch

A top-class chaser, winner of the Gold Cup in 1999, he returned to winning ways at Wincanton in February 2002. A fine third in the Gold Cup next time, he stays three miles two furlongs. Acts on soft and good but does not want the ground too fast.

See More Snow

83f

5-y-o b g Seymour Hicks (FR)-Snow Child (Mandrake Major)
W G M Turner E Goody

Placings:64-6 (3613)
2001/02: 16^{6}S

	Starts	1st	2nd	3rd	Win & Pl
NH Flat	1	0	0	0	0
Career Total	**3**	**0**	**0**	**0**	**0**

Going: Sf: 0-1 GS: 0-0 Gd: 0-0 GF: - Fm: 0-0
Distance: 2m/2m3: 0-1 2m4-2m7: 0-0 3m+: 0-0
Track: LH: 0-0 RH: 0-1 Tight: 0-1 Gall: 0-0
Aids: Bl: 0-0 Vi: 0-0 Tstrap: 0-0
Best Rating: 83 4/01 Winc 2m soft NHF

See More Stars

84 — 76

5-y-o b g Seymour Hicks (FR)-China's Way (USA) (Native Uproar (USA))

J Mackie Fools Who Dream

Placings:P **(4842)**

2001/02: 20^{P}G

	Starts	1st	2nd	3rd	Win & Pl
Hurdles	1	0	0	0	
Career Total	**1**	**0**	**0**	**0**	

Going: Sf: 0-0 GS: 0-0 Gd: 0-1 GF: - Fm: 0-0
Distance: 2m/2m3: 0-0 2m4-2m7: 0-1 3m+: 0-0
Track: LH: 0-1 RH: 0-0 Tight: 0-1 Gall: 0-0
Aids: Bl: 0-0 Vi: 0-0 Tstrap: 0-0
Best Rating:

See More Tricks

75 — 40

7-y-o b m Seymour Hicks (FR)-Jolejester (Relkino)

W Jenks Michael Stoddart

Placings:*0/0*-00 **(0777)**

2001/02: 20^{0}G, 16^{0}GF

	Starts	1st	2nd	3rd	Win & Pl
Hurdles	2	0	0	0	
Career Total	**4**	**0**	**0**	**0**	

Going: Sf: 0-0 GS: 0-0 Gd: 0-1 GF: - Fm: 0-1
Distance: 2m/2m3: 0-1 2m4-2m7: 0-1 3m+: 0-0
Track: LH: 0-2 RH: 0-0 Tight: 0-0 Gall: 0-0
Aids: Bl: 0-0 Vi: 0-0 Tstrap: 0-0
Best Rating: 49 3/00 Ludl 2m good NHF

See You Around

99(101h) — (94h)110

7-y-o b g Sharp Deal-Seeborg (Lepanto (GER))

C Tizzard The Infamous Five

Placings:*0320*P25P-4SP64U22P **(4634)**

2001/02: 22^{4}HY, 19^{S}G, 21^{P}G, 18^{6}S, 26^{4}HY, 21^{U}G, 19^{2}S, 21^{2}S, 24^{P}GF

	Starts	1st	2nd	3rd	Win & Pl
Hurdles	2	0	0	0	0
Chases	7	0	2	0	2561
Career Total	**17**	**0**	**4**	**1**	**4125**

Going: Sf: 0-5 GS: 0-0 Gd: 0-3 GF: - Fm: 0-1
Distance: 2m/2m3: 0-2 2m4-2m7: 0-5 3m+: 0-2
Track: LH: 0-3 RH: 0-5 Tight: 0-5 Gall: 0-0
Aids: Bl: 0-5 Vi: 0-0 Tstrap: 0-0
Best Rating: 110 3/02 Chep 2m3f110y soft Ch

Modest hurdler, novice chaser. Suited by soft/heavy ground and trips around two and a half miles.

See You Sometime

112 — 140

7-y-o b g Sharp Deal-Shepani (New Member)

J W Mullins J A G Meaden

Placings:*43435*-3111132 **(3232)**

2001/02: 17^{3}G, 20^{1}GF, 22^{1}GF, 21^{1}G, 21^{1}GS, 21^{3}G, 26^{2}GS

	Starts	1st	2nd	3rd	Win & Pl
Hurdles	7	4	1	2	41196
Career Total	**12**	**4**	**1**	**4**	**41857**

140	12/01	Newb	2m5f	B Hdl	G-S	£9993
132	11/01	Chel	2m5f	C(0-135)HHdl	GD	£18118
121	6/01	Strf	2m6f110y	D Hdl	G-F	£3796
118	5/01	Folk	2m4f110y	F(0-100)HHdl	G-F	£2037

Total win prize-money £33946

Going: Sf: 0-0 GS: 1-2 Gd: 1-3 GF: - Fm: 2-2
Distance: 2m/2m3: 0-1 **2m4-2m7: 4-5** 3m+: 0-1
Track: **LH: 3-4** RH: 1-3 Tight: 2-2 Gall: 2-4
Aids: Bl: 0-0 Vi: 0-0 Tstrap: 0-0
Best Rating: 140 12/01 Newb 2m5f gd-sft Hdl

Fair placed form in bumpers before scoring over hurdles at Folkestone in May of 2001, and won his next three starts before finishing second to Classified in a grade one event at Newbury in December 2001. Effective over two miles four to two miles six furlongs. Acts on a sound surface.

Seebald (GER)

119(104h) — 168

7-y-o b g Mulberry (FR)-Spartina (USA) (Northern Baby (CAN))

M C Pipe The Macca & Growler Partnership

Placings:110/2630-**111111122** **(4675)**

2001/02: 16^{1}G, 16^{1}F, 17^{1}GF, 16^{1}G, 16^{1}G, 19^{1}G, 20^{1}S, 16^{2}GS, 16^{2}G

	Starts	1st	2nd	3rd	Win & Pl
Chases	9	7	2	0	109533
Career Total	**16**	**9**	**3**	**1**	**128523**

165	1/02	Wwck	2m4f110y	C Ch	SFT	£8385
163	12/01	Asct	2m3f110y	A Ch	GD	£16375
163	11/01	Chel	2m	A Ch	GD	£18000
141	10/01	Chel	2m	C Ch	GD	£10272
133	6/01	MRas	2m1f110y	D Ch	G-F	£6045
127	6/01	Hrfd	2m	E Ch	FRM	£3159
127	5/01	Hrfd	2m	E Ch	GD	£3297
133	2/00	Newb	2m110y	C Hdl	G-S	£5226
123	1/00	Tntn	2m1f	E Hdl	G-S	£2513

Total win prize-money £73273

Going: Sf: 1-1 GS: 0-1 Gd: 4-5 GF: - Fm: 2-2
Distance: **2m/2m3: 5-7** 2m4-2m7: 2-2 3m+: 0-0
Track: LH: 3-5 **RH: 4-4** Tight: 1-2 **Gall: 2-3**
Aids: Bl: 0-0 Vi: 0-0 Tstrap: 0-0
Best Rating: 168 3/02 Chel 2m gd-sft Ch

He has done very well over fences, winning his first seven races from two to two and a half miles before a good second in the Arkle. Unable to confirm the form with Armaturk at Aintree. Acts on good and soft ground, but still has room for improvement in his jumping.

Seef

106(86h) — (67h)90

8-y-o b g Slip Anchor-Compton Lady (USA) (Sovereign Dancer (USA))

J S King Mrs S Horton

Placings:*20*/*6*0006/*1435*/*35324*-002352 **(4641)**

2001/02: 21^{0}G, 24^{0}GF, 25^{2}G, 24^{3}G, 24^{5}GF, 24^{2}G

	Starts	1st	2nd	3rd	Win & Pl
Hurdles	2	0	0	0	0
Chases	4	0	2	1	3428
Career Total	**22**	**1**	**4**	**4**	**9647**

99	5/99	Extr	2m6f	E Hdl	G-F	£2915

Total win prize-money £2915

Going: Sf: 0-0 GS: 0-0 Gd: 0-4 GF: - Fm: 0-2
Distance: 2m/2m3: 0-0 2m4-2m7: 0-1 3m+: 0-5
Track: LH: 0-0 RH: 0-6 Tight: 0-3 Gall: 0-1
Aids: Bl: 0-0 Vi: 0-0 Tstrap: 0-0
Best Rating: 99 10/99 Winc 2m6f gd-fm Hdl

Modest hurdler/chaser. Best over staying distances. Acts on a sound surface.

Seek

106 — 113

6-y-o br g Rainbow Quest (USA)-Souk (IRE) (Ahonoora)

J A B Old W E Sturt

Placings:013501 **(4764)**

2001/02: 16^{0}G, 17^{1}GF, 19^{3}S, 19^{5}G, 17^{0}HY, 16^{1}GF

	Starts	1st	2nd	3rd	Win & Pl
Hurdles	6	2	0	1	8409
Career Total	**6**	**2**	**0**	**1**	**8409**

113	4/02	Asct	2m110y	D(0-115)HHdl	G-F	£4420
109	11/01	Extr	2m1f	E Hdl	G-F	£3465

Total win prize-money £7885

Going: Sf: 0-2 GS: 0-0 Gd: 0-2 GF: - Fm: 2-2
Distance: **2m/2m3: 2-6** 2m4-2m7: 0-0 3m+: 0-0
Track: LH: 0-3 **RH: 2-3** Tight: 0-0 Gall: 0-1
Aids: Bl: 0-0 Vi: 0-0 Tstrap: 0-0
Best Rating: 113 4/02 Asct 2m110y gd-fm Hdl

Seek The Faith (USA)

93(91h) — (81h)111

13-y-o ch g Pilgrim (USA)-Bundler (USA) (Raise A Native)

J G M O'Shea R H F Matthews

Placings:130/0/**14355**/**521**/**3210**/**U44500**/**P-20PPP** **(4824)**

2001/02: 20^{2}GF, 16^{0}GS, 16^{P}HY, 16^{P}G, 16^{P}G

	Starts	1st	2nd	3rd	Win & Pl
Hurdles	1	0	0	0	0
Chases	4	0	1	0	1000
Career Total	**28**	**4**	**3**	**3**	**23658**

134	2/98	Newb	2m1f	C(0-135)HCh	GD	£4857
117	4/97	Chel	2m110y	C(0-130)HCh	G-F	£5121
121	11/95	Chep	2m110y	E Ch	G-S	£2882
110	1/94	Naas	2m	Hdl	SFT	£2957

Total win prize-money £15818

Going: Sf: 0-1 GS: 0-1 Gd: 0-2 GF: - Fm: 0-1
Distance: 2m/2m3: 0-4 2m4-2m7: 0-1 3m+: 0-0
Track: LH: 0-4 RH: 0-1 Tight: 0-1 Gall: 0-2
Aids: Bl: 0-0 Vi: 0-0 Tstrap: 0-0
Best Rating: 134 2/98 Newb 2m1f good Ch

Formerly useful veteran chaser, but lightly-raced of late and now very modest. Does not want the ground too soft.

Seek The Light (USA)

84 — 48

5-y-o b g Seeking The Gold (USA)-Jolypha (USA) (Lyphard (USA))

C J Gray (G L Moore 11/7) D J Staddon

Placings:40 **(1034)**

2001/02: 16^{4}GF, 17^{0}G

	Starts	1st	2nd	3rd	Win & Pl
Hurdles	2	0	0	0	395
Career Total	**2**	**0**	**0**	**0**	**395**

Going: Sf: 0-0 GS: 0-0 Gd: 0-1 GF: - Fm: 0-1
Distance: 2m/2m3: 0-2 2m4-2m7: 0-0 3m+: 0-0
Track: LH: 0-2 RH: 0-0 Tight: 0-2 Gall: 0-0
Aids: Bl: 0-0 Vi: 0-0 Tstrap: 0-0
Best Rating: 48 7/01 NAbb 2m1f good Hdl

Seem Of Gold

94 **85**

6-y-o b m Gold Dust-Shepani (New Member)

J W Mullins J A G Meaden

Placings:00-B160506 **(4881)**

2001/02: 17^{B}GF, 17^{1}G, 17^{6}GF, 17^{0}GS, 16^{5}G, 17^{0}G, 18^{6}GF

	Starts	1st	2nd	3rd	Win & Pl
NH Flat	2	1	0	0	2282
Hurdles	5	0	0	0	0
Career Total	**9**	**1**	**0**	**0**	**2282**

84	6/01	NAbb	2m1f	H NHF	GD	£2282

Total win prize-money £2282

Going: Sf: 0-0 GS: 0-1 Gd: 1-3 GF: - Fm: 0-3
Distance: **2m/2m3: 1-7** 2m4-2m7: 0-0 3m+: 0-0
Track: **LH: 1-2** RH: 0-4 **Tight: 1-4** Gall: 0-0
Aids: Bl: 0-0 Vi: 0-0 Tstrap: 0-0
Best Rating: 85 12/01 Tntn 2m1f gd-sft Hdl

Sefton Blake

98(53c) **71**

8-y-o b g Roscoe Blake-Rainbow Lady (Jaazeiro (USA))

R D Wylie M R Johnson

Placings:404P6/55243616/112P0/**415P56-0P46** **(1234)**

2001/02: 22^{0}GF, 25^{P}G, 24^{4}F, 22^{6}GS

	Starts	1st	2nd	3rd	Win & Pl
Hurdles	3	0	0	0	0
Chases	1	0	0	0	0
Career Total	**28**	**4**	**2**	**1**	**12549**

103	8/00	Sthl	3m110y	E Ch	G-F	£3133
93	11/99	Catt	3m1f110y	E(0-115)HHdl	G-F	£2304
93	5/99	Ctml	2m6f	F(0-95)HHdl	GD	£3100
84	4/99	Sedg	2m5f110y	G(0-100)HHdl	FRM	£2164

Total win prize-money £10702

Going: Sf: 0-0 GS: 0-1 Gd: 0-1 GF: - Fm: 0-2
Distance: 2m/2m3: 0-0 2m4-2m7: 0-2 3m+: 0-2
Track: LH: 0-2 RH: 0-2 Tight: 0-2 Gall: 0-0
Aids: Bl: 0-1 Vi: 0-0 Tstrap: 0-0
Best Rating: 103 8/00 Sthl 3m110y gd-fm Ch

Segsbury Belle

78f **56f**

7-y-o b m Petoski-Rolling Dice (Balinger)

Miss G Browne R A Instone

Placings:0O-0 **(2341)**

2001/02: 16^{0}GF

	Starts	1st	2nd	3rd	Win & Pl
NH Flat	1	0	0	0	
Career Total	**3**	**0**	**0**	**0**	

Going: Sf: 0-0 GS: 0-0 Gd: 0-0 GF: - Fm: 0-1
Distance: 2m/2m3: 0-1 2m4-2m7: 0-0 3m+: 0-0
Track: LH: 0-0 RH: 0-1 Tight: 0-0 Gall: 0-0
Aids: Bl: 0-0 Vi: 0-0 Tstrap: 0-0
Best Rating: 56 11/01 Ludl 2m gd-fm NHF

Seize The Day (IRE)

94 **79**

14-y-o b g Lomond (USA)-Cheerful Heart (Petingo)

M J Coombe Mrs N M Coombe

Placings:000/51211/550123/0 **(3659)**

2001/02: 16^{0}S

	Starts	1st	2nd	3rd	Win & Pl
Hurdles	1	0	0	0	
Career Total	**15**	**4**	**2**	**1**	**11266**

114	1/99	Winc	2m6f	E(0-115)HHdl	SFT	£2878
112	4/98	Hntg	2m5f110y	E(0-115)HHdl	G-S	£2390
104	4/98	Winc	2m6f	F(0-105)HHdl	G-S	£2374
95	3/98	Hntg	2m5f110y	G(0-90)HHdl	GD	£1968

Total win prize-money £9610

Going: Sf: 0-1 GS: 0-0 Gd: 0-0 GF: - Fm: 0-0
Distance: 2m/2m3: 0-1 2m4-2m7: 0-0 3m+: 0-0
Track: LH: 0-0 RH: 0-1 Tight: 0-0 Gall: 0-0
Aids: Bl: 0-0 Vi: 0-0 Tstrap: 0-0
Best Rating: 119 3/99 Hntg 3m2f gd-sft Hdl

Veteran handicap hurdler. Has won at up to two miles six furlongs. Acts on soft ground.

Sel

109 **95**

4-y-o b f Salse (USA)-Frog (Akarad (FR))

G L Moore John Hetherington

Placings:403225 **(4881)**

2001/02: 17^{4}S, 16^{0}S, 16^{3}S, 16^{2}GF, 16^{2}GF, 18^{5}GF

	Starts	1st	2nd	3rd	Win & Pl
Hurdles	6	0	2	1	1928
Career Total	**6**	**0**	**2**	**1**	**1928**

Going: Sf: 0-3 GS: 0-0 Gd: 0-0 GF: - Fm: 0-3
Distance: 2m/2m3: 0-6 2m4-2m7: 0-0 3m+: 0-0
Track: LH: 0-3 RH: 0-3 Tight: 0-4 Gall: 0-2
Aids: Bl: 0-6 Vi: 0-0 Tstrap: 0-0
Best Rating: 95 4/02 Plum 2m gd-fm Hdl

Modest hurdler, handles soft ground but suited by faster. Usually wears blinkers.

Selatan (IRE)

103(97h) **101**

10-y-o ch g Shernazar-Seleret (USA) (Lear Fan (USA))

D R Gandolfo Starlight Racing

Placings:0414210/0331/**3422P323/F21P/4F4313/F06 4P-24PP** **(2465)**

2001/02: 24^{2}S, 26^{4}S, 25^{P}S, 25^{P}G

	Starts	1st	2nd	3rd	Win & Pl
Chases	4	0	1	0	1380
Career Total	**38**	**5**	**6**	**7**	**27384**

120	1/00	Folk	3m2f	F(0-105)HCh	G-S	£2450
112	2/99	Font	3m2f110y	D(0-120)HCh	GD	£3733
113	3/97	Bang	3m	E(0-115)HHdl	GD	£2957
105	3/96	Towc	2m5f	D(0-120)HHdl	G-S	£2973
102	2/96	Towc	2m	E Hdl	HVY	£2431

Total win prize-money £14546

Going: Sf: 0-3 GS: 0-0 Gd: 0-1 GF: - Fm: 0-0
Distance: 2m/2m3: 0-0 2m4-2m7: 0-0 3m+: 0-4
Track: LH: 0-2 RH: 0-2 Tight: 0-3 Gall: 0-0
Aids: Bl: 0-0 Vi: 0-0 Tstrap: 0-0
Best Rating: 120 1/00 Folk 3m2f gd-sft Ch

Staying chaser who ran well when runner-up at Bangor in October 2001, although he was well held at Newton Abbot after that.

Selberry

114(107h) (103h)**122**

8-y-o b g Selkirk (USA)-Choke Cherry (Connaught)

E L James Mr & Mrs D W H Bell

Placings:66/5011142424/4260/3104114005-23525221 **(3589)**

2001/02: 16^{2}GS, 17^{3}G, 16^{5}S, 16^{2}G, 20^{5}GS, 16^{2}G, 16^{2}GS, 16^{1}HY

	Starts	1st	2nd	3rd	Win & Pl
Chases	8	1	4	1	11021
Career Total	**34**	**7**	**7**	**2**	**33330**

122	2/02	Uttx	2m	D(0-120)HCh	HVY	£5109
112	1/01	Chep	2m110y	D(0-125)HHdl	G-S	£3160
112	1/01	Winc	2m	F(0-110)HHdl	G-S	£2982
110	10/00	Wwck	2m	D(0-125)HHdl	SFT	£2879
110	12/98	Hrfd	2m1f	E(0-100)HHdl	SFT	£2920
95	12/98	MRas	2m1f110y	D(0-120)HHdl	SFT	£2798
107	12/98	Extr	2m1f110y	F(0-100)HHdl	GD	£1975

Total win prize-money £21825

Going: Sf: 1-2 GS: 0-3 Gd: 0-3 GF: - Fm: 0-0
Distance: **2m/2m3: 1-7** 2m4-2m7: 0-1 3m+: 0-0
Track: **LH: 1-2** RH: 0-6 Tight: 0-1 Gall: 0-1
Aids: **Bl: 1-5** Vi: 0-0 Tstrap: 0-0
Best Rating: 122 2/02 Uttx 2m heavy Ch

Multiple hurdles winner who got off the mark over fences in Febraury 2002. He is suited by cut in the ground and has been fitted with blinkers. Best at around two miles.

Selshion Moss

75f **49f**

7-y-o b m Young Senor (USA)-Tommys Dream (Le Bavard (FR))

A B Mulholland J Mulholland

Placings:0000 **(1753)**

2001/02: 16^{0}GF, 18^{0}GF, 17^{0}GF, 17^{0}G

	Starts	1st	2nd	3rd	Win & Pl
NH Flat	4	0	0	0	
Career Total	**4**	**0**	**0**	**0**	

Going: Sf: 0-0 GS: 0-0 Gd: 0-1 GF: - Fm: 0-3
Distance: 2m/2m3: 0-4 2m4-2m7: 0-0 3m+: 0-0
Track: LH: 0-1 RH: 0-3 Tight: 0-1 Gall: 0-1
Aids: Bl: 0-0 Vi: 0-0 Tstrap: 0-2
Best Rating: 49 9/01 Hrfd 2m1f gd-fm NHF

Semliki

9-y-o b g Nearly A Hand-River Culm (Royal Salmon)

A D Peachey J H Cooke

Placings:P **(0231)**

2001/02: 24^{P}GF

	Starts	1st	2nd	3rd	Win & Pl
Chases	1	0	0	0	
Career Total	**1**	**0**	**0**	**0**	

Going: Sf: 0-0 GS: 0-0 Gd: 0-0 GF: - Fm: 0-1
Distance: 2m/2m3: 0-0 2m4-2m7: 0-0 3m+: 0-1
Track: LH: 0-0 RH: 0-1 Tight: 0-0 Gall: 0-1
Aids: Bl: 0-0 Vi: 0-0 Tstrap: 0-0
Best Rating:

Send It To Penny (IRE)

87 **72**

5-y-o b m Marju (IRE)-Sparkish (IRE) (Persian Bold)

W Storey W Storey

Placings:05F0P **(2723)**

2001/02: 16^{0}GS, 16^{5}G, 20^{F}G, 16^{0}GS, 17^{P}GF

	Starts	1st	2nd	3rd	Win & Pl
Hurdles	5	0	0	0	0
Career Total	**5**	**0**	**0**	**0**	**0**

Going: Sf: 0-0 GS: 0-2 Gd: 0-2 GF: - Fm: 0-1
Distance: 2m/2m3: 0-4 2m4-2m7: 0-1 3m+: 0-0
Track: LH: 0-4 RH: 0-0 Tight: 0-2 Gall: 0-2
Aids: Bl: 0-0 Vi: 0-0 Tstrap: 0-0
Best Rating: 72 11/01 Kels 2m110y good Hdl

Send Me An Angel (IRE)

74 **46**

5-y-o ch m Lycius (USA)-Niamh Cinn Oir (IRE) (King Of Clubs)
M Mullineaux Miss Gill Quincey

Placings:0 **(2208)**
2001/02: 16^{0}GS

	Starts	1st	2nd	3rd	Win & Pl
Hurdles	1	0	0	0	
Career Total	**1**	**0**	**0**	**0**	

Going: Sf: 0-0 GS: 0-1 Gd: 0-0 GF: - Fm: 0-0
Distance: 2m/2m3: 0-1 2m4-2m7: 0-0 3m+: 0-0
Track: LH: 0-0 RH: 0-1 Tight: 0-0 Gall: 0-0
Aids: Bl: 0-0 Vi: 0-0 Tstrap: 0-0
Best Rating: 46 11/01 Leic 2m gd-sft Hdl

Senhora Da Rocha

91f **71f**

6-y-o ch m Karinga Bay-Sea Challenger (Seaepic (USA))
J Neville T G B Racing Club

Placings:*000* **(4743)**
2001/02: 16^{0}G, 16^{0}S, 16^{0}GF

	Starts	1st	2nd	3rd	Win & Pl
NH Flat	3	0	0	0	
Career Total	**3**	**0**	**0**	**0**	

Going: Sf: 0-1 GS: 0-0 Gd: 0-1 GF: - Fm: 0-1
Distance: 2m/2m3: 0-3 2m4-2m7: 0-0 3m+: 0-0
Track: LH: 0-1 RH: 0-2 Tight: 0-0 Gall: 0-0
Aids: Bl: 0-0 Vi: 0-0 Tstrap: 0-0
Best Rating: 71 4/02 Ludl 2m gd-fm NHF

Senor Eduardo

88f **98f**

5-y-o gr g Terimon-Jasmin Path (Warpath)
S Gollings R L Houlton

Placings:*005* **(4317)**
2001/02: 16^{0}S, 17^{0}GS, 16^{5}HY

	Starts	1st	2nd	3rd	Win & Pl
NH Flat	3	0	0	0	0
Career Total	**3**	**0**	**0**	**0**	**0**

Going: Sf: 0-2 GS: 0-1 Gd: 0-0 GF: - Fm: 0-0
Distance: 2m/2m3: 0-3 2m4-2m7: 0-0 3m+: 0-0
Track: LH: 0-2 RH: 0-1 Tight: 0-2 Gall: 0-0
Aids: Bl: 0-0 Vi: 0-0 Tstrap: 0-0
Best Rating: 98 2/02 Wwck 2m soft NHF

Senor El Betrutti (IRE)

13-y-o gr g Roselier (FR)-Rambling Gold (Little Buskins)
Mrs Susan Nock Gerard Nock

Placings:0/61300/61P12P16/5P361116/F211P334P/4 F00200/65200F/5-0 **(0075)**
2001/02: 24^{0}G

	Starts	1st	2nd	3rd	Win & Pl
Hurdles	1	0	0	0	
Career Total	**46**	**9**	**4**	**4**	**175969**

163	12/97	Chel	2m5f	A HCh	GD	£37574
157	11/97	Chel	2m4f110y	A HCh	GD	£37690
145	3/97	Newb	3m	B HCh	GD	£6853
145	3/97	Winc	2m5f	C(0-135)HCh	GD	£5410
150	2/97	Wwck	2m4f110y	B HCh	GD	£6498
145	4/96	Asct	2m3f110y	C Ch	G-S	£5590
134	2/96	Sand	2m4f110y	A Ch	G-F	£21556
137	12/95	Asct	2m3f110y	A Ch	GD	£11544
105	11/94	Wind	2m	Hdl	G-S	£2127

Total win prize-money £134843

Going: Sf: 0-0 GS: 0-0 Gd: 0-1 GF: - Fm: 0-0
Distance: 2m/2m3: 0-0 2m4-2m7: 0-0 3m+: 0-1
Track: LH: 0-0 RH: 0-1 Tight: 0-0 Gall: 0-0
Aids: Bl: 0-0 Vi: 0-0 Tstrap: 0-0
Best Rating: 163 2/99 Asct 2m3f110y good Ch

He hit the headlines by completing the Murphy's/Tripleprint Gold Cup double in '97, but never quite reached the same heights again. Reportedly retired.

Sense Of Duty (IRE)

7-y-o b g Supreme Leader-Armagale (IRE) (Strong Gale)
A G Hobbs Mrs M David

Placings:*00*/U0-PP **(3357)**
2001/02: 19^{P}G, 24^{P}HY

	Starts	1st	2nd	3rd	Win & Pl
Hurdles	2	0	0	0	
Career Total	**6**	**0**	**0**	**0**	

Going: Sf: 0-1 GS: 0-0 Gd: 0-1 GF: - Fm: 0-0
Distance: 2m/2m3: 0-0 2m4-2m7: 0-1 3m+: 0-1
Track: LH: 0-1 RH: 0-1 Tight: 0-0 Gall: 0-0
Aids: Bl: 0-0 Vi: 0-0 Tstrap: 0-0
Best Rating: 73 2/01 Ludl 2m good Hdl

Sentry Duty

73 **52**

7-y-o b g Nashwan (USA)-Third Watch (Slip Anchor)
Mrs V C Ward Mrs V C Ward

Placings:063P/5-0P **(3553)**
2001/02: 16^{0}GS, 19^{P}S

	Starts	1st	2nd	3rd	Win & Pl
Hurdles	2	0	0	0	
Career Total	**7**	**0**	**0**	**1**	**315**

Going: Sf: 0-1 GS: 0-1 Gd: 0-0 GF: - Fm: 0-0
Distance: 2m/2m3: 0-2 2m4-2m7: 0-0 3m+: 0-0
Track: LH: 0-2 RH: 0-0 Tight: 0-2 Gall: 0-0
Aids: Bl: 0-0 Vi: 0-0 Tstrap: 0-0
Best Rating: 97 11/98 Uttx 2m soft Hdl

September Harvest (USA)

92 **68**

6-y-o ch g Mujtahid (USA)-Shawgatny (USA) (Danzig Connection (USA))
Mrs S Lamyman P Lamyman

Placings:4/600664F-0060646 **(2947)**
2001/02: 17^{0}GF, 16^{0}GF, 24^{6}GS, 16^{0}G, 17^{6}G, 20^{4}S, 20^{6}G

	Starts	1st	2nd	3rd	Win & Pl
Hurdles	7	0	0	0	0
Career Total	**15**	**0**	**0**	**0**	**209**

Going: Sf: 0-1 GS: 0-1 Gd: 0-3 GF: - Fm: 0-2
Distance: 2m/2m3: 0-4 2m4-2m7: 0-2 3m+: 0-1
Track: LH: 0-4 RH: 0-3 Tight: 0-7 Gall: 0-0
Aids: Bl: 0-3 Vi: 0-0 Tstrap: 0-0
Best Rating: 84 12/00 Donc 2m110y heavy Hdl

Serdal (USA)

89 **78**

6-y-o b g Gulch (USA)-Ginnydare (USA) (Pilgrim (USA))
J Mackie Exors Of The Late P B Short

Placings:2160006/5-0 **(0081)**
2001/02: 17^{0}G

	Starts	1st	2nd	3rd	Win & Pl
Hurdles	1	0	0	0	
Career Total	**9**	**1**	**1**	**0**	**4438**

96	11/99	Wwck	2m	D Hdl	GD	£3496

Total win prize-money £3496

Going: Sf: 0-0 GS: 0-0 Gd: 0-1 GF: - Fm: 0-0
Distance: 2m/2m3: 0-1 2m4-2m7: 0-0 3m+: 0-0
Track: LH: 0-0 RH: 0-1 Tight: 0-0 Gall: 0-0
Aids: Bl: 0-0 Vi: 0-0 Tstrap: 0-0
Best Rating: 96 11/99 Wwck 2m good Hdl

Serenus (USA)

102(116h) (138h)**132**

9-y-o b g Sunshine Forever (USA)-Curl And Set (USA) (Nijinsky (CAN))
D R C Elsworth W V M W & Mrs E S Robins

Placings:3511F60/114304/21304/**1322U14**/420465-534**060443** **(4401)**
2001/02: 16^{5}GS, 20^{3}GS, 16^{4}S, 16^{0}G, 16^{6}GS, 20^{0}S, 20^{4}GS, 21^{4}G, 18^{3}GS

	Starts	1st	2nd	3rd	Win & Pl
Hurdles	4	0	0	1	6250
Chases	5	0	0	1	2495
Career Total	**40**	**7**	**4**	**6**	**88818**

147	2/00	Kemp	2m4f110y	A Ch	G-S	£13200
131	11/99	Newb	2m1f	D Ch	G-F	£4500
147	12/98	Kemp	2m	B(0-145)HHdl	SFT	£6957
133	12/97	Kemp	2m	B HHdl	SFT	£6768
122	12/97	Hntg	2m110y	D(0-125)HHdl	GD	£2735
115	12/96	Ling	2m110y	A Hdl	G-S	£9735
110	12/96	Font	2m2f110y	E Hdl	GD	£2364

Total win prize-money £46260

Going: Sf: 0-2 GS: 0-5 Gd: 0-2 GF: - Fm: 0-0
Distance: 2m/2m3: 0-5 2m4-2m7: 0-4 3m+: 0-0
Track: LH: 0-2 RH: 0-7 Tight: 0-0 Gall: 0-1
Aids: Bl: 0-0 Vi: 0-0 Tstrap: 0-0
Best Rating: 149 12/00 Kemp 2m gd-sft Hdl

A Kempton specialist, having won on the Flat, over hurdles and fences there, he was a smart novice chaser in

1999/2000, but did not go on from there. He acts on most types of ground. Has won at up to two and a half miles. Appears to be on the downgrade.

Serenze (IRE)

68 **34**

9-y-o b g Jolly Jake (NZ)-Strong Language (Formidable (USA))
R Lee W D Edwards

Placings:006PPP (0925)
2001/02: 17^{0}GS, 19^{0}G, 16^{6}G, 25^{P}F, 16^{P}G, 20^{P}GF

	Starts	1st	2nd	3rd	Win & Pl
Chases	6	0	0	0	0
Career Total	**6**	**0**	**0**	**0**	**0**

Going: Sf: 0-0 GS: 0-1 Gd: 0-3 GF: - Fm: 0-2
Distance: 2m/2m3: 0-4 2m4-2m7: 0-1 3m+: 0-1
Track: LH: 0-2 RH: 0-4 Tight: 0-1 Gall: 0-0
Aids: Bl: 0-1 Vi: 0-0 Tstrap: 0-0
Best Rating: 34 5/01 Extr 2m1f110y gd-sft Ch

Sergeant's Inn

102 **94**

5-y-o b g Sabrehill (USA)-Pink Brief (IRE) (Ela-Mana-Mou)
G Brown John W Barnard

Placings:204260 (4327)
2001/02: 16^{2}S, 16^{0}S, 17^{4}HY, 16^{2}HY, 16^{6}S, 19^{0}S

	Starts	1st	2nd	3rd	Win & Pl
Hurdles	6	0	2	0	1313
Career Total	**6**	**0**	**2**	**0**	**1313**

Going: Sf: 0-6 GS: 0-0 Gd: 0-0 GF: - Fm: 0-0
Distance: 2m/2m3: 0-5 2m4-2m7: 0-1 3m+: 0-0
Track: LH: 0-3 RH: 0-3 Tight: 0-4 Gall: 0-0
Aids: Bl: 0-0 Vi: 0-0 Tstrap: 0-0
Best Rating: 94 4/01 Plum 2m soft Hdl

Moderate hurdler, suited by soft ground.

Serious

12-y-o b g Shadeed (USA)-Azallya (FR) (Habitat)
S Dow Tony And Dee Lousada

Placings:1/01F0/43/000/2/P-P (0241)
2001/02: 16^{P}GF

	Starts	1st	2nd	3rd	Win & Pl
Hurdles	1	0	0	0	
Career Total	**13**	**2**	**1**	**1**	**8864**

110	4/97	Uttx	2m	B(0-140)HHdl	G-F	£4756
102	12/95	Uttx	2m	E Hdl	G-F	£2333

Total win prize-money £7090

Going: Sf: 0-0 GS: 0-0 Gd: 0-0 GF: - Fm: 0-1
Distance: 2m/2m3: 0-1 2m4-2m7: 0-0 3m+: 0-0
Track: LH: 0-1 RH: 0-0 Tight: 0-0 Gall: 0-0
Aids: Bl: 0-0 Vi: 0-0 Tstrap: 0-0
Best Rating: 110 4/97 Uttx 2m gd-fm Hdl

Serious Position (IRE)

100 **91**

7-y-o ch g Orchestra-Lady Temba (Callernish)
D R Stoddart D R Stoddart

Placings:5P6P4P-0PP336P (4848)
2001/02: 21^{0}GS, 18^{P}HY, 21^{P}HY, 16^{3}S, 16^{3}GS, 16^{6}GF, 16^{P}G

	Starts	1st	2nd	3rd	Win & Pl
Hurdles	7	0	0	2	1074
Career Total	**13**	**0**	**0**	**2**	**1344**

Going: Sf: 0-3 GS: 0-2 Gd: 0-1 GF: - Fm: 0-1
Distance: 2m/2m3: 0-5 2m4-2m7: 0-2 3m+: 0-0
Track: LH: 0-3 RH: 0-3 Tight: 0-2 Gall: 0-2
Aids: Bl: 0-0 Vi: 0-0 Tstrap: 0-0
Best Rating: 91 4/02 Wwck 2m gd-fm Hdl

Pulled up five times from first nine starts over hurdles, but showed a measure of ability in the spring of 2002.

Serious Trust

99 **68**

9-y-o b g Alzao (USA)-Mill Line (Mill Reef (USA))
Mrs L C Jewell Peter J Allen

Placings:0-020 (1353)
2001/02: 19^{0}GF, 20^{2}GF, 22^{0}GF

	Starts	1st	2nd	3rd	Win & Pl
Hurdles	3	0	1	0	449
Career Total	**4**	**0**	**1**	**0**	**449**

Going: Sf: 0-0 GS: 0-0 Gd: 0-0 GF: - Fm: 0-3
Distance: 2m/2m3: 0-1 2m4-2m7: 0-2 3m+: 0-0
Track: LH: 0-3 RH: 0-0 Tight: 0-3 Gall: 0-0
Aids: Bl: 0-0 Vi: 0-1 Tstrap: 0-0
Best Rating: 60 7/01 Wolv 2m4f110y gd-fm Hdl

Seriously Now (IRE)

67

7-y-o b g Fresh Breeze (USA)-Croziers Glimmer (Crozier)
D M Grissell D Curtis

Placings:PPP1/PO (4507)
2001/02: 22^{P}S, 21^{0}G

	Starts	1st	2nd	3rd	Win & Pl
Hurdles	2	0	0	0	
Career Total	**6**	**1**	**0**	**0**	**2520**

76	3/00	Font	2m6f110y	F(0-100)HHdl	G-F	£2520

Total win prize-money £2520

Going: Sf: 0-1 GS: 0-0 Gd: 0-1 GF: - Fm: 0-0
Distance: 2m/2m3: 0-0 2m4-2m7: 0-2 3m+: 0-0
Track: LH: 0-1 RH: 0-1 Tight: 0-2 Gall: 0-0
Aids: Bl: 0-0 Vi: 0-0 Tstrap: 0-0
Best Rating: 76 3/00 Font 2m6f110y gd-fm Hdl

Serraval (FR)

97 **86**

4-y-o ch f Sanglamore (USA)-Saone (USA) (Bering)
B S Rothwell (H Van De Poele 26/11) J T Brown

Placings:F (4237)
2001/02: 16^{F}GF

	Starts	1st	2nd	3rd	Win & Pl
Hurdles	1	0	0	0	
Career Total	**1**	**0**	**0**	**0**	

Going: Sf: 0-0 GS: 0-0 Gd: 0-0 GF: - Fm: 0-1
Distance: 2m/2m3: 0-1 2m4-2m7: 0-0 3m+: 0-0
Track: LH: 0-0 RH: 0-1 Tight: 0-0 Gall: 0-1
Aids: Bl: 0-0 Vi: 0-0 Tstrap: 0-0
Best Rating: 84 3/02 Hntg 2m110y gd-fm Hdl

Modest mile winner on the Flat in France. Looked a shade unlucky when runner-up in maiden hurdle at Worcester July 2002. Can go one better in similar company.

Sertorius (IRE)

5-y-o b g Sharifabad (IRE)-Nomun Nofun (Creative Plan (USA))
P T Dalton Mrs Julie Martin

Placings:*0*-P0 (4594)
2001/02: 20^{P}S, 16^{0}G

	Starts	1st	2nd	3rd	Win & Pl
Hurdles	2	0	0	0	
Career Total	**3**	**0**	**0**	**0**	

Going: Sf: 0-1 GS: 0-0 Gd: 0-1 GF: - Fm: 0-0
Distance: 2m/2m3: 0-1 2m4-2m7: 0-1 3m+: 0-0
Track: LH: 0-2 RH: 0-0 Tight: 0-0 Gall: 0-0
Aids: Bl: 0-0 Vi: 0-0 Tstrap: 0-1
Best Rating: 20 3/01 MRas 2m1f110y good NHF

Set Dance (IRE)

101 **76**

6-y-o b g Suave Dancer (USA)-La Courant (USA) (Little Current (USA))
E L James Miss Helen Pease

Placings:000PP (4035)
2001/02: 17^{0}GS, 22^{0}G, 17^{0}G, 22^{P}S, 22^{P}S

	Starts	1st	2nd	3rd	Win & Pl
NH Flat	1	0	0	0	0
Hurdles	4	0	0	0	0
Career Total	**5**	**0**	**0**	**0**	

Going: Sf: 0-2 GS: 0-1 Gd: 0-2 GF: - Fm: 0-0
Distance: 2m/2m3: 0-2 2m4-2m7: 0-3 3m+: 0-0
Track: LH: 0-1 RH: 0-4 Tight: 0-3 Gall: 0-0
Aids: Bl: 0-1 Vi: 0-0 Tstrap: 0-0
Best Rating: 52 12/01 Hrfd 2m1f good Hdl

Seul Moi (IRE)

8-y-o b m Denel (FR)-No Reason (Kemal (FR))
K F Clutterbuck K F Clutterbuck

Placings:P0 (1258)
2001/02: 24^{P}G, 20^{0}GF

	Starts	1st	2nd	3rd	Win & Pl
Hurdles	2	0	0	0	
Career Total	**2**	**0**	**0**	**0**	

Going: Sf: 0-0 GS: 0-0 Gd: 0-1 GF: - Fm: 0-1
Distance: 2m/2m3: 0-0 2m4-2m7: 0-1 3m+: 0-1
Track: LH: 0-1 RH: 0-1 Tight: 0-0 Gall: 0-1
Aids: Bl: 0-0 Vi: 0-0 Tstrap: 0-0
Best Rating:

Seven Bays

49

6-y-o b g Seven Hearts-Priory Bay (Petong)
J C Fox Mrs J A Cleary

Placings:*0000*P (2429)
2001/02: 17^{0}GF, 16^{0}G, 16^{0}G, 19^{0}G, 24^{P}G

	Starts	1st	2nd	3rd	Win & Pl
NH Flat	3	0	0	0	0
Hurdles	2	0	0	0	0

	Starts	1st	2nd	3rd	Win & Pl
Career Total	5	0	0	0	

Going: Sf: 0-0 GS: 0-0 Gd: 0-4 GF: - Fm: 0-1
Distance: 2m/2m3: 0-4 2m4-2m7: 0-0 3m+: 0-1
Track: LH: 0-5 RH: 0-0 Tight: 0-1 Gall: 0-2
Aids: Bl: 0-0 Vi: 0-0 Tstrap: 0-0
Best Rating: 74 5/01 NAbb 2m1f gd-fm NHF

Moderate over hurdles and in bumpers.

Seven Leagues (IRE)

13-y-o b g Runnett-Linbury Lady (Royal Palace)
G P Enright J G Armstrong

Placings:P (4508)
2001/02: 17^{P}G

	Starts	1st	2nd	3rd	Win & Pl
Chases	1	0	0	0	
Career Total	1	0	0	0	

Going: Sf: 0-0 GS: 0-0 Gd: 0-1 GF: - Fm: 0-0
Distance: 2m/2m3: 0-1 2m4-2m7: 0-0 3m+: 0-0
Track: LH: 0-1 RH: 0-0 Tight: 0-1 Gall: 0-0
Aids: Bl: 0-0 Vi: 0-0 Tstrap: 0-0
Best Rating:

Seven Towers (IRE)

(71h)
13-y-o b g Roselier (FR)-Ramble Bramble (Random Shot)
Mrs M Reveley Mrs E A Murray

Placings:3/121P/51/11011F/51111/51P0U2/545130P-P (0069)
2001/02: 28^{P}G

	Starts	1st	2nd	3rd	Win & Pl
Chases	1	0	0	0	
Career Total	32	13	2	2	131082

135	1/01	Newc	3m6f	D(0-125)HCh	SFT	£4065
157	11/98	Ayr	3m1f	B HCh	G-S	£10861
154	3/97	Uttx	4m2f	A HCh	GD	£30867
141	2/97	Newc	4m1f	B(0-140)HCh	GD	£22053
135	1/97	Kels	4m	B HCh	GD	£20902
121	12/96	Kels	3m4f	B HCh	GD	£10172
122	3/96	Carl	3m2f	D(0-120)HCh	GD	£3856
119	2/96	Ayr	3m1f	F(0-105)HCh	GD	£3938
96	12/95	Chel	3m1f110y	C Ch	GD	£4891
122	11/95	Newc	2m4f	D Ch	GD	£3615
121	12/94	Hayd	2m7f110y	(0-135)HHdl	SFT	£3290
102	1/94	Ayr	2m6f	Hdl	SFT	£1955
84	10/93	Hexm	2m	Hdl	SFT	£1856

Total win prize-money £122325

Going: Sf: 0-0 GS: 0-0 Gd: 0-1 GF: - Fm: 0-0
Distance: 2m/2m3: 0-0 2m4-2m7: 0-0 3m+: 0-1
Track: LH: 0-1 RH: 0-0 Tight: 0-1 Gall: 0-0
Aids: Bl: 0-1 Vi: 0-0 Tstrap: 0-0
Best Rating: 157 11/98 Ayr 3m1f gd-sft Ch

Severn Belle (IRE)

82 75
6-y-o ch m Executive Perk-Our Siveen (Deep Run)
Mrs S J Smith Worcester Racing Club

Placings:30603 (1251)
2001/02: 16^{3}GS, 16^{0}G, 16^{6}GF, 24^{0}GF, 17^{3}G

	Starts	1st	2nd	3rd	Win & Pl
NH Flat	2	0	0	1	230
Hurdles	3	0	0	1	435
Career Total	5	0	0	2	665

Going: Sf: 0-0 GS: 0-1 Gd: 0-2 GF: - Fm: 0-2
Distance: 2m/2m3: 0-4 2m4-2m7: 0-0 3m+: 0-1
Track: LH: 0-4 RH: 0-1 Tight: 0-3 Gall: 0-0
Aids: Bl: 0-0 Vi: 0-0 Tstrap: 0-0
Best Rating: 83 6/01 Hexm 2m gd-sft NHF

Severn Gale

107 110
12-y-o b m Strong Gale-Miss Apex (Wolverlife)
John Allen Mrs Carol Allen

Placings:100/0PP24/20312113F/3F/P/006152112/400421225-0400P025PF (3228)
2001/02: 16^{0}GF, 16^{4}G, 16^{0}GF, 17^{0}GF, 16^{P}GS, 16^{0}G, 16^{2}GF, 19^{5}S, 16^{P}G, 16^{F}G

	Starts	1st	2nd	3rd	Win & Pl
Hurdles	10	0	1	0	1084
Career Total	48	8	9	3	30160

112	8/00	Strf	2m110y	F(0-105)HHdl	G-F	£1918
102	11/99	Uttx	2m	F(0-110)HHdl	G-S	£2571
103	11/99	Kemp	2m	E(0-110)HHdl	GD	£2221
98	9/99	Hntg	2m110y	E(0-115)HHdl	G-F	£2250
102	12/96	Wwck	2m	D(0-125)HHdl	G-F	£2786
96	12/96	Wind	2m	D(0-120)HHdl	GD	£2747
95	10/96	Strf	2m110y	G Hdl	GD	£1940
84	11/94	Uttx	2m	Hdl	G-S	£2813

Total win prize-money £19248

Going: Sf: 0-1 GS: 0-1 Gd: 0-4 GF: - Fm: 0-4
Distance: 2m/2m3: 0-10 2m4-2m7: 0-0 3m+: 0-0
Track: LH: 0-4 RH: 0-6 Tight: 0-4 Gall: 0-1
Aids: Bl: 0-0 Vi: 0-0 Tstrap: 0-10
Best Rating: 112 9/00 Worc 2m gd-fm Hdl

Inonsistent handicap hurdler who showed his best form in autumn 2000. Best at around two miles on a sound surface.

Severn Magic

9-y-o b m Buckley-La Margarite (Bonne Noel)
M G Hazell (D Thomas 17/3) M G Hazell

Placings:P (0063)
2001/02: 26^{P}G

	Starts	1st	2nd	3rd	Win & Pl
Chases	1	0	0	0	
Career Total	1	0	0	0	

Going: Sf: 0-0 GS: 0-0 Gd: 0-1 GF: - Fm: 0-0
Distance: 2m/2m3: 0-0 2m4-2m7: 0-0 3m+: 0-1
Track: LH: 0-0 RH: 0-1 Tight: 0-1 Gall: 0-0
Aids: Bl: 0-0 Vi: 0-0 Tstrap: 0-0
Best Rating:

Seviche (IRE)

4-y-o ch f College Chapel-Smeraldina (USA) (Night Shift (USA))
F Jordan The Bhiss Partnership

Placings:P (2066)
2001/02: 16^{P}G

	Starts	1st	2nd	3rd	Win & Pl
Hurdles	1	0	0	0	
Career Total	1	0	0	0	

Going: Sf: 0-0 GS: 0-0 Gd: 0-1 GF: - Fm: 0-0
Distance: 2m/2m3: 0-1 2m4-2m7: 0-0 3m+: 0-0
Track: LH: 0-0 RH: 0-1 Tight: 0-0 Gall: 0-1
Aids: Bl: 0-0 Vi: 0-0 Tstrap: 0-0
Best Rating:

Sex Bomb

85 68
5-y-o gr h Bob Back (USA)-Lucky Starkist (Lucky Wednesday)
J Neville J Neville

Placings:0-0560P (4565)
2001/02: 17^{0}G, 16^{5}GF, 18^{6}S, 17^{0}S, 16^{P}G

	Starts	1st	2nd	3rd	Win & Pl
NH Flat	1	0	0	0	0
Hurdles	4	0	0	0	0
Career Total	6	0	0	0	0

Going: Sf: 0-2 GS: 0-0 Gd: 0-2 GF: - Fm: 0-1
Distance: 2m/2m3: 0-5 2m4-2m7: 0-0 3m+: 0-0
Track: LH: 0-3 RH: 0-2 Tight: 0-4 Gall: 0-0
Aids: Bl: 0-0 Vi: 0-2 Tstrap: 0-0
Best Rating: 82 4/01 MRas 1m5f110y gd-sft NHF

Seymour Chance

89f 75f
6-y-o ch m Seymour Hicks (FR)-City's Sister (Maystreak)
Mrs G S Rees Mrs C J Black

Placings:0 (4860)
2001/02: 16^{0}G

	Starts	1st	2nd	3rd	Win & Pl
NH Flat	1	0	0	0	
Career Total	1	0	0	0	

Going: Sf: 0-0 GS: 0-0 Gd: 0-1 GF: - Fm: 0-0
Distance: 2m/2m3: 0-1 2m4-2m7: 0-0 3m+: 0-0
Track: LH: 0-0 RH: 0-0 Tight: 0-0 Gall: 0-0
Aids: Bl: 0-0 Vi: 0-0 Tstrap: 0-0
Best Rating: 54 4/02 Hexm 2m110y good NHF

Seymour Of Me

61 15
7-y-o ch g Riverwise (USA)-Seymour Lady (Malicious)
N R Mitchell Michael Green

Placings:0/0P000-0 (0122)
2001/02: 19^{0}F

	Starts	1st	2nd	3rd	Win & Pl
Hurdles	1	0	0	0	
Career Total	7	0	0	0	

Going: Sf: 0-0 GS: 0-0 Gd: 0-0 GF: - Fm: 0-1
Distance: 2m/2m3: 0-0 2m4-2m7: 0-1 3m+: 0-0
Track: LH: 0-0 RH: 0-1 Tight: 0-1 Gall: 0-0
Aids: Bl: 0-0 Vi: 0-0 Tstrap: 0-0
Best Rating: 57 5/00 Worc 2m gd-fm NHF

Seymours Bobby

79 58
6-y-o b m Seymour Hicks (FR)-Gibraltar Girl (True Song)
A Hollingsworth D H Godfrey

Placings:0-00 (0580)
2001/02: 22^{0}G, 22^{0}GF

	Starts	1st	2nd	3rd	Win & Pl
Hurdles	2	0	0	0	

	Starts	1st	2nd	3rd	Win & Pl
Career Total	**3**	**0**	**0**	**0**	

Going: Sf: 0-0 GS: 0-0 Gd: 0-1 GF: - Fm: 0-1
Distance: 2m/2m3: 0-0 2m4-2m7: 0-2 3m+: 0-0
Track: LH: 0-2 RH: 0-0 Tight: 0-2 Gall: 0-0
Aids: Bl: 0-0 Vi: 0-0 Tstrap: 0-0
Best Rating: **58** 6/01 Strf 2m6f110y gd-fm Hdl

Sh Boom

104f 98f

4-y-o b g Alderbrook-Muznah (Royal And Regal (USA))
K C Bailey E Pick

Placings:*61* (4571)
2001/02: 16^{6}S, 16^{1}G

	Starts	1st	2nd	3rd	Win & Pl
NH Flat	2	1	0	0	1722
Career Total	**2**	**1**	**0**	**0**	**1722**

98 4/02 Towc 2m H NHF GD £1722
Total win prize-money £1722

Going: Sf: 0-1 GS: 0-0 Gd: 1-1 GF: - Fm: 0-0
Distance: **2m/2m3: 1-2** 2m4-2m7: 0-0 3m+: 0-0
Track: LH: 0-1 **RH: 1-1** Tight: 0-0 Gall: 0-0
Aids: Bl: 0-0 Vi: 0-0 Tstrap: 0-0
Best Rating: **98** 4/02 Towc 2m good NHF

Half-brother to smart staying hurdler Anzum. Has shown up well on both bumper starts, winning the second on good ground at Towcester. Look sure to pay his way over hurdles.

Shade Lucky

77f 67f

6-y-o ch g Gildoran-Snowy Autumn (Deep Run)
B J M Ryall J F Tucker

Placings:*00* (2487)
2001/02: 16^{0}G, 17^{0}HY

	Starts	1st	2nd	3rd	Win & Pl
NH Flat	2	0	0	0	
Career Total	**2**	**0**	**0**	**0**	

Going: Sf: 0-1 GS: 0-0 Gd: 0-1 GF: - Fm: 0-0
Distance: 2m/2m3: 0-2 2m4-2m7: 0-0 3m+: 0-0
Track: LH: 0-1 RH: 0-1 Tight: 0-1 Gall: 0-0
Aids: Bl: 0-0 Vi: 0-0 Tstrap: 0-0
Best Rating: **67** 12/01 NAbb 2m1f heavy NHF

Shaded (IRE)

97 75

8-y-o b g Night Shift (USA)-Sarsaparilla (FR) (Shirley Heights)
D J Minty D J Minty

Placings:06FP0/00P200P/00P0434534P/0-000301 (1728)
2001/02: 17^{0}GF, 17^{0}G, 17^{0}G, 16^{3}GF, 17^{0}GF, 19^{1}F

	Starts	1st	2nd	3rd	Win & Pl
Hurdles	6	1	0	1	2040
Career Total	**30**	**1**	**1**	**3**	**3192**

75 10/01 Tntn 2m3f110y G(0-90)HHdl FRM £1690
Total win prize-money £1691

Going: Sf: 0-0 GS: 0-0 Gd: 0-2 GF: - Fm: 1-4
Distance: 2m/2m3: 0-5 **2m4-2m7: 1-1** 3m+: 0-0
Track: LH: 0-4 **RH: 1-2 Tight: 1-4** Gall: 0-0
Aids: Bl: 0-0 Vi: 0-0 Tstrap: 0-0
Best Rating: **75** 10/01 Tntn 2m3f110y firm Hdl

Finished lame when winning a modest Taunton seller in October 2001.

Shadow Catcher

5-y-o b g Missed Flight-Welgenco (Welsh Saint)
P Winkworth Tim Davis

Placings:*00* (2139)
2001/02: 17^{0}S, 17^{0}G

	Starts	1st	2nd	3rd	Win & Pl
NH Flat	1	0	0	0	0
Hurdles	1	0	0	0	0
Career Total	**2**	**0**	**0**	**0**	

Going: Sf: 0-1 GS: 0-0 Gd: 0-1 GF: - Fm: 0-0
Distance: 2m/2m3: 0-2 2m4-2m7: 0-0 3m+: 0-0
Track: LH: 0-1 RH: 0-1 Tight: 0-2 Gall: 0-0
Aids: Bl: 0-0 Vi: 0-0 Tstrap: 0-0
Best Rating: **26** 10/01 Bang 2m1f soft NHF

Shady Affair (IRE)

97 92

11-y-o b g Black Minstrel-Golden Ice (Golden Love)
R N Bevis Miss S J Done

Placings:PP-**25516UP** (3649)
2001/02: 19^{2}G, 17^{5}S, 16^{5}S, 17^{1}S, 19^{6}G, 20^{U}S, 20^{P}S

	Starts	1st	2nd	3rd	Win & Pl
Chases	7	1	1	0	4528
Career Total	**9**	**1**	**1**	**0**	**4528**

92 11/01 Bang 2m1f110y E(0-105)HCh SFT £3607
Total win prize-money £3608

Going: Sf: 1-5 GS: 0-0 Gd: 0-2 GF: - Fm: 0-0
Distance: **2m/2m3: 1-5** 2m4-2m7: 0-2 3m+: 0-0
Track: **LH: 1-3** RH: 0-4 **Tight: 1-2** Gall: 0-1
Aids: Bl: 0-0 Vi: 0-0 Tstrap: 0-0
Best Rating: **92** 11/01 Bang 2m1f110y soft Ch

Shady Emma

10-y-o ch m Gunner B-Shady Legacy (Rymer)
F Jordan D Pugh

Placings:*0/6PP/11/PPP* (0422)
2001/02: 25^{P}G, 20^{P}GS, 30^{P}G

	Starts	1st	2nd	3rd	Win & Pl
Chases	3	0	0	0	
Career Total	**9**	**2**	**0**	**0**	**4462**

102 3/99 Bang 3m110y H Ch HVY £1674
102 5/98 Bang 3m110y H Ch GD £2788
Total win prize-money £4462

Going: Sf: 0-0 GS: 0-1 Gd: 0-2 GF: - Fm: 0-0
Distance: 2m/2m3: 0-0 2m4-2m7: 0-1 3m+: 0-2
Track: LH: 0-2 RH: 0-1 Tight: 0-2 Gall: 0-0
Aids: Bl: 0-0 Vi: 0-0 Tstrap: 0-0
Best Rating: **102** 3/99 Bang 3m110y heavy Ch

Shady Man

84f 66f

4-y-o b g Shaamit (IRE)-Miss Hardy (Formidable (USA))
Miss H C Knight Trevor Hemmings

Placings:*0* (3661)
2001/02: 16^{0}S

	Starts	1st	2nd	3rd	Win & Pl
NH Flat	1	0	0	0	
Career Total	**1**	**0**	**0**	**0**	

Going: Sf: 0-1 GS: 0-0 Gd: 0-0 GF: - Fm: 0-0
Distance: 2m/2m3: 0-1 2m4-2m7: 0-0 3m+: 0-0
Track: LH: 0-0 RH: 0-1 Tight: 0-0 Gall: 0-0
Aids: Bl: 0-0 Vi: 0-0 Tstrap: 0-0
Best Rating: **66** 2/02 Winc 2m soft NHF

Shaffishayes

90 95

10-y-o ch g Clantime-Mischievous Miss (Niniski (USA))
Mrs M Reveley P Davidson-Brown

Placings:F4 (2182)
2001/02: 16^{F}G, 16^{4}GS

	Starts	1st	2nd	3rd	Win & Pl
Hurdles	2	0	0	0	0
Career Total	**2**	**0**	**0**	**0**	**0**

Going: Sf: 0-0 GS: 0-1 Gd: 0-1 GF: - Fm: 0-0
Distance: 2m/2m3: 0-2 2m4-2m7: 0-0 3m+: 0-0
Track: LH: 0-2 RH: 0-0 Tight: 0-1 Gall: 0-0
Aids: Bl: 0-0 Vi: 0-0 Tstrap: 0-0
Best Rating: **95** 10/01 Aint 2m110y good Hdl

A faller when in contention on his hurdling debut at Aintree but made no show next time.

Shafi (IRE)

11-y-o b g Reference Point-Azyaa (Kris)
S Flook Glyn Byard

Placings:40P/**22324/12UP-P223** (4638)
2001/02: 24^{P}GS, 16^{2}S, 19^{2}G, 19^{3}GF

	Starts	1st	2nd	3rd	Win & Pl
Chases	4	0	2	1	1706
Career Total	**16**	**1**	**6**	**2**	**7512**

111 5/00 Chel 2m110y H Ch GD £2821
Total win prize-money £2821

Going: Sf: 0-1 GS: 0-1 Gd: 0-1 GF: 0-1 Fm: 0-1
Distance: 2m/2m3: 0-2 2m4-2m7: 0-1 3m+: 0-1
Track: LH: 0-0 RH: 0-4 Tight: 0-1 Gall: 0-0
Aids: Bl: 0-0 Vi: 0-0 Tstrap: 0-0
Best Rating: **111** 3/02 Leic 2m soft Ch

He is pacey for a hunter chaser, and is effective on decent ground.

Shafqan

86 59

7-y-o ch g Sharpo-Rani (IRE) (Groom Dancer (USA))
P T Dalton Mrs Julie Martin

Placings:02/000-P00P (1039)
2001/02: 21^{P}GF, 19^{0}G, 20^{0}G, 20^{P}GF

	Starts	1st	2nd	3rd	Win & Pl
Hurdles	4	0	0	0	
Career Total	**9**	**0**	**1**	**0**	**703**

Going: Sf: 0-0 GS: 0-0 Gd: 0-2 GF: - Fm: 0-2
Distance: 2m/2m3: 0-0 2m4-2m7: 0-4 3m+: 0-0
Track: LH: 0-2 RH: 0-1 Tight: 0-1 Gall: 0-0
Aids: Bl: 0-0 Vi: 0-0 Tstrap: 0-0
Best Rating: **71** 11/00 Uttx 2m heavy Hdl

Shagreen (IRE)

92 104

9-y-o b g Buckskin (FR)-Laiton Peni (Laurence O)

J Howard Johnson Mrs M W Bird

Placings:*0521*/21/1B43/0P202P-2050 **(2769)**
2001/02: 27^{2}GS, 25^{0}G, 20^{5}GS, 25^{0}G

	Starts	1st	2nd	3rd	Win & Pl
Chases	4	0	1	0	1036
Career Total	**20**	**3**	**5**	**1**	**14152**

125	12/99	Newc	3m	D Ch	SFT	£3940
115	1/99	Uttx	2m4f110y	D Hdl	SFT	£3022
112	4/98	Chel	2m1f	H NHF	HVY	£1870

Total win prize-money £8832

Going: Sf: 0-0 GS: 0-2 Gd: 0-2 GF: - Fm: 0-0
Distance: 2m/2m3: 0-0 2m4-2m7: 0-1 3m+: 0-3
Track: LH: 0-4 RH: 0-0 Tight: 0-3 Gall: 0-1
Aids: Bl: 0-1 Vi: 0-0 Tstrap: 0-2
Best Rating: 125 12/99 Newc 3m soft Ch

Effective on most types of ground, he needs at least three miles, is not the most consistent sort.

Shah (IRE)

98 **92**

9-y-o b g King Persian-Gay And Sharp (Fine Blade (USA))
P Kelsall Peter Kelsall

Placings:*00P0P*/1-45 **(1953)**
2001/02: 16^{4}G, 16^{5}G

	Starts	1st	2nd	3rd	Win & Pl
Chases	2	0	0	0	261
Career Total	**8**	**1**	**0**	**0**	**3972**

88	10/00	Ludl	2m4f	D(0-110)HCh	G-F	£3711

Total win prize-money £3712

Going: Sf: 0-0 GS: 0-0 Gd: 0-2 GF: - Fm: 0-0
Distance: 2m/2m3: 0-2 2m4-2m7: 0-0 3m+: 0-0
Track: LH: 0-1 RH: 0-0 Tight: 0-1 Gall: 0-0
Aids: Bl: 0-0 Vi: 0-0 Tstrap: 0-0
Best Rating: 92 10/01 Sthl 2m good Ch

Won weak novices handicap chase at Ludlow October 2000. Scored on second start for new trainer at Worcester May 2002. Effective at up to two and a half miles. Likes fast ground.

Shahboor (USA)

105(106h) (123h) **110**

8-y-o b g Zilzal (USA)-Iva Reputation (USA) (Sir Ivor)
Mrs P Robeson Sir Evelyn De Rothschild

Placings:0/24160/12104233/325F3435 **(2410)**
2001/02: 16^{3}G, 19^{2}G, 16^{5}GF, 20^{F}G, 20^{3}G, 17^{4}S, 16^{3}GF, 19^{5}GS

	Starts	1st	2nd	3rd	Win & Pl
Hurdles	3	0	1	1	2152
Chases	5	0	0	2	1369
Career Total	**22**	**3**	**4**	**5**	**21672**

125	5/99	Uttx	2m	C(0-135)HHdl	GD	£4440
125	5/99	Strf	2m110y	D(0-120)HHdl	G-S	£3860
106	5/98	Uttx	2m	E(0-100)HHdl	G-F	£2547

Total win prize-money £10847

Going: Sf: 0-1 GS: 0-1 Gd: 0-4 GF: - Fm: 0-2
Distance: 2m/2m3: 0-5 2m4-2m7: 0-3 3m+: 0-0
Track: LH: 0-5 RH: 0-3 Tight: 0-7 Gall: 0-0
Aids: Bl: 0-0 Vi: 0-0 Tstrap: 0-0
Best Rating: 125 5/99 Uttx 2m good Hdl

A fair handicap hurdler, he has shown ability over fences. Stays two and a half miles.

Shake Eddie Shake (IRE)

5-y-o b g Blues Traveller (IRE)-Fortune Teller (Troy)
H S Howe C I A Slocock

Placings:*05*-PPP **(4479)**
2001/02: 19^{P}G, 20^{P}GS, 19^{P}G

	Starts	1st	2nd	3rd	Win & Pl
Hurdles	3	0	0	0	
Career Total	**5**	**0**	**0**	**0**	**0**

Going: Sf: 0-0 GS: 0-1 Gd: 0-2 GF: - Fm: 0-0
Distance: 2m/2m3: 0-2 2m4-2m7: 0-1 3m+: 0-0
Track: LH: 0-1 RH: 0-2 Tight: 0-0 Gall: 0-0
Aids: Bl: 0-1 Vi: 0-0 Tstrap: 0-0
Best Rating: 25 3/01 Newb 2m110y heavy NHF

Shalaal (USA)

92(72h) **114**

8-y-o b g Sheikh Albadou-One Fine Day (USA) (Quadratic (USA))
M C Chapman Eric Knowles

Placings:620/1P/000050500/51114203300-54 **(1749)**
2001/02: 16^{5}GS, 17^{4}G

	Starts	1st	2nd	3rd	Win & Pl
Chases	2	0	0	0	526
Career Total	**27**	**4**	**2**	**2**	**20065**

116	6/00	Hrfd	2m1f	F(0-105)HHdl	G-F	£3627
106	6/00	Uttx	2m	F(0-110)HHdl	G-F	£1932
97	5/00	Ctml	2m1f110y	D(0-120)HHdl	G-S	£3185
97	5/98	Ctml	2m1f110y	D Hdl	G-F	£2736

Total win prize-money £11480

Going: Sf: 0-0 GS: 0-1 Gd: 0-1 GF: - Fm: 0-0
Distance: 2m/2m3: 0-2 2m4-2m7: 0-0 3m+: 0-0
Track: LH: 0-1 RH: 0-1 Tight: 0-1 Gall: 0-0
Aids: Bl: 0-0 Vi: 0-0 Tstrap: 0-0
Best Rating: 116 8/00 Ctml 2m1f110y gd-sft Ch

Completed a hat-trick over hurdles in the summer of 2000 but, after a promising start over fences has not really progressed. Does not want extremes of going.

Shalbeblue (IRE)

105 **111**

5-y-o b g Shalford (IRE)-Alberjas (IRE) (Sure Blade (USA))
B Ellison Four Clubs

Placings:3534P-16632116 **(4524)**
2001/02: 17^{1}GS, 16^{6}G, 16^{6}G, 16^{3}GS, 16^{2}G, 17^{1}S, 17^{1}S, 17^{6}G

	Starts	1st	2nd	3rd	Win & Pl
Hurdles	8	3	1	1	8962
Career Total	**13**	**3**	**1**	**3**	**11887**

108	3/02	Sedg	2m1f	E(0-110)HHdl	SFT	£2548
110	2/02	Sedg	2m1f	E Hdl	SFT	£2583
111	10/01	Sedg	2m1f	E Hdl	G-S	£2576

Total win prize-money £7707

Going: Sf: 2-2 GS: 1-2 Gd: 0-4 GF: - Fm: 0-0
Distance: **2m/2m3: 3-8** 2m4-2m7: 0-0 3m+: 0-0
Track: **LH: 3-6** RH: 0-2 **Tight: 3-5** Gall: 0-0
Aids: **Bl: 2-5** Vi: 1-3 Tstrap: 0-0
Best Rating: 112 1/01 Donc 2m110y good Hdl

He got off the mark over hurdles in an uncompetitive event at Sedgefield in October, but was held in better company until scoring again twice at the same track in early 2002. Suited by cut in the ground.

Sham Sharif

81 **49**

5-y-o b m Be My Chief (USA)-Syrian Queen (Slip Anchor)
C J Gray Gordon James Cossey

Placings:606 **(1103)**
2001/02: 17^{6}GF, 17^{0}G, 17^{6}G

	Starts	1st	2nd	3rd	Win & Pl
Hurdles	3	0	0	0	0
Career Total	**3**	**0**	**0**	**0**	**0**

Going: Sf: 0-0 GS: 0-0 Gd: 0-2 GF: - Fm: 0-1
Distance: 2m/2m3: 0-3 2m4-2m7: 0-0 3m+: 0-0
Track: LH: 0-3 RH: 0-0 Tight: 0-3 Gall: 0-0
Aids: Bl: 0-0 Vi: 0-1 Tstrap: 0-0
Best Rating: 49 7/01 NAbb 2m1f good Hdl

Shamawan (IRE)

105 **139**

7-y-o b g Kris-Shamawna (IRE) (Darshaan)
J J O'Neill J P McManus

Placings:050/020/3P632-2112 **(4960a)**
2001/02: 17^{2}S, 16^{1}S, 17^{1}GS, 16^{2}GY

	Starts	1st	2nd	3rd	Win & Pl
Chases	4	2	2	0	13854
Career Total	**15**	**2**	**4**	**2**	**16028**

129	3/02	MRas	2m1f110y	D Ch	G-S	£5936
139	3/02	Hntg	2m110y	D(0-115)HCh	SFT	£3893

Total win prize-money £9830

Going: Sf: 1-2 GS: 1-1 Gd: 0-0 GF: - Fm: 0-0
Distance: **2m/2m3: 2-4** 2m4-2m7: 0-0 3m+: 0-0
Track: LH: 0-1 **RH: 2-3** Tight: 1-2 Gall: 1-1
Aids: Bl: 0-0 Vi: 0-0 Tstrap: 0-0
Best Rating: 139 3/02 Hntg 2m110y soft Ch

Ex-Irish maiden over hurdles, he showed signs of improvement over the larger obstacles and won a fair handicap on his second start in this country for new trainer Jonjo O'Neill. Followed up with an easy win at Market Rasen and looks a decent chasing prospect.

Shameless

84f **89f**

5-y-o ch g Prince Daniel (USA)-Level Edge (Beveled (USA))
H Alexander Mrs L Lever

Placings:*4025* **(4790)**
2001/02: 16^{4}S, 16^{0}GS, 16^{2}HY, 16^{5}F

	Starts	1st	2nd	3rd	Win & Pl
NH Flat	4	0	1	0	506
Career Total	**4**	**0**	**1**	**0**	**506**

Going: Sf: 0-2 GS: 0-1 Gd: 0-0 GF: - Fm: 0-1
Distance: 2m/2m3: 0-4 2m4-2m7: 0-0 3m+: 0-0
Track: LH: 0-2 RH: 0-0 Tight: 0-2 Gall: 0-0
Aids: Bl: 0-0 Vi: 0-0 Tstrap: 0-0
Best Rating: 89 3/02 Sthl 2m heavy NHF

Modest form in bumpers.

Shamokin

10-y-o b g Green Desert (USA)-Shajan (Kris)

F Watson F Watson

Placings:0 **(0475)**
2001/02: 17^{0}G

	Starts	1st	2nd	3rd	Win & Pl
Hurdles	1	0	0	0	
Career Total	**1**	**0**	**0**	**0**	

Going: Sf: 0-0 GS: 0-0 Gd: 0-1 GF: - Fm: 0-0
Distance: 2m/2m3: 0-1 2m4-2m7: 0-0 3m+: 0-0
Track: LH: 0-0 RH: 0-1 Tight: 0-1 Gall: 0-0
Aids: Bl: 0-0 Vi: 0-0 Tstrap: 0-0
Best Rating:

Shampooed (IRE)

100(108h) (100h)**121**
8-y-o b m Law Society (USA)-White Cap'S (Shirley Heights)
R Dickin Warwick Members Racing Club

Placings:001/200/010511/114561300-**4102553641** **(4598)**
2001/02: 19^{4}G, 17^{1}GS, 16^{0}GF, 16^{2}S, 20^{5}G, 20^{5}S, 20^{3}S, 16^{6}S, 16^{4}S, 16^{1}GF

	Starts	1st	2nd	3rd	Win & Pl
Hurdles	1	0	0	0	0
Chases	9	2	1	1	11130
Career Total	**31**	**9**	**2**	**2**	**35418**

109	4/02	Wwck	2m110y	E Ch	G-F	£3458
121	5/01	Strf	2m1f110y	D Ch	G-S	£4403
113	2/01	Wwck	2m	C(0-130)HHdl	SFT	£5135
110	5/00	Hntg	2m3f110y	D(0-120)HHdl	G-S	£3071
116	5/00	Towc	2m	D(0-125)HHdl	SFT	£3211
109	4/00	Strf	2m110y	D(0-120)HHdl	GD	£3568
92	3/00	Wwck	2m	F(0-100)HHdl	SFT	£1960
98	12/99	Wwck	2m	F(0-110)HHdl	SFT	£1996
94	3/98	Clon	2m	Hdl	YLD	£2382

Total win prize-money £29187

Going: Sf: 0-5 GS: 1-1 Gd: 0-2 GF: - Fm: 1-2
Distance: **2m/2m3: 2-6** 2m4-2m7: 0-4 3m+: 0-0
Track: **LH: 1-4** RH: 0-4 **Tight: 1-2** Gall: 0-0
Aids: Bl: 0-0 Vi: 0-0 Tstrap: 0-0
Best Rating: 121 5/01 Strf 2m1f110y gd-sft Ch

Tough handicap hurdler at up to two and a half miles, she successfully turned to chasing last season. Effective on a sound surface but best when the mud is flying. Has worn a visor.

Shamrock

94f **85f**
5-y-o ch m Sanglamore (USA)-Rockfest (USA) (Stagedoor Johnny)
Lady Herries Lady Herries

Placings:2 **(1545)**
2001/02: 17^{2}G

	Starts	1st	2nd	3rd	Win & Pl
NH Flat	1	0	1	0	456
Career Total	**1**	**0**	**1**	**0**	**456**

Going: Sf: 0-0 GS: 0-0 Gd: 0-1 GF: - Fm: 0-0
Distance: 2m/2m3: 0-1 2m4-2m7: 0-0 3m+: 0-0
Track: LH: 0-0 RH: 0-1 Tight: 0-0 Gall: 0-0
Aids: Bl: 0-0 Vi: 0-0 Tstrap: 0-0
Best Rating: 85 10/01 Hrfd 2m1f good NHF

Shamsan (IRE)

90(111h) (121h)**105+**
5-y-o ch g Night Shift (USA)-Awayil (USA) (Woodman (USA))
J Joseph (P J Hobbs 29/7) Jack Joseph

Placings:03-1212116600 **(4550)**
2001/02: 16^{1}F, 16^{2}GF, 17^{1}F, 16^{2}GS, 16^{1}G, 17^{1}G, 21^{6}HY, 21^{6}HY, 16^{0}S, 21^{0}GF

	Starts	1st	2nd	3rd	Win & Pl
Hurdles	10	4	2	0	15086
Career Total	**12**	**4**	**2**	**1**	**15692**

118	7/01	NAbb	2m1f	D Hdl	GD	£3376
106	7/01	Strf	2m110y	D Hdl	GD	£3472
110	6/01	Hrfd	2m1f	E Hdl	FRM	£2712
113	5/01	Sthl	2m	D Hdl	FRM	£3662

Total win prize-money £13224

Going: Sf: 0-3 GS: 0-1 Gd: 2-2 GF: - Fm: 2-4
Distance: **2m/2m3: 4-7** 2m4-2m7: 0-3 3m+: 0-0
Track: **LH: 3-6** RH: 1-3 **Tight: 3-6** Gall: 0-1
Aids: Bl: 0-0 Vi: 0-0 **Tstrap: 3-7**
Best Rating: 121 6/01 Strf 2m110y gd-fm Hdl

Multiple novice hurdle winner but has struggled in handicap company. Won Class E handicap at Hereford June 2002. Needs ground good or faster. Stays two and a half miles.

Shanavogh

11-y-o b g Idiots Delight-Honeybuzzard (FR) (Sea Hawk II)
Mrs Caroline Bailey R S Hunnisett

Placings:00530/121413/**2F1/3332/2/O44** **(0579)**
2001/02: 21°GF, 21^{4}G, 24^{4}GF

	Starts	1st	2nd	3rd	Win & Pl
Chases	3	0	0	0	0
Career Total	**22**	**4**	**4**	**5**	**22557**

103	2/98	Sedg	2m5f	E Ch	GD	£3179
108	2/97	Muss	2m4f	D Hdl	GD	£3105
110	11/96	Hayd	2m4f	C Hdl	GD	£3875
93	10/96	Carl	2m4f110y	E Hdl	GD	£2556

Total win prize-money £12715

Going: Sf: 0-0 GS: 0-0 Gd: 0-1 GF: - Fm: 0-2
Distance: 2m/2m3: 0-0 2m4-2m7: 0-2 3m+: 0-1
Track: LH: 0-2 RH: 0-0 Tight: 0-2 Gall: 0-0
Aids: Bl: 0-0 Vi: 0-0 Tstrap: 0-0
Best Rating: 127 5/99 Chep 3m good Ch

Shane

4-y-o ch g Aragon-Angel Fire (Nashwan (USA))
F P Murtagh (C W Thornton 25/9) Callaghans Racing Syndicate

Placings:PPP **(2512)**
2001/02: 16^{P}GS, 16^{P}GF, 16^{P}S

	Starts	1st	2nd	3rd	Win & Pl
Hurdles	3	0	0	0	
Career Total	**3**	**0**	**0**	**0**	

Going: Sf: 0-1 GS: 0-1 Gd: 0-0 GF: - Fm: 0-1
Distance: 2m/2m3: 0-3 2m4-2m7: 0-0 3m+: 0-0
Track: LH: 0-3 RH: 0-0 Tight: 0-2 Gall: 0-0
Aids: Bl: 0-0 Vi: 0-0 Tstrap: 0-0
Best Rating:

Shank's Pony (IRE)

10-y-o b m Jolly Jake (NZ)-Flachra's Kumar (Le Moss)
E M Caine Mrs Karen Woodhead

Placings:P00-0 **(1099)**
2001/02: 19^{0}GF

	Starts	1st	2nd	3rd	Win & Pl
Hurdles	1	0	0	0	
Career Total	**4**	**0**	**0**	**0**	

Going: Sf: 0-0 GS: 0-0 Gd: 0-0 GF: - Fm: 0-1
Distance: 2m/2m3: 0-0 2m4-2m7: 0-1 3m+: 0-0
Track: LH: 0-0 RH: 0-1 Tight: 0-1 Gall: 0-0
Aids: Bl: 0-0 Vi: 0-0 Tstrap: 0-0
Best Rating:

Shankar (IRE)

11-y-o gr g Shareef Dancer (USA)-Sibelle D'Oa (FR) (Kenmare (FR))
A King International Plywood Plc

Placings:F422/12315/**F**0312/3/U400P/01**03613320U2/UF**500-PPP **(1026)**
2001/02: 24^{P}GF, 21^{P}GF, 22^{P}G

	Starts	1st	2nd	3rd	Win & Pl
Hurdles	3	0	0	0	
Career Total	**40**	**5**	**6**	**6**	**53795**

131	11/99	Hntg	2m4f110y	D Ch	GD	£4159
128	7/99	Worc	2m	E Ch	G-F	£3039
135	4/97	Aint	2m110y	B HHdl	GD	£19870
103	2/96	Ludl	2m	E Hdl	GD	£2234
110	11/95	Newb	2m110y	C Hdl	HVY	£4435

Total win prize-money £33738

Going: Sf: 0-0 GS: 0-0 Gd: 0-1 GF: - Fm: 0-2
Distance: 2m/2m3: 0-0 2m4-2m7: 0-2 3m+: 0-1
Track: LH: 0-2 RH: 0-1 Tight: 0-2 Gall: 0-1
Aids: Bl: 0-0 Vi: 0-0 Tstrap: 0-1
Best Rating: 146 5/97 Hayd 2m gd-fm Hdl

Shannon Gale (IRE)

105 **130**
10-y-o b g Strong Gale-Shannon Spray (Le Bavard (FR))
C Roche J P McManus

Placings:00/0002*1*/14P/**252F/231P2**02-02P046 **(4955a)**
2001/02: 29^{0}G, 16^{2}Y, 24^{P}Y, 24^{0}YS, 21^{4}G, 25^{6}G

	Starts	1st	2nd	3rd	Win & Pl
Chases	6	0	1	0	5565
Career Total	**27**	**3**	**7**	**1**	**63785**

127	11/00	Navn	2m4f	Ch	SFT	£4968
116	12/98	Leop	3m	HHdl	HVY	£8445
108	12/96	Leop	2m	NHF	YLD	£3177

Total win prize-money £16592

Going: Sf: 0-0 GS: 0-0 Gd: 0-3 GF: - Fm: 0-0
Distance: 2m/2m3: 0-1 2m4-2m7: 0-1 3m+: 0-4
Track: LH: 0-4 RH: 0-1 Tight: 0-1 Gall: 0-0
Aids: Bl: 0-0 Vi: 0-0 Tstrap: 0-0
Best Rating: 142 4/01 Leop 3m sft-hvy Ch

Useful Irish performer over hurdles and fences. Stays three miles plus, effective on soft ground.

Shannon Light (IRE)

104 **100**
10-y-o b/br g Electric-Shannon Lass (Callernish)
N R Mitchell N R Mitchell

Placings:00202/3/0/0P-2506410F (4885)
2001/02: 21^{2}G, 21^{5}S, 25^{0}HY, 22^{6}S, 19^{4}G, 24^{1}S, 22^{0}G, 27^{F}GF

	Starts	1st	2nd	3rd	Win & Pl
Hurdles	8	1	1	0	4275
Career Total	**17**	**1**	**3**	**1**	**6038**

100	3/02	Chep	3m	D(0-120)HHdl	SFT	£3575

Total win prize-money £3575

Going: Sf: 1-4 GS: 0-0 Gd: 0-3 GF: - Fm: 0-1
Distance: 2m/2m3: 0-1 2m4-2m7: 0-4 **3m+: 1-3**
Track: **LH: 1-4** RH: 0-2 Tight: 0-4 Gall: 0-0
Aids: Bl: 0-0 Vi: 0-0 Tstrap: 0-0
Best Rating: 102 5/97 Tipp 2m4f yld-sft NHF

Modest form over hurdles. Gained his first success at Chepstow over three miles. Has won on heavy ground, handles faster.

Shannon Quest (IRE)

107(96h) (94h)106
6-y-o b/br g Zaffaran (USA)-Carrick Shannon (Green Shoon)
O Sherwood Ledwidge Best Dellal Forde

Placings:0-030436F (4551)
2001/02: 17^{0}G, 16^{3}G, 19^{0}G, 16^{4}S, 16^{3}GS, 16^{6}G, 16^{F}GF

	Starts	1st	2nd	3rd	Win & Pl
NH Flat	1	0	0	0	0
Hurdles	5	0	0	2	1177
Chases	1	0	0	0	0
Career Total	**8**	**0**	**0**	**2**	**1177**

Going: Sf: 0-1 GS: 0-1 Gd: 0-4 GF: - Fm: 0-1
Distance: 2m/2m3: 0-6 2m4-2m7: 0-1 3m+: 0-0
Track: LH: 0-2 RH: 0-5 Tight: 0-2 Gall: 0-1
Aids: Bl: 0-0 Vi: 0-0 Tstrap: 0-0
Best Rating: 94 3/02 Winc 2m good Hdl

Placed over hurdles and fences but has not been getting home. Pulled up lame in May 2002.

Shannon's Dream

70 26
6-y-o gr m Anshan-Jenny's Call (Petong)
Mrs Barbara Waring Hugh J Shapter

Placings:00PP (2134)
2001/02: 16^{0}GF, 22^{0}G, 24^{P}G, 21^{P}GF

	Starts	1st	2nd	3rd	Win & Pl
Hurdles	4	0	0	0	
Career Total	**4**	**0**	**0**	**0**	

Going: Sf: 0-0 GS: 0-0 Gd: 0-2 GF: - Fm: 0-2
Distance: 2m/2m3: 0-1 2m4-2m7: 0-2 3m+: 0-1
Track: LH: 0-3 RH: 0-1 Tight: 0-2 Gall: 0-0
Aids: Bl: 0-0 Vi: 0-0 Tstrap: 0-0
Best Rating: 26 6/01 Worc 2m gd-fm Hdl

Shannon's Pride (IRE)

98 99
6-y-o gr g Roselier (FR)-Spanish Flame (IRE) (Spanish Place (USA))
N G Richards J Hales

Placings:3 (4832)
2001/02: 20^{3}G

	Starts	1st	2nd	3rd	Win & Pl
Hurdles	1	0	0	1	857
Career Total	**1**	**0**	**0**	**1**	**857**

Going: Sf: 0-0 GS: 0-0 Gd: 0-1 GF: - Fm: 0-0
Distance: 2m/2m3: 0-0 2m4-2m7: 0-1 3m+: 0-0
Track: LH: 0-1 RH: 0-0 Tight: 0-0 Gall: 0-0
Aids: Bl: 0-0 Vi: 0-0 Tstrap: 0-0
Best Rating: 99 4/02 Ayr 2m4f good Hdl

Shantarini (IRE)

100 119
8-y-o gr g Pharly (FR)-Shanjarina (USA) (Blushing Groom (FR))
D J Wintle L & P Partnership

Placings:0533010/413102060/F4534004/0165335540-1F3P (1281)
2001/02: 21^{1}GF, 27^{F}G, 22^{3}G, 20^{P}GF

	Starts	1st	2nd	3rd	Win & Pl
Hurdles	4	1	0	1	3552
Career Total	**38**	**5**	**1**	**7**	**42424**

119	5/01	Wwck	2m5f	F(0-110)HHdl	G-F	£2802
130	5/00	Worc	3m	C(0-130)HHdl	G-F	£5388
130	9/98	List	2m	HHdl	GD	£11304
121	5/98	Leop	2m	(0-116)Hdl	G-F	£3573
118	4/98	Fair	2m	Hdl	YLD	£5956

Total win prize-money £29027

Going: Sf: 0-0 GS: 0-0 Gd: 0-2 GF: - Fm: 1-2
Distance: 2m/2m3: 0-0 **2m4-2m7: 1-3** 3m+: 0-1
Track: LH: 0-3 RH: 0-0 Tight: 0-2 Gall: 0-0
Aids: **Bl: 1-3** Vi: 0-0 Tstrap: 0-0
Best Rating: 132 3/99 Chel 2m1f gd-sft Hdl

Sharazan (IRE)

120
9-y-o b g Akarad (FR)-Sharaniya (USA) (Alleged (USA))
O O'Neill Merry Fellows

Placings:04/2/323051112/442035-5 (0075)
2001/02: 24^{5}G

	Starts	1st	2nd	3rd	Win & Pl
Hurdles	1	0	0	0	0
Career Total	**19**	**3**	**4**	**3**	**15045**

110	3/00	Hntg	3m2f	E(0-115)HHdl	G-F	£2520
117	3/00	Towc	3m	F(0-100)HHdl	SFT	£2394
117	3/00	Newb	2m3f	E(0-105)HHdl	SFT	£3331

Total win prize-money £8245

Going: Sf: 0-0 GS: 0-0 Gd: 0-1 GF: - Fm: 0-0
Distance: 2m/2m3: 0-0 2m4-2m7: 0-0 3m+: 0-1
Track: LH: 0-0 RH: 0-1 Tight: 0-0 Gall: 0-0
Aids: Bl: 0-0 Vi: 0-0 Tstrap: 0-0
Best Rating: 120 5/01 Extr 3m110y good Hdl

Fairly useful handicap hurdler who stays very well but is hard to win with. Effective on good/heavy.

Shardam (IRE)

110 115
5-y-o b g Shardari-Knockea Hill (Buckskin (FR))
N A Twiston-Davies Howard Parker

Placings:2526262 (4530)
2001/02: 17^{2}G, 17^{5}G, 20^{2}S, 20^{6}GS, 16^{2}HY, 21^{6}HY, 20^{2}GS

	Starts	1st	2nd	3rd	Win & Pl
NH Flat	2	0	1	0	510
Hurdles	5	0	3	0	2630
Career Total	**7**	**0**	**4**	**0**	**3140**

Going: Sf: 0-3 GS: 0-2 Gd: 0-2 GF: - Fm: 0-0
Distance: 2m/2m3: 0-3 2m4-2m7: 0-4 3m+: 0-0
Track: LH: 0-5 RH: 0-1 Tight: 0-1 Gall: 0-0
Aids: Bl: 0-0 Vi: 0-0 Tstrap: 0-0
Best Rating: 115 4/02 Chep 2m4f gd-sft Hdl

Out of a prolific pointer, he has shown ability in bumpers and over hurdles. He stays two and a half miles and handles soft and good ground.

Shardante (IRE)

88 85
9-y-o ch g Phardante (FR)-Shirabas (Karabas)
J M Jefferson W A Bethell

Placings:0P/304524402P/152541-5 (1656)
2001/02: 24^{5}G

	Starts	1st	2nd	3rd	Win & Pl
Chases	1	0	0	0	0
Career Total	**19**	**2**	**3**	**1**	**12142**

127	2/01	Hntg	3m	D(0-120)HCh	G-S	£4426
120	9/00	Bang	2m4f110y	D Ch	G-F	£4173

Total win prize-money £8600

Going: Sf: 0-0 GS: 0-0 Gd: 0-1 GF: - Fm: 0-0
Distance: 2m/2m3: 0-0 2m4-2m7: 0-0 3m+: 0-1
Track: LH: 0-1 RH: 0-0 Tight: 0-1 Gall: 0-0
Aids: Bl: 0-0 Vi: 0-0 Tstrap: 0-0
Best Rating: 127 2/01 Hntg 3m gd-sft Ch

He won his first start of last season at Bangor and his last start of the campaign at Huntingdon. Useful form in between and, although he has won on easy ground, he looks best on soft.

Shared Expectation (IRE)

70f 62f
6-y-o ch g Husyan (USA)-Calmount (IRE) (Callernish)
J M Jefferson R E Williams

Placings:0 (2055)
2001/02: 17^{0}S

	Starts	1st	2nd	3rd	Win & Pl
NH Flat	1	0	0	0	
Career Total	**1**	**0**	**0**	**0**	

Going: Sf: 0-1 GS: 0-0 Gd: 0-0 GF: - Fm: 0-0
Distance: 2m/2m3: 0-1 2m4-2m7: 0-0 3m+: 0-0
Track: LH: 0-0 RH: 0-1 Tight: 0-0 Gall: 0-0
Aids: Bl: 0-0 Vi: 0-0 Tstrap: 0-0
Best Rating: 62 11/01 Carl 2m1f soft NHF

Shared-Interest

75 13
8-y-o ch m Interrex (CAN)-La Campagnola (Hubble Bubble)
Jane Southcombe David J Adams

Placings:0/P0 (1239)
2001/02: 22^{P}G, 20^{0}GF

	Starts	1st	2nd	3rd	Win & Pl
Hurdles	2	0	0	0	
Career Total	**3**	**0**	**0**	**0**	

Going: Sf: 0-0 GS: 0-0 Gd: 0-1 GF: - Fm: 0-1
Distance: 2m/2m3: 0-0 2m4-2m7: 0-2 3m+: 0-0
Track: LH: 0-2 RH: 0-0 Tight: 0-1 Gall: 0-0
Aids: Bl: 0-0 Vi: 0-0 Tstrap: 0-0
Best Rating: 32 2/99 Winc 2m gd-sft NHF

Shareef (FR)

103 **123**

5-y-o b g Port Lyautey (FR)-Saralik (Salse (USA))
J W Mullins Mrs Jeni Fisher

Placings: *1-5*U12P44 **(4586)**
2001/02: 17^{5}G, 17^{U}GF, 22^{1}G, 22^{2}GF, 20^{P}S, 22^{4}S, 22^{4}G

	Starts	1st	2nd	3rd	Win & Pl
NH Flat	1	0	0	0	0
Hurdles	6	1	1	0	3919
Career Total	**8**	**2**	**1**	**0**	**5669**

114	10/01	Winc	2m6f	E Hdl	GD	£2275
91	4/01	Newb	2m110y	H NHF	SFT	£1750

Total win prize-money £4025

Going: Sf: 0-2 GS: 0-0 Gd: 1-3 GF: - Fm: 0-2
Distance: 2m/2m3: 0-2 **2m4-2m7: 1-5** 3m+: 0-0
Track: LH: 0-1 **RH: 1-6** Tight: 0-1 Gall: 0-0
Aids: Bl: 0-0 Vi: 0-0 Tstrap: 0-0
Best Rating: 118 11/01 Winc 2m6f gd-fm Hdl

Showed a nice change of gear when winning below-par Newbury bumper in April 2001. Got off the mark over hurdles on good ground at Wincanton but held since. Best on a soundish surface.

Shareton

11-y-o br g Lighter-Share (Khalkis)
C Tizzard J H Green

Placings: PP **(0596)**
2001/02: 22^{P}GF, 17^{P}G

	Starts	1st	2nd	3rd	Win & Pl
Hurdles	2	0	0	0	
Career Total	**2**	**0**	**0**	**0**	

Going: Sf: 0-0 GS: 0-0 Gd: 0-1 GF: - Fm: 0-1
Distance: 2m/2m3: 0-1 2m4-2m7: 0-1 3m+: 0-0
Track: LH: 0-1 RH: 0-1 Tight: 0-1 Gall: 0-0
Aids: Bl: 0-1 Vi: 0-0 Tstrap: 0-0
Best Rating:

Shark (IRE)

104 **84**

9-y-o b g Tirol-Gay Appeal (Star Appeal)
K A Morgan M J Harmer

Placings: 42034/52/U524 **(2947)**
2001/02: 17^{U}G, 19^{5}GS, 19^{2}S, 20^{4}G

	Starts	1st	2nd	3rd	Win & Pl
Hurdles	4	0	1	0	450
Career Total	**11**	**0**	**3**	**1**	**1930**

Going: Sf: 0-1 GS: 0-1 Gd: 0-2 GF: - Fm: 0-0
Distance: 2m/2m3: 0-1 2m4-2m7: 0-3 3m+: 0-0
Track: LH: 0-1 RH: 0-3 Tight: 0-4 Gall: 0-0
Aids: Bl: 0-0 Vi: 0-0 Tstrap: 0-0
Best Rating: 98 9/98 MRas 2m1f110y good Hdl

A dual-purpose horse on the Flat and over hurdles, he has never imposed himself since a two year lay-off.

Sharlom (IRE)

(93h) (74h)**74**

5-y-o br g Shardari-Sarahs Music (IRE) (Orchestra)
Mrs M Stirk Mrs M Stirk

Placings: *0*5PF0P **(4871)**
2001/02: 17^{0}GF, 16^{5}G, 17^{P}G, 20^{F}G, 23^{0}G, 25^{P}GF

	Starts	1st	2nd	3rd	Win & Pl
NH Flat	1	0	0	0	0
Hurdles	5	0	0	0	0
Career Total	**6**	**0**	**0**	**0**	**0**

Going: Sf: 0-0 GS: 0-0 Gd: 0-4 GF: - Fm: 0-2
Distance: 2m/2m3: 0-3 2m4-2m7: 0-2 3m+: 0-1
Track: LH: 0-5 RH: 0-1 Tight: 0-3 Gall: 0-0
Aids: Bl: 0-0 Vi: 0-0 Tstrap: 0-0
Best Rating: 74 10/01 Sthl 2m good Hdl

Sharmadan (FR)

75f **65f**

6-y-o ch g Zayyani-Sharmada (FR) (Zeddaan)
K A Morgan H A Blenkhorn

Placings: *0* **(0843)**
2001/02: 16^{0}G

	Starts	1st	2nd	3rd	Win & Pl
NH Flat	1	0	0	0	
Career Total	**1**	**0**	**0**	**0**	

Going: Sf: 0-0 GS: 0-0 Gd: 0-1 GF: - Fm: 0-0
Distance: 2m/2m3: 0-1 2m4-2m7: 0-0 3m+: 0-0
Track: LH: 0-1 RH: 0-0 Tight: 0-0 Gall: 0-0
Aids: Bl: 0-0 Vi: 0-0 Tstrap: 0-0
Best Rating: 65 6/01 Worc 2m good NHF

Sharmy (IRE)

108 **116**

6-y-o b g Caerleon (USA)-Petticoat Lane (Ela-Mana-Mou)
Ian Williams T J And Mrs H Parrott

Placings: 525224 **(4662)**
2001/02: 16^{5}GS, 16^{2}G, 16^{5}GS, 16^{2}S, 16^{2}GS, 16^{4}G

	Starts	1st	2nd	3rd	Win & Pl
Hurdles	6	0	3	0	4734
Career Total	**6**	**0**	**3**	**0**	**4734**

Going: Sf: 0-1 GS: 0-3 Gd: 0-2 GF: - Fm: 0-0
Distance: 2m/2m3: 0-6 2m4-2m7: 0-0 3m+: 0-0
Track: LH: 0-4 RH: 0-2 Tight: 0-2 Gall: 0-1
Aids: Bl: 0-0 Vi: 0-0 Tstrap: 0-0
Best Rating: 116 4/02 Aint 2m110y good Hdl

Decent novice hurdler, effective over two miles and on good ground or softer.

Sharon's Touch (IRE)

111 **118**

7-y-o b m Mandalus-Russell's Touch (Deep Run)
L J Archdeacon J A O'Sullivan

Placings: *0500400*/16446640502-36301U0U0 **(4084a)**
2001/02: 20^{3}GY, 24^{6}G, 16^{3}Y, 18^{0}S, 21^{1}G, 20^{U}S, 19^{0}SH, 20^{U}S, 24^{0}S

	Starts	1st	2nd	3rd	Win & Pl
Hurdles	9	1	0	2	11825
Career Total	**27**	**2**	**1**	**2**	**17733**

118	11/01	Chel	2m5f	E(0-115)HHdl	GD	£9438
94	5/00	Klny	2m4f	Hdl	Y-S	£3864

Total win prize-money £13302

Going: Sf: 0-4 GS: 0-0 Gd: 1-2 GF: - Fm: 0-0
Distance: 2m/2m3: 0-3 **2m4-2m7: 1-4** 3m+: 0-2
Track: **LH: 1-2** RH: 0-2 Tight: 0-0 **Gall: 1-1**
Aids: Bl: 0-0 Vi: 0-0 Tstrap: 0-0
Best Rating: 118 11/01 Chel 2m5f good Hdl

A fair Irish handicapper, won a handicap hurdle in good style at the Thomas Pink meeting.

Sharp Belline (IRE)

109 **114**

5-y-o b g Robellino (USA)-Moon Watch (Night Shift (USA))
John A Harris (J L Harris 26/5) Townville C C Racing Club

Placings: 01402-063304624 **(4636)**
2001/02: 19^{0}G, 16^{6}GF, 21^{3}G, 20^{3}G, 20^{0}G, 24^{4}G, 24^{6}S, 21^{2}GS, 24^{4}GF

	Starts	1st	2nd	3rd	Win & Pl
Hurdles	9	0	1	2	3877
Career Total	**14**	**1**	**2**	**2**	**7596**

117	2/01	Donc	2m4f	E Hdl	GD	£2508

Total win prize-money £2509

Going: Sf: 0-1 GS: 0-1 Gd: 0-5 GF: - Fm: 0-2
Distance: 2m/2m3: 0-1 2m4-2m7: 0-5 3m+: 0-3
Track: LH: 0-5 RH: 0-4 Tight: 0-3 Gall: 0-3
Aids: Bl: 0-0 Vi: 0-0 Tstrap: 0-0
Best Rating: 117 2/01 Donc 2m4f good Hdl

She is only small but she is all heart. Stays three miles and acts on a sound surface, has won on good to soft ground, but does not have much in the way of a turn of foot.

Sharp Command

88(86h) (62h)**52**

9-y-o ch g Sharpo-Bluish (USA) (Alleged (USA))
R M Stronge A P Holland

Placings: U04141/P123442P0/110P010131420F/1063 0P3P045/06PP0-0P00 **(1138)**
2001/02: 20^{0}GF, 23^{P}G, 23^{0}G, 24^{0}G

	Starts	1st	2nd	3rd	Win & Pl
Hurdles	1	0	0	0	0
Chases	3	0	0	0	0
Career Total	**49**	**9**	**3**	**4**	**45534**

114	5/99	Ctml	3m2f	E Ch	GD	£2084
114	2/99	Catt	3m1f110y	E(0-115)HHdl	GD	£5641
130	12/98	Catt	3m1f110y	E(0-110)HCh	GD	£7587
113	10/98	Sedg	2m5f110y	E(0-110)HHdl	G-S	£5316
123	5/98	Prth	3m	D Ch	G-F	£3566
95	5/98	Sthl	3m110y	E Ch	GD	£3516
111	9/97	Sedg	2m5f110y	D(0-120)HHdl	G-F	£2838
111	4/97	Towc	2m5f	E(0-100)HHdl	G-F	£2132
106	4/97	Sedg	2m5f110y	E Hdl	G-F	£2740

Total win prize-money £36322

Going: Sf: 0-0 GS: 0-0 Gd: 0-3 GF: - Fm: 0-1
Distance: 2m/2m3: 0-0 2m4-2m7: 0-1 3m+: 0-3
Track: LH: 0-4 RH: 0-0 Tight: 0-1 Gall: 0-0
Aids: Bl: 0-0 Vi: 0-0 Tstrap: 0-0
Best Rating: 130 4/99 Tntn 3m firm Ch

Sharp Embrace

9-y-o ch g Broadsword (USA)-Running Kiss (Deep Run)
Miss Susan Rodman (Trainer Unknown 7/4) Miss Susan Rodman

Placings: 40P/005P032FP/3 **(4777)**
2001/02: 25^{3}G

	Starts	1st	2nd	3rd	Win & Pl

	Starts	1st	2nd	3rd	Win & Pl
Chases	1	0	0	1	168
Career Total	**13**	**0**	**1**	**2**	**1532**

Going: Sf: 0-0 GS: 0-0 Gd: 0-1 GF: - Fm: 0-0
Distance: 2m/2m3: 0-0 2m4-2m7: 0-0 3m+: 0-1
Track: LH: 0-0 RH: 0-1 Tight: 0-1 Gall: 0-0
Aids: Bl: 0-0 Vi: 0-0 Tstrap: 0-0
Best Rating: 90 9/98 Bang 3m110y good Ch

Sharp Monkey

7-y-o b g Man Among Men (IRE)-Sharp Thistle (Sharpo)
I J Hooper I J Hooper

Placings:4000/0PP-PU0 **(0430)**
2001/02: 20^{P}GF, 28^{U}GF, 16^{0}G

	Starts	1st	2nd	3rd	Win & Pl
Chases	3	0	0	0	
Career Total	**10**	**0**	**0**	**0**	**320**

Going: Sf: 0-0 GS: 0-0 Gd: 0-1 GF: - Fm: 0-2
Distance: 2m/2m3: 0-1 2m4-2m7: 0-1 3m+: 0-1
Track: LH: 0-2 RH: 0-0 Tight: 0-1 Gall: 0-0
Aids: Bl: 0-1 Vi: 0-0 Tstrap: 0-0
Best Rating: 71 11/99 Sedg 2m1f good Hdl

Sharp Seal

8-y-o b g Broadsword (USA)-Little Beaver (Privy Seal)
M Madgwick J D Brownrigg

Placings:P **(0490)**
2001/02: 27^{P}GF

	Starts	1st	2nd	3rd	Win & Pl
Hurdles	1	0	0	0	
Career Total	**1**	**0**	**0**	**0**	

Going: Sf: 0-0 GS: 0-0 Gd: 0-0 GF: - Fm: 0-1
Distance: 2m/2m3: 0-0 2m4-2m7: 0-0 3m+: 0-1
Track: LH: 0-0 RH: 0-0 Tight: 0-1 Gall: 0-0
Aids: Bl: 0-0 Vi: 0-0 Tstrap: 0-0
Best Rating:

Sharp Shooter (IRE)

(81h) (35h)**53**
7-y-o b g Sabrehill (USA)-Kermesse (IRE) (Reference Point)
W G Young W G Young

Placings:03315040P0/0-BFP0P00P **(1460)**
2001/02: 21^{B}G, 16^{F}GF, 24^{P}F, 16^{0}GS, 20^{P}G, 16^{0}G, 17^{0}G, 16^{P}G

	Starts	1st	2nd	3rd	Win & Pl
Hurdles	5	0	0	0	0
Chases	3	0	0	0	0
Career Total	**19**	**1**	**0**	**2**	**3607**

101 10/99 MRas 2m1f110y E Hdl GD £2878
Total win prize-money £2878

Going: Sf: 0-0 GS: 0-1 Gd: 0-5 GF: - Fm: 0-2
Distance: 2m/2m3: 0-5 2m4-2m7: 0-2 3m+: 0-1
Track: LH: 0-6 RH: 0-2 Tight: 0-2 Gall: 0-0
Aids: Bl: 0-0 Vi: 0-0 Tstrap: 0-8
Best Rating: 101 10/99 MRas 2m1f110y good Hdl

Sharp Steel

87 **85**
7-y-o ch g Beveled (USA)-Shift Over (USA) (Night Shift (USA))
Miss S J Wilton John Pointon And Sons

Placings:400 **(4774)**
2001/02: 16^{4}S, 16^{0}G, 17^{0}G

	Starts	1st	2nd	3rd	Win & Pl
Hurdles	3	0	0	0	0
Career Total	**3**	**0**	**0**	**0**	**0**

Going: Sf: 0-1 GS: 0-0 Gd: 0-2 GF: - Fm: 0-0
Distance: 2m/2m3: 0-3 2m4-2m7: 0-0 3m+: 0-0
Track: LH: 0-1 RH: 0-2 Tight: 0-1 Gall: 0-0
Aids: Bl: 0-0 Vi: 0-0 Tstrap: 0-0
Best Rating: 85 4/02 Uttx 2m good Hdl

Sharpastrizam (NZ)

107(85h) (57h)**122**
7-y-o b g Try To Stop Me-Atristazam (NZ) (Zamazaan (FR))
P Beaumont Trevor Hemmings

Placings:2F060P-11P1211551 **(4891)**
2001/02: 16^{1}F, 17^{1}G, 16^{P}S, 16^{1}G, 16^{2}S, 16^{1}G, 16^{1}G, 16^{5}S, 20^{5}G, 16^{1}G

	Starts	1st	2nd	3rd	Win & Pl
Chases	10	6	1	0	24971
Career Total	**16**	**6**	**2**	**0**	**25417**

122	4/02	Prth	2m	C(0-130)HCh	GD	£7111
119	1/02	Donc	2m110y	E(0-105)HCh	GD	£3201
106	12/01	Catt	2m	F(0-105)HCh	GD	£3024
106	11/01	Weth	2m	D(0-110)HCh	GD	£4153
102	5/01	Bang	2m1f110y	F(0-95)HCh	GD	£3486
101	5/01	Sthl	2m	F(0-100)HCh	FRM	£2775

Total win prize-money £23752

Going: Sf: 0-3 GS: 0-0 Gd: 5-6 GF: - Fm: 1-1
Distance: 2m/2m3: 6-9 2m4-2m7: 0-1 3m+: 0-0
Track: LH: 5-8 RH: 1-2 **Tight: 3-5** Gall: 1-2
Aids: Bl: 0-0 Vi: 0-0 Tstrap: 0-0
Best Rating: 122 4/02 Prth 2m good Ch

Enjoying a fine season in novice chases, he is suited to around two miles on a sound surface.

Sharpe's Lady

75 **67**
4-y-o b f Prince Des Coeurs (USA)-To The Point (Sharpen Up)
Miss K M George (Nick Williams 18/10) Stableline

Placings:01 **(3356)**
2001/02: 17^{0}F, 16^{1}HY

	Starts	1st	2nd	3rd	Win & Pl
Hurdles	2	1	0	0	1897
Career Total	**2**	**1**	**0**	**0**	**1897**

67 1/02 Uttx 2m F Hdl HVY £1897
Total win prize-money £1897

Going: Sf: 1-1 GS: 0-0 Gd: 0-0 GF: - Fm: 0-1
Distance: 2m/2m3: 1-2 2m4-2m7: 0-0 3m+: 0-0
Track: LH: 1-1 RH: 0-1 Tight: 0-1 Gall: 0-0
Aids: Bl: 0-0 Vi: 0-0 Tstrap: 0-0
Best Rating: 67 1/02 Uttx 2m heavy Hdl

Suited by testing conditions. Won a claiming hurdle at Uttoxeter on he rsecond start over flights.

Sharpical

10-y-o b g Sharpo-Magical Spirit (Top Ville)
J F Panvert J F Panvert

Placings:1212F/2261/P/32/P **(0581)**
2001/02: 16^{P}GF

	Starts	1st	2nd	3rd	Win & Pl
Hurdles	1	0	0	0	
Career Total	**13**	**3**	**5**	**1**	**80573**

148	2/98	Newb	2m110y	A HHdl	GD	£57375
117	3/97	Folk	2m1f110y	E Hdl	GD	£2566
111	12/96	Hntg	2m110y	E Hdl	G-S	£2652

Total win prize-money £62595

Going: Sf: 0-0 GS: 0-0 Gd: 0-0 GF: - Fm: 0-1
Distance: 2m/2m3: 0-1 2m4-2m7: 0-0 3m+: 0-0
Track: LH: 0-1 RH: 0-0 Tight: 0-1 Gall: 0-0
Aids: Bl: 0-1 Vi: 0-0 Tstrap: 0-0
Best Rating: 148 12/99 Kemp 2m soft Hdl

Shaws Cross (IRE)

11-y-o ch g Ashmolean (USA)-Dandy Vision (Quayside)
S G Griffiths S G Griffiths

Placings:00/F00/00004F15/P6/PP **(1018)**
2001/02: 24^{P}G, 23^{P}G

	Starts	1st	2nd	3rd	Win & Pl
Hurdles	1	0	0	0	0
Chases	1	0	0	0	0
Career Total	**17**	**1**	**0**	**0**	**2317**

96 3/97 Tram 2m6f Ch GD £2204
Total win prize-money £2204

Going: Sf: 0-0 GS: 0-0 Gd: 0-2 GF: - Fm: 0-0
Distance: 2m/2m3: 0-0 2m4-2m7: 0-0 3m+: 0-2
Track: LH: 0-2 RH: 0-0 Tight: 0-0 Gall: 0-0
Aids: Bl: 0-0 Vi: 0-0 Tstrap: 0-0
Best Rating: 96 3/97 Tram 2m6f good Ch

Shays Lane (IRE)

93 **78**
8-y-o b g The Bart (USA)-Continuity Lass (Continuation)
Ferdy Murphy Mrs C McKeane

Placings:0000 **(2920)**
2001/02: 16^{0}G, 16^{0}GS, 23^{0}S, 20^{0}G

	Starts	1st	2nd	3rd	Win & Pl
Hurdles	4	0	0	0	
Career Total	**4**	**0**	**0**	**0**	

Going: Sf: 0-1 GS: 0-1 Gd: 0-2 GF: - Fm: 0-0
Distance: 2m/2m3: 0-2 2m4-2m7: 0-2 3m+: 0-0
Track: LH: 0-3 RH: 0-1 Tight: 0-1 Gall: 0-1
Aids: Bl: 0-0 Vi: 0-0 Tstrap: 0-0
Best Rating: 78 11/01 Weth 2m good Hdl

Shayzara (IRE)

112 **116**
5-y-o b m Turtle Island (IRE)-Shayraz (Darshaan)
N J Henderson Peter E Clinton

Placings:214-13640 **(4721a)**
2001/02: 16^{1}G, 16^{3}GS, 16^{6}S, 16^{4}GS, 20^{0}GY

	Starts	1st	2nd	3rd	Win & Pl
Hurdles	5	1	0	1	4328
Career Total	**8**	**2**	**1**	**1**	**7435**

101	11/01	Wwck	2m	E Hdl	GD	£2775
81	4/01	Fknm	2m	H NHF	G-S	£1526

Total win prize-money £4302

Going: Sf: 0-1 GS: 0-2 Gd: 1-1 GF: - Fm: 0-0
Distance: 2m/2m3: 1-4 2m4-2m7: 0-1 3m+: 0-0
Track: LH: 1-2 RH: 0-3 Tight: 0-0 Gall: 0-0
Aids: Bl: 0-0 Vi: 0-0 Tstrap: 0-0
Best Rating: 116 2/02 Kemp 2m gd-sft Hdl

Made a winning hurdles debut at Warwick but her limitations have been exposed since. Best at two miles. Acts on good or slightly softer.

Shazal

69f 56f

5-y-o b m Afzal-Isolationist (Welsh Pageant)
J N R Billinge Mr & Mrs D Nimmo

Placings: 0 **(4841)**
2001/02: 16^{0}G

	Starts	1st	2nd	3rd	Win & Pl
NH Flat	1	0	0	0	
Career Total	**1**	**0**	**0**	**0**	

Going: Sf: 0-0 GS: 0-0 Gd: 0-1 GF: - Fm: 0-0
Distance: 2m/2m3: 0-1 2m4-2m7: 0-0 3m+: 0-0
Track: LH: 0-1 RH: 0-0 Tight: 0-0 Gall: 0-0
Aids: Bl: 0-0 Vi: 0-0 Tstrap: 0-0
Best Rating: 56 4/02 Ayr 2m good NHF

She's All Heart

99 87

9-y-o b m Broken Hearted-Tina's Brig (Majestic Streak)
L Lungo D Griffiths

Placings: 050/000606000/15150F255/1-P2U252P **(4898)**
2001/02: 20^{P}G, 18^{2}GS, 20^{U}S, 16^{2}S, 20^{5}HY, 16^{2}G, 16^{P}G

	Starts	1st	2nd	3rd	Win & Pl
Hurdles	7	0	3	0	2528
Career Total	**29**	**3**	**4**	**0**	**19531**

101	5/00	Uttx	2m4f110y	G(0-100)HHdl	GD	£10725
84	6/99	Prth	2m110y	F(0-100)HHdl	SFT	£2592
78	5/99	Prth	2m110y	G(0-100)HHdl	SFT	£2905

Total win prize-money £16223

Going: Sf: 0-3 GS: 0-1 Gd: 0-3 GF: - Fm: 0-0
Distance: 2m/2m3: 0-4 2m4-2m7: 0-3 3m+: 0-0
Track: LH: 0-5 RH: 0-1 Tight: 0-1 Gall: 0-2
Aids: Bl: 0-0 Vi: 0-0 Tstrap: 0-0
Best Rating: 101 5/00 Uttx 2m4f110y good Hdl

Modest hurdler, returned from injury late in 2001 and has shown she retains ability. Stays two and a half miles, possibly does not want the ground too soft nowadays.

She's My Girl (IRE)

104 86

7-y-o ch m Arctic Cider (USA)-Sinead's Princess (Sun Prince)
John G Carr J Stanley

Placings: 62430000/0B420U30560-565505P **(2735a)**
2001/02: 20^{5}G, 22^{6}G, 20^{5}GF, 20^{5}GF, 21^{0}G, 21^{5}G, 24^{P}Y

	Starts	1st	2nd	3rd	Win & Pl
Hurdles	7	0	0	0	0
Career Total	**26**	**0**	**2**	**2**	**4781**

Going: Sf: 0-0 GS: 0-0 Gd: 0-4 GF: - Fm: 0-2
Distance: 2m/2m3: 0-0 2m4-2m7: 0-6 3m+: 0-1
Track: LH: 0-4 RH: 0-1 Tight: 0-0 Gall: 0-2
Aids: Bl: 0-1 Vi: 0-0 Tstrap: 0-0
Best Rating: 89 11/99 Punc 2m yield NHF

Shebang (IRE)

10-y-o b g Be My Native (USA)-Polly's Cottage (Pollerton)
J Howard Johnson Maurice Hutchinson

Placings: 2232/53/0/U25-P **(0066)**
2001/02: 21^{P}G

	Starts	1st	2nd	3rd	Win & Pl
Chases	1	0	0	0	
Career Total	**11**	**0**	**4**	**2**	**2650**

Going: Sf: 0-0 GS: 0-0 Gd: 0-1 GF: - Fm: 0-0
Distance: 2m/2m3: 0-0 2m4-2m7: 0-1 3m+: 0-0
Track: LH: 0-1 RH: 0-0 Tight: 0-1 Gall: 0-0
Aids: Bl: 0-0 Vi: 0-0 Tstrap: 0-0
Best Rating: 99 12/00 Sedg 2m5f soft Ch

Sheer Genius (IRE)

100(94c) (119c)131

6-y-o b g Insan (USA)-Mulberry (IRE) (Denel (FR))
M Pitman Malcolm C Denmark

Placings: 430/111332-30 **(3887)**
2001/02: 16^{3}G, 24^{0}GS

	Starts	1st	2nd	3rd	Win & Pl
Hurdles	1	0	0	0	0
Chases	1	0	0	1	593
Career Total	**11**	**3**	**1**	**4**	**19879**

129	11/00	Chel	2m5f	B Hdl	G-S	£7377
101	10/00	Towc	2m	D Hdl	GD	£2977
110	10/00	Font	2m2f110y	E Hdl	GD	£1858

Total win prize-money £12214

Going: Sf: 0-0 GS: 0-1 Gd: 0-1 GF: - Fm: 0-0
Distance: 2m/2m3: 0-1 2m4-2m7: 0-0 3m+: 0-1
Track: LH: 0-0 RH: 0-2 Tight: 0-0 Gall: 0-0
Aids: Bl: 0-0 Vi: 0-0 Tstrap: 0-0
Best Rating: 131 4/01 Ayr 3m110y good Hdl

He notched up a hat-trick of successes over hurdles in 2000/01 in game fashion at two miles and two miles five on a sound surface. He either did not stay three miles or raced on unsuitably heavy ground subsequently. A shade disappointing on his chasing debut in October 2001.

Sheila McKenzie

5-y-o b m Aragon-Lady Quachita (USA) (Sovereign Dancer (USA))
C O King C O King

Placings: P **(4416)**
2001/02: 20^{P}S

	Starts	1st	2nd	3rd	Win & Pl
Chases	1	0	0	0	
Career Total	**1**	**0**	**0**	**0**	

Going: Sf: 0-1 GS: 0-0 Gd: 0-0 GF: - Fm: 0-0
Distance: 2m/2m3: 0-0 2m4-2m7: 0-1 3m+: 0-0
Track: LH: 0-0 RH: 0-0 Tight: 0-1 Gall: 0-0
Aids: Bl: 0-0 Vi: 0-0 Tstrap: 0-0
Best Rating:

Sheilas Dream

81 60

9-y-o b m Inca Chief (USA)-Windlass (Persian Bold)
H S Howe George Searle

Placings: 0400315/002/6U1202/4P65 **(4182)**
2001/02: 19^{4}G, 19^{P}S, 16^{6}GS, 19^{5}S

	Starts	1st	2nd	3rd	Win & Pl
Chases	4	0	0	0	301
Career Total	**20**	**2**	**3**	**1**	**7572**

95	8/99	NAbb	2m1f	F(0-100)HHdl	GD	£2403
95	4/98	Tntn	2m1f	F Hdl	GD	£1616

Total win prize-money £4019

Going: Sf: 0-2 GS: 0-1 Gd: 0-1 GF: - Fm: 0-0
Distance: 2m/2m3: 0-3 2m4-2m7: 0-1 3m+: 0-0
Track: LH: 0-0 RH: 0-4 Tight: 0-2 Gall: 0-0
Aids: Bl: 0-0 Vi: 0-0 Tstrap: 0-0
Best Rating: 95 8/99 NAbb 2m1f good Hdl

Moderate handicap hurdler at around two miles on a sound surface. Handles soft ground. Modest efforts over fences so far. Modest efforts over fences so far. Has a tendency to race too keenly.

Shekels (IRE)

11-y-o ch g Orchestra-Rare Currency (Rarity)
Nick Gifford Mrs Sarah Dunsdon

Placings: 1/0311U/P1FP11P/4P033/U1/4-6 **(4638)**
2001/02: 19^{6}GF

	Starts	1st	2nd	3rd	Win & Pl
Chases	1	0	0	0	0
Career Total	**22**	**5**	**1**	**3**	**18452**

117	4/00	Strf	2m5f110y	H Ch	GD	£2660
127	3/98	Strf	2m4f	D Ch	GD	£4718
130	3/98	Leic	2m4f110y	E Ch	GD	£3132
115	11/97	Kemp	2m4f110y	D Ch	G-F	£3371
113	3/97	Uttx	2m	E Hdl	GD	£2389

Total win prize-money £16271

Going: Sf: 0-0 GS: 0-0 Gd: 0-0 GF: - Fm: 0-1
Distance: 2m/2m3: 0-0 2m4-2m7: 0-1 3m+: 0-0
Track: LH: 0-0 RH: 0-1 Tight: 0-0 Gall: 0-0
Aids: Bl: 0-0 Vi: 0-0 Tstrap: 0-0
Best Rating: 130 3/98 Leic 2m4f110y good Ch

Shelayly (IRE)

102 102

6-y-o b m Zaffaran (USA)-Dim Drums (Proverb)
N A Twiston-Davies Mrs S Tainton

Placings: 230-12P **(2914)**
2001/02: 21^{1}G, 21^{2}G, 23^{P}HY

	Starts	1st	2nd	3rd	Win & Pl
Hurdles	3	1	1	0	4382
Career Total	**6**	**1**	**2**	**1**	**5319**

97	11/01	Wwck	2m5f	D Hdl	GD	£3601

Total win prize-money £3601

Going: Sf: 0-1 GS: 0-0 Gd: 1-2 GF: - Fm: 0-0
Distance: 2m/2m3: 0-0 2m4-2m7: 1-2 3m+: 0-1
Track: LH: 0-1 RH: 0-1 Tight: 0-0 Gall: 0-0
Aids: Bl: 0-0 Vi: 0-0 Tstrap: 0-0
Best Rating: 102 12/01 Ludl 2m5f good Hdl

Modest hurdler, suited by two miles-five and a sound surface.

Shellin Hill (IRE)

107(86h) (87h)107

8-y-o ch g Sharp Victor (USA)-Queenspay (Sandhurst Prince)

R J Price (M Sheppard 18/7) My Left Foot Racing Syndicate

Placings:000/*0532*00402P6-0423424F0P622 **(4551)**

2001/02: 17^{0}F, 17^{4}GS, 16^{2}G, 16^{3}GF, 16^{4}F, 16^{2}G, 16^{4}GF, 16^{F}S, 20^{0}G, 16^{P}HY, 16^{6}G, 16^{2}S, 16^{2}GF

	Starts	1st	2nd	3rd	Win & Pl
Hurdles	1	0	0	0	0
Chases	12	0	4	1	5339
Career Total	**27**	**0**	**6**	**2**	**7087**

Going: Sf: 0-3 GS: 0-1 Gd: 0-4 GF: - Fm: 0-5
Distance: 2m/2m3: 0-12 2m4-2m7: 0-1 3m+: 0-0
Track: LH: 0-5 RH: 0-8 Tight: 0-5 Gall: 0-1
Aids: Bl: 0-0 Vi: 0-0 Tstrap: 0-7
Best Rating: 107 6/01 Worc 2m good Ch

Modest chaser, suited by two miles and fast ground.

Sheltering (IRE)

110 150

10-y-o b g Strong Gale-Lady Brenda (IRE) (Crash Course)

E J O'Grady Mrs Stewart Catherwood

Placings:5/1112/1131F/1111-312U41 **(4949a)**

2001/02: 29^{3}G, 25^{1}SH, 24^{2}HY, 26^{U}G, 21^{4}G, 25^{1}G

	Starts	1st	2nd	3rd	Win & Pl
Chases	6	2	1	1	29307
Career Total	**20**	**12**	**2**	**2**	**87744**

123	4/02	Punc	3m1f	Ch	GD	£9969
150	1/02	Punc	3m1f	Ch	SH	£5503
145	4/01	Fair	3m1f	Ch	SH	£10483
156	2/01	Fair	3m1f	Ch	YLD	£4173
160	2/01	Leop	3m	Ch	HVY	£6677
149	5/00	Punc	3m1f	Ch	GD	£10400
137	2/00	Fair	3m1f	Ch	HVY	£3312
137	1/00	Fair	3m1f	Ch	SFT	£3312
113	5/99	Gowr	3m	Ch	YLD	£3683
134	4/99	Fair	3m1f	Ch	G-Y	£6138
127	3/99	Wxfd	3m	Ch	Y-S	£3069
109	3/99	Limk	2m6f	Ch	SFT	£3222

Total win prize-money £69943

Going: Sf: 0-1 GS: 0-0 Gd: 1-4 GF: - Fm: 0-0
Distance: 2m/2m3: 0-0 2m4-2m7: 0-1 **3m+: 2-5**
Track: LH: 0-3 **RH: 2-2** Tight: 0-1 Gall: 0-1
Aids: Bl: 0-0 Vi: 0-0 Tstrap: 0-0
Best Rating: 160 2/01 Leop 3m heavy Ch

Prolific irish hunter chaser who has also finished third in the Irish National. Stays well, acts on any ground. best going right-handed.

Shelu

46f

4-y-o b g Good Thyne (USA)-Nearly Married (Nearly A Hand)

Ferdy Murphy Raj Patel

Placings:0 **(4860)**

2001/02: 16^{0}G

	Starts	1st	2nd	3rd	Win & Pl
NH Flat	1	0	0	0	
Career Total	**1**	**0**	**0**	**0**	

Going: Sf: 0-0 GS: 0-0 Gd: 0-1 GF: - Fm: 0-0
Distance: 2m/2m3: 0-1 2m4-2m7: 0-0 3m+: 0-0
Track: LH: 0-0 RH: 0-0 Tight: 0-0 Gall: 0-0
Aids: Bl: 0-0 Vi: 0-0 Tstrap: 0-0
Best Rating: 46 4/02 Hexm 2m110y good NHF

Shemardi

93 82

5-y-o b g Jumbo Hirt (USA)-Masirah (Dunphy)

M Madgwick J D Brownrigg

Placings:000-05005640 **(4033)**

2001/02: 18^{0}GF, 18^{5}GS, 20^{0}GS, 19^{0}G, 21^{5}G, 22^{6}G, 17^{4}S, 20^{0}S

	Starts	1st	2nd	3rd	Win & Pl
Hurdles	8	0	0	0	0
Career Total	**11**	**0**	**0**	**0**	**0**

Going: Sf: 0-2 GS: 0-2 Gd: 0-3 GF: - Fm: 0-1
Distance: 2m/2m3: 0-4 2m4-2m7: 0-4 3m+: 0-0
Track: LH: 0-4 RH: 0-2 Tight: 0-6 Gall: 0-0
Aids: Bl: 0-0 Vi: 0-4 Tstrap: 0-0
Best Rating: 82 3/02 Font 2m4f soft Hdl

Shemdani (IRE)

111 133

5-y-o b g Unfuwain (USA)-Shemaka (IRE) (Nishapour (FR))

M C Pipe (F-X De Watrigant 1/12) Mr & Mrs M Bovingdon & C Langley

Placings:112 **(4764)**

2001/02: 16^{1}S, 17^{1}GS, 16^{2}GF

	Starts	1st	2nd	3rd	Win & Pl
Hurdles	3	2	1	0	8136
Career Total	**3**	**2**	**1**	**0**	**8136**

133	3/02	MRas	2m1f110y	E Hdl	G-S	£3304
102	1/02	Donc	2m110y	D Hdl	SFT	£3472

Total win prize-money £6776

Going: Sf: 1-1 GS: 1-1 Gd: 0-0 GF: - Fm: 0-1
Distance: **2m/2m3: 2-3** 2m4-2m7: 0-0 3m+: 0-0
Track: LH: 1-1 RH: 1-2 Tight: 1-1 Gall: 1-1
Aids: Bl: 0-0 Vi: 0-0 Tstrap: 0-0
Best Rating: 133 3/02 MRas 2m1f110y gd-sft Hdl

A winner on the Flat in France, he made a successful debut over hurdles in Britain on soft ground and proved different class under a positive ride in a similar event next time before being narrowly beaten on fast ground at Ascot. He is effective over two miles.

Shemill

64f 70f

4-y-o b g Spectrum (IRE)-Shemaleyah (Lomond (USA))

D Eddy I R Clements

Placings:0 **(4526)**

2001/02: 17^{0}G

	Starts	1st	2nd	3rd	Win & Pl
NH Flat	1	0	0	0	
Career Total	**1**	**0**	**0**	**0**	

Going: Sf: 0-0 GS: 0-0 Gd: 0-1 GF: - Fm: 0-0
Distance: 2m/2m3: 0-1 2m4-2m7: 0-0 3m+: 0-0
Track: LH: 0-0 RH: 0-1 Tight: 0-0 Gall: 0-0
Aids: Bl: 0-0 Vi: 0-0 Tstrap: 0-0
Best Rating: 70 4/02 Carl 2m1f good NHF

Shepherds Rest (IRE)

108(97h) (57h)120

10-y-o b g Accordion-Mandy's Last (Krayyan)

C P Morlock (S Mellor 27/10) The Odd Dozen

Placings:062640223/231U220/0322/P45P02/5332211 2215P01/346P003PP0-PP02324133143411 **(4753)**

2001/02: 19^{P}GS, 21^{P}GF, 22^{0}GF, 23^{2}G, 20^{3}G, 24^{2}G, 20^{4}GF, 21^{1}G, 24^{3}G, 20^{3}S, 21^{1}G, 20^{4}G, 20^{3}G, 20^{4}S, 24^{1}GF, 26^{1}GF

	Starts	1st	2nd	3rd	Win & Pl
Hurdles	1	0	0	0	0
Chases	15	4	2	4	20098
Career Total	**66**	**9**	**15**	**11**	**58150**

120	4/02	Uttx	3m2f	E(0-110)HCh	G-F	£3601
110	4/02	Wwck	3m110y	E(0-105)HCh	G-F	£4078
112	10/01	Folk	2m5f	F(0-95)HCh	GD	£3406
99	8/01	Ctml	2m5f110y	F(0-110)HCh	GD	£4192
107	4/00	Uttx	2m4f110y	E(0-115)HHdl	SFT	£2824
127	3/00	Newb	2m4f	D(0-125)HCh	SFT	£7097
129	1/00	Kemp	2m4f110y	E(0-115)HCh	GD	£3477
126	1/00	Wwck	2m4f	E(0-115)HCh	SFT	£3198
104	12/96	Ling	2m110y	E(0-110)HHdl	G-S	£2364

Total win prize-money £34235

Going: Sf: 0-2 GS: 0-1 Gd: 2-8 GF: - Fm: 2-5
Distance: 2m/2m3: 0-0 2m4-2m7: 2-11 3m+: 2-5
Track: **LH: 2-9** RH: 1-6 **Tight: 2-10** Gall: 0-0
Aids: Bl: 0-0 **Vi: 4-14** Tstrap: 0-0
Best Rating: 129 2/00 Wwck 2m4f soft Ch

A modest handicap chaser, he has developed stamina with age and now gets three and a quarter miles. He likes to be held up, finds little off the bridle, and seems best on a sound surface these days although he handles cut. Won back to back chases for A.P. McCoy in April 2002.

Sherbet Fizz (IRE)

6-y-o b m Petardia-Skiddaw (USA) (Grey Dawn Ii)

J A Moore J A Moore

Placings:P **(1305)**

2001/02: 19^{P}GF

	Starts	1st	2nd	3rd	Win & Pl
Hurdles	1	0	0	0	
Career Total	**1**	**0**	**0**	**0**	

Going: Sf: 0-0 GS: 0-0 Gd: 0-0 GF: - Fm: 0-1
Distance: 2m/2m3: 0-0 2m4-2m7: 0-1 3m+: 0-0
Track: LH: 0-0 RH: 0-1 Tight: 0-1 Gall: 0-0
Aids: Bl: 0-0 Vi: 0-0 Tstrap: 0-0
Best Rating:

Sherbet Lad (IRE)

101f 88f

6-y-o b g Cataldi-She's Foolish (IRE) (Callernish)

V R A Dartnall Lisa Mackenzie, M Foxon & J Darbishire

Placings:*02U3* **(1263)**

2001/02: 18^{0}GF, 17^{2}G, 17^{U}GF, 16^{3}GF

	Starts	1st	2nd	3rd	Win & Pl
NH Flat	4	0	1	1	862
Career Total	**4**	**0**	**1**	**1**	**862**

Going: Sf: 0-0 GS: 0-0 Gd: 0-1 GF: - Fm: 0-3
Distance: 2m/2m3: 0-4 2m4-2m7: 0-0 3m+: 0-0
Track: LH: 0-3 RH: 0-1 Tight: 0-3 Gall: 0-1
Aids: Bl: 0-0 Vi: 0-0 Tstrap: 0-0

Best Rating: 88 8/01 Hntg 2m110y gd-fm NHF

Sherdon Water

69f 57f

6-y-o b m Petoski-Sherdon Hutch (New Member)

N R Mitchell Mrs Sarah Faulks

Placings:00 (2480)

2001/02: 16^{0}G, 17^{0}S

	Starts	1st	2nd	3rd	Win & Pl
NH Flat	2	0	0	0	
Career Total	2	0	0	0	

Going: Sf: 0-1 GS: 0-0 Gd: 0-1 GF: - Fm: 0-0
Distance: 2m/2m3: 0-2 2m4-2m7: 0-0 3m+: 0-0
Track: LH: 0-1 RH: 0-1 Tight: 0-0 Gall: 0-0
Aids: Bl: 0-0 Vi: 0-0 Tstrap: 0-0
Best Rating: 57 10/01 Chep 2m110y good NHF

Sheriff Song

94 89

4-y-o br g Hernando (FR)-Zippy Zoe (Rousillon (USA))

M W Easterby Yorkshire Racing Club Iii

Placings:3 (1246)

2001/02: 17^{3}G

	Starts	1st	2nd	3rd	Win & Pl
Hurdles	1	0	0	1	378
Career Total	1	0	0	1	378

Going: Sf: 0-0 GS: 0-0 Gd: 0-1 GF: - Fm: 0-0
Distance: 2m/2m3: 0-1 2m4-2m7: 0-0 3m+: 0-0
Track: LH: 0-1 RH: 0-0 Tight: 0-1 Gall: 0-0
Aids: Bl: 0-0 Vi: 0-0 Tstrap: 0-0
Best Rating: 89 8/01 Ctml 2m1f110y good Hdl

Shermi (IRE)

87 92

8-y-o b g Beau Sher-Woodland Theory (Sheer Grit)

C Grant Mrs H Scotto

Placings:000/F4FP-UP0 (3366)

2001/02: 22^{U}GS, 19^{P}G, 25^{0}GS

	Starts	1st	2nd	3rd	Win & Pl
Chases	3	0	0	0	
Career Total	10	0	0	0	293

Going: Sf: 0-0 GS: 0-2 Gd: 0-1 GF: - Fm: 0-0
Distance: 2m/2m3: 0-1 2m4-2m7: 0-1 3m+: 0-1
Track: LH: 0-3 RH: 0-0 Tight: 0-3 Gall: 0-0
Aids: Bl: 0-0 Vi: 0-0 Tstrap: 0-1
Best Rating: 92 12/01 Kels 2m6f110y gd-sft Ch

Sherpas (IRE)

9-y-o b g Shirley Heights-Ala Mahlik (Ahonoora)

K R Pearce Keith R Pearce

Placings:0000/04-P (0979)

2001/02: 27^{P}G

	Starts	1st	2nd	3rd	Win & Pl
Hurdles	1	0	0	0	
Career Total	7	0	0	0	160

Going: Sf: 0-0 GS: 0-0 Gd: 0-1 GF: - Fm: 0-0
Distance: 2m/2m3: 0-0 2m4-2m7: 0-0 3m+: 0-1
Track: LH: 0-1 RH: 0-0 Tight: 0-1 Gall: 0-0
Aids: Bl: 0-0 Vi: 0-0 Tstrap: 0-0
Best Rating: 61 7/00 Bell 2m4f gd-fm Hdl

Sherwood Rose (IRE)

74f 70f

6-y-o gr m Mandalus-Cronlier (Roselier (FR))

K C Bailey Peter Granger

Placings:0-0 (3896)

2001/02: 16^{0}HY

	Starts	1st	2nd	3rd	Win & Pl
NH Flat	1	0	0	0	
Career Total	2	0	0	0	

Going: Sf: 0-1 GS: 0-0 Gd: 0-0 GF: - Fm: 0-0
Distance: 2m/2m3: 0-1 2m4-2m7: 0-0 3m+: 0-0
Track: LH: 0-1 RH: 0-0 Tight: 0-0 Gall: 0-0
Aids: Bl: 0-0 Vi: 0-0 Tstrap: 0-0
Best Rating: 70 2/02 Wwck 2m heavy NHF

Sheskinqueen (IRE)

106 103

7-y-o b m Black Monday-Our Lady Sofie (Ile De Bourbon (USA))

M G Quinlan Twincroft Partnerships

Placings:50142060 (4013)

2001/02: 17^{5}G, 17^{0}G, 16^{1}S, 16^{4}G, 16^{2}S, 20^{0}GS, 16^{6}GS, 16^{0}GS

	Starts	1st	2nd	3rd	Win & Pl
NH Flat	2	0	0	0	0
Hurdles	6	1	1	0	3303
Career Total	8	1	1	0	3303

95	7/01	Worc	2m	E Hdl	SFT	£2513

Total win prize-money £2513

Going: Sf: 1-2 GS: 0-3 Gd: 0-3 GF: - Fm: 0-0
Distance: 2m/2m3: 1-7 2m4-2m7: 0-1 3m+: 0-0
Track: LH: 1-6 RH: 0-2 Tight: 0-3 Gall: 0-2
Aids: Bl: 0-0 Vi: 0-0 Tstrap: 0-1
Best Rating: 103 1/02 Hntg 2m110y gd-sft Hdl

Won at Worcester in the summer of 2001, but found a subsequent step up in company a little overfacing. She likes to get her toe in and stays two miles.

Shifting Moon

109(80c) (83c)100

10-y-o b g Night Shift (USA)-Moonscape (Ribero)

F Jordan Mrs K Roberts-Hindle

Placings:2104500/0PP204031F/61211233P/0631/P0 0140633634/00610534446-0P22050U3P (2511)

2001/02: 17^{0}G, 21^{P}GF, 20^{2}G, 21^{2}GF, 20^{0}G, 20^{5}G, 20^{0}G, 21^{U}S, 24^{3}GF, 25^{P}S

	Starts	1st	2nd	3rd	Win & Pl
Hurdles	5	0	2	0	1713
Chases	5	0	0	1	766
Career Total	63	8	6	9	32321

100	9/00	Bang	2m4f	F(0-110)HHdl	G-F	£4251
95	11/99	NAbb	2m1f	E(0-115)HHdl	G-S	£2906
108	7/98	Strf	2m110y	D(0-125)HHdl	G-F	£3496
91	8/97	Ctml	2m1f110y	D(0-120)HHdl	G-F	£2784
89	8/97	NAbb	2m1f	E(0-110)HHdl	G-F	£2179
89	8/97	NAbb	2m1f	E(0-110)HHdl	G-F	£2116
75	4/97	Tntn	2m1f	E(0-115)HHdl	FRM	£2200
98	8/95	NAbb	2m1f	D Hdl	G-F	£2532

Total win prize-money £22468

Going: Sf: 0-2 GS: 0-0 Gd: 0-5 GF: - Fm: 0-3
Distance: 2m/2m3: 0-1 2m4-2m7: 0-7 3m+: 0-2
Track: LH: 0-8 RH: 0-1 Tight: 0-7 Gall: 0-1
Aids: Bl: 0-1 Vi: 0-0 Tstrap: 0-10
Best Rating: 108 7/98 Strf 2m110y gd-fm Hdl

Modest handicap hurdler who stays two miles six furlongs. Suited by hold up tactics. A flop over fences.

Shii-Take's Girl

70 58

4-y-o ch f Deploy-Super Sally (Superlative)

M E Sowersby (Mrs A J Perrett 8/10) The Wolds Partnership

Placings:50 (4493)

2001/02: 16^{5}S, 16^{0}G

	Starts	1st	2nd	3rd	Win & Pl
Hurdles	2	0	0	0	0
Career Total	2	0	0	0	0

Going: Sf: 0-1 GS: 0-0 Gd: 0-1 GF: - Fm: 0-0
Distance: 2m/2m3: 0-2 2m4-2m7: 0-0 3m+: 0-0
Track: LH: 0-1 RH: 0-1 Tight: 0-1 Gall: 0-0
Aids: Bl: 0-0 Vi: 0-0 Tstrap: 0-0
Best Rating: 59 3/02 Hayd 2m good Hdl

Has bled on both starts over hurdles.

Shikanne Surely (IRE)

6-y-o b/br m Religiously (USA)-Shikanne (Spin Of A Coin)

N G Richards Greystoke Stables Ltd

Placings:0 (0744)

2001/02: 16^{0}GS

	Starts	1st	2nd	3rd	Win & Pl
NH Flat	1	0	0	0	
Career Total	1	0	0	0	

Going: Sf: 0-0 GS: 0-1 Gd: 0-0 GF: - Fm: 0-0
Distance: 2m/2m3: 0-1 2m4-2m7: 0-0 3m+: 0-0
Track: LH: 0-1 RH: 0-0 Tight: 0-0 Gall: 0-0
Aids: Bl: 0-0 Vi: 0-0 Tstrap: 0-0
Best Rating:

Shilling (IRE)

101(64h) 96

8-y-o b m Bob Back (USA)-Quiche (Formidable (USA))

P J Hobbs Mrs Anona Taylor

Placings:0330/3554/F1/P0**F200-652** (0555)

2001/02: 19^{6}GS, 20^{5}GF, 20^{2}GF

	Starts	1st	2nd	3rd	Win & Pl
Chases	3	0	1	0	920
Career Total	19	1	2	3	5462

103	12/99	Wwck	2m2f110y	F(0-100)HHdl	SFT	£2136

Total win prize-money £2136

Going: Sf: 0-0 GS: 0-1 Gd: 0-0 GF: 0-2
Distance: 2m/2m3: 0-0 2m4-2m7: 0-3 3m+: 0-0
Track: LH: 0-1 RH: 0-2 Tight: 0-1 Gall: 0-1
Aids: Bl: 0-3 Vi: 0-0 Tstrap: 0-0
Best Rating: 105 1/01 Extr 2m1f110y heavy Ch

Shinerolla

104(57c) 107

10-y-o b g Thatching-Primrolla (Relko)

A Parker Mr & Mrs Raymond Anderson Green

Placings:2250/1/2414/3/3340-221436 **(1742)**
2001/02: 16^{2}GF, 16^{2}F, 16^{1}F, 16^{4}GF, 16^{3}G, 16^{6}G

	Starts	1st	2nd	3rd	Win & Pl
Hurdles	6	1	2	1	7220
Career Total	**20**	**3**	**5**	**4**	**19004**

107	6/01	Prth	2m110y	E(0-115)HHdl	FRM	£3513
106	4/99	Kels	2m110y	D(0-125)HHdl	G-F	£2762
93	10/97	Kels	2m110y	D(0-120)HHdl	FRM	£2920

Total win prize-money £9195

Going: Sf: 0-0 GS: 0-0 Gd: 0-2 GF: - Fm: 1-4
Distance: **2m/2m3: 1-6** 2m4-2m7: 0-0 3m+: 0-0
Track: LH: 0-4 **RH: 1-2** Tight: 0-2 Gall: 0-0
Aids: Bl: 0-0 Vi: 0-0 Tstrap: 0-0
Best Rating: 112 11/00 Ayr 2m soft Ch

Shining Fountain (IRE)

13-y-o b g Royal Fountain-Ever Shining (Indigenous)
D M Forster D M Forster

Placings:1/1/PP5P0/PFPP/P50/0-PP **(4892)**
2001/02: 25^{P}HY, 31^{P}G

	Starts	1st	2nd	3rd	Win & Pl
Chases	2	0	0	0	
Career Total	**17**	**2**	**0**	**0**	**6104**

102	12/95	Fair	2m6f	Ch	GD	£3391
103	5/95	Limk	2m4f	NHF	G-Y	£2712

Total win prize-money £6104

Going: Sf: 0-1 GS: 0-0 Gd: 0-1 GF: - Fm: 0-0
Distance: 2m/2m3: 0-0 2m4-2m7: 0-0 3m+: 0-2
Track: LH: 0-1 RH: 0-0 Tight: 0-1 Gall: 0-0
Aids: Bl: 0-0 Vi: 0-0 Tstrap: 0-0
Best Rating: 103 5/95 Limk 2m4f gd-yld NHF

Shining Light (IRE)

13-y-o b g Crash Course-Arumah (Arapaho)
S J Robinson S J Robinson

Placings:0060/11P406/53132U5/12153P/3161P/5235 1RP/55 **(4672)**
2001/02: 21^{5}GF, 27^{5}GF

	Starts	1st	2nd	3rd	Win & Pl
Chases	2	0	0	0	0
Career Total	**37**	**8**	**3**	**5**	**45098**

132	1/99	Leic	2m4f110y	D(0-120)HCh	G-S	£7327
130	12/97	Leic	2m4f110y	C(0-135)HCh	G-S	£9520
122	11/97	Hntg	2m4f110y	C(0-130)HCh	G-F	£4370
121	1/97	Leic	2m4f110y	D(0-125)HCh	G-F	£3850
115	11/96	Hntg	2m4f110y	C(0-130)HCh	GD	£4597
104	1/96	Ludl	2m4f	E Ch	GD	£3420
100	12/94	Extr	2m2f	Hdl	GD	£2373
104	11/94	Towc	2m	Hdl	G-S	£2217

Total win prize-money £37677

Going: Sf: 0-0 GS: 0-0 Gd: 0-0 GF: - Fm: 0-2
Distance: 2m/2m3: 0-0 2m4-2m7: 0-1 3m+: 0-1
Track: LH: 0-2 RH: 0-0 Tight: 0-2 Gall: 0-0
Aids: Bl: 0-0 Vi: 0-0 Tstrap: 0-0
Best Rating: 132 1/99 Leic 2m4f110y gd-sft Ch

Shining Oasis (IRE)

85 51

4-y-o b f Mujtahid (USA)-Desert Maiden (Green Desert (USA))

N Tinkler (P F I Cole 9/10) Elite Racing Club

Placings:05U0 **(4546)**
2001/02: 16^{0}G, 16^{5}HY, 16^{U}S, 16^{0}GF

	Starts	1st	2nd	3rd	Win & Pl
Hurdles	4	0	0	0	0
Career Total	**4**	**0**	**0**	**0**	**0**

Going: Sf: 0-2 GS: 0-0 Gd: 0-1 GF: - Fm: 0-1
Distance: 2m/2m3: 0-4 2m4-2m7: 0-0 3m+: 0-0
Track: LH: 0-2 RH: 0-2 Tight: 0-0 Gall: 0-2
Aids: Bl: 0-0 Vi: 0-0 Tstrap: 0-0
Best Rating: 51 1/02 Uttx 2m heavy Hdl

Shining Tyne

95 101

8-y-o b g Primitive Rising (USA)-Shining Bann (Bargello)
R Johnson David Blythe

Placings:0/00F/6RPP03-6423F **(3549)**
2001/02: 25^{6}S, 20^{4}G, 20^{2}GS, 20^{3}S, 20^{F}S

	Starts	1st	2nd	3rd	Win & Pl
Chases	5	0	1	1	3964
Career Total	**15**	**0**	**1**	**2**	**5020**

Going: Sf: 0-3 GS: 0-1 Gd: 0-1 GF: - Fm: 0-0
Distance: 2m/2m3: 0-0 2m4-2m7: 0-4 3m+: 0-1
Track: LH: 0-5 RH: 0-0 Tight: 0-0 Gall: 0-4
Aids: Bl: 0-0 Vi: 0-0 Tstrap: 0-1
Best Rating: 101 1/02 Newc 2m4f soft Ch

Fair placed form over fences. Acts on a soft surface and is effective at around two miles four furlongs.

Shipley Mill

91 71

6-y-o b g St Ninian-Shipley Bridge (Town And Country)
J T Gifford Mrs J T Gifford

Placings:5P0 **(3340)**
2001/02: 16^{5}GS, 16^{P}S, 17^{0}S

	Starts	1st	2nd	3rd	Win & Pl
NH Flat	1	0	0	0	0
Hurdles	2	0	0	0	0
Career Total	**3**	**0**	**0**	**0**	**0**

Going: Sf: 0-2 GS: 0-1 Gd: 0-0 GF: - Fm: 0-0
Distance: 2m/2m3: 0-3 2m4-2m7: 0-0 3m+: 0-0
Track: LH: 0-1 RH: 0-2 Tight: 0-2 Gall: 0-0
Aids: Bl: 0-0 Vi: 0-0 Tstrap: 0-0
Best Rating: 92 11/01 Sand 2m110y gd-sft NHF

Shobrooke Mill

9-y-o ch g Shaab-Jubilee Leigh (Hubble Bubble)
Mrs S Prouse Mrs S Prouse

Placings:U/U342 **(4735)**
2001/02: 21^{U}G, 26^{3}GF, 19^{4}G, 23^{2}F

	Starts	1st	2nd	3rd	Win & Pl
Chases	4	0	1	1	853
Career Total	**5**	**0**	**1**	**1**	**853**

Going: Sf: 0-0 GS: 0-0 Gd: 0-2 GF: - Fm: 0-2
Distance: 2m/2m3: 0-0 2m4-2m7: 0-2 3m+: 0-2
Track: LH: 0-1 RH: 0-2 Tight: 0-1 Gall: 0-0
Aids: Bl: 0-0 Vi: 0-0 Tstrap: 0-0
Best Rating: 105 4/02 Extr 2m7f110y firm Ch

Fair hunter/point-to-pointer. Stays three miles, handles most ground.

Shoemaker (IRE)

8-y-o b g Good Thyne (USA)-Kalanshoe (Random Shot)
W J Warner Mrs Judy Wilson

Placings:P1 **(0231)**
2001/02: 25^{P}S, 24^{1}GF

	Starts	1st	2nd	3rd	Win & Pl
Chases	2	1	0	0	2022
Career Total	**2**	**1**	**0**	**0**	**2022**

110	5/01	Hntg	3m	H Ch	G-F	£2021

Total win prize-money £2022

Going: Sf: 0-1 GS: 0-0 Gd: 0-0 GF: - Fm: 1-1
Distance: 2m/2m3: 0-0 2m4-2m7: 0-0 **3m+: 1-2**
Track: LH: 0-1 **RH: 1-1** Tight: 0-0 **Gall: 1-1**
Aids: Bl: 0-0 Vi: 0-0 Tstrap: 0-0
Best Rating: 110 5/01 Hntg 3m gd-fm Ch

Shooting Light (IRE)

118(107h) (130h)179

9-y-o b g Shernazar-Church Light (Caerleon (USA))
M C Pipe J M Brown & M J Blackburn

Placings:1213/24004/526/36B2365/3132350-111P **(4252)**
2001/02: 20^{1}G, 20^{1}G, 24^{1}G, 26^{P}G

	Starts	1st	2nd	3rd	Win & Pl
Chases	4	3	0	0	103513
Career Total	**30**	**6**	**5**	**6**	**173601**

179	12/01	Asct	3m110y	A HCh	GD	£32500
171	11/01	Chel	2m4f110y	A HCh	GD	£58000
165	10/01	Chel	2m4f110y	C(0-135)HCh	GD	£13013
142	11/00	Asct	2m3f110y	B Ch	SFT	£9350
124	1/97	Chel	2m1f	A Hdl	G-F	£9779
112	11/96	Sand	2m110y	D Hdl	GD	£2801

Total win prize-money £125444

Going: Sf: 0-0 GS: 0-0 Gd: 3-4 GF: - Fm: 0-0
Distance: 2m/2m3: 0-0 **2m4-2m7: 2-2** 3m+: 1-2
Track: **LH: 2-3** RH: 1-1 Tight: 0-0 **Gall: 2-3**
Aids: Bl: 0-0 **Vi: 3-4** Tstrap: 0-0
Best Rating: 179 12/01 Asct 3m110y good Ch

He received a vintage ride from Tony McCoy when winning at Ascot in November 2000, but was basically frustrating in novice chases. Joined Martin Pipe at the start of 2001/02, and looked an improved performer when trotting up on his reappearance in a Cheltenham handicap in October 2001, and when making light work of his rivals in the Thomas Pink Gold Cup and Tote Silver Cup. Out of his depth in the Gold Cup. Has won on good ground and soft, usually wears a visor.

Shoplatch

9-y-o ch g Phardante (FR)-Ethels Course (Crash Course)
Mrs Edward Crow Gareth Samuel

Placings:60P/4PF-P **(0056)**
2001/02: 24^{P}GS

	Starts	1st	2nd	3rd	Win & Pl
Chases	1	0	0	0	
Career Total	**7**	**0**	**0**	**0**	**550**

Going: Sf: 0-0 GS: 0-1 Gd: 0-0 GF: - Fm: 0-0
Distance: 2m/2m3: 0-0 2m4-2m7: 0-0 3m+: 0-1
Track: LH: 0-1 RH: 0-0 Tight: 0-1 Gall: 0-0
Aids: Bl: 0-0 Vi: 0-0 Tstrap: 0-0
Best Rating: 88 1/00 Leic 2m4f110y good Ch

Shosen (IRE)

101 121

6-y-o b g Persian Mews-Lugnagullagh (Pitpan)
A King Mrs M C Sweeney

Placings:341 **(4400)**
2001/02: 19^{3}G, 20^{4}G, 21^{1}S

	Starts	1st	2nd	3rd	Win & Pl
Hurdles	3	1	0	1	7722
Career Total	**3**	**1**	**0**	**1**	**7722**

121	3/02	Newb	2m5f	D Hdl	SFT	£6318

Total win prize-money £6318

Going: Sf: 1-1 GS: 0-0 Gd: 0-2 GF: - Fm: 0-0
Distance: 2m/2m3: 0-1 **2m4-2m7: 1-2** 3m+: 0-0
Track: **LH: 1-2** RH: 0-1 Tight: 0-0 **Gall: 1-2**
Aids: Bl: 0-0 Vi: 0-0 Tstrap: 0-0
Best Rating: 121 3/02 Newb 2m5f soft Hdl

Ran well on his hurdling debut at Newbury in November 2001, but failed to improve on that next time. Made light of a 91-day absence when easily winning at Newbury in March 2002. Chasing will be his game.

Shotacross The Bow (IRE)

90 81

5-y-o b g Warning-Nordica (Northfields (USA))
M Blanshard The Wardroom Boys

Placings:44 **(1617)**
2001/02: 16^{4}GF, 17^{4}GF

	Starts	1st	2nd	3rd	Win & Pl
Hurdles	2	0	0	0	0
Career Total	**2**	**0**	**0**	**0**	**0**

Going: Sf: 0-0 GS: 0-0 Gd: 0-0 GF: - Fm: 0-2
Distance: 2m/2m3: 0-2 2m4-2m7: 0-0 3m+: 0-0
Track: LH: 0-1 RH: 0-1 Tight: 0-1 Gall: 0-0
Aids: Bl: 0-0 Vi: 0-0 Tstrap: 0-0
Best Rating: 81 8/01 Worc 2m gd-fm Hdl

A sprinter on the Flat, has shown a little ability over hurdles.

Shotgun Willy (IRE)

112 175

8-y-o ch g Be My Native (USA)-Minorettes Girl (Strong Gale)
P F Nicholls C G Roach

Placings:*52*/1111/**11312-32P2** **(4839)**
2001/02: 25^{3}G, 24^{2}S, 26^{P}G, 33^{2}G

	Starts	1st	2nd	3rd	Win & Pl
Chases	4	0	2	1	41700
Career Total	**15**	**7**	**4**	**2**	**151924**

170	2/01	Newb	3m	B Ch	SFT	£29750
162	11/00	Newb	3m	A Ch	G-S	£29750
150	10/00	Winc	3m1f110y	D Ch	G-S	£4192
144	3/00	Chep	3m	A Hdl	HVY	£9600
147	2/00	Uttx	3m110y	C Hdl	SFT	£5466
135	1/00	Uttx	3m110y	D Hdl	SFT	£3997
126	11/99	Winc	2m6f	C Hdl	GD	£5303

Total win prize-money £88061

Going: Sf: 0-1 GS: 0-0 Gd: 0-3 GF: - Fm: 0-0
Distance: 2m/2m3: 0-0 2m4-2m7: 0-0 3m+: 0-4
Track: LH: 0-4 RH: 0-0 Tight: 0-0 Gall: 0-2
Aids: Bl: 0-0 Vi: 0-0 Tstrap: 0-0
Best Rating: 175 4/02 Ayr 4m1f good Ch

A high-class chaser who beat First Gold in the Aon Chase at Newbury in 2001, he was in need of the run when disappointing in the Charlie Hall Chase on his return in 2001/02, but ran much better when runner-up in the Aon at Newbury. Out of his depth in the Gold Cup, but ran a blinder in the Scottish National in 2002 when second. Suited b y soft ground.

Shoulton (IRE)

82f 64f

5-y-o br g Aristocracy-Jay Joy (Double U Jay)
G H Yardley Mrs S Tainton

Placings:*05* **(4410)**
2001/02: 16^{0}S, 17^{5}S

	Starts	1st	2nd	3rd	Win & Pl
NH Flat	2	0	0	0	0
Career Total	**2**	**0**	**0**	**0**	**0**

Going: Sf: 0-2 GS: 0-0 Gd: 0-0 GF: - Fm: 0-0
Distance: 2m/2m3: 0-2 2m4-2m7: 0-0 3m+: 0-0
Track: LH: 0-1 RH: 0-1 Tight: 0-1 Gall: 0-0
Aids: Bl: 0-0 Vi: 0-0 Tstrap: 0-0
Best Rating: 64 3/02 Bang 2m1f soft NHF

Show The Way

90 82

4-y-o ch g Hernando (FR)-Severine (USA) (Trempolino (USA))
J R Jenkins (A P Jarvis 19/8) Uk Packaging Supplies Ltd

Placings:40 **(4237)**
2001/02: 16^{4}GS, 16^{0}GF

	Starts	1st	2nd	3rd	Win & Pl
Hurdles	2	0	0	0	0
Career Total	**2**	**0**	**0**	**0**	**0**

Going: Sf: 0-0 GS: 0-1 Gd: 0-0 GF: - Fm: 0-1
Distance: 2m/2m3: 0-2 2m4-2m7: 0-0 3m+: 0-0
Track: LH: 0-1 RH: 0-1 Tight: 0-1 Gall: 0-1
Aids: Bl: 0-0 Vi: 0-1 Tstrap: 0-0
Best Rating: 76 3/02 Hntg 2m110y gd-fm Hdl

Showtime Shirley

85 55

4-y-o ch f First Trump-Wollow Maid (Wollow)
A Bailey Showtime Ice Cream Concessionaire

Placings:0006 **(3363)**
2001/02: 16^{0}GF, 16^{0}S, 16^{0}G, 16^{6}GS

	Starts	1st	2nd	3rd	Win & Pl
Hurdles	4	0	0	0	0
Career Total	**4**	**0**	**0**	**0**	**0**

Going: Sf: 0-1 GS: 0-1 Gd: 0-1 GF: - Fm: 0-1
Distance: 2m/2m3: 0-4 2m4-2m7: 0-0 3m+: 0-0
Track: LH: 0-2 RH: 0-2 Tight: 0-2 Gall: 0-0
Aids: Bl: 0-0 Vi: 0-0 Tstrap: 0-0
Best Rating: 55 12/01 Catt 2m soft Hdl

Shropshire Gale (IRE)

11-y-o b g Strong Gale-Willow Fashion (Quayside)
Miss E Morton (P J Hobbs 7/4) Miss E Morton

Placings:*200*/P/P **(4777)**
2001/02: 25^{P}G

	Starts	1st	2nd	3rd	Win & Pl
Chases	1	0	0	0	
Career Total	**5**	**0**	**1**	**0**	**434**

Going: Sf: 0-0 GS: 0-0 Gd: 0-1 GF: - Fm: 0-0
Distance: 2m/2m3: 0-0 2m4-2m7: 0-0 3m+: 0-1
Track: LH: 0-0 RH: 0-1 Tight: 0-1 Gall: 0-0
Aids: Bl: 0-0 Vi: 0-0 Tstrap: 0-0
Best Rating: 105 2/97 Hayd 2m good NHF

Shu Gaa (IRE)

9-y-o ch g Salse (USA)-River Reem (USA) (Irish River (FR))
J Mackie R M Kirkland

Placings:10411/3/**4F3F**4F0/**545630/14P43-0P** **(0356)**
2001/02: 20^{0}GS, 20^{P}GS

	Starts	1st	2nd	3rd	Win & Pl
Chases	2	0	0	0	
Career Total	**26**	**4**	**0**	**4**	**24646**

122	5/00	Bang	2m4f110y	D(0-120)HCh	GD	£7475
114	4/97	Ayr	2m	C HHdl	GD	£4402
104	3/97	Chep	2m110y	C HHdl	G-S	£3488
99	12/96	Hayd	2m	D Hdl	G-S	£2955

Total win prize-money £18321

Going: Sf: 0-0 GS: 0-2 Gd: 0-0 GF: - Fm: 0-0
Distance: 2m/2m3: 0-0 2m4-2m7: 0-2 3m+: 0-0
Track: LH: 0-2 RH: 0-0 Tight: 0-2 Gall: 0-0
Aids: Bl: 0-0 Vi: 0-2 Tstrap: 0-0
Best Rating: 122 1/01 Donc 2m3f110y good Ch

Shuil Americo (IRE)

68 60

9-y-o br g Lord Americo-Shuil Ard (Quayside)
P Monteith (Gerard Cully 12/5) P Monteith

Placings:*0*/F0-0 **(0660)**
2001/02: 16^{0}F

	Starts	1st	2nd	3rd	Win & Pl
Chases	1	0	0	0	
Career Total	**4**	**0**	**0**	**0**	

Going: Sf: 0-0 GS: 0-0 Gd: 0-0 GF: - Fm: 0-1
Distance: 2m/2m3: 0-1 2m4-2m7: 0-0 3m+: 0-0
Track: LH: 0-0 RH: 0-1 Tight: 0-0 Gall: 0-0
Aids: Bl: 0-0 Vi: 0-0 Tstrap: 0-0
Best Rating: 89 7/98 Gowr 2m good NHF

Shuil Back (IRE)

95f 82f

5-y-o b m Bob Back (USA)-Shuil Ar Aghaidh (The Parson)
A J Lidderdale George Ward

Placings:3 **(4571)**
2001/02: 16^{3}G

	Starts	1st	2nd	3rd	Win & Pl
NH Flat	1	0	0	1	246
Career Total	**1**	**0**	**0**	**1**	**246**

Going: Sf: 0-0 GS: 0-0 Gd: 0-1 GF: - Fm: 0-0
Distance: 2m/2m3: 0-1 2m4-2m7: 0-0 3m+: 0-0
Track: LH: 0-0 RH: 0-1 Tight: 0-0 Gall: 0-0
Aids: Bl: 0-0 Vi: 0-0 Tstrap: 0-0
Best Rating: 82 4/02 Towc 2m good NHF

Daughter of a smart staying mare, likely to need a test of stamina in time.

Shuil's Star (IRE)

103 127

11-y-o b g Henbit (USA)-Shuil Run (Deep Run)

G Prodromou L Cohen

Placings:3P/0/54/2642641P-11P322 **(1225)**

2001/02: 20^{1}GF, 24^{1}GF, 20^{P}GF, 20^{3}G, 17^{2}GF, 22^{2}GF

	Starts	1st	2nd	3rd	Win & Pl
Chases	6	2	2	1	13190
Career Total	**19**	**3**	**4**	**2**	**20617**

127	6/01	Fknm	3m110y	E(0-115)HCh	G-F	£6175
124	5/01	Font	2m4f	F(0-110)HCh	G-F	£3640
109	1/01	Fknm	2m5f110y	F(0-100)HCh	SFT	£2374

Total win prize-money £12189

Going: Sf: 0-0 GS: 0-0 Gd: 0-1 GF: - Fm: 2-5
Distance: 2m/2m3: 0-1 2m4-2m7: 1-4 3m+: 1-1
Track: **LH: 1-3** RH: 0-1 **Tight: 2-6** Gall: 0-0
Aids: Bl: 0-0 **Vi: 2-6** Tstrap: 0-0
Best Rating: 127 6/01 Fknm 3m110y gd-fm Ch

Shuildante (IRE)

111(100h) (110h)112

8-y-o br m Phardante (FR)-Shuil Tapaidh (Strong Gale)

J M Jefferson Mrs K S Gaffney & Mrs Alix Stevenson

Placings:*24/*550222/P15**P**232-4352P0410P112 **(4918)**

2001/02: 24^{4}GS, 20^{3}GF, 22^{5}GF, 21^{2}G, 24^{P}S, 22^{0}GS, 21^{4}G, 21^{1}S, 24^{0}HY, 27^{P}HY, 25^{1}HY, 25^{1}GF, 28^{2}GF

	Starts	1st	2nd	3rd	Win & Pl
Hurdles	7	1	1	0	2854
Chases	6	2	1	1	14789
Career Total	**28**	**4**	**8**	**2**	**32868**

107	4/02	Kels	3m1f	D Ch	G-F	£4166
112	3/02	Kels	3m1f	D Ch	HVY	£5362
106	11/01	Sedg	2m5f110y	F(0-105)HHdl	SFT	£1827
114	5/00	Prth	3m110y	E Hdl	G-S	£2788

Total win prize-money £14145

Going: Sf: 2-5 GS: 0-2 Gd: 0-2 GF: - Fm: 1-4
Distance: 2m/2m3: 0-0 2m4-2m7: 1-6 **3m+: 2-7**
Track: **LH: 3-8** RH: 0-5 **Tight: 3-11** Gall: 0-0
Aids: Bl: 0-0 Vi: 0-1 **Tstrap: 3-6**
Best Rating: 117 3/00 Weth 2m4f110y gd-sft Hdl

Effective mare over hurdles and fences. Stays three miles plus and seems best suited by cut in the ground.

Shuttleworth (IRE)

98 115

8-y-o br g Be My Native (USA)-Cool Princess (Proverb)

C C Bealby (Edward U Hales 10/5) Michael Hill

Placings:*453*214600-01U32 **(2554)**

2001/02: 24^{0}GF, 24^{1}G, 25^{U}G, 25^{3}GS, 24^{2}S

	Starts	1st	2nd	3rd	Win & Pl
Hurdles	1	0	0	0	0
Chases	4	1	1	1	4670
Career Total	**14**	**2**	**2**	**2**	**10438**

97	10/01	Sthl	3m110y	E Ch	GD	£3149
116	11/00	Thur	2m6f110y	Hdl	HVY	£3864

Total win prize-money £7013

Going: Sf: 0-1 GS: 0-1 Gd: 1-2 GF: - Fm: 0-1
Distance: 2m/2m3: 0-0 2m4-2m7: 0-0 **3m+: 1-5**
Track: **LH: 1-2** RH: 0-2 **Tight: 1-4** Gall: 0-0
Aids: Bl: 0-0 Vi: 0-0 Tstrap: 0-0
Best Rating: 116 11/00 Thur 2m6f110y heavy Hdl

Fair chaser, stays three miles, acts on good or softer.

Siberian Gale (IRE)

113 154

10-y-o b g Strong Gale-Siberian Princess (Northfields (USA))

J J O'Neill J P McManus

Placings:*12146*/1141/11131/20 **(3371)**

2001/02: 24^{2}G, 24^{0}S

	Starts	1st	2nd	3rd	Win & Pl
Chases	2	0	1	0	10000
Career Total	**16**	**9**	**2**	**1**	**65032**

150	11/99	DRoy	2m2f	Ch	SFT	£11607
146	8/99	Tral	2m4f	HCh	YLD	£13928
142	6/99	Rosc	2m5f	Ch	FRM	£3683
129	5/99	Rosc	2m5f	Ch	Y-S	£4296
123	10/98	Navn	2m1f	Ch	HVY	£2989
112	5/98	Fair	2m	Hdl	G-F	£2680
137	5/98	Fair	2m	Hdl	Y-S	£2680
131	1/98	Leop	2m2f	NHF	Y-S	£2978
111	5/97	Fair	2m	NHF	YLD	£3051

Total win prize-money £47895

Going: Sf: 0-1 GS: 0-0 Gd: 0-1 GF: - Fm: 0-0
Distance: 2m/2m3: 0-0 2m4-2m7: 0-0 3m+: 0-2
Track: LH: 0-1 RH: 0-1 Tight: 0-0 Gall: 0-0
Aids: Bl: 0-0 Vi: 0-0 Tstrap: 0-0
Best Rating: 154 12/01 Asct 3m110y good Ch

A high-class, if lightly-raced, chaser. Reappeared after a two-year absence to finish runner-up at Ascot in December 2001 for Jonjo O'Neill and showed he still retains plenty of ability. Most of his wins have come from two to two miles five. Acts on most ground but does not want it too soft.

Sidbury Girl

89 74

5-y-o b m Presidium-Busted Love (Busted)

Miss E C Lavelle Cornelius Lysaght

Placings:0P **(3470)**

2001/02: 16^{0}G, 17^{P}HY

	Starts	1st	2nd	3rd	Win & Pl
Hurdles	2	0	0	0	
Career Total	**2**	**0**	**0**	**0**	

Going: Sf: 0-1 GS: 0-0 Gd: 0-1 GF: - Fm: 0-0
Distance: 2m/2m3: 0-2 2m4-2m7: 0-0 3m+: 0-0
Track: LH: 0-0 RH: 0-2 Tight: 0-1 Gall: 0-0
Aids: Bl: 0-0 Vi: 0-0 Tstrap: 0-0
Best Rating: 74 1/02 Winc 2m good Hdl

Sideliner

14-y-o ch g Green Shoon-Emmalina (Doubtless Ii)

A Hollingsworth A Hollingsworth

Placings:5P/P0P-0 **(0256)**

2001/02: 28^{0}GF

	Starts	1st	2nd	3rd	Win & Pl
Chases	1	0	0	0	
Career Total	**6**	**0**	**0**	**0**	**0**

Going: Sf: 0-0 GS: 0-0 Gd: 0-0 GF: - Fm: 0-1
Distance: 2m/2m3: 0-0 2m4-2m7: 0-0 3m+: 0-1
Track: LH: 0-1 RH: 0-0 Tight: 0-1 Gall: 0-0
Aids: Bl: 0-0 Vi: 0-0 Tstrap: 0-0
Best Rating: 75 5/00 Strf 3m gd-fm Ch

Siena (GER)

72 56

7-y-o ch m Platini (GER)-Smeralda (GER) (Nebos (GER))

Miss K M George Miss K George

Placings:0652405/3000042222364/0F **(0072)**

2001/02: 20^{0}G, 17^{F}G

	Starts	1st	2nd	3rd	Win & Pl
Hurdles	2	0	0	0	
Career Total	**22**	**0**	**5**	**2**	**3373**

Going: Sf: 0-0 GS: 0-0 Gd: 0-2 GF: - Fm: 0-0
Distance: 2m/2m3: 0-1 2m4-2m7: 0-1 3m+: 0-0
Track: LH: 0-0 RH: 0-2 Tight: 0-0 Gall: 0-1
Aids: Bl: 0-0 Vi: 0-2 Tstrap: 0-0
Best Rating: 81 9/99 Worc 3m gd-fm Hdl

Sierra Bay (IRE)

12-y-o b g Castle Keep-Beau's Trout (Beau Charmeur (FR))

Mat Barnard Miss Alice Camp

Placings:*2/3P/***R11FFP/P1P14P4P/664/PP **(4638)**

2001/02: 20^{P}S, 19^{P}GF

	Starts	1st	2nd	3rd	Win & Pl
Chases	2	0	0	0	
Career Total	**22**	**4**	**1**	**1**	**17040**

121	12/98	Towc	2m110y	D(0-125)HCh	SFT	£3488
116	11/98	Hntg	2m4f110y	C(0-130)HCh	G-S	£4926
119	1/98	Hntg	2m110y	D(0-120)HCh	G-S	£3439
109	1/98	Folk	2m	E(0-100)HCh	G-S	£2924

Total win prize-money £14777

Going: Sf: 0-1 GS: 0-0 Gd: 0-0 GF: - Fm: 0-1
Distance: 2m/2m3: 0-0 2m4-2m7: 0-2 3m+: 0-0
Track: LH: 0-0 RH: 0-2 Tight: 0-0 Gall: 0-0
Aids: Bl: 0-0 Vi: 0-0 Tstrap: 0-0
Best Rating: 121 12/98 Towc 2m110y soft Ch

Sierra Storm

76(79h) (56h)43

7-y-o gr m Gods Solution-Iberian Start (King Of Spain)

C Grant J Howard

Placings:*5000F/0*-000P **(1502)**

2001/02: 17^{0}GF, 17^{0}GF, 16^{0}G, 21^{P}G

	Starts	1st	2nd	3rd	Win & Pl
Hurdles	2	0	0	0	0
Chases	2	0	0	0	0
Career Total	**10**	**0**	**0**	**0**	**0**

Going: Sf: 0-0 GS: 0-0 Gd: 0-2 GF: - Fm: 0-2
Distance: 2m/2m3: 0-3 2m4-2m7: 0-1 3m+: 0-0
Track: LH: 0-4 RH: 0-0 Tight: 0-4 Gall: 0-0
Aids: Bl: 0-1 Vi: 0-0 Tstrap: 0-0
Best Rating: 69 6/99 Hexm 2m soft NHF

Sifat

87 55

7-y-o b m Marju (IRE)-Reine Maid (USA) (Mr Prospector (USA))

J R Jenkins Mr C N & Mrs J C Wright

Placings:246/00 **(2275)**

2001/02: 16^{0}G, 16^{0}GF

	Starts	1st	2nd	3rd	Win & Pl
Hurdles	2	0	0	0	

Career Total	5	0	1	0	1000

Going: Sf: 0-0 GS: 0-0 Gd: 0-1 GF: - Fm: 0-1
Distance: 2m/2m3: 0-2 2m4-2m7: 0-0 3m+: 0-0
Track: LH: 0-0 RH: 0-2 Tight: 0-0 Gall: 0-1
Aids: Bl: 0-0 Vi: 0-1 Tstrap: 0-0
Best Rating: 106 12/99 Leic 2m good Hdl

Sigma Comms (IRE)

90 118

9-y-o b/br g Don't Forget Me-River Serenade (USA) (Riverman (USA))
R Lee The Another Comedy Partnership

Placings:000/522112210/014200200/0/000P-314P (4009)
2001/02: 17³S, 22¹S, 19⁴HY, 22ᴾS

	Starts	1st	2nd	3rd	Win & Pl
Chases	4	1	0	1	7239
Career Total	**30**	**5**	**6**	**1**	**25423**

118	12/01	Hayd	2m6f	D(0-115)HCh	SFT	£6435
112	10/98	Rosc	2m	(0-109)HHdl	Y-S	£2540
105	12/97	Leop	2m	(0-116)HHdl	HVY	£5086
102	11/97	Naas	2m	(0-102)HHdl	Y-S	£3051
99	10/97	Dpat	2m1f172y	(0-102)HHdl	G-Y	£1695

Total win prize-money £18811

Going: Sf: 1-4 GS: 0-0 Gd: 0-0 GF: - Fm: 0-0
Distance: 2m/2m3: 0-2 **2m4-2m7: 1-2** 3m+: 0-0
Track: LH: 0-2 RH: 0-1 Tight: 0-1 Gall: 0-1
Aids: Bl: 0-0 Vi: 0-0 **Tstrap: 1-2**
Best Rating: 118 12/01 Hayd 2m6f soft Ch

Sigma Run (IRE)

108(79h) (65h)100

13-y-o b g The Parson-Splendid Run (Deep Run)
Dr P Pritchard The Shooting Stars

Placings:54/1F63FUB/350F56U/01531FP4/1213F553 123/0F364261P6/412P2P0430/P32123240445O-02603343P1P04U44203 (4740)
2001/02: 19⁰F, 18²GF, 16⁶G, 16⁰GF, 17³GF, 17³G, 16⁴GF, 20³GF, 19ᴾG, 16¹GF, 18ᴾGS, 19⁰GF, 19⁴GS, 16ᵁG, 16⁴G, 16⁴S, 20²G, 20⁰GF, 20³GF

	Starts	1st	2nd	3rd	Win & Pl
Hurdles	2	0	0	0	0
Chases	17	1	2	4	8556
Career Total	**87**	**10**	**10**	**14**	**51947**

100	10/01	Ludl	2m	G(0-95)HCh	G-F	£2926
107	7/00	MRas	2m1f110y	F(0-110)HCh	GD	£3510
98	6/99	MRas	2m1f110y	D(0-125)HCh	GD	£3764
111	10/98	Extr	2m1f	E(0-115)HCh	GD	£3485
110	10/97	Hrfd	2m	F(0-105)HCh	GD	£2710
97	6/97	Sthl	2m	E(0-115)HCh	G-F	£3842
93	5/97	Ludl	2m	E Ch	G-F	£2892
91	11/96	Leic	2m1f	E Ch	G-F	£3246
65	10/96	Ludl	2m	E Hdl	FRM	£2192
88	11/94	MRas	1m5f110y	NHF	GD	£1940

Total win prize-money £30508

Going: Sf: 0-1 GS: 0-2 Gd: 0-6 GF: - Fm: 1-10
Distance: **2m/2m3: 1-13** 2m4-2m7: 0-6 3m+: 0-0
Track: LH: 0-6 **RH: 1-11 Tight: 1-13** Gall: 0-1
Aids: Bl: 0-0 Vi: 0-0 Tstrap: 0-0
Best Rating: 111 7/99 NAbb 2m110y gd-fm Ch

A fair sort in modest handicap chases at up to two and a half miles, but needs a sound surface and is not altogether consistent. Best going right-handed.

Signora Zipporah

7-y-o b m Teamster-Chatty Corner (Le Bavard (FR))
M J Weeden Mrs Maureen Shenkin

Placings:5/PP2P (2712)
2001/02: 22ᴾGS, 24ᴾGS, 21²S, 21ᴾHY

	Starts	1st	2nd	3rd	Win & Pl
Hurdles	4	0	1	0	627
Career Total	**5**	**0**	**1**	**0**	**627**

Going: Sf: 0-2 GS: 0-2 Gd: 0-0 GF: - Fm: 0-0
Distance: 2m/2m3: 0-0 2m4-2m7: 0-3 3m+: 0-1
Track: LH: 0-2 RH: 0-1 Tight: 0-1 Gall: 0-0
Aids: Bl: 0-0 Vi: 0-0 Tstrap: 0-0
Best Rating: 87 3/00 Towc 2m soft NHF

Sigy Point

54 27

5-y-o b m King's Signet (USA)-Red Point (Reference Point)
J W Mullins Mrs Maureen Emery

Placings:F0PP (3514)
2001/02: 17ᶠGF, 19⁰GS, 21ᴾHY, 24ᴾS

	Starts	1st	2nd	3rd	Win & Pl
Hurdles	4	0	0	0	
Career Total	**4**	**0**	**0**	**0**	

Going: Sf: 0-2 GS: 0-1 Gd: 0-0 GF: - Fm: 0-1
Distance: 2m/2m3: 0-1 2m4-2m7: 0-2 3m+: 0-1
Track: LH: 0-1 RH: 0-3 Tight: 0-3 Gall: 0-0
Aids: Bl: 0-0 Vi: 0-0 Tstrap: 0-0
Best Rating: 27 12/01 Tntn 2m3f110y gd-sft Hdl

Sijujama (IRE)

93 83

7-y-o b g Torus-Knights Bounty (IRE) (Henbit (USA))
Miss Lucinda V Russell Major R B H Young

Placings:00000/P0F-P3 (0467)
2001/02: 16ᴾS, 20³GF

	Starts	1st	2nd	3rd	Win & Pl
Chases	2	0	0	1	326
Career Total	**10**	**0**	**0**	**1**	**326**

Going: Sf: 0-1 GS: 0-0 Gd: 0-0 GF: - Fm: 0-1
Distance: 2m/2m3: 0-1 2m4-2m7: 0-1 3m+: 0-0
Track: LH: 0-1 RH: 0-1 Tight: 0-0 Gall: 0-0
Aids: Bl: 0-0 Vi: 0-0 Tstrap: 0-0
Best Rating: 102 11/99 Naas 2m yld-sft Hdl

Poor form when placed twice over fences so far.

Sikander A Azam

106 135

9-y-o b g Arctic Lord-Shanlaragh (Gaberdine)
C Grant Lord Daresbury & J E Greenall

Placings:32140/F51106/61163/514-32003 (4831)
2001/02: 17³GS, 16²G, 19⁰G, 16⁰G, 20³G

	Starts	1st	2nd	3rd	Win & Pl
Chases	5	0	1	2	4090
Career Total	**24**	**6**	**2**	**4**	**25805**

143	5/00	Ctml	2m1f110y	D(0-125)HCh	G-F	£3867
134	11/99	Ayr	2m	D Ch	GD	£4055
143	10/99	MRas	2m1f110y	D Ch	GD	£4435
115	12/98	Donc	2m110y	E Hdl	GD	£2182
121	11/98	Aint	2m110y	C Hdl	G-S	£3818
103	1/98	Muss	2m	H NHF	G-S	£1175

Total win prize-money £19534

Going: Sf: 0-0 GS: 0-1 Gd: 0-4 GF: - Fm: 0-0
Distance: 2m/2m3: 0-3 2m4-2m7: 0-2 3m+: 0-0
Track: LH: 0-5 RH: 0-0 Tight: 0-2 Gall: 0-1
Aids: Bl: 0-0 Vi: 0-0 Tstrap: 0-0
Best Rating: 143 5/00 Ctml 2m1f110y gd-fm Ch

Decent free-running chaser at around two miles on fast ground.

Silence Reigns

109(113h) 149

8-y-o b g Saddlers' Hall (IRE)-Rensaler (USA) (Stop The Music (USA))
P F Nicholls C G Roach

Placings:0/16310/0-1412P (3905)
2001/02: 16¹S, 16⁴GS, 19¹GS, 20²GS, 20ᴾG

	Starts	1st	2nd	3rd	Win & Pl
Chases	5	2	1	0	18429
Career Total	**12**	**4**	**1**	**1**	**32675**

136	12/01	Chep	2m3f110y	D Ch	G-S	£4163
149	11/01	Chep	2m110y	E Ch	SFT	£3415
127	3/00	Ludl	2m	E Hdl	G-S	£2880
127	11/99	Chel	2m110y	A Hdl	GD	£9525

Total win prize-money £19985

Going: Sf: 1-1 GS: 1-3 Gd: 0-1 GF: - Fm: 0-0
Distance: 2m/2m3: 1-2 2m4-2m7: 1-3 3m+: 0-0
Track: **LH: 2-2** RH: 0-3 Tight: 0-0 Gall: 0-0
Aids: Bl: 0-0 Vi: 0-0 Tstrap: 0-0
Best Rating: 149 2/02 Sand 2m4f110y gd-sft Ch

Group placed on the Flat, he took quite well to hurdles but was sidelined after finishing unplaced at Haydock in May 2000. Made a winning debut over fences at Chepstow on his reappearance in November 2001, and ran well in better class next time. Jumped better when winning over two and a half miles at Chepstow in December. Suited by give underfoot and two/two and a half miles.

Silent Action (USA)

89(90c) (68c)63

10-y-o b/br g Greinton-Heather Bee (USA) (Drone (USA))
N A Smith Mrs G C List

Placings:25/00036/334/63P/03F53-0P5000060 (3325)
2001/02: 22⁰GF, 21ᴾG, 20⁵GF, 23⁰GF, 25⁰GF, 25⁰G, 20⁰G, 19⁶G, 20⁰GS

	Starts	1st	2nd	3rd	Win & Pl
Hurdles	2	0	0	0	0
Chases	7	0	0	0	0
Career Total	**27**	**0**	**1**	**6**	**2856**

Going: Sf: 0-0 GS: 0-1 Gd: 0-4 GF: - Fm: 0-4
Distance: 2m/2m3: 0-1 2m4-2m7: 0-5 3m+: 0-3
Track: LH: 0-5 RH: 0-4 Tight: 0-3 Gall: 0-2
Aids: Bl: 0-0 Vi: 0-0 Tstrap: 0-9
Best Rating: 92 2/96 Punc 2m soft NHF

Silent Auction

92 57

7-y-o b m Petoski-Lady Rosanna (Kind Of Hush)
Countess Goess-Saurau Count K Goess-Saurau

Placings:0/0000 (3332)
2001/02: 17⁰G, 18⁰GS, 17⁰G, 21⁰G

	Starts	1st	2nd	3rd	Win & Pl
NH Flat	2	0	0	0	0

	Starts	1st	2nd	3rd	Win & Pl
Hurdles	2	0	0	0	0
Career Total	**5**	**0**	**0**	**0**	

Going: Sf: 0-0 GS: 0-1 Gd: 0-3 GF: - Fm: 0-0
Distance: 2m/2m3: 0-3 2m4-2m7: 0-1 3m+: 0-0
Track: LH: 0-1 RH: 0-2 Tight: 0-2 Gall: 0-0
Aids: Bl: 0-0 Vi: 0-0 Tstrap: 0-0
Best Rating: 80 10/99 Chel 2m110y good NHF

Silent Cracker

(97h) (94h)
10-y-o br g Teenoso (USA)-Silent Surrender (Nearly A Hand)
M Pitman Silent Partners

Placings:*60*/2614P034/**321314P/2P/PP**64 **(1226)**
2001/02: 22^{P}GF, 21^{P}GF, 16^{6}G, 22^{4}GF

	Starts	1st	2nd	3rd	Win & Pl
Hurdles	2	0	0	0	0
Chases	2	0	0	0	0
Career Total	**23**	**3**	**3**	**3**	**14953**

127 12/98 Sand 2m4f110y D Ch GD £4143
114 10/98 Plum 2m5f E Ch G-F £3062
108 12/97 Folk 2m1f110y E Hdl GD £2406
Total win prize-money £9612

Going: Sf: 0-0 GS: 0-0 Gd: 0-1 GF: - Fm: 0-3
Distance: 2m/2m3: 0-1 2m4-2m7: 0-3 3m+: 0-0
Track: LH: 0-3 RH: 0-1 Tight: 0-4 Gall: 0-0
Aids: Bl: 0-0 Vi: 0-2 Tstrap: 0-0
Best Rating: 127 12/98 Sand 2m4f110y good Ch

Silent Guest (IRE)

87 55
9-y-o b g Don't Forget Me-Guest House (What A Guest)
J D Frost (R G Frost 28/12) R C Burridge

Placings:2164/53P/565/0200224-60 **(4657)**
2001/02: 24^{6}GS, 24^{0}G

	Starts	1st	2nd	3rd	Win & Pl
Hurdles	2	0	0	0	0
Career Total	**19**	**1**	**4**	**1**	**5770**

85 11/96 Newc 2m E Hdl G-F £2274
Total win prize-money £2274

Going: Sf: 0-0 GS: 0-1 Gd: 0-1 GF: - Fm: 0-0
Distance: 2m/2m3: 0-0 2m4-2m7: 0-0 3m+: 0-2
Track: LH: 0-0 RH: 0-2 Tight: 0-2 Gall: 0-0
Aids: Bl: 0-0 Vi: 0-0 Tstrap: 0-0
Best Rating: 85 11/96 Newc 2m gd-fm Hdl

Silent Hunter

(70h) (40h)
6-y-o ch g Lion Cavern (USA)-Zealous Kitten (USA) (The Minstrel (CAN))
M J Ryan The Beach Boys

Placings:*0-00*PPPP **(4751)**
2001/02: 16^{0}GS, 16^{0}GS, 21^{P}S, 24^{P}GS, 20^{P}GS, 20^{P}GF

	Starts	1st	2nd	3rd	Win & Pl
NH Flat	1	0	0	0	0
Hurdles	2	0	0	0	0
Chases	3	0	0	0	0
Career Total	**7**	**0**	**0**	**0**	**0**

Going: Sf: 0-1 GS: 0-4 Gd: 0-0 GF: - Fm: 0-1
Distance: 2m/2m3: 0-2 2m4-2m7: 0-3 3m+: 0-1
Track: LH: 0-2 RH: 0-4 Tight: 0-1 Gall: 0-3
Aids: Bl: 0-0 Vi: 0-0 Tstrap: 0-0

Best Rating: 54 3/01 Hntg 2m110y soft NHF

Poor chase/hurdles form.

Silent Snipe

107(93h) (51h)95
9-y-o ch g Jendali (USA)-Sasol (Bustino)
Miss L C Siddall Mrs D Ibbotson

Placings:P665P60P30**10** **(4856)**
2001/02: 25^{P}S, 20^{6}G, 20^{6}GF, 24^{5}S, 25^{P}GS, 20^{6}S, 20^{0}G, 24^{P}S, 27^{3}S, 26^{0}GF, 25^{1}GF, 25^{0}G

	Starts	1st	2nd	3rd	Win & Pl
Hurdles	7	0	0	1	263
Chases	5	1	0	0	3218
Career Total	**12**	**1**	**0**	**1**	**3481**

90 4/02 Hexm 3m1f E Ch G-F £3217
Total win prize-money £3218

Going: Sf: 0-5 GS: 0-1 Gd: 0-3 GF: - Fm: 1-3
Distance: 2m/2m3: 0-0 2m4-2m7: 0-4 **3m+: 1-8**
Track: **LH: 1-8** RH: 0-4 Tight: 0-3 Gall: 0-2
Aids: Bl: 0-0 Vi: 0-0 Tstrap: 0-2
Best Rating: 90 4/02 Hexm 3m1f gd-fm Ch

Winning pointer but only plating class over hurdles. Won on his chasing reappearance in April on firm ground, but only in modest company.

Silent Voice (IRE)

10
5-y-o ch g Unfuwain (USA)-Symeterie (USA) (Seattle Song (USA))
Sir John Barlow Bt Sir John & Lady Barlow

Placings:0 **(4520)**
2001/02: 20^{0}G

	Starts	1st	2nd	3rd	Win & Pl
Hurdles	1	0	0	0	
Career Total	**1**	**0**	**0**	**0**	

Going: Sf: 0-0 GS: 0-0 Gd: 0-1 GF: - Fm: 0-0
Distance: 2m/2m3: 0-0 2m4-2m7: 0-1 3m+: 0-0
Track: LH: 0-0 RH: 0-0 Tight: 0-0 Gall: 0-0
Aids: Bl: 0-0 Vi: 0-0 Tstrap: 0-0
Best Rating: 10 4/02 Carl 2m4f good Hdl

Siljan (GER)

84 54
5-y-o b g Darshaan-Schwarzmeer (GER) (King's Lake (USA))
C R Egerton Seven Wayward Lads

Placings:0 **(4152)**
2001/02: 20^{0}GS

	Starts	1st	2nd	3rd	Win & Pl
Hurdles	1	0	0	0	
Career Total	**1**	**0**	**0**	**0**	

Going: Sf: 0-0 GS: 0-1 Gd: 0-0 GF: - Fm: 0-0
Distance: 2m/2m3: 0-0 2m4-2m7: 0-1 3m+: 0-0
Track: LH: 0-1 RH: 0-0 Tight: 0-0 Gall: 0-0
Aids: Bl: 0-0 Vi: 0-0 Tstrap: 0-0
Best Rating: 59 3/02 Chep 2m4f gd-sft Hdl

Silk St John

101 91
8-y-o b g Damister (USA)-Silk St James (Pas De Seul)
M J Ryan C R S Partners

Placings:0-2 **(2063)**
2001/02: 16^{2}G

	Starts	1st	2nd	3rd	Win & Pl
Hurdles	1	0	1	0	694
Career Total	**2**	**0**	**1**	**0**	**694**

Going: Sf: 0-0 GS: 0-0 Gd: 0-1 GF: - Fm: 0-0
Distance: 2m/2m3: 0-1 2m4-2m7: 0-0 3m+: 0-0
Track: LH: 0-0 RH: 0-1 Tight: 0-0 Gall: 0-1
Aids: Bl: 0-0 Vi: 0-0 Tstrap: 0-0
Best Rating: 91 11/01 Hntg 2m110y good Hdl

Has shown ability over hurdles and should be capable of scoring over two miles on good ground.

Silk Trader

111 113
7-y-o b g Nomadic Way (USA)-Money Run (Deep Run)
J Mackie The Festival Dream Partnership

Placings:*40/6*1U3-31400403163110 **(4950a)**
2001/02: 20^{3}G, 19^{1}G, 19^{4}GF, 20^{0}G, 21^{0}G, 20^{4}S, 16^{0}S, 16^{3}HY, 16^{1}S, 16^{6}GS, 16^{3}S, 16^{1}GS, 16^{1}GS, 16^{0}G

	Starts	1st	2nd	3rd	Win & Pl
Hurdles	14	4	0	3	16510
Career Total	**20**	**5**	**0**	**4**	**19829**

113 3/02 Towc 2m D(0-125)HHdl G-S £5174
104 3/02 Sand 2m110y D(0-115)HHdl G-S £4231
108 12/01 Leic 2m F(0-100)HHdl SFT £3146
113 5/01 Wwck 2m3f E(0-115)HHdl GD £2660
100 2/01 Uttx 2m D Hdl SFT £2849
Total win prize-money £18062

Going: Sf: 1-5 GS: 2-3 Gd: 1-5 GF: - Fm: 0-1
Distance: **2m/2m3: 4-9** 2m4-2m7: 0-5 3m+: 0-0
Track: LH: 1-5 **RH: 3-9** Tight: 0-3 Gall: 0-1
Aids: Bl: 0-0 Vi: 0-0 Tstrap: 0-2
Best Rating: 113 3/02 Towc 2m gd-sft Hdl

Acts on good and soft ground and is effective at around two miles to two miles three furlongs. Regained winning form at Leicester in December 2001. Won the amateur hurdle at Sandown in March 2002 and followed up the same month in handicap company. Goes well for an inexperienced rider.

Silken Lady

73 3
6-y-o br m Rock Hopper-Silk St James (Pas De Seul)
M J Ryan Sez Les Partnership

Placings:00P-P40 **(1747)**
2001/02: 20^{P}GS, 22^{4}HY, 17^{0}G

	Starts	1st	2nd	3rd	Win & Pl
Hurdles	3	0	0	0	0
Career Total	**6**	**0**	**0**	**0**	**0**

Going: Sf: 0-1 GS: 0-1 Gd: 0-1 GF: - Fm: 0-0
Distance: 2m/2m3: 0-1 2m4-2m7: 0-2 3m+: 0-0
Track: LH: 0-0 RH: 0-2 Tight: 0-3 Gall: 0-0
Aids: Bl: 0-2 Vi: 0-0 Tstrap: 0-0
Best Rating: 8 10/01 MRas 2m1f110y good Hdl

Silken Pearls

79f 103f
6-y-o b m Leading Counsel (USA)-River Pearl (Oats)
L Lungo P E Truscott

Placings:4 **(4526)**
2001/02: 17^{4}G

Starts	1st	2nd	3rd	Win & Pl
NH Flat	1	0	0	0	0
Career Total	1	0	0	0	0

Going: Sf: 0-0 GS: 0-0 Gd: 0-1 GF: - Fm: 0-0
Distance: 2m/2m3: 0-1 2m4-2m7: 0-0 3m+: 0-0
Track: LH: 0-0 RH: 0-1 Tight: 0-0 Gall: 0-0
Aids: Bl: 0-0 Vi: 0-0 Tstrap: 0-0
Best Rating: 103 4/02 Carl 2m1f good NHF

Out of a winning hurdler/chaser, she ran well on her debut in a bumper in the spring of 2002.

Silken Thomas

101(96h) (79h)99

7-y-o b g King's Ride-Padykin (Bustino)
N J Hawke Mrs G Watkinson-Yull

Placings: *02*/3030-435PU40 (4502)
2001/02: 17^{4}G, 16^{3}G, 16^{5}GF, 19^{P}G, 20^{U}G, 20^{4}GS, 22^{0}G

	Starts	1st	2nd	3rd	Win & Pl
Hurdles	2	0	0	0	0
Chases	5	0	0	1	699
Career Total	13	0	1	3	1838

Going: Sf: 0-0 GS: 0-1 Gd: 0-5 GF: - Fm: 0-1
Distance: 2m/2m3: 0-4 2m4-2m7: 0-3 3m+: 0-0
Track: LH: 0-3 RH: 0-3 Tight: 0-3 Gall: 0-0
Aids: Bl: 0-0 Vi: 0-0 Tstrap: 0-0
Best Rating: 103 4/00 NAbb 2m1f heavy NHF

Moderate individual over hurdles and fences. Not a natural jumper of obstacles. Has only been tried at up to two and a half miles.

Silva Venture (IRE)

63f

5-y-o b m Mandalus-Miss The Post (Bustino)
L Lungo Elite Racing Club

Placings: *0* (4860)
2001/02: 16^{0}G

	Starts	1st	2nd	3rd	Win & Pl
NH Flat	1	0	0	0	
Career Total	1	0	0	0	

Going: Sf: 0-0 GS: 0-0 Gd: 0-1 GF: - Fm: 0-0
Distance: 2m/2m3: 0-1 2m4-2m7: 0-0 3m+: 0-0
Track: LH: 0-0 RH: 0-0 Tight: 0-0 Gall: 0-0
Aids: Bl: 0-0 Vi: 0-0 Tstrap: 0-0
Best Rating: 63 4/02 Hexm 2m110y good NHF

Silvaani (USA)

67 37

4-y-o gr g Dumaani (USA)-Ruby Silver (USA) (Silver Hawk (USA))
Mrs A J Perrett (Miss Gay Kelleway 3/11) Lingfield Breakfast Club

Placings: 0 (1925)
2001/02: 16^{0}G

	Starts	1st	2nd	3rd	Win & Pl
Hurdles	1	0	0	0	
Career Total	1	0	0	0	

Going: Sf: 0-0 GS: 0-0 Gd: 0-1 GF: - Fm: 0-0
Distance: 2m/2m3: 0-1 2m4-2m7: 0-0 3m+: 0-0
Track: LH: 0-0 RH: 0-1 Tight: 0-0 Gall: 0-0
Aids: Bl: 0-0 Vi: 0-0 Tstrap: 0-0
Best Rating: 37 11/01 Asct 2m110y good Hdl

Silver Bullet

77 59

6-y-o gr g Grey Desire-Spanish Realm (King Of Spain)
B Mactaggart Des Redhead

Placings: 0P00 (4785)
2001/02: 16^{0}GS, 16^{P}GS, 16^{0}S, 16^{0}F

	Starts	1st	2nd	3rd	Win & Pl
Hurdles	4	0	0	0	
Career Total	4	0	0	0	

Going: Sf: 0-1 GS: 0-2 Gd: 0-0 GF: - Fm: 0-1
Distance: 2m/2m3: 0-4 2m4-2m7: 0-0 3m+: 0-0
Track: LH: 0-3 RH: 0-1 Tight: 0-2 Gall: 0-1
Aids: Bl: 0-0 Vi: 0-0 Tstrap: 0-0
Best Rating: 59 11/01 Ayr 2m gd-sft Hdl

Silver Button

8-y-o b g Silver Kite (USA)-Klairover (Smackover)
Graham Smith Graham Smith

Placings: FP (2684)
2001/02: 16^{F}G, 16^{P}G

	Starts	1st	2nd	3rd	Win & Pl
Hurdles	2	0	0	0	
Career Total	2	0	0	0	

Going: Sf: 0-0 GS: 0-0 Gd: 0-2 GF: - Fm: 0-0
Distance: 2m/2m3: 0-2 2m4-2m7: 0-0 3m+: 0-0
Track: LH: 0-2 RH: 0-0 Tight: 0-0 Gall: 0-1
Aids: Bl: 0-0 Vi: 0-0 Tstrap: 0-0
Best Rating:

Silver Challenge

98

6-y-o gr m Norton Challenger-Gold Caste (USA) (Singh (USA))
J L Harris Nigel Stokes

Placings: *0*P-0 (0372)
2001/02: 16^{0}GF

	Starts	1st	2nd	3rd	Win & Pl
Hurdles	1	0	0	0	
Career Total	3	0	0	0	

Going: Sf: 0-0 GS: 0-0 Gd: 0-0 GF: - Fm: 0-1
Distance: 2m/2m3: 0-1 2m4-2m7: 0-0 3m+: 0-0
Track: LH: 0-0 RH: 0-1 Tight: 0-0 Gall: 0-1
Aids: Bl: 0-0 Vi: 0-0 Tstrap: 0-0
Best Rating: 36 3/01 Hntg 2m110y soft NHF

Silver Chevalier (IRE)

96 80

4-y-o gr g Petong-Princess Eurolink (Be My Guest (USA))
B Llewellyn (C N Allen 13/11) Mrs M Llewellyn

Placings: 06P5 (4737)
2001/02: 16^{0}GF, 16^{6}GF, 16^{P}G, 16^{5}GF

	Starts	1st	2nd	3rd	Win & Pl
Hurdles	4	0	0	0	0
Career Total	4	0	0	0	0

Going: Sf: 0-0 GS: 0-0 Gd: 0-1 GF: - Fm: 0-3
Distance: 2m/2m3: 0-4 2m4-2m7: 0-0 3m+: 0-0
Track: LH: 0-1 RH: 0-3 Tight: 0-1 Gall: 0-1
Aids: Bl: 0-0 Vi: 0-0 Tstrap: 0-0
Best Rating: 80 4/02 Ludl 2m gd-fm Hdl

Silver Gift

103 81

5-y-o b m Rakaposhi King-Kellsboro Kate (Paddy's Stream)
G Fierro G Fierro

Placings: *0040*-PP360P3 (4176)
2001/02: 17^{P}GS, 21^{P}G, 16^{3}GF, 19^{6}G, 20^{0}GS, 24^{P}S, 19^{3}GS

	Starts	1st	2nd	3rd	Win & Pl
Hurdles	7	0	0	2	964
Career Total	11	0	0	2	964

Going: Sf: 0-1 GS: 0-3 Gd: 0-2 GF: - Fm: 0-1
Distance: 2m/2m3: 0-3 2m4-2m7: 0-3 3m+: 0-1
Track: LH: 0-3 RH: 0-4 Tight: 0-3 Gall: 0-0
Aids: Bl: 0-0 Vi: 0-0 Tstrap: 0-0
Best Rating: 81 3/02 Strf 2m3f gd-sft Hdl

A very modest performer over hurdles. has only had one outing over fences where he fell. Improved form when runner up in two novice handicap hurdles when stepped up to three miles.

Silver Grey Annie

5-y-o gr m Arzanni-Celtic Berry (Celtic Cone)
F P Murtagh Norman Furness

Placings: *0* (3680)
2001/02: 16^{0}HY

	Starts	1st	2nd	3rd	Win & Pl
NH Flat	1	0	0	0	
Career Total	1	0	0	0	

Going: Sf: 0-1 GS: 0-0 Gd: 0-0 GF: - Fm: 0-0
Distance: 2m/2m3: 0-1 2m4-2m7: 0-0 3m+: 0-0
Track: LH: 0-1 RH: 0-0 Tight: 0-0 Gall: 0-0
Aids: Bl: 0-0 Vi: 0-0 Tstrap: 0-0
Best Rating:

Silver Groom (IRE)

12-y-o gr g Shy Groom (USA)-Rustic Lawn (Rusticaro (FR))
P R Webber T D Rose & Miss K P Barron

Placings: 132P/14020/14350/06/254/5P (0786)
2001/02: 24^{5}GF, 17^{P}GF

	Starts	1st	2nd	3rd	Win & Pl
Chases	2	0	0	0	0
Career Total	21	3	3	2	29293

138	11/96	Asct	2m110y	B HHdl	G-F	£4992
136	11/95	Sand	2m110y	B(0-145)HHdl	G-F	£4947
107	11/94	Strf	2m110y	Hdl	G-S	£2164

Total win prize-money £12104

Going: Sf: 0-0 GS: 0-0 Gd: 0-0 GF: - Fm: 0-2
Distance: 2m/2m3: 0-1 2m4-2m7: 0-0 3m+: 0-1
Track: LH: 0-1 RH: 0-1 Tight: 0-2 Gall: 0-0
Aids: Bl: 0-0 Vi: 0-0 Tstrap: 0-0
Best Rating: 143 2/97 Newb 2m110y good Hdl

Silver Howe

99 99

9-y-o gr g Move Off-Vinovia (Ribston)

D Moffatt The C J G Partnership

Placings:*0000600*/6065O2466/402P42/46222P-102340640 **(4896)**
2001/02: 20^{1}G, 17^{0}GS, 18^{2}G, 20^{3}GS, 19^{4}S, 20^{0}GS, 22^{6}HY, 17^{4}G, 20^{0}G

	Starts	1st	2nd	3rd	Win & Pl
Hurdles	9	1	1	1	4236
Career Total	**37**	**1**	**7**	**1**	**10039**

97 5/01 Bang 2m4f E Hdl GD £3104
Total win prize-money £3105

Going: Sf: 0-2 GS: 0-3 Gd: 1-4 GF: - Fm: 0-0
Distance: 2m/2m3: 0-4 **2m4-2m7: 1-5** 3m+: 0-0
Track: **LH: 1-6** RH: 0-3 **Tight: 1-4** Gall: 0-0
Aids: Bl: 0-0 Vi: 0-2 Tstrap: 0-0
Best Rating: 99 11/01 Kels 2m2f good Hdl

He has shown some ability and has made the frame often, but has only ever won once and now looks well past his best.

Silver Joy

7-y-o b m Silver Kite (USA)-Oh My Joy (Grundy)
D Burchell M G Jones

Placings:P/P **(3643)**
2001/02: 16^{P}S

	Starts	1st	2nd	3rd	Win & Pl
Hurdles	1	0	0	0	
Career Total	**2**	**0**	**0**	**0**	

Going: Sf: 0-1 GS: 0-0 Gd: 0-0 GF: - Fm: 0-0
Distance: 2m/2m3: 0-1 2m4-2m7: 0-0 3m+: 0-0
Track: LH: 0-0 RH: 0-1 Tight: 0-0 Gall: 0-0
Aids: Bl: 0-0 Vi: 0-0 Tstrap: 0-0
Best Rating:

Silver Knight

115f 114f

4-y-o gr g Simply Great (FR)-Hysteria (Prince Bee)
T D Easterby C H Stevens

Placings:*16* **(4679)**
2001/02: 16^{1}GS, 17^{6}G

	Starts	1st	2nd	3rd	Win & Pl
NH Flat	2	1	0	0	2187
Career Total	**2**	**1**	**0**	**0**	**2187**

109 3/02 Donc 2m110y H NHF G-S £2186
Total win prize-money £2187

Going: Sf: 0-0 GS: 1-1 Gd: 0-1 GF: - Fm: 0-0
Distance: **2m/2m3: 1-2** 2m4-2m7: 0-0 3m+: 0-0
Track: **LH: 1-1** RH: 0-0 Tight: 0-0 **Gall: 1-1**
Aids: Bl: 0-0 Vi: 0-0 Tstrap: 0-0
Best Rating: 114 4/02 Aint 2m1f good NHF

A tall, unfurnished type, he won going away on his bumper debut at Doncaster in March 2002. Not disgraced in top company at Aintree and looks to have a fair bit of potential.

Silver Pot Black

7-y-o gr g Ron's Victory (USA)-Haunting (Lord Gayle (USA))
P J Hobbs (Miss L Day 3/3) Pot Black Racing

Placings:543/F2000-0 **(0560)**
2001/02: 21^{0}GF

	Starts	1st	2nd	3rd	Win & Pl
Chases	1	0	0	0	
Career Total	**9**	**0**	**1**	**1**	**891**

Going: Sf: 0-0 GS: 0-0 Gd: 0-0 GF: - Fm: 0-1
Distance: 2m/2m3: 0-0 2m4-2m7: 0-1 3m+: 0-0
Track: LH: 0-1 RH: 0-0 Tight: 0-1 Gall: 0-0
Aids: Bl: 0-0 Vi: 0-0 Tstrap: 0-0
Best Rating: 102 3/00 Tntn 3m110y good Hdl

Silver Rebel

(86h) (57h)

8-y-o gr g Scallywag-Melfio Miss (Town Crier)
A Crook G Heap

Placings:*100*/004PP-**0FP0P** **(4578)**
2001/02: 20^{0}S, 24^{F}S, 20^{P}GS, 16^{0}S, 23^{P}G

	Starts	1st	2nd	3rd	Win & Pl
Hurdles	2	0	0	0	0
Chases	3	0	0	0	0
Career Total	**13**	**1**	**0**	**0**	**1716**

95 10/99 Hexm 2m H NHF GD £1716
Total win prize-money £1716

Going: Sf: 0-3 GS: 0-1 Gd: 0-1 GF: - Fm: 0-0
Distance: 2m/2m3: 0-1 2m4-2m7: 0-3 3m+: 0-1
Track: LH: 0-4 RH: 0-1 Tight: 0-1 Gall: 0-1
Aids: Bl: 0-1 Vi: 0-1 Tstrap: 0-2
Best Rating: 95 2/01 Hayd 2m heavy Hdl

Silver Risks (FR)

80 57

4-y-o gr f Take Risks (FR)-Turkansa (FR) (Baby Turk)
D R Gandolfo (M J Grassick 11/11) Starlight Racing

Placings:0 **(4504)**
2001/02: 17^{0}G

	Starts	1st	2nd	3rd	Win & Pl
Hurdles	1	0	0	0	
Career Total	**1**	**0**	**0**	**0**	

Going: Sf: 0-0 GS: 0-0 Gd: 0-1 GF: - Fm: 0-0
Distance: 2m/2m3: 0-1 2m4-2m7: 0-0 3m+: 0-0
Track: LH: 0-1 RH: 0-0 Tight: 0-1 Gall: 0-0
Aids: Bl: 0-0 Vi: 0-0 Tstrap: 0-0
Best Rating: 22 3/02 NAbb 2m1f good Hdl

Silver Samuel (NZ)

78f 80f

5-y-o gr g Hula Town (NZ)-Offrande (NZ) (Decies)
S A Brookshaw S A Brookshaw

Placings:*0* **(3777)**
2001/02: 16^{0}S

	Starts	1st	2nd	3rd	Win & Pl
NH Flat	1	0	0	0	
Career Total	**1**	**0**	**0**	**0**	

Going: Sf: 0-1 GS: 0-0 Gd: 0-0 GF: - Fm: 0-0
Distance: 2m/2m3: 0-1 2m4-2m7: 0-0 3m+: 0-0
Track: LH: 0-0 RH: 0-1 Tight: 0-0 Gall: 0-0
Aids: Bl: 0-0 Vi: 0-0 Tstrap: 0-0
Best Rating: 80 2/02 Sand 2m110y soft NHF

Silver Sapphire

8-y-o gr m Carlingford Castle-Silver Snow (Abwah)
Graham Smith Graham Smith

Placings:6 **(1584)**
2001/02: 19^{6}GS

	Starts	1st	2nd	3rd	Win & Pl
Hurdles	1	0	0	0	0
Career Total	**1**	**0**	**0**	**0**	**0**

Going: Sf: 0-0 GS: 0-1 Gd: 0-0 GF: - Fm: 0-0
Distance: 2m/2m3: 0-0 2m4-2m7: 0-1 3m+: 0-0
Track: LH: 0-0 RH: 0-1 Tight: 0-1 Gall: 0-0
Aids: Bl: 0-0 Vi: 0-0 Tstrap: 0-0
Best Rating:

Silver Secret

75 45

8-y-o ro g Absalom-Secret Dance (Sadler's Wells (USA))
S Gollings Mrs Jayne M Gollings

Placings:32400/5/60 **(1667)**
2001/02: 16^{6}GS, 16^{0}G

	Starts	1st	2nd	3rd	Win & Pl
Hurdles	1	0	0	0	0
Chases	1	0	0	0	0
Career Total	**8**	**0**	**1**	**1**	**1118**

Going: Sf: 0-0 GS: 0-1 Gd: 0-1 GF: - Fm: 0-0
Distance: 2m/2m3: 0-2 2m4-2m7: 0-0 3m+: 0-0
Track: LH: 0-2 RH: 0-0 Tight: 0-1 Gall: 0-0
Aids: Bl: 0-0 Vi: 0-0 Tstrap: 0-0
Best Rating: 93 11/97 Hntg 2m110y gd-fm Hdl

Silver Sirocco (IRE)

10-y-o gr g Razzo Forte-Oronocco Gift (Camden Town)
S Kelly (Mrs Merrita Jones 7/4) Mrs A P Kelly

Placings:*33/4U6/4U60/6234/5PPP-P* **(4846)**
2001/02: 24^{P}G

	Starts	1st	2nd	3rd	Win & Pl
Chases	1	0	0	0	
Career Total	**18**	**0**	**1**	**3**	**2192**

Going: Sf: 0-0 GS: 0-0 Gd: 0-1 GF: - Fm: 0-0
Distance: 2m/2m3: 0-0 2m4-2m7: 0-0 3m+: 0-1
Track: LH: 0-1 RH: 0-0 Tight: 0-1 Gall: 0-0
Aids: Bl: 0-0 Vi: 0-0 Tstrap: 0-0
Best Rating: 103 2/00 Folk 2m5f good Ch

Silver Sleeve (IRE)

10-y-o b g Taufan (USA)-Sable Coated (Caerleon (USA))
Mrs H M Bridges (Jane Southcombe 27/9) Mrs H M Bridges

Placings:F0002035/4124430/P-0060 **(4638)**
2001/02: 20^{0}G, 24^{0}GF, 19^{6}G, 19^{0}GF

	Starts	1st	2nd	3rd	Win & Pl
Hurdles	1	0	0	0	0
Chases	3	0	0	0	0
Career Total	**20**	**1**	**2**	**2**	**4003**

82 7/96 Strf 2m3f E(0-100)HHdl G-F £2178
Total win prize-money £2178

Going: Sf: 0-0 GS: 0-0 Gd: 0-2 GF: - Fm: 0-2
Distance: 2m/2m3: 0-0 2m4-2m7: 0-3 3m+: 0-1
Track: LH: 0-0 RH: 0-4 Tight: 0-1 Gall: 0-0

Aids: Bl: 0-2 Vi: 0-0 Tstrap: 0-0
Best Rating: 100 3/02 Extr 2m3f110y good Ch

Silver Smoke

5-y-o gr m Perpendicular-Smoke (Rusticaro (FR))
D G Bridgwater Mucky Duck Partnership

Placings:*00* **(2655)**
2001/02: 17^{0}G, 16^{0}G

	Starts	1st	2nd	3rd	Win & Pl
NH Flat	2	0	0	0	
Career Total	**2**	**0**	**0**	**0**	

Going: Sf: 0-0 GS: 0-0 Gd: 0-2 GF: - Fm: 0-0
Distance: 2m/2m3: 0-2 2m4-2m7: 0-0 3m+: 0-0
Track: LH: 0-0 RH: 0-2 Tight: 0-0 Gall: 0-0
Aids: Bl: 0-0 Vi: 0-0 Tstrap: 0-0
Best Rating:

Silver Socks

112 **111**
5-y-o gr g Petong-Tasmim (Be My Guest (USA))
M W Easterby Mrs Angela K Geraghty

Placings:054-313143 **(3997)**
2001/02: 16^{3}G, 16^{1}S, 20^{3}S, 16^{1}G, 16^{4}S, 16^{3}S

	Starts	1st	2nd	3rd	Win & Pl
Hurdles	6	2	0	3	7787
Career Total	**9**	**2**	**0**	**3**	**8087**

110	1/02	Muss	2m	E Hdl	GD	£2730
111	12/01	Hayd	2m	E(0-105)HHdl	SFT	£3052

Total win prize-money £5782

Going: Sf: 1-4 GS: 0-0 Gd: 1-2 GF: - Fm: 0-0
Distance: 2m/2m3: 2-5 2m4-2m7: 0-1 3m+: 0-0
Track: LH: 1-5 RH: 1-1 **Tight: 1-1** Gall: 0-2
Aids: Bl: 2-5 Vi: 0-0 Tstrap: 0-0
Best Rating: 112 2/02 Newc 2m soft Hdl

Fitted with blinkers he scored on his second start over timber in soft ground and again in similarly modest company in January.

Silver Steel

115 (123h) **137**
7-y-o b g Shernazar-Yldizlar (Star Appeal)
C Roche Thomas Harty

Placings:*524/323*14-5F11F1U53 **(4233)**
2001/02: 20^{5}YS, 16^{F}Y, 24^{1}HY, 20^{1}Y, 24^{F}Y, 21^{1}YS, 21^{U}HY, 20^{5}HY, 32^{3}GS

	Starts	1st	2nd	3rd	Win & Pl
Hurdles	1	0	0	0	0
Chases	8	3	0	1	30431
Career Total	**17**	**4**	**2**	**3**	**39198**

137	1/02	Leop	2m5f	Ch	Y-S	£11963
137	12/01	Navn	2m4f	Ch	YLD	£7790
131	12/01	Thur	3m	Ch	HVY	£6677
120	12/00	Leop	2m2f	Hdl	SH	£5520

Total win prize-money £31950

Going: Sf: 1-3 GS: 0-1 Gd: 0-0 GF: - Fm: 0-0
Distance: 2m/2m3: 0-1 **2m4-2m7: 2-5** 3m+: 1-3
Track: LH: 2-6 RH: 1-1 Tight: 0-0 Gall: 0-1
Aids: Bl: 0-0 Vi: 0-0 Tstrap: 0-0
Best Rating: 137 1/02 Leop 2m5f yld-sft Ch

He ran well in novice chases in 2001/02 including the National Hunt Chase, winning three from two and a half to three miles, showing a preference for soft ground.

Silver Strand (IRE)

83 **55**
7-y-o b m Waajib-Jendeal (Troy)
Mrs D Thomas Mrs D Thomas

Placings:0UP0/0P050 **(4654)**
2001/02: 17^{0}GS, 22^{P}G, 16^{0}G, 17^{5}G, 17^{0}GS

	Starts	1st	2nd	3rd	Win & Pl
Hurdles	5	0	0	0	0
Career Total	**9**	**0**	**0**	**0**	**0**

Going: Sf: 0-0 GS: 0-2 Gd: 0-3 GF: - Fm: 0-0
Distance: 2m/2m3: 0-4 2m4-2m7: 0-1 3m+: 0-0
Track: LH: 0-3 RH: 0-2 Tight: 0-3 Gall: 0-0
Aids: Bl: 0-0 Vi: 0-0 Tstrap: 0-1
Best Rating: 55 7/01 NAbb 2m1f good Hdl

Silver Streak (IRE)

105 **142**
8-y-o gr g Roselier (FR)-Vulcash (IRE) (Callernish)
J T Gifford Mrs Timothy Pilkington

Placings:*2/422013/33P5*-52411P2 **(4825)**
2001/02: 19^{5}G, 20^{2}GS, 22^{4}GS, 25^{1}G, 25^{1}G, 24^{P}GS, 25^{2}G

	Starts	1st	2nd	3rd	Win & Pl
Chases	7	2	2	0	21033
Career Total	**18**	**3**	**5**	**3**	**32808**

142	12/01	Chel	3m1f110y	B Ch	GD	£12018
130	11/01	Weth	3m1f	D Ch	GD	£4069
128	3/00	Sand	2m4f110y	D Hdl	GD	£4426

Total win prize-money £20515

Going: Sf: 0-0 GS: 0-3 Gd: 2-4 GF: - Fm: 0-0
Distance: 2m/2m3: 0-0 2m4-2m7: 0-3 **3m+: 2-4**
Track: LH: 2-5 RH: 0-0 Tight: 0-2 **Gall: 1-3**
Aids: Bl: 0-0 Vi: 0-0 Tstrap: 0-0
Best Rating: 142 12/01 Chel 3m1f110y good Ch

A winner over hurdles, but struggled in better company over fences until hitting form late in 2001. Stays three miles plus and best on good ground.

Silver Top (FR)

7-y-o b g Sheyrann-Mary De L'Orne (FR) (Son Of Silver)
Miss Venetia Williams Sir Robert Ogden

Placings:1422111151/2150P/PP **(3792)**
2001/02: 25^{P}GS, 25^{P}S

	Starts	1st	2nd	3rd	Win & Pl
Hurdles	1	0	0	0	0
Chases	1	0	0	0	0
Career Total	**17**	**7**	**3**	**0**	**250651**

	6/99	Autl	2m3f110y	Hdl	VS	£26911
	5/99	Autl	2m4f110y	Ch	VS	£43057
	11/98	Autl	2m1f110y	Hdl	VS	£35353
	11/98	Autl	2m2f	Hdl	HVY	£60606
	10/98	Engh	2m1f	Ch	HLD	£20202
	10/98	Autl	2m1f110y	Ch	HLD	£12121
	5/98	Autl	1m7f	Hdl	SFT	£12121

Total win prize-money £210372

Going: Sf: 0-1 GS: 0-1 Gd: 0-0 GF: - Fm: 0-0
Distance: 2m/2m3: 0-0 2m4-2m7: 0-0 3m+: 0-2
Track: LH: 0-0 RH: 0-1 Tight: 0-0 Gall: 0-0
Aids: Bl: 0-1 Vi: 0-0 Tstrap: 0-1
Best Rating: 126 4/00 Asct 2m3f110y soft Ch

Silverdale Lad

(44h)
11-y-o b g Presidium-Its My Turn (Palm Track)
Miss Kate Milligan R A W Racing

Placings:*5/200/23/331225/41433/0P0/***6UP**0-P **(0224)**
2001/02: 16^{P}GF

	Starts	1st	2nd	3rd	Win & Pl
Hurdles	1	0	0	0	
Career Total	**25**	**2**	**4**	**5**	**10199**

100	5/98	MRas	2m3f110y	D(0-120)HHdl	G-F	£3088
91	6/97	MRas	2m1f110y	E Hdl	GD	£2495

Total win prize-money £5583

Going: Sf: 0-0 GS: 0-0 Gd: 0-0 GF: - Fm: 0-1
Distance: 2m/2m3: 0-1 2m4-2m7: 0-0 3m+: 0-0
Track: LH: 0-1 RH: 0-0 Tight: 0-0 Gall: 0-0
Aids: Bl: 0-0 Vi: 0-0 Tstrap: 0-0
Best Rating: 100 8/98 Prth 2m4f110y gd-fm Hdl

Silverdalesureshot

10-y-o b g Wace (USA)-Upshot (Marcus Superbus)
Mrs W D Sykes Mrs P Evans

Placings:1/34122/3152U-1P **(0426)**
2001/02: 25^{1}G, 26^{P}G

	Starts	1st	2nd	3rd	Win & Pl
Chases	2	1	0	0	2100
Career Total	**10**	**4**	**0**	**2**	**9097**

138	5/01	Hrfd	3m1f110y	H Ch	GD	£2100
129	5/00	Hrfd	3m1f110y	H Ch	GD	£2257
118	3/00	Bang	3m110y	H Ch	SFT	£1554
122	4/99	Bang	3m110y	H Ch	G-S	£1450

Total win prize-money £7363

Going: Sf: 0-0 GS: 0-0 Gd: 1-2 GF: - Fm: 0-0
Distance: 2m/2m3: 0-0 2m4-2m7: 0-0 **3m+: 1-2**
Track: LH: 0-0 **RH: 1-1** Tight: 0-0 Gall: 0-0
Aids: Bl: 0-0 Vi: 0-0 Tstrap: 0-0
Best Rating: 138 5/01 Hrfd 3m1f110y good Ch

Silvertown

105 **105**
7-y-o b g Danehill (USA)-Docklands (USA) (Theatrical)
L Lungo R J Gilbert & Sw Transport (Swindon) Ltd

Placings:5106P **(4434)**
2001/02: 16^{5}GF, 16^{1}GF, 16^{0}GS, 17^{6}HY, 20^{P}HY

	Starts	1st	2nd	3rd	Win & Pl
Hurdles	5	1	0	0	2968
Career Total	**5**	**1**	**0**	**0**	**2968**

105	5/01	Newc	2m	E Hdl	G-F	£2968

Total win prize-money £2968

Going: Sf: 0-2 GS: 0-1 Gd: 0-0 GF: - Fm: 1-2
Distance: 2m/2m3: 1-4 2m4-2m7: 0-1 3m+: 0-0
Track: LH: 1-3 RH: 0-2 Tight: 0-1 **Gall: 1-2**
Aids: Bl: 0-0 Vi: 0-0 Tstrap: 0-0
Best Rating: 105 5/01 Newc 2m gd-fm Hdl

He was an enigma on the Flat and even his talented trainer is finding it hard to get any consistency from him over hurdles. Suited by two miles and fast ground.

Silverwyche

65 **16**
8-y-o gr m Arzanni-Vonnage (Levanter)
A King Roger Allsop

Placings: *0/0* **(0580)**
2001/02: 22^{0}GF

	Starts	1st	2nd	3rd	Win & Pl
Hurdles	1	0	0	0	
Career Total	**2**	**0**	**0**	**0**	

Going: Sf: 0-0 GS: 0-0 Gd: 0-0 GF: - Fm: 0-1
Distance: 2m/2m3: 0-0 2m4-2m7: 0-1 3m+: 0-0
Track: LH: 0-1 RH: 0-0 Tight: 0-1 Gall: 0-0
Aids: Bl: 0-0 Vi: 0-0 Tstrap: 0-0
Best Rating: 71 12/99 Wwck 2m soft NHF

Simber Hill (IRE)

110 131+

8-y-o ch g Phardante (FR)-Princess Wager (Pollerton)
A King J E Brown

Placings: *105*/25213/**3F33354** **(4600)**
2001/02: 25^{3}S, 26^{F}G, 26^{3}G, 24^{3}GS, 25^{3}G, 25^{5}S, 24^{4}GF

	Starts	1st	2nd	3rd	Win & Pl
Chases	7	0	0	4	2850
Career Total	**15**	**2**	**2**	**5**	**10131**

108	3/00	Newb	3m110y	D Hdl	G-F	£3770
108	12/98	Bang	2m1f	H NHF	G-S	£1266

Total win prize-money £5036

Going: Sf: 0-2 GS: 0-1 Gd: 0-3 GF: - Fm: 0-1
Distance: 2m/2m3: 0-0 2m4-2m7: 0-0 3m+: 0-7
Track: LH: 0-2 RH: 0-4 Tight: 0-1 Gall: 0-1
Aids: Bl: 0-0 Vi: 0-0 Tstrap: 0-0
Best Rating: 108 12/01 Hntg 3m gd-sft Ch

Lightly-raced bumper and hurdle winner, he stays three miles and acts on most types of ground, but appreciates fast. Has won both his starts in easy fashion in handicap chases since joining Philip Hobbs.

Simlet

108 121

7-y-o b g Forzando-Besito (Wassl)
E W Tuer E Tuer

Placings: 0P3603/62102F5442124/F1430-5131 **(1469)**
2001/02: 21^{5}GF, 20^{1}G, 21^{3}GF, 24^{1}G

	Starts	1st	2nd	3rd	Win & Pl
Hurdles	4	2	0	1	7712
Career Total	**28**	**5**	**4**	**4**	**22816**

121	9/01	Prth	3m110y	D(0-125)HHdl	GD	£4036
112	8/01	Prth	2m4f110y	E(0-115)HHdl	GD	£3386
111	5/00	Prth	2m4f110y	F(0-110)HHdl	G-S	£3591
99	3/00	Muss	2m	D(0-120)HHdl	G-F	£3526
97	6/99	Sthl	2m	E Hdl	G-F	£2410

Total win prize-money £16952

Going: Sf: 0-0 GS: 0-0 Gd: 2-2 GF: - Fm: 0-2
Distance: 2m/2m3: 0-0 2m4-2m7: 1-3 3m+: 1-1
Track: LH: 0-2 **RH: 2-2** Tight: 0-2 Gall: 0-0
Aids: Bl: 0-0 Vi: 0-0 **Tstrap: 2-3**
Best Rating: 121 9/01 Prth 3m110y good Hdl

Fair staying hurdler, suited by any ground. Goes very well at Perth.

Simons Castle (IRE)

95(84h) (54h)97

9-y-o b g Scenic-Miss Toot (Ardross)
J D Frost (R G Frost 13/2) Ides Of March Racing

Placings: *13*/202123/13630/**3U0P/542623** **(4505)**
2001/02: 16^{5}GF, 16^{4}GF, 21^{2}S, 21^{6}HY, 16^{2}S, 21^{3}G

	Starts	1st	2nd	3rd	Win & Pl
Chases	6	0	2	1	2439
Career Total	**23**	**3**	**5**	**6**	**21664**

133	10/98	Towc	2m	C(0-135)HHdl	G-S	£4096
124	2/98	Ling	2m110y	F Hdl	G-S	£2262
113	1/97	Punc	2m	NHF	YLD	£3051

Total win prize-money £9410

Going: Sf: 0-3 GS: 0-0 Gd: 0-1 GF: - Fm: 0-2
Distance: 2m/2m3: 0-3 2m4-2m7: 0-3 3m+: 0-0
Track: LH: 0-5 RH: 0-1 Tight: 0-5 Gall: 0-0
Aids: Bl: 0-0 Vi: 0-0 Tstrap: 0-0
Best Rating: 133 10/98 Towc 2m gd-sft Hdl

Modest performer, has failed to win since 1998.

Simoski

5-y-o b g Petoski-Miss Simone (Ile De Bourbon (USA))
N A Twiston-Davies Jamtr Racing Club

Placings: *0-0* **(0240)**
2001/02: 16^{0}GF

	Starts	1st	2nd	3rd	Win & Pl
NH Flat	1	0	0	0	
Career Total	**2**	**0**	**0**	**0**	

Going: Sf: 0-0 GS: 0-0 Gd: 0-0 GF: - Fm: 0-1
Distance: 2m/2m3: 0-1 2m4-2m7: 0-0 3m+: 0-0
Track: LH: 0-1 RH: 0-0 Tight: 0-1 Gall: 0-0
Aids: Bl: 0-0 Vi: 0-0 Tstrap: 0-0
Best Rating:

Simply Da Best (IRE)

84f 100f

4-y-o b g Lake Coniston (IRE)-Sakala (NZ) (Gold And Ivory (USA))
S Magnier Marcus Reeder And J G Rafferty

Placings: *1* **(4242)**
2001/02: 16^{1}GF

	Starts	1st	2nd	3rd	Win & Pl
NH Flat	1	1	0	0	1590
Career Total	**1**	**1**	**0**	**0**	**1590**

100	3/02	Hntg	2m110y	H NHF	G-F	£1590

Total win prize-money £1590

Going: Sf: 0-0 GS: 0-0 Gd: 0-0 GF: - Fm: 1-1
Distance: **2m/2m3: 1-1** 2m4-2m7: 0-0 3m+: 0-0
Track: LH: 0-0 **RH: 1-1** Tight: 0-0 **Gall: 1-1**
Aids: Bl: 0-0 Vi: 0-0 Tstrap: 0-0
Best Rating: 100 3/02 Hntg 2m110y gd-fm NHF

Sprint-bred. Landed an old fashioned gamble on his debut at Huntingdon in March.

Simply Dashing (IRE)

11-y-o br g Simply Great (FR)-Qurrat Al Ain (Wolver Hollow)
T D Easterby Steve Hammond

Placings: *2/3*21111115/**11F111F2/116462/322P26/24 3P/2PP-30** **(0584)**
2001/02: 25^{3}G, 28^{0}GF

	Starts	1st	2nd	3rd	Win & Pl
Chases	2	0	0	1	290
Career Total	**39**	**13**	**9**	**4**	**186390**

169	11/97	Asct	2m3f110y	A HCh	G-S	£25840
160	11/97	Weth	2m4f110y	B HCh	G-F	£7335
150	1/97	Hayd	2m4f	B Ch	G-F	£11715
150	12/96	Asct	2m3f110y	A Ch	G-F	£12320
148	12/96	Weth	2m4f110y	D Ch	G-S	£4107
136	11/96	MRas	2m4f	D Ch	GD	£3977
99	10/96	MRas	2m4f	D Ch	GD	£3968
134	2/96	Wwck	2m4f110y	C Hdl	GD	£7880
129	1/96	Weth	2m4f110y	D Hdl	G-S	£3057
129	12/95	Hayd	2m	D Hdl	GD	£3243
114	12/95	Sand	2m110y	B HHdl	GD	£7360
101	11/95	Aint	2m4f	B HHdl	G-F	£5389
94	10/95	Weth	2m	D Hdl	GD	£2966

Total win prize-money £99159

Going: Sf: 0-0 GS: 0-0 Gd: 0-1 GF: - Fm: 0-1
Distance: 2m/2m3: 0-0 2m4-2m7: 0-0 3m+: 0-2
Track: LH: 0-2 RH: 0-0 Tight: 0-1 Gall: 0-0
Aids: Bl: 0-2 Vi: 0-0 Tstrap: 0-0
Best Rating: 175 1/99 Hayd 3m soft Ch

Simply Gifted

115(113c) (147c)147

7-y-o b g Simply Great (FR)-Souveniers (Relko)
T D Easterby Steve Hammond

Placings: 1F21104/**331315333-P403** **(2452)**
2001/02: 20^{P}G, 16^{4}G, 16^{0}G, 16^{3}GS

	Starts	1st	2nd	3rd	Win & Pl
Hurdles	3	0	0	1	4670
Chases	1	0	0	0	0
Career Total	**20**	**5**	**1**	**7**	**46159**

147	1/01	Hayd	2m	C Ch	SFT	£7150
134	11/00	Leic	2m	E Ch	G-S	£3022
147	2/99	Hayd	2m	C HHdl	SFT	£5173
140	12/98	Weth	2m	D Hdl	SFT	£3008
118	10/98	Weth	2m	D Hdl	GD	£3037

Total win prize-money £21392

Going: Sf: 0-0 GS: 0-1 Gd: 0-3 GF: - Fm: 0-0
Distance: 2m/2m3: 0-3 2m4-2m7: 0-1 3m+: 0-0
Track: LH: 0-4 RH: 0-0 Tight: 0-0 Gall: 0-1
Aids: Bl: 0-2 Vi: 0-0 Tstrap: 0-0
Best Rating: 147 12/01 Newc 2m gd-sft Hdl

Decent hurdler/chaser. He has won twice over fences, including at Haydock in January 2001. Has run well since, although he has found getting his head in front a problem. Acts well with cut in the ground. Has won in blinkers.

Simply Silver Lady

7-y-o ch m Push On-Pentwd Mundy (Vital Season)
C Grant Girsonfield Stud Racing

Placings: *0*PP **(4875)**
2001/02: 17^{0}S, 16^{P}GF, 24^{P}G

	Starts	1st	2nd	3rd	Win & Pl
NH Flat	1	0	0	0	0
Hurdles	2	0	0	0	0
Career Total	**3**	**0**	**0**	**0**	

Going: Sf: 0-1 GS: 0-0 Gd: 0-1 GF: - Fm: 0-1
Distance: 2m/2m3: 0-2 2m4-2m7: 0-0 3m+: 0-1
Track: LH: 0-0 RH: 0-2 Tight: 0-0 Gall: 0-0
Aids: Bl: 0-0 Vi: 0-0 Tstrap: 0-0
Best Rating: 2 11/01 Carl 2m1f soft NHF

Simply Supreme (IRE)

103f 118f

5-y-o b g Supreme Leader-Some Gift (Avocat)

Mrs S J Smith Trevor Hemmings

Placings: *130* **(4679)**
2001/02: 17^{1}GS, 16^{3}S, 17^{0}G

	Starts	1st	2nd	3rd	Win & Pl
NH Flat	3	1	0	1	2081
Career Total	**3**	**1**	**0**	**1**	**2081**

111	12/01	Bang	2m1f	H NHF	G-S	£1746

Total win prize-money £1747

Going: Sf: 0-1 GS: 1-1 Gd: 0-1 GF: - Fm: 0-0
Distance: **2m/2m3: 1-3** 2m4-2m7: 0-0 3m+: 0-0
Track: **LH: 1-2** RH: 0-0 **Tight: 1-1** Gall: 0-0
Aids: Bl: 0-0 Vi: 0-0 Tstrap: 0-0
Best Rating: 118 1/02 Hayd 2m soft NHF

A brother to winning Irish three-mile hurdler Mega Deal.Easy bumper winner on racecourse debut on soft ground. Not disgraced under penalty next time out.

Simply The One (IRE)

93 **80**
5-y-o ch g Simply Great (FR)-Lady Mearlane (Giolla Mear)
Mrs H Dalton A J Brazier

Placings:45 **(4025)**
2001/02: 19^{4}GS, 16^{5}S

	Starts	1st	2nd	3rd	Win & Pl
Hurdles	2	0	0	0	353
Career Total	**2**	**0**	**0**	**0**	**353**

Going: Sf: 0-1 GS: 0-1 Gd: 0-0 GF: - Fm: 0-0
Distance: 2m/2m3: 0-2 2m4-2m7: 0-0 3m+: 0-0
Track: LH: 0-1 RH: 0-1 Tight: 0-0 Gall: 0-2
Aids: Bl: 0-0 Vi: 0-0 Tstrap: 0-0
Best Rating: 80 12/01 Newb 2m3f gd-sft Hdl

Sing Solo (IRE)

102(95h) (76h)**116**
7-y-o ch g Be My Native (USA)-Caesonia (Buckskin (FR))
P J Hobbs T A Curran

Placings:*5240*/3P0-**B1FP0** **(3335)**
2001/02: 19^{B}S, 19^{1}G, 19^{F}G, 19^{P}GS, 20^{0}G

	Starts	1st	2nd	3rd	Win & Pl
Chases	5	1	0	0	5398
Career Total	**12**	**1**	**1**	**1**	**6616**

116	11/01	Tntn	2m3f	E(0-105)HCh	GD	£5398

Total win prize-money £5398

Going: Sf: 0-1 GS: 0-1 Gd: 1-3 GF: - Fm: 0-0
Distance: **2m/2m3: 1-4** 2m4-2m7: 0-1 3m+: 0-0
Track: LH: 0-0 **RH: 1-5 Tight: 1-3** Gall: 0-0
Aids: Bl: 0-0 Vi: 0-0 Tstrap: 0-0
Best Rating: 116 11/01 Tntn 2m3f good Ch

He justified market support next time with a convincing win over two miles three furlongs at Taunton in November 2001.

Singing Sand

104 **115**
12-y-o b g Orchestra-Noss Head (New Brig)
P Monteith Hamilton House Limited

Placings:*06*/036203/033F1122/23P3P4/0/52F33222/0 3531U6P4-030121F32 **(1930)**

2001/02: 16^{0}GF, 17^{3}G, 16^{0}GF, 17^{1}G, 17^{2}G, 16^{1}GF, 16^{F}G, 16^{3}GS, 17^{2}G

	Starts	1st	2nd	3rd	Win & Pl
Chases	9	2	2	2	10331
Career Total	**49**	**5**	**10**	**12**	**32994**

115	9/01	Uttx	2m	F(0-100)HCh	G-F	£2933
110	7/01	MRas	2m1f110y	F(0-110)HCh	GD	£3607
111	10/00	Kels	2m1f	E(0-115)HCh	SFT	£3250
126	3/97	Ayr	2m	E Ch	SFT	£3119
98	2/97	Muss	2m	E(0-100)HCh	G-F	£2976

Total win prize-money £15886

Going: Sf: 0-0 GS: 0-1 Gd: 1-5 GF: - Fm: 1-3
Distance: **2m/2m3: 2-9** 2m4-2m7: 0-0 3m+: 0-0
Track: LH: 1-4 RH: 1-5 **Tight: 1-4** Gall: 0-0
Aids: Bl: 0-0 Vi: 0-0 Tstrap: 0-0
Best Rating: 126 4/97 Ayr 2m good Ch

He is an effective sort in modest handicap chases over two miles in the north, but is no world-beater and is not too easy to predict.

Singing Scally

70(86h) (50h)**40**
11-y-o gr m Scallywag-Singing Kettle (True Song)
W Clay Patrick Chesters

Placings:*000/00PP0/406U5P/00* **(1097)**
2001/02: 20^{0}G, 20^{0}GF

	Starts	1st	2nd	3rd	Win & Pl
Hurdles	1	0	0	0	0
Chases	1	0	0	0	0
Career Total	**16**	**0**	**0**	**0**	**0**

Going: Sf: 0-0 GS: 0-0 Gd: 0-1 GF: - Fm: 0-1
Distance: 2m/2m3: 0-0 2m4-2m7: 0-2 3m+: 0-0
Track: LH: 0-1 RH: 0-1 Tight: 0-1 Gall: 0-0
Aids: Bl: 0-0 Vi: 0-0 Tstrap: 0-0
Best Rating: 71 7/99 Worc 2m gd-fm Ch

Single Currency

(86h) (47h)
6-y-o b g Barathea (IRE)-Kithanga (IRE) (Darshaan)
P Butler Christopher W Wilson

Placings:2P-00F **(4508)**
2001/02: 17^{0}S, 22^{0}S, 17^{F}G

	Starts	1st	2nd	3rd	Win & Pl
Hurdles	2	0	0	0	0
Chases	1	0	0	0	0
Career Total	**5**	**0**	**1**	**0**	**651**

Going: Sf: 0-2 GS: 0-0 Gd: 0-1 GF: - Fm: 0-0
Distance: 2m/2m3: 0-2 2m4-2m7: 0-1 3m+: 0-0
Track: LH: 0-2 RH: 0-1 Tight: 0-3 Gall: 0-0
Aids: Bl: 0-0 Vi: 0-0 Tstrap: 0-2
Best Rating: 76 11/00 Plum 2m heavy Hdl

Single Sourcing (IRE)

109 **111**
11-y-o b g Good Thyne (USA)-Lady Albron (Royal Match)
A C Whillans G Harrow

Placings:*142*/P/P1PP3P/F304241/FPPP3-41146 **(3256)**
2001/02: 24^{4}S, 25^{1}G, 28^{1}GS, 25^{4}S, 30^{6}S

	Starts	1st	2nd	3rd	Win & Pl
Chases	5	2	0	0	10403
Career Total	**27**	**5**	**2**	**3**	**28610**

111	11/01	Kels	3m4f	F(0-110)HCh	G-S	£4212
108	10/01	Aint	3m1f	F(0-105)HCh	GD	£5232
108	1/99	Ayr	2m5f110y	C HCh	HVY	£10480
92	5/97	Uttx	2m	E Hdl	G-S	£2389
99	5/95	Uttx	2m	H NHF	G-F	£1805

Total win prize-money £24120

Going: Sf: 0-3 GS: 1-1 Gd: 1-1 GF: - Fm: 0-0
Distance: 2m/2m3: 0-0 2m4-2m7: 0-0 **3m+: 2-5**
Track: **LH: 2-4** RH: 0-1 **Tight: 2-2** Gall: 0-1
Aids: Bl: 0-0 Vi: 0-0 Tstrap: 0-0
Best Rating: 111 11/01 Kels 3m4f gd-sft Ch

Handicap chaser. Stays three and a half miles and acts on most types of ground.

Sipowitz

92 **56**
8-y-o b g Warrshan (USA)-Springs Welcome (Blakeney)
J Mackie Trying To Buy Fun Partnership

Placings:U45P **(3553)**
2001/02: 23^{U}S, 21^{4}GS, 16^{5}G, 19^{P}S

	Starts	1st	2nd	3rd	Win & Pl
Hurdles	4	0	0	0	0
Career Total	**4**	**0**	**0**	**0**	**0**

Going: Sf: 0-2 GS: 0-1 Gd: 0-1 GF: - Fm: 0-0
Distance: 2m/2m3: 0-2 2m4-2m7: 0-2 3m+: 0-0
Track: LH: 0-2 RH: 0-2 Tight: 0-1 Gall: 0-1
Aids: Bl: 0-0 Vi: 0-0 Tstrap: 0-0
Best Rating: 56 12/01 Leic 2m good Hdl

Sir Alf

88 **95**
6-y-o ch g Alflora (IRE)-D'Egliere (FR) (Port Etienne (FR))
M Pitman Howard Spooner & Partners Ii

Placings:*P*-PP0 **(3696)**
2001/02: 17^{P}S, 16^{P}G, 16^{0}S

	Starts	1st	2nd	3rd	Win & Pl
Hurdles	3	0	0	0	
Career Total	**4**	**0**	**0**	**0**	

Going: Sf: 0-2 GS: 0-0 Gd: 0-1 GF: - Fm: 0-0
Distance: 2m/2m3: 0-3 2m4-2m7: 0-0 3m+: 0-0
Track: LH: 0-1 RH: 0-2 Tight: 0-0 Gall: 0-1
Aids: Bl: 0-0 Vi: 0-0 Tstrap: 0-1
Best Rating: 95 2/02 Newb 2m110y soft Hdl

Sir Bob (IRE)

107 **138**
10-y-o br g Aristocracy-Wilden (Will Somers)
K C Bailey Mrs Lucia Farmer

Placings:*02/4200/313112*/F342/2U5-124P4 **(4107)**
2001/02: 22^{1}S, 22^{2}HY, 24^{4}G, 26^{P}HY, 22^{4}S

	Starts	1st	2nd	3rd	Win & Pl
Chases	5	1	1	0	7991
Career Total	**24**	**4**	**6**	**3**	**22581**

138	11/01	Towc	2m6f	D Ch	SFT	£5304
128	3/99	Carl	3m110y	E Hdl	SFT	£2318
128	2/99	Carl	3m110y	E Hdl	HVY	£2472
108	11/98	Newc	3m	E Hdl	G-S	£2379

Total win prize-money £12473

Going: Sf: 1-4 GS: 0-0 Gd: 0-1 GF: - Fm: 0-0
Distance: 2m/2m3: 0-0 **2m4-2m7: 1-3** 3m+: 0-2

Track: LH: 0-1 **RH: 1-4** Tight: 0-0 Gall: 0-0
Aids: Bl: 0-0 Vi: 0-0 Tstrap: 0-0
Best Rating: 138 11/01 Towc 2m6f soft Ch

Stays well and likes soft ground. Landed a Towcester novices' chase in November 2001.

Sir Cador (IRE)

(91h) (67h)
7-y-o b g Waajib-Seaworthy (IRE) (Slip Anchor)
Miss M E Rowland Miss M E Rowland

Placings:00/336002/00-00006 (1143)
2001/02: 19^{0}GF, 21^{0}G, 17^{0}GF, 17^{0}GF, 16^{6}GF

	Starts	1st	2nd	3rd	Win & Pl
Hurdles	4	0	0	0	0
Chases	1	0	0	0	0
Career Total	**15**	**0**	**1**	**2**	**1053**

Going: Sf: 0-0 GS: 0-0 Gd: 0-1 GF: - Fm: 0-4
Distance: 2m/2m3: 0-3 2m4-2m7: 0-2 3m+: 0-0
Track: LH: 0-2 RH: 0-3 Tight: 0-5 Gall: 0-0
Aids: Bl: 0-2 Vi: 0-0 Tstrap: 0-0
Best Rating: 90 4/00 DRoy 2m gd-fm Hdl

Sir D'Orton (FR)

106(110h) (120h)133
6-y-o ch g Beyssac (FR)-Prime Target (FR) (Ti King (FR))
P F Nicholls Mrs J Stewart

Placings:332/23P4233-2112232 (3808)
2001/02: 18^{2}GF, 20^{1}S, 20^{1}GS, 20^{2}S, 21^{2}G, 22^{3}S, 26^{2}S

	Starts	1st	2nd	3rd	Win & Pl
Hurdles	3	0	2	1	6755
Chases	4	2	2	0	11605
Career Total	**17**	**2**	**7**	**6**	**22419**

129	11/01	Plum	2m4f	D(0-120)HCh	G-S	£5392
130	10/01	Plum	2m4f	D(0-120)HCh	SFT	£4111

Total win prize-money £9503

Going: Sf: 1-4 GS: 1-1 Gd: 0-1 GF: - Fm: 0-1
Distance: 2m/2m3: 0-1 **2m4-2m7: 2-5** 3m+: 0-1
Track: **LH: 2-3** RH: 0-2 **Tight: 2-5** Gall: 0-0
Aids: Bl: 0-1 Vi: 0-0 Tstrap: 0-0
Best Rating: 133 2/02 Font 3m2f110y soft Ch

He has done well since switching to fences. Handles soft ground and may prove best at three miles.

Sir Dante (IRE)

103(41h) 128
11-y-o ch g Phardante (FR)-Tumvella (Tumble Wind (USA))
R Rowe Peter R Wilby

Placings:6401/0030P111/01F2215/1/41F1044/0055-62 (0362)
2001/02: 20^{6}GF, 24^{2}GF

	Starts	1st	2nd	3rd	Win & Pl
Chases	2	0	1	0	2280
Career Total	**33**	**9**	**3**	**1**	**70569**

148	1/00	Kemp	2m4f110y	B(0-145)HCh	GD	£14092
142	11/99	Kemp	2m4f110y	B(0-140)HCh	G-F	£8533
131	5/98	Worc	2m4f110y	E Ch	GD	£3406
126	3/98	Hntg	2m4f110y	E Ch	GD	£2929
119	12/97	Folk	2m5f	E Ch	GD	£4449
122	4/97	Chel	2m4f110y	A HHdl	G-F	£16200
106	3/97	Fknm	2m4f	F(0-100)HHdl	GD	£3755
88	3/97	Sand	2m110y	D(0-110)HHdl	GD	£2885
100	4/96	Folk	2m1f110y	H NHF	G-F	£1316

Total win prize-money £57568

Going: Sf: 0-0 GS: 0-0 Gd: 0-0 GF: - Fm: 0-2
Distance: 2m/2m3: 0-0 2m4-2m7: 0-1 3m+: 0-1
Track: LH: 0-2 RH: 0-0 Tight: 0-2 Gall: 0-0
Aids: Bl: 0-0 Vi: 0-0 Tstrap: 0-1
Best Rating: 148 3/00 Chel 2m4f110y good Ch

Fair chaser at around two and ahalf miles. Best on a sound surface.

Sir Edward Burrow (IRE)

100 93
4-y-o b g Distinctly North (USA)-Alalja (IRE) (Entitled)
W Storey (R F Fisher 20/10) W Storey

Placings:450 (3251)
2001/02: 16^{4}S, 16^{5}GS, 16^{0}S

	Starts	1st	2nd	3rd	Win & Pl
Hurdles	3	0	0	0	308
Career Total	**3**	**0**	**0**	**0**	**308**

Going: Sf: 0-2 GS: 0-1 Gd: 0-0 GF: - Fm: 0-0
Distance: 2m/2m3: 0-3 2m4-2m7: 0-0 3m+: 0-0
Track: LH: 0-3 RH: 0-0 Tight: 0-1 Gall: 0-1
Aids: Bl: 0-0 Vi: 0-0 Tstrap: 0-0
Best Rating: 93 12/01 Weth 2m gd-sft Hdl

Sir Frosty

118 132
9-y-o b g Arctic Lord-Snowy Autumn (Deep Run)
B J M Ryall J F Tucker

Placings:1341 (3341)
2001/02: 25^{1}S, 24^{3}S, 24^{4}S, 27^{1}S

	Starts	1st	2nd	3rd	Win & Pl
Chases	4	2	0	1	10998
Career Total	**4**	**2**	**0**	**1**	**10998**

132	1/02	Tntn	3m3f	C(0-130)HCh	SFT	£7020
132	10/01	Hrfd	3m1f110y	E Ch	SFT	£2941

Total win prize-money £9961

Going: Sf: 2-4 GS: 0-0 Gd: 0-0 GF: - Fm: 0-0
Distance: 2m/2m3: 0-0 2m4-2m7: 0-0 **3m+: 2-4**
Track: LH: 0-2 **RH: 2-2 Tight: 1-2** Gall: 0-0
Aids: Bl: 0-0 Vi: 0-0 **Tstrap: 2-4**
Best Rating: 132 1/02 Tntn 3m3f soft Ch

Stays three miles three furlongs and acts on soft ground, he likes to be raced prominently and often wears a tongue tie.

Sir Galeforce (IRE)

12-y-o br g Mister Lord (USA)-Forest Gale (Strong Gale)
R Curtis & Mrs Michael J Low

Placings:3/224252P0PP00/444P12/440-P (0723)
2001/02: 25^{P}F

	Starts	1st	2nd	3rd	Win & Pl
Chases	1	0	0	0	
Career Total	**23**	**1**	**5**	**1**	**9590**

96	3/00	Folk	2m5f	E(0-115)HCh	G-F	£3796

Total win prize-money £3797

Going: Sf: 0-0 GS: 0-0 Gd: 0-0 GF: - Fm: 0-1
Distance: 2m/2m3: 0-0 2m4-2m7: 0-0 3m+: 0-1
Track: LH: 0-0 RH: 0-1 Tight: 0-0 Gall: 0-0
Aids: Bl: 0-0 Vi: 0-0 Tstrap: 0-0
Best Rating: 104 9/98 Hntg 2m4f110y gd-fm Ch

Sir Hamelin (IRE)

89 80
5-y-o b g Hernando (FR)-Georgia Stephens (USA) (The Minstrel (CAN))
M C Pipe A S Helaissi

Placings:P-4000 (0976)
2001/02: 16^{4}F, 17^{0}G, 16^{0}GF, 16^{0}GF

	Starts	1st	2nd	3rd	Win & Pl
Hurdles	4	0	0	0	0
Career Total	**5**	**0**	**0**	**0**	**0**

Going: Sf: 0-0 GS: 0-0 Gd: 0-1 GF: - Fm: 0-3
Distance: 2m/2m3: 0-4 2m4-2m7: 0-0 3m+: 0-0
Track: LH: 0-3 RH: 0-1 Tight: 0-4 Gall: 0-0
Aids: Bl: 0-0 Vi: 0-3 Tstrap: 0-3
Best Rating: 80 5/01 Sthl 2m firm Hdl

Sir Harry Henbit

5-y-o ch g Henbit (USA)-Debbigene (Royal Vulcan)
J R Turner M R Clarke

Placings:0 (4900)
2001/02: 16^{0}G

	Starts	1st	2nd	3rd	Win & Pl
NH Flat	1	0	0	0	
Career Total	**1**	**0**	**0**	**0**	

Going: Sf: 0-0 GS: 0-0 Gd: 0-1 GF: - Fm: 0-0
Distance: 2m/2m3: 0-1 2m4-2m7: 0-0 3m+: 0-0
Track: LH: 0-0 RH: 0-1 Tight: 0-0 Gall: 0-0
Aids: Bl: 0-0 Vi: 0-0 Tstrap: 0-0
Best Rating:

Sir Henbue

76f 63f
6-y-o ch g Henbit (USA)-Owena Deep (Deep Run)
Mark Campion The Sir Henbue Partnership

Placings:P0 (0911)
2001/02: 16^{P}GF, 16^{0}G

	Starts	1st	2nd	3rd	Win & Pl
NH Flat	2	0	0	0	
Career Total	**2**	**0**	**0**	**0**	

Going: Sf: 0-0 GS: 0-0 Gd: 0-1 GF: - Fm: 0-1
Distance: 2m/2m3: 0-2 2m4-2m7: 0-0 3m+: 0-0
Track: LH: 0-2 RH: 0-0 Tight: 0-0 Gall: 0-0
Aids: Bl: 0-0 Vi: 0-0 Tstrap: 0-0
Best Rating: 63 7/01 Worc 2m good NHF

Sir Homo (IRE)

8-y-o b g Homo Sapien-Deise Lady (Le Bavard (FR))
Mrs A M Naughton (Paul Nolan 11/7) W M Wanless

Placings:00660P-F0P (4785)
2001/02: 17^{F}GF, 16^{0}G, 16^{P}F

	Starts	1st	2nd	3rd	Win & Pl
Hurdles	3	0	0	0	
Career Total	**9**	**0**	**0**	**0**	

Going: Sf: 0-0 GS: 0-0 Gd: 0-1 GF: - Fm: 0-2
Distance: 2m/2m3: 0-3 2m4-2m7: 0-0 3m+: 0-0
Track: LH: 0-1 RH: 0-0 Tight: 0-0 Gall: 0-1
Aids: Bl: 0-1 Vi: 0-0 Tstrap: 0-0
Best Rating: 98 6/00 Naas 2m3f yield NHF

Sir Humph

97 96

7-y-o b g Miners Lamp-New Game (New Member)
Simon Earle Mrs E W Pegna

Placings:0-54F0 **(4502)**
2001/02: 19^5G, 21^4S, 21^FGS, 22^0G

	Starts	1st	2nd	3rd	Win & Pl
Hurdles	4	0	0	0	0
Career Total	**5**	**0**	**0**	**0**	**0**

Going: Sf: 0-1 GS: 0-1 Gd: 0-2 GF: - Fm: 0-0
Distance: 2m/2m3: 0-1 2m4-2m7: 0-3 3m+: 0-0
Track: LH: 0-3 RH: 0-1 Tight: 0-1 Gall: 0-2
Aids: Bl: 0-0 Vi: 0-0 Tstrap: 0-0
Best Rating: 96 2/02 Ludl 2m5f soft Hdl

Some promise on his second start over hurdles. Seems best at short of two and a half miles.

Sir Lamb

104 98+

6-y-o gr g Rambo Dancer (CAN)-Caroline Lamb (Hotfoot)
Miss S E Hall C Platts

Placings:*130-0*2056 **(4194)**
2001/02: 17^0GF, 17^2G, 20^0GF, 20^5S, 17^6S

	Starts	1st	2nd	3rd	Win & Pl
NH Flat	1	0	0	0	0
Hurdles	4	0	1	0	951
Career Total	**8**	**1**	**1**	**1**	**3212**

109 10/00 Carl 2m1f H NHF G-S £2023
Total win prize-money £2023

Going: Sf: 0-2 GS: 0-0 Gd: 0-1 GF: - Fm: 0-2
Distance: 2m/2m3: 0-3 2m4-2m7: 0-2 3m+: 0-0
Track: LH: 0-3 RH: 0-2 Tight: 0-4 Gall: 0-1
Aids: Bl: 0-0 Vi: 0-0 Tstrap: 0-0
Best Rating: 109 10/00 Carl 2m1f gd-sft NHF

Made a successful debut in a bumper in October 2000, although he has failed to add to that since. Acts on good to soft ground and has looked less than keen on occasions.

Sir Lunchalot (IRE)

94 93

9-y-o b g Homo Sapien-Halpin (Yashgan)
M C Pipe P W A Westerman

Placings: 1/P0/P26/541P/60PP0 **(1041)**
2001/02: 19^6G, 21^0G, 22^PGF, 16^PGF, 22^0GF

	Starts	1st	2nd	3rd	Win & Pl
Hurdles	4	0	0	0	0
Chases	1	0	0	0	0
Career Total	**15**	**2**	**1**	**0**	**4544**

108 6/99 Worc 2m F(0-100)HCh G-F £2485
101 3/97 Towc 2m H NHF G-F £1413
Total win prize-money £3899

Going: Sf: 0-0 GS: 0-0 Gd: 0-2 GF: - Fm: 0-3
Distance: 2m/2m3: 0-2 2m4-2m7: 0-3 3m+: 0-0
Track: LH: 0-3 RH: 0-1 Tight: 0-2 Gall: 0-0
Aids: Bl: 0-0 Vi: 0-2 Tstrap: 0-0
Best Rating: 108 6/99 Worc 2m gd-fm Ch

Sir Lupin

107 112

7-y-o gr g Scallywag-Sentimental Me (Precipice Wood)
C J Mann The Whitcoombe Partnership

Placings:22 **(4762)**
2001/02: 19^2GS, 20^2GF

	Starts	1st	2nd	3rd	Win & Pl
Hurdles	2	0	2	0	7964
Career Total	**2**	**0**	**2**	**0**	**7964**

Going: Sf: 0-0 GS: 0-1 Gd: 0-0 GF: - Fm: 0-1
Distance: 2m/2m3: 0-1 2m4-2m7: 0-1 3m+: 0-0
Track: LH: 0-1 RH: 0-1 Tight: 0-0 Gall: 0-1
Aids: Bl: 0-0 Vi: 0-0 Tstrap: 0-0
Best Rating: 112 1/02 Newb 2m3f gd-sft Hdl

Runner-up on hurdling debut at Newbury over two miles three furlongs on good to soft ground, and at Ascot on fast ground. Looks sure to win races and stay farther.

Sir Mouse

87 102

6-y-o gr g Phardante (FR)-Place Stephanie (IRE) (Hatim (USA))
R Rowe Capt A Pratt

Placings:2 **(2061)**
2001/02: 20^2GS

	Starts	1st	2nd	3rd	Win & Pl
Hurdles	1	0	1	0	682
Career Total	**1**	**0**	**1**	**0**	**682**

Going: Sf: 0-0 GS: 0-1 Gd: 0-0 GF: - Fm: 0-0
Distance: 2m/2m3: 0-0 2m4-2m7: 0-1 3m+: 0-0
Track: LH: 0-0 RH: 0-0 Tight: 0-1 Gall: 0-0
Aids: Bl: 0-0 Vi: 0-0 Tstrap: 0-0
Best Rating: 102 11/01 Font 2m4f gd-sft Hdl

He gave encouragement for the future when runner-up to easy winner Haafel at Fontwell on his debut over hurdles.

Sir Ninja (IRE)

76(86h) (94h)84

5-y-o b g Turtle Island (IRE)-The Poachers Lady (IRE) (Salmon Leap (USA))
G Brown (D J S Ffrench Davis 8/11) Hargood Limited

Placings:5003 **(4765)**
2001/02: 16^5GS, 17^0S, 16^0G, 16^3GF

	Starts	1st	2nd	3rd	Win & Pl
Hurdles	4	0	0	1	396
Career Total	**4**	**0**	**0**	**1**	**396**

Going: Sf: 0-1 GS: 0-1 Gd: 0-1 GF: - Fm: 0-1
Distance: 2m/2m3: 0-4 2m4-2m7: 0-0 3m+: 0-0
Track: LH: 0-3 RH: 0-0 Tight: 0-2 Gall: 0-0
Aids: Bl: 0-1 Vi: 0-0 Tstrap: 0-0
Best Rating: 94 4/02 Hexm 2m110y gd-fm Hdl

Useful ten-furlong handicapper on the Flat on his day. Has yet to show the same level of form over hurdles.

Sir Norman

90 78

7-y-o b g Arctic Lord-Moy Ran Lady (Black Minstrel)
R D E Woodhouse M A Sawyer

Placings:*0-000*P6PP **(4577)**
2001/02: 17^0GS, 16^0G, 20^0G, 16^PGS, 20^6G, 24^PS, 24^PG

	Starts	1st	2nd	3rd	Win & Pl
NH Flat	1	0	0	0	0
Hurdles	6	0	0	0	0
Career Total	**8**	**0**	**0**	**0**	**0**

Going: Sf: 0-1 GS: 0-2 Gd: 0-4 GF: - Fm: 0-0
Distance: 2m/2m3: 0-3 2m4-2m7: 0-2 3m+: 0-2
Track: LH: 0-7 RH: 0-0 Tight: 0-2 Gall: 0-3
Aids: Bl: 0-0 Vi: 0-0 Tstrap: 0-2
Best Rating: 78 12/01 Donc 2m4f good Hdl

Little show in bumpers, and over hurdles.

Sir Pelinore

64f 55f

7-y-o b g Caerleon (USA)-Soemba (General Assembly (USA))
Mrs A M Woodrow Mrs Ann Woodrow

Placings:*0* **(0064)**
2001/02: 17^0GS

	Starts	1st	2nd	3rd	Win & Pl
NH Flat	1	0	0	0	
Career Total	**1**	**0**	**0**	**0**	

Going: Sf: 0-0 GS: 0-1 Gd: 0-0 GF: - Fm: 0-0
Distance: 2m/2m3: 0-1 2m4-2m7: 0-0 3m+: 0-0
Track: LH: 0-0 RH: 0-0 Tight: 0-1 Gall: 0-0
Aids: Bl: 0-0 Vi: 0-0 Tstrap: 0-1
Best Rating: 55 5/01 Folk 2m1f110y gd-sft NHF

Sir Prize (IRE)

9-y-o b g Prince Rupert (FR)-Banasiya (Mill Reef (USA))
R Rowe C Cornwell

Placings:*300/60/0/*65363PP-P **(0103)**
2001/02: 26^PGF

	Starts	1st	2nd	3rd	Win & Pl
Chases	1	0	0	0	
Career Total	**14**	**0**	**0**	**3**	**960**

Going: Sf: 0-0 GS: 0-0 Gd: 0-0 GF: - Fm: 0-1
Distance: 2m/2m3: 0-0 2m4-2m7: 0-0 3m+: 0-1
Track: LH: 0-0 RH: 0-0 Tight: 0-1 Gall: 0-0
Aids: Bl: 0-1 Vi: 0-0 Tstrap: 0-1
Best Rating: 87 2/97 Kemp 2m good NHF

Sir Rembrandt (IRE)

106 113

6-y-o b g Mandalus-Sue's A Lady (Le Moss)
R H Alner A & D Enterprises (poole) Ltd

Placings:*32*021 **(4398)**
2001/02: 18^3GS, 17^2G, 16^0G, 19^2S, 24^1S

	Starts	1st	2nd	3rd	Win & Pl
NH Flat	3	0	1	1	890
Hurdles	2	1	1	0	6087
Career Total	**5**	**1**	**2**	**1**	**6977**

113 3/02 Newb 3m110y D Hdl SFT £4563
Total win prize-money £4563

Going: Sf: 1-2 GS: 0-1 Gd: 0-2 GF: - Fm: 0-0
Distance: 2m/2m3: 0-4 2m4-2m7: 0-0 **3m+: 1-1**
Track: **LH: 1-4** RH: 0-0 Tight: 0-1 **Gall: 1-3**
Aids: Bl: 0-0 Vi: 0-0 Tstrap: 0-0
Best Rating: 113 3/02 Newb 3m110y soft Hdl

Showed promise in bumpers and has since shown himself a good stayer over hurdles. Sure to make a fine chaser.

Sir Robbo (IRE)

103 **109**

8-y-o b g Glacial Storm (USA)-Polly's Slipper (Pollerton)
N A Twiston-Davies Melton Pets Direct Ltd

Placings:*U03/01*P1005546/**1-525FP** **(4328)**
2001/02: 17^{5}GS, 25^{2}G, 19^{5}S, 27^{F}G, 25^{P}S

	Starts	1st	2nd	3rd	Win & Pl
Chases	5	0	1	0	799
Career Total	**19**	**3**	**1**	**1**	**10597**

109	5/00	Hrfd	2m3f	D Ch	GD	£3900
96	10/99	Hrfd	2m1f	D Hdl	G-F	£2892
96	6/99	Hrfd	2m1f	D Hdl	GD	£2801

Total win prize-money £9593

Going: Sf: 0-2 GS: 0-1 Gd: 0-2 GF: - Fm: 0-0
Distance: 2m/2m3: 0-2 2m4-2m7: 0-0 3m+: 0-3
Track: LH: 0-1 RH: 0-4 Tight: 0-2 Gall: 0-0
Aids: Bl: 0-0 Vi: 0-0 Tstrap: 0-0
Best Rating: 109 11/01 Hrfd 3m1f110y good Ch

All his wins over hurdles and fences have come at Hereford. Stays three miles plus, likes fast ground.

Sir Ruscott (IRE)

103 **101**

8-y-o b g Mister Lord (USA)-Clash Moss (Le Moss)
J R Norton Mrs Y Ruscoe

Placings:0412505 **(4513)**
2001/02: 20^{0}G, 24^{4}S, 27^{1}S, 24^{2}S, 24^{5}S, 27^{0}HY, 24^{5}GS

	Starts	1st	2nd	3rd	Win & Pl
Hurdles	7	1	1	0	3035
Career Total	**7**	**1**	**1**	**0**	**3035**

101	11/01	Sedg	3m3f110y	E Hdl	SFT	£2338

Total win prize-money £2338

Going: Sf: 1-5 GS: 0-1 Gd: 0-1 GF: - Fm: 0-0
Distance: 2m/2m3: 0-0 2m4-2m7: 0-1 **3m+: 1-6**
Track: **LH: 1-5** RH: 0-2 **Tight: 1-2** Gall: 0-1
Aids: Bl: 0-0 **Vi: 1-6** Tstrap: 0-0
Best Rating: 101 12/01 Hexm 3m soft Hdl

Modest hurdler, stays very well and appreciates soft ground. Wears a visor.

Sir Storm (IRE)

110 **114**

6-y-o b g Ore-Yonder Bay (IRE) (Trimmingham)
G M Moore J R F (management Consultants) Ltd

Placings:*301*P2P **(4404)**
2001/02: 17^{3}GS, 17^{0}G, 17^{1}GS, 16^{P}S, 19^{2}S, 17^{P}S

	Starts	1st	2nd	3rd	Win & Pl
NH Flat	2	0	0	1	226
Hurdles	4	1	1	0	3788
Career Total	**6**	**1**	**1**	**1**	**4014**

114	11/01	Bang	2m1f	E Hdl	G-S	£2828

Total win prize-money £2828

Going: Sf: 0-3 GS: 1-2 Gd: 0-1 GF: - Fm: 0-0
Distance: **2m/2m3: 1-6** 2m4-2m7: 0-0 3m+: 0-0
Track: **LH: 1-5** RH: 0-1 **Tight: 1-5** Gall: 0-0
Aids: Bl: 0-0 Vi: 0-0 Tstrap: 0-0
Best Rating: 114 11/01 Bang 2m1f gd-sft Hdl

He made a winning debut over hurdles at Bangor in November 2001, but has not built on it. Has been known to break blood vessels.

Sir Talbot

105 **145**

8-y-o b g Ardross-Bermuda Lily (Dunbeath (USA))
J A B Old W E Sturt

Placings:12/15215/4F2/45FF5 **(4760)**
2001/02: 16^{4}GS, 21^{5}HY, 24^{F}GS, 24^{F}G, 24^{5}GF

	Starts	1st	2nd	3rd	Win & Pl
Hurdles	5	0	0	0	2270
Career Total	**15**	**3**	**3**	**0**	**47052**

152	3/99	Chel	2m1f	A HHdl	G-S	£29750
142	10/98	Chep	2m110y	C Hdl	G-S	£3740
109	1/98	Hntg	2m110y	E Hdl	G-S	£2080

Total win prize-money £35570

Going: Sf: 0-1 GS: 0-2 Gd: 0-1 GF: - Fm: 0-1
Distance: 2m/2m3: 0-1 2m4-2m7: 0-1 3m+: 0-3
Track: LH: 0-2 RH: 0-2 Tight: 0-0 Gall: 0-2
Aids: Bl: 0-0 Vi: 0-0 Tstrap: 0-0
Best Rating: 159 11/99 Chel 2m110y good Hdl

Alightly-raced, useful hurdler. In the past seemed best at around two miles with give in the ground, but was in the process of running a promising race over three miles when taking a tumble at Kempton in February and again at the Festival the following month.

Sir Toby (IRE)

102(94h) (86h)**110**

9-y-o bl g Strong Gale-Petite Deb (Cure The Blues (USA))
R Rowe Capt A Pratt

Placings:*0430/530*-3F2 **(2127)**
2001/02: 20^{3}G, 24^{F}G, 24^{2}G

	Starts	1st	2nd	3rd	Win & Pl
Chases	3	0	1	1	2228
Career Total	**10**	**0**	**1**	**3**	**3212**

Going: Sf: 0-0 GS: 0-0 Gd: 0-3 GF: - Fm: 0-0
Distance: 2m/2m3: 0-0 2m4-2m7: 0-1 3m+: 0-2
Track: LH: 0-1 RH: 0-2 Tight: 0-0 Gall: 0-2
Aids: Bl: 0-0 Vi: 0-0 Tstrap: 0-0
Best Rating: 110 11/01 Kemp 3m good Ch

A maiden over hurdles and fences, he showed potential in chases in 2001/02. Suited by good ground.

Sir Valentine (IRE)

110 **109**

8-y-o b g Be My Native (USA)-Tumvella (Tumble Wind (USA))
R Rowe Capt A Pratt

Placings:*0/0530P/121004/***0130-U13** **(4414)**
2001/02: 26^{U}HY, 26^{1}S, 28^{3}S

	Starts	1st	2nd	3rd	Win & Pl
Chases	3	1	0	1	6084
Career Total	**19**	**4**	**1**	**3**	**16383**

109	3/02	Font	3m2f110y	E(0-110)HCh	SFT	£3374
109	10/00	Plum	3m2f	D(0-110)HCh	SFT	£4060
96	12/99	Plum	3m1f110y	E(0-105)HHdl	GD	£2285
96	11/99	Plum	2m5f	F(0-100)HHdl	G-F	£2355

Total win prize-money £12074

Going: Sf: 1-3 GS: 0-0 Gd: 0-0 GF: - Fm: 0-0
Distance: 2m/2m3: 0-0 2m4-2m7: 0-0 **3m+: 1-3**
Track: LH: 0-0 RH: 0-0 **Tight: 1-1** Gall: 0-0
Aids: Bl: 0-0 Vi: 0-0 Tstrap: 0-0
Best Rating: 109 3/02 Font 3m4f soft Ch

Fair handicap chaser, stays well and likes soft ground. Goes well fresh.

Sir Walter (IRE)

108(105h) (105h)**90**

9-y-o b g The Bart (USA)-Glenbalda (Kambalda)
A G Hobbs (D Burchell 24/8) J Parfitt

Placings:*0000/0/044346F023/0304-*
PFF0200U64123613446134 **(4853)**
2001/02: 24^{P}GF, 16^{F}G, 21^{F}GF, 20^{0}GF, 16^{2}GF, 20^{0}G, 17^{0}G, 16^{U}GF, 22^{6}GF, 20^{4}GF, 17^{1}G, 16^{2}S, 16^{3}G, 16^{6}S, 16^{1}G, 16^{3}GS, 17^{4}HY, 17^{4}HY, 16^{6}GS, 16^{1}GS, 19^{3}G, 16^{4}G

	Starts	1st	2nd	3rd	Win & Pl
Hurdles	19	3	2	3	9970
Chases	3	0	0	0	0
Career Total	**41**	**3**	**3**	**6**	**11451**

105	3/02	Wwck	2m	F(0-100)HHdl	G-S	£2159
97	12/01	Ludl	2m	F Hdl	GD	£2383
91	10/01	MRas	2m1f110y	G(0-95)HHdl	GD	£1680

Total win prize-money £6224

Going: Sf: 0-4 GS: 1-3 Gd: 2-8 GF: - Fm: 0-7
Distance: **2m/2m3: 3-15** 2m4-2m7: 0-6 3m+: 0-1
Track: LH: 1-15 **RH: 2-6 Tight: 1-6** Gall: 0-3
Aids: Bl: 0-0 Vi: 0-0 **Tstrap: 2-7**
Best Rating: 105 3/02 Wwck 2m gd-sft Hdl

A hold-up hurdler, he took a seller and a claimer before making his mark in open handicap company at Warwick in March 2002. Suited by two miles and a sound surface, travels well in his races. Runner-up over fences in May 2002.

Sir William

(85h) (63h)

8-y-o ch g Karlinsky (USA)-Charmezzo (Remezzo)
R J Baker R G Westacott

Placings:0P **(0735)**
2001/02: 22^{0}GF, 21^{P}GS

	Starts	1st	2nd	3rd	Win & Pl
Hurdles	1	0	0	0	0
Chases	1	0	0	0	0
Career Total	**2**	**0**	**0**	**0**	

Going: Sf: 0-0 GS: 0-1 Gd: 0-0 GF: - Fm: 0-1
Distance: 2m/2m3: 0-0 2m4-2m7: 0-2 3m+: 0-0
Track: LH: 0-2 RH: 0-0 Tight: 0-2 Gall: 0-0
Aids: Bl: 0-0 Vi: 0-0 Tstrap: 0-2
Best Rating: 63 5/01 NAbb 2m6f gd-fm Hdl

Sir Williamwallace (IRE)

103 **89**

9-y-o br g Strong Gale-Kemchee (Kemal (FR))
J G M O'Shea Mrs Ruth Nelmes

Placings:0*0*560000/F133F0/14626633-4P0PPP **(4268)**
2001/02: 20^{4}GF, 22^{P}GF, 17^{0}G, 24^{P}GF, 19^{P}G, 16^{P}S

	Starts	1st	2nd	3rd	Win & Pl
Hurdles	2	0	0	0	0
Chases	4	0	0	0	265
Career Total	**28**	**2**	**1**	**4**	**9540**

87	5/00	Dpat	2m2f	(0-95)HCh	GD	£3174
85	7/99	Wxfd	2m	(0-95)HCh	FRM	£3683

Total win prize-money £6857

Going: Sf: 0-1 GS: 0-0 Gd: 0-2 GF: - Fm: 0-3
Distance: 2m/2m3: 0-2 2m4-2m7: 0-3 3m+: 0-1

Track: LH: 0-4 RH: 0-2 Tight: 0-4 Gall: 0-0
Aids: Bl: 0-0 Vi: 0-1 Tstrap: 0-1
Best Rating: 94 9/00 Dpat 2m2f good Ch

Modest ex-Irish chaser who is more effective on a sound surface, has a tendency to be pulled up.

Sire De Brumetz (FR)

7-y-o b g Nashamaa-La Beaumont (FR) (Hellios (USA))
N J Pewter N J Pewter

Placings:P (0228)
2001/02: 20PGF

	Starts	1st	2nd	3rd	Win & Pl
Chases	1	0	0	0	
Career Total	**1**	**0**	**0**	**0**	

Going: Sf: 0-0 GS: 0-0 Gd: 0-0 GF: - Fm: 0-1
Distance: 2m/2m3: 0-0 2m4-2m7: 0-1 3m+: 0-0
Track: LH: 0-0 RH: 0-1 Tight: 0-0 Gall: 0-1
Aids: Bl: 0-0 Vi: 0-0 Tstrap: 0-0
Best Rating:

Siren Song (IRE)

82 35
11-y-o b g Warning-Nazwa (Tarboosh (USA))
T A K Cuthbert Mrs Joyce Cuthbert

Placings:11/23/221150656/435F24/50-0 (2766)
2001/02: 190G

	Starts	1st	2nd	3rd	Win & Pl
Hurdles	1	0	0	0	
Career Total	**22**	**4**	**4**	**2**	**17263**

124	12/98	Ling	2m110y	C(0-130)HHdl	SFT	£3841
111	11/98	Worc	2m	E Hdl	HVY	£2302
	8/95	Gway	2m	NHF	G-F	£4069
	7/95	Gowr	2m	NHF	YLD	£2712

Total win prize-money £12927

Going: Sf: 0-0 GS: 0-0 Gd: 0-1 GF: - Fm: 0-0
Distance: 2m/2m3: 0-1 2m4-2m7: 0-0 3m+: 0-0
Track: LH: 0-1 RH: 0-0 Tight: 0-1 Gall: 0-0
Aids: Bl: 0-0 Vi: 0-0 Tstrap: 0-0
Best Rating: 124 12/98 Ling 2m110y soft Hdl

Sireric (IRE)

101 110
12-y-o b g Asir-Twice Regal (Royal Prerogative)
R Johnson C H P Bell

Placings:0321/000/03/316213/F4U0P0/4221P2-33243 (4437)
2001/02: 243S, 293S, 302S, 244S, 243HY

	Starts	1st	2nd	3rd	Win & Pl
Chases	5	0	1	3	3335
Career Total	**32**	**4**	**6**	**7**	**26125**

107	1/01	Newc	3m	E(0-115)HCh	HVY	£3391
110	3/98	Hexm	4m	D(0-120)HCh	SFT	£4272
110	12/97	Sedg	3m3f	E(0-110)HCh	SFT	£3738
105	4/95	Hexm	3m	E Hdl	HVY	£2578

Total win prize-money £13982

Going: Sf: 0-5 GS: 0-0 Gd: 0-0 GF: - Fm: 0-0
Distance: 2m/2m3: 0-0 2m4-2m7: 0-0 3m+: 0-5
Track: LH: 0-4 RH: 0-1 Tight: 0-0 Gall: 0-3
Aids: Bl: 0-0 Vi: 0-0 Tstrap: 0-0
Best Rating: 110 1/02 Newc 3m soft Ch

Fair handicap chaser. Stays three miles six and acts on a soft surface. Goes well at Newcastle.

Sirinndi (IRE)

(76c) (50c)72
8-y-o b g Shahrastani (USA)-Sinntara (IRE) (Lashkari)
Miss K Marks Nick Shutts

Placings:0/630/0/54100654-00 (1629)
2001/02: 170GS, 210GF

	Starts	1st	2nd	3rd	Win & Pl
Hurdles	1	0	0	0	0
Chases	1	0	0	0	0
Career Total	**15**	**1**	**0**	**1**	**1937**

90	12/00	Chep	2m4f	G Hdl	HVY	£1526

Total win prize-money £1526

Going: Sf: 0-0 GS: 0-1 Gd: 0-0 GF: - Fm: 0-1
Distance: 2m/2m3: 0-1 2m4-2m7: 0-1 3m+: 0-0
Track: LH: 0-1 RH: 0-0 Tight: 0-1 Gall: 0-0
Aids: Bl: 0-0 Vi: 0-0 Tstrap: 0-0
Best Rating: 90 12/00 Chep 2m4f heavy Hdl

Sirmoor Rifles (IRE)

88(90c) 115
8-y-o b g Be My Native (USA)-Bale Out (Shackleton)
P F Nicholls T G A Chappell

Placings:00/212F411-5 (0250)
2001/02: 175GF

	Starts	1st	2nd	3rd	Win & Pl
Hurdles	1	0	0	0	0
Career Total	**10**	**3**	**2**	**0**	**9720**

115	4/01	Winc	2m	F(0-105)HHdl	SFT	£2765
115	4/01	Winc	2m	F(0-110)HHdl	SFT	£2380
110	10/00	Winc	2m	F(0-100)HHdl	G-S	£2527

Total win prize-money £7672

Going: Sf: 0-0 GS: 0-0 Gd: 0-0 GF: - Fm: 0-1
Distance: 2m/2m3: 0-1 2m4-2m7: 0-0 3m+: 0-0
Track: LH: 0-1 RH: 0-0 Tight: 0-1 Gall: 0-0
Aids: Bl: 0-0 Vi: 0-0 Tstrap: 0-0
Best Rating: 115 4/01 Winc 2m soft Hdl

Sirrah Aris (IRE)

101(106c) (104c)84
11-y-o b g Buckskin (FR)-Sirrah Madam (Tug Of War)
P Bowen (R Curtis 11/7) R Owen

Placings:2/P61/P-P462P65240P (2338)
2001/02: 21PGF, 224GF, 196F, 232G, 23PG, 226GF, 275GF, 262G, 244GS, 240GF, 24PGF

	Starts	1st	2nd	3rd	Win & Pl
Hurdles	4	0	1	0	584
Chases	7	0	1	0	1465
Career Total	**16**	**1**	**3**	**0**	**5423**

97	10/99	Ludl	3m	F(0-110)HCh	G-F	£2762

Total win prize-money £2762

Going: Sf: 0-0 GS: 0-1 Gd: 0-3 GF: - Fm: 0-7
Distance: 2m/2m3: 0-1 2m4-2m7: 0-3 3m+: 0-7
Track: LH: 0-4 RH: 0-5 Tight: 0-5 Gall: 0-1
Aids: Bl: 0-7 Vi: 0-0 Tstrap: 0-0
Best Rating: 104 5/01 Font 2m6f gd-fm Ch

Sissinghurst Flyer (IRE)

101 109
10-y-o gr m Celio Rufo-Jeanarie (Reformed Character)
R Dickin Brian Clifford

Placings:0F/P003F6F3222/U1U11PF13F/2/P461125-F6F2 (0776)
2001/02: 24FF, 206GS, 22FGF, 202GF

	Starts	1st	2nd	3rd	Win & Pl
Chases	4	0	1	0	1266
Career Total	**35**	**6**	**6**	**3**	**30115**

107	3/01	MRas	2m4f	F(0-110)HCh	G-S	£3542
109	2/01	Leic	2m4f110y	F(0-105)HCh	SFT	£3360
105	4/99	Weth	2m	E(0-115)HCh	G-F	£3353
100	12/98	Winc	2m	D Ch	G-S	£3988
95	11/98	Ludl	2m	E(0-105)HCh	GD	£2840
91	10/98	Hrfd	2m	F(0-105)HCh	G-F	£3503

Total win prize-money £20586

Going: Sf: 0-0 GS: 0-1 Gd: 0-0 GF: - Fm: 0-3
Distance: 2m/2m3: 0-0 2m4-2m7: 0-3 3m+: 0-1
Track: LH: 0-3 RH: 0-1 Tight: 0-3 Gall: 0-0
Aids: Bl: 0-0 Vi: 0-0 Tstrap: 0-0
Best Rating: 109 6/01 Worc 2m4f110y gd-fm Ch

Sissinghurst Star (IRE)

72(90h) (74h)97
7-y-o b g Moscow Society (USA)-Raplist (Arapaho)
R Dickin Brian Clifford

Placings:0/60P0-60305 (3739)
2001/02: 166G, 200G, 163S, 160S, 165S

	Starts	1st	2nd	3rd	Win & Pl
Hurdles	4	0	0	1	462
Chases	1	0	0	0	0
Career Total	**10**	**0**	**0**	**1**	**462**

Going: Sf: 0-3 GS: 0-0 Gd: 0-2 GF: - Fm: 0-0
Distance: 2m/2m3: 0-4 2m4-2m7: 0-1 3m+: 0-0
Track: LH: 0-3 RH: 0-2 Tight: 0-2 Gall: 0-0
Aids: Bl: 0-2 Vi: 0-0 Tstrap: 0-0
Best Rating: 80 3/00 Chep 2m110y good NHF

Sister Charlotte

7-y-o ch m Gildoran-Sharlinda (Deep Run)
J C Tuck M J Howard

Placings:00P (4485)
2001/02: 160G, 170GF, 19PG

	Starts	1st	2nd	3rd	Win & Pl
NH Flat	2	0	0	0	0
Hurdles	1	0	0	0	0
Career Total	**3**	**0**	**0**	**0**	

Going: Sf: 0-0 GS: 0-0 Gd: 0-2 GF: - Fm: 0-1
Distance: 2m/2m3: 0-3 2m4-2m7: 0-0 3m+: 0-0
Track: LH: 0-1 RH: 0-2 Tight: 0-0 Gall: 0-0
Aids: Bl: 0-0 Vi: 0-0 Tstrap: 0-0
Best Rating: 68 11/01 Extr 2m1f gd-fm NHF

Sister Superior (IRE)

103 101
7-y-o b m Supreme Leader-Nicat (Wolver Hollow)

S Gollings The High Five Partnership

Placings:0*2263500516*-35P (4636)
2001/02: 22^{3}HY, 25^{5}S, 24^{P}GF

	Starts	1st	2nd	3rd	Win & Pl
Hurdles	3	0	0	1	1616
Career Total	**14**	**1**	**2**	**2**	**21239**

109	3/01	Newb	2m5f	HHdl	HVY	£17400

Total win prize-money £17400

Going: Sf: 0-2 GS: 0-0 Gd: 0-0 GF: - Fm: 0-1
Distance: 2m/2m3: 0-0 2m4-2m7: 0-1 3m+: 0-2
Track: LH: 0-1 RH: 0-1 Tight: 0-0 Gall: 0-0
Aids: Bl: 0-0 Vi: 0-0 Tstrap: 0-0
Best Rating: 111 6/00 Uttx 2m good NHF

In the frame in bumpers and on her hurdles debut, she caused a bit of a surprise when scoring in the valuable mares' final at Newbury in March 2001 on heavy ground. Lightly raced since, she has stamina in abundance.

Sister Valenthyne (IRE)

78f **72f**

5-y-o ch m Good Thyne (USA)-Coteri Run (Deep Run)
S Gollings Mrs M A Hall

Placings:0P (4289)
2001/02: 16^{0}S, 17^{P}GS

	Starts	1st	2nd	3rd	Win & Pl
NH Flat	2	0	0	0	
Career Total	**2**	**0**	**0**	**0**	

Going: Sf: 0-1 GS: 0-1 Gd: 0-0 GF: - Fm: 0-0
Distance: 2m/2m3: 0-2 2m4-2m7: 0-0 3m+: 0-0
Track: LH: 0-1 RH: 0-1 Tight: 0-1 Gall: 0-1
Aids: Bl: 0-0 Vi: 0-0 Tstrap: 0-0
Best Rating: 72 2/02 Donc 2m110y soft NHF

Six Clerks (IRE)

9-y-o b g Shadeed (USA)-Skidmore Girl (USA) (Vaguely Noble)
Mrs S M Odell W J Odell

Placings:0421330/5232**5263**/6P5P46/30**F3FP**/055305 35 (4763)
2001/02: 24^{0}GS, 24^{5}GF, 16^{5}G, 21^{3}GF, 19^{0}S, 24^{5}GS, 22^{3}G, 24^{5}GF

	Starts	1st	2nd	3rd	Win & Pl
Chases	8	0	0	2	777
Career Total	**35**	**1**	**4**	**8**	**8100**

87	2/97	Catt	2m	F Hdl	GD	£2029

Total win prize-money £2029

Going: Sf: 0-1 GS: 0-2 Gd: 0-2 GF: - Fm: 0-3
Distance: 2m/2m3: 0-1 2m4-2m7: 0-3 3m+: 0-4
Track: LH: 0-5 RH: 0-2 Tight: 0-4 Gall: 0-1
Aids: Bl: 0-0 Vi: 0-1 Tstrap: 0-0
Best Rating: 104 3/00 Donc 2m3f110y gd-sft Ch

Modest hunter chaser on a long losing run.

Sixmile River (IRE)

9-y-o b m Zaffaran (USA)-Flickers Image Vii (Damsire Unregistered)
S J Gilmore H Barrons

Placings:0PP (0556)
2001/02: 20^{0}GF, 20^{P}GF, 24^{P}GF

	Starts	1st	2nd	3rd	Win & Pl
Chases	3	0	0	0	
Career Total	**3**	**0**	**0**	**0**	

Going: Sf: 0-0 GS: 0-0 Gd: 0-0 GF: - Fm: 0-3
Distance: 2m/2m3: 0-0 2m4-2m7: 0-2 3m+: 0-1
Track: LH: 0-1 RH: 0-2 Tight: 0-1 Gall: 0-2
Aids: Bl: 0-0 Vi: 0-0 Tstrap: 0-0
Best Rating:

Sixties Melody

8-y-o b g Merdon Melody-Balidilemma (Balidar)
Mrs K Bewley (Mrs M Reveley 14/4) Mrs D H Clyde

Placings:0-P (4859)
2001/02: 25^{P}G

	Starts	1st	2nd	3rd	Win & Pl
Chases	1	0	0	0	
Career Total	**2**	**0**	**0**	**0**	

Going: Sf: 0-0 GS: 0-0 Gd: 0-1 GF: - Fm: 0-0
Distance: 2m/2m3: 0-0 2m4-2m7: 0-0 3m+: 0-1
Track: LH: 0-1 RH: 0-0 Tight: 0-0 Gall: 0-0
Aids: Bl: 0-0 Vi: 0-0 Tstrap: 0-0
Best Rating:

Ski Pass

100 **95**

7-y-o b g Petoski-Cover Your Money (Precipice Wood)
M C Pipe David Jenks

Placings:046-200P6 (4730)
2001/02: 24^{2}G, 17^{0}GS, 24^{0}GS, 20^{P}GS, 20^{6}GF

	Starts	1st	2nd	3rd	Win & Pl
Hurdles	5	0	1	0	1504
Career Total	**8**	**0**	**1**	**0**	**1504**

Going: Sf: 0-0 GS: 0-3 Gd: 0-1 GF: - Fm: 0-1
Distance: 2m/2m3: 0-1 2m4-2m7: 0-2 3m+: 0-2
Track: LH: 0-3 RH: 0-2 Tight: 0-1 Gall: 0-1
Aids: Bl: 0-0 Vi: 0-0 Tstrap: 0-0
Best Rating: 95 11/01 Asct 3m good Hdl

Modest hurdler, he improved for the step up to three miles, and should be capable of scoring at one of the lesser tracks.

Skiddaw Gale

80(81h) (56h)**69+**

8-y-o b g Strong Gale-Whimbrel (Dara Monarch)
M A Barnes (P Monteith 27/8) M Barnes

Placings:0/56560-4P04P0P6 (4868)
2001/02: 20^{4}F, 20^{P}GF, 21^{0}GF, 21^{4}GF, 24^{P}G, 17^{0}G, 17^{P}S, 20^{6}GF

	Starts	1st	2nd	3rd	Win & Pl
Hurdles	7	0	0	0	0
Chases	1	0	0	0	0
Career Total	**14**	**0**	**0**	**0**	**0**

Going: Sf: 0-1 GS: 0-0 Gd: 0-2 GF: - Fm: 0-5
Distance: 2m/2m3: 0-2 2m4-2m7: 0-5 3m+: 0-1
Track: LH: 0-5 RH: 0-3 Tight: 0-4 Gall: 0-0
Aids: Bl: 0-3 Vi: 0-0 Tstrap: 0-2
Best Rating: 74 6/00 Hexm 2m gd-fm Hdl

Of little account.

Skiddaw Rose (IRE)

86 **53**

6-y-o gr m Terimon-Whimbrel (Dara Monarch)
M A Barnes John Wills

Placings:06-00PP (2917)
2001/02: 16^{0}G, 16^{0}GS, 16^{P}S, 20^{P}G

	Starts	1st	2nd	3rd	Win & Pl
NH Flat	2	0	0	0	0
Hurdles	2	0	0	0	0
Career Total	**6**	**0**	**0**	**0**	**0**

Going: Sf: 0-1 GS: 0-1 Gd: 0-2 GF: - Fm: 0-0
Distance: 2m/2m3: 0-3 2m4-2m7: 0-1 3m+: 0-0
Track: LH: 0-2 RH: 0-2 Tight: 0-1 Gall: 0-0
Aids: Bl: 0-0 Vi: 0-0 Tstrap: 0-0
Best Rating: 57 2/01 Muss 2m good NHF

Skiffle Man

107 **84**

6-y-o b g Alhijaz-Laundry Maid (Forzando)
A G Hobbs (B I Case 6/12) Miss Jayne Brace & Mr Gwyn Brace

Placings:050016/056-3601P (4733)
2001/02: 20^{3}S, 20^{6}HY, 19^{0}S, 22^{1}S, 24^{P}F

	Starts	1st	2nd	3rd	Win & Pl
Hurdles	5	1	0	1	2258
Career Total	**14**	**2**	**0**	**1**	**5027**

84	3/02	Font	2m6f110y	G(0-95)HHdl	SFT	£1991
78	3/00	Strf	2m3f	G Hdl	GD	£2769

Total win prize-money £4761

Going: Sf: 1-4 GS: 0-0 Gd: 0-0 GF: - Fm: 0-1
Distance: 2m/2m3: 0-0 **2m4-2m7: 1-4** 3m+: 0-1
Track: **LH: 1-2** RH: 0-3 **Tight: 1-3** Gall: 0-0
Aids: Bl: 0-0 Vi: 0-0 Tstrap: 0-0
Best Rating: 84 4/02 Extr 3m110y firm Hdl

Plating-class hurdler, stays two miles-six. Suited by good ground or softer.

Skillwise

109 **136**

10-y-o b g Buckley-Calametta (Oats)
T D Easterby Chris D Calvert

Placings:0/012252U51/3/02142P5/412264U16-432P34100U (4839)
2001/02: 25^{4}G, 26^{3}S, 25^{2}G, 27^{P}S, 25^{3}GS, 24^{4}HY, 26^{1}GS, 32^{0}HY, 21^{0}G, 33^{U}G

	Starts	1st	2nd	3rd	Win & Pl
Chases	10	1	1	2	24740
Career Total	**37**	**6**	**8**	**3**	**58513**

136	3/02	Donc	3m2f	B(0-145)HCh	G-S	£20640
133	4/01	Hayd	2m6f	B(0-140)HCh	SFT	£10093
124	11/00	Newc	3m	D(0-125)HCh	SFT	£3809
130	11/99	Weth	3m1f	D Ch	GD	£3925
114	4/98	Ayr	2m4f	C HHdl	GD	£4289
107	10/97	Sedg	2m1f	H NHF	GD	£1035

Total win prize-money £43792

Going: Sf: 0-4 GS: 1-2 Gd: 0-4 GF: - Fm: 0-0
Distance: 2m/2m3: 0-0 2m4-2m7: 0-1 **3m+: 1-9**
Track: **LH: 1-9** RH: 0-1 Tight: 0-4 **Gall: 1-1**
Aids: Bl: 0-0 Vi: 0-0 Tstrap: 0-0
Best Rating: 136 3/02 Donc 3m2f gd-sft Ch

Decent handicap chaser. Seemingly effective on any ground, he stays beyond three miles.

Skimabit (IRE)

11-y-o b/br g Henbit (USA)-Mauras Cross (Deep Run)
R H P Williams (P W Hiatt 24/3) Robert A Jones

Placings:00P/PPU0/P0FPUP6/U (4727)
2001/02: 24^{U}GF

	Starts	1st	2nd	3rd	Win & Pl
Chases	1	0	0	0	
Career Total	**15**	**0**	**0**	**0**	**0**

Going: Sf: 0-0 GS: 0-0 Gd: 0-0 GF: - Fm: 0-1
Distance: 2m/2m3: 0-0 2m4-2m7: 0-0 3m+: 0-1
Track: LH: 0-1 RH: 0-0 Tight: 0-0 Gall: 0-0
Aids: Bl: 0-0 Vi: 0-0 Tstrap: 0-1
Best Rating: 105 11/98 Ludl 3m good Ch

Skiora

81f 82f
5-y-o br m Petoski-Coral Delight (Idiots Delight)
A J Wilson The Up And Running Partnership

Placings:0 (4377)
2001/02: 16^{0}S

	Starts	1st	2nd	3rd	Win & Pl
NH Flat	1	0	0	0	
Career Total	**1**	**0**	**0**	**0**	

Going: Sf: 0-1 GS: 0-0 Gd: 0-0 GF: - Fm: 0-0
Distance: 2m/2m3: 0-1 2m4-2m7: 0-0 3m+: 0-0
Track: LH: 0-0 RH: 0-1 Tight: 0-0 Gall: 0-0
Aids: Bl: 0-0 Vi: 0-0 Tstrap: 0-0
Best Rating: mfy

Has shown ability in bumpers on varying ground.

Skip'N'Time

101 128
12-y-o b g Idiots Delight-Skipton Bridge (Harwell)
R H Buckler M S Rose

Placings:3112/20/20P4-022P (0848)
2001/02: 25^{0}GF, 26^{2}G, 28^{2}GF, 32^{P}GF

	Starts	1st	2nd	3rd	Win & Pl
Chases	4	0	2	0	8040
Career Total	**14**	**2**	**5**	**1**	**15869**

121	4/99	Asct	3m110y	H Ch	G-F	£2762
115	3/99	Winc	3m1f110y	H Ch	G-S	£1469

Total win prize-money £4231

Going: Sf: 0-0 GS: 0-0 Gd: 0-1 GF: - Fm: 0-3
Distance: 2m/2m3: 0-0 2m4-2m7: 0-0 3m+: 0-4
Track: LH: 0-1 RH: 0-1 Tight: 0-1 Gall: 0-0
Aids: Bl: 0-0 Vi: 0-0 Tstrap: 0-0
Best Rating: 128 6/01 Strf 3m4f gd-fm Ch

Useful hunter chaser, chasing Blanville home in a valuable hunter chase at Cheltenham in May, and runner-up in the Intrum Justicia Cup. A thorough stayer, he is best on decent ground.

Skipmantoo (IRE)

65f 50f
7-y-o ch g Pips Pride-Sports Post Lady (IRE) (M Double M (USA))
Miss C Dyson Miss C Dyson

Placings:U0 (0377)
2001/02: 17^{U}GS, 16^{0}GF

	Starts	1st	2nd	3rd	Win & Pl
NH Flat	2	0	0	0	
Career Total	**2**	**0**	**0**	**0**	

Going: Sf: 0-0 GS: 0-1 Gd: 0-0 GF: - Fm: 0-1
Distance: 2m/2m3: 0-2 2m4-2m7: 0-0 3m+: 0-0
Track: LH: 0-0 RH: 0-1 Tight: 0-1 Gall: 0-1
Aids: Bl: 0-0 Vi: 0-0 Tstrap: 0-0
Best Rating: 50 5/01 Hntg 2m110y gd-fm NHF

Skram

108 (33h)126
9-y-o b g Rambo Dancer (CAN)-Skarberg (FR) (Noir Et Or)
R Dickin Mr W P Evans & Mrs D L Weaver

Placings:F14552P20/122236224412/16010P/P20034252245/11U21113245-250F51204 (4824)
2001/02: 17^{2}G, 20^{5}G, 16^{0}GF, 20^{F}GF, 20^{5}GF, 20^{1}G, 20^{2}G, 17^{0}G, 16^{4}G

	Starts	1st	2nd	3rd	Win & Pl
Hurdles	1	0	0	0	0
Chases	8	1	2	0	11084
Career Total	**59**	**11**	**16**	**3**	**63413**

123	7/01	Strf	2m4f	D(0-125)HCh	GD	£7280
125	9/00	Strf	2m4f	D(0-120)HCh	GD	£4017
125	8/00	Worc	2m4f110y	D Ch	G-F	£4147
127	7/00	Strf	2m1f110y	E Ch	G-F	£3103
122	6/00	Worc	2m4f110y	D(0-110)HCh	G-F	£4069
115	5/00	Wwck	2m	E Ch	G-F	£2948
101	2/99	Font	2m2f110y	E(0-115)HHdl	SFT	£7007
107	5/98	Hntg	2m5f110y	E(0-125)HHdl	G-F	£2931
107	4/98	Font	2m2f110y	E(0-110)HHdl	G-S	£2427
97	9/97	Font	2m2f110y	F(0-105)HHdl	GD	£2048
75	8/96	Font	2m2f110y	E Hdl	G-F	£2175

Total win prize-money £42475

Going: Sf: 0-0 GS: 0-0 Gd: 1-6 GF: - Fm: 0-3
Distance: 2m/2m3: 0-4 **2m4-2m7: 1-5** 3m+: 0-0
Track: **LH: 1-7** RH: 0-2 **Tight: 1-6** Gall: 0-1
Aids: Bl: 0-0 Vi: 0-0 Tstrap: 0-0
Best Rating: 127 9/00 MRas 2m6f110y gd-fm Ch

Fair handicap chaser from two-two and a half miles, he likes fast ground and shows his best form in the summer months.

Skyber Breeze

6-y-o gr/ro g Safawan-Shrood Biddy (Sharrood (USA))
P Bowen T W Raymond

Placings:060 (3157)
2001/02: 17^{0}G, 17^{6}GS, 17^{0}S

	Starts	1st	2nd	3rd	Win & Pl
NH Flat	2	0	0	0	0
Hurdles	1	0	0	0	0
Career Total	**3**	**0**	**0**	**0**	**0**

Going: Sf: 0-1 GS: 0-1 Gd: 0-1 GF: - Fm: 0-0
Distance: 2m/2m3: 0-3 2m4-2m7: 0-0 3m+: 0-0
Track: LH: 0-1 RH: 0-2 Tight: 0-2 Gall: 0-0
Aids: Bl: 0-0 Vi: 0-0 Tstrap: 0-0
Best Rating: 70 10/01 MRas 2m1f110y gd-sft NHF

Skycab (IRE)

108 137
10-y-o b g Montelimar (USA)-Sams Money (Pry)
J T Gifford P H Betts (holdings) Ltd

Placings:4/522411/4225/2162140115/P0P4P-51 (1665)
2001/02: 25^{5}GF, 20^{1}G

	Starts	1st	2nd	3rd	Win & Pl
Chases	2	1	0	0	6841
Career Total	**28**	**7**	**6**	**0**	**56253**

137	10/01	Sthl	2m4f110y	D(0-120)HCh	GD	£6841
145	4/00	Strf	2m4f	C(0-130)HCh	GD	£6500
145	4/00	Asct	2m3f110y	C(0-130)HCh	SFT	£13812
139	12/99	Hntg	2m4f110y	E Ch	G-S	£3613
137	11/99	Sand	2m	D Ch	GD	£4401
127	4/98	MRas	2m3f110y	D Hdl	SFT	£3315
127	4/98	Fknm	2m	E(0-100)HHdl	G-S	£3001

Total win prize-money £41485

Going: Sf: 0-0 GS: 0-0 Gd: 1-1 GF: - Fm: 0-1
Distance: 2m/2m3: 0-0 **2m4-2m7: 1-1** 3m+: 0-1
Track: **LH: 1-1** RH: 0-1 **Tight: 1-1** Gall: 0-0
Aids: Bl: 0-0 Vi: 0-0 Tstrap: 0-0
Best Rating: 145 4/00 Strf 2m4f good Ch

Useful two and a half-mile chaser. best on good ground or easier.

Skye Blue (IRE)

105 113
5-y-o b g Blues Traveller (IRE)-Hitopah (Bustino)
N J Henderson (D W P Arbuthnot 28/8) W H Ponsonby

Placings:23-1P450 (4403)
2001/02: 16^{1}S, 17^{P}HY, 22^{4}S, 20^{5}S, 19^{0}S

	Starts	1st	2nd	3rd	Win & Pl
Hurdles	5	1	0	0	3053
Career Total	**7**	**1**	**1**	**1**	**4042**

113	4/01	Plum	2m	F Hdl	SFT	£2646

Total win prize-money £2646

Going: Sf: 1-5 GS: 0-0 Gd: 0-0 GF: - Fm: 0-0
Distance: **2m/2m3: 1-3** 2m4-2m7: 0-2 3m+: 0-0
Track: **LH: 1-5** RH: 0-0 **Tight: 1-2** Gall: 0-3
Aids: Bl: 0-0 Vi: 0-0 Tstrap: 0-0
Best Rating: 113 4/01 Plum 2m soft Hdl

Won a claimer at Plumpton last year but has cut little ice since.

Skyers A Kite

86 49
7-y-o b m Deploy-Milady Jade (IRE) (Drumalis)
Ronald Thompson G A W Racing Partnership

Placings:630040/1-0 (0028)
2001/02: 16^{0}G

	Starts	1st	2nd	3rd	Win & Pl
Hurdles	1	0	0	0	
Career Total	**8**	**1**	**0**	**1**	**2321**

93	2/01	Catt	2m	F(0-95)HHdl	SFT	£2065

Total win prize-money £2065

Going: Sf: 0-0 GS: 0-0 Gd: 0-1 GF: - Fm: 0-0
Distance: 2m/2m3: 0-1 2m4-2m7: 0-0 3m+: 0-0
Track: LH: 0-0 RH: 0-1 Tight: 0-0 Gall: 0-1
Aids: Bl: 0-0 Vi: 0-0 Tstrap: 0-0
Best Rating: 93 2/01 Catt 2m soft Hdl

Skyjack

66 37
8-y-o b g Skyliner-Cottagers Lane (Farm Walk)
N M L Ewart N M L Ewart

Placings:000-0 (1746)
2001/02: 16^{0}GS

	Starts	1st	2nd	3rd	Win & Pl
Hurdles	1	0	0	0	
Career Total	**4**	**0**	**0**	**0**	

Going: Sf: 0-0 GS: 0-1 Gd: 0-1 GF: - Fm: 0-0
Distance: 2m/2m3: 0-1 2m4-2m7: 0-0 3m+: 0-0
Track: LH: 0-1 RH: 0-0 Tight: 0-1 Gall: 0-0
Aids: Bl: 0-0 Vi: 0-0 Tstrap: 0-0
Best Rating: **70** 12/00 Muss 2m good NHF

Skylander

79 **55**

6-y-o b g Thethingaboutitis (USA)-Mesembryanthemum (Warpath)
B J Llewellyn G I Isaac

Placings:*0* **(4639)**
2001/02: 16^{0}GF

	Starts	1st	2nd	3rd	Win & Pl
NH Flat	1	0	0	0	
Career Total	**1**	**0**	**0**	**0**	

Going: Sf: 0-0 GS: 0-0 Gd: 0-0 GF: - Fm: 0-1
Distance: 2m/2m3: 0-1 2m4-2m7: 0-0 3m+: 0-0
Track: LH: 0-0 RH: 0-1 Tight: 0-0 Gall: 0-0
Aids: Bl: 0-0 Vi: 0-0 Tstrap: 0-0
Best Rating: **59** 4/02 Asct 2m110y gd-fm NHF

Slaney Boy (IRE)

99 **102**

4-y-o b g Woods Of Windsor (USA)-Madam Slaney (Prince Tenderfoot (USA))
Ms Joanna Morgan Denis John O'Brien

Placings:06000 **(3890)**
2001/02: 16^{0}Y, 16^{6}YS, 16^{0}Y, 17^{0}S, 16^{0}HY

	Starts	1st	2nd	3rd	Win & Pl
Hurdles	5	0	0	0	
Career Total	**5**	**0**	**0**	**0**	

Going: Sf: 0-2 GS: 0-0 Gd: 0-0 GF: - Fm: 0-0
Distance: 2m/2m3: 0-5 2m4-2m7: 0-0 3m+: 0-0
Track: LH: 0-2 RH: 0-2 Tight: 0-1 Gall: 0-0
Aids: Bl: 0-0 Vi: 0-0 Tstrap: 0-0
Best Rating: **102** 11/01 Navn 2m yld-sft Hdl

Slaney Lass

75 **62**

8-y-o b m Arctic Lord-Deep Cut (Deep Run)
Miss K Marks Nick Shutts

Placings:*00*P/O5250-66F **(0841)**
2001/02: 23^{6}GF, 26^{6}F, 16^{F}G

	Starts	1st	2nd	3rd	Win & Pl
Hurdles	3	0	0	0	0
Career Total	**11**	**0**	**1**	**0**	**540**

Going: Sf: 0-0 GS: 0-0 Gd: 0-1 GF: - Fm: 0-2
Distance: 2m/2m3: 0-1 2m4-2m7: 0-0 3m+: 0-2
Track: LH: 0-2 RH: 0-1 Tight: 0-1 Gall: 0-0
Aids: Bl: 0-0 Vi: 0-0 Tstrap: 0-1
Best Rating: **77** 9/00 Strf 2m6f110y good Hdl

Slaneyside (IRE)

80 **43**

5-y-o ch g Project Manager-Erneside (Lomond (USA))
I Semple Gordon McDowall

Placings:0 **(0800)**
2001/02: 16^{0}GF

	Starts	1st	2nd	3rd	Win & Pl
Hurdles	1	0	0	0	
Career Total	**1**	**0**	**0**	**0**	

Going: Sf: 0-0 GS: 0-0 Gd: 0-0 GF: - Fm: 0-1
Distance: 2m/2m3: 0-1 2m4-2m7: 0-0 3m+: 0-0
Track: LH: 0-0 RH: 0-1 Tight: 0-0 Gall: 0-0
Aids: Bl: 0-0 Vi: 0-0 Tstrap: 0-0
Best Rating: **43** 6/01 Prth 2m110y gd-fm Hdl

Slasher Jack (IRE)

83(97h) (77h)**76**

11-y-o b g Alzao (USA)-Sherkraine (Shergar)
Mrs D Thomson The Boozers Brigade

Placings:24/1550/60510PP06P-6**50634P5** **(4899)**
2001/02: 16^{6}GF, 16^{5}G, 21^{0}GF, 16^{6}G, 16^{3}S, 16^{4}HY, 17^{P}S, 16^{5}G

	Starts	1st	2nd	3rd	Win & Pl
Hurdles	1	0	0	0	0
Chases	7	0	0	1	691
Career Total	**24**	**2**	**1**	**1**	**6614**

97	11/00	Kels	2m2f	F(0-90)HHdl	SFT	£2873
97	1/00	Muss	2m	E Hdl	GD	£2415

Total win prize-money £5288

Going: Sf: 0-3 GS: 0-0 Gd: 0-3 GF: - Fm: 0-2
Distance: 2m/2m3: 0-7 2m4-2m7: 0-1 3m+: 0-0
Track: LH: 0-3 RH: 0-5 Tight: 0-2 Gall: 0-0
Aids: Bl: 0-0 Vi: 0-0 Tstrap: 0-1
Best Rating: **97** 11/00 Kels 2m2f soft Hdl

He has ability, but also has a mind of his own.

Sledmere (IRE)

7-y-o ch g Shalford (IRE)-Jazirah (Main Reef)
George R Moscrop (Mrs E Moscrop 20/1) George R Moscrop

Placings:005PP-F **(3861)**
2001/02: 19^{F}S

	Starts	1st	2nd	3rd	Win & Pl
Chases	1	0	0	0	
Career Total	**6**	**0**	**0**	**0**	**0**

Going: Sf: 0-1 GS: 0-0 Gd: 0-0 GF: - Fm: 0-0
Distance: 2m/2m3: 0-0 2m4-2m7: 0-1 3m+: 0-0
Track: LH: 0-1 RH: 0-0 Tight: 0-0 Gall: 0-1
Aids: Bl: 0-0 Vi: 0-0 Tstrap: 0-1
Best Rating: **72** 7/00 Uttx 2m4f110y gd-fm Hdl

Sleeping Music (FR)

91 **76**

5-y-o b g Sleeping Car (FR)-Music Sobre (FR) (Crowned Music (USA))
J R Best Edward Charles Brooke

Placings:P504-23054 **(2591)**
2001/02: 17^{2}G, 17^{3}GS, 20^{0}GS, 17^{5}HY, 17^{4}S

	Starts	1st	2nd	3rd	Win & Pl
Hurdles	3	0	0	0	0
Chases	2	0	1	1	3395
Career Total	**9**	**0**	**1**	**1**	**4802**

Going: Sf: 0-2 GS: 0-2 Gd: 0-1 GF: - Fm: 0-0
Distance: 2m/2m3: 0-4 2m4-2m7: 0-1 3m+: 0-0
Track: LH: 0-0 RH: 0-2 Tight: 0-3 Gall: 0-0
Aids: Bl: 0-5 Vi: 0-0 Tstrap: 0-0
Best Rating:

Sleeping Night (FR)

118(108h) (146h)**173**

6-y-o b g Sleeping Car (FR)-Doll Night (FR) (Karkour (FR))
Mrs M Reveley David J Jackson

Placings:613141/3121213-2424 **(4648)**
2001/02: 25^{2}G, 20^{4}GS, 24^{2}GS, 25^{4}G

	Starts	1st	2nd	3rd	Win & Pl
Hurdles	1	0	1	0	5750
Chases	3	0	1	0	19750
Career Total	**17**	**6**	**4**	**3**	**196294**

11/00	Autl	2m4f110y	Ch	HVY	£28818
10/00	Autl	2m4f110y	Ch	VS	£28818
6/00	Autl	2m4f110y	Ch	VS	£28818
4/00	Autl	2m1f110y	Ch	HVY	£11527
2/00	Autl	2m1f110y	Hdl	VS	£10567
12/99	Pau	2m110y	Hdl	HVY	£6459

Total win prize-money £115007

Going: Sf: 0-0 GS: 0-2 Gd: 0-2 GF: - Fm: 0-0
Distance: 2m/2m3: 0-0 2m4-2m7: 0-1 3m+: 0-3
Track: LH: 0-2 RH: 0-2 Tight: 0-1 Gall: 0-1
Aids: Bl: 0-0 Vi: 0-0 Tstrap: 0-0
Best Rating: **173** 11/01 Weth 3m1f good Ch

Formerly trained in France, he specialised at Auteuil, winning four chases and two hurdle races there in 2000. Now with Mary Reveley, he ran a brilliant race on his British debut to chase home Sackville in the Charlie Hall at Wetherby in November 2001, but disappointed over a shorter trip next time. Returned to beat all except Baracouda over hurdles in February 2002 and well beaten at aintreestill looks a useful prospect but will need to jump better. A mudlark who stays three miles.

Sleepy River (IRE)

100 **114**

11-y-o ch g Over The River (FR)-Shreelane (Laurence O)
Miss Kate Milligan The Aunts

Placings:0103/005010/0050/1F14/36**P3606/11-15P34** **(4437)**
2001/02: 24^{1}G, 25^{5}G, 25^{P}GS, 28^{3}S, 24^{4}HY

	Starts	1st	2nd	3rd	Win & Pl
Chases	5	1	0	1	4692
Career Total	**32**	**7**	**0**	**4**	**24348**

114	11/01	Newc	3m	D(0-125)HCh	GD	£4075
106	11/00	Wwck	3m110y	E(0-105)HCh	HVY	£2886
106	10/00	Wwck	3m2f	F(0-105)HCh	SFT	£2467
109	11/98	Kels	2m6f110y	D(0-125)HHdl	HVY	£2749
114	10/98	Kels	2m6f110y	D(0-125)HHdl	SFT	£2871
111	3/97	Tipp	2m4f	(0-123)HHdl	G-Y	£4069
104	1/96	Tram	2m	Hdl	SFT	£2295

Total win prize-money £21414

Going: Sf: 0-2 GS: 0-1 Gd: 1-2 GF: - Fm: 0-0
Distance: 2m/2m3: 0-0 2m4-2m7: 0-0 **3m+: 1-5**
Track: **LH: 1-5** RH: 0-0 Tight: 0-2 **Gall: 1-2**
Aids: Bl: 0-0 Vi: 0-0 Tstrap: 0-0
Best Rating: **114** 11/01 Newc 3m good Ch

A fair staying chaser, he goes well at Warwick and likes cut in the ground.

Sleepytime Tim

33f **19f**

6-y-o b g Henbit (USA)-Cloncoose (IRE) (Remainder

Man)
J A Moore J A Moore

Placings:0 **(1753)**
2001/02: 17^{0}G

	Starts	1st	2nd	3rd	Win & Pl
NH Flat	1	0	0	0	
Career Total	**1**	**0**	**0**	**0**	

Going: Sf: 0-0 GS: 0-0 Gd: 0-1 GF: - Fm: 0-0
Distance: 2m/2m3: 0-1 2m4-2m7: 0-0 3m+: 0-0
Track: LH: 0-0 RH: 0-1 Tight: 0-1 Gall: 0-0
Aids: Bl: 0-0 Vi: 0-0 Tstrap: 0-0
Best Rating:

Sleeting

100(104h) (89h)79
9-y-o ch g Lycius (USA)-Pluvial (Habat)
J Gallagher Horses Away Racing Club

Placings:3505060/2F443604/133000/01403-62060306554 **(2654)**
2001/02: 17^{6}F, 18^{2}GF, 20^{0}GF, 16^{6}GF, 22^{0}G, 17^{3}GF, 17^{0}GF, 16^{6}G, 16^{5}GS, 16^{5}GF, 20^{4}G

	Starts	1st	2nd	3rd	Win & Pl
Hurdles	9	0	1	1	1002
Chases	2	0	0	0	326
Career Total	**37**	**2**	**2**	**6**	**7892**

90	11/00	Tntn	2m1f	G(0-90)HHdl	GD	£1599
98	9/99	Sedg	2m1f	E Hdl	GD	£2267

Total win prize-money £3868

Going: Sf: 0-0 GS: 0-1 Gd: 0-3 GF: - Fm: 0-7
Distance: 2m/2m3: 0-8 2m4-2m7: 0-3 3m+: 0-0
Track: LH: 0-6 RH: 0-5 Tight: 0-8 Gall: 0-0
Aids: Bl: 0-0 Vi: 0-1 Tstrap: 0-0
Best Rating: 98 10/99 Sedg 2m1f gd-fm Hdl

moderate hurdler/chaser, acts on well on good ground and is suited by around two miles.

Sleight Of Hand (IRE)

84(87h) (69h)72
9-y-o b g Hollow Hand-Marand (Prefairy)
J S King Alan Lee

Placings:60/3060/33/P5P-5P45 **(2654)**
2001/02: 21^{5}GF, 20^{P}S, 20^{4}GF, 20^{5}G

	Starts	1st	2nd	3rd	Win & Pl
Hurdles	2	0	0	0	0
Chases	2	0	0	0	313
Career Total	**15**	**0**	**0**	**3**	**1252**

Going: Sf: 0-1 GS: 0-0 Gd: 0-1 GF: - Fm: 0-2
Distance: 2m/2m3: 0-0 2m4-2m7: 0-4 3m+: 0-0
Track: LH: 0-0 RH: 0-4 Tight: 0-3 Gall: 0-0
Aids: Bl: 0-0 Vi: 0-0 Tstrap: 0-0
Best Rating: 92 10/99 Font 2m6f110y good Hdl

Sliabh Foy (IRE)

78 52
9-y-o b g Electric-Lily Gale (IRE) (Strong Gale)
D M Grissell F Marshall

Placings:0/000/U-0 **(0431)**
2001/02: 17^{0}GF

	Starts	1st	2nd	3rd	Win & Pl
Hurdles	1	0	0	0	
Career Total	**6**	**0**	**0**	**0**	

Going: Sf: 0-0 GS: 0-0 Gd: 0-0 GF: - Fm: 0-1
Distance: 2m/2m3: 0-1 2m4-2m7: 0-0 3m+: 0-0
Track: LH: 0-0 RH: 0-1 Tight: 0-1 Gall: 0-0
Aids: Bl: 0-0 Vi: 0-0 Tstrap: 0-0
Best Rating: 52 5/01 Folk 2m1f110y gd-fm Hdl

Slide On

69 67
12-y-o b g Seymour Hicks (FR)-Star Alliance (Big Morton)
W M Brisbourne R W Morris

Placings:6/1P/043P/142350/03P3440-0 **(0052)**
2001/02: 20^{0}G

	Starts	1st	2nd	3rd	Win & Pl
Hurdles	1	0	0	0	
Career Total	**21**	**2**	**1**	**4**	**5706**

99	12/99	Hrfd	2m1f	G Hdl	HVY	£2071
111	12/96	Hayd	2m	H NHF	G-S	£1292

Total win prize-money £3363

Going: Sf: 0-0 GS: 0-0 Gd: 0-1 GF: - Fm: 0-0
Distance: 2m/2m3: 0-0 2m4-2m7: 0-1 3m+: 0-0
Track: LH: 0-1 RH: 0-0 Tight: 0-1 Gall: 0-0
Aids: Bl: 0-0 Vi: 0-0 Tstrap: 0-0
Best Rating: 111 12/96 Hayd 2m gd-sft NHF

Sliema (IRE)

85 60
4-y-o b g Desert Style (IRE)-Ascoli (Skyliner)
O Sherwood John Marks

Placings:00 **(4873)**
2001/02: 17^{0}G, 16^{0}GF

	Starts	1st	2nd	3rd	Win & Pl
NH Flat	2	0	0	0	
Career Total	**2**	**0**	**0**	**0**	

Going: Sf: 0-0 GS: 0-0 Gd: 0-1 GF: - Fm: 0-1
Distance: 2m/2m3: 0-2 2m4-2m7: 0-0 3m+: 0-0
Track: LH: 0-2 RH: 0-0 Tight: 0-1 Gall: 0-0
Aids: Bl: 0-0 Vi: 0-0 Tstrap: 0-0
Best Rating: 85 4/02 Weth 2m gd-fm NHF

Sliema Creek

8-y-o gr g Beveled (USA)-Sea Farer Lake (Gairloch)
V Thompson V Thompson

Placings:U3221600160/0010300PB50P/P **(4920)**
2001/02: 21^{P}GF

	Starts	1st	2nd	3rd	Win & Pl
Chases	1	0	0	0	
Career Total	**24**	**3**	**2**	**2**	**9333**

81	10/98	Sedg	2m5f	E Ch	GD	£3176
94	3/98	Hntg	2m110y	G Hdl	SFT	£1870
94	10/97	Worc	2m	E Hdl	SFT	£2279

Total win prize-money £7326

Going: Sf: 0-0 GS: 0-0 Gd: 0-0 GF: - Fm: 0-1
Distance: 2m/2m3: 0-0 2m4-2m7: 0-1 3m+: 0-0
Track: LH: 0-1 RH: 0-0 Tight: 0-1 Gall: 0-0
Aids: Bl: 0-1 Vi: 0-0 Tstrap: 0-0
Best Rating: 94 3/98 Hntg 2m110y soft Hdl

Slim Prior

95 77

7-y-o gr g Norton Challenger-Hopeful Katie (Full Of Hope)
D W Whillans Chas N Whillans

Placings:P4422/2000426/0000-24340065 **(2920)**
2001/02: 16^{2}GF, 16^{4}GS, 20^{3}F, 16^{4}G, 16^{0}GS, 17^{0}G, 17^{6}GF, 20^{5}G

	Starts	1st	2nd	3rd	Win & Pl
Hurdles	8	0	1	1	942
Career Total	**24**	**0**	**5**	**1**	**4266**

Going: Sf: 0-0 GS: 0-2 Gd: 0-3 GF: - Fm: 0-3
Distance: 2m/2m3: 0-6 2m4-2m7: 0-2 3m+: 0-0
Track: LH: 0-5 RH: 0-2 Tight: 0-3 Gall: 0-0
Aids: Bl: 0-0 Vi: 0-0 Tstrap: 0-8
Best Rating: 92 1/00 Kels 2m110y good Hdl

Slip Away

94(91h) (39h)60
9-y-o gr g Jumbo Hirt (USA)-Au Pair (Runnymede)
Mrs M Haughan David Alan Harrison

Placings:40/5/2P **(1388)**
2001/02: 26^{2}G, 26^{P}GF

	Starts	1st	2nd	3rd	Win & Pl
Chases	2	0	1	0	1055
Career Total	**5**	**0**	**1**	**0**	**1055**

Going: Sf: 0-0 GS: 0-0 Gd: 0-1 GF: - Fm: 0-1
Distance: 2m/2m3: 0-0 2m4-2m7: 0-0 3m+: 0-2
Track: LH: 0-2 RH: 0-0 Tight: 0-1 Gall: 0-0
Aids: Bl: 0-0 Vi: 0-0 Tstrap: 0-0
Best Rating: 72 10/97 Carl 2m1f firm NHF

Slip Killick

5-y-o b m Cosmonaut-Killick (Slip Anchor)
M Mullineaux Frank Chadwick

Placings:P **(3979)**
2001/02: 16^{P}G

	Starts	1st	2nd	3rd	Win & Pl
Hurdles	1	0	0	0	
Career Total	**1**	**0**	**0**	**0**	

Going: Sf: 0-0 GS: 0-0 Gd: 0-1 GF: - Fm: 0-0
Distance: 2m/2m3: 0-1 2m4-2m7: 0-0 3m+: 0-0
Track: LH: 0-0 RH: 0-1 Tight: 0-0 Gall: 0-0
Aids: Bl: 0-0 Vi: 0-0 Tstrap: 0-0
Best Rating:

Slip The Ring

79 79
8-y-o ch g Belmez (USA)-Sixslip (USA) (Diesis)
Miss K Marks Nick Shutts

Placings:S52250-565 **(0671)**
2001/02: 20^{5}G, 21^{6}G, 24^{5}G

	Starts	1st	2nd	3rd	Win & Pl
Hurdles	3	0	0	0	0
Career Total	**9**	**0**	**2**	**0**	**1532**

Going: Sf: 0-0 GS: 0-0 Gd: 0-3 GF: - Fm: 0-0
Distance: 2m/2m3: 0-0 2m4-2m7: 0-2 3m+: 0-1
Track: LH: 0-1 RH: 0-1 Tight: 0-0 Gall: 0-1
Aids: Bl: 0-0 Vi: 0-0 Tstrap: 0-0
Best Rating: 108 10/00 MRas 2m3f110y good Hdl

Slipper Rose

71 **32**

4-y-o ch f Democratic (USA)-Brown Taw (Whistlefield)
J J Quinn (R Hollinshead 12/9) Mrs B J Boocock

Placings:P6P (1381)
2001/02: 17^{P}G, 16^{6}GF, 17^{P}GF

	Starts	1st	2nd	3rd	Win & Pl
Hurdles	3	0	0	0	0
Career Total	**3**	**0**	**0**	**0**	**0**

Going: Sf: 0-0 GS: 0-0 Gd: 0-1 GF: - Fm: 0-2
Distance: 2m/2m3: 0-3 2m4-2m7: 0-0 3m+: 0-0
Track: LH: 0-2 RH: 0-1 Tight: 0-1 Gall: 0-0
Aids: Bl: 0-0 Vi: 0-0 Tstrap: 0-0
Best Rating: 32 8/01 Uttx 2m gd-fm Hdl

Slipstream

93 **60**

8-y-o b g Slip Anchor-Butosky (Busted)
S G Chadwick S Chadwick

Placings:00/0/0P0065 (4786)
2001/02: 16^{0}G, 16^{P}GS, 17^{0}S, 20^{0}GS, 16^{6}GF, 20^{5}F

	Starts	1st	2nd	3rd	Win & Pl
Hurdles	6	0	0	0	0
Career Total	**9**	**0**	**0**	**0**	**0**

Going: Sf: 0-1 GS: 0-2 Gd: 0-1 GF: - Fm: 0-2
Distance: 2m/2m3: 0-4 2m4-2m7: 0-2 3m+: 0-0
Track: LH: 0-4 RH: 0-0 Tight: 0-2 Gall: 0-1
Aids: Bl: 0-0 Vi: 0-0 Tstrap: 0-0
Best Rating: 60 4/02 Hexm 2m110y gd-fm Hdl

Modest hurdler.

Slooghy (FR)

6-y-o br g Missolonghi (USA)-Lady Charrecey (FR) (Fin Bon)
N J Henderson P A Deal

Placings:4-0 (3497)
2001/02: 21^{0}S

	Starts	1st	2nd	3rd	Win & Pl
Hurdles	1	0	0	0	
Career Total	**2**	**0**	**0**	**0**	**2910**

Going: Sf: 0-1 GS: 0-0 Gd: 0-0 GF: - Fm: 0-0
Distance: 2m/2m3: 0-0 2m4-2m7: 0-1 3m+: 0-0
Track: LH: 0-0 RH: 0-1 Tight: 0-0 Gall: 0-0
Aids: Bl: 0-0 Vi: 0-0 Tstrap: 0-0
Best Rating:

Smackwater Jack (IRE)

94 **78**

9-y-o ch g Montelimar (USA)-Liberties (Don)
R H Alner H John Irish

Placings:P-2 (2479)
2001/02: 25^{2}S

	Starts	1st	2nd	3rd	Win & Pl
Chases	1	0	1	0	978
Career Total	**2**	**0**	**1**	**0**	**978**

Going: Sf: 0-1 GS: 0-0 Gd: 0-0 GF: - Fm: 0-0
Distance: 2m/2m3: 0-0 2m4-2m7: 0-0 3m+: 0-1
Track: LH: 0-0 RH: 0-1 Tight: 0-0 Gall: 0-0
Aids: Bl: 0-0 Vi: 0-0 Tstrap: 0-0
Best Rating: 78 12/01 Hrfd 3m1f110y soft Ch

A winning pointer, he collapsed and died after finishing second in a novices' chase in December. (DEAD)

Smart Guy

98 **91**

10-y-o ch g Gildoran-Talahache Bridge (New Brig)
Mrs L C Jewell Mrs P S Donkin

Placings:*0/0P0F/0P0003U6U02U0/5U65P/3P343263 3-U210P5P* (4312)
2001/02: 18^{U}GS, 24^{2}GF, 20^{1}G, 22^{0}G, 20^{P}S, 20^{5}S, 20^{P}HY

	Starts	1st	2nd	3rd	Win & Pl
Chases	7	1	1	0	4587
Career Total	**39**	**1**	**3**	**6**	**9174**

89	12/01	Font	2m4f	F(0-100)HCh	GD	£3055

Total win prize-money £3055

Going: Sf: 0-3 GS: 0-1 Gd: 1-2 GF: - Fm: 0-1
Distance: 2m/2m3: 0-1 **2m4-2m7: 1-5** 3m+: 0-1
Track: LH: 0-2 RH: 0-1 **Tight: 1-7** Gall: 0-0
Aids: Bl: 0-0 Vi: 0-0 Tstrap: 0-0
Best Rating: 97 6/00 Hrfd 2m gd-fm Ch

Modest chaser, stays two miles four furlongs and acts on good ground.

Smart In Blue

9-y-o br g Roscoe Blake-Cool Down (Warpath)
Mrs E Slack Mrs Evelyn Slack

Placings:P (2070)
2001/02: 17^{P}S

	Starts	1st	2nd	3rd	Win & Pl
Hurdles	1	0	0	0	
Career Total	**1**	**0**	**0**	**0**	

Going: Sf: 0-1 GS: 0-0 Gd: 0-0 GF: - Fm: 0-0
Distance: 2m/2m3: 0-1 2m4-2m7: 0-0 3m+: 0-0
Track: LH: 0-1 RH: 0-0 Tight: 0-1 Gall: 0-0
Aids: Bl: 0-0 Vi: 0-0 Tstrap: 0-0
Best Rating:

Smart Lord

103(88h) (60h)**85**

11-y-o br g Arctic Lord-Lady Catcher (Free Boy)
M R Bosley The Blowingstone Partnership

Placings:*5050/303545P/20FP/0/***43/3**-36223 (2138)
2001/02: 16^{3}G, 20^{6}GF, 19^{2}G, 16^{2}GF, 19^{3}G

	Starts	1st	2nd	3rd	Win & Pl
Chases	5	0	2	2	3158
Career Total	**24**	**0**	**3**	**6**	**5724**

Going: Sf: 0-0 GS: 0-0 Gd: 0-3 GF: - Fm: 0-2
Distance: 2m/2m3: 0-4 2m4-2m7: 0-1 3m+: 0-0
Track: LH: 0-2 RH: 0-3 Tight: 0-3 Gall: 0-0
Aids: Bl: 0-0 Vi: 0-0 Tstrap: 0-2
Best Rating: 93 11/00 Ludl 2m good Ch

A modest performer over hurdles, he is regularly in the frame over fences, but is proving hard to win with.

Smart Savannah

109 **107**

6-y-o b g Primo Dominie-High Savannah (Rousillon (USA))
E Stanners George Ward

Placings:4-2122220 (2413)
2001/02: 16^{2}G, 16^{1}GF, 16^{2}GF, 16^{2}G, 16^{2}GS, 19^{2}GF, 19^{0}GS

	Starts	1st	2nd	3rd	Win & Pl
Hurdles	7	1	5	0	8127
Career Total	**8**	**1**	**5**	**0**	**8127**

97	8/01	Worc	2m	E Hdl	G-F	£3230

Total win prize-money £3231

Going: Sf: 0-0 GS: 0-2 Gd: 0-2 GF: - Fm: 1-3
Distance: **2m/2m3: 1-6** 2m4-2m7: 0-1 3m+: 0-0
Track: **LH: 1-5** RH: 0-2 Tight: 0-3 Gall: 0-0
Aids: Bl: 0-0 Vi: 0-0 Tstrap: 0-0
Best Rating: 107 11/01 Extr 2m3f gd-fm Hdl

Showed fair novice hurdle form in the summer of 2001, on good or fast ground, but has subsequently been runner-up more times than he deserves. He needs producing late and is best on a sound surface over two miles.

Smarty (IRE)

108(101h) (102h)**148**

9-y-o b g Royal Fountain-Cahernane Girl (Bargello)
M Pitman Mrs T Brown

Placings:*0036P/***45F11P11/132P2-12035PP** (4955a)
2001/02: 21^{1}GS, 27^{2}S, 25^{0}G, 24^{3}S, 21^{5}GS, 36^{P}G, 25^{P}G

	Starts	1st	2nd	3rd	Win & Pl
Hurdles	3	1	0	1	3157
Chases	4	0	1	0	11000
Career Total	**25**	**6**	**3**	**3**	**167969**

91	11/01	Plum	2m5f	E Hdl	G-S	£2387
143	12/00	Leic	2m7f110y	D(0-125)HCh	G-S	£4192
146	3/99	Uttx	3m2f	C HCh	G-S	£18643
141	2/99	Hntg	3m	D(0-120)HCh	G-S	£5836
129	1/99	Leic	2m7f110y	F(0-110)HCh	SFT	£3262
124	12/98	Wwck	3m2f	E Ch	G-S	£2846

Total win prize-money £37168

Going: Sf: 0-2 GS: 1-2 Gd: 0-3 GF: - Fm: 0-0
Distance: 2m/2m3: 0-0 **2m4-2m7: 1-2** 3m+: 0-5
Track: **LH: 1-5** RH: 0-2 **Tight: 1-4** Gall: 0-1
Aids: Bl: 0-3 Vi: 0-1 Tstrap: 0-0
Best Rating: 148 11/01 Aint 3m3f soft Ch

Useful staying chaser, he ran a blinder when narrowly beaten under 12st in the Sussex National and topped that effort when runner-up in the Grand National to Red Marauder. He made a winning return to hurdles in November 2001, before finishing second over the National fences again in the Becher Chase. Suited by good to soft ground, often wears blinkers or visor. Had a couple of spins over hurdles earlier this year but right out of luck in his repeat National bid.

Smile Pleeze (IRE)

10-y-o b g Naheez (USA)-Harkin Park (Pollerton)
M R Daniell Miss S Troughton

Placings:*66F/50/5-40P* (4763)
2001/02: 19^{4}S, 26^{0}G, 24^{P}GF

	Starts	1st	2nd	3rd	Win & Pl
Chases	3	0	0	0	
Career Total	**9**	**0**	**0**	**0**	**0**

Going: Sf: 0-1 GS: 0-0 Gd: 0-1 GF: - Fm: 0-1
Distance: 2m/2m3: 0-0 2m4-2m7: 0-1 3m+: 0-2
Track: LH: 0-2 RH: 0-1 Tight: 0-0 Gall: 0-2
Aids: Bl: 0-0 Vi: 0-0 Tstrap: 0-0
Best Rating: 103 3/02 Chel 3m2f110y good Ch

Winning pointer, best on a sound surface although has

won on good to soft.

Smiling Thru

10-y-o b g Reference Point-Ever Genial (Brigadier Gerard)
T H Caldwell Manton Hire Ltd

Placings:P (0568)
2001/02: 20^{P}F

	Starts	1st	2nd	3rd	Win & Pl
Hurdles	1	0	0	0	
Career Total	**1**	**0**	**0**	**0**	

Going: Sf: 0-0 GS: 0-0 Gd: 0-0 GF: - Fm: 0-1
Distance: 2m/2m3: 0-0 2m4-2m7: 0-1 3m+: 0-0
Track: LH: 0-1 RH: 0-0 Tight: 0-0 Gall: 0-0
Aids: Bl: 0-0 Vi: 0-0 Tstrap: 0-0
Best Rating:

Smokestack (IRE)

98 91
6-y-o b g Lord Americo-Chiminee Fly (Proverb)
J A B Old M Lovatt/c Jenkins

Placings:054 (4134)
2001/02: 16^{0}G, 20^{5}GS, 20^{4}GS

	Starts	1st	2nd	3rd	Win & Pl
NH Flat	1	0	0	0	0
Hurdles	2	0	0	0	332
Career Total	**3**	**0**	**0**	**0**	**332**

Going: Sf: 0-0 GS: 0-2 Gd: 0-1 GF: - Fm: 0-0
Distance: 2m/2m3: 0-1 2m4-2m7: 0-2 3m+: 0-0
Track: LH: 0-0 RH: 0-3 Tight: 0-0 Gall: 0-0
Aids: Bl: 0-0 Vi: 0-0 Tstrap: 0-0
Best Rating: 91 3/02 Sand 2m4f110y gd-sft Hdl

Smokey Robot (IRE)

82 46
9-y-o b g Riberetto-Smokey Queen (Proverb)
C Weedon Bbb Computer Services

Placings:00/3463/PU/253-0 (1897)
2001/02: 26^{0}GS

	Starts	1st	2nd	3rd	Win & Pl
Chases	1	0	0	0	
Career Total	**12**	**0**	**1**	**3**	**2120**

Going: Sf: 0-0 GS: 0-1 Gd: 0-0 GF: - Fm: 0-0
Distance: 2m/2m3: 0-0 2m4-2m7: 0-0 3m+: 0-1
Track: LH: 0-0 RH: 0-0 Tight: 0-1 Gall: 0-0
Aids: Bl: 0-0 Vi: 0-0 Tstrap: 0-1
Best Rating: 105 11/00 Font 2m6f heavy Ch

Smolensk (IRE)

10-y-o b g Ela-Mana-Mou-Merry Twinkle (Martinmas)
A Berry Chris & Antonia Deuters

Placings:60/32213P/13**F5341/5116/5/PPP** (1542)
2001/02: 16^{P}GS, 16^{P}GF, 16^{P}G

	Starts	1st	2nd	3rd	Win & Pl
Chases	3	0	0	0	
Career Total	**23**	**5**	**2**	**4**	**19852**

136	12/98	Donc	2m110y	C(0-130)HCh	GD	£4973
129	5/98	Hrfd	2m3f	D Ch	GD	£3582
129	3/98	Hrfd	2m	E Ch	G-F	£3156
	5/97	Hayd	2m	D Hdl	G-F	£3004
	12/96	Muss	2m4f	E Hdl	G-F	£1878

Total win prize-money £16595

Going: Sf: 0-0 GS: 0-1 Gd: 0-1 GF: - Fm: 0-1
Distance: 2m/2m3: 0-3 2m4-2m7: 0-0 3m+: 0-0
Track: LH: 0-2 RH: 0-1 Tight: 0-2 Gall: 0-0
Aids: Bl: 0-0 Vi: 0-0 Tstrap: 0-0
Best Rating: 136 12/98 Donc 2m110y good Ch

Smooth Sailing

100 104
7-y-o gr g Beveled (USA)-Sea Farer Lake (Gairloch)
K McAuliffe A R Parrish

Placings:10/PP451 (4509)
2001/02: 16^{P}G, 17^{P}S, 16^{4}HY, 16^{5}S, 16^{1}G

	Starts	1st	2nd	3rd	Win & Pl
Hurdles	5	1	0	0	2342
Career Total	**7**	**2**	**0**	**0**	**5670**
99 3/02 Plum	2m	F(0-90)Hdl	GD		£2341
90 1/00 Leic	2m	E Hdl	SFT		£3328

Total win prize-money £5670

Going: Sf: 0-3 GS: 0-0 Gd: 1-2 GF: - Fm: 0-0
Distance: **2m/2m3: 1-5** 2m4-2m7: 0-0 3m+: 0-0
Track: **LH: 1-2** RH: 0-3 **Tight: 1-2** Gall: 0-0
Aids: Bl: 0-0 Vi: 0-0 Tstrap: 0-0
Best Rating: 99 3/02 Plum 2m good Hdl

Fair hurdler, suited by fast ground and two miles.

Smudge (IRE)

83f 76f
5-y-o br g Be My Native (USA)-Crash Call (Crash Course)
R Ford Mrs Brenda Siddall

Placings:0 (4046)
2001/02: 17^{0}GS

	Starts	1st	2nd	3rd	Win & Pl
NH Flat	1	0	0	0	
Career Total	**1**	**0**	**0**	**0**	

Going: Sf: 0-0 GS: 0-1 Gd: 0-0 GF: - Fm: 0-0
Distance: 2m/2m3: 0-1 2m4-2m7: 0-0 3m+: 0-0
Track: LH: 0-0 RH: 0-1 Tight: 0-1 Gall: 0-0
Aids: Bl: 0-0 Vi: 0-0 Tstrap: 0-0
Best Rating: 76 3/02 MRas 2m1f110y gd-sft NHF

Smudger Smith

99 105
5-y-o ch g Deploy-Parfait Amour (Clantime)
B S Rothwell S P Hudson

Placings:1140-001P (3406)
2001/02: 20^{0}G, 20^{0}HY, 16^{1}S, 20^{P}S

	Starts	1st	2nd	3rd	Win & Pl
Hurdles	4	1	0	0	2744
Career Total	**8**	**3**	**0**	**0**	**10471**
105 1/02 Leic	2m	E(0-110)HHdl	SFT		£2744
110 11/00 Newc	2m	D Hdl	SFT		£3090
89 11/00 Hayd	2m	D Hdl	HVY		£3136

Total win prize-money £8971

Going: Sf: 1-3 GS: 0-0 Gd: 0-1 GF: - Fm: 0-0
Distance: **2m/2m3: 1-1** 2m4-2m7: 0-3 3m+: 0-0
Track: LH: 0-2 **RH: 1-2** Tight: 0-0 Gall: 0-0
Aids: Bl: 0-0 Vi: 0-0 Tstrap: 0-0
Best Rating: 110 11/00 Newc 2m soft Hdl

Suited by two miles and cut in the ground, he won a weak handicap hurdle at Leicester in January 2002.

Smyslov

101 90
4-y-o b g Rainbow Quest (USA)-Vlaanderen (IRE) (In The Wings)
P R Webber (J L Dunlop 25/10) Trevor Sharman

Placings:553 (4737)
2001/02: 17^{5}GS, 16^{5}G, 16^{3}GF

	Starts	1st	2nd	3rd	Win & Pl
Hurdles	3	0	0	1	432
Career Total	**3**	**0**	**0**	**1**	**432**

Going: Sf: 0-0 GS: 0-1 Gd: 0-1 GF: - Fm: 0-1
Distance: 2m/2m3: 0-3 2m4-2m7: 0-0 3m+: 0-0
Track: LH: 0-1 RH: 0-2 Tight: 0-1 Gall: 0-0
Aids: Bl: 0-0 Vi: 0-0 Tstrap: 0-0
Best Rating: 90 4/02 Ludl 2m gd-fm Hdl

Fair handicapper on the Flat but disappointing over hurdles until a better effort on his third attempt.

Snake Goddess

84 51
4-y-o b f Primo Dominie-Shoshone (Be My Chief (USA))
D W P Arbuthnot (H Morrison 30/9) The Sfs Partnership

Placings:0P00 (4881)
2001/02: 16^{0}HY, 19^{P}GS, 20^{0}S, 18^{0}GF

	Starts	1st	2nd	3rd	Win & Pl
Hurdles	4	0	0	0	
Career Total	**4**	**0**	**0**	**0**	

Going: Sf: 0-2 GS: 0-1 Gd: 0-0 GF: - Fm: 0-1
Distance: 2m/2m3: 0-3 2m4-2m7: 0-1 3m+: 0-0
Track: LH: 0-4 RH: 0-0 Tight: 0-2 Gall: 0-0
Aids: Bl: 0-2 Vi: 0-0 Tstrap: 0-0
Best Rating: 51 4/02 Font 2m2f110y gd-fm Hdl

Snapper

93(92h) (70h)75
11-y-o b g Gunner B-Fortalice (Saucy Kit)
Mrs L B Normile L B N Racing Club

Placings:6/4036/143/56P61UP0-0505PU (4260)
2001/02: 26^{0}GF, 24^{5}S, 24^{0}S, 24^{5}S, 27^{P}S, 32^{U}HY

	Starts	1st	2nd	3rd	Win & Pl
Hurdles	3	0	0	0	0
Chases	3	0	0	0	0
Career Total	**22**	**2**	**0**	**2**	**5874**
104 12/00 Ayr	3m5f	E(0-115)HCh	SFT		£2834
109 5/99 Prth	2m4f110y	H Ch	HVY		£2190

Total win prize-money £5024

Going: Sf: 0-5 GS: 0-0 Gd: 0-0 GF: - Fm: 0-1
Distance: 2m/2m3: 0-0 2m4-2m7: 0-3 3m+: 0-6
Track: LH: 0-2 RH: 0-3 Tight: 0-2 Gall: 0-0
Aids: Bl: 0-5 Vi: 0-0 Tstrap: 0-0
Best Rating: 109 4/00 Newc 3m gd-sft Ch

Modest staying handicapper, seems better over hurdles. Acts on any ground and has run his better races on galloping tracks. Usually wears blinkers.

Sneeze

7-y-o ch m Cotation-Gardella (Garnered)
J F Coupland J F Coupland

Placings:*0* **(2181)**
2001/02: 16^{0}G

	Starts	1st	2nd	3rd	Win & Pl
NH Flat	1	0	0	0	
Career Total	**1**	**0**	**0**	**0**	

Going: Sf: 0-0 GS: 0-0 Gd: 0-1 GF: - Fm: 0-0
Distance: 2m/2m3: 0-1 2m4-2m7: 0-0 3m+: 0-0
Track: LH: 0-1 RH: 0-0 Tight: 0-0 Gall: 0-0
Aids: Bl: 0-0 Vi: 0-0 Tstrap: 0-0
Best Rating:

Sniper

103 **86**

10-y-o ch g Gunner B-Highfrith (Deep Run)
F P Murtagh Hurst Farm Racing

Placings:00P/64S3P362U00/21122445P/P356PPP/1P0P66P-20P32PP4 **(4769)**
2001/02: 26^{2}GF, 24^{0}G, 27^{P}G, 27^{3}S, 25^{2}GS, 24^{P}S, 26^{P}GS, 25^{4}GF

	Starts	1st	2nd	3rd	Win & Pl
Chases	8	0	2	1	2573
Career Total	**45**	**3**	**6**	**4**	**20292**
86 10/00 Sedg	3m3f	F(0-90)HCh		G-S	£2808
116 11/98 Kels	3m1f	D Ch		SFT	£5107
113 10/98 Kels	3m1f	D Ch		SFT	£3468
					Total win prize-money £11384

Going: Sf: 0-2 GS: 0-2 Gd: 0-2 GF: - Fm: 0-2
Distance: 2m/2m3: 0-0 2m4-2m7: 0-0 3m+: 0-8
Track: LH: 0-4 RH: 0-3 Tight: 0-4 Gall: 0-0
Aids: Bl: 0-0 Vi: 0-0 Tstrap: 0-1
Best Rating: **116** 11/98 Kels 3m1f soft Ch

Modest staying chaser. Best on good to soft.

Snob Wells (IRE)

(96h) (125h)**119+**

5-y-o b h Sadler's Wells (USA)-Galitizine (USA) (Riverman (USA))
Noel Meade D P Sharkey

Placings:433-311160000 **(4950a)**
2001/02: 16^{3}Y, 16^{1}S, 16^{1}G, 16^{1}GF, 16^{6}Y, 16^{0}YS, 16^{0}GS, 16^{0}GY, 16^{0}G

	Starts	1st	2nd	3rd	Win & Pl
Hurdles	9	3	0	1	34601
Career Total	**12**	**3**	**0**	**3**	**35911**
125 9/01 List	2m	HHdl		G-F	£19657
119 9/01 Tral	2m	HHdl		GD	£10483
106 8/01 Rosc	2m	Hdl		SFT	£3895
					Total win prize-money £34036

Going: Sf: 1-1 GS: 0-1 Gd: 1-2 GF: - Fm: 1-1
Distance: **2m/2m3: 3-9** 2m4-2m7: 0-0 3m+: 0-0
Track: **LH: 1-4** RH: 0-2 Tight: 0-0 Gall: 0-0
Aids: Bl: 0-2 Vi: 0-0 Tstrap: 0-2
Best Rating: **125** 4/02 Fair 2m gd-yld Hdl

Irish hurdler, a winner three times on varying ground in the autumn of 2001, before limitations exposed in better class after break.

Snooty Eskimo (IRE)

10-y-o ch g Aristocracy-Over The Arctic (Over The River (FR))
J S Haldane A Fraser

Placings:*0050*/PP2060/P05P00/6P0P/P43-P006P **(4678)**
2001/02: 25^{P}S, 16^{0}G, 17^{0}G, 20^{6}S, 25^{P}G

	Starts	1st	2nd	3rd	Win & Pl
Chases	5	0	0	0	0
Career Total	**28**	**0**	**1**	**1**	**1014**

Going: Sf: 0-2 GS: 0-0 Gd: 0-3 GF: - Fm: 0-0
Distance: 2m/2m3: 0-2 2m4-2m7: 0-1 3m+: 0-2
Track: LH: 0-3 RH: 0-1 Tight: 0-2 Gall: 0-0
Aids: Bl: 0-0 Vi: 0-0 Tstrap: 0-0
Best Rating: **90** 2/01 Kels 3m1f soft Ch

Snowboy (IRE)

10-y-o br g Celio Rufo-Laurestown Rose (Derring Rose)
J W Mullins (Mrs J M Bailey 16/5) Mrs J M Bailey

Placings:*56P0U0*/43P/3PU/54F **(0796)**
2001/02: 21^{5}G, 20^{4}GF, 16^{F}GF

	Starts	1st	2nd	3rd	Win & Pl
Chases	3	0	0	0	230
Career Total	**15**	**0**	**0**	**2**	**1392**

Going: Sf: 0-0 GS: 0-0 Gd: 0-1 GF: - Fm: 0-2
Distance: 2m/2m3: 0-1 2m4-2m7: 0-2 3m+: 0-0
Track: LH: 0-1 RH: 0-2 Tight: 0-2 Gall: 0-1
Aids: Bl: 0-0 Vi: 0-0 Tstrap: 0-0
Best Rating: **95** 9/98 Hntg 2m110y gd-fm Ch

Snowmore

99 **89**

6-y-o ch m Glacial Storm (USA)-Royal Typhoon (Royal Fountain)
Mrs S J Smith Paul J Dixon

Placings:*4622*412P0 **(4198)**
2001/02: 16^{4}GF, 16^{6}GF, 17^{2}GS, 16^{2}G, 16^{4}S, 19^{1}GF, 17^{2}S, 20^{P}GS, 21^{0}S

	Starts	1st	2nd	3rd	Win & Pl
NH Flat	3	0	1	0	452
Hurdles	6	1	2	0	3534
Career Total	**9**	**1**	**3**	**0**	**3986**
83 11/01 Catt	2m3f	F Hdl		G-F	£1907
					Total win prize-money £1908

Going: Sf: 0-3 GS: 0-2 Gd: 0-1 GF: - Fm: 1-3
Distance: **2m/2m3: 1-7** 2m4-2m7: 0-2 3m+: 0-0
Track: **LH: 1-6** RH: 0-3 **Tight: 1-6** Gall: 0-0
Aids: Bl: 0-0 Vi: 0-0 Tstrap: 0-0
Best Rating: **89** 12/01 MRas 2m1f110y soft Hdl

modest hurdler, stays two miles-five, suited by a sound surface and positive tactcis.

Snuggle Under

8-y-o b g Mazilier (USA)-Gleaning (Sovereign Gleam)
P T Dalton Mrs Christina M Griffin

Placings:*00*/P0 **(4591)**
2001/02: 16^{P}HY, 16^{0}G

	Starts	1st	2nd	3rd	Win & Pl
Hurdles	2	0	0	0	
Career Total	**4**	**0**	**0**	**0**	

Going: Sf: 0-1 GS: 0-0 Gd: 0-1 GF: - Fm: 0-0
Distance: 2m/2m3: 0-2 2m4-2m7: 0-0 3m+: 0-0
Track: LH: 0-2 RH: 0-0 Tight: 0-0 Gall: 0-0
Aids: Bl: 0-0 Vi: 0-0 Tstrap: 0-0
Best Rating: **80** 3/00 Strf 2m110y good NHF

So Keen

(51h)

9-y-o ch g Keen-Diana's Bow (Great Nephew)
Mrs H Dalton Ray Bailey

Placings:F506/501226/4624F210/U00-PPP **(4043)**
2001/02: 23^{P}G, 20^{P}S, 25^{P}S

	Starts	1st	2nd	3rd	Win & Pl
Hurdles	2	0	0	0	0
Chases	1	0	0	0	0
Career Total	**24**	**2**	**4**	**0**	**8593**
110 12/99 Donc	2m4f	E(0-115)HHdl		G-S	£2918
86 7/98 Bang	2m1f	E Hdl		GD	£2221
					Total win prize-money £5140

Going: Sf: 0-2 GS: 0-0 Gd: 0-1 GF: - Fm: 0-0
Distance: 2m/2m3: 0-0 2m4-2m7: 0-1 3m+: 0-2
Track: LH: 0-1 RH: 0-2 Tight: 0-1 Gall: 0-0
Aids: Bl: 0-1 Vi: 0-0 Tstrap: 0-0
Best Rating: **110** 12/99 Donc 2m4f gd-sft Hdl

So Money (IRE)

102 **106**

8-y-o b g Supreme Leader-Money No Object (Goldhill)
G Prodromou Andreas Andoniou

Placings:*2*-2230 **(3142)**
2001/02: 20^{2}S, 22^{2}S, 21^{3}G, 23^{0}S

	Starts	1st	2nd	3rd	Win & Pl
Hurdles	4	0	2	1	2160
Career Total	**5**	**0**	**3**	**1**	**2604**

Going: Sf: 0-3 GS: 0-0 Gd: 0-1 GF: - Fm: 0-0
Distance: 2m/2m3: 0-0 2m4-2m7: 0-3 3m+: 0-1
Track: LH: 0-3 RH: 0-1 Tight: 0-4 Gall: 0-0
Aids: Bl: 0-0 Vi: 0-1 Tstrap: 0-0
Best Rating: **106** 11/01 Folk 2m6f110y soft Hdl

He has kept on finding one too good in his early starts, but should win a staying hurdle somewhere.

So Peaceful

68 **18**

8-y-o b m Prince Of Peace-Indian Election (Sula Bula)
R E Pocock T E Pocock

Placings:0 **(1849)**
2001/02: 22^{0}G

	Starts	1st	2nd	3rd	Win & Pl
Hurdles	1	0	0	0	
Career Total	**1**	**0**	**0**	**0**	

Going: Sf: 0-0 GS: 0-0 Gd: 0-1 GF: - Fm: 0-0
Distance: 2m/2m3: 0-0 2m4-2m7: 0-1 3m+: 0-0
Track: LH: 0-0 RH: 0-1 Tight: 0-0 Gall: 0-0
Aids: Bl: 0-0 Vi: 0-0 Tstrap: 0-0
Best Rating: **18** 10/01 Winc 2m6f good Hdl

So Precious (IRE)

96 93

5-y-o b m Batshoof-Golden Form (Formidable (USA))
Ian Williams (N P Littmoden 2/6) M Murphy

Placings:313-606 **(4239)**
2001/02: 16^6GF, 16^0GF, 16^6GF

	Starts	1st	2nd	3rd	Win & Pl
Hurdles	3	0	0	0	0
Career Total	**6**	**1**	**0**	**2**	**4415**

103 12/00 Fknm 2m D Hdl G-S £2850
Total win prize-money £2850

Going: Sf: 0-0 GS: 0-0 Gd: 0-0 GF: - Fm: 0-3
Distance: 2m/2m3: 0-3 2m4-2m7: 0-0 3m+: 0-0
Track: LH: 0-1 RH: 0-2 Tight: 0-1 Gall: 0-2
Aids: Bl: 0-0 Vi: 0-2 Tstrap: 0-0
Best Rating: 103 12/00 Fknm 2m gd-sft Hdl

Not very big and best under lighter weights.

Soaring Monarch

92 100

7-y-o b g Rakaposhi King-Flying Faith (Rymer)
J T Gifford Ivybrook Partners

Placings:0/0-00F30P0 **(4850)**
2001/02: 17^0GS, 17^0G, 22^FS, 21^3S, 19^0S, 21^PGS, 22^0G

	Starts	1st	2nd	3rd	Win & Pl
Hurdles	7	0	0	1	610
Career Total	**9**	**0**	**0**	**1**	**610**

Going: Sf: 0-3 GS: 0-2 Gd: 0-2 GF: - Fm: 0-0
Distance: 2m/2m3: 0-3 2m4-2m7: 0-4 3m+: 0-0
Track: LH: 0-4 RH: 0-3 Tight: 0-3 Gall: 0-2
Aids: Bl: 0-0 Vi: 0-0 Tstrap: 0-0
Best Rating: 102 12/00 Kemp 2m gd-sft Hdl

Third in a novice hurdle in January 2002 and acts on soft ground. Stays two and a half miles.

Sober As A Judge

93 77

5-y-o b g Mon Tresor-Flicker Toa Flame (USA) (Empery (USA))
C A Dwyer M M Foulger

Placings:00P **(2899)**
2001/02: 16^0GS, 16^0G, 16^PG

	Starts	1st	2nd	3rd	Win & Pl
Hurdles	3	0	0	0	
Career Total	**3**	**0**	**0**	**0**	

Going: Sf: 0-0 GS: 0-1 Gd: 0-2 GF: - Fm: 0-0
Distance: 2m/2m3: 0-3 2m4-2m7: 0-0 3m+: 0-0
Track: LH: 0-1 RH: 0-2 Tight: 0-0 Gall: 0-1
Aids: Bl: 0-0 Vi: 0-0 Tstrap: 0-0
Best Rating: 77 11/01 Leic 2m gd-sft Hdl

Sober Hill

98 83

4-y-o b g Komaite (USA)-Mamoda (Good Times (ITY))
N B Mason (D Shaw 23/1) N B Mason

Placings:50022 **(4904)**
2001/02: 17^5S, 16^0G, 17^0GS, 16^2GF, 17^2G

	Starts	1st	2nd	3rd	Win & Pl
Hurdles	5	0	2	0	1056
Career Total	**5**	**0**	**2**	**0**	**1056**

Going: Sf: 0-1 GS: 0-1 Gd: 0-2 GF: - Fm: 0-1
Distance: 2m/2m3: 0-5 2m4-2m7: 0-0 3m+: 0-0
Track: LH: 0-2 RH: 0-3 Tight: 0-3 Gall: 0-0
Aids: Bl: 0-0 Vi: 0-0 Tstrap: 0-0
Best Rating: 83 4/02 MRas 2m1f110y good Hdl

In the frame in selling hurdles, but looks an awkward ride.

Socialist (USA)

95 67

6-y-o b g Hermitage (USA)-Social Missy (USA) (Raised Socially (USA))
G Brown Mrs Carol Ann Brown

Placings:500-50FP **(1068)**
2001/02: 16^5GF, 17^0GF, 21^FG, 17^PGF

	Starts	1st	2nd	3rd	Win & Pl
Hurdles	3	0	0	0	0
Chases	1	0	0	0	0
Career Total	**7**	**0**	**0**	**0**	**0**

Going: Sf: 0-0 GS: 0-0 Gd: 0-1 GF: - Fm: 0-3
Distance: 2m/2m3: 0-3 2m4-2m7: 0-1 3m+: 0-0
Track: LH: 0-2 RH: 0-2 Tight: 0-3 Gall: 0-1
Aids: Bl: 0-2 Vi: 0-0 Tstrap: 0-0
Best Rating: 67 5/01 Hntg 2m110y gd-fm Hdl

Society Buck (IRE)

99f 89f

5-y-o b g Moscow Society (USA)-Bucks Grove (IRE) (Buckskin (FR))
M W Easterby Abbots Salford Caravan Park

Placings:0 **(4873)**
2001/02: 16^0GF

	Starts	1st	2nd	3rd	Win & Pl
NH Flat	1	0	0	0	
Career Total	**1**	**0**	**0**	**0**	

Going: Sf: 0-0 GS: 0-0 Gd: 0-0 GF: - Fm: 0-1
Distance: 2m/2m3: 0-1 2m4-2m7: 0-0 3m+: 0-0
Track: LH: 0-1 RH: 0-0 Tight: 0-0 Gall: 0-0
Aids: Bl: 0-0 Vi: 0-0 Tstrap: 0-0
Best Rating: 89 4/02 Weth 2m gd-fm NHF

Unplaced on his debut, he got off the mark second time out at Sedgefield in July 2002. Bred to stay. Acts on good to firm ground.

Sodelk

(100h) (81h)

8-y-o ch m Interrex (CAN)-Summoned By Bells (Stanford)
J E Long (Julian Poulton 19/2) Mick Robinson

Placings:000/L4/50F2P60-PP3RU54PU55P **(4760)**
2001/02: 17^PHY, 16^PG, 17^3S, 16^RG, 16^UG, 16^5S, 17^4HY, 17^PS, 16US, 21^5GF, 16^5G, 24^PGF

	Starts	1st	2nd	3rd	Win & Pl
Hurdles	12	0	0	1	383
Career Total	**24**	**0**	**1**	**1**	**1067**

Going: Sf: 0-6 GS: 0-0 Gd: 0-4 GF: - Fm: 0-2
Distance: 2m/2m3: 0-10 2m4-2m7: 0-1 3m+: 0-1
Track: LH: 0-2 RH: 0-10 Tight: 0-5 Gall: 0-2
Aids: Bl: 0-0 Vi: 0-0 Tstrap: 0-2
Best Rating: 81 1/02 Leic 2m soft Hdl

Modest maiden hurdler whose best effort was on heavy ground. Has shown signs of temperament.

Soeur Fontenail (FR)

107(98h) (101h)111

5-y-o b m Turgeon (USA)-Fontanalia (FR) (Rex Magna (FR))
N J Hawke La Connection Francaise

Placings:P65-2432310 **(4764)**
2001/02: 17^2G, 17^4GS, 16^3G, 16^2S, 16^3S, 17^1G, 16^0GF

	Starts	1st	2nd	3rd	Win & Pl
Hurdles	2	1	0	0	3052
Chases	5	0	2	2	3676
Career Total	**10**	**1**	**2**	**2**	**7064**

101 3/02 NAbb 2m1f E Hdl GD £3052
Total win prize-money £3052

Going: Sf: 0-2 GS: 0-1 Gd: 1-3 GF: - Fm: 0-1
Distance: **2m/2m3: 1-7** 2m4-2m7: 0-0 3m+: 0-0
Track: **LH: 1-2** RH: 0-5 **Tight: 1-2** Gall: 0-1
Aids: Bl: 0-0 Vi: 0-0 Tstrap: 0-0
Best Rating: 111 12/01 Extr 2m1f110y gd-sft Ch

A French import, she has shown ability in this country over fences at around two miles. Has shown her best form on decent ground. Successful on her first run over timber in this country at Newton Abbot in March 2002.

Sofisio

107 93

5-y-o ch g Efisio-Legal Embrace (CAN) (Legal Bid (USA))
Miss S J Wilton John Pointon And Sons

Placings:0-5U543 **(2784)**
2001/02: 16^5G, 17^UG, 17^5S, 19^4G, 16^3G

	Starts	1st	2nd	3rd	Win & Pl
Hurdles	5	0	0	1	623
Career Total	**6**	**0**	**0**	**1**	**623**

Going: Sf: 0-1 GS: 0-0 Gd: 0-4 GF: - Fm: 0-0
Distance: 2m/2m3: 0-4 2m4-2m7: 0-1 3m+: 0-0
Track: LH: 0-3 RH: 0-2 Tight: 0-3 Gall: 0-0
Aids: Bl: 0-0 Vi: 0-0 Tstrap: 0-2
Best Rating: 93 12/01 Ludl 2m good Hdl

Moderate hurdler who races in tongue tie and blinkers.

Sol Music

10-y-o ch g Southern Music-Tyqueen (Tycoon Ii)
Mrs V M Graham (M Hill 15/6) Peter Thomas

Placings:0/55/245212/0**3551120**/5P55600/131 **(4483)**
2001/02: 16^1GF, 16^3GS, 19^1G

	Starts	1st	2nd	3rd	Win & Pl
Chases	3	2	0	1	6047
Career Total	**27**	**5**	**4**	**2**	**18716**

117 3/02 Extr 2m3f110y H Ch GD £2156
117 5/01 NAbb 2m110y E(0-115)HCh G-F £3410
132 3/99 Hrfd 2m E Ch G-S £3160
124 3/99 Tntn 2m110y F(0-100)HCh SFT £3241
113 4/98 Hrfd 2m1f E Hdl SFT £2641
Total win prize-money £14610

Going: Sf: 0-0 GS: 0-1 Gd: 1-1 GF: - Fm: 1-1
Distance: 2m/2m3: 1-2 2m4-2m7: 1-1 3m+: 0-0
Track: LH: 1-2 RH: 1-1 **Tight: 1-2** Gall: 0-0
Aids: Bl: 0-0 Vi: 0-0 Tstrap: 0-0
Best Rating: 132 3/99 Hrfd 2m gd-sft Ch

A front-running chaser, seems best in the spring on a

right-handed track. Suited by two miles and handles any ground.

Solar Dove

84 **91**

6-y-o b g Jupiter Island-Celtic Dove (Celtic Cone)
C J Price Ryan Price

Placings: *00*F41-0PP**U**0 **(4599)**
2001/02: 20^{0}S, 20^{P}S, 23^{P}HY, 19^{U}S, 25^{0}GF

	Starts	1st	2nd	3rd	Win & Pl
Hurdles	4	0	0	0	0
Chases	1	0	0	0	0
Career Total	**10**	**1**	**0**	**0**	**2304**

91	4/01	Extr	2m6f110y	E Hdl	SFT	£2304

Total win prize-money £2304

Going: Sf: 0-4 GS: 0-0 Gd: 0-0 GF: - Fm: 0-1
Distance: 2m/2m3: 0-1 2m4-2m7: 0-2 3m+: 0-2
Track: LH: 0-3 RH: 0-1 Tight: 0-0 Gall: 0-0
Aids: Bl: 0-0 Vi: 0-0 Tstrap: 0-0
Best Rating: **91** 4/01 Extr 2m6f110y soft Hdl

Soldier Mak

102(102h) **117**

9-y-o ch g Infantry-Truly Blest (So Blessed)
J Mackie Rose And Crown, Boylestone

Placings:350/232336155/22216504/14/0504-53 **(0424)**
2001/02: 19^{5}G, 20^{3}G

	Starts	1st	2nd	3rd	Win & Pl
Chases	2	0	0	1	518
Career Total	**28**	**3**	**5**	**5**	**15146**

107	8/99	Uttx	2m4f110y	D(0-125)HHdl	G-F	£3123
112	10/98	Uttx	2m	D(0-120)HHdl	GD	£3501
97	2/98	Catt	2m3f	F(0-105)HHdl	GD	£1996

Total win prize-money £8620

Going: Sf: 0-0 GS: 0-0 Gd: 0-2 GF: - Fm: 0-0
Distance: 2m/2m3: 0-1 2m4-2m7: 0-1 3m+: 0-0
Track: LH: 0-1 RH: 0-1 Tight: 0-1 Gall: 0-0
Aids: Bl: 0-0 Vi: 0-0 Tstrap: 0-0
Best Rating: **117** 5/01 Bang 2m4f110y good Ch

Soldier Of Rome (IRE)

100 **103**

5-y-o b g Satco (FR)-Queens Tricks (Le Bavard (FR))
M Pitman Howard Spooner

Placings: *F*33P **(4303)**
2001/02: 16^{F}G, 16^{3}GS, 20^{3}S, 16^{P}HY

	Starts	1st	2nd	3rd	Win & Pl
NH Flat	1	0	0	0	0
Hurdles	3	0	0	2	1053
Career Total	**4**	**0**	**0**	**2**	**1053**

Going: Sf: 0-2 GS: 0-1 Gd: 0-1 GF: - Fm: 0-0
Distance: 2m/2m3: 0-3 2m4-2m7: 0-1 3m+: 0-0
Track: LH: 0-3 RH: 0-1 Tight: 0-0 Gall: 0-3
Aids: Bl: 0-0 Vi: 0-0 Tstrap: 0-0
Best Rating: **103** 1/02 Donc 2m4f soft Hdl

A lightly-raced maiden over hurdles, he has run with credit, including when third at Doncaster in January 2002. Should stay further. Acts on an easy surface.

Soldier's Song

9-y-o b m Infantry-Top Soprano (High Top)
R J Hodges Lt Col E L Stocker

Placings:00/PP **(4504)**
2001/02: 22^{P}S, 17^{P}G

	Starts	1st	2nd	3rd	Win & Pl
Hurdles	2	0	0	0	
Career Total	**4**	**0**	**0**	**0**	

Going: Sf: 0-1 GS: 0-0 Gd: 0-1 GF: - Fm: 0-0
Distance: 2m/2m3: 0-1 2m4-2m7: 0-1 3m+: 0-0
Track: LH: 0-1 RH: 0-1 Tight: 0-1 Gall: 0-0
Aids: Bl: 0-0 Vi: 0-0 Tstrap: 0-0
Best Rating: **55** 3/98 Winc 2m good Hdl

Soldiered Again (IRE)

(106h) (109h)

7-y-o b g Be My Native (USA)-She's Tough (Deep Run)
Niall Madden J P McManus

Placings:0/600-2P0*1*10215**0** **(2731a)**
2001/02: 16^{2}GF, 16^{P}G, 19^{0}G, 16^{1}GY, 20^{1}SH, 16^{0}G, 22^{2}GY, 20^{1}YS, 21^{5}G, 18^{0}Y

	Starts	1st	2nd	3rd	Win & Pl
NH Flat	1	1	0	0	3339
Hurdles	8	2	2	0	11377
Chases	1	0	0	0	0
Career Total	**14**	**3**	**2**	**0**	**14715**

109	10/01	Wxfd	2m4f	(0-109)HHdl	Y-S	£5008
101	8/01	Slig	2m4f	(0-95)HHdl	SH	£4451
104	7/01	Wxfd	2m	NHF	G-Y	£3338

Total win prize-money £12799

Going: Sf: 0-0 GS: 0-0 Gd: 0-4 GF: - Fm: 0-1
Distance: 2m/2m3: 1-6 **2m4-2m7: 2-4** 3m+: 0-0
Track: LH: 0-1 RH: 0-2 Tight: 0-0 Gall: 0-1
Aids: Bl: 0-0 Vi: 0-0 Tstrap: 0-0
Best Rating: **109** 11/01 Chel 2m5f good Hdl

Solitary

5-y-o b g Sanglamore (USA)-Set Fair (USA) (Alleged (USA))
J G Given Mrs Jo Hardy

Placings:P **(1581)**
2001/02: 24^{P}GS

	Starts	1st	2nd	3rd	Win & Pl
Hurdles	1	0	0	0	
Career Total	**1**	**0**	**0**	**0**	

Going: Sf: 0-0 GS: 0-1 Gd: 0-0 GF: - Fm: 0-0
Distance: 2m/2m3: 0-0 2m4-2m7: 0-0 3m+: 0-1
Track: LH: 0-0 RH: 0-1 Tight: 0-1 Gall: 0-0
Aids: Bl: 0-0 Vi: 0-0 Tstrap: 0-0
Best Rating:

Solo Dancer

96 **70**

4-y-o ch f Sayaarr (USA)-Oiseval (National Trust)
Jane Southcombe (W G M Turner 17/5) Mrs H M Bridges

Placings:0F630P **(4011)**
2001/02: 16^{0}G, 16^{F}G, 16^{6}G, 16^{3}G, 24^{0}S, 21^{P}S

	Starts	1st	2nd	3rd	Win & Pl
Hurdles	6	0	0	1	349
Career Total	**6**	**0**	**0**	**1**	**349**

Going: Sf: 0-2 GS: 0-0 Gd: 0-4 GF: - Fm: 0-0
Distance: 2m/2m3: 0-4 2m4-2m7: 0-1 3m+: 0-1
Track: LH: 0-4 RH: 0-2 Tight: 0-2 Gall: 0-2
Aids: Bl: 0-0 Vi: 0-0 Tstrap: 0-0
Best Rating: **70** 12/01 Winc 2m good Hdl

Modest form over hurdles so far.

Solo Gent

102 **116**

13-y-o br g Le Bavard (FR)-Go-It-Alone (Linacre)
A P Jones A A King

Placings: *50*03025/21643/6**521P4P**P60**414/2140P36P /1120/5443312P5P/332/11P2UP1P04-0P1PP** **(2065)**
2001/02: 24^{0}G, 25^{P}G, 24^{1}GF, 25^{P}GS, 24^{P}G

	Starts	1st	2nd	3rd	Win & Pl
Chases	5	1	0	0	2975
Career Total	**65**	**11**	**8**	**7**	**52287**

116	9/01	Hntg	3m	F(0-110)HCh	G-F	£2975
121	12/00	Ludl	3m3f110y	E(0-115)HCh	SFT	£8209
108	5/00	Hntg	3m	H Ch	G-F	£1225
114	5/00	Hntg	3m	H Ch	GD	£1603
115	11/98	Hntg	3m6f110y	C(0-130)HCh	GD	£7067
115	10/97	Towc	3m1f	E(0-110)HCh	GD	£2864
108	9/97	Hntg	3m	E(0-110)HCh	G-F	£2795
108	11/96	Hntg	3m	E(0-110)HCh	G-S	£3036
98	4/96	Hntg	3m	E Ch	FRM	£3059
92	11/95	Hntg	2m4f110y	E Ch	G-F	£2964
112	10/94	Chel	2m5f110y	Hdl	G-F	£2368

Total win prize-money £38170

Going: Sf: 0-0 GS: 0-1 Gd: 0-3 GF: - Fm: 1-1
Distance: 2m/2m3: 0-0 2m4-2m7: 0-0 **3m+: 1-5**
Track: LH: 0-0 **RH: 1-4** Tight: 0-0 **Gall: 1-3**
Aids: Bl: 0-0 Vi: 0-0 Tstrap: 0-0
Best Rating: **121** 12/00 Ludl 3m3f110y soft Ch

Veteran staying chaser. He is not a fluent jumper, nor consistent. One to ignore unless he is at Huntingdon.

Solo Lord (USA)

10-y-o b g Assault Landing (USA)-Lady Demon (USA) (Solo Performance (USA))
F Bruce Miller Mr And Mrs Michael E Hoffman

Placings:4/F31-P **(4191)**
2001/02: 24^{P}GS

	Starts	1st	2nd	3rd	Win & Pl
Chases	1	0	0	0	
Career Total	**5**	**1**	**0**	**1**	**28982**

	4/01	Glyn	4m	Ch	YLD	£26000

Total win prize-money £26000

Going: Sf: 0-0 GS: 0-1 Gd: 0-0 GF: - Fm: 0-0
Distance: 2m/2m3: 0-0 2m4-2m7: 0-0 3m+: 0-1
Track: LH: 0-1 RH: 0-0 Tight: 0-0 Gall: 0-1
Aids: Bl: 0-0 Vi: 0-0 Tstrap: 0-1
Best Rating:

Winner of 2001 Maryland Hunt Cup. Prefers fast ground. Jumps soundly. Stays four miles.

Soloman (IRE)

115 **122**

9-y-o br g Mandalus-Solo Player (Blue Refrain)
J T Gifford R F Eliot

Placings:32132/34433/123521/5-0P402 **(3870)**
2001/02: 24^{0}GS, 24^{P}G, 21^{4}G, 24^{0}GS, 24^{2}GS

	Starts	1st	2nd	3rd	Win & Pl
Chases	5	0	1	0	2527
Career Total	**22**	**3**	**5**	**6**	**28546**

126	4/00	Plum	3m2f	E Ch	G-S	£3168
132	10/99	Chel	2m4f110y	D(0-110)HCh	GD	£5550
123	2/98	Towc	2m	E Hdl	GD	£2652

Total win prize-money £11372

Going: Sf: 0-0 GS: 0-3 Gd: 0-2 GF: - Fm: 0-0
Distance: 2m/2m3: 0-0 2m4-2m7: 0-1 3m+: 0-4
Track: LH: 0-1 RH: 0-4 Tight: 0-0 Gall: 0-2
Aids: Bl: 0-0 Vi: 0-0 Tstrap: 0-0
Best Rating: **138** 11/99 Newb 3m good Ch

One-time decent chaser who has not reached the heights that were expected of him. Stays three miles plus and does not want the ground too soft.

Solomans Sister

79 **76**

12-y-o ch m Lir-Cornish Princess (True Code)
G F H Charles-Jones Mrs Jessica Charles-Jones

Placings:P635 **(4864)**
2001/02: 26^{P}HY, 24^{6}S, 23^{3}F, 25^{5}F

	Starts	1st	2nd	3rd	Win & Pl
Chases	4	0	0	1	560
Career Total	**4**	**0**	**0**	**1**	**560**

Going: Sf: 0-2 GS: 0-0 Gd: 0-0 GF: - Fm: 0-2
Distance: 2m/2m3: 0-0 2m4-2m7: 0-0 3m+: 0-4
Track: LH: 0-1 RH: 0-2 Tight: 0-1 Gall: 0-0
Aids: Bl: 0-0 Vi: 0-0 Tstrap: 0-0
Best Rating: **76** 4/02 Extr 2m7f110y firm Ch

Veteran ex-pointer, has shown modest form over fences.

Solsgirth

99(86h) (35h)**99**

11-y-o br g Ardross-Lillie's Brig (New Brig)
J Barclay Alexander Family

Placings:0P/013P/13F5P3P53/1112F36263/6001F3U/P523PP4-0024PP **(4310)**
2001/02: 16^{0}S, 20^{0}S, 16^{2}S, 20^{4}HY, 16^{P}HY, 16^{P}S

	Starts	1st	2nd	3rd	Win & Pl
Hurdles	1	0	0	0	0
Chases	5	0	1	0	1919
Career Total	**45**	**6**	**4**	**8**	**33778**

105	1/00	Ayr	2m	E(0-115)HCh	SFT	£3211
115	11/98	Hexm	2m4f110y	F(0-105)HCh	HVY	£3063
105	11/98	Kels	2m1f	D(0-120)HCh	SFT	£3387
104	10/98	Kels	2m1f	E(0-115)HCh	SFT	£3139
90	11/97	Ayr	2m4f	D(0-110)HCh	G-S	£3636
90	2/97	Ayr	2m	E(0-100)HHdl	SFT	£2626

Total win prize-money £19065

Going: Sf: 0-6 GS: 0-0 Gd: 0-0 GF: - Fm: 0-0
Distance: 2m/2m3: 0-4 2m4-2m7: 0-2 3m+: 0-0
Track: LH: 0-6 RH: 0-0 Tight: 0-0 Gall: 0-1
Aids: Bl: 0-0 Vi: 0-0 Tstrap: 0-0
Best Rating: **121** 12/98 Ayr 3m1f gd-sft Ch

Moderate ability over hurdles and fences, he stays three miles, but his wins in recent seasons have been over shorter. Very much suited by soft ground.

Soltero (IRE)

109 **129**

6-y-o ch g Good Thyne (USA)-Golden Ambition (Torus)
Mrs John Harrington Augustus Moon Syndicate

Placings:2/12-12423104 **(4717a)**
2001/02: 16^{1}GY, 16^{2}S, 20^{4}SH, 20^{2}YS, 16^{3}S, 16^{1}HY, 16^{0}GS, 20^{4}GY

	Starts	1st	2nd	3rd	Win & Pl
Hurdles	8	2	2	1	22030
Career Total	**11**	**3**	**4**	**1**	**27861**

129	2/02	Thur	2m	Hdl	HVY	£5079
121	5/01	Fair	2m	Hdl	G-Y	£7790
117	11/00	Punc	2m	NHF	SFT	£3450

Total win prize-money £16320

Going: Sf: 1-3 GS: 0-1 Gd: 0-0 GF: - Fm: 0-0
Distance: **2m/2m3: 2-5** 2m4-2m7: 0-3 3m+: 0-0
Track: LH: 0-1 **RH: 1-5** Tight: 0-0 Gall: 0-0
Aids: Bl: 0-0 Vi: 0-0 Tstrap: 0-0
Best Rating: **129** 2/02 Thur 2m heavy Hdl

An Irish bumper winner, he scored on his hurdling debut and has run consistently well since. Suited by cut.

Solvang (IRE)

95 **98**

10-y-o b g Carlingford Castle-Bramble Bird (Pitpan)
C C Bealby P F H Stephens

Placings:10/1132FP3PP/10201613/232125/45F6-05 **(0878)**
2001/02: 23^{0}GF, 22^{5}G

	Starts	1st	2nd	3rd	Win & Pl
Chases	2	0	0	0	0
Career Total	**31**	**7**	**5**	**4**	**46451**

140	11/99	Aint	2m4f	C(0-130)HCh	GD	£7067
110	10/98	Winc	2m6f	E Hdl	G-F	£2206
132	8/98	Tral	2m4f	HCh	GD	£11260
127	6/98	Rosc	3m100y	Ch	G-Y	£2382
127	7/97	Klny	2m4f	Ch	Y-S	£3391
115	6/97	Clon	2m2f	Ch	GD	£2712
107	4/97	Fair	2m2f	NHF	G-F	£6287

Total win prize-money £35309

Going: Sf: 0-0 GS: 0-0 Gd: 0-1 GF: - Fm: 0-1
Distance: 2m/2m3: 0-0 2m4-2m7: 0-1 3m+: 0-1
Track: LH: 0-1 RH: 0-1 Tight: 0-1 Gall: 0-0
Aids: Bl: 0-0 Vi: 0-0 Tstrap: 0-2
Best Rating: **140** 12/99 Leic 2m4f110y good Ch

Modest chaser, suited by a sound surface.

Solway Breeze (IRE)

99 **105**

9-y-o b m King's Ride-Spicey Cut (Cut Above)
Ms Liz Harrison David Alan Harrison

Placings:225/331P10/**F4UP-3312** **(4426)**
2001/02: 20^{3}HY, 25^{3}HY, 25^{1}S, 26^{2}HY

	Starts	1st	2nd	3rd	Win & Pl
Chases	4	1	1	2	7618
Career Total	**17**	**3**	**3**	**4**	**15689**

108	3/02	Ayr	3m1f	D Ch	SFT	£4367
116	1/00	Hayd	2m6f	D Hdl	SFT	£3666
97	12/99	Hexm	3m	E Hdl	HVY	£2658

Total win prize-money £10691

Going: Sf: 1-4 GS: 0-0 Gd: 0-0 GF: - Fm: 0-0
Distance: 2m/2m3: 0-0 2m4-2m7: 0-1 **3m+: 1-3**
Track: **LH: 1-4** RH: 0-0 Tight: 0-0 Gall: 0-0
Aids: Bl: 0-0 Vi: 0-0 Tstrap: 0-0
Best Rating: **116** 1/00 Hayd 2m6f soft Hdl

Not the most fluent of hurdlers, stays three miles plus and acts on soft ground. Got off the mark over fences at Ayr in March.

Solway Dawn

9

7-y-o ch m Minster Son-Oh Dear (Paico)
Ms Liz Harrison David Alan Harrison

Placings:5110/53P-0 **(1639)**
2001/02: 20^{0}GS

	Starts	1st	2nd	3rd	Win & Pl
Hurdles	1	0	0	0	
Career Total	**8**	**2**	**0**	**1**	**3813**

102	3/00	Ludl	2m	H NHF	GD	£1683
100	3/00	Catt	2m	H NHF	G-F	£1652

Total win prize-money £3336

Going: Sf: 0-0 GS: 0-1 Gd: 0-0 GF: - Fm: 0-0
Distance: 2m/2m3: 0-0 2m4-2m7: 0-1 3m+: 0-0
Track: LH: 0-0 RH: 0-0 Tight: 0-0 Gall: 0-0
Aids: Bl: 0-0 Vi: 0-0 Tstrap: 0-0
Best Rating: **102** 3/00 Ludl 2m good NHF

Solway Donal (IRE)

101(44h) (73h)**90**

9-y-o b m Celio Rufo-Knockaville (Crozier)
Ms Liz Harrison (Mrs M Haughan 7/9) David Alan Harrison

Placings:0FP/00 00P40PU010P **(3912)**
2001/02: 22^{0}GS, 21^{6}GF, 24^{P}G, 24^{4}S, 24^{0}S, 20^{P}HY, 22^{U}GS, 25^{3}GS, 16^{1}HY, 24^{6}S, 24^{P}GS

	Starts	1st	2nd	3rd	Win & Pl
Hurdles	5	0	0	0	0
Chases	6	1	0	1	3001
Career Total	**16**	**1**	**0**	**1**	**3001**

82	1/02	Sedg	2m110y	F(0-90)HCh	HVY	£2499

Total win prize-money £2499

Going: Sf: 1-5 GS: 0-4 Gd: 0-1 GF: - Fm: 0-1
Distance: **2m/2m3: 1-1** 2m4-2m7: 0-4 3m+: 0-6
Track: **LH: 1-5** RH: 0-6 **Tight: 1-7** Gall: 0-0
Aids: Bl: 0-0 Vi: 0-0 Tstrap: 0-0
Best Rating: **90** 1/02 Catt 3m1f110y gd-sft Ch

Modest dual-purpose stayer who handles heavy ground and has won on good in the past.

Solway Gale (IRE)

77f **77f**

5-y-o b m Husyan (USA)-Some Gale (Strong Gale)
Ms Liz Harrison David Alan Harrison

Placings:60 **(4750)**
2001/02: 16^{6}S, 17^{0}G

	Starts	1st	2nd	3rd	Win & Pl
NH Flat	2	0	0	0	0
Career Total	**2**	**0**	**0**	**0**	**0**

Going: Sf: 0-1 GS: 0-0 Gd: 0-1 GF: - Fm: 0-0
Distance: 2m/2m3: 0-2 2m4-2m7: 0-0 3m+: 0-0
Track: LH: 0-0 RH: 0-2 Tight: 0-1 Gall: 0-0
Aids: Bl: 0-0 Vi: 0-0 Tstrap: 0-0
Best Rating: **77** 2/02 Muss 2m soft NHF

Solway Plain

(97h) (76h)

8-y-o b g King's Ride-Oh Dear (Paico)

Ms Liz Harrison David Alan Harrison

Placings:5635400 (4745)
2001/02: 20⁵G, 25⁶GS, 24³HY, 24⁵GS, 22⁴HY, 20⁰GS, 24⁰G

	Starts	1st	2nd	3rd	Win & Pl
Hurdles	7	0	0	1	440
Career Total	**7**	**0**	**0**	**1**	**440**

Going: Sf: 0-2 GS: 0-3 Gd: 0-2 GF: - Fm: 0-0
Distance: 2m/2m3: 0-0 2m4-2m7: 0-3 3m+: 0-4
Track: LH: 0-3 RH: 0-3 Tight: 0-3 Gall: 0-0
Aids: Bl: 0-0 Vi: 0-0 Tstrap: 0-0
Best Rating: 76 3/02 Ayr 2m6f heavy Hdl

Modest staying hurdler.

Solway Rose

110(48h) **115**

8-y-o ch m Minster Son-Lady Mag (Silver Season)
Ms Liz Harrison David Alan Harrison

Placings:346/31P/3F301-PUP1U4 (4489)
2001/02: 24PS, 25UHY, 27PS, 25¹HY, 32UHY, 26⁴GS

	Starts	1st	2nd	3rd	Win & Pl
Chases	6	1	0	0	5171
Career Total	**17**	**3**	**0**	**4**	**13311**

115	3/02	Ayr	3m1f	D(0-125)HCh	HVY	£4745
115	10/00	Carl	3m2f	D(0-120)HCh	G-S	£3786
100	6/99	Prth	3m110y	E Hdl	G-S	£2724

Total win prize-money £11255

Going: Sf: 1-5 GS: 0-1 Gd: 0-0 GF: - Fm: 0-0
Distance: 2m/2m3: 0-0 2m4-2m7: 0-0 **3m+: 1-6**
Track: **LH: 1-5** RH: 0-1 Tight: 0-2 Gall: 0-1
Aids: Bl: 0-0 Vi: 0-0 Tstrap: 0-0
Best Rating: 115 3/02 Ayr 3m1f heavy Ch

Fair staying chaser, handles the mud.

Solway Saffy

7-y-o b m Safawan-Out On A Flyer (Comedy Star (USA))
Ms Liz Harrison David Alan Harrison

Placings:300-0PPPP (4898)
2001/02: 16⁰S, 20PHY, 19PS, 20PS, 16PG

	Starts	1st	2nd	3rd	Win & Pl
Hurdles	4	0	0	0	0
Chases	1	0	0	0	0
Career Total	**8**	**0**	**0**	**1**	**224**

Going: Sf: 0-4 GS: 0-0 Gd: 0-1 GF: - Fm: 0-0
Distance: 2m/2m3: 0-3 2m4-2m7: 0-2 3m+: 0-0
Track: LH: 0-2 RH: 0-2 Tight: 0-1 Gall: 0-1
Aids: Bl: 0-0 Vi: 0-0 Tstrap: 0-4
Best Rating: 101 6/00 MRas 2m1f110y gd-fm NHF

Somayda (IRE)

64 **25**

7-y-o b g Last Tycoon-Flame Of Tara (Artaius (USA))
Miss Jacqueline S Doyle The Somayda Partnership

Placings:0P (4422)
2001/02: 16⁰G, 16PGS

	Starts	1st	2nd	3rd	Win & Pl
Hurdles	2	0	0	0	
Career Total	**2**	**0**	**0**	**0**	

Going: Sf: 0-0 GS: 0-1 Gd: 0-1 GF: - Fm: 0-0
Distance: 2m/2m3: 0-2 2m4-2m7: 0-0 3m+: 0-0
Track: LH: 0-1 RH: 0-1 Tight: 0-0 Gall: 0-1
Aids: Bl: 0-0 Vi: 0-0 Tstrap: 0-0
Best Rating: 28 3/02 Winc 2m good Hdl

Some Go West (IRE)

8-y-o b g Un Desperado (FR)-Costly Lady (Bold Lad (IRE))
Neil King Simon Bullimore

Placings:5/520P614/0255P-332 (0585)
2001/02: 24³GF, 25³G, 24²GF

	Starts	1st	2nd	3rd	Win & Pl
Chases	3	0	1	2	1642
Career Total	**16**	**1**	**3**	**2**	**6765**

112	2/00	Donc	2m3f110y	E(0-105)HCh	GD	£3055

Total win prize-money £3055

Going: Sf: 0-0 GS: 0-0 Gd: 0-1 GF: - Fm: 0-2
Distance: 2m/2m3: 0-0 2m4-2m7: 0-0 3m+: 0-3
Track: LH: 0-2 RH: 0-1 Tight: 0-3 Gall: 0-0
Aids: Bl: 0-0 Vi: 0-0 Tstrap: 0-0
Best Rating: 112 5/01 Folk 3m1f good Ch

Some Operator (IRE)

101 **80**

8-y-o b g Lord Americo-Rathvilly Flier (Peacock (FR))
N A Twiston-Davies Lock Cottage Racing

Placings:50/UU434U0/00300 (2454)
2001/02: 16⁰G, 19⁰GF, 16³G, 16⁰G, 16⁰S

	Starts	1st	2nd	3rd	Win & Pl
Hurdles	5	0	0	1	389
Career Total	**14**	**0**	**0**	**2**	**1404**

Going: Sf: 0-1 GS: 0-0 Gd: 0-3 GF: - Fm: 0-1
Distance: 2m/2m3: 0-5 2m4-2m7: 0-0 3m+: 0-0
Track: LH: 0-3 RH: 0-2 Tight: 0-1 Gall: 0-0
Aids: Bl: 0-0 Vi: 0-0 Tstrap: 0-0
Best Rating: 99 10/99 Chep 2m110y soft Hdl

Showed ability in 1999, but has not had much racing mainly due to an 18 month absence. Showed signs of a revival at Towcester in October 2001.

Some Trainer (IRE)

(99c) (93c)**73**

6-y-o b g Leading Counsel (USA)-Miss Polymer (Doulab (USA))
J G Cromwell (Denis J Reddan 29/8) Denis J Reddan

Placings:00/640050-006642PP2 (4926a)
2001/02: 17⁰F, 17⁰GF, 20⁶SH, 17⁶G, 16⁴GF, 24²S, 24PS, 25PG, 20²Y

	Starts	1st	2nd	3rd	Win & Pl
NH Flat	1	0	0	0	0
Hurdles	2	0	0	0	0
Chases	6	0	2	0	2531
Career Total	**17**	**0**	**2**	**0**	**2739**

Going: Sf: 0-2 GS: 0-0 Gd: 0-2 GF: - Fm: 0-3
Distance: 2m/2m3: 0-4 2m4-2m7: 0-2 3m+: 0-3
Track: LH: 0-1 RH: 0-1 Tight: 0-1 Gall: 0-0
Aids: Bl: 0-0 Vi: 0-0 Tstrap: 0-8
Best Rating: 117 5/00 Punc 2m yield NHF

Somemanforoneman (IRE)

108 **143**

8-y-o b g Asir-Wintry Shower (Strong Gale)
C J Mann Bryan & Ann Beacham

Placings:4500/352430/63301F646263/011232F-055P420 (4661)
2001/02: 20⁰G, 24⁵S, 19⁵GS, 24PS, 20⁴GS, 24²GS, 25⁰G

	Starts	1st	2nd	3rd	Win & Pl
Chases	7	0	1	0	7469
Career Total	**36**	**3**	**5**	**6**	**32377**

155	11/00	Asct	3m110y	C(0-130)HCh	G-S	£6646
140	10/00	Wwck	2m4f110y	D Ch	SFT	£4030
105	12/99	Clon	2m6f	(0-95)Hdl	SH	£3388

Total win prize-money £14064

Going: Sf: 0-2 GS: 0-3 Gd: 0-2 GF: - Fm: 0-0
Distance: 2m/2m3: 0-0 2m4-2m7: 0-3 3m+: 0-4
Track: LH: 0-6 RH: 0-1 Tight: 0-2 Gall: 0-1
Aids: Bl: 0-7 Vi: 0-0 Tstrap: 0-0
Best Rating: 155 11/00 Asct 3m110y gd-sft Ch

A front-running ex-Irish chaser, he did well in novice chases in this country in 2001, but struggled somewhat in 2001/02. Suited by cut in the ground. Stays three miles, effective at two and a half.

Somerton Reef

8-y-o gr g Mystiko (USA)-Lady Reef (Mill Reef (USA))
N M Babbage Magor Golden Boys

Placings:0620/0 (4680)
2001/02: 17⁰GF

	Starts	1st	2nd	3rd	Win & Pl
Hurdles	1	0	0	0	
Career Total	**5**	**0**	**1**	**0**	**890**

Going: Sf: 0-0 GS: 0-0 Gd: 0-0 GF: - Fm: 0-1
Distance: 2m/2m3: 0-1 2m4-2m7: 0-0 3m+: 0-0
Track: LH: 0-0 RH: 0-1 Tight: 0-0 Gall: 0-0
Aids: Bl: 0-0 Vi: 0-0 Tstrap: 0-0
Best Rating: 94 9/98 List 2m good Hdl

Something Dandy (IRE)

102(104h) (90h)**114**

9-y-o b g Brush Aside (USA)-Hawthorn Dandy (Deep Run)
J A B Old Blomeley/lovatt Partnership

Placings:00/F0U/2240-520 (3226)
2001/02: 23⁵G, 20²GF, 21⁰G

	Starts	1st	2nd	3rd	Win & Pl
Chases	3	0	1	0	1004
Career Total	**12**	**0**	**3**	**0**	**3181**

Going: Sf: 0-0 GS: 0-0 Gd: 0-2 GF: - Fm: 0-1
Distance: 2m/2m3: 0-0 2m4-2m7: 0-2 3m+: 0-1
Track: LH: 0-0 RH: 0-3 Tight: 0-0 Gall: 0-0
Aids: Bl: 0-0 Vi: 0-0 Tstrap: 0-0
Best Rating: 114 12/01 Leic 2m4f110y gd-fm Ch

Fair novice hurdler/chaser at around two and a half/three miles. Acts on good or faster ground.

Something Happened (NZ)

96 88

9-y-o b g Cache Of Gold (USA)-Iseki (NZ) (Brazen Bay (AUS))

O Brennan Michael Lowe

Placings:5/0-3 **(0451)**

2001/02: 23^{3}F

	Starts	1st	2nd	3rd	Win & Pl
Hurdles	1	0	0	1	507
Career Total	**3**	**0**	**0**	**1**	**507**

Going: Sf: 0-0 GS: 0-0 Gd: 0-0 GF: - Fm: 0-1
Distance: 2m/2m3: 0-0 2m4-2m7: 0-1 3m+: 0-0
Track: LH: 0-1 RH: 0-0 Tight: 0-0 Gall: 0-0
Aids: Bl: 0-0 Vi: 0-0 Tstrap: 0-0
Best Rating: 88 5/01 Weth 2m7f firm Hdl

Somosierra (IRE)

7-y-o gr g Paris House-Island Heather (IRE) (Salmon Leap (USA))

V Thompson V Thompson

Placings:00/P **(4857)**

2001/02: 20^{P}G

	Starts	1st	2nd	3rd	Win & Pl
Hurdles	1	0	0	0	
Career Total	**3**	**0**	**0**	**0**	

Going: Sf: 0-0 GS: 0-0 Gd: 0-1 GF: - Fm: 0-0
Distance: 2m/2m3: 0-0 2m4-2m7: 0-1 3m+: 0-0
Track: LH: 0-1 RH: 0-0 Tight: 0-0 Gall: 0-0
Aids: Bl: 0-0 Vi: 0-0 Tstrap: 0-0
Best Rating: 34 4/99 Kels 2m110y gd-fm Hdl

Son Gancho

77 77

6-y-o ch g Arzanni-Early Morn (Sassafras (FR))

Miss D Cole Mrs Marilyn Cook

Placings:0U0P/0P-B0F **(1996)**

2001/02: 20^{B}GF, 16^{0}G, 17^{F}S

	Starts	1st	2nd	3rd	Win & Pl
Hurdles	3	0	0	0	
Career Total	**9**	**0**	**0**	**0**	

Going: Sf: 0-1 GS: 0-0 Gd: 0-1 GF: - Fm: 0-1
Distance: 2m/2m3: 0-2 2m4-2m7: 0-1 3m+: 0-0
Track: LH: 0-3 RH: 0-0 Tight: 0-1 Gall: 0-0
Aids: Bl: 0-0 Vi: 0-0 Tstrap: 0-0
Best Rating: 77 11/01 NAbb 2m1f soft Hdl

Son Of A Gun

110 108

8-y-o b g Gunner B-Sola Mia (Tolomeo)

J Neville Mrs P A Barratt

Placings:312223/330 **(3641)**

2001/02: 16^{3}G, 20^{3}G, 16^{0}S

	Starts	1st	2nd	3rd	Win & Pl
Hurdles	3	0	0	2	930
Career Total	**9**	**1**	**3**	**4**	**6814**

101	9/99	MRas	1m5f110y	H NHF	G-F	£1595

Total win prize-money £1595

Going: Sf: 0-1 GS: 0-0 Gd: 0-2 GF: - Fm: 0-0

Distance: 2m/2m3: 0-2 2m4-2m7: 0-1 3m+: 0-0
Track: LH: 0-2 RH: 0-1 Tight: 0-0 Gall: 0-2
Aids: Bl: 0-0 Vi: 0-0 Tstrap: 0-0
Best Rating: 126 12/99 Chep 2m110y heavy NHF

A former decent bumper horse, he has shown promise over hurdles following a spell on the Flat.

Son Of Anshan

9-y-o b g Anshan-Anhaar (Ela-Mana-Mou)

G Tuer G Tuer

Placings:0321F11/33P/314P3223/4450/P4-5213 **(4650)**

2001/02: 19^{5}S, 24^{2}S, 27^{1}S, 21^{3}G

	Starts	1st	2nd	3rd	Win & Pl
Chases	4	1	1	1	5256
Career Total	**28**	**5**	**4**	**7**	**25509**

95	3/02	Sedg	3m3f	H Ch	SFT	£1498
119	11/98	Uttx	3m	D Ch	GD	£4370
131	3/97	Kels	2m2f	D Hdl	GD	£2815
119	3/97	Ayr	2m	E Hdl	SFT	£2134
107	12/96	Newc	2m	E Hdl	GD	£2337

Total win prize-money £13156

Going: Sf: 1-3 GS: 0-0 Gd: 0-1 GF: - Fm: 0-0
Distance: 2m/2m3: 0-0 2m4-2m7: 0-2 **3m+: 1-2**
Track: **LH: 1-3** RH: 0-0 **Tight: 1-2** Gall: 0-1
Aids: Bl: 0-0 Vi: 0-0 **Tstrap: 1-2**
Best Rating: 131 4/99 Chel 2m5f good Ch

A one-time decent novice over fences, he is now a modest hunter chaser, tongue tied when successful at Sedgefield in March 2002.

Son Of Chaos (IRE)

83(87h) (68h)73

6-y-o b g Eurobus-Castle Otway (IRE) (Jeu De Paille (FR))

Mrs S C Bradburne Lord Cochrane And Partners

Placings:00FF/0330P-4540 **(1814)**

2001/02: 24^{4}G, 20^{5}G, 25^{4}G, 20^{0}S

	Starts	1st	2nd	3rd	Win & Pl
Hurdles	1	0	0	0	261
Chases	3	0	0	0	246
Career Total	**13**	**0**	**0**	**2**	**1129**

Going: Sf: 0-1 GS: 0-0 Gd: 0-3 GF: - Fm: 0-0
Distance: 2m/2m3: 0-0 2m4-2m7: 0-2 3m+: 0-2
Track: LH: 0-1 RH: 0-3 Tight: 0-1 Gall: 0-0
Aids: Bl: 0-0 Vi: 0-0 Tstrap: 0-0
Best Rating: 91 12/00 Ayr 2m4f soft Hdl

Son Of Courage

80 62

9-y-o br g Straight Knight-Fort Courage (Cash And Carry)

Miss D Cole M G Smale

Placings:5-P62 **(1063)**

2001/02: 22^{P}GS, 22^{6}G, 22^{2}G

	Starts	1st	2nd	3rd	Win & Pl
Hurdles	3	0	1	0	917
Career Total	**4**	**0**	**1**	**0**	**917**

Going: Sf: 0-0 GS: 0-1 Gd: 0-2 GF: - Fm: 0-0
Distance: 2m/2m3: 0-0 2m4-2m7: 0-3 3m+: 0-0
Track: LH: 0-2 RH: 0-0 Tight: 0-2 Gall: 0-0
Aids: Bl: 0-0 Vi: 0-0 Tstrap: 0-0
Best Rating: 62 8/01 NAbb 2m6f good Hdl

Son Of Light (IRE)

106(101h) (113h)117+

7-y-o br g Hollow Hand-Leaney Kamscort (Kambalda)

A Streeter Mrs Rosemary Bateman

Placings:432420/114-304P660 **(4778)**

2001/02: 16^{3}F, 16^{0}GF, 17^{4}GF, 21^{P}G, 17^{6}G, 20^{6}GS, 17^{0}G

	Starts	1st	2nd	3rd	Win & Pl
Hurdles	3	0	0	1	366
Chases	4	0	0	0	465
Career Total	**16**	**2**	**2**	**2**	**7917**

106	10/00	Sthl	2m	E Hdl	G-S	£2226
107	9/00	Strf	2m110y	E Hdl	GD	£2743

Total win prize-money £4969

Going: Sf: 0-0 GS: 0-1 Gd: 0-3 GF: - Fm: 0-3
Distance: 2m/2m3: 0-5 2m4-2m7: 0-2 3m+: 0-0
Track: LH: 0-5 RH: 0-2 Tight: 0-4 Gall: 0-0
Aids: Bl: 0-0 Vi: 0-1 Tstrap: 0-0
Best Rating: 113 5/01 Weth 2m firm Hdl

Won twice over hurdles in the autumn of 2000 and after many attempts finally broke his duck over fences at Uttoxeter in the summer of 2002. Stays well, acts on fast ground.

Son Of Ross

97 59

8-y-o b g Minster Son-Nancy Ardross (Ardross)

R W Thomson R W Thomson

Placings:0/00/4005-41PP00 **(4745)**

2001/02: 24^{4}GF, 24^{1}GF, 27^{P}S, 20^{P}S, 27^{0}S, 24^{0}G

	Starts	1st	2nd	3rd	Win & Pl
Hurdles	6	1	0	0	2898
Career Total	**13**	**1**	**0**	**0**	**2898**

70	6/01	Prth	3m110y	E Hdl	G-F	£2898

Total win prize-money £2898

Going: Sf: 0-3 GS: 0-0 Gd: 0-1 GF: - Fm: 1-2
Distance: 2m/2m3: 0-0 2m4-2m7: 0-1 **3m+: 1-5**
Track: LH: 0-2 **RH: 1-4** Tight: 0-3 Gall: 0-0
Aids: Bl: 0-0 Vi: 0-0 Tstrap: 0-0
Best Rating: 70 6/01 Prth 3m110y gd-fm Hdl

Son Of Sam

8-y-o b g Minster Son-Samonia (Rolfe (USA))

C Grant J W Barker

Placings:00/F-F **(0088)**

2001/02: 25^{F}S

	Starts	1st	2nd	3rd	Win & Pl
Chases	1	0	0	0	
Career Total	**4**	**0**	**0**	**0**	

Going: Sf: 0-1 GS: 0-0 Gd: 0-0 GF: - Fm: 0-0
Distance: 2m/2m3: 0-0 2m4-2m7: 0-0 3m+: 0-1
Track: LH: 0-1 RH: 0-0 Tight: 0-0 Gall: 0-0
Aids: Bl: 0-0 Vi: 0-0 Tstrap: 0-0
Best Rating: 52 3/98 Newc 2m gd-fm NHF

Sonevafushi (FR)

100 115

4-y-o b g Ganges (USA)-For Kicks (FR) (Top Ville)

Miss Venetia Williams (H-A Pantall 30/6) B C Dice

Placings:130 **(3979)**

2001/02: 16^{1}GS, 17^{3}GS, 16^{0}G

	Starts	1st	2nd	3rd	Win & Pl
Hurdles	3	1	0	1	4696
Career Total	**3**	**1**	**0**	**1**	**4696**

115 1/02 Newb 2m110y D Hdl G-S £4179
Total win prize-money £4180

Going: Sf: 0-0 GS: 1-2 Gd: 0-1 GF: - Fm: 0-0
Distance: **2m/2m3: 1-3** 2m4-2m7: 0-0 3m+: 0-0
Track: **LH: 1-1** RH: 0-2 Tight: 0-1 **Gall: 1-1**
Aids: Bl: 0-0 Vi: 0-0 Tstrap: 0-0
Best Rating: **115** 1/02 Newb 2m110y gd-sft Hdl

Winning form at nine-ten furlongs on the Flat in France. He got off the mark on his hurdling debut at Newbury in January 2002. Disappointing subsequently, was given time to come back to himself before winning a weakly contested event over two and a half miles at Southwell in May. Seems to act on most types of ground.

Song For Jess (IRE)

101 **88**

9-y-o b m Accordion-Ritual Girl (Ballad Rock)
F Jordan F K Jennings

Placings:UF524P0466423/553P/0241005F2/3001P-4P25P00 **(2926)**
2001/02: 20⁴G, 22ᴾGF, 25²GF, 22⁵GF, 24ᴾGF, 17⁰G, 24⁰GS

	Starts	1st	2nd	3rd	Win & Pl
Hurdles	7	0	1	0	561
Career Total	**38**	**2**	**5**	**3**	**10602**

88 6/00 Uttx 3m110y F(0-105)HHdl G-F £2674
85 8/99 Bang 2m4f F(0-105)HHdl GD £3777
Total win prize-money £6452

Going: Sf: 0-0 GS: 0-1 Gd: 0-2 GF: - Fm: 0-4
Distance: 2m/2m3: 0-1 2m4-2m7: 0-3 3m+: 0-3
Track: LH: 0-4 RH: 0-3 Tight: 0-4 Gall: 0-0
Aids: Bl: 0-0 Vi: 0-0 Tstrap: 0-0
Best Rating: **88** 7/01 Wolv 3m1f gd-fm Hdl

Songino (IRE)

98 **85**

6-y-o ch g Perugino (USA)-Sonbere (Electric)
J Clements J Clements

Placings:0000/0-0030000 **(4709a)**
2001/02: 20⁰F, 16⁰GY, 22³GF, 16⁰GF, 17⁰GY, 21⁰G, 20⁰Y

	Starts	1st	2nd	3rd	Win & Pl
Hurdles	7	0	0	1	353
Career Total	**12**	**0**	**0**	**1**	**353**

Going: Sf: 0-0 GS: 0-0 Gd: 0-1 GF: - Fm: 0-3
Distance: 2m/2m3: 0-3 2m4-2m7: 0-4 3m+: 0-0
Track: LH: 0-2 RH: 0-2 Tight: 0-0 Gall: 0-1
Aids: Bl: 0-0 Vi: 0-0 Tstrap: 0-0
Best Rating: **85** 10/01 Dpat 2m1f172y gd-yld Hdl

Sonic Girl (IRE)

33

7-y-o ch m Boyne Valley-So Ladylike (Malinowski (USA))
N M Babbage Mrs Joan Nelson

Placings:0406004002000-0 **(1398)**
2001/02: 16⁰GF

	Starts	1st	2nd	3rd	Win & Pl
Hurdles	1	0	0	0	
Career Total	**14**	**0**	**1**	**0**	**1368**

Going: Sf: 0-0 GS: 0-0 Gd: 0-0 GF: - Fm: 0-1
Distance: 2m/2m3: 0-1 2m4-2m7: 0-0 3m+: 0-0
Track: LH: 0-1 RH: 0-0 Tight: 0-0 Gall: 0-0
Aids: Bl: 0-0 Vi: 0-0 Tstrap: 0-0
Best Rating: **84** 8/00 Rosc 2m firm NHF

Sonny Jim

101 **89**

4-y-o b g Timeless Times (USA)-Allesca (Alleging (USA))
J J O'Neill (M D I Usher 11/2) The Cartmel Syndicate

Placings:0F622010440 **(4871)**
2001/02: 16⁰G, 16ᶠG, 18⁶G, 16²G, 16²G, 16⁰S, 16¹HY, 16⁰S, 16⁴HY, 20⁴GF, 25⁰GF

	Starts	1st	2nd	3rd	Win & Pl
Hurdles	11	1	2	0	5380
Career Total	**11**	**1**	**2**	**0**	**5380**

89 2/02 Plum 2m F Hdl HVY £2247
Total win prize-money £2247

Going: Sf: 1-4 GS: 0-0 Gd: 0-5 GF: - Fm: 0-2
Distance: **2m/2m3: 1-9** 2m4-2m7: 0-1 3m+: 0-1
Track: **LH: 1-6** RH: 0-5 **Tight: 1-2** Gall: 0-0
Aids: Bl: 0-2 Vi: 0-0 Tstrap: 0-0
Best Rating: **89** 4/02 Asct 2m4f gd-fm Hdl

Plating-class hurdler. Suited by good ground but handles heavy. Best at around two miles.

Sooprima (IRE)

86 **68**

9-y-o ch m Montelimar (USA)-Golden Rapid (Over The River (FR))
R Curtis Eddie Gloyne

Placings:35/0500/P/53-5 **(0374)**
2001/02: 26⁵GF

	Starts	1st	2nd	3rd	Win & Pl
Hurdles	1	0	0	0	0
Career Total	**10**	**0**	**0**	**2**	**381**

Going: Sf: 0-0 GS: 0-0 Gd: 0-0 GF: - Fm: 0-1
Distance: 2m/2m3: 0-0 2m4-2m7: 0-0 3m+: 0-1
Track: LH: 0-0 RH: 0-1 Tight: 0-0 Gall: 0-1
Aids: Bl: 0-0 Vi: 0-0 Tstrap: 0-0
Best Rating: **91** 1/98 Folk 2m1f110y gd-sft NHF

Sorbiere

15-y-o b g Deep Run-Irish Mint (Dusky Boy)
D M Grissell Mrs R A Proctor

Placings:023/3223/12331/33/5P511U/44F2PF503/35 23/0633310214/345162/6642-F **(0107)**
2001/02: 22ᶠGF

	Starts	1st	2nd	3rd	Win & Pl
Hurdles	1	0	0	0	
Career Total	**54**	**7**	**9**	**14**	**36780**

102 2/00 Plum 2m5f E(0-115)HHdl HVY £5083
97 4/99 Plum 2m4f D(0-120)HHdl GD £3062
90 12/98 Folk 2m6f110y F(0-105)HHdl SFT £2143
105 4/96 Folk 3m2f E Ch G-F £3206
101 3/96 Folk 3m2f D Ch G-F £3661
93 3/93 Newb 2m5f Hdl G-F £2652
6/92 Naas 2m3f NHF G-F £2901
Total win prize-money £22713

Going: Sf: 0-0 GS: 0-0 Gd: 0-0 GF: - Fm: 0-1
Distance: 2m/2m3: 0-0 2m4-2m7: 0-1 3m+: 0-0
Track: LH: 0-1 RH: 0-0 Tight: 0-1 Gall: 0-0
Aids: Bl: 0-0 Vi: 0-0 Tstrap: 0-0
Best Rating: **109** 4/94 Asct 3m good Hdl

Sorcerer's Drum (IRE)

11-y-o b g Orchestra-Pearly Miss (Space King)
Simon J Stearn (A L T Moore 10/3) Simon J Stearn

Placings:P/016P/014P0/P251/40-6 **(4538)**
2001/02: 24⁶G

	Starts	1st	2nd	3rd	Win & Pl
Chases	1	0	0	0	0
Career Total	**17**	**3**	**1**	**0**	**14235**

134 3/00 Navn 2m1f (0-116)HCh YLD £4692
117 2/99 Fair 2m2f Ch HVY £4603
108 1/97 Navn 2m Hdl G-Y £3051
Total win prize-money £12348

Going: Sf: 0-0 GS: 0-0 Gd: 0-1 GF: - Fm: 0-0
Distance: 2m/2m3: 0-0 2m4-2m7: 0-0 3m+: 0-1
Track: LH: 0-1 RH: 0-0 Tight: 0-1 Gall: 0-0
Aids: Bl: 0-0 Vi: 0-0 Tstrap: 0-0
Best Rating: **134** 3/00 Navn 2m1f yield Ch

Sorely Missed (IRE)

(102h) (86h)

7-y-o br g Yashgan-Well Honey (Al Sirat (USA))
R Dickin Mrs M Payne

Placings:60P-0P613334 **(4599)**
2001/02: 16⁰G, 16ᴾG, 21⁶G, 19¹G, 16³S, 16³S, 19³S, 25⁴GF

	Starts	1st	2nd	3rd	Win & Pl
Hurdles	7	1	0	3	4759
Chases	1	0	0	0	0
Career Total	**11**	**1**	**0**	**3**	**4759**

78 11/01 Wwck 2m3f F(0-100)HHdl GD £2059
Total win prize-money £2059

Going: Sf: 0-3 GS: 0-0 Gd: 1-4 GF: - Fm: 0-1
Distance: **2m/2m3: 1-6** 2m4-2m7: 0-1 3m+: 0-1
Track: **LH: 1-5** RH: 0-2 Tight: 0-1 Gall: 0-1
Aids: Bl: 0-0 Vi: 0-0 Tstrap: 0-0
Best Rating: **87** 10/00 Chep 2m110y gd-sft NHF

Modest hurdler. Stays two miles-three and may get further. Acts on good ground.

Sorrento

97 **84**

6-y-o b g Neltino-Lunabelle (Idiots Delight)
N J Henderson Queen Elizabeth

Placings:13-35 **(0844)**
2001/02: 20³GF, 19⁵GF

	Starts	1st	2nd	3rd	Win & Pl
Hurdles	2	0	0	1	414
Career Total	**4**	**1**	**0**	**2**	**2216**

108 5/00 Worc 2m H NHF GD £1477
Total win prize-money £1477

Going: Sf: 0-0 GS: 0-0 Gd: 0-0 GF: - Fm: 0-2
Distance: 2m/2m3: 0-1 2m4-2m7: 0-1 3m+: 0-0
Track: LH: 0-2 RH: 0-0 Tight: 0-2 Gall: 0-0
Aids: Bl: 0-0 Vi: 0-0 Tstrap: 0-0
Best Rating: **108** 5/00 Worc 2m good NHF

Sorrento King

98(105h) (99h)**100**

5-y-o ch g First Trump-Star Face (African Sky)
Mrs M Reveley (M W Easterby 5/8) B Padgett, K Bennett & A Davies

Placings:4203U3102 (4788)
2001/02: 16[4]GS, 19[2]G, 19[0]GF, 17[3]G, 20[U]G, 20[3]G, 16[1]GS, 16[0]GS, 20[2]F

	Starts	1st	2nd	3rd	Win & Pl
Hurdles	9	1	2	2	5990
Career Total	9	1	2	2	5990

99 12/01 Kels 2m110y E Hdl G-S £3346
Total win prize-money £3346

Going: Sf: 0-0 GS: 1-3 Gd: 0-4 GF: - Fm: 0-2
Distance: 2m/2m3: 1-4 2m4-2m7: 0-5 3m+: 0-0
Track: LH: 1-7 RH: 0-2 Tight: 1-4 Gall: 0-1
Aids: Bl: 0-1 Vi: 0-0 Tstrap: 0-0
Best Rating: 99 4/02 Newc 2m4f firm Hdl

Fair novice hurdler, successful at Kelso in December. Probably best at two miles. Made a satisfactory first start over fences.

Soso Gold

8-y-o b m Scallywag-Golden Valley (Hotfoot)
Mrs S J Smith Mrs S Smith

Placings:6-RP (2558)
2001/02: 19[R]GF, 16[P]S

	Starts	1st	2nd	3rd	Win & Pl
Hurdles	2	0	0	0	
Career Total	3	0	0	0	0

Going: Sf: 0-1 GS: 0-0 Gd: 0-0 GF: - Fm: 0-1
Distance: 2m/2m3: 0-2 2m4-2m7: 0-0 3m+: 0-0
Track: LH: 0-2 RH: 0-0 Tight: 0-2 Gall: 0-0
Aids: Bl: 0-0 Vi: 0-0 Tstrap: 0-0
Best Rating: 71 6/00 Worc 2m good NHF

Sossus Vlei

108 141
6-y-o b g Inchinor-Sassalya (Sassafras (FR))
P Winkworth (R Gibson 1/12) P Winkworth

Placings:300 (4188)
2001/02: 16[3]S, 16[0]GS, 16[0]GS

	Starts	1st	2nd	3rd	Win & Pl
Hurdles	3	0	0	1	976
Career Total	3	0	0	1	976

Going: Sf: 0-1 GS: 0-2 Gd: 0-0 GF: - Fm: 0-0
Distance: 2m/2m3: 0-3 2m4-2m7: 0-0 3m+: 0-0
Track: LH: 0-2 RH: 0-1 Tight: 0-0 Gall: 0-1
Aids: Bl: 0-0 Vi: 0-0 Tstrap: 0-0
Best Rating: 141 2/02 Newb 2m110y soft Hdl

A one-time decent performer on the Flat in France, he ran a blinder on his hurdles debut in February 2002, and ran another decent race in a Grade Two next time. Suited by soft ground.

Soul King (IRE)

(83h) (15h)
7-y-o b g King's Ride-Soul Lucy (Lucifer (USA))
N J Hawke (G M McCourt 24/2) N J Hawke

Placings:40005-0FP (4590)
2001/02: 24[0]G, 25[F]S, 24[P]G

	Starts	1st	2nd	3rd	Win & Pl
Hurdles	1	0	0	0	0
Chases	2	0	0	0	0
Career Total	8	0	0	0	0

Going: Sf: 0-1 GS: 0-0 Gd: 0-2 GF: - Fm: 0-0
Distance: 2m/2m3: 0-0 2m4-2m7: 0-0 3m+: 0-3
Track: LH: 0-2 RH: 0-1 Tight: 0-0 Gall: 0-0
Aids: Bl: 0-0 Vi: 0-1 Tstrap: 0-1
Best Rating: 85 5/00 Worc 2m gd-fm NHF

Modest hurdler. Winning pointer. Fell in a handicap chase at Hereford in March 2002. Stays three miles. Acts on soft ground.

Sound Of Cheers

103 109
5-y-o br g Zilzal (USA)-Martha Stevens (USA) (Super Concorde (USA))
F Kirby (P W D'Arcy 8/5) Fred Kirby

Placings:061023 (4492)
2001/02: 16[0]GS, 20[6]G, 20[1]S, 20[0]GS, 17[2]S, 17[3]GS

	Starts	1st	2nd	3rd	Win & Pl
Hurdles	6	1	1	1	3837
Career Total	6	1	1	1	3837

105 1/02 Newc 2m4f E Hdl SFT £2667
Total win prize-money £2667

Going: Sf: 1-2 GS: 0-3 Gd: 0-1 GF: - Fm: 0-0
Distance: 2m/2m3: 0-3 **2m4-2m7: 1-3** 3m+: 0-0
Track: **LH: 1-5** RH: 0-1 Tight: 0-1 **Gall: 1-4**
Aids: Bl: 0-0 Vi: 0-0 Tstrap: 0-0
Best Rating: 109 3/02 Sedg 2m1f soft Hdl

Chaser in the making. Stays two and a half miles. Acts on soft/heavy ground.

Sounds Cool

100 85
6-y-o b g Savahra Sound-Lucky Candy (Lucky Wednesday)
A Streeter Formula One Racing

Placings:0/00500F-U126P33 (1473)
2001/02: 16[U]GF, 17[1]GF, 17[2]G, 17[6]G, 16[P]GF, 16[3]G, 17[3]S

	Starts	1st	2nd	3rd	Win & Pl
Hurdles	7	1	1	2	3238
Career Total	14	1	1	2	3238

74 6/01 MRas 2m1f110y G(0-90)HHdl G-F £1645
Total win prize-money £1645

Going: Sf: 0-1 GS: 0-0 Gd: 0-3 GF: - Fm: 1-3
Distance: **2m/2m3: 1-7** 2m4-2m7: 0-0 3m+: 0-0
Track: LH: 0-4 **RH: 1-3 Tight: 1-6** Gall: 0-0
Aids: Bl: 0-0 Vi: 0-2 Tstrap: 0-0
Best Rating: 82 9/01 Uttx 2m good Hdl

Sounds Special

5-y-o b m Savahra Sound-Sola Mia (Tolomeo)
Mrs S J Smith Paul J Dixon

Placings:P (0976)
2001/02: 16[P]GF

	Starts	1st	2nd	3rd	Win & Pl
Hurdles	1	0	0	0	
Career Total	1	0	0	0	

Going: Sf: 0-0 GS: 0-0 Gd: 0-0 GF: - Fm: 0-1
Distance: 2m/2m3: 0-1 2m4-2m7: 0-0 3m+: 0-0
Track: LH: 0-1 RH: 0-0 Tight: 0-1 Gall: 0-0
Aids: Bl: 0-0 Vi: 0-0 Tstrap: 0-0
Best Rating:

Soundtrack (IRE)

93 113
9-y-o b g Orchestra-Misty Boosh (Tarboosh (USA))
Miss Venetia Williams J M Kinnear

Placings:22/11125/34111F-P0P (3982)
2001/02: 24[P]GS, 26[0]S, 24[P]GS

	Starts	1st	2nd	3rd	Win & Pl
Chases	3	0	0	0	
Career Total	17	7	3	1	27884

131 3/01 Plum 3m2f E Ch HVY £3055
140 2/01 Tntn 3m D Ch HVY £5715
150 1/01 Plum 3m2f E Ch HVY £3318
123 10/99 Strf 2m6f110y D Hdl G-F £3717
120 10/99 Bang 2m4f E Hdl G-S £2295
119 9/99 Hrfd 2m3f110y E Hdl GD £2472
98 9/99 Carl 2m1f H NHF G-F £1647
Total win prize-money £22221

Going: Sf: 0-1 GS: 0-2 Gd: 0-0 GF: - Fm: 0-0
Distance: 2m/2m3: 0-0 2m4-2m7: 0-0 3m+: 0-3
Track: LH: 0-1 RH: 0-2 Tight: 0-1 Gall: 0-0
Aids: Bl: 0-0 Vi: 0-0 Tstrap: 0-0
Best Rating: 150 1/01 Plum 3m2f heavy Ch

He is an out-and-out stayer and did well in novice chases at the beginning of 2001, winning three times on heavy ground. Well below form during 2001/02.

South West Express (IRE)

95(91h) 87
10-y-o ch g Executive Perk-Bohemian Girl (Pardao)
Mrs D Thomas Mrs D Thomas

Placings:0/500/5521030/3022U1/12263FP/PP56-P00PF304356 (4505)
2001/02: 16[P]GF, 19[0]G, 19[0]S, 24[F]G, 21[F]G, 19[3]G, 22[0]G, 20[4]S, 16[3]HY, 16[5]S, 21[6]G

	Starts	1st	2nd	3rd	Win & Pl
Hurdles	1	0	0	0	0
Chases	10	0	0	2	1071
Career Total	39	3	5	5	14893

99 11/99 Leic 2m4f110y F(0-100)HCh G-F £3379
94 3/99 Tntn 2m110y F(0-105)HCh SFT £2775
72 12/97 Leic 2m4f110y G(0-90)HHdl SFT £2108
Total win prize-money £8262

Going: Sf: 0-4 GS: 0-0 Gd: 0-6 GF: - Fm: 0-1
Distance: 2m/2m3: 0-5 2m4-2m7: 0-5 3m+: 0-1
Track: LH: 0-5 RH: 0-4 Tight: 0-2 Gall: 0-0
Aids: Bl: 0-0 Vi: 0-0 Tstrap: 0-0
Best Rating: 102 3/00 Tntn 2m110y good Ch

Very modest handicap chaser these days.

Southampton

103(90h) (67h)104
12-y-o b g Ballacashtal (CAN)-Petingo Gold (Pitskelly)
G B Balding Mrs E A Haycock

Placings:1102/5212125F2311P302P/641013053315 3212/223203/3664250/610313236/24P-002FF (1138)
2001/02: 19[0]GS, 22[0]GF, 23[2]G, 23[F]G, 24[F]G

	Starts	1st	2nd	3rd	Win & Pl
Hurdles	1	0	0	0	0
Chases	4	0	1	0	917
Career Total	67	12	15	12	76125

110 9/99 Plum 2m5f E(0-120)HHdl GD £2786
106 7/99 NAbb 2m6f D(0-120)HHdl G-S £2848
122 4/96 Asct 2m3f110y C HCh G-F £14655
121 2/96 Sand 2m C(0-135)HCh G-S £4554

110 11/95 Worc 2m C(0-130)HHdl G-F £3601
107 10/95 Chel 2m110y C(0-130)HHdl G-F £3420
105 12/94 Wind 2m (0-125)HHdl G-S £2948
108 11/94 Strf 2m110y (0-120)HHdl G-S £2635
90 8/94 Ctml 2m1f110y (0-115)HHdl GD £2901
90 6/94 Strf 2m110y HHdl G-F £1716
85 12/93 Wwck 2m Hdl SFT £1473
74 9/93 Hntg 2m110y Hdl G-F £1480
Total win prize-money £45021

Going: Sf: 0-0 GS: 0-1 Gd: 0-3 GF: - Fm: 0-1
Distance: 2m/2m3: 0-0 2m4-2m7: 0-2 3m+: 0-3
Track: LH: 0-4 RH: 0-1 Tight: 0-2 Gall: 0-0
Aids: Bl: 0-0 Vi: 0-5 Tstrap: 0-0
Best Rating: **124** 2/97 Wwck 2m4f110y good Ch

Prolific hurdler/chaser. (DEAD)

Southdown Lad

98 **94**
8-y-o b g Henbit (USA)-Stupid Cupid (Idiots Delight)
R Rowe The Exclusive Partnership

Placings: *040/5*004/05/**5FP-P2033** **(1255)**
2001/02: 26^{P}G, 24^{2}GF, 23^{0}G, 20^{3}GF, 22^{3}GF

	Starts	1st	2nd	3rd	Win & Pl
Chases	5	0	1	2	1985
Career Total	**17**	**0**	**1**	**2**	**2195**

Going: Sf: 0-0 GS: 0-0 Gd: 0-2 GF: - Fm: 0-3
Distance: 2m/2m3: 0-0 2m4-2m7: 0-2 3m+: 0-3
Track: LH: 0-2 RH: 0-2 Tight: 0-2 Gall: 0-1
Aids: Bl: 0-0 Vi: 0-0 Tstrap: 0-5
Best Rating: **96** 5/98 Chep 2m110y gd-fm NHF

Southern Cross

10-y-o ch g Buckley-Muznah (Royal And Regal (USA))
A Hollingsworth M Stephenson

Placings: *U13/5*4323/F6005424/00/0/P **(0246)**
2001/02: 21^{P}GF

	Starts	1st	2nd	3rd	Win & Pl
Hurdles	1	0	0	0	
Career Total	**20**	**1**	**2**	**3**	**4809**

99 3/96 Newc 2m H NHF SFT £1637
Total win prize-money £1637

Going: Sf: 0-0 GS: 0-0 Gd: 0-0 GF: - Fm: 0-1
Distance: 2m/2m3: 0-0 2m4-2m7: 0-1 3m+: 0-0
Track: LH: 0-0 RH: 0-0 Tight: 0-0 Gall: 0-0
Aids: Bl: 0-0 Vi: 0-0 Tstrap: 0-0
Best Rating: **102** 3/97 Hexm 2m soft Hdl

Southern Dunes

90 **55**
6-y-o b g Ardkinglass-Leprechaun Lady (Royal Blend)
G Fierro G Fierro

Placings: PP-0P0P0P **(4236)**
2001/02: 16^{0}G, 25^{P}GS, 16^{0}GF, 16^{P}G, 16^{0}G, 21^{P}GF

	Starts	1st	2nd	3rd	Win & Pl
Hurdles	6	0	0	0	
Career Total	**8**	**0**	**0**	**0**	

Going: Sf: 0-0 GS: 0-1 Gd: 0-3 GF: - Fm: 0-2
Distance: 2m/2m3: 0-4 2m4-2m7: 0-1 3m+: 0-1
Track: LH: 0-3 RH: 0-3 Tight: 0-1 Gall: 0-2
Aids: Bl: 0-6 Vi: 0-0 Tstrap: 0-0
Best Rating: **55** 12/01 Donc 2m110y good Hdl

Southern Ridge

99(66c) (40c)**69**
11-y-o b g Indian Ridge-Southern Sky (Comedy Star (USA))
Anthony Holdsworth N J Holdsworth

Placings: 60066/22145/66/00P/0F02 **(4565)**
2001/02: 16^{0}S, 17^{F}GF, 17^{0}G, 16^{2}G

	Starts	1st	2nd	3rd	Win & Pl
Hurdles	3	0	1	0	574
Chases	1	0	0	0	0
Career Total	**19**	**1**	**3**	**0**	**4032**

95 9/96 NAbb 2m1f E Hdl GD £2326
Total win prize-money £2327

Going: Sf: 0-1 GS: 0-0 Gd: 0-2 GF: - Fm: 0-1
Distance: 2m/2m3: 0-4 2m4-2m7: 0-0 3m+: 0-0
Track: LH: 0-1 RH: 0-3 Tight: 0-1 Gall: 0-0
Aids: Bl: 0-0 Vi: 0-0 Tstrap: 0-0
Best Rating: **95** 9/96 NAbb 2m1f good Hdl

Plating class hurdler, suited by two miles and good ground.

Southern Star (IRE)

110(107h) (128h)**150**
7-y-o ch g Montelimar (USA)-Flying Pegus (Beau Chapeau)
Miss H C Knight Southern Brick & Tile Co Ltd

Placings: *13/2*3113-**11U34P2** **(4666)**
2001/02: 20^{1}G, 24^{1}G, 24^{U}G, 24^{3}G, 25^{4}G, 24^{P}GS, 25^{2}G

	Starts	1st	2nd	3rd	Win & Pl
Chases	7	2	1	1	33380
Career Total	**14**	**5**	**2**	**4**	**51628**

150 10/01 Chel 3m110y C Ch GD £8346
124 10/01 Bang 2m4f110y D Ch GD £4309
132 2/01 Hntg 2m4f110y B Hdl G-S £8970
133 1/01 Winc 2m E Hdl G-S £2047
123 10/99 Hntg 2m110y H NHF G-F £1842
Total win prize-money £25516

Going: Sf: 0-0 GS: 0-1 Gd: 2-6 GF: - Fm: 0-0
Distance: 2m/2m3: 0-0 2m4-2m7: 1-1 3m+: 1-6
Track: **LH: 2-7** RH: 0-0 Tight: 1-2 Gall: 1-5
Aids: Bl: 0-0 Vi: 0-0 Tstrap: 0-0
Best Rating: **150** 4/02 Aint 3m1f good Ch

A promising novice chaser last season, he acts on most types of ground. A good second to Barton at Aintree, he needs a left-handed track.

Southern-Be-George

93(106h) (95h)**86**
7-y-o b g Be My Chief (USA)-Southern Sky (Comedy Star (USA))
W G M Turner A Wilkinson

Placings: P435/0P44P/215-11 **(1380)**
2001/02: 20^{1}GF, 19^{1}GF

	Starts	1st	2nd	3rd	Win & Pl
Hurdles	2	2	0	0	5849
Career Total	**14**	**3**	**1**	**1**	**10070**

95 9/01 Hrfd 2m3f110y F(0-100)HHdl G-F £2901
87 8/01 Sthl 2m4f110y F(0-110)HHdl G-F £2947
89 5/00 Extr 2m6f E(0-105)HHdl G-F £2957
Total win prize-money £8807

Going: Sf: 0-0 GS: 0-0 Gd: 0-0 GF: - Fm: 2-2
Distance: 2m/2m3: 0-0 **2m4-2m7: 2-2** 3m+: 0-0
Track: LH: 1-1 RH: 1-1 **Tight: 1-1** Gall: 0-0
Aids: Bl: 0-0 Vi: 0-0 Tstrap: 0-0
Best Rating: **95** 9/01 Hrfd 2m3f110y gd-fm Hdl

Modest hurdler, suited by two and a half miles and easy ground.

Southerncrosspatch

107 **103**
11-y-o ch g Ra Nova-Southern Bird (Shiny Tenth)
Mrs Barbara Waring E S Chivers

Placings: *0/040/*0125**F3P/111P/3PP**204**P**4/03422**P**-1334244022 **(4754)**
2001/02: 27^{1}G, 22^{3}G, 22^{3}GF, 24^{4}GF, 24^{2}GF, 24^{4}G, 24^{4}GF, 21^{0}G, 25^{2}GF, 24^{2}GF

	Starts	1st	2nd	3rd	Win & Pl
Hurdles	10	1	3	2	8187
Career Total	**39**	**5**	**7**	**5**	**27259**

101 6/01 NAbb 3m3f E(0-115)HHdl GD £3038
107 6/98 Strf 2m4f E(0-115)HCh G-S £2921
92 6/98 Sthl 3m110y F(0-105)HCh GD £3777
113 6/98 Worc 2m4f110y E(0-100)HCh G-F £3315
87 8/97 Sthl 3m110y E Hdl G-F £2322
Total win prize-money £15375

Going: Sf: 0-0 GS: 0-0 Gd: 1-4 GF: - Fm: 0-6
Distance: 2m/2m3: 0-0 2m4-2m7: 0-3 **3m+: 1-7**
Track: **LH: 1-7** RH: 0-1 **Tight: 1-4** Gall: 0-1
Aids: Bl: 0-0 Vi: 0-0 Tstrap: 0-0
Best Rating: **113** 6/98 Worc 2m4f110y gd-fm Ch

A one-tme fair dual-purpose performer, he needs extreme distances. Runner-up in first two starts of 2002.

Southerndown (IRE)

110(97h) (82h)**97**
9-y-o ch g Montelimar (USA)-Country Melody (IRE) (Orchestra)
R Lee Mrs Bill Neale And John Jackson

Placings: *05/6*2265504/**P**5261055/040-**4**00**2260**553033 **(4501)**
2001/02: 24^{4}GF, 24^{0}GF, 25^{0}GF, 24^{2}GF, 24^{2}GF, 24^{6}G, 25^{0}G, 27^{5}G, 27^{5}S, 26^{3}G, 22^{0}HY, 24^{3}HY, 27^{3}G

	Starts	1st	2nd	3rd	Win & Pl
Hurdles	6	0	0	3	1016
Chases	7	0	2	0	2361
Career Total	**34**	**1**	**5**	**3**	**7964**

80 9/99 Hntg 3m2f F(0-90)HHdl GD £1955
Total win prize-money £1956

Going: Sf: 0-3 GS: 0-0 Gd: 0-5 GF: - Fm: 0-5
Distance: 2m/2m3: 0-0 2m4-2m7: 0-1 3m+: 0-12
Track: LH: 0-11 RH: 0-2 Tight: 0-11 Gall: 0-1
Aids: Bl: 0-0 Vi: 0-6 Tstrap: 0-0
Best Rating: **97** 5/01 Sthl 3m110y gd-fm Ch

Plating-class staying hurdler and chaser. Suited by good ground or faster and stays extreme distances.

Southwold (IRE)

72 **38**
5-y-o ch g Moscow Society (USA)-Rose Miller (Roselier (FR))
B G Powell P H Betts

Placings: *0*P0 **(4548)**
2001/02: 16^{0}S, 22^{P}GS, 21^{0}GF

	Starts	1st	2nd	3rd	Win & Pl
NH Flat	1	0	0	0	0
Hurdles	2	0	0	0	0
Career Total	**3**	**0**	**0**	**0**	

Going: Sf: 0-1 GS: 0-1 Gd: 0-0 GF: - Fm: 0-1
Distance: 2m/2m3: 0-1 2m4-2m7: 0-2 3m+: 0-0

Track: LH: 0-1 RH: 0-2 Tight: 0-1 Gall: 0-1
Aids: Bl: 0-0 Vi: 0-0 Tstrap: 0-0
Best Rating: **77** 2/02 Winc 2m soft NHF

Sovereign

106 92

8-y-o b m Interrex (CAN)-Shiny Penny (Glint Of Gold)
J F Panvert J F Panvert

Placings:5524342/6220604060P5/60P6P6655050002 3303/610015-0 **(4911)**
2001/02: $24^{0}G$

	Starts	1st	2nd	3rd	Win & Pl
Hurdles	1	0	0	0	
Career Total	**45**	**2**	**5**	**4**	**9670**

92 9/00 Hrfd 2m3f110y E Hdl G-F £2992
90 5/00 Fknm 2m7f110y E Hdl FRM £2229
Total win prize-money £5222

Going: Sf: 0-0 GS: 0-0 Gd: 0-1 GF: - Fm: 0-0
Distance: 2m/2m3: 0-0 2m4-2m7: 0-0 3m+: 0-1
Track: LH: 0-0 RH: 0-0 Tight: 0-0 Gall: 0-0
Aids: Bl: 0-0 Vi: 0-0 Tstrap: 0-0
Best Rating: **92** 9/00 Hrfd 2m3f110y gd-fm Hdl

Modest hurdler. Absent from October 2000 until April 2002, and scored in June back at Hereford. Stays two and a half miles.

Sovereign Gale (IRE)

(95h) (73h)

8-y-o b m Strong Gale-Sovereign Sox (Don)
Mrs H Dalton Miss Julia Oakey

Placings:045F **(1802)**
2001/02: $20^{0}G$, $20^{4}GF$, $19^{0}G$, $16^{F}GF$

	Starts	1st	2nd	3rd	Win & Pl
Hurdles	3	0	0	0	0
Chases	1	0	0	0	0
Career Total	**4**	**0**	**0**	**0**	**0**

Going: Sf: 0-0 GS: 0-0 Gd: 0-2 GF: - Fm: 0-2
Distance: 2m/2m3: 0-1 2m4-2m7: 0-3 3m+: 0-0
Track: LH: 0-2 RH: 0-2 Tight: 0-1 Gall: 0-0
Aids: Bl: 0-0 Vi: 0-0 Tstrap: 0-0
Best Rating: **73** 10/01 Hrfd 2m3f110y good Hdl

Sovereign Gold

87f 88f

5-y-o b g Rakaposhi King-Page Of Gold (Goldhill)
D R Gandolfo A E Smith

Placings:0 **(2041)**
2001/02: $16^{0}GS$

	Starts	1st	2nd	3rd	Win & Pl
NH Flat	1	0	0	0	
Career Total	**1**	**0**	**0**	**0**	

Going: Sf: 0-0 GS: 0-1 Gd: 0-0 GF: - Fm: 0-0
Distance: 2m/2m3: 0-1 2m4-2m7: 0-0 3m+: 0-0
Track: LH: 0-0 RH: 0-1 Tight: 0-0 Gall: 0-0
Aids: Bl: 0-0 Vi: 0-0 Tstrap: 0-0
Best Rating: **88** 11/01 Sand 2m110y gd-sft NHF

Sovereign Grit (IRE)

94 51

12-y-o ch g Sheer Grit-Gorryelm (Arctic Slave)
Mrs L C Jewell Mrs A Greengrow

Placings:20/40/P63 **(4779)**
2001/02: $20^{P}S$, $17^{6}G$, $21^{3}GF$

	Starts	1st	2nd	3rd	Win & Pl
Hurdles	2	0	0	1	400
Chases	1	0	0	0	0
Career Total	**7**	**0**	**1**	**1**	**1219**

Going: Sf: 0-1 GS: 0-0 Gd: 0-1 GF: - Fm: 0-1
Distance: 2m/2m3: 0-1 2m4-2m7: 0-2 3m+: 0-0
Track: LH: 0-2 RH: 0-0 Tight: 0-3 Gall: 0-0
Aids: Bl: 0-0 Vi: 0-0 Tstrap: 0-0
Best Rating: **92** 4/96 Thur 2m gd-yld NHF

Poor form over both types of obstacle.

Sovereign's Gift

96 77

6-y-o ch m Elegant Monarch-Cadeau D'Aragon (Aragon)
Miss D Cole B W Gillbard

Placings:000/05030 **(1544)**
2001/02: $17^{0}GS$, $17^{5}G$, $20^{0}G$, $17^{3}GF$, $17^{0}G$

	Starts	1st	2nd	3rd	Win & Pl
Hurdles	5	0	0	1	381
Career Total	**8**	**0**	**0**	**1**	**381**

Going: Sf: 0-0 GS: 0-1 Gd: 0-3 GF: - Fm: 0-1
Distance: 2m/2m3: 0-4 2m4-2m7: 0-1 3m+: 0-0
Track: LH: 0-3 RH: 0-2 Tight: 0-3 Gall: 0-0
Aids: Bl: 0-0 Vi: 0-0 Tstrap: 0-0
Best Rating: **77** 8/01 NAbb 2m1f gd-fm Hdl

A winning plater on the Flat. Moderate form in novice hurdles.

Soviet Lady (IRE)

8-y-o b m Soviet Lad (USA)-La Vosgienne (Ashmore (FR))
L A Dace Simply Poyle & Pragnell

Placings:3504/40/P **(2711)**
2001/02: $16^{P}HY$

	Starts	1st	2nd	3rd	Win & Pl
Hurdles	1	0	0	0	
Career Total	**7**	**0**	**0**	**1**	**350**

Going: Sf: 0-1 GS: 0-0 Gd: 0-0 GF: - Fm: 0-0
Distance: 2m/2m3: 0-1 2m4-2m7: 0-0 3m+: 0-0
Track: LH: 0-0 RH: 0-1 Tight: 0-0 Gall: 0-0
Aids: Bl: 0-0 Vi: 0-0 Tstrap: 0-0
Best Rating: **90** 3/99 Font 2m2f110y soft Hdl

Spa Gulch (USA)

80 53

4-y-o ch g Gulch (USA)-Carezza (USA) (Caro)
M E Sowersby (S C Williams 12/7) The Southwold Set

Placings:06P060 **(1718)**
2001/02: $17^{0}GS$, $16^{6}G$, $17^{P}G$, $17^{0}G$, $17^{6}S$, $16^{0}G$

	Starts	1st	2nd	3rd	Win & Pl
Hurdles	6	0	0	0	0
Career Total	**6**	**0**	**0**	**0**	**0**

Going: Sf: 0-1 GS: 0-1 Gd: 0-4 GF: - Fm: 0-0
Distance: 2m/2m3: 0-6 2m4-2m7: 0-0 3m+: 0-0
Track: LH: 0-4 RH: 0-1 Tight: 0-4 Gall: 0-0
Aids: Bl: 0-1 Vi: 0-0 Tstrap: 0-5
Best Rating: **53** 9/01 Sedg 2m1f good Hdl

Space Hopper (IRE)

86f 76f

7-y-o ch g Mister Lord (USA)-Kilmalooda Lass (Prince Rheingold)
H E Haynes N D Edden

Placings:06 **(0684)**
2001/02: $17^{0}F$, $17^{6}G$

	Starts	1st	2nd	3rd	Win & Pl
NH Flat	2	0	0	0	0
Career Total	**2**	**0**	**0**	**0**	**0**

Going: Sf: 0-0 GS: 0-0 Gd: 0-1 GF: - Fm: 0-1
Distance: 2m/2m3: 0-2 2m4-2m7: 0-0 3m+: 0-0
Track: LH: 0-1 RH: 0-1 Tight: 0-1 Gall: 0-0
Aids: Bl: 0-0 Vi: 0-0 Tstrap: 0-0
Best Rating: **76** 6/01 NAbb 2m1f good NHF

Spandau (NZ)

8-y-o br g Fiesta Star (AUS)-Koru (NZ) (Diplomatic Agent (USA))
J C Tuck James R Tuck

Placings:00P/2600/1-P **(1085)**
2001/02: $20^{P}G$

	Starts	1st	2nd	3rd	Win & Pl
Hurdles	1	0	0	0	
Career Total	**9**	**1**	**1**	**0**	**3417**

95 5/00 Hrfd 2m1f D(0-110)HHdl GD £2762
Total win prize-money £2763

Going: Sf: 0-0 GS: 0-0 Gd: 0-1 GF: - Fm: 0-0
Distance: 2m/2m3: 0-0 2m4-2m7: 0-1 3m+: 0-0
Track: LH: 0-1 RH: 0-0 Tight: 0-1 Gall: 0 0
Aids: Bl: 0-0 Vi: 0-0 Tstrap: 0-0
Best Rating: **95** 5/00 Hrfd 2m1f good Hdl

Spanish Archer (IRE)

100(102h) 80

7-y-o b g Spanish Place (USA)-Bow Gello (Bargello)
P J Hobbs Waterloo

Placings:610000/02213-P **(4588)**
2001/02: $22^{P}G$

	Starts	1st	2nd	3rd	Win & Pl
Hurdles	1	0	0	0	
Career Total	**12**	**2**	**2**	**1**	**6593**

97 10/00 Folk 2m5f F(0-95)HCh G-F £2387
99 11/99 Tntn 2m1f H NHF GD £1680
Total win prize-money £4068

Going: Sf: 0-0 GS: 0-0 Gd: 0-1 GF: - Fm: 0-0
Distance: 2m/2m3: 0-0 2m4-2m7: 0-1 3m+: 0-0
Track: LH: 0-0 RH: 0-1 Tight: 0-0 Gall: 0-0
Aids: Bl: 0-0 Vi: 0-0 Tstrap: 0-0
Best Rating: **99** 11/99 Tntn 2m1f good NHF

Only third best when gifted a modest handicap chase at Uttoxeter in June 2002.

Spanish Light (IRE)

13-y-o b g Spanish Place (USA)-Arconist (Welsh Pageant)
Sir John Barlow Bt Sir John Barlow

Placings:051/421**U122141F/P2425/33U5P/363444/1P643U/056-5** (1629)
2001/02: 21^{5}GF

	Starts	1st	2nd	3rd	Win & Pl
Hurdles	1	0	0	0	0
Career Total	**40**	**6**	**5**	**5**	**36428**

113	5/99	Bang	2m4f110y	D(0-120)HCh	GD	£5288
127	2/96	Hayd	2m	C Ch	SFT	£4475
128	12/95	Hayd	2m4f	C Ch	GD	£4970
120	11/95	Hayd	3m	D Ch	G-F	£4962
103	10/95	Carl	2m4f110y	D Ch	G-F	£2853
99	4/95	Bang	2m1f	D Hdl	G-F	£2752

Total win prize-money £25301

Going: Sf: 0-0 GS: 0-0 Gd: 0-0 GF: - Fm: 0-1
Distance: 2m/2m3: 0-0 2m4-2m7: 0-1 3m+: 0-0
Track: LH: 0-0 RH: 0-0 Tight: 0-0 Gall: 0-0
Aids: Bl: 0-0 Vi: 0-0 Tstrap: 0-0
Best Rating: 128 12/95 Hayd 2m4f good Ch

Spanish Main (IRE)

109 **139**

8-y-o b g Spanish Place (USA)-Willow Grouse (Giolla Mear)
N A Twiston-Davies C B Sanderson

Placings:454/21U3111/1333F1U0-3U0P5 (4163)
2001/02: 25^{3}G, 27^{U}G, 28^{0}S, 24^{P}GS, 29^{5}G

	Starts	1st	2nd	3rd	Win & Pl
Chases	5	0	0	1	1572
Career Total	**23**	**6**	**1**	**5**	**40487**

141	2/01	Uttx	3m2f	B HCh	HVY	£12640
117	10/00	Extr	2m7f110y	D Ch	GD	£3789
124	4/00	Chel	3m	D(0-120)HHdl	SFT	£7247
111	3/00	Font	3m3f	E Hdl	G-S	£2394
112	1/00	Asct	3m	C HHdl	G-S	£5694
93	10/99	Strf	2m6f110y	E Hdl	G-S	£2057

Total win prize-money £33824

Going: Sf: 0-1 GS: 0-1 Gd: 0-3 GF: - Fm: 0-0
Distance: 2m/2m3: 0-0 2m4-2m7: 0-0 3m+: 0-5
Track: LH: 0-3 RH: 0-2 Tight: 0-2 Gall: 0-1
Aids: Bl: 0-0 Vi: 0-3 Tstrap: 0-2
Best Rating: 141 2/01 Uttx 3m2f heavy Ch

A dogged stayer, he faced some stiff tasks in his first season over fences in 2000/2001, running in both the English and Scottish Nationals. Not at his best last season, he needs soft ground to perform at his best.

Sparebit

8-y-o b m Henbit (USA)-Sparticone (Celtic Cone)
W J Warner Mrs Judy Wilson

Placings:P (4274)
2001/02: 21^{P}G

	Starts	1st	2nd	3rd	Win & Pl
Chases	1	0	0	0	
Career Total	**1**	**0**	**0**	**0**	

Going: Sf: 0-0 GS: 0-0 Gd: 0-1 GF: - Fm: 0-0
Distance: 2m/2m3: 0-0 2m4-2m7: 0-1 3m+: 0-0
Track: LH: 0-1 RH: 0-0 Tight: 0-1 Gall: 0-0
Aids: Bl: 0-0 Vi: 0-0 Tstrap: 0-0
Best Rating:

Spark Of Life

100 **95**

5-y-o b m Rainbows For Life (CAN)-Sparkly Girl (IRE) (Danehill (USA))
T D McCarthy A D Spence

Placings:3 (2289)
2001/02: 17^{3}GF

	Starts	1st	2nd	3rd	Win & Pl
Hurdles	1	0	0	1	495
Career Total	**1**	**0**	**0**	**1**	**495**

Going: Sf: 0-0 GS: 0-0 Gd: 0-0 GF: - Fm: 0-1
Distance: 2m/2m3: 0-1 2m4-2m7: 0-0 3m+: 0-0
Track: LH: 0-0 RH: 0-1 Tight: 0-0 Gall: 0-0
Aids: Bl: 0-0 Vi: 0-0 Tstrap: 0-0
Best Rating: 95 11/01 Extr 2m1f gd-fm Hdl

Sparkling Cascade (IRE)

90 **97**

10-y-o b m Royal Fountain-Yukon Law (Goldhill)
A G Newcombe M G Tootell

Placings:320-P62 (4505)
2001/02: 21^{P}HY, 16^{6}S, 21^{2}G

	Starts	1st	2nd	3rd	Win & Pl
Chases	3	0	1	0	652
Career Total	**6**	**0**	**2**	**1**	**2360**

Going: Sf: 0-2 GS: 0-0 Gd: 0-1 GF: - Fm: 0-0
Distance: 2m/2m3: 0-1 2m4-2m7: 0-2 3m+: 0-0
Track: LH: 0-2 RH: 0-1 Tight: 0-3 Gall: 0-0
Aids: Bl: 0-0 Vi: 0-0 Tstrap: 0-0
Best Rating: 102 8/00 NAbb 2m110y good Ch

A moderate point to pointer. She showed fair form in novice chases in the autumn of 2000. Stays three miles. Probably best suited by a sound surface.

Sparkling Embers

7-y-o b g Regal Embers (IRE)-Lady Pia (Pia Fort)
C J Price Gerald Davies

Placings:PPU (4682)
2001/02: 16^{P}G, 16^{P}S, 17^{U}GF

	Starts	1st	2nd	3rd	Win & Pl
Hurdles	3	0	0	0	
Career Total	**3**	**0**	**0**	**0**	

Going: Sf: 0-1 GS: 0-0 Gd: 0-1 GF: - Fm: 0-1
Distance: 2m/2m3: 0-3 2m4-2m7: 0-0 3m+: 0-0
Track: LH: 0-1 RH: 0-2 Tight: 0-1 Gall: 0-0
Aids: Bl: 0-0 Vi: 0-0 Tstrap: 0-0
Best Rating:

Sparkling Gift (IRE)

9-y-o b m Naheez (USA)-Northern Gift (Northern Guest (USA))
Miss S Robertson Mrs Phyl Robertson

Placings:P (4053)
2001/02: 20^{P}S

	Starts	1st	2nd	3rd	Win & Pl
Chases	1	0	0	0	
Career Total	**1**	**0**	**0**	**0**	

Going: Sf: 0-1 GS: 0-0 Gd: 0-0 GF: - Fm: 0-0
Distance: 2m/2m3: 0-0 2m4-2m7: 0-1 3m+: 0-0
Track: LH: 0-0 RH: 0-1 Tight: 0-0 Gall: 0-0
Aids: Bl: 0-0 Vi: 0-0 Tstrap: 0-0
Best Rating:

Sparkling Lass

73(95h) (88h)**56**

8-y-o gr m Nicholas Bill-Sparkling Time (USA) (Olden Times)
N G Ayliffe R A Bimson

Placings:050P/06F52/00450544-04P004 (4732)
2001/02: 16^{0}S, 22^{4}HY, 22^{P}G, 21^{0}HY, 24^{0}S, 23^{4}F

	Starts	1st	2nd	3rd	Win & Pl
Hurdles	5	0	0	0	0
Chases	1	0	0	0	280
Career Total	**23**	**0**	**1**	**0**	**924**

Going: Sf: 0-4 GS: 0-0 Gd: 0-1 GF: - Fm: 0-1
Distance: 2m/2m3: 0-1 2m4-2m7: 0-3 3m+: 0-2
Track: LH: 0-2 RH: 0-2 Tight: 0-3 Gall: 0-0
Aids: Bl: 0-0 Vi: 0-0 Tstrap: 0-0
Best Rating: 88 4/01 Winc 2m6f soft Hdl

Moderate hurdler/chaser.

Sparkling Spring (IRE)

11-y-o b g Strong Gale-Cherry Jubilee (Le Bavard (FR))
Evan Williams R Mason

Placings:12216/F25/13/21/3U-P (0256)
2001/02: 28^{P}GF

	Starts	1st	2nd	3rd	Win & Pl
Chases	1	0	0	0	
Career Total	**15**	**4**	**4**	**2**	**17592**

133	10/99	Strf	3m4f	D(0-120)HCh	G-S	£3977
117	7/98	NAbb	3m2f110y	E Ch	G-F	£2818
106	3/97	Plum	2m4f	E Hdl	G-F	£2826
96	11/96	Wind	2m4f	D Hdl	GD	£2581

Total win prize-money £12203

Going: Sf: 0-0 GS: 0-0 Gd: 0-0 GF: - Fm: 0-1
Distance: 2m/2m3: 0-0 2m4-2m7: 0-0 3m+: 0-1
Track: LH: 0-1 RH: 0-0 Tight: 0-1 Gall: 0-0
Aids: Bl: 0-0 Vi: 0-0 Tstrap: 0-0
Best Rating: 133 10/99 Strf 3m4f gd-sft Ch

Sparkling Sword

91 **56**

7-y-o gr m Broadsword (USA)-Sparkling Time (USA) (Olden Times)
Miss Venetia Williams Mrs M Horton

Placings:12-3 (4112)
2001/02: 16^{3}S

	Starts	1st	2nd	3rd	Win & Pl
NH Flat	1	0	0	1	329
Career Total	**3**	**1**	**1**	**1**	**5354**

107	10/00	Wwck	2m	H NHF	SFT	£1575

Total win prize-money £1575

Going: Sf: 0-1 GS: 0-0 Gd: 0-0 GF: - Fm: 0-0
Distance: 2m/2m3: 0-1 2m4-2m7: 0-0 3m+: 0-0
Track: LH: 0-0 RH: 0-1 Tight: 0-0 Gall: 0-0
Aids: Bl: 0-0 Vi: 0-0 Tstrap: 0-0
Best Rating: 120 12/00 Chep 2m110y soft NHF

A half-sister to the stayers Sparkling Buck and Sparkling Cone, she has shown plenty of ability in bumpers. Suited by soft ground.

Sparky Gayle (IRE)

12-y-o b g Strong Gale-Baybush (Boreen (FR))
A Parker Mr & Mrs Raymond Anderson Green

Placings:*2/12*221001/13254/**111111/4342/3P31/0602 U/P20-01** **(4692)**
2001/02: 25^{0}F, 25^{1}GF

	Starts	1st	2nd	3rd	Win & Pl
Chases	2	1	0	0	2671
Career Total	**38**	**12**	**8**	**4**	**115537**

138	4/02	Kels	3m1f	H Ch	G-F	£2670
156	4/99	Ayr	2m4f	B HCh	HVY	£10328
145	4/97	Ayr	2m4f	A Ch	GD	£14490
153	3/97	Chel	2m5f	B Ch	GD	£32850
138	2/97	Ayr	2m4f	D Ch	SFT	£3808
124	1/97	Carl	2m	D Ch	G-F	£3707
133	11/96	Newc	2m4f	C Ch	GD	£5340
112	11/96	Ayr	2m	D Ch	GD	£3675
123	11/95	Ayr	2m4f	D(0-120)HHdl	GD	£3615
103	4/95	Carl	2m4f110y	E Hdl	FRM	£2480
117	1/95	Ayr	2m4f	D Hdl	SFT	£2983
	5/94	Dpat	2m1f172y	NHF	GD	£1479

Total win prize-money £87429

Going: Sf: 0-0 GS: 0-0 Gd: 0-0 GF: - Fm: 1-2
Distance: 2m/2m3: 0-0 2m4-2m7: 0-0 **3m+: 1-2**
Track: **LH: 1-2** RH: 0-0 **Tight: 1-1** Gall: 0-0
Aids: Bl: 0-0 Vi: 0-0 **Tstrap: 1-2**
Best Rating: 100 4/00 Ayr 2m4f heavy Ch

One-time high-class chaser, now at the veteran stage and running in hunter chases. Best on a sound surface although handles cut.

Spartan Point

71f 26f

5-y-o b m Spartan Monarch-Altar Point (Persian Bold)
J R Best Broomdown Racing 2

Placings:*0* **(0108)**
2001/02: 18^{0}GF

	Starts	1st	2nd	3rd	Win & Pl
NH Flat	1	0	0	0	
Career Total	**1**	**0**	**0**	**0**	

Going: Sf: 0-0 GS: 0-0 Gd: 0-0 GF: - Fm: 0-1
Distance: 2m/2m3: 0-1 2m4-2m7: 0-0 3m+: 0-0
Track: LH: 0-1 RH: 0-0 Tight: 0-1 Gall: 0-0
Aids: Bl: 0-0 Vi: 0-0 Tstrap: 0-0
Best Rating: 26 5/01 Font 2m2f110y gd-fm NHF

Spartan Royale

8-y-o b g Shareef Dancer (USA)-Cormorant Creek (Gorytus (USA))
P Monteith Allan W Melville

Placings:*P/6/11*30**P21/PF** **(3364)**
2001/02: 22^{P}GS, 16^{F}GS

	Starts	1st	2nd	3rd	Win & Pl
Hurdles	2	0	0	0	
Career Total	**11**	**3**	**1**	**1**	**13271**

117	4/00	Carl	2m1f	D(0-120)HHdl	G-S	£2912
118	1/00	Ayr	2m	C(0-135)HHdl	SFT	£4758
106	11/99	Newc	2m	D Hdl	G-S	£3087

Total win prize-money £10757

Going: Sf: 0-0 GS: 0-2 Gd: 0-0 GF: - Fm: 0-0
Distance: 2m/2m3: 0-1 2m4-2m7: 0-1 3m+: 0-0
Track: LH: 0-2 RH: 0-0 Tight: 0-2 Gall: 0-0
Aids: Bl: 0-0 Vi: 0-0 Tstrap: 0-0
Best Rating: 126 4/00 Ayr 2m good Hdl

Won a handicap hurdle at Carlisle in April 2000 and was then absent for a long time. Suited by two miles and soft ground.

Spear Of Destiny (IRE)

4-y-o ch g Rainbows For Life (CAN)-Theda (Mummy's Pet)
T P McGovern N Boyle

Placings:*0U*0 **(4559)**
2001/02: 18^{0}S, 16^{U}GS, 16^{0}GF

	Starts	1st	2nd	3rd	Win & Pl
NH Flat	1	0	0	0	0
Hurdles	2	0	0	0	0
Career Total	**3**	**0**	**0**	**0**	

Going: Sf: 0-1 GS: 0-1 Gd: 0-0 GF: - Fm: 0-1
Distance: 2m/2m3: 0-3 2m4-2m7: 0-0 3m+: 0-0
Track: LH: 0-3 RH: 0-0 Tight: 0-3 Gall: 0-0
Aids: Bl: 0-0 Vi: 0-0 Tstrap: 0-0
Best Rating: 49 2/02 Font 2m2f110y soft NHF

Special Agenda (IRE)

111 (46h) 134

8-y-o b g Torus-Easter Blade (IRE) (Fine Blade (USA))
C J Mann Mrs L G Turner

Placings:445/**P1132O3F2-222PU202P6** **(4901)**
2001/02: 16^{2}G, 17^{2}GS, 17^{2}GS, 17^{P}S, 16^{U}S, 17^{2}S, 17^{0}G, 17^{2}S, 17^{P}S, 16^{6}G

	Starts	1st	2nd	3rd	Win & Pl
Chases	10	0	5	0	7807
Career Total	**22**	**2**	**7**	**2**	**18128**

132	11/00	Hrfd	2m	E(0-105)HCh	SFT	£2804
129	11/00	Plum	2m1f	E Ch	SFT	£3346

Total win prize-money £6151

Going: Sf: 0-5 GS: 0-2 Gd: 0-3 GF: - Fm: 0-0
Distance: 2m/2m3: 0-10 2m4-2m7: 0-0 3m+: 0-0
Track: LH: 0-7 RH: 0-3 Tight: 0-5 Gall: 0-3
Aids: Bl: 0-0 Vi: 0-0 Tstrap: 0-0
Best Rating: 134 12/01 Strf 2m1f110y soft Ch

Won back-to-back novice chases in the mud in November 2000 and has continued to run with credit since then, although completing a frustrating run of seconds. Won a Class D handicap at Newton Abbot in May 2002. His best races have been in the mud over two miles. Considered best when conceding weight to inferior rivals.

Special Present

96f 106f

4-y-o ch g Presenting-Pitts Special (Pitpan)
L Wells Mrs Carrie Zetter-Wells

Placings:*220* **(4235)**
2001/02: 16^{2}S, 16^{2}G, 16^{0}GS

	Starts	1st	2nd	3rd	Win & Pl
NH Flat	3	0	2	0	1304
Career Total	**3**	**0**	**2**	**0**	**1304**

Going: Sf: 0-1 GS: 0-1 Gd: 0-1 GF: - Fm: 0-0
Distance: 2m/2m3: 0-3 2m4-2m7: 0-0 3m+: 0-0
Track: LH: 0-1 RH: 0-2 Tight: 0-0 Gall: 0-0
Aids: Bl: 0-0 Vi: 0-0 Tstrap: 0-0
Best Rating: 100 3/02 Chel 2m110y gd-sft NHF

Just touched off in two of his four bumpers, deserves a change of luck.

Special Promise (IRE)

103 99

5-y-o ch g Anjiz (USA)-Woodenitbenice (USA) (Nasty And Bold (USA))
I Semple (P C Haslam 19/8) Mrs D Santonocito

Placings:11 **(1021)**
2001/02: 20^{1}GF, 21^{1}GF

	Starts	1st	2nd	3rd	Win & Pl
Hurdles	2	2	0	0	2366
Career Total	**2**	**2**	**0**	**0**	**2366**

99	7/01	Sedg	2m5f110y	E Hdl	G-F	£2366

Total win prize-money £2366

Going: Sf: 0-0 GS: 0-0 Gd: 0-0 GF: - Fm: 2-2
Distance: 2m/2m3: 0-0 **2m4-2m7: 2-2** 3m+: 0-0
Track: LH: 1-1 RH: 1-1 **Tight: 1-1** Gall: 0-0
Aids: Bl: 0-0 Vi: 0-0 Tstrap: 0-0
Best Rating: 99 7/01 Sedg 2m5f110y gd-fm Hdl

Better known as an All-Weather performer, but won twice over hurdles on fast ground in the summer of 2001.

Specialize

107 129d

10-y-o b g Faustus (USA)-Scholastika (GER) (Alpenkonig (GER))
K R Burke P A Brazier

Placings:606/PP3/11124302**P5212/112130650220/P1 43100P-P0011163** **(1503)**
2001/02: 24^{P}GS, 20^{0}GF, 20^{0}GF, 21^{1}GF, 20^{1}G, 21^{1}GF, 20^{6}G, 21^{3}G

	Starts	1st	2nd	3rd	Win & Pl
Chases	8	3	0	1	13726
Career Total	**47**	**12**	**7**	**5**	**64199**

129	8/01	Sedg	2m5f	D(0-125)HCh	G-F	£4056
128	7/01	Strf	2m4f	E(0-115)HCh	GD	£4707
117	7/01	Sedg	2m5f	F(0-110)HCh	G-F	£4348
129	12/00	Fknm	3m110y	D(0-120)HCh	G-S	£4260
129	10/00	Strf	2m4f	F(0-110)HCh	SFT	£4257
134	6/99	Uttx	2m5f	C(0-135)HCh	G-S	£6905
127	5/99	Fknm	3m110y	D(0-120)HCh	G-F	£6602
127	5/99	Uttx	2m4f	D(0-125)HCh	G-F	£4396
127	4/99	Uttx	2m5f	D(0-110)HCh	G-S	£4513
95	5/98	Worc	2m	F(0-105)HHdl	G-F	£2285
97	5/98	Hrfd	2m1f	E(0-100)HHdl	GD	£2442
91	5/98	Uttx	2m	G(0-95)HHdl	GD	£1710

Total win prize-money £50488

Going: Sf: 0-0 GS: 0-1 Gd: 1-3 GF: - Fm: 2-4
Distance: 2m/2m3: 0-0 **2m4-2m7: 3-7** 3m+: 0-1
Track: **LH: 3-7** RH: 0-1 **Tight: 3-6** Gall: 0-0
Aids: Bl: 0-3 **Vi: 3-5** Tstrap: 0-0
Best Rating: 134 6/99 Uttx 2m5f gd-sft Ch

Decent two and a half-mile chaser, suited by a sound surface. Usually wears headgear.

Speckles (IRE)

8-y-o b m Brush Aside (USA)-Daring Duchess (Brave

Invader (USA))
F P Murtagh Peter Diggle

Placings:00/P0 **(4522)**
2001/02: 24^{P}HY, 17^{0}G

	Starts	1st	2nd	3rd	Win & Pl
Hurdles	2	0	0	0	
Career Total	**4**	**0**	**0**	**0**	

Going: Sf: 0-1 GS: 0-0 Gd: 0-1 GF: - Fm: 0-0
Distance: 2m/2m3: 0-1 2m4-2m7: 0-0 3m+: 0-1
Track: LH: 0-1 RH: 0-1 Tight: 0-0 Gall: 0-0
Aids: Bl: 0-0 Vi: 0-0 Tstrap: 0-0
Best Rating: 43 12/98 Catt 2m good NHF

Spectacle (IRE)

12-y-o gr g Peacock (FR)-Aunty Babs (Sexton Blake)
Cecil Mahon Coleman Rooney

Placings:00000/4600/55F20000F624P6/2UU/0P/0500/0R0-0B0 **(4608a)**
2001/02: 24^{0}GS, 20^{B}S, 24^{0}S

	Starts	1st	2nd	3rd	Win & Pl
Chases	3	0	0	0	
Career Total	**38**	**0**	**3**	**0**	**1696**

Going: Sf: 0-2 GS: 0-1 Gd: 0-0 GF: - Fm: 0-0
Distance: 2m/2m3: 0-0 2m4-2m7: 0-1 3m+: 0-2
Track: LH: 0-1 RH: 0-0 Tight: 0-1 Gall: 0-0
Aids: Bl: 0-2 Vi: 0-0 Tstrap: 0-3
Best Rating: 90 5/97 Dpat 2m2f gd-fm Ch

Spectacular View (IRE)

7-y-o b g Scenic-La Petruschka (Ballad Rock)
C Dawson (Mrs K Walton 21/4) C Dawson

Placings:B-PP **(0338)**
2001/02: 21^{P}G, 20^{P}S

	Starts	1st	2nd	3rd	Win & Pl
Chases	2	0	0	0	
Career Total	**3**	**0**	**0**	**0**	

Going: Sf: 0-1 GS: 0-0 Gd: 0-1 GF: - Fm: 0-0
Distance: 2m/2m3: 0-0 2m4-2m7: 0-2 3m+: 0-0
Track: LH: 0-1 RH: 0-1 Tight: 0-1 Gall: 0-0
Aids: Bl: 0-0 Vi: 0-0 Tstrap: 0-0
Best Rating:

Spectre Brown

83(63h) **52**
12-y-o b g Respect-My Goddess (Palm Track)
D A Nolan Mrs J McFadyen-Murray

Placings:PFF0UU/4/25P0/450P/PPF05450/U5-P006P **(3505)**
2001/02: 16^{P}G, 16^{0}GF, 20^{0}G, 16^{6}G, 16^{P}S

	Starts	1st	2nd	3rd	Win & Pl
Hurdles	1	0	0	0	0
Chases	4	0	0	0	0
Career Total	**30**	**0**	**1**	**0**	**1533**

Going: Sf: 0-1 GS: 0-0 Gd: 0-3 GF: - Fm: 0-1
Distance: 2m/2m3: 0-4 2m4-2m7: 0-1 3m+: 0-0
Track: LH: 0-1 RH: 0-4 Tight: 0-4 Gall: 0-0
Aids: Bl: 0-0 Vi: 0-0 Tstrap: 0-0
Best Rating: 86 2/00 Muss 2m gd-sft Ch

Mixes hurdles, jumps and Flat, but has had no success in any of these disciplines.

Spectrometer

109 **125**
5-y-o ch g Rainbow Quest (USA)-Selection Board (Welsh Pageant)
P J Hobbs Concertina Racing

Placings:21124 **(1888)**
2001/02: 16^{2}GF, 19^{1}GF, 16^{1}G, 16^{2}GF, 16^{4}G

	Starts	1st	2nd	3rd	Win & Pl
Hurdles	5	2	2	0	8217
Career Total	**5**	**2**	**2**	**0**	**8217**

117	7/01	Worc	2m	D Hdl	GD	£3307
104	7/01	Strf	2m3f	E Hdl	G-F	£2415

Total win prize-money £5723

Going: Sf: 0-0 GS: 0-0 Gd: 1-2 GF: - Fm: 1-3
Distance: **2m/2m3: 2-5** 2m4-2m7: 0-0 3m+: 0-0
Track: **LH: 2-5** RH: 0-0 **Tight: 1-1** Gall: 0-0
Aids: Bl: 0-0 Vi: 0-0 Tstrap: 0-0
Best Rating: 117 7/01 Worc 2m good Hdl

A winning stayer on the Flat, he won twice over hurdles in the summer of 2001 and ran well after an eight-month break in June 2002. Likes fast ground but also handles softer.

Speed Venture

100 **99**
5-y-o b g Owington-Jade Venture (Never So Bold)
J Mackie Wall Racing Partners

Placings:13345 **(3268)**
2001/02: 16^{1}S, 16^{3}HY, 16^{3}S, 16^{4}GS, 20^{5}G

	Starts	1st	2nd	3rd	Win & Pl
Hurdles	5	1	0	2	3534
Career Total	**5**	**1**	**0**	**2**	**3534**

99	11/01	Uttx	2m	E Hdl	SFT	£2758

Total win prize-money £2758

Going: Sf: 1-3 GS: 0-1 Gd: 0-1 GF: - Fm: 0-0
Distance: **2m/2m3: 1-4** 2m4-2m7: 0-1 3m+: 0-0
Track: **LH: 1-5** RH: 0-0 Tight: 0-0 Gall: 0-1
Aids: Bl: 0-0 Vi: 0-0 **Tstrap: 1-5**
Best Rating: 99 11/01 Uttx 2m soft Hdl

Fair handicap hurdler who is not very big but won on his debut and has been placed since over two miles on soft/heavy ground.

Speedy

9-y-o b g Teenoso (USA)-Onaway (Commanche Run)
Miss M Bayliss Miss M Bayliss

Placings:6/36/U **(0271)**
2001/02: 25^{U}G

	Starts	1st	2nd	3rd	Win & Pl
Chases	1	0	0	0	
Career Total	**4**	**0**	**0**	**1**	**167**

Going: Sf: 0-0 GS: 0-0 Gd: 0-1 GF: - Fm: 0-0
Distance: 2m/2m3: 0-0 2m4-2m7: 0-0 3m+: 0-1
Track: LH: 0-0 RH: 0-1 Tight: 0-0 Gall: 0-0
Aids: Bl: 0-0 Vi: 0-0 Tstrap: 0-0
Best Rating: 89 5/98 Hrfd 2m1f good NHF

Speedy Snaps Image

93 **52**
11-y-o ch g Ballacashtal (CAN)-Lillicara (FR) (Caracolero (USA))
P R Rodford P R Rodford

Placings:U21/22/453FP5/P324435/64343-50 **(0910)**
2001/02: 21^{5}GS, 16^{0}G

	Starts	1st	2nd	3rd	Win & Pl
Chases	2	0	0	0	0
Career Total	**25**	**1**	**4**	**5**	**8832**

68	10/94	Font	2m2f	Hdl	FRM	£1879

Total win prize-money £1880

Going: Sf: 0-0 GS: 0-1 Gd: 0-1 GF: - Fm: 0-0
Distance: 2m/2m3: 0-1 2m4-2m7: 0-1 3m+: 0-0
Track: LH: 0-2 RH: 0-0 Tight: 0-1 Gall: 0-0
Aids: Bl: 0-1 Vi: 0-0 Tstrap: 0-0
Best Rating: 91 7/00 NAbb 2m5f110y gd-fm Ch

Spendid (IRE)

121(66c) **152**
10-y-o b g Tidaro (USA)-Spendapromise (Goldhill)
A King Mrs Stewart Catherwood

Placings:201311/11642321/11122P1/F225154/0P-23224616 **(4954a)**
2001/02: 25^{2}G, 25^{3}G, 24^{2}S, 25^{2}S, 24^{4}GS, 24^{6}G, 24^{1}GF, 24^{6}G

	Starts	1st	2nd	3rd	Win & Pl
Hurdles	8	1	3	1	38210
Career Total	**38**	**12**	**10**	**3**	**176257**

152	4/02	Asct	3m	A Hdl	G-F	£17400
167	2/00	Winc	3m1f110y	B Ch	GD	£17306
167	4/99	Aint	3m1f	A Ch	GD	£26775
150	12/98	Chel	3m1f110y	C Ch	GD	£7230
140	11/98	Chel	3m110y	B Ch	G-S	£9530
130	10/98	Weth	3m1f	C Ch	GD	£4770
144	4/98	Chel	2m5f110y	B HHdl	HVY	£6208
132	11/97	Chel	2m5f	E(0-130)HHdl	GD	£2788
130	11/97	Towc	2m5f	D(0-125)HHdl	G-S	£2912
117	2/97	Towc	2m	E Hdl	SFT	£1976
114	1/97	MRas	2m3f110y	E Hdl	GD	£2700
109	9/96	List	2m	NHF	GD	£3884

Total win prize-money £103482

Going: Sf: 0-2 GS: 0-1 Gd: 0-4 GF: - Fm: 1-1
Distance: 2m/2m3: 0-0 2m4-2m7: 0-0 **3m+: 1-8**
Track: LH: 0-3 **RH: 1-3** Tight: 0-0 Gall: 0-2
Aids: Bl: 0-0 Vi: 0-0 Tstrap: 0-0
Best Rating: 167 2/00 Winc 3m1f110y good Ch

Winner of a valuable event at Aintree as a novice chaser, he developed into a decent staying handicapper. However, his last win was in February 2000 and he was absent for nearly a year after suffering a stress fracture in the 2000 Hennessy. Delighted connections when second to Boss Doyle in the John Smiths Hurdle at Wetherby in November of 2001 on his reappearance and has run good races in decent company over timber subsequently. Stays three miles plus. Does not want the ground too fast or too soft.

Speriamo (IRE)

70f
6-y-o b g Mandalus-Mares Eat Oats (Ovac (ITY))
G Brown The Ever Smiling Partnership

Placings:0 **(0272)**
2001/02: 17^{0}G

	Starts	1st	2nd	3rd	Win & Pl
NH Flat	1	0	0	0	
Career Total	**1**	**0**	**0**	**0**	

Going: Sf: 0-0 GS: 0-0 Gd: 0-1 GF: - Fm: 0-0
Distance: 2m/2m3: 0-1 2m4-2m7: 0-0 3m+: 0-0
Track: LH: 0-0 RH: 0-1 Tight: 0-0 Gall: 0-0
Aids: Bl: 0-0 Vi: 0-0 Tstrap: 0-0
Best Rating:

Spey Cast (IRE)

72 72

8-y-o b m Brush Aside (USA)-Arctic Match (Royal Match)
J K Magee (N J Henderson 23/6) J K Magee

Placings:045/P-604 (1457a)
2001/02: 22^{6}GF, 17^{0}GF, 20^{4}F

	Starts	1st	2nd	3rd	Win & Pl
NH Flat	1	0	0	0	0
Hurdles	2	0	0	0	290
Career Total	**7**	**0**	**0**	**0**	**290**

Going: Sf: 0-0 GS: 0-0 Gd: 0-0 GF: - Fm: 0-3
Distance: 2m/2m3: 0-1 2m4-2m7: 0-2 3m+: 0-0
Track: LH: 0-1 RH: 0-0 Tight: 0-1 Gall: 0-0
Aids: Bl: 0-0 Vi: 0-0 Tstrap: 0-2
Best Rating: 91 3/00 Towc 2m soft NHF

Spiocy Marble (IRE)

87 55

6-y-o ch m Houmayoun (FR)-Red Marble (Le Bavard (FR))
Mrs Merrita Jones The Rockfel Racers

Placings:063PP (4871)
2001/02: 16^{0}G, 17^{6}G, 20^{3}GF, 20^{P}S, 25^{P}GF

	Starts	1st	2nd	3rd	Win & Pl
NH Flat	1	0	0	0	0
Hurdles	4	0	0	1	480
Career Total	**5**	**0**	**0**	**1**	**480**

Going: Sf: 0-1 GS: 0-0 Gd: 0-2 GF: - Fm: 0-2
Distance: 2m/2m3: 0-2 2m4-2m7: 0-2 3m+: 0-1
Track: LH: 0-5 RH: 0-0 Tight: 0-1 Gall: 0-0
Aids: Bl: 0-0 Vi: 0-0 Tstrap: 0-0
Best Rating: 72 6/01 Worc 2m good NHF

Spider Boy

74f 77f

5-y-o b g Jupiter Island-Great Dilemma (Vaigly Great)
Miss Z C Davison Highly Charged Partnership

Placings:00 (4887)
2001/02: 16^{0}G, 18^{0}GF

	Starts	1st	2nd	3rd	Win & Pl
NH Flat	2	0	0	0	
Career Total	**2**	**0**	**0**	**0**	

Going: Sf: 0-0 GS: 0-0 Gd: 0-1 GF: - Fm: 0-1
Distance: 2m/2m3: 0-2 2m4-2m7: 0-0 3m+: 0-0
Track: LH: 0-1 RH: 0-1 Tight: 0-1 Gall: 0-0
Aids: Bl: 0-0 Vi: 0-0 Tstrap: 0-0
Best Rating: 77 4/02 Towc 2m good NHF

Spider Music

102f 102f

6-y-o ch g Orchestra-Muffet's Spider (Rymer)
Ferdy Murphy Mrs F D McInnes Skinner

Placings:03 (4166)
2001/02: 16^{0}G, 16^{3}GS

	Starts	1st	2nd	3rd	Win & Pl
NH Flat	2	0	0	1	283
Career Total	**2**	**0**	**0**	**1**	**283**

Going: Sf: 0-0 GS: 0-1 Gd: 0-1 GF: - Fm: 0-0
Distance: 2m/2m3: 0-2 2m4-2m7: 0-0 3m+: 0-0
Track: LH: 0-1 RH: 0-1 Tight: 0-1 Gall: 0-0
Aids: Bl: 0-0 Vi: 0-0 Tstrap: 0-0
Best Rating: 102 2/02 Kemp 2m good NHF

Has shown ability in bumpers.

Spike Barnes

7-y-o b g Bedford (USA)-Ballintava (Better By Far)
G M McCourt D A N Ross

Placings:0-00 (2168)
2001/02: 17^{0}S, 16^{0}S

	Starts	1st	2nd	3rd	Win & Pl
NH Flat	1	0	0	0	0
Hurdles	1	0	0	0	0
Career Total	**3**	**0**	**0**	**0**	

Going: Sf: 0-2 GS: 0-0 Gd: 0-0 GF: - Fm: 0-0
Distance: 2m/2m3: 0-2 2m4-2m7: 0-0 3m+: 0-0
Track: LH: 0-2 RH: 0-0 Tight: 0-1 Gall: 0-0
Aids: Bl: 0-0 Vi: 0-0 Tstrap: 0-0
Best Rating: 51 2/01 Towc 2m heavy NHF

Spilaw (FR)

103(92h) (73h)105

6-y-o b g Sky Lawyer (FR)-Spinage (FR) (Village Star (FR))
John Allen Avon Estates Ltd

Placings:1/045/2614200400F-000040U0130 (2647)
2001/02: 16^{0}S, 19^{0}G, 19^{0}GF, 22^{0}GF, 16^{4}GF, 18^{0}GF, 16^{U}GS, 16^{0}GS, 16^{1}G, 16^{3}S, 16^{0}GS

	Starts	1st	2nd	3rd	Win & Pl
Hurdles	8	0	0	0	0
Chases	3	1	0	1	3141
Career Total	**26**	**3**	**2**	**1**	**23380**

105	11/01	Folk	2m	F(0-95)HCh	GD	£2541
	11/00	Engh	2m2f	Ch	HLD	£6244
	4/99	Toul	1m7f	Hdl	VS	£3229

Total win prize-money £12014

Going: Sf: 0-2 GS: 0-3 Gd: 1-2 GF: - Fm: 0-4
Distance: 2m/2m3: 1-9 2m4-2m7: 0-2 3m+: 0-0
Track: LH: 0-7 **RH: 1-4 Tight: 1-6** Gall: 0-1
Aids: Bl: 0-1 Vi: 0-0 Tstrap: 0-0
Best Rating: 105 11/01 Folk 2m good Ch

He had shown little since arriving from France until winning an amateur riders' chase at Folkestone in November 2001.

Spiney Norman

4-y-o gr g Petong-Fairy Ballerina (Fairy King (USA))
Jamie Poulton Robert Townsend

Placings:00 (2597)
2001/02: 16^{0}GS, 18^{0}G

	Starts	1st	2nd	3rd	Win & Pl
Hurdles	2	0	0	0	
Career Total	**2**	**0**	**0**	**0**	

Going: Sf: 0-0 GS: 0-1 Gd: 0-1 GF: - Fm: 0-0
Distance: 2m/2m3: 0-2 2m4-2m7: 0-0 3m+: 0-0
Track: LH: 0-1 RH: 0-1 Tight: 0-1 Gall: 0-0
Aids: Bl: 0-0 Vi: 0-0 Tstrap: 0-0
Best Rating:

Spinning Silver

77 53

7-y-o b g Nearly A Hand-Paid Elation (Pia Fort)
P R Rodford Mrs C A Lewis-Jones

Placings:00-FP (1995)
2001/02: 24^{F}G, 16^{P}S

	Starts	1st	2nd	3rd	Win & Pl
Chases	2	0	0	0	
Career Total	**4**	**0**	**0**	**0**	

Going: Sf: 0-1 GS: 0-0 Gd: 0-1 GF: - Fm: 0-0
Distance: 2m/2m3: 0-1 2m4-2m7: 0-0 3m+: 0-1
Track: LH: 0-2 RH: 0-0 Tight: 0-1 Gall: 0-1
Aids: Bl: 0-0 Vi: 0-0 Tstrap: 0-0
Best Rating: 51 9/00 Worc 2m gd-fm NHF

Spinofski

106 136

7-y-o b g Petoski-Spin Again (Royalty)
P R Webber D R Stoddart

Placings:45/RF3131-4R434110 (4192)
2001/02: 20^{4}GS, 19^{R}S, 21^{4}G, 20^{3}G, 26^{4}G, 24^{1}GS, 24^{1}GS, 24^{0}GS

	Starts	1st	2nd	3rd	Win & Pl
Chases	8	2	0	1	14760
Career Total	**16**	**4**	**0**	**3**	**27824**

136	2/02	Kemp	3m	D(0-125)HCh	G-S	£7085
127	1/02	Hntg	3m	D(0-120)HCh	G-S	£3991
128	4/01	MRas	2m4f	F(0-105)HCh	HVY	£4158
114	3/01	Newb	2m2f110y	D(0-110)HCh	HVY	£7345

Total win prize-money £22579

Going: Sf: 0-1 **GS: 2-4** Gd: 0-3 GF: - Fm: 0-0
Distance: 2m/2m3: 0-0 2m4-2m7: 0-4 **3m+: 2-4**
Track: LH: 0-5 **RH: 2-3** Tight: 0-1 **Gall: 1-4**
Aids: Bl: 0-0 Vi: 0-0 Tstrap: 0-0
Best Rating: 136 2/02 Kemp 3m gd-sft Ch

Decent chaser, won at Huntingdon in January and Kempton the following month.Travelling well in the Kim Muir until hampered by a faller. Effective on most types of ground and stays three miles.

Spirit Of Destiny

75f 63f

5-y-o ch m Riverwise (USA)-Tearful Sarah (Rugantino)
C W Mitchell C W Mitchell

Placings:00 (4391)
2001/02: 16^{0}S, 16^{0}S

	Starts	1st	2nd	3rd	Win & Pl
NH Flat	2	0	0	0	
Career Total	**2**	**0**	**0**	**0**	

Going: Sf: 0-2 GS: 0-0 Gd: 0-0 GF: - Fm: 0-0
Distance: 2m/2m3: 0-2 2m4-2m7: 0-0 3m+: 0-0
Track: LH: 0-0 RH: 0-2 Tight: 0-0 Gall: 0-0
Aids: Bl: 0-0 Vi: 0-0 Tstrap: 0-0
Best Rating: 63 3/02 Winc 2m soft NHF

Spirit Of Love (USA)

106 100

7-y-o ch g Trempolino (USA)-Dream Mary (USA) (Marfa (USA))
E W Tuer (J G Given 14/2) E Tuer

Placings:45 (4880)
2001/02: 20^{4}S, 20^{5}G

	Starts	1st	2nd	3rd	Win & Pl
Hurdles	2	0	0	0	274
Career Total	**2**	**0**	**0**	**0**	**274**

Going: Sf: 0-1 GS: 0-0 Gd: 0-1 GF: - Fm: 0-0
Distance: 2m/2m3: 0-0 2m4-2m7: 0-2 3m+: 0-0
Track: LH: 0-0 RH: 0-2 Tight: 0-0 Gall: 0-0
Aids: Bl: 0-0 Vi: 0-0 Tstrap: 0-0
Best Rating: 87 4/02 Prth 2m4f110y good Hdl

Formerly high-class stayer on the Flat. Effortless winner at Cartmel in June 2002, but fell fatally at Market Rasen later in the month. (DEAD)

Spirit Of May

8-y-o ch m Broadsword (USA)-Spartan Sprite (Country Retreat)
J C McConnochie Lord Somerleyton

Placings:FPF-P (0061)
2001/02: 26^{P}G

	Starts	1st	2nd	3rd	Win & Pl
Chases	1	0	0	0	
Career Total	**4**	**0**	**0**	**0**	

Going: Sf: 0-0 GS: 0-0 Gd: 0-1 GF: - Fm: 0-0
Distance: 2m/2m3: 0-0 2m4-2m7: 0-0 3m+: 0-1
Track: LH: 0-0 RH: 0-1 Tight: 0-1 Gall: 0-0
Aids: Bl: 0-0 Vi: 0-0 Tstrap: 0-0
Best Rating:

Spirit Of Tenby (IRE)

106 97

5-y-o b g Tenby-Asturiana (Julio Mariner)
C J Mann Tony Stapleton

Placings:3210 (0881)
2001/02: 16^{3}GF, 17^{2}GF, 16^{1}GF, 17^{0}G

	Starts	1st	2nd	3rd	Win & Pl
Hurdles	4	1	1	1	5001
Career Total	**4**	**1**	**1**	**1**	**5001**

97	6/01	Prth	2m110y	D Hdl	G-F	£3493

Total win prize-money £3494

Going: Sf: 0-0 GS: 0-0 Gd: 0-1 GF: - Fm: 1-3
Distance: **2m/2m3: 1-4** 2m4-2m7: 0-0 3m+: 0-0
Track: LH: 0-1 **RH: 1-3** Tight: 0-3 Gall: 0-0
Aids: Bl: 0-0 Vi: 0-0 Tstrap: 0-0
Best Rating: 97 6/01 Prth 2m110y gd-fm Hdl

Spirito

7-y-o b g Mystiko (USA)-Classic Beam (Cut Above)
D D Scott Mrs D D Scott

Placings:0/6000-P0PP (4501)
2001/02: 24^{P}HY, 19^{0}HY, 22^{P}S, 27^{P}G

	Starts	1st	2nd	3rd	Win & Pl
Hurdles	4	0	0	0	

Career Total	**9**	**0**	**0**	**0**	**0**

Going: Sf: 0-3 GS: 0-0 Gd: 0-1 GF: - Fm: 0-0
Distance: 2m/2m3: 0-0 2m4-2m7: 0-2 3m+: 0-2
Track: LH: 0-3 RH: 0-1 Tight: 0-2 Gall: 0-0
Aids: Bl: 0-0 Vi: 0-0 Tstrap: 0-0
Best Rating: 22 9/00 Worc 3m gd-fm Hdl

Spiritual Dancer (IRE)

95 102

7-y-o b g King's Ride-Arctic Tartan (Deep Run)
L Wells D W Cox & Paul Zetter

Placings:2F2P-3 (1898)
2001/02: 22^{3}GS

	Starts	1st	2nd	3rd	Win & Pl
Hurdles	1	0	0	1	359
Career Total	**5**	**0**	**2**	**1**	**2015**

Going: Sf: 0-0 GS: 0-1 Gd: 0-0 GF: - Fm: 0-0
Distance: 2m/2m3: 0-0 2m4-2m7: 0-1 3m+: 0-0
Track: LH: 0-1 RH: 0-0 Tight: 0-1 Gall: 0-0
Aids: Bl: 0-0 Vi: 0-0 Tstrap: 0-0
Best Rating: 102 10/01 Font 2m6f110y gd-sft Hdl

A keen sort, he has stamina in abundance and should be capable of winning an ordinary novice hurdle.

Spizzichino

49f

6-y-o b g Lancastrian-Garjun (IRE) (Orchestra)
R F Fisher Great Head House Estates Limited

Placings:*0* (3257)
2001/02: 16^{0}S

	Starts	1st	2nd	3rd	Win & Pl
NH Flat	1	0	0	0	
Career Total	**1**	**0**	**0**	**0**	

Going: Sf: 0-1 GS: 0-0 Gd: 0-0 GF: - Fm: 0-0
Distance: 2m/2m3: 0-1 2m4-2m7: 0-0 3m+: 0-0
Track: LH: 0-0 RH: 0-0 Tight: 0-0 Gall: 0-0
Aids: Bl: 0-0 Vi: 0-0 Tstrap: 0-0
Best Rating: 49 1/02 Newc 2m soft NHF

Splendid Thyne

10-y-o ch g Good Thyne (USA)-Mrs Jennifer (River Knight (FR))
A Ennis John Galvanoni

Placings:*51*/21313/611112/P1/P-P (2442)
2001/02: 24^{P}S

	Starts	1st	2nd	3rd	Win & Pl
Hurdles	1	0	0	0	
Career Total	**17**	**8**	**2**	**2**	**62410**

155	1/99	Chel	3m	B Hdl	G-S	£7300
152	2/98	Chep	2m4f110y	B HHdl	G-S	£6729
137	1/98	Wwck	2m4f110y	B HHdl	SFT	£8168
139	12/97	Hayd	2m7f110y	C(0-130)HHdl	SFT	£3533
140	11/97	Wwck	2m3f	B(0-140)HHdl	G-S	£4812
124	2/97	Newb	2m110y	C Hdl	G-S	£4068
109	1/97	Ling	2m110y	D Hdl	SFT	£3091
107	3/96	Newb	2m110y	H NHF	G-S	£1782

Total win prize-money £39486

Going: Sf: 0-1 GS: 0-0 Gd: 0-0 GF: - Fm: 0-0
Distance: 2m/2m3: 0-0 2m4-2m7: 0-0 3m+: 0-1
Track: LH: 0-1 RH: 0-0 Tight: 0-0 Gall: 0-1
Aids: Bl: 0-0 Vi: 0-0 Tstrap: 0-0
Best Rating: 160 3/98 Chel 3m good Hdl

Formerly high-class staying hurdler, plagued with injury in recent seasons.

Splodge

92 89

11-y-o b g Oedipus Complex-Gardella (Garnered)
N A Callaghan Miss Sarah L Judge

Placings:F-P5PP (4882)
2001/02: 26^{P}GS, 26^{5}GF, 26^{P}G, 26^{P}GF

	Starts	1st	2nd	3rd	Win & Pl
Chases	4	0	0	0	0
Career Total	**5**	**0**	**0**	**0**	**0**

Going: Sf: 0-0 GS: 0-1 Gd: 0-1 GF: - Fm: 0-2
Distance: 2m/2m3: 0-0 2m4-2m7: 0-0 3m+: 0-4
Track: LH: 0-1 RH: 0-0 Tight: 0-2 Gall: 0-0
Aids: Bl: 0-0 Vi: 0-0 Tstrap: 0-0
Best Rating: 89 5/01 Font 3m2f110y gd-fm Ch

Sponsor

40f

5-y-o b h Cadeaux Genereux-Pevna (USA) (Danzig (USA))
D A Nolan Gary Harrison

Placings:*0* (1471)
2001/02: 16^{0}G

	Starts	1st	2nd	3rd	Win & Pl
NH Flat	1	0	0	0	
Career Total	**1**	**0**	**0**	**0**	

Going: Sf: 0-0 GS: 0-0 Gd: 0-1 GF: - Fm: 0-0
Distance: 2m/2m3: 0-1 2m4-2m7: 0-0 3m+: 0-0
Track: LH: 0-0 RH: 0-1 Tight: 0-0 Gall: 0-0
Aids: Bl: 0-0 Vi: 0-0 Tstrap: 0-0
Best Rating:

Spontaneity (IRE)

52

6-y-o ch m Shalford (IRE)-Mariyda (IRE) (Vayrann)
P D Evans Colin G R Booth

Placings:4315321F0-P (0081)
2001/02: 17^{P}G

	Starts	1st	2nd	3rd	Win & Pl
Hurdles	1	0	0	0	
Career Total	**10**	**2**	**1**	**2**	**5097**

93	1/01	Ludl	2m	G Hdl	SFT	£1918
89	10/00	Strf	2m110y	G Hdl	G-S	£1918

Total win prize-money £3836

Going: Sf: 0-0 GS: 0-0 Gd: 0-1 GF: - Fm: 0-0
Distance: 2m/2m3: 0-1 2m4-2m7: 0-0 3m+: 0-0
Track: LH: 0-0 RH: 0-1 Tight: 0-0 Gall: 0-0
Aids: Bl: 0-0 Vi: 0-0 Tstrap: 0-1
Best Rating: 93 1/01 Tntn 2m3f110y soft Hdl

Spoof (IRE)

105 105

7-y-o b g Good Thyne (USA)-Wraparound Sue (Touch Paper)
L Lungo The Hookers

Placings:*503060*/511-4F00214 (4877)

2001/02: 22^{4}G, 24^{F}GS, 20^{0}S, 25^{0}S, 24^{2}S, 22^{1}HY, 24^{4}G

	Starts	1st	2nd	3rd	Win & Pl
Hurdles	7	1	1	0	3615
Career Total	**16**	**3**	**1**	**1**	**13725**

105	3/02	Ayr	2m6f	E(0-110)HHdl	HVY	£2712
105	4/01	Prth	2m4f110y	D(0-110)HHdl	HVY	£6474
104	1/01	Ayr	3m110y	D(0-110)HHdl	G-S	£3409

Total win prize-money £12596

Going: Sf: 1-4 GS: 0-1 Gd: 0-2 GF: - Fm: 0-0
Distance: 2m/2m3: 0-0 **2m4-2m7: 1-3** 3m+: 0-4
Track: **LH: 1-5** RH: 0-1 Tight: 0-2 Gall: 0-1
Aids: Bl: 0-0 Vi: 0-0 Tstrap: 0-0
Best Rating: 105 3/02 Ayr 2m6f heavy Hdl

Fair hurdler. Likes to get his toe in. Stays three miles.

Sporting Chance

96 **89+**

10-y-o ch g Ikdam-Tumbling Ego (Abednego)
Ms J Channon H S Channon

Placings:5000P/P **(4735)**
2001/02: 23^{P}F

	Starts	1st	2nd	3rd	Win & Pl
Chases	1	0	0	0	
Career Total	**6**	**0**	**0**	**0**	**0**

Going: Sf: 0-0 GS: 0-0 Gd: 0-0 GF: - Fm: 0-1
Distance: 2m/2m3: 0-0 2m4-2m7: 0-0 3m+: 0-1
Track: LH: 0-0 RH: 0-1 Tight: 0-0 Gall: 0-0
Aids: Bl: 0-0 Vi: 0-0 Tstrap: 0-0
Best Rating: 38 12/97 Tntn 2m1f good Hdl

Sports Express

106 **92**

4-y-o ch f Then Again-Lady St Lawrence (USA) (Bering)
G A Swinbank Tim Hawkins

Placings:2222 **(3860)**
2001/02: 16^{2}G, 16^{2}S, 16^{2}S, 20^{2}S

	Starts	1st	2nd	3rd	Win & Pl
Hurdles	4	0	4	0	3308
Career Total	**4**	**0**	**4**	**0**	**3308**

Going: Sf: 0-3 GS: 0-0 Gd: 0-1 GF: - Fm: 0-0
Distance: 2m/2m3: 0-3 2m4-2m7: 0-1 3m+: 0-0
Track: LH: 0-4 RH: 0-0 Tight: 0-1 Gall: 0-3
Aids: Bl: 0-0 Vi: 0-0 Tstrap: 0-0
Best Rating: 92 2/02 Donc 2m4f soft Hdl

Moderate form on the Flat, has shaped much better over hurdles. Effective over two miles.

Spot The Native (IRE)

61

6-y-o ch g Be My Native (USA)-Shannon Foam (Le Bavard (FR))
Miss H C Knight Trevor Hemmings

Placings:*0*-500 **(3647)**
2001/02: 21^{5}GS, 17^{0}GS, 21^{0}S

	Starts	1st	2nd	3rd	Win & Pl
Hurdles	3	0	0	0	0
Career Total	**4**	**0**	**0**	**0**	**0**

Going: Sf: 0-1 GS: 0-2 Gd: 0-0 GF: - Fm: 0-0
Distance: 2m/2m3: 0-1 2m4-2m7: 0-2 3m+: 0-0
Track: LH: 0-1 RH: 0-2 Tight: 0-1 Gall: 0-0
Aids: Bl: 0-0 Vi: 0-0 Tstrap: 0-0
Best Rating: 93 4/01 Ayr 2m gd-fm NHF

Spot Thedifference (IRE)

(61h)**145**

9-y-o b g Lafontaine (USA)-Spotted Choice (IRE) (Callernish)
E Bolger J P McManus

Placings:P13F/220/4142-311126UP **(4955a)**
2001/02: 24^{3}G, 25^{1}G, 24^{1}G, 25^{1}G, 23^{2}G, 22^{6}S, 36^{U}G, 25^{P}G

	Starts	1st	2nd	3rd	Win & Pl
Hurdles	1	0	0	0	0
Chases	7	3	1	1	26577
Career Total	**19**	**5**	**4**	**2**	**42502**

140	6/01	Kbgn	3m1f	(0-123)HCh	GD	£10483
129	6/01	Rosc	3m100y	(0-116)HCh	GD	£5564
120	5/01	Kbgn	3m1f	Ch	GD	£3895
118	2/01	Thur	3m	Ch	SFT	£4729
106	2/99	Clon	3m	Ch	SFT	£2455

Total win prize-money £27129

Going: Sf: 0-1 GS: 0-0 Gd: 3-7 GF: - Fm: 0-0
Distance: 2m/2m3: 0-0 2m4-2m7: 0-2 **3m+: 3-6**
Track: LH: 0-1 RH: 0-1 Tight: 0-1 Gall: 0-0
Aids: Bl: 0-0 Vi: 0-0 Tstrap: 0-0
Best Rating: 145 7/01 Kbgn 2m7f good Ch

Useful irish staying chaser, suited by good ground.

Spree Vision

103 **89**

6-y-o b g Suave Dancer (USA)-Regent's Folly (IRE) (Touching Wood (USA))
P Monteith I Bell

Placings:6/30620-653 **(2472)**
2001/02: 17^{6}G, 16^{5}GS, 16^{3}GS

	Starts	1st	2nd	3rd	Win & Pl
Hurdles	3	0	0	1	478
Career Total	**9**	**0**	**1**	**2**	**1328**

Going: Sf: 0-0 GS: 0-2 Gd: 0-1 GF: - Fm: 0-0
Distance: 2m/2m3: 0-3 2m4-2m7: 0-0 3m+: 0-0
Track: LH: 0-2 RH: 0-1 Tight: 0-3 Gall: 0-0
Aids: Bl: 0-0 Vi: 0-0 Tstrap: 0-0
Best Rating: 88 12/00 Muss 2m good Hdl

Modest novice hurdler, in good form on the Flat and just denied at Perth in August 2002.

Sprig Muslin

98 **72**

10-y-o br m Ra Nova-Wood Heath (Heres)
D R Gandolfo Peter Melotti & Andy Chalmers

Placings:*13/0*236P/P5234/51/41000-600 **(0983)**
2001/02: 22^{6}GF, 20^{0}S, 19^{0}G

	Starts	1st	2nd	3rd	Win & Pl
Hurdles	3	0	0	0	0
Career Total	**22**	**3**	**2**	**3**	**7810**

87	11/00	Font	2m6f110y	F(0-110)HHdl	HVY	£2352
87	6/98	Worc	2m4f	E(0-100)HHdl	GD	£2355
87	2/96	Towc	2m	H NHF	HVY	£1264

Total win prize-money £5971

Going: Sf: 0-1 GS: 0-0 Gd: 0-1 GF: - Fm: 0-1
Distance: 2m/2m3: 0-1 2m4-2m7: 0-2 3m+: 0-0
Track: LH: 0-3 RH: 0-0 Tight: 0-2 Gall: 0-0
Aids: Bl: 0-0 Vi: 0-3 Tstrap: 0-1
Best Rating: 87 11/00 Font 2m6f110y heavy Hdl

Sprightley Pip (IRE)

11-y-o gr g Roselier (FR)-Owen's Rose (Master Owen)
P Williams Mrs D J Hughes

Placings:*500*/4/20/103 **(4727)**
2001/02: 24^{1}GF, 21^{0}G, 24^{3}GF

	Starts	1st	2nd	3rd	Win & Pl
Chases	3	1	0	1	2444
Career Total	**9**	**1**	**1**	**1**	**3353**

101	5/01	Strf	3m	H Ch	G-F	£1904

Total win prize-money £1905

Going: Sf: 0-0 GS: 0-0 Gd: 0-1 GF: - Fm: 1-2
Distance: 2m/2m3: 0-0 2m4-2m7: 0-1 **3m+: 1-2**
Track: **LH: 1-3** RH: 0-0 **Tight: 1-2** Gall: 0-0
Aids: Bl: 0-0 Vi: 0-0 Tstrap: 0-0
Best Rating: 106 11/97 Chep 2m4f110y gd-sft Hdl

A lightly raced individual who won a maiden point to point on good ground in February 2001. He has apparently had back problems in the past. A fortunate winner of a fast ground Stratford hunter chase in the spring of 2001, decent efforts since.

Spring Double (IRE)

104 **110**

11-y-o br g Seclude (USA)-Solar Jet (Mandalus)
N A Twiston-Davies Mrs Lorna Berryman

Placings:*06/13*40511P2/4333/22P313/63432PP43/10 00P **(4599)**
2001/02: 24^{1}G, 24^{0}S, 24^{0}S, 25^{0}S, 25^{P}GF

	Starts	1st	2nd	3rd	Win & Pl
Hurdles	5	1	0	0	4446
Career Total	**35**	**5**	**4**	**9**	**28898**

104	11/01	Kemp	3m110y	D(0-120)HHdl	GD	£4446
116	4/99	Uttx	3m	D(0-125)HCh	G-S	£4416
124	3/97	Newb	2m5f	D Hdl	G-S	£3467
103	2/97	Hrfd	2m3f110y	E(0-105)HHdl	SFT	£2337
106	5/96	Uttx	2m	H NHF	GD	£1763

Total win prize-money £16429

Going: Sf: 0-3 GS: 0-0 Gd: 1-1 GF: - Fm: 0-1
Distance: 2m/2m3: 0-0 2m4-2m7: 0-0 **3m+: 1-5**
Track: LH: 0-1 **RH: 1-2** Tight: 0-0 Gall: 0-0
Aids: Bl: 0-0 Vi: 0-0 Tstrap: 0-0
Best Rating: 124 3/97 Newb 2m5f gd-sft Hdl

Fair staying hurdler/chaser, he returned from a layoff to score at Kempton in November 2001, but did not build on that. Stays three miles and is effective on good ground or softer.

Spring Gale (IRE)

11-y-o b g Strong Gale-Orospring (Tesoro Mio)
J M Turner J M Turner

Placings:*3/0*12151P/2121243/22523P32/62/124-21 **(0323)**
2001/02: 24^{2}GF, 25^{1}G

	Starts	1st	2nd	3rd	Win & Pl
Chases	2	1	1	0	2386
Career Total	**30**	**7**	**11**	**4**	**38590**

125	5/01	Folk	3m1f	H Ch	GD	£1934
115	5/00	Fknm	3m110y	H Ch	FRM	£1473
129	12/97	Strf	2m5f110y	D Ch	SFT	£4770
134	11/97	Uttx	2m4f	D(0-125)HCh	G-S	£3468
113	3/97	Donc	2m4f	E Hdl	G-F	£2679

109	1/97	Tntn	2m3f110y	D Hdl	G-F	£3137
108	10/96	Font	2m6f110y	E Hdl	GD	£2595

Total win prize-money £20059

Going: Sf: 0-0 GS: 0-0 Gd: 1-1 GF: - Fm: 0-1
Distance: 2m/2m3: 0-0 2m4-2m7: 0-0 **3m+: 1-2**
Track: LH: 0-1 **RH: 1-1 Tight: 1-2** Gall: 0-0
Aids: Bl: 0-0 Vi: 0-0 Tstrap: 0-0
Best Rating: 134 10/98 Plum 3m1f110y good Ch

Decent pointer/hunter chaser, but is sometimes reluctant to start.

Spring Gift

5-y-o b m Slip Anchor-Belmez Melody (Belmez (USA))
R J Hodges (P W D'Arcy 15/1) Marinos Ioannou

Placings:F **(4504)**
2001/02: 17^{F}G

	Starts	1st	2nd	3rd	Win & Pl
Hurdles	1	0	0	0	
Career Total	**1**	**0**	**0**	**0**	

Going: Sf: 0-0 GS: 0-0 Gd: 0-1 GF: - Fm: 0-0
Distance: 2m/2m3: 0-1 2m4-2m7: 0-0 3m+: 0-0
Track: LH: 0-1 RH: 0-0 Tight: 0-1 Gall: 0-0
Aids: Bl: 0-0 Vi: 0-0 Tstrap: 0-0
Best Rating:

Spring Grove (IRE)

108 **142**

7-y-o b g Mandalus-Lucy Lorraine (IRE) (Buckskin (FR))
R H Alner H V Perry

Placings: 1/52153/**123313-FUPP34** **(4759)**
2001/02: 21^{F}G, 20^{U}S, 22^{P}GS, 19^{P}GS, 20^{3}S, 19^{4}GF

	Starts	1st	2nd	3rd	Win & Pl
Hurdles	1	0	0	0	0
Chases	5	0	0	1	3070
Career Total	**18**	**4**	**2**	**5**	**20874**

142	2/01	Leic	2m	E Ch	SFT	£3413
134	10/00	Kemp	2m	D Ch	G-S	£4959
125	2/00	Font	2m2f110y	E Hdl	SFT	£2537
108	3/99	Chep	2m110y	H NHF	G-S	£1856

Total win prize-money £12768

Going: Sf: 0-2 GS: 0-2 Gd: 0-1 GF: - Fm: 0-1
Distance: 2m/2m3: 0-0 2m4-2m7: 0-6 3m+: 0-0
Track: LH: 0-2 RH: 0-4 Tight: 0-1 Gall: 0-0
Aids: Bl: 0-0 Vi: 0-0 Tstrap: 0-0
Best Rating: 142 12/01 Winc 2m5f good Ch

Looked useful in 2001 over fences but has not progressed as expected since. Acts well on a soft surface and is effective at around two to two and a half miles.

Spring Margot (FR)

103(110h) (129h)**156**

6-y-o b g Kadalko (FR)-La Brunante (FR) (Chaparral (FR))
Miss Venetia Williams Sir Robert Ogden

Placings: *161*U1213-**11311P** **(4836)**
2001/02: 17^{1}G, 20^{1}GS, 19^{3}GS, 20^{1}G, 20^{1}G, 20^{P}G

	Starts	1st	2nd	3rd	Win & Pl
Chases	6	4	0	1	36247
Career Total	**14**	**8**	**1**	**2**	**51339**

156	4/02	Aint	2m4f	B HCh	GD	£21775
144	1/02	Ludl	2m4f	E Ch	GD	£3513
133	10/01	Font	2m4f	E Ch	G-S	£3081
144	10/01	MRas	2m1f110y	C Ch	GD	£6838
127	4/01	Ayr	2m4f	C Hdl	GD	£5479
127	3/01	Extr	2m3f	E Hdl	HVY	£2287
128	1/01	Plum	2m5f	E Hdl	SFT	£2513
120	10/00	Sthl	2m	H NHF	SFT	£1501

Total win prize-money £46990

Going: Sf: 0-0 GS: 1-2 Gd: 3-4 GF: - Fm: 0-0
Distance: 2m/2m3: 1-2 **2m4-2m7: 3-4** 3m+: 0-0
Track: LH: 1-2 **RH: 2-3 Tight: 4-5** Gall: 0-0
Aids: Bl: 0-0 Vi: 0-0 Tstrap: 0-0
Best Rating: 156 4/02 Aint 2m4f good Ch

A useful novice chaser, he stays two miles-five, but is effective at shorter and acts on good or easier ground. Despite his four wins in the 2001/2002 season, he is not the best of jumpers.

Spring Song

5-y-o b m Petong-Naturally Fresh (Thatching)
M E Sowersby Racing Ladies

Placings:PP **(3492)**
2001/02: 19^{P}GF, 24^{P}S

	Starts	1st	2nd	3rd	Win & Pl
Hurdles	2	0	0	0	
Career Total	**2**	**0**	**0**	**0**	

Going: Sf: 0-1 GS: 0-0 Gd: 0-0 GF: - Fm: 0-1
Distance: 2m/2m3: 0-1 2m4-2m7: 0-0 3m+: 0-1
Track: LH: 0-2 RH: 0-0 Tight: 0-1 Gall: 0-1
Aids: Bl: 0-0 Vi: 0-0 Tstrap: 0-0
Best Rating:

Spring To Glory

15-y-o b g Teenoso (USA)-English Spring (USA) (Grey Dawn Ii)
P Hayward Mrs C A Davies

Placings:4PU0/302510/341252/31F/0F42**403/34P15/ 23F/633302F/1PPP-P0** **(0908)**
2001/02: 23^{P}G, 23^{0}G

	Starts	1st	2nd	3rd	Win & Pl
Chases	2	0	0	0	
Career Total	**47**	**5**	**6**	**9**	**23202**

102	5/00	Hrfd	3m1f110y	F(0-95)HCh	GD	£4208
98	2/98	Tntn	3m	E(0-115)HCh	G-F	£3680
110	8/94	Worc	3m	(0-115)HHdl	G-F	£1975
97	10/93	Tntn	2m3f110y	(0-115)HHdl	GD	£2400
102	3/92	Tntn	2m110y	Hdl	G-F	£1369

Total win prize-money £13633

Going: Sf: 0-0 GS: 0-0 Gd: 0-2 GF: - Fm: 0-0
Distance: 2m/2m3: 0-0 2m4-2m7: 0-0 3m+: 0-2
Track: LH: 0-2 RH: 0-0 Tight: 0-0 Gall: 0-0
Aids: Bl: 0-0 Vi: 0-2 Tstrap: 0-0
Best Rating: 999 11/91 Nott 2m gd-fm Hdl

Springbok Attitude

96 **84**

5-y-o b g Pharly (FR)-Tugra (FR) (Baby Turk)
B Llewellyn (D Eddy 9/5) Mrs M Llewellyn

Placings: *000-00*042P0P **(1755)**
2001/02: 16^{0}GF, 16^{0}GF, 20^{0}G, 16^{4}GF, 16^{2}GF, 16^{P}GF, 16^{0}GF, 16^{P}GS

	Starts	1st	2nd	3rd	Win & Pl
NH Flat	1	0	0	0	0
Hurdles	7	0	1	0	848
Career Total	**11**	**0**	**1**	**0**	**848**

Going: Sf: 0-0 GS: 0-1 Gd: 0-1 GF: - Fm: 0-6
Distance: 2m/2m3: 0-7 2m4-2m7: 0-1 3m+: 0-0
Track: LH: 0-7 RH: 0-1 Tight: 0-3 Gall: 0-0
Aids: Bl: 0-0 Vi: 0-1 Tstrap: 0-1
Best Rating: 84 9/01 Strf 2m110y gd-fm Hdl

Springer The Lad

94 **90**

5-y-o ch g Carlton (GER)-Also Kirsty (Twilight Alley)
D M Grissell Mrs Christine Notley

Placings:04P6 **(4167)**
2001/02: 16^{0}GS, 21^{4}S, 22^{P}HY, 21^{6}GS

	Starts	1st	2nd	3rd	Win & Pl
NH Flat	1	0	0	0	0
Hurdles	3	0	0	0	0
Career Total	**4**	**0**	**0**	**0**	**0**

Going: Sf: 0-2 GS: 0-2 Gd: 0-0 GF: - Fm: 0-0
Distance: 2m/2m3: 0-1 2m4-2m7: 0-3 3m+: 0-0
Track: LH: 0-2 RH: 0-2 Tight: 0-3 Gall: 0-1
Aids: Bl: 0-0 Vi: 0-0 Tstrap: 0-0
Best Rating: 90 1/02 Plum 2m5f soft Hdl

Springfield Chorse

7-y-o ch g Weld-Ledee (Le Bavard (FR))
J R Cornwall Nick Sarson

Placings: *0*-0P **(1842)**
2001/02: 19^{0}G, 24^{P}S

	Starts	1st	2nd	3rd	Win & Pl
Hurdles	2	0	0	0	
Career Total	**3**	**0**	**0**	**0**	

Going: Sf: 0-1 GS: 0-0 Gd: 0-1 GF: - Fm: 0-0
Distance: 2m/2m3: 0-0 2m4-2m7: 0-1 3m+: 0-1
Track: LH: 0-0 RH: 0-2 Tight: 0-1 Gall: 0-0
Aids: Bl: 0-0 Vi: 0-0 Tstrap: 0-0
Best Rating: 13 12/00 Hntg 2m110y soft NHF

Springfield Gilda (IRE)

94f **83f**

4-y-o b f Gildoran-Ledee (Le Bavard (FR))
S Gollings Mrs M A Hall

Placings: *052* **(4289)**
2001/02: 16^{0}GS, 16^{5}S, 17^{2}GS

	Starts	1st	2nd	3rd	Win & Pl
NH Flat	3	0	1	0	462
Career Total	**3**	**0**	**1**	**0**	**462**

Going: Sf: 0-1 GS: 0-2 Gd: 0-0 GF: - Fm: 0-0
Distance: 2m/2m3: 0-3 2m4-2m7: 0-0 3m+: 0-0
Track: LH: 0-2 RH: 0-1 Tight: 0-2 Gall: 0-1
Aids: Bl: 0-0 Vi: 0-0 Tstrap: 0-0
Best Rating: 87 3/02 MRas 2m1f110y gd-sft NHF

Has shown progressive if modest form in bumpers.

Springfield Rex

97 **100**

11-y-o ch g Oedipus Complex-Scarlet Coon (Tycoon Ii)
D E Ingle The Extreme Team

Placings:15-300 (4814)
2001/02: 24^{3}GF, 21^{0}G, 21^{0}GF

	Starts	1st	2nd	3rd	Win & Pl
Chases	3	0	0	1	482
Career Total	**5**	**1**	**0**	**1**	**2234**

100	5/00	Aint	3m1f	H Ch	G-F	£1751

Total win prize-money £1752

Going: Sf: 0-0 GS: 0-0 Gd: 0-1 GF: - Fm: 0-2
Distance: 2m/2m3: 0-0 2m4-2m7: 0-2 3m+: 0-1
Track: LH: 0-3 RH: 0-0 Tight: 0-2 Gall: 0-1
Aids: Bl: 0-0 Vi: 0-0 Tstrap: 0-0
Best Rating: 100 5/01 Strf 3m gd-fm Ch

Springfield Scally

100 **138**

9-y-o ch g Scallywag-Ledee (Le Bavard (FR))
S Gollings Mrs M A Hall

Placings:*2111411324 6/222U33616/*5324541220-F00 (4647)
2001/02: 24^{F}GS, 21^{0}GS, 24^{0}G

	Starts	1st	2nd	3rd	Win & Pl
Hurdles	3	0	0	0	
Career Total	**33**	**7**	**8**	**4**	**61694**

145	2/01	Uttx	2m6f110y	C(0-135)HHdl	HVY	£10426
132	3/00	Uttx	2m6f110y	B(0-140)HHdl	GD	£10692
112	1/99	MRas	3m	E Hdl	SFT	£2337
96	12/98	MRas	2m3f110y	F Hdl	SFT	£2304
108	10/98	Fknm	2m	H NHF	SFT	£1143
103	9/98	MRas	1m5f110y	H NHF	GD	£1255
103	9/98	Worc	2m	H NHF	G-F	£1116

Total win prize-money £29876

Going: Sf: 0-0 GS: 0-2 Gd: 0-1 GF: - Fm: 0-0
Distance: 2m/2m3: 0-0 2m4-2m7: 0-1 3m+: 0-2
Track: LH: 0-3 RH: 0-0 Tight: 0-1 Gall: 0-2
Aids: Bl: 0-0 Vi: 0-0 Tstrap: 0-0
Best Rating: 145 2/01 Uttx 2m6f110y heavy Hdl

A tremendously genuine front-runner, he enjoyed a profitable 2000/2001 campaign in staying handicap hurdles but did not show much in a brief 2001/2002 campaign. Best when able to dominate. Stays three miles. Acts on soft/heavy ground.

Springfieldsparky

6-y-o ch m Cotation-Scarlet Coon (Tycoon Ii)
D E Ingle The Extreme Team

Placings:*00* (4046)
2001/02: 17^{0}S, 17^{0}GS

	Starts	1st	2nd	3rd	Win & Pl
NH Flat	2	0	0	0	
Career Total	**2**	**0**	**0**	**0**	

Going: Sf: 0-1 GS: 0-1 Gd: 0-0 GF: - Fm: 0-0
Distance: 2m/2m3: 0-2 2m4-2m7: 0-0 3m+: 0-0
Track: LH: 0-1 RH: 0-1 Tight: 0-2 Gall: 0-0
Aids: Bl: 0-0 Vi: 0-0 Tstrap: 0-0
Best Rating:

Springford (IRE)

10-y-o b g King's Ride-Tickenor Wood (Le Bavard (FR))
M R Bosley Mrs Jean M O'Connor

Placings:*00P/224521P/*3006 (1383)
2001/02: 25^{3}G, 22^{0}G, 25^{0}GF, 26^{6}GF

	Starts	1st	2nd	3rd	Win & Pl
Hurdles	1	0	0	0	0
Chases	3	0	0	1	668
Career Total	**14**	**1**	**3**	**1**	**8004**

102	3/00	Towc	2m6f	D Ch	GD	£4143

Total win prize-money £4144

Going: Sf: 0-0 GS: 0-0 Gd: 0-2 GF: - Fm: 0-2
Distance: 2m/2m3: 0-0 2m4-2m7: 0-1 3m+: 0-3
Track: LH: 0-0 RH: 0-4 Tight: 0-2 Gall: 0-0
Aids: Bl: 0-0 Vi: 0-0 Tstrap: 0-0
Best Rating: 116 11/99 Hrfd 3m1f110y good Ch

Springhill

107 **111**

7-y-o b g Relief Pitcher-Early Call (Kind Of Hush)
Mrs Mary Hambro Richard Hambro

Placings:*2132/*25-335 (2683)
2001/02: 16^{3}G, 16^{3}GS, 16^{5}G

	Starts	1st	2nd	3rd	Win & Pl
Hurdles	3	0	0	2	3523
Career Total	**9**	**1**	**3**	**3**	**7736**

113	10/99	Sedg	2m1f	H NHF	G-F	£1605

Total win prize-money £1606

Going: Sf: 0-0 GS: 0-1 Gd: 0-2 GF: - Fm: 0-0
Distance: 2m/2m3: 0-3 2m4-2m7: 0-0 3m+: 0-0
Track: LH: 0-3 RH: 0-0 Tight: 0-1 Gall: 0-1
Aids: Bl: 0-0 Vi: 0-0 Tstrap: 0-0
Best Rating: 113 11/99 Winc 2m good NHF

Looks every inch a chaser in the making. Needs decent ground to be seen to best effect.

Springlea Tower

85 **86**

9-y-o b g Meadowbrook-Tringa (GER) (Kaiseradler)
R Nixon G R S Nixon

Placings:P/64FU40/PP646PU5/445U25323/35144FP 3P52-5460P (1577)
2001/02: 26^{5}GF, 24^{4}GF, 24^{6}F, 24^{0}G, 25^{P}G

	Starts	1st	2nd	3rd	Win & Pl
Chases	5	0	0	0	0
Career Total	**40**	**1**	**3**	**4**	**13072**

80	5/00	Ctml	3m2f	E Ch	G-S	£3720

Total win prize-money £3720

Going: Sf: 0-0 GS: 0-0 Gd: 0-2 GF: - Fm: 0-3
Distance: 2m/2m3: 0-0 2m4-2m7: 0-0 3m+: 0-5
Track: LH: 0-2 RH: 0-2 Tight: 0-1 Gall: 0-1
Aids: Bl: 0-0 Vi: 0-0 Tstrap: 0-0
Best Rating: 101 2/01 Kels 3m1f soft Ch

Springside (IRE)

70 **25**

8-y-o b m Brush Aside (USA)-Springphar (IRE) (Phardante (FR))
R H Buckler Mrs P J Buckler

Placings:*0*-00P (2358)
2001/02: 17^{0}GS, 16^{0}GS, 21^{P}S

	Starts	1st	2nd	3rd	Win & Pl
Hurdles	3	0	0	0	
Career Total	**4**	**0**	**0**	**0**	

Going: Sf: 0-1 GS: 0-2 Gd: 0-0 GF: - Fm: 0-0
Distance: 2m/2m3: 0-2 2m4-2m7: 0-1 3m+: 0-0
Track: LH: 0-1 RH: 0-2 Tight: 0-1 Gall: 0-0
Aids: Bl: 0-0 Vi: 0-0 Tstrap: 0-0

Best Rating: 52 12/00 Tntn 2m1f soft NHF

Springtime Lady

72 **32**

6-y-o ch m Desert Dirham (USA)-Affaire De Coeur (Imperial Fling (USA))
J G M O'Shea Graham Brown

Placings:55-0 (0493)
2001/02: 17^{0}G

	Starts	1st	2nd	3rd	Win & Pl
Hurdles	1	0	0	0	
Career Total	**3**	**0**	**0**	**0**	**0**

Going: Sf: 0-0 GS: 0-0 Gd: 0-1 GF: - Fm: 0-0
Distance: 2m/2m3: 0-1 2m4-2m7: 0-0 3m+: 0-0
Track: LH: 0-0 RH: 0-1 Tight: 0-0 Gall: 0-0
Aids: Bl: 0-0 Vi: 0-0 Tstrap: 0-0
Best Rating: 84 9/00 Worc 2m gd-fm Hdl

Springwell Albert (IRE)

6-y-o ch g Alphabatim (USA)-Red Bit (IRE) (Henbit (USA))
C Grant Birotex

Placings:00UP (4673)
2001/02: 16^{0}G, 16^{0}G, 16^{U}GS, 17^{P}GF

	Starts	1st	2nd	3rd	Win & Pl
NH Flat	2	0	0	0	0
Hurdles	2	0	0	0	0
Career Total	**4**	**0**	**0**	**0**	

Going: Sf: 0-0 GS: 0-1 Gd: 0-2 GF: - Fm: 0-1
Distance: 2m/2m3: 0-4 2m4-2m7: 0-0 3m+: 0-0
Track: LH: 0-3 RH: 0-1 Tight: 0-3 Gall: 0-1
Aids: Bl: 0-0 Vi: 0-0 Tstrap: 0-0
Best Rating: 83 1/02 Muss 2m good NHF

Springwood White

81 **60**

8-y-o gr g Sharkskin Suit (USA)-Kale Brig (New Brig)
J L Gledson J L Gledson

Placings:P (4859)
2001/02: 25^{P}G

	Starts	1st	2nd	3rd	Win & Pl
Chases	1	0	0	0	
Career Total	**1**	**0**	**0**	**0**	

Going: Sf: 0-0 GS: 0-0 Gd: 0-1 GF: - Fm: 0-0
Distance: 2m/2m3: 0-0 2m4-2m7: 0-0 3m+: 0-1
Track: LH: 0-1 RH: 0-0 Tight: 0-0 Gall: 0-0
Aids: Bl: 0-0 Vi: 0-0 Tstrap: 0-0
Best Rating:

Spumante

88(63h) (67h)**56**

10-y-o ch g Executive Man-Midler (Comedy Star (USA))
Mrs L Williamson The Charleston Partnership

Placings:03/24060/**P-00500** (1191)
2001/02: 20^{0}GF, 25^{0}G, 20^{5}GF, 24^{0}GF, 20^{0}G

	Starts	1st	2nd	3rd	Win & Pl
Hurdles	2	0	0	0	0

	Starts	1st	2nd	3rd	Win & Pl
Chases	3	0	0	0	0
Career Total	**13**	**0**	**1**	**1**	**1000**

Going: Sf: 0-0 GS: 0-0 Gd: 0-2 GF: - Fm: 0-3
Distance: 2m/2m3: 0-0 2m4-2m7: 0-3 3m+: 0-2
Track: LH: 0-4 RH: 0-1 Tight: 0-4 Gall: 0-0
Aids: Bl: 0-0 Vi: 0-0 Tstrap: 0-0
Best Rating: 82 5/96 Chep 2m110y gd-fm Hdl

Spunkie

99 **111**

9-y-o ch g Jupiter Island-Super Sol (Rolfe (USA))
R F Johnson Houghton Jim Short

Placings:21/3F/301160-06 **(2485)**
2001/02: 21^{0}G, 22^{6}HY

	Starts	1st	2nd	3rd	Win & Pl
Hurdles	2	0	0	0	0
Career Total	**12**	**3**	**1**	**2**	**9831**

131	1/01	Fknm	2m4f	D(0-120)HHdl	SFT	£3471
129	1/01	Fknm	2m4f	D Hdl	SFT	£3360
107	3/97	Font	2m2f	H NHF	GD	£1255

Total win prize-money £8087

Going: Sf: 0-1 GS: 0-0 Gd: 0-1 GF: - Fm: 0-0
Distance: 2m/2m3: 0-0 2m4-2m7: 0-2 3m+: 0-0
Track: LH: 0-2 RH: 0-0 Tight: 0-1 Gall: 0-1
Aids: Bl: 0-0 Vi: 0-0 Tstrap: 0-0
Best Rating: 131 1/01 Fknm 2m4f soft Hdl

fair hurdler in 2000/01, but he has been disappointing since. Likes to front run.

Spy Boy (IRE)

91(96h) (80h)**72+**

6-y-o b g Balla Cove-Spy Girl (Tanfirion)
Simon T Lewis (J S Moore 31/10) Simon T Lewis

Placings:3/F04440-53301U005 **(4127)**
2001/02: 16^{5}YS, 18^{3}GF, 16^{3}GF, 17^{0}S, 20^{1}GS, 19^{U}GS, 20^{0}GS, 19^{0}S, 17^{5}G

	Starts	1st	2nd	3rd	Win & Pl
NH Flat	1	0	0	0	0
Hurdles	8	1	1	2	3141
Career Total	**16**	**1**	**0**	**3**	**3891**

80	10/01	Font	2m4f	F Hdl	G-S	£2373

Total win prize-money £2373

Going: Sf: 0-2 GS: **1-3** Gd: 0-1 GF: - Fm: 0-2
Distance: 2m/2m3: 0-5 **2m4-2m7: 1-4** 3m+: 0-0
Track: LH: 0-2 RH: 0-4 **Tight: 1-6** Gall: 0-0
Aids: Bl: 0-0 **Vi: 1-3** Tstrap: 0-0
Best Rating: 88 7/00 Worc 2m gd-fm NHF

Plating-class hurdler, all out to win a claiming hurdle at Fontwell in October but well held subsequently.

Spy Knoll

103 **115**

8-y-o b g Shirley Heights-Garden Pink (FR) (Bellypha)
Jamie Poulton M K George

Placings:30/P30/5/3022 **(4636)**
2001/02: 20^{3}G, 24^{0}G, 22^{2}GS, 24^{2}GF

	Starts	1st	2nd	3rd	Win & Pl
Hurdles	4	0	2	1	4934
Career Total	**10**	**0**	**2**	**3**	**5626**

Going: Sf: 0-0 GS: 0-1 Gd: 0-2 GF: - Fm: 0-1
Distance: 2m/2m3: 0-0 2m4-2m7: 0-2 3m+: 0-2
Track: LH: 0-0 RH: 0-4 Tight: 0-0 Gall: 0-0
Aids: Bl: 0-2 Vi: 0-0 Tstrap: 0-0
Best Rating: 115 4/02 Asct 3m gd-fm Hdl

Frustrating maiden hurdler who ran a blinder at Sandown in March 2002 and again at Ascot the following month. Suited by a test of stamina and good ground.

Squaddie

10-y-o ch g Infantry-Mendelita (Kings Company)
Mrs C Lawrence (P J Millington 27/1) Mrs C & Miss K E Lawrence

Placings:3/253660/434006/03P50 **(4483)**
2001/02: 20^{0}GF, 25^{3}G, 25^{P}G, 24^{5}S, 19^{0}G

	Starts	1st	2nd	3rd	Win & Pl
Chases	5	0	0	1	291
Career Total	**18**	**0**	**1**	**4**	**1491**

Going: Sf: 0-1 GS: 0-0 Gd: 0-3 GF: - Fm: 0-1
Distance: 2m/2m3: 0-0 2m4-2m7: 0-2 3m+: 0-3
Track: LH: 0-1 RH: 0-4 Tight: 0-2 Gall: 0-1
Aids: Bl: 0-0 Vi: 0-0 Tstrap: 0-0
Best Rating: 102 5/98 Hntg 2m4f110y gd-fm Hdl

Squandamania

93 **71**

9-y-o b g Ela-Mana-Mou-Garden Pink (FR) (Bellypha)
J R Norton Jaffa Racing Syndicate

Placings:3005/3522/5644213/F261311-P00P060 **(4432)**
2001/02: 17^{P}S, 16^{0}S, 16^{0}GS, 16^{P}GS, 17^{0}S, 21^{6}GS, 20^{0}HY

	Starts	1st	2nd	3rd	Win & Pl
Hurdles	7	0	0	0	0
Career Total	**29**	**4**	**4**	**4**	**17463**

108	2/01	Sedg	2m1f	F(0-110)HHdl	G-S	£3038
101	2/01	Sedg	2m1f	D(0-120)HHdl	SFT	£5193
104	12/00	Sedg	2m1f	F(0-110)HHdl	SFT	£2383
101	2/00	Sedg	2m1f	F(0-110)HHdl	G-S	£2775

Total win prize-money £13392

Going: Sf: 0-4 GS: 0-3 Gd: 0-0 GF: - Fm: 0-0
Distance: 2m/2m3: 0-5 2m4-2m7: 0-2 3m+: 0-0
Track: LH: 0-6 RH: 0-1 Tight: 0-4 Gall: 0-1
Aids: Bl: 0-1 Vi: 0-0 Tstrap: 0-0
Best Rating: 108 2/01 Sedg 2m1f gd-sft Hdl

Suited by a strongly-run two miles, he goes very well at Sedgefield. Not at his best in 2001/02.

Square One (IRE)

91 **89**

8-y-o b m Mandalus-Deep Dollar (Deep Run)
C C Bealby Mrs C Price

Placings:1-033PP **(4426)**
2001/02: 24^{0}GS, 24^{3}S, 22^{3}HY, 25^{P}S, 26^{P}HY

	Starts	1st	2nd	3rd	Win & Pl
Chases	5	0	0	2	1430
Career Total	**6**	**1**	**0**	**2**	**2810**

99	3/01	MRas	3m1f	H Ch	HVY	£1380

Total win prize-money £1381

Going: Sf: 0-4 GS: 0-1 Gd: 0-0 GF: - Fm: 0-0
Distance: 2m/2m3: 0-0 2m4-2m7: 0-1 3m+: 0-4
Track: LH: 0-3 RH: 0-2 Tight: 0-3 Gall: 0-0
Aids: Bl: 0-0 Vi: 0-0 Tstrap: 0-0
Best Rating: 99 3/01 MRas 3m1f heavy Ch

Winning hunter chaser, stays three miles.

Squeaky

101f **94f**

5-y-o ch m Infantry-Steady Saunter Vii (Damsire Unregistered)
Miss K M George R E Baskerville

Placings:5 **(0506)**
2001/02: 16^{5}GF

	Starts	1st	2nd	3rd	Win & Pl
NH Flat	1	0	0	0	0
Career Total	**1**	**0**	**0**	**0**	**0**

Going: Sf: 0-0 GS: 0-0 Gd: 0-0 GF: - Fm: 0-1
Distance: 2m/2m3: 0-1 2m4-2m7: 0-0 3m+: 0-0
Track: LH: 0-0 RH: 0-1 Tight: 0-0 Gall: 0-1
Aids: Bl: 0-0 Vi: 0-0 Tstrap: 0-0
Best Rating: 94 5/01 Hntg 2m110y gd-fm NHF

Squire Shandy

108f **108f**

5-y-o ch g Afzal-Hatherley (Deep Run)
Noel T Chance Mrs Jane Lane

Placings:1 **(2394)**
2001/02: 16^{1}S

	Starts	1st	2nd	3rd	Win & Pl
NH Flat	1	1	0	0	1638
Career Total	**1**	**1**	**0**	**0**	**1638**

108	11/01	Chep	2m110y	H NHF	SFT	£1638

Total win prize-money £1638

Going: Sf: 1-1 GS: 0-0 Gd: 0-0 GF: - Fm: 0-0
Distance: **2m/2m3: 1-1** 2m4-2m7: 0-0 3m+: 0-0
Track: **LH: 1-1** RH: 0-0 Tight: 0-0 Gall: 0-0
Aids: Bl: 0-0 Vi: 0-0 Tstrap: 0-0
Best Rating: 108 11/01 Chep 2m110y soft NHF

Made a winning debut in a Chepstow bumper.

Squirrel

50f

5-y-o gr g Prince Daniel (USA)-Hanim (IRE) (Hatim (USA))
R D E Woodhouse Miss J M Slater

Placings:0 **(2675)**
2001/02: 16^{0}G

	Starts	1st	2nd	3rd	Win & Pl
NH Flat	1	0	0	0	
Career Total	**1**	**0**	**0**	**0**	

Going: Sf: 0-0 GS: 0-0 Gd: 0-1 GF: - Fm: 0-0
Distance: 2m/2m3: 0-1 2m4-2m7: 0-0 3m+: 0-0
Track: LH: 0-1 RH: 0-0 Tight: 0-0 Gall: 0-1
Aids: Bl: 0-0 Vi: 0-0 Tstrap: 0-0
Best Rating:

Squirrel Nutkin (IRE)

73 **68**

4-y-o gr g Bluebird (USA)-Saltoki (Ballad Rock)
Jedd O'Keeffe The Squirrel Fanclub Partnership

Placings:6F **(1718)**
2001/02: 16^{6}G, 16^{F}G

	Starts	1st	2nd	3rd	Win & Pl
Hurdles	2	0	0	0	0
Career Total	**2**	**0**	**0**	**0**	**0**

Going: Sf: 0-0 GS: 0-0 Gd: 0-2 GF: - Fm: 0-0
Distance: 2m/2m3: 0-2 2m4-2m7: 0-0 3m+: 0-0
Track: LH: 0-2 RH: 0-0 Tight: 0-1 Gall: 0-0
Aids: Bl: 0-0 Vi: 0-0 Tstrap: 0-0
Best Rating: 68 10/01 Kels 2m110y good Hdl

St George's Boy

5-y-o b g Inchinor-Deanta In Eirinn (Red Sunset)
M A Barnes (H Morrison 27/6) Thirdtimelucky

Placings:PP **(2182)**
2001/02: 16^{P}G, 16^{P}GS

	Starts	1st	2nd	3rd	Win & Pl
Hurdles	2	0	0	0	
Career Total	**2**	**0**	**0**	**0**	

Going: Sf: 0-0 GS: 0-1 Gd: 0-1 GF: - Fm: 0-0
Distance: 2m/2m3: 0-2 2m4-2m7: 0-0 3m+: 0-0
Track: LH: 0-2 RH: 0-0 Tight: 0-1 Gall: 0-0
Aids: Bl: 0-0 Vi: 0-0 Tstrap: 0-1
Best Rating:

St Helensfield

101 **105**

7-y-o ch g Kris-On Credit (FR) (No Pass No Sale)
M C Pipe Paul Dean

Placings:20165 **(4502)**
2001/02: 17^{2}GF, 16^{0}G, 17^{4}S, 17^{6}S, 22^{5}G

	Starts	1st	2nd	3rd	Win & Pl
Hurdles	5	0	1	0	990
Career Total	**5**	**0**	**1**	**0**	**990**

Going: Sf: 0-2 GS: 0-0 Gd: 0-2 GF: - Fm: 0-1
Distance: 2m/2m3: 0-4 2m4-2m7: 0-1 3m+: 0-0
Track: LH: 0-1 RH: 0-4 Tight: 0-3 Gall: 0-0
Aids: Bl: 0-0 Vi: 0-2 Tstrap: 0-0
Best Rating: 105 11/01 Extr 2m1f gd-fm Hdl

St Lawrence (CAN)

8-y-o gr g With Approval (CAN)-Mingan Isle (USA) (Lord Avie (USA))
B S Rothwell Northern Cladding Ltd

Placings:434-P **(1913)**
2001/02: 23^{P}G

	Starts	1st	2nd	3rd	Win & Pl
Hurdles	1	0	0	0	
Career Total	**4**	**0**	**0**	**1**	**530**

Going: Sf: 0-0 GS: 0-0 Gd: 0-1 GF: - Fm: 0-0
Distance: 2m/2m3: 0-0 2m4-2m7: 0-1 3m+: 0-0
Track: LH: 0-1 RH: 0-0 Tight: 0-0 Gall: 0-0
Aids: Bl: 0-0 Vi: 0-0 Tstrap: 0-0
Best Rating: 96 5/00 Weth 2m gd-fm Hdl

St Mellion Par (IRE)

93 **94**

8-y-o ch g Glacial Storm (USA)-Tenerife Sunset (Boreen (FR))
P J Hobbs St Mellion Estates Ltd

Placings:21350/1340-P5P **(4388)**
2001/02: 24^{P}HY, 21^{5}GS, 25^{P}S

	Starts	1st	2nd	3rd	Win & Pl
Chases	3	0	0	0	0
Career Total	**12**	**2**	**1**	**2**	**10261**

131	1/01	Hayd	2m6f	D(0-110)HCh	SFT	£4134
107	1/00	Plum	2m5f	E Hdl	HVY	£2695

Total win prize-money £6829

Going: Sf: 0-2 GS: 0-1 Gd: 0-0 GF: - Fm: 0-0
Distance: 2m/2m3: 0-0 2m4-2m7: 0-1 3m+: 0-2
Track: LH: 0-1 RH: 0-2 Tight: 0-0 Gall: 0-0
Aids: Bl: 0-0 Vi: 0-0 Tstrap: 0-0
Best Rating: 131 1/01 Hayd 2m6f soft Ch

A front runner, he has been held in handicap company since winning a novice chase at Haydock in January 2001. Stays two miles-six, suited by soft ground.

St Mellion Wood (IRE)

(91c) (78c)

7-y-o b g Insan (USA)-Home In The Glen (Furry Glen)
C Weedon Paul Rafferty,Godfrey Hyde,Pete McKay

Placings:566/0000P/434-5P **(0671)**
2001/02: 20^{5}GF, 24^{P}G

	Starts	1st	2nd	3rd	Win & Pl
Hurdles	1	0	0	0	0
Chases	1	0	0	0	0
Career Total	**13**	**0**	**0**	**1**	**683**

Going: Sf: 0-0 GS: 0-0 Gd: 0-1 GF: - Fm: 0-1
Distance: 2m/2m3: 0-0 2m4-2m7: 0-1 3m+: 0-1
Track: LH: 0-1 RH: 0-0 Tight: 0-1 Gall: 0-0
Aids: Bl: 0-0 Vi: 0-0 Tstrap: 0-0
Best Rating: 84 1/01 Ludl 2m4f soft Ch

St Pacokise (IRE)

61 **13**

5-y-o b m Brief Truce (USA)-Classic Opera (Lomond (USA))
R J Smith Silent Running Syndicate

Placings:0 **(1381)**
2001/02: 17^{0}GF

	Starts	1st	2nd	3rd	Win & Pl
Hurdles	1	0	0	0	
Career Total	**1**	**0**	**0**	**0**	

Going: Sf: 0-0 GS: 0-0 Gd: 0-0 GF: - Fm: 0-1
Distance: 2m/2m3: 0-1 2m4-2m7: 0-0 3m+: 0-0
Track: LH: 0-0 RH: 0-1 Tight: 0-0 Gall: 0-0
Aids: Bl: 0-0 Vi: 0-0 Tstrap: 0-0
Best Rating: 13 9/01 Hrfd 2m1f gd-fm Hdl

St Pirran (IRE)

112(113h) (119h)**142**

7-y-o b/br g Be My Native (USA)-Guess Twice (Deep Run)
P F Nicholls C G Roach

Placings:3211214-1U23264 **(4675)**
2001/02: 17^{1}G, 16^{U}G, 17^{2}GS, 19^{3}G, 18^{2}GS, 21^{6}G, 16^{4}G

	Starts	1st	2nd	3rd	Win & Pl
Chases	7	1	2	1	15694
Career Total	**14**	**4**	**4**	**2**	**45902**

127	10/01	Extr	2m1f110y	D Ch	GD	£4329
136	2/01	Kemp	2m	A Hdl	G-S	£12000
137	12/00	Chel	2m1f	B Hdl	SFT	£7280
120	11/00	Extr	2m1f	E Hdl	G-S	£3080

Total win prize-money £26689

Going: Sf: 0-0 GS: 0-2 Gd: 1-5 GF: - Fm: 0-0
Distance: **2m/2m3: 1-5** 2m4-2m7: 0-2 3m+: 0-0
Track: LH: 0-4 **RH: 1-3** Tight: 0-1 Gall: 0-3
Aids: Bl: 0-2 Vi: 0-0 Tstrap: 0-0
Best Rating: 142 3/02 Newb 2m2f110y gd-sft Ch

Progressed well over hurdles and made light work of his rivals to land his chasing debut in promising style at Exeter in the latter part of 2001, but was not totally convinced subsequently. He ideally needs a strongly-run race in yielding ground, and should stay further than two miles.

Stack The Pack (IRE)

97f **105f**

5-y-o ch g Good Thyne (USA)-Game Trix (Buckskin (FR))
T R George Mrs Christine Davies

Placings:01 **(4506)**
2001/02: 16^{0}GS, 17^{1}G

	Starts	1st	2nd	3rd	Win & Pl
NH Flat	2	1	0	0	2415
Career Total	**2**	**1**	**0**	**0**	**2415**

105	3/02	NAbb	2m1f	H NHF	GD	£2415

Total win prize-money £2415

Going: Sf: 0-0 GS: 0-1 Gd: 1-1 GF: - Fm: 0-0
Distance: **2m/2m3: 1-2** 2m4-2m7: 0-0 3m+: 0-0
Track: **LH: 1-1** RH: 0-1 **Tight: 1-1** Gall: 0-0
Aids: Bl: 0-0 Vi: 0-0 Tstrap: 0-0
Best Rating: 105 3/02 NAbb 2m1f good NHF

Benefited from Sandown debut when winning a bumper at Newton Abbot in March 2002.

Stacky Light (FR)

9-y-o b g Conquistacky (USA)-Lumineuse (BEL) (Lisaro)
D Pipe (M C Pipe 20/1) C M Batterham

Placings:1P/F **(4826)**
2001/02: 26^{F}G

	Starts	1st	2nd	3rd	Win & Pl
Chases	1	0	0	0	
Career Total	**3**	**1**	**0**	**0**	**1235**

107	5/99	Hrfd	3m1f110y	H Ch	G-S	£1234

Total win prize-money £1235

Going: Sf: 0-0 GS: 0-0 Gd: 0-1 GF: - Fm: 0-0
Distance: 2m/2m3: 0-0 2m4-2m7: 0-0 3m+: 0-1
Track: LH: 0-1 RH: 0-0 Tight: 0-0 Gall: 0-1
Aids: Bl: 0-0 Vi: 0-1 Tstrap: 0-0
Best Rating: 107 5/99 Hrfd 3m1f110y gd-sft Ch

Stag Fight

12-y-o b g Primitive Rising (USA)-Gamewood (Ascertain (USA))
M Sheppard Mr & Mrs J S Scott

Placings:P/35-3P4 **(0497)**
2001/02: 25^{3}G, 25^{P}G, 25^{4}G

	Starts	1st	2nd	3rd	Win & Pl
Chases	3	0	0	1	738
Career Total	**6**	**0**	**0**	**2**	**1497**

Going: Sf: 0-0 GS: 0-0 Gd: 0-3 GF: - Fm: 0-0

Distance: 2m/2m3: 0-0 2m4-2m7: 0-0 3m+: 0-3
Track: LH: 0-0 RH: 0-3 Tight: 0-0 Gall: 0-0
Aids: Bl: 0-3 Vi: 0-0 Tstrap: 0-0
Best Rating: 95 5/01 Hrfd 3m1f110y good Ch

Stage Direction (USA)

100 **83**

5-y-o b g Theatrical-Carya (USA) (Northern Dancer)
B J Llewellyn (A Crook 6/2) The Welsh Valleys Syndicate

Placings:405 **(4820)**
2001/02: 16^{4}GF, 17^{0}G, 17^{5}G

	Starts	1st	2nd	3rd	Win & Pl
Hurdles	3	0	0	0	0
Career Total	**3**	**0**	**0**	**0**	**0**

Going: Sf: 0-0 GS: 0-0 Gd: 0-2 GF: - Fm: 0-1
Distance: 2m/2m3: 0-3 2m4-2m7: 0-0 3m+: 0-0
Track: LH: 0-3 RH: 0-0 Tight: 0-1 Gall: 0-1
Aids: Bl: 0-0 Vi: 0-0 Tstrap: 0-0
Best Rating: 83 8/01 Worc 2m gd-fm Hdl

Won two-mile novices' claimer at Worcester June 2002. Likes fast ground.

Stage Door (IRE)

97 **51**

5-y-o b g Sadler's Wells (USA)-Dancing Shadow (Dancer's Image (USA))
S Dow S Dow

Placings:0P065 **(4035)**
2001/02: 18^{0}GF, 20^{P}GS, 18^{0}G, 20^{6}S, 22^{5}S

	Starts	1st	2nd	3rd	Win & Pl
NH Flat	1	0	0	0	0
Hurdles	4	0	0	0	0
Career Total	**5**	**0**	**0**	**0**	**0**

Going: Sf: 0-2 GS: 0-1 Gd: 0-1 GF: - Fm: 0-1
Distance: 2m/2m3: 0-2 2m4-2m7: 0-3 3m+: 0-0
Track: LH: 0-4 RH: 0-0 Tight: 0-5 Gall: 0-0
Aids: Bl: 0-0 Vi: 0-0 Tstrap: 0-2
Best Rating: 51 3/02 Font 2m6f110y soft Hdl

Stakeholder (IRE)

89f **95f**

4-y-o ch g Priolo (USA)-Island Goddess (Godswalk (USA))
R A Fahey R A Fahey

Placings:035 **(4526)**
2001/02: 16^{0}S, 16^{3}HY, 17^{5}G

	Starts	1st	2nd	3rd	Win & Pl
NH Flat	3	0	0	1	256
Career Total	**3**	**0**	**0**	**1**	**256**

Going: Sf: 0-2 GS: 0-0 Gd: 0-1 GF: - Fm: 0-0
Distance: 2m/2m3: 0-3 2m4-2m7: 0-0 3m+: 0-0
Track: LH: 0-2 RH: 0-1 Tight: 0-0 Gall: 0-1
Aids: Bl: 0-0 Vi: 0-0 Tstrap: 0-0
Best Rating: 95 4/02 Carl 2m1f good NHF

Shaped with promise in bumpers, one of which was a Graded event. Handles the mud.

Stamford Hill

(91h) (46h)

7-y-o ch g Jendali (USA)-Laxay (Laxton)
G P Kelly (M E Sowersby 6/7) A M McArdle

Placings:03101/005550/0-0000P0PP **(3554)**
2001/02: 17^{0}G, 19^{0}GF, 16^{0}S, 20^{0}G, 23^{P}G, 16^{0}S, 16^{P}GS, 19^{P}S

	Starts	1st	2nd	3rd	Win & Pl
Hurdles	7	0	0	0	0
Chases	1	0	0	0	0
Career Total	**20**	**2**	**0**	**1**	**4867**

86	4/99	Towc	2m	G Hdl	SFT	£1786
82	3/99	Strf	2m3f	G Hdl	HVY	£2843

Total win prize-money £4629

Going: Sf: 0-3 GS: 0-1 Gd: 0-3 GF: - Fm: 0-1
Distance: 2m/2m3: 0-5 2m4-2m7: 0-2 3m+: 0-1
Track: LH: 0-5 RH: 0-3 Tight: 0-5 Gall: 0-1
Aids: Bl: 0-1 Vi: 0-0 Tstrap: 0-0
Best Rating: 86 4/99 Towc 2m soft Hdl

Stamparland Hill

99(107h) (112h)**140**

7-y-o b g Gildoran-Woodland Flower (Furry Glen)
J M Jefferson Ashleybank Investments Limited

Placings:355-1321FP3P **(4899)**
2001/02: 17^{1}G, 16^{3}G, 16^{2}S, 16^{1}GS, 16^{F}S, 16^{P}HY, 17^{3}G, 16^{P}G

	Starts	1st	2nd	3rd	Win & Pl
Hurdles	5	1	1	2	4509
Chases	3	1	0	0	3343
Career Total	**11**	**2**	**1**	**3**	**8368**

140	1/02	Weth	2m	E Ch	G-S	£3342
93	9/01	Sedg	2m1f	E Hdl	GD	£2380

Total win prize-money £5723

Going: Sf: 0-3 GS: 1-1 Gd: 1-4 GF: - Fm: 0-0
Distance: **2m/2m3: 2-8** 2m4-2m7: 0-0 3m+: 0-0
Track: **LH: 2-6** RH: 0-2 **Tight: 1-1** Gall: 0-2
Aids: Bl: 0-0 Vi: 0-0 Tstrap: 0-0
Best Rating: 140 1/02 Weth 2m gd-sft Ch

A keen sort, won a novice hurdle at Sedgefield in September 2001, and was an impressive winner at Wetherby on his chasing debut, before reverting to the smaller obstacles.

Stan's Your Man

107 **146**

12-y-o b g Young Man (FR)-Charlotte's Festival (Gala Performance (USA))
Ferdy Murphy Mrs J D Goodfellow

Placings:141/411U4/361/1/11P **(2165)**
2001/02: 20^{1}GS, 25^{1}GS, 20^{P}G

	Starts	1st	2nd	3rd	Win & Pl
Chases	3	2	0	0	12324
Career Total	**15**	**8**	**0**	**1**	**32575**

146	11/01	Kels	3m1f	C(0-130)HCh	G-S	£6760
143	5/01	Prth	2m4f110y	E(0-115)HCh	G-S	£5564
141	5/99	Uttx	3m2f	D(0-125)HCh	GD	£4013
146	4/99	Carl	2m4f110y	F(0-110)HCh	G-S	£3365
101	3/98	Newc	2m4f	E Ch	G-F	£2957
111	12/97	Muss	3m	D(0-125)HHdl	GD	£2723
111	3/97	Newc	2m4f	C HHdl	GD	£3550
100	11/96	Newc	2m4f	E Hdl	G-F	£2274

Total win prize-money £31206

Going: Sf: 0-0 GS: 2-2 Gd: 0-1 GF: - Fm: 0-0
Distance: 2m/2m3: 0-0 2m4-2m7: 1-2 3m+: 1-1
Track: LH: 1-2 RH: 1-1 **Tight: 1-1** Gall: 0-1
Aids: Bl: 0-0 Vi: 0-0 Tstrap: 0-0
Best Rating: 146 11/01 Kels 3m1f gd-sft Ch

Showed decent form over hurdles and fences but after winning twice in the spring of 1999, he did not race again until making a winning reappearance at Perth in May 2001 and scored again at Kelso in November. Has won at up to three miles two and, though he has won on soft ground, is considered a better horse on a sounder surface.

Stand Easy (IRE)

109 **119**

9-y-o b g Buckskin (FR)-Geeaway (Gala Performance (USA))
J G Portman Christopher Shankland

Placings:1/3355222/25303 **(4585)**
2001/02: 23^{2}G, 22^{5}G, 25^{3}S, 24^{0}G, 25^{3}G

	Starts	1st	2nd	3rd	Win & Pl
Chases	5	0	1	2	2906
Career Total	**13**	**1**	**4**	**4**	**9052**

98	4/99	NAbb	2m1f	H NHF	SFT	£1397

Total win prize-money £1397

Going: Sf: 0-1 GS: 0-0 Gd: 0-4 GF: - Fm: 0-0
Distance: 2m/2m3: 0-0 2m4-2m7: 0-1 3m+: 0-4
Track: LH: 0-1 RH: 0-4 Tight: 0-0 Gall: 0-1
Aids: Bl: 0-0 Vi: 0-0 Tstrap: 0-0
Best Rating: 119 12/01 Extr 2m7f110y good Ch

Standiford Girl (IRE)

90 **59**

5-y-o b m Standiford (USA)-Pennine Girl (IRE) (Pennine Walk)
L A Dace Noel Monaghan

Placings:0 **(1727)**
2001/02: 17^{0}F

	Starts	1st	2nd	3rd	Win & Pl
Hurdles	1	0	0	0	
Career Total	**1**	**0**	**0**	**0**	

Going: Sf: 0-0 GS: 0-0 Gd: 0-0 GF: - Fm: 0-1
Distance: 2m/2m3: 0-1 2m4-2m7: 0-0 3m+: 0-0
Track: LH: 0-0 RH: 0-1 Tight: 0-1 Gall: 0-0
Aids: Bl: 0-0 Vi: 0-0 Tstrap: 0-0
Best Rating: 59 10/01 Tntn 2m1f firm Hdl

Standing Bloom

92 **92**

6-y-o ch m Presidium-Rosie Cone (Celtic Cone)
Mrs P Sly Piquet Racing Partners

Placings:4536-065P **(4772)**
2001/02: 16^{0}G, 16^{6}G, 21^{5}G, 21^{P}G

	Starts	1st	2nd	3rd	Win & Pl
Hurdles	4	0	0	0	0
Career Total	**8**	**0**	**0**	**1**	**237**

Going: Sf: 0-0 GS: 0-0 Gd: 0-4 GF: - Fm: 0-0
Distance: 2m/2m3: 0-2 2m4-2m7: 0-2 3m+: 0-0
Track: LH: 0-2 RH: 0-2 Tight: 0-1 Gall: 0-0
Aids: Bl: 0-0 Vi: 0-0 Tstrap: 0-0
Best Rating: 102 4/01 Kemp 2m good NHF

Stanmore (IRE)

103 **114**

10-y-o b g Aristocracy-Lady Go Marching (USA) (Go Marching (USA))
Mrs J A Saunders & Mrs Simon E Bown

Placings:*500*/3U21P51F0/313PF2P1/423/6153-1P4010 **(2526)**
2001/02: 24^{1}GF, 21^{P}GF, 20^{4}G, 24^{0}GF, 20^{1}GF, 20^{0}G

	Starts	1st	2nd	3rd	Win & Pl
Chases	6	2	0	0	5472
Career Total	**33**	**7**	**3**	**5**	**28158**

114	11/01	Leic	2m4f110y	F(0-100)HCh	G-F	£3125
98	5/01	Hntg	3m	H Ch	G-F	£1820
109	5/00	MRas	2m6f110y	H Ch	G-S	£1976
106	5/99	Hrfd	2m3f110y	E Hdl	GD	£2560
132	5/98	Strf	2m5f110y	C(0-135)HCh	G-F	£5182
114	12/97	Wwck	2m4f110y	D(0-120)HCh	G-S	£3551
105	10/97	Chel	2m4f110y	D(0-110)HCh	GD	£3876

Total win prize-money £22095

Going: Sf: 0-0 GS: 0-0 Gd: 0-2 GF: - Fm: 2-4
Distance: 2m/2m3: 0-0 2m4-2m7: 1-4 3m+: 1-2
Track: LH: 0-2 **RH: 2-4** Tight: 0-3 **Gall: 1-1**
Aids: Bl: 0-0 Vi: 0-0 Tstrap: 0-0
Best Rating: 132 5/98 Strf 2m5f110y gd-fm Ch

A fair handicap chaser, but is not altogether consistent these days. Suited by forcing tactics, stays three miles and acts on fast ground.

Staple Sound

77f 67f

5-y-o b g Alflora (IRE)-Loch Scavaig (IRE) (The Parson)
W McKeown The Northumberland Group Racing Club

Placings:*00* **(3550)**
2001/02: 16^{0}G, 16^{0}S

	Starts	1st	2nd	3rd	Win & Pl
NH Flat	2	0	0	0	
Career Total	**2**	**0**	**0**	**0**	

Going: Sf: 0-1 GS: 0-0 Gd: 0-1 GF: - Fm: 0-0
Distance: 2m/2m3: 0-2 2m4-2m7: 0-0 3m+: 0-0
Track: LH: 0-0 RH: 0-1 Tight: 0-1 Gall: 0-0
Aids: Bl: 0-0 Vi: 0-0 Tstrap: 0-0
Best Rating: 67 1/02 Newc 2m soft NHF

Star Blakeney

(101h) (78+h)

9-y-o b g Blakeney-Trikkala Star (Tachypous)
B D Leavy Barry Leavy

Placings:*00/600/0***P530P-P** **(2316)**
2001/02: 20^{P}GS

	Starts	1st	2nd	3rd	Win & Pl
Hurdles	1	0	0	0	
Career Total	**12**	**0**	**0**	**1**	**564**

Going: Sf: 0-0 GS: 0-1 Gd: 0-0 GF: - Fm: 0-0
Distance: 2m/2m3: 0-0 2m4-2m7: 0-1 3m+: 0-0
Track: LH: 0-1 RH: 0-0 Tight: 0-1 Gall: 0-0
Aids: Bl: 0-0 Vi: 0-0 Tstrap: 0-1
Best Rating: 88 11/00 Uttx 2m heavy Ch

Star Catcher (IRE)

6-y-o b g Toulon-Paper Merchant (Hays)
B G Powell L J Brotherton

Placings:*00*-PP **(4861)**
2001/02: 19^{P}GF, 22^{P}F

	Starts	1st	2nd	3rd	Win & Pl
Hurdles	2	0	0	0	
Career Total	**4**	**0**	**0**	**0**	

Going: Sf: 0-0 GS: 0-0 Gd: 0-0 GF: - Fm: 0-2
Distance: 2m/2m3: 0-0 2m4-2m7: 0-2 3m+: 0-0
Track: LH: 0-0 RH: 0-1 Tight: 0-0 Gall: 0-0
Aids: Bl: 0-0 Vi: 0-0 Tstrap: 0-0
Best Rating: 54 10/00 Fknm 2m good NHF

Star Changes

9-y-o b g Derrylin-Sweet Linda (Saucy Kit)
A Hollingsworth A Hollingsworth

Placings:*0/6*-00 **(0585)**
2001/02: 24^{0}GF, 24^{0}GF

	Starts	1st	2nd	3rd	Win & Pl
Chases	2	0	0	0	
Career Total	**4**	**0**	**0**	**0**	**0**

Going: Sf: 0-0 GS: 0-0 Gd: 0-0 GF: - Fm: 0-2
Distance: 2m/2m3: 0-0 2m4-2m7: 0-0 3m+: 0-2
Track: LH: 0-2 RH: 0-0 Tight: 0-2 Gall: 0-0
Aids: Bl: 0-0 Vi: 0-0 Tstrap: 0-0
Best Rating: 90 6/01 Strf 3m gd-fm Ch

Star Control (IRE)

104(93c) (71c)77

8-y-o gr m Phardante (FR)-Grey Star (General Ironside)
H J Evans Mrs Jane Evans

Placings:*0U0/66*-**0F0P3** **(4730)**
2001/02: 21^{0}GF, 24^{F}GS, 24^{0}S, 20^{P}S, 20^{3}GF

	Starts	1st	2nd	3rd	Win & Pl
Hurdles	3	0	0	1	382
Chases	2	0	0	0	0
Career Total	**10**	**0**	**0**	**1**	**382**

Going: Sf: 0-2 GS: 0-1 Gd: 0-0 GF: - Fm: 0-2
Distance: 2m/2m3: 0-0 2m4-2m7: 0-3 3m+: 0-2
Track: LH: 0-4 RH: 0-1 Tight: 0-3 Gall: 0-1
Aids: Bl: 0-0 Vi: 0-0 Tstrap: 0-0
Best Rating: 87 5/00 Uttx 2m4f110y gd-fm Hdl

Star Diva (IRE)

99f 105f

6-y-o b m Toulon-Kerris Melody (Furry Glen)
M Bradstock Dorchester On Thames Syndicate

Placings:*010* **(4823)**
2001/02: 17^{0}GF, 18^{1}HY, 17^{0}G

	Starts	1st	2nd	3rd	Win & Pl
NH Flat	3	1	0	0	1554
Career Total	**3**	**1**	**0**	**0**	**1554**

105	2/02	Font	2m2f110y	H NHF	HVY	£1554

Total win prize-money £1554

Going: Sf: 1-1 GS: 0-0 Gd: 0-1 GF: - Fm: 0-1
Distance: **2m/2m3: 1-3** 2m4-2m7: 0-0 3m+: 0-0
Track: **LH: 1-2** RH: 0-1 **Tight: 1-2** Gall: 0-1
Aids: Bl: 0-0 Vi: 0-0 Tstrap: 0-0
Best Rating: 105 2/02 Font 2m2f110y heavy NHF

Made all to win bumper second time out in the mud.

Star Dynasty (IRE)

104 94

5-y-o b g Bering-Siwaayib (Green Desert (USA))
D McCain (E A L Dunlop 24/7) Clayton Bigley Partnership Ltd

Placings:042 **(4404)**
2001/02: 16^{0}HY, 16^{4}S, 17^{2}S

	Starts	1st	2nd	3rd	Win & Pl
Hurdles	3	0	1	0	932
Career Total	**3**	**0**	**1**	**0**	**932**

Going: Sf: 0-3 GS: 0-0 Gd: 0-0 GF: - Fm: 0-0
Distance: 2m/2m3: 0-3 2m4-2m7: 0-0 3m+: 0-0
Track: LH: 0-2 RH: 0-1 Tight: 0-1 Gall: 0-1
Aids: Bl: 0-0 Vi: 0-0 Tstrap: 0-0
Best Rating: 94 3/02 Bang 2m1f soft Hdl

Above average maiden on the Flat who is finding his feet over hurdles. Handles soft ground.

Star Jack (FR)

115 134

7-y-o b g Epervier Bleu-Little Point (FR) (Le Nain Jaune (FR))
J G Fitzgerald Mr & Mrs Raymond Anderson Green

Placings:1115/3213/**PF-PP1P** **(4891)**
2001/02: 17^{P}HY, 20^{P}GS, 20^{1}G, 16^{P}G

	Starts	1st	2nd	3rd	Win & Pl
Hurdles	1	0	0	0	0
Chases	3	1	0	0	10397
Career Total	**14**	**5**	**1**	**2**	**46390**

134	4/02	Ayr	2m4f	B HCh	GD	£10397
	1/00	Pau	2m110y	Hdl	GD	£6244
	2/99	Pau	2m2f110y	Ch	HVY	£15070
	1/99	Pau	2m1f	Ch	GD	£6459
	10/98	Toul	2m1f110y	Hdl	HVY	£4041

Total win prize-money £42211

Going: Sf: 0-1 GS: 0-1 Gd: 1-2 GF: - Fm: 0-0
Distance: 2m/2m3: 0-2 **2m4-2m7: 1-2** 3m+: 0-0
Track: **LH: 1-1** RH: 0-3 Tight: 0-1 Gall: 0-0
Aids: Bl: 0-0 Vi: 0-0 **Tstrap: 1-3**
Best Rating: 134 4/02 Ayr 2m4f good Ch

A fair handicap chaser, but tends to have two ways of running these days. Best over two and a half miles. Effective on most ground.

Star Man (IRE)

93f

7-y-o ch g Phardante (FR)-Hansel's Lady (IRE) (The Parson)
Ferdy Murphy Kbro Racing Group

Placings:*0*-0P4U5 **(4547)**
2001/02: 21^{0}G, 24^{P}S, 21^{4}GS, 20^{U}G, 20^{5}GF

	Starts	1st	2nd	3rd	Win & Pl
Hurdles	3	0	0	0	
Chases	2	0	0	0	
Career Total	**6**	**0**	**0**	**0**	**0**

Going: Sf: 0-1 GS: 0-1 Gd: 0-2 GF: - Fm: 0-1
Distance: 2m/2m3: 0-0 2m4-2m7: 0-4 3m+: 0-1
Track: LH: 0-1 RH: 0-4 Tight: 0-1 Gall: 0-2
Aids: Bl: 0-0 Vi: 0-0 Tstrap: 0-0
Best Rating: 93 4/01 Ayr 2m gd-fm NHF

Star Marshall (IRE)

45

10-y-o b g Bustomi-Marshallstown (Callernish)
P A Pritchard Thomas D Goodman

Placings:*000/0F5/6*-0 **(0246)**

2001/02: 21^{0}GF

	Starts	1st	2nd	3rd	Win & Pl
Hurdles	1	0	0	0	
Career Total	**8**	**0**	**0**	**0**	**0**

Going: Sf: 0-0 GS: 0-0 Gd: 0-0 GF: - Fm: 0-1
Distance: 2m/2m3: 0-0 2m4-2m7: 0-1 3m+: 0-0
Track: LH: 0-0 RH: 0-0 Tight: 0-0 Gall: 0-0
Aids: Bl: 0-0 Vi: 0-0 Tstrap: 0-0
Best Rating: 53 5/98 Slig 2m4f good Ch

Star Of Wonder

102 **104**

4-y-o b f Celtic Swing-Meant To Be (Morston (FR))
Lady Herries Lady Mary Mumford

Placings:1125 **(4764)**
2001/02: 18^{1}GF, 16^{1}GF, 16^{2}GS, 16^{5}GF

	Starts	1st	2nd	3rd	Win & Pl
Hurdles	4	2	1	0	6796
Career Total	**4**	**2**	**1**	**0**	**6796**

99	10/01	Winc	2m	D Hdl	G-F	£3283
95	9/01	Font	2m2f110y	E Hdl	G-F	£2408

Total win prize-money £5691

Going: Sf: 0-0 GS: 0-1 Gd: 0-0 GF: - Fm: 2-3
Distance: **2m/2m3: 2-4** 2m4-2m7: 0-0 3m+: 0-0
Track: LH: 1-1 RH: 1-3 **Tight: 1-1** Gall: 0-0
Aids: Bl: 0-0 Vi: 0-0 Tstrap: 0-0
Best Rating: 104 4/02 Asct 2m110y gd-fm Hdl

No great shakes on the Flat, but made a winning debut over hurdles in a modest event at Fontwell in September and followed up with another victory at Wincanton. Ran well in defeat under a double penalty. Two miles on fast ground are her ideal conditions.

Star Of Wonder (FR)

(90h) (79h)

7-y-o ch m The Wonder (FR)-Teardrops Fall (FR) (Law Society (USA))
John Allen John Allen, Michael Gray, Vicki Jameson

Placings:F600501P/P63U5 **(4371)**
2001/02: 16^{P}S, 16^{6}S, 16^{3}S, 16^{U}GS, 16^{5}GS

	Starts	1st	2nd	3rd	Win & Pl
Hurdles	4	0	0	1	295
Chases	1	0	0	0	0
Career Total	**13**	**1**	**0**	**1**	**3106**

89	4/00	Plum	2m	D Hdl	G-S	£2811

Total win prize-money £2811

Going: Sf: 0-3 GS: 0-2 Gd: 0-0 GF: - Fm: 0-0
Distance: 2m/2m3: 0-5 2m4-2m7: 0-0 3m+: 0-0
Track: LH: 0-2 RH: 0-3 Tight: 0-1 Gall: 0-0
Aids: Bl: 0-0 Vi: 0-0 Tstrap: 0-0
Best Rating: 89 4/00 Plum 2m gd-sft Hdl

Modest hurdler, a staying-on third in a seller in February 2002.

Star Selection

102 **92**

11-y-o b g Rainbow Quest (USA)-Selection Board (Welsh Pageant)
J Mackie R M Mitchell

Placings:6310121/5343303/**143F/PU0**05666/0211445 6-0P036150F03 **(4847)**
2001/02: 16^{0}G, 19^{P}GF, 20^{0}GF, 20^{3}G, 20^{6}G, 20^{1}G, 19^{5}S, 20^{0}S, 20^{F}S, 17^{0}S, 20^{3}G

	Starts	1st	2nd	3rd	Win & Pl
Hurdles	11	1	0	2	6647
Career Total	**45**	**7**	**2**	**8**	**38619**

92	9/01	Bang	2m4f	F(0-110)HHdl	GD	£5209
118	6/00	MRas	2m3f110y	D(0-120)HHdl	GD	£3461
113	5/00	MRas	2m3f110y	C(0-130)HHdl	G-S	£5746
108	5/98	Bang	2m1f110y	D Ch	GD	£3582
126	3/97	Carl	2m1f	E Hdl	G-S	£2136
122	2/97	Ayr	2m	D(0-125)HHdl	SFT	£2777
105	12/96	Hrfd	2m1f	E Hdl	G-S	£2192

Total win prize-money £25105

Going: Sf: 0-4 GS: 0-0 Gd: 1-5 GF: - Fm: 0-2
Distance: 2m/2m3: 0-2 **2m4-2m7: 1-9** 3m+: 0-0
Track: **LH: 1-7** RH: 0-4 **Tight: 1-7** Gall: 0-2
Aids: Bl: 0-0 Vi: 0-0 Tstrap: 0-0
Best Rating: 130 12/98 Ayr 2m gd-sft Ch

Just a modest handicap hurdler nowadays and likes decent ground now.

Star To The North (IRE)

108 **131**

7-y-o br g Distinctly North (USA)-Star With A Glimer (Montekin)
Ferdy Murphy Mrs H J Clarke

Placings:410F/045510110P0/**3136-154** **(0803)**
2001/02: 21^{1}GF, 21^{5}GF, 24^{4}GF

	Starts	1st	2nd	3rd	Win & Pl
Chases	3	1	0	0	8025
Career Total	**22**	**6**	**0**	**2**	**28799**

131	5/01	Ayr	2m5f110y	C(0-130)HCh	G-F	£6950
126	12/00	Muss	2m4f	E Ch	GD	£2944
106	9/99	Fair	2m4f	(0-116)HHdl	G-Y	£3080
100	9/99	Baln	2m4f	(0-109)HHdl	G-F	£3265
107	7/99	Gway	2m4f	(0-116)HHdl	G-F	£6138
105	9/98	List	2m	Hdl	G-Y	£3885

Total win prize-money £26264

Going: Sf: 0-0 GS: 0-0 Gd: 0-0 GF: - Fm: 1-3
Distance: 2m/2m3: 0-0 **2m4-2m7: 1-2** 3m+: 0-1
Track: **LH: 1-2** RH: 0-1 Tight: 0-1 Gall: 0-0
Aids: Bl: 0-0 Vi: 0-0 Tstrap: 0-0
Best Rating: 131 5/01 Ayr 2m5f110y gd-fm Ch

Decent handicap chaser, stays two miles-five, best on a sound surface. (DEAD)

Starbuck

90 **74**

8-y-o b g Brush Aside (USA)-Clonmello (Le Bavard (FR))
Mrs Dianne Sayer R P Heffering,E B Smith,A Slack,D Sayer

Placings:0/2604-4P **(2770)**
2001/02: 18^{4}G, 25^{P}G

	Starts	1st	2nd	3rd	Win & Pl
Hurdles	2	0	0	0	0
Career Total	**7**	**0**	**1**	**0**	**730**

Going: Sf: 0-0 GS: 0-0 Gd: 0-2 GF: - Fm: 0-0
Distance: 2m/2m3: 0-1 2m4-2m7: 0-0 3m+: 0-1
Track: LH: 0-2 RH: 0-0 Tight: 0-2 Gall: 0-0
Aids: Bl: 0-0 Vi: 0-0 Tstrap: 0-0
Best Rating: 90 10/99 Carl 2m1f good NHF

Staroski

92f **83f**

5-y-o b m Petoski-Olnistar (FR) (Balsamo (FR))
C C Bealby E Wilmott

Placings:503 **(3770)**
2001/02: 16^{5}S, 16^{0}G, 16^{3}GS

	Starts	1st	2nd	3rd	Win & Pl
NH Flat	3	0	0	1	221
Career Total	**3**	**0**	**0**	**1**	**221**

Going: Sf: 0-1 GS: 0-1 Gd: 0-1 GF: - Fm: 0-0
Distance: 2m/2m3: 0-3 2m4-2m7: 0-0 3m+: 0-0
Track: LH: 0-3 RH: 0-0 Tight: 0-1 Gall: 0-1
Aids: Bl: 0-0 Vi: 0-0 Tstrap: 0-0
Best Rating: 83 2/02 Fknm 2m gd-sft NHF

Starpath (NZ)

10-y-o ch g Starjo (NZ)-Centa Belle (NZ) (Centurius)
P F Nicholls (J J Boulter 3/3) J J Boulter/f J Wilkins/k J Pearce

Placings:F1-2 **(0427)**
2001/02: 33^{2}G

	Starts	1st	2nd	3rd	Win & Pl
Chases	1	0	1	0	1701
Career Total	**3**	**1**	**1**	**0**	**5005**

113	4/01	Prth	3m7f	H Ch	HVY	£3304

Total win prize-money £3304

Going: Sf: 0-0 GS: 0-0 Gd: 0-1 GF: - Fm: 0-0
Distance: 2m/2m3: 0-0 2m4-2m7: 0-0 3m+: 0-1
Track: LH: 0-0 RH: 0-0 Tight: 0-0 Gall: 0-0
Aids: Bl: 0-0 Vi: 0-0 Tstrap: 0-0
Best Rating: 117 5/01 Chel 4m1f good Ch

Fair pointer who stays particularly well. Has won on good ground and heavy and stays three miles seven.

Stars

11-y-o b g Neltino-Celia's Halo (Mountain Call)
Mrs J A Saunders Mrs M E Thompson

Placings:PP4 **(2326)**
2001/02: 21^{P}S, 24^{P}S, 21^{4}S

	Starts	1st	2nd	3rd	Win & Pl
Chases	3	0	0	0	290
Career Total	**3**	**0**	**0**	**0**	**290**

Going: Sf: 0-3 GS: 0-0 Gd: 0-0 GF: - Fm: 0-0
Distance: 2m/2m3: 0-0 2m4-2m7: 0-2 3m+: 0-1
Track: LH: 0-3 RH: 0-0 Tight: 0-2 Gall: 0-0
Aids: Bl: 0-0 Vi: 0-0 Tstrap: 0-0
Best Rating:

A staying ex-pointer, he has a habit of pulling up but is usually in the frame when he does complete. Best on a sound surface.

Stars Delight (IRE)

93f **82f**

5-y-o ch g Fourstars Allstar (USA)-Celtic Cygnet (Celtic Cone)
Mrs L C Jewell Leon Best

Placings:050 **(4552)**
2001/02: 16^{0}G, 16^{5}S, 16^{0}GF

	Starts	1st	2nd	3rd	Win & Pl
NH Flat	3	0	0	0	0
Career Total	**3**	**0**	**0**	**0**	**0**

Going: Sf: 0-1 GS: 0-0 Gd: 0-1 GF: - Fm: 0-1
Distance: 2m/2m3: 0-3 2m4-2m7: 0-0 3m+: 0-0

Track: LH: 0-0 RH: 0-3 Tight: 0-0 Gall: 0-1
Aids: Bl: 0-0 Vi: 0-0 Tstrap: 0-0
Best Rating: 82 4/02 Hntg 2m110y gd-fm NHF

Stars Out Tonight (IRE)

107 **137**

5-y-o b g Insan (USA)-Go And Tell (Kemal (FR))
Miss H C Knight Jim Lewis

Placings: *0-1*1004 **(4820)**
2001/02: 16^{1}G, 16^{1}G, 16^{0}S, 16^{0}GS, 17^{4}G

	Starts	1st	2nd	3rd	Win & Pl
NH Flat	1	1	0	0	3949
Hurdles	4	1	0	0	4106
Career Total	**6**	**2**	**0**	**0**	**8054**

115	11/01	Kemp	2m	D Hdl	GD	£3412
108	10/01	Chel	2m110y	H NHF	GD	£3948

Total win prize-money £7362

Going: Sf: 0-1 GS: 0-1 Gd: 2-3 GF: - Fm: 0-0
Distance: **2m/2m3: 2-5** 2m4-2m7: 0-0 3m+: 0-0
Track: LH: 1-4 RH: 1-1 Tight: 0-0 Gall: 0-1
Aids: Bl: 0-0 Vi: 0-0 Tstrap: 0-0
Best Rating: 137 3/02 Chel 2m110y gd-sft Hdl

Looked a decent recruit in the autumn of 2001, but his limitations were exposed in better company. Needs a sound surface.

Starting Again

105(90h) **130**

8-y-o b g Petoski-Lynemore (Nearly A Hand)
H D Daly Mr & Mrs M P Wiggin

Placings: *1/32*-**21PF2313** **(4843)**
2001/02: 17^{2}GF, 20^{1}GF, 16^{P}HY, 20^{F}G, 20^{2}GS, 20^{3}GS, 20^{1}G, 17^{3}G

	Starts	1st	2nd	3rd	Win & Pl
Chases	8	2	2	2	14127
Career Total	**11**	**3**	**3**	**3**	**16809**

130	4/02	Ludl	2m4f	D(0-115)HCh	GD	£6500
116	10/01	Ludl	2m4f	E Ch	G-F	£3386
105	12/98	Ludl	2m	H NHF	G-S	£1318

Total win prize-money £11206

Going: Sf: 0-1 GS: 0-2 Gd: 1-3 GF: - Fm: 1-2
Distance: 2m/2m3: 0-3 **2m4-2m7: 2-5** 3m+: 0-0
Track: LH: 0-3 **RH: 2-5 Tight: 2-6** Gall: 0-0
Aids: Bl: 0-0 Vi: 0-0 Tstrap: 0-0
Best Rating: 130 4/02 Ludl 2m4f good Ch

Bumper winner and ex-pointer. Placed over hurdles, he made a good start to his chasing career, winning at Ludlow twice.

State Casino

38f

5-y-o b m State Diplomacy (USA)-Nod And A Wink (Casino Boy)
Miss L C Siddall Podso Racing

Placings: *0* **(2675)**
2001/02: 16^{0}G

	Starts	1st	2nd	3rd	Win & Pl
NH Flat	1	0	0	0	
Career Total	**1**	**0**	**0**	**0**	

Going: Sf: 0-0 GS: 0-0 Gd: 0-1 GF: - Fm: 0-0
Distance: 2m/2m3: 0-1 2m4-2m7: 0-0 3m+: 0-0
Track: LH: 0-1 RH: 0-0 Tight: 0-0 Gall: 0-1
Aids: Bl: 0-0 Vi: 0-0 Tstrap: 0-0
Best Rating:

Stateley Lord (IRE)

87 **65**

6-y-o b/br g Good Thyne (USA)-Sixfoursix (Balinger)
Mrs L Richards Mrs Betty Hobbs

Placings: UP0P **(4400)**
2001/02: 18^{U}G, 22^{P}S, 19^{0}S, 21^{P}S

	Starts	1st	2nd	3rd	Win & Pl
Hurdles	4	0	0	0	
Career Total	**4**	**0**	**0**	**0**	

Going: Sf: 0-3 GS: 0-0 Gd: 0-1 GF: - Fm: 0-0
Distance: 2m/2m3: 0-2 2m4-2m7: 0-2 3m+: 0-0
Track: LH: 0-3 RH: 0-1 Tight: 0-1 Gall: 0-2
Aids: Bl: 0-0 Vi: 0-0 Tstrap: 0-4
Best Rating: 65 3/02 Newb 2m3f soft Hdl

Little sign of ability in three novice hurdles at up to two miles six furlongs.

Stately Home (IRE)

106 **129**

11-y-o b/br g Fool's Holme (USA)-Water Splash (USA) (Little Current (USA))
P Bowen P Bowen

Placings: 300555/40041P22325/31111114U2241211P 632/2F11030425/246P4066353/13P00/5F **(0435)**
2001/02: 20^{5}GF, 21^{F}GF

	Starts	1st	2nd	3rd	Win & Pl
Chases	2	0	0	0	0
Career Total	**65**	**13**	**10**	**8**	**109070**

149	7/99	Strf	2m4f	C(0-135)HCh	GD	£6775
149	6/97	MRas	2m4f	C(0-135)HCh	G-F	£10308
149	5/97	Strf	2m5f110y	C(0-135)HCh	GD	£4532
149	2/97	Sand	2m4f110y	A Ch	G-F	£22032
129	12/96	Sand	2m4f110y	B HCh	GD	£6775
125	11/96	Weth	2m4f110y	B(0-145)HCh	GD	£6710
121	8/96	Ctml	2m1f110y	C(0-130)HCh	GD	£4419
107	8/96	Strf	2m1f110y	D(0-120)HCh	G-F	£3731
113	8/96	Worc	2m	E Ch	GD	£3136
101	7/96	Strf	2m1f110y	D(0-120)HCh	G-F	£3847
116	7/96	Strf	2m1f110y	E Ch	G-F	£3051
105	7/96	Worc	2m	E Ch	G-F	£3036
101	1/96	Sedg	2m1f110y	G(0-95)HHdl	G-F	£2094

Total win prize-money £80448

Going: Sf: 0-0 GS: 0-0 Gd: 0-0 GF: - Fm: 0-2
Distance: 2m/2m3: 0-0 2m4-2m7: 0-2 3m+: 0-0
Track: LH: 0-1 RH: 0-1 Tight: 0-2 Gall: 0-0
Aids: Bl: 0-0 Vi: 0-0 Tstrap: 0-0
Best Rating: 149 7/99 MRas 2m4f gd-fm Ch

Formerly useful chaser and prolific winner. Now at the veteran stage.

Steady Eddy

107(57h) **97**

10-y-o ch g Scorpio (FR)-Moaning Jenny (Privy Seal)
N A Twiston-Davies The Double Octagon Partnership

Placings: *13/4O21*-**UPU031P** **(4738)**
2001/02: 20^{U}S, 24^{P}S, 26^{U}S, 24^{0}S, 24^{3}S, 24^{1}G, 24^{P}GF

	Starts	1st	2nd	3rd	Win & Pl
Chases	7	1	0	1	2968
Career Total	**13**	**3**	**1**	**2**	**6984**

97	4/02	Uttx	3m	G(0-90)HCh	GD	£2317
99	9/00	Worc	3m	F Hdl	G-F	£1869
108	8/98	Worc	2m	H NHF	GD	£1203

Total win prize-money £5389

Going: Sf: 0-5 GS: 0-0 Gd: 1-1 GF: - Fm: 0-1
Distance: 2m/2m3: 0-0 2m4-2m7: 0-1 **3m+: 1-6**
Track: **LH: 1-4** RH: 0-2 Tight: 0-4 Gall: 0-0
Aids: Bl: 0-0 Vi: 0-0 Tstrap: 0-0
Best Rating: 108 8/98 Worc 2m good NHF

Lightly-raced winner over hurdles, he ran his best race to date over fences when winning a selling handicap at Uttoxeter. Likes good ground, stays three miles.

Steel Mill (IRE)

82 **77**

7-y-o gr g Roselier (FR)-Chatmando (IRE) (Mandalus)
D J Caro Mrs J F Billington

Placings: *000*-**PP63** **(4742)**
2001/02: 23^{P}G, 24^{P}GS, 21^{6}GS, 24^{3}GF

	Starts	1st	2nd	3rd	Win & Pl
Hurdles	2	0	0	1	374
Chases	2	0	0	0	0
Career Total	**7**	**0**	**0**	**1**	**374**

Going: Sf: 0-0 GS: 0-2 Gd: 0-1 GF: - Fm: 0-1
Distance: 2m/2m3: 0-0 2m4-2m7: 0-1 3m+: 0-3
Track: LH: 0-0 RH: 0-4 Tight: 0-0 Gall: 0-1
Aids: Bl: 0-0 Vi: 0-0 Tstrap: 0-0
Best Rating: 86 3/01 Wwck 2m heavy NHF

Moderate form in bumpers, over hurdles and over fences.

Steel Rose

82 **41**

8-y-o gr m Scottish Reel-Rosewater (Waterfall)
N A Twiston-Davies Mrs S Tainton

Placings: *240/3F06/00* **(4131)**
2001/02: 20^{0}HY, 26^{0}G

	Starts	1st	2nd	3rd	Win & Pl
Hurdles	2	0	0	0	
Career Total	**9**	**0**	**1**	**1**	**895**

Going: Sf: 0-1 GS: 0-0 Gd: 0-1 GF: - Fm: 0-0
Distance: 2m/2m3: 0-0 2m4-2m7: 0-1 3m+: 0-1
Track: LH: 0-0 RH: 0-1 Tight: 0-0 Gall: 0-0
Aids: Bl: 0-0 Vi: 0-0 Tstrap: 0-0
Best Rating: 95 11/99 Wwck 2m4f110y good Hdl

Steel The Day

35f

6-y-o ch m Weld-Gain The Day (Bivouac)
Mrs T M Gibson Mrs T M Gibson

Placings: *0* **(3331)**
2001/02: 16^{0}S

	Starts	1st	2nd	3rd	Win & Pl
NH Flat	1	0	0	0	
Career Total	**1**	**0**	**0**	**0**	

Going: Sf: 0-1 GS: 0-0 Gd: 0-0 GF: - Fm: 0-0
Distance: 2m/2m3: 0-1 2m4-2m7: 0-0 3m+: 0-0
Track: LH: 0-0 RH: 0-0 Tight: 0-0 Gall: 0-0
Aids: Bl: 0-0 Vi: 0-0 Tstrap: 0-0
Best Rating: 35 1/02 Newc 2m soft NHF

Steeples Lad (IRE)

9-y-o b g Brush Aside (USA)-Awbeg Lady (The

Parson)
N A Twiston-Davies Mrs Lorna Berryman

Placings: *25/0*360P0/012044/**P**0 **(0575)**
2001/02: 25^{P}G, 27^{0}GF

	Starts	1st	2nd	3rd	Win & Pl
Hurdles	1	0	0	0	0
Chases	1	0	0	0	0
Career Total	**16**	**1**	**2**	**1**	**3783**

94	6/99	Strf	2m6f110y	F(0-95)HHdl	G-F	£2150

Total win prize-money £2150

Going: Sf: 0-0 GS: 0-0 Gd: 0-1 GF: - Fm: 0-1
Distance: 2m/2m3: 0-0 2m4-2m7: 0-0 3m+: 0-2
Track: LH: 0-1 RH: 0-1 Tight: 0-1 Gall: 0-0
Aids: Bl: 0-1 Vi: 0-0 Tstrap: 0-2
Best Rating: 112 2/98 Sand 2m110y good NHF

Stellissima (IRE)

91 **97**

7-y-o ch m Persian Bold-Ruffling Point (Gorytus (USA))
Lindsay Woods Patrick Doherty

Placings:00/02136/420-000P50000 **(3018a)**
2001/02: 16^{0}G, 20^{0}G, 16^{0}G, 24^{P}F, 16^{5}F, 17^{0}GY, 16^{0}S, 18^{0}GS, 20^{0}YS

	Starts	1st	2nd	3rd	Win & Pl
Hurdles	9	0	0	0	
Career Total	**19**	**1**	**2**	**1**	**5278**

83	8/99	Prth	2m110y	E Hdl	G-F	£2905

Total win prize-money £2905

Going: Sf: 0-1 GS: 0-1 Gd: 0-3 GF: - Fm: 0-2
Distance: 2m/2m3: 0-6 2m4-2m7: 0-2 3m+: 0-1
Track: LH: 0-1 RH: 0-3 Tight: 0-1 Gall: 0-0
Aids: Bl: 0-0 Vi: 0-0 Tstrap: 0-5
Best Rating: 97 11/01 Punc 2m soft Hdl

Stennikov (IRE)

101 **114**

6-y-o b g Good Thyne (USA)-Belle Bavard (Le Bavard (FR))
P F Nicholls B C Marshall

Placings: *41*603 **(4530)**
2001/02: 17^{4}G, 16^{1}S, 16^{6}GS, 21^{0}G, 20^{3}GS

	Starts	1st	2nd	3rd	Win & Pl
NH Flat	3	1	0	0	1722
Hurdles	2	0	0	1	423
Career Total	**5**	**1**	**0**	**1**	**2145**

108	10/01	Chep	2m110y	H NHF	SFT	£1722

Total win prize-money £1722

Going: Sf: 1-1 GS: 0-2 Gd: 0-2 GF: - Fm: 0-0
Distance: **2m/2m3: 1-3** 2m4-2m7: 0-2 3m+: 0-0
Track: **LH: 1-3** RH: 0-2 Tight: 0-0 Gall: 0-0
Aids: Bl: 0-0 Vi: 0-0 Tstrap: 0-0
Best Rating: 114 2/02 Kemp 2m5f good Hdl

Landed a Chepstow bumper in October. Yet to prove his stamina over two and a half miles over hurdles.

Step In Line (IRE)

10-y-o gr g Step Together (USA)-Ballycahan Girl (Bargello)
R G Frost Mrs B M Blake

Placings:00/3P0**P3/4**462243464**P1/33132330FP**/003 **03214**P-**6503**65 **(1794)**
2001/02: 16^{6}GF, 21^{5}GF, 16^{0}GF, 22^{3}G, 22^{6}GF, 19^{5}S

	Starts	1st	2nd	3rd	Win & Pl
Hurdles	2	0	0	1	321
Chases	4	0	0	0	0
Career Total	**44**	**3**	**4**	**11**	**19132**

105	8/00	NAbb	2m5f110y	F(0-105)HCh	GD	£3454
105	6/99	NAbb	2m110y	F(0-105)HCh	GD	£4396
105	3/99	NAbb	2m110y	F Ch	SFT	£2362

Total win prize-money £10214

Going: Sf: 0-1 GS: 0-0 Gd: 0-1 GF: - Fm: 0-4
Distance: 2m/2m3: 0-2 2m4-2m7: 0-4 3m+: 0-0
Track: LH: 0-6 RH: 0-0 Tight: 0-5 Gall: 0-0
Aids: Bl: 0-0 Vi: 0-0 Tstrap: 0-0
Best Rating: 105 8/00 NAbb 2m5f110y good Ch

Step In Silver (IRE)

95 **87**

6-y-o gr g Step Together (USA)-Seagate (IRE) (Decent Fellow)
J J O'Neill Ray & Sue Dodd Partnership

Placings: *0*604 **(4842)**
2001/02: 16^{0}S, 24^{6}S, 16^{0}G, 20^{4}G

	Starts	1st	2nd	3rd	Win & Pl
NH Flat	1	0	0	0	0
Hurdles	3	0	0	0	0
Career Total	**4**	**0**	**0**	**0**	**0**

Going: Sf: 0-2 GS: 0-0 Gd: 0-2 GF: - Fm: 0-0
Distance: 2m/2m3: 0-2 2m4-2m7: 0-1 3m+: 0-1
Track: LH: 0-2 RH: 0-2 Tight: 0-1 Gall: 0-0
Aids: Bl: 0-0 Vi: 0-0 Tstrap: 0-1
Best Rating: 87 4/02 Bang 2m4f good Hdl

Showed definite promise on hurdling bow over three miles in soft ground, and looks to have a future especially over fences in due course.

Step On Eyre (IRE)

110 **140**

12-y-o b g Step Together (USA)-Jane Eyre (Master Buck)
H D Daly Anne Duchess Of Westminster

Placings: *00/115*/151/22**2P331/22111P/042435/6P16-641P2** **(4089)**
2001/02: 23^{6}GS, 24^{4}S, 33^{1}S, 25^{P}HY, 24^{2}S

	Starts	1st	2nd	3rd	Win & Pl
Chases	5	1	1	0	6506
Career Total	**36**	**10**	**7**	**3**	**70881**

140	12/01	Bang	4m1f	D(0-120)HCh	SFT	£4494
144	2/01	Bang	3m6f	D(0-120)HCh	HVY	£5209
160	2/99	Hayd	3m	B(0-145)HCh	SFT	£12518
154	1/99	Weth	3m1f	B HCh	HVY	£8130
133	12/98	Bang	2m4f110y	D(0-120)HCh	G-S	£4299
119	4/98	Towc	2m6f	E Ch	G-S	£2921
121	4/97	Punc	2m	Hdl	GD	£4747
109	11/96	Tipp	2m	Hdl	SFT	£2824
117	6/95	Tipp	2m	NHF	Y-S	£2712
108	5/95	Tipp	2m4f	NHF	GD	£2712

Total win prize-money £50571

Going: Sf: 1-4 GS: 0-1 Gd: 0-0 GF: - Fm: 0-0
Distance: 2m/2m3: 0-0 2m4-2m7: 0-0 **3m+: 1-5**
Track: **LH: 1-3** RH: 0-2 **Tight: 1-3** Gall: 0-0
Aids: Bl: 0-0 Vi: 0-0 Tstrap: 0-0
Best Rating: 160 2/99 Hayd 3m soft Ch

Handicap chaser, he goes well under testing conditions but is inconsistent. Stays four miles plus. Goes well at Bangor.

Stepasideboy

108 **101**

12-y-o b g Idiots Delight-Waterside (Shackleton)
Miss D Cole E Wonnacott

Placings:P651/01**PP/PP/24** **(1496)**
2001/02: 26^{2}GF, 23^{4}GF

	Starts	1st	2nd	3rd	Win & Pl
Chases	2	0	1	0	1171
Career Total	**12**	**2**	**1**	**0**	**6496**

107	12/98	Wind	3m	E Ch	G-S	£3020
97	4/98	Plum	2m4f	E(0-100)HHdl	G-S	£2305

Total win prize-money £5326

Going: Sf: 0-0 GS: 0-0 Gd: 0-0 GF: - Fm: 0-2
Distance: 2m/2m3: 0-0 2m4-2m7: 0-0 3m+: 0-2
Track: LH: 0-1 RH: 0-1 Tight: 0-1 Gall: 0-0
Aids: Bl: 0-0 Vi: 0-0 Tstrap: 0-0
Best Rating: 107 12/98 Wind 3m gd-sft Ch

Won on his chasing debut at Windsor, the last steeplechase to be held at the Berkshire track. Has his problems and has been lightly-raced since.

Stephen's Brae

10-y-o b g Scorpio (FR)-Pendella (Pendragon)
N G Richards Dr Kenneth S Fraser

Placings: *00*PPF/1/44**02P-P** **(0277)**
2001/02: 26^{P}GF

	Starts	1st	2nd	3rd	Win & Pl
Chases	1	0	0	0	
Career Total	**12**	**1**	**1**	**0**	**3749**

88	8/99	Ctml	3m2f	E Ch	GD	£2877

Total win prize-money £2877

Going: Sf: 0-0 GS: 0-0 Gd: 0-0 GF: - Fm: 0-1
Distance: 2m/2m3: 0-0 2m4-2m7: 0-0 3m+: 0-1
Track: LH: 0-0 RH: 0-0 Tight: 0-0 Gall: 0-0
Aids: Bl: 0-0 Vi: 0-0 Tstrap: 0-0
Best Rating: 91 11/98 Ayr 2m gd-sft NHF

Steppintyme

93f **74f**

7-y-o ch m Bandmaster (USA)-Letitica (Deep Run)
E L James Mrs M M Stobart

Placings: *0*-6 **(0320)**
2001/02: 17^{6}F

	Starts	1st	2nd	3rd	Win & Pl
NH Flat	1	0	0	0	0
Career Total	**2**	**0**	**0**	**0**	**0**

Going: Sf: 0-0 GS: 0-0 Gd: 0-0 GF: - Fm: 0-1
Distance: 2m/2m3: 0-1 2m4-2m7: 0-0 3m+: 0-0
Track: LH: 0-0 RH: 0-1 Tight: 0-0 Gall: 0-0
Aids: Bl: 0-0 Vi: 0-0 Tstrap: 0-0
Best Rating: 74 5/01 Extr 2m1f firm NHF

Sterling Dot Com (IRE)

96 **116**

6-y-o b g Roselier (FR)-Daddy's Folly (Le Moss)
P J Hobbs Sterling Racing Syndicate

Placings: *3*-134 **(3585)**
2001/02: 21^{1}S, 22^{3}G, 22^{4}S

Starts		1st	2nd	3rd	Win & Pl
Hurdles	3	1	0	1	3790
Career Total	**4**	**1**	**0**	**2**	**4071**

116 12/01 Wwck 2m5f E Hdl SFT £2844
Total win prize-money £2845

Going: Sf: 1-2 GS: 0-0 Gd: 0-1 GF: - Fm: 0-0
Distance: 2m/2m3: 0-0 **2m4-2m7: 1-3** 3m+: 0-0
Track: LH: 0-1 RH: 0-1 Tight: 0-1 Gall: 0-0
Aids: Bl: 0-0 Vi: 0-0 Tstrap: 0-0
Best Rating: 116 12/01 Wwck 2m5f soft Hdl

Confirmed the promise of his racecourse debut with a win first time over hurdles on soft ground. Stays two miles five, acts on soft ground.

Sterling Stewart (IRE)

105(109h) (112h)**127**
7-y-o b g Insan (USA)-Kyle Eile (IRE) (Callernish)
M Pitman Ron George

Placings:03U3F2P/61PF30U15 **(4956a)**
2001/02: 20^{6}HY, 19^{1}GS, 24^{P}G, 20^{F}S, 20^{3}G, 24^{0}G, 20^{U}GF, 19^{1}GF, 18^{5}G

	Starts	1st	2nd	3rd	Win & Pl
Hurdles	3	1	0	0	5376
Chases	6	1	0	1	8888
Career Total	**16**	**2**	**1**	**3**	**16064**

124 4/02 Asct 2m3f110y C Ch G-F £6012
112 12/01 Newb 2m3f D(0-105)HHdl G-S £5375
Total win prize-money £11389

Going: Sf: 0-2 GS: 1-1 Gd: 0-4 GF: - Fm: 1-2
Distance: 2m/2m3: 1-2 2m4-2m7: 1-5 3m+: 0-2
Track: LH: 1-3 RH: 1-6 Tight: 0-1 **Gall: 1-2**
Aids: Bl: 0-1 Vi: 0-0 Tstrap: 0-0
Best Rating: 125 2/02 Kemp 2m4f110y good Ch

Fair hurdler around middle distances. Of similar ability over fences. Stays two and a half miles, acts on any ground.

Steve Ford

13-y-o gr g Another Realm-Sky Miss (Skymaster)
P W Hiatt P J Morgan

Placings:60/P/30F0V3/5140450/U632/15**223**/**11**23/U5 P/P0P **(0721)**
2001/02: 21^{P}GF, 24^{0}GF, 19^{P}F

	Starts	1st	2nd	3rd	Win & Pl
Chases	3	0	0	0	
Career Total	**35**	**4**	**4**	**5**	**19259**

112 5/98 Worc 2m4f110y D(0-125)HCh G-F £4235
107 5/98 Winc 2m5f E(0-100)HCh GD £3480
97 5/97 Uttx 2m4f110y D(0-125)HHdl GD £2913
93 5/95 Worc 2m E(0-110)HHdl GD £2547
Total win prize-money £13176

Going: Sf: 0-0 GS: 0-0 Gd: 0-0 GF: - Fm: 0-3
Distance: 2m/2m3: 0-1 2m4-2m7: 0-1 3m+: 0-1
Track: LH: 0-1 RH: 0-2 Tight: 0-1 Gall: 0-1
Aids: Bl: 0-0 Vi: 0-0 Tstrap: 0-0
Best Rating: 112 4/99 Strf 2m4f gd-sft Ch

Steve The Fish (IRE)

100 **98**
6-y-o ch g Dry Dock-Country Clothing (Salluceva)
J A B Old W E Sturt

Placings:06-05FF2 **(4519)**
2001/02: 16^{0}G, 22^{5}S, 17^{F}G, 21^{F}HY, 21^{2}GS

	Starts	1st	2nd	3rd	Win & Pl
Hurdles	5	0	1	0	558
Career Total	**7**	**0**	**1**	**0**	**558**

Going: Sf: 0-2 GS: 0-1 Gd: 0-2 GF: - Fm: 0-0
Distance: 2m/2m3: 0-2 2m4-2m7: 0-3 3m+: 0-0
Track: LH: 0-3 RH: 0-1 Tight: 0-1 Gall: 0-0
Aids: Bl: 0-0 Vi: 0-0 Tstrap: 0-0
Best Rating: 98 3/02 Towc 2m5f gd-sft Hdl

Stewart's Lad

91 **95**
5-y-o b g Well Beloved-Moneyacre (Veloski)
B D Leavy (D McCain 17/11) S H Riley

Placings:0453F **(4906)**
2001/02: 16^{0}S, 16^{4}GS, 16^{5}HY, 16^{3}G, 19^{F}G

	Starts	1st	2nd	3rd	Win & Pl
NH Flat	1	0	0	0	0
Hurdles	4	0	0	1	386
Career Total	**5**	**0**	**0**	**1**	**386**

Going: Sf: 0-2 GS: 0-1 Gd: 0-2 GF: - Fm: 0-0
Distance: 2m/2m3: 0-4 2m4-2m7: 0-1 3m+: 0-0
Track: LH: 0-3 RH: 0-2 Tight: 0-1 Gall: 0-0
Aids: Bl: 0-0 Vi: 0-0 Tstrap: 0-0
Best Rating: 97 4/02 Uttx 2m good Hdl

Has shown ability in novice hurdles.

Stewarts Pride

113 **122**
9-y-o b g Henbit (USA)-Pennyazena (Pamroy)
B D Leavy S H Riley

Placings:10/04155320/12F20P/F0U06PU-2111 **(0848)**
2001/02: 25^{2}G, 25^{1}G, 28^{1}GF, 32^{1}GF

	Starts	1st	2nd	3rd	Win & Pl
Chases	4	3	1	0	19683
Career Total	**27**	**6**	**4**	**1**	**30721**

122 7/01 Strf 4m B(0-140)HCh G-F £10075
112 6/01 Strf 3m4f D(0-120)HCh G-F £4403
114 5/01 Hrfd 3m1f110y F(0-95)HCh GD £4004
131 11/99 Uttx 3m E Ch SFT £3230
107 11/98 Towc 3m D Hdl SFT £2901
103 3/98 Sand 2m110y H NHF SFT £1444
Total win prize-money £26060

Going: Sf: 0-0 GS: 0-0 Gd: 1-2 GF: - Fm: 2-2
Distance: 2m/2m3: 0-0 2m4-2m7: 0-0 **3m+: 3-4**
Track: LH: 1-1 RH: 1-2 **Tight: 1-1** Gall: 0-0
Aids: **Bl: 3-4** Vi: 0-0 Tstrap: 0-0
Best Rating: 131 11/99 Uttx 3m soft Ch

Fair staying chaser, acted on easy ground but also went well on fast. Ran up a hat-trick in the summer of 2001. (DEAD)

Sticiboots

74 **47**
5-y-o b g Batshoof-Satiric (IRE) (Doyoun)
F Jordan F Jordan

Placings:0PP **(3979)**
2001/02: 17^{0}GS, 24^{P}HY, 16^{P}G

	Starts	1st	2nd	3rd	Win & Pl
Hurdles	3	0	0	0	
Career Total	**3**	**0**	**0**	**0**	

Going: Sf: 0-1 GS: 0-1 Gd: 0-1 GF: - Fm: 0-0
Distance: 2m/2m3: 0-2 2m4-2m7: 0-0 3m+: 0-1
Track: LH: 0-1 RH: 0-2 Tight: 0-1 Gall: 0-0
Aids: Bl: 0-0 Vi: 0-0 Tstrap: 0-3
Best Rating: 47 12/01 Tntn 2m1f gd-sft Hdl

Still In Business

14-y-o b g Don Enrico (USA)-Mill Miss (Typhoon)
R W Gardiner A Ayers

Placings:1235/3U/1/43/6/P55 **(0556)**
2001/02: 24^{P}GF, 21^{5}G, 24^{5}GF

	Starts	1st	2nd	3rd	Win & Pl
Chases	3	0	0	0	0
Career Total	**13**	**2**	**1**	**3**	**4261**

110 4/98 Tntn 3m H Ch GD £1523
102 5/95 NAbb 2m5f H Ch GD £1444
Total win prize-money £2967

Going: Sf: 0-0 GS: 0-0 Gd: 0-1 GF: - Fm: 0-2
Distance: 2m/2m3: 0-0 2m4-2m7: 0-1 3m+: 0-2
Track: LH: 0-0 RH: 0-3 Tight: 0-1 Gall: 0-2
Aids: Bl: 0-0 Vi: 0-0 Tstrap: 0-0
Best Rating: 111 4/99 Tntn 3m firm Ch

Still Waters

68 **43**
7-y-o b g Rainbow Quest (USA)-Krill (Kris)
B A Pearce A Leg Each Partnership

Placings:0/0-0 **(0673)**
2001/02: 16^{0}GF

	Starts	1st	2nd	3rd	Win & Pl
Hurdles	1	0	0	0	
Career Total	**3**	**0**	**0**	**0**	

Going: Sf: 0-0 GS: 0-0 Gd: 0-0 GF: - Fm: 0-1
Distance: 2m/2m3: 0-1 2m4-2m7: 0-0 3m+: 0-0
Track: LH: 0-1 RH: 0-0 Tight: 0-0 Gall: 0-0
Aids: Bl: 0-0 Vi: 0-0 Tstrap: 0-0
Best Rating: 78 5/00 Hntg 2m110y good Hdl

Stillmore Business

80 **82**
11-y-o ch g Don Enrico (USA)-Mill Miss (Typhoon)
P F Nicholls R G Williams

Placings:0-04 **(0123)**
2001/02: 17^{0}GS, 19^{4}F

	Starts	1st	2nd	3rd	Win & Pl
Chases	2	0	0	0	389
Career Total	**3**	**0**	**0**	**0**	**389**

Going: Sf: 0-0 GS: 0-1 Gd: 0-0 GF: - Fm: 0-1
Distance: 2m/2m3: 0-2 2m4-2m7: 0-0 3m+: 0-0
Track: LH: 0-0 RH: 0-2 Tight: 0-1 Gall: 0-0
Aids: Bl: 0-0 Vi: 0-0 Tstrap: 0-0
Best Rating: 82 5/01 Tntn 2m3f firm Ch

Stinging Bee

11-y-o b g Respect-Regal Bee (Royal Fountain)
Mrs A Bell Mrs A Bell

Placings:00/PFP65/563646P4/4/0P-45P6 **(4859)**
2001/02: 24^{4}S, 21^{5}G, 21^{P}G, 25^{6}G

	Starts	1st	2nd	3rd	Win & Pl
Chases	4	0	0	0	83
Career Total	**22**	**0**	**0**	**1**	**1098**

Going: Sf: 0-1 GS: 0-0 Gd: 0-3 GF: - Fm: 0-0
Distance: 2m/2m3: 0-0 2m4-2m7: 0-2 3m+: 0-2
Track: LH: 0-3 RH: 0-1 Tight: 0-2 Gall: 0-1
Aids: Bl: 0-0 Vi: 0-0 Tstrap: 0-0
Best Rating: 97 3/01 MRas 3m1f gd-sft Ch

Stitch-B (IRE)

(94h) (74h)
9-y-o ch g Naheez (USA)-Sea View (Quayside)
P Beaumont The Foulrice Twenty

Placings:0000/013/3002-00 **(0419)**
2001/02: 17^{0}G, 20^{0}G

	Starts	1st	2nd	3rd	Win & Pl
Hurdles	2	0	0	0	
Career Total	**13**	**1**	**1**	**2**	**3963**
79 6/99 Wxfd 2m4f Hdl				G-F	£2639
					Total win prize-money £2640

Going: Sf: 0-0 GS: 0-0 Gd: 0-2 GF: - Fm: 0-0
Distance: 2m/2m3: 0-1 2m4-2m7: 0-1 3m+: 0-0
Track: LH: 0-2 RH: 0-0 Tight: 0-2 Gall: 0-0
Aids: Bl: 0-0 Vi: 0-0 Tstrap: 0-0
Best Rating: 99 5/00 Klny 2m1f gd-fm Ch

Stockers Pride

97 **106**
7-y-o b g Sula Bula-Fille De Soleil (Sunyboy)
S Woodman J D Sells

Placings:*06*2313 **(4039)**
2001/02: 18^{0}GF, 18^{6}GS, 17^{2}HY, 21^{3}G, 25^{1}HY, 27^{3}S

	Starts	1st	2nd	3rd	Win & Pl
NH Flat	2	0	0	0	0
Hurdles	4	1	1	2	3968
Career Total	**6**	**1**	**1**	**2**	**3968**
106 1/02 Plum 3m1f110y E Hdl				HVY	£2572
					Total win prize-money £2573

Going: Sf: 1-3 GS: 0-1 Gd: 0-1 GF: - Fm: 0-1
Distance: 2m/2m3: 0-3 2m4-2m7: 0-1 **3m+: 1-2**
Track: LH: 0-2 RH: 0-1 Tight: 0-4 Gall: 0-0
Aids: Bl: 0-0 Vi: 0-0 Tstrap: 0-0
Best Rating: 106 1/02 Plum 3m1f110y heavy Hdl

Modest novice hurdler, stays well and acts in the mud.

Stone Cold

103(106h) (97h)**107**
5-y-o ch g Inchinor-Vaula (Henbit (USA))
T D Easterby Six Diamonds Partnership

Placings:45551040-0525P0**21F51** **(4905)**
2001/02: 17^{0}G, 21^{5}G, 23^{2}G, 25^{5}G, 23^{P}HY, 20^{0}G, 19^{2}S, 16^{1}S, 20^{F}GS, 21^{5}GF, 17^{1}GF

	Starts	1st	2nd	3rd	Win & Pl
Hurdles	6	0	1	0	1150
Chases	5	2	1	0	8962
Career Total	**19**	**3**	**2**	**0**	**12665**
107 4/02 MRas 2m1f110y E(0-105)HCh				G-F	£3786
107 3/02 Donc 2m110y D(0-110)HCh				SFT	£4160
97 2/01 Sedg 2m1f F(0-95)HHdl				SFT	£2009
					Total win prize-money £9955

Going: Sf: 1-3 GS: 0-1 Gd: 0-5 GF: - Fm: 1-2
Distance: **2m/2m3: 2-3** 2m4-2m7: 0-5 3m+: 0-3
Track: LH: 1-9 RH: 1-2 Tight: 1-4 Gall: 1-4
Aids: Bl: 0-3 Vi: 0-0 Tstrap: 0-0
Best Rating: 107 4/02 MRas 2m1f110y gd-fm Ch

Took well to fences in 2001/02 and opened his account in a novices' handicap at Doncaster in March on only his second attempt before following up later at Market Rasen.

Stone Crop

11-y-o br g Kefaah (USA)-Sweet Pleasure (Sweet Revenge)
P W Hiatt S C Clark

Placings:00/45/PPP/5 **(0490)**
2001/02: 27^{5}GF

	Starts	1st	2nd	3rd	Win & Pl
Hurdles	1	0	0	0	0
Career Total	**8**	**0**	**0**	**0**	**0**

Going: Sf: 0-0 GS: 0-0 Gd: 0-0 GF: - Fm: 0-1
Distance: 2m/2m3: 0-0 2m4-2m7: 0-0 3m+: 0-1
Track: LH: 0-0 RH: 0-0 Tight: 0-1 Gall: 0-0
Aids: Bl: 0-0 Vi: 0-0 Tstrap: 0-0
Best Rating: 57 6/95 Strf 2m6f110y good Hdl

Stone's Throw

(88h)
9-y-o b g Roscoe Blake-Lampstone (Ragstone)
Miss Z C Davison The Merry Monks

Placings:*00*/0433F/44343/005P-P **(0061)**
2001/02: 26^{P}G

	Starts	1st	2nd	3rd	Win & Pl
Chases	1	0	0	0	
Career Total	**17**	**0**	**0**	**4**	**2490**

Going: Sf: 0-0 GS: 0-0 Gd: 0-1 GF: - Fm: 0-0
Distance: 2m/2m3: 0-0 2m4-2m7: 0-0 3m+: 0-1
Track: LH: 0-0 RH: 0-1 Tight: 0-1 Gall: 0-0
Aids: Bl: 0-0 Vi: 0-0 Tstrap: 0-0
Best Rating: 108 1/99 Towc 2m heavy Hdl

Stonehenge (IRE)

90(100h) (95h)**87**
5-y-o b g Caerleon (USA)-Sharata (IRE) (Darshaan)
J W Mullins Mrs Jeni Fisher

Placings:5P0-512535P**P05** **(4602)**
2001/02: 17^{5}GF, 22^{1}G, 22^{2}GF, 20^{5}G, 22^{3}GF, 22^{5}GF, 22^{P}GF, 17^{P}GS, 23^{0}G, 20^{5}GF

	Starts	1st	2nd	3rd	Win & Pl
Hurdles	7	1	1	1	4155
Chases	3	0	0	0	0
Career Total	**13**	**1**	**1**	**1**	**4155**
95 6/01 NAbb 2m6f F(0-105)HHdl				GD	£2793
					Total win prize-money £2793

Going: Sf: 0-0 GS: 0-1 Gd: 1-3 GF: - Fm: 0-6
Distance: 2m/2m3: 0-2 **2m4-2m7: 1-7** 3m+: 0-1
Track: **LH: 1-3** RH: 0-5 **Tight: 1-3** Gall: 0-1
Aids: Bl: 0-0 Vi: 0-0 Tstrap: 0-0
Best Rating: 95 6/01 NAbb 2m6f gd-fm Hdl

Stonehill

105 **97**
9-y-o b g Bustino-B A Poundstretcher (Laser Light)
J Howard Johnson The Braw Partnership

Placings:*5*/P245/5/4U1-6U61 **(4554)**
2001/02: 19^{6}S, 24^{U}S, 16^{6}HY, 17^{1}G

	Starts	1st	2nd	3rd	Win & Pl
Chases	4	1	0	0	4696
Career Total	**13**	**2**	**1**	**0**	**10131**
97 4/02 MRas 2m1f110y D(0-115)HCh				GD	£4696
97 1/01 Catt 2m E(0-105)HCh				G-S	£4478
					Total win prize-money £9175

Going: Sf: 0-3 GS: 0-0 Gd: 1-1 GF: - Fm: 0-0
Distance: **2m/2m3: 1-3** 2m4-2m7: 0-0 3m+: 0-1
Track: LH: 0-2 **RH: 1-2 Tight: 1-3** Gall: 0-1
Aids: Bl: 0-0 Vi: 0-0 Tstrap: 0-0
Best Rating: 97 4/02 MRas 2m1f110y good Ch

Modest chaser, best at around two miles, likes good ground.

Stonehill Prospect

76 **39**
8-y-o b m Lightning Dealer-Ditchling Beacon (High Line)
J Cullinan Mrs F Kehoe

Placings:0-04 **(0594)**
2001/02: 17^{0}G, 20^{4}GF

	Starts	1st	2nd	3rd	Win & Pl
Hurdles	2	0	0	0	0
Career Total	**3**	**0**	**0**	**0**	**0**

Going: Sf: 0-0 GS: 0-0 Gd: 0-1 GF: - Fm: 0-1
Distance: 2m/2m3: 0-1 2m4-2m7: 0-1 3m+: 0-0
Track: LH: 0-1 RH: 0-1 Tight: 0-1 Gall: 0-0
Aids: Bl: 0-0 Vi: 0-0 Tstrap: 0-0
Best Rating: 60 4/01 Font 2m2f110y good Hdl

Stoney Path

108 **94**
7-y-o b m Petoski-Lampstone (Ragstone)
A King The Golden Anorak Partnership

Placings:*450*/2-P001 **(4540)**
2001/02: 21^{P}S, 22^{0}G, 16^{0}S, 19^{1}G

	Starts	1st	2nd	3rd	Win & Pl
Hurdles	4	1	0	0	3430
Career Total	**8**	**1**	**1**	**0**	**4217**
89 4/02 Hrfd 2m3f110y E(0-105)HHdl				GD	£3430
					Total win prize-money £3430

Going: Sf: 0-2 GS: 0-0 Gd: 1-2 GF: - Fm: 0-0
Distance: 2m/2m3: 0-1 **2m4-2m7: 1-3** 3m+: 0-0
Track: LH: 0-0 **RH: 1-3** Tight: 0-0 Gall: 0-0
Aids: Bl: 0-0 Vi: 0-0 Tstrap: 0-0
Best Rating: 93 4/00 Chel 2m1f soft NHF

Modest hurdler, effective on fast ground. Won novices handicap at Hereford April 2002. Finished lame when following up at Worcester.

Stoney River (IRE)

8-y-o b g Riverhead (USA)-Another Space (Brave Invader (USA))
R H Alner C W W Dupont

Placings:U-33P **(0835)**

2001/02: 26^{3}GF, 23^{3}F, 26^{P}GF

	Starts	1st	2nd	3rd	Win & Pl
Chases	3	0	0	2	1134
Career Total	**4**	**0**	**0**	**2**	**1134**

Going: Sf: 0-0 GS: 0-0 Gd: 0-0 GF: - Fm: 0-3
Distance: 2m/2m3: 0-0 2m4-2m7: 0-0 3m+: 0-3
Track: LH: 0-1 RH: 0-1 Tight: 0-2 Gall: 0-0
Aids: Bl: 0-0 Vi: 0-0 Tstrap: 0-0
Best Rating: 100 5/01 Font 3m2f110y gd-fm Ch

Stop The Gossip (IRE)

98

8-y-o br g Cataldi-Rosie Owen (IRE) (Roselier (FR))
W F Treacy (M Todhunter 15/1) W F Treacy

Placings: *3010*/F041O50P/2F0150R1-PPPR0 **(4933a)**
2001/02: 19^{P}G, 16^{P}G, 22^{P}G, 17^{R}S, 16^{0}S

	Starts	1st	2nd	3rd	Win & Pl
Hurdles	4	0	0	0	0
Chases	1	0	0	0	0
Career Total	**25**	**4**	**1**	**1**	**11561**

98	4/01	Prth	2m110y	D(0-120)HHdl	HVY	£3601
98	10/00	Carl	2m1f	E(0-115)HHdl	SFT	£2821
98	11/99	Carl	2m4f110y	F(0-100)HHdl	SFT	£2332
101	3/99	Muss	2m	H NHF	GD	£1388

Total win prize-money £10143

Going: Sf: 0-2 GS: 0-0 Gd: 0-3 GF: - Fm: 0-0
Distance: 2m/2m3: 0-3 2m4-2m7: 0-2 3m+: 0-0
Track: LH: 0-1 RH: 0-3 Tight: 0-2 Gall: 0-0
Aids: Bl: 0-0 Vi: 0-0 Tstrap: 0-0
Best Rating: 101 3/99 Muss 2m good NHF

Stop The Music (IRE)

83f 86f

6-y-o b g Lord Americo-Brace Yourself (Castle Keep)
S E H Sherwood The Hon Mrs S Sherwood

Placings: *45* **(3338)**
2001/02: 17^{4}G, 16^{5}G

	Starts	1st	2nd	3rd	Win & Pl
NH Flat	2	0	0	0	0
Career Total	**2**	**0**	**0**	**0**	**0**

Going: Sf: 0-0 GS: 0-0 Gd: 0-2 GF: - Fm: 0-0
Distance: 2m/2m3: 0-2 2m4-2m7: 0-0 3m+: 0-0
Track: LH: 0-0 RH: 0-1 Tight: 0-0 Gall: 0-0
Aids: Bl: 0-0 Vi: 0-0 Tstrap: 0-0
Best Rating: 86 1/02 Ludl 2m good NHF

Stopwatch (IRE)

104 88

7-y-o b g Lead On Time (USA)-Rose Bonbon (FR) (High Top)
Mrs L C Jewell The Stopwatch Partnership

Placings: 03015/5P40/3542500-64360016 **(4509)**
2001/02: 16^{6}G, 21^{4}GF, 18^{3}GF, 17^{6}HY, 21^{0}GS, 17^{0}S, 16^{1}GF, 16^{6}G

	Starts	1st	2nd	3rd	Win & Pl
Hurdles	8	1	0	1	2204
Career Total	**24**	**2**	**1**	**3**	**7622**

80	3/02	Hntg	2m110y	F(0-100)HHdl	G-F	£1848
104	4/99	Plum	2m1f	E(0-105)HHdl	GD	£2302

Total win prize-money £4151

Going: Sf: 0-2 GS: 0-1 Gd: 0-2 GF: - Fm: 1-3
Distance: **2m/2m3: 1-6** 2m4-2m7: 0-2 3m+: 0-0
Track: LH: 0-3 **RH: 1-5** Tight: 0-5 **Gall: 1-3**
Aids: Bl: 0-1 Vi: 0-0 Tstrap: 0-0
Best Rating: 104 4/99 Chel 2m1f good Hdl

Emerged from the doldrums to take a ladies' handicap hurdle at Huntingdon in March 2002. Suited by two miles and a sound surface.

Storm A Brewing

89f 98f

6-y-o ch g Glacial Storm (USA)-Southern Squaw (Buckskin (FR))
R M Stronge Peter J Douglas Engineering

Placings: *20* **(3883)**
2001/02: 16^{2}G, 16^{0}GS

	Starts	1st	2nd	3rd	Win & Pl
NH Flat	2	0	1	0	632
Career Total	**2**	**0**	**1**	**0**	**632**

Going: Sf: 0-0 GS: 0-1 Gd: 0-1 GF: - Fm: 0-0
Distance: 2m/2m3: 0-2 2m4-2m7: 0-0 3m+: 0-0
Track: LH: 0-0 RH: 0-2 Tight: 0-0 Gall: 0-0
Aids: Bl: 0-0 Vi: 0-0 Tstrap: 0-0
Best Rating: 98 1/02 Ludl 2m good NHF

Out of half-sister to Docklands Express, a runner-up in bumper on racecourse debut.

Storm Ahead (IRE)

104 88

8-y-o b g Glacial Storm (USA)-Little Slip (Super Slip)
N G Richards (Michael McNeilly 20/10) It's A Bargain Syndicate

Placings: *04320*/0000-F425P **(4093)**
2001/02: 17^{F}YS, 16^{4}GS, 20^{2}S, 20^{5}G, 25^{P}GS

	Starts	1st	2nd	3rd	Win & Pl
Hurdles	4	0	1	0	872
Chases	1	0	0	0	0
Career Total	**14**	**0**	**2**	**1**	**1930**

Going: Sf: 0-1 GS: 0-2 Gd: 0-1 GF: - Fm: 0-0
Distance: 2m/2m3: 0-2 2m4-2m7: 0-2 3m+: 0-1
Track: LH: 0-3 RH: 0-2 Tight: 0-2 Gall: 0-1
Aids: Bl: 0-0 Vi: 0-0 Tstrap: 0-3
Best Rating: 101 11/99 Dpat 2m1f87y yield NHF

Storm Call

11-y-o b m Celestial Storm (USA)-Right Mall (Pall Mall)
D W Whillans Chas N Whillans

Placings: *05*/606/1130/**34FB/1P2F4351/P34-P** **(0336)**
2001/02: 24^{P}S

	Starts	1st	2nd	3rd	Win & Pl
Chases	1	0	0	0	
Career Total	**25**	**4**	**1**	**4**	**18235**

113	4/00	Carl	2m4f110y	F(0-100)HCh	G-S	£3403
103	5/99	Prth	2m	D Ch	HVY	£4260
91	3/98	Hexm	2m	E(0-110)HHdl	SFT	£2646
93	3/98	Ayr	2m	F Hdl	SFT	£2320

Total win prize-money £12630

Going: Sf: 0-1 GS: 0-0 Gd: 0-0 GF: - Fm: 0-0
Distance: 2m/2m3: 0-0 2m4-2m7: 0-0 3m+: 0-1
Track: LH: 0-0 RH: 0-1 Tight: 0-0 Gall: 0-0
Aids: Bl: 0-0 Vi: 0-0 Tstrap: 0-0
Best Rating: 113 4/00 Carl 2m4f110y gd-sft Ch

Storm Castle (IRE)

10-y-o b g Carlingford Castle-Strong Rum (Strong Gale)
Miss J Wickens Noel Cronin

Placings: 21P2/034P630/0-2 **(4172)**
2001/02: 26^{2}GS

	Starts	1st	2nd	3rd	Win & Pl
Chases	1	0	1	0	328
Career Total	**13**	**1**	**3**	**2**	**10149**

116	2/99	Tntn	3m110y	D Hdl	G-S	£2644

Total win prize-money £2644

Going: Sf: 0-0 GS: 0-1 Gd: 0-0 GF: - Fm: 0-0
Distance: 2m/2m3: 0-0 2m4-2m7: 0-0 3m+: 0-1
Track: LH: 0-0 RH: 0-0 Tight: 0-0 Gall: 0-0
Aids: Bl: 0-0 Vi: 0-0 Tstrap: 0-0
Best Rating: 120 4/99 Chel 2m5f110y good Hdl

A useful pointer/hunter chaser, suited by a sound surface.

Storm Clipper (IRE)

6-y-o gr g Roscoe Blake-Bissie's Jayla (Zambrano)
M Pitman Peter Bonner

Placings: *0P* **(3222)**
2001/02: 16^{0}S, 22^{P}G

	Starts	1st	2nd	3rd	Win & Pl
NH Flat	1	0	0	0	0
Hurdles	1	0	0	0	0
Career Total	**2**	**0**	**0**	**0**	

Going: Sf: 0-1 GS: 0-0 Gd: 0-1 GF: - Fm: 0-0
Distance: 2m/2m3: 0-1 2m4-2m7: 0-1 3m+: 0-0
Track: LH: 0-1 RH: 0-1 Tight: 0-0 Gall: 0-0
Aids: Bl: 0-0 Vi: 0-0 Tstrap: 0-0
Best Rating: 60 12/01 Wwck 2m soft NHF

Storm Cry (USA)

7-y-o b g Hermitage (USA)-Doonesbury Lady (USA) (Doonesbury (USA))
M S Saunders B McFadzean

Placings: 0P-P **(2277)**
2001/02: 22^{P}GF

	Starts	1st	2nd	3rd	Win & Pl
Hurdles	1	0	0	0	
Career Total	**3**	**0**	**0**	**0**	

Going: Sf: 0-0 GS: 0-0 Gd: 0-0 GF: - Fm: 0-1
Distance: 2m/2m3: 0-0 2m4-2m7: 0-1 3m+: 0-0
Track: LH: 0-0 RH: 0-1 Tight: 0-0 Gall: 0-0
Aids: Bl: 0-0 Vi: 0-0 Tstrap: 0-0
Best Rating: 36 1/01 Tntn 2m1f soft Hdl

Storm Damage (IRE)

120 145

10-y-o b g Waajib-Connaught Lace (Connaught)
P F Nicholls T Curry,C Lewis,Penny Mitchell & J Olds

Placings: 65113/00/**F21245/33112334/3132305/34221 50-2064B10** **(4897)**
2001/02: 24^{2}GS, 24^{0}G, 20^{6}S, 24^{4}GS, 24^{B}GS, 24^{1}G, 24^{0}G

	Starts	1st	2nd	3rd	Win & Pl
Chases	7	1	1	0	11664
Career Total	**42**	**8**	**7**	**9**	**103303**

145	3/02	Sand	3m110y	C(0-135)HCh	GD	£6987
145	2/01	Sand	3m110y	B(0-145)HCh	HVY	£20825
145	11/99	Chep	2m3f110y	C(0-130)HCh	GD	£6006
145	1/99	Kemp	2m4f110y	B(0-145)HCh	SFT	£10386
145	12/98	Chep	2m3f110y	C(0-130)HCh	HVY	£4955
118	1/98	Wind	2m	E Ch	GD	£2921
115	2/96	Clon	2m	Hdl	SFT	£2295
113	2/96	Gowr	2m	Hdl	Y-S	£3177

Total win prize-money £57556

Going: Sf: 0-1 GS: 0-3 Gd: 1-3 GF: - Fm: 0-0
Distance: 2m/2m3: 0-0 2m4-2m7: 0-1 **3m+: 1-6**
Track: LH: 0-2 **RH: 1-5** Tight: 0-0 Gall: 0-1
Aids: Bl: 0-0 Vi: 0-0 Tstrap: 0-0
Best Rating: 145 3/02 Sand 3m110y good Ch

He goes well on soft ground and had conditions in his favour when winning a sub-standard renewal of the Agfa Chase at Sandown in February 2001. A shade disappointing after that success, but won back at Sandown in March 2002. Stays three miles.

Storm Drum

13-y-o ch g Celestial Storm (USA)-Bushti Music (Bustino)
K D Giles K D Giles

Placings:4312/1262135503F021/20P/6F624540/0344 55/P **(0323)**
2001/02: 25^{P}G

	Starts	1st	2nd	3rd	Win & Pl
Chases	1	0	0	0	
Career Total	**36**	**4**	**6**	**4**	**15216**

109	4/94	Weth	3m1f	(0-125)HHdl	GD	£2965
111	9/93	Uttx	3m110y	(0-115)HHdl	G-F	£2778
89	5/93	Ludl	2m	Hdl	FRM	£1861
75	4/93	Plum	2m1f	Hdl	SFT	£1481

Total win prize-money £9086

Going: Sf: 0-0 GS: 0-0 Gd: 0-1 GF: - Fm: 0-0
Distance: 2m/2m3: 0-0 2m4-2m7: 0-0 3m+: 0-1
Track: LH: 0-0 RH: 0-1 Tight: 0-1 Gall: 0-0
Aids: Bl: 0-1 Vi: 0-0 Tstrap: 0-0
Best Rating: 111 10/93 Chep 3m good Hdl

Storm Kitten (IRE)

67f

4-y-o br f Catrail (USA)-Mbunda (Mtoto)
Miss K M George Miss K George

Placings:600 **(4506)**
2001/02: 17^{6}S, 16^{0}S, 17^{0}G

	Starts	1st	2nd	3rd	Win & Pl
NH Flat	3	0	0	0	0
Career Total	**3**	**0**	**0**	**0**	**0**

Going: Sf: 0-2 GS: 0-0 Gd: 0-1 GF: - Fm: 0-0
Distance: 2m/2m3: 0-3 2m4-2m7: 0-0 3m+: 0-0
Track: LH: 0-2 RH: 0-0 Tight: 0-1 Gall: 0-0
Aids: Bl: 0-0 Vi: 0-0 Tstrap: 0-0
Best Rating: 67 1/02 Tntn 2m1f soft NHF

Storm Of Gold (IRE)

9-y-o b g Glacial Storm (USA)-Tipperary Tartan (Rarity)
Miss C F Elliott (M C Pipe 20/1) Mrs Pippa Cook

Placings:235/11320/21F/0020-61PP **(4892)**
2001/02: 24^{6}S, 31^{1}GS, 24^{P}G, 31^{P}G

	Starts	1st	2nd	3rd	Win & Pl
Chases	4	1	0	0	2618
Career Total	**19**	**4**	**4**	**2**	**23588**

111	2/02	Ludl	3m7f	H Ch	G-S	£2618
134	12/99	MRas	3m1f	E Ch	G-S	£3070
124	12/98	Uttx	2m4f110y	E Hdl	G-S	£1966
121	11/98	Hayd	2m4f	D Hdl	G-S	£2885

Total win prize-money £10540

Going: Sf: 0-1 GS: 1-1 Gd: 0-2 GF: - Fm: 0-0
Distance: 2m/2m3: 0-0 2m4-2m7: 0-0 **3m+: 1-4**
Track: LH: 0-0 RH: 0-2 Tight: 0-1 Gall: 0-0
Aids: Bl: 0-0 Vi: 0-0 Tstrap: 0-0
Best Rating: 143 12/00 Newb 2m6f110y soft Ch

A fortunate winner of a hunter chase at Ludlow in February 2002, he stays very well but may not be the most hearty.

Storm Run (IRE)

(84h) (72h)

12-y-o b g Strong Gale-Summerville Lass (Deep Run)
Miss J Wormall Mrs R Wormall

Placings:1/222B3/31F/1F1BP6U3/3/0 **(0582)**
2001/02: 19^{0}GF

	Starts	1st	2nd	3rd	Win & Pl
Hurdles	1	0	0	0	
Career Total	**19**	**4**	**3**	**4**	**21515**

123	11/97	Aint	2m	D(0-115)HCh	G-S	£11212
125	10/97	Hrfd	2m3f	E(0-100)HCh	GD	£2996
81	9/96	NAbb	2m6f	E Hdl	GD	£2200
80	10/94	Extr	2m1f110y	NHF	GD	£1938

Total win prize-money £18348

Going: Sf: 0-0 GS: 0-0 Gd: 0-0 GF: - Fm: 0-1
Distance: 2m/2m3: 0-1 2m4-2m7: 0-0 3m+: 0-0
Track: LH: 0-1 RH: 0-0 Tight: 0-1 Gall: 0-0
Aids: Bl: 0-0 Vi: 0-0 Tstrap: 0-0
Best Rating: 125 3/98 Tntn 2m3f gd-sft Ch

Storm Tiger (IRE)

108(106h) (101h)123

11-y-o b g Strong Gale-Happy Party (Invited (USA))
C G Cox (S Mellor 28/10) Mrs Sara Warren

Placings:4000/0042P1/05641122/350645F2/412643F 13514F3321/1431431522-50422F44233PU **(4872)**
2001/02: 17^{5}GF, 17^{0}G, 16^{4}GF, 16^{2}G, 17^{2}G, 17^{F}G, 17^{4}GF, 16^{4}G, 16^{2}G, 16^{3}GS, 20^{3}G, 20^{P}S, 16^{U}GF

	Starts	1st	2nd	3rd	Win & Pl
Hurdles	2	0	0	0	415
Chases	11	0	3	2	7446
Career Total	**66**	**10**	**11**	**9**	**54431**

118	8/00	Ctml	2m1f110y	D(0-120)HCh	G-S	£3809
123	7/00	Sthl	2m	F(0-105)HCh	G-F	£4056
123	5/00	Hntg	2m110y	F(0-105)HCh	G-S	£2846
114	4/00	Hayd	2m	D(0-120)HCh	GD	£7215
106	12/99	Hntg	2m110y	F(0-105)HCh	G-S	£2565
106	11/99	Ludl	2m	E(0-105)HCh	GD	£3485
102	5/99	Worc	2m	F(0-105)HHdl	G-F	£2031
92	2/98	Towc	2m	E(0-110)HHdl	GD	£2460
89	1/98	Wind	2m	F(0-105)HHdl	GD	£2076
85	3/97	Wind	2m	F(0-105)HHdl	GD	£2104

Total win prize-money £32649

Going: Sf: 0-1 GS: 0-1 Gd: 0-7 GF: - Fm: 0-4
Distance: 2m/2m3: 0-11 2m4-2m7: 0-2 3m+: 0-0
Track: LH: 0-8 RH: 0-5 Tight: 0-9 Gall: 0-0
Aids: Bl: 0-0 Vi: 0-9 Tstrap: 0-0

Best Rating: 123 10/01 Hrfd 2m good Ch

A consistent handicapper chaser around two miles on the smaller tracks, he won four times in the middle of 2000, but has tended to find one or two to beat him since. Prefers decent ground and jumps soundly. Usually wears a visor.

Storm Valley (IRE)

95 105

10-y-o b g Strong Gale-Windy Run (Deep Run)
J R Cornwall J R Cornwall

Placings:0P0/56/650UP5P4/133-P1PP **(2320)**
2001/02: 28^{P}GS, 24^{1}G, 20^{P}G, 20^{P}GS

	Starts	1st	2nd	3rd	Win & Pl
Chases	4	1	0	0	2940
Career Total	**20**	**2**	**0**	**2**	**7877**

105	10/01	Sthl	3m110y	F(0-100)HCh	GD	£2940
96	9/00	Plum	2m4f	D(0-110)HCh	G-F	£3770

Total win prize-money £6710

Going: Sf: 0-0 GS: 0-2 Gd: 1-2 GF: - Fm: 0-0
Distance: 2m/2m3: 0-0 2m4-2m7: 0-2 **3m+: 1-2**
Track: **LH: 1-3** RH: 0-1 **Tight: 1-4** Gall: 0-0
Aids: Bl: 0-0 Vi: 0-0 **Tstrap: 1-4**
Best Rating: 105 10/01 Sthl 3m110y good Ch

Storm Wizard (IRE)

73 83

5-y-o b g Catrail (USA)-Society Ball (Law Society (USA))
C J Mann Bel Leisure Limited

Placings:0 **(0102)**
2001/02: 18^{0}GF

	Starts	1st	2nd	3rd	Win & Pl
Hurdles	1	0	0	0	
Career Total	**1**	**0**	**0**	**0**	

Going: Sf: 0-0 GS: 0-0 Gd: 0-0 GF: - Fm: 0-1
Distance: 2m/2m3: 0-1 2m4-2m7: 0-0 3m+: 0-0
Track: LH: 0-1 RH: 0-0 Tight: 0-1 Gall: 0-0
Aids: Bl: 0-0 Vi: 0-0 Tstrap: 0-0
Best Rating: 83 5/01 Font 2m2f110y gd-fm Hdl

Stormez (FR)

103(108h) (140h)150

5-y-o b g Ezzoud (IRE)-Stormy Scene (USA) (Storm Bird (CAN))
M C Pipe (C Aubert 30/11) D A Johnson

Placings:02163011541033 **(4830)**
2001/02: 17^{0}S, 18^{2}VS, 19^{1}GS, 18^{6}VS, 18^{3}VS, 19^{0}VS, 18^{1}HY, 19^{1}HY, 16^{5}S, 16^{4}S, 24^{1}S, 21^{0}GS, 24^{3}G, 24^{3}G

	Starts	1st	2nd	3rd	Win & Pl
Hurdles	14	4	1	3	95751
Career Total	**14**	**4**	**1**	**3**	**95751**

134	2/02	Asct	3m	C Hdl	SFT	£5005
140	11/01	Engh	2m3f	Hdl	HVY	£31038
	11/01	Engh	2m2f	Hdl	HVY	£17459
	7/01	Autl	2m3f110y	Hdl	G-S	£19399

Total win prize-money £72901

Going: Sf: 3-6 GS: 1-2 Gd: 0-2 GF: - Fm: 0-0
Distance: **2m/2m3: 2-8** 2m4-2m7: 1-3 3m+: 1-3
Track: LH: 0-6 **RH: 1-1** Tight: 0-1 Gall: 0-2
Aids: Bl: 0-0 Vi: 0-1 Tstrap: 0-3
Best Rating: 140 4/02 Aint 3m110y good Hdl

A smart hurdler in France, he was disappointing on his

British debut at Warwick in January 2002, but the step up to three miles at Ascot brought about the required improvement. Made an impressive start to his chasing career in two low-grade affairs in May 2002 before winning a valuable handicap over four miles at Uttoxeter in June. Acts on any ground.

Stormhill Stag

106(90h) **130**

10-y-o b g Buckley-Sweet Sirenia (Al Sirat (USA))

R Lee R Taylor

Placings:*2112*/426431F/534**P**0/22**30F-1220113** **(4146)**

2001/02: 19^{1}GS, 16^{2}S, 16^{2}S, 20^{0}GS, 16^{1}HY, 20^{1}GS, 19^{3}GS

	Starts	1st	2nd	3rd	Win & Pl
Chases	7	3	2	1	22694
Career Total	**28**	**6**	**7**	**4**	**33506**

128	3/02	Newb	2m4f	D(0-125)HCh	G-S	£9512
126	1/02	Towc	2m110y	D(0-120)HCh	HVY	£5083
116	5/01	Extr	2m3f110y	F(0-95)HCh	G-S	£3248
110	1/99	Font	2m6f110y	F(0-110)HHdl	SFT	£2845
113	6/97	Sthl	2m	H NHF	G-S	£1203
113	5/97	Uttx	2m	H NHF	G-F	£1287

Total win prize-money £23178

Going: Sf: 1-3 GS: 2-4 Gd: 0-0 GF: - Fm: 0-0
Distance: 2m/2m3: 1-3 **2m4-2m7: 2-4** 3m+: 0-0
Track: LH: 1-2 **RH: 2-5** Tight: 0-0 **Gall: 1-2**
Aids: Bl: 0-0 Vi: 0-0 Tstrap: 0-0
Best Rating: **130** 3/02 Chep 2m3f110y gd-sft Ch

Often in the frame, he has not always been the most reliable jumper but has looked improved in that respect early in 2002, winning twice over fences. Improving, he is effective at up to two and a half miles. Best with give.

Stormin' Native (IRE)

105(113h) (112h)**142**

7-y-o b/br g Be My Native (USA)-Vermont Angel (Lucifer (USA))

A Crook Turner Technology Ltd

Placings:2133-**312351F** **(4878)**

2001/02: 17^{3}G, 20^{1}GS, 20^{2}S, 20^{3}HY, 20^{5}S, 22^{1}G, 24^{F}G

	Starts	1st	2nd	3rd	Win & Pl
Chases	7	2	1	2	14424
Career Total	**11**	**3**	**2**	**4**	**18921**

142	3/02	Hayd	2m6f	D Ch	GD	£5791
129	11/01	Ayr	2m4f	D Ch	G-S	£5080
112	2/01	Catt	2m3f	D Hdl	SFT	£2905

Total win prize-money £13776

Going: Sf: 0-3 GS: 1-1 Gd: 1-3 GF: - Fm: 0-0
Distance: 2m/2m3: 0-1 **2m4-2m7: 2-5** 3m+: 0-1
Track: **LH: 1-5** RH: 0-1 Tight: 0-1 Gall: 0-1
Aids: Bl: 0-0 Vi: 0-0 Tstrap: 0-0
Best Rating: **142** 3/02 Hayd 2m6f good Ch

A winner over fences, he acted on a soft surface andwas suited by two miles four furlongs. A bold jumper, he sadly broke a knee at Perth in April 2002. (DEAD)

Stormy Affair (IRE)

94 **72**

7-y-o br m Glacial Storm (USA)-Elect (New Member)

R M Beckett The Half Monty Partnership

Placings:*66*060P4 **(4236)**

2001/02: 16^{6}S, 17^{6}GF, 16^{0}G, 16^{6}S, 19^{0}HY, 22^{P}G, 21^{4}GF

	Starts	1st	2nd	3rd	Win & Pl
NH Flat	2	0	0	0	0
Hurdles	5	0	0	0	0
Career Total	**7**	**0**	**0**	**0**	**0**

Going: Sf: 0-3 GS: 0-0 Gd: 0-2 GF: - Fm: 0-2
Distance: 2m/2m3: 0-4 2m4-2m7: 0-3 3m+: 0-0
Track: LH: 0-1 RH: 0-6 Tight: 0-0 Gall: 0-1
Aids: Bl: 0-0 Vi: 0-0 Tstrap: 0-0
Best Rating: **95** 11/01 Hayd 2m soft NHF

Has achieved little over hurdles to date.

Stormy Beech

79 **42**

6-y-o b g Glacial Storm (USA)-Cheeny's Brig (New Brig)

B Mactaggart R J Cowper

Placings:*0*-P00 **(4689)**

2001/02: 20^{P}HY, 20^{0}GF, 16^{0}GF

	Starts	1st	2nd	3rd	Win & Pl
Hurdles	3	0	0	0	
Career Total	**4**	**0**	**0**	**0**	

Going: Sf: 0-1 GS: 0-0 Gd: 0-0 GF: - Fm: 0-2
Distance: 2m/2m3: 0-1 2m4-2m7: 0-2 3m+: 0-0
Track: LH: 0-1 RH: 0-1 Tight: 0-2 Gall: 0-0
Aids: Bl: 0-0 Vi: 0-0 Tstrap: 0-0
Best Rating: **45** 4/02 Kels 2m110y gd fm Hdl

Stormy Glen (IRE)

72f **63f**

6-y-o b/br g Glacial Storm (USA)-Glenwood Lass (Furry Glen)

Ms A E Embiricos The Rogerson Partnership

Placings:*0* **(0032)**

2001/02: 16^{0}G

	Starts	1st	2nd	3rd	Win & Pl
NH Flat	1	0	0	0	
Career Total	**1**	**0**	**0**	**0**	

Going: Sf: 0-0 GS: 0-0 Gd: 0-1 GF: - Fm: 0-0
Distance: 2m/2m3: 0-1 2m4-2m7: 0-0 3m+: 0-0
Track: LH: 0-0 RH: 0-1 Tight: 0-0 Gall: 0-1
Aids: Bl: 0-0 Vi: 0-0 Tstrap: 0-0
Best Rating: **63** 5/01 Hntg 2m110y good NHF

Stormy Lord (IRE)

103 **105**

6-y-o br g Lord Americo-Decent Shower (Decent Fellow)

J Wade John Wade

Placings:00-323 **(4894)**

2001/02: 16^{3}S, 17^{2}GS, 16^{3}G

	Starts	1st	2nd	3rd	Win & Pl
Hurdles	3	0	1	2	1955
Career Total	**5**	**0**	**1**	**2**	**1955**

Going: Sf: 0-1 GS: 0-1 Gd: 0-1 GF: - Fm: 0-0
Distance: 2m/2m3: 0-3 2m4-2m7: 0-0 3m+: 0-0
Track: LH: 0-1 RH: 0-2 Tight: 0-0 Gall: 0-0
Aids: Bl: 0-0 Vi: 0-0 Tstrap: 0-0
Best Rating: **105** 3/02 Carl 2m1f gd-sft Hdl

Stormy Pass

81 **36**

5-y-o b g Dolphin Street (FR)-Noble Choice (Dahar (USA))

P R Webber Mrs P Sherwood

Placings:*00*0P **(2332)**

2001/02: 17^{0}GS, 17^{0}GF, 20^{0}G, 21^{P}G

	Starts	1st	2nd	3rd	Win & Pl
NH Flat	2	0	0	0	0
Hurdles	2	0	0	0	0
Career Total	**4**	**0**	**0**	**0**	

Going: Sf: 0-0 GS: 0-1 Gd: 0-2 GF: - Fm: 0-1
Distance: 2m/2m3: 0-2 2m4-2m7: 0-2 3m+: 0-0
Track: LH: 0-2 RH: 0-0 Tight: 0-3 Gall: 0-0
Aids: Bl: 0-0 Vi: 0-0 Tstrap: 0-0
Best Rating: **86** 5/01 Folk 2m1f110y gd-sft NHF

Stormy Session

79(90c) (64c)**22**

12-y-o b g Celestial Storm (USA)-No Jazz (Jaazeiro (USA))

M F Harris (R Williams 13/6) M Harris

Placings:*60*/P/40P6/25420/**2PPF/312306/UR0F-S0**0 **(2926)**

2001/02: 24^{S}GF, 24^{0}GF, 24^{0}GS

	Starts	1st	2nd	3rd	Win & Pl
Hurdles	1	0	0	0	0
Chases	2	0	0	0	0
Career Total	**29**	**1**	**4**	**2**	**10502**

109	5/99	Strf	2m5f110y	D(0-110)HCh	GD	£4315

Total win prize-money £4315

Going: Sf: 0-0 GS: 0-1 Gd: 0-0 GF: - Fm: 0-2
Distance: 2m/2m3: 0-0 2m4-2m7: 0-0 3m+: 0-3
Track: LH: 0-2 RH: 0-1 Tight: 0-3 Gall: 0-0
Aids: Bl: 0-0 Vi: 0-1 Tstrap: 0-0
Best Rating: **109** 5/99 Uttx 3m2f gd-fm Ch

Stormy Skye (IRE)

106 **122**

6-y-o b g Bluebird (USA)-Canna (Caerleon (USA))

G L Moore Mrs J Moore,Mrs J Agnew,T Pollock

Placings:435122/102P-36300536 **(4136)**

2001/02: 19^{3}GF, 16^{6}G, 18^{3}G, 21^{0}G, 20^{0}G, 21^{5}GS, 22^{3}S, 22^{6}GS

	Starts	1st	2nd	3rd	Win & Pl
Hurdles	8	0	0	3	2993
Career Total	**18**	**2**	**3**	**4**	**20368**

122	11/00	Asct	2m110y	C(0-135)HHdl	SFT	£8365
108	2/00	Plum	2m	E Hdl	SFT	£2534

Total win prize-money £10900

Going: Sf: 0-1 GS: 0-2 Gd: 0-4 GF: - Fm: 0-1
Distance: 2m/2m3: 0-2 2m4-2m7: 0-6 3m+: 0-0
Track: LH: 0-3 RH: 0-4 Tight: 0-4 Gall: 0-0
Aids: Bl: 0-7 Vi: 0-0 Tstrap: 0-8
Best Rating: **125** 2/01 Kemp 2m5f gd-sft Hdl

A formerly useful handicap hurdler who has become slightly disappointing. Stays two and three-quarter miles, acts on soft ground.

Stormy Voyage

73 **13**

4-y-o b g Storm Bird (CAN)-Vividimagination (USA) (Raise A Man (USA))

J M Bradley (K R Burke 30/6) John Brookman

Placings:P0 (4724)
2001/02: 17PGF, 160GF

	Starts	1st	2nd	3rd	Win & Pl
Hurdles	2	0	0	0	
Career Total	**2**	**0**	**0**	**0**	

Going: Sf: 0-0 GS: 0-0 Gd: 0-0 GF: - Fm: 0-2
Distance: 2m/2m3: 0-2 2m4-2m7: 0-0 3m+: 0-0
Track: LH: 0-1 RH: 0-1 Tight: 0-0 Gall: 0-0
Aids: Bl: 0-0 Vi: 0-0 Tstrap: 0-0
Best Rating: 13 4/02 Chep 2m110y gd-fm Hdl

Straffan Gold (USA)

96 **72**

8-y-o b g Lear Fan (USA)-Oro Bianco (USA) (Lyphard's Wish (FR))
J C Fox Shirley M & Peter G Palmer

Placings:P0P/01F220P4/00PP060 (2711)
2001/02: 160G, 190GS, 24PGF, 24PS, 200HY, 166GS, 160HY

	Starts	1st	2nd	3rd	Win & Pl
Hurdles	7	0	0	0	0
Career Total	**18**	**1**	**2**	**0**	**3037**

83 11/98 MRas 2m3f110y G(0-90)HHdl HVY £1548
Total win prize-money £1548

Going: Sf: 0-3 GS: 0-2 Gd: 0-1 GF: - Fm: 0-1
Distance: 2m/2m3: 0-4 2m4-2m7: 0-1 3m+: 0-2
Track: LH: 0-1 RH: 0-6 Tight: 0-1 Gall: 0-0
Aids: Bl: 0-5 Vi: 0-0 Tstrap: 0-0
Best Rating: 85 12/98 Catt 2m good Hdl

Straight On (IRE)

11-y-o b/br g Tremblant-Maybird (Royalty)
Mrs A Hodge Gerard Cashin

Placings:0/00003/104O0612/2U31/4P (4852)
2001/02: 244G, 24PG

	Starts	1st	2nd	3rd	Win & Pl
Chases	2	0	0	0	0
Career Total	**20**	**3**	**2**	**2**	**8770**

107 2/98 Fknm 3m110y D Ch GD £3313
96 9/96 Dpat 2m1f172y (0-102)HHdl FRM £1765
94 5/96 Dpat 2m6f Hdl G-F £1588
Total win prize-money £6667

Going: Sf: 0-0 GS: 0-0 Gd: 0-2 GF: - Fm: 0-0
Distance: 2m/2m3: 0-0 2m4-2m7: 0-0 3m+: 0-2
Track: LH: 0-2 RH: 0-0 Tight: 0-2 Gall: 0-0
Aids: Bl: 0-0 Vi: 0-0 Tstrap: 0-0
Best Rating: 111 1/98 Hntg 3m gd-sft Ch

Straighttothebar

94 **90**

6-y-o b g Perpendicular-Willow Path (Farm Walk)
Miss Lucinda V Russell The Onefortheroad Partnership

Placings:00P-0P2P0P (4880)
2001/02: 200GS, 22PGS, 162GS, 16PGS, 160GF, 20PG

	Starts	1st	2nd	3rd	Win & Pl
Hurdles	6	0	1	0	742
Career Total	**9**	**0**	**1**	**0**	**742**

Going: Sf: 0-0 GS: 0-4 Gd: 0-1 GF: - Fm: 0-1
Distance: 2m/2m3: 0-3 2m4-2m7: 0-3 3m+: 0-0
Track: LH: 0-3 RH: 0-2 Tight: 0-2 Gall: 0-0
Aids: Bl: 0-0 Vi: 0-0 Tstrap: 0-0
Best Rating: 94 10/00 Sedg 2m1f gd-sft NHF

Modest hurdler.

Strain The Rein

90 **92**

7-y-o b g Petoski-Valls D'Andorra (Free State)
Ian Williams Mrs Belinda Harvey

Placings:061/20-00 (2282)
2001/02: 160G, 200G

	Starts	1st	2nd	3rd	Win & Pl
Hurdles	2	0	0	0	
Career Total	**7**	**1**	**1**	**0**	**2500**

107 4/00 Hexm 2m H NHF GD £1883
Total win prize-money £1883

Going: Sf: 0-0 GS: 0-0 Gd: 0-2 GF: - Fm: 0-0
Distance: 2m/2m3: 0-1 2m4-2m7: 0-1 3m+: 0-0
Track: LH: 0-1 RH: 0-1 Tight: 0-0 Gall: 0-0
Aids: Bl: 0-0 Vi: 0-0 Tstrap: 0-1
Best Rating: 114 2/01 Hayd 2m soft NHF

Strait Talking (FR)

93 **88**

4-y-o b g Bering-Servia (Le Marmot (FR))
Jedd O'Keeffe (S Dow 6/9) E Rider

Placings:040 (3552)
2001/02: 160GS, 164S, 160S

	Starts	1st	2nd	3rd	Win & Pl
Hurdles	3	0	0	0	0
Career Total	**3**	**0**	**0**	**0**	**0**

Going: Sf: 0-2 GS: 0-1 Gd: 0-0 GF: - Fm: 0-0
Distance: 2m/2m3: 0-3 2m4-2m7: 0-0 3m+: 0-0
Track: LH: 0-3 RH: 0-0 Tight: 0-1 Gall: 0-1
Aids: Bl: 0-0 Vi: 0-0 Tstrap: 0-0
Best Rating: 88 1/02 Newc 2m soft Hdl

Novice hurdler, he failed to trouble the judges in his first three starts on soft ground.

Stratco (IRE)

103(99h) (111h)**138**

8-y-o b/br g Satco (FR)-No Slow (King's Ride)
W W Dennis W W Dennis

Placings:000/25/P0-03102140 (3483)
2001/02: 220F, 223G, 221GF, 200G, 222G, 191GF, 194GF, 170HY

	Starts	1st	2nd	3rd	Win & Pl
Hurdles	8	2	1	1	7642
Career Total	**15**	**2**	**2**	**1**	**8282**

111 10/01 Extr 2m3f E(0-105)HHdl G-F £2730
110 6/01 NAbb 2m6f D Hdl G-F £3241
Total win prize-money £5972

Going: Sf: 0-1 GS: 0-0 Gd: 0-3 GF: - Fm: 2-4
Distance: 2m/2m3: 1-3 2m4-2m7: 1-5 3m+: 0-0
Track: LH: 1-5 RH: 1-2 Tight: 1-3 Gall: 0-1
Aids: Bl: 0-0 Vi: 0-0 Tstrap: 0-0
Best Rating: 111 10/01 Extr 2m3f gd-fm Hdl

Fair staying hurdler. Made quite an impressive start over fences when winning at Exeter May 2002 over two miles seven and a half furlong.. Acts on fast ground.

Stratford House (IRE)

(54h)

8-y-o ch g Good Thyne (USA)-Keep The Faith (Furry Glen)
C Grant Mrs J D Percy

Placings:30P/0-P (4856)
2001/02: 25PG

	Starts	1st	2nd	3rd	Win & Pl
Chases	1	0	0	0	
Career Total	**5**	**0**	**0**	**1**	**455**

Going: Sf: 0-0 GS: 0-0 Gd: 0-1 GF: - Fm: 0-0
Distance: 2m/2m3: 0-0 2m4-2m7: 0-0 3m+: 0-1
Track: LH: 0-1 RH: 0-0 Tight: 0-0 Gall: 0-0
Aids: Bl: 0-0 Vi: 0-0 Tstrap: 0-0
Best Rating: 62 11/99 Hayd 2m4f good Hdl

Strath Fillan

91 **73**

4-y-o b f Dolphin Street (FR)-Adarama (IRE) (Persian Bold)
W J Musson Mrs P A Linton

Placings:0 (4237)
2001/02: 160GF

	Starts	1st	2nd	3rd	Win & Pl
Hurdles	1	0	0	0	
Career Total	**1**	**0**	**0**	**0**	

Going: Sf: 0-0 GS: 0-0 Gd: 0-0 GF: - Fm: 0-1
Distance: 2m/2m3: 0-1 2m4-2m7: 0-0 3m+: 0-0
Track: LH: 0-0 RH: 0-1 Tight: 0-0 Gall: 0-1
Aids: Bl: 0-0 Vi: 0-0 Tstrap: 0-0
Best Rating: 73 3/02 Hntg 2m110y gd-fm Hdl

Stravmour

70f **80f**

6-y-o ch h Seymour Hicks (FR)-La Stravaganza (Slip Anchor)
R Hollinshead E Bennion

Placings:0-0 (0239)
2001/02: 160GF

	Starts	1st	2nd	3rd	Win & Pl
NH Flat	1	0	0	0	
Career Total	**2**	**0**	**0**	**0**	

Going: Sf: 0-0 GS: 0-0 Gd: 0-0 GF: - Fm: 0-1
Distance: 2m/2m3: 0-1 2m4-2m7: 0-0 3m+: 0-0
Track: LH: 0-1 RH: 0-0 Tight: 0-1 Gall: 0-0
Aids: Bl: 0-0 Vi: 0-0 Tstrap: 0-0
Best Rating: 80 4/01 MRas 1m5f110y gd-sft NHF

Strawberry Hill (IRE)

95 **82**

8-y-o b g Lancastrian-Tudor Lady (Green Shoon)
A Scott Andy Scott

Placings:546P (4307)
2001/02: 205G, 274GS, 276S, 24PS

	Starts	1st	2nd	3rd	Win & Pl
Hurdles	4	0	0	0	0
Career Total	**4**	**0**	**0**	**0**	**0**

Going: Sf: 0-2 GS: 0-1 Gd: 0-1 GF: - Fm: 0-0
Distance: 2m/2m3: 0-0 2m4-2m7: 0-1 3m+: 0-3
Track: LH: 0-3 RH: 0-1 Tight: 0-2 Gall: 0-0
Aids: Bl: 0-0 Vi: 0-0 Tstrap: 0-0
Best Rating: 82 9/01 Prth 2m4f110y good Hdl

Strawman

90(96h) (79h)79

5-y-o b g Ela-Mana-Mou-Oatfield (Great Nephew)
J G Given J E Titley

Placings:44P4P-60660 (4162)
2001/02: 19^6GF, 17^0G, 21^6GS, 16^6GS, 20^0G

	Starts	1st	2nd	3rd	Win & Pl
Hurdles	4	0	0	0	0
Chases	1	0	0	0	0
Career Total	**10**	**0**	**0**	**0**	**462**

Going: Sf: 0-0 GS: 0-2 Gd: 0-2 GF: - Fm: 0-1
Distance: 2m/2m3: 0-2 2m4-2m7: 0-3 3m+: 0-0
Track: LH: 0-2 RH: 0-2 Tight: 0-3 Gall: 0-0
Aids: Bl: 0-0 Vi: 0-0 Tstrap: 0-0
Best Rating: 90 12/00 Fknm 2m gd-sft Hdl

Well held in modest company over hurdles and on his chasing debut.

Streamsforth Lad (IRE)

77f 88f

5-y-o b g Be My Native (USA)-Protrial (Proverb)
S A Brookshaw T G K Construction Ltd

Placings:*00* (4713a)
2001/02: 16^0GF, 16^0Y

	Starts	1st	2nd	3rd	Win & Pl
NH Flat	2	0	0	0	
Career Total	**2**	**0**	**0**	**0**	

Going: Sf: 0-0 GS: 0-0 Gd: 0-0 GF: - Fm: 0-1
Distance: 2m/2m3: 0-2 2m4-2m7: 0-0 3m+: 0-0
Track: LH: 0-0 RH: 0-2 Tight: 0-0 Gall: 0-1
Aids: Bl: 0-0 Vi: 0-0 Tstrap: 0-0
Best Rating: 88 3/02 Hntg 2m110y gd-fm NHF

Streamstown (IRE)

111 159

8-y-o b/br g Rashar (USA)-Lady Torsil (Torus)
Ferdy Murphy Haydock Park National Hunt Partnership

Placings:*3104*100/540551212/4F21115-56P1P0 (4677)
2001/02: 25^5G, 26^6S, 25^PGS, 28^1HY, 34^PHY, 36^0G

	Starts	1st	2nd	3rd	Win & Pl
Chases	6	1	0	0	43350
Career Total	**29**	**8**	**3**	**1**	**87969**

159	2/02	Uttx	3m4f	A HCh	HVY	£40600
154	1/01	Weth	3m1f	B HCh	G-S	£10056
153	11/00	Hayd	3m	E(0-115)HCh	HVY	£3510
138	11/00	Aint	2m4f	D(0-125)HCh	G-S	£7280
112	3/00	Clon	2m6f	Ch	G-Y	£4416
108	2/00	Punc	2m4f	(0-116)HCh	SFT	£4968
110	3/99	Gowr	2m4f	Hdl	YLD	£2700
104	1/99	Naas	2m	NHF	HVY	£2762

Total win prize-money £76294

Going: Sf: 1-3 GS: 0-1 Gd: 0-2 GF: - Fm: 0-0
Distance: 2m/2m3: 0-0 2m4-2m7: 0-0 **3m+: 1-6**
Track: **LH: 1-6** RH: 0-0 Tight: 0-1 Gall: 0-1
Aids: Bl: 0-0 Vi: 0-0 Tstrap: 0-0
Best Rating: 159 2/02 Uttx 3m4f heavy Ch

A useful ex-Irish chaser, after falling at Aintree on his British debut in 2000, he improved to win three in a row, including a valuable Wetherby handicap. His limitations were exposedin top handicaps, but testing conditions saw him win the National Trial at Uttoxeter in February 2002. Stays three miles plus. Acts on soft ground.

Street Fighter (FR)

7-y-o b g Subotica (FR)-American Order (USA) (Slew O'Gold (USA))
Ian Williams Tony Eaves

Placings:2P/0 (0341)
2001/02: 16^0G

	Starts	1st	2nd	3rd	Win & Pl
Hurdles	1	0	0	0	
Career Total	**3**	**0**	**1**	**0**	**681**

Going: Sf: 0-0 GS: 0-0 Gd: 0-1 GF: - Fm: 0-0
Distance: 2m/2m3: 0-1 2m4-2m7: 0-0 3m+: 0-0
Track: LH: 0-1 RH: 0-0 Tight: 0-1 Gall: 0-0
Aids: Bl: 0-0 Vi: 0-0 Tstrap: 0-0
Best Rating: 95 1/99 Tntn 2m1f soft Hdl

Street Magic (IRE)

87 62

5-y-o br m Jolly Jake (NZ)-Corrie's Duchess (IRE) (Burslem)
N A Twiston-Davies The Alchemists

Placings:*60*F5 (4575)
2001/02: 17^6G, 16^0GS, 24^FG, 20^5G

	Starts	1st	2nd	3rd	Win & Pl
NH Flat	2	0	0	0	0
Hurdles	2	0	0	0	0
Career Total	**4**	**0**	**0**	**0**	**0**

Going: Sf: 0-0 GS: 0-1 Gd: 0-3 GF: - Fm: 0-0
Distance: 2m/2m3: 0-2 2m4-2m7: 0-1 3m+: 0-1
Track: LH: 0-1 RH: 0-3 Tight: 0-0 Gall: 0-1
Aids: Bl: 0-0 Vi: 0-0 Tstrap: 0-0
Best Rating: 80 11/01 Hrfd 2m1f good NHF

Keen sort, poor form over hurdles.

Street Walker (IRE)

96 63

6-y-o b m Dolphin Street (FR)-Foolish Dame (USA) (Foolish Pleasure (USA))
W Storey D O Cremin

Placings:P500/05-646 (2510)
2001/02: 17^6G, 17^4S, 16^6S

	Starts	1st	2nd	3rd	Win & Pl
Hurdles	3	0	0	0	0
Career Total	**9**	**0**	**0**	**0**	**0**

Going: Sf: 0-2 GS: 0-0 Gd: 0-1 GF: - Fm: 0-0
Distance: 2m/2m3: 0-3 2m4-2m7: 0-0 3m+: 0-0
Track: LH: 0-3 RH: 0-0 Tight: 0-3 Gall: 0-0
Aids: Bl: 0-0 Vi: 0-0 Tstrap: 0-0
Best Rating: 63 11/01 Sedg 2m1f soft Hdl

Stretchit

102 99

12-y-o b g Full Extent (USA)-Snippet (Ragstone)
M Tate Mrs N J Bird

Placings:0/4052FFP/06/232/5/0530050 (1804)
2001/02: 25^0G, 28^5GF, 30^3G, 23^0GF, 25^0GF, 25^5G, 24^0GF

	Starts	1st	2nd	3rd	Win & Pl
Chases	7	0	0	1	854
Career Total	**21**	**0**	**3**	**2**	**2706**

Going: Sf: 0-0 GS: 0-0 Gd: 0-3 GF: - Fm: 0-4
Distance: 2m/2m3: 0-0 2m4-2m7: 0-0 3m+: 0-7
Track: LH: 0-3 RH: 0-4 Tight: 0-4 Gall: 0-0
Aids: Bl: 0-5 Vi: 0-0 Tstrap: 0-0
Best Rating: 99 5/01 Bang 3m6f good Ch

Strictly Hard

8-y-o b m Reprimand-Formidable Dancer (Formidable (USA))
P Monteith P Monteith

Placings:P/PP (3554)
2001/02: 16^PS, 19^PS

	Starts	1st	2nd	3rd	Win & Pl
Chases	2	0	0	0	
Career Total	**3**	**0**	**0**	**0**	

Going: Sf: 0-2 GS: 0-0 Gd: 0-0 GF: - Fm: 0-0
Distance: 2m/2m3: 0-2 2m4-2m7: 0-0 3m+: 0-0
Track: LH: 0-2 RH: 0-0 Tight: 0-1 Gall: 0-1
Aids: Bl: 0-0 Vi: 0-0 Tstrap: 0-0
Best Rating:

Strictly Speaking (IRE)

106 112

5-y-o b g Sri Pekan (USA)-Gaijin (Caerleon (USA))
P F I Cole P F I Cole Ltd

Placings:0340 (3882)
2001/02: 16^0G, 19^3GS, 20^4S, 16^0GS

	Starts	1st	2nd	3rd	Win & Pl
Hurdles	4	0	0	1	682
Career Total	**4**	**0**	**0**	**1**	**682**

Going: Sf: 0-1 GS: 0-2 Gd: 0-1 GF: - Fm: 0-0
Distance: 2m/2m3: 0-3 2m4-2m7: 0-1 3m+: 0-0
Track: LH: 0-2 RH: 0-2 Tight: 0-0 Gall: 0-2
Aids: Bl: 0-0 Vi: 0-0 Tstrap: 0-0
Best Rating: 112 1/02 Newb 2m3f gd-sft Hdl

A winner on the Flat, he stays two miles three furlongs over hurdles and acts on good to soft ground.

Stride To Glory (IRE)

11-y-o b g Superpower-Damira (FR) (Pharly (FR))
Miss Joanne Tremain (Mrs H M Arnold 2/4) Nigel Hooper

Placings:2P (4852)
2001/02: 20^2GF, 24^PG

	Starts	1st	2nd	3rd	Win & Pl
Chases	2	0	1	0	382
Career Total	**2**	**0**	**1**	**0**	**382**

Going: Sf: 0-0 GS: 0-0 Gd: 0-1 GF: - Fm: 0-1
Distance: 2m/2m3: 0-0 2m4-2m7: 0-1 3m+: 0-1
Track: LH: 0-2 RH: 0-0 Tight: 0-1 Gall: 0-0

Aids: Bl: 0-2 Vi: 0-0 Tstrap: 0-0
Best Rating: 88 5/01 Hexm 2m4f110y gd-fm Ch

Strike Accord (IRE)

103(91h) (68h)**103**

8-y-o br g Accordion-Ritual Girl (Ballad Rock)
I A Wood A Rybak

Placings:*0*/0-PP0**24PP00** **(4849)**
2001/02: 25^{P}G, 24^{P}G, 17^{0}G, 17^{2}S, 17^{4}G, 21^{P}S, 20^{P}HY, 20^{0}GF, 24^{0}G

	Starts	1st	2nd	3rd	Win & Pl
Hurdles	3	0	0	0	0
Chases	6	0	1	0	1262
Career Total	**11**	**0**	**1**	**0**	**1262**

Going: Sf: 0-3 GS: 0-0 Gd: 0-5 GF: - Fm: 0-1
Distance: 2m/2m3: 0-3 2m4-2m7: 0-3 3m+: 0-3
Track: LH: 0-5 RH: 0-3 Tight: 0-6 Gall: 0-0
Aids: Bl: 0-0 Vi: 0-0 Tstrap: 0-0
Best Rating: 103 12/01 Plum 2m1f good Ch

Moderate over hurdles, although he has shaped with a little promise over fences.

Strike Camp

8-y-o b/br g Nomadic Way (USA)-Purple Streak (Majestic Streak)
Mrs P Sly Sir Stephen Hastings

Placings:P **(0641)**
2001/02: 24^{P}GF

	Starts	1st	2nd	3rd	Win & Pl
Hurdles	1	0	0	0	
Career Total	**1**	**0**	**0**	**0**	

Going: Sf: 0-0 GS: 0-0 Gd: 0-0 GF: - Fm: 0-1
Distance: 2m/2m3: 0-0 2m4-2m7: 0-0 3m+: 0-1
Track: LH: 0-0 RH: 0-1 Tight: 0-1 Gall: 0-0
Aids: Bl: 0-0 Vi: 0-0 Tstrap: 0-0
Best Rating:

Strip Search

77 **46**

6-y-o b m Bluebird (USA)-Swift Pursuit (Posse (USA))
J G Smyth-Osbourne J G Smyth-Osbourne

Placings:400/03450-6 **(0122)**
2001/02: 19^{6}F

	Starts	1st	2nd	3rd	Win & Pl
Hurdles	1	0	0	0	0
Career Total	**9**	**0**	**0**	**1**	**483**

Going: Sf: 0-0 GS: 0-0 Gd: 0-0 GF: - Fm: 0-1
Distance: 2m/2m3: 0-0 2m4-2m7: 0-1 3m+: 0-0
Track: LH: 0-0 RH: 0-1 Tight: 0-1 Gall: 0-0
Aids: Bl: 0-0 Vi: 0-0 Tstrap: 0-0
Best Rating: 78 8/00 Sedg 2m1f good Hdl

Stromian House (IRE)

72

6-y-o br g Rock Hopper-Strike Home (Be My Guest (USA))
A D Smith (Miss Venetia Williams 11/6) David M Williams

Placings:*00*-0P **(4861)**
2001/02: 17^{0}G, 22^{P}F

	Starts	1st	2nd	3rd	Win & Pl
NH Flat	1	0	0	0	0
Hurdles	1	0	0	0	0
Career Total	**4**	**0**	**0**	**0**	

Going: Sf: 0-0 GS: 0-0 Gd: 0-1 GF: - Fm: 0-1
Distance: 2m/2m3: 0-1 2m4-2m7: 0-1 3m+: 0-0
Track: LH: 0-1 RH: 0-0 Tight: 0-1 Gall: 0-0
Aids: Bl: 0-0 Vi: 0-0 Tstrap: 0-0
Best Rating: 81 5/00 Hntg 2m110y gd-sft NHF

Stromness (USA)

113 **147**

5-y-o ch g Trempolino (USA)-Caithness (USA) (Roberto (USA))
A King Lady Harris

Placings:5225-25112241 **(4665)**
2001/02: 20^{2}G, 20^{5}GS, 22^{1}G, 21^{1}GS, 24^{2}S, 20^{2}S, 21^{4}GS, 24^{1}G

	Starts	1st	2nd	3rd	Win & Pl
Hurdles	8	3	3	0	56825
Career Total	**12**	**3**	**5**	**0**	**61662**

147	4/02	Aint	3m110y	A Hdl	GD	£34800
130	1/02	Kemp	2m5f	D Hdl	G-S	£5073
121	1/02	Font	2m6f110y	E Hdl	GD	£2730

Total win prize-money £42603

Going: Sf: 0-2 GS: 1-3 Gd: 2-3 GF: - Fm: 0-0
Distance: 2m/2m3: 0-0 **2m4-2m7: 2-6** 3m+: 1-2
Track: **LH: 2-6** RH: 1-1 **Tight: 2-4** Gall: 0-2
Aids: Bl: 0-0 Vi: 0-0 Tstrap: 0-0
Best Rating: 147 4/02 Aint 3m110y good Hdl

A small individual, he improved for a step up in trip, getting off the mark over two miles-six at Fontwell early in 2002 and following up at Kempton. Good efforts in defeat subsequently including when fourth in the Coral Cup at the Festival and was stepped up to three miles when successful in a Grade One novice event at Aintree. Handles most types of ground.

Strong Arrow (IRE)

101(79c) **95**

9-y-o b g Strong Gale-Caesonia (Buckskin (FR))
Ferdy Murphy Exors Of The Late Mr G A Hubbard

Placings:*2*/6P2/4F21P3F5/P100F-3 **(2110)**
2001/02: 22^{3}S

	Starts	1st	2nd	3rd	Win & Pl
Hurdles	1	0	0	1	429
Career Total	**18**	**2**	**3**	**2**	**11361**

131	10/00	Sthl	2m4f110y	F(0-110)HCh	SFT	£2723
131	1/00	Wwck	2m4f	D Ch	SFT	£4631

Total win prize-money £7355

Going: Sf: 0-1 GS: 0-0 Gd: 0-0 GF: - Fm: 0-0
Distance: 2m/2m3: 0-0 2m4-2m7: 0-1 3m+: 0-0
Track: LH: 0-0 RH: 0-1 Tight: 0-1 Gall: 0-0
Aids: Bl: 0-0 Vi: 0-0 Tstrap: 0-0
Best Rating: 131 10/00 Sthl 2m4f110y soft Ch

An unreliable jumper of fences, he stays three miles and goes well on soft ground.

Strong Brew (IRE)

10-y-o br g Strong Gale-Teapot Hall (Royal Buck)
J Porter J Perriss

Placings:3/46/0P0056/0F0-P **(0321)**
2001/02: 26^{P}G

	Starts	1st	2nd	3rd	Win & Pl
Chases	1	0	0	0	
Career Total	**13**	**0**	**0**	**1**	**164**

Going: Sf: 0-0 GS: 0-0 Gd: 0-1 GF: - Fm: 0-0
Distance: 2m/2m3: 0-0 2m4-2m7: 0-0 3m+: 0-1
Track: LH: 0-0 RH: 0-1 Tight: 0-1 Gall: 0-0
Aids: Bl: 0-0 Vi: 0-0 Tstrap: 0-1
Best Rating: 96 10/98 Strf 2m110y good Hdl

Strong Chairman (IRE)

11-y-o br g Strong Gale-The Furnituremaker (Mandalus)
R Waley-Cohen Robert Waley-Cohen

Placings:214P/2400/45/3-P **(4826)**
2001/02: 26^{P}G

	Starts	1st	2nd	3rd	Win & Pl
Chases	1	0	0	0	
Career Total	**12**	**1**	**2**	**1**	**13699**

132	11/97	Newb	3m	C Ch	G-S	£5672

Total win prize-money £5672

Going: Sf: 0-0 GS: 0-0 Gd: 0-1 GF: - Fm: 0-0
Distance: 2m/2m3: 0-0 2m4-2m7: 0-0 3m+: 0-1
Track: LH: 0-1 RH: 0-0 Tight: 0-0 Gall: 0-1
Aids: Bl: 0-0 Vi: 0-0 Tstrap: 0-0
Best Rating: 134 11/98 Chel 3m3f110y good Ch

Strong Decision (IRE)

99f **108f**

5-y-o br g Mandalus-Francois's Crumpet (IRE) (Strong Gale)
W Jarvis M C Banks

Placings:*504* **(3368)**
2001/02: 16^{5}S, 16^{0}G, 16^{4}GS

	Starts	1st	2nd	3rd	Win & Pl
NH Flat	3	0	0	0	0
Career Total	**3**	**0**	**0**	**0**	**0**

Going: Sf: 0-1 GS: 0-1 Gd: 0-1 GF: - Fm: 0-0
Distance: 2m/2m3: 0-3 2m4-2m7: 0-0 3m+: 0-0
Track: LH: 0-3 RH: 0-0 Tight: 0-1 Gall: 0-1
Aids: Bl: 0-0 Vi: 0-0 Tstrap: 0-0
Best Rating: 108 12/01 Newb 2m110y good NHF

Has shown ability in bumpers. Looks suited by a sound surface.

Strong Finish

96 **77**

7-y-o ch g Montelimar (USA)-Atlantic View (Crash Course)
P W Hiatt Paul Porter

Placings:*00*P-0400 **(1492)**
2001/02: 22^{0}G, 22^{4}GF, 22^{0}G, 26^{0}G

	Starts	1st	2nd	3rd	Win & Pl
Hurdles	4	0	0	0	0
Career Total	**7**	**0**	**0**	**0**	**0**

Going: Sf: 0-0 GS: 0-0 Gd: 0-3 GF: - Fm: 0-1
Distance: 2m/2m3: 0-0 2m4-2m7: 0-3 3m+: 0-1
Track: LH: 0-3 RH: 0-1 Tight: 0-3 Gall: 0-1
Aids: Bl: 0-0 Vi: 0-0 Tstrap: 0-1
Best Rating: 77 8/01 Strf 2m6f110y gd-fm Hdl

Strong King (IRE)

(91h) (2h)

8-y-o b/br g Strong Gale-Mrs Simpson (Kinglet)
R Ford (Mrs Carrie Ford 21/4) D W Watson

Placings:00/0-P (0276)
2001/02: 24^{P}GF

	Starts	1st	2nd	3rd	Win & Pl
Hurdles	1	0	0	0	
Career Total	**4**	**0**	**0**	**0**	

Going: Sf: 0-0 GS: 0-0 Gd: 0-0 GF: - Fm: 0-1
Distance: 2m/2m3: 0-0 2m4-2m7: 0-0 3m+: 0-1
Track: LH: 0-0 RH: 0-1 Tight: 0-0 Gall: 0-0
Aids: Bl: 0-0 Vi: 0-0 Tstrap: 0-0
Best Rating: 69 1/01 Ayr 2m4f gd-sft Hdl

Strong Magic (IRE)

108 114

10-y-o br g Strong Gale-Baybush (Boreen (FR))
J R Cornwall J R Cornwall

Placings:00/5/503040/4536F542/30-B3FB1123220 (4635)
2001/02: 22^{B}GS, 22^{3}G, 20^{F}G, 24^{B}G, 24^{1}G, 25^{1}GS, 24^{2}GS, 22^{3}S, 24^{2}GS, 22^{2}GS, 19^{0}GF

	Starts	1st	2nd	3rd	Win & Pl
Chases	11	2	3	2	21125
Career Total	**30**	**2**	**4**	**5**	**24813**

110	11/01	Aint	3m1f	D(0-115)HCh	G-S	£10627
114	11/01	Hntg	3m	F(0-105)HCh	GD	£2625

Total win prize-money £13253

Going: Sf: 0-1 GS: 1-5 Gd: 1-4 GF: - Fm: 0-1
Distance: 2m/2m3: 0-0 2m4-2m7: 0-6 **3m+: 2-5**
Track: LH: 1-4 RH: 1-7 Tight: 1-5 Gall: 1-3
Aids: Bl: 0-0 Vi: 0-0 Tstrap: 0-0
Best Rating: 114 12/01 Sand 3m110y gd-sft Ch

Progressed well in the autumn of 2001, winning at Huntingdon and Aintree. Stays three miles. Best on a sound surface. Jumps well generally.

Strong Paladin (IRE)

115 137

11-y-o b g Strong Gale-Kalanshoe (Random Shot)
N A Gaselee Mrs Angela Brodie

Placings:50/6011/F53332/3F233/32334/312-1224 (3493)
2001/02: 22^{1}GS, 24^{2}G, 24^{2}G, 24^{4}S

	Starts	1st	2nd	3rd	Win & Pl
Chases	4	1	2	0	23190
Career Total	**29**	**4**	**6**	**10**	**51163**

137	10/01	Font	2m6f	D(0-120)HCh	G-S	£6922
119	10/00	Folk	3m1f	F(0-100)HCh	G-F	£2656
108	3/97	Font	2m2f110y	E Hdl	G-F	£2385
95	2/97	Tntn	2m3f110y	D Hdl	G-S	£2567

Total win prize-money £14531

Going: Sf: 0-1 GS: 1-1 Gd: 0-2 GF: - Fm: 0-0
Distance: 2m/2m3: 0-0 **2m4-2m7: 1-1** 3m+: 0-3
Track: LH: 0-1 RH: 0-2 **Tight: 1-1** Gall: 0-1
Aids: Bl: 0-0 Vi: 0-0 Tstrap: 0-0

Best Rating: 137 12/01 Kemp 3m good Ch

Fair chaser, he is a little one-paced, but he is an honest sort who generally jumps well, and improved during 2001. Acts on a fast and easy surface.

Strong Red Pine (IRE)

10-y-o br g Electric-Red Pine (Khalkis)
Mrs C Maude E D Bailey

Placings:0 (0227)
2001/02: 24^{0}GF

	Starts	1st	2nd	3rd	Win & Pl
Chases	1	0	0	0	
Career Total	**1**	**0**	**0**	**0**	

Going: Sf: 0-0 GS: 0-0 Gd: 0-0 GF: - Fm: 0-1
Distance: 2m/2m3: 0-0 2m4-2m7: 0-0 3m+: 0-1
Track: LH: 0-0 RH: 0-1 Tight: 0-0 Gall: 0-1
Aids: Bl: 0-0 Vi: 0-0 Tstrap: 0-0
Best Rating:

Strong Resolve (IRE)

101 100

6-y-o gr g Roselier (FR)-Farmerette (Teofane)
J Barclay Nigel Shepherd

Placings:62F3UP50 (4890)
2001/02: 16^{6}GS, 16^{2}S, 24^{F}HY, 20^{3}GS, 24^{U}HY, 24^{P}S, 20^{5}G, 24^{0}G

	Starts	1st	2nd	3rd	Win & Pl
NH Flat	1	0	0	0	0
Hurdles	7	0	1	1	1267
Career Total	**8**	**0**	**1**	**1**	**1267**

Going: Sf: 0-4 GS: 0-2 Gd: 0-2 GF: - Fm: 0-0
Distance: 2m/2m3: 0-2 2m4-2m7: 0-2 3m+: 0-4
Track: LH: 0-6 RH: 0-2 Tight: 0-1 Gall: 0-0
Aids: Bl: 0-0 Vi: 0-0 Tstrap: 0-0
Best Rating: 100 12/01 Ayr 2m soft Hdl

Has shown ability in hurdles on soft ground. Stays two and a half miles.

Strong Run (IRE)

115 (114h) 150

9-y-o b g Strong Gale-Arctic Run (Deep Run)
Noel Meade M D McGrath

Placings:225/33411/11FF/0010-1F411 (4938a)
2001/02: 17^{1}YS, 20^{F}S, 20^{4}GS, 16^{1}GY, 16^{1}YS

	Starts	1st	2nd	3rd	Win & Pl
Chases	5	3	0	0	65018
Career Total	**21**	**8**	**2**	**2**	**99345**

150	4/02	Punc	2m	Ch	Y-S	£38159
148	4/02	Fair	2m100y	HCh	G-Y	£15950
139	1/02	Navn	2m1f	(0-123)HCh	Y-S	£7407
137	2/01	Fair	2m4f	(0-140)HHdl	Y-S	£6677
115	11/99	Naas	2m	Ch	Y-S	£6589
133	10/99	Punc	2m	Ch	GD	£4312
125	4/99	Punc	2m	(0-135)HHdl	YLD	£8671
123	4/99	Fair	2m	Hdl	YLD	£6138

Total win prize-money £93908

Going: Sf: 0-1 GS: 0-1 Gd: 0-0 GF: - Fm: 0-0
Distance: **2m/2m3: 3-3** 2m4-2m7: 0-2 3m+: 0-0
Track: LH: 1-3 RH: 1-1 Tight: 0-0 Gall: 0-1
Aids: Bl: 0-0 Vi: 0-0 **Tstrap: 2-4**

Best Rating: 150 4/02 Punc 2m yld-sft Ch

Lightly-raced Irish chaser, stays two and a half miles, suited by cut in the ground. Progressive early in 2002, fourth in the Mildmay of Flete at Cheltenham, then won a good handicap at Fairyhouse before taking the grade One BMW Chase at Punchestown in April. Progressive.

Strong Tartan (IRE)

110 113

8-y-o br g Strong Gale-Kemchee (Kemal (FR))
A Parker Mr & Mrs Raymond Anderson Green

Placings:0153F/132F (4687)
2001/02: 21^{1}G, 24^{3}GF, 24^{2}S, 25^{F}GF

	Starts	1st	2nd	3rd	Win & Pl
Chases	4	1	1	1	5835
Career Total	**9**	**2**	**1**	**2**	**7885**

113	11/01	Ayr	2m5f110y	D(0-110)HCh	GD	£4251
100	1/00	Muss	2m	H NHF	SFT	£1599

Total win prize-money £5851

Going: Sf: 0-1 GS: 0-0 Gd: 1-1 GF: - Fm: 0-2
Distance: 2m/2m3: 0-0 **2m4-2m7: 1-1** 3m+: 0-3
Track: **LH: 1-2** RH: 0-2 Tight: 0-3 Gall: 0-0
Aids: Bl: 0-0 Vi: 0-0 Tstrap: 0-0
Best Rating: 113 1/02 Muss 3m soft Ch

He won a bumper on soft ground and won on his chasing debut on good ground. Stays three miles.

Strong Tel (IRE)

114

12-y-o b g Strong Gale-Arctic Snow Cat (Raise You Ten)
M C Pipe Terry Neill

Placings:00/33O/1320P4/3U1P4P/11111U/0FP-P0P (4266)
2001/02: 24^{P}G, 24^{0}GS, 29^{P}S

	Starts	1st	2nd	3rd	Win & Pl
Chases	3	0	0	0	
Career Total	**29**	**7**	**1**	**4**	**46834**

161	12/99	Chel	3m2f110y	B(0-140)HCh	SFT	£17993
153	12/99	Ling	3m	D(0-125)HCh	G-S	£3798
146	5/99	Uttx	3m2f	D Ch	G-F	£3712
148	5/99	Worc	2m7f110y	E Ch	G-F	£3500
137	5/99	Worc	2m7f110y	E Ch	G-S	£3661
116	2/99	Plum	3m1f110y	E Ch	G-S	£2835
117	11/97	Chep	2m4f110y	C Hdl	SFT	£3826

Total win prize-money £39328

Going: Sf: 0-1 GS: 0-1 Gd: 0-1 GF: - Fm: 0-0
Distance: 2m/2m3: 0-0 2m4-2m7: 0-0 3m+: 0-3
Track: LH: 0-3 RH: 0-0 Tight: 0-0 Gall: 0-2
Aids: Bl: 0-1 Vi: 0-0 Tstrap: 0-0
Best Rating: 161 12/99 Chel 3m2f110y soft Ch

Useful handicapper at best, he has been lightly raced in recent seasons and looks on the wane. Best at beyond three miles on fast ground.

Strong Vision (IRE)

91 119

11-y-o b g Strong Gale-Deep Vision (Deep Run)
K C Bailey I F W Buchan

Placings:2/F22/32/4PP (3360)
2001/02: 22^{4}HY, 25^{P}GS, 26^{P}HY

	Starts	1st	2nd	3rd	Win & Pl
Chases	3	0	0	0	446
Career Total	**9**	**0**	**4**	**1**	**7559**

Going: Sf: 0-2 GS: 0-1 Gd: 0-0 GF: - Fm: 0-0
Distance: 2m/2m3: 0-0 2m4-2m7: 0-1 3m+: 0-2
Track: LH: 0-2 RH: 0-1 Tight: 0-0 Gall: 0-0
Aids: Bl: 0-0 Vi: 0-0 Tstrap: 0-0
Best Rating: 130 12/99 Wwck 3m1f110y soft Ch

Fair chaser, stays three miles. Acts on soft, handles faster ground.

Strongtrooper (IRE)

99(74h) **116**

7-y-o b g Doubletour (USA)-Moss Gale (Strong Gale)
O Sherwood Beckwith, Milne, Munro Partnership

Placings:4/10-**FPF341F** (4851)
2001/02: 20^{F}G, 21^{P}G, 24^{F}G, 24^{3}G, 24^{4}GS, 21^{1}GS, 20^{F}G

	Starts	1st	2nd	3rd	Win & Pl
Chases	7	1	0	1	5627
Career Total	**10**	**2**	**0**	**1**	**8350**

99	4/02	Uttx	2m5f	E Ch	G-S	£4264
106	11/00	Ludl	2m5f	E Hdl	GD	£2723

Total win prize-money £6987

Going: Sf: 0-0 GS: 1-2 Gd: 0-5 GF: - Fm: 0-0
Distance: 2m/2m3: 0-0 **2m4-2m7: 1-4** 3m+: 0-3
Track: **LH: 1-4** RH: 0-3 Tight: 0-4 Gall: 0-0
Aids: Bl: 0-0 Vi: 0-0 Tstrap: 0-0
Best Rating: 116 12/01 Sthl 3m110y good Ch

Looked made for chasing when winning his hurdles debut in November 2000, but has not looked a natural over fences. Made the most of an easy opening at Uttoxeter at Easter 2002.

Struggles Glory (IRE)

109 **149**

11-y-o b g Kamehameha (USA)-Another Struggle (Cheval)
D C Robinson D C Robinson

Placings:11/2/2/41F/114-56100B (4677)
2001/02: 20^{5}GS, 24^{6}G, 25^{1}GS, 24^{0}S, 24^{0}GS, 36^{B}G

	Starts	1st	2nd	3rd	Win & Pl
Chases	6	1	0	0	9330
Career Total	**16**	**6**	**2**	**0**	**43691**

149	1/02	Winc	3m1f110y	C(0-135)HCh	G-S	£8580
149	1/01	Kemp	3m	D(0-125)HCh	SFT	£7247
137	12/00	Kemp	2m4f110y	D(0-120)HCh	G-S	£14950
110	3/00	Plum	3m2f	H Ch	GD	£1141
116	4/97	Hntg	3m	H Ch	GD	£1548
108	4/97	Asct	3m110y	H Ch	G-F	£2879

Total win prize-money £36346

Going: Sf: 0-1 GS: 1-3 Gd: 0-2 GF: - Fm: 0-0
Distance: 2m/2m3: 0-0 2m4-2m7: 0-1 **3m+: 1-5**
Track: LH: 0-2 **RH: 1-4** Tight: 0-1 Gall: 0-1
Aids: Bl: 0-0 Vi: 0-0 Tstrap: 0-0
Best Rating: 149 1/02 Winc 3m1f110y gd-sft Ch

A lightly-raced chaser, he ran disappointingly in late 2001, but redeemed himself when winning at Wincanton at the start of 2002, although he was well beaten at Cheltenham in hot company in March 2002. Stays three miles. Acts on good to soft/soft ground.

Strumpet

87 **77**

4-y-o gr f Tragic Role (USA)-Fee (Mandamus)
M Todhunter (P W D'Arcy 15/10) Mrs J Mandle

Placings:054P (4094)
2001/02: 16^{0}GS, 16^{5}S, 16^{4}G, 16^{P}GS

	Starts	1st	2nd	3rd	Win & Pl
Hurdles	4	0	0	0	0
Career Total	**4**	**0**	**0**	**0**	**0**

Going: Sf: 0-1 GS: 0-2 Gd: 0-1 GF: - Fm: 0-0
Distance: 2m/2m3: 0-4 2m4-2m7: 0-0 3m+: 0-0
Track: LH: 0-3 RH: 0-1 Tight: 0-2 Gall: 0-1
Aids: Bl: 0-0 Vi: 0-0 Tstrap: 0-0
Best Rating: 77 1/02 Newc 2m soft Hdl

Headstrong sort who will need to settle if she is to make her mark even in selling company.

Studio Thirty

105 **93**

10-y-o gr g Rock City-Chepstow Vale (USA) (Key To The Mint (USA))
R J Price Derek & Cheryl Holder

Placings:5F0P/1165546/146224243/**534460PP**/05P0-4220 (0672)
2001/02: 16^{4}G, 16^{2}GF, 19^{2}G, 20^{0}GF

	Starts	1st	2nd	3rd	Win & Pl
Hurdles	4	0	2	0	1637
Career Total	**36**	**3**	**5**	**2**	**15153**

89	12/98	Hrfd	2m1f	D(0-120)HHdl	G-S	£2731
85	12/97	Hrfd	2m1f	E(0-100)HHdl	SFT	£2934
79	12/97	Hrfd	2m3f110y	F(0-100)HHdl	GD	£2122

Total win prize-money £7787

Going: Sf: 0-0 GS: 0-0 Gd: 0-2 GF: - Fm: 0-2
Distance: 2m/2m3: 0-2 2m4-2m7: 0-2 3m+: 0-0
Track: LH: 0-2 RH: 0-2 Tight: 0-1 Gall: 0-1
Aids: Bl: 0-0 Vi: 0-0 Tstrap: 0-0
Best Rating: 103 11/99 Hrfd 2m good Ch

Sturm Und Drang

90(99h) (90h)**89**

8-y-o ch g Selkirk (USA)-Historiette (Chief's Crown (USA))
J D Frost R G Frost

Placings:*0006/02* (4736)
2001/02: 19^{0}G, 17^{2}F

	Starts	1st	2nd	3rd	Win & Pl
Hurdles	2	0	1	0	876
Career Total	**6**	**0**	**1**	**0**	**876**

Going: Sf: 0-0 GS: 0-0 Gd: 0-1 GF: - Fm: 0-1
Distance: 2m/2m3: 0-2 2m4-2m7: 0-0 3m+: 0-0
Track: LH: 0-0 RH: 0-2 Tight: 0-0 Gall: 0-0
Aids: Bl: 0-0 Vi: 0-0 Tstrap: 0-0
Best Rating: 90 4/02 Extr 2m1f firm Hdl

Modest, lightly-raced hurdler, suited by a sound surface.

Stylish Fella (USA)

83 **65**

4-y-o b g Irish River (FR)-Dariela (USA) (Manila (USA))
Ian Williams Horses For Courses Partnership

Placings:4P0 (2204)
2001/02: 16^{4}GF, 16^{P}G, 16^{0}GS

	Starts	1st	2nd	3rd	Win & Pl
Hurdles	3	0	0	0	0
Career Total	**3**	**0**	**0**	**0**	**0**

Going: Sf: 0-0 GS: 0-1 Gd: 0-1 GF: - Fm: 0-1
Distance: 2m/2m3: 0-3 2m4-2m7: 0-0 3m+: 0-0
Track: LH: 0-1 RH: 0-2 Tight: 0-0 Gall: 0-0
Aids: Bl: 0-1 Vi: 0-0 Tstrap: 0-0
Best Rating: 54 10/01 Ludl 2m gd-fm Hdl

Stylish Interval

107 **102**

10-y-o ch g Interrex (CAN)-Super Style (Artaius (USA))
Denys Smith Ian Darling

Placings:05/634501001025/313320F56/1134**1235**/F4/0P-01F4U2P3P (1236)
2001/02: 16^{0}S, 16^{1}GF, 25^{F}GF, 20^{4}GS, 22^{U}G, 21^{2}GF, 16^{P}GF, 21^{3}GF, 26^{P}GS

	Starts	1st	2nd	3rd	Win & Pl
Chases	9	1	1	1	4832
Career Total	**44**	**7**	**4**	**7**	**27104**

94	5/01	Hexm	2m110y	F(0-95)HCh	G-F	£2870
102	9/98	Sedg	2m5f	E Ch	GD	£2960
104	5/98	Hexm	2m4f110y	E(0-110)HHdl	G-F	£1952
104	5/98	Hexm	2m4f110y	E(0-115)HHdl	GD	£2546
93	5/97	Ctml	2m6f	F(0-95)HHdl	GD	£2542
87	3/97	Sedg	2m1f	E Hdl	G-F	£2253
79	11/96	Kels	2m110y	G Hdl	G-F	£2316

Total win prize-money £17440

Going: Sf: 0-1 GS: 0-2 Gd: 0-1 GF: - Fm: 1-5
Distance: **2m/2m3: 1-3** 2m4-2m7: 0-4 3m+: 0-2
Track: **LH: 1-8** RH: 0-1 Tight: 0-5 Gall: 0-0
Aids: Bl: 0-1 Vi: 0-0 Tstrap: 0-0
Best Rating: 110 9/98 Carl 2m4f110y good Ch

Sualamar (IRE)

81 **54**

6-y-o b g Magical Strike (USA)-Annagh Trust (Jester)
G M Moore Mrs Mary And Miss Susan Hatfield

Placings:*O/0006*-P5P0 (2070)
2001/02: 20^{P}GF, 16^{5}G, 17^{P}GS, 17^{0}S

	Starts	1st	2nd	3rd	Win & Pl
Hurdles	4	0	0	0	0
Career Total	**9**	**0**	**0**	**0**	**0**

Going: Sf: 0-1 GS: 0-1 Gd: 0-1 GF: - Fm: 0-1
Distance: 2m/2m3: 0-3 2m4-2m7: 0-1 3m+: 0-0
Track: LH: 0-4 RH: 0-0 Tight: 0-2 Gall: 0-0
Aids: Bl: 0-0 Vi: 0-0 Tstrap: 0-0
Best Rating: 72 11/00 Newc 2m gd-sft NHF

Suanda

71f **68f**

5-y-o ch m Factual (USA)-Sue Clare (Busted)
H J Manners Mrs T Fitzgerald O'Connor

Placings:*00* (4570)
2001/02: 16^{0}GF, 16^{0}G

	Starts	1st	2nd	3rd	Win & Pl
NH Flat	2	0	0	0	
Career Total	**2**	**0**	**0**	**0**	

Going: Sf: 0-0 GS: 0-0 Gd: 0-1 GF: - Fm: 0-1
Distance: 2m/2m3: 0-2 2m4-2m7: 0-0 3m+: 0-0
Track: LH: 0-0 RH: 0-2 Tight: 0-0 Gall: 0-1
Aids: Bl: 0-0 Vi: 0-0 Tstrap: 0-0
Best Rating: 68 3/02 Hntg 2m110y gd-fm NHF

Suave Frankie

106 **77**

6-y-o ch g Suave Dancer (USA)-Francia (Legend Of France (USA))
I W McInnes (A Smith 21/5) I W McInnes

Placings:P6460620 **(3856)**
2001/02: 19^{P}G, 16^{6}GF, 16^{4}GF, 19^{6}GF, 16^{0}GF, 17^{6}GF, 21^{2}G, 16^{0}S

	Starts	1st	2nd	3rd	Win & Pl
Hurdles	8	0	1	0	548
Career Total	**8**	**0**	**1**	**0**	**548**

Going: Sf: 0-1 GS: 0-0 Gd: 0-2 GF: - Fm: 0-5
Distance: 2m/2m3: 0-5 2m4-2m7: 0-3 3m+: 0-0
Track: LH: 0-6 RH: 0-2 Tight: 0-7 Gall: 0-1
Aids: Bl: 0-0 Vi: 0-0 Tstrap: 0-0
Best Rating: 73 9/01 Sedg 2m5f110y good Hdl

Suaverof (IRE)

102 110

7-y-o ch g Suave Dancer (USA)-Mild Intrigue (USA) (Sir Ivor)
M Pitman Martin Van Doorne

Placings:4-3P31122P **(1280)**
2001/02: 17^{3}GS, 25^{P}G, 20^{3}G, 20^{1}GF, 24^{1}G, 24^{2}S, 20^{2}GF, 24^{P}GF

	Starts	1st	2nd	3rd	Win & Pl
Hurdles	8	2	2	2	7323
Career Total	**9**	**2**	**2**	**2**	**7724**

110	6/01	Worc	3m	E Hdl	GD	£2562
110	6/01	Worc	2m4f	E Hdl	G-F	£2597

Total win prize-money £5159

Going: Sf: 0-1 GS: 0-1 Gd: 1-3 GF: - Fm: 1-3
Distance: 2m/2m3: 0-1 2m4-2m7: 1-3 3m+: 1-4
Track: **LH: 2-6** RH: 0-1 Tight: 0-2 Gall: 0-0
Aids: Bl: 0-0 Vi: 0-0 Tstrap: 0-0
Best Rating: 110 8/01 Sthl 2m4f110y gd-fm Hdl

Subadar Major

82 68

5-y-o b g Komaite (USA)-Rather Gorgeous (Billion (USA))
Mrs G S Rees Major P Bailey

Placings:0P **(3369)**
2001/02: 16^{0}S, 20^{P}S

	Starts	1st	2nd	3rd	Win & Pl
Hurdles	2	0	0	0	
Career Total	**2**	**0**	**0**	**0**	

Going: Sf: 0-2 GS: 0-0 Gd: 0-0 GF: - Fm: 0-0
Distance: 2m/2m3: 0-1 2m4-2m7: 0-1 3m+: 0-0
Track: LH: 0-2 RH: 0-0 Tight: 0-0 Gall: 0-0
Aids: Bl: 0-0 Vi: 0-0 Tstrap: 0-0
Best Rating: 68 12/01 Hayd 2m soft Hdl

Such Phun

4-y-o b f Karinga Bay-Bugsy's Sister (Aragon)
J Hetherton Peter Urquhart

Placings:6 **(4771)**
2001/02: 16^{6}GF

	Starts	1st	2nd	3rd	Win & Pl
NH Flat	1	0	0	0	0
Career Total	**1**	**0**	**0**	**0**	**0**

Going: Sf: 0-0 GS: 0-0 Gd: 0-0 GF: - Fm: 0-1
Distance: 2m/2m3: 0-1 2m4-2m7: 0-0 3m+: 0-0
Track: LH: 0-0 RH: 0-0 Tight: 0-0 Gall: 0-0
Aids: Bl: 0-0 Vi: 0-0 Tstrap: 0-0
Best Rating: 72 4/02 Hexm 2m110y gd-fm NHF

Suck Your Thumb

8-y-o b m Teenoso (USA)-Onaway (Commanche Run)
Mrs A Barclay Mrs Althea Barclay

Placings:5-PPP **(4504)**
2001/02: 22^{P}S, 16^{P}HY, 17^{P}G

	Starts	1st	2nd	3rd	Win & Pl
Hurdles	3	0	0	0	
Career Total	**4**	**0**	**0**	**0**	**0**

Going: Sf: 0-2 GS: 0-0 Gd: 0-1 GF: - Fm: 0-0
Distance: 2m/2m3: 0-2 2m4-2m7: 0-1 3m+: 0-0
Track: LH: 0-2 RH: 0-1 Tight: 0-2 Gall: 0-0
Aids: Bl: 0-0 Vi: 0-0 Tstrap: 0-0
Best Rating: 100 5/00 Bang 2m1f good NHF

Sud Bleu (FR)

106 116

4-y-o b g Pistolet Bleu (IRE)-Sudaka (FR) (Garde Royale)
P F Nicholls (E Lellouche 10/10) Barry Marshall & Terry Warner

Placings:043200 **(4651)**
2001/02: 18^{0}VS, 18^{4}VS, 16^{3}S, 16^{2}G, 17^{0}G, 16^{0}G

	Starts	1st	2nd	3rd	Win & Pl
Hurdles	6	0	1	1	8078
Career Total	**6**	**0**	**1**	**1**	**8078**

Going: Sf: 0-1 GS: 0-0 Gd: 0-3 GF: - Fm: 0-0
Distance: 2m/2m3: 0-6 2m4-2m7: 0-0 3m+: 0-0
Track: LH: 0-3 RH: 0-1 Tight: 0-1 Gall: 0-1
Aids: Bl: 0-0 Vi: 0-0 Tstrap: 0-0
Best Rating: 116 2/02 Kemp 2m good Hdl

Placed on the level and over hurdles in France in the mud, he has shown promise over hurdles in this country, but does not find much off the bridle.

Sudden Shock (GER)

106 150

7-y-o br g Motley (USA)-Santalina (Relko)
J J O'Neill Darren C Mercer

Placings:11/312212/122216126-06PP12 **(4911)**
2001/02: 25^{0}G, 24^{6}GS, 25^{P}S, 20^{P}S, 24^{1}G, 24^{2}G

	Starts	1st	2nd	3rd	Win & Pl
Hurdles	6	1	1	0	34200
Career Total	**23**	**8**	**8**	**1**	**146504**

134	4/02	Aint	3m110y	A HHdl	GD	£23200
	11/00	Siro	2m4f	Hdl	HVY	£16266
	9/00	Maia	2m4f110y	Hdl	GD	£35785
	5/00	Badn	2m4f165y	Hdl	HVY	£9677
	11/99	Turi	2m2f	Hdl	SFT	£10935
	8/99	Gels	2m1f	Hdl	SFT	£2708
	4/99	Gels	2m	Hdl	HVY	£2166
	3/99	Gels	2m	Hdl	HVY	£2166

Total win prize-money £102903

Going: Sf: 0-2 GS: 0-1 Gd: 1-3 GF: - Fm: 0-0
Distance: 2m/2m3: 0-0 2m4-2m7: 0-1 **3m+: 1-5**
Track: **LH: 1-4** RH: 0-0 **Tight: 1-1** Gall: 0-0
Aids: Bl: 0-0 Vi: 0-0 Tstrap: 0-0
Best Rating: 150 4/02 Sand 3m good Hdl

Useful hurdler, he won seven times between two miles and two and a half miles in Germany and Italy before changing stables in the spring of 2001. He has tumbled in the ratings and landed a bit of a touch at Aintree, his first outing after a wind operation, before running well at Sandown in April. Stays three miles acts on good ground or softer.

Suez Tornado (IRE)

91(100h) 79

9-y-o ch g Mujtahid (USA)-So Stylish (Great Nephew)
P J Hobbs Mr & Mrs Don Last & Mr & Mrs Bill Yates

Placings:06/B200-02 **(0317)**
2001/02: 16^{0}F, 23^{2}F

	Starts	1st	2nd	3rd	Win & Pl
Chases	2	0	1	0	1282
Career Total	**8**	**0**	**2**	**0**	**2260**

Going: Sf: 0-0 GS: 0-0 Gd: 0-0 GF: - Fm: 0-2
Distance: 2m/2m3: 0-1 2m4-2m7: 0-0 3m+: 0-1
Track: LH: 0-1 RH: 0-1 Tight: 0-1 Gall: 0-0
Aids: Bl: 0-0 Vi: 0-0 Tstrap: 0-0
Best Rating: 84 12/00 Ludl 2m soft Hdl

Suggest

106 91

7-y-o b g Midyan (USA)-Awham (USA) (Lear Fan (USA))
W Storey Mrs M Tindale

Placings:066/03110025/01110PP-35 **(1504)**
2001/02: 20^{3}GF, 21^{5}G

	Starts	1st	2nd	3rd	Win & Pl
Hurdles	2	0	0	1	279
Career Total	**20**	**5**	**1**	**2**	**15245**

112	5/00	Ctml	3m2f	D(0-125)HHdl	GD	£4170
106	5/00	Hexm	2m4f110y	E(0-115)HHdl	GD	£2039
87	5/00	Hexm	2m4f110y	D(0-125)HHdl	G-F	£3230
107	2/00	Newc	3m	F(0-100)HHdl	SFT	£2023
93	1/00	Sedg	2m5f110y	E(0-115)HHdl	SFT	£2380

Total win prize-money £13844

Going: Sf: 0-0 GS: 0-0 Gd: 0-1 GF: - Fm: 0-1
Distance: 2m/2m3: 0-0 2m4-2m7: 0-2 3m+: 0-0
Track: LH: 0-2 RH: 0-0 Tight: 0-1 Gall: 0-0
Aids: Bl: 0-0 Vi: 0-0 Tstrap: 0-0
Best Rating: 112 5/00 Ctml 3m2f good Hdl

Sulaban

78f 66f

6-y-o b m Sula Bula-Mariban (Mummy's Pet)
B J M Ryall B J M Ryall

Placings:0 **(2294)**
2001/02: 17^{0}GF

	Starts	1st	2nd	3rd	Win & Pl
NH Flat	1	0	0	0	
Career Total	**1**	**0**	**0**	**0**	

Going: Sf: 0-0 GS: 0-0 Gd: 0-0 GF: - Fm: 0-1
Distance: 2m/2m3: 0-1 2m4-2m7: 0-0 3m+: 0-0
Track: LH: 0-0 RH: 0-1 Tight: 0-0 Gall: 0-0
Aids: Bl: 0-0 Vi: 0-0 Tstrap: 0-0
Best Rating: 66 11/01 Extr 2m1f gd-fm NHF

Sullys Hope

112 **115**

5-y-o b g Rock Hopper-Super Sally (Superlative)
Nick Williams Mrs Jane Kelly

Placings:PP0F-0202321341010 **(4500)**
2001/02: 17^{0}GF, 17^{2}GF, 17^{0}GF, 16^{2}GF, 16^{3}GF, 16^{2}GS, 16^{1}S, 17^{3}G, 16^{4}S, 16^{1}S, 18^{0}S, 16^{1}GS, 17^{0}G

	Starts	1st	2nd	3rd	Win & Pl
Hurdles	13	3	3	2	17007
Career Total	**17**	**3**	**3**	**2**	**17007**

115	3/02	Strf	2m110y	D(0-125)HHdl	G-S	£7514
115	12/01	Strf	2m110y	D Hdl	SFT	£3822
106	11/01	Strf	2m110y	F(0-100)HHdl	SFT	£2765

Total win prize-money £14101

Going: Sf: 2-4 GS: 1-2 Gd: 0-2 GF: - Fm: 0-5
Distance: **2m/2m3: 3-13** 2m4-2m7: 0-0 3m+: 0-0
Track: **LH: 3-13** RH: 0-0 **Tight: 3-12** Gall: 0-0
Aids: Bl: 0-0 Vi: 0-1 Tstrap: 0-0
Best Rating: 115 3/02 Strf 2m110y gd-sft Hdl

He is a different horse at Stratford and has gained all three of his wins there. Suited by two miles and soft ground.

Sulphur Springs (IRE)

107 **155**

10-y-o ch g Don't Forget Me-Short Wave (FR) (Trepan (FR))
M C Pipe P A D Scouller

Placings:0/056P25/22F3P22/45533/066/1-PS1111161 **(4851)**
2001/02: 24^{P}GS, 24^{S}GF, 24^{1}GF, 22^{1}GF, 24^{1}G, 26^{1}GF, 22^{1}S, 24^{6}GS, 20^{1}G

	Starts	1st	2nd	3rd	Win & Pl
Chases	9	6	0	0	29654
Career Total	**32**	**7**	**5**	**3**	**112361**

155	4/02	Strf	2m4f	C(0-130)HCh	GD	£7124
150	9/01	MRas	2m6f110y	C Ch	SFT	£7665
140	9/01	NAbb	3m2f110y	D(0-120)HCh	G-F	£3997
140	7/01	Strf	3m	E(0-115)HCh	GD	£4920
145	6/01	MRas	2m6f110y	E(0-105)HCh	G-F	£4160
131	6/01	Strf	3m	H Ch	G-F	£1337
110	4/01	MRas	2m6f110y	H Ch	G-S	£1266

Total win prize-money £30471

Going: Sf: 1-1 GS: 0-2 Gd: 2-2 GF: - Fm: 3-4
Distance: 2m/2m3: 0-0 2m4-2m7: 3-3 3m+: 3-6
Track: **LH: 4-6** RH: 2-3 **Tight: 6-8** Gall: 0-0
Aids: Bl: 0-0 Vi: 0-0 **Tstrap: 6-8**
Best Rating: 155 4/02 Strf 2m4f good Ch

Handicap chaser. Won six times in 2001, and has continued in good form in 2002. Acts on most types of ground and stays three miles.

Sum Leader (IRE)

107 **125**

6-y-o b g Leading Counsel (USA)-Greenodd (Green Shoon)
Gerard Keane John E Smyth

Placings:*00*-00P0S1124 **(2145)**
2001/02: 16^{0}YS, 16^{0}GY, 19^{P}G, 16^{0}G, 16^{S}GF, 16^{1}GF, 16^{1}G, 16^{2}HY, 16^{4}G

	Starts	1st	2nd	3rd	Win & Pl
Hurdles	9	2	1	0	13133
Career Total	**11**	**2**	**1**	**0**	**13133**

114	10/01	Fair	2m	(67-102)HHdl	GD	£4729
107	9/01	Gowr	2m	Hdl	G-F	£4729

Total win prize-money £9460

Going: Sf: 0-1 GS: 0-0 Gd: 1-4 GF: - Fm: 1-2
Distance: **2m/2m3: 2-9** 2m4-2m7: 0-0 3m+: 0-0
Track: LH: 0-1 **RH: 1-1** Tight: 0-0 Gall: 0-0
Aids: Bl: 0-0 Vi: 0-0 Tstrap: 0-0
Best Rating: 114 11/01 Chel 2m110y good Hdl

A decent Irish-trained novice, he has won at Gowran Park and Fairyhouse so far this season and looks best on fast ground.

Sumbawa (IRE)

7-y-o ch m Magic Ring (IRE)-Tittlemouse (Castle Keep)
K Goldsworthy Greenacre Racing Partnership Ltd

Placings:P0/P **(4545)**
2001/02: 19^{P}G

	Starts	1st	2nd	3rd	Win & Pl
Chases	1	0	0	0	
Career Total	**3**	**0**	**0**	**0**	

Going: Sf: 0-0 GS: 0-0 Gd: 0-1 GF: - Fm: 0-0
Distance: 2m/2m3: 0-1 2m4-2m7: 0-0 3m+: 0-0
Track: LH: 0-0 RH: 0-1 Tight: 0-0 Gall: 0-0
Aids: Bl: 0-0 Vi: 0-0 Tstrap: 0-0
Best Rating: 23 8/99 Worc 2m soft Hdl

Sumboy (IRE)

8-y-o gr g Aristocracy-Sign O'The Season (Strong Gale)
J F Panvert J F Panvert

Placings:5PPBPP **(4170)**
2001/02: 24^{5}S, 21^{P}G, 23^{P}S, 25^{B}HY, 26^{P}S, 26^{P}GS

	Starts	1st	2nd	3rd	Win & Pl
Hurdles	5	0	0	0	0
Chases	1	0	0	0	0
Career Total	**6**	**0**	**0**	**0**	**0**

Going: Sf: 0-4 GS: 0-1 Gd: 0-1 GF: - Fm: 0-0
Distance: 2m/2m3: 0-0 2m4-2m7: 0-1 3m+: 0-5
Track: LH: 0-2 RH: 0-2 Tight: 0-2 Gall: 0-1
Aids: Bl: 0-0 Vi: 0-0 Tstrap: 0-0
Best Rating:

Summer Bounty

94 **77**

6-y-o b g Lugana Beach-Tender Moment (IRE) (Caerleon (USA))
F Jordan F Jordan

Placings:55P/24-000 **(1908)**
2001/02: 17^{0}GF, 16^{0}G, 16^{0}S

	Starts	1st	2nd	3rd	Win & Pl
Hurdles	3	0	0	0	
Career Total	**8**	**0**	**1**	**0**	**775**

Going: Sf: 0-1 GS: 0-0 Gd: 0-1 GF: - Fm: 0-1
Distance: 2m/2m3: 0-3 2m4-2m7: 0-0 3m+: 0-0
Track: LH: 0-2 RH: 0-1 Tight: 0-3 Gall: 0-0
Aids: Bl: 0-0 Vi: 0-0 Tstrap: 0-0
Best Rating: 81 6/00 Hrfd 2m1f gd-fm Hdl

Ineffective over hurdles.

Summer Break (IRE)

91 **98**

5-y-o ch m Foxhound (USA)-Out In The Sun (USA) (It's Freezing (USA))
Ian Williams (S Dow 7/1) K A Cosby

Placings:131-5000000 **(4908)**
2001/02: 16^{5}G, 21^{0}GS, 16^{0}GS, 16^{0}G, 16^{0}S, 16^{0}S, 21^{0}G

	Starts	1st	2nd	3rd	Win & Pl
Hurdles	7	0	0	0	0
Career Total	**10**	**2**	**0**	**1**	**7658**

111	1/01	Fknm	2m	D Hdl	SFT	£3265
110	11/00	Clon	2m	Hdl	HVY	£3312

Total win prize-money £6578

Going: Sf: 0-2 GS: 0-2 Gd: 0-3 GF: - Fm: 0-0
Distance: 2m/2m3: 0-5 2m4-2m7: 0-2 3m+: 0-0
Track: LH: 0-3 RH: 0-4 Tight: 0-2 Gall: 0-1
Aids: Bl: 0-0 Vi: 0-0 Tstrap: 0-0
Best Rating: 111 1/01 Fknm 2m soft Hdl

Modest hurdler, acts on well on a soft surface and is effective at around two miles, but well beaten in 2001/2.

Summer Cherry (USA)

79 **77**

5-y-o b g Summer Squall (USA)-Cherryrob (USA) (Roberto (USA))
Jamie Poulton Jamie Poulton

Placings:0-0 **(1556)**
2001/02: 16^{0}G

	Starts	1st	2nd	3rd	Win & Pl
Hurdles	1	0	0	0	
Career Total	**2**	**0**	**0**	**0**	

Going: Sf: 0-0 GS: 0-0 Gd: 0-1 GF: - Fm: 0-0
Distance: 2m/2m3: 0-1 2m4-2m7: 0-0 3m+: 0-0
Track: LH: 0-1 RH: 0-0 Tight: 0-0 Gall: 0-0
Aids: Bl: 0-0 Vi: 0-0 Tstrap: 0-1
Best Rating: 82 1/01 Kemp 2m soft Hdl

Summer Villa

85 **34**

10-y-o b m Nomination-Maravilla (Mandrake Major)
K G Wingrove A F Maiden

Placings:00/33202532/235501442306/5U2060/00 **(2952)**
2001/02: 16^{0}GF, 16^{0}S

	Starts	1st	2nd	3rd	Win & Pl
Hurdles	2	0	0	0	
Career Total	**30**	**1**	**6**	**5**	**6509**

79	8/97	MRas	2m1f110y	F(0-100)HHdl	G-F	£1982

Total win prize-money £1982

Going: Sf: 0-1 GS: 0-0 Gd: 0-0 GF: - Fm: 0-1
Distance: 2m/2m3: 0-2 2m4-2m7: 0-0 3m+: 0-0
Track: LH: 0-1 RH: 0-1 Tight: 0-1 Gall: 0-0
Aids: Bl: 0-2 Vi: 0-0 Tstrap: 0-0
Best Rating: 79 10/97 Plum 2m1f good Hdl

Summerville Wood

78(56c) **43**

8-y-o b g Nomination-Four Love (Pas De Seul)
P Bowen L L Rees

Placings:00/6U55606/62045P/60-0P (0977)
2001/02: 18⁰GF, 24ᴾGF

	Starts	1st	2nd	3rd	Win & Pl
Hurdles	2	0	0	0	
Career Total	**19**	**0**	**1**	**0**	**458**

Going: Sf: 0-0 GS: 0-0 Gd: 0-0 GF: - Fm: 0-2
Distance: 2m/2m3: 0-1 2m4-2m7: 0-0 3m+: 0-1
Track: LH: 0-2 RH: 0-0 Tight: 0-2 Gall: 0-0
Aids: Bl: 0-0 Vi: 0-0 Tstrap: 0-0
Best Rating: 74 6/00 Uttx 2m4f110y gd-fm Hdl

Sumo

9-y-o ch g Superlative-Model Lady (Le Bavard (FR))
C N Kellett Mrs Jennifer Woodward

Placings:005065/334601/0P4632/3-0 (1752)
2001/02: 22⁰G

	Starts	1st	2nd	3rd	Win & Pl
Chases	1	0	0	0	
Career Total	**20**	**1**	**1**	**4**	**5192**
88 3/99 Donc 2m110y E(0-105)HHdl				G-S	£2722

Total win prize-money £2723

Going: Sf: 0-0 GS: 0-0 Gd: 0-1 GF: - Fm: 0-0
Distance: 2m/2m3: 0-0 2m4-2m7: 0-1 3m+: 0-0
Track: LH: 0-0 RH: 0-1 Tight: 0-1 Gall: 0-0
Aids: Bl: 0-0 Vi: 0-0 Tstrap: 0-0
Best Rating: 88 4/00 MRas 2m1f110y gd-fm Hdl

Sumthyne Special (IRE)

110 (90c) 119
10-y-o b g Good Thyne (USA)-Condonstown Rose (Giolla Mear)
L Lungo J M Crichton

Placings:2312/P6/4F2-2112FP1 (4392)
2001/02: 24²S, 24¹S, 24¹S, 24²GS, 25ᶠHY, 25ᴾS, 22¹HY

	Starts	1st	2nd	3rd	Win & Pl
Hurdles	5	3	2	0	10440
Chases	2	0	0	0	0
Career Total	**16**	**4**	**5**	**1**	**13798**
119 3/02 Kels 2m6f110y E Hdl				HVY	£3178
116 11/01 Carl 3m110y E Hdl				SFT	£2765
114 10/01 Carl 3m110y E Hdl				SFT	£2564
97 3/98 Carl 2m1f H NHF				HVY	£1245

Total win prize-money £9753

Going: Sf: 3-6 GS: 0-1 Gd: 0-0 GF: - Fm: 0-0
Distance: 2m/2m3: 0-0 2m4-2m7: 1-1 **3m+: 2-6**
Track: LH: 1-4 **RH: 2-3 Tight: 1-1** Gall: 0-1
Aids: Bl: 0-0 Vi: 0-0 Tstrap: 0-0
Best Rating: 119 3/02 Kels 2m6f110y heavy Hdl

Novice hurdler. Stays three miles. Acts on soft ground.

Sun King

106 107
5-y-o ch g Zilzal (USA)-Opus One (Slip Anchor)
Mrs M Reveley Sir Robert Ogden

Placings:4-21S015 (4828)
2001/02: 16²GF, 16¹GF, 17ˢGF, 17⁰GF, 19¹GF, 16⁵G

	Starts	1st	2nd	3rd	Win & Pl
NH Flat	2	1	1	0	2031
Hurdles	4	1	0	0	3780

	Starts	1st	2nd	3rd	Win & Pl
Career Total	**7**	**2**	**1**	**0**	**5811**
96 4/02 MRas 2m3f110y D Hdl				G-F	£3780
94 6/01 Worc 2m H NHF				G-F	£1536

Total win prize-money £5317

Going: Sf: 0-0 GS: 0-0 Gd: 0-1 GF: - Fm: 2-5
Distance: 2m/2m3: 1-5 2m4-2m7: 1-1 3m+: 0-0
Track: LH: 1-4 RH: 1-2 **Tight: 1-3** Gall: 0-1
Aids: Bl: 0-0 Vi: 0-0 Tstrap: 0-0
Best Rating: 103 4/02 Ayr 2m good Hdl

Fair novice hurdler, effective on fast ground and stays two and a half miles.

Sunburnt

95(94h) (77h)81
8-y-o b g Henbit (USA)-Sunshine Gal (Alto Volante)
R H Buckler Melplash Racing

Placings:45/05PP03/0P12-P34400P5 (4560)
2001/02: 19ᴾGF, 19³GF, 16⁴S, 24⁴G, 19⁰GS, 24⁰GS, 21ᴾG, 17⁵GF

	Starts	1st	2nd	3rd	Win & Pl
Hurdles	3	0	0	1	390
Chases	5	0	0	0	0
Career Total	**20**	**1**	**1**	**2**	**4310**
96 8/00 Sthl 2m F(0-100)HCh				G-F	£2707

Total win prize-money £2707

Going: Sf: 0-1 GS: 0-2 Gd: 0-2 GF: - Fm: 0-3
Distance: 2m/2m3: 0-5 2m4-2m7: 0-1 3m+: 0-2
Track: LH: 0-0 RH: 0-5 Tight: 0-3 Gall: 0-0
Aids: Bl: 0-0 Vi: 0-0 Tstrap: 0-0
Best Rating: 102 2/99 Winc 2m gd-sft NHF

Moderate hurdler/chaser, best on fast ground.

Sundance Sid (IRE)

96 65
6-y-o b g Phardante (FR)-The Kid's Sister (Black Minstrel)
Miss E C Lavelle Remenham Racing

Placings:0PF0060 (4731)
2001/02: 22⁰GS, 22ᴾS, 22ᶠHY, 20⁰S, 17⁰S, 16⁶G, 17⁰F

	Starts	1st	2nd	3rd	Win & Pl
Hurdles	7	0	0	0	0
Career Total	**7**	**0**	**0**	**0**	**0**

Going: Sf: 0-4 GS: 0-1 Gd: 0-1 GF: - Fm: 0-1
Distance: 2m/2m3: 0-3 2m4-2m7: 0-4 3m+: 0-0
Track: LH: 0-1 RH: 0-6 Tight: 0-4 Gall: 0-1
Aids: Bl: 0-0 Vi: 0-0 Tstrap: 0-0
Best Rating: 65 4/02 Extr 2m1f firm Hdl

Sunday Rain (USA)

105 103
5-y-o b g Summer Squall (USA)-Oxava (FR) (Antheus (USA))
Miss Lucinda V Russell (J J O'Neill 10/5) Peter K Dale Ltd

Placings:233P0-352400 (3624)
2001/02: 20³G, 20⁵G, 20²S, 20⁴HY, 24⁰S, 21⁰GS

	Starts	1st	2nd	3rd	Win & Pl
Hurdles	6	0	1	1	1551
Career Total	**11**	**0**	**2**	**3**	**7646**

Going: Sf: 0-3 GS: 0-1 Gd: 0-2 GF: - Fm: 0-0
Distance: 2m/2m3: 0-0 2m4-2m7: 0-5 3m+: 0-1
Track: LH: 0-5 RH: 0-1 Tight: 0-1 Gall: 0-2
Aids: Bl: 0-1 Vi: 0-0 Tstrap: 0-0
Best Rating: 111 12/00 Chel 2m1f soft Hdl

Novice hurdler. Suited by front running, he stays beyond two miles.

Sungates (IRE)

94f 95f
6-y-o ch g Glacial Storm (USA)-Live It Up (Le Coq D'Or)
E Stanners Team George Ii

Placings:2 (0272)
2001/02: 17²G

	Starts	1st	2nd	3rd	Win & Pl
NH Flat	1	0	1	0	559
Career Total	**1**	**0**	**1**	**0**	**559**

Going: Sf: 0-0 GS: 0-0 Gd: 0-1 GF: - Fm: 0-0
Distance: 2m/2m3: 0-1 2m4-2m7: 0-0 3m+: 0-0
Track: LH: 0-0 RH: 0-1 Tight: 0-0 Gall: 0-0
Aids: Bl: 0-0 Vi: 0-0 Tstrap: 0-0
Best Rating: 95 5/01 Hrfd 2m1f good NHF

Sungio

88 87
4-y-o b g Halling (USA)-Time Or Never (FR) (Dowsing (USA))
B G Powell (L M Cumani 17/9) Mrs Rachel A Powell

Placings:660 (3668)
2001/02: 16⁶G, 16⁶GS, 16⁰S

	Starts	1st	2nd	3rd	Win & Pl
Hurdles	3	0	0	0	0
Career Total	**3**	**0**	**0**	**0**	**0**

Going: Sf: 0-1 GS: 0-1 Gd: 0-1 GF: - Fm: 0-0
Distance: 2m/2m3: 0-3 2m4-2m7: 0-0 3m+: 0-0
Track: LH: 0-2 RH: 0-1 Tight: 0-0 Gall: 0-1
Aids: Bl: 0-0 Vi: 0-0 Tstrap: 0-0
Best Rating: 87 10/01 Chel 2m110y good Hdl

Sunley Way

87(84h) (41h)70
8-y-o b m Sunley Builds-Borotown (Treboro (USA))
Mrs D Thomson Area Eight

Placings:0P-3006P (4487)
2001/02: 24³GF, 20⁰GS, 20⁰S, 25⁶GS, 26ᴾGS

	Starts	1st	2nd	3rd	Win & Pl
Hurdles	1	0	0	1	414
Chases	4	0	0	0	0
Career Total	**7**	**0**	**0**	**1**	**414**

Going: Sf: 0-1 GS: 0-3 Gd: 0-0 GF: - Fm: 0-1
Distance: 2m/2m3: 0-0 2m4-2m7: 0-2 3m+: 0-3
Track: LH: 0-1 RH: 0-3 Tight: 0-1 Gall: 0-0
Aids: Bl: 0-0 Vi: 0-0 Tstrap: 0-0
Best Rating: 78 11/00 Ayr 2m soft NHF

Sunny Leith

75 47
11-y-o b g Feelings (FR)-Pinkie Hill (Le Coq D'Or)
P Monteith G M Cowan

Placings:500424/01F/35FP40/2233P24F40/310P-U0P (0551)
2001/02: 21ᵁGF, 24⁰GF, 24ᴾGF

	Starts	1st	2nd	3rd	Win & Pl

	Starts	1st	2nd	3rd	Win & Pl
Chases	3	0	0	0	
Career Total	**32**	**2**	**4**	**4**	**14754**

102 2/01 Kels 3m1f H Ch SFT £2268
95 1/98 Ayr 3m1f E(0-105)HCh SFT £3197
Total win prize-money £5465

Going: Sf: 0-0 GS: 0-0 Gd: 0-0 GF: - Fm: 0-3
Distance: 2m/2m3: 0-0 2m4-2m7: 0-1 3m+: 0-2
Track: LH: 0-2 RH: 0-1 Tight: 0-0 Gall: 0-1
Aids: Bl: 0-0 Vi: 0-0 Tstrap: 0-0
Best Rating: 112 1/00 Kels 3m1f good Ch

Sunnycliff

91 **95**

9-y-o b g Dancing High-Nicolini (Nicholas Bill)
Miss R Brewis R Brewis

Placings:1-3 **(2726)**
2001/02: 20^{3}GF

	Starts	1st	2nd	3rd	Win & Pl
Chases	1	0	0	1	657
Career Total	**2**	**1**	**0**	**1**	**2718**

112 5/00 Prth 2m4f110y H Ch G-S £2060
Total win prize-money £2061

Going: Sf: 0-0 GS: 0-0 Gd: 0-0 GF: - Fm: 0-1
Distance: 2m/2m3: 0-0 2m4-2m7: 0-1 3m+: 0-0
Track: LH: 0-0 RH: 0-1 Tight: 0-1 Gall: 0-0
Aids: Bl: 0-0 Vi: 0-0 Tstrap: 0-1
Best Rating: 112 5/00 Prth 2m4f110y gd-sft Ch

Sunridge Rose

80 **42**

4-y-o b f Piccolo-Floral Spark (Forzando)
Andrew Reid A S Reid

Placings:P **(3709)**
2001/02: 16^{P}HY

	Starts	1st	2nd	3rd	Win & Pl
Hurdles	1	0	0	0	
Career Total	**1**	**0**	**0**	**0**	

Going: Sf: 0-1 GS: 0-0 Gd: 0-0 GF: - Fm: 0-0
Distance: 2m/2m3: 0-1 2m4-2m7: 0-0 3m+: 0-0
Track: LH: 0-1 RH: 0-0 Tight: 0-1 Gall: 0-0
Aids: Bl: 0-0 Vi: 0-0 Tstrap: 0-0
Best Rating:

Sunshade (USA)

103 **101**

6-y-o b g Alleged (USA)-Sunny Bay (USA) (Northern Bay (USA))
G A Swinbank Elsa Crankshaw & G Allan Ii

Placings:*225500*-146P **(3393)**
2001/02: 17^{1}G, 17^{4}GS, 20^{6}GS, 20^{P}GS

	Starts	1st	2nd	3rd	Win & Pl
Hurdles	4	1	0	0	2548
Career Total	**10**	**1**	**2**	**0**	**3553**

93 10/01 Sedg 2m1f E Hdl GD £2548
Total win prize-money £2548

Going: Sf: 0-0 GS: 0-3 Gd: 1-1 GF: - Fm: 0-0
Distance: **2m/2m3: 1-2** 2m4-2m7: 0-2 3m+: 0-0
Track: **LH: 1-3** RH: 0-1 **Tight: 1-2** Gall: 0-0
Aids: Bl: 0-0 Vi: 0-0 Tstrap: 0-0
Best Rating: 101 10/01 Carl 2m1f gd-sft Hdl

Showed the right attitude to land a poor novice hurdle at Sedgefield in October 2001.

Sunshine Boy

80 **100**

6-y-o b g Cadeaux Genereux-Sahara Baladee (USA) (Shadeed (USA))
G M McCourt D M Huglin

Placings:P0/51122-26 **(1137)**
2001/02: 24^{2}G, 22^{6}G

	Starts	1st	2nd	3rd	Win & Pl
Hurdles	2	0	1	0	1236
Career Total	**9**	**2**	**3**	**0**	**8283**

100 6/00 Fknm 2m7f110y F(0-100)HHdl GD £2671
93 5/00 Worc 2m4f F(0-100)HHdl GD £2065
Total win prize-money £4737

Going: Sf: 0-0 GS: 0-0 Gd: 0-2 GF: - Fm: 0-0
Distance: 2m/2m3: 0-0 2m4-2m7: 0-1 3m+: 0-1
Track: LH: 0-2 RH: 0-0 Tight: 0-1 Gall: 0-0
Aids: Bl: 0-0 Vi: 0-0 Tstrap: 0-0
Best Rating: 100 7/01 Worc 3m good Hdl

Sunshine Leader (IRE)

106 **100**

7-y-o b m Supreme Leader-Cherry Run (Deep Run)
E L James Mrs D C Samworth

Placings:*1232*-231330 **(4420)**
2001/02: 19^{2}G, 21^{3}S, 20^{1}S, 16^{3}S, 21^{3}S, 21^{0}GS

	Starts	1st	2nd	3rd	Win & Pl
Hurdles	6	1	1	3	6904
Career Total	**10**	**2**	**3**	**4**	**12666**

100 12/01 Leic 2m4f110y D Hdl SFT £3562
87 6/00 Cork 2m4f NHF GD £3864
Total win prize-money £7426

Going: Sf: 1-4 GS: 0-1 Gd: 0-1 GF: - Fm: 0-0
Distance: 2m/2m3: 0-2 **2m4-2m7: 1-4** 3m+: 0-0
Track: LH: 0-2 **RH: 1-4** Tight: 0-0 Gall: 0-2
Aids: Bl: 0-1 Vi: 0-0 Tstrap: 0-0
Best Rating: 100 2/02 Kemp 2m5f soft Hdl

A strongly-made mare, very consistent, but has only a solitary victory ay Leicester in December 2001 to her name since arriving from Ireland. Stays two and a half miles. Has won on good and acts on soft ground.

Suntas (IRE)

113(112h) (98h)**125**

7-y-o b m Riberetto-Shuil (IRE) (Meneval (USA))
T R George Mr & Mrs D A Gamble

Placings:0/32244-**42214P2** **(4541)**
2001/02: 17^{4}S, 20^{2}S, 22^{2}S, 24^{1}GS, 33^{4}S, 26^{P}HY, 25^{2}G

	Starts	1st	2nd	3rd	Win & Pl
Hurdles	1	0	0	0	0
Chases	6	1	3	0	11231
Career Total	**13**	**1**	**5**	**1**	**15032**

125 1/02 Hntg 3m E Ch G-S £3164
Total win prize-money £3164

Going: Sf: 0-5 GS: 1-1 Gd: 0-1 GF: - Fm: 0-0
Distance: 2m/2m3: 0-1 2m4-2m7: 0-2 **3m+: 1-4**
Track: LH: 0-3 **RH: 1-4** Tight: 0-1 **Gall: 1-2**
Aids: Bl: 0-0 Vi: 0-0 Tstrap: 0-0
Best Rating: 125 4/02 Hrfd 3m1f110y good Ch

An ex-Irish point-to-pointer, she won over fences in January 2002. Stays three miles over fences, but did not get home over four when a creditable fourth in the Eider. Suited by good to soft ground.

Sunuvugun

100 **74**

10-y-o b g Gunner B-Final Melody (Final Straw)
Mrs D Thomson Discounted Cashflow

Placings:*3PP/2043/15P/PFP24P*-PPP **(4769)**
2001/02: 21^{P}GF, 20^{P}HY, 25^{P}GF

	Starts	1st	2nd	3rd	Win & Pl
Chases	3	0	0	0	
Career Total	**19**	**1**	**2**	**2**	**6053**

98 9/99 Kels 3m1f E Ch G-F £2786
Total win prize-money £2786

Going: Sf: 0-1 GS: 0-0 Gd: 0-0 GF: - Fm: 0-2
Distance: 2m/2m3: 0-0 2m4-2m7: 0-2 3m+: 0-1
Track: LH: 0-3 RH: 0-0 Tight: 0-0 Gall: 0-0
Aids: Bl: 0-0 Vi: 0-0 Tstrap: 0-0
Best Rating: 98 10/99 Kels 3m1f good Ch

Supelo

5-y-o b m Superlative-Enchanteur (Damister (USA))
D McCain D McCain

Placings:*0* **(0744)**
2001/02: 16^{0}GS

	Starts	1st	2nd	3rd	Win & Pl
NH Flat	1	0	0	0	
Career Total	**1**	**0**	**0**	**0**	

Going: Sf: 0-0 GS: 0-1 Gd: 0-0 GF: - Fm: 0-0
Distance: 2m/2m3: 0-1 2m4-2m7: 0-0 3m+: 0-0
Track: LH: 0-1 RH: 0-0 Tight: 0-0 Gall: 0-0
Aids: Bl: 0-0 Vi: 0-0 Tstrap: 0-0
Best Rating:

Super Dollar (IRE)

100(104h) (104h)**115**

6-y-o ch g Great Commotion (USA)-L'Americaine (USA) (Verbatim (USA))
K C Bailey The Not Over Big Partnership

Placings:66441/B230043-51505 **(1026)**
2001/02: 16^{5}G, 19^{1}GF, 20^{5}GF, 20^{0}GF, 22^{5}G

	Starts	1st	2nd	3rd	Win & Pl
Hurdles	5	1	0	0	3262
Career Total	**17**	**2**	**1**	**2**	**8984**

104 6/01 Strf 2m3f F(0-110)HHdl G-F £3262
105 4/00 Fknm 2m D(0-110)HHdl GD £2837
Total win prize-money £6099

Going: Sf: 0-0 GS: 0-0 Gd: 0-2 GF: - Fm: 1-3
Distance: **2m/2m3: 1-2** 2m4-2m7: 0-3 3m+: 0-0
Track: **LH: 1-4** RH: 0-1 **Tight: 1-2** Gall: 0-1
Aids: Bl: 0-0 Vi: 0-0 Tstrap: 0-0
Best Rating: 105 4/00 Fknm 2m good Hdl

A winner over hurdles and acts on a sound surface. Effective at around two and a half miles.

Super Franky (IRE)

78(89h) (130h)**147**

9-y-o ch g Lanfranco-Teazle (Quayside)
Charles Byrnes Stayers Syndicate

Placings:*4/203/31*0131215145U1P/**3203F11**00-420010F **(4677)**
2001/02: 24^{4}GF, 24^{2}Y, 16^{0}Y, 24^{0}G, 22^{1}Y, 16^{0}S, 36^{F}G

	Starts	1st	2nd	3rd	Win & Pl
Hurdles	3	0	0	0	452

	Starts	1st	2nd	3rd	Win & Pl
Chases	4	1	1	0	16833
Career Total	**35**	**9**	**4**	**5**	**69098**

134	1/02	Tram	2m6f	Ch	YLD	£9171
142	10/00	Cork	3m	HCh	Y-S	£13000
130	10/00	Cork	2m5f	Ch	YLD	£4968
131	11/99	Cork	2m6f	Ch	SFT	£6160
105	9/99	List	2m4f	Hdl	HVY	£5616
119	8/99	Tral	2m6f	(0-123)HHdl	YLD	£4620
114	7/99	Gway	2m2f	(0-116)HHdl	G-F	£5217
94	7/99	Tipp	2m	Hdl	G-F	£3069
91	6/99	Tral	2m4f	NHF	GD	£2455

Total win prize-money £54280

Going: Sf: 0-1 GS: 0-0 Gd: 0-2 GF: - Fm: 0-1
Distance: 2m/2m3: 0-2 **2m4-2m7: 1-1** 3m+: 0-4
Track: LH: 0-1 **RH: 1-3** Tight: 0-1 Gall: 0-0
Aids: Bl: 0-2 Vi: 0-0 Tstrap: 0-0
Best Rating: 147 10/01 Limk 3m yield Ch

A game front runner, he was successful over fences at Tramore in January 2002. Possibly at his best around three miles, he is probably best with a bit of give underfoot.

Super Nomad

107(107h) **135**

7-y-o b g Nomadic Way (USA)-Super Sue (Lochnager)
M W Easterby T A Hughes & B Hutchinson

Placings:_245_/05315136123/214P-**1F452123** **(4421)**
2001/02: 17^{1}G, 20^{F}GS, 20^{4}S, 25^{5}GS, 19^{2}S, 16^{1}S, 16^{2}S, 18^{0}GS

	Starts	1st	2nd	3rd	Win & Pl
Chases	8	2	2	1	10872
Career Total	**26**	**6**	**5**	**4**	**34469**

135	2/02	Newc	2m110y	E Ch	SFT	£3055
116	11/01	Kels	2m1f	E Ch	GD	£3445
128	11/00	Aint	2m4f	C(0-135)HHdl	G-S	£10871
121	3/00	Newc	2m4f	D(0-110)HHdl	GD	£3256
112	1/00	Donc	2m110y	F(0-100)HHdl	G-F	£2138
107	12/99	Newc	2m4f	E Hdl	SFT	£2690

Total win prize-money £25458

Going: Sf: 1-4 GS: 0-3 Gd: 1-1 GF: - Fm: 0-0
Distance: **2m/2m3: 2-5** 2m4-2m7: 0-2 3m+: 0-1
Track: **LH: 2-7** RH: 0-1 Tight: 1-4 Gall: 1-2
Aids: Bl: 0-0 Vi: 0-0 **Tstrap: 1-4**
Best Rating: 135 2/02 Newc 2m110y soft Ch

Fair novice chaser, he acts on most types of ground and is effective at up to two miles four furlongs. Jumps soundly.

Super Rapier (IRE)

99(71c) (22c)**82+**

10-y-o b g Strong Gale-Misty Venture (Foggy Bell)
Ferdy Murphy Exors Of The Late Mr G A Hubbard

Placings:46343/3052**F33**/5**113**/3634/0P6-60006 **(4871)**
2001/02: 20^{6}G, 22^{0}G, 23^{0}G, 24^{0}G, 25^{6}GF

	Starts	1st	2nd	3rd	Win & Pl
Hurdles	4	0	0	0	0
Chases	1	0	0	0	0
Career Total	**28**	**2**	**1**	**8**	**12706**

109	5/98	Uttx	2m5f	E(0-115)HCh	G-F	£2866
109	5/98	Fknm	2m5f110y	E(0-110)HCh	GD	£4298

Total win prize-money £7164

Going: Sf: 0-0 GS: 0-0 Gd: 0-4 GF: - Fm: 0-1
Distance: 2m/2m3: 0-0 2m4-2m7: 0-3 3m+: 0-2
Track: LH: 0-3 RH: 0-1 Tight: 0-2 Gall: 0-0
Aids: Bl: 0-0 Vi: 0-0 Tstrap: 0-0
Best Rating: 109 9/98 Plum 2m5f gd-fm Ch

Handicap hurdler. Stays beyond three miles and acts on a sound surface.

Super Sammy

100 **103**

6-y-o br m Mesleh-Super Sue (Lochnager)
M W Easterby Whitestonecliffe Racing Partnership

Placings:_0-311_642 **(4315)**
2001/02: 16^{3}G, 16^{1}G, 16^{1}S, 20^{6}S, 16^{4}GS, 16^{2}HY

	Starts	1st	2nd	3rd	Win & Pl
NH Flat	3	2	0	1	4887
Hurdles	3	0	1	0	744
Career Total	**7**	**2**	**1**	**1**	**5631**

110	1/02	Newc	2m	H NHF	SFT	£1988
96	12/01	Donc	2m110y	H NHF	GD	£2562

Total win prize-money £4550

Going: Sf: 1-3 GS: 0-1 Gd: 1-2 GF: - Fm: 0-0
Distance: **2m/2m3: 2-5** 2m4-2m7: 0-1 3m+: 0-0
Track: **LH: 1-5** RH: 0-0 Tight: 0-2 **Gall: 1-2**
Aids: Bl: 0-0 Vi: 0-0 Tstrap: 0-0
Best Rating: 110 1/02 Newc 2m soft NHF

Successful in bumpers, she acts on good and soft ground but has shown lesser form over hurdles.

Super Sonic Sonia (IRE)

83 **25**

7-y-o b m Tirol-Lunulae (Tumble Wind (USA))
K A Morgan John Sheridan

Placings:00/000/00 **(1747)**
2001/02: 17^{0}GF, 17^{0}G

	Starts	1st	2nd	3rd	Win & Pl
Hurdles	2	0	0	0	
Career Total	**7**	**0**	**0**	**0**	

Going: Sf: 0-0 GS: 0-0 Gd: 0-1 GF: - Fm: 0-1
Distance: 2m/2m3: 0-2 2m4-2m7: 0-0 3m+: 0-0
Track: LH: 0-0 RH: 0-2 Tight: 0-2 Gall: 0-0
Aids: Bl: 0-0 Vi: 0-0 Tstrap: 0-0
Best Rating: 57 3/99 Navn 2m heavy Hdl

Super Tactics (IRE)

115(103h) **158**

14-y-o b g Furry Glen-Hilarys Pet (Bonne Noel)
R H Alner H V Perry

Placings:56302/62034123451/**321035**/5**0432413231**/**211411F42**/**3113U21**/**155P161**/**P**336364**220-U2224510** **(4914)**
2001/02: 24^{U}G, 20^{2}G, 20^{2}GS, 19^{2}G, 24^{4}G, 20^{5}G, 19^{1}GF, 20^{0}G

	Starts	1st	2nd	3rd	Win & Pl
Chases	8	1	3	0	26525
Career Total	**74**	**16**	**14**	**13**	**177082**

158	4/02	Asct	2m3f110y	C(0-130)HCh	G-F	£13780
164	4/99	Sand	2m4f110y	A Ch	GD	£19200
160	2/99	Kemp	2m	B Ch	SFT	£8208
170	10/98	Winc	2m5f	A HCh	G-S	£19050
160	2/98	Kemp	3m	A HCh	G-F	£29600
160	11/97	Kemp	2m4f110y	B(0-145)HCh	G-S	£4760
145	11/97	Newb	2m4f	B HCh	G-F	£7429
143	1/97	Kemp	2m	C(0-135)HCh	G-F	£4463
144	12/96	Uttx	2m	C(0-135)HCh	SFT	£4448
127	11/96	Newb	2m1f	E(0-125)HCh	GD	£3395
125	10/96	Kemp	2m	B(0-145)HCh	GD	£4351
119	5/96	Extr	2m3f110y	D(0-125)HCh	G-S	£3586
115	2/96	Kemp	2m4f110y	C(0-135)HCh	G-S	£4690
105	12/94	Thur	2m	(0-120)HCh	G-Y	£2120
103	4/94	Baln	2m4f	Ch	YLD	£2136
102	12/93	Limk	2m	Hdl	HVY	£3709

Total win prize-money £134931

Going: Sf: 0-0 GS: 0-1 Gd: 0-6 GF: - Fm: 1-1
Distance: 2m/2m3: 0-0 **2m4-2m7: 1-6** 3m+: 0-2
Track: LH: 0-0 **RH: 1-8** Tight: 0-0 Gall: 0-0
Aids: Bl: 0-0 Vi: 0-0 Tstrap: 0-0
Best Rating: 170 10/98 Winc 2m5f gd-sft Ch

A useful chaser at the veteran stage of his career, he rolled back the years when easily winning a valuable chase at Ascot in April 2002. He has a tremendous record at Kempton, goes well fresh, and appreciates a right-handed track. He acts on most types of ground and is effective from two to three miles.

Supercharmer

8-y-o ch g Charmer-Surpassing (Superlative)
M A Humphreys M A Humphreys

Placings:00/6-F **(0474)**
2001/02: 22^{F}G

	Starts	1st	2nd	3rd	Win & Pl
Chases	1	0	0	0	
Career Total	**4**	**0**	**0**	**0**	**0**

Going: Sf: 0-0 GS: 0-0 Gd: 0-1 GF: - Fm: 0-0
Distance: 2m/2m3: 0-0 2m4-2m7: 0-1 3m+: 0-0
Track: LH: 0-0 RH: 0-1 Tight: 0-1 Gall: 0-0
Aids: Bl: 0-0 Vi: 0-0 Tstrap: 0-0
Best Rating: 80 5/00 MRas 2m6f110y gd-sft Ch

Superior Risk (IRE)

109(109c) (129c)**129**

13-y-o b g Mandalus-Hal's Pauper (Official)
T R George Silkword Racing Partnership

Placings: 1/2F112/P/1/133U14P-1225 **(3894)**
2001/02: 20^{1}GS, 20^{2}S, 20^{2}HY, 21^{5}HY

	Starts	1st	2nd	3rd	Win & Pl
Hurdles	3	1	1	0	3235
Chases	1	0	1	0	1205
Career Total	**19**	**7**	**4**	**2**	**34429**

129	12/01	Hayd	2m4f	F Hdl	G-S	£2341
140	1/01	Plum	2m4f	D(0-125)HCh	HVY	£3867
134	11/00	Chep	2m110y	E(0-115)HCh	SFT	£3328
117	9/99	Worc	2m4f110y	D Ch	SFT	£3949
132	2/96	Tntn	3m110y	E Hdl	G-S	£2766
129	2/96	Ling	2m7f	E Hdl	HVY	£3078
111	4/95	Limk	2m4f	NHF	GD	£2712

Total win prize-money £22045

Going: Sf: 0-3 GS: 1-1 Gd: 0-0 GF: - Fm: 0-0
Distance: 2m/2m3: 0-0 **2m4-2m7: 1-4** 3m+: 0-0
Track: **LH: 1-2** RH: 0-1 Tight: 0-1 Gall: 0-0
Aids: Bl: 0-0 Vi: 0-0 Tstrap: 0-0
Best Rating: 140 1/01 Plum 2m4f heavy Ch

An enthusiastic veteran, effective over fences and hurdles, he goes well fresh and seems best when ridden aggressively at around two and a half miles in the mud.

Superior Weapon (IRE)

104 **108**

8-y-o b g Riverhead (USA)-Ballytrustan Maid (IRE)

(Orchestra)
F P Murtagh Hendy And Hammy Partnership

Placings:P-6353100 **(4872)**
2001/02: 20^{6}G, 16^{3}S, 16^{5}S, 16^{3}S, 17^{1}S, 20^{0}GF, 16^{0}GF

	Starts	1st	2nd	3rd	Win & Pl
Chases	7	1	0	2	4694
Career Total	**8**	**1**	**0**	**2**	**4694**

108	3/02	Kels	2m1f	E Ch	SFT	£3796

Total win prize-money £3796

Going: Sf: 1-4 GS: 0-0 Gd: 0-1 GF: - Fm: 0-2
Distance: **2m/2m3: 1-5** 2m4-2m7: 0-2 3m+: 0-0
Track: **LH: 1-6** RH: 0-1 **Tight: 1-1** Gall: 0-3
Aids: Bl: 0-0 Vi: 0-0 **Tstrap: 1-6**
Best Rating: 108 3/02 Kels 2m1f soft Ch

A winner twice in point-to-points up to three miles in the mud. Showed his first sign of form on similar ground at Newcastle in January and won a novice chase at Kelso in March. Handles any ground, usually tongue tied.

Supermick

86 **70**
11-y-o ch g Faustus (USA)-Lardana (Burglar)
M C Pipe P Clarke

Placings:6F0/1222206/3621034/2**31FF**14312/33122/F0644045/342020-000 **(1493)**
2001/02: 17^{0}G, 17^{0}G, 17^{0}GF

	Starts	1st	2nd	3rd	Win & Pl
Hurdles	3	0	0	0	
Career Total	**49**	**6**	**11**	**7**	**25002**

110	7/98	Strf	2m110y	E(0-115)HHdl	G-F	£2276
110	2/98	Winc	2m	E(0-110)HHdl	G-F	£2416
101	12/97	Hrfd	2m1f	G Hdl	GD	£1800
99	11/97	Plum	2m	E(0-115)HCh	G-F	£2890
84	11/96	Wind	2m	E(0-110)HHdl	GD	£2997
79	11/95	NAbb	2m1f	G(0-95)HHdl	G-S	£1989

Total win prize-money £14369

Going: Sf: 0-0 GS: 0-0 Gd: 0-2 GF: - Fm: 0-1
Distance: 2m/2m3: 0-3 2m4-2m7: 0-0 3m+: 0-0
Track: LH: 0-2 RH: 0-1 Tight: 0-2 Gall: 0-0
Aids: Bl: 0-0 Vi: 0-3 Tstrap: 0-0
Best Rating: 110 7/98 Strf 2m110y gd-fm Hdl

Superstar Express (IRE)

74f **80f**
5-y-o br g Jurado (USA)-Easter Bee (IRE) (Phardante (FR))
J I A Charlton J I A Charlton

Placings:*000* **(4526)**
2001/02: 16^{0}HY, 16^{0}GF, 17^{0}G

	Starts	1st	2nd	3rd	Win & Pl
NH Flat	3	0	0	0	
Career Total	**3**	**0**	**0**	**0**	

Going: Sf: 0-1 GS: 0-0 Gd: 0-1 GF: - Fm: 0-1
Distance: 2m/2m3: 0-3 2m4-2m7: 0-0 3m+: 0-0
Track: LH: 0-1 RH: 0-2 Tight: 0-0 Gall: 0-1
Aids: Bl: 0-0 Vi: 0-0 Tstrap: 0-2
Best Rating: 80 3/02 Hntg 2m110y gd-fm NHF

Supertop

101 **110**
14-y-o b/br g High Top-Myth (Troy)
L Lungo Mrs Barbara Lungo

Placings:0244/**11F**/2112151332/3113/10446F5F006/035501P/F4360-105005 **(4143)**
2001/02: 24^{1}GF, 20^{0}S, 16^{5}GS, 20^{0}GS, 20^{0}GS, 20^{5}HY

	Starts	1st	2nd	3rd	Win & Pl
Hurdles	6	1	0	0	3598
Career Total	**50**	**11**	**4**	**6**	**40004**

110	5/01	Prth	3m110y	F(0-100)HHdl	G-F	£3598
102	4/00	Newc	2m4f	G(0-95)HHdl	G-S	£1617
129	5/98	Prth	2m4f110y	D(0-120)HHdl	G-F	£3468
123	10/97	Carl	2m1f	D(0-120)HHdl	FRM	£2689
120	10/97	Kels	2m110y	D(0-125)HHdl	G-F	£2633
113	12/96	Muss	3m	D(0-125)HHdl	FRM	£2705
117	11/96	Aint	2m4f	E(0-110)HHdl	GD	£2626
104	10/96	Hexm	2m	B Hdl	G-F	£6192
96	10/96	Hexm	2m	G Hdl	FRM	£2067
98	11/95	Hexm	2m110y	F(0-100)HCh	G-F	£2490
93	10/95	Weth	2m	D Ch	GD	£4216

Total win prize-money £34302

Going: Sf: 0-2 GS: 0-3 Gd: 0-0 GF: - Fm: 1-1
Distance: 2m/2m3: 0-1 2m4-2m7: 0-4 **3m+: 1-1**
Track: LH: 0-5 **RH: 1-1** Tight: 0-0 Gall: 0-1
Aids: Bl: 0-0 Vi: 0-0 Tstrap: 0-0
Best Rating: 129 5/98 Prth 2m4f110y gd-fm Hdl

Modest handicap hurdler, stays three miles on a sound surface.

Supreme Attraction (IRE)

88f **101f**
5-y-o b m Supreme Leader-Tourist Attraction (IRE) (Pollerton)
Noel T Chance Mrs Norma Kelly

Placings:*01* **(3896)**
2001/02: 17^{0}G, 16^{1}HY

	Starts	1st	2nd	3rd	Win & Pl
NH Flat	2	1	0	0	1897
Career Total	**2**	**1**	**0**	**0**	**1897**

101	2/02	Wwck	2m	H NHF	HVY	£1897

Total win prize-money £1897

Going: Sf: 1-1 GS: 0-0 Gd: 0-1 GF: - Fm: 0-0
Distance: **2m/2m3: 1-2** 2m4-2m7: 0-0 3m+: 0-0
Track: **LH: 1-1** RH: 0-1 Tight: 0-0 Gall: 0-0
Aids: Bl: 0-0 Vi: 0-0 Tstrap: 0-0
Best Rating: 101 2/02 Wwck 2m heavy NHF

Out of a useful racemare, she has shown promise in bumpers.

Supreme Bramble (IRE)

105 **97**
6-y-o b m Supreme Leader-Bramble Bird (Pitpan)
Mrs M Reveley Andy Peake & David Jackson

Placings:*3320*-200F **(3785)**
2001/02: 20^{2}G, 20^{0}G, 20^{0}S, 20^{F}S

	Starts	1st	2nd	3rd	Win & Pl
Hurdles	4	0	1	0	1086
Career Total	**8**	**0**	**2**	**2**	**2056**

Going: Sf: 0-2 GS: 0-0 Gd: 0-2 GF: - Fm: 0-0
Distance: 2m/2m3: 0-0 2m4-2m7: 0-4 3m+: 0-0
Track: LH: 0-4 RH: 0-0 Tight: 0-0 Gall: 0-2
Aids: Bl: 0-0 Vi: 0-0 Tstrap: 0-0
Best Rating: 108 3/01 Hntg 2m110y soft NHF

Showed ability in bumpers and over hurdles but was sadly killed at Newcastle in February. (DEAD)

Supreme Breeze (IRE)

107(59h) **99**
7-y-o b g Supreme Leader-Merry Breeze (Strong Gale)
Ferdy Murphy The Supreme Three

Placings:*0*/21530-**PF252F2** **(4521)**
2001/02: 25^{P}G, 19^{F}GS, 19^{2}S, 16^{5}S, 25^{2}S, 21^{F}S, 20^{2}GS

	Starts	1st	2nd	3rd	Win & Pl
Chases	7	0	3	0	3322
Career Total	**13**	**1**	**4**	**1**	**7871**

95	11/00	Newc	2m4f	E Hdl	SFT	£2478

Total win prize-money £2478

Going: Sf: 0-4 GS: 0-2 Gd: 0-1 GF: - Fm: 0-0
Distance: 2m/2m3: 0-2 2m4-2m7: 0-3 3m+: 0-2
Track: LH: 0-5 RH: 0-2 Tight: 0-4 Gall: 0-2
Aids: Bl: 0-2 Vi: 0-0 Tstrap: 0-0
Best Rating: 99 4/02 Carl 2m4f gd-sft Ch

Winner over hurdles but only modest form over fences.

Supreme Buccaneer (IRE)

8-y-o b g Supreme Leader-Night Blade (Fine Blade (USA))
Mrs S M Johnson I K Johnson

Placings:*0*/*0*-P **(2388)**
2001/02: 20^{P}S

	Starts	1st	2nd	3rd	Win & Pl
Hurdles	1	0	0	0	
Career Total	**3**	**0**	**0**	**0**	

Going: Sf: 0-1 GS: 0-0 Gd: 0-0 GF: - Fm: 0-0
Distance: 2m/2m3: 0-0 2m4-2m7: 0-1 3m+: 0-0
Track: LH: 0-1 RH: 0-0 Tight: 0-0 Gall: 0-0
Aids: Bl: 0-0 Vi: 0-0 Tstrap: 0-0
Best Rating: 75 5/99 Chep 2m110y good NHF

Supreme Catch (IRE)

103 **121**
5-y-o b g Supreme Leader-Lucky Trout (Beau Charmeur (FR))
Miss H C Knight Bicknall Street Partnership

Placings:12 **(4300)**
2001/02: 20^{1}S, 20^{2}HY

	Starts	1st	2nd	3rd	Win & Pl
Hurdles	2	1	1	0	3672
Career Total	**2**	**1**	**1**	**0**	**3672**

121	3/02	Font	2m4f	E Hdl	SFT	£2530

Total win prize-money £2531

Going: Sf: 1-2 GS: 0-0 Gd: 0-0 GF: - Fm: 0-0
Distance: 2m/2m3: 0-0 **2m4-2m7: 1-2** 3m+: 0-0
Track: LH: 0-1 RH: 0-0 **Tight: 1-1** Gall: 0-0
Aids: Bl: 0-0 Vi: 0-0 Tstrap: 0-0
Best Rating: 121 3/02 Uttx 2m4f110y heavy Hdl

Ex-Irish pointer, made a winning debut over hurdles at Fontwell. Effective over two and a half miles, should get further.

Supreme Charm (IRE)

107 **146**

10-y-o b g Sovereign Water (FR)-Welsh Charmer (Welsh Captain)
K C Bailey P J Vogt

Placings: *114506*/212111121/**211316/420413FP/3163 U6-24U2214650** **(4913)**
2001/02: 25^{2}F, 23^{4}GF, 34^{U}GF, 24^{2}G, 23^{2}GF, 26^{1}G, 24^{4}G, 24^{6}GS, 36^{5}G, 29^{0}G

	Starts	1st	2nd	3rd	Win & Pl
Chases	10	1	3	0	31765
Career Total	**45**	**14**	**8**	**4**	**124687**

146	12/01	Donc	3m2f	B(0-140)HCh	GD	£11242
148	11/00	Chel	3m7f	B Ch	SFT	£21255
145	2/00	Leic	2m7f110y	D(0-125)HCh	G-S	£7085
137	3/99	Asct	2m3f110y	C HCh	G-F	£13810
130	1/99	Ludl	2m	E Ch	G-S	£2866
114	12/98	Ludl	2m	D Ch	GD	£3581
130	4/98	Asct	2m4f	D Hdl	SFT	£3777
128	4/98	Asct	3m	C(0-135)HHdl	GD	£5152
123	12/97	Extr	2m2f	D Hdl	SFT	£3841
118	11/97	Asct	2m4f	C Hdl	SFT	£3582
114	11/97	Asct	2m4f	E(0-105)HHdl	GD	£3598
96	9/97	Strf	2m6f110y	D Hdl	G-F	£3038
100	7/96	Bell	2m1f	NHF	GD	£3685
96	6/96	Slig	2m	NHF	YLD	£2824

Total win prize-money £89341

Going: Sf: 0-0 GS: 0-1 Gd: 1-5 GF: - Fm: 0-4
Distance: 2m/2m3: 0-0 2m4-2m7: 0-0 **3m+: 1-10**
Track: **LH: 1-8** RH: 0-2 Tight: 0-1 **Gall: 1-4**
Aids: Bl: 0-0 Vi: 0-0 Tstrap: 0-0
Best Rating: 148 11/00 Chel 3m7f soft Ch

A sound jumper, he won the Sporting Index Chase over Cheltenham's cross-country course in November 2000. A thorough stayer, he won over three miles two at Doncaster in December 2001 and finished a fine fifth in the 2002 National. Acts on any ground and is probably best with patient tactics employed.

Supreme Confidence (IRE)

93f **98f**

6-y-o b g Lord Americo-Ceoltoir Dubh (Black Minstrel)
Ferdy Murphy S L & M A Hubbard Rodwell

Placings: *6-3* (0181)
2001/02: 16^{3}GF

	Starts	1st	2nd	3rd	Win & Pl
NH Flat	1	0	0	1	234
Career Total	**2**	**0**	**0**	**1**	**234**

Going: Sf: 0-0 GS: 0-0 Gd: 0-0 GF: - Fm: 0-1
Distance: 2m/2m3: 0-1 2m4-2m7: 0-0 3m+: 0-0
Track: LH: 0-1 RH: 0-0 Tight: 0-0 Gall: 0-0
Aids: Bl: 0-0 Vi: 0-0 Tstrap: 0-0
Best Rating: 98 5/01 Ayr 2m gd-fm NHF

Supreme Dawn (IRE)

84f **96f**

5-y-o b g Supreme Leader-Tudor Dawn (Deep Run)
A J Lidderdale George Ward

Placings: *4* **(4570)**
2001/02: 16^{4}G

	Starts	1st	2nd	3rd	Win & Pl
NH Flat	1	0	0	0	0
Career Total	**1**	**0**	**0**	**0**	**0**

Going: Sf: 0-0 GS: 0-0 Gd: 0-1 GF: - Fm: 0-0
Distance: 2m/2m3: 0-1 2m4-2m7: 0-0 3m+: 0-0
Track: LH: 0-0 RH: 0-1 Tight: 0-0 Gall: 0-0
Aids: Bl: 0-0 Vi: 0-0 Tstrap: 0-0
Best Rating: 96 4/02 Towc 2m good NHF

Half-brother to smart hurdler Dawn Leader amongst others, ran a creditable race on his bumper debut and should improve for the experience

Supreme Day (IRE)

9-y-o g Supreme Leader-Autumn Spirit (Deep Run)
Miss J M Furness J C Clark

Placings: *032125*/340/P **(4396)**
2001/02: 25^{P}HY

	Starts	1st	2nd	3rd	Win & Pl
Chases	1	0	0	0	
Career Total	**10**	**1**	**2**	**2**	**5040**

99	1/99	Fknm	2m7f110y	E Hdl	G-S	£2168

Total win prize-money £2169

Going: Sf: 0-1 GS: 0-0 Gd: 0-0 GF: - Fm: 0-0
Distance: 2m/2m3: 0-0 2m4-2m7: 0-0 3m+: 0-1
Track: LH: 0-1 RH: 0-0 Tight: 0-1 Gall: 0-0
Aids: Bl: 0-0 Vi: 0-0 Tstrap: 0-0
Best Rating: 107 5/99 Towc 3m gd-fm Hdl

Supreme Developer (IRE)

113f **126f**

5-y-o b g Supreme Leader-Bettys The Boss (IRE) (Deep Run)
Anthony Mullins Mrsandurkan

Placings: *161* **(4948a)**
2001/02: 16^{1}YS, 16^{6}GS, 16^{1}G

	Starts	1st	2nd	3rd	Win & Pl
NH Flat	3	2	0	0	16408
Career Total	**3**	**2**	**0**	**0**	**16408**

125	4/02	Punc	2m	NHF	GD	£11963
118	1/02	Fair	2m	NHF	Y-S	£4444

Total win prize-money £16408

Going: Sf: 0-0 GS: 0-1 Gd: 1-1 GF: - Fm: 0-0
Distance: **2m/2m3: 2-3** 2m4-2m7: 0-0 3m+: 0-0
Track: LH: 0-1 **RH: 2-2** Tight: 0-0 Gall: 0-0
Aids: Bl: 0-0 Vi: 0-0 Tstrap: 0-0
Best Rating: 126 3/02 Chel 2m110y gd-sft NHF

Useful Irish bumper horse. Won at Fairyhouse before running well in the Festival bumper, and won a good race at Punchestown in April. Suited by cut in the ground.

Supreme Fortune (IRE)

113 **127**

8-y-o b g Supreme Leader-Lucylet (Kinglet)
Mrs M Reveley The Supreme Partnership

Placings: *2034*/133515113555/02U14P-003352066 **(4010)**
2001/02: 16^{0}G, 16^{0}G, 16^{3}G, 16^{3}G, 16^{5}S, 20^{2}S, 20^{0}S, 20^{6}S, 16^{6}S

	Starts	1st	2nd	3rd	Win & Pl
Hurdles	9	0	1	2	5028
Career Total	**31**	**5**	**3**	**6**	**32028**

124	1/01	Hayd	2m	B(0-140)HHdl	SFT	£8392
117	2/00	Catt	2m3f	D Hdl	GD	£3198
121	1/00	Newc	2m	B Hdl	SFT	£6857
124	12/99	Newc	2m	F(0-105)HHdl	SFT	£2305
110	5/99	Aint	2m110y	D Hdl	G-S	£2905

Total win prize-money £23660

Going: Sf: 0-5 GS: 0-0 Gd: 0-4 GF: - Fm: 0-0
Distance: 2m/2m3: 0-6 2m4-2m7: 0-3 3m+: 0-0
Track: LH: 0-9 RH: 0-0 Tight: 0-0 Gall: 0-2
Aids: Bl: 0-0 Vi: 0-0 Tstrap: 0-0
Best Rating: 127 12/01 Hayd 2m4f soft Hdl

Fair hurdler, he likes to come late off a strong pace. Has shown a tendency to hang left under pressure. Acts well with cut in the ground and is effective at around two miles.

Supreme Glory (IRE)

113 **160**

9-y-o b g Supreme Leader-Pentlows (Sheer Grit)
P G Murphy C J L Moorsom

Placings: 221FP4/521343-1415 (3699)
2001/02: 28^{1}S, 28^{4}S, 29^{1}GS, 24^{5}S

	Starts	1st	2nd	3rd	Win & Pl
Chases	4	2	0	0	50144
Career Total	**16**	**4**	**3**	**2**	**90033**

160	12/01	Chep	3m5f110y	A HCh	G-S	£43500
150	11/01	Strf	3m4f	D(0-125)HCh	SFT	£4160
148	12/00	Extr	4m	D(0-120)HCh	HVY	£8352
133	12/99	Wwck	3m1f110y	D Ch	SFT	£6222

Total win prize-money £62236

Going: Sf: 1-3 GS: 1-1 Gd: 0-0 GF: - Fm: 0-0
Distance: 2m/2m3: 0-0 2m4-2m7: 0-0 **3m+: 2-4**
Track: **LH: 2-4** RH: 0-0 **Tight: 1-1** Gall: 0-1
Aids: Bl: 0-0 Vi: 0-0 Tstrap: 0-0
Best Rating: 160 12/01 Chep 3m5f110y gd-sft Ch

A dour stayer, he has a good record when racing over marathon distances and took the Welsh National at Chepstow in December. Ran an eyecatching Grand National trial in a conditions race at Newbury. Suited by testing conditions, he jumps soundly and acts on soft ground.

Supreme Hill (IRE)

101f **121f**

5-y-o br g Supreme Leader-Regents Prancer (Prince Regent (FR))
C J Mann J E Brown

Placings: *1522* **(3798)**
2001/02: 16^{1}S, 16^{5}GS, 16^{2}S, 16^{2}S

	Starts	1st	2nd	3rd	Win & Pl
NH Flat	4	1	2	0	4839
Career Total	**4**	**1**	**2**	**0**	**4839**

121	12/01	Wwck	2m	H NHF	SFT	£1708

Total win prize-money £1708

Going: Sf: 1-3 GS: 0-1 Gd: 0-0 GF: - Fm: 0-0
Distance: **2m/2m3: 1-4** 2m4-2m7: 0-0 3m+: 0-0
Track: **LH: 1-3** RH: 0-1 Tight: 0-0 Gall: 0-0
Aids: Bl: 0-0 Vi: 0-0 Tstrap: 0-0
Best Rating: 121 12/01 Wwck 2m soft NHF

Showed an encouraging turn of foot to land his racecourse debut in a Warwick bumper, and was held subsequently.

Supreme Irony (IRE)

106(93h) (101h)105

9-y-o b g Supreme Leader-Florenanti (Floriferous)

M J Roberts Mike Roberts

Placings:0051/004/B4-5PP36 **(4761)**

2001/02: 20^{5}G, 20^{P}S, 21^{P}S, 19^{3}GS, 19^{6}GF

	Starts	1st	2nd	3rd	Win & Pl
Hurdles	3	0	0	0	0
Chases	2	0	0	1	724
Career Total	**14**	**1**	**0**	**1**	**2919**
105 4/99 Folk 2m1f110y H NHF G-F					£1483

Total win prize-money £1483

Going: Sf: 0-2 GS: 0-1 Gd: 0-1 GF: - Fm: 0-1
Distance: 2m/2m3: 0-1 2m4-2m7: 0-4 3m+: 0-0
Track: LH: 0-2 RH: 0-3 Tight: 0-3 Gall: 0-0
Aids: Bl: 0-0 Vi: 0-0 Tstrap: 0-0
Best Rating: 105 4/02 Tntn 2m3f gd-sft Ch

A fast ground bumper winner, has shown limited ability both over hurdles and fences on softer ground subsequently. Needs three miles.

Supreme Lad (IRE)

98 115

8-y-o b g Supreme Leader-April Shade (Harwell)

M W Easterby Lord Daresbury & The Hon Mrs E Greenall

Placings:24311/5 **(4895)**

2001/02: 20^{5}G

	Starts	1st	2nd	3rd	Win & Pl
Chases	1	0	0	0	0
Career Total	**6**	**2**	**1**	**1**	**7344**
124 3/00 Donc 2m4f E Hdl G-S					£2688
124 1/00 Weth 2m4f110y D Hdl SFT					£3367

Total win prize-money £6055

Going: Sf: 0-0 GS: 0-0 Gd: 0-1 GF: - Fm: 0-0
Distance: 2m/2m3: 0-0 2m4-2m7: 0-1 3m+: 0-0
Track: LH: 0-0 RH: 0-1 Tight: 0-0 Gall: 0-0
Aids: Bl: 0-0 Vi: 0-0 Tstrap: 0-0
Best Rating: 124 3/00 Donc 2m4f gd-sft Hdl

Supreme Lass (IRE)

96f 99f

6-y-o b m Supreme Leader-Falas Lass (Belfalas)

G M Moore Ean Muller

Placings:*2401* **(3999)**

2001/02: 17^{2}GS, 16^{4}G, 16^{0}GS, 16^{1}S

	Starts	1st	2nd	3rd	Win & Pl
NH Flat	4	1	1	0	2129
Career Total	**4**	**1**	**1**	**0**	**2129**
99 3/02 Donc 2m110y H NHF SFT					£1666

Total win prize-money £1666

Going: Sf: 1-1 GS: 0-2 Gd: 0-1 GF: - Fm: 0-0
Distance: **2m/2m3: 1-4** 2m4-2m7: 0-0 3m+: 0-0
Track: **LH: 1-4** RH: 0-0 Tight: 0-2 **Gall: 1-1**
Aids: Bl: 0-0 Vi: 0-0 Tstrap: 0-0
Best Rating: 99 3/02 Donc 2m110y soft NHF

Took a mares' only bumper at Doncaster in March.

Supreme Native (IRE)

104 109

6-y-o b g Be My Native (USA)-Ballough Bui (IRE) (Supreme Leader)

P F Nicholls Mrs Angela Tincknell

Placings:*2-233* **(4479)**

2001/02: 16^{2}G, 19^{3}G, 19^{3}G

	Starts	1st	2nd	3rd	Win & Pl
NH Flat	1	0	1	0	460
Hurdles	2	0	0	2	824
Career Total	**4**	**0**	**2**	**2**	**1284**

Going: Sf: 0-0 GS: 0-0 Gd: 0-3 GF: - Fm: 0-0
Distance: 2m/2m3: 0-3 2m4-2m7: 0-0 3m+: 0-0
Track: LH: 0-0 RH: 0-3 Tight: 0-0 Gall: 0-0
Aids: Bl: 0-0 Vi: 0-0 Tstrap: 0-0
Best Rating: 109 3/02 Extr 2m3f good Hdl

Placed in all starts in bumpers and hurdles. Suited by good ground, but seems a little short of pace.

Supreme Optimist (IRE)

5-y-o b g Supreme Leader-Armagale (IRE) (Strong Gale)

N G Richards H R C Catherwood

Placings:50 **(4874)**

2001/02: 16^{5}S, 20^{0}G

	Starts	1st	2nd	3rd	Win & Pl
NH Flat	1	0	0	0	0
Hurdles	1	0	0	0	0
Career Total	**2**	**0**	**0**	**0**	**0**

Going: Sf: 0-1 GS: 0-0 Gd: 0-1 GF: - Fm: 0-0
Distance: 2m/2m3: 0-1 2m4-2m7: 0-1 3m+: 0-0
Track: LH: 0-1 RH: 0-1 Tight: 0-0 Gall: 0-0
Aids: Bl: 0-0 Vi: 0-0 Tstrap: 0-0
Best Rating: 96 3/02 Ayr 2m soft NHF

Supreme Prince (IRE)

97f 117f

5-y-o b g Supreme Leader-Strong Serenade (IRE) (Strong Gale)

P J Hobbs Mrs Karola Vann

Placings:*1* **(1773)**

2001/02: 17^{1}GS

	Starts	1st	2nd	3rd	Win & Pl
NH Flat	1	1	0	0	1810
Career Total	**1**	**1**	**0**	**0**	**1810**
117 10/01 Extr 2m1f H NHF G-S					£1809

Total win prize-money £1810

Going: Sf: 0-0 GS: 1-1 Gd: 0-0 GF: - Fm: 0-0
Distance: **2m/2m3: 1-1** 2m4-2m7: 0-0 3m+: 0-0
Track: LH: 0-0 **RH: 1-1** Tight: 0-0 Gall: 0-0
Aids: Bl: 0-0 Vi: 0-0 Tstrap: 0-0
Best Rating: 117 10/01 Extr 2m1f gd-sft NHF

Well regarded at home and bred for the job, stayed on strongly, albeit running green, to score at first time of asking in an two miles one Exeter bumper on soft ground. Should make a lovely chaser in time.

Supreme Quest (IRE)

112 116

6-y-o b g Supreme Leader-Hazy River (Over The River (FR))

J J O'Neill Exors Of The Late Robert Hitchins

Placings:*1/002PB1U* **(4817)**

2001/02: 16^{0}GS, 22^{0}G, 24^{2}HY, 24^{P}HY, 24^{B}S, 24^{1}G, 24^{U}GF

	Starts	1st	2nd	3rd	Win & Pl
NH Flat	1	0	0	0	0
Hurdles	6	1	1	0	3744
Career Total	**8**	**2**	**1**	**0**	**9632**
114 4/02 Uttx 3m110y E(0-100)HHdl GD					£3178
94 4/00 Fair 2m2f NHF G-Y					£5888

Total win prize-money £9066

Going: Sf: 0-3 GS: 0-1 Gd: 1-2 GF: - Fm: 0-1
Distance: 2m/2m3: 0-1 2m4-2m7: 0-1 **3m+: 1-5**
Track: **LH: 1-5** RH: 0-1 Tight: 0-1 Gall: 0-0
Aids: Bl: 0-0 Vi: 0-0 Tstrap: 0-0
Best Rating: 114 4/02 Uttx 3m110y good Hdl

Fair novice hurdler around three miles who lacks scope. Wears a visor and acts on most types of ground.

Supreme Silence (IRE)

103 88

5-y-o b g Bluebird (USA)-Why So Silent (Mill Reef (USA))

Jedd O'Keeffe Wetherby Racing Bureau 50

Placings:P-5651PPP0 **(4858)**

2001/02: 16^{5}GF, 20^{6}GS, 16^{5}F, 20^{1}G, 22^{P}GS, 24^{P}GS, 20^{P}G, 16^{0}G

	Starts	1st	2nd	3rd	Win & Pl
Hurdles	8	1	0	0	2398
Career Total	**9**	**1**	**0**	**0**	**2398**
88 6/01 Hexm 2m4f110y E Hdl GD					£2397

Total win prize-money £2398

Going: Sf: 0-0 GS: 0-3 Gd: 1-3 GF: - Fm: 0-2
Distance: 2m/2m3: 0-3 **2m4-2m7: 1-4** 3m+: 0-1
Track: **LH: 1-6** RH: 0-1 Tight: 0-1 Gall: 0-1
Aids: Bl: 0-1 Vi: 0-0 Tstrap: 0-1
Best Rating: 88 6/01 Hexm 2m4f110y good Hdl

Won a novice hurdle at Hexham in the summer of 2001 over two and a half miles. Should stay further and will make a chaser in time. Has won on a sound surface.

Supreme Soviet

108 108

12-y-o ch g Presidium-Sylvan Song (Song)

A C Whillans Mrs L M Whillans

Placings:050/46/F32220/24204/16203/114014/5350P141/564P03000P-3202201OP **(4142)**

2001/02: 26^{3}GF, 20^{2}GF, 20^{0}GS, 24^{2}G, 27^{2}G, 25^{0}GS, 24^{1}S, 24°S, 25^{P}HY

	Starts	1st	2nd	3rd	Win & Pl
Chases	9	1	3	1	8230
Career Total	**54**	**7**	**9**	**5**	**37487**
108 2/02 Muss 3m E(0-105)HCh SFT					£3396
119 3/00 Carl 2m4f110y F(0-110)HCh G-S					£4738
114 2/00 Muss 3m F(0-95)HCh G-S					£2938
119 12/98 Ayr 2m4f E(0-105)HCh HVY					£3187
122 6/98 Prth 2m4f110y E(0-115)HCh G-F					£4143
113 5/98 Kels 2m6f110y E Ch G-F					£2424
88 5/97 Prth 2m4f110y E Hdl SFT					£2747

Total win prize-money £23575

Going: Sf: 1-3 GS: 0-2 Gd: 0-2 GF: 0-2 Fm: 0-2
Distance: 2m/2m3: 0-0 2m4-2m7: 0-2 **3m+: 1-7**
Track: LH: 0-4 **RH: 1-4 Tight: 1-4** Gall: 0-0
Aids: Bl: 0-0 Vi: 0-0 Tstrap: 0-0
Best Rating: 122 6/98 Prth 2m4f110y gd-fm Ch

Moderate three-mile chaser, acts on any ground.

Supreme Storm (IRE)

99(98h) (92h)118+

7-y-o b g Supreme Leader-Angolass (Al Sirat (USA))

B G Powell P Keane

Placings:*40/0*030 (4398)

2001/02: 17^{0}G, 21^{0}S, 20^{3}GS, 24^{0}S

	Starts	1st	2nd	3rd	Win & Pl
NH Flat	1	0	0	0	0
Hurdles	3	0	0	1	663
Career Total	**6**	**0**	**0**	**1**	**663**

Going: Sf: 0-2 GS: 0-1 Gd: 0-1 GF: - Fm: 0-0
Distance: 2m/2m3: 0-1 2m4-2m7: 0-2 3m+: 0-1
Track: LH: 0-3 RH: 0-1 Tight: 0-2 Gall: 0-1
Aids: Bl: 0-0 Vi: 0-0 Tstrap: 0-0
Best Rating: 100 11/99 Chep 2m110y gd-sft NHF

Supreme Toss (IRE)

104f 98f

6-y-o b g Supreme Leader-Sleemana (Prince Hansel)

R T Phillips The Coin Tossers

Placings:*31* (4166)

2001/02: 10^{3}G, 10^{1}GS

	Starts	1st	2nd	3rd	Win & Pl
NH Flat	2	1	0	1	2229
Career Total	**2**	**1**	**0**	**1**	**2229**
98 3/02 Wwck 2m	H NHF			G-S	£1981

Total win prize-money £1981

Going: Sf: 0-1 GS: 1-1 Gd: 0-0 GF: - Fm: 0-0
Distance: **2m/2m3: 1-2** 2m4-2m7: 0-0 3m+: 0-0
Track: **LH: 1-1** RH: 0-1 Tight: 0-0 Gall: 0-0
Aids: Bl: 0-0 Vi: 0-0 Tstrap: 0-0
Best Rating: 98 3/02 Wwck 2m gd-sft NHF

Off the mark on only his second ever outing in a bumper at Warwick in March.

Supremely Red (IRE)

84 89+

5-y-o b g Supreme Leader-Her Name Was Lola (Pitskelly)

M C Pipe D Rees

Placings:*4* (4506)

2001/02: 17^{4}G

	Starts	1st	2nd	3rd	Win & Pl
NH Flat	1	0	0	0	0
Career Total	**1**	**0**	**0**	**0**	**0**

Going: Sf: 0-0 GS: 0-0 Gd: 0-1 GF: - Fm: 0-0
Distance: 2m/2m3: 0-1 2m4-2m7: 0-0 3m+: 0-0
Track: LH: 0-1 RH: 0-0 Tight: 0-1 Gall: 0-0
Aids: Bl: 0-0 Vi: 0-0 Tstrap: 0-0
Best Rating: 86 3/02 NAbb 2m1f good NHF

Looked doubtful stayer when tried over two and three-quarter miles on hurdling debut.

Supremism

8-y-o b g Be My Chief (USA)-Ever Welcome (Be My Guest (USA))

Mrs H E Rees (C J Mann 30/6) Mrs H E Rees

Placings:5240634/230/0/4-133**10** (4483)

2001/02: 19^{1}G, 19^{3}GF, 20^{3}G, 24^{1}S, 19^{0}G

	Starts	1st	2nd	3rd	Win & Pl
Hurdles	3	1	0	2	4915
Chases	2	1	0	0	3038
Career Total	**17**	**2**	**2**	**4**	**10352**
118 3/02 Tntn 3m	H Ch			SFT	£3038
123 5/01 Hrfd 2m3f110y	D(0-120)HHdl			GD	£3552

Total win prize-money £6590

Going: Sf: 1-1 GS: 0-0 Gd: 1-3 GF: - Fm: 0-1
Distance: 2m/2m3: 0-0 2m4-2m7: 1-4 3m+: 1-1
Track: LH: 0-1 **RH: 2-4 Tight: 1-2** Gall: 0-0
Aids: Bl: 0-0 Vi: 0-0 Tstrap: 0-0
Best Rating: 123 5/01 Hrfd 2m3f110y good Hdl

A winning hurdler, he has become a useful sort in points/hunter chases. Acts on good and soft ground.

Sur Le Fil (IRE)

98 75

5-y-o b m Funambule (USA)-Best Choice (FR) (Rainbow Quest (USA))

Nick Williams Mrs Jane Kelly

Placings:0433 (1131)

2001/02: 17^{0}GS, 17^{4}G, 17^{3}G, 16^{3}GF

	Starts	1st	2nd	3rd	Win & Pl
Hurdles	4	0	0	2	749
Career Total	**4**	**0**	**0**	**2**	**749**

Going: Sf: 0-0 GS: 0-1 Gd: 0-2 GF: - Fm: 0-1
Distance: 2m/2m3: 0-4 2m4-2m7: 0-0 3m+: 0-0
Track: LH: 0-2 RH: 0-2 Tight: 0-1 Gall: 0-0
Aids: Bl: 0-0 Vi: 0-0 Tstrap: 0-0
Best Rating: 75 8/01 Worc 2m gd-fm Hdl

Surabaya (FR)

97(83h) 75

7-y-o ch m Galetto (FR)-Silver Sea (FR) (Gay Mecene (USA))

F Jordan Supercraft Structures Limited

Placings:23P0P/P0200/40P5**4P-5PF46FPP** (2174)

2001/02: 20^{5}GF, 23^{P}G, 26^{F}GF, 23^{4}GF, 25^{6}GF, 26^{F}GF, 25^{P}G, 26^{P}S

	Starts	1st	2nd	3rd	Win & Pl
Chases	8	0	0	0	275
Career Total	**24**	**0**	**2**	**1**	**1012**

Going: Sf: 0-1 GS: 0-0 Gd: 0-2 GF: - Fm: 0-5
Distance: 2m/2m3: 0-0 2m4-2m7: 0-1 3m+: 0-7
Track: LH: 0-4 RH: 0-3 Tight: 0-1 Gall: 0-1
Aids: Bl: 0-0 Vi: 0-0 Tstrap: 0-0
Best Rating: 100 9/99 Hrfd 2m1f good Hdl

Sure Future

102 95

6-y-o b g Kylian (USA)-Lady Ever-So-Sure (Malicious)

R M Stronge (J R Best 22/1) The Test Valley Partnership

Placings:34046/336-5450122 (4403)

2001/02: 16^{5}G, 20^{4}S, 16^{5}S, 22^{0}S, 21^{1}S, 22^{2}G, 19^{2}S

	Starts	1st	2nd	3rd	Win & Pl
Hurdles	7	1	2	0	5567
Career Total	**15**	**1**	**2**	**3**	**6571**
92 3/02 Newb 2m5f	E(0-105)HHdl			SFT	£3640

Total win prize-money £3640

Going: Sf: 1-5 GS: 0-0 Gd: 0-2 GF: - Fm: 0-0
Distance: 2m/2m3: 0-3 **2m4-2m7: 1-4** 3m+: 0-0
Track: **LH: 1-4** RH: 0-3 Tight: 0-2 **Gall: 1-2**
Aids: Bl: 0-0 Vi: 0-0 Tstrap: 0-0
Best Rating: 99 9/00 Hntg 2m4f110y gd-fm Hdl

Finally won his first race in a 'hands and heels' race at Newbury in March 2002. Stays well and looks best on soft ground.

Sure Touch

90f 92f

5-y-o ch g Sure Blade (USA)-Welsh Lustre (IRE) (Mandalus)

J J O'Neill Mrs L R Lovell

Placings:*03* (4603)

2001/02: 16^{0}GS, 16^{3}GF

	Starts	1st	2nd	3rd	Win & Pl
NH Flat	2	0	0	1	308
Career Total	**2**	**0**	**0**	**1**	**308**

Going: Sf: 0-0 GS: 0-1 Gd: 0-0 GF: - Fm: 0-1
Distance: 2m/2m3: 0-2 2m4-2m7: 0-0 3m+: 0-0
Track: LH: 0-1 RH: 0-1 Tight: 0-0 Gall: 0-0
Aids: Bl: 0-0 Vi: 0-0 Tstrap: 0-0
Best Rating: 92 4/02 Wwck 2m gd-fm NHF

Showed ability in bumpers in the spring of 2002.

Surefast

92(99h) (80h)90

7-y-o ch g Nearly A Hand-Meldon Lady (Ballymoss)

P R Rodford B A Derrick

Placings:*0/00*-60**F0U55** (4656)

2001/02: 20^{6}GF, 17^{0}GF, 19^{F}GF, 19^{0}GF, 19^{U}GS, 24^{5}S, 19^{5}GS

	Starts	1st	2nd	3rd	Win & Pl
Hurdles	2	0	0	0	0
Chases	5	0	0	0	0
Career Total	**10**	**0**	**0**	**0**	**0**

Going: Sf: 0-1 GS: 0-2 Gd: 0-0 GF: - Fm: 0-4
Distance: 2m/2m3: 0-3 2m4-2m7: 0-3 3m+: 0-1
Track: LH: 0-1 RH: 0-6 Tight: 0-3 Gall: 0-0
Aids: Bl: 0-0 Vi: 0-0 Tstrap: 0-0
Best Rating: 90 4/02 Tntn 2m3f gd-sft Ch

Very modest novice hurdler, stays two and a half miles.

Surprise Gunner

(101h) (97h)

12-y-o b g Gunner B-Heckley Loch (Lochnager)

K McAuliffe (Mrs Merrita Jones 1/11) Mrs T Lewis

Placings:5/020001/1P-24P (3386)

2001/02: 19^{2}GF, 27^{4}G, 21^{P}GS

	Starts	1st	2nd	3rd	Win & Pl
Hurdles	2	0	1	0	932
Chases	1	0	0	0	0
Career Total	**12**	**2**	**2**	**0**	**6481**
94 1/01 Leic 2m	F(0-110)HHdl			HVY	£2733
97 2/99 Folk 2m4f110y	F(0-100)HHdl			SFT	£1953

Total win prize-money £4687

Going: Sf: 0-0 GS: 0-1 Gd: 0-1 GF: - Fm: 0-1

Distance: 2m/2m3: 0-1 2m4-2m7: 0-1 3m+: 0-1
Track: LH: 0-2 RH: 0-1 Tight: 0-2 Gall: 0-0
Aids: Bl: 0-0 Vi: 0-0 Tstrap: 0-0
Best Rating: 97 6/01 Strf 2m3f gd-fm Hdl

Lightly raced, modest hurdler, he did not seem to get the trip when tried over an extended three miles three furlongs at Sedgefield in November.

Surprising

116 142
7-y-o b g Primitive Rising (USA)-Ascot Lass (Touching Wood (USA))
P J Hobbs M G St Quinton

Placings:4/212P-1133221 **(4890)**
2001/02: 21[1]S, 21[1]G, 21[3]G, 22[3]G, 22[2]S, 25[2]GS, 24[1]G

	Starts	1st	2nd	3rd	Win & Pl
Hurdles	7	3	2	2	40103
Career Total	**12**	**4**	**4**	**2**	**48835**

135	4/02	Prth	3m110y	B Hdl	GD	£8978
121	11/01	Kemp	2m5f	D Hdl	GD	£3558
112	10/01	Plum	2m5f	E Hdl	SFT	£2481
118	10/00	Extr	2m1f	H NHF	GD	£1652

Total win prize-money £16671

Going: Sf: 1-2 GS: 0-1 Gd: 2-4 GF: - Fm: 0-0
Distance: 2m/2m3: 0-0 **2m4-2m7: 2-5** 3m+: 1-2
Track: LH: 1-3 **RH: 2-4 Tight: 1-1** Gall: 0-2
Aids: **Bl: 1-3** Vi: 0-0 Tstrap: 0-0
Best Rating: 137 3/02 Chel 3m1f110y gd-sft Hdl

Useful staying hurdler, regularly in the frame including when second in the Pertemps Final at Cheltenham, he seemed improved by the fitting of blinkers, and finished the season with a win at Perth. Defied a 6lb rise in the weights in better company at Haydock the following week. Described as a stuffy sort, he idles in front.

Sursum Corda

101 136
11-y-o b g Idiots Delight-Childhay (Roi Soleil)
John Wall M Ward-Thomas

Placings:4/2/342F3211/4252R14/2112330/030-P1P231 **(4638)**
2001/02: 24[P]GF, 21[1]G, 21[P]GS, 20[2]G, 20[3]S, 19[1]GF

	Starts	1st	2nd	3rd	Win & Pl
Chases	6	2	1	1	6287
Career Total	**33**	**7**	**8**	**6**	**41021**

117	4/02	Asct	2m3f110y	H Ch	G-F	£2947
100	5/01	Folk	2m5f	H Ch	GD	£1909
133	12/99	Hayd	2m	B(0-140)HCh	HVY	£10113
130	11/99	Wwck	2m	D(0-125)HCh	GD	£4042
118	3/99	Hntg	2m4f110y	E Ch	SFT	£2997
94	4/98	Hntg	2m110y	E Hdl	G-S	£2425
116	4/98	Extr	2m3f110y	E Hdl	SFT	£2889

Total win prize-money £27324

Going: Sf: 0-1 GS: 0-1 Gd: 1-2 GF: - Fm: 1-2
Distance: 2m/2m3: 0-0 **2m4-2m7: 2-5** 3m+: 0-1
Track: LH: 0-2 **RH: 2-4 Tight: 1-4** Gall: 0-0
Aids: Bl: 0-0 Vi: 0-0 **Tstrap: 2-4**
Best Rating: 136 2/00 Sand 2m4f110y gd-sft Ch

Formerly a decent hurdler/chaser, he is now a modest hunter though he has won a couple of races of that type. Suited by two and a half miles.

Susan Wintour (IRE)

83f 66f
5-y-o gr m Roselier (FR)-Fine Artist (Fine Blade (USA))
H D Daly M Ward-Thomas

Placings:*04* **(4429)**
2001/02: 16[0]HY, 16[4]HY

	Starts	1st	2nd	3rd	Win & Pl
NH Flat	2	0	0	0	0
Career Total	**2**	**0**	**0**	**0**	**0**

Going: Sf: 0-2 GS: 0-0 Gd: 0-0 GF: - Fm: 0-0
Distance: 2m/2m3: 0-2 2m4-2m7: 0-0 3m+: 0-0
Track: LH: 0-2 RH: 0-0 Tight: 0-0 Gall: 0-0
Aids: Bl: 0-0 Vi: 0-0 Tstrap: 0-0
Best Rating: 66 3/02 Uttx 2m heavy NHF

Poor form in bumpers.

Susan's Boy

92 74
6-y-o b g Minster Son-Nancy Ardross (Ardross)
R Dickin T Joyce

Placings:54 **(2023)**
2001/02: 17[5]GF, 16[4]S

	Starts	1st	2nd	3rd	Win & Pl
NH Flat	1	0	0	0	0
Hurdles	1	0	0	0	0
Career Total	**2**	**0**	**0**	**0**	**0**

Going: Sf: 0-1 GS: 0-0 Gd: 0-0 GF: - Fm: 0-1
Distance: 2m/2m3: 0-2 2m4-2m7: 0-0 3m+: 0-0
Track: LH: 0-2 RH: 0-0 Tight: 0-1 Gall: 0-0
Aids: Bl: 0-0 Vi: 0-0 Tstrap: 0-0
Best Rating: 82 5/01 NAbb 2m1f gd-fm NHF

Susie Sinatra

89 78
6-y-o ch m Jupiter Island-Noire Small (USA) (Elocutionist (USA))
Ian Williams M Murphy

Placings:*3/45-6P* **(4854)**
2001/02: 16[6]S, 22[P]G

	Starts	1st	2nd	3rd	Win & Pl
NH Flat	1	0	0	0	0
Hurdles	1	0	0	0	0
Career Total	**5**	**0**	**0**	**1**	**251**

Going: Sf: 0-1 GS: 0-0 Gd: 0-1 GF: - Fm: 0-0
Distance: 2m/2m3: 0-1 2m4-2m7: 0-1 3m+: 0-0
Track: LH: 0-2 RH: 0-0 Tight: 0-1 Gall: 0-1
Aids: Bl: 0-0 Vi: 0-0 Tstrap: 0-0
Best Rating: 89 11/00 Hrfd 2m1f gd-sft NHF

Susie's Sonny

8-y-o ch g Timeless Times (USA)-Pickwood Sue (Right Boy)
B J Llewellyn R Mason

Placings:P **(1088)**
2001/02: 16[P]GF

	Starts	1st	2nd	3rd	Win & Pl
Hurdles	1	0	0	0	
Career Total	**1**	**0**	**0**	**0**	

Going: Sf: 0-0 GS: 0-0 Gd: 0-0 GF: - Fm: 0-1

Distance: 2m/2m3: 0-1 2m4-2m7: 0-0 3m+: 0-0
Track: LH: 0-1 RH: 0-0 Tight: 0-0 Gall: 0-0
Aids: Bl: 0-0 Vi: 0-0 Tstrap: 0-0
Best Rating:

Suspendid (IRE)

110(63h) 131
9-y-o b g Yashgan-Spendapromise (Goldhill)
C R Egerton Stockton Heath Racing

Placings:*10/11P0-143* **(4814)**
2001/02: 20[1]G, 20[4]GF, 21[3]GF

	Starts	1st	2nd	3rd	Win & Pl
Chases	3	1	0	1	7164
Career Total	**9**	**4**	**0**	**1**	**14491**

124	9/01	Prth	2m4f110y	E Ch	GD	£4901
113	9/00	Hrfd	2m3f110y	E Hdl	G-S	£2170
106	6/00	Strf	2m110y	E Hdl	G-S	£2702
94	6/99	Rosc	2m	NHF	G-F	£2455

Total win prize-money £12228

Going: Sf: 0-0 GS: 0-0 Gd: 1-1 GF: - Fm: 0-2
Distance: 2m/2m3: 0-0 **2m4-2m7: 1-3** 3m+: 0-0
Track: LH: 0-1 **RH: 1-2** Tight: 0-1 Gall: 0-1
Aids: Bl: 0-0 Vi: 0-0 Tstrap: 0-0
Best Rating: 131 4/02 Chel 2m5f gd-fm Ch

A fair novice hurdler in 2000, he has had blood-vessel problems but made a winning chasing debut at Perth in September 2001. Held next time but ran well after a break. Jumps well, stays two and a half miles but looks as though he would not be inconvenienced by shorter. Acts on a sound surface.

Susy In The Summer (IRE)

80f 84f
6-y-o b m Be My Native (USA)-Rock Solid (Hard Boy)
Ferdy Murphy Not For Friends

Placings:*00* **(0550)**
2001/02: 17[0]GS, 16[0]GF

	Starts	1st	2nd	3rd	Win & Pl
NH Flat	2	0	0	0	
Career Total	**2**	**0**	**0**	**0**	

Going: Sf: 0-0 GS: 0-1 Gd: 0-0 GF: - Fm: 0-1
Distance: 2m/2m3: 0-2 2m4-2m7: 0-0 3m+: 0-0
Track: LH: 0-1 RH: 0-0 Tight: 0-1 Gall: 0-0
Aids: Bl: 0-0 Vi: 0-0 Tstrap: 0-0
Best Rating: 84 5/01 Newc 2m gd-fm NHF

Swaldo

90 68
5-y-o ch g Muhtarram (USA)-Ethel Knight (Thatch (USA))
O O'Neill London Bridge Ii

Placings:666-056 **(1908)**
2001/02: 17[0]S, 16[5]G, 16[6]S

	Starts	1st	2nd	3rd	Win & Pl
Hurdles	3	0	0	0	0
Career Total	**6**	**0**	**0**	**0**	**0**

Going: Sf: 0-2 GS: 0-0 Gd: 0-1 GF: - Fm: 0-0
Distance: 2m/2m3: 0-3 2m4-2m7: 0-0 3m+: 0-0
Track: LH: 0-2 RH: 0-1 Tight: 0-3 Gall: 0-0
Aids: Bl: 0-0 Vi: 0-0 Tstrap: 0-0
Best Rating: 68 11/01 Strf 2m110y soft Hdl

He has shown nothing over hurdles in modest company.

Swallow Jaz

72 **35**

5-y-o b g Alhijaz-Marguerite Bay (IRE) (Darshaan)

J J O'Neill Foreneish Racing

Placings:00 **(1274)**

2001/02: 20^{0}GS, 16^{0}GF

	Starts	1st	2nd	3rd	Win & Pl
Hurdles	2	0	0	0	
Career Total	**2**	**0**	**0**	**0**	

Going: Sf: 0-0 GS: 0-1 Gd: 0-0 GF: - Fm: 0-1

Distance: 2m/2m3: 0-1 2m4-2m7: 0-1 3m+: 0-0

Track: LH: 0-2 RH: 0-0 Tight: 0-2 Gall: 0-0

Aids: Bl: 0-0 Vi: 0-1 Tstrap: 0-0

Best Rating: 35 8/01 Sthl 2m gd-fm Hdl

Swan Knight (USA)

104 **123**

6-y-o b/br g Sadler's Wells (USA)-Shannkara (IRE) (Akarad (FR))

R J White (B Moreno 2/9) Littleton Manor Racing

Placings:1P2-0 **(0080)**

2001/02: 16^{0}G

	Starts	1st	2nd	3rd	Win & Pl
Hurdles	1	0	0	0	
Career Total	**4**	**1**	**1**	**0**	**5644**

127 2/01 Winc 2m D Hdl GD £3969

Total win prize-money £3969

Going: Sf: 0-0 GS: 0-0 Gd: 0-1 GF: - Fm: 0-0

Distance: 2m/2m3: 0-1 2m4-2m7: 0-0 3m+: 0-0

Track: LH: 0-1 RH: 0-0 Tight: 0-0 Gall: 0-0

Aids: Bl: 0-0 Vi: 0-0 Tstrap: 0-0

Best Rating: 127 2/01 Winc 2m good Hdl

Won impressively over hurdles on his debut for Pipe. Lightly-raced since.

Swaneys Hill (IRE)

76f **75f**

6-y-o b g Shernazar-Why Me Linda (IRE) (Nashamaa)

F Lloyd F Lloyd

Placings:*0* **(3798)**

2001/02: 16^{0}S

	Starts	1st	2nd	3rd	Win & Pl
NH Flat	1	0	0	0	
Career Total	**1**	**0**	**0**	**0**	

Going: Sf: 0-1 GS: 0-0 Gd: 0-0 GF: - Fm: 0-0

Distance: 2m/2m3: 0-1 2m4-2m7: 0-0 3m+: 0-0

Track: LH: 0-1 RH: 0-0 Tight: 0-0 Gall: 0-0

Aids: Bl: 0-0 Vi: 0-0 Tstrap: 0-0

Best Rating: 75 2/02 Wwck 2m soft NHF

Swansea Bay

111(103h) (89h)**109**

6-y-o b g Jurado (USA)-Slave's Bangle (Prince Rheingold)

P Bowen Peter Bowling

Placings:*26244*-130 **(2058)**

2001/02: 24^{1}GF, 24^{3}GS, 22^{0}GS

	Starts	1st	2nd	3rd	Win & Pl
Hurdles	3	1	0	1	2365
Career Total	**8**	**1**	**2**	**1**	**3263**

89 9/01 Worc 3m F Hdl G-F £1883

Total win prize-money £1883

Going: Sf: 0-0 GS: 0-2 Gd: 0-0 GF: - Fm: 1-1

Distance: 2m/2m3: 0-0 2m4-2m7: 0-1 **3m+: 1-2**

Track: **LH: 1-2** RH: 0-1 Tight: 0-2 Gall: 0-0

Aids: Bl: 0-0 Vi: 0-0 Tstrap: 0-0

Best Rating: 106 1/01 Font 2m2f110y soft NHF

Moderate hurdler. Progressive over fences and landed handicaps at Worcester in July 2002 and at Bangor the following month. Stays three miles. Acts on fast ground but has won on soft.

Sweet Bird (FR)

90 **99**

5-y-o ch g Epervier Bleu-Sweet Virginia (FR) (Tapioca Ii)

A M Hales Andrew L Cohen

Placings:*3*-40 **(4014)**

2001/02: 16^{4}HY, 20^{0}GS

	Starts	1st	2nd	3rd	Win & Pl
Hurdles	2	0	0	0	0
Career Total	**3**	**0**	**0**	**1**	**210**

Going: Sf: 0-1 GS: 0-1 Gd: 0-0 GF: - Fm: 0-0

Distance: 2m/2m3: 0-1 2m4-2m7: 0-1 3m+: 0-0

Track: LH: 0-1 RH: 0-1 Tight: 0-0 Gall: 0-1

Aids: Bl: 0-0 Vi: 0-0 Tstrap: 0-0

Best Rating: 99 1/02 Towc 2m heavy Hdl

A half-brother to useful chaser and hurdler Sweet Duke, he has run well to date.

Sweet Ciseaux (IRE)

84 **70**

9-y-o b g Be My Guest (USA)-Wild Abandon (USA) (Graustark)

C J Gray G P Cox

Placings:04562F10PPP/21F250**P**4/5P0 **(0979)**

2001/02: 19^{5}F, 27^{P}G, 27^{0}G

	Starts	1st	2nd	3rd	Win & Pl
Hurdles	3	0	0	0	0
Career Total	**22**	**2**	**3**	**0**	**7944**

90 5/98 Ctml 3m2f E(0-115)HHdl G-F £3436

86 10/97 Sedg 3m3f110y F(0-100)HHdl GD £2267

Total win prize-money £5704

Going: Sf: 0-0 GS: 0-0 Gd: 0-2 GF: - Fm: 0-1

Distance: 2m/2m3: 0-0 2m4-2m7: 0-1 3m+: 0-2

Track: LH: 0-2 RH: 0-1 Tight: 0-3 Gall: 0-0

Aids: Bl: 0-1 Vi: 0-0 Tstrap: 0-0

Best Rating: 90 5/98 Ctml 3m2f gd-fm Hdl

Sweet Environment

5-y-o gr m Environment Friend-Sweets (IRE) (Persian Heights)

D G Bridgwater R W Neale

Placings:P **(3641)**

2001/02: 16^{P}S

	Starts	1st	2nd	3rd	Win & Pl
Hurdles	1	0	0	0	
Career Total	**1**	**0**	**0**	**0**	

Going: Sf: 0-1 GS: 0-0 Gd: 0-0 GF: - Fm: 0-0

Distance: 2m/2m3: 0-1 2m4-2m7: 0-0 3m+: 0-0

Track: LH: 0-0 RH: 0-1 Tight: 0-0 Gall: 0-0

Aids: Bl: 0-0 Vi: 0-0 Tstrap: 0-0

Best Rating:

Sweet Kari (IRE)

7-y-o b g Lashkari-Sucre Fan (IRE) (Lear Fan (USA))

B G Powell Mrs Rachel A Powell

Placings:PPP/P-P **(1226)**

2001/02: 22^{P}GF

	Starts	1st	2nd	3rd	Win & Pl
Hurdles	1	0	0	0	
Career Total	**5**	**0**	**0**	**0**	

Going: Sf: 0-0 GS: 0-0 Gd: 0-0 GF: - Fm: 0-1

Distance: 2m/2m3: 0-0 2m4-2m7: 0-1 3m+: 0-0

Track: LH: 0-1 RH: 0-0 Tight: 0-1 Gall: 0-0

Aids: Bl: 0-0 Vi: 0-0 Tstrap: 0-0

Best Rating:

Sweet Minuet

90 **80**

5-y-o b m Minshaanshu Amad (USA)-Sweet N' Twenty (High Top)

M Madgwick W E Baird

Placings:*3000*-**P**4306 **(3150)**

2001/02: 16^{P}S, 22^{4}GF, 21^{3}G, 22^{0}G, 18^{6}G

	Starts	1st	2nd	3rd	Win & Pl
Hurdles	5	0	0	1	554
Career Total	**9**	**0**	**0**	**2**	**768**

Going: Sf: 0-1 GS: 0-0 Gd: 0-3 GF: - Fm: 0-1

Distance: 2m/2m3: 0-2 2m4-2m7: 0-3 3m+: 0-0

Track: LH: 0-2 RH: 0-2 Tight: 0-2 Gall: 0-0

Aids: Bl: 0-0 Vi: 0-0 Tstrap: 0-0

Best Rating: 80 1/02 Font 2m2f110y good Hdl

Sweet Reward

7-y-o ch g Beveled (USA)-Sweet Revival (Claude Monet (USA))

H Morrison (J G Smyth-Osbourne 16/10) Mrs Andria Dorler & Partners

Placings:*5/55*-P **(1473)**

2001/02: 17^{P}S

	Starts	1st	2nd	3rd	Win & Pl
Hurdles	1	0	0	0	
Career Total	**4**	**0**	**0**	**0**	**0**

Going: Sf: 0-1 GS: 0-0 Gd: 0-0 GF: - Fm: 0-0

Distance: 2m/2m3: 0-1 2m4-2m7: 0-0 3m+: 0-0

Track: LH: 0-0 RH: 0-1 Tight: 0-1 Gall: 0-0

Aids: Bl: 0-0 Vi: 0-0 Tstrap: 0-0

Best Rating: 97 1/00 Tntn 2m1f gd-sft Hdl

Sweet Senorita

83(106c) (146c)**107**

7-y-o b m Young Senor (USA)-Sweet N' Twenty (High Top)

M C Pipe D A Johnson

Placings:1P21141151211/212-611 **(0910)**
2001/02: 16^{6}G, 16^{1}G, 16^{1}G

	Starts	1st	2nd	3rd	Win & Pl
Hurdles	1	0	0	0	0
Chases	2	2	0	0	6351
Career Total	**19**	**11**	**4**	**0**	**35666**

127	7/01	Worc	2m	E Ch	GD	£2999
146	6/01	NAbb	2m110y	E Ch	GD	£3351
133	5/00	Uttx	2m	D(0-125)HHdl	GD	£3432
135	4/00	Strf	2m110y	D(0-110)HHdl	GD	£3024
117	3/00	Bang	2m1f	F Hdl	GD	£2331
131	2/00	Leic	2m	F Hdl	G-S	£2793
93	1/00	Plum	2m	F Hdl	HVY	£2485
111	12/99	MRas	2m1f110y	G Hdl	GD	£1616
115	10/99	Ludl	2m	G Hdl	G-F	£2113
108	9/99	Extr	2m1f	G(0-95)HHdl	G-S	£1798
99	8/99	NAbb	2m1f	G Hdl	G-F	£1987

Total win prize-money £27930

Going: Sf: 0-0 GS: 0-0 Gd: 2-3 GF: - Fm: 0-0
Distance: **2m/2m3: 2-3** 2m4-2m7: 0-0 3m+: 0-0
Track: **LH: 2-3** RH: 0-0 **Tight: 1-2** Gall: 0-0
Aids: Bl: 0-0 Vi: 0-0 Tstrap: 0-0
Best Rating: 146 6/01 NAbb 2m110y good Ch

A prolific front-running hurdler, she made a successful switch to fences in the summer of 2001. Best around two miles, she handles most types of ground and is notably tough.

Sweet Sensation

94f 99f

7-y-o ch m Carlingford Castle-Pink Sensation (Sagaro)
C Grant Mrs A Meller

Placings:*0434* **(1044)**
2001/02: 16^{0}GF, 16^{4}GF, 17^{3}GF, 16^{4}GF

	Starts	1st	2nd	3rd	Win & Pl
NH Flat	4	0	0	1	227
Career Total	**4**	**0**	**0**	**1**	**227**

Going: Sf: 0-0 GS: 0-0 Gd: 0-0 GF: - Fm: 0-4
Distance: 2m/2m3: 0-4 2m4-2m7: 0-0 3m+: 0-0
Track: LH: 0-2 RH: 0-1 Tight: 0-1 Gall: 0-0
Aids: Bl: 0-0 Vi: 0-0 Tstrap: 0-0
Best Rating: 99 5/01 Newc 2m gd-fm NHF

Sweet Serenata

89 65

7-y-o gr m Keen-Serenata (Larrinaga)
M E Sowersby R D Seldon

Placings:4P35/0PF022-504050 **(4578)**
2001/02: 19^{5}GF, 21^{0}HY, 19^{4}S, 24^{0}S, 24^{5}HY, 23^{0}G

	Starts	1st	2nd	3rd	Win & Pl
Hurdles	6	0	0	0	0
Career Total	**16**	**0**	**2**	**1**	**1268**

Going: Sf: 0-4 GS: 0-0 Gd: 0-1 GF: - Fm: 0-1
Distance: 2m/2m3: 0-2 2m4-2m7: 0-2 3m+: 0-2
Track: LH: 0-6 RH: 0-0 Tight: 0-3 Gall: 0-1
Aids: Bl: 0-0 Vi: 0-0 Tstrap: 0-0
Best Rating: 78 11/00 Catt 2m3f good Hdl

Sweetski

6-y-o b m Petoski-Sweetcal (Caliban)
P C Ritchens M Blandford

Placings:*0* **(4391)**
2001/02: 16^{0}S

	Starts	1st	2nd	3rd	Win & Pl
NH Flat	1	0	0	0	
Career Total	**1**	**0**	**0**	**0**	

Going: Sf: 0-1 GS: 0-0 Gd: 0-0 GF: - Fm: 0-0
Distance: 2m/2m3: 0-1 2m4-2m7: 0-0 3m+: 0-0
Track: LH: 0-0 RH: 0-1 Tight: 0-0 Gall: 0-0
Aids: Bl: 0-0 Vi: 0-0 Tstrap: 0-0
Best Rating:

Swemby

5-y-o ch m Mizoram (USA)-Equilibrium (Statoblest)
K Bell North Farm Stud

Placings:P **(1103)**
2001/02: 17^{P}G

	Starts	1st	2nd	3rd	Win & Pl
Hurdles	1	0	0	0	
Career Total	**1**	**0**	**0**	**0**	

Going: Sf: 0-0 GS: 0-0 Gd: 0-1 GF: - Fm: 0-0
Distance: 2m/2m3: 0-1 2m4-2m7: 0-0 3m+: 0-0
Track: LH: 0-1 RH: 0-0 Tight: 0-1 Gall: 0-0
Aids: Bl: 0-0 Vi: 0-0 Tstrap: 0-0
Best Rating:

Swiftmar

90 60

4-y-o b f Marju (IRE)-Swift Spring (FR) (Bluebird (USA))
K A Morgan (P F I Cole 20/10) Joe Casey

Placings:P55U **(3856)**
2001/02: 16^{P}GF, 17^{5}S, 16^{5}G, 16^{U}S

	Starts	1st	2nd	3rd	Win & Pl
Hurdles	4	0	0	0	0
Career Total	**4**	**0**	**0**	**0**	**0**

Going: Sf: 0-2 GS: 0-0 Gd: 0-1 GF: - Fm: 0-1
Distance: 2m/2m3: 0-4 2m4-2m7: 0-0 3m+: 0-0
Track: LH: 0-2 RH: 0-2 Tight: 0-2 Gall: 0-1
Aids: Bl: 0-0 Vi: 0-0 Tstrap: 0-0
Best Rating: 60 12/01 Ludl 2m good Hdl

Swiftway

89(92h) (69h)97

8-y-o ch g Anshan-Solemn Occasion (USA) (Secreto (USA))
Mrs E Slack (K W Hogg 20/10) A Slack

Placings:121/1P4/P503 **(4592)**
2001/02: 24^{P}S, 21^{5}G, 21^{0}G, 26^{3}G

	Starts	1st	2nd	3rd	Win & Pl
Hurdles	3	0	0	0	0
Chases	1	0	0	1	530
Career Total	**10**	**3**	**1**	**1**	**11538**

126	9/99	MRas	3m	C(0-130)HHdl	G-F	£5151
111	4/99	Carl	2m4f110y	E(0-105)HHdl	G-S	£2486
97	12/98	Muss	2m4f	E Hdl	G-F	£1996

Total win prize-money £9634

Going: Sf: 0-1 GS: 0-0 Gd: 0-3 GF: - Fm: 0-0
Distance: 2m/2m3: 0-0 2m4-2m7: 0-2 3m+: 0-2
Track: LH: 0-2 RH: 0-2 Tight: 0-3 Gall: 0-0
Aids: Bl: 0-1 Vi: 0-0 Tstrap: 0-0
Best Rating: 126 9/99 MRas 3m gd-fm Hdl

A fair hurdler, he ran with credit on his chasing debut in April 2002. He stays particularly well.

Swindle

105 101

6-y-o b m Sir Harry Lewis (USA)-Pilfer (Vaigly Great)
C R Egerton Bloomsbury Stud

Placings:*10*-6212 **(4536)**
2001/02: 16^{6}G, 16^{2}G, 19^{1}GS, 16^{2}G

	Starts	1st	2nd	3rd	Win & Pl
Hurdles	4	1	2	0	7383
Career Total	**6**	**2**	**2**	**0**	**9049**

98	11/01	Tntn	2m3f110y	C Hdl	G-S	£5398
115	2/01	Font	2m2f110y	H NHF	G-S	£1666

Total win prize-money £7064

Going: Sf: 0-0 GS: 1-1 Gd: 0-3 GF: - Fm: 0-0
Distance: 2m/2m3: 0-3 **2m4-2m7: 1-1** 3m+: 0-0
Track: LH: 0-2 **RH: 1-2 Tight: 1-2** Gall: 0-0
Aids: Bl: 0-0 Vi: 0-0 **Tstrap: 1-3**
Best Rating: 115 2/01 Font 2m2f110y gd-sft NHF

Winner of a bumper on easy ground early in 2001, she progressed to score over hurdles at Taunton when staying two miles three on similar ground. Wears a tongue strap.

Swing Bar

96 85

9-y-o b m Sadeem (USA)-Murex (Royalty)
J M Bradley Miss S Howell

Placings:4/2660/13/5460 **(2056)**
2001/02: 16^{5}GF, 19^{4}S, 19^{6}G, 18^{0}GS

	Starts	1st	2nd	3rd	Win & Pl
Hurdles	4	0	0	0	0
Career Total	**11**	**1**	**1**	**1**	**2894**

84	6/99	Worc	2m	G(0-90)HHdl	G-F	£2094

Total win prize-money £2094

Going: Sf: 0-1 GS: 0-1 Gd: 0-1 GF: - Fm: 0-1
Distance: 2m/2m3: 0-2 2m4-2m7: 0-2 3m+: 0-0
Track: LH: 0-2 RH: 0-2 Tight: 0-2 Gall: 0-0
Aids: Bl: 0-0 Vi: 0-0 Tstrap: 0-0
Best Rating: 85 9/01 Worc 2m gd-fm Hdl

Swinging The Blues (IRE)

96 69

8-y-o b g Bluebird (USA)-Winsong Melody (Music Maestro)
C A Dwyer Mrs Shelley Dwyer

Placings:55/030 **(4898)**
2001/02: 16^{0}S, 16^{3}G, 16^{0}G

	Starts	1st	2nd	3rd	Win & Pl
Hurdles	3	0	0	1	270
Career Total	**5**	**0**	**0**	**1**	**270**

Going: Sf: 0-1 GS: 0-0 Gd: 0-2 GF: - Fm: 0-0
Distance: 2m/2m3: 0-3 2m4-2m7: 0-0 3m+: 0-0
Track: LH: 0-1 RH: 0-2 Tight: 0-1 Gall: 0-1
Aids: Bl: 0-0 Vi: 0-1 Tstrap: 0-0
Best Rating: 89 11/98 Hntg 2m110y gd-sft Hdl

Middle-distance Flat winner, very lightly raced over hurdles.

Swiss Alps (IRE)

81 **43**

5-y-o b g Common Grounds-Lady Of Zurich (IRE) (Danehill (USA))
Mrs N S Sharpe (Miss K Marks 15/5) B Owen

Placings:30-P0 **(1544)**
2001/02: 19^{PG}, $17^{0}G$

	Starts	1st	2nd	3rd	Win & Pl
Hurdles	2	0	0	0	
Career Total	**4**	**0**	**0**	**1**	**304**

Going: Sf: 0-0 GS: 0-0 Gd: 0-2 GF: - Fm: 0-0
Distance: 2m/2m3: 0-1 2m4-2m7: 0-1 3m+: 0-0
Track: LH: 0-0 RH: 0-2 Tight: 0-0 Gall: 0-0
Aids: Bl: 0-1 Vi: 0-0 Tstrap: 0-1
Best Rating: 81 2/01 Ludl 2m gd-sft Hdl

Swiss Comfort (IRE)

61 **59**

11-y-o b m Henbit (USA)-Malozza Brig (New Brig)
E M Caine Mrs Karen Woodhead

Placings:P/P/PP/P0U0PP/0PPUPP-5 **(2183)**
2001/02: $16^{5}G$

	Starts	1st	2nd	3rd	Win & Pl
Chases	1	0	0	0	0
Career Total	**17**	**0**	**0**	**0**	**0**

Going: Sf: 0-0 GS: 0-0 Gd: 0-1 GF: - Fm: 0-0
Distance: 2m/2m3: 0-1 2m4-2m7: 0-0 3m+: 0-0
Track: LH: 0-1 RH: 0-0 Tight: 0-0 Gall: 0-0
Aids: Bl: 0-0 Vi: 0-0 Tstrap: 0-0
Best Rating: 59 11/01 Ayr 2m good Ch

Swoosh

93 **71**

7-y-o gr g Absalom-Valldemosa (Music Boy)
T Needham T Needham

Placings:PP/O400 **(2291)**
2001/02: $17^{O}GF$, $16^{4}G$, $19^{0}F$, $19^{0}GF$

	Starts	1st	2nd	3rd	Win & Pl
Chases	4	0	0	0	296
Career Total	**6**	**0**	**0**	**0**	**296**

Going: Sf: 0-0 GS: 0-0 Gd: 0-1 GF: - Fm: 0-3
Distance: 2m/2m3: 0-3 2m4-2m7: 0-1 3m+: 0-0
Track: LH: 0-0 RH: 0-4 Tight: 0-1 Gall: 0-0
Aids: Bl: 0-0 Vi: 0-0 Tstrap: 0-0
Best Rating: 71 11/01 Extr 2m3f110y gd-fm Ch

Sylcan Express

98 **76**

9-y-o br g Sylvan Express-Dercanny (Derek H)
C N Kellett Vince, Ady, Bob And Rich

Placings:300/0P40P/105/00U0P-0000440P3 **(4573)**
2001/02: $20^{0}G$, $21^{0}GF$, $19^{0}GF$, $16^{0}GF$, $20^{4}GF$, $21^{4}G$, $16^{0}S$, $24^{P}S$, $20^{3}G$

	Starts	1st	2nd	3rd	Win & Pl
Hurdles	8	0	0	1	283
Chases	1	0	0	0	0
Career Total	**25**	**1**	**0**	**2**	**2887**

89 10/99 Towc 2m5f E(0-105)HHdl GD £2390
Total win prize-money £2390

Going: Sf: 0-2 GS: 0-0 Gd: 0-3 GF: - Fm: 0-4
Distance: 2m/2m3: 0-2 2m4-2m7: 0-6 3m+: 0-1
Track: LH: 0-3 RH: 0-6 Tight: 0-2 Gall: 0-2
Aids: Bl: 0-0 Vi: 0-2 Tstrap: 0-0
Best Rating: 92 2/98 Muss 2m good NHF

Selling hurdler, has not won for over two years.

Sylphide

85 **58**

7-y-o b m Ballet Royal (USA)-Shafayif (Ela-Mana-Mou)
H J Manners H J Manners

Placings:P033052/00/F0300-P55P4 **(4742)**
2001/02: $21^{P}G$, $16^{5}S$, $20^{5}S$, $16^{P}HY$, $24^{4}GF$

	Starts	1st	2nd	3rd	Win & Pl
Hurdles	5	0	0	0	0
Career Total	**19**	**0**	**1**	**3**	**1194**

Going: Sf: 0-3 GS: 0-0 Gd: 0-1 GF: - Fm: 0-1
Distance: 2m/2m3: 0-2 2m4-2m7: 0-2 3m+: 0-1
Track: LH: 0-2 RH: 0-3 Tight: 0-0 Gall: 0-1
Aids: Bl: 0-0 Vi: 0-0 Tstrap: 0-0
Best Rating: 64 1/01 Folk 2m1f110y heavy Hdl

Sylva Legend (USA)

104 **102**

6-y-o b g Lear Fan (USA)-Likeashot (CAN) (Gun Shot)
R J Baker M A Swift, A J Chapman And T Warden

Placings:2322566 **(4848)**
2001/02: $17^{2}F$, $17^{3}G$, $17^{2}GS$, $17^{2}GF$, $17^{5}GF$, $17^{6}G$, $16^{6}G$

	Starts	1st	2nd	3rd	Win & Pl
Hurdles	7	0	3	1	3371
Career Total	**7**	**0**	**3**	**1**	**3371**

Going: Sf: 0-0 GS: 0-1 Gd: 0-3 GF: - Fm: 0-3
Distance: 2m/2m3: 0-7 2m4-2m7: 0-0 3m+: 0-0
Track: LH: 0-6 RH: 0-1 Tight: 0-6 Gall: 0-0
Aids: Bl: 0-0 Vi: 0-0 Tstrap: 0-0
Best Rating: 102 4/02 Strf 2m110y good Hdl

Fair efforts in novice hurdles, winning a minor handicap at Chepstow in May 2002, and a 22-furlong novice hurdle at Newton Abbot June. Handles most types of ground.

Sylvia's Dream

7-y-o gr m Thethingaboutitis (USA)-Koritsaki (Strong Gale)
B P J Baugh Mrs Sylvia Knobbs

Placings:0-P0 **(4842)**
2001/02: $20^{P}G$, $20^{0}G$

	Starts	1st	2nd	3rd	Win & Pl
Hurdles	2	0	0	0	
Career Total	**3**	**0**	**0**	**0**	

Going: Sf: 0-0 GS: 0-0 Gd: 0-2 GF: - Fm: 0-0
Distance: 2m/2m3: 0-0 2m4-2m7: 0-2 3m+: 0-0
Track: LH: 0-2 RH: 0-0 Tight: 0-1 Gall: 0-0
Aids: Bl: 0-0 Vi: 0-0 Tstrap: 0-0
Best Rating: 50 1/01 Donc 2m110y good NHF

Syrah

86 **51**

6-y-o b m Minshaanshu Amad (USA)-La Domaine (Dominion)
W Storey Steve Howard And Tony Peters

Placings:0200-06PP66 **(3553)**
2001/02: $23^{0}G$, $24^{6}GS$, $20^{P}S$, $25^{P}GS$, $21^{6}HY$, $19^{6}S$

	Starts	1st	2nd	3rd	Win & Pl
Hurdles	6	0	0	0	0
Career Total	**10**	**0**	**1**	**0**	**411**

Going: Sf: 0-3 GS: 0-2 Gd: 0-1 GF: - Fm: 0-0
Distance: 2m/2m3: 0-1 2m4-2m7: 0-3 3m+: 0-2
Track: LH: 0-6 RH: 0-0 Tight: 0-2 Gall: 0-1
Aids: Bl: 0-0 Vi: 0-0 Tstrap: 0-0
Best Rating: 77 11/00 Catt 2m3f good Hdl

Ta Ta For Now

104 **101+**

5-y-o b g Ezzoud (IRE)-Exit Laughing (Shaab)
P Beaumont Mrs V M Stewart

Placings:05F0P **(4880)**
2001/02: $16^{0}G$, $16^{5}S$, $19^{F}S$, $20^{0}S$, $20^{P}G$,

	Starts	1st	2nd	3rd	Win & Pl
NH Flat	2	0	0	0	0
Hurdles	3	0	0	0	0
Career Total	**5**	**0**	**0**	**0**	**0**

Going: Sf: 0-3 GS: 0-0 Gd: 0-2 GF: - Fm: 0-0
Distance: 2m/2m3: 0-3 2m4-2m7: 0-2 3m+: 0-0
Track: LH: 0-3 RH: 0-1 Tight: 0-1 Gall: 0-2
Aids: Bl: 0-0 Vi: 0-0 Tstrap: 0-0
Best Rating: 90 1/02 Newc 2m soft NHF

Moderate form in bumpers and over hurdles so far, winner of a novice hurdle at Hexham early in the new season.

Taakid (USA)

105 **105+**

7-y-o b g Diesis-Tanwi (Vision (USA))
Mrs S J Smith Daggers Drawn

Placings:660/360305/301P-55F **(4872)**
2001/02: $17^{5}G$, $17^{5}G$, $16^{F}GF$

	Starts	1st	2nd	3rd	Win & Pl
Chases	3	0	0	0	0
Career Total	**16**	**1**	**0**	**3**	**4434**

105 7/00 Wolv 2m4f110y E Ch GD £3386
Total win prize-money £3387

Going: Sf: 0-0 GS: 0-0 Gd: 0-2 GF: - Fm: 0-1
Distance: 2m/2m3: 0-3 2m4-2m7: 0-0 3m+: 0-0
Track: LH: 0-1 RH: 0-2 Tight: 0-2 Gall: 0-0
Aids: Bl: 0-0 Vi: 0-0 Tstrap: 0-0
Best Rating: 105 7/00 Wolv 2m4f110y good Ch

He held a clear lead when falling late on at Wetherby in April 2002, but made amends at Hexham next time. Best on fast ground and does not stay much beyond two miles.

Tabbetinna Blue

5-y-o b m Interrex (CAN)-True Is Blue (Gabitat)
J C McConnochie Dingley Dell Racing Ltd

Placings:P **(3320)**
2001/02: $16^{P}GS$

	Starts	1st	2nd	3rd	Win & Pl
Hurdles	1	0	0	0	
Career Total	**1**	**0**	**0**	**0**	

Going: Sf: 0-0 GS: 0-1 Gd: 0-0 GF: - Fm: 0-0
Distance: 2m/2m3: 0-1 2m4-2m7: 0-0 3m+: 0-0
Track: LH: 0-0 RH: 0-1 Tight: 0-0 Gall: 0-1
Aids: Bl: 0-0 Vi: 0-0 Tstrap: 0-0

Best Rating:

Tabernacle

7-y-o ch g Selkirk (USA)-Tabyan (USA) (Topsider (USA))
R G Frost P Tosh

Placings:0050/P/000FP-P (2560)
2001/02: 20^{P}S

	Starts	1st	2nd	3rd	Win & Pl
Hurdles	1	0	0	0	
Career Total	**11**	**0**	**0**	**0**	**0**

Going: Sf: 0-1 GS: 0-0 Gd: 0-0 GF: - Fm: 0-0
Distance: 2m/2m3: 0-0 2m4-2m7: 0-1 3m+: 0-0
Track: LH: 0-1 RH: 0-0 Tight: 0-0 Gall: 0-0
Aids: Bl: 0-0 Vi: 0-0 Tstrap: 0-0
Best Rating: 82 2/99 Donc 2m4f gd-fm Hdl

Table For Five

82 **109**
8-y-o b g Sunley Builds-Prying Nell (Pry)
C J Mann Il Buon Gustaio Partnership

Placings:F54/21224P1-PR0P (3700)
2001/02: 24^{P}S, 24^{R}G, 24^{0}GS, 24^{P}S

	Starts	1st	2nd	3rd	Win & Pl
Hurdles	2	0	0	0	0
Chases	2	0	0	0	0
Career Total	**14**	**2**	**3**	**0**	**9801**

109	4/01	Winc	2m6f	E Hdl	SFT	£2422
112	11/00	Newb	2m5f	D Hdl	SFT	£4316

Total win prize-money £6738

Going: Sf: 0-2 GS: 0-1 Gd: 0-1 GF: - Fm: 0-0
Distance: 2m/2m3: 0-0 2m4-2m7: 0-0 3m+: 0-4
Track: LH: 0-4 RH: 0-0 Tight: 0-0 Gall: 0-3
Aids: Bl: 0-0 Vi: 0-0 Tstrap: 0-0
Best Rating: 112 11/00 Newb 2m5f soft Hdl

Fair staying hurdler, stays two miles-six and is suited by soft ground. Did not take to fences in late 2001.

Table For Four

100 **102**
6-y-o b g Sunley Builds-Prying Nell (Pry)
C J Mann Table For Four Partnership

Placings:*0*343 (4425)
2001/02: 18^{0}GS, 24^{3}S, 24^{4}S, 24^{3}HY

	Starts	1st	2nd	3rd	Win & Pl
NH Flat	1	0	0	0	0
Hurdles	3	0	0	2	1103
Career Total	**4**	**0**	**0**	**2**	**1103**

Going: Sf: 0-3 GS: 0-1 Gd: 0-0 GF: - Fm: 0-0
Distance: 2m/2m3: 0-1 2m4-2m7: 0-0 3m+: 0-3
Track: LH: 0-1 RH: 0-2 Tight: 0-1 Gall: 0-0
Aids: Bl: 0-0 Vi: 0-0 Tstrap: 0-0
Best Rating: 102 2/02 Kemp 3m110y soft Hdl

Half-brother to fair staying novice hurdler Table For Five. Showed plenty of promise on his hurdle debut, and looks capable of winning races. Likely to prove best suited by a test of stamina but is not suited by heavy ground.

Table Mountain

6-y-o ch g Rock Hopper-Comtec Princess (Gulf Pearl)
C Weedon Atlantic Foods Ltd

Placings:*3222*-P (3402)
2001/02: 20^{P}S

	Starts	1st	2nd	3rd	Win & Pl
Hurdles	1	0	0	0	
Career Total	**5**	**0**	**3**	**1**	**2376**

Going: Sf: 0-1 GS: 0-0 Gd: 0-0 GF: - Fm: 0-0
Distance: 2m/2m3: 0-0 2m4-2m7: 0-1 3m+: 0-0
Track: LH: 0-0 RH: 0-1 Tight: 0-0 Gall: 0-0
Aids: Bl: 0-0 Vi: 0-0 Tstrap: 0-0
Best Rating: 120 4/01 Asct 2m110y heavy NHF

Taboo Tee

(102h) (94h)
6-y-o br m Teenoso (USA)-Temporary Affair (Mandalus)
O Sherwood The Taboo Team

Placings:*4*-044256 (4420)
2001/02: 17^{0}GS, 16^{4}S, 17^{4}GS, 16^{2}G, 20^{5}S, 21^{6}GS

	Starts	1st	2nd	3rd	Win & Pl
NH Flat	1	0	0	0	0
Hurdles	5	0	1	0	1386
Career Total	**7**	**0**	**1**	**0**	**1386**

Going: Sf: 0-2 GS: 0-3 Gd: 0-1 GF: - Fm: 0-0
Distance: 2m/2m3: 0-4 2m4-2m7: 0-2 3m+: 0-0
Track: LH: 0-2 RH: 0-3 Tight: 0-2 Gall: 0-1
Aids: Bl: 0-0 Vi: 0-0 Tstrap: 0-0
Best Rating: 94 12/01 Winc 2m good Hdl

Fair maiden hurdler who stays two and a half miles and is effective on good/soft ground.

Tacita

104 **80**
7-y-o ch m Gunner B-Taco (High Season)
M D McMillan M D McMillan

Placings:*40*-3P (3655)
2001/02: 22^{3}S, 22^{P}S

	Starts	1st	2nd	3rd	Win & Pl
Hurdles	2	0	0	1	376
Career Total	**4**	**0**	**0**	**1**	**376**

Going: Sf: 0-2 GS: 0-0 Gd: 0-0 GF: - Fm: 0-0
Distance: 2m/2m3: 0-0 2m4-2m7: 0-2 3m+: 0-0
Track: LH: 0-1 RH: 0-1 Tight: 0-1 Gall: 0-0
Aids: Bl: 0-0 Vi: 0-0 Tstrap: 0-0
Best Rating: 89 12/00 Ludl 2m soft NHF

She showed promise in bumpers in soft ground at Ludlow and did not disgrace herself on her debut over hurdles in November at Stratford.

Taffs Well

94 **103**
9-y-o b g Dowsing (USA)-Zahiah (So Blessed)
B Ellison Ronald McCulloch

Placings:F2 (4275)
2001/02: 16^{F}GF, 16^{2}G

	Starts	1st	2nd	3rd	Win & Pl
Hurdles	2	0	1	0	748
Career Total	**2**	**0**	**1**	**0**	**748**

Going: Sf: 0-0 GS: 0-0 Gd: 0-1 GF: - Fm: 0-1
Distance: 2m/2m3: 0-2 2m4-2m7: 0-0 3m+: 0-0
Track: LH: 0-2 RH: 0-0 Tight: 0-2 Gall: 0-0
Aids: Bl: 0-0 Vi: 0-0 Tstrap: 0-0
Best Rating: 103 3/02 Fknm 2m good Hdl

On the downgrade on the level, he has twice finished runner-up in novices' hurdles.

Tagar (FR)

104 **131**
5-y-o b g Fijar Tango (FR)-Fight For Arfact (Salmon Leap (USA))
N J Henderson P J Orme

Placings:3640-522 (4422)
2001/02: 16^{5}S, 20^{2}S, 16^{2}GS

	Starts	1st	2nd	3rd	Win & Pl
Hurdles	3	0	2	0	2109
Career Total	**7**	**0**	**2**	**1**	**8257**

Going: Sf: 0-2 GS: 0-1 Gd: 0-0 GF: - Fm: 0-0
Distance: 2m/2m3: 0-2 2m4-2m7: 0-1 3m+: 0-0
Track: LH: 0-2 RH: 0-0 Tight: 0-1 Gall: 0-2
Aids: Bl: 0-0 Vi: 0-0 Tstrap: 0-0
Best Rating: 131 2/02 Newb 2m110y soft Hdl

Ex-French hurdler, made a promising debut at Newbury in February 2002 over two miles. Held over a longer trip next time before a better effort dropped in trip. Suited by soft ground.

Tagula Sun (IRE)

90f **80f**
4-y-o b g Tagula (IRE)-Dee-Lady (Deploy)
Jean-Rene Auvray Mrs Christine Fennell

Placings:*00* (4552)
2001/02: 16^{0}GS, 16^{0}GF

	Starts	1st	2nd	3rd	Win & Pl
NH Flat	2	0	0	0	
Career Total	**2**	**0**	**0**	**0**	

Going: Sf: 0-0 GS: 0-1 Gd: 0-0 GF: - Fm: 0-1
Distance: 2m/2m3: 0-2 2m4-2m7: 0-0 3m+: 0-0
Track: LH: 0-0 RH: 0-2 Tight: 0-0 Gall: 0-1
Aids: Bl: 0-0 Vi: 0-0 Tstrap: 0-1
Best Rating: 78 4/02 Hntg 2m110y gd-fm NHF

Taillefer (FR)

89 **108**
6-y-o b g Cyborg (FR)-Tourka (FR) (Rose Laurel)
M E D Francis Mrs Merrick Francis Iii

Placings:0F503123126-0 (2126)
2001/02: 20^{0}G

	Starts	1st	2nd	3rd	Win & Pl
Chases	1	0	0	0	
Career Total	**12**	**2**	**2**	**2**	**13627**

132	3/01	Hntg	2m4f110y	E Ch	SFT	£3276
	9/00	Fntb	2m3f	Ch	GD	£3362

Total win prize-money £6638

Going: Sf: 0-0 GS: 0-0 Gd: 0-1 GF: - Fm: 0-0
Distance: 2m/2m3: 0-0 2m4-2m7: 0-1 3m+: 0-0
Track: LH: 0-1 RH: 0-0 Tight: 0-0 Gall: 0-1
Aids: Bl: 0-0 Vi: 0-0 Tstrap: 0-0
Best Rating: 132 3/01 Hayd 2m6f heavy Ch

Successful in France, he made a good impression on his first two starts over fences here but ran moderately subsequently.

Taity Tony (IRE)

55 9

4-y-o gr g Up And At 'Em-Angie (Prince Bee)

J L Eyre Sunpak Potatoes

Placings:0 (1718)

2001/02: 16^{0}G

	Starts	1st	2nd	3rd	Win & Pl
Hurdles	1	0	0	0	
Career Total	1	0	0	0	

Going: Sf: 0-0 GS: 0-0 Gd: 0-1 GF: - Fm: 0-0
Distance: 2m/2m3: 0-1 2m4-2m7: 0-0 3m+: 0-0
Track: LH: 0-1 RH: 0-0 Tight: 0-0 Gall: 0-0
Aids: Bl: 0-0 Vi: 0-0 Tstrap: 0-0
Best Rating: 9 10/01 Weth 2m good Hdl

Take A Rain Check (IRE)

5-y-o b m Rainbows For Life (CAN)-Just A Second (Jimsun)

C J Drewe Miss J A Leek

Placings:PP (4048)

2001/02: 20^{P}GS, 19^{P}G

	Starts	1st	2nd	3rd	Win & Pl
Hurdles	2	0	0	0	
Career Total	2	0	0	0	

Going: Sf: 0-0 GS: 0-1 Gd: 0-1 GF: - Fm: 0-0
Distance: 2m/2m3: 0-1 2m4-2m7: 0-1 3m+: 0-0
Track: LH: 0-0 RH: 0-2 Tight: 0-0 Gall: 0-1
Aids: Bl: 0-0 Vi: 0-0 Tstrap: 0-0
Best Rating:

Take A Turn

99 68

7-y-o br g Forzando-Honeychurch (USA) (Bering)

M J Wilkinson The Dann, Gomersall & Pullan Partnership

Placings:1144PF/34/500P-4042664 (2952)

2001/02: 18^{4}GF, 17^{0}G, 19^{4}G, 20^{2}S, 24^{6}S, 17^{0}GS, 16^{4}S

	Starts	1st	2nd	3rd	Win & Pl
Hurdles	7	0	1	0	909
Career Total	19	2	1	1	7446

112	10/98	Plum	2m1f	E Hdl	G-F	£2460
108	10/98	Tntn	2m1f	E Hdl	FRM	£2253

Total win prize-money £4713

Going: Sf: 0-3 GS: 0-1 Gd: 0-2 GF: - Fm: 0-1
Distance: 2m/2m3: 0-5 2m4-2m7: 0-1 3m+: 0-1
Track: LH: 0-6 RH: 0-1 Tight: 0-5 Gall: 0-1
Aids: Bl: 0-2 Vi: 0-4 Tstrap: 0-2
Best Rating: 114 10/98 Weth 2m good Hdl

Plating-class front-running hurdler, seems to handle any ground.

Take Action (IRE)

5-y-o b g Shalford (IRE)-Action Belle (Auction Ring (USA))

F Jordan D Pugh

Placings:43060-PP (0929)

2001/02: 20^{P}G, 20^{P}GF

	Starts	1st	2nd	3rd	Win & Pl
Hurdles	2	0	0	0	
Career Total	7	0	0	1	488

Going: Sf: 0-0 GS: 0-0 Gd: 0-1 GF: - Fm: 0-1
Distance: 2m/2m3: 0-0 2m4-2m7: 0-2 3m+: 0-0
Track: LH: 0-1 RH: 0-1 Tight: 0-1 Gall: 0-1
Aids: Bl: 0-1 Vi: 0-0 Tstrap: 0-0
Best Rating: 77 9/00 Bang 2m1f gd-fm Hdl

Take Control (IRE)

113 163

8-y-o b g Roselier (FR)-Frosty Fairy (Paddy's Stream)

M C Pipe D A Johnson

Placings:0501/113101/11225130-36P4P51 (4839)

2001/02: 26^{3}S, 29^{6}GS, 26^{P}S, 24^{4}S, 24^{P}GS, 25^{5}G, 33^{1}G

	Starts	1st	2nd	3rd	Win & Pl
Chases	7	1	0	1	75125
Career Total	25	9	2	3	150752

163	4/02	Ayr	4m1f	A HCh	GD	£60000
141	2/01	Wwck	3m2f	C Ch	SFT	£7046
148	11/00	NAbb	3m2f110y	C Ch	HVY	£5768
153	10/00	Extr	2m3f110y	D Ch	SFT	£5655
145	4/00	Chel	3m	B(0-145)HHdl	SFT	£10582
126	2/00	Plum	2m5f	D Hdl	SFT	£3797
117	12/99	Hayd	2m7f110y	D(0-110)HHdl	SFT	£3257
112	12/99	Winc	2m6f	F(0-100)HHdl	GD	£2472
118	2/99	Naas	2m3f	NHF	SFT	£3069

Total win prize-money £101649

Going: Sf: 0-0 GS: 0-2 Gd: 1-2 GF: - Fm: 0-0
Distance: 2m/2m3: 0-0 2m4-2m7: 0-0 3m+: 1-7
Track: LH: 1-7 RH: 0-0 Tight: 0-1 Gall: 0-3
Aids: Bl: 0-0 Vi: 0-2 Tstrap: 0-0
Best Rating: 163 4/02 Ayr 4m1f good Ch

A useful staying novice chaser in 2000/2001, he had the Singer & Friedlander Trial at Uttoxeter sewn up when coming down. Third in the Hennessy on his return in December 2001, he put in a couple of disappointing efforts but ran better at Newbury in February. However, he was below his best at both, Cheltenham in March and Aintree in April, but he bounced back to form when landing the Scottish National at Ayr in April 2001. Relishes testing conditions, but also effective on a sound surface. Stays three and a quarter miles.

Take Heed

93 71+

6-y-o b g Warning-Tunaria (USA) (Lyphard (USA))

K A Morgan Roemex Ltd

Placings:U-0FP (4880)

2001/02: 16^{0}GS, 17^{F}GS, 20^{P}G

	Starts	1st	2nd	3rd	Win & Pl
Hurdles	3	0	0	0	
Career Total	4	0	0	0	

Going: Sf: 0-0 GS: 0-2 Gd: 0-1 GF: - Fm: 0-0
Distance: 2m/2m3: 0-2 2m4-2m7: 0-1 3m+: 0-0
Track: LH: 0-1 RH: 0-2 Tight: 0-0 Gall: 0-0
Aids: Bl: 0-0 Vi: 0-0 Tstrap: 0-0
Best Rating: 32 1/02 Weth 2m gd-sft Hdl

Take My Side (IRE)

10-y-o b g Be My Native (USA)-Fight For It (Strong Gale)

Mrs P Townsley Paul Townsley

Placings:6501U43/35353U0/P/PP (2464)

2001/02: 21^{P}G, 22^{P}HY

	Starts	1st	2nd	3rd	Win & Pl
Hurdles	1	0	0	0	0
Chases	1	0	0	0	0
Career Total	17	1	0	4	4572

111	1/98	Plum	2m4f	E Hdl	HVY	£2637

Total win prize-money £2637

Going: Sf: 0-1 GS: 0-0 Gd: 0-1 GF: - Fm: 0-0
Distance: 2m/2m3: 0-0 2m4-2m7: 0-2 3m+: 0-0
Track: LH: 0-0 RH: 0-2 Tight: 0-2 Gall: 0-0
Aids: Bl: 0-1 Vi: 0-0 Tstrap: 0-1
Best Rating: 116 3/98 Sand 2m4f110y good Ch

Take The Brush (IRE)

8-y-o b m Brush Aside (USA)-Ballywilliam Girl (Royal Match)

J White Nick Quesnel

Placings:0/P (4058)

2001/02: 16^{P}S

	Starts	1st	2nd	3rd	Win & Pl
Chases	1	0	0	0	
Career Total	2	0	0	0	

Going: Sf: 0-1 GS: 0-0 Gd: 0-0 GF: - Fm: 0-0
Distance: 2m/2m3: 0-1 2m4-2m7: 0-0 3m+: 0-0
Track: LH: 0-0 RH: 0-1 Tight: 0-0 Gall: 0-0
Aids: Bl: 0-0 Vi: 0-0 Tstrap: 0-0
Best Rating:

Take The Stand (IRE)

100 97

6-y-o b g Witness Box (USA)-Denys Daughter (IRE) (Crash Course)

Ian Williams C M Kinane

Placings:00-64224135 (1886)

2001/02: 19^{6}GF, 17^{4}GS, 20^{2}GF, 20^{2}GF, 19^{4}GF, 24^{1}GF, 22^{3}G, 21^{5}G

	Starts	1st	2nd	3rd	Win & Pl
Hurdles	8	1	2	1	4550
Career Total	10	1	2	1	4550

92	9/01	Worc	3m	F Hdl	G-F	£1876

Total win prize-money £1876

Going: Sf: 0-0 GS: 0-1 Gd: 0-2 GF: - Fm: 1-5
Distance: 2m/2m3: 0-2 2m4-2m7: 0-5 3m+: 1-1
Track: LH: 1-6 RH: 0-1 Tight: 0-3 Gall: 0-1
Aids: Bl: 0-0 Vi: 0-0 Tstrap: 0-0
Best Rating: 97 10/01 Kels 2m6f110y good Hdl

Takeyourtime

103 95

7-y-o b m Hatim (USA)-Wand Of Youth (Mandamus)

A Scott Andy Scott

Placings:0664062-024 (4392)

2001/02: 20^{0}S, 25^{2}F, 22^{4}HY

	Starts	1st	2nd	3rd	Win & Pl
Hurdles	3	0	1	0	984
Career Total	10	0	2	0	11984

Going: Sf: 0-2 GS: 0-0 Gd: 0-0 GF: - Fm: 0-1
Distance: 2m/2m3: 0-0 2m4-2m7: 0-2 3m+: 0-1

Track: LH: 0-3 RH: 0-0 Tight: 0-1 Gall: 0-0
Aids: Bl: 0-0 Vi: 0-0 Tstrap: 0-0
Best Rating: 112 4/01 Aint 2m4f soft Hdl

Very moderate novice hurdler. Stays three miles, acts on most types of ground.

Taking (FR)

109(110h) **102**

6-y-o gr g Take Risks (FR)-Sonning (FR) (Moulin)
C N Kellett Sean A Taylor

Placings:P265033/565640364621-**P0F22** **(4872)**
2001/02: 16^{PS}, 16^{0}G, 16^{F}G, 17^{2}G, 16^{2}GF

	Starts	1st	2nd	3rd	Win & Pl
Chases	5	0	2	0	2016
Career Total	**24**	**1**	**4**	**3**	**31381**

97	2/01	Folk	2m	F(0-90)HCh	SFT	£2926

Total win prize-money £2926

Going: Sf: 0-1 GS: 0-0 Gd: 0-3 GF: - Fm: 0-1
Distance: 2m/2m3: 0-5 2m4-2m7: 0-0 3m+: 0-0
Track: LH: 0-2 RH: 0-3 Tight: 0-2 Gall: 0-1
Aids: Bl: 0-0 Vi: 0-0 Tstrap: 0-0
Best Rating: 102 4/02 Weth 2m gd-fm Ch

A French import, he failed to win over hurdles, but looked a decent prospect when making a successful chasing debut at Folkestone in February 2001. Unfortunately he was off for a year after that. Improved form since tried in blinkers and won Class F handicap over an extended 21 furlongs at Southwell July 2002. Seems to act on any ground.

Talama Lady (IRE)

104f **109f**

5-y-o b m Persian Bold-Talama (FR) (Shakapour)
G A Swinbank Miss Sally R Haynes

Placings: *1-1* **(0506)**
2001/02: 16^{1}GF

	Starts	1st	2nd	3rd	Win & Pl
NH Flat	1	1	0	0	1687
Career Total	**2**	**2**	**0**	**0**	**3556**

109	5/01	Hntg	2m110y	H NHF	G-F	£1687
97	4/01	MRas	1m5f110y	H NHF	G-S	£1869

Total win prize-money £3556

Going: Sf: 0-0 GS: 0-0 Gd: 0-0 GF: - Fm: 1-1
Distance: **2m/2m3: 1-1** 2m4-2m7: 0-0 3m+: 0-0
Track: LH: 0-0 **RH: 1-1** Tight: 0-0 **Gall: 1-1**
Aids: Bl: 0-0 Vi: 0-0 Tstrap: 0-0
Best Rating: 109 5/01 Hntg 2m110y gd-fm NHF

Talathath (FR)

97(74h) (33h)**103**

10-y-o b g Soviet Star (USA)-Mashmoon (USA) (Habitat)
M J Wilkinson R G & R A Whitehead

Placings:321411/2124265**U055**/0P0404**P20**/**30F**5311/42P30-0022 **(1477)**
2001/02: 20^{0}G, 20^{0}GF, 21^{2}GF, 20^{2}S

	Starts	1st	2nd	3rd	Win & Pl
Hurdles	1	0	0	0	0
Chases	3	0	2	0	2500
Career Total	**42**	**6**	**8**	**4**	**31907**

97	11/99	Tntn	2m3f110y	D(0-120)HHdl	GD	£2913
89	11/99	Kemp	2m5f	E(0-115)HHdl	G-F	£5277
127	9/97	Worc	2m4f	B(0-140)HHdl	G-F	£4948
112	4/97	MRas	2m3f110y	D Hdl	GD	£3156
116	4/97	Chel	2m1f	D Hdl	G-F	£2957
114	3/97	Winc	2m	F Hdl	GD	£1917

Total win prize-money £21171

Going: Sf: 0-1 GS: 0-0 Gd: 0-1 GF: - Fm: 0-2
Distance: 2m/2m3: 0-0 2m4-2m7: 0-4 3m+: 0-0
Track: LH: 0-3 RH: 0-1 Tight: 0-2 Gall: 0-0
Aids: Bl: 0-0 Vi: 0-0 Tstrap: 0-3
Best Rating: 127 9/97 Worc 2m4f gd-fm Hdl

Talbot Lad

99 **102**

6-y-o b g Weld-Greenacres Girl (Tycoon Ii)
S A Brookshaw M J Thomas & Sali Thomas

Placings:*2022*55020 **(4848)**
2001/02: 16^{2}GF, 17^{0}S, 16^{2}GF, 16^{2}GF, 19^{5}G, 16^{5}S, 16^{0}GS, 16^{2}G, 16^{0}G

	Starts	1st	2nd	3rd	Win & Pl
NH Flat	4	0	3	0	1370
Hurdles	5	0	1	0	1200
Career Total	**9**	**0**	**4**	**0**	**2570**

Going: Sf: 0-2 GS: 0-1 Gd: 0-3 GF: - Fm: 0-3
Distance: 2m/2m3: 0-8 2m4-2m7: 0-1 3m+: 0-0
Track: LH: 0-4 RH: 0-5 Tight: 0-3 Gall: 0-1
Aids: Bl: 0-0 Vi: 0-0 Tstrap: 0-7
Best Rating: 102 4/02 Ludl 2m good Hdl

Placed in bumpers and over hurdles.

Taleban

71 **26**

7-y-o b g Alleged (USA)-Triode (USA) (Sharpen Up)
J Wade John Wade

Placings:6/044320/000 **(2342)**
2001/02: 19^{0}G, 21^{0}S, 16^{0}GS

	Starts	1st	2nd	3rd	Win & Pl
Hurdles	3	0	0	0	
Career Total	**10**	**0**	**1**	**1**	**1334**

Going: Sf: 0-1 GS: 0-1 Gd: 0-1 GF: - Fm: 0-0
Distance: 2m/2m3: 0-1 2m4-2m7: 0-2 3m+: 0-0
Track: LH: 0-2 RH: 0-1 Tight: 0-2 Gall: 0-1
Aids: Bl: 0-0 Vi: 0-0 Tstrap: 0-0
Best Rating: 108 1/00 Ludl 2m gd-sft Hdl

Taleca Son (IRE)

71 **20**

7-y-o b g Conquering Hero (USA)-Lady Taleca (IRE) (Exhibitioner)
Mrs L Williamson Miss Judy Eaton

Placings:00F00/101-00 **(0775)**
2001/02: 19^{0}GF, 20^{0}GF

	Starts	1st	2nd	3rd	Win & Pl
Hurdles	2	0	0	0	
Career Total	**10**	**2**	**0**	**0**	**2968**

92	8/00	Sthl	2m	G Hdl	GD	£1445
90	7/00	Sthl	2m	G Hdl	G-F	£1522

Total win prize-money £2969

Going: Sf: 0-0 GS: 0-0 Gd: 0-0 GF: - Fm: 0-2
Distance: 2m/2m3: 0-0 2m4-2m7: 0-2 3m+: 0-0
Track: LH: 0-1 RH: 0-1 Tight: 0-1 Gall: 0-0
Aids: Bl: 0-0 Vi: 0-0 Tstrap: 0-0
Best Rating: 92 8/00 Sthl 2m good Hdl

Talents Little Gem

94 **85**

5-y-o b m Democratic (USA)-Le Saule D'Or (Sonnen Gold)
A W Carroll Group 1 Racing (1994) Ltd

Placings:4-305P **(2952)**
2001/02: 16^{3}S, 16^{0}GS, 17^{5}S, 16^{P}S

	Starts	1st	2nd	3rd	Win & Pl
Hurdles	4	0	0	1	292
Career Total	**5**	**0**	**0**	**1**	**292**

Going: Sf: 0-3 GS: 0-1 Gd: 0-0 GF: - Fm: 0-0
Distance: 2m/2m3: 0-4 2m4-2m7: 0-0 3m+: 0-0
Track: LH: 0-2 RH: 0-2 Tight: 0-2 Gall: 0-0
Aids: Bl: 0-0 Vi: 0-0 Tstrap: 0-0
Best Rating: 85 11/01 Strf 2m110y soft Hdl

Tales Of Bounty (IRE)

123

7-y-o b g Ela-Mana-Mou-Tales Of Wisdom (Rousillon (USA))
P F Nicholls H B Geddes

Placings:36532/100/31-2 **(0075)**
2001/02: 24^{2}G

	Starts	1st	2nd	3rd	Win & Pl
Hurdles	1	0	1	0	1743
Career Total	**11**	**2**	**2**	**3**	**12184**

123	4/01	Winc	2m6f	D(0-120)HHdl	SFT	£4225
116	11/99	Extr	2m1f	E Hdl	G-S	£3297

Total win prize-money £7522

Going: Sf: 0-0 GS: 0-0 Gd: 0-1 GF: - Fm: 0-0
Distance: 2m/2m3: 0-0 2m4-2m7: 0-0 3m+: 0-1
Track: LH: 0-0 RH: 0-1 Tight: 0-0 Gall: 0-0
Aids: Bl: 0-0 Vi: 0-0 Tstrap: 0-0
Best Rating: 123 4/01 Winc 2m6f soft Hdl

Fairly useful handicap hurdler who stays very well. Handles most ground.

Talkasha (IRE)

97 **91**

7-y-o br m Doyoun-Talwara (USA) (Diesis)
John Allen J Allen

Placings:131/131111120/30500P-0056P0 **(2778)**
2001/02: 17^{0}GS, 22^{0}GF, 24^{5}G, 24^{6}G, 20^{P}S, 22^{0}G

	Starts	1st	2nd	3rd	Win & Pl
Hurdles	6	0	0	0	0
Career Total	**24**	**8**	**1**	**3**	**77972**

10/99	Lyrh	2m1f	Ch	HLD	£6459
10/99	Autl	2m2f	HHdl	VS	£21529
10/99	Lyrh	2m1f	Ch	HVY	£4844
9/99	Nanc	2m3f	Ch	SFT	£4306
8/99	Diep	2m1f110y	Ch	SFT	£3445
5/99	Autl	2m2f	Hdl	VS	£6997
4/99	Engh	2m1f110y	Hdl	HLD	£6997
3/99	Engh	2m	Hdl	HVY	£6997

Total win prize-money £61574

Going: Sf: 0-1 GS: 0-1 Gd: 0-3 GF: - Fm: 0-1
Distance: 2m/2m3: 0-1 2m4-2m7: 0-3 3m+: 0-2
Track: LH: 0-3 RH: 0-2 Tight: 0-4 Gall: 0-0
Aids: Bl: 0-0 Vi: 0-0 Tstrap: 0-0
Best Rating: 91 10/01 Sthl 3m110y good Hdl

Tall Story

80(79h) (30h)79

7-y-o gr m Arzanni-Corny Story (Oats)

E L James Mrs J Heywood Lonsdale

Placings:0/5632/144010-5P0P (4089)

2001/02: 21^{5}S, 22^{P}G, 21^{0}G, 24^{P}S

	Starts	1st	2nd	3rd	Win & Pl
Hurdles	1	0	0	0	0
Chases	3	0	0	0	0
Career Total	**15**	**2**	**1**	**1**	**10115**

121	2/01	Hntg	2m4f110y	D Ch	G-S	£5980
100	9/00	Hrfd	2m3f110y	E Hdl	G-S	£2170

Total win prize-money £8150

Going: Sf: 0-2 GS: 0-0 Gd: 0-2 GF: - Fm: 0-0
Distance: 2m/2m3: 0-0 2m4-2m7: 0-3 3m+: 0-1
Track: LH: 0-3 RH: 0-1 Tight: 0-1 Gall: 0-1
Aids: Bl: 0-2 Vi: 0-0 Tstrap: 0-0
Best Rating: 121 2/01 Hntg 2m4f110y gd-sft Ch

Well held over hurdles after winning a modest novice event in September 2000. She fought hard to win her chasing debut in February the following year, but has failed to trouble the judge since then.

Tall Tale (IRE)

106 89

10-y-o b g Tale Quale-Prudent Rose (IRE) (Strong Gale)

R Johnson Mrs H Gwin

Placings:52/34P/PP0425520/03UP4-345340F34 (4856)

2001/02: 21^{3}G, 25^{4}G, 28^{5}GS, 24^{3}GS, 24^{4}S, 27^{0}S, 25^{F}S, 20^{3}HY, 25^{4}G

	Starts	1st	2nd	3rd	Win & Pl
Chases	9	0	0	3	2484
Career Total	**28**	**0**	**3**	**5**	**7115**

Going: Sf: 0-4 GS: 0-2 Gd: 0-3 GF: - Fm: 0-0
Distance: 2m/2m3: 0-0 2m4-2m7: 0-2 3m+: 0-7
Track: LH: 0-8 RH: 0-1 Tight: 0-5 Gall: 0-3
Aids: Bl: 0-0 Vi: 0-0 Tstrap: 0-0
Best Rating: 108 10/01 Kels 3m1f good Ch

Staying maiden chaser. Acts on most types of ground.

Tallaburn

6-y-o br m Mutamarrid-Make The Grade (Last Fandango)

J I A Charlton J C Thomson

Placings:40 (0678)

2001/02: 16^{4}S, 16^{0}GF

	Starts	1st	2nd	3rd	Win & Pl
NH Flat	2	0	0	0	0
Career Total	**2**	**0**	**0**	**0**	**0**

Going: Sf: 0-1 GS: 0-0 Gd: 0-0 GF: - Fm: 0-1
Distance: 2m/2m3: 0-2 2m4-2m7: 0-0 3m+: 0-0
Track: LH: 0-1 RH: 0-1 Tight: 0-0 Gall: 0-0
Aids: Bl: 0-0 Vi: 0-0 Tstrap: 0-2
Best Rating:

Tallison

84f 73f

4-y-o ch g First Trump-Clare Celeste (Coquelin (USA))

P F Nicholls Neil Smith

Placings:5 (4910)

2001/02: 17^{5}G

	Starts	1st	2nd	3rd	Win & Pl
NH Flat	1	0	0	0	0
Career Total	**1**	**0**	**0**	**0**	**0**

Going: Sf: 0-0 GS: 0-0 Gd: 0-1 GF: - Fm: 0-0
Distance: 2m/2m3: 0-1 2m4-2m7: 0-0 3m+: 0-0
Track: LH: 0-0 RH: 0-1 Tight: 0-1 Gall: 0-0
Aids: Bl: 0-0 Vi: 0-0 Tstrap: 0-0
Best Rating: 73 4/02 MRas 2m1f110y good NHF

Tallow Bay (IRE)

109(98h) (51h)116

7-y-o b g Glacial Storm (USA)-Minimum Choice (IRE) (Miners Lamp)

Mrs S Wall Mrs S Wall

Placings:000/5054600-243F25U2P (4634)

2001/02: 16^{2}S, 20^{4}G, 26^{3}G, 25^{F}G, 21^{2}S, 24^{5}S, 23^{U}S, 22^{2}S, 24^{P}GF

	Starts	1st	2nd	3rd	Win & Pl
Chases	9	0	3	1	5482
Career Total	**19**	**0**	**3**	**1**	**5482**

Going: Sf: 0-5 GS: 0-0 Gd: 0-3 GF: - Fm: 0-1
Distance: 2m/2m3: 0-1 2m4-2m7: 0-3 3m+: 0-5
Track: LH: 0-1 RH: 0-7 Tight: 0-2 Gall: 0-0
Aids: Bl: 0-0 Vi: 0-0 Tstrap: 0-0
Best Rating: 116 3/02 Towc 2m6f soft Ch

Fair handicap chaser. Prefers stiff tracks and soft ground. Stays three miles.

Tam O'Shanter

98(107h) (97h)97

8-y-o gr g Persian Bold-No More Rosies (Warpath)

J G M O'Shea (A P James 13/6) Gary Roberts

Placings:F220/0/035112025635325/2F3331143-5P3152 (1137)

2001/02: 24^{5}G, 25^{P}G, 25^{3}F, 27^{1}GF, 24^{5}G, 22^{2}G

	Starts	1st	2nd	3rd	Win & Pl
Hurdles	2	1	1	0	3474
Chases	4	0	0	1	469
Career Total	**35**	**5**	**7**	**8**	**25793**

97	7/01	Sedg	3m3f110y	F(0-110)HHdl	G-F	£2814
103	8/00	NAbb	3m2f110y	E Ch	G-S	£3347
103	7/00	Sedg	3m3f	D Ch	G-F	£3757
103	7/99	Worc	2m4f	D Hdl	G-F	£3104
108	6/99	Uttx	2m4f110y	C(0-95)HHdl	G-S	£2186

Total win prize-money £15211

Going: Sf: 0-0 GS: 0-0 Gd: 0-4 GF: - Fm: 1-2
Distance: 2m/2m3: 0-0 2m4-2m7: 0-1 **3m+: 1-5**
Track: **LH: 1-3** RH: 0-3 **Tight: 1-3** Gall: 0-1
Aids: Bl: 0-0 Vi: 0-1 Tstrap: 0-0
Best Rating: 108 6/99 Uttx 2m4f110y gd-sft Hdl

Tamango (FR)

102 103

5-y-o ch g Klimt (FR)-Tipmosa (FR) (Tip Moss (FR))

P J Hobbs The Brushmakers

Placings:32401 (4654)

2001/02: 18^{3}G, 18^{2}S, 20^{4}GS, 21^{0}S, 17^{1}GS

	Starts	1st	2nd	3rd	Win & Pl
NH Flat	2	0	1	1	708
Hurdles	3	1	0	0	3073
Career Total	**5**	**1**	**1**	**1**	**3781**

103	4/02	Tntn	2m1f	E Hdl	G-S	£2800

Total win prize-money £2800

Going: Sf: 0-2 GS: 1-2 Gd: 0-1 GF: - Fm: 0-0
Distance: **2m/2m3: 1-3** 2m4-2m7: 0-2 3m+: 0-0
Track: LH: 0-4 **RH: 1-1 Tight: 1-3** Gall: 0-1
Aids: Bl: 0-0 Vi: 0-0 Tstrap: 0-0
Best Rating: 118 2/02 Font 2m2f110y soft NHF

Useful placed form in bumpers, made all to get off the mark over hurdles in a Taunton maiden. Looks a staying chaser in the making. Three miles should suit over hurdles.

Tambo (IRE)

90 121

7-y-o b g Shardari-Carmen Lady (Torus)

M Bradstock Mark Tamburro

Placings:040221/40-3P (2428)

2001/02: 22^{3}GS, 22^{P}G

	Starts	1st	2nd	3rd	Win & Pl
Chases	2	0	0	1	490
Career Total	**10**	**1**	**2**	**1**	**4835**

113	3/00	Plum	2m5f	E Hdl	GD	£2450

Total win prize-money £2450

Going: Sf: 0-0 GS: 0-1 Gd: 0-1 GF: - Fm: 0-0
Distance: 2m/2m3: 0-0 2m4-2m7: 0-2 3m+: 0-0
Track: LH: 0-1 RH: 0-0 Tight: 0-1 Gall: 0-1
Aids: Bl: 0-0 Vi: 0-0 Tstrap: 0-0
Best Rating: 121 11/01 Font 2m6f gd-sft Ch

Came back with a pleasing run over the larger obstacles in November 2001 after a year off, but pulled up next time and not seen after.

Taming (IRE)

109 135+

6-y-o ch g Lycius (USA)-Black Fighter (USA) (Secretariat (USA))

Miss Venetia Williams Oakview Racing

Placings:6F2/P003-5 (4848)

2001/02: 16^{5}G

	Starts	1st	2nd	3rd	Win & Pl
Hurdles	1	0	0	0	0
Career Total	**8**	**0**	**1**	**1**	**1279**

Going: Sf: 0-0 GS: 0-0 Gd: 0-1 GF: - Fm: 0-0
Distance: 2m/2m3: 0-1 2m4-2m7: 0-0 3m+: 0-0
Track: LH: 0-1 RH: 0-0 Tight: 0-1 Gall: 0-0
Aids: Bl: 0-0 Vi: 0-0 Tstrap: 0-0
Best Rating: 101 3/00 Catt 2m gd-fm Hdl

A fair hurdler, but was finding it hard to force his head in front until found some easy opportunities in the summer of 2002. Suited by two to two and a half miles and a sound surface.

Tango Royal (FR)

109(97h) (106h)139

6-y-o gr g Royal Charter (FR)-Nazia (FR) (Zino)

M C Pipe B A Kilpatrick

Placings:01310112/03154F4-600 (4649)

2001/02: 16^{6}GS, 20^{0}GS, 16^{0}G

	Starts	1st	2nd	3rd	Win & Pl
Hurdles	1	0	0	0	0
Chases	2	0	0	0	0
Career Total	**18**	**5**	**1**	**2**	**115392**

9/00	Comp	2m1f110y	Hdl	G-S	£3362
3/00	Autl	2m4f110y	Ch	VS	£28818

3/00	Autl	2m1f110y	Ch	HVY	£28818
11/99	Engh	2m1f	Ch	HLD	£10764
10/99	Toul	2m1f110y	Ch	SFT	£4844

Total win prize-money £76606

Going: Sf: 0-0 GS: 0-2 Gd: 0-1 GF: - Fm: 0-0
Distance: 2m/2m3: 0-2 2m4-2m7: 0-1 3m+: 0-0
Track: LH: 0-2 RH: 0-1 Tight: 0-1 Gall: 0-1
Aids: Bl: 0-0 Vi: 0-0 Tstrap: 0-0
Best Rating: **139** 3/02 Chel 2m4f110y gd-sft Ch

A useful ex-French import, successful over both hurdles and fences, he joined Martin Pipe in December 2000. Subsequently off the track for over a year, he was well held on his comeback run but ran well at the Festival. Looks best suited by trips around two miles on soft ground.

Tanshan

70 **31**

7-y-o ch g Anshan-Nafla (FR) (Arctic Tern (USA))
R Rowe Richard Rowe

Placings:0/00 **(0365)**
2001/02: 17⁰GS, 19⁰GF

	Starts	1st	2nd	3rd	Win & Pl
Hurdles	2	0	0	0	
Career Total	**3**	**0**	**0**	**0**	

Going: Sf: 0-0 GS: 0-1 Gd: 0-0 GF: - Fm: 0-1
Distance: 2m/2m3: 0-1 2m4-2m7: 0-1 3m+: 0-0
Track: LH: 0-1 RH: 0-1 Tight: 0-2 Gall: 0-0
Aids: Bl: 0-0 Vi: 0-0 Tstrap: 0-0
Best Rating: **88** 11/99 Hntg 2m110y good Hdl

Tantivy Bay (IRE)

8-y-o b g Good Thyne (USA)-Swiftly Belle (Deep Run)
P J Hobbs D R Peppiatt

Placings:1/42144P/3PP-PP **(2545)**
2001/02: 24PG, 23PGS

	Starts	1st	2nd	3rd	Win & Pl
Chases	2	0	0	0	
Career Total	**12**	**2**	**1**	**1**	**5441**

112	12/99	Font	2m4f	E Hdl	G-S	£2092
102	4/99	Towc	2m	H NHF	GD	£1525

Total win prize-money £3618

Going: Sf: 0-0 GS: 0-1 Gd: 0-1 GF: - Fm: 0-0
Distance: 2m/2m3: 0-0 2m4-2m7: 0-0 3m+: 0-2
Track: LH: 0-1 RH: 0-1 Tight: 0-0 Gall: 0-1
Aids: Bl: 0-1 Vi: 0-0 Tstrap: 0-0
Best Rating: **114** 12/99 Hrfd 2m3f110y soft Hdl

Tap Dance

103 **85**

4-y-o ch g Dancing Spree (USA)-Trachelium (Formidable (USA))
Miss S E Hall C Platts

Placings:20P2P **(4522)**
2001/02: 17²G, 16⁰G, 17PS, 18⁰HY, 17PG

	Starts	1st	2nd	3rd	Win & Pl
Hurdles	5	0	2	0	1478
Career Total	**5**	**0**	**2**	**0**	**1478**

Going: Sf: 0-2 GS: 0-0 Gd: 0-3 GF: - Fm: 0-0
Distance: 2m/2m3: 0-5 2m4-2m7: 0-0 3m+: 0-0
Track: LH: 0-3 RH: 0-2 Tight: 0-3 Gall: 0-0
Aids: Bl: 0-0 Vi: 0-0 Tstrap: 0-0
Best Rating: **85** 9/01 Sedg 2m1f good Hdl

Novice hurdler. Effective at two miles two furlongs and acts on heavy ground.

Tap Dancer (IRE)

75 **56**

4-y-o b g Sadler's Wells (USA)-Watch Out (USA) (Mr Prospector (USA))
B G Powell (J T Gorman 11/10) The A T P Racing Partnership

Placings:006 **(4371)**
2001/02: 16⁰GS, 16⁰G, 16⁶GS

	Starts	1st	2nd	3rd	Win & Pl
Hurdles	3	0	0	0	0
Career Total	**3**	**0**	**0**	**0**	**0**

Going: Sf: 0-0 GS: 0-2 Gd: 0-1 GF: - Fm: 0-0
Distance: 2m/2m3: 0-3 2m4-2m7: 0-0 3m+: 0-0
Track: LH: 0-0 RH: 0-3 Tight: 0-0 Gall: 0-0
Aids: Bl: 0-0 Vi: 0-0 Tstrap: 0-0
Best Rating: **48** 2/02 Winc 2m gd-sft Hdl

Tapping Tam (IRE)

111(98h) (93h)**99**

6-y-o b g King's Ride-Jeanarie (Reformed Character)
N A Twiston-Davies H R Mould

Placings:00P-P3252P5P **(4233)**
2001/02: 26PG, 22³GS, 23²G, 22⁵G, 24²GS, 24PHY, 24⁵G, 32PGS

	Starts	1st	2nd	3rd	Win & Pl
Hurdles	3	0	1	1	1466
Chases	5	0	1	0	956
Career Total	**11**	**0**	**2**	**1**	**2422**

Going: Sf: 0-1 GS: 0-3 Gd: 0-4 GF: - Fm: 0-0
Distance: 2m/2m3: 0-0 2m4-2m7: 0-3 3m+: 0-5
Track: LH: 0-4 RH: 0-3 Tight: 0-1 Gall: 0-2
Aids: Bl: 0-0 Vi: 0-0 Tstrap: 0-0
Best Rating: **99** 12/01 Hntg 3m gd-sft Ch

Tappingthecoffin

15

5-y-o br g Afzal-Crimson Sol (Crimson Beau)
P W Hiatt Phil Kelly

Placings:00-06 **(0486)**
2001/02: 21⁰GF, 18⁶GF

	Starts	1st	2nd	3rd	Win & Pl
Hurdles	2	0	0	0	0
Career Total	**4**	**0**	**0**	**0**	**0**

Going: Sf: 0-0 GS: 0-0 Gd: 0-0 GF: - Fm: 0-2
Distance: 2m/2m3: 0-1 2m4-2m7: 0-1 3m+: 0-0
Track: LH: 0-1 RH: 0-0 Tight: 0-1 Gall: 0-0
Aids: Bl: 0-0 Vi: 0-0 Tstrap: 0-0
Best Rating: **15** 5/01 Wwck 2m5f gd-fm Hdl

Tara-Brogan

105 **135**

9-y-o b g Jupiter Island-Princess Semele (Imperial Fling (USA))
Ian Williams Patrick Kelly

Placings:45/1153203/F232U/2-111 **(1487)**
2001/02: 24¹GF, 23¹F, 24¹GF

	Starts	1st	2nd	3rd	Win & Pl
Chases	3	3	0	0	15158
Career Total	**18**	**5**	**4**	**3**	**28376**

130	9/01	Hntg	3m	E Ch	G-F	£3753
135	5/01	Weth	2m7f110y	D Ch	FRM	£4108
133	5/01	Sthl	3m110y	C Ch	G-F	£7296
118	6/98	MRas	2m3f110y	D Hdl	GD	£3140
112	6/98	Worc	2m4f	E Hdl	G-F	£2005

Total win prize-money £20303

Going: Sf: 0-0 GS: 0-0 Gd: 0-0 GF: - Fm: 3-3
Distance: 2m/2m3: 0-0 2m4-2m7: 0-0 **3m+: 3-3**
Track: LH: 1-1 RH: 1-1 Tight: 1-1 Gall: 1-1
Aids: Bl: 0-0 Vi: 0-0 Tstrap: 0-0
Best Rating: **135** 5/01 Weth 2m7f110y firm Ch

He injured a foot after winning two novice chases during May 2001 but bounced back to form when taking a novice chase at Huntingdon in September. Best on decent ground, he stays well.

Tarajan (USA)

10-y-o ch g Shahrastani (USA)-Tarafa (Akarad (FR))
Tim Butt (Miss Lucinda V Russell 20/1) Tim Butt

Placings:43425/321154511425500/50533/144340520 44/2335532/54 **(3916)**
2001/02: 22⁵HY, 24⁴GS

	Starts	1st	2nd	3rd	Win & Pl
Chases	2	0	0	0	0
Career Total	**45**	**5**	**6**	**8**	**27345**

100	5/98	Prth	2m	D Ch	G-F	£3566
117	10/96	Gway	2m4f	(0-116)HHdl	SFT	£3530
117	10/96	Rosc	2m	(0-109)HHdl	YLD	£2824
100	8/96	Tipp	2m	Hdl	YLD	£3707
108	7/96	Klny	2m1f	Hdl	G-F	£3530

Total win prize-money £17160

Going: Sf: 0-1 GS: 0-1 Gd: 0-0 GF: - Fm: 0-0
Distance: 2m/2m3: 0-0 2m4-2m7: 0-1 3m+: 0-1
Track: LH: 0-0 RH: 0-1 Tight: 0-1 Gall: 0-0
Aids: Bl: 0-0 Vi: 0-0 Tstrap: 0-0
Best Rating: **124** 12/96 Leop 2m2f yield Hdl

Taransay

4-y-o b g Contract Law (USA)-Homemaker (Homeboy)
Brendan W Duke Miss A C Telling

Placings:6P **(2209)**
2001/02: 16⁶GS, 17PG

	Starts	1st	2nd	3rd	Win & Pl
Hurdles	2	0	0	0	0
Career Total	**2**	**0**	**0**	**0**	**0**

Going: Sf: 0-0 GS: 0-1 Gd: 0-1 GF: - Fm: 0-0
Distance: 2m/2m3: 0-2 2m4-2m7: 0-0 3m+: 0-0
Track: LH: 0-0 RH: 0-2 Tight: 0-0 Gall: 0-0
Aids: Bl: 0-0 Vi: 0-0 Tstrap: 0-0
Best Rating:

Tarasco (FR)

105 **133**

6-y-o b g Deploy-Moucha (FR) (Fabulous Dancer (USA))
P R Webber Mrs D Ridley

Placings:13205 **(4418)**
2001/02: 17¹GS, 16³S, 20²HY, 16⁰GS, 16⁵GS

Starts	1st	2nd	3rd	Win & Pl
Hurdles	5	1	1	1	11018
Career Total	**5**	**1**	**1**	**1**	**11018**

130	12/01	Bang	2m1f	E Hdl	G-S	£2807

Total win prize-money £2807

Going: Sf: 0-2 GS: 1-3 Gd: 0-0 GF: - Fm: 0-0
Distance: **2m/2m3: 1-4** 2m4-2m7: 0-1 3m+: 0-0
Track: **LH: 1-4** RH: 0-1 **Tight: 1-1** Gall: 0-1
Aids: Bl: 0-0 Vi: 0-0 Tstrap: 0-0
Best Rating: 133 1/02 Wwck 2m soft Hdl

Ex-French, he was an easy winner of hurdles debut in this country on soft ground over the minimum trip, and ran well in decent company subsequently.

Tarashani (IRE)

85 **70**

4-y-o ch c Primo Dominie-Tarakana (USA) (Shahrastani (USA))
B Ellison (Sir Michael Stoute 10/6) Eddie Kirtland/r W L Bowden

Placings:006 **(2512)**
2001/02: 16^{0}G, 16^{0}G, 16^{6}S

	Starts	1st	2nd	3rd	Win & Pl
Hurdles	3	0	0	0	0
Career Total	**3**	**0**	**0**	**0**	**0**

Going: Sf: 0-1 GS: 0-0 Gd: 0-2 GF: - Fm: 0-0
Distance: 2m/2m3: 0-3 2m4-2m7: 0-0 3m+: 0-0
Track: LH: 0-3 RH: 0-0 Tight: 0-1 Gall: 0-0
Aids: Bl: 0-0 Vi: 0-1 Tstrap: 0-0
Best Rating: 70 11/01 Weth 2m good Hdl

Tarbolton Moss

104 **101**

7-y-o b m Le Moss-Priceless Peril (Silly Prices)
M Todhunter Mrs David Marshall

Placings:*05*05-40331212 **(4875)**
2001/02: 24^{4}S, 20^{0}G, 22^{3}GS, 24^{3}G, 24^{1}S, 24^{2}HY, 27^{1}S, 24^{2}G

	Starts	1st	2nd	3rd	Win & Pl
Hurdles	8	2	2	2	8102
Career Total	**12**	**2**	**2**	**2**	**8102**

101	3/02	Kels	3m3f	F(0-95)HHdl	SFT	£2999
93	2/02	Newc	3m	F(0-100)HHdl	SFT	£1904

Total win prize-money £4904

Going: Sf: 2-4 GS: 0-1 Gd: 0-3 GF: - Fm: 0-0
Distance: 2m/2m3: 0-0 2m4-2m7: 0-2 **3m+: 2-6**
Track: **LH: 2-5** RH: 0-3 Tight: 1-3 Gall: 1-2
Aids: Bl: 0-0 Vi: 0-0 Tstrap: 0-0
Best Rating: 101 4/02 Prth 3m110y good Hdl

Modest hurdler, stays three miles plus. Appreciated the soft ground when winning at Newcastle in February and Kelso in March 2002.

Taro Prince (IRE)

101 **82**

8-y-o b g Dragon Palace (USA)-Carlys Bank (Saucy Kit)
J L Spearing Carl Spate

Placings:00/UPP42PP-O03PF **(1669)**
2001/02: 24^{0}G, 22^{0}G, 24^{3}GF, 26^{P}G, 24^{F}G

	Starts	1st	2nd	3rd	Win & Pl
Hurdles	5	0	0	1	353
Career Total	**14**	**0**	**1**	**1**	**1382**

Going: Sf: 0-0 GS: 0-0 Gd: 0-4 GF: - Fm: 0-1
Distance: 2m/2m3: 0-0 2m4-2m7: 0-1 3m+: 0-4
Track: LH: 0-4 RH: 0-1 Tight: 0-2 Gall: 0-1
Aids: Bl: 0-0 Vi: 0-0 Tstrap: 0-0
Best Rating: 82 8/01 Uttx 3m110y gd-fm Hdl

Tarongo (FR)

4-y-o b g Tel Quel (FR)-Rainbow Rainbow (Vision (USA))
Mrs L C Taylor Mrs L C Taylor

Placings:PP **(4263)**
2001/02: 17^{P}GS, 16^{P}S

	Starts	1st	2nd	3rd	Win & Pl
Hurdles	2	0	0	0	
Career Total	**2**	**0**	**0**	**0**	

Going: Sf: 0-1 GS: 0-1 Gd: 0-0 GF: - Fm: 0-0
Distance: 2m/2m3: 0-2 2m4-2m7: 0-0 3m+: 0-0
Track: LH: 0-1 RH: 0-1 Tight: 0-0 Gall: 0-0
Aids: Bl: 0-0 Vi: 0-0 Tstrap: 0-0
Best Rating: mfy

Pulled up when tailed off on hurdles debut.

Tarongoshy (IRE)

5-y-o ch m Over The River (FR)-October Lady (Lucifer (USA))
M Pitman B R L Racing

Placings:24P0 **(4138)**
2001/02: 17^{2}S, 22^{4}HY, 22^{P}S, 16^{0}GS

	Starts	1st	2nd	3rd	Win & Pl
NH Flat	1	0	1	0	460
Hurdles	3	0	0	0	0
Career Total	**4**	**0**	**1**	**0**	**460**

Going: Sf: 0-3 GS: 0-1 Gd: 0-0 GF: - Fm: 0-0
Distance: 2m/2m3: 0-2 2m4-2m7: 0-2 3m+: 0-0
Track: LH: 0-0 RH: 0-3 Tight: 0-2 Gall: 0-0
Aids: Bl: 0-0 Vi: 0-0 Tstrap: 0-0
Best Rating: 94 1/02 Folk 2m1f110y soft NHF

A half-sister to winning hurdlers. Runner-up on her bumper debut at Folkestone in January, but no show over hurdles.

Tarski

98 **93**

8-y-o ch g Polish Precedent (USA)-Illusory (King's Lake (USA))
W S Kittow Midd Shire Racing

Placings:66 **(1996)**
2001/02: 17^{6}G, 17^{6}S

	Starts	1st	2nd	3rd	Win & Pl
Hurdles	2	0	0	0	0
Career Total	**2**	**0**	**0**	**0**	**0**

Going: Sf: 0-1 GS: 0-0 Gd: 0-1 GF: - Fm: 0-0
Distance: 2m/2m3: 0-2 2m4-2m7: 0-0 3m+: 0-0
Track: LH: 0-1 RH: 0-1 Tight: 0-1 Gall: 0-0
Aids: Bl: 0-0 Vi: 0-1 Tstrap: 0-0
Best Rating: 83 10/01 Extr 2m1f good Hdl

Sprang 25/1 shock when winning two mile maiden hurdle at Worcester July 2002.

Tartan Thyne (IRE)

(96h) (85h)

8-y-o ro g Good Thyne (USA)-Lady Trissie (Politico (USA))
P Beaumont Exors Of The Late J N Yeadon

Placings:0050/0PP **(4195)**
2001/02: 20^{0}G, 24^{P}HY, 21^{P}S

	Starts	1st	2nd	3rd	Win & Pl
Hurdles	2	0	0	0	0
Chases	1	0	0	0	0
Career Total	**7**	**0**	**0**	**0**	**0**

Going: Sf: 0-2 GS: 0-0 Gd: 0-1 GF: - Fm: 0-0
Distance: 2m/2m3: 0-0 2m4-2m7: 0-2 3m+: 0-1
Track: LH: 0-3 RH: 0-0 Tight: 0-1 Gall: 0-1
Aids: Bl: 0-0 Vi: 0-0 Tstrap: 0-0
Best Rating: 85 11/01 Newc 2m4f good Hdl

Has shown nothing so far.

Tarxien

109 **142**

8-y-o b g Kendor (FR)-Tanz (IRE) (Sadler's Wells (USA))
M C Pipe (Mrs Merrita Jones 12/5) B A Kilpatrick

Placings:4/443/54302-4111111B2 **(4665)**
2001/02: 24^{4}GF, 22^{1}G, 19^{1}GF, 22^{1}GF, 20^{1}GF, 21^{1}G, 24^{1}G, 21^{B}GS, 24^{2}G

	Starts	1st	2nd	3rd	Win & Pl
Hurdles	9	6	1	0	53273
Career Total	**18**	**6**	**2**	**2**	**57504**

134	12/01	Asct	3m	B Hdl	GD	£11340
140	11/01	Chel	2m5f	B Hdl	GD	£8736
136	9/01	Worc	2m4f	C(0-135)HHdl	G-F	£5554
126	8/01	NAbb	2m6f	E Hdl	G-F	£2954
130	8/01	MRas	2m3f110y	C(0-130)HHdl	G-F	£6179
125	7/01	NAbb	2m6f	C(0-130)HHdl	GD	£4867

Total win prize-money £39632

Going: Sf: 0-0 GS: 0-1 Gd: 3-4 GF: - Fm: 3-4
Distance: 2m/2m3: 0-0 **2m4-2m7: 5-6** 3m+: 1-3
Track: **LH: 4-7** RH: 2-2 **Tight: 3-5** Gall: 1-2
Aids: Bl: 0-0 Vi: 0-0 **Tstrap: 6-8**
Best Rating: 142 4/02 Aint 3m110y good Hdl

Notched up four easy wins in handicap hurdles in the summer of 2001 at up to two miles six and was 17lb higher by the end of that purple patch. After running on the Flat in the Cesarewitch, he bolted up on his return to hurdles and completed the six-timer over timber at Ascot before being brought down at the Festival. Good effort at Aintree. Likes a sound surface and wears a tongue strap. Stays three miles and is most progressive.

Tasbok (IRE)

104 **95**

7-y-o b g Posen (USA)-Go Honey Go (General Assembly (USA))
R Rowe (W P Mullins 14/10) R Stillwell

Placings:605023 **(4764)**
2001/02: 16^{6}Y, 16^{0}G, 17^{5}HY, 17^{0}S, 16^{2}GF, 16^{3}GF

	Starts	1st	2nd	3rd	Win & Pl
Hurdles	6	0	1	1	1533
Career Total	**6**	**0**	**1**	**1**	**1533**

Going: Sf: 0-2 GS: 0-0 Gd: 0-1 GF: - Fm: 0-2
Distance: 2m/2m3: 0-6 2m4-2m7: 0-0 3m+: 0-0
Track: LH: 0-1 RH: 0-4 Tight: 0-2 Gall: 0-0
Aids: Bl: 0-0 Vi: 0-0 Tstrap: 0-3

Best Rating: 95 4/02 Asct 2m110y gd-fm Hdl

Ex-Irish Flat winner, showed best form over hurdles when faced with fast ground. Has worn a tongue tie.

Tashreef

(59h)

12-y-o b g Shareef Dancer (USA)-Lune De Minuit (USA) (Caro)

Mrs S J Smith George Joseph Larkin

Placings:00/3R056RP0/11F43400/62034RPL/21/046 2622134233141/432640024414045-PPR **(3393)**

2001/02: 24^{P}GS, 16^{P}S, 20^{R}GS

	Starts	1st	2nd	3rd	Win & Pl
Hurdles	2	0	0	0	0
Chases	1	0	0	0	0
Career Total	**62**	**7**	**8**	**7**	**41940**

117	1/01	Catt	2m3f	D Ch	G-S	£3802
118	12/99	MRas	2m3f110y	D(0-125)HHdl	GD	£4601
118	11/99	Newc	2m4f	D(0-125)HHdl	G-S	£5226
108	8/99	MRas	2m3f110y	C(0-130)HHdl	G-F	£5064
96	11/98	MRas	2m1f110y	E(0-110)HHdl	SFT	£2262
83	5/95	Prth	2m100y	F(0-100)HHdl	SFT	£2709
83	5/95	Hexm	2m	G(0-95)HHdl	FRM	£2143

Total win prize-money £25809

Going: Sf: 0-1 GS: 0-1 Gd: 0-1 GF: - Fm: 0-0
Distance: 2m/2m3: 0-1 2m4-2m7: 0-1 3m+: 0-1
Track: LH: 0-2 RH: 0-1 Tight: 0-0 Gall: 0-1
Aids: Bl: 0-0 Vi: 0-0 Tstrap: 0-0
Best Rating: 122 1/01 Catt 2m3f gd-sft Ch

Taskmaster

89f 83f

5-y-o b g Alflora (IRE)-Travail Girl (Forties Field (FR))

P J Hobbs Andrew P Wyer

Placings:0 **(3502)**

2001/02: 16^{0}S

	Starts	1st	2nd	3rd	Win & Pl
NH Flat	1	0	0	0	
Career Total	**1**	**0**	**0**	**0**	

Going: Sf: 0-1 GS: 0-0 Gd: 0-0 GF: - Fm: 0-0
Distance: 2m/2m3: 0-1 2m4-2m7: 0-0 3m+: 0-0
Track: LH: 0-0 RH: 0-1 Tight: 0-0 Gall: 0-0
Aids: Bl: 0-0 Vi: 0-0 Tstrap: 0-0
Best Rating: 83 1/02 Kemp 2m soft NHF

Tasmin Tyrant (NZ)

13-y-o b g Church Parade-Lovela (NZ) (Rapier Ii)

Mrs C Egalton Mrs C Egalton

Placings:P **(4253)**

2001/02: 26^{P}G

	Starts	1st	2nd	3rd	Win & Pl
Chases	1	0	0	0	
Career Total	**1**	**0**	**0**	**0**	

Going: Sf: 0-0 GS: 0-0 Gd: 0-1 GF: - Fm: 0-0
Distance: 2m/2m3: 0-0 2m4-2m7: 0-0 3m+: 0-1
Track: LH: 0-1 RH: 0-0 Tight: 0-0 Gall: 0-1
Aids: Bl: 0-0 Vi: 0-0 Tstrap: 0-0
Best Rating: mfy

Prolific winning pointer who ran up sequences in 1996 and 1999. Suited by most going bar extremes of ground.

Tate Tirol (IRE)

(87c) 110

5-y-o b g Tirol-Lovely Deise (IRE) (Tate Gallery (USA))

R T Phillips (C F Swan 23/7) Ford Associated Racing Team

Placings:11F4650-20P **(4164)**

2001/02: 17^{2}GF, 16^{0}GS, 21^{P}GS

	Starts	1st	2nd	3rd	Win & Pl
Hurdles	2	0	0	0	0
Chases	1	0	1	0	1484
Career Total	**10**	**2**	**1**	**0**	**10858**

115	10/00	Gowr	2m	Hdl	SFT	£5520
110	9/00	Fair	2m	Hdl	G-F	£3312

Total win prize-money £8832

Going: Sf: 0-0 GS: 0-2 Gd: 0-0 GF: - Fm: 0-1
Distance: 2m/2m3: 0-2 2m4-2m7: 0-1 3m+: 0-0
Track: LH: 0-1 RH: 0-0 Tight: 0-1 Gall: 0-0
Aids: Bl: 0-0 Vi: 0-0 Tstrap: 0-0
Best Rating: 117 2/01 Navn 2m soft Hdl

A winner twice in juvenile events in Ireland but has achieved little so far here.

Tathmin

103(103h) (102h) 112

9-y-o b g Weldnaas (USA)-Alcassa (FR) (Satingo)

A King Miss J M Bodycote

Placings:0053/10/000-1105212 **(2259)**

2001/02: 22^{1}GF, 19^{1}G, 22^{0}GF, 24^{5}GF, 24^{2}G, 24^{1}GF, 24^{2}G

	Starts	1st	2nd	3rd	Win & Pl
Hurdles	7	3	2	0	13178
Career Total	**16**	**4**	**2**	**1**	**15742**

102	11/01	Extr	3m110y	E(0-115)HHdl	G-F	£3234
95	5/01	Hrfd	2m3f110y	F(0-110)HHdl	GD	£3643
98	5/01	Winc	2m6f	F(0-100)HHdl	G-F	£3584
76	5/97	Hrfd	2m1f	E(0-100)HHdl	GD	£2332

Total win prize-money £12794

Going: Sf: 0-0 GS: 0-0 Gd: 1-3 GF: - Fm: 2-4
Distance: 2m/2m3: 0-0 **2m4-2m7: 2-3** 3m+: 1-4
Track: LH: 0-3 **RH: 3-4** Tight: 0-2 Gall: 0-0
Aids: **Bl: 3-7** Vi: 0-0 Tstrap: 0-0
Best Rating: 102 11/01 Kemp 3m110y good Hdl

A moderate handicapper over hurdles, he made a satisfactory start over fences when runner-up over three miles at Wetherby in May but was only second when odds-on next time. May need blinkers.

Tatty The Tank

95 83

4-y-o b g Tragic Role (USA)-Springfield Girl (Royal Vulcan)

M C Pipe Sandicroft Stud Syndicate

Placings:3 **(1080)**

2001/02: 17^{3}G

	Starts	1st	2nd	3rd	Win & Pl
Hurdles	1	0	0	1	436
Career Total	**1**	**0**	**0**	**1**	**436**

Going: Sf: 0-0 GS: 0-0 Gd: 0-1 GF: - Fm: 0-0
Distance: 2m/2m3: 0-1 2m4-2m7: 0-0 3m+: 0-0
Track: LH: 0-1 RH: 0-0 Tight: 0-1 Gall: 0-0
Aids: Bl: 0-0 Vi: 0-0 Tstrap: 0-0
Best Rating: 83 8/01 Bang 2m1f good Hdl

Taw Park

100 92

8-y-o b g Inca Chief (USA)-Parklands Belle (Stanford)

R J Baker R P Maddock

Placings:5560 **(2928)**

2001/02: 17^{5}F, 17^{5}G, 17^{6}GS, 19^{0}GS

	Starts	1st	2nd	3rd	Win & Pl
Hurdles	4	0	0	0	0
Career Total	**4**	**0**	**0**	**0**	**0**

Going: Sf: 0-0 GS: 0-2 Gd: 0-1 GF: - Fm: 0-1
Distance: 2m/2m3: 0-3 2m4-2m7: 0-1 3m+: 0-0
Track: LH: 0-0 RH: 0-4 Tight: 0-4 Gall: 0-0
Aids: Bl: 0-0 Vi: 0-0 Tstrap: 0-0
Best Rating: 92 11/01 Tntn 2m1f good Hdl

Tawafek (USA)

100 97

9-y-o br g Silver Hawk (USA)-Tippy Tippy Toe (USA) (Nureyev (USA))

J Mackie A J Winterton

Placings:22413/3/P-330 **(1795)**

2001/02: 20^{3}G, 20^{3}G, 20^{0}S

	Starts	1st	2nd	3rd	Win & Pl
Hurdles	3	0	0	2	1168
Career Total	**10**	**1**	**2**	**4**	**6564**

114	12/98	Weth	2m7f	D Hdl	GD	£2966

Total win prize-money £2966

Going: Sf: 0-1 GS: 0-0 Gd: 0-2 GF: - Fm: 0-0
Distance: 2m/2m3: 0-0 2m4-2m7: 0-3 3m+: 0-0
Track: LH: 0-3 RH: 0-0 Tight: 0-2 Gall: 0-0
Aids: Bl: 0-0 Vi: 0-0 Tstrap: 0-0
Best Rating: 114 5/99 Uttx 3m110y gd-fm Hdl

A useful staying hurdler. Apparently had breathing problems at Bangor in September 2001. Best on a sound surface.

Taxbuster

(95h) (75h)

10-y-o b g Welsh Captain-Indian Cash (Indian Ruler)

N B Thomson Taxbusters

Placings:43/2/0P0036/46-0000 **(4866)**

2001/02: 16^{0}GF, 21^{0}G, 17^{0}G, 17^{0}F

	Starts	1st	2nd	3rd	Win & Pl
Hurdles	4	0	0	0	
Career Total	**15**	**0**	**1**	**2**	**854**

Going: Sf: 0-0 GS: 0-0 Gd: 0-2 GF: - Fm: 0-2
Distance: 2m/2m3: 0-3 2m4-2m7: 0-1 3m+: 0-0
Track: LH: 0-0 RH: 0-4 Tight: 0-0 Gall: 0-0
Aids: Bl: 0-0 Vi: 0-0 Tstrap: 0-0
Best Rating: 110 3/00 Winc 2m gd-sft Hdl

Te Akau Dan (NZ)

8-y-o b g Dance Floor (USA)-Bellandaan (NZ) (Standaan (FR))

G W Lewis (G M McCourt 7/10) G W Lewis

Placings:P040/0PF0P/PP-PP **(4727)**

2001/02: 18^{P}GS, 24^{P}GF

	Starts	1st	2nd	3rd	Win & Pl
Hurdles	1	0	0	0	0
Chases	1	0	0	0	0
Career Total	**13**	**0**	**0**	**0**	**0**

Going: Sf: 0-0 GS: 0-1 Gd: 0-0 GF: - Fm: 0-1
Distance: 2m/2m3: 0-1 2m4-2m7: 0-0 3m+: 0-1
Track: LH: 0-2 RH: 0-0 Tight: 0-1 Gall: 0-0
Aids: Bl: 0-0 Vi: 0-0 Tstrap: 0-0
Best Rating: 66 2/99 Hrfd 2m3f110y good Hdl

Te Quiero (FR)

89 **69**

6-y-o gr g Turgeon (USA)-Passerene (FR) (Persepolis (FR))
Mrs L C Jewell (P Mitchell 6/6) Mrs A Emanuel

Placings:6 (4762)
2001/02: 20^6GF

	Starts	1st	2nd	3rd	Win & Pl
Hurdles	1	0	0	0	450
Career Total	**1**	**0**	**0**	**0**	**450**

Going: Sf: 0-0 GS: 0-0 Gd: 0-0 GF: - Fm: 0-1
Distance: 2m/2m3: 0-0 2m4-2m7: 0-1 3m+: 0-0
Track: LH: 0-0 RH: 0-1 Tight: 0-0 Gall: 0-0
Aids: Bl: 0-0 Vi: 0-0 Tstrap: 0-0
Best Rating: 69 4/02 Asct 2m4f gd-fm Hdl

Tea Box (IRE)

11-y-o b g Meneval (USA)-Elteetee (Paddy's Stream)
M A Kemp (Miss Pauline Robson 17/3) M A Kemp

Placings:00/U0405/1/31-1FP (4852)
2001/02: 24^1G, 23^FGF, 24^PG

	Starts	1st	2nd	3rd	Win & Pl
Chases	3	1	0	0	2162
Career Total	**13**	**3**	**0**	**1**	**5668**

120	4/02	Fknm	3m110y	H Ch	GD	£2161
100	5/00	Hexm	2m4f110y	H Ch	GD	£1237
103	4/00	Newc	2m4f	H Ch	G-S	£1813

Total win prize-money £5214

Going: Sf: 0-0 GS: 0-0 Gd: 1-2 GF: - Fm: 0-1
Distance: 2m/2m3: 0-0 2m4-2m7: 0-1 **3m+: 1-2**
Track: **LH: 1-3** RH: 0-0 **Tight: 1-2** Gall: 0-0
Aids: Bl: 0-0 Vi: 0-0 Tstrap: 0-0
Best Rating: 120 4/02 Fknm 3m110y good Ch

Useful pointer/hunter chaser with high strike rate. Stays three miles, does not want the ground too soft.

Tea Time (IRE)

7-y-o b g Glacial Storm (USA)-Blaze Of Hope (IRE) (Le Moss)
R T Phillips Colin Pocock

Placings:P (4530)
2001/02: 20^PGS

	Starts	1st	2nd	3rd	Win & Pl
Hurdles	1	0	0	0	
Career Total	**1**	**0**	**0**	**0**	

Going: Sf: 0-0 GS: 0-1 Gd: 0-0 GF: - Fm: 0-0
Distance: 2m/2m3: 0-0 2m4-2m7: 0-1 3m+: 0-0
Track: LH: 0-1 RH: 0-0 Tight: 0-0 Gall: 0-0
Aids: Bl: 0-0 Vi: 0-0 Tstrap: 0-0
Best Rating:

Teaatral

114 **157**

8-y-o b g Saddlers' Hall (IRE)-La Cabrilla (Carwhite)
C R Egerton Bernard Gover Bloodstock Trading Ltd

Placings:210112/013110/U3111/P412P56-5430PP (4251)
2001/02: 24^5S, 23^4S, 16^3S, 20^0S, 16^PGS, 24^PG

	Starts	1st	2nd	3rd	Win & Pl
Hurdles	6	0	0	1	3485
Career Total	**30**	**10**	**3**	**3**	**132122**

164	2/01	Sand	2m110y	B Hdl	HVY	£13468
164	4/00	Asct	3m	A Hdl	GD	£18600
158	2/00	Kemp	3m110y	A HHdl	SFT	£13200
162	2/00	Asct	2m4f	B(0-150)HHdl	SFT	£20579
150	2/99	Sand	2m6f	A HHdl	G-S	£26800
148	1/99	Kemp	2m5f	C(0-135)HHdl	HVY	£5628
131	12/98	Leic	2m4f110y	D(0-120)HHdl	SFT	£3002
105	4/98	Hrfd	2m1f	E Hdl	G-S	£2624
110	4/98	Tntn	2m1f	E(0-115)HHdl	GD	£2710
111	1/98	Folk	2m1f110y	E Hdl	G-S	£1976

Total win prize-money £108588

Going: Sf: 0-4 GS: 0-1 Gd: 0-1 GF: - Fm: 0-0
Distance: 2m/2m3: 0-2 2m4-2m7: 0-1 3m+: 0-3
Track: LH: 0-2 RH: 0-3 Tight: 0-0 Gall: 0-1
Aids: Bl: 0-6 Vi: 0-0 Tstrap: 0-0
Best Rating: 164 2/01 Kemp 3m110y gd-sft Hdl

A high-class staying hurdler, he showed his versatility when winning over the minimum trip at Sandown in February 2001. Disappointing in 2001/2. He has been beaten each time he has contested a Grade One race since and has only ever won on right-handed tracks. Suited by soft ground, he usually wears blinkers.

Tealby

101 **99**

5-y-o b m Efisio-Al Raja (King's Lake (USA))
Mrs L Wadham The Dyball Partnership

Placings:21214 (3320)
2001/02: 16^2G, 17^1GF, 16^2G, 16^1G, 16^4GS

	Starts	1st	2nd	3rd	Win & Pl
NH Flat	4	2	2	0	4031
Hurdles	1	0	0	0	0
Career Total	**5**	**2**	**2**	**0**	**4031**

95	7/01	Worc	2m	H NHF	GD	£1494
109	6/01	MRas	2m1f110y	H NHF	G-F	£1589

Total win prize-money £3084

Going: Sf: 0-0 GS: 0-1 Gd: 1-3 GF: - Fm: 1-1
Distance: **2m/2m3: 2-5** 2m4-2m7: 0-0 3m+: 0-0
Track: LH: 1-2 RH: 1-3 **Tight: 1-1** Gall: 0-2
Aids: Bl: 0-0 Vi: 0-0 Tstrap: 0-0
Best Rating: 109 6/01 MRas 2m1f110y gd-fm NHF

Team Captain

8-y-o ch g Teamster-Silly Sausage (Silly Answer)
C J Down (L G Cottrell 20/6) P J Hickman

Placings:0/P-2PF2122 (4865)
2001/02: 21^2GF, 21^PG, 23^FG, 23^2GF, 25^1G, 24^2G, 23^2F

	Starts	1st	2nd	3rd	Win & Pl
Chases	7	1	4	0	4705
Career Total	**9**	**1**	**4**	**0**	**4705**

110	3/02	Winc	3m1f110y	H Ch	GD	£1684

Total win prize-money £1684

Going: Sf: 0-0 GS: 0-0 Gd: 1-4 GF: - Fm: 0-3
Distance: 2m/2m3: 0-0 2m4-2m7: 0-2 **3m+: 1-5**
Track: LH: 0-2 **RH: 1-4** Tight: 0-1 Gall: 0-0
Aids: Bl: 0-0 Vi: 0-0 Tstrap: 0-0
Best Rating: 115 4/02 Tntn 3m good Ch

A fair hunter/pointer, he stays three miles and acts on fast ground.

Teardrop Mick (IRE)

95f **104f**

6-y-o b/br g Malmsey (USA)-Random Bay (Mandalus)
N A Twiston-Davies The 'Yes' - 'No' - 'Wait'....Sorries

Placings:2 (2655)
2001/02: 16^2G

	Starts	1st	2nd	3rd	Win & Pl
NH Flat	1	0	1	0	458
Career Total	**1**	**0**	**1**	**0**	**458**

Going: Sf: 0-0 GS: 0-0 Gd: 0-1 GF: - Fm: 0-0
Distance: 2m/2m3: 0-1 2m4-2m7: 0-0 3m+: 0-0
Track: LH: 0-0 RH: 0-1 Tight: 0-0 Gall: 0-0
Aids: Bl: 0-0 Vi: 0-0 Tstrap: 0-0
Best Rating: 104 12/01 Ludl 2m good NHF

Teddy Boy

77 **68**

6-y-o b g Midyan (USA)-Likeable Lady (Piaffer (USA))
D E Cantillon Mrs P K J Brightwell

Placings:00 (3702)
2001/02: 16^6S, 19^0HY

	Starts	1st	2nd	3rd	Win & Pl
Hurdles	2	0	0	0	0
Career Total	**2**	**0**	**0**	**0**	**0**

Going: Sf: 0-2 GS: 0-0 Gd: 0-0 GF: - Fm: 0-0
Distance: 2m/2m3: 0-1 2m4-2m7: 0-1 3m+: 0-0
Track: LH: 0-1 RH: 0-1 Tight: 0-0 Gall: 0-1
Aids: Bl: 0-0 Vi: 0-0 Tstrap: 0-0
Best Rating: 68 1/02 Donc 2m110y soft Hdl

Teddy Ruckster (IRE)

91 **45**

8-y-o ch g Commanche Run-Snuggle (Music Boy)
Miss Venetia Williams Six Diamonds Partnership

Placings:6/0-0000 (4877)
2001/02: 20^0HY, 20^0GS, 17^0S, 24^0G

	Starts	1st	2nd	3rd	Win & Pl
Hurdles	4	0	0	0	
Career Total	**6**	**0**	**0**	**0**	**0**

Going: Sf: 0-2 GS: 0-1 Gd: 0-1 GF: - Fm: 0-0
Distance: 2m/2m3: 0-1 2m4-2m7: 0-2 3m+: 0-1
Track: LH: 0-2 RH: 0-2 Tight: 0-0 Gall: 0-0
Aids: Bl: 0-0 Vi: 0-0 Tstrap: 0-0
Best Rating: 102 4/00 Hntg 2m110y good NHF

Tedo (IRE)

4-y-o ch g Beveled (USA)-Gunner Girl (Gunner B)
J Neville J Neville

Placings:P (3621)
2001/02: 17^PGS

	Starts	1st	2nd	3rd	Win & Pl
Hurdles	1	0	0	0	

	Starts	1st	2nd	3rd	Win & Pl
Career Total	1	0	0	0	

Going: Sf: 0-0 GS: 0-1 Gd: 0-0 GF: - Fm: 0-0
Distance: 2m/2m3: 0-1 2m4-2m7: 0-0 3m+: 0-0
Track: LH: 0-0 RH: 0-1 Tight: 0-1 Gall: 0-0
Aids: Bl: 0-0 Vi: 0-0 Tstrap: 0-0
Best Rating:

Tedstone Fox

10-y-o b g Bold Fox-Royal Wren (Blast)
Mrs E Weaver Mrs E Weaver

Placings:P/FFP0 **(0577)**
2001/02: 24^{F}GF, 20^{F}GF, 21^{P}G, 21^{0}GF

	Starts	1st	2nd	3rd	Win & Pl
Chases	4	0	0	0	
Career Total	5	0	0	0	

Going: Sf: 0-0 GS: 0-0 Gd: 0-1 GF: - Fm: 0-3
Distance: 2m/2m3: 0-0 2m4-2m7: 0-3 3m+: 0-1
Track: LH: 0-2 RH: 0-2 Tight: 0-3 Gall: 0-1
Aids: Bl: 0-0 Vi: 0-0 Tstrap: 0-0
Best Rating: 85 6/01 Strf 2m5f110y gd-fm Ch

Tee-Jay (IRE)

103 **111**

6-y-o ch g Un Desperado (FR)-N T Nad (Welsh Pageant)
A Crook T J Equestrian Ltd

Placings:03-5131PP **(4555)**
2001/02: 16^{5}G, 19^{1}S, 20^{3}HY, 20^{1}GS, 20^{P}GS, 19^{P}GF

	Starts	1st	2nd	3rd	Win & Pl
NH Flat	1	0	0	0	0
Hurdles	5	2	0	1	6594
Career Total	8	2	0	2	6846

111	2/02	Muss	2m4f	D Hdl	G-S	£3510
108	12/01	Catt	2m3f	E Hdl	SFT	£2492

Total win prize-money £6002

Going: Sf: 1-2 GS: 1-2 Gd: 0-1 GF: - Fm: 0-1
Distance: 2m/2m3: 1-2 2m4-2m7: 1-4 3m+: 0-0
Track: LH: 1-3 RH: 1-3 **Tight: 2-3** Gall: 0-0
Aids: Bl: 0-0 Vi: 0-0 Tstrap: 0-0
Best Rating: 111 2/02 Muss 2m4f gd-sft Hdl

Fair hurdler, stays two and a half miles, suited by soft ground. Has run well in decent company.

Teejay'N'Aitch (IRE)

(78h)

10-y-o b g Maelstrom Lake-Middle Verde (USA) (Sham (USA))
J S Goldie Mrs Alice S Goldie

Placings:00053535/323356P4U211/1111022U6034U 00/5FP553P5/2P60P5655/30354PPP0P-R **(0277)**
2001/02: 26^{R}GF

	Starts	1st	2nd	3rd	Win & Pl
Chases	1	0	0	0	
Career Total	63	6	5	9	27193

109	6/97	Prth	2m110y	E(0-115)HHdl	G-F	£2558
101	5/97	Weth	2m	D(0-120)HHdl	G-F	£2600
100	5/97	Prth	2m110y	E(0-105)HHdl	G-S	£2710
97	5/97	Weth	2m	D(0-120)HHdl	G-S	£2705
88	4/97	Prth	2m110y	D(0-110)HHdl	GD	£3824
89	4/97	Ayr	2m	E(0-110)HHdl	GD	£3291

Total win prize-money £17690

Going: Sf: 0-0 GS: 0-0 Gd: 0-0 GF: - Fm: 0-1
Distance: 2m/2m3: 0-0 2m4-2m7: 0-0 3m+: 0-1
Track: LH: 0-0 RH: 0-0 Tight: 0-0 Gall: 0-0
Aids: Bl: 0-0 Vi: 0-1 Tstrap: 0-0
Best Rating: 109 6/97 Prth 2m110y gd-fm Hdl

Teelin Bay (IRE)

10-y-o b g Be My Native (USA)-Fahy Quay (Quayside)
Miss Pauline Robson Mr & Mrs Raymond Anderson Green

Placings:00/0/21P/42PP/1-U1 **(4833)**
2001/02: 21^{U}G, 27^{1}G

	Starts	1st	2nd	3rd	Win & Pl
Chases	2	1	0	0	3038
Career Total	13	3	2	0	11313

125	4/02	Ayr	3m3f110y	H Ch	GD	£3038
123	4/01	Ayr	3m3f110y	H Ch	GD	£3900
90	11/98	Kels	2m6f110y	E Hdl	HVY	£2374

Total win prize-money £9312

Going: Sf: 0-0 GS: 0-0 Gd: 1-2 GF: - Fm: 0-0
Distance: 2m/2m3: 0-0 2m4-2m7: 0-1 **3m+: 1-1**
Track: **LH: 1-2** RH: 0-0 Tight: 0-1 Gall: 0-0
Aids: Bl: 0-0 Vi: 0-0 **Tstrap: 1-2**
Best Rating: 125 4/02 Ayr 3m3f110y good Ch

Hunter chaser. Stays three miles three furlongs and is effective on a soft surface.

Teen Desert (IRE)

73(70h) (51h)**84**

6-y-o b g Teenoso (USA)-Five And Four (IRE) (Green Desert (USA))
J Wade John Wade

Placings:00-0PPF0F **(4868)**
2001/02: 20^{0}GS, 16^{P}S, 27^{P}HY, 21^{F}S, 16^{0}GS, 20^{F}GF

	Starts	1st	2nd	3rd	Win & Pl
Hurdles	2	0	0	0	0
Chases	4	0	0	0	0
Career Total	8	0	0	0	

Going: Sf: 0-3 GS: 0-2 Gd: 0-0 GF: - Fm: 0-1
Distance: 2m/2m3: 0-2 2m4-2m7: 0-3 3m+: 0-1
Track: LH: 0-6 RH: 0-0 Tight: 0-3 Gall: 0-1
Aids: Bl: 0-1 Vi: 0-0 Tstrap: 0-0
Best Rating: 84 4/02 Weth 2m4f110y gd-fm Ch

Modest hurdler, yet to complete over fences.(DEAD)

Tees Components

95f **134f**

7-y-o b g Risk Me (FR)-Lady Warninglid (Ela-Mana-Mou)
Mrs M Reveley Tees Components Ltd

Placings:211/11 **(2887)**
2001/02: 16^{1}G, 16^{1}GS

	Starts	1st	2nd	3rd	Win & Pl
NH Flat	2	2	0	0	11359
Career Total	5	4	1	0	15351

134	12/01	Chep	2m110y	A NHF	G-S	£9000
123	11/01	Weth	2m	H NHF	GD	£2359
120	2/00	Weth	2m	H NHF	SFT	£1862
129	11/99	Weth	2m	H NHF	GD	£1618

Total win prize-money £14839

Going: Sf: 0-0 GS: 1-1 Gd: 1-1 GF: - Fm: 0-0
Distance: **2m/2m3: 2-2** 2m4-2m7: 0-0 3m+: 0-0
Track: **LH: 2-2** RH: 0-0 Tight: 0-0 Gall: 0-0
Aids: Bl: 0-0 Vi: 0-0 Tstrap: 0-0
Best Rating: 134 12/01 Chep 2m110y gd-sft NHF

Very useful bumper horse, winner of a Grade One event at Chepstow in December having missed a season due to injury.

Teeton Bubbley

101 **79**

9-y-o b m Neltino-Teeton Frolic (Sunley Builds)
K C Bailey A Sansome

Placings:4 **(2358)**
2001/02: 21^{4}S

	Starts	1st	2nd	3rd	Win & Pl
Hurdles	1	0	0	0	301
Career Total	1	0	0	0	301

Going: Sf: 0-1 GS: 0-0 Gd: 0-0 GF: - Fm: 0-0
Distance: 2m/2m3: 0-0 2m4-2m7: 0-1 3m+: 0-0
Track: LH: 0-0 RH: 0-1 Tight: 0-0 Gall: 0-0
Aids: Bl: 0-0 Vi: 0-0 Tstrap: 0-0
Best Rating: 79 11/01 Towc 2m5f soft Hdl

Telemoss (IRE)

117 **154**

8-y-o b g Montelimar (USA)-Shan's Moss (Le Moss)
N G Richards Ashleybank Investments Limited

Placings:15/021-1121244 **(4834)**
2001/02: 20^{1}S, 16^{1}G, 21^{2}G, 20^{1}S, 23^{2}S, 24^{4}G, 22^{4}G

	Starts	1st	2nd	3rd	Win & Pl
Hurdles	7	3	2	0	39004
Career Total	12	5	3	0	44829

140	12/01	Hayd	2m4f	B HHdl	SFT	£11921
130	10/01	Weth	2m	C(0-135)HHdl	GD	£5430
127	5/01	Hexm	2m4f110y	D(0-125)HHdl	SFT	£3570
124	2/01	Kels	2m2f	E Hdl	SFT	£2912
105	11/99	Hayd	2m	H NHF	GD	£1934

Total win prize-money £25769

Going: Sf: 2-3 GS: 0-0 Gd: 1-4 GF: - Fm: 0-0
Distance: 2m/2m3: 1-1 **2m4-2m7: 2-4** 3m+: 0-2
Track: **LH: 3-6** RH: 0-0 Tight: 0-0 Gall: 0-1
Aids: Bl: 0-0 Vi: 0-0 Tstrap: 0-0
Best Rating: 154 3/02 Chel 3m good Hdl

He is a promising hurdler who completed a hat-trick between February and October 2001. Scored in the mud at Haydock in December and has run well since, finishing a good fourth in the Cheltenham Stayers' in 2002. Acts on good or softer ground and is suited by two and a half miles plus. Should make a nice chaser in time.

Telimar Prince (IRE)

108 **124**

6-y-o b g Montelimar (USA)-Blakica (Sexton Blake)
J T Gifford Mrs Angela Brodie

Placings:0-61 **(4033)**
2001/02: 16^{6}G, 20^{1}S

	Starts	1st	2nd	3rd	Win & Pl
Hurdles	2	1	0	0	2531
Career Total	3	1	0	0	2531

124	3/02	Font	2m4f	E Hdl	SFT	£2530

Total win prize-money £2531

Going: Sf: 1-1 GS: 0-0 Gd: 0-1 GF: - Fm: 0-0
Distance: 2m/2m3: 0-1 **2m4-2m7: 1-1** 3m+: 0-0
Track: LH: 0-1 RH: 0-0 **Tight: 1-1** Gall: 0-1
Aids: Bl: 0-0 Vi: 0-0 Tstrap: 0-0
Best Rating: 124 3/02 Font 2m4f soft Hdl

Promising novice hurdler, stays two and a half miles.

Tell Me Why (IRE)

99 97

6-y-o b g Roselier (FR)-Clonarctic Slave (Sir Mordred)
P R Webber Mrs C A Waters

Placings:5 **(3672)**
2001/02: 24^{5}S

	Starts	1st	2nd	3rd	Win & Pl
Hurdles	1	0	0	0	0
Career Total	**1**	**0**	**0**	**0**	**0**

Going: Sf: 0-1 GS: 0-0 Gd: 0-0 GF: - Fm: 0-0
Distance: 2m/2m3: 0-0 2m4-2m7: 0-0 3m+: 0-1
Track: LH: 0-0 RH: 0-1 Tight: 0-0 Gall: 0-0
Aids: Bl: 0-0 Vi: 0-0 Tstrap: 0-0
Best Rating: **97** 2/02 Kemp 3m110y soft Hdl

Tell The Nipper (IRE)

11-y-o b g Riberetto-Divine Dibs (Raise You Ten)
Mrs C M Gorman Mrs C M Gorman

Placings:04124545/06524466124/1333F1455/P22000 2P/0/001P5-35 **(3895)**
2001/02: 26^{3}HY, 26^{5}HY

	Starts	1st	2nd	3rd	Win & Pl
Chases	2	0	0	1	164
Career Total	**44**	**5**	**6**	**4**	**56008**

121	2/01	Wwck	3m2f	H Ch	SFT	£1288
129	2/98	Fair	3m1f	HCh	Y-S	£8413
127	9/97	List	2m4f	(0-123)HCh	G-Y	£4069
111	3/97	Limk	2m6f	Ch	Y-S	£3391
113	1/96	Naas	2m3f	Hdl	Y-S	£3177

Total win prize-money £20339

Going: Sf: 0-2 GS: 0-0 Gd: 0-0 GF: - Fm: 0-0
Distance: 2m/2m3: 0-0 2m4-2m7: 0-0 3m+: 0-2
Track: LH: 0-1 RH: 0-0 Tight: 0-0 Gall: 0-0
Aids: Bl: 0-1 Vi: 0-0 Tstrap: 0-0
Best Rating: **136** 4/98 Fair 3m5f yield Ch

Formerly decent Irish handicap chaser, has not looked as good in points and hunter chases recently.

Tell The Troops (IRE)

93 83

7-y-o b g Soviet Lad (USA)-Are You Sure (Lepanto (GER))
H D Daly S R B Holdings Ltd

Placings:3140-5 **(0421)**
2001/02: 24^{5}G

	Starts	1st	2nd	3rd	Win & Pl
Hurdles	1	0	0	0	0
Career Total	**5**	**1**	**0**	**1**	**2097**

102	12/00	Hrfd	2m1f	H NHF	HVY	£1788

Total win prize-money £1789

Going: Sf: 0-0 GS: 0-0 Gd: 0-1 GF: - Fm: 0-0
Distance: 2m/2m3: 0-0 2m4-2m7: 0-0 3m+: 0-1
Track: LH: 0-1 RH: 0-0 Tight: 0-1 Gall: 0-0
Aids: Bl: 0-0 Vi: 0-0 Tstrap: 0-0
Best Rating: **102** 12/00 Hrfd 2m1f heavy NHF

Tellaporky

13-y-o b g Bold Fort-Ab Dabh (Spanish Gold)
H H G Owen (James Owen 5/3) Mrs J Owen

Placings:PP/U466/4344552230/5U3030/PP/405 **(4685)**
2001/02: 16^{4}S, 16^{0}GF, 16^{5}GF

	Starts	1st	2nd	3rd	Win & Pl
Chases	3	0	0	0	0
Career Total	**27**	**0**	**2**	**4**	**3268**

Going: Sf: 0-1 GS: 0-0 Gd: 0-0 GF: - Fm: 0-2
Distance: 2m/2m3: 0-3 2m4-2m7: 0-0 3m+: 0-0
Track: LH: 0-0 RH: 0-2 Tight: 0-0 Gall: 0-0
Aids: Bl: 0-3 Vi: 0-0 Tstrap: 0-0
Best Rating: **87** 1/98 Sand 2m6f soft Hdl

Teller Of Tales

101 103

6-y-o ch g Arazi (USA)-Water Splash (USA) (Little Current (USA))
C J Mann The Teller Of Tales Partnership

Placings:0F-11 **(1039)**
2001/02: 20^{1}GF, 20^{1}GF

	Starts	1st	2nd	3rd	Win & Pl
Hurdles	2	2	0	0	5995
Career Total	**4**	**2**	**0**	**0**	**5995**

103	7/01	Uttx	2m4f110y	D Hdl	G-F	£3318
103	5/01	Hntg	2m4f110y	E Hdl	G-F	£2676

Total win prize-money £5995

Going: Sf: 0-0 GS: 0-0 Gd: 0-0 GF: - Fm: 2-2
Distance: 2m/2m3: 0-0 **2m4-2m7: 2-2** 3m+: 0-0
Track: LH: 1-1 RH: 1-1 Tight: 0-0 **Gall: 1-1**
Aids: **Bl: 2-2** Vi: 0-0 Tstrap: 0-0
Best Rating: **103** 7/01 Uttx 2m4f110y gd-fm Hdl

Tellion

96 83

8-y-o b g Mystiko (USA)-Salchow (Niniski (USA))
J R Jenkins Mrs Jean Hale

Placings:0F203/R41355/0111-0500 **(4110)**
2001/02: 16^{0}G, 16^{5}HY, 20^{0}S, 16^{0}S

	Starts	1st	2nd	3rd	Win & Pl
Hurdles	4	0	0	0	0
Career Total	**19**	**4**	**1**	**2**	**10863**

106	12/00	Folk	2m1f110y	F(0-100)HHdl	HVY	£2289
98	11/00	Leic	2m	F(0-110)HHdl	HVY	£2240
99	10/00	Sthl	2m	E(0-115)HHdl	G-S	£2704
94	11/99	Kemp	2m	F(0-100)HHdl	G-F	£2305

Total win prize-money £9539

Going: Sf: 0-3 GS: 0-0 Gd: 0-1 GF: - Fm: 0-0
Distance: 2m/2m3: 0-3 2m4-2m7: 0-1 3m+: 0-0
Track: LH: 0-0 RH: 0-4 Tight: 0-0 Gall: 0-1
Aids: Bl: 0-0 Vi: 0-3 Tstrap: 0-0
Best Rating: **109** 1/99 Ling 2m110y heavy Hdl

Telmar Flyer

5-y-o gr m Neltino-Flying Mistress (Lear Jet)
J Cullinan Dodson & Partners

Placings:0 **(4158)**
2001/02: 16^{0}GS

	Starts	1st	2nd	3rd	Win & Pl
NH Flat	1	0	0	0	
Career Total	**1**	**0**	**0**	**0**	

Going: Sf: 0-0 GS: 0-1 Gd: 0-0 GF: - Fm: 0-0
Distance: 2m/2m3: 0-1 2m4-2m7: 0-0 3m+: 0-0
Track: LH: 0-0 RH: 0-1 Tight: 0-0 Gall: 0-0
Aids: Bl: 0-0 Vi: 0-0 Tstrap: 0-0
Best Rating:

Teme Valley

103 111

8-y-o br g Polish Precedent (USA)-Sudeley (Dancing Brave (USA))
J Howard Johnson Eddie Shotton

Placings:065U01/0F60132211/550150-00020016 **(4858)**
2001/02: 16^{0}G, 16^{0}G, 16^{0}G, 17^{2}S, 16^{0}GS, 17^{0}S, 17^{1}GF, 16^{6}G

	Starts	1st	2nd	3rd	Win & Pl
Hurdles	8	1	1	0	3944
Career Total	**30**	**6**	**3**	**1**	**19138**

110	4/02	Sedg	2m1f	D(0-115)HHdl	G-F	£3276
115	1/01	Catt	2m3f	F(0-110)HHdl	G-S	£2373
121	4/00	Sedg	2m1f	E(0-115)HHdl	GD	£2394
116	3/00	Sedg	2m1f	F(0-110)HHdl	G-F	£2677
110	12/99	Sedg	2m1f	F(0-110)HHdl	G-S	£2460
96	4/99	Sedg	2m1f	E Hdl	G-S	£2495

Total win prize-money £15676

Going: Sf: 0-2 GS: 0-1 Gd: 0-4 GF: - Fm: 1-1
Distance: **2m/2m3: 1-8** 2m4-2m7: 0-0 3m+: 0-0
Track: **LH: 1-7** RH: 0-0 **Tight: 1-4** Gall: 0-0
Aids: Bl: 0-0 Vi: 0-0 **Tstrap: 1-8**
Best Rating: **121** 4/00 Sedg 2m1f good Hdl

Fair hurdler and a Sedgefield specialist, he does not want the ground too soft. Regularly tongue tied.

Temper Lad (USA)

105 100

7-y-o b g Riverman (USA)-Dokki (USA) (Northern Dancer)
J Joseph Jack Joseph

Placings:P11331/6210P3404/00-5404 **(4415)**
2001/02: 22^{5}GF, 20^{4}GF, 24^{0}GF, 22^{4}S

	Starts	1st	2nd	3rd	Win & Pl
Hurdles	4	0	0	0	0
Career Total	**21**	**4**	**1**	**3**	**18140**

129	10/99	Chep	2m110y	C Hdl	GD	£4658
116	4/99	Strf	2m110y	D(0-110)HHdl	GD	£2612
110	9/98	Hntg	2m110y	E Hdl	G-F	£2326
105	9/98	Strf	2m110y	E Hdl	GD	£2318

Total win prize-money £11915

Going: Sf: 0-1 GS: 0-0 Gd: 0-0 GF: - Fm: 0-3
Distance: 2m/2m3: 0-0 2m4-2m7: 0-3 3m+: 0-1
Track: LH: 0-4 RH: 0-0 Tight: 0-3 Gall: 0-0
Aids: Bl: 0-0 Vi: 0-0 Tstrap: 0-4
Best Rating: **130** 1/00 Kemp 2m5f good Hdl

Temple Dog (IRE)

103f 131f

6-y-o ch g Un Desperado (FR)-Shower (King's Lake (USA))
T P Tate The Ivy Syndicate

Placings:4-103 **(4526)**
2001/02: 16^{1}HY, 16^{0}GS, 17^{3}GS

	Starts	1st	2nd	3rd	Win & Pl
NH Flat	3	1	0	1	2002
Career Total	**4**	**1**	**0**	**1**	**2002**

131	2/02	Ayr	2m	H NHF	HVY	£1739

Total win prize-money £1740

Going: Sf: 1-1 GS: 0-1 Gd: 0-1 GF: - Fm: 0-0
Distance: **2m/2m3: 1-3** 2m4-2m7: 0-0 3m+: 0-0
Track: **LH: 1-2** RH: 0-1 Tight: 0-0 Gall: 0-0
Aids: Bl: 0-0 Vi: 0-0 Tstrap: 0-0
Best Rating: 131 2/02 Ayr 2m heavy NHF

Promising bumper horse, an easy winner in heavy ground at Ayr in February, ran well at Cheltenham, but beaten on faster ground under a penalty next time.

Temple Garth

13-y-o b g Baron Blakeney-Future Chance (Hopeful Venture)
Miss Freya Hartley Miss Freya Hartley

Placings:40211/300P0/5312PF5/1P60664/3111F3/4P 5P35/20P/0/10-060 **(0556)**
2001/02: 25^{0}G, 22^{6}G, 24^{0}GF

	Starts	1st	2nd	3rd	Win & Pl
Chases	3	0	0	0	0
Career Total	**45**	**8**	**3**	**5**	**26358**

105	5/00	Ctml	3m2f	H Ch	G-F	£2977
105	6/96	Prth	3m	E Ch	G-F	£3178
100	5/96	Weth	3m110y	D Ch	GD	£3499
99	5/96	Prth	3m	E Ch	G-F	£3615
99	5/95	Prth	3m110y	G(0-95)HHdl	GD	£2295
99	1/95	Catt	3m1f110y	E(0-115)HHdl	SFT	£2265
97	4/93	Carl	2m4f110y	Hdl	G-S	£1457
90	3/93	Sedg	2m5f110y	Hdl	GD	£1484

Total win prize-money £20772

Going: Sf: 0-0 GS: 0-0 Gd: 0-2 GF: - Fm: 0-1
Distance: 2m/2m3: 0-0 2m4-2m7: 0-1 3m+: 0-2
Track: LH: 0-1 RH: 0-2 Tight: 0-1 Gall: 0-1
Aids: Bl: 0-0 Vi: 0-0 Tstrap: 0-0
Best Rating: 105 5/00 Ctml 3m2f gd-fm Ch

Templenoe Hare (IRE)

9-y-o b g Lafontaine (USA)-Bellalma (Belfalas)
Mrs W D Sykes Mrs P Sykes

Placings:0*6*/00/0P*00*/04 **(0577)**
2001/02: 20^{0}G, 21^{4}GF

	Starts	1st	2nd	3rd	Win & Pl
Hurdles	1	0	0	0	0
Chases	1	0	0	0	0
Career Total	**10**	**0**	**0**	**0**	**0**

Going: Sf: 0-0 GS: 0-0 Gd: 0-1 GF: - Fm: 0-1
Distance: 2m/2m3: 0-0 2m4-2m7: 0-2 3m+: 0-0
Track: LH: 0-2 RH: 0-0 Tight: 0-1 Gall: 0-0
Aids: Bl: 0-0 Vi: 0-0 Tstrap: 0-0
Best Rating: 89 6/01 Strf 2m5f110y gd-fm Ch

Temples Time (IRE)

91 **74**
4-y-o b f Distinctly North (USA)-Midnight Patrol (Ashmore (FR))
R Brotherton (R Hannon 8/5) W M Rollett

Placings:5 **(4504)**
2001/02: 17^{5}G

	Starts	1st	2nd	3rd	Win & Pl
Hurdles	1	0	0	0	0
Career Total	**1**	**0**	**0**	**0**	**0**

Going: Sf: 0-0 GS: 0-0 Gd: 0-1 GF: - Fm: 0-0
Distance: 2m/2m3: 0-1 2m4-2m7: 0-0 3m+: 0-0
Track: LH: 0-1 RH: 0-0 Tight: 0-1 Gall: 0-0
Aids: Bl: 0-0 Vi: 0-0 Tstrap: 0-0
Best Rating: 65 3/02 NAbb 2m1f good Hdl

Has yet to prove she gets the trip over hurdles.

Tempo (IRE)

103(67h) (39h)**93**
10-y-o b g Satco (FR)-Arabian Sands (Pollerton)
Ian Williams C N Barnes

Placings:5/*1224*/2313142F/230U/5/FP-0P0FP6651UP **(4872)**
2001/02: 19^{0}G, 20^{P}G, 19^{0}F, 20^{F}GF, 20^{P}G, 21^{6}G, 21^{6}G, 19^{5}G, 17^{1}GF, 17^{U}G, 16^{P}GF

	Starts	1st	2nd	3rd	Win & Pl
Hurdles	1	0	0	0	0
Chases	10	1	0	0	2268
Career Total	**31**	**4**	**5**	**3**	**23752**

93	4/02	Plum	2m1f	G(0-90)HCh	G-F	£2268
134	2/98	Thur	2m	Ch	YLD	£2382
132	2/98	Clon	2m4f	Ch	Y-S	£2978
115	5/96	Gowr	2m	NHF	GD	£2824

Total win prize-money £10454

Going: Sf: 0-0 GS: 0-0 Gd: 0-7 GF: - Fm: 1-4
Distance: **2m/2m3: 1-6** 2m4-2m7: 0-5 3m+: 0-0
Track: **LH: 1-5** RH: 0-6 **Tight: 1-5** Gall: 0-0
Aids: Bl: 0-0 Vi: 0-0 Tstrap: 0-0
Best Rating: 138 4/98 Fair 2m4f gd-yld Ch

Ex-Irish chaser, now selling class. Seems best when making the running.

Tempo D'Or (FR)

114 **137**
4-y-o b g Esprit Du Nord (USA)-Peau D'Or (FR) (Pot D'Or (FR))
G Macaire Mrs F Montauban

Placings:6-1111131133 **(3906)**
2001/02: 16^{1}G, 15^{1}GS, 17^{1}S, 17^{1}S, 17^{1}HY, 15^{3}HO, 17^{1}HY, 16^{1}GS, 17^{3}HY, 16^{3}G

	Starts	1st	2nd	3rd	Win & Pl
Hurdles	8	5	0	3	48279
Chases	2	2	0	0	15034
Career Total	**11**	**7**	**0**	**3**	**63313**

137	12/01	Chep	2m110y	A Hdl	G-S	£17400
	11/01	Engh	2m1f110y	Hdl	HVY	£10669
	11/01	Engh	2m1f	Ch	HVY	£11639
	10/01	Pina	2m1f110y	Ch	SFT	£3395
	10/01	Stma	2m1f	Hdl	SFT	£4074
	9/01	Buch	1m7f	Hdl	G-S	£4365
	8/01	Stma	2m	Hdl	GD	£3395

Total win prize-money £54937

Going: Sf: 4-5 GS: 2-2 Gd: 1-2 GF: - Fm: 0-0
Distance: **2m/2m3: 6-8** 2m4-2m7: 0-0 3m+: 0-0
Track: **LH: 1-2** RH: 0-1 Tight: 0-0 Gall: 0-1
Aids: Bl: 0-0 Vi: 0-0 Tstrap: 0-0
Best Rating: 137 12/01 Chep 2m110y gd-sft Hdl

Already a multiple winner over hurdles and fences in his native France, he landed Chepstow's Finale Hurdle over two miles at Christmas 2001. Suited by soft ground and looks to have plenty of stamina.

Ten Commanches

102f
5-y-o ch h Commanche Run-Deep Pier (Deep Run)
Ferdy Murphy The Sgs Partnership

Placings:*3* **(3257)**
2001/02: 16^{3}S

	Starts	1st	2nd	3rd	Win & Pl
NH Flat	1	0	0	1	284
Career Total	**1**	**0**	**0**	**1**	**284**

Going: Sf: 0-1 GS: 0-0 Gd: 0-0 GF: - Fm: 0-0
Distance: 2m/2m3: 0-1 2m4-2m7: 0-0 3m+: 0-0
Track: LH: 0-0 RH: 0-0 Tight: 0-0 Gall: 0-0
Aids: Bl: 0-0 Vi: 0-0 Tstrap: 0-0
Best Rating: 102 1/02 Newc 2m soft NHF

Potential chaser, third in a bumper on his racecourse debut. Acts on soft ground.

Ten Mile Hill

101(99h) (109h)**118**
11-y-o b g Teenoso (USA)-Okavamba (Wollow)
Mrs S J Smith Mrs Enid Brindle

Placings:221/412/0/452-31F4 **(2557)**
2001/02: 19^{3}S, 22^{1}GS, 20^{F}G, 20^{4}S

	Starts	1st	2nd	3rd	Win & Pl
Hurdles	2	0	0	1	721
Chases	2	1	0	0	3754
Career Total	**14**	**3**	**4**	**1**	**16259**

118	10/01	MRas	2m6f110y	E Ch	G-S	£3753
116	4/98	Weth	2m4f110y	C(0-135)HHdl	GD	£4739
91	9/95	Prth	2m110y	D Hdl	GD	£2710

Total win prize-money £11203

Going: Sf: 0-2 GS: 1-1 Gd: 0-1 GF: - Fm: 0-0
Distance: 2m/2m3: 0-0 **2m4-2m7: 1-4** 3m+: 0-0
Track: LH: 0-2 **RH: 1-2 Tight: 1-3** Gall: 0-0
Aids: Bl: 0-0 Vi: 0-0 Tstrap: 0-0
Best Rating: 118 10/01 MRas 2m6f110y gd-sft Ch

Fair chaser, won at Market Rasen in October of 2001. Acts on good and good to soft, and is effective from two miles to two miles seven.

Ten Poundsworth (IRE)

9-y-o ch g Orchestra-Rush For Gold (Mugatpura)
George Stewart R T McLoughlin

Placings:4-102 **(4949a)**
2001/02: 24^{1}HY, 26^{0}G, 25^{2}G

	Starts	1st	2nd	3rd	Win & Pl
Chases	3	1	1	0	10890
Career Total	**4**	**1**	**1**	**0**	**11277**

132	2/02	Leop	3m	Ch	HVY	£7975

Total win prize-money £7975

Going: Sf: 1-1 GS: 0-0 Gd: 0-2 GF: - Fm: 0-0
Distance: 2m/2m3: 0-0 2m4-2m7: 0-0 **3m+: 1-3**
Track: **LH: 1-2** RH: 0-1 Tight: 0-0 Gall: 0-1
Aids: Bl: 0-0 Vi: 0-0 Tstrap: 0-0
Best Rating: 132 2/02 Leop 3m heavy Ch

Irish hunter chaser, who loves the mud. Beat Sheltering to win at Leopardstown at the start of 2002.

Tenacious Melody

73 **48**

6-y-o b g Tina's Pet-High Run (HOL) (Runnymede)
Mrs L Williamson L & Mrs A Chamberlain

Placings:0P **(3469)**
2001/02: 16^{0}S, 16^{P}S

	Starts	1st	2nd	3rd	Win & Pl
Hurdles	2	0	0	0	
Career Total	**2**	**0**	**0**	**0**	

Going: Sf: 0-2 GS: 0-0 Gd: 0-0 GF: - Fm: 0-0
Distance: 2m/2m3: 0-2 2m4-2m7: 0-0 3m+: 0-0
Track: LH: 0-2 RH: 0-0 Tight: 0-0 Gall: 0-1
Aids: Bl: 0-0 Vi: 0-0 Tstrap: 0-0
Best Rating: 48 12/01 Hayd 2m soft Hdl

Tender Cove (IRE)

108 **118**

4-y-o b g Balla Cove-Fair Tender (Tender King)
P Mullins Cabin Hill Syndicate

Placings:100 **(4952a)**
2001/02: 16^{1}Y, 17^{0}G, 16^{0}G

	Starts	1st	2nd	3rd	Win & Pl
Hurdles	3	1	0	0	4656
Career Total	**3**	**1**	**0**	**0**	**4656**

118	1/02	Naas	2m	Hdl	YLD	£4656

Total win prize-money £4656

Going: Sf: 0-0 GS: 0-0 Gd: 0-2 GF: - Fm: 0-0
Distance: **2m/2m3: 1-3** 2m4-2m7: 0-0 3m+: 0-0
Track: **LH: 1-2** RH: 0-1 Tight: 0-0 Gall: 0-1
Aids: Bl: 0-0 Vi: 0-0 Tstrap: 0-0
Best Rating: 118 1/02 Naas 2m yield Hdl

Winning Irish sprinter. Maiden hurdle winner on his debut in easy fashion. Suited by two miles and easy ground.

Tender Tangle

81 **63**

7-y-o ch g Crested Lark-Red Tango (Legal Tender)
F Jordan F Jordan

Placings:P **(4174)**
2001/02: 22^{P}GS

	Starts	1st	2nd	3rd	Win & Pl
Hurdles	1	0	0	0	
Career Total	**1**	**0**	**0**	**0**	

Going: Sf: 0-0 GS: 0-1 Gd: 0-0 GF: - Fm: 0-0
Distance: 2m/2m3: 0-0 2m4-2m7: 0-1 3m+: 0-0
Track: LH: 0-1 RH: 0-0 Tight: 0-1 Gall: 0-0
Aids: Bl: 0-0 Vi: 0-0 Tstrap: 0-0
Best Rating:

Tender Touch (IRE)

98 **84**

7-y-o gr m Weldnaas (USA)-Moments Peace (Adonijah)
Miss Kate Milligan J D Gordon

Placings:23545/B00/6632322054-105464 **(4898)**
2001/02: 16^{1}G, 18^{0}GS, 16^{5}GS, 17^{4}GS, 21^{6}G, 16^{4}G

	Starts	1st	2nd	3rd	Win & Pl
Hurdles	6	1	0	0	2986
Career Total	**24**	**1**	**4**	**3**	**6507**

84	11/01	Kels	2m110y	G Hdl	GD	£2702

Total win prize-money £2702

Going: Sf: 0-0 GS: 0-3 Gd: 1-3 GF: - Fm: 0-0
Distance: **2m/2m3: 1-5** 2m4-2m7: 0-1 3m+: 0-0
Track: **LH: 1-3** RH: 0-3 **Tight: 1-5** Gall: 0-0
Aids: Bl: 0-0 Vi: 0-0 Tstrap: 0-0
Best Rating: 84 11/01 Kels 2m110y good Hdl

Plating class hurdler.

Tenerife Flyer

81 **53**

4-y-o ch f Rock City-Nobleata (Dunbeath (USA))
J R Norton K Swift

Placings:000P **(4330)**
2001/02: 16^{0}S, 16^{0}GS, 17^{0}GS, 17^{P}S

	Starts	1st	2nd	3rd	Win & Pl
Hurdles	4	0	0	0	
Career Total	**4**	**0**	**0**	**0**	

Going: Sf: 0-2 GS: 0-2 Gd: 0-0 GF: - Fm: 0-0
Distance: 2m/2m3: 0-4 2m4-2m7: 0-0 3m+: 0-0
Track: LH: 0-3 RH: 0-1 Tight: 0-2 Gall: 0-0
Aids: Bl: 0-0 Vi: 0-0 Tstrap: 0-0
Best Rating: 53 12/01 Weth 2m gd-sft Hdl

Tennessee (IRE)

5-y-o b g Blues Traveller (IRE)-Valiant Friend (USA) (Shahrastani (USA))
S P C Woods B Allen/r Hine/r Dawson/a Duke

Placings:U **(0844)**
2001/02: 19^{U}GF

	Starts	1st	2nd	3rd	Win & Pl
Hurdles	1	0	0	0	
Career Total	**1**	**0**	**0**	**0**	

Going: Sf: 0-0 GS: 0-0 Gd: 0-0 GF: - Fm: 0-1
Distance: 2m/2m3: 0-1 2m4-2m7: 0-0 3m+: 0-0
Track: LH: 0-1 RH: 0-0 Tight: 0-1 Gall: 0-0
Aids: Bl: 0-0 Vi: 0-0 Tstrap: 0-0
Best Rating:

Tennessee Twist (IRE)

12-y-o b g Buckskin (FR)-Darjoy (Darantus)
M Williamson M Williamson

Placings:*420*/2141/**P1/FP/31F/U/0PPPP-3** **(4091)**
2001/02: 24^{3}S

	Starts	1st	2nd	3rd	Win & Pl
Chases	1	0	0	1	214
Career Total	**21**	**4**	**2**	**2**	**24553**

134	11/98	Chel	3m3f110y	B HCh	GD	£10191
138	2/97	Chep	3m	C Ch	GD	£5411
120	2/96	Towc	3m	E Hdl	HVY	£2452
113	11/95	Newb	3m110y	C Hdl	GD	£3603

Total win prize-money £21661

Going: Sf: 0-1 GS: 0-0 Gd: 0-0 GF: - Fm: 0-0
Distance: 2m/2m3: 0-0 2m4-2m7: 0-0 3m+: 0-1
Track: LH: 0-0 RH: 0-0 Tight: 0-0 Gall: 0-0
Aids: Bl: 0-0 Vi: 0-0 Tstrap: 0-0
Best Rating: 138 2/97 Chep 3m good Ch

One-time decent handicapper, now hunter chaser. Stays well. Acts on a sound surface.

Tenseesee (FR)

104 **116**

7-y-o ch g Murmure (FR)-Chattanooga Choo (FR) (In The Mood (FR))
N J Henderson Raymond Tooth

Placings:111511P0/P02 **(2763)**
2001/02: 20^{P}G, 20^{0}G, 19^{2}GS

	Starts	1st	2nd	3rd	Win & Pl
Hurdles	2	0	1	0	1654
Chases	1	0	0	0	0
Career Total	**11**	**5**	**1**	**0**	**21442**

132	1/00	Donc	2m4f	E Hdl	GD	£2996
	9/99	Crao	2m2f	Ch	GD	£6997
	7/99	Rcpp	2m1f	Ch	GD	£3767
	7/99	Sart	2m110y	Hdl	GD	£2906
	6/99	Jall	2m2f	Ch	SFT	£2691

Total win prize-money £19357

Going: Sf: 0-0 GS: 0-1 Gd: 0-2 GF: - Fm: 0-0
Distance: 2m/2m3: 0-1 2m4-2m7: 0-2 3m+: 0-0
Track: LH: 0-3 RH: 0-0 Tight: 0-0 Gall: 0-1
Aids: Bl: 0-0 Vi: 0-0 Tstrap: 0-0
Best Rating: 132 1/00 Donc 2m4f good Hdl

A winner over both hurdles and fences in France, he won a Doncaster novice hurdle easily on his British debut early in 2000 but flopped in soft ground next time. Returned from injury in the autumn of 2001, running well at Newbury. Stays two and a half miles, does not want the ground too soft.

Tensile (IRE)

105(115h) (139h)**131+**

7-y-o b g Tenby-Bonnie Isle (Pitcairn)
P J Hobbs (M C Pipe 7/6) D Charlesworth

Placings:1/1211P-343P201 **(4496)**
2001/02: 24^{3}G, 20^{4}GS, 20^{3}G, 20^{P}S, 22^{2}GS, 21^{0}GS, 22^{1}G

	Starts	1st	2nd	3rd	Win & Pl
Hurdles	7	1	1	2	13730
Career Total	**13**	**5**	**2**	**2**	**42206**

139	3/02	Hayd	2m6f	C(0-135)HHdl	GD	£6929
144	12/00	Hayd	2m4f	B HHdl	HVY	£12174
144	12/00	Chep	2m4f	C(0-130)HHdl	HVY	£8716
132	11/00	Tntn	2m3f110y	F(0-110)HHdl	GD	£2564
110	11/99	Leic	2m	E Hdl	G-S	£2945

Total win prize-money £33331

Going: Sf: 0-1 GS: 0-3 Gd: 1-3 GF: - Fm: 0-0
Distance: 2m/2m3: 0-0 **2m4-2m7: 1-6** 3m+: 0-1
Track: **LH: 1-5** RH: 0-2 Tight: 0-0 Gall: 0-1
Aids: Bl: 0-0 Vi: 0-0 Tstrap: 0-2
Best Rating: 144 12/00 Hayd 2m4f heavy Hdl

A useful handicap hurdler who loves the mud and stays well. Regained the winning thread at Haydock in March 2002. Made successful debut over fences at Newton Abbot in May 2002 and followed up at Stratford, but still not the best of jumpers.

Tentsmuir

73f **95f**

6-y-o b m Arctic Lord-Deep Pier (Deep Run)
D W Whillans D McComb

Placings:*10* **(3999)**
2001/02: 16^{1}S, 16^{0}S

	Starts	1st	2nd	3rd	Win & Pl
NH Flat	2	1	0	0	1932
Career Total	**2**	**1**	**0**	**0**	**1932**

95	1/02	Newc	2m	H NHF	SFT	£1932

Total win prize-money £1932

Going: Sf: 1-2 GS: 0-0 Gd: 0-0 GF: - Fm: 0-0
Distance: **2m/2m3: 1-2** 2m4-2m7: 0-0 3m+: 0-0
Track: LH: 0-1 RH: 0-0 Tight: 0-0 Gall: 0-1
Aids: Bl: 0-0 Vi: 0-0 Tstrap: 0-0
Best Rating: 95 1/02 Newc 2m soft NHF

A surprise winner of a soft-ground bumper on her debut in January 2002.

Teofilio (IRE)

91 **88**

8-y-o ch h Night Shift (USA)-Rivoltade (USA) (Sir Ivor)
Andrew Reid (Miss Venetia Williams 15/9) L R Gotch

Placings:0040 **(1409)**
2001/02: 17^{0}GS, 16^{0}GF, 16^{4}GF, 16^{0}GF

	Starts	1st	2nd	3rd	Win & Pl
Hurdles	4	0	0	0	0
Career Total	**4**	**0**	**0**	**0**	**0**

Going: Sf: 0-0 GS: 0-1 Gd: 0-0 GF: - Fm: 0-3
Distance: 2m/2m3: 0-4 2m4-2m7: 0-0 3m+: 0-0
Track: LH: 0-4 RH: 0-0 Tight: 0-1 Gall: 0-0
Aids: Bl: 0-0 Vi: 0-0 Tstrap: 0-2
Best Rating: 88 8/01 Uttx 2m gd-fm Hdl

Terdad (USA)

114 **119**

9-y-o ch g Lomond (USA)-Istiska (FR) (Irish River (FR))
Mrs M Reveley Tremousser Partnership

Placings:1142/1040/332116336/052062203-0001551615 **(2689)**
2001/02: 19^{0}G, 19^{0}GF, 21^{0}GF, 17^{1}GF, 16^{5}G, 17^{5}GF, 17^{1}G, 21^{6}G, 19^{1}S, 20^{5}G

	Starts	1st	2nd	3rd	Win & Pl
Hurdles	10	3	0	0	5649
Career Total	**36**	**8**	**5**	**5**	**27949**

119	12/01	Catt	2m3f	F(0-110)HHdl	SFT	£1890
111	10/01	Sedg	2m1f	F Hdl	GD	£1974
106	8/01	MRas	2m1f110y	G(0-95)HHdl	G-F	£1785
118	12/99	Hntg	2m110y	D(0-125)HHdl	GD	£5204
111	11/99	Wwck	2m	G Hdl	GD	£1637
109	5/98	Prth	2m110y	E(0-105)HHdl	G-F	£2892
93	9/97	Prth	2m110y	E Hdl	G-F	£2633
91	8/97	Sedg	2m1f	E Hdl	G-F	£2304

Total win prize-money £20320

Going: Sf: 1-1 GS: 0-0 Gd: 1-5 GF: - Fm: 1-4
Distance: **2m/2m3: 3-5** 2m4-2m7: 0-5 3m+: 0-0
Track: **LH: 2-6** RH: 1-4 **Tight: 3-8** Gall: 0-1
Aids: Bl: 1-3 **Vi: 2-5** Tstrap: 0-0
Best Rating: 119 12/01 Catt 2m3f soft Hdl

Terek (GER)

96 **100**

6-y-o ch g Irish River (FR)-Turbaine (USA) (Trempolino (USA))
R T Phillips (P Schiergen 23/9) Mrs Claire Smith

Placings:2P **(4662)**
2001/02: 17^{2}S, 16^{P}G

	Starts	1st	2nd	3rd	Win & Pl
Hurdles	2	0	1	0	814
Career Total	**2**	**0**	**1**	**0**	**814**

Going: Sf: 0-1 GS: 0-0 Gd: 0-1 GF: - Fm: 0-0
Distance: 2m/2m3: 0-2 2m4-2m7: 0-0 3m+: 0-0
Track: LH: 0-1 RH: 0-1 Tight: 0-1 Gall: 0-0
Aids: Bl: 0-0 Vi: 0-0 Tstrap: 0-0
Best Rating: 100 3/02 Hrfd 2m1f soft Hdl

Group Three winner on the Flat in Germany, suited by cut in the ground. Runner-up on his hurdles debut, faced a stiff task next time.

Terino

80 **75**

6-y-o b g Terimon-Ashmo (Ashmore (FR))
A E Jessop A Jessop

Placings:*500* **(4166)**
2001/02: 16^{5}GS, 18^{0}G, 16^{0}GS

	Starts	1st	2nd	3rd	Win & Pl
NH Flat	3	0	0	0	0
Career Total	**3**	**0**	**0**	**0**	**0**

Going: Sf: 0-0 GS: 0-2 Gd: 0-1 GF: - Fm: 0-0
Distance: 2m/2m3: 0-3 2m4-2m7: 0-0 3m+: 0-0
Track: LH: 0-2 RH: 0-1 Tight: 0-1 Gall: 0-1
Aids: Bl: 0-0 Vi: 0-0 Tstrap: 0-0
Best Rating: 91 12/01 Hntg 2m110y gd-sft NHF

Modest bumper form.

Test Of Loyalty

106(94h) (71h)**100**

8-y-o b g Niniski (USA)-River Chimes (Forlorn River)
J N R Billinge Hilton Racing Partnership

Placings:0/P-0364P206 **(4829)**
2001/02: 20^{0}G, 16^{3}G, 19^{6}G, 16^{4}G, 24^{P}S, 16^{2}S, 17^{0}GF, 16^{6}G

	Starts	1st	2nd	3rd	Win & Pl
Hurdles	1	0	0	0	0
Chases	7	0	1	1	1797
Career Total	**10**	**0**	**1**	**1**	**1797**

Going: Sf: 0-2 GS: 0-0 Gd: 0-5 GF: - Fm: 0-1
Distance: 2m/2m3: 0-5 2m4-2m7: 0-2 3m+: 0-1
Track: LH: 0-6 RH: 0-2 Tight: 0-3 Gall: 0-1
Aids: Bl: 0-0 Vi: 0-0 Tstrap: 0-0
Best Rating: 100 11/01 Ayr 2m good Ch

Texas Ranger

103 **128+**

4-y-o b c Mtoto-Favorable Exchange (USA) (Exceller (USA))
C J Mann (J W Hills 30/10) The Whitcoombe Partnership

Placings:2 **(4813)**
2001/02: 17^{2}GF

	Starts	1st	2nd	3rd	Win & Pl
Hurdles	1	0	1	0	2628
Career Total	**1**	**0**	**1**	**0**	**2628**

Going: Sf: 0-0 GS: 0-0 Gd: 0-0 GF: - Fm: 0-1
Distance: 2m/2m3: 0-1 2m4-2m7: 0-0 3m+: 0-0
Track: LH: 0-1 RH: 0-0 Tight: 0-0 Gall: 0-1
Aids: Bl: 0-0 Vi: 0-0 Tstrap: 0-0
Best Rating: 117 4/02 Chel 2m1f gd-fm Hdl

Progressive novice hurdler. Stays two miles four furlongs and acts on a sound surface. Has shown form with cut in the ground.

Thalys (GER)

95 **107+**

4-y-o bl c Gold And Ivory (USA)-Tachira (Faraway Times (USA))
Mrs H Dalton J Hales

Placings:0 **(3621)**
2001/02: 17^{0}GS

	Starts	1st	2nd	3rd	Win & Pl
Hurdles	1	0	0	0	
Career Total	**1**	**0**	**0**	**0**	

Going: Sf: 0-0 GS: 0-1 Gd: 0-0 GF: - Fm: 0-0
Distance: 2m/2m3: 0-1 2m4-2m7: 0-0 3m+: 0-0
Track: LH: 0-0 RH: 0-1 Tight: 0-1 Gall: 0-0
Aids: Bl: 0-0 Vi: 0-0 Tstrap: 0-0
Best Rating: 72 2/02 MRas 2m1f110y gd-sft Hdl

Winner on the Flat in native Germany. Has opened his account over hurdles at Market Rasen in July.

Thanks Keith

105 **122**

7-y-o ch g Risk Me (FR)-Nannie Annie (Persian Bold)
F P Murtagh (J J O'Neill 29/6) Clayton Bigley Partnership Ltd

Placings:264211242/**2223FP-1412PP** **(2197)**
2001/02: 20^{1}G, 20^{4}GF, 24^{1}GF, 21^{2}G, 23^{P}GF, 22^{P}G

	Starts	1st	2nd	3rd	Win & Pl
Chases	6	2	1	0	9884
Career Total	**21**	**4**	**8**	**1**	**23790**

108	6/01	Strf	3m	E Ch	G-F	£3328
122	5/01	Aint	2m4f	D Ch	GD	£5120
112	2/99	Ayr	2m4f	D(0-110)HHdl	SFT	£2875
112	1/99	Ayr	2m4f	E Hdl	HVY	£2745

Total win prize-money £14068

Going: Sf: 0-0 GS: 0-0 Gd: 1-3 GF: - Fm: 1-3
Distance: 2m/2m3: 0-0 2m4-2m7: 1-4 3m+: 1-2
Track: **LH: 2-4** RH: 0-1 **Tight: 2-4** Gall: 0-0
Aids: Bl: 1-3 Vi: 1-3 Tstrap: 0-0
Best Rating: 122 7/01 Strf 2m5f110y good Ch

He won two novice hurdles at Ayr in 1999, but he did not win again until May 2001, when he won chases at Aintree and at Stratford in June. Acts on any ground.

Thanx Mr Smallman (IRE)

5-y-o b g Erin's Isle-Treasure (IRE) (Treasure Kay)
A Dickman Mike Smallman

Placings:P **(3856)**
2001/02: 16^{P}S

	Starts	1st	2nd	3rd	Win & Pl
Hurdles	1	0	0	0	
Career Total	**1**	**0**	**0**	**0**	

Going: Sf: 0-1 GS: 0-0 Gd: 0-0 GF: - Fm: 0-0
Distance: 2m/2m3: 0-1 2m4-2m7: 0-0 3m+: 0-0
Track: LH: 0-1 RH: 0-0 Tight: 0-0 Gall: 0-1
Aids: Bl: 0-0 Vi: 0-0 Tstrap: 0-0
Best Rating:

Thari (USA)

117 **145**

5-y-o b g Silver Hawk (USA)-Magic Slipper (Habitat)
Noel Meade (B Hanbury 18/10) D P Sharkey

Placings:124012 **(4944a)**
2001/02: 16^{1}Y, 20^{2}Y, 18^{4}HY, 21^{0}GS, 20^{1}GY, 20^{2}G

	Starts	1st	2nd	3rd	Win & Pl
Hurdles	6	2	2	0	38310
Career Total	**6**	**2**	**2**	**0**	**38310**

129 4/02 Fair 2m4f Hdl G-Y £13957
122 12/01 Leop 2m Hdl YLD £7512
Total win prize-money £21469

Going: Sf: 0-1 GS: 0-1 Gd: 0-1 GF: - Fm: 0-0
Distance: 2m/2m3: 1-2 2m4-2m7: 1-4 3m+: 0-0
Track: LH: 1-3 RH: 1-2 Tight: 0-0 Gall: 0-1
Aids: Bl: 0-0 Vi: 0-0 **Tstrap: 1-3**
Best Rating: 145 4/02 Punc 2m4f good Hdl

Decent Irish hurdler, stays two and a half miles, suited by cut in the ground.

That's Fine

104 **104**

7-y-o ch g Good Thyne (USA)-Wing On (Quayside)
R T Phillips The After Eights

Placings:53-123 **(4518)**
2001/02: 17^{1}S, 21^{2}S, 21^{3}GS

	Starts	1st	2nd	3rd	Win & Pl
NH Flat	1	1	0	0	1568
Hurdles	2	0	1	1	1172
Career Total	**5**	**1**	**1**	**2**	**3046**

96 12/01 Folk 2m1f110y H NHF SFT £1568
Total win prize-money £1568

Going: Sf: 1-2 GS: 0-1 Gd: 0-0 GF: - Fm: 0-0
Distance: **2m/2m3: 1-1** 2m4-2m7: 0-2 3m+: 0-0
Track: LH: 0-0 RH: 0-0 **Tight: 1-1** Gall: 0-0
Aids: Bl: 0-0 Vi: 0-0 Tstrap: 0-0
Best Rating: 104 3/02 Towc 2m5f gd-sft Hdl

Improved to win his third start in a Folkestone bumper. Has subsequently run with credit over hurdles.

That's The Goose (IRE)

104 **112**

6-y-o br m Be My Native (USA)-Black Pit (Black Minstrel)
P A Fahy Malachys Island Syndicate

Placings:2055500211-50P50 **(2148)**
2001/02: 20^{5}GY, 16^{0}G, 16^{P}G, 18^{5}S, 21^{0}G

	Starts	1st	2nd	3rd	Win & Pl
Hurdles	5	0	0	0	
Career Total	**15**	**2**	**2**	**0**	**11498**

112 4/01 Gowr 2m4f Hdl Y-S £5008
114 2/01 Thur 2m NHF Y-S £3895
Total win prize-money £8903

Going: Sf: 0-1 GS: 0-0 Gd: 0-3 GF: - Fm: 0-0
Distance: 2m/2m3: 0-3 2m4-2m7: 0-2 3m+: 0-0
Track: LH: 0-1 RH: 0-1 Tight: 0-0 Gall: 0-1
Aids: Bl: 0-0 Vi: 0-0 Tstrap: 0-1
Best Rating: 114 2/01 Thur 2m yld-sft NHF

Thatcher Rock

86 **89**

6-y-o b g High Estate-Bellifontaine (FR) (Bellypha)
C J Mann D J Deer

Placings:0-406 **(4485)**
2001/02: 17^{4}S, 16^{0}GS, 19^{6}G

	Starts	1st	2nd	3rd	Win & Pl
NH Flat	2	0	0	0	0
Hurdles	1	0	0	0	0
Career Total	**4**	**0**	**0**	**0**	**0**

Going: Sf: 0-1 GS: 0-1 Gd: 0-1 GF: - Fm: 0-0
Distance: 2m/2m3: 0-3 2m4-2m7: 0-0 3m+: 0-0
Track: LH: 0-1 RH: 0-1 Tight: 0-1 Gall: 0-0
Aids: Bl: 0-0 Vi: 0-0 Tstrap: 0-0
Best Rating: 89 3/02 Extr 2m3f good Hdl

Thats All Folks

110(99h) (107h)**124**

5-y-o b g Alhijaz-So It Goes (Free State)
P F Nicholls Arron F A Banks & D J Nichols

Placings:3100-04F2315 **(4886)**
2001/02: 16^{0}G, 16^{4}G, 19^{F}S, 17^{2}S, 16^{3}S, 19^{1}GF, 18^{5}GF

	Starts	1st	2nd	3rd	Win & Pl
Hurdles	2	0	0	0	401
Chases	5	1	1	1	6058
Career Total	**11**	**2**	**1**	**2**	**9205**

124 4/02 Hrfd 2m3f D Ch G-F £4153
114 1/01 Tntn 2m1f E Hdl HVY £2046
Total win prize-money £6200

Going: Sf: 0-3 GS: 0-0 Gd: 0-2 GF: - Fm: 1-2
Distance: **2m/2m3: 1-7** 2m4-2m7: 0-0 3m+: 0-0
Track: LH: 0-1 **RH: 1-5** Tight: 0-3 Gall: 0-0
Aids: Bl: 0-0 Vi: 0-0 Tstrap: 0-0
Best Rating: 124 4/02 Hrfd 2m3f gd-fm Ch

Fair chaser, effective at around two miles but stays further.

Thats No Answer (IRE)

106(98h) (70h)**85**

9-y-o b g Rich Rebel (USA)-Reprieved Run (Deep Run)
G L Moore R Goad

Placings:0PF/P2/333 **(1224)**
2001/02: 20^{3}GF, 16^{3}GF, 20^{3}GF

	Starts	1st	2nd	3rd	Win & Pl
Hurdles	1	0	0	1	329
Chases	2	0	0	2	871
Career Total	**8**	**0**	**1**	**3**	**2224**

Going: Sf: 0-0 GS: 0-0 Gd: 0-0 GF: - Fm: 0-3
Distance: 2m/2m3: 0-1 2m4-2m7: 0-2 3m+: 0-0
Track: LH: 0-2 RH: 0-0 Tight: 0-3 Gall: 0-0
Aids: Bl: 0-0 Vi: 0-0 Tstrap: 0-0
Best Rating: 85 8/01 Sthl 2m gd-fm Ch

Thats The Crack (IRE)

101 **106**

8-y-o b g King's Ride-Mighty Crack (Deep Run)
R H Alner M Worcester

Placings:4PP6/2-1 **(0364)**
2001/02: 20^{1}GF

	Starts	1st	2nd	3rd	Win & Pl
Chases	1	1	0	0	3486
Career Total	**6**	**1**	**1**	**0**	**4996**

106 5/01 Ling 2m4f110y F(0-90)HCh G-F £3486
Total win prize-money £3486

Going: Sf: 0-0 GS: 0-0 Gd: 0-0 GF: - Fm: 1-1
Distance: 2m/2m3: 0-0 **2m4-2m7: 1-1** 3m+: 0-0
Track: **LH: 1-1** RH: 0-0 **Tight: 1-1** Gall: 0-0
Aids: Bl: 0-0 Vi: 0-0 Tstrap: 0-0
Best Rating: 106 5/01 Ling 2m4f110y gd-fm Ch

Thatsforeel

104 **122**

9-y-o b g Scottish Reel-That Space (Space King)
A G Hobbs Hill Fuels Limited

Placings:2-32PPP0 **(3405)**
2001/02: 24^{3}G, 24^{2}S, 24^{P}G, 25^{P}HY, 27^{P}G, 23^{0}G

	Starts	1st	2nd	3rd	Win & Pl
Chases	6	0	1	1	1757
Career Total	**7**	**0**	**2**	**1**	**2913**

Going: Sf: 0-2 GS: 0-0 Gd: 0-4 GF: - Fm: 0-0
Distance: 2m/2m3: 0-0 2m4-2m7: 0-0 3m+: 0-6
Track: LH: 0-1 RH: 0-4 Tight: 0-1 Gall: 0-1
Aids: Bl: 0-2 Vi: 0-0 Tstrap: 0-0
Best Rating: 122 4/01 Winc 3m1f110y soft Ch

A winning pointer, he has been placed in staying novice chases.

The Airy Man (IRE)

24

13-y-o ch g Roselier (FR)-Turnpike Lass (Indigenous)
Miss D Cole R A B Brassey

Placings:U/0 **(1494)**
2001/02: 22^{0}GF

	Starts	1st	2nd	3rd	Win & Pl
Hurdles	1	0	0	0	
Career Total	**2**	**0**	**0**	**0**	

Going: Sf: 0-0 GS: 0-0 Gd: 0-0 GF: - Fm: 0-1
Distance: 2m/2m3: 0-0 2m4-2m7: 0-1 3m+: 0-0
Track: LH: 0-0 RH: 0-0 Tight: 0-0 Gall: 0-0
Aids: Bl: 0-0 Vi: 0-0 Tstrap: 0-0
Best Rating: 24 10/01 Extr 2m6f110y gd-fm Hdl

The Alleycat (IRE)

107 **102**

11-y-o b g Tidaro (USA)-Allitess (Mugatpura)
J S Haldane (R Ford 26/7) J S Haldane

Placings:0F-61152150 **(1420)**
2001/02: 24^{6}GF, 20^{1}GF, 16^{1}GF, 20^{5}GF, 16^{2}GF, 16^{1}GF, 20^{5}G, 16^{0}G

	Starts	1st	2nd	3rd	Win & Pl
Chases	8	3	1	0	12449
Career Total	**10**	**3**	**1**	**0**	**12449**

102 7/01 Sedg 2m110y E(0-115)HCh G-F £3363
96 6/01 Prth 2m F(0-100)HCh G-F £4823
90 5/01 Hntg 2m4f110y F(0-100)HCh G-F £2990
Total win prize-money £11177

Going: Sf: 0-0 GS: 0-0 Gd: 0-2 GF: - Fm: 3-6
Distance: **2m/2m3: 2-4** 2m4-2m7: 1-3 3m+: 0-1
Track: LH: 1-4 **RH: 2-4** Tight: 1-4 Gall: 1-1
Aids: Bl: 0-0 Vi: 0-0 Tstrap: 0-0
Best Rating: 102 7/01 Sedg 2m110y gd-fm Ch

The Artful Dodger

7-y-o b g Alhijaz-Madam Millie (Milford)
Mrs V C Ward Colin Linney

Placings:00/P **(4553)**
2001/02: 17^{P}GF

	Starts	1st	2nd	3rd	Win & Pl

Hurdles	1	0	0	0
Career Total	**3**	**0**	**0**	**0**

Going: Sf: 0-0 GS: 0-0 Gd: 0-0 GF: - Fm: 0-1
Distance: 2m/2m3: 0-1 2m4-2m7: 0-0 3m+: 0-0
Track: LH: 0-0 RH: 0-1 Tight: 0-1 Gall: 0-0
Aids: Bl: 0-0 Vi: 0-0 Tstrap: 0-0
Best Rating: 80 11/99 Uttx 2m gd-sft Hdl

The Auctioneer

12-y-o gr g Neltino-Floral Palm (Floribunda)
Mrs Caroline Bailey Mrs P Rowe

Placings:6-2U **(0497)**
2001/02: 20^{2}GF, 25^{U}G

	Starts	1st	2nd	3rd	Win & Pl
Chases	2	0	1	0	510
Career Total	**3**	**0**	**1**	**0**	**510**

Going: Sf: 0-0 GS: 0-0 Gd: 0-1 GF: - Fm: 0-1
Distance: 2m/2m3: 0-0 2m4-2m7: 0-1 3m+: 0-1
Track: LH: 0-1 RH: 0-1 Tight: 0-1 Gall: 0-0
Aids: Bl: 0-0 Vi: 0-0 Tstrap: 0-0
Best Rating: 100 5/01 Strf 2m4f gd-fm Ch

The Bailiff (IRE)

6-y-o b g Lashkari-Salote (USA) (Forli (ARG))
Ian Williams Mr & Mrs John Poynton

Placings:00P **(4174)**
2001/02: 16^{0}S, 16^{0}G, 22^{P}GS

	Starts	1st	2nd	3rd	Win & Pl
NH Flat	1	0	0	0	0
Hurdles	2	0	0	0	0
Career Total	**3**	**0**	**0**	**0**	

Going: Sf: 0-1 GS: 0-1 Gd: 0-1 GF: - Fm: 0-0
Distance: 2m/2m3: 0-2 2m4-2m7: 0-1 3m+: 0-0
Track: LH: 0-3 RH: 0-0 Tight: 0-1 Gall: 0-1
Aids: Bl: 0-0 Vi: 0-0 Tstrap: 0-0
Best Rating: 77 11/01 Hayd 2m soft NHF

The Bajan Bandit (IRE)

104 **134**

7-y-o b g Commanche Run-Sunrise Highway Vii (Damsire Unregistered)
L Lungo Ashleybank Investments Limited

Placings:1/111-11101 **(4832)**
2001/02: 16^{1}GS, 17^{1}HY, 20^{1}HY, 21^{0}GS, 20^{1}G

	Starts	1st	2nd	3rd	Win & Pl
Hurdles	5	4	0	0	13807
Career Total	**9**	**8**	**0**	**0**	**44237**

131	4/02	Ayr	2m4f	C Hdl	GD	£5570
134	2/02	Ayr	2m4f	E Hdl	HVY	£3108
126	11/01	Carl	2m1f	E Hdl	HVY	£2531
115	11/01	Ayr	2m	E Hdl	G-S	£2597
147	4/01	Aint	2m1f	A NHF	HVY	£18000
142	12/00	Chep	2m110y	A NHF	SFT	£9000
129	11/00	Ayr	2m	H NHF	SFT	£1767
108	4/00	Carl	2m1f	H NHF	G-S	£1662

Total win prize-money £44238

Going: Sf: 2-2 GS: 1-2 Gd: 1-1 GF: - Fm: 0-0
Distance: 2m/2m3: 2-2 2m4-2m7: 2-3 3m+: 0-0
Track: **LH: 3-4** RH: 1-1 Tight: 0-0 Gall: 0-1
Aids: Bl: 0-0 Vi: 0-0 Tstrap: 0-0
Best Rating: 147 4/01 Aint 2m1f heavy NHF

Unbeaten in four bumpers, including the Martell Weatherbys Champion Bumper at Aintree in April, he won his first three over hurdles before finishing unplaced at the Festival. However, he bounced back to form in an ordinary novice event at Ayr. Stays two and a half miles and has raced mainly on an easy surface. A high-class chasing prospect.

The Bandit (IRE)

88f **102f**

5-y-o b g Un Desperado (FR)-Sweet Friendship (Alleging (USA))
Miss E C Lavelle R J Lavelle

Placings:0 **(3910)**
2001/02: 16^{0}G

	Starts	1st	2nd	3rd	Win & Pl
NH Flat	1	0	0	0	
Career Total	**1**	**0**	**0**	**0**	

Going: Sf: 0-0 GS: 0-0 Gd: 0-1 GF: - Fm: 0-0
Distance: 2m/2m3: 0-1 2m4-2m7: 0-0 3m+: 0-0
Track: LH: 0-0 RH: 0-1 Tight: 0-0 Gall: 0-0
Aids: Bl: 0-0 Vi: 0-0 Tstrap: 0-0
Best Rating: 102 2/02 Kemp 2m good NHF

The Barge (IRE)

87 **103**

9-y-o b g Un Desperado (FR)-Marble Owen (Master Owen)
J White Jim Kelly

Placings:3/B3100/0000/P5P-P6623 **(2592)**
2001/02: 27^{P}G, 22^{6}GF, 23^{6}G, 26^{2}G, 25^{3}G

	Starts	1st	2nd	3rd	Win & Pl
Hurdles	1	0	0	0	0
Chases	4	0	1	1	1675
Career Total	**18**	**1**	**1**	**3**	**4686**

115	2/99	Thur	2m6f	Hdl	HVY	£2455

Total win prize-money £2455

Going: Sf: 0-0 GS: 0-0 Gd: 0-4 GF: - Fm: 0-1
Distance: 2m/2m3: 0-0 2m4-2m7: 0-1 3m+: 0-4
Track: LH: 0-2 RH: 0-1 Tight: 0-3 Gall: 0-0
Aids: Bl: 0-3 Vi: 0-0 Tstrap: 0-0
Best Rating: 115 2/99 Thur 2m6f heavy Hdl

Irish staying hurdler, handles soft ground.

The Bedouin

62 **24**

7-y-o br g Nomadic Way (USA)-Bramcote Centenary (Alleging (USA))
Miss K Marks Nick Shutts

Placings:460-000 **(1748)**
2001/02: 16^{0}GF, 16^{0}GF, 19^{0}G

	Starts	1st	2nd	3rd	Win & Pl
NH Flat	1	0	0	0	0
Hurdles	2	0	0	0	0
Career Total	**6**	**0**	**0**	**0**	**0**

Going: Sf: 0-0 GS: 0-0 Gd: 0-1 GF: - Fm: 0-2
Distance: 2m/2m3: 0-2 2m4-2m7: 0-1 3m+: 0-0
Track: LH: 0-2 RH: 0-1 Tight: 0-1 Gall: 0-0
Aids: Bl: 0-0 Vi: 0-0 Tstrap: 0-0
Best Rating: 94 10/00 MRas 2m1f110y good NHF

The Beeches (IRE)

9-y-o ch g Be My Native (USA)-Red Bit (IRE) (Henbit (USA))
C L Popham Mrs C R Hayton

Placings:26/1P/060PPP-PP **(0981)**
2001/02: 17^{P}G, 22^{P}G

	Starts	1st	2nd	3rd	Win & Pl
Hurdles	2	0	0	0	
Career Total	**12**	**1**	**1**	**0**	**2687**

102	11/99	Dpat	2m1f87y	NHF	YLD	£2002

Total win prize-money £2002

Going: Sf: 0-0 GS: 0-0 Gd: 0-2 GF: - Fm: 0-0
Distance: 2m/2m3: 0-1 2m4-2m7: 0-1 3m+: 0-0
Track: LH: 0-2 RH: 0-0 Tight: 0-2 Gall: 0-0
Aids: Bl: 0-0 Vi: 0-0 Tstrap: 0-0
Best Rating: 102 11/99 Dpat 2m1f87y yield NHF

The Beyton Bear (IRE)

89f **79f**

6-y-o b g Dromod Hill-Reffian (IRE) (Henbit (USA))
Mrs L Wadham R B Holt

Placings:0 **(1832)**
2001/02: 16^{0}G

	Starts	1st	2nd	3rd	Win & Pl
NH Flat	1	0	0	0	
Career Total	**1**	**0**	**0**	**0**	

Going: Sf: 0-0 GS: 0-0 Gd: 0-1 GF: - Fm: 0-0
Distance: 2m/2m3: 0-1 2m4-2m7: 0-0 3m+: 0-0
Track: LH: 0-1 RH: 0-0 Tight: 0-1 Gall: 0-0
Aids: Bl: 0-0 Vi: 0-0 Tstrap: 0-1
Best Rating: 79 10/01 Sthl 2m good NHF

The Big Lad (IRE)

9-y-o b g Montelimar (USA)-Amelioras Daughter (General Ironside)
Graham Smith Graham Smith

Placings:P/4 **(1582)**
2001/02: 22^{4}GS

	Starts	1st	2nd	3rd	Win & Pl
Chases	1	0	0	0	289
Career Total	**2**	**0**	**0**	**0**	**289**

Going: Sf: 0-0 GS: 0-1 Gd: 0-0 GF: - Fm: 0-0
Distance: 2m/2m3: 0-0 2m4-2m7: 0-1 3m+: 0-0
Track: LH: 0-0 RH: 0-1 Tight: 0-1 Gall: 0-0
Aids: Bl: 0-0 Vi: 0-0 Tstrap: 0-1
Best Rating:

The Big'Un

93 **94**

8-y-o b g Green-Fingered-Lismore (Relkino)
G L Moore The P G Partnership

Placings:P243/46 **(3235)**
2001/02: 20^{4}GS, 20^{6}GS

	Starts	1st	2nd	3rd	Win & Pl
Chases	2	0	0	0	438
Career Total	**6**	**0**	**1**	**1**	**2240**

Going: Sf: 0-0 GS: 0-2 Gd: 0-0 GF: - Fm: 0-0
Distance: 2m/2m3: 0-0 2m4-2m7: 0-2 3m+: 0-0
Track: LH: 0-0 RH: 0-2 Tight: 0-0 Gall: 0-1
Aids: Bl: 0-0 Vi: 0-0 Tstrap: 0-0
Best Rating: 113 3/00 Font 2m4f gd-sft Ch

The Bigwig (NZ)

11-y-o ch g Wiganthorpe-Appraisal (NZ) (Centurius)
G B Balding The Cleric Partnership

Placings:1325/00P/0-P (1241)
2001/02: 20^{P}GF

	Starts	1st	2nd	3rd	Win & Pl
Chases	1	0	0	0	
Career Total	**9**	**1**	**1**	**1**	**1810**

	8/98		1m5f	Hdl	HVY	£1144

Total win prize-money £1144

Going: Sf: 0-0 GS: 0-0 Gd: 0-0 GF: - Fm: 0-1
Distance: 2m/2m3: 0-0 2m4-2m7: 0-1 3m+: 0-0
Track: LH: 0-1 RH: 0-0 Tight: 0-0 Gall: 0-0
Aids: Bl: 0-0 Vi: 0-0 Tstrap: 0-1
Best Rating: 100 11/99 Wwck 2m good Ch

The Biscuit

87 **71**
9-y-o ch m Nomadic Way (USA)-Not To Worry (USA) (Stevward)
B Mactaggart K Bruce

Placings:0-00 (2917)
2001/02: 20^{0}GF, 20^{0}G

	Starts	1st	2nd	3rd	Win & Pl
Hurdles	2	0	0	0	
Career Total	**3**	**0**	**0**	**0**	

Going: Sf: 0-0 GS: 0-0 Gd: 0-1 GF: - Fm: 0-1
Distance: 2m/2m3: 0-0 2m4-2m7: 0-2 3m+: 0-0
Track: LH: 0-0 RH: 0-2 Tight: 0-2 Gall: 0-0
Aids: Bl: 0-0 Vi: 0-0 Tstrap: 0-2
Best Rating: 71 12/01 Muss 2m4f gd-fm Hdl

The Black Bishop (IRE)

14-y-o b g The Parson-Darkina (Tarqogan)
Miss P A Williams Martin F Edgar

Placings:053505P/P-40 (0278)
2001/02: 25^{4}S, 24^{0}GF

	Starts	1st	2nd	3rd	Win & Pl
Chases	2	0	0	0	0
Career Total	**10**	**0**	**0**	**1**	**621**

Going: Sf: 0-1 GS: 0-0 Gd: 0-0 GF: - Fm: 0-1
Distance: 2m/2m3: 0-0 2m4-2m7: 0-0 3m+: 0-2
Track: LH: 0-1 RH: 0-1 Tight: 0-0 Gall: 0-0
Aids: Bl: 0-0 Vi: 0-0 Tstrap: 0-0
Best Rating: 56 5/01 Hexm 3m1f soft Ch

The Boiler White (IRE)

14-y-o ch g Deep Run-Cill Dara (Lord Gayle (USA))
E W Froggatt E W Froggatt

Placings:00/101240301316F0/P2F006P2/P/P-CP (0427)
2001/02: 24^{C}GS, 33^{P}G

	Starts	1st	2nd	3rd	Win & Pl
Chases	2	0	0	0	
Career Total	**28**	**4**	**3**	**2**	**15456**

104	3/95	Nott	3m3f110y	F(0-105)HCh	SFT	£2684
104	2/95	Hayd	2m4f	D Ch	HVY	£4105
111	11/94	Wind	2m6f110y	Hdl	G-S	£2024
103	10/94	Uttx	2m4f110y	Hdl	G-F	£2421

Total win prize-money £11237

Going: Sf: 0-0 GS: 0-1 Gd: 0-1 GF: - Fm: 0-0
Distance: 2m/2m3: 0-0 2m4-2m7: 0-0 3m+: 0-2
Track: LH: 0-1 RH: 0-0 Tight: 0-1 Gall: 0-0
Aids: Bl: 0-0 Vi: 0-0 Tstrap: 0-0
Best Rating: 111 11/94 Chel 3m1f110y gd-sft Hdl

The Bold Abbot

12-y-o b g Derring Rose-Canford Abbas (Hasty Word)
Miss Sarah West (Miss Sheena West 24/3) Miss S West

Placings:0P0/54/U3-4 (4741)
2001/02: 24^{4}GF

	Starts	1st	2nd	3rd	Win & Pl
Chases	1	0	0	0	0
Career Total	**8**	**0**	**0**	**1**	**212**

Going: Sf: 0-0 GS: 0-0 Gd: 0-0 GF: - Fm: 0-1
Distance: 2m/2m3: 0-0 2m4-2m7: 0-0 3m+: 0-1
Track: LH: 0-0 RH: 0-1 Tight: 0-1 Gall: 0-0
Aids: Bl: 0-0 Vi: 0-0 Tstrap: 0-0
Best Rating: 99 4/00 Towc 2m6f good Ch

The Bongo Man (IRE)

92 **118**
9-y-o b g Be My Native (USA)-Fight For It (Strong Gale)
D J Wintle (Anthony Mullins 20/5) Hugh M Duffy

Placings: 1/3360/6123350/064412124F/016-2P0PF (2788)
2001/02: 17^{2}G, 19^{P}GS, 21^{0}G, 20^{P}GS, 20^{F}G

	Starts	1st	2nd	3rd	Win & Pl
Hurdles	5	0	1	0	5363
Career Total	**32**	**5**	**4**	**4**	**37036**

118	9/00	Clon	2m4f	(0-109)HHdl	GD	£2760
127	11/99	Tram	2m	(0-109)HCh	YLD	£6160
119	9/99	Tram	2m	Ch	G-Y	£2926
118	9/98	Clon	2m	(0-102)HHdl	G-F	£2540
113	4/97	Punc	2m	NHF	GD	£6782

Total win prize-money £21170

Going: Sf: 0-0 GS: 0-2 Gd: 0-3 GF: - Fm: 0-0
Distance: 2m/2m3: 0-2 2m4-2m7: 0-3 3m+: 0-0
Track: LH: 0-3 RH: 0-1 Tight: 0-2 Gall: 0-1
Aids: Bl: 0-0 Vi: 0-0 Tstrap: 0-0
Best Rating: 127 12/99 Punc 2m soft Ch

A winner on the flat, over hurdles, over fences and has won a bumper. Acts on most types of ground and is effective at two miles to two miles four furlongs.

The Bould Vic (IRE)

87 **76**
10-y-o b g Bold Arrangement-Silojoka (Home Guard (USA))
Miss M E Rowland Goldliner Racing Club

Placings:4224/331264/22450444/2503P/42PP445065 P/0UP-U5P (0879)
2001/02: 20^{U}G, 21^{5}GF, 20^{P}G

	Starts	1st	2nd	3rd	Win & Pl
Chases	3	0	0	0	0
Career Total	**40**	**1**	**7**	**3**	**9920**

101	7/96	Kbgn	2m3f	Hdl	G-F	£2295

Total win prize-money £2295

Going: Sf: 0-0 GS: 0-0 Gd: 0-2 GF: - Fm: 0-1
Distance: 2m/2m3: 0-0 2m4-2m7: 0-3 3m+: 0-0
Track: LH: 0-1 RH: 0-2 Tight: 0-3 Gall: 0-0
Aids: Bl: 0-0 Vi: 0-0 Tstrap: 0-3
Best Rating: 108 5/97 Kbgn 2m3f good Hdl

The Boy King (IRE)

110 **97**
10-y-o ch g Roi Danzig (USA)-Susie Spangles (USA) (Solford (USA))
P R Chamings R V Shaw

Placings:2204300335/P/61PP/531/P544-3030 (0908)
2001/02: 16^{3}G, 20^{0}GF, 20^{3}GF, 23^{0}G

	Starts	1st	2nd	3rd	Win & Pl
Chases	4	0	0	2	877
Career Total	**26**	**2**	**2**	**6**	**10984**

117	11/00	Clon	2m1f	Ch	YLD	£1160
81	6/98	Tram	2m	Hdl	G-Y	£2531

Total win prize-money £6690

Going: Sf: 0-0 GS: 0-0 Gd: 0-2 GF: - Fm: 0-2
Distance: 2m/2m3: 0-1 2m4-2m7: 0-2 3m+: 0-1
Track: LH: 0-3 RH: 0-1 Tight: 0-3 Gall: 0-0
Aids: Bl: 0-0 Vi: 0-0 Tstrap: 0-0
Best Rating: 117 11/99 Clon 2m1f yld-sft Ch

The Brewer

97(42c) **77**
10-y-o ch g Dunbeath (USA)-Bell Cord (Beldale Flutter (USA))
J C Tuck J C T Racing Club

Placings:024/00003022/33111313/5440332U0/3FF40 2-004002 (4657)
2001/02: 16^{0}G, 16^{0}S, 16^{4}S, 16^{0}G, 22^{0}G, 24^{2}G

	Starts	1st	2nd	3rd	Win & Pl
Hurdles	6	0	1	0	500
Career Total	**40**	**4**	**6**	**8**	**19209**

107	3/98	Extr	2m2f	D(0-120)HHdl	SFT	£2804
107	11/97	Extr	2m3f	E(0-100)HHdl	G-S	£2700
93	10/97	Extr	2m3f	F(0-105)HHdl	GD	£2766
87	10/97	Hrfd	2m3f110y	F(0-95)HHdl	G-F	£2094

Total win prize-money £10364

Going: Sf: 0-2 GS: 0-0 Gd: 0-4 GF: - Fm: 0-0
Distance: 2m/2m3: 0-4 2m4-2m7: 0-1 3m+: 0-1
Track: LH: 0-0 RH: 0-6 Tight: 0-1 Gall: 0-0
Aids: Bl: 0-1 Vi: 0-0 Tstrap: 0-0
Best Rating: 107 3/98 Extr 2m2f soft Hdl

The Brixham Boys (IRE)

61f **25f**
5-y-o b g Un Desperado (FR)-Paper Merchant (Hays)
M C Pipe D A Johnson

Placings: 00 (4269)
2001/02: 18^{0}G, 16^{0}S

	Starts	1st	2nd	3rd	Win & Pl
NH Flat	2	0	0	0	
Career Total	**2**	**0**	**0**	**0**	

Going: Sf: 0-1 GS: 0-0 Gd: 0-1 GF: - Fm: 0-0
Distance: 2m/2m3: 0-2 2m4-2m7: 0-0 3m+: 0-0
Track: LH: 0-2 RH: 0-0 Tight: 0-1 Gall: 0-0
Aids: Bl: 0-0 Vi: 0-0 Tstrap: 0-0
Best Rating: 25 3/02 Chep 2m110y soft NHF

The Bunny Boiler (IRE)

113 (122h) **155**

8-y-o b g Tremblant-Danny's Charm (IRE) (Arapahos (FR))
Noel Meade Usual Suspects Syndicate

Placings: 2/15210/**FU00U21-5312F11** (4705a)
2001/02: 24^{5}YS, 28^{3}Y, 22^{1}HY, 24^{2}Y, 24^{F}HY, 34^{1}HY, 29^{1}GY

	Starts	1st	2nd	3rd	Win & Pl
Hurdles	1	1	0	0	5008
Chases	6	2	1	1	137995
Career Total	**20**	**6**	**4**	**1**	**159218**

155	4/02	Fair	3m5f	HCh	G-Y	£65693
155	3/02	Uttx	4m2f	A HCh	HVY	£49600
122	12/01	Thur	2m6f	Hdl	HVY	£5008
128	1/01	DRoy	3m	Ch	G-Y	£6677
113	3/00	Naas	3m	Hdl	Y-S	£3588
84	5/99	Dpat	2m4f110y	NHF	GD	£1994

Total win prize-money £132561

Going: Sf: 2-3 GS: 0-0 Gd: 0-0 GF: - Fm: 0-0
Distance: 2m/2m3: 0-0 2m4-2m7: 1-1 **3m+: 2-6**
Track: LH: 1-2 **RH: 2-4** Tight: 0-0 Gall: 0-0
Aids: Bl: 0-0 Vi: 0-0 Tstrap: 0-0
Best Rating: 155 4/02 Fair 3m5f gd-yld Ch

A decent Irish-trained handicap chaser, he had his big day when winning the Midlands Grand National at Uttoxeter in March 2002. Stays extreme distances and acts on soft and heavy ground.

The Burglar (IRE)

(84h) (61h)

10-y-o b g Denel (FR)-Night Invader (Brave Invader (USA))
R Tate K Needham

Placings: 0/0505/00540/**5P6P/0** (0093)
2001/02: 24^{0}S

	Starts	1st	2nd	3rd	Win & Pl
Hurdles	1	0	0	0	
Career Total	**15**	**0**	**0**	**0**	**193**

Going: Sf: 0-1 GS: 0-0 Gd: 0-0 GF: - Fm: 0-0
Distance: 2m/2m3: 0-0 2m4-2m7: 0-0 3m+: 0-1
Track: LH: 0-1 RH: 0-0 Tight: 0-0 Gall: 0-0
Aids: Bl: 0-0 Vi: 0-0 Tstrap: 0-0
Best Rating: 96 3/98 Ayr 2m gd-sft NHF

The Bushkeeper (IRE)

119 **153**

8-y-o b g Be My Native (USA)-Our Little Lamb (Prince Regent (FR))
N J Henderson B T Stewart-Brown

Placings: 3313/11 (4192)
2001/02: 24^{1}GS, 24^{1}GS

	Starts	1st	2nd	3rd	Win & Pl
Chases	2	2	0	0	32955
Career Total	**6**	**3**	**0**	**3**	**37766**

153	3/02	Chel	3m110y	B(0-140)HCh	G-S	£26000
144	2/02	Hntg	3m	D(0-120)HCh	G-S	£6955
111	1/00	Plum	3m2f	E Ch	G-S	£3290

Total win prize-money £36245

Going: Sf: 0-0 GS: 2-2 Gd: 0-0 GF: - Fm: 0-0
Distance: 2m/2m3: 0-0 2m4-2m7: 0-0 **3m+: 2-2**
Track: LH: 1-1 RH: 1-1 Tight: 0-0 **Gall: 2-2**
Aids: Bl: 0-0 Vi: 0-0 Tstrap: 0-0
Best Rating: 153 3/02 Chel 3m110y gd-sft Ch

He looked a horse with a future when winning a Plumpton novice chase in January 2000, but did not jump well next time and was absent for a long time afterwards. Returned to the track in February 2002 with a win and followed up with a convincing win in the Kim Muir at the Cheltenham Festival. He stays three miles well. Acts on a sound surface.

The Butterwick Kid

109(101h) (109h)**133**

9-y-o ch g Interrex (CAN)-Ville Air (Town Crier)
R A Fahey Mr Robert Chambers & Mrs M W Kenyon

Placings: 4/2134/4152PR/**2631U2636**-60113610 (4946a)
2001/02: 20^{6}GS, 16^{0}S, 20^{1}S, 20^{1}GS, 20^{3}HY, 19^{6}GS, 20^{1}GS, 20^{0}G

	Starts	1st	2nd	3rd	Win & Pl
Hurdles	3	0	0	1	543
Chases	5	3	0	0	12386
Career Total	**28**	**6**	**4**	**4**	**32565**

132	3/02	Carl	2m4f	E(0-110)HCh	G-S	£3688
132	1/02	Sthl	2m4f110y	D(0-115)HCh	G-S	£4193
133	1/02	Carl	2m4f	D(0-120)HCh	SFT	£4503
120	12/00	Weth	3m1f	D Ch	SFT	£4043
127	12/98	Weth	2m7f	B(0-140)HHdl	SFT	£5052
120	12/97	Hexm	2m	E Hdl	SFT	£2106

Total win prize-money £23588

Going: Sf: 1-3 GS: 2-4 Gd: 0-1 GF: - Fm: 0-0
Distance: 2m/2m3: 0-1 **2m4-2m7: 3-7** 3m+: 0-0
Track: LH: 1-5 **RH: 2-3 Tight: 1-2** Gall: 0-1
Aids: Bl: 0-1 **Vi: 3-5** Tstrap: 0-0
Best Rating: 133 1/02 Carl 2m4f soft Ch

A winner on the Flat, over hurdles and over fences. Acts on soft ground and is effective between two miles and three miles one furlong over hurdles and fences.

The Byedein (IRE)

88f **71f**

5-y-o b m Alflora (IRE)-Southern Squaw (Buckskin (FR))
A H Mactaggart A H Mactaggart

Placings: 00 (4750)
2001/02: 16^{0}G, 17^{0}G

	Starts	1st	2nd	3rd	Win & Pl
NH Flat	2	0	0	0	
Career Total	**2**	**0**	**0**	**0**	

Going: Sf: 0-0 GS: 0-0 Gd: 0-2 GF: - Fm: 0-0
Distance: 2m/2m3: 0-2 2m4-2m7: 0-0 3m+: 0-0
Track: LH: 0-1 RH: 0-1 Tight: 0-1 Gall: 0-0
Aids: Bl: 0-0 Vi: 0-0 Tstrap: 0-0
Best Rating: 65 4/02 Carl 2m1f good NHF

Has shown some ability in bumpers.

The Camden Blower (IRE)

(75h) (43h)

9-y-o b g Camden Town-Winola (USA) (Windsor Ruler (USA))
J C McConnochie (Miss H M Irving 13/6) J C McConnochie

Placings: 0/PP0-0**30PPP** (2068)
2001/02: 17^{0}G, 16^{3}GF, 16^{0}F, 26^{P}GF, 24^{P}G, 20^{P}G

	Starts	1st	2nd	3rd	Win & Pl
Hurdles	1	0	0	0	0
Chases	5	0	0	1	470
Career Total	**10**	**0**	**0**	**1**	**470**

Going: Sf: 0-0 GS: 0-0 Gd: 0-3 GF: - Fm: 0-3
Distance: 2m/2m3: 0-3 2m4-2m7: 0-1 3m+: 0-2
Track: LH: 0-2 RH: 0-4 Tight: 0-2 Gall: 0-2
Aids: Bl: 0-0 Vi: 0-0 Tstrap: 0-3
Best Rating: 43 5/01 MRas 2m1f110y good Hdl

The Campdonian (IRE)

86 **56**

11-y-o ch g Clearly Bust-Not At All (Royal Highway)
O O'Neill P J R Gardner

Placings: 0665/56/**F2/442021/0P1PP532/5-P0P** (4184)
2001/02: 24^{P}S, 24^{0}G, 24^{P}S

	Starts	1st	2nd	3rd	Win & Pl
Chases	3	0	0	0	
Career Total	**26**	**2**	**4**	**1**	**12339**

98	1/00	Ludl	3m	F(0-105)HCh	GD	£3172
92	4/99	Towc	2m6f	E Ch	SFT	£2635

Total win prize-money £5807

Going: Sf: 0-2 GS: 0-0 Gd: 0-1 GF: - Fm: 0-0
Distance: 2m/2m3: 0-0 2m4-2m7: 0-0 3m+: 0-3
Track: LH: 0-0 RH: 0-3 Tight: 0-3 Gall: 0-0
Aids: Bl: 0-0 Vi: 0-0 Tstrap: 0-0
Best Rating: 103 4/00 Hrfd 3m1f110y good Ch

The Cardiff Bay

69 **33**

8-y-o b g St Ninian-Comarch (Ancient Monro)
Mrs Merrita Jones G J Hicks

Placings: 03P0/P-5 (4530)
2001/02: 20^{5}GS

	Starts	1st	2nd	3rd	Win & Pl
Hurdles	1	0	0	0	0
Career Total	**6**	**0**	**0**	**1**	**235**

Going: Sf: 0-0 GS: 0-1 Gd: 0-0 GF: - Fm: 0-0
Distance: 2m/2m3: 0-0 2m4-2m7: 0-1 3m+: 0-0
Track: LH: 0-1 RH: 0-0 Tight: 0-0 Gall: 0-0
Aids: Bl: 0-0 Vi: 0-0 Tstrap: 0-0
Best Rating: 78 1/00 Towc 2m heavy NHF

The Come Back Kid

5-y-o b g Shareef Dancer (USA)-Clockwatch (USA) (Alleged (USA))
B Ellison B Batey

Placings:CP (1385)
2001/02: 16^{C}G, 16^{P}G

	Starts	1st	2nd	3rd	Win & Pl
Hurdles	2	0	0	0	
Career Total	**2**	**0**	**0**	**0**	

Going: Sf: 0-0 GS: 0-0 Gd: 0-2 GF: - Fm: 0-0
Distance: 2m/2m3: 0-2 2m4-2m7: 0-0 3m+: 0-0
Track: LH: 0-2 RH: 0-0 Tight: 0-0 Gall: 0-0
Aids: Bl: 0-0 Vi: 0-0 Tstrap: 0-0
Best Rating:

The Cottonwool Kid

90 81

10-y-o b g Blakeney-Relatively Smart (Great Nephew)
Mrs Merrita Jones Stephen Appelbee

Placings:50/0/5005000/F000/610-6 (0213)
2001/02: 24^{6}F

	Starts	1st	2nd	3rd	Win & Pl
Hurdles	1	0	0	0	0
Career Total	**18**	**1**	**0**	**0**	**2984**

90 10/00 Tntn 3m110y F(0-110)HHdl GD £2983
Total win prize-money £2984

Going: Sf: 0-0 GS: 0-0 Gd: 0-0 GF: - Fm: 0-1
Distance: 2m/2m3: 0-0 2m4-2m7: 0-0 3m+: 0-1
Track: LH: 0-1 RH: 0-0 Tight: 0-1 Gall: 0-0
Aids: Bl: 0-1 Vi: 0-0 Tstrap: 0-0
Best Rating: 90 10/00 Tntn 3m110y good Hdl

The Crooked Oak

10-y-o ch g Fearless Action (USA)-Life Goes On (Pharly (FR))
Keith Thomas (F P Murtagh 26/7) Keith Thomas

Placings:2/400P/0343/0U4/PU5/56-41410U040 (4855)
2001/02: 20^{4}GF, 20^{1}GF, 24^{4}GF, 25^{1}G, 20^{0}G, 27^{U}GF, 20^{0}G, 25^{4}GF, 20^{0}G

	Starts	1st	2nd	3rd	Win & Pl
Hurdles	2	0	0	0	0
Chases	7	2	0	0	5883
Career Total	**26**	**2**	**1**	**2**	**7544**

106 6/01 Hexm 3m1f E(0-105)HCh GD £3204
85 5/01 Hexm 2m4f110y F Ch G-F £2115
Total win prize-money £5321

Going: Sf: 0-0 GS: 0-0 Gd: 1-4 GF: - Fm: 1-5
Distance: 2m/2m3: 0-0 2m4-2m7: 1-5 3m+: 1-4
Track: **LH: 2-6** RH: 0-2 Tight: 0-2 Gall: 0-0
Aids: Bl: 0-0 Vi: 0-0 Tstrap: 0-0
Best Rating: 106 6/01 Hexm 3m1f good Ch

Modest stayer winning over fences, held over hurdles. Best on a sound surface.

The Croppy

6-y-o b g Arctic Lord-Deep Cut (Deep Run)
J Neville Quarrington Plant Ltd

Placings:0P-P (3892)
2001/02: 21^{P}HY

	Starts	1st	2nd	3rd	Win & Pl
Hurdles	1	0	0	0	
Career Total	**3**	**0**	**0**	**0**	

Going: Sf: 0-1 GS: 0-0 Gd: 0-0 GF: - Fm: 0-0
Distance: 2m/2m3: 0-0 2m4-2m7: 0-1 3m+: 0-0
Track: LH: 0-0 RH: 0-0 Tight: 0-0 Gall: 0-0
Aids: Bl: 0-0 Vi: 0-0 Tstrap: 0-1
Best Rating:

The Croppy Boy

10-y-o b g Arctic Lord-Deep Cut (Deep Run)
Mrs N S Sharpe J V C Davenport

Placings:5400/0/454P/F4P (2273)
2001/02: 23^{F}GF, 24^{4}GS, 24^{P}G

	Starts	1st	2nd	3rd	Win & Pl
Chases	3	0	0	0	318
Career Total	**12**	**0**	**0**	**0**	**318**

Going: Sf: 0-0 GS: 0-1 Gd: 0-1 GF: - Fm: 0-1
Distance: 2m/2m3: 0-0 2m4-2m7: 0-0 3m+: 0-3
Track: LH: 0-2 RH: 0-0 Tight: 0-1 Gall: 0-0
Aids: Bl: 0-0 Vi: 0-0 Tstrap: 0-0
Best Rating: 83 11/96 Wwck 2m good NHF

The Dangler (IRE)

98(76h) (79h)103

9-y-o b g Feelings (FR)-Royal Typhoon (Royal Fountain)
R G Frost Mrs J McCormack

Placings:550P02P/222U-2132066 (2929)
2001/02: 16^{2}G, 16^{1}GS, 21^{3}G, 26^{2}GF, 22^{0}G, 19^{6}GS, 24^{6}GS

	Starts	1st	2nd	3rd	Win & Pl
Hurdles	1	0	0	0	0
Chases	6	1	2	1	5834
Career Total	**18**	**1**	**6**	**1**	**10827**

96 6/01 NAbb 2m110y F(0-105)HCh G-S £3360
Total win prize-money £3360

Going: Sf: 0-0 GS: 1-3 Gd: 0-3 GF: - Fm: 0-1
Distance: **2m/2m3: 1-3** 2m4-2m7: 0-2 3m+: 0-2
Track: **LH: 1-4** RH: 0-3 **Tight: 1-6** Gall: 0-0
Aids: Bl: 0-0 Vi: 0-0 Tstrap: 0-0
Best Rating: 103 6/00 NAbb 3m2f110y gd-fm Ch

Fair handicap chaser. Stays 21 furlongs and needs soft ground to be effective at around two miles.

The Dark Flasher (IRE)

107 118

5-y-o b h Lucky Guest-Perpignan (Rousillon (USA))
C F Swan N O'Flaherty

Placings:1343204F (4674)
2001/02: 16^{1}YS, 16^{3}Y, 16^{4}S, 16^{3}YS, 16^{2}HY, 16^{0}HY, 16^{4}HY, 16^{F}G

	Starts	1st	2nd	3rd	Win & Pl
Hurdles	8	1	1	2	8256
Career Total	**8**	**1**	**1**	**2**	**8256**

111 11/01 Naas 2m Hdl Y-S £4729
Total win prize-money £4730

Going: Sf: 0-4 GS: 0-0 Gd: 0-1 GF: - Fm: 0-0
Distance: **2m/2m3: 1-8** 2m4-2m7: 0-0 3m+: 0-0
Track: **LH: 1-5** RH: 0-2 Tight: 0-1 Gall: 0-0
Aids: Bl: 0-0 Vi: 0-0 Tstrap: 0-0
Best Rating: 118 3/02 Leop 2m heavy Hdl

Useful Irish handicap hurdler at two miles. Acts on good ground, handles heavy.

The Deacon

6-y-o b g Seymour Hicks (FR)-Deaconess (The Parson)
Mrs H Dalton & Mrs P Huxley

Placings:00P (3592)
2001/02: 16^{0}G, 21^{0}S, 24^{P}HY

	Starts	1st	2nd	3rd	Win & Pl
NH Flat	1	0	0	0	0
Hurdles	2	0	0	0	0
Career Total	**3**	**0**	**0**	**0**	

Going: Sf: 0-2 GS: 0-0 Gd: 0-1 GF: - Fm: 0-0
Distance: 2m/2m3: 0-1 2m4-2m7: 0-1 3m+: 0-1
Track: LH: 0-3 RH: 0-0 Tight: 0-1 Gall: 0-1
Aids: Bl: 0-0 Vi: 0-0 Tstrap: 0-0
Best Rating: 65 12/01 Donc 2m110y good NHF

The Dream Lives On (IRE)

6-y-o ch g Phardante (FR)-Rare Dream (Pollerton)
T P McGovern B & M McHugh Ltd Civil Engineering

Placings:05P (2332)
2001/02: 17^{0}S, 16^{5}G, 21^{P}G

	Starts	1st	2nd	3rd	Win & Pl
NH Flat	2	0	0	0	0
Hurdles	1	0	0	0	0
Career Total	**3**	**0**	**0**	**0**	**0**

Going: Sf: 0-1 GS: 0-0 Gd: 0-2 GF: - Fm: 0-0
Distance: 2m/2m3: 0-2 2m4-2m7: 0-1 3m+: 0-0
Track: LH: 0-1 RH: 0-2 Tight: 0-2 Gall: 0-1
Aids: Bl: 0-0 Vi: 0-0 Tstrap: 0-0
Best Rating: 75 10/01 Hntg 2m110y good NHF

The Duckpond (IRE)

91f 107f

5-y-o ch g Bob's Return (IRE)-Miss Gosling (Prince Bee)
J A B Old W E Sturt

Placings:4 (3777)
2001/02: 16^{4}S

	Starts	1st	2nd	3rd	Win & Pl
NH Flat	1	0	0	0	0
Career Total	**1**	**0**	**0**	**0**	**0**

Going: Sf: 0-1 GS: 0-0 Gd: 0-0 GF: - Fm: 0-0
Distance: 2m/2m3: 0-1 2m4-2m7: 0-0 3m+: 0-0
Track: LH: 0-0 RH: 0-1 Tight: 0-0 Gall: 0-0
Aids: Bl: 0-0 Vi: 0-0 Tstrap: 0-0
Best Rating: 107 2/02 Sand 2m110y soft NHF

The Dust Buster

9-y-o ch g Primitive Rising (USA)-Potterway (Velvet Prince)
Miss Lucinda V Russell A R Trotter

Placings:P6P (0782)
2001/02: 16^{P}S, 20^{6}GF, 20^{P}G

	Starts	1st	2nd	3rd	Win & Pl
Chases	3	0	0	0	0
Career Total	**3**	**0**	**0**	**0**	**0**

Going: Sf: 0-1 GS: 0-0 Gd: 0-1 GF: - Fm: 0-1
Distance: 2m/2m3: 0-1 2m4-2m7: 0-2 3m+: 0-0
Track: LH: 0-2 RH: 0-1 Tight: 0-0 Gall: 0-0
Aids: Bl: 0-0 Vi: 0-0 Tstrap: 0-3
Best Rating:

The Eens

109(72h) (18h)**100**

10-y-o b g Rakaposhi King-Snippet (Ragstone)
D McCain Shaw Hill Golf Club (sage Cott Props Ltd

Placings:5064/26P4P1/124231U0/4P440522143/462 3P5P-03623541313 **(4870)**
2001/02: 20^{0}G, 27^{3}GS, 27^{6}G, 22^{2}G, 24^{3}S, 24^{5}S, 16^{4}HY, 25^{1}S, 20^{3}HY, 26^{1}GS, 23^{3}GF

	Starts	1st	2nd	3rd	Win & Pl
Hurdles	2	0	0	0	0
Chases	9	2	1	4	10709
Career Total	**47**	**6**	**7**	**7**	**34156**

100	4/02	Uttx	3m2f	E(0-110)HCh	G-S	£4221
95	3/02	MRas	3m1f	F(0-95)HCh	SFT	£3031
101	3/00	Carl	2m1f	E(0-115)HHdl	HVY	£2436
101	3/99	Uttx	3m2f	F(0-110)HCh	HVY	£3631
111	11/98	Hayd	2m	C(0-130)HCh	SFT	£4697
96	3/98	Bang	2m4f110y	D Ch	G-S	£3598

Total win prize-money £21616

Going: Sf: 1-5 GS: 1-2 Gd: 0-3 GF: - Fm: 0-1
Distance: 2m/2m3: 0-1 2m4-2m7: 0-3 **3m+: 2-7**
Track: LH: 1-7 RH: 1-2 **Tight: 1-4** Gall: 0-1
Aids: Bl: 0-0 Vi: 0-0 Tstrap: 0-0
Best Rating: 111 11/98 Hayd 2m soft Ch

A modest chaser/hurdler, he is normally a sound jumper. Needs cut in the ground to be seen at his best. Stays three miles.

The Extra Man (IRE)

106(115h) **128**

8-y-o b g Sayaarr (USA)-Chez Georges (Welsh Saint)
M J Ryan Extraman Ltd

Placings:610P/011520/12131-**23P2** **(4634)**
2001/02: 20^{0}G, 22^{3}S, 24^{P}S, 24^{2}GF

	Starts	1st	2nd	3rd	Win & Pl
Chases	4	0	2	1	5517
Career Total	**19**	**6**	**4**	**2**	**72346**

131	2/01	Sand	2m6f	A HHdl	HVY	£29000
122	11/00	Chel	2m5f	C(0-135)HHdl	G-S	£19337
116	10/00	MRas	2m5f110y	D(0-125)HHdl	GD	£7312
110	10/99	Asct	2m4f	E(0-105)HHdl	GD	£3647
100	9/99	Hntg	2m4f110y	E(0-105)HHdl	GD	£2582
99	1/99	Kemp	2m	H NHF	SFT	£1661

Total win prize-money £63543

Going: Sf: 0-2 GS: 0-0 Gd: 0-1 GF: - Fm: 0-1
Distance: 2m/2m3: 0-0 2m4-2m7: 0-2 3m+: 0-2
Track: LH: 0-1 RH: 0-3 Tight: 0-0 Gall: 0-2
Aids: Bl: 0-4 Vi: 0-0 Tstrap: 0-0
Best Rating: 131 2/01 Sand 2m6f heavy Hdl

He had a fine season over hurdles in 2000/2001. Can go well fresh, and has shown ability over fences. Acts on soft ground and stays well.

The Fairy Flag (IRE)

108 **97**

4-y-o ch f Inchinor-Good Reference (IRE) (Reference Point)
A Bailey (J Hetherton 15/10) Mrs V Farrington

Placings:115 **(2295)**
2001/02: 16^{1}S, 16^{1}GS, 16^{5}G

	Starts	1st	2nd	3rd	Win & Pl
Hurdles	3	2	0	0	7817
Career Total	**3**	**2**	**0**	**0**	**7817**

97	11/01	Sand	2m110y	D Hdl	G-S	£4212
97	11/01	Hayd	2m	D Hdl	SFT	£3605

Total win prize-money £7817

Going: Sf: 1-1 GS: 1-1 Gd: 0-1 GF: - Fm: 0-0
Distance: **2m/2m3: 2-3** 2m4-2m7: 0-0 3m+: 0-0
Track: LH: 1-1 RH: 1-2 Tight: 0-0 Gall: 0-0
Aids: Bl: 0-0 Vi: 0-0 Tstrap: 0-0
Best Rating: 97 11/01 Sand 2m110y gd-sft Hdl

Made a winning hurdling debut at Haydock in November and followed up at Sandown 48 hours later, but her penalties will be a major obstacle from now on. Suited by two miles on soft ground.

The Fear Of God (IRE)

98f **103f**

5-y-o b g Supreme Leader-Angel's Dream (King's Ride)
J G Fitzgerald R Burridge, H Burridge, J H W Lloyd

Placings:*4-4* **(1892)**
2001/02: 16^{4}G

	Starts	1st	2nd	3rd	Win & Pl
NH Flat	1	0	0	0	304
Career Total	**2**	**0**	**0**	**0**	**304**

Going: Sf: 0-0 GS: 0-0 Gd: 0-1 GF: - Fm: 0-0
Distance: 2m/2m3: 0-1 2m4-2m7: 0-0 3m+: 0-0
Track: LH: 0-1 RH: 0-0 Tight: 0-0 Gall: 0-0
Aids: Bl: 0-0 Vi: 0-0 Tstrap: 0-0
Best Rating: 103 10/01 Chel 2m110y good NHF

The Fenman

89 **82**

4-y-o b g Mazaad-Dalgorian (IRE) (Lancastrian)
C N Kellett D H & Mrs R E Muir

Placings:*000* **(4552)**
2001/02: 16^{0}GS, 17^{0}GS, 16^{0}GF

	Starts	1st	2nd	3rd	Win & Pl
NH Flat	3	0	0	0	
Career Total	**3**	**0**	**0**	**0**	

Going: Sf: 0-0 GS: 0-2 Gd: 0-0 GF: - Fm: 0-1
Distance: 2m/2m3: 0-3 2m4-2m7: 0-0 3m+: 0-0
Track: LH: 0-1 RH: 0-2 Tight: 0-2 Gall: 0-1
Aids: Bl: 0-0 Vi: 0-0 Tstrap: 0-0
Best Rating: 72 4/02 Hntg 2m110y gd-fm NHF

Has yet to show much over hurdles.

The Flyer (IRE)

110 **101**

5-y-o b g Blues Traveller (IRE)-National Ballet (Shareef Dancer (USA))
Miss S J Wilton John Pointon And Sons

Placings:1314-0301201320 **(4593)**
2001/02: 17^{0}G, 16^{3}S, 16^{0}S, 17^{1}G, 20^{2}G, 20^{0}S, 17^{1}HY, 16^{3}S, 18^{2}S, 16^{0}G

	Starts	1st	2nd	3rd	Win & Pl
Hurdles	10	2	2	2	9410
Career Total	**14**	**4**	**2**	**3**	**13641**

101	2/02	Hrfd	2m1f	D(0-115)HHdl	HVY	£3381
101	12/01	Hrfd	2m1f	E(0-115)HHdl	GD	£2968
97	11/00	Uttx	2m	E Hdl	HVY	£2303
97	9/00	MRas	2m1f110y	G Hdl	G-F	£1561

Total win prize-money £10213

Going: Sf: 1-6 GS: 0-0 Gd: 1-4 GF: - Fm: 0-0
Distance: **2m/2m3: 2-8** 2m4-2m7: 0-2 3m+: 0-0
Track: LH: 0-7 **RH: 2-3** Tight: 0-3 Gall: 0-2
Aids: Bl: 0-0 Vi: 0-0 Tstrap: 0-0
Best Rating: 101 3/02 Font 2m2f110y soft Hdl

Fair handicap hurdler, stays two and a half miles, twice a winner at Hereford in 2001/2.

The French Furze (IRE)

118 **153**

8-y-o ch g Be My Guest (USA)-Exciting (Mill Reef (USA))
N G Richards Jim Ennis

Placings:1261131PP/P2060/2110P/222065-2222304 **(4837)**
2001/02: 16^{2}G, 16^{2}GS, 16^{2}GS, 16^{2}S, 16^{3}HY, 20^{0}G, 16^{4}G

	Starts	1st	2nd	3rd	Win & Pl
Hurdles	7	0	4	1	39966
Career Total	**32**	**6**	**10**	**2**	**103126**

146	1/00	Chel	2m1f	B(0-145)HHdl	G-S	£10140
141	1/00	Hayd	2m	B(0-145)HHdl	SFT	£6652
134	2/98	Hntg	2m110y	C Hdl	GD	£4202
137	11/97	Chel	2m110y	B Hdl	GD	£5121
135	11/97	Plum	2m1f	E Hdl	G-F	£2385
96	8/97	Tram	2m	Hdl	GD	£2712

Total win prize-money £31214

Going: Sf: 0-2 GS: 0-2 Gd: 0-3 GF: - Fm: 0-0
Distance: 2m/2m3: 0-6 2m4-2m7: 0-1 3m+: 0-0
Track: LH: 0-7 RH: 0-0 Tight: 0-1 Gall: 0-2
Aids: Bl: 0-0 Vi: 0-0 Tstrap: 0-0
Best Rating: 153 1/02 Leop 2m heavy Hdl

Smart handicap hurdler at two miles over the years. Ran some fine races in defeat in the 2001/02 season when chasing home the likes of Landing Light in the Fighting Fifth and Valiramix in the Bula Hurdle. Suited by soft ground and likes to front run. Two miles is his trip.

The Frisky Farmer

84 **55**

9-y-o b g Emarati (USA)-Farceuse (Comedy Star (USA))
Ian Williams The Four Musketeers

Placings:6P **(1146)**
2001/02: 16^{6}GF, 16^{P}GF

	Starts	1st	2nd	3rd	Win & Pl
Hurdles	2	0	0	0	0
Career Total	**2**	**0**	**0**	**0**	**0**

Going: Sf: 0-0 GS: 0-0 Gd: 0-0 GF: - Fm: 0-2
Distance: 2m/2m3: 0-2 2m4-2m7: 0-0 3m+: 0-0
Track: LH: 0-2 RH: 0-0 Tight: 0-2 Gall: 0-0
Aids: Bl: 0-0 Vi: 0-0 Tstrap: 0-0
Best Rating: 55 8/01 Strf 2m110y gd-fm Hdl

The Fuelologist

7-y-o b g Skyliner-Munequita (Marching On)
L Lungo Dennis Hutchinson

Placings:F **(0545)**
2001/02: 16^{F}GF

	Starts	1st	2nd	3rd	Win & Pl

	Starts	1st	2nd	3rd	Win & Pl
Hurdles	1	0	0	0	
Career Total	1	0	0	0	

Going: Sf: 0-0 GS: 0-0 Gd: 0-0 GF: - Fm: 0-1
Distance: 2m/2m3: 0-1 2m4-2m7: 0-0 3m+: 0-0
Track: LH: 0-1 RH: 0-0 Tight: 0-0 Gall: 0-1
Aids: Bl: 0-0 Vi: 0-0 Tstrap: 0-0
Best Rating:

The Funky Monkey (IRE)

85f 68f

6-y-o gr g Roselier (FR)-Rumups Debut (IRE) (Good Thyne (USA))
A Parker Mr & Mrs Raymond Anderson Green

Placings:00 **(4860)**
2001/02: 16^{0}G, 16^{0}G

	Starts	1st	2nd	3rd	Win & Pl
NH Flat	2	0	0	0	
Career Total	2	0	0	0	

Going: Sf: 0-0 GS: 0-0 Gd: 0-2 GF: - Fm: 0-0
Distance: 2m/2m3: 0-2 2m4-2m7: 0-0 3m+: 0-0
Track: LH: 0-1 RH: 0-0 Tight: 0-1 Gall: 0-0
Aids: Bl: 0-0 Vi: 0-0 Tstrap: 0-0
Best Rating: 68 4/02 Hexm 2m110y good NHF

The Gadfly

10-y-o br g Welsh Captain-Spartan Imp (Spartan General)
G Lavis D L Evans

Placings:0/04050/P/6 **(0563)**
2001/02: 26^{6}GF

	Starts	1st	2nd	3rd	Win & Pl
Chases	1	0	0	0	0
Career Total	8	0	0	0	0

Going: Sf: 0-0 GS: 0-0 Gd: 0-0 GF: - Fm: 0-1
Distance: 2m/2m3: 0-0 2m4-2m7: 0-0 3m+: 0-1
Track: LH: 0-1 RH: 0-0 Tight: 0-1 Gall: 0-0
Aids: Bl: 0-0 Vi: 0-0 Tstrap: 0-0
Best Rating:

The Gambling Lady

6-y-o b/br m General Gambul-Coach Rd Express (Pony Express)
C Tizzard G F Gingell

Placings:P **(3384)**
2001/02: 16^{P}GS

	Starts	1st	2nd	3rd	Win & Pl
Hurdles	1	0	0	0	
Career Total	1	0	0	0	

Going: Sf: 0-0 GS: 0-1 Gd: 0-0 GF: - Fm: 0-0
Distance: 2m/2m3: 0-1 2m4-2m7: 0-0 3m+: 0-0
Track: LH: 0-0 RH: 0-1 Tight: 0-0 Gall: 0-0
Aids: Bl: 0-0 Vi: 0-0 Tstrap: 0-0
Best Rating:

The Gamboller (USA)

102 100

7-y-o b g Irish Tower (USA)-Lady Limbo (USA) (Dance Spell (USA))
M E Sowersby The Wolds Partnership

Placings:6P1/0433131P45/03-0042P **(1069)**
2001/02: 19^{0}GF, 19^{0}GF, 21^{4}GF, 21^{2}GF, 27^{P}GF

	Starts	1st	2nd	3rd	Win & Pl
Hurdles	5	0	1	0	936
Career Total	20	3	1	4	10509

107	10/99	Sedg	2m5f110y	D(0-125)HHdl	G-F	£3226
108	9/99	Sedg	2m5f110y	D(0-120)HHdl	G-F	£2856
88	4/99	Sedg	2m1f	E Hdl	FRM	£2022

Total win prize-money £8106

Going: Sf: 0-0 GS: 0-0 Gd: 0-0 GF: - Fm: 0-5
Distance: 2m/2m3: 0-0 2m4-2m7: 0-4 3m+: 0-1
Track: LH: 0-3 RH: 0-2 Tight: 0-5 Gall: 0-0
Aids: Bl: 0-0 Vi: 0-0 Tstrap: 0-0
Best Rating: 108 9/99 Sedg 2m5f110y gd-fm Hdl

The Gatherer (IRE)

116 145

8-y-o b g Be My Native (USA)-Reaper's Run (Deep Run)
A L T Moore J P McManus

Placings:332/5120/145-42F1620 **(4674)**
2001/02: 16^{4}G, 16^{2}GY, 20^{F}G, 16^{1}YS, 16^{6}S, 17^{2}G, 16^{0}G

	Starts	1st	2nd	3rd	Win & Pl
Hurdles	7	1	2	0	41288
Career Total	17	3	4	2	68359

142	1/02	Leop	2m	Hdl	Y-S	£7975
139	10/00	Gowr	2m	(0-135)HHdl	SFT	£10400
103	2/00	Punc	2m	Hdl	Y-S	£4140

Total win prize-money £22515

Going: Sf: 0-1 GS: 0-0 Gd: 0-4 GF: - Fm: 0-0
Distance: **2m/2m3: 1-6** 2m4-2m7: 0-1 3m+: 0-0
Track: **LH: 1-4** RH: 0-0 Tight: 0-1 Gall: 0-2
Aids: Bl: 0-0 Vi: 0-0 Tstrap: 0-0
Best Rating: 145 3/02 Chel 2m1f good Hdl

Irish handicap hurdler, runner-up in the County Hurdle at Cheltenham in 2002. Usually held up, he is best at two miles and acts on soft ground.

The Gene Genie

105 104

7-y-o b g Syrtos-Sally Maxwell (Roscoe Blake)
R J Hodges K Small

Placings:32506/13230-21232243P **(4389)**
2001/02: 16^{2}S, 16^{1}G, 17^{2}G, 22^{3}GS, 18^{2}HY, 19^{2}S, 16^{4}G, 16^{3}GS, 16^{P}S

	Starts	1st	2nd	3rd	Win & Pl
Hurdles	9	1	4	2	10904
Career Total	19	2	6	5	15229

103	12/01	Winc	2m	D(0-120)HHdl	GD	£5213
91	12/00	Hrfd	2m1f	G Hdl	HVY	£2023

Total win prize-money £7236

Going: Sf: 0-4 GS: 0-2 Gd: 1-3 GF: - Fm: 0-0
Distance: **2m/2m3: 1-7** 2m4-2m7: 0-2 3m+: 0-0
Track: LH: 0-2 **RH: 1-7** Tight: 0-2 Gall: 0-0
Aids: Bl: 0-0 Vi: 0-2 Tstrap: 0-0
Best Rating: 113 1/01 Tntn 2m1f soft Hdl

A consistent handicap hurdler, acts on good ground or softer and is best at around two miles.

The Gopher (IRE)

102 113

13-y-o ch g General View-Egg Shells (Miami Springs)
D J Wintle John W Egan Philip Banks Mrs B Grainger

Placings:*50*/0006*00*215/**B103P341P/031U22414/11B31S33/44122160F/3332F240PP-40641F** **(1489)**
2001/02: 28^{4}GF, 24^{0}GF, 23^{6}G, 21^{4}GF, 19^{1}GF, 24^{F}GF

	Starts	1st	2nd	3rd	Win & Pl
Chases	6	1	0	0	4847
Career Total	62	11	7	9	75709

113	9/01	Hrfd	2m3f	F(0-110)HCh	G-F	£4056
145	8/99	Sthl	3m110y	D(0-125)HCh	G-F	£4513
138	6/99	MRas	2m4f	C(0-135)HCh	GD	£7035
135	8/98	Worc	2m7f110y	D(0-125)HCh	G-F	£3685
130	6/98	MRas	3m1f	D(0-120)HCh	GD	£4648
124	5/98	Uttx	3m2f	C(0-130)HCh	G-F	£4947
116	11/97	Wwck	3m2f	C(0-135)HCh	GD	£5014
108	9/97	NAbb	3m2f110y	D(0-120)HCh	SFT	£3338
108	4/97	Fair	2m6f110y	(0-109)HCh	G-F	£4069
108	9/96	List	2m6f	Ch	GD	£4237
104	4/95	Baln	3m	Hdl	YLD	£2204

Total win prize-money £47749

Going: Sf: 0-0 GS: 0-0 Gd: 0-1 GF: - Fm: 1-5
Distance: **2m/2m3: 1-1** 2m4-2m7: 0-1 3m+: 0-4
Track: LH: 0-4 **RH: 1-2** Tight: 0-2 Gall: 0-1
Aids: **Bl: 1-6** Vi: 0-0 Tstrap: 0-0
Best Rating: 145 8/99 Sthl 3m110y gd-fm Ch

He is consistent but slow. Has won over trips of around two and a half miles, but looks better suited by further.

The Granby (IRE)

105 145

8-y-o b g Insan (USA)-Elteetee (Paddy's Stream)
Mrs M Reveley Revival Racing Ltd

Placings:4063/2F11111/3311U **(4582)**
2001/02: 17^{3}GF, 19^{3}G, 24^{1}G, 24^{1}S, 25^{U}G

	Starts	1st	2nd	3rd	Win & Pl
Chases	5	2	0	2	9194
Career Total	16	7	1	3	27307

145	2/02	Donc	3m	E Ch	SFT	£3354
127	12/01	Muss	3m	D Ch	GD	£4231
135	4/00	Ayr	2m4f	C Hdl	GD	£5572
135	1/00	Donc	2m4f	D Hdl	G-F	£3493
124	1/00	Catt	2m	E Hdl	GD	£2835
127	12/99	Catt	2m3f	E Hdl	G-F	£1940
112	10/99	Sedg	2m1f	D Hdl	GD	£3168

Total win prize-money £24595

Going: Sf: 1-1 GS: 0-0 Gd: 1-3 GF: - Fm: 0-1
Distance: 2m/2m3: 0-1 2m4-2m7: 0-1 **3m+: 2-3**
Track: LH: 1-3 RH: 1-2 Tight: 1-2 Gall: 1-2
Aids: Bl: 0-0 Vi: 0-0 Tstrap: 0-0
Best Rating: 145 2/02 Donc 3m soft Ch

Won a string of ordinary novice hurdles in the 1999/2000 season but was absent the following campaign. Had shown decent form over fences before winning at Musselburgh in December 2001 and came out to win two months later at Doncaster. Stays three miles. Did most of his winning over hurdles on a sound surface but has won both chase starts on good to soft/soft ground.

The Grandson (IRE)

52 14

7-y-o b g Husyan (USA)-Tarary (Boreen (FR))
Simon T Lewis Simon T Lewis

Placings:P0P (4726)
2001/02: 20^{P}HY, 17^{0}GS, 20^{P}GF

	Starts	1st	2nd	3rd	Win & Pl
Hurdles	3	0	0	0	
Career Total	**3**	**0**	**0**	**0**	

Going: Sf: 0-1 GS: 0-1 Gd: 0-0 GF: - Fm: 0-1
Distance: 2m/2m3: 0-1 2m4-2m7: 0-2 3m+: 0-0
Track: LH: 0-2 RH: 0-1 Tight: 0-2 Gall: 0-0
Aids: Bl: 0-0 Vi: 0-0 Tstrap: 0-0
Best Rating: 17 4/02 Tntn 2m1f gd-sft Hdl

The Great O'Malley (IRE)

6-y-o br m Mandalus-Another Miller (Gala Performance (USA))
Miss Venetia Williams Austin O'Malley

Placings:*6*-P (2358)
2001/02: 21^{P}S

	Starts	1st	2nd	3rd	Win & Pl
Hurdles	1	0	0	0	
Career Total	**2**	**0**	**0**	**0**	**0**

Going: Sf: 0-1 GS: 0-0 Gd: 0-0 GF: - Fm: 0-0
Distance: 2m/2m3: 0-0 2m4-2m7: 0-1 3m+: 0-0
Track: LH: 0-0 RH: 0-1 Tight: 0-0 Gall: 0-0
Aids: Bl: 0-0 Vi: 0-0 Tstrap: 0-0
Best Rating:

The Greenkeeper (IRE)

9-y-o b g Beau Sher-Hurricane Hattie (Strong Gale)
C Tizzard Mrs N G Smyth

Placings:P/P6 (4656)
2001/02: 19^{P}G, 19^{6}GS

	Starts	1st	2nd	3rd	Win & Pl
Chases	2	0	0	0	0
Career Total	**3**	**0**	**0**	**0**	**0**

Going: Sf: 0-0 GS: 0-1 Gd: 0-1 GF: - Fm: 0-0
Distance: 2m/2m3: 0-1 2m4-2m7: 0-1 3m+: 0-0
Track: LH: 0-0 RH: 0-2 Tight: 0-1 Gall: 0-0
Aids: Bl: 0-0 Vi: 0-0 Tstrap: 0-0
Best Rating:

The Grey Dyer (IRE)

108(108h) (120h)119
8-y-o gr g Roselier (FR)-Tawny Kate (IRE) (Crash Course)
L Lungo Ashleybank Investments Limited

Placings:05/52/421-UF132 (3279)
2001/02: 24^{U}S, 20^{F}S, 20^{1}G, 16^{3}S, 26^{2}HY

	Starts	1st	2nd	3rd	Win & Pl
Hurdles	2	1	0	0	2478
Chases	3	0	1	1	1988
Career Total	**12**	**2**	**3**	**1**	**8804**

109 11/01 Weth 2m4f110y F(0-110)HHdl GD £2478
105 4/01 Prth 2m4f110y D Hdl HVY £2828
Total win prize-money £5306

Going: Sf: 0-4 GS: 0-0 Gd: 1-1 GF: - Fm: 0-0
Distance: 2m/2m3: 0-1 **2m4-2m7: 1-2** 3m+: 0-2
Track: **LH: 1-3** RH: 0-2 Tight: 0-0 Gall: 0-0
Aids: Bl: 0-0 Vi: 0-0 Tstrap: 0-0
Best Rating: 122 12/01 Hexm 2m110y soft Ch

Lightly-raced hurdler/chaser, jumped well prior to exiting on chasing debut, and received a confidence booster when successful back over timber before further good efforts back over fences.

The Hazel Harrier (IRE)

78 48
9-y-o ch g Denel (FR)-Golden Echo (Golden Love)
A J Lockwood A J Lockwood

Placings:*04*/P0-55P60P (1419)
2001/02: 20^{5}F, 20^{5}GF, 21^{P}GF, 24^{6}GF, 21^{0}GF, 21^{P}G

	Starts	1st	2nd	3rd	Win & Pl
Hurdles	6	0	0	0	0
Career Total	**10**	**0**	**0**	**0**	**0**

Going: Sf: 0-0 GS: 0-0 Gd: 0-1 GF: - Fm: 0-5
Distance: 2m/2m3: 0-0 2m4-2m7: 0-5 3m+: 0-1
Track: LH: 0-5 RH: 0-1 Tight: 0-5 Gall: 0-0
Aids: Bl: 0-0 Vi: 0-0 Tstrap: 0-0
Best Rating: 82 6/99 Sthl 2m gd-fm NHF

The Hearty Joker (IRE)

93(80h) 98
7-y-o b g Broken Hearted-Furryway (Furry Glen)
B G Powell Mrs Marygold O'Kelly

Placings:P0-P6P42 (4734)
2001/02: 24^{P}G, 25^{6}G, 21^{P}S, 20^{4}GF, 19^{2}F

	Starts	1st	2nd	3rd	Win & Pl
Hurdles	1	0	0	0	0
Chases	4	0	1	0	1422
Career Total	**7**	**0**	**1**	**0**	**1422**

Going: Sf: 0-1 GS: 0-0 Gd: 0-2 GF: - Fm: 0-2
Distance: 2m/2m3: 0-0 2m4-2m7: 0-3 3m+: 0-2
Track: LH: 0-1 RH: 0-4 Tight: 0-2 Gall: 0-1
Aids: Bl: 0-0 Vi: 0-0 Tstrap: 0-0
Best Rating: 98 4/02 Hntg 2m4f110y gd-fm Ch

Modest, lightly-raced chaser, suited by two and a half miles and a sound surface.

The Hen Hut

114
8-y-o b g Henbit (USA)-Caithness Dawn (Deep Run)
Eugene M O'Sullivan (A Crook 18/5) Eugene M O'Sullivan

Placings:*35520130*/4F-F044 (4934a)
2001/02: 20^{F}G, 16^{0}YS, 20^{4}GF, 24^{4}YS

	Starts	1st	2nd	3rd	Win & Pl
Chases	4	0	0	0	748
Career Total	**14**	**1**	**1**	**2**	**5133**

90 3/00 Thur 2m Hdl SFT £2760
Total win prize-money £2760

Going: Sf: 0-0 GS: 0-0 Gd: 0-1 GF: - Fm: 0-1
Distance: 2m/2m3: 0-1 2m4-2m7: 0-2 3m+: 0-1
Track: LH: 0-2 RH: 0-0 Tight: 0-1 Gall: 0-0
Aids: Bl: 0-0 Vi: 0-0 Tstrap: 0-0
Best Rating: 125 10/00 Hntg 2m110y gd-fm Ch

The Hobbit (IRE)

9-y-o ch g Mister Lord (USA)-Sustentation (The Parson)
P F Nicholls Mrs Susan Humphreys

Placings:322-4P (0427)
2001/02: 26^{4}GF, 33^{P}G

	Starts	1st	2nd	3rd	Win & Pl
Chases	2	0	0	0	246
Career Total	**5**	**0**	**2**	**1**	**1969**

Going: Sf: 0-0 GS: 0-0 Gd: 0-1 GF: - Fm: 0-1
Distance: 2m/2m3: 0-0 2m4-2m7: 0-0 3m+: 0-2
Track: LH: 0-0 RH: 0-0 Tight: 0-1 Gall: 0-0
Aids: Bl: 0-0 Vi: 0-0 Tstrap: 0-0
Best Rating: 121 3/01 Asct 3m110y soft Ch

The Indispensable (IRE)

103 108
6-y-o ch g College Chapel-Fanellan (Try My Best (USA))
J J O'Neill (C Roche 12/1) J P McManus

Placings:00/246-4050 (4147)
2001/02: 16^{4}YS, 16^{0}HY, 21^{5}G, 16^{0}GS

	Starts	1st	2nd	3rd	Win & Pl
Hurdles	4	0	0	0	270
Career Total	**9**	**0**	**1**	**0**	**2278**

Going: Sf: 0-1 GS: 0-1 Gd: 0-1 GF: - Fm: 0-0
Distance: 2m/2m3: 0-3 2m4-2m7: 0-1 3m+: 0-0
Track: LH: 0-2 RH: 0-2 Tight: 0-0 Gall: 0-0
Aids: Bl: 0-0 Vi: 0-0 Tstrap: 0-0
Best Rating: 108 2/02 Ludl 2m5f good Hdl

Placed over hurdles in Ireland, but has not shone so far in this country.

The Jam Saheb

84 65
5-y-o b g Petong-Reem El Fala (FR) (Fabulous Dancer (USA))
N J Hawke N J Hawke

Placings:05-PP0U0 (2657)
2001/02: 16^{P}GF, 16^{P}GF, 19^{0}F, 17^{U}GF, 19^{0}GS

	Starts	1st	2nd	3rd	Win & Pl
Hurdles	5	0	0	0	
Career Total	**7**	**0**	**0**	**0**	**0**

Going: Sf: 0-0 GS: 0-1 Gd: 0-0 GF: - Fm: 0-4
Distance: 2m/2m3: 0-3 2m4-2m7: 0-2 3m+: 0-0
Track: LH: 0-1 RH: 0-4 Tight: 0-2 Gall: 0-0
Aids: Bl: 0-0 Vi: 0-0 Tstrap: 0-0
Best Rating: 65 11/01 Extr 2m1f gd-fm Hdl

The Kerry Rebel (IRE)

85(91h) (66h)62
9-y-o b g Gallant Knight-Symphony Orchestra (Orchestra)
C G Cox Mrs Rhona Alexander

Placings:P/*P0000/0/0/00*P-0 (0073)
2001/02: 19^{0}G

	Starts	1st	2nd	3rd	Win & Pl

	Starts	1st	2nd	3rd	Win & Pl
Hurdles	1	0	0	0	[illegible]
Career Total	**12**	**0**	**0**	**0**	[illegible]

Going: Sf: 0-0 GS: 0-0 Gd: 0-1 GF: - Fm: 0-0
Distance: 2m/2m3: 0-1 2m4-2m7: 0-0 3m+: 0-0
Track: LH: 0-0 RH: 0-1 Tight: 0-0 Gall: 0-0
Aids: Bl: 0-0 Vi: 0-0 Tstrap: 0-0
Best Rating: 72 5/97 Gowr 2m good NHF

The King's Doctor (IRE)

74 **88**

8-y-o gr g Glacial Storm (USA)-Grandpa's River (Over The River (FR))
J D Frost (R G Frost 24/1) C Johnston

Placings:*300/12024*U203B4-060 **(4011)**
2001/02: 22^{0}GF, 21^{6}HY, 21^{0}S

	Starts	1st	2nd	3rd	Win & Pl
Hurdles	3	0	0	0	0
Career Total	**17**	**1**	**3**	**2**	**4260**

Going: Sf: 0-2 GS: 0-0 Gd: 0-0 GF: - Fm: 0-1
Distance: 2m/2m3: 0-0 2m4-2m7: 0-3 3m+: 0-0
Track: LH: 0-1 RH: 0-0 Tight: 0-0 Gall: 0-1
Aids: Bl: 0-0 Vi: 0-0 Tstrap: 0-0
Best Rating: 114 9/00 DRoy 2m4f good Hdl

The Lady Scores (IRE)

102(109h) (103h)**113**

10-y-o br m Orchestra-Lysanders Lady (Saulingo)
S Dow Tony And Dee Lousada

Placings:004F004/0030P**53103043/131F1P36P6/3P1325P13424-3P3** **(1656)**
2001/02: 24^{3}GF, 28^{P}GF, 24^{3}G

	Starts	1st	2nd	3rd	Win & Pl
Chases	3	0	0	2	2190
Career Total	**45**	**6**	**2**	**11**	**34998**

100	1/01	Leic	2m4f110y	F(0-110)HHdl	HVY	£5999
103	9/00	Uttx	3m2f	E(0-115)HCh	G-S	£5148
117	12/99	Plum	3m2f	D(0-120)HCh	SFT	£3740
110	11/99	Hntg	3m	F(0-110)HCh	G-F	£3155
98	10/99	Fknm	2m5f110y	F(0-100)HCh	GD	£3323
97	12/98	Ling	2m	F(0-95)HCh	SFT	£2288

Total win prize-money £23656

Going: Sf: 0-0 GS: 0-0 Gd: 0-1 GF: - Fm: 0-2
Distance: 2m/2m3: 0-0 2m4-2m7: 0-0 3m+: 0-3
Track: LH: 0-3 RH: 0-0 Tight: 0-3 Gall: 0-0
Aids: Bl: 0-0 Vi: 0-0 Tstrap: 0-0
Best Rating: 117 11/00 Hntg 3m6f110y gd-sft Ch

Fair chaser, stays well and has won on fast ground, but particularly likes soft ground.

The Laird's Entry (IRE)

105 **111**

7-y-o b g King's Ride-Balancing Act (Balinger)
L Lungo Ashleybank Investments Limited

Placings:3315 **(4141)**
2001/02: 17^{3}S, 20^{3}GS, 19^{1}S, 24^{5}HY

	Starts	1st	2nd	3rd	Win & Pl
NH Flat	1	0	0	1	230
Hurdles	3	1	0	1	3836
Career Total	**4**	**1**	**0**	**2**	**4066**

111	1/02	Catt	2m3f	D Hdl	SFT	£3360

Total win prize-money £3360

Going: Sf: 1-3 GS: 0-1 Gd: 0-0 GF: - Fm: 0-0
Distance: **2m/2m3: 1-2** 2m4-2m7: 0-1 3m+: 0-1
Track: **LH: 1-3** RH: 0-1 **Tight: 1-1** Gall: 0-1
Aids: Bl: 0-0 Vi: 0-0 Tstrap: 0-0
Best Rating: 111 1/02 Catt 2m3f soft Hdl

A lovely big chasing type from the family of Granville Again and Morley Street, he got off the mark on his second start over hurdles at Catterick in February 2002. Highly regarded, he is suited by two and a half miles and give in the ground.

The Lambton Worm

(97h) (88h)

8-y-o b g Superpower-Springwell (Miami Springs)
G F Edwards G F Edwards

Placings:054035/00/4050-500 **(0922)**
2001/02: 16^{5}GF, 17^{0}G, 17^{0}GF

	Starts	1st	2nd	3rd	Win & Pl
Hurdles	3	0	0	0	0
Career Total	**15**	**0**	**0**	**1**	**395**

Going: Sf: 0-0 GS: 0-0 Gd: 0-1 GF: - Fm: 0-2
Distance: 2m/2m3: 0-3 2m4-2m7: 0-0 3m+: 0-0
Track: LH: 0-3 RH: 0-0 Tight: 0-3 Gall: 0-0
Aids: Bl: 0-0 Vi: 0-0 Tstrap: 0-0
Best Rating: 93 1/99 Catt 2m soft Hdl

The Land Agent

105 **123**

11-y-o b g Town And Country-Notinhand (Nearly A Hand)
J W Mullins D I Bare

Placings:*31/20/53424311*/PP431224U5/U2441453/2U4P-56F004 **(4851)**
2001/02: 24^{5}GS, 20^{6}GS, 24^{F}G, 24^{0}G, 24^{0}GS, 20^{4}G

	Starts	1st	2nd	3rd	Win & Pl
Hurdles	1	0	0	0	0
Chases	5	0	0	0	548
Career Total	**40**	**5**	**6**	**5**	**89594**

155	2/00	Winc	2m5f	B Ch	G-S	£10432
150	1/99	Winc	2m5f	B Ch	G-S	£10162
141	4/98	Sand	2m4f110y	C HCh	G-S	£14975
141	4/98	Asct	2m3f110y	C Ch	G-S	£5924
124	4/96	NAbb	2m1f	H NHF	SFT	£1509

Total win prize-money £43004

Going: Sf: 0-0 GS: 0-3 Gd: 0-3 GF: - Fm: 0-0
Distance: 2m/2m3: 0-0 2m4-2m7: 0-2 3m+: 0-4
Track: LH: 0-3 RH: 0-3 Tight: 0-2 Gall: 0-1
Aids: Bl: 0-0 Vi: 0-0 Tstrap: 0-0
Best Rating: 155 2/00 Winc 2m5f gd-sft Ch

A formerly useful chaser but now at the veteran stage and on the downgrade. He goes especially well at Wincanton, and is generally best on a right-handed track. He looks suited by two and a half miles with give in the ground.

The Last Fling (IRE)

111 **150**

12-y-o ch g Avocat-Highway's Last (Royal Highway)
Mrs S J Smith Trevor Hemmings

Placings:11121150/**11U13F3U2/2FUF05/13F2P40U0/4U14211P0/46U0U0U-1U2P10F** **(4677)**
2001/02: 25^{1}G, 27^{U}S, 28^{2}S, 25^{P}GS, 26^{1}S, 26^{0}GS, 36^{F}G

	Starts	1st	2nd	3rd	Win & Pl
Chases	7	2	1	0	57561
Career Total	**55**	**14**	**6**	**3**	**247644**

150	1/02	Wwck	3m2f	B HCh	SFT	£43407
148	10/01	MRas	3m1f	C(0-130)HCh	GD	£10218
172	2/00	Hayd	3m4f110y	A HCh	SFT	£59500
158	1/00	Hayd	3m	A HCh	SFT	£25500
160	11/99	Hayd	3m	A HCh	GD	£25000
147	10/98	Weth	3m1f	B(0-140)HCh	SFT	£7249
132	12/96	Weth	2m4f110y	B(0-145)HCh	G-S	£6742
126	11/96	Weth	3m1f	C Ch	GD	£4523
116	10/96	Bang	2m4f110y	D Ch	G-F	£3663
124	1/96	Newc	3m	D(0-120)HHdl	GD	£2970
123	11/95	Hayd	2m6f	B HHdl	GD	£5083
107	10/95	Kels	2m6f110y	D Hdl	G-F	£2931
104	9/95	Chep	2m4f110y	F(0-100)HHdl	GD	£3601
92	9/95	Bang	2m1f	D Hdl	GD	£2612

Total win prize-money £203004

Going: Sf: 1-3 GS: 0-2 Gd: 1-2 GF: - Fm: 0-0
Distance: 2m/2m3: 0-0 2m4-2m7: 0-0 **3m+: 2-7**
Track: LH: 1-6 RH: 1-1 **Tight: 1-3** Gall: 0-1
Aids: Bl: 0-0 Vi: 0-0 Tstrap: 0-0
Best Rating: 172 2/00 Hayd 3m4f110y soft Ch

Adopting front-running tactics seemed to concentrate his mind in the 1999/2000 season as he ran up a hat-trick of victories in top-class staying chases at Haydock, but was not in anything like the same form the following season. Suited by soft ground, he took advantage of a lenient mark to win a valuable handicap at Warwick in January 2002. Stays three miles plus. Suited by soft ground. Met an untimely end in the Grand National after making much of the running. (DEAD)

The Leader

106 **115**

9-y-o b g Ardross-Leading Line (Leading Man)
P R Chamings Inhurst Farm Stables Partnership

Placings:546P/**31U644/2541355-P2P441200** **(4268)**
2001/02: 19^{P}GS, 16^{2}G, 16^{P}S, 19^{4}G, 16^{4}GS, 16^{1}S, 16^{2}HY, 16^{0}S, 16^{0}S

	Starts	1st	2nd	3rd	Win & Pl
Chases	9	1	2	0	5460
Career Total	**26**	**3**	**3**	**2**	**13286**

115	1/02	Folk	2m	F(0-100)HCh	SFT	£3250
115	1/01	Folk	2m	F(0-100)HCh	HVY	£2478
112	1/00	Folk	2m	E Ch	SFT	£2866

Total win prize-money £8596

Going: Sf: 1-5 GS: 0-2 Gd: 0-2 GF: - Fm: 0-0
Distance: **2m/2m3: 1-8** 2m4-2m7: 0-1 3m+: 0-0
Track: LH: 0-1 **RH: 1-8 Tight: 1-2** Gall: 0-2
Aids: Bl: 0-0 Vi: 0-0 Tstrap: 0-0
Best Rating: 115 1/02 Folk 2m soft Ch

He runs by far his best races at Folkestone and has gained all three of his wins there. Suited by two miles and soft ground.

The Lyme Volunteer (IRE)

86f **78f**

5-y-o b m Zaffaran (USA)-Dooley O'Brien (The Parson)
O Sherwood The Chamberlain Addiscott Partnership

Placings:6 **(4887)**
2001/02: 18^{6}GF

	Starts	1st	2nd	3rd	Win & Pl
NH Flat	1	0	0	0	0
Career Total	**1**	**0**	**0**	**0**	**0**

Going: Sf: 0-0 GS: 0-0 Gd: 0-0 GF: - Fm: 0-1

Distance: 2m/2m3: 0-1 2m4-2m7: 0-0 3m+: 0-0
Track: LH: 0-1 RH: 0-0 Tight: 0-1 Gall: 0-0
Aids: Bl: 0-0 Vi: 0-0 Tstrap: 0-0
Best Rating: 78 4/02 Font 2m2f110y gd-fm NHF

Modest form in bumpers.

The Major (NZ)

107 **143**

9-y-o ch g Try To Stop Me-Equation (NZ) (Palatable (USA))
Mrs M Reveley Sir Robert Ogden

Placings:232U1-444P11113 **(3675)**
2001/02: 16^{4}GF, 21^{4}GF, 20^{4}GF, 20^{P}S, 21^{1}GS, 24^{1}G, 20^{1}GS, 20^{1}GS, 20^{3}HY

	Starts	1st	2nd	3rd	Win & Pl
Chases	9	4	0	1	22733
Career Total	**14**	**5**	**2**	**2**	**30945**

143	12/01	Newc	2m4f	D(0-125)HCh	G-S	£4085
135	11/01	Ayr	2m4f	D(0-120)HCh	G-S	£4111
128	10/01	Bang	3m110y	D(0-120)HCh	GD	£6825
128	10/01	Uttx	2m5f	D(0-125)HCh	G-S	£4875
130	2/01	Uttx	2m	D(0-120)HCh	HVY	£5070

Total win prize-money £24966

Going: Sf: 0-2 GS: 3-3 Gd: 1-1 GF: - Fm: 0-3
Distance: 2m/2m3: 0-1 **2m4-2m7: 3-7** 3m+: 1-1
Track: **LH: 4-7** RH: 0-2 Tight: 1-4 Gall: 1-1
Aids: Bl: 0-0 Vi: 0-0 Tstrap: 0-0
Best Rating: 143 12/01 Newc 2m4f gd-sft Ch

Fair chaser, in good form in late 2001. He does not like fast ground or heavy, best on good/good to soft. Probably best at two and a half miles but stays three.

The Manse Brae (IRE)

103 **110**

6-y-o b g Roselier (FR)-Decent Preacher (Decent Fellow)
J M Jefferson Ashleybank Investments Limited

Placings:04411 **(4857)**
2001/02: 23^{0}S, 24^{4}HY, 24^{4}HY, 20^{1}GS, 20^{1}G

	Starts	1st	2nd	3rd	Win & Pl
Hurdles	5	2	0	0	7043
Career Total	**5**	**2**	**0**	**0**	**7043**

107	4/02	Hexm	2m4f110y	E Hdl	GD	£3276
110	3/02	Carl	2m4f	E(0-105)HHdl	G-S	£3486

Total win prize-money £6762

Going: Sf: 0-3 GS: 1-1 Gd: 1-1 GF: - Fm: 0-0
Distance: 2m/2m3: 0-0 **2m4-2m7: 2-3** 3m+: 0-2
Track: **LH: 1-4** RH: 0-0 Tight: 0-0 Gall: 0-0
Aids: Bl: 0-0 Vi: 0-0 Tstrap: 0-0
Best Rating: 110 3/02 Carl 2m4f gd-sft Hdl

Lightly-raced hurdler, stays two and a half miles and should get further. Won twice in the spring of 2002 and seems to appreciate good ground or slightly softer.

The Masareti Kid (IRE)

90f **104f**

5-y-o b g Commanche Run-Little Crack (IRE) (Lancastrian)
G A Swinbank Ward And Gartzon

Placings:*501* **(4771)**
2001/02: 17^{5}GS, 16^{0}HY, 16^{1}GF

	Starts	1st	2nd	3rd	Win & Pl
NH Flat	3	1	0	0	2443
Career Total	**3**	**1**	**0**	**0**	**2443**

104	4/02	Hexm	2m110y	H NHF	G-F	£2443

Total win prize-money £2443

Going: Sf: 0-1 GS: 0-1 Gd: 0-0 GF: - Fm: 1-1
Distance: **2m/2m3: 1-3** 2m4-2m7: 0-0 3m+: 0-0
Track: LH: 0-0 RH: 0-1 Tight: 0-1 Gall: 0-0
Aids: Bl: 0-0 Vi: 0-0 Tstrap: 0-0
Best Rating: 104 4/02 Hexm 2m110y gd-fm NHF

Bumper winner. Acts on a fast surface and is effective over two miles.

The Matrix (IRE)

107 **116**

6-y-o b g Toulon-Neasham (Nishapour (FR))
Miss H C Knight Ken Liscombe

Placings:*500*122PP **(4154)**
2001/02: 16^{5}G, 16^{0}G, 16^{0}G, 19^{1}S, 19^{2}G, 16^{2}GS, 17^{P}HY, 20^{P}GS

	Starts	1st	2nd	3rd	Win & Pl
NH Flat	2	0	0	0	0
Hurdles	6	1	2	0	4547
Career Total	**8**	**1**	**2**	**0**	**4547**

116	12/01	Hrfd	2m3f110y	E Hdl	SFT	£2670

Total win prize-money £2671

Going: Sf: 1-2 GS: 0-2 Gd: 0-4 GF: - Fm: 0-0
Distance: 2m/2m3: 0-6 **2m4-2m7: 1-2** 3m+: 0-0
Track: LH: 0-2 **RH: 1-6** Tight: 0-0 Gall: 0-3
Aids: Bl: 0-0 Vi: 0-0 Tstrap: 0-1
Best Rating: 116 12/01 Hrfd 2m3f110y soft Hdl

Not impressive when winning a Hereford novices' hurdle in December but useful placed form since. Acts on soft ground but might prefer a sounder surface. Has had breathing problems. Should stay two and a half miles.

The Merry Mason (IRE)

87 **76**

6-y-o b g Roselier (FR)-Busters Lodge (Antwerp City)
J M Jefferson Ashleybank Investments Limited

Placings:06P **(4063)**
2001/02: 20^{0}S, 24^{6}HY, 27^{P}S

	Starts	1st	2nd	3rd	Win & Pl
Hurdles	3	0	0	0	0
Career Total	**3**	**0**	**0**	**0**	**0**

Going: Sf: 0-3 GS: 0-0 Gd: 0-0 GF: - Fm: 0-0
Distance: 2m/2m3: 0-0 2m4-2m7: 0-1 3m+: 0-2
Track: LH: 0-3 RH: 0-0 Tight: 0-1 Gall: 0-0
Aids: Bl: 0-0 Vi: 0-0 Tstrap: 0-0
Best Rating: 76 12/01 Hayd 2m4f soft Hdl

The Monkey (IRE)

8-y-o ch g Long Pond-Carrig Lady (Menelek)
R Allan R Allan

Placings:*0504*/P/PP **(3507)**
2001/02: 20^{P}G, 20^{P}S

	Starts	1st	2nd	3rd	Win & Pl
Hurdles	2	0	0	0	
Career Total	**7**	**0**	**0**	**0**	**0**

Going: Sf: 0-1 GS: 0-0 Gd: 0-1 GF: - Fm: 0-0
Distance: 2m/2m3: 0-0 2m4-2m7: 0-2 3m+: 0-0
Track: LH: 0-0 RH: 0-2 Tight: 0-2 Gall: 0-0
Aids: Bl: 0-0 Vi: 0-1 Tstrap: 0-0
Best Rating: 78 3/99 Kels 2m6f110y good Hdl

The Murphy Meister (IRE)

6-y-o b/br g Cardinal Flower-Kilbrien Star (Goldhill)
E W Tuer G Tuer

Placings:*0* **(1593)**
2001/02: 17^{0}GS

	Starts	1st	2nd	3rd	Win & Pl
NH Flat	1	0	0	0	
Career Total	**1**	**0**	**0**	**0**	

Going: Sf: 0-0 GS: 0-1 Gd: 0-0 GF: - Fm: 0-0
Distance: 2m/2m3: 0-1 2m4-2m7: 0-0 3m+: 0-0
Track: LH: 0-1 RH: 0-0 Tight: 0-1 Gall: 0-0
Aids: Bl: 0-0 Vi: 0-0 Tstrap: 0-0
Best Rating:

The Names Bond

97 **87**

4-y-o b g Tragic Role (USA)-Artistic Licence (High Top)
Andrew Turnell Mrs Claire Hollowood

Placings:25322 **(1800)**
2001/02: 17^{2}G, 17^{5}G, 17^{3}G, 16^{2}G, 16^{2}GF

	Starts	1st	2nd	3rd	Win & Pl
Hurdles	5	0	3	1	2727
Career Total	**5**	**0**	**3**	**1**	**2727**

Going: Sf: 0-0 GS: 0-0 Gd: 0-4 GF: - Fm: 0-1
Distance: 2m/2m3: 0-5 2m4-2m7: 0-0 3m+: 0-0
Track: LH: 0-4 RH: 0-1 Tight: 0-4 Gall: 0-0
Aids: Bl: 0-0 Vi: 0-0 Tstrap: 0-0
Best Rating: 87 10/01 Ludl 2m gd-fm Hdl

Regularly in the frame in early-season juvenile hurdles.

The Negotiator

107(102h) (98h)**129**

8-y-o ch g Nebos (GER)-Baie Des Anges (Pas De Seul)
M A Barnes T A Barnes

Placings:444P/04422/123/4401331330-5213442213236 **(4836)**
2001/02: 16^{5}GF, 20^{2}F, 16^{1}F, 16^{3}GF, 16^{4}GF, 20^{4}GF, 17^{2}G, 17^{2}G, 16^{1}G, 16^{3}S, 16^{2}GS, 17^{3}GF, 20^{6}G

	Starts	1st	2nd	3rd	Win & Pl
Hurdles	1	0	0	0	0
Chases	12	2	4	3	19167
Career Total	**35**	**5**	**7**	**8**	**34756**

120	11/01	Ayr	2m	C(0-130)HCh	GD	£6045
110	6/01	Prth	2m	D Ch	FRM	£4186
102	10/00	Kels	2m110y	E(0-115)HHdl	G-S	£2737
103	8/00	Prth	2m110y	G Hdl	GD	£2717
100	5/99	Bang	2m4f	D(0-110)HHdl	GD	£3243

Total win prize-money £18928

Going: Sf: 0-1 GS: 0-1 Gd: 1-4 GF: - Fm: 1-7
Distance: **2m/2m3: 2-10** 2m4-2m7: 0-3 3m+: 0-0
Track: LH: 1-10 RH: 1-3 Tight: 0-5 Gall: 0-0
Aids: Bl: 0-0 Vi: 0-0 Tstrap: 0-0
Best Rating: 127 4/02 Kels 2m1f gd-fm Ch

Fair chaser at up to two and a half miles. Handles most types of ground.

The Nelson Touch

85 **86**

5-y-o b g Past Glories-Kellys Special (Netherkelly)

J W Mullins F G Matthews

Placings:04P6 **(4726)**

2001/02: 17^{0}GS, 27^{4}S, 19^{P}G, 20^{6}GF

	Starts	1st	2nd	3rd	Win & Pl
NH Flat	1	0	0	0	0
Hurdles	3	0	0	0	0
Career Total	**4**	**0**	**0**	**0**	**0**

Going: Sf: 0-1 GS: 0-1 Gd: 0-1 GF: - Fm: 0-1
Distance: 2m/2m3: 0-2 2m4-2m7: 0-1 3m+: 0-1
Track: LH: 0-1 RH: 0-2 Tight: 0-1 Gall: 0-0
Aids: Bl: 0-0 Vi: 0-0 Tstrap: 0-0
Best Rating: 86 4/02 Chep 2m4f gd-fm Hdl

The Newsman (IRE)

106 **111**

10-y-o b g Homo Sapien-Miller Fall'S (Stubbs Gazette)

Miss S Edwards Maurice E Pinto

Placings:041/405006/201/4343 **(4886)**

2001/02: 20^{4}S, 20^{3}GS, 20^{4}GF, 18^{3}GF

	Starts	1st	2nd	3rd	Win & Pl
Chases	4	0	0	2	1722
Career Total	**16**	**2**	**1**	**2**	**13092**

	4/00	Fntb	2m4f	Hdl	SFT	£3074
107	3/98	Font	2m2f110y	E Hdl	G-F	£2659

Total win prize-money £5734

Going: Sf: 0-1 GS: 0-1 Gd: 0-0 GF: - Fm: 0-2
Distance: 2m/2m3: 0-1 2m4-2m7: 0-3 3m+: 0-0
Track: LH: 0-2 RH: 0-0 Tight: 0-3 Gall: 0-0
Aids: Bl: 0-1 Vi: 0-0 Tstrap: 0-0
Best Rating: 111 2/02 Font 2m4f soft Ch

Lightly raced type, he mixes hurdling and chasing. Seems most effective at up to two and a half miles. Has worn blinkers.

The Next Waltz (IRE)

105(104h) **126**

11-y-o b g Buckskin (FR)-Loge (Orchestra)

L Lungo Mrs Michael Royds

Placings:006/3600/P2110/F51124111312212110 6/3P 05523/4P0601055-1P3 **(0743)**

2001/02: 27^{1}G, 24^{P}S, 20^{3}GS

	Starts	1st	2nd	3rd	Win & Pl
Chases	3	1	0	1	4432
Career Total	**50**	**13**	**6**	**5**	**49418**

126	5/01	Sedg	3m3f	F(0-110)HCh	GD	£3932
110	11/00	Weth	2m4f110y	F(0-110)HHdl	SFT	£1939
130	3/99	Carl	3m2f	D(0-125)HCh	SFT	£3538
129	2/99	Carl	3m2f	C(0-135)HCh	HVY	£5524
124	12/98	Catt	3m1f110y	E(0-110)HCh	GD	£3766
118	11/98	Ayr	3m110y	D(0-125)HHdl	G-S	£3470
112	10/98	Kels	2m6f110y	E(0-115)HHdl	SFT	£2304
111	10/98	Kels	2m6f110y	F(0-105)HHdl	G-S	£2416
107	9/98	Carl	2m4f110y	E(0-115)HHdl	GD	£2220
104	6/98	Hexm	2m4f110y	E(0-100)HHdl	HVY	£2448
96	6/98	Prth	2m4f110y	E(0-110)HHdl	G-F	£2775
104	3/98	Uttx	2m4f	E(0-100)HCh	GD	£3009
98	11/97	Bang	2m4f110y	E(0-105)HCh	SFT	£3615

Total win prize-money £40958

Going: Sf: 0-1 GS: 0-1 Gd: 1-1 GF: - Fm: 0-0
Distance: 2m/2m3: 0-0 2m4-2m7: 0-1 **3m+: 1-2**
Track: **LH: 1-2** RH: 0-1 **Tight: 1-1** Gall: 0-0
Aids: Bl: 0-0 Vi: 0-0 Tstrap: 0-0
Best Rating: 130 3/99 Carl 3m2f soft Ch

The Noble Moor (IRE)

86f **86f**

6-y-o br g Euphemism-Who Says (IRE) (Amazing Bust)

T R George Mrs Sharon C Nelson

Placings:00 **(2655)**

2001/02: 16^{0}GS, 16^{0}G

	Starts	1st	2nd	3rd	Win & Pl
NH Flat	2	0	0	0	
Career Total	**2**	**0**	**0**	**0**	

Going: Sf: 0-0 GS: 0-1 Gd: 0-1 GF: - Fm: 0-0
Distance: 2m/2m3: 0-2 2m4-2m7: 0-0 3m+: 0-0
Track: LH: 0-0 RH: 0-2 Tight: 0-0 Gall: 0-0
Aids: Bl: 0-0 Vi: 0-0 Tstrap: 0-0
Best Rating: 86 11/01 Sand 2m110y gd-sft NHF

The Nobleman (USA)

92 **86**

6-y-o b g Quiet American (USA)-Furajet (USA) (The Minstrel (CAN))

T J Etherington Mrs J E Todd

Placings:5/0650-0414P05 **(0977)**

2001/02: 17^{0}G, 16^{4}GF, 20^{1}F, 24^{4}G, 17^{P}GF, 16^{0}GF, 24^{5}GF

	Starts	1st	2nd	3rd	Win & Pl
Hurdles	7	1	0	0	2366
Career Total	**12**	**1**	**0**	**0**	**2366**

86	5/01	Hexm	2m4f110y	E(0-105)HHdl	FRM	£2366

Total win prize-money £2366

Going: Sf: 0-0 GS: 0-0 Gd: 0-2 GF: - Fm: 1-5
Distance: 2m/2m3: 0-4 **2m4-2m7: 1-1** 3m+: 0-2
Track: **LH: 1-6** RH: 0-1 Tight: 0-5 Gall: 0-0
Aids: Bl: 0-0 Vi: 0-0 Tstrap: 0-0
Best Rating: 86 5/01 Hexm 2m4f110y firm Hdl

The Nomad

99 **102**

6-y-o b g Nomadic Way (USA)-Bubbling (Tremblant)

M W Easterby S J Brewer & D Sugars

Placings:35-2O55622 **(4579)**

2001/02: 17^{2}GF, 16°G, 16^{5}GS, 19^{5}S, 16^{6}HY, 21^{2}S, 16^{2}G

	Starts	1st	2nd	3rd	Win & Pl
NH Flat	2	0	1	0	452
Hurdles	5	0	2	0	1404
Career Total	**9**	**0**	**3**	**1**	**2218**

Going: Sf: 0-3 GS: 0-1 Gd: 0-2 GF: - Fm: 0-1
Distance: 2m/2m3: 0-6 2m4-2m7: 0-1 3m+: 0-0
Track: LH: 0-5 RH: 0-1 Tight: 0-3 Gall: 0-0
Aids: Bl: 0-0 Vi: 0-0 Tstrap: 0-0
Best Rating: 103 12/01 Muss 2m1f gd-fm NHF

Fair if fragile gelding. Has shown moderate form in ordinary bumpers and over hurdles.

The O'Malley

5-y-o b m Risk Me (FR)-Farrh Nouriya (IRE) (Lomond (USA))

M Mullineaux Mrs N O'Malley

Placings:P **(2755)**

2001/02: 17^{P}GS

	Starts	1st	2nd	3rd	Win & Pl
Hurdles	1	0	0	0	
Career Total	**1**	**0**	**0**	**0**	

Going: Sf: 0-0 GS: 0-1 Gd: 0-0 GF: - Fm: 0-0
Distance: 2m/2m3: 0-1 2m4-2m7: 0-0 3m+: 0-0
Track: LH: 0-1 RH: 0-0 Tight: 0-1 Gall: 0-0
Aids: Bl: 0-0 Vi: 0-0 Tstrap: 0-0
Best Rating:

The Only Option (IRE)

86 **66**

7-y-o b m Phardante (FR)-Sirrah Madam (Tug Of War)

R Tate R Tate

Placings:5P **(0451)**

2001/02: 21^{5}G, 23^{P}F

	Starts	1st	2nd	3rd	Win & Pl
Hurdles	2	0	0	0	0
Career Total	**2**	**0**	**0**	**0**	**0**

Going: Sf: 0-0 GS: 0-0 Gd: 0-1 GF: - Fm: 0-1
Distance: 2m/2m3: 0-0 2m4-2m7: 0-2 3m+: 0-0
Track: LH: 0-2 RH: 0-0 Tight: 0-1 Gall: 0-0
Aids: Bl: 0-0 Vi: 0-0 Tstrap: 0-0
Best Rating: 66 5/01 Sedg 2m5f110y good Hdl

The Optician

57 **35**

8-y-o b/br g Scorpio (FR)-Star Connection (Faustus (USA))

C N Kellett Frank Hutchinson

Placings:P-0P **(0191)**

2001/02: 20^{0}G, 23^{P}GF

	Starts	1st	2nd	3rd	Win & Pl
Hurdles	2	0	0	0	
Career Total	**3**	**0**	**0**	**0**	

Going: Sf: 0-0 GS: 0-0 Gd: 0-1 GF: - Fm: 0-1
Distance: 2m/2m3: 0-0 2m4-2m7: 0-1 3m+: 0-1
Track: LH: 0-1 RH: 0-1 Tight: 0-1 Gall: 0-1
Aids: Bl: 0-0 Vi: 0-0 Tstrap: 0-0
Best Rating: 35 5/01 Hntg 2m4f110y good Hdl

The Other Half

10-y-o ch g Alias Smith (USA)-Water Eaton Gal (Legal Eagle)

R Johnson The Border Terriers

Placings:5006/620F3P00P/43/6P **(1818)**

2001/02: 25^{6}G, 16^{P}S

	Starts	1st	2nd	3rd	Win & Pl
Chases	2	0	0	0	0
Career Total	**17**	**0**	**1**	**2**	**1485**

Going: Sf: 0-1 GS: 0-0 Gd: 0-1 GF: - Fm: 0-0
Distance: 2m/2m3: 0-1 2m4-2m7: 0-0 3m+: 0-1

Track: LH: 0-1 RH: 0-1 Tight: 0-1 Gall: 0-0
Aids: Bl: 0-0 Vi: 0-0 Tstrap: 0-0
Best Rating: 72 12/98 Ayr 2m5f110y gd-sft Ch

The Parsons Dingle

94 90

7-y-o ch g Le Moss-Not Enough (Balinger)
P R Webber Tavern Racing

Placings: 41/66-2 (0201)
2001/02: 16^{2}G

	Starts	1st	2nd	3rd	Win & Pl
Hurdles	1	0	1	0	816
Career Total	**5**	**1**	**1**	**0**	**2720**

110	3/00	Bang	2m1f	H NHF	GD	£1904

Total win prize-money £1904

Going: Sf: 0-0 GS: 0-0 Gd: 0-1 GF: - Fm: 0-0
Distance: 2m/2m3: 0-1 2m4-2m7: 0-0 3m+: 0-0
Track: LH: 0-1 RH: 0-0 Tight: 0-0 Gall: 0-0
Aids: Bl: 0-0 Vi: 0-0 Tstrap: 0-0
Best Rating: 110 3/00 Bang 2m1f good NHF

The Pecker Dunn (IRE)

100 65

8-y-o b g Be My Native (USA)-Riversdale Shadow (Kemal (FR))
Mrs N S Sharpe The Illiney Group

Placings: 0/300/3-5 (4730)
2001/02: 20^{5}GF

	Starts	1st	2nd	3rd	Win & Pl
Hurdles	1	0	0	0	0
Career Total	**6**	**0**	**0**	**2**	**650**

Going: Sf: 0-0 GS: 0-0 Gd: 0-0 GF: - Fm: 0-1
Distance: 2m/2m3: 0-0 2m4-2m7: 0-1 3m+: 0-0
Track: LH: 0-1 RH: 0-0 Tight: 0-0 Gall: 0-0
Aids: Bl: 0-0 Vi: 0-0 Tstrap: 0-0
Best Rating: 92 6/99 Navn 2m gd-fm NHF

The Pennys Dropped (IRE)

85f 93f

5-y-o ch g Bob's Return (IRE)-Shuil Alainn (Levanter)
J J O'Neill J P McManus

Placings: 0 (4032)
2001/02: 16^{0}GS

	Starts	1st	2nd	3rd	Win & Pl
NH Flat	1	0	0	0	
Career Total	**1**	**0**	**0**	**0**	

Going: Sf: 0-0 GS: 0-1 Gd: 0-0 GF: - Fm: 0-0
Distance: 2m/2m3: 0-1 2m4-2m7: 0-0 3m+: 0-0
Track: LH: 0-1 RH: 0-0 Tight: 0-0 Gall: 0-1
Aids: Bl: 0-0 Vi: 0-0 Tstrap: 0-0
Best Rating: 93 3/02 Newb 2m110y gd-sft NHF

The Phair Crier (IRE)

109 133

7-y-o ch g Phardante (FR)-Maul-More (Deep Run)
L Lungo Ashleybank Investments Limited

Placings: 13-F14P (4890)
2001/02: 20^{F}HY, 24^{1}S, 24^{4}HY, 24^{P}G

	Starts	1st	2nd	3rd	Win & Pl
Hurdles	4	1	0	0	6939
Career Total	**6**	**2**	**0**	**1**	**8920**

133	1/02	Newc	3m	B Hdl	SFT	£6938
104	1/01	Ayr	2m	H NHF	G-S	£1673

Total win prize-money £8612

Going: Sf: 1-3 GS: 0-0 Gd: 0-1 GF: - Fm: 0-0
Distance: 2m/2m3: 0-0 2m4-2m7: 0-1 **3m+: 1-3**
Track: **LH: 1-2** RH: 0-1 Tight: 0-0 **Gall: 1-1**
Aids: Bl: 0-0 Vi: 0-0 Tstrap: 0-0
Best Rating: 133 1/02 Newc 3m soft Hdl

Useful Northern-trained staying hurdler, stays three miles and acts on soft ground, but suffered breathing problems at Ayr in February.

The Pickled Duke (IRE)

105(110h) (112h)121

10-y-o gr g Duky-Silk Empress (Young Emperor)
T R George Timothy N Chick

Placings: 225R/2/P4110U/1PU111-P245PP (4301)
2001/02: 24^{P}GS, 24^{2}S, 24^{4}HY, 22^{5}HY, 33^{P}S, 22^{P}HY

	Starts	1st	2nd	3rd	Win & Pl
Hurdles	2	0	0	0	0
Chases	4	0	1	0	2637
Career Total	**23**	**6**	**4**	**0**	**28405**

135	3/01	Hayd	2m7f110y	C(0-130)HHdl	HVY	£7477
135	3/01	Wwck	3m1f	E Hdl	HVY	£2926
114	2/01	Bang	2m4f	E(0-105)HHdl	HVY	£2870
128	11/00	Uttx	2m4f	F(0-110)HCh	HVY	£2919
128	2/00	Sand	3m110y	D(0-115)HCh	G-S	£4959
109	2/00	Font	2m6f	F(0-95)HCh	SFT	£3006

Total win prize-money £24159

Going: Sf: 0-5 GS: 0-1 Gd: 0-0 GF: - Fm: 0-0
Distance: 2m/2m3: 0-0 2m4-2m7: 0-2 3m+: 0-4
Track: LH: 0-5 RH: 0-1 Tight: 0-1 Gall: 0-1
Aids: Bl: 0-0 Vi: 0-0 Tstrap: 0-0
Best Rating: 135 3/01 Hayd 2m7f110y heavy Hdl

Useful handicap hurdler/chaser. Ended the 2000/1 season with a hat-trick of hurdle wins. Placed over fences last term. Stays three miles plus. Loves the mud.

The Piewacket

92(89h) (57h)61

7-y-o b g Rock Hopper-Early Gales (Precocious)
B De Haan Duncan Heath

Placings: 65P6-5P (2113)
2001/02: 25^{5}G, 25^{P}G

	Starts	1st	2nd	3rd	Win & Pl
Chases	2	0	0	0	0
Career Total	**6**	**0**	**0**	**0**	**0**

Going: Sf: 0-0 GS: 0-0 Gd: 0-2 GF: - Fm: 0-0
Distance: 2m/2m3: 0-0 2m4-2m7: 0-0 3m+: 0-2
Track: LH: 0-0 RH: 0-2 Tight: 0-1 Gall: 0-0
Aids: Bl: 0-1 Vi: 0-0 Tstrap: 0-0
Best Rating: 81 12/00 Folk 2m1f110y heavy Hdl

The President

100(82c) (77c)104

7-y-o b g Yaheeb (USA)-When The Saints (Bay Express)
Mrs M Reveley North Racing Partnership

Placings: 051/4321/36562 (4693)
2001/02: 21^{3}GF, 20^{6}GS, 20^{5}G, 22^{6}GS, 22^{2}GF

	Starts	1st	2nd	3rd	Win & Pl
Hurdles	3	0	1	1	1455
Chases	2	0	0	0	0
Career Total	**12**	**2**	**2**	**2**	**8049**

105	10/99	Kels	2m110y	E(0-115)HHdl	GD	£2773
103	4/99	Kels	2m110y	E Hdl	G-F	£2661

Total win prize-money £5434

Going: Sf: 0-0 GS: 0-2 Gd: 0-1 GF: - Fm: 0-2
Distance: 2m/2m3: 0-0 2m4-2m7: 0-5 3m+: 0-0
Track: LH: 0-4 RH: 0-0 Tight: 0-3 Gall: 0-1
Aids: Bl: 0-0 Vi: 0-0 Tstrap: 0-0
Best Rating: 105 10/99 Kels 2m110y good Hdl

The Prince

98 110

8-y-o b g Machiavellian (USA)-Mohican Girl (Dancing Brave (USA))
Ian Williams Patrick Kelly

Placings: 16F13-00 (0975)
2001/02: 16^{0}G, 16^{0}GF

	Starts	1st	2nd	3rd	Win & Pl
Hurdles	2	0	0	0	
Career Total	**7**	**2**	**0**	**1**	**6315**

124	1/01	Catt	2m	E Hdl	G-S	£2891
120	7/00	NAbb	2m1f	D Hdl	G-F	£2957

Total win prize-money £5849

Going: Sf: 0-0 GS: 0-0 Gd: 0-1 GF: - Fm: 0-1
Distance: 2m/2m3: 0-2 2m4-2m7: 0-0 3m+: 0-0
Track: LH: 0-2 RH: 0-0 Tight: 0-1 Gall: 0-0
Aids: Bl: 0-0 Vi: 0-0 Tstrap: 0-2
Best Rating: 124 1/01 Catt 2m gd-sft Hdl

The Project

66f 55f

6-y-o b g Prince Of Darkness (IRE)-Kerry Calluna (Celtic Cone)
J C Fox Shirley M & Peter G Palmer

Placings: 0 (4158)
2001/02: 16^{0}GS

	Starts	1st	2nd	3rd	Win & Pl
NH Flat	1	0	0	0	
Career Total	**1**	**0**	**0**	**0**	

Going: Sf: 0-0 GS: 0-1 Gd: 0-0 GF: - Fm: 0-0
Distance: 2m/2m3: 0-1 2m4-2m7: 0-0 3m+: 0-0
Track: LH: 0-0 RH: 0-1 Tight: 0-0 Gall: 0-0
Aids: Bl: 0-0 Vi: 0-0 Tstrap: 0-0
Best Rating: 55 3/02 Sand 2m110y gd-sft NHF

The Proof

90 73

5-y-o b g Rudimentary (USA)-Indubitable (Sharpo)
G B Balding Miss B Swire

Placings: 0 (4400)
2001/02: 21^{0}S

	Starts	1st	2nd	3rd	Win & Pl
Hurdles	1	0	0	0	
Career Total	**1**	**0**	**0**	**0**	

Going: Sf: 0-1 GS: 0-0 Gd: 0-0 GF: - Fm: 0-0

Distance: 2m/2m3: 0-0 2m4-2m7: 0-1 3m+: 0-0
Track: LH: 0-1 RH: 0-0 Tight: 0-0 Gall: 0-1
Aids: Bl: 0-0 Vi: 0-0 Tstrap: 0-0
Best Rating: 51 3/02 Newb 2m5f soft Hdl

The Prosecutor

79 44

5-y-o b h Contract Law (USA)-Elsocko (Swing Easy (USA))
P Winkworth (B A McMahon 7/5) Whiston Management Ltd

Placings:0 (2064)
2001/02: 16^{0}G

	Starts	1st	2nd	3rd	Win & Pl
Hurdles	1	0	0	0	
Career Total	**1**	**0**	**0**	**0**	

Going: Sf: 0-0 GS: 0-0 Gd: 0-1 GF: - Fm: 0-0
Distance: 2m/2m3: 0-1 2m4-2m7: 0-0 3m+: 0-0
Track: LH: 0-0 RH: 0-1 Tight: 0-0 Gall: 0-1
Aids: Bl: 0-0 Vi: 0-0 Tstrap: 0-0
Best Rating: 44 11/01 Hntg 2m110y good Hdl

The Puffin Man (IRE)

39

9-y-o b g Roselier (FR)-Move Along Gypsy (Menelek)
J W Payne T J Wyatt

Placings:000/06/FP0-P (0374)
2001/02: 26^{P}GF

	Starts	1st	2nd	3rd	Win & Pl
Hurdles	1	0	0	0	
Career Total	**9**	**0**	**0**	**0**	**0**

Going: Sf: 0-0 GS: 0-0 Gd: 0-0 GF: - Fm: 0-1
Distance: 2m/2m3: 0-0 2m4-2m7: 0-0 3m+: 0-1
Track: LH: 0-0 RH: 0-1 Tight: 0-0 Gall: 0-1
Aids: Bl: 0-0 Vi: 0-0 Tstrap: 0-0
Best Rating: 95 2/99 Newb 2m110y good NHF

The Purple Penguin

95f 98f

5-y-o ch m Rock Hopper-Corn Lily (Aragon)
Mrs M Reveley Mrs Susan McDonald

Placings:0-2 (2401)
2001/02: 16^{2}G

	Starts	1st	2nd	3rd	Win & Pl
NH Flat	1	0	1	0	436
Career Total	**2**	**0**	**1**	**0**	**436**

Going: Sf: 0-0 GS: 0-0 Gd: 0-1 GF: - Fm: 0-0
Distance: 2m/2m3: 0-1 2m4-2m7: 0-0 3m+: 0-0
Track: LH: 0-1 RH: 0-0 Tight: 0-0 Gall: 0-0
Aids: Bl: 0-0 Vi: 0-0 Tstrap: 0-0
Best Rating: 98 11/01 Weth 2m good NHF

The Quads

113 (113h)135

10-y-o b g Tinoco-Queen's Royale (Tobrouk (FR))
Ferdy Murphy (A L T Moore 6/5) John Duddy

Placings:430064/531131/605302231300/050124264/P00/403240106-03104P40P (4497)
2001/02: 22^{0}G, 26^{3}GS, 26^{1}S, 27^{0}G, 28^{4}S, 28^{P}HY, 28^{4}S, 24^{0}GS, 24^{P}G

	Starts	1st	2nd	3rd	Win & Pl
Hurdles	1	0	0	0	0
Chases	8	1	0	1	5673
Career Total	**54**	**7**	**5**	**8**	**79273**

135	10/01	Carl	3m2f	D(0-120)HCh	SFT	£4290
125	1/01	Navn	2m4f	HHdl	SFT	£13104
120	10/98	Gowr	3m	HHdl	SH	£14076
123	1/98	Leop	2m3f	HCh	Y-S	£7147
106	4/97	Punc	2m2f	HHdl	GD	£8138
103	3/97	Navn	3m	HHdl	SFT	£5425
97	1/97	Leop	2m6f	(0-130)HHdl	G-Y	£3051

Total win prize-money £55236

Going: Sf: 1-4 GS: 0-2 Gd: 0-3 GF: - Fm: 0-0
Distance: 2m/2m3: 0-0 2m4-2m7: 0-1 **3m+: 1-8**
Track: LH: 0-5 **RH: 1-2** Tight: 0-1 Gall: 0-2
Aids: Bl: 0-0 Vi: 0-0 **Tstrap: 1-9**
Best Rating: 135 10/01 Carl 3m2f soft Ch

A winner of several races in Ireland, he is now with Ferdy Murphy. Stays well and likes to get his toe in. Regularly tongue tied.

The Real Murphy (IRE)

95f 73f

7-y-o ch g Hamas (IRE)-Rocket Alert (Red Alert)
R H Buckler R H Buckler

Placings:0/3 (1630)
2001/02: 16^{0}GF

	Starts	1st	2nd	3rd	Win & Pl
NH Flat	1	0	0	1	250
Career Total	**2**	**0**	**0**	**1**	**250**

Going: Sf: 0-0 GS: 0-0 Gd: 0-0 GF: - Fm: 0-1
Distance: 2m/2m3: 0-1 2m4-2m7: 0-0 3m+: 0-0
Track: LH: 0-0 RH: 0-1 Tight: 0-0 Gall: 0-0
Aids: Bl: 0-0 Vi: 0-0 Tstrap: 0-0
Best Rating: 74 2/00 Winc 2m gd-sft NHF

The Red Rector (IRE)

88 102

9-y-o b g Moscow Society (USA)-Parson's Dream (The Parson)
D M Grissell John Grist

Placings:25/020/22/2-164 (3925)
2001/02: 20^{1}HY, 25^{6}HY, 21^{4}HY

	Starts	1st	2nd	3rd	Win & Pl
Hurdles	3	1	0	0	1848
Career Total	**11**	**1**	**5**	**0**	**4629**

102	12/01	Folk	2m4f110y	F Hdl	HVY	£1848

Total win prize-money £1848

Going: Sf: 1-3 GS: 0-0 Gd: 0-0 GF: - Fm: 0-0
Distance: 2m/2m3: 0-0 **2m4-2m7: 1-2** 3m+: 0-1
Track: LH: 0-1 **RH: 1-1 Tight: 1-2** Gall: 0-0
Aids: Bl: 0-0 Vi: 0-0 Tstrap: 0-0
Best Rating: 105 11/99 Folk 2m4f110y gd-sft Hdl

The Right Cue (IRE)

88 66

8-y-o b g Torus-Bo Reynella (IRE) (Le Bavard (FR))
P R Rodford Mrs Christine Priest

Placings:P/0/5-P05 (4736)
2001/02: 22^{P}G, 19^{0}G, 17^{5}F

	Starts	1st	2nd	3rd	Win & Pl
Hurdles	3	0	0	0	0
Career Total	**6**	**0**	**0**	**0**	**0**

Going: Sf: 0-0 GS: 0-0 Gd: 0-2 GF: - Fm: 0-1
Distance: 2m/2m3: 0-2 2m4-2m7: 0-1 3m+: 0-0
Track: LH: 0-1 RH: 0-2 Tight: 0-1 Gall: 0-0
Aids: Bl: 0-1 Vi: 0-0 Tstrap: 0-0
Best Rating: 66 4/02 Extr 2m1f firm Hdl

The Rile (IRE)

88 105

8-y-o ch g Alphabatim (USA)-Donna Chimene (Royal Gunner (USA))
L Lungo Mrs Barbara Lungo

Placings:0212/64010-0000100 (4432)
2001/02: 22^{0}GS, 16^{0}G, 17^{0}HY, 16^{0}GS, 20^{1}S, 20^{0}HY, 20^{0}HY

	Starts	1st	2nd	3rd	Win & Pl
Hurdles	7	1	0	0	3526
Career Total	**16**	**3**	**2**	**0**	**9378**

105	1/02	Carl	2m4f	D(0-125)HHdl	SFT	£3526
105	2/01	Carl	2m4f110y	E Hdl	SFT	£1964
111	3/00	Carl	2m1f	H NHF	HVY	£1704

Total win prize-money £7195

Going: Sf: 1-4 GS: 0-2 Gd: 0-1 GF: - Fm: 0-0
Distance: 2m/2m3: 0-3 **2m4-2m7: 1-4** 3m+: 0-0
Track: LH: 0-5 RH: 0-1 Tight: 0-1 Gall: 0-1
Aids: Bl: 0-0 Vi: 0-0 Tstrap: 0-0
Best Rating: 111 3/00 Carl 2m1f gd-sft NHF

Two and a half mile handicapper who loves the mud. All his wins have come at Carlisle.

The River Joker (IRE)

97 83

6-y-o ch g Over The River (FR)-Augustaeliza (IRE) (Callernish)
John R Upson Graeme P McPherson

Placings:000-FB50P (4131)
2001/02: 27^{F}G, 21^{B}GS, 22^{5}G, 26^{0}S, 26^{P}G

	Starts	1st	2nd	3rd	Win & Pl
Hurdles	5	0	0	0	0
Career Total	**8**	**0**	**0**	**0**	**0**

Going: Sf: 0-1 GS: 0-1 Gd: 0-3 GF: - Fm: 0-0
Distance: 2m/2m3: 0-0 2m4-2m7: 0-2 3m+: 0-3
Track: LH: 0-2 RH: 0-3 Tight: 0-1 Gall: 0-2
Aids: Bl: 0-0 Vi: 0-0 Tstrap: 0-0
Best Rating: 83 12/01 Winc 2m6f good Hdl

The Roundsills

99 94

8-y-o ch g Handsome Sailor-Eye Sight (Roscoe Blake)
M Mullineaux R Williamson

Placings:25/0004/4256142/0-00 (0478)
2001/02: 16^{0}GF, 17^{0}G

	Starts	1st	2nd	3rd	Win & Pl
Chases	2	0	0	0	
Career Total	**16**	**1**	**3**	**0**	**6022**

105	12/99	Hrfd	2m	E(0-105)HCh	GD	£3243

Total win prize-money £3243

Going: Sf: 0-0 GS: 0-0 Gd: 0-1 GF: - Fm: 0-1
Distance: 2m/2m3: 0-2 2m4-2m7: 0-0 3m+: 0-0
Track: LH: 0-1 RH: 0-1 Tight: 0-1 Gall: 0-0

Aids: Bl: 0-0 Vi: 0-0 Tstrap: 0-0
Best Rating: 105 2/00 Ludl 2m good Ch

The Rum Mariner

15-y-o gr g Julio Mariner-Decorum (Quorum)
Richard Mathias T A Rogers

Placings:P2/24P2P/4U-1 **(0271)**
2001/02: 25^{1}G

	Starts	1st	2nd	3rd	Win & Pl
Chases	1	1	0	0	2373
Career Total	**10**	**1**	**3**	**0**	**3944**

92 5/01 Hrfd 3m1f110y H Ch GD £2373
Total win prize-money £2373

Going: Sf: 0-0 GS: 0-0 Gd: 1-1 GF: - Fm: 0-0
Distance: 2m/2m3: 0-0 2m4-2m7: 0-0 **3m+: 1-1**
Track: LH: 0-0 **RH: 1-1** Tight: 0-0 Gall: 0-0
Aids: Bl: 0-0 Vi: 0-0 Tstrap: 0-0
Best Rating: 97 3/98 Hrfd 3m1f110y gd-fm Ch

The Sawdust Kid

98(96h) (104h)98
8-y-o ch g River God (USA)-Susie's Money (Seymour Hicks (FR))
R H Buckler Golden Cap

Placings:3/1323P-1654P0 **(4817)**
2001/02: 22^{1}GF, 22^{6}G, 24^{5}G, 22^{4}GF, 24^{P}F, 24^{0}GF

	Starts	1st	2nd	3rd	Win & Pl
Hurdles	6	1	0	0	2886
Career Total	**12**	**2**	**1**	**3**	**6256**

104 10/01 Winc 2m6f E Hdl G-F £2474
98 8/00 Worc 2m H NHF G-F £1473
Total win prize-money £3949

Going: Sf: 0-0 GS: 0-0 Gd: 0-2 GF: - Fm: 1-4
Distance: 2m/2m3: 0-0 **2m4-2m7: 1-3** 3m+: 0-3
Track: LH: 0-0 **RH: 1-4** Tight: 0-0 Gall: 0-0
Aids: Bl: 0-0 Vi: 0-0 Tstrap: 0-0
Best Rating: 111 10/00 Chel 3m1f110y good Hdl

A strong galloper, he got off the mark over hurdles at Wincanton in October 2001. Stays three miles, acts on fast ground. Well beaten on chasing debut.

The Screamer (IRE)

86
5-y-o b m Insan (USA)-Augusta Victoria (Callernish)
Michael Hourigan P Trant

Placings:*150* **(4235)**
2001/02: 16^{1}GF, 16^{5}Y, 16^{0}GS

	Starts	1st	2nd	3rd	Win & Pl
NH Flat	3	1	0	0	5565
Career Total	**3**	**1**	**0**	**0**	**5565**

106 9/01 List 2m NHF G-F £5564
Total win prize-money £5565

Going: Sf: 0-0 GS: 0-1 Gd: 0-0 GF: - Fm: 1-1
Distance: **2m/2m3: 1-3** 2m4-2m7: 0-0 3m+: 0-0
Track: LH: 0-1 RH: 0-0 Tight: 0-0 Gall: 0-0
Aids: Bl: 0-0 Vi: 0-0 Tstrap: 0-0
Best Rating: 106 9/01 List 2m gd-fm NHF

The Sea Club (IRE)

97 74
7-y-o b g Be My Native (USA)-Furry Slipper (Furry Glen)
H Alexander The Sea Club (marjorca)

Placings:*00*-4P5P5 **(2306)**
2001/02: 20^{4}GS, 20^{P}GF, 20^{5}F, 22^{P}GS, 16^{5}GF

	Starts	1st	2nd	3rd	Win & Pl
Hurdles	5	0	0	0	0
Career Total	**7**	**0**	**0**	**0**	**0**

Going: Sf: 0-0 GS: 0-2 Gd: 0-0 GF: - Fm: 0-3
Distance: 2m/2m3: 0-1 2m4-2m7: 0-4 3m+: 0-0
Track: LH: 0-3 RH: 0-2 Tight: 0-2 Gall: 0-0
Aids: Bl: 0-0 Vi: 0-0 Tstrap: 0-0
Best Rating: 74 5/01 Prth 2m4f110y gd-sft Hdl

The Silver Surfer (IRE)

104 98
7-y-o gr g Sexton Blake-Ballinkillen (Levmoss)
J Mackie A J Winterton

Placings:*0*/254-00422155 **(2941)**
2001/02: 19^{0}G, 24^{0}G, 22^{4}GF, 20^{2}GF, 16^{2}G, 20^{1}G, 19^{5}G, 19^{5}G

	Starts	1st	2nd	3rd	Win & Pl
Hurdles	8	1	2	0	5709
Career Total	**12**	**1**	**3**	**0**	**6240**

98 11/01 Asct 2m4f E(0-105)HHdl GD £4329
Total win prize-money £4329

Going: Sf: 0-0 GS: 0-0 Gd: 1-6 GF: - Fm: 0-2
Distance: 2m/2m3: 0-2 **2m4-2m7: 1-5** 3m+: 0-1
Track: LH: 0-3 **RH: 1-5** Tight: 0-0 Gall: 0-2
Aids: Bl: 0-0 **Vi: 1-6** Tstrap: 0-0
Best Rating: 104 10/00 Font 2m2f110y good Hdl

Stays two and a half miles. Acts on good ground.

The Sky Is Blue

6-y-o ch g Alflora (IRE)-Mistress Boreen (Boreen (FR))
S E H Sherwood David Knox

Placings:30P-FPP **(4585)**
2001/02: 24^{F}GS, 22^{P}S, 25^{P}G

	Starts	1st	2nd	3rd	Win & Pl
Hurdles	1	0	0	0	0
Chases	2	0	0	0	0
Career Total	**6**	**0**	**0**	**1**	**220**

Going: Sf: 0-1 GS: 0-1 Gd: 0-1 GF: - Fm: 0-0
Distance: 2m/2m3: 0-0 2m4-2m7: 0-1 3m+: 0-2
Track: LH: 0-1 RH: 0-2 Tight: 0-2 Gall: 0-0
Aids: Bl: 0-0 Vi: 0-0 Tstrap: 0-1
Best Rating: 92 10/00 Tntn 2m1f good NHF

The Sleeper

83f 62f
6-y-o b g Perpendicular-Distant Cherry (General Ironside)
H P Hogarth H P Hogarth

Placings:*00* **(3368)**
2001/02: 16^{0}G, 16^{0}GS

	Starts	1st	2nd	3rd	Win & Pl
NH Flat	2	0	0	0	
Career Total	2	0	0	0	

Going: Sf: 0-0 GS: 0-1 Gd: 0-1 GF: - Fm: 0-0
Distance: 2m/2m3: 0-2 2m4-2m7: 0-0 3m+: 0-0
Track: LH: 0-2 RH: 0-0 Tight: 0-2 Gall: 0-0
Aids: Bl: 0-0 Vi: 0-0 Tstrap: 0-0
Best Rating: 62 12/01 Catt 2m good NHF

The Staggery Boy (IRE)

105 104
6-y-o b g Shalford (IRE)-Murroe Star (Glenstal (USA))
Mrs V C Ward (F Flood 27/7) The Late Mrs R F Key & Mrs V C Ward

Placings:00/000-61056P443 **(2306)**
2001/02: 16^{6}GF, 16^{1}G, 16^{0}GF, 17^{5}G, 16^{6}G, 22^{P}GS, 17^{4}G, 17^{4}G, 16^{3}GF

	Starts	1st	2nd	3rd	Win & Pl
Hurdles	9	1	0	1	5937
Career Total	**14**	**1**	**0**	**1**	**5937**

91 6/01 Navn 2m (0-102)HHdl GD £5564
Total win prize-money £5565

Going: Sf: 0-0 GS: 0-1 Gd: 1-5 GF: - Fm: 0-3
Distance: **2m/2m3: 1-8** 2m4-2m7: 0-1 3m+: 0-0
Track: LH: 0-4 RH: 0-0 Tight: 0-3 Gall: 0-0
Aids: Bl: 0-0 Vi: 0-0 **Tstrap: 1-7**
Best Rating: 104 11/01 Sedg 2m1f good Hdl

The Stirrer (IRE)

49f 20f
6-y-o b g Warcraft (USA)-Lawlors Stile (Buckskin (FR))
M Todhunter C J Cookson

Placings:*0* **(2181)**
2001/02: 16^{0}G

	Starts	1st	2nd	3rd	Win & Pl
NH Flat	1	0	0	0	
Career Total	**1**	**0**	**0**	**0**	

Going: Sf: 0-0 GS: 0-0 Gd: 0-1 GF: - Fm: 0-0
Distance: 2m/2m3: 0-1 2m4-2m7: 0-0 3m+: 0-0
Track: LH: 0-1 RH: 0-0 Tight: 0-0 Gall: 0-0
Aids: Bl: 0-0 Vi: 0-0 Tstrap: 0-0
Best Rating: 20 11/01 Weth 2m good NHF

The Tall Guy (IRE)

74 21
6-y-o b/br g Zaffaran (USA)-Mullangale (Strong Gale)
N A Twiston-Davies Mrs Jill Scott & Mrs Sarah Macechern

Placings:*1*-40P **(2284)**
2001/02: 17^{4}GS, 20^{0}S, 24^{P}G

	Starts	1st	2nd	3rd	Win & Pl
NH Flat	1	0	0	0	0
Hurdles	2	0	0	0	0
Career Total	**4**	**1**	**0**	**0**	**3308**

100 4/01 Ayr 2m H NHF G-F £3307
Total win prize-money £3308

Going: Sf: 0-1 GS: 0-1 Gd: 0-1 GF: - Fm: 0-0
Distance: 2m/2m3: 0-1 2m4-2m7: 0-1 3m+: 0-1
Track: LH: 0-1 RH: 0-2 Tight: 0-0 Gall: 0-0
Aids: Bl: 0-0 Vi: 0-0 Tstrap: 0-3
Best Rating: 106 10/01 Carl 2m1f gd-sft NHF

The Ten Amigos (IRE)

11-y-o b g Tremblant-Light Foot (Little Buskins)
T P McGovern The Hove Racing Club

Placings:050/F3P/FFU3-SP (0374)
2001/02: 25^{S}S, 26^{P}GF

	Starts	1st	2nd	3rd	Win & Pl
Hurdles	2	0	0	0	
Career Total	**12**	**0**	**0**	**2**	**831**

Going: Sf: 0-1 GS: 0-0 Gd: 0-0 GF: - Fm: 0-1
Distance: 2m/2m3: 0-0 2m4-2m7: 0-0 3m+: 0-2
Track: LH: 0-0 RH: 0-1 Tight: 0-0 Gall: 0-1
Aids: Bl: 0-0 Vi: 0-0 Tstrap: 0-0
Best Rating: 82 3/01 Ling 2m heavy Ch

The Texan (NZ)

94(88c) (82c)91
10-y-o gr g Oak Ridge (FR)-Sorority (NZ) (Standaan (FR))
H W Lavis (H D Daly 1/5) R & P Goldsworthy, L Parry & R Burks

Placings:6102/0PP-P00036 (4646)
2001/02: 24^{P}G, 16^{0}S, 20^{0}G, 26^{0}S, 20^{3}S, 21^{6}G

	Starts	1st	2nd	3rd	Win & Pl
Hurdles	3	0	0	1	288
Chases	3	0	0	0	0
Career Total	**13**	**1**	**1**	**1**	**14400**
6/99 Autl 2m2f110y Ch				VS	£12917

Total win prize-money £12917

Going: Sf: 0-3 GS: 0-0 Gd: 0-3 GF: - Fm: 0-0
Distance: 2m/2m3: 0-1 2m4-2m7: 0-3 3m+: 0-2
Track: LH: 0-2 RH: 0-3 Tight: 0-2 Gall: 0-2
Aids: Bl: 0-1 Vi: 0-0 Tstrap: 0-0
Best Rating: 101 11/99 Uttx 2m soft Ch

The Tile Baron (IRE)

82f
5-y-o b g Little Bighorn-Elegant Miss (Prince Tenderfoot (USA))
L Lungo The Tile Barons

Placings:5 (4436)
2001/02: 16^{5}HY

	Starts	1st	2nd	3rd	Win & Pl
NH Flat	1	0	0	0	0
Career Total	**1**	**0**	**0**	**0**	**0**

Going: Sf: 0-1 GS: 0-0 Gd: 0-0 GF: - Fm: 0-0
Distance: 2m/2m3: 0-1 2m4-2m7: 0-0 3m+: 0-0
Track: LH: 0-0 RH: 0-0 Tight: 0-0 Gall: 0-0
Aids: Bl: 0-0 Vi: 0-0 Tstrap: 0-0
Best Rating: 82 3/02 Newc 2m heavy NHF

The Timberman

10-y-o gr g Grey Desire-Heldigvis (Hot Grove)
Tim Butt (R Johnson 17/3) Tim Butt

Placings:P5360-F (4859)
2001/02: 25^{F}G

	Starts	1st	2nd	3rd	Win & Pl
Chases	1	0	0	0	
Career Total	**6**	**0**	**0**	**1**	**449**

Going: Sf: 0-0 GS: 0-0 Gd: 0-1 GF: - Fm: 0-0
Distance: 2m/2m3: 0-0 2m4-2m7: 0-0 3m+: 0-1
Track: LH: 0-1 RH: 0-0 Tight: 0-0 Gall: 0-0
Aids: Bl: 0-0 Vi: 0-0 Tstrap: 0-1
Best Rating: 52 8/00 Ctml 2m1f110y gd-sft Hdl

The Tinker

97(72h) (45h)109
7-y-o b g Nomadic Way (USA)-Miss Tino (Relkino)
Mrs S C Bradburne Mrs S Irwin

Placings:00P-600P2P6 (4521)
2001/02: 24^{6}S, 22^{0}GS, 16^{0}G, 20^{P}GS, 20^{2}GF, 24^{P}S, 20^{6}GS

	Starts	1st	2nd	3rd	Win & Pl
Hurdles	4	0	0	0	0
Chases	3	0	1	0	1314
Career Total	**10**	**0**	**1**	**0**	**1314**

Going: Sf: 0-2 GS: 0-3 Gd: 0-1 GF: - Fm: 0-1
Distance: 2m/2m3: 0-1 2m4-2m7: 0-4 3m+: 0-2
Track: LH: 0-3 RH: 0-4 Tight: 0-4 Gall: 0-0
Aids: Bl: 0-0 Vi: 0-0 Tstrap: 0-0
Best Rating: 109 12/01 Muss 2m4f gd-fm Ch

A modest performer over hurdles,acts on fast ground.

The Tippler (IRE)

100I
8-y-o b g Alphabatim (USA)-La Tortue (Lafontaine (USA))
Lindsay Woods Patrick Blee

Placings:4P/P00000 (4610a)
2001/02: 16^{P}GS, 18^{0}S, 18^{0}YS, 17^{0}S, 16^{0}S, 17^{0}S

	Starts	1st	2nd	3rd	Win & Pl
NH Flat	2	0	0	0	0
Hurdles	4	0	0	0	0
Career Total	**8**	**0**	**0**	**0**	**134**

Going: Sf: 0-4 GS: 0-1 Gd: 0-0 GF: - Fm: 0-0
Distance: 2m/2m3: 0-6 2m4-2m7: 0-0 3m+: 0-0
Track: LH: 0-1 RH: 0-2 Tight: 0-1 Gall: 0-0
Aids: Bl: 0-0 Vi: 0-0 Tstrap: 0-1
Best Rating: 63 5/99 DRoy 2m gd-fm NHF

The Toiseach (IRE)

11-y-o b g Phardante (FR)-Owens Toi (Master Owen)
J R Fanshawe T & J Vestey

Placings:01/330412/12113111/1PP1/PP-P (2296)
2001/02: 24^{P}G

	Starts	1st	2nd	3rd	Win & Pl
Chases	1	0	0	0	
Career Total	**23**	**10**	**2**	**3**	**77124**

161	3/99	Newb	3m	B HCh	G-F	£9981
157	11/98	Asct	3m110y	B HCh	GD	£10221
152	3/98	Donc	3m2f	B(0-145)HCh	SFT	£13511
151	2/98	Asct	3m110y	A Ch	GD	£18840
145	1/98	Donc	3m	D(0-115)HCh	GD	£4258
110	12/97	Hntg	2m4f110y	E(0-110)HCh	GD	£2795
112	11/97	Hntg	2m4f110y	D Ch	G-F	£3552
126	5/97	Worc	3m	D(0-125)HHdl	G-S	£2903
119	3/97	Towc	2m5f	D(0-120)HHdl	G-F	£2945
116	3/96	Newb	2m5f	D Hdl	SFT	£3891

Total win prize-money £72899

Going: Sf: 0-0 GS: 0-0 Gd: 0-1 GF: - Fm: 0-0
Distance: 2m/2m3: 0-0 2m4-2m7: 0-0 3m+: 0-1
Track: LH: 0-0 RH: 0-1 Tight: 0-0 Gall: 0-0
Aids: Bl: 0-0 Vi: 0-1 Tstrap: 0-1
Best Rating: 161 3/99 Newb 3m gd-fm Ch

The Tube (IRE)

94 60
4-y-o b f Royal Abjar (USA)-Grandeur And Grace (USA) (Septieme Ciel (USA))
P Bowen (Andrew Reid 20/10) D R James

Placings:5P (4737)
2001/02: 17^{5}G, 16^{P}GF

	Starts	1st	2nd	3rd	Win & Pl
Hurdles	2	0	0	0	0
Career Total	**2**	**0**	**0**	**0**	**0**

Going: Sf: 0-0 GS: 0-0 Gd: 0-1 GF: - Fm: 0-1
Distance: 2m/2m3: 0-2 2m4-2m7: 0-0 3m+: 0-0
Track: LH: 0-0 RH: 0-2 Tight: 0-0 Gall: 0-0
Aids: Bl: 0-0 Vi: 0-0 Tstrap: 0-0
Best Rating: 60 4/02 Hrfd 2m1f good Hdl

The Villager (IRE)

100 125
6-y-o br g Zaffaran (USA)-Kitty Wren (Warpath)
N A Twiston-Davies Mrs S Tainton

Placings:210-131140 (4229)
2001/02: 16^{1}G, 21^{3}G, 20^{1}G, 20^{1}S, 21^{4}S, 21^{0}GS

	Starts	1st	2nd	3rd	Win & Pl
NH Flat	1	1	0	0	1453
Hurdles	5	2	0	1	9836
Career Total	**9**	**4**	**1**	**1**	**13540**

121	12/01	Hayd	2m4f	D Hdl	SFT	£3770
115	11/01	Hayd	2m4f	D Hdl	GD	£3861
109	10/01	Hntg	2m110y	H NHF	GD	£1452
109	1/01	Donc	2m110y	H NHF	GD	£1771

Total win prize-money £10855

Going: Sf: 1-2 GS: 0-1 Gd: 2-3 GF: - Fm: 0-0
Distance: 2m/2m3: 1-1 **2m4-2m7: 2-5** 3m+: 0-0
Track: **LH: 2-4** RH: 1-1 Tight: 0-0 **Gall: 1-3**
Aids: Bl: 0-0 Vi: 0-0 Tstrap: 0-1
Best Rating: 125 1/02 Wwck 2m5f soft Hdl

Winner of bumpers, he looked to be crying out for a greater test of stamina when making his debut over obstacles at Cheltenham in October, and scored twice over two miles four before a fair effort at Warwick when fourth to Classified. Appreciates good ground and, at this stage, looks a similar type to Beau, who is by the same sire and races in the same colours.

The Warrior (IRE)

79 59
6-y-o gr g Willie Joe (IRE)-Fast And Straight (IRE) (Shirley Heights)
T P McGovern A J Loader

Placings:0-0 (3272)
2001/02: 16^{0}S

	Starts	1st	2nd	3rd	Win & Pl
Hurdles	1	0	0	0	
Career Total	**2**	**0**	**0**	**0**	

Going: Sf: 0-1 GS: 0-0 Gd: 0-0 GF: - Fm: 0-0
Distance: 2m/2m3: 0-1 2m4-2m7: 0-0 3m+: 0-0
Track: LH: 0-1 RH: 0-0 Tight: 0-1 Gall: 0-0
Aids: Bl: 0-0 Vi: 0-0 Tstrap: 0-0
Best Rating: 59 1/02 Plum 2m soft Hdl

The Wasp (IRE)

10-y-o gr g Lancastrian-Moll Of Kintire (Politico (USA))
C C Bealby Miss Mary Samworth

Placings:0/3P/P/PPP6/P **(3857)**
2001/02: 24^{P}S

	Starts	1st	2nd	3rd	Win & Pl
Chases	1	0	0	0	
Career Total	9	0	0	1	471

Going: Sf: 0-1 GS: 0-0 Gd: 0-0 GF: - Fm: 0-0
Distance: 2m/2m3: 0-0 2m4-2m7: 0-0 3m+: 0-1
Track: LH: 0-1 RH: 0-0 Tight: 0-0 Gall: 0-1
Aids: Bl: 0-0 Vi: 0-0 Tstrap: 0-0
Best Rating: 72 12/97 Sedg 3m3f good Ch

The Welder

8-y-o b g Buckley-Crystal Run Vii (Damsire Unregistered)
V Y Gethin (N A Twiston-Davies 9/6) V Y Gethin

Placings:503/P60F **(4741)**
2001/02: 19^{P}G, 17^{6}GS, 20^{0}G, 24^{F}GF

	Starts	1st	2nd	3rd	Win & Pl
Hurdles	3	0	0	0	0
Chases	1	0	0	0	0
Career Total	7	0	0	1	241

Going: Sf: 0-0 GS: 0-1 Gd: 0-2 GF: - Fm: 0-1
Distance: 2m/2m3: 0-1 2m4-2m7: 0-2 3m+: 0-1
Track: LH: 0-2 RH: 0-2 Tight: 0-2 Gall: 0-0
Aids: Bl: 0-0 Vi: 0-0 Tstrap: 0-1
Best Rating: 91 3/00 Ludl 2m good NHF

The Whole Hog (IRE)

13-y-o b g Cataldi-Beeston (Our Babu)
D E Ingle J M B Cookson

Placings:00/5PPP/U2121/1413414/F3PP/56/F-0 **(0205)**
2001/02: 25^{0}G

	Starts	1st	2nd	3rd	Win & Pl
Chases	1	0	0	0	
Career Total	26	5	2	2	19148

100 11/97 Leic 2m7f110y E(0-110)HCh G-F £3464
101 10/97 Towc 3m1f E(0-115)HCh G-F £2852
92 5/97 Sedg 3m3f E Ch G-F £3059
4/97 NAbb 3m2f110y E Ch FRM £2846
79 3/97 Font 3m2f110y E Ch G-F £3132
Total win prize-money £15355

Going: Sf: 0-0 GS: 0-0 Gd: 0-1 GF: - Fm: 0-0
Distance: 2m/2m3: 0-0 2m4-2m7: 0-0 3m+: 0-1
Track: LH: 0-1 RH: 0-0 Tight: 0-0 Gall: 0-0
Aids: Bl: 0-0 Vi: 0-0 Tstrap: 0-0
Best Rating: 101 9/98 Hntg 3m gd-fm Ch

The Wiley Kalmuck (IRE)

101(103c) (103c)73
8-y-o b g Be My Native (USA)-Beecom Silk (English Prince)
A Crook Noel O'Brien

Placings:0500020530/001026400/0P0U0F0010-250P44050 **(4578)**
2001/02: 25^{2}GF, 24^{5}F, 22^{0}GS, 27^{P}S, 25^{4}GF, 25^{4}G, 24^{0}S, 21^{5}S, 23^{0}G

	Starts	1st	2nd	3rd	Win & Pl
Hurdles	7	0	0	0	0
Chases	2	0	1	0	776
Career Total	38	2	3	1	8659

104 12/00 Muss 3m F(0-90)HHdl GD £1813
96 9/99 Gowr 3m (0-102)HHdl Y-S £4312
Total win prize-money £6126

Going: Sf: 0-3 GS: 0-1 Gd: 0-2 GF: - Fm: 0-3
Distance: 2m/2m3: 0-0 2m4-2m7: 0-3 3m+: 0-6
Track: LH: 0-8 RH: 0-1 Tight: 0-5 Gall: 0-1
Aids: Bl: 0-7 Vi: 0-0 Tstrap: 0-0
Best Rating: 104 12/00 Muss 3m good Hdl

Selling-class hurdler.

The Winkster (IRE)

8-y-o b/br g Black Minstrel-Oremus (Marisco)
D M Grissell Cockerell Cowing Racing

Placings:0-0 **(0039)**
2001/02: 22^{0}GS

	Starts	1st	2nd	3rd	Win & Pl
Hurdles	1	0	0	0	
Career Total	2	0	0	0	

Going: Sf: 0-0 GS: 0-1 Gd: 0-0 GF: - Fm: 0-0
Distance: 2m/2m3: 0-0 2m4-2m7: 0-1 3m+: 0-0
Track: LH: 0-0 RH: 0-0 Tight: 0-0 Gall: 0-0
Aids: Bl: 0-0 Vi: 0-0 Tstrap: 0-0
Best Rating:

The Woodstock Lady

107 100
5-y-o ch m Barathea (IRE)-Howlin' (USA) (Alleged (USA))
P J Hobbs Richard Green (fine Paintings)

Placings:32112 **(1952)**
2001/02: 17^{3}G, 18^{2}GF, 19^{1}GF, 22^{1}GF, 22^{2}GF

	Starts	1st	2nd	3rd	Win & Pl
Hurdles	5	2	2	1	6997
Career Total	5	2	2	1	6997

98 10/01 Extr 2m6f110y F(0-100)HHdl G-F £2548
96 9/01 Hrfd 2m3f110y E Hdl G-F £2646
Total win prize-money £5194

Going: Sf: 0-0 GS: 0-0 Gd: 0-1 GF: - Fm: 2-4
Distance: 2m/2m3: 0-2 **2m4-2m7: 2-3** 3m+: 0-0
Track: LH: 0-1 **RH: 1-2** Tight: 0-1 Gall: 0-0
Aids: Bl: 0-0 Vi: 0-0 Tstrap: 0-0
Best Rating: 100 11/01 Extr 2m6f110y gd-fm Hdl

Has improved with experience over hurdles, and helped by the step up in trip scored at Hereford and Exeter in the autumn of 2001. Stays two miles six plus, acts on fast ground, although she won on soft on the Flat.

Theatreland (USA)

(101h) (112h)
5-y-o b g Dynaformer (USA)-Mime (Cure The Blues (USA))
S E H Sherwood (P J Hobbs 21/11) Knightsbridge Bc Glos Ltd & A Clift

Placings:13-0223P **(2391)**
2001/02: 16^{0}GF, 19^{2}G, 24^{2}GF, 24^{3}G, 24^{P}S

	Starts	1st	2nd	3rd	Win & Pl
Hurdles	5	0	2	1	2623
Career Total	7	1	2	2	5835

105 8/00 Worc 2m E Hdl G-F £2785
Total win prize-money £2785

Going: Sf: 0-1 GS: 0-0 Gd: 0-2 GF: - Fm: 0-2
Distance: 2m/2m3: 0-1 2m4-2m7: 0-1 3m+: 0-3
Track: LH: 0-2 RH: 0-3 Tight: 0-0 Gall: 0-0
Aids: Bl: 0-1 Vi: 0-0 Tstrap: 0-0
Best Rating: 112 11/01 Kemp 3m110y good Hdl

Made a successful debut over hurdles, but has since found life a little harder. Acts on good to firm and stays three miles.

Thebwlboy

85(92h) (63h)82
9-y-o ch g Interrex (CAN)-Super Melody (Song)
J Neville D C Gibbs

Placings:0013220300-00 **(0679)**
2001/02: 17^{0}GF, 17^{0}G

	Starts	1st	2nd	3rd	Win & Pl
Hurdles	2	0	0	0	
Career Total	12	1	2	2	5348

85 6/00 NAbb 2m1f E Hdl G-F £2359
Total win prize-money £2359

Going: Sf: 0-0 GS: 0-0 Gd: 0-1 GF: - Fm: 0-1
Distance: 2m/2m3: 0-2 2m4-2m7: 0-0 3m+: 0-0
Track: LH: 0-1 RH: 0-1 Tight: 0-2 Gall: 0-0
Aids: Bl: 0-0 Vi: 0-0 Tstrap: 0-0
Best Rating: 89 9/00 Bang 2m1f gd-fm Hdl

Thegift

93(104h) (79h)92
9-y-o b g Say Primula-Fair Echo (Quality Fair)
J Howard Johnson G F Bear

Placings:00/33/1-P66 **(4487)**
2001/02: 24^{P}GF, 23^{6}G, 26^{6}GS

	Starts	1st	2nd	3rd	Win & Pl
Hurdles	1	0	0	0	0
Chases	2	0	0	0	0
Career Total	8	1	0	2	4048

89 1/01 Muss 3m F(0-110)HHdl G-S £3038
Total win prize-money £3038

Going: Sf: 0-0 GS: 0-1 Gd: 0-1 GF: - Fm: 0-1
Distance: 2m/2m3: 0-0 2m4-2m7: 0-0 3m+: 0-3
Track: LH: 0-0 RH: 0-2 Tight: 0-0 Gall: 0-0
Aids: Bl: 0-0 Vi: 0-0 Tstrap: 0-0
Best Rating: 92 3/02 Carl 3m2f gd-sft Ch

Thelonius (IRE)

108 128
7-y-o ch g Statoblest-Little Sega (FR) (Bellypha)
P J Hobbs Michael C Morris

Placings:01120/53 **(0581)**
2001/02: 16^{5}G, 16^{3}GF

	Starts	1st	2nd	3rd	Win & Pl
Hurdles	2	0	0	1	891
Career Total	7	2	1	1	9059

122 11/99 Winc 2m D(0-125)HHdl GD £3454
96 10/99 Tntn 2m1f E Hdl G-F £3151

Total win prize-money £6605

Going: Sf: 0-0 GS: 0-0 Gd: 0-1 GF: - Fm: 0-1
Distance: 2m/2m3: 0-2 2m4-2m7: 0-0 3m+: 0-0
Track: LH: 0-2 RH: 0-0 Tight: 0-1 Gall: 0-0
Aids: Bl: 0-0 Vi: 0-0 Tstrap: 0-0
Best Rating: 128 5/01 Hayd 2m good Hdl

Themanfromcarlisle

91f 79f

6-y-o br g Jupiter Island-Country Mistress (Town And Country)
M Pitman Mrs Elizabeth Pearce

Placings:*4* (4571)
2001/02: 16^{4}G

	Starts	1st	2nd	3rd	Win & Pl
NH Flat	1	0	0	0	0
Career Total	**1**	**0**	**0**	**0**	**0**

Going: Sf: 0-0 GS: 0-0 Gd: 0-1 GF: - Fm: 0-0
Distance: 2m/2m3: 0-1 2m4-2m7: 0-0 3m+: 0-0
Track: LH: 0-0 RH: 0-1 Tight: 0-0 Gall: 0-0
Aids: Bl: 0-0 Vi: 0-0 Tstrap: 0-0
Best Rating: 79 4/02 Towc 2m good NHF

Won a maiden point over two and a half miles in January. Well held but shaped with promise on bumper debut in April.

Theydon Star (NZ)

74 49

5-y-o b g Classic Fame (USA)-Hilarity (NZ) (St Hilarion (USA))
Mrs N Smith Tony Hayward

Placings:*60U* (4637)
2001/02: 16^{6}GF, 18^{0}GS, 20^{U}GF

	Starts	1st	2nd	3rd	Win & Pl
NH Flat	1	0	0	0	0
Hurdles	2	0	0	0	0
Career Total	**3**	**0**	**0**	**0**	**0**

Going: Sf: 0-0 GS: 0-1 Gd: 0-0 GF: - Fm: 0-2
Distance: 2m/2m3: 0-2 2m4-2m7: 0-1 3m+: 0-0
Track: LH: 0-2 RH: 0-1 Tight: 0-1 Gall: 0-0
Aids: Bl: 0-0 Vi: 0-0 Tstrap: 0-0
Best Rating: 79 8/01 Worc 2m gd-fm NHF

Thieves'Glen

93f 112f

4-y-o b g Teenoso (USA)-Hollow Creek (Tarqogan)
H Morrison Panda Wilson & Stephanie Gore

Placings:*4* (4900)
2001/02: 16^{4}G

	Starts	1st	2nd	3rd	Win & Pl
NH Flat	1	0	0	0	0
Career Total	**1**	**0**	**0**	**0**	**0**

Going: Sf: 0-0 GS: 0-0 Gd: 0-1 GF: - Fm: 0-0
Distance: 2m/2m3: 0-1 2m4-2m7: 0-0 3m+: 0-0
Track: LH: 0-0 RH: 0-1 Tight: 0-0 Gall: 0-0
Aids: Bl: 0-0 Vi: 0-0 Tstrap: 0-0
Best Rating: 112 4/02 Prth 2m110y good NHF

Think Again (IRE)

8-y-o b g Long Pond-Either Or (Boreen (FR))
R Craggs Ray Craggs

Placings:P/0/6P/PSF-P (1588)
2001/02: 17^{P}GS

	Starts	1st	2nd	3rd	Win & Pl
Hurdles	1	0	0	0	
Career Total	**8**	**0**	**0**	**0**	**0**

Going: Sf: 0-0 GS: 0-1 Gd: 0-0 GF: - Fm: 0-0
Distance: 2m/2m3: 0-1 2m4-2m7: 0-0 3m+: 0-0
Track: LH: 0-1 RH: 0-0 Tight: 0-1 Gall: 0-0
Aids: Bl: 0-0 Vi: 0-0 Tstrap: 0-0
Best Rating: 73 9/00 Sedg 2m1f good Hdl

Think On

96 84

6-y-o b g Then Again-Its My Turn (Palm Track)
J Mackie Mrs Sue Adams

Placings:*4030* (3271)
2001/02: 17^{4}G, 16^{0}S, 20^{3}S, 16^{0}G

	Starts	1st	2nd	3rd	Win & Pl
NH Flat	2	0	0	0	0
Hurdles	2	0	0	1	383
Career Total	**4**	**0**	**0**	**1**	**383**

Going: Sf: 0-2 GS: 0-0 Gd: 0-2 GF: - Fm: 0-0
Distance: 2m/2m3: 0-3 2m4-2m7: 0-1 3m+: 0-0
Track: LH: 0-3 RH: 0-1 Tight: 0-1 Gall: 0-1
Aids: Bl: 0-0 Vi: 0-0 Tstrap: 0-0
Best Rating: 91 11/01 Hayd 2m soft NHF

A half-brother to winning hurdlers Silverdale Fox and Silverdale Knight, as well as Prince Nicholas, showed some ability in bumpers.

Thinkaboutthat (IRE)

13-y-o br g Roselier (FR)-Rossian (Silent Spring)
J F W Muir J F W Muir

Placings:046/0P/P-P (0094)
2001/02: 25^{P}S

	Starts	1st	2nd	3rd	Win & Pl
Chases	1	0	0	0	
Career Total	**7**	**0**	**0**	**0**	**73**

Going: Sf: 0-1 GS: 0-0 Gd: 0-0 GF: - Fm: 0-0
Distance: 2m/2m3: 0-0 2m4-2m7: 0-0 3m+: 0-1
Track: LH: 0-1 RH: 0-0 Tight: 0-0 Gall: 0-0
Aids: Bl: 0-0 Vi: 0-0 Tstrap: 0-0
Best Rating: 81 4/98 Carl 3m2f good Ch

Thirkleby Alissica

70 38

6-y-o ch m Nomadic Way (USA)-Thirkleby Skeena (Marching On)
P Beaumont Peter Beaumont

Placings:*00P*040P0 (4871)
2001/02: 16^{0}G, 16^{0}G, 16^{P}GS, 19^{0}S, 16^{4}HY, 17^{0}GS, 21^{P}G, 25^{0}GF

	Starts	1st	2nd	3rd	Win & Pl
NH Flat	3	0	0	0	0
Hurdles	5	0	0	0	0
Career Total	**8**	**0**	**0**	**0**	**0**

Going: Sf: 0-2 GS: 0-2 Gd: 0-3 GF: - Fm: 0-1
Distance: 2m/2m3: 0-6 2m4-2m7: 0-1 3m+: 0-1
Track: LH: 0-6 RH: 0-2 Tight: 0-5 Gall: 0-0
Aids: Bl: 0-0 Vi: 0-0 Tstrap: 0-0
Best Rating: 65 11/01 Weth 2m good NHF

Thirty Below (IRE)

13-y-o b g Strong Gale-Arctic Bavard (Le Bavard (FR))
Miss J Wickens Miss J Wickens

Placings:006P/102523610006330/342P**010P0P0/000 334400P6P0/0UPP-P** (0323)
2001/02: 25^{P}G

	Starts	1st	2nd	3rd	Win & Pl
Chases	1	0	0	0	
Career Total	**48**	**3**	**3**	**6**	**13777**

87	8/98	MRas	3m1f	E(0-100)HCh	GD	£3185
	10/97	Weth	3m1f	F(0-105)HHdl	G-F	£2092
	8/97	NAbb	2m6f	E Hdl	G-F	£2232

Total win prize-money £7511

Going: Sf: 0-0 GS: 0-0 Gd: 0-1 GF: - Fm: 0-0
Distance: 2m/2m3: 0-0 2m4-2m7: 0-0 3m+: 0-1
Track: LH: 0-0 RH: 0-1 Tight: 0-1 Gall: 0-0
Aids: Bl: 0-0 Vi: 0-0 Tstrap: 0-0
Best Rating: 92 8/99 MRas 3m1f gd-fm Ch

This Is Serious (IRE)

110 (86h)146

8-y-o ch g Broken Hearted-Lady Virtue (IRE) (Oats)
C F Swan Granit City Syndicate

Placings:0000/*0*030S22125/0**0001F140**P3-00113011P (4299)
2001/02: 16^{0}S, 24^{0}G, 24^{1}YS, 28^{1}Y, 25^{3}Y, 24^{0}Y, 24^{1}HY, 33^{1}S, 34^{P}HY

	Starts	1st	2nd	3rd	Win & Pl
Hurdles	2	0	0	0	0
Chases	7	4	0	1	107846
Career Total	**34**	**7**	**3**	**3**	**127226**

146	2/02	Newc	4m1f	B(0-150)HCh	SFT	£37700
143	1/02	Gowr	3m	HCh	HVY	£33895
118	11/01	Cork	3m4f	(0-140)HCh	YLD	£18346
111	10/01	Wxfd	3m	HCh	Y-S	£15726
97	12/00	Muss	3m	D(0-120)HCh	GD	£4329
114	11/00	Navn	3m	HHdl	SFT	£6624
110	3/00	Ludl	3m	F(0-105)HHdl	SFT	£3718

Total win prize-money £120340

Going: Sf: 2-4 GS: 0-0 Gd: 0-1 GF: - Fm: 0-0
Distance: 2m/2m3: 0-1 2m4-2m7: 0-0 **3m+: 4-8**
Track: LH: 1-3 **RH: 2-3** Tight: 0-0 **Gall: 1-1**
Aids: Bl: 0-0 Vi: 0-0 Tstrap: 0-0
Best Rating: 146 2/02 Newc 4m1f soft Ch

Useful Irish staying chaser, successful in the Thyestes at Gowran Park and the Eider at Newcastle. Stays four miles plus, acts on testing ground.

This One Is A Boy (IRE)

78 35

6-y-o b g Executive Perk-Belinda Vard (Le Bavard (FR))
J J O'Neill Darren C Mercer

Placings:*0P-0P* (1651)
2001/02: 22^{0}GS, 20^{P}GS

	Starts	1st	2nd	3rd	Win & Pl
Hurdles	2	0	0	0	
Career Total	**4**	**0**	**0**	**0**	

Going: Sf: 0-0 GS: 0-1 Gd: 0-1 GF: - Fm: 0-0
Distance: 2m/2m3: 0-0 2m4-2m7: 0-2 3m+: 0-0
Track: LH: 0-2 RH: 0-0 Tight: 0-1 Gall: 0-0
Aids: Bl: 0-0 Vi: 0-0 Tstrap: 0-0
Best Rating: 69 4/01 Muss 2m1f gd-fm NHF

This Thyne

87 65

6-y-o b m Good Thyne (USA)-Dalkey Sound (Crash Course)
Mrs M Reveley G S Brown

Placings:*50*P0 **(4522)**
2001/02: 16^{5}G, 16^{0}S, 22^{P}HY, 17^{0}G

	Starts	1st	2nd	3rd	Win & Pl
NH Flat	2	0	0	0	0
Hurdles	2	0	0	0	0
Career Total	**4**	**0**	**0**	**0**	**0**

Going: Sf: 0-2 GS: 0-0 Gd: 0-2 GF: - Fm: 0-0
Distance: 2m/2m3: 0-3 2m4-2m7: 0-1 3m+: 0-0
Track: LH: 0-2 RH: 0-1 Tight: 0-1 Gall: 0-0
Aids: Bl: 0-0 Vi: 0-0 Tstrap: 0-0
Best Rating: 90 11/01 Weth 2m good NHF

Thisthatandtother (IRE)

109f 135f

6-y-o b g Bob Back (USA)-Baden (IRE) (Furry Glen)
P F Nicholls C G Roach

Placings:*2145* **(4679)**
2001/02: 16^{2}G, 16^{1}S, 16^{4}GS, 17^{5}G

	Starts	1st	2nd	3rd	Win & Pl
NH Flat	4	1	1	0	3386
Career Total	**4**	**1**	**1**	**0**	**3386**

115 2/02 Winc 2m H NHF SFT £1736
Total win prize-money £1736

Going: Sf: 1-1 GS: 0-1 Gd: 0-2 GF: - Fm: 0-0
Distance: **2m/2m3: 1-4** 2m4-2m7: 0-0 3m+: 0-0
Track: LH: 0-1 **RH: 1-2** Tight: 0-0 Gall: 0-0
Aids: Bl: 0-0 Vi: 0-0 Tstrap: 0-0
Best Rating: 135 3/02 Chel 2m110y gd-sft NHF

Out of a winning hurdler, made an encouraging debut at Ascot before scoring at Wincanton. Ran fourth in the Festival bumper at Cheltenham and fifth at Aintree. Should make a top novice hurdler next season.

Thistle Do

92f 61f

4-y-o b g College Chapel-Fishki (Niniski (USA))
L Lungo S T Brankin

Placings:*0* **(4019)**
2001/02: 16^{0}GS

	Starts	1st	2nd	3rd	Win & Pl
NH Flat	1	0	0	0	
Career Total	**1**	**0**	**0**	**0**	

Going: Sf: 0-0 GS: 0-1 Gd: 0-0 GF: - Fm: 0-0
Distance: 2m/2m3: 0-1 2m4-2m7: 0-0 3m+: 0-0
Track: LH: 0-1 RH: 0-0 Tight: 0-0 Gall: 0-1
Aids: Bl: 0-0 Vi: 0-0 Tstrap: 0-0
Best Rating: 61 3/02 Donc 2m110y gd-sft NHF

Thistlekicker (IRE)

103 81

10-y-o b g Mandalus-Miss Ranova (Giacometti)
Mrs D Thomson Mrs Jean McGregor

Placings:*00/04*OP/P2P0-34F0034P2650 **(4898)**
2001/02: 16^{3}GF, 16^{4}F, 20^{F}F, 16^{0}GF, 16^{0}GF, 16^{3}GF, 20^{4}G, 16^{P}G, 17^{2}GF, 17^{6}G, 16^{5}GF, 16^{0}G

	Starts	1st	2nd	3rd	Win & Pl
Hurdles	11	0	1	1	1057
Chases	1	0	0	1	448
Career Total	**22**	**0**	**2**	**2**	**2439**

Going: Sf: 0-0 GS: 0-0 Gd: 0-4 GF: - Fm: 0-8
Distance: 2m/2m3: 0-10 2m4-2m7: 0-2 3m+: 0-0
Track: LH: 0-4 RH: 0-6 Tight: 0-2 Gall: 0-0
Aids: Bl: 0-0 Vi: 0-0 Tstrap: 0-0
Best Rating: 80 5/01 Hexm 2m firm Hdl

Moderate hurdler, suited by fast ground.

Thornaby Girl (IRE)

6-y-o b m Fayruz-Anita's Love (IRE) (Anita's Prince)
Mrs L B Normile L B N Racing Club

Placings:0-PU **(0800)**
2001/02: 16^{P}GS, 16^{U}GF

	Starts	1st	2nd	3rd	Win & Pl
Hurdles	2	0	0	0	
Career Total	**3**	**0**	**0**	**0**	

Going: Sf: 0-0 GS: 0-1 Gd: 0-0 GF: - Fm: 0-1
Distance: 2m/2m3: 0-2 2m4-2m7: 0-0 3m+: 0-0
Track: LH: 0-0 RH: 0-2 Tight: 0-0 Gall: 0-0
Aids: Bl: 0-0 Vi: 0-0 Tstrap: 0-0
Best Rating:

Thornhill (FR)

(98h) (80h)

6-y-o b g Tel Quel (FR)-The Dream I Dream (USA) (Theatrical)
John Allen Avon Estates Ltd

Placings:4/06304354-55 **(0372)**
2001/02: 17^{5}GS, 16^{5}GF

	Starts	1st	2nd	3rd	Win & Pl
Hurdles	2	0	0	0	0
Career Total	**11**	**0**	**0**	**2**	**9936**

Going: Sf: 0-0 GS: 0-1 Gd: 0-0 GF: - Fm: 0-1
Distance: 2m/2m3: 0-2 2m4-2m7: 0-0 3m+: 0-0
Track: LH: 0-0 RH: 0-2 Tight: 0-1 Gall: 0-1
Aids: Bl: 0-0 Vi: 0-0 Tstrap: 0-0
Best Rating: 80 5/01 Folk 2m1f110y gd-sft Hdl

Thorntoun House (IRE)

(89h) (58h)

9-y-o b g Durgam (USA)-Commanche Song (Commanche Run)
J S Goldie W M Johnstone

Placings:005/100P2**P**52P4F5/210F132F114160/FUP U-P0UP **(3789)**
2001/02: 25^{P}S, 24^{0}S, 25^{U}HY, 33^{P}S

	Starts	1st	2nd	3rd	Win & Pl
Hurdles	1	0	0	0	0
Chases	3	0	0	0	0
Career Total	**37**	**6**	**4**	**1**	**34932**

125	2/00	Ayr	2m5f110y	C HCh	HVY	£9016
125	1/00	Ayr	3m1f	E(0-105)HCh	SFT	£3217
120	12/99	Ayr	2m4f	E(0-105)HCh	HVY	£3246
112	9/99	Prth	3m	F(0-100)HCh	SFT	£5810
105	6/99	Prth	3m	D Ch	G-S	£4506
96	9/98	Prth	2m4f110y	D Hdl	GD	£2866

Total win prize-money £28662

Going: Sf: 0-4 GS: 0-0 Gd: 0-0 GF: - Fm: 0-0
Distance: 2m/2m3: 0-0 2m4-2m7: 0-0 3m+: 0-4
Track: LH: 0-4 RH: 0-0 Tight: 0-0 Gall: 0-2
Aids: Bl: 0-0 Vi: 0-3 Tstrap: 0-0
Best Rating: 125 2/00 Ayr 2m5f110y heavy Ch

Thorpey's Thriller

6-y-o br m Homo Sapien-Inbisat (Beldale Flutter (USA))
Mrs A M Thorpe Don Jenkins

Placings:*0*-S **(0684)**
2001/02: 17^{S}G

	Starts	1st	2nd	3rd	Win & Pl
NH Flat	1	0	0	0	
Career Total	**2**	**0**	**0**	**0**	

Going: Sf: 0-0 GS: 0-0 Gd: 0-1 GF: - Fm: 0-0
Distance: 2m/2m3: 0-1 2m4-2m7: 0-0 3m+: 0-0
Track: LH: 0-1 RH: 0-0 Tight: 0-1 Gall: 0-0
Aids: Bl: 0-0 Vi: 0-0 Tstrap: 0-0
Best Rating:

Thosewerethedays

110(104h) (101h)143

9-y-o b g Past Glories-Charlotte's Festival (Gala Performance (USA))
Ferdy Murphy Mrs J D Goodfellow

Placings:3131FP **(4298)**
2001/02: 16^{3}GS, 16^{1}G, 16^{3}GS, 20^{1}S, 20^{F}G, 26^{P}HY

	Starts	1st	2nd	3rd	Win & Pl
Hurdles	1	0	0	1	447
Chases	5	2	0	1	8209
Career Total	**6**	**2**	**0**	**2**	**8656**

143	2/02	Kemp	2m4f110y	D Ch	SFT	£5300
125	12/01	Hrfd	2m	F Ch	GD	£2431

Total win prize-money £7732

Going: Sf: 1-2 GS: 0-2 Gd: 1-2 GF: - Fm: 0-0
Distance: 2m/2m3: 1-3 2m4-2m7: 1-2 3m+: 0-1
Track: LH: 0-3 **RH: 2-3** Tight: 0-1 Gall: 0-0
Aids: Bl: 0-0 Vi: 0-0 Tstrap: 0-0
Best Rating: 143 2/02 Kemp 2m4f110y soft Ch

Was running for the first time in two and a half years when a promising third in a novice hurdle at Kelso in November 2001. Won a maiden chase next time. Acts on good to heavy ground. Suited by two and a half miles.

Thrashing

105 97

7-y-o b g Kahyasi-White-Wash (Final Straw)
Simon Earle Graham Brown

Placings:06365300/022F32P5U-221 **(0927)**
2001/02: 19^{2}G, 22^{2}GF, 25^{1}GF

	Starts	1st	2nd	3rd	Win & Pl
Hurdles	3	1	2	0	3333
Career Total	**20**	**1**	**5**	**3**	**6682**

87 7/01 Wolv 3m1f F Hdl G-F £1962
Total win prize-money £1963

Going: Sf: 0-0 GS: 0-0 Gd: 0-1 GF: - Fm: 1-2
Distance: 2m/2m3: 0-0 2m4-2m7: 0-2 **3m+: 1-1**
Track: **LH: 1-2** RH: 0-1 **Tight: 1-2** Gall: 0-0
Aids: Bl: 0-0 Vi: 0-0 **Tstrap: 1-3**
Best Rating: 106 7/00 Sedg 2m5f110y gd-fm Hdl

Three Angels (IRE)

89 **90**

7-y-o b g Houmayoun (FR)-Mullaghroe (Tarboosh (USA))
A W Carroll (M H Tompkins 5/6) R T C Racing

Placings:6-2P (1769)
2001/02: 16²GF, 17ᴾG

	Starts	1st	2nd	3rd	Win & Pl
Hurdles	2	0	1	0	456
Career Total	**3**	**0**	**1**	**0**	**456**

Going: Sf: 0-0 GS: 0-0 Gd: 0-1 GF: - Fm: 0-1
Distance: 2m/2m3: 0-2 2m4-2m7: 0-0 3m+: 0-0
Track: LH: 0-1 RH: 0-1 Tight: 0-1 Gall: 0-0
Aids: Bl: 0-2 Vi: 0-0 Tstrap: 0-0
Best Rating: 90 5/01 Fknm 2m gd-fm Hdl

Three Cherries

86 **70**

6-y-o ch m Formidable (USA)-Mistral's Dancer (Shareef Dancer (USA))
R E Barr P Cartmell

Placings:U0-R5P (1505)
2001/02: 16ᴿS, 17⁵GF, 17ᴾG

	Starts	1st	2nd	3rd	Win & Pl
Hurdles	3	0	0	0	0
Career Total	**5**	**0**	**0**	**0**	**0**

Going: Sf: 0-1 GS: 0-0 Gd: 0-1 GF: - Fm: 0-1
Distance: 2m/2m3: 0-3 2m4-2m7: 0-0 3m+: 0-0
Track: LH: 0-3 RH: 0-0 Tight: 0-2 Gall: 0-0
Aids: Bl: 0-0 Vi: 0-0 Tstrap: 0-0
Best Rating: 70 9/01 Sedg 2m1f gd-fm Hdl

Three Clouds

77 **53**

5-y-o b g Rainbow Quest (USA)-Three Tails (Blakeney)
G L Moore George Smith Ltd

Placings:P6 (4781)
2001/02: 16ᴾG, 16⁶GF

	Starts	1st	2nd	3rd	Win & Pl
Hurdles	2	0	0	0	0
Career Total	**2**	**0**	**0**	**0**	**0**

Going: Sf: 0-0 GS: 0-0 Gd: 0-1 GF: - Fm: 0-1
Distance: 2m/2m3: 0-2 2m4-2m7: 0-0 3m+: 0-0
Track: LH: 0-1 RH: 0-1 Tight: 0-1 Gall: 0-0
Aids: Bl: 0-0 Vi: 0-0 Tstrap: 0-0
Best Rating: 53 4/02 Plum 2m gd-fm Hdl

Three Days Reign (IRE)

88 **91**

8-y-o br g Camden Town-Little Treat (Miners Lamp)
S E H Sherwood Entre-Nous

Placings:2/500-30 (1923)
2001/02: 21³GF, 20⁰G

	Starts	1st	2nd	3rd	Win & Pl
Hurdles	2	0	0	1	400
Career Total	**6**	**0**	**1**	**1**	**873**

Going: Sf: 0-0 GS: 0-0 Gd: 0-1 GF: - Fm: 0-1
Distance: 2m/2m3: 0-0 2m4-2m7: 0-2 3m+: 0-0
Track: LH: 0-0 RH: 0-1 Tight: 0-0 Gall: 0-0
Aids: Bl: 0-2 Vi: 0-0 Tstrap: 0-0
Best Rating: 107 5/99 Chep 2m110y good NHF

Three Eagles (USA)

108 **107**

5-y-o ch g Eagle Eyed (USA)-Tertiary (USA) (Vaguely Noble)
A Bailey Granite By Design Ltd

Placings:50-414026F504P435 (4896)
2001/02: 20⁴G, 20¹GS, 17⁴GF, 20⁰G, 24²G, 24⁶G, 23ᶠG, 23⁵HY, 25⁰GS, 23⁴GS, 20ᴾS, 20⁴S, 17³S, 20⁵G

	Starts	1st	2nd	3rd	Win & Pl
Hurdles	14	1	1	1	4616
Career Total	**16**	**1**	**1**	**1**	**4616**

101 8/01 Bang 2m4f F Hdl G-S £2268
Total win prize-money £2268

Going: Sf: 0-4 GS: 1-3 Gd: 0-6 GF: - Fm: 0-1
Distance: 2m/2m3: 0-2 **2m4-2m7: 1-7** 3m+: 0-5
Track: **LH: 1-10** RH: 0-4 **Tight: 1-7** Gall: 0-1
Aids: Bl: 0-0 Vi: 0-0 Tstrap: 0-0
Best Rating: 107 11/01 Hayd 2m7f110y good Hdl

A fair front-running hurdler. Handles most ground and goes well at Bangor.

Three Lions

106 **118**

5-y-o ch g Jupiter Island-Super Sol (Rolfe (USA))
R S Brookhouse (R F Johnson Houghton 14/2) R S Brookhouse

Placings:32F5 (4762)
2001/02: 17³S, 16²G, 16ᶠGS, 20⁵GF

	Starts	1st	2nd	3rd	Win & Pl
Hurdles	4	0	1	1	2251
Career Total	**4**	**0**	**1**	**1**	**2251**

Going: Sf: 0-1 GS: 0-1 Gd: 0-1 GF: - Fm: 0-1
Distance: 2m/2m3: 0-3 2m4-2m7: 0-1 3m+: 0-0
Track: LH: 0-1 RH: 0-3 Tight: 0-1 Gall: 0-0
Aids: Bl: 0-0 Vi: 0-0 Tstrap: 0-0
Best Rating: 118 2/02 Tntn 2m1f soft Hdl

A fair stayer on the Flat, he has shown ability over hurdles.

Three Saints (IRE)

13-y-o b g Rising-Oh Dora (Even Money)
W G Dutton (H D Daly 24/3) V Dutton

Placings:42/3F14/52U4/5P0P/5 (4846)
2001/02: 24⁵G

	Starts	1st	2nd	3rd	Win & Pl
Chases	1	0	0	0	0
Career Total	**15**	**1**	**2**	**1**	**6114**

103 3/96 Bang 2m4f110y E Ch HVY £3649
Total win prize-money £3649

Going: Sf: 0-0 GS: 0-0 Gd: 0-1 GF: - Fm: 0-0
Distance: 2m/2m3: 0-0 2m4-2m7: 0-0 3m+: 0-1
Track: LH: 0-1 RH: 0-0 Tight: 0-1 Gall: 0-0
Aids: Bl: 0-0 Vi: 0-0 Tstrap: 0-0
Best Rating: 103 3/96 Bang 2m4f110y heavy Ch

Three Weeks

100 **100**

9-y-o ch g Formidable (USA)-Zilda (FR) (Zino)
M J Wilkinson Edgcote Yacht Club

Placings:02/560/6413550/03150-2514 (2454)
2001/02: 17²G, 18⁵GS, 19¹G, 16⁴S

	Starts	1st	2nd	3rd	Win & Pl
Hurdles	4	1	1	0	4312
Career Total	**21**	**3**	**2**	**2**	**11447**

100 11/01 Tntn 2m3f110y F(0-110)HHdl GD £2520
93 12/00 Ludl 2m E(0-115)HHdl SFT £3532
113 11/99 Wwck 2m F(0-100)HHdl GD £2080
Total win prize-money £8133

Going: Sf: 0-1 GS: 0-1 Gd: 1-2 GF: - Fm: 0-0
Distance: 2m/2m3: 0-3 **2m4-2m7: 1-1** 3m+: 0-0
Track: LH: 0-3 **RH: 1-1 Tight: 1-3** Gall: 0-0
Aids: Bl: 0-0 Vi: 0-0 Tstrap: 0-0
Best Rating: 113 11/99 Wwck 2m good Hdl

Only a modest hurdler, his wins have come in ordinary handicap company. Has won on good and soft ground and stays up to two and a half miles.

Threefortycash (IRE)

5-y-o b g Balla Cove-Tigeen (Habitat)
Miss Kate Milligan A F Monk

Placings:6-PP (4094)
2001/02: 17ᴾGF, 16ᴾGS

	Starts	1st	2nd	3rd	Win & Pl
Hurdles	2	0	0	0	
Career Total	**3**	**0**	**0**	**0**	**0**

Going: Sf: 0-0 GS: 0-1 Gd: 0-0 GF: - Fm: 0-1
Distance: 2m/2m3: 0-2 2m4-2m7: 0-0 3m+: 0-0
Track: LH: 0-1 RH: 0-1 Tight: 0-2 Gall: 0-0
Aids: Bl: 0-0 Vi: 0-0 Tstrap: 0-0
Best Rating: 51 8/00 Ctml 2m1f110y gd-sft Hdl

Threes Company (IRE)

7-y-o b g Torus-Doonaree Belle (IRE) (Duky)
Mrs L C Jewell Bray Partners

Placings:6/000-PP (0983)
2001/02: 25ᴾGS, 19ᴾG

	Starts	1st	2nd	3rd	Win & Pl
Hurdles	2	0	0	0	
Career Total	**6**	**0**	**0**	**0**	**0**

Going: Sf: 0-0 GS: 0-1 Gd: 0-1 GF: - Fm: 0-0
Distance: 2m/2m3: 0-1 2m4-2m7: 0-0 3m+: 0-1
Track: LH: 0-2 RH: 0-0 Tight: 0-2 Gall: 0-0
Aids: Bl: 0-0 Vi: 0-0 Tstrap: 0-1
Best Rating: 47 1/01 Winc 2m gd-sft Hdl

Thrill A Minute (IRE)

99(101h) (85h)**120**

8-y-o b g Be My Native (USA)-Fairy Run (Deep Run)
J J O'Neill C D Carr

Placings:0/25P/02-46114PPP **(3893)**
2001/02: 20^{4}GF, 20^{6}G, 24^{1}S, 26^{1}HY, 22^{4}S, 25^{P}S, 23^{P}S, 29^{P}HY

	Starts	1st	2nd	3rd	Win & Pl
Hurdles	2	0	0	0	0
Chases	6	2	0	0	7020
Career Total	**14**	**2**	**2**	**0**	**8437**

120	11/01	Uttx	3m2f	F(0-100)HCh	HVY	£2982
100	10/01	Bang	3m110y	F(0-105)HCh	SFT	£3542

Total win prize-money £6525

Going: Sf: 2-6 GS: 0-0 Gd: 0-1 GF: - Fm: 0-1
Distance: 2m/2m3: 0-0 2m4-2m7: 0-3 **3m+: 2-5**
Track: **LH: 2-4** RH: 0-3 **Tight: 1-3** Gall: 0-0
Aids: Bl: 0-0 Vi: 0-0 Tstrap: 0-1
Best Rating: 120 11/01 Uttx 3m2f heavy Ch

Effective over three miles plus in soft ground.

Thrillofthechase

5-y-o ch m Saddlers' Hall (IRE)-General Chase (Scottish Reel)
D McCain Eamonn O'Malley

Placings:0000-P **(0499)**
2001/02: 17^{P}G

	Starts	1st	2nd	3rd	Win & Pl
Hurdles	1	0	0	0	
Career Total	**5**	**0**	**0**	**0**	

Going: Sf: 0-0 GS: 0-0 Gd: 0-1 GF: - Fm: 0-0
Distance: 2m/2m3: 0-1 2m4-2m7: 0-0 3m+: 0-0
Track: LH: 0-0 RH: 0-1 Tight: 0-0 Gall: 0-0
Aids: Bl: 0-1 Vi: 0-0 Tstrap: 0-0
Best Rating: 51 1/01 Donc 2m110y good Hdl

Through The Rye

112 **133**

6-y-o ch g Sabrehill (USA)-Baharlilys (Green Dancer (USA))
E W Tuer (W J Haggas 4/7) G Tuer

Placings:116F/011141 **(4393)**
2001/02: 19^{0}G, 16^{1}S, 17^{1}S, 16^{1}S, 16^{4}GS, 18^{1}HY

	Starts	1st	2nd	3rd	Win & Pl
Hurdles	6	4	0	0	22944
Career Total	**10**	**6**	**0**	**0**	**27970**

133	3/02	Kels	2m2f	C(0-135)HHdl	HVY	£8515
124	3/02	Donc	2m110y	D(0-120)HHdl	SFT	£3486
130	2/02	Sedg	2m1f	E(0-110)HHdl	SFT	£2947
115	2/02	Muss	2m	E(0-110)HHdl	SFT	£5746
122	2/00	Folk	2m1f110y	E Hdl	G-S	£2604
122	1/00	Folk	2m1f110y	E Hdl	SFT	£2422

Total win prize-money £25720

Going: Sf: 4-4 GS: 0-1 Gd: 0-1 GF: - Fm: 0-0
Distance: **2m/2m3: 4-6** 2m4-2m7: 0-0 3m+: 0-0
Track: **LH: 3-4** RH: 1-2 **Tight: 3-4** Gall: 1-1
Aids: Bl: 0-0 Vi: 0-0 Tstrap: 0-0
Best Rating: 133 3/02 Kels 2m2f heavy Hdl

A decent sort as a juvenile, he took advantage of a fair mark to win at Musselburgh in February 2002 and followed at the same track before completing the hat-trick at Doncaster. He was a good fourth in the Imperial Cup at Sandown, before gaining his fourth success of the year at Kelso in March 2002. Suited by soft ground.

Throw The Deuce (IRE)

75 **101**

5-y-o b g Desert Style (IRE)-Baileys Bride (IRE) (Shy Groom (USA))
G F Edwards (Michael Hourigan 24/8) G F Edwards

Placings:0000-6100F000 **(1615)**
2001/02: 16^{6}GF, 16^{1}GF, 17^{0}G, 16^{0}Y, 16^{F}G, 25^{0}G, 17^{0}GF, 17^{0}GF

	Starts	1st	2nd	3rd	Win & Pl
Hurdles	6	1	0	0	6121
Chases	2	0	0	0	0
Career Total	**12**	**1**	**0**	**0**	**6121**

101	7/01	Cork	2m	Hdl	G-F	£6120

Total win prize-money £6121

Going: Sf: 0-0 GS: 0-0 Gd: 0-3 GF: - Fm: 1-4
Distance: **2m/2m3: 1-7** 2m4-2m7: 0-0 3m+: 0-1
Track: LH: 0-0 RH: 0-2 Tight: 0-0 Gall: 0-0
Aids: Bl: 0-2 Vi: 0-0 Tstrap: 0-0
Best Rating: 101 7/01 Cork 2m gd-fm Hdl

Throwaline

97f **104f**

6-y-o b g Thowra (FR)-Stockline (Capricorn Line)
P J Hobbs Yusof Sepiuddin

Placings:1 **(3883)**
2001/02: 16^{1}GS

	Starts	1st	2nd	3rd	Win & Pl
NH Flat	1	1	0	0	1708
Career Total	**1**	**1**	**0**	**0**	**1708**

104	2/02	Winc	2m	H NHF	G-S	£1708

Total win prize-money £1708

Going: Sf: 0-0 GS: 1-1 Gd: 0-0 GF: - Fm: 0-0
Distance: **2m/2m3: 1-1** 2m4-2m7: 0-0 3m+: 0-0
Track: LH: 0-0 **RH: 1-1** Tight: 0-0 Gall: 0-0
Aids: Bl: 0-0 Vi: 0-0 Tstrap: 0-0
Best Rating: 104 2/02 Winc 2m gd-sft NHF

Fought hard to get his head in front on his bumper debut.

Thrower

106 **107**

11-y-o b g Thowra (FR)-Atlantic Line (Capricorn Line)
W M Brisbourne C M & S J Owen

Placings:4006/5U2444/113131/0/3U053 **(4128)**
2001/02: 20^{3}GS, 24^{U}GS, 25^{0}HY, 24^{5}G, 19^{3}G

	Starts	1st	2nd	3rd	Win & Pl
Hurdles	5	0	0	2	866
Career Total	**22**	**4**	**1**	**4**	**20260**

135	12/97	Hayd	2m4f	B HHdl	SFT	£6820
132	11/97	Hayd	2m4f	C(0-135)HHdl	GD	£3403
123	11/97	Hayd	2m	D(0-120)HHdl	GD	£2773
130	10/97	Bang	2m1f	E(0-110)HHdl	GD	£3533

Total win prize-money £16532

Going: Sf: 0-1 GS: 0-2 Gd: 0-2 GF: - Fm: 0-0
Distance: 2m/2m3: 0-0 2m4-2m7: 0-2 3m+: 0-3
Track: LH: 0-2 RH: 0-2 Tight: 0-1 Gall: 0-0
Aids: Bl: 0-0 Vi: 0-0 Tstrap: 0-0
Best Rating: 135 12/97 Hayd 2m4f soft Hdl

One-time useful hurdler at up to two and a half miles. He has been lightly-raced over hurdles in recent seasons and, although not as good as he was, retains some ability. Appreciates cut in the ground.

Thundered (USA)

4-y-o gr g Thunder Gulch (USA)-Lady Lianga (USA) (Secretariat (USA))
G A Swinbank (Mrs J R Ramsden 11/6) Scotnorth Racing Ltd

Placings:P **(1472)**
2001/02: 17^{P}S

	Starts	1st	2nd	3rd	Win & Pl
Hurdles	1	0	0	0	
Career Total	**1**	**0**	**0**	**0**	

Going: Sf: 0-1 GS: 0-0 Gd: 0-0 GF: - Fm: 0-0
Distance: 2m/2m3: 0-1 2m4-2m7: 0-0 3m+: 0-0
Track: LH: 0-0 RH: 0-1 Tight: 0-1 Gall: 0-0
Aids: Bl: 0-0 Vi: 0-0 Tstrap: 0-1
Best Rating:

Thunderpoint (IRE)

104 **99**

10-y-o b g Glacial Storm (USA)-Urdite (FR) (Concertino (FR))
R J Price P E Shock

Placings:035/2155P25/1FF1300PP/RP00FP/04R022 032F424P-0F6041344 **(1594)**
2001/02: 16^{0}GF, 16^{F}G, 21^{6}G, 16^{0}S, 20^{4}G, 20^{1}G, 20^{3}GF, 19^{4}GF, 16^{4}G

	Starts	1st	2nd	3rd	Win & Pl
Chases	9	1	0	1	5745
Career Total	**48**	**4**	**6**	**4**	**18454**

96	8/01	Bang	2m4f110y	F(0-100)HCh	GD	£4348
107	8/98	MRas	2m1f110y	F(0-105)HHdl	G-F	£1912
101	5/98	Hexm	2m	E Hdl	GD	£2033
110	10/97	Sedg	2m1f	D Hdl	GD	£2847

Total win prize-money £11142

Going: Sf: 0-1 GS: 0-0 Gd: 1-5 GF: - Fm: 0-3
Distance: 2m/2m3: 0-5 **2m4-2m7: 1-4** 3m+: 0-0
Track: **LH: 1-8** RH: 0-1 **Tight: 1-4** Gall: 0-0
Aids: **Bl: 1-9** Vi: 0-0 Tstrap: 0-0
Best Rating: 110 2/98 Sedg 2m1f good Hdl

Thursday-Fourball (IRE)

80(96h) (94h)**50**

8-y-o b g Phardante (FR)-Ashville Lady (IRE) (Le Bavard (FR))
R Curtis Eddie Gloyne

Placings:34FPP/U-26PUP0 **(4686)**
2001/02: 25^{2}S, 23^{6}GS, 26^{P}S, 24^{U}S, 25^{P}S, 26^{0}GF

	Starts	1st	2nd	3rd	Win & Pl
Hurdles	2	0	1	0	1085
Chases	4	0	0	0	0
Career Total	**12**	**0**	**1**	**1**	**1269**

Going: Sf: 0-4 GS: 0-1 Gd: 0-0 GF: - Fm: 0-1
Distance: 2m/2m3: 0-0 2m4-2m7: 0-0 3m+: 0-6
Track: LH: 0-0 RH: 0-4 Tight: 0-1 Gall: 0-0
Aids: Bl: 0-0 Vi: 0-0 Tstrap: 0-0
Best Rating: 94 10/01 Plum 3m1f110y soft Hdl

Lightly-raced sort, had shown ability in bumpers and hurdles but struggled in chases. Best effort came over three and a quarter miles over hurdles on soft ground in winter of 2001.

Thyne Will Tell (IRE)

112(105h) (126h)130

7-y-o ch g Good Thyne (USA)-Deep Khaletta (Deep Run)

P J Hobbs R J B Partners

Placings:1/220-111221 **(1354)**

2001/02: 19^{1}G, 22^{1}GF, 22^{1}GF, 22^{2}G, 21^{2}G, 21^{1}GF

Starts	1st	2nd	3rd	Win & Pl
Hurdles	4	3	1	0	10626
Chases	2	1	1	0	5354
Career Total	**10**	**5**	**4**	**0**	**20745**

128	9/01	Strf	2m5f110y	D Ch	G-F	£4208
116	5/01	NAbb	2m6f	E Hdl	G-F	£3045
120	5/01	Winc	2m6f	E Hdl	G-F	£3283
118	5/01	Hrfd	2m3f110y	E Hdl	GD	£2800
110	10/99	Gway	2m	NHF	SFT	£3234

Total win prize-money £16571

Going: Sf: 0-0 GS: 0-0 Gd: 1-3 GF: - Fm: 3-3
Distance: 2m/2m3: 0-0 **2m4-2m7: 4-6** 3m+: 0-0
Track: LH: 2-4 RH: 2-2 **Tight: 2-4** Gall: 0-0
Aids: Bl: 0-0 Vi: 0-0 Tstrap: 0-0
Best Rating: 130 8/01 NAbb 2m5f110y good Ch

Tianyi (IRE)

92 70+

6-y-o b g Mujadil (USA)-Okinily (Rally)

F Jordan Eddie Moss

Placings:P0PP **(4772)**

2001/02: 19^{P}S, 16^{0}S, 16^{P}S, 21^{P}G

	Starts	1st	2nd	3rd	Win & Pl
Hurdles	4	0	0	0	
Career Total	**4**	**0**	**0**	**0**	

Going: Sf: 0-3 GS: 0-0 Gd: 0-1 GF: - Fm: 0-0
Distance: 2m/2m3: 0-3 2m4-2m7: 0-1 3m+: 0-0
Track: LH: 0-2 RH: 0-2 Tight: 0-1 Gall: 0-0
Aids: Bl: 0-0 Vi: 0-0 Tstrap: 0-0
Best Rating: 50 12/01 Hayd 2m soft Hdl

Tibbie Lugs

6-y-o ch g Turbo Speed-Tina's Song (Tina's Pet)

F P Murtagh Miss Shelley Johnstone

Placings:0-0 **(2729)**

2001/02: 17^{0}GF

	Starts	1st	2nd	3rd	Win & Pl
NH Flat	1	0	0	0	
Career Total	**2**	**0**	**0**	**0**	

Going: Sf: 0-0 GS: 0-0 Gd: 0-0 GF: - Fm: 0-1
Distance: 2m/2m3: 0-1 2m4-2m7: 0-0 3m+: 0-0
Track: LH: 0-0 RH: 0-0 Tight: 0-0 Gall: 0-0
Aids: Bl: 0-0 Vi: 0-0 Tstrap: 0-0
Best Rating:

Tibetan

(106h) (120h)

10-y-o b g Reference Point-Winter Queen (Welsh Pageant)

Lady Herries Mrs Wendy Brown

Placings:21/440/P11200523/34F1-3 **(3908)**

2001/02: 21^{3}G

	Starts	1st	2nd	3rd	Win & Pl
Hurdles	1	0	0	1	2145
Career Total	**19**	**4**	**3**	**3**	**27062**

114	9/00	Strf	2m5f110y	D Ch	GD	£4043
139	12/97	Chel	2m1f	C(0-135)HHdl	GD	£3452
136	11/97	Hntg	2m110y	C(0-130)HHdl	GD	£5320
134	1/96	Sand	2m110y	C Hdl	G-S	£4240

Total win prize-money £17058

Going: Sf: 0-0 GS: 0-0 Gd: 0-1 GF: - Fm: 0-0
Distance: 2m/2m3: 0-0 2m4-2m7: 0-1 3m+: 0-0
Track: LH: 0-0 RH: 0-1 Tight: 0-0 Gall: 0-0
Aids: Bl: 0-0 Vi: 0-0 Tstrap: 0-0
Best Rating: 145 4/98 Asct 2m110y good Hdl

He was again off the track for a long time after struggling home from inferior opponents at Stratford in September of 2000, but ran well on his return at Kempton in February 2002. Probably best up to two and a half miles.

Tickerty's Gift

84 55

12-y-o b g Formidable (USA)-Handy Dancer (Green God)

Dr J R J Naylor C D May

Placings:2/26U00/5031312115/54431311/535641444 4/432123456/053P/P0-0 **(0564)**

2001/02: 17^{0}GF

	Starts	1st	2nd	3rd	Win & Pl
Hurdles	1	0	0	0	
Career Total	**50**	**9**	**5**	**8**	**32998**

117	12/98	Ling	2m110y	E(0-110)HHdl	SFT	£2183
115	2/98	Ling	2m110y	E(0-110)HHdl	GD	£2305
117	3/97	Ling	2m110y	F(0-115)HHdl	G-F	£2343
112	3/97	Ling	2m3f110y	C(0-130)HHdl	G-S	£4441
112	1/97	Ling	2m3f110y	E(0-110)HHdl	SFT	£2251
110	3/96	Ling	2m3f110y	C(0-130)HHdl	SFT	£4347
105	3/96	Ling	2m110y	D(0-120)HHdl	SFT	£2795
112	2/96	Ling	2m3f110y	F(0-100)HHdl	HVY	£2447
106	1/96	Ling	2m3f110y	F(0-95)HHdl	HVY	£2265

Total win prize-money £25382

Going: Sf: 0-0 GS: 0-0 Gd: 0-0 GF: - Fm: 0-1
Distance: 2m/2m3: 0-1 2m4-2m7: 0-0 3m+: 0-0
Track: LH: 0-1 RH: 0-0 Tight: 0-1 Gall: 0-0
Aids: Bl: 0-0 Vi: 0-0 Tstrap: 0-0
Best Rating: 118 1/99 Ling 2m110y heavy Hdl

Ticket To The Moon

12-y-o b m Pollerton-Spring Rocket (Harwell)

Mrs Janita Scott Mrs Janita Scott

Placings:22/12/3F/3P **(3991)**

2001/02: 25^{3}HY, 24^{P}S

	Starts	1st	2nd	3rd	Win & Pl
Chases	2	0	0	1	267
Career Total	**8**	**1**	**3**	**2**	**2987**

96	3/99	NAbb	2m5f110y	H Ch	SFT	£1446

Total win prize-money £1446

Going: Sf: 0-2 GS: 0-0 Gd: 0-0 GF: - Fm: 0-0
Distance: 2m/2m3: 0-0 2m4-2m7: 0-0 3m+: 0-2
Track: LH: 0-0 RH: 0-2 Tight: 0-1 Gall: 0-0
Aids: Bl: 0-0 Vi: 0-0 Tstrap: 0-0
Best Rating: 97 3/98 NAbb 2m5f110y soft Ch

Tickton Flyer

107f 101+f

4-y-o b g Sovereign Water (FR)-Contradictory (Reprimand)

M W Easterby T D Rose & A P Foreman

Placings:2 **(4873)**

2001/02: 16^{2}GF

	Starts	1st	2nd	3rd	Win & Pl
NH Flat	1	0	1	0	554
Career Total	**1**	**0**	**1**	**0**	**554**

Going: Sf: 0-0 GS: 0-0 Gd: 0-0 GF: - Fm: 0-1
Distance: 2m/2m3: 0-1 2m4-2m7: 0-0 3m+: 0-0
Track: LH: 0-1 RH: 0-0 Tight: 0-0 Gall: 0-0
Aids: Bl: 0-0 Vi: 0-0 Tstrap: 0-0
Best Rating: 101 4/02 Weth 2m gd-fm NHF

Runner-up to a well regarded winner in a bumper at Wetherby in April. Prefers a sound surface.

Tidal Force (IRE)

97(65h) (46h)96

11-y-o br g Strong Gale-Liffey Travel (Le Bavard (FR))

Mrs S M Johnson Mrs J E Symonds And Cross & James

Placings:1006/O11110/2F/032/F242-0F66403P4U **(1670)**

2001/02: 27^{0}G, 21^{F}GF, 22^{6}GF, 24^{6}G, 23^{4}G, 24^{0}GF, 23^{3}GF, 25^{P}GF, 24^{4}GF, 21^{U}G

	Starts	1st	2nd	3rd	Win & Pl
Hurdles	1	0	0	0	0
Chases	9	0	0	1	838
Career Total	**29**	**5**	**4**	**2**	**25334**

124	11/97	Chel	2m5f	C Hdl	GD	£3615
114	11/97	NAbb	2m6f	C(0-135)HHdl	G-F	£5524
118	10/97	Chep	2m4f110y	D(0-120)HHdl	GD	£2843
110	10/97	Chep	2m4f110y	D(0-110)HHdl	G-F	£4357
85	10/96	Chel	2m110y	H NHF	FRM	£1604

Total win prize-money £17943

Going: Sf: 0-0 GS: 0-0 Gd: 0-4 GF: - Fm: 0-6
Distance: 2m/2m3: 0-0 2m4-2m7: 0-3 3m+: 0-7
Track: LH: 0-6 RH: 0-4 Tight: 0-6 Gall: 0-1
Aids: Bl: 0-1 Vi: 0-0 Tstrap: 0-0
Best Rating: 129 10/98 Chep 2m3f110y gd-fm Ch

Tidal Reef (IRE)

90(38c) 60

10-y-o br g Tidaro (USA)-Windsor Reef (Take A Reef)

R Fielder R Fielder

Placings:14-PP5P0056 **(1671)**

2001/02: 21^{P}G, 20^{P}GF, 23^{5}GF, 20^{P}G, 24^{0}GF, 24^{0}GF, 22^{5}GF, 25^{6}G

	Starts	1st	2nd	3rd	Win & Pl
Hurdles	3	0	0	0	0
Chases	5	0	0	0	0
Career Total	**10**	**1**	**0**	**0**	**2116**

97	5/00	Folk	2m5f	H Ch	GD	£2115

Total win prize-money £2116

Going: Sf: 0-0 GS: 0-0 Gd: 0-3 GF: - Fm: 0-5
Distance: 2m/2m3: 0-0 2m4-2m7: 0-4 3m+: 0-4
Track: LH: 0-2 RH: 0-4 Tight: 0-5 Gall: 0-0
Aids: Bl: 0-0 Vi: 0-0 Tstrap: 0-0
Best Rating: 97 5/00 Folk 2m5f good Ch

Tied For Time (IRE)

10-y-o b g Montelimar (USA)-Cornamucla (Lucky Guy)

A J Walker S Birkinshaw

Placings:0/05P/015 (0578)

2001/02: 21^{0}G, 25^{1}G, 28^{5}GF

	Starts	1st	2nd	3rd	Win & Pl
Chases	3	1	0	0	1888
Career Total	**7**	**1**	**0**	**0**	**1888**

96	5/01	Aint	3m1f	H Ch	GD	£1888

Total win prize-money £1888

Going: Sf: 0-0 GS: 0-0 Gd: 1-2 GF: - Fm: 0-1
Distance: 2m/2m3: 0-0 2m4-2m7: 0-1 **3m+: 1-2**
Track: **LH: 1-3** RH: 0-0 **Tight: 1-3** Gall: 0-0
Aids: Bl: 0-0 Vi: 0-0 Tstrap: 0-0
Best Rating: 96 5/01 Aint 3m1f good Ch

Tierna's Respect

86 77

10-y-o b g Respect-Tierna's Pet (Laurence O)
M Wellings J R Sutcliffe

Placings:54P-U0PF (0971)

2001/02: 20^{U}G, 22^{0}GF, 20^{P}G, 20^{F}GF

	Starts	1st	2nd	3rd	Win & Pl
Hurdles	1	0	0	0	0
Chases	3	0	0	0	0
Career Total	**7**	**0**	**0**	**0**	**254**

Going: Sf: 0-0 GS: 0-0 Gd: 0-2 GF: - Fm: 0-2
Distance: 2m/2m3: 0-0 2m4-2m7: 0-4 3m+: 0-0
Track: LH: 0-3 RH: 0-1 Tight: 0-3 Gall: 0-0
Aids: Bl: 0-0 Vi: 0-0 Tstrap: 0-0
Best Rating: 77 6/01 MRas 2m6f110y gd-fm Ch

Tifasi (IRE)

99 71

12-y-o b g Shardari-Tikrara (USA) (Assert)
M J Wilkinson Mark Wilkinson

Placings:0/4214/6P0432/2/P2613/1322340/040-34P (2952)

2001/02: 20^{3}S, 19^{4}S, 16^{P}S

	Starts	1st	2nd	3rd	Win & Pl
Hurdles	3	0	0	1	234
Career Total	**30**	**3**	**6**	**5**	**12429**

103	11/99	Wwck	2m2f110y	G(0-100)HHdl	GD	£1660
88	3/99	Catt	2m3f	G(0-90)HHdl	SFT	£2262
	7/94	Rosc	2m	NHF	YLD	£2611

Total win prize-money £6533

Going: Sf: 0-3 GS: 0-0 Gd: 0-0 GF: - Fm: 0-0
Distance: 2m/2m3: 0-1 2m4-2m7: 0-2 3m+: 0-0
Track: LH: 0-2 RH: 0-1 Tight: 0-2 Gall: 0-0
Aids: Bl: 0-0 Vi: 0-0 Tstrap: 0-0
Best Rating: 103 1/00 Plum 2m soft Hdl

Tiger Grass (IRE)

97 101+

6-y-o gr g Ezzoud (IRE)-Rustic Lawn (Rusticaro (FR))
W R Muir M J Caddy

Placings:31P/553231106-P0633PP066 (4164)

2001/02: 24^{P}S, 20^{0}G, 25^{6}S, 22^{3}S, 22^{3}G, 24^{P}GF, 24^{P}GS, 26^{0}S, 26^{6}GS, 21^{6}GS

	Starts	1st	2nd	3rd	Win & Pl
Hurdles	10	0	0	2	1208
Career Total	**22**	**3**	**1**	**5**	**12022**

119	10/00	Plum	3m1f110y	D(0-120)HHdl	SFT	£3136
116	10/00	Sthl	2m4f110y	E(0-115)HHdl	G-S	£2289
115	12/99	Plum	2m	E Hdl	HVY	£2582

Total win prize-money £8008

Going: Sf: 0-4 GS: 0-3 Gd: 0-2 GF: - Fm: 0-1
Distance: 2m/2m3: 0-0 2m4-2m7: 0-4 3m+: 0-6
Track: LH: 0-3 RH: 0-5 Tight: 0-5 Gall: 0-0
Aids: Bl: 0-5 Vi: 0-3 Tstrap: 0-0
Best Rating: 119 10/00 Plum 3m1f110y soft Hdl

Slipping down the ratings before taking a Market Rasen seller in July 2002 on his first run for Pipe.

Tiger Lake

(82h)

9-y-o ch g Nashwan (USA)-Tiger Flower (Sadler's Wells (USA))
S Dow Brian Solomon And Miss Jo-Ann Wood

Placings:00/11/0P-P (0061)

2001/02: 26^{P}G

	Starts	1st	2nd	3rd	Win & Pl
Chases	1	0	0	0	
Career Total	**7**	**2**	**0**	**0**	**4658**

95	10/98	Hntg	2m4f110y	E Hdl	GD	£2320
101	9/98	Font	2m6f110y	E Hdl	G-F	£2337

Total win prize-money £4658

Going: Sf: 0-0 GS: 0-0 Gd: 0-1 GF: - Fm: 0-0
Distance: 2m/2m3: 0-0 2m4-2m7: 0-0 3m+: 0-1
Track: LH: 0-0 RH: 0-1 Tight: 0-1 Gall: 0-0
Aids: Bl: 0-0 Vi: 0-0 Tstrap: 0-0
Best Rating: 101 9/98 Font 2m6f110y gd-fm Hdl

Tiger Loose

91f 77f

6-y-o b g Tigerwood-My Bid (Cleon)
D Brace David Brace

Placings:50 (1263)

2001/02: 17^{5}GF, 16^{0}GF

	Starts	1st	2nd	3rd	Win & Pl
NH Flat	2	0	0	0	0
Career Total	**2**	**0**	**0**	**0**	**0**

Going: Sf: 0-0 GS: 0-0 Gd: 0-0 GF: - Fm: 0-2
Distance: 2m/2m3: 0-2 2m4-2m7: 0-0 3m+: 0-0
Track: LH: 0-1 RH: 0-1 Tight: 0-1 Gall: 0-1
Aids: Bl: 0-0 Vi: 0-0 Tstrap: 0-0
Best Rating: 77 8/01 NAbb 2m1f gd-fm NHF

Tiger Rouge

61 5

7-y-o ch g Kinglet-Lake View Lady (Little Buskins)
M Pitman Mrs Kay Birchenhough

Placings:0P0 (4597)

2001/02: 16^{0}HY, 18^{P}S, 19^{0}GF

	Starts	1st	2nd	3rd	Win & Pl
NH Flat	1	0	0	0	0
Hurdles	2	0	0	0	0
Career Total	**3**	**0**	**0**	**0**	

Going: Sf: 0-2 GS: 0-0 Gd: 0-0 GF: - Fm: 0-1
Distance: 2m/2m3: 0-3 2m4-2m7: 0-0 3m+: 0-0
Track: LH: 0-2 RH: 0-1 Tight: 0-1 Gall: 0-0
Aids: Bl: 0-0 Vi: 0-0 Tstrap: 0-0
Best Rating: 63 1/02 Towc 2m heavy NHF

Tiger Talk

100 93

6-y-o ch g Sabrehill (USA)-Tebre (USA) (Sir Ivor)

M E Sowersby M E Sowersby

Placings:U453604P0-2630300063 (4867)

2001/02: 16^{2}G, 17^{6}G, 16^{3}F, 16^{0}G, 17^{3}S, 16^{0}S, 16^{0}S, 17^{0}S, 16^{6}G, 16^{3}GF

	Starts	1st	2nd	3rd	Win & Pl
Hurdles	10	0	1	3	2122
Career Total	**19**	**0**	**1**	**4**	**3176**

Going: Sf: 0-4 GS: 0-0 Gd: 0-4 GF: - Fm: 0-2
Distance: 2m/2m3: 0-10 2m4-2m7: 0-0 3m+: 0-0
Track: LH: 0-8 RH: 0-2 Tight: 0-5 Gall: 0-0
Aids: Bl: 0-3 Vi: 0-0 Tstrap: 0-0
Best Rating: 98 11/00 Newc 2m gd-sft Hdl

Moderate hurdler, suited by a sound surface. Has worn blinkers.

Tiger Typhoon (IRE)

84f 80f

6-y-o b g Cataldi-Churchtown Breeze (Tarqogan)
R J Hodges Mrs Anna L Sanders

Placings:0-3 (1155)

2001/02: 17^{3}GF

	Starts	1st	2nd	3rd	Win & Pl
NH Flat	1	0	0	1	310
Career Total	**2**	**0**	**0**	**1**	**310**

Going: Sf: 0-0 GS: 0-0 Gd: 0-0 GF: - Fm: 0-1
Distance: 2m/2m3: 0-1 2m4-2m7: 0-0 3m+: 0-0
Track: LH: 0-1 RH: 0-0 Tight: 0-1 Gall: 0-0
Aids: Bl: 0-0 Vi: 0-0 Tstrap: 0-0
Best Rating: 80 8/01 NAbb 2m1f gd-fm NHF

Tigre Bois

83 71

5-y-o b g Mon Tresor-Gentle Star (Comedy Star (USA))
B R Millman Victor G Palmer

Placings:06 (1615)

2001/02: 16^{0}GF, 17^{6}GF

	Starts	1st	2nd	3rd	Win & Pl
Hurdles	2	0	0	0	0
Career Total	**2**	**0**	**0**	**0**	**0**

Going: Sf: 0-0 GS: 0-0 Gd: 0-0 GF: - Fm: 0-2
Distance: 2m/2m3: 0-2 2m4-2m7: 0-0 3m+: 0-0
Track: LH: 0-1 RH: 0-1 Tight: 0-0 Gall: 0-0
Aids: Bl: 0-0 Vi: 0-0 Tstrap: 0-0
Best Rating: 71 9/01 Worc 2m gd-fm Hdl

Tik-A-Tai (IRE)

110 135

7-y-o b g Alphabatim (USA)-Carrig Ross (Lord Ha Ha)
O Sherwood The Chamberlain Addiscott Partnership

Placings:1PP-14221P (4661)

2001/02: 21^{1}S, 22^{4}G, 24^{2}S, 24^{2}G, 20^{1}GS, 25^{P}G

	Starts	1st	2nd	3rd	Win & Pl
Chases	6	2	2	0	15498
Career Total	**9**	**3**	**2**	**0**	**17836**

135	2/02	Ludl	2m4f	D(0-125)HCh	G-S	£5369
124	10/01	Fknm	2m5f110y	C Ch	SFT	£6776
123	10/00	Font	2m6f110y	E Hdl	G-S	£2338

Total win prize-money £14483

Going: Sf: 1-2 GS: 1-1 Gd: 0-3 GF: - Fm: 0-0
Distance: 2m/2m3: 0-0 **2m4-2m7: 2-3** 3m+: 0-3
Track: LH: 1-5 RH: 1-1 **Tight: 2-4** Gall: 0-2
Aids: Bl: 0-0 Vi: 0-0 Tstrap: 0-0

Best Rating: **135** 2/02 Ludl 2m4f gd-sft Ch

Fair novice chaser, suited by up to three miles, but not the best of jumpers.

Tikopia

100 **94**

8-y-o b g Saddlers' Hall (IRE)-Shesadelight (Shirley Heights)

M E Sowersby A Milner

Placings:00/324/2/P0P54**F**-1540 **(1095)**

2001/02: 20^{1}F, 24^{5}GF, 19^{4}G, 24^{0}GF

	Starts	1st	2nd	3rd	Win & Pl
Hurdles	4	1	0	0	3822
Career Total	**16**	**1**	**2**	**1**	**5680**

94 5/01 Weth 2m4f110y D Hdl FRM £3549

Total win prize-money £3549

Going: Sf: 0-0 GS: 0-0 Gd: 0-1 GF: - Fm: 1-3
Distance: 2m/2m3: 0-0 **2m4-2m7: 1-2** 3m+: 0-2
Track: **LH: 1-1** RH: 0-3 Tight: 0-3 Gall: 0-0
Aids: Bl: 0-0 **Vi: 1-4** Tstrap: 0-0
Best Rating: **104** 12/98 Weth 2m7f good Hdl

Tikram

113 **140**

5-y-o ch g Lycius (USA)-Black Fighter (USA) (Secretariat (USA))

G L Moore Mike Charlton And Rodger Sargent

Placings:2316-22360 **(4256)**

2001/02: 16^{2}S, 17^{2}G, 16^{3}G, 16^{6}GS, 17^{0}G

	Starts	1st	2nd	3rd	Win & Pl
Hurdles	5	0	2	1	22675
Career Total	**9**	**1**	**3**	**2**	**32154**

120 1/01 Donc 2m110y C Hdl GD £6305

Total win prize-money £6305

Going: Sf: 0-1 GS: 0-1 Gd: 0-3 GF: - Fm: 0-0
Distance: 2m/2m3: 0-5 2m4-2m7: 0-0 3m+: 0-0
Track: LH: 0-3 RH: 0-2 Tight: 0-0 Gall: 0-3
Aids: Bl: 0-0 Vi: 0-1 Tstrap: 0-0
Best Rating: **140** 12/01 Asct 2m110y good Hdl

A winner on the Flat and over hurdles, he is suited by around two miles and acts on good and soft ground. He has been knocking on the door over hurdles, being placed in some good handicaps.

Tilanjani (IRE)

87 **60**

5-y-o ch g Indian Ridge-Tijara (IRE) (Darshaan)

K A Morgan S Giles

Placings:*0-462*50005 **(4640)**

2001/02: 16^{4}GF, 16^{6}GF, 16^{2}GF, 17^{5}G, 16^{0}G, 16^{0}S, 16^{0}G, 16^{5}G

	Starts	1st	2nd	3rd	Win & Pl
NH Flat	3	0	1	0	420
Hurdles	5	0	0	0	0
Career Total	**9**	**0**	**1**	**0**	**420**

Going: Sf: 0-1 GS: 0-0 Gd: 0-4 GF: - Fm: 0-3
Distance: 2m/2m3: 0-8 2m4-2m7: 0-0 3m+: 0-0
Track: LH: 0-4 RH: 0-4 Tight: 0-3 Gall: 0-3
Aids: Bl: 0-0 Vi: 0-0 Tstrap: 0-0
Best Rating: **80** 7/01 Uttx 2m gd-fm NHF

Tilt And Turn

95 **98**

8-y-o b g Syrtos-Sally Maxwell (Roscoe Blake)

B N Doran West Mercia Fork Trucks Ltd

Placings:*00/22*43/2431344F00/**UP-FP53** **(4905)**

2001/02: 19^{F}S, 16^{P}S, 16^{5}GF, 17^{3}GF

	Starts	1st	2nd	3rd	Win & Pl
Chases	4	0	0	1	583
Career Total	**22**	**1**	**3**	**4**	**7702**

104 9/99 Strf 2m110y E Hdl G-F £2901

Total win prize-money £2902

Going: Sf: 0-2 GS: 0-0 Gd: 0-0 GF: - Fm: 0-2
Distance: 2m/2m3: 0-3 2m4-2m7: 0-1 3m+: 0-0
Track: LH: 0-1 RH: 0-2 Tight: 0-2 Gall: 0-1
Aids: Bl: 0-0 Vi: 0-0 Tstrap: 0-0
Best Rating: **109** 10/99 Chel 2m110y good Hdl

Tim Soldier (FR)

91 **71**

15-y-o ch g Tip Moss (FR)-Pali Dancer (FR) (Green Dancer (USA))

M F Barraclough M F Barraclough

Placings:2111232/26P0/**65F15F4PP**/0013/**645**045/3**P** P112421/P**44/03P**/**F0065/P-P5U** **(0590)**

2001/02: 21^{P}GF, 24^{5}GF, 24^{U}GF

	Starts	1st	2nd	3rd	Win & Pl
Chases	3	0	0	0	0
Career Total	**54**	**8**	**6**	**4**	**32427**

100 3/97 Fknm 2m5f110y F(0-100)HCh GD £4712
91 1/97 Catt 3m1f110y E(0-110)HCh GD £3159
90 12/96 Catt 2m3f F(0-105)HCh GD £2786
101 1/94 Catt 2m3f (0-110)HCh G-S £2820
85 2/93 Bang 2m4f110y HCh SFT £2866
2/91 Sthl 2m Ch STD £1866
2/91 Sthl 2m4f Ch STD £1763
1/91 Nott 2m Hdl G-S £2372

Total win prize-money £22346

Going: Sf: 0-0 GS: 0-0 Gd: 0-0 GF: - Fm: 0-3
Distance: 2m/2m3: 0-0 2m4-2m7: 0-1 3m+: 0-2
Track: LH: 0-2 RH: 0-1 Tight: 0-2 Gall: 0-1
Aids: Bl: 0-0 Vi: 0-0 Tstrap: 0-0
Best Rating: **101** 3/97 Hntg 3m gd-fm Ch

Timber Broker

11-y-o ch g Jalmood (USA)-La Petite Noblesse (Thatching)

J L Spearing Barry Adams

Placings:0P0P-PP **(1624)**

2001/02: 16^{P}G, 16^{P}GF

	Starts	1st	2nd	3rd	Win & Pl
Hurdles	2	0	0	0	
Career Total	**6**	**0**	**0**	**0**	

Going: Sf: 0-0 GS: 0-0 Gd: 0-1 GF: - Fm: 0-1
Distance: 2m/2m3: 0-2 2m4-2m7: 0-0 3m+: 0-0
Track: LH: 0-1 RH: 0-1 Tight: 0-0 Gall: 0-0
Aids: Bl: 0-0 Vi: 0-0 Tstrap: 0-0
Best Rating: **26** 8/00 Strf 2m110y gd-fm Hdl

Timber King (IRE)

112 **146**

6-y-o b g Brief Truce (USA)-Shanntabariya (IRE) (Shernazar)

C Roche Mrs John Magnier

Placings:*21*132-1F1450 **(4712a)**

2001/02: 16^{1}G, 16^{F}GY, 17^{1}GF, 16^{4}GF, 17^{5}G, 16^{0}Y

	Starts	1st	2nd	3rd	Win & Pl
Hurdles	6	2	0	0	24435
Career Total	**11**	**4**	**2**	**1**	**39503**

143 8/01 Tral 2m1f HHdl G-F £13104
143 5/01 Fair 2m Hdl GD £10483
131 12/00 Leop 2m Hdl SH £5520
117 10/00 Cork 2m NHF YLD £5520

Total win prize-money £34629

Going: Sf: 0-0 GS: 0-0 Gd: 1-2 GF: - Fm: 1-2
Distance: **2m/2m3: 2-6** 2m4-2m7: 0-0 3m+: 0-0
Track: LH: 0-2 RH: 0-1 Tight: 0-0 Gall: 0-1
Aids: Bl: 0-0 Vi: 0-0 Tstrap: 0-0
Best Rating: **146** 9/01 List 2m gd-fm Hdl

Decent Irish handicap hurdler at around two miles on a sound surface. Put in a sound effort to finish fifth in the County Hurdle at Cheltenham.

Timbera (IRE)

114 **148**

8-y-o b/br g Commanche Run-Morry's Lady (The Parson)

D T Hughes Mrs J M Breen

Placings:*1/234155*/**000-411112F** **(4705a)**

2001/02: 18^{4}Y, 20^{1}HY, 25^{1}GY, 25^{1}YS, 25^{1}S, 32^{2}GS, 29^{F}GY

	Starts	1st	2nd	3rd	Win & Pl
Chases	7	4	1	0	43058
Career Total	**17**	**6**	**2**	**1**	**51262**

135 2/02 Fair 3m1f HCh SFT £11165
133 1/02 Fair 3m1f (0-109)HCh Y-S £6773
113 1/02 Fair 3m1f (0-116)HCh G-Y £6773
109 12/01 Limk 2m4f (0-116)HCh HVY £9959
112 2/00 Clon 2m4f Hdl SH £3036
97 4/99 Cork 2m4f NHF HVY £3683

Total win prize-money £41391

Going: Sf: 2-2 GS: 0-1 Gd: 0-0 GF: - Fm: 0-0
Distance: 2m/2m3: 0-1 2m4-2m7: 1-1 **3m+: 3-5**
Track: LH: 0-1 **RH: 4-6** Tight: 0-0 Gall: 0-1
Aids: Bl: 0-0 Vi: 0-0 **Tstrap: 4-7**
Best Rating: **148** 3/02 Chel 4m gd-sft Ch

Useful Irish staying chaser, acts on soft ground, stays really well. Usually wears a tongue tie. Just beaten in the four-miler at the Cheltenham Festival.

Time After Thyne

9-y-o b g Good Thyne (USA)-Lady Solstice (Vital Season)

Ferdy Murphy Edward Birkbeck

Placings:4/06/0/**F5P-0** **(0273)**

2001/02: 20^{0}GF

	Starts	1st	2nd	3rd	Win & Pl
Hurdles	1	0	0	0	
Career Total	**8**	**0**	**0**	**0**	**0**

Going: Sf: 0-0 GS: 0-0 Gd: 0-0 GF: - Fm: 0-1
Distance: 2m/2m3: 0-0 2m4-2m7: 0-1 3m+: 0-0
Track: LH: 0-0 RH: 0-1 Tight: 0-0 Gall: 0-0
Aids: Bl: 0-0 Vi: 0-0 Tstrap: 0-0
Best Rating: **99** 3/98 Ayr 2m gd-sft NHF

Time Can Tell

94 **83**

8-y-o ch g Sylvan Express-Stellaris (Star Appeal)
A G Juckes A C W Price

Placings:5/6/3P **(3357)**
2001/02: 19^{3}G, 24^{P}HY

	Starts	1st	2nd	3rd	Win & Pl
Hurdles	2	0	0	1	359
Career Total	4	0	0	1	359

Going: Sf: 0-1 GS: 0-0 Gd: 0-1 GF: - Fm: 0-0
Distance: 2m/2m3: 0-0 2m4-2m7: 0-1 3m+: 0-1
Track: LH: 0-1 RH: 0-1 Tight: 0-0 Gall: 0-0
Aids: Bl: 0-0 Vi: 0-0 Tstrap: 0-0
Best Rating: **83** 12/01 Hrfd 2m3f110y good Hdl

Time Enough (IRE)

74 **36**

13-y-o ch g Callernish-Easter Gazette (London Gazette)
Mrs P Townsley Paul Townsley

Placings:56P/01U/02FPF3031P3/22114/PPP/0/2U54/40-0 **(0107)**
2001/02: 22^{0}GF

	Starts	1st	2nd	3rd	Win & Pl
Hurdles	1	0	0	0	
Career Total	33	4	4	3	20739

114	11/96	Chel	3m110y	C(0-135)HCh	GD	£4856
107	11/96	Wwck	3m2f	C(0-130)HCh	G-F	£4692
107	3/96	Leic	2m4f110y	F(0-105)HCh	G-S	£3070
96	3/95	Towc	2m110y	E Ch	HVY	£2860

Total win prize-money £15479

Going: Sf: 0-0 GS: 0-0 Gd: 0-0 GF: - Fm: 0-1
Distance: 2m/2m3: 0-0 2m4-2m7: 0-1 3m+: 0-0
Track: LH: 0-1 RH: 0-0 Tight: 0-1 Gall: 0-0
Aids: Bl: 0-1 Vi: 0-0 Tstrap: 0-0
Best Rating: **114** 11/96 Chel 3m110y good Ch

Time For A Glass

9-y-o b m Timeless Times (USA)-Marie Zephyr (Treboro (USA))
Mrs A L M King Mrs D Mitchell

Placings:40301504/665P4/P **(0582)**
2001/02: 19^{P}GF

	Starts	1st	2nd	3rd	Win & Pl
Hurdles	1	0	0	0	
Career Total	14	1	0	1	2985

91	11/98	Worc	2m	E Hdl	HVY	£2250

Total win prize-money £2250

Going: Sf: 0-0 GS: 0-0 Gd: 0-0 GF: - Fm: 0-1
Distance: 2m/2m3: 0-1 2m4-2m7: 0-0 3m+: 0-0
Track: LH: 0-1 RH: 0-0 Tight: 0-1 Gall: 0-0
Aids: Bl: 0-0 Vi: 0-0 Tstrap: 0-0
Best Rating: **91** 11/98 Worc 2m heavy Hdl

Time For Action (IRE)

99 **94**

10-y-o b g Alzao (USA)-Beyond Words (Ballad Rock)
H J Evans Mrs Jane Evans

Placings:23/13260314355/36/60-400 **(0918)**
2001/02: 19^{4}G, 22^{0}G, 22^{0}GF

	Starts	1st	2nd	3rd	Win & Pl
Hurdles	3	0	0	0	273
Career Total	20	2	2	5	10039

116	12/98	Tntn	2m1f	E(0-115)HHdl	G-S	£2274
100	5/98	Bang	2m1f	E Hdl	GD	£2578

Total win prize-money £4853

Going: Sf: 0-0 GS: 0-0 Gd: 0-2 GF: - Fm: 0-1
Distance: 2m/2m3: 0-0 2m4-2m7: 0-3 3m+: 0-0
Track: LH: 0-2 RH: 0-1 Tight: 0-2 Gall: 0-0
Aids: Bl: 0-0 Vi: 0-0 Tstrap: 0-3
Best Rating: **116** 2/99 Donc 2m110y gd-fm Hdl

Time He Went

82 **55**

13-y-o b g Blakeney-Fast Asleep (Hotfoot)
G Wareham G Wareham

Placings:351/P/5/P/5UPP **(4415)**
2001/02: 20^{5}GS, 22^{U}GS, 22^{P}S, 22^{P}S

	Starts	1st	2nd	3rd	Win & Pl
Hurdles	4	0	0	0	0
Career Total	10	1	0	1	1557

107	6/94	Uttx	2m	NHF	G-F	£1339

Total win prize-money £1340

Going: Sf: 0-2 GS: 0-2 Gd: 0-0 GF: - Fm: 0-0
Distance: 2m/2m3: 0-0 2m4-2m7: 0-4 3m+: 0-0
Track: LH: 0-3 RH: 0-0 Tight: 0-4 Gall: 0-0
Aids: Bl: 0-0 Vi: 0-0 Tstrap: 0-0
Best Rating: **107** 6/94 Uttx 2m gd-fm NHF

Time N Tide (IRE)

102 **106**

6-y-o b g Namaqualand (USA)-Now Then (Sandford Lad)
G M McCourt Mccourt Fine Meats Ltd

Placings:6512312/500-53 **(1145)**
2001/02: 20^{5}GF, 16^{3}GF

	Starts	1st	2nd	3rd	Win & Pl
Hurdles	2	0	0	1	740
Career Total	12	2	2	2	14626

104	4/00	Ludl	2m	D Hdl	GD	£2925
117	1/00	Donc	2m110y	C Hdl	GD	£5876

Total win prize-money £8801

Going: Sf: 0-0 GS: 0-0 Gd: 0-0 GF: - Fm: 0-2
Distance: 2m/2m3: 0-1 2m4-2m7: 0-1 3m+: 0-0
Track: LH: 0-2 RH: 0-0 Tight: 0-1 Gall: 0-0
Aids: Bl: 0-0 Vi: 0-0 Tstrap: 0-0
Best Rating: **117** 4/00 Chel 2m1f soft Hdl

Fair hurdler, suited by two miles and a sound surface.

Time Of Flight (IRE)

115 **139**

9-y-o ch g Over The River (FR)-Icy Lou (Blue Rullah)
Mrs M Reveley Andy Peake & David Jackson

Placings:150/33UP41/215P4P-25112233F **(4254)**
2001/02: 24^{2}GF, 20^{5}GF, 16^{1}GS, 16^{1}G, 16^{2}G, 16^{2}G, 20^{3}S, 16^{3}S, 16^{F}G

	Starts	1st	2nd	3rd	Win & Pl
Chases	9	2	3	2	18896
Career Total	24	5	4	4	31908

130	11/01	Weth	2m	C(0-135)HCh	GD	£7085
119	10/01	Carl	2m	D(0-125)HCh	G-S	£3900
137	10/00	Weth	2m4f110y	C(0-130)HCh	HVY	£5882
110	3/00	Newc	2m	E Hdl	GD	£2684
111	12/98	Newc	2m	H NHF	SFT	£1318

Total win prize-money £20872

Going: Sf: 0-2 GS: 1-1 Gd: 1-4 GF: - Fm: 0-2
Distance: **2m/2m3: 2-6** 2m4-2m7: 0-2 3m+: 0-1
Track: LH: 1-6 RH: 1-3 Tight: 0-1 Gall: 0-3
Aids: Bl: 0-0 Vi: 0-0 Tstrap: 0-0
Best Rating: **139** 11/01 Weth 2m good Ch

Fair handicap chaser, although inconsistent, he ran well in the autumn of 2001 after being dropped to two miles, winning twice at that trip at Carlise and wetherby. He has continued to run well since then off higher marks. Does not want the ground too soft.

Time Temptress

95 **66**

6-y-o b m Timeless Times (USA)-Tangalooma (Hotfoot)
I W McInnes (A Crook 1/8) I W McInnes

Placings:4543P-02565 **(4917)**
2001/02: 17^{0}G, 23^{2}G, 19^{5}S, 25^{6}G, 21^{5}GF

	Starts	1st	2nd	3rd	Win & Pl
Hurdles	5	0	1	0	668
Career Total	10	0	1	1	874

Going: Sf: 0-1 GS: 0-0 Gd: 0-3 GF: - Fm: 0-1
Distance: 2m/2m3: 0-1 2m4-2m7: 0-3 3m+: 0-1
Track: LH: 0-4 RH: 0-1 Tight: 0-4 Gall: 0-0
Aids: Bl: 0-0 Vi: 0-0 Tstrap: 0-0
Best Rating: **74** 11/01 Weth 2m7f good Hdl

Small mare, poor selling hurdler.

Time To Parlez

103 **96**

11-y-o b g Amboise-Image Of War (Warpath)
C J Drewe Mrs J Strange

Placings:00/6/PPP44/P02250/B532P1PP-021UPP4P **(4514)**
2001/02: 24^{0}GS, 25^{2}S, 25^{1}HY, 26^{U}S, 26^{P}S, 26^{P}S, 25^{4}S, 25^{P}GS

	Starts	1st	2nd	3rd	Win & Pl
Chases	8	1	1	0	5961
Career Total	30	2	4	1	13047

96	12/01	Towc	3m1f	F(0-110)HCh	HVY	£4438
96	1/01	Font	3m2f110y	F(0-100)HCh	SFT	£2847

Total win prize-money £7285

Going: Sf: 1-6 GS: 0-2 Gd: 0-0 GF: - Fm: 0-0
Distance: 2m/2m3: 0-0 2m4-2m7: 0-0 **3m+: 1-8**
Track: LH: 0-2 **RH: 1-4** Tight: 0-1 Gall: 0-0
Aids: Bl: 0-1 Vi: 0-0 Tstrap: 0-0
Best Rating: **96** 3/02 Towc 3m1f soft Ch

Moderate front-running chaser. A mudlark who stays three miles two furlongs, goes well at Towcester.

Time To Wyn

99 **86**

6-y-o b g Timeless Times (USA)-Wyn-Bank (Green God)
J G Fitzgerald Mike Browne

Placings:0424400 **(2723)**
2001/02: 16^{0}G, 17^{4}G, 17^{2}GF, 17^{4}S, 17^{4}S, 16^{0}S, 17^{0}GF

	Starts	1st	2nd	3rd	Win & Pl
Hurdles	7	0	1	0	717
Career Total	7	0	1	0	717

Going: Sf: 0-3 GS: 0-0 Gd: 0-2 GF: - Fm: 0-2
Distance: 2m/2m3: 0-7 2m4-2m7: 0-0 3m+: 0-0
Track: LH: 0-3 RH: 0-3 Tight: 0-6 Gall: 0-0
Aids: Bl: 0-0 Vi: 0-5 Tstrap: 0-5
Best Rating: **86** 6/01 MRas 2m1f110y gd-fm Hdl

Time Warrior (IRE)

11-y-o ch g Decent Fellow-Oonagh's Teddy (Quayside)
G M Moore Mrs Susan Moore

Placings:*62/*340P/1/P **(0091)**
2001/02: 20^{PS}

	Starts	1st	2nd	3rd	Win & Pl
Hurdles	1	0	0	0	
Career Total	8	1	1	1	3068

96 12/98 Ayr 2m4f E Hdl G-S £2318
Total win prize-money £2318

Going: Sf: 0-1 GS: 0-0 Gd: 0-0 GF: - Fm: 0-0
Distance: 2m/2m3: 0-0 2m4-2m7: 0-1 3m+: 0-0
Track: LH: 0-1 RH: 0-0 Tight: 0-0 Gall: 0-0
Aids: Bl: 0-0 Vi: 0-0 Tstrap: 0-0
Best Rating: 96 12/98 Ayr 2m4f gd-sft Hdl

Timeless Chick

100 **84**
5-y-o ch m Timeless Times (USA)-Be My Bird (Be My Chief (USA))
J L Spearing (B A McMahon 29/6) Be Luckies

Placings:55343P0 **(0004)**
2001/02: 16^{5}GS, 17^{5}S, 16^{3}GS, 20^{4}S, 17^{3}G, 16^{P}S, 16^{0}G

	Starts	1st	2nd	3rd	Win & Pl
Hurdles	7	0	0	2	554
Career Total	7	0	0	2	554

Going: Sf: 0-3 GS: 0-2 Gd: 0-2 GF: - Fm: 0-0
Distance: 2m/2m3: 0-6 2m4-2m7: 0-1 3m+: 0-0
Track: LH: 0-4 RH: 0-3 Tight: 0-3 Gall: 0-0
Aids: Bl: 0-1 Vi: 0-0 Tstrap: 0-0
Best Rating: 84 12/01 Hrfd 2m1f good Hdl

Timely Magic (IRE)

63(86c) **19**
10-y-o b g Good Thyne (USA)-Magic Quiz (Quisling)
J Neville Park Industrial Supplies (wales) Ltd

Placings:*3/24/20/*633300/44-0 **(3876)**
2001/02: 20^{0}S

	Starts	1st	2nd	3rd	Win & Pl
Hurdles	1	0	0	0	
Career Total	14	0	2	4	2452

Going: Sf: 0-1 GS: 0-0 Gd: 0-0 GF: - Fm: 0-0
Distance: 2m/2m3: 0-0 2m4-2m7: 0-1 3m+: 0-0
Track: LH: 0-0 RH: 0-1 Tight: 0-0 Gall: 0-1
Aids: Bl: 0-0 Vi: 0-0 Tstrap: 0-0
Best Rating: 114 12/99 Ling 2m3f110y gd-sft Hdl

Timidjar (IRE)

92 **72**
9-y-o b g Doyoun-Timissara (USA) (Shahrastani (USA))
Mrs D Thomas Mrs D Thomas

Placings:603/236P/2006/26011/1440-0040000 **(1493)**
2001/02: 17^{0}F, 16^{0}G, 17^{4}G, 17^{0}GF, 16^{0}GF, 16^{0}GF, 17^{0}GF

	Starts	1st	2nd	3rd	Win & Pl
Hurdles	7	0	0	0	0
Career Total	27	3	3	2	8829

100 5/00 Hrfd 2m1f G(0-95)HHdl GD £2100
99 4/00 Hrfd 2m1f G Hdl GD £2159
95 3/00 NAbb 2m1f F(0-100)HHdl GD £1862
Total win prize-money £6122

Going: Sf: 0-0 GS: 0-0 Gd: 0-2 GF: - Fm: 0-5
Distance: 2m/2m3: 0-7 2m4-2m7: 0-0 3m+: 0-0
Track: LH: 0-4 RH: 0-3 Tight: 0-3 Gall: 0-0
Aids: Bl: 0-0 Vi: 0-0 Tstrap: 0-0
Best Rating: 100 5/00 Hrfd 2m1f good Hdl

Timpani (IRE)

59
6-y-o b g Broken Hearted-Queen Kam (IRE) (Kambalda)
N A Twiston-Davies Mr John Duggan & Mr Michael Purtill

Placings:*06*-P5 **(1767)**
2001/02: 24^{P}G, 22^{5}G

	Starts	1st	2nd	3rd	Win & Pl
Hurdles	2	0	0	0	0
Career Total	4	0	0	0	0

Going: Sf: 0-0 GS: 0-0 Gd: 0-2 GF: - Fm: 0-0
Distance: 2m/2m3: 0-0 2m4-2m7: 0-1 3m+: 0-1
Track: LH: 0-1 RH: 0-0 Tight: 0-1 Gall: 0-0
Aids: Bl: 0-0 Vi: 0-0 Tstrap: 0-0
Best Rating: 95 1/01 Kemp 2m soft NHF

Tin Cup

81 **65**
10-y-o b g Broadsword (USA)-Osmium (Petong)
J N R Billinge J N R Billinge

Placings:*0/6P/*04P **(4874)**
2001/02: 16^{0}GS, 16^{4}GS, 20^{P}G

	Starts	1st	2nd	3rd	Win & Pl
Hurdles	3	0	0	0	0
Career Total	6	0	0	0	0

Going: Sf: 0-0 GS: 0-2 Gd: 0-1 GF: - Fm: 0-0
Distance: 2m/2m3: 0-2 2m4-2m7: 0-1 3m+: 0-0
Track: LH: 0-2 RH: 0-1 Tight: 0-1 Gall: 0-0
Aids: Bl: 0-0 Vi: 0-0 Tstrap: 0-0
Best Rating: 67 4/00 Newc 2m4f gd-sft Ch

Tina Cooke

6-y-o gr m Tina's Pet-Up Cooke (Deep Run)
Miss Kate Milligan Mrs J M L Milligan

Placings:*50* **(3354)**
2001/02: 17^{5}GS, 16^{0}G

	Starts	1st	2nd	3rd	Win & Pl
NH Flat	2	0	0	0	0
Career Total	2	0	0	0	0

Going: Sf: 0-0 GS: 0-1 Gd: 0-1 GF: - Fm: 0-0
Distance: 2m/2m3: 0-2 2m4-2m7: 0-0 3m+: 0-0
Track: LH: 0-0 RH: 0-1 Tight: 0-1 Gall: 0-0
Aids: Bl: 0-0 Vi: 0-0 Tstrap: 0-0
Best Rating: 85 1/02 Muss 2m good NHF

Held in bumpers and hurdles.

Tina Thyne (IRE)

99 **89**
8-y-o b m Good Thyne (USA)-Tiny Tina (Deep Run)
T P Tate The Ivy Syndicate

Placings:*12/*0042326 **(4875)**
2001/02: 22^{0}G, 24^{0}S, 24^{4}S, 21^{2}HY, 27^{3}S, 20^{2}G, 24^{6}G

	Starts	1st	2nd	3rd	Win & Pl
Hurdles	7	0	2	1	1885
Career Total	9	1	3	1	7765

107 3/00 Uttx 2m H NHF GD £1610
Total win prize-money £1610

Going: Sf: 0-4 GS: 0-0 Gd: 0-3 GF: - Fm: 0-0
Distance: 2m/2m3: 0-0 2m4-2m7: 0-3 3m+: 0-4
Track: LH: 0-5 RH: 0-2 Tight: 0-3 Gall: 0-0
Aids: Bl: 0-2 Vi: 0-0 Tstrap: 0-0
Best Rating: 119 4/00 Chel 2m1f soft NHF

Winner of a bumper in 2000, she is still a maiden over hurdles despite being tried over various trips and surfaces.

Tindles Bible

10-y-o b g Le Coq D'Or-Wedderburn (Royalty)
J S Wainwright Keith Jackson

Placings:2262/3F **(4396)**
2001/02: 21^{3}HY, 25^{F}HY

	Starts	1st	2nd	3rd	Win & Pl
Chases	2	0	0	1	227
Career Total	6	0	3	1	2768

Going: Sf: 0-2 GS: 0-0 Gd: 0-0 GF: - Fm: 0-0
Distance: 2m/2m3: 0-0 2m4-2m7: 0-1 3m+: 0-1
Track: LH: 0-2 RH: 0-0 Tight: 0-1 Gall: 0-0
Aids: Bl: 0-0 Vi: 0-0 Tstrap: 0-0
Best Rating: 103 3/98 Bang 3m gd-sft Hdl

Well-related and lightly raced, he proved frustrating over hurdles and was not very fluent over fences.

Tino (IRE)

108(73h) (72h)**84**
6-y-o ch g Torus-Delphic Thunder (Viking (USA))
J S King Robert Skillen

Placings:*0-*00P3536 **(4511)**
2001/02: 19^{0}G, 22^{0}G, 24^{P}G, 20^{3}G, 23^{5}G, 20^{3}GF, 20^{6}G

	Starts	1st	2nd	3rd	Win & Pl
Hurdles	3	0	0	0	0
Chases	4	0	0	2	1119
Career Total	8	0	0	2	1119

Going: Sf: 0-0 GS: 0-0 Gd: 0-6 GF: - Fm: 0-1
Distance: 2m/2m3: 0-0 2m4-2m7: 0-5 3m+: 0-2
Track: LH: 0-1 RH: 0-6 Tight: 0-3 Gall: 0-1
Aids: Bl: 0-0 Vi: 0-0 Tstrap: 0-0
Best Rating: 84 3/02 Hntg 2m4f110y gd-fm Ch

Has taken time to get his eye in over fences but seemed to turn in a much improved effort on latest start.

Tinstre (IRE)

58 **44**
4-y-o ch g Dolphin Street (FR)-Satin Poppy (Satin Wood)
P W Hiatt P W Hiatt

Placings:5 **(1027)**

2001/02: 16^{5}G

	Starts	1st	2nd	3rd	Win & Pl
Hurdles	1	0	0	0	0
Career Total	**1**	**0**	**0**	**0**	**0**

Going: Sf: 0-0 GS: 0-0 Gd: 0-1 GF: - Fm: 0-0
Distance: 2m/2m3: 0-1 2m4-2m7: 0-0 3m+: 0-0
Track: LH: 0-1 RH: 0-0 Tight: 0-1 Gall: 0-0
Aids: Bl: 0-0 Vi: 0-0 Tstrap: 0-0
Best Rating: 44 7/01 Strf 2m110y good Hdl

Tiny Mind

4-y-o b g Factual (USA)-Lady Louise (IRE) (Lord Americo)
A Crook A Saccomando

Placings:P (2156)
2001/02: 16^{P}GS

	Starts	1st	2nd	3rd	Win & Pl
Hurdles	1	0	0	0	
Career Total	**1**	**0**	**0**	**0**	

Going: Sf: 0-0 GS: 0-1 Gd: 0-0 GF: - Fm: 0-0
Distance: 2m/2m3: 0-1 2m4-2m7: 0-0 3m+: 0-0
Track: LH: 0-1 RH: 0-0 Tight: 0-0 Gall: 0-0
Aids: Bl: 0-0 Vi: 0-0 Tstrap: 0-0
Best Rating:

Tip Image (FR)

86 **77**

5-y-o gr m Badolato (USA)-Yvolene (FR) (Tip Moss (FR))
T Needham T Needham

Placings:6435/40000-P2 (0122)
2001/02: 16^{P}S, 19^{2}F

	Starts	1st	2nd	3rd	Win & Pl
Hurdles	2	0	1	0	464
Career Total	**11**	**0**	**1**	**1**	**4509**

Going: Sf: 0-1 GS: 0-0 Gd: 0-0 GF: - Fm: 0-1
Distance: 2m/2m3: 0-1 2m4-2m7: 0-1 3m+: 0-0
Track: LH: 0-1 RH: 0-1 Tight: 0-2 Gall: 0-0
Aids: Bl: 0-1 Vi: 0-0 Tstrap: 0-0
Best Rating: 77 5/01 Tntn 2m3f110y firm Hdl

Tip Kash (FR)

98f **107f**

5-y-o ch g Kashtan (FR)-Tipas (FR) (Tip Moss (FR))
A M Hales Andrew L Cohen

Placings:0 (2942)
2001/02: 16^{0}G

	Starts	1st	2nd	3rd	Win & Pl
NH Flat	1	0	0	0	
Career Total	**1**	**0**	**0**	**0**	

Going: Sf: 0-0 GS: 0-0 Gd: 0-1 GF: - Fm: 0-0
Distance: 2m/2m3: 0-1 2m4-2m7: 0-0 3m+: 0-0
Track: LH: 0-1 RH: 0-0 Tight: 0-0 Gall: 0-1
Aids: Bl: 0-0 Vi: 0-0 Tstrap: 0-0
Best Rating: 107 12/01 Newb 2m110y good NHF

Tip The Scales

89 **92**

4-y-o b g Dancing Spree (USA)-Keen Melody (USA) (Sharpen Up)
Mrs T J McInnes Skinner (R M Whitaker 1/9) Mrs T J McInnes Skinner

Placings:344 (2531)
2001/02: 16^{3}G, 16^{4}G, 17^{4}S

	Starts	1st	2nd	3rd	Win & Pl
Hurdles	3	0	0	1	541
Career Total	**3**	**0**	**0**	**1**	**541**

Going: Sf: 0-1 GS: 0-0 Gd: 0-2 GF: - Fm: 0-0
Distance: 2m/2m3: 0-3 2m4-2m7: 0-0 3m+: 0-0
Track: LH: 0-1 RH: 0-2 Tight: 0-1 Gall: 0-1
Aids: Bl: 0-0 Vi: 0-0 Tstrap: 0-0
Best Rating: 92 11/01 Hntg 2m110y good Hdl

Little ability on the Flat, but ran with some promise on his hurdling debut.

Tipping Along (IRE)

13-y-o ch g Rising-Gone (Whistling Wind)
Miss M I Macgregor (Trainer Unknown 17/2) Miss M I Macgregor

Placings:*060*/C53/BP34/P/P (3991)
2001/02: 24^{P}S

	Starts	1st	2nd	3rd	Win & Pl
Chases	1	0	0	0	
Career Total	**12**	**0**	**0**	**2**	**604**

Going: Sf: 0-1 GS: 0-0 Gd: 0-0 GF: - Fm: 0-0
Distance: 2m/2m3: 0-0 2m4-2m7: 0-0 3m+: 0-1
Track: LH: 0-0 RH: 0-1 Tight: 0-1 Gall: 0-0
Aids: Bl: 0-1 Vi: 0-0 Tstrap: 0-0
Best Rating: 80 12/95 Towc 2m5f soft Hdl

Tipstaff (FR)

90 **82**

9-y-o b g Kendor (FR)-Spanish Sparrow (Ile De Bourbon (USA))
M C Pipe D A Johnson

Placings:002P05/1111/FF/00/40 (2413)
2001/02: 22^{4}G, 19^{0}GS

	Starts	1st	2nd	3rd	Win & Pl
Hurdles	2	0	0	0	0
Career Total	**16**	**4**	**1**	**0**	**56980**

Date	Course	Distance	Race	Going	Prize
11/97	Autl	2m4f110y	Ch	HVY	£13468
11/97	Autl	2m1f110y	Ch	VS	£11223
9/97	Autl	2m2f	Hdl	SFT	£12346
7/97	Autl	2m2f	Hdl	HVY	£11223

Total win prize-money £48260

Going: Sf: 0-0 GS: 0-1 Gd: 0-1 GF: - Fm: 0-0
Distance: 2m/2m3: 0-0 2m4-2m7: 0-2 3m+: 0-0
Track: LH: 0-1 RH: 0-1 Tight: 0-2 Gall: 0-0
Aids: Bl: 0-0 Vi: 0-0 Tstrap: 0-0
Best Rating: 95 8/99 MRas 2m3f110y gd-fm Hdl

Tiraldo (FR)

100 **84**

9-y-o b g Royal Charter (FR)-Tamilda (FR) (Rose Laurel)
A G Juckes Whistlejacket Partnership

Placings:4/5/22F1F1/23142P2F/40-PP444 (4783)
2001/02: 21^{P}S, 24^{P}HY, 29^{4}S, 26^{4}GS, 29^{4}GF

	Starts	1st	2nd	3rd	Win & Pl
Chases	5	0	0	0	1039
Career Total	**23**	**3**	**5**	**1**	**36799**

Rating	Date	Course	Distance	Race	Going	Prize
132	11/99	Towc	3m1f	D(0-120)HCh	GD	£6905
127	2/99	Hntg	2m4f110y	D Ch	G-S	£5160
118	12/98	Strf	2m5f110y	D Ch	SFT	£4224

Total win prize-money £16289

Going: Sf: 0-3 GS: 0-1 Gd: 0-0 GF: - Fm: 0-1
Distance: 2m/2m3: 0-0 2m4-2m7: 0-1 3m+: 0-4
Track: LH: 0-4 RH: 0-0 Tight: 0-0 Gall: 0-0
Aids: Bl: 0-0 Vi: 0-0 Tstrap: 0-0
Best Rating: 132 3/00 Strf 3m good Ch

Formerly decent chaser, tumbling down the ratings but remains largely out of form.

Tirley Gale

10-y-o b g Strong Gale-Mascara Vii (Damsire Unregistered)
Miss N Brookes (J S Smith 20/1) Donald Smith

Placings:*000*P/0FP35/153P5R6F/04P-04PR (4892)
2001/02: 24^{0}G, 24^{4}GS, 31^{P}GS, 31^{R}G

	Starts	1st	2nd	3rd	Win & Pl
Hurdles	1	0	0	0	0
Chases	3	0	0	0	0
Career Total	**24**	**1**	**0**	**2**	**4713**

Rating	Date	Course	Distance	Race	Going	Prize
104	5/99	Worc	2m7f110y	F(0-105)HCh	G-S	£3002

Total win prize-money £3003

Going: Sf: 0-0 GS: 0-2 Gd: 0-2 GF: - Fm: 0-0
Distance: 2m/2m3: 0-0 2m4-2m7: 0-0 3m+: 0-4
Track: LH: 0-1 RH: 0-1 Tight: 0-2 Gall: 0-0
Aids: Bl: 0-0 Vi: 0-0 Tstrap: 0-0
Best Rating: 110 3/99 Wwck 2m4f110y good Ch

Tirley Storm

(89h) (66h)**79**

7-y-o b g Tirley Gale-Random Select (Random Shot)
J S Smith Mrs J A Benson

Placings:6-P0044P2P (4878)
2001/02: 20^{P}G, 22^{0}G, 24^{0}GS, 19^{4}G, 21^{4}GS, 24^{P}GS, 19^{2}GF, 24^{P}G

	Starts	1st	2nd	3rd	Win & Pl
Hurdles	4	0	0	0	0
Chases	4	0	1	0	1616
Career Total	**9**	**0**	**1**	**0**	**1616**

Going: Sf: 0-0 GS: 0-3 Gd: 0-4 GF: - Fm: 0-1
Distance: 2m/2m3: 0-1 2m4-2m7: 0-4 3m+: 0-3
Track: LH: 0-1 RH: 0-7 Tight: 0-1 Gall: 0-1
Aids: Bl: 0-0 Vi: 0-0 Tstrap: 0-0
Best Rating: 81 1/01 Donc 2m110y good NHF

Moderate form over hurdles and fences so far. Has shown his best form over two and a half miles on good to soft ground.

Tis Gromit

101 **75**

8-y-o b m Bedford (USA)-Lac Royale (Lochnager)
Miss Sheena West Gerald West

Placings:0/6P/56323 (4568)
2001/02: 22^{5}HY, 22^{6}S, 24^{3}S, 22^{2}S, 24^{3}G

	Starts	1st	2nd	3rd	Win & Pl
Hurdles	5	0	1	2	1482
Career Total	**8**	**0**	**1**	**2**	**1482**

Going: Sf: 0-4 GS: 0-0 Gd: 0-1 GF: - Fm: 0-0
Distance: 2m/2m3: 0-0 2m4-2m7: 0-3 3m+: 0-2
Track: LH: 0-3 RH: 0-2 Tight: 0-3 Gall: 0-0
Aids: Bl: 0-0 Vi: 0-0 Tstrap: 0-0

Best Rating: 90 4/00 Plum 2m5f gd-sft Hdl

Lightly-raced eight-year-old. Running consistently well in a modest handicap hurdles around three miles in the spring of 2002.

Tissifer

106 **124**

6-y-o b g Polish Precedent (USA)-Ingozi (Warning)
M C Pipe (M Johnston 4/10) Richard Abbott & Mario Stavrou li

Placings:1132000 **(4674)**
2001/02: 16^{1}GS, 17^{1}S, 16^{3}GS, 17^{2}GS, 25^{0}S, 17^{0}G, 16^{0}G

	Starts	1st	2nd	3rd	Win & Pl
Hurdles	7	2	1	1	7518
Career Total	**7**	**2**	**1**	**1**	**7518**

111	11/01	NAbb	2m1f	E Hdl	SFT	£2961
110	10/01	Strf	2m110y	E Hdl	G-S	£3293

Total win prize-money £6255

Going: Sf: 1-2 GS: 1-3 Gd: 0-2 GF: - Fm: 0-0
Distance: **2m/2m3: 2-6** 2m4-2m7: 0-0 3m+: 0-1
Track: **LH: 2-5** RH: 0-1 **Tight: 2-4** Gall: 0-1
Aids: Bl: 0-0 Vi: 0-0 Tstrap: 0-0
Best Rating: 124 12/01 Bang 2m1f gd-sft Hdl

Useful on the Flat, he was claimed by Martin Pipe and duly won his first two over hurdles before his limitations were exposed. Two miles is his trip, and he is suited by soft ground. Now with Lydia Pearce.

Titatium (IRE)

10-y-o ch g Lancastrian-Argu Ironside (General Ironside)
Mrs P Grainger B Hawkins

Placings:F/*000*/F/5 **(0271)**
2001/02: 25^{5}G

	Starts	1st	2nd	3rd	Win & Pl
Chases	1	0	0	0	0
Career Total	**6**	**0**	**0**	**0**	**0**

Going: Sf: 0-0 GS: 0-0 Gd: 0-1 GF: - Fm: 0-0
Distance: 2m/2m3: 0-0 2m4-2m7: 0-0 3m+: 0-1
Track: LH: 0-0 RH: 0-1 Tight: 0-0 Gall: 0-0
Aids: Bl: 0-0 Vi: 0-0 Tstrap: 0-1
Best Rating: 34 5/01 Hrfd 3m1f110y good Ch

Titian Angel (IRE)

97 **77**

5-y-o ch m Brief Truce (USA)-Kuwah (IRE) (Be My Guest (USA))
A B Coogan A B Coogan

Placings:606000 **(4565)**
2001/02: 16^{6}G, 16^{0}GS, 16^{6}S, 16^{0}S, 21^{0}GF, 16^{0}G

	Starts	1st	2nd	3rd	Win & Pl
Hurdles	6	0	0	0	0
Career Total	**6**	**0**	**0**	**0**	**0**

Going: Sf: 0-2 GS: 0-1 Gd: 0-2 GF: - Fm: 0-1
Distance: 2m/2m3: 0-5 2m4-2m7: 0-1 3m+: 0-0
Track: LH: 0-1 RH: 0-5 Tight: 0-0 Gall: 0-4
Aids: Bl: 0-0 Vi: 0-0 Tstrap: 0-0
Best Rating: 77 11/01 Hntg 2m110y good Hdl

Headstrong selling-class hurdler.

Titian Charmer

71f **35f**

4-y-o ch f Charmer-Titian Beauty (Auction Ring (USA))
Mrs L C Jewell Mrs Val Morgan

Placings:*00* **(4539)**
2001/02: 17^{0}S, 16^{0}G

	Starts	1st	2nd	3rd	Win & Pl
NH Flat	2	0	0	0	
Career Total	**2**	**0**	**0**	**0**	

Going: Sf: 0-1 GS: 0-0 Gd: 0-1 GF: - Fm: 0-0
Distance: 2m/2m3: 0-2 2m4-2m7: 0-0 3m+: 0-0
Track: LH: 0-1 RH: 0-0 Tight: 0-2 Gall: 0-0
Aids: Bl: 0-0 Vi: 0-0 Tstrap: 0-0
Best Rating: 35 4/02 Fknm 2m good NHF

Titus Bramble

108(86h) (66h)**95**

5-y-o b g Puissance-Norska (Northfields (USA))
P C Ritchens Mrs B D Adams

Placings:54431330-UP00**PF2254P5** **(4761)**
2001/02: 22^{U}GF, 24^{P}GF, 18^{0}GF, 21^{0}G, 17^{P}G, 20^{F}G, 22^{2}S, 18^{2}HY, 20^{5}S, 16^{4}S, 21^{P}G, 19^{5}GF

	Starts	1st	2nd	3rd	Win & Pl
Hurdles	4	0	0	0	0
Chases	8	0	2	0	2248
Career Total	**20**	**1**	**2**	**3**	**7867**

80	1/01	Tntn	2m1f	E(0-105)HHdl	HVY	£3082

Total win prize-money £3083

Going: Sf: 0-4 GS: 0-0 Gd: 0-4 GF: - Fm: 0-4
Distance: 2m/2m3: 0-4 2m4-2m7: 0-7 3m+: 0-1
Track: LH: 0-5 RH: 0-3 Tight: 0-9 Gall: 0-0
Aids: Bl: 0-2 Vi: 0-6 Tstrap: 0-1
Best Rating: 95 4/02 Asct 2m3f110y gd-fm Ch

A fair handicap hurdler. Has worn blinkers. Looks best around two and a half miles. Likes to get his toe in.

Tiutchev

118 **180**

9-y-o b g Soviet Star (USA)-Cut Ahead (Kalaglow)
N J Henderson The Liars Poker Partnership

Placings:4FU/U2311/21F1662/**111**/1061U5-3154 **(4663)**
2001/02: 16^{3}GF, 16^{1}GS, 16^{5}GS, 20^{4}G

	Starts	1st	2nd	3rd	Win & Pl
Chases	4	1	0	1	23364
Career Total	**28**	**10**	**3**	**2**	**218332**

180	2/02	Sand	2m	B HCh	G-S	£10179
180	2/01	Asct	2m3f110y	A Ch	SFT	£42575
172	5/00	Punc	2m	Ch	GD	£24800
174	3/00	Chel	2m	A Ch	GD	£66700
155	1/00	Sand	2m4f110y	C Ch	SFT	£7785
154	12/99	Extr	2m1f110y	C Ch	G-S	£7220
152	1/99	Kemp	2m	B(0-145)HHdl	HVY	£21280
142	12/98	Chel	2m1f	C(0-135)HHdl	GD	£4622
113	11/97	Chel	2m110y	D(0-110)HHdl	G-F	£7490
117	10/97	Extr	2m1f110y	E Hdl	GD	£2326

Total win prize-money £194979

Going: Sf: 0-0 GS: 1-2 Gd: 0-1 GF: - Fm: 0-1
Distance: **2m/2m3: 1-3** 2m4-2m7: 0-1 3m+: 0-0
Track: LH: 0-2 **RH: 1-1** Tight: 0-1 Gall: 0-1
Aids: Bl: 0-0 Vi: 0-0 Tstrap: 0-0
Best Rating: 180 2/02 Sand 2m gd-sft Ch

Top-class chaser, he was unbeaten over fences in 1999/2000, highlighted by a clear-cut victory in the Arkle. He has not quite reached the heights that seemed likely since, despite a couple of fine victories including the 2001 Ascot Chase, and has been prone to bouts of colic. Suited by two to two and a half miles. Has reportedly joined Martin Pipe

Tiye

82 **53**

7-y-o b m Salse (USA)-Kiya (USA) (Dominion)
D L Williams P F Moore

Placings:356/00020005-00 **(0788)**
2001/02: 16^{0}S, 17^{0}GF

	Starts	1st	2nd	3rd	Win & Pl
Hurdles	2	0	0	0	
Career Total	**13**	**0**	**1**	**1**	**1169**

Going: Sf: 0-1 GS: 0-0 Gd: 0-0 GF: - Fm: 0-1
Distance: 2m/2m3: 0-2 2m4-2m7: 0-0 3m+: 0-0
Track: LH: 0-1 RH: 0-1 Tight: 0-2 Gall: 0-0
Aids: Bl: 0-0 Vi: 0-0 Tstrap: 0-0
Best Rating: 92 2/99 Newb 2m110y gd-sft Hdl

To Be The Best

81(79h) (61h)**64**

12-y-o ch g Superlative-Early Call (Kind Of Hush)
D A Lamb D A Lamb

Placings:P/P5506/5604**0PP**/4012/P02333/300044P56 04050/5 **(1024)**
2001/02: 16^{5}GF

	Starts	1st	2nd	3rd	Win & Pl
Chases	1	0	0	0	0
Career Total	**38**	**1**	**2**	**4**	**6423**

94	9/96	Carl	2m	E Ch	FRM	£2099

Total win prize-moncy £2099

Going: Sf: 0-0 GS: 0-0 Gd: 0-0 GF: - Fm: 0-1
Distance: 2m/2m3: 0-1 2m4-2m7: 0-0 3m+: 0-0
Track: LH: 0-1 RH: 0-0 Tight: 0-1 Gall: 0-0
Aids: Bl: 0-0 Vi: 0-0 Tstrap: 0-0
Best Rating: 96 7/99 Sedg 2m110y gd-fm Ch

To The Future (IRE)

6-y-o ch g Bob Back (USA)-Lady Graduate (IRE) (Le Bavard (FR))
Miss Pauline Robson (A Parker 10/3) Mr & Mrs Raymond Anderson Green

Placings:4454-1 **(4525)**
2001/02: 26^{1}GS

	Starts	1st	2nd	3rd	Win & Pl
Chases	1	1	0	0	1430
Career Total	**5**	**1**	**0**	**0**	**1430**

107	4/02	Carl	3m2f	H Ch	G-S	£1430

Total win prize-money £1430

Going: Sf: 0-0 GS: 1-1 Gd: 0-0 GF: - Fm: 0-0
Distance: 2m/2m3: 0-0 2m4-2m7: 0-0 **3m+: 1-1**
Track: LH: 0-0 **RH: 1-1** Tight: 0-0 Gall: 0-0
Aids: Bl: 0-0 Vi: 0-0 Tstrap: 0-0
Best Rating: 107 4/02 Carl 3m2f gd-sft Ch

Hunter chaser, won twice in points before completing the hat-trick in a Carlisle hunter chase in April 2002.

To-Day To-Day (IRE)

105(89h) **114**

9-y-o b g Waajib-Balela (African Sky)

L Lungo Mrs S J Matthews

Placings: *263332/P4611P/635654054/U0-025311* **(4308)**

2001/02: 17^{0}G, 16^{2}S, 21^{5}G, 16^{3}S, 21^{1}S, 21^{1}S

	Starts	1st	2nd	3rd	Win & Pl
Chases	6	2	1	1	8810
Career Total	**29**	**4**	**3**	**5**	**17276**

114	3/02	Ayr	2m5f110y	D(0-110)HCh	SFT	£4121
107	3/02	Sedg	2m5f	F(0-95)HCh	SFT	£3318
101	3/99	Newc	2m4f	D(0-110)HHdl	SFT	£2866
94	3/99	Catt	3m1f110y	F(0-100)HHdl	SFT	£2472

Total win prize-money £12777

Going: Sf: 2-4 GS: 0-0 Gd: 0-2 GF: - Fm: 0-0
Distance: 2m/2m3: 0-3 **2m4-2m7: 2-3** 3m+: 0-0
Track: **LH: 2-5** RH: 0-1 **Tight: 1-2** Gall: 0-1
Aids: Bl: 0-0 **Vi: 2-2** Tstrap: 0-0
Best Rating: 114 3/02 Ayr 2m5f110y soft Ch

A winner over hurdles from two miles four furlongs to three miles. Scored twice over fences over two miles five furlongs. Acts on soft ground.

Tobago (IRE)

102(105h) (108h)**120**

7-y-o b g Phardante (FR)-Portia's Delight (IRE) (The Parson)

P F Nicholls Hunt & Co (bournemouth) Ltd

Placings: *2-2341F* **(4835)**

2001/02: 22^{2}GF, 22^{3}G, 24^{4}GS, 25^{1}G, 25^{F}G

	Starts	1st	2nd	3rd	Win & Pl
Hurdles	3	0	1	1	1533
Chases	2	1	0	0	3445
Career Total	**6**	**1**	**2**	**1**	**5741**

120	4/02	Winc	3m1f110y	E Ch	GD	£3445

Total win prize-money £3445

Going: Sf: 0-0 GS: 0-1 Gd: 1-3 GF: - Fm: 0-1
Distance: 2m/2m3: 0-0 2m4-2m7: 0-2 **3m+: 1-3**
Track: LH: 0-1 **RH: 1-4** Tight: 0-1 Gall: 0-0
Aids: Bl: 0-0 Vi: 0-0 Tstrap: 0-0
Best Rating: 120 4/02 Winc 3m1f110y good Ch

Fair hurdler, he made all to land his chasing debut with ease, but fell when in front next time. Effective on good ground. Stays three miles.

Tobesure (IRE)

95(96c) (109c)**100**

8-y-o b g Asir-Princess Citrus (IRE) (Auction Ring (USA))

J I A Charlton Richard Nixon

Placings: *250352/64124460-4024P32F* **(4395)**

2001/02: 20^{4}GF, 21^{0}G, 20^{2}G, 20^{4}G, 20^{P}S, 24^{3}S, 25^{2}GS, 25^{F}HY

	Starts	1st	2nd	3rd	Win & Pl
Hurdles	1	0	0	1	272
Chases	7	0	2	0	2454
Career Total	**22**	**1**	**5**	**2**	**8173**

96	10/00	Kels	2m6f110y	E Hdl	GD	£2800

Total win prize-money £2800

Going: Sf: 0-3 GS: 0-1 Gd: 0-3 GF: - Fm: 0-1
Distance: 2m/2m3: 0-0 2m4-2m7: 0-5 3m+: 0-3
Track: LH: 0-7 RH: 0-1 Tight: 0-4 Gall: 0-3
Aids: Bl: 0-0 Vi: 0-0 Tstrap: 0-1
Best Rating: 109 11/01 Newc 2m4f good Ch

A fair novice hurdler, he was switched to fences in May 2001 but did not really take to them. Decent effort back over hurdles in February, but is a weak finisher and one to have reservations about overall.

Tobia's Ting

52f **25f**

5-y-o b g Savahra Sound-Lucky Relikon (Lucky Wednesday)

D Shaw L Dickson

Placings: *0* **(3338)**

2001/02: 16^{0}G

	Starts	1st	2nd	3rd	Win & Pl
NH Flat	1	0	0	0	
Career Total	**1**	**0**	**0**	**0**	

Going: Sf: 0-0 GS: 0-0 Gd: 0-1 GF: - Fm: 0-0
Distance: 2m/2m3: 0-1 2m4-2m7: 0-0 3m+: 0-0
Track: LH: 0-0 RH: 0-1 Tight: 0-0 Gall: 0-0
Aids: Bl: 0-0 Vi: 0-0 Tstrap: 0-0
Best Rating: 25 1/02 Ludl 2m good NHF

Toby Brown

88(98h) (123h)**105**

9-y-o b g Arzanni-Forest Nymph (NZ) (Oak Ridge (FR))

A King Mr A Stennett & Mrs J M Stennett

Placings: *F2053/112U22/42/PP3-360P* **(4301)**

2001/02: 21^{3}GS, 23^{6}HY, 22^{0}GS, 22^{P}HY

	Starts	1st	2nd	3rd	Win & Pl
Hurdles	4	0	0	1	498
Career Total	**20**	**2**	**5**	**3**	**13981**

116	11/97	MRas	2m5f110y	E(0-115)HHdl	GD	£2337
107	9/97	Worc	2m4f	E Hdl	GD	£2495

Total win prize-money £4833

Going: Sf: 0-2 GS: 0-2 Gd: 0-0 GF: - Fm: 0-0
Distance: 2m/2m3: 0-0 2m4-2m7: 0-3 3m+: 0-1
Track: LH: 0-2 RH: 0-2 Tight: 0-0 Gall: 0-1
Aids: Bl: 0-0 Vi: 0-0 Tstrap: 0-0
Best Rating: 137 12/98 Sand 2m6f good Hdl

Handicap hurdler, but lightly raced in recent seasons and has not won since November 1997. Effective at two and a half to three miles and acts on good ground. Pulled up lame on his second chase run in May 2002.

Todays Man

50

5-y-o b g Bigstone (IRE)-Snowgirl (IRE) (Mazaad)

Mrs Dianne Sayer A Slack

Placings: *0P* **(1576)**

2001/02: 17^{0}G, 22^{P}G

	Starts	1st	2nd	3rd	Win & Pl
Hurdles	2	0	0	0	
Career Total	**2**	**0**	**0**	**0**	

Going: Sf: 0-0 GS: 0-0 Gd: 0-2 GF: - Fm: 0-0
Distance: 2m/2m3: 0-1 2m4-2m7: 0-1 3m+: 0-0
Track: LH: 0-2 RH: 0-0 Tight: 0-2 Gall: 0-0
Aids: Bl: 0-0 Vi: 0-0 Tstrap: 0-0
Best Rating:

Toddeano

6-y-o b g Perpendicular-Phisus (Henbit (USA))

G Fierro G Fierro

Placings: *00* **(0843)**

2001/02: 16^{0}GS, 16^{0}G

	Starts	1st	2nd	3rd	Win & Pl
NH Flat	2	0	0	0	
Career Total	**2**	**0**	**0**	**0**	

Going: Sf: 0-0 GS: 0-1 Gd: 0-1 GF: - Fm: 0-0
Distance: 2m/2m3: 0-2 2m4-2m7: 0-0 3m+: 0-0
Track: LH: 0-2 RH: 0-0 Tight: 0-0 Gall: 0-0
Aids: Bl: 0-0 Vi: 0-0 Tstrap: 0-0
Best Rating:

Tohunga

7-y-o b/br g Rudimentary (USA)-Refinancing (USA) (Forli (ARG))

J M Turner J M Turner

Placings: *1/2022/0-P* **(0321)**

2001/02: 26^{P}G

	Starts	1st	2nd	3rd	Win & Pl
Chases	1	0	0	0	
Career Total	**7**	**1**	**3**	**0**	**4019**

99	4/99	MRas	1m5f110y	H NHF	GD	£1567

Total win prize-money £1567

Going: Sf: 0-0 GS: 0-0 Gd: 0-1 GF: - Fm: 0-0
Distance: 2m/2m3: 0-0 2m4-2m7: 0-0 3m+: 0-1
Track: LH: 0-0 RH: 0-1 Tight: 0-1 Gall: 0-0
Aids: Bl: 0-0 Vi: 0-0 Tstrap: 0-0
Best Rating: 116 10/99 Chel 2m110y good NHF

Toi Express (IRE)

99(101h) (100h)**119**

6-y-o ch g Phardante (FR)-Toi Figures (Deep Run)

P J Hobbs J & B Gibbs & Sons Ltd

Placings: *5S-2563* **(4731)**

2001/02: 16^{2}G, 20^{5}GS, 19^{6}G, 17^{3}F

	Starts	1st	2nd	3rd	Win & Pl
Hurdles	4	0	1	1	1410
Career Total	**6**	**0**	**1**	**1**	**1410**

Going: Sf: 0-0 GS: 0-1 Gd: 0-2 GF: - Fm: 0-1
Distance: 2m/2m3: 0-3 2m4-2m7: 0-1 3m+: 0-0
Track: LH: 0-0 RH: 0-3 Tight: 0-1 Gall: 0-0
Aids: Bl: 0-0 Vi: 0-0 Tstrap: 0-0
Best Rating: 100 4/02 Extr 2m1f firm Hdl

Lightly-raced hurdler, has shown ability on a sound surface.

Tollbrae (IRE)

100f **123f**

5-y-o gr g Supreme Leader-Miss Henrietta (IRE) (Step Together (USA))

N J Henderson R A Bartlett

Placings: *14* **(4841)**

2001/02: 17^{1}S, 16^{4}G

	Starts	1st	2nd	3rd	Win & Pl
NH Flat	2	1	0	0	1701
Career Total	**2**	**1**	**0**	**0**	**1701**

123	3/02	Hrfd	2m1f	H NHF	SFT	£1701

Total win prize-money £1701

Going: Sf: 1-1 GS: 0-0 Gd: 0-1 GF: - Fm: 0-0
Distance: **2m/2m3: 1-2** 2m4-2m7: 0-0 3m+: 0-0
Track: LH: 0-1 **RH: 1-1** Tight: 0-0 Gall: 0-0
Aids: Bl: 0-0 Vi: 0-0 Tstrap: 0-0
Best Rating: 123 3/02 Hrfd 2m1f soft NHF

Impressive winner on his bumper debut, before a fair effort at Ayr on good ground.

Tom Brodie

88 110

12-y-o b g Ardross-Deep Line (Deep Run)

J Howard Johnson Mrs M W Bird

Placings:*214/2*131444/111144230/0333313145/1211 34P/22245P/05-4 **(0330)**

2001/02: 20^{4}GS

	Starts	1st	2nd	3rd	Win & Pl
Chases	1	0	0	0	428
Career Total	**45**	**12**	**7**	**8**	**70579**

137	11/98	Weth	2m	B(0-150)HCh	GD	£6989
126	11/98	Ayr	2m	C(0-130)HCh	G-S	£7586
133	9/98	Prth	2m	E(0-115)HCh	GD	£5012
123	2/98	Muss	2m4f	E(0-115)HCh	GD	£3220
112	1/98	Muss	2m	E(0-115)HCh	G-S	£3562
132	11/96	Aint	2m110y	B(0-140)HHdl	GD	£10377
120	11/96	Newc	2m	D(0-125)HHdl	G-F	£2752
112	10/96	Kels	2m110y	E(0-115)HHdl	FRM	£2206
112	5/96	Weth	2m	D(0-120)HHdl	G-F	£2847
100	1/96	Newc	2m	E Hdl	GD	£2593
89	11/95	Newc	2m	E Hdl	FRM	£2071
96	1/95	Muss	2m	H NHF	G-S	£1208

Total win prize-money £50426

Going: Sf: 0-0 GS: 0-1 Gd: 0-0 GF: - Fm: 0-0
Distance: 2m/2m3: 0-0 2m4-2m7: 0-1 3m+: 0-0
Track: LH: 0-0 RH: 0-1 Tight: 0-0 Gall: 0-0
Aids: Bl: 0-0 Vi: 0-0 Tstrap: 0-0
Best Rating: 137 11/98 Weth 2m good Ch

Tom Cobbler (IRE)

89(97c) (92c)103

8-y-o ch g Zaffaran (USA)-Po Bo Pu (Pollerton)

N A Twiston-Davies I Guest

Placings:*6213*/133144/**1U244**505-005 **(1644)**

2001/02: 27^{0}G, 23^{0}GF, 26^{5}G

	Starts	1st	2nd	3rd	Win & Pl
Hurdles	2	0	0	0	0
Chases	1	0	0	0	0
Career Total	**21**	**4**	**2**	**3**	**15274**

124	9/00	Worc	2m7f110y	D Ch	G-F	£4056
114	1/00	Folk	2m6f110y	E Hdl	SFT	£2573
102	9/99	Worc	2m	E Hdl	SFT	£2455
110	4/99	NAbb	2m1f	H NHF	SFT	£1397

Total win prize-money £10481

Going: Sf: 0-0 GS: 0-0 Gd: 0-2 GF: - Fm: 0-1
Distance: 2m/2m3: 0-0 2m4-2m7: 0-0 3m+: 0-3
Track: LH: 0-1 RH: 0-2 Tight: 0-1 Gall: 0-1
Aids: Bl: 0-2 Vi: 0-0 Tstrap: 0-0
Best Rating: 124 9/00 Worc 2m7f110y gd-fm Ch

Tom Collins

9-y-o b g Broadsword (USA)-Special Venture (Giolla Mear)

Miss S E Forster J P Seymour

Placings:P-PF **(0782)**

2001/02: 20^{P}GF, 20^{F}G

	Starts	1st	2nd	3rd	Win & Pl
Hurdles	1	0	0	0	0
Chases	1	0	0	0	0
Career Total	**3**	**0**	**0**	**0**	

Going: Sf: 0-0 GS: 0-0 Gd: 0-1 GF: - Fm: 0-1
Distance: 2m/2m3: 0-0 2m4-2m7: 0-2 3m+: 0-0
Track: LH: 0-2 RH: 0-0 Tight: 0-0 Gall: 0-0
Aids: Bl: 0-0 Vi: 0-0 Tstrap: 0-0
Best Rating:

Tom Costalot (IRE)

104(100h) (84h)129

7-y-o gr g Black Minstrel-Hop Picker (USA) (Plugged Nickle (USA))

Mrs Susan Nock Gerard Nock

Placings:*6055/B420*-35**1112** **(4117)**

2001/02: 19^{3}G, 21^{5}G, 21^{1}G, 20^{1}G, 19^{1}S, 21^{2}G

	Starts	1st	2nd	3rd	Win & Pl
Hurdles	1	0	0	1	304
Chases	5	3	1	0	16672
Career Total	**14**	**3**	**2**	**1**	**17839**

129	2/02	Donc	2m3f110y	E(0-105)HCh	SFT	£3302
119	12/01	Leic	2m4f110y	D(0-125)HCh	GD	£7672
121	12/01	Winc	2m5f	F(0-105)HCh	GD	£3588

Total win prize-money £14562

Going: Sf: 1-1 GS: 0-0 Gd: 2-5 GF: - Fm: 0-0
Distance: 2m/2m3: 0-1 **2m4-2m7: 3-5** 3m+: 0-0
Track: LH: 1-2 **RH: 2-4** Tight: 0-1 **Gall: 1-1**
Aids: Bl: 0-0 Vi: 0-0 Tstrap: 0-0
Best Rating: 129 3/02 Winc 2m5f good Ch

Improved no end when switched to chasing at the end of 2001 and completed a hat trick at Wincanton, Leicester and Doncaster. Suited by trips of around two and a half miles and is probably best on a sound surface, but handles soft.

Tom De Savoie (IRE)

9-y-o br g War Hero-Black Pilot (Linacre)

Mrs Caroline Bailey W G N Barber

Placings:1/2-2F **(4288)**

2001/02: 24^{2}S, 25^{F}GS

	Starts	1st	2nd	3rd	Win & Pl
Chases	2	0	1	0	548
Career Total	**4**	**1**	**2**	**0**	**3136**

108	4/00	Fknm	3m110y	H Ch	GD	£2131

Total win prize-money £2132

Going: Sf: 0-1 GS: 0-1 Gd: 0-0 GF: - Fm: 0-0
Distance: 2m/2m3: 0-0 2m4-2m7: 0-0 3m+: 0-2
Track: LH: 0-1 RH: 0-1 Tight: 0-1 Gall: 0-1
Aids: Bl: 0-0 Vi: 0-0 Tstrap: 0-0
Best Rating: 114 3/02 Newb 3m soft Ch

A successful pointer and hunter chaser, he is suited by a sound surface and three miles.

Tom Pinch (IRE)

106 84

13-y-o b g Mandalus-Spanish Royale (Royal Buck)

J R Cornwall J R Cornwall

Placings:2/00/53FF3331U/P4/P23-P6P3 **(4590)**

2001/02: 23^{P}G, 20^{6}S, 20^{P}GS, 24^{3}G

	Starts	1st	2nd	3rd	Win & Pl
Chases	4	0	0	1	331
Career Total	**21**	**1**	**2**	**6**	**7210**

101	4/99	Uttx	3m	G(0-90)HCh	G-S	£2207

Total win prize-money £2208

Going: Sf: 0-1 GS: 0-1 Gd: 0-2 GF: - Fm: 0-0
Distance: 2m/2m3: 0-0 2m4-2m7: 0-2 3m+: 0-2
Track: LH: 0-1 RH: 0-3 Tight: 0-1 Gall: 0-0
Aids: Bl: 0-0 Vi: 0-0 Tstrap: 0-0
Best Rating: 110 4/99 MRas 2m4f soft Ch

Tom Tailor (GER)

110 110

8-y-o b g Beldale Flutter (USA)-Thoughtful (Northfields (USA))

D R C Elsworth The A A Partnership

Placings:1012432/P0/5/1-231231630 **(4500)**

2001/02: 18^{2}GS, 18^{3}G, 16^{1}GS, 16^{2}G, 22^{3}S, 21^{1}HY, 22^{6}HY, 17^{3}S, 17^{0}G

	Starts	1st	2nd	3rd	Win & Pl
Hurdles	9	2	2	3	6566
Career Total	**20**	**5**	**4**	**4**	**17904**

105	1/02	Plum	2m5f	G Hdl	HVY	£2352
99	12/01	Leic	2m	G Hdl	G-S	£1883
120	11/00	Font	2m2f110y	F Hdl	HVY	£2446
109	1/98	Extr	2m2f	E Hdl	HVY	£2565
109	11/97	Sand	2m110y	D Hdl	GD	£2723

Total win prize-money £11970

Going: Sf: 1-4 GS: 1-2 Gd: 0-3 GF: - Fm: 0-0
Distance: 2m/2m3: 1-6 2m4-2m7: 1-3 3m+: 0-0
Track: LH: 1-5 RH: 1-4 **Tight: 1-7** Gall: 0-0
Aids: Bl: 0-0 Vi: 0-0 Tstrap: 0-0
Best Rating: 120 11/00 Font 2m2f110y heavy Hdl

Modest hurdler, stays two and a half miles plus. Acts on an easy surface.

Tom Tod (IRE)

8-y-o ch g Be My Native (USA)-Deep Hansel (Deep Run)

D Burchell M G Jones

Placings:*0*/PP **(4127)**

2001/02: 21^{P}S, 17^{P}G

	Starts	1st	2nd	3rd	Win & Pl
Hurdles	2	0	0	0	
Career Total	**3**	**0**	**0**	**0**	

Going: Sf: 0-1 GS: 0-0 Gd: 0-1 GF: - Fm: 0-0
Distance: 2m/2m3: 0-1 2m4-2m7: 0-1 3m+: 0-0
Track: LH: 0-0 RH: 0-2 Tight: 0-0 Gall: 0-0
Aids: Bl: 0-0 Vi: 0-0 Tstrap: 0-0
Best Rating: 63 5/99 Extr 2m1f110y gd-fm NHF

Tom's Man

66 87

8-y-o ch g Milieu-Lorna's Choice (Oats)

G F White F V White

Placings:*B0P/0*/**P04-P3PPP** **(1681)**

2001/02: 20^{P}S, 20^{3}GF, 20^{P}GF, 20^{P}G, 21^{P}G

	Starts	1st	2nd	3rd	Win & Pl
Chases	5	0	0	1	191
Career Total	**12**	**0**	**0**	**1**	**477**

Going: Sf: 0-1 GS: 0-0 Gd: 0-2 GF: - Fm: 0-2
Distance: 2m/2m3: 0-0 2m4-2m7: 0-5 3m+: 0-0
Track: LH: 0-2 RH: 0-3 Tight: 0-2 Gall: 0-0
Aids: Bl: 0-0 Vi: 0-0 Tstrap: 0-4
Best Rating: 87 4/01 Weth 2m gd-sft Ch

Tom's Prize

104(84h) (80h)126

7-y-o ch g Gunner B-Pandora's Prize (Royal Vulcan)

J L Spearing Mrs P Joynes

Placings:0054/U-2514241 **(4849)**

2001/02: 22^{2}S, 17^{5}G, 22^{1}HY, 26^{4}HY, 24^{2}S, 20^{4}GS, 24^{1}G

	Starts	1st	2nd	3rd	Win & Pl
Hurdles	1	0	1	0	748
Chases	6	2	1	0	11179
Career Total	**12**	**2**	**2**	**0**	**11927**

126 4/02 Strf 3m D Ch GD £4322
119 12/01 Towc 2m6f D Ch HVY £5089
Total win prize-money £9413

Going: Sf: 1-4 GS: 0-1 Gd: 1-2 GF: - Fm: 0-0
Distance: 2m/2m3: 0-1 2m4-2m7: 1-3 3m+: 1-3
Track: LH: 1-4 RH: 1-2 **Tight: 1-5** Gall: 0-0
Aids: Bl: 0-0 Vi: 0-0 Tstrap: 0-0
Best Rating: 126 4/02 Strf 3m good Ch

Stays well and has won novice chases over two miles and six furlongs on heavy ground at Towcester and three miles at Stratford on good.

Tom's River (IRE)

113(97h) (82h)116

10-y-o ch g Over The River (FR)-Nesford (Walshford)

Mrs M Reveley Jemm Partnership

Placings:*120/200/*U11P4/4213F/023UU-45415P **(4394)**

2001/02: 24^{4}G, 25^{5}S, 25^{4}G, 25^{1}GS, 24^{5}GS, 32^{P}HY

	Starts	1st	2nd	3rd	Win & Pl
Chases	6	1	0	0	4211
Career Total	**27**	**5**	**4**	**2**	**22604**

114 1/02 Catt 3m1f110y F(0-100)HCh G-S £3514
132 12/99 Catt 3m1f110y F(0-110)HCh GD £5004
126 1/99 Catt 3m1f110y F(0-110)HCh SFT £3096
107 1/99 Catt 3m1f110y E Ch GD £2814
97 2/97 Carl 2m1f H NHF SFT £1035
Total win prize-money £15464

Going: Sf: 0-2 GS: 1-2 Gd: 0-2 GF: - Fm: 0-0
Distance: 2m/2m3: 0-0 2m4-2m7: 0-0 **3m+: 1-6**
Track: **LH: 1-5** RH: 0-1 **Tight: 1-4** Gall: 0-2
Aids: Bl: 0-0 Vi: 0-0 Tstrap: 0-0
Best Rating: 132 10/00 Kels 2m6f110y soft Ch

A decent staying chaser, he goes well at Catterick and is suited to ground on the easy side.

Tombazaan (IRE)

97 89

6-y-o b m Good Thyne (USA)-Master Nidee (Master Owen)

N J Henderson F T Wilson

Placings:*31-*P4 **(3705)**

2001/02: 19^{P}S, 19^{4}HY

	Starts	1st	2nd	3rd	Win & Pl
Hurdles	2	0	0	0	273
Career Total	**4**	**1**	**0**	**1**	**2105**

107 1/01 Weth 2m H NHF HVY £1610
Total win prize-money £1610

Going: Sf: 0-2 GS: 0-0 Gd: 0-0 GF: - Fm: 0-0
Distance: 2m/2m3: 0-0 2m4-2m7: 0-2 3m+: 0-0
Track: LH: 0-0 RH: 0-2 Tight: 0-1 Gall: 0-0
Aids: Bl: 0-0 Vi: 0-0 Tstrap: 0-0
Best Rating: 107 1/01 Weth 2m heavy NHF

Tomcappagh (IRE)

99 103

11-y-o br g Riberetto-Shuil Suas (Menelek)

Mrs S Wall Mrs S Wall

Placings:F3P3P/4312/F55P/P0UP323P3-0045133U2CP3 **(4563)**

2001/02: 24^{0}GF, 26^{0}G, 21^{4}G, 25^{5}S, 26^{1}S, 25^{3}HY, 26^{3}S, 26^{U}S, 24^{2}S, 24^{C}GS, 26^{P}HY, 26^{3}GF

	Starts	1st	2nd	3rd	Win & Pl
Chases	12	1	1	3	6900
Career Total	**34**	**2**	**3**	**9**	**12252**

96 12/01 Plum 3m2f F(0-100)HCh SFT £4127
109 2/99 Folk 2m5f H Ch G-S £1096
Total win prize-money £5224

Going: Sf: 1-7 GS: 0-1 Gd: 0-2 GF: - Fm: 0-2
Distance: 2m/2m3: 0-0 2m4-2m7: 0-1 **3m+: 1-11**
Track: LH: 0-1 RH: 0-7 Tight: 0-2 Gall: 0-1
Aids: Bl: 0-0 Vi: 0-0 Tstrap: 0-0
Best Rating: 116 3/99 Strf 3m heavy Ch

Moderate staying chaser, effective in soft ground, stays three miles-two.

Tomenoso

101 97

4-y-o b g Teenoso (USA)-Guarded Expression (Siberian Express (USA))

Mrs S J Smith (W G M Turner 24/11) Keith Nicholson

Placings:44223 **(3251)**

2001/02: 16^{4}GF, 16^{4}G, 16^{2}GF, 16^{2}GS, 16^{3}S

	Starts	1st	2nd	3rd	Win & Pl
Hurdles	5	0	2	1	2309
Career Total	**5**	**0**	**2**	**1**	**2309**

Going: Sf: 0-1 GS: 0-1 Gd: 0-1 GF: - Fm: 0-2
Distance: 2m/2m3: 0-5 2m4-2m7: 0-0 3m+: 0-0
Track: LH: 0-3 RH: 0-2 Tight: 0-1 Gall: 0-2
Aids: Bl: 0-0 Vi: 0-0 Tstrap: 0-0
Best Rating: 97 12/01 Weth 2m gd-sft Hdl

Still a maiden over hurdles. Effective over two miles, he acts on most types of ground.

Tomfoolary (IRE)

85 74

5-y-o ch g Erin's Isle-Liberty Bird (USA) (Danzatore (CAN))

J A B Old (E Sheehy 16/7) Mrs C H Antrobus

Placings:*30350* **(3657)**

2001/02: 16^{3}HY, 16^{0}GF, 19^{3}G, 17^{5}G, 22^{0}S

	Starts	1st	2nd	3rd	Win & Pl
NH Flat	4	0	0	2	677
Hurdles	1	0	0	0	0
Career Total	**5**	**0**	**0**	**2**	**677**

Going: Sf: 0-2 GS: 0-0 Gd: 0-2 GF: - Fm: 0-1
Distance: 2m/2m3: 0-4 2m4-2m7: 0-1 3m+: 0-0
Track: LH: 0-0 RH: 0-1 Tight: 0-0 Gall: 0-0
Aids: Bl: 0-0 Vi: 0-0 Tstrap: 0-0
Best Rating: 94 4/01 Slig 2m heavy NHF

Tomich (IRE)

102(101h) (87h)124

7-y-o b/br g Lord Americo-Gilt Course (Crash Course)

Miss A M Newton-Smith Julian Smith

Placings:*0P-*363P1FF **(4849)**

2001/02: 20^{3}G, 19^{6}G, 22^{3}G, 22^{P}GS, 21^{1}G, 22^{F}G, 24^{F}G

	Starts	1st	2nd	3rd	Win & Pl
Hurdles	4	0	0	2	754
Chases	3	1	0	0	4310
Career Total	**9**	**1**	**0**	**2**	**5064**

124 3/02 Winc 2m5f D Ch GD £4309
Total win prize-money £4310

Going: Sf: 0-0 GS: 0-1 Gd: 1-6 GF: - Fm: 0-0
Distance: 2m/2m3: 0-1 **2m4-2m7: 1-5** 3m+: 0-1
Track: LH: 0-3 **RH: 1-3** Tight: 0-2 Gall: 0-1
Aids: Bl: 0-0 Vi: 0-0 Tstrap: 0-0
Best Rating: 124 3/02 Winc 2m5f good Ch

Shock winner at Wincanton in March but a keen sort and not a reliable jumper.

Tommie Swift

51 25

6-y-o b g Karinga Bay-Marie Swift (Main Reef)

B J Llewellyn B J Llewellyn

Placings:*0000* **(3157)**

2001/02: 16^{0}GF, 16^{0}S, 19^{0}GS, 17^{0}S

	Starts	1st	2nd	3rd	Win & Pl
NH Flat	2	0	0	0	0
Hurdles	2	0	0	0	0
Career Total	**4**	**0**	**0**	**0**	

Going: Sf: 0-2 GS: 0-1 Gd: 0-0 GF: - Fm: 0-1
Distance: 2m/2m3: 0-3 2m4-2m7: 0-1 3m+: 0-0
Track: LH: 0-2 RH: 0-2 Tight: 0-1 Gall: 0-0
Aids: Bl: 0-0 Vi: 0-0 Tstrap: 0-0
Best Rating: 60 6/01 Worc 2m gd-fm NHF

Tommy Carson

109 108

7-y-o b g Last Tycoon-Ivory Palm (USA) (Sir Ivor)

Jamie Poulton J Logan

Placings:035P/5424P3045/24-3013352P1344 **(4814)**

2001/02: 16^{3}GF, 20^{0}G, 20^{1}GF, 17^{3}GS, 19^{3}G, 20^{5}G, 24^{2}G, 22^{P}G, 20^{1}S, 20^{3}HY, 20^{4}G, 21^{4}GF

	Starts	1st	2nd	3rd	Win & Pl
Chases	12	2	1	4	12636
Career Total	**27**	**2**	**3**	**6**	**15253**

108 1/02 Plum 2m4f E(0-105)HCh SFT £3360
105 9/01 Plum 2m4f D(0-115)HCh G-F £4075
Total win prize-money £7436

Going: Sf: 1-2 GS: 0-1 Gd: 0-6 GF: - Fm: 1-3
Distance: 2m/2m3: 0-2 **2m4-2m7: 2-9** 3m+: 0-1
Track: **LH: 2-11** RH: 0-1 **Tight: 2-6** Gall: 0-3
Aids: Bl: 0-0 Vi: 0-0 Tstrap: 0-0
Best Rating: 108 1/02 Plum 2m4f soft Ch

A maiden on the Flat and over hurdles, he has won a couple of minor chases. Seems to handle any ground stays two and a half miles.

Tommy Cooper

11-y-o br h Macmillion-My Charade (Cawston's Clown)

Mrs Barbara Waring E Davies, J McDonnell, A West, H Shapter

Placings:5F/2P/0PP14B4/U6U/3/PP **(1770)**

2001/02: 25^{P}G, 23^{P}GS

Starts 1st 2nd 3rd Win & Pl

	Starts	1st	2nd	3rd	Win & Pl
Chases	2	0	0	0	
Career Total	**17**	**1**	**1**	**1**	**3078**

68	9/97	Hntg	3m2f	G(0-95)HHdl	G-F	£1880

Total win prize-money £1881

Going: Sf: 0-0 GS: 0-1 Gd: 0-1 GF: - Fm: 0-0
Distance: 2m/2m3: 0-0 2m4-2m7: 0-0 3m+: 0-2
Track: LH: 0-0 RH: 0-2 Tight: 0-0 Gall: 0-0
Aids: Bl: 0-0 Vi: 0-0 Tstrap: 0-0
Best Rating: 72 11/97 NAbb 3m3f gd-fm Hdl

Tommy Tickle

10-y-o b g Rustingo-Ruths Magic (Current Magic)
C M Price Colin M Price

Placings: *40/066/P/0* **(1405)**
2001/02: 16^{0}GF

	Starts	1st	2nd	3rd	Win & Pl
Hurdles	1	0	0	0	
Career Total	**7**	**0**	**0**	**0**	**0**

Going: Sf: 0-0 GS: 0-0 Gd: 0-0 GF: - Fm: 0-1
Distance: 2m/2m3: 0-1 2m4-2m7: 0-0 3m+: 0-0
Track: LH: 0-1 RH: 0-0 Tight: 0-0 Gall: 0-0
Aids: Bl: 0-0 Vi: 0-0 Tstrap: 0-0
Best Rating: 83 3/97 Winc 2m gd-fm NHF

Tommy Trooper

107 116

7-y-o ch g Infantry-Steady Saunter Vii (Damsire Unregistered)
P F Nicholls Paul K Barber, Mick Coburn & Colin Lewis

Placings: *6316/14* **(4167)**
2001/02: 18^{1}HY, 21^{4}GS

	Starts	1st	2nd	3rd	Win & Pl
Hurdles	2	1	0	0	2615
Career Total	**6**	**2**	**0**	**1**	**4436**

116	2/02	Font	2m2f110y	E Hdl	HVY	£2614
120	2/00	Winc	2m	H NHF	GD	£1575

Total win prize-money £4190

Going: Sf: 1-1 GS: 0-1 Gd: 0-0 GF: - Fm: 0-0
Distance: **2m/2m3: 1-1** 2m4-2m7: 0-1 3m+: 0-0
Track: **LH: 1-2** RH: 0-0 **Tight: 1-2** Gall: 0-0
Aids: Bl: 0-0 Vi: 0-0 Tstrap: 0-0
Best Rating: 120 4/00 Aint 2m110y good NHF

A useful bumper horse. He missed all of 2001 due to leg trouble. Won his hurdles bow at Fontwell in February 2002. Stays two and a quarter miles. Has won on good ground and heavy.

Tone Mist

7-y-o gr m Absalom-Connie's Pet (National Trust)
R J Baker Trefusis Farm

Placings: S **(4504)**
2001/02: 17^{S}G

	Starts	1st	2nd	3rd	Win & Pl
Hurdles	1	0	0	0	
Career Total	**1**	**0**	**0**	**0**	

Going: Sf: 0-0 GS: 0-0 Gd: 0-1 GF: - Fm: 0-0
Distance: 2m/2m3: 0-1 2m4-2m7: 0-0 3m+: 0-0
Track: LH: 0-1 RH: 0-0 Tight: 0-1 Gall: 0-0
Aids: Bl: 0-0 Vi: 0-0 Tstrap: 0-0
Best Rating:

Tongita

89f 75f

4-y-o b f Petong-Bonita Bee (King Of Spain)
J C McConnochie Mrs R E Stocks

Placings: *60* **(4539)**
2001/02: 16^{6}GF, 16^{0}G

	Starts	1st	2nd	3rd	Win & Pl
NH Flat	2	0	0	0	0
Career Total	**2**	**0**	**0**	**0**	**0**

Going: Sf: 0-0 GS: 0-0 Gd: 0-1 GF: - Fm: 0-1
Distance: 2m/2m3: 0-2 2m4-2m7: 0-0 3m+: 0-0
Track: LH: 0-1 RH: 0-1 Tight: 0-1 Gall: 0-1
Aids: Bl: 0-0 Vi: 0-0 Tstrap: 0-0
Best Rating: 75 3/02 Hntg 2m110y gd-fm NHF

Toni's Tiger

8-y-o b g Shere Khan-Miss Jay-Are (Bunny Boy)
Mrs M B Stephens Mrs M B Stephens

Placings: P **(0322)**
2001/02: 21^{P}G

	Starts	1st	2nd	3rd	Win & Pl
Chases	1	0	0	0	
Career Total	**1**	**0**	**0**	**0**	

Going: Sf: 0-0 GS: 0-0 Gd: 0-1 GF: - Fm: 0-0
Distance: 2m/2m3: 0-0 2m4-2m7: 0-1 3m+: 0-0
Track: LH: 0-0 RH: 0-1 Tight: 0-1 Gall: 0-0
Aids: Bl: 0-0 Vi: 0-0 Tstrap: 0-0
Best Rating:

Tonka

105 110

10-y-o b g Mazilier (USA)-Royal Meeting (Dara Monarch)
D R Gandolfo M F Cartwright

Placings: 32/203140/F1F4223503/14/24540-0F13600 **(4550)**
2001/02: 16^{0}S, 19^{F}G, 21^{1}G, 21^{3}S, 20^{6}GS, 22^{0}GS, 21^{0}GF

	Starts	1st	2nd	3rd	Win & Pl
Hurdles	7	1	0	1	7069
Career Total	**32**	**4**	**5**	**5**	**26177**

110	10/01	MRas	2m5f110y	D(0-125)HHdl	GD	£5993
110	2/00	Wwck	2m4f110y	C(0-130)HHdl	GD	£5135
106	11/98	Chep	2m110y	D(0-125)HHdl	G-S	£2737
107	12/97	Font	2m2f110y	D(0-120)HHdl	SFT	£2889

Total win prize-money £16756

Going: Sf: 0-2 GS: 0-2 Gd: 1-2 GF: - Fm: 0-1
Distance: 2m/2m3: 0-1 **2m4-2m7: 1-6** 3m+: 0-0
Track: LH: 0-1 **RH: 1-6 Tight: 1-2** Gall: 0-1
Aids: Bl: 0-0 Vi: 0-0 Tstrap: 0-0
Best Rating: 110 10/01 MRas 2m5f110y good Hdl

A game front-runner. He had reportedly lost his confidence before scoring at Market Rasen in October 2001, although he has been well held since then. Best at around two miles five furlongs. Has won on various goings but probably appreciates a bit of cut in the ground.

Tonoco

122

9-y-o b g Teenoso (USA)-Lady Shoco (Montekin)
Mrs S J Smith Trevor Hemmings

Placings: 1/41116P/50211F2-PPP **(4197)**
2001/02: 17^{P}S, 20^{P}G, 21^{P}S

	Starts	1st	2nd	3rd	Win & Pl
Chases	3	0	0	0	
Career Total	**17**	**6**	**2**	**0**	**31309**

142	3/01	MRas	2m1f110y	D Ch	G-S	£5027
142	2/01	Carl	2m	D Ch	SFT	£4536
138	2/99	Weth	2m	A Hdl	GD	£9509
133	1/99	Hntg	2m110y	D Hdl	SFT	£2762
132	12/98	Hayd	2m	D Hdl	SFT	£2866
106	4/98	Ayr	2m	H NHF	GD	£3598

Total win prize-money £28301

Going: Sf: 0-2 GS: 0-0 Gd: 0-1 GF: - Fm: 0-0
Distance: 2m/2m3: 0-1 2m4-2m7: 0-2 3m+: 0-0
Track: LH: 0-2 RH: 0-1 Tight: 0-2 Gall: 0-1
Aids: Bl: 0-0 Vi: 0-0 Tstrap: 0-1
Best Rating: 142 3/01 MRas 2m1f110y gd-sft Ch

A decent hurdler, he did well in novice chases last season in 2000/2001 but has now been pulled up on his last three outings and is one to have severe reservations about at present.

Tony The Piler (IRE)

94 82

6-y-o br g Tidaro (USA)-Adabiya (IRE) (Akarad (FR))
N G Richards Taranto De Pol

Placings: U660100B **(4745)**
2001/02: 20^{0}G, 20^{6}G, 24^{6}S, 26^{0}S, 24^{1}S, 24^{0}G, 27^{0}S, 24^{B}G

	Starts	1st	2nd	3rd	Win & Pl
Hurdles	8	1	0	0	0
Career Total	**8**	**1**	**0**	**0**	

Going: Sf: 1-4 GS: 0-0 Gd: 0-4 GF: - Fm: 0-0
Distance: 2m/2m3: 0-0 2m4-2m7: 0-2 **3m+: 1-6**
Track: LH: 0-2 **RH: 1-6 Tight: 1-3** Gall: 0-0
Aids: Bl: 0-0 Vi: 0-0 Tstrap: 0-0
Best Rating: 82 4/02 Carl 3m110y good Hdl

Showed his first sign of ability over hurdles when dead-heating in a seller at Musselburgh in February 2002. Stays well and acts on soft ground.

Tony's Time

8-y-o b g Tina's Pet-Time Warp (Town And Country)
Miss D Cole Mrs Sarah Faulks

Placings: P-P **(0489)**
2001/02: 20^{P}GF

	Starts	1st	2nd	3rd	Win & Pl
Chases	1	0	0	0	
Career Total	**2**	**0**	**0**	**0**	

Going: Sf: 0-0 GS: 0-0 Gd: 0-0 GF: - Fm: 0-1
Distance: 2m/2m3: 0-0 2m4-2m7: 0-1 3m+: 0-0
Track: LH: 0-0 RH: 0-0 Tight: 0-1 Gall: 0-0
Aids: Bl: 0-0 Vi: 0-0 Tstrap: 0-0
Best Rating:

Too Cool (IRE)

94 76

6-y-o b/br g Un Desperado (FR)-Daraniyda (Mouktar)
J Howard Johnson Chris Heron

Placings: 30000P **(4491)**
2001/02: 17^{3}GS, 20^{0}G, 16^{0}GS, 20^{0}GF, 20^{0}G, 20^{P}GS

	Starts	1st	2nd	3rd	Win & Pl

	Starts	1st	2nd	3rd	Win & Pl
NH Flat	1	0	0	1	232
Hurdles	5	0	0	0	0
Career Total	**6**	**0**	**0**	**1**	**232**

Going: Sf: 0-0 GS: 0-3 Gd: 0-2 GF: - Fm: 0-1
Distance: 2m/2m3: 0-2 2m4-2m7: 0-4 3m+: 0-0
Track: LH: 0-3 RH: 0-2 Tight: 0-4 Gall: 0-0
Aids: Bl: 0-1 Vi: 0-0 Tstrap: 0-0
Best Rating: 91 10/01 Sedg 2m1f gd-sft NHF

Too Forward (IRE)

111 **137**

6-y-o ch g Toulon-One Back (IRE) (Meneval (USA))
M Pitman T L Gibson & D Mathias

Placings:*233*-F4122100 **(4665)**
2001/02: 16^{F}GF, 19^{4}G, 17^{1}HY, 17^{2}S, 21^{2}G, 24^{1}S, 21^{0}GS, 24^{0}G

	Starts	1st	2nd	3rd	Win & Pl
Hurdles	8	2	2	0	20046
Career Total	**11**	**2**	**3**	**2**	**21911**

137	1/02	Donc	3m110y	A Hdl	SFT	£10800
117	12/01	Folk	2m1f110y	E Hdl	HVY	£2355

Total win prize-money £13156

Going: Sf: 2-3 GS: 0-1 Gd: 0-3 GF: - Fm: 0-1
Distance: 2m/2m3: 1-3 2m4-2m7: 0-3 3m+: 1-2
Track: LH: 1-5 RH: 1-3 Tight: 1-4 Gall: 1-3
Aids: Bl: 0-0 Vi: 0-0 Tstrap: 0-0
Best Rating: 137 1/02 Donc 3m110y soft Hdl

Useful bumper form in the 2000/2001 season. He improved to win a Grade Two novice hurdle at the start of 2002, but was well held in the Royal & SunAlliance at Cheltenham next time. Handles heavy but does not want it too tacky. Acts on a sounder surface and stays three miles. Does not find a lot at the business end.

Toorak (USA)

99 **98**

5-y-o b g Irish River (FR)-Just Juliet (USA) (What A Pleasure (USA))
C J Mann D J Deer

Placings:4300 **(3771)**
2001/02: 17^{4}GF, 16^{3}S, 16^{0}GS, 16^{0}S

	Starts	1st	2nd	3rd	Win & Pl
Hurdles	4	0	0	1	523
Career Total	**4**	**0**	**0**	**1**	**523**

Going: Sf: 0-2 GS: 0-1 Gd: 0-0 GF: - Fm: 0-1
Distance: 2m/2m3: 0-4 2m4-2m7: 0-0 3m+: 0-0
Track: LH: 0-1 RH: 0-3 Tight: 0-0 Gall: 0-1
Aids: Bl: 0-0 Vi: 0-0 Tstrap: 0-0
Best Rating: 98 12/01 Hayd 2m soft Hdl

Top Buck (IRE)

105 **118**

8-y-o b/br g Top Of The World-Orlita (Master Buck)
K C Bailey A N Solomons

Placings:*2F*/235-1331430 **(4893)**
2001/02: 17^{1}G, 16^{3}G, 19^{3}G, 22^{1}G, 24^{4}S, 22^{3}GS, 20^{0}G

	Starts	1st	2nd	3rd	Win & Pl
Hurdles	7	2	0	3	9417
Career Total	**12**	**2**	**2**	**4**	**11204**

114	1/02	Winc	2m6f	E Hdl	GD	£2859
118	10/01	Extr	2m1f	D Hdl	GD	£4238

Total win prize-money £7098

Going: Sf: 0-1 GS: 0-1 Gd: 2-5 GF: - Fm: 0-0
Distance: 2m/2m3: 1-3 2m4-2m7: 1-3 3m+: 0-1
Track: LH: 0-1 **RH: 2-6** Tight: 0-0 Gall: 0-0
Aids: Bl: 0-0 Vi: 0-0 Tstrap: 0-0
Best Rating: 118 3/02 Sand 2m6f gd-sft Hdl

Lightly-raced, dual hurdle winner. Stays two miles six. Acts on a sound surface.

Top Hand

86 **68**

5-y-o ch m First Trump-Gold Luck (USA) (Slew O'Gold (USA))
E W Tuer E Tuer

Placings:B-30P **(4332)**
2001/02: 19^{3}GF, 20^{0}GF, 21^{P}S

	Starts	1st	2nd	3rd	Win & Pl
Hurdles	3	0	0	1	273
Career Total	**4**	**0**	**0**	**1**	**273**

Going: Sf: 0-1 GS: 0-0 Gd: 0-0 GF: - Fm: 0-2
Distance: 2m/2m3: 0-1 2m4-2m7: 0-2 3m+: 0-0
Track: LH: 0-2 RH: 0-1 Tight: 0-3 Gall: 0-0
Aids: Bl: 0-0 Vi: 0-0 Tstrap: 0-0
Best Rating: 68 12/01 Muss 2m4f gd-fm Hdl

Top Light

6-y-o b g Miners Lamp-Myrtilla (Beldale Flutter (USA))
R H Buckler Robert Long

Placings:*0-300*PP **(4883)**
2001/02: 17^{3}GF, 16^{0}G, 19^{0}S, 20^{P}GF, 22^{P}GF

	Starts	1st	2nd	3rd	Win & Pl
NH Flat	2	0	0	1	224
Hurdles	3	0	0	0	0
Career Total	**6**	**0**	**0**	**1**	**224**

Going: Sf: 0-1 GS: 0-0 Gd: 0-1 GF: - Fm: 0-3
Distance: 2m/2m3: 0-3 2m4-2m7: 0-2 3m+: 0-0
Track: LH: 0-3 RH: 0-2 Tight: 0-1 Gall: 0-1
Aids: Bl: 0-0 Vi: 0-0 Tstrap: 0-0
Best Rating: 76 10/01 Chep 2m110y good NHF

Top Note (IRE)

(89h) (70h)**84**

10-y-o ch g Orchestra-Clarrie (Ballyciptic)
J T Gifford Mrs S N J Embiricos

Placings:*10*/F32415/**F3F2R**/S600-3 **(0215)**
2001/02: 21^{3}GF

	Starts	1st	2nd	3rd	Win & Pl
Chases	1	0	0	1	640
Career Total	**18**	**2**	**2**	**3**	**7563**

116	3/98	Towc	2m5f	E Hdl	G-S	£2670
93	1/97	Folk	2m1f110y	H NHF	G-S	£1182

Total win prize-money £3852

Going: Sf: 0-0 GS: 0-0 Gd: 0-0 GF: - Fm: 0-1
Distance: 2m/2m3: 0-0 2m4-2m7: 0-1 3m+: 0-0
Track: LH: 0-0 RH: 0-1 Tight: 0-0 Gall: 0-0
Aids: Bl: 0-0 Vi: 0-0 Tstrap: 0-0
Best Rating: 122 11/98 Wind 2m5f gd-sft Ch

Top Of The Charts

74(89h) (74h)**66**

6-y-o b g Salse (USA)-Celebrity (Troy)
D L Williams Wentworths Racing Group

Placings:405045-032604**PF**0 **(2926)**
2001/02: 17^{0}GF, 22^{3}GF, 20^{2}GS, 22^{6}HY, 22^{0}G, 20^{4}GF, 24^{P}G, 24^{F}G, 24^{0}GS

	Starts	1st	2nd	3rd	Win & Pl
Hurdles	6	0	1	1	1030
Chases	3	0	0	0	290
Career Total	**15**	**0**	**1**	**1**	**1320**

Going: Sf: 0-1 GS: 0-2 Gd: 0-3 GF: - Fm: 0-3
Distance: 2m/2m3: 0-1 2m4-2m7: 0-5 3m+: 0-3
Track: LH: 0-1 RH: 0-5 Tight: 0-5 Gall: 0-1
Aids: Bl: 0-0 Vi: 0-1 Tstrap: 0-0
Best Rating: 80 11/00 Ludl 2m5f good Hdl

Plating-class staying hurdler. Seems to handle any ground.

Top Of The Class (IRE)

104 **73**

5-y-o b m Rudimentary (USA)-School Mum (Reprimand)
P D Evans P D Evans

Placings:40-5U456 **(4127)**
2001/02: 16^{5}G, 17^{U}S, 16^{4}GF, 16^{5}HY, 17^{6}G

	Starts	1st	2nd	3rd	Win & Pl
Hurdles	5	0	0	0	0
Career Total	**7**	**0**	**0**	**0**	**207**

Going: Sf: 0-2 GS: 0-0 Gd: 0-2 GF: - Fm: 0-1
Distance: 2m/2m3: 0-5 2m4-2m7: 0-0 3m+: 0-0
Track: LH: 0-3 RH: 0-2 Tight: 0-2 Gall: 0-0
Aids: Bl: 0-0 Vi: 0-1 Tstrap: 0-0
Best Rating: 73 10/01 Aint 2m110y good Hdl

A winner on the Flat, but only of moderate ability over hurdles.

Top Of The Dee

89 **78**

5-y-o ch m Rakaposhi King-Lavenham's Last (Rymer)
Mrs L Williamson Bangor-On-Dee Racing Club

Placings:*600* **(3332)**
2001/02: 17^{6}GS, 17^{0}GS, 21^{0}G

	Starts	1st	2nd	3rd	Win & Pl
NH Flat	2	0	0	0	0
Hurdles	1	0	0	0	0
Career Total	**3**	**0**	**0**	**0**	**0**

Going: Sf: 0-0 GS: 0-2 Gd: 0-1 GF: - Fm: 0-0
Distance: 2m/2m3: 0-2 2m4-2m7: 0-1 3m+: 0-0
Track: LH: 0-1 RH: 0-1 Tight: 0-1 Gall: 0-0
Aids: Bl: 0-0 Vi: 0-0 Tstrap: 0-0
Best Rating: 66 11/01 Aint 2m1f gd-sft NHF

Top Of The Snobs (IRE)

60 **18**

8-y-o b g Top Of The World-Little Snob (Aristocracy)
C Grant P Bamford

Placings:*004/0/*PF0P **(4583)**
2001/02: 17^{P}HY, 17^{F}S, 16^{0}S, 20^{P}G

	Starts	1st	2nd	3rd	Win & Pl

Hurdles	4	0	0	0	
Career Total	**8**	**0**	**0**	**0**	**0**

Going: Sf: 0-3 GS: 0-0 Gd: 0-1 GF: - Fm: 0-0
Distance: 2m/2m3: 0-3 2m4-2m7: 0-1 3m+: 0-0
Track: LH: 0-3 RH: 0-1 Tight: 0-1 Gall: 0-0
Aids: Bl: 0-0 Vi: 0-0 Tstrap: 0-0
Best Rating: 89 5/99 Uttx 2m good NHF

Top Quality

104 85

4-y-o br f Simply Great (FR)-Qurrat Al Ain (Wolver Hollow)
T D Easterby T H Bennett

Placings:5463 **(3356)**
2001/02: 16^{5}G, 16^{4}S, 16^{6}GS, 16^{3}HY

	Starts	1st	2nd	3rd	Win & Pl
Hurdles	4	0	0	1	271
Career Total	**4**	**0**	**0**	**1**	**271**

Going: Sf: 0-2 GS: 0-1 Gd: 0-1 GF: - Fm: 0-0
Distance: 2m/2m3: 0-4 2m4-2m7: 0-0 3m+: 0-0
Track: LH: 0-4 RH: 0-0 Tight: 0-0 Gall: 0-1
Aids: Bl: 0-0 Vi: 0-0 Tstrap: 0-3
Best Rating: 85 11/01 Hayd 2m soft Hdl

A full-sister to top-class chaser Simply Dashing, she lacks physical scope but has shown some ability in moderate company.

Top Saint (IRE)

100 86

8-y-o gr g Topanoora-God's Kiss (Godswalk (USA))
Mrs M Reveley Brennan And Rodden

Placings:*0/04/005/030-54* **(4786)**
2001/02: 23^{5}G, 20^{4}F

	Starts	1st	2nd	3rd	Win & Pl
Hurdles	2	0	0	0	0
Career Total	**11**	**0**	**0**	**1**	**573**

Going: Sf: 0-0 GS: 0-0 Gd: 0-1 GF: - Fm: 0-1
Distance: 2m/2m3: 0-0 2m4-2m7: 0-2 3m+: 0-0
Track: LH: 0-2 RH: 0-0 Tight: 0-0 Gall: 0-1
Aids: Bl: 0-0 Vi: 0-0 Tstrap: 0-0
Best Rating: 91 1/00 Sedg 2m1f soft Hdl

Selling-class hurdler, stays well.

Top Skipper (IRE)

101(86h) (53h)67

10-y-o b g Nordico (USA)-Scarlet Slipper (Gay Mecene (USA))
Mrs S Gardner D V Gardner

Placings:54004110P/50625P/453103/556/PP-P0006 **(1076)**
2001/02: 19^{P}F, 16^{0}GF, 25^{0}F, 26^{0}GF, 24^{6}GF

	Starts	1st	2nd	3rd	Win & Pl
Hurdles	2	0	0	0	0
Chases	3	0	0	0	0
Career Total	**31**	**3**	**1**	**2**	**7360**

97	12/98	Tntn	3m110y	G(0-90)HHdl	G-S	£1637
78	12/96	Extr	2m2f	F Hdl	SFT	£2102
72	11/96	Sedg	3m3f110y	G(0-95)HHdl	GD	£1877

Total win prize-money £5616

Going: Sf: 0-0 GS: 0-0 Gd: 0-0 GF: - Fm: 0-5
Distance: 2m/2m3: 0-1 2m4-2m7: 0-1 3m+: 0-3
Track: LH: 0-3 RH: 0-2 Tight: 0-4 Gall: 0-0
Aids: Bl: 0-1 Vi: 0-0 Tstrap: 0-0

Best Rating: 97 2/99 Font 3m2f110y good Ch

Top Team

6-y-o b m Teamster-Highly Inflammable (USA) (Wind And Wuthering (USA))
C R Barwell Lady Maria Coventry

Placings:*0/0-0*PPP00 **(2411)**
2001/02: 16^{0}G, 20^{P}GF, 19^{P}G, 25^{P}G, 20^{0}GS, 19^{0}GS

	Starts	1st	2nd	3rd	Win & Pl
NH Flat	1	0	0	0	0
Hurdles	5	0	0	0	0
Career Total	**8**	**0**	**0**	**0**	

Going: Sf: 0-0 GS: 0-2 Gd: 0-3 GF: - Fm: 0-1
Distance: 2m/2m3: 0-1 2m4-2m7: 0-4 3m+: 0-1
Track: LH: 0-2 RH: 0-3 Tight: 0-1 Gall: 0-0
Aids: Bl: 0-0 Vi: 0-2 Tstrap: 0-0
Best Rating: 54 7/01 Worc 2m good NHF

Topaz

74 47

7-y-o b g Alhijaz-Daisy Topper (Top Ville)
H J Collingridge The Topaz Partnership

Placings:00R **(2896)**
2001/02: 20^{0}S, 16^{0}G, 20^{R}S

	Starts	1st	2nd	3rd	Win & Pl
Hurdles	3	0	0	0	
Career Total	**3**	**0**	**0**	**0**	

Going: Sf: 0-2 GS: 0-0 Gd: 0-1 GF: - Fm: 0-0
Distance: 2m/2m3: 0-1 2m4-2m7: 0-2 3m+: 0-0
Track: LH: 0-2 RH: 0-1 Tight: 0-1 Gall: 0-0
Aids: Bl: 0-0 Vi: 0-0 Tstrap: 0-0
Best Rating: 47 10/01 Fknm 2m4f soft Hdl

Topical Times (IRE)

92 99

10-y-o ch m Executive Perk-Sonlaru (Deep Run)
S A Brookshaw G F Cheney

Placings:504/450P3P0/**5F4050-42P642P** **(4514)**
2001/02: 24^{4}GF, 26^{2}S, 26^{P}HY, 25^{6}G, 26^{4}S, 25^{2}G, 25^{P}GS

	Starts	1st	2nd	3rd	Win & Pl
Chases	7	0	2	0	2189
Career Total	**23**	**0**	**2**	**1**	**2817**

Going: Sf: 0-3 GS: 0-1 Gd: 0-2 GF: - Fm: 0-1
Distance: 2m/2m3: 0-0 2m4-2m7: 0-0 3m+: 0-7
Track: LH: 0-3 RH: 0-4 Tight: 0-1 Gall: 0-0
Aids: Bl: 0-0 Vi: 0-0 Tstrap: 0-0
Best Rating: 99 11/01 Uttx 3m2f soft Ch

Very modest novice chaser, stays three miles.

Topman

5-y-o ch g Komaite (USA)-Top Yard (Teekay)
A P Jones George W Smith

Placings:P **(0365)**
2001/02: 19^{P}GF

	Starts	1st	2nd	3rd	Win & Pl
Hurdles	1	0	0	0	
Career Total	**1**	**0**	**0**	**0**	

Going: Sf: 0-0 GS: 0-0 Gd: 0-0 GF: - Fm: 0-1
Distance: 2m/2m3: 0-0 2m4-2m7: 0-1 3m+: 0-0
Track: LH: 0-1 RH: 0-0 Tight: 0-1 Gall: 0-0
Aids: Bl: 0-0 Vi: 0-0 Tstrap: 0-1
Best Rating:

Topol (IRE)

84f 82f

4-y-o br g Topanoora-Kislev (IRE) (Be My Guest (USA))
Miss H C Knight Top Brass Partnership

Placings:*0* **(4032)**
2001/02: 16^{0}GS

	Starts	1st	2nd	3rd	Win & Pl
NH Flat	1	0	0	0	
Career Total	**1**	**0**	**0**	**0**	

Going: Sf: 0-0 GS: 0-1 Gd: 0-0 GF: - Fm: 0-0
Distance: 2m/2m3: 0-1 2m4-2m7: 0-0 3m+: 0-0
Track: LH: 0-1 RH: 0-0 Tight: 0-0 Gall: 0-1
Aids: Bl: 0-0 Vi: 0-0 Tstrap: 0-0
Best Rating: 82 3/02 Newb 2m110y gd-sft NHF

Toraness (IRE)

6-y-o b g Cataldi-Ardnasagh Rose (Crash Course)
Ian Williams M S Turl

Placings:*0P*-PP **(0968)**
2001/02: 22^{P}GF, 17^{P}GS

	Starts	1st	2nd	3rd	Win & Pl
Hurdles	2	0	0	0	
Career Total	**4**	**0**	**0**	**0**	

Going: Sf: 0-0 GS: 0-1 Gd: 0-0 GF: - Fm: 0-1
Distance: 2m/2m3: 0-1 2m4-2m7: 0-1 3m+: 0-0
Track: LH: 0-1 RH: 0-0 Tight: 0-1 Gall: 0-0
Aids: Bl: 0-0 Vi: 0-0 Tstrap: 0-0
Best Rating: 70 10/00 Chel 2m110y good NHF

Torduff Express (IRE)

11-y-o b g Kambalda-Marhabtain (Touching Wood (USA))
P F Nicholls Two Plus Two

Placings:121321/12104/33F/1562P-2131 **(4650)**
2001/02: 25^{2}S, 26^{1}S, 26^{3}G, 21^{1}G

	Starts	1st	2nd	3rd	Win & Pl
Chases	4	2	1	1	32906
Career Total	**23**	**8**	**5**	**4**	**101102**

141	4/02	Aint	2m5f110y	B Ch	GD	£21645
136	2/02	Font	3m2f110y	H Ch	SFT	£6922
112	10/00	Extr	2m6f110y	E Hdl	GD	£2540
150	12/98	Asct	3m110y	B HCh	G-S	£27230
134	10/98	Plum	3m1f110y	C(0-130)HCh	GD	£5257
124	4/98	Sand	3m110y	C Ch	G-S	£4598
105	2/98	Font	3m2f110y	E Ch	GD	£3116
105	12/97	Hrfd	3m1f110y	E Ch	GD	£2697

Total win prize-money £74007

Going: Sf: 1-2 GS: 0-0 Gd: 1-2 GF: - Fm: 0-0
Distance: 2m/2m3: 0-0 2m4-2m7: 1-1 3m+: 1-3
Track: **LH: 1-2** RH: 0-1 **Tight: 2-2** Gall: 0-1
Aids: **Bl: 1-2** Vi: 0-0 Tstrap: 0-0
Best Rating: 150 12/98 Asct 3m110y gd-sft Ch

A formerly useful staying chaser, he has taken well to hunter chasing in 2002 and gave Polly Curling a memorable success in the Fox Hunters' at Aintree. Goes well in soft ground, effective in blinkers.

Tormentoso

99 **77**

5-y-o b g Catrail (USA)-Chita Rivera (Chief Singer)
A G Hobbs (B G Powell 1/4) Furnish With Abbey

Placings:00P4PP5-5F06000502350225 **(4731)**
2001/02: 17^{5}GF, 17^{F}G, 17^{0}G, 16^{6}GF, 16^{0}G, 20^{0}S, 17^{0}G, 17^{5}GF, 17^{0}GF, 17^{2}G, 17^{3}S, 19^{5}GS, 16^{0}G, 16^{2}G, 17^{2}G, 17^{5}F

	Starts	1st	2nd	3rd	Win & Pl
Hurdles	16	0	3	1	1843
Career Total	**23**	**0**	**3**	**1**	**1843**

Going: Sf: 0-2 GS: 0-1 Gd: 0-8 GF: - Fm: 0-5
Distance: 2m/2m3: 0-14 2m4-2m7: 0-2 3m+: 0-0
Track: LH: 0-8 RH: 0-8 Tight: 0-7 Gall: 0-0
Aids: Bl: 0-0 Vi: 0-3 Tstrap: 0-0
Best Rating: 77 4/02 Hrfd 2m1f good Hdl

Plating-class hurdler, suited by good ground.

Tormoss Lady

73f **46f**

6-y-o ch m Le Moss-Torus Queen (Torus)
R Williams R Williams

Placings:*00* **(2341)**
2001/02: 17^{0}G, 16^{0}GF

	Starts	1st	2nd	3rd	Win & Pl
NH Flat	2	0	0	0	
Career Total	**2**	**0**	**0**	**0**	

Going: Sf: 0-0 GS: 0-0 Gd: 0-1 GF: - Fm: 0-1
Distance: 2m/2m3: 0-2 2m4-2m7: 0-0 3m+: 0-0
Track: LH: 0-0 RH: 0-2 Tight: 0-0 Gall: 0-0
Aids: Bl: 0-0 Vi: 0-0 Tstrap: 0-0
Best Rating: 46 11/01 Ludl 2m gd-fm NHF

Torn Silk

106 **139**

8-y-o b g Top Ville-Cut Velvet (USA) (Northern Dancer)
P F Nicholls Tim Chappell,Roger Eddy & Mrs F Jackson

Placings:01533/05331**UF/P**421**PF2/144564-014F52F1** **(1730)**
2001/02: 17^{0}G, 20^{1}GF, 20^{4}GF, 20^{F}GS, 23^{5}GF, 21^{2}GF, 21^{F}G, 24^{1}F

	Starts	1st	2nd	3rd	Win & Pl
Chases	8	2	1	0	11914
Career Total	**33**	**6**	**3**	**4**	**51004**

135	10/01	Tntn	3m	D(0-120)HCh	FRM	£5538
139	6/01	Worc	2m4f110y	D(0-120)HCh	G-F	£4114
133	5/00	Worc	2m4f110y	B(0-145)HCh	G-F	£10380
133	12/99	Uttx	2m	C(0-135)HCh	SFT	£7048
117	1/99	Muss	2m	D Ch	SFT	£3762
114	2/98	MRas	2m1f110y	C Hdl	GD	£4458

Total win prize-money £35303

Going: Sf: 0-0 GS: 0-1 Gd: 0-2 GF: - Fm: 2-5
Distance: 2m/2m3: 0-1 2m4-2m7: 1-5 3m+: 1-2
Track: LH: 1-5 RH: 1-2 **Tight: 1-2** Gall: 0-0
Aids: **Bl: 2-8** Vi: 0-0 Tstrap: 0-0
Best Rating: 139 6/01 Worc 2m4f110y gd-fm Ch

He has not fulfilled his early promise and needs to do things on the bridle. Successful at Taunton in October, he likes top of the ground.

Torpica

98 **77**

6-y-o br g Be My Native (USA)-Irish Mint (Dusky Boy)
P Winkworth Miss Jessica Winkworth

Placings:*0*-03062P **(4686)**
2001/02: 16^{0}S, 21^{3}GS, 21^{0}G, 20^{6}GS, 25^{2}GS, 26^{P}GF

	Starts	1st	2nd	3rd	Win & Pl
Hurdles	6	0	1	1	992
Career Total	**7**	**0**	**1**	**1**	**992**

Going: Sf: 0-1 GS: 0-3 Gd: 0-1 GF: - Fm: 0-1
Distance: 2m/2m3: 0-1 2m4-2m7: 0-3 3m+: 0-2
Track: LH: 0-3 RH: 0-2 Tight: 0-2 Gall: 0-1
Aids: Bl: 0-0 Vi: 0-0 Tstrap: 0-0
Best Rating: 77 3/02 Plum 3m1f110y gd-sft Hdl

He showed the first signs of promise in a low-grade novice hurdle at Plumpton when finishing third behind Smarty over two miles five furlongs. Stayed an extended three miles one furlong at the same track in March.

Torrid Kentavr (USA)

104 **96**

5-y-o b g Trempolino (USA)-Torrid Tango (USA) (Green Dancer (USA))
B Ellison (T G Mills 8/7) Henry Rix

Placings:226 **(2149)**
2001/02: 17^{2}G, 17^{2}G, 20^{6}G

	Starts	1st	2nd	3rd	Win & Pl
Hurdles	3	0	2	0	1426
Career Total	**3**	**0**	**2**	**0**	**1426**

Going: Sf: 0-0 GS: 0-0 Gd: 0-3 GF: - Fm: 0-0
Distance: 2m/2m3: 0-2 2m4-2m7: 0-1 3m+: 0-0
Track: LH: 0-3 RH: 0-0 Tight: 0-2 Gall: 0-1
Aids: Bl: 0-0 Vi: 0-0 Tstrap: 0-0
Best Rating: 96 10/01 Sedg 2m1f good Hdl

Has shown ability over hurdles.

Tortugas (FR)

91 **78**

5-y-o b g Subotica (FR)-Northern Whisper (FR) (Vacarme (USA))
G M McCourt Miss Julia Oakey

Placings:01206-P3P50 **(2525)**
2001/02: 19^{P}G, 19^{3}GS, 16^{P}S, 16^{5}GF, 20^{0}HY

	Starts	1st	2nd	3rd	Win & Pl
Hurdles	5	0	0	1	279
Career Total	**10**	**1**	**1**	**1**	**2735**

97	11/00	Tntn	2m1f	G Hdl	G-S	£1578

Total win prize-money £1579

Going: Sf: 0-2 GS: 0-1 Gd: 0-1 GF: - Fm: 0-1
Distance: 2m/2m3: 0-2 2m4-2m7: 0-3 3m+: 0-0
Track: LH: 0-0 RH: 0-5 Tight: 0-0 Gall: 0-0
Aids: Bl: 0-0 Vi: 0-0 Tstrap: 0-0
Best Rating: 97 11/00 Tntn 2m1f gd-sft Hdl

Best effort to date is a win in a moderately-contested Taunton seller on good to soft ground, he has since been well held.

Torus Spa (IRE)

11-y-o ch g Torus-Deep Spa (Deep Run)
J M Turner J M Turner

Placings:23FP1/P/22/340-5 **(0194)**
2001/02: 24^{5}GF

	Starts	1st	2nd	3rd	Win & Pl
Chases	1	0	0	0	0
Career Total	**12**	**1**	**3**	**2**	**5863**

88	3/98	Hexm	3m1f	G(0-90)HCh	GD	£2528

Total win prize-money £2529

Going: Sf: 0-0 GS: 0-0 Gd: 0-0 GF: - Fm: 0-1
Distance: 2m/2m3: 0-0 2m4-2m7: 0-0 3m+: 0-1
Track: LH: 0-1 RH: 0-0 Tight: 0-1 Gall: 0-0
Aids: Bl: 0-0 Vi: 0-0 Tstrap: 0-0
Best Rating: 109 4/00 Fknm 3m110y good Ch

Tory Boy

106 **100**

7-y-o b g Deploy-Mukhayyalah (Dancing Brave (USA))
Ian Williams Mary Ann Properties Ltd

Placings:P0/121150/65243-06315 **(1353)**
2001/02: 25^{0}GF, 22^{6}G, 24^{3}GF, 20^{1}GF, 22^{5}GF

	Starts	1st	2nd	3rd	Win & Pl
Hurdles	5	1	0	1	1775
Career Total	**18**	**4**	**2**	**2**	**12237**

82	8/01	Hntg	2m4f110y	G Hdl	G-F	£1549
101	9/99	Sedg	2m5f110y	E Hdl	G-F	£2617
72	8/99	Sthl	3m110y	E Hdl	G-F	£2221
93	8/99	Strf	2m110y	E Hdl	GD	£2557

Total win prize-money £8947

Going: Sf: 0-0 GS: 0-0 Gd: 0-1 GF: - Fm: 1-4
Distance: 2m/2m3: 0-0 **2m4-2m7: 1-3** 3m+: 0-2
Track: LH: 0-4 **RH: 1-1** Tight: 0-4 **Gall: 1-1**
Aids: Bl: 0-1 Vi: 0-2 Tstrap: 0-0
Best Rating: 111 7/00 Strf 2m6f110y gd-fm Hdl

Transferred the form that saw him win on the Flat when beating an in form rival in a two-mile handicap at Southwell July 2002. Followed up at Stratford next time.

Tosawi (IRE)

105 **109**

6-y-o b g Commanche Run-Deep Satisfaction (Deep Run)
R J Hodges S J Norman

Placings:*5/030*-04P1421PP **(4479)**
2001/02: 16^{0}G, 16^{4}G, 21^{P}G, 17^{1}G, 16^{4}G, 19^{2}S, 19^{1}S, 21^{P}G, 19^{P}G

	Starts	1st	2nd	3rd	Win & Pl
Hurdles	9	2	1	0	6415
Career Total	**13**	**2**	**1**	**1**	**6651**

109	1/02	Tntn	2m3f110y	F(0-100)HHdl	SFT	£2714
97	12/01	Extr	2m1f	F(0-100)HHdl	GD	£2520

Total win prize-money £5235

Going: Sf: 1-2 GS: 0-0 Gd: 1-7 GF: - Fm: 0-0
Distance: 2m/2m3: 1-5 2m4-2m7: 1-4 3m+: 0-0
Track: LH: 0-1 **RH: 2-8 Tight: 1-3** Gall: 0-0
Aids: Bl: 0-0 Vi: 0-0 Tstrap: 0-0
Best Rating: 109 1/02 Tntn 2m3f110y soft Hdl

Novice hurdler. Effective on good ground and softer at around two miles, stays two miles three.

Toscanini (GER)

100 **104**

6-y-o b g Goofalik (USA)-Tosca Stella (GER) (Surumu (GER))
D R Gandolfo Mrs John Lee

Placings:3404 **(4128)**
2001/02: 20^{3}S, 16^{4}HY, 16^{0}GS, 19^{4}G

	Starts	1st	2nd	3rd	Win & Pl
Hurdles	4	0	0	1	814
Career Total	**4**	**0**	**0**	**1**	**814**

Going: Sf: 0-2 GS: 0-1 Gd: 0-1 GF: - Fm: 0-0
Distance: 2m/2m3: 0-2 2m4-2m7: 0-2 3m+: 0-0
Track: LH: 0-1 RH: 0-3 Tight: 0-0 Gall: 0-0
Aids: Bl: 0-0 Vi: 0-0 Tstrap: 0-0
Best Rating: 104 2/02 Hayd 2m heavy Hdl

Toshiba Times

101 **98**

6-y-o b g Persian Bold-Kirkby Belle (Bay Express)
B Ellison B Batey

Placings:60P-202132 **(1505)**
2001/02: 17^{2}GF, 17^{0}GF, 16^{2}G, 17^{1}GF, 17^{3}G, 17^{2}G

Starts		1st	2nd	3rd	Win & Pl
Hurdles	6	1	3	1	5055
Career Total	**9**	**1**	**3**	**1**	**5055**

98	9/01	Sedg	2m1f	E Hdl	G-F	£2436

Total win prize-money £2436

Going: Sf: 0-0 GS: 0-0 Gd: 0-3 GF: - Fm: 1-3
Distance: **2m/2m3: 1-6** 2m4-2m7: 0-0 3m+: 0-0
Track: **LH: 1-5** RH: 0-1 **Tight: 1-5** Gall: 0-0
Aids: Bl: 0-0 Vi: 0-0 Tstrap: 0-0
Best Rating: 98 10/01 Sedg 2m1f good Hdl

Won a novice hurdle at Sedgefield, but looked less than keen when beaten there in October 2001.

Toskano

113 **124**

10-y-o b g Salse (USA)-Kukri (Kris)
D L Williams Berkshire Commercial Components Ltd

Placings:0P0600501/**2120/21113/U422-5133F14** **(1190)**
2001/02: 28^{5}G, 24^{1}GF, 22^{3}G, 20^{3}GS, 24^{F}G, 25^{1}GF, 20^{4}G

	Starts	1st	2nd	3rd	Win & Pl
Chases	7	2	0	2	17234
Career Total	**29**	**7**	**5**	**3**	**39688**

124	8/01	MRas	3m1f	F(0-110)HCh	G-F	£7020
122	5/01	Hntg	3m	F(0-100)HCh	G-F	£3346
79	5/98	Weth	3m1f	D Ch	G-F	£3434
118	5/98	Towc	3m1f	E(0-115)HCh	G-F	£3088
116	5/98	Aint	3m1f	D(0-125)HCh	G-F	£3568
101	10/97	Weth	3m1f	E(0-105)HCh	G-F	£3688
	4/96	Hrfd	3m2f	G Hdl	G-F	£2080

Total win prize-money £26226

Going: Sf: 0-0 GS: 0-1 Gd: 0-4 GF: - Fm: 2-2
Distance: 2m/2m3: 0-0 2m4-2m7: 0-3 **3m+: 2-4**
Track: LH: 0-3 **RH: 2-3** Tight: 1-5 Gall: 1-1
Aids: Bl: 0-0 Vi: 0-0 Tstrap: 0-0
Best Rating: 124 8/01 MRas 3m1f gd-fm Ch

He jumps and stays well and has an excellent record when the ground is riding fast..

Toss Of A Coin

76f **53f**

5-y-o b g Syrtos-By Chance (Le Johnstan)
F Kirby (C G Cox 10/11) Fred Kirby

Placings:00 **(2772)**
2001/02: 16^{0}G, 16^{0}G

	Starts	1st	2nd	3rd	Win & Pl
NH Flat	2	0	0	0	
Career Total	**2**	**0**	**0**	**0**	

Going: Sf: 0-0 GS: 0-0 Gd: 0-2 GF: - Fm: 0-0
Distance: 2m/2m3: 0-2 2m4-2m7: 0-0 3m+: 0-0
Track: LH: 0-1 RH: 0-1 Tight: 0-1 Gall: 0-0
Aids: Bl: 0-0 Vi: 0-0 Tstrap: 0-0
Best Rating: 53 11/01 Winc 2m good NHF

Tosti (FR)

6-y-o b g Beyssac (FR)-Madame Flibuste (FR) (Rahotep (FR))
C R Egerton K Blackham, T Gould & E De Giles

Placings:1/P **(3275)**
2001/02: 20^{P}S

	Starts	1st	2nd	3rd	Win & Pl
Chases	1	0	0	0	
Career Total	**2**	**1**	**0**	**0**	**3362**

	4/00	Fntb	2m	Hdl	SFT	£3362

Total win prize-money £3362

Going: Sf: 0-1 GS: 0-0 Gd: 0-0 GF: - Fm: 0-0
Distance: 2m/2m3: 0-0 2m4-2m7: 0-1 3m+: 0-0
Track: LH: 0-1 RH: 0-0 Tight: 0-1 Gall: 0-0
Aids: Bl: 0-0 Vi: 0-0 Tstrap: 0-0
Best Rating:

Total Delight

91 **99**

6-y-o b g Mtoto-Shesadelight (Shirley Heights)
P R Webber D Heath

Placings:10 **(0431)**
2001/02: 16^{1}GF, 17^{0}GF

	Starts	1st	2nd	3rd	Win & Pl
Hurdles	2	1	0	0	3073
Career Total	**2**	**1**	**0**	**0**	**3073**

99	5/01	Winc	2m	E Hdl	G-F	£3073

Total win prize-money £3073

Going: Sf: 0-0 GS: 0-0 Gd: 0-0 GF: - Fm: 1-2
Distance: **2m/2m3: 1-2** 2m4-2m7: 0-0 3m+: 0-0
Track: LH: 0-0 **RH: 1-2** Tight: 0-1 Gall: 0-0
Aids: Bl: 0-0 Vi: 0-0 Tstrap: 0-0
Best Rating: 99 5/01 Winc 2m gd-fm Hdl

Totally Scottish

110 **103**

6-y-o b g Mtoto-Glenfinlass (Lomond (USA))
Mrs M Reveley The Phoenix Racing C O

Placings:0002-32451164464402 **(4785)**
2001/02: 16^{3}GF, 16^{2}GF, 19^{4}GF, 17^{5}S, 20^{1}GS, 16^{1}GS, 17^{6}HY, 20^{4}GS, 16^{4}GS, 16^{6}S, 19^{4}GS, 16^{4}S, 19^{0}GF, 16^{2}F

	Starts	1st	2nd	3rd	Win & Pl
Hurdles	14	2	2	1	7859
Career Total	**18**	**2**	**3**	**1**	**8379**

103	11/01	Kels	2m110y	D(0-125)HHdl	G-S	£3325
99	10/01	Carl	2m4f	F(0-100)HHdl	G-S	£2108

Total win prize-money £5433

Going: Sf: 0-4 GS: 2-5 Gd: 0-0 GF: - Fm: 0-5
Distance: 2m/2m3: 1-10 2m4-2m7: 1-4 3m+: 0-0
Track: **LH: 1-7** RH: 0-6 **Tight: 1-7** Gall: 0-2
Aids: Bl: 0-0 Vi: 0-0 Tstrap: 0-0
Best Rating: 103 1/02 Catt 2m gd-sft Hdl

He is not most the reliable of sorts, but did nothing wrong when winning modest events at Carlisle and Kelso in the autumn of 2001. Held off higher marks subsequently.

Totem Dancer

53

9-y-o b m Mtoto-Ballad Opera (Sadler's Wells (USA))
J L Eyre Graham Lloyd & Dean Kiely

Placings:0/6P-4 **(2161)**
2001/02: 20^{4}GS

	Starts	1st	2nd	3rd	Win & Pl
Hurdles	1	0	0	0	0
Career Total	**4**	**0**	**0**	**0**	**0**

Going: Sf: 0-0 GS: 0-1 Gd: 0-0 GF: - Fm: 0-0
Distance: 2m/2m3: 0-0 2m4-2m7: 0-1 3m+: 0-0
Track: LH: 0-1 RH: 0-0 Tight: 0-0 Gall: 0-0
Aids: Bl: 0-0 Vi: 0-0 Tstrap: 0-1
Best Rating: 82 2/00 Muss 2m gd-sft Hdl

Totland Bay (IRE)

104 **86**

6-y-o br g Phardante (FR)-Seanaphobal Lady (Kambalda)
J W Mullins Ian M McGready

Placings:43040P2 **(4730)**
2001/02: 16^{4}GF, 17^{3}G, 18^{0}GS, 16^{4}GF, 17^{0}GS, 22^{P}G, 20^{2}GF

	Starts	1st	2nd	3rd	Win & Pl
NH Flat	4	0	0	1	228
Hurdles	3	0	1	0	764
Career Total	**7**	**0**	**1**	**1**	**992**

Going: Sf: 0-0 GS: 0-2 Gd: 0-2 GF: - Fm: 0-3
Distance: 2m/2m3: 0-5 2m4-2m7: 0-2 3m+: 0-0
Track: LH: 0-3 RH: 0-3 Tight: 0-1 Gall: 0-0
Aids: Bl: 0-0 Vi: 0-0 Tstrap: 0-0
Best Rating: 86 11/01 Ludl 2m gd-fm NHF

Bounced back after apparently making a noise on his previous start to win 22-furlong maiden hurdle at Newton Abbot July 2002.

Toto Taleca

75f

5-y-o b m Mtoto-Miss Taleca (Pharly (FR))
M E Sowersby M E Sowersby

Placings:00-4 **(2321)**
2001/02: 17^{4}GS

	Starts	1st	2nd	3rd	Win & Pl
NH Flat	1	0	0	0	0
Career Total	**3**	**0**	**0**	**0**	**0**

Going: Sf: 0-0 GS: 0-1 Gd: 0-0 GF: - Fm: 0-0
Distance: 2m/2m3: 0-1 2m4-2m7: 0-0 3m+: 0-0
Track: LH: 0-0 RH: 0-0 Tight: 0-0 Gall: 0-0
Aids: Bl: 0-0 Vi: 0-0 Tstrap: 0-0
Best Rating: 75 11/01 Aint 2m1f gd-sft NHF

Touch Closer

97f **135f**

5-y-o b g Inchinor-Ryewater Dream (Touching Wood (USA))
G A Swinbank C N Barnes

Placings:13 **(4679)**
2001/02: 16^{1}S, 17^{3}G

	Starts	1st	2nd	3rd	Win & Pl
NH Flat	2	1	0	1	5123
Career Total	**2**	**1**	**0**	**1**	**5123**

115	3/02	Ayr	2m	H NHF	SFT	£1673

Total win prize-money £1673

Going: Sf: 1-1 GS: 0-0 Gd: 0-1 GF: - Fm: 0-0
Distance: **2m/2m3: 1-2** 2m4-2m7: 0-0 3m+: 0-0
Track: **LH: 1-1** RH: 0-0 Tight: 0-0 Gall: 0-0
Aids: Bl: 0-0 Vi: 0-0 Tstrap: 0-0
Best Rating: 135 4/02 Aint 2m1f good NHF

Flat-bred. Won on his debut at Ayr and was third in top bumper company at Aintree.

Touching Down (IRE)

72 **29**

10-y-o ch g Buckskin (FR)-Got To Fly (IRE) (Kemal (FR))
P York (C P Morlock 17/2) Miss C Llewellin

Placings:5/PPP/2P50/0 **(4135)**
2001/02: 24^{0}G

	Starts	1st	2nd	3rd	Win & Pl
Chases	1	0	0	0	
Career Total	**9**	**0**	**1**	**0**	**959**

Going: Sf: 0-0 GS: 0-0 Gd: 0-1 GF: - Fm: 0-0
Distance: 2m/2m3: 0-2 2m4-2m7: 0-0 3m+: 0-1
Track: LH: 0-0 RH: 0-1 Tight: 0-0 Gall: 0-0
Aids: Bl: 0-0 Vi: 0-0 Tstrap: 0-0
Best Rating: 93 7/99 Worc 2m7f110y gd-fm Ch

Toulon D'Or (IRE)

58f **37f**

5-y-o b g Toulon-Rare Currency (Rarity)
M Pitman Mrs D Salmon

Placings:*00* **(3338)**
2001/02: 16^{0}G, 16^{0}G

	Starts	1st	2nd	3rd	Win & Pl
NH Flat	2	0	0	0	
Career Total	**2**	**0**	**0**	**0**	

Going: Sf: 0-0 GS: 0-0 Gd: 0-2 GF: - Fm: 0-0
Distance: 2m/2m3: 0-2 2m4-2m7: 0-0 3m+: 0-0
Track: LH: 0-1 RH: 0-1 Tight: 0-0 Gall: 0-0
Aids: Bl: 0-0 Vi: 0-0 Tstrap: 0-0
Best Rating: 37 1/02 Ludl 2m good NHF

Toulon Rouge (IRE)

87f **103f**

5-y-o b m Toulon-Master Nidee (Master Owen)
Ferdy Murphy Racegoers Club Owners Group

Placings:*140* **(4823)**
2001/02: 17^{1}S, 16^{4}S, 17^{0}G

	Starts	1st	2nd	3rd	Win & Pl
NH Flat	3	1	0	0	1561
Career Total	**3**	**1**	**0**	**0**	**1561**

89	1/02	Sedg	2m1f	H NHF	SFT	£1561

Total win prize-money £1561

Going: Sf: 1-2 GS: 0-0 Gd: 0-1 GF: - Fm: 0-0
Distance: **2m/2m3: 1-3** 2m4-2m7: 0-0 3m+: 0-0
Track: **LH: 1-2** RH: 0-1 **Tight: 1-1** Gall: 0-1
Aids: Bl: 0-0 Vi: 0-0 Tstrap: 0-0
Best Rating: 103 3/02 Towc 2m soft NHF

Worked hard to win bumper on heavy ground on racecourse debut and ran well under a penalty subsequently.

Toulouse-Lautrec (IRE)

90 **87**

6-y-o ch g Toulon-Bucks Slave (Buckskin (FR))
T R George John French

Placings:*6500* **(3892)**
2001/02: 17^{6}S, 21^{5}S, 16^{0}HY, 21^{0}HY

	Starts	1st	2nd	3rd	Win & Pl
NH Flat	1	0	0	0	0
Hurdles	3	0	0	0	0
Career Total	**4**	**0**	**0**	**0**	**0**

Going: Sf: 0-4 GS: 0-0 Gd: 0-0 GF: - Fm: 0-0
Distance: 2m/2m3: 0-2 2m4-2m7: 0-2 3m+: 0-0
Track: LH: 0-1 RH: 0-1 Tight: 0-2 Gall: 0-0
Aids: Bl: 0-0 Vi: 0-0 Tstrap: 0-0
Best Rating: 87 1/02 Plum 2m5f soft Hdl

Touring-Turtle (IRE)

105 **97**

10-y-o gr g Roselier (FR)-Rossian (Silent Spring)
C Tizzard Summer Fun Racing

Placings:0000/0*023003100203/PPP/P/33P-432P13P* **(3762)**
2001/02: 25^{4}G, 25^{3}G, 19^{2}G, 23^{P}GS, 19^{1}GS, 19^{3}S, 24^{P}S

	Starts	1st	2nd	3rd	Win & Pl
Chases	7	1	1	2	6500
Career Total	**31**	**2**	**3**	**7**	**11041**

97	12/01	Tntn	2m3f	F(0-95)HCh	G-S	£3181
89	8/97	Dpat	2m6f	(0-102)HHdl	G-F	£1695

Total win prize-money £4877

Going: Sf: 0-2 GS: 1-2 Gd: 0-3 GF: - Fm: 0-0
Distance: **2m/2m3: 1-3** 2m4-2m7: 0-0 3m+: 0-4
Track: LH: 0-0 **RH: 1-7 Tight: 1-5** Gall: 0-0
Aids: Bl: 0-0 Vi: 0-0 Tstrap: 0-0
Best Rating: 102 6/00 NAbb 3m2f110y gd-fm Ch

Moderate novice chaser, winner at Taunton in December. Stays three miles plus.

Town Gossip (IRE)

101 **92**

5-y-o ch m Indian Ridge-Only Gossip (USA) (Trempolino (USA))
J L Eyre Sunpak Potatoes

Placings:33F555 **(3363)**
2001/02: 19^{3}GF, 21^{3}G, 20^{F}G, 16^{5}G, 20^{5}S, 16^{5}GS

	Starts	1st	2nd	3rd	Win & Pl
Hurdles	6	0	0	2	756
Career Total	**6**	**0**	**0**	**2**	**756**

Going: Sf: 0-1 GS: 0-1 Gd: 0-3 GF: - Fm: 0-1
Distance: 2m/2m3: 0-2 2m4-2m7: 0-4 3m+: 0-0
Track: LH: 0-4 RH: 0-2 Tight: 0-3 Gall: 0-1
Aids: Bl: 0-0 Vi: 0-0 Tstrap: 0-0
Best Rating: 92 10/01 Sedg 2m5f110y good Hdl

An All-Weather winer, she has shown ability over hurdles. Races prominently.

Townleyhall (IRE)

101 **94**

10-y-o ch g Phardante (FR)-Arctic Tartan (Deep Run)
M R Bosley G Kingston

Placings:*0/00225F4/41011/64/056-0350* **(2140)**
2001/02: 21^{0}GF, 19^{3}G, 20^{5}S, 19^{0}G

	Starts	1st	2nd	3rd	Win & Pl
Hurdles	4	0	0	1	438
Career Total	**23**	**3**	**2**	**1**	**9445**

103	10/98	Plum	2m4f	E Hdl	GD	£2495
113	10/98	Hrfd	2m3f110y	E Hdl	GD	£2374
97	7/98	Bell	2m1f	NHF	GD	£2391

Total win prize-money £7260

Going: Sf: 0-1 GS: 0-0 Gd: 0-2 GF: - Fm: 0-1
Distance: 2m/2m3: 0-0 2m4-2m7: 0-4 3m+: 0-0
Track: LH: 0-1 RH: 0-2 Tight: 0-1 Gall: 0-0
Aids: Bl: 0-0 Vi: 0-0 Tstrap: 0-0
Best Rating: 113 10/98 Hrfd 2m3f110y good Hdl

Toy Story (FR)

27

6-y-o b g Fijar Tango (FR)-Grundygold (FR) (Grundy)
M E Sowersby Paul Clifton

Placings:R0/0-P **(0222)**
2001/02: 20^{P}GF

	Starts	1st	2nd	3rd	Win & Pl
Hurdles	1	0	0	0	
Career Total	**4**	**0**	**0**	**0**	

Going: Sf: 0-0 GS: 0-0 Gd: 0-0 GF: - Fm: 0-1
Distance: 2m/2m3: 0-0 2m4-2m7: 0-1 3m+: 0-0
Track: LH: 0-1 RH: 0-0 Tight: 0-0 Gall: 0-0
Aids: Bl: 0-0 Vi: 0-0 Tstrap: 0-0
Best Rating: 27 4/01 Hayd 2m soft Hdl

Track O' Profit (IRE)

10-y-o ch g Kambalda-Teazle (Quayside)
Ms Kate Rogers (Miss S Young 17/3) Exors Of The Late R J S Linne

Placings:3*0/P44253632/42P-1U* **(4483)**
2001/02: 21^{1}GF, 19^{U}G

	Starts	1st	2nd	3rd	Win & Pl
Chases	2	1	0	0	10291
Career Total	**16**	**1**	**3**	**3**	**13608**

108	5/01	NAbb	2m5f110y	B HCh	G-F	£10290

Total win prize-money £10291

Going: Sf: 0-0 GS: 0-0 Gd: 0-1 GF: - Fm: 1-1
Distance: 2m/2m3: 0-0 **2m4-2m7: 1-2** 3m+: 0-0
Track: **LH: 1-1** RH: 0-1 **Tight: 1-1** Gall: 0-0
Aids: Bl: 0-0 Vi: 0-0 Tstrap: 0-0
Best Rating: 108 5/01 NAbb 2m5f110y gd-fm Ch

Trade Dispute (IRE)

10-y-o ro g Ela-Mana-Mou-Safety Feature (Be My Guest (USA))
E W Tuer G Tuer

Placings:1110/4/1311U/1F31/2-11 **(3916)**
2001/02: 24^{1}S, 24^{1}GS

	Starts	1st	2nd	3rd	Win & Pl
Chases	2	2	0	0	4578
Career Total	**17**	**10**	**1**	**2**	**31160**

127	2/02	Muss	3m	H Ch	G-S	£2247
127	2/02	Muss	3m	H Ch	SFT	£2331
131	4/00	Newc	3m	H Ch	G-S	£2681
138	2/00	Catt	3m4f110y	H Ch	GD	£3477
131	4/99	Weth	3m1f	H Ch	G-F	£1203
130	3/99	Sedg	3m3f	H Ch	SFT	£1276
119	2/99	Catt	3m4f110y	H Ch	GD	£3485
126	9/95	List	2m	Hdl	GD	£3730

104	8/95	Tral	2m	Hdl	G-F	£3730
99	8/95	Rosc	2m	Hdl	G-F	£2373

Total win prize-money £26537

Going: Sf: 1-1 GS: 1-1 Gd: 0-0 GF: - Fm: 0-0
Distance: 2m/2m3: 0-0 2m4-2m7: 0-0 **3m+: 2-2**
Track: LH: 0-0 **RH: 2-2 Tight: 2-2** Gall: 0-0
Aids: Bl: 0-0 Vi: 0-0 Tstrap: 0-0
Best Rating: 145 3/00 Chel 3m2f110y gd-fm Ch

He has a solid record in hunter chases and finished a close third in the Christie's Foxhunter Chase at the Cheltenham Festival in 2000. A sound jumper, he gets three miles plus.

Tradescant

64f 51f

6-y-o b m Alflora (IRE)-Cooks Lawn (The Parson)
E L James Lady Cobham

Placings:*00* **(4570)**
2001/02: 16^{0}HY, 16^{0}G

	Starts	1st	2nd	3rd	Win & Pl
NH Flat	2	0	0	0	
Career Total	**2**	**0**	**0**	**0**	

Going: Sf: 0-1 GS: 0-0 Gd: 0-1 GF: - Fm: 0-0
Distance: 2m/2m3: 0-2 2m4-2m7: 0-0 3m+: 0-0
Track: LH: 0-1 RH: 0-1 Tight: 0-0 Gall: 0-0
Aids: Bl: 0-0 Vi: 0-0 Tstrap: 0-0
Best Rating: 51 4/02 Towc 2m good NHF

Trading Trouble

108 125

5-y-o b g Petoski-Marielou (FR) (Carwhite)
J M Jefferson Richard Collins

Placings:*261*-22116 **(4890)**
2001/02: 16^{2}GS, 17^{2}GS, 20^{1}HY, 20^{1}HY, 24^{6}G

	Starts	1st	2nd	3rd	Win & Pl
Hurdles	5	2	2	0	9411
Career Total	**8**	**3**	**3**	**0**	**11849**

116	3/02	Uttx	2m4f110y	D Hdl	HVY	£3484
125	3/02	Uttx	2m4f110y	D Hdl	HVY	£3993
98	3/01	Hntg	2m110y	H NHF	SFT	£1960

Total win prize-money £9438

Going: Sf: 2-2 GS: 0-2 Gd: 0-1 GF: - Fm: 0-0
Distance: 2m/2m3: 0-2 **2m4-2m7: 2-2** 3m+: 0-1
Track: **LH: 2-4** RH: 0-1 Tight: 0-2 Gall: 0-0
Aids: Bl: 0-0 Vi: 0-0 Tstrap: 0-0
Best Rating: 125 3/02 Uttx 2m4f110y heavy Hdl

Showed promise over hurdles before successfully returning from a break at Uttoxeter in March 2002 and followed up there a week later. Suited by two and a half miles and soft ground.

Tragic Belle

60f 33f

5-y-o b m Tragic Role (USA)-Pokey's Belle (Uncle Pokey)
D L Williams Miss B W Palmer

Placings:*0* **(2215)**
2001/02: 17^{0}G

	Starts	1st	2nd	3rd	Win & Pl
NH Flat	1	0	0	0	
Career Total	**1**	**0**	**0**	**0**	

Going: Sf: 0-0 GS: 0-0 Gd: 0-1 GF: - Fm: 0-0
Distance: 2m/2m3: 0-1 2m4-2m7: 0-0 3m+: 0-0
Track: LH: 0-0 RH: 0-1 Tight: 0-0 Gall: 0-0
Aids: Bl: 0-0 Vi: 0-0 Tstrap: 0-0
Best Rating: 33 11/01 Hrfd 2m1f good NHF

Tragic Dancer

6-y-o b g Tragic Role (USA)-Chantallee's Pride (Mansooj)
K McAuliffe E Treadwell/miss M Butler

Placings:PP **(4113)**
2001/02: 21^{P}S, 16^{P}G

	Starts	1st	2nd	3rd	Win & Pl
Hurdles	2	0	0	0	
Career Total	**2**	**0**	**0**	**0**	

Going: Sf: 0-1 GS: 0-0 Gd: 0-1 GF: - Fm: 0-0
Distance: 2m/2m3: 0-1 2m4-2m7: 0-1 3m+: 0-0
Track: LH: 0-0 RH: 0-1 Tight: 0-0 Gall: 0-0
Aids: Bl: 0-0 Vi: 0-0 Tstrap: 0-0
Best Rating:

Tragic Lady

88 72

6-y-o b m Tragic Role (USA)-Rainbow Lady (Jaazeiro (USA))
C J Hemsley Mark Hoaren

Placings:P00 **(0797)**
2001/02: 18^{0}GF, 17^{0}GF

	Starts	1st	2nd	3rd	Win & Pl
Hurdles	2	0	0	0	
Career Total	**3**	**0**	**0**	**0**	

Going: Sf: 0-0 GS: 0-0 Gd: 0-0 GF: - Fm: 0-2
Distance: 2m/2m3: 0-2 2m4-2m7: 0-0 3m+: 0-0
Track: LH: 0-2 RH: 0-0 Tight: 0-2 Gall: 0-0
Aids: Bl: 0-0 Vi: 0-0 Tstrap: 0-2
Best Rating: 72 6/01 NAbb 2m1f gd-fm Hdl

Train Lover (NZ)

12-y-o br g Beau Zephyr (AUS)-Belle Rail (NZ) (Man The Rail (USA))
Graham Smith Graham Smith

Placings:P **(1397)**
2001/02: 24^{P}GF

	Starts	1st	2nd	3rd	Win & Pl
Hurdles	1	0	0	0	
Career Total	**1**	**0**	**0**	**0**	

Going: Sf: 0-0 GS: 0-0 Gd: 0-0 GF: - Fm: 0-1
Distance: 2m/2m3: 0-0 2m4-2m7: 0-0 3m+: 0-1
Track: LH: 0-1 RH: 0-0 Tight: 0-0 Gall: 0-0
Aids: Bl: 0-0 Vi: 0-0 Tstrap: 0-0
Best Rating:

Trained Bythe Best

106 113

4-y-o b f Alderbrook-Princess Moodyshoe (Jalmood (USA))
M C Pipe Mrs Alison C Farrant

Placings:13P3 **(4660)**
2001/02: 18^{1}G, 16^{3}GS, 17^{P}G, 17^{3}G

	Starts	1st	2nd	3rd	Win & Pl
Hurdles	4	1	0	2	3238
Career Total	**4**	**1**	**0**	**2**	**3238**

113	12/01	Font	2m2f110y	E Hdl	GD	£2502

Total win prize-money £2503

Going: Sf: 0-0 GS: 0-1 Gd: 1-3 GF: - Fm: 0-0
Distance: **2m/2m3: 1-4** 2m4-2m7: 0-0 3m+: 0-0
Track: **LH: 1-3** RH: 0-1 **Tight: 1-3** Gall: 0-1
Aids: Bl: 0-0 Vi: 0-0 Tstrap: 0-0
Best Rating: 113 12/01 Font 2m2f110y good Hdl

Showed a little on the Flat, but bolted up on her hurdling debut at Fontwell in December. Suited by good ground.

Travellers Heir (IRE)

67f 89f

4-y-o ch g Montelimar (USA)-Allaracket (IRE) (The Parson)
H D Daly Mrs Strachan, Griffith, Lewis & Graham

Placings:3 **(4499)**
2001/02: 16^{3}G

	Starts	1st	2nd	3rd	Win & Pl
NH Flat	1	0	0	1	276
Career Total	**1**	**0**	**0**	**1**	**276**

Going: Sf: 0-0 GS: 0-0 Gd: 0-1 GF: - Fm: 0-0
Distance: 2m/2m3: 0-1 2m4-2m7: 0-0 3m+: 0-0
Track: LH: 0-1 RH: 0-0 Tight: 0-0 Gall: 0-0
Aids: Bl: 0-0 Vi: 0-0 Tstrap: 0-0
Best Rating: 89 3/02 Hayd 2m good NHF

Stoutly-bred on dams's side and looked a stayer when third on his debut in a bumper at Haydock in March.

Travellers Rest

5-y-o b g Nomadic Way (USA)-Rest (Dance In Time (CAN))
J S Moore (J G Smyth-Osbourne 6/7) Ernest H Moore

Placings:PP **(1755)**
2001/02: 21^{P}G, 16^{P}GS

	Starts	1st	2nd	3rd	Win & Pl
Hurdles	2	0	0	0	
Career Total	**2**	**0**	**0**	**0**	

Going: Sf: 0-0 GS: 0-1 Gd: 0-1 GF: - Fm: 0-0
Distance: 2m/2m3: 0-1 2m4-2m7: 0-1 3m+: 0-0
Track: LH: 0-1 RH: 0-1 Tight: 0-1 Gall: 0-0
Aids: Bl: 0-0 Vi: 0-0 Tstrap: 0-0
Best Rating:

Travelling Jack

7-y-o ch g Lyphento (USA)-Lady Magenta (Rolfe (USA))
Mrs Laura J Young M Rowe

Placings:P **(4763)**
2001/02: 24^{P}GF

	Starts	1st	2nd	3rd	Win & Pl
Chases	1	0	0	0	
Career Total	**1**	**0**	**0**	**0**	

Going: Sf: 0-0 GS: 0-0 Gd: 0-0 GF: - Fm: 0-1
Distance: 2m/2m3: 0-0 2m4-2m7: 0-0 3m+: 0-1
Track: LH: 0-0 RH: 0-1 Tight: 0-0 Gall: 0-0
Aids: Bl: 0-0 Vi: 0-0 Tstrap: 0-0

Best Rating:

Treasure Chest (IRE)

103 **98**

7-y-o b g Last Tycoon-Sought Out (IRE) (Rainbow Quest (USA))
M C Pipe S A Helaissi

Placings:PP00/3P200F3/4P436R142P3106-26 **(4844)**
2001/02: 18^{2}S, 24^{6}G

	Starts	1st	2nd	3rd	Win & Pl
Hurdles	2	0	1	0	1656
Career Total	**27**	**2**	**3**	**4**	**8114**

98	2/01	Ludl	2m5f	G Hdl	G-S	£1960
98	11/00	Wwck	2m3f	G(0-95)HHdl	SFT	£1617

Total win prize-money £3577

Going: Sf: 0-1 GS: 0-0 Gd: 0-1 GF: - Fm: 0-0
Distance: 2m/2m3: 0-1 2m4-2m7: 0-0 3m+: 0-1
Track: LH: 0-2 RH: 0-0 Tight: 0-2 Gall: 0-0
Aids: Bl: 0-0 Vi: 0-0 Tstrap: 0-0
Best Rating: 98 3/02 Font 2m2f110y soft Hdl

Bred to stay and placed on the Flat, he has shown bits and pieces of form over hurdles in modest company. He has ability but is not very reliable and has run some of his better races when amateur or conditional ridden. Stays three miles. Acts on an easy surface. Runs well fresh.

Treasure Dome (IRE)

8-y-o b g Treasure Kay-Royal Saint (USA) (Crimson Satan)
John Whyte John Whyte

Placings:025/441006240/U **(3769)**
2001/02: 21^{U}GS

	Starts	1st	2nd	3rd	Win & Pl
Chases	1	0	0	0	
Career Total	**13**	**1**	**2**	**0**	**4006**

90	7/98	Bell	2m1f	Hdl	G-F	£2391

Total win prize-money £2391

Going: Sf: 0-0 GS: 0-1 Gd: 0-0 GF: - Fm: 0-0
Distance: 2m/2m3: 0-0 2m4-2m7: 0-1 3m+: 0-0
Track: LH: 0-1 RH: 0-0 Tight: 0-1 Gall: 0-0
Aids: Bl: 0-0 Vi: 0-0 Tstrap: 0-0
Best Rating: 101 11/97 Navn 2m gd-yld Hdl

Treasured Coin

85 **60**

4-y-o b g Overbury (IRE)-Slip A Coin (Slip Anchor)
Mrs D A Hamer (D Burchell 25/10) Eamonn O'Malley

Placings:004P0 **(3987)**
2001/02: 17^{0}G, 16^{0}G, 16^{4}HY, 16^{P}HY, 19^{0}S

	Starts	1st	2nd	3rd	Win & Pl
Hurdles	5	0	0	0	0
Career Total	**5**	**0**	**0**	**0**	**0**

Going: Sf: 0-3 GS: 0-0 Gd: 0-2 GF: - Fm: 0-0
Distance: 2m/2m3: 0-4 2m4-2m7: 0-1 3m+: 0-0
Track: LH: 0-2 RH: 0-3 Tight: 0-1 Gall: 0-0
Aids: Bl: 0-0 Vi: 0-0 Tstrap: 0-0
Best Rating: 60 1/02 Uttx 2m heavy Hdl

Treaty (USA)

85 **75**

8-y-o b g Trempolino (USA)-Zonda (Fabulous Dancer (USA))
Miss D Cole E Wonnacott

Placings:00RP **(0832)**
2001/02: 17^{0}F, 17^{0}G, 17^{R}GS, 17^{P}GF

	Starts	1st	2nd	3rd	Win & Pl
Hurdles	4	0	0	0	
Career Total	**4**	**0**	**0**	**0**	

Going: Sf: 0-0 GS: 0-1 Gd: 0-1 GF: - Fm: 0-2
Distance: 2m/2m3: 0-4 2m4-2m7: 0-0 3m+: 0-0
Track: LH: 0-3 RH: 0-1 Tight: 0-3 Gall: 0-0
Aids: Bl: 0-0 Vi: 0-0 Tstrap: 0-0
Best Rating: 75 6/01 NAbb 2m1f good Hdl

Treble Six (IRE)

76 **72**

6-y-o ch m Zaffaran (USA)-Ascot Princess (Prince Hansel)
N A Twiston-Davies Mr F J Mills & Mr W Mills

Placings:*00066*P **(2928)**
2001/02: 17^{0}GS, 17^{0}G, 19^{0}G, 25^{6}G, 20^{6}GS, 19^{P}GS

	Starts	1st	2nd	3rd	Win & Pl
NH Flat	2	0	0	0	0
Hurdles	4	0	0	0	0
Career Total	**6**	**0**	**0**	**0**	**0**

Going: Sf: 0-0 GS: 0-3 Gd: 0-3 GF: - Fm: 0-0
Distance: 2m/2m3: 0-2 2m4-2m7: 0-3 3m+: 0-1
Track: LH: 0-1 RH: 0-3 Tight: 0-4 Gall: 0-1
Aids: Bl: 0-0 Vi: 0-0 Tstrap: 0-0
Best Rating: 85 5/01 Folk 2m1f110y gd-sft NHF

Treble Trouble

85

6-y-o b g Minster Son-Ferneyhill Lady (Menelek)
C C Bealby (C Grant 10/2) C C Bealby

Placings:*0*/F **(4534)**
2001/02: 21^{F}G

	Starts	1st	2nd	3rd	Win & Pl
Chases	1	0	0	0	
Career Total	**2**	**0**	**0**	**0**	

Going: Sf: 0-0 GS: 0-0 Gd: 0-1 GF: - Fm: 0-0
Distance: 2m/2m3: 0-0 2m4-2m7: 0-1 3m+: 0-0
Track: LH: 0-1 RH: 0-0 Tight: 0-1 Gall: 0-0
Aids: Bl: 0-0 Vi: 0-0 Tstrap: 0-0
Best Rating: 85 4/02 Fknm 2m5f110y good Ch

Trefelyn Snowdrop

(87h) (68h)

9-y-o ch m Buckley-Trefelyn Rose (Tom Noddy)
P Bowen Pobl Ardderchog

Placings:*21100*P/6FF05F-0P **(0318)**
2001/02: 20^{0}GF, 22^{P}F

	Starts	1st	2nd	3rd	Win & Pl
Hurdles	2	0	0	0	
Career Total	**14**	**2**	**1**	**0**	**3351**

106	7/99	Sedg	2m1f	H NHF	G-F	£1574
88	6/99	Worc	2m	H NHF	G-F	£1388

Total win prize-money £2963

Going: Sf: 0-0 GS: 0-0 Gd: 0-0 GF: - Fm: 0-2
Distance: 2m/2m3: 0-0 2m4-2m7: 0-2 3m+: 0-0
Track: LH: 0-1 RH: 0-0 Tight: 0-1 Gall: 0-0
Aids: Bl: 0-0 Vi: 0-0 Tstrap: 0-0
Best Rating: 106 7/99 Sedg 2m1f gd-fm NHF

Tremallt (IRE)

116(102h) (102h)**154**

11-y-o b g Henbit (USA)-Secret Romance (Gala Performance (USA))
T R George Silkword Racing Partnership

Placings:*2/226/***U12FF1F11/16UP/5146FF-10616** **(3907)**
2001/02: 24^{1}GS, 24^{0}GS, 25^{6}G, 24^{1}G, 24^{6}G

	Starts	1st	2nd	3rd	Win & Pl
Hurdles	1	1	0	0	3374
Chases	4	1	0	0	30350
Career Total	**28**	**8**	**4**	**0**	**79500**

154	12/01	Kemp	3m	C(0-135)HCh	GD	£29000
102	10/01	MRas	3m	E Hdl	G-S	£3374
154	10/00	Kemp	3m	B(0-145)HCh	G-S	£14794
154	10/99	Worc	2m7f110y	C(0-135)HCh	GD	£6807
148	4/99	Uttx	2m4f	D(0-125)HCh	G-S	£4455
140	3/99	Uttx	2m4f	F(0-100)HCh	HVY	£3009
120	2/99	Uttx	2m5f	C HCh	HVY	£7002
113	11/98	Bang	2m4f110y	E(0-105)HCh	SFT	£3598

Total win prize-money £72042

Going: Sf: 0-0 GS: 1-2 Gd: 1-3 GF: - Fm: 0-0
Distance: 2m/2m3: 0-0 2m4-2m7: 0-0 **3m+: 2-5**
Track: LH: 0-0 **RH: 2-5 Tight: 1-1** Gall: 0-0
Aids: Bl: 0-0 Vi: 0-1 Tstrap: 0-0
Best Rating: 154 12/01 Kemp 3m good Ch

A useful front-running chaser, he returned to winning form at Kempton in October of the 2000/2001 season. He ran a blinder in the Racing Post Chase at the same track and had just been headed when falling at the last. He appreciated the drop in class to win his only run over hurdles this term at Market Rasen in October 2001, and picked up a big prize over fences at Kempton over Christmas in game fashion. He is prone to the odd jumping error. Stays three miles. Best with a little cut in the ground.

Tremendisto

89 **71**

12-y-o b g Petoski-Misty Halo (High Top)
T Wall D P Constable

Placings:*2/342/1630P/5***LFP/1R412RR/R/0P4-6P65** **(1043)**
2001/02: 17^{6}G, 20^{P}GS, 20^{6}S, 20^{5}GF

	Starts	1st	2nd	3rd	Win & Pl
Chases	4	0	0	0	0
Career Total	**28**	**3**	**3**	**2**	**10956**

96	2/99	Hrfd	2m1f	E(0-115)HHdl	GD	£2944
92	12/98	Hrfd	2m1f	G Hdl	G-S	£1646
97	11/96	Aint	2m110y	D Hdl	GD	£3009

Total win prize-money £7599

Going: Sf: 0-1 GS: 0-1 Gd: 0-1 GF: - Fm: 0-1
Distance: 2m/2m3: 0-1 2m4-2m7: 0-3 3m+: 0-0
Track: LH: 0-4 RH: 0-0 Tight: 0-2 Gall: 0-0
Aids: Bl: 0-0 Vi: 0-1 Tstrap: 0-0
Best Rating: 100 3/99 Hrfd 2m3f110y gd-sft Hdl

Tremezzo

94 **75**

4-y-o b g Mind Games-Rosa Van Fleet (Sallust)
B R Millman G Battocchi

Placings:0413432 (4589)
2001/02: 16^{0}G, 17^{4}F, 17^{1}GS, 16^{3}G, 16^{4}HY, 17^{3}S, 16^{2}G

	Starts	1st	2nd	3rd	Win & Pl
Hurdles	7	1	1	2	3015
Career Total	**7**	**1**	**1**	**2**	**3015**

75	11/01	Tntn	2m1f	G Hdl	G-S	£1669

Total win prize-money £1670

Going: Sf: 0-2 GS: 1-1 Gd: 0-3 GF: - Fm: 0-1
Distance: **2m/2m3: 1-7** 2m4-2m7: 0-0 3m+: 0-0
Track: LH: 0-2 **RH: 1-5 Tight: 1-4** Gall: 0-0
Aids: Bl: 0-0 Vi: 0-0 **Tstrap: 1-6**
Best Rating: 75 4/02 Winc 2m good Hdl

Fair sort in selling hurdles, rather a fortunate winner at Taunton.

Trencrom Hill

60f **38f**

5-y-o b g Homo Sapien-Sweet On Willie (USA) (Master Willie)
P J Hobbs D F P Racing

Placings:0 (4032)
2001/02: 16^{0}GS

	Starts	1st	2nd	3rd	Win & Pl
NH Flat	1	0	0	0	
Career Total	**1**	**0**	**0**	**0**	

Going: Sf: 0-0 GS: 0-1 Gd: 0-0 GF: - Fm: 0-0
Distance: 2m/2m3: 0-1 2m4-2m7: 0-0 3m+: 0-0
Track: LH: 0-1 RH: 0-0 Tight: 0-0 Gall: 0-1
Aids: Bl: 0-0 Vi: 0-0 Tstrap: 0-0
Best Rating: 38 3/02 Newb 2m110y gd-sft NHF

Tres Touche (USA)

108 **139**

5-y-o b g Poles Apart (USA)-Princess Smoggy (USA) (Smoggy)
R Hendriks Contrarian Stables

Placings:21P1-2561103 (2759)
2001/02: 16^{2}F, 17^{5}F, 20^{6}F, 16^{1}F, 20^{1}F, 10^{0}F, 21^{3}GS

	Starts	1st	2nd	3rd	Win & Pl
Hurdles	7	2	1	1	68543
Career Total	**11**	**4**	**2**	**1**	**102446**

	10/01	Fars	2m4f	Hdl	FRM	£30000
	8/01	Sara	2m110y	Hdl	FRM	£19200
	4/01	Ahnt	2m	Hdl	FRM	£20000
	10/00	Fars	2m1f	Hdl	FRM	£12805

Total win prize-money £82005

Going: Sf: 0-0 GS: 0-1 Gd: 0-0 GF: - Fm: 2-6
Distance: 2m/2m3: 1-4 2m4-2m7: 1-3 3m+: 0-0
Track: LH: 0-1 RH: 0-0 Tight: 0-0 Gall: 0-1
Aids: **Bl: 1-1** Vi: 0-0 Tstrap: 0-1
Best Rating: 139 12/01 Newb 2m5f gd-sft Hdl

Useful American hurdler.

Tresor De Mai (FR)

117 **170**

8-y-o ch g Grand Tresor (FR)-Lady Night (FR) (Pompon Rouge)
M C Pipe Joe Moran

Placings:1112/151225/4F1334/P224UFP-1P1 (3780)
2001/02: 19^{1}G, 24^{P}S, 19^{1}GS

	Starts	1st	2nd	3rd	Win & Pl
Chases	3	2	0	0	47951
Career Total	**26**	**8**	**5**	**2**	**146130**

170	2/02	Asct	2m3f110y	A Ch	G-S	£37700
160	1/02	Asct	2m3f110y	B HCh	GD	£10250
161	12/99	Asct	3m110y	B HCh	G-S	£29050
148	1/99	Ling	2m	E Ch	HVY	£2684
	10/98	Segr	2m3f	Ch	SFT	£2727
	3/98	Vire	2m1f	Hdl	HLD	£2525
	11/97	Vire	2m1f	Hdl	GD	£3143

Total win prize-money £88080

Going: Sf: 0-1 GS: 1-1 Gd: 1-1 GF: - Fm: 0-0
Distance: 2m/2m3: 0-0 **2m4-2m7: 2-2** 3m+: 0-1
Track: LH: 0-1 **RH: 2-2** Tight: 0-0 Gall: 0-1
Aids: Bl: 0-0 Vi: 0-0 Tstrap: 0-0
Best Rating: 170 2/02 Asct 2m3f110y gd-sft Ch

High-class chaser at up to three miles, He won twice at Ascot, where he is unbeaten, in 2001/02, including the Ritz Club Chase. Best suited by an easy surface.

Tribal Dancer (IRE)

109 **118**

8-y-o ch g Commanche Run-Cute Play (Salluceva)
Miss Venetia Williams You Can Be Sure

Placings: 1/P5-0423115210 (4136)
2001/02: 19^{0}G, 20^{4}GF, 22^{2}G, 19^{3}G, 24^{1}GF, 21^{1}G, 24^{5}G, 24^{2}G, 20^{1}S, 22^{0}GS

	Starts	1st	2nd	3rd	Win & Pl
Hurdles	10	3	2	1	13028
Career Total	**13**	**4**	**2**	**1**	**14743**

118	2/02	Sand	2m4f110y	D(0-120)HHdl	SFT	£4405
104	12/01	Ludl	2m5f	E(0-105)HHdl	GD	£2733
105	11/01	Ludl	3m	F(0-105)HHdl	G-F	£3513
118	4/00	Hntg	2m110y	H NHF	GD	£1715

Total win prize-money £12420

Going: Sf: 1-1 GS: 0-1 Gd: 1-6 GF: - Fm: 1-2
Distance: 2m/2m3: 0-0 **2m4-2m7: 2-7** 3m+: 1-3
Track: LH: 0-3 **RH: 3-7** Tight: 0-3 Gall: 0-0
Aids: Bl: 0-0 Vi: 0-0 Tstrap: 0-0
Best Rating: 118 2/02 Sand 2m4f110y soft Hdl

Fair handicap hurdler. Stays three miles. Acts on a sound surface, but has been successful on soft ground.

Tribal Dispute

95f **87f**

5-y-o b g Primitive Rising (USA)-Coral Princess (Imperial Fling (USA))
T D Easterby Mrs Jennifer E Pallister

Placings:4 (2772)
2001/02: 16^{4}G

	Starts	1st	2nd	3rd	Win & Pl
NH Flat	1	0	0	0	0
Career Total	**1**	**0**	**0**	**0**	**0**

Going: Sf: 0-0 GS: 0-0 Gd: 0-1 GF: - Fm: 0-0
Distance: 2m/2m3: 0-1 2m4-2m7: 0-0 3m+: 0-0
Track: LH: 0-1 RH: 0-0 Tight: 0-1 Gall: 0-0
Aids: Bl: 0-0 Vi: 0-0 Tstrap: 0-0
Best Rating: 87 12/01 Catt 2m good NHF

Tribal King (IRE)

107(110h) **124**

7-y-o b/br g Be My Native (USA)-Island Bridge (Mandalus)
Miss H C Knight Mrs Peter Andrews

Placings:461/15455-23 (2163)
2001/02: 17^{2}GS, 20^{3}G

	Starts	1st	2nd	3rd	Win & Pl
Chases	2	0	1	1	2877
Career Total	**10**	**2**	**1**	**1**	**9600**

103	10/00	Winc	2m	D Hdl	G-S	£3250
122	2/00	Asct	2m110y	H NHF	SFT	£2373

Total win prize-money £5623

Going: Sf: 0-0 GS: 0-1 Gd: 0-1 GF: - Fm: 0-0
Distance: 2m/2m3: 0-1 2m4-2m7: 0-1 3m+: 0-0
Track: LH: 0-1 RH: 0-1 Tight: 0-0 Gall: 0-1
Aids: Bl: 0-0 Vi: 0-0 Tstrap: 0-0
Best Rating: 131 1/01 Asct 2m110y soft Hdl

Missed the second half of the 2001/2 season after breaking a blood vessel , but was successful on his return at Aintree in May. Should stay three miles.

Tribal Tract (IRE)

98 **110**

8-y-o b g Alphabatim (USA)-Wiji Damar (Laurence O)
J J O'Neill Anne Duchess Of Westminster

Placings:432-3P52P (4043)
2001/02: 24^{3}S, 26^{P}S, 26^{5}HY, 26^{2}HY, 25^{P}S

	Starts	1st	2nd	3rd	Win & Pl
Chases	5	0	1	1	1485
Career Total	**8**	**0**	**2**	**2**	**3224**

Going: Sf: 0-5 GS: 0-0 Gd: 0-0 GF: - Fm: 0-0
Distance: 2m/2m3: 0-0 2m4-2m7: 0-0 3m+: 0-5
Track: LH: 0-1 RH: 0-3 Tight: 0-2 Gall: 0-0
Aids: Bl: 0-1 Vi: 0-0 Tstrap: 0-2
Best Rating: 110 10/01 Bang 3m110y soft Ch

Lightly raced chaser who stays three miles. Has become disappointing. Handles soft/heavy ground. Has raced in a tongue tie and blinkers on latest start but to little effect.

Tribal Venture (FR)

89f **99f**

4-y-o gr g Dom Alco (FR)-Babacha (FR) (Latnahc (USA))
Ferdy Murphy Network Training Iii

Placings: 1 (4570)
2001/02: 16^{1}G

	Starts	1st	2nd	3rd	Win & Pl
NH Flat	1	1	0	0	1729
Career Total	**1**	**1**	**0**	**0**	**1729**

99	4/02	Towc	2m	H NHF	GD	£1729

Total win prize-money £1729

Going: Sf: 0-0 GS: 0-0 Gd: 1-1 GF: - Fm: 0-0
Distance: **2m/2m3: 1-1** 2m4-2m7: 0-0 3m+: 0-0
Track: LH: 0-0 **RH: 1-1** Tight: 0-0 Gall: 0-0
Aids: Bl: 0-0 Vi: 0-0 Tstrap: 0-0
Best Rating: 99 4/02 Towc 2m good NHF

Ran on with some purpose up the straight at Towcester to win a bumper and looks a promising recruit.

Tribal Warrior (IRE)

104(96c) (91c)**87**

7-y-o b m Muharib (USA)-War Saint (Tug Of War)
N B Mason (John A Quinn 12/7) N B Mason

Placings:000/44260-0065060305012P (4877)
2001/02: 20^{0}G, 16^{0}G, 17^{6}GF, 16^{5}F, 16^{0}GF, 17^{6}S, 24^{0}GS, 19^{3}G, 21^{0}GS, 24^{5}S, 19^{0}GS, 23^{1}G, 20^{2}GF, 24^{P}G

	Starts	1st	2nd	3rd	Win & Pl

	Starts	1st	2nd	3rd	Win & Pl
NH Flat	2	0	0	0	0
Hurdles	11	1	0	1	2606
Chases	1	0	1	0	1038
Career Total	**22**	**1**	**2**	**1**	**4620**

82 4/02 Weth 2m7f G(0-90)HHdl GD £2317

Total win prize-money £2317

Going: Sf: 0-2 GS: 0-3 Gd: 1-5 GF: - Fm: 0-4
Distance: 2m/2m3: 0-7 **2m4-2m7: 1-4** 3m+: 0-3
Track: **LH: 1-5** RH: 0-5 Tight: 0-5 Gall: 0-1
Aids: Bl: 0-0 Vi: 0-0 Tstrap: 0-4
Best Rating: **97** 7/00 Gway 2m good NHF

Short head winner of 23 furlong Wetherby seller on Easter Monday 2002. Probably found two and a half miles inadequate when well beaten second on chasing debut next time.

Trillionaire

93 **72**

4-y-o ch g Dilum (USA)-Madam Trilby (Grundy)
Miss C J E Caroe (D W Chapman 23/11) Miss N F Thesiger

Placings:05 **(4781)**
2001/02: 17^{0}GS, 16^{5}GF

	Starts	1st	2nd	3rd	Win & Pl
Hurdles	2	0	0	0	0
Career Total	**2**	**0**	**0**	**0**	**0**

Going: Sf: 0-0 GS: 0-1 Gd: 0-0 GF: - Fm: 0-1
Distance: 2m/2m3: 0-2 2m4-2m7: 0-0 3m+: 0-0
Track: LH: 0-1 RH: 0-1 Tight: 0-2 Gall: 0-0
Aids: Bl: 0-0 Vi: 0-0 Tstrap: 0-0
Best Rating: **56** 4/02 Plum 2m gd-fm Hdl

Trina Bawden

11-y-o ch m Remezzo-Stonybridge (Perhapsburg)
J L Spearing Miss Tammy Potter

Placings:P-P **(0087)**
2001/02: 26^{P}G

	Starts	1st	2nd	3rd	Win & Pl
Hurdles	1	0	0	0	
Career Total	**2**	**0**	**0**	**0**	

Going: Sf: 0-0 GS: 0-0 Gd: 0-1 GF: - Fm: 0-0
Distance: 2m/2m3: 0-0 2m4-2m7: 0-0 3m+: 0-1
Track: LH: 0-0 RH: 0-1 Tight: 0-0 Gall: 0-0
Aids: Bl: 0-0 Vi: 0-0 Tstrap: 0-0
Best Rating:

Trinity Buoy (IRE)

99(87c) (46c)**86**

7-y-o b g Phardante (FR)-Vinegar Hill (Pauper)
G M McCourt Mrs Margaret Turner

Placings:006P/300**FP**-003200200 **(1611)**
2001/02: 17^{0}F, 26^{0}GF, 26^{3}F, 22^{2}GF, 24^{0}GF, 20^{0}GF, 16^{2}GF, 19^{0}GF, 19^{0}GF

	Starts	1st	2nd	3rd	Win & Pl
Hurdles	8	0	2	1	1601
Chases	1	0	0	0	0
Career Total	**18**	**0**	**2**	**2**	**1994**

Going: Sf: 0-0 GS: 0-0 Gd: 0-0 GF: - Fm: 0-9
Distance: 2m/2m3: 0-3 2m4-2m7: 0-3 3m+: 0-3
Track: LH: 0-4 RH: 0-5 Tight: 0-4 Gall: 0-1
Aids: Bl: 0-2 Vi: 0-0 Tstrap: 0-9
Best Rating: **93** 3/00 Newb 2m110y gd-fm NHF

Trink Hill

80f **60f**

4-y-o ch f Good Times (ITY)-Sweet On Willie (USA) (Master Willie)
R J Hodges D F P Racing

Placings:0 **(3503)**
2001/02: 16^{0}S

	Starts	1st	2nd	3rd	Win & Pl
NH Flat	1	0	0	0	
Career Total	**1**	**0**	**0**	**0**	

Going: Sf: 0-1 GS: 0-0 Gd: 0-0 GF: - Fm: 0-0
Distance: 2m/2m3: 0-1 2m4-2m7: 0-0 3m+: 0-0
Track: LH: 0-0 RH: 0-1 Tight: 0-0 Gall: 0-0
Aids: Bl: 0-0 Vi: 0-0 Tstrap: 0-0
Best Rating: **60** 1/02 Kemp 2m soft NHF

Trinket (IRE)

90f **101+f**

4-y-o b g Definite Article-Alamiya (IRE) (Doyoun)
H D Daly Mrs Strachan, Mrs Gabb & Jim Morris

Placings:5 **(3910)**
2001/02: 16^{5}G

	Starts	1st	2nd	3rd	Win & Pl
NH Flat	1	0	0	0	0
Career Total	**1**	**0**	**0**	**0**	**0**

Going: Sf: 0-0 GS: 0-0 Gd: 0-1 GF: - Fm: 0-0
Distance: 2m/2m3: 0-1 2m4-2m7: 0-0 3m+: 0-0
Track: LH: 0-0 RH: 0-1 Tight: 0-0 Gall: 0-0
Aids: Bl: 0-0 Vi: 0-0 Tstrap: 0-0
Best Rating: **94** 2/02 Kemp 2m good NHF

Showed promise on his bumper debut in good company at Kempton. Impressive winner at Worcester in May 2002.

Triona's Hope (IRE)

80 **70**

13-y-o br g Rising-Quinpool (Royal Highway)
E M Caine Mrs Karen Woodhead

Placings:0/P000004003P/055653U34/362554/0P4P/5 3P54003U0654-6P00P **(2344)**
2001/02: 20^{6}F, 24^{P}GF, 20^{0}GF, 20^{0}G, 24^{P}GS

	Starts	1st	2nd	3rd	Win & Pl
Hurdles	1	0	0	0	0
Chases	4	0	0	0	0
Career Total	**49**	**0**	**1**	**6**	**6416**

Going: Sf: 0-0 GS: 0-1 Gd: 0-1 GF: - Fm: 0-3
Distance: 2m/2m3: 0-0 2m4-2m7: 0-3 3m+: 0-2
Track: LH: 0-4 RH: 0-1 Tight: 0-3 Gall: 0-1
Aids: Bl: 0-0 Vi: 0-0 Tstrap: 0-0
Best Rating: **87** 7/00 Sedg 3m3f gd-fm Ch

Trios Venture

63(97c) (93c)

7-y-o ch g Bedford (USA)-Hunting Cottage (Pyjama Hunt)
Miss E C Lavelle Mrs R J Lavelle

Placings:450P2/203PU-2F0P **(4731)**
2001/02: 17^{2}GS, 16^{F}GF, 17^{0}G, 17^{P}F

	Starts	1st	2nd	3rd	Win & Pl
Hurdles	2	0	0	0	0
Chases	2	0	1	0	1380
Career Total	**14**	**0**	**3**	**1**	**2722**

Going: Sf: 0-0 GS: 0-1 Gd: 0-1 GF: - Fm: 0-2
Distance: 2m/2m3: 0-4 2m4-2m7: 0-0 3m+: 0-0
Track: LH: 0-2 RH: 0-2 Tight: 0-2 Gall: 0-1
Aids: Bl: 0-0 Vi: 0-0 Tstrap: 0-0
Best Rating: **93** 5/01 Hntg 2m110y gd-fm Ch

Trip The Switch (IRE)

67 **21**

4-y-o b f Imperial Frontier (USA)-Brite Mist (IRE) (Shy Groom (USA))
B S Rothwell Jim Browne

Placings:0 **(1800)**
2001/02: 16^{0}GF

	Starts	1st	2nd	3rd	Win & Pl
Hurdles	1	0	0	0	
Career Total	**1**	**0**	**0**	**0**	

Going: Sf: 0-0 GS: 0-0 Gd: 0-0 GF: - Fm: 0-1
Distance: 2m/2m3: 0-1 2m4-2m7: 0-0 3m+: 0-0
Track: LH: 0-0 RH: 0-1 Tight: 0-0 Gall: 0-0
Aids: Bl: 0-0 Vi: 0-0 Tstrap: 0-0
Best Rating: **21** 10/01 Ludl 2m gd-fm Hdl

Triple Crown (IRE)

9-y-o b/br g Tidaro (USA)-Noreen Beag (Thatching)
R M Bluck R M Bluck

Placings:0000/00P/P **(4852)**
2001/02: 24^{P}G

	Starts	1st	2nd	3rd	Win & Pl
Chases	1	0	0	0	
Career Total	**8**	**0**	**0**	**0**	

Going: Sf: 0-0 GS: 0-0 Gd: 0-1 GF: - Fm: 0-0
Distance: 2m/2m3: 0-0 2m4-2m7: 0-0 3m+: 0-1
Track: LH: 0-1 RH: 0-0 Tight: 0-1 Gall: 0-0
Aids: Bl: 0-0 Vi: 0-0 Tstrap: 0-0
Best Rating: **59** 7/99 Bell 2m1f good Hdl

Triple Dash

87 **77**

6-y-o ch g Nashwan (USA)-Triple Joy (Most Welcome)
Miss Venetia Williams Mr Derek D & Mrs Jean P Clee

Placings:40-0 **(0201)**
2001/02: 16^{0}G

	Starts	1st	2nd	3rd	Win & Pl
Hurdles	1	0	0	0	
Career Total	**3**	**0**	**0**	**0**	**0**

Going: Sf: 0-0 GS: 0-0 Gd: 0-1 GF: - Fm: 0-0
Distance: 2m/2m3: 0-1 2m4-2m7: 0-0 3m+: 0-0
Track: LH: 0-1 RH: 0-0 Tight: 0-0 Gall: 0-0
Aids: Bl: 0-0 Vi: 0-0 Tstrap: 0-0
Best Rating: **102** 2/01 Kemp 2m gd-sft Hdl

Triple Sharp

93 **86**

5-y-o ch m Selkirk (USA)-Drei (USA) (Lyphard (USA))
Mrs L Wadham Mrs Julia Scott

Placings:000-10 **(0587)**
2001/02: 20^{1}GF, 16^{0}GF

	Starts	1st	2nd	3rd	Win & Pl
Hurdles	2	1	0	0	1862
Career Total	**5**	**1**	**0**	**0**	**1862**

86	5/01	Fknm	2m4f	F(0-95)HHdl	G-F	£1862

Total win prize-money £1862

Going: Sf: 0-0 GS: 0-0 Gd: 0-0 GF: - Fm: 1-2
Distance: 2m/2m3: 0-1 **2m4-2m7: 1-1** 3m+: 0-0
Track: **LH: 1-2** RH: 0-0 **Tight: 1-2** Gall: 0-0
Aids: Bl: 0-0 **Vi: 1-2** Tstrap: 0-0
Best Rating: 86 5/01 Fknm 2m4f gd-fm Hdl

Tristan Ludlow (IRE)

101 **99**

6-y-o gr g Roselier (FR)-Surely Madam (Torenaga)
J J O'Neill The Blue And White Partnership

Placings:*0606* **(4594)**
2001/02: 18^{0}S, 19^{6}S, 24^{0}S, 16^{6}G

	Starts	1st	2nd	3rd	Win & Pl
NH Flat	1	0	0	0	0
Hurdles	3	0	0	0	0
Career Total	**4**	**0**	**0**	**0**	**0**

Going: Sf: 0-3 GS: 0-0 Gd: 0-1 GF: - Fm: 0-0
Distance: 2m/2m3: 0-3 2m4-2m7: 0-0 3m+: 0-1
Track: LH: 0-4 RH: 0-0 Tight: 0-1 Gall: 0-2
Aids: Bl: 0-0 Vi: 0-0 Tstrap: 0-0
Best Rating: 99 3/02 Newb 2m3f soft Hdl

Trivial (IRE)

104 **88**

10-y-o b m Rakaposhi King-Miss Rubbish (Hubor)
J E Brockbank T Brockbank

Placings:54UP623 **(4745)**
2001/02: 16^{5}GS, 20^{4}GF, 17^{U}HY, 24^{P}S, 24^{6}S, 20^{2}G, 24^{3}G

	Starts	1st	2nd	3rd	Win & Pl
Hurdles	6	0	1	1	1342
Chases	1	0	0	0	0
Career Total	**7**	**0**	**1**	**1**	**1342**

Going: Sf: 0-3 GS: 0-1 Gd: 0-2 GF: - Fm: 0-1
Distance: 2m/2m3: 0-2 2m4-2m7: 0-2 3m+: 0-3
Track: LH: 0-2 RH: 0-4 Tight: 0-3 Gall: 0-0
Aids: Bl: 0-0 Vi: 0-0 Tstrap: 0-0
Best Rating: 88 4/02 Carl 2m4f good Hdl

Former winning pointer, had shown ability over hurdles before scoring at Perth in May 2002. Seems to need decent ground.

Trochilidae (IRE)

77f **55f**

6-y-o b m Alphabatim (USA)-Quincy Bay (Buckskin (FR))
A J Wilson Mrs M J Wilson

Placings:*000* **(3502)**
2001/02: 16^{0}G, 17^{0}S, 16^{0}S

	Starts	1st	2nd	3rd	Win & Pl
NH Flat	3	0	0	0	
Career Total	**3**	**0**	**0**	**0**	

Going: Sf: 0-2 GS: 0-0 Gd: 0-1 GF: - Fm: 0-0
Distance: 2m/2m3: 0-3 2m4-2m7: 0-0 3m+: 0-0
Track: LH: 0-1 RH: 0-2 Tight: 0-0 Gall: 0-0
Aids: Bl: 0-0 Vi: 0-0 Tstrap: 0-0
Best Rating: 55 12/01 Hrfd 2m1f soft NHF

Trois Elles

6-y-o b g Elmaamul (USA)-Ca Ira (IRE) (Dancing Dissident (USA))
R C Spicer Mrs A Grayson

Placings:425-PP **(3648)**
2001/02: 16^{P}S, 16^{P}S

	Starts	1st	2nd	3rd	Win & Pl
Hurdles	2	0	0	0	
Career Total	**5**	**0**	**1**	**0**	**657**

Going: Sf: 0-2 GS: 0-0 Gd: 0-0 GF: - Fm: 0-0
Distance: 2m/2m3: 0-2 2m4-2m7: 0-0 3m+: 0-0
Track: LH: 0-0 RH: 0-2 Tight: 0-0 Gall: 0-1
Aids: Bl: 0-1 Vi: 0-0 Tstrap: 0-0
Best Rating: 82 7/00 Wolv 2m gd-sft Hdl

Trooper

106(99h) (95h)**93**

8-y-o b g Rock Hopper-Silica (USA) (Mr Prospector (USA))
A Crook Sunstar Racing Ltd

Placings:14/2P015/2662212-543530 **(4490)**
2001/02: 25^{5}S, 20^{4}F, 24^{3}GF, 21^{5}S, 21^{3}S, 20^{0}GS

	Starts	1st	2nd	3rd	Win & Pl
Chases	6	0	0	2	1436
Career Total	**20**	**3**	**5**	**2**	**12825**

103	12/00	Leic	2m	G Hdl	HVY	£1876
98	3/00	Catt	2m	G Hdl	G-F	£1578
107	1/98	Muss	2m	E Hdl	GD	£2402

Total win prize-money £5857

Going: Sf: 0-3 GS: 0-1 Gd: 0-0 GF: - Fm: 0-2
Distance: 2m/2m3: 0-0 2m4-2m7: 0-4 3m+: 0-2
Track: LH: 0-4 RH: 0-2 Tight: 0-2 Gall: 0-0
Aids: Bl: 0-3 Vi: 0-0 Tstrap: 0-0
Best Rating: 107 2/98 Weth 2m good Hdl

Not without ability but has a mind of his own.

Trooper Collins (IRE)

90 **99**

4-y-o b c Dolphin Street (FR)-Born To Fly (IRE) (Last Tycoon)
J J O'Neill Mrs J Carrington

Placings:653P0 **(4813)**
2001/02: 16^{6}S, 16^{5}GS, 16^{3}GS, 18^{P}S, 17^{0}GF

	Starts	1st	2nd	3rd	Win & Pl
Hurdles	5	0	0	1	643
Career Total	**5**	**0**	**0**	**1**	**643**

Going: Sf: 0-2 GS: 0-2 Gd: 0-0 GF: - Fm: 0-1
Distance: 2m/2m3: 0-5 2m4-2m7: 0-0 3m+: 0-0
Track: LH: 0-4 RH: 0-1 Tight: 0-1 Gall: 0-3
Aids: Bl: 0-1 Vi: 0-0 Tstrap: 0-3
Best Rating: 99 1/02 Newb 2m110y gd-sft Hdl

A maiden on the Flat, he has shown a little bit of form over hurdles.

Tropical Flame

7-y-o ch m Desert Dirham (USA)-Yen (AUS) (Biscay (AUS))
G A Ham Mrs S Hutchings

Placings:*0-P* **(0348)**
2001/02: 16^{P}G

	Starts	1st	2nd	3rd	Win & Pl
Hurdles	1	0	0	0	
Career Total	**2**	**0**	**0**	**0**	

Going: Sf: 0-0 GS: 0-0 Gd: 0-1 GF: - Fm: 0-0
Distance: 2m/2m3: 0-1 2m4-2m7: 0-0 3m+: 0-0
Track: LH: 0-1 RH: 0-0 Tight: 0-1 Gall: 0-0
Aids: Bl: 0-0 Vi: 0-0 Tstrap: 0-0
Best Rating:

Tropnevad

14-y-o ch g Alias Smith (USA)-Confident Girl (Quorum)
Paul Morris Paul Morris

Placings:*46000/3U/P334600/05005/6/0/*PUR **(0358)**
2001/02: 20^{P}GF, 24^{U}GF, 24^{R}GS

	Starts	1st	2nd	3rd	Win & Pl
Chases	3	0	0	0	
Career Total	**24**	**0**	**0**	**3**	**956**

Going: Sf: 0-0 GS: 0-1 Gd: 0-0 GF: - Fm: 0-2
Distance: 2m/2m3: 0-0 2m4-2m7: 0-1 3m+: 0-2
Track: LH: 0-2 RH: 0-1 Tight: 0-2 Gall: 0-1
Aids: Bl: 0-2 Vi: 0-0 Tstrap: 0-0
Best Rating: 72 11/94 Hexm 2m good Hdl

Trouble Ahead (IRE)

105(84h) **144**

11-y-o b g Cataldi-Why 'O' Why (Giolla Mear)
Miss Venetia Williams Mrs Sharon C Nelson

Placings:*5/3/22111/UP2F11R/330-*P1RP **(4897)**
2001/02: 24^{P}G, 21^{1}G, 29^{R}GY, 24^{P}G

	Starts	1st	2nd	3rd	Win & Pl
Chases	4	1	0	0	6858
Career Total	**21**	**6**	**3**	**3**	**49732**

144	3/02	Winc	2m5f	C(0-130)HCh	GD	£6857
161	3/00	Sand	3m110y	C(0-135)HCh	GD	£7085
147	2/00	Sand	3m110y	B(0-145)HCh	GD	£19140
137	5/99	Hrfd	2m3f	D Ch	GD	£3850
142	3/99	Hntg	2m4f110y	E Ch	G-S	£2815
139	3/99	Tntn	3m	E Ch	SFT	£3192

Total win prize-money £42941

Going: Sf: 0-0 GS: 0-0 Gd: 1-3 GF: - Fm: 0-0
Distance: 2m/2m3: 0-0 **2m4-2m7: 1-1** 3m+: 0-3
Track: LH: 0-0 **RH: 1-4** Tight: 0-0 Gall: 0-0
Aids: Bl: 0-0 Vi: 0-0 Tstrap: 0-0
Best Rating: 161 3/00 Sand 3m110y good Ch

Decent chaser who has had his problems, but bounced back to wining ways at Wincanton in March 2001. Best right-handed, he is prone to mistakes and is suited by the ground good or softer.

Trouble Next Door (IRE)

97 **85**

4-y-o b g Persian Bold-Adjacent (IRE) (Doulab (USA))
N P Littmoden Mrs Linda Francis

Placings:11 **(1626)**
2001/02: 16^{1}GS, 16^{1}GF

	Starts	1st	2nd	3rd	Win & Pl
Hurdles	2	2	0	0	6370
Career Total	**2**	**2**	**0**	**0**	**6370**

85	10/01	Ludl	2m	E Hdl	G-F	£2957
83	9/01	Plum	2m	D Hdl	G-S	£3412

Total win prize-money £6371

Going: Sf: 0-0 GS: 1-1 Gd: 0-0 GF: - Fm: 1-1
Distance: **2m/2m3: 2-2** 2m4-2m7: 0-0 3m+: 0-0
Track: LH: 1-1 RH: 1-1 **Tight: 1-1** Gall: 0-0
Aids: Bl: 0-0 Vi: 0-0 Tstrap: 0-0
Best Rating: 85 10/01 Ludl 2m gd-fm Hdl

A maiden on the Flat, he proved he has taken well to hurdling with back-to-back wins at Plumpton and Ludlow on different going.

Trouble'N'Strife

66 **42**

5-y-o b m Endoli (USA)-Midsummer Breeze (Tumble Wind (USA))
Mrs S D Williams Mrs Sarah D Williams

Placings:0 **(2487)**
2001/02: 17^{0}HY

	Starts	1st	2nd	3rd	Win & Pl
NH Flat	1	0	0	0	
Career Total	**1**	**0**	**0**	**0**	

Going: Sf: 0-1 GS: 0-0 Gd: 0-0 GF: - Fm: 0-0
Distance: 2m/2m3: 0-1 2m4-2m7: 0-0 3m+: 0-0
Track: LH: 0-1 RH: 0-0 Tight: 0-1 Gall: 0-0
Aids: Bl: 0-0 Vi: 0-0 Tstrap: 0-0
Best Rating: 17 12/01 NAbb 2m1f heavy NHF

Trout Secrets (NZ)

8-y-o b g Sir Trout (NZ)-Tuna Jill (NZ) (Alvaro)
N J Henderson Trevor Hemmings

Placings:611-P **(2916)**
2001/02: 20^{P}HY

	Starts	1st	2nd	3rd	Win & Pl
Hurdles	1	0	0	0	
Career Total	**4**	**2**	**0**	**0**	**5374**

6/00	Elle	2m4f165y	Ch	HVY	£3981
5/00	Mata	2m4f	Ch	HVY	£1393

Total win prize-money £5374

Going: Sf: 0-1 GS: 0-0 Gd: 0-0 GF: - Fm: 0-0
Distance: 2m/2m3: 0-0 2m4-2m7: 0-1 3m+: 0-0
Track: LH: 0-1 RH: 0-0 Tight: 0-0 Gall: 0-0
Aids: Bl: 0-0 Vi: 0-0 Tstrap: 0-0
Best Rating:

Truancy

102 **110**

9-y-o b g Polar Falcon (USA)-Zalfa (Luthier)
S Woodman Mrs Sally Woodman

Placings:1/51/42506/42 **(2538)**

2001/02: 16^{4}G, 16^{2}G

	Starts	1st	2nd	3rd	Win & Pl
Hurdles	2	0	1	0	1604
Career Total	**10**	**2**	**2**	**0**	**8706**

108	12/97	Wwck	2m	D(0-125)HHdl	GD	£2765
93	10/96	Kemp	2m	D Hdl	G-F	£2897

Total win prize-money £5663

Going: Sf: 0-0 GS: 0-0 Gd: 0-2 GF: - Fm: 0-0
Distance: 2m/2m3: 0-2 2m4-2m7: 0-0 3m+: 0-0
Track: LH: 0-1 RH: 0-1 Tight: 0-1 Gall: 0-0
Aids: Bl: 0-0 Vi: 0-0 Tstrap: 0-0
Best Rating: 114 4/99 Folk 2m1f110y gd-fm Hdl

Truckers Tavern (IRE)

113(54h) **158**

7-y-o ch g Phardante (FR)-Sweet Tulip (Beau Chapeau)
Ferdy Murphy Mrs M B Scholey

Placings:1-111246 **(4711a)**
2001/02: 16^{1}S, 16^{1}S, 16^{1}HY, 21^{2}HY, 16^{4}GS, 20^{6}Y

	Starts	1st	2nd	3rd	Win & Pl
Chases	6	3	1	0	39622
Career Total	**7**	**4**	**1**	**0**	**44728**

158	1/02	Towc	2m110y	B Ch	HVY	£13552
125	1/02	Newc	2m110y	E Ch	SFT	£3110
125	12/01	Ayr	2m	D Ch	SFT	£3887
120	10/00	Weth	2m	C Hdl	HVY	£5105

Total win prize-money £25656

Going: Sf: 3-4 GS: 0-1 Gd: 0-0 GF: - Fm: 0-0
Distance: **2m/2m3: 3-4** 2m4-2m7: 0-2 3m+: 0-0
Track: **LH: 2-4** RH: 1-2 Tight: 0-0 **Gall: 1-2**
Aids: Bl: 0-0 Vi: 0-0 Tstrap: 0-0
Best Rating: 158 1/02 Towc 2m110y heavy Ch

An old-fashioned chasing type, he won three points in Ireland before changing hands for 50,000gns. Won a novice hurdle on his British debut at Wetherby, his only start of 2000/01, and his first three races over fences in 2001/02. Runner-up in a Grade One at Leopardstown in February, before a good fourth in the Arkle at Cheltenham in March. Acts on an easy surface. Stays two and a half miles.

True Chimes

11-y-o ch g True Song-Ballytina (Rugantino)
James Owen (H H G Owen 10/2) Mrs E V Cardew

Placings:000/4/35/4 **(3817)**
2001/02: 21^{4}S

	Starts	1st	2nd	3rd	Win & Pl
Chases	1	0	0	0	83
Career Total	**7**	**0**	**0**	**1**	**539**

Going: Sf: 0-1 GS: 0-0 Gd: 0-0 GF: - Fm: 0-0
Distance: 2m/2m3: 0-0 2m4-2m7: 0-1 3m+: 0-0
Track: LH: 0-0 RH: 0-1 Tight: 0-1 Gall: 0-0
Aids: Bl: 0-0 Vi: 0-0 Tstrap: 0-0
Best Rating: 90 2/99 Folk 2m5f gd-sft Ch

True Lies

84 **63**

5-y-o ch m King's Signet (USA)-Lysithea (Imperial Fling (USA))
W G M Turner (C Tizzard 12/9) Richard Hedditch

Placings:00-256 **(1381)**
2001/02: 17^{2}GF, 16^{5}GF, 17^{6}GF

	Starts	1st	2nd	3rd	Win & Pl
NH Flat	2	0	1	0	620
Hurdles	1	0	0	0	0
Career Total	**5**	**0**	**1**	**0**	**620**

Going: Sf: 0-0 GS: 0-0 Gd: 0-0 GF: - Fm: 0-3
Distance: 2m/2m3: 0-3 2m4-2m7: 0-0 3m+: 0-0
Track: LH: 0-2 RH: 0-1 Tight: 0-1 Gall: 0-0
Aids: Bl: 0-0 Vi: 0-0 Tstrap: 0-0
Best Rating: 76 8/01 Worc 2m gd-fm NHF

True North (IRE)

80 **90**

7-y-o b g Black Monday-Slip A Loop (The Parson)
L Lungo M W Chapman

Placings:4/33 **(4888)**
2001/02: 20^{3}HY, 16^{3}G

	Starts	1st	2nd	3rd	Win & Pl
Hurdles	2	0	0	2	1040
Career Total	**3**	**0**	**0**	**2**	**1040**

Going: Sf: 0-1 GS: 0-0 Gd: 0-1 GF: - Fm: 0-0
Distance: 2m/2m3: 0-1 2m4-2m7: 0-1 3m+: 0-0
Track: LH: 0-1 RH: 0-1 Tight: 0-0 Gall: 0-0
Aids: Bl: 0-0 Vi: 0-0 Tstrap: 0-0
Best Rating: 95 2/00 Carl 2m1f heavy NHF

Looked a stayer in the making on his only outing in a bumper. Showed ability over hurdles after missing a season.

Trueway Two

80 **48**

9-y-o br m True Song-Portway (Pardigras)
Mrs S Gardner D V Gardner

Placings:PP0F **(1063)**
2001/02: 26^{P}F, 22^{P}GF, 17^{0}G, 22^{F}G

	Starts	1st	2nd	3rd	Win & Pl
Hurdles	4	0	0	0	
Career Total	**4**	**0**	**0**	**0**	

Going: Sf: 0-0 GS: 0-0 Gd: 0-2 GF: - Fm: 0-2
Distance: 2m/2m3: 0-1 2m4-2m7: 0-2 3m+: 0-1
Track: LH: 0-3 RH: 0-1 Tight: 0-3 Gall: 0-0
Aids: Bl: 0-0 Vi: 0-0 Tstrap: 0-0
Best Rating: 48 7/01 NAbb 2m1f good Hdl

Truicear

72 **37**

5-y-o b g Petoski-Fit For A King (Royalty)
A Ennis The A T P Racing Partnership

Placings:00 **(4548)**
2001/02: 18^{0}S, 21^{0}GF

	Starts	1st	2nd	3rd	Win & Pl
NH Flat	1	0	0	0	0
Hurdles	1	0	0	0	0
Career Total	**2**	**0**	**0**	**0**	

Going: Sf: 0-1 GS: 0-0 Gd: 0-0 GF: - Fm: 0-1
Distance: 2m/2m3: 0-1 2m4-2m7: 0-1 3m+: 0-0
Track: LH: 0-1 RH: 0-1 Tight: 0-1 Gall: 0-1
Aids: Bl: 0-0 Vi: 0-0 Tstrap: 0-1
Best Rating: 37 4/02 Hntg 2m5f110y gd-fm Hdl

Truly Madly

10-y-o b g Regal Steel-Truly Hot (True Song)
B I Case Gone To Ground

Placings:P (3321)
2001/02: 24^{P}GS

	Starts	1st	2nd	3rd	Win & Pl
Chases	1	0	0	0	
Career Total	**1**	**0**	**0**	**0**	

Going: Sf: 0-0 GS: 0-1 Gd: 0-0 GF: - Fm: 0-0
Distance: 2m/2m3: 0-0 2m4-2m7: 0-0 3m+: 0-1
Track: LH: 0-0 RH: 0-1 Tight: 0-0 Gall: 0-1
Aids: Bl: 0-0 Vi: 0-0 Tstrap: 0-0
Best Rating:

Trump

70 **59**
13-y-o b g Last Tycoon-Fleeting Affair (Hotfoot)
A Parker Mr & Mrs Raymond Anderson Green

Placings:4001113/10500/52311112603/634401PP/31
4334/PP/0000/0U14/313U00-004 (3608)
2001/02: 20^{0}S, 20^{0}GS, 24^{4}S

	Starts	1st	2nd	3rd	Win & Pl
Hurdles	3	0	0	0	0
Career Total	**56**	**12**	**2**	**9**	**36087**

101	5/00	Kels	3m3f	F(0-110)HHdl	G-F	£2756
101	3/00	Muss	3m	G(0-95)HHdl	G-F	£2254
113	12/96	Muss	3m	D(0-125)HHdl	G-F	£2633
116	2/96	Weth	2m4f110y	D(0-125)HHdl	G-S	£3020
107	1/95	Muss	3m	E(0-115)HHdl	GD	£2827
98	12/94	Muss	3m	(0-120)HHdl	GD	£2671
89	12/94	Muss	2m4f	(0-115)HHdl	GD	£2253
88	11/94	Carl	3m110y	(0-110)HHdl	G-S	£2075
99	11/93	Ayr	2m4f	(0-135)HHdl	GD	£2584
88	4/93	Carl	2m4f110y	(0-100)HHdl	GD	£1912
78	2/93	Muss	2m4f	HHdl	GD	£2305
76	1/93	Muss	2m	HHdl	GD	£1997

Total win prize-money £29290

Going: Sf: 0-2 GS: 0-1 Gd: 0-0 GF: - Fm: 0-0
Distance: 2m/2m3: 0-0 2m4-2m7: 0-2 3m+: 0-1
Track: LH: 0-2 RH: 0-1 Tight: 0-1 Gall: 0-0
Aids: Bl: 0-1 Vi: 0-0 Tstrap: 0-3
Best Rating: 116 2/96 Weth 2m4f110y gd-sft Hdl

Trump Appeal

97 **93**
4-y-o b g First Trump-Appelania (Star Appeal)
J G Portman Simon Skinner

Placings:03F (3890)
2001/02: 16^{0}G, 17^{3}S, 16^{F}HY

	Starts	1st	2nd	3rd	Win & Pl
Hurdles	3	0	0	1	414
Career Total	**3**	**0**	**0**	**1**	**414**

Going: Sf: 0-2 GS: 0-0 Gd: 0-1 GF: - Fm: 0-0
Distance: 2m/2m3: 0-3 2m4-2m7: 0-0 3m+: 0-0
Track: LH: 0-2 RH: 0-1 Tight: 0-1 Gall: 0-1
Aids: Bl: 0-0 Vi: 0-0 Tstrap: 0-0
Best Rating: 93 12/01 Folk 2m1f110y soft Hdl

Trumper

96 **91**
6-y-o b g First Trump-Sayida-Shahira (Record Run)
J T Gifford Mrs D Day

Placings:0/003400-04502P0 (3756)
2001/02: 19^{0}GF, 18^{4}GS, 21^{5}GS, 16^{0}G, 25^{2}S, 25^{P}HY, 20^{0}HY

	Starts	1st	2nd	3rd	Win & Pl
Hurdles	7	0	1	0	691
Career Total	**14**	**0**	**1**	**1**	**1149**

Going: Sf: 0-3 GS: 0-2 Gd: 0-1 GF: - Fm: 0-1
Distance: 2m/2m3: 0-2 2m4-2m7: 0-3 3m+: 0-2
Track: LH: 0-4 RH: 0-1 Tight: 0-3 Gall: 0-0
Aids: Bl: 0-0 Vi: 0-0 Tstrap: 0-0
Best Rating: 91 12/01 Plum 3m1f110y soft Hdl

Modest maiden hurdler, stays three miles.

Trumpington

101 **92**
4-y-o ch f First Trump-Brockton Flame (Emarati (USA))
D G Bridgwater (J A R Toller 22/10) R Paul Russell

Placings:6532 (4881)
2001/02: 16^{6}HY, 16^{5}S, 16^{3}G, 18^{2}GF

	Starts	1st	2nd	3rd	Win & Pl
Hurdles	4	0	1	1	1160
Career Total	**4**	**0**	**1**	**1**	**1160**

Going: Sf: 0-2 GS: 0-0 Gd: 0-1 GF: - Fm: 0-1
Distance: 2m/2m3: 0-4 2m4-2m7: 0-0 3m+: 0-0
Track: LH: 0-4 RH: 0-0 Tight: 0-1 Gall: 0-0
Aids: Bl: 0-0 Vi: 0-0 Tstrap: 0-0
Best Rating: 92 4/02 Font 2m2f110y gd-fm Hdl

Has shown ability in novice hurdles. Stays well.

Trusanba

6-y-o gr m Gran Alba (USA)-True Finesse (True Song)
J W Mullins Miss C A James

Placings:0P-PP (4385)
2001/02: 22^{P}GF, 22^{P}S

	Starts	1st	2nd	3rd	Win & Pl
Hurdles	2	0	0	0	
Career Total	**4**	**0**	**0**	**0**	

Going: Sf: 0-1 GS: 0-0 Gd: 0-0 GF: - Fm: 0-1
Distance: 2m/2m3: 0-0 2m4-2m7: 0-2 3m+: 0-0
Track: LH: 0-1 RH: 0-1 Tight: 0-1 Gall: 0-0
Aids: Bl: 0-0 Vi: 0-0 Tstrap: 0-0
Best Rating:

Trusted Mole (IRE)

79 **85**
4-y-o b g Eagle Eyed (USA)-Orient Air (Prince Sabo)
R M Stronge (S Kirk 6/3) Peter J Douglas Engineering

Placings:U3 (4756)
2001/02: 16^{U}G, 20^{3}GF

	Starts	1st	2nd	3rd	Win & Pl
Hurdles	2	0	0	1	572
Career Total	**2**	**0**	**0**	**1**	**572**

Going: Sf: 0-0 GS: 0-0 Gd: 0-1 GF: - Fm: 0-1
Distance: 2m/2m3: 0-1 2m4-2m7: 0-1 3m+: 0-0
Track: LH: 0-2 RH: 0-0 Tight: 0-0 Gall: 0-0
Aids: Bl: 0-0 Vi: 0-0 Tstrap: 0-0
Best Rating: 85 4/02 Uttx 2m4f110y gd-fm Hdl

Could be best at around two miles over hurdles.

Trusting Paddy (IRE)

89f **87f**
5-y-o b g Synefos (USA)-Homefield Girl (IRE) (Rahotep (FR))
L A Dace D Newman

Placings:5 (4639)
2001/02: 16^{5}GF

	Starts	1st	2nd	3rd	Win & Pl
NH Flat	1	0	0	0	0
Career Total	**1**	**0**	**0**	**0**	**0**

Going: Sf: 0-0 GS: 0-0 Gd: 0-0 GF: - Fm: 0-1
Distance: 2m/2m3: 0-1 2m4-2m7: 0-0 3m+: 0-0
Track: LH: 0-0 RH: 0-1 Tight: 0-0 Gall: 0-0
Aids: Bl: 0-0 Vi: 0-0 Tstrap: 0-0
Best Rating: 87 4/02 Asct 2m110y gd-fm NHF

Trusting Tom

104 **108**
7-y-o b g Teamster-Florista (Oats)
C C Bealby (Miss Elizabeth Doyle 6/5) T P Radford

Placings:3F2P (4133)
2001/02: 21^{3}S, 24^{F}S, 24^{2}GS, 24^{P}G

	Starts	1st	2nd	3rd	Win & Pl
Chases	4	0	1	1	2235
Career Total	**1**	**0**	**1**	**1**	**2235**

Going: Sf: 0-2 GS: 0-1 Gd: 0-1 GF: - Fm: 0-0
Distance: 2m/2m3: 0-0 2m4-2m7: 0-1 3m+: 0-3
Track: LH: 0-3 RH: 0-1 Tight: 0-2 Gall: 0-0
Aids: Bl: 0-0 Vi: 0-0 Tstrap: 0-0
Best Rating: 108 2/02 Fknm 3m110y gd-sft Ch

Modest form over fences, stays three miles.

Truvaro (IRE)

85 **66**
11-y-o b g Corvaro (USA)-Trudy Belle (Furry Glen)
A Streeter Mrs Sue Adams

Placings:02/0024F33/0405UP (3437)
2001/02: 17^{0}GS, 16^{4}GS, 20^{0}S, 20^{5}S, 24^{U}HY, 27^{P}HY

	Starts	1st	2nd	3rd	Win & Pl
Hurdles	6	0	0	0	250
Career Total	**15**	**0**	**2**	**2**	**2527**

Going: Sf: 0-4 GS: 0-2 Gd: 0-0 GF: - Fm: 0-0
Distance: 2m/2m3: 0-2 2m4-2m7: 0-2 3m+: 0-2
Track: LH: 0-6 RH: 0-0 Tight: 0-3 Gall: 0-0
Aids: Bl: 0-0 Vi: 0-1 Tstrap: 0-0
Best Rating: 110 11/96 Navn 2m yield Hdl

Try A Bluff (IRE)

103 **94**
10-y-o b g Hollow Hand-Happy Hereford (Bonne Noel)
Miss Lucinda V Russell J & J McCann Ltd

Placings:4/3/3/14P24P-P3664P (2434)
2001/02: 24^{P}S, 24^{3}GF, 25^{6}G, 25^{6}G, 28^{4}GS, 24^{P}S

	Starts	1st	2nd	3rd	Win & Pl
Chases	6	0	0	1	848
Career Total	**15**	**1**	**1**	**3**	**7195**

109	10/00	Kels	3m1f	E Ch	GD	£3087

Total win prize-money £3088

Going: Sf: 0-2 GS: 0-1 Gd: 0-2 GF: - Fm: 0-1

Distance: 2m/2m3: 0-0 2m4-2m7: 0-0 3m+: 0-6
Track: LH: 0-5 RH: 0-1 Tight: 0-3 Gall: 0-1
Aids: Bl: 0-0 Vi: 0-2 Tstrap: 0-0
Best Rating: 116 4/99 Fair 3m1f gd-yld Ch

Try Me And See

58 **15**

8-y-o ch g Rock City-Al Raja (King's Lake (USA))
J R Bewley R Bewley

Placings:*250*/0 **(4304)**
2001/02: 16^{0}S

	Starts	1st	2nd	3rd	Win & Pl
Hurdles	1	0	0	0	
Career Total	**4**	**0**	**1**	**0**	**354**

Going: Sf: 0-1 GS: 0-0 Gd: 0-0 GF: - Fm: 0-0
Distance: 2m/2m3: 0-1 2m4-2m7: 0-0 3m+: 0-0
Track: LH: 0-1 RH: 0-0 Tight: 0-0 Gall: 0-0
Aids: Bl: 0-0 Vi: 0-0 Tstrap: 0-1
Best Rating: 113 3/98 Chel 2m110y good NHF

Try Paris (IRE)

6-y-o b g Paris House-Try My Rosie (Try My Best (USA))
Mrs L C Jewell (H J Collingridge 30/5) The Headquarters Partnership Ii

Placings:P-0 **(1414)**
2001/02: 16^{0}GF

	Starts	1st	2nd	3rd	Win & Pl
Hurdles	1	0	0	0	
Career Total	**2**	**0**	**0**	**0**	

Going: Sf: 0-0 GS: 0-0 Gd: 0-0 GF: - Fm: 0-1
Distance: 2m/2m3: 0-1 2m4-2m7: 0-0 3m+: 0-0
Track: LH: 0-1 RH: 0-0 Tight: 0-1 Gall: 0-0
Aids: Bl: 0-1 Vi: 0-0 Tstrap: 0-0
Best Rating:

Tsanga

92(88h) (59h)**84**

10-y-o b g Rakaposhi King-Audrina (Young Generation)
C Grant Garry E West

Placings:*00*/00043/130/153011130/0016023/PP3-PPP **(3823)**
2001/02: 24^{P}GF, 24^{P}G, 27^{P}S

	Starts	1st	2nd	3rd	Win & Pl
Hurdles	3		0	0	0
Career Total	**32**	**6**	**1**	**6**	**20702**

107	7/99	Sedg	3m3f110y	E(0-115)HHdl	G-F	£2687
107	9/98	Prth	3m110y	E(0-115)HHdl	GD	£3468
107	9/98	Prth	2m4f110y	F(0-100)HHdl	GD	£3485
89	8/98	Prth	2m4f110y	F(0-100)HHdl	G-F	£2788
92	5/98	Ctml	2m1f110y	G(0-90)HHdl	G-F	£3475
75	5/97	Hexm	2m	G(0-95)HHdl	FRM	£2008

Total win prize-money £17913

Going: Sf: 0-1 GS: 0-0 Gd: 0-1 GF: - Fm: 0-1
Distance: 2m/2m3: 0-0 2m4-2m7: 0-0 3m+: 0-3
Track: LH: 0-1 RH: 0-2 Tight: 0-3 Gall: 0-0
Aids: Bl: 0-0 Vi: 0-0 Tstrap: 0-0
Best Rating: 107 7/99 Sedg 3m3f110y gd-fm Hdl

Lightly-raced, former multiple selling hurdle winner, but has had a habit of pulling up more often than not over the past few seasons.

Tsunami

101(92c) (89c)**87**

6-y-o b m Beveled (USA)-Alvecote Lady (Touching Wood (USA))
B D Leavy (P D Evans 20/6) K J Condliffe

Placings:042322320-33154345614 **(3406)**
2001/02: 16^{3}G, 16^{3}F, 16^{1}GF, 16^{5}S, 16^{4}GF, 17^{3}GS, 20^{4}G, 19^{5}G, 21^{6}GF, 20^{1}GS, 20^{4}S

	Starts	1st	2nd	3rd	Win & Pl
Hurdles	8	2	0	1	7913
Chases	3	0	0	2	1002
Career Total	**20**	**2**	**4**	**5**	**11910**

87	11/01	Aint	2m4f	F(0-100)HHdl	G-S	£4602
85	6/01	Worc	2m	F Hdl	G-F	£2030

Total win prize-money £6632

Going: Sf: 0-2 GS: 1-2 Gd: 0-3 GF: - Fm: 1-4
Distance: 2m/2m3: 1-6 2m4-2m7: 1-5 3m+: 0-0
Track: **LH: 2-7** RH: 0-4 **Tight: 1-4** Gall: 0-0
Aids: Bl: 0-0 Vi: 0-1 Tstrap: 0-0
Best Rating: 89 6/01 Hrfd 2m firm Ch

A fair handicap hurdler. Stays two and a half miles. Has won on good to firm and soft.

Tuba (IRE)

103 **89**

7-y-o b g Orchestra-Princess Paula (Smoggy)
Mrs S J Smith Trevor Hemmings

Placings:*0*/0000-FF0340 **(0930)**
2001/02: 20^{F}G, 20^{F}G, 20^{0}G, 17^{3}GF, 16^{4}GF, 16^{0}GF

	Starts	1st	2nd	3rd	Win & Pl
Hurdles	5	0	0	1	415
Chases	1	0	0	0	0
Career Total	**11**	**0**	**0**	**1**	**415**

Going: Sf: 0-0 GS: 0-0 Gd: 0-3 GF: - Fm: 0-3
Distance: 2m/2m3: 0-3 2m4-2m7: 0-3 3m+: 0-0
Track: LH: 0-4 RH: 0-2 Tight: 0-4 Gall: 0-0
Aids: Bl: 0-0 Vi: 0-0 Tstrap: 0-2
Best Rating: 83 7/01 Strf 2m110y gd-fm Hdl

Tubber Roads (IRE)

9-y-o b g Un Desperado (FR)-Node (Deep Run)
M G Hazell W F Caudwell

Placings:*30/431/30U0*-5631110 **(4650)**
2001/02: 21^{5}GF, 21^{6}G, 24^{3}GS, 21^{1}GS, 24^{1}S, 22^{1}GS, 21^{0}G

	Starts	1st	2nd	3rd	Win & Pl
Chases	7	3	0	1	6538
Career Total	**16**	**4**	**0**	**4**	**9637**

127	3/02	Newb	2m6f110y	H Ch	G-S	£2077
121	3/02	Newb	3m	H Ch	SFT	£1918
121	2/02	Fknm	2m5f110y	H Ch	G-S	£2167
121	4/00	Fknm	2m5f110y	H Ch	GD	£2008

Total win prize-money £8172

Going: Sf: 1-1 GS: 2-3 Gd: 0-2 GF: - Fm: 0-1
Distance: 2m/2m3: 0-0 **2m4-2m7: 2-5** 3m+: 1-2
Track: **LH: 3-5** RH: 0-1 Tight: 1-4 **Gall: 2-2**
Aids: Bl: 0-0 Vi: 0-0 Tstrap: 0-0
Best Rating: 127 3/02 Newb 2m6f110y gd-sft Ch

Hunter chaser, suited by two and a half/three miles, should stay further. Suited by good or good to soft ground. In fine fettlein 2001/02, scoring a hat-trick at the start of the year.

Tucacas (FR)

111 **142**

5-y-o gr m Highest Honor (FR)-Three Well (FR) (Sicyos (USA))
M C Pipe (M Rolland 2/12) Mrs Belinda Harvey

Placings:611311012 **(4822)**
2001/02: 18^{6}VS, 17^{1}HO, 18^{1}HY, 18^{3}HY, 16^{1}S, 16^{1}S, 21^{0}GS, 20^{1}GF, 21^{2}G

	Starts	1st	2nd	3rd	Win & Pl
Hurdles	9	5	1	1	50240
Career Total	**9**	**5**	**1**	**1**	**50240**

142	4/02	Asct	2m4f	C(0-130)HHdl	G-F	£6418
125	2/02	Sand	2m110y	D Hdl	SFT	£4543
130	1/02	Leic	2m	E Hdl	SFT	£3178
	11/01	Engh	2m2f	Hdl	HVY	£13579
	10/01	Engh	2m1f110y	Hdl	HLD	£12124

Total win prize-money £39844

Going: Sf: 3-4 GS: 0-1 Gd: 0-1 GF: - Fm: 1-1
Distance: **2m/2m3: 4-6** 2m4-2m7: 1-3 3m+: 0-0
Track: LH: 0-2 **RH: 3-3** Tight: 0-0 Gall: 0-2
Aids: Bl: 0-0 Vi: 0-0 Tstrap: 0-0
Best Rating: 142 4/02 Chel 2m5f110y good Hdl

A winner over hurdles in France, she made a successful British debut at Leicester in January 2002 and followed up at Sandown before her limitations were exposed at the Festival. She found the fast ground no problem when regaining winning form over two and a half miles at Ascot and running well at Cheltenham and still has improvement in her.

Tuck In

96f **115f**

5-y-o b g Good Thyne (USA)-Always Shining (Tug Of War)
P Winkworth Help-Yourself

Placings:*44* **(4158)**
2001/02: 16^{4}S, 16^{4}GS

	Starts	1st	2nd	3rd	Win & Pl
NH Flat	2	0	0	0	0
Career Total	**2**	**0**	**0**	**0**	**0**

Going: Sf: 0-1 GS: 0-1 Gd: 0-0 GF: - Fm: 0-0
Distance: 2m/2m3: 0-2 2m4-2m7: 0-0 3m+: 0-0
Track: LH: 0-0 RH: 0-2 Tight: 0-0 Gall: 0-0
Aids: Bl: 0-0 Vi: 0-0 Tstrap: 0-0
Best Rating: 115 2/02 Asct 2m110y soft NHF

Some ability in well-contested bumpers at the top tracks.

Tudor Arch (IRE)

73f **47f**

6-y-o ch g Archway (IRE)-Halpin (Yashgan)
Mark Campion Faulkner West & Co Ltd (building Contrs)

Placings:*00* **(1044)**
2001/02: 17^{0}G, 16^{0}GF

	Starts	1st	2nd	3rd	Win & Pl
NH Flat	2	0	0	0	
Career Total	**2**	**0**	**0**	**0**	

Going: Sf: 0-0 GS: 0-0 Gd: 0-1 GF: - Fm: 0-1
Distance: 2m/2m3: 0-2 2m4-2m7: 0-0 3m+: 0-0
Track: LH: 0-2 RH: 0-0 Tight: 0-1 Gall: 0-0
Aids: Bl: 0-0 Vi: 0-0 Tstrap: 0-0
Best Rating: 47 6/01 NAbb 2m1f good NHF

Tudor Falcon

70 40

9-y-o b g Midyan (USA)-Tudorealm (USA) (Palace Music (USA))

M A Barnes Thirdtimelucky

Placings: 00/P1P/P6PP46/0 (0204)

2001/02: 20^{0}G

	Starts	1st	2nd	3rd	Win & Pl
Chases	1	0	0	0	
Career Total	**12**	**1**	**0**	**0**	**1788**

68	12/97	MRas	2m1f110y	G(0-95)HHdl	HVY	£1590

Total win prize-money £1590

Going: Sf: 0-0 GS: 0-0 Gd: 0-1 GF: - Fm: 0-0
Distance: 2m/2m3: 0-0 2m4-2m7: 0-1 3m+: 0-0
Track: LH: 0-1 RH: 0-0 Tight: 0-0 Gall: 0-0
Aids: Bl: 0-0 Vi: 0-0 Tstrap: 0-1
Best Rating: 85 4/99 MRas 2m1f110y soft Ch

Tudor Gale (IRE)

(62h)

9-y-o br m Strong Gale-Orra Beg (Dear Gazelle)

A G Juckes Graham Brown

Placings: 0/004P6040/0P/060656R-P (4646)

2001/02: 21^{P}G

	Starts	1st	2nd	3rd	Win & Pl
Hurdles	1	0	0	0	
Career Total	**19**	**0**	**0**	**0**	**1425**

Going: Sf: 0-0 GS: 0-0 Gd: 0-1 GF: - Fm: 0-0
Distance: 2m/2m3: 0-0 2m4-2m7: 0-1 3m+: 0-0
Track: LH: 0-0 RH: 0-1 Tight: 0-0 Gall: 0-0
Aids: Bl: 0-0 Vi: 0-0 Tstrap: 0-0
Best Rating: 90 12/98 Chep 2m110y heavy Hdl

Tudor King (IRE)

101(93h) (62h)100

8-y-o br g Orchestra-Jane Bond (Good Bond)

J S King J R Kinloch

Placings: 0/00000/4430/06U421FU-4401P260 (2291)

2001/02: 20^{4}F, 16^{4}GF, 20^{0}G, 24^{1}GF, 25^{P}G, 25^{2}G, 24^{6}G, 19^{0}GF

	Starts	1st	2nd	3rd	Win & Pl
Hurdles	2	0	0	0	0
Chases	6	1	1	0	4075
Career Total	**26**	**2**	**2**	**1**	**8957**

98	8/01	Uttx	3m	F(0-100)HCh	G-F	£3045
100	10/00	Font	2m2f	E(0-105)HCh	G-S	£3395

Total win prize-money £6440

Going: Sf: 0-0 GS: 0-0 Gd: 0-4 GF: - Fm: 1-4
Distance: 2m/2m3: 0-1 2m4-2m7: 0-3 3m+: 1-4
Track: LH: 1-3 RH: 0-5 Tight: 0-3 Gall: 0-1
Aids: Bl: 0-0 Vi: 0-0 Tstrap: 0-0
Best Rating: 100 10/01 Folk 3m1f good Ch

A low-grade handicapper with a disappointing career record. Stays three miles, acts on any ground.

Tudor Nickola

10-y-o ch m Nicholas Bill-Cottage Melody (Super Song)

P D Purdy P D Purdy

Placings: 00/00U/PPP/060-P (2779)

2001/02: 19^{P}G

	Starts	1st	2nd	3rd	Win & Pl
Hurdles	1	0	0	0	
Career Total	**12**	**0**	**0**	**0**	**0**

Going: Sf: 0-0 GS: 0-0 Gd: 0-1 GF: - Fm: 0-0
Distance: 2m/2m3: 0-1 2m4-2m7: 0-0 3m+: 0-0
Track: LH: 0-0 RH: 0-1 Tight: 0-0 Gall: 0-0
Aids: Bl: 0-0 Vi: 0-0 Tstrap: 0-1
Best Rating: 43 1/98 Ling 2m110y gd-sft NHF

Tufamore (USA)

6-y-o ch g Mt. Livermore (USA)-Tufa (Warning)

E W Tuer E Tuer

Placings: 005-P (0741)

2001/02: 16^{P}GS

	Starts	1st	2nd	3rd	Win & Pl
Hurdles	1	0	0	0	
Career Total	**4**	**0**	**0**	**0**	**0**

Going: Sf: 0-0 GS: 0-1 Gd: 0-0 GF: - Fm: 0-0
Distance: 2m/2m3: 0-1 2m4-2m7: 0-0 3m+: 0-0
Track: LH: 0-1 RH: 0-0 Tight: 0-0 Gall: 0-0
Aids: Bl: 0-0 Vi: 0-0 Tstrap: 0-1
Best Rating: 18 7/00 Sedg 2m1f firm Hdl

Tui

96(97c) (87c)81

7-y-o b m Tina's Pet-Curious Feeling (Nishapour (FR))

P Bowen Dragon Racing

Placings: 44326/101014560/P0P06-02F44643PF (1940)

2001/02: 19^{0}G, 16^{2}S, 20^{F}GF, 20^{4}GF, 20^{4}G, 23^{6}GF, 21^{4}GF, 24^{3}F, 24^{P}GF, 21^{F}GS

	Starts	1st	2nd	3rd	Win & Pl
Hurdles	5	0	0	1	494
Chases	5	0	1	0	1451
Career Total	**29**	**3**	**2**	**2**	**11228**

101	8/99	Worc	2m4f	F(0-110)HHdl	SFT	£2565
90	7/99	Sedg	2m5f110y	E Hdl	G-F	£2250
98	5/99	Worc	2m	F(0-110)HHdl	G-S	£2528

Total win prize-money £7343

Going: Sf: 0-1 GS: 0-1 Gd: 0-2 GF: - Fm: 0-6
Distance: 2m/2m3: 0-2 2m4-2m7: 0-5 3m+: 0-3
Track: LH: 0-0 RH: 0-3 Tight: 0-3 Gall: 0-0
Aids: Bl: 0-1 Vi: 0-0 Tstrap: 0-0
Best Rating: 101 8/99 Worc 2m4f soft Hdl

An honest sort in moderate hurdles company but a little small for chasing.

Tukano (CAN)

63

11-y-o ch g Halo (USA)-Northern Prancer (USA) (Northern Dancer)

J R Jenkins The B C W Partnership

Placings: 630/00022/131P/460/000/42P60F/0P0P-0P (0552)

2001/02: 16^{0}GF, 21^{P}GF

	Starts	1st	2nd	3rd	Win & Pl
Hurdles	2	0	0	0	
Career Total	**30**	**2**	**3**	**2**	**9403**

98	8/96	Bang	2m4f	E Hdl	G-F	£2612
98	6/96	Prth	2m110y	E Hdl	G-F	£2332

Total win prize-money £4944

Going: Sf: 0-0 GS: 0-0 Gd: 0-0 GF: - Fm: 0-2
Distance: 2m/2m3: 0-1 2m4-2m7: 0-1 3m+: 0-0
Track: LH: 0-0 RH: 0-2 Tight: 0-0 Gall: 0-2
Aids: Bl: 0-0 Vi: 0-1 Tstrap: 0-1
Best Rating: 102 3/96 Ling 2m3f110y soft Hdl

Tulach Ard (IRE)

102 100

7-y-o b g Erdelistan (FR)-Noon Hunting (Green Shoon)

A Parker And Mrs M C Mackenzie

Placings: 3/6-432P2 (4747)

2001/02: 17^{4}HY, 20^{3}S, 16^{2}S, 20^{P}HY, 20^{2}G

	Starts	1st	2nd	3rd	Win & Pl
Hurdles	5	0	2	1	1932
Career Total	**7**	**0**	**2**	**2**	**2159**

Going: Sf: 0-4 GS: 0-0 Gd: 0-1 GF: - Fm: 0-0
Distance: 2m/2m3: 0-2 2m4-2m7: 0-3 3m+: 0-0
Track: LH: 0-3 RH: 0-1 Tight: 0-0 Gall: 0-1
Aids: Bl: 0-0 Vi: 0-0 Tstrap: 0-0
Best Rating: 100 4/02 Carl 2m4f good Hdl

A lightly-raced sort with form on heavy ground in modest hurdles.

Tullimoss (IRE)

90 77

7-y-o b m Husyan (USA)-Ballynattin Moss (Le Moss)

J N R Billinge Mrs S E Billinge

Placings: 4060 (4875)

2001/02: 16^{4}G, 16^{0}GS, 16^{6}GF, 24^{0}G

	Starts	1st	2nd	3rd	Win & Pl
NH Flat	2	0	0	0	0
Hurdles	2	0	0	0	0
Career Total	**4**	**0**	**0**	**0**	**0**

Going: Sf: 0-0 GS: 0-1 Gd: 0-2 GF: - Fm: 0-1
Distance: 2m/2m3: 0-3 2m4-2m7: 0-0 3m+: 0-1
Track: LH: 0-2 RH: 0-2 Tight: 0-1 Gall: 0-0
Aids: Bl: 0-0 Vi: 0-0 Tstrap: 0-2
Best Rating: 71 9/01 Prth 2m110y good NHF

Modest form in bumpers and novice hurdles.

Tullons Lane

89(91h) (73h)91

7-y-o b g Riverwise (USA)-Pallanda (Pablond)

N R Mitchell Mrs E Mitchell

Placings: 0/05P550-0F45P (4734)

2001/02: 19^{0}G, 17^{F}G, 19^{4}G, 16^{5}S, 19^{P}F

	Starts	1st	2nd	3rd	Win & Pl
Hurdles	1	0	0	0	0
Chases	4	0	0	0	309
Career Total	**12**	**0**	**0**	**0**	**309**

Going: Sf: 0-1 GS: 0-0 Gd: 0-3 GF: - Fm: 0-1
Distance: 2m/2m3: 0-3 2m4-2m7: 0-2 3m+: 0-0
Track: LH: 0-0 RH: 0-5 Tight: 0-0 Gall: 0-0
Aids: Bl: 0-0 Vi: 0-0 Tstrap: 0-0
Best Rating: 93 11/00 Winc 2m gd-sft NHF

Tulsa (IRE)

79 56

8-y-o b g Priolo (USA)-Lagrion (USA) (Diesis)

L Montague Hall A D Green

Placings: 6/3456-0 (0375)

2001/02: 16^{0}GF

	Starts	1st	2nd	3rd	Win & Pl
Hurdles	1	0	0	0	
Career Total	**6**	**0**	**0**	**1**	**362**

Going: Sf: 0-0 GS: 0-0 Gd: 0-0 GF: - Fm: 0-1
Distance: 2m/2m3: 0-1 2m4-2m7: 0-0 3m+: 0-0
Track: LH: 0-0 RH: 0-1 Tight: 0-0 Gall: 0-1
Aids: Bl: 0-0 Vi: 0-0 Tstrap: 0-0
Best Rating: 96 5/00 Towc 2m gd-fm Hdl

Tumbleweed Glen (IRE)

100(83h) (85h)95
6-y-o ch g Mukaddamah (USA)-Mistic Glen (IRE) (Mister Majestic)
P Kelsall Peter Kelsall

Placings:524335U23/34U0000-P50**230** **(2640)**
2001/02: 24^{P}GF, 16^{5}G, 16^{0}G, 16^{2}GF, 20^{3}GF, 16^{0}GF

	Starts	1st	2nd	3rd	Win & Pl
Hurdles	3	0	0	0	0
Chases	3	0	1	1	1571
Career Total	**22**	**0**	**3**	**5**	**7115**

Going: Sf: 0-0 GS: 0-0 Gd: 0-2 GF: - Fm: 0-4
Distance: 2m/2m3: 0-4 2m4-2m7: 0-1 3m+: 0-1
Track: LH: 0-3 RH: 0-3 Tight: 0-1 Gall: 0-0
Aids: Bl: 0-1 Vi: 0-0 Tstrap: 0-0
Best Rating: 106 4/00 Chel 2m1f soft Hdl

Moderate hurdler who acts on good ground.

Tupgill Turbo

79 41
4-y-o ch g Rudimentary (USA)-Persian Alexandra (Persian Bold)
S E Kettlewell The Tupgill Partnership

Placings:02 **(2794)**
2001/02: 16^{0}G, 16^{2}S

	Starts	1st	2nd	3rd	Win & Pl
Hurdles	2	0	1	0	542
Career Total	**2**	**0**	**1**	**0**	**542**

Going: Sf: 0-1 GS: 0-0 Gd: 0-1 GF: - Fm: 0-0
Distance: 2m/2m3: 0-2 2m4-2m7: 0-0 3m+: 0-0
Track: LH: 0-2 RH: 0-0 Tight: 0-0 Gall: 0-1
Aids: Bl: 0-0 Vi: 0-0 Tstrap: 0-0
Best Rating: 41 12/01 Donc 2m110y good Hdl

Turaath (IRE)

108 94
6-y-o b g Sadler's Wells (USA)-Diamond Field (USA) (Mr Prospector (USA))
G M McCourt Mrs Kathy Stuart

Placings:05P**11** **(4908)**
2001/02: 17^{0}F, 17^{5}GF, 24^{P}S, 21^{1}G, 21^{1}G

	Starts	1st	2nd	3rd	Win & Pl
Hurdles	5	2	0	0	4981
Career Total	**5**	**2**	**0**	**0**	**4981**

94	4/02	MRas	2m5f110y	F(0-100)HHdl	GD	£2579
85	4/02	MRas	2m5f110y	F(0-95)HHdl	GD	£2401

Total win prize-money £4981

Going: Sf: 0-1 GS: 0-0 Gd: 2-2 GF: - Fm: 0-2
Distance: 2m/2m3: 0-2 **2m4-2m7: 2-2** 3m+: 0-1
Track: LH: 0-1 **RH: 2-4 Tight: 2-4** Gall: 0-0
Aids: Bl: 0-0 Vi: 0-0 **Tstrap: 1-1**
Best Rating: 94 4/02 MRas 2m5f110y good Hdl

A fair hurdler, he stays two miles five and is effective on good and fast ground. In good heart in the spring of 2002.

Turbo Mower

4-y-o b g Turbo Speed-Fruids Park (Royal Fountain)
W G Young W G Young

Placings:*0* **(4841)**
2001/02: 16^{0}G

	Starts	1st	2nd	3rd	Win & Pl
NH Flat	1	0	0	0	
Career Total	**1**	**0**	**0**	**0**	

Going: Sf: 0-0 GS: 0-0 Gd: 0-1 GF: - Fm: 0-0
Distance: 2m/2m3: 0-1 2m4-2m7: 0-0 3m+: 0-0
Track: LH: 0-1 RH: 0-0 Tight: 0-0 Gall: 0-0
Aids: Bl: 0-0 Vi: 0-0 Tstrap: 0-0
Best Rating:

Turgeonev (FR)

121(96h) 165
7-y-o gr g Turgeon (USA)-County Kerry (FR) (Comrade In Arms)
T D Easterby D F Sills

Placings:05/56121/31P25-4**1111**P0U2 **(4838)**
2001/02: 16^{4}G, 16^{1}G, 16^{1}G, 16^{1}GS, 16^{1}G, 21^{P}HY, 16^{0}GS, 16^{U}G, 16^{2}G

	Starts	1st	2nd	3rd	Win & Pl
Chases	9	4	1	0	65225
Career Total	**21**	**7**	**3**	**1**	**78484**

160	1/02	Asct	2m	A HCh	GD	£34800
148	12/01	Weth	2m	A HCh	G-S	£13500
143	11/01	Weth	2m	B(0-150)HCh	GD	£8895
139	11/01	Newc	2m110y	E(0-115)HCh	GD	£3360
141	11/00	MRas	2m1f110y	E Ch	SFT	£3096
122	4/00	MRas	2m1f110y	D Hdl	G-F	£3212
126	2/00	Kels	2m110y	D Hdl	G-S	£3721

Total win prize-money £70587

Going: Sf: 0-1 GS: 1-2 Gd: 3-6 GF: - Fm: 0-0
Distance: **2m/2m3: 4-8** 2m4-2m7: 0-1 3m+: 0-0
Track: **LH: 3-8** RH: 1-1 Tight: 0-1 **Gall: 1-3**
Aids: Bl: 0-0 Vi: 0-0 Tstrap: 0-0
Best Rating: 165 3/02 Chel 2m gd-sft Ch

Formerly headstrong, he has settled better for his new trainer and completed a fine hat-trick towards the end of 2001 with a win at Newcastle and two at Wetherby including the Castleford Chase. Easy winner of the 2002 Victor Chandler, but could not handle the heavy ground at Cheltenham next time and was outclassed in the Queen Mother Champion Chase. Out of luck at Aintree next time, before a good second in at Ayr in a tough handicap chase. Suited by two miles, he does not want the ground too soft.

Turkestan (FR)

110 130
5-y-o b/br g Petit Loup (USA)-Turkeina (FR) (Kautokeino (FR))
M C Pipe (J Bertran De Balanda 6/5) Gerald Myers

Placings:5424-**511121**500 **(4480)**
2001/02: 18^{5}HY, 16^{1}GF, 16^{1}GF, 16^{1}GF, 18^{2}S, 16^{1}G, 16^{5}G, 16^{0}GS, 22^{0}G

	Starts	1st	2nd	3rd	Win & Pl
Hurdles	9	4	1	0	21082
Career Total	**13**	**4**	**2**	**0**	**31412**

124	11/01	Asct	2m110y	C Hdl	GD	£4953
120	9/01	Plum	2m	E Hdl	G-F	£2646
102	8/01	Worc	2m	E Hdl	G-F	£3178
120	8/01	Strf	2m110y	E Hdl	G-F	£3062

Total win prize-money £13840

Going: Sf: 0-2 GS: 0-1 Gd: 1-3 GF: - Fm: 3-3
Distance: **2m/2m3: 4-8** 2m4-2m7: 0-1 3m+: 0-0
Track: **LH: 3-6** RH: 1-1 **Tight: 2-3** Gall: 0-0
Aids: Bl: 0-0 Vi: 0-0 Tstrap: 0-0
Best Rating: 130 3/02 Chel 2m110y gd-sft Hdl

He showed ability over hurdles in France and scored an easy win at Stratford on his British debut in August 2001. He scored a further three times in 2001 and looked especially suited by fast ground and two miles. Will make a nice chaser in time.

Turn Of The Tide

(72h) (50h)
9-y-o ch g Riverwise (USA)-Cut Above The Rest (Indiaro)
Mrs John Harrington (N R Mitchell 5/6) Piers Butler

Placings:*00/05*0P/54F6PPP/0P0PP0F-0P **(4448a)**
2001/02: 17^{0}G, 16^{P}S

	Starts	1st	2nd	3rd	Win & Pl
Hurdles	1	0	0	0	0
Chases	1	0	0	0	0
Career Total	**22**	**0**	**0**	**0**	**302**

Going: Sf: 0-1 GS: 0-0 Gd: 0-1 GF: - Fm: 0-0
Distance: 2m/2m3: 0-2 2m4-2m7: 0-0 3m+: 0-0
Track: LH: 0-1 RH: 0-0 Tight: 0-1 Gall: 0-0
Aids: Bl: 0-1 Vi: 0-0 Tstrap: 0-1
Best Rating: 81 10/00 Tntn 2m3f good Ch

Turn The Tide

83 67
5-y-o b m Derrylin-Mermaid Bay (Jupiter Island)
A King The Octomists

Placings:*5*F0 **(4584)**
2001/02: 18^{5}HY, 16^{F}G, 16^{0}G

	Starts	1st	2nd	3rd	Win & Pl
NH Flat	1	0	0	0	0
Hurdles	2	0	0	0	0
Career Total	**3**	**0**	**0**	**0**	**0**

Going: Sf: 0-1 GS: 0-0 Gd: 0-2 GF: - Fm: 0-0
Distance: 2m/2m3: 0-3 2m4-2m7: 0-0 3m+: 0-0
Track: LH: 0-1 RH: 0-2 Tight: 0-1 Gall: 0-0
Aids: Bl: 0-0 Vi: 0-0 Tstrap: 0-0
Best Rating: 63 4/02 Winc 2m good Hdl

Turnpole (IRE)

109 140
11-y-o br g Satco (FR)-Mountain Chase (Mount Hagen (FR))
Mrs M Reveley Mr & Mrs W J Williams

Placings:1116/3U2/33/20110/4 **(1935)**
2001/02: 25^{4}G

	Starts	1st	2nd	3rd	Win & Pl
Hurdles	1	0	0	0	1210
Career Total	**15**	**5**	**2**	**3**	**36598**

125	2/99	Sedg	3m3f	D Ch	GD	£3900
117	2/99	Catt	3m1f110y	D Ch	GD	£4432
132	2/96	Newc	2m4f	B(0-140)HHdl	SFT	£11283
116	11/95	Newc	2m	E Hdl	GD	£2270
112	11/95	Weth	2m	D Hdl	GD	£3008

Total win prize-money £24896

Going: Sf: 0-0 GS: 0-0 Gd: 0-1 GF: - Fm: 0-0
Distance: 2m/2m3: 0-0 2m4-2m7: 0-0 3m+: 0-1
Track: LH: 0-1 RH: 0-0 Tight: 0-0 Gall: 0-0
Aids: Bl: 0-0 Vi: 0-0 Tstrap: 0-0
Best Rating: 150 11/98 Asct 2m4f gd-sft Hdl

He won a couple of novice chases in 1999, but has been returned to concentrate on the Flat since then, although he returned to no success over hurdles at Wetherby in November.

Turtle Soup (IRE)

110 129

6-y-o b g Turtle Island (IRE)-Lisa's Favourite (Gorytus (USA))
Mrs L Richards M K George

Placings:43-41234 **(4398)**
2001/02: 16^4G, 19^1GS, 22^2S, 21^3G, 24^4S

	Starts	1st	2nd	3rd	Win & Pl
Hurdles	5	1	1	1	8562
Career Total	7	1	1	2	9291

119 1/02 Newb 2m3f D Hdl G-S £4433
Total win prize-money £4433

Going: Sf: 0-2 GS: 1-1 Gd: 0-2 GF: - Fm: 0-0
Distance: **2m/2m3: 1-2** 2m4-2m7: 0-2 3m+: 0-1
Track: **LH: 1-2** RH: 0-3 Tight: 0-0 **Gall: 1-2**
Aids: Bl: 0-0 Vi: 0-0 Tstrap: 0-0
Best Rating: 129 2/02 Sand 2m6f soft Hdl

Useful hurdler, he got off the mark in January and ran a good races in decent company subsequently. Appreciates cut in the ground and stays two miles three furlongs plus.

Turtleback (IRE)

109 128

4-y-o b g Turtle Island (IRE)-Mimicry (Thatch (USA))
E J O'Grady (P Mullins 27/12) D F Desmond

Placings:13621 **(4962a)**
2001/02: 16^1Y, 16^3HY, 17^6G, 16^2GY, 16^1GY

	Starts	1st	2nd	3rd	Win & Pl
Hurdles	5	2	1	1	22452
Career Total	5	2	1	1	22452

128 4/02 Punc 2m Hdl G-Y £7975
128 12/01 Leop 2m Hdl YLD £8068
Total win prize-money £16044

Going: Sf: 0-1 GS: 0-0 Gd: 0-1 GF: - Fm: 0-0
Distance: **2m/2m3: 2-5** 2m4-2m7: 0-0 3m+: 0-0
Track: LH: 1-3 RH: 1-2 Tight: 0-0 Gall: 0-1
Aids: Bl: 0-0 Vi: 0-0 Tstrap: 0-0
Best Rating: 128 4/02 Punc 2m gd-yld Hdl

He won his hurdles debut easily in December 2001 but was hampered next time out in heavy ground. Won on good to soft ground over two miles.

Tuska Ridge (IRE)

107(107c) (102c)95

9-y-o b g Zaffaran (USA)-Mcbrides Reject (Avocat)
J J Lambe (Stephen McConville 24/10) Stephen McConville

Placings:4/2213 1356105P3P/0/2321P53FFU-0FU001400 **(3411a)**
2001/02: 27^0G, 18^FGF, 20^UY, 24^0YS, 24^0Y, 22^1YS, 22^4GY, 20^0YS, 20^0S

	Starts	1st	2nd	3rd	Win & Pl
Hurdles	8	1	0	0	5933
Chases	1	0	0	0	0
Career Total	35	5	4	5	21754

95 12/01 Navn 2m6f (0-109)HHdl Y-S £5564
123 6/00 Strf 3m E Ch G-S £3354
111 10/98 DRoy 2m4f Hdl GD £1494
104 7/98 Klny 2m1f NHF G-F £2989
100 6/98 Tipp 2m1f NHF Y-S £2382
Total win prize-money £15786

Going: Sf: 0-1 GS: 0-0 Gd: 0-1 GF: - Fm: 0-1
Distance: 2m/2m3: 0-1 **2m4-2m7: 1-5** 3m+: 0-3
Track: **LH: 1-5** RH: 0-2 Tight: 0-1 Gall: 0-0
Aids: Bl: 0-0 Vi: 0-0 Tstrap: 0-0
Best Rating: 123 6/00 Strf 3m gd-sft Ch

Tweed

92 88

5-y-o ch g Barathea (IRE)-In Perpetuity (Great Nephew)
J R Best (J M Jefferson 10/1) Paul J Dixon

Placings:204P-2PP **(2751)**
2001/02: 17^2GF, 16^PGS, 17^PGS

	Starts	1st	2nd	3rd	Win & Pl
Hurdles	3	0	1	0	696
Career Total	7	0	2	0	1666

Going: Sf: 0-0 GS: 0-2 Gd: 0-0 GF: - Fm: 0-1
Distance: 2m/2m3: 0-3 2m4-2m7: 0-0 3m+: 0-0
Track: LH: 0-3 RH: 0-0 Tight: 0-2 Gall: 0-0
Aids: Bl: 0-0 Vi: 0-0 Tstrap: 0-0
Best Rating: 94 1/01 Muss 2m good Hdl

Twenty Bucks

85 122

8-y-o b g Buckley-Sweet N' Twenty (High Top)
M Madgwick W E Baird

Placings:0/60/2454351/2F-3U **(2057)**
2001/02: 20^3GS, 22^UGS

	Starts	1st	2nd	3rd	Win & Pl
Chases	2	0	0	1	474
Career Total	14	1	2	2	5866

105 4/00 Winc 2m6f E Hdl G-S £2968
Total win prize-money £2968

Going: Sf: 0-0 GS: 0-2 Gd: 0-0 GF: - Fm: 0-0
Distance: 2m/2m3: 0-0 2m4-2m7: 0-2 3m+: 0-0
Track: LH: 0-0 RH: 0-0 Tight: 0-2 Gall: 0-0
Aids: Bl: 0-0 Vi: 0-0 Tstrap: 0-0
Best Rating: 122 10/01 Font 2m4f gd-sft Ch

Fair novice chaser, ran encouragingly on return from a year off. Should stay three miles and is suited by cut although handles faster.

Twice As Good (IRE)

83 97

8-y-o b g Good Thyne (USA)-Twice As Fluffy (Pollerton)
K C Bailey Graham And Alison Jelley

Placings:1/0-3324 **(4850)**
2001/02: 25^3G, 16^3HY, 23^2S, 22^4G

	Starts	1st	2nd	3rd	Win & Pl
Hurdles	4	0	1	2	1620
Career Total	6	1	1	2	3335

115 4/00 Hntg 2m110y H NHF GD £1715
Total win prize-money £1715

Going: Sf: 0-2 GS: 0-0 Gd: 0-2 GF: - Fm: 0-0
Distance: 2m/2m3: 0-1 2m4-2m7: 0-1 3m+: 0-2
Track: LH: 0-2 RH: 0-1 Tight: 0-2 Gall: 0-0
Aids: Bl: 0-0 Vi: 0-0 Tstrap: 0-0
Best Rating: 115 4/00 Hntg 2m110y good NHF

Winner of a bumper in the 2000/2001 season, he was running for the first time in a year when a creditable third on his hurdling debut at Warwick in November. Just touched off at Fakenham two months later.

Twin Falls (IRE)

11-y-o b g Trempolino (USA)-Twice A Fool (USA) (Foolish Pleasure (USA))
Mrs P M Stevens Mrs P M Stevens

Placings:346162544/2360550/246225121531336/F6/1140306/263213UP414/4PPP-6 **(0229)**
2001/02: 30^6GF

	Starts	1st	2nd	3rd	Win & Pl
Chases	1	0	0	0	0
Career Total	56	8	8	8	36268

114 1/00 Font 3m2f110y D(0-125)HCh G-S £3711
106 8/99 Prth 3m110y E(0-115)HHdl G-F £3485
112 10/98 Font 2m3f F(0-105)HCh G-S £2617
119 10/98 Font 2m3f D(0-120)HCh GD £3371
110 2/97 Catt 2m3f E Ch G-S £2894
97 12/96 Catt 2m F(0-105)HCh GFT £2005
103 11/96 Catt 2m E Ch G-F £2816
90 11/94 Catt 2m3f Hdl GD £1380
Total win prize-money £22912

Going: Sf: 0-0 GS: 0-0 Gd: 0-0 GF: - Fm: 0-1
Distance: 2m/2m3: 0-0 2m4-2m7: 0-0 3m+: 0-1
Track: LH: 0-0 RH: 0-1 Tight: 0-0 Gall: 0-1
Aids: Bl: 0-0 Vi: 0-0 Tstrap: 0-0
Best Rating: 119 10/98 Font 2m3f good Ch

Twin Pleasures

102 88

8-y-o b m Rolfe (USA)-Moment's Pleasure (USA) (What A Pleasure (USA))
J R Bewley R Bewley

Placings:006/01541 **(2471)**
2001/02: 17^0G, 17^1G, 16^5G, 16^4GF, 18^1GS

	Starts	1st	2nd	3rd	Win & Pl
Hurdles	5	2	0	0	4809
Career Total	10	2	0	0	4809

88 12/01 Kels 2m2f F(0-90)HHdl G-S £3150
88 11/01 Sedg 2m1f G(0-90)HHdl GD £1659
Total win prize-money £4809

Going: Sf: 0-0 GS: 1-1 Gd: 1-3 GF: - Fm: 0-1
Distance: **2m/2m3: 2-5** 2m4-2m7: 0-0 3m+: 0-0
Track: **LH: 2-5** RH: 0-0 **Tight: 2-4** Gall: 0-0
Aids: Bl: 0-0 Vi: 0-0 Tstrap: 0-0
Best Rating: 88 12/01 Kels 2m2f gd-sft Hdl

Lightly-raced, she got off the mark when finding plenty under pressure in an ordinary Sedgefield seller over two miles one furlong, coming home at a massive 50/1. Has since added a weak Kelso handicap.

Twin Time

104 88

8-y-o b m Syrtos-Carramba (CZE) (Tumble Wind (USA))

J S King Dajam Ltd

Placings:P/00/20-4 (1260)
2001/02: 16^{4}GF

	Starts	1st	2nd	3rd	Win & Pl
Hurdles	1	0	0	0	0
Career Total	**6**	**0**	**1**	**0**	**826**

Going: Sf: 0-0 GS: 0-0 Gd: 0-0 GF: - Fm: 0-1
Distance: 2m/2m3: 0-1 2m4-2m7: 0-0 3m+: 0-0
Track: LH: 0-0 RH: 0-1 Tight: 0-0 Gall: 0-1
Aids: Bl: 0-0 Vi: 0-0 Tstrap: 0-0
Best Rating: 93 10/00 Tntn 2m1f good Hdl

Twinnings Grove (IRE)

95 **95**
9-y-o b m Lord Americo-Mary Deen (Avocat)
T R George Mrs Sharon C Nelson

Placings:*302/02/*333P41-FP2 (1812)
2001/02: 19^{F}G, 21^{P}G, 21^{2}S

	Starts	1st	2nd	3rd	Win & Pl
Chases	3	0	1	0	1057
Career Total	**14**	**1**	**3**	**4**	**8004**

95	4/01	Prth	2m	D Ch	HVY	£3718

Total win prize-money £3718

Going: Sf: 0-1 GS: 0-0 Gd: 0-2 GF: - Fm: 0-0
Distance: 2m/2m3: 0-0 2m4-2m7: 0-3 3m+: 0-0
Track: LH: 0-1 RH: 0-2 Tight: 0-2 Gall: 0-0
Aids: Bl: 0-0 Vi: 0-0 Tstrap: 0-0
Best Rating: 99 3/99 Tntn 2m3f110y soft Hdl

Modest chaser who goes well in the mud.

Twiscombe

7-y-o br m Arctic Lord-Flying Cherub (Osiris)
Mrs J G Retter Mrs J G Retter

Placings:*60* (4823)
2001/02: 18^{6}HY, 17^{0}G

	Starts	1st	2nd	3rd	Win & Pl
NH Flat	2	0	0	0	0
Career Total	**2**	**0**	**0**	**0**	**0**

Going: Sf: 0-1 GS: 0-0 Gd: 0-1 GF: - Fm: 0-0
Distance: 2m/2m3: 0-2 2m4-2m7: 0-0 3m+: 0-0
Track: LH: 0-2 RH: 0-0 Tight: 0-1 Gall: 0-1
Aids: Bl: 0-0 Vi: 0-0 Tstrap: 0-0
Best Rating: 29 4/02 Chel 2m1f good NHF

Twisted Logic (IRE)

109(95h) **141**
9-y-o b g Tremblant-Logical View (Mandalus)
R H Alner P M De Wilde

Placings:533P3/1P2110151/F63U5-451410U (4819)
2001/02: 23^{4}GS, 30^{5}G, 24^{1}G, 24^{4}G, 25^{1}G, 24^{0}GS, 26^{U}GF

	Starts	1st	2nd	3rd	Win & Pl
Chases	7	2	0	0	15419
Career Total	**26**	**7**	**1**	**4**	**40959**

141	12/01	Extr	3m1f110y	C(0-135)HCh	GD	£6994
136	10/01	Chel	3m110y	E(0-125)HCh	GD	£7247
146	4/00	Bang	3m110y	C(0-135)HCh	G-S	£7410
137	3/00	Font	3m2f110y	D(0-125)HCh	G-S	£4616
128	1/00	Wwck	3m1f110y	E(0-115)HCh	SFT	£3000
129	12/99	Tntn	3m	F(0-105)HCh	SFT	£3395
112	5/99	Towc	2m6f	E Ch	G-F	£3042

Total win prize-money £35706

Going: Sf: 0-0 GS: 0-2 Gd: 2-4 GF: - Fm: 0-1
Distance: 2m/2m3: 0-0 2m4-2m7: 0-0 **3m+: 2-7**
Track: **LH: 1-5** RH: 0-1 Tight: 0-1 **Gall: 1-4**
Aids: Bl: 0-0 Vi: 0-0 Tstrap: 0-0
Best Rating: 146 4/00 Bang 3m110y gd-sft Ch

A fair stayer at his best, he has dropped in the ratings and scored his first success for 18 months in an amateur chase at Cheltenham in October. He went on to defy the firm grasp of the Handicapper when beating Atavistic in December. Has won on good and good to soft ground.

Two By Four

9-y-o ch g Sunley Builds-Zenaida (Lear Jet)
Miss Z C Davison Mrs J A C Lundgren

Placings:P (0720)
2001/02: 26^{P}F

	Starts	1st	2nd	3rd	Win & Pl
Hurdles	1	0	0	0	
Career Total	**1**	**0**	**0**	**0**	

Going: Sf: 0-0 GS: 0-0 Gd: 0-0 GF: - Fm: 0-1
Distance: 2m/2m3: 0-0 2m4-2m7: 0-0 3m+: 0-1
Track: LH: 0-0 RH: 0-1 Tight: 0-0 Gall: 0-0
Aids: Bl: 0-0 Vi: 0-0 Tstrap: 0-0
Best Rating:

Two For Joy (IRE)

(106h) (115h)**95**
7-y-o br m Mandalus-Misty Joy (General Ironside)
C R Egerton Ian Jacombs Sarah Macechern & Partners

Placings:*13*-121510 (4822)
2001/02: 20^{1}G, 22^{2}S, 19^{1}G, 21^{5}GS, 24^{1}GS, 21^{0}G

	Starts	1st	2nd	3rd	Win & Pl
Hurdles	6	3	1	0	12663
Career Total	**8**	**4**	**1**	**1**	**14739**

115	3/02	Towc	3m	D Hdl	G-S	£3507
110	3/02	Extr	2m3f	D Hdl	GD	£3815
100	1/02	Donc	2m4f	E Hdl	GD	£3220
110	11/00	Hrfd	2m1f	H NHF	G-S	£1617

Total win prize-money £12160

Going: Sf: 0-1 GS: 1-2 Gd: 2-3 GF: - Fm: 0-0
Distance: 2m/2m3: 1-1 2m4-2m7: 1-4 3m+: 1-1
Track: LH: 1-3 **RH: 2-3** Tight: 0-0 **Gall: 1-3**
Aids: Bl: 0-0 Vi: 0-0 Tstrap: 0-0
Best Rating: 115 3/02 Towc 3m gd-sft Hdl

A bumper winner, she landed a Doncaster novice hurdle in January 2002 after an 11-month absence and has landed a couple of better novice events since. Stays three miles and is best on a sound surface but out of luck over fences so far.

Two Lords

101 **86**
10-y-o b g Arctic Lord-Doddycross (Deep Run)
Mrs A C Tate (M Tate 24/1) O I F Davies

Placings:*00*/PP00P/P54140/005224306P0/624U11P4 P-PPP000 (4599)
2001/02: 23^{P}G, 25^{P}HY, 26^{P}GS, 24^{0}G, 26^{0}GF, 25^{0}GF

	Starts	1st	2nd	3rd	Win & Pl
Hurdles	6	0	0	0	
Career Total	**39**	**3**	**3**	**1**	**15921**

108	11/00	Hayd	2m7f110y	E(0-115)HHdl	SFT	£3623
108	10/00	Ludl	3m	F(0-95)HHdl	G-F	£2765
106	3/99	Ludl	2m5f110y	E(0-115)HHdl	SFT	£5454

Total win prize-money £11844

Going: Sf: 0-1 GS: 0-1 Gd: 0-2 GF: - Fm: 0-2
Distance: 2m/2m3: 0-0 2m4-2m7: 0-0 3m+: 0-6
Track: LH: 0-1 RH: 0-3 Tight: 0-0 Gall: 0-1
Aids: Bl: 0-3 Vi: 0-0 Tstrap: 0-6
Best Rating: 108 11/00 Hayd 2m7f110y soft Hdl

Two Paddies (IRE)

48
9-y-o b g Lord Americo-Reardans Fancy (Dramatic Bid (USA))
T P McGovern N Benstead And Mrs J Peake

Placings:*065*/P0 (0778)
2001/02: 21^{P}G, 20^{0}GF

	Starts	1st	2nd	3rd	Win & Pl
Hurdles	1	0	0	0	0
Chases	1	0	0	0	0
Career Total	**5**	**0**	**0**	**0**	**0**

Going: Sf: 0-0 GS: 0-0 Gd: 0-1 GF: - Fm: 0-1
Distance: 2m/2m3: 0-0 2m4-2m7: 0-2 3m+: 0-0
Track: LH: 0-1 RH: 0-1 Tight: 0-1 Gall: 0-0
Aids: Bl: 0-0 Vi: 0-0 Tstrap: 0-0
Best Rating: 91 12/98 Wwck 2m soft NHF

Two Tears

(34h)
8-y-o gr g Silver Owl-Vomero (NZ) (Church Parade)
N J Hawke M J Disney

Placings:40/2P-4U (1887)
2001/02: 23^{4}GF, 20^{U}G

	Starts	1st	2nd	3rd	Win & Pl
Chases	2	0	0	0	318
Career Total	**6**	**0**	**1**	**0**	**1402**

Going: Sf: 0-0 GS: 0-0 Gd: 0-1 GF: - Fm: 0-1
Distance: 2m/2m3: 0-0 2m4-2m7: 0-1 3m+: 0-1
Track: LH: 0-1 RH: 0-1 Tight: 0-0 Gall: 0-1
Aids: Bl: 0-0 Vi: 0-0 Tstrap: 0-0
Best Rating: 89 9/00 Chep 2m110y good Hdl

Twoforten

88 **76**
7-y-o b g Robellino (USA)-Grown At Rowan (Gabitat)
P Butler P Butler

Placings:P/40-6 (1414)
2001/02: 16^{6}GF

	Starts	1st	2nd	3rd	Win & Pl
Hurdles	1	0	0	0	0
Career Total	**4**	**0**	**0**	**0**	**0**

Going: Sf: 0-0 GS: 0-0 Gd: 0-0 GF: - Fm: 0-1
Distance: 2m/2m3: 0-1 2m4-2m7: 0-0 3m+: 0-0
Track: LH: 0-1 RH: 0-0 Tight: 0-1 Gall: 0-0
Aids: Bl: 0-0 Vi: 0-0 Tstrap: 0-0
Best Rating: 76 9/01 Plum 2m gd-fm Hdl

Twotensforafive

101 **94**
9-y-o b g Arctic Lord-Sister Of Gold (The Parson)
P R Rodford Mrs Christine Priest

Placings:0000/000300/*602*P0/F443 (1035)

2001/02: 26^{F}G, 21^{4}GF, 23^{4}G, 21^{3}G

	Starts	1st	2nd	3rd	Win & Pl
Chases	4	0	0	1	801
Career Total	**19**	**0**	**1**	**2**	**2110**

Going: Sf: 0-0 GS: 0-0 Gd: 0-3 GF: - Fm: 0-1
Distance: 2m/2m3: 0-0 2m4-2m7: 0-2 3m+: 0-2
Track: LH: 0-4 RH: 0-0 Tight: 0-3 Gall: 0-0
Aids: Bl: 0-0 Vi: 0-0 Tstrap: 0-0
Best Rating: 94 7/01 Worc 2m7f110y good Ch

Tyglyns Folly

82f **59f**

7-y-o ch m Out Of Hand-My Home (Homing)
Mrs S D Williams J W Haydon

Placings:0 **(2048)**
2001/02: 16^{0}G

	Starts	1st	2nd	3rd	Win & Pl
NH Flat	1	0	0	0	
Career Total	**1**	**0**	**0**	**0**	

Going: Sf: 0-0 GS: 0-0 Gd: 0-1 GF: - Fm: 0-0
Distance: 2m/2m3: 0-1 2m4-2m7: 0-0 3m+: 0-0
Track: LH: 0-0 RH: 0-1 Tight: 0-0 Gall: 0-0
Aids: Bl: 0-0 Vi: 0-0 Tstrap: 0-0
Best Rating: 59 11/01 Winc 2m good NHF

Tyke Gale (IRE)

83 **73**

9-y-o br g Strong Gale-Relkissimo (Relkino)
Mrs A Price Mrs A Price

Placings:U0/25U **(0670)**
2001/02: 25^{2}G, 25^{5}G, 23^{U}G

	Starts	1st	2nd	3rd	Win & Pl
Chases	3	0	1	0	678
Career Total	**5**	**0**	**1**	**0**	**678**

Going: Sf: 0-0 GS: 0-0 Gd: 0-3 GF: - Fm: 0-0
Distance: 2m/2m3: 0-0 2m4-2m7: 0-0 3m+: 0-3
Track: LH: 0-1 RH: 0-2 Tight: 0-0 Gall: 0-0
Aids: Bl: 0-0 Vi: 0-0 Tstrap: 0-0
Best Rating: 73 5/01 Hrfd 3m1f110y good Ch

Tylo Steamer (IRE)

84 **110**

10-y-o b g King's Ride-Chatty Actress (Le Bavard (FR))
D L Williams D L Williams

Placings:2/446021265P/05053P4P43/11PP1P-1PP **(3893)**
2001/02: 26^{1}HY, 25^{P}HY, 29^{P}HY

	Starts	1st	2nd	3rd	Win & Pl
Chases	3	1	0	0	2898
Career Total	**30**	**5**	**3**	**2**	**20018**

110	12/01	NAbb	3m2f110y	F(0-105)HCh	HVY	£2898
107	3/01	Ling	3m4f110y	D(0-120)HCh	HVY	£6929
107	1/01	Wwck	3m2f	F(0-95)HCh	HVY	£2674
90	5/00	Towc	3m1f	F(0-90)HCh	SFT	£2654
90	2/99	Font	2m6f110y	G(0-95)HHdl	SFT	£2110

Total win prize-money £17265

Going: Sf: 1-3 GS: 0-0 Gd: 0-0 GF: - Fm: 0-0
Distance: 2m/2m3: 0-0 2m4-2m7: 0-0 **3m+: 1-3**
Track: **LH: 1-2** RH: 0-1 **Tight: 1-1** Gall: 0-0
Aids: Bl: 0-0 Vi: 0-0 Tstrap: 0-0
Best Rating: 110 12/01 NAbb 3m2f110y heavy Ch

Moderate staying chaser. Loves the mud.

Tyndarius (IRE)

108 **132**

11-y-o b g Mandalus-Lady Rerico (Pamroy)
B Ellison Alex Shaw

Placings:0/0101P/**03U0/2211F/01450P-150** **(4234)**
2001/02: 17^{1}S, 19^{5}GS, 20^{0}GS

	Starts	1st	2nd	3rd	Win & Pl
Chases	3	1	0	0	4144
Career Total	**24**	**6**	**2**	**1**	**34519**

132	2/02	MRas	2m1f110y	D(0-115)HCh	SFT	£4143
132	12/00	Fair	3m1f	HCh	Y-S	£10400
114	3/00	Leop	2m2f	HCh	GD	£5520
114	3/00	Navn	2m1f	Ch	Y-S	£3864
116	4/98	List	2m4f	(0-109)HHdl	Y-S	£2978
103	2/98	Clon	2m4f	Hdl	Y-S	£1935

Total win prize-money £28842

Going: Sf: 1-1 GS: 0-2 Gd: 0-0 GF: - Fm: 0-0
Distance: **2m/2m3: 1-1** 2m4-2m7: 0-2 3m+: 0-0
Track: LH: 0-2 **RH: 1-1 Tight: 1-1** Gall: 0-2
Aids: Bl: 0-0 Vi: 0-0 Tstrap: 0-0
Best Rating: 132 2/02 MRas 2m1f110y soft Ch

Ex-Irish handicap chaser. Had his first run for new connections when winning over a trip short of his best at Market Rasen in February 2002. Stays three miles. Has won on good ground and heavy. Runs well fresh.

Tyneandthyneagain

100 **140**

7-y-o b g Good Thyne (USA)-Radical Lady (Radical)
N B Mason N B Mason

Placings:222333122121-PP10 **(4193)**
2001/02: 20^{P}S, 23^{P}HY, 24^{1}GS, 25^{0}GS

	Starts	1st	2nd	3rd	Win & Pl
Hurdles	3	1	0	0	13546
Chases	1	0	0	0	0
Career Total	**16**	**4**	**6**	**3**	**43983**

135	3/02	Donc	3m110y	B(0-140)HHdl	G-S	£13546
140	4/01	Prth	3m110y	B Hdl	HVY	£8814
128	3/01	Hayd	2m4f	C Hdl	HVY	£6136
107	1/01	Sthl	2m4f110y	E(0-105)HHdl	HVY	£2597

Total win prize-money £31093

Going: Sf: 0-2 GS: 1-2 Gd: 0-0 GF: - Fm: 0-0
Distance: 2m/2m3: 0-0 2m4-2m7: 0-1 **3m+: 1-3**
Track: **LH: 1-4** RH: 0-0 Tight: 0-1 **Gall: 1-2**
Aids: Bl: 0-0 Vi: 0-0 Tstrap: 0-0
Best Rating: 140 4/01 Prth 3m110y heavy Hdl

Mud lover. Admirably consistent over hurdles in the 2000/2001 season and developed into a high-class handicapper. Was pulled up as if something was amiss on his chasing debut and again when returned to hurdles. Returned to winning ways next time out at Doncaster. Stays three miles. Acts on soft/heavy ground.

Typhoon Tilly

94 **87**

5-y-o b g Hernando (FR)-Meavy (Kalaglow)
C R Egerton Mrs Evelyn Hankinson

Placings:0-200P **(1809)**
2001/02: 16^{2}GF, 16^{0}G, 16^{0}GF, 16^{P}S

	Starts	1st	2nd	3rd	Win & Pl
Hurdles	4	0	1	0	698
Career Total	**5**	**0**	**1**	**0**	**698**

Going: Sf: 0-1 GS: 0-0 Gd: 0-1 GF: - Fm: 0-2
Distance: 2m/2m3: 0-4 2m4-2m7: 0-0 3m+: 0-0
Track: LH: 0-2 RH: 0-2 Tight: 0-1 Gall: 0-0
Aids: Bl: 0-2 Vi: 0-0 Tstrap: 0-0
Best Rating: 87 9/01 Worc 2m gd-fm Hdl

Tyre Hill Lilly

5-y-o br m Jupiter Island-The Howlet (New Brig)
A G Hobbs Hill Fuels Limited

Placings:0F0PP **(4542)**
2001/02: 16^{0}G, 16^{F}GF, 16^{0}G, 21^{P}G, 17^{P}G

	Starts	1st	2nd	3rd	Win & Pl
NH Flat	3	0	0	0	0
Hurdles	2	0	0	0	0
Career Total	**5**	**0**	**0**	**0**	

Going: Sf: 0-0 GS: 0-0 Gd: 0-4 GF: - Fm: 0-1
Distance: 2m/2m3: 0-4 2m4-2m7: 0-1 3m+: 0-0
Track: LH: 0-0 RH: 0-5 Tight: 0-0 Gall: 0-1
Aids: Bl: 0-0 Vi: 0-0 Tstrap: 0-1
Best Rating: 63 12/01 Ludl 2m good NHF

Tyrolean Dream (IRE)

100 **127**

8-y-o b g Tirol-Heavenly Hope (Glenstal (USA))
M H Tompkins P Heath

Placings:1320/1126510/**024/312** **(0802)**
2001/02: 16^{3}GF, 20^{1}F, 16^{2}GF

	Starts	1st	2nd	3rd	Win & Pl
Chases	3	1	1	1	6518
Career Total	**17**	**5**	**4**	**2**	**40514**

127	5/01	Weth	2m4f110y	D Ch	FRM	£3935
143	3/99	Asct	2m110y	B(0-145)HHdl	G-F	£6152
127	10/98	Weth	2m	C(0-135)HHdl	GD	£3821
134	10/98	Chep	2m110y	B HHdl	GD	£6869
105	1/98	Wind	2m	D Hdl	G-S	£3246

Total win prize-money £24025

Going: Sf: 0-0 GS: 0-0 Gd: 0-0 GF: - Fm: 1-3
Distance: 2m/2m3: 0-2 **2m4-2m7: 1-1** 3m+: 0-0
Track: **LH: 1-1** RH: 0-1 Tight: 0-0 Gall: 0-0
Aids: Bl: 0-0 Vi: 0-0 Tstrap: 0-0
Best Rating: 150 12/99 Sand 2m good Ch

Tysou (FR)

108(84c) (139c)**146**

5-y-o b/br g Ajdayt (USA)-Pretty Point (Crystal Glitters (USA))
N J Henderson W J Brown

Placings:2155612110-421300 **(4674)**
2001/02: 19^{4}GS, 16^{2}G, 16^{1}G, 16^{3}GS, 16^{0}S, 16^{0}G

	Starts	1st	2nd	3rd	Win & Pl
Hurdles	4	1	0	1	12512
Chases	2	0	1	0	3453
Career Total	**16**	**5**	**3**	**1**	**37952**

146	12/01	Donc	2m110y	B(0-140)HHdl	GD	£8112
133	2/01	Muss	2m	D Hdl	GD	£3444
128	2/01	Catt	2m	E Hdl	SFT	£2775
107	11/00	Catt	2m	D Hdl	G-S	£3900
	7/00	Claf	2m	Hdl	SFT	£5764

Total win prize-money £23996

Going: Sf: 0-1 GS: 0-2 Gd: 1-3 GF: - Fm: 0-0
Distance: **2m/2m3: 1-5** 2m4-2m7: 0-1 3m+: 0-0

Track: LH: 1-4 RH: 0-1 Tight: 0-1 **Gall: 1-2**
Aids: Bl: 0-0 Vi: 0-0 Tstrap: 0-0
Best Rating: 146 1/02 Kemp 2m gd-sft Hdl

He successfully returned to hurdles at Doncaster in December 2001 and ran well in defeat at Kempton, but then lost his form. Suited by two miles.

Ultimate Gold (IRE)

(104h) (103h)
8-y-o b g Good Thyne (USA)-Golden Mela (Golden Love)
K C Bailey John White

Placings:2623 **(4854)**
2001/02: 16^{2}HY, 22^{6}S, 21^{2}GS, 22^{3}G

	Starts	1st	2nd	3rd	Win & Pl
Hurdles	4	0	2	1	1956
Career Total	**4**	**0**	**2**	**1**	**1956**

Going: Sf: 0-2 GS: 0-1 Gd: 0-1 GF: - Fm: 0-0
Distance: 2m/2m3: 0-1 2m4-2m7: 0-3 3m+: 0-0
Track: LH: 0-1 RH: 0-3 Tight: 0-2 Gall: 0-0
Aids: Bl: 0-0 Vi: 0-0 Tstrap: 0-0
Best Rating: 103 3/02 Towc 2m5f gd-sft Hdl

Made a fair racecourse debut when second over two miles at Towcester in January 2002. Not the best of hurdlers and held subsequently.

Ultra Calm (IRE)

97 **75**
6-y-o ch g Doubletour (USA)-Shyonn (IRE) (Shy Groom (USA))
Miss K M George Stableline

Placings:33-0050 **(0930)**
2001/02: 16^{0}GF, 17^{0}G, 17^{5}G, 16^{0}GF

	Starts	1st	2nd	3rd	Win & Pl
Hurdles	4	0	0	0	0
Career Total	**6**	**0**	**0**	**2**	**665**

Going: Sf: 0-0 GS: 0-0 Gd: 0-2 GF: - Fm: 0-2
Distance: 2m/2m3: 0-4 2m4-2m7: 0-0 3m+: 0-0
Track: LH: 0-3 RH: 0-1 Tight: 0-4 Gall: 0-0
Aids: Bl: 0-0 Vi: 0-0 Tstrap: 0-0
Best Rating: 90 8/00 Sedg 2m1f good Hdl

Ultra Pontem

80 **36**
10-y-o b m Governor General-Rocquelle (Coquelin (USA))
P Hayward The Welsh Connection

Placings:500603/0-00P **(1013)**
2001/02: 22^{0}GF, 20^{0}G, 20^{P}G

	Starts	1st	2nd	3rd	Win & Pl
Hurdles	3	0	0	0	
Career Total	**10**	**0**	**0**	**1**	**651**

Going: Sf: 0-0 GS: 0-0 Gd: 0-2 GF: - Fm: 0-1
Distance: 2m/2m3: 0-0 2m4-2m7: 0-3 3m+: 0-0
Track: LH: 0-3 RH: 0-0 Tight: 0-1 Gall: 0-0
Aids: Bl: 0-0 Vi: 0-0 Tstrap: 0-0
Best Rating: 98 3/99 Newb 2m4f gd-fm Ch

Ulundi

106 **145**
7-y-o b g Rainbow Quest (USA)-Flit (USA) (Lyphard (USA))
P R Webber D Heath

Placings:3111510/51-063 **(2043)**
2001/02: 16^{0}GY, 16^{6}GS, 16^{3}G

	Starts	1st	2nd	3rd	Win & Pl
Hurdles	3	0	0	1	2875
Career Total	**12**	**5**	**0**	**2**	**31966**

145	4/01	Ayr	2m	A HHdl	G-F	£15600
122	10/99	Chel	2m110y	B HHdl	GD	£6872
111	9/99	Font	2m2f110y	E Hdl	GD	£2285
124	8/99	NAbb	2m1f	H NHF	GD	£2263
101	7/99	NAbb	2m1f	H NHF	G-S	£1871

Total win prize-money £28894

Going: Sf: 0-0 GS: 0-1 Gd: 0-1 GF: - Fm: 0-0
Distance: 2m/2m3: 0-3 2m4-2m7: 0-0 3m+: 0-0
Track: LH: 0-0 RH: 0-2 Tight: 0-0 Gall: 0-0
Aids: Bl: 0-0 Vi: 0-0 Tstrap: 0-0
Best Rating: 145 11/01 Winc 2m good Hdl

A fast-ground performer, he improved last year to win the Scottish Champion Hurdle. He disappointed in the Galway Hurdle in August and his subsequent performances appear to reinforce the view that he is totally dependent on a fast surface.

Ulusaba

100(106h) (106h)**90**
6-y-o b g Alflora (IRE)-Mighty Fly (Comedy Star (USA))
N B Mason N B Mason

Placings:06P/22124-002313 **(4858)**
2001/02: 18^{0}GS, 17^{0}GS, 20^{2}G, 20^{3}S, 16^{1}GS, 16^{3}G

	Starts	1st	2nd	3rd	Win & Pl
Hurdles	6	1	1	2	3247
Career Total	**14**	**2**	**4**	**2**	**7453**

106	3/02	Catt	2m	G Hdl	G-S	£1708
88	3/01	MRas	2m1f110y	G(0-95)HHdl	GD	£1561

Total win prize-money £3269

Going: Sf: 0-1 GS: 1-3 Gd: 0-2 GF: - Fm: 0-0
Distance: **2m/2m3: 1-4** 2m4-2m7: 0-2 3m+: 0-0
Track: **LH: 1-3** RH: 0-2 **Tight: 1-5** Gall: 0-0
Aids: Bl: 0-1 Vi: 1-3 Tstrap: 1-3
Best Rating: 106 3/02 Catt 2m gd-sft Hdl

Plating-class hurdler, best on good ground.

Ulvick Star (IRE)

89(43c) **71**
10-y-o b g Lord Americo-She's Approaching (Ragapan)
Mrs Julie Read Mrs P King

Placings:0/3-P **(4053)**
2001/02: 20^{P}S

	Starts	1st	2nd	3rd	Win & Pl
Chases	1	0	0	0	
Career Total	**3**	**0**	**0**	**1**	**247**

Going: Sf: 0-1 GS: 0-0 Gd: 0-0 GF: - Fm: 0-0
Distance: 2m/2m3: 0-0 2m4-2m7: 0-1 3m+: 0-0
Track: LH: 0-0 RH: 0-1 Tight: 0-0 Gall: 0-0
Aids: Bl: 0-0 Vi: 0-0 Tstrap: 0-0
Best Rating: 104 5/00 Hntg 3m good Ch

Very modest hurdler, stays three miles.

Umbrella Man (IRE)

112 **109**
6-y-o ch g Insan (USA)-Askasilla (IRE) (Lucky Mickmooch)
Miss H C Knight Mrs J Dollar & Mrs M Hall

Placings:00-2424 **(4479)**
2001/02: 16^{2}S, 16^{4}S, 19^{2}S, 19^{4}G

	Starts	1st	2nd	3rd	Win & Pl
Hurdles	4	0	2	0	1927
Career Total	**6**	**0**	**2**	**0**	**1927**

Going: Sf: 0-3 GS: 0-0 Gd: 0-1 GF: - Fm: 0-0
Distance: 2m/2m3: 0-3 2m4-2m7: 0-1 3m+: 0-0
Track: LH: 0-1 RH: 0-3 Tight: 0-0 Gall: 0-0
Aids: Bl: 0-0 Vi: 0-0 Tstrap: 0-0
Best Rating: 109 1/02 Hrfd 2m3f110y soft Hdl

Fair form in novice hurdles in 2001/02. Appreciates cut in the ground.

Un Jour A Vassy (FR)

114(105h) (115h)**136**
7-y-o b g Video Rock (FR)-Bayalika (FR) (Kashtan (FR))
P F Nicholls Mrs Bunty Millard

Placings:64/532F/33U11-1P15330P **(4876)**
2001/02: 20^{1}GF, 20^{P}G, 24^{1}G, 24^{5}G, 25^{3}G, 25^{3}G, 23^{0}G, 20^{P}G

	Starts	1st	2nd	3rd	Win & Pl
Hurdles	2	1	0	0	5889
Chases	6	1	0	2	13056
Career Total	**19**	**4**	**1**	**5**	**27531**

115	11/01	Tntn	3m110y	D Hdl	GD	£5889
136	5/01	Sthl	2m4f110y	B(0-145)HCh	G-F	£10790
125	4/01	Tntn	3m	D(0-110)HCh	G-F	£4046
124	4/01	Fknm	2m5f110y	H Ch	G-S	£2298

Total win prize-money £23023

Going: Sf: 0-0 GS: 0-0 Gd: 1-7 GF: - Fm: 1-1
Distance: 2m/2m3: 0-0 2m4-2m7: 1-3 3m+: 1-5
Track: LH: 1-2 RH: 1-6 **Tight: 2-2** Gall: 0-0
Aids: Bl: 0-0 Vi: 0-0 Tstrap: 0-0
Best Rating: 136 5/01 Sthl 2m4f110y gd-fm Ch

He was switched to Paul Nicholls after winning a maiden point last season and soon rattled up a hat-trick under Polly Gundry, one hunter chase and two handicaps. Pulled up as though something was amiss at Warwick in May 2001, but came back to win a three-mile hurdle at Taunton after a six-month break. Reported to have finished distressed at Ascot and has struggled subsequently. Has won from two and a half to three miles.

Uncle Mick (IRE)

105 (104c)**112**
7-y-o b g Ikdam-Kandy Kate (Pry)
R H Alner Mrs W H Walter

Placings:5/015-FUF2033 **(4885)**
2001/02: 25^{F}G, 24^{U}S, 23^{F}G, 24^{2}S, 25^{0}S, 24^{3}S, 27^{3}GF

	Starts	1st	2nd	3rd	Win & Pl
Hurdles	4	0	1	2	2602
Chases	3	0	0	0	0
Career Total	**11**	**1**	**1**	**2**	**4989**

100	1/01	Plum	3m1f110y	E Hdl	HVY	£2387

Total win prize-money £2387

Going: Sf: 0-4 GS: 0-0 Gd: 0-2 GF: - Fm: 0-1
Distance: 2m/2m3: 0-0 2m4-2m7: 0-0 3m+: 0-7
Track: LH: 0-2 RH: 0-3 Tight: 0-2 Gall: 0-0
Aids: Bl: 0-0 Vi: 0-0 Tstrap: 0-0
Best Rating: 112 3/02 Chep 3m soft Hdl

He had trouble completing over fences, but ran much better back over hurdles at the start of 2002. Stays well and appreciates soft ground.

Uncle Oberon

6-y-o b g Distant Relative-Fairy Story (IRE) (Persian Bold)
H J Manners H J Manners

Placings:P **(0841)**
2001/02: 16^{P}G

	Starts	1st	2nd	3rd	Win & Pl
Hurdles	1	0	0	0	
Career Total	**1**	**0**	**0**	**0**	

Going: Sf: 0-0 GS: 0-0 Gd: 0-1 GF: - Fm: 0-0
Distance: 2m/2m3: 0-1 2m4-2m7: 0-0 3m+: 0-0
Track: LH: 0-1 RH: 0-0 Tight: 0-0 Gall: 0-0
Aids: Bl: 0-0 Vi: 0-0 Tstrap: 0-0
Best Rating:

Uncle Teddy (IRE)

101(97h) (82h)107
9-y-o b g Arctic Cider (USA)-Ishtar (Dike (USA))
Miss E C Lavelle (N A Twiston-Davies 23/6) Miss N Henton

Placings:551/P-50CP41 **(4863)**
2001/02: 20^{5}G, 22^{0}GF, 22^{C}GF, 22^{P}S, 19^{4}F, 19^{1}F

	Starts	1st	2nd	3rd	Win & Pl
Hurdles	4	0	0	0	0
Chases	2	1	0	0	1050
Career Total	**10**	**2**	**0**	**0**	**5820**

107	4/02	Extr	2m3f110y	E Ch	FRM	£3962
85	10/99	Towc	2m5f	G Hdl	GD	£1562

Total win prize-money £5524

Going: Sf: 0-1 GS: 0-0 Gd: 0-1 GF: - Fm: 1-4
Distance: 2m/2m3: 0-0 **2m4-2m7: 1-6** 3m+: 0-0
Track: LH: 0-4 **RH: 1-2** Tight: 0-4 Gall: 0-0
Aids: Bl: 0-3 Vi: 0-1 Tstrap: 0-0
Best Rating: 107 4/02 Extr 2m3f110y firm Ch

Moderate lightly-raced hurdler/chaser. Suited by a sound surface. Took advantage of the odds-on favourite's mistake when winning three runner novice chase at Exeter April 2002.

Uncle Wallace

109 114
6-y-o b g Neltino-Auntie Dot (Hallodri (ATA))
P R Webber Mrs John Webber

Placings:40-60420 **(4154)**
2001/02: 16^{6}G, 20^{0}S, 16^{4}G, 20^{2}S, 20^{0}GS

	Starts	1st	2nd	3rd	Win & Pl
NH Flat	1	0	0	0	0
Hurdles	4	0	1	0	1443
Career Total	**7**	**0**	**1**	**0**	**1443**

Going: Sf: 0-2 GS: 0-1 Gd: 0-2 GF: - Fm: 0-0
Distance: 2m/2m3: 0-2 2m4-2m7: 0-3 3m+: 0-0
Track: LH: 0-4 RH: 0-1 Tight: 0-0 Gall: 0-2
Aids: Bl: 0-0 Vi: 0-0 Tstrap: 0-0
Best Rating: 114 12/01 Newb 2m110y good Hdl

A son of the useful Auntie Dot. He is still a maiden but has run with credit in decent company, including when second in bad ground at Doncaster in January 2002. Stays two and a half miles. A chaser in the making.

Undeniable

97 102
4-y-o b g Unfuwain (USA)-Shefoog (Kefaah (USA))
J L Eyre (J L Dunlop 4/9) The Kamnac/manfast Partnership

Placings:160P **(4330)**
2001/02: 16^{1}S, 16^{6}S, 17^{0}GS, 17^{P}S

	Starts	1st	2nd	3rd	Win & Pl
Hurdles	4	1	0	0	2989
Career Total	**4**	**1**	**0**	**0**	**2989**

102	1/02	Newc	2m	E Hdl	SFT	£2989

Total win prize-money £2989

Going: Sf: 1-3 GS: 0-1 Gd: 0-0 GF: - Fm: 0-0
Distance: **2m/2m3: 1-4** 2m4-2m7: 0-0 3m+: 0-0
Track: **LH: 1-3** RH: 0-1 Tight: 0-2 **Gall: 1-2**
Aids: Bl: 0-0 Vi: 0-0 Tstrap: 0-1
Best Rating: 102 1/02 Newc 2m soft Hdl

Juvenile hurdler, has gone the wrong way since winning on his debut at Newcastle.

Under The Sand (IRE)

113 129
5-y-o b g Turtle Island (IRE)-Occupation (Homing)
P J Hobbs R Triple H

Placings:140-2 **(1920)**
2001/02: 16^{2}G

	Starts	1st	2nd	3rd	Win & Pl
Hurdles	1	0	1	0	2191
Career Total	**4**	**1**	**1**	**0**	**10124**

122	3/01	Hntg	2m110y	E Hdl	SFT	£2933

Total win prize-money £2933

Going: Sf: 0-0 GS: 0-0 Gd: 0-1 GF: - Fm: 0-0
Distance: 2m/2m3: 0-1 2m4-2m7: 0-0 3m+: 0-0
Track: LH: 0-0 RH: 0-1 Tight: 0-0 Gall: 0-0
Aids: Bl: 0-0 Vi: 0-0 Tstrap: 0-0
Best Rating: 129 11/01 Asct 2m110y good Hdl

A useful middle-distance performer on the Flat, he showed a nice turn of foot on his hurdles debut at Huntingdon in March 2001 when he rather surprised connections by beating stable-mate Fait Le Jojo. Fair effort in a bog at Aintree when raised in class. Made a good return at Ascot in November 2001 when second.

Under The Thumb

101(105h) (85h)104
8-y-o b g Sunley Builds-Solhoon (Tycoon Ii)
C P Morlock The Two Gingas

Placings:000/04365/01F10-53P32500 **(4872)**
2001/02: 17^{5}G, 16^{3}GF, 20^{P}GF, 16^{3}G, 20^{2}GF, 20^{5}GF, 17^{0}G, 16^{0}GF

	Starts	1st	2nd	3rd	Win & Pl
Hurdles	2	0	1	1	837
Chases	6	0	0	1	416
Career Total	**21**	**2**	**1**	**3**	**7728**

110	11/00	Ludl	2m	E(0-105)HCh	GD	£3406
111	5/00	Worc	2m	F(0-110)HCh	G-F	£2499

Total win prize-money £5905

Going: Sf: 0-0 GS: 0-0 Gd: 0-3 GF: - Fm: 0-5
Distance: 2m/2m3: 0-5 2m4-2m7: 0-3 3m+: 0-0
Track: LH: 0-5 RH: 0-3 Tight: 0-1 Gall: 0-1
Aids: Bl: 0-0 Vi: 0-0 Tstrap: 0-0
Best Rating: 111 5/00 Worc 2m gd-fm Ch

Under Wraps (IRE)

86(71h) 103
8-y-o b g In The Wings-Wrapping (Kris)
J J O'Neill G Brown

Placings:400/542122146/11122-0P0 **(2776)**
2001/02: 20^{0}G, 24^{P}S, 25^{0}G

	Starts	1st	2nd	3rd	Win & Pl
Chases	3	0	0	0	
Career Total	**20**	**5**	**5**	**0**	**25062**

130	10/00	Carl	2m4f110y	D Ch	GD	£4557
121	5/00	Prth	3m110y	D(0-120)HHdl	GD	£3464
121	5/00	Towc	2m5f	D(0-125)HHdl	SFT	£3334
101	2/00	Ayr	2m6f	E Hdl	HVY	£2905
121	12/99	Uttx	3m110y	F(0-100)HHdl	SFT	£2379

Total win prize-money £16641

Going: Sf: 0-1 GS: 0-0 Gd: 0-2 GF: - Fm: 0-0
Distance: 2m/2m3: 0-0 2m4-2m7: 0-1 3m+: 0-2
Track: LH: 0-2 RH: 0-0 Tight: 0-0 Gall: 0-0
Aids: Bl: 0-3 Vi: 0-0 Tstrap: 0-0
Best Rating: 139 11/00 Hayd 2m4f heavy Ch

He was progressing well over fences but sprung a ligament in a hind leg in November 2000. Reported to have made a full recovery, he was disappointing on his return. Stays beyond three miles and is suited by easy ground.

Underley Park (IRE)

8-y-o ch g Aristocracy-Even Bunny VII (Damsire Unregistered)
F P Murtagh (R Ford 30/5) Kirkby Lonsdale Racing

Placings:650/56/U-PPP **(3439)**
2001/02: 27^{P}S, 24^{P}S, 27^{P}HY

	Starts	1st	2nd	3rd	Win & Pl
Hurdles	2	0	0	0	0
Chases	1	0	0	0	0
Career Total	**9**	**0**	**0**	**0**	**0**

Going: Sf: 0-3 GS: 0-0 Gd: 0-0 GF: - Fm: 0-0
Distance: 2m/2m3: 0-0 2m4-2m7: 0-0 3m+: 0-3
Track: LH: 0-3 RH: 0-0 Tight: 0-2 Gall: 0-0
Aids: Bl: 0-0 Vi: 0-0 Tstrap: 0-0
Best Rating: 95 3/99 Hexm 2m gd-sft NHF

Uneven Line

87 56
6-y-o b m Jurado (USA)-Altovise (Black Minstrel)
Miss S E Forster C Storey (should Be Fun Syndicate)

Placings:00 **(1465)**
2001/02: 22^{0}GS, 20^{0}G

	Starts	1st	2nd	3rd	Win & Pl
Hurdles	2	0	0	0	
Career Total	**2**	**0**	**0**	**0**	

Going: Sf: 0-0 GS: 0-1 Gd: 0-1 GF: - Fm: 0-0
Distance: 2m/2m3: 0-0 2m4-2m7: 0-2 3m+: 0-0
Track: LH: 0-1 RH: 0-1 Tight: 0-1 Gall: 0-0
Aids: Bl: 0-0 Vi: 0-0 Tstrap: 0-0
Best Rating: 56 9/01 Prth 2m4f110y good Hdl

Unforgotten Star (IRE)

62
9-y-o b g Don't Forget Me-Murroe Star (Glenstal (USA))

Mrs V C Ward (F Flood 4/5) Mrs V C Ward

Placings:6032/*3*106031/0056F361P3/20520-0P0 **(1677)**

2001/02: 25^{0}GY, 26^{P}GS, 27^{0}G

	Starts	1st	2nd	3rd	Win & Pl
Chases	3	0	0	0	
Career Total	**29**	**3**	**3**	**5**	**17932**

92 3/00 DRoy 2m4f (0-109)HCh G-Y £4140
107 4/99 Clon 2m4f Hdl HVY £2455
101 11/98 Navn 2m NHF SH £3586
Total win prize-money £10182

Going: Sf: 0-0 GS: 0-1 Gd: 0-1 GF: - Fm: 0-0
Distance: 2m/2m3: 0-0 2m4-2m7: 0-0 3m+: 0-3
Track: LH: 0-2 RH: 0-0 Tight: 0-1 Gall: 0-0
Aids: Bl: 0-0 Vi: 0-0 Tstrap: 0-1
Best Rating: **107** 4/99 Clon 2m4f heavy Hdl

Ungaretti (GER)

100 **105**

5-y-o b g Law Society (USA)-Urena (GER) (Dschingis Khan)
Ian Williams Pel Project Management

Placings:30-3032120 **(4164)**

2001/02: 20^{3}G, 20^{0}G, 19^{3}G, 21^{2}GS, 20^{1}S, 21^{2}HY, 21^{0}GS

	Starts	1st	2nd	3rd	Win & Pl
Hurdles	7	1	2	2	4299
Career Total	**9**	**1**	**2**	**3**	**4675**

105 2/02 Hntg 2m4f110y F(0-100)HHdl SFT £2018
Total win prize-money £2019

Going: Sf: 1-2 GS: 0-2 Gd: 0-3 GF: - Fm: 0-0
Distance: 2m/2m3: 0-1 **2m4-2m7: 1-6** 3m+: 0-0
Track: LH: 0-1 **RH: 1-4** Tight: 0-0 **Gall: 1-3**
Aids: Bl: 0-0 Vi: 0-0 **Tstrap: 1-3**
Best Rating: **105** 2/02 Hntg 2m4f110y soft Hdl

A winner on the Flat in Germany, and has taken time to get his act together over hurdles. Seems best suited by distances around two and a half miles on good to soft ground.

Unicorn Star (IRE)

5-y-o b g Persian Bold-Highland Warning (Warning)
J S Wainwright Ms Julie French

Placings:P **(1748)**

2001/02: 19^{P}G

	Starts	1st	2nd	3rd	Win & Pl
Hurdles	1	0	0	0	
Career Total	**1**	**0**	**0**	**0**	

Going: Sf: 0-0 GS: 0-0 Gd: 0-1 GF: - Fm: 0-0
Distance: 2m/2m3: 0-0 2m4-2m7: 0-1 3m+: 0-0
Track: LH: 0-0 RH: 0-1 Tight: 0-1 Gall: 0-0
Aids: Bl: 0-0 Vi: 0-0 Tstrap: 0-0
Best Rating:

Union Man

9-y-o ch g Teamster-Cobusino (Bustino)
Miss H C Knight Philip Newton

Placings:*0*/1-P **(3875)**

2001/02: 24^{P}GS

	Starts	1st	2nd	3rd	Win & Pl
Chases	1	0	0	0	
Career Total	**3**	**1**	**0**	**0**	**3010**

121 2/01 Kemp 3m H Ch GD £3010
Total win prize-money £3010

Going: Sf: 0-0 GS: 0-1 Gd: 0-0 GF: - Fm: 0-0
Distance: 2m/2m3: 0-0 2m4-2m7: 0-0 3m+: 0-1
Track: LH: 0-0 RH: 0-1 Tight: 0-0 Gall: 0-1
Aids: Bl: 0-0 Vi: 0-0 Tstrap: 0-0
Best Rating: **121** 2/01 Kemp 3m good Ch

Union Town (IRE)

8-y-o b g Generous (IRE)-Exclusive Life (USA) (Exclusive Native (USA))
V Thompson V Thompson

Placings:5F/23162300550/06/P **(4097)**

2001/02: 25^{P}GS

	Starts	1st	2nd	3rd	Win & Pl
Chases	1	0	0	0	
Career Total	**16**	**1**	**2**	**2**	**5449**

101 7/98 Klny 2m1f Hdl G-Y £2989
Total win prize-money £2989

Going: Sf: 0-0 GS: 0-1 Gd: 0-0 GF: - Fm: 0-0
Distance: 2m/2m3: 0-0 2m4-2m7: 0-0 3m+: 0-1
Track: LH: 0-0 RH: 0-0 Tight: 0-0 Gall: 0-0
Aids: Bl: 0-0 Vi: 0-0 Tstrap: 0-0
Best Rating: **116** 8/98 Tral 2m good Hdl

Union Wood (IRE)

106 (111h)**124**

9-y-o ch g Un Desperado (FR)-Miss Leone (Milford)
A J Martin A B C D Syndicate

Placings:*03/43*1234**F0**/003F2P305-42310 **(2088a)**

2001/02: 16^{4}G, 17^{2}GF, 17^{3}GF, 16^{1}G, 16^{0}Y

	Starts	1st	2nd	3rd	Win & Pl
Hurdles	3	0	1	1	1450
Chases	2	1	0	0	4810
Career Total	**24**	**2**	**3**	**6**	**11283**

124 9/01 Prth 2m D Ch GD £4810
80 9/99 Dpat 2m1f87y NHF GD £2002
Total win prize-money £6812

Going: Sf: 0-0 GS: 0-0 Gd: 1-2 GF: - Fm: 0-2
Distance: **2m/2m3: 1-5** 2m4-2m7: 0-0 3m+: 0-0
Track: LH: 0-0 **RH: 1-2** Tight: 0-0 Gall: 0-0
Aids: Bl: 0-0 Vi: 0-0 **Tstrap: 1-5**
Best Rating: **124** 9/01 Prth 2m good Ch

Unlimited Free (IRE)

97(104h) (84h)**119**

8-y-o ch g Ile De Chypre-Merry Madness (Raise You Ten)
O Sherwood B T Stewart-Brown

Placings:*0365*-502125P23 **(4753)**

2001/02: 24^{5}G, 24^{0}G, 24^{2}G, 23^{1}G, 24^{2}S, 24^{5}GS, 32^{P}GS, 25^{2}G, 26^{3}GF

	Starts	1st	2nd	3rd	Win & Pl
Hurdles	1	0	0	0	0
Chases	8	1	3	1	10322
Career Total	**13**	**1**	**3**	**2**	**10727**

119 1/02 Leic 2m7f110y D(0-110)HCh GD £5882
Total win prize-money £5883

Going: Sf: 0-1 GS: 0-2 Gd: 1-5 GF: - Fm: 0-1
Distance: 2m/2m3: 0-0 2m4-2m7: 0-0 **3m+: 1-9**
Track: LH: 0-5 **RH: 1-4** Tight: 0-2 Gall: 0-3
Aids: Bl: 0-0 Vi: 0-0 Tstrap: 0-0
Best Rating: **119** 1/02 Donc 3m soft Ch

Lightly raced gelding, built for chasing. Modest form over hurdles. Has appeared to be in the grip of the Handicapper after winning a three-mile novices handicap chase at Leicester in January 2002. Acts on good and soft ground.

Unmasked

87 **66**

6-y-o ch m Safawan-Unveiled (Sayf El Arab (USA))
A Scott R McClelland

Placings:000 **(3347)**

2001/02: 16^{0}S, 16^{0}S, 16^{0}G

	Starts	1st	2nd	3rd	Win & Pl
Hurdles	3	0	0	0	
Career Total	**3**	**0**	**0**	**0**	

Going: Sf: 0-2 GS: 0-0 Gd: 0-1 GF: - Fm: 0-0
Distance: 2m/2m3: 0-3 2m4-2m7: 0-0 3m+: 0-0
Track: LH: 0-2 RH: 0-1 Tight: 0-1 Gall: 0-1
Aids: Bl: 0-0 Vi: 0-0 Tstrap: 0-0
Best Rating: **66** 1/02 Newc 2m soft Hdl

Unveil

69 **28**

4-y-o b f Rudimentary (USA)-Magical Veil (Majestic Light (USA))
G M McCourt Graham McCourt

Placings:0 **(1231)**

2001/02: 16^{0}GF

	Starts	1st	2nd	3rd	Win & Pl
Hurdles	1	0	0	0	
Career Total	**1**	**0**	**0**	**0**	

Going: Sf: 0-0 GS: 0-0 Gd: 0-0 GF: - Fm: 0-1
Distance: 2m/2m3: 0-1 2m4-2m7: 0-0 3m+: 0-0
Track: LH: 0-1 RH: 0-0 Tight: 0-0 Gall: 0-0
Aids: Bl: 0-0 Vi: 0-0 Tstrap: 0-0
Best Rating: **28** 8/01 Uttx 2m gd-fm Hdl

Up And Over (IRE)

98(76h) (15h)**106**

11-y-o b g Henbit (USA)-Tell-Em-All (Le Bavard (FR))
C J Hemsley (M W Easterby 31/7) W E Dudley

Placings:5F4F6320/00/435PP0P **(1886)**

2001/02: 25^{4}G, 24^{3}GF, 25^{5}G, 24^{P}GF, 26^{P}GF, 24^{0}GF, 21^{P}G

	Starts	1st	2nd	3rd	Win & Pl
Hurdles	2	0	0	0	0
Chases	5	0	0	1	442
Career Total	**17**	**0**	**1**	**2**	**2011**

Going: Sf: 0-0 GS: 0-0 Gd: 0-3 GF: - Fm: 0-4
Distance: 2m/2m3: 0-0 2m4-2m7: 0-1 3m+: 0-6
Track: LH: 0-7 RH: 0-0 Tight: 0-1 Gall: 0-2
Aids: Bl: 0-2 Vi: 0-0 Tstrap: 0-3
Best Rating: **106** 5/01 Weth 3m1f good Ch

Up For Ransome (IRE)

13-y-o b g Boyne Valley-Fauvette (USA) (Youth (USA))
Mrs A M Naughton Mrs C T Woodley

Placings:0/0000/006/0/0543F22/5U03330/224/4-P (0340)
2001/02: $25^{P}G$

	Starts	1st	2nd	3rd	Win & Pl
Chases	1	0	0	0	
Career Total	**28**	**0**	**4**	**4**	**5374**

Going: Sf: 0-0 GS: 0-0 Gd: 0-1 GF: - Fm: 0-0
Distance: 2m/2m3: 0-0 2m4-2m7: 0-0 3m+: 0-1
Track: LH: 0-1 RH: 0-0 Tight: 0-1 Gall: 0-0
Aids: Bl: 0-0 Vi: 0-0 Tstrap: 0-1
Best Rating: 103 4/97 Hexm 3m1f firm Ch

Up The Clarets (IRE)

100 82
7-y-o b g Petardia-Madeira Lady (On Your Mark)
D McCain (E J Alston 24/10) Valley Paddocks Racing Limited

Placings:U41515/554404500/6520 (4917)
2001/02: $16^{6}S$, $17^{5}S$, $16^{2}GF$, $21^{0}GF$

	Starts	1st	2nd	3rd	Win & Pl
Hurdles	4	0	1	0	792
Career Total	**19**	**2**	**1**	**0**	**6646**

114	10/98	Hexm	2m	E Hdl	G-S	£2385
106	9/98	Bang	2m1f	D Hdl	GD	£2840

Total win prize-money £5225

Going: Sf: 0-2 GS: 0-0 Gd: 0-0 GF: - Fm: 0-2
Distance: 2m/2m3: 0-3 2m4-2m7: 0-1 3m+: 0-0
Track: LH: 0-3 RH: 0-0 Tight: 0-2 Gall: 0-0
Aids: Bl: 0-1 Vi: 0-0 Tstrap: 0-0
Best Rating: 114 10/98 Hexm 2m gd-sft Hdl

Lightly-raced handicap hurdler, best at around the minimum trip on a sound surface.

Up The Glen (IRE)

95 79
8-y-o b g Tale Quale-Etrenne (Happy New Year)
R T Phillips Jock Strap Partners

Placings:16664P-5P (2546)
2001/02: $19^{5}G$, $19^{P}GS$

	Starts	1st	2nd	3rd	Win & Pl
Hurdles	2	0	0	0	0
Career Total	**8**	**1**	**0**	**0**	**1659**

104	11/00	Wwck	2m	H NHF	HVY	£1659

Total win prize-money £1659

Going: Sf: 0-0 GS: 0-1 Gd: 0-1 GF: - Fm: 0-0
Distance: 2m/2m3: 0-2 2m4-2m7: 0-0 3m+: 0-0
Track: LH: 0-1 RH: 0-1 Tight: 0-0 Gall: 0-0
Aids: Bl: 0-0 Vi: 0-0 Tstrap: 0-0
Best Rating: 104 11/00 Wwck 2m heavy NHF

Up The Kyber

86 72
5-y-o b g Missed Flight-Najariya (Northfields (USA))
A Crook The Adbrokes Partnership

Placings:30 (2671)
2001/02: $16^{3}GF$, $16^{0}G$

	Starts	1st	2nd	3rd	Win & Pl
Hurdles	2	0	0	1	429
Career Total	**2**	**0**	**0**	**1**	**429**

Going: Sf: 0-0 GS: 0-0 Gd: 0-1 GF: - Fm: 0-1
Distance: 2m/2m3: 0-2 2m4-2m7: 0-0 3m+: 0-0
Track: LH: 0-1 RH: 0-1 Tight: 0-0 Gall: 0-1
Aids: Bl: 0-0 Vi: 0-0 Tstrap: 0-0
Best Rating: 72 6/01 Prth 2m110y gd-fm Hdl

Up The Slaney (IRE)

93 78
10-y-o b m Over The River (FR)-Twice As Fluffy (Pollerton)
B G Powell R B Felmingham

Placings:35/3P/4-443 (0378)
2001/02: $26^{4}GS$, $21^{4}GF$, $24^{3}GF$

	Starts	1st	2nd	3rd	Win & Pl
Chases	3	0	0	1	1053
Career Total	**8**	**0**	**0**	**3**	**1766**

Going: Sf: 0-0 GS: 0-1 Gd: 0-0 GF: - Fm: 0-2
Distance: 2m/2m3: 0-0 2m4-2m7: 0-1 3m+: 0-2
Track: LH: 0-0 RH: 0-2 Tight: 0-0 Gall: 0-1
Aids: Bl: 0-0 Vi: 0-0 Tstrap: 0-0
Best Rating: 84 2/98 Winc 2m6f good Hdl

Up Your Street

106 93
7-y-o b m Petoski-Air Streak (Air Trooper)
J Neville F J Ayres

Placings:5S0-2006PUP22 (4686)
2001/02: $20^{2}G$, $20^{0}GF$, $19^{0}GF$, $24^{6}GF$, $26^{P}S$, $22^{U}S$, $19^{P}S$, $24^{2}G$, $26^{2}GF$

	Starts	1st	2nd	3rd	Win & Pl
Hurdles	9	0	3	0	2452
Career Total	**12**	**0**	**3**	**0**	**2452**

Going: Sf: 0-3 GS: 0-0 Gd: 0-2 GF: - Fm: 0-4
Distance: 2m/2m3: 0-1 2m4-2m7: 0-4 3m+: 0-4
Track: LH: 0-6 RH: 0-3 Tight: 0-4 Gall: 0-0
Aids: Bl: 0-0 Vi: 0-0 Tstrap: 0-0
Best Rating: 93 6/01 Worc 2m4f good Hdl

Returned to form when narrowly denied under a low weight at Uttoxeter and Hereford in April 2002.

Upgrade

113 168
8-y-o b g Be My Guest (USA)-Cantanta (Top Ville)
M C Pipe Matt Archer & Miss Jean Broadhurst

Placings:P15111P/3F0F30/26F126F1/210-6531251 (4759)
2001/02: $24^{6}G$, $19^{5}G$, $21^{3}GS$, $21^{1}S$, $25^{2}GS$, $20^{5}G$, $19^{1}GF$

	Starts	1st	2nd	3rd	Win & Pl
Chases	7	2	1	1	45339
Career Total	**31**	**9**	**4**	**3**	**199275**

168	4/02	Asct	2m3f110y	B HCh	G-F	£24900
168	2/02	Winc	2m5f	B Ch	SFT	£10188
168	11/00	Asct	2m3f110y	A HCh	SFT	£30000
164	4/00	Chel	2m5f	A Ch	SFT	£21000
168	2/00	Sand	2m4f110y	A Ch	GD	£24000
147	3/98	Chel	2m1f	A Hdl	GD	£43460
127	2/98	Sand	2m110y	D Hdl	GD	£2853
140	2/98	Wwck	2m	E Hdl	GD	£2827
133	12/97	Kemp	2m	B Hdl	SFT	£5288

Total win prize-money £164519

Going: Sf: 1-1 GS: 0-2 Gd: 0-3 GF: - Fm: 1-1
Distance: 2m/2m3: 0-0 **2m4-2m7: 2-5** 3m+: 0-2
Track: LH: 0-1 **RH: 2-6** Tight: 0-1 Gall: 0-0
Aids: Bl: 0-0 Vi: 0-0 Tstrap: 0-0
Best Rating: 168 4/02 Asct 2m3f110y gd-fm Ch

A high-class chaser but a lazy type, suited by forcing tactics, he won the First National Gold Cup at Ascot in 2000. Reluctant to start at Wincanton in January 2002, but won back over course and distance the following month and at Ascot in April. Best at around two and a half miles and acts on soft ground.

Upham Lord (IRE)

94 120
9-y-o b g Lord Americo-Top O The Mall (Don)
P Beaumont Mrs E W Wilson

Placings:3/3242/51F40104F1/4-3 (0208)
2001/02: $24^{3}F$

	Starts	1st	2nd	3rd	Win & Pl
Chases	1	0	0	1	586
Career Total	**17**	**3**	**2**	**3**	**17569**

120	4/00	Chep	2m4f	E Hdl	HVY	£2716
120	2/00	Sand	2m4f110y	D(0-120)HHdl	SFT	£5369
127	11/99	Newb	3m	D(0-120)HCh	G-F	£5670

Total win prize-money £10750

Going: Sf: 0-0 GS: 0-0 Gd: 0-0 GF: - Fm: 0-1
Distance: 2m/2m3: 0-0 2m4-2m7: 0-0 3m+: 0-1
Track: LH: 0-1 RH: 0-0 Tight: 0-1 Gall: 0-0
Aids: Bl: 0-0 Vi: 0-0 Tstrap: 0-0
Best Rating: 127 11/99 Newb 3m gd-fm Ch

Urban Hymn (IRE)

101 114
6-y-o ch g College Chapel-Soltura (IRE) (Sadler's Wells (USA))
Ferdy Murphy D A Johnson

Placings:140/5P-3053 (1903)
2001/02: $16^{3}GF$, $16^{0}GF$, $20^{5}G$, $21^{3}G$

	Starts	1st	2nd	3rd	Win & Pl
Hurdles	4	0	0	2	983
Career Total	**9**	**1**	**0**	**2**	**5728**

103	2/00	Sand	2m110y	D Hdl	G-S	£4329

Total win prize-money £4329

Going: Sf: 0-0 GS: 0-0 Gd: 0-2 GF: - Fm: 0-2
Distance: 2m/2m3: 0-2 2m4-2m7: 0-2 3m+: 0-0
Track: LH: 0-4 RH: 0-0 Tight: 0-1 Gall: 0-1
Aids: Bl: 0-0 Vi: 0-0 Tstrap: 0-0
Best Rating: 114 5/01 Newc 2m gd-fm Hdl

Fair hurdler, suited by cut in the ground.

Uron V (FR)

16-y-o b g Cap Martin (FR)-Jolivette (FR) (Laniste)
Mrs E M Bousquet-Payne Mrs E M Bousquet-Payne

Placings:20/121P3/33232/4UU11322/11152462P/400/O30/112F2/UP0 (0474)
2001/02: $30^{U}GF$, $31^{P}G$, $22^{0}G$

	Starts	1st	2nd	3rd	Win & Pl
Chases	3	0	0	0	
Career Total	**43**	**9**	**10**	**6**	**35791**

101	5/98	Towc	3m1f	E(0-110)HCh	G-F	£3224
94	5/98	Hrfd	3m1f110y	F(0-105)HCh	GD	£3255
112	6/95	Prth	3m	D(0-120)HCh	GD	£4006
108	5/95	Ctml	3m2f	E Ch	GD	£2762
110	5/95	Prth	3m	E Ch	GD	£3111
109	3/95	Ayr	3m110y	E(0-115)HHdl	HVY	£2626
103	2/95	Nott	3m110y	E(0-110)HHdl	SFT	£2559
113	1/92	Carl	2m4f	Hdl	SFT	£1235
113	11/91	Kels	2m6f	Hdl	G-F	£1856

Total win prize-money £24636

Going: Sf: 0-0 GS: 0-0 Gd: 0-2 GF: - Fm: 0-1
Distance: 2m/2m3: 0-0 2m4-2m7: 0-1 3m+: 0-2
Track: LH: 0-0 RH: 0-3 Tight: 0-2 Gall: 0-1
Aids: Bl: 0-0 Vi: 0-0 Tstrap: 0-0
Best Rating: **118** 12/95 Sedg 3m3f110y good Hdl

Us And Them (IRE)

5-y-o ch m Pips Pride-Tasskeen (FR) (Lyphard (USA))
G A Ham Corey M Gardner

Placings:UP (2924)
2001/02: 17^{U}HY, 17^{P}GS

	Starts	1st	2nd	3rd	Win & Pl
Hurdles	2	0	0	0	
Career Total	**2**	**0**	**0**	**0**	

Going: Sf: 0-1 GS: 0-1 Gd: 0-0 GF: - Fm: 0-0
Distance: 2m/2m3: 0-2 2m4-2m7: 0-0 3m+: 0-0
Track: LH: 0-1 RH: 0-1 Tight: 0-2 Gall: 0-0
Aids: Bl: 0-0 Vi: 0-0 Tstrap: 0-0
Best Rating:

Usk Valley (IRE)

92 **76**

7-y-o b g Tenby-Penultimate (USA) (Roberto (USA))
P R Chamings Peter Oldfield

Placings:*2/20/3*-3P05 (4327)
2001/02: 20^{3}S, 22^{P}S, 24^{0}GS, 19^{5}S

	Starts	1st	2nd	3rd	Win & Pl
Hurdles	4	0	0	1	436
Career Total	**8**	**0**	**2**	**2**	**1745**

Going: Sf: 0-3 GS: 0-1 Gd: 0-0 GF: - Fm: 0-0
Distance: 2m/2m3: 0-0 2m4-2m7: 0-3 3m+: 0-1
Track: LH: 0-1 RH: 0-3 Tight: 0-1 Gall: 0-1
Aids: Bl: 0-0 Vi: 0-0 Tstrap: 0-0
Best Rating: **109** 2/00 Sand 2m110y soft NHF

He has shown ability in bumpers and over hurdles, but his runs have been well spread out and he is still very lightly raced.

Uther Pendragon (IRE)

82 **55**

7-y-o b g Petardia-Mountain Stage (IRE) (Pennine Walk)
M Bradstock Miss J C Blackwell

Placings:0-0060P (1228)
2001/02: 16^{0}GF, 16^{0}GF, 16^{6}G, 16^{0}GF, 16^{P}GF

	Starts	1st	2nd	3rd	Win & Pl
Hurdles	5	0	0	0	0
Career Total	**6**	**0**	**0**	**0**	**0**

Going: Sf: 0-0 GS: 0-0 Gd: 0-1 GF: - Fm: 0-4
Distance: 2m/2m3: 0-5 2m4-2m7: 0-0 3m+: 0-0
Track: LH: 0-5 RH: 0-0 Tight: 0-1 Gall: 0-0
Aids: Bl: 0-0 Vi: 0-0 Tstrap: 0-0
Best Rating: **55** 6/01 Worc 2m gd-fm Hdl

Vague Hope (IRE)

10-y-o b g Strong Gale-Misty's Wish (Furry Glen)
Mrs A L M King Mrs A L M King

Placings:*2/0464U224P0/064*-0 (1135)
2001/02: 20^{0}GF

	Starts	1st	2nd	3rd	Win & Pl
Hurdles	1	0	0	0	
Career Total	**15**	**0**	**3**	**0**	**2538**

Going: Sf: 0-0 GS: 0-0 Gd: 0-0 GF: - Fm: 0-1
Distance: 2m/2m3: 0-0 2m4-2m7: 0-1 3m+: 0-0
Track: LH: 0-1 RH: 0-0 Tight: 0-0 Gall: 0-0
Aids: Bl: 0-0 Vi: 0-0 Tstrap: 0-0
Best Rating: **104** 5/97 NAbb 2m1f gd-fm NHF

Vague Idea

92 **102**

9-y-o gr g Tout Ensemble-Roodle Doodle (Rugantino)
O J Carter O J Carter

Placings:P6RP-P30 (4678)
2001/02: 21^{P}GF, 23^{3}S, 25^{0}G

	Starts	1st	2nd	3rd	Win & Pl
Chases	3	0	0	1	329
Career Total	**7**	**0**	**0**	**1**	**329**

Going: Sf: 0-1 GS: 0-0 Gd: 0-1 GF: - Fm: 0-1
Distance: 2m/2m3: 0-0 2m4-2m7: 0-1 3m+: 0-2
Track: LH: 0-1 RH: 0-2 Tight: 0-1 Gall: 0-0
Aids: Bl: 0-0 Vi: 0-0 Tstrap: 0-0
Best Rating: **88** 3/02 Leic 2m7f110y soft Ch

A bit of a character, he was a fortunate winner at Hereford in May 2002. Acts on a sound surface.

Vaguely Blazing

5-y-o b g Blaze O'Gold (USA)-Vaguely Fair (Royal And Regal (USA))
Mrs L B Normile Dr Julie Farrar

Placings:*00* (4526)
2001/02: 16^{0}GS, 17^{0}G

	Starts	1st	2nd	3rd	Win & Pl
NH Flat	2	0	0	0	
Career Total	**2**	**0**	**0**	**0**	

Going: Sf: 0-0 GS: 0-1 Gd: 0-1 GF: - Fm: 0-0
Distance: 2m/2m3: 0-2 2m4-2m7: 0-0 3m+: 0-0
Track: LH: 0-1 RH: 0-1 Tight: 0-0 Gall: 0-0
Aids: Bl: 0-0 Vi: 0-0 Tstrap: 0-0
Best Rating:

Vale Of Leven (IRE)

6-y-o b g Fayruz-Speedy Action (Horage)
R Williams R Williams

Placings:PU-0P (0725)
2001/02: 20^{0}GF, 17^{P}F

	Starts	1st	2nd	3rd	Win & Pl
Hurdles	2	0	0	0	
Career Total	**4**	**0**	**0**	**0**	

Going: Sf: 0-0 GS: 0-0 Gd: 0-0 GF: - Fm: 0-2
Distance: 2m/2m3: 0-1 2m4-2m7: 0-1 3m+: 0-0
Track: LH: 0-0 RH: 0-2 Tight: 0-0 Gall: 0-1
Aids: Bl: 0-0 Vi: 0-0 Tstrap: 0-0
Best Rating:

Valentines Vision

61 **18**

5-y-o b g Distinctly North (USA)-Sharp Anne (Belfort (FR))
Mrs S Lamyman P Lamyman & N Underwood

Placings:0 (2399)
2001/02: 16^{0}G

	Starts	1st	2nd	3rd	Win & Pl
Hurdles	1	0	0	0	
Career Total	**1**	**0**	**0**	**0**	

Going: Sf: 0-0 GS: 0-0 Gd: 0-1 GF: - Fm: 0-0
Distance: 2m/2m3: 0-1 2m4-2m7: 0-0 3m+: 0-0
Track: LH: 0-1 RH: 0-0 Tight: 0-0 Gall: 0-0
Aids: Bl: 0-0 Vi: 0-0 Tstrap: 0-0
Best Rating: **18** 11/01 Weth 2m good Hdl

Valerio

110 **129**

6-y-o b g Be My Native (USA)-Laurello (Bargello)
N J Henderson Nicholas Cooper

Placings:*1*-2210 (4154)
2001/02: 16^{2}G, 18^{2}G, 19^{1}GS, 20^{0}GS

	Starts	1st	2nd	3rd	Win & Pl
Hurdles	4	1	2	0	5932
Career Total	**5**	**2**	**2**	**0**	**7661**

115	2/02	MRas	2m3f110y	D Hdl	G-S	£3640
106	2/01	Winc	2m	H NHF	GD	£1729

Total win prize-money £5369

Going: Sf: 0-0 GS: 1-2 Gd: 0-2 GF: - Fm: 0-0
Distance: 2m/2m3: 0-2 **2m4-2m7: 1-2** 3m+: 0-0
Track: LH: 0-1 **RH: 1-3 Tight: 1-2** Gall: 0-0
Aids: Bl: 0-0 Vi: 0-0 Tstrap: 0-0
Best Rating: **129** 11/01 Asct 2m110y good Hdl

Won his only bumper start and shaped well in decent races prior to winning at Market Rasen in February 2002. Stays two and a half miles. Acts on soft ground. A potential chaser.

Valeureux

102 **107**

4-y-o ch g Cadeaux Genereux-La Strada (Niniski (USA))
J Hetherton Eureka Racing

Placings:620 (4250)
2001/02: 16^{6}S, 17^{2}GS, 17^{0}G

	Starts	1st	2nd	3rd	Win & Pl
Hurdles	3	0	1	0	790
Career Total	**3**	**0**	**1**	**0**	**790**

Going: Sf: 0-1 GS: 0-1 Gd: 0-1 GF: - Fm: 0-0
Distance: 2m/2m3: 0-3 2m4-2m7: 0-0 3m+: 0-0
Track: LH: 0-1 RH: 0-2 Tight: 0-2 Gall: 0-1
Aids: Bl: 0-0 Vi: 0-0 Tstrap: 0-0
Best Rating: **107** 3/02 MRas 2m1f110y gd-sft Hdl

Valfonic

101 111

4-y-o b g Zafonic (USA)-Valbra (Dancing Brave (USA))
M C Pipe (Mrs A J Perrett 8/10) Done It Again

Placings:60U1 **(4601)**
2001/02: 16^{6}S, 16^{0}HY, 16^{U}HY, 16^{1}GF

	Starts	1st	2nd	3rd	Win & Pl
Hurdles	4	1	0	0	2986
Career Total	**4**	**1**	**0**	**0**	**2986**

89	4/02	Wwck	2m	F(0-95)HHdl	G-F	£2985

Total win prize-money £2986

Going: Sf: 0-3 GS: 0-0 Gd: 0-0 GF: - Fm: 1-1
Distance: **2m/2m3: 1-4** 2m4-2m7: 0-0 3m+: 0-0
Track: **LH: 1-4** RH: 0-0 Tight: 0-2 Gall: 0-0
Aids: Bl: 0-0 Vi: 0-0 **Tstrap: 1-1**
Best Rating: 89 4/02 Wwck 2m gd-fm Hdl

Modest hurdler, won on his handicap debut at Warwick in April when encountering fast ground and being fitted with a tongue tie, and followed up next time at Southwell. Showed signs of temperament when overcoming an attempt to head for the paddock at the final flight when completing a hat-trick at Worcester. Disappointing when tried in a visor, may now be in the Handicapper's grip.

Valhalla (IRE)

97 83

9-y-o b g Bush Acido (USA)-Fimore Pot (Daddy's Stream)
R F Fisher Mrs D Miller

Placings:3/16/5FP0/**44F4**/3-6F03 **(4486)**
2001/02: 17^{6}G, 17^{F}G, 20^{0}G, 17^{3}GS

	Starts	1st	2nd	3rd	Win & Pl
Hurdles	4	0	0	1	442
Career Total	**16**	**1**	**0**	**3**	**3554**

101	5/97	Uttx	2m	H NHF	GD	£1609

Total win prize-money £1609

Going: Sf: 0-0 GS: 0-1 Gd: 0-3 GF: - Fm: 0-0
Distance: 2m/2m3: 0-3 2m4-2m7: 0-1 3m+: 0-0
Track: LH: 0-2 RH: 0-2 Tight: 0-3 Gall: 0-0
Aids: Bl: 0-0 Vi: 0-0 Tstrap: 0-0
Best Rating: 101 5/97 Uttx 2m good NHF

Modest handicap hurdler at two/two and a half miles. Not a natural jumper of fences. Acts on a sound surface.

Valiant Warrior

14-y-o br g Valiyar-Jouvencelle (Rusticaro (FR))
Jedd O'Keeffe Paul Sellars

Placings:364400/166/1121/3211221/22511/25530/43 36R41/52F/P402-P **(0277)**
2001/02: 26^{P}GF

	Starts	1st	2nd	3rd	Win & Pl
Chases	1	0	0	0	
Career Total	**45**	**10**	**9**	**5**	**65967**

124	3/98	Newc	3m	D(0-125)HCh	GD	£3473
138	3/96	Donc	2m3f110y	C(0-130)HCh	GD	£7100
133	2/96	Newc	2m4f	B(0-140)HCh	G-S	£10942
127	3/95	Fknm	2m5f110y	D(0-120)HCh	G-S	£4699
116	1/95	Catt	2m3f	D(0-120)HCh	SFT	£3557
118	12/94	Newc	2m4f	(0-115)HCh	GD	£3192
105	11/93	Hayd	2m4f	HCh	GD	£3322
90	9/93	Bang	2m4f110y	Ch	GD	£2762
91	8/93	Prth	2m4f110y	Ch	G-F	£2671
102	10/92	Weth	2m4f110y	Hdl	G-F	£1952

Total win prize-money £43676

Going: Sf: 0-0 GS: 0-0 Gd: 0-0 GF: - Fm: 0-1
Distance: 2m/2m3: 0-0 2m4-2m7: 0-0 3m+: 0-1
Track: LH: 0-0 RH: 0-0 Tight: 0-0 Gall: 0-0
Aids: Bl: 0-0 Vi: 0-0 Tstrap: 0-0
Best Rating: 138 3/96 Donc 2m3f110y good Ch

Valigan (IRE)

115 140

9-y-o gr g Roselier (FR)-Wonderful Lilly (Prince Hansel)
L Lungo Ronald Thorburn/andrew W B Duncan

Placings:6/310231/641150/42F1-241004 **(4870)**
2001/02: 25^{2}GS, 25^{4}GS, 24^{1}GF, 24^{0}S, 24^{0}GS, 23^{4}GF

	Starts	1st	2nd	3rd	Win & Pl
Chases	6	1	1	0	6365
Career Total	**23**	**6**	**3**	**2**	**28164**

140	12/01	Muss	3m	D(0-120)HCh	G-F	£4134
118	2/01	Sedg	3m3f	D Ch	SFT	£4010
127	12/99	Muss	3m	D(0-125)HHdl	G-S	£5498
135	12/99	Hexm	3m	F(0-105)HHdl	HVY	£2343
120	3/99	Ayr	3m110y	D(0-115)HHdl	SFT	£3574
106	11/98	Sedg	3m3f110y	E Hdl	G-S	£2302

Total win prize-money £21864

Going: Sf: 0-1 GS: 0-3 Gd: 0-0 GF: - Fm: 1-2
Distance: 2m/2m3: 0-0 2m4-2m7: 0-0 **3m+: 1-6**
Track: LH: 0-4 **RH: 1-1 Tight: 1-2** Gall: 0-2
Aids: Bl: 0-0 Vi: 0-1 Tstrap: 0-0
Best Rating: 140 12/01 Muss 3m gd-fm Ch

Decent chaser, proved he acts on a sounder surface when conceding two stone to his rivals to romp home in a three-mile chase at Musselburgh but disappointing since including when tried in a visor.

Valignani (IRE)

94 114

10-y-o b g Law Society (USA)-When Lit (Northfields (USA))
M C Pipe (T Civel 27/5) Codan Trust Company Limited

Placings:1/111/4212P2P/112FB23302/2F011325054 F135-0UPRP500 **(4193)**
2001/02: 21^{0}S, 16^{U}G, 21^{P}G, 20^{R}GF, 21^{P}GF, 20^{5}G, 25^{0}S, 25^{0}GS

	Starts	1st	2nd	3rd	Win & Pl
Hurdles	4	0	0	0	0
Chases	4	0	0	0	0
Career Total	**44**	**10**	**8**	**4**	**166807**

	4/01	Comp	2m4f	Hdl	HVY	£6790
	8/00	Claf	2m1f	Hdl	SFT	£6244
	7/00	Vich	2m3f110y	Hdl	GD	£5283
	6/99	Maia	2m1f110y	Hdl	GD	£3645
	5/99	Maia	2m110y	Hdl	GD	£3281
	8/98	Maia	2m1f110y	Hdl	GD	£7736
	11/97	Turi	2m2f	HHdl	VS	£13500
	8/97	Maia	2m1f110y	Hdl	GD	£7714
	5/97	Siro	2m2f	HHdl	GD	£11571
	11/96	Turi	2m2f	HHdl	G-S	£12180

Total win prize-money £77944

Going: Sf: 0-2 GS: 0-1 Gd: 0-3 GF: - Fm: 0-2
Distance: 2m/2m3: 0-1 2m4-2m7: 0-5 3m+: 0-2
Track: LH: 0-6 RH: 0-0 Tight: 0-3 Gall: 0-1
Aids: Bl: 0-4 Vi: 0-0 Tstrap: 0-0
Best Rating: 114 11/01 Hayd 2m4f good Hdl

Winner over hurdles in France and Italy, not half as good in England, failing to complete on all starts over fences, and reverting to hurdles late in 2001.

Valiramix (FR)

116 170

6-y-o gr g Linamix (FR)-Valira (USA) (Nijinsky (CAN))
M C Pipe Jim Weeden

Placings:1012/1123-1S **(4190)**
2001/02: 16^{1}GS, 16^{S}GS

	Starts	1st	2nd	3rd	Win & Pl
Hurdles	2	1	0	0	18848
Career Total	**10**	**5**	**2**	**1**	**60935**

170	12/01	Newb	2m110y	A Hdl	G-S	£18848
151	12/00	Asct	2m110y	B Hdl	HVY	£8092
157	11/00	Newb	2m110y	C(0-130)HHdl	G-S	£9750
127	4/00	Chep	2m110y	E Hdl	SFT	£2639
129	2/00	Tntn	2m1f	E Hdl	SFT	£2485

Total win prize-money £41815

Going: Sf: 0-0 GS: 1-2 Gd: 0-0 GF: - Fm: 0-0
Distance: **2m/2m3: 1-2** 2m4-2m7: 0-0 3m+: 0-0
Track: **LH: 1-2** RH: 0-0 Tight: 0-0 **Gall: 1-1**
Aids: Bl: 0-0 Vi: 0-0 Tstrap: 0-0
Best Rating: 170 12/01 Newb 2m110y gd-sft Hdl

High-classl hurdler, he won his first two starts of the 2000/01 season at Newbury and Ascot, and lost no caste in defeat when runner-up under 12 stone in desperate conditions in Sandown's Imperial Cup. Ran a cracker when third to Landing Light and Geos in Sandown's consolation Champion Hurdle. Made a winning reappearance at Newbury in December 2001, winning hard held. Travelling like a winner when taking a crashing fall in the 2002 Champion Hurdle, breaking a shoulder.He was well suited by soft ground. (DEAD)

Valjean (IRE)

73 44

6-y-o b g Alzao (USA)-Escape Path (Wolver Hollow)
W M Brisbourne (R J Price 28/12) John Richards

Placings:0-0U **(4752)**
2001/02: 17^{0}GS, 16^{U}GF

	Starts	1st	2nd	3rd	Win & Pl
Hurdles	2	0	0	0	
Career Total	**3**	**0**	**0**	**0**	

Going: Sf: 0-0 GS: 0-1 Gd: 0-0 GF: - Fm: 0-1
Distance: 2m/2m3: 0-2 2m4-2m7: 0-0 3m+: 0-0
Track: LH: 0-1 RH: 0-1 Tight: 0-1 Gall: 0-0
Aids: Bl: 0-0 Vi: 0-0 Tstrap: 0-0
Best Rating: 44 12/01 Tntn 2m1f gd-sft Hdl

Valley Henry (IRE)

118(106h) (88h)168

7-y-o b g Step Together (USA)-Pineway Vii (Damsire Unregistered)
P F Nicholls Paul K Barber

Placings:15/1134-11FU2F11 **(4836)**
2001/02: 19^{1}G, 24^{1}G, 24^{F}G, 20^{U}S, 19^{2}GS, 24^{F}GS, 25^{1}G, 20^{1}G

	Starts	1st	2nd	3rd	Win & Pl
Chases	8	4	1	0	48618
Career Total	**14**	**7**	**1**	**1**	**74410**

168	4/02	Ayr	2m4f	A Ch	GD	£15600
109	3/02	Extr	3m1f110y	D Ch	GD	£5304
159	11/01	Newb	3m	A Ch	GD	£17850
134	10/01	Chep	2m3f110y	C Ch	GD	£6776
140	11/00	Winc	2m6f	C Hdl	SFT	£6286
134	11/00	Chep	2m4f	A Hdl	SFT	£12000
122	3/00	Leop	2m	NHF	Y-S	£3588

Total win prize-money £67404

Going: Sf: 0-1 GS: 0-2 Gd: 4-5 GF: - Fm: 0-0
Distance: 2m/2m3: 0-0 2m4-2m7: 2-4 3m+: 2-4
Track: LH: 3-4 RH: 0-3 Tight: 0-0 Gall: 1-2
Aids: Bl: 0-0 Vi: 0-0 Tstrap: 0-0
Best Rating: 168 4/02 Ayr 2m4f good Ch

Useful chaser, he won in impressive style on his chasing debut at Chepstow in October 2001 and followed up with victory in a Grade Two event at Newbury when stepped up to three miles. He had his jumping problems afterwards, but had a confidence booster in a small chase at Exeter in March and jumped well to win at Ayr. Best on good ground.

Vallingale (IRE)

82 **64**

11-y-o b m Strong Gale-Knockarctic (Quayside)
Miss M Bragg W H Whitley

Placings: 030/532P0/4PP/25123/565-60 (0494)
2001/02: 24^{6}F, 25^{0}G

	Starts	1st	2nd	3rd	Win & Pl
Chases	2	0	0	0	0
Career Total	**21**	**1**	**3**	**3**	**7875**

107 10/99 Extr 2m6f110y D Ch GD £3857
Total win prize-money £3857

Going: Sf: 0-0 GS: 0-0 Gd: 0-1 GF: - Fm: 0-1
Distance: 2m/2m3: 0-0 2m4-2m7: 0-0 3m+: 0-2
Track: LH: 0-0 RH: 0-2 Tight: 0-1 Gall: 0-0
Aids: Bl: 0-0 Vi: 0-0 Tstrap: 0-0
Best Rating: 107 11/99 Winc 3m1f110y good Ch

Vals Castle (IRE)

8-y-o b m Ala Hounak-Church Brae (The Parson)
Jedd O'Keeffe S Clark

Placings: PP (2450)
2001/02: 22^{P}GS, 24^{P}GS

	Starts	1st	2nd	3rd	Win & Pl
Hurdles	2	0	0	0	
Career Total	**2**	**0**	**0**	**0**	

Going: Sf: 0-0 GS: 0-2 Gd: 0-0 GF: - Fm: 0-0
Distance: 2m/2m3: 0-0 2m4-2m7: 0-1 3m+: 0-1
Track: LH: 0-2 RH: 0-0 Tight: 0-0 Gall: 0-1
Aids: Bl: 0-0 Vi: 0-0 Tstrap: 0-0
Best Rating:

Vals Well (IRE)

52 **13**

7-y-o b g Be My Native (USA)-Castle-Lady (Little Buskins)
B J Llewellyn R Mason

Placings: 0 (0674)
2001/02: 16^{0}GF

	Starts	1st	2nd	3rd	Win & Pl
Hurdles	1	0	0	0	
Career Total	**1**	**0**	**0**	**0**	

Going: Sf: 0-0 GS: 0-0 Gd: 0-0 GF: - Fm: 0-1
Distance: 2m/2m3: 0-1 2m4-2m7: 0-0 3m+: 0-0
Track: LH: 0-1 RH: 0-0 Tight: 0-0 Gall: 0-0
Aids: Bl: 0-0 Vi: 0-0 Tstrap: 0-0
Best Rating: 13 6/01 Worc 2m gd-fm Hdl

Vanishing Dancer (SWI)

110 **107**

5-y-o ch g Llandaff (USA)-Vanishing Prairie (USA) (Alysheba (USA))
A Dickman Mike Smallman

Placings: 126004-230430 (3348)
2001/02: 16^{2}G, 20^{3}F, 20^{0}G, 20^{4}G, 20^{3}G, 24^{0}G

	Starts	1st	2nd	3rd	Win & Pl
Hurdles	6	0	1	2	1763
Career Total	**12**	**1**	**2**	**2**	**5640**

105 11/00 Weth 2m D Hdl SFT £3152
Total win prize-money £3153

Going: Sf: 0-0 GS: 0-0 Gd: 0-5 GF: - Fm: 0-1
Distance: 2m/2m3: 0-1 2m4-2m7: 0-4 3m+: 0-1
Track: LH: 0-5 RH: 0-1 Tight: 0-1 Gall: 0-1
Aids: Bl: 0-0 Vi: 0-0 Tstrap: 0-0
Best Rating: 107 5/01 Weth 2m4f110y firm Hdl

He got off the mark on his hurdling debut at Wetherby in November 2000, displaying an ability to handle soft ground in the process. He has not added to that victory, but ran with credit during the spring of 2001.

Varykinov (IRE)

13-y-o b/br g Roselier (FR)-Royal Handful (Some Hand)
Mark G Rimell Mark G Rimell

Placings: 5/34/0P/12/10FB/5-3P (4402)
2001/02: 26^{3}HY, 22^{P}GS

	Starts	1st	2nd	3rd	Win & Pl
Chases	2	0	0	1	190
Career Total	**14**	**2**	**1**	**2**	**9099**

132 2/99 Hayd 3m H Ch SFT £7035
109 4/98 Worc 2m7f110y H Ch G-S £1021
Total win prize-money £8057

Going: Sf: 0-1 GS: 0-1 Gd: 0-0 GF: - Fm: 0-0
Distance: 2m/2m3: 0-0 2m4-2m7: 0-1 3m+: 0-1
Track: LH: 0-2 RH: 0-0 Tight: 0-0 Gall: 0-1
Aids: Bl: 0-2 Vi: 0-0 Tstrap: 0-0
Best Rating: 132 2/99 Hayd 3m soft Ch

Modest hunter chaser these days.

Velcro Girl (IRE)

95(105h) **110**

8-y-o b m Be My Native (USA)-Daddy's Folly (Le Moss)
Miss H C Knight R F Sayer & R G Dear

Placings: 5/F610P-414P (3333)
2001/02: 19^{4}GF, 20^{1}GF, 20^{4}GS, 24^{P}G

	Starts	1st	2nd	3rd	Win & Pl
Chases	4	1	0	0	4788
Career Total	**10**	**2**	**0**	**0**	**8655**

110 11/01 Ludl 2m4f E(0-105)HCh G-F £4065
98 12/00 Ludl 2m5f D Hdl SFT £3867
Total win prize-money £7934

Going: Sf: 0-0 GS: 0-1 Gd: 0-1 GF: - Fm: 1-2
Distance: 2m/2m3: 0-0 2m4-2m7: 1-3 3m+: 0-1
Track: LH: 0-0 RH: 1-4 Tight: 1-2 Gall: 0-1
Aids: Bl: 0-0 Vi: 0-0 Tstrap: 0-0
Best Rating: 110 11/01 Ludl 2m4f gd-fm Ch

Is suited by around two miles four furlongs and acts on most types of ground.

Velmez

102(70c) (45c)**78**

9-y-o ch g Belmez (USA)-Current Raiser (Filiberto (USA))
B J Llewellyn Thomas Leonard

Placings: 6006544P/046050/6F02122-P06P (4316)
2001/02: 26^{P}S, 22^{0}S, 19^{6}S, 24^{P}HY

	Starts	1st	2nd	3rd	Win & Pl
Hurdles	4	0	0	0	0
Career Total	**25**	**1**	**3**	**0**	**8451**

105 6/00 NAbb 2m6f E Hdl G-F £2464
Total win prize-money £2464

Going: Sf: 0-4 GS: 0-0 Gd: 0-0 GF: - Fm: 0-0
Distance: 2m/2m3: 0-0 2m4-2m7: 0-2 3m+: 0-2
Track: LH: 0-1 RH: 0-3 Tight: 0-3 Gall: 0-0
Aids: Bl: 0-4 Vi: 0-0 Tstrap: 0-0
Best Rating: 105 7/00 Worc 3m gd-fm Hdl

Velsheda (IRE)

101 **115**

9-y-o b m Royal Vulcan-Premier Susan (Murrayfield)
C P Morlock Mrs Z S Clark

Placings: 5060/203302/1543-1112 (1090)
2001/02: 19^{1}G, 20^{1}GF, 20^{1}GS, 24^{2}GF

	Starts	1st	2nd	3rd	Win & Pl
Hurdles	4	3	1	0	9453
Career Total	**18**	**4**	**3**	**3**	**14637**

112 7/01 Wolv 2m4f110y F(0-110)HHdl G-S £3385
107 6/01 Worc 2m4f F(0-100)HHdl G-F £2289
96 5/01 Extr 2m3f F(0-100)HHdl GD £2128
98 5/00 Extr 2m1f E Hdl GD £2058
Total win prize-money £9860

Going: Sf: 0-0 GS: 1-1 Gd: 1-1 GF: - Fm: 1-2
Distance: 2m/2m3: 1-1 2m4-2m7: 2-2 3m+: 0-1
Track: LH: 2-3 RH: 1-1 Tight: 1-1 Gall: 0-0
Aids: Bl: 0-0 Vi: 0-0 Tstrap: 0-0
Best Rating: 115 8/01 Worc 3m gd-fm Hdl

Modest handicap hurdler who excels on a sound surface. Best on right-handed tracks and goes well fresh.

Veneguera (IRE)

104(97c) (123c)**106**

9-y-o b g Satco (FR)-Orlita (Master Buck)
K C Bailey The Sporting Has Beens

Placings: 4006P60/5441440412140/4-025362341130464 (4535)
2001/02: 20^{0}G, 22^{2}GF, 24^{5}GF, 23^{3}G, 20^{6}GF, 24^{2}GF, 26^{3}GF, 24^{4}GF, 26^{1}G, 21^{1}GS, 22^{3}G, 21^{0}G, 22^{4}HY, 20^{6}G, 20^{4}G

	Starts	1st	2nd	3rd	Win & Pl
Hurdles	11	2	1	2	9405
Chases	4	0	1	1	1596
Career Total	**36**	**5**	**3**	**3**	**21162**

106 10/01 Kemp 2m5f D(0-125)HHdl G-S £5073
106 10/01 Hntg 3m2f F(0-110)HHdl GD £1862
103 3/00 Dpat 2m4f110y (0-95)HHdl G-F £2345
93 11/99 Dpat 2m6f (0-95)HHdl YLD £2002
81 8/99 Naas 2m4f Hdl G-F £3696
Total win prize-money £14979

Going: Sf: 0-1 GS: 1-1 Gd: 1-7 GF: - Fm: 0-6
Distance: 2m/2m3: 0-0 2m4-2m7: 1-9 3m+: 1-6
Track: LH: 0-8 RH: 2-6 Tight: 0-5 Gall: 1-3
Aids: Bl: 0-3 Vi: 0-0 Tstrap: 0-0
Best Rating: 123 6/01 MRas 2m6f110y gd-fm Ch

An out-and-out stayer, he scored over three and a quarter miles at Huntingdon in October 2001 after having run only 24 hours earlier. Good effort to follow up at Kempton over five furlongs shorter. Suited by decent ground. A little quirky.

Venn Ottery

86(71h) (42h)**80**

7-y-o b g Access Ski-Tom's Comedy (Comedy Star (USA))

O J Carter O J Carter

Placings:P/P-PF **(4675)**

2001/02: 17^{P}GS, 16^{F}G

	Starts	1st	2nd	3rd	Win & Pl
Chases	2	0	0	0	
Career Total	**4**	**0**	**0**	**0**	

Going: Sf: 0-0 GS: 0-1 Gd: 0-1 GF: - Fm: 0-0
Distance: 2m/2m3: 0-2 2m4-2m7: 0-0 3m+: 0-0
Track: LH: 0-1 RH: 0-1 Tight: 0-1 Gall: 0-0
Aids: Bl: 0-0 Vi: 0-0 Tstrap: 0-0
Best Rating:

Headstrong maiden pointer/hunter chaser. Acts on a sound surface.

Vent D'Aout (IRE)

(96h) (119h)

8-y-o ch m Imp Society (USA)-Barncogue (Monseigneur (USA))

M C Pipe Elite Racing Club

Placings:1166/04100P/41222F/5211314FUP-2 **(0238)**

2001/02: 24^{2}GF

	Starts	1st	2nd	3rd	Win & Pl
Hurdles	1	0	1	0	1764
Career Total	**27**	**7**	**5**	**1**	**28970**

132	9/00	Sedg	2m5f	E Ch	GD	£3087
132	8/00	NAbb	2m5f110y	D Ch	GD	£3653
112	7/00	NAbb	2m5f110y	E Ch	G-F	£3435
131	11/99	Wwck	2m	D(0-125)HHdl	GD	£3002
131	1/99	Tntn	2m1f	D(0-120)HHdl	SFT	£2710
123	12/97	Leic	2m	E Hdl	SFT	£2574
124	11/97	Hrfd	2m1f	E Hdl	G-S	£2304

Total win prize-money £20766

Going: Sf: 0-0 GS: 0-0 Gd: 0-0 GF: - Fm: 0-1
Distance: 2m/2m3: 0-0 2m4-2m7: 0-0 3m+: 0-1
Track: LH: 0-1 RH: 0-0 Tight: 0-1 Gall: 0-0
Aids: Bl: 0-0 Vi: 0-1 Tstrap: 0-1
Best Rating: 136 6/00 Worc 2m4f good Hdl

Venture More

75 **66+**

6-y-o br g Green Adventure (USA)-Admire-A-More (Le Coq D'Or)

P Monteith Mrs A F Tullie

Placings:*00* **(4841)**

2001/02: 16^{0}G, 16^{0}G

	Starts	1st	2nd	3rd	Win & Pl
NH Flat	2	0	0	0	
Career Total	**2**	**0**	**0**	**0**	

Going: Sf: 0-0 GS: 0-0 Gd: 0-2 GF: - Fm: 0-0
Distance: 2m/2m3: 0-2 2m4-2m7: 0-0 3m+: 0-0
Track: LH: 0-1 RH: 0-1 Tight: 0-0 Gall: 0-0
Aids: Bl: 0-0 Vi: 0-0 Tstrap: 0-0
Best Rating:

Venture To Fly (IRE)

(102h) (95h)

8-y-o ch g Roselier (FR)-Fly Run (Deep Run)

N G Richards Ashleybank Investments Limited

Placings:*2*325/1134-F **(2159)**

2001/02: 20^{F}GS

	Starts	1st	2nd	3rd	Win & Pl
Chases	1	0	0	0	
Career Total	**9**	**2**	**2**	**2**	**8464**

108	1/01	Ayr	2m6f	E Hdl	SFT	£2954
117	11/00	Newc	3m	E Hdl	SFT	£2583

Total win prize-money £5537

Going: Sf: 0-0 GS: 0-1 Gd: 0-0 GF: - Fm: 0-0
Distance: 2m/2m3: 0-0 2m4-2m7: 0-1 3m+: 0-0
Track: LH: 0-1 RH: 0-0 Tight: 0-0 Gall: 0-0
Aids: Bl: 0-0 Vi: 0-0 Tstrap: 0-0
Best Rating: 117 1/01 Ayr 3m110y gd-sft Hdl

A fair novice hurdler, he has won at up to three miles at Ayr and Newcastle, but was disappointing when stepped up in class at Perth in April 2001. He was making a good start to his chasing career at Ayr in November 2001, when he fell five from home.

Veredarius (FR)

11-y-o b g Le Nain Jaune (FR)-Villa Verde (FR) (Top Ville)

P J Millington P J Millington

Placings:*0*0610/00440051/U01P25/P0044460/00600 P/0PP-UP4PP **(0579)**

2001/02: 25^{U}G, 24^{P}GF, 24^{4}GF, 26^{P}G, 24^{P}GF

	Starts	1st	2nd	3rd	Win & Pl
Chases	5	0	0	0	0
Career Total	**41**	**3**	**1**	**0**	**12837**

12/97	Leop	2m5f	(0-116)HCh	HVY	£4069
4/97	Slig	2m4f	Ch	HVY	£2712
3/96	Navn	2m	Hdl	SFT	£3177

Total win prize-money £9960

Going: Sf: 0-0 GS: 0-0 Gd: 0-2 GF: - Fm: 0-3
Distance: 2m/2m3: 0-0 2m4-2m7: 0-0 3m+: 0-5
Track: LH: 0-3 RH: 0-1 Tight: 0-2 Gall: 0-1
Aids: Bl: 0-3 Vi: 0-2 Tstrap: 0-0
Best Rating: 114 12/98 Leop 2m5f soft Ch

Veridian

99(110h) (126h)**105+**

9-y-o b g Green Desert (USA)-Alik (FR) (Targowice (USA))

B J Llewellyn (N J Henderson 28/7) John Marks And Dave Allsopp

Placings:F42126/5/14025/15-045006 **(4853)**

2001/02: 16^{0}GS, 17^{4}HY, 16^{5}S, 21^{0}G, 17^{0}G, 16^{6}G

	Starts	1st	2nd	3rd	Win & Pl
Hurdles	6	0	0	0	789
Career Total	**20**	**3**	**3**	**0**	**26355**

136	9/00	Bang	2m1f	C(0-135)HHdl	G-F	£6825
137	12/99	Kemp	2m	B(0-145)HHdl	SFT	£10259
116	3/98	Folk	2m1f110y	E Hdl	GD	£2630

Total win prize-money £19714

Going: Sf: 0-2 GS: 0-1 Gd: 0-3 GF: - Fm: 0-0
Distance: 2m/2m3: 0-5 2m4-2m7: 0-1 3m+: 0-0
Track: LH: 0-4 RH: 0-2 Tight: 0-1 Gall: 0-2
Aids: Bl: 0-0 Vi: 0-0 Tstrap: 0-0
Best Rating: 137 12/99 Kemp 2m soft Hdl

He stays two and a half miles but is probably better at shorter. Has a fair turn of foot when on song but seems to be on the downgrade. Handles any ground.

Verrazano Bridge (IRE)

10-y-o b/br g Be My Native (USA)-Shannon Ville (Deep Run)

B G Powell D A Rees

Placings: 1/2612114/314P/P1-2P0 **(0428)**

2001/02: 20^{2}GS, 25^{P}GF, 21^{0}G

	Starts	1st	2nd	3rd	Win & Pl
Chases	3	0	1	0	1035
Career Total	**17**	**6**	**3**	**1**	**32921**

128	4/01	Hntg	2m5f110y	F(0-110)HHdl	SFT	£2371
119	2/00	Gowr	2m2f	Ch	SFT	£5520
128	4/98	Fair	2m4f	Hdl	GD	£5956
121	4/98	Cork	2m4f	(0-123)HHdl	HVY	£5956
107	12/97	Leop	2m4f	Hdl	HVY	£5086
110	3/97	Naas	2m	NHF	Y-S	£3051

Total win prize-money £27945

Going: Sf: 0-0 GS: 0-1 Gd: 0-1 GF: - Fm: 0-1
Distance: 2m/2m3: 0-0 2m4-2m7: 0-2 3m+: 0-1
Track: LH: 0-1 RH: 0-1 Tight: 0-1 Gall: 0-0
Aids: Bl: 0-0 Vi: 0-0 Tstrap: 0-0
Best Rating: 133 4/01 Plum 2m4f gd-sft Ch

Versicium (FR)

103(101h) (109h)**128**

8-y-o ch g Mister Sicy (FR)-Verdurine (FR) (General Holme (USA))

M C Pipe The Arthur White Partnership

Placings:3322U2-120F023U **(1495)**

2001/02: 17^{1}GF, 17^{2}G, 17^{0}F, 16^{F}GF, 16^{0}GF, 16^{2}G, 17^{3}GF, 17^{U}GF

	Starts	1st	2nd	3rd	Win & Pl
Hurdles	4	1	0	1	3153
Chases	4	0	2	0	2196
Career Total	**14**	**1**	**5**	**3**	**9454**

109	5/01	NAbb	2m1f	F(0-100)HHdl	G-F	£2775

Total win prize-money £2776

Going: Sf: 0-0 GS: 0-0 Gd: 0-2 GF: - Fm: 1-6
Distance: **2m/2m3: 1-8** 2m4-2m7: 0-0 3m+: 0-0
Track: **LH: 1-5** RH: 0-3 **Tight: 1-6** Gall: 0-0
Aids: Bl: 0-0 **Vi: 1-8** Tstrap: 0-0
Best Rating: 128 6/01 NAbb 2m110y gd-fm Ch

Front-running low grade handicap hurdler and chaser. Best at two miles and is suited by fast ground.

Vert Espere

103 **89**

9-y-o ch g Green Adventure (USA)-Celtic Dream (Celtic Cone)

A Streeter P S Daly

Placings:*P/0*P000F0/40P5406-2310 **(1913)**

2001/02: 20^{2}G, 22^{3}F, 24^{1}G, 23^{0}G

	Starts	1st	2nd	3rd	Win & Pl
Hurdles	4	1	1	1	3245
Career Total	**19**	**1**	**1**	**1**	**3245**

90	6/01	Worc	3m	F(0-100)HHdl	GD	£2037

Total win prize-money £2037

Going: Sf: 0-0 GS: 0-0 Gd: 1-3 GF: - Fm: 0-1
Distance: 2m/2m3: 0-0 2m4-2m7: 0-3 **3m+: 1-1**

Track: LH: 1-2 RH: 0-1 Tight: 0-0 Gall: 0-1
Aids: Bl: 0-0 Vi: 0-0 Tstrap: 0-0
Best Rating: 90 6/01 Worc 3m good Hdl

Verulam (IRE)

9-y-o b/br g Marju (IRE)-Hot Curry (USA) (Sharpen Up)
R J Barrett (C J Hemsley 17/2) R J Barrett

Placings:21F00/05P/**PP0** (4638)
2001/02: 20PGF, 23PGF, 190GF

	Starts	1st	2nd	3rd	Win & Pl
Chases	3	0	0	0	
Career Total	11	1	1	0	2871

78	8/96	Plum	2m1f	E Hdl		FRM	£2259

Total win prize-money £2259

Going: Sf: 0-0 GS: 0-0 Gd: 0-0 GF: - Fm: 0-3
Distance: 2m/2m3: 0-0 2m4-2m7: 0-2 3m+: 0-1
Track: LH: 0-1 RH: 0-2 Tight: 0-0 Gall: 0-1
Aids: Bl: 0-0 Vi: 0-0 Tstrap: 0-0
Best Rating: 80 9/97 Plum 2m4f gd-fm Hdl

Very Daring

12-y-o b g Derring Rose-La Verite (Vitiges (FR))
Miss N L Elliott Miss N L Elliott

Placings:P6/B4364P/03/600545000000-P (4846)
2001/02: 24PG

	Starts	1st	2nd	3rd	Win & Pl
Chases	1	0	0	0	
Career Total	24	0	0	2	835

Going: Sf: 0-0 GS: 0-0 Gd: 0-1 GF: - Fm: 0-0
Distance: 2m/2m3: 0-0 2m4-2m7: 0-0 3m+: 0-1
Track: LH: 0-1 RH: 0-0 Tight: 0-1 Gall: 0-0
Aids: Bl: 0-0 Vi: 0-0 Tstrap: 0-0
Best Rating: 85 5/98 Uttx 2m5f gd-fm Ch

Very Tasty (IRE)

5-y-o ch g Be My Native (USA)-Jasmine Melody (Jasmine Star)
Mrs E Slack A Slack

Placings:0U (4857)
2001/02: 170G, 20UG

	Starts	1st	2nd	3rd	Win & Pl
NH Flat	1	0	0	0	0
Hurdles	1	0	0	0	0
Career Total	2	0	0	0	

Going: Sf: 0-0 GS: 0-0 Gd: 0-2 GF: - Fm: 0-0
Distance: 2m/2m3: 0-1 2m4-2m7: 0-1 3m+: 0-0
Track: LH: 0-1 RH: 0-1 Tight: 0-0 Gall: 0-0
Aids: Bl: 0-0 Vi: 0-0 Tstrap: 0-0
Best Rating: 57 4/02 Carl 2m1f good NHF

Very Very Noble (IRE)

103 131

8-y-o ch g Aristocracy-Hills Angel (IRE) (Salluceva)
A M Hales Andrew L Cohen

Placings:12F/0-13113 (2939)
2001/02: 201G, 243GS, 241G, 251G, 243G

	Starts	1st	2nd	3rd	Win & Pl
Chases	5	3	0	2	11082
Career Total	9	4	1	2	14708

127	12/01	Folk	3m1f	F(0-110)HCh	GD	£2947
121	11/01	Wwck	3m110y	F(0-95)HCh	GD	£2656
125	10/01	Sthl	2m4f110y	F(0-110)HCh	GD	£3391
99	3/00	Dpat	3m	Ch	SFT	£2345

Total win prize-money £11342

Going: Sf: 0-0 GS: 0-1 Gd: 3-4 GF: - Fm: 0-0
Distance: 2m/2m3: 0-0 2m4-2m7: 1-1 **3m+: 2-4**
Track: LH: 1-3 RH: 1-1 **Tight: 2-2** Gall: 0-1
Aids: Bl: 0-0 Vi: 0-0 **Tstrap: 3-5**
Best Rating: 131 12/01 Newb 3m good Ch

Lightly-raced handicap chaser. Stays three miles plus, likes good ground but handles softer. Wears a tongue tie.

Verywell (IRE)

(88h) (55h)

11-y-o b g Torus-Merrywell (Mugatpura)
Mrs T J McInnes Skinner Mrs T J McInnes Skinner

Placings:0005000300/0**FB0262526464/53F/0P** (0971)
2001/02: 190G, 20PGF

	Starts	1st	2nd	3rd	Win & Pl
Hurdles	1	0	0	0	0
Chases	1	0	0	0	0
Career Total	28	0	3	2	3192

Going: Sf: 0-0 GS: 0-0 Gd: 0-1 GF: - Fm: 0-1
Distance: 2m/2m3: 0-0 2m4-2m7: 0-2 3m+: 0-0
Track: LH: 0-1 RH: 0-1 Tight: 0-2 Gall: 0-0
Aids: Bl: 0-0 Vi: 0-0 Tstrap: 0-0
Best Rating: 108 11/99 Weth 2m4f110y good Ch

Vexford Deltic

7-y-o b m Deltic (USA)-Suchong (No Mercy)
V G Greenway V G Greenway

Placings:00/U (2411)
2001/02: 19UGS

	Starts	1st	2nd	3rd	Win & Pl
Hurdles	1	0	0	0	
Career Total	3	0	0	0	

Going: Sf: 0-0 GS: 0-1 Gd: 0-0 GF: - Fm: 0-0
Distance: 2m/2m3: 0-0 2m4-2m7: 0-1 3m+: 0-0
Track: LH: 0-0 RH: 0-1 Tight: 0-1 Gall: 0-0
Aids: Bl: 0-0 Vi: 0-0 Tstrap: 0-0
Best Rating: 36 2/00 Winc 2m gd-sft NHF

Via Del Quatro (IRE)

90 57

10-y-o b m Posen (USA)-Gulistan (Sharpen Up)
M R Bosley Mrs Jean M O'Connor

Placings:0/2035P6/4263622413062/15P/21-645 (1344)
2001/02: 266G, 264GF, 265GF

	Starts	1st	2nd	3rd	Win & Pl
Chases	3	0	0	0	273
Career Total	28	3	6	3	14627

95	7/00	Worc	2m7f110y	F(0-110)HCh	G-F	£2352
100	5/99	Font	3m2f110y	E Ch	FRM	£2883
87	10/98	Font	3m2f110y	F(0-95)HCh	GD	£2445

Total win prize-money £7681

Going: Sf: 0-0 GS: 0-0 Gd: 0-1 GF: - Fm: 0-2
Distance: 2m/2m3: 0-0 2m4-2m7: 0-0 3m+: 0-3
Track: LH: 0-2 RH: 0-0 Tight: 0-3 Gall: 0-0
Aids: Bl: 0-0 Vi: 0-0 Tstrap: 0-0
Best Rating: 100 5/99 Font 3m2f110y firm Ch

Vic's Girl

8-y-o b m Jester-Porto Irene (Porto Bello)
W G M Turner Donald C Tucker

Placings:50-0 (0007)
2001/02: 160S

	Starts	1st	2nd	3rd	Win & Pl
Hurdles	1	0	0	0	
Career Total	3	0	0	0	0

Going: Sf: 0-1 GS: 0-0 Gd: 0-0 GF: - Fm: 0-0
Distance: 2m/2m3: 0-1 2m4-2m7: 0-0 3m+: 0-0
Track: LH: 0-1 RH: 0-0 Tight: 0-1 Gall: 0-0
Aids: Bl: 0-0 Vi: 0-0 Tstrap: 0-0
Best Rating: 83 7/00 Worc 2m gd-fm NHF

Vicars Destiny

93f 79f

4-y-o b f Sir Harry Lewis (USA)-Church Leap (Pollerton)
Mrs S Lamyman Terence Deal

Placings:4 (4539)
2001/02: 164G

	Starts	1st	2nd	3rd	Win & Pl
NH Flat	1	0	0	0	0
Career Total	1	0	0	0	0

Going: Sf: 0-0 GS: 0-0 Gd: 0-1 GF: - Fm: 0-0
Distance: 2m/2m3: 0-1 2m4-2m7: 0-0 3m+: 0-0
Track: LH: 0-1 RH: 0-0 Tight: 0-1 Gall: 0-0
Aids: Bl: 0-0 Vi: 0-0 Tstrap: 0-0
Best Rating: 79 4/02 Fknm 2m good NHF

A half-sister to a hurdles winner, showed promise on bumper debut.

Vicky Scarlett

5-y-o gr m Missed Flight-Just Greenwich (Chilibang)
P A Pritchard P A Pritchard

Placings:PPP (2476)
2001/02: 16PS, 16PGS, 17PS

	Starts	1st	2nd	3rd	Win & Pl
Hurdles	3	0	0	0	
Career Total	3	0	0	0	

Going: Sf: 0-2 GS: 0-1 Gd: 0-0 GF: - Fm: 0-0
Distance: 2m/2m3: 0-3 2m4-2m7: 0-0 3m+: 0-0
Track: LH: 0-0 RH: 0-3 Tight: 0-0 Gall: 0-0
Aids: Bl: 0-1 Vi: 0-0 Tstrap: 0-0
Best Rating:

Victor Laszlo

100 91

10-y-o b g Ilium-Report 'Em (USA) (Staff Writer (USA))
R Allan Mrs L A Ogilvie

Placings:6/63064/1205/000/04334P5P0P-

2600325454 (2726)
2001/02: 16²G, 17⁶GS, 21⁰GF, 16⁰G, 16³G, 25²G, 17⁵G, 22⁴G, 16⁵G, 20⁴GF

	Starts	1st	2nd	3rd	Win & Pl
Chases	10	0	2	1	3698
Career Total	33	1	3	4	8958

93 5/98 Prth 2m4f110y E Hdl G-F £2835
Total win prize-money £2835

Going: Sf: 0-0 GS: 0-1 Gd: 0-7 GF: - Fm: 0-2
Distance: 2m/2m3: 0-6 2m4-2m7: 0-3 3m+: 0-1
Track: LH: 0-7 RH: 0-3 Tight: 0-7 Gall: 0-0
Aids: Bl: 0-0 Vi: 0-1 Tstrap: 0-6
Best Rating: 99 5/98 Kels 2m110y gd-fm Hdl

Modest form over fences.

Victoria's Boy (IRE)

111 94

9-y-o b g Denel (FR)-Cloghroe Lady (Hard Boy)
T D Walford David Dickson

Placings:00/00/1526-P50654320 (4521)
2001/02: 24ᴾG, 23⁵G, 27⁰G, 24⁶G, 16⁵S, 16⁴GS, 19³S, 24²GF, 20⁰GS

	Starts	1st	2nd	3rd	Win & Pl
Chases	9	0	1	1	1739
Career Total	17	1	2	1	5215

112 5/00 Hexm 3m1f H Ch G-F £2366
Total win prize-money £2366

Going: Sf: 0-2 GS: 0-2 Gd: 0-4 GF: - Fm: 0-1
Distance: 2m/2m3: 0-2 2m4-2m7: 0-2 3m+: 0-5
Track: LH: 0-5 RH: 0-2 Tight: 0-4 Gall: 0-2
Aids: Bl: 0-2 Vi: 0-0 Tstrap: 0-0
Best Rating: 112 5/00 Hexm 3m1f gd-fm Ch

A winning pointer and hunter chaser. Best at three miles on fast ground.

Victory Marble (NZ)

9-y-o b g Le Belvedere (USA)-Happy Hostess (NZ) (Takearisk (FR))
H D Daly Mrs L Greenway & Miss A Lakin

Placings:P4 (4086)
2001/02: 24ᴾG, 17⁴S

	Starts	1st	2nd	3rd	Win & Pl
Chases	2	0	0	0	318
Career Total	2	0	0	0	318

Going: Sf: 0-1 GS: 0-0 Gd: 0-1 GF: - Fm: 0-0
Distance: 2m/2m3: 0-1 2m4-2m7: 0-0 3m+: 0-1
Track: LH: 0-1 RH: 0-1 Tight: 0-2 Gall: 0-0
Aids: Bl: 0-0 Vi: 0-0 Tstrap: 0-0
Best Rating:

Victory Roll

108 110

6-y-o b g In The Wings-Persian Victory (IRE) (Persian Bold)
Miss E C Lavelle Sir Gordon Brunton

Placings:004143-01131320 (3781)
2001/02: 19⁰G, 17¹HY, 17¹S, 16³GS, 16¹GS, 16³G, 16²S, 16⁰S

	Starts	1st	2nd	3rd	Win & Pl
Hurdles	8	3	1	2	17462
Career Total	14	4	1	3	20469

107 12/01 Hntg 2m110y D(0-125)HHdl G-S £8287
110 11/01 Folk 2m1f110y F(0-105)HHdl SFT £2681
104 10/01 Folk 2m1f110y F(0-110)HHdl HVY £2919
82 1/01 Folk 2m1f110y E(0-115)HHdl HVY £2387
Total win prize-money £16275

Going: Sf: 2-4 GS: 1-2 Gd: 0-2 GF: - Fm: 0-0
Distance: **2m/2m3: 3-7** 2m4-2m7: 0-1 3m+: 0-0
Track: LH: 0-1 **RH: 3-7 Tight: 2-2** Gall: 1-2
Aids: Bl: 0-0 Vi: 0-0 Tstrap: 0-0
Best Rating: 110 2/02 Winc 2m soft Hdl

Goes particularly well over the extended two miles one furlong on heavy ground at Folkestone, but has shown decent form on other right-handed tracks and acts on a faster surface.

Viking Moss

79f 68f

7-y-o b g Le Moss-Saxon Gift (Saxon Farm)
A Hollingsworth M Stephenson

Placings:00 (0911)
2001/02: 16⁰GF, 16⁰G

	Starts	1st	2nd	3rd	Win & Pl
NH Flat	2	0	0	0	
Career Total	2	0	0	0	

Going: Sf: 0-0 GS: 0-0 Gd: 0-1 GF: - Fm: 0-1
Distance: 2m/2m3: 0-2 2m4-2m7: 0-0 3m+: 0-0
Track: LH: 0-2 RH: 0-0 Tight: 0-0 Gall: 0-0
Aids: Bl: 0-0 Vi: 0-0 Tstrap: 0-0
Best Rating: 68 7/01 Worc 2m good NHF

Viking Rod (IRE)

89 93

10-y-o b g Mandalus-Deep Link (Deep Run)
Mrs J A Saunders (M J Wilkinson 13/6) John Nicholls (banbury) Ltd

Placings:U454U6/43P/2U-506U (2524)
2001/02: 25⁵G, 25⁰F, 22⁶S, 23ᵁG

	Starts	1st	2nd	3rd	Win & Pl
Chases	4	0	0	0	0
Career Total	15	0	1	1	2407

Going: Sf: 0-1 GS: 0-0 Gd: 0-2 GF: - Fm: 0-1
Distance: 2m/2m3: 0-0 2m4-2m7: 0-1 3m+: 0-3
Track: LH: 0-0 RH: 0-4 Tight: 0-0 Gall: 0-0
Aids: Bl: 0-0 Vi: 0-0 Tstrap: 0-0
Best Rating: 98 5/00 Hntg 3m gd-sft Ch

Villa

102f 108f

6-y-o b g Jupiter Island-Spoonhill Wood (Celtic Cone)
M C Pipe Matt Archer & Miss Jean Broadhurst

Placings:61 (3563)
2001/02: 16⁶G, 16¹HY

	Starts	1st	2nd	3rd	Win & Pl
NH Flat	2	1	0	0	2317
Career Total	2	1	0	0	2317

108 1/02 Towc 2m H NHF HVY £2317
Total win prize-money £2317

Going: Sf: 1-1 GS: 0-0 Gd: 0-1 GF: - Fm: 0-0
Distance: **2m/2m3: 1-2** 2m4-2m7: 0-0 3m+: 0-0
Track: LH: 0-1 **RH: 1-1** Tight: 0-0 Gall: 0-1
Aids: Bl: 0-0 Vi: 0-0 Tstrap: 0-0
Best Rating: 108 1/02 Towc 2m heavy NHF

Bumper winner on heavy ground.

Village Copper

10-y-o b g Town And Country-Culm Valley (Port Corsair)
Mrs Ruth Hayter A Howland Jackson

Placings:06-5 (0325)
2001/02: 21⁵G

	Starts	1st	2nd	3rd	Win & Pl
Chases	1	0	0	0	0
Career Total	3	0	0	0	0

Going: Sf: 0-0 GS: 0-0 Gd: 0-1 GF: - Fm: 0-0
Distance: 2m/2m3: 0-0 2m4-2m7: 0-1 3m+: 0-0
Track: LH: 0-0 RH: 0-1 Tight: 0-1 Gall: 0-0
Aids: Bl: 0-0 Vi: 0-0 Tstrap: 0-0
Best Rating: 97 4/01 Fknm 3m110y gd-sft Ch

Village Kid

13-y-o br g Another Realm-Village Lass (No Mercy)
D J Wintle D J Renney

Placings:0/B-PP0 (0673)
2001/02: 18ᴾGF, 19ᴾG, 16⁰GF

	Starts	1st	2nd	3rd	Win & Pl
Hurdles	3	0	0	0	
Career Total	5	0	0	0	

Going: Sf: 0-0 GS: 0-0 Gd: 0-1 GF: - Fm: 0-2
Distance: 2m/2m3: 0-2 2m4-2m7: 0-1 3m+: 0-0
Track: LH: 0-2 RH: 0-1 Tight: 0-1 Gall: 0-0
Aids: Bl: 0-0 Vi: 0-0 Tstrap: 0-0
Best Rating:

Village King (IRE)

107 145

9-y-o b g Roi Danzig (USA)-Honorine (USA) (Blushing Groom (FR))
P J Hobbs Capt E J Edwards-Heathcote

Placings:45210320/111123122/1336F0/0223F0-001P1 (4819)
2001/02: 31⁰G, 27⁰S, 26¹S, 24ᴾGS, 26¹GF

	Starts	1st	2nd	3rd	Win & Pl
Chases	5	2	0	0	17225
Career Total	34	9	7	5	84296

145 4/02 Chel 3m2f110y C(0-135)HCh G-F £13071
138 2/02 Font 3m2f110y D(0-125)HCh SFT £4153
157 12/99 Chel 2m5f C(0-130)HCh SFT £10796
145 3/99 Extr 2m3f E(0-115)HCh GD £4040
140 10/98 Chel 2m4f110y D(0-110)HCh GD £4856
113 10/98 NAbb 2m5f110y E(0-120)Ch GD £3126
113 9/98 Worc 2m7f110y D Ch G-F £3556
105 8/98 NAbb 2m110y D Ch G-F £3501
112 1/98 Ludl 2m5f110y F Hdl SFT £2095
Total win prize-money £49198

Going: Sf: 1-2 GS: 0-1 Gd: 0-1 GF: - Fm: 1-1
Distance: 2m/2m3: 0-0 2m4-2m7: 0-0 **3m+: 2-5**
Track: **LH: 1-4** RH: 0-0 Tight: 1-2 Gall: 1-2
Aids: Bl: 0-0 Vi: 0-0 Tstrap: 0-0
Best Rating: 157 12/99 Chel 2m5f soft Ch

A useful handicap chaser who stays well, he is a somewhat quirky individual and not one to place too much trust in. Successful at Fontwell in February 2002. Pulled up at the Festival, but bounced back at Cheltenham's April meeting. Stays three and a quarter miles. Acts on soft and fast ground.

Villair (IRE)

103(82c) (66c)84

7-y-o b g Valville (FR)-Brackenair (Fairbairn)

D R Stoddart D R Stoddart

Placings:3004-00526 **(4566)**

2001/02: 16^{0}G, 16^{0}GS, 20^{5}S, 16^{2}S, 16^{6}G

	Starts	1st	2nd	3rd	Win & Pl
Hurdles	4	0	1	0	542
Chases	1	0	0	0	0
Career Total	**9**	**0**	**1**	**1**	**822**

Going: Sf: 0-2 GS: 0-1 Gd: 0-2 GF: - Fm: 0-0
Distance: 2m/2m3: 0-4 2m4-2m7: 0-1 3m+: 0-0
Track: LH: 0-1 RH: 0-4 Tight: 0-0 Gall: 0-3
Aids: Bl: 0-0 Vi: 0-0 Tstrap: 0-0
Best Rating: 84 2/02 Hntg 2m110y soft Hdl

Modest hurdler, best over two miles with cut in the ground.

Ville D'Or (IRE)

90 74

8-y-o b g Montelimar (USA)-Blaze Gold (Arizona Duke)

K C Bailey K C Bailey

Placings:0/00P **(4127)**

2001/02: 16^{0}S, 16^{0}S, 17^{P}G

	Starts	1st	2nd	3rd	Win & Pl
Hurdles	3	0	0	0	
Career Total	**4**	**0**	**0**	**0**	

Going: Sf: 0-2 GS: 0-0 Gd: 0-1 GF: - Fm: 0-0
Distance: 2m/2m3: 0-3 2m4-2m7: 0-0 3m+: 0-0
Track: LH: 0-0 RH: 0-3 Tight: 0-0 Gall: 0-2
Aids: Bl: 0-0 Vi: 0-0 Tstrap: 0-0
Best Rating: 74 2/02 Hntg 2m110y soft Hdl

Vilprano

110 114

11-y-o b g Ra Nova-Village Princess (Rolfe (USA))

D Moffatt The Vilprano Partnership

Placings:0603/313/P012/223625342201/321366/5432 321656-0450141 **(3555)**

2001/02: 20^{0}S, 27^{4}G, 27^{5}GF, 22^{0}G, 24^{1}GS, 24^{4}S, 25^{1}S

	Starts	1st	2nd	3rd	Win & Pl
Hurdles	7	2	0	0	8872
Career Total	**46**	**7**	**9**	**9**	**38611**

114	1/02	Catt	3m1f110y	D(0-115)HHdl	SFT	£5122
107	11/01	Ayr	3m110y	D(0-125)HHdl	G-S	£3477
120	12/00	Newc	3m	C(0-135)HHdl	SFT	£5086
113	11/99	Ayr	3m110y	D(0-125)HHdl	GD	£3574
103	4/99	Bang	3m	D(0-125)HHdl	GD	£4474
87	2/98	Newc	3m	F(0-105)HHdl	GD	£2102
84	5/96	Ctml	2m6f	F(0-95)HHdl	G-F	£2528

Total win prize-money £26366

Going: Sf: 1-3 GS: 1-1 Gd: 0-2 GF: - Fm: 0-1
Distance: 2m/2m3: 0-0 2m4-2m7: 0-2 **3m+: 2-5**
Track: **LH: 2-7** RH: 0-0 **Tight: 1-4** Gall: 0-1
Aids: Bl: 0-0 Vi: 0-0 Tstrap: 0-0
Best Rating: 120 12/00 Newc 3m soft Hdl

A useful staying handicap hurdler who is suited by a strong pace. Effective at around three miles, he acts on a soft surface.

Vincent Van Gogh (IRE)

106(46h) 110

7-y-o b g Executive Perk-Rare Picture (Pollerton)

R J Hodges The Trojan Partnership

Placings:00/P0U2246F1-006521P143P6 **(4658)**

2001/02: 17^{0}GS, 21^{0}GF, 21^{6}G, 19^{5}GF, 21^{2}G, 24^{1}G, 25^{P}S, 24^{1}S, 24^{4}GS, 21^{3}S, 26^{P}G, 24^{6}G

	Starts	1st	2nd	3rd	Win & Pl
Chases	12	2	1	1	11863
Career Total	**23**	**3**	**3**	**1**	**17647**

110	2/02	Tntn	3m	D(0-115)HCh	SFT	£4771
108	12/01	Ludl	3m	F(0-100)HCh	GD	£4550
100	4/01	Tntn	2m110y	E(0-105)HCh	GD	£3029

Total win prize-money £12350

Going: Sf: 1-3 GS: 0-2 Gd: 1-5 GF: - Fm: 0-2
Distance: 2m/2m3: 0-1 2m4-2m7: 0-5 **3m+: 2-6**
Track: LH: 0-3 **RH: 2-9 Tight: 2-8** Gall: 0-0
Aids: Bl: 0-0 Vi: 0-0 Tstrap: 0-0
Best Rating: 110 3/02 Winc 2m5f soft Ch

Moderate chaser. Effective between two and a half and three miles, he goes well on fast ground, but acts on soft and must go right-handed. Has broken blood-vessels in the past.

Vino Tinto (IRE)

8-y-o b g Glacial Storm (USA)-Pure Spec (Fine Blade (USA))

Mrs C M Mulhall (Robert John Osborne 10/2) Mrs C M Mulhall

Placings:00/000000/6640004/0-2 **(3824)**

2001/02: 21^{2}S

	Starts	1st	2nd	3rd	Win & Pl
Chases	1	0	1	0	444
Career Total	**17**	**0**	**1**	**0**	**1020**

Going: Sf: 0-1 GS: 0-0 Gd: 0-0 GF: - Fm: 0-0
Distance: 2m/2m3: 0-0 2m4-2m7: 0-1 3m+: 0-0
Track: LH: 0-1 RH: 0-0 Tight: 0-1 Gall: 0-0
Aids: Bl: 0-0 Vi: 0-0 Tstrap: 0-1
Best Rating: 94 2/02 Sedg 2m5f soft Ch

Violent

78 33

4-y-o b f Deploy-Gentle Irony (Mazilier (USA))

Jamie Poulton (Andrew Reid 8/5) Chris Steward

Placings:5 **(4171)**

2001/02: 16^{5}GS

	Starts	1st	2nd	3rd	Win & Pl
Hurdles	1	0	0	0	0
Career Total	**1**	**0**	**0**	**0**	**0**

Going: Sf: 0-0 GS: 0-1 Gd: 0-0 GF: - Fm: 0-0
Distance: 2m/2m3: 0-1 2m4-2m7: 0-0 3m+: 0-0
Track: LH: 0-1 RH: 0-0 Tight: 0-1 Gall: 0-0
Aids: Bl: 0-0 Vi: 0-0 Tstrap: 0-0
Best Rating: 33 3/02 Plum 2m gd-sft Hdl

Virbius (IRE)

93 86

6-y-o ch g Wolfhound (USA)-Virelai (Kris)

R D E Woodhouse R D E Woodhouse

Placings:46000P/F6-00 **(1918)**

2001/02: 16^{0}G, 16^{0}G

	Starts	1st	2nd	3rd	Win & Pl
Hurdles	2	0	0	0	
Career Total	**10**	**0**	**0**	**0**	**0**

Going: Sf: 0-0 GS: 0-0 Gd: 0-2 GF: - Fm: 0-0
Distance: 2m/2m3: 0-2 2m4-2m7: 0-0 3m+: 0-0
Track: LH: 0-2 RH: 0-0 Tight: 0-1 Gall: 0-0
Aids: Bl: 0-0 Vi: 0-0 Tstrap: 0-0
Best Rating: 86 5/01 Aint 2m110y good Hdl

Virgin Soldier (IRE)

108 118

6-y-o ch g Waajib-Never Been Chaste (Posse (USA))

G A Swinbank (M Johnston 11/8) J David Abell

Placings:414 **(3915)**

2001/02: 16^{4}GS, 20^{1}G, 20^{4}GS

	Starts	1st	2nd	3rd	Win & Pl
Hurdles	3	1	0	0	3726
Career Total	**3**	**1**	**0**	**0**	**3726**

116	12/01	Donc	2m4f	E Hdl	GD	£3402

Total win prize-money £3402

Going: Sf: 0-0 GS: 0-2 Gd: 1-1 GF: - Fm: 0-0
Distance: 2m/2m3: 0-1 **2m4-2m7: 1-2** 3m+: 0-0
Track: **LH: 1-2** RH: 0-1 Tight: 0-1 **Gall: 1-2**
Aids: Bl: 0-0 Vi: 0-0 Tstrap: 0-0
Best Rating: 118 2/02 Muss 2m4f gd-sft Hdl

A useful stayer on the Flat, he has taken well to hurdles. Won on his second start at Doncaster in December 2001. Suited by two and a half miles. Looks most effective on a sound surface.

Virginian (FR)

89(81c) 46

6-y-o b g Al Nasr (FR)-Violet Dancer (FR) (Fabulous Dancer (USA))

Miss Kate Milligan (A Crook 8/8) A G Chappell

Placings:0P565/0443P50P-PP5P **(4443)**

2001/02: 24^{P}GF, 19^{P}G, 27^{5}S, 27^{P}S

	Starts	1st	2nd	3rd	Win & Pl
Hurdles	4	0	0	0	0
Career Total	**17**	**0**	**0**	**1**	**1317**

Going: Sf: 0-2 GS: 0-0 Gd: 0-1 GF: - Fm: 0-1
Distance: 2m/2m3: 0-1 2m4-2m7: 0-0 3m+: 0-3
Track: LH: 0-4 RH: 0-0 Tight: 0-3 Gall: 0-0
Aids: Bl: 0-0 Vi: 0-0 Tstrap: 0-0
Best Rating: 83 11/00 Hntg 2m4f110y good Ch

Plating class hurdler who is frequently pulled up.

Virtuoso

100(98h) (100h)125

8-y-o ch g Suave Dancer (USA)-Creake (Derring Do)

C J Mann Mrs M Devine

Placings:4115/2F5/254402562/2113040641 5-3144645 **(4401)**

2001/02: 16^{3}G, 16^{1}S, 16^{4}S, 16^{4}HY, 16^{6}S, 16^{4}S, 18^{5}GS

	Starts	1st	2nd	3rd	Win & Pl
Hurdles	1	0	0	0	0
Chases	6	1	0	1	5762
Career Total	**34**	**6**	**5**	**2**	**31991**

125	12/01	Wwck	2m110y	D(0-125)HCh	SFT	£3900
125	4/01	Newb	2m2f110y	D Ch	SFT	£3978

125	10/00	Sthl	2m	E(0-115)HCh	SFT	£3454
125	10/00	Sthl	2m	E Ch	HVY	£4192
114	12/97	Wwck	2m	E Hdl	GD	£2773
117	11/97	Uttx	2m	E Hdl	G-S	£2442

Total win prize-money £20741

Going: Sf: 1-5 GS: 0-1 Gd: 0-1 GF: - Fm: 0-0
Distance: **2m/2m3: 1-7** 2m4-2m7: 0-0 3m+: 0-0
Track: LH: 0-4 RH: 0-2 Tight: 0-1 Gall: 0-2
Aids: Bl: 0-0 Vi: 0-0 Tstrap: 0-0
Best Rating: 131 10/98 Weth 2m good Hdl

Fair handicap chaser, he is effective at trips of around two miles and goes well on ground ranging from good to heavy.

Virtuous Circle

99(106h) **134**

8-y-o b g Rolfe (USA)-Bubbling (Tremblant)
B Ellison Ffwd Precision Marketing Ltd

Placings:000/340P/22F141011-01P1PP **(4272)**
2001/02: 20^{0}S, 25^{1}GS, 22^{P}HY, 19^{1}G, 22^{P}S, 21^{P}G

	Starts	1st	2nd	3rd	Win & Pl
Chases	6	2	0	0	10674
Career Total	**22**	**6**	**2**	**1**	**30187**

134	1/02	Donc	2m3f110y	C(0-130)HCh	GD	£7245
130	11/01	MRas	3m1f	E(0-115)HCh	G-S	£3428
134	3/01	MRas	2m6f110y	F(0-110)HCh	HVY	£7767
126	3/01	Wwck	2m4f110y	E(0-105)HCh	SFT	£4023
120	12/00	Sedg	2m5f110y	F(0-110)HHdl	SFT	£2744
106	10/00	Kels	2m6f110y	E Hdl	SFT	£2422

Total win prize-money £27632

Going: Sf: 0-3 GS: 1-1 Gd: 1-2 GF: - Fm: 0-0
Distance: 2m/2m3: 0-0 2m4-2m7: 1-5 3m+: 1-1
Track: LH: 1-2 RH: 1-4 Tight: 1-3 Gall: 1-1
Aids: Bl: 0-1 Vi: 0-0 Tstrap: 0-0
Best Rating: 134 1/02 Donc 2m3f110y good Ch

Successfully switched to fences during the 2000/2001 season with wins at Warwick and Market Rasen and made a successful reappearance at the latter track last term. A laboured winner at Doncaster in January 2002, he is suited by soft ground and stays three miles.

Viscount Bankes

77 **33**

4-y-o ch g Clantime-Bee Dee Dancer (Ballacashtal (CAN))
W G M Turner T Lightbowne

Placings:60 **(4682)**
2001/02: 17^{6}S, 17^{0}GF

	Starts	1st	2nd	3rd	Win & Pl
Hurdles	2	0	0	0	0
Career Total	**2**	**0**	**0**	**0**	**0**

Going: Sf: 0-1 GS: 0-0 Gd: 0-0 GF: - Fm: 0-1
Distance: 2m/2m3: 0-2 2m4-2m7: 0-0 3m+: 0-0
Track: LH: 0-0 RH: 0-2 Tight: 0-1 Gall: 0-0
Aids: Bl: 0-0 Vi: 0-0 Tstrap: 0-0
Best Rating: 33 4/02 Hrfd 2m1f gd-fm Hdl

Vislink (IRE)

4-y-o br g Shalford (IRE)-Wide Outside (IRE) (Don't Forget Me)
K A Ryan Mrs K E Fletcher

Placings:0 **(2397)**
2001/02: 16^{0}G

	Starts	1st	2nd	3rd	Win & Pl
Hurdles	1	0	0	0	
Career Total	**1**	**0**	**0**	**0**	

Going: Sf: 0-0 GS: 0-0 Gd: 0-1 GF: - Fm: 0-0
Distance: 2m/2m3: 0-1 2m4-2m7: 0-0 3m+: 0-0
Track: LH: 0-1 RH: 0-0 Tight: 0-0 Gall: 0-0
Aids: Bl: 0-0 Vi: 0-0 Tstrap: 0-0
Best Rating:

Vivaldi Rose (IRE)

81 **65**

7-y-o b m Cataldi-Peaceful Rose (Roselier (FR))
L Lungo Mrs S J Matthews

Placings:0600 **(4438)**
2001/02: 16^{0}GF, 16^{6}GS, 16^{0}G, 16^{0}S

	Starts	1st	2nd	3rd	Win & Pl
NH Flat	1	0	0	0	0
Hurdles	3	0	0	0	0
Career Total	**4**	**0**	**0**	**0**	**0**

Going: Sf: 0-1 GS: 0-1 Gd: 0-1 GF: - Fm: 0-1
Distance: 2m/2m3: 0-4 2m4-2m7: 0-0 3m+: 0-0
Track: LH: 0-3 RH: 0-1 Tight: 0-3 Gall: 0-0
Aids: Bl: 0-0 Vi: 0-0 Tstrap: 0-0
Best Rating: 87 5/01 Ayr 2m gd-fm NHF

Modest hurdler, held in weak company.

Vivo (IRE)

(106h) (139h)**100**

9-y-o b g Shaadi (USA)-Gay Nocturne (Lord Gayle (USA))
C Roche J P McManus

Placings:40/606105/300/135-213500F **(3307a)**
2001/02: 16^{2}GF, 17^{1}YS, 16^{3}GY, 17^{5}GF, 18^{0}YS, 16^{0}YS, 17^{F}YS

	Starts	1st	2nd	3rd	Win & Pl
Hurdles	4	1	1	1	28357
Chases	3	0	0	0	0
Career Total	**21**	**3**	**1**	**3**	**55067**

134	7/01	Klny	2m1f	(0-137)HHdl	Y-S	£15725
128	6/00	Worc	2m	B(0-140)HHdl	G-F	£14121
108	12/98	Leop	2m	Hdl	SH	£4184

Total win prize-money £34032

Going: Sf: 0-0 GS: 0-0 Gd: 0-0 GF: - Fm: 0-2
Distance: **2m/2m3: 1-7** 2m4-2m7: 0-0 3m+: 0-0
Track: LH: 0-2 RH: 0-1 Tight: 0-0 Gall: 0-0
Aids: Bl: 0-0 Vi: 0-0 Tstrap: 0-3
Best Rating: 139 8/01 Gway 2m gd-yld Hdl

Vodka Inferno (IRE)

94f **97f**

5-y-o ch g Moscow Society (USA)-Corrie Lough (IRE) (The Parson)
C R Egerton Madgenta

Placings:03 **(4506)**
2001/02: 16^{0}G, 17^{3}G

	Starts	1st	2nd	3rd	Win & Pl
NH Flat	2	0	0	1	345
Career Total	**2**	**0**	**0**	**1**	**345**

Going: Sf: 0-0 GS: 0-0 Gd: 0-2 GF: - Fm: 0-0
Distance: 2m/2m3: 0-2 2m4-2m7: 0-0 3m+: 0-0
Track: LH: 0-2 RH: 0-0 Tight: 0-1 Gall: 0-1
Aids: Bl: 0-0 Vi: 0-0 Tstrap: 0-0
Best Rating: 97 3/02 NAbb 2m1f good NHF

Voice Of Hope (IRE)

60 **28**

5-y-o b g Magical Strike (USA)-Glendee (Boreen (FR))
Mrs N Macauley (Mrs M Reveley 25/11) Andy Peake

Placings:060P **(3590)**
2001/02: 17^{0}GS, 16^{6}GF, 16^{0}GS, 16^{P}HY

	Starts	1st	2nd	3rd	Win & Pl
NH Flat	2	0	0	0	0
Hurdles	2	0	0	0	0
Career Total	**4**	**0**	**0**	**0**	**0**

Going: Sf: 0-1 GS: 0-2 Gd: 0-0 GF: - Fm: 0-1
Distance: 2m/2m3: 0-4 2m4-2m7: 0-0 3m+: 0-0
Track: LH: 0-2 RH: 0-2 Tight: 0-1 Gall: 0-0
Aids: Bl: 0-0 Vi: 0-0 Tstrap: 0-0
Best Rating: 90 10/01 Carl 2m1f gd-sft NHF

Vol Solitaire (FR)

107 **141**

4-y-o b g Loup Solitaire (USA)-Vol Sauvage (FR) (Always Fair (USA))
P F Nicholls (T Civel 11/9) B C Marshall

Placings:4-324315130125 **(4902)**
2001/02: 15^{3}HO, 15^{2}VS, 17^{4}S, 18^{3}S, 16^{1}HY, 16^{5}GS, 17^{1}HY, 16^{3}S, 17^{0}G, 16^{1}GS, 16^{2}G, 16^{5}G

	Starts	1st	2nd	3rd	Win & Pl
Hurdles	12	3	2	3	58546
Career Total	**13**	**3**	**2**	**3**	**60971**

131	4/02	Chep	2m110y	B HHdl	G-S	£10172
133	1/02	Chel	2m1f	A Hdl	HVY	£15000
113	12/01	Leic	2m	E Hdl	HVY	£3052

Total win prize-money £28225

Going: Sf: 2-5 GS: 1-2 Gd: 0-3 GF: - Fm: 0-0
Distance: **2m/2m3: 3-10** 2m4-2m7: 0-0 3m+: 0-0
Track: **LH: 2-5** RH: 1-3 Tight: 0-0 **Gall: 1-3**
Aids: Bl: 0-0 Vi: 0-0 Tstrap: 0-0
Best Rating: 141 4/02 Ayr 2m good Hdl

Formerly trained in France, he has won three times since arriving in this country including a battling victory over Copeland in the Welsh Champion Hurdle and went down by a short-head in the Scottish version. Acts on soft and good ground and is suited by two miles.

Volano (FR)

105 **126**

4-y-o b g Pistolet Bleu (IRE)-Vouivre (FR) (Matahawk)
N J Henderson (Mme C De La Soudiere-Niault 9/9) Thurloe Finsbury

Placings:12P **(4250)**
2001/02: 16^{1}S, 16^{2}HY, 17^{P}G

	Starts	1st	2nd	3rd	Win & Pl
Hurdles	3	1	1	0	5705
Career Total	**3**	**1**	**1**	**0**	**5705**

126	2/02	Sand	2m110y	D Hdl	SFT	£4348

Total win prize-money £4349

Going: Sf: 1-2 GS: 0-0 Gd: 0-1 GF: - Fm: 0-0
Distance: **2m/2m3: 1-3** 2m4-2m7: 0-0 3m+: 0-0
Track: LH: 0-1 **RH: 1-2** Tight: 0-0 Gall: 0-1
Aids: Bl: 0-0 Vi: 0-0 Tstrap: 0-0
Best Rating: 126 2/02 Sand 2m110y soft Hdl

Showed an impressive turn of foot to win his hurdle debut on soft ground in fine style, but was beaten in a muddling race next time.

Vrin (IRE)

111 132

7-y-o b g Mukaddamah (USA)-Traumerei (GER) (Surumu (GER))

Miss Venetia Williams T Cooper, P Kent & R Stevenson

Placings:31-341631P (4647)

2001/02: 20^{3}S, 20^{4}G, 24^{1}GS, 22^{6}S, 24^{3}GS, 22^{1}HY, 24^{P}G

	Starts	1st	2nd	3rd	Win & Pl
Hurdles	7	2	0	2	19070
Career Total	**9**	**3**	**0**	**3**	**24389**

132	3/02	Uttx	2m6f110y	B(0-140)HHdl	HVY	£10595
130	1/02	Newb	3m110y	D(0-120)HHdl	G-S	£4563
125	4/01	Prth	2m110y	D Hdl	HVY	£4917

Total win prize-money £20076

Going: Sf: 1-3 GS: 1-2 Gd: 0-2 GF: - Fm: 0-0
Distance: 2m/2m3: 0-0 2m4-2m7: 1-4 3m+: 1-3
Track: **LH: 2-5** RH: 0-2 Tight: 0-2 **Gall: 1-2**
Aids: Bl: 0-0 Vi: 0-0 Tstrap: 0-0
Best Rating: **132** 3/02 Uttx 2m6f110y heavy Hdl

Lightly raced handicap hurdler, suited by soft ground and effective at up to three miles.

Waddy Peytona (IRE)

(90c)

8-y-o ch g Denel (FR)-Who Says (IRE) (Amazing Bust)

J G Given The G-Guck Group

Placings:F44-P (2581)

2001/02: 23^{P}S

	Starts	1st	2nd	3rd	Win & Pl
Hurdles	1	0	0	0	
Career Total	4	0	0	0	244

Going: Sf: 0-1 GS: 0-0 Gd: 0-0 GF: - Fm: 0-0
Distance: 2m/2m3: 0-0 2m4-2m7: 0-1 3m+: 0-0
Track: LH: 0-1 RH: 0-0 Tight: 0-0 Gall: 0-0
Aids: Bl: 0-0 Vi: 0-0 Tstrap: 0-0
Best Rating: **89** 12/00 Sedg 2m5f soft Ch

Wadenhoe (IRE)

66

5-y-o b m Persian Bold-Frill (Henbit (USA))

M S Saunders Mrs Margaret Hall

Placings:0 (1378)

2001/02: 19^{0}GF

	Starts	1st	2nd	3rd	Win & Pl
Hurdles	1	0	0	0	
Career Total	1	0	0	0	

Going: Sf: 0-0 GS: 0-0 Gd: 0-0 GF: - Fm: 0-1
Distance: 2m/2m3: 0-0 2m4-2m7: 0-1 3m+: 0-0
Track: LH: 0-0 RH: 0-1 Tight: 0-0 Gall: 0-0
Aids: Bl: 0-0 Vi: 0-0 Tstrap: 0-0
Best Rating:

Waders (IRE)

84 41

8-y-o b g Good Thyne (USA)-Lochda (Crash Course)

Mrs A M Thorpe Mrs A M Thorpe

Placings:*446P*/R3P1P-UP0F (4049)

2001/02: 24^{U}G, 26^{P}S, 24^{0}G, 30^{F}G

	Starts	1st	2nd	3rd	Win & Pl
Chases	4	0	0	0	
Career Total	**13**	**1**	**0**	**1**	**4010**

90	8/00	Ctml	3m2f	E Ch	G-S	£3560

Total win prize-money £3560

Going: Sf: 0-1 GS: 0-0 Gd: 0-3 GF: - Fm: 0-0
Distance: 2m/2m3: 0-0 2m4-2m7: 0-0 3m+: 0-4
Track: LH: 0-0 RH: 0-2 Tight: 0-2 Gall: 0-0
Aids: Bl: 0-0 Vi: 0-0 Tstrap: 0-0
Best Rating: **100** 11/99 Worc 2m gd-sft NHF

Wadsworth (NZ)

103 101

9-y-o br g Kirmann-Guard The Gold (NZ) (Imperial Guard)

B P J Baugh M W & A N Harris

Placings:30/006P-2311363 (1556)

2001/02: 17^{2}F, 16^{3}GF, 16^{1}GS, 16^{1}GF, 18^{3}GY, 17^{6}GF, 16^{3}G

	Starts	1st	2nd	3rd	Win & Pl
Hurdles	7	2	1	3	8993
Career Total	**13**	**2**	**1**	**4**	**9493**

101	7/01	Wolv	2m	E(0-105)HHdl	G-F	£2940
90	7/01	Wolv	2m	E Hdl	G-S	£2374

Total win prize-money £5314

Going: Sf: 0-0 GS: 1-1 Gd: 0-1 GF: - Fm: 1-4
Distance: **2m/2m3: 2-7** 2m4-2m7: 0-0 3m+: 0-0
Track: **LH: 2-4** RH: 0-2 **Tight: 2-4** Gall: 0-1
Aids: Bl: 0-0 Vi: 0-0 Tstrap: 0-0
Best Rating: **101** 8/01 Gway 2m2f gd-yld Hdl

Fair hurdler, won twice in the summer of 2001 at Wolverhampton, and ran a big race in a £30,000 handicap at Galway. Stays two miles, acts on any ground.

Wag The Brush

89(96c) (95c)105

10-y-o br g Scallywag-Foxy Fort (Ampney Prince)

Mrs M Reveley P A Tylor

Placings:006/2F4/4313P2-4FF4 (1309)

2001/02: 20^{4}G, 20^{F}GF, 19^{F}GF, 19^{4}GF

	Starts	1st	2nd	3rd	Win & Pl
Hurdles	2	0	0	0	0
Chases	2	0	0	0	392
Career Total	**16**	**1**	**2**	**2**	**5922**

110	11/00	Catt	2m	F(0-100)HHdl	GD	£2607

Total win prize-money £2608

Going: Sf: 0-0 GS: 0-0 Gd: 0-1 GF: - Fm: 0-3
Distance: 2m/2m3: 0-0 2m4-2m7: 0-4 3m+: 0-0
Track: LH: 0-0 RH: 0-4 Tight: 0-4 Gall: 0-0
Aids: Bl: 0-0 Vi: 0-0 Tstrap: 0-0
Best Rating: **110** 2/01 Catt 2m3f soft Hdl

Wager

74 21

8-y-o b g Formidable (USA)-Petty Purse (Petingo)

M Sheppard K Jones

Placings:*0/0*P605-P0 (0500)

2001/02: 19^{P}G, 16^{0}GF

	Starts	1st	2nd	3rd	Win & Pl
Hurdles	1	0	0	0	0
Chases	1	0	0	0	0
Career Total	**8**	**0**	**0**	**0**	**0**

Going: Sf: 0-0 GS: 0-0 Gd: 0-1 GF: - Fm: 0-1
Distance: 2m/2m3: 0-2 2m4-2m7: 0-0 3m+: 0-0
Track: LH: 0-0 RH: 0-2 Tight: 0-0 Gall: 0-1
Aids: Bl: 0-2 Vi: 0-0 Tstrap: 0-0
Best Rating: **75** 5/98 Worc 2m gd-fm NHF

Wahiba Sands

116 171

9-y-o b g Pharly (FR)-Lovely Noor (USA) (Fappiano (USA))

M C Pipe D A Johnson

Placings:11230/12/112U6/P2125-110022 (4815)

2001/02: 19^{1}G, 16^{1}G, 16^{0}G, 16^{0}GS, 20^{2}G, 21^{2}GF

	Starts	1st	2nd	3rd	Win & Pl
Chases	6	2	2	0	81850
Career Total	**23**	**8**	**7**	**1**	**187904**

171	12/01	Asct	2m	B HCh	GD	£16825
164	11/01	Asct	2m3f110y	A HCh	GD	£30000
151	1/01	Donc	2m110y	D Ch	GD	£4088
159	11/99	Asct	2m4f	A Hdl	GD	£15475
161	11/99	Winc	2m	A HHdl	GD	£14875
155	11/98	Newb	2m110y	A(0-145)HHdl	SFT	£19290
131	12/97	Asct	2m110y	A Hdl	G-S	£8918
123	12/97	Leic	2m	E Hdl	SFT	£2784

Total win prize-money £112256

Going: Sf: 0-0 GS: 0-1 Gd: 2-4 GF: - Fm: 0-1
Distance: 2m/2m3: 1-3 2m4-2m7: 1-3 3m+: 0-0
Track: LH: 0-3 **RH: 2-3** Tight: 0-1 Gall: 0-2
Aids: Bl: 0-0 Vi: 0-0 Tstrap: 0-0
Best Rating: **171** 4/02 Aint 2m4f good Ch

He has developed into a very smart handicap chaser at two to two and a half miles and beat Best Mate in the First National Gold Cup on his reappearance in November 2001. Disappointing later in the season, but bounced back better than ever when runner-up to Native Upmanship at Aintree. Best on good ground.

Wahkeena (IRE)

7-y-o ch g Commanche Run-Le Sept (Le Bavard (FR))

Ferdy Murphy K Henderson

Placings:FP (4785)

2001/02: 20^{F}G, 16^{P}F

	Starts	1st	2nd	3rd	Win & Pl
Hurdles	2	0	0	0	
Career Total	2	0	0	0	

Going: Sf: 0-0 GS: 0-0 Gd: 0-1 GF: - Fm: 0-1
Distance: 2m/2m3: 0-1 2m4-2m7: 0-1 3m+: 0-0
Track: LH: 0-1 RH: 0-0 Tight: 0-0 Gall: 0-1
Aids: Bl: 0-1 Vi: 0-0 Tstrap: 0-0
Best Rating:

Wain Mountain

110(112h) (114h)143

6-y-o b g Unfuwain (USA)-Mountain Memory (High Top)

J A B Old W J Smith And M D Dudley

Placings:1/5321P-1122 (4298)

2001/02: 21^{1}S, 26^{1}HY, 26^{2}S, 26^{2}HY

	Starts	1st	2nd	3rd	Win & Pl
Chases	4	2	2	0	14869
Career Total	**10**	**4**	**3**	**1**	**29128**

140	1/02	Uttx	3m2f	E Ch	HVY	£3207
138	12/01	Uttx	2m5f	D Ch	SFT	£4104
136	2/01	Hayd	2m7f110y	B HHdl	HVY	£8767
120	2/00	Leic	2m	E Hdl	HVY	£2800

Total win prize-money £18880

Going: Sf: 2-4 GS: 0-0 Gd: 0-0 GF: - Fm: 0-0
Distance: 2m/2m3: 0-0 2m4-2m7: 1-1 3m+: 1-3
Track: LH: 2-4 RH: 0-0 Tight: 0-0 Gall: 0-0
Aids: Bl: 0-0 Vi: 0-0 Tstrap: 0-0
Best Rating: 143 2/02 Wwck 3m2f soft Ch

A tough staying hurdler, he developed into a good chaser last season. He revels in heavy ground, recording three of his four wins over obstacles in such conditions.

Wainak (USA)

105 **83**

4-y-o b g Silver Hawk (USA)-Cask (Be My Chief (USA))
M H Tompkins P A & D G Sakal

Placings:50 **(2597)**
2001/02: 16^{5}G, 18^{0}G

	Starts	1st	2nd	3rd	Win & Pl
Hurdles	2	0	0	0	0
Career Total	2	0	0	0	0

Going: Sf: 0-0 GS: 0-0 Gd: 0-2 GF: - Fm: 0-0
Distance: 2m/2m3: 0-2 2m4-2m7: 0-0 3m+: 0-0
Track: LH: 0-2 RH: 0-0 Tight: 0-1 Gall: 0-0
Aids: Bl: 0-2 Vi: 0-0 Tstrap: 0-0
Best Rating: 83 11/01 Weth 2m good Hdl

Wait For The Will (USA)

101 **98**

6-y-o ch g Seeking The Gold (USA)-You'd Be Surprised (USA) (Blushing Groom (FR))
G L Moore Rdm Racing

Placings:3/3 **(1146)**
2001/02: 16^{3}GF

	Starts	1st	2nd	3rd	Win & Pl
Hurdles	1	0	0	1	350
Career Total	2	0	0	2	816

Going: Sf: 0-0 GS: 0-0 Gd: 0-0 GF: - Fm: 0-1
Distance: 2m/2m3: 0-1 2m4-2m7: 0 0 3m+: 0-0
Track: LH: 0-1 RH: 0-0 Tight: 0-1 Gall: 0-0
Aids: Bl: 0-1 Vi: 0-0 Tstrap: 0-0
Best Rating: 104 10/99 Kemp 2m gd-fm Hdl

Wait For This (IRE)

7-y-o b g Torus-Bar You Try (Bargello)
C J Down (L G Cottrell 30/6) J B Radford

Placings:0442-41PP21 **(4763)**
2001/02: 22^{4}GS, 24^{1}F, 27^{P}G, 24^{P}G, 19^{2}G, 24^{1}GF

	Starts	1st	2nd	3rd	Win & Pl
Hurdles	4	1	0	0	3087
Chases	2	1	1	0	3366
Career Total	10	2	2	0	7358

115	4/02	Asct	3m110y	H Ch	G-F	£2749
105	5/01	Tntn	3m110y	E Hdl	FRM	£3087

Total win prize-money £5837

Going: Sf: 0-0 GS: 0-1 Gd: 0-3 GF: - Fm: 2-2
Distance: 2m/2m3: 0-0 2m4-2m7: 0-2 **3m+: 2-4**
Track: LH: 0-2 **RH: 2-3 Tight: 1-2** Gall: 0-0
Aids: Bl: 0-0 Vi: 0-0 **Tstrap: 2-6**
Best Rating: 115 4/02 Asct 3m110y gd-fm Ch

A winner over hurdles in 2001, hunter chasing in 2002. Stays three miles, appreciates a sound surface.

Walcot Lad (IRE)

90 **70**

6-y-o b g Jurado (USA)-Butty Miss (Menelek)
Miss Z C Davison Five Men And A Horse

Placings:300-0U0000040 **(3229)**
2001/02: 16^{0}G, 22^{U}GF, 22^{0}G, 24^{0}GF, 16^{0}G, 20^{0}GS, 21^{0}GS, 18^{4}G, 21^{0}GS

	Starts	1st	2nd	3rd	Win & Pl
NH Flat	1	0	0	0	0
Hurdles	8	0	0	0	0
Career Total	12	0	0	1	212

Going: Sf: 0-0 GS: 0-3 Gd: 0-4 GF: - Fm: 0-2
Distance: 2m/2m3: 0-3 2m4-2m7: 0-5 3m+: 0-1
Track: LH: 0-6 RH: 0-2 Tight: 0-5 Gall: 0-1
Aids: Bl: 0-3 Vi: 0-1 Tstrap: 0-0
Best Rating: 102 1/01 Chep 2m110y gd-sft NHF

Walk On By

102 **105**

8-y-o gr g Terimon-Try G'S (Hotfoot)
J S King Mrs R M Hill

Placings:2362/30P35040/**U23243652/1533453-2** **(4886)**
2001/02: 10^{2}GF

	Starts	1st	2nd	3rd	Win & Pl
Chases	1	0	1	0	1045
Career Total	29	1	6	8	13956

105	5/00	Font	2m2f	F Ch	GD	£2340

Total win prize-money £2340

Going: Sf: 0-0 GS: 0-0 Gd: 0-0 GF: - Fm: 0-1
Distance: 2m/2m3: 0-1 2m4-2m7: 0-0 3m+: 0-0
Track: LH: 0-0 RH: 0-0 Tight: 0-1 Gall: 0-0
Aids: Bl: 0-0 Vi: 0-0 Tstrap: 0-0
Best Rating: 107 11/99 Tntn 2m3f good Ch

Modest handicap chaser, effective up to two and a half miles, and best suited by a sound surface.

Walkabout

59 **23**

8-y-o ch g Generous (IRE)-Nomadic Pleasure (Habitat)
H W Lavis C H Warner

Placings:05P **(2474)**
2001/02: 17^{0}G, 22^{5}GF, 19^{P}S

	Starts	1st	2nd	3rd	Win & Pl
Hurdles	3	0	0	0	0
Career Total	3	0	0	0	0

Going: Sf: 0-1 GS: 0-0 Gd: 0-1 GF: - Fm: 0-1
Distance: 2m/2m3: 0-1 2m4-2m7: 0-2 3m+: 0-0
Track: LH: 0-0 RH: 0-3 Tight: 0-1 Gall: 0-0
Aids: Bl: 0-0 Vi: 0-0 Tstrap: 0-0
Best Rating: 23 11/01 Tntn 2m1f good Hdl

Walkaway (IRE)

9-y-o b g Un Desperado (FR)-Hooch (Warpath)
O Sherwood I A Low

Placings:PP **(4285)**
2001/02: 20^{P}GS, 17^{P}GS

	Starts	1st	2nd	3rd	Win & Pl
Chases	2	0	0	0	
Career Total	2	0	0	0	

Going: Sf: 0-0 GS: 0-2 Gd: 0-0 GF: - Fm: 0-0
Distance: 2m/2m3: 0-1 2m4-2m7: 0-1 3m+: 0-0
Track: LH: 0-0 RH: 0-2 Tight: 0-1 Gall: 0-1
Aids: Bl: 0-0 Vi: 0-0 Tstrap: 0-0
Best Rating:

Tubed novice chaser, yet to complete.

Walking Tall (IRE)

72(62h) **39**

11-y-o ch g Hatim (USA)-Futility (Tower Walk)
T P McGovern The Walking Tall Partnership

Placings:10323211P0/3P2/**30P5140/301/2560U2511 200/P6-U0P** **(0874)**
2001/02: 20^{U}G, 22^{0}GF, 20^{P}GS

	Starts	1st	2nd	3rd	Win & Pl
Hurdles	1	0	0	0	0
Chases	2	0	0	0	0
Career Total	40	7	6	5	28326

116	2/00	Plum	2m	B HHdl	SFT	£6615
120	1/00	Plum	2m	E(0-115)HHdl	SFT	£2811
115	4/99	Worc	2m	D(0-125)HHdl	G-S	£3338
107	8/97	Worc	2m4f	E(0-110)HHdl	GD	£2232
102	12/95	Sthl	2m4f110y	E Hdl	GD	£2427
102	11/95	Plum	2m4f	E Hdl	G-F	£2226
74	5/95	Towc	2m	G Hdl	FRM	£1975

Total win prize-money £21020

Going: Sf: 0-0 GS: 0-1 Gd: 0-1 GF: - Fm: 0-1
Distance: 2m/2m3: 0-0 2m4-2m7: 0-3 3m+: 0-0
Track: LH: 0-2 RH: 0-1 Tight: 0-2 Gall: 0-0
Aids: Bl: 0-0 Vi: 0-0 Tstrap: 0-0
Best Rating: 120 3/00 Plum 2m good Hdl

Walter Plinge

108(105h) (75h)**86**

6-y-o b g Theatrical Charmer-Carousel Zingira (Reesh)
A G Juckes Tony Cocum

Placings:36/5-F0615300 **(4572)**
2001/02: 19^{F}F, 21^{0}GF, 17^{6}GF, 20^{1}GF, 20^{5}GF, 20^{3}GF, 20^{0}GF, 20^{0}G

	Starts	1st	2nd	3rd	Win & Pl
Hurdles	8	1	0	1	1992
Career Total	11	1	0	2	2245

72	7/01	Wolv	2m4f110y	G Hdl	G-F	£1570

Total win prize-money £1571

Going: Sf: 0-0 GS: 0-0 Gd: 0-1 GF: - Fm: 1-7
Distance: 2m/2m3: 0-1 **2m4-2m7: 1-7** 3m+: 0-0
Track: **LH: 1-4** RH: 0-4 **Tight: 1-4** Gall: 0-2
Aids: Bl: 0-0 Vi: 0-0 Tstrap: 0-0
Best Rating: 75 4/02 Uttx 2m4f110y good Hdl

Modest hurdler, suited by fast ground. Ran with credit on his chasing debut.

Walter's Destiny

112 **125**

10-y-o ch g White Prince (USA)-Tearful Sarah (Rugantino)
C W Mitchell C W Mitchell

Placings:60/0505/22P1144/3263401/**F3/3U1UP4P-341** **(1951)**
2001/02: 25^{3}GF, 25^{4}G, 23^{1}GF

	Starts	1st	2nd	3rd	Win & Pl

	Starts	1st	2nd	3rd	Win & Pl
Chases	3	1	0	1	6191
Career Total	**32**	**5**	**3**	**5**	**28616**

125	11/01	Extr	2m7f110y	D(0-125)HCh	G-F	£5050
124	12/00	Winc	3m1f110y	D(0-125)HCh	G-S	£9441
101	4/99	Extr	2m7f	D(0-125)HHdl	G-S	£3078
95	2/98	Ling	2m3f110y	F(0-100)HHdl	GD	£2126
86	1/98	Winc	2m6f	F(0-105)HHdl	GD	£2122

Total win prize-money £21819

Going: Sf: 0-0 GS: 0-0 Gd: 0-1 GF: - Fm: 1-2
Distance: 2m/2m3: 0-0 2m4-2m7: 0-0 **3m+: 1-3**
Track: LH: 0-0 **RH: 1-3** Tight: 0-0 Gall: 0-0
Aids: Bl: 0-0 Vi: 0-0 Tstrap: 0-0
Best Rating: 125 11/01 Extr 2m7f110y gd-fm Ch

Fair handicap chaser, stays three miles, does not want extremes of ground.

Waltham Dove

85 **43**

7-y-o br g Gypsy Castle-Dovetail (Brigadier Gerard)
K A Morgan Hall Farm Syndicate

Placings:*650420/0* **(4286)**
2001/02: 21^{0}GS

	Starts	1st	2nd	3rd	Win & Pl
Hurdles	1	0	0	0	
Career Total	**7**	**0**	**1**	**0**	**1269**

Going: Sf: 0-0 GS: 0-1 Gd: 0-0 GF: - Fm: 0-0
Distance: 2m/2m3: 0-0 2m4-2m7: 0-1 3m+: 0-0
Track: LH: 0-0 RH: 0-1 Tight: 0-1 Gall: 0-0
Aids: Bl: 0-0 Vi: 0-0 Tstrap: 0-0
Best Rating: 100 2/00 MRas 2m3f110y gd-sft Hdl

Waltham Kingfisher

73 **24**

7-y-o b m Presidium-Lindrake's Pride (Mandrake Major)
P R Rodford Les Trott

Placings:*0/0-00*P **(2277)**
2001/02: 16^{0}G, 17^{0}F, 22^{P}GF

	Starts	1st	2nd	3rd	Win & Pl
NH Flat	1	0	0	0	0
Hurdles	2	0	0	0	0
Career Total	**5**	**0**	**0**	**0**	

Going: Sf: 0-0 GS: 0-0 Gd: 0-1 GF: - Fm: 0-2
Distance: 2m/2m3: 0-2 2m4-2m7: 0-1 3m+: 0-0
Track: LH: 0-1 RH: 0-2 Tight: 0-1 Gall: 0-0
Aids: Bl: 0-1 Vi: 0-0 Tstrap: 0-0
Best Rating: 60 7/99 Sedg 2m1f gd-fm NHF

Wandering Light (IRE)

99 **128**

13-y-o b g Royal Fountain-Pleaseme (Javelot)
H D Daly Anne Duchess Of Westminster

Placings:5/00/111/30/12-45P **(4177)**
2001/02: 30^{4}G, 24^{5}HY, 24^{P}GS

	Starts	1st	2nd	3rd	Win & Pl
Chases	3	0	0	0	427
Career Total	**13**	**4**	**1**	**1**	**37699**

136	3/01	Hayd	3m	D(0-125)HCh	HVY	£7735
132	3/98	Chel	4m	B Ch	GD	£21135
110	11/97	Ludl	3m	E(0-100)HCh	GD	£3178
111	11/97	Worc	2m7f110y	D Ch	GD	£3550

Total win prize-money £35598

Going: Sf: 0-1 GS: 0-1 Gd: 0-1 GF: - Fm: 0-0
Distance: 2m/2m3: 0-0 2m4-2m7: 0-0 3m+: 0-3
Track: LH: 0-3 RH: 0-0 Tight: 0-2 Gall: 0-0
Aids: Bl: 0-0 Vi: 0-0 Tstrap: 0-0
Best Rating: 136 3/01 Hayd 3m heavy Ch

Lightly raced since winning the National Hunt Chase at the Cheltenham Festival in 1998, he returned from a two-year absence to score at Haydock in March 2001. Not disgraced since, he jumps well.

Wandering Wild

76 **38**

7-y-o ch m Nomadic Way (USA)-Wild Child (Grey Ghost)
R E Barr A Jackson

Placings:00-00 **(0568)**
2001/02: 21^{0}G, 20^{0}F

	Starts	1st	2nd	3rd	Win & Pl
Hurdles	2	0	0	0	
Career Total	**4**	**0**	**0**	**0**	

Going: Sf: 0-0 GS: 0-0 Gd: 0-1 GF: - Fm: 0-1
Distance: 2m/2m3: 0-0 2m4-2m7: 0-2 3m+: 0-0
Track: LH: 0-2 RH: 0-0 Tight: 0-1 Gall: 0-0
Aids: Bl: 0-0 Vi: 0-0 Tstrap: 0-2
Best Rating: 38 4/01 Ayr 2m4f good Hdl

Wanna Shout

80 **51**

4-y-o b f Missed Flight-Lulu (Polar Falcon (USA))
R Dickin E R C Beech & B Wilkinson

Placings:6 **(1956)**
2001/02: 16^{6}G

	Starts	1st	2nd	3rd	Win & Pl
Hurdles	1	0	0	0	0
Career Total	**1**	**0**	**0**	**0**	**0**

Going: Sf: 0-0 GS: 0-0 Gd: 0-1 GF: - Fm: 0-0
Distance: 2m/2m3: 0-1 2m4-2m7: 0-0 3m+: 0-0
Track: LH: 0-1 RH: 0-0 Tight: 0-0 Gall: 0-0
Aids: Bl: 0-0 Vi: 0-0 Tstrap: 0-0
Best Rating: 51 11/01 Wwck 2m good Hdl

Wansford Lady

84 **56**

6-y-o b m Michelozzo (USA)-Marnie's Girl (Crooner)
A W Carroll Mrs J Webster

Placings:0 **(0044)**
2001/02: 17^{0}GS

	Starts	1st	2nd	3rd	Win & Pl
Hurdles	1	0	0	0	
Career Total	**1**	**0**	**0**	**0**	

Going: Sf: 0-0 GS: 0-1 Gd: 0-0 GF: - Fm: 0-0
Distance: 2m/2m3: 0-1 2m4-2m7: 0-0 3m+: 0-0
Track: LH: 0-0 RH: 0-1 Tight: 0-0 Gall: 0-0
Aids: Bl: 0-0 Vi: 0-0 Tstrap: 0-0
Best Rating: 56 5/01 Extr 2m1f gd-sft Hdl

War Bride

64 **51**

4-y-o ch f Deploy-Dom One (Dominion)
Miss K M George Exterior Profiles Ltd

Placings:0 **(4504)**
2001/02: 17^{0}G

	Starts	1st	2nd	3rd	Win & Pl
Hurdles	1	0	0	0	
Career Total	**1**	**0**	**0**	**0**	

Going: Sf: 0-0 GS: 0-0 Gd: 0-1 GF: - Fm: 0-0
Distance: 2m/2m3: 0-1 2m4-2m7: 0-0 3m+: 0-0
Track: LH: 0-1 RH: 0-0 Tight: 0-1 Gall: 0-0
Aids: Bl: 0-0 Vi: 0-0 Tstrap: 0-0
Best Rating: 51 3/02 NAbb 2m1f good Hdl

War Paint (IRE)

10-y-o gr g Zaffaran (USA)-Rosy Posy (IRE) (Roselier (FR))
Mrs Nicola Sheppard (Mrs J Pitman 10/2) The Autofour/haven Partnership

Placings:*40/6/4/4* **(4179)**
2001/02: 24^{4}GS

	Starts	1st	2nd	3rd	Win & Pl
Chases	1	0	0	0	216
Career Total	**5**	**0**	**0**	**0**	**216**

Going: Sf: 0-0 GS: 0-1 Gd: 0-0 GF: - Fm: 0-0
Distance: 2m/2m3: 0-0 2m4-2m7: 0-0 3m+: 0-1
Track: LH: 0-1 RH: 0-0 Tight: 0-1 Gall: 0-0
Aids: Bl: 0-0 Vi: 0-0 Tstrap: 0-0
Best Rating: 103 1/99 Donc 2m4f gd-sft Hdl

War Tune

107 **99**

6-y-o b g Warrshan (USA)-Keen Melody (USA) (Sharpen Up)
G F Edwards G F Edwards

Placings:*04/63*-056F32FP20 **(4400)**
2001/02: 17^{0}GF, 17^{5}GF, 16^{6}S, 16^{F}G, 16^{3}G, 19^{2}S, 19^{F}S, 17^{P}S, 20^{2}GS, 21^{0}S

	Starts	1st	2nd	3rd	Win & Pl
Hurdles	10	0	2	1	2170
Career Total	**14**	**0**	**2**	**2**	**2399**

Going: Sf: 0-5 GS: 0-1 Gd: 0-2 GF: - Fm: 0-2
Distance: 2m/2m3: 0-6 2m4-2m7: 0-4 3m+: 0-0
Track: LH: 0-5 RH: 0-5 Tight: 0-5 Gall: 0-2
Aids: Bl: 0-0 Vi: 0-0 Tstrap: 0-0
Best Rating: 95 3/02 Chep 2m4f gd-sft Hdl

Plating class hurdler. Stays two and a half miles, seems effective on most ground.

Warjan (FR)

106

5-y-o b g Beaudelaire (USA)-Twilight Mood (USA) (Devil's Bag (USA))
R T Phillips Graeme Love

Placings:325155-0P **(3858)**
2001/02: 16^{0}S, 16^{P}S

	Starts	1st	2nd	3rd	Win & Pl
Hurdles	2	0	0	0	
Career Total	**8**	**1**	**1**	**1**	**16625**

128	3/01	MRas	2m1f110y	D Hdl	GD	£3654

Total win prize-money £3654

Going: Sf: 0-2 GS: 0-0 Gd: 0-0 GF: - Fm: 0-0
Distance: 2m/2m3: 0-2 2m4-2m7: 0-0 3m+: 0-0
Track: LH: 0-1 RH: 0-1 Tight: 0-0 Gall: 0-1
Aids: Bl: 0-0 Vi: 0-0 Tstrap: 0-0
Best Rating: 128 3/01 MRas 2m1f110y good Hdl

Ex-French import, showed a nice turn of foot when winning at Market Rasen in March 2001 found life a lot tougher at Aintree on heavy ground. Well held since. Best at around two miles on a sound surface.

Warner For Players (IRE)

103 120

11-y-o b g Good Thyne (USA)-Bramble Hatch (Pry)

J M Bradley Terry Warner

Placings: *331/5451/36P/200/* **2-115234** (4596)

2001/02: 20[1]GS, 25[1]S, 24[5]S, 24[2]HY, 19[3]S, 20[4]G

	Starts	1st	2nd	3rd	Win & Pl
Chases	6	2	1	1	9487
Career Total	**20**	**4**	**3**	**4**	**18771**

115	12/01	Hrfd	3m1f110y	E Ch	SFT	£3178
120	11/01	MRas	2m4f	E Ch	G-S	£4200
117	2/97	Ling	2m7f	E Hdl	HVY	£2729
107	4/96	NAbb	2m1f	H NHF	G-S	£1313

Total win prize-money £11421

Going: Sf: 1-4 GS: 1-1 Gd: 0-1 GF: - Fm: 0-0
Distance: 2m/2m3: 0-0 2m4-2m7: 1-3 3m+: 1-3
Track: LH: 0-4 **RH: 2-2 Tight: 1-2** Gall: 0-1
Aids: Bl: 0-0 Vi: 0-0 Tstrap: 0-0
Best Rating: 137 2/00 Hayd 2m7f110y heavy Hdl

A relatively lightly-raced stayer who loves the mud, he has landed two weak novice chases since switching to Milton Bradley. Held in handicaps since.

Warren Hill

7-y-o ch g Triune-The Warreness (Gargoor)

T Needham T Needham

Placings: 0 (3340)

2001/02: 17[0]S

	Starts	1st	2nd	3rd	Win & Pl
Hurdles	1	0	0	0	
Career Total	**1**	**0**	**0**	**0**	

Going: Sf: 0-1 GS: 0-0 Gd: 0-0 GF: - Fm: 0-0
Distance: 2m/2m3: 0-1 2m4-2m7: 0-0 3m+: 0-0
Track: LH: 0-0 RH: 0-1 Tight: 0-1 Gall: 0-0
Aids: Bl: 0-0 Vi: 0-0 Tstrap: 0-0
Best Rating:

Warrlin

106(103h) (70h)116

8-y-o b g Warrshan (USA)-Lahin (Rainbow Quest (USA))

C W Fairhurst Glasgow House Racing Syndicate

Placings: 202562360/1523123F/044031134/03200030 U0-02P3343 (4761)

2001/02: 17[0]G, 21[2]G, 20[P]GS, 19[3]GS, 19[3]S, 19[4]S, 19[3]GF

	Starts	1st	2nd	3rd	Win & Pl
Chases	7	0	1	3	3763
Career Total	**43**	**4**	**7**	**10**	**25481**

107	2/00	MRas	2m1f110y	F(0-110)HHdl	G-S	£1858
100	2/00	Kels	2m2f	E(0-115)HHdl	G-S	£5850
103	12/98	Sedg	2m1f	E(0-110)HHdl	SFT	£2757
93	8/98	Ctml	2m1f110y	E Hdl	G-S	£2477

Total win prize-money £12945

Going: Sf: 0-2 GS: 0-2 Gd: 0-2 GF: - Fm: 0-1
Distance: 2m/2m3: 0-3 2m4-2m7: 0-4 3m+: 0-0
Track: LH: 0-5 RH: 0-2 Tight: 0-5 Gall: 0-1
Aids: Bl: 0-0 Vi: 0-0 Tstrap: 0-0
Best Rating: 116 4/02 Asct 2m3f110y gd-fm Ch

A winner over hurdles, he has shown fair form over fences. Acts on most types of ground and is effective at around two miles.

Warton Crag

6-y-o b g Tina's Pet-Majestic Form (IRE) (Double Schwartz)

D Moffatt Mrs G A Turnbull

Placings: *0* (4771)

2001/02: 16[0]GF

	Starts	1st	2nd	3rd	Win & Pl
NH Flat	1	0	0	0	
Career Total	**1**	**0**	**0**	**0**	

Going: Sf: 0-0 GS: 0-0 Gd: 0-0 GF: - Fm: 0-1
Distance: 2m/2m3: 0-1 2m4-2m7: 0-0 3m+: 0-0
Track: LH: 0-0 RH: 0-0 Tight: 0-0 Gall: 0-0
Aids: Bl: 0-0 Vi: 0-0 Tstrap: 0-0
Best Rating:

Wartorn (IRE)

94 83

7-y-o b g Warcraft (USA)-Alice Minkthorn (Party Mink)

J S King Miss S Douglas-Pennant

Placings: 450 (3989)

2001/02: 19[4]G, 22[5]G, 24[0]S

	Starts	1st	2nd	3rd	Win & Pl
Hurdles	3	0	0	0	0
Career Total	**3**	**0**	**0**	**0**	**0**

Going: Sf: 0-1 GS: 0-0 Gd: 0-2 GF: - Fm: 0-0
Distance: 2m/2m3: 0-0 2m4-2m7: 0-2 3m+: 0-1
Track: LH: 0-0 RH: 0-3 Tight: 0-1 Gall: 0-0
Aids: Bl: 0-0 Vi: 0-0 Tstrap: 0-0
Best Rating: 83 1/02 Winc 2m6f good Hdl

Was A Drive (IRE)

106 99

8-y-o b g Yashgan-Alan's Rosalinda (Prefairy)

Miss Kate Milligan E C Gordon

Placings: PP-30P14P (4889)

2001/02: 19[3]G, 24[0]S, 24[P]S, 20[1]HY, 20[4]GS, 26[P]G

	Starts	1st	2nd	3rd	Win & Pl
Chases	6	1	0	1	3794
Career Total	**8**	**1**	**0**	**1**	**3794**

99	3/02	Hexm	2m4f110y	F(0-100)HCh	HVY	£3066

Total win prize-money £3066

Going: Sf: 1-3 GS: 0-1 Gd: 0-2 GF: - Fm: 0-0
Distance: 2m/2m3: 0-1 **2m4-2m7: 1-2** 3m+: 0-3
Track: **LH: 1-3** RH: 0-2 Tight: 0-2 Gall: 0-1
Aids: Bl: 0-0 Vi: 0-0 Tstrap: 0-0
Best Rating: 99 3/02 Carl 2m4f gd-sft Ch

Moderate chaser, suited by two and a half miles, handles good ground and has won on heavy.

Waseyla (IRE)

5-y-o b m Sri Pekan (USA)-Lady Windley (Baillamont (USA))

Miss E C Lavelle (Julian Poulton 1/5) At Leisure Racing

Placings: P (3340)

2001/02: 17[P]S

	Starts	1st	2nd	3rd	Win & Pl
Hurdles	1	0	0	0	
Career Total	**1**	**0**	**0**	**0**	

Going: Sf: 0-1 GS: 0-0 Gd: 0-0 GF: - Fm: 0-0
Distance: 2m/2m3: 0-1 2m4-2m7: 0-0 3m+: 0-0
Track: LH: 0-0 RH: 0-1 Tight: 0-1 Gall: 0-0
Aids: Bl: 0-0 Vi: 0-0 Tstrap: 0-0
Best Rating:

Wassiwopped

8-y-o ch g Joli Wasfi (USA)-Shades Of Autumn (Double Form)

J W Mullins Brian S Heath

Placings: P0P (1842)

2001/02: 22[P]GF, 22[0]GF, 24[P]S

	Starts	1st	2nd	3rd	Win & Pl
Hurdles	3	0	0	0	
Career Total	**3**	**0**	**0**	**0**	

Going: Sf: 0-1 GS: 0-0 Gd: 0-0 GF: - Fm: 0-2
Distance: 2m/2m3: 0-0 2m4-2m7: 0-2 3m+: 0-1
Track: LH: 0-0 RH: 0-2 Tight: 0-0 Gall: 0-0
Aids: Bl: 0-0 Vi: 0-0 Tstrap: 0-0
Best Rating:

Watch It

80f 80f

4-y-o b g Sea Raven (IRE)-Magic Penny (Sharrood (USA))

M Todhunter Mrs Allison Stamper

Placings: 6 (3354)

2001/02: 16[6]G

	Starts	1st	2nd	3rd	Win & Pl
NH Flat	1	0	0	0	0
Career Total	**1**	**0**	**0**	**0**	**0**

Going: Sf: 0-0 GS: 0-0 Gd: 0-1 GF: - Fm: 0-0
Distance: 2m/2m3: 0-1 2m4-2m7: 0-0 3m+: 0-0
Track: LH: 0-0 RH: 0-1 Tight: 0-1 Gall: 0-0
Aids: Bl: 0-0 Vi: 0-0 Tstrap: 0-0
Best Rating: 80 1/02 Muss 2m good NHF

Watch The Dove

94f 100f

5-y-o b g Afzal-Spot The Dove (Riberetto)

C Tizzard L G Tizzard

Placings: *024* (4887)

2001/02: 16[0]S, 17[2]G, 18[4]GF

	Starts	1st	2nd	3rd	Win & Pl
NH Flat	3	0	1	0	690
Career Total	**3**	**0**	**1**	**0**	**690**

Going: Sf: 0-1 GS: 0-0 Gd: 0-1 GF: - Fm: 0-1
Distance: 2m/2m3: 0-3 2m4-2m7: 0-0 3m+: 0-0
Track: LH: 0-2 RH: 0-1 Tight: 0-2 Gall: 0-0
Aids: Bl: 0-0 Vi: 0-0 Tstrap: 0-0
Best Rating: 100 3/02 NAbb 2m1f good NHF

From the same family as 1994 Champion Hurdler Flakey Dove. Has shown ability in bumpers on a sound surface.

Water Font (IRE)

115 125

10-y-o b g Lafontaine (USA)-Belle Savenay (Coquelin

(USA))
J J O'Neill G & P Barker Ltd/globe Engineering

Placings: *4P03*P/0043121/1/03**FP011P/P24PPU342-P111P** **(0848)**
2001/02: 26^{P}GF, 24^{1}GF, 24^{1}F, 24^{1}GF, 32^{P}GF

	Starts	1st	2nd	3rd	Win & Pl
Chases	5	3	0	0	22048
Career Total	**35**	**8**	**3**	**4**	**42337**

125	6/01	Prth	3m	C(0-135)HCh	G-F	£13975
115	6/01	Prth	3m	E(0-115)HCh	FRM	£4979
115	5/01	Newc	3m	F(0-90)HCh	G-F	£3094
115	3/00	Catt	3m1f110y	F(0-100)HCh	G-F	£2626
97	2/00	Muss	3m	E(0-105)HCh	GD	£4290
97	5/98	Uttx	3m110y	E(0-105)HHdl	G-F	£2442
97	4/98	Sedg	2m5f110y	E(0-100)HHdl	GD	£4034
90	3/98	Newc	2m4f	G(0-95)HHdl	G-F	£1668

Total win prize-money £37109

Going: Sf: 0-0 GS: 0-0 Gd: 0-0 GF: - Fm: 3-5
Distance: 2m/2m3: 0-0 2m4-2m7: 0-0 **3m+: 3-5**
Track: LH: 1-1 **RH: 2-2** Tight: 0-0 **Gall: 1-1**
Aids: Bl: 0-1 Vi: 0-0 Tstrap: 0-0
Best Rating: 125 6/01 Prth 3m gd-fm Ch

Fair staying chaser. Acts on fast ground. In good form in the summer of 2001. Likes to dominate.

Water Stratford (IRE)

107 117
9-y-o b m Jurado (USA)-Decent Lady (Decent Fellow)
P R Webber C W Booth

Placings: *131*/1261/0104-F5**U013P** **(4844)**
2001/02: 17^{F}GS, 17^{5}S, 20^{U}S, 16^{0}S, 16^{1}S, 16^{3}GS, 24^{P}G

	Starts	1st	2nd	3rd	Win & Pl
Hurdles	6	1	0	1	4306
Chases	1	0	0	0	0
Career Total	**18**	**6**	**1**	**2**	**15450**

117	3/02	Winc	2m	D(0-125)HHdl	SFT	£3510
117	3/01	Hntg	2m110y	F(0-110)HHdl	SFT	£1974
95	3/00	Bang	2m1f	E Hdl	G-S	£2847
106	11/99	Worc	2m	E Hdl	G-S	£2512
107	2/99	Fknm	2m	H NHF	G-S	£1283
109	11/98	Hrfd	2m1f	H NHF	GD	£1234

Total win prize-money £13362

Going: Sf: 1-4 GS: 0-2 Gd: 0-1 GF: - Fm: 0-0
Distance: **2m/2m3: 1-5** 2m4-2m7: 0-1 3m+: 0-1
Track: LH: 0-3 **RH: 1-4** Tight: 0-4 Gall: 0-1
Aids: Bl: 0-0 Vi: 0-0 Tstrap: 0-0
Best Rating: 117 3/02 Towc 2m gd-sft Hdl

Winning bumper and novice hurdler, she landed a weak event in handicap company in March 2001, but unseated her rider on her chasing debut. Got off the mark in 2002 when landing a fair handicap over the minimum trip. Acts with cut.

Water Wheels Lass

4-y-o b f Sovereign Water (FR)-Miss Marjorie (Swing Easy (USA))
R D E Woodhouse Mrs S J Gale And M P Gale

Placings: *P0* **(3862)**
2001/02: 17^{P}S, 16^{0}S

	Starts	1st	2nd	3rd	Win & Pl
NH Flat	2	0	0	0	
Career Total	**2**	**0**	**0**	**0**	

Going: Sf: 0-2 GS: 0-0 Gd: 0-0 GF: - Fm: 0-0
Distance: 2m/2m3: 0-2 2m4-2m7: 0-0 3m+: 0-0
Track: LH: 0-2 RH: 0-0 Tight: 0-1 Gall: 0-1
Aids: Bl: 0-0 Vi: 0-0 Tstrap: 0-0
Best Rating:

Waterberg (IRE)

105(105h) (116h)136
7-y-o b g Sadler's Wells (USA)-Pretoria (Habitat)
H D Daly R M Kirkland

Placings: *1/142*/122-**161311** **(4878)**
2001/02: 20^{1}G, 20^{6}GS, 24^{1}GS, 24^{3}S, 20^{1}GF, 24^{1}G

	Starts	1st	2nd	3rd	Win & Pl
Hurdles	1	1	0	0	3892
Chases	5	3	0	1	18925
Career Total	**13**	**7**	**3**	**1**	**32736**

136	4/02	Prth	3m	C Ch	GD	£7241
117	4/02	Carl	2m4f	C Ch	G-F	£6987
128	2/02	Ludl	3m	D Ch	G-S	£4134
116	5/01	Hntg	2m4f110y	D Hdl	GD	£3892
119	1/01	Leic	2m4f110y	D Hdl	HVY	£3510
119	12/99	Uttx	2m	H NHF	SFT	£1742
112	4/99	MRas	1m5f110y	H NHF	SFT	£1517

Total win prize-money £29024

Going: Sf: 0-1 GS: 1-2 Gd: 2-2 GF: - Fm: 1-1
Distance: 2m/2m3: 0-0 2m4-2m7: 2-3 3m+: 2-3
Track: LH: 0-0 **RH: 4-6** Tight: 1-2 Gall: 1-2
Aids: Bl: 0-0 Vi: 0-0 Tstrap: 0-0
Best Rating: 136 4/02 Prth 3m good Ch

He put a poor run on his chasing debut behind him to win at Ludlow in February 2002 and added to that with two wins on a sound surface in April. Stays three miles, acts on any ground, is suited by a right-handed track.

Waterfront (IRE)

6-y-o b g Turtle Island (IRE)-Rising Tide (Red Alert)
G P Kelly G P Kelly

Placings: P-P **(0976)**
2001/02: 16^{P}GF

	Starts	1st	2nd	3rd	Win & Pl
Hurdles	1	0	0	0	
Career Total	**2**	**0**	**0**	**0**	

Going: Sf: 0-0 GS: 0-0 Gd: 0-0 GF: - Fm: 0-1
Distance: 2m/2m3: 0-1 2m4-2m7: 0-0 3m+: 0-0
Track: LH: 0-1 RH: 0-0 Tight: 0-1 Gall: 0-0
Aids: Bl: 0-0 Vi: 0-0 Tstrap: 0-1
Best Rating:

Waterlaw (IRE)

99(63h) 109
8-y-o b g Kahyasi-Shuss (USA) (Princely Native (USA))
E Stanners Waterlaw Limited

Placings: *1023110/00/22-1445* **(2126)**
2001/02: 20^{1}G, 20^{4}GF, 19^{4}F, 20^{5}G

	Starts	1st	2nd	3rd	Win & Pl
Chases	4	1	0	0	4839
Career Total	**15**	**4**	**3**	**1**	**13355**

104	8/01	Bang	2m4f110y	D Ch	GD	£4173
97	9/98	Plum	2m4f	E Hdl	GD	£2337
91	8/98	Bang	2m4f	E Hdl	GD	£2410
93	5/98	Uttx	2m	H NHF	G-F	£1222

Total win prize-money £10144

Going: Sf: 0-0 GS: 0-0 Gd: 1-2 GF: - Fm: 0-2
Distance: 2m/2m3: 0-1 **2m4-2m7: 1-3** 3m+: 0-0
Track: **LH: 1-2** RH: 0-1 **Tight: 1-3** Gall: 0-1
Aids: Bl: 0-0 Vi: 0-0 **Tstrap: 1-4**
Best Rating: 112 8/00 Bang 2m4f good Hdl

Won a Bangor novice event on his chasing debut but has jumped sketchily in defeat since.

Waterloo Park (IRE)

6-y-o b m Alphabatim (USA)-Waterloo Sunset (Deep Run)
Noel T Chance Mrs M Chance

Placings: *100* **(4823)**
2001/02: 16^{1}G, 16^{0}G, 17^{0}G

	Starts	1st	2nd	3rd	Win & Pl
NH Flat	3	1	0	0	1561
Career Total	**3**	**1**	**0**	**0**	**1561**

112	11/01	Wwck	2m	H NHF	GD	£1561

Total win prize-money £1561

Going: Sf: 0-0 GS: 0-0 Gd: 1-3 GF: - Fm: 0-0
Distance: **2m/2m3: 1-3** 2m4-2m7: 0-0 3m+: 0-0
Track: **LH: 1-2** RH: 0-1 Tight: 0-0 Gall: 0-1
Aids: Bl: 0-0 Vi: 0-0 Tstrap: 0-0
Best Rating: 112 11/01 Wwck 2m good NHF

She made an impressive debut when easily winning a Warwick bumper in November 2001, but was held subsequently.

Watership Down (IRE)

102(97h) (70h)97
5-y-o b g Dolphin Street (FR)-Persian Myth (Persian Bold)
B G Powell D & J Newell

Placings: 6-064155 **(2336)**
2001/02: 20^{0}G, 20^{6}GF, 20^{4}G, 21^{1}G, 21^{5}S, 20^{5}GF

	Starts	1st	2nd	3rd	Win & Pl
Hurdles	2	0	0	0	0
Chases	4	1	0	0	3351
Career Total	**7**	**1**	**0**	**0**	**3351**

97	10/01	Sedg	2m5f	E Ch	GD	£3019

Total win prize-money £3019

Going: Sf: 0-1 GS: 0-0 Gd: 1-3 GF: - Fm: 0-2
Distance: 2m/2m3: 0-0 **2m4-2m7: 1-6** 3m+: 0-0
Track: **LH: 1-5** RH: 0-1 **Tight: 1-4** Gall: 0-0
Aids: Bl: 0-0 Vi: 0-0 Tstrap: 0-0
Best Rating: 97 10/01 Sedg 2m5f good Ch

Got off the mark in a novice chase in October 2001, but has struggled since then. Acts on good ground.

Watkins

97(81c) (85c)80
7-y-o ch g King's Signet (USA)-Windbound Lass (Crofter (USA))
Miss D Cole R W Savery

Placings: 60/1/460P-6500F450 **(1395)**
2001/02: 22^{6}GF, 27^{5}G, 24^{0}GF, 24^{0}G, 27^{F}G, 27^{4}G, 26^{5}GF, 24^{0}GF

	Starts	1st	2nd	3rd	Win & Pl
Hurdles	6	0	0	0	0
Chases	2	0	0	0	0
Career Total	**15**	**1**	**0**	**0**	**2481**

76	7/99	NAbb	3m3f	E Hdl	G-F	£2266

Total win prize-money £2266

Going: Sf: 0-0 GS: 0-0 Gd: 0-4 GF: - Fm: 0-4
Distance: 2m/2m3: 0-0 2m4-2m7: 0-1 3m+: 0-7
Track: LH: 0-7 RH: 0-1 Tight: 0-6 Gall: 0-0
Aids: Bl: 0-1 Vi: 0-0 Tstrap: 0-2
Best Rating: 85 7/01 Strf 3m good Ch

Wave Rock

119(107h) (124h)**154**

7-y-o br g Tragic Role (USA)-Moonscape (Ribero)
P J Hobbs Sterling Racing Syndicate

Placings:23223413/23U1312F3211F3/141332P1-6523552 **(4914)**
2001/02: 18^{6}S, 16^{5}G, 16^{2}G, 16^{3}GS, 16^{5}G, 16^{5}G, 20^{2}G

	Starts	1st	2nd	3rd	Win & Pl
Hurdles	1	0	0	0	319
Chases	6	0	2	1	21366
Career Total	**37**	**8**	**9**	**10**	**95079**

144	4/01	Ayr	2m	B HCh	G-F	£13474
144	11/00	Chel	2m	B(0-145)HCh	G-S	£14088
134	5/00	Punc	2m2f	Ch	GD	£6072
139	3/00	Hntg	2m110y	E Ch	SFT	£2983
132	2/00	Chep	2m110y	D Ch	SFT	£4134
124	11/99	Wwck	2m	D Ch	GD	£4290
110	8/99	Worc	2m	D(0-125)HHdl	G-S	£3029
109	2/99	Sand	2m110y	D Hdl	G-S	£2853

Total win prize-money £50928

Going: Sf: 0-1 GS: 0-1 Gd: 0-5 GF: - Fm: 0-0
Distance: 2m/2m3: 0-6 2m4-2m7: 0-1 3m+: 0-0
Track: LH: 0-3 RH: 0-4 Tight: 0-1 Gall: 0-2
Aids: Bl: 0-7 Vi: 0-0 Tstrap: 0-0
Best Rating: 154 4/02 Sand 2m4f110y good Ch

A winner on the Flat, over hurdles and over fences, he is an effective performer in two-mile handicap chases. He ran some fine races last season including when runner-up in the Victor Chandler. Just caught when stepped up to two and a half miles at Sandown in April. Reverted to hurdles in May 2002, fortunate winner at Hereford. Usually blinkered, he tends to carry his head awkwardly but is genuine.

Way Home

76 **38**

7-y-o b m La Grange Music-Good Way (Good Apple)
N G Richards Mrs Julia Young And Partners

Placings:20-00 **(2070)**
2001/02: 17^{0}G, 17^{0}S

	Starts	1st	2nd	3rd	Win & Pl
NH Flat	1	0	0	0	0
Hurdles	1	0	0	0	0
Career Total	**4**	**0**	**1**	**0**	**425**

Going: Sf: 0-1 GS: 0-0 Gd: 0-1 GF: - Fm: 0-0
Distance: 2m/2m3: 0-2 2m4-2m7: 0-0 3m+: 0-0
Track: LH: 0-2 RH: 0-0 Tight: 0-2 Gall: 0-0
Aids: Bl: 0-0 Vi: 0-0 Tstrap: 0-0
Best Rating: 94 7/00 Worc 2m gd-fm NHF

Waylaid (IRE)

(39c) **60**

7-y-o b g Grand Plaisir (IRE)-No Notice (Mandalus)
Mrs D Haine Mrs Solna Thomson Jones

Placings:05U04/05UP5-0P **(0979)**
2001/02: 22^{0}GF, 27^{P}G

	Starts	1st	2nd	3rd	Win & Pl
Hurdles	2	0	0	0	
Career Total	**12**	**0**	**0**	**0**	**250**

Going: Sf: 0-0 GS: 0-0 Gd: 0-1 GF: - Fm: 0-1
Distance: 2m/2m3: 0-0 2m4-2m7: 0-1 3m+: 0-1
Track: LH: 0-2 RH: 0-0 Tight: 0-2 Gall: 0-0
Aids: Bl: 0-0 Vi: 0-0 Tstrap: 0-0
Best Rating: 78 4/00 MRas 2m3f110y soft Hdl

Wayward Buttons

109(90h) (76h)**118**

8-y-o b g Nomadic Way (USA)-Lady Buttons (New Brig)
M Todhunter Mrs A W Scott-Harden And Mrs A Nicholson

Placings:06145PP **(4521)**
2001/02: 17^{0}GS, 21^{6}G, 21^{1}S, 24^{4}GF, 20^{5}G, 20^{P}HY, 20^{P}GS

	Starts	1st	2nd	3rd	Win & Pl
Hurdles	1	0	0	0	0
Chases	6	1	0	0	3409
Career Total	**7**	**1**	**0**	**0**	**3409**

105	11/01	Sedg	2m5f	E Ch	SFT	£3090

Total win prize-money £3091

Going: Sf: 1-2 GS: 0-2 Gd: 0-2 GF: - Fm: 0-1
Distance: 2m/2m3: 0-1 **2m4-2m7: 1-5** 3m+: 0-1
Track: **LH: 1-3** RH: 0-4 **Tight: 1-4** Gall: 0-0
Aids: Bl: 0-0 Vi: 0-0 Tstrap: 0-0
Best Rating: 118 12/01 Muss 3m gd-fm Ch

Showed some sign of ability in decent novice chase won by Man On The Hill and jumped soundly next time when picking up a small race over the same course and distance. Stays two miles-five, probably best with cut.

Wayward Cove

83f **72f**

5-y-o b m Karinga Bay-Wayward Pam (Pamroy)
R J Hodges Mrs E M Charlton

Placings:0 **(2294)**
2001/02: 17^{0}GF

	Starts	1st	2nd	3rd	Win & Pl
NH Flat	1	0	0	0	
Career Total	**1**	**0**	**0**	**0**	

Going: Sf: 0-0 GS: 0-0 Gd: 0-0 GF: - Fm: 0-1
Distance: 2m/2m3: 0-1 2m4-2m7: 0-0 3m+: 0-0
Track: LH: 0-0 RH: 0-1 Tight: 0-0 Gall: 0-0
Aids: Bl: 0-0 Vi: 0-0 Tstrap: 0-0
Best Rating: 72 11/01 Extr 2m1f gd-fm NHF

We Have Him (IRE)

85(80h) (28h)**66**

9-y-o ch g Orange Reef-Corrib Agreement (Lucifer (USA))
G Brown Mrs Rhona Alexander

Placings:060450-0 **(0207)**
2001/02: 16^{0}F

	Starts	1st	2nd	3rd	Win & Pl
Chases	1	0	0	0	
Career Total	**7**	**0**	**0**	**0**	**160**

Going: Sf: 0-0 GS: 0-0 Gd: 0-0 GF: - Fm: 0-1
Distance: 2m/2m3: 0-1 2m4-2m7: 0-0 3m+: 0-0
Track: LH: 0-1 RH: 0-0 Tight: 0-1 Gall: 0-0
Aids: Bl: 0-0 Vi: 0-0 Tstrap: 0-0
Best Rating: 69 7/00 Dund 2m4f153y gd-fm Hdl

We'Ll Make It (IRE)

105 **109**

4-y-o b g Spectrum (IRE)-Walliser (Niniski (USA))
G L Moore Mrs Charles Sparrowhawk

Placings:4342430 **(4417)**
2001/02: 16^{4}GS, 16^{3}GS, 16^{4}G, 18^{2}G, 16^{4}G, 17^{3}S, 16^{0}GS

	Starts	1st	2nd	3rd	Win & Pl
Hurdles	7	0	1	2	2977
Career Total	**7**	**0**	**1**	**2**	**2977**

Going: Sf: 0-1 GS: 0-3 Gd: 0-3 GF: - Fm: 0-0
Distance: 2m/2m3: 0-7 2m4-2m7: 0-0 3m+: 0-0
Track: LH: 0-3 RH: 0-4 Tight: 0-2 Gall: 0-2
Aids: Bl: 0-1 Vi: 0-0 Tstrap: 0-0
Best Rating: 109 12/01 Kemp 2m good Hdl

Modest form over hurdles so far and looks to need a step up to two and a half miles. Flatters to deceive.

Weather Wise

76 **90**

10-y-o b g Town And Country-Sunshine Gal (Alto Volante)
W G M Turner David Chown

Placings:0043/33612012PPP/6116P512002P/231033 6/60-00 **(0562)**
2001/02: 22^{0}GS, 22^{0}GF

	Starts	1st	2nd	3rd	Win & Pl
Hurdles	2	0	0	0	
Career Total	**38**	**6**	**5**	**6**	**15331**

104	12/99	Sthl	2m4f110y	G Hdl	SFT	£1537
104	12/98	Hrfd	3m2f	G(0-95)HHdl	SFT	£1976
100	10/98	Sthl	2m4f110y	G(0-95)HHdl	GD	£1672
98	9/98	Hntg	3m2f	G(0-95)HHdl	G-F	£1632
82	12/97	Hrfd	3m2f	G(0-95)HHdl	SFT	£1772
90	12/97	Font	2m2f110y	G Hdl	SFT	£1832

Total win prize-money £10423

Going: Sf: 0-0 GS: 0-1 Gd: 0-0 GF: - Fm: 0-1
Distance: 2m/2m3: 0-0 2m4-2m7: 0-2 3m+: 0-0
Track: LH: 0-1 RH: 0-0 Tight: 0-1 Gall: 0-0
Aids: Bl: 0-0 Vi: 0-0 Tstrap: 0-2
Best Rating: 104 12/99 Sthl 2m4f110y soft Hdl

Weaver George (IRE)

108(99h) (94h)**135**

12-y-o b g Flash Of Steel-Nephrite (Godswalk (USA))
W Storey Regent Decorators Ltd

Placings:F0233241/1100342U/3403F015/152412111 23/11223/33F612241/52P26324/64621245-604211111F50 **(3493)**
2001/02: 24^{6}S, 21^{0}GF, 21^{4}G, 21^{2}G, 21^{1}G, 25^{1}G, 26^{1}GS, 25^{1}GS, 25^{1}GS, 25^{F}S, 26^{5}G, 24^{0}S

	Starts	1st	2nd	3rd	Win & Pl
Chases	12	5	1	0	28117
Career Total	**77**	**19**	**16**	**10**	**104182**

135	12/01	Kels	3m1f	B(0-145)HCh	G-S	£10707
135	10/01	Kels	3m1f	D(0-125)HCh	G-S	£4173
131	10/01	Carl	3m2f	E(0-115)HCh	G-S	£3477
120	10/01	Kels	3m1f	D(0-125)HCh	GD	£4290
115	10/01	Sedg	2m5f	E(0-115)HCh	GD	£3987
129	11/00	Newc	2m4f	D(0-125)HCh	SFT	£5404
127	4/99	Sedg	2m5f	D(0-125)HCh	G-S	£4432
135	3/99	Newc	2m4f	D(0-125)HCh	SFT	£3694
116	5/97	Prth	2m4f110y	D(0-125)HCh	SFT	£3436

116	5/97	Sedg	2m5f	D(0-125)HCh	G-F	£3821
116	2/97	Catt	2m	E(0-115)HCh	G-S	£2842
114	2/97	Catt	2m3f	E(0-110)HCh	GD	£2706
113	1/97	Catt	2m3f	D(0-120)HCh	GD	£3470
106	12/96	Sedg	2m110y	E(0-115)HCh	GD	£2877
103	5/96	Sedg	2m110y	E Ch	FRM	£2945
103	3/96	Sedg	2m1f	E Ch	GD	£3185
103	12/94	Weth	2m	(0-135)HHdl	GD	£2565
98	5/94	Weth	2m	Hdl	G-F	£2075
87	4/94	Weth	2m	Hdl	GD	£2337

Total win prize-money £72430

Going: Sf: 0-3 GS: 3-3 Gd: 2-5 GF: - Fm: 0-1
Distance: 2m/2m3: 0-0 2m4-2m7: 1-4 **3m+: 4-8**
Track: **LH: 4-10** RH: 1-2 **Tight: 4-7** Gall: 0-2
Aids: Bl: 0-0 Vi: 0-0 Tstrap: 0-0
Best Rating: 135 12/01 Kels 3m1f gd-sft Ch

Enjoyed a purple patch towards the end of 2001 when stepped up to three miles and equipped with sheepskin cheekpieces, completing a fine nap-hand including three wins at Kelso. Handles easy ground.

Weaver Sam

71 24

7-y-o ch g Ron's Victory (USA)-Grove Star (Upper Case (USA))
Ferdy Murphy (P S McEntee 18/7) J Wightman

Placings:*203/*100/6P0 **(1419)**
2001/02: 17^{6}GF, 24^{P}G, 21^{0}G

	Starts	1st	2nd	3rd	Win & Pl
Hurdles	3	0	0	0	0
Career Total	**9**	**1**	**1**	**1**	**2023**

100 6/99 Hexm 2m H NHF SFT £1367
Total win prize-money £1368

Going: Sf: 0-0 GS: 0-0 Gd: 0-2 GF: - Fm: 0-1
Distance: 2m/2m3: 0-1 2m4-2m7: 0-1 3m+: 0-1
Track: LH: 0-2 RH: 0-1 Tight: 0-2 Gall: 0-0
Aids: Bl: 0-1 Vi: 0-0 Tstrap: 0-0
Best Rating: 109 4/99 Aint 2m110y good NHF

Weavers Choice

9-y-o ch g Sunley Builds-Wedding Song (True Song)
Mrs Joan Tice (Trainer Unknown 24/2) Mrs Joan Tice

Placings:4 **(4057)**
2001/02: 23^{4}S

	Starts	1st	2nd	3rd	Win & Pl
Chases	1	0	0	0	165
Career Total	**1**	**0**	**0**	**0**	**165**

Going: Sf: 0-1 GS: 0-0 Gd: 0-0 GF: - Fm: 0-0
Distance: 2m/2m3: 0-0 2m4-2m7: 0-0 3m+: 0-1
Track: LH: 0-0 RH: 0-1 Tight: 0-0 Gall: 0-0
Aids: Bl: 0-0 Vi: 0-0 Tstrap: 0-0
Best Rating: 85 3/02 Leic 2m7f110y soft Ch

Webbswood

69f 57f

7-y-o b g Newski (USA)-Miss Inigo (Sagaro)
C J Hemsley Alan Love

Placings:*0-0* **(0377)**
2001/02: 16^{0}GF

	Starts	1st	2nd	3rd	Win & Pl
NH Flat	1	0	0	0	
Career Total	**2**	**0**	**0**	**0**	

Going: Sf: 0-0 GS: 0-0 Gd: 0-0 GF: - Fm: 0-1
Distance: 2m/2m3: 0-1 2m4-2m7: 0-0 3m+: 0-0
Track: LH: 0-0 RH: 0-1 Tight: 0-0 Gall: 0-1
Aids: Bl: 0-0 Vi: 0-0 Tstrap: 0-0
Best Rating: 57 5/01 Hntg 2m110y gd-fm NHF

Wedidthat (IRE)

(72h) (55h)

6-y-o ch m Moscow Society (USA)-Vesper Time (The Parson)
M C Pipe G L Phippen

Placings:*0-0***P** **(0317)**
2001/02: 18^{0}GF, 23^{P}F

	Starts	1st	2nd	3rd	Win & Pl
Hurdles	1	0	0	0	0
Chases	1	0	0	0	0
Career Total	**3**	**0**	**0**	**0**	

Going: Sf: 0-0 GS: 0-0 Gd: 0-0 GF: - Fm: 0-2
Distance: 2m/2m3: 0-1 2m4-2m7: 0-0 3m+: 0-1
Track: LH: 0-1 RH: 0-1 Tight: 0-1 Gall: 0-0
Aids: Bl: 0-0 Vi: 0-2 Tstrap: 0-0
Best Rating: 55 5/01 Font 2m2f110y gd-fm Hdl

Wee Barney

88 33

5-y-o b g Balnibarbi-Never So True (Never So Bold)
C Grant B Ayre

Placings:200-00 **(4917)**
2001/02: 21^{0}S, 21^{0}GF

	Starts	1st	2nd	3rd	Win & Pl
Hurdles	2	0	0	0	
Career Total	**5**	**0**	**1**	**0**	**888**

Going: Sf: 0-1 GS: 0-0 Gd: 0-0 GF: - Fm: 0-1
Distance: 2m/2m3: 0-0 2m4-2m7: 0-2 3m+: 0-0
Track: LH: 0-2 RH: 0-0 Tight: 0-2 Gall: 0-0
Aids: Bl: 0-0 Vi: 0-0 Tstrap: 0-0
Best Rating: 82 8/00 Bang 2m1f good Hdl

Wee Jimmy

87 57

6-y-o b g Lugana Beach-Cutlass Princess (USA) (Cutlass (USA))
B A McMahon Michael Sturgess

Placings:6042/06P0053-4PP0 **(4160)**
2001/02: 16^{4}HY, 16^{P}GS, 24^{P}HY, 16^{0}GS

	Starts	1st	2nd	3rd	Win & Pl
Hurdles	4	0	0	0	0
Career Total	**15**	**0**	**1**	**1**	**724**

Going: Sf: 0-2 GS: 0-2 Gd: 0-0 GF: - Fm: 0-0
Distance: 2m/2m3: 0-3 2m4-2m7: 0-0 3m+: 0-1
Track: LH: 0-3 RH: 0-1 Tight: 0-0 Gall: 0-0
Aids: Bl: 0-1 Vi: 0-0 Tstrap: 0-0
Best Rating: 83 3/00 Uttx 2m good Hdl

Wee Nel

81 67

4-y-o ch f Imp Society (USA)-Eskimo Nel (IRE) (Shy Groom (USA))
N P Littmoden First Chance Racing

Placings:600 **(2512)**
2001/02: 16^{6}G, 17^{0}GS, 16^{0}S

	Starts	1st	2nd	3rd	Win & Pl
Hurdles	3	0	0	0	0
Career Total	**3**	**0**	**0**	**0**	**0**

Going: Sf: 0-1 GS: 0-1 Gd: 0-1 GF: - Fm: 0-0
Distance: 2m/2m3: 0-3 2m4-2m7: 0-0 3m+: 0-0
Track: LH: 0-3 RH: 0-0 Tight: 0-2 Gall: 0-1
Aids: Bl: 0-0 Vi: 0-0 Tstrap: 0-0
Best Rating: 67 11/01 Newb 2m110y good Hdl

Wee River (IRE)

(64h)

13-y-o b g Over The River (FR)-Mahe Reef (Be Friendly)
J Barclay Miss L Wood

Placings:*0006*/605*00*/PF11211113/13412/541243/4P6/P5600/33564/0-PP **(0650)**
2001/02: 20^{P}S, 16^{P}GF

	Starts	1st	2nd	3rd	Win & Pl
Hurdles	1	0	0	0	0
Chases	1	0	0	0	0
Career Total	**46**	**9**	**3**	**5**	**48140**

130	1/97	Kels	2m1f	C(0-135)HCh	GD	£4421
130	3/96	Newb	2m1f	C(0-135)HCh	G-S	£4349
127	10/95	Worc	2m	D(0-125)HCh	GD	£3465
108	4/95	Sedg	2m1f	C Ch	FRM	£5507
98	3/95	Kels	2m1f	D Ch	G-F	£3501
112	1/95	Muss	2m	E Ch	G-S	£3061
87	1/95	Muss	2m	E Ch	GD	£2801
98	12/94	Sedg	2m1f110y	(0-100)HHdl	G-S	£1992
93	11/94	Kels	2m110y	(0-100)HHdl	G-F	£2775

Total win prize-money £31874

Going: Sf: 0-1 GS: 0-0 Gd: 0-0 GF: - Fm: 0-1
Distance: 2m/2m3: 0-1 2m4-2m7: 0-1 3m+: 0-0
Track: LH: 0-0 RH: 0-2 Tight: 0-0 Gall: 0-0
Aids: Bl: 0-0 Vi: 0-0 Tstrap: 0-0
Best Rating: 130 4/97 Aint 2m good Ch

Wee Willow

84 46

8-y-o b m Minster Son-Peak Princess (Charlottown)
D W Whillans Chas N Whillans

Placings:050 **(4520)**
2001/02: 20^{0}S, 22^{5}HY, 20^{0}G

	Starts	1st	2nd	3rd	Win & Pl
Hurdles	3	0	0	0	
Career Total	**3**	**0**	**0**	**0**	**0**

Going: Sf: 0-2 GS: 0-0 Gd: 0-1 GF: - Fm: 0-0
Distance: 2m/2m3: 0-0 2m4-2m7: 0-3 3m+: 0-0
Track: LH: 0-2 RH: 0-0 Tight: 0-1 Gall: 0-1
Aids: Bl: 0-0 Vi: 0-0 Tstrap: 0-0
Best Rating: 46 2/02 Newc 2m4f soft Hdl

Wee Windy (IRE)

93(76h) (29h)104

13-y-o b g Cheval-Vulrain (Raincheck)
J T Gifford W E Gale

Placings:0310/5P2133/31124/2223U012P/4/F0/3462P41F0/65014P0-50 **(0362)**
2001/02: 20^{5}GF, 24^{0}GF

	Starts	1st	2nd	3rd	Win & Pl
Chases	2	0	0	0	0
Career Total	**45**	**7**	**7**	**6**	**38424**

119	11/00	Folk	3m2f	F(0-110)HCh	SFT	£2707
117	2/00	Font	3m2f110y	D(0-120)HCh	SFT	£3848
116	3/97	Ling	3m	E Ch	G-F	£3316
126	11/95	Font	2m6f	D(0-120)HHdl	G-F	£3548
115	11/95	Kemp	3m110y	C(0-135)HHdl	G-F	£3485
100	2/95	Hntg	2m5f110y	F(0-105)HHdl	SFT	£2635
96	3/94	Plum	2m1f	Hdl	GD	£1543

Total win prize-money £21083

Going: Sf: 0-0 GS: 0-0 Gd: 0-0 GF: - Fm: 0-2
Distance: 2m/2m3: 0-0 2m4-2m7: 0-1 3m+: 0-1
Track: LH: 0-1 RH: 0-0 Tight: 0-2 Gall: 0-0
Aids: Bl: 0-2 Vi: 0-0 Tstrap: 0-0
Best Rating: 127 12/95 Chel 3m good Hdl

Weejumpawud

99 **100**

12-y-o b m Jumbo Hirt (USA)-Weewumpawud (King Log)
Miss S E Forster C Storey

Placings:F000/0/4253-132 **(4669)**
2001/02: 21^{1}G, 16^{3}S, 21^{2}GF

	Starts	1st	2nd	3rd	Win & Pl
Chases	3	1	1	1	3553
Career Total	**12**	**1**	**2**	**2**	**4518**
98 5/01 Sedg 2m5f	H Ch		GD		£1620

Total win prize-money £1621

Going: Sf: 0-1 GS: 0-0 Gd: 1-1 GF: - Fm: 0-1
Distance: 2m/2m3: 0-1 **2m4-2m7: 1-2** 3m+: 0-0
Track: **LH: 1-2** RH: 0-1 **Tight: 1-2** Gall: 0-0
Aids: Bl: 0-0 Vi: 0-0 Tstrap: 0-0
Best Rating: 100 4/02 Sedg 2m5f gd-fm Ch

Modest front-running chaser, suited by a sharp track and a sound surface, stays two miles-five.

Weet And See

103(90c) (86c)**95**

8-y-o b g Lochnager-Simply Style (Bairn (USA))
T Wall Ed Weetman (haulage & Storage) Ltd

Placings:5F003/F034056553/026011310661/03600**F**0 0-06350160P06**P**3 **(4546)**
2001/02: 16^{0}F, 16^{6}F, 16^{3}GS, 16^{5}GS, 16^{0}S, 16^{1}S, 16^{6}S, 16^{0}G, 16^{P}S, 16^{0}HY, 16^{0}S, 20^{P}G, 16^{3}GF

	Starts	1st	2nd	3rd	Win & Pl
Hurdles	12	1	0	2	3235
Chases	1	0	0	0	0
Career Total	**48**	**5**	**1**	**7**	**16004**

95	11/01	Uttx	2m	F(0-100)HHdl	SFT	£2737
110	4/00	Uttx	2m	E(0-105)HHdl	HVY	£2663
112	9/99	NAbb	2m1f	F(0-110)HHdl	G-F	£2621
109	7/99	Worc	2m	F(0-110)HHdl	G-F	£1987
102	7/99	NAbb	2m1f	F(0-105)HHdl	G-S	£2779

Total win prize-money £12789

Going: Sf: 1-6 GS: 0-2 Gd: 0-2 GF: - Fm: 0-3
Distance: **2m/2m3: 1-12** 2m4-2m7: 0-1 3m+: 0-0
Track: **LH: 1-8** RH: 0-5 Tight: 0-4 Gall: 0-1
Aids: Bl: 0-0 Vi: 0-0 Tstrap: 0-0
Best Rating: 112 9/99 NAbb 2m1f gd-fm Hdl

Still capable in modest company over hurdles as he showed when winning a seller at Wolverhampton in July 2002.

Weet U There (IRE)

91 **75**

6-y-o b g Forest Wind (USA)-Lady Aladdin (Persian Bold)
T Wall Ed Weetman (haulage & Storage) Ltd

Placings:554602/360-0P00 **(3334)**
2001/02: 17^{0}G, 16^{P}HY, 17^{0}G, 16^{0}G

	Starts	1st	2nd	3rd	Win & Pl
Hurdles	4	0	0	0	0
Career Total	**13**	**0**	**1**	**1**	**1133**

Going: Sf: 0-1 GS: 0-0 Gd: 0-3 GF: - Fm: 0-0
Distance: 2m/2m3: 0-4 2m4-2m7: 0-0 3m+: 0-0
Track: LH: 0-1 RH: 0-3 Tight: 0-0 Gall: 0-0
Aids: Bl: 0-3 Vi: 0-0 Tstrap: 0-0
Best Rating: 80 4/00 Uttx 2m heavy Hdl

Welburn Boy

83(83h) (47h)**85**

10-y-o b g Kalaglow-Teevano (Blakeney)
M Sheppard K Jones

Placings:030/60P/440P6FF1450/23PU510P/433-003P **(4590)**
2001/02: 17^{0}G, 20^{0}S, 25^{3}S, 24^{P}G

	Starts	1st	2nd	3rd	Win & Pl
Hurdles	2	0	0	0	0
Chases	2	0	0	1	442
Career Total	**32**	**2**	**1**	**5**	**10049**

100	2/00	Ludl	3m	F(0-95)HCh	GD	£3965
83	3/99	Hrfd	3m2f	F(0-95)HHdl	G-S	£2472

Total win prize-money £6437

Going: Sf: 0-2 GS: 0-0 Gd: 0-2 GF: - Fm: 0-0
Distance: 2m/2m3: 0-1 2m4-2m7: 0-1 3m+: 0-2
Track: LH: 0-2 RH: 0-2 Tight: 0-0 Gall: 0-0
Aids: Bl: 0-4 Vi: 0-0 Tstrap: 0-4
Best Rating: 103 1/00 Ludl 3m good Ch

A winning pointer, he is only of moderate ability over hurdles and fences.

Welcome

96 **105**

5-y-o b g Be My Guest (USA)-Cantanta (Top Ville)
Miss Venetia Williams O P Dakin

Placings:5-4 **(0341)**
2001/02: 16^{4}G

	Starts	1st	2nd	3rd	Win & Pl
Hurdles	1	0	0	0	0
Career Total	**2**	**0**	**0**	**0**	**0**

Going: Sf: 0-0 GS: 0-0 Gd: 0-1 GF: - Fm: 0-0
Distance: 2m/2m3: 0-1 2m4-2m7: 0-0 3m+: 0-0
Track: LH: 0-1 RH: 0-0 Tight: 0-1 Gall: 0-0
Aids: Bl: 0-0 Vi: 0-0 Tstrap: 0-1
Best Rating: 105 4/01 Ayr 2m good Hdl

Welcome Heights

83 **43**

8-y-o b g Most Welcome-Mount Ida (USA) (Conquistador Cielo (USA))
R C Spicer Sean Michael Toynton

Placings:546/P-00P **(1353)**
2001/02: 16^{0}GF, 17^{0}GF, 22^{P}GF

	Starts	1st	2nd	3rd	Win & Pl
Hurdles	3	0	0	0	
Career Total	**7**	**0**	**0**	**0**	**256**

Going: Sf: 0-0 GS: 0-0 Gd: 0-0 GF: - Fm: 0-3
Distance: 2m/2m3: 0-2 2m4-2m7: 0-1 3m+: 0-0
Track: LH: 0-2 RH: 0-1 Tight: 0-2 Gall: 0-0
Aids: Bl: 0-1 Vi: 0-2 Tstrap: 0-0
Best Rating: 83 1/00 Leic 2m soft Hdl

Welcome To Due's (USA)

5-y-o gr g Cozzene (USA)-Etoile D'Amore (USA) (The Minstrel (CAN))
G M Moore J & M Leisure / Unos Restaurant

Placings:0 **(0744)**
2001/02: 16^{0}GS

	Starts	1st	2nd	3rd	Win & Pl
NH Flat	1	0	0	0	
Career Total	**1**	**0**	**0**	**0**	

Going: Sf: 0-0 GS: 0-1 Gd: 0-0 GF: - Fm: 0-0
Distance: 2m/2m3: 0-1 2m4-2m7: 0-0 3m+: 0-0
Track: LH: 0-1 RH: 0-0 Tight: 0-0 Gall: 0-0
Aids: Bl: 0-0 Vi: 0-0 Tstrap: 0-0
Best Rating:

Weldunfrank

106 **74**

9-y-o br g Weld-Damsong (Petong)
W M Brisbourne Mrs J P McCormack

Placings:600/6P6/P05U406 **(4546)**
2001/02: 16^{P}G, 16^{0}G, 16^{5}S, 16^{U}S, 16^{4}G, 16^{0}S, 16^{6}GF

	Starts	1st	2nd	3rd	Win & Pl
Hurdles	7	0	0	0	0
Career Total	**13**	**0**	**0**	**0**	**0**

Going: Sf: 0-3 GS: 0-0 Gd: 0-3 GF: - Fm: 0-1
Distance: 2m/2m3: 0-7 2m4-2m7: 0-0 3m+: 0-0
Track: LH: 0-1 RH: 0-6 Tight: 0-1 Gall: 0-1
Aids: Bl: 0-0 Vi: 0-0 Tstrap: 0-0
Best Rating: 89 5/98 Ludl 2m gd-fm NHF

Well Armed (IRE)

11-y-o b g Moscow Society (USA)-Sales Centre (Deep Run)
D Pipe (M C Pipe 17/3) Denis Williams

Placings:634000/32640/PU/U/52P30P **(4659)**
2001/02: 22^{5}GS, 22^{2}F, 26^{P}GF, 24^{3}GF, 20^{0}GF, 24^{P}G

	Starts	1st	2nd	3rd	Win & Pl
Hurdles	4	0	1	1	1150
Chases	2	0	0	0	0
Career Total	**20**	**0**	**2**	**3**	**3132**

Going: Sf: 0-0 GS: 0-1 Gd: 0-1 GF: - Fm: 0-4
Distance: 2m/2m3: 0-0 2m4-2m7: 0-3 3m+: 0-3
Track: LH: 0-2 RH: 0-2 Tight: 0-3 Gall: 0-0
Aids: Bl: 0-6 Vi: 0-0 Tstrap: 0-0
Best Rating: 106 7/96 Naas 2m3f gd-fm NHF

Well Gone

91f **79f**

5-y-o b g Sanglamore (USA)-Well Away (IRE) (Sadler's Wells (USA))
Ian Williams A L R Morton

Placings:0 **(0506)**
2001/02: 16^{0}GF

	Starts	1st	2nd	3rd	Win & Pl
NH Flat	1	0	0	0	

	Starts	1st	2nd	3rd
Career Total	1	0	0	0

Going: Sf: 0-0 GS: 0-0 Gd: 0-0 GF: - Fm: 0-1
Distance: 2m/2m3: 0-1 2m4-2m7: 0-0 3m+: 0-0
Track: LH: 0-0 RH: 0-1 Tight: 0-0 Gall: 0-1
Aids: Bl: 0-0 Vi: 0-0 Tstrap: 0-0
Best Rating: **79** 5/01 Hntg 2m110y gd-fm NHF

Well Sir (IRE)

105

7-y-o ch g Denel (FR)-Rare Vermilion (Rakaposhi King)
N A Twiston-Davies (J K Magee 2/6) G M Powell

Placings:3P **(1631)**
2001/02: 22^{3}F, 22^{P}GF

	Starts	1st	2nd	3rd	Win & Pl
Hurdles	2	0	0	1	353
Career Total	**2**	**0**	**0**	**1**	**353**

Going: Sf: 0-0 GS: 0-0 Gd: 0-0 GF: - Fm: 0-2
Distance: 2m/2m3: 0-0 2m4-2m7: 0-2 3m+: 0-0
Track: LH: 0-0 RH: 0-1 Tight: 0-0 Gall: 0-0
Aids: Bl: 0-0 Vi: 0-0 Tstrap: 0-0
Best Rating: **105** 6/01 Dpat 2m6f firm Hdl

Well Ted (IRE)

96 **85**

10-y-o ch g Carlingford Castle-Pollyfane (Pollerton)
T R George Fisher, Gallivan, Riley & Seabourne

Placings:*40005*0/3 **(0421)**
2001/02: 24^{3}G

	Starts	1st	2nd	3rd	Win & Pl
Hurdles	1	0	0	1	427
Career Total	**7**	**0**	**0**	**1**	**566**

Going: Sf: 0-0 GS: 0-0 Gd: 0-1 GF: - Fm: 0-0
Distance: 2m/2m3: 0-0 2m4-2m7: 0-0 3m+: 0-1
Track: LH: 0-1 RH: 0-0 Tight: 0-1 Gall: 0-0
Aids: Bl: 0-0 Vi: 0-0 Tstrap: 0-0
Best Rating: **86** 6/97 Slig 2m gd-fm NHF

Well Then Now Then (IRE)

100 **100**

7-y-o b m Supreme Leader-Northern Dandy (The Parson)
H D Daly Mrs A L Wood

Placings:*2232*-23 **(2411)**
2001/02: 16^{2}S, 19^{3}GS

	Starts	1st	2nd	3rd	Win & Pl
Hurdles	2	0	1	1	1579
Career Total	**6**	**0**	**4**	**2**	**3686**

Going: Sf: 0-1 GS: 0-1 Gd: 0-0 GF: - Fm: 0-0
Distance: 2m/2m3: 0-1 2m4-2m7: 0-1 3m+: 0-0
Track: LH: 0-0 RH: 0-2 Tight: 0-1 Gall: 0-0
Aids: Bl: 0-0 Vi: 0-0 Tstrap: 0-0
Best Rating: **100** 11/01 Towc 2m soft Hdl

A very useful ex-Irish point to pointer who finished eight lengths second to Best Mate on her first outing in Ireland in 2000, she has since run well against healthy competition and is knocking at the door. She is suited to the mud.

Well Timed

94 **91**

12-y-o ch g Relkino-Cherry Meringue (Birdbrook)
R G Frost Mrs G A Robarts

Placings:62P/3122P/3121U3/164UF33/5PFF610/404-3P **(0683)**
2001/02: 21^{3}GF, 26^{P}G

	Starts	1st	2nd	3rd	Win & Pl
Chases	2	0	0	1	574
Career Total	**33**	**5**	**4**	**6**	**27694**

112	3/00	NAbb	3m2f110y	F(0-100)HCh	GD	£2625
125	5/98	Chep	3m	B(0-145)HCh	GD	£7520
121	1/98	Winc	3m1f110y	E(0-115)HCh	GD	£3610
119	12/97	NAbb	2m110y	E(0-115)HCh	HVY	£2842
97	11/96	NAbb	2m110y	E(0-115)HCh	HVY	£2831

Total win prize-money £19430

Going: Sf: 0-0 GS: 0-0 Gd: 0-1 GF: - Fm: 0-1
Distance: 2m/2m3: 0-0 2m4-2m7: 0-1 3m+: 0-1
Track: LH: 0-2 RH: 0-0 Tight: 0-2 Gall: 0-0
Aids: Bl: 0-2 Vi: 0-0 Tstrap: 0-0
Best Rating: **125** 5/98 Chep 3m good Ch

Wellfranko (IRE)

100 **97**

7-y-o b g Camden Town-Electana (Electrify)
Ferdy Murphy (T P McGovern 14/11) Anthony O'Gorman

Placings:U0001P **(4896)**
2001/02: 16^{U}GF, 16^{0}GF, 20^{0}GF, 19^{0}G, 16^{1}GF, 20^{P}G

	Starts	1st	2nd	3rd	Win & Pl
Hurdles	6	1	0	0	2667
Career Total	**6**	**1**	**0**	**0**	**2667**

97	4/02	Uttx	2m	E(0-100)HHdl	G-F	£2667

Total win prize-money £2667

Going: Sf: 0-0 GS: 0-0 Gd: 0-2 GF: - Fm: 1-4
Distance: **2m/2m3: 1-4** 2m4-2m7: 0-2 3m+: 0-0
Track: **LH: 1-2** RH: 0-1 Tight: 0-0 Gall: 0-1
Aids: Bl: 0-0 Vi: 0-0 Tstrap: 0-0
Best Rating: **97** 4/02 Uttx 2m gd-fm Hdl

Showed improved form when winning novices' handicap at Uttoxeter in April 2002. Can continue on the upgrade.

Wellie (IRE)

96 **103**

9-y-o b/br g Aristocracy-Sweet View (King's Ride)
M J Wilkinson D Ancil

Placings:06*000*UP523/54-54U30F4 **(4549)**
2001/02: 16^{5}GF, 16^{4}G, 16^{U}G, 16^{3}GS, 20^{0}S, 23^{F}S, 24^{4}GF

	Starts	1st	2nd	3rd	Win & Pl
Chases	7	0	0	1	1685
Career Total	**19**	**0**	**1**	**2**	**3111**

Going: Sf: 0-2 GS: 0-1 Gd: 0-2 GF: - Fm: 0-2
Distance: 2m/2m3: 0-4 2m4-2m7: 0-1 3m+: 0-2
Track: LH: 0-0 RH: 0-7 Tight: 0-0 Gall: 0-2
Aids: Bl: 0-0 Vi: 0-0 Tstrap: 0-0
Best Rating: **113** 1/01 Donc 2m110y good Ch

Front-running chaser, prone to the odd mistake. Seems to act on any ground

Wellow (IRE)

102 (24c)**85**

6-y-o b g Unblest-Alpine Sunset (Auction Ring (USA))
Miss C J E Caroe D Fish

Placings:P-0PP04000006P055 **(4518)**
2001/02: 16^{0}GF, 16^{P}GF, 16^{P}GF, 16^{0}GF, 16^{4}GS, 16^{0}GF, 16^{0}G, 20^{0}S, 16^{0}S, 16^{0}S, 16^{6}S, 16^{P}S, 16^{0}S, 19^{5}GS, 21^{5}GS

	Starts	1st	2nd	3rd	Win & Pl
Hurdles	12	0	0	0	0
Chases	3	0	0	0	0
Career Total	**16**	**0**	**0**	**0**	**0**

Going: Sf: 0-6 GS: 0-3 Gd: 0-1 GF: - Fm: 0-5
Distance: 2m/2m3: 0-13 2m4-2m7: 0-2 3m+: 0-0
Track: LH: 0-9 RH: 0-5 Tight: 0-8 Gall: 0-1
Aids: Bl: 0-0 Vi: 0-0 Tstrap: 0-0
Best Rating: **85** 3/02 Towc 2m5f gd-sft Hdl

Wellswood (IRE)

92(85h) **95**

9-y-o ch g Montelimar (USA)-Many Views (Bargello)
J M Jefferson R G Marshall

Placings:*63/300*/04P0150/262P240/504P-5P3 **(1022)**
2001/02: 22^{5}GF, 21^{P}G, 27^{3}GF

	Starts	1st	2nd	3rd	Win & Pl
Chases	3	0	0	1	585
Career Total	**26**	**1**	**3**	**3**	**7404**

81	3/99	Towc	3m	F(0-100)HHdl	SFT	£2337

Total win prize-money £2338

Going: Sf: 0-0 GS: 0-0 Gd: 0-1 GF: - Fm: 0-2
Distance: 2m/2m3: 0-0 2m4-2m7: 0-2 3m+: 0-1
Track: LH: 0-2 RH: 0-1 Tight: 0-3 Gall: 0-0
Aids: Bl: 0-2 Vi: 0-1 Tstrap: 0-0
Best Rating: **116** 2/00 MRas 3m4f110y gd-sft Ch

Welody

92 **75**

6-y-o ch g Weldnaas (USA)-The Boozy News (USA) (L'Emigrant (USA))
G Prodromou A Georgiou

Placings:400650 **(4904)**
2001/02: 17^{4}S, 16^{0}G, 19^{0}G, 16^{6}G, 16^{5}G, 17^{0}G

	Starts	1st	2nd	3rd	Win & Pl
Hurdles	6	0	0	0	0
Career Total	**6**	**0**	**0**	**0**	**0**

Going: Sf: 0-1 GS: 0-0 Gd: 0-5 GF: - Fm: 0-0
Distance: 2m/2m3: 0-6 2m4-2m7: 0-0 3m+: 0-0
Track: LH: 0-5 RH: 0-1 Tight: 0-6 Gall: 0-0
Aids: Bl: 0-0 Vi: 0-1 Tstrap: 0-0
Best Rating: **75** 3/02 Fknm 2m good Hdl

Welsh Border

114 **120**

4-y-o ch g Zafonic (USA)-Welsh Daylight (Welsh Pageant)
G Prodromou (H R A Cecil 28/9) L Cohen

Placings:6 **(4651)**
2001/02: 16^{6}G

	Starts	1st	2nd	3rd	Win & Pl
Hurdles	1	0	0	0	1500
Career Total	**1**	**0**	**0**	**0**	**1500**

Going: Sf: 0-0 GS: 0-0 Gd: 0-1 GF: - Fm: 0-0
Distance: 2m/2m3: 0-1 2m4-2m7: 0-0 3m+: 0-0
Track: LH: 0-1 RH: 0-0 Tight: 0-1 Gall: 0-0
Aids: Bl: 0-0 Vi: 0-0 Tstrap: 0-0
Best Rating: **120** 4/02 Aint 2m110y good Hdl

Wide-margin winner of a novices' hurdle at Market

Rasen in August 2002.

Welsh Dream

109 101

5-y-o b g Mtoto-Morgannwg (IRE) (Simply Great (FR))
P C Haslam Mrs B M Hawkins & Mrs C Barclay

Placings:3 **(2342)**
2001/02: 16^{3}GS

	Starts	1st	2nd	3rd	Win & Pl
Hurdles	1	0	0	1	510
Career Total	**1**	**0**	**0**	**1**	**510**

Going: Sf: 0-0 GS: 0-1 Gd: 0-0 GF: - Fm: 0-0
Distance: 2m/2m3: 0-1 2m4-2m7: 0-0 3m+: 0-0
Track: LH: 0-1 RH: 0-0 Tight: 0-0 Gall: 0-1
Aids: Bl: 0-0 Vi: 0-0 Tstrap: 0-0
Best Rating: 101 11/01 Newc 2m gd-sft Hdl

Welsh Harvest

10-y-o b g Weld-Swift Messenger (Giolla Mear)
D L Williams Reliance Car Hire Services Ltd

Placings:6PP3R60P/P5P50/P-PP **(0490)**
2001/02: 24^{P}GF, 27^{P}GF

	Starts	1st	2nd	3rd	Win & Pl
Hurdles	1	0	0	0	0
Chases	1	0	0	0	0
Career Total	**16**	**0**	**0**	**1**	**711**

Going: Sf: 0-0 GS: 0-0 Gd: 0-0 GF: - Fm: 0-2
Distance: 2m/2m3: 0-0 2m4-2m7: 0-0 3m+: 0-2
Track: LH: 0-0 RH: 0-1 Tight: 0-1 Gall: 0-1
Aids: Bl: 0-1 Vi: 0-0 Tstrap: 0-0
Best Rating: 89 1/99 Kemp 2m soft Ch

Welsh Lad (IRE)

99(93c) (94c)101

10-y-o b g Welsh Term-Aubretia (USA) (Hatchet Man (USA))
D R Gandolfo Mr Stephen Freud & Friends

Placings:*L6/0*013U1/416023-F5P1600 **(4480)**
2001/02: 20^{F}G, 16^{5}S, 19^{P}G, 20^{1}G, 21^{6}GS, 21^{0}GS, 22^{0}G

	Starts	1st	2nd	3rd	Win & Pl
Hurdles	4	1	0	0	1960
Chases	3	0	0	0	0
Career Total	**21**	**4**	**1**	**2**	**12929**

101	12/01	Sthl	2m4f110y	G Hdl	GD	£1960
112	11/00	Extr	2m3f	D(0-125)HHdl	G-S	£3237
115	12/99	Ludl	2m5f	E(0-105)HHdl	GD	£2640
87	7/99	Dund	2m4f153y	Hdl	G-F	£2209

Total win prize-money £10047

Going: Sf: 0-1 GS: 0-2 Gd: 1-4 GF: - Fm: 0-0
Distance: 2m/2m3: 0-2 **2m4-2m7: 1-5** 3m+: 0-0
Track: **LH: 1-3** RH: 0-3 **Tight: 1-3** Gall: 0-2
Aids: Bl: 0-0 Vi: 0-0 Tstrap: 0-0
Best Rating: 120 2/01 Ludl 2m4f good Ch

Handicap hurdler, who goes well on right-handed track, and seems especially effective at Ludlow. Lost his way over fences and made a winning return to hurdles at Southwell in December 2001. Acts on most types of ground and is effective at around two miles four furlongs.

Welsh Main

103 106

5-y-o br g Zafonic (USA)-Welsh Daylight (Welsh Pageant)
S Magnier (H R A Cecil 5/5) Marcus Reeder

Placings:1U **(4888)**
2001/02: 16^{1}GS, 16^{U}G

	Starts	1st	2nd	3rd	Win & Pl
Hurdles	2	1	0	0	3332
Career Total	**2**	**1**	**0**	**0**	**3332**

102	3/02	Catt	2m	E Hdl	G-S	£3332

Total win prize-money £3332

Going: Sf: 0-0 GS: 1-1 Gd: 0-1 GF: - Fm: 0-0
Distance: **2m/2m3: 1-2** 2m4-2m7: 0-0 3m+: 0-0
Track: **LH: 1-1** RH: 0-1 **Tight: 1-1** Gall: 0-0
Aids: Bl: 0-0 Vi: 0-0 Tstrap: 0-0
Best Rating: 102 3/02 Catt 2m gd-sft Hdl

Useful if lightly-raced on the Flat for Henry Cecil. Off the mark in a weak, slowly-run event at Catterick in March 2002. Acts on any ground.

Welsh March (IRE)

93 124

10-y-o b g Over The River (FR)-Welsh Tan (Welsh Saint)
G M Moore John Robson

Placings:22112/2F15PP/3532/3232121060-253 **(2187)**
2001/02: 16^{2}G, 16^{5}S, 16^{3}G

	Starts	1st	2nd	3rd	Win & Pl
Chases	3	0	1	1	1972
Career Total	**28**	**5**	**9**	**5**	**40960**

128	1/01	Ayr	2m	E(0-115)HCh	G-S	£3416
128	12/00	Hayd	2m	C(0-135)HCh	HVY	£8807
133	11/98	Bang	2m4f110y	C(0-130)HCh	SFT	£4879
126	3/98	Ayr	2m	E Ch	SFT	£2872
114	12/97	Ayr	2m	E Ch	SFT	£2784

Total win prize-money £22760

Going: Sf: 0-1 GS: 0-0 Gd: 0-2 GF: - Fm: 0-0
Distance: 2m/2m3: 0-3 2m4-2m7: 0-0 3m+: 0-0
Track: LH: 0-3 RH: 0-0 Tight: 0-1 Gall: 0-0
Aids: Bl: 0-0 Vi: 0-0 Tstrap: 0-0
Best Rating: 136 11/98 Ayr 2m gd-sft Ch

Fair chaser who was in good form in the middle of the 2000/2001season with wins at Haydock and Ayr. Best at two miles with cut in the ground and goes especially well at the latter track.

Welsh Park (IRE)

97 62

9-y-o ch g Balinger-Welsh Escort (Welsh Captain)
A P James The Festival Racing Partnership

Placings:0000*0*/4065005313P0/3F036600/UUP0R-FP30040 **(1806)**
2001/02: 16^{F}F, 25^{P}GF, 27^{3}G, 27^{0}GF, 26^{0}GF, 26^{4}G, 24^{0}GF

	Starts	1st	2nd	3rd	Win & Pl
Hurdles	6	0	0	1	435
Chases	1	0	0	0	0
Career Total	**37**	**1**	**0**	**5**	**4091**

98	10/98	Font	2m6f110y	F Hdl	GD	£2267

Total win prize-money £2268

Going: Sf: 0-0 GS: 0-0 Gd: 0-2 GF: - Fm: 0-5
Distance: 2m/2m3: 0-1 2m4-2m7: 0-0 3m+: 0-6
Track: LH: 0-3 RH: 0-4 Tight: 0-3 Gall: 0-1
Aids: Bl: 0-7 Vi: 0-0 Tstrap: 0-0
Best Rating: 98 10/98 Font 2m6f110y good Hdl

Welsh Silk

103(93h) 92

10-y-o b g Weld-Purple Silk (Belfalas)
D R Gandolfo Starlight Racing

Placings:*22*0002/3114346/512420P0/63U63/36P424-00 **(0268)**
2001/02: 19^{0}GS, 25^{0}G

	Starts	1st	2nd	3rd	Win & Pl
Chases	2	0	0	0	
Career Total	**34**	**3**	**6**	**5**	**16152**

108	10/98	Chep	2m4f110y	D(0-120)HHdl	G-S	£3018
98	11/97	Newb	2m5f	E(0-110)HHdl	SFT	£2757
99	11/97	Hrfd	2m3f110y	E(0-100)HHdl	G-S	£2374

Total win prize-money £8151

Going: Sf: 0-0 GS: 0-1 Gd: 0-1 GF: - Fm: 0-0
Distance: 2m/2m3: 0-0 2m4-2m7: 0-1 3m+: 0-1
Track: LH: 0-0 RH: 0-2 Tight: 0-0 Gall: 0-0
Aids: Bl: 0-1 Vi: 0-1 Tstrap: 0-0
Best Rating: 111 3/01 Extr 2m3f110y heavy Ch

Welsh Wind (IRE)

80 54

6-y-o b g Tenby-Bavaria (Top Ville)
M Wigham (B G Powell 20/9) D Hassan

Placings:0 **(1032)**
2001/02: 17^{0}G

	Starts	1st	2nd	3rd	Win & Pl
Hurdles	1	0	0	0	
Career Total	**1**	**0**	**0**	**0**	

Going: Sf: 0-0 GS: 0-0 Gd: 0-1 GF: - Fm: 0-0
Distance: 2m/2m3: 0-1 2m4-2m7: 0-0 3m+: 0-0
Track: LH: 0-1 RH: 0-0 Tight: 0-1 Gall: 0-0
Aids: Bl: 0-0 Vi: 0-0 Tstrap: 0-0
Best Rating: 54 7/01 NAbb 2m1f good Hdl

Wemyss Quest

104(116h) (129h)106+

7-y-o b g Rainbow Quest (USA)-Wemyss Bight (Dancing Brave (USA))
Ferdy Murphy Four Blokes

Placings:*2515*223-21110P0 **(4890)**
2001/02: 17^{2}G, 24^{1}GF, 20^{1}G, 25^{1}G, 25^{0}G, 22^{P}S, 24^{0}G

	Starts	1st	2nd	3rd	Win & Pl
Hurdles	7	3	1	0	14366
Career Total	**14**	**4**	**4**	**1**	**19847**

129	10/01	Chel	3m1f110y	B Hdl	GD	£7117
109	10/01	Weth	2m4f110y	D Hdl	GD	£3801
116	6/01	MRas	3m	E Hdl	G-F	£2614
86	8/00	Rosc	2m	NHF	FRM	£3036

Total win prize-money £16570

Going: Sf: 0-1 GS: 0-0 Gd: 2-5 GF: - Fm: 1-1
Distance: 2m/2m3: 0-1 2m4-2m7: 1-2 **3m+: 2-4**
Track: **LH: 2-3** RH: 1-4 Tight: 1-2 Gall: 1-2
Aids: Bl: 0-0 Vi: 0-0 **Tstrap: 1-3**
Best Rating: 129 10/01 Chel 3m1f110y good Hdl

Scored over three miles at Market Rasen in June and successfully returned from a four-month break when winning at Wetherby next time out. Completed the hat-trick at Cheltenham at the end of October in fine style. Stays well, is best on a sound surface and will make a chaser.

Were Not Stoppin

105 **85**

7-y-o b g Mystiko (USA)-Power Take Off (Aragon)
R Bastiman I B Barker

Placings:5/46 **(4867)**
2001/02: 17^{4}G, 16^{6}GF

	Starts	1st	2nd	3rd	Win & Pl
Hurdles	2	0	0	0	0
Career Total	**3**	**0**	**0**	**0**	**0**

Going: Sf: 0-0 GS: 0-0 Gd: 0-1 GF: - Fm: 0-1
Distance: 2m/2m3: 0-2 2m4-2m7: 0-0 3m+: 0-0
Track: LH: 0-2 RH: 0-0 Tight: 0-1 Gall: 0-0
Aids: Bl: 0-0 Vi: 0-0 Tstrap: 0-0
Best Rating: 69 10/01 Sedg 2m1f good Hdl

Modest novice hurdler, suited by hold up tactics around two miles. Awarded a race at Uttoxeter in June.

Wesley Snype (FR)

107 **116**

4-y-o b g Passing Sale (FR)-Falcon Crest (FR) (Cadoudal (FR))
F Doumen (E Lellouche 25/11) Ecurie Passing

Placings:0040230P **(1644)**
2001/02: 15^{0}VS, 18^{0}VS, 15^{4}VS, 18^{0}HO, 16^{2}G, 16^{3}HY, 17^{0}G, 19^{P}VS

	Starts	1st	2nd	3rd	Win & Pl
Hurdles	8	0	1	1	5273
Career Total	**8**	**0**	**1**	**1**	**5273**

Going: Sf: 0-1 GS: 0-0 Gd: 0-2 GF: - Fm: 0-0
Distance: 2m/2m3: 0-5 2m4-2m7: 0-1 3m+: 0-0
Track: LH: 0-2 RH: 0-2 Tight: 0-0 Gall: 0-1
Aids: Bl: 0-0 Vi: 0-0 Tstrap: 0-0
Best Rating: 116 3/02 Chel 2m1f good Hdl

A French hurdler who showed improved form on his first run for Francois Doumen when second at Kempton in December 2001. Acts on soft ground.

Wesley's Lad (IRE)

8-y-o b/br g Classic Secret (USA)-Galouga (FR) (Lou Piguet (FR))
D Burchell Brian Williams

Placings:043151/262425321/2P/30 **(1920)**
2001/02: 16^{3}G, 16^{0}G

	Starts	1st	2nd	3rd	Win & Pl
Hurdles	2	0	0	1	776
Career Total	**19**	**3**	**5**	**3**	**17933**

127	3/99	Strf	2m110y	C(0-135)HHdl	HVY	£4930
115	3/98	Plum	2m1f	E Hdl	SFT	£2490
114	1/98	Folk	2m1f110y	E Hdl	G-S	£1976

Total win prize-money £9397

Going: Sf: 0-0 GS: 0-0 Gd: 0-2 GF: - Fm: 0-0
Distance: 2m/2m3: 0-2 2m4-2m7: 0-0 3m+: 0-0
Track: LH: 0-0 RH: 0-2 Tight: 0-0 Gall: 0-1
Aids: Bl: 0-0 Vi: 0-0 Tstrap: 0-0
Best Rating: 130 11/99 Leic 2m gd-sft Hdl

Wesperada (IRE)

10-y-o ch g Waajib-Divine Apsara (Godswalk (USA))
Miss S E Forster A G & Mrs E J Bell

Placings:2353/31115554/F64/P **(4688)**
2001/02: 16^{P}GF

	Starts	1st	2nd	3rd	Win & Pl
Hurdles	1	0	0	0	
Career Total	**16**	**3**	**1**	**3**	**11176**

107	7/96	Bell	2m1f	Hdl	G-F	£3001
111	6/96	Gowr	2m	Hdl	YLD	£3530
100	6/96	Gowr	2m	Hdl	G-F	£2824

Total win prize-money £9357

Going: Sf: 0-0 GS: 0-0 Gd: 0-0 GF: - Fm: 0-1
Distance: 2m/2m3: 0-1 2m4-2m7: 0-0 3m+: 0-0
Track: LH: 0-1 RH: 0-0 Tight: 0-1 Gall: 0-0
Aids: Bl: 0-0 Vi: 0-0 Tstrap: 0-1
Best Rating: 111 10/96 Rosc 2m yield Hdl

West Aside (IRE)

86 **66**

8-y-o b g Brush Aside (USA)-Chancy Belle (Le Bavard (FR))
T P McGovern B C J Enterprise

Placings:06-00 **(1644)**
2001/02: 20^{0}G, 26^{0}G

	Starts	1st	2nd	3rd	Win & Pl
Hurdles	2	0	0	0	
Career Total	**4**	**0**	**0**	**0**	**0**

Going: Sf: 0-0 GS: 0-0 Gd: 0-2 GF: - Fm: 0-0
Distance: 2m/2m3: 0-0 2m4-2m7: 0-1 3m+: 0-1
Track: LH: 0-0 RH: 0-2 Tight: 0-0 Gall: 0-2
Aids: Bl: 0-0 Vi: 0-0 Tstrap: 0-0
Best Rating: 66 5/01 Hntg 2m4f110y good Hdl

West Coaster (IRE)

86f **89f**

4-y-o gr g Be My Native (USA)-Donegal Grey (IRE) (Roselier (FR))
Miss H C Knight White Rabbit Partnership

Placings:*00* **(4423)**
2001/02: 16^{0}G, 16^{0}GS

	Starts	1st	2nd	3rd	Win & Pl
NH Flat	2	0	0	0	
Career Total	**2**	**0**	**0**	**0**	

Going: Sf: 0-0 GS: 0-1 Gd: 0-1 GF: - Fm: 0-0
Distance: 2m/2m3: 0-2 2m4-2m7: 0-0 3m+: 0-0
Track: LH: 0-1 RH: 0-1 Tight: 0-0 Gall: 0-1
Aids: Bl: 0-0 Vi: 0-0 Tstrap: 0-0
Best Rating: 89 2/02 Kemp 2m good NHF

West Hill Rose (IRE)

105 **115**

7-y-o gr m Roselier (FR)-Clonmeen Official (Official)
V R A Dartnall D G Staddon

Placings:*0/0*35-2114 **(4150)**
2001/02: 24^{2}GS, 24^{1}HY, 24^{1}S, 24^{4}GS

	Starts	1st	2nd	3rd	Win & Pl
Hurdles	4	2	1	0	8793
Career Total	**8**	**2**	**1**	**1**	**9419**

115	2/02	Newb	3m110y	C(0-130)HHdl	SFT	£6006
113	1/02	Uttx	3m110y	F Hdl	HVY	£1981

Total win prize-money £7987

Going: Sf: 2-2 GS: 0-2 Gd: 0-0 GF: - Fm: 0-0
Distance: 2m/2m3: 0-0 2m4-2m7: 0-0 **3m+: 2-4**
Track: **LH: 2-4** RH: 0-0 Tight: 0-0 **Gall: 1-1**
Aids: Bl: 0-0 Vi: 0-0 Tstrap: 0-0
Best Rating: 115 2/02 Newb 3m110y soft Hdl

A mud-loving staying mare. Relatively lightly raced. Stays three miles.

West Hope

69 **28**

8-y-o b m Wace (USA)-Just A Whisper (Humdoleila)
G F Edwards G F Edwards

Placings:0P65 **(0873)**
2001/02: 16^{0}GF, 20^{P}GF, 17^{6}GS, 25^{5}GS

	Starts	1st	2nd	3rd	Win & Pl
Hurdles	4	0	0	0	0
Career Total	**4**	**0**	**0**	**0**	**0**

Going: Sf: 0-0 GS: 0-2 Gd: 0-0 GF: - Fm: 0-2
Distance: 2m/2m3: 0-2 2m4-2m7: 0-1 3m+: 0-1
Track: LH: 0-3 RH: 0-1 Tight: 0-3 Gall: 0-1
Aids: Bl: 0-1 Vi: 0-0 Tstrap: 0-0
Best Rating: 28 5/01 Hntg 2m110y gd-fm Hdl

Westcoast

101 **88**

11-y-o b g Handsome Sailor-Pichon (Formidable (USA))
M Tate M Tate

Placings:4/3/0/00600452/5006F45100/B2215015/6PP-00336 **(3337)**
2001/02: 20^{0}G, 24^{0}G, 23^{3}G, 24^{3}GF, 24^{6}G

	Starts	1st	2nd	3rd	Win & Pl
Hurdles	5	0	0	2	1116
Career Total	**37**	**3**	**3**	**3**	**14370**

107	3/00	Bang	3m	D(0-120)HHdl	GD	£4719
96	1/00	Ludl	3m	E(0-115)HHdl	GD	£3591
96	3/99	Ludl	2m5f110y	E Hdl	SFT	£2542

Total win prize-money £10852

Going: Sf: 0-0 GS: 0-0 Gd: 0-4 GF: - Fm: 0-1
Distance: 2m/2m3: 0-0 2m4-2m7: 0-1 3m+: 0-4
Track: LH: 0-3 RH: 0-2 Tight: 0-2 Gall: 0-0
Aids: Bl: 0-4 Vi: 0-0 Tstrap: 0-0
Best Rating: 107 3/00 Bang 3m good Hdl

Fair staying hurdler, approaching the veteran stage. Suited by good ground and a flat track.

Westcountry Lad

12-y-o b g General Surprise-Charmezzo (Remezzo)
Mrs P Bond L Bond

Placings:5/UP/0-U **(4118)**
2001/02: 25^{U}G

	Starts	1st	2nd	3rd	Win & Pl
Chases	1	0	0	0	
Career Total	**5**	**0**	**0**	**0**	**0**

Going: Sf: 0-0 GS: 0-0 Gd: 0-1 GF: - Fm: 0-0
Distance: 2m/2m3: 0-0 2m4-2m7: 0-0 3m+: 0-1
Track: LH: 0-0 RH: 0-1 Tight: 0-0 Gall: 0-0
Aids: Bl: 0-0 Vi: 0-0 Tstrap: 0-0
Best Rating: 60 4/99 Worc 2m7f110y gd-sft Ch

Westender (FR)

119 **151**

6-y-o b g In The Wings-Trude (GER) (Windwurf (GER))
M C Pipe Matt Archer & Miss Jean Broadhurst

Placings:P11111022 (4662)
2001/02: 16^{P}GF, 16^{1}GF, 16^{1}G, 16^{1}G, 16^{1}G, 16^{1}G, 16^{0}G, 16^{2}GS, 16^{2}G

				Starts	1st	2nd	3rd	Win & Pl
Hurdles				9	5	2	0	84724
Career Total				**9**	**5**	**2**	**0**	**84724**
151	11/01	Chel	2m110y	A HHdl		GD		£32500
147	10/01	Chel	2m110y	B HHdl		GD		£10432
128	10/01	Chep	2m110y	D Hdl		GD		£3552
119	9/01	Uttx	2m	D Hdl		GD		£3591
125	6/01	Strf	2m110y	D Hdl		G-F		£3848

Total win prize-money £53924

Going: Sf: 0-0 GS: 0-1 Gd: 4-6 GF: - Fm: 1-2
Distance: 2m/2m3: 5-9 2m4-2m7: 0-0 3m+: 0-0
Track: LH: 5-7 RH: 0-2 Tight: 1-2 Gall: 0-0
Aids: Bl: 4-7 Vi: 0-0 Tstrap: 0-0
Best Rating: 151 3/02 Chel 2m110y gd-sft Hdl

A useful middle-distance handicapper on the level, he blotted his copybook when attempting to run out on his hurdles debut and nearly repeated the trick before winning comfortably at Stratford next time.Went on to complete a five-timer in the autumn, culminating a valuable handicap at Cheltenham and was runner-up in the Supreme Novices' at the Cheltenham Festival and a valuable event at Aintree. Seems to concentrate better with blinkers. Suited by good ground.

Westerdunes

100f

5-y-o b g Petoski-Olympian Princess (Master Owen)
P Monteith Mrs R M Wood

Placings:1 (4790)
2001/02: 16^{1}F

				Starts	1st	2nd	3rd	Win & Pl
NH Flat				1	1	0	0	1792
Career Total				**1**	**1**	**0**	**0**	**1792**
100	4/02	Newc	2m	NHF		FRM		£1792

Total win prize-money £1792

Going: Sf: 0-0 GS: 0-0 Gd: 0-0 GF: - Fm: 1-1
Distance: 2m/2m3: 1-1 2m4-2m7: 0-0 3m+: 0-0
Track: LH: 0-0 RH: 0-0 Tight: 0-0 Gall: 0-0
Aids: Bl: 0-0 Vi: 0-0 Tstrap: 0-0
Best Rating: 100 4/02 Newc 2m firm NHF

Won a weak firm-ground bumper on his debut.

Westerly Gale (IRE)

72

12-y-o br g Strong Gale-Alix (Malinowski (USA))
R Hollinshead Mrs B L Shaw

Placings:00/3005/45UUF04/0 (0552)
2001/02: 21^{0}GF

	Starts	1st	2nd	3rd	Win & Pl
Hurdles	1	0	0	0	
Career Total	**14**	**0**	**0**	**1**	**607**

Going: Sf: 0-0 GS: 0-0 Gd: 0-0 GF: - Fm: 0-1
Distance: 2m/2m3: 0-0 2m4-2m7: 0-1 3m+: 0-0
Track: LH: 0-0 RH: 0-1 Tight: 0-0 Gall: 0-1
Aids: Bl: 0-0 Vi: 0-0 Tstrap: 0-0
Best Rating: 84 5/95 Strf 2m6f110y good Hdl

Western Bay (IRE)

89 83

6-y-o b g Midhish-Redington Belle (Ahonoora)
D W P Arbuthnot Eastwind Racing Ltd

Placings:430 (1406)
2001/02: 16^{4}GF, 17^{3}GF, 16^{0}GF

	Starts	1st	2nd	3rd	Win & Pl
Hurdles	3	0	0	1	350
Career Total	**3**	**0**	**0**	**1**	**350**

Going: Sf: 0-0 GS: 0-0 Gd: 0-0 GF: - Fm: 0-3
Distance: 2m/2m3: 0-3 2m4-2m7: 0-0 3m+: 0-0
Track: LH: 0-3 RH: 0-0 Tight: 0-2 Gall: 0-0
Aids: Bl: 0-0 Vi: 0-0 Tstrap: 0-0
Best Rating: 83 9/01 Sedg 2m1f gd-fm Hdl

Western Bluebird (IRE)

76 70

4-y-o b g Bluebird (USA)-Arrastra (Bustino)
H Morrison Hugh Scott-Barrett And Partners

Placings:0 (3210)
2001/02: 16^{0}GS

	Starts	1st	2nd	3rd	Win & Pl
Hurdles	1	0	0	0	
Career Total	**1**	**0**	**0**	**0**	

Going: Sf: 0-0 GS: 0-1 Gd: 0-0 GF: - Fm: 0-0
Distance: 2m/2m3: 0-1 2m4-2m7: 0-0 3m+: 0-0
Track: LH: 0-1 RH: 0-0 Tight: 0-0 Gall: 0-1
Aids: Bl: 0-0 Vi: 0-0 Tstrap: 0-0
Best Rating: 70 1/02 Newb 2m110y gd-sft Hdl

Western Chief (IRE)

92 116

8-y-o b h Caerleon (USA)-Go Honey Go (General Assembly (USA))
D L Williams Miss B W Palmer

Placings:460006/06033524/31111U2/2-2PP (0787)
2001/02: 20^{2}GF, 28^{P}GF, 20^{P}GF

				Starts	1st	2nd	3rd	Win & Pl
Chases				3	0	1	0	1040
Career Total				**25**	**4**	**4**	**3**	**18655**
127	5/99	Uttx	2m5f	F(0-100)HCh		GD		£3022
118	5/99	MRas	2m4f	D Ch		G-F		£4580
97	5/99	Uttx	2m	F(0-100)HHdl		G-F		£2515
98	5/99	Fknm	2m	G(0-95)HHdl		G-F		£1895

Total win prize-money £12014

Going: Sf: 0-0 GS: 0-0 Gd: 0-0 GF: - Fm: 0-3
Distance: 2m/2m3: 0-0 2m4-2m7: 0-2 3m+: 0-1
Track: LH: 0-1 RH: 0-1 Tight: 0-3 Gall: 0-0
Aids: Bl: 0-0 Vi: 0-0 Tstrap: 0-3
Best Rating: 127 7/99 Wolv 2m gd-sft Ch

Western Fort (IRE)

93 85

12-y-o ch g Saher-Moon Away (Mount Hagen (FR))
R J Baker (K Cumings 16/5) R G Westacott

Placings:0/U060 (0796)
2001/02: 20^{0}GF, 19^{0}F, 21^{6}GF, 16^{0}GF

	Starts	1st	2nd	3rd	Win & Pl
Chases	4	0	0	0	0
Career Total	**5**	**0**	**0**	**0**	**0**

Going: Sf: 0-0 GS: 0-0 Gd: 0-0 GF: - Fm: 0-4
Distance: 2m/2m3: 0-1 2m4-2m7: 0-3 3m+: 0-0
Track: LH: 0-3 RH: 0-1 Tight: 0-3 Gall: 0-0
Aids: Bl: 0-0 Vi: 0-0 Tstrap: 0-0
Best Rating: 85 5/01 NAbb 2m5f110y gd-fm Ch

Western Ridge (FR)

73 44

5-y-o b g Darshaan-Helvellyn (USA) (Gone West (USA))
B J Llewellyn (P Mitchell 3/9) D H Driscoll

Placings:0 (2924)
2001/02: 17^{0}GS

	Starts	1st	2nd	3rd	Win & Pl
Hurdles	1	0	0	0	
Career Total	**1**	**0**	**0**	**0**	

Going: Sf: 0-0 GS: 0-1 Gd: 0-0 GF: - Fm: 0-0
Distance: 2m/2m3: 0-1 2m4-2m7: 0-0 3m+: 0-0
Track: LH: 0-0 RH: 0-1 Tight: 0-1 Gall: 0-0
Aids: Bl: 0-0 Vi: 0-0 Tstrap: 0-0
Best Rating: 44 12/01 Tntn 2m1f gd-sft Hdl

Western Sun

12-y-o b g Sunyboy-Running Valley (Buckskin (FR))
J L Needham J L Needham

Placings:0/00/P/0U0P/R-P0 (4543)
2001/02: 16^{P}GF, 19^{0}G

	Starts	1st	2nd	3rd	Win & Pl
Chases	2	0	0	0	
Career Total	**11**	**0**	**0**	**0**	

Going: Sf: 0-0 GS: 0-0 Gd: 0-1 GF: - Fm: 0-1
Distance: 2m/2m3: 0-2 2m4-2m7: 0-0 3m+: 0-0
Track: LH: 0-0 RH: 0-2 Tight: 0-1 Gall: 0-0
Aids: Bl: 0-0 Vi: 0-0 Tstrap: 0-0
Best Rating: 55 9/99 Gway 2m6f soft Ch

Westernmost

105 105

4-y-o b g Most Welcome-Dakota Girl (Northern State (USA))
M Todhunter (T D Barron 29/8) Steve Baron

Placings:S3F52 (4330)
2001/02: 16^{S}G, 16^{3}GS, 16^{F}S, 16^{5}GS, 17^{2}S

	Starts	1st	2nd	3rd	Win & Pl
Hurdles	5	0	1	1	1479
Career Total	**5**	**0**	**1**	**1**	**1479**

Going: Sf: 0-2 GS: 0-2 Gd: 0-1 GF: - Fm: 0-0
Distance: 2m/2m3: 0-5 2m4-2m7: 0-0 3m+: 0-0
Track: LH: 0-5 RH: 0-0 Tight: 0-1 Gall: 0-2
Aids: Bl: 0-0 Vi: 0-0 Tstrap: 0-0
Best Rating: 105 3/02 Sedg 2m1f soft Hdl

Modest middle-distance maiden on the Flat. Took a weak novices' hurdle at Cartmel in June.

Westfield Cockney (IRE)

88 100

9-y-o b g Mulhollande (USA)-Cockney Bug (Torus)
M C Pipe D A Johnson

Placings:32/S3P312/6-3P (1026)
2001/02: 20^{3}S, 22^{P}G

	Starts	1st	2nd	3rd	Win & Pl
Hurdles	2	0	0	1	540
Career Total	**11**	**1**	**2**	**4**	**5483**

110 3/00 Tntn 2m3f110y E Hdl GD £2655
Total win prize-money £2655

Going: Sf: 0-1 GS: 0-0 Gd: 0-1 GF: - Fm: 0-0
Distance: 2m/2m3: 0-0 2m4-2m7: 0-2 3m+: 0-0
Track: LH: 0-2 RH: 0-0 Tight: 0-1 Gall: 0-0
Aids: Bl: 0-0 Vi: 0-1 Tstrap: 0-1
Best Rating: 114 3/00 Tntn 2m3f110y good Hdl

Westfield John

81(88h) (51h)64
7-y-o ch g Little Wolf-Moonbreaker (Twilight Alley)
Ferdy Murphy The Westfielders

Placings: *00-0*O0 (4857)
2001/02: 16^{0}S, 20°G, 20^{0}G

	Starts	1st	2nd	3rd	Win & Pl
NH Flat	1	0	0	0	0
Hurdles	2	0	0	0	0
Career Total	**5**	**0**	**0**	**0**	

Going: Sf: 0-1 GS: 0-0 Gd: 0-2 GF: - Fm: 0-0
Distance: 2m/2m3: 0-1 2m4-2m7: 0-2 3m+: 0-0
Track: LH: 0-3 RH: 0-0 Tight: 0-0 Gall: 0-0
Aids: Bl: 0-0 Vi: 0-0 Tstrap: 0-0
Best Rating: 96 10/00 Chel 2m110y good NHF

Westfield Max

90f 91f
7-y-o b g Teenoso (USA)-Manenda (Mandalus)
R A Fahey W S Wright

Placings: *0*-4 (1019)
2001/02: 16^{4}G

	Starts	1st	2nd	3rd	Win & Pl
NH Flat	1	0	0	0	0
Career Total	**2**	**0**	**0**	**0**	**0**

Going: Sf: 0-0 GS: 0-0 Gd: 0-1 GF: - Fm: 0-0
Distance: 2m/2m3: 0-1 2m4-2m7: 0-0 3m+: 0-0
Track: LH: 0-1 RH: 0-0 Tight: 0-0 Gall: 0-0
Aids: Bl: 0-0 Vi: 0-0 Tstrap: 0-0
Best Rating: 91 4/01 MRas 1m5f110y gd-sft NHF

Westmeath Flyer

113(93c) (113c)129
7-y-o b g Deploy-Re-Release (Baptism)
M Todhunter Jim Ennis

Placings: *2/22221*-**2F**312 (3373)
2001/02: 16^{2}S, 21^{F}S, 16^{3}S, 20^{1}HY, 20^{2}S

	Starts	1st	2nd	3rd	Win & Pl
Hurdles	3	1	1	1	9678
Chases	2	0	1	0	1484
Career Total	**11**	**2**	**7**	**1**	**17688**

124 12/01 Hayd 2m4f C(0-135)HHdl HVY £5343
110 2/01 Catt 2m3f E Hdl SFT £3262
Total win prize-money £8605

Going: Sf: 1-5 GS: 0-0 Gd: 0-0 GF: - Fm: 0-0
Distance: 2m/2m3: 0-2 **2m4-2m7: 1-3** 3m+: 0-0
Track: **LH: 1-4** RH: 0-1 Tight: 0-1 Gall: 0-0
Aids: Bl: 0-0 Vi: 0-0 Tstrap: 0-0
Best Rating: 129 1/02 Hayd 2m4f soft Hdl

A winner over hurdles, he acts well on a soft surface and is effective at around two and a half miles.

Westmeath Lad

72
5-y-o ch g Primo Dominie-Re-Release (Baptism)
M Todhunter Jim Ennis

Placings: *60* (4750)
2001/02: 16^{6}HY, 17^{0}G

	Starts	1st	2nd	3rd	Win & Pl
NH Flat	2	0	0	0	
Career Total	**2**	**0**	**0**	**0**	

Going: Sf: 0-1 GS: 0-0 Gd: 0-1 GF: - Fm: 0-0
Distance: 2m/2m3: 0-2 2m4-2m7: 0-0 3m+: 0-0
Track: LH: 0-0 RH: 0-1 Tight: 0-0 Gall: 0-0
Aids: Bl: 0-0 Vi: 0-0 Tstrap: 0-0
Best Rating: 79 4/02 Carl 2m1f good NHF

Westminster City (USA)

94 75
6-y-o b g Alleged (USA)-Promanade Fan (USA) (Timeless Moment (USA))
B J Llewellyn (Ian Williams 11/9) Miss S Rudge

Placings: P30 (1943)
2001/02: 16^{P}GF, 17^{3}GF, 16^{0}GS

	Starts	1st	2nd	3rd	Win & Pl
Hurdles	3	0	0	1	395
Career Total	**3**	**0**	**0**	**1**	**395**

Going: Sf: 0-0 GS: 0-1 Gd: 0-0 GF: - Fm: 0-2
Distance: 2m/2m3: 0-3 2m4-2m7: 0-0 3m+: 0-0
Track: LH: 0-2 RH: 0-1 Tight: 0-2 Gall: 0-0
Aids: Bl: 0-0 Vi: 0-0 Tstrap: 0-0
Best Rating: 75 11/01 Plum 2m gd-sft Hdl

Changed trainers frequently in 2001, fair effort when third at Exeter in October.

Westmorland (IRE)

109 108+
6-y-o b g Phardante (FR)-Ticking Over (IRE) (Decent Fellow)
L Lungo M W Chapman

Placings: *000P*-001F1 (4745)
2001/02: 17^{0}HY, 20^{0}S, 21^{1}S, 20^{F}GS, 24^{1}G

	Starts	1st	2nd	3rd	Win & Pl
Hurdles	5	2	0	0	4872
Career Total	**9**	**2**	**0**	**0**	**4872**

97 4/02 Carl 3m110y E(0-105)HHdl GD £3108
85 3/02 Sedg 2m5f110y G(0-90)HHdl SFT £1764
Total win prize-money £4872

Going: Sf: 1-3 GS: 0-1 Gd: 1-1 GF: - Fm: 0-0
Distance: 2m/2m3: 0-1 2m4-2m7: 1-3 3m+: 1-1
Track: LH: 1-3 RH: 1-1 **Tight: 1-2** Gall: 0-1
Aids: Bl: 0-0 Vi: 0-0 Tstrap: 0-0
Best Rating: 97 4/02 Carl 3m110y good Hdl

He has improved no end since being faced with a test of stamina with wins at Sedgefield, Carlisle and Hexham in the spring of 2002 despite rising in the handicap. Acts on any ground.

Westwinds

88 92
10-y-o b g Vital Season-April's Crook (Crozier)
M J Coombe Mrs N M Coombe

Placings: 4U-15P4 (4849)
2001/02: 26^{1}G, 23^{5}GS, 21^{P}S, 24^{4}G

	Starts	1st	2nd	3rd	Win & Pl
Chases	4	1	0	0	3999
Career Total	**6**	**1**	**0**	**0**	**4339**

92 5/01 Folk 3m2f E Ch GD £3666
Total win prize-money £3666

Going: Sf: 0-1 GS: 0-1 Gd: 1-2 GF: - Fm: 0-0
Distance: 2m/2m3: 0-0 2m4-2m7: 0-1 **3m+: 1-3**
Track: LH: 0-1 **RH: 1-3 Tight: 1-3** Gall: 0-0
Aids: Bl: 0-0 Vi: 0-0 Tstrap: 0-0
Best Rating: 101 1/01 Donc 3m good Ch

Modest chaser, stays three miles, acts on good ground.

Wethaab (USA)

62
5-y-o b g Pleasant Colony (USA)-Binntastic (USA) (Lyphard's Wish (FR))
Mrs A M Naughton (G M Moore 27/8) Mrs S E Cooper

Placings: P-P0 (1839)
2001/02: 17^{P}G, 16^{0}G

	Starts	1st	2nd	3rd	Win & Pl
Hurdles	2	0	0	0	
Career Total	**3**	**0**	**0**	**0**	

Going: Sf: 0-0 GS: 0-0 Gd: 0-2 GF: - Fm: 0-0
Distance: 2m/2m3: 0-2 2m4-2m7: 0-0 3m+: 0-0
Track: LH: 0-2 RH: 0-0 Tight: 0-2 Gall: 0-0
Aids: Bl: 0-0 Vi: 0-0 Tstrap: 0-1
Best Rating:

What A Beauty

5-y-o b m Perpendicular-Jane's Affair (Alleging (USA))
Ronald Thompson Mrs K Morrell

Placings: *0* (0240)
2001/02: 16^{0}GF

	Starts	1st	2nd	3rd	Win & Pl
NH Flat	1	0	0	0	
Career Total	**1**	**0**	**0**	**0**	

Going: Sf: 0-0 GS: 0-0 Gd: 0-0 GF: - Fm: 0-1
Distance: 2m/2m3: 0-1 2m4-2m7: 0-0 3m+: 0-0
Track: LH: 0-1 RH: 0-0 Tight: 0-1 Gall: 0-0
Aids: Bl: 0-0 Vi: 0-0 Tstrap: 0-0
Best Rating:

What A Cracker

70 37
5-y-o b m Bustino-Moon Spin (Night Shift (USA))
Miss H M Irving The Nap Hand Partnership

Placings: *06P*-0 (0348)
2001/02: 16^{0}G

	Starts	1st	2nd	3rd	Win & Pl
Hurdles	1	0	0	0	
Career Total	**4**	**0**	**0**	**0**	**0**

Going: Sf: 0-0 GS: 0-0 Gd: 0-1 GF: - Fm: 0-0
Distance: 2m/2m3: 0-1 2m4-2m7: 0-0 3m+: 0-0
Track: LH: 0-1 RH: 0-0 Tight: 0-1 Gall: 0-0
Aids: Bl: 0-1 Vi: 0-0 Tstrap: 0-0
Best Rating: 37 5/01 Strf 2m110y good Hdl

What A Fiddler (IRE)

9-y-o ch g Orchestra-Crowenstown Miss (Over The River (FR))
J S Haldane J S Haldane

Placings:*2/24/5P***23/15** (4396)
2001/02: 25^{1}S, 25^{5}HY

	Starts	1st	2nd	3rd	Win & Pl
Chases	2	1	0	0	2483
Career Total	**9**	**1**	**3**	**1**	**4930**

115	5/01	Hexm	3m1f	H Ch	SFT	£2483

Total win prize-money £2483

Going: Sf: 1-2 GS: 0-0 Gd: 0-0 GF: - Fm: 0-0
Distance: 2m/2m3: 0-0 2m4-2m7: 0-0 **3m+: 1-2**
Track: **LH: 1-2** RH: 0-0 Tight: 0-1 Gall: 0-0
Aids: Bl: 0-0 Vi: 0-0 Tstrap: 0-0
Best Rating: 115 5/01 Hexm 3m1f soft Ch

What A Fuss

100 111

9-y-o b g Great Commotion (USA)-Hafwah (Gorytus (USA))
P J Hobbs Mrs D A Winton

Placings:304566/0P1F5P/**0P**114P**2244/3510** (1441)
2001/02: 20^{3}GS, 20^{5}G, 18^{1}GF, 20^{0}GF

	Starts	1st	2nd	3rd	Win & Pl
Chases	1	1	0	1	4005
Career Total	**26**	**4**	**2**	**2**	**14784**

110	8/01	Font	2m2f	E Ch	G-F	£3120
118	11/99	Hexm	2m	F(0-105)HHdl	GD	£2247
115	11/99	MRas	2m5f110y	E(0-115)HHdl	G-S	£2721
107	2/99	Hrfd	2m1f	F(0-100)HHdl	GD	£2556

Total win prize-money £10645

Going: Sf: 0-0 GS: 0-1 Gd: 0-1 GF: - Fm: 1-2
Distance: **2m/2m3: 1-1** 2m4-2m7: 0-3 3m+: 0-0
Track: LH: 0-2 RH: 0-0 **Tight: 1-3** Gall: 0-0
Aids: Bl: 0-0 Vi: 0-0 Tstrap: 0-0
Best Rating: 118 2/00 Newc 2m4f soft Ch

Fair fast-ground chaser, stays two and a half miles.

What A Gem

89f 89f

5-y-o br m Karinga Bay-Scarlet Dymond (Rymer)
Nick Williams The Brendon Toffs

Placings:*50* (3345)
2001/02: 17^{5}GF, 17^{0}S

	Starts	1st	2nd	3rd	Win & Pl
NH Flat	2	0	0	0	0
Career Total	**2**	**0**	**0**	**0**	**0**

Going: Sf: 0-1 GS: 0-0 Gd: 0-0 GF: - Fm: 0-1
Distance: 2m/2m3: 0-2 2m4-2m7: 0-0 3m+: 0-0
Track: LH: 0-0 RH: 0-1 Tight: 0-0 Gall: 0-0
Aids: Bl: 0-0 Vi: 0-0 Tstrap: 0-0
Best Rating: 89 11/01 Extr 2m1f gd-fm NHF

What A Tale (IRE)

109 106

10-y-o b g Tale Quale-Cherish (Bargello)
Mrs M Reveley Jemm Partnership

Placings:*6/65*406/4116/63P0/**2333-164** (3508)
2001/02: 21^{1}G, 21^{6}G, 24^{4}S

	Starts	1st	2nd	3rd	Win & Pl
Chases	3	1	0	0	3308
Career Total	**21**	**3**	**1**	**4**	**12223**

110	10/01	Sedg	2m5f	E Ch	GD	£3071
106	1/99	Catt	3m1f110y	E Hdl	SFT	£2486
102	6/98	Prth	3m110y	E Hdl	G-F	£2696

Total win prize-money £8253

Going: Sf: 0-1 GS: 0-0 Gd: 1-2 GF: - Fm: 0-0
Distance: 2m/2m3: 0-0 **2m4-2m7: 1-2** 3m+: 0-1
Track: **LH: 1-2** RH: 0-1 **Tight: 1-3** Gall: 0-0
Aids: Bl: 0-0 Vi: 0-0 Tstrap: 0-0
Best Rating: 119 12/00 Donc 3m heavy Ch

Staying novice chaser, successful at Sedgefield in October.

What A Wonder (IRE)

104(109h) (120h)112

7-y-o gr g Roselier (FR)-Lady Abednego Vii (Damsire Unregistered)
Ferdy Murphy The Sheepscar Syndicate

Placings:*0/*222121-24U4P01 (4877)
2001/02: 21^{2}S, 25^{4}GS, 24^{U}GS, 24^{4}GS, 25^{P}HY, 25^{0}GF, 24^{1}G

	Starts	1st	2nd	3rd	Win & Pl
Hurdles	2	1	0	0	4654
Chases	5	0	1	0	2067
Career Total	**14**	**3**	**5**	**0**	**17025**

116	4/02	Prth	3m110y	E(0-105)HHdl	GD	£4654
120	4/01	Prth	3m110y	F(0-105)HHdl	HVY	£3514
106	2/01	Muss	3m	D(0-110)HHdl	GD	£3458

Total win prize-money £11626

Going: Sf: 0-2 GS: 0-3 Gd: 1-1 GF: - Fm: 0-1
Distance: 2m/2m3: 0-0 2m4-2m7: 0-1 **3m+: 1-6**
Track: LH: 0-5 **RH: 1-1** Tight: 0-4 Gall: 0-0
Aids: Bl: 0-0 Vi: 0-0 Tstrap: 0-0
Best Rating: 120 4/01 Prth 3m110y heavy Hdl

A winner twice over hurdles and has made a good start to his chasing career at Sedgefield in November. Jumping has let him down after and he reverted to hurdles, scoring at Perth in April. Suited by a sharp right-handed track, acts on any ground.

What Jim Wants (IRE)

91 74

9-y-o b g Magical Strike (USA)-Sally Gone (IRE) (Last Tycoon)
P Wegmann R Koniger

Placings:5026P4/P6P6224162/45000/04664640/5-00P (1101)
2001/02: 22^{0}G, 20^{0}S, 22^{P}G

	Starts	1st	2nd	3rd	Win & Pl
Hurdles	3	0	0	0	
Career Total	**33**	**1**	**4**	**0**	**5722**

94	3/98	Catt	3m1f110y	E(0-100)HHdl	G-S	£2472

Total win prize-money £2472

Going: Sf: 0-1 GS: 0-0 Gd: 0-2 GF: - Fm: 0-0
Distance: 2m/2m3: 0-0 2m4-2m7: 0-3 3m+: 0-0
Track: LH: 0-3 RH: 0-0 Tight: 0-2 Gall: 0-0
Aids: Bl: 0-0 Vi: 0-1 Tstrap: 0-0
Best Rating: 94 4/98 Worc 3m gd-sft Hdl

What You Mean

97 86

7-y-o ch g Kasakov-Lonely Lass (Headin' Up)
J R Norton Michael Ng

Placings:*60/32*U256/0-050 (2630)
2001/02: 20^{0}G, 20^{5}G, 24^{0}S

	Starts	1st	2nd	3rd	Win & Pl
Hurdles	3	0	0	0	0
Career Total	**12**	**0**	**2**	**1**	**1450**

Going: Sf: 0-1 GS: 0-0 Gd: 0-2 GF: - Fm: 0-0
Distance: 2m/2m3: 0-0 2m4-2m7: 0-2 3m+: 0-1
Track: LH: 0-3 RH: 0-0 Tight: 0-0 Gall: 0-0
Aids: Bl: 0-0 Vi: 0-0 Tstrap: 0-0
Best Rating: 94 6/99 Worc 2m gd-fm NHF

What's The Count

6-y-o gr g Theatrical Charmer-Yankee Silver (Yankee Gold)
B R Johnson The Twenty Five Club

Placings:*0/500*-P (0365)
2001/02: 19^{P}GF

	Starts	1st	2nd	3rd	Win & Pl
Hurdles	1	0	0	0	
Career Total	**5**	**0**	**0**	**0**	**0**

Going: Sf: 0-0 GS: 0-0 Gd: 0-0 GF: - Fm: 0-1
Distance: 2m/2m3: 0-0 2m4-2m7: 0-1 3m+: 0-0
Track: LH: 0-1 RH: 0-0 Tight: 0-1 Gall: 0-0
Aids: Bl: 0-0 Vi: 0-0 Tstrap: 0-0
Best Rating: 80 2/00 Kemp 2m soft NHF

What's Up Boys (IRE)

114 170

8-y-o gr g Supreme Leader-Maryville Bick (Malacate (USA))
P J Hobbs R J B Partners

Placings:*62126*/11P313/**12F1112-14P52** (4677)
2001/02: 26^{1}S, 29^{4}GS, 24^{P}S, 26^{5}G, 36^{2}G

	Starts	1st	2nd	3rd	Win & Pl
Chases	5	1	1	0	179250
Career Total	**23**	**9**	**5**	**2**	**352390**

167	12/01	Newb	3m2f110y	A HCh	SFT	£58000
165	4/01	Aint	3m1f	A Ch	SFT	£50250
151	2/01	Ludl	3m	E Ch	G-S	£3750
133	12/00	Muss	2m4f	D Ch	GD	£4641
149	5/00	Punc	2m4f	Hdl	GD	£24800
149	3/00	Chel	2m5f	A HHdl	GD	£39000
146	12/99	Sand	2m6f	A Hdl	G-S	£9525
119	11/99	Folk	2m4f110y	F Hdl	G-S	£1499
104	12/98	Punc	2m	NHF	SH	£2989

Total win prize-money £194455

Going: Sf: 1-2 GS: 0-1 Gd: 0-2 GF: - Fm: 0-0
Distance: 2m/2m3: 0-0 2m4-2m7: 0-0 **3m+: 1-5**
Track: **LH: 1-5** RH: 0-0 Tight: 0-1 **Gall: 1-3**
Aids: Bl: 0-2 Vi: 0-0 Tstrap: 0-0
Best Rating: 170 4/02 Aint 4m4f good Ch

He was a very smart hurdler, including winning the Coral Cup at Cheltenham in 2000 and also winning at Punchestown. He did little wrong over fences last season, despite not jumping all that well in his first three starts, but there was no hint of an error when he beat Shotgun Willy by a distance at Aintree and he ran a fine race for a novice to finish second in the Whitbread. Game winner of the Hennessy on his return, he stays well and is especially effective in soft ground. Fourth in the Welsh National at Christmas, but ran poorly at Newbury next time. Ran a staying-on race in the Gold

Cup and finished a fine second in the Grand National. Always seems to run well at the big meetings.

Whataboutit

8-y-o gr g Thethingaboutitis (USA)-Baltic Call (Czarist)
W M Brisbourne Cecil W Wardle

Placings:P **(2426)**
2001/02: 17^{P}GS

	Starts	1st	2nd	3rd	Win & Pl
Hurdles	1	0	0	0	
Career Total	**1**	**0**	**0**	**0**	

Going: Sf: 0-0 GS: 0-1 Gd: 0-0 GF: - Fm: 0-0
Distance: 2m/2m3: 0-1 2m4-2m7: 0-0 3m+: 0-0
Track: LH: 0-1 RH: 0-0 Tight: 0-1 Gall: 0-0
Aids: Bl: 0-0 Vi: 0-0 Tstrap: 0-0
Best Rating:

Whatadeal

104 105

6-y-o b g Then Again-Close The Deal (Nicholas Bill)
M W Easterby Abbots Salford Caravan Park

Placings:23/11P010214-5 **(0206)**
2001/02: 16^{5}G

	Starts	1st	2nd	3rd	Win & Pl
Hurdles	1	0	0	0	0
Career Total	**12**	**4**	**2**	**1**	**8534**

108	1/01	Newc	2m	F(0-100)HHdl	HVY	£2226
95	11/00	Catt	2m3f	E Hdl	G-S	£1869
110	10/00	MRas	2m1f110y	H NHF	GD	£1610
104	9/00	MRas	1m5f110y	H NHF	G-F	£1547

Total win prize-money £7252

Going: Sf: 0-0 GS: 0-0 Gd: 0-1 GF: - Fm: 0-0
Distance: 2m/2m3: 0-1 2m4-2m7: 0-0 3m+: 0-0
Track: LH: 0-1 RH: 0-0 Tight: 0-0 Gall: 0-0
Aids: Bl: 0-0 Vi: 0-0 Tstrap: 0-0
Best Rating: **110** 1/01 Donc 2m110y good Hdl

Whatafellow (IRE)

12-y-o ch g Arapahos (FR)-Dara's March (March Parade)
Mrs Edward Crow Gareth Samuel

Placings:20F/1P-F **(4826)**
2001/02: 26^{F}G

	Starts	1st	2nd	3rd	Win & Pl
Chases	1	0	0	0	
Career Total	**6**	**1**	**1**	**0**	**3009**

115	5/00	Ctml	3m2f	H Ch	G-S	£1964

Total win prize-money £1964

Going: Sf: 0-0 GS: 0-0 Gd: 0-1 GF: - Fm: 0-0
Distance: 2m/2m3: 0-0 2m4-2m7: 0-0 3m+: 0-1
Track: LH: 0-1 RH: 0-0 Tight: 0-0 Gall: 0-1
Aids: Bl: 0-1 Vi: 0-0 Tstrap: 0-0
Best Rating: **118** 3/00 Chel 3m2f110y gd-fm Ch

A multiple winner in points, albeit in easy races. Not as effective under Rules. Acts on a sound surface.

Whatashot

105 83

12-y-o ch g Gunner B-Lady Letitia (Le Bavard (FR))
D McCain D McCain

Placings:646PP/422/0**0242P**/**R**560**P**21240-0341F0P0 **(1353)**
2001/02: 20^{0}G, 20^{3}GF, 24^{4}F, 20^{1}G, 27^{F}GF, 27^{0}GF, 22^{P}GS, 22^{0}GF

	Starts	1st	2nd	3rd	Win & Pl
Hurdles	8	1	0	1	2569
Career Total	**32**	**2**	**6**	**1**	**10870**

83	6/01	Hexm	2m4f110y	G(0-95)HHdl	GD	£2102
83	8/00	Ctml	2m6f	G(0-90)HHdl	GD	£2730

Total win prize-money £4833

Going: Sf: 0-0 GS: 0-1 Gd: 1-2 GF: - Fm: 0-5
Distance: 2m/2m3: 0-0 **2m4-2m7: 1-5** 3m+: 0-3
Track: **LH: 1-7** RH: 0-1 Tight: 0-5 Gall: 0-0
Aids: Bl: 0-0 **Vi: 1-8** Tstrap: 0-0
Best Rating: **97** 2/00 Muss 3m good Ch

Whatasucker (IRE)

8-y-o ch g Meneval (USA)-Tuney Blade (Fine Blade (USA))
E Haddock E Haddock

Placings:0/PUF/P **(0367)**
2001/02: 24^{P}G

	Starts	1st	2nd	3rd	Win & Pl
Chases	1	0	0	0	
Career Total	**5**	**0**	**0**	**0**	

Going: Sf: 0-0 GS: 0-0 Gd: 0-1 GF: - Fm: 0-0
Distance: 2m/2m3: 0-0 2m4-2m7: 0-0 3m+: 0-1
Track: LH: 0-0 RH: 0-0 Tight: 0-0 Gall: 0-0
Aids: Bl: 0-0 Vi: 0-0 Tstrap: 0-0
Best Rating:

Whats Money

97(83h) (20h)86

11-y-o gr m Scallywag-What A Coup (Malicious)
Mrs J G Retter Mrs J G Retter

Placings:4/6P4PP5/632F00-3U **(0574)**
2001/02: 18^{3}GF, 21^{U}GF

	Starts	1st	2nd	3rd	Win & Pl
Chases	2	0	0	1	412
Career Total	**15**	**0**	**1**	**2**	**2081**

Going: Sf: 0-0 GS: 0-0 Gd: 0-0 GF: - Fm: 0-2
Distance: 2m/2m3: 0-1 2m4-2m7: 0-1 3m+: 0-0
Track: LH: 0-1 RH: 0-0 Tight: 0-2 Gall: 0-0
Aids: Bl: 0-0 Vi: 0-0 Tstrap: 0-0
Best Rating: **93** 12/99 Font 2m4f good Ch

Whats Up Maid

5-y-o b m Emperor Fountain-Roman Maid (Roman Warrior)
G F H Charles-Jones H S Channon

Placings:0 **(1545)**
2001/02: 17^{0}G

	Starts	1st	2nd	3rd	Win & Pl
NH Flat	1	0	0	0	
Career Total	**1**	**0**	**0**	**0**	

Going: Sf: 0-0 GS: 0-0 Gd: 0-1 GF: - Fm: 0-0
Distance: 2m/2m3: 0-1 2m4-2m7: 0-0 3m+: 0-0
Track: LH: 0-0 RH: 0-1 Tight: 0-0 Gall: 0-0
Aids: Bl: 0-0 Vi: 0-0 Tstrap: 0-0
Best Rating:

Whenwilliemetharry

5-y-o b m Sabrehill (USA)-William's Bird (USA) (Master Willie)
M E Sowersby (A Bailey 20/7) M E Sowersby

Placings:P **(3856)**
2001/02: 16^{P}S

	Starts	1st	2nd	3rd	Win & Pl
Hurdles	1	0	0	0	
Career Total	**1**	**0**	**0**	**0**	

Going: Sf: 0-1 GS: 0-0 Gd: 0-0 GF: - Fm: 0-0
Distance: 2m/2m3: 0-1 2m4-2m7: 0-0 3m+: 0-0
Track: LH: 0-1 RH: 0-0 Tight: 0-0 Gall: 0-1
Aids: Bl: 0-0 Vi: 0-0 Tstrap: 0-0
Best Rating:

Whether The Storm (IRE)

6-y-o b g Glacial Storm (USA)-Minimum Choice (IRE) (Miners Lamp)
Miss H C Knight Executive Racing

Placings:3/441-0 **(3378)**
2001/02: 21^{0}GS

	Starts	1st	2nd	3rd	Win & Pl
Hurdles	1	0	0	0	
Career Total	**5**	**1**	**0**	**1**	**3869**

109	12/00	Newb	2m3f	D Hdl	SFT	£3623

Total win prize-money £3624

Going: Sf: 0-0 GS: 0-1 Gd: 0-0 GF: - Fm: 0-0
Distance: 2m/2m3: 0-0 2m4-2m7: 0-1 3m+: 0-0
Track: LH: 0-0 RH: 0-1 Tight: 0-0 Gall: 0-0
Aids: Bl: 0-0 Vi: 0-0 Tstrap: 0-0
Best Rating: **109** 12/00 Newb 2m3f soft Hdl

Whinholme Lad

6-y-o ch g My Generation-Broken Paws (Busted)
F Kirby Fred Kirby

Placings:OP0 **(3271)**
2001/02: 16^{0}G, 19^{P}G, 16^{0}G

	Starts	1st	2nd	3rd	Win & Pl
Hurdles	3	0	0	0	
Career Total	**3**	**0**	**0**	**0**	

Going: Sf: 0-0 GS: 0-0 Gd: 0-3 GF: - Fm: 0-0
Distance: 2m/2m3: 0-3 2m4-2m7: 0-0 3m+: 0-0
Track: LH: 0-3 RH: 0-0 Tight: 0-1 Gall: 0-1
Aids: Bl: 0-0 Vi: 0-0 Tstrap: 0-0
Best Rating:

Whippers Delight (IRE)

14-y-o ch g King Persian-Crashing Juno (Crash Course)
G F H Charles-Jones S P Tindall

Placings:561426510124/44022222214/4P241226322 3/61334**F213U2/63U0051F2/PPP513232/2O/U16462P /4P**/0 **(3453)**

2001/02: 21^{0}HY

	Starts	1st	2nd	3rd	Win & Pl
Hurdles	1	0	0	0	
Career Total	**76**	**10**	**20**	**8**	**43867**

101	12/98	Plum	3m1f110y	E(0-120)HCh	G-S	£2705
97	1/97	Plum	2m	F(0-105)HCh	GD	£2733
103	3/96	Plum	2m5f	E(0-110)HCh	G-S	£3206
91	3/95	Plum	2m	E Ch	G-S	£2742
103	11/94	Wind	2m	(0-120)HHdl	G-S	£3886
108	12/93	Font	2m2f	(0-130)HHdl	HVY	£2092
100	3/93	Uttx	2m	Hdl	GD	£2180
89	4/92	Bang	2m	HHdl	SFT	£1982
95	2/92	Uttx	2m	Hdl	GD	£1595
110	11/91	Bang	2m	Hdl	G-S	£1603

Total win prize-money £24728

Going: Sf: 0-1 GS: 0-0 Gd: 0-0 GF: - Fm: 0-0
Distance: 2m/2m3: 0-0 2m4-2m7: 0-1 3m+: 0-0
Track: LH: 0-1 RH: 0-0 Tight: 0-1 Gall: 0-0
Aids: Bl: 0-0 Vi: 0-0 Tstrap: 0-0
Best Rating: 110 11/91 Bang 2m gd-sft Hdl

Whisky Chaser

93 **98**

5-y-o ch m Never So Bold-Highland Spirit (Scottish Reel)
M C Pipe G H Senior, T Richmond & A Robertson

Placings:1540-1 **(0773)**
2001/02: 16^{1}GF

	Starts	1st	2nd	3rd	Win & Pl
Hurdles	1	1	0	0	1813
Career Total	**5**	**2**	**0**	**0**	**3742**

98	6/01	Worc	2m	G(0-90)HHdl	G-F	£1813
85	9/00	Hrfd	2m1f	G Hdl	G-F	£1928

Total win prize-money £3742

Going: Sf: 0-0 GS: 0-0 Gd: 0-0 GF: - Fm: 1-1
Distance: **2m/2m3: 1-1** 2m4-2m7: 0-0 3m+: 0-0
Track: **LH: 1-1** RH: 0-0 Tight: 0-0 Gall: 0-0
Aids: Bl: 0-0 Vi: 0-0 Tstrap: 0-0
Best Rating: 98 6/01 Worc 2m gd-fm Hdl

Whispering Pines (NZ)

10-y-o b g Cache Of Gold (USA)-Woodhill (NZ) (Zamazaan (FR))
B J M Ryall J J Boulter/f J Wilkins/k J Pearce

Placings:4-PF **(0585)**
2001/02: 23^{P}GS, 24^{F}GF

	Starts	1st	2nd	3rd	Win & Pl
Chases	2	0	0	0	
Career Total	**3**	**0**	**0**	**0**	**0**

Going: Sf: 0-0 GS: 0-1 Gd: 0-0 GF: - Fm: 0-1
Distance: 2m/2m3: 0-0 2m4-2m7: 0-0 3m+: 0-2
Track: LH: 0-1 RH: 0-1 Tight: 0-1 Gall: 0-0
Aids: Bl: 0-0 Vi: 0-0 Tstrap: 0-0
Best Rating: 86 4/01 Hrfd 3m2f good Hdl

Whistful Suzie (IRE)

80 **55**

5-y-o ch m Eurobus-Ah Suzie (IRE) (King's Ride)
Mrs S C Bradburne Lord Cochrane And Partners

Placings:*006* **(4894)**
2001/02: 16^{0}HY, 16^{0}HY, 16^{6}G

	Starts	1st	2nd	3rd	Win & Pl
NH Flat	2	0	0	0	0
Hurdles	1	0	0	0	0
Career Total	**3**	**0**	**0**	**0**	**0**

Going: Sf: 0-2 GS: 0-0 Gd: 0-1 GF: - Fm: 0-0
Distance: 2m/2m3: 0-3 2m4-2m7: 0-0 3m+: 0-0
Track: LH: 0-1 RH: 0-1 Tight: 0-0 Gall: 0-0
Aids: Bl: 0-0 Vi: 0-0 Tstrap: 0-0
Best Rating: 78 3/02 Ayr 2m heavy NHF

Whistlewell Lady

98 **72**

8-y-o b m Blow The Whistle-Indian Wells (Reliance Ii)
M J Wilkinson Mrs Elizabeth Young & Mrs Hilary Pye

Placings:*0/540*/00-04 **(0981)**
2001/02: 16^{0}GF, 22^{4}G

	Starts	1st	2nd	3rd	Win & Pl
Hurdles	2	0	0	0	0
Career Total	**8**	**0**	**0**	**0**	**0**

Going: Sf: 0-0 GS: 0-0 Gd: 0-1 GF: - Fm: 0-1
Distance: 2m/2m3: 0-1 2m4-2m7: 0-1 3m+: 0-0
Track: LH: 0-1 RH: 0-1 Tight: 0-1 Gall: 0-1
Aids: Bl: 0-0 Vi: 0-0 Tstrap: 0-0
Best Rating: 72 7/01 Strf 2m6f110y good Hdl

Whistling Dixie (IRE)

114 **138**

6-y-o ch g Forest Wind (USA)-Camdens Gift (Camden Town)
Mrs M Reveley Mrs P D Savill

Placings:12113-216 **(2192)**
2001/02: 17^{2}GS, 16^{1}S, 16^{6}G

	Starts	1st	2nd	3rd	Win & Pl
Hurdles	3	1	1	0	32384
Career Total	**8**	**4**	**2**	**1**	**48141**

131	11/01	DRoy	2m	(0-135)HHdl	SFT	£26209
127	2/01	Muss	2m	F(0-110)HHdl	GD	£5668
115	1/01	Donc	2m110y	C(0-130)HHdl	GD	£5980
103	12/00	Muss	2m	E Hdl	GD	£1792

Total win prize-money £39650

Going: Sf: 1-1 GS: 0-1 Gd: 0-1 GF: - Fm: 0-0
Distance: **2m/2m3: 1-3** 2m4-2m7: 0-0 3m+: 0-0
Track: LH: 0-1 RH: 0-0 Tight: 0-0 Gall: 0-0
Aids: Bl: 0-0 Vi: 0-0 Tstrap: 0-0
Best Rating: 131 11/01 DRoy 2m soft Hdl

Useful hurdler, he has won four times over hurdles, including at Down Royal in November 2001. Acts on most types of ground.

Whistling Song

87 **85**

7-y-o ch m True Song-Sancal (Whistlefield)
R Dickin Mrs C M Dickin

Placings:04P **(4541)**
2001/02: 16^{0}S, 25^{4}G, 25^{P}G

	Starts	1st	2nd	3rd	Win & Pl
Chases	3	0	0	0	258
Career Total	**3**	**0**	**0**	**0**	**258**

Going: Sf: 0-1 GS: 0-0 Gd: 0-2 GF: - Fm: 0-0
Distance: 2m/2m3: 0-1 2m4-2m7: 0-0 3m+: 0-2
Track: LH: 0-0 RH: 0-3 Tight: 0-0 Gall: 0-0
Aids: Bl: 0-0 Vi: 0-0 Tstrap: 0-0
Best Rating: 85 3/02 Hrfd 3m1f110y good Ch

White Amit

4-y-o b f Shaamit (IRE)-White African (Carwhite)
A G Newcombe (J A Gilbert 13/8) A G Newcombe

Placings:P **(2409)**
2001/02: 17^{P}GS

	Starts	1st	2nd	3rd	Win & Pl
Hurdles	1	0	0	0	
Career Total	**1**	**0**	**0**	**0**	

Going: Sf: 0-0 GS: 0-1 Gd: 0-0 GF: - Fm: 0-0
Distance: 2m/2m3: 0-1 2m4-2m7: 0-0 3m+: 0-0
Track: LH: 0-0 RH: 0-1 Tight: 0-1 Gall: 0-0
Aids: Bl: 0-0 Vi: 0-0 Tstrap: 0-1
Best Rating:

White In Front

110(84h) (69h)**105**

11-y-o ch g Tina's Pet-Lyaaric (Privy Seal)
Mrs A Price Mrs A Price

Placings:P/20F5P5FF/2240465F43/5062353434-0P50362565314 **(4683)**
2001/02: 17^{0}GS, 19^{P}G, 17^{5}GS, 17^{0}G, 20^{3}GF, 20^{6}GF, 16^{2}GF, 16^{5}G, 20^{6}G, 20^{5}G, 16^{3}G, 16^{1}S, 19^{4}GF

	Starts	1st	2nd	3rd	Win & Pl
Hurdles	1	0	0	0	0
Chases	12	1	1	2	6800
Career Total	**42**	**1**	**5**	**6**	**12959**

105	3/02	Hrfd	2m	E(0-105)HCh	SFT	£4108

Total win prize-money £4108

Going: Sf: 1-1 GS: 0-2 Gd: 0-6 GF: - Fm: 0-4
Distance: **2m/2m3: 1-9** 2m4-2m7: 0-4 3m+: 0-0
Track: LH: 0-3 **RH: 1-10** Tight: 0-9 Gall: 0-0
Aids: Bl: 0-1 Vi: 0-0 Tstrap: 0-0
Best Rating: 105 3/02 Hrfd 2m soft Ch

Regularly placed in Ludlow novice chases before getting off the mark at Hereford. Best at two miles.

White Van Man (IRE)

79f

7-y-o ch g Wakashan-Mrs Mac (General Ironside)
J S Haldane Mrs Hugh Fraser

Placings:*00-0* **(1905)**
2001/02: 17^{0}G

	Starts	1st	2nd	3rd	Win & Pl
NH Flat	1	0	0	0	
Career Total	**3**	**0**	**0**	**0**	

Going: Sf: 0-0 GS: 0-0 Gd: 0-1 GF: - Fm: 0-0
Distance: 2m/2m3: 0-1 2m4-2m7: 0-0 3m+: 0-0
Track: LH: 0-1 RH: 0-0 Tight: 0-1 Gall: 0-0
Aids: Bl: 0-0 Vi: 0-0 Tstrap: 0-0
Best Rating: 79 4/01 Ayr 2m gd-fm NHF

Whitebonnet (IRE)

97 **61**

12-y-o b g Rainbow Quest (USA)-Dawn Is Breaking (Import)
C F C Jackson Bogs Hole Racing

Placings:0200P/22501323/20F02500/00P4352/P1515

F35/46P0/6342-P0000 **(4568)**
2001/02: 20^{P}GS, 20^{0}S, 26^{0}GS, 24^{0}G, 24^{0}G

	Starts	1st	2nd	3rd	Win & Pl
Hurdles	5	0	0	0	
Career Total	**49**	**3**	**8**	**5**	**14453**

90	1/99	Extr	2m3f110y	E(0-115)HHdl	HVY	£2495
81	6/98	NAbb	3m3f	F(0-105)HHdl	GD	£1802
85	1/96	Towc	2m5f	G(0-95)HHdl	SFT	£2052

Total win prize-money £6349

Going: Sf: 0-1 GS: 0-2 Gd: 0-2 GF: - Fm: 0-0
Distance: 2m/2m3: 0-0 2m4-2m7: 0-2 3m+: 0-3
Track: LH: 0-0 RH: 0-5 Tight: 0-0 Gall: 0-1
Aids: Bl: 0-5 Vi: 0-0 Tstrap: 0-0
Best Rating: 91 1/95 Plum 2m1f soft Hdl

Whitegates Beauty

35

6-y-o ch m Minster Son-Whitegates Lady (Le Coq D'Or)
J Howard Johnson R W L Bowden

Placings:0PP0 **(4768)**
2001/02: 21^{0}G, 19^{P}GF, 22^{P}HY, 16^{0}GF

	Starts	1st	2nd	3rd	Win & Pl
Hurdles	4	0	0	0	
Career Total	**4**	**0**	**0**	**0**	

Going: Sf: 0-1 GS: 0-0 Gd: 0-1 GF: - Fm: 0-2
Distance: 2m/2m3: 0-2 2m4-2m7: 0-2 3m+: 0-0
Track: LH: 0-3 RH: 0-0 Tight: 0-3 Gall: 0-0
Aids: Bl: 0-0 Vi: 0-0 Tstrap: 0-0
Best Rating: 35 4/02 Hexm 2m110y gd-fm Hdl

Whitegates Prince

7-y-o b g Teenoso (USA)-Whitegates Lady (Le Coq D'Or)
B Ellison R W L Bowden

Placings:*000*/P/**PF-PP** **(4768)**
2001/02: 17^{P}GS, 16^{P}GF

	Starts	1st	2nd	3rd	Win & Pl
Hurdles	1	0	0	0	0
Chases	1	0	0	0	0
Career Total	**8**	**0**	**0**	**0**	

Going: Sf: 0-0 GS: 0-1 Gd: 0-0 GF: - Fm: 0-1
Distance: 2m/2m3: 0-2 2m4-2m7: 0-0 3m+: 0-0
Track: LH: 0-0 RH: 0-1 Tight: 0-1 Gall: 0-0
Aids: Bl: 0-0 Vi: 0-1 Tstrap: 0-0
Best Rating: 69 2/99 Sedg 2m1f good NHF

Whitegates Willie

10-y-o b g Buckskin (FR)-Whitegates Lady (Le Coq D'Or)
G D Hanmer W Puddifer

Placings:*000*/P002P/**3F26244/4P/P-P** **(4650)**
2001/02: 21^{P}G

	Starts	1st	2nd	3rd	Win & Pl
Chases	1	0	0	0	
Career Total	**19**	**0**	**3**	**1**	**4103**

Going: Sf: 0-0 GS: 0-0 Gd: 0-1 GF: - Fm: 0-0
Distance: 2m/2m3: 0-0 2m4-2m7: 0-1 3m+: 0-0
Track: LH: 0-1 RH: 0-0 Tight: 0-1 Gall: 0-0
Aids: Bl: 0-0 Vi: 0-0 Tstrap: 0-0
Best Rating: 96 2/98 Catt 2m good Ch

Lightly-raced winning pointer. Acts with cut. Has worn a tongue-strap.

Whitenzo (FR)

105(115c) (160c)140

6-y-o b g Lesotho (USA)-Whitengy (FR) (Olantengy (FR))
P F Nicholls Malcolm Pearce & Gerry Mizel Ii

Placings:00544/5**P221112-644251**425 **(4911)**
2001/02: 16^{6}G, 16^{4}GS, 21^{4}GS, 21^{2}S, 19^{5}GS, 24^{1}G, 24^{4}G, 24^{2}G, 24^{5}G

	Starts	1st	2nd	3rd	Win & Pl
Hurdles	4	1	1	0	9505
Chases	5	0	1	0	7511
Career Total	**22**	**4**	**5**	**0**	**71699**

114	3/02	Extr	3m110y	E Hdl	GD	£3024
157	2/01	Wwck	2m110y	A Ch	SFT	£15000
159	1/01	Tntn	2m110y	D Ch	HVY	£5292
124	1/01	Font	2m6f	D Ch	SFT	£4494

Total win prize-money £27810

Going: Sf: 0-1 GS: 0-3 Gd: 1-5 GF: - Fm: 0-0
Distance: 2m/2m3: 0-2 2m4-2m7: 0-3 **3m+: 1-4**
Track: LH: 0-3 **RH: 1-5** Tight: 0-1 Gall: 0-0
Aids: Bl: 0-0 Vi: 0-0 Tstrap: 0-0
Best Rating: 160 1/02 Winc 2m5f gd-sft Ch

Notched up a handful of hurdle victories in France and was runner-up twice over fences. He won his first three starts over fences in this country and was just worn down in desperate conditions at Aintree in April 2001. He was a little below par until returning to hurdling at Exeter in March 2002. Stays three miles and the softer the better for him.

Whitestone

6-y-o b m Sula Bula-Flying Cherub (Osiris)
Mrs J G Retter Mrs J G Retter

Placings:*0* **(3701)**
2001/02: 16^{0}S

	Starts	1st	2nd	3rd	Win & Pl
NH Flat	1	0	0	0	
Career Total	**1**	**0**	**0**	**0**	

Going: Sf: 0-1 GS: 0-0 Gd: 0-0 GF: - Fm: 0-0
Distance: 2m/2m3: 0-1 2m4-2m7: 0-0 3m+: 0-0
Track: LH: 0-1 RH: 0-0 Tight: 0-0 Gall: 0-1
Aids: Bl: 0-0 Vi: 0-0 Tstrap: 0-0
Best Rating:

Whitley Grange Boy

84 55

9-y-o b g Hubbly Bubbly (USA)-Choir (High Top)
J L Eyre Mrs Carole Sykes

Placings:103/P0 **(3748)**
2001/02: 25^{P}S, 16^{0}S

	Starts	1st	2nd	3rd	Win & Pl
Hurdles	2	0	0	0	
Career Total	**5**	**1**	**0**	**1**	**3525**

107	10/99	Weth	2m4f110y	D Hdl	G-F	£3187

Total win prize-money £3188

Going: Sf: 0-2 GS: 0-0 Gd: 0-0 GF: - Fm: 0-0
Distance: 2m/2m3: 0-1 2m4-2m7: 0-0 3m+: 0-1
Track: LH: 0-1 RH: 0-1 Tight: 0-2 Gall: 0-0
Aids: Bl: 0-0 Vi: 0-0 Tstrap: 0-0
Best Rating: 107 10/99 Weth 2m4f110y gd-fm Hdl

Whitleygrange Girl

5-y-o b m Rudimentary (USA)-Choir's Image (Lochnager)
J L Eyre Mrs Carole Sykes

Placings:P **(2767)**
2001/02: 19^{P}G

	Starts	1st	2nd	3rd	Win & Pl
Hurdles	1	0	0	0	
Career Total	**1**	**0**	**0**	**0**	

Going: Sf: 0-0 GS: 0-0 Gd: 0-1 GF: - Fm: 0-0
Distance: 2m/2m3: 0-1 2m4-2m7: 0-0 3m+: 0-0
Track: LH: 0-1 RH: 0-0 Tight: 0-1 Gall: 0-0
Aids: Bl: 0-0 Vi: 0-0 Tstrap: 0-0
Best Rating:

Who Am I (IRE)

12-y-o b g Supreme Leader-Bonny Joe (Derring Rose)
M J Bloom Mrs C Barratt

Placings:4634/565/**1442F212/111FP46/3UP0/33** **(4538)**
2001/02: 21^{3}GS, 24^{3}G

	Starts	1st	2nd	3rd	Win & Pl
Chases	2	0	0	2	618
Career Total	**28**	**5**	**3**	**4**	**22656**

125	11/98	Towc	2m5f	D(0-125)HHdl	SFT	£2910
116	10/98	Extr	2m6f	E Hdl	GD	£2347
119	10/98	Uttx	2m6f110y	C Hdl	GD	£4182
112	3/98	Leic	2m4f110y	E(0-110)HCh	GD	£3431
	5/97	Worc	2m4f110y	E Ch	G-S	£2977

Total win prize-money £15849

Going: Sf: 0-0 GS: 0-1 Gd: 0-1 GF: - Fm: 0-0
Distance: 2m/2m3: 0-0 2m4-2m7: 0-1 3m+: 0-1
Track: LH: 0-2 RH: 0-0 Tight: 0-2 Gall: 0-0
Aids: Bl: 0-0 Vi: 0-0 Tstrap: 0-0
Best Rating: 125 11/98 Towc 2m5f soft Hdl

Veteran pointer/hunter chaser, suited by good ground.

Who Cares Wins

100 100

6-y-o ch g Kris-Anne Bonny (Ajdal (USA))
J R Jenkins The B C W Partnership

Placings:44-1 **(0981)**
2001/02: 22^{1}G

	Starts	1st	2nd	3rd	Win & Pl
Hurdles	1	1	0	0	3374
Career Total	**3**	**1**	**0**	**0**	**3374**

100	7/01	Strf	2m6f110y	D Hdl	GD	£3374

Total win prize-money £3374

Going: Sf: 0-0 GS: 0-0 Gd: 1-1 GF: - Fm: 0-0
Distance: 2m/2m3: 0-0 **2m4-2m7: 1-1** 3m+: 0-0
Track: **LH: 1-1** RH: 0-0 **Tight: 1-1** Gall: 0-0
Aids: Bl: 0-0 Vi: 0-0 Tstrap: 0-0
Best Rating: 105 3/01 Hntg 2m110y soft Hdl

Who Dares Wins

105(103h) (112h)105

9-y-o b g Kala Shikari-Sarah's Venture (Averof)
T R George Mrs A Meller

Placings:322/32202/331363/31-23UP3023 (4576)
2001/02: 21^{2}S, 29^{3}S, 28^{U}S, 30^{P}S, 24^{3}HY, 24^{0}GS, 29^{2}S, 26^{3}GS

	Starts	1st	2nd	3rd	Win & Pl
Hurdles	2	0	1	1	2714
Chases	6	0	1	2	2640
Career Total	**24**	**2**	**7**	**10**	**22810**

122	11/00	Uttx	3m2f	F(0-100)HCh	HVY	£2961
116	2/00	Carl	3m2f	D Ch	HVY	£4368

Total win prize-money £7329

Going: Sf: 0-6 GS: 0-2 Gd: 0-0 GF: - Fm: 0-0
Distance: 2m/2m3: 0-0 2m4-2m7: 0-1 3m+: 0-7
Track: LH: 0-5 RH: 0-2 Tight: 0-0 Gall: 0-2
Aids: Bl: 0-0 Vi: 0-0 Tstrap: 0-0
Best Rating: 122 11/00 Uttx 3m2f heavy Ch

Modest staying chaser, suited by marathon trips and very soft ground.

Who Is Equiname (IRE)

12-y-o b g Bob Back (USA)-Instanter (Morston (FR))
W J Warner Mrs J Wilson

Placings:2203/410203/6/43321/FP1/P (0094)
2001/02: 25^{P}S

	Starts	1st	2nd	3rd	Win & Pl
Chases	1	0	0	0	
Career Total	**20**	**3**	**4**	**4**	**21883**

115	12/97	Leic	2m7f110y	D(0-125)HCh	GD	£4080
93	4/97	Towc	2m6f	E Ch	G-F	£2560
114	12/94	Kemp	2m	Hdl	SFT	£6555

Total win prize-money £13195

Going: Sf: 0-1 GS: 0-0 Gd: 0-0 GF: - Fm: 0-0
Distance: 2m/2m3: 0-0 2m4-2m7: 0-0 3m+: 0-1
Track: LH: 0-1 RH: 0-0 Tight: 0-0 Gall: 0-0
Aids: Bl: 0-1 Vi: 0-0 Tstrap: 0-0
Best Rating: 118 5/97 Worc 2m7f110y soft Ch

Who Tells Jan

9-y-o b m Royal Fountain-Constant Rose (Confusion)
Mrs P Ford W E Donohue

Placings:4P/P (0929)
2001/02: 20^{P}GF

	Starts	1st	2nd	3rd	Win & Pl
Hurdles	1	0	0	0	
Career Total	**3**	**0**	**0**	**0**	**0**

Going: Sf: 0-0 GS: 0-0 Gd: 0-0 GF: - Fm: 0-1
Distance: 2m/2m3: 0-0 2m4-2m7: 0-1 3m+: 0-0
Track: LH: 0-1 RH: 0-0 Tight: 0-1 Gall: 0-0
Aids: Bl: 0-0 Vi: 0-0 Tstrap: 0-0
Best Rating: 69 9/97 Worc 2m gd-fm Hdl

Who's The Man

68(81h) 26
8-y-o gr g Arzanni-Tommys Dream (Le Bavard (FR))
N M L Ewart N M L Ewart

Placings:0-55 (4433)
2001/02: 24^{5}S, 20^{5}HY

	Starts	1st	2nd	3rd	Win & Pl
Chases	2	0	0	0	0
Career Total	**3**	**0**	**0**	**0**	**0**

Going: Sf: 0-2 GS: 0-0 Gd: 0-0 GF: - Fm: 0-0
Distance: 2m/2m3: 0-0 2m4-2m7: 0-1 3m+: 0-1
Track: LH: 0-1 RH: 0-1 Tight: 0-1 Gall: 0-1
Aids: Bl: 0-0 Vi: 0-0 Tstrap: 0-0
Best Rating: 65 1/01 Catt 2m gd-sft Hdl

Who's To Say

90(98c) (88c)57
16-y-o b g Saher-Whisht (Raise You Ten)
Dr P Pritchard Mrs T Pritchard

Placings:25600/0331UF/6U5335514/02P413600U353 6510/140241303230/345344363/5PP3222614F06323 5P/014PU/0-6005465U0PP (4505)
2001/02: 16^{6}GF, 18^{0}GF, 16^{0}GF, 16^{5}GF, 16^{4}G, 21^{6}GF, 16^{5}G, 16^{U}S, 17^{0}G, 16^{P}HY, 21^{P}G

	Starts	1st	2nd	3rd	Win & Pl
Chases	11	0	0	0	286
Career Total	**103**	**11**	**8**	**17**	**61973**

107	9/98	Hntg	2m110y	E(0-115)HCh	G-F	£2860
103	11/97	Wwck	2m	E(0-115)HCh	GD	£2977
125	11/95	Thur	2m	(0-120)HCh	YLD	£2204
121	5/95	Rosc	2m	(0-130)HCh	G-F	£2712
125	4/95	Fair	2m	HCh	G-F	£6782
118	10/94	Punc	2m	(0-123)HCh	YLD	£2935
122	3/94	Navn	2m	HCh	SH	£6571
104	1/93	Punc	2m	Ch	HVY	£4021
	1/92	Fair	2m2f	HHdl	YLD	£2901
	10/91	Gowr	2m	Hdl	Y-S	£2555
	9/91	Gowr	2m	NHF	GD	£2555

Total win prize-money £39081

Going: Sf: 0-2 GS: 0-0 Gd: 0-4 GF: - Fm: 0-5
Distance: 2m/2m3: 0-9 2m4-2m7: 0-2 3m+: 0-0
Track: LH: 0-8 RH: 0-1 Tight: 0-9 Gall: 0-1
Aids: Bl: 0-0 Vi: 0-0 Tstrap: 0-0
Best Rating: 128 5/96 Weth 2m gd-fm Ch

Wicked Crack (IRE)

109(101h) (128h)154
9-y-o b m King's Ride-Mighty Crack (Deep Run)
Edward U Hales Liam Queally

Placings:00/00600/61F5112133-1222F123F5 (4945a)
2001/02: 21^{1}S, 24^{2}YS, 24^{2}YS, 24^{2}S, 24^{F}Y, 21^{1}YS, 20^{2}HY, 24^{3}S, 36^{F}G, 25^{5}G

	Starts	1st	2nd	3rd	Win & Pl
Hurdles	1	0	0	1	2761
Chases	9	2	4	0	58668
Career Total	**27**	**6**	**5**	**3**	**88340**

132	1/02	Punc	2m5f	Ch	Y-S	£7975
118	10/01	Tipp	2m5f	Ch	SFT	£18346
129	1/01	Leop	3m	HHdl	SFT	£10483
113	12/00	Fair	3m	(0-109)HHdl	SFT	£3864
105	11/00	Dpat	2m6f	(0-95)HHdl	SFT	£2345
103	10/00	Navn	3m	(0-116)HHdl	YLD	£4416

Total win prize-money £47432

Going: Sf: 1-4 GS: 0-0 Gd: 0-2 GF: - Fm: 0-0
Distance: 2m/2m3: 0-0 **2m4-2m7: 2-3** 3m+: 0-7
Track: LH: 0-4 **RH: 1-4** Tight: 0-1 Gall: 0-0
Aids: Bl: 0-0 Vi: 0-0 Tstrap: 0-0
Best Rating: 154 11/01 DRoy 3m yld-sft Ch

A thorough stayer, she revels in the mud and is very tough. She had a superb season in 2000/2001 over hurdles, and developed into a very useful chaser last season, running a cracker to split Foxchapel King and Florida Pearl at Down Royal, finishing runner-up in the Rehearsal Chase and winning at Punchestown in January. Stays three miles. Acts on soft ground.

Wicked Imp

95 83
10-y-o ch g Scallywag-Naughty Niece (Bribe)
Miss D Cole (V R A Dartnall 5/5) Mrs Marilyn Cook

Placings:202/05/450-4P056 (1397)
2001/02: 26^{4}G, 27^{P}G, 20^{0}G, 22^{5}GF, 24^{6}GF

	Starts	1st	2nd	3rd	Win & Pl
Hurdles	5	0	0	0	0
Career Total	**13**	**0**	**2**	**0**	**1158**

Going: Sf: 0-0 GS: 0-0 Gd: 0-3 GF: - Fm: 0-2
Distance: 2m/2m3: 0-0 2m4-2m7: 0-2 3m+: 0-3
Track: LH: 0-4 RH: 0-1 Tight: 0-3 Gall: 0-0
Aids: Bl: 0-0 Vi: 0-0 Tstrap: 0-0
Best Rating: 111 12/98 Wwck 2m3f gd-sft Hdl

Wide Awake (NZ)

91 53
9-y-o ch g Watchman (NZ)-Dewi (NZ) (Roi Lear (FR))
M D I Usher The Ridgeway Partnership

Placings:225/0/0P6 (4657)
2001/02: 16^{0}S, 17^{P}HY, 24^{6}G

	Starts	1st	2nd	3rd	Win & Pl
Hurdles	3	0	0	0	0
Career Total	**7**	**0**	**2**	**0**	**741**

Going: Sf: 0-2 GS: 0-0 Gd: 0-1 GF: - Fm: 0-0
Distance: 2m/2m3: 0-2 2m4-2m7: 0-0 3m+: 0-1
Track: LH: 0-1 RH: 0-2 Tight: 0-2 Gall: 0-0
Aids: Bl: 0-0 Vi: 0-0 Tstrap: 0-0
Best Rating: 98 5/98 Uttx 2m gd-fm NHF

Wilby Willie

66 27
6-y-o bl g Bob's Return (IRE)-Kev's Lass (IRE) (Kemal (FR))
Ferdy Murphy Exors Of The Late Mr G A Hubbard

Placings:00-066 (2322)
2001/02: 20^{0}S, 16^{6}S, 20^{6}S

	Starts	1st	2nd	3rd	Win & Pl
Hurdles	3	0	0	0	0
Career Total	**5**	**0**	**0**	**0**	**0**

Going: Sf: 0-3 GS: 0-0 Gd: 0-0 GF: - Fm: 0-0
Distance: 2m/2m3: 0-1 2m4-2m7: 0-2 3m+: 0-0
Track: LH: 0-2 RH: 0-1 Tight: 0-2 Gall: 0-0
Aids: Bl: 0-0 Vi: 0-0 Tstrap: 0-1
Best Rating: 34 11/00 Wwck 2m soft Hdl

Wild Blade (IRE)

88(97h) (68h)50
9-y-o ch g Meneval (USA)-Tuney Blade (Fine Blade (USA))
Noel T Chance Middleham Park Racing Xvi

Placings:14036/50106/P4006 (4909)
2001/02: 17^{P}S, 16^{4}HY, 16^{0}G, 19^{0}S, 20^{6}GF

	Starts	1st	2nd	3rd	Win & Pl
Hurdles	4	0	0	0	0
Chases	1	0	0	0	0
Career Total	**15**	**2**	**0**	**1**	**3568**

94	8/99	Worc	2m4f	F(0-100)HHdl	G-F	£1900
104	5/98	Ludl	2m	H NHF	G-F	£1236

Total win prize-money £3136

Going: Sf: 0-0 GS: 0-0 Gd: 0-1 GF: - Fm: 0-1
Distance: 2m/2m3: 0-3 2m4-2m7: 0-2 3m+: 0-0
Track: LH: 0-0 RH: 0-5 Tight: 0-3 Gall: 0-0
Aids: Bl: 0-0 Vi: 0-0 Tstrap: 0-0
Best Rating: 104 5/98 Ludl 2m gd-fm NHF

Wild Colonial Boy (IRE)

(97h) (26h)

7-y-o b g Warning-Loch Clair (IRE) (Lomond (USA))
G P Enright The Jack Duggan Trio

Placings:230-0P (4562)
2001/02: 21^{0}GS, 20^{P}GF

	Starts	1st	2nd	3rd	Win & Pl
Hurdles	1	0	0	0	0
Chases	1	0	0	0	0
Career Total	**5**	**0**	**1**	**1**	**1145**

Going: Sf: 0-0 GS: 0-1 Gd: 0-0 GF: - Fm: 0-1
Distance: 2m/2m3: 0-0 2m4-2m7: 0-2 3m+: 0-0
Track: LH: 0-1 RH: 0-1 Tight: 0-1 Gall: 0-1
Aids: Bl: 0-2 Vi: 0-0 Tstrap: 0-0
Best Rating: 91 10/00 Hntg 2m4f110y gd-fm Hdl

Modest maiden hurdler, pulled up on his only run over fences.

Wild Dream

115f 126f

7-y-o b m Derrylin-Vedra (IRE) (Carlingford Castle)
S Pike Stewart Pike

Placings:3-12 (2194)
2001/02: 16^{1}G, 16^{2}G

	Starts	1st	2nd	3rd	Win & Pl
NH Flat	2	1	1	0	4228
Career Total	**3**	**1**	**1**	**1**	**4504**

100 6/01 Worc 2m H NHF GD £1515
Total win prize-money £1516

Going: Sf: 0-0 GS: 0-0 Gd: 1-2 GF: - Fm: 0-0
Distance: **2m/2m3: 1-2** 2m4-2m7: 0-0 3m+: 0-0
Track: **LH: 1-2** RH: 0-0 Tight: 0-0 Gall: 0-0
Aids: Bl: 0-0 Vi: 0-0 Tstrap: 0-0
Best Rating: 126 11/01 Chel 2m110y good NHF

Tough and useful bumper performer, suited by fast ground.

Wild Hadeer

101 93

8-y-o ch g Hadeer-Wild Moon (USA) (Arctic Tern (USA))
John R Upson The Nap Hand Partnership

Placings:51464/24512/PP00210 (4847)
2001/02: 24^{P}S, 20^{P}S, 21^{0}HY, 21^{0}GS, 16^{2}S, 16^{1}G, 20^{0}G

	Starts	1st	2nd	3rd	Win & Pl
Hurdles	7	1	1	0	2760
Career Total	**17**	**3**	**3**	**0**	**10244**

93 4/02 Towc 2m G(0-95)HHdl GD £2009
99 3/00 Towc 2m5f D(0-120)HHdl GD £3133
94 3/99 Catt 2m E Hdl SFT £2915
Total win prize-money £8057

Going: Sf: 0-4 GS: 0-1 Gd: 1-2 GF: - Fm: 0-0
Distance: **2m/2m3: 1-2** 2m4-2m7: 0-4 3m+: 0-1
Track: LH: 0-1 **RH: 1-5** Tight: 0-2 Gall: 0-0
Aids: Bl: 1-5 Vi: 0-0 Tstrap: 0-0
Best Rating: 104 4/00 Hexm 2m4f110y good Hdl

Moderate hurdler, stays two miles-five, and is effective on good ground or softer. Usually wears blinkers.

Wild Native (IRE)

10-y-o br g Be My Native (USA)-Wild Justice (Sweet Revenge)
Mrs G M S Slater (N J Hawke 24/3) Mrs G M S Slater

Placings:0/5/PPP (4735)
2001/02: 21^{P}GF, 26^{P}G, 23^{P}F

	Starts	1st	2nd	3rd	Win & Pl
Chases	3	0	0	0	
Career Total	**5**	**0**	**0**	**0**	**0**

Going: Sf: 0-0 GS: 0-0 Gd: 0-1 GF: - Fm: 0-2
Distance: 2m/2m3: 0-0 2m4-2m7: 0-1 3m+: 0-2
Track: LH: 0-2 RH: 0-1 Tight: 0-2 Gall: 0-0
Aids: Bl: 0-0 Vi: 0-0 Tstrap: 0-0
Best Rating: 69 2/97 Winc 2m good NHF

Wild Nettle

72 47

8-y-o ch m Beveled (USA)-Pink Pumpkin (Tickled Pink)
J C Fox Mrs J A Cleary

Placings:PP-0 (0348)
2001/02: 16^{0}G

	Starts	1st	2nd	3rd	Win & Pl
Hurdles	1	0	0	0	
Career Total	**3**	**0**	**0**	**0**	

Going: Sf: 0-0 GS: 0-0 Gd: 0-1 GF: - Fm: 0-0
Distance: 2m/2m3: 0-1 2m4-2m7: 0-0 3m+: 0-0
Track: LH: 0-1 RH: 0-0 Tight: 0-1 Gall: 0-0
Aids: Bl: 0-0 Vi: 0-0 Tstrap: 0-0
Best Rating: 47 5/01 Strf 2m110y good Hdl

Wild Spice (IRE)

99 121

7-y-o b g Mandalus-Curry Lunch (Pry)
Miss Venetia Williams M Crabb, B Ead, P May, M Moore

Placings:5330/1-0 (4413)
2001/02: 18^{0}S

	Starts	1st	2nd	3rd	Win & Pl
Hurdles	1	0	0	0	
Career Total	**6**	**1**	**0**	**2**	**3629**

114 5/00 Hrfd 3m2f E Hdl GD £2600
Total win prize-money £2600

Going: Sf: 0-1 GS: 0-0 Gd: 0-0 GF: - Fm: 0-0
Distance: 2m/2m3: 0-1 2m4-2m7: 0-0 3m+: 0-0
Track: LH: 0-1 RH: 0-0 Tight: 0-1 Gall: 0-0
Aids: Bl: 0-0 Vi: 0-0 Tstrap: 0-0
Best Rating: 114 5/00 Hrfd 3m2f good Hdl

Suffered a tendon injury and found the ground too soft on comeback race at Fontwell in March 2002. Appreciated better ground when winning handicaps at Exeter and Stratford in May 2002. Considered a chaser in the making.

Wildfield Rufo (IRE)

7-y-o b g Celio Rufo-Jersey Girl (Hard Boy)
Mrs K Walton Mrs K Walton

Placings:14 (4678)
2001/02: 25^{1}GS, 25^{4}G

	Starts	1st	2nd	3rd	Win & Pl
Chases	2	1	0	0	2308
Career Total	**2**	**1**	**0**	**0**	**2308**

124 3/02 Catt 3m1f110y H Ch G-S £1475
Total win prize-money £1476

Going: Sf: 0-0 GS: 1-1 Gd: 0-1 GF: - Fm: 0-0
Distance: 2m/2m3: 0-0 2m4-2m7: 0-0 **3m+: 1-2**
Track: LH: 0-1 RH: 0-0 Tight: 0-1 Gall: 0-0
Aids: Bl: 0-0 Vi: 0-0 Tstrap: 0-0
Best Rating: 124 3/02 Catt 3m1f110y gd-sft Ch

Winner of his only outing in an Irish point. Impressive on his hunter chase bow at Catterick in March and looks a bargain buy.

Wilemmgeo

74 60

5-y-o b m Emarati (USA)-Floral Spark (Forzando)
Mrs N Macauley (P D Evans 10/8) R J Hayward

Placings:05P0 (1136)
2001/02: 19^{0}GF, 16^{5}S, 16^{P}G, 16^{0}GF

	Starts	1st	2nd	3rd	Win & Pl
Hurdles	4	0	0	0	0
Career Total	**4**	**0**	**0**	**0**	**0**

Going: Sf: 0-1 GS: 0-0 Gd: 0-1 GF: - Fm: 0-2
Distance: 2m/2m3: 0-4 2m4-2m7: 0-0 3m+: 0-0
Track: LH: 0-4 RH: 0-0 Tight: 0-2 Gall: 0-0
Aids: Bl: 0-0 Vi: 0-0 Tstrap: 0-0
Best Rating: 60 8/01 Worc 2m gd-fm Hdl

Will He Wish

82 58

6-y-o b g Winning Gallery-More To Life (Northern Tempest (USA))
Miss M E Rowland Mrs D Dukes, Mrs C D Buckland

Placings:00 (2674)
2001/02: 16^{0}GF, 20^{0}G

	Starts	1st	2nd	3rd	Win & Pl
NH Flat	1	0	0	0	0
Hurdles	1	0	0	0	0
Career Total	**2**	**0**	**0**	**0**	

Going: Sf: 0-0 GS: 0-0 Gd: 0-1 GF: - Fm: 0-1
Distance: 2m/2m3: 0-1 2m4-2m7: 0-1 3m+: 0-0
Track: LH: 0-2 RH: 0-0 Tight: 0-0 Gall: 0-1
Aids: Bl: 0-0 Vi: 0-0 Tstrap: 0-1
Best Rating: 59 6/01 Worc 2m gd-fm NHF

Will Of The People (IRE)

104 109

7-y-o b g Supreme Leader-Another Partner (Le Bavard (FR))
Miss H C Knight Dr's D Silk,M Gillard,P Walker,R Purkis

Placings:2-4135 (4586)
2001/02: 21^{4}G, 19^{1}G, 19^{3}S, 22^{5}G

	Starts	1st	2nd	3rd	Win & Pl
Hurdles	4	1	0	1	3114
Career Total	**5**	**1**	**1**	**1**	**3592**

95 12/01 Hrfd 2m3f110y E Hdl GD £2523

Total win prize-money £2524

Going: Sf: 0-1 GS: 0-0 Gd: 1-3 GF: - Fm: 0-0
Distance: 2m/2m3: 0-0 **2m4-2m7: 1-4** 3m+: 0-0
Track: LH: 0-1 **RH: 1-3** Tight: 0-2 Gall: 0-0
Aids: Bl: 0-0 Vi: 0-0 Tstrap: 0-0
Best Rating: 109 4/02 Winc 2m6f good Hdl

Novice hurdler, effective on good ground and is effective over two miles three furlongs.

Will'Sillyshankers

84 **47**

7-y-o b g Silly Prices-Hannah's Song (Saintly Song)
G A Ham D M Drury

Placings: 06-00P00P (4657)
2001/02: 17^{0}G, 16^{0}G, 24^{P}HY, 21^{0}S, 24^{0}S, 24^{P}G

	Starts	1st	2nd	3rd	Win & Pl
NH Flat	2	0	0	0	0
Hurdles	4	0	0	0	0
Career Total	**8**	**0**	**0**	**0**	**0**

Going: Sf: 0-3 GS: 0-0 Gd: 0-3 GF: - Fm: 0-0
Distance: 2m/2m3: 0-2 2m4-2m7: 0-1 3m+: 0-3
Track: LH: 0-3 RH: 0-3 Tight: 0-3 Gall: 0-0
Aids: Bl: 0-0 Vi: 0-0 Tstrap: 0-0
Best Rating: 85 4/01 Winc 2m soft NHF

Willa Thyne (IRE)

86 **26**

8-y-o br m Good Thyne (USA)-Florella (Royal Fountain)
R Allan Mrs V Scott Watson

Placings: 03320P/500/0P6-0P0 (4766)
2001/02: 22^{0}GS, 22^{P}GS, 20^{0}GF

	Starts	1st	2nd	3rd	Win & Pl
Hurdles	3	0	0	0	
Career Total	**15**	**0**	**1**	**2**	**747**

Going: Sf: 0-0 GS: 0-2 Gd: 0-0 GF: - Fm: 0-1
Distance: 2m/2m3: 0-0 2m4-2m7: 0-3 3m+: 0-0
Track: LH: 0-3 RH: 0-0 Tight: 0-2 Gall: 0-0
Aids: Bl: 0-0 Vi: 0-0 Tstrap: 0-3
Best Rating: 81 11/98 Hexm 2m heavy NHF

Lightly-raced long-standing maiden hurdler.

William O'Dee (NZ)

13-y-o br g Exceptionnel-Fiducia O'Dee (NZ) (Sir Godfrey (FR))
G Chambers R H Pedrick

Placings: 0PP/2F436/4533-03F (4186)
2001/02: 23^{0}G, 21^{3}GF, 24^{F}S

	Starts	1st	2nd	3rd	Win & Pl
Chases	3	0	0	1	1583
Career Total	**15**	**0**	**1**	**4**	**5430**

Going: Sf: 0-1 GS: 0-0 Gd: 0-1 GF: - Fm: 0-1
Distance: 2m/2m3: 0-0 2m4-2m7: 0-1 3m+: 0-2
Track: LH: 0-1 RH: 0-2 Tight: 0-2 Gall: 0-0
Aids: Bl: 0-0 Vi: 0-0 Tstrap: 0-0
Best Rating: 122 12/99 Chel 2m5f good Ch

Willie Wallace (IRE)

10-y-o b g Torus-Gothic Model (Salluceva)
O O'Neill John McKenna

Placings: 4003P/P/P-P0P (1379)
2001/02: 24^{P}GF, 21^{0}GF, 25^{P}GF

	Starts	1st	2nd	3rd	Win & Pl
Chases	3	0	0	0	
Career Total	**10**	**0**	**0**	**1**	**470**

Going: Sf: 0-0 GS: 0-0 Gd: 0-0 GF: - Fm: 0-3
Distance: 2m/2m3: 0-0 2m4-2m7: 0-1 3m+: 0-2
Track: LH: 0-2 RH: 0-1 Tight: 0-2 Gall: 0-0
Aids: Bl: 0-0 Vi: 0-0 Tstrap: 0-0
Best Rating: 75 11/98 Ludl 2m good NHF

Willoughby Moss

10-y-o b g Le Moss-Willow Wood (Precipice Wood)
Mrs B K Thomson Mrs B K Thomson

Placings: P (4690)
2001/02: 25^{P}GF

	Starts	1st	2nd	3rd	Win & Pl
Chases	1	0	0	0	
Career Total	**1**	**0**	**0**	**0**	

Going: Sf: 0-0 GS: 0-0 Gd: 0-0 GF: - Fm: 0-1
Distance: 2m/2m3: 0-0 2m4-2m7: 0-0 3m+: 0-1
Track: LH: 0-1 RH: 0-0 Tight: 0-1 Gall: 0-0
Aids: Bl: 0-0 Vi: 0-0 Tstrap: 0-0
Best Rating:

Willow Run (NZ)

99 **89**

8-y-o b g Conquistarose (USA)-Crazy Lady (NZ) (One Pound Sterling)
B Ellison (L Lungo 1/11) Brian Ellison

Placings: 6560-1252503 (4271)
2001/02: 17^{1}GS, 16^{2}G, 17^{5}G, 16^{2}S, 20^{5}G, 17^{0}S, 16^{3}G

	Starts	1st	2nd	3rd	Win & Pl
Hurdles	7	1	2	1	3671
Career Total	**11**	**1**	**2**	**1**	**3671**

89	10/01	Sedg	2m1f	F(0-95)HHdl	G-S	£2299

Total win prize-money £2300

Going: Sf: 0-2 GS: 1-1 Gd: 0-4 GF: - Fm: 0-0
Distance: **2m/2m3: 1-6** 2m4-2m7: 0-1 3m+: 0-0
Track: **LH: 1-6** RH: 0-1 **Tight: 1-7** Gall: 0-0
Aids: Bl: 0-0 Vi: 0-0 Tstrap: 0-4
Best Rating: 89 10/01 Sedg 2m1f gd-sft Hdl

Willows Roulette

107 **99**

10-y-o b g High Season-Willows Casino (Olympic Casino)
A G Hobbs Miss Jayne Brace & Mr Gwyn Brace

Placings: 40044/2U304/41005/P/635321124-P352F04 (1804)
2001/02: 20^{P}GF, 20^{3}G, 21^{5}G, 20^{2}GF, 19^{F}GF, 21^{0}GF, 24^{4}GF

	Starts	1st	2nd	3rd	Win & Pl
Chases	7	0	1	1	1775
Career Total	**32**	**3**	**4**	**4**	**16409**

108	8/00	Worc	2m4f110y	F(0-100)HCh	G-F	£3513
102	8/00	Worc	2m4f110y	E(0-105)HCh	G-F	£3523
82	5/98	Extr	2m7f	E(0-100)HHdl	FRM	£2640

Total win prize-money £9676

Going: Sf: 0-0 GS: 0-0 Gd: 0-2 GF: - Fm: 0-5
Distance: 2m/2m3: 0-1 2m4-2m7: 0-5 3m+: 0-1
Track: LH: 0-4 RH: 0-3 Tight: 0-4 Gall: 0-0
Aids: Bl: 0-1 Vi: 0-0 Tstrap: 0-0
Best Rating: 108 9/00 MRas 2m4f gd-fm Ch

Wills Perk (IRE)

92 **79**

7-y-o ch m Executive Perk-Brandy Hill Girl (Green Shoon)
N B Mason N B Mason

Placings: F05PF05 (4889)
2001/02: 20^{F}G, 21^{0}G, 20^{5}S, 25^{P}S, 25^{F}G, 24^{0}S, 26^{5}G

	Starts	1st	2nd	3rd	Win & Pl
Chases	7	0	0	0	0
Career Total	**7**	**0**	**0**	**0**	**0**

Going: Sf: 0-3 GS: 0-0 Gd: 0-4 GF: - Fm: 0-0
Distance: 2m/2m3: 0-0 2m4-2m7: 0-3 3m+: 0-4
Track: LH: 0-3 RH: 0-3 Tight: 0-3 Gall: 0-0
Aids: Bl: 0-0 Vi: 0-0 Tstrap: 0-2
Best Rating: 79 10/01 Carl 2m4f soft Ch

Willy Willy

101(64c) **93**

9-y-o ch g Master Willie-Monsoon (Royal Palace)
G Brown (D L Williams 27/7) Berkshire Commercial Components Ltd

Placings: 00411663420/113F00-PP551 (1629)
2001/02: 19^{P}GF, 17^{P}G, 19^{5}GF, 21^{5}GS, 21^{1}GF

	Starts	1st	2nd	3rd	Win & Pl
Hurdles	4	1	0	0	2671
Chases	1	0	0	0	0
Career Total	**22**	**5**	**1**	**2**	**19205**

93	10/01	Ludl	2m5f	F(0-90)Hdl	G-F	£2670
114	8/00	MRas	2m4f	D Ch	G-F	£5331
119	7/00	MRas	2m1f110y	F(0-105)HCh	G-F	£4056
109	10/99	Winc	2m	F(0-100)HHdl	GD	£2374
109	9/99	MRas	2m1f110y	F(0-100)HHdl	G-F	£2318

Total win prize-money £16751

Going: Sf: 0-0 GS: 0-1 Gd: 0-1 GF: - Fm: 1-3
Distance: 2m/2m3. 0-1 **2m4-2m7: 1-4** 3m+: 0-0
Track: LH: 0-1 RH: 0-3 Tight: 0-3 Gall: 0-0
Aids: Bl: 0-0 Vi: 0-0 Tstrap: 0-0
Best Rating: 119 7/00 MRas 2m1f110y gd-fm Ch

Wilmer (SWE)

8-y-o b g Wildvogel (GER)-Winnymere (IRE) (Persian Bold)
Mrs V C Ward Miss A S Rosengren

Placings: 05-P (0211)
2001/02: 20^{P}F

	Starts	1st	2nd	3rd	Win & Pl
Hurdles	1	0	0	0	
Career Total	**3**	**0**	**0**	**0**	

Going: Sf: 0-0 GS: 0-0 Gd: 0-0 GF: - Fm: 0-1
Distance: 2m/2m3: 0-0 2m4-2m7: 0-1 3m+: 0-0
Track: LH: 0-1 RH: 0-0 Tight: 0-1 Gall: 0-0
Aids: Bl: 0-0 Vi: 0-0 Tstrap: 0-0
Best Rating:

Wilton

73 **53**

7-y-o ch g Sharpo-Poyle Amber (Sharrood (USA))
Miss S J Wilton John Pointon And Sons

Placings:456-00 **(2025)**
2001/02: 17^{0}G, 16^{0}S

	Starts	1st	2nd	3rd	Win & Pl
Hurdles	2	0	0	0	
Career Total	**5**	**0**	**0**	**0**	**0**

Going: Sf: 0-1 GS: 0-0 Gd: 0-1 GF: - Fm: 0-0
Distance: 2m/2m3: 0-2 2m4-2m7: 0-0 3m+: 0-0
Track: LH: 0-2 RH: 0-0 Tight: 0-1 Gall: 0-0
Aids: Bl: 0-1 Vi: 0-0 Tstrap: 0-1
Best Rating: 98 12/00 Donc 2m110y gd-sft Hdl

Win Alot

101 **79+**

4-y-o b g Aragon-Having Fun (Hard Fought)
D Burchell (J Hetherton 2/7) Mrs Linda Cognet

Placings:P0R531 **(4904)**
2001/02: 17^{P}GS, 16^{0}S, 17^{R}S, 16^{5}GS, 16^{3}GF, 17^{1}G

	Starts	1st	2nd	3rd	Win & Pl
Hurdles	6	1	0	1	2028
Career Total	**6**	**1**	**0**	**1**	**2028**

79	4/02	MRas	2m1f110y	G(0-95)HHdl	GD	£1750

Total win prize-money £1750

Going: Sf: 0-2 GS: 0-2 Gd: 1-1 GF: - Fm: 0-1
Distance: **2m/2m3: 1-6** 2m4-2m7: 0-0 3m+: 0-0
Track: LH: 0-4 **RH: 1-2 Tight: 1-2** Gall: 0-1
Aids: Bl: 0-0 Vi: 0-0 Tstrap: 0-0
Best Rating: 79 4/02 MRas 2m1f110y good Hdl

Selling hurdler.

Win The Toss

10-y-o b g Idiots Delight-Mayfield (USA) (Alleged (USA))
R M Stronge R M Green

Placings:0/0/220554P201/442UP/6004-0 **(0052)**
2001/02: 20^{0}G

	Starts	1st	2nd	3rd	Win & Pl
Hurdles	1	0	0	0	
Career Total	**22**	**1**	**4**	**0**	**4609**

94	5/99	Uttx	2m4f110y	G(0-100)HHdl	GD	£1784

Total win prize-money £1784

Going: Sf: 0-0 GS: 0-0 Gd: 0-1 GF: - Fm: 0-0
Distance: 2m/2m3: 0-0 2m4-2m7: 0-1 3m+: 0-0
Track: LH: 0-1 RH: 0-0 Tight: 0-1 Gall: 0-0
Aids: Bl: 0-0 Vi: 0-0 Tstrap: 0-0
Best Rating: 111 5/98 Uttx 2m gd-sft NHF

Windle Brook

102 **108**

10-y-o b g Gildoran-Minigale (Strong Gale)
K C Bailey Peter Granger

Placings:0/05U63U/422F01-423P1 **(4734)**
2001/02: 24^{4}G, 20^{2}S, 24^{3}GS, 24^{P}S, 19^{1}F

	Starts	1st	2nd	3rd	Win & Pl
Chases	5	1	1	1	5257
Career Total	**18**	**2**	**3**	**2**	**11404**

108	4/02	Extr	2m3f110y	F(0-95)HCh	FRM	£3851
106	9/00	Hntg	3m	F(0-110)HCh	G-F	£3250

Total win prize-money £7101

Going: Sf: 0-2 GS: 0-1 Gd: 0-1 GF: - Fm: 1-1
Distance: 2m/2m3: 0-0 **2m4-2m7: 1-2** 3m+: 0-3
Track: LH: 0-1 **RH: 1-4** Tight: 0-1 Gall: 0-3
Aids: Bl: 0-0 Vi: 0-0 Tstrap: 0-2
Best Rating: 108 4/02 Extr 2m3f110y firm Ch

Moderate chaser, he stays three miles on a lively surface.

Windmill Lane

15

5-y-o b m Saddlers' Hall (IRE)-Alpi Dora (Valiyar)
B S Rothwell John H Price

Placings:606-P0 **(1639)**
2001/02: 24^{P}F, 20^{0}GS

	Starts	1st	2nd	3rd	Win & Pl
Hurdles	2	0	0	0	
Career Total	**5**	**0**	**0**	**0**	**0**

Going: Sf: 0-0 GS: 0-1 Gd: 0-0 GF: - Fm: 0-1
Distance: 2m/2m3: 0-0 2m4-2m7: 0-1 3m+: 0-1
Track: LH: 0-1 RH: 0-0 Tight: 0-1 Gall: 0-0
Aids: Bl: 0-0 Vi: 0-0 Tstrap: 0-0
Best Rating: 79 12/00 Newc 2m soft Hdl

Windross

105 **150**

10-y-o b g Ardross-Dans Le Vent (Pollerton)
A King Mrs Peter Prowting

Placings:221140/221F12/3P60-1 **(2939)**
2001/02: 24^{1}G

	Starts	1st	2nd	3rd	Win & Pl
Chases	1	1	0	0	11193
Career Total	**17**	**5**	**5**	**1**	**37914**

150	12/01	Newb	3m	D(0-125)HCh	GD	£11193
155	2/00	Kemp	3m	C Ch	G-S	£7595
140	12/99	Uttx	2m5f	D Ch	SFT	£4102
124	1/99	Hayd	2m4f	E Hdl	SFT	£2340
123	12/98	Wwck	2m3f	E Hdl	G-S	£2897

Total win prize-money £28130

Going: Sf: 0-0 GS: 0-0 Gd: 1-1 GF: - Fm: 0-0
Distance: 2m/2m3: 0-0 2m4-2m7: 0-0 **3m+: 1-1**
Track: **LH: 1-1** RH: 0-0 Tight: 0-0 **Gall: 1-1**
Aids: Bl: 0-0 Vi: 0-0 Tstrap: 0-0
Best Rating: 155 2/00 Kemp 3m gd-sft Ch

Lightly-raced, useful chaser, came back to form on his return in 2001/02 when dropped in the handicap. Three miles looks as far as he wants, and he needs cut in the ground.

Windshift (IRE)

94 **78**

6-y-o b g Forest Wind (USA)-Beautyofthepeace (IRE) (Exactly Sharp (USA))
I A Wood (D Shaw 5/12) G E Griffiths

Placings:PP-6040 **(2175)**
2001/02: 16^{6}G, 16^{0}GS, 16^{4}S, 16^{0}G

	Starts	1st	2nd	3rd	Win & Pl
Hurdles	4	0	0	0	257
Career Total	**6**	**0**	**0**	**0**	**257**

Going: Sf: 0-1 GS: 0-1 Gd: 0-2 GF: - Fm: 0-0
Distance: 2m/2m3: 0-4 2m4-2m7: 0-0 3m+: 0-0
Track: LH: 0-4 RH: 0-0 Tight: 0-2 Gall: 0-0
Aids: Bl: 0-0 Vi: 0-2 Tstrap: 0-0
Best Rating: 78 10/01 Fknm 2m soft Hdl

Windsor Beauty (IRE)

88 **69**

4-y-o b/br g Woods Of Windsor (USA)-Tumble Dale (Tumble Wind (USA))
R Rowe (Kevin Prendergast 16/7) Capt A Pratt

Placings:505 **(4654)**
2001/02: 18^{5}S, 16^{0}S, 17^{5}GS

	Starts	1st	2nd	3rd	Win & Pl
Hurdles	3	0	0	0	0
Career Total	**3**	**0**	**0**	**0**	**0**

Going: Sf: 0-2 GS: 0-1 Gd: 0-0 GF: - Fm: 0-0
Distance: 2m/2m3: 0-3 2m4-2m7: 0-0 3m+: 0-0
Track: LH: 0-2 RH: 0-1 Tight: 0-2 Gall: 0-1
Aids: Bl: 0-0 Vi: 0-0 Tstrap: 0-0
Best Rating: 69 1/02 Font 2m2f110y soft Hdl

Poor hurdle form to date.

Windy Valley (IRE)

107(97h) (99h)**107**

9-y-o gr g Roi Guillaume (FR)-My Bonny Girl (Bonne Noel)
Mrs A J Hamilton-Fairley Runs In The Family

Placings:0000/000532321322U5/254222/12036U-1032355242024 **(4884)**
2001/02: 18^{1}GF, 20^{0}GF, 20^{3}G, 21^{2}G, 24^{3}GF, 22^{5}GF, 20^{5}GF, 20^{2}G, 19^{4}G, 20^{2}GF, 20^{0}G, 24^{2}GF, 22^{4}GF

	Starts	1st	2nd	3rd	Win & Pl
Hurdles	2	1	0	0	2489
Chases	11	0	4	2	6918
Career Total	**43**	**3**	**13**	**6**	**22168**

99	5/01	Font	2m2f110y	F(0-105)HHdl	G-F	£2488
93	5/00	Wwck	2m4f110y	E(0-115)HHdl	G-F	£2710
89	10/98	Dpat	2m1f172y	Hdl	GD	£1494

Total win prize-money £6694

Going: Sf: 0-0 GS: 0-0 Gd: 0-5 GF: - Fm: 1-8
Distance: **2m/2m3: 1-2** 2m4-2m7: 0-9 3m+: 0-2
Track: **LH: 1-7** RH: 0-4 **Tight: 1-9** Gall: 0-0
Aids: Bl: 1-13 Vi: 0-0 Tstrap: 1-13
Best Rating: 107 11/01 Ludl 2m4f gd-fm Ch

An ex-Irish hurdler/novice chaser, he stays three miles and is effective on fast ground, but is proving very hard to win with.

Wing Fat (IRE)

7-y-o ch g Torus-Rareitess (Rarity)
P Butler Lau, McElroy & Warren

Placings:0-4P0 **(1485)**
2001/02: 20^{4}GF, 16^{P}GF, 16^{0}GS

	Starts	1st	2nd	3rd	Win & Pl
Hurdles	3	0	0	0	0
Career Total	**4**	**0**	**0**	**0**	**0**

Going: Sf: 0-0 GS: 0-1 Gd: 0-0 GF: - Fm: 0-2
Distance: 2m/2m3: 0-2 2m4-2m7: 0-1 3m+: 0-0
Track: LH: 0-2 RH: 0-0 Tight: 0-3 Gall: 0-0
Aids: Bl: 0-0 Vi: 0-0 Tstrap: 0-0
Best Rating: 71 9/00 Worc 2m gd-fm NHF

Winged Angel

103 **104+**

5-y-o ch g Prince Sabo-Silky Heights (IRE) (Head For Heights)
Miss J A Camacho Four Up One Down Partnership

Placings:0P (2399)
2001/02: 17^{0}S, 16^{P}G

	Starts	1st	2nd	3rd	Win & Pl
Hurdles	2	0	0	0	
Career Total	**2**	**0**	**0**	**0**	

Going: Sf: 0-1 GS: 0-0 Gd: 0-1 GF: - Fm: 0-0
Distance: 2m/2m3: 0-2 2m4-2m7: 0-0 3m+: 0-0
Track: LH: 0-2 RH: 0-0 Tight: 0-1 Gall: 0-0
Aids: Bl: 0-0 Vi: 0-0 Tstrap: 0-0
Best Rating: 60 11/01 Sedg 2m1f soft Hdl

Improving hurdler, successful twice at Hexham in the summer of 2002. Stays two and a half miles.

Winged Hussar

110 **106**

9-y-o b g In The Wings-Akila (FR) (Top Ville)
D R Gandolfo A E Frost

Placings:2PF2P4 (4147)
2001/02: 16^{2}GS, 19^{P}G, 19^{F}S, 16^{2}S, 21^{P}G, 16^{4}GS

	Starts	1st	2nd	3rd	Win & Pl
Hurdles	6	0	2	0	2517
Career Total	**6**	**0**	**2**	**0**	**2517**

Going: Sf: 0-2 GS: 0-2 Gd: 0-2 GF: - Fm: 0-0
Distance: 2m/2m3: 0-4 2m4-2m7: 0-2 3m+: 0-0
Track: LH: 0-4 RH: 0-2 Tight: 0-1 Gall: 0-1
Aids: Bl: 0-0 Vi: 0-0 Tstrap: 0-0
Best Rating: 106 3/02 Chep 2m110y gd-sft Hdl

A useful handicapper on the Flat in Ireland, he is still a maiden over hurdles in Britain, but has run some fair races, including when second at Doncaster in January 2002.

Wings Of Hope (IRE)

102 **102**

6-y-o b g Treasure Hunter-She's Got Wings (Bulldozer)
C R Egerton Hon Mrs J Greenall

Placings:22535P (3816)
2001/02: 20^{2}HY, 22^{2}S, 24^{5}HY, 25^{3}HY, 20^{5}HY, 22^{P}S

	Starts	1st	2nd	3rd	Win & Pl
Hurdles	6	0	2	1	2020
Career Total	**6**	**0**	**2**	**1**	**2020**

Going: Sf: 0-6 GS: 0-0 Gd: 0-0 GF: - Fm: 0-0
Distance: 2m/2m3: 0-0 2m4-2m7: 0-4 3m+: 0-2
Track: LH: 0-3 RH: 0-2 Tight: 0-2 Gall: 0-0
Aids: Bl: 0-4 Vi: 0-0 Tstrap: 0-0
Best Rating: 102 12/01 Strf 2m6f110y soft Hdl

Ordinary novice hurdler, stays well but does not find much off the bridle.

Wink And Whisper

101(100h) (90h)**114**

7-y-o b m Gunner B-Lady Hannah (Daring March)
A King Mrs V A Tory

Placings:2302016 (3501)

2001/02: 17^{2}GS, 21^{3}GF, 22^{0}S, 20^{2}GS, 22^{0}G, 19^{1}S, 20^{6}S

	Starts	1st	2nd	3rd	Win & Pl
Hurdles	5	0	2	1	1920
Chases	2	1	0	0	4693
Career Total	**7**	**1**	**2**	**1**	**6613**

114 1/02 Tntn 2m3f D(0-110)HCh SFT £4693
Total win prize-money £4693

Going: Sf: 1-3 GS: 0-2 Gd: 0-1 GF: - Fm: 0-1
Distance: **2m/2m3: 1-2** 2m4-2m7: 0-5 3m+: 0-0
Track: LH: 0-1 **RH: 1-5 Tight: 1-2** Gall: 0-0
Aids: Bl: 0-0 Vi: 0-0 Tstrap: 0-0
Best Rating: 114 1/02 Tntn 2m3f soft Ch

Handicap chaser, acts on soft ground and is effective at two miles three furlongs.

Winn's Pride (IRE)

110 **124**

11-y-o b g Indian Ridge-Blue Bell Girl (Blakeney)
R Hollinshead Mrs W L Bailey

Placings:3241460/10/13/3030405/441434252005/**U6/U1-1063** (4596)
2001/02: 20^{1}GS, 20^{0}G, 20^{6}G, 20^{3}G

	Starts	1st	2nd	3rd	Win & Pl
Chases	4	1	0	1	6597
Career Total	**38**	**6**	**3**	**6**	**26378**

124	5/01	Bang	2m4f110y	D(0-120)HCh	G-S	£6006
124	2/01	Donc	2m3f110y	E(0-105)HCh	GD	£3368
111	6/98	Uttx	2m4f110y	E(0-110)HHdl	GD	£2389
107	3/97	Uttx	2m6f110y	C(0-135)HHdl	GD	£3501
102	5/95	Aint	2m4f	F(0-105)HHdl	FRM	£2247
90	2/95	Ludl	2m	F Hdl	G-S	£2290

Total win prize-money £19802

Going: Sf: 0-0 GS: 1-1 Gd: 0-3 GF: - Fm: 0-0
Distance: 2m/2m3: 0-0 **2m4-2m7: 1-4** 3m+: 0-0
Track: **LH: 1-2** RH: 0-2 **Tight: 1-3** Gall: 0-0
Aids: Bl: 0-0 Vi: 0-0 Tstrap: 0-0
Best Rating: 124 4/02 Uttx 2m4f good Ch

Fair chaser, best at around two and a half miles, suited by decent ground.

Winnick (IRE)

90 **77**

8-y-o b/br g Fool's Holme (USA)-Injection (On Your Mark)
D McCain D McCain

Placings:*00*202044/464-3003 (1073)
2001/02: 16^{3}F, 20^{0}GS, 16^{0}GF, 21^{3}GF

	Starts	1st	2nd	3rd	Win & Pl
Hurdles	4	0	0	2	680
Career Total	**15**	**0**	**2**	**2**	**2577**

Going: Sf: 0-0 GS: 0-1 Gd: 0-0 GF: - Fm: 0-3
Distance: 2m/2m3: 0-2 2m4-2m7: 0-2 3m+: 0-0
Track: LH: 0-4 RH: 0-0 Tight: 0-2 Gall: 0-0
Aids: Bl: 0-0 Vi: 0-0 Tstrap: 0-0
Best Rating: 82 6/00 MRas 2m1f110y gd-fm Hdl

Winnie

99 **82**

7-y-o br m Presidium-Sindur (Rolfe (USA))
Miss A M Newton-Smith John Grist

Placings:*00*PP0-600334P000 (4509)
2001/02: 20^{6}GF, 22^{0}GS, 20^{0}GS, 17^{3}HY, 20^{3}S, 22^{4}G, 20^{P}S, 17^{0}S, 22^{0}G, 16^{0}G

	Starts	1st	2nd	3rd	Win & Pl
Hurdles	10	0	0	2	597
Career Total	**15**	**0**	**0**	**2**	**597**

Going: Sf: 0-4 GS: 0-2 Gd: 0-3 GF: - Fm: 0-1
Distance: 2m/2m3: 0-3 2m4-2m7: 0-7 3m+: 0-0
Track: LH: 0-2 RH: 0-6 Tight: 0-8 Gall: 0-0
Aids: Bl: 0-1 Vi: 0-0 Tstrap: 0-1
Best Rating: 82 1/02 Winc 2m6f good Hdl

Winnie Flies Again

77 **51**

6-y-o b m Phardante (FR)-Winnie The Witch (Leading Man)
D G Bridgwater Abracadabra

Placings:*0*-P0 (4237)
2001/02: 16^{P}S, 16^{0}GF

	Starts	1st	2nd	3rd	Win & Pl
Hurdles	2	0	0	0	
Career Total	**3**	**0**	**0**	**0**	

Going: Sf: 0-1 GS: 0-0 Gd: 0-0 GF: - Fm: 0-1
Distance: 2m/2m3: 0-2 2m4-2m7: 0-0 3m+: 0-0
Track: LH: 0-0 RH: 0-2 Tight: 0-0 Gall: 0-1
Aids: Bl: 0-0 Vi: 0-0 Tstrap: 0-0
Best Rating: 51 3/02 Hntg 2m110y gd-fm Hdl

Winnie The Pooh

92(87c) (73c)**82**

8-y-o br g Landyap (USA)-Moorland Nell (Neltino)
R G Frost J E Blake

Placings:*024*P-F600 (2291)
2001/02: 17^{F}GF, 17^{6}GF, 17^{0}G, 19^{0}GF

	Starts	1st	2nd	3rd	Win & Pl
Hurdles	3	0	0	0	0
Chases	1	0	0	0	0
Career Total	**8**	**0**	**1**	**0**	**650**

Going: Sf: 0-0 GS: 0-0 Gd: 0-1 GF: - Fm: 0-3
Distance: 2m/2m3: 0-3 2m4-2m7: 0-1 3m+: 0-0
Track: LH: 0-3 RH: 0-1 Tight: 0-3 Gall: 0-0
Aids: Bl: 0-0 Vi: 0-0 Tstrap: 0-0
Best Rating: 92 8/00 NAbb 2m1f good NHF

Winning Town

9-y-o ch g Jester-Lurex Girl (Camden Town)
Mrs J S Lewis (Miss S H Talbot 10/2) Miss S H Talbot

Placings:*00F/56*/P (4545)
2001/02: 19^{P}G

	Starts	1st	2nd	3rd	Win & Pl
Chases	1	0	0	0	
Career Total	**6**	**0**	**0**	**0**	**0**

Going: Sf: 0-0 GS: 0-0 Gd: 0-1 GF: - Fm: 0-0
Distance: 2m/2m3: 0-1 2m4-2m7: 0-0 3m+: 0-0
Track: LH: 0-0 RH: 0-1 Tight: 0-0 Gall: 0-0
Aids: Bl: 0-0 Vi: 0-0 Tstrap: 0-0
Best Rating: 85 12/97 Ludl 2m good NHF

Winsford Hill

11-y-o ch g Nearly A Hand-Gay Ticket (New Member)
J Groucott (R S Kendall 14/4) C D Harrison

Placings: 10/455/10135F2/152232U21F/532P/F13034 2-P (0086)
2001/02: 25^{P}G

	Starts	1st	2nd	3rd	Win & Pl
Chases	1	0	0	0	
Career Total	**34**	**6**	**7**	**5**	**29169**

134	6/00	Hrfd	2m3f	F(0-110)HCh	G-F	£3575
121	4/99	Hntg	2m4f110y	E Ch	G-F	£3135
112	5/98	Ludl	2m	E(0-115)HHdl	G-F	£2931
112	9/97	Worc	2m4f	C(0-130)HHdl	GD	£3367
96	5/97	Bang	2m1f	F(0-105)HHdl	GD	£2905
95	9/95	NAbb	2m1f	E Hdl	GD	£2122

Total win prize-money £18037

Going: Sf: 0-0 GS: 0-0 Gd: 0-1 GF: - Fm: 0-0
Distance: 2m/2m3: 0-0 2m4-2m7: 0-0 3m+: 0-1
Track: LH: 0-0 RH: 0-1 Tight: 0-0 Gall: 0-0
Aids: Bl: 0-0 Vi: 0-0 Tstrap: 0-0
Best Rating: **134** 6/00 Hrfd 2m3f gd-fm Ch

Winsome George

104 **81**

7-y-o b g Marju (IRE)-June Moon (IRE) (Sadler's Wells (USA))
N B Mason N B Mason

Placings: 000045 (3216)
2001/02: 16^{0}GS, 16^{0}GS, 16^{0}GS, 16^{0}GS, 19^{4}G, 20^{5}GS

	Starts	1st	2nd	3rd	Win & Pl
Hurdles	6	0	0	0	0
Career Total	**6**	**0**	**0**	**0**	**0**

Going: Sf: 0-0 GS: 0-5 Gd: 0-1 GF: - Fm: 0-0
Distance: 2m/2m3: 0-5 2m4-2m7: 0-1 3m+: 0-0
Track: LH: 0-5 RH: 0-1 Tight: 0-3 Gall: 0-1
Aids: Bl: 0-1 Vi: 0-0 Tstrap: 0-2
Best Rating: **81** 12/01 Catt 2m3f good Hdl

Modest hurdler, stays two and a half miles. Has worn sheepskin cheekpieces.

Winsome Wallace (IRE)

8-y-o ch g Montelimar (USA)-Gleann Ard (Deep Run)
Mrs S Shirley-Beavan (C Grant 20/1) H Crook, V Fletcher, C Sample

Placings: 53P-0P (4892)
2001/02: 20^{0}S, 31^{P}G

	Starts	1st	2nd	3rd	Win & Pl
Chases	2	0	0	0	
Career Total	**5**	**0**	**0**	**1**	**633**

Going: Sf: 0-1 GS: 0-0 Gd: 0-1 GF: - Fm: 0-0
Distance: 2m/2m3: 0-0 2m4-2m7: 0-1 3m+: 0-1
Track: LH: 0-0 RH: 0-1 Tight: 0-0 Gall: 0-0
Aids: Bl: 0-0 Vi: 0-0 Tstrap: 0-0
Best Rating: **83** 10/01 Carl 2m4f soft Ch

Winsome Winnie

96 **82**

7-y-o b m Teamster-G W Supermare (Rymer)
M J Weeden Mrs S Frost

Placings: 0/0065 (4385)
2001/02: 17^{0}G, 22^{0}S, 19^{6}G, 22^{5}S

	Starts	1st	2nd	3rd	Win & Pl
NH Flat	1	0	0	0	0
Hurdles	3	0	0	0	0
Career Total	**5**	**0**	**0**	**0**	**0**

Going: Sf: 0-2 GS: 0-0 Gd: 0-2 GF: - Fm: 0-0
Distance: 2m/2m3: 0-2 2m4-2m7: 0-2 3m+: 0-0
Track: LH: 0-1 RH: 0-3 Tight: 0-1 Gall: 0-0
Aids: Bl: 0-0 Vi: 0-0 Tstrap: 0-0
Best Rating: **82** 3/02 Winc 2m6f soft Hdl

Winston Run

91(86c) **118**

10-y-o ch g Derrylin-Craftsmans Made (Jimsun)
Ian Williams Mr & Mrs John Poynton

Placings: *312*/34133/3/35-60 (3499)
2001/02: 24^{6}G, 24^{0}S

	Starts	1st	2nd	3rd	Win & Pl
Hurdles	2	0	0	0	0
Career Total	**13**	**2**	**1**	**6**	**17108**

125	12/98	Chep	2m4f110y	D Hdl	HVY	£3241
111	11/97	Sand	2m110y	H NHF	GD	£1392

Total win prize-money £4633

Going: Sf: 0-1 GS: 0-0 Gd: 0-1 GF: - Fm: 0-0
Distance: 2m/2m3: 0-0 2m4-2m7: 0-0 3m+: 0-2
Track: LH: 0-0 RH: 0-1 Tight: 0-0 Gall: 0-0
Aids: Bl: 0-0 Vi: 0-0 Tstrap: 0-0
Best Rating: **146** 3/99 Chel 2m5f gd-sft Hdl

He ran a wonderful race in the Royal & SunAlliance Novices' Hurdle at Cheltenham in 1999, keeping on strongly to finish third behind Barton. He subsequently suffered a stress fracture of a hind leg, and has been lightly-raced and has failed to shine since.

Winter Gale (IRE)

103(46h) **98**

10-y-o b/br g Strong Gale-Winter Fox (Martinmas)
M W Easterby Mrs M E Curtis

Placings: *00/4330*/P30/11123-02F66 (4778)
2001/02: 22^{0}G, 20^{2}GF, 20^{F}GF, 16^{6}GS, 17^{6}G

	Starts	1st	2nd	3rd	Win & Pl
Chases	5	0	1	0	1227
Career Total	**19**	**3**	**2**	**4**	**15325**

116	7/00	Wolv	3m1f	E(0-115)HCh	GD	£3978
110	7/00	MRas	2m6f110y	F(0-105)HCh	GD	£3770
103	7/00	Worc	2m	F(0-95)HCh	GD	£2463

Total win prize-money £10212

Going: Sf: 0-0 GS: 0-1 Gd: 0-2 GF: - Fm: 0-2
Distance: 2m/2m3: 0-2 2m4-2m7: 0-3 3m+: 0-0
Track: LH: 0-2 RH: 0-3 Tight: 0-4 Gall: 0-0
Aids: Bl: 0-0 Vi: 0-0 Tstrap: 0-0
Best Rating: **118** 8/00 MRas 3m1f gd-fm Ch

Winter Rose

90(79h) (40h)**83**

11-y-o br g Derring Rose-Eleri (Rolfe (USA))
Mrs P Ford W E Donohue, R Herbert & K Marritt

Placings: *00*436P6/335P260241/25530/0604/01006F4 25/0-045P60 (1379)
2001/02: 20^{0}GF, 23^{4}GF, 21^{5}GF, 20^{P}GF, 22^{6}GF, 25^{0}GF

	Starts	1st	2nd	3rd	Win & Pl
Hurdles	1	0	0	0	0
Chases	5	0	0	0	245
Career Total	**42**	**2**	**4**	**4**	**9932**

92	5/99	Font	2m6f110y	E(0-115)HHdl	G-F	£2477
91	3/97	Towc	3m	E(0-100)HHdl	SFT	£2460

Total win prize-money £4938

Going: Sf: 0-0 GS: 0-0 Gd: 0-0 GF: - Fm: 0-6
Distance: 2m/2m3: 0-0 2m4-2m7: 0-4 3m+: 0-2
Track: LH: 0-4 RH: 0-2 Tight: 0-4 Gall: 0-0
Aids: Bl: 0-0 Vi: 0-0 Tstrap: 0-0
Best Rating: **92** 2/00 Towc 2m heavy Hdl

Wise Advice (IRE)

12-y-o b g Duky-Down The Aisle (Godswalk (USA))
M A Kemp (M D Hammond 17/2) M A Kemp

Placings: *2P12*/3301F2P/206433FF1/5112354235/131 30305P/235/0 (4638)
2001/02: 19^{0}GF

	Starts	1st	2nd	3rd	Win & Pl
Chases	1	0	0	0	
Career Total	**43**	**7**	**7**	**10**	**36707**

115	5/98	Ctml	2m1f110y	D(0-125)HCh	G-F	£3516
117	5/98	Prth	2m4f110y	E(0-115)HCh	G-F	£4240
106	7/97	MRas	2m4f	D(0-120)HCh	G-F	£3764
110	7/97	Sthl	2m4f110y	D(0-120)HCh	G-F	£4198
105	10/96	Hexm	2m4f110y	E(0-110)HCh	G-F	£3175
100	2/96	Muss	2m4f	F(0-100)HCh	G-F	£3143
92	3/95	Newc	2m110y	E Hdl	G-F	£2333

Total win prize-money £24371

Going: Sf: 0-0 GS: 0-0 Gd: 0-0 GF: - Fm: 0-1
Distance: 2m/2m3: 0-0 2m4-2m7: 0-1 3m+: 0-0
Track: LH: 0-0 RH: 0-1 Tight: 0-0 Gall: 0-0
Aids: Bl: 0-0 Vi: 0-0 Tstrap: 0-0
Best Rating: **117** 5/98 Prth 2m4f110y gd-fm Ch

Wise Examiner (IRE)

84 **69**

9-y-o b g Homo Sapien-Fountains Glory (IRE) (Royal Fountain)
L Wells R A Gadd

Placings: 0/0/0500/6P (1092)
2001/02: 16^{6}S, 20^{P}GF

	Starts	1st	2nd	3rd	Win & Pl
Chases	2	0	0	0	0
Career Total	**8**	**0**	**0**	**0**	**0**

Going: Sf: 0-1 GS: 0-0 Gd: 0-0 GF: - Fm: 0-1
Distance: 2m/2m3: 0-1 2m4-2m7: 0-1 3m+: 0-0
Track: LH: 0-2 RH: 0-0 Tight: 0-0 Gall: 0-0
Aids: Bl: 0-0 Vi: 0-0 Tstrap: 0-2
Best Rating: **77** 7/99 Gway 2m1f gd-fm Ch

Wise King

111 **140**

12-y-o b g Rakaposhi King-Sunwise (Roi Soleil)
J A B Old Denis Milne

Placings: *412*/3F2/2311/311/542/520-5325 (2892)
2001/02: 20^{5}G, 20^{3}GS, 20^{2}G, 24^{5}G

	Starts	1st	2nd	3rd	Win & Pl
Chases	4	0	1	1	3788
Career Total	**23**	**5**	**6**	**4**	**39905**

150	4/99	Asct	2m3f110y	B HCh	G-F	£9885
155	2/99	Kemp	2m4f110y	D(0-125)HCh	GD	£5038
133	12/97	Sand	2m4f110y	D Ch	GD	£4065
124	11/97	Newb	2m110y	D(0-110)HHdl	GD	£4810
107	3/96	Uttx	2m	H NHF	GD	£1551

Total win prize-money £25350

Going: Sf: 0-0 GS: 0-1 Gd: 0-3 GF: - Fm: 0-0
Distance: 2m/2m3: 0-0 2m4-2m7: 0-3 3m+: 0-1

Track: LH: 0-1 RH: 0-3 Tight: 0-0 Gall: 0-1
Aids: Bl: 0-0 Vi: 0-0 Tstrap: 0-0
Best Rating: 159 4/00 Asct 2m3f110y good Ch

Lightly raced, his last win came on fast ground at Ascot in April 1999 and, although he has not won since then, he has been running well. At his best at around two and a half miles on good ground, but is getting on a bit now.

Wise Prince (IRE)

10-y-o b g Denel (FR)-Kissowen (Pitpan)
Mrs Edward Crow David Rogers

Placings:223 **(4179)**
2001/02: 20^{2}GF, 25^{2}G, 24^{3}GS

	Starts	1st	2nd	3rd	Win & Pl
Chases	3	0	2	1	1320
Career Total	**3**	**0**	**2**	**1**	**1320**

Going: Sf: 0-0 GS: 0-1 Gd: 0-1 GF: - Fm: 0-1
Distance: 2m/2m3: 0-0 2m4-2m7: 0-1 3m+: 0-2
Track: LH: 0-1 RH: 0-2 Tight: 0-1 Gall: 0-1
Aids: Bl: 0-0 Vi: 0-0 Tstrap: 0-0
Best Rating: 111 3/02 Strf 3m gd-sft Ch

Threw away a hunter chase at Hereford in May when jumping badly left at the last.

Wise Reflection (IRE)

102 **126**
8-y-o b g Detroit Sam (FR)-Hester Ann (Proverb)
A King Mrs M C Sweeney

Placings:2P1545/3352P-2 **(0233)**
2001/02: 24^{2}GF

	Starts	1st	2nd	3rd	Win & Pl
Chases	1	0	1	0	2245
Career Total	**12**	**1**	**3**	**2**	**11598**

107 11/99 Asct 2m4f E Hdl GD £5015
Total win prize-money £5016

Going: Sf: 0-0 GS: 0-0 Gd: 0-0 GF: - Fm: 0-1
Distance: 2m/2m3: 0-0 2m4-2m7: 0-0 3m+: 0-1
Track: LH: 0-1 RH: 0-0 Tight: 0-1 Gall: 0-0
Aids: Bl: 0-0 Vi: 0-0 Tstrap: 0-0
Best Rating: 126 5/01 Sthl 3m110y gd-fm Ch

Wise Tom

6-y-o br g Homo Sapien-Linn Falls (Royal Fountain)
Mrs L B Normile Mrs V Gilmour

Placings:00P **(4874)**
2001/02: 16^{0}GS, 20^{0}G, 20^{P}G

	Starts	1st	2nd	3rd	Win & Pl
NH Flat	1	0	0	0	0
Hurdles	2	0	0	0	0
Career Total	**3**	**0**	**0**	**0**	

Going: Sf: 0-0 GS: 0-1 Gd: 0-2 GF: - Fm: 0-0
Distance: 2m/2m3: 0-1 2m4-2m7: 0-2 3m+: 0-0
Track: LH: 0-1 RH: 0-1 Tight: 0-0 Gall: 0-0
Aids: Bl: 0-0 Vi: 0-0 Tstrap: 0-0
Best Rating: 67 11/01 Ayr 2m gd-sft NHF

Wishbone (IRE)

104(116h) (124h)**136**
9-y-o b g Lord Americo-C C Meade (Paddy's Stream)
N A Twiston-Davies The Big Bone Partnership

Placings:F21464-2224536F **(4839)**
2001/02: 24^{2}GS, 24^{2}S, 24^{2}G, 22^{4}G, 25^{5}S, 24^{3}GS, 24^{6}GF, 33^{F}G

	Starts	1st	2nd	3rd	Win & Pl
Chases	8	0	3	1	10556
Career Total	**14**	**1**	**4**	**1**	**18126**

126 11/00 Newb 3m110y C Hdl G-S £4550
Total win prize-money £4550

Going: Sf: 0-2 GS: 0-2 Gd: 0-3 GF: - Fm: 0-1
Distance: 2m/2m3: 0-0 2m4-2m7: 0-1 3m+: 0-7
Track: LH: 0-6 RH: 0-2 Tight: 0-1 Gall: 0-3
Aids: Bl: 0-0 Vi: 0-1 Tstrap: 0-0
Best Rating: 136 11/01 Chel 3m110y good Ch

Successful between the flags in Ireland, he ran some fair races over fences before being killed at Ayr in April. (DEAD)

Wishbone Alley (IRE)

84 **61**
7-y-o b g Common Grounds-Dul Dul (USA) (Shadeed (USA))
R Wilman Century Racing

Placings:00P **(1669)**
2001/02: 16^{0}GF, 16^{0}G, 24^{P}G

	Starts	1st	2nd	3rd	Win & Pl
Hurdles	3	0	0	0	
Career Total	**3**	**0**	**0**	**0**	

Going: Sf: 0-0 GS: 0-0 Gd: 0-2 GF: - Fm: 0-1
Distance: 2m/2m3: 0-2 2m4-2m7: 0-0 3m+: 0-1
Track: LH: 0-2 RH: 0-1 Tight: 0-1 Gall: 0-1
Aids: Bl: 0-0 Vi: 0-0 Tstrap: 0-0
Best Rating: 66 9/01 Uttx 2m good Hdl

Wishful Valentine

75 **50**
6-y-o ch g Riverwise (USA)-Wishful Dream (Crawter)
C W Mitchell C W Mitchell

Placings:*0*-000 **(3384)**
2001/02: 16^{0}G, 17^{0}HY, 16^{0}GS

	Starts	1st	2nd	3rd	Win & Pl
Hurdles	3	0	0	0	
Career Total	**4**	**0**	**0**	**0**	

Going: Sf: 0-1 GS: 0-1 Gd: 0-1 GF: - Fm: 0-0
Distance: 2m/2m3: 0-3 2m4-2m7: 0-0 3m+: 0-0
Track: LH: 0-1 RH: 0-2 Tight: 0-1 Gall: 0-0
Aids: Bl: 0-0 Vi: 0-0 Tstrap: 0-0
Best Rating: 82 1/01 Kemp 2m soft NHF

Wisley Warrior

11-y-o b g Derring Rose-Miss Topem (Mossberry)
N A Twiston-Davies The Wisley Golf Partnership

Placings:*66*/4530/F1FF/25P23P/B34-P **(0059)**
2001/02: 16^{P}G

	Starts	1st	2nd	3rd	Win & Pl
Chases	1	0	0	0	
Career Total	**20**	**1**	**2**	**3**	**11225**

120 3/99 Newb 3m D(0-115)HCh SFT £3727
Total win prize-money £3727

Going: Sf: 0-0 GS: 0-0 Gd: 0-1 GF: - Fm: 0-0
Distance: 2m/2m3: 0-1 2m4-2m7: 0-0 3m+: 0-0
Track: LH: 0-0 RH: 0-1 Tight: 0-1 Gall: 0-0
Aids: Bl: 0-0 Vi: 0-0 Tstrap: 0-0
Best Rating: 120 3/99 Newb 3m soft Ch

Witchtime

7-y-o b m Lyphento (USA)-Dusty Chimes (Foggy Bell)
P R Webber H J H Reynolds

Placings:P-P **(0214)**
2001/02: 22^{P}GF

	Starts	1st	2nd	3rd	Win & Pl
Hurdles	1	0	0	0	
Career Total	**2**	**0**	**0**	**0**	

Going: Sf: 0-0 GS: 0-0 Gd: 0-0 GF: - Fm: 0-1
Distance: 2m/2m3: 0-0 2m4-2m7: 0-1 3m+: 0-0
Track: LH: 0-0 RH: 0-1 Tight: 0-0 Gall: 0-0
Aids: Bl: 0-0 Vi: 0-0 Tstrap: 0-0
Best Rating:

With A Twist (GER)

100 **120**
4-y-o ch g Alwuhush (USA)-Walkona (IRE) (Local Suitor (USA))
C J Mann The Dunnkirk Partnership

Placings:13U2 **(3651)**
2001/02: 16^{1}HY, 16^{3}GS, 17^{U}GS, 16^{2}S

	Starts	1st	2nd	3rd	Win & Pl
Hurdles	4	1	1	1	4960
Career Total	**4**	**1**	**1**	**1**	**4960**

10/01 Brem 2m Hdl HVY £1629
Total win prize-money £1629

Going: Sf: 1-2 GS: 0-2 Gd: 0-0 GF: - Fm: 0-0
Distance: **2m/2m3: 1-4** 2m4-2m7: 0-0 3m+: 0-0
Track: LH: 0-0 RH: 0-3 Tight: 0-1 Gall: 0-1
Aids: Bl: 0-0 Vi: 0-0 Tstrap: 0-0
Best Rating: 120 2/02 Hntg 2m110y soft Hdl

A winner on the Flat and over hurdles in Germany, he just missed out in a decent race at Huntingdon on his third outing over hurdles in this country.

Witness Time (IRE)

94f **97f**
6-y-o b g Witness Box (USA)-Lisnacoilla (Beau Chapeau)
B J Eckley Brian Eckley

Placings:*304* **(4329)**
2001/02: 17^{3}G, 16^{0}S, 17^{4}S

	Starts	1st	2nd	3rd	Win & Pl
NH Flat	3	0	0	1	238
Career Total	**3**	**0**	**0**	**1**	**238**

Going: Sf: 0-2 GS: 0-0 Gd: 0-1 GF: - Fm: 0-0
Distance: 2m/2m3: 0-3 2m4-2m7: 0-0 3m+: 0-0
Track: LH: 0-2 RH: 0-1 Tight: 0-1 Gall: 0-0
Aids: Bl: 0-0 Vi: 0-0 Tstrap: 0-0

Best Rating: 97 3/02 Hrfd 2m1f soft NHF

Witney (IRE)

85 73

8-y-o b m Strong Gale-Euroblend (IRE) (The Parson)
P T Dalton Mrs Lucia Farmer

Placings:30/6-0P (4106)
2001/02: 20^{0}GS, 21^{P}S

	Starts	1st	2nd	3rd	Win & Pl
Hurdles	2	0	0	0	
Career Total	5	0	0	1	230

Going: Sf: 0-1 GS: 0-1 Gd: 0-0 GF: - Fm: 0-0
Distance: 2m/2m3: 0-0 2m4-2m7: 0-2 3m+: 0-0
Track: LH: 0-0 RH: 0-2 Tight: 0-0 Gall: 0-1
Aids: Bl: 0-0 Vi: 0-0 Tstrap: 0-0
Best Rating: 101 3/00 Uttx 2m good NHF

Witney O'Grady (IRE)

64 68

9-y-o ch g Ring Of Ford-C B M Girl (Diamonds Are Trump (USA))
Miss L V Davis (R G Frost 31/5) Miss Louise Davis

Placings:0/0/0P5 (4555)
2001/02: 22^{0}GF, 16^{P}S, 19^{5}GF

	Starts	1st	2nd	3rd	Win & Pl
Hurdles	3	0	0	0	0
Career Total	5	0	0	0	0

Going: Sf: 0-1 GS: 0-0 Gd: 0-0 GF: - Fm: 0-2
Distance: 2m/2m3: 0-1 2m4-2m7: 0-2 3m+: 0-0
Track: LH: 0-2 RH: 0-1 Tight: 0-2 Gall: 0-1
Aids: Bl: 0-0 Vi: 0-0 Tstrap: 0-0
Best Rating: 68 4/02 MRas 2m3f110y gd-fm Hdl

Witney Royale (IRE)

91 92

4-y-o ch g Royal Abjar (USA)-Collected (IRE) (Taufan (USA))
J S Moore Ernie Houghton

Placings:4 (1863)
2001/02: 16^{4}G

	Starts	1st	2nd	3rd	Win & Pl
Hurdles	1	0	0	0	528
Career Total	1	0	0	0	528

Going: Sf: 0-0 GS: 0-0 Gd: 0-1 GF: - Fm: 0-0
Distance: 2m/2m3: 0-1 2m4-2m7: 0-0 3m+: 0-0
Track: LH: 0-1 RH: 0-0 Tight: 0-0 Gall: 0-0
Aids: Bl: 0-0 Vi: 0-0 Tstrap: 0-0
Best Rating: 92 10/01 Chel 2m110y good Hdl

Wizadora

7-y-o gr m Safawan-Shrood Biddy (Sharrood (USA))
Mrs S Davies (Paul Morris 20/1) Mrs S Davies

Placings:0PP/P0P00/**P4PP-0UPPR** (4685)
2001/02: 20^{0}GF, 16^{U}G, 19^{P}S, 20^{P}S, 16^{R}GF

	Starts	1st	2nd	3rd	Win & Pl
Chases	5	0	0	0	
Career Total	17	0	0	0	134

Going: Sf: 0-2 GS: 0-0 Gd: 0-1 GF: - Fm: 0-2
Distance: 2m/2m3: 0-2 2m4-2m7: 0-3 3m+: 0-0
Track: LH: 0-1 RH: 0-3 Tight: 0-1 Gall: 0-2
Aids: Bl: 0-2 Vi: 0-0 Tstrap: 0-0
Best Rating: 79 3/99 Ludl 2m good NHF

Wonder Weasel (IRE)

109(102h) (101h)150

9-y-o b g Lancastrian-The She Weasel (Gulf Pearl)
K C Bailey D A Halsall

Placings:513/1-511PP5U (4839)
2001/02: 24^{5}G, 24^{1}S, 24^{1}HY, 28^{P}HY, 24^{P}GS, 24^{5}S, 33^{U}G

	Starts	1st	2nd	3rd	Win & Pl
Hurdles	1	0	0	0	0
Chases	6	2	0	0	10023
Career Total	11	4	0	1	26241

150	12/01	Hayd	3m	D(0-125)HCh	HVY	£6464
150	12/01	Hayd	3m	E(0-115)HCh	SFT	£3558
133	1/01	Donc	2m3f110y	C(0-130)HCh	GD	£7182
130	4/00	Hayd	2m6f	D Ch	GD	£5655

Total win prize-money £22861

Going: Sf: 2-4 GS: 0-1 Gd: 0-2 GF: - Fm: 0-0
Distance: 2m/2m3: 0-0 2m4-2m7: 0-0 **3m+: 2-7**
Track: **LH: 2-6** RH: 0-1 Tight: 0-0 Gall: 0-2
Aids: Bl: 0-1 Vi: 0-0 Tstrap: 0-0
Best Rating: 150 12/01 Hayd 3m heavy Ch

Handicap chaser. Stays well. Suited by good and soft ground.

Wonderboy (IRE)

94 80

8-y-o ch g Arazi (USA)-Alsaaybah (USA) (Diesis)
Jamie Poulton Chris Steward

Placings:50/0300/25423314220/0P**040P00** (3286)
2001/02: 16^{0}GF, 21^{P}GS, 16^{0}GS, 17^{4}GS, 17^{0}G, 26^{P}S, 20^{0}G, 16^{0}S

	Starts	1st	2nd	3rd	Win & Pl
Hurdles	2	0	0	0	0
Chases	6	0	0	0	0
Career Total	25	1	4	3	3994

80	11/99	Tntn	2m1f	G(0-90)HHdl	GD	£1553

Total win prize-money £1553

Going: Sf: 0-2 GS: 0-3 Gd: 0-2 GF: - Fm: 0-1
Distance: 2m/2m3: 0-5 2m4-2m7: 0-2 3m+: 0-1
Track: LH: 0-4 RH: 0-2 Tight: 0-6 Gall: 0-0
Aids: Bl: 0-0 Vi: 0-0 Tstrap: 0-8
Best Rating: 83 1/00 Plum 2m heavy Hdl

Wonderful Man

102 84

6-y-o ch g Magical Wonder (USA)-Gleeful (Sayf El Arab (USA))
R D E Woodhouse M K Oldham

Placings:P640-00 (2669)
2001/02: 16^{0}G, 16^{0}G

	Starts	1st	2nd	3rd	Win & Pl
Hurdles	2	0	0	0	
Career Total	6	0	0	0	0

Going: Sf: 0-0 GS: 0-0 Gd: 0-2 GF: - Fm: 0-0
Distance: 2m/2m3: 0-2 2m4-2m7: 0-0 3m+: 0-0
Track: LH: 0-2 RH: 0-0 Tight: 0-0 Gall: 0-1
Aids: Bl: 0-0 Vi: 0-0 Tstrap: 0-0
Best Rating: 84 12/00 Fknm 2m gd-sft Hdl

Modest, lightly-raced hurdler, suited by fast ground. Best when held up.

Wonderful Remark

90 63

6-y-o b m Golden Heights-Queen Of Dreams (Ti King (FR))
J A Pickering Mrs Joanne Woods

Placings:00/0P60 (4597)
2001/02: 16^{0}HY, 21^{P}S, 16^{6}HY, 19^{0}GF

	Starts	1st	2nd	3rd	Win & Pl
NH Flat	1	0	0	0	0
Hurdles	3	0	0	0	0
Career Total	6	0	0	0	0

Going: Sf: 0-3 GS: 0-0 Gd: 0-0 GF: - Fm: 0-1
Distance: 2m/2m3: 0-3 2m4-2m7: 0-1 3m+: 0-0
Track: LH: 0-3 RH: 0-1 Tight: 0-1 Gall: 0-0
Aids: Bl: 0-0 Vi: 0-0 Tstrap: 0-0
Best Rating: 59 4/00 Fknm 2m good NHF

Wontcostalotbut

100(111h) (121h)98

8-y-o b m Nicholas Bill-Brave Maiden (Three Legs)
M J Wilkinson Wontcostalot Partnership

Placings:U36230210/432041532444/22112640/0PP0-**306033** (4412)
2001/02: 24^{3}S, 22^{0}S, 24^{6}G, 25^{0}HY, 20^{3}S, 20^{3}S

	Starts	1st	2nd	3rd	Win & Pl
Hurdles	4	0	0	1	836
Chases	2	0	0	2	1089
Career Total	39	4	7	7	33301

135	12/99	Kemp	3m110y	B(0-140)HHdl	SFT	£7061
118	11/99	Newb	3m110y	C(0-135)HHdl	G-F	£4695
108	12/98	NAbb	2m6f	(0-125)HHdl	SFT	£2684
106	4/98	Uttx	2m4f110y	E Hdl	SFT	£2211

Total win prize-money £16651

Going: Sf: 0-5 GS: 0-0 Gd: 0-1 GF: - Fm: 0-0
Distance: 2m/2m3: 0-0 2m4-2m7: 0-3 3m+: 0-3
Track: LH: 0-1 RH: 0-2 Tight: 0-2 Gall: 0-0
Aids: Bl: 0-0 Vi: 0-2 Tstrap: 0-0
Best Rating: 135 1/00 Uttx 3m110y soft Hdl

A game staying mare who loves the mud and enjoyed a fine season in 1999/2000. She has since lost her sparkle.

Woodfield Gale (IRE)

103 125

9-y-o b g Strong Gale-Excitable Lady (Buckskin (FR))
Ferdy Murphy Mrs M B Scholey

Placings:43402/311120/23F1310/**453-36PF0** (4941a)
2001/02: 25^{3}F, 24^{6}G, 24^{P}S, 24^{F}GF, 25^{0}Y

	Starts	1st	2nd	3rd	Win & Pl
Chases	5	0	0	1	1398
Career Total	26	5	3	6	26609

117	2/00	Catt	2m3f	D Ch	GD	£4368
125	1/00	Catt	3m1f110y	E Ch	GD	£3159
123	12/98	Newc	2m4f	C HHdl	SFT	£5147
110	11/98	Newc	2m4f	D(0-125)HHdl	GD	£2836
116	10/98	Weth	2m4f110y	D Hdl	SFT	£2575

Total win prize-money £18085

Going: Sf: 0-1 GS: 0-0 Gd: 0-1 GF: - Fm: 0-2
Distance: 2m/2m3: 0-0 2m4-2m7: 0-0 3m+: 0-5
Track: LH: 0-3 RH: 0-2 Tight: 0-1 Gall: 0-2
Aids: Bl: 0-1 Vi: 0-0 Tstrap: 0-0
Best Rating: 125 5/01 Weth 3m1f firm Ch

Fair chaser, stays three miles, suited by good ground.

Woodland Park (USA)

100 **86**

4-y-o b g Woodman (USA)-Yemanja (USA) (Alleged (USA))
Mrs D Haine Mrs Solna Thomson Jones

Placings:000 (3558)
2001/02: 16^{0}S, 16^{0}GS, 16^{0}HY

	Starts	1st	2nd	3rd	Win & Pl
Hurdles	3	0	0	0	
Career Total	**3**	**0**	**0**	**0**	

Going: Sf: 0-2 GS: 0-1 Gd: 0-0 GF: - Fm: 0-0
Distance: 2m/2m3: 0-3 2m4-2m7: 0-0 3m+: 0-0
Track: LH: 0-0 RH: 0-3 Tight: 0-0 Gall: 0-1
Aids: Bl: 0-0 Vi: 0-0 Tstrap: 0-0
Best Rating: 59 1/02 Hntg 2m110y gd-sft Hdl

Woodland Warrior

88 **77**

5-y-o b g Lyphento (USA)-Dutch Majesty (Homing)
A Ennis Mrs J Sjoblom

Placings:5600PS0 (4546)
2001/02: 17^{5}F, 20^{6}GS, 18^{0}HY, 22^{0}S, 22^{P}G, 21^{S}G, 16^{0}GF

	Starts	1st	2nd	3rd	Win & Pl
NH Flat	1	0	0	0	0
Hurdles	6	0	0	0	0
Career Total	**7**	**0**	**0**	**0**	**0**

Going: Sf: 0-2 GS: 0-1 Gd: 0-2 GF: - Fm: 0-2
Distance: 2m/2m3: 0-3 2m4-2m7: 0-4 3m+: 0-0
Track: LH: 0-3 RH: 0-2 Tight: 0-4 Gall: 0-1
Aids: Bl: 0-0 Vi: 0-2 Tstrap: 0-0
Best Rating: 77 11/01 Font 2m4f gd-sft Hdl

Woodlands Beau (IRE)

108 **123**

10-y-o b g Beau Sher-Never Intended (Sayyaf)
R H Alner Club Ten

Placings:2U130U22U/234P25PP23U6/2241521U0-03U555552 (4864)
2001/02: 25^{0}GF, 25^{3}G, 25^{U}GF, 25^{5}G, 24^{5}S, 23^{5}S, 25^{5}S, 25^{5}S, 25^{2}F

	Starts	1st	2nd	3rd	Win & Pl
Chases	9	0	1	1	2432
Career Total	**39**	**3**	**10**	**4**	**30287**

123 1/01 Folk 3m1f F(0-110)HCh HVY £6838
123 10/00 Winc 3m1f110y F(0-110)HCh G-S £5362
123 11/98 Towc 3m1f D Ch G-S £3692

Total win prize-money £15894

Going: Sf: 0-4 GS: 0-0 Gd: 0-2 GF: - Fm: 0-3
Distance: 2m/2m3: 0-0 2m4-2m7: 0-0 3m+: 0-9
Track: LH: 0-0 RH: 0-8 Tight: 0-1 Gall: 0-0
Aids: Bl: 0-7 Vi: 0-0 Tstrap: 0-0
Best Rating: 123 10/01 Winc 3m1f110y good Ch

Moderate handicap chaser, suited by three miles plus, soft ground and a right-handed track. Usually wears blinkers.

Woodlands Energy

(69h)

11-y-o b m Risk Me (FR)-Hallowed (Wolver Hollow)
P A Pritchard Woodlands (worcestershire) Ltd

Placings:P6P004/0000PP0PP/002430/00/0F (1415)
2001/02: 22^{0}G, 20^{F}GF

	Starts	1st	2nd	3rd	Win & Pl
Hurdles	1	0	0	0	0
Chases	1	0	0	0	0
Career Total	**25**	**0**	**1**	**1**	**921**

Going: Sf: 0-0 GS: 0-0 Gd: 0-1 GF: - Fm: 0-1
Distance: 2m/2m3: 0-0 2m4-2m7: 0-2 3m+: 0-0
Track: LH: 0-2 RH: 0-0 Tight: 0-2 Gall: 0-0
Aids: Bl: 0-0 Vi: 0-0 Tstrap: 0-0
Best Rating: 64 10/97 Hrfd 2m3f110y good Hdl

Woodlands Lass

6-y-o ch m Nearly A Hand-Maranzi (Jimmy Reppin)
P A Pritchard Woodlands (worcestershire) Ltd

Placings:0000P (4854)
2001/02: 17^{0}G, 16^{0}HY, 16^{0}HY, 16^{0}GF, 22^{P}G

	Starts	1st	2nd	3rd	Win & Pl
NH Flat	4	0	0	0	0
Hurdles	1	0	0	0	0
Career Total	**5**	**0**	**0**	**0**	

Going: Sf: 0-2 GS: 0-0 Gd: 0-2 GF: - Fm: 0-1
Distance: 2m/2m3: 0-4 2m4-2m7: 0-1 3m+: 0-0
Track: LH: 0-3 RH: 0-2 Tight: 0-1 Gall: 0-0
Aids: Bl: 0-0 Vi: 0-0 Tstrap: 0-1
Best Rating: 59 4/02 Wwck 2m gd-fm NHF

Woodside

5-y-o b m Terimon-Misowni (Niniski (USA))
Miss K M George Exterior Profiles Ltd

Placings:P (2134)
2001/02: 21^{P}GF

	Starts	1st	2nd	3rd	Win & Pl
Hurdles	1	0	0	0	
Career Total	**1**	**0**	**0**	**0**	

Going: Sf: 0-0 GS: 0-0 Gd: 0-0 GF: - Fm: 0-1
Distance: 2m/2m3: 0-0 2m4-2m7: 0-1 3m+: 0-0
Track: LH: 0-0 RH: 0-1 Tight: 0-0 Gall: 0-0
Aids: Bl: 0-0 Vi: 0-0 Tstrap: 0-0
Best Rating:

Woodward Street (AUS)

100 **115**

7-y-o b g Coronation Day (AUS)-Super Unicorn (AUS) (Ksar)
N J Henderson Mrs Margaret Turner

Placings:1P-46P5P (4418)
2001/02: 16^{4}G, 17^{6}S, 16^{P}S, 16^{5}S, 16^{P}GS

	Starts	1st	2nd	3rd	Win & Pl
Hurdles	5	0	0	0	535
Career Total	**7**	**1**	**0**	**0**	**3866**

106 11/00 Hayd 2m D Hdl HVY £3331

Total win prize-money £3331

Going: Sf: 0-3 GS: 0-1 Gd: 0-1 GF: - Fm: 0-0
Distance: 2m/2m3: 0-5 2m4-2m7: 0-0 3m+: 0-0
Track: LH: 0-2 RH: 0-3 Tight: 0-1 Gall: 0-2
Aids: Bl: 0-0 Vi: 0-0 Tstrap: 0-0
Best Rating: 115 12/01 Kemp 2m good Hdl

Ex-New Zealand recruit who won his hurdles debut in this country at Haydock in convincing style in heavy ground, but pulled up next time and was absent for over a year before returning at Kempton over Christmas 2001, he has been disappointing since. Suited by two miles and soft/heavy ground.

Woodwind Down

105(101h) (80h)**112+**

5-y-o b m Piccolo-Bint El Oumara (Al Nasr (FR))
M Todhunter Domino Racing

Placings:066-01P03 (1463)
2001/02: 17^{0}G, 16^{1}F, 17^{P}GF, 17^{0}GF, 16^{3}G

	Starts	1st	2nd	3rd	Win & Pl
Hurdles	5	1	0	1	3425
Career Total	**8**	**1**	**0**	**1**	**3425**

80 6/01 Prth 2m110y F(0-90)HHdl FRM £2999

Total win prize-money £3000

Going: Sf: 0-0 GS: 0-0 Gd: 0-2 GF: - Fm: 1-3
Distance: **2m/2m3: 1-5** 2m4-2m7: 0-0 3m+: 0-0
Track: LH: 0-1 **RH: 1-4** Tight: 0-3 Gall: 0-0
Aids: Bl: 0-0 Vi: 0-1 Tstrap: 0-0
Best Rating: 80 9/01 Prth 2m110y good Hdl

Moderate hurdler, suited by a sound surface. Won on her debut over fences at Sedgefield in July 2002.

Woody Dare

12-y-o b g Phardante (FR)-Woodland Pit (Pitpan)
P Needham P Needham

Placings:21/0P/F4240/P (0071)
2001/02: 21^{P}G

	Starts	1st	2nd	3rd	Win & Pl
Hurdles	1	0	0	0	
Career Total	**10**	**1**	**2**	**0**	**2041**

89 3/97 Newc 2m4f H Ch G-F £1047

Total win prize-money £1048

Going: Sf: 0-0 GS: 0-0 Gd: 0-1 GF: - Fm: 0-0
Distance: 2m/2m3: 0-0 2m4-2m7: 0-1 3m+: 0-0
Track: LH: 0-1 RH: 0-0 Tight: 0-1 Gall: 0-0
Aids: Bl: 0-0 Vi: 0-0 Tstrap: 0-0
Best Rating: 94 5/99 Weth 2m4f110y good Hdl

Woody's Mop

10-y-o b g Supreme Leader-Dishcloth (Fury Royal)
J S Swindells Mrs J Wood

Placings:3P (0497)
2001/02: 24^{3}GS, 25^{P}G

	Starts	1st	2nd	3rd	Win & Pl
Chases	2	0	0	1	420
Career Total	**2**	**0**	**0**	**1**	**420**

Going: Sf: 0-0 GS: 0-1 Gd: 0-1 GF: - Fm: 0-0
Distance: 2m/2m3: 0-0 2m4-2m7: 0-0 3m+: 0-2
Track: LH: 0-1 RH: 0-1 Tight: 0-1 Gall: 0-0
Aids: Bl: 0-0 Vi: 0-0 Tstrap: 0-0
Best Rating: 97 5/01 Bang 3m110y gd-sft Ch

Woodyates

95 **91**

5-y-o b m Naheez (USA)-Night Mission (IRE) (Night Shift (USA))
D R C Elsworth D Watson

Placings:5P-500 **(4504)**
2001/02: 16^{5}GS, 19^{0}GS, 17^{0}G

	Starts	1st	2nd	3rd	Win & Pl
Hurdles	3	0	0	0	0
Career Total	**5**	**0**	**0**	**0**	**0**

Going: Sf: 0-0 GS: 0-2 Gd: 0-1 GF: - Fm: 0-0
Distance: 2m/2m3: 0-2 2m4-2m7: 0-1 3m+: 0-0
Track: LH: 0-1 RH: 0-2 Tight: 0-2 Gall: 0-0
Aids: Bl: 0-0 Vi: 0-0 Tstrap: 0-0
Best Rating: 91 12/01 Leic 2m gd-sft Hdl

Woodys Blue Lagoon (IRE)

111 **133**

8-y-o b g Buckskin (FR)-Picton Lass (Rymer)
Noel Meade Mrs P Sloan

Placings:*236/6/0-6*1114402056 **(4944a)**
2001/02: 16^{6}G, 20^{1}S, 20^{1}SH, 20^{1}YS, 20^{4}YS, 20^{4}Y, 24^{0}YS, 20^{2}HY, 21^{0}GS, 20^{5}GY, 20^{6}G

	Starts	1st	2nd	3rd	Win & Pl
NH Flat	1	0	0	0	0
Hurdles	10	3	1	0	28911
Career Total	**16**	**3**	**2**	**1**	**30362**

129	11/01	Punc	2m4f	Hdl	Y-S	£7862
125	10/01	Gway	2m4f	Hdl	SH	£8387
110	10/01	Punc	2m4f	Hdl	SFT	£6677

Total win prize-money £22927

Going: Sf: 1-2 GS: 0-1 Gd: 0-2 GF: - Fm: 0-0
Distance: 2m/2m3: 0-1 **2m4-2m7: 3-9** 3m+: 0-1
Track: LH: 0-2 **RH: 3-6** Tight: 0-0 Gall: 0-1
Aids: Bl: 0-0 Vi: 0-0 Tstrap: 0-0
Best Rating: 133 1/02 Naas 2m4f yield Hdl

Fair Irish novice hurdler, winner three times on easy ground in the autumn of 2001. Stays two and a half miles.

Woolley

102 **79**

8-y-o b g Welsh Captain-Singing Hills (Crash Course)
John Allen J Allen

Placings:*00*F6245/B63243-U0P **(4572)**
2001/02: 24^{U}GS, 21^{0}S, 20^{P}G

	Starts	1st	2nd	3rd	Win & Pl
Hurdles	2	0	0	0	0
Chases	1	0	0	0	0
Career Total	**16**	**0**	**2**	**2**	**3366**

Going: Sf: 0-1 GS: 0-1 Gd: 0-1 GF: - Fm: 0-0
Distance: 2m/2m3: 0-0 2m4-2m7: 0-2 3m+: 0-1
Track: LH: 0-2 RH: 0-1 Tight: 0-1 Gall: 0-0
Aids: Bl: 0-0 Vi: 0-0 Tstrap: 0-0
Best Rating: 109 3/00 Strf 2m6f110y good Hdl

Woolly Winsome

70 **40**

6-y-o br g Lugana Beach-Gay Ming (Gay Meadow)
G Brown Mrs S Clifford

Placings:0P0U0 **(4752)**
2001/02: 16^{0}GS, 16^{P}HY, 17^{0}S, 16^{U}GF, 16^{0}GF

	Starts	1st	2nd	3rd	Win & Pl
Hurdles	5	0	0	0	
Career Total	**5**	**0**	**0**	**0**	

Going: Sf: 0-2 GS: 0-1 Gd: 0-0 GF: - Fm: 0-2
Distance: 2m/2m3: 0-5 2m4-2m7: 0-0 3m+: 0-0
Track: LH: 0-2 RH: 0-3 Tight: 0-1 Gall: 0-2
Aids: Bl: 0-0 Vi: 0-0 Tstrap: 0-0
Best Rating: 40 3/02 Hrfd 2m1f soft Hdl

Word Of Honour (IRE)

105 **113**

6-y-o br g Supreme Leader-Shaping (Deep Run)
M Pitman Malcolm C Denmark

Placings:623 **(4007)**
2001/02: 16^{6}GS, 21^{2}S, 19^{3}S

	Starts	1st	2nd	3rd	Win & Pl
Hurdles	3	0	1	1	1982
Career Total	**3**	**0**	**1**	**1**	**1982**

Going: Sf: 0-2 GS: 0-1 Gd: 0-0 GF: - Fm: 0-0
Distance: 2m/2m3: 0-2 2m4-2m7: 0-1 3m+: 0-0
Track: LH: 0-1 RH: 0-2 Tight: 0-0 Gall: 0-1
Aids: Bl: 0-0 Vi: 0-0 Tstrap: 0-0
Best Rating: 113 1/02 Kemp 2m5f soft Hdl

By the leading jump sire, Supreme Leader, he is a chasing type who has already shown promise over hurdles.

Workaway

86 **81**

6-y-o b g Alflora (IRE)-Annicombe Run (Deep Run)
A Parker Mr & Mrs Raymond Anderson Green

Placings:*14-*540 **(4522)**
2001/02: 17^{5}GS, 20^{4}GS, 17^{0}G

	Starts	1st	2nd	3rd	Win & Pl
NH Flat	1	0	0	0	0
Hurdles	2	0	0	0	270
Career Total	**5**	**1**	**0**	**0**	**2248**

104	11/00	Carl	2m1f	H NHF	HVY	£1977

Total win prize-money £1978

Going: Sf: 0-0 GS: 0-2 Gd: 0-1 GF: - Fm: 0-0
Distance: 2m/2m3: 0-2 2m4-2m7: 0-1 3m+: 0-0
Track: LH: 0-0 RH: 0-3 Tight: 0-1 Gall: 0-0
Aids: Bl: 0-0 Vi: 0-0 Tstrap: 0-0
Best Rating: 105 10/01 Carl 2m1f gd-sft NHF

Worlaby Dale

6-y-o b g Terimon-Restandbethankful (Random Shot)
Mrs S Lamyman P Lamyman

Placings:*00030-*P **(1830)**
2001/02: 20^{P}G

	Starts	1st	2nd	3rd	Win & Pl
Hurdles	1	0	0	0	
Career Total	**6**	**0**	**0**	**1**	**248**

Going: Sf: 0-0 GS: 0-0 Gd: 0-1 GF: - Fm: 0-0
Distance: 2m/2m3: 0-0 2m4-2m7: 0-1 3m+: 0-0
Track: LH: 0-1 RH: 0-0 Tight: 0-1 Gall: 0-0
Aids: Bl: 0-0 Vi: 0-0 Tstrap: 0-0
Best Rating: 94 3/01 MRas 2m1f110y good NHF

Worthahand

7-y-o ch g Nearly A Hand-Worth Matravers (National Trust)
R J Hodges M H Dare

Placings:*6-*0P00 **(4586)**
2001/02: 16^{0}G, 19^{P}S, 24^{0}G, 22^{0}G

	Starts	1st	2nd	3rd	Win & Pl
NH Flat	1	0	0	0	0
Hurdles	3	0	0	0	0
Career Total	**5**	**0**	**0**	**0**	**0**

Going: Sf: 0-1 GS: 0-0 Gd: 0-3 GF: - Fm: 0-0
Distance: 2m/2m3: 0-1 2m4-2m7: 0-2 3m+: 0-1
Track: LH: 0-0 RH: 0-4 Tight: 0-1 Gall: 0-0
Aids: Bl: 0-0 Vi: 0-0 Tstrap: 0-0
Best Rating: 96 4/01 Tntn 2m1f gd-fm NHF

Worthy Man

68f **55f**

5-y-o b g Homo Sapien-Marnworth (Funny Man)
Miss H C Knight Mrs W H Walter

Placings:*0* **(3784)**
2001/02: 16^{0}S

	Starts	1st	2nd	3rd	Win & Pl
NH Flat	1	0	0	0	
Career Total	**1**	**0**	**0**	**0**	

Going: Sf: 0-1 GS: 0-0 Gd: 0-0 GF: - Fm: 0-0
Distance: 2m/2m3: 0-1 2m4-2m7: 0-0 3m+: 0-0
Track: LH: 0-0 RH: 0-1 Tight: 0-0 Gall: 0-0
Aids: Bl: 0-0 Vi: 0-0 Tstrap: 0-0
Best Rating: 55 2/02 Asct 2m110y soft NHF

Wortley Boy

100(108h) **120**

8-y-o ch g Zambrano-Blue Empress (Blue Cashmere)
T R George Three Of A Kind Racing

Placings:*000/*460413-423 **(2554)**
2001/02: 20^{4}S, 22^{2}G, 24^{3}S

	Starts	1st	2nd	3rd	Win & Pl
Chases	3	0	1	1	3332
Career Total	**12**	**1**	**1**	**2**	**6304**

110	3/01	Wwck	2m	F(0-100)HHdl	HVY	£2170

Total win prize-money £2170

Going: Sf: 0-2 GS: 0-0 Gd: 0-1 GF: - Fm: 0-0
Distance: 2m/2m3: 0-0 2m4-2m7: 0-2 3m+: 0-1
Track: LH: 0-2 RH: 0-0 Tight: 0-2 Gall: 0-0
Aids: Bl: 0-0 Vi: 0-0 Tstrap: 0-0
Best Rating: 120 11/01 Hayd 2m6f good Ch

He could have done with even more cut in the ground when tried over fences in November 2001, but ran reasonable races nonetheless.

Wot About Me (IRE)

7-y-o b g Jolly Jake (NZ)-Time Please (Welsh Saint)
Ian Williams M R Parkes

Placings:*00*/F0-FPP (0780)
2001/02: 20^{F}G, 26^{P}GF, 20^{P}G

	Starts	1st	2nd	3rd	Win & Pl
Hurdles	3	0	0	0	
Career Total	**7**	**0**	**0**	**0**	

Going: Sf: 0-0 GS: 0-0 Gd: 0-2 GF: - Fm: 0-1
Distance: 2m/2m3: 0-0 2m4-2m7: 0-2 3m+: 0-1
Track: LH: 0-1 RH: 0-2 Tight: 0-0 Gall: 0-2
Aids: Bl: 0-0 Vi: 0-0 Tstrap: 0-0
Best Rating: 80 11/99 Hayd 2m good NHF

Wot No Cash

106 **94**

10-y-o gr g Ballacashtal (CAN)-Madame Non (My Swanee)
R C Harper (P W Hiatt 30/6) R C Harper

Placings:P5P/F5-P012005PP (4886)
2001/02: 19^{P}GS, 20^{0}GF, 18^{1}GF, 16^{2}GS, 16^{0}G, 16^{0}S, 16^{5}G, 20^{P}GF, 18^{P}GF

	Starts	1st	2nd	3rd	Win & Pl
Hurdles	1	0	0	0	0
Chases	8	1	1	0	3344
Career Total	**11**	**1**	**1**	**0**	**0044**
87 5/01 Font	2m2f	G(0-90)HCh		G-F	£2383

Total win prize-money £2384

Going: Sf: 0-1 GS: 0-2 Gd: 0-2 GF: - Fm: 1-4
Distance: **2m/2m3: 1-6** 2m4-2m7: 0-3 3m+: 0-0
Track: LH: 0-4 RH: 0-3 **Tight: 1-4** Gall: 0-0
Aids: Bl: 0-0 Vi: 0-0 Tstrap: 0-0
Best Rating: 94 6/01 NAbb 2m110y gd-sft Ch

Inconsistent chaser, who often pulls up. Won over two miles two on a sound surface in May 2001.

Wot No Gin

13-y-o b g Broadsword (USA)-Lawnswood Miss (Grey Mirage)
A J Wilson The Up And Running Partnership

Placings:*00*/663/FF50/331600/320154F/0/0425-P (0125)
2001/02: 24^{P}F

	Starts	1st	2nd	3rd	Win & Pl
Chases	1	0	0	0	
Career Total	**28**	**2**	**2**	**4**	**9925**
92 10/98 Winc	3m1f110y	F(0-100)HCh		G-F	£2700
96 5/97 Uttx	2m5f	E(0-100)HCh		GD	£2927

Total win prize-money £5629

Going: Sf: 0-0 GS: 0-0 Gd: 0-0 GF: - Fm: 0-1
Distance: 2m/2m3: 0-0 2m4-2m7: 0-0 3m+: 0-1
Track: LH: 0-0 RH: 0-1 Tight: 0-1 Gall: 0-0
Aids: Bl: 0-0 Vi: 0-0 Tstrap: 0-0
Best Rating: 103 12/96 Hrfd 2m3f gd-sft Ch

Wotan (IRE)

81 **53**

4-y-o ch g Wolfhound (USA)-Triple Tricks (IRE) (Royal Academy (USA))
R Curtis A J J Racing

Placings:P0 (2597)
2001/02: 16^{P}G, 18^{0}G

	Starts	1st	2nd	3rd	Win & Pl
Hurdles	2	0	0	0	
Career Total	**2**	**0**	**0**	**0**	

Going: Sf: 0-0 GS: 0-0 Gd: 0-2 GF: - Fm: 0-0
Distance: 2m/2m3: 0-2 2m4-2m7: 0-0 3m+: 0-0
Track: LH: 0-1 RH: 0-1 Tight: 0-1 Gall: 0-0
Aids: Bl: 0-0 Vi: 0-0 Tstrap: 0-0
Best Rating: 53 12/01 Font 2m2f110y good Hdl

Wrangel (FR)

101 **100**

8-y-o ch g Tropular-Swedish Princess (Manado)
B J Llewellyn Miss Emily Jane Jones

Placings:*0*/P62/4061320UF0/064210-34 (0375)
2001/02: 16^{3}F, 16^{4}GF

	Starts	1st	2nd	3rd	Win & Pl
Hurdles	2	0	0	1	340
Career Total	**22**	**2**	**3**	**2**	**8907**
100 10/00 Fknm	2m	F(0-105)HHdl		GD	£3331
100 10/99 Strf	2m110y	F(0-100)HHdl		G-S	£2495

Total win prize-money £5826

Going: Sf: 0-0 GS: 0-0 Gd: 0-0 GF: - Fm: 0-2
Distance: 2m/2m3: 0-2 2m4-2m7: 0-0 3m+: 0-0
Track: LH: 0-1 RH: 0-1 Tight: 0-1 Gall: 0-1
Aids: Bl: 0-0 Vi: 0-0 Tstrap: 0-0
Best Rating: 101 12/99 Donc 2m110y gd-fm Hdl

Wrekengale (IRE)

12-y-o br g Strong Gale-Wrekenogan (Tarqogan)
Neil King Mrs Jill McVay

Placings:*00*/06/600111/1P/35124P6/32P6330/6PP-32P (0584)
2001/02: 30^{3}GF, 31^{2}G, 28^{P}GF

	Starts	1st	2nd	3rd	Win & Pl
Chases	3	0	1	1	1329
Career Total	**32**	**5**	**3**	**5**	**27226**
112 7/98 Worc	2m7f110y	D(0-125)HCh		G-F	£3579
116 5/96 Uttx	3m2f	C(0-130)HCh		G-F	£4429
104 4/96 Asct	3m110y	C HCh		G-F	£7035
91 4/96 Hrfd	3m1f110y	F(0-100)HCh		G-F	£3403
99 3/96 Uttx	2m5f	F(0-100)HCh		GD	£2579

Total win prize-money £21026

Going: Sf: 0-0 GS: 0-0 Gd: 0-1 GF: - Fm: 0-2
Distance: 2m/2m3: 0-0 2m4-2m7: 0-0 3m+: 0-3
Track: LH: 0-1 RH: 0-2 Tight: 0-2 Gall: 0-1
Aids: Bl: 0-0 Vi: 0-0 Tstrap: 0-2
Best Rating: 116 5/96 Uttx 3m2f gd-fm Ch

Modest pointer/hunter chaser, suited by fast ground, has worn a tongue tie.

Wrens Island (IRE)

104 **112**

8-y-o br g Yashgan-Tipiton (Balboa)
R Dickin Wholebuild Ltd

Placings:P-P1162P5450 (4905)
2001/02: 17^{P}GS, 20^{1}GF, 16^{1}G, 21^{6}GF, 20^{2}G, 20^{P}G, 16^{5}G, 16^{4}S, 20^{5}GF, 17^{0}GF

	Starts	1st	2nd	3rd	Win & Pl
Chases	10	2	1	0	6087
Career Total	**11**	**2**	**1**	**0**	**6087**
112 5/01 Chel	2m110y	H Ch		GD	£3178
110 5/01 Strf	2m4f	H Ch		G-F	£1657

Total win prize-money £4836

Going: Sf: 0-1 GS: 0-1 Gd: 1-4 GF: - Fm: 1-4
Distance: 2m/2m3: 1-5 2m4-2m7: 1-5 3m+: 0-0
Track: **LH: 1-5** RH: 0-3 **Tight: 1-3** Gall: 0-3
Aids: Bl: 0-0 Vi: 0-0 Tstrap: 0-0
Best Rating: 112 10/01 Hntg 2m4f110y good Ch

Novice chaser. Stays two miles four furlongs and is effective on a sound surface.

Wychnor King (IRE)

(82h) (27h)

8-y-o b/br g Torus-Eva's Fancy (Distinctly (USA))
M Mullineaux (A Streeter 17/10) Frank Chadwick

Placings:*60*/0-04 (4641)
2001/02: 20^{0}G, 24^{4}G

	Starts	1st	2nd	3rd	Win & Pl
Hurdles	1	0	0	0	0
Chases	1	0	0	0	400
Career Total	**5**	**0**	**0**	**0**	**400**

Going: Sf: 0-0 GS: 0-0 Gd: 0-2 GF: - Fm: 0-0
Distance: 2m/2m3: 0-2 2m4-2m7: 0-1 3m+: 0-1
Track: LH: 0-1 RH: 0-1 Tight: 0-1 Gall: 0-0
Aids: Bl: 0-0 Vi: 0-0 Tstrap: 0-0
Best Rating: 80 2/00 Weth 2m soft NHF

Wychnor Princess (IRE)

93 **51**

7-y-o ch m Montelimar (USA)-Forty One (IRE) (Over The River (FR))
L R James C Raine

Placings:*0*/*00*0P-0U (3363)
2001/02: 16^{0}GF, 16^{U}GS

	Starts	1st	2nd	3rd	Win & Pl
Hurdles	2	0	0	0	
Career Total	**7**	**0**	**0**	**0**	

Going: Sf: 0-0 GS: 0-1 Gd: 0 0 GF: - Fm: 0-1
Distance: 2m/2m3: 0-2 2m4-2m7: 0-0 3m+: 0-0
Track: LH: 0-2 RH: 0-0 Tight: 0-2 Gall: 0-0
Aids: Bl: 0-0 Vi: 0-0 Tstrap: 0-0
Best Rating: 73 4/00 MRas 1m5f110y soft NHF

Wynbury Flyer

87 **93**

7-y-o ch g Risk Me (FR)-Woolcana (Some Hand)
C J Mann Mrs G P Seymour

Placings:45031443/43614FU1342/0543-F4F (2356)
2001/02: 20^{F}GS, 16^{4}GS, 16^{F}S

	Starts	1st	2nd	3rd	Win & Pl
Chases	3	0	0	0	0
Career Total	**26**	**3**	**1**	**5**	**15050**
119 2/00 Carl	2m	D Ch		HVY	£4173
119 12/99 Donc	2m3f110y	D Ch		G-S	£4261
93 1/99 Catt	2m	G Hdl		GD	£1646

Total win prize-money £10080

Going: Sf: 0-1 GS: 0-2 Gd: 0-0 GF: - Fm: 0-0
Distance: 2m/2m3: 0-2 2m4-2m7: 0-1 3m+: 0-0
Track: LH: 0-2 RH: 0-1 Tight: 0-1 Gall: 0-0
Aids: Bl: 0-0 Vi: 0-0 Tstrap: 0-0
Best Rating: 119 3/00 Kels 2m1f gd-sft Ch

Wyndham (IRE)

6-y-o b g Executive Perk-Bid For Fun (IRE) (Auction Ring (USA))
R J Smith S McConville

Placings:0 **(0506)**
2001/02: 16^{0}GF

	Starts	1st	2nd	3rd	Win & Pl
NH Flat	1	0	0	0	
Career Total	**1**	**0**	**0**	**0**	

Going: Sf: 0-0 GS: 0-0 Gd: 0-0 GF: - Fm: 0-1
Distance: 2m/2m3: 0-1 2m4-2m7: 0-0 3m+: 0-0
Track: LH: 0-0 RH: 0-1 Tight: 0-0 Gall: 0-1
Aids: Bl: 0-0 Vi: 0-0 Tstrap: 0-0
Best Rating:

Wynsey Helen (IRE)

79 **43**

6-y-o b m Presidium-Sindur (Rolfe (USA))
M Sheppard R K Arrowsmith

Placings:3/000P400-0P **(3702)**
2001/02: 16^{0}G, 19^{P}HY

	Starts	1st	2nd	3rd	Win & Pl
Hurdles	2	0	0	0	
Career Total	**10**	**0**	**0**	**1**	**214**

Going: Sf: 0-1 GS: 0-0 Gd: 0-1 GF: - Fm: 0-0
Distance: 2m/2m3: 0-1 2m4-2m7: 0-1 3m+: 0-0
Track: LH: 0-0 RH: 0-2 Tight: 0-0 Gall: 0-0
Aids: Bl: 0-0 Vi: 0-0 Tstrap: 0-0
Best Rating: 73 2/00 Ayr 2m heavy NHF

Wynyard Knight

102(75h) **119**

10-y-o b g Silly Prices-The White Lion (Flying Tyke)
Mrs M Reveley G S Brown

Placings:202/1341/111014/4052/333-353 **(4029)**
2001/02: 20^{3}G, 20^{5}GS, 20^{3}GS

	Starts	1st	2nd	3rd	Win & Pl
Chases	3	0	0	2	2538
Career Total	**23**	**6**	**3**	**6**	**27128**

133	4/99	Weth	2m4f110y	D Ch	GD	£3925
146	1/99	Donc	2m110y	D Ch	GD	£4561
132	12/98	Ayr	2m	D Ch	G-S	£3610
113	5/98	Weth	2m	D(0-120)HHdl	GD	£3020
107	3/98	Newc	2m	E Hdl	GD	£2515
110	11/97	Weth	2m	H NHF	GD	£1360

Total win prize-money £18993

Going: Sf: 0-0 GS: 0-2 Gd: 0-1 GF: - Fm: 0-0
Distance: 2m/2m3: 0-0 2m4-2m7: 0-3 3m+: 0-0
Track: LH: 0-1 RH: 0-2 Tight: 0-0 Gall: 0-1
Aids: Bl: 0-0 Vi: 0-0 Tstrap: 0-0
Best Rating: 146 1/99 Donc 2m110y good Ch

A multiple winner over hurdles and in novice chases, he has been well held in handicap company over both hurdles and fences since his last win in 1999. Suited by good ground.

Xaipete (IRE)

(107h) (119h)**132**

10-y-o b g Jolly Jake (NZ)-Rolfete (USA) (Tom Rolfe)
N B Mason N B Mason

Placings:000513/5/02341253/43622114211352U/112 2320152244U5301/1641133434045300 3F-3262F **(1917)**
2001/02: 16^{3}GF, 17^{2}G, 16^{6}GF, 16^{2}G, 16^{F}G

	Starts	1st	2nd	3rd	Win & Pl
Hurdles	4	0	2	1	4752
Chases	1	0	0	0	0
Career Total	**71**	**13**	**13**	**13**	**79123**

120	8/00	Ctml	2m1f110y	D(0-125)HHdl	GD	£3581
144	8/00	Bang	2m4f110y	D(0-125)HCh	GD	£5642
123	5/00	Kels	2m110y	D(0-125)HHdl	GD	£4706
112	4/00	Kels	2m110y	D(0-125)HHdl	SFT	£2941
137	8/99	Bang	2m4f110y	D(0-125)HCh	GD	£4810
140	5/99	Aint	2m	D(0-125)HCh	G-S	£4485
133	5/99	Weth	2m	C(0-135)HCh	G-F	£5572
119	1/99	Muss	2m	D(0-125)HCh	G-S	£3597
115	12/98	Sedg	2m110y	E(0-110)HCh	G-S	£3488
116	11/98	Sedg	2m110y	E(0-110)HCh	G-S	£3397
105	10/98	Fknm	2m	F(0-105)HHdl	G-S	£3326
95	11/97	Sedg	2m110y	F(0-100)HCh	GD	£2784
73	3/96	Sedg	2m1f	E Hdl	G-F	£2372

Total win prize-money £50707

Going: Sf: 0-0 GS: 0-0 Gd: 0-3 GF: - Fm: 0-2
Distance: 2m/2m3: 0-5 2m4-2m7: 0-0 3m+: 0-0
Track: LH: 0-5 RH: 0-0 Tight: 0-3 Gall: 0-0
Aids: Bl: 0-0 Vi: 0-0 Tstrap: 0-0
Best Rating: 144 9/00 Worc 2m gd-fm Ch

A fair hurdler/chaser, he keeps a hectic schedule and holds his form well. Effective between two and two and a half miles, he is thoroughly genuine and will pay his way again at a minor level.

Xpres Lady (IRE)

94 **97**

7-y-o b m Commanche Run-Chalk It Down (Cheval)
J Mackie Charterhouse Holdings Plc

Placings:1-33266 **(3994)**
2001/02: 16^{3}S, 17^{3}G, 20^{2}S, 24^{6}HY, 20^{6}S

	Starts	1st	2nd	3rd	Win & Pl
NH Flat	2	0	0	2	479
Hurdles	3	0	1	0	1120
Career Total	**6**	**1**	**1**	**2**	**3363**

95	4/01	MRas	2m1f110y	H NHF	HVY	£1764

Total win prize-money £1764

Going: Sf: 0-4 GS: 0-0 Gd: 0-1 GF: - Fm: 0-0
Distance: 2m/2m3: 0-2 2m4-2m7: 0-2 3m+: 0-1
Track: LH: 0-4 RH: 0-1 Tight: 0-0 Gall: 0-1
Aids: Bl: 0-0 Vi: 0-0 Tstrap: 0-0
Best Rating: 103 11/01 Hrfd 2m1f good NHF

Fair bumper performer in the mud. Has shown ability over hurdles.

Y-Dug (IRE)

7-y-o b g Wakashan-Jerpoint Sparkle (Roselier (FR))
B J Llewellyn Miss Jo Fowler

Placings:0U **(0674)**
2001/02: 16^{0}GF, 16^{U}GF

	Starts	1st	2nd	3rd	Win & Pl
NH Flat	1	0	0	0	0
Hurdles	1	0	0	0	0
Career Total	**2**	**0**	**0**	**0**	

Going: Sf: 0-0 GS: 0-0 Gd: 0-0 GF: - Fm: 0-2
Distance: 2m/2m3: 0-2 2m4-2m7: 0-0 3m+: 0-0
Track: LH: 0-1 RH: 0-1 Tight: 0-0 Gall: 0-1
Aids: Bl: 0-0 Vi: 0-0 Tstrap: 0-0
Best Rating: 57 5/01 Hntg 2m110y gd-fm NHF

Yafa

86 **71**

6-y-o ch g Elmaamul (USA)-Mousaiha (USA) (Shadeed (USA))
Miss M Bragg Friends Of Rock Park

Placings:06 **(2716)**
2001/02: 17^{0}GF, 19^{6}G

	Starts	1st	2nd	3rd	Win & Pl
Hurdles	2	0	0	0	0
Career Total	**2**	**0**	**0**	**0**	**0**

Going: Sf: 0-0 GS: 0-0 Gd: 0-1 GF: - Fm: 0-1
Distance: 2m/2m3: 0-1 2m4-2m7: 0-1 3m+: 0-0
Track: LH: 0-0 RH: 0-2 Tight: 0-0 Gall: 0-0
Aids: Bl: 0-0 Vi: 0-0 Tstrap: 0-0
Best Rating: 71 11/01 Extr 2m1f gd-fm Hdl

Yaheska (IRE)

93 **84**

5-y-o b m Prince Of Birds (USA)-How Ya Been (IRE) (Last Tycoon)
J M Bradley N Savage

Placings:10F0P **(1996)**
2001/02: 17^{1}GF, 18^{0}GF, 17^{F}S, 16^{0}S, 17^{P}S

	Starts	1st	2nd	3rd	Win & Pl
Hurdles	5	1	0	0	1960
Career Total	**5**	**1**	**0**	**0**	**1960**

84	9/01	Hrfd	2m1f	G Hdl	G-F	£1960

Total win prize-money £1960

Going: Sf: 0-3 GS: 0-0 Gd: 0-0 GF: - Fm: 1-2
Distance: **2m/2m3: 1-5** 2m4-2m7: 0-0 3m+: 0-0
Track: LH: 0-3 **RH: 1-2** Tight: 0-4 Gall: 0-0
Aids: Bl: 0-0 Vi: 0-0 Tstrap: 0-0
Best Rating: 84 9/01 Hrfd 2m1f gd-fm Hdl

Yakareem (IRE)

99(108h) (101h)**103**

6-y-o b g Rainbows For Life (CAN)-Brandywell (Skyliner)
D G Bridgwater Terry & Sarah Amos

Placings:0-2120050 **(3380)**
2001/02: 16^{2}GF, 16^{1}GF, 17^{2}G, 17^{0}G, 16^{0}GS, 17^{5}GS, 16^{0}GS

	Starts	1st	2nd	3rd	Win & Pl
Hurdles	7	1	2	0	3731
Career Total	**8**	**1**	**2**	**0**	**3731**

101	8/01	Hntg	2m110y	F Hdl	G-F	£2128

Total win prize-money £2128

Going: Sf: 0-0 GS: 0-3 Gd: 0-2 GF: - Fm: 1-2
Distance: **2m/2m3: 1-7** 2m4-2m7: 0-0 3m+: 0-0
Track: LH: 0-3 **RH: 1-4** Tight: 0-3 **Gall: 1-1**
Aids: Bl: 0-0 Vi: 0-0 **Tstrap: 1-6**
Best Rating: 101 9/01 Sedg 2m1f good Hdl

Group Three placed on the Flat, he improved on his hurdles debut given fast ground. A winner at Huntingdon in August 2001, his limitations have been exposed since then.

Yancy Tucker

7-y-o b g Broadsword (USA)-Mazza (Mazilier (USA))
H M Kavanagh Mrs S Kavanagh

Placings:0P-P **(0246)**
2001/02: 21^{P}GF

	Starts	1st	2nd	3rd	Win & Pl
Hurdles	1	0	0	0	
Career Total	**3**	**0**	**0**	**0**	

Going: Sf: 0-0 GS: 0-0 Gd: 0-0 GF: - Fm: 0-1
Distance: 2m/2m3: 0-0 2m4-2m7: 0-1 3m+: 0-0
Track: LH: 0-0 RH: 0-0 Tight: 0-0 Gall: 0-0
Aids: Bl: 0-0 Vi: 0-0 Tstrap: 0-0
Best Rating: 41 10/00 Gway 2m heavy Hdl

Yankee Jamie (IRE)

106 **102**

8-y-o b g Strong Gale-Sparkling Opera (Orchestra)
L Lungo R J Gilbert

Placings:6660/P11 **(2467)**
2001/02: 22PGS, 221GS, 221GS

	Starts	1st	2nd	3rd	Win & Pl
Hurdles	3	2	0	0	6090
Career Total	**7**	**2**	**0**	**0**	**6090**

102	12/01	Kels	2m6f110y	E(0-105)HHdl	G-S	£3080
84	11/01	Kels	2m6f110y	F(0-100)HHdl	G-S	£3010

Total win prize-money £6090

Going: Sf: 0-0 GS: 2-3 Gd: 0-0 GF: - Fm: 0-0
Distance: 2m/2m3: 0-0 **2m4-2m7: 2-3** 3m+: 0-0
Track: **LH: 2-3** RH: 0-0 **Tight: 2-3** Gall: 0-0
Aids: Bl: 0-0 Vi: 0-0 Tstrap: 0-0
Best Rating: 102 12/01 Kels 2m6f110y gd-sft Hdl

Difficult to train, he was beginning to look disappointing over hurdles, but was well backed before winning a modest event at Kelso in November. Followed up at the same track. Stays well.

Yankie Lord (IRE)

103 **110**

10-y-o b g Lord Americo-Coolstutt (Over The River (FR))
Mrs D Thomson The Good To Soft Firm

Placings:12/P1212/P2301/55FFP-0PFPU5431 (3914)
2001/02: 250G, 25PGS, 22FG, 20PGS, 24UGS, 245GF, 204G, 203S, 201GS

	Starts	1st	2nd	3rd	Win & Pl
Chases	9	1	0	1	6619
Career Total	**26**	**5**	**4**	**2**	**32695**

110	2/02	Muss	2m4f	D(0-115)HCh	G-S	£5694
141	4/00	Hayd	3m	D(0-125)HCh	GD	£7572
124	3/99	Fknm	2m5f110y	D(0-120)HCh	GD	£4281
136	1/99	Hntg	2m4f110y	F(0-105)HCh	SFT	£2600
96	2/97	Naas	2m	Ch	SFT	£3051

Total win prize-money £23201

Going: Sf: 0-1 GS: 1-4 Gd: 0-3 GF: - Fm: 0-1
Distance: 2m/2m3: 0-0 **2m4-2m7: 1-5** 3m+: 0-4
Track: LH: 0-5 **RH: 1-4 Tight: 1-7** Gall: 0-1
Aids: Bl: 0-0 Vi: 0-0 Tstrap: 0-0
Best Rating: 141 4/00 Hayd 3m good Ch

Taught to jump by the top eventer Ginny Elliot, he won at Haydock in April 2000, but was very disappointing until winning at a long price at Musselburgh in February 2002. Probably best when able to dictate over two and a half miles, and looks best suited by a sound surface.

Yann's (FR)

102 **125**

6-y-o b g Hellios (USA)-Listen Gyp (USA) (Advocator)
R T Phillips Darren Bloom & Matthew Miller

Placings:0/1103-206S **(4893)**
2001/02: 182S, 210GS, 226G, 20SG

	Starts	1st	2nd	3rd	Win & Pl
Hurdles	4	0	1	0	1264
Career Total	**9**	**2**	**1**	**1**	**7277**

125	1/01	Ludl	2m	E(0-105)HHdl	SFT	£3041
109	11/00	Wwck	2m	E Hdl	SFT	£2119

Total win prize-money £5162

Going: Sf: 0-1 GS: 0-1 Gd: 0-2 GF: - Fm: 0-0
Distance: 2m/2m3: 0-1 2m4-2m7: 0-3 3m+: 0-0
Track: LH: 0-2 RH: 0-1 Tight: 0-1 Gall: 0-1
Aids: Bl: 0-0 Vi: 0-0 Tstrap: 0-0
Best Rating: 125 1/02 Font 2m2f110y soft Hdl

Formerly trained in France, he won his first two starts over here at Warwick and Ludlow before being found out in better company. Fair reappearance at Fontwell in January 2002 after nearly a year off . Needs soft ground and has given the impression that he should stay further than two miles.

Yanus

96 **101**

4-y-o b g Inchinor-Birsay (Bustino)
J S Goldie M Wassall

Placings:25205 **(4840)**
2001/02: 162GS, 165GS, 162S, 160S, 165G

	Starts	1st	2nd	3rd	Win & Pl
Hurdles	5	0	2	0	1711
Career Total	**5**	**0**	**2**	**0**	**1711**

Going: Sf: 0-2 GS: 0-2 Gd: 0-1 GF: - Fm: 0-0
Distance: 2m/2m3: 0-5 2m4-2m7: 0-0 3m+: 0-0
Track: LH: 0-5 RH: 0-0 Tight: 0-0 Gall: 0-3
Aids: Bl: 0-0 Vi: 0-0 Tstrap: 0-0
Best Rating: 101 4/02 Ayr 2m good Hdl

Novice hurdler, stays two and a half miles and acts on any ground.

Yasheva (IRE)

65 **16**

7-y-o b m Yashgan-Eva's Fancy (Distinctly (USA))
O Brennan O Brennan

Placings:0406/0 **(0475)**
2001/02: 170G

	Starts	1st	2nd	3rd	Win & Pl
Hurdles	1	0	0	0	
Career Total	**5**	**0**	**0**	**0**	**0**

Going: Sf: 0-0 GS: 0-0 Gd: 0-1 GF: - Fm: 0-0
Distance: 2m/2m3: 0-1 2m4-2m7: 0-0 3m+: 0-0
Track: LH: 0-0 RH: 0-1 Tight: 0-1 Gall: 0-0
Aids: Bl: 0-0 Vi: 0-0 Tstrap: 0-0
Best Rating: 92 3/00 MRas 1m5f110y gd-fm NHF

Yashwell (IRE)

8-y-o b g Yashgan-Shesadream (Green Shoon)
J M Turner J M Turner

Placings:P **(0322)**
2001/02: 21PG

	Starts	1st	2nd	3rd	Win & Pl
Chases	1	0	0	0	
Career Total	**1**	**0**	**0**	**0**	

Going: Sf: 0-0 GS: 0-0 Gd: 0-1 GF: - Fm: 0-0
Distance: 2m/2m3: 0-0 2m4-2m7: 0-1 3m+: 0-0
Track: LH: 0-0 RH: 0-1 Tight: 0-1 Gall: 0-0
Aids: Bl: 0-0 Vi: 0-0 Tstrap: 0-0
Best Rating:

Yaspleezdo (IRE)

75 **57**

8-y-o ch g Yashgan-By All Means (Pitpan)
G Brown Mel Davies

Placings:0P **(4405)**
2001/02: 210S, 17PS

	Starts	1st	2nd	3rd	Win & Pl
Chases	2	0	0	0	
Career Total	**2**	**0**	**0**	**0**	

Going: Sf: 0-2 GS: 0-0 Gd: 0-0 GF: - Fm: 0-0
Distance: 2m/2m3: 0-1 2m4-2m7: 0-1 3m+: 0-0
Track: LH: 0-2 RH: 0-0 Tight: 0-2 Gall: 0-0
Aids: Bl: 0-0 Vi: 0-0 Tstrap: 0-0
Best Rating:

Well held in novice event on chasing debut.

Yazain (IRE)

6-y-o b g Pips Pride-Trust Sally (Sallust)
P S McEntee (G Prodromou 30/7) Racing Thoroughbreds Plc

Placings:P **(1755)**
2001/02: 16PGS

	Starts	1st	2nd	3rd	Win & Pl
Hurdles	1	0	0	0	
Career Total	**1**	**0**	**0**	**0**	

Going: Sf: 0-0 GS: 0-1 Gd: 0-0 GF: - Fm: 0-0
Distance: 2m/2m3: 0-1 2m4-2m7: 0-0 3m+: 0-0
Track: LH: 0-1 RH: 0-0 Tight: 0-1 Gall: 0-0
Aids: Bl: 0-0 Vi: 0-0 Tstrap: 0-0
Best Rating:

Yelapa Prince (IRE)

102 **65**

11-y-o b g Buckskin (FR)-Ballyoran Princess (The Parson)
F Kirby Fred Kirby

Placings:0/3041600/623FF05P/FP0F2/6P06FP0P/06-02200 **(4578)**
2001/02: 200G, 192S, 172S, 210S, 230G

	Starts	1st	2nd	3rd	Win & Pl
Hurdles	5	0	2	0	1100
Career Total	**36**	**1**	**4**	**2**	**8084**

113	11/96	Naas	2m4f	Hdl	Y-S	£4237

Total win prize-money £4237

Going: Sf: 0-3 GS: 0-0 Gd: 0-2 GF: - Fm: 0-0
Distance: 2m/2m3: 0-2 2m4-2m7: 0-3 3m+: 0-0
Track: LH: 0-4 RH: 0-1 Tight: 0-4 Gall: 0-0
Aids: Bl: 0-0 Vi: 0-0 Tstrap: 0-0
Best Rating: 113 11/96 Naas 2m4f yld-sft Hdl

Acts on soft ground and is effective from two to two miles-four, usually runs in selling company.

Yeoman's Point (IRE)

114 **133**

6-y-o b g Sadler's Wells (USA)-Truly Bound (USA) (In

Reality)
C Roche J P McManus

Placings:325/1120F **(4667)**
2001/02: 17^{1}G, 18^{1}Y, 16^{2}Y, 21^{0}GS, 20^{F}G

	Starts	1st	2nd	3rd	Win & Pl
Hurdles	5	2	1	0	19206
Career Total	**8**	**2**	**2**	**1**	**24893**

123	12/01	Fair	2m2f	Hdl	YLD	£7233
118	10/01	Gowr	2m1f	Hdl	GD	£5842

Total win prize-money £13077

Going: Sf: 0-0 GS: 0-1 Gd: 1-2 GF: - Fm: 0-0
Distance: **2m/2m3: 2-3** 2m4-2m7: 0-2 3m+: 0-0
Track: LH: 0-3 **RH: 1-1** Tight: 0-1 Gall: 0-1
Aids: Bl: 0-0 Vi: 0-0 Tstrap: 0-0
Best Rating: 133 12/01 Leop 2m yield Hdl

A good performer on the Flat, he has shown useful form in novice hurdles. He acts on most types of ground and is effective at around two miles.

York Rite (AUS)

6-y-o ch g Grand Lodge (USA)-Amazaan (NZ) (Zamazaan (FR))
S G Griffiths S G Griffiths

Placings:P00 **(3369)**
2001/02: 17^{P}GS, 16^{0}GS, 20^{0}S

	Starts	1st	2nd	3rd	Win & Pl
Hurdles	3	0	0	0	
Career Total	**3**	**0**	**0**	**0**	

Going: Sf: 0-1 GS: 0-2 Gd: 0-0 GF: - Fm: 0-0
Distance: 2m/2m3: 0-2 2m4-2m7: 0-1 3m+: 0-0
Track: LH: 0-2 RH: 0-1 Tight: 0-1 Gall: 0-0
Aids: Bl: 0-0 Vi: 0-0 Tstrap: 0-0
Best Rating:

Yorkshire Edition (IRE)

110 **114**

9-y-o br g Strong Gale-Rent A Card (Raise You Ten)
P F Nicholls Sir Robert Ogden

Placings:541P10/**114UP/4FP-3** **(4918)**
2001/02: 28^{3}GF

	Starts	1st	2nd	3rd	Win & Pl
Chases	1	0	0	1	2170
Career Total	**15**	**4**	**0**	**1**	**18642**

137	11/99	Winc	3m1f110y	E(0-105)HCh	GD	£7035
128	10/99	Winc	3m1f110y	D Ch	G-F	£3798
91	4/99	Winc	2m6f	E Hdl	GD	£2738
102	12/98	Winc	2m6f	E Hdl	G-S	£2066

Total win prize-money £15638

Going: Sf: 0-0 GS: 0-0 Gd: 0-0 GF: - Fm: 0-1
Distance: 2m/2m3: 0-0 2m4-2m7: 0-0 3m+: 0-1
Track: LH: 0-1 RH: 0-0 Tight: 0-1 Gall: 0-0
Aids: Bl: 0-0 Vi: 0-0 Tstrap: 0-0
Best Rating: 137 11/99 Winc 3m1f110y good Ch

Staying handicap chaser, third after a year off over three and a half miles at Sedgefield in April 2002. Appreciated return to a slightly shorter trip when successful at Wincanton next time. Acts on fast ground.

You Make Me Laugh (IRE)

77 **61**

10-y-o ch g Doubletour (USA)-Bold Sea Reef (Main Reef)
G Prodromou L Cohen

Placings:4004/20015*0*/4514000/FP6/5PP-P0 **(0791)**
2001/02: 21^{P}GF, 22^{0}GF

	Starts	1st	2nd	3rd	Win & Pl
Chases	2	0	0	0	
Career Total	**25**	**2**	**1**	**0**	**4873**

101	7/98	Wxfd	2m	Hdl	GD	£2241
98	10/97	DRoy	2m	NHF	G-F	£1695

Total win prize-money £3938

Going: Sf: 0-0 GS: 0-0 Gd: 0-0 GF: - Fm: 0-2
Distance: 2m/2m3: 0-0 2m4-2m7: 0-2 3m+: 0-0
Track: LH: 0-1 RH: 0-1 Tight: 0-2 Gall: 0-0
Aids: Bl: 0-0 Vi: 0-0 Tstrap: 0-1
Best Rating: 105 8/98 Cork 2m firm Hdl

You Never Learn

8-y-o b g Aydimour-Briglen (Swing Easy (USA))
R Curtis Dingley Dell Racing Ltd

Placings:*00*/5/P6R **(2645)**
2001/02: 21^{P}S, 21^{6}GS, 24^{R}GS

	Starts	1st	2nd	3rd	Win & Pl
Hurdles	2	0	0	0	0
Chases	1	0	0	0	0
Career Total	**6**	**0**	**0**	**0**	**0**

Going: Sf: 0-1 GS: 0-2 Gd: 0-0 GF: - Fm: 0-0
Distance: 2m/2m3: 0-0 2m4-2m7: 0-2 3m+: 0-1
Track: LH: 0-2 RH: 0-1 Tight: 0-2 Gall: 0-1
Aids: Bl: 0-0 Vi: 0-0 Tstrap: 0-0
Best Rating: 81 3/99 Ludl 2m good NHF

You're Agoodun

116 **156**

10-y-o ch g Derrylin-Jennie Pat (Rymer)
M C Pipe J S Lammiman

Placings:*00000*/2R53211/104F2003/**114UU2B0-143540P** **(4913)**
2001/02: 24^{1}G, 27^{4}G, 24^{3}G, 29^{5}GS, 24^{4}GS, 36^{0}G, 29^{P}G

	Starts	1st	2nd	3rd	Win & Pl
Chases	7	1	0	1	22729
Career Total	**35**	**6**	**4**	**3**	**52251**

156	11/01	Asct	3m110y	B(0-150)HCh	GD	£9854
142	10/00	Hrfd	3m1f110y	E Ch	GD	£3493
142	9/00	Hrfd	3m1f110y	D Ch	G-S	£3701
142	10/99	Towc	3m	C(0-135)HHdl	GD	£4840
138	4/99	Chel	3m	D(0-120)HHdl	GD	£5425
130	12/98	Hayd	2m7f110y	D(0-110)HHdl	SFT	£2997

Total win prize-money £30311

Going: Sf: 0-0 GS: 0-2 Gd: 1-5 GF: - Fm: 0-0
Distance: 2m/2m3: 0-0 2m4-2m7: 0-0 **3m+: 1-7**
Track: LH: 0-4 **RH: 1-3** Tight: 0-1 Gall: 0-2
Aids: Bl: 0-0 **Vi: 1-7** Tstrap: 0-0
Best Rating: 156 3/02 Chel 3m110y gd-sft Ch

He won his first two starts over fences in the autumn of 2000, but struggled in better company. Made a successful return at Ascot in November 2001 and ran well in decent company afterwards. Stays three miles plus, suited by good ground or softer.

You're Special (USA)

106 **122**

5-y-o b g Northern Flagship (USA)-Pillow Mint (USA) (Stagedoor Johnny)
P C Haslam Les Buckley

Placings:123P14 **(4817)**
2001/02: 20^{1}G, 21^{2}GS, 24^{3}S, 24^{P}HY, 20^{1}G, 24^{4}GF

	Starts	1st	2nd	3rd	Win & Pl
Hurdles	6	2	1	1	8191
Career Total	**6**	**2**	**1**	**1**	**8191**

110	4/02	Weth	2m4f110y	E Hdl	GD	£3143
122	11/01	Newc	2m4f	E Hdl	GD	£2625

Total win prize-money £5768

Going: Sf: 0-2 GS: 0-1 Gd: 2-2 GF: - Fm: 0-1
Distance: 2m/2m3: 0-0 **2m4-2m7: 2-3** 3m+: 0-3
Track: **LH: 2-4** RH: 0-1 Tight: 0-1 **Gall: 1-2**
Aids: Bl: 0-0 Vi: 0-0 Tstrap: 0-1
Best Rating: 122 11/01 MRas 2m5f110y gd-sft Hdl

Won over two and a half miles at Newcastle in good ground on his hurdling debut in November 2001 and has continued to run well since then except when tried on very heavy ground.

You're The Man (IRE)

61f

5-y-o b g Lapierre-Another Advantage (IRE) (Roselier (FR))
M Todhunter A Slack

Placings:*0* **(4436)**
2001/02: 16^{0}HY

	Starts	1st	2nd	3rd	Win & Pl
NH Flat	1	0	0	0	
Career Total	**1**	**0**	**0**	**0**	

Going: Sf: 0-1 GS: 0-0 Gd: 0-0 GF: - Fm: 0-0
Distance: 2m/2m3: 0-1 2m4-2m7: 0-0 3m+: 0-0
Track: LH: 0-0 RH: 0-0 Tight: 0-0 Gall: 0-0
Aids: Bl: 0-0 Vi: 0-0 Tstrap: 0-0
Best Rating: 61 3/02 Newc 2m heavy NHF

Youaskhim

87f **76f**

6-y-o b g Primitive Rising (USA)-Hardwick Sun (Dieu Soleil)
J M Jefferson J M Jefferson

Placings:*B-53* **(1025)**
2001/02: 16^{5}GS, 17^{3}GF

	Starts	1st	2nd	3rd	Win & Pl
NH Flat	2	0	0	1	220
Career Total	**3**	**0**	**0**	**1**	**220**

Going: Sf: 0-0 GS: 0-1 Gd: 0-0 GF: - Fm: 0-1
Distance: 2m/2m3: 0-2 2m4-2m7: 0-0 3m+: 0-0
Track: LH: 0-2 RH: 0-0 Tight: 0-1 Gall: 0-0
Aids: Bl: 0-0 Vi: 0-0 Tstrap: 0-0
Best Rating: 76 7/01 Sedg 2m1f gd-fm NHF

Youbetterbelieveit (IRE)

102 (74h)**114**

13-y-o ch g The Parson-Emperors Twinkle (King

Emperor (USA))
Mrs D Thomson The Kelso Connection

Placings:2301/2/**P253/11113F5/4541455453/0PPP05-43P603P** **(1198)**
2001/02: 16^{4}GF, 16^{3}GF, 24^{P}GF, 20^{6}GF, 23^{0}G, 24^{3}G, 20^{P}G

	Starts	1st	2nd	3rd	Win & Pl
Chases	7	0	0	2	1499
Career Total	**39**	**6**	**3**	**6**	**34462**

124	11/99	Ayr	2m	C(0-130)HCh	GD	£5819
133	9/98	Worc	2m	C Ch	GD	£5225
133	9/98	Strf	2m1f110y	D(0-125)HCh	GD	£3470
124	8/98	Strf	2m1f110y	D(0-120)HCh	G-F	£3548
130	8/98	Worc	2m	E Ch	G-F	£3163
110	4/96	Worc	2m	E Hdl	G-F	£3440

Total win prize-money £24665

Going: Sf: 0-0 GS: 0-0 Gd: 0-3 GF: - Fm: 0-4
Distance: 2m/2m3: 0-2 2m4-2m7: 0-2 3m+: 0-3
Track: LH: 0-4 RH: 0-3 Tight: 0-2 Gall: 0-0
Aids: Bl: 0-0 Vi: 0-0 Tstrap: 0-0
Best Rating: 133 9/98 Worc 2m good Ch

Youlneverwalkalone (IRE)

119(117h) (154h)**157**
8-y-o b g Montelimar (USA)-In My Time (Levmoss)
C Roche J P McManus

Placings:1/1113/21PF1-3221320 **(4189)**
2001/02: 16^{3}S, 16^{2}Y, 17^{2}Y, 17^{1}YS, 21^{3}HY, 20^{2}HY, 16^{0}GS

	Starts	1st	2nd	3rd	Win & Pl
Hurdles	1	0	0	1	2540
Chases	6	1	3	1	31220
Career Total	**17**	**7**	**4**	**3**	**131725**

133	1/02	Navn	2m1f	Ch	Y-S	£6773
163	2/01	Gowr	2m	Hdl	HVY	£18346
169	12/00	Fair	2m4f	Hdl	Y-S	£23400
156	2/00	Leop	2m2f	Hdl	YLD	£15600
146	12/99	Leop	2m	Hdl	SH	£14508
123	11/99	Naas	2m4f	Hdl	Y-S	£4004
106	12/98	Leop	2m	NHF	HVY	£4184

Total win prize-money £86818

Going: Sf: 0-3 GS: 0-1 Gd: 0-0 GF: - Fm: 0-0
Distance: **2m/2m3: 1-5** 2m4-2m7: 0-2 3m+: 0-0
Track: **LH: 1-4** RH: 0-1 Tight: 0-0 Gall: 0-1
Aids: Bl: 0-0 Vi: 0-0 Tstrap: 0-0
Best Rating: 169 12/00 Fair 2m4f yld-sft Hdl

A top-class novice in the 1999/2000, winning three times and finishing third in the Supreme Novices', he went through a sticky patch in the middle of the 2000/2001 campaign, but still won twice against top-class rivals. Sent novice chasing last term, he won at Navan in January. Held since, including in the Arkle at Cheltenham in March. He travels well in his races and is at his best around two miles on soft ground.

Youmeandhim (IRE)

60 **24**
10-y-o b g Balinger-November Bloom (Camden Town)
Miss D Cole R Rawle

Placings:00/00 **(0596)**
2001/02: 22^{0}GF, 17^{0}G

	Starts	1st	2nd	3rd	Win & Pl
Hurdles	2	0	0	0	
Career Total	**4**	**0**	**0**	**0**	

Going: Sf: 0-0 GS: 0-0 Gd: 0-1 GF: - Fm: 0-1
Distance: 2m/2m3: 0-1 2m4-2m7: 0-1 3m+: 0-0
Track: LH: 0-2 RH: 0-0 Tight: 0-2 Gall: 0-0
Aids: Bl: 0-1 Vi: 0-0 Tstrap: 0-0
Best Rating: 25 6/99 Cork 2m1f gd-fm Hdl

Young American (IRE)

114 **128**
6-y-o br h Hamas (IRE)-Banana Peel (Green Dancer (USA))
J J O'Neill (C Roche 12/1) J P McManus

Placings:51402/0402-06P03031 **(4844)**
2001/02: 24^{0}G, 24^{6}Y, 20^{P}YS, 20^{0}S, 21^{3}GS, 16^{0}GS, 16^{3}G, 24^{1}G

	Starts	1st	2nd	3rd	Win & Pl
Hurdles	8	1	0	2	7158
Career Total	**17**	**2**	**2**	**2**	**15034**

123	4/02	Bang	3m	D(0-120)HHdl	GD	£5687
116	12/99	Leop	2m	Hdl	SH	£4620

Total win prize-money £10309

Going: Sf: 0-1 GS: 0-2 Gd: 1-3 GF: - Fm: 0-0
Distance: 2m/2m3: 0-2 2m4-2m7: 0-3 **3m+: 1-3**
Track: **LH: 1-5** RH: 0-2 **Tight: 1-2** Gall: 0-1
Aids: Bl: 0-1 Vi: 0-0 Tstrap: 0-0
Best Rating: 129 11/00 Naas 2m sft-hvy Hdl

Showed useful form as a juvenile hurdler when trained in Ireland, but rather lost his way. Has joined Jonjo O'Neill and is gradually slipping down the handicap. Appreciated the step up to three miles when regaining the winning thread at Bangor in April 2002.

Young Annie

66 **24**
4-y-o b f Young Ern-Snugfit Annie (Midyan (USA))
M J Ryan Mrs A M Byrne

Placings:0 **(1956)**
2001/02: 16^{0}G

	Starts	1st	2nd	3rd	Win & Pl
Hurdles	1	0	0	0	
Career Total	**1**	**0**	**0**	**0**	

Going: Sf: 0-0 GS: 0-0 Gd: 0-1 GF: - Fm: 0-0
Distance: 2m/2m3: 0-1 2m4-2m7: 0-0 3m+: 0-0
Track: LH: 0-1 RH: 0-0 Tight: 0-0 Gall: 0-0
Aids: Bl: 0-0 Vi: 0-0 Tstrap: 0-0
Best Rating: 24 11/01 Wwck 2m good Hdl

Young Archie (IRE)

9-y-o b g Yashgan-Fatal Hesitation (Torus)
I McMath (Miss Venetia Williams 20/1) Mrs A J McMath

Placings:40/053-0 **(4525)**
2001/02: 26^{0}GS

	Starts	1st	2nd	3rd	Win & Pl
Chases	1	0	0	0	
Career Total	**6**	**0**	**0**	**1**	**332**

Going: Sf: 0-0 GS: 0-1 Gd: 0-0 GF: - Fm: 0-0
Distance: 2m/2m3: 0-0 2m4-2m7: 0-0 3m+: 0-1
Track: LH: 0-0 RH: 0-1 Tight: 0-0 Gall: 0-0
Aids: Bl: 0-0 Vi: 0-0 Tstrap: 0-0
Best Rating: 85 2/01 Tntn 2m1f heavy Hdl

Young Buck (IRE)

104(97c) (58c)**115**
8-y-o ch g Glacial Storm (USA)-Lady Buck (Pollerton)
T P McGovern (Noel Meade 6/5) Anthony O'Gorman

Placings:12/21360/1PP0-06006 **(2334)**
2001/02: 22^{0}G, 20^{6}G, 18^{0}GS, 21^{0}S, 16^{6}G

	Starts	1st	2nd	3rd	Win & Pl
Hurdles	5	0	0	0	0
Career Total	**16**	**3**	**2**	**1**	**16680**

119	11/00	DRoy	2m	Hdl	Y-S	£7800
120	11/99	Navn	2m	Hdl	Y-S	£4004
100	10/98	Fair	2m	NHF	YLD	£2690

Total win prize-money £14494

Going: Sf: 0-1 GS: 0-1 Gd: 0-3 GF: - Fm: 0-0
Distance: 2m/2m3: 0-2 2m4-2m7: 0-3 3m+: 0-0
Track: LH: 0-3 RH: 0-1 Tight: 0-3 Gall: 0-0
Aids: Bl: 0-3 Vi: 0-0 Tstrap: 0-0
Best Rating: 126 12/99 Punc 2m soft Hdl

Modest ex-Irish hurdler/chaser. Suited by cut in the ground.

Young Chevalier

87 **78**
5-y-o b g Alflora (IRE)-Mrs Teasdale (Idiots Delight)
J R Adam James R Adam

Placings:00-0506 **(4555)**
2001/02: 16^{0}GF, 16^{5}GS, 16^{0}S, 19^{6}GF

	Starts	1st	2nd	3rd	Win & Pl
Hurdles	4	0	0	0	0
Career Total	**6**	**0**	**0**	**0**	**0**

Going: Sf: 0-1 GS: 0-1 Gd: 0-0 GF: - Fm: 0-2
Distance: 2m/2m3: 0-3 2m4-2m7: 0-1 3m+: 0-0
Track: LH: 0-3 RH: 0-1 Tight: 0-1 Gall: 0-1
Aids: Bl: 0-0 Vi: 0-0 Tstrap: 0-0
Best Rating: 78 11/01 Ayr 2m gd-sft Hdl

Young Dalesman

114 **121**
9-y-o br g Teenoso (USA)-Fabulous Molly (Whitstead)
A Streeter Mrs D F Garrett

Placings:14632/1/02510330-126F14 **(4821)**
2001/02: 24^{1}S, 24^{2}G, 25^{6}G, 21^{F}GS, 24^{1}S, 24^{4}G

	Starts	1st	2nd	3rd	Win & Pl
Hurdles	6	2	1	0	18567
Career Total	**20**	**5**	**3**	**3**	**30069**

121	3/02	Bang	3m	C(0-135)HHdl	SFT	£5216
112	9/01	MRas	3m	C(0-135)HHdl	SFT	£10400
109	8/00	Bang	2m4f	E(0-115)HHdl	GD	£4309
93	5/98	Towc	2m5f	E(0-110)HHdl	G-F	£2547
88	8/97	Bang	2m1f	E Hdl	GD	£2211

Total win prize-money £24685

Going: Sf: 2-2 GS: 0-1 Gd: 0-3 GF: - Fm: 0-0
Distance: 2m/2m3: 0-0 2m4-2m7: 0-1 **3m+: 2-5**
Track: LH: 1-3 RH: 1-2 **Tight: 2-4** Gall: 0-1
Aids: Bl: 0-0 Vi: 0-0 Tstrap: 0-0
Best Rating: 121 3/02 Bang 3m soft Hdl

A useful handicap hurdler, he stays three miles and acts on soft ground. He scored on his reappearance at Market Rasen in September 2001 with a runaway success, and nearly followed it up at Aintree. Goes well at Bangor and won there for the third time in March 2002.

Young Devereaux (IRE)

111 **145**

9-y-o b/br g Lord Americo-Miss Iverk (Torus)

P F Nicholls Paul K Barber,Mick Coburn,Colin Lewis 2

Placings: *45*/31/**F11/2** **(2443)**

2001/02: 20^{2}S

	Starts	1st	2nd	3rd	Win & Pl
Chases	1	0	1	0	7700
Career Total	**8**	**3**	**1**	**1**	**20147**

145	1/00	Folk	2m	E Ch	G-S	£3217
154	1/00	Uttx	2m	D Ch	SFT	£5330
115	12/98	Chep	2m110y	D Hdl	GD	£3116

Total win prize-money £11664

Going: Sf: 0-1 GS: 0-0 Gd: 0-0 GF: - Fm: 0-0
Distance: 2m/2m3: 0-0 2m4-2m7: 0-1 3m+: 0-0
Track: LH: 0-1 RH: 0-0 Tight: 0-0 Gall: 0-1
Aids: Bl: 0-0 Vi: 0-0 Tstrap: 0-0
Best Rating: 154 1/00 Uttx 2m soft Ch

Looked a useful novice chaser in 1999/2000, but injury then kept him off the track. Returned at Newbury in December 2001 when he found only Cyfor Malta too good. All of his wins have come over two miles, though he does stay further.

Young Douglas (IRE)

7-y-o ch g Alphabatim (USA)-Strong Language (Formidable (USA))

R M Stronge Peter J Douglas Engineering

Placings: *0*/03 **(0952)**

2001/02: 16^{0}G, 24^{3}S

	Starts	1st	2nd	3rd	Win & Pl
NH Flat	1	0	0	0	0
Hurdles	1	0	0	1	344
Career Total	**3**	**0**	**0**	**1**	**344**

Going: Sf: 0-1 GS: 0-0 Gd: 0-1 GF: - Fm: 0-0
Distance: 2m/2m3: 0-1 2m4-2m7: 0-0 3m+: 0-1
Track: LH: 0-2 RH: 0-0 Tight: 0-0 Gall: 0-0
Aids: Bl: 0-0 Vi: 0-0 Tstrap: 0-0
Best Rating: 86 5/99 Chep 2m110y good NHF

Young Joker (IRE)

111(95h) (85h)**140**

6-y-o b g Jolly Jake (NZ)-Ara View (Rontino)

N A Twiston-Davies Gavin Macechern

Placings: *00*-33231F **(4683)**

2001/02: 16^{3}S, 16^{3}G, 16^{2}G, 19^{3}HY, 19^{1}G, 19^{F}GF

	Starts	1st	2nd	3rd	Win & Pl
Hurdles	1	0	0	1	384
Chases	5	1	1	2	5958
Career Total	**8**	**1**	**1**	**3**	**6342**

135	4/02	Hrfd	2m3f	E(0-110)HCh	GD	£4231

Total win prize-money £4232

Going: Sf: 0-2 GS: 0-0 Gd: 1-3 GF: - Fm: 0-1
Distance: **2m/2m3: 1-6** 2m4-2m7: 0-0 3m+: 0-0
Track: LH: 0-1 **RH: 1-5** Tight: 0-1 Gall: 0-0
Aids: Bl: 0-0 Vi: 0-0 Tstrap: 0-0
Best Rating: 140 4/02 Hrfd 2m3f gd-fm Ch

Modest placed form over hurdles and fences before winning a Hereford handicap chase by a distance at Easter 2002. Unlucky not to follow up over course and distance next time. Stays two miles three, likes to bowl along in front.

Young Lirrup

70f **58f**

4-y-o ch g Lir-Blue-Bird Express (Pony Express)

W S Kittow W G Kittow

Placings: *0* **(4391)**

2001/02: 16^{0}S

	Starts	1st	2nd	3rd	Win & Pl
NH Flat	1	0	0	0	
Career Total	**1**	**0**	**0**	**0**	

Going: Sf: 0-1 GS: 0-0 Gd: 0-0 GF: - Fm: 0-0
Distance: 2m/2m3: 0-1 2m4-2m7: 0-0 3m+: 0-0
Track: LH: 0-0 RH: 0-1 Tight: 0-0 Gall: 0-0
Aids: Bl: 0-0 Vi: 0-0 Tstrap: 0-0
Best Rating: 58 3/02 Winc 2m soft NHF

Young Lorcan

92 **91**

6-y-o ch g Bay Tern (USA)-Naughty Nessie (Celtic Cone)

A Dickman Mike Smallman

Placings: *2142600*-P140 **(2306)**

2001/02: 17^{P}G, 17^{1}GF, 17^{4}G, 16^{0}GF

	Starts	1st	2nd	3rd	Win & Pl
Hurdles	4	1	0	0	2450
Career Total	**11**	**2**	**2**	**0**	**5097**

91	9/01	Sedg	2m1f	E Hdl	G-F	£2450
105	6/00	MRas	2m1f110y	H NHF	G-F	£1568

Total win prize-money £4018

Going: Sf: 0-0 GS: 0-0 Gd: 0-2 GF: - Fm: 1-2
Distance: **2m/2m3: 1-4** 2m4-2m7: 0-0 3m+: 0-0
Track: **LH: 1-4** RH: 0-0 **Tight: 1-4** Gall: 0-0
Aids: Bl: 0-0 Vi: 0-0 Tstrap: 0-0
Best Rating: 105 7/00 Worc 2m gd-fm NHF

Young Magoo

4-y-o ch g Lycius (USA)-Fataana (USA) (El Gran Senor (USA))

R Johnson M N Emmerson

Placings: *0* **(4098)**

2001/02: 16^{0}GS

	Starts	1st	2nd	3rd	Win & Pl
NH Flat	1	0	0	0	
Career Total	**1**	**0**	**0**	**0**	

Going: Sf: 0-0 GS: 0-1 Gd: 0-0 GF: - Fm: 0-0
Distance: 2m/2m3: 0-1 2m4-2m7: 0-0 3m+: 0-0
Track: LH: 0-1 RH: 0-0 Tight: 0-1 Gall: 0-0
Aids: Bl: 0-0 Vi: 0-0 Tstrap: 0-0
Best Rating:

Young Monash (IRE)

4-y-o b g General Monash (USA)-Sound Pet (Runnett)

B S Rothwell John H Price

Placings: P **(1934)**

2001/02: 16^{P}G

	Starts	1st	2nd	3rd	Win & Pl
Hurdles	1	0	0	0	
Career Total	**1**	**0**	**0**	**0**	

Going: Sf: 0-0 GS: 0-0 Gd: 0-1 GF: - Fm: 0-0
Distance: 2m/2m3: 0-1 2m4-2m7: 0-0 3m+: 0-0
Track: LH: 0-1 RH: 0-0 Tight: 0-0 Gall: 0-0
Aids: Bl: 0-0 Vi: 0-0 Tstrap: 0-0
Best Rating:

Young Ottoman (IRE)

101 **125**

6-y-o b g Mandalus-Lone Run (Kemal (FR))

V R A Dartnall D G Staddon

Placings: *0562*-1123 **(4051)**

2001/02: 22^{1}GS, 21^{1}S, 24^{2}S, 24^{3}G

	Starts	1st	2nd	3rd	Win & Pl
Hurdles	4	2	1	1	7488
Career Total	**8**	**2**	**2**	**1**	**8142**

118	1/02	Plum	2m5f	E Hdl	SFT	£2730
101	5/01	Extr	2m6f110y	F Hdl	G-S	£2786

Total win prize-money £5516

Going: Sf: 1-2 GS: 1-1 Gd: 0-1 GF: - Fm: 0-0
Distance: 2m/2m3: 0-0 **2m4-2m7: 2-2** 3m+: 0-2
Track: **LH: 1-1** RH: 0-2 **Tight: 1-1** Gall: 0-0
Aids: Bl: 0-0 Vi: 0-0 Tstrap: 0-0
Best Rating: 125 2/02 Asct 3m soft Hdl

An improver over hurdles, he stays an extended two miles six furlongs on an easy surface, jumps well and looks an exciting chasing prospect.

Young Owen

81f **58f**

4-y-o b g Balnibarbi-Polly Potter (Pollerton)

R A Fahey Alf Chadwick

Placings: *60* **(4910)**

2001/02: 17^{6}S, 17^{0}G

	Starts	1st	2nd	3rd	Win & Pl
NH Flat	2	0	0	0	0
Career Total	**2**	**0**	**0**	**0**	**0**

Going: Sf: 0-1 GS: 0-0 Gd: 0-1 GF: - Fm: 0-0
Distance: 2m/2m3: 0-2 2m4-2m7: 0-0 3m+: 0-0
Track: LH: 0-1 RH: 0-1 Tight: 0-2 Gall: 0-0
Aids: Bl: 0-0 Vi: 0-0 Tstrap: 0-0
Best Rating: 58 4/02 MRas 2m1f110y good NHF

Young Radical (IRE)

93 **100**

10-y-o b g Radical-Fountain Blue (Le Tricolore)

John R Upson Sir Nicholas Wilson

Placings: 22315/6/4P1/1315202**P/0-3P3** **(0849)**

2001/02: 24^{3}GF, 20^{P}GF, 21^{3}GF

	Starts	1st	2nd	3rd	Win & Pl
Chases	3	0	0	2	1761
Career Total	**21**	**4**	**4**	**4**	**26249**

123	11/99	Newb	2m5f	C(0-135)HHdl	G-F	£5569
119	10/99	Strf	2m3f	C(0-135)HHdl	G-F	£4955
107	2/99	Wwck	2m4f110y	E(0-115)HHdl	G-S	£2637
63	10/96	Towc	2m	D Hdl	G-F	£2889

Total win prize-money £16050

Going: Sf: 0-0 GS: 0-0 Gd: 0-0 GF: - Fm: 0-3

Distance: 2m/2m3: 0-0 2m4-2m7: 0-2 3m+: 0-1
Track: LH: 0-2 RH: 0-1 Tight: 0-3 Gall: 0-0
Aids: Bl: 0-0 Vi: 0-0 Tstrap: 0-0
Best Rating: 127 3/00 Uttx 2m6f110y good Hdl

Young Sandy

4-y-o b g Bin Ajwaad (IRE)-Lady Keyser (Le Johnstan)
H D Daly Paul Sandy

Placings:0 **(4263)**
2001/02: 16⁰S

	Starts	1st	2nd	3rd	Win & Pl
Hurdles	1	0	0	0	
Career Total	**1**	**0**	**0**	**0**	

Going: Sf: 0-1 GS: 0-0 Gd: 0-0 GF: - Fm: 0-0
Distance: 2m/2m3: 0-1 2m4-2m7: 0-0 3m+: 0-0
Track: LH: 0-1 RH: 0-0 Tight: 0-0 Gall: 0-0
Aids: Bl: 0-0 Vi: 0-0 Tstrap: 0-0
Best Rating: mfy

Young Spartacus

103(92h) **148**
9-y-o b g Teenoso (USA)-Celtic Slave (Celtic Cone)
H D Daly B G Hellyer

Placings:6161/15102/**11222F/13211U-306** **(3264)**
2001/02: 20³GS, 24⁰S, 26⁶G

	Starts	1st	2nd	3rd	Win & Pl
Chases	3	0	0	1	5750
Career Total	**24**	**9**	**5**	**2**	**140128**

167	2/01	Kemp	3m	A HCh	GD	£46400
162	1/01	Chel	2m5f	B HCh	SFT	£20800
148	11/00	Chep	2m4f	B HHdl	SFT	£22750
157	12/99	Chep	2m3f110y	D Ch	SFT	£3891
146	11/99	Towc	2m110y	E Ch	GD	£3265
133	2/99	Wwck	2m	C(0-135)HHdl	G-S	£4828
128	12/98	Wwck	2m	C(0-130)HHdl	SFT	£5487
119	4/98	Ludl	2m	E Hdl	GD	£2836
120	12/97	Strf	2m110y	E Hdl	SFT	£2710

Total win prize-money £112969

Going: Sf: 0-2 GS: 0-1 Gd: 0-0 GF: - Fm: 0-0
Distance: 2m/2m3: 0-0 2m4-2m7: 0-1 3m+: 0-2
Track: LH: 0-2 RH: 0-1 Tight: 0-0 Gall: 0-1
Aids: Bl: 0-0 Vi: 0-0 Tstrap: 0-0
Best Rating: 167 2/01 Kemp 3m good Ch

Tough and genuine, he landed three valuable handicaps in the 2000/2001season, the Tote Silver Trophy over hurdles at Chepstow, the Ladbroke Trophy Chase at Cheltenham and the Racing Post Chase at Kempton, but generally below-par in 2001/02. Handles good ground or softer.

Young Steven

11-y-o b g Singing Steven-Adoration (FR) (Dancer's Image (USA))
Mrs J M Hollands (Mrs S C Bradburne 10/2) Mrs J M Hollands

Placings:003024P/40/3233532/**2361/43341/P3P0-5P** **(4124)**
2001/02: 24⁵S, 21ᴾHY

	Starts	1st	2nd	3rd	Win & Pl
Chases	2	0	0	0	0
Career Total	**31**	**2**	**4**	**9**	**13000**

117	4/00	Kels	3m1f	D Ch	SFT	£3906
105	3/99	Newc	2m4f	H Ch	SFT	£1746

Total win prize-money £5654

Going: Sf: 0-2 GS: 0-0 Gd: 0-0 GF: - Fm: 0-0
Distance: 2m/2m3: 0-0 2m4-2m7: 0-1 3m+: 0-1
Track: LH: 0-1 RH: 0-1 Tight: 0-0 Gall: 0-0
Aids: Bl: 0-0 Vi: 0-1 Tstrap: 0-0
Best Rating: 117 4/00 Kels 3m1f soft Ch

Young Thruster (IRE)

107 **121**
9-y-o b g Over The River (FR)-Bit Of Fashion (Master Owen)
N A Twiston-Davies Gavin Macechern

Placings:*326*/01231033/11/**F-46225P2** **(4576)**
2001/02: 26⁴S, 24⁶GS, 30²GS, 22ᴾHY, 24⁵HY, 25ᴾHY, 26²GS

	Starts	1st	2nd	3rd	Win & Pl
Chases	7	0	3	0	8313
Career Total	**21**	**4**	**5**	**4**	**25141**

107	10/99	Hexm	3m1f	E Ch	GD	£3162
114	5/99	Worc	3m	C(0-130)HHdl	G-S	£5203
107	12/98	Hntg	3m2f	E Hdl	SFT	£2740
105	11/98	NAbb	3m3f	E Hdl	SFT	£2697

Total win prize-money £13804

Going: Sf: 0-4 GS: 0-3 Gd: 0-0 GF: - Fm: 0-0
Distance: 2m/2m3: 0-0 2m4-2m7: 0-1 3m+: 0-6
Track: LH: 0-3 RH: 0-4 Tight: 0-0 Gall: 0-1
Aids: Bl: 0-0 Vi: 0-0 Tstrap: 0-0
Best Rating: 127 10/00 MRas 3m1f good Ch

A fair hurdler/chaser, he has had his problems with injury. Returned in good form in the autumn of 2001, he likes marathon trips on good or easy ground.

Young Tomo (IRE)

105 **112**
10-y-o b g Lafontaine (USA)-Siege Queen (Tarqogan)
J Howard Johnson Michael Thompson

Placings:20151/**241FP2/4F1/20P-5331FP2** **(4787)**
2001/02: 24⁵GF, 28³GS, 25³GS, 27¹G, 27ᶠS, 24ᴾGF, 24²F

	Starts	1st	2nd	3rd	Win & Pl
Chases	7	1	1	2	5590
Career Total	**24**	**5**	**5**	**2**	**20637**

112	11/01	Sedg	3m3f	F(0-90)HCh	GD	£2947
100	10/99	Sedg	3m3f	F(0-110)HCh	GD	£2882
104	12/98	Muss	3m	E Ch	G-F	£2901
99	2/98	Muss	2m4f	D Hdl	GD	£2895
71	12/97	Sedg	2m5f110y	E Hdl	GD	£2022

Total win prize-money £13649

Going: Sf: 0-1 GS: 0-2 Gd: 1-1 GF: - Fm: 0-3
Distance: 2m/2m3: 0-0 2m4-2m7: 0-0 **3m+: 1-7**
Track: **LH: 1-4** RH: 0-3 **Tight: 1-5** Gall: 0-1
Aids: **Bl: 1-7** Vi: 0-0 Tstrap: 0-0
Best Rating: 112 11/01 Sedg 3m3f good Ch

A fair novice chaser at a modest level during the 1998-99 season, he needs fast ground. Scored his first win for two years at Sedgefield in November 2001. Stays well.

Young Tycoon (NZ)

11-y-o br g Young Runaway-Spare Money (NZ) (Moss Trooper (USA))
A J Wilson Mrs Sylvia Darlington

Placings:00/PP000/P32405P/1B40/0P-P **(0219)**
2001/02: 22ᴾGF

	Starts	1st	2nd	3rd	Win & Pl
Hurdles	1	0	0	0	
Career Total	**21**	**1**	**1**	**1**	**4171**

86	1/00	Winc	2m	F(0-110)HHdl	G-S	£2834

Total win prize-money £2834

Going: Sf: 0-0 GS: 0-0 Gd: 0-0 GF: - Fm: 0-1
Distance: 2m/2m3: 0-0 2m4-2m7: 0-1 3m+: 0-0
Track: LH: 0-0 RH: 0-1 Tight: 0-0 Gall: 0-0
Aids: Bl: 0-0 Vi: 0-0 Tstrap: 0-1
Best Rating: 86 2/00 Winc 2m gd-sft Hdl

Younico

7-y-o b g Nordico (USA)-Young Wilkie (Callernish)
R G Frost Paul O J Hosgood

Placings:530364**604/6-63** **(0248)**
2001/02: 17⁶GS, 21³GF

	Starts	1st	2nd	3rd	Win & Pl
Chases	2	0	0	1	556
Career Total	**12**	**0**	**0**	**3**	**1608**

Going: Sf: 0-0 GS: 0-1 Gd: 0-0 GF: - Fm: 0-1
Distance: 2m/2m3: 0-1 2m4-2m7: 0-1 3m+: 0-0
Track: LH: 0-1 RH: 0-1 Tight: 0-1 Gall: 0-0
Aids: Bl: 0-0 Vi: 0-0 Tstrap: 0-0
Best Rating: 99 3/01 Extr 2m3f110y heavy Ch

Youpeeveecee (IRE)

93f **97f**
6-y-o b g Little Bighorn-Godlike (Godswalk (USA))
A Streeter Green Card Golfers

Placings:*042* **(4910)**
2001/02: 16⁰GS, 17⁴S, 17²G

	Starts	1st	2nd	3rd	Win & Pl
NH Flat	3	0	1	0	514
Career Total	**3**	**0**	**1**	**0**	**514**

Going: Sf: 0-1 GS: 0-1 Gd: 0-1 GF: - Fm: 0 0
Distance: 2m/2m3: 0-3 2m4-2m7: 0-0 3m+: 0-0
Track: LH: 0-2 RH: 0-1 Tight: 0-2 Gall: 0-1
Aids: Bl: 0-0 Vi: 0-0 Tstrap: 0-0
Best Rating: 97 4/02 MRas 2m1f110y good NHF

Your Punishment (IRE)

104(106h) (95h)**113**
8-y-o b m Montelimar (USA)-Black Dale (IRE) (Burslem)
N A Twiston-Davies Mrs Ian McKie

Placings:*2140*-63221232P4 **(4551)**
2001/02: 17⁶GF, 16³G, 16²GF, 20²GF, 20¹GF, 16²G, 17³G, 16²G, 16ᴾS, 16⁴GF

	Starts	1st	2nd	3rd	Win & Pl
Hurdles	5	1	2	1	4459
Chases	5	0	2	1	5106
Career Total	**14**	**2**	**5**	**2**	**11478**

94	9/01	Worc	2m4f	E Hdl	G-F	£2576
102	7/00	Worc	2m	H NHF	G-F	£1487

Total win prize-money £4064

Going: Sf: 0-1 GS: 0-0 Gd: 0-4 GF: - Fm: 1-5
Distance: 2m/2m3: 0-8 **2m4-2m7: 1-2** 3m+: 0-0
Track: **LH: 1-7** RH: 0-3 Tight: 0-2 Gall: 0-2

Aids: Bl: 0-0 Vi: 0-0 Tstrap: 0-0
Best Rating: 113 10/01 Chel 2m good Ch

A front-runner, she ran well in her first two starts over fences but jumped poorly at Cheltenham in October, jumping to her right, and eventually fell but was remounted to claim second prize. Could need a return to right-handed tracks. Acts on a sound surface.

Your So Cool

73f 53f

5-y-o ch g Karinga Bay-Laurel Diver (Celtic Cone)
M C Pipe Matt Archer & Miss Jean Broadhurst

Placings: 0 (3661)
2001/02: 16^{0}S

	Starts	1st	2nd	3rd	Win & Pl
NH Flat	1	0	0	0	
Career Total	**1**	**0**	**0**	**0**	

Going: Sf: 0-1 GS: 0-0 Gd: 0-0 GF: - Fm: 0-0
Distance: 2m/2m3: 0-1 2m4-2m7: 0-0 3m+: 0-0
Track: LH: 0-0 RH: 0-1 Tight: 0-0 Gall: 0-0
Aids: Bl: 0-0 Vi: 0-0 Tstrap: 0-0
Best Rating: 53 2/02 Winc 2m soft NHF

Your Turn Rosie

79 43

7-y-o b m Relief Pitcher-Bremhill Rosie (Celtic Cone)
I R Brown I R Brown

Placings: 0 (2215)
2001/02: 17^{0}G

	Starts	1st	2nd	3rd	Win & Pl
NH Flat	1	0	0	0	
Career Total	**1**	**0**	**0**	**0**	

Going: Sf: 0-0 GS: 0-0 Gd: 0-1 GF: - Fm: 0-0
Distance: 2m/2m3: 0-1 2m4-2m7: 0-0 3m+: 0-0
Track: LH: 0-0 RH: 0-1 Tight: 0-0 Gall: 0-0
Aids: Bl: 0-0 Vi: 0-0 Tstrap: 0-0
Best Rating:

Yours Truly (IRE)

10-y-o ch g Salluceva-Precious Petra (Bing Ii)
Jane Southcombe A G Varney

Placings: PPP (3656)
2001/02: 25^{P}S, 26^{P}HY, 25^{P}S

	Starts	1st	2nd	3rd	Win & Pl
Chases	3	0	0	0	
Career Total	**3**	**0**	**0**	**0**	

Going: Sf: 0-3 GS: 0-0 Gd: 0-0 GF: - Fm: 0-0
Distance: 2m/2m3: 0-0 2m4-2m7: 0-0 3m+: 0-3
Track: LH: 0-1 RH: 0-2 Tight: 0-0 Gall: 0-0
Aids: Bl: 0-0 Vi: 0-0 Tstrap: 0-0
Best Rating:

Yquem (IRE)

12-y-o ch g Henbit (USA)-Silent Run (Deep Run)
B J M Ryall (J J Boulter 17/2) J J Boulter/f J Wilkins/k J Pearce

Placings: 15PP/1P-1 (0428)
2001/02: 21^{1}G

	Starts	1st	2nd	3rd	Win & Pl
Chases	1	1	0	0	3486
Career Total	**7**	**3**	**0**	**0**	**7239**

123	5/01	Chel	2m5f	H Ch	GD	£3486
115	4/01	NAbb	2m5f110y	G(0-95)HCh	SFT	£2373
102	5/97	Hrfd	2m3f	H Ch	GD	£1380

Total win prize-money £7239

Going: Sf: 0-0 GS: 0-0 Gd: 1-1 GF: - Fm: 0-0
Distance: 2m/2m3: 0-0 **2m4-2m7: 1-1** 3m+: 0-0
Track: LH: 0-0 RH: 0-0 Tight: 0-0 Gall: 0-0
Aids: Bl: 0-0 Vi: 0-0 Tstrap: 0-0
Best Rating: 123 5/01 Chel 2m5f good Ch

Zaajer (USA)

99 90

6-y-o ch g Silver Hawk (USA)-Crown Quest (USA) (Chief's Crown (USA))
J A B Old W E Sturt

Placings: 244P (4011)
2001/02: 17^{2}S, 16^{4}HY, 16^{4}GS, 21^{P}S

	Starts	1st	2nd	3rd	Win & Pl
Hurdles	4	0	1	0	846
Career Total	**4**	**0**	**1**	**0**	**846**

Going: Sf: 0-3 GS: 0-1 Gd: 0-0 GF: - Fm: 0-0
Distance: 2m/2m3: 0-3 2m4-2m7: 0-1 3m+: 0-0
Track: LH: 0-3 RH: 0-1 Tight: 0-1 Gall: 0-2
Aids: Bl: 0-0 Vi: 0-0 Tstrap: 0-0
Best Rating: 90 1/02 Hntg 2m110y gd-sft Hdl

A Listed winner on the Flat, but modest form over hurdles.

Zabadi (IRE)

105 129

10-y-o b g Shahrastani (USA)-Zerzaya (Beldale Flutter (USA))
Miss Venetia Williams Festival Racing (uk) Limited

Placings: 051101/1005052/**32F3332F3/52/221222223 P2063-2212111P3** (3269)
2001/02: 21^{2}G, 19^{2}GF, 21^{1}S, 17^{2}GS, 16^{1}S, 20^{1}S, 16^{1}HY, 19^{P}GS, 19^{3}G

	Starts	1st	2nd	3rd	Win & Pl
Chases	9	4	3	1	20575
Career Total	**47**	**9**	**15**	**8**	**100255**

129	12/01	Towc	2m110y	D(0-120)HCh	HVY	£5486
123	12/01	Plum	2m4f	D(0-125)HCh	SFT	£3802
129	11/01	Towc	2m110y	F(0-105)HCh	SFT	£3900
127	10/01	Fknm	2m5f110y	F(0-100)HCh	SFT	£3435
101	6/00	Uttx	2m4f	D Ch	G-F	£4225
147	11/96	Newb	2m110y	A Hdl	GD	£12120
134	3/96	Aint	2m110y	A Hdl	GD	£28424
135	2/96	Kemp	2m	A Hdl	SFT	£9002
131	1/96	Kemp	2m	D Hdl	GD	£3061

Total win prize-money £73457

Going: Sf: 4-4 GS: 0-2 Gd: 0-2 GF: - Fm: 0-1
Distance: 2m/2m3: 2-4 2m4-2m7: 2-5 3m+: 0-0
Track: LH: 2-6 RH: 2-3 **Tight: 2-4** Gall: 0-1
Aids: Bl: 0-0 Vi: 0-0 Tstrap: 0-0
Best Rating: 148 4/97 Ayr 2m good Hdl

A one-time smart hurdler, he has proved expensive to follow over fences, though he showed a better attitude in the winter of 2001/2 winning four times. Suited by two to two and a half miles and soft ground.

Zabionic (IRE)

77 39

5-y-o ch g Zafonic (USA)-Scene Galante (FR) (Sicyos (USA))
M Hill (M E Sowersby 12/5) Martin Hill

Placings: 5563F0F0-00 (1611)
2001/02: 24^{0}GF, 19^{0}GF

	Starts	1st	2nd	3rd	Win & Pl
Hurdles	2	0	0	0	
Career Total	**10**	**0**	**0**	**1**	**244**

Going: Sf: 0-0 GS: 0-0 Gd: 0-0 GF: - Fm: 0-2
Distance: 2m/2m3: 0-1 2m4-2m7: 0-0 3m+: 0-1
Track: LH: 0-1 RH: 0-1 Tight: 0-0 Gall: 0-0
Aids: Bl: 0-0 Vi: 0-0 Tstrap: 0-0
Best Rating: 76 11/00 Catt 2m good Hdl

Zacopani (IRE)

(105h) (91h)

10-y-o b g Lafontaine (USA)-Take A Dare (Pragmatic)
R Ford Williams Thompson Partnership

Placings: 0P0P/041616132/**5PF04000P5P/P3300/1F1 -P4P24** (1644)
2001/02: 26^{P}GS, 27^{4}GF, 24^{P}G, 24^{2}G, 26^{4}G

	Starts	1st	2nd	3rd	Win & Pl
Hurdles	2	0	1	0	1242
Chases	3	0	0	0	273
Career Total	**37**	**5**	**2**	**3**	**20034**

98	7/00	Sedg	3m3f110y	F(0-110)HHdl	FRM	£2618
105	5/00	Hexm	3m1f	E Ch	G-F	£3159
101	8/97	Cork	3m	(0-116)HHdl	Y-S	£4069
96	7/97	Klny	2m6f	(0-109)HHdl	G-Y	£3051
101	6/97	Tral	2m	NHF	FRM	£3391

Total win prize-money £16289

Going: Sf: 0-0 GS: 0-1 Gd: 0-3 GF: - Fm: 0-1
Distance: 2m/2m3: 0-0 2m4-2m7: 0-0 3m+: 0-5
Track: LH: 0-2 RH: 0-3 Tight: 0-2 Gall: 0-1
Aids: Bl: 0-5 Vi: 0-0 Tstrap: 0-0
Best Rating: 108 10/99 Sedg 2m5f good Ch

A real stayer who won on soft ground in Ireland, has looked better suited to fast ground since coming to Britain.

Zafarabad (IRE)

110(89h) (134h)150

8-y-o gr g Shernazar-Zarafa (Blushing Groom (FR))
P J Hobbs Mrs Elaine Baines

Placings: 11141/1323F4/**12221U/P03133** (4897)
2001/02: 21^{P}GS, 24^{0}G, 20^{3}G, 20^{1}GS, 19^{3}GF, 24^{3}G

	Starts	1st	2nd	3rd	Win & Pl
Hurdles	2	0	0	0	0
Chases	4	1	0	3	20067
Career Total	**23**	**8**	**4**	**5**	**106834**

150	2/02	Kemp	2m4f110y	C(0-130)HCh	G-S	£11212
145	1/00	Hntg	3m	D Ch	GD	£4381
142	11/99	Extr	2m3f	C Ch	G-S	£6385
150	11/98	Newb	2m110y	B Hdl	G-S	£5095
143	4/98	Punc	2m	Hdl	HVY	£26956
142	2/98	Newb	2m110y	C Hdl	GD	£4272
137	1/98	Chel	2m1f	A Hdl	G-S	£9645
134	1/98	Kemp	2m	D Hdl	SFT	£2996

Total win prize-money £70945

Going: Sf: 0-0 GS: 1-2 Gd: 0-3 GF: - Fm: 0-1
Distance: 2m/2m3: 0-0 **2m4-2m7: 1-4** 3m+: 0-2
Track: LH: 0-0 **RH: 1-5** Tight: 0-1 Gall: 0-0

Aids: Bl: 1-5 Vi: 0-0 Tstrap: 0-0
Best Rating: 156 1/99 Leop 2m heavy Hdl

A very useful sort over hurdles in his younger days, he was pulled up over hurdles on return from a nine-month break in November 2001. Better effort back over fences at Kempton before making all there in February. Stays three miles over fences. Acts on soft ground.

Zafarelli

105 90

8-y-o gr g Nishapour (FR)-Voltigeuse (USA) (Filiberto (USA))
J R Jenkins The East India Dock Partnership

Placings:403305/400P115P0/PUP665025/142-P056 **(4240)**
2001/02: 21PGS, 20OS, 265S, 266GF

	Starts	1st	2nd	3rd	Win & Pl
Hurdles	4	0	0	0	0
Career Total	**31**	**3**	**2**	**2**	**12034**

98	5/00	Hntg	2m5f110y	D(0-125)HHdl	G-S	£3146
98	1/99	Plum	2m1f	E(0-115)HHdl	HVY	£2740
93	12/98	Folk	2m1f110y	E(0-105)HHdl	SFT	£2508

Total win prize-money £8395

Going: Sf: 0-2 GS: 0-1 Gd: 0-0 GF: - Fm: 0-1
Distance: 2m/2m3: 0-0 2m4-2m7: 0-2 3m+: 0-2
Track: LH: 0-0 RH: 0-4 Tight: 0-0 Gall: 0-4
Aids: Bl: 0-0 Vi: 0-2 Tstrap: 0-0
Best Rating: 98 9/00 Plum 2m5f good Hdl

In-and-out perfromer who is not genuine.

Zaffamore (IRE)

104 97

6-y-o ch g Zaffaran (USA)-Furmore (Furry Glen)
Miss H C Knight Martin Broughton

Placings:0/4-52 **(2340)**
2001/02: 225G, 212GF

	Starts	1st	2nd	3rd	Win & Pl
Hurdles	2	0	1	0	801
Career Total	**4**	**0**	**1**	**0**	**801**

Going: Sf: 0-0 GS: 0-0 Gd: 0-1 GF: - Fm: 0-1
Distance: 2m/2m3: 0-0 2m4-2m7: 0-2 3m+: 0-0
Track: LH: 0-0 RH: 0-2 Tight: 0-0 Gall: 0-0
Aids: Bl: 0-0 Vi: 0-0 Tstrap: 0-0
Best Rating: 97 11/01 Ludl 2m5f gd-fm Hdl

Zaffaran Winds (IRE)

7-y-o b m Zaffaran (USA)-Sharp Winds (Tumble Wind (USA))
N A Twiston-Davies M Scudamore

Placings:00605-6F **(1736)**
2001/02: 216GF, 19FS

	Starts	1st	2nd	3rd	Win & Pl
Chases	2	0	0	0	0
Career Total	**7**	**0**	**0**	**0**	**0**

Going: Sf: 0-1 GS: 0-0 Gd: 0-0 GF: - Fm: 0-1
Distance: 2m/2m3: 0-1 2m4-2m7: 0-1 3m+: 0-0
Track: LH: 0-0 RH: 0-2 Tight: 0-0 Gall: 0-0
Aids: Bl: 0-0 Vi: 0-0 Tstrap: 0-1
Best Rating: 91 4/01 Hayd 2m soft Ch

Winning pointer.

Zaffaranni (IRE)

108 103

6-y-o ch m Zaffaran (USA)-Nimbi (Orchestra)
N A Twiston-Davies Mrs S Tainton

Placings:0240-321530 **(4420)**
2001/02: 163G, 162GS, 211G, 245G, 213G, 210GS

	Starts	1st	2nd	3rd	Win & Pl
Hurdles	6	1	1	2	5920
Career Total	**10**	**1**	**2**	**2**	**6473**

103	12/01	Ludl	2m5f	D Hdl	GD	£3711

Total win prize-money £3712

Going: Sf: 0-0 GS: 0-2 Gd: 1-4 GF: - Fm: 0-0
Distance: 2m/2m3: 0-2 **2m4-2m7: 1-3** 3m+: 0-1
Track: LH: 0-2 **RH: 1-4** Tight: 0-0 Gall: 0-1
Aids: Bl: 0-0 Vi: 0-0 Tstrap: 0-0
Best Rating: 103 12/01 Ludl 2m5f good Hdl

A half-sister to Santabless, she has shown ability in bumpers and novice hurdles. Appreciated step up to two miles five when scoring at Ludlow in December 2001. Likely to appreciate a longer trip in time.

Zaffrax (IRE)

6-y-o ch g Zaffaran (USA)-Ardtana (IRE) (Cidrax (FR))
R J Smith R Smith

Placings:6-0 **(1245)**
2001/02: 10OOF

	Starts	1st	2nd	3rd	Win & Pl
NH Flat	1	0	0	0	
Career Total	**2**	**0**	**0**	**0**	**0**

Going: Sf: 0-0 GS: 0-0 Gd: 0-0 GF: - Fm: 0-1
Distance: 2m/2m3: 0-1 2m4-2m7: 0-0 3m+: 0-0
Track: LH: 0-1 RH: 0-0 Tight: 0-0 Gall: 0-0
Aids: Bl: 0-0 Vi: 0-0 Tstrap: 0-0
Best Rating: 80 5/00 Worc 2m good NHF

Zaffre Noir (IRE)

104 120

6-y-o b g Zaffaran (USA)-Maccinetta (Bold Lad (IRE))
M Pitman Mrs D Salmon

Placings:260/261F31-3054 **(4760)**
2001/02: 213G, 23OHY, 225G, 244GF

	Starts	1st	2nd	3rd	Win & Pl
Hurdles	4	0	0	1	2640
Career Total	**13**	**2**	**2**	**2**	**10643**

120	4/01	Winc	2m6f	E Hdl	SFT	£2408
118	12/00	Newb	2m3f	D Hdl	SFT	£3607

Total win prize-money £6016

Going: Sf: 0-1 GS: 0-0 Gd: 0-2 GF: - Fm: 0-1
Distance: 2m/2m3: 0-0 2m4-2m7: 0-2 3m+: 0-2
Track: LH: 0-1 RH: 0-2 Tight: 0-0 Gall: 0-0
Aids: Bl: 0-0 Vi: 0-0 Tstrap: 0-0
Best Rating: 120 12/01 Kemp 2m5f good Hdl

Fair hurdler, gets two miles-six but not much further, and appreciates cut in the ground.

Zaggy Lane

111 129

10-y-o b g Prince Of Peace-Meldon Lady (Ballymoss)
P R Rodford E T Wey

Placings:6/006/5F422/3F111F2/P56/FP306153-3462423P **(4299)**
2001/02: 263S, 304GS, 266S, 332S, 274S, 292HY, 293G, 34PHY

	Starts	1st	2nd	3rd	Win & Pl
Chases	8	0	2	2	5403
Career Total	**35**	**4**	**5**	**5**	**31149**

129	2/01	Wwck	3m5f	F(0-110)HCh	SFT	£3558
129	1/99	Tntn	3m3f	C(0-130)HCh	SFT	£7197
123	12/98	Uttx	3m	D(0-120)HCh	SFT	£3598
118	12/98	NAbb	2m5f110y	(0-100)HCh	SFT	£3080

Total win prize-money £17436

Going: Sf: 0-6 GS: 0-1 Gd: 0-1 GF: - Fm: 0-0
Distance: 2m/2m3: 0-0 2m4-2m7: 0-0 3m+: 0-8
Track: LH: 0-6 RH: 0-2 Tight: 0-3 Gall: 0-1
Aids: Bl: 0-0 Vi: 0-0 Tstrap: 0-0
Best Rating: 129 4/01 Newb 3m soft Ch

Fair staying chaser, suited by marathon trips and soft ground, but does not win very often these days.

Zaidaan

101 46

6-y-o b g Ezzoud (IRE)-River Maiden (USA) (Riverman (USA))
G M McCourt 'It Might Be Ten' Partnership

Placings:45-P **(0039)**
2001/02: 22PGS

	Starts	1st	2nd	3rd	Win & Pl
Hurdles	1	0	0	0	
Career Total	**3**	**0**	**0**	**0**	**0**

Going: Sf: 0-0 GS: 0-1 Gd: 0-0 GF: - Fm: 0-0
Distance: 2m/2m3: 0-0 2m4-2m7: 0-1 3m+: 0-0
Track: LH: 0-0 RH: 0-0 Tight: 0-0 Gall: 0-0
Aids: Bl: 0-0 Vi: 0-0 Tstrap: 0-0
Best Rating: 90 9/00 Worc 2m gd-fm Hdl

Landed a gamble in a selling hurdle at Worcester in June but lame when well beaten next time.

Zaitoon (IRE)

88 65

11-y-o b g Waajib-Sawlah (Known Fact (USA))
A King Cheltenham Racing Ltd

Placings:410442033/1F5442022/6U3F/02P3364/4232 120221223/24121253U53/0065P-P044 **(1595)**
2001/02: 26PG, 240GF, 264GS, 244G

	Starts	1st	2nd	3rd	Win & Pl
Chases	4	0	0	0	297
Career Total	**62**	**6**	**15**	**9**	**49754**

127	7/99	Worc	2m7f110y	D(0-125)HCh	G-F	£3790
122	6/99	Worc	2m7f110y	E(0-115)HCh	G-F	£3065
107	10/98	Worc	2m7f110y	E Ch	GD	£2906
112	7/98	Worc	2m7f110y	F(0-100)HCh	G-F	£2840
101	5/95	Hayd	2m	B HHdl	G-F	£10455
82	10/94	Wwck	2m	Hdl	GD	£2145

Total win prize-money £25202

Going: Sf: 0-0 GS: 0-1 Gd: 0-2 GF: - Fm: 0-1
Distance: 2m/2m3: 0-0 2m4-2m7: 0-0 3m+: 0-4
Track: LH: 0-3 RH: 0-0 Tight: 0-2 Gall: 0-0
Aids: Bl: 0-2 Vi: 0-0 Tstrap: 0-0
Best Rating: 127 8/99 Worc 2m7f110y gd-fm Ch

A veteran Worcester specialist, he goes well on fast ground and is the ideal sort for summer jumping.

Zaleem (IRE)

97f 94f

5-y-o b g Kahyasi-Zallaka (IRE) (Shardari)
A Streeter Martin Jump

Placings: *034* (3338)
2001/02: 16^{0}GF, 16^{3}G, 16^{4}G

	Starts	1st	2nd	3rd	Win & Pl
NH Flat	3	0	0	1	283
Career Total	**3**	**0**	**0**	**1**	**283**

Going: Sf: 0-0 GS: 0-0 Gd: 0-2 GF: - Fm: 0-1
Distance: 2m/2m3: 0-3 2m4-2m7: 0-0 3m+: 0-0
Track: LH: 0-0 RH: 0-3 Tight: 0-0 Gall: 0-1
Aids: Bl: 0-0 Vi: 0-1 Tstrap: 0-0
Best Rating: 94 12/01 Ludl 2m good NHF

Zalotto (IRE)

102 **105**

8-y-o b g Polish Patriot (USA)-Honest Penny (USA) (Honest Pleasure (USA))
Ian Williams N Jinks & G Edmunds

Placings:221/U50-02113 (2941)
2001/02: 19^{0}G, 16^{2}S, 17^{1}G, 17^{1}S, 19^{3}G

	Starts	1st	2nd	3rd	Win & Pl
Hurdles	5	2	1	1	2806
Career Total	**11**	**3**	**3**	**1**	**6210**

105	12/01	Hrfd	2m1f	G Hdl	SFT	£1781
95	7/99	Wolv	3m1f	E Hdl	G-S	£2196

Total win prize-money £3979

Going: Sf: 1-2 GS: 0-0 Gd: 1-3 GF: - Fm: 0-0
Distance: **2m/2m3: 2-4** 2m4-2m7: 0-1 3m+: 0-0
Track: LH: 0-1 **RH: 2-4** Tight: 0-0 Gall: 0-1
Aids: Bl: 0-0 Vi: 0-0 Tstrap: 0-0
Best Rating: 105 12/01 Hrfd 2m1f soft Hdl

Modest chaser, stays three miles one, suited by soft ground.

Zamat

103 **94+**

6-y-o b g Slip Anchor-Khandjar (Kris)
P Monteith I Bell

Placings:4360 (2342)
2001/02: 16^{4}GS, 16^{3}G, 16^{6}GS, 16^{0}GS

	Starts	1st	2nd	3rd	Win & Pl
Hurdles	4	0	0	1	464
Career Total	**4**	**0**	**0**	**1**	**464**

Going: Sf: 0-0 GS: 0-3 Gd: 0-1 GF: - Fm: 0-0
Distance: 2m/2m3: 0-4 2m4-2m7: 0-0 3m+: 0-0
Track: LH: 0-4 RH: 0-0 Tight: 0-3 Gall: 0-1
Aids: Bl: 0-0 Vi: 0-0 Tstrap: 0-0
Best Rating: 93 10/01 Aint 2m110y good Hdl

He has shown some ability in his early starts over hurdles without setting the world alight.

Zamhareer (USA)

105 **90**

11-y-o b g Lear Fan (USA)-Awenita (Rarity)
R Ford R Burgess

Placings:1336/2F21056/0P**53**/**21**F**1**U**3**1**5**0/**2334**00**24**/ 545-1P524F (4889)
2001/02: 28^{1}GS, 27^{P}G, 25^{5}G, 29^{2}S, 32^{4}HY, 26^{F}G

	Starts	1st	2nd	3rd	Win & Pl
Chases	6	1	1	0	5031
Career Total	**41**	**6**	**6**	**6**	**28300**

90	10/01	MRas	3m4f110y	F(0-100)HCh	G-S	£3461
109	3/99	Hexm	3m	F(0-110)HHdl	SFT	£2022
112	11/98	Sedg	3m3f	F(0-105)HCh	G-S	£2882
113	10/98	Sedg	3m3f110y	F(0-100)HHdl	G-S	£2495
116	3/96	Donc	3m110y	B HHdl	G-F	£5114
92	11/94	Newc	2m110y	Hdl	GD	£2736

Total win prize-money £18711

Going: Sf: 0-2 GS: 1-1 Gd: 0-3 GF: - Fm: 0-0
Distance: 2m/2m3: 0-0 2m4-2m7: 0-0 **3m+: 1-6**
Track: LH: 0-3 **RH: 1-1 Tight: 1-3** Gall: 0-0
Aids: Bl: 0-0 Vi: 0-0 Tstrap: 0-0
Best Rating: 118 3/96 Aint 3m110y good Hdl

Moderate staying chaser, appreciates marathon trips and easy ground.

Zanariann (FR)

5-y-o b g Indian Ridge-Zanadiyka (FR) (Akarad (FR))
A Berry Alan Berry

Placings:*0* (4860)
2001/02: 16^{0}G

	Starts	1st	2nd	3rd	Win & Pl
NH Flat	1	0	0	0	
Career Total	**1**	**0**	**0**	**0**	

Going: Sf: 0-0 GS: 0-0 Gd: 0-1 GF: - Fm: 0-0
Distance: 2m/2m3: 0-1 2m4-2m7: 0-0 3m+: 0-0
Track: LH: 0-0 RH: 0-0 Tight: 0-0 Gall: 0-0
Aids: Bl: 0-0 Vi: 0-0 Tstrap: 0-0
Best Rating:

Zapata Highway

5-y-o ch g Bold Arrangement-Trailing Rose (Undulate (USA))
D R C Elsworth R & H Burridge, M Matheson, A S Wing

Placings:*0* (3701)
2001/02: 16^{0}S

	Starts	1st	2nd	3rd	Win & Pl
NH Flat	1	0	0	0	
Career Total	**1**	**0**	**0**	**0**	

Going: Sf: 0-1 GS: 0-0 Gd: 0-0 GF: - Fm: 0-0
Distance: 2m/2m3: 0-1 2m4-2m7: 0-0 3m+: 0-0
Track: LH: 0-1 RH: 0-0 Tight: 0-0 Gall: 0-1
Aids: Bl: 0-0 Vi: 0-0 Tstrap: 0-0
Best Rating:

Zapateado (FR)

(98h)

7-y-o b g Galetto (FR)-Zinarelle (FR) (Zino)
M C Pipe Matt Archer & Miss Jean Broadhurst

Placings:F00143/32015/05244-F (0243)
2001/02: 16^{F}GF

	Starts	1st	2nd	3rd	Win & Pl
Chases	1	0	0	0	
Career Total	**17**	**2**	**2**	**2**	**10137**

114	2/00	Towc	2m	F(0-110)HHdl	HVY	£2590
107	2/99	Sand	2m110y	D Hdl	G-S	£3387

Total win prize-money £5978

Going: Sf: 0-0 GS: 0-0 Gd: 0-0 GF: - Fm: 0-1
Distance: 2m/2m3: 0-1 2m4-2m7: 0-0 3m+: 0-0
Track: LH: 0-0 RH: 0-0 Tight: 0-0 Gall: 0-0
Aids: Bl: 0-0 Vi: 0-0 Tstrap: 0-0
Best Rating: 116 1/01 Chep 2m110y gd-sft Hdl

Zedium

102 **85**

7-y-o b m Presidium-Zamandra (Foggy Bell)
J G Fitzgerald N F And F Racing

Placings:*30/06*0-50 (2343)
2001/02: 20^{5}G, 20^{0}GS

	Starts	1st	2nd	3rd	Win & Pl
Hurdles	2	0	0	0	0
Career Total	**7**	**0**	**0**	**1**	**248**

Going: Sf: 0-0 GS: 0-1 Gd: 0-1 GF: - Fm: 0-0
Distance: 2m/2m3: 0-0 2m4-2m7: 0-2 3m+: 0-0
Track: LH: 0-2 RH: 0-0 Tight: 0-0 Gall: 0-1
Aids: Bl: 0-0 Vi: 0-0 Tstrap: 0-0
Best Rating: 94 3/00 MRas 1m5f110y gd-fm NHF

Zen (IRE)

104 **99**

7-y-o b g Shernazar-Mary Mary (Moulton)
T P McGovern Ahmed Abdel-Khaleq

Placings:*2155*-544 (2429)
2001/02: 21^{5}S, 22^{4}S, 24^{4}G

	Starts	1st	2nd	3rd	Win & Pl
Hurdles	3	0	0	0	421
Career Total	**7**	**1**	**1**	**0**	**2579**

111	12/00	Folk	2m1f110y	H NHF	HVY	£1725

Total win prize-money £1726

Going: Sf: 0-2 GS: 0-0 Gd: 0-1 GF: - Fm: 0-0
Distance: 2m/2m3: 0-0 2m4-2m7: 0-2 3m+: 0-1
Track: LH: 0-2 RH: 0-1 Tight: 0-2 Gall: 0-1
Aids: Bl: 0-0 Vi: 0-0 Tstrap: 0-0
Best Rating: 111 12/00 Folk 2m1f110y heavy NHF

Winner of a bumper and has shown moderate form over hurdles. Acts on heavy ground.

Zero Risk (IRE)

104 **103**

6-y-o ch g Insan (USA)-Serenade Run (Deep Run)
L Wells Paul Zetter

Placings:*16U3*-0133 (1737)
2001/02: 16^{0}GF, 17^{1}G, 16^{3}GS, 17^{3}S

	Starts	1st	2nd	3rd	Win & Pl
Hurdles	4	1	0	2	4378
Career Total	**8**	**2**	**0**	**3**	**9490**

101	9/01	Bang	2m1f	D Hdl	GD	£3542
112	12/00	Folk	2m1f110y	H NHF	HVY	£1662

Total win prize-money £5205

Going: Sf: 0-1 GS: 0-1 Gd: 1-1 GF: - Fm: 0-1
Distance: **2m/2m3: 1-4** 2m4-2m7: 0-0 3m+: 0-0
Track: **LH: 1-3** RH: 0-1 **Tight: 1-3** Gall: 0-0
Aids: Bl: 0-0 Vi: 0-0 Tstrap: 0-2
Best Rating: 114 4/01 Aint 2m1f heavy NHF

Modest hurdler, acts on well with cut in the ground and is effective at around two miles and one furlong.

Zetagalopon

67 **30**

4-y-o b f Petong-Azola (IRE) (Alzao (USA))
C L Popham (J A Osborne 12/7) Miss Deborah Bullion

Placings:560 (1725)
2001/02: 17^{5}GF, 16^{6}GS, 17^{0}F

	Starts	1st	2nd	3rd	Win & Pl
Hurdles	3	0	0	0	0
Career Total	**3**	**0**	**0**	**0**	**0**

Going: Sf: 0-0 GS: 0-1 Gd: 0-0 GF: - Fm: 0-2
Distance: 2m/2m3: 0-3 2m4-2m7: 0-0 3m+: 0-0
Track: LH: 0-2 RH: 0-1 Tight: 0-3 Gall: 0-0
Aids: Bl: 0-1 Vi: 0-0 Tstrap: 0-0
Best Rating: 30 9/01 NAbb 2m1f gd-fm Hdl

Zieting (IRE)

81 60

4-y-o b g Zieten (USA)-Ball Cat (FR) (Cricket Ball (USA))
P W Hiatt (K R Burke 29/6) P W Hiatt

Placings:P0P6 (1626)
2001/02: 17^{P}G, 17^{0}G, 17^{P}S, 16^{6}GF

	Starts	1st	2nd	3rd	Win & Pl
Hurdles	4	0	0	0	0
Career Total	**4**	**0**	**0**	**0**	**0**

Going: Sf: 0-1 GS: 0-0 Gd: 0-2 GF: - Fm: 0-1
Distance: 2m/2m3: 0-4 2m4-2m7: 0-0 3m+: 0-0
Track: LH: 0-2 RH: 0-2 Tight: 0-3 Gall: 0-0
Aids: Bl: 0-0 Vi: 0-0 Tstrap: 0-0
Best Rating: 60 9/01 Sedg 2m1f good Hdl

Ziggy's Way

102 85

7-y-o b g Teenoso (USA)-Onaway (Commanche Run)
Mrs A Barclay Mrs Althea Barclay

Placings:54P-40 (2883)
2001/02: 21^{4}HY, 20^{0}GS

	Starts	1st	2nd	3rd	Win & Pl
Hurdles	2	0	0	0	323
Career Total	**5**	**0**	**0**	**0**	**323**

Going: Sf: 0-1 GS: 0-1 Gd: 0-0 GF: - Fm: 0-0
Distance: 2m/2m3: 0-0 2m4-2m7: 0-2 3m+: 0-0
Track: LH: 0-1 RH: 0-1 Tight: 0-0 Gall: 0-0
Aids: Bl: 0-0 Vi: 0-0 Tstrap: 0-0
Best Rating: 99 2/01 Towc 2m heavy NHF

Zilarator (USA)

112 123

6-y-o b g Zilzal (USA)-Allegedly (USA) (Sir Ivor)
P J Hobbs (W J Haggas 11/10) Jay Dee Bloodstock Limited

Placings:5 (3886)
2001/02: 16^{5}GS

	Starts	1st	2nd	3rd	Win & Pl
Hurdles	1	0	0	0	0
Career Total	**1**	**0**	**0**	**0**	**0**

Going: Sf: 0-0 GS: 0-1 Gd: 0-0 GF: - Fm: 0-0
Distance: 2m/2m3: 0-1 2m4-2m7: 0-0 3m+: 0-0
Track: LH: 0-0 RH: 0-1 Tight: 0-0 Gall: 0-0
Aids: Bl: 0-0 Vi: 0-0 Tstrap: 0-0
Best Rating: 123 2/02 Kemp 2m gd-sft Hdl

A useful middle-distance handicapper on the Flat, but not the easiest of rides. He ran a strange race on his hurdles debut at Kempton, jumping badly before flying late on. Suited by cut in the ground.

Zincalo (USA)

82 78

6-y-o gr g Zilzal (USA)-Silver Glitz (USA) (Grey Dawn Ii)
Mrs D Haine (C E Brittain 28/7) Mrs Diana Haine

Placings:00 (1567)
2001/02: 16^{0}GF, 20^{0}GS

	Starts	1st	2nd	3rd	Win & Pl
Hurdles	2	0	0	0	
Career Total	**2**	**0**	**0**	**0**	

Going: Sf: 0-0 GS: 0-1 Gd: 0-0 GF: - Fm: 0-1
Distance: 2m/2m3: 0-1 2m4-2m7: 0-1 3m+: 0-0
Track: LH: 0-1 RH: 0-0 Tight: 0-2 Gall: 0-0
Aids: Bl: 0-0 Vi: 0-0 Tstrap: 0-0
Best Rating: 78 9/01 Plum 2m gd-fm Hdl

Zoes Pet

11-y-o ch m Cisto (FR)-Pat's Pet (Autre Prince)
G Prodromou Major M S Edwards

Placings:0 (0230)
2001/02: 16^{0}GF

	Starts	1st	2nd	3rd	Win & Pl
Hurdles	1	0	0	0	
Career Total	**1**	**0**	**0**	**0**	

Going: Sf: 0-0 GS: 0-0 Gd: 0-0 GF: - Fm: 0-1
Distance: 2m/2m3: 0-1 2m4-2m7: 0-0 3m+: 0-0
Track: LH: 0-0 RH: 0-1 Tight: 0-0 Gall: 0-1
Aids: Bl: 0-0 Vi: 0-0 Tstrap: 0-0
Best Rating:

Zolaran (IRE)

6-y-o b m Zaffaran (USA)-Nelly Don (Shackleton)
M Bradstock The Old Manor Racing Club

Placings:F (0436)
2001/02: 17^{F}GF

	Starts	1st	2nd	3rd	Win & Pl
NH Flat	1	0	0	0	
Career Total	**1**	**0**	**0**	**0**	

Going: Sf: 0-0 GS: 0-0 Gd: 0-0 GF: - Fm: 0-1
Distance: 2m/2m3: 0-1 2m4-2m7: 0-0 3m+: 0-0
Track: LH: 0-0 RH: 0-0 Tight: 0-1 Gall: 0-0
Aids: Bl: 0-0 Vi: 0-0 Tstrap: 0-0
Best Rating:

Zoot Money

10-y-o gr m Scallywag-Moonduster (Sparkler)
F P Murtagh D Sundin

Placings:P/P5/00P-0 (0333)
2001/02: 24^{0}S

	Starts	1st	2nd	3rd	Win & Pl
Hurdles	1	0	0	0	
Career Total	**7**	**0**	**0**	**0**	**0**

Going: Sf: 0-1 GS: 0-0 Gd: 0-0 GF: - Fm: 0-0
Distance: 2m/2m3: 0-0 2m4-2m7: 0-0 3m+: 0-1
Track: LH: 0-0 RH: 0-1 Tight: 0-0 Gall: 0-0
Aids: Bl: 0-0 Vi: 0-0 Tstrap: 0-0
Best Rating: 32 5/00 Hexm 3m gd-fm Hdl

Zoralo (IRE)

6-y-o gr g Toulon-Another Yankee (Le Moss)
J Howard Johnson J Howard Johnson

Placings:0-P (1902)
2001/02: 17^{P}G

	Starts	1st	2nd	3rd	Win & Pl
Hurdles	1	0	0	0	
Career Total	**2**	**0**	**0**	**0**	

Going: Sf: 0-0 GS: 0-0 Gd: 0-1 GF: - Fm: 0-0
Distance: 2m/2m3: 0-1 2m4-2m7: 0-0 3m+: 0-0
Track: LH: 0-1 RH: 0-0 Tight: 0-1 Gall: 0-0
Aids: Bl: 0-0 Vi: 0-0 Tstrap: 0-0
Best Rating:

Zorro Real

66f 39f

5-y-o b g Rakaposhi King-Sharp Vixen (Laurence O)
Miss S Edwards Coldharbour Racing Ltd

Placings:0 (3236)
2001/02: 16^{0}GS

	Starts	1st	2nd	3rd	Win & Pl
NH Flat	1	0	0	0	
Career Total	**1**	**0**	**0**	**0**	

Going: Sf: 0-0 GS: 0-1 Gd: 0-0 GF: - Fm: 0-0
Distance: 2m/2m3: 0-1 2m4-2m7: 0-0 3m+: 0-0
Track: LH: 0-0 RH: 0-1 Tight: 0-0 Gall: 0-1
Aids: Bl: 0-0 Vi: 0-0 Tstrap: 0-0
Best Rating: 39 1/02 Hntg 2m110y gd-sft NHF

Zorya

4-y-o br f Henbit (USA)-Whirlwind Romance (IRE) (Strong Gale)
Miss K M George Exterior Profiles Ltd

Placings:U (2209)
2001/02: 17^{U}G

	Starts	1st	2nd	3rd	Win & Pl
Hurdles	1	0	0	0	
Career Total	**1**	**0**	**0**	**0**	

Going: Sf: 0-0 GS: 0-0 Gd: 0-1 GF: - Fm: 0-0
Distance: 2m/2m3: 0-1 2m4-2m7: 0-0 3m+: 0-0
Track: LH: 0-0 RH: 0-1 Tight: 0-0 Gall: 0-0
Aids: Bl: 0-0 Vi: 0-0 Tstrap: 0-0
Best Rating:

Zsarabak

97(105h) (111h)90+

5-y-o br g Soviet Lad (USA)-Moorefield Girl (IRE) (Gorytus (USA))
J J O'Neill C D Carr

Placings:331P0-3223P (1398)
2001/02: 16^{3}GF, 16^{2}G, 20^{2}G, 20^{3}G, 16^{P}GF

	Starts	1st	2nd	3rd	Win & Pl
Hurdles	5	0	2	2	3388
Career Total	**10**	**1**	**2**	**4**	**7392**

97 9/00 Bang 2m1f D Hdl G-F £3172
Total win prize-money £3172

Going: Sf: 0-0 GS: 0-0 Gd: 0-3 GF: - Fm: 0-2
Distance: 2m/2m3: 0-3 2m4-2m7: 0-2 3m+: 0-0
Track: LH: 0-4 RH: 0-1 Tight: 0-2 Gall: 0-0
Aids: Bl: 0-0 Vi: 0-2 Tstrap: 0-0
Best Rating: **105** 8/01 Prth 2m4f110y good Hdl

Fair handicap hurdler between two and two and a half miles who goes well at Bangor. At his best on good or faster.

Zurs (IRE)

(113h) (121h)

9-y-o b g Tirol-Needy (High Top)
J J O'Neill (Jamie Poulton 29/6) Mrs M Liston

Placings:0/50/213/4-00031134430 **(4515)**
2001/02: 16^{0}GF, 16^{0}GF, 16^{0}GF, 16^{3}GF, 17^{1}G, 16^{1}G, 16^{3}GS, 17^{4}G, 21^{4}GS, 16^{3}GS, 16^{0}GS

	Starts	1st	2nd	3rd	Win & Pl
Hurdles	11	2	0	3	18377
Career Total	**18**	**3**	**1**	**4**	**23609**

118	10/01	Chel	2m110y	E(0-135)HHdl	GD	£7182
112	10/01	Bang	2m1f	F(0-110)HHdl	GD	£5824
112	11/99	Plum	2m	F(0-110)HHdl	G-F	£2818

Total win prize-money £15826

Going: Sf: 0-0 GS: 0-4 Gd: 2-3 GF: - Fm: 0-4
Distance: **2m/2m3: 2-10** 2m4-2m7: 0-1 3m+: 0-0
Track: **LH: 2-7** RH: 0-4 **Tight: 1-3** Gall: 0-1
Aids: Bl: 0-0 Vi: 0-0 Tstrap: 0-0
Best Rating: **121** 2/02 Kemp 2m gd-sft Hdl

A change of stable and a drop in the handicap helped him regain winning form at Bangor in October 2001, and he followed up in impressive style at Cheltenham. Continued to run well in competitive handicaps without winning. His best form over hurdles has come on a sound surface.

Zweitausender (IRE)

93f

6-y-o b m Leading Counsel (USA)-Pass Thurn (Trimmingham)
Patrick Morris (R H Alner 29/9) C P Byrne

Placings:*200* **(2089a)**
2001/02: 16^{2}GF, 17^{0}S, 16^{0}Y

	Starts	1st	2nd	3rd	Win & Pl
NH Flat	3	0	1	0	774
Career Total	**3**	**0**	**1**	**0**	**774**

Going: Sf: 0-1 GS: 0-0 Gd: 0-0 GF: - Fm: 0-1
Distance: 2m/2m3: 0-3 2m4-2m7: 0-0 3m+: 0-0
Track: LH: 0-0 RH: 0-1 Tight: 0-1 Gall: 0-0
Aids: Bl: 0-0 Vi: 0-0 Tstrap: 0-0
Best Rating: 93 6/01 DRoy 2m gd-fm NHF

WINNING TRAINERS 2001-2002

		Wins	Stakes (£)
1.	M C Pipe	234	2,689,643
2.	P F Nicholls	135	1,438,882
3.	P J Hobbs	119	1,359,416
4.	J J O'Neill	113	979,239
5.	N J Henderson	93	861,667
6.	Miss H C Knight	48	817,512
7.	N A Twiston-Davies	35	593,582
8.	Miss Venetia Williams	55	591,831
9.	Mrs M Reveley	90	542,686
10.	Ferdy Murphy	68	498,872
11.	L Lungo	61	326,451
12.	Ian Williams	46	313,957
13.	A King	34	310,513
14.	T R George	30	296,143
15.	C J Mann	34	279,748
16.	W P Mullins (IRE)	4	268,925
17.	F Doumen (FR)	9	261,468
18.	H D Daly	28	260,803
19.	P R Webber	33	257,865
20.	R H Alner	29	256,422
21.	K C Bailey	36	243,863
22.	T D Easterby	19	243,252
23.	Mrs S J Smith	27	236,647
24.	H Morrison	6	219,502
25.	J R Fanshawe	3	217,148
26.	M Pitman	25	214,870
27.	N B Mason	30	213,417
28.	A L T Moore (IRE)	2	186,700
29.	M W Easterby	26	173,887
30.	J T Gifford	20	172,928

WINNING OWNERS 2001-2002

		Wins	Stakes (£)
1.	D A Johnson	49	726,762
2.	Sir Robert Ogden	34	516,024
3.	J P McManus	25	469,247
4.	Jim Lewis	5	336,775
5.	H R Mould	3	334,019
6.	Paul Green	5	234,931
7.	R J B Partners	13	231,526
8.	Trevor Hemmings	21	198,224
9.	E Gutner & M Krysztofiak Racing	2	192,064
10.	Matt Archer & Miss Jean Broadhurst	18	191,331
11.	N B Mason	27	190,371
12.	Joe Moran	5	164,343
13.	Mrs J Stewart	9	158,575
14.	The Macca & Growler Partnership	14	143,191
15.	Ashleybank Investments Limited	23	139,414
16.	B C Marshall	8	139,392
17.	The Winning Line	13	138,354
18.	Mrs John Magnier	2	130,475
19.	Terry Warner	9	130,402
20.	Dr D B A & Mrs Heather Silk	3	129,737
21.	Stanley W Clarke	10	128,522
22.	M S Wilson, R Sweet, Mrs Mary Wilson	2	127,150
23.	C G Roach	9	121,089
24.	Mrs Belinda Harvey	5	118,909
25.	Mr & Mrs Raymond Anderson Green	16	116,980
26.	P A Deal	4	112,521
27.	C D Carr	8	106,834
28.	Anne Duchess Of Westminster	7	105,446
29.	J M Brown & M J Blackburn	3	103,513
30.	Lady Harris	5	99,797

LEADING JUMP JOCKEYS 2001-2002

	Stakes (£)	1st	2nd	3rd	Unpl	Mounts	per cent	£1 stake
A P McCoy	1956742	288	184	133	401	1006	28.6	- 76.85
R Johnson	862784	133	99	87	284	603	22.0	+ **22.79**
M A Fitzgerald	603139	109	85	47	324	565	19.2	- 146.08
A Dobbin	637890	108	54	61	314	537	20.1	- 14.32
T J Murphy	595347	97	66	65	296	524	18.5	+ **57.34**
N Williamson	682663	82	55	47	230	414	19.8	+ **48.17**
G Lee	208998	58	54	50	277	439	13.2	+ **6.42**
R Thornton	304662	56	61	55	373	545	10.2	- 180.67
A Thornton	235469	54	63	59	306	482	11.2	- 161.99
A Maguire	324895	53	63	55	317	488	10.8	- 196.71
J Culloty	765073	51	58	36	194	339	15.0	- 51.93
H Oliver	175707	47	45	34	336	462	10.1	- 30.83
J Tizzard	261753	44	53	30	236	363	12.1	- 128.69
A Dempsey	180951	43	27	34	178	282	15.2	- 2.36
L Cooper	234355	42	27	21	124	214	19.6	+ **40.93**
L Aspell	227986	42	55	54	329	480	8.7	- 166.40
R Garritty	212388	40	43	28	178	289	13.8	- 20.74
W Marston	209790	39	47	51	366	503	7.7	- 162.53
M Bradburne	173262	38	40	45	272	395	9.6	+ **43.32**
C Llewellyn	153909	36	51	47	425	559	6.4	- 323.24
N Fehily	140654	35	31	34	209	309	11.3	- 10.84
J A McCarthy	156400	35	42	39	266	382	9.1	- 87.56
R Wakley	135482	35	43	41	336	455	7.6	- 143.42
D R Dennis	174773	34	33	29	219	315	10.7	- 34.78
R McGrath	182376	34	45	49	312	440	7.7	- 141.63
Richard Guest	164188	33	27	28	119	207	15.9	- 47.27
J P McNamara	131383	33	45	45	227	350	9.4	- 171.34
T Scudamore	173189	32	39	43	269	383	8.3	- 227.74
F Keniry	129810	31	37	41	322	431	7.1	- 72.27
D Gallagher	299480	30	34	36	266	366	8.1	- 95.63
R Greene	161261	29	22	38	275	364	7.9	- 130.14
B Hitchcott	104455	29	26	20	224	299	9.6	- 10.73
P Flynn	160682	26	25	29	185	265	9.8	- 121.87
B Fenton	171996	26	39	35	208	308	8.4	- 87.76
B Storey	109987	25	45	32	250	352	7.1	- 166.48
J Crowley	88713	24	21	23	160	228	10.5	- 27.33
A S Smith	95514	24	26	31	263	344	6.9	- 180.86
T Doyle	99598	24	45	33	276	378	6.3	- 100.76
J M Maguire	160644	23	33	22	180	258	8.9	- 65.38
R Widger	134735	22	18	23	157	220	10.0	- 121.91
C Rafter	70284	21	12	20	146	199	10.5	+ **33.05**
V T Keane	102156	20	18	12	154	204	9.8	- 76.85
K Renwick	80043	20	25	35	185	265	7.5	- 104.17
S Stronge	62694	20	26	20	196	262	7.6	- 95.07
J R Kavanagh	126873	20	27	18	227	292	6.8	- 93.86
S Durack	106174	20	27	23	256	326	6.1	- 139.75
M Foley	138212	19	18	24	168	229	8.2	- 73.97
Mr D Crosse	101257	19	18	16	131	184	10.3	+ **11.20**
M Batchelor	59644	17	17	19	184	237	7.1	- 72.44
W Worthington	65178	17	19	18	181	235	7.2	- 41.00
L Cummins	72960	15	12	13	106	146	10.2	- 14.16

RACEFORM JUMP MEDIAN TIMES 2001-2002

Some new distances have been omitted where insufficient data exists to establish a reliable median time.

AINTREE

Chase (Mildmay)

2m 3m58.7
2m4f 5m5.4
3m1f........................ 6m27.1

Chase (National)

2m 6f........................ 5m40.1
3m3f........................ 7m15.7
4m4f........................ 9m6.4

Hurdles

2m110y 4m6.4
2m4f........................ 4m54.4
3m110y 6m7.5

ASCOT

Chase

2m 3m59.9
2m3f110y 4m57.1
3m110y 6m22.7

Hurdles

2m110y 4m0.8
2m4f........................ 4m59.0
3m 5m54.9
3m1f 110y 6m22.3

AYR

Chase

2m 4m4.2
2m4f........................ 5m18.4
2m5f110y 6m0.6
3m1f........................ 6m37.8
3m3f110y 7m12.1
4m1f........................ 8m21.8

Hurdles

2m........................ 3m53.1
2m4f........................ 5m4.7
2m6f........................ 5m41.5
3m110y 6m18.4

BANGOR

Chase

2m1f110y 4m24.4
2m4f110y 5m16.4
3m110y........................ 6m22.3
3m6f........................ 8m10.4
4m1f........................ 9m16.7

Hurdles

2m1f........................ 4m7.8
2m4f........................ 4m53.5
3m 5m54.3

CARLISLE

Chase

2m........................ 4m9.4
2m4f110y........................ 5m18.6
3m 6m23.9
3m2f........................ 7m7.9

Hurdles

2m1f........................ 4m22.2
2m4f110y 5m10.3
3m110y 6m19.6

CARTMEL

Chase

2m1f110y 4m19.3
2m5f110y 5m21.7
3m2f 6m36.5

Hurdles

2m1f110y 4m9.3
2m6f........................ 5m26.8
3m2f........................ 6m18.6

CATTERICK

Chase

2m 4m1.7
2m3f........................ 4m57
3m1f110y 6m45.0
3m4f110y 7m27.6
3m6f........................ 7m57

Hurdles

2m........................ 3m55.2
2m3f........................ 4m47.3
3m1f110y........................ 6m33.4

CHELTENHAM (NEW)

Chase

2m110y 4m11.0
2m5f 5m28.9
3m2f110y........................ 6m50.8
4m1f........................ 8m55.7

Hurdles

2m1f........................ 4m14.0
2m4f........................ 5m10.9
2m5f110y 5m28.6
3m110y 6m0.7

CHELTENHAM (OLD)

Chase

2m........................ 3m59.4
2m4f110y 5m12.3
3m1f........................ 6m26.0
3m3f110y 7m19.2
4m 8m23.6

Cross Country Chases

3m 7m0.7
3m7f........................ 8m25.9

Hurdles

2m110y........................ 4m1.5
2m5f........................ 5m14.3
3m2f........................ 6m39.8

CHEPSTOW

Chase

2m110y 4m19.6
2m3f110y 5m13.6
3m 6m17.0
3m2f110y 7m22.8
3m5f110y 8m11.0

Hurdles

2m110y 4m12.8
2m4f 5m6.6
3m 6m18.5

DONCASTER

Chase

2m110y 4m5.5
2m3f110y 4m57.6
3m 6m9.5
3m2f........................ 6m35.2

Hurdles

2m110y 4m1.3
2m4f 4m52.6
3m110y 6m1.1

EXETER

Chase

2m1f 4m10.1
2m1f110y 4m21.8
2m3f........................ 4m44.5
2m6f110y 5m43.6
3m1f 6m29.3
3m2f........................ 6m52.3
3m6f 8m19.1

Hurdles

2m1f 4m6.6
2m1f110y 4m12.6
2m3f 4m31.4
2m3f110y 4m49.3
2m6f........................ 5m26.2
2m7f 5m49.2
3m2f........................ 6m42.3

FAKENHAM

Chase

2m110y 4m13.2
2m5f110y 5m33.1
3m110y 6m26.9

Hurdles

2m 4m0.6
2m4f 4m58.8
2m7f110y 5m42.6

FOLKESTONE

Chase

2m 4m7.7
2m5f 5m30.1
3m2f 6m44.0
3m7f 7m58.1

Hurdles

2m1f110y 4m27.5
2m4f110y 5m12.9
2m6f110y 5m55.1

FONTWELL

Chase

2m2f 4m39.1
3m2f110y 7m3.1

Hurdles

2m2f110y 4m32.8
2m6f110y 5m37.7
3m2f110y 6m32.7

HAYDOCK

Chase

2m 4m14.8
2m4f 5m28.3
3m 6m33.5
3m4f110y 7m39.9
4m110y 9m11.2

Hurdles

2m 3m59.0
2m4f 5m5.2
2m6f 5m49.8
2m7f110y 6m5.9

HEREFORD

Chase

2m 4m4.6
2m3f 4m48.5
3m1f110y 6m33.7

Hurdles

2m1f 4m3.2
2m3f110y 4m48.4
3m2f 6m29.0

HEXHAM

Chase

2m110y 4m10.1
2m4f110y 5m14.2
3m1f 6m32.8
4m 9m6.6

Hurdles

2m 4m3.6
2m4f110y 5m7.5
3m 6m11.0

HUNTINGDON

Chase

2m110y 4m9.1
2m4f110y 5m4.8
3m 6m12.0
3m6f110y 8m7.4

Hurdles

2m110y 3m55.7
2m4f110y 4m46.8
2m5f110y 5m10.0
3m2f 6m20.4

KELSO

Chase

2m1f 4m20.0
2m6f110y 5m54.5
3m1f 6m26.9
3m4f 7m24.1
4m 8m39.0

Hurdles

2m110y 3m59.8
2m2f 4m30.7
2m6f110y 5m37.6

KEMPTON

Chase

2m 3m57.0
2m4f110y 5m16.7
3m 6m13.3

Hurdles

2m 3m57.5
2m5f 5m16.7
3m110y 6m10.9

LEICESTER

Chase

2m1f 4m22.4
2m4f110y 5m24.5
2m7f110y 6m12.5

Hurdles

2m 4m5.1
2m4f110y 5m15.1
3m 6m19.7

LINGFIELD

Chase

2m 4m20.5
2m4f110y 5m34.8
3m 6m36.1

Hurdles

2m110y 4m14.3
2m3f110y 5m11.1
2m7f 6m13.4

LUDLOW

Chase

2m 4m 4.1
2m4f 5m4.6
3m 6m8.2

Hurdles

2m 3m46.5

MARKET RASEN

Chase

2m1f110y 4m28.5
2m4f 5m6.5
2m6f110y 5m43.5
3m1f 6m31.7
3m4f110y 7m46.5
4m1f 9m6.5

Hurdles

2m1f110y 4m16.0
2m3f110y 4m48.6
2m5f110y 5m24.6
3m 6m6.8

MUSSELBURGH

Chase

2m 3m58.2
2m4f 5m4.8
3m 6m9.3

Hurdles

2m 3m49.4
2m4f 4m53.1
3m 6m9.3

NEWBURY

Chase

2m1f 4m15.9
2m4f 5m12.1
3m 6m12.1
3m2f110y 6m51.9

Hurdles

2m110y 4m3.5
2m3f 4m48.0
2m5f 5m15.2
3m110y 6m9.5

NEWCASTLE

Chase

2m110y 4m13.7
2m4f 5m13.4
3m 6m6.8
3m6f 8m0.1
4m1f 8m37.5

Hurdles

2m 4m1.9
2m4f 5m6.4
3m 6m2.5

NEWTON ABBOT

Chase

2m110y 4m9.6
2m5f110y 5m28.6
3m2f110y 6m51.2

Hurdles

2m1f 4m8.0
2m6f 5m23.6
3m3f 6m45.6

PERTH

Chase

2m 3m59.7
2m4f110y 5m9.8
3m 6m13.5

Hurdles
2m110y 3m55.8
2m4f110y 5m1.1
3m110y 6m4.3

PLUMPTON
Chase
2m 4m5.9
2m1f 4m23.8
2m2f 4m35.4
2m4f 5m22.9
2m5f 5m33.0
3m1f110y 6m45.2
Hurdles
2m 3m46.3
2m1f 4m22.6
2m4f 5m5.7
2m5f 5m26.8
3m110y 6m23.7

SANDOWN
Chase
2m 4m2.9
2m4f110y 5m21.1
3m110y 6m30.4
3m5f110y 7m41.6
Hurdles
2m110y 4m5.9
2m4f110y 5m24.8
2m6f 5m32.8

SEDGEFIELD
Chase
2m110y 4m7.5
2m5f 5m18.7
3m3f 7m2.3
3m4f 7m11.6
Hurdles
2m1f 4m0.7
2m5f110y 5m10.3
3m3f110y 6m54.6

SOUTHWELL
Chase
2m 4m9.2
2m4f110y 5m22.1
3m110y 6m31.6
Hurdles
2m 3m37.2
2m4f110y 5m14.3
3m110y 6m21.3

STRATFORD
Chase
2m1f110y 4m14.0
2m4f 5m2.8
2m5f110y 5m24.2
3m 6m4.2
3m4f 7m9.6

Hurdles
2m110y 4m0.6
2m3f 4m37.8
2m6f110y 5m33.8
3m3f 6m32.0

TAUNTON
Chase
2m110y 4m9.1
2m3f 4m55.0
3m 6m14.4
3m3f 7m22.8
4m2f110y 9m38.9
Hurdles
2m1f 4m1.8
2m3f110y 4m40.8
3m110y 6m7.2

TOWCESTER
Chase
2m110y 4m15.2
2m6f 5m50.3
3m1f 6m40.8
Hurdles
2m 4m1.4
2m5f 5m31.9
3m 6m13.1

UTTOXETER
Chase
2m 3m59.6
2m4f 5m14.5
2m5f 5m18.0
2m7f 5m53.2
3m 6m20.8
3m2f 6m51.4
3m4f 7m45.1
4m2f 8m51.6
Hurdles
2m 3m50.9
2m4f110y 4m59.4
2m6f110y 5m28.8
3m110y 5m56.3

WARWICK
Chase
2m 4m5.2
2m4f110y 5m14.5
3m2f 6m47.5
3m5f 7m47.3
4m1f110y 8m48.9
Hurdles
2m 3m53.5
2m3f 4m35.1
2m4f110y 5m7.2

WETHERBY
Chase
2m 4m2.7

2m4f110y 5m19.3
3m1f 6m32.6
3m5f 7m23.1
Hurdles
2m 3m57.1
2m4f110y 5m8.1
2m7f 5m55.8
3m1f 6m16.3

WINCANTON
Chase
2m 4m4.4
2m5f 5m22.5
3m1f110y 6m45.3
Hurdles
2m 3m47.7
2m6f 5m23.6

WOLVERHAMPTON
Chase
2m 3m57.2
2m4f110y 5m7.5
3m1f 6m35.1
Hurdles
2m 3m51.6
2m4f110y 5m2.2
3m1f 6m14.7

WORCESTER
Chase
2m 3m58.8
2m4f110y 5m16.9
2m7f110y 6m6.5
Hurdles
2m 3m50.7
2m2f 4m22.4
2m4f 4m55.2
3m 5m52.5

WINNERS OF PRINCIPAL RACES (LAST TEN YEARS)

THOMAS PINK GOLD CUP (HANDICAP CHASE)
formerly Murphy's & Mackeson Gold Cup
Cheltenham 2m 4f 110y

1992	Tipping Tim	7-10-10	16
1993	Bradbury Star	8-11-08	15
1994	Bradbury Star	9-11-11	14
1995	Dublin Flyer	9-11-08	12
1996	Challenger du Luc	6-10-02	12
1997	Senor El Betrutti	8-10-00	9
1998	Cyfor Malta	5-11-03	12
1999	The Outback Way	9-10-00	14
2000	Lady Cricket	6-10-13	15
2001	Shooting Light	8-11-3	14

FIRST NATIONAL BANK GOLD CUP (HANDICAP CHASE)
formerly H & T Walker Gold Cup
Ascot 2m 4f

1992	Deep Sensation	7-11-02	10
1993	Abandoned due to frost		
1994	Raymylette	7-11-10	11
1995	Sound Man	7-12-00	5
1996	Strong Promise	5-10-05	8
1997	Simply Dashing	9-10-05	15
1998	Red Marauder	8-10-11	11
1999	Nordance Prince	8-10-09	11
2000	Upgrade	6-11-08	4
2001	Wahiba Sands	8-10-4	4

HENNESSY COGNAC GOLD CUP (HANDICAP CHASE)
Newbury 3m 2f 110y

1992	Sibton Abbey	7-10-00	13
1993	Cogent	9-10-01	9
1994	One Man	6-10-00	16
1995	Couldnt Be Better	8-10-08	11
1996	Coome Hill	7-10-00	11
1997	Suny Bay	8-11-08	14
1998	Teeton Mill	9-10-05	16
1999	Ever Blessed	7-10-00	13
2000	King's Road	7-10-07	17
2001	What's Up Boys	7-10-12	14

TRIPLEPRINT GOLD CUP (HANDICAP CHASE)
Cheltenham 2m 4f

1992	Another Coral	9-11-04	10
1993	Fragrant Dawn	9-10-02	11
1994	Dublin Flyer	8-10-02	11
1995	Abandoned due to frost		
1996	Addington Boy	8-11-10	10
1997	Senor El Betrutti	8-11-03	9
1998	Northern Starlight	7-10-01	13
1999	Legal Right	6-10-13	9
2000	Go Roger Go	8-11-00	12
2001	Abandoned due to frost		

BONUSPRINT CHRISTMAS HURDLE
Kempton 2m

1992	Mighty Mogul	5-11-07	8
1993	Muse	6-11-07	5
1994	Absaloms's Lady	6-11-02	6
1995	Abandoned due to frost		
1996	Abandoned due to frost		
1997	Kerawi	4-11-07	5
1998	French Holly	7-11-07	5
1999	Dato Star	8-11-07	4
2000	Geos	5-11-07	7
2001	Landing Light	6-11-7	5

PERTEMPS KING GEORGE VI CHASE
Kempton 3m

1992	The Fellow (FR)	7-11-10	8
1993	Barton Bank	7-11-10	10
1994	Algan (FR)	6-11-10	9
1995	*One Man	8-11-10	11
1996	One Man	8-11-10	5
1997	See More Business	7-11-10	8
1998	Teeton Mill	9-11-10	9
1999	See More Business	9-11-10	9
2000	First Gold	7-11-10	9
2001	Florida Pearl	9-11-10	8

(*Run at Sandown Jan 6th 1996)

CORAL WELSH NATIONAL (HANDICAP CHASE)
Chepstow 3m 6f

1992	Run For Free	8-10-09	11
1993	Riverside Boy	10-10-00	8
1994	*Master Oats	8-11-06	8
1995	Abandoned due to frost		
1996	Abandoned due to frost		
1997	Earth Summit	9-10-13	14
1998	Kendal Cavalier	8-10-08	14
1999	Edmond	7-10-00	16
2000	Jocks Cross	9-10-04	19
2001	Supreme Glory	8-10-00	13

(*Run at Newbury)

PIERSE HANDICAP HURDLE
(formerly Ladbroke Handicap Hurdle)
Leopardstown 2m

1993	Glencloud	5-10-13	25
1994	Atone	7-10-08	25
1995	Anusha	5-10-02	17
1996	Dance Beat	5-09-12	22
1997	Master Tribe	7-10-04	23
1998	Graphic Equaliser	6-10-00	20
1999	Archieve Footage	7-11-08	25
2000	Mantles Prince	6-9-12	14
2001	Grinkov	6-10-07	24
2002	Adamant Approach	8-11-1	26

VICTOR CHANDLER HANDICAP CHASE
Ascot 2m

1993	Sybillin	7-10-10	11
1994	*Viking Flagship	7-10-10	4
1995	Martha's Son	8-10-09	8
1996	Big Matt	9-10-04	11
1997	**Ask Tom	8-10-10	8
1998	Jeffell	8-10-11	9
1999	**Call Equiname	9-11-03	7
2000	Nordance Prince	9-10-00	10
2001	Function Dream	9-10-11	10
2002	Turgeonev	7-10-4	8

(* Run at Warwick)
(**Run at Kempton)

AGFA DIAMOND (HANDICAP) CHASE
Sandown 3m 110y

1993	Country Member	8-10-07	3

1994 Second Schedual 9-10-07 5
1995 Deep Bramble 8-11-10 11
1996 Amtrak Express 9-10-07 3
1997 Dextra Dove 10-11-02 6
1998 Court Melody 10-10-05 6
1999 Clever Remark 10-10-05 5
2000 Trouble Ahead 9-11-04 8
2001 Storm Damage 9-10-07 9
2002 Billingsgate 10-11-01 9

TOTE GOLD TROPHY (HANDICAP HURDLE)
Newbury 2m 110y

1993 King Credo 8-10-00 16
1994 Large Action 6-10-08 11
1995 Mysilv 5-10-08 8
1996 Squire Silk 7-10-12 18
1997 Make a Stand 6-11-07 18
1998 Sharpical 6-11-01 14
1999 Decoupage 7-11-10 18
2000 Geos 5-11-03 17
2001 Landing Light 6-10-02 20
2002 Copeland 7-11-07 16

HENNESSY COGNAC GOLD CUP
Leopardstown 3m

1993 Jodami 8-12-00 7
1994 Jodami 9-12-00 6
1995 Jodami 10-12-00 6
1996 Imperial Call 7-12-00 8
1997 Danoli 9-12-00 8
1998 Dorans Pride 9-12-00 8
1999 Florida Pearl 7-12-00 7
2000 Florida Pearl 8-12-00 7
2001 Florida Pearl 9-12-00 7
2002 Alexander Banquet 9-12-00 5

RACING POST HANDICAP CHASE
Kempton 3m

1993 Zeta's Lad 10-10-10 12
1994 Antonin 6-10-04 16
1995 Val D'Alene 8-11-02 9
1996 Rough Quest 10-10-08 9
1997 Mudahim 11-10-02 9
1998 Super Tactics 10-10-10 7
1999 Dr. Leunt 8-11-05 8
2000 Gloria Victis 6-11-10 13
2001 Young Spartacus 8-11-03 15
2002 Gunther McBride 7-10-03 14

SUNDERLANDS IMPERIAL CUP (HANDICAP) HURDLE
Sandown 2m 110y

1993 Olympian 6-10-00 15
1994 Precious Boy 8-11-07 13
1995 Collier Bay 5-10-02 10
1996 Amancio 5-10-08 11
1997 Carlito Brigante 5-10-00 18
1998 Blowing Wind 5-11-10 15
1999 Regency Rake 7-10-07 9
2000 Magic Combination 7-10-00 18
2001 Ibal 5-9-09 23
2002 Polar Red 5-11-01 16

IRISH INDEPENDENT ARKLE CHALLENGE TROPHY (NOVICES) CHASE
(formerly Guinness Arkle Challenge Trophy)
Cheltenham 2m

1993 Travado 7-11-08 8
1994 Nakir 6-11-08 11
1995 Klairon Davis 6-11-08 11
1996 Ventana Canyon 7-11-08 16
1997 Or Royal 6-11-08 9
1998 Champleve 5-11-00 16
1999 Flagship Uberalles 5-11-00 14
2000 Tiutchev 7-11-08 12
2001 Abandoned- Foot & Mouth
2002 Moscow Flyer 8-11-08 12

SMURFIT CHAMPION HURDLE
Cheltenham 2m 110y

1993 Granville Again 7-12-00 18
1994 Flakey Dove 8-11-09 15
1995 Alderbrook 6-12-00 14
1996 Collier Bay 6-12-00 16
1997 Make a Stand 6-12-00 17
1998 Istabraq 6-12-00 18
1999 Istabraq 7-12-00 14
2000 Istabraq 8-12-00 12
2001 Abandoned - Foot & Mouth
2002 Hors La Loi III 7-12-00 15

QUEEN MOTHER CHAMPION CHASE
Cheltenham 2m

1993 Deep Sensation 8-12-00 9
1994 Viking Flagship 7-12-00 8
1995 Viking Flagship 8-12-00 10
1996 Klairon Davis 7-12-00 7
1997 Martha's Son 10-12-00 6
1998 One Man 10-12-00 8
1999 Call Equiname 9-12-00 13
2000 Edredon Bleu 8-12-00 13
2001 Abandoned - Foot & Mouth
2002 Flagship Uberalles 8-12-00 12

ROYAL & SUNALLIANCE (NOVICES') CHASE
Cheltenham 3m

1993 Young Hustler 6-11-04 8
1994 Monsieur Le Cure 8-11-04 18
1995 Brief Gale 8-10-13 13
1996 Nahthen Lad 7-11-04 12
1997 Hanakham 8-11-04 14
1998 Florida Pearl 6-11-04 10
1999 Looks Like Touble 7-11-04 14
2000 Lord Noelie 7-11-04 9
2001 Abandoned - Foot & Mouth
2002 Hussard Collonges 7-11-04 19

JCB TRIUMPH HURDLE
(formerly Daily Express & Elite Racing Club Triumph Hurdle) Cheltenham 2m 1f (4-y-o)

1993 Shawiya 10-09 25
1994 Mysilv 10-09 28
1995 Kissair 11-00 26
1996 Paddy's Return 11-00 29
1997 Commanche Court 11-00 28
1998 Upgrade 11-00 25
1999 Katarino 11-00 23
2000 Snow Drop 10-09 28
2001 Abandoned - Foot & Mouth
2002 Scolardy 11-00 28

TOTE CHELTENHAM GOLD CUP (CHASE)
Cheltenham 3m 2f

1993 Jodami 8-12-00 16
1994 The Fellow 9-12-00 15
1995 Master Oats 9-12-00 15
1996 Imperial Call 7-12-00 10

1997	Mr Mulligan	9-12-00	14
1998	Cool Dawn	10-12-00	17
1999	See More Business	9-12-00	12
2000	Looks Like Trouble	8-12-00	12
2001	Abandoned - Foot & Mouth		
2002	Best Mate	7-12-00	18

MARTELL CUP CHASE
Aintree 3m 1f

1993	Docklands Express	11-11-05	4
1994	Docklands Express	12-11-05	4
1995	Merry Gale	7-11-09	6
1996	Scotton Banks	7-11-05	6
1997	Barton Bank	11-11-05	5
1998	Escartefigue	6-11-13	8
1999	Macgeorge	9-11-05	5
2000	See More Business	10-12-00	4
2001	First Gold	8-12-00	7
2002	Florida Pearl	10-11-12	6

MARTELL XO ANNIVERSARY HURDLE
(formerly GLENLIVETANNIVERSARY HURDLE
(4-y-o) Aintree 2m 110y

1993	Titled Dancer	10-09	8
1994	Tropical Lake	10-09	12
1995	Stompin	11-00	18
1996	Zabadi	11-00	11
1997	Quakers Field	11-00	12
1998	Deep Water	11-00	14
1999	Hors La Loi III	11-04	6
2000	Lord Brex	11-00	12
2001	Bilboa	10-13	14
2002	Quazar	11-04	17

MARTELL MELLING CHASE
Aintree 2m 4f

1993	Deep Sensation	8-11-10	4
1994	Katabatic	11-11-10	5
1995	Viking Flagship	8-11-10	6
1996	Viking Flagship	9-11-10	4
1997	Martha's Son	10-11-10	4
1998	Opera Hat	10-11-05	5
1999	Direct Route	8-11-10	6
2000	Direct Route	9-11-10	5
2001	Fadalko	8-11-10	7
2002	Native Upmanship	9-11-10	8

MARTELL RED RUM CHASE
(LIMITED HANDICAP)
Aintree 2m

1993	Boutzdaroff	11-10-07	6
1994	Uncle Ernie	9-10-08	8
1995	Coulton	8-11-08	12
1996	Arctic Kinsman	8-11-00	10
1997	Down the Fell	8-10-07	10
1998	Jeffell	8-12-00	5
1999	Flying Instructor	9-11-05	7
2000	Jungli	7-10-07	7
2001	Aghawadda Gold	9-11-02	12
2002	Dark'n Sharp	7-10-08	15

MARTELL AINTREE HURDLE
Aintree 2m 4f

1993	Morley Street	9-11-07	6
1994	Danoli	6-11-07	9
1995	Danoli	7-11-07	6
1996	Urubande	6-11-07	8
1997	Bimsey	7-11-07	7
1998	Pridwell	8-11-07	6
1999	Istabraq	7-11-7	7
2000	Mister Morose	10-11-07	10
2001	Barton	8-11-07	8
2002	Ilnamar	6-11-07	14

MARTELL GRAND NATIONAL
(HANDICAP CHASE) 4m 4f

1971	Specify	9-10-13	42
1972	Well To Do	9-10-01	42
1973	Red Rum	8-10-05	38
1974	Red Rum	9-12-00	42
1975	L'Escargot	12-11-03	31
1976	Rag Trade	10-10-12	32
1977	Red Rum	12-11-08	42
1978	Lucius	9-10-09	37
1979	Rubstic	10-10-00	34
1980	Ben Nevis	12-10-12	30
1981	Aldaniti	11-10-13	39
1982	Grittar	9-11-05	39
1983	Corbiere	8-11-04	41
1984	Hallo Dandy	10-10-02	40
1985	Last Suspect	11-10-05	40
1986	West Tip	9-10-11	40
1987	Maori Venture	11-10-13	40
1988	Rhyme 'N Reason	9-11-00	40
1989	Little Polveir	12-10-03	40
1990	Mr Frisk	11-10-06	38
1991	Seagram	11-10-06	40
1992	Party Politics	8-10-07	40
1993	Void Race		
1994	Miinnehoma	11-10-08	36
1995	Royal Athlete	12-10-06	35
1996	Rough Quest	10-10-07	27
1997	Lord Gyllene	9-10-00	36
1998	Earth Summit	10-10-05	37
1999	Bobbyjo	9-10-00	32
2000	Papillon	9-10-12	40
2001	Red Marauder	11-10-11	40
2002	Bindaree	8-10-04	14

GALA CASINOS DAILY RECORD SCOTTISH GRAND NATIONAL (HANDICAP CHASE)
Ayr 4m 1f

1993	Run For Free	9-11-10	21
1994	Earth Summit	6-10-00	22
1995	Willsford	12-10-12	22
1996	Moorcroft Boy	11-10-02	20
1997	Belmont King	9-11-10	17
1998	Baronet	8-10-00	18
1999	Young Kenny	8-11-10	15
2000	Paris Pike	8-11-0	18
2001	Gingembre	7-11-02	30
2002	Take Control	8-10-06	18

ATTHERACES GOLD CUP (HANDICAP CHASE)
(formerly WHITBREAD GOLD CUP)
Sandown 3m 5f 110y

1993	**Topsham Bay	10-10-01	13
1994	Ushers Island	8-10-00	12
1995	Cache Fleur	9-10-01	14
1996	Life of a Lord	10-11-10	17
1997	Harwell Lad	8-10-0	9
1998	Call It A Day	8-10-10	19
1999	Eulogy	9-10-00	19
2000	Beau	7-10-9	20
2001	Ad Hoc	7-10-04	25
2002	Bounce Back	6-10-09	20

(** Givus A Buck 10-10-00 disqualified from 1st)